JAPAN
An Illustrated Encyclopedia

1
A······L

JAPAN
An Illustrated Encyclopedia

1

A ······▸ L

KODANSHA

Distributed in the United States and Canada by Kodansha America, Inc., 114
Fifth Avenue, New York, N.Y., 10011, and in the United Kingdom and continental
Europe by Kodansha Europe Ltd., Gillingham House, 38-44 Gillingham Street,
London, SW1V 1HU, and in Asia, Australia, and New Zealand by Kodansha
International Ltd., 17-14, Otowa 1-chome, Bunkyo-ku, Tokyo 112.

Published by Kodansha Ltd., 12-21, Otowa 2-chome, Bunkyo-ku, Tokyo 112.

Library of Congress Cataloging-in-Publication Data

Japan: an illustrated encyclopedia / Kodansha—1st ed.
  p.   cm.
  Includes bibliographical references and indexes.
  ISBN 4-06-931098-3
  1. Japan—Encyclopedias. I. Kōdansha.
DS805.J263 1993
952'.003—dc20   93-20512
                                           CIP

ISBN 4-06-206489-8 (Volume 1)
ISBN 4-06-931098-3 (Set)

CONTENTS

PUBLISHER'S FOREWORD

We are living in a period of great historic change. The collapse of the Soviet Union, the end of the Cold War, and the integration of the European Community are harbingers of this new era. Various problems and tensions persist, but the road toward a new global community lies open before us.

In these times, it is crucial that all peoples and nations come to understand and respect one another's historical and cultural traditions. To this end, each nation and people must tell its story to the world—a mission that is, to my mind, the greatest one facing today's publishers.

Beginning in 1949 under the leadership of my father, Noma Shōichi, Kōdansha, Ltd, has striven to internationalize Japanese publishing. The company has engaged in a variety of cooperative publishing ventures with North American, European, and Asian publishers and has lent financial and other support to the growth of the publishing industry in the developing nations of Africa and Asia. In 1963 Kōdansha International was established to produce books introducing Japanese culture to a global audience, and in the last few years Kōdansha America and Kōdansha Europe have been set up in New York and London, respectively, to broaden and deepen Kōdansha's commitment to international publishing operations.

One of the major accomplishments of this dedication to an international perspective was the publication in 1983 of the nine-volume *Kodansha Encyclopedia of Japan*. Ten years of labor went into producing this work, under the direction of Edwin O. Reischauer and Tsuru Shigeto, with Gen Itasaka as editor in chief. It has met with critical acclaim and found a secure place in universities and libraries throughout the world as a basic reference source for Japanese studies.

Japan: An Illustrated Encyclopedia builds upon this legacy to meet the increasing worldwide interest in Japan with a new, more compact, and completely revised edition that incorporates many features not included in its nine-volume predecessor. Perhaps the most noteworthy innovation is the use of full color throughout these pages and the employment of more than 4,000 photographs and illustrations (including charts, graphs, and tables) to help introduce Japan and its people to the reader in a vivid and enjoyable way. Nearly 100 feature articles and pictorial essays also enliven the text and expand on subjects of particular interest. In addition to the specialized maps that accompany many articles, the use of full color has permitted the inclusion of a detailed atlas of Japan. Other supplementary materials include a topical reader's guide to the encyclopedia, a chronological table of Japanese history, a bibliography of major works in English on Japan, and a bilingual index of entry titles. The sum of all these elements is an encyclopedia that affords the reader a comprehensive overview of Japanese society and culture from prehistoric times to the rapidly changing present.

My father often said that books are silent ambassadors. Books, with their ability to transmit thought and culture with precision and accuracy, are one of the most powerful vehicles for international communication and ultimately for world peace and global development. I hope that this encyclopedia will serve as a silent but capable ambassador from Japan to the peoples of the world.

May 1993

Noma Sawako
President, Kōdansha, Ltd

ADVISORY COMMITTEE

EDITORIAL STAFF

INTRODUCTION TO THE ENCYCLOPEDIA

In the course of the past decade Japan's power to affect the rest of our planet has grown at an astonishing rate. The global reach of Japanese industry and finance and the transformative impact of Japanese technology have been felt in almost every country. Yet Japan remains an enigma to most people, inspiring unease and distrust in addition to admiration and curiosity. In part this is because Japan has faced more formidable barriers to the export of its cultural, artistic, and intellectual accomplishments than it has to the products of its industries. Even today, the volume of information on Japan that reaches other countries is pitifully small in comparison to the rapidly increasing demand.

This book is an attempt to redress this imbalance. It is conceived as a single, comprehensive resource that will give the interested reader a key to unlocking the complex society of late-20th-century Japan. It contains a wealth of hard data on Japanese politics, government, economics, and corporate behavior, but it is also a treasury of Japanese art, culture, and history and a guide to the more subtle traditions that have shaped Japanese life and thought through the centuries. Our hope is that this encyclopedia will serve not only as a ready reference for those seeking specific information but also as an enjoyable and instructive tool for those who wish to add depth and perspective to their image of Japan and the Japanese.

Japan: An Illustrated Encyclopedia has its own history, of course, and a word here seems appropriate. This encyclopedia is based on the nine-volume *Kodansha Encyclopedia of Japan,* published in 1983. The nine-volume encyclopedia has been widely acknowledged as a landmark in English-language writing and scholarship on Japan, but the eventful decade that has passed since its publication seemed to demand a thorough updating and revision of its contents, as well as a new format and manner of presentation that would reach out to a broader audience of readers. The result is the book you hold in your hands.

In total number of words—two million—it is about half the size of its nine-volume predecessor, the product of a lengthy process of selection and condensation. Many entries have been rewritten in their entirety; all have been reviewed and revised when necessary; and hundreds of new entries have been added on contemporary subjects. The goal throughout has been to present the most current knowledge about Japan in as concise a form as possible.

There are many new features that distinguish the present encyclopedia from its predecessor, making it in many ways an entirely new work. These will be introduced below. Before proceeding, however, the editors of *Japan: An Illustrated Encyclopedia* wish to acknowledge the foundations of scholarship and prior editorial labor upon which we have built and express the hope that we have created a reference book on Japan that will prove as useful in the decade to come as the *Kodansha Encyclopedia of Japan* has been in the 10 years since its publication.

PRINCIPAL FEATURES OF THE ENCYCLOPEDIA

Main Text and Related Illustrations

The core of the encyclopedia is formed by more than 11,000 **main-text entries,** ranging in length from 50 words to more than 4,000. Arranged alphabetically, they cover every area of Japanese culture and society from prehistory to contemporary science and technology. These entries are the work of some 1,400 scholars and specialists from Japan and 27 other countries as well as an international editorial staff. Individual main-text entries in this encyclopedia are unsigned, but the names of all contributors are presented on pages 1913–1918.

These main-text entries are supplemented by more than 4,000 **illustrations,** most of them in full color. There are thousands of photographs and hundreds of drawings and paintings, diagrams, charts, graphs, tables, and maps. All of these are keyed by title to the entries they accompany and in almost all cases appear on the same page as the entry or on the facing page.

Pictorial Essays and Feature Articles

An entirely new aspect of this encyclopedia is the inclusion of nearly 100 special features keyed to selected main-text entries and appearing on nearby pages.

The **pictorial essays,** ranging from one to eight pages, provide readers with glimpses of aspects of Japanese life, history, society, and culture that seemed especially suited to an integrated visual presentation. Compiled by the editorial staff, many of these essays were shaped and guided by specialists who contributed their expertise and judgment and whose names appear at the end of the introductory texts.

The **feature articles,** each contained within a single double-page spread, are the work of dozens of writers and scholars who were invited by the editors to contribute signed articles that would provide more in-depth, interpretive, and personal treatments of particular facets of Japan than was possible in the main-text entries.

Rather than being arranged in alphabetical order, each pictorial essay or feature article is placed near the main-text entry to which it is most closely related. The link between the two is indicated by the appearance of the relevant main-text entry title at the top of each pictorial-essay or feature-article page and by a cross-reference at the end of the main-text entry. This cross-reference takes the form of an icon (☛ for pictorial essays and ▣▷ for feature articles) followed by the page numbers where these special features may be found. Readers should consult the **List of Pictorial Essays and Feature Articles** on pages xiv–xv for a complete guide to these parts of the book.

Navigational Aids

The alphabetical arrangement of the main text of this encyclopedia, together with the linking of special features to individual main-text entries, makes finding information on a specific subject quite easy—*if you know what you are looking for*. Yet there are times when it is difficult to guess what entry title might be used for a given subject of interest or to imagine the full range of articles addressing a particular topic that might be contained in the encyclopedia but scattered onto unrelated pages as a consequence of alphabetical ordering.

These problems, common to most modern reference works, are compounded in a book about Japan by the fact that many readers will be unfamiliar with various aspects of Japanese language, culture, and thought. With this in mind, we have provided several alternatives to aid the reader in locating information.

The first is the topical **Reader's Guide to the Encyclopedia** beginning on page xvi. The Reader's Guide divides the encyclopedia into seven major areas of knowledge and scores of subsidiary fields, arranging major articles according to subject and content. Look to the guide if you are interested in, say, Japanese architecture, but do not know where to begin in terms of finding specific items on this subject. The Reader's Guide is not a comprehensive list of all entries, but it does provide a highly structured overview of the contents of this book and the topics that it covers.

The encyclopedia's plentiful **cross-references** are a further aid to locating related articles on a particular subject. Within main-text entries, words in SMALL CAPITALS represent the title of a related (and relevant) entry. A second type of cross-reference is the entry-title cross-reference, which directs the reader from a variant entry title to the active entry title under which the text actually appears. There are about 1,000 of these entry-title cross-references throughout the book. (A more extensive discussion of cross-referencing is given below in the section on Editorial Conventions.)

In addition to these features, a **Bilingual Index of Entry Titles** has also been provided in the **Appendix** to the book. Every entry in the encyclopedia is listed here with the page on which it may be found. Cross-references are provided from the Japanese equivalents of all English entry titles and from the English equivalents for Japanese entry titles when appropriate.

Other Supplementary Materials

Heading the supplementary materials appearing in the **Appendix** to the encyclopedia is a detailed **Atlas of Japan**. Fourteen pages of full-color maps of the country's regions, natural features, and political and administrative units are accompanied by a comprehensive index of place names. Nearly 3,000 place names are represented in this atlas and its index, and many of them have also been assigned main-text entries.

Following the atlas is a 22-page **Chronology of Japanese History** listing major events in Japan's political, social, and cultural development. Major events in world history are listed in a separate parallel column for comparison and reference. In addition to providing a concise overview of the course of Japanese history, the chronology also functions by means of copious cross-references as a convenient guide to the history entries in the main text, as well as to entries in other fields such as international relations, literature, and religion. The main chronology is followed by a **Table of Japanese Era Names (Nengō)**.

For readers interested in pursuing a particular subject in greater depth and detail than this book can provide, **For Further Reading** is a useful point of departure. Compiled by a specialist in East Asian bibliography, this guide is a topical listing of over 700 books and periodicals representing the most accessible and up-to-date writing on Japan available in English, as well as English translations of Japanese literary and scholarly works.

EDITORIAL CONVENTIONS

The following section details the conventions adopted in editing this book, beginning with the ones that most affect the arrangement of the entries and the reader's efforts to locate information.

Entry Titles

The rule governing entry titles in this encyclopedia has been to use English whenever possible. Given the nature of the material, however, many titles are in romanized Japanese, including personal names, place names, and words with no exact or appropriate English equivalent. As an aid to readers and students of Japanese, each entry title is also given in Japanese characters (as it might appear in a Japanese reference book). In most cases, a romanization of this Japanese title appears in parentheses at the head of the entry. In cases in which the main entry is already in romanized Japanese, a parenthetical English translation has been given when appropriate.

Alphabetization

Main-text entry titles are arranged in alphabetical order on a letter-by-letter basis. All word breaks, punctuation, and diacritical marks such as macrons are ignored. As a consequence of this arrangement, entries on people with the same surname are not always grouped together. For example, MORI ARINORI and MORI SOSEN are separated by entries on MORIMOTO KAORU and MORINAGA & CO, LTD, among others. Nor are entries whose titles begin with the same English word necessarily grouped together: for example, JAPAN DEVELOPMENT BANK and JAPAN FEDERATION OF BAR ASSOCIATIONS are separated by a host of entries whose titles begin with the word "Japanese." Numbers and abbreviations are alphabetized as if they were spelled out, so that ST. ANDREW'S UNIVERSITY precedes SAIONJI FAMILY, and MARCH 15TH INCIDENT appears before MARCH INCIDENT. However, exceptions include entries referring to events of the same name distinguished only by date, which are arranged in chronological order. Thus EXPO '75 appears before EXPO '85.

For other factors affecting the alphabetical ordering of entries, please consult the following sections on Romanization and Personal Names.

Romanization

Japanese words are spelled in this encyclopedia according to the Hepburn system of romanization used in most English-language publications on Japan. Long vowels are indicated by macrons on all words, including well-known place names (Tōkyō, Ōsaka). The encyclopedia follows the older Hepburn practice of using *m* instead of *n* before *p, b,* or *m* (e.g., Shimbashi, not Shinbashi). An apostrophe is used to distinguish syllable-final *n* from *n* at the beginning of a syllable (e.g., *ken'in* "seal of approval" versus *kenin* "vassal"). The spelling of non-Japanese words that have been incorporated into Japanese reflects the way these words are pronounced by Japanese speakers.

Word division in romanized Japanese is problematic given the frequency with which individual words and characters combine to form compounds in Japanese. The principle followed in this encyclopedia is to divide words so as to make semantic and grammatical relationships clear, breaking down longer Japanese words and expressions into smaller units in a way that shows how the parts relate to one another. Occasionally, this results in an apparent inconsistency. One example is the word *shi* (history), which often appears in compound words: the compound *keizaishi* (economic history) is spelled as a single word, but the more complex compound *shihon shugi shi* (history of capitalism) is spelled as three words.

The five vowels of Japanese—*a, i, u, e, o*—are similar to those of Spanish or Italian. Long vowels are pronounced the same as short vowels but given approximately twice the duration. Consecutive vowels are pronounced as sequences of discrete vowels. Japanese consonants are similar to those in English, except that *g* is always hard, pronounced as in "go," never as in "gender," and the Japanese *r* is pronounced in a way that falls somewhere between the English *r* and *l* sounds.

In the main-text entries, Chinese words and names are given in the official *pinyin* system of romanization, followed in parentheses by the spelling in the Wade-Giles system or, for a handful of well-established place names, the old Chinese post office system spelling. A few personal names are given in the dialect spelling that has become established in English (e.g., Chiang Kai-shek, Sun Yat-sen). Chinese words appearing in photo captions, illustrations, pictorial essays, and feature articles are given solely in the *pinyin* spelling.

The system of romanization used for Korean is the McCune-Reischauer system. Sanskrit and Russian are transliterated in the systems most widely used in English-language scholarly publications.

Personal Names

In entry titles and throughout the rest of the encyclopedia, Japanese, Chinese, and Korean personal names are given surname first, the normal order used in those languages (e.g., Kawabata Yasunari rather than Yasunari Kawabata or Kawabata, Yasunari).

After their first appearance, most modern personages in this book are referred to by their surnames, in accordance with contemporary Japanese usage. Conventions of usage also dictate, however, the use of a pen name, sobriquet, or stage name for many literary or artistic figures (e.g., Sōseki for the writer Natsume Sōseki) and personal names for most premodern historical and cultural figures (e.g., Ieyasu for Tokugawa Ieyasu).

For ancient Japanese names, it is the policy of this encyclopedia to include the particle *no* in the names of persons born before 1193 (e.g., Fujiwara no Sadaie) and to omit it in all later names except when Japanese common usage includes it, as in Kamo no Mabuchi.

Cross-References

As noted above, two types of cross-references are provided in order to help the reader locate a given entry under its proper title.

Entry-title cross-references, some 1,000 of which appear among the regular entry titles in the same bold-faced type, use arrows to direct the reader to the appropriate active entries.

Cross-references of another sort are included within the entries themselves in the form of words set in SMALL CAPITALS to inform the reader that the encyclopedia contains an entry on the subject named. As a rule the words set in small capitals indicate the exact wording of the entry title, as in the sentence, "The family's fortunes were established by TOKUGAWA IEYASU, who founded the TOKUGAWA SHOGUNATE." Exceptions include Western personal names (for which only the surname is marked) and battles and treaties named after a place (for which only the place is marked). Thus, in the sentence, "He fought at the Battle of SEKIGAHARA," the cross-reference is to the entry SEKIGAHARA, BATTLE OF. These textual

cross-references are selective rather than all-inclusive; in other words, entry titles have not necessarily been set in small capitals every time they appear in the text.

Another type of cross-reference that has already been mentioned consists of the icons, followed by page numbers, that appear at the end of a main-text entry for which there is a corresponding pictorial essay or feature article. The same icon, accompanied by the main-text entry title, appears at the top of each special-feature page.

Dates

Dates prior to Japan's adoption of the Western calendar on 1 January 1873 have been converted from the old Japanese lunar civil calendar. Every effort has been made to give precise conversions, accounting for the discrepancy between the beginning of the year in the lunar calendar and that in the Western solar calendar. Thus the dates given in this encyclopedia will sometimes differ from those found in many other reference sources, both Japanese and Western, which frequently assign a date at the beginning or end of the lunar year to the wrong solar year. Occasionally, the lunar calendar equivalent, using an era name, may appear in parentheses after a Western date, as in 31 January 1703 (Genroku 15.12.15). In this example, the date in parentheses is the 15th day of the 12th month of the 15th year of Genroku. For information on the premodern Japanese calendrical system, see the main-text entry CALENDAR, DATES, AND TIME and the **Table of Japanese Era Names (Nengō)** on pages 1830–1831.

Money

Premodern measures of value are given in the monetary or nonmonetary units (e.g., measures of rice) in use at the time. No attempt has been made to give modern monetary equivalents for these units. The yen was established as Japan's official unit of currency in 1871. However, because of the great difference between the value of pre–World War II yen and the postwar yen, no dollar equivalents are given. Post-1945 yen values are followed by their US dollar equivalents, with the dollar figure based on the average exchange rate pertaining during the year or years in question. For information on the value of the postwar yen, including a table of exchange rates, see the main-text entry YEN.

Weights and Measures

Japan has used the metric system officially since 1959, and weights and measures are given in metric units throughout this book. In the main text, these are usually followed in parentheses by the US equivalents; in captions, illustrations, pictorial essays, and feature articles, the metric units stand alone. When traditional Japanese weights and measures are mentioned, they are given approximate metric equivalents. For a discussion and table of premodern units and their modern equivalents, see the main-text entry WEIGHTS AND MEASURES.

Population and Other Figures

Figures for the populations of Japanese prefectures, cities, towns, and villages are based on the official Japanese census of 1990. Other quantitative information is drawn from a variety of governmental and nongovernmental sources, and every effort has been made to provide the most current figures available. As a rule, charts, graphs, tables, and other presentations of statistical data include notes on their sources. Sales figures and other data for Japanese businesses and corporations are based primarily on information provided by the companies themselves.

Paleolithic	pre-10,000 BC
Jōmon	ca 10,000 BC–ca 300 BC
Yayoi	ca 300 BC–ca AD 300
Kofun	ca 300–710
Asuka	593–710
Nara	710–794
Heian	794–1185
Fujiwara	894–1185
Kamakura	1185–1333
Muromachi	1333–1568
Northern and Southern Courts	1337–1392
Sengoku	1467–1568
Azuchi-Momoyama	1568–1600
Edo	1600–1868
Meiji	1868–1912
Taishō	1912–1926
Shōwa	1926–1989
Heisei	1989–

a acre
AB Artium Baccalaureus, Bachelor of Arts
AD anno Domini, year of our Lord
AM ante meridiem, before noon
AM Artium Magister, Master of Arts
art. article
b born
BA Bachelor of Arts
BC before Christ
Bldg. Building
BS Bachelor of Science
bu bushel
C Centigrade
ca circa
cc cubic centimeter
cg centigram
Ch Chinese
chap. chapter
cm centimeter
Co Company
c/o care of
Corp. Corporation
cu cubic
d died
DC District of Columbia
Dept. Department
Dr Doctor
E east
ed editor(s), edited
e.g. *exempli gratia*, for example
Eng English
et al *et alii*, and others
etc *et cetera*
F Fahrenheit
fl *floruit*, flourished
fl oz fluid ounce
ft foot

g, gm gram
gal gallon
gr grain
ha hectare
i.e. *id est*, that is
in inch
Inc Incorporated
Inst. Institute
Int'l International
J Japanese
Jr Junior
kg kilogram
KK Kabushiki Kaisha, joint-stock company
kl kiloliter
km kilometer
Kor Korean
l liter
lat latitude
lb pound
long longitude
Ltd Limited
m meter
MA Master of Arts
Met. Metropolitan
Mfg Manufacturing
mg milligram
mi mile
ml milliliter
mm millimeter
Mt. Mount, Mountain
N north
NE northeast
no. number
NW northwest
oz ounce
p page
para. paragraph

PhD Philosophiae Doctor, Doctor of Philosophy
pk peck
PM post meridiem, afternoon
pop population
Port Portuguese
pp pages
Pref. Prefecture
pt pint, part
pt. part (of legal documents, laws, etc)
qt quart
r reigned
repr reprinted
rev ed revised edition
S south
SE southeast
ser series
Skt Sanskrit
sq cm square centimeter
sq ft square foot
sq in square inch
sq km square kilometer
sq m square meter
sq mi square mile
sq yd square yard
Sr Senior
St. Street, Saint
supp. supplement
SW southwest
Tbsp tablespoon
Tel. telephone
tr translator, translated
trad traditionally
tsp teaspoon
v versus
vol volume
W west
yd yard

LIST OF PICTORIAL ESSAYS AND FEATURE ARTICLES

PICTORIAL ESSAYS

▶ **FEATURE ARTICLES**

READER'S GUIDE
TO THE ENCYCLOPEDIA

The Reader's Guide is intended as an aid to the reader who wants a more integrated approach to the information contained in this book. It divides the encyclopedia into seven major areas of knowledge and scores of subsidiary fields, arranging a selected number of the entries according to subject and content. The Reader's Guide is not a comprehensive list of all entries, but it provides a highly structured overview of the contents of the encyclopedia and may be used as a study guide as well as a topical index.

Listed below are seven major subject areas and the fields they incorporate. In the pages that follow, these are further subdivided into various topical groupings which list actual main-text entry titles. All topical headings and subheadings are set in bold; actual entry titles appear in plain type. Icons appear beside

entry titles that are accompanied by a pictorial essay (☞) or feature article (▶). See the Introduction to the Encyclopedia for a discussion of these features.

Within the various topical groups, entries are ordered in several different ways. Many groups are arranged alphabetically or by some other explicitly stated criterion (such as chronological order, population, size, etc). The remainder are organized more subjectively, according to the editors' sense of their interrelationship or relative importance. For further exploration of a subject, the reader is advised to consult the numerous cross-references contained within the individual main-text entries listed in this guide.

1. Japan's Natural Setting
- Geography
- Plants and Animals
- Environment

2. History of Japan
- An Overview of Japanese History
- Prehistory and Archaeology
- Early History (593–1185)
- Medieval History (1185–1600)
- Edo Period (1600–1868)
- Meiji Period (1868–1912)
- Taishō and Early Shōwa Periods (1912–1945)
- Late Shōwa and Heisei Periods (1945–Present)

3. Society
- Government and Politics
- Law
- International Relations
- Military
- Mass Communications
- Education
- Social Structure and Social Relations

4. Economy
- An Overview of the Japanese Economy
- Government and the Economy
- Industry
- Finance
- Agriculture and Fishery
- Transportation
- Corporate Management
- Labor and Labor Unions
- International Economic Relations

5. Science and Technology
- Science
- Technology and Engineering
- Medicine

6. Culture
- Folklore
- Philosophy and Thought
- Religion
- Literature
- Language
- Fine Arts
- Architecture
- Performing Arts

7. Daily Life
- Manners and Customs
- Clothing and Fashion
- Food
- Housing
- Leisure

1. Japan's Natural Setting

■GEOGRAPHY

2. History of Japan

3. Society

4. Economy

5. Science and Technology

6. Culture

Some 85 entries on individual temples can be found in the encyclopedia.

xxxiii

7. Daily Life

■ MANNERS AND CUSTOMS

▶ Etiquette

See also under Ceremonies, Customs, and Practices, p. xxviii.

JAPAN
An Illustrated Encyclopedia

A

abacus 算盤

(*soroban*). Traditional manual calculator. The abacus was introduced to Japan from China in the 16th century, and by the mid-17th century it had become an important tool in commerce and finance. Abacus arithmetic (*shuzan*) was, with reading and writing, a central element in traditional education, and was made a part of the official school curriculum in 1926.

The typical Japanese abacus has a rectangular frame containing either 23 or 27 parallel vertical rods divided by a crossbar into two sections. The upper section of each rod has one bead and the lower section four beads, which are manipulated as counters. Rods to the left of a point chosen by the operator designate units, 10s, 100s, and so forth, while rods to the right of the point indicate decimal places. Skilled abacus users can carry out fairly complex computations at high speeds. The Japanese believe that learning the abacus develops children's abilities to handle figures, and there are special schools (JUKU) for instruction in its use. Nowadays electronic calculators are widely used in Japan, but some people, both on the job and in the home, still prefer to do their figuring on an abacus.

abalones 鮑

(*awabi*). *Awabi* is the common name for large marine snails of the family Haliotidae, class Gastropoda. Ten species of *awabi* are distributed in the coastal waters of Japan. Of these, three large species, namely the *madakaawabi* (giant abalone or *madaka* abalone; *Haliotis gigantea*), *megaiawabi* (*megai* abalone; *H. sieboldii*), and *kuroawabi* (Japanese abalone; *H. discus*), are important to Japan's fishing industry. The first two species occur in the warm current regions of Japan and the Korean peninsula. Some giant abalones attain a shell length of 30 centimeters (12 in). The *kuroawabi* has an exceptionally wide breeding distribution, extending as far as the coast of the Shandong (Shantung) Peninsula. The small *tokobushi* (*H. aquatilis*) is a common edible species found in the warm currents of Japan. Abalones are now actively cultivated.

The Japanese have known the abalone since ancient times. Judging from Jōmon-period (ca 10,000 BC–ca 300 BC) archaeological remains and shell mounds, prehistoric man in Japan ate abalone and utilized its shell for various purposes. It has long been an auspicious symbol when used as NOSHI, which were originally flattened, dried strips of the flesh fastened to offerings to the gods. Today abalone is eaten boiled or as *mizugai*, raw with a dip.

Abashiri 網走[市]

City in northeastern Hokkaidō on the coast of the Sea of Okhotsk. Abashiri has been a flourishing fishing port since the beginning of the 19th century. The harbor is closed every winter from January to March because of ice floes. Its principal industries are food processing, dairy farming, and lumber. The main agricultural products are potatoes, legumes, and beets. Part of the city is situated within Abashiri Quasi-National Park, the location of the MOYORO SHELL MOUND, a Jōmon-period (ca 10,000 BC–ca 300 BC) archaeological site. There is a maximum security prison here. Pop: 44,416.

Abashirigawa 網走川

River that originates at the Sempoku Pass north of Lake AKAN in eastern Hokkaidō and flows to the northeast, emptying into the Sea of Okhotsk. There is virgin forestland along the upper reaches. Lake ABASHIRI on the lower reaches acts to regulate the water flow. Length: 169 km (105 mi). Area of drainage basin: 1,380 sq km (533 sq mi).

Abashiri, Lake 網走湖

(Abashiriko). Brackish lake in the city of Abashiri, northeastern Hokkaidō. Pond smelt are the principal catch. Area: 34 sq km (13 sq mi); circumference: 42 km (26 mi); depth: 16 m (52 ft).

Abe Akira 阿部昭

(1934–89). Author. Born in Hiroshima Prefecture; graduate of Tōkyō University. He worked in radio and television production until he became a full-time professional writer in 1971. Abe wrote in the tradition of the I-NOVEL (*watakushi shōsetsu*). Two of his highly regarded works are *Miseinen* (1968, The Adolescent), a collection of short stories, and *Shirei no kyūka* (1970, Commander on Leave), his first major novel.

Abe family 阿倍氏・安倍氏

(Abeshi). 1. Influential family (UJI) of ancient Japan, based in Yamato Province (now Nara Prefecture). The chronicle NIHON SHOKI (720) and the 9th-century genealogy SHINSEN SHŌJIROKU claim, improbably, the family's descent from the legendary 8th emperor Kōgen. Both the general ABE NO HIRAFU and the poet ABE NO NAKAMARO are said to have descended from this famous family.

2. A family claiming descent from a certain Abi (the pronunciation later changed to Abe), elder brother of the chieftain Nagasunehiko, who resisted the conquest of Yamato by the legendary emperor JIMMU. The family achieved great power in northern Honshū by the mid-Heian period (794–1185). See ABE NO YORITOKI; EARLIER NINE YEARS' WAR; LATER THREE YEARS' WAR.

Abe Isoo 安部磯雄

(1865–1949). Socialist and Christian educator; member of the Meiji-period (1868–1912) group who were led to socialism through Christianity. Born in the Fukuoka domain (now Fukuoka Prefecture), he graduated from Dōshisha University (Kyōto), where he became a Christian under the influence of NIIJIMA JŌ. He studied in the United States from 1891 to 1894. With KATAYAMA SEN, KŌTOKU SHŪSUI, and Murai Tomoyoshi (1861–1944), he founded the SHAKAI SHUGI KENKYŪKAI (Society for the Study of Socialism) in 1898. This organization was parent to the SHAKAI MINSHUTŌ (Socialist Democratic Party), formed in 1901. In 1899 he became a professor at Waseda University.

Abe opposed the Russo-Japanese War (1904–05) and voiced his opinions through publication and other activities. He published the magazine *Shin kigen* (New Era) in 1905 with KINOSHITA NAOE and ISHIKAWA SANSHIRŌ and helped to revive the newspaper HEIMIN SHIMBUN in 1907. However, after the arrest and execution of Kōtoku Shūsui for an alleged plot to assassinate the emperor Meiji (see HIGH TREASON INCIDENT OF 1910), he disassociated himself from those radicals advocating violent action to overthrow the state and joined the more moderate elements of the socialist and labor movements. In 1924 Abe was a founder of the Japan Fabian Society. He also formed the Seijigaku Kenkyūkai (Political Study Association) with such socialist leaders as ŌYAMA IKUO and

KAGAWA TOYOHIKO. In 1926 Abe helped organize the moderate SHAKAI MINSHŪTŌ (Socialist People's Party). He was elected to the Diet in 1928. In 1932, with ASŌ HISASHI and others, he formed the SHAKAI TAISHŪTŌ (Socialist Masses Party). In 1940 he and others resigned to form the Kinrō Kokumintō (Nationalist Labor Party). After World War II, he served as an adviser to the JAPAN SOCIALIST PARTY.

Abe Jirō 阿部次郎

(1883–1959). Philosopher, critic, and educator. Born in Yamagata Prefecture; graduate of Tōkyō University. In 1923 he became professor of aesthetics at Tōhoku University in Sendai. Abe was much influenced by German idealism and introduced Neo-Kantian philosophy to Japan. An important early work is *Santarō no nikki* (1914–15, Santarō's Diary). He founded the Nihon Bunka Kenkyūjo (Japanese Culture Research Institute).

Abekawa 安倍川

Also known as Abegawa. River in Shizuoka Prefecture, central Honshū, originating in the Minobu Mountains and flowing south through the Shizuoka Plain to the city of Shizuoka, where it flows into Suruga Bay. There are numerous landslides at the riverhead. Hot springs are found on the upper reaches. The river is the main source of water for irrigating the fertile Shizuoka Plain. Length: 51 km (32 mi); area of drainage basin: 567 sq km (219 sq mi).

Abe Kōbō 安部公房

(1924–93). Novelist and playwright. Real name Abe Kimifusa. Abe was one of the best-known Japanese literary personalities in the second half of the 20th century.

Abe was born in Tōkyō but grew up in Manchuria, where his father was a physician. The concept of the *furusato* (hometown), so prominent in the writings of many Japanese authors, seemed to have no place in Abe's fiction. "I am," said Abe, "a man without a hometown," a sentiment that finds expression in the barren landscapes and deracinated figures that appear in his fiction. In 1943 he enrolled at Tōkyō University as a medical student. Although Abe found his studies uninspiring, he later incorporated his medical knowledge into his writing, particularly works of science fiction such as *Daiyon kampyōki* (1959; tr *Inter Ice Age 4*, 1970). Abe married while still a student. His wife, Machi, an accomplished artist and stage designer, provided illustrations for many of his works.

Abe's singular style of writing, distinguished by its peculiar characters, absurd plots, and abstract settings, won acclaim in 1951 when he received the Akutagawa Prize for "Kabe—S. Karuma shi no hanzai" (1951; partial tr "The Crime of S. Karma," 1991), one of Abe's many Kafka-inspired works. Alienation and loss of identity are central to almost all of his fiction. *Tanin no kao* (1964; tr *The Face of Another*, 1966) describes a scientist who, badly disfigured by a laboratory explosion, finds himself estranged from society. Fashioning a mask to conceal his scars, he creates a new identity. Abe gave special attention to the problem of identity as it relates to the urban environment. The city, as in *Moetsukita chizu* (1967; tr *The Ruined Map*, 1969), often appears as a labyrinth in which characters are reduced to mere objects in the metropolitan agglomeration. In SUNA

NO ONNA (1962; tr *The Woman in the Dunes*, 1964) and *Hako otoko* (1973; tr *The Box Man*, 1974) characters escape from the stultifying urban scene. The protagonist of *Hako otoko*, a novel of the absurd, takes up residence in a box that provides anonymity and a sense of liberation denied in everyday life.

Abe's 1984 novel *Hakobune sakura maru* (tr *The Ark Sakura*, 1988) continues in the absurdist vein. In this novel, a character named Mole has built a vast underground complex, the so-called ark, that will serve as a shelter in case of nuclear war. A confusing maze of underground tunnels and a collection of bizarre characters mark this novel as a product of Abe's distinctive imagination.

Over the years, Abe was an active playwright, creating such works as *Omae ni mo tsumi ga aru* (1965; tr *You, Too, Are Guilty*, 1979) and *Tomodachi* (1967; tr *Friends*, 1969). His plays, like his novels and short stories, have an allegorical feel. Abe formed his own theater group in 1973 and staged productions of his plays. He also wrote for radio, television, and cinema.

Abe Masahiro 阿部正弘

(1819–57). *Daimyō* of the Fukuyama domain (now part of Hiroshima Prefecture) and senior councillor (*rōjū*) of the Tokugawa shogunate from 1843 to 1857. As chief senior councillor (*rōjū shuseki*) from 1845 to 1855, he was responsible for the shogunate's drastic change in diplomatic policy toward Western nations. When Commodore Matthew PERRY arrived in 1853, demanding that Japan end its policy of seclusion, Abe took the unprecedented step of soliciting opinions from the daimyō and other officials, Confucian scholars, and even the imperial court. Without receiving clear answers, he established a dangerous precedent by allowing others to participate in the shogunate's decision-making process.

Under pressure from Perry, he concluded a treaty of friendship with the United States (see KANAGAWA TREATY). Similar pacts with Great Britain, Russia, and the Netherlands followed shortly. Abe's policy was attacked by TOKUGAWA NARIAKI and others who thought the shogunate should attempt to "expel the barbarians." His domestic policies also met opposition, notably from II NAOSUKE. Although Abe resigned his position as chief senior councillor in 1855, he remained influential within the shogunate until his death.

Abe Nobuyuki 阿部信行

(1875–1953). General and politician; prime minister (1939–40). Born in Ishikawa Prefecture, he graduated from the Army Academy and the Army War College. Abe served as chief of the Military Affairs Bureau (Gummukyoku) and army vice-minister before being appointed minister of state in 1930 to carry out the duties of ailing war minister UGAKI KAZUSHIGE. In 1939 he formed a cabinet after the resignation of HIRANUMA KIICHIRŌ. Abe sought to end the SINO-JAPANESE WAR OF

1937–1945 and to maintain neutrality in the European conflict. Unsupported by the political parties and the military, he resigned in January 1940. Three months later he was sent to Nanjing (Nanking) to advise the puppet regime of WANG JINGWEI (Wang Ching-wei) to negotiate a treaty ensuring Japan's military and economic rights in occupied China. He was appointed governor-general of Korea in 1944. After World War II, Abe was listed as a war criminal but was never indicted.

Abe no Hirafu 阿倍比羅夫

(fl mid-7th century). General of the Yamato court. The chronicle NIHON SHOKI (720) records that during the reign of Empress SAIMEI, Abe was sent on three occasions between 658 and 660 to subdue the EZO tribesmen of northern Japan. Some scholars believe that he may have gone as far north as present-day Hokkaidō. In 663, during the reign of Emperor TENJI, Abe led an expeditionary force to defend the Korean kingdom of PAEKCHE from conquest by its neighbor SILLA. The Japanese were routed, however, by the combined forces of Silla and the Chinese Tang (T'ang) dynasty in the naval battle of HAKUSUKINOE. Abe was later appointed commander of DAZAIFU, the military headquarters in Kyūshū, in anticipation of a retaliatory invasion from the continent.

Abe no Munetō 安倍宗任

(fl mid-11th century). Warrior of Mutsu Province (now Aomori, Iwate, Miyagi, and Fukushima prefectures); son of ABE NO YORITOKI and younger brother of ABE NO SADATŌ. During the EARLIER NINE YEARS' WAR (1051–62), Munetō defeated the forces of the court in the Battle of Torinomi Palisade (1057) but surrendered in 1062 after Sadatō was killed. Munetō was exiled to Iyo Province (now Ehime Prefecture) in 1064 and later to Dazaifu in Chikuzen Province (now part of Fukuoka Prefecture).

Abe no Nakamaro 阿倍仲麻呂

(698–770). Poet and Chinese government official. In 717, with KIBI NO MAKIBI and the priest GEMBŌ, he accompanied a Japanese embassy to Tang (T'ang) China. He remained in the Chinese capital, Chang'an (Ch'ang-an), where he took a Chinese name and accepted an official post. He also established a literary reputation and was befriended by such poets as Li Bo (Li Po; 701–763) and Wang Wei (701–761). In 753 he attempted to return to Japan with the embassy of FUJIWARA NO KIYOKAWA but was prevented by shipwreck. He eventually became governor-general of Vietnam (then under Chinese control). He died in Chang'an after 54 years' absence from home. In Japan, Nakamaro is best re-

Abe Kōbō Many of the works by this prolific novelist and playwright, such as *The Woman in the Dunes*, are written in a surreal and absurdist vein.

Aburatsubo The name of this Miura Peninsula resort area translates as "oil bottle," a reference to the shape of the coastline and the bay's calm waters.

membered for a WAKA poem, included in the anthology HYAKUNIN ISSHU, that expresses his longing for his native land.

Abe no Sadatō 安倍貞任

(1019–62). Magnate in Mutsu Province (now Aomori, Iwate, Miyagi, and Fukushima prefectures). With his father, ABE NO YORITOKI, he fought against the court in the EARLIER NINE YEARS' WAR (1051–62). In the Battle of Kinomi (1057) Sadatō destroyed the forces of Minamoto no Yoriyoshi (988–1075), but in 1062 Yoriyoshi defeated and killed him at Kuriyagawa Palisade.

Abe no Yoritoki 安倍頼時

(?–1057). Magnate in Mutsu Province (now Aomori, Iwate, Miyagi, and Fukushima prefectures); father of ABE NO SADATŌ and ABE NO MUNETŌ. The Abe were local commanders in charge of aborigines (the so-called *fushū*) who had submitted to the court. By Yoritoki's time the family controlled six districts of Mutsu. He invaded neighboring territories and refused to pay taxes to the central government. In 1051 the court dispatched Minamoto no Yoriyoshi (988–1075) and his son MINAMOTO NO YOSHIIE to suppress him in the campaign known as the EARLIER NINE YEARS' WAR (1051–62). Yoritoki was killed in the Battle of Torinomi Palisade in 1057; however, his sons continued their resistance for another five years.

Abe Shigetaka 阿部重孝

(1890–1939). Educator. Born in Niigata Prefecture, he graduated from Tōkyō University and was a professor there from 1934. Abe introduced empirical, statistical methods in educational research to Japan. He used American methods in his extensive research and proposed various educational reforms. Among his works is *Kyōiku kaikaku ron* (1937, Educational Reform).

Abe Shinnosuke 阿部真之助

(1884–1964). Newspaperman and critic. Born in Saitama Prefecture. After graduation from Tōkyō University he was employed by the *Manshū nichinichi shimbun*, a Japanese-language daily published in Manchuria. He became chief editor and director of the *Ōsaka mainichi shimbun* (later the MAINICHI SHIMBUN), gaining popularity for his critical sketches of statesmen. He acted as chairman of the board of Nippon Hōsō Kyōkai (NHK; Japan Broadcasting Corporation) from 1960 until his death.

Abe Shōō 阿部将翁

(?–1753). Specialist in *honzōgaku* (traditional pharmacognosy), who traveled around Japan collecting animal, plant, and mineral specimens of medicinal value. Born in Morioka (now in Iwate Prefecture). He first studied medicine and later pharmacognosy. He collected medicinal materials by order of the Tokugawa shogunate and advised local districts about the cultivation of sugarcane,

cotton, and other crops. He also cultivated medicinal plants in Edo (now Tōkyō).

Abe Tadaaki 阿部忠秋

(1602–75). *Daimyō* of the Edo period (1600–1868). Tadaaki entered the service of TOKUGAWA IEMITSU as a child. In 1633 he was appointed RŌJŪ (senior councillor). In 1639 he was named daimyō of Oshi Castle in northern Musashi Province (now Saitama Prefecture). Known for his integrity and administrative skill, he devised a plan for useful employment of *rōnin* (masterless *samurai*) after the KEIAN INCIDENT of 1651.

Abe Tomoji 阿部知二

(1903–73). Novelist, critic, and translator. Born in Okayama Prefecture; studied English literature at Tōkyō University. He associated with such writers as FUNAHASHI SEIICHI, IBUSE MASUJI, and KITAGAWA FUYUHIKO. His first book, *Koi to Afurika* (1930), was a collection of short stories. With *Shuchiteki bungakuron* (1930, On Subjective Literary Criticism), Abe emerged as one of the strongest opponents of the PROLETARIAN LITERATURE MOVEMENT. His major novel, *Fuyu no yado* (1936), depicts Japanese intellectuals as suffering from skepticism and unable to deal with the looming threat of militarism. After World War II, he wrote liberal political novels and translated works by Byron, Shakespeare, Melville, the Brontës, and Austen.

Abe Yoshishige 安倍能成

(1883–1966). Philosopher and educator. Born in Ehime Prefecture, Abe studied philosophy at Tōkyō University. Early in his career he became a disciple of NATSUME SŌSEKI and wrote literary criticism from an idealist point of view. He introduced Kantian philosophy to Japan. After two years of study at the University of Heidelberg, Germany, he became a professor at Keijō University in Seoul in 1926. He became principal of the First Higher School in Tōkyō in 1940, maintaining his liberal educational policies even under wartime conditions.

After World War II, Abe served briefly as minister of education in the SHIDEHARA KIJŪRŌ cabinet. He was a leading figure in the various postwar educational reforms. He urgently requested the US Education Mission to Japan not to enforce any policies disregarding Japan's traditions and circumstances. In 1947 Abe became head of the Peers' School (see GAKUSHŪIN UNIVERSITY) and served in that capacity for almost 20 years.

Abiko 我孫子[市]

City in northwestern Chiba Prefecture, central Honshū, located between the river TONEGAWA and the marshland known as TEGANUMA. Abiko developed as a post-station town on the Mito Kaidō, a highway that connected Edo (now Tōkyō) and Mito. It is now a satellite city of Tōkyō, with some horticulture, mainly flowers. Pop: 120,628.

Abō Pass 安房峠

(Abō Tōge). Located on the border between Nagano and Gifu prefectures, central Honshū. A bus road through Abō Pass is a major tourist route in this area famous for its rugged mountain scenery. The HIRAYU HOT SPRING is found at the western end. The pass lies within the Chūbu Sangaku National Park. Altitude: 1,812 m (5,945 ft).

abortion 人工妊娠中絶

(*jinkō ninshin chūzetsu*). Abortion was illegal in Japan until the EUGENIC PROTECTION LAW of 1948, which legalized the termination of a

pregnancy for medical, eugenic, economic, or ethical reasons. Although the Penal Code still carries a penalty for the performance of an illegal abortion, the terms of the Eugenic Protection Law have, in effect, allowed abortion on demand whenever, in the opinion of any doctor, there is concern that childbirth or pregnancy would substantially endanger the mother either physically or economically.

Under the law, abortions are performed by designated physicians whose competence has been reviewed by prefectural branches of the Japan Medical Association. Reported abortions increased rapidly after 1949, reaching a peak of 1,170,143 in 1955. The annual number then gradually decreased, falling to 466,876 in 1989. A proposed amendment to the Eugenic Protection Law that would have eliminated economic reasons as a justification for abortion was rejected by the Diet. See also FAMILY PLANNING.

Abugawa 阿武川

River in Yamaguchi and Shimane prefectures, western Honshū, flowing from the Abu Mountains to the Sea of Japan at the city of Hagi. It has been harnessed for electric power by the Abugawa Dam at the village of Kawakami. The area surrounding the gorge called CHŌMONKYŌ, a 12-km (7-mi) stretch of spectacular precipices and crags in the middle reaches of the river, is a prefectural natural park. Length: 82 km (51 mi).

Abukumagawa 阿武隈川

River in Fukushima and Miyagi prefectures, northern Honshū, flowing north from the volcano Kasshizan to the Pacific Ocean at Sendai Bay. It passes between the Abukuma and the Ōu mountains and through the cities of Kōriyama and Fukushima. It is the second longest river in the Tōhoku region, the longest being the Kitakamigawa. Length: 239 km (148 mi); area of drainage basin: 5,400 sq km (2,084 sq mi).

Abukuma Mountains 阿武隈山地

(Abukuma Sanchi). A range of mountains running north to south mainly in eastern Fukushima Prefecture, northern Honshū. The mountains are an elevated peneplain with an average height of 300–500 m (1,000–1,600 ft). The highest peak is Ōtakineyama (1,193 m; 3,914 ft), a monadnock.

Aburatsubo 油壺

Resort area in the city of MIURA, western Miura Peninsula, eastern Kanagawa Prefecture, central Honshū. Aburatsubo has a yacht harbor, swimming areas, an aquarium, and the Marine Biological Station of Tōkyō University.

abuse of right 権利濫用

(*kenri ran'yō*). The exercise of rights by a property owner beyond reasonable social limits. In 1947 the Civil Code was amended to establish that individual rights shall yield to the PUBLIC WELFARE (art. 1[1]), that rights and duties shall be exercised in accordance with the principles of fidelity and good faith (art. 1[2]), and that abuse of right shall be prohibited (art. 1[3]). The theory of the prohibition of abuses of rights, however, had been acknowledged judicially and academically since the 1920s, when it became clear that the 19th-century theory of the free exercise of rights could not be applied to the differing social conditions of the 20th century.

Abuses of rights may become tortious behavior toward another person. For example, if an owner of land significantly cuts off the sunlight from a neighbor's house by constructing a building, it has been held by the court that even where there is no statutory illegality, the landowner will bear liability for compensation for damages to the party whose sunlight has been blocked. See also OWNERSHIP RIGHTS; PROPERTY RIGHTS.

Abutsu Ni 阿仏尼

(?–1283; Abutsu the Nun). WAKA poet and author of the poetic travel diary IZAYOI NIKKI (Diary of the Waning Moon). She served as lady-in-waiting to the princess later known as former empress Anka Mon'in. Abutsu Ni was known variously as Anka Mon'in no Shijō and Anka Mon'in Emon no Suke. Around 1250 she became the secondary wife of FUJIWARA NO TAMEIE. Tameie was the son of FUJIWARA NO SADAIE (Fujiwara no Teika) and head of the foremost poetic family at court. She became a nun upon the death of her husband in 1275. She also wrote *Yoru no tsuru* (The Night Crane) and is generally accepted as the author of *Utatane no ki* (Record of a Nap).

academic degrees 学位

(*gakui*). The 1953 Ministry of Education ordinance on academic degrees officially established only the master's degree (*shūshi*) and doctor's degree (*hakushi*) as legitimate academic degrees. It made no provision for the bachelor's degree (*gakushi*), which in Japan is not a formally recognized degree.

The academic degree system was instituted by the Academic Degree Order (Gakuirei) of 1887. Prior to World War II, the doctorate was the only degree conferred and was awarded by the minister of education. The master's degree was instituted as part of the educational reform that followed World War II. It is awarded to those who have completed an integrated course of study at an advanced level and generally requires two years of research work beyond university graduation. The doctor's degree is awarded to those who have completed academic course work at the highest level, usually involving extensive research and the presentation of a thesis. See also GRADUATE SCHOOLS.

academic freedom 学問の自由

(*gakumon no jiyū*). Civil right guaranteed by article 23 of the 1947 CONSTITUTION OF JAPAN. It refers to the freedom of academicians to engage in research and present their findings. It also provides the right to teach one's beliefs and to disagree with established views or government authorities. Academic freedom is unique to institutions of higher learning and thus is accorded only to those within such institutions. Academic freedom was not mentioned in the Meiji Constitution of 1889, and it was always under the threat of interference by the government, particularly in the 1930s. Since World War II, this newly acquired constitutional right, along with the expansion of UNIVERSITY AUTONOMY, has provided scholars with unprecedented freedom of academic activity. Widespread student movements in the late 1960s expanded the rights of students to academic freedom and participation in university decision making.

accent in the Japanese language
日本語のアクセント

(*nihongo no akusento*). In Japanese the system of accent (phonetic characteristics that give prominence to one syllable of a word or phrase) is one of pitch accent: words are differentiated with regard to the place where pitch drops.

Accent in the Modern Standard Language—The Japanese words for "oyster," "fence," and "persimmon" are identical as far as their consonants and vowels are concerned but differ in pitch: *káki ga, kakí ga, kakí gá* (given here with the case marker *ga*). The acute accent here indicates high pitch: the vowels so marked are higher in pitch than the unmarked vowels by a small but perceptible amount, ranging from a semitone to a major third. Not all combinations of high and low pitch are possible; for example, no word has a high-low-high melody. The place, if any, at which pitch drops determines which syllables are high pitched and which low pitched: the syllables are high pitched up to the drop in pitch, if any, and low thereafter, except that the first syllable is low if the second is high.

Modern Japanese has both short and long syllables. A short syllable consists of either a short vowel alone or a consonant plus a short vowel; thus the word *atama'*, "head," consists of three short syllables. A long syllable consists of either a long vowel, a diphthong, or a syllable-final consonant (either a nasal, as in *sense'i*, "teacher," or the onset of a double consonant, as in *gappei*, "merger").

Both the syllable and the mora (a unit of relative meter like a beat in music) play roles in the Japanese accent system. A short syllable contains one mora; a long syllable contains two. The syllable is the unit that bears the accent, the mora the unit in which length and distance are measured. These roles of syllable and mora are illustrated in the rule for accent in recent loanwords: put accent on the syllable containing the third from last mora, e.g., *sokura'tesu*, "Socrates"; *poke'tto*, "pocket"; *washi'nton*, "Washington."

The various parts of speech differ with regard to the range of accentual distinctions they allow. Nouns exhibit the maximum possible range of accentual distinctions. Verbs and adjectives show only a two-way accent distinction: if a verb or adjective root contributes an accent, the place of that accent is predictable. Derived verb forms share the accentedness or unaccentedness of the basic verb, although the accent will necessarily be on a different syllable.

Superimposed on the Japanese accentual system is an intonational system that can make certain Japanese speech melodies liable to misinterpretation by nonnative speakers. For example, in Japanese a fall in pitch followed by a rise on the final syllable is simply an accent combined with the question intonation, but the melody is often identical with the English intonation that conveys irritation.

Accent is the domain in which Japanese dialects show the greatest diversity. It is also the domain in which Japanese dialects have been studied in the most detail. Strong evidence exists that the various dialects are descendants of a common ancestral language. The ancestral Japanese accentual system is thought by some scholars to be similar to that recorded in the RUIJU MYŌGI SHŌ, an extensive word list compiled in Kyōto in approximately 1100.

accounting for business enterprises 企業会計

(*kigyō kaikei*). Accounting in Japan, which is based largely on procedures required by law, can be divided into accounting for business enterprises (also called financial accounting) and TAX ACCOUNTING. Accounting for business enterprises falls under two jurisdictions: the accounting laws and regulations defined in the Commercial Code (Shō Hō), and those defined in the Securities Exchange Law (Shōken Torihiki Hō).

Commercial Code accounting provides for accountability of company management to stockholders and creditors through the confirmation and approval of financial statements at the general stockholders' meeting. Laws and regulations covering accounting requirements under the Commercial Code include laws for special exceptions to the Commercial Code for corporate audits and regulations concerning the format and preparation methods of financial statements such as the balance sheet, income statement, and supplementary schedules. An audit of the financial statements is required by one or more statutory auditors elected by the stockholders. In addition, an independent audit by a certified public accountant or audit corporation is required for corporations with capital stock of ¥500 million (US $3.6 million) or more, or debt of ¥20 billion (US $142.0 million) or more.

Accounting under the Commercial Code was at one time based on balance-sheet-oriented accounting principles with the objective of protection of creditors. However, through several revisions that took place after World War II, profit-and-loss-oriented accounting principles have been added with the objective of protection of stockholders. Balance-sheet-oriented accounting is primarily concerned with revealing the status of company assets and liabilities. The balance sheet compares assets, which show ownership claims, with liabilities to be repaid and stockholders' equity. The balance sheet can be characterized as the statement that shows the company's financial condition.

In contrast, profit-and-loss-oriented accounting emphasizes the assessment of periodic income in order to measure the company's earning power in response to concerns of stockholders about the company's operating results. Here the income statement is considered the primary financial statement, while the balance sheet is used as a tool for measuring asset and liability changes.

While elements of balance-sheet-oriented accounting remain in Commercial Code accounting to a certain extent, a significant number of regulations have been introduced covering accounting methods in accord with profit-and-loss-oriented principles. Examples of the former include regulations concerning accumulation of legal reserves appropriated from retained earnings (Commercial Code, art. 288) and regulations specifying the way legal reserves can be used (art. 289). Examples of profit-and-loss-oriented principles include regulations concerning deferral accounting, such as deferring of organization costs (art. 286) and deferring of preparation costs for starting a business (art. 286-2), and regulations concerning reserves and accruals (art. 287-2). Consideration has also been given in provisions relating to accounting under the Commercial Code to reconciling the need for protecting creditors with that for protecting stockholders. This can be seen in regulations concerning methods for amortization of deferred charges (art. 286-3) and those concerning calculation of retained earnings available for dividends (art. 290).

acupuncture
1 Acupuncture needles in place for treatment of a gastric disorder. The needles transmit heat from the infrared lamp at left into the patient's body.
2 Needles used for acupuncture treatment. These examples are 0.1 to 0.3 mm in diameter and 3 to 9 cm in length.

Only the major aspects of financial accounting are provided in the Commercial Code. For points not covered in these regulations, accounting methods are to comply with generally accepted accounting principles (art. 32[2]).

The primary purpose of the accounting provisions of the Securities Exchange Law is to promote protection of investors by insuring fairness in the issuing, buying, and selling of securities. Companies subject to the Securities Exchange Law accounting requirements include those listed on STOCK EXCHANGES, certain of those that have issued over ¥500 million in stocks or corporate bonds, and those that have issued stocks registered for over-the-counter trading. Such companies must also submit an annual securities report to the minister of finance. This report contains the financial statements and describes the company's financial and business conditions as well as other important matters concerning its operations. The financial statements consist of a balance sheet, an income statement, a statement of appropriation of retained earnings, and footnotes. The Securities Exchange Law requires the financial statements to be audited by an independent auditor (certified public accountant or audit corporation) who then expresses an opinion as to the fairness of presentation of the financial statements.

Acheson statement   アチソン声明

(Achison *seimei*). Major policy statement concerning the Far East made by US Secretary of State Dean G. Acheson on 12 January 1950 before the National Press Club in Washington, DC. Discussing military policy in the Far East, he said that the US defense line was along a perimeter defined by the Aleutian archipelago, Japan, Okinawa, and the Philippines. He stated that the United States would make a direct response to any threats to Japan or the Philippines. Acheson added that countries beyond the perimeter, if attacked, must first expect to defend themselves, but could hope for help from other countries under the terms of the United Nations Charter.

Acheson's statement was generally taken to indicate that the United States had abandoned Korea and Taiwan. The KOREAN WAR started in June 1950, and it is often claimed that the North Koreans had been encouraged by the Acheson statement in their decision to attack the South.

achievement tests   学力テスト

(*gakuryoku tesuto*). Standardized scholastic tests have been employed in Japan on the prefectural level as part of the entrance examinations for public high schools since 1948 and for all national and prefectural universities since 1979. Testing in primary and middle schools on the national level was discontinued in 1967 because of public opposition.

Achilles Corporation   アキレス[株]

(Akiresu). Manufacturer and vendor of Achilles-brand products, including urethane and rubber products, footwear, and resin. Incorporated in 1947, it was formerly called Kohkoku Chemical Industry Co, Ltd. The firm has a nationwide computer-connected network of 55 sales bases. It has a subsidiary in the United States (Kohkoku USA, Inc) and business offices in Hong Kong and Amsterdam. Total sales for the fiscal year ending March 1991 were ¥119.8 billion (US $873.2 million), and capitalization was ¥14.6 billion (US $106.4 million). Headquarters are in Tōkyō.

acid rain   酸性雨

(*sanseiu*). Damage from acid rain (precipitation whose increased acidity is caused by such environmental factors as pollution) has not been as severe in Japan as in other industrialized countries, but acid rain conditions have been observed. A 1980 study in eastern Honshū showed small-scale acid rain damage to *sugi* (Japanese cedar) groves in that area, and in 1990 the first thorough study of acid rain conditions on a national scale found the pH level of rainfall in Japan averaged 4.3–5.3 annually. These figures are similar to those for Europe and North America, and they definitely indicate the presence of acid rain. The low incidence of damage from acid rain in Japan is attributed to the neutralizing properties of Japanese soil.

ACOM Co, Ltd   アコム[株]

(Akomu). Consumer finance company providing credit to individuals. Incorporated in 1978. Now diversifying into the rental video and compact disc business, ACOM has the largest automated teller machine (ATM) system nationwide. Revenue for the fiscal year ending March 1990 totaled ¥108.3 billion (US $789.4 million). Capitalization stood at ¥2.5 billion (US $18.2 million) in the same year. Headquarters are in Tōkyō.

acupuncture   鍼

(*hari*). Ancient East Asian medical technique that consists of puncturing the body at designated points with special needles; together with *kyū* (MOXA TREATMENT), it has been practiced for more than 2,000 years in East Asia. Acupuncture is said to have originated in China or India. Since its introduction to Japan in the 6th century, it has been popularly regarded as an effective means of medical treatment and health maintenance. In accordance with the traditional Asian concept of disease as an imbalance caused by the strain of internal and external stress, acupuncture aims to "cure" disease by correcting the body's balance. The acupuncturist decides the size and kind of needle, the depth and direction of insertion, and the method of handling the needles after puncture according to the physical strength of the patient and the tissue condition at the points to be punctured. There are many methods of applying acupuncture, established after centuries of practical experience and theorizing. The most effective method still remains undetermined, requiring further scientific research.

Adachi Buntarō   足立文太郎

(1865–1945). Anthropologist and physician. Born in Izu Province (now part of Shizuoka Prefecture); graduate of Tōkyō University

School of Medicine in 1894. Adachi studied anatomy in Germany and became a professor at Kyōto University. He pioneered comparative anatomical studies of the Japanese and other peoples and in 1928–33 published a two-volume study in German on the physical characteristics of the Japanese.

Adachi Kagemori   安達景盛

(?–1248). Warlord of the early Kamakura period (1185–1333). Born in Sagami Province (now part of Kanagawa Prefecture), Adachi was politically influential as the maternal grandfather of Hōjō Tsunetoki (1224–46) and HŌJŌ TOKIYORI, the fourth and fifth Kamakura regents (SHIKKEN), and held high office. In 1247 Kagemori joined with Tokiyori to destroy the MIURA FAMILY in the HŌJI CONFLICT.

Adachi Kenzō   安達謙蔵

(1864–1948). Politician. Born in Higo Province (now Kumamoto Prefecture). Adachi worked as a reporter and founded several newspapers in Korea. In 1895 he was implicated in the assassination of Queen MIN, but was acquitted. He was elected to the Diet in 1902 and reelected 14 times. A member of the RIKKEN DŌSHIKAI (later known as the KENSEIKAI and the RIKKEN MINSEITŌ), he served as minister of communications and home minister. After the MANCHURIAN INCIDENT in 1931, Adachi cooperated with the militarists in their call for a "national unity" cabinet, which led to the collapse of the second WAKATSUKI REIJIRŌ cabinet, in which he was home minister. He withdrew from the Rikken Minseitō in 1931 and formed the ultranationalistic KOKUMIN DŌMEI party with NAKANO SEIGŌ. After serving as councillor in the second KONOE FUMIMARO cabinet (1940), he retired.

Adachi Museum of Art   足立美術館

(Adachi Bijutsukan). Located in the city of Yasugi, Shimane Prefecture. Opened in 1970. The museum holds the collection of the entrepreneur Adachi Zenkō (1899–1990) and is known for its modern Japanese-style paintings (NIHONGA) and its spacious Japanese gardens, the latter extending over 3.3 hectares (8.2 acres). The museum houses the largest collection of paintings by YOKOYAMA TAIKAN (130 works), as well as paintings by UEMURA SHŌEN, ITŌ SHINSUI, and TAKEUCHI SEIHŌ. A ceramics exhibition hall contains many pieces by KAWAI KANJIRŌ and KITAŌJI ROSANJIN.

Adachi Tadashi   足立正

(1883–1973). Businessman and business community leader. Born in Tottori Prefecture. Graduated from Tōkyō Higher School of Commerce (now Hitotsubashi University). Adachi joined Mitsui & Co in 1905 but moved in 1907 to Ōji Paper Co, of which he became president in 1942, retiring in 1946. He later served in a variety of positions, including the chairmanships of the National Association of Commercial Broadcasters and the Japan Productivity Center and the presidency of the Japan Chamber of Commerce and Industry.

Adachi Ward   足立区

(Adachi Ku). One of the 23 wards of Tōkyō. In the Edo period (1600–1868) one of the important post-station towns on the highway Ōshū Kaidō. During World War II, factories were concentrated here; today the ward is increasingly residential. Pop: 631,163.

Adams, William

アダムズ, W.

(1564–1620). English mariner who lived in Japan in the early 17th century. He was also known as Miura Anjin (Miura Pilot) from the location, on the Miura Peninsula, near Edo (now Tōkyō), of the estate granted him by TOKUGAWA IEYASU. Adams was born in Gillingham, Kent, and apprenticed as a shipwright. In 1598 he sailed as a pilot in a Dutch fleet, and after a series of mishaps his disabled ship, the LIEFDE, reached Kyūshū in April 1600. He was befriended by Ieyasu, who employed him as commercial agent, informant, pilot, shipbuilder, and interpreter. Adams thus became a man of influence and renown, owning a large estate with some 80 servants and traveling around the country on official business. He made several commercial voyages from Japan by junk, trading in Okinawa, Cochin China, and Siam. He died in or near the port town of Hirado (the site of the English and Dutch trading posts) on 26 May 1620. His adventurous life has been the subject of several books in both English and Japanese, including James Clavell's novel *Shōgun* (1976).

Adatarasan

安達太良山

Volcanic mountain group in northern Fukushima Prefecture, northern Honshū, part of the Nasu Volcanic Zone. Consisting of the mountains Minowayama (the highest; 1,719 m or 5,640 ft), Kimenzan, Tetsuzan, and Adatarayama. Located within the Bandai-Asahi National Park, Adatarasan has numerous hot springs and ski areas.

Administrative Court

行政裁判所

(Gyōsei Saibansho). A special court instituted under the Meiji Constitution of 1889. Also called the Court of Administrative Litigation. It was separate from the judicial system, with jurisdiction only over administrative cases. The Administrative Court was abolished with the enactment of the 1947 constitution.

administrative guidance

行政指導

(gyōsei shidō). Method employed by agencies of the Japanese government to obtain the adherence of individuals and enterprises to policies or practices deemed desirable by the government. Such guidance is not legally binding, although informal sanctions are sometimes imposed on those who do not voluntarily cooperate; it must be confined to the duties and functions of the agency concerned; and where matters fall within the purview of the ANTIMONOPOLY LAW, the guidance must accord with one of the laws that specifically allows for exemptions to that statute. Administrative guidance is not unique to Japan, although it has probably been more widely accepted there as a style of government administration than in other democracies.

Bureaucrats in Japan have traditionally exercised broad administrative powers, usually drafting and implementing legislation designed to carry out major national goals and objectives. This was particularly true during the post–World War II reconstruction in the 1950s, when Japan embarked upon an extensive program of industrial development. At that time, the economic affairs ministries were given more general responsibility for guiding the economy in desired directions. In addition to officially sanctioned administrative decisions, the responsible agencies also resorted to the practice of administrative guidance without specific legal authority.

The MINISTRY OF INTERNATIONAL TRADE AND INDUSTRY (MITI) has made extensive use of administrative guidance, especially after Japan began the progressive liberalization of trade and investment controls in 1964. Prior to this time the government had been able to implement INDUSTRIAL POLICY by controlling allocations of foreign exchange for capital equipment and technology imports (see FOREIGN EXCHANGE CONTROLS). After restrictions on the use of foreign exchange were lifted, administrative guidance was increasingly relied upon. Administrative guidance also has been used to implement "voluntary" restrictions on Japanese exports, such as those negotiated under orderly marketing agreements with the United States and other countries. Administrative guidance may consist of direction, requests, warnings, suggestions, or encouragement. In addition, the huge number of directives, notifications, and opinions emanating from the economic affairs ministries often constitute administrative guidance in a broad sense. Numerous ad hoc and informal channels are used for the communication of guidance. It is often conveyed in the form of recommendations from a *shingikai*, or MINISTERIAL DELIBERATIVE COUNCIL. These councils, made up of representatives of industry, trade associations and business organizations, banking and financial interests, academics, and other groups, meet to discuss and pass on actions usually proposed by appropriate government officials.

The effectiveness of administrative guidance, never very great, has been diminishing. For example, MITI has had a long string of guidance failures, mainly in cases where there was little consensus between the government and the private sector or between the various ministries or government agencies involved. The reduced dependence on government aid and protection of many of the now fully developed industries has made them critical of government interference, particularly that of MITI, and less susceptible to informal pressures. There have also been legal challenges that could result in strict limitations on the use of guidance.

administrative law

行政法

(gyōsei hō). In Japan as elsewhere, the rubric of administrative law covers the bundle of legal theories and principles that defines the organization and functions of the executive branch of government (see GOVERNMENT, EXECUTIVE BRANCH), the administrative process, and direct JUDICIAL REVIEW of governmental actions. These principles in Japanese administrative law derive primarily from continental (especially German) ideas. Although there is no specific code or basic statute as in the substantive (civil, criminal, and commercial) or procedural (criminal and civil) codes or the 1947 CONSTITUTION OF JAPAN, the statutory materials are numerous and diffuse. They include the Cabinet Law (Naikaku Hō); the National Administrative Organization Law (Kokka Gyōsei Soshiki Hō); the Administrative Case Litigation Law (Gyōsei Jiken Soshō Hō); various statutes concerning the civil service, local government, and the police; and social and economic regulatory legislation.

Under the Meiji Constitution of 1889 the cabinet was responsible solely to the emperor and not to the Diet. Also, the judicial courts were denied jurisdiction to hear direct appeals from administrative decisions. Instead, the 15-member ADMINISTRATIVE COURT, located in Tōkyō, was established with limited jurisdiction as the exclusive forum to adjudicate appeals from administrative decisions.

In contrast, the postwar constitution is premised on the "dual" sovereignty of the legislature and the courts. The cabinet and, through it, the ministries are accountable to the Diet. There is express provision for judicial review.

The central organizing concept of Japanese administrative law is the notion of "administrative act" (gyōsei kōi; Verwaltungsakt; acte administratif), which parallels the concept of JURISTIC ACT (hōritsu kōi) in the CIVIL CODE. Typical administrative acts or dispositions include the various types of governmental approval (kyoka, ninka, menkyo), decisions (kettei, saitei, shinketsu), orders (meirei), prohibitions (kinshi), acknowledgments (kakunin), and public notices (kōnin, tsūchi, kokuji).

administrative litigation

行政訴訟

(gyōsei soshō). Procedure whereby a court makes an examination and decision concerning an objection to an action by a government agency or disputes about legal relationships under administrative law. In response to significant public interest in these administrative cases, the Administrative Litigation Law (Gyōsei Jiken Soshō Hō) was enacted in 1962. Administrative litigation is divided into four types: (1) appeal litigation or other exercises of public power; (2) litigation between concerned parties, in regard to legal relationships based on public law; (3) class action litigation, which is filed in order to rectify administrative illegalities for the benefit of the common public; and (4) institutional litigation between national or public institutions.

administrative procedure

行政手続

(gyōsei tetsuzuki). Procedures to be followed by government agencies when making administrative decisions. Included are procedures for administrative regulations, dispositions, guidance, execution, judgments, complaint investigation, and grievances. Administrative procedures are divided into those for prior review, which cover requirements for notification, hearings, and information access, and those covering complaints and grievances after an administrative act has gone into effect. The Administrative Complaint Investigation Law specifies procedures for after-the-fact relief.

In recent years attention has focused on prior review in order to protect against violation of the public's rights and guarantee public participation in the administrative process. By giving the affected parties an opportunity to voice their opinions, prior review promotes just administration and protects the public interest. See also ADMINISTRATIVE LITIGATION.

administrative scrivener

行政書士

(gyōsei shoshi). A legal functionary who drafts, on behalf of the public, documents that are to be submitted to government and other public offices and documents that evidence rights and duties or facts. Administrative scriveners are often utilized in drafting documents of incorporation, building permit applications, informal dispute settlements, and contracts.

▶ Passengers in commuter trains and subways are a captive audience for hanging advertisements placed throughout the cars.

▲ Magazine advertising is the fastest growing advertising medium, with expenditures growing fivefold between 1980 and 1990. Shown are ads for whiskey, a bank, blue jeans, and film.

◀ The huge screen at the Studio Alta building, near Shinjuku Station in Tōkyō, displays advertising, music videos, and weather forecasts. Outdoor video screens and neon signs account for a large portion of advertising expenses.

▲ A scene from the pit during a formula car race. Corporate sponsorship of various sporting events is common, with formula racing providing the best opportunity to display a company logo.

▲ Corporations often cooperate with television networks in charity telethons like the one shown. Such events result in publicity for both the corporation and the network.

Adogawa
安曇川

River in Shiga Prefecture, central Honshū, flowing from northeastern Kyōto to Lake Biwa. It runs between the Hira Mountains and the Tamba Mountains in its upper reaches. Small *ayu* (sweetfish) are caught at the river's mouth. Length: 57 km (35 mi).

adoption
養子

(*yōshi*). Unlike American or European adoption practice, which is aimed at providing homes for orphans and foundlings and at providing childless couples with children, Japanese adoption is concerned with providing for the continuity of a household (IE) over time; adoption may also be used among elite families to create political or economic alliances. Japanese adoptees are almost always adult or adolescent relatives of the adopting house; thus, their natal families and social history are known, and relations between the houses continue. The adoption of an infant or older child whose background cannot be traced is rare in Japan.

The Ie—Traditionally, the household was the basic social unit in Japan. It was legally recognized both as a group of people who existed in a particular generation and as an institution enduring over time. It included the property and the professional enterprise of the group, as well as the house name, ancestors, and genealogy. The continuation of the house was considered extremely important. When no natural heir (by preference a male) existed, or when an existing natural heir was considered unfit for succession, adoption was the only way to maintain house continuity.

Adoption in History—Adoption appears to have been practiced in Japan as early as the Nara period (710–794). Japanese practices of that time included the adoption of younger brothers and of people of a different surname. During the Kamakura period (1185–1333), the practice of adopting males (even when the family had natural sons) to form household alliances began. Adoptive practices were highly elaborated during the Edo period (1600–1868), employing detailed distinctions of type and status.

Adoption in the Modern Period—The legal status of the house (and its role in adoption) remained largely unchanged until after World War II. The 1948 revisions to the CIVIL CODE eliminated the legal status of the *ie* and placed more emphasis on the rights of the individual over the house, in theory establishing adoption as an institution more for the welfare of the adoptee than for household continuity. Actual adoption law, however, remained largely unchanged: an adopted person was recognized as such in the adopting family's *koseki* (see HOUSEHOLD REGISTERS), the legal relationship between the natal parents and the adoptee continued, and the adoption could at any time and for various reasons be "voided" and the adoptee "returned" to the natal family. An alternative form of legal adoption was provided in 1987, when the SPECIAL ADOPTION SYSTEM was created. Under this system, which affects only children under the age of six, all legal ties between the child and the natural parents are severed, and dissolution of the adoption is in principle prohibited. However, such adoptions are only a tiny minority of all Japanese adoptions.

Types of Adoption—The most prevalent form of Japanese adoption today involves the adoption of a son-in-law (*muko yōshi*) by his in-laws. Here, the husband of a daughter of a house takes his wife's surname and becomes the successor to his wife's father as head of the household. A man who consents to be adopted as a son-in-law usually has at least one brother to ensure the continuity of his own house.

An heirless house may also adopt a relative's second son or grandson. This brings a young man who would have had to establish his own house (through marriage) into the correct sequence for succession. This type of adoption may take place when the boy is quite young or after he has reached adulthood.

The adoption of a married couple, although rare, is still legally possible. The husband of the adopted couple (*fūfu yōshi*) succeeds as head of the adopting house. The couple may already have a son, or they may be adopted with the hope that they will produce an heir.

Japanese infants and children who are orphaned through accident or illness are almost always adopted and brought up by their relatives. This sort of intrafamily adoption carries little or no social stigma for either party, since the background of the child is clearly known. Abandoned children, on the other hand, are at a great disadvantage. Strong social sanctions in Japan prevent the adoption of nonrelatives and of strangers of unknown social background. Abandoned children are usually cared for by a series of foster families until they reach legal adulthood, although some are now adopted under the new special adoption system.

adultery
姦通罪

(*kantsūzai*). Until the 1947 revision of the Penal Code, Japan's adultery laws punished women far more severely than they punished men. Behind this reluctance to criminalize a husband's act of adultery lay the traditional tolerance of husbands' extramarital sexual affairs as well as a recognition that few wives had the economic re-

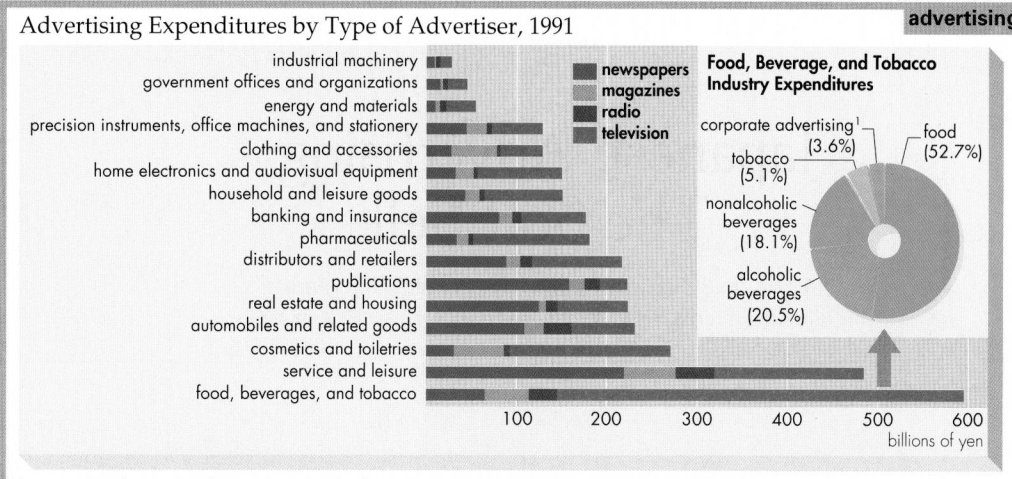

Advertising Expenditures by Type of Advertiser, 1991

industrial machinery
government offices and organizations
energy and materials
precision instruments, office machines, and stationery
clothing and accessories
home electronics and audiovisual equipment
household and leisure goods
banking and insurance
pharmaceuticals
distributors and retailers
publications
real estate and housing
automobiles and related goods
cosmetics and toiletries
service and leisure
food, beverages, and tobacco

newspapers
magazines
radio
television

100 200 300 400 500 600
billions of yen

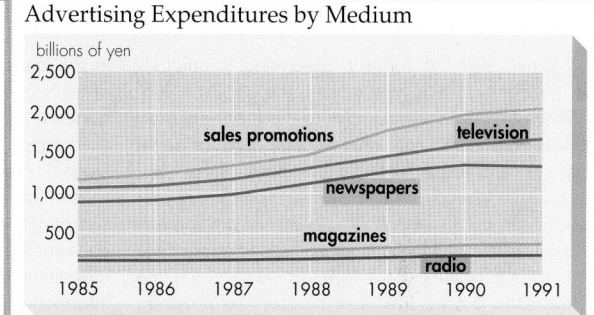

Food, Beverage, and Tobacco Industry Expenditures

corporate advertising[1] (3.6%)
tobacco (5.1%)
nonalcoholic beverages (18.1%)
alcoholic beverages (20.5%)
food (52.7%)

[1] "Corporate advertising" refers to advertising that features a corporation rather than specific products made by a corporation.
SOURCE: Dentsū, Inc, *1991 Advertising Expenditures in Japan* (1992).

sources to allow them to live independently after bringing a complaint against their husbands. Consistent with the principle of sexual equality in the postwar constitution, however, the Diet declared adultery by either husband or wife no longer a criminal offense. Adultery is still considered grounds for DIVORCE.

adult, legal definition of
成年（法律上の）

(*seinen, hōritsujō no*). In Japan adulthood is legally defined as the age at which a person becomes entitled to manage his or her own affairs. The CIVIL CODE (art. 3) specifies 20 years as the age of adulthood, except for some members of the imperial family, for whom the age is 18. Upon reaching adulthood, one can vote, execute contracts, and marry without parental approval. See AGE, LEGAL DEFINITION OF.

advanced ceramics ファインセラミックス

(*fain seramikkusu*). A general term for exotic materials that result from a sophisticated reaction-bonding calcination of chemically synthesized inorganic compounds. The term refers to high-grade ceramics used for electronics and structural and medical materials, as distinguished from traditional ceramic products such as cement, glass, pottery, and china.

Japan's long tradition of CERAMICS has formed the basis for later outstanding achievements in the field of advanced ceramics. Japanese research began in the 1950s, but the MINISTRY OF INTERNATIONAL TRADE AND INDUSTRY's 1981 designation of advanced ceramics as a basic, new-generation industrial technology and its encouragement of research and development in the field led to a tremendous surge in Japanese advanced-ceramics technology during the 1980s. Japan currently leads the world in the industrial standards and practical application of this technology. Sales of advanced-ceramics products in 1990 amounted to US $5.7 billion.

Almina-ceramic, used for forming integrated circuit boards, is an example of an advanced ceramic. Other examples are silicon carbide, silicon nitride, and partially stabilized zirconia. Since these advanced ceramics have excellent heat resistance and good impact resistance and are also extremely strong, they are expected to lead to innovations in engineering technology, particularly in engine construction where, until recently, only metal parts were used. Japanese automobiles are already powered by engines using ceramic turbocharger rotors. Ceramic parts make it possible to raise the engine's operating temperature to over 1,300°C (2,372°F), allowing fuel consumption to be reduced by more than 30 percent.

Advantest Corporation
[株]アドバンテスト

(Adobantesuto). Electronic measuring and automatic test equipment manufacturer. Incorporated in 1954. Advantest holds the largest market share in the global sale of semiconductor test systems. For the fiscal year ending March 1991, the company had annual sales of ¥81.5 billion (US $594.0 million). Capitalization was ¥30.0 billion (US $218.7 million) in the same year. Headquarters are in Tōkyō.

advertising 広告

(*kōkoku*). Japan has the world's second largest advertising industry, with expenditures in 1991 of ¥5.7 trillion (US $42.5 billion), an amount constituting 1.3 percent of the gross national product (GNP) that year. On a per capita basis approximately ¥46,000 (US $341) was spent in 1991. The major media—newspapers, magazines, television, and radio—typically account for about 64 percent of advertising revenues. Television, with 29 percent in 1991, has been the dominant medium since 1974, when it surpassed newspapers. Newspapers, with 23 percent in 1991, usually allocate about 40 percent of their space to advertising and consistently earn more from advertising than from circulation revenue.

The largest spender on advertising and promotion in 1991, HITACHI, LTD, an electrical machinery manufacturer, spent ¥53 billion (US $366 million). The largest category of advertised items was food and beverages. In 1990 there were 4,858 advertising agencies, almost 40 percent of which were located in either Tōkyō or Ōsaka.

Large agencies plan advertising campaigns, conduct market and advertising research, create the advertisements, and select and buy media time or space; they may also provide the ancillary services of sales promotion, public relations, and outdoor and direct mail advertising. Smaller agencies tend to concentrate on one or two services, deal with smaller clients, and handle only regional or specialized media.

History——The earliest reference in Japan to what seems to be a signboard, or *kamban*, dates from 833. The growing commercialization of the Edo period (1600–1868) brought forth more aggressive forms of promotion, such as handbills and advertisements bound into popular books. Nonetheless, advertising as a modern industry had to await the development of mass media and a broadly based commercial economy. Those conditions began to emerge in the Meiji period (1868–1912). The first newspaper advertisement placed by a Japanese firm in a Japanese-language newspaper appeared in 1867, and the first advertising agency is said to have been founded in 1873.

The first documented agency, Kōhōdō, was founded in 1886. In the next decade and a half, dozens of agencies sprang up, many of them under the auspices of newspapers. In 1892 an existing news wire service added an advertising agency. Its growth demonstrated the potential of this combination, and it was widely imitated, most successfully by the forerunner of DENTSŪ, INC, which was founded in 1901. Local papers eventually became quite dependent upon these firms, which simultaneously provided them with news and revenue.

Media and agency concentration was al-

Advertising Expenditures by Medium

billions of yen
2,500
2,000
1,500
1,000
500

sales promotions
television
newspapers
magazines
radio

1985 1986 1987 1988 1989 1990 1991

NOTE: Sales promotions include direct mail, inserts in newspapers, billboards and other signs, telephone directory and mass transit advertisements, point-of-purchase displays, and promotional films and videos.

Expenditures on various new media such as cable television, teletext, and videotex services totaled ¥10.9 billion in 1991, 0.2 percent of total expenditures.
SOURCE: Dentsū, Inc, *1991 Advertising Expenditures in Japan* (1992).

ready pronounced by the 1920s. Large agencies, such as Dentsū, Hakuhōdō, and Mannensha, dominated the larger accounts and relationships with the major urban dailies. In this period the agencies operated as space brokers, providing no services to advertisers other than access to media through exclusive arrangements that still persist today.

Postwar History——The advent of commercial broadcasting in 1951 and the recovery of the Japanese economy after the war-induced shortages set the stage for advertising's impressive postwar growth. Agencies took up marketing; they built creative divisions, taking over from advertisers the task of creative planning and execution. From the mid-1960s, sales promotion divisions became a feature of these new "full service agencies." Then, in the late 1960s, Japanese agencies began incorporating functions performed by other kinds of firms in the United States. Agencies designed and managed exposition pavilions, organized street festivals, produced television specials, designed urban shopping complexes, promoted sports events, and shaped national celebrations.

Industry Structure——While Japanese agencies have expanded their services to advertisers, they have not abandoned their original function as media representatives. This has had certain consequences for industry structure. First and foremost, it has meant that those advertisers, including competitors, seeking access to a particular medium have had to call upon the services of the agency or agencies that can offer that access. It is thus possible for an agency to obtain as clients all the major producers in an industry. One agency, Dentsū, has used this feature of

Continued on page 12——

Japanese Advertising: The Soft Sell

Japan's image-oriented advertising reflects the country's cultural preference for subtle, indirect forms of expression.

How much of Japan's advertising is uniquely Japanese and how much is the application of universal advertising principles to the Japanese market? Like so many other aspects of modern Japanese culture, Japanese advertising has many of the trappings of its Western counterpart. The process of producing an ad, for example, is basically the same in Japan as it is in the West. The creative team at the advertising agency must have an idea of (1) the target (the prospective customer for the product); (2) how features of the product can benefit the target by filling a need or solving some problem; (3) the medium, such as newspaper, television, or radio, that will carry the ad; and (4) competing products.

The creative team typically consists of a copywriter, who thinks up the words for the ad, and an art director, who is responsible for the pictorial aspects. Illustrators, photographers, jingle composers, and the like are brought in as needed. The team tries to come up with ways of communicating the product's benefits that will be meaningful to the target, taking into account the characteristics of the medium. (You can't put many words into a 15-second television commercial, for instance.)

In creating an ad, both Japanese and Western advertising professionals follow certain general guidelines. Japanese advertising texts even use the same acronym that is used in the United States—AIDMA, which stands for Attention, Interest, Desire, Memory, and Action. In other words, the ad should attract the target's Attention, then hold the target's Interest long enough to arouse a Desire for the product, the Memory of which will lead to the Action of buying it. Another universal principle is the use of the "three Bs" (Beauty, Baby, or Beast) as emotional attention-getters. In Japan, if the creative team cannot agree on one of the three Bs, they will use a foreigner in the ad instead!

Although Japanese advertising agencies subscribe to basic universal advertising principles, their ads tend to be more suggestive and less direct than American ads. Japanese advertising has been characterized as emotionally oriented or image oriented—in other words, soft sell as opposed to the aggressive American hard sell with its emphasis on logical persuasion.

In advertising in general, the question of whether to appeal to reason or emotion usually depends on the product. The less a product can be differentiated from other similar products, the more effective an emotional appeal is. Emotional appeals are also used in the later stages of market growth, when there is already a high awareness of the product's intrinsic benefits.

In Japan, however, one sees image advertising even for products that are clearly differentiated. One reason for this is that Japanese buyers tend to have surprisingly detailed knowledge of a wide variety of consumer goods. There are a number of specialized magazines that cater to prospective buyers eager for information. Separate magazines on new products target male or female consumers. There are also television programs and videocassettes (available at convenience stores) on the features of the latest automobiles. This kind of "editorial" product coverage in the media reduces the need for ads to communicate facts. Another reason is that, while products such as VCRs may be adequately differentiated in terms of features, many of the features are mere bells and whistles and are unlikely to entice new buyers on their merits alone.

So the function of the commercial or print ad is often less to push the selling point than it is to establish brand image and product personality. Owning a particular consumer product is like wearing a particular style of clothing—a person is making a statement about his or her taste. Hence the effectiveness of Sony's "It's a Sony" slogan.

Whereas Westerners provide reasons in their ads for people to try their products and attempt to convince them or cajole them into buying, their Japanese counterparts aim for harmony with the target audience. Japanese advertisers believe it is more desirable to gain "mind share" and to blend their message into the target's environment. They do not find it necessary to convey an understandable meaning in the Western sense. It is enough to trigger mental associations that create the desired mood. The Japanese are accustomed to drawing conclusions from bits and pieces of information. In the Japanese language, for example, you do not need to specify the subject of a sentence; a verb or adjective alone is frequently sufficient. *Rikutsuppoi* is a derogatory Japanese term meaning overly logical. Related to this is *kudoi*, or tedious, a term that is applied to aggressive, hard-sell messages.

The Abstract Approach In advertising, as in any situation in which you are trying to influence someone, the more thought or initiative supplied by the other party, the better—but only when the other party trusts his or her own judg-

ment. Japanese advertisers often let prospective buyers draw their own conclusions about a product. In a television commercial for a sporty Nissan Cefiro, for instance, a well-known folksinger appeared on screen and said simply, *"Ogenki desu ka"* ("How are you doing?"). The car was expensive and targeted toward an upwardly mobile, think-for-yourself crowd.

The tendency toward indirectness is a deep-seated cultural preference that helps to explain the preponderance of soft-sell, image advertising in Japan. The Japanese have always preferred to communicate through intuition, indirect hints, and subtle suggestions rather than through words and logic. This cultural propensity for indirect expression reached the level of high art in *haiku*, ink painting, and Nō drama. Even advertising can take on aspects of surrealism, replete with subconscious imagery. A case in point, and one of the most remarkable ads in recent years, was a TV commercial for the Kira Kira Pole, a stainless-steel clothing pole. (In Japan, laundry is typically hung out on horizontal poles rather than clotheslines.)

Entrance to rural maternity clinic. A 35-ish farmer-type man waiting outside. A woman comes out, obviously pregnant.
Man: "What did he say?"
Woman: "Six months pregnant."
Man: "Don't remember how that happened."
Woman starts singing strange jingle.
Shot of clothing pole thrust horizontally across screen. Then the claim: "Stainless-steel clothing poles—they don't rust."

The pole is a phallic symbol that suggests "how that happened." It also hints of an impending problem

An advertisement for Toshimaen, an amusement park. The copy for the ad hails Toshimaen as "the thinker's amusement park."

NOTICE
1 Do not rest articles on top of the dryer as it is a major heat source.
2 Articles should be thoroughly spun dry before being placed in the dryer. (Water leakage may result in an electrical shortage thus putting dryers out of commission.)
3 Machine coin slots accept 100 yen coins only.

考える遊園地。としまえん

(increased laundry) and offers itself as a solution. The claim for stainless steel being long-lasting is not made until the final cut, when the viewer is shown the pole. The symbolism is so well integrated that the audience does not have to figure out what the buildup has to do with the punch line. The creative team could have demonstrated how the stainless-steel pole withstands corrosion better than an ordinary pole. Instead, they created a minicomedy that tied the product into the emotional lives of the viewers.

This kind of advertising is effective in Japan because the Japanese are raised to expect the surface message (*tatemae*) to conceal a deeper layer of meaning (*honne*). Unlike Westerners, the Japanese do not feel the need to communicate ideas explicitly. Some Westerners find the intuitive approach to advertising a bit strange. Consider, for example, a print advertisement for Kirin Beer in which the headline reads, "Somehow it's Kirin Beer." A photo shows a man sitting at a table, with a woman standing behind him sipping a glass of beer. Above the couple is a line saying, "Somehow we're husband and wife."

Advertising as Entertainment

Another aspect of the soft sell in Japanese advertising is the emphasis on entertainment. Indeed, many Japanese ads seem designed more to entertain than to sell or inform.

As the need for information in advertising diminishes, the demand for entertainment increases. As of 1991, at least four out of five Japanese homes had VCRs. Entertainment value becomes critical when your audience is capable of "zapping" commercials by means of a remote control. Song-and-dance numbers that run throughout television commercials

are popular for this reason. Another more recent tactic is the "miniseries" TV commercial, which makes the audience wonder what will happen in the next dramatic installment.

The need to prevent zapping has given rise to a spate of TV commercials featuring conflict-based, slice-of-life situations such as employee versus boss, wife versus husband, and child versus parents. While certainly not harmonious, these ads involve the viewer at a gut level, creating the immediacy necessary to hold interest. Humor is used to offset the sense of conflict, as in the following commercial for a Panasonic camcorder: A husband arrives home late—drunk and disheveled. His wife appears with a camcorder and points it at her husband, who immediately tries to put on his best behavior.

Sociologically this commercial involves a play on the Japanese theme of the private home situation (*uchi*) versus interaction with the outside world (*soto*). In the home situation the man is not ashamed of coming in drunk and unruly, but once an outside party is introduced (represented by the video camera and its association with seeing other people's lives on TV), he automatically switches back to his public face. Such Japanese commercials using slice-of-life situations can serve as lighthearted vehicles for social commentary. This is one role of humor in any society—to provide an outlet for thoughts and feelings that must otherwise be suppressed in daily life. Although few wives would use a camcorder to embarrass their husbands, how many would like to?

Sometimes advertising's role is to stimulate the target to actually act on suppressed, culturally forbidden desires. This was the case with a series of TV commercials for a job-placement magazine called *Dyūda*. The aim of the ads was to show people happily quitting their jobs, or at least considering the idea. In one of the commercials, a pesky superior wants to see what an employee is reading (it is *Dyūda* magazine). The employee blocks him, saying, "It's my life," which is just the opposite of the traditional "company first" attitude.

The same approach—appealing to suppressed

impulses—was used with a peculiar twist in a TV commercial for a bug spray called Kinchōru. In the commercial, a pop star appears as a member of a bizarre religious sect chanting, "Bugs, bugs, roll over, roll over, Kinchōru!" In many urban areas of Japan today, fervent proponents of new faiths can be seen on street corners trying to recruit members for their sects. Since these proselytizers, like insects, are often viewed as an annoyance, the analogy was effective. In all likelihood, it stuck in the minds of viewers far better than a straightforward sales pitch would have. In fact, it is doubtful whether people would have continued to watch an informational commercial at all.

Future Trends

As we have seen, clear communication of product benefits in Japanese advertising often takes a back seat to simply getting noticed. Ads concentrate more on the Attention, Interest, and Memory of AIDMA and less on the Desire and Action. But getting noticed is not easy when there are some 2,500 different commercials on television every month and hundreds of thousands of print ads. The consumer quickly develops an immunity to eye-catching devices and may even become immune to appeals that play on the consumer's aspirations and self-image.

Fujioka Wakao, a producer of television commercials and veteran of the Japanese advertising industry, predicts that the informational content of ads will decline still further and that we may soon be seeing ads with such messages as, "Our company doesn't rely on 'image' advertising," or even, "We're lousy at making commercials."

It is possible that the rules of the advertising game may be changed over the long run by revolutionary manufacturing techniques that permit almost infinite product variations. If this trend continues and market segmentation increases to the degree that flexible manufacturing and distribution permit, the advertising industry will have to adapt its strategies accordingly. This means developing new point-of-purchase advertising technology like Videocart, the American-designed shopping cart equipped with a video screen that promotes various supermarket products. At the same time, one can expect traditional avenues of advertising—television, newspaper, radio, magazine, etc—to continue in the direction of the subtle soft sell.

Stephen Benfey

the industry to make itself the preponderant force in Japanese advertising, with 20 percent of the market in 1990. Two others, Hakuhōdō and Tōkyū Agency, took another 12 percent between them; the top five together accounted for 37 percent. Once established, the competitive strength of the large agencies has had self-perpetuating mechanisms: (1) greater resources, both financial and personal, available to provide more diversified and innovative services to clients; (2) greater dependence of the media on a continued good relationship with the large agencies; and (3) greater dependence of advertisers on the large agencies for access to the most desirable media.

A second consequence stems from the fact that, historically, the Japanese agency had close relationships with some media and weaker ties with others. As a result, advertisers became accustomed to using one agency for one set of media and another agency for a different set. As services in addition to media buying began to be provided by agencies, most advertisers extended this custom of split accounts to the new services.

Some advertisers have attempted to adopt the American system, under which one agency handles all aspects of the campaign for its assigned brands. However, the strong agencies' grip on the most desirable television time and newspaper space virtually requires major advertisers to give at least some of their business to those agencies.

Future Prospects—Major change will undoubtedly accompany the ongoing telecommunications revolution, which could link home computers and television screens to central data bases and other homes and businesses. Although the full impact of these developments may not be felt for several decades, each move toward the "wired nation" will be certain to have incremental effects on the advertising industry.

▶▶ 10–11

advertising agencies   広告代理店

(kōkoku dairiten). The first advertising agency in Japan was established in 1873. The first agencies developed as representatives of early newspapers, seeking patrons for the advertising space made available in the new medium. The industry expanded rapidly after World War II in conjunction with the rapid growth of the Japanese economy and the proliferation of media and promotional outlets.

In 1990 there were 4,858 advertising agencies in Japan. Most of these were quite small; 87 percent had fewer than 30 employees. On the other hand, DENTSŪ, INC, the largest agency, handled about one-fifth of the total advertising business, and the top five agencies controlled 37 percent of the market. Thus Japanese advertising exhibits aspects of both oligopoly and dual structure (the coexistence of a small number of giant firms with large numbers of small and medium-size enterprises), characteristics of the Japanese economy as a whole.

Because Japanese advertising agencies developed as sales representatives of the media rather than as marketing representatives for clients, many agencies handle the accounts of firms that compete within an industry. Some advertising interests have advocated the reform of the industry through introducing the account-executive system used in the United States and elsewhere. Adoption of this system would give advertising clients

more complete service, it is argued, since comprehensive media strategies could be provided. Under such a system agencies could, of course, no longer represent competing enterprises.

Today advertising agencies not only perform market research and promote products, but they set trends and shape public opinion. They also work for political campaigns and organize international conferences.

Advisory Council on Social Security   社会保障制度審議会

(Shakai Hoshō Seido Shingikai). Prime ministerial advisory council established in 1949 to examine Japan's social security (or social welfare) system and make recommendations about it. The members of the council, who are appointed by the prime minister, consist of members of the Diet and related government agencies, scholars in the field, and members of labor and management, medical, social insurance, and other concerned groups. Because proposals for new social security laws cannot be submitted to the Diet without being first put before this council, its findings, recommendations, and suggestions have a significant influence on the development of Japan's social security system.

Aeba Kōson   饗庭篁村

(1855–1922). Novelist and theater critic. Real name Aeba Yosaburō. Born in Edo (now Tōkyō). He worked for the newspapers Yomiuri shimbun and Asahi shimbun. He published novels and adaptations from US and European literary works. Aeba's writing reflects his study of the great 17th-century novelist Ihara SAIKAKU. His most representative novel is Tōsei shōnin katagi (1886).

Aeba Takao   饗庭孝男

(1930–). Literary critic and scholar of French literature; born in Shiga Prefecture. Graduated from Nanzan University. Aeba first appeared on the literary scene in 1966 with the publication of Sengo bungaku ron (On Postwar Literature), a reappraisal of postwar literature from an existentialist point of view. In Hihyō to hyōgen (1979, Criticism and Expression), Aeba considered the watakushi shōsetsu (I-NOVEL) from a new perspective.

aesthetics   美学

(bigaku). Aesthetics as a clearly defined field of study was introduced to Japan from the West in the Meiji period (1868–1912), but a considerable amount of writing on the nature of art existed before then in the fields of poetry, drama, painting, calligraphy, music, the tea ceremony, flower arrangement, and landscape gardening. The authors were mainly artists who wished to hand down the secrets of their art. Consequently their remarks tended to be pedagogic, intuitive, and technical, often lacking a philosophical frame of reference and a logical analysis of aesthetic problems. Yet in many cases they were able to give coherence to their ideas by stressing spiritual discipline and relating them to Buddhism, Confucianism, or Shintō.

Before and during the Heian period (794–1185), conceptions of art were very much influenced by Chinese aesthetic ideas contained in the Confucian classics. The only exception was in the realm of literature, which soon asserted its independence from Chinese models. Women writers of the Heian court, such as MURASAKI SHIKIBU and SEI SHŌNAGON, also expressed a penchant for a

type of beauty uniquely their own. Medieval writings on art were characterized by an especially strong tendency to merge art with religion. Common to these writings was the belief that ultimately all arts are one and in harmony with Buddhist teachings. In this view, art is a means by which to glimpse a higher reality. Inevitably these ideas pointed toward symbolism of one kind or another.

In the Edo period (1600–1868) aesthetic thinking became more diverse. The promotion of Neo-Confucianism by the Tokugawa shogunate (1603–1867) gave rise to more pragmatic theories of art. Many writings emerged, especially on JŌRURI and KABUKI, that had little to do with Buddhism, Confucianism, or Shintō. By and large aesthetic thought in the Edo period was more humanistic than in previous ages, emphasizing the role of emotion in both the artist's creation and the spectator's appreciation.

A distinctive feature of premodern aesthetic thought in Japan was the tendency to value symbolic representation more highly than realistic delineation. Another characteristic was the assumption that true art involves a selective presentation of the beautiful and avoidance of the humble and vulgar. Consequently the artist tended to choose nature for his subject, avoiding the depiction of everyday occurrences in the lives of common people. As the Heian court taste for grace and refinement exerted a lasting impact on the later cultural tradition, elegance was one of the main types of beauty favored. Such important concepts as OKASHI, FŪRYŪ, YŪGEN, and iki (see IKI AND SUI) all included a connotation of elegance. Another highly valued quality was impermanence, which could be considered a variation of elegance, for exquisite beauty was considered fragile and fleeting. Buddhism, with its emphasis on life's mutability, merged with this ideal and provided philosophical depth. Such aesthetic principles as aware (and its later elaboration, MONO NO AWARE), yūgen, WABI, and sabi all had perishability as part of their meaning. Simplicity was a corollary to the concept of mimesis, which stressed symbolic representation. The mystery of nature could never be presented through description; it could only be suggested, and the terser the suggestion, the greater its effectiveness.

The modern Japanese term for aesthetics, bigaku, was coined around 1883 by NAKAE CHŌMIN. In 1886 Tōkyō University established a course in aesthetics with a Western scholar as its first instructor. Inevitably, early Japanese specialists in the field were all students of Western aesthetics who paid little attention to the native tradition. The trend began to change when KUKI SHŪZŌ and Ōnishi Yoshinori (1888–1959) pioneered in philosophical studies of premodern Japanese aesthetic thought. Today the gap is narrower, although it still exists, between academic aestheticians who are primarily interested in defining the nature of beauty through Western methodologies and professional critics who try to appraise individual works of art according to traditional criteria. A synthesis of Japanese and Western aesthetics still remains the ultimate challenge for both groups.

Africa and Japan   アフリカと日本

(Afurika to Nihon). Japanese interest in Africa remains relatively low, due mainly to the fact that possibilities for political, economic, and cultural cooperation remain unrecognized in many areas.

Japan's first diplomatic mission in Africa

was established in Capetown (Union of South Africa) in 1918, followed by missions in Port Said and Alexandria (Egypt) and Mombasa (Kenya). Japan's interests were principally in trade, which was facilitated by the opening up of regular routes to East Africa by the Ōsaka Shōsen Kaisha shipping line in 1926 and a similar route to West Africa in 1933.

Trade relations between Africa and Japan were temporarily severed during World War II, but were slowly resumed in the postwar years. Diplomatic relations developed during the 1960s and in the 1970s permanent consulates and embassies increased as Japan made a strong push toward establishing local contact in Africa.

Japan traditionally took the stance of advising African nations to be more trusting toward the former colonial powers and abstained when resolutions denouncing South Africa's apartheid policies were brought before the United Nations. However, after 1974 Japan made known its support for anticolonial movements in Africa and demanded a quick end to apartheid policies in South Africa.

Japan has also taken a sympathetic position toward African expressions of economic nationalism, and economic and technical assistance for Africa has been expanded. Since 1964 Japanese aid to Africa has constituted approximately 10 percent of its total foreign aid disbursements; in 1988 Japan's aid to sub-Saharan Africa stood at $884 million. Japan Overseas Cooperation Volunteers have also been stationed in a number of African nations.

In 1988 Japan's trade with Africa as a whole accounted for 3.2 percent of its exports and 2.3 percent of its imports. South Africa took 44.9 percent of Japan's exports to Africa and provided 33.8 percent of total imports from Africa. Owing to Japan's large export surpluses with the countries of black Africa, such as Nigeria and Kenya, some 20 countries have been the recipients of yen loans. Japan has also made significant donations to the African Development Fund run by the African Development Bank.

Afro-Asian Conferences
アジア・アフリカ会議

(Ajia Afurika Kaigi). Meetings to promote the ideas of sovereignty, equality, and solidarity among the nations of Africa and Asia, beginning with the Afro-Asian Conference held in Bandung, Indonesia, in April 1955. Official representatives of 29 countries attended the Bandung Conference and declared 10 principles for the promotion of world peace and cooperation. Japan sent Takasaki Tatsunosuke (1885–1964) as its representative. A second Afro-Asian Conference was scheduled to be held in Algiers in 1965, but several circumstances, including Sino-Soviet tensions, disagreements among the African nations, and a coup d'état in the host country of Algeria, led to its cancellation.

AFS Japan Association, Inc
エイ・エフ・エス日本協会

(Ei Efu Esu Nihon Kyōkai). Japanese branch of the American Field Service, an organization for international educational exchange tracing its origins back to 1914. The AFS Japan Association was created in 1955 to administer an AFS high school exchange program for Japanese students initiated the previous year. By 1990 over 4,700 Japanese students had completed a one-year course of

study in 1 of 20 or so of the 72 AFS member countries; nearly 1,200 students had participated in shorter programs. Over the same period more than 3,200 foreign students came to Japan for similar courses of study. Since 1985 the AFS Japan Association has also offered a special program for Chinese teachers of Japanese.

afterlife
あの世

(ano yo; literally, "that world"). Also referred to as shigo no sekai, "the world after death," and Yomi no Kuni, "the Land of Darkness." The traditional, fundamental Japanese belief about life after death has been that the spirits of the dead gradually lose individuality and finally, after the 33rd anniversary of death, merge with the spirits of the ancestors and reside in mountains (see YAMA NO KAMI). The spirits then keep watch over the living, visit kinsmen over the NEW YEAR holidays, and at the summer BON FESTIVAL come to protect the rice crop (see TA NO KAMI). An exceptional individual, especially if he has died a tragic or violent death, is believed to become a vengeful god (onryō or GORYŌ) who needs to be placated.

Buddhism modified this traditional view, introducing such notions as reincarnation and different realms of being into which the dead might be reborn. Especially from the Kamakura period (1185–1333) on, belief in various hells as well as in the paradise of the Buddha AMIDA's Pure Land became popular. It was believed that during the 49 days after death—the period of intermediate existence—the dead passed through mountains and crossed a river before being judged by the lord Emma (Skt: Yama) or the Ten Lords (J: Jūō) and assigned to a realm for the next life. Today only a minority of Japanese people believe in the afterlife.

After the Banquet case
「宴のあと」裁判

(Utage no ato saiban). Case in which the right of privacy was first recognized by the Japanese judiciary. The Tōkyō District Court decided on 28 September 1964 that MISHIMA YUKIO in his novel Utage no ato (1960; tr After the Banquet, 1963) violated the privacy of politician ARITA HACHIRŌ. The fame of both the politician and the novelist made this one of the most discussed cases in Japan's history. See also PRIVACY, RIGHT TO.

Aganogawa
阿賀野川

River in Niigata Prefecture, central Honshū. It has its source in three rivers: the Nippashigawa, originating in Lake Inawashiro; the Agagawa (or Ōkawa), originating in the southern Aizu Mountains; and the Tadamigawa, originating in the lake called Ozenuma. It flows west through the Niigata Plain and enters the Sea of Japan at the city of Niigata. Three dams were constructed after World War II. In 1965 the waters of the Aganogawa were found to be contaminated with methyl-mercury pollutants (see POLLUTION-RELATED DISEASES). Length: 210 km (130 mi).

Agano ware
上野焼

(agano-yaki). Pottery produced near the mountain Fukuchiyama in northern Kyūshū from the early 17th century. Most prized by connoisseurs is the Old Agano ware produced from 1602 to 1632 under the supervision of the Korean potter Chon'gye (J: Sonkai; also known as Agano Kizo; d 1654) and his family for the Hosokawa family, lords of Kokura (now part of Fukuoka Prefecture).

The products were mainly tea utensils and pieces for everyday use with relatively thick, creamy white ash glazes and dark brown iron glazes, which resembled the Old KARATSU WARE and TAKATORI WARE from adjacent areas. The main innovations were the introduction of RAKU WARE in the early 18th century and a characteristic bluish-green copper glaze in the late 18th century. As a result of archaeological research, some old-style kilns have been reconstructed and the once almost extinct tradition of Agano ware is being revived.

Agata no Inukai no Tachibana no Michiyo
県犬養橘三千代

(?–733). A court lady during the reigns of six sovereigns. Also known as Tachibana no Michiyo. First married to the imperial prince Minu, she was the mother of TACHIBANA NO MOROE. By her second husband, FUJIWARA NO FUHITO, the statesman and compiler of the TAIHŌ CODE, she bore a daughter who became Empress KŌMYŌ. One of her poems is included in the 8th-century anthology Man'yōshū, and the so-called Shrine of Lady Tachibana at the temple HŌRYŪJI in Nara is said to have been donated by her.

agatanushi
県主

The head (nushi means "chief") of an agata, a political unit smaller than a kuni (province) in the kuniagata system of local administration instituted by the YAMATO COURT (ca 4th century–ca mid-7th century). It is believed that agatanushi were originally the hereditary chieftains of small tribal states (buzoku kokka). Tribal chieftains of larger territories were titled KUNI NO MIYATSUKO.

Agatsumagawa
吾妻川

River in northern Gumma Prefecture, central Honshū, originating near the Torii Pass on the border with Nagano Prefecture and flowing east to empty into the river Tonegawa near the city of Shibukawa. Because of its strongly acid waters, a neutralization plant was built at the town of Kusatsu in 1963. It is a source of hydroelectric power. Length: 74 km (46 mi); area of drainage basin: 1,364 sq km (527 sq mi).

Agawa Hiroyuki
阿川弘之

(1920–). Novelist. Born in Hiroshima. Upon graduation from Tōkyō University he was drafted into the Imperial Navy. After World War II, Agawa made his debut as an ardent follower of SHIGA NAOYA with the short story "Nennen saisai" (1946), about a soldier who returns to Hiroshima after the atomic blast. Many of his stories reflect his experiences as a naval officer. Other notable works include Haru no shiro (1952, Spring Castle), for which he received the Yomiuri Literary Prize in 1952, and Yamamoto Isoroku (1964– 65; tr The Reluctant Admiral: Yamamoto and the Imperial Navy, 1980), a novelization of the life of the admiral who planned the attack on Pearl Harbor. In 1979 Agawa received the Japan Academy Prize. In 1986 he published Inoue Seibi, a historical novel dealing with the life of the naval officer INOUE SHIGEYOSHI.

Agechirei
上知令

(Land Requisition Orders). An ordinance issued in 1843 by MIZUNO TADAKUNI decreeing the return of certain lands to the shogunate or daimyō. Part of the TEMPŌ REFORMS, the ordinance was intended to consolidate

Agawa Hiroyuki This World War II naval officer began writing fiction after the war; much of his work reflects his military experience.

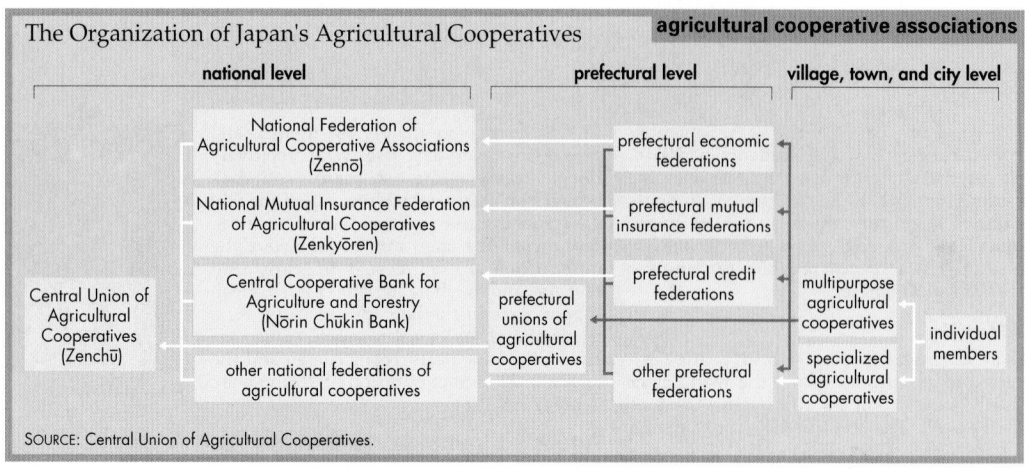

The Organization of Japan's Agricultural Cooperatives

agricultural cooperative associations

national level	prefectural level	village, town, and city level

National Federation of Agricultural Cooperative Associations (Zennō)

National Mutual Insurance Federation of Agricultural Cooperatives (Zenkyōren)

Central Cooperative Bank for Agriculture and Forestry (Nōrin Chūkin Bank)

other national federations of agricultural cooperatives

Central Union of Agricultural Cooperatives (Zenchū)

prefectural economic federations

prefectural mutual insurance federations

prefectural credit federations

prefectural unions of agricultural cooperatives

other prefectural federations

multipurpose agricultural cooperatives

specialized agricultural cooperatives

individual members

SOURCE: Central Union of Agricultural Cooperatives.

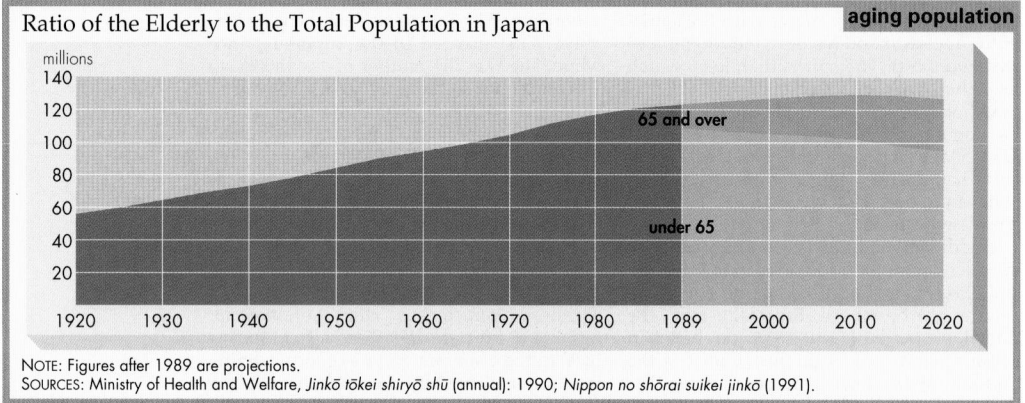

Ratio of the Elderly to the Total Population in Japan

aging population

millions

140 / 120 / 100 / 80 / 60 / 40 / 20

65 and over

under 65

1920 1930 1940 1950 1960 1970 1980 1989 2000 2010 2020

NOTE: Figures after 1989 are projections.
SOURCES: Ministry of Health and Welfare, *Jinkō tōkei shiryō shū* (annual): 1990; *Nippon no shōrai suikei jinkō* (1991).

Tokugawa house lands that had been dispersed over the years. It designated all lands within 10 *ri* (40 km; 25 mi) of Edo (now Tōkyō) and 5 *ri* (20 km; 12 mi) of Ōsaka as TENRYŌ, or land under direct shogunal control. Private holdings within the designated areas were to be restored to the shogunate, and the fief holders transferred to other lands. The order immediately incurred criticism from Tokugawa Nariyuki, the powerful daimyō of Wakayama. Tadakuni was forced to rescind the ordinance and two days later resigned from office.

age, legal definition of 年齢（法律上の）

(*nenrei, hōritsujō no*). In present-day Japan, age is legally reckoned from the date of birth and is calculated according to the Western calendar. In many cases, attainment of a particular age is deemed a condition for the obtaining of legal capacities, qualifications, rights, and duties. Some of the most important of these are as follows. The parent or guardian of a child must provide for the education of that child from 6 through 15 years of age (School Education Law, art. 22). A child who has reached 15 may independently make a will and enter into an employment contract. An adoptive child of 15

or over may no longer be required to furnish the consent of a parent or guardian instead of his or her own. However, there are still cases in which the permission of the family court is required.

Women reach the age of eligibility to marry at 16, men at 18. A minor who has reached the age of eligibility to marry, however, still requires parental consent to do so. A married minor is the same as an adult with respect to legal relations with others. Accordingly, for instance, such a person may, without the agreement of his or her parent or guardian, independently perform valid juristic acts. Furthermore, upon attaining the age of 20, the person is free of parental authority and obtains the right to vote.

agency → dairi

Agency of Industrial Science and Technology 工業技術院

(*Kōgyō Gijutsu In*). Government research institution administered by the MINISTRY OF INTERNATIONAL TRADE AND INDUSTRY (MITI). Located in Tōkyō, it was established in 1948. Its activities include conducting experiments and research on mining, performing geological surveys, establishing standards for weights and measures, preserving devices used to maintain those standards, and enforcing industrial standards. Under this agency are 16 research centers, including the National Research Laboratory of Metrology, the GEOLOGICAL SURVEY OF JAPAN, and the National Chemical Laboratory for Industry.

Ageo 上尾〔市〕

City in eastern Saitama Prefecture, central Honshū. Ageo developed as a post-station town on the NAKASENDŌ, one of the major highways during the Edo period (1600–1868). It was long known for its wheat and sweet potatoes, but since World War II, it has become a center for the automobile, nonferrous-metal, and machine industries. It is also a residential district for workers commuting to Tōkyō. Pop: 194,947.

aging population 高齢化社会

(*kōreika shakai*). Increase in the number of elderly within a nation's population and the socioeconomic changes associated with such growth. The aging of Japan's population became an important issue in the early 1980s and is expected to become increasingly acute as the number of elderly grows at the rate of approximately 650,000 per year. In 1989, 12 percent of Japan's population was aged 65 or over. By 2020 the proportion of elderly is expected to reach 25 percent, giving Japan the largest elderly population in the world.

In the last decade of the 19th century average life expectancy was about 43 years for men and 44 years for women. Longevity for both sexes first exceeded 50 years in 1947, 60 years in 1952, and 70 years in 1971. Figures for 1989 show a life expectancy of 82 years for women and 76 years for men. These figures are expected to increase to 84 years for women and 78 years for men by 2025. Due to the growing number of elderly within the working population, most large corporations have raised their mandatory retirement age to 60 years or above since the mid-1980s, and, increasingly, Japanese are working beyond what was once considered the mandatory retirement age of 55. In 1986 a more unified pension system, based on revisions of the National Pension Law, the Employees' Pension Insurance Law, and laws affecting other types of public pensions, was put into effect to respond to problems created by the aging population (see PENSIONS). Revisions were designed to assure the long-term stability of the nation's pension system and establish 65 as the uniform starting age for public pensions.

It is estimated that by 2020 there will be only three workers for each retiree. Supporting such a large, nonproductive population will require major adjustments to the financing and structure of public services, such as national health and welfare programs. Due to the disproportionately large burden that health care for the elderly was beginning to place on the medical care system as a whole, existing provisions for a national system of free health care for the elderly were replaced in 1983 by the LAW CONCERNING HEALTH AND MEDICAL SERVICES FOR THE AGED. The law stipulated that health care expenses for the elderly were to be covered partly by fixed rate contributions from prefectures, municipalities, the NATIONAL HEALTH INSURANCE program, employee insurance plans, and the individual. A 1986 amendment further increased costs borne by the elderly for health care. These changes temporarily stabilized medical care expenditure. In 1986 and 1988, however, expenses began to rise again, and by 1989 more than 25 percent of national medical care expenditure was devoted to caring for the elderly.

Other issues that are expected to accompany Japan's growing elderly population include the development of facilities and resources to care adequately for the senile and bedridden and the projected drop in economic vitality and tax revenues. Finding acceptable solutions to these problems will be one of Japan's greatest challenges as it approaches the 21st century.

Ago Bay 英虞湾

(*Ago Wan*). Inlet of the Pacific Ocean on the coast of Shima Peninsula, eastern Mie Prefecture, central Honshū. Part of the Ise-Shima National Park, the bay is also known

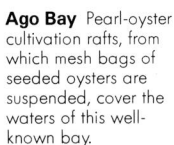

Ago Bay Pearl-oyster cultivation rafts, from which mesh bags of seeded oysters are suspended, cover the waters of this well-known bay.

for its pearl industry, begun by MIKIMOTO KŌKICHI in 1893.

agrarian nationalism→nōhon shugi

agricultural cooperative associations 農業協同組合

(*nōgyō kyōdō kumiai;* abbreviated *nōkyō*). The first agricultural cooperative associations in Japan were established in 1900. These *sangyō kumiai* (production unions) served rural communities as credit unions, sales and purchase cooperatives, and cooperative farming unions. The cooperatives were disbanded in 1943, but the movement was revived in 1947 and has flourished throughout the post–World War II period.

Prewar Cooperatives——The establishment of agricultural credit unions was first proposed in the Diet in 1891 by SHINAGAWA YAJIRŌ and HIRATA TŌSUKE. Enabling legislation was passed by the Diet and implemented in 1900. The organization of cooperatives was considered to be a means for modernizing Japanese agriculture and adapting it to a capitalist economy.

Prefectural federations were established early in the Taishō period (1912–26), completing a three-tiered, pyramidal structure of the associations (local, prefectural, and national bodies). Sales cooperatives, centered on rice sales, grew rapidly at this time, and they gained increased importance as nationwide markets were consolidated in the aftermath of the RICE RIOTS OF 1918 and the general economic crisis of the early 1920s. TENANT FARMER DISPUTES reflected a breakdown in the system of LANDLORDISM, and in response the government passed numerous measures to regulate and modernize agriculture. By 1924 just under half of all farms belonged to the cooperatives.

The early part of the Shōwa period (1926–89) was characterized by the consolidation of the national networks of cooperative organizations. After the SHŌWA DEPRESSION of the 1930s, cooperatives figured in government recovery plans and organizational activity was intensified.

The *sangyō kumiai* were disbanded in 1943, when the wartime government established the centrally controlled Nōgyōkai (Agricultural Association) in their place. Much of the organizational structure of the cooperatives was revived after the war, however, and a number of prewar institutions (such as the NŌRIN CHŪKIN BANK) have survived.

Postwar Cooperatives——Postwar agricultural cooperatives (called *nōgyō kyōdō kumiai* or *nōkyō*) were formed under the provisions of a special law enacted in 1947 as part of the Allied Occupation reforms. The cooperative movement's activities include the marketing of products, large-scale purchases, the extension of credit, mutual aid insurance, and joint production. Agricultural cooperatives had a nationwide membership of 8.5 million in 1991; this membership represented 3.8 million farming households, or an effective organization rate of 100 percent. As such, the cooperative movement can be counted as one of the giant organizations of Japan. At the same time, the cooperatives are facing a number of serious problems. Most threatening to their future is the narrowing of the agricultural base by the progressive urbanization of the country. This threatens not only cooperative movement membership levels but also the very existence of the rural household

inheritance system as farming households struggle to secure spouses for their heirs. A second problem is that rice farming, which has provided a stable base for the business operations of cooperatives, now suffers from surplus production. The adjustment of rice production levels could jeopardize the financial solvency of the cooperatives. A third major problem is that because of mergers (reinforced by the centralization of the nation's DISTRIBUTION SYSTEM), some local cooperatives have become so large that their power rivals that of the prefectural federation, causing a rethinking of the three-tiered structure of the movement.

agricultural policy 農業政策

(*nōgyō seisaku*). From the Meiji Restoration (1868) until the LAND REFORMS OF 1946, Japan had a tenant farming system under which landowners collected high amounts of rent in kind. In the early Meiji period (1868–1912) landowners played an important role in the maintenance and development of agriculture, since it was difficult for tenants to accumulate capital. Following the stabilization of Japanese capitalism after 1897, however, landowners rapidly lost their role in production. The government took over this role, providing subsidies, low-interest loans, education in agricultural operations, and other measures.

Agricultural policy and administration immediately after World War II focused on the resolution of problems associated with land reform. After 1955, economic recovery and the national INCOME-DOUBLING PLAN, which placed top priority on commerce, industry, and urban development, neglected the development of agriculture and farming villages. In order to cope with the resulting stagnation in agricultural income, the Basic Agriculture Law (Nōgyō Kihon Hō) was promulgated in 1961 to foster self-supporting owner-farmers, selective expansion of production, and structural improvements in agricultural labor productivity. The law was characterized by excessive emphasis on rice production and income elevation measures based on price manipulation. Among the programs it mandated were various subsidized projects, the promotion of large-scale single-crop farming, and the encouragement of highly mechanized modern agricultural practices aimed at agricultural land readjustment. These measures failed, partly because the rapid development of manufacturing led to a sharp increase in the price of land, reducing the availability of agricultural land and preventing the development of large-scale mechanized farms. Farming households turned to other forms of employment and food imports increased, lowering Japan's self-sufficiency in food. See also FOOD SUPPLY.

After the OIL CRISIS OF 1973 Japan made a quick turnabout and reemphasized the necessity of attaining self-sufficiency in food. Since that time, however, self-sufficiency rates (except in rice) have continued to decrease. In the early 1990s the main problems facing Japanese agricultural policymakers were as follows: First, much of Japan's food supply was imported, and decreasing self-sufficiency in food continued. This was partly because the high value of the yen made it less expensive to import food than to grow it domestically. Pressure from foreign countries to import agricultural products also played a role. Second, small-scale, relatively unproductive farms still predominated. Third, urbanization and industrialization, coupled with steep land prices, were

agricultural rites

Rice cultivation is the main focus of the various agricultural rites and ceremonies carried out in Japan.

In Ishikawa Prefecture, the rite called *aenokoto* begins in December with the head of a farming household donning traditional clothes and laying out a feast to welcome the *ta no kami*, or god of the rice paddies.

Toward evening the household head goes out to the fields to greet the *ta no kami*. Here he breaks up the ground with a hoe to help the god make its way out of the paddy and to the house.

At the ceremonial banquet, the household head welcomes the god to partake of the feast and gives thanks for the year's harvest. A small, freshly cut pine or a *sakaki* tree decorates the ceremonial spread. Trees are thought to be the dwelling places of various deities, including the *ta no kami*.

As the *ta no kami* is thought to be blind, each item of food must be carefully described by the household head.

agriculture This detail from a late-16th-century sliding-door painting at Nagoya Castle shows farmers planting rice.

steadily reducing the amount of land available for farming. Fourth, there was a chronic shortage of agricultural labor due to the gradual decrease of farming households and the shrinking size of farming communities. The Basic Agricultural Law was still at the heart of Japanese agricultural policy, but there were calls for new measures to deal with persistent agricultural policy problems.

agricultural rites　　　農耕儀礼

(*nōkō girei*). Rites and ceremonies connected with the growth cycle of cultivated food plants. In Japan agricultural rites have focused on rice growing since rice is the staple food crop. The sowing of rice grain in spring is followed by the transplanting of seedlings during the rainy season in early summer and by harvest in the fall. There are ceremonies for encouraging growth, supplications for rain and insect removal, and harvest rites. Sowing and harvest rites involve the arrival and departure of the TA NO KAMI, the traditional guardian deity of the rice fields. According to folk religious beliefs, during spring sowing the *ta no kami* comes from the sky, the mountains, or the farmhouse to dwell in the fields and watch over the rice plants until the autumn harvest, whereupon the deity returns home.

When the rice seeds are sown, a tree branch inserted in the rice-seedling bed serves as a symbol that trees are the dwelling places (*yorishiro*) of deities. Seedling-transplanting (*taue*) ceremonies take place before and after the actual transplanting of the rice shoots. Offerings are placed in the field or in the house. These always include three bundles of rice seedlings, which function as the resting place for the *ta no kami.*

At harvest time, farmhouses set up offerings to honor the *ta no kami.* In northern Kyūshū the head of the family gathers left-over rice plants into sheaves and brings them to the house on the day the *ta no kami* is believed to leave the rice paddies. He builds an altar to display the rice sheaves along with offerings for the *ta no kami.* This practice stems from the belief that the *ta no kami* actually dwells within the rice plants. In central Japan, the head of the household goes out to the fields to greet the *ta no kami* and guides the god back to the house for a bath and a ceremonial banquet.

The Okinawa and Amami island chains to the southwest of the Japanese mainland have developed their own rites, which show marked differences from those in Honshū, Shikoku, and Kyūshū. Rites accompanying transplanting are rarely seen in the southwest islands, and great emphasis is placed on rites for barley, millet, taro, and sweet potatoes, rather than on rice cultivation rites. There are a number of other basic differences between agricultural rites in the two regions. Ceremonies in the southwest islands place little emphasis on the *ta no kami.* Further, rites on the Japanese mainland tend to take place within the individual family, but rites in the southwest islands involve the entire hamlet. — *See photos, previous page.*

agriculture　　　農業

(*nōgyō*). Prior to the Meiji Restoration of 1868, as much as 80 percent of the population of Japan was engaged in farming. Although Japan has always had a great variety of crops in relation to its size, RICE has been overwhelmingly dominant as the main crop. Animal husbandry has remained relatively undeveloped; instead the emphasis has always been on improving productivity per unit of land area in rice and other plant crops. Highly labor-intensive farming methods were developed as a result of the limited acreage allotted to each farm household. These agricultural characteristics gave rise to farming practices and folk customs that in turn profoundly affected the nature of Japanese culture as a whole. Since the Meiji Restoration, industrialization and urbanization have had a significant impact on Japanese agriculture. The proportion of farmers to the total population, the proportion of cultivated acreage to the total area of the country, and the relative importance of agriculture in the total economy have all declined, while the importation of foodstuffs has increased (see FOOD SUPPLY). The country's tendency toward urbanization has led to a cultural transformation, and many of the events and customs of Japanese rural life have begun to lose their importance.

History of Agriculture— Japanese agriculture began about 2,000 years ago with the cultivation of rice. The rice plant and other important crops were introduced from abroad; very few indigenous plants have been cultivated in Japan. Crops cultivated in Japan since ancient times include wheat, barley, *awa* (Italian millet), *hie* (barnyard millet), SOYBEANS, AZUKI, *daikon* (see RADISHES), and CUCURBITS.

The oldest farm tools were made of wood or stone. When technology from the continent brought the manufacture of iron tools, rapid progress in agriculture was made for the first time. Yield per unit of area increased, and much wasteland was brought under cultivation.

From the end of the Heian period (794–1185) influential families emerged in the provinces. They assumed increasing political power and accumulated wealth through agricultural production. Taking control of the government in the Kamakura period (1185–1333), they showed greater concern about agriculture than did former rulers and encouraged improvements. Early in the Edo period (1600–1868) the first Japanese agricultural treatise, volume 7 of the military chronicle known as the SEIRYŌKI, was written. A number of agricultural books were published, the most famous being MIYAZAKI YASUSADA's NŌGYŌ ZENSHO (1696). With the emergence of a large number of cities and towns, predominant among them Edo (now Tōkyō) and Ōsaka, the percentage of the population not engaged in agriculture increased, and farmers were required to produce more and more. Although hard work was lauded as a virtue, more than half of the rice produced was collected as land tax, and farmers were frequently left with insufficient amounts for their own needs. They made do with wheat, barley, or millet. Agricultural output was increased with endeavors in three major areas: reclaimed lands, fertilizers, and plant breeding. The cultivation of crops for direct sale in the marketplace also flourished in the Edo period, and this brought agriculture and commerce closer together.

During Japan's drive toward modernization after the Meiji Restoration, European and American practices in agriculture, as in other areas, were studied closely. However, since the natural condition of the land in Japan is quite different from the West, mere transplantation of foreign technology often did not work well in agriculture. Emphasis was shifted, therefore, back to rice as the main crop and to the development of intensive farming methods. Since the introduction and employment of new technologies required facilities beyond the capacity of most farmers, agriculture experimental stations were built by the state to conduct most of the plant breeding of important crops. Fertilizers

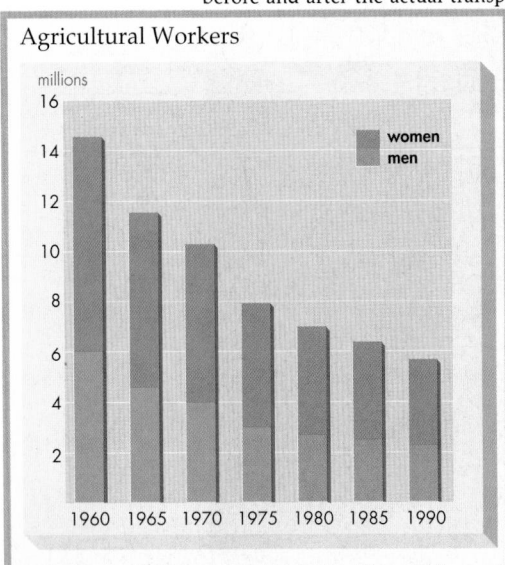

Agricultural Workers

millions

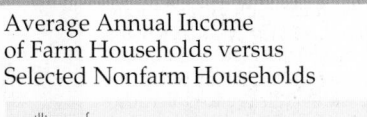

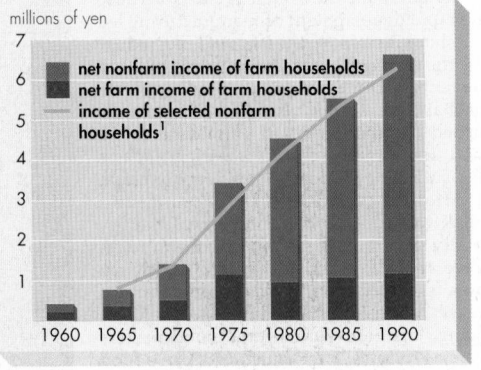

Average Annual Income of Farm Households versus Selected Nonfarm Households

millions of yen

■ net nonfarm income of farm households
■ net farm income of farm households
— income of selected nonfarm households[1]

1960　1965　1970　1975　1980　1985　1990

[1] The households of nonmanagerial employees of private companies and public corporations.
NOTE: Income figures for farm households do not include grants, subsidies, or income sent home by household members living and working away from the farm (*dekasegi* income). Data for farm households in 1990 is estimated.
SOURCES: Ministry of Agriculture, Forestry, and Fisheries, *Poketto nōrin suisan tōkei* (annual): 1975, 1989, 1991; Management and Coordination Agency, *Kakei chōsa hōkoku* (annual): 1991.

NOTE: Data for 1990 is estimated. Agricultural workers are defined as those who work exclusively or primarily on their own farms.
SOURCE: Ministry of Agriculture, Forestry, and Fisheries, *Poketto nōrin suisan tōkei* (annual): 1975, 1989, 1991.

were in great demand, and they became highly profitable commodities.

Agricultural Modernization—The impressive rationalization and modernization of agriculture has been largely a "quiet revolution." Since World War II, the most significant changes have included the introduction of millions of farming machines; the hybridization of crops, especially rice; and the development of a large and advanced agricultural chemical industry.

Of all the reform programs that followed World War II, the LAND REFORMS OF 1946 were perhaps the most successful in bringing about basic and far-reaching changes in Japan. A sweeping redistribution of land largely eliminated tenancy by 1949 and resulted in about 90 percent of cultivated land being farmed by owners. Confiscated land was sold at very low prices with long-term, low-interest mortgages. Postwar food shortages, high prices, an active black market in rice, and general inflation all worked to the advantage of Japan's farmers. In most cases they were able to pay off the debts on their new land with relative ease and to begin investing the capital that was needed for the rationalization of agriculture. The government aided farmers by establishing price support programs, especially for rice (see RICE PRICE CONTROLS). It also gave strong support to agricultural technical schools, experimental stations, and extension programs. AGRICULTURAL COOPERATIVE ASSOCIATIONS enhanced these government initiatives by extending low-interest loans and developing group marketing at the village level. The end result was a relatively affluent farming population with the education, incentive, and access to capital needed to purchase the new crop strains and fertilizers to increase yields, as well as the machinery to ease labor demand and increase capacity and flexibility.

Japan began to experience labor shortages by the late 1950s after the beginning of rapid economic growth. The demand for labor in the urban-industrial centers resulted in a growing exodus of people, especially the young, from rural areas. The decline of the farm population has led to serious and chronic labor shortages in the agricultural sector. A large part of the present agricultural labor force is over 45 years of age. Part-time farmers are numerous, and well over half the labor force is female.

It seems unlikely that Japanese agriculture could have succeeded without the spread of machines, chemicals, and other labor-saving devices that paralleled the explosive growth of manufacturing and commerce. Virtually all land is now cultivated by machine. Traditional methods of farming are rapidly giving way to power cultivators, tractors, and other machines, including pickup trucks. Due to all of these factors Japan's total rice crop increased from about 9.5 million metric tons (10.5 million short tons) in 1950 to over 13 million metric tons (14.3 million short tons) in 1975. Per capita rice consumption, however, has declined, and the government is now concerned with problems of overproduction and surplus storage. Farmers are being encouraged, and in some cases subsidized, to convert their rice fields to other crops. Accompanying changes in Japanese eating habits, production of meat, dairy products, fruits, and vegetables has increased.

Japan's traditional labor-intensive agriculture has been transformed into a highly mechanized and capital-intensive system in less than a generation. It remains one of the most productive systems in the world, and much of its new technology serves as a model for other developing Asian nations. There also has been a dramatic improvement in the standard of living of the Japanese farmer, yet some problems and questions remain for the future. Production costs, especially for rice, are very high, and Japanese agriculture requires heavy subsidies. Most farms are too small in scale for maximum utilization of land and capital, and operating units should be larger. When and how Japanese farms will reach a more efficient size remains a question for the future. ☎ 18-19

Agriculture, White Paper on
農業白書

(*Nōgyō hakusho*). An annual report submitted by the government to the Diet in accordance with provisions of the Basic Agriculture Law (*Nōgyō Kihon Hō*, 1961). The document provides public information concerning recent economic developments in agriculture and existing government measures. The government is explicitly required to include its views on trends in agricultural productivity. The views of the Agricultural Administration Council (*Nōsei Shingikai*) must be incorporated in these judgments. Finally, the report informs the Diet and the public of the government's intentions with respect to future policy and legislation.

Aguinaldo, Emilio
アギナルド, E.

(1869–1964). Nationalist leader of the Philippine Revolution against the Spanish and US colonial governments; president of the Philippine republic, 1899–1901. Born in the town of Kawit, Cavite Province. He became the leader of the revolutionary underground organization Katipunan in May 1897 but was exiled to Hong Kong under terms of a pact signed in December with the Spanish governor-general. After he returned home with US assistance at the outbreak of the Spanish-American War, his revolutionary government declared the Philippines independent on 12 June 1898 and established the Constitutional Republic of the Philippines. Aguinaldo was inaugurated as its president on 23 January 1899. In February he declared war against the United States, which had assumed sovereignty over the Philippines. His capture by US forces in 1901 ended his public career until World War II. Following the occupation of the Philippines by Japan in 1942, Aguinaldo collaborated with the Japanese military government, which had promised "independence with honor." When a puppet republican government was declared on 14 October 1943, however, Aguinaldo was not given the leading role he had anticipated. See also PHILIPPINES AND JAPAN.

Aichi Canal
愛知用水

(Aichi Yōsui). Canal in Gifu and Aichi prefectures, central Honshū, extending from the river Kisogawa in southern Gifu Prefecture to the southern tip of the Chita Peninsula in Aichi Prefecture. The completion of this canal in 1961 brought irrigation to the uplands of the Chita Peninsula for the first time. The canal supplies water to farms, factories, and residences in the Nagoya area. Length: 112 km (70 mi); total length of branch canals: 1,135 km (705 mi).

Aichi Machine Industry Co, Ltd
愛知機械工業[株]

(Aichi Kikai Kōgyō). Manufacturer, principally of automobile engines, transmissions,
Continued on page 20►

Production of Selected Crops, 1989 — agriculture

Crop	Production (metric tons)	Area harvested (hectares)
Grains		
Rice	10,347,000	2,097,000
Wheat	985,000	284,000
Vegetables		
White potato	3,586,500	119,740
Japanese white radish (daikon)[1]	2,448,000	62,300
Cabbage	1,623,000	41,400
Sweet potato	1,431,000	61,900
Chinese cabbage (hakusai)[2]	1,334,000	29,900
Onion	1,269,000	28,200
Cucumber	975,000	20,900
Tomato	773,000	14,500
Carrot	684,700	24,000
Eggplant	567,400	17,700
Welsh onion (negi)[3]	542,100	24,000
Lettuce	520,900	22,500
Green corn	386,600	39,300
Spinach	378,000	27,500
Taro (satoimo)[4]	363,700	26,800
Pumpkin and squash	296,500	19,300
Burdock (gobō)[5]	274,300	15,200
Soybean	221,700	151,600
Turnip	210,200	7,610
Sweet pepper	182,400	4,770
Azuki bean[6]	106,200	66,700
Green soybean (edamame)	104,000	14,100
Kidney bean	95,300	11,900
Fruits		
Satsuma or mandarin orange (mikan)	2,015,000	78,800
Apple	1,075,000	49,800
Watermelon	763,500	23,200
Japanese pear (nashi)[7]	439,100	18,600
Melon	415,600	17,950
Grape	275,100	24,600
Persimmon	268,100	26,300
Iyokan orange[8]	217,300	11,300
Strawberry	215,500	10,300
Natsumikan orange[9]	200,700	8,880
Peach	180,200	12,800
Hassaku orange[10]	142,900	6,750
Japanese plum (ume)[11]	66,100	15,200
Navel orange	54,400	3,800
Chestnut	39,500	35,100
Plum (sumomo)[12]	30,700	3,370
Cherry	14,500	2,420
Loquat	12,800	2,370
Pear	8,820	595

[1] *Raphanus sativus.* [2] *Brassica pekinensis.* [3] *Allium fistulosum.* [4] *Colocasia esculenta.* [5] *Arctium lappa.* [6] *Phaseolus angularis.* [7] *Pyrus serotina.* [8] *Citrus iyo.* [9] *Citrus natsudaidai.* [10] *Citrus hassaku.* [11] *Prunus mume.* [12] *Prunus salicina.*
SOURCE: Ministry of Agriculture, Forestry, and Fisheries, *Poketto nōrin suisan tōkei* (annual): 1991.

Agricultural Machinery in Use

Year	Tractors and cultivators	Power rice-planting machines	Power reapers	Combines
1970	3,452,300	32,400	263,000	45,400
1975	3,927,400	740,300	1,327,100	344,100
1980	4,223,100	1,746,100	1,619,100	883,900
1985	4,432,800	1,992,600	1,518,300	1,109,500
1990	4,328,000	1,983,000	1,298,000	1,215,000

NOTE: Figures for 1990 are estimates.
SOURCE: Ministry of Agriculture, Forestry, and Fisheries, *Poketto nōrin suisan tōkei* (annual): 1989 and 1991.

Aichi Machine Industry Co, Ltd

Farming Today: Adapting to New Conditions

Production of rice, Japan's staple crop, has been the basis of the country's agriculture for some 2,000 years. Over half the nation's arable land is devoted to paddies, and the transformations wrought upon them to meet the demands of each season have shaped Japan's terrain and colored its landscape since ancient times. Many of the nation's rituals and festivals are related to the planting, cultivation, or harvesting of rice. The traditional method of rice farming was highly labor-intensive; this fact fostered an emphasis on the interdependence of households in Japanese rural community life.

Although rice is still the predominant crop, Japanese agriculture has now entered a complex era of transition. Rice consumption is on the decline. There is increasing demand from consumers for a wider variety of produce. Members of the younger rural generation are reluctant to follow in their parents' footsteps and remain on the farm. Faced with such challenges, a significant number of farming households are finding it a struggle to keep their farms going.

In response, many have begun to specialize in particular fruit and vegetable crops suited to local growing conditions. The hope that they can increase the viability of their farming operations by improving quality and productivity is spurring a growing number of farmers to make use of the latest research in agronomy and biotechnology.

Mechanized rice-planting is now commonplace on Japan's small farms, with their chronic shortages of labor.

Paddies still dominate much of the rural landscape. In Toyama Prefecture, farmhouses are interspersed among them.

Apples are a vital crop in Nagano and Aomori prefectures, being well suited to cold mountain climates.

Mikan (Satsuma oranges), grown in Japan's warmer regions, are cultivated here in a greenhouse to make them ripen faster and fetch higher values.

Night lighting is used to control the blooming of chrysanthemums, a popular flower in Japan.

Raising strawberries indoors enables growers to make them available virtually year-round.

Demand for flower crops is on the rise. Here women pick lavender in Hokkaidō.

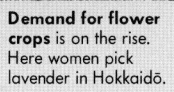

Food industry giants, applying the same quality-control principles as other industries, have begun to computerize their operations.

Picking the buds of green tea bushes in Kyōto Prefecture. Many regions of Japan produce their own local varieties of tea.

Ōta Market, Tōkyō. Each day buyers line up to make their bids on the newly arrived produce.

Cabbages being harvested on a mountain plateau in Gumma Prefecture. Proximity to major markets like Tōkyō and Ōsaka is vital for vegetable growers.

The "Super Tomato" plant displayed at Expo '85 in Tsukuba, Ibaraki Prefecture. Hydroponically cultivated, it produced 15,000 tomatoes in a year.

aikidō In this art of self-defense developed by Ueshiba Morihei, the attacker's own strength and momentum are used against him. Here, an opponent is thrown after attempting an attack to the head during a formal practice exercise.

small-size commercial vehicles, and machine tools. Established in 1943 when the aircraft division of Aichi Tokei Denki became independent of its parent firm. It started production of automobiles after World War II and in 1965 became affiliated with the NISSAN MOTOR CO, LTD, whose cars it produces on consignment. Sales for the fiscal year ending March 1991 totaled ¥252.6 billion (US $1.8 billion), and the company was capitalized at ¥8.5 billion (US $62.0 million). Headquarters are in Nagoya.

Aichi Prefecture   愛知県

(Aichi Ken). Located in central Honshū; bordered by Gifu and Nagano prefectures to the north, Shizuoka Prefecture to the east, the Pacific Ocean to the south, and Mie Prefecture to the west. The eastern section is largely covered by the Mikawa Highland. To the west, on the Nōbi Plain, lies the city of NAGOYA, which contains over one-third of the prefecture's population. Principal rivers are the KISOGAWA and YAHAGIGAWA.

In feudal times the prefecture was composed of the two provinces of Mikawa and Owari. During the 16th century three warlords from these provinces succeeded in unifying the country: ODA NOBUNAGA, TOYOTOMI HIDEYOSHI, and TOKUGAWA IEYASU. The present prefectural boundaries were established in 1872.

In the modern age the prefecture has seen a steady growth in the size and number of industrial cities. Located at the center of the PACIFIC COASTAL BELT, it has become one of the major industrial centers of Japan (see CHŪKYŌ INDUSTRIAL ZONE), ranking first among all prefectures in annual production. Textiles, steel, chemicals, automobiles, and ceramics are its leading industries. Lumber also continues to be a major industry. Farm products include rice, vegetables, and chickens. Area: 5,139 sq km (1,984 sq mi); pop: 6,690,603; capital: Nagoya. Other major cities include TOYOHASHI, TOYOTA, ICHINOMIYA, and OKAZAKI.

Aichi Prefecture
Location and
Prefectural Crest

Aichi Steel Works, Ltd   愛知製鋼[株]

(Aichi Seikō). Company engaged in the production and sale of special steel materials and forged steel products. It is a leader in the manufacture of spring steel and stainless steel shapes. A member of the Toyota group, the company was established as the steel manufacturing department of TOYODA AUTOMATIC LOOM WORKS, LTD, in 1934. It exports spring steel to about 60 countries. In 1990 the company's annual sales were ¥178.9 billion (US $1.3 billion), and capitalization was ¥24.8 billion (US $180.8 million). Headquarters are in the city of Tōkai, Aichi Prefecture.

AIDS   エイズ

(acquired immune deficiency syndrome; J: eizu). The first confirmed case of AIDS in Japan was reported in May 1985. As of February 1991 the Ministry of Health and Welfare had confirmed the existence of 374 AIDS patients and 1,640 carriers of the

virus. Among patients, 280 were hemophiliacs who had contracted AIDS through infected blood preparations that had been imported, largely from the United States. Blood preparations are now sterilized by heating and are no longer a source of infection. Medical costs of hemophiliac patients of AIDS are borne by the firms that sold the infected blood preparations. The Law concerning the Prevention of AIDS, effective in 1989, was created as a part of efforts to arrest the spread of the disease. See also AIDS, LAW CONCERNING THE PREVENTION OF.

AIDS, Law concerning the Prevention of   エイズ予防法

(Eizu Yobō Hō). Law enacted in 1988 to prevent the spread of the AIDS virus in Japan. It became effective in 1989. The law requires doctors to explain to anyone who tests positive for the AIDS virus, and who, in the judgment of the doctor, is considered likely to spread the disease, the methods necessary to prevent its transmission. Doctors are further required to report the patient's name, age, and address, and information about the manner in which the virus was contracted, to the prefectural governor within seven days. If a patient fails to follow the doctor's instructions, the governor will urge or order the patient to undergo a second medical examination, during which methods to prevent transmission will again be explained. A report to the prefectural governor is not required in the case of a patient who has contracted the AIDS virus from imported blood preparations, which are presently the cause of the majority of reported AIDS cases in Japan. Critics have, however, pointed out that the law represents a danger to the human rights and to the right to privacy of AIDS patients.

Aikawa   愛川[町]

Town on the river Nakatsugawa in northern Kanagawa Prefecture, central Honshū. Long a sericultural center, Aikawa flourished during the Taishō period (1912–26) as a producer of thrown silk; today, the textile industry continues to prosper here. Pop: 40,424.

Aikawa   相川[町]

Town on the island of Sado off the coast of northwestern Honshū; administratively part of Niigata Prefecture. Aikawa developed as a mining town when gold was discovered in 1601. With the decline in mining, its population, as high as 100,000 in the early 1600s, decreased. The annual mine festival in July is a popular tourist attraction. Pop: 11,121.

Aikawa Yoshisuke   鮎川義介

(1880–1967). Also known as Ayukawa Gisuke. Businessman and founder of the Nissan zaibatsu, a major financial and industrial combine before World War II. Born in Yamaguchi Prefecture, he graduated from Tōkyō University and later studied malleable cast-iron technology in the United States. In 1910 he established the Tobata Foundry in Kyūshū, which later grew into NISSAN MOTOR CO, LTD. In 1928 he took over Kuhara Mining, formerly run by his brother-in-law KUHARA FUSANOSUKE, and turned it into a holding company called Nihon Sangyō (Nissan). Taking advantage of a major stock market boom after the MANCHURIAN INCIDENT of 1931, he forged 148 of Nissan's subsidiaries into a powerful zaibatsu. Aikawa moved Nissan to Manchuria in 1937 and reorganized it as the Manchuria

Heavy Industry Co. He served as its president until the end of World War II when Occupation forces dissolved the Nissan group, forcing him to resign. He later turned to politics and was elected to the House of Councillors in 1953.

aikidō   合気道

One of the Japanese MARTIAL ARTS; a system of pure self-defense derived from the traditional weaponless fighting techniques of jūjutsu (see JŪDŌ) in its use of immobilizing holds and twisting throws whereby an attacker's own momentum and strength are used against him. UESHIBA MORIHEI (1883–1969) is credited with the modern systematization of aikidō. After schooling in the various martial arts Ueshiba drew upon the teachings of Takeda Sōkaku (1860–1943), who taught the daitō aiki system of jūjutsu, and his own religious experiences as a convert to the ŌMOTO sect of Shintō in formulating the basic skills of aikidō self-defense as distinct from jūjutsu or jūdō. Since the 1960s aikidō has rapidly gained in popularity throughout Japan and in many countries of the world.

Practice usually takes an established form, or kata: one partner takes the offensive role dealing blows or holds and the other deflects these using aikidō moves. Since two persons cannot practice defensive techniques against each other, aikidō does not lend itself to a contest situation. However, in the Tomiki form of aikidō "free-fight" (randori) matches, points are scored for defensive technique by contestants who alternate in taking the role of the attacker. Students are ranked according to skill level.

Aikoku Fujinkai   愛国婦人会

(Patriotic Women's Association). Founded in 1901 by OKUMURA IOKO to aid and comfort Japanese soldiers and their families. Its membership expanded dramatically during the Russo-Japanese War of 1904–05. By 1919 membership reached over 1 million; in the 1930s it reached over 3 million. In 1942 the Aikoku Fujinkai, DAI NIPPON KOKUBŌ FUJINKAI, and other women's groups were merged by the government to form a new group, the DAI NIPPON FUJINKAI.

Aikoku Kōtō   愛国公党

(Public Party of Patriots). Political society founded in January 1874 by ITAGAKI TAISUKE, GOTŌ SHŌJIRŌ, ETŌ SHIMPEI, and others. Spearheading the FREEDOM AND PEOPLE'S RIGHTS MOVEMENT, it petitioned the government to establish a national assembly. The society soon disbanded, fearing government suppression after the SAGA REBELLION. In May 1890 Itagaki revived the Aikoku Kōtō, which later merged with other political groups to form the JIYŪTŌ.

Aikokusha   愛国社

(Society of Patriots). One of Japan's first political coalitions, formed by ITAGAKI TAISUKE in February 1875 to associate his RISSHISHA with other groups in the FREEDOM AND PEOPLE'S RIGHTS MOVEMENT. The small group was dissolved when Itagaki accepted the promise of ŌKUBO TOSHIMICHI at the ŌSAKA CONFERENCE OF 1875 that the government would draft a constitution. When no constitution emerged, Itagaki withdrew from the government and revived the Aikokusha in September 1878. Two years later the group renamed itself the LEAGUE FOR ESTABLISHING A NATIONAL ASSEMBLY. It was a predecessor of the JIYŪTŌ (Liberal

Party), which Itagaki founded in October 1881.

aikyōgen 間狂言

Performances by KYŌGEN players within a NŌ play. There are two main types of *aikyōgen: katariai* and *ashiraiai*. In *katariai* the player provides a kind of colloquial commentary, which makes the story more easily understood and bridges the interval between acts, allowing the main Nō actor to change costumes. Representative examples can be seen in the Nō plays TAKASAGO, IZUTSU, and YASHIMA. In *ashiraiai*, the *aikyōgen* player shares the stage with the Nō actors, performing an integral role in the play. Examples of *ashiraiai* are found in the Nō plays ATAKA and *Dōjōji*.

Aikyōjuku 愛郷塾

Small private school near the city of Mito, Ibaraki Prefecture, founded by agrarian nationalist TACHIBANA KŌZABURŌ in April 1931. Its two-and-a-half-year course for primary-school graduates and its youth-group lectures focused on mathematics, bookkeeping, natural history, and farm management. Regular talks were also given on the importance of village community life and traditional rural virtues. The school's name was literally "Academy for the Love of One's Community." When it was discovered that Tachibana and several students were implicated in the MAY 15TH INCIDENT of 1932, the school was closed. It reopened in June but survived only until March 1933.

Ai Mitsu 靉光

(1907–46). Western-style painter. Real name Ishimura Nichirō. Born in Mibu, Hiroshima Prefecture. Ai worked for a time as a designer in a printing firm. In 1925 he went to Tōkyō, where he studied Western-style painting at the Pacific Art Society Institute (Taiheiyō Gakai Kenkyūjo). An admirer of Chinese painting based on detailed realism as well as of Western surrealism, Ai portrayed the inner dimensions of humanity under the shadow of war.

Ai no korīda → In the Realm of the Senses

Ainu アイヌ

The term Ainu is now used to refer to an indigenous people of Hokkaidō and adjacent islands as a single integrated population, although formerly a number of ethnically distinct groups were recognized. (Originally *ainu* meant man [human being or male] in the Ainu language of Hokkaidō.) It is generally assumed that the Ainu are descendants of the people referred to as the Emishi or Ezo in ancient Japanese documents, but exact identification remains unclear. The gradual integration of the separate so-called Ainu groups resulted from collective resistance to encroachment over the centuries by Japanese and other neighboring ethnic groups. In 1878 these integrated groups came to be officially referred to in Japanese as *kyūdojin* (former indigenous people), which accelerated among them the growth of a strong group identity.

Population—At present, the majority of Ainu live in Hokkaidō, although at least a small number live in southern Sakhalin in Russian territory. During much of the Edo period (1600–1868) many of their ancestors also resided in the northern part of Honshū, in the southern Kuril Islands, along the lower reaches of the Amur River, and in

southern Kamchatka.

Treated as aliens by the Japanese and affected by disease and other factors, the Ainu population declined considerably in the middle of the 19th century. In a survey conducted in 1807 the total Ainu population of Hokkaidō and Sakhalin numbered 23,797; by 1854 the number had dropped to 18,805. It is reported that by the first quarter of the 20th century mixed marriages between Ainu and Japanese had increased to approximately 36 percent. By the 1960s mixed marriages had increased to 43 percent and the mixed population to 88 percent. Unmixed births dropped from approximately 70 percent in 1902 to zero by 1957. In 1986 the total number of people in Hokkaidō identifying themselves as Ainu was 24,381.

Origins—The Ainu have often been referred to as Caucasoid or Australoid, but such speculations are based largely upon occasional resemblances in facial features, body

hair, etc. Recent intensive skeletal, anthropometric, serological, and other genetic studies suggest closer racial ties with some of the neighboring Tungusic, Altaic, and Uralic populations of Siberia. Despite these descriptive data, a precise distinction between the Japanese and the Ainu cannot be made from the standpoint of physical anthropology.

Traditional Lifestyle—The traditional Ainu culture was supported by hunting, fishing, and gathering. Village communities (*kotan*) of up to 20 houses were located along riverbanks or near game trails to take advantage of food and water resources. Dwellings were rectangular and pole-framed, consisting of a main room next to a smaller room with an entryway, enclosed with a thatched roof and walls made of miscanthus or bamboo grass. In the middle of the roof was a covered opening to allow

Ainu

Every September, Ainu elders in Kushiro, Hokkaidō, make offerings at Lake Harutori to the gods of the village, fire, and lake to ensure a successful fishing season.

This Ainu ankle-length robe is made of cotton cloth overlaid with patterns cut from different-colored fabric.

An Ainu woman demonstrates a handloom, weaving cloth from thread made by spinning elm and other tree bark fibers. The cloth is used to make clothing and bags.

In an effort to help preserve the steadily disappearing Ainu culture, the city of Asahikawa, Hokkaidō, has restored this traditional Ainu dwelling (*chise*) in Arashiyama Park.

Artist's Rendering of a 19th-Century Ainu Dwelling

treasure platform (Ainu: *iyoykir*)
seat of honor
master sleeping area
hearth
inner entryway
vestibule
outer entryway
cooking area

fencelike row of sticks (Ainu: *nusasan*)
raised storehouse
ceremonial altar (Ainu: *rorunso*)
spirit window (Ainu: *rorunpuyar*)
ritual bear cage (Ainu: *heperset*)
side window
family sleeping area
cooking area window

smoke to escape; the doorway was protected by a woven hanging. For sitting and sleeping, mats of woven grass or animal pelts were used to cover the earthen floor of the main room.

An interesting feature of Ainu social organization was a bilineal descent system: males tracing descent through male descent groups (patrilineages) symbolized by different animal crests (*itokpa*) and females tracing descent through comparable matrilines symbolized by hereditary chastity belts (*ponkut* or *upsor*).

Among the Hokkaidō Ainu traditional dress for a man was a calf-length coatlike garment made of *attus*, a woven textile of shredded and softened inner elm bark fibers, worn with a woven belt, and in winter a short sleeveless jacket of deer or other animal fur. Women's clothing was similar but ankle length. A custom formerly followed by all women was the tattooing of a circle around the mouth. Started at puberty and completed before marriage, the tattoo was both a sign of adulthood and of preparedness for marriage.

Language, Religion, and Culture—Although three major dialects have been recognized (Hokkaidō, Sakhalin, and Kuril), the relationship of Ainu to other languages has not been clearly established. Although the Ainu possess no system of writing (see AINU LANGUAGE), there is a rich oral tradition including songs, epic poems (*yukar*), and stories with formalized expressions in prose and poetry.

Ainu religious beliefs focus on the existence of another world composed of the spirit essences of all former earthly beings and inanimate objects, subject to the same spirit forces (*kamuy*) that control the visible universe: wind, rain, hail, and, above all, fire (*ape-huci*). Homage must be paid to the spirits of the ancestors and their divine protection implored. The people's prayers to the gods are believed to be transmitted by means of tufted wooden poles; special prayer sticks are also used in offering wine to the gods. Shamans predict good or bad luck in hunting and take charge of the treatment of ailing people.

A number of animal gods, including those of the bear, the large striped owl, and the killer whale, play a prominent part in Ainu religion and ritual. One of the most important Ainu rituals is the Bear Festival, held to express gratitude to the bear deity for providing the Ainu with his gifts of bearskin and meat. The ritual features an actual bear, brought up by the community and thought to be inhabited by the bear deity. After three days of profound reverence, the bear is killed, so that the deity may return to the other world divested of its early form. More superficial versions of such rituals, known as *i-omante*, are currently carried out every year in Ainu communities as tourist attractions.

The Modern Ainu—Since the beginning of the Meiji period (1868–1912) traditional hunting, fishing, and gathering of wild plants have been gradually replaced by rice and dry-crop cultivation, commercial fishing, and other activities. There has also been a shift toward Japanese practice in housing, clothing, food, and other aspects of family life and economy, with traditional dress and religious objects reserved for ceremonial occasions. The compulsory educational system has also resulted in an emphasis on the use of Japanese by the younger generations.

Ainu language　アイヌ語

(*ainugo*). The language originally spoken by the Ainu people of northeastern Asia. There is evidence that the Ainu language was originally spoken in the Tōhoku region of northern Honshū, Hokkaidō, the Kuril Islands, and Sakhalin. Although no record remains of the Tōhoku Ainu dialect, traces can be found in local place names. The last of the Kuril Ainu were moved to Hokkaidō before World War II, and after the war most of the Sakhalin Ainu were repatriated to Hokkaidō, too, so that today the Ainu language is spoken only on that island.

The Ainu language is no longer in daily use, and few living persons have actually spoken Ainu as their primary language. Linguists first became interested in the language at the turn of the century, but then only two major dialect groups of Ainu were left: those of Hokkaidō and Sakhalin. These two groups differ and are virtually mutually unintelligible. Both can be subdivided into many minor dialects, of which the Hokkaidō group is the better recorded. The British missionary John BATCHELOR, the Japanese scholar KINDAICHI KYŌSUKE, and the linguist Chiri Mashiho (1909–61), an Ainu, conducted early linguistic studies of the language.

Phonology—The Ainu language has a very simple phoneme inventory. Like Japanese it has only 5 vowels (/i/, /e/, /a/, /o/, and /u/), and it has even fewer consonants than Japanese, only 12: the plosives /p/, /t/, /k/; the affricate /c/; the sibilant /s/; the glottal fricative /h/; the liquid /r/; the nasals /m/ and /n/; the semivowels /y/ and /w/; and the glottal plosive /'/. The syllabic structure for the Hokkaidō dialect is $CV(C)$ (C = consonant, V = vowel) and in Sakhalin, $CV(V)(C)$, in which case the vowels must be identical. A pitch accent system is found in most Hokkaidō dialects, but in the Sakhalin Ainu dialect, there is instead an opposition between short and long (double) vowels.

Syntax, Grammar, and Vocabulary—Ainu word order is similar to that of Japanese. Both are so-called SOV (subject-object-verb word order) languages. Affixing is one of the distinctive aspects of the Ainu language. By adding prefixes and suffixes very long words can be produced, often so long that they correspond to whole sentences in English or Japanese. There are many compounds and derivatives, and this feature has sometimes been pointed to as a resemblance to the polysynthetic languages (such as a number of Native American languages). In addition, Ainu is extremely rich in words for natural phenomena. Ainu nouns do not distinguish gender, case, or number, but some nouns have in addition to their conceptual form a "belonging" form, which expresses that the noun in question is owned by, or is part of, somebody or something.

Ainu Literature—Although the Ainu have no written language, their epics, songs, and stories have been orally transmitted from generation to generation, preserving classical forms of speech, which have disappeared from the colloquial language. The *yukar* (hero epics) form the essence of Ainu literature. A typical *yukar* consists mainly of stock phrases and descriptions, but since the choice of these as well as the framework of the epic is left to each individual reciter to determine, the same story is never repeated exactly. One telling equals one story with the plot remaining the same.

Affinities—The origin and affinities of the Ainu language have been much discussed, but there is no consensus. Many similarities exist between Japanese and Ainu, which naturally reflect mutual linguistic influences resulting from centuries of close contact between the Ainu and Japanese people. The question of a genetic relationship to other languages also remains in doubt, although a number of theories have been proposed. Until sounder evidence is produced, however, Ainu will continue to be grouped with certain other languages of northeastern Asia as either Paleosiberian or Paleoasiatic.

Ainu Museum　アイヌ民族博物館

(Ainu Minzoku Hakubutsukan). Museum established in 1984 in the district of Shiraoi in Hokkaidō to preserve and transmit the culture of the AINU, an indigenous people of the island. Among the items on exhibit are traditional articles of clothing, such as the *attush* (a coatlike garment made of tree fibers), and hunting equipment. There are exhibits illustrating traditional Ainu ceremonies, and ritual dances, such as the *i-omante rimse*, are performed. Outside the museum are several restored Ainu dwellings.

Ainu music　アイヌ音楽

(Ainu *ongaku*). Ainu music, like other aspects of AINU culture, is distinct from that of Japan as a whole. Among the many types of Ainu song the oldest is the *yukar*, long epics about the totemic gods and ancestral heroes of the race. The former are called *kamui-yukar*, the latter *oina*; there are also other subtypes. Apart from *yukar*, the two main kinds of Ainu song are *upopo* (festival songs) and *rimse* (group dance-songs). The former are performed sitting down, to the accompaniment of rhythmical taps on a chest; the latter are sung antiphonally, are faster, and have partly meaningless repeated texts. Another kind of dance-song is the *tapkar*, a slow stamping dance, performed solo by men. The Ainu also have work songs, especially for brewing *sake* (*sake-haw*) and for pounding flour, lullabies (*ihumke*) characterized by a special high trilling, and many songs that incorporate imitations of animals or birds. Ainu musical instruments include a straw whistle (*wakka-ku-kutu* or *chi-rekte-kuttar*); a coiled-bark horn (*kosa-bue*); a wide, flat skin drum (*kaco*); a guimbarde (*mukkuri*); a five-string zither (*tonkori*); and a type of lute.

Aioi　相生〔市〕

City in southwestern Hyōgo Prefecture, western Honshū, on the INLAND SEA. Originally a fishing village, Aioi developed as a post-station town on the highway San'yōdō. Since a shipbuilding industry was established in 1907, it has become an industrial center. The Peiron Festival for boat racing is held here in May. Pop: 36,871.

aircraft industry　航空機工業

(*kōkūki kōgyō*). The Japanese aircraft industry got its start after World War I, when such companies as Mitsubishi Shipbuilding Co, Ltd, Nakajima Aircraft Co, and Kawasaki Shipyard Co began producing aircraft engines and fuselages. By the beginning of World War II, Japan had developed advanced aircraft technology, which it put to use in the production of such aircraft as the ZERO FIGHTER. Immediately after the war, however, US Occupation authorities prohibited the development and production of aircraft in Japan.

New Tōkyō International Airport, popularly called Narita Airport, is located 66 km east of Tōkyō in Chiba Prefecture. Tōkyō's chief international airport, it was opened in 1978 and now handles some 20 million passengers annually.

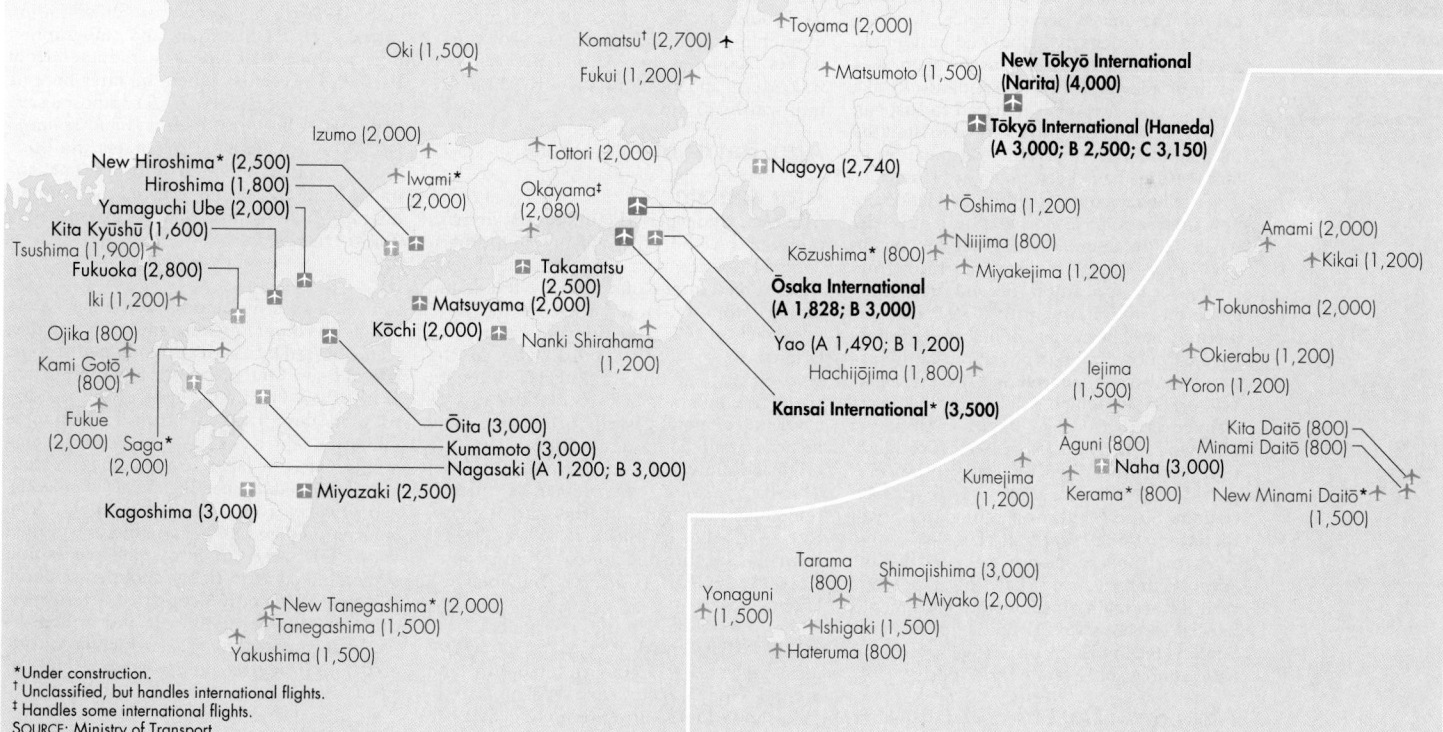

Commercial Airports in 1992

🛪 class 1 airports (primarily handling international flights)

🛪 class 2a airports (primarily handling domestic flights)

🛪 class 2b airports (primarily handling domestic flights but also some international flights)

✈ class 3 airports (airports primarily handling regional flights)

Airport names are followed by their runway lengths in meters.

Rebun (800)
Rishiri (800)
Wakkanai (2,000)
Mombetsu (1,200)
Memambetsu (2,000)
Asahikawa (2,000)
Naka Shibetsu (1,800)
Kushiro (2,300)
New Chitose (3,000)
Obihiro (2,500)
Okushiri (800)
Hakodate (2,500)
Aomori (2,500)
Akita (2,500)
Hanamaki (2,000)
Shōnai (2,000)
Yamagata (2,000)
Sendai (A 1,200; B 2,000)
Sado (890)
Niigata (A 1,314; B 2,000)
Fukushima* (2,000)
Oki (1,500)
Komatsu† (2,700)
Toyama (2,000)
Fukui (1,200)
Matsumoto (1,500)
New Tōkyō International (Narita) (4,000)
Tōkyō International (Haneda) (A 3,000; B 2,500; C 3,150)
Izumo (2,000)
Tottori (2,000)
Nagoya (2,740)
New Hiroshima* (2,500)
Hiroshima (1,800)
Iwami* (2,000)
Okayama‡ (2,080)
Ōshima (1,200)
Amami (2,000)
Yamaguchi Ube (2,000)
Kōzushima* (800)
Niijima (800)
Kikai (1,200)
Kita Kyūshū (1,600)
Miyakejima (1,200)
Tsushima (1,900)
Takamatsu (2,500)
Tokunoshima (2,000)
Fukuoka (2,800)
Matsuyama (2,000)
Ōsaka International (A 1,828; B 3,000)
Iki (1,200)
Kōchi (2,000)
Nanki Shirahama (1,200)
Yao (A 1,490; B 1,200)
Okierabu (1,200)
Ojika (800)
Iejima (1,500)
Yoron (1,200)
Kami Gotō (800)
Hachijōjima (1,800)
Kansai International* (3,500)
Fukue (2,000)
Aguni (800)
Kita Daitō (800)
Minami Daitō (800)
Saga* (2,000)
Ōita (3,000)
Kumejima (1,200)
Naha (3,000)
Kumamoto (3,000)
Kerama* (800)
New Minami Daitō* (1,500)
Nagasaki (A 1,200; B 3,000)
Miyazaki (2,500)
Kagoshima (3,000)
Tarama (800)
Shimojishima (3,000)
Yonaguni (1,500)
Miyako (2,000)
New Tanegashima* (2,000)
Ishigaki (1,500)
Tanegashima (1,500)
Yakushima (1,500)
Hateruma (800)

*Under construction.
† Unclassified, but handles international flights.
‡ Handles some international flights.
SOURCE: Ministry of Transport.

Japan's aircraft industry was revived after the signing of the SAN FRANCISCO PEACE TREATY in 1951. After a period of mainly providing maintenance for US military aircraft, the industry expanded its development and production capacities. The licensed production of the Lockheed T-33A jet trainer was begun in 1956 with technology acquired from the United States, and in 1962 independent Japanese aircraft development culminated in the YS-11, a prototype twin-turboprop transport plane.

In the early 1990s the Japanese aircraft industry still depended heavily on licenses from US companies. Major tie-ups included the joint production of the B-767 and B-777 passenger aircraft with the Boeing Co and the further development of the F-16 fighter with General Dynamics. In terms of sales the Japanese industry is still small compared to its US counterpart. Sales in 1991 totaled ¥851 billion (US $6.3 billion), about one-fifteenth of the US sales figures. Approximately 80 percent of Japan's aircraft industry sales goes to meet national defense needs. The industry is competitive in the production of new materials and electronic components but remains behind in engine technology.

airports
空港

(kūkō). Commercial airports in Japan are classified by the government into three categories based on size and use. As of 1992, class 1 consisted of Japan's 3 major international airports: TŌKYŌ INTERNATIONAL AIRPORT (Haneda), NEW TŌKYŌ INTERNATIONAL AIRPORT (Narita), and Ōsaka International Airport.

Akagisan Much of the area around this conical double volcano is used as farmland.

Aizu Yaichi This award-winning *tanka* poet was also a professor of art history at Waseda University and a noted calligrapher.

Class 2 comprised 25 major domestic airports (some with international service), and class 3 was composed of 45 smaller domestic airports. Besides these, there were 10 unclassified airports used jointly by commercial and military aircraft or for other purposes. Of these 83 commercial and semicommercial airports, 49 had facilities for jet passenger aircraft.

Both Haneda and Ōsaka International airports have 3,000-meter (10,000-ft) main runways, but they have very limited areas (408 hectares or 1,008 acres for Haneda and 317 hectares or 783 acres for Ōsaka) and poor terminal facilities in proportion to the number of passengers served. Since they are located near densely populated residential areas, noise has been a serious problem. As a result of a lawsuit filed by residents, Ōsaka International Airport is required to suspend flights between 9 PM and 7 AM and to limit the number of aircraft operating per hour. Similar measures have been taken at Haneda.

To alleviate overcrowding at Haneda, a new international airport was built at Narita in Chiba Prefecture. It was finally opened in 1978 after a lengthy delay resulting from strong local opposition. Second-stage construction was initiated in 1987, but its completion has been postponed indefinitely because of continuing opposition. Construction has also commenced on KANSAI INTERNATIONAL AIRPORT, which will be situated on reclaimed land in Ōsaka Bay; completion is planned for the summer of 1994. A reclamation project in Tōkyō Bay, due to be completed in 1995, is also under way to increase by some 50 percent the operating capacity of the international airport at Haneda.

Airport operations are regulated by the Airport Improvement Law of 1956, and facilities are maintained by the government's Special Account for Airport Improvement. Landing fees and a tax on aircraft fuel are the chief sources of revenue for airports.

Aisin Seiki Co, Ltd　アイシン精機[株]

(Aishin Seiki). Manufacturer and seller of automotive components. It also produces and distributes beds, sewing machines, and knitting machines. Incorporated in 1949. It is a member of the Toyota group. The company has 8 overseas offices and 12 subsidiaries and affiliates in the United States, Mexico, Brazil, Belgium, the Netherlands, France, Germany, England, Singapore, Australia, and Taiwan. Sales for the fiscal year ending March 1991 totaled ¥525.0 billion (US $3.8 billion), of which automotive parts accounted for 94

percent. The company was capitalized at ¥31.9 billion (US $232.5 million) in the same year. Headquarters are in Kariya, Aichi Prefecture.

Aizawa Seishisai　会沢正志斎

(1782–1863). Scholar of the MITO SCHOOL, a nationalist school of Confucian study. Real name Aizawa Yasushi. Born in Hitachi Province (now Ibaraki Prefecture). He became a pupil of FUJITA YŪKOKU, a noted Neo-Confucian scholar. Aizawa served TOKUGAWA NARIAKI, the lord of the Mito domain (now part of Ibaraki Prefecture), and helped reform his government. He also helped establish a new domain school, Kōdōkan, and influenced the domain's policies toward the end of the Tokugawa shogunate (1603–1867). His book on national policy, *Shinron* (1825), inspired many proimperial activists.

Aizawa Tadahiro　相沢忠洋

(1926–89). Amateur archaeologist known for his 1946 discovery of the first paleolithic STONE TOOLS in Japan. Born in Tōkyō. Aizawa's discovery in a partly exposed stratum of the so-called KANTŌ LOAM in Gumma Prefecture led to a full-scale investigation of the now-famous IWAJUKU SITE, confirming that PALEOLITHIC CULTURE existed in Japan more than 30,000 years ago.

Aizu Basin　会津盆地

(Aizu Bonchi). In western Fukushima Prefecture, northern Honshū. Bounded by the Ōu Mountains on the east and the Echigo Mountains on the west. A rice- and vegetable-producing region, it is also known for its lacquer ware. Major cities are AIZU WAKAMATSU and KITAKATA. Length: 35 km (22 mi); width: 13 km (8 mi).

Aizu, Battle of　→Byakkotai

Aizu domain　会津藩

(Aizu han). Edo-period (1600–1868) domain centered on the Aizu Basin in southern Mutsu Province; part of present-day Fukushima Prefecture. Ruled first by the Gamō family (from 1601) and then by the Katō family (from 1627), the domain was in 1643 granted to HOSHINA MASAYUKI, who, as the son of the second Tokugawa shōgun, TOKUGAWA HIDETADA, received the status of SHIMPAN (collateral vassal). In 1696, the family was granted the name Matsudaira, the original family name of TOKUGAWA IEYASU. The last *daimyō*, MATSUDAIRA KATAMORI, fought on the side of the anti-imperial forces in the BOSHIN CIVIL WAR (1868). OMOTEDAKA (estimated annual production of rice): 230,000 KOKU (1 *koku* = 180 liters or 5 US bushels).

Aizu Hongō ware　会津本郷焼

(aizu-hongō-yaki). Ceramics made in and around Hongō, near Aizu Wakamatsu in Fukushima Prefecture. Production dates to 1645. At first folk-style stoneware of reddish brown, gritty clay was made. The rims or shoulders were covered with slip glazes and glossy black overglazes, or with off-white glazes with a gray-green or blue tinge.

Underglaze-blue porcelains were most typical of 19th century Aizu Hongō work, the folk-style stonewares having been relegated to second place. This flourishing porcelain industry was practically destroyed in 1868 when many potters fought for the Tokugawa shogunate in the Boshin Civil War. At the end of the century the industry was revived to meet the demand for electrical

insulators and other commercial products. Today both stoneware and porcelain are mass-produced as well as handmade.

Aizu Komagatake　→Komagatake

Aizu nōsho　会津農書

(Aizu Book of Agriculture). One of the earliest Japanese agricultural treatises; three volumes. Written in 1684 by Sase Yojiemon (1630–1711), a rich farmer of the Aizu domain (now part of Fukushima Prefecture), and revised and expanded by his adopted son, Sase Rin'emon, its wide range of agricultural topics includes cultivation, irrigation, rice planting, and weed removal. It was based primarily on the author's experience rather than on Chinese works, which made it noteworthy for its time.

Aizu Wakamatsu　会津若松[市]

City in western Fukushima Prefecture, northern Honshū. Established as a castle town of the Aizu domain in the late 16th century, much of the city burned in the BOSHIN CIVIL WAR accompanying the Meiji Restoration (1868). Famous for its lacquer ware, the city also produces *sake*, textiles, and lumber. There is an emerging electronics industry. Attractions include the remains of Wakamatsu Castle and IIMORIYAMA, the hill where the BYAKKOTAI, a band of youths, died in a last effort to save the Tokugawa shogunate. Pop: 119,080.

Aizu Yaichi　会津八一

(1881–1956). Also known as Shūsō Dōjin. TANKA poet, art historian, and calligrapher. Born in the city of Niigata. Graduated from Waseda University, where he later became professor of art history. Aizu composed several *tanka* collections, such as *Nankyō shinshō* (1924), which lyrically celebrates the Buddhist art and architecture of the ancient capital of Nara. In 1951 he received the Yomiuri Literary Prize for his collected poems, *Aizu Yaichi zen kashū*.

aji　鰺

(saurel; also translated as horse mackerel). Fish of the order Percida, family Carangidae, characterized by a series of bony plates on its lateral lines. One of Japan's most important food fishes. Over 40 species of *aji* are distributed along the coast from Hokkaidō to Okinawa. The three types of *aji* most commonly eaten in Japan are *ma aji* (Trachurus japonicus), *muro aji* (Decapterus muroadsi), and *shima aji* (Caranx delicatissimus). *Ma aji* is often prepared as a type of SASHIMI called *tataki*: fillets are cut into small pieces and served mixed with finely chopped scallion. It is also commonly deep-fried. *Muro aji* is dried or seasoned with salt and grilled directly over a fire. *Shima aji*, which is considered a delicacy, is prepared as *sashimi* or SUSHI.

Ajikawa　安治川

Also known as Ajigawa. Canal in the city of Ōsaka, Ōsaka Prefecture, central Honshū. It links the river Yodogawa with Ōsaka Bay. The Ajikawa was constructed in the late 17th century by KAWAMURA ZUIKEN. During the Edo period (1600–1868) it was used for transporting rice and other products to markets in Ōsaka. Today its many piers service vessels importing petroleum and coal.

Ajinomoto Co, Inc　味の素[株]

(Ajinomoto). Diversified manufacturer and distributor of food products and one of the leading producers of amino acids, pharmaceuticals, and fine chemicals in the world. The company dates from 1909, when Suzuki Saburōsuke II placed Aji-no-moto brand monosodium glutamate seasoning on commercial sale. International activities began in 1917 with the establishment of an office in New York. In 1988 the company had 45 subsidiaries, affiliates, plants, and representative offices in 20 foreign countries. Ajinomoto's joint ventures include those with CPC International, General Foods, and Gervais Danone. Sales for the fiscal year ending March 1991 totaled ¥504.0 billion (US $3.7 billion), of which processed foods accounted for 47 percent; seasonings, 20 percent; amino acids, pharmaceuticals, and fine chemicals, 14 percent; and edible oils and other products, 19 percent. The company was capitalized at ¥79.3 billion (US $577.8 million) in the same year. Headquarters are in Tōkyō.

Ajinomoto General Foods, Inc
味の素ゼネラルフーヅ[株]

(Ajinomoto Zeneraru Fūzu). Manufacturer of beverages, foods, and animal feed. Incorporated in 1954. It is a joint venture between General Mills of the United States and Ajinomoto Co, Inc. For the fiscal year ending March 1990, sales totaled ¥79.5 billion (US $579.4 million) and capitalization stood at ¥3.9 billion (US $28.4 million). Headquarters are in Tōkyō.

ajisai → hydrangea, Japanese

Akabane Kōsaku Bunkyoku
赤羽工作分局

(Akabane Manufacturing Branch). A government-operated factory established in the Akabane section of Tōkyō in 1871. The factory adopted technology from Europe and manufactured steam boilers and light machinery. It was transferred to the Ordnance Department of the Navy Ministry in 1883.

Akabira
赤平[市]

City in central Hokkaidō, on the river Sorachigawa. First settled in 1891, Akabira became an important mining town after the opening of a railway line to the ISHIKARI COALFIELD in 1913. Since 1960 many mines have closed down. Pop: 19,409.

Akabori Shirō
赤堀四郎

(1900–1992). Biochemist known for his research on the synthesis of amino acids. Born in Shizuoka Prefecture, he graduated from Chiba Medical College (now a part of Chiba University) and studied chemistry at Tōhoku University. He studied in Germany and the United States and became professor at Ōsaka University after his return. In 1958 he became the first director of Ōsaka University's Institute for Protein Research and, in 1960, university president. He received the Order of Culture in 1965.

Akaezo fūsetsu kō
赤蝦夷風説考

(Report on the Ezo Lands). A report in two volumes presented to the Tokugawa shogunate in 1783 by the physician and scholar KUDŌ HEISUKE concerning Russia's advance toward Japan's northern frontier regions, then called EZO. He suggested official trade with Russia to avert potential aggression and noted the vast resources of Ezo. *Akaezo fūsetsu kō* was a forerunner of works that further attacked the shogunate's NATIONAL SECLUSION policy, including HAYASHI SHIHEI's *Kaikoku heidan* (1786) and HONDA TOSHIAKI's *Keisei hisaku* (1798).

Akagawa Jirō
赤川次郎

(1948–). Novelist. Born in Fukuoka Prefecture; graduate of Tōhō High School. His debut novel, *Yūrei ressha* (Ghost Train), was published in 1976. Akagawa has attracted a following of young readers with his light, humorous mysteries, such as *Mikeneko Hōmuzu no suiri* (1978, The Deductions of Calico Cat Holmes). His other works include *Sanshimai tanteidan* (1982; tr *Three Sisters Investigate*, 1985) and *Mayonaka no tame no kumikyoku* (1981; tr *Midnight Suite*, 1984).

Akagi Masao
赤木正雄

(1887–1972). Civil engineer and specialist in erosion control. Born in Hyōgo Prefecture. Akagi graduated from Tōkyō University in 1914 and entered the Home Ministry. After studying in Austria in 1923, he introduced advanced erosion control technology to Japan and worked to modernize Japanese flood and erosion control operations. Akagi was awarded the Order of Culture in 1971.

Akagisan
赤城山

Conical double volcano in eastern Gumma Prefecture, central Honshū. It is part of the Akagi Prefectural Park. At the summit are two crater lakes, Ono and Kono. The lower slopes are used as farmland. Height: 1,828 m (5,997 ft).

Akahata
赤旗

(Red Flag). Newspaper; principal organ of the JAPAN COMMUNIST PARTY. It is the oldest extant party newspaper in Japan, having been launched in 1928 under the name *Sekki*; it was renamed *Akahata* in 1946. (*Sekki* and *akahata* are two different pronunciations of the same Chinese characters meaning "red flag.") It was suppressed from 1935 to 1945, and publication was suspended during the Korean War, resuming in 1952. In 1959 a Sunday edition was added and the format changed to one with more general appeal. With a circulation of about 3 million (1990), it has considerable impact on public opinion in Japan.

Akahata Jiken → Red Flag Incident
of 1908

akahon → kusazōshi

Akai Electric Co, Ltd
赤井電機[株]

(Akai Denki). Manufacturer of high-fidelity audio and video equipment. Incorporated in 1929. In 1978 Akai adopted the video home system (VHS) format in the home video market. Future plans call for an increased share in domestic markets and expansion in the US

market. Akai has overseas subsidiaries in Australia, the United Kingdom, France, and Germany. Sales for the fiscal year ending November 1990 totaled ¥62.7 billion (US $485.7 million). For that same year, the export ratio was 91 percent, and the company was capitalized at ¥4.3 billion (US $33.3 million). Headquarters are in Tōkyō.

Akaishidake
赤石岳

Mountain on the border of Nagano and Shizuoka prefectures, central Honshū; a major peak of the AKAISHI MOUNTAINS in the JAPANESE ALPS. The name Akaishi ("red stone") derives from the color of the quartzite rocks found near its peak. Height: 3,120 m (10,236 ft).

Akaishi Mountains
赤石山脈

(Akaishi Sammyaku). Mountain range on the border of Shizuoka, Yamanashi, and Nagano prefectures, central Honshū. The southernmost of the three ranges that form the JAPANESE ALPS, this range is often called the Southern Alps, and most of its peaks are included in the SOUTHERN ALPS NATIONAL PARK. Some of its peaks are KITADAKE (3,192 m; 10,472 ft), Ainotake (3,189 m; 10,462 ft), KOMAGATAKE (2,966 m; 9,731 ft), AKAISHIDAKE (3,120 m; 10,236 ft), and Nōtoridake (3,026 m; 9,928 ft).

Akai tori
赤い鳥

(Red Bird). Children's literary magazine published from July 1918 to October 1936 (publication was temporarily halted from March 1929 to January 1931). Founder and editor SUZUKI MIEKICHI called on numerous established writers to help modernize and improve the quality of children's literature and turned *Akai tori* into one of the most important juvenile publications of its day. It had the backing of intellectuals and educators as well as virtually the entire Japanese literary world. Among the many writers and poets who contributed to its pages were such prominent figures as MORI ŌGAI, SHIMAZAKI TŌSON, NOGAMI YAEKO, AKUTAGAWA RYŪNOSUKE, and KITAHARA HAKUSHŪ. *Akai tori* is noted for having pioneered the concept of soliciting contributions by child readers. The success of *Akai tori* spawned other children's magazines; its peak circulation exceeded 30,000. Other writers who participated in its publication included OGAWA MIMEI, SAIJŌ YASO, KUME MASAO, and UNO CHIYO.

Akaji Yūsai
赤地友哉

(1906–84). Lacquer ware craftsman. Real name Akaji Sotoji. Born in Kanazawa, Ishi-

Akaishi Mountains The mist-shrouded peak of Komagatake, seen from the vicinity of a climbers' hut on the upper slopes of the peak Kitadake.

Akagawa Jirō This best-selling author's light, humorous mysteries have attracted a large following among young readers.

Akama Shrine
Women in ancient costume parade across a bridge on the grounds of this shrine during its annual festival, the Senteisai.

akebi The light purple flowers of this vine appear in spring. The edible, oblong fruit of the *akebi* splits lengthwise at maturity.

48 Falls of Akame
Ninaidaki (pictured) is known as the most beautiful of the waterfalls—actually more than 50 in number—on this tributary of the river Nabarigawa.

kawa Prefecture. Akaji studied the traditional art of lacquer ware in the city of Kanazawa and in Tōkyō. He produced contemporary works by applying the *magewazukuri* technique of bending thin pieces of wood to form vessels and other implements. He was designated a Living National Treasure in 1974.

Akakura Hot Spring   赤倉温泉

(Akakura Onsen). Located at the foot of the mountain Myōkōsan in southwestern Niigata Prefecture, central Honshū. An earthy, carbonated spring; water temperature 55°–60°C (131°–140°F).

Akama Shrine   赤間神宮

(Akama Jingū). Shintō shrine in the city of Shimonoseki, Yamaguchi Prefecture; dedicated to the spirit of the boy emperor ANTOKU (1178–85), who died in the naval battle of DANNOURA. Antoku's remains are buried within the precincts of a Buddhist temple that was located here. In 1191 Emperor GO-TOBA renamed the temple Amidaji and ordered the construction of a memorial hall. In 1875 the government ordered that the temple be converted to a Shintō shrine, which was called Akama Shrine. Among its many treasures is an early manuscript of the 13th-century HEIKE MONOGATARI (The Tale of the Heike), known as the *Nagato-bon.* The regular annual festival is held on 7 October; the colorful Senteisai festival is held annually on 2–4 May to pay reverence to the deceased emperor.

Akamatsu family   赤松氏

(Akamatsushi). Warlords of the Muromachi period (1333–1568). Descendants of the Murakami Genji branch of the MINAMOTO FAMILY. In 1336 Akamatsu Norimura (1277–1350) allied himself with ASHIKAGA TAKAUJI

and was made military governor (*shugo*) of Harima Province (now part of Hyōgo Prefecture). From the end of the 14th century, the Akamatsu were one of the four families eligible to head the Board of Retainers (Samurai-dokoro) of the Muromachi shogunate. In 1441 AKAMATSU MITSUSUKE assassinated the shōgun ASHIKAGA YOSHINORI and was in turn destroyed by the YAMANA FAMILY and the HOSOKAWA FAMILY. The Akamatsu later regained power but finally lost their domains in 1521 after defeat by their vassals, the URAGAMI FAMILY.

Akamatsu Katsumaro   赤松克麿

(1894–1955). Political activist. Born in Yamaguchi Prefecture. He helped to form the political study group SHINJINKAI at Tōkyō University. After graduation in 1919 he worked as a journalist for the *Tōyō keizai shimpō* until he joined the staff of the Nihon Rōdō Sōdōmei (Japan Federation of Labor) in 1921. In 1922 he joined the newly organized JAPAN COMMUNIST PARTY, and in 1926 he helped form the SHAKAI MINSHŪTŌ (Socialist People's Party), becoming its secretary-general in 1930. After 1931 he began to espouse right-wing state socialism. In 1932 he organized the Nihon Kokka Shakaitō (Japan State Socialist Party) and the next year helped create the KOKUMIN KYŌKAI (Nationalist Association). He was elected to the Diet in 1937 and helped organize the Nihon Kakushintō (Japan Reform Party). During World War II, he headed the planning section of the IMPERIAL RULE ASSISTANCE ASSOCIATION. After the war he was barred from political office by Occupation authorities.

Akamatsu Mitsusuke   赤松満祐

(1373–1441). Warlord. In the MUROMACHI SHOGUNATE, he served as military governor (SHUGO) of three provinces in western Honshū. In 1441, angered by the attempts of the shōgun ASHIKAGA YOSHINORI to reallocate some of his lands, Mitsusuke assassinated him. Shogunal forces led by YAMANA SŌZEN defeated Mitsusuke later that year, forcing him to commit suicide. The events are known as the Kakitsu Incident.

Akame, 48 Falls of   赤目四十八滝

(Akame Shijūhattaki). Waterfalls located on a small tributary of the river Nabarigawa, in the southern part of the city of Nabari, Mie Prefecture, central Honshū. Contrary to the name, there are more than 50 waterfalls, noted for their natural beauty and for spring and autumn foliage. A hiking trail and camping grounds are nearby.

Akan, Lake   阿寒湖

(Akanko). In eastern Hokkaidō. Located west of the mountain Oakandake within Akan National Park. It was created by an eruption of Oakandake, and islands formed by lava flows dot the lake. Caldera cliffs covered with primeval forests extend on its eastern side. Smelt, trout, crucian carp, and carp are found in the lake. Balls of algae called *marimo,* which rise to the surface in the morning and sink at night because of photosynthesis, are an unusual natural phenomenon of the lake. Area: 12.7 sq km (4.9 sq mi); circumference: 31 km (19 mi); depth: 45 m (148 ft); altitude: 420 m (1,378 ft).

Akan National Park   阿寒国立公園

(Akan Kokuritsu Kōen). Situated in eastern Hokkaidō, the park is set in rugged mountain terrain with volcanoes, some of which are ac-

tive; subarctic forests; and numerous caldera lakes. The largest lake in the area is Lake KUSSHARO in the north; the area surrounding Lake AKAN in the southwest contains the volcanic cones of MEAKANDAKE (1,503 m; 4,931 ft) and OAKANDAKE (1,371 m; 4,498 ft). To the east lies Lake MASHŪ, the second major lake, which has a transparency depth of 35.8 m (117.4 ft), one of the greatest in the world. The forests consist largely of white birch (*shirakaba*), Yeddo spruce (*ezomatsu*), and Sakhalin fir (*todomatsu*). Two famous hot-spring resorts are Akankohan by Lake Akan and Kawayu by Lake Kussharo. Area: 905 sq km (349 sq mi).

Akasaka   赤坂

Business, entertainment, and high-income residential district in the northern part of Minato Ward, Tōkyō. During the Edo period (1600–1868), there were numerous DAIMYŌ residences here. In the eastern part of Akasaka there are now elegant Japanese-style restaurants (*ryōtei*) catering to politicians and businesspeople, and many office buildings, hotels, and nightclubs. The Geihinkan (the official state guesthouse and former imperial residence; see AKASAKA DETACHED PALACE) and the US embassy are located in Akasaka.

Akasaka Detached Palace   赤坂離宮

(Akasaka Rikyū). Officially known as the Geihinkan (State Guesthouse). Distinguished example of late-Meiji-period (1868–1912) Western-style architecture; located in Minato Ward, Tōkyō. Designed by Katayama Tōkuma (1854–1917), with the palace at Versailles and the Louvre in Paris serving as his models. Built in 1909 as a residence for the crown prince, the palace was symbolic of the Meiji government's desire to demonstrate Japan's attainment of equality with the West. Most of the building materials and furnishings were imported. KURODA SEIKI is among the many collaborating artists whose works decorate the interior. In the late 1960s a plan was presented for its restoration, and in 1974 it was converted into an official state guesthouse for visiting foreign dignitaries.

Akashi   明石[市]

City in southern Hyōgo Prefecture, western Honshū. A castle town and post-station town on the San'yōdō highway during the Edo period (1600–1868), it is now a heavy industry center, with steel and machinery plants built on reclaimed land. It is a major transportation center for the INLAND SEA area and a commuter suburb of both Ōsaka and Kōbe. Much of the coastal beauty, celebrated in literary works, has been lost. Pop: 270,722.

Akashi Strait   明石海峡

(Akashi Kaikyō). Narrow strait in the Inland Sea between the island of Awajishima and the city of Akashi in Hyōgo Prefecture, Honshū. It links Ōsaka Bay and the Harima Sea and is part of the most convenient route between Honshū and Shikoku. A bridge over the strait connecting Honshū and Awajishima (see HONSHŪ-SHIKOKU BRIDGES) is scheduled for completion in 1998. The Akashi Strait is noted for its strong currents. Deepest point: 135 m (443 ft).

Akashi Yasushi   明石康

(1931–). Diplomat and United Nations official. Born in Akita Prefecture. A graduate of Tōkyō University, Akashi also received a master's degree at the University of Virginia.

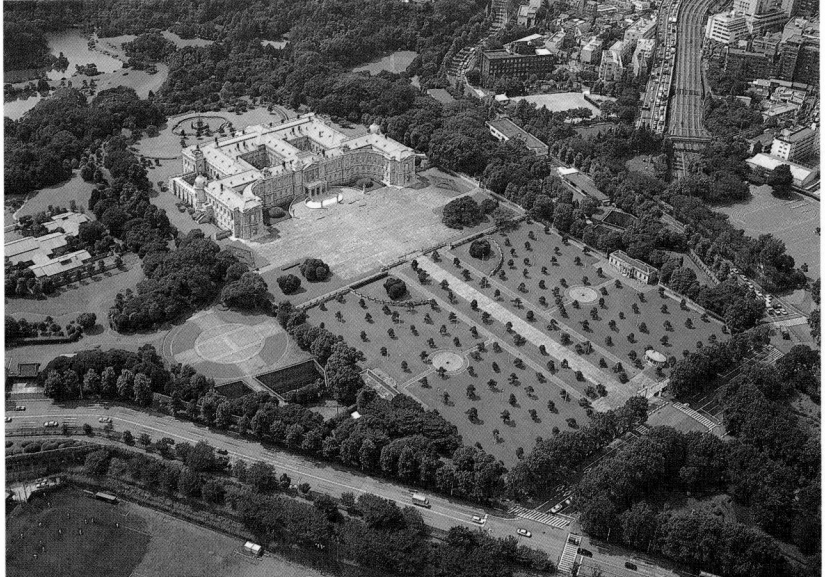

In 1957 he joined the United Nations Secretariat as a political affairs officer, becoming the first Japanese to serve as a permanent member of the United Nations staff. In 1974 he joined Japan's Ministry of Foreign Affairs and became Japan's ambassador to the United Nations. In 1992 Akashi headed UN peacekeeping operations in Cambodia, the largest peacekeeping effort in UN history. His publications include *Kokusai rengō* (1965, The United Nations) and *Kokuren biru no mado kara* (1984, From the Windows of the United Nations).

Akayu Hot Spring   赤湯温泉

(Akayu Onsen). Located on the northern edge of the YONEZAWA BASIN in the city of Nan'yō, Yamagata Prefecture, northern Honshū. A common salt spring; maximum temperature 56°C (133°F). Many skiers lodge here in the winter.

Akazome Emon   赤染衛門

(ca 957–1041). Court lady and WAKA poet. She served Rinshi, wife of FUJIWARA NO MICHINAGA, and perhaps later Rinshi's daughter, Empress Shōshi (JŌTŌ MON'IN). Akazome Emon was one of the foremost female court poets of her day; 93 of her poems are found in IMPERIAL ANTHOLOGIES, beginning with the SHŪI WAKASHŪ (ca 1000, Collection of Gleanings). Her personal anthology, *Akazome Emon shū*, contains more than 600 poems. Akazome Emon is also traditionally credited with having written part (chapters 1–30?) of the historical tale EIGA MONOGATARI (mid-11th century; tr *A Tale of Flowering Fortunes*, 1980).

akebi   木通

Akebia quinata. A deciduous, woody vine of the family Lardizabalaceae growing wild in Honshū, Shikoku, and Kyūshū; also found in Korea and China and cultivated in Europe and the United States. The compound leaves have five leaflets. Clusters of male and female flowers appear in the spring. The light purple fruit has edible white flesh with black seeds. The vines of a three-leaved variety called *mitsuba akebi* (*A. trifoliata*) are used in handicrafts. See also MUBE.

Akebono   曙

(1969–). SUMŌ wrestler. The 64th grand *sumō* champion (*yokozuna*) and the first non-Japanese to hold that rank. Born in Hawaii. Real name Chad George Rowan. Akebono entered the Azumazeki stable in 1988 and set a *sumō* record by becoming *yokozuna* in 1993 after just 30 tournaments.

Akebono Brake Industry Co, Ltd   曙ブレーキ工業[株]

(Akebono Burēki Kōgyō). Manufacturer of brake mechanisms for automobiles, railway cars, and industrial machinery. Incorporated in 1936. Among the company's major stockholders are Japanese automakers and Bosch of Germany. Akebono has a joint venture with General Motors of the United States. Sales for the fiscal year ending March 1991 totaled ¥104.5 billion (US $761.7 million), and capitalization stood at ¥7.8 billion (US $56.9 million) in the same year. Headquarters are in Tōkyō.

Akechi Mitsuhide   明智光秀

(?–1582). Also known as Koretō Hyūga no Kami. One of the principal captains of and the assassin of ODA NOBUNAGA, Japan's 16th-century unifier. Mitsuhide first appears in history in 1569 as one of Nobunaga's military and administrative deputies in Kyōto; for the next three years he occupied the difficult position of intermediary between Nobunaga and the shōgun ASHIKAGA YOSHIAKI. Between 1570 and 1573 Mitsuhide also took part in Nobunaga's campaigns in Ōmi (now Shiga Prefecture) and was awarded Sakamoto Castle and two districts in that province. In 1580 Mitsuhide was assigned Tamba Province (now part of Kyōto and Hyōgo prefectures) and was appointed one of two special commissioners to conduct a provincewide cadastral survey (see KENCHI) in Yamato Province (now Nara Prefecture), and in 1581 he performed a similar task in Tango Province (now the northern part of Kyōto Prefecture). In 1582 he turned against Nobunaga for reasons that remain unclear and destroyed him in the HONNŌJI INCIDENT. Defeated 11 days later by TOYOTOMI HIDEYOSHI in the Battle of YAMAZAKI, he was killed in flight by marauding peasants.

Aki   安芸[市]

City in southeastern Kōchi Prefecture, Shikoku, located on Tosa Bay. Aki is the political, economic, and cultural center of southeastern Kōchi. Forestry is a thriving industry in the nearby mountains, and on the Aki Plain rice and vegetables are grown. The coast is known for its fishing. Special products of the city include roof tiles and cutlery. Pop: 23,739.

Akiba Shrine   秋葉神社

(Akiba Jinja; formally Akibasan Hongū Akiba Jinja). Shintō shrine on Akihasan, a

Akasaka Detached Palace Now an official state guesthouse, this Tōkyō palace was built in 1909 as a residence for the crown prince.

Akan National Park Lake Kussharo is visible in the distance behind the volcanic cone of Iōzan.

mountain in the Shūchi district of Shizuoka Prefecture; dedicated to Kagutsuchi no Kami, the deity of fire. Founded in the early 8th century, the shrine was believed to afford protection from calamities related to fire. There is a legend that the deity Izanagi used his sword to kill the fire god worshiped here. Veneration of this shrine gradually spread throughout eastern Japan in the Edo period (1600–1868). The shrine is noted for its annual Fire Festival (Hi Matsuri), held on 16 December.

Akigawa   秋川[市]

City in northwestern Tōkyō Prefecture at the confluence of the rivers Akigawa and Tamagawa. Formerly a rural village, Akigawa is now a residential suburb of Tōkyō. Pop: 50,387.

Akihabara   秋葉原

District in the northeastern part of Chiyoda Ward, Tōkyō. The name derives from the Akiba Shrine, built there in 1870. It is famous

Akihabara Shoppers flock to the Akihabara district of Tōkyō, known for its high concentration of electronics stores.

for its hundreds of wholesale and discount stores specializing in electrical and electronic products, which had their origins in the black market that flourished in the area after World War II. Akihabara is also a major transportation hub served by several rail and subway lines.

Akihito, Emperor　　　　明仁天皇

(1933– ; Akihito Tennō). The present emperor and the 125th sovereign (*tennō*) in the traditional count (which includes several legendary emperors). Eldest son of Emperor SHŌWA and Empress NAGAKO, the present empress dowager. His princely title was Tsugu no Miya. He entered Gakushūin Elementary School in April 1940 and went on to study at Gakushūin Junior and Senior High schools. From 1946 to 1950 he was also privately tutored in the English language and Western culture by Elizabeth Gray VINING, an American teacher known for her authorship of children's books. In 1952 he entered the Department of Politics at Gakushūin University, and in November of that year his coming-of-age ceremony and his investiture as crown prince were conducted. While still a college student, he left Japan in the spring of 1953 for a state visit to the United Kingdom to act as his father's representative at the coronation of Queen Elizabeth II. On his tour, the first overseas trip by a member of the imperial household in the postwar period, he visited 13 countries in Europe and North America before returning to Japan in October. He completed his course of studies at Gakushūin University in March 1956.

In April 1959 Crown Prince Akihito married Shōda Michiko (see MICHIKO, EMPRESS), eldest daughter of SHŌDA HIDESABURŌ, then president of the Nisshin Flour Milling Co, Ltd, breaking with the long-established tradition that the wife of the crown prince should be chosen from among the ranks of the imperial family or the former peerage. In their family life they have achieved a relative freedom from the restrictive precedents of court tradition, becoming symbols of the democratization of the imperial household.

While still crown prince, Akihito represented Emperor Shōwa on a number of state visits overseas, visiting 37 countries in the course of 22 separate trips. He also served as the honorary president of the 11th Pacific Science Congress in 1966, of Universiade 1967 in Tōkyō, and of EXPO '70 in Ōsaka. During Emperor Shōwa's tour of Europe in September 1971 and his tour of the United States in 1975, Crown Prince Akihito conducted affairs of state in his absence. In 1975, as the honorary president of the International Ocean Exposition (EXPO '75) in Okinawa, he attended the opening ceremonies and was the first member of the imperial family to

officially visit Okinawa after its reversion to Japan in 1972.

In September 1988, as a result of Emperor Shōwa's illness, Crown Prince Akihito was charged with conducting affairs of state in his name. On 7 January 1989 he became Emperor Akihito, succeeding to the throne after his father's death. The following day he adopted the formal reign title Heisei ("Establishing Peace"), based on two passages from the Chinese classics implying the achievement of peace throughout the world. This was the first reign title (*gengō*; see NENGŌ) to be determined in accordance with the Gengō Law of 1979.

Like his father, Emperor Akihito is known as a scholar of marine biology and ichthyology and for his research into the fishes of the family Gobiidae. He also enjoys sports such as tennis, skiing, and horseback riding and is a lover of music, playing cello in impromptu performances with other members of the royal family. He and Empress Michiko have three children: Crown Prince NARUHITO, Prince AKISHINO, and Princess Sayako.

Akimoto Matsuyo　　　　秋元松代

(1911–). Playwright. Born in Kanagawa Prefecture. Debuting in 1947 with the one-act play *Keijin*, she established herself as a major dramatist within a decade. Her plays interweave folklore and legend with the sufferings of those who inhabit society's lowest levels. Akimoto also wrote many popular radio and television dramas. Her important plays include *Hitachibō Kaison* (1964; tr *Kaison, the Priest of Hitachi*, 1973) and *Kasabuta Shikibu kō* (1969), both based on popular local legends, and *Chikamatsu shinjū monogatari* (1979).

akirame　　　　諦め

(renunciation, resignation). An important behavioral concept in traditional Japanese popular psychology. Until recently the Japanese have tended to emphasize the virtue of enduring pain and deprivation with patience. It was a part of the warrior's code (reflecting the influence of Confucian ethics), which taught the importance of self-control and perseverance. The willingness to endure and suffer the unavoidable in a spirit of resignation also reflected a kind of fatalism derived in part from Buddhist thought (and perhaps Taoism). This fatalism contained a certain optimism as expressed in the popular saying, "Pain is followed by pleasure." Like all of nature, human life, with its pain and hardships, was accepted as transient. Because of this almost stoic resignation, many Japanese endured hardships without protest and accepted their place in a rigidly hierarchical society with a sense of *akirame*.

Akishima　　　　昭島[市]

City in western Tōkyō Prefecture, east of the confluence of the rivers Akigawa and

Tamagawa. Before World War II, it was a silk- and vegetable-producing village. Because it was the site of the Japanese army's Tachikawa Airfield, munition plants were relocated here during the war. After the war the airfield became a United States Air Force base; it now is the site of Shōwa Kinen Kōen (SHŌWA MEMORIAL PARK). Today, Akishima is both a residential and industrial city. Pop: 105,372.

Akishinodera　　　　秋篠寺

A nonsectarian Buddhist temple in Nara; formerly affiliated with the Seizan branch of the JŌDO SECT. Akishinodera was founded in 780 by the HOSSŌ SECT scholar Zenju (723–797). With cells to accommodate over a thousand monks, it was comparable to SAIDAIJI in size. Patronized by the imperial court from the outset, Akishinodera was designated a *chokuganji*, a temple at which prayers were offered for the well-being of the emperor. In 834, after the introduction of esoteric Buddhism, it was transformed into a SHINGON SECT temple by imperial decree. The monastery was destroyed in 1135 by a fire that left only the *kōdō* (lecture hall) standing.

Akishino, Prince　　　　秋篠宮文仁親王

(1965– ; Akishino no Miya Fumihito Shinnō). Second son of Emperor AKIHITO and Empress MICHIKO. Graduated from Gakushūin University in 1988; studied zoology at Oxford University (1988–90). In 1990 he married Kawashima Kiko (b 1966), eldest daughter of Kawashima Tatsuhiko, professor of economics at Gakushūin University, and established the new princely house of Akishino. Prince Akishino is president of several associations concerned with wildlife and conservation. Following Crown Prince NARUHITO, he is second in line of succession to the throne.

Akita　　　　秋田[市]

Capital of Akita Prefecture, located at the mouth of the river OMONOGAWA, northern Honshū. A fortification called AKITAJŌ was constructed in 733 (its remains can be seen), and from the 1600s the city flourished as a castle town of the SATAKE FAMILY. Akita is the political and cultural center of the prefecture and part of the Akita Bay Industrial Area. Principal manufactures are petrochemicals, fertilizer, machinery, pulp, and zinc. The city is also a distribution center for agricultural produce. Five universities, including Akita University, are here. The KANTŌ, a lantern festival, is held here in August. Pop: 302,362.

Akita Incident　　　　秋田事件

(Akita Jiken). An incident in 1881 in which members of the Akita Risshikai (Self-Help Society of Akita Prefecture) were arrested and imprisoned for plotting to overthrow the government. The Akita Risshikai, composed

Akiyoshidai Karst outcroppings dot the landscape of this limestone tableland, the largest in Japan.

of farmers and former *samurai* disenchanted with the Meiji government, had been formed in 1880 in response to the FREEDOM AND PEOPLE'S RIGHTS MOVEMENT.

Akitajō 秋田城

One of a series of fortified outposts in Dewa Province (now Akita and Yamagata prefectures) in northeastern Honshū, used between the 8th and 10th centuries for the pacification of EZO tribesmen. Construction began in 733 at what is now the city of Akita to replace an earlier outpost located farther south. The fort was abandoned sometime after the 9th century but was replaced by newer fortifications nearby, for the area long remained strategically important. The only remains of the original structures are parts of a palisade surrounding the keep and the foundation of a temple.

Akita Oil Fields 秋田油田

(Akita Yuden). Situated along the Sea of Japan coast in western Akita Prefecture, northern Honshū. At their peak in 1959, these oil fields produced 294 million liters (1,849,057 barrels) of crude oil, totaling 70 percent of nationwide production for that year. An offshore oil field was also developed in 1960. In 1988 crude oil production was 124 million liters (779,874 barrels).

Akita Plain 秋田平野

(Akita Heiya). Coastal alluvial plain in central Akita Prefecture, northern Honshū. Bounded on the west by the Sea of Japan and on the east by the DEWA MOUNTAINS, it is a major agricultural region with a large annual rice crop. Oil wells are located near the city of Akita, and the coastal area near Akita is being developed into an industrial and commercial region. Length: 30 km (19 mi); width: 6 km (4 mi).

Akita Prefecture 秋田県

(Akita Ken). Located in northern Honshū and bounded by Aomori Prefecture on the north, Iwate Prefecture on the east, Miyagi and Yamagata prefectures on the south, and the Sea of Japan on the west. Largely mountainous, its principal ranges include the ŌU MOUNTAINS in the east and the DEWA MOUNTAINS running down the center from north to south. Major rivers are the OMONOGAWA and YONESHIROGAWA. The OGA PENINSULA juts out into the Sea of Japan north of the city of AKITA. Lake TAZAWA is located within the prefecture, whereas Lake TOWADA extends across its border into Aomori Prefecture. The climate is marked by heavy precipitation, especially in winter when snow accumulates to depths of 1.5 m (5 ft) in the inland districts.

Under the ancient provincial system (KOKUGUN SYSTEM), Akita Prefecture was the Ugo section of Dewa Province. A military outpost, AKITAJŌ, was established in 733 at the present site of Akita. The area was ruled by the SATAKE FAMILY and other *daimyō* during the Edo period (1600–1868). The present prefectural name and boundaries were established in 1871.

Its economy has traditionally been dominated by agriculture, especially rice and forestry. It also produces petroleum and copper; other minerals include gold, silver, lead, and zinc. *Sake* brewing and the pulp and plywood industries are active as well. Transportation difficulties caused by its mountainous terrain and snowy winters have long retarded industrial development and led to an outflow of population to urban centers such as Tōkyō and Yokohama. Tourist attractions include TOWADA-HACHIMANTAI NATIONAL PARK, Oga Peninsula, Lake Tazawa, and the mountain KURIKOMAYAMA. There are also numerous hot-spring resorts. Area: 11,613 sq km (4,484 sq mi); pop: 1,227,478; capital: Akita. Other major cities include NOSHIRO, YOKOTE, ŌDATE, and KAZUNO.

Akita school 秋田派

(Akitaha). Also known as Akita *ranga* (Akita Dutch painting). A school of Japanese painting of the mid-18th century that flourished in Akita in northern Honshū. Developed by the *daimyō* of Akita, SATAKE SHOZAN, and his chief retainer, ODANO NAOTAKE, Akita painting used traditional Japanese pigments on silk or paper with an overall surface coating of oil and resin. Composition focused on the unexpectedly large foreground subject, generally a bird or flower arrangement modeled in light and shade, and often juxtaposed against a distant landscape in Western perspective.

The style may be said to date from 1773, the year HIRAGA GENNAI traveled to Akita to give advice on the fief's copper mines. While there Gennai taught the principles of Western painting, which he had learned from the Dutch at Nagasaki, to Shozan and Naotake. The three major painters of the school were Shozan, Naotake, and Satake Yoshimi (1749–1800). The main principles of the Akita school are stated in Shozan's essays, "Gahō kōryō" (1778, Art of Painting) and "Gato rikai" (1778, Understanding Painting and Composition). See also WESTERN-STYLE PICTURES, EARLY.

Akitsu 安芸津[町]

Port town in southern Hiroshima Prefecture, western Honshū, on the Inland Sea. Long known for its *sake* brewing. The town's modern industries include brick firing, shipbuilding, and sodium sulfide production. Rice, potatoes, mandarin oranges, loquats, and other crops are grown on the surrounding hills. The cultivation of edible oysters and pearl oysters is a major occupation. Pop: 13,002.

Akiyama Saneyuki 秋山真之

(1868–1918). Naval officer and architect of modern Japanese naval doctrine. Also called Akiyama Masayuki. Born in Matsuyama, Iyo Province (now Ehime Prefecture), of a *samurai* family. Graduating in 1890 from the Naval Academy, Akiyama made an early mark as a perceptive analyst of naval matters. He was sent to study in the United States (1897–99).

As lieutenant commander, Akiyama was appointed instructor at the Naval Staff College (1902–03), where he revolutionized instruction. During these years Akiyama put together a comprehensive tactical doctrine for the naval defense of Japan. As a member of the senior staff of the First Fleet under TŌGŌ HEIHACHIRŌ, Akiyama put his genius for tactical planning and organization to stunning effect during the RUSSO-JAPANESE WAR of 1904–05 in the Battle of TSUSHIMA. Again instructor at the Staff College (1905–08 and 1912–14) Akiyama exercised a decisive influence in the navy's expansion.

Akiyama Shōtarō 秋山庄太郎

(1920–). Photographer. Born in Tōkyō. Graduate of Waseda University. Known for his portraits of women, Akiyama is a prominent advertising photographer. Among his publications is the collection of photographs titled *Onna* (1976, Woman).

Akiyama Shun 秋山駿

(1930–). Literary critic. Born in Tōkyō; graduated from Waseda University. Received the Gunzō Prize for New Talent in 1960 for *Kobayashi Hideo*, a book-length critical study of the famous man of letters. In addition to his literary criticism, Akiyama is known for his contemplative essays on broader questions of human experience, such as those collected in *Naibu no ningen* (1967, The Person Inside). His other works include *Shirezaru honoo: Hyōden Nakahara Chūya* (1977, The Unknown Flame: A Critical Biography of Nakahara Chūya).

Akiyama Teisuke 秋山定輔

(1868–1950). Politician; publisher of the popular Meiji-period (1868–1912) newspaper *Niroku shimpō*. Born in Kurashiki, Bizen Province (now Okayama Prefecture). After graduation from Tōkyō University he became a government official, but grew displeased with the exclusive control of the government by men from the former Satsuma and Chōshū domains (now Kagoshima and Yamaguchi prefectures; see HAMBATSU) and resigned. In 1893 he launched the *Niroku shimpō*. The paper went bankrupt in a year and a half, but publication was resumed in 1900. Its rapidly growing readership made it, along with the YOROZU CHŌHŌ, one of the most important newspapers of the first decade of the 20th century.

Akiyoshidai 秋吉台

Upland in central western Yamaguchi Prefecture, western Honshū. The largest limestone tableland in Japan, known for its karst topography. AKIYOSHIDŌ, a lime grotto, is a popular attraction for tourists. Average elevation: 300 m (1,000 ft); area: 130 sq km (50 sq mi).

Akiyoshidō 秋芳洞

Also known as Shūhōdō. Limestone cave in the AKIYOSHIDAI upland, western Yamaguchi

Akiyoshidō Inside the cave, the formation called *hyakumaizara* ("100 saucers") was created through the action of limestone-rich water on a gentle slope. Actually, more than 500 pools can be counted.

Akita Prefecture Location and Prefectural Crest

Akutagawa Ryūnosuke The preeminent short-story writer of the Taishō period (1912–26), Akutagawa is shown here in the last photograph taken before his suicide on 24 July 1927.

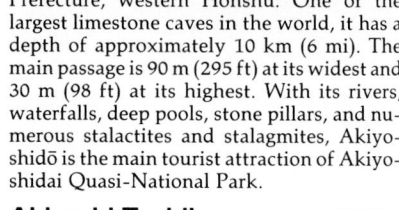

Akiyoshi Toshiko Shown here in a 1989 photograph, Akiyoshi is well established in the international jazz world as a pianist, band leader, and composer.

Prefecture, western Honshū. One of the largest limestone caves in the world, it has a depth of approximately 10 km (6 mi). The main passage is 90 m (295 ft) at its widest and 30 m (98 ft) at its highest. With its rivers, waterfalls, deep pools, stone pillars, and numerous stalactites and stalagmites, Akiyoshidō is the main tourist attraction of Akiyoshidai Quasi-National Park.

Akiyoshi Toshiko   秋吉敏子

(1929–). Jazz pianist, band leader, and composer. Highly regarded artist active in American jazz circles. Born in Dairen (Ch: Dalian or Ta-lien) in Manchuria. She was inspired by the pianist Hampton Hawes, an American military officer stationed in Japan after World War II, and from 1956 to 1959 studied at Berklee College of Music in Boston. The big band she organized with her husband, Lew Tabackin, has won a loyal following among jazz fans. Among Akiyoshi's many jazz pieces is the award-winning "Kogun" (The Lost Battalion) of 1974.

Akizuki Rebellion of 1876

秋月の乱

(Akizuki no Ran). Rebellion by former *samurai* in Akizuki, Fukuoka Prefecture, on 27 October 1876. Angered by government decrees terminating samurai stipends (see CHITSUROKU SHOBUN) and prohibiting the wearing of swords (HAITŌREI), several hundred warriors of the former Akizuki domain, led by Iso Jun (1827?–76) and Miyazaki Kurumanosuke (1835–76), attacked the prefectural office. They planned to combine forces with MAEBARA ISSEI, who revolted simultaneously at Hagi, Yamaguchi Prefecture (see HAGI REBELLION). The Akizuki rebels were quickly captured by government troops. Iso and Miyazaki committed suicide. This armed revolt was sparked by the JIMPŪREN REBELLION in Kumamoto three days earlier. See also SAGA REBELLION; SATSUMA REBELLION.

Akkadō   安家洞

Limestone caves in the town of Iwaizumi, eastern Iwate Prefecture, northern Honshū. Said to be the largest group of such caves in Japan. According to a 1961 survey, the total length of the caves was 7.6 km (4.7 mi); the longest single cave, 2.3 km (1.4 mi); the widest, 17 m (56 ft); the highest, 25 m (82 ft); with a total of 40 branch caves. Primitive oceanic life, such as the *horaanagokai (Nerillidae)*, inhabits the caves.

Akō   赤穂［市］

City in southwestern Hyōgo Prefecture, western Honshū, located on the INLAND SEA. Akō developed as a castle town in the Edo period (1600–1868). The town was early known for its salt and cotton. Today the major industries are textiles, steel, chemicals, and brick. Akō has long been associated in the popular imagination with the FORTY-SEVEN RŌNIN INCIDENT (1703), in which a band of local retainers avenged the death of their

lord; a festival is held in December to commemorate the event. The coastal area is part of the Inland Sea National Park. Pop: 51,131.

Akogiura   阿漕浦

Also known as Akogigaura. Coastal area in the city of Tsu, Mie Prefecture, central Honshū. Located on Ise Bay, it is famous for its scenic coastal views and its association with the ISE SHRINE. Because of its religious affiliation, the coast was formerly regarded as sacred, and there was a historic prohibition against any fishing. It is part of Isenoumi Prefectural Natural Park.

Akō Incident of 887   阿衡事件

(Akō Jiken or Akō no Fungi). A conflict between Fujiwara no Mototsune (836–891) and Emperor UDA on the latter's accession in 887. Mototsune expected to be reconfirmed as regent (KAMPAKU), but an edict was drafted naming him *akō* (the title of an ancient Chinese regent), an attempt, he insisted, to deprive him of power. Because of Mototsune's influence, Uda was forced to rescind the edict and reappoint him as *kampaku*. Only after Mototsune's death was Uda able to free himself of Fujiwara REGENCY GOVERNMENT.

Akō Incident of 1703 → Forty-Seven Rōnin Incident

Akune   阿久根［市］

City in northwestern Kagoshima Prefecture, Kyūshū. Principal industries are farming and fishing; it is particularly noted for its citrus fruits. Akune Hot Spring and a beautiful seacoast make this a popular tourist area. Pop: 27,869.

Akutagawa Prize   芥川賞

(Akutagawa Shō). A literary prize awarded twice annually to works by relatively unknown writers of prose fiction. The prize was established in 1935 by BUNGEI SHUNJŪ, LTD, at the suggestion of KIKUCHI KAN, to commemorate the writer AKUTAGAWA RYŪNOSUKE. The NAOKI PRIZE, which was established by Bungei Shunjū in the same year, is for works by seasoned writers, while the Akutagawa Prize is generally intended to encourage new talent. Until 1938 the prize was awarded by Bungei Shunjū; since then it has been awarded by the Society for the Promotion of Japanese Literature (Nihon Bungaku Shinkōkai). It was not awarded from 1945 to 1948. The Akutagawa Prize is considered a gateway to prominence for new writers in Japan. The winning works are published in the magazine *Bungei shunjū*. See also LITERARY PRIZES.

Akutagawa Ryūnosuke   芥川竜之介

(1892–1927). Short-story writer, poet, and essayist; noted for the superb style of his finely crafted stories that explore the darker side of human nature. Born in Tōkyō, he was the eldest son of Niihara Toshizō. Soon after his birth his mother, Fuku, went insane. Subsequently he was adopted as a son by his maternal uncle, Akutagawa Michiaki, taking the latter's family name.

Akutagawa's talent was fostered by the study of Chinese classics, Western authors, and contemporary Japanese novelists, especially MORI ŌGAI and NATSUME SŌSEKI, the two greatest writers of his time. While majoring in English literature at Tōkyō University, he began to publish a series of remarkable stories. They are based on Japanese tales of the 12th and 13th centuries, but they are given sharp twists of modern psychological in-

sight and rendered in a finely polished style. "Hana" (1916; tr "The Nose," 1930), for example, portrays a high-ranking Buddhist priest who is troubled by the gigantic proportions of his nose. While outwardly calm, he suffers deeply from embarrassment. The priest stumbles on an esoteric method for shrinking his nose to ordinary size. The transformation, however, unexpectedly invites derision, now more open and unsparing. One morning, much to his relief, he wakes up to discover his nose returned to its former monstrous size. "Now, nobody will laugh at me any more," he sighs to himself, as his long dangling nose sways in the morning breeze. The story caught the attention of Natsume Sōseki, who praised it highly in a letter to the author.

After his graduation in 1916, Akutagawa taught briefly at the Naval Engineering School and then decided to devote himself full time to writing. In 1918 he married Tsukamoto Fumiko. These early years were the most productive of Akutagawa's career; he published some of his most accomplished works, including "Rashōmon" (1915; tr "Rashomon," 1930), "Imogayu" (1916; tr "Yam Gruel," 1952), "Hankechi" (1916; tr "A Handkerchief," 1930), "Hōkyōnin no shi" (1918; tr "The Martyr," 1952), "Kumo no ito" (1918; tr "The Spider's Thread," 1930), and "Jigokuhen" (1918; tr "Hell Screen," 1948), a macabre tale of an eccentric artist who values art over life.

Akutagawa, firmly established in literary circles by 1918, was regarded as a major opponent of NATURALISM (*shizen shugi*), which dominated Japanese literature in the early 1900s with its rather sordid confessional tone. From 1919 to 1922 he continued to write stories as before, borrowing material from old tales and giving them a complex modern interpretation dressed in a superbly tailored prose. Representative works dating from this middle period include "Nankin no Kirisuto" (1920, Christ in Nanjing [Nanking]), "Toshishun" (1920; tr "Tu Tzechun," 1944), "Shūzanzu" (1921; tr "The Painting of an Autumn Mountain," 1962), and "Yabu no naka" (1922; tr "In a Grove," 1952), which, along with "Rashōmon," provided the material for KUROSAWA AKIRA's brilliant film RASHŌMON (1950).

The final period of Akutagawa's literary career, 1923 to 1927, was marred by his deteriorating health. Much of the work in this period was autobiographical in tone; some even resembled embellished diary entries. Despite worsening health he engaged in a celebrated literary dispute with TANIZAKI JUN'ICHIRŌ, in which Akutagawa upheld lyricism as the primary value in the novel and discredited the role of structure. The most significant fictional work from this final period is *Kappa* (1927; tr *Kappa*, 1947), a satirical tale about amphibious elves, known as KAPPA, who appear in the folklore of Japan. "Haguruma" (1927; tr "Cogwheel," 1965), another of his late works, is a terrifying account of an extraordinarily sensitive mind that is gradually losing its hold on reality and breaking down.

Worn out and haunted by the fear that he had inherited his mother's mental disorder, Akutagawa committed suicide in 1927 at the age of 35. He left behind approximately 100 beautifully wrought stories. Eight years after his death the AKUTAGAWA PRIZE, a yearly award for outstanding works by promising new writers, was established in his honor. It became and remains the most prestigious literary award in Japan.

akutō 悪党

(bands of evildoers). A manifestation of social disturbance during the Kamakura period (1185–1333) and subsequent decades. The term occurs in official documents from the late Heian period (794–1185) onward, its use becoming frequent after the mid-13th century. These lawless groups included not only brigands, looters, and pirates, but also estate stewards (JITŌ) and local landholders (MYŌSHU) who coalesced for forcible seizure of rents and wealth from estate (SHŌEN) proprietors. The Kamakura shogunate took steps against them but was forced to call on them for aid during the MONGOL INVASIONS OF JAPAN in the 1270s. Many akutō used this opportunity to make raids on estates, seize tax rice, and even build fortifications. Some historians believe that the akutō evolved into the local lords (KOKUJIN) of the Muromachi period (1333–1568).

Alcock, Rutherford オールコック, R.

(1809–97). First British minister to Japan. In 1858 Alcock was appointed British consul general in Japan. Arriving in Edo (now Tōkyō) in 1859, he pressed for the opening of trade between Britain and Japan and for shogunal protection of Westerners from Japanese radicals eager to expel them. Later that year he was appointed minister to Japan. In 1862 he returned to London and wrote an account of his experiences in Japan, *The Capital of the Tycoon* (1863). Returning to Edo the following year, he arranged for British, American, French, and Dutch ships to bombard shore batteries of the Chōshū domain (now Yamaguchi Prefecture) that had attacked Western ships passing through the Shimonoseki Strait (see SHIMONOSEKI BOMBARDMENT). Differences with Foreign Secretary Lord Russell led to his recall to London in 1864.

alcoholic beverages in Japanese society 酒と日本人

(*sake to nihonjin*). Alcoholic beverages are an integral part of many social and business activities in Japanese life, and many traditional rites and customs include the consumption of Japanese SAKE (rice wine).

Premodern Practices and Customs—The earliest mention in writing of alcoholic beverages in connection with the Japanese is in the section on Japan in the Chinese historical work WEI ZHI (*Wei chih*). According to this record, which refers to the 3rd century AD, the inhabitants of YAMATAI (the ancient Japanese state) were fond of liquor and drank at funeral ceremonies while they sang and danced. Other ancient sources that mention the use of alcohol are the Japanese regional gazetteers known as FUDOKI; these record the existence of establishments called *sakadono* and *sakaya* where *sake* was produced. In Japanese tradition there are rice wine deities similar to the Greek god Bacchus. The chronicle NIHON SHOKI (compiled in 720) tells how people venerated the wine deity Ōmiwa no Kami during the reign of the legendary emperor SUJIN. Shrines dedicated to deities of wine included the ŌMIWA SHRINE (in what is now Nara Prefecture) as well as Matsuo Shrine and Umemiya Shrine in Kyōto. The three deities of these shrines are known as the Sanshujin (Three Wine Deities).

By the time the RITSURYŌ SYSTEM was instituted in the late 7th century, the court had set up a Sake Production Bureau (Sake no Tsukasa) within the palace, which made rice wine for the court. In the Nara period (710–794), *sake* production moved to Buddhist temples. Several temples, notably Kongōji in Kawachi (in what is now Ōsaka Prefecture), achieved reputations as *sake* producers.

In rural areas people produced their own *sake* for the New Year and other festivals at which offerings of rice wine were traditionally made to the deities. Following the festivals, there was a banquet called NAORAI at which the participants drank the *sake* that had been offered to the deities. During the Edo period (1600–1868) the commercial production of *sake* flourished.

Although in ancient times there were fewer occasions on which alcoholic beverages were drunk, people evidently drank large amounts when they did drink. *Jōgo* (strong drinker) was a term of admiration, and *geko* (weak drinker), a label of scorn. In the Edo period the drinking of liquor became a common form of socializing and entertaining.

Present-Day Customs—In present-day Japan it is customary to offer both traditional *sake* and Western alcoholic beverages on public occasions such as New Year's parties, congratulatory occasions, and religious rites. When people return home after work, they often enjoy a drink before or after dinner; this is known as the *banshaku* (evening cup). Others join coworkers at a bar or cabaret or at one of the many kinds of typically Japanese small drinking establishments. These are known by generic names such as *akachōchin* (red lantern), *izakaya* (sit and drink), and *nawanoren* (rope curtain), but all of them are similar in offering both Japanese and Western beverages along with light meals at cheap prices. Many people drink at *yatai*, a kind of movable, roofed stall on wheels that is set up or pulled along the streets at night. These usually offer some particular food, such as noodles or chicken on skewers, along with *sake*. When a group stops at several places during an evening, it is called *hashigozake* (ladder drinking). A general term for the business of providing food, drink, and entertainment, including such traditional establishments as *geisha* houses, is *mizu shōbai* (literally, "the water trade").

A wedding custom in existence since ancient times is for a bride and groom to exchange three cups of *sake* three times in succession in the ceremony known as *sansankudo* ("three-three-nine times"). Members of the wedding party also partake of *sake*. At banquets there is a custom known as *kenshū*, in which one guest pours a cup of *sake* and offers it to another guest, who then uses the same cup to make a return offering.

At present the Japanese enjoy several varieties of alcoholic beverages. *Seishu* or clear *sake* is the most representative type of domestic liquor, but other native beverages include SHŌCHŪ (distilled spirits), *doburoku* (unrefined *sake*), *shirozake* (white *sake*), and *awamori* (Okinawan *shōchū*). Popular Western alcoholic beverages include beer, whiskey, wine, and brandy. Western drinks were introduced to Japan during the Muromachi period (1333–1568) when wines were brought from Portugal. Beer production had its start in 1873, and with the introduction of beer halls on the Ginza in Tōkyō in 1899, beer drinking began to rival *sake* drinking in popularity. Before World War II, *seishu* accounted for 60 percent of consumption figures, and beer 20 percent. Recent years have seen a reverse trend; as of the late 1980s beer accounted for 70 percent, and *seishu* had dropped to 20 percent.

akutō Detail of a 1309 handscroll depicting fighting between akutō who have stolen sacred mirrors from the Kasuga Shrine and warriors sent to retrieve them.

Alexander, Wallace McKinney アレクサンダー, W. M.

(1869–1939). American businessman who worked to improve Japanese-American relations. Born of American parents on the island of Maui, Hawaii; educated at Yale (BA, 1892). He took an interest in the welfare of his employees, many of whom were Japanese. When relations between the United States and Japan deteriorated in the early 1900s over the question of Japanese immi-

alcoholic beverages in Japanese society
A typical evening in an informal drinking establishment. In recent years, working women as well as men have begun to frequent these small bars.

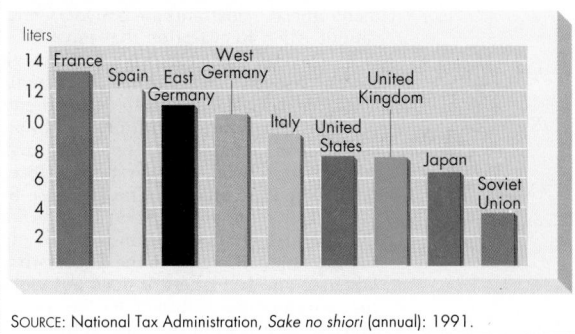

alcoholic beverages in Japanese society

Total Annual Alcohol Consumption in Japan

billions of liters

legend:
- beer
- sake (seishu)
- other[1]

years: 1965, 1970, 1975, 1980, 1985, 1989

[1]Includes such beverages as *shōchū*, whiskey, brandy, wine, liqueurs, and unrefined *sake*.

Per Capita Consumption of Alcoholic Beverages in Selected Countries, 1988

liters

France, Spain, West Germany, East Germany, Italy, United States, United Kingdom, Japan, Soviet Union

SOURCE: National Tax Administration, *Sake no shiori* (annual): 1991.

ama Female divers, carrying wooden tubs to hold their abalone catch, step into the waters of Toba Bay in Mie Prefecture.

gration, he founded the Japanese-American Relations Committee with Japanese entrepreneur SHIBUSAWA EIICHI and others.

Alien Land Acts 排日土地法

(Hainichi Tochi Hō). Acts passed by the state of California in 1913 and 1920, as well as similar acts passed by most other far-western states, that were efforts to stop the acquisition of agricultural land by Japanese immigrants. The California acts and those modeled on them aimed at only one kind of alien, the "alien ineligible to citizenship," that is, Asian immigrants who from 1870 to 1952 were ineligible for naturalization.

The 1913 act was passed under the leadership of California's governor, Hiram W. Johnson. The law had little real effect, since its intentions could be legally evaded by land-leasing and sharecropping contracts and by land purchases by US-born children of Japanese immigrants, who had US citizenship. The 1920 California act, however, made leasing and sharecropping by "aliens ineligible to citizenship" illegal.

In California the laws stayed on the books until they were declared unconstitutional in a state court decision (*Fujii v State of California*, 1952). That same year the federal Immigration and Nationality Act (the so-called McCarran-Walter Act) abolished the status of "aliens ineligible to citizenship." See also UNITED STATES IMMIGRATION ACTS OF 1924, 1952, AND 1965.

alien registration 外国人登録

(*gaikokujin tōroku*). Registration of personal identity is required of all persons residing in Japan for more than one year who do not hold Japanese citizenship. The Alien Registration Law (Gaikokujin Tōroku Hō, 1952) requires these residents to apply for such registration to the mayor or headman of the village, town, or city (in the case of a large city, the head of the ward) where they live and to present a passport and copies of a photograph within 90 days from the date of entry into Japan. The information required on the application form includes the applicant's name, date and place of birth, sex, nationality, occupation, port of entry, passport number, and address while in Japan.

Upon registration by the local government official, registrants are issued a Certificate of Alien Registration that must be renewed every five years or whenever visa status changes. Each registrant, excluding children under the age of 16, is required to carry this certificate at all times and to present it upon demand to police officers, maritime safety officials, railway police officers, or other public officials. The Japanese Supreme Court has ruled (1955) that because the alien registration system is based on a fundamental difference in the legal status of Japanese and foreigners, it does not violate the guarantee of equality under the law provided in article 14 of the constitution.

A growing number of noncitizens in Japan have objected strongly to the requirement that fingerprints be taken as part of the registration procedure, arguing that fingerprinting is the treatment given to criminals and that it constitutes an infringement of their human rights. By December 1991, 156 people had refused to be fingerprinted, and several prosecutions had resulted in guilty verdicts and fines. In response to growing protests the Ministry of Justice abolished the fingerprinting requirement for persons with permanent resident status, effective January 1993. See also FOREIGNERS IN JAPAN; FOREIGNERS, LEGAL STATUS OF; REFUSAL TO BE FINGERPRINTED.

Allied Council for Japan 対日理事会

(ACJ; J: Tainichi Rijikai). Four-power body charged with advising the supreme commander for the Allied powers (SCAP) on the implementation of the surrender terms for Japan. It was established along with the FAR EASTERN COMMISSION (FEC) at Moscow on 27 December 1945 by the foreign ministers of the United States, the United Kingdom, and the USSR, with the concurrence of China. Its membership consisted of the supreme commander, or his deputy, as chairman (and as US member); representatives of the USSR and China; and a member representing jointly the United Kingdom, Australia, New Zealand, and India. The supreme commander's decisions were controlling, and he acted as the sole executive authority of the Allied powers in Japan. The council met 162 times from early 1946 to the end of the OCCUPATION in 1952.

All-Japan Student Music Competition 全日本学生音楽コンクール

(Zen Nihon Gakusei Ongaku Konkūru). A music competition for students, held once a year since 1947. Sponsored by the daily newspaper *Mainichi shimbun* with the assistance of NHK (Japan Broadcasting Corporation), the contest has three age divisions (elementary school, middle school, and high school). All ages may compete in piano and violin, while solo voice and flute (added in 1988) are open only to high school students. Every autumn, preliminary and main competitions are held in four regional centers: Tōkyō, Nagoya, Ōsaka, and Fukuoka. The winners from each of the four regions then compete for the national top place in their divisions. Some of Japan's best musicians are past champions.

All Nippon Airways Co, Ltd 全日本空輸[株]

(Zen Nippon Kūyu). Second largest airline company in Japan. Incorporated in 1952 as the Nippon Helicopter Transport Co, it merged with Far Eastern Airlines in 1958 and adopted its current name. Its operations are centered on domestic passenger flights, but as of 1990 it was operating 13 scheduled international routes. In addition to passenger flights, the company provides cargo transportation and operates hotel, leisure, and food service facilities. Operating revenues for the fiscal year ending March 1991 totaled ¥733.4 billion (US $5.3 billion), and capitalization was ¥72.1 billion (US $525.5 million). Headquarters are in Tōkyō.

Alps Electric Co, Ltd アルプス電気[株]

(Arupusu Denki). Manufacturer of various types of electronic parts, including tuners, switches, variable resistors, and keyboards, for televisions, videocassette recorders, and

office automation equipment. Incorporated in 1948. It has subsidiary manufacturing companies in the United States, the United Kingdom, Ireland, Germany, South Korea, Taiwan, and Brazil. Sales for the fiscal year ending March 1991 totaled ¥355.2 billion (US $2.6 billion). The company's export ratio was 30 percent, and capitalization stood at ¥21.2 billion (US $153.8 million) in the same year. Headquarters are in Tōkyō.

ama 海人

Sea divers who catch fish and shellfish and gather seaweed. At present, women *ama* are more common in central Japan, while men predominate in the northeastern and southwestern regions of the country. This is the only area in the Japanese fishing industry in which women are directly involved. The *ama* fish principally for *awabi* (abalone), *sazae* (wreath shell), *tengusa* (agar-agar), and *egonori* (a kind of seaweed).

There are three methods employed by male *ama*, depending on the local tradition. One is for the *ama* to dive directly into the sea. Another is to use a long stick to gather seaweed while standing in a boat. The third involves the use of a glass-bottomed boat, from which the *ama* brings the abalone up with a long spear. Female *ama* use floating wooden tubs, in which they place the shellfish they catch by diving. The *ama*'s method of diving was recorded by Chinese observers in Japan in the 3rd century.

Amache Relocation Center アマチ収容所

(Amachi Shūyōjo). Wartime relocation facility for Japanese Americans from California; located near Granada, Powers County, Colorado. In operation from 27 August 1942 until 15 October 1945, it held a maximum of 7,318 inmates at any one time; in all, 10,295 persons were confined there. See also JAPANESE AMERICANS, WARTIME RELOCATION OF; WAR RELOCATION AUTHORITY.

Amada Co, Ltd [株]アマダ

(Amada). Leading builder of metal-working machines. Incorporated in 1948. Amada develops and produces band-sawing machines, blades, precision sheet-metal-working machines, presses, tooling processing machines, and related machinery. The company has overseas subsidiaries in the United Kingdom (Amada UK), the United States (Amada Engineering & Services, Inc, and Amada MFG America), Taiwan (Amada Taiwan), France (Amada SA), and Austria (Amada Austria). Sales for the fiscal year ending March 1991 totaled ¥165.2 billion (US $1.2 billion), and capitalization stood at ¥57.3 billion (US $381.2 million) in the same year. Headquarters are in the city of Isehara, Kanagawa Prefecture.

amae 甘え

Amae, which can be translated as "dependency wishes," is the noun form of a commonly used Japanese verb, *amaeru*, that has no true equivalent in English but refers to the desire to depend upon the love, patience, and tolerance of others. *Amaeru* can be translated as "to play baby," "to behave like a spoiled child," "to coax," or "to coquet," although in Japanese it derives from the same root as the adjective for "sweet" (*amai*) and possesses an aura of sweetness and permissiveness not conveyed by the pejorative tone of translations into English.

Amae arises from feelings of helplessness

and the need to be loved and, stated in Freudian terminology, expresses the longing for restoration of the lost quasi-union of mother and child. Since the parent-child relationship is reflected in Japanese society in many adult relationships, including those of husband-wife, teacher-pupil, and leader-follower (see OYABUN-KOBUN), *amae* tends to be prolonged and diffused throughout adult life.

Doi Takeo (b 1920), one of Japan's pioneers in psychiatry, defines *amaeru* as the desire "to presume upon another's love," "to bask in another's indulgence," or "to indulge in another's kindness." He holds that *amae* is a key to understanding the psychodynamics of Japanese culture, which is relatively tolerant of dependency feelings and relations. In his writings, especially his bestselling *Amae no kōzō* (1971; tr *Anatomy of Dependence*, 1973), he sees it as the core of a constellation of *amae*-related words and feelings and as the key to understanding the traditional Japanese dilemma between obligations (*giri*) and feelings (*ninjō*). In Doi's definition, Japanese-style *ninjō* is the art of knowing how to *amaeru* and how to respond to the call of *amae* in others; *giri*, or social obligations, exists to be pervaded by *ninjō* (see GIRI AND NINJŌ).

Amae also explains for Doi the centrality of the mother-child relationship in Japanese society; the importance attached to the ability to "merge" (*tokekomu*) with others; less distinct notions of subject and object, self and other; differently defined concepts of privacy and individual rights; a dislike for cut-and-dried logic and businesslike relationships; the high degree of nonverbal communication; and the strong aesthetic orientation of the culture.

Amagasaki 尼崎[市]

City in southeastern Hyōgo Prefecture. Situated on ŌSAKA BAY and with river access to Kyōto, Amagasaki has been an important port since the Heian period (794–1185). A castle town during the Edo period (1600–1868), in modern times its proximity to Ōsaka has made Amagasaki a major industrial center. Steel, electrical goods, and chemicals are the principal industries. The remains of Tano, a Yayoi-period (ca 300 BC–ca AD 300) settlement, are here. Pop: 498,999.

Amagase Hot Spring 天ケ瀬温泉

(Amagase Onsen). Hot spring in the town of Amagase in the northwestern part of Ōita Prefecture, Kyūshū. A simple thermal spring with a water temperature of 80°–100°C (176°–212°F), its source is located in the upper reaches of the river CHIKUGOGAWA.

Amagi 甘木[市]

City in central Fukuoka Prefecture, Kyūshū. It developed as one of the post-station towns on the highway Bungo Kaidō and as an agricultural market center. Rice and vegetables are still grown in Amagi. It is also a producer of lumber, beer, rubber tires, chemical fertilizers, and Amagi *shibori* (tie-dyed fabrics). Pop: 43,034.

Amagi Pass 天城峠

(Amagi Tōge). Located along the Shimoda highway, central Izu Peninsula, Shizuoka Prefecture, central Honshū. A toll road including the new Amagi Tunnel runs through this pass. The surrounding land is covered with cedar groves. YUGASHIMA HOT SPRING is found on the northern side. The pass is famous as part of the setting of Kawabata

Yasunari's *Izu no odoriko* (The Izu Dancer). Altitude: 820 m (2,690 ft).

Amagisan 天城山

Mountain group in central Izu Peninsula, Shizuoka Prefecture, central Honshū. Its volcanic peaks belong to the FUJI VOLCANIC ZONE. The mountains are part of the Fuji-Hakone-Izu National Park. The hot springs at Yuga-shima and Yugano are popular. Principal peaks include: Manjirōdake (1,300 m; 4,265 ft), Manzaburōdake (1,406 m; 4,613 ft), and Tōgasayama (1,197 m; 3,927 ft).

amagoi→ rain, rituals for

Amako family 尼子氏

(Amakoshi). *Daimyō* family of the Sengoku period (1467–1568); descendants of the KYŌGOKU FAMILY. In 1392 Amako Mochihisa became deputy military governor (*shugodai*) of Izumo Province (now part of Shimane Prefecture). His grandson Tsunehisa (1458–1541) extended his power into Aki and Bingo provinces (now Hiroshima Prefecture), conflicting with the ŌUCHI FAMILY and the MŌRI FAMILY. The defeat in 1566 of Tsunehisa's great-grandson Yoshihisa (d 1610) by Mōri forces ended the Amako power. Not long afterward, Yoshihisa's kinsman Amako Katsuhisa (1553–78) attempted to revive the family's fortunes with the aid of YAMANAKA SHIKANOSUKE; as a vassal of ODA NOBUNAGA, Katsuhisa enjoyed brief military success but committed suicide while under siege by the Mōri in 1578.

amakudari 天下り

The practice of reemploying former high-level bureaucrats in private-sector positions after their retirement from government work. At times the term also applies to the movement of former bureaucrats into service with public corporations. Literally, *amakudari* means "descent from heaven," in recognition of the elite status that bureaucrats have traditionally held in Japanese society. Although the practice of *amakudari* began before World War II, it flourished during the late 1960s and early 1970s. *Amakudari* grows out of complementary public- and private-sector motivations: the desire of bureaucrats, forced to retire at 47–55 years of age with relatively modest financial pensions, for second careers and the desire of private corporations for access to government contacts and information, which they can obtain from ex-bureaucrats. Former bureaucrats are concentrated most heavily in such highly regulated industries as banking and transportation. See also BUREAUCRACY.

Amakusa 天草[町]

Town on Amakusa Shimoshima, one of the AMAKUSA ISLANDS off southern Kyūshū; part of Kumamoto Prefecture. Primarily a fishing port, it also produces clay for porcelain. During the 17th century many Japanese Christians hid in the area to avoid persecution (see KAKURE KIRISHITAN); a church memorializes those who died in the SHIMABARA UPRISING, a rebellion of Christians in 1637. The town is within the Unzen-Amakusa National Park. Pop: 5,563.

Amakusa Islands 天草諸島

(Amakusa Shotō). Island group west of Kumamoto Prefecture, Kyūshū. The group consists of more than 100 islands, divided between Kumamoto and Kagoshima prefectures, with most belonging to the former. Most important are Amakusa Kamishima

and Amakusa Shimoshima. Wheat, sweet potatoes, flowers, and mandarin oranges are cultivated. There is offshore fishing, and pearls, shrimp, and yellowtail are cultivated. Underground resources include coal, building stone, and clay for pottery. The islands form part of the UNZEN-AMAKUSA NATIONAL PARK. Tourist attractions include relics of early Christians who lived here. The islands are connected to Kyūshū by the Five Amakusa Bridges. Area: 882 sq km (341 sq mi).

Amakusa Sea 天草灘

(Amakusa Nada). Sea off the Amakusa Islands and the western coast of Kumamoto Prefecture, western Kyūshū. Bounded on the north by the Nagasaki Peninsula and on the south by the Koshikijima Islands.

Amakusa Shirō→ Shimabara Uprising

Amami Islands 奄美諸島

(Amami Shotō). Group of islands between Kyūshū and the Okinawa Islands; part of Kagoshima Prefecture. Includes the islands of AMAMI ŌSHIMA, KIKAISHIMA, TOKUNOSHIMA, OKINOERABUJIMA, and YORONJIMA. In ancient days the Amami Islands belonged to the Ryūkyū kingdom in Okinawa. In 1609 they came under the control of the SHIMAZU FAMILY and after 1871 were administered by Kagoshima Prefecture, except during American military rule (1946–53). The islands are chiefly agricultural, the main crop being sugarcane. Other produce includes bananas and pineapples. Ōshima *tsumugi* (pongee) is a special local product. Area: 1,237 sq km (478 sq mi).

Amami Ōshima 奄美大島

Also known as Ōshima. Island 400 km (250 mi) southwest of Kyūshū, largest of the AMAMI ISLANDS. It is administratively part of Kagoshima Prefecture. The main city is Naze. The island is hilly with little level land and surrounded by coral reefs. About 40 percent of the island is arable; the principal agricultural products are sugarcane, sweet potatoes, and subtropical fruits. The principal product of the island is Ōshima *tsumugi* (pongee). Area: 710 sq km (274 sq mi); pop: 79,302.

Amanohashidate 天橋立

Sandbar in western Wakasa Bay near Tango Peninsula, northwestern Kyōto Prefecture, central Honshū; known for the beauty of its gnarled pine trees. Along with Matsushima and Itsukushima, it is one of the "three most famous views in Japan" (Nihon Sankei).

Amami Ōshima
Storehouses similar to those once used throughout Japan for the storage of rice remain in use in Amami Ōshima. A platform directly beneath the roof keeps crops away from the damp.

Amanohashidate
This pine-covered sandbar, whose name literally means "bridge of heaven," separates Miyazu Bay (left) and the lagoon Asokai, both of which are in the inner reaches of Wakasa Bay.

Length: 3.3 km (2 mi); width: 40–110 m (130–360 ft).

Amanojaku 天邪鬼

Also known as Amanojakko or Amanosagume.

1. Supernatural creature described in various folktales who acts contrary to the desires of others and is skilled at impersonation. It is thought to have assumed features of Amanosagume, a mythical female deity.

2. In common parlance, a person whose statements or actions perversely contradict accepted notions or the express desires of others.

3. In Buddhist art, the creature or creatures trampled underfoot by the guardian deity groups Niō and Shitennō.

Amanokaguyama →Yamato Sanzan

Amano Tameyuki 天野為之

(1861–1938). Economist and educator. Born in Edo (now Tōkyō). In 1882, after graduating from Tōkyō University, he joined ŌKUMA SHIGENOBU in establishing Tōkyō Semmon Gakkō (now WASEDA UNIVERSITY), where he later became a professor. He joined the RIKKEN KAISHINTŌ political party the same year and was elected to the House of Representatives in the first Japanese general election (1890). After losing the next election he returned to Waseda University, where he served as president from 1915 to 1917. From 1897 to 1907 he was editor in chief of the magazine TŌYŌ KEIZAI SHIMPŌ. His *Keizai genron* (1886) was the first book on the principles of economics published in Japan that adhered to J. S. Mill's laissez-faire theories.

Amano Teiyū 天野貞祐

(1884–1980). Philosopher and educator; noted for his studies of Kant and advocacy of democracy in education. Born in Kanagawa Prefecture. After graduating from Kyōto University, he studied philosophy at the University of Heidelberg, Germany, in 1923–24. On his return to Japan he was appointed to the faculty of Kyōto University. In 1937 he published *Dōri no kankaku* (The Sense of Right), a highly controversial book that was denounced by military and right-wing groups for its antiwar theme and was eventually suppressed by the government.

In the post–World War II period, he was a member of the Japanese committee that dealt with the first of the UNITED STATES EDUCATION MISSIONS TO JAPAN. He was minister of education in the YOSHIDA SHIGERU cabinet from 1950 to 1952, during which time he criticized the left-wing tendencies then prevalent in educational circles and stressed the necessity of moral education in the schools (see KOKUMIN JISSEN YŌRYŌ). After retiring as minister of education he founded Dokkyō University. From 1955 to 1963 he served as chairman of the CENTRAL COUNCIL FOR EDUCATION (Chūō Kyōiku Shingikai).

Amano Tōkage 天野遠景

(fl 1180–1203). General of the early Kamakura period (1185–1333). Tōkage joined MINAMOTO NO YORITOMO in 1180 and fought under him in the TAIRA-MINAMOTO WAR. When Yoritomo established his regime at Kamakura in 1185, Tōkage was made military commander in Kyūshū; however, he was dismissed around 1193 because of local opposition, returned to Kamakura, and eventually became a monk. In 1203, on the orders of the shogunal regent HŌJŌ TOKIMASA, Tōkage assassinated HIKI YOSHIKAZU, the father-in-law of the shōgun MINAMOTO NO YORIIE.

Amaterasu Ōmikami 天照大神

(Great Divinity Illuminating Heaven). The principal female deity of SHINTŌ mythology, identified with the sun and regarded as the progenitrix of the imperial line. According to the chronicle *Kojiki* (712) she was born from Izanagi when he used water to purify his left eye after a visit to the netherworld; according to the *Nihon shoki* (720) she was born after intercourse between IZANAGI AND IZANAMI. She was assigned to rule the High Celestial Plain (TAKAMAGAHARA). Deeply offended by the misdeeds of her younger brother SUSANOO NO MIKOTO, Amaterasu hid herself in a cave (*ama no iwaya*), leaving the universe in complete darkness and chaos. Lured out of the cave by the merrymaking of the other divinities, she shone forth again and order was restored. Later she dispatched her grandson NINIGI NO MIKOTO to pacify the Japanese islands, having given him the sacred mirror, sword, and jewels that became the IMPERIAL REGALIA; his great-grandson became the first emperor, JIMMU.

Amaterasu is worshiped at the Inner Shrine (Naikū) of the ancient ISE SHRINE, the central shrine of the Shintō religion that was the object of mass pilgrimages (OKAGE MAIRI) throughout the Edo period (1600–1868).

Amatsu Kominato 天津小湊〔町〕

Town in southern Chiba Prefecture, central Honshū. Located on the BŌSŌ PENINSULA, it serves as a base for Pacific fishing. An important temple of the Nichiren sect, Tanjōji, is situated in the town. Other attractions are TAINOURA, a coastal area noted for sea-bream watching, and KIYOSUMIYAMA, the mountain where NICHIREN studied and prayed. Pop: 8,640.

Amazawa Taijirō 天沢退二郎

(1936–). Poet. Born in Tōkyō. Graduate of Tōkyō University. Following the publication of his first poetry collection, *Michimichi* (1957, On the Way), Amazawa's work began to appear regularly in poetry magazines, and he is now generally considered to be the representative poet of the 1960s in Japan. His poems have a surreal narrative quality, visible in such collections as *Asa no kawa* (1961, Morning River) and *les invisibles* (1976, Invisible Men). Also known for his writings about the poet MIYAZAWA KENJI, Amazawa published *Miyazawa Kenji no kanata e* (Beyond Miyazawa Kenji) in 1968.

AMeDAS 地域気象観測システム

(Automated Meteorological Data Acquisition System; J: Chiiki Kishō Kansoku Shisutemu). Automated weather observation system put in place by the Meteorological Agency in 1974. Data on weather conditions are transmitted hourly from over 1,300 AMeDAS observation points to a main processing center and then sent by computer to meteorological observatories throughout Japan.

Amenomori Hōshū 雨森芳洲

(1668–1755). Scholar of Neo-Confucianism (see SHUSHIGAKU). Born in Ōmi Province (now Shiga Prefecture), he studied under KINOSHITA JUN'AN in Edo (now Tōkyō). In 1689 he entered the service of the *daimyō* of Tsushima, an island domain (now part of Nagasaki Prefecture), and distinguished himself in diplomatic relations with Korea. He was an orthodox follower of the Zhu Xi (Chu Hsi; J: Shushi) school of Neo-Confucianism and concerned himself primarily with proper conduct of individuals and the moral relationship between emperor and subject. He criticized ARAI HAKUSEKI's designation of the shōgun as king (*kokuō*) in official documents addressed to Korea (see SHUGŌ INCIDENT).

Amerika Hikozō →Hamada Hikozō

Amerika Mura アメリカ村

Popular name for Mio, a hamlet in the town of Mihama, Wakayama Prefecture, central Honshū. Situated on the western tip of the Kii Peninsula, Amerika Mura ("American Village") is known as the home of emigrants who have returned from the United States and Canada and retained their Western way of life.

Amida 阿弥陀

A Buddha of cardinal importance in the Mahāyāna tradition who presides over the Western Paradise of the Pure Land (J: Jōdo); central to the evolution of PURE LAND BUDDHISM in East Asia. The term Amida, or Amita, is the Japanese pronunciation of the Chinese transliteration of the Sanskrit titles for this Buddha (Skt: Amitābha, immeasurable light; Amitāyus, immeasurable life). The bodhisattva Dharmākara (the future Amida) made 48 vows, the most important being the 18th vow, called the Primal Vow of Amida, to satisfy every conceivable need of humankind. When these vows were fulfilled, he achieved Buddhahood and realized his Pure Land.

Amida worship can be classified into three general types: Amida as the object of contemplative practice found in early sects such as the TENDAI SECT and the SHINGON SECT; Amida as a savior who welcomes the dying into his Pure Land, promising eternal life (this was the popular Pure Land belief in China and during the Heian period [794–1185] in Japan); and Amida as the salvific power that affirms the value of human life and the Buddhahood of all beings, even the lowliest of sinners. This latter tradition, taught by HŌNEN and SHINRAN in the Kamakura period (1185–1333), stresses the recitation of the NEMBUTSU (*Namu Amida Butsu:* "I entrust myself to the Buddha Amida"), which is both the call of Amida to authentic life and the human response to that call, both to be realized here and now. Statues of Amida were produced in great numbers from the Nara period (710–794) onward, as were Amida halls (*amidadō*) dedicated to the worship of this deity, the most famous of which is the Hōōdō of the temple BYŌDŌIN at Uji.

Amino Kiku　　　網野菊

(1900–1978). Novelist. Born in Tōkyō; graduate of Japan Women's University, where she majored in English literature. She became a follower of novelist SHIGA NAOYA, whose autobiographical fiction (see I-NOVEL) she imitated. Amino's reputation rests on moving fictionalized accounts of her unhappy life as a divorced working woman. Her works include the short-story collections *Kisha no naka de* (1940, On the Train) and *Sakura no hana* (1961, Cherry Blossoms) and a long autobiographical novel, *Yureru ashi* (1964, Trembling Reed). In 1967 she received the Yomiuri Literary Prize for *Ichigo ichie* (1967, Once in a Lifetime), a collection of short stories.

Ami school　　　阿弥派

(Amiha). School chiefly of INK PAINTING of the 15th and 16th centuries. The term refers to three generations of painters, NŌAMI (1397–1471), GEIAMI (1431–85), and SŌAMI (ca 1455–1525), and others who painted under their influence. The three Ami (*san'ami*) served the Muromachi shogunate (1338–1573) as curators of Chinese paintings (see DŌBŌSHŪ) and also taught their techniques to students. Among schools of painting of the time that worked in the Chinese tradition of ink painting, their influence is considered to have been exceeded only by the group of painters that surrounded SHŪBUN (d ca 1460) and his student SESSHŪ TŌYŌ (1420–1506).

The most widely accepted attribution to Nōami is the *Byakue Kannon* (1468, White-Robed Kannon), which blends the styles of the academic painters Xia Gui (Hsia Kuei) and Ma Yuan (Ma Yüan) of the Chinese Southern Song (Sung) dynasty (1127–1279). Sōami painted both in the "hard-edge" Xia Gui style, which influenced the work of both Nōami and Geiami, and, as in the sliding-screen landscape at the temple DAITOKUJI, in the "soft" style developed by the Southern Song painter Muqi (Mu-ch'i; J: MOKKEI). The style of the Ami school, transmitted from Kyōto to Kamakura by SHŌKEI, was influential in providing new directions for Japanese secular painting of the 16th and 17th centuries.

amma　　　按摩

Method of massage derived from Chinese medical practice; the term also refers to its practitioners. The earliest records regarding *amma* are found in the TAIHŌ CODE (701), which provided for the establishment of a Medical Bureau (Ten'yakuryō), whose officials included *amma*. The massage style practiced by *amma* of that time included methods common today, as well as methods for setting bones. ACUPUNCTURE was also involved. During the Edo period (1600–1868) various schools appeared, such as Hanaokaryū, Tōdōryū, and Ishizakaryū. It was probably at this time that *amma* therapy came to be performed largely by the blind. Partly because of the introduction of Western medical practice, in the Meiji period (1868–1912) *amma* were no longer regarded as physicians. Nevertheless, *amma* survives today as both an occupation and a massage technique. The practice has been regulated by a licensing system since 1947. See also SHIATSU; ZATŌ.

Amō statement　　　天羽声明

(Amō *seimei*). Declaration concerning Japan's East Asia policy made by Amō Eiji (1887–1968), chief of the Information Bureau of the Ministry of Foreign Affairs, on 17 April 1934. Amō asserted that Japan would maintain a close relation with China and Manchukuo (the puppet state set up in Manchuria by the Japanese) and reject all interference from other countries; relations between Japan and China were to be handled by those two countries alone. Any moves by other nations to supply China with arms or assistance for political purposes would have a divisive effect on relations between China and Japan and hence could not be ignored by Japan. This statement provoked a strong reaction from several countries, and the United States immediately issued a denunciation. Under the guise of a reinterpretation of its content, the Japanese government withdrew the Amō statement in an attempt to maintain peaceful relations with the United States.

amphibians　　　両生類

(*ryōseirui*). About 40 species of amphibians inhabit Japan. Among them, only about half of the FROGS and toads (order Salientia) are endemic, while 15 out of the 16 species of the tailed amphibians (order Caudata) are endemic. Of the 18 species of Asian land SALAMANDERS (family Hynobiidae), 12 inhabit Japan. On the mainland are found 9 species of 2 genera including the *kasumi sanshōuo*, which inhabits ponds in the lowlands, and the Hakone *sanshōuo*, which inhabits mountain streams; 1 species is found in Tsushima, and 2 species of different genera in Hokkaidō. Only the swamp-dwelling *kita sanshōuo* (Siberian salamander; *Salamandrella keyserlingii*) of Hokkaidō is distributed extensively on the continent, while the others are endemic to Japan. The *ō sanshōuo* (Japanese giant salamander), which grows to a length of 1.2 meters (47 in) and to a weight of over 10.5 kilograms (23 lb), is the largest living amphibian in the world. It inhabits streams in the mountains of Honshū and Shikoku and emerges from underwater holes to hunt water animals by night. In the Tertiary period its family, Cryptobranchidae, was widely distributed over Eurasia and North America, but it is today a living fossil with the only other species of the same genus inhabiting China and a species of another genus inhabiting the United States.

The red-bellied IMORI (Japanese newt) is indigenous to the mainland and the Ryūkyū Islands and is commonly found in still water.

The grotesque *iboimori* (crocodile salamander; *Tylototriton andersoni*) of the Ryūkyū Islands usually conceals itself under fallen leaves in dark, humid places. Of the frogs and toads on the mainland, endemic species include the following: the *mori aogaeru* (Japanese arboreal rhacophorid; *Rhacophorus arboreus*); the *kajikagaeru*, often kept as a pet for its charming voice; the cave-dwelling *tagogaeru* (*Rana tagoi*); and the *ottongaeru* (*Rana subaspera*), with spiny first fingers on the forelegs. The beautifully colored *ishikawa-gaeru* (*Rana ishikawae*), whose body is covered with conical pustules, inhabits the Ryūkyū Islands.

Amur River Society　　　黒竜会

(Kokuryūkai; literally, "Black Dragon Society"). Ultranationalist association. An offshoot of the ultranationalist society GEN'YŌSHA, it was founded in 1901 by UCHIDA RYŌHEI to drive Russia out of the East Asian sphere south of the Amur River. The society published a journal, *Kokuryū* (later *Ajia jiron*), dispatched agents trained at its own school to gather intelligence on Russian activities in Siberia and Manchuria, and pressured government leaders to adopt a strong foreign policy. Espousing PAN-ASIANISM, it supported revolutionaries such as SUN YAT-SEN and Emilio AGUINALDO. At the time of the Russo-Japanese War (1904–05), the annexation of Korea (1910), and the SIBERIAN INTERVENTION (1918–22), it sent members to engage in covert political activities. During the late 1920s and early 1930s the society attacked liberal and leftist thought and called for an emperor-centered national reconstruction. Though it never had more than several dozen members at one time, the close ties of leading members such as TŌYAMA MITSURU to the military, government officials, and powerful businessmen gave the society greater influence than other ultranationalist groups. It was disbanded by the OCCUPATION authorities in 1946.

Anami Korechika　　　阿南惟幾

(1887–1945). Army general and army minister at the end of World War II. Native of Ōita Prefecture. He graduated from the Army Academy in 1905. He was appointed to the position of army minister in the SUZUKI KANTARŌ cabinet in April 1945. At the 14 August imperial conference to discuss the surrender terms of the POTSDAM DECLARATION, Anami insisted on fighting to the end. He killed himself that night, after the imperial decision to surrender was made.

Anan　　　阿南[市]

City in eastern Tokushima Prefecture, Shikoku; situated on the river Nakagawa. Formerly a rice-producing area, the city has been industrialized; there are thermoelectric generating plants on Tachibana Bay at the mouth of the Nakagawa. Pop: 59,044.

Anan Coast　　　阿南海岸

(Anan Kaigan). South of the city of Anan, southeastern Tokushima Prefecture, Shikoku. Characterized by its numerous sea cliffs, sea caves, and tiny islets, it is one of the centers of Muroto-Anan Coast Quasi-National Park.

anarchism　　　無政府主義

(*museifu shugi*). Anarchistic elements appear in the Chinese Taoist philosophies of Laozi

(Lao-tzu) and Zhuangzi (Chuang-tzu), as well as that of the Japanese thinker ANDŌ SHŌEKI (1703?–62). In the Meiji period (1868–1912) the ideas of Russian anarchists Kropotkin and Bakunin, mixed with socialist and communist philosophies, were introduced to Japan, perhaps inspiring the short-lived TŌYŌ SHAKAITŌ (Oriental Socialist Party) founded by TARUI TŌKICHI (1850–1922) in 1882.

Anarchism as a separate theory rooted in Western philosophy was first introduced to Japan by KŌTOKU SHŪSUI (1871–1911) and ŌSUGI SAKAE (1885–1923). In 1906 Kōtoku advocated direct action by the proletariat to overthrow the power structure. After Kōtoku's execution in 1911 for involvement in the HIGH TREASON INCIDENT OF 1910, the leadership of the anarchist movement passed to Ōsugi Sakae, but the movement lost momentum, especially after Ōsugi's death in 1923. Besides this violent anarchist movement, there was also the nonviolent anarchist philosophy of ISHIKAWA SANSHIRŌ (1876–1956) based on Christian humanism.

ancestor worship   祖先崇拝

(sosen sūhai). The Japanese regularly conduct rites on behalf of the souls of the dead of their households. Sutras are recited before Buddhist family altars (BUTSUDAN) that contain memorial tablets (ihai) for the individual dead and on which candles and incense are burned and flowers and food are offered.

Since the 7th century ceremonies have been conducted to comfort the dead, to solicit their beneficence and prevent vengeful acts by them, and to secure their safe passage into paradise. Since the mid-17th century domestic ancestral rites have been inextricably linked to the fortunes of the Buddhist temple and its clergy. By 1665 the domainal lords (daimyō) were required by the central government to establish a household registry system. Partly in order to ascertain that Christianity had been completely eradicated, every household was required to register as a DANKA (parishioner-household) of a Buddhist temple, whose priests would then certify the accuracy of the annual enumeration of its members (see TERAUKE). Among the many responsibilities of the temple was the overseeing of the performance of ancestral rites by its parishioners, and the contributions received in return for this remains the chief source of revenue for temples today.

When a person dies, the Buddhist priest is asked to devise an appropriate posthumous name, which is written with a brush or incised on the face of the memorial tablet. On the 49th day after death the tablet is placed with others in the altar in the main room of the family home of the deceased.

Ceremonies are held and offerings are made to the dead of the household on a number of occasions. The ancestors are venerated as a group at the New Year, 1–3 January; at the vernal and autumnal equinoxes (HIGAN), approximately 21 March and 23 September; and at the Festival of the Dead (see BON FESTIVAL), 13–16 July (in some localities 13–16 August).

One of the major purposes of the ancestral rites is to move the soul of the newly dead from its ritually polluting, still-earthbound state, into the purified collectivity of the long-dead ancestors of the house and community. At the 33rd or 50th (far more rarely at the 100th) anniversary of death, a transition is marked that obliterates the concept of the individual soul altogether. In some parts of Japan, the posthumous and real-life names are shaved from the tablet and it is burned, cast into the sea, or left in a temple or at the grave by the head of the household. From that anniversary of his or her death—known as tomurai age or toikiri (the final rites)—the individual has merged with the collectivity of deities that protect the community and its residents, and no further rites are directed to it alone.

Since the reforms of the post–World War II period, the household (IE) has ceased to be a legal entity, and the nuclear family has emerged as a dominant domestic form. A husband and wife may well have an altar (or its equivalent) in which they venerate the parents of both rather than the traditional patrilineal altar.

An Chung-gŭn   安重根

(1879–1910; J: An Jūkon). Korean nationalist who assassinated the Japanese statesman ITŌ HIROBUMI. The son of a well-to-do provincial family, he was baptized a Catholic at age 15 and then traveled to Seoul and Shanghai where he engaged in Western studies. In 1905, just as he took over his family's trade business in the port of Chinnamp'o, Japan took over responsibility for Korea's foreign affairs (see KOREAN-JAPANESE CONVENTION OF 1905). He sold the business and established a school to prepare Koreans in Western skills needed for the nation's defense. He also participated in Korean nationalist activities in Vladivostok. Focusing his wrath and frustration upon Itō Hirobumi, who in 1906 had become resident general of Japan's advisory administration in Korea, An shot him at a railway station in Harbin, Manchuria, on 26 October 1909. He was executed in 1910 and became a permanent hero to Koreans.

Ancient Learning →Kogaku

ando   安堵

(literally, "undisturbed possession"). Formal confirmation by a lord of vassals' rights of proprietorship, governance, or usufruct over real property, a key element in the lord-vassal relationship in medieval Japan. One important type was honryō ando, confirmation of a family's hereditary tenure of an estate, granted by the shōguns of the Kamakura (1185–1333) and Muromachi (1333–1568) periods to warriors who became their direct vassals (gokenin). In the sense of ratification by shogunal authorities, ando was generally required to formalize the sale or other transfer by a vassal of land or proprietary rights (see YUZURIJŌ).

Andō Hiroshige →Hiroshige

Andō Hirotarō   安藤広太郎

(1871–1958). Scholar of agriculture and agricultural technologist. Born in Hyōgo Prefecture. After graduation from Tōkyō University in 1895, he entered the Agricultural Experiment Station of the Ministry of Agriculture and Commerce (later the Ministry of Agriculture and Forestry) and made many contributions to the improvement of various rice plant varieties as well as to the study of damage due to cold weather and frost. He was director of the Agricultural Experiment Station for 21 years, beginning in 1920, while also serving as a professor at Tōkyō University. He was the author of Nihon kodai inasakushi zakkō (1951, Studies on the Cultivation of Rice in Ancient Japan). He was awarded the Order of Culture in 1956.

andon →lanterns

Andō Nobumasa   安藤信正

(1820–71). Daimyō of Iwaki Taira domain (now part of Fukushima Prefecture); senior councillor (rōjū) of the Tokugawa shogunate from 1860 to 1862. In the wake of II NAOSUKE's assassination, Andō and KUZE HIROCHIKA assumed leadership of the senior council. Andō attempted to strengthen the shogunate's position politically, economically, and diplomatically in its dealings with the Western powers. He hoped to counter the antiforeign, proimperial movement by uniting the court and the shogunate (see MOVEMENT FOR UNION OF COURT AND SHOGUNATE), and in 1862 he effected the marriage of Princess KAZU, sister of Emperor KŌMEI, to the shōgun TOKUGAWA IEMOCHI. This so incensed a group of imperial loyalists that they tried to assassinate him (see SAKASHITAMONGAI INCIDENT). Although Andō survived, his efforts to strengthen the shogunate failed. Andō was forced to resign (1862) and placed under house arrest for the next four years. He supported shogunal loyalists in the BOSHIN CIVIL WAR. After their defeat he was again placed under house arrest, but was soon pardoned by the new Meiji government.

Andō Shōeki   安藤昌益

(1703?–62). Physician and thinker unique in the pre-Meiji history of Japanese thought for advocating a thoroughgoing egalitarianism. Shōeki was completely unknown until his works were discovered around 1899 by the philosopher KANŌ KŌKICHI. Much about his life is still unknown. It appears that he practiced medicine in the town of Hachinohe (in present-day Aomori Prefecture). Shōeki's chief works, SHIZEN SHIN'EIDŌ and Tōdō shinden, were probably written or published around 1752–55.

Shōeki was unique in his opposition to the feudal class system; he said that because all men are equal, each should work to grow his own food (chokkō). The natural order of human society is for people to feed and clothe themselves through agricultural labor, for men and women to join together on equal terms in monogamous bonds, and for them to give birth to and raise the next generation. Shōeki called this ideal society the "natural world" (shizen no yo). In opposition to this he placed the "legal world" (hōsei) of man-made laws and institutions, through which social class distinction is born and the emperor and feudal lords can live in luxury by stealing and devouring the fruits of the labor of others. Those of lower social rank become envious and revolt.

Shōeki's own metaphysical view of nature, which formed the foundation for his social thought, was that there is truth in action (katsushin) at the source of all things; the katsushin is manifested in the forward and backward movement of the elements (ki; Ch: qi or ch'i) of wood, fire, metal, and water, which together form the eight elements (hakki). The harmonious creation and action of all things is carried out through the synergy (gosei) of these elements opposing and supplementing each other in their interactions. In opposition to this synergy is the concept of dichotomy (nibetsu), or the placing of value distinctions such as upper and lower or good and bad, the process by which people of the "legal world" disrupt the harmony of the "natural world."

Andō Tadao 安藤忠雄

(1941–). Architect. Born in Ōsaka. After studying architectural design on his own through firsthand observation in various parts of Japan as well as in Europe and the United States, Andō set up his own firm in Ōsaka in 1969. He was awarded the Architectural Institute of Japan's annual prize for Row House in Sumiyoshi (1979), a box-like concrete dwelling in Ōsaka replacing an old-style row house (*nagaya*). The design, emphasizing the concrete walls and combining Japanese sensibility and Western architectural techniques, attracted attention in Japan and abroad. Other major works are Rokkō Housing I (1983), Church on the Water (1989), and Church with the Light (1989). Andō designed the Japanese Government Pavilion for the 1992 Seville International Exposition.

Andō Tsuguo 安藤次男

(1919–). Poet and critic. Born in Okayama Prefecture. Graduate of Tōkyō University. Andō made his debut with the poetry collection *Rokugatsu no midori no yoru wa* (1950, A Green Night in June). More recently he has turned to the origins of Japanese poetry, conveying in his verses a *haiku*-like seasonal awareness. Among his works of criticism are *Bashō shichibushū hyōshaku* (1973, Commentaries on the Collected Haiku of the Bashō School) and *Fujiwara no Teika* (1977), on the *waka* poet FUJIWARA NO SADAIE.

Anegawa, Battle of 姉川の戦い

(Anegawa no Tatakai). Major engagement fought on 30 July 1570 near the river Anegawa in northern Ōmi Province (now Azai Chō, Shiga Prefecture). The allied armies of ODA NOBUNAGA and TOKUGAWA IEYASU defeated the combined forces of ASAI NAGAMASA, the *daimyō* of northern Ōmi, who was Nobunaga's brother-in-law, and Asakura Kagetake (d 1575), a general of the daimyō ASAKURA YOSHIKAGE of Echizen (now part of Fukui Prefecture). Nobunaga carried the day against an army he himself estimated at 20,000 men, largely because of Ieyasu's efforts in leading the van. Kinoshita Tōkichirō (later called TOYOTOMI HIDEYOSHI) also participated in this campaign. Nobunaga failed to capture Asai's nearby stronghold, Odani Castle, but his victory broke the cordon that had barred his way to the strategic Kyōto-Ōsaka area.

anemone, Japanese 秋明菊

(*shūmeigiku*). *Anemone japonica* or *A. hupehensis* var. *japonica*. Also known as *kibunegiku*. A large perennial herb of the buttercup family (Ranunculaceae) thought to be of Chinese origin. It grows wild in mountainous areas of Honshū, Kyūshū, and Shikoku. Height about 70 centimeters (about 30 in). Long-stalked, three-part leaves grow from the root; ovate leaflets have three to five lobes. Branched flower stalks with pinkish-purple double flowers (about 5 cm [2 in] across) appear in autumn. Numerous garden varieties of this herb have been developed, and its cut flowers are popular. See also ICHIRINSŌ; MISUMISŌ.

An Encouragement of Learning
→ Gakumon no susume

Anesaki Masaharu 姉崎政治

(1873–1949). Pen name Anesaki Chōfū. Scholar of religion and literary critic who laid the foundation for modern religious scholarship in Japan. Born in Kyōto Prefecture. A graduate of Tōkyō University in 1896, he studied, and later lectured, abroad. He was closely associated with the writer TAKAYAMA CHOGYŪ. In 1904 Anesaki was appointed professor at his alma mater and in 1905 founded Japan's first university department for the study of religion. He insisted upon an empathetic approach to religion, free of sectarian bias. As the director of the Tōkyō University Library, he reconstructed and restored collections destroyed in the TŌKYŌ EARTHQUAKE OF 1923. Two of his major works, *Nichiren: The Buddhist Prophet* (1916) and *History of Japanese Religion* (1930), helped introduce Japanese religion to Western readers.

anglerfishes 鮟鱇

(*ankō*). In Japanese, *ankō* is the general name for bottom-dwelling saltwater fish of the family Lophiidae, order Lophiiformes, class Osteichthyes. In Japan the *hon'ankō* (*Lophius litulon*), 1.5 meters (5 ft) long, and the *kutsuankō* (*Liphiomus setigerus*), 1 meter (3 ft) long, are caught for food. The body is soft, and the head and mouth are large. The fish moves the tip of its first dorsal spine, which looks like a baited fishing rod, to lure small fish. It inhabits continental shelf areas off Japan. Its liver is considered a delicacy, and its meat is exported. In premodern times the common people, especially of Edo (now Tōkyō), greeted the arrival of winter by eating *ankō* served in a pot.

Anglo-Japanese Alliance 日英同盟

(Nichiei Dōmei). A military alliance between Great Britain and Japan, concluded in 1902 and lasting until 1923. It helped mark Japan's emergence as a major power in the Far East.

Both Britain and Japan shared a concern with protecting their interests on the Asian mainland in the face of Russian expansion in Manchuria and northeast China. Japan's leaders, however, were divided over priorities. One faction within the Japanese government, led by ITŌ HIROBUMI, wanted to reach an accommodation with Russia whereby Japan would acknowledge Russia's paramount position in Manchuria in return for recognition of Japanese hegemony over Korea. Another faction, led by YAMAGATA ARITOMO and Prime Minister KATSURA TARŌ, argued that Japanese interests would be better served by an alliance with Britain, and it was this policy that ultimately prevailed.

Original Agreement and Revisions—The treaty of alliance was signed in London on 30 January 1902. It was to continue in force for a period of five years and provided for joint action in the event of encroachment against either of the allies by Russia in concert with any fourth power. The two nations affirmed their recognition of each other's special interests and privileges in China, as well as of Japan's special interests in Korea.

The provisions of the treaty did not come into full effect during the RUSSO-JAPANESE WAR of 1904–05, since the Russians fought alone. Nevertheless, while the peace negotiations were in progress at Portsmouth, New Hampshire, in August 1905, the alliance was revised and extended for 10 years. The alliance was renewed prematurely for 10 years in July 1911, but with a considerably narrowed scope. Britain had implicitly accepted Japan's annexation of Korea in the previous year, but Japan acknowledged that the alliance did not imply any British obligation to aid Japan against the United States.

Dissatisfaction and Termination—Some Japanese statesmen used the British alliance as a pretext for Japan's joining the Allies in World War I, although Japan was not obligated to do so under the terms of the alliance. Japanese campaigns against German-leased territory in China and Germany's Pacific islands were among the first Allied victories of the war. The British, however, became dissatisfied with the alliance, fearing Japan would usurp British markets in the Pacific and Indian oceans. Britain, China, and the United States all condemned Japan's expansion in China.

The issue of renewing or abandoning the alliance was brought to a head in private discussions held at the time of the WASHINGTON CONFERENCE in 1921. Britain and Japan both realized that in the altered circumstances of the postwar period they would need the naval, financial, and political cooperation of the United States to maintain security in the Pacific. In effect, Britain and Japan gave up their fairly precise contract in favor of the ambiguous FOUR-POWER TREATY (signed 13 December 1921, effective 17 August 1923) with the United States and France.

Andō Tadao The architect's Church on the Water (1989) in the Yūfutsu district of Hokkaidō. A cross rises from an artificial lake situated directly in front of the pews.

Japanese anemone This autumn-blooming perennial herb grows in the wild and is also cultivated.

Anglo-Japanese Commercial Treaty of 1894　日英通商航海条約

(Nichiei Tsūshō Kōkai Jōyaku). Signed in London on 16 July 1894 by the Japanese ambassador to Great Britain, AOKI SHŪZŌ, and the British foreign secretary, John W. Kimberley. The treaty was Japan's first important success in its efforts to remove inequities imposed by the Western powers in 1858 (see ANSEI COMMERCIAL TREATIES). Effective on 17 July 1899, the agreement ended British extraterritorial rights and partly restored Japan's rights of tariff autonomy. Other Western powers soon concluded similar agreements. See also UNEQUAL TREATIES, REVISION OF.

Angyō　安行

District in the northeastern part of the city of Kawaguchi, Saitama Prefecture, central Honshū. Plants, seedlings, and cut flowers have been produced here since the Edo period (1600–1868), and today Angyō is one of the three largest producers of garden plants in Japan. It is becoming progressively urbanized.

animal experimentation, ethical guidelines for　動物実験の倫理綱領

(dōbutsu jikken no rinri kōryō). In recent years both scientists and animal welfare advocates have been increasingly concerned about the issue of animal experimentation. On 25 May 1987 the Ministry of Education issued an official notification calling on institutions involved in animal experimentation to establish guidelines for research based on a report submitted by the Science Council, one of the ministry's advisory bodies. The report contained the following six principles: (1) Specialists in laboratory animals should be consulted in the preparation of research proposals to ensure that the experiments involved are both effective and appropriate. Efforts should be made to employ experimental methods that do not require the use of animals. (2) Selection of test animals should be guided by consideration of the species most appropriate to experimental goals, the number of animals necessary to ensure accuracy and reproducibility of results, the genetic and microbiological quality of the specimens, and the conditions required for their care. (Specimens should be subjected to quarantine when necessary.) (3) In order to conduct experiments appropriate from the standpoint of both scientific accuracy and animal welfare, attention must be given to the proper management and maintenance of facilities and equipment, and to the provision of adequate food, water, and other care. (4) Experimental procedures should be designed to avoid causing animals unnecessary pain. (5) Use of physical, chemical, or pathogenic materials in experiments must be monitored with care in order to ensure human safety, prevent injury to the animals due to environmental contamination, and guarantee the reliability of the experimental data. (6) Animal experimentation committees should be created at each research facility to implement the established guidelines. These committees should be composed of specialists in laboratory animals, experimenters, and other relevant personnel.

animals　動物

(dōbutsu). The Japanese islands are inhabited by Southeast Asiatic tropical animals, Korean and Chinese temperate-zone animals, and Siberian subarctic animals. Japan's fauna includes many species and relicts not found in neighboring areas. Some of these relicts are found on Honshū, but a larger number inhabit the Ogasawara Islands and the islands south of Kyūshū.

Overall Characteristics——In zoogeographic terms, the sea south of central Honshū belongs to the Indo-Western Pacific region, which is part of the tropical kingdom; it abounds in bright coral fish, sea snakes, and turtles and is inhabited by the dugong and the black finless porpoise. The sea north of central Honshū belongs to the Northern Pacific region, part of the northern kingdom, which extends along the southern coast of the Aleutian Islands and the west coast of the United States down to California and is inhabited by the fur seal, Steller's sea lion, and Baird's beaked whale. Finally, Hokkaidō, which largely faces the Sea of Okhotsk in the Arctic region, is visited occasionally by animals indigenous to the Arctic region, such as the walrus.

In the zoogeographical division of the Japanese islands by land animals, the Ryūkyū Islands south of Amami Ōshima are sometimes regarded as part of the Oriental region extending from the Malayan Peninsula to India and sometimes as a transition zone from this region to the Palaearctic region; the area north of Yakushima off southern Kyūshū is considered part of the Palaearctic region. The Ryūkyū Islands are inhabited mostly by tropical animals, such as the flying fox, crested serpent eagle, variable lizard, and butterflies of the family Danaidae. In mainland Japan (Honshū, Shikoku, and Kyūshū) and Hokkaidō, which belong to the Palaearctic region, two groups of animals are predominant: those of deciduous forests of Korea and central and northern China, such as the raccoon dog, sika deer, Japanese crested ibis, mandarin duck, and hairstreak; and those of coniferous forests of Siberia, such as the brown bear, pika, hazel grouse, common lizard, and nine-spined stickleback.

Of these animals, those of the Korean and Chinese group are confined mostly to the Japanese mainland and those of the Siberian group to Hokkaidō. Consequently, it is common to include the mainland in the Manchurian subregion of the Palaearctic region and Hokkaidō in the Siberian subregion. However, the geological history of the Japanese islands, marked by repeated separation from and reunion with the Asian continent, is exceedingly complex, giving rise to a corresponding complexity of animal migration and, as a result, noncontinuous distribution. The fauna of Japan differs slightly from those found in corresponding areas of the continent and not a few species are endemic to Japan. Among possible relicts of species that migrated in the remote past are insects of the order Grylloblattodea found only in Japan, Russia, and Canada; the Himalayan water shrew, distributed in the Japanese mainland, southern China, Taiwan, Southeast Asia, and the Himalayas; and the eastern barbastelle, distributed in Hokkaidō, Honshū, western China, the Himalayas, and the Caucasus. The distribution of the Japanese serow is analogous when the genus as a whole is considered. The Japanese mainland is inhabited by many endemic species, such as the Japanese macaque, Japanese dormouse, copper pheasant, Japanese giant salamander, and primitive dragonfly (Epiophlebia superstes). The Ryūkyū Islands, presumed to have separated from the continent long before the mainland, are inhabited by such endemic genera as Pryer's woodpecker and the Amami spiny mouse. The Amami rabbit and Iriomote cat belong to endemic genera but also have characteristics that differ from the standards of higher taxonomic ranks and may be said to be living fossils.

Other examples of living fossils are found in the deep sea and include the slit shell, horseshoe crab, and frilled shark. The giant spider crab, the world's largest crustacean; the (freshwater) Japanese giant salamander, the largest amphibian of the Recent epoch; and the ōgusokumushi (genus Bathynomus), one of the largest species of the order Isopoda, are also noteworthy Japanese aquatic animals.

There are many forms of Asian land salamanders, dragonflies, and cicadas. Large swallowtail butterflies number eight species in the mainland alone, which is remarkable for such a small temperate-zone area.

For the protection of endangered species, countermeasures such as the conservation of habitats, artificial breeding, and feeding have been reviewed by the ENVIRONMENT AGENCY, and some proposals already have been implemented. In order to protect animals and insects, in 1979 the agency started a quinquennial survey of the status of animal populations.

Animals in Japanese Culture——Many of the beliefs and views held in Japan about various animals stem from native traditions, Buddhist sources, and the classic works of Chinese literature. Such traditional animal symbols as cranes and turtles (for felicity and long life) and swallows (for faithful return) were adopted from the Chinese by the Japanese ruling class in the protohistoric and ancient periods. It was not until the late medieval period (mid-12th–16th centuries) that a set of animal symbols that were truly Japanese evolved.

Until the late 19th century, the vast majority of Japanese refrained from slaughtering four-legged animals and relied chiefly on fish for animal protein. This practice derived mainly from Buddhist teachings. The Japanese view of animals includes the role played by the JIKKAN JŪNISHI, or the sexagenary cycle of the ancient Chinese calendrical system. The cycle is broken down into subcycles of 12 years, each of which is represented by an animal. Even today, it is common practice to associate a person's character and fortune—based on his or her birth date—with those of the corresponding animal in the sexagenary cycle (e.g., "the year of the dragon"). In addition, animals and flowers are often used in artistic and poetic descriptions to elicit a sense of time and season. See also AMPHIBIANS; BIRDS; FISHES; INSECTS; MAMMALS; REPTILES.

For individual entries on amphibians, see FROGS; IMORI; SALAMANDERS.

For entries on birds, see BUSH WARBLER; CHICKEN, JAPANESE; CRANES; CROWS; CUCKOOS; GEESE; GULLS; HAWKS AND EAGLES; HERONS; KITE, BLACK; KOMADORI; LARKS; MANDARIN DUCK; OWLS; PHEASANTS; PLOVERS; PTARMIGAN; RAILS; REED WARBLERS; SHRIKES; SPARROWS; SWALLOWS; THRUSHES; WAGTAILS; WILD DUCKS; WOODPECKERS.

For entries on fishes, see ANGLERFISHES; AYU; BONITO; CARP; EEL, JAPANESE; GLOBEFISHES; GOBIES; GOLDFISH; HERRING; MACKEREL; SALMONS; SAMMA; SARDINES; SEA BREAM; TUNA; WHITEBAIT; YELLOWTAIL.

For entries on insects, see ANTS; BEES AND WASPS; BUTTERFLIES; CICADAS; CRICKETS; DRAGONFLIES; FIREFLIES; GOLD BEETLE; KIRIGIRISU.

For entries on mammals, see BATS; BEARS; CATS; CATTLE; DEER, JAPANESE; DOG, JAPANESE; DORMOUSE, JAPANESE; FLYING SQUIRRELS; FOXES;

HORSES; JAPANESE SPANIEL; JAPANESE TERRIER; KAMOSHIKA; KAWAUSO; MARINE MAMMALS; MOLES; MONKEYS; RABBITS; RATS AND MICE; TANUKI; TOSA DOG; WEASELS; WHALES; WILD BOAR; WILDCATS; WOLF, JAPANESE.

For entries on reptiles, see SNAKES; TOKAGE; TURTLES.

For other animal articles, see ABALONES; CRABS; EARTHWORMS; HORSESHOE CRAB; JELLYFISH; LEECHES; OCTOPUSES; SEA CUCUMBERS; SEA URCHINS; SHELLFISH; SHRIMPS, PRAWNS, AND LOBSTERS; SPIDERS; SQUID AND CUTTLEFISH.

animated films アニメーション映画

(*animēshon eiga*). The first animated films produced in Japan date from around 1916 and were heavily influenced by the techniques of such early French animators as Emile Cohl. Ōfuji Noburō (1900–1961), who pioneered a technique of cut-out silhouette animation in the 1920s, was the first Japanese animator to achieve international recognition. In 1932 Masaoka Kenzō (1898–1988) produced the first Japanese animated film with sound. Masaoka, who is known as the father of Japanese animation, is also credited with realizing the commercial potential of animation in Japan and turning what had been a group of small-scale, private animators into the beginnings of an organized industry. Among Masaoka's followers were Seo Michiyo (b 1911) and Yabushita Taiji (1903–86). Seo produced the first Japanese feature-length, cell-animation film, a representation of the attack on Pearl Harbor entitled *Momotarō no umiwashi* (1943, Momotarō and His Eagles of the Sea). It is regarded as an animated film classic.

The Japanese animation industry grew, albeit slowly, in the immediate postwar period. In 1958 the Tōei Animation Co, Ltd, released the first Japanese color feature-length animated film, Yabushita Taiji's *Hakujaden* (White Snake Enchantress). The company has released an animated feature film almost every year since. Later, the animation group Animēshon Sannin no Kai, formed by Kuri Yōji (b 1928) and two fellow animators in 1960, experimented with various types of comedic themes, including adult-oriented black humor. The group's work was praised abroad for its adult appeal but received comparatively little notice in Japan.

The most important event in postwar Japanese animation circles occurred in 1963, when the MANGA (comic strip) artist TEZUKA OSAMU formed his own animation production company and released an animated version of his long-running series *Astro Boy* (*Tetsuwan Atomu*) for television broadcast. The huge popularity of the animated *Astro Boy* among Japanese youngsters sparked the production of a number of other 30-minute, made-for-television animated serials in Japan, nearly all of which were based on comic-magazine serials. Some (like *Astro Boy*) were later dubbed in foreign languages for broadcast in other countries. Among these were *Janguru taitei* (1965, shown abroad as *Kimba the White Lion*) and *Mahha gōgō* (1967, shown abroad as *Speed Racer*). In the late 1960s sports stories, such as *Kyojin no hoshi* (1968, Star of the Giants), became popular for their portrayals of "fighting spirit" on the playing field. The animated version of *Sazae san* (1969), from the comic strip created by HASEGAWA MACHIKO, portrayed the everyday life of a typical Japanese woman and her family and proved popular with viewers of all ages. It was still being aired in 1991.

The cycle of comic magazine to animated television series continued through the 1970s and 1980s. A notable example is FUJIKO FUJIO's *Doraemon* (1979), the adventures of a futuristic robot cat. *Kyandī Kyandī* (1976, Candy Candy), a sentimental series aimed at young girls, was dubbed for broadcast abroad and became a hit in Italy. Old Japanese folktales and Western children's classics have also been mined for treatment in animation, as in a popular version of *Heidi* entitled *Arupusu no shōjo Haiji* (1974). Some of the more successful animated television series have been adapted for feature-film release. The best examples of this Japanese method of "recycling" story ideas through different media are Matsumoto Reiji's (b 1938) string of science fiction comics with animation tie-ins. When his *Uchū senkan Yamato* (Space Cruiser Yamato; shown abroad as *Star Blazers*) was released to Japanese theaters in 1977 it met with huge success, thanks largely to a generation of youngsters who had grown up with televised animated series. It was followed by a flood of animated feature films, including a number of other Matsumoto productions, such as *Ginga tetsudō 999* (1979, Galaxy Express 999). MIYAZAKI HAYAO, who is recognized as one of Japan's top feature film animators, produced TONARI NO TOTORO (My Neighbor Totoro) in 1988. The story of a friendly woodland ghost that can be seen only by children, *Tonari no Totoro* carried a message of environmental protection. The film was popular among children and praised by adults for its theme and artistic merits. Two other notable figures in Japanese animation are KAWAMOTO KIHACHIRŌ and OKAMOTO TADANARI, who are internationally known for their puppet animation. Important Japanese animation productions of the late 1980s and early 1990s included Ōtomo Katsuhiro's (b 1954) dark postapocalypse adventure *Akira* (1988), an animated feature film, and *Chibi Maruko chan* (1990), a television series created by Sakura Momoko (b 1965) that portrays the everyday life of a little Japanese girl. 🐦40

animism アニミズム

(*animizumu*). Belief in the existence of a spiritual life in natural objects, natural phenomena, and the universe itself that is capable of exercising an influence on human beings. The Japanese have apparently believed in spirits called *chi*, *mi*, or *tama*—which, although not clearly defined, were associated with natural phenomena—since prehistoric times. The chronicle KOJIKI and the poetry anthology MAN'YŌSHŪ (both 8th century) refer to the sun god Ōhirume no Nu*chi*, the moon god Tsukiyo*mi*, the mountain god Yamatsu*mi*, and the ocean god Wadatsu*mi*. There was also a belief in such *tama* as *kodama* (the spirit of the trees) and KOTODAMA (the spirit of words). Gods given individual designations and characteristics were called *kami* or *mikoto*. These gods and less clearly defined spirits were thought to have control over natural and human phenomena. Such beliefs have continued to endow the Japanese relationship to nature with a particular spiritual quality. See also RELIGION; SHINTŌ.

Anjō 安城[市]

City in central Aichi Prefecture, central Honshū. Before World War II, its main activity was rice cultivation, utilizing the MEIJI CANAL for water. More recently it has become a satellite city of NAGOYA. Anjō has a growing machine industry. Pop: 142,251.

Ankokuji Ekei 安国寺恵瓊

(?–1600). Buddhist warrior-monk of the Azuchi-Momoyama period (1568–1600). Born in the province of Aki (now part of Hiroshima Prefecture), he became abbot of the monastery Ankokuji in Aki in 1579. Ekei served in the invasion of Korea in 1592 (see INVASIONS OF KOREA IN 1592 AND 1597). He made extensive repairs to Ankokuji and to the temple Tōfukuji in Kyōto, where he became chief abbot in 1598. He also received a substantial fief in Iyo Province (now Ehime Prefecture) from his patron TOYOTOMI HIDEYOSHI. In 1600 Ekei fought against TOKUGAWA IEYASU at the Battle of SEKIGAHARA. After Ieyasu's victory Ekei was captured and beheaded.

Anna Incident 安和の変

(Anna no Hen). A conspiracy at the time of the abdication of Emperor Reizei (r 967–969) in 969 (the year Anna 2 in Japanese reckoning) whereby the FUJIWARA FAMILY discredited Minamoto no Takaakira (914–982), son of the late emperor DAIGO and the chief political obstacle to the ambitious Fujiwara no Saneyori (900–970). A Fujiwara ally, Minamoto no Mitsunaka (912–997), reported a plot to depose Crown Prince Morihira and elevate Takaakira's son-in-law Prince Tamehira. Takaakira was disgraced and banished to Kyūshū, and Crown Prince Morihira was enthroned as Emperor En'yū (r 969–984) with Saneyori as his regent. Thus the Fujiwara consolidated their control of the court and established their REGENCY GOVERNMENT as a permanent institution, while Mitsunaka's branch of the MINAMOTO FAMILY began its rise.

Annaka 安中[市]

City in southwestern Gumma Prefecture, central Honshū, situated on the river Usuigawa. In premodern times Annaka was a post-station town and a castle town on the highway Nakasendō. Its principal industry is zinc refining. Isobe Hot Spring is located in the western section of the city. Annaka is also known as the onetime home of NIIJIMA JŌ, a Christian educator. Pop: 45,525.

Anno Mitsumasa 安野光雅

(1926–). Author-illustrator, essayist, and painter. Born in Shimane Prefecture. Graduate of Yamaguchi University. Anno began to write and illustrate his own books with *Fushigi na e* (1968; tr *Topsy-Turvies*, 1970). In his picture books he creates a unique world of delicately colored landscapes. His major works are *Tabi no ehon* (1977; tr *Anno's Journey*, 1978) and *Tendōsetsu no ehon* (1979; tr *Anno's Medieval World*, 1980).

annual events→nenchū gyōji

Anotsu 安濃津

Former seaport in Ise Province (now the city of Tsu in Mie Prefecture). With Hakata (see HAKATA MERCHANTS) and BŌ NO TSU, it was one of Japan's three principal ports during the Muromachi period (1333–1568) and a major entrepôt of the TALLY TRADE with Ming China. Though ruined for shipping by a 1498 earthquake, the town prospered throughout the Edo period (1600–1868) as a stopping place for pilgrims traveling to the ISE SHRINE.

Anrakuan Sakuden 安楽庵策伝

(1554–1642). Prelate of the JŌDO SECT (Pure Land sect) of Buddhism, devotee of the tea cult, and poet, who presumably compiled the

The World of Japanese Animation

Like the ubiquitous comic books from which many of their characters are taken, animated features are enormously popular in Japan with both children and adults. Appealing characters and technical virtuosity have made animation one of the few aspects of Japanese popular culture to be successfully exported. Ever since the 1963 debut of Astro Boy (Tetsuwan Atomu), Japan's first animated TV star, Japanese animated TV programs and feature films have been shown around the world. The examples here illustrate the development of modern Japanese animation.

Hakujaden (1958, White Snake Enchantress). A white snake is rescued by a boy and transformed into a beautiful girl. This tale of romance and adventure is based on a story from Ming-dynasty (1368–1644) China.

Momotarō no umiwashi (1943, Momotarō and His Eagles of the Sea). Japan's first feature-length animated film, made during World War II under the direction of the Navy Ministry. In this scene, planes departing to attack Pearl Harbor are given a send-off.

Tetsuwan Atomu (1963, shown abroad as *Astro Boy*). Originally comic-book heroes and later TV characters, the robot Astro Boy and his sister Uran continued their fight for peace and justice on the big screen.

Arupusu no shōjo Haiji (1974, Heidi). A popular adaptation of the Swiss story of Heidi, an orphan taken in by her grandfather. Animated versions of many classic Japanese and Western children's stories were made during the 1970s.

Kyandī Kyandī (1976, Candy Candy). Starring the popular girls' comic-book heroine Candy, this story was a great hit in Italy—where children were surprised to learn that the story of the blond orphan with huge sparkling eyes was made in Japan.

Ginga tetsudō 999 (1979, Galaxy Express 999). This science-fiction fantasy about Tetsurō (left), a boy seeking revenge for the murder of his mother, was inspired by Miyazawa Kenji's well-known story "Ginga tetsudō no yoru" (Night Train to the Stars).

Doraemon (1979). This film follows the adventures of Doraemon (right), a robot cat from the future, and his friend Nobita. Doraemon continues to be one of Japan's best-loved animated characters. The desk drawer in the picture serves as the entrance to his time machine.

Tonari no Totoro (1988, My Neighbor Totoro). Set in rural Japan in the 1950s, this fantasy about a gentle woodland ghost who befriends children was a great success.

Akira (1988). This apocalyptic science-fiction story is set in a post-nuclear "Neo-Tōkyō" in the year 2019. The film won critical acclaim for the complexity and sophistication of its animation techniques and artwork.

collection of anecdotes *Seisuishō* (Laughs to Wake You Up), a major precursor of the popular Edo-period (1600–1868) genre called *hanashibon* (books of humorous stories).

Sakuden was adept at *mandara etoki*, a form of religious instruction through which works such as the *Jōdo hen mandara* (a mandala depicting the Pure Land of Amida) are explained. He became chief priest of several temples, the last of which was the Pure Land temple Seiganji in Kyōto. Granted high imperial honors, he retired at 70 to Anrakuan (Hermitage of Peace and Comfort) and prepared the *Seisuishō.* Two other Sakuden works survive: *Hyakuchinshū* (Collection of One Hundred Camellias), a descriptive catalogue of camellia varieties, and *Sakuden oshō sōtōhikae* (Memorandum of the Correspondence of the Priest Sakuden), his collected correspondence in verse—chiefly KYŌKA and *hokku* (see HAIKU)—with, among others, the landscape architect KOBORI ENSHŪ and the literary figures MATSUNAGA TEITOKU, KARASUMARU MITSUHIRO, and KINOSHITA CHŌSHŌSHI.

Anritsu Corporation アンリツ[株]

(Anritsu). Electronic appliance manufacturer; affiliated with NEC Corporation. Incorporated in 1950, the company assumed its current name in 1985. It is engaged in the manufacture of communications equipment as well as measuring instruments for fiberoptic communications. Overseas sales subsidiaries are located in the United States, Brazil, the United Kingdom, and Germany. Sales for the fiscal year ending March 1991 totaled ¥100.0 billion (US $728.9 million), and capitalization stood at ¥9.5 billion (US $69.2 million). Headquarters are in Tōkyō.

Ansei commercial treaties 安政五箇国条約

(Ansei *gokakoku jōyaku;* literally, "Ansei five-power treaties"). Trade agreements concluded between the Tokugawa shogunate and the United States, Russia, the Netherlands, Great Britain, and France in 1858, only five years after Commodore Matthew PERRY ended Japan's policy of NATIONAL SECLUSION. The US treaty (HARRIS TREATY) served as a model for the treaties with the other nations. These treaties opened several Japanese cities to trade, including Kanagawa (later changed to nearby Yokohama), Niigata, Hyōgo (now Kōbe), Hakodate, Nagasaki, Edo (now Tōkyō), and Ōsaka. The treaties also provided for the exchange of diplomatic representatives, assigned living and recreational areas for foreign residents, set tariff rates, and sanctioned extraterritoriality. These unequal arrangements drew Japan, for the first time in 250 years, into a network of economic and political relationships with the West. The shogunate, headed by the great elder (*tairō*) II NAOSUKE, attempted to eliminate the treaties' critics with the ANSEI PURGE but was constrained to adopt a more conciliatory posture after Ii's assassination in 1860. Amendment of the treaties remained an important diplomatic issue throughout the Meiji period (1868–1912). See also UNEQUAL TREATIES, REVISION OF.

Ansei Purge 安政の大獄

(Ansei no Taigoku). Widespread purge, occurring from 1858 to 1860 (Ansei 5–7), of political leaders and court nobles who opposed the Tokugawa shogunate's policy of opening Japan to diplomatic and trade relations with

the West. The purge was carried out by *tairō* (great elder) II NAOSUKE as soon as he assumed office in June 1858. All told, more than 100 were involved in the purge. Leading *daimyō* were placed under house arrest or forced to retire, antiforeign court nobles were dismissed from office, and proimperial activists such as HASHIMOTO SANAI and YOSHIDA SHŌIN were executed. Retaliation was swift: on 24 March 1860 Ii was murdered by *samurai* from Mito (now part of Ibaraki Prefecture) and Satsuma (now Kagoshima Prefecture), areas whose *daimyō* opposed any plan to deal with the West (see SAKURADAMONGAI INCIDENT). His assassination at the hands of outraged followers of the purge's victims signaled the end of the purge. Ostensibly the purge reaffirmed shogunate authority in the face of open challenge to its decisions regarding shogunal succession and the signing of the HARRIS TREATY; it also represented a vendetta by Ii against his enemies. Culminating in utter failure, it served to hurry the shogunate's demise in 1867 and affected the nature of the MEIJI RESTORATION in 1868.

Antarctic research 南極観測

(Nankyoku *kansoku*). After a pioneering expedition in 1912, Japan's Antarctic research got its real start in 1957, when Shōwa Station was established and wintering-over research expeditions became possible.

In January 1912 the Shirase party, Japan's first successful Antarctic research expedition, under SHIRASE NOBU, penetrated the ice belt in the Ross Sea in the ship *Kainan maru* and landed on the Ross Ice Shelf in the Bay of Whales. The party traveled over the ice shelf to a latitude of 80°05′ S. It is credited with the discovery of Kainan Bay and Ōkuma Bay, and it explored the coast of the northeastern limit of the Ross Sea, now known as the Shirase Coast.

After a long period of no research or exploration by Japanese in the Antarctic, Japan participated in scientific exploration of the Antarctic during the International Geophysical Year (IGY) of 1957–58, establishing the Japanese Antarctic Research Expedition (JARE), an adjunct of the Ministry of Education. Shōwa Station was established in January 1957 on East Ongul Island at 69°00′ S, 39°35′ E, on the northeastern edge of Lützow-Holm Bay in eastern Queen Maud Land, and it remains the principal base for Japanese Antarctic research. In 1970 Mizuho Station was set upon the ice sheet at 70°42′ S, 44°18′ E, at an altitude of 2,170 meters (7,118 ft) above sea level. As of 1991 a total of 32 research teams had been sent to the Antarctic.

Research conducted at Shōwa Station includes surface meteorological observations, aerological observations, observations of auroras and geomagnetism, ionospheric observations, tidal observations, seismological observations, and geodesy. At Mizuho Station, observations of ice and snow, the atmosphere, and the upper atmosphere are conducted. In 1991, the five-year Japanese Dome Ice Coring Project was initiated to study the composition of the ice on the Antarctic polar cap.

anti-Christian edicts 禁教令

(*kinkyōrei*). Anti-Christian directives of the Azuchi-Momoyama (1568–1600) and Edo (1600–1868) periods. After the introduction of CHRISTIANITY into Japan by Jesuits in 1549, Japan's fragmented political condition facilitated the religion's regional spread, es-

Antarctic research
Built on the exposed rock of the Ongul Islands, Shōwa Station, pictured here during the brief summer season, is the main base for Japanese Antarctic research.

pecially in Kyūshū, where CHRISTIAN DAIMYŌ such as ŌMURA SUMITADA compelled the populace of their domains to convert to Christianity. TOYOTOMI HIDEYOSHI moved against Christianity immediately upon completing his conquest of Kyūshū. He issued a notice in Hakata (now Fukuoka) on 23 July 1587 condemning forced conversions. The notice was followed a day later by a decree that the Jesuit missionaries (BATEREN) must leave Japan "within 20 days." Although some Christian churches were destroyed, no missionaries left Japan permanently as a result of these edicts. In the aftermath of the SAN FELIPE INCIDENT of 1596, Hideyoshi renewed his proscription of Christian missionaries, an action that was followed by the death of the TWENTY-SIX MARTYRS of Japan on 5 February 1597. TOKUGAWA IEYASU issued anti-Christian directives in 1612 after the MADRE DE DEUS INCIDENT. The Tokugawa shogunate's anti-Christian rationale was elaborated in the Statement on the Expulsion of the Bateren, drafted by the Zen monk Konchiin SŪDEN at Ieyasu's behest and dated 1 February 1614.

By 1663 a clause requiring the strict prohibition of Christianity "in all provinces and localities" was incorporated in the BUKE SHOHATTO (Laws for the Military Houses). From 1640 to 1792 the shogunate's table of organization included an Office of the Inquisition (see SHŪMON ARATAME). The anti-Christian element was one of the most prominent constituents of the policy of NATIONAL SECLUSION. Christianity survived in a gradually deteriorating form as a syncretic folk religion among the KAKURE KIRISHITAN (Hidden Christians) until the edicts were voided by the Meiji government's declaration of religious freedom in 1873.

Anti-Comintern Pact 日独伊三国防共協定

(Nichidokui Sangoku Bōkyō Kyōtei). Also known as the Tripartite Anti-Comintern Pact. A treaty signed by Japan, Germany, and Italy to oppose the Soviet Union. Japan and Germany initially concluded the pact in Berlin on 25 November 1936, and Italy joined them as an equal partner on 6 November 1937. The signatories committed themselves to exchanging information on Comintern activities and to collaborating closely on preventive measures. A secret supplementary protocol identified the Soviet Union as the signatories' common enemy. The signatories also secretly agreed to conclude no political treaties with the Soviet Union except by mutual consent. The treaty, drawn up largely by Japanese military attaché ŌSHIMA HIROSHI and German diplomat Joachim von Ribbentrop, was the first step toward an alliance between Japan and Germany. In 1939 Hungary, Spain, and the Japanese puppet state of MANCHUKUO signed the pact; in 1941 the treaty was re-

Aoi Festival An oxcart on its way from the southern gate (Kenreimon) of the Kyōto Imperial Palace to the Kamo Shrines. The participants wear Heian-period costumes.

Antimonopoly Law 独占禁止法

(Dokusen Kinshi Hō; popular abbreviation of Shiteki Dokusen no Kinshi oyobi Kōsei Torihiki no Kakuho ni kansuru Hōritsu, or Law concerning the Prohibition of Private Monopoly and the Preservation of Fair Trade). Japan's first antimonopoly law, enacted in 1947 as part of the economic democratization of Japan begun under the Allied OCCUPATION. The law, "by prohibiting private monopolization, unreasonable restraint of trade, and unfair business practices, . . . aims to promote free and fair competition, to stimulate the initiative of entrepreneurs, to encourage business activities of entrepreneurs, to heighten the level of employment and people's real income, and thereby to promote the democratic and wholesome development of the national economy as well as to assure the interests of consumers in general."

The development of the antimonopoly law in Japan since its inception may be divided into three periods that reflect varying degrees of enforcement. The first period, from 1947 to 1952, was marked by strict enforcement, due largely to the vigorous support of the Occupation. The second period, from 1952 until the mid-1960s, was marked by more relaxed enforcement. The first reason for this relaxation was a 1952 amendment to the law that eliminated the per se illegality of cartels and other provisions dissolving all businesses above certain size limits (see ZAIBATSU DISSOLUTION); the second was a shift in Allied strategy regarding Japan during the Korean War. In the third period, from the mid-1960s until the present, the law has been enforced with renewed vigor. Among factors contributing to renewed enforcement are steady inflation, rising consumerism, the liberalization of trade and capital transactions, and a shift in Japan's national economic policy goal from high growth toward welfare. Furthermore, the year 1977 saw another amendment to the law, this time strengthening its antimonopoly provisions and providing for stricter enforcement.

Although the interpretation and enforcement of the law reflect to a large extent the influence of the US antitrust laws after which the Japanese law was modeled, there are substantive and procedural differences. For example, the private suit for damages has yet to play a large role in enforcement of the law. Similarly, there have been very few criminal prosecutions under the law. Enforcement of the law is left primarily to the jurisdiction of an administrative agency, the Fair Trade Commission (FTC). Substantively, the three main areas of regulation under the law are private monopolization, unreasonable restraint of trade, and unfair business practices.

Private Monopolization——"Private monopolization" is defined in section 2(5) of the law as "business activities by which any entrepreneur, individually, by combination or conspiracy with other entrepreneurs, or in any other manner, excludes or controls the business activities of other entrepreneurs, thereby causing, contrary to the public interest, a substantial restraint of competition in any particular field of trade." Section 2(1) of the law defines "entrepreneur" as any "person who carries on a commercial, industrial, financial, or any other business."

Unreasonable Restraint of Trade——Section 2(6) of the law defines "unreasonable restraint of trade" as "such business activities, by which entrepreneurs by contract, agreement, or by other concerted activities mutually restrict or conduct their business activities in such a manner as to fix, maintain, or enhance prices, or to limit production, technology, products, facilities, or customers, or suppliers, thereby causing, contrary to the public interest, a substantial restraint of competition in any particular field of trade." Under this definition, "unreasonable restraint of trade" is essentially the activity of a cartel. It should be noted that the prohibition of cartels applies only to horizontal agreements among competitors. A vertical agreement such as that between seller and purchaser does not fall within the prohibition.

Unfair Business Practices——Section 2(9) of the law defines "unfair business practices" as "any act coming under any one of the following paragraphs which tends to impede fair competition and which is designated by the Fair Trade Commission: unduly discriminating against other entrepreneurs; dealing at undue prices; unreasonably inducing or coercing customers of a competitor to deal with oneself; trading with another party on such conditions as will restrict unjustly the business activities of the said party; dealing with another party by unwarranted use of one's bargaining position. . . ."

Enforcement Procedures——Primary enforcement of the law is left to the FTC. A violation may be brought to the attention of the FTC in one of three ways. First, a private citizen may report information he or she considers a violation of the law. The FTC must then investigate and decide whether to initiate an action. Second, the prosecutor-general must report to the FTC any violations of which he is aware. Third, the FTC may initiate an investigation *ex officio*. Of these three means of commencing an investigation, the first is by far the most common.

If the results of the investigation indicate that a violation has been committed, the FTC may either recommend that the violator cease the illegal behavior and, if this recommendation is accepted, hand down a decision without a hearing, or it may institute formal proceedings against the violator. In most cases, the FTC first makes a recommendation and then, depending on whether the recommendation is accepted, institutes formal proceedings. These proceedings are conducted in an adversarial manner with administrative law judges presiding. During the course of the proceedings, the respondent may accept the statement of facts and application of the law as presented by the FTC and propose to eliminate the violations. If the respondent's proposal is in turn accepted by the FTC, what is referred to as a "consent decision" is handed down. Otherwise the proceedings will continue, and a formal decision will be handed down. There is no difference in the legal effect of these different types of decisions.

After the decision of the FTC, a party dissatisfied with that decision may bring an appeal directly to the Tōkyō High Court. The High Court then reviews the findings of the FTC as to the correctness of the commission's application of the law. No new findings of fact are made by the High Court unless the facts as found by the FTC are totally without evidentiary support. After the decision of the High Court an appeal may be taken to the Supreme Court.

Antoku, Emperor 安徳天皇

(1178–85; Antoku Tennō). The 81st sovereign (*tennō*) in the traditional count (which includes several legendary emperors); reigned 1180–85. Son of Emperor Takakura (1161–81; r 1168–80) and Tokuko (Kenrei Mon'in; 1155–1213?), a daughter of TAIRA NO KIYOMORI. Only a month after Antoku's enthronement, the TAIRA-MINAMOTO WAR (1180–85) began, in which the Minamoto destroyed the Taira. The Taira abandoned Kyōto in 1183, taking Antoku with them. The rival emperor GO-TOBA was installed in his place. Antoku died in the naval battle of DANNOURA, when Kiyomori's widow, Tokiko (Nii no Ama; 1126–85), plunged into the sea with the young emperor in her arms.

ants 蟻

(*ari*). In Japanese, *ari* is the common name for insects of the family Formicidae, or ants, which together with bees and wasps form the order Hymenoptera. Of the several thousand species known worldwide, about 160 species of 6 subfamilies have been identified in Japan. Among these are the *ōhariari* (*Brachyponera chinensis*), the *amimeari* (*Pristomyrmex pungens*), the *ōari* (genus *Camponotus*), and the *samuraiari* (*Polyergus samurai*). The last enslave the *kuroyamaari* (*Formica fusca japonica*) to gather their food and raise their young.

There are very few popular beliefs and legends about ants in Japan. References to the ant are found in the MAKURA NO SŌSHI (ca 1000) and TSUREZUREGUSA (ca 1330). In the Meiji period (1868–1912), two stories dealing with ants appear in Lafcadio HEARN's *Kwaidan*, both of which probably derive from Chinese sources.

An'ya kōro 暗夜行路

(tr *A Dark Night's Passing*, 1976). Celebrated novel by SHIGA NAOYA (1883–1971); his only full-length work of fiction, written sporadically over a quarter of a century and published 1921–37. Considered to be largely autobiographical, it depicts the psychological crises experienced by its protagonist, Tokitō Kensaku, who is profoundly disturbed by the discovery that his birth was the result of a liaison between his mother and grandfather while his father was traveling abroad. He leads a life of dissipation and solitary travel in an effort to throw off his obsession, and eventually enters into a marriage that appears to provide him with a tranquility he had not previously known. This is shattered, however, when he learns that his wife has betrayed him with his cousin. The end of the novel sees Kensaku immersing himself in the contemplation of nature and attaining a spiritual peace that may be more enduring. The novel is prized for its acuity in depicting the psychological states of its protagonist and for the beautiful lucidity of its prose style.

The development of the antimonopoly law. . . . newed for five years. See also GERMANY AND JAPAN.

Anzai Fuyue 安西冬衛

(1898–1965). Poet. Real name Anzai Masaru. Born in Nara Prefecture. Anzai attracted attention with his first collection of prose poems, *Gunkan Mari* (1929, The Battleship Mari). An avant-garde 1930s poet who, along with KITAGAWA FUYUHIKO, helped establish prose poetry in Japan, his poems are noted for their conciseness and rich imagery. His poetry is collected in *Anzai Fuyue zen shishū* (1966).

Anzai Hiroshi 安西浩

(1901–90). Businessman; chairman of TŌKYŌ GAS CO, LTD (1972–89). Born in Chiba Prefecture. After graduating from Tōhoku University, Anzai joined Tōkyō Gas Co in 1928, becoming its president in 1967. He saw great potential in liquefied natural gas (LNG) as a clean energy source, and in 1969 he made Tōkyō Gas Co the first city gas supplier in Japan to convert to LNG. Anzai was chairman of the Tōkyō Metropolitan Public Safety Commission (1979–89) and chairman of the Japan-Soviet Business Corporation Committee of KEIDANREN (Federation of Economic Organizations; 1984–90).

Aōdō Denzen 亜欧堂田善

(1748–1822). Western-style artist known especially for copperplate etching, in which he followed the initiative of his contemporary SHIBA KŌKAN. Real name Nagata Zenkichi. Born in Iwashiro Province (now part of Fukushima Prefecture). The decisive moment in Denzen's career came in 1794, when he was summoned to the court of MATSUDAIRA SADANOBU. Impressed by Denzen's work, Sadanobu ordered the then 47-year-old artist to study with TANI BUNCHŌ. In 1796 Denzen was appointed official painter to Sadanobu and in 1797 he was sent to Edo (now Tōkyō), where he mastered the technique of copperplate etching. Sadanobu later bestowed on him the name Aōdō ("Hall of Asia and Europe"), underscoring Denzen's interest in European and Asian art styles.

aohon →kusazōshi

Aoi Festival 葵祭

(Aoi Matsuri). Festival of the KAMO SHRINES in Kyōto; held on 15 May. Its name derives from the leaves of the *futaba aoi* plant (*Asarum caulescens;* wild ginger), which decorate the headgear of the participants, the oxcarts in the procession, and the houses along the path of the procession. It is said to have originated sometime in the 7th century. On the morning of the festival, the participants gather at the Kyōto Imperial Palace, dressed like nobles of the late Heian period (794–1185). The procession makes its way across Aoi Bridge to Shimo-Gamo Sha, one of the two Kamo Shrines. After rites are conducted, the procession moves to Kami-Gamo Sha, the other shrine, farther north, where a similar ceremony is held. It then returns to the palace.

Aoi Library 葵文庫

(Aoi Bunko). Also known as the Shizuoka Library (Shizuoka Bunko). A collection of books and documents of the TOKUGAWA SHOGUNATE (1603–1867) housed in the Shizuoka Prefecture Central Library in the city of Shizuoka. The collection contains several thousand Dutch, French, German, and English books from various departments of the Tokugawa shogunate, including the BANSHO SHIRABESHO, as well as Chinese and Japanese books from private collections and from the SHŌHEIKŌ, the shogunate academy. Among some 100 Japanese manuscripts is the official Tokugawa record of its relations with the Dutch.

Aoi no Ue 葵上

(Lady Aoi). NŌ play. Author unknown; adapted by ZEAMI. Classified as a *yobammemono* ("part-four play"), it is based on the TALE OF GENJI. Lady Aoi, wife of Prince Genji, has a mysterious illness, so a medium (the *tsure* or "companion" character) is summoned. As she begins to divine the source of illness by plucking her catalpa bow (*azusayumi*), the ghost of Genji's former lover Lady Rokujō (the *maejite* or main character at the beginning of a play) appears. The ghost bewails the loss of Genji's love and attacks his stricken wife. A Buddhist mountain ascetic priest (the *waki* or subordinate character) is sent for and struggles with the enraged ghost, which later takes the form of a female demon (the *nochijite* or main character at the end of a play). The ghost fades away as the prayers of the priest begin to take effect.

aoki 青木

(Japanese laurel). *Aucuba japonica.* An evergreen shrub of the dogwood family (Cornaceae) that grows wild in forested areas of Kyūshū, Shikoku, and Honshū, from the Kantō district westward. It grows to a height of about 2 meters (6.6 ft). The glossy leaves (10–15 cm [4–6 in] long) are opposite, thick, and elliptical. Tiny green to purple-brown flowers appear in spring. Male and female flowers grow on separate trees; female trees bear coral-colored fruits from autumn through spring. The *aoki* tolerates cold, shade, and urban pollution and is valuable as a firebreak or windbreak. Widely cultivated, its horticultural varieties include narrow-leaf and mottled-leaf forms. *Aoki* leaves were roasted as a folk remedy for boils and wounds.

Aoki Corporation [株]青木建設

(Aoki Kensetsu). General construction firm specializing in civil engineering projects. Incorporated in 1947. It also owns and operates 76 hotels in 14 countries, including Brazil, Panama, Taiwan, the United States, and China and is developing a gold mine in Brazil. Sales for the fiscal year ending March 1991 totaled ¥323.6 billion (US $2.4 billion), and capitalization stood at ¥92.8 billion (US $676.4 million). Headquarters are in Ōsaka.

Aoki Isao 青木功

(1942–). Professional golfer. Born in Chiba Prefecture. Aoki entered the ranks of professional golf in 1964. He won the Japan Professional Golf Championship in 1973, 1981, and 1986. As of August 1990 he had won a total of 52 Japanese tournaments. In 1989 he added the Coca-Cola Classic in Melbourne to his list of overseas victories, which also includes the Hawaiian Open in the United States, the European Open in England, and the Pacific Open in Australia. He acquired an American tour license in 1981. Aoki is known particularly for his ability in approach shots.

Aoki Kon'yō 青木昆陽

(1698–1769). Confucian and WESTERN LEARNING scholar. Probably born in Edo (now Tōkyō), he studied Confucianism with ITŌ TŌGAI. In 1719–20 ŌOKA TADASUKE recommended him to the shōgun TOKUGAWA YOSHIMUNE. In 1739 Kon'yō was given a position supervising the official archives, and in the following year Yoshimune ordered him to take up Western studies. In 1747 he was appointed Confucian scholar of the shogunate's Judicial Council (Hyōjōsho) and in 1767 became head of the Momijiyama Bunko, the shogunal library. His book *Banshokō* (1735, Studies on the Sweet Potato) urged cultivation of this easily grown tuber to alleviate famine and earned him the nickname of Sweet Potato Professor (Kansho Sensei). Other works include *Oranda kaheikō* (1745, Notes on Dutch Currency) and *Oranda moji ryakkō* (1746, Notes on the Dutch Language).

Aoki Mokubei 青木木米

(1767–1833). Potter and BUNJINGA painter. Real name Aoki Sahei. Born in Kyōto. At an early age he studied with the great scholar and seal carver Kō Fuyō (1722–84). He later studied pottery under OKUDA EISEN (1753–1811) and soon became famous for his reproductions of classic Chinese-style ceramics, including polychrome enamel, blue-and-white ware, and celadon. He established kilns at Kasugayama in Kanazawa and at Awata in Kyōto. In his later years he also gained fame for his paintings in the *bunjinga* style. He produced mainly landscapes, generally in a tall, narrow, hanging-scroll format in ink, reddish-brown ocher, and indigo, which were much admired by TANOMURA CHIKUDEN. Mokubei's characteristically vibrant landscapes, such as *Autumn Landscape* (1824), employ dry texture strokes and a wash that frequently lends fluidity to the land forms interacting with the atmosphere around them.

Aoki Shigeru 青木繁

(1882–1911). Western-style painter identified with the romantic school. Born in the city of Kurume, Fukuoka Prefecture. In 1899 he entered the Fudōsha, a Tōkyō school operated by Koyama Shōtarō (1857–1916). In 1900 he also enrolled in the Tōkyō Bijutsu Gakkō (now Tōkyō University of Fine Arts and Music), where he studied under KURODA SEIKI and FUJISHIMA TAKEJI. While a student there he was greatly influenced by the En-

Aoyama A number of the many fashionable boutiques and galleries that characterize this Tōkyō district are housed in one of Japan's first Western-style public apartment buildings (pictured), built in 1925.

glish pre-Raphaelites and became deeply interested in ancient Indian and Japanese legends. This led to his two series *Yomotsu Hirasaka* (Pass to the Land of the Dead) and *Jaimini*, which took first place in the eighth HAKUBAKAI exhibition. In the summer of his graduation year, he painted several masterpieces. One of them, *Umi no sachi* (Gifts of the Sea), created a sensation because of its depiction of vigorous nude fishermen hauling in their catch. His works, many of which are held by the ISHIBASHI MUSEUM OF ART, were highly acclaimed after his death.

Aoki Shūzō   青木周蔵

(1844–1914). Diplomat prominent in the effort to revise the so-called Unequal Treaties contracted between Japan and the Western powers in the 1850s. Born into a *samurai* family of the Chōshū domain (now Yamaguchi Prefecture), he studied Western science and medicine. On the eve of the MEIJI RESTORATION (1868) he was sent by his domain to study law in Germany. During his career Aoki was foreign minister in the cabinets of YAMAGATA ARITOMO and MATSUKATA MASAYOSHI; ambassador to Germany, the United States, and Great Britain; and privy councillor and special consultant on revising the Unequal Treaties. As foreign minister, he assumed responsibility for the ŌTSU INCIDENT (1891) and resigned. In 1894, as minister to England, he assisted Foreign Minister MUTSU MUNEMITSU in renegotiating Japan's treaty with Britain (see ANGLO–JAPANESE COMMERCIAL TREATY OF 1894). See also UNEQUAL TREATIES, REVISION OF.

Aomori   青森[市]

City on Aomori Bay, northern Honshū; capital of Aomori Prefecture. Since the establishment of harbor facilities in 1624, Aomori has been an important shipping and fishing center. Its role as a terminal for ferries between Honshū and Hokkaidō ceased in 1988 when the SEIKAN TUNNEL (Aomori–Hakodate Tunnel) opened. It is also the gateway to the Towada-Hachimantai National Park. Industries include lumber, food products, metal, and machinery. The NEBUTA FESTIVAL (3–7 August) and a museum commemorating the artist MUNAKATA SHIKŌ draw visitors. Pop: 287,808.

Aomori Prefectural Museum

青森県立郷土館

(Aomori Kenritsu Kyōdokan). A collection of archaeological and ethnographical material of Aomori; opened in 1973. Jōmon-period (ca 10,000 BC–ca 300 BC) implements and figurines are in the archaeological section; the ethnographical section includes a number of *oshirasama* (local gods represented by colorfully draped sticks of wood).

Aomori Prefecture   青森県

(Aomori Ken). Located at the northern tip of Honshū, and bounded on the north by Tsugaru Strait, on the east by the Pacific Ocean, on the south by Iwate and Akita

prefectures, and on the west by the Sea of Japan. The western and central portions are dominated by the Dewa and Ōu mountains, respectively, while the eastern area is relatively level, with some hills at the foot of the Ōu Mountains. The TSUGARU PENINSULA on the west and the SHIMOKITA PENINSULA on the east jut out from the northern coast, cradling Mutsu Bay. Major rivers include the IWAKIGAWA in the west and OIRASEGAWA in the east. The latter is fed by Lake Towada, located on the common border with Akita Prefecture. The climate is marked by short summers and long winters, with heavy snowfall in the western section. Like Hokkaidō, it is largely free from the rainy season common to the rest of Japan.

Inhabited at an early date, the western part of this region formed the Tsugaru district and the eastern region the Nambu district. These were combined in 1871 into the prefecture of Hirosaki; later the name was changed to Aomori.

The economy has traditionally been dominated by agriculture, forestry, and fishing. The entire prefecture is famous as a leading producer of rice, grains, and apples. Horses were formerly bred in great numbers, but since the end of World War II have gradually been replaced by dairy cattle and other livestock. Aomori's fisheries produce large amounts of mackerel, pollack, and squid. Industry has developed slowly because of the prefecture's remote location and has traditionally been connected with agricultural products and lumber, but in recent years there has been a growth of modern industries centered on the city of HACHINOHE. Lacquer ware continues as a traditional industry in the cities of AOMORI and HIROSAKI. Aomori was important as the transportation gateway to Hokkaidō, but an undersea railway tunnel (see SEIKAN TUNNEL), which was opened in 1988, now connects Mimmaya on the Tsugaru Peninsula with the southern tip of Hokkaidō.

Traditional festivals, such as the NEBUTA FESTIVAL of the cities of Aomori and Hirosaki, attract visitors from throughout the country. OSOREZAN, a volcano on the Shimokita Peninsula, is famous as a center of traditional Japanese shamanism. Major tourist areas include Towada-Hachimantai National Park and numerous hot-spring resorts. Area: 9,619 sq km (3,714 sq mi); pop: 1,482,935; capital: Aomori. Other major cities include HACHINOHE, Hirosaki, MISAWA, and TOWADA.

Aonodōmon   青ノ洞門

Tunnel dug into the rock beside the Yamakunigawa, a river in northern Ōita Prefecture, northeastern Kyūshū. It reputedly was dug single-handedly through an almost impassable area in the gorge known as YABA-KEI by the priest Zenkai over a 30-year period in the mid-Edo period (1600–1868). Kyō-shūhō, a famous scenic area and Yabakei's most noted sight-seeing spot, is in this area. Length: 337 m (1,106 ft); width: approximately 3 m (9.8 ft).

Aono Sō   青野聰

(1943–). Novelist. Born in Tōkyō; son of literary critic AONO SUEKICHI. Attended Waseda University. Aono Sō won the Akutagawa Prize in 1979 with *Gusha no yoru* (A Fool's Night). Having traveled extensively abroad, Aono pursues through his writing the implications of nationality, identity, and rootlessness. He won the Noma Prize for New Talent with *Onna kara no koe* (Voice from a Woman) in 1984.

Aono Suekichi   青野季吉

(1890–1961). Critic. Born in Niigata Prefecture; graduate of Waseda University. In 1923 he joined Japan's first so-called proletarian literary magazine, *Tane maku hito*, contributing essays on social and political issues. Active as a Communist Party member, he became the central figure of *Bungei sensen*, the successor to *Tane maku hito*. His *Shizen seichō to mokuteki ishiki* (1926), in which he elaborated on the ideas of Lenin's essay *What Is to Be Done?*, exerted considerable influence on Japanese socialist writing of the late 1920s. After the POPULAR FRONT INCIDENT of 1938, his activities were restricted. Following World War II, he became president of the Japan Writers' Association (Nihon Bungeika Kyōkai) and was active in the postwar rebirth of the JAPAN P.E.N. CLUB. His principal works include *Shirabeta geijutsu* (1925) and *Tenkanki no bungaku* (1927), both collections of critical essays, and his memoirs, *Bungaku gojūnen* (1957).

Aoshima   青島

Island approximately 1.7 km (1.0 mi) south of the city of Miyazaki, Miyazaki Prefecture, southeastern Kyūshū; part of the city of Miyazaki. It is connected with the mainland at low tide. The erosive action of waves on the island's rocky shore has given it the name Ogre's Washboard. The island supports 230 species of subtropical plants. It is part of the Nichinan Coast Quasi-National Park. Area: 0.04 sq km (0.02 sq mi).

Aoto Fujitsuna   青砥藤綱

(fl mid-13th century). A legendary warrior and wise man of the Kamakura period (1185–1333). According to the 14th-century military chronicle TAIHEIKI, he was a retainer of the shogunal regent (SHIKKEN) HŌJŌ TOKIYORI and served as a judge of the Council of State (HYŌJŌSHŪ), becoming famous for his sound decisions.

Aoto-zōshi hana no nishiki-e

青砥稿花紅彩画

(Benten the Thief). KABUKI play; popular title *Benten Kozō*. A *sewa-mono* (domestic play) written by Kawatake MOKUAMI (1816–93); first performed in 1862. The play recounts the exploits of Benten Kozō Kikunosuke, a handsome young rogue skilled at disguises, and the rest of his gang, the Five Thieves (Shiranami Gonin Otoko, an alternative title of the play). The high point of the play is the Hamamatsuya Scene of Act III, one of kabuki's most famous "extortion scenes" (*yusuriba*). Other famous scenes are the Inasegawa Riverbank Scene of Act IV, with its lineup of the Five Thieves declaiming their identities, and the Gokurakuji Scene of Act V, a spectacular acrobatic fight (*tachi-mawari*) of one against many that takes place on the rooftop of a temple and ends with Benten's suicide.

Aoyama   青山

District in the northwestern part of Minato Ward, Tōkyō. During the Edo period (1600–1868) it was the site of *samurai* residences, temples, and shrines. Today, much of Aoyama is devoted to high-income housing and commercial use, and the area has become a fashion center, where major designers such as MORI HANAE and MIYAKE ISSEI have their headquarters. A principal landmark is the Aoyama Cemetery, dating from 1872, where many famous personages are interred.

Aomori Prefecture Location and Prefectural Crest

Aoyama Gakuin University
青山学院大学

(Aoyama Gakuin Daigaku). Private, coeducational university; main campus located in Shibuya Ward, Tōkyō. Founded as a school for girls in 1874 by a group of young Japanese Christians and Robert S. Maclay, an American Methodist missionary. In 1883 the school was renamed Tōkyō Eiwa Gakkō (Tōkyo Anglo-Japanese School) and expanded. In 1894 the school adopted its present name and in 1904 it became a college. University status was granted in 1948. In keeping with its original spirit, the school strives to instill in the students a strong Christian character. The university has affiliated schools from kindergarten through senior high school and a two-year junior college for women. It maintains faculties of letters, economics, business administration, law, and science and engineering, as well as international politics, economics, and business. Enrollment was 18,973 in 1989.

Aoyama Tanemichi
青山胤通

(1859–1917). Internist. Born in Edo (now Tōkyō). A graduate of Tōkyō University, Aoyama studied at the University of Berlin and was named professor at Tōkyō University in 1887. He studied the bubonic plague in Hong Kong and worked on beriberi and other diseases. Aoyama was head of the clinic attached to Tōkyō University and of its medical faculty. He was also director of the Institute for Infectious Diseases after it was placed under the jurisdiction of the Ministry of Education. He greatly influenced internal medicine and medical education in Japan.

apples
林檎

(ringo). *Malus pumila.* The cultivation of apples in Japan began early in the Meiji period (1868–1912), when 75 American varieties and 106 French varieties were introduced. At the outset lack of knowledge of the plant's optimum growing conditions caused repeated failures, but it was later found that places with a cool climate and little rainfall in summer were most suitable for apple cultivation, and the prefectures of Aomori, Nagano, Hokkaidō, Iwate, Yamagata, Akita, and Fukushima became the main centers of production. In addition to the Iwai (American Summer Pearmain), Asahi (McIntosh Red), Kōgyoku (Jonathan), Kokkō (Rall's Janet), Golden Delicious, and Delicious strains introduced from abroad, the Mutsu, Fuji, and Tsugaru, which were developed in Japan after World War II, are now widely grown. Although a wide range of early- to late-ripening varieties are cultivated, the great majority of Japan's production consists of late-ripening varieties. Only about 10 percent of the total crop is processed.

apprentice system
徒弟制度

(totei seido). The traditional Japanese apprentice system, which evolved among handicraft artisans, became socially and economically significant during the Edo period (1600–1868). Such a master-apprentice relation had already existed in medieval guilds (ZA), but the apprentice (totei) was often a bondman rather than hired help. With the formation of merchant guilds (KABUNAKAMA) in the Edo period, the arrangement became formalized, resulting in a contractual relationship that mutually bound the individual master (oyakata) and the hired apprentice. Regulations governing

this relationship were observed by all *kabunakama.*

The apprentice was usually 10 to 12 years old, and his term of indenture lasted about 10 years, although this was later shortened. Upon completion of his apprenticeship, the new artisan could apply for membership in the artisans' guild and, if accepted, become an *oyakata* himself. But as the number of artisans increased, the guilds limited membership, causing much hardship. With the dissolution of the *kabunakama* in the Meiji period (1868–1912), the apprentice system declined.

April 16th Incident
四・一六事件

(Yon'ichiroku Jiken). Nationwide arrest of 600 to 700 suspected communists in 1929. Most of those arrested were party members who had escaped apprehension in the MARCH 15TH INCIDENT a year earlier. Approximately half of the arrested suspects were tried and found guilty, including such important party leaders as ICHIKAWA SHŌICHI, Nabeyama Sadachika (1901–79), and Mitamura Shirō (1906–64). See also COMMUNISTS, PUBLIC TRIAL OF (1931–1932).

aquariums
水族館

(suizokukan). Most of the approximately 100 aquariums in Japan are located near the seacoast. Geographically they range from subtropical Okinawa in the south to Hokkaidō in the north, and their range of marine specimens is correspondingly broad.

Japan's first aquarium was built in 1882 on the grounds of the Ueno Zoological Gardens in Tōkyō. By the end of the 19th century, a total of seven public aquariums had been built, all located at the seashore and equipped with tanks of the so-called open system, in which seawater was pumped through the aquarium once and then discarded. At the time only the municipal aquarium in the city of Sakai in Ōsaka Prefecture used a closed system, in which water is continuously recirculated. In recent years aquariums have been designed in a variety of distinctive new styles. One such innovation is an endless waterway, in which schools of fish swim in a circulating current within a doughnut-shaped tank.

Arabian Oil Co, Ltd
アラビア石油[株]

(Arabia Sekiyu). Japan's largest crude oil producer. Incorporated in 1958 by YAMASHITA TARŌ with the support of the Japanese government and business leaders. Granted offshore oil concessions by Saudi Arabia and Kuwait, the company discovered the Khafji Oil Field in 1960 and the Hout Oil Field in 1963. Since then, the crude oil produced from these fields has been sold mainly to the Japanese market, but some has been exported to other countries. The company's refining plant at Ras al-Khafji (capacity: 30,000 barrels per day) produces naphtha, diesel oil, and fuel oil. In the fiscal year ending Decem-

ber 1990 annual sales totaled ¥249.0 billion (US \$1.9 billion). Capitalization as of December 1990 was ¥30.0 billion (US \$218.7 million), 10 percent of which was held by the government of Saudi Arabia and 10 percent by Kuwait. Headquarters are in Tōkyō.

Aragaki Hideo
荒垣秀雄

(1903–89). Journalist and social critic. Born in Gifu Prefecture, Aragaki graduated from Waseda University. In 1926 he went to work at the newspaper *Tōkyō asahi shimbun* (now ASAHI SHIMBUN), where he held such positions as editorial writer. From 1946 to 1963 he was the writer of the *Asahi*'s front-page column "Tensei Jingo" ("Vox Populi, Vox Dei"). An active member of Japan's conservation movement, Aragaki was president of the Nature Conservation Society of Japan from 1981 to 1989. His books include a four-volume compilation of his "Tensei Jingo" columns that was published in 1981.

Arahata Kanson
荒畑寒村

(1887–1981). Journalist; socialist and labor activist. Born Arahata Katsuzō in Yokohama, Kanagawa Prefecture. In 1903 he began an apprenticeship in the Yokosuka Naval Arsenal. His experiences as a worker there and antiwar pamphlets by KŌTOKU SHŪSUI, SAKAI TOSHIHIKO, and others converted him to socialism. He established a branch of the socialist association HEIMINSHA in Yokohama and wrote for socialist publications. His account of the ASHIO COPPER MINE INCIDENT is considered a journalistic classic. He was arrested in the RED FLAG INCIDENT OF 1908.

In 1918 he formed the Labor Unions Research Group. In 1922 he joined YAMAKAWA HITOSHI in publishing the left-wing magazine *Zen'ei* (Vanguard) and helped found the JAPAN COMMUNIST PARTY. He left the party in 1927 to join the RŌNŌHA (Labor-Farmer faction) and help publish its magazine *Rōnō.* Jailed in the government crackdown on its critics (see POPULAR FRONT INCIDENT) in 1937, he was released in 1939. After World War II, Arahata became the first chairman of the National Trade Union of Metal and Engineering Workers. He also helped found the JAPAN SOCIALIST PARTY, winning election to the Diet on its slate in 1946 and 1947. Ideological differences led him to leave the party in 1948; by 1951 he withdrew from active political involvement. The most famous of his literary achievements—which included essays, novels, translations, and historical studies—is his autobiography, *Kanson jiden* (1948; revised 1965).

Arai
新井[市]

City in central Niigata Prefecture, central Honshū. Arai developed as a post-station and market town. In 1935 a chemical plant was set up, and since then the city has

apples

1 The Iwai variety is often harvested and sold while still green.
2 Apples of the Kōgyoku (Jonathan) variety are a deep red with a tart taste and can be stored from harvest in mid-October until the following June.
3 The Tsugaru apple is a cross between Golden Delicious and Kōgyoku and was developed in Japan in 1973.
4 The Fuji apple is a cross between two American varieties, Rall's Janet and Delicious.
5 An orchard of Mutsu apples in Aomori Prefecture, with the mountain Iwakisan in the background. A cross between Golden Delicious and another strain, the Mutsu was developed in Japan in 1949.

Arahata Kanson This pillar of Japanese left-wing politics is also remembered as an accomplished writer.

become the center of an electrical-appliance and precision-instrument industry. Pop: 28,325.

Arai 新居[町]

Town located at the mouth of the channel that connects Lake HAMANA to the Pacific Ocean, in western Shizuoka Prefecture, central Honshū. During the Edo period (1600–1868) there was a *sekisho* (barrier station) here, and Arai was an important post-station town. Today there is commercial fishing on Lake Hamana and neighboring seas, and *unagi* (Japanese eels) are raised. Pop: 16,871.

Arai Hakuseki 新井白石

(1657–1725). Confucian scholar, historian, poet, geographer, and statesman. Influential adviser to the Tokugawa shōguns during the second decade of the 18th century. Born to a *samurai* family in a small domain in Kazusa Province (now part of Chiba Prefecture). He entered samurai service as a Confucian tutor, serving the family of HOTTA MASATOSHI from 1682 to 1691 and in 1694 becoming personal tutor to Tokugawa Tsunatoyo, who later ruled as TOKUGAWA IENOBU, the sixth Tokugawa shōgun. During Ienobu's rule from 1709 to 1712 and that of his young son Tokugawa Ietsugu (1709–16) from 1713 to 1716, Hakuseki served as a key adviser to the shōguns and their chamberlain MANABE AKIFUSA.

Hakuseki wanted to transform the shogunate from a military government into a Confucian kingship guided by an upright adviser. On the occasion of the Korean embassy of 1711 Hakuseki did succeed in changing the shōgun's title in the diplomatic correspondence from "great ruler" (*taikun*) to "king" (*kokuō*), but it was never used officially within Japan (see SHUGŌ INCIDENT). Hakuseki also urged reform of the currency, reorganization and limitation of Nagasaki's foreign trade (see SHŌTOKU NAGASAKI SHINREI), and improvement of the judicial system.

Hakuseki's works include HANKANPU (1702), a history of the *daimyō* houses; *Koshitsū* (1716), a study of the myths and early history of Japan; and *Tokushi yoron* (1712–24), a history of Japan. *Seiyō kibun* (1715) is a geographical account of the West based on his interrogations of the Italian Jesuit Giovanni Battista SIDOTTI. Hakuseki also wrote an autobiography, *Oritaku shiba no ki* (ca 1716; tr *Told Round a Brushwood Fire*, 1980).

Arai Ōsui 新井奥邃

(1846–1922). Christian community leader. Born to a *samurai* family of the Sendai domain (now Miyagi Prefecture), Arai studied at the domainal school and in Edo (now Tōkyō). Learning of the shogunal army's defeat in the Battle of TOBA-FUSHIMI (1868), Arai returned to Sendai and helped form a coalition of northeastern domains (ŌUETSU REPPAN DŌMEI) loyal to the shogunate.

In 1871 Arai went to the United States with MORI ARINORI, the new minister to that country. Mori entrusted Arai to Thomas Lake HARRIS, an unorthodox Christian utopian. Arai stayed for 30 years in Harris's community, the Brotherhood of the New Life, and became the brotherhood's spiritual mainstay after Harris's retirement in 1892. He returned to Japan in 1899 to propagate Harris's teachings. By 1903 Arai's teachings had attracted a number of university students and intellectuals. One of his followers,

the reformer TANAKA SHŌZŌ, championed the beleaguered villagers of Yanaka in the ASHIO COPPER MINE INCIDENT. After Arai's death his collected writings were published as *Ōsui kōroku* (5 vols, 1930–31) by one of his disciples.

Arakawa 荒川

River in Saitama and Tōkyō prefectures, central Honshū, originating in the Kantō Mountains and flowing through the Kantō Plain into Tōkyō Bay. A multipurpose dam was constructed on the upper reaches, creating Lake Chichibu. The lower reaches are known as the SUMIDAGAWA. The Arakawa Canal, constructed in 1930 on the lower reaches to prevent floods, split the river's course in two. Length: 169 km (105 mi); area of drainage basin: 2,940 sq km (1,135 sq mi).

Arakawa Shūsaku 荒川修作

(1936–). Western-style painter and a pioneer of conceptual art. Born in Aichi Prefecture. Arakawa attended Musashino Art School (now Musashino Art University). He exhibited works at the Yomiuri Salon des Artistes Indépendants between 1958 and 1961. Around 1960 he became active in the antiart movement, producing works consisting of masses of cement and fabric and establishing a group called the "Neo-DADA Organizers." In 1961 he moved to New York City, where he began producing paintings in which diagrammatic lines and symbols and English words appear in precise detail on a milk-white background. In 1979 Arakawa coauthored a book entitled *The Mechanism of Meaning*, with his wife, the poet Madeline H. Gins.

Arakawa Toyozō 荒川豊蔵

(1894–1985). Potter in the Shino-Oribe (see MINO WARE) tradition. Born in Tajimi, Gifu Prefecture. He studied painting in Kyōto but in 1922 decided to study ceramics under Miyanaga Tōzan (1868–1941). In 1930 Arakawa began working as an assistant to KITAŌJI ROSANJIN. That same year Arakawa found the ruins of the Mutabora kiln, the greatest of the Shino-ware kilns, near Ōkaya in Gifu Prefecture (formerly Mino Province). Other Shino, Seto, and Oribe kiln sites were subsequently discovered, inspiring Arakawa to undertake the arduous task of reinventing the original Shino, Seto, and Oribe techniques. Arakawa built a Shino-type kiln directly on the remains of the old Mutabora kiln and began producing tea-ceremony freshwater jars, teabowls, and other Shino-ware pieces with the characteristic thick, rich, translucent white glaze and lively underglaze iron-oxide painted designs. His efforts were so successful that the Japanese government designated him one of the LIVING NATIONAL TREASURES in 1955. He was awarded the Order of Culture in 1971.

Arakawa Ward 荒川区

(Arakawa Ku). One of the 23 wards of Tōkyō. Many retail shops and metal, furniture, leather, and confectionery industries are located here. Pop: 184,809.

Arakawa Yōji 荒川洋治

(1949–). Poet and essayist. Born in Fukui Prefecture. Arakawa studied creative writing at Waseda University, where he first attracted public notice with his graduation thesis, a collection of poems entitled *Shōfuron* (1971, On Prostitutes). He won the H-Shi Prize for his second collection, *Suieki* (1975, Water Station).

Arakida Moritake 荒木田守武

(1473–1549). RENGA and *haikai* (see HAIKU) poet of the late Muromachi period (1333–1568). With YAMAZAKI SŌKAN, he is considered to be the father of *haikai*. Members of his family had for many generations served as priests at the Ise Shrine, where Moritake himself became chief priest at age 69. He studied with the *renga* poets SŌGI, SŌCHŌ, and INAWASHIRO KENSAI. Moritake was known chiefly for his *haikai*, written before conventions of *haikai* composition became fixed. The radical DANRIN SCHOOL poets later hailed Moritake and Sōkan as their predecessors.

Arakida Reijo 荒木田麗女

(1732–1806). Also known as Arakida Rei. Writer known for her poetry and historical fiction. As a young woman she took up RENGA (linked verse) poetry, remaining active in *renga* circles to the end of her life. She achieved fame for her mastery of WAKA, HAIKU, and verse written in Chinese. She is chiefly remembered, however, for her historical novels. In 1768 she produced a collated text of the UTSUBO MONOGATARI, and in 1771 she wrote her two best-known historical novels, *Ike no mokuzu* and *Tsuki no yukue*. She also produced collections of short stories, travel diaries, and historical works of a scholarly nature.

Araki Sadao 荒木貞夫

(1877–1966). General and politician; a leader of the ultranationalist Imperial Way faction (KŌDŌHA). Native of Tōkyō; graduate of the Army Academy and the Army War College. He was a military attaché in Russia during World War I and took part in the SIBERIAN INTERVENTION of 1918. From 1928 to 1929 he served as principal of the Army War College. After Araki was appointed chief of the Army Educational Administration in August 1931, there was an attempted military coup d'état (see OCTOBER INCIDENT), intended in part to make Araki prime minister. To soothe the insurgent officers, Araki was named army minister in the INUKAI TSUYOSHI and SAITŌ MAKOTO cabinets; he was promoted to full general in 1933. In 1936 junior Kōdōha officers staged an armed rebellion in central Tōkyō (see FEBRUARY 26TH INCIDENT); because Araki had given them tacit support, he was forced to retire. In 1938, as minister of education in the first KONOE FUMIMARO cabinet, he promoted military instruction in the schools. Tried as a class-A war criminal after World War II, Araki was sentenced to life imprisonment, but was paroled in 1954 because of ill health and later pardoned.

Araki Sōtarō 荒木宗太郎

(?–1636). Merchant and trader. Born into a *samurai* family in Higo Province (now Kumamoto Prefecture), he moved to Nagasaki about 1588 and became a trader. Licensed to engage in the VERMILION SEAL SHIP TRADE, early in the 17th century Araki led several commercial expeditions to Southeast Asia, in particular to Annam (now central Vietnam) and Siam (now Thailand).

Ara Masahito 荒正人

(1913–79). Literary critic. Born in Fukushima Prefecture; graduate of Tōkyō University. Ara became an influential critic as a writer for *Kindai bungaku*, a progressive literary magazine he launched with HIRANO KEN, ODAGIRI HIDEO, and others in 1946. Influenced as a youth by the Marxist movement of the 1930s, he later, in his criticism of prewar and wartime literature, questioned the intellectual's role in society. The first Japanese critic to apply Freudian theory to literature, he was noted for ground-breaking studies of the novelist NATSUME SŌSEKI. His works include *Daini no seishun* (1946), an essay collection; and *Sōseki kenkyū nempyō* (1974), an annotated chronology of Sōseki's life.

Arao 荒尾[市]

City in northwestern Kumamoto Prefecture, Kyūshū, contiguous with the city of Ōmuta in Fukuoka Prefecture. In the Meiji period (1868–1912) Arao developed with the exploitation of the MIIKE COAL MINES, closed after World War II. Principal products are chemicals, pears, oranges, and *nori* (a type of seaweed). Pop: 59,507.

Araragi アララギ

Leading TANKA poetry magazine launched in 1908 by ITŌ SACHIO and followers of the poet MASAOKA SHIKI. It succeeded an earlier magazine, *Ashibi*, which ceased publication that same year, as the official organ of the Negishi Tanka Kai, a group of poets. Itō wanted the magazine to reflect his traditionalist view that the best source for poetic inspiration was the MAN'YŌSHŪ, the great 8th-century anthology of Japanese verse. Younger poets such as SHIMAKI AKAHIKO and SAITŌ MOKICHI soon pressed for changes as *tanka* poetry took new directions, and convinced Itō to include critical essays, pieces on Western art theories, translations, and works by opposing schools. Shimaki took over after Itō's death and went even further in shedding the magazine's conventional image. Saitō succeeded Shimaki as editor and was followed by TSUCHIYA BUMMEI. Still an influential poetry magazine, *Araragi* has continued to emphasize the Man'yō style and realistic description.

Arashi Kanjūrō 嵐寛寿郎

(1903–80). Actor. Born in Kyōto. Originally a KABUKI actor, Arashi began acting in silent films in 1927. Through his roles as swordsman and sleuth in two period-film movie series, respectively titled *Kurama Tengu* (1927–56) and *Umon torimonochō* (1929–55), Arashi became a box-office star. By the end of World War II, he had appeared in some 100 films. He played the leading role as the emperor Meiji in the film *Meiji tennō to nichiro daisensō* (1957, The Emperor Meiji and the Great Russo-Japanese War). In the early 1960s Arashi began acting in supporting roles.

Arashiyama 嵐山

Also known as Ranzan. Hill in the western section of the city of Kyōto beside the river Hozugawa. Favored early on as a recreational area by the Kyōto nobility, it is known for its cherry blossoms and autumn foliage. Togetsukyō (a bridge on the Hozugawa) and several temples in the area are important sightseeing attractions. Height: 382 m (1,253 ft).

arbitration 仲裁

(*chūsai*). Method of dispute resolution in which both parties agree to submit to a decision (arbitral award) made by an arbitrator of their own choice. The Code of Civil Procedure (Minji Soshō Hō) recognizes arbitration and gives the arbitral award the same *res judicata* effect as the judgment of a court. The arbitrator determines the procedure to be followed unless the parties agree otherwise. The arbitrator is not generally bound by substantive law in making an award but

must always hear both parties' sides, and the award must be reasonable and not contrary to public policy. If any of these requirements is violated, the award can be set aside by a court, but the court is not allowed to review the merits of the award.

Arbitration is used in maritime business matters, international trade, and labor disputes. See also DISPUTE RESOLUTION SYSTEMS OTHER THAN LITIGATION.

archaeology 考古学

(*kōkogaku*). Japan's archaeological record is one of the most intensely studied in the world. Excavations are required prior to any large public works or construction projects, and Japanese archaeologists investigate and report thousands of sites annually. In most Japanese universities archaeology is considered a highly specialized branch of Japanese history. Because of this, Japanese archaeologists have brought to their work a historical or particularistic approach, rather than the social scientific approach adopted in some other countries. Important archaeological sites are often preserved as public parks, and archaeological findings are frequently presented in the mass media, so that there is considerable popular awareness of and support for the discipline. Responsibility for the preservation of prehistoric sites and the supervision of archaeological research rests with the Agency for Cultural Affairs (Bunkachō), part of the Ministry of Education. See CULTURAL PROPERTIES LAW.

Archaeology became established as a scholarly discipline in Japan in the late 19th century, but its roots go back to the Edo period (1600–1868), when stone tools and prehistoric pottery attracted the attention of rock collectors, herbalists, and historians. Their interest did not result in archaeological research, however, because the concept of a "prehistoric" past had not developed in Japan. That concept, and the understanding of what the excavation of ancient sites could reveal about the time before written history, were introduced to Japan by the American zoologist Edward S. MORSE, who excavated the ŌMORI SHELL MOUNDS in 1877.

Throughout the Meiji (1868–1912) and Taishō (1912–26) periods, Japanese archaeologists worked to identify the major varieties of ancient materials present in their country. JŌMON PERIOD, YAYOI PERIOD, and protohistoric cultural complexes were all identified during this time. Archaeologists of the early Shōwa period (1926–89), led by YAMANOUCHI SUGAO, faced the challenge of typing and ordering the diverse archaeological complexes that had been revealed. The discovery of true paleolithic material in 1949 introduced a new set of chronological problems. Publication in 1965 of a six-volume series entitled *Nihon no kōkogaku* (The Archaeology of Japan) marked the culmination of this chronological research.

Although typology of prehistoric sites and cultural complexes remains a key concern of Japanese archaeologists, current research stresses analysis of ancient settlement and economic patterns. Japanese archaeologists are also becoming world leaders in the technical analysis and dating of ancient materials. Industrial expansion, urban sprawl, and a generally booming economy have kept Japanese archaeologists very busy since the 1960s with salvage excavations, but these efforts, along with the cultural preservation projects of recent years, have made it possible to gather valuable additional information from archaeological sites representing all

periods of Japan's past. See also PREHISTORY; JŌMON POTTERY; YAYOI POTTERY; KOFUN PERIOD.

archery → kyūdō

archery, mounted → yabusame

Architectural Standards Law 建築基準法

(Kenchiku Kijun Hō). Law enacted in 1950 to protect the lives, health, and property of citizens by establishing minimum standards for building sites, structures, facilities, and use. The law provides that a permit be obtained for new construction or large-scale repairs or alterations within city planning areas. The law also covers permitted uses in designated areas, the height and capacity of buildings, and other architectural standards. The law has been much criticized for its ineffective enforcement, and some favor a full-scale revision or updating to meet widespread building violations.

architecture, modern 近現代の建築

(*kingendai no kenchiku*). As Japan launched its modernization drive following the MEIJI RESTORATION of 1868 and began to import Western science and technology as part of its national policy, the government invited foreign engineers and experts to train Japanese and oversee initial construction projects. Official bodies responsible for the development of architecture were the Department of Civil Engineering of the Ministry of Finance, the Department of Architecture and the Department of Railroads of the Ministry of Industry, and the Industrial College (forerunner of the Department of Engineering at Tōkyō University). Thomas James WATERS of Britain and François VERNY of France were two of the central figures responsible for introducing modern architectural techniques.

At first, Western methods and designs were incorporated into traditional Japanese methods of wood construction. As exemplified by the Kaichi Elementary School (1876) in the city of Matsumoto, Nagano Prefecture, this approach was adopted for the schools built throughout the country after the establishment of a new educational system in 1872.

In 1877 Josiah CONDER of Britain arrived in Japan to teach at the Industrial College; he trained many architects, including TATSUNO KINGO and Katayama Tōkuma (1854–1917). The AKASAKA DETACHED PALACE (1909) by Katayama and the main office of the Bank of Japan (1896) and TŌKYŌ STATION (1914) by Tatsuno are typical of the kind of Western-style buildings designed by Japanese at this time.

In the 1880s there was a general reaction against excessive Westernization in many

Arashiyama Cherry blossoms along the Hozugawa, with the bridge Togetsukyō in the background—a view long considered one of the most picturesque in Kyōto.

Arashi Kanjūrō This actor is best known for his role as the *samurai* swordsman in the long-running *Kurama Tengu* movie series (1927–56).

modern architecture
The Kaichi Elementary School (1876) is typical of the early modern period of Japanese architecture, when Western styles were often combined with traditional Japanese building materials and techniques.

fields, including architecture. Architect and art historian ITŌ CHŪTA was among the first to advocate Asian models for Japanese architecture; he was later responsible for the design of the MEIJI SHRINE (1920). After World War I architects like Frank Lloyd WRIGHT and Antonin RAYMOND of the United States and Bruno TAUT of Germany came to Japan, contributing to the reevaluation of traditional Japanese architecture. Through their work, Japanese architecture influenced Western architecture, in much the same way that UKIYO-E had influenced Western painting. The renewed interest in tradition also led to the development by YOSHIDA ISOYA of a new style in residential architecture that assimilated traditional SUKIYA-ZUKURI techniques.

At the same time, during the 1920s and 1930s, the so-called international style and other European trends influenced Japanese architecture, as evidenced by the Wakasa House (1939) in Tōkyō by HORIGUCHI SUTEMI. The modern architectural movement clashed, however, with nationalistic tendencies in the 1930s, and as a result MAEKAWA KUNIO's design for the Imperial Household Museum was rejected in favor of a more traditionalist entry.

Since World War II the activities of Japanese architects have increasingly attracted attention overseas. The reconciliation of modern and traditional architectural forms was one of the major issues during the postwar years. TANIGUCHI YOSHIRŌ designed the Tōson Memorial Hall (1948) as a monument to the writer SHIMAZAKI TŌSON, making innovative use of traditional architectural forms, and became in 1949 the first recipient of the Architectural Institute of Japan Award, the most prestigious prize of its kind in Japan.

One of the best-known and most influential modern Japanese architects is TANGE KENZŌ. He developed a methodology linking Japanese traditional elements with the achievements of science and technology in architectural form and established his reputation with a number of dramatic buildings in the 1950s and 1960s such as the futuristic YOYOGI NATIONAL STADIUM (1963), built for the 1964 Tōkyō Olympics, and the Dentsū head office building (1967). These were built at a time when there was a rush, propelled by a new wave of technological innovation and the dynamism of rapid economic growth, to construct very large buildings. The 1960s were a period both of pioneering work by individual architects and of the industrialization and depersonalization of architecture, as fast-working design and construction companies specializing in building groups of standardized, characterless structures came to dominate the field. Cities in Japan as in many other countries were rapidly filled with boxlike buildings.

By the early 1970s, the heavy costs of

rapid industrialization had become apparent. Citizens' movements motivated by the determination to oppose industrial pollution and protect the quality of life became a major force in society, and mass-produced architecture came under severe attack as a force contributing to the barrenness and impersonality of urban life.

The reevaluation of architectural priorities was led by ISOZAKI ARATA, who worked under Tange early in his career. Rejecting the tendency toward the total commercialization of architecture and construction, Isozaki argued that architecture had to regain its independence from commercial and technological imperatives. Examples of his work such as the Museum of Modern Art in Gumma Prefecture (1975) and his many critical writings had an immense impact on the rising younger generation of architects in the 1970s. It was about this time that architects who regarded themselves primarily as artists (as opposed to technicians or builders) began to make their appearance, among the most distinguished being ANDŌ TADAO, Shinohara Kazuo (b 1925), and KUROKAWA KISHŌ. During this period Japanese architects were preoccupied with reassessing the functional and utilitarian aspects of postwar Japanese architecture and its relationship to Japanese traditions. These more introspective concerns paralleled the relative contraction in the growth and dynamism of the Japanese economy as a whole after the expansion of the 1960s.

In the 1980s, however, the economy once again began to boom, and this was reflected in architectural circles by a union between new commercial imperatives, prompted by government deregulation of the construction industry, and the emphasis on pure design that had resulted from the introspection of the 1970s. The demand of business for imposing buildings with the power to impress customers—which had, for example, led to the construction of the first skyscrapers in the Shinjuku area of downtown Tōkyō in the early 1970s—reasserted itself in the 1980s, but now architects responded with buildings that incorporated more artistic design features. Tange Kenzō's TŌKYŌ METROPOLITAN GOVERNMENT OFFICES (1991) are a good example of the monumental style that resulted.

While the construction boom of the 1980s provided more opportunities for younger Japanese architects, the strong yen also made it economically feasible to invite major architects from overseas to work in Japan. Among those who came to Japan during the 1980s and early 1990s were Renzo Piano of Italy (Kansai International Airport Passenger Terminal, mid-1990s), and Christopher Alexander (Eishin Higashino High School, 1985) and Peter Eisenmann (Koizumi Sangyō Building, 1991) of the United States.

The 1980s and early 1990s also saw a rapid increase in the number of works by Japanese architects being built in other countries. Works like Isozaki's Museum of Contemporary Art in Los Angeles (1986) and Tange Kenzō's OUB Center in Singapore (1986) marked the advent of active two-way international exchange in the field of architecture.

☎ 50–51

architecture, traditional domestic
伝統的日本建築

(*dentōteki* Nihon *kenchiku*). Traditional residential architecture in Japan is perhaps best viewed as a response to the natural environment. Traditional Japan was a primarily agricultural society, centering on activities as-

sociated with rice planting. A feeling of cooperation, rather than an antagonistic relationship, developed between the Japanese and their natural surroundings. Instead of resistance or defense, accommodation and adaptation became the basic stance. Traditional Japanese architecture is characterized by the same attitude toward the natural environment, responding in particular to climatic and geographical conditions.

Japan's climate is distinguished by long, hot, humid summers and relatively short, cold, dry winters, and the Japanese house has evolved accordingly to make the summers more bearable. Since in the past the only relief from the oppressive heat and humidity was found in the cooling movement of air, the choice was toward light and open structures much like those found in Malaysia and other tropical areas. The traditional Japanese house was raised slightly off the ground and the interior opened up to allow for unrestricted movement of air around and below the living spaces. Associated with the heat and humidity of summer were sun and frequent rain. This necessitated a substantial roof structure with long, low overhangs to protect the interior.

With its open structure, the traditional Japanese house is vulnerable to all kinds of intrusion, including dirt, dust, and insects. Noise and lack of privacy are also problems, though screens and SHŌJI (translucent paper-covered sliding panels) offer a measure of visual privacy to the inhabitants.

Materials and Construction—The choice of building materials has been determined by the climate, wood being preferred to stone. Stone is uncomfortable and unhealthy in hot, humid weather, restricting airflow and closing off the structure; it also requires a longer period of time in preparing materials and in building. In contrast, wood responds more sensitively to the climate, being much cooler and absorbing moisture in summer and not as cold to the touch in winter. Wood is also more suited to withstand earthquakes, almost daily occurrences in Japan.

The choice of wood and an open structure allows for flexibility in living arrangements according to seasonal changes and the needs of the family. Inner partitions such as *shōji* and *fusuma* (opaque paper-covered sliding panels) can be removed to open up the interior, and, except for the roof's supporting columns, a clear space can be exposed.

The actual building of a house was traditionally entrusted to a carpenter (*daiku*). With specialized skills, the *daiku* was more than a carpenter; he was actually an architect, capable of designing and building an entire structure according to the wishes of the family. The construction of houses by a special occupational group soon led to a standardization of materials and design. There were also social strictures against extravagance in both design and the use of materials. The *daiku* prepared all the supporting columns and beams in his shop area, and in one day erected columns and roof structure with the help of the family or laborers. The position of *daiku* was thus very important, and certain secrets of his craft, such as intricate joinery methods, were closely guarded and passed down through his family. This accounts for the regional variation in building techniques. *Daiku* practiced exclusively in one area and seldom moved about except by order of some authority. For this reason, it is not uncommon to find a very different style of traditional architecture after crossing a mountain pass or another natural barrier.

Apart from the use of wood, the apparently little consideration given to earthquake protection in the structure itself is striking. Diagonal bracing, for example, is hardly ever seen in walls or roof structure. Rigidity, however, is not the only way of protecting a structure against earthquakes. Wood is flexible and can take more shear and torque for its weight than most other materials. The joinery makes use of the strengths of wood. The walls, consisting essentially of bamboo lattices heavily plastered with clay, are not at all substantial by Western standards but are surprisingly resistant to earthquakes. One room of the traditional house is plastered heavily on four walls in this way, with only a minimal entrance in one. This is directly connected to some of the main supports and helps to strengthen the building. The diagonal was not unknown, for wood diagonal compression braces have been found beneath the plaster walls of a few very old structures, but for some reason it was not used generally. In older structures the joint between a foundation stone and the support post or column was not fixed, so that when the earth moved, the column sometimes simply slid off its foundation stone. After the earthquake, the house could be lifted up and the support placed on another stone with no real damage to the structure.

Spatial Concepts in Architecture—A basic spatial concept in Japan is *ma* (written with a Chinese character that is also pronounced *ken* or *aida*). It has no exact English equivalent, variously meaning space, relationship, interval, period, luck, or pause, depending on the context. In architecture the term is applicable to the distance between two posts or the space between two or more walls, rocks in a garden, buildings, people, or other things with a possible relationship.

In constructing a house, the first step is to raise posts and beams until a skeletal structure stable enough to support a roof is completed. The space is organized by the roof and by the modular placement of the posts and columns. From this point on, design concerns itself with filling in the spaces or intervals between the posts and columns. Two things happen as this filling-in process occurs. First, a relationship is developed between the filled-in wall planes, and subdivisions—rooms—are created. Second, the wall itself alters the relationship of the posts by the kinds of materials used in its construction and its value as a barrier. In both cases, one is adjusting *ma*, or relationships that already exist—a process that lies at the heart of traditional Japanese design. Once the structure is given, design is concerned with the realignment and alteration of already existing relationships. Consequently, in Japanese design the wall has a different conceptual basis than that of Western design. Japanese walls are not defensive. In the West, by contrast, the wall is conceived as defensive, acting as a barrier between two opposing environments, such as winter cold and house warmth.

An important aspect of traditional design is the relationship of the house to its specific environment, particularly the garden; the two are continuous. The Japanese do not see exterior and interior as two separate entities; in other words, there is no definite point at which exterior ends and interior begins. The lack of barriers in Japanese designs has already been discussed. The Japanese veranda (*engawa*) is a concrete expression of this con-

cept, serving as a transition space from inside to outside. Its function is further expressed by the materials used in its construction. Whereas the floors of the interior of the house are covered with TATAMI mats and the exterior is made of earth and rock, the *engawa* is made of unfinished wood planks, belonging neither to the soft and accommodating interior nor to the harsh and more primitive materials on the outside.

The development of the individual spaces within the house was a gradual process of breaking down the larger open space that was available into smaller, more human-scaled spaces. This has already been mentioned with regard to *ma* and the "choosing" of space for a particular function. In the past the Japanese house was even more open, with no interior screens and only a few fixed walls. The space was large, too large for the individual, and self-standing screens—very often no more than wooden racks draped with fabric—were introduced. Later, folding paper screens came to be used. These, and such furnishings as tables, arm rests, and lamps, were placed to designate a space for a specific function—sleeping, eating, or dressing. Individual rooms were later defined by *shōji* and *fusuma*, "sliding doors" that could still be removed to form a single large space.

It would be a misconception to describe the rooms as multipurpose; although they are not as specific as Western rooms, each usually has a special function. In a traditional Japanese house, certain rooms are set aside for members of the family to sleep in, eat in, and so forth.

Unit of Measure—The module, if it can be called one, since it varied depending on time and place, was the *ken* (written with the same Chinese character as *ma*), or interpost distance. The interpost distance varied from district to district but was generally between 6 and 6.5 feet (1.8 and 2 m). The interpost distance was eventually standardized at 1.8 meters, however, if only because of the advantage of having a standard *tatami* size (generally 3 by 6 ft; 0.9 ft by 1.8 m) based on interpost measurement. The important aspect of *ken* is not that it was standardized in all buildings—it was not—but that it became the standard for all other measurements in the building (columns, beams, ceiling, *shōji*, etc), resulting in a harmonious balance of proportion.

The standardization of *ken* also led to the standardization of such construction materials as lumber. Carpenters could focus on the creation of space itself without concern for structure or detailing. The *ken* itself was subordinate to the average human height. The traditional house was designed for a Japanese height of 5.5 feet (1.7 m), although in aesthetic terms it was designed not for a standing person but for one sitting (seated height is a little more than 36 in or about 1 m for a tall Japanese). The garden and the artwork on display are meant to be viewed from a sitting or kneeling position, and the placement of doors, windows, and alcoves is adjusted accordingly.

Archives and Mausolea Department, Imperial Household Agency 宮内庁書陵部

(Kunaichō Shoryōbu). Established in 1884 as the Kunaichō Zushoryō, the department was merged with the Shoryōryō (Bureau of Imperial Mausolea) in 1949 and is located within the palace grounds in Tōkyō. Besides

traditional domestic architecture The veranda of a 250-year-old farmhouse that once served as a village headman's residence.

compiling imperial family records and maintaining the imperial tombs, the department administers the collections of the SHŌSŌIN in Nara.

Arechi 荒地

(Waste Land). Influential poetry magazine. Founded before World War II by a small group of Waseda University students led by AYUKAWA NOBUO and Morikawa Yoshinobu (1918–42), the first series of *Arechi*, which took its name from T. S. Eliot's poem "The Waste Land," appeared briefly between 1939 and 1940. Revived after the war, the second series (1947–48) was published by a group of young poets who best represent the development of modern poetry in the first postwar decade. Collectively known as the *Arechi* poets (although not a coterie per se), the group's central figures were Ayukawa Nobuo and TAMURA RYŪICHI. Contributors included Kitamura Tarō (b 1922), Kuroda Saburō (1919–80), Miyoshi Toyoichirō (b 1920), Nakagiri Masao (1919–83), and, later, YOSHIMOTO TAKAAKI. The third series of *Arechi* took the form of an annual anthology of poetry and criticism, the *Arechi shishū* (1951–58).

Argentina and Japan アルゼンチンと日本

(Aruzenchin to Nihon). Japan and Argentina established diplomatic relations in 1898. Before World War II, Japanese emigration was an important aspect of contact. By 1941 approximately 5,400 Japanese had emigrated to Argentina, mostly as agricultural laborers. Diplomatic relations were severed as a result of the war but restored by the San Francisco Peace Treaty in 1952. Due to the relaxation of immigration conditions by an accord signed in 1961 during President Arturo Frondizi's visit to Japan, emigration to Argentina became easier. Currently there are more than 30,000 Japanese immigrants and their descendants in Argentina.

In addition to emigration, trade and investment have increased in importance over the last decades. In 1966 a joint economic council was set up to expand economic ties. Argentina's recent debt problems have had an adverse effect on the growth of economic relations. Trade volume, particularly Argentina's imports, and Japanese direct investment tended to decrease in the late 1980s. In 1990 Japan's imports from Argentina were valued at US $539 million, and exports from Japan totaled US $196 million. Japan's major imports were foodstuffs and raw materials while exports were mostly machinery and tools. The fishing industry is currently the most active area of Japanese direct investment.

Contemporary Japanese Architecture

Before Japan's business "bubble" burst at the start of the 1990s, the powerful economy of the previous decade had led Japanese consumers to demand more goods than ever before. Capital investment skyrocketed in the latter half of the 1980s as the industrial sector went into high gear to satisfy these desires. Much of the money was earmarked for factories, business offices, and new corporate headquarters, particularly in larger metropolitan areas such as Tōkyō and Ōsaka. At the same time, the leisure industry was investing in tourist facilities and hotels throughout Japan, and regional governments were moving to realize their own plans for infrastructure development. All this activity created an epic building boom.

With so many opportunities at hand, the country's architects were quick to assimilate technological innovations into their already formidable architectural arsenal. Major architectural firms and construction conglomerates took on assignments ranging from huge urban projects to buildings that incorporated some radical technologies, raising expectations that the future would be marked by a completely new approach to design. During this period, Japanese architects were accumulating the wealth of experience needed to confront the challenges of postmodernism and the 21st century.

Miyawaki Mayumi

Centennial Hall, Tōkyō Institute of Technology, 1987

In this building, erected to commemorate the Tōkyō Institute of Technology's 100th anniversary, architect Shinohara Kazuo has used large, simple shapes to embody the monumental nature of the occasion. The massive semicircular tube at the top of the building, which houses a lounge and restaurant, refracts slightly in the middle; twin blocklike portions of the main structure support it from below. As the architect intended, the hall stands out from the cramped confusion of Tōkyō and the surrounding environment. Its singularity is enhanced by highly reflective aluminum and stainless steel surfaces.

Tōkyō Metropolitan Government Offices, 1991

Though nearly 80 years old, Tange Kenzō, one of Japan's leading postwar architects, remains as influential as ever. His plan for Tōkyō's metropolitan government offices was chosen unanimously over entries from some of Japan's best-known architects. The huge, twin-towered building, reminiscent of Notre Dame, is neither in the functionalist style formerly championed by Tange nor postmodern. The silhouette and grandeur of its marble classical facade sparked a clamorous debate about the skyscraper that went beyond the confines of the architectural world and into the public arena, with the controversy centering on whether the metropolitan government needed such a domineering structure.

Yamato International, Inc, Tōkyō Head Office, 1987

The renowned avant-garde architect and architectural theorist Hara Hiroshi rejected the standard four-corner design for the headquarters-cum-warehouse of Yamato, an apparel firm. Entrusted with both its construction and design, Hara used several design elements and building techniques in his

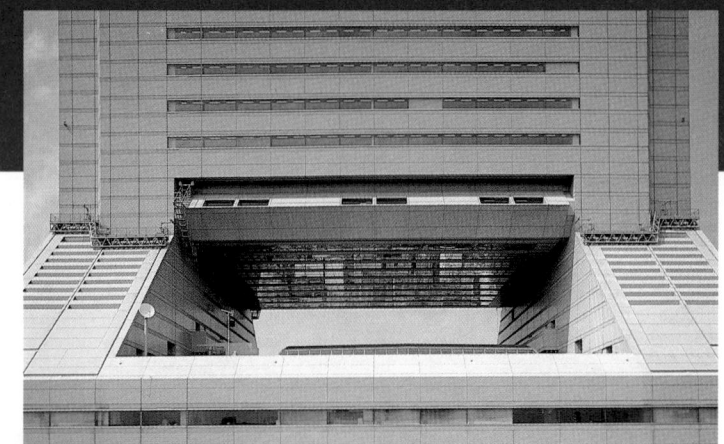

NEC Corporation Headquarters, Tōkyō, 1990

One of the world's largest architectural firms, Nikken Sekkei, Ltd, matured during Japan's postwar technological revolution. The company's design for this skyscraper (left), headquarters for electronics giant NEC, marks a great advance over previous high-rise buildings. The open space in the structure's center (above) dampens the bothersome wind currents characteristically generated in the vicinity of tall buildings, and it also provides natural ventilation and lighting.

Ōsaka Tokio Kaijō Building, 1990

Separate companies usually handle the planning and execution of architectural projects in the West. In Japan, however, large construction companies have the architectural staffs and design, capital, and technological resources to do it all. Here, a Kajima Construction architect uses a mundane office building as a foil for sophisticated building technology, creating a groundbreaking office design and a new Ōsaka landmark. Its pillars and crossbeams (right) bring to mind traditional Japanese construction, while the lobby's sashless glass windows (below) create a sense of continuity with its surroundings.

plan, which incorporates both etched window glass and an aluminum-covered exterior in an attempt to integrate the surroundings into the Yamato building's motifs. A multidimensional form adds to its allure. Amid the stark landscape of a Tōkyō Bay landfill, this structure stands out prominently.

Shōnandai Culture Center, Fujisawa, 1989

The young postmodernist architect Hasegawa Itsuko won the design competition for this facility in Kanagawa Prefecture. Her plan is notable both for its use of aluminum and because it puts the main facilities underground. The upper level is a virtual forest of futuristic forms—such as a "tree" of clocks—that seem to come from another universe, creating what Hasegawa calls a "second nature" of architectural origin. The resulting environment, despite its artificial elements, does not feel alien.

Ariake Sea Sunset over the tidal flats at the edge of the Ariake Sea.

Arishima Takeo Years of study in the United States exposed this Taishō-period (1912–26) writer to Western humanist and socialist thought and left a permanent imprint on his style.

Ariake Sea 有明海

(Ariake Kai). Inlet of Shimabara Bay, off Nagasaki, Saga, Fukuoka, and Kumamoto prefectures, in central-western Kyūshū. Known for its large difference in tide levels, this is a shallow sea; mud flats extend 4–6 km (2–4 mi) offshore at low tide. Seaweed (nori) and shellfish are produced here, and the shoal areas are being reclaimed. Two major rivers, the Chikugogawa and Yabegawa, empty into the Ariake Sea. Area: approximately 1,600 sq km (620 sq mi).

Arida 有田[市]

City in northwestern Wakayama Prefecture, central Honshū, located at the mouth of the river Aridagawa. Arida is known for its mandarin oranges and mosquito-repellent incense and herbicides. There is an oil-refining industry in the Hatsushima district. The coastal region to the southwest of the city is noted for its beauty. Pop: 34,810.

Aridagawa 有田川

River in north-central Wakayama Prefecture, central Honshū, flowing west from the Jingamine area of the Kii Mountains to the Kii Channel in the city of Arida. The Futagawa Dam provides flood control and hydroelectric power. Length: 67 km (42 mi).

Arima Harunobu 有馬晴信

(1567–1612). Prominent CHRISTIAN DAIMYŌ of the Azuchi-Momoyama (1568–1600) and early Edo (1600–1868) periods. Lord of the Takaku region of Hizen Province (now part of Nagasaki Prefecture) that became solidly Christian. In 1580 Harunobu became a Christian, taking the name Protasio. He was one of the sponsors of the "Tenshō Embassy" (see MISSION TO EUROPE OF 1582) of Japanese youths to Catholic Europe.

Harunobu served TOYOTOMI HIDEYOSHI in his INVASIONS OF KOREA in 1592 and 1597, and later supported TOKUGAWA IEYASU. He was active in the VERMILION SEAL SHIP TRADE in the South China Sea. He destroyed a Portuguese trading ship in the MADRE DE DEUS INCIDENT. He later became involved in a bribery scandal and was forced to commit suicide. In the wake of this affair the Tokugawa shogunate (1603–1867) issued the first of its ANTI-CHRISTIAN EDICTS.

Arima Hot Spring 有馬温泉

(Arima Onsen). Located on the northern slope of the mountain ROKKŌSAN, in the city of Kōbe, Hyōgo Prefecture, western Honshū. A common salt spring; maximum water temperature reaches 95°C (203°F). One of the few spas in the Kansai region, it has historically been favored by emperors and Buddhist clergy. It is popular with residents of the Kyōto-Ōsaka-Kōbe metropolitan area.

Arima Ineko 有馬稲子

(1932–). Film star popular from the late 1950s through the early 1960s for performances as a glamorous leading lady. Real name Nakanishi Mitsuko. Born in Ōsaka, she joined the Takarazuka Girls' Operetta Company (TAKARAZUKA KAGEKIDAN) after graduation from high school. She began making films in 1951. Her important films include ICHIKAWA KON's *Aijin* (1953, Lovers), OZU YASUJIRŌ's *Tōkyō boshoku* (1957, Tōkyō Twilight) and *Higambana* (1958, Equinox Flower), and HANI SUSUMU's *Mitasareta seikatsu* (1962, Full Life). Since the mid-1960s she has mostly acted on stage and television.

Arima, Prince 有間皇子

(640–658; Arima no Miko). Imperial prince of the late Kofun period (ca 300–710); son of Emperor KŌTOKU. After his father's death, he was critical of his aunt Empress SAIMEI for delegating all authority to her son Prince Naka no Ōe (later Emperor TENJI), and he feigned madness to escape the political intrigues of the late 650s. However, Soga no Akae (623?–672?), a confidant of Naka no Ōe, duped him into joining an ostensible plot against the government. Arima was charged with treason and put to death. Two valedictory poems composed by the young prince shortly before his execution are included in the 8th-century anthology MAN'YŌSHŪ.

Arima Shinshichi 有馬新七

(1825–62). *Samurai* of Satsuma domain (now Kagoshima Prefecture) active in the movement to overthrow the Tokugawa shogunate (1603–1867). In 1860 he helped to plot the assassination of the great elder (tairō) II NAOSUKE but was in Satsuma when it took place (see SAKURADAMONGAI INCIDENT). When SHIMAZU HISAMITSU, father of the *daimyō* of Satsuma, was visiting Kyōto in 1862, Arima made plans to organize an antishogunate army there and assassinate high Tokugawa officials. Hisamitsu sent men to persuade Arima and his cohorts to abandon their plans, but they resisted, and Arima and six others were killed in the ensuing fight (see TERADAYA INCIDENT).

Arima Yoriyasu 有馬頼寧

(1884–1957). Politician. Born in Tōkyō; scion of the Arima family, formerly the *daimyō* family of the Kurume domain (now part of Fukuoka Prefecture). He studied agricultural science at Tōkyō University and taught there. He formed the Nihon Nōmin Kumiai (Japan Farmers' Union) together with KAGAWA TOYOHIKO and others. He was elected to the House of Representatives in 1924 as a member of the RIKKEN SEIYŪKAI, and in 1929, after succeeding to the family title of count, he was named to the House of Peers. A confidant of KONOE FUMIMARO, he served as minister of agriculture and forestry in the first Konoe cabinet (1937) and assumed the directorship of the IMPERIAL RULE ASSISTANCE ASSOCIATION in 1940, but resigned after five

months in the face of opposition from rightists. He was detained as a war criminal after World War II but was not prosecuted.

Arisaka Hideyo 有坂秀世

(1908–52). Linguist and historical phonologist of Japanese. Born in the city of Kure, Hiroshima Prefecture; raised in Tōkyō. The son of an engineering professor, he graduated from Tōkyō University in 1931, majoring in linguistics. Arisaka's most noted contribution to Japanese-language studies was his observation of restrictions on the distribution of the Old Japanese vowels reconstructed by HASHIMOTO SHINKICHI. He suggested that these restrictions could be understood as vestiges of an earlier vowel harmony system. Arisaka was also a pioneer in applying the results of Chinese historical phonology to Japanese.

Arisaka was also involved in the development of structuralist phonological theory. His book *On'inron* (1940, Phonological Theory) was in part a critique of Prague School phonology. Arisaka's ideas, especially on the application of phonemic theory to historical phonology, were very influential in Japan.

Arisawa Hiromi 有沢広巳

(1896–1988). Economist and statistician. Born in Kōchi Prefecture. A graduate of Tōkyō University, Arisawa later joined the faculty there. After World War II, he formulated an economic recovery plan, known as the *keisha seisan hōshiki* (PRIORITY PRODUCTION PROGRAM), that was instrumental in the early stages of Japan's postwar economic recovery. He later became president of Hōsei University and served as a member of the Atomic Energy Commission. He was a pioneer in introducing dialectical methods to statistics.

Arishima Takeo 有島武郎

(1878–1923). Novelist, short-story writer, and essayist. Born in Tōkyō of a *samurai* background; attended a mission school in Yokohama, where he learned English. Later he attended the Peers' School (see GAKUSHŪIN UNIVERSITY). With his brothers Arishima Ikuma and SATOMI TON, Arishima was a member of the humanist SHIRAKABA SCHOOL.

Education——While a student at Sapporo Nōgakkō (Sapporo Agricultural College; now Hokkaidō University), he made a serious commitment to the modified Calvinism preached by UCHIMURA KANZŌ. He later espoused a kind of secular humanism whose central figures included Walt Whitman, Tolstoy, and Prince Kropotkin. His three and a half years of study at Haverford College and Harvard University in the United States put him in touch with socialist and progressive thinkers and gave him a keen understanding of the social and spiritual problems in modern European and American history. The experience apparently also led to his permanent dislocation from the Japanese literary and social scene.

Works——ARU ONNA (1919; tr *A Certain Woman*, 1978), his best-known novel, is essentially a psychological and moral melodrama. Its heroine is a strong-willed woman who in important respects is superior to her hypocritical male-dominated society but afflicted with the fatal flaw of true "passion." In this work and in most of his short fiction and nonfiction, Arishima was transfixed by the Christian and post-Christian dilemmas rooted in a deeply dualistic view of human nature and the world. In *Kain no matsuei* (1917; tr *The Descendants of Cain*, 1955) he showed, through the figure of a self-destructive tenant farmer, how God's primal curse lies on both man and nature. Such characters and themes did not appeal even to the more Westernized readers in Japan. Of Arishima's style, which was erratic though often moving, AKUTAGAWA RYŪNOSUKE remarked that reading it was like listening to Western phonograph records; it made him want to hear the real thing.

Later Life——In "Sengen hitotsu," a manifesto published in 1922, Arishima renounced ownership of a large tenant farm in Hokkaidō that his father had left him. At the same time, he despaired of the possibility of playing a progressive role in the "coming revolution" because he was a *"petit bourgeois."* Despite the seeming extremity of his renunciation, the cooperative management consequently instituted by the tenants lasted until recent times. Its survival was in sharp contrast to the short-lived communal experiment of MUSHANOKŌJI SANEATSU. In 1923 Arishima committed double suicide with his mistress, a married woman who was a reporter for the *Fujin kōron*, a popular women's magazine.

Arisugawa, Prince　有栖川宮熾仁親王

(1835–95; Arisugawa no Miya Taruhito Shinnō). Member of the imperial family (adopted son of Emperor Ninkō, 1800–1846; r 1817–46). Before the Meiji Restoration of 1868 he was active in the movement to overthrow the Tokugawa shogunate (1603–1867) and restore imperial rule. He was the first president appointed under the SANSHOKU system of the early Meiji government, and he commanded Imperial Army troops against the shogunate in the BOSHIN CIVIL WAR (1868–69). He was named to the GENRŌIN (Chamber of Elders) in 1875. Prince Arisugawa again led troops, this time against SAIGŌ TAKAMORI, during the SATSUMA REBELLION of 1877 in Kyūshū. He traveled through Europe and the United States in 1882 and was appointed chief of the general staff of the army in 1889.

Arita　有田［町］

Town in western Saga Prefecture, Kyūshū, noted for its porcelain (ARITA WARE). The porcelain industry was introduced to Arita by Yi Sam-p'yong (J: RI SAMPEI) from Korea in 1616 and was later perfected by Sakaida Kakiemon (1596–1666; see KAKIEMON WARE). There are numerous porcelain factories, a museum, and a porcelain inspection station. A ceramic fair is held in May. Pop: 13,826.

Arita Hachirō　有田八郎

(1884–1965). Diplomat and politician. Born on the island of Sado in Niigata Prefecture. Upon graduation from Tōkyō University, he joined the Ministry of Foreign Affairs. Establishing himself as an authority on Asian affairs, Arita rose to the position of vice-minister in 1932. He became minister of foreign affairs in the HIROTA KŌKI cabinet of 1936 and went on to serve in that post in the first KONOE FUMIMARO cabinet and then the HIRANUMA KIICHIRŌ and YONAI MITSUMASA cabinets. He opposed close ties with the Axis powers and advocated friendly relations with the United States but was forced to make repeated compromises with the increasingly powerful militarist faction in the government. In his late years he brought a suit against the writer MISHIMA YUKIO for invasion of privacy (see AFTER THE BANQUET CASE).

Arita ware　有田焼

(*arita-yaki*). Ceramics made in the Arita region in Saga Prefecture, Kyūshū. Also known as Imari ware after the port of Imari, the shipping point for the ware. KAKIEMON WARE and NABESHIMA WARE are also classified as Arita ware. In the early 17th century, a naturalized Korean potter, Ri Sampei, discovered clay for ceramics at Izumiyama, Arita, and started the first domestic porcelain production in Japan. Originally an underglaze blue and white porcelain, Arita ware largely changed to a colorful enameled porcelain after Sakaida Kakiemon perfected an enamel overglaze in the 1640s. Arita ware was produced in large quantities by the first half of the 17th century. Its use spread widely, and from the mid-17th to the mid-18th century it was exported to Europe. Factory production began in the Meiji period (1868–1912). Along with SETO, Arita is one of the largest ceramic production centers in Japan today. See also CERAMICS.

Ariwara family　在原氏

(Ariwarashi). Court nobles of the Heian period (794–1185); descended from two sons of Emperor Heizei (774–824; r 806–809). Emperor SAGA (r 809–823) first granted the surname to the children of Takaoka (799–865), the deposed crown prince (see KUSUKO INCIDENT). In 826 Emperor Junna (786–840; r 823–833) granted the name to four sons of Takaoka's brother Prince Abo (792–842), including the poet ARIWARA NO NARIHIRA.

Ariwara no Narihira　在原業平

(825–880). WAKA poet of the early Heian period (794–1185). Great-grandson of Emperor Kammu (r 781–806). Narihira was a minor official who held a number of posts, chiefly in the provinces. He is counted as one of the ROKKASEN (Six Poetic Geniuses) and SANJŪROKKASEN (Thirty-Six Poetic Geniuses). Due to spurious attributions it is difficult to ascertain the exact number of his poems in the 21 imperial poetry collections (*chokusenshū*). He has often been mentioned as the author of ISE MONOGATARI (10th century; tr *The Tales of Ise*, 1968). Although this theory is no longer accepted, the majority of the *Ise* tales center on him, and more than a third of the poems in the collection are accepted as his compositions. His poetry is collected in the *Narihira shū*.

In the preface to the KOKINSHŪ, the celebrated early-10th-century *waka* collection, KI NO TSURAYUKI criticizes Narihira as follows: "As for Ariwara no Narihira, his feelings are too strong; his words, insufficient. His poetry is, so to speak, a faded flower in which the fragrance lingers." In the *Kokinshū* we find many poems that embody Tsurayuki's ideals of verbal grace but few that, like Narihira's, overflow with passion. Narihira's importance as a poet is indicated by the fact that the *Ise monogatari*, in which so many of his poems are included, was used throughout the ages as a manual for the study of poetry.

Ariyoshi Sawako　有吉佐和子

(1931–84). Novelist. Born in Wakayama Prefecture; graduate of Tōkyō Women's Christian University. Recognized for her adept handling of contemporary social issues, Ariyoshi was one of Japan's most popular woman writers. Early stories, such as "Jiuta" (1956), brought to life the traditional world of Japanese entertainers and artists. *Kinokawa* (1959; tr *The River Ki*, 1980), her first

novel, is a sensitive record of four generations of women of Kii Province (now Wakayama Prefecture). In a similar vein, *Hanaoka Seishū no tsuma* (1966; tr *The Doctor's Wife*, 1978) is the story of an 18th-century surgeon, Hanaoka Seishū, and his devoted wife. *Kōkotsu no hito* (1972), a novel about problems of the elderly, and *Fukugō osen* (1974–75), a look at pollution in Japan, were both best sellers.

armed forces, imperial Japanese　帝国陸海軍

(*teikoku rikukaigun*). Created from the forces of the southwestern domains that overthrew the TOKUGAWA SHOGUNATE in 1867–68, the new imperial Japanese armed forces grew into one of the largest and most powerful military establishments in the world before they were abolished in 1945. The founders of the modern armed forces, many of them of *samurai* background, incorporated the organizational principles and training methods of Western military systems and created for the army and the navy prerogatives that were to profoundly affect the history of modern Japan.

Founding of the Imperial Army——Following the MEIJI RESTORATION (1868) the new government put its first emphasis on the slogan FUKOKU KYŌHEI (Enrich the Nation, Strengthen the Military) and embarked on a wide-scale program to import the technology of advanced Western nations. At the instigation of ŌMURA MASUJIRŌ, the first vice-minister of the new Ministry of Military Affairs, the effort to found a modern army was begun in 1869. The KIHEITAI militia that he and TAKASUGI SHINSAKU organized from lower-ranking samurai and peasants had destroyed the shogunate forces sent against his home domain of Chōshū (now Yamaguchi Prefecture) in the second of the CHŌSHŪ EXPEDITIONS, and because of this experience Ōmura sought to found a nationally conscripted army that would include all four classes of people—samurai, farmers, artisans, and merchants. Under his successor, YAMAGATA ARITOMO, the conscription system was finally implemented in 1873 (see CONSCRIPTION ORDINANCE OF 1873). Uprisings against the system, efforts to avoid induction, and incidents of desertion were common (see KETSUZEI IKKI). However, universal conscription was eventually put into effect.

The Prussia of the Far East——For reasons of convenience and because of Ōmura's idealized image of Napoleonic France, the decision was made to organize the new Japanese military on the French model. The navy, however, adopted the British system.

After France was defeated in the Franco-Prussian War of 1870–71, Yamagata Aritomo and ŌYAMA IWAO proposed that the Japanese military system should be modeled on the Prussian system. The power of the pro-French faction in the Ministry of Military Affairs was deeply rooted, however,

and it took more than 10 years to accomplish this change.

KATSURA TARŌ, who had studied and served as a military attaché in Germany, played a very large part in this transition. He was familiar with and espoused the Prussian military system, which included independence of the military from civilian organs of government. The ARMY GENERAL STAFF OFFICE became independent in December 1878, largely as a result of Katsura's maneuvering. This autonomy was later formalized in the Meiji Constitution of 1889 (see TŌSUIKEN).

Until about 1870 Japan's armed forces were designed primarily for domestic security. The military leaders of the Meiji government, however, soon began to think in terms of foreign wars. In 1874 some government leaders urged an invasion of Korea (see SEIKANRON), and an expeditionary force was sent to Taiwan to chastise aborigines who had murdered Ryukyuan fishermen (see TAIWAN EXPEDITION OF 1874). Large-scale military expansion and reorganization began in 1884.

In 1885 the Japanese government extended an invitation to Major Klemens W. J. MECKEL, the favorite pupil of Field Marshal Helmuth von Moltke, chief of the Great General Staff of Prussia, to teach at the new Army War College and to advise the General Staff. A total conversion to the Prussian military system was now embarked upon. Of all the aspects of the Prussian military system, the concept of the "independence of the supreme command" was to have the greatest repercussions in Japan. Moreover, a provision was made that only active-duty officers would be allowed to hold the posts of service ministers in the cabinet (see GUMBU DAIJIN GEN'EKI BUKAN SEI). During the SINO-JAPANESE WAR of 1894–1895 and the RUSSO-JAPANESE WAR of 1904–05, the "right of supreme command" was asserted ever more strongly against civil authority.

The Naval General Staff Office became independent in 1893. Soon after, the office of the inspector general of military education, which ranked equal to that of the army minister and the chief of general staff, was created. Coordination between state affairs and military command, and between politics and military strategy, thus became even more difficult. When the Imperial Headquarters (Daihon'ei), the central command structure, was established during the Sino-Japanese War of 1894–95, Prime Minister Itō Hirobumi was allowed to attend its meetings at the order of Emperor Meiji. But during the Russo-Japanese War, Prime Minister Katsura Tarō, in spite of his military background, never attended Daihon'ei meetings.

Split in a National Defense Policy— Victory in the Russo-Japanese War raised Japan to a position of international importance, but it altered the attitude of the United States, which had hitherto been favorable to Japan. The Japanese military became divided over the issue of strategic priorities. The so-called advance-to-the-north (hokushinron) group, mainly supported by the army, advocated aggressive action on the Asian continent, using Korea as a base. It saw Russia as the hypothetical enemy. The advance-to-the-south (nanshinron; see SOUTHERN EXPANSION DOCTRINE) group, supported by the navy, called for the extension of Japanese interests in Southeast Asia and the Pacific and saw the United States as the potential enemy. In 1907 the Teikoku Kokubō Hōshin (Imperial National Defense Policy) was adopted with imperial approval. It represented a compromise, in which the hypothetical enemy was determined to be "first Russia, then the United States, Germany, and France." The army focused on "taking the offensive against Russian military strength deployed in the Far East," and the navy prepared for "taking the offensive against the US Navy in the Far East."

World War I—In WORLD WAR I (1914–18), in keeping with its commitments under the ANGLO-JAPANESE ALLIANCE, Japan belatedly entered the war on the Allied side, but it also enlarged its sphere of influence in the Far East and the Pacific Basin and made great profits by monopolizing trade in military materials while the Allies were locked in war with Germany. By the end of World War I, the navy's share of the total national budget had risen to over 30 percent, and it was moving ahead with plans for a new fleet (see HACHIHACHI KANTAI), while the army was unable to break away from its outdated emphasis on infantry.

The unprecedented bloodshed in World War I brought calls for pacifism and disarmament. The WASHINGTON NAVAL TREATY OF 1922 fixed the ratio of capital ship tonnage for the United States, Great Britain, and Japan at 10:10:6 and declared a 10-year moratorium on naval construction. Public sentiment for disarmament grew. The prestige of the military declined.

The Era of Militarism—The worldwide depression, beginning in 1929, destroyed the international economic order that had been reestablished after World War I and caused a severe crisis in the capitalist system. Germany, Italy, and Japan chose the course of totalitarian government and foreign aggression (see SHŌWA DEPRESSION).

The first overt sign of MILITARISM was the MANCHURIAN INCIDENT, a virtual coup d'état by field grade officers in the GUANDONG (KWANTUNG) ARMY in Manchuria and the central headquarters of the army. When the Washington Naval Treaty expired in 1935, Japan began unlimited military expansion. Domestically, several aborted coups culminated in the FEBRUARY 26TH INCIDENT of 1936, in which young officers attempted to take over the Japanese government. Army discipline of these officers paradoxically led to a larger political role for the military; generals and admirals were now regularly named to form cabinets. It was largely at the instigation of the military that the ANTI-COMINTERN PACT (1936) of Germany, Italy, and Japan and the subsequent TRIPARTITE PACT (1940) were signed.

The China War—The China War broke out in July 1937 (see SINO-JAPANESE WAR OF 1937–1945). The army, which had begun the conflict, assumed that China would soon capitulate, but the Chinese army retreated further into the interior and refused to negotiate for peace. By 1939, almost 1 million fighting men were tied down on the Asian continent. In contrast to Japan's initial victories in China, its confrontation with the Soviet Union in the NOMONHAN INCIDENT (1939) on the Mongolian-Manchurian border proved disastrous.

The Pacific War and the Dissolution of the Military—At the brink of the Pacific War, Japan had an army of 2 million men and a naval force with 1.6 million gross tons. The Japanese fleet had reached a ratio of 70.6 percent in total tonnage and 94 percent in aircraft carriers as against the US Navy. Japan decided that, given the differences in production capabilities between the two nations, any delay in starting hostilities would be only to its disadvantage. The surprise attack on Pearl Harbor on 7 December 1941 destroyed the main power of the US Pacific Fleet. Within six months Japan had occupied Indochina, Malaya, and the Dutch East Indies and had pushed far westward through Burma to the Indian frontier and southward to the Solomon Islands. However, following a major defeat at the Battle of MIDWAY in June 1942, Japan found itself on the defensive. By the spring of 1945 most of its cities and industrial facilities had been destroyed by firebomb raids. Hiroshima and Nagasaki were obliterated by atomic bombs, Soviet troops moved into Manchuria, and Japan surrendered on 15 August 1945. In accordance with the POTSDAM DECLARATION the imperial Japanese forces were abolished on 30 November 1945. See also WORLD WAR II.

arms and armor　　　　武具

(bugu). The broad spectrum of Japanese offensive and defensive paraphernalia including hand weapons, projectiles, various types of body armor, and other battle accessories is collectively known as bugu. Japanese weapons and armor were often also objects of artistic and symbolic significance.

Early weapons. The earliest objects in Japan that may be tentatively classified as weapons are the stone implements, including axheads and spearheads, of the prehistoric Jōmon period (ca 10,000 BC–ca 300 BC). Japanese arms changed drastically in the 5th century AD with the introduction of mounted warfare and bronze and iron weapons from the Asian continent. As iron gradually replaced bronze in the 6th century, the tachi appeared. It was a long sword with a straight blade and a single, unbeveled cutting edge.

Swords, naginata, spears, bows, and shields. Swords with beveled edges appeared in the 7th century. In the mid-Heian period (794–1185) the blade developed an elegant curve, becoming the distinctive Japanese sword, both functional and aesthetic. (See also SWORDS.) The NAGINATA has a curved blade like a sword, but with a longer and more acutely curved tip, attached to a long wooden handle. The spear came in two types—the hoko and the yari—that were identical in function. The hoko was in use until the end of the Nara period (710–794). The yari was adopted by the Japanese after the 14th century, along with the use of massed troops in battle. Bows were made of laminated wood and bamboo by the 9th century. Arrows of two, three, and four vanes were used, and quivers were developed in a variety of forms. Shields were made in great numbers and designed to ward off arrows. Although few remain from ancient times, some lacquered ceremonial shields have been preserved at Shintō shrines.

Armor. Keikō and tankō armor based on mainland prototypes was used in the Kofun period (ca 300–710). The keikō was a flexible but extremely heavy suit of armor made of long, narrow pieces of iron or bronze joined together edge to edge by cords or strips of leather. The inflexible and restrictive tankō reached only to the hips and was made of fitted metal panels riveted together. Two different types of helmet were also used: the mabisashitsuki kabuto and the shōkakutsuki kabuto. The former had a flat, crescent-shaped brim; the latter was distinguished by a protruding front part like the prow of a ship. In the 9th century a distinctly Japanese style of armor known as *ōyoroi* came into being. *Ōyoroi* were designed to accommodate mounted archers and were decorated with bright ornaments of gold and silver. Their numerous segments were joined by cords woven of richly colored threads. The iron helmet was studded with raised decorative rivets and usually topped with the *kuwagata*, a large, flat metal piece resembling a stylized pair of horns. By the 14th century, when mounted warfare gave way to battles between massed ranks of foot soldiers, lighter types or armor called *dōmaru* or *haramaki* gradually replaced the *ōyoroi*. The introduction of firearms in the 16th century necessitated the development of a new type of armor modeled on Western styles, the *tōsei gusoku*.

Saddlery. Wooden saddles (*kura*) are in general classified as either Chinese-style (*karakura*) or Japanese-style (*yamatogura*). The latter are further divided into two types: a formal court saddle, the *suikangura*, used by members of the nobility, and a war saddle, the *gunjingura*. Most saddles and stirrups were sumptuously decorated.

Firearms. Firearms (*teppō*) were introduced into Japan by the Portuguese in 1543 (see FIREARMS, INTRODUCTION OF). They were immediately adopted and effected a revolution in battle tactics and strategy. The Tokugawa shogunate (1603–1867) restricted the production of *teppō*, and no advances in design were made. Cannons (*ōzutsu* or *taihō*) were not used effectively until the early 19th century.

Arms Export, Three Principles of
武器輸出三原則

(Buki Yushutsu Sangensoku). Policy of the Japanese government since 1967 establishing three specific areas to which Japan is forbidden to export arms: communist countries; countries under embargoes mandated by the United Nations; and countries currently, or likely to be in the near future, involved in military conflicts.

During the Korean War (1950–53) the government passed the Ordnance Manufacturing Law (1953), under which arms trade was permitted (see DEFENSE INDUSTRY). Subsequently, exports of weapons and ammunition to Southeast Asia increased, until in 1962 the Ministry of International Trade and Industry, in accordance with the Export Trade Control Order, first laid down the aforementioned prohibitions. In 1967 Prime Minister SATŌ EISAKU presented these principles to the Diet as the official policy of the government. In February 1976 the MIKI TAKEO cabinet not only refused to allow the export of arms to the three areas but expressed reluctance to export to other countries as well.

When the United States in 1981 expressed a desire for the exchange of defense-related technologies with Japan, the policy began to be relaxed. In January 1983 the Japanese government announced its approval of the transfer of Japanese military technology to the United States as an exception to the three principles. This was followed in July 1987 by a US-Japanese agreement defining Japan's participation in research for the US government's Strategic Defense Initiative (SDI).

Army Academy   陸軍士官学校
(Rikugun Shikan Gakkō). Principal school of the Imperial Japanese Army for the study of military science and the training of officers. First established as the Heigakkō in 1868 in Kyōto. In 1874 the school, then known as the Rikugun Shikan Gakkō, was put under the

arms and armor

Foot soldiers wield longbows (*yumi*) and spears (*yari*) in this panel from a screen painting depicting the Battle of Shizugatake in 1583.

Ōyoroi

hoshikabuto (iron helmet)

shōji no ita (crescent-shaped neck guards)

sendan no ita (right chest guard)

fukikaeshi ("rolled back" helmet flaps)

keshō no ita (decorative wooden panel)

ōsode (arm guards)

waidate (right rib guard)

kyūbi no ita (left chest guard)

wakiita (left underarm guard)

tsurubashiri (smooth leather covering)

substructure of *tsurubashiri*

leather substructure for *kusazuri* cording

inside back of *ōyoroi*

kusazuri (corded, segmented leather hip and thigh guards)

The style of armor known as *ōyoroi* came into use in the 9th century. Independent plates were joined to segmented shields of leather with cords, providing maneuverability for mounted archers.

NOTE: In this cutaway view, some outer surfaces are removed to show the substructure of the armor.

direct supervision of the Army Ministry and located at Ichigaya, Tōkyō. After 1898 it came under the supervision of the newly established Army Educational Administration. The academy was moved to Sagamihara in Kanagawa Prefecture in 1937.

After several changes two programs were put into effect from 1887: a junior course for graduates of the army cadet schools and for those who had completed the first four years of middle school, and a senior course for officer candidates. In 1938 the program for air force officers was established as a separate school. The academy disappeared along with the imperial army after World War II.

Army General Staff Office 参謀本部

(Sambō Hombu). Highest organization of the Imperial Japanese Army. Established in 1878 after the Prussian model. The chief of the General Staff Office was responsible to the emperor for national defense and strategic planning. See also ARMED FORCES, IMPERIAL JAPANESE.

Army Ministry 陸軍省

(Rikugunshō). Central government office established on 5 April 1872 along with the NAVY MINISTRY to replace the Hyōbushō (Ministry of Military Affairs). YAMAGATA ARITOMO was the first minister. The ministry initially had control of both administration and military command, but the latter function was taken over by the ARMY GENERAL STAFF OFFICE in December 1878. The politically powerful post of ministry head was usually filled by an army officer on active service (see GUMBU DAIJIN GEN'EKI BUKAN SEI). After the cabinet system was established in 1885, he was responsible directly to the emperor. The ministry was dissolved in December 1945. See also ARMED FORCES, IMPERIAL JAPANESE.

art 日本美術

(Nihon *bijutsu*). Over the centuries, a wide variety of social, economic, political, cultural, and environmental factors have had an influence on the development of Japanese art. The temperate climate and four distinct seasons provided an abundance of seasonal symbols and motifs, such as the plum, the cherry, the maple, and the chrysanthemum, which appear again and again in Japanese art. The Japanese love of nature is reflected in the use of such raw materials as lacquer, wood, bamboo, and paper throughout Japanese architecture. The high humidity and frequent earthquakes and typhoons common to Japan discouraged the use of more permanent materials such as stone in architecture and ensured the preference for the more readily mendable and available materials that dominate the Japanese aesthetic.

At the same time, the influence of China, whose culture rests at the heart of East Asian creativity, was particularly felt in Japan; Chinese artistic styles and larger segments of Chinese culture, including the great international tradition of Buddhist art, reached Japan either directly or filtered through the Korean peninsula. Even the famous secular style of the Heian court (794–1185) received notable inspiration from continental shores.

In the face of this continuing influence from continental culture, yet another characteristic of Japanese art came to the fore—its ability to absorb continental influences and produce an aesthetic all its own. Despite its proximity to the Asian continent, its position as an isolated island nation enabled Japan to mold enormously varied continental styles into a markedly indigenous expression. In other words, over the years the Japanese have been able to take generations of heterogeneous continental influence and form it into what must be considered a homogeneous whole that is "Japanese."

Despite Japan's contact with and absorption of foreign aesthetics from prehistoric times to the present, Japanese art had little, if any, influence on outside cultures, especially Western cultures, until the last half of the 19th century, when European artists discovered its beauties and developed a passion for *japonaiserie*. Exposure to and consciousness of Japanese art through, for example, Japanese ceramics and woodblock prints played a major role in the development of a modern European painting aesthetic, as well as influencing the aesthetic course of the decorative arts. Present-day Japanese artists are making an increasingly active contribution to the development of contemporary international art. See also BUDDHIST ART; BUDDHIST SCULPTURE; CERAMICS; PAINTING; UKIYO-E.

☛ 58–61

Aruga Kizaemon 有賀喜左衛門

(1897–1979). Sociologist. Born in Nagano Prefecture. A graduate of Tōkyō University, he served as professor at Tōkyō University of Education and as president of Japan Women's University (1965–73). He began his career as a student of folklore under YANAGITA KUNIO, later becoming a sociologist. In his studies of the social structure of Japanese rural communities, he maintained that there is a close historical and social connection between the landlord–tenant farmer relationship and the rural main family–branch family relationship (see IE). He believed that the vertical kinship relationship found in a clan or large family is the basic form of social relationship in Japanese society and that it is also found in urban communities and within corporations. His writings include *Nihon kazoku seido to kosaku seido* (1943, The Japanese Family and Tenant Farmer Systems).

Aru onna 或る女

(tr *A Certain Woman*, 1978). Novel by ARISHIMA TAKEO (1878–1923); published 1919. *Aru onna* describes the spiral toward self-destruction of the passionate Satsuki Yōko, a rebellious, intelligent, and beautiful woman from a bourgeois Meiji-period (1868–1912) family. The work is indebted to 19th-century European realism: the strong-willed Yōko, at odds with the restrictive society in which she lives, resolves to defeat that society and move toward greater freedom. Despite Yōko's strength of character, however, the novel slips into ever greater chaos as the heroine, feverishly involved in a scandalous romance, gradually loses her hold on reality. Time becomes confused, and space, which has an unstable and threatening quality throughout (a large portion of the book takes place at sea), loses its boundaries. *Aru onna*, Arishima's masterpiece, stands in marked contrast to much of the literature of the same era, which chose more familiar and comforting settings. Through Yōko's madness and the nightmarish setting, Arishima suggests the intellectual turmoil of the times and the sense of dislocation that arose in a rapidly changing urban environment.

asa 麻

Usually referring to hemp or ramie, *asa* is a comprehensive term that in its broadest sense includes almost all plant-derived fibers except cotton. Thus it can refer to fibers taken from the inner bark of trees and shrubs, such as *fuji* (wisteria), *kōzo*, *kaji*, and *shina* (types of mulberry), and *bashō* (a fiber-producing plantain), as well as to bast fibers, such as hemp, ramie, jute, various nettles, and linen. Of these, all but jute and linen have traditionally been used in Japan.

Uncultivated strands of wisteria, mulberry, hemp, and nettle were probably used in the Jōmon period (ca 10,000 BC–ca 300 BC). Ramie was brought to Japan from the Asian continent during the Yayoi period (ca 300 BC–ca AD 300). Ramie is known in Japanese as *choma* or *karamushi* (China grass). Hemp (*taima*), one of the oldest and most widely used *asa* fibers, is sometimes referred to as *hon'asa* (the original, most basic form of *asa*). Flax was not grown in Japan until modern times. Linen is sometimes called *seiyō asa* (Western *asa*). *Asa* fibers were the only fibers available to the general populace until the important introduction of cotton late in the Muromachi period (1333–1568).

Asabuki Eiji 朝吹英二

(1849–1918). Businessman associated with the MITSUBISHI and MITSUI conglomerates. Born in Bungo Province (now part of Ōita Prefecture); graduate of Keiō Gijuku (now Keiō University). He joined Mitsubishi Shōkai (later Mitsubishi Corporation) in 1878; in 1891 he became director of Kanegafuchi Bōseki (later KANEBŌ, LTD), a textile company controlled by Mitsui. In 1894 he joined Mitsui and by 1902 was in charge of the entire Mitsui group.

Asada Gōryū 麻田剛立

(1734–99). Astronomer. Born in the Kitsuki domain (now part of Ōita Prefecture). He succeeded his father, Ayabe Keisai (1676–1750), as domainal physician in 1767. However, in order to study astronomy he abandoned the post and went to Ōsaka, where he changed his surname to Asada. Using Chinese translations of Western scientific works he studied mathematics, calendar science, and astronomy. Asada improved existing astronomical instruments and formulated several fundamental laws of astronomy. He is credited with having arrived independently at Kepler's third law.

Asada Sōhaku 浅田宗伯

(1815–94). Prominent physician of traditional Chinese medicine (*kampō*). Real name Asada Koretsune. Born in Shinano Province (now Nagano Prefecture), he studied *kampō* in Kyōto and later practiced in Edo (now Tōkyō). He served as a physician to the shogunal household and, after the Meiji Restoration (1868), to the imperial court. Asada is credited with having systematized *kampō*, insisting that research and therapy go hand in hand.

asagao → morning glories

asagaoichi → morning glory fair

Asagiri Kōgen 朝霧高原

Plateau on the western slope of Mt. Fuji in the northern part of the city of Fujinomiya in Shizuoka Prefecture, central Honshū. Asagiri Kōgen was formed by lava flowing from Mt. Fuji. Dairy farming and cattle raising are conducted on a large scale. Elevation: 500–900 m (1,640–2,953 ft).

Asahi
旭[市]

City in northeastern Chiba Prefecture, central Honshū. It developed as a market town for agricultural produce and marine produce from nearby KUJŪKURIHAMA. The processing of marine products is an important industry. Pop: 38,906.

Asahi Bank, Ltd
[株]あさひ銀行

(Asahi Ginkō). City bank created in April 1991 through the merger of the Kyōwa Bank, Ltd, and the Saitama Bank, Ltd, and named Saitama Kyōwa Bank, Ltd, until September 1992. The percentage of Asahi's loan business catering to individual borrowers is higher than that of any other Japanese city bank. The bank maintains 449 branches in Japan and 23 branches overseas. In the fiscal year ending April 1991 total deposits were ¥24.3 trillion (US $177.2 billion), total assets were ¥32.7 trillion (US $238.5 billion), and capitalization stood at ¥280.7 billion (US $2.0 billion). Headquarters are in Tōkyō.

Asahi Breweries, Ltd
アサヒビール[株]

(Asahi Bīru). Company producing and distributing beer, soft drinks, and wines. Incorporated in 1949. Asahi ranks second in sales behind Kirin Brewing Co, Ltd, among Japanese beer brewers. The company also operates restaurants and manufactures pharmaceuticals and glass products. Sales for 1991 were ¥730.8 billion (US $5.5 billion), of which 82 percent came from beer. The company was capitalized at ¥125.7 billion (US $941.2 million) the same year. Headquarters are in Tōkyō.

Asahi Broadcasting Corporation (ABC)
朝日放送[株]

(Asahi Hōsō). A commercial radio and television broadcasting company serving the greater Ōsaka area. The company's offices are located in Ōsaka and its main transmitters in Ikoma, Nara Prefecture. Funded by the ASAHI SHIMBUN, one of Japan's largest national daily newspapers, the company began operation as a radio station in 1951 and initiated television broadcasting in 1956. In 1975 it became one of the major stations in the All Nippon News Network (ANN). ANN is a division of the ASAHI NATIONAL BROADCASTING CO, LTD, which is controlled by the *Asahi shimbun.* ABC programs featuring humor of the Ōsaka area have become popular nationwide.

Asahi Chemical Industry Co, Ltd
旭化成工業[株]

(Asahi Kasei Kōgyō). General chemical firm engaged in the manufacture of chemical fibers, petrochemicals, foods, pharmaceutical and medical products, and housing and construction materials. Founded in 1923 as a producer of ammonia, it assumed its present name in 1946. Asahi Chemical leads a group of approximately 200 related companies, including Asahi Organic Chemical Industry Co, Ltd. It has 14 overseas joint-venture companies in 12 nations in Asia, North America, Central and South America, and Europe. Long-term plans call for developing such growth areas as fermentation, food products, construction materials, and housing. Sales for the fiscal year ending March 1991 totaled ¥965.2 billion (US $7.3 billion). In the same year the company was

capitalized at ¥99.2 billion (US $723.0 million). Headquarters are in Ōsaka and Tōkyō.

Asahi Denka Kōgyō KK
旭電化工業[株]

(Asahi Denka Kōgyō). Chemical company producing various types of goods, including oils, fats, and foodstuffs. Incorporated in 1917. Affiliated with the FURUKAWA group. The company has recently devoted considerable energy to the development and sale of high value-added products, such as high purity gases for the electronics industry, processed foods, and food-product materials utilizing biotechnology. Sales for the fiscal year ending March 1991 totaled ¥98.9 billion (US $720.8 million), and the company was capitalized at ¥12.3 billion (US $89.7 million). Headquarters are in Tōkyō.

Asahi Diamond Industrial Co, Ltd
旭ダイヤモンド工業[株]

(Asahi Daiyamondo Kōgyō). Manufacturer of diamond-tipped tools. Incorporated in 1937. Sales for the fiscal year ending March 1991 totaled ¥41.4 billion (US $301.7 million), of which diamond wheels accounted for 58 percent; diamond dies, 7 percent; diamond tools, 18 percent; and diamond-related equipment and other revenues, 17 percent. The company was capitalized at ¥3.9 billion (US $28.4 million) in the same year. Headquarters are in Tōkyō.

Asahigawa
旭川

River in central Okayama Prefecture, western Honshū, flowing south from the Hiruzen Mountains to the Inland Sea. There are many deep gorges in its upper reaches, and the broad Okayama Plain is in its lower reaches. A multipurpose dam has been constructed to harness its waters for agriculture, industry, and other uses. Length: 142 km (88 mi).

Asahi Glass Co, Ltd
旭硝子[株]

(Asahi Garasu). Manufacturer of glass products used in construction, automobiles, and television sets as well as chemical and ceramic products. The largest Japanese manufacturer of glass products. Founded in 1907, it was the first Japanese firm to succeed in the commercial production of plate glass. At the end of December 1990 total sales were ¥1.0 trillion (US $7.5 billion), of which glass products accounted for 52 percent; chemical products, 36 percent; ceramics, 3 percent; and other products, 9 percent. In 1990 the export rate was 13 percent, and the firm was capitalized at ¥86.6 billion (US $648.4 million). Headquarters are in Tōkyō.

Asahikawa
旭川[市]

City in central Hokkaidō; located on the river Ishikarigawa. Asahikawa developed during the Meiji period (1868–1912) as a government-sponsored farmer-militia (TONDENHEI) settlement. It has developed as an industrial city since World War II, the principal industries being lumber, furniture production, paper pulp, and brewing. There is an airport, and the city is a gateway to Daisetsuzan National Park. Pop: 359,071.

Asahi Mountains
朝日山地

(Asahi Sanchi). Mountain range on the border between Yamagata and Niigata prefectures, northern Honshū, extending about 60 km (40 mi) north to south. Its highest peak is Ōasahidake (1,870 m; 6,134 ft). Largely granite, with many scenic gorges and rushing streams, the mountains have both alpine

plants and virgin growth of Japanese beech. Wildlife includes bears, monkeys, and antelopes. Located within the Bandai-Asahi National Park.

Asahi Mutual Life Insurance Co
朝日生命保険[相]

(Asahi Seimei Hoken). Major life insurance company. Incorporated in 1888. Asahi Mutual provides individual and group insurance and is also known for property insurance. Assets for the fiscal year ending March 1990 totaled ¥8.0 trillion (US $52.0 billion), and premiums received totaled ¥1.8 trillion (US $11.8 billion). Headquarters are in Tōkyō.

Asahi National Broadcasting Co, Ltd
全国朝日放送[株]

(Zenkoku Asahi Hōsō). A Tōkyō-based commercial broadcasting company serving the Kantō (eastern Honshū) area. Established in 1957 as an educational station with support from the ASAHI SHIMBUN (one of Japan's largest daily newspapers) and other sources, it was known as Nippon Educational Television (NET). Because of operational problems and because the public-operated Japan Broadcasting Corporation (Nippon Hōsō Kyōkai or NHK) also had an educational network, it switched to general programming in 1973. Funding by the *Asahi shimbun* increased over the years, and the firm adopted its present name in 1977. It is affiliated with the All Nippon News Network (ANN), which comprises 22 commercial stations (1992).

Asahina Yasuhiko
朝比奈泰彦

(1881–1975). Pharmacologist. His research in plant chemistry and pharmacognosy, particularly in relation to drugs used in traditional Chinese medicine (*kampō*), contributed to the development of pharmacology in Japan. Born in Tōkyō, he graduated from Tōkyō University. He studied in Germany and Switzerland and taught at Tōkyō University from 1918 to 1941. He received the Order of Culture in 1943.

Asahi Optical Co, Ltd
旭光学工業[株]

(Asahi Kōgaku Kōgyō). Manufacturer of cameras and optical and medical equipment; uses the trade name Pentax. Incorporated in 1938. In 1954 the firm invented the world's first mechanism for the quick return of a camera mirror, ushering in the era of the single-lens reflex camera. It controls 11 overseas subsidiaries. Sales for the fiscal year ending March 1991 totaled ¥75.7 billion (US $551.7 million), and capitalization stood at ¥6.1 billion (US $44.5 million). Headquarters are in Tōkyō.

Asahi shimbun
朝日新聞

One of Japan's oldest national daily newspapers. It began publication in Ōsaka in 1879 as the *Ōsaka asahi shimbun,* a small illustrated paper headed by MURAYAMA RYŌHEI. In 1881 the *Asahi* adopted an all-news format, growing into an influential commercial daily with a large circulation. The paper branched out to Tōkyō in 1888 as the *Tōkyō asahi shimbun.*

Because of its liberal position, the paper's offices were vandalized at the time of the FEBRUARY 26TH INCIDENT (1936). Prior to World War II, when controls over free speech were tightened and many papers were forced to merge, the Tōkyō and Ōsaka papers joined under the present banner.

Continued on page 62 ➤

Contemporary Art in Japan: Departing for the Unknown

Modern Japanese art originated in response to Western influences introduced during the Meiji period (1868–1912). Despite a decisive break with their aesthetic tradition, most Japanese artists confined their innovations to assimilating and imitating the styles and techniques of Western art. It was not until after World War II that Japan's artists began to strive for forms of expression that were uniquely their own. At the same time they maintained an active interest in artistic developments outside Japan.

Japan's first postwar avant-garde movement began in 1954—the short-lived but highly influential Gutai ("definite" or "concrete") movement. The Gutai artists sought to establish new modes for creative expression, including live performances and works incorporating movement, sound, and film, but after 1957 the movement was largely eclipsed by the influence of the European *informel* style of painting. A number of artists, resisting the spell of *informel*, elected to carry on the Gutai movement's original principles. Their efforts produced contemporary Japanese art's second major movement—the neo-dadaist antiart movement, which flourished from 1958 until the early 1960s, yielding offshoots like pop art and Japanese conceptual art. The third major movement, formed in 1968, took a separate path entirely. This was the Monoha (literally, "thing group"), whose proponents emphasized the material aspects of their subjects, exerting a strong influence on contemporary Japanese art. Fresh currents emerging since the late 1970s—the so-called New Painting and New Sculpture movements—reveal the continuing efforts of Japanese artists to challenge conventional forms and ideas.

Chiba Shigeo

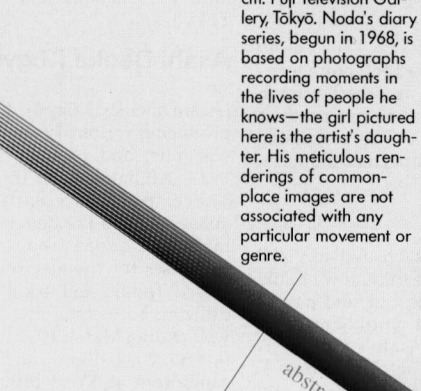

Noda Tetsuya (b 1940). *Diary; August 10th, '77.* 1977. Woodcut and silkscreen on Japanese paper. 79 × 43 cm. Fuji Television Gallery, Tōkyō. Noda's diary series, begun in 1968, is based on photographs recording moments in the lives of people he knows—the girl pictured here is the artist's daughter. His meticulous renderings of commonplace images are not associated with any particular movement or genre.

abstract painting

1950

abstract sculpture

Gutai

1955

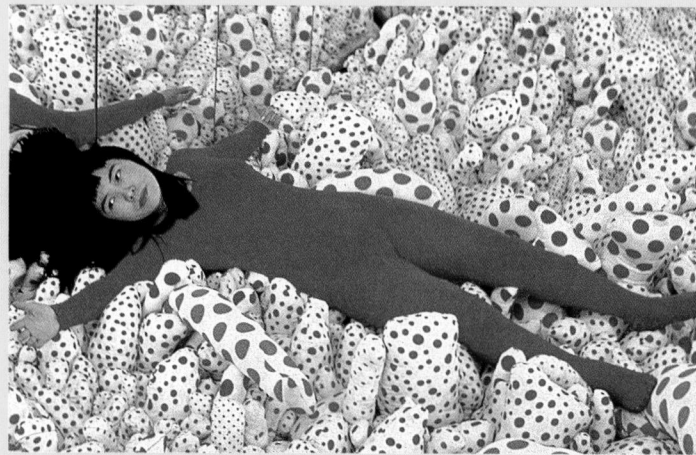

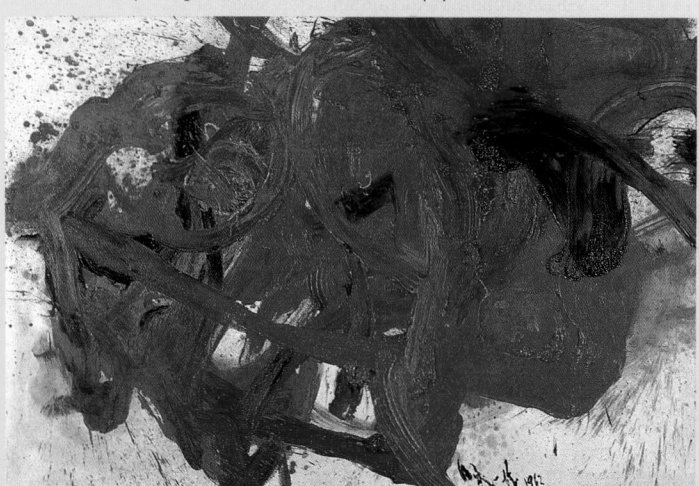

Above, **Kusama Yayoi** (b 1929). *Infinity Mirrored Room—Phalli's Field.* 1963. Mixed media performance at the Castellane Gallery, New York. Kusama has experimented with the phenomenon of multiplicity in her abstract paintings and sculpture. Here she is pictured in a performance-art piece in a mirrored room filled with stuffed polka-dotted phalluses.

Below, **Shiraga Kazuo** (b 1924). *The Second (Tenkōsei Rōshi).* 1962. Oil on canvas. 181 × 276 cm. Tōkyō Metropolitan Art Museum. Associated with the Gutai movement since its inception, Shiraga attracted attention in 1955 for a performance in which he immersed himself in one ton of wet cement. In paintings like this one he focuses on the physical characteristics of the work.

Kuwayama Tadaaki (b 1932). *Metallic Dark Blue, in 3 Sections; Metallic Dark Gray, in 3 Sections.* 1990. Oil and beeswax on fiberboard. Six pieces, 243 × 117 cm each. Gallery Yamaguchi, Ōsaka. A representative of the minimalist school of abstract painting, Kuwayama emphasizes modularity by using groups of identical pieces to create his spatial compositions. Since 1990 he has been erasing all traces of his own hand from his earlier works, leaving only the texture.

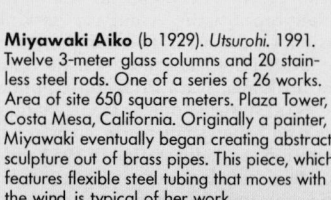

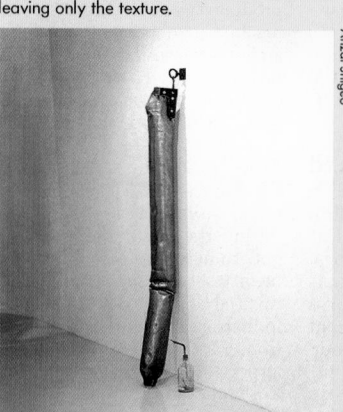

Anzai Shigeo

Muraoka Saburō (b 1928). *Bent Oxygen.* 1985. Lead, oxygen, natural gas, glass bottle. Diameter of pipe 20 cm; length 180 cm. Akiyama Gallery, Tōkyō. Formless materials like water, oxygen, and heat take on physical dimensions in Muraoka's abstract sculptures, which explore the concepts of content and containment.

Miyawaki Aiko (b 1929). *Utsurohi.* 1991. Twelve 3-meter glass columns and 20 stainless steel rods. One of a series of 26 works. Area of site 650 square meters. Plaza Tower, Costa Mesa, California. Originally a painter, Miyawaki eventually began creating abstract sculpture out of brass pipes. This piece, which features flexible steel tubing that moves with the wind, is typical of her work.

Sakurai Tadahisa

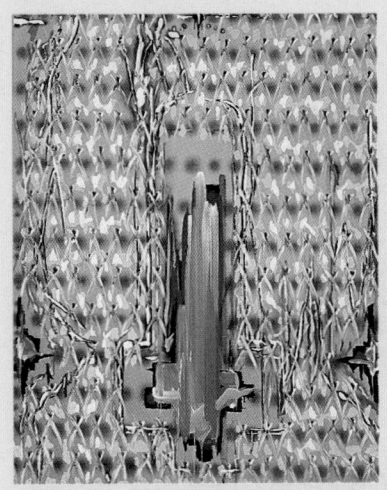

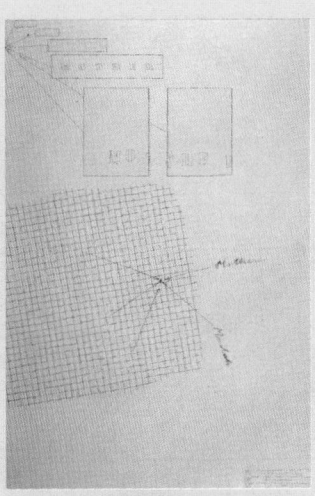

Ishimatsu Takeo

Nakanishi Natsuyuki (b 1935). *MURASAKI·MURASAKI XVII.* 1983. Oil on canvas. 227 × 182 cm. The National Museum of Modern Art, Tōkyō. Formerly associated with antiart, Nakanishi often fills his paintings with complicated dappled patterns and meticulously devised tableaux. He has also designed sets for the avant-garde dance group Sankai Juku.

Arakawa Shūsaku (b 1936). *Portrait No. 1.* 1961–62. Oil, acrylic, and pencil on canvas. 183 × 122 cm. Collection of the artist. Cofounder (with Shinohara Ushio) of an influential neo-dadaist group in 1960, Arakawa was an early proponent of antiart. He has since moved on to conceptual art, using words and mathematical symbols—presented as compositional elements devoid of inherent meaning—as his principal motif.

Shinohara Ushio (b 1932). *Boxing Painting.* 1991 performance at the National Museum of Art, Ōsaka. One of the original standard-bearers of antiart, Shinohara also participated in the pop art movement. He is known for his powerful use of color and his unorthodox performances. For this one he revived a technique he invented in the early 1960s.

Miyajima Tatsuo (b 1957). *Counter Line No. 2.* 1989. Light-emitting diodes (LEDs), integrated circuit, electric wire, and aluminum panel. 11 × 470 × 4 cm. Gallery Takagi, Nagoya. Numbers displayed by pulsing LEDs stand out against darkness and silence in Miyajima's conceptual art installation. Zero is represented not as a number but as an interval of darkness.

Suzuki Mitsuhiko

Matsuzawa Yutaka (b 1922). *EXPEDIENT 9.* 1990. Silkscreen. 25 × 18 cm. Okazaki Tamako Gallery, Tōkyō. Matsuzawa was one of Japan's first conceptual artists. Since the 1960s he has employed various media to examine the possibility of reducing language and symbols to their essential elements.

TOWARD QUANTUM ART
[EXPEDIENT 9]

informel
antiart
1960
conceptual art
pop art
1965
1970
Monoha

Nomura Hitoshi (b 1945). In the foreground, *The Genesis Out of the Vacuum Glass.* 1989. Glass. 39 × 24 × 24 cm. In the background, *The Sun on the Equator.* 1989. Photographs and plastic. 140 × 352 × 60 cm. Collection of the artist. In these two conceptual works, Nomura employs a series of photographs to depict the sun's apparent yearly movement around the earth and presents his unusual vision of the cosmos in glass.

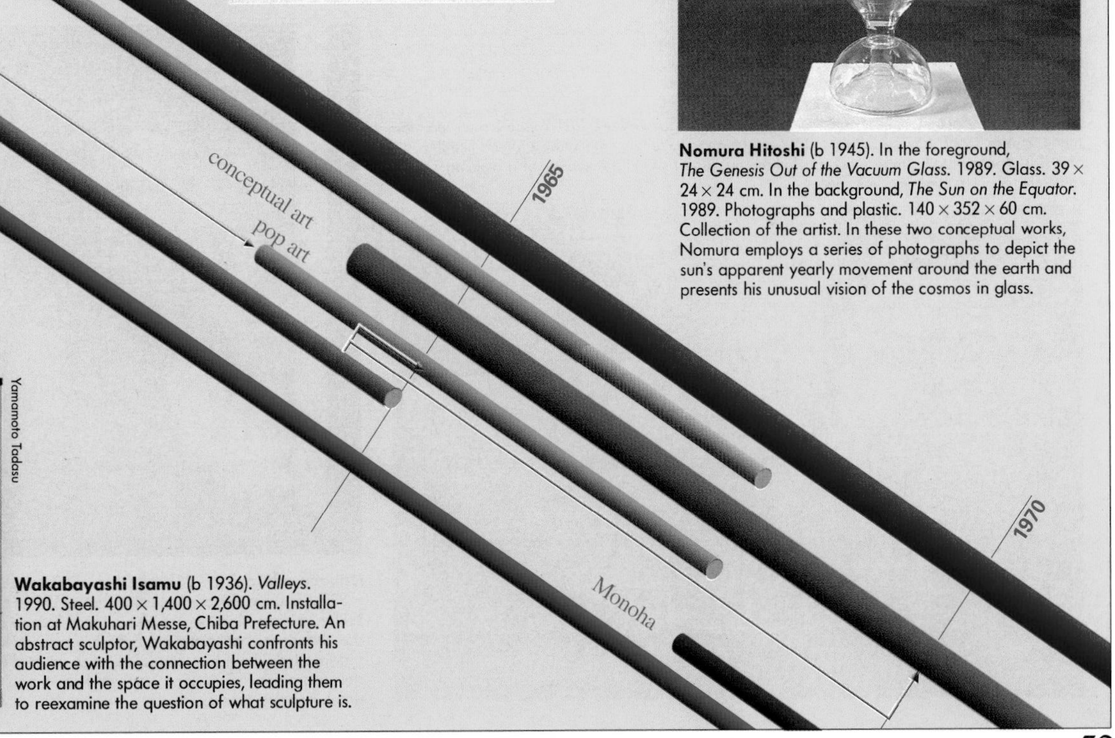

Yamamoto Tadasu

Wakabayashi Isamu (b 1936). *Valleys.* 1990. Steel. 400 × 1,400 × 2,600 cm. Installation at Makuhari Messe, Chiba Prefecture. An abstract sculptor, Wakabayashi confronts his audience with the connection between the work and the space it occupies, leading them to reexamine the question of what sculpture is.

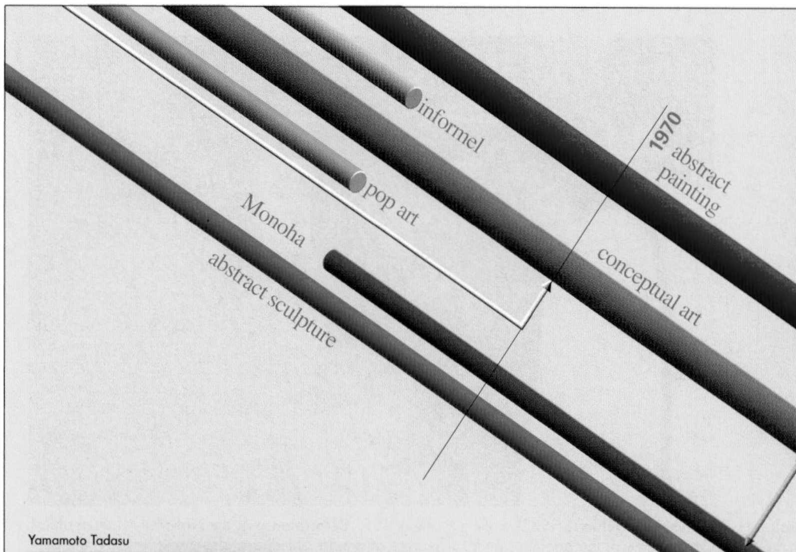

informel

1970

abstract painting

pop art

Monoha

conceptual art

abstract sculpture

Suga Kishio (b 1944). *Kainyūsa.* 1979. Stone, zinc, and plate. 1,000 × 400 × 45 cm. Private collection. In his stark displays of contrasting elements Suga eschews the attempt to create an integrated work, instead deriving structure from disparities among the materials themselves—a classic Monoha technique.

Yamamoto Sōroku

1975

New Sculpture

New Painting

1980

Yamamoto Tadasu

Kawashima Kiyoshi (b 1951). *Observation 26.* 1989–90. Wood, steel, lead, and acrylic. 450 × 388 × 244 cm. Collection of the artist. Confronted with this heap of acid-etched lead, rusty iron, and scrap wood, viewers are compelled to consider its relationship to its surroundings and its claim to the space it occupies. Unusual materials are typical in Kawashima's New Sculpture works.

Yamamoto Tadasu

Toya Shigeo (b 1947). *Woods II.* 1989–90. Wood, ash, and acrylic. Thirty pieces, 220 × 31 × 31 cm each. Hara Museum of Contemporary Art, Tōkyō. Fashioned with a chainsaw rather than a chisel, Toya's work evokes images of a crowded dead forest. His New Sculpture creations are often related thematically.

Endō Toshikatsu (b 1950). *Untitled.* 1983. Wood, water, and tar. Twenty-two pieces, each 140 cm high and 35 cm in diameter. 1989 installation at the Nordic Arts Centre, Finland. Another artist associated with New Sculpture, Endō employs elemental materials—earth, water, wood, and fire—that lend a mystical touch to his creations. This one is composed of water-filled wooden columns arranged in a circle 4 meters in diameter.

Kawamata Tadashi (b 1953). *Toronto Project: Colonial Tavern Park, 201 Yonge Street, Toronto.* July–October 1989. 1,372 × 3,200 × 1,829 cm. In large-scale New Sculpture projects like this one, Kawamata installs timberwork around the outside or within the interior of a building, radically reconstructing familiar spaces.

Narita Hiromu

© Tadashi Kawamata

Uematsu Keiji (b 1947). *Calm Time—Red Form/Inclination.* 1989. Granite and iron. 500 × 230 × 100 cm. Setoda, Hiroshima Prefecture. Uematsu's principal aim is to make visible the relationship between objects that come into contact with one another. The cone is a motif that occurs in many of his New Sculpture works.

Nakahara Kōdai (b 1961). *Untitled.* 1990. Legos. 280 × 320 × 210 cm. Private collection. In the 1980s, New Sculpture artist Nakahara worked with relatively orthodox techniques and materials, but more recently he has produced playful pieces employing such unusual materials as trampolines, knitting wool, and—as here—children's building blocks.

Murai Osamu

Sekine Nobuo (b 1942). *Phase—Mother Earth*. 1968. Earth and hole. Installation. Suma Palace Park, Kōbe. Sekine acquired his reputation as a Monoha artist for works such as this—a column of earth standing next to the hole from which the earth was dug. The "positive" column's shape and dimensions correspond to those of the "negative" space created by its excavation.

Lee U-Fan (b 1936). *Relatum*. 1968. Glass and stone. 140 × 180 × 40 cm. Collection of the artist. With works like this one that explore the juxtaposition of dissimilar materials—cotton and iron, rope and wood—Lee contributed to the theoretical foundations of the Monoha movement. His more recent, two-dimensional works focus on the physical qualities of points and lines.

Murai Osamu

1985

1990

Hori Kōsai (b 1947). *Voice of Wind—24*. 1989. Chinese ink, acrylic, and stone pigment on canvas and Japanese paper. 91 × 65 cm. Collection of the artist. A participant in the New Painting movement, Hori has long worked with saturated, multilayered coloring. Many of his works feature a contrapuntal arrangement of wide brush strokes and fine lines, conveying an impression of great depth.

The artists whose works are displayed here were selected by Chiba Shigeo and Sakai Tadayasu.

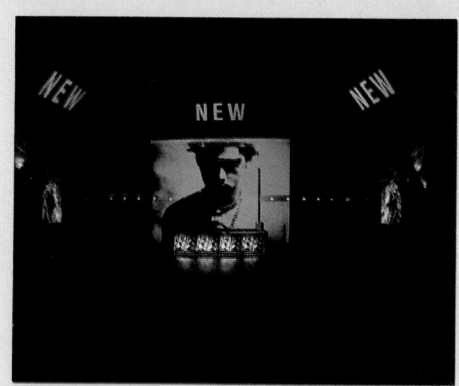

Complesso Plastico (Hirano Jirō [b 1963] and Matsukage Hiroyuki [b 1965]). *Everybody Knows New Life*. 1990. Mixed media. Installation. Tōkō Museum of Contemporary Art, Tōkyō. This duo combines photographic, video, and motion-picture images to create its New Sculpture installations, many of which are provocatively adorned with altars and crosses.

Tanaka Noriyuki (b 1959). *X DEPARTMENT (Fruits No. 91–3.4)*. 1991. Mixed media. Installation. Isetan Museum of Art. A graphic designer who also produces New Sculpture works, Tanaka refuses to recognize restrictions on the selection of materials, techniques, or subjects. His paintings and installations reflect his fascination with the city of Tōkyō.

Koyama Hotarō (b 1955). *Space/Road Under the Ground/Sight No. 3*. 1989. Gelatin silver print. 142 × 306 cm. Ishiyachō Gallery, Kyōto. Koyama photographs wooded areas, marshes, and the like and then transforms the prints by bleaching, scorching, or sanding them. His work defies categorization.

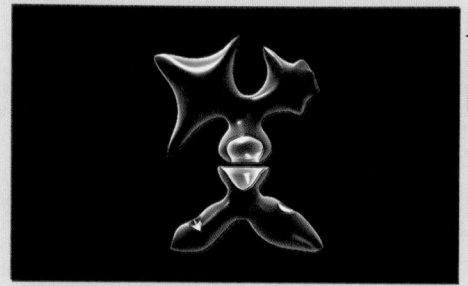

© Fujihata Masaki

Fujihata Masaki (b 1956). *Forbidden Fruits*. 1990. Computer image. 4,096 × 4,096 pixels. Collection of the artist. Fujihata's strangely erotic computer images transcend genre distinctions and disregard conventional notions of form. He has also produced three-dimensional pieces based on computer-generated imagery.

Asai Chū *Harvest.* 1890. Oil on canvas. 70 × 99 cm. Tōkyō University of Fine Arts and Music.

► *Continued from page 57*

The *Asahi* also publishes an English-language daily, the *Asahi Evening News;* Japan's oldest weekly magazine, *Shūkan asahi* (Weekly Asahi, established in 1922); an English-language weekly magazine, *Japan Access,* established in 1990; other periodicals; and books. It has special affiliations with the Associated Press (AP), Reuters, and Tass wire services and subscribes to the *New York Times* and *The Times* (London) news services. Since 1980 the head office of the *Asahi shimbun* has used a computerized system known as the New Editing and Layout System of Newspapers (NELSON). Circulation was 8.3 million in 1991.

Asahi ware 朝日焼

(*asahi-yaki*). Pottery made since the early 17th century at Uji, Kyōto Prefecture. Most products were tea-ceremony wares and reflected the influence of Korean pottery, perhaps by way of KARATSU WARE and HAGI WARE. Asahi ware tends to be heavy and is made of a coarse, sandy clay. A characteristic mottled pink "deer-spotting" can often be seen on the uneven surface of the clay under a translucent glaze that fires with greenish or bluish tones. Perhaps the best wares were produced in the mid- to late 17th century, but identification is difficult as early pieces were neither dated nor stamped. The kiln is still in production and is well known for its modern, computer-controlled technology.

Asai Chū 浅井忠

(1856–1907). Western-style painter known for his lyrical watercolors. Artist name (*gō*) Mokugo or Mokugyo. Born in Edo (now Tōkyō). In 1875 he entered the Shōgidō, a school of Western-style painting sponsored by Kunisawa Shinkurō (1847–77). In 1876 he began studying with Antonio FONTANESI at the Technical Fine Arts School (Kōbu Bijutsu Gakkō). Asai later taught at the Tōkyō Normal School and in 1889 helped to establish the Meiji Bijutsukai (Meiji Art Society), Japan's first group of Western-style painters. Representative works by Asai are *Shumpo* (Fields in Spring) and *Shūkaku* (Harvest). He became professor at the Tōkyō Bijutsu Gakkō (now Tōkyō University of Fine Arts and Music) in 1898. Beginning in 1900, greatly influenced by the impressionists, he completed numerous paintings in oil and watercolor. He was then appointed professor at the Kyōto Kōtō Kōgei Gakkō (Kyōto Higher School of Design). In 1903 he founded the Shōgoin Institute of Western Art, which was reorganized in 1905 as the Kansai Art School, where he trained Ishii Hakutei (1882–1958), YASUI SŌTARŌ, and UMEHARA RYŪZABURŌ.

Asai family 浅井氏

(Asaishi). *Daimyō* family of the Sengoku period (1467–1568); more properly called Azai. The Asai had served the KYŌGOKU FAMILY of northern Ōmi Province (now Shiga Prefecture) since the mid-1400s, but early in the 16th century Asai Sukemasa (d 1542) seized their domain. He built a castle at Odani (now Kohoku Chō, Shiga Prefecture) and formed alliances with the ASAKURA FAMILY of Echizen (now part of Fukui Prefecture) and the Saitō family of Mino (now part of Gifu Prefecture). Although ASAI NAGAMASA, Sukemasa's grandson, was married to the sister of ODA NOBUNAGA, he fought against Nobunaga in the Battle of ANEGAWA (1570). He was forced to commit suicide while under siege by Nobunaga's forces in 1573, in effect ending the Asai line.

Asai Nagamasa 浅井長政

(1545–73). Sometimes called Azai Nagamasa. Prominent *daimyō* of the Sengoku period (1467–1568); lord of Odani Castle in northern Ōmi Province (now Kohoku Chō, Shiga Prefecture). Although married to ODA NOBUNAGA's sister Oichi (ODANI NO KATA), Nagamasa turned against him in 1570, forcing Nobunaga to break off an invasion of the domains of ASAKURA YOSHIKAGE. In 1570 the armies of Nagamasa and Yoshikage were defeated in the Battle of ANEGAWA by Nobunaga and the future shōgun TOKUGAWA IEYASU. Nagamasa's strategic domains in northern Ōmi became the scene of three years of warfare as Nobunaga moved from one front to another to frustrate the attempt of a coalition to encircle and eliminate him. After driving the shōgun ASHIKAGA YOSHIAKI, the coalition's presumed leader, out of Kyōto in the summer of 1573, Nobunaga invaded Yoshikage's home territory and destroyed him. Deprived of his ally, and assaulted by one of Nobunaga's armies, Asai Nagamasa committed suicide.

Asai Ryōi 浅井了意

(?–1691). Writer of KANA-ZŌSHI, a kind of popular prose fiction, in the early Edo period (1600–1868). A RŌNIN (masterless *samurai*), he later became a priest at the Honjōji, a temple in Kyōto. Although an erudite, serious scholar, he wrote on a wide variety of subjects in a simple, direct style, aiming to reach as wide an audience as possible. His principal works include the *Tōkaidō meisho ki* (ca 1660, A Record of Famous Spots along the Tōkaidō), a descriptive travel guide; *Otogibōko* (1666) and *Inuhariko* (1692), collections of ghost stories, many of which are adaptations of Chinese and Korean tales; *Kanninki* (1659, Notes on Patience), a didactic treatise; and *Ukiyo monogatari* (ca 1661, Tales of the Floating World), a satirical, episodic account of the life of a bumbling priest named Ukiyobō. Asai also wrote scholarly books, including many commentaries on Buddhist texts and studies of the Japanese classics. He is considered to be Japan's first professional writer.

Asaka 朝霞[市]

City in southeastern Saitama Prefecture, located about 20 km (12 mi) northwest of Tōkyō. Asaka developed as a post-station town during the Edo period (1600–1868). Long associated with the copper-rolling industry, more recently it has become a satellite city of Tōkyō. A former US Army camp in Asaka currently serves as a base for the Japanese Self Defense Forces. Pop: 103,617.

Asaka Canal 安積疏水

(Asaka Sosui). Canal in central Fukushima Prefecture, northern Honshū, running from Lake Inawashiro through the Kōriyama Basin. It provides water for irrigation, hydroelectric power, drinking, and industry. It was opened in 1882, and a new section was completed in 1951. Length (main canal): 95 km (59 mi).

Asakasha あさ香社

Coterie of TANKA poets. Asakasha was formed in 1893 by OCHIAI NAOBUMI, among whose pupils were YOSANO TEKKAN, Ayukai Kaien (1864–1946), Utsumi Getsujō (1872–1935), Shioi Ukō (1869–1913), KANEKO KUN'EN, Kubo Inokichi (1874–1939), Takeshima Hagoromo (1872–1967), and ONOE SAISHŪ. Their poems appeared in the daily newspapers *Nihon, Jiyū shimbun,* and *Niroku shimpō.* Although they had no specific rules and no coterie publication, the reforms they initiated helped free *tanka* from traditional WAKA conventions. Their works tended to reflect Ochiai's inclinations.

Asaka Tampaku 安積澹泊

(1656–1737). Confucian scholar of the Edo period (1600–1868); an early leader of the MITO SCHOOL. Born in the domain of Mito (now part of Ibaraki Prefecture), he studied with SHU SHUNSUI. In 1693 he was named head of the SHŌKŌKAN, the bureau established by TOKUGAWA MITSUKUNI, the *daimyō* of Mito, for the compilation of the history of Japan, DAI NIHON SHI. An adherent of the Zhu Xi (Chu Hsi) school of Neo-Confucianism (see SHUSHIGAKU) and a friend of ARAI HAKUSEKI, he also corresponded with Confucian scholars, including OGYŪ SORAI.

Asakawa Kan'ichi 朝河貫一

(1873–1948). Historian. Born in Fukushima Prefecture; graduate of Tōkyō Semmon Gakkō (now Waseda University). He received his PhD in 1902 from Yale University for his study of the TAIKA REFORM. From 1910 to 1942 he taught history at Yale and became noted for his comparisons of Japanese and European feudal institutions. Among his numerous English publications is *The Documents of Iriki* (1929; rev ed, 1953), a summary and translation of some 250 documents covering the period 1135 to 1870, in the possession of the Irikiin family of Iriki, Kagoshima Prefecture.

Asakura family 朝倉氏

(Asakurashi). Warrior family of the Muromachi period (1333–1568). Asakura Hirokage (1255–1352) helped Ashikaga general Shiba Takatsune (1305–67) defeat NITTA YOSHISADA in 1338 and established himself at Kuromaru Castle in Echizen Province (now part of Fukui Prefecture) as a vassal of the SHIBA FAMILY. His son Masakage (1314–72) expanded Asakura holdings in Echizen, becoming a powerful local lord (KOKUJIN). Asakura Toshikage (or Takakage; 1428–81) later seized all of Echizen. For his services in the ŌNIN WAR (1467–77) Toshikage was made SHUGO of Echizen in 1471 and gained the status of SHUGO DAIMYŌ. Toshikage built a large fortification near Ichijōdani (now part of the city of Fukui) and established "house laws" for governance of his domain (see ASAKURA TOSHIKAGE, 17-ARTICLE CODE OF). The Asakura family line ended in 1573, when ODA NOBUNAGA devastated Ichijōdani Castle and Toshikage's grandson ASAKURA YOSHIKAGE committed suicide.

Asakura Fumio 朝倉文夫

(1883–1964). Western-style sculptor. Born in Ōita Prefecture; graduate of the Tōkyō Bijutsu Gakkō (now Tōkyō University of Fine Arts and Music) where he later taught. Noted for his disciplined technique and realistic style, he was a frequent prizewinner in the annual government-sponsored Bunten exhibitions. He received the Order of Culture in 1948. Important works include *Hakamori* (1910, Grave Keeper) and *Ebamu neko* (1942, Cat Consuming Its Prey).

Asakura Toshikage, 17-Article Code of 朝倉敏景十七箇条

(Asakura Toshikage Jūshichikajō). Also known as Asakura Takakage Jōjō; some variants have 16 articles. A set of household precepts (KAKUN) attributed to Asakura Toshikage (more properly called Takakage; 1428–81), who became military governor (*shugo*) of Echizen Province (now part of Fukui Prefecture) in 1471. The ASAKURA FAMILY continued to rule the province as SENGOKU DAIMYŌ until 1573, when ASAKURA YOSHIKAGE was destroyed by the national unifier ODA NOBUNAGA. The injunctions are meant to guide successive heads of the Asakura family in their demeanor and the government of their domain. Particularly famous is article 14 (15), which is often cited as ahead of its time. However, it reflects the conditions that prevailed in Japan from the late 16th century onward, rather than the actuality of the early Sengoku period (1467–1568), and thus renders the attribution of authorship suspect.

Asakura Yoshikage 朝倉義景

(1533–73). Prominent *daimyō* of the Sengoku period (1467–1568). The fifth and last lord of the ASAKURA FAMILY of Echizen Province (now part of Fukui Prefecture), where the Asakura had displaced the SHIBA FAMILY as military governors (SHUGO) in 1471. Their castle town of Ichijōdani (now part of the city of Fukui) became a cultural center that emulated Kyōto. Yoshikage became master of this realm in 1548. In 1570 his domains were invaded by ODA NOBUNAGA, and Yoshikage became active in a coalition intent on checking him. The armies of Yoshikage and his ally ASAI NAGAMASA were defeated by Nobunaga in the Battle of ANEGAWA in 1570. For three years Yoshikage was able to avoid a decisive encounter, but in 1573, when he went to Nagamasa's assistance, he was defeated and chased back to Echizen by Nobunaga. Forced to abandon Ichijōdani and betrayed by a kinsman, Asakura Kageaki (d 1574), Yoshikage committed suicide at Rokubō Kenshōji (now the city of Ōno).

Asakusa 浅草

District in the eastern part of Taitō Ward, Tōkyō, on the west bank of the river Sumidagawa. The district came into being during the Edo period (1600–1868) as a commercial and entertainment area centered on the temple SENSŌJI, popularly called the Asakusa Kannon. The YOSHIWARA pleasure quarter was once located just to the north. Asakusa still retains the distinctive atmosphere of Tōkyō's SHITAMACHI, with attractions that include the Nakamise and Shin Nakamise shopping arcades and the movie theaters and entertainment halls of the Rokku area. A number of traditional fairs and festivals are held in Asakusa, among them the SANJA FESTIVAL.

Asakusa Bunko 浅草文庫

(Asakusa Library). Name of five separate libraries formed during the Edo (1600–1868) and Meiji (1868–1912) periods in the Asakusa section of Tōkyō. The earliest, also known as the Bokusai Bunko, was the personal collection of Itazaka Bokusai (1578–1655). Reputedly the first private library in Japan to be opened to the public (1655?), it was destroyed in the great fire of 1657. Three private libraries, all named Asakusa Bunko, were subsequently founded by the *daimyō* Hotta Masamori (1608–51), the Tokugawa vassal Kimura Shigesuke, and the scholar Ōtsuki Joden (1845–1931). The fifth Asakusa Bunko, consisting of collections of Japanese and foreign books in the Ministry of Education's former Shojakukan Library, was opened to the public in 1875. Its books have since been kept at the CABINET LIBRARY of the National Archives.

Asakusa Kannon →Sensōji

Asakusa Shrine 浅草神社

(Asakusa Jinja). Also called Sanja Gongen. Shintō shrine located on the grounds of the temple SENSŌJI in the Asakusa section of Taitō Ward, Tōkyō. The souls of three people are enshrined here: the brothers Hinokuma Hamanari and Hinokuma Takenari, who are said to have found the Sensōji's statue of the bodhisattva Kannon in 628, and the village headman Haji no Nakatomo, said to have built the temple. The date of the shrine's construction is unknown, but Tokugawa Iemitsu (1604–51), the third Tokugawa shōgun, built the main shrine building in 1649. The SANJA FESTIVAL takes place at Asakusa Shrine annually on the weekend that falls the closest to 18 May, and the HAGOITA ICHI festival is held here on 17 and 18 December.

Asama Hot Spring 浅間温泉

(Asama Onsen). Located in the city of Matsumoto, Nagano Prefecture, central Honshū. A simple thermal spring; temperature approximately 50°C (122°F). Established around the beginning of the 17th century by the lords of the Matsumoto domain. Located in an area serving as a base for mountain climbers in the HIDA MOUNTAINS.

Asamayama 浅間山

Triple active volcano on the border of Gumma and Nagano prefectures, central Honshū. It has erupted 50 times in recorded history. On its northern slope is ONIOSHIDASHI, a rock formation, formed by lava flows at the time of the 1783 eruption. A Tōkyō University volcano observation station is located on its eastern slope. Karuizawa, on the southern slope, is a popular summer resort. Part of JŌSHIN'ETSU KŌGEN NATIONAL PARK. Height: 2,568 m (8,425 ft).

Asami Keisai 浅見絅斎

(1652–1712). Scholar of Neo-Confucianism (see SHUSHIGAKU). Born in Ōmi Province (now Shiga Prefecture), Keisai initially was a physician. He became a disciple of YAMAZAKI ANSAI in Kyōto, but he disagreed with Ansai's Shintō doctrines (SUIKA SHINTŌ). After Ansai's death, however, Keisai became the most faithful transmitter of his master's teaching. A severe disciplinarian, Keisai severed ties with his students and friends over the slightest omission of *giri* (righteous duty; see GIRI AND NINJŌ). For Keisai *giri* was the basis of scholarship, indeed of life itself; he praised the FORTY-SEVEN RŌNIN INCIDENT as a display of loyalty. He lived in poverty, steadfastly refusing all offers of official employment. His treatise SEIKEN IGEN influenced members

Asanuma Inejirō
A founding member and later chairman of the Japan Socialist Party, Asanuma fell victim to a right-wing assassin in October 1960.

of the proimperial, antishogunate movement (see SONNŌ JŌI) in the late Edo period (1600–1868).

Asamushi Hot Spring　浅虫温泉

(Asamushi Onsen). Located in the city of Aomori, Aomori Prefecture, northern Honshū. A weak, common salt spring containing gypsum; water temperature 30°–78°C (86°–172°F). Facing Aomori Bay, this scenic hot spring is part of the Asamushi-Natsudomari Peninsula Prefectural Natural Park. It is surrounded by a resort area.

Asano Nagamasa　浅野長政

(1547–1611). Military commander and one of the Five Commissioners (Gobugyō) of the Azuchi-Momoyama period (1568–1600). Born in Owari Province (now part of Aichi Prefecture), Nagamasa served as both general and administrator for ODA NOBUNAGA and his successor TOYOTOMI HIDEYOSHI. A brother-in-law of Hideyoshi, in 1585 he was appointed senior member of the Gobugyō and two years later became lord of Obama Castle. After participating in Hideyoshi's invasion of Korea in 1592, he was made *daimyō* of Kai Province (now Yamanashi Prefecture). Nagamasa resigned his posts after Hideyoshi's death in 1598 but fought, with his son ASANO YOSHINAGA, under TOKUGAWA IEYASU in the Battle of SEKIGAHARA (1600).

Asano Sōichirō　浅野総一郎

(1848–1930). Businessman and founder of the Asano *zaibatsu*, a financial and industrial combine. Born in what is now Toyama Prefecture, Asano moved to Tōkyō in 1871. After attempting a number of other businesses he made his fortune in coal and coke. In 1884, with the help of entrepreneur SHIBUSAWA EIICHI, he bought a government-built cement factory and established the Asano Cement Co (later the NIHON CEMENT CO, LTD). From this base he expanded into many other areas of business, including coal, oil, shipping, trading, and shipbuilding. Closely linked with powerful banker YASUDA ZENJIRŌ, Asano eventually formed the Asano *zaibatsu* by placing 30 direct subsidiaries and 50 affiliates under the control of Asano Dōzoku Kaisha, a holding company created in 1918.

Asano Yoshinaga　浅野幸長

(1576–1613). *Daimyō* of the Azuchi-Momoyama period (1568–1600). Son of ASANO NAGAMASA, a trusted general of TOYOTOMI HIDEYOSHI. Yoshinaga participated in Hideyoshi's ODAWARA CAMPAIGN (1590) and the INVASIONS OF KOREA in 1592 and 1597. At the Battle of SEKIGAHARA (1600), he took the side of TOKUGAWA IEYASU and was rewarded with a fief in Kii Province (now Wakayama Prefecture) for his services.

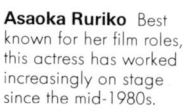

Asaoka Ruriko Best known for her film roles, this actress has worked increasingly on stage since the mid-1980s.

Asanuma Corporation　[株]浅沼組

(Asanuma-Gumi). Construction company. Founded in Nara Prefecture in 1892. Before World War II, the company constructed Japanese military installations and, after the war, US military bases on Okinawa. In the 1970s the company began to build concrete, prefabricated houses. It has a subsidiary firm in Guam. Sales for the fiscal year ending March 1991 totaled ¥248.6 billion (US $1.8 billion), of which the share of architecture and building was 79 percent; civil engineering, 20 percent; and real estate, 1 percent. The company was capitalized at ¥8.1 billion (US

$59.0 million) in the same year. Headquarters are in Ōsaka.

Asanuma Inejirō　浅沼稲次郎

(1898–1960). Socialist politician. Born in Miyakejima, Tōkyō Prefecture; graduated from Waseda University in 1923. While still a student, he joined the fledgling Japan Communist Party. In 1924 he was sentenced to five months' hard labor for participating in a violent demonstration during a labor dispute. Later he helped to form several prewar socialist parties, including the RŌDŌ NŌMINTŌ (Labor-Farmer Party). Elected to the House of Representatives on the SHAKAI TAISHŪTŌ (Socialist Masses Party) slate in 1936, he served in the Diet for 20 years. Immediately after World War II, he helped to organize the JAPAN SOCIALIST PARTY, eventually becoming its secretary-general and chairman. In 1959 he denounced American imperialism as the common enemy of Japan and China, arousing controversy in Japan. On 12 October 1960 he was stabbed to death at a televised political rally by a right-wing youth.

Asaoka Ruriko　浅丘ルリ子

(1940–). Actress. Born in Changchun (Ch'ang-ch'un), China. In 1954, while in middle school, she auditioned for and was chosen to play the starring role in the NIKKATSU CORPORATION film *Midori haruka ni* (1955, released abroad as *The Green Music Box*). She specializes in portraying women of keen sensibility, some of them almost neurotically intense. Among her major films are *Shūen* (1964, The Flame of Devotion) and *Ai no kawaki* (1967, Thirst for Love).

Asari Keita　浅利慶太

(1933–). Theatrical producer and leader of the Shiki Theatrical Company. Born in Tōkyō. Asari attended Keiō University but withdrew without graduating. He formed the Shiki Theatrical Company in 1953 while still at the university. Asari has been active in the staging of a repertory of modern French plays in the orthodox style known as the "new classicism." He began staging musicals in 1970 and was responsible for the Japanese productions of a succession of Broadway hits, including *Applause* (1972), *A Chorus Line* (1979), *Cats* (1984), and *West Side Story* (1990). His production of *Madame Butterfly* for La Scala in Milan in December 1985 was a great success.

Asayama Bontō　朝山梵燈

(1349–ca 1427). RENGA (linked verse) poet and Buddhist priest. Also known as Bontō An. His lay name was Morotsuna. He studied under NIJŌ YOSHIMOTO and was a teacher of TAKAYAMA SŌZEI. His most important treatise is *Bontō anshu hentō sho* (1417, Master Bontō's Answers to Questions on Renga).

Asayama Nichijō　朝山日乗

(?–1577). Buddhist priest and political adviser of the Sengoku (1467–1568) and Azuchi-Momoyama (1568–1600) periods. He was supposedly born in Asayama, Izumo Province (now part of Shimane Prefecture). Nichijō became ODA NOBUNAGA's adviser and commissioner of rebuilding (*shūzen bugyō*), overseeing the reconstruction of the Imperial Palace. In 1569 he engaged in a doctrinal dispute with the Jesuit priest Luis FROIS. Nichijō lost the debate and became the Jesuits' most implacable enemy. His excessive hatred of the Jesuits eventually caused him to lose Nobunaga's patronage.

asceticism　修行・苦行

(*shugyō; kugyō*). The English term "asceticism" corresponds to either of two Japanese terms. *Shugyō* refers to spiritual exercises undertaken for the attainment of a particular religious goal, while *kugyō*, a category of *shugyō*, is a religious practice in which suffering is considered a way to attain a religious goal. In SHINTŌ, man is understood to be originally pure in nature, and TSUMI (sin) is an adventitious or ritual impurity that may be swept away by a ritual act of cleansing. Under such conditions, there is no need for what is commonly understood as asceticism in the West. In BUDDHISM, however, man is considered capable of attaining enlightenment by following a set of spiritual exercises, including *kugyō*. The exercises differ from one sect to another; for example, recitation of the NEMBUTSU for the JŌDO SECT and JŌDO SHIN SECT.

Various kinds of self-mortification have been used as spiritual exercises in Japanese religions. Many such practices, known as *aragyō* (literally, "harsh practices") as well as *kugyō*, were undertaken as an integral part of ESOTERIC BUDDHISM and mountain religions (SHUGENDŌ; YAMABUSHI). One of the most common traditional practices still performed today is waterfall austerities (*taki no gyō*), in which the practitioner performs ablutions under a waterfall. Other examples are fasting (*danjiki*) and walking over hot coals (*hiwatari*).

ASEAN and Japan →Southeast Asia and Japan

asebi　馬酔木

(Japanese andromeda). *Pieris japonica*. Also known as *ashibi* or *asebo*. An evergreen shrub of the heath family (Ericaceae) that grows wild in hilly areas of western Honshū, Shikoku, and Kyūshū and is often cultivated in gardens and parks. It reaches a height of 1.5–3 meters (5–10 ft). The leaves are broad, lance-shaped, leathery, and glossy, with serrated edges. In early spring, small, urn-shaped, white flowers appear in clusters at the ends of the branches. Long admired by the Japanese, the shrub is mentioned (as *ashibi*) in 10 poems of the 8th-century poetry collection *Man'yōshū*. Many horticultural varieties have been developed, including the *fuiri asebi*, with mottled leaves; the *usubeni asebi*, with pink flowers; the *fukurin asebi*, with white-edged leaves; and the *hime asebi*, a miniature variety. *Asebi* leaves and stems contain a toxin that causes numbness in cattle; a garden insecticide is made from the boiled leaves.

aseismatic engineering　耐震工法

(*taishin kōhō*). Aseismatic (earthquake-resistant) design is in special demand in Japan, especially for such structures as nuclear power plants and hospitals. Research on aseismatic engineering began in 1891, following a major earthquake that struck Gifu and Aichi prefectures. The devastating TŌKYŌ EARTHQUAKE OF 1923 further stimulated research. The basic principles of the most common type of aseismatic construction were established by around 1940 and have been in wide use since then. These principles include strengthening such basic structural members as posts and beams, and also reinforcing floors and walls.

In 1970, revisions to the ARCHITECTURAL STANDARDS LAW called for earthquake resistance studies at two stages in a building's design, taking into account Japan's frequent small- and medium-scale tremors as well as its less frequent major earthquakes.

In the early 1990s, all of Japan's large construction firms were researching an alternate aseismatic construction method known as the base isolation method (*menshin kōhō*). This method involves constructing a building so that the cycle at which it shakes in an earthquake is longer than the cycle of the earthquake, thereby absorbing tremors. Although this principle has been known since the 1920s, it was not applied to aseismatic construction until quite recently because of the precise and detailed analysis necessary to employ it successfully.

ashi
葦

(common reed). *Phragmites communis.* A perennial herb of the family Gramineae that grows in clusters in marshes and on riverbanks throughout Japan. Also called *yoshi.* The culm (hollow stem) grows to a height of 2–3 meters (6.6–9.8 ft). The leaf is alternate, rather stiff, and lanceolate. During summer and autumn, the flowers bloom in dark brown spikes 20–40 centimeters (7.9–15.8 in) long. The young sprout is edible. The mature culm is used to make blinds and screens (*yoshizu* and *sudare*), and the rhizome is used as a medicine. The alternative name *yoshi,* which means "good," is said to have been adopted to counter *ashi,* which means "bad."

Ashibetsu
芦別[市]

City in central Hokkaidō, at the confluence of the rivers Sorachigawa and Ashibetsugawa. Its proximity to the ISHIKARI COALFIELD once made Ashibetsu the center of a flourishing coal-mining industry. Today mining operations are minimal, food processing and lumber being the major industries. Agricultural products include rice and potatoes. Pop: 25,078.

Ashibetsudake
芦別岳

Mountain in central Hokkaidō; highest peak of the Yūbari Mountains. The eastern slope faces the Furano Basin; the western is separated from the Sorachi Mountains by the river Ashibetsugawa. The mountain is popular with climbers and skiers. Height: 1,727 m (5,666 ft).

Ashida Enosuke
芦田恵之助

(1873–1951). Educator. Born in Hyōgo Prefecture. Ashida taught from 1905 to 1921 at the elementary school attached to the Tōkyō Higher Normal School. After this period he accepted no official positions; instead he traveled throughout the country demonstrating his teaching methods. Ashida encouraged students to select their own topics for composition; this was in marked contrast to traditional Japanese methods of teaching composition, which relied upon assigned topics. See SEIKATSU TSUZURIKATA UNDŌ.

Ashida Hitoshi
芦田均

(1887–1959). Politician; prime minister in 1948. Born in Kyōto Prefecture, Ashida graduated from Tōkyō University in 1912. In 1932 he resigned from the Ministry of Foreign Affairs in protest over the MANCHURIAN INCIDENT. He joined the RIKKEN SEIYŪKAI (Friends of Constitutional Government Party) and was elected to the Diet in 1932 and in 10 subsequent elections. As head of the JAPAN TIMES from 1933 to 1940, he spoke out against military involvement in political affairs. In October 1945 Ashida joined the first postwar cabinet as minister of health and welfare. A month later, with HATOYAMA ICHIRŌ, he formed the Nihon Jiyūtō (Japan Liberal Party) but in March 1947 organized his own party, the MINSHUTŌ (Democratic Party). In June he became foreign minister in the KATAYAMA TETSU cabinet, and after Katayama's resignation he formed a coalition cabinet in March 1948. As prime minister he denied government employees the right to strike. Implicated in the SHOWA DENKŌ SCANDAL, he was forced to resign in October 1948.

Ashida Jun
芦田淳

(1930–). Fashion designer. Real name Ashida Atsushi. Born in Korea. He studied under the fashion designer Nakahara Jun'ichi (1913–83). Ashida's creations, elegantly orthodox in design, yet comfortable to wear, have won him a following among affluent women.

ashide
葦手

Decorative style of calligraphy developed during the Heian period (794–1185) in which the shapes and lines of the indigenous Japanese KANA syllabary were rendered as pictures of reeds (hence the name *ashide,* "reed script"), waterfowl, streams, rocks, and other objects associated with waterside scenery. The use of the *ashide* calligraphic style as an integral compositional element in a painting or as part of the ornamental background of fine writing paper is known as *ashide-e,* or "reed script painting," and was often employed in the decoration of poetic anthologies or Buddhist sutras. *Ashide-e* designs later came to be employed solely for their playful visual effect as decorative designs on women's embroidered trains, fans, and finely crafted lacquer ware. Occasionally KANJI (Chinese characters used for writing Japanese) were also depicted in this manner.

ashigaru
足軽

Foot soldiers of the Muromachi (1333–1568) through Edo (1600–1868) periods; they first achieved notoriety during the ŌNIN WAR (1467–77) when miscellaneous soldiery (*zōhyō*), variously called NOBUSHI (armed peasants), AKUTŌ (bandits), and *hayaashi* or *ashigaru* (the "light of foot"), ravaged Kyōto.

Equipped with little or no armor, they were highly mobile; their characteristic weapon was the lance or the bow. *Ashigaru* played an increasingly important role in warfare after the introduction of European firearms in 1543; *daimyō* organized large units of musketeers (*teppō ashigaru*). The hegemon ODA NOBUNAGA put as many as 3,000 musketeers in the field; they gained him victory in the Battle of NAGASHINO in 1575. His successor as hegemon, TOYOTOMI HIDEYOSHI, is said to have been the son of an *ashigaru.* The "light of foot" attained *samurai* status in the Edo period, being ranked as the lowest of that class.

Ashihara Yoshishige
芦原義重

(1901–). Electric company executive and business leader in the Kansai (Ōsaka-Kōbe-Kyōto) area. Born in Kagawa Prefecture. A graduate of Kyōto University, Ashihara first worked for the HANKYŪ CORPORATION. After World War II, when the KANSAI ELECTRIC POWER CO, INC, was established, Ashihara became its managing director; he assumed its presidency in 1959. Ashihara helped to create the Kansai Keizai Rengō Kai, a business organization dealing primarily with the interests of the Kansai area, and was its president from 1966 to 1977.

ashi This reed grows in marshes and on riverbanks throughout Japan. Pictured is a grove of dry ashi on the snowy lakeshore of Nishinoko in Shiga Prefecture.

Ashikaga
足利[市]

City in southwestern Tochigi Prefecture, central Honshū. It was the original base of the ASHIKAGA FAMILY, the founders of the Muromachi shogunate (1338–1573). The weaving of Ashikaga *meisen,* a silk fabric, dates to the 8th century. The city now mainly produces tricot, chemicals, and machinery. The remains of the ASHIKAGA GAKKŌ, the largest school in medieval Japan, are here. Pop: 167,686.

Ashikaga family
足利氏

(Ashikagashi). Warrior family of the 12th to 16th centuries; with the NITTA FAMILY, one of two major offshoots of the Seiwa Genji branch of the MINAMOTO FAMILY. The Ashikaga rose to prominence in the 14th century under ASHIKAGA TAKAUJI (1305–58), who established the MUROMACHI SHOGUNATE (1338–1573). Fifteen shōguns of the Ashikaga family ruled during two and a half centuries of political and social disorder.

asebi One of the horticultural varieties of the Japanese andromeda, usubeni asebi.

Origins of the Ashikaga Family—The Ashikaga family was founded by Yoshiyasu (d 1157), a grandson of MINAMOTO NO YOSHIIE (1039–1106). They took the name of their family seat, the Ashikaga estate (*shōen*) in Shimotsuke Province (now Tochigi Prefecture). Yoshiyasu's son Yoshikane (d 1199) distinguished himself in the TAIRA-MINAMOTO WAR (1180–85) and allied himself with MINAMOTO NO YORITOMO (1147–99), founder of the Kamakura shogunate (1192–1333). The Ashikaga intermarried with the HŌJŌ FAMILY, powerful shogunal regents (SHIKKEN) and the real rulers at Kamakura after Yoritomo's death in 1199.

The Muromachi Shogunate—When in 1333 Emperor GO-DAIGO (1288–1339; r 1318–39), who had left the Oki Islands to which he had been exiled for plotting against the Kamakura shogunate, again moved to overthrow the shogunate, the shogunate dispatched an army under Ashikaga Takauji to the central provinces where forces loyal to Go-Daigo had risen. However, Takauji changed sides, seizing the shogunate offices in Kyōto. Go-Daigo's KEMMU RESTORATION lasted scarcely three years; a contest between Takauji and NITTA YOSHISADA (1301–38) for military hegemony led Takauji to turn against the restoration government in 1335–36, and in 1338 he established the Muromachi shogunate in Kyōto.

The Ashikaga received legitimacy from the Northern Court in Kyōto while Go-Daigo and his descendants ruled the Southern Court at Yoshino (see NORTHERN AND SOUTHERN COURTS). The schism ended in 1392, when the Ashikaga promised to reinstate the practice of alternate succession to the throne by the two rival branches of the imperial family.

Under the third shōgun, ASHIKAGA YOSHIMITSU (1358–1408; r 1369–95), the shogun-

Genealogy of the Ashikaga Family

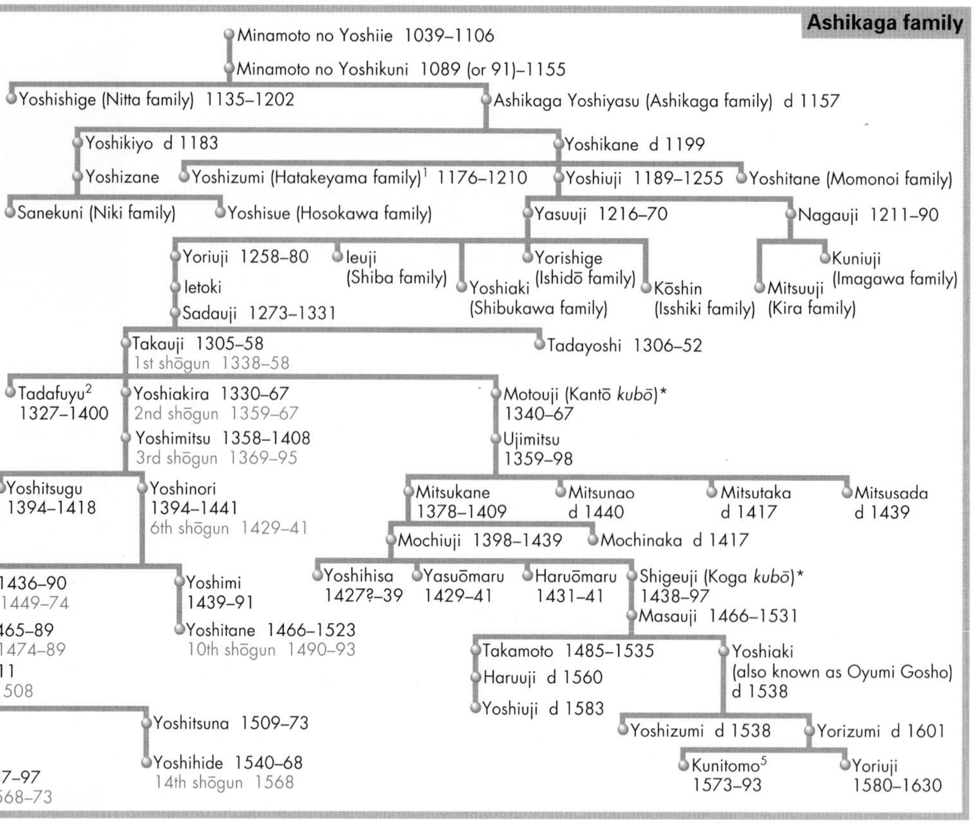

[1]Yoshizumi succeeded to the headship of the Hatakeyama family when he married the widow of Hatakeyama Shigetada.
[2]Tadafuyu was also the adopted son of Tadayoshi.
[3]Yoshimochi ruled from retirement after his son's death.
[4]This encyclopedia considers the Muromachi shogunate to have ended in 1573, when Oda Nobunaga ousted Yoshiaki from Kyōto.
[5]Kunitomo, founder of the collateral family Kitsuregawa, was also the adopted son of Yoshiuji.
*The Kantō kubō (or Kamakura kubō) and the Koga kubō were offices established during the Muromachi period (1333–1568), being held, respectively, by Motouji and three of his descendants and Shigeuji and four of his descendants.
NOTE: Time gaps in shogunal rule indicate the lack of a formally invested shōgun. Collateral family names appear in parentheses after founder names.

Minamoto no Yoshiie 1039–1106
Minamoto no Yoshikuni 1089 (or 91)–1155
Yoshishige (Nitta family) 1135–1202
Ashikaga Yoshiyasu (Ashikaga family) d 1157
Yoshikiyo d 1183
Yoshikane d 1199
Yoshizane
Yoshizumi (Hatakeyama family)[1] 1176–1210
Yoshiuji 1189–1255
Yoshitane (Momonoi family)
Sanekuni (Niki family)
Yoshisue (Hosokawa family)
Yasuuji 1216–70
Nagauji 1211–90
Yoriuji 1258–80
Ieuji (Shiba family)
Yorishige (Ishidō family)
Kuniuji (Imagawa family)
Ietoki
Yoshiaki (Shibukawa family)
Kōshin (Isshiki family)
Mitsuuji (Kira family)
Sadauji 1273–1331
Takauji 1305–58 1st shōgun 1338–58
Tadayoshi 1306–52
Tadafuyu[2] 1327–1400
Yoshiakira 1330–67 2nd shōgun 1359–67
Motouji (Kantō kubō)* 1340–67
Yoshimitsu 1358–1408 3rd shōgun 1369–95
Ujimitsu 1359–98
Yoshimochi[3] 1386–1428 4th shōgun 1395–1423
Yoshitsugu 1394–1418
Yoshinori 1394–1441 6th shōgun 1429–41
Mitsukane 1378–1409
Mitsunao d 1440
Mitsutaka d 1417
Mitsusada d 1439
Yoshikazu 1407–25 5th shōgun 1423–25
Mochiuji 1398–1439
Mochinaka d 1417
Yoshikatsu 1434–43 7th shōgun 1442–43
Masatomo (also known as Horikoshi Kubō) 1435–91
Yoshimasa 1436–90 8th shōgun 1449–74
Yoshimi 1439–91
Yoshihisa 1427?–39
Yasuōmaru 1429–41
Haruōmaru 1431–41
Shigeuji (Koga kubō)* 1438–97
Yoshihisa 1465–89 9th shōgun 1474–89
Yoshitane 1466–1523 10th shōgun 1490–93
Masauji 1466–1531
Chachamaru d 1491
Yoshizumi 1480–1511 11th shōgun 1495–1508
Takamoto 1485–1535
Yoshiaki (also known as Oyumi Gosho) d 1538
Yoshiharu 1511–50 12th shōgun 1522–47
Yoshitsuna 1509–73
Haruuji d 1560
Yoshiuji d 1583
Yoshizumi d 1538
Yorizumi d 1601
Yoshiteru 1536–65 13th shōgun 1547–65
Yoshiaki[4] 1537–97 15th shōgun 1568–73
Yoshihide 1540–68 14th shōgun 1568
Kunitomo[5] 1573–93
Yoriuji 1580–1630

Ashikaga Takauji
This 14th-century painting is thought to portray Takauji, founder of the Muromachi shogunate.

ate achieved its greatest authority and stability. Ashikaga vassals holding the title of SHUGO, or military governor, had established territorial domains, but Yoshimitsu was able to maintain a balance of power between these SHUGO DAIMYŌ and the shogunate. The principal link between the Ashikaga shōgun and *shugo* was the office of shogunal deputy (KANREI), held in rotation by the chieftains of three *shugo* houses collateral to the Ashikaga: the HOSOKAWA FAMILY, the HATAKEYAMA FAMILY, and the SHIBA FAMILY.

Yoshimitsu's sons Ashikaga Yoshimochi (1386–1428) and ASHIKAGA YOSHINORI (1394–1441) provided firm leadership in the early 15th century. The Kantō region was administered by the head of a branch line of the Ashikaga who styled himself Kantō *kubō* (literally, "shōgun of the east"; see KUBŌ). However, during Yoshinori's time the Kantō region slipped from Ashikaga control. Moreover, succession disputes plagued some *shugo* houses, including the *kanrei* houses of Shiba and Hatakeyama, and the

balance of power between shōgun and *shugo* became precarious.

Decline of the Shogunate—The ŌNIN WAR (1467–77) hastened the end of the Ashikaga hegemony. It was precipitated by a dispute within the Ashikaga family over the successor to the eighth shōgun, ASHIKAGA YOSHIMASA (1436–90), and at its close the Ashikaga hegemony had been destroyed. During the century of disunion known as the "Warring States" or SENGOKU PERIOD the Ashikaga were essentially puppets of their leading *shugo*. A new class of barons or DAIMYŌ arose to set the stage for military unification in the late 16th century. In 1573 ODA NOBUNAGA (1534–82) finally deposed the 15th shōgun, ASHIKAGA YOSHIAKI (1537–97).

As patrons of such arts as the NŌ theater, linked verse (see RENGA), monochrome INK PAINTING, and the TEA CEREMONY, the Ashikaga shōguns showed themselves far more gifted than as military despots (see also KITAYAMA CULTURE; HIGASHIYAMA CULTURE).

Ashikaga Gakkō　　足利学校

(Ashikaga School). A major educational facility of the Muromachi period (1333–1568), located in what is now the city of Ashikaga, Tochigi Prefecture. The date of its founding is unknown. It was the site of one of the two most highly regarded libraries in Japan by the time of the Muromachi period. It was formally established as a school in 1439, when UESUGI NORIZANE installed Kaigen, a monk from the temple Engakuji in Kamakura, as the first director and drew up a set of regulations. Monks made up a large part of the student body, and the curriculum concentrated on Confucian learning. Military science was the other major subject.

The school reached its zenith during the Sengoku period (1467–1568). In the mid-Edo period (1600–1868) it went into decline, finally closing in 1872. The library also went into decline in the Edo period, and many of its best holdings were lost. It was closed after the Meiji Restoration of 1868 and was preserved, along with other school property, by a historic site committee established in 1897. In 1903 the library was reestablished as the

Ashikaga Gakkō Iseki Toshokan (Ashikaga School Historic Site Library), and 77 of its 13,000 manuscripts have been designated National Treasures.

Ashikaga shogunate→Muromachi shogunate

Ashikaga Tadayoshi　　足利直義

(1306–52). General of the Northern and Southern Courts period (1337–92) and associate of his elder brother ASHIKAGA TAKAUJI, the first Muromachi shōgun. After helping Emperor GO-DAIGO in the KEMMU RESTORATION of 1333, Tadayoshi was made governor (*kami*) of Sagami Province (now part of Kanagawa Prefecture). In 1335, during the NAKASENDAI REBELLION led by Hōjō Tokiyuki (d 1353), Tadayoshi killed Go-Daigo's son Prince MORINAGA. Turning against Go-Daigo, Tadayoshi and Takauji set up a rival emperor in 1336 (see NORTHERN AND SOUTHERN COURTS) and founded the Muromachi shogunate in 1338. In their "dual shogunate" (*ryōgosho*) system Takauji took charge of military affairs and Tadayoshi of judicial and administrative matters. In 1350, however, because of conflict with Takauji's deputy KŌ NO MORONAO, Tadayoshi rebelled; in 1351 he occupied Kyōto (see KANNŌ DISTURBANCE). A reconciliation between the brothers proved to be brief. Tadayoshi fled to Kamakura, but Takauji pursued him there with an army. In March 1352, shortly after an ostensible second reconciliation, Tadayoshi died suddenly, perhaps by poisoning.

Ashikaga Takauji　　足利尊氏

(1305–58). Warrior chieftain; head of the ASHIKAGA FAMILY and founder of the MUROMACHI SHOGUNATE (1338–1573). After the accession of Emperor GO-DAIGO in 1318, opposition to the KAMAKURA SHOGUNATE (1192–1333) led to antishogunate plots in 1324 and 1331. Go-Daigo was exiled as a conspirator (see GENKŌ INCIDENT), but his son Prince MORINAGA and KUSUNOKI MASASHIGE kept the loyalists' aspirations alive. In May 1333 the shogunate dispatched an army under Ashikaga Takauji to destroy them. Takauji instead supported

Go-Daigo and captured the shogunate offices in Kyōto. The general NITTA YOSHISADA also rebelled and destroyed the heart of the shogunal regime at Kamakura.

Go-Daigo attempted to institute direct imperial rule, but his KEMMU RESTORATION was undermined by competition between Takauji and Yoshisada, and Takauji was driven into rebellion. In July 1336 he captured Kyōto and forced Go-Daigo to flee to Yoshino, south of the capital. Takauji installed Emperor Kōmyō (1322–80; r 1336–48) and founded the Muromachi shogunate in Kyōto. Go-Daigo established the Southern Court at Yoshino, which lasted until 1392 (see NORTHERN AND SOUTHERN COURTS).

Takauji received the title of SHŌGUN from the Northern Court in 1338, and Ashikaga shōguns were to rule Japan for the next 235 years. In 1351–52 Takauji found himself at odds with his brother ASHIKAGA TADAYOSHI. The latter was apparently murdered by Takauji's men early in 1352 (see KANNŌ DISTURBANCE). At his own death in 1358 Takauji bequeathed to his son and successor Yoshiakira (1330–67; r 1359–67) a regime that had effectively neutralized its potential enemy, the Southern Court. Though he had brought a measure of stability to Japan in a troubled age, Takauji was vilified by generations of historians before World War II for having mistreated Go-Daigo, a rightful emperor.

Ashikaga Yoshiaki 足利義昭

(1537–97). The 15th and last shōgun of the MUROMACHI SHOGUNATE (1338–1573); ruled 1568–73. Second son of the 12th shōgun, Ashikaga Yoshiharu (1511–50; r 1522–47). Yoshiaki became abbot of the Buddhist monastery Ichijōin at Nara in 1562. After his brother Yoshiteru (1536–65; r 1547–65) was assassinated in 1565, Yoshiaki renounced the priesthood and sought *daimyō* support for the succession. ODA NOBUNAGA seized control of Kyōto and installed Yoshiaki as shōgun in 1568, but Yoshiaki soon banded with secular and religious lords intent on destroying Nobunaga. In 1573 Nobunaga burned the greater part of Kyōto to intimidate Yoshiaki, who withdrew to Makinoshima, south of the city. Nobunaga took that fortress on 15 August 1573 and drove Yoshiaki into exile. Yoshiaki entertained hopes of a return to power until TOYOTOMI HIDEYOSHI attained paramount leadership. In 1588 Yoshiaki formally abdicated, took the priestly name Shōzan Dōkyū, and accepted a stipend from Hideyoshi.

Ashikaga Yoshimasa 足利義政

(1436–90). The eighth shōgun of the MUROMACHI SHOGUNATE (1338–1573); ruled 1449–74. Son of the sixth shōgun, ASHIKAGA YOSHINORI. Born in Kyōto. After Yoshinori's assassination in 1441, his eldest son, Yoshikatsu (1434–43), became shōgun but died two years later. Yoshimasa succeeded him in 1449 (there was no shōgun in the interval). In 1465 a succession dispute arose involving Yoshimasa's younger brother Yoshimi (1439–91), his designated successor, and Yoshihisa (1465–89), the son his wife, HINO TOMIKO, had unexpectedly borne him. The dispute intensified in 1467 into the ŌNIN WAR, which ended inconclusively 10 years later, destroying the shogunate's authority and inaugurating the century of civil strife known as the SENGOKU PERIOD (1467–1568). On 7 January 1474 Yoshimasa—who cared little for affairs of state and devoted most of his time to the arts—abdicated in favor of

Yoshihisa and retired to the Higashiyama section of Kyōto, where he built the villa that later became the temple GINKAKUJI. See HIGASHIYAMA CULTURE.

Ashikaga Yoshimitsu 足利義満

(1358–1408). Third shōgun of the Muromachi shogunate (1338–1573). Yoshimitsu was 10 when he succeeded his father Yoshiakira (1330–67) in 1369 after an interval with no shōgun. He was guided by the KANREI (shogunate deputy) Hosokawa Yoriyuki (1329–92). As the first Muromachi shōgun with sufficient authority to control the powerful SHUGO families, Yoshimitsu succeeded in consolidating the power of the shogunate and extending military control over most of the country. He also worked at ending the schism between the NORTHERN AND SOUTHERN COURTS, persuading the southern emperor in 1392 to return to Kyōto.

Yoshimitsu crushed Yamana Ujikiyo (1344–92; see MEITOKU REBELLION), and in 1400 he destroyed Ōuchi Yoshihiro (1356–1400; see ŌEI REBELLION). In 1395 he relinquished the shogunal office to his son Yoshimochi (1386–1428), but he remained in control, living in the Kitayama section of Kyōto, where he surrounded himself with artists and learned priests and lived in lavish style (see also KITAYAMA CULTURE). In 1401 Yoshimitsu established trade relations with China (see TALLY TRADE). He entered into a tributary arrangement with the Ming ruler for this purpose and in a letter to the Ming court signed himself as the "King of Japan." Yoshimitsu obtained huge profits and monopolized the import of copper currency.

Ashikaga Yoshinori 足利義教

(1394–1441). The sixth shōgun of the Muromachi shogunate (1338–1573); ruled 1429–41. Fourth son of ASHIKAGA YOSHIMITSU. Yoshinori, who had become a Buddhist monk at an early age and eventually rose to head of the Tendai sect, returned to secular life and succeeded his older brother, Ashikaga Yoshimochi, as shōgun after the latter's death in 1428. A decisive and overbearing leader who was determined to restore the shogunate's authority, he revitalized the judiciary system, strengthened his military organization, and punished or destroyed many vassals, including his kinsman Ashikaga Mochiuji (1398–1439), who was forced to commit suicide. Yoshinori's dictatorship caused disaffection among his vassals, and he was assassinated by AKAMATSU MITSUSUKE, a military leader of central Honshū.

Ashinoko 芦ノ湖

Lake in southwestern Kanagawa Prefecture, central Honshū. Located within the Fuji-Hakone-Izu National Park, Ashinoko is a popular tourist area. Area: 6.8 sq km (2.6 sq mi); circumference: 21 km (13 mi); depth: 41 m (135 ft); altitude: 725 m (2,378 ft).

Ashio 足尾[町]

Town in western Tochigi Prefecture, central Honshū. Major copper-mining center from early in the Edo period (1600–1868) until 1973, when the mine closed. In the 1890s the mine was the center of a pollution controversy. See ASHIO COPPER MINE INCIDENT; ASHIO COPPER MINE LABOR DISPUTE. Pop: 4,934.

Ashio Copper Mine Incident 足尾鉱毒事件

(Ashio Kōdoku Jiken). Early environmental disaster. Beginning in 1877 the Furukawa Mining Co, headed by FURUKAWA ICHIBEI, ex-

panded the Ashio Copper Mine in Tochigi Prefecture, causing acidic pollutants to contaminate the nearby rivers Watarasegawa and Tonegawa. From 1890 floods regularly polluted over 50,000 fertile acres in the north Kantō Plain. Local farmers began protests and petitions; and their cause was championed in the Diet by TANAKA SHŌZŌ and SHIMADA SABURŌ and was supported by a wide range of prominent journalists, socialists, and Christian humanists. In 1897 the government directed installation of expensive pollution controls, but these were not strictly enforced. The government declared the lands around the village of Yanaka "a flood overflow area" and had the village razed in 1907. Pollution continued until the mine's closure in 1973, and in 1974 farmers were awarded the equivalent of US $7 million in the first major case successfully litigated through the Environmental Disputes Coordination Commission. See also ENVIRONMENTAL QUALITY; POLLUTION LITIGATION.

Ashio Copper Mine labor dispute 足尾銅山争議

(Ashio Dōzan *sōgi*). Labor disturbance of 1907 at the Furukawa Mining Co's Ashio Copper Mine in Tochigi Prefecture. In the previous year some 600 miners, led by the labor organizers Nagaoka Tsuruzō (1864–1914) and Minami Sukematsu (1873–1964), had formed an Ashio branch of the Dai Nihon Rōdō Shiseikai, a miners' union. Violence erupted on 4 February 1907 (telephone lines were cut and buildings set on fire), and on the seventh the government sent militia units to quell the disturbance. Of the 181 miners charged with instigating a riot, 82 were convicted and jailed. After further troubles at the mine in 1919 and 1921, the miners succeeded in ridding themselves of the labor-boss system (HAMBA SEIDO). The Ashio riots inspired similar disturbances throughout Japan (see BESSHI COPPER MINE LABOR DISPUTES).

Ashio Kōdoku Jiken → Ashio Copper Mine Incident

Ashiya 芦屋[市]

City in southeastern Hyōgo Prefecture at the foot of the Rokkō Mountains. It commands a view of Ōsaka Bay and is convenient to Kōbe and Ōsaka. Ashiya has been a home to the famous and the rich; the city was the setting for TANIZAKI JUN'ICHIRŌ's novel *Sasameyuki* (1943–48; tr *The Makioka Sisters*, 1957). The ARIMA HOT SPRING is nearby. Pop: 87,524.

Ashizuri-Uwakai National Park
A lighthouse stands atop the 80-meter cliffs at Ashizurimisaki, the cape that is the centerpiece of the park.

Ashiya　　　　　　　　芦屋[町]

Town in northern Fukuoka Prefecture, Kyūshū, at the mouth of the river Ongagawa on Hibiki Bay. It has been an entrepôt for rice, coal, and salt since ancient times. The American military base established here after World War II is today a base for the Japanese Air Self Defense Force. Pop: 17,398.

Ashizurimisaki　　　　　足摺岬

Cape in southern Kōchi Prefecture, southwestern Shikoku. It is the southernmost point of the island of Shikoku. Noted for its towering cliffs, its palm trees and other subtropical vegetation, and its magnificent scenery, Ashizurimisaki is the main point of interest of ASHIZURI-UWAKAI NATIONAL PARK.

Ashizuri-Uwakai National Park
足摺宇和海国立公園

(Ashizuri-Uwakai Kokuritsu Kōen). Situated in southeastern Shikoku, in Kōchi and Ehime prefectures. It consists of several small regions scattered about the island's western side. The chief features are coastal stretches of granite cliffs, sandstone rock formations, coral reefs, and an irregular coastline with many small bays and islets. The focus of the park is the cape of ASHIZURIMISAKI, a narrow promontory at the southernmost tip of the island, famed for panoramic views of the Pacific Ocean. The area around the cape is rich in subtropical vegetation. The coastline between Minokoshi and Tatsukushi, north of the cape, is noted for its coral reefs and unusual rock formations. Southeast of the city of Uwajima is the gorge Nametoko, with fantastically shaped rocks and waterfalls. Area: 110 sq km (42 sq mi).

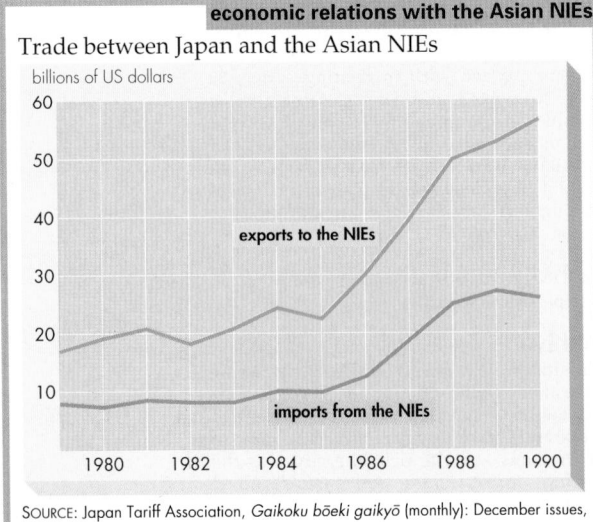

economic relations with the Asian NIEs

Trade between Japan and the Asian NIEs

billions of US dollars

[Line chart showing exports to the NIEs and imports from the NIEs from 1980 to 1990, with y-axis from 10 to 60 billions of US dollars. Exports to the NIEs rising to about 57 by 1990; imports from the NIEs rising to about 27 by 1990.]

SOURCE: Japan Tariff Association, *Gaikoku bōeki gaikyō* (monthly): December issues, 1979–90.

Asia Development Board　　興亜院

(Kōain). Cabinet agency established in December 1938 to coordinate the Japanese government's China policy. The SINO-JAPANESE WAR OF 1937–1945 had not been quickly resolved as promised by the military, and in the fall of 1938 Prime Minister KONOE FUMIMARO decided to set up a separate agency that would coordinate all government activities related to China apart from formal diplomacy, which would continue to be conducted by the Ministry of Foreign Affairs. The prime minister assumed the presidency of the board, which opened branch offices in occupied China to supervise Japanese enterprises engaged in development. It is thought that the Kōain was set up largely at the instigation of the army, which hoped to outmaneuver the Ministry of Foreign Affairs, and the board did in fact become an instrument of the military. The Kōain was absorbed by the Dai Tōa Shō (Greater East Asia Ministry; see GREATER EAST ASIA COPROSPERITY SPHERE) when that organ was created in November 1942.

Asian Development Bank
アジア開発銀行

(Ajia Kaihatsu Ginkō). Intergovernmental finance institution established to promote the economic growth of developing Asian and South Pacific countries. Founded in 1965, the bank began operations in 1966. Its headquarters are in Manila. As of 1991 the bank had 51 member countries. In 1990 the bank's two largest contributors were Japan and the United States, each of which contributed close to 15 percent of the bank's total capital. In addition, Japan contributed some 37 percent of the capital for the bank's Asian Development Fund, an interest-free fund for countries with low gross national products (below US $780 per capita). Since the bank's establishment, all of its presidents have been Japanese.

Asian Games　　　　アジア競技大会

(Ajia Kyōgi Taikai). First held in 1951 in New Delhi, an amateur sports competition among Asian nations held every four years (since 1954) midway between the Olympic Games, under the auspices of the Olympic Council of Asia. These meets are based on the ideals of the Olympics. Japan's first participation in an international meet after World War II took place at the 1951 games. Tōkyō was the site of the games in 1958. Besides the usual Olympic events, the games include sports particularly popular in the host nation. The first (1986) and second (1990) Winter Asian Games were held in Sapporo.

Asian NIEs, economic relations with　　日本・アジアNIEs経済関係

(Nihon Ajia Nīzu *keizai kankei*). The term Asian NIEs (newly industrializing economies) refers to the Republic of Korea (ROK or South Korea), the Republic of China (ROC or Taiwan), Hong Kong, and Singapore. Together with Japan, the Asian NIEs account for an increasing percentage of manufactured exports within the global economy. For the most part, economic relations between Japan and the Asian NIEs are complementary in that they are able to meet each other's needs because of differences in their relative stages of economic development. For instance, Japan's import preferences are for labor-intensive, nondurable consumer goods, an area in which the Asian

NIEs hold a comparative advantage. Japan holds an advantage in the manufacture of capital goods, which it exports to the Asian NIEs. But there are some sectors in which both are competitive, and trade disputes occasionally flare up in these areas. A dispute over growing imports of knitted textile products into Japan in 1989 is one example of growing frictions, although Japan is working to alleviate such conflicts through the restructuring of its domestic economy.

Japan-NIEs Trade—In 1990 the total value of trade between Japan and the Asian NIEs was US $82.6 billion, with Japan exporting US $56.7 billion and importing US $25.9 billion. The Asian NIEs accounted for 15.8 percent of Japan's total trade (purchasing 9.0 percent of Japan's exports and supplying 24.1 percent of Japan's imports). Japan was the second largest market for Asian NIEs exports, accounting for 11.5 percent of their 1990 total exports (the United States was the largest, at 27.4 percent). Japan was the largest single supplier for the Asian NIEs, accounting for 23.5 percent of their total imports in 1990, with the United States accounting for 17.4 percent.

Japan has run a consistent trade surplus with the Asian NIEs, making expansion of exports to the Japanese market a keen economic and political issue in these countries. Until the mid-1980s the trade pattern between Japan and the Asian NIEs was one in which Japan exported capital equipment to the Asian NIEs, which was then used to manufacture goods for export to the United States. In the late 1980s, however, the Japanese market became a destination for manufactured goods from the Asian NIEs.

Japanese Investments in the Asian NIEs—By fiscal year 1990 there were 10,549 cases of Japanese direct investment in the Asian NIEs. These were cumulatively valued at US $23.3 billion and accounted for 7.5 percent of Japan's total worldwide investments. On a country basis, direct investment stood at US $9.9 billion in Hong Kong; US $6.6 billion in Singapore; US $4.1 billion in South Korea; and US $2.7 billion in Taiwan. Rising exchange rates and labor costs have begun to erase some of the relative advantages of the Asian NIEs as a manufacturing base, resulting in a recent decline in investments by Japanese manufacturing firms.

As the Asian NIEs continue to industrialize, economic aid from Japan increasingly will shift from developmental assistance to more advanced technical cooperation projects. South Korea was the second largest recipient of bilateral official development assistance through the mid-1970s, reflecting its political and strategic importance to Japan, but the bulk of Japan's assistance now takes the form of technical cooperation. South Korea has repaid all of the development loans it received under Japan's program of financial cooperation. Technical cooperation is also the main form of assistance to Singapore, which, like South Korea, is no longer receiving developmental loans from Japan and is in the process of repaying its existing obligations.

Asics Corporation　　[株]アシックス

(Ashikkusu). Manufacturer of sporting and leisure goods. Its origins date back to 1943, but the current company was created through the merger of Onitsuka Co, Ltd, GTO Co, Ltd, and Jelenk Co, Ltd in 1977. It is known for its cooperation in international sporting events such as the Olympics. Asics has manufacturing and sales subsidiaries in

10 countries. Sales for the fiscal year ending January 1991 totaled ¥127.5 billion (US $952.3 million), and the company was capitalized at ¥23.9 billion (US $178.5 million) in the same year. Headquarters are in Kōbe.

ASMO Co, Ltd   アスモ[株]

(Asumo). Manufacturer of small motors for automobiles. Incorporated in 1979. It also is engaged in the development of electronics systems for motor vehicles. For the fiscal year ending December 1990, sales totaled ¥169.0 billion (US $1.3 billion) and capitalization stood at ¥4.5 billion (US $33.7 million). Headquarters are in Kosai, Shizuoka Prefecture.

Aso   阿蘇[町]

Town in northeastern Kumamoto Prefecture, Kyūshū. Located on the river Kurokawa and part of the ASO-KUJŪ NATIONAL PARK, it serves as a base camp for climbing Mt. Aso (ASOSAN). Aso (Uchinomaki) Hot Spring is a popular resort. Pop: 19,876.

Asō Hisashi   麻生久

(1891–1940). Socialist activist and politician. Born in Ōita Prefecture, he graduated from Tōkyō University. Joining the labor group YŪAIKAI in 1919, he led several strikes as head of its mining section. In 1923 he became secretary of the political office of the Japan Federation of Labor (see SŌDŌMEI). In 1926 he helped form the NIHON RŌNŌTŌ (Japan Labor-Farmer Party). In 1932 he helped to found the anticommunist SHAKAI TAISHŪTŌ (Socialist Masses Party), and in 1936 and 1937 was elected to the House of Representatives. Later he began to show sympathy for the military-dominated government and became involved in 1940 in the NEW ORDER MOVEMENT of Prime Minister KONOE FUMI-MARO.

Aso Hot Spring   阿蘇温泉

(Aso Onsen). Located in the town of Aso, northeastern Kumamoto Prefecture, Kyūshū. It is situated in the northern reaches of the caldera of ASOSAN, one of the world's largest volcanoes. A simple thermal spring; water temperature 25°–48°C (77°–118°F).

Aso-Kujū National Park
阿蘇くじゅう国立公園

(Aso-Kujū Kokuritsu Kōen). Situated in central Kyūshū, in Ōita and Kumamoto prefectures. The park, known as Aso National Park until 1986, is renowned for its hot-spring resorts, but its most notable feature is the volcano ASOSAN, which has one of the world's largest calderas. Within the caldera lie five central cones, one of which, Nakadake (1,520 m; 4,987 ft), is still active. The highest of the five is Takadake (1,592 m; 5,223 ft). Northeast of Asosan lies the extinct volcano KUJŪSAN (1,787 m; 5,863 ft), whose summit is covered with alpine flora and which is thickly wooded on its lower slopes. Both Asosan and Kujūsan have plateaus with good pastures for cattle. Colorful wild Kirishima azaleas (*miyama kirishima*), found only in Kyūshū, are abundant in early summer. Area: 727 sq km (281 sq mi).

ason   朝臣

Also pronounced *asomi.* The second highest of the YAKUSA NO KABANE, a system of eight hereditary titles (KABANE) established in 684 by Emperor TEMMU. The rank was bestowed upon 52 lineage groups (UJI) that claimed kinship to the Yamato imperial line. Later it was granted to virtually all prominent clans, and, with the rise of the *ason*-ranked FUJIWARA FAMILY in the late 8th century, *ason* in effect replaced the rank *mahito* as the highest position. The *kabane* system subsequently declined, and *ason* became a general honorific title for court officials of the fourth rank or higher. See also UJI-KABANE SYSTEM.

Asosan   阿蘇山

Volcano in central Kyūshū. The Aso caldera, one of the world's largest, has a circumference of 80 km (50 mi), running about 18 km (11 mi) from east to west and about 24 km (15 mi) from north to south. The Five Peaks of Aso, which are all central cones, are Takadake, Nakadake, Nekodake, Kishimadake, and Eboshidake. The radius of the lava flow created by eruptions of Asosan over the years is about 100 km (62 mi), covering the greater part of the island of Kyūshū. Nakadake still spews out volcanic ash, damaging nearby crops. Past eruptions, the most recent in 1979, have killed many people. Uchinomaki Hot Spring is located within the caldera. Asosan forms the center of Aso-Kujū National Park. Takadake is the highest point (1,592 m; 5,223 ft).

Aso Shrine   阿蘇神社

(Aso Jinja). Shintō shrine in the district of Aso, Kumamoto Prefecture; dedicated to Takeiwatatsu no Mikoto and 11 other dei-

ties. The actual date of its establishment is unknown. The deities enshrined here were associated with the ancestors of the Aso clan, the hereditary governors (*kuni no miyatsuko*) of Higo Province (now Kumamoto Prefecture). It was decreed in 1017 that each emperor would make an offering there once during his reign, and the shrine has enjoyed both imperial and popular veneration. The major festival, a rice-planting ritual known as Mitaue Matsuri, is held annually on 28 July.

Assembly of Prefectural
Governors   地方官会議

(Chihōkan Kaigi). Name given to a series of conferences of prefectural governors that played an important part in determining the structure of local government in the Meiji period (1868–1912). These conferences were planned at the ŌSAKA CONFERENCE OF 1875 as a first step toward a representative assembly. In three sessions convened between 1875 and 1880, the Assembly of Prefectural Governors discussed local administrative and tax laws and the creation of elected prefectural assemblies. It was formally abolished at the time of the 1881 edict promising the establishment of a national parliament within nine years.

Association of International
Education, Japan   日本国際教育協会

(Nihon Kokusai Kyōiku Kyōkai). An association established in 1957 with public funds

Aso-Kujū National Park
1 Morning mist across the Handa Plateau, a high plain (elevation up to 1,200 m) formed by a lava flow from the now-extinct volcano Kujūsan.
2 Snow dusts the deep crater of Nakadake, an active volcano within the Aso caldera.

astronomical observatories An array of radio telescopes at the Nobeyama Radio Observatory in Nagano Prefecture, a substation of the National Astronomical Observatory.

as an auxiliary of the Ministry of Education. It provides financial support for the educational and living expenses of foreign students in Japan. It also administers a Japanese language proficiency test for nonnative speakers and publishes English language guides to student life and study in Japan. In 1989 total assets were ¥2.9 billion (US $21.0 million). Headquarters are in Tōkyō.

Association of Japanese Geographers   日本地理学会

(Nihon Chiri Gakkai). A leading Japanese geographical society formed in 1925 by YAMASAKI NAOMASA. Its monthly organ, the *Chirigaku hyōron* (series A), publishes articles and research reports on geographical studies in Japan. The association also publishes an English-language periodical, *Geographical Review of Japan* (series B), twice a year. The association has published a number of critical studies of Japanese geography, which include English works such as *Geography in Japan* (1976) and *Geography of Japan* (1980). The number of association members is about 3,000.

Association of Private Universities in Japan   日本私立大学協会

(APUJ; J: Nihon Shiritsu Daigaku Kyōkai). Organization formed by private universities in December 1946 to promote private higher education and scholarship in general. In 1990 the APUJ had 219 member schools, making it the largest such association in Japan. The APUJ sponsors faculty training programs, engages in public relations and opinion sampling, and lobbies to influence new legislation affecting private universities. Unlike its American counterparts, the APUJ plays no role in accreditation. See also JAPAN ASSOCIATION OF PRIVATE COLLEGES AND UNIVERSITIES.

assumption of risk in contracts   危険負担

(*kiken futan*). Legal term referring to whether, in a bilateral contract such as a sales-purchase agreement, the obligations of one party can be terminated when the other party is unable to fulfill its obligations for causes beyond its control. For example, suppose A and B have concluded a contract whereby A agrees to sell something to B for a sum of money, but A's ability to transfer the item is terminated for reasons not attributable to A. If B's obligation (to pay for the object) is also terminated, A cannot receive payment in return for his obligation, and the obligor bears the risk resulting from the termination of his own obligation. This is called the doctrine of the obligor assuming the risk (*saimusha shugi*). If, on the contrary, B's obligation continues to exist, and B must pay for the item, even though he does not

obtain it, the obligee bears the risk resulting from A's obligation being terminated. This is called the doctrine of the obligee assuming the risk (*saikensha shugi*).

In general, Japan's CIVIL CODE subscribes to the doctrine of the obligor assuming the risk. If the obligation of one party is terminated for reasons not attributable to either party, the obligation of the other party (B in the example) is also terminated (art. 536 [1]). There is, however, an important exception to this doctrine: when the purpose of a contract is the establishment or transfer of real rights to a specific thing and that thing ceases to exist from causes not attributable to the parties concerned, the obligatory duty of the other party does not terminate. Also, in contracts concerned with nonspecific things, as soon as the identity of the thing is fixed, the risk is transferred to the obligee (art. 534). See also CONTRACTS.

Aston, William George   アストン, W. G.

(1841–1911). British diplomat and Japanologist. Born in Northern Ireland. Arriving in Japan in 1864, he worked for the British legation during the late Edo (1600–1868) and early Meiji (1868–1912) periods, first serving as an interpreter and later as Hyōgo (now Kōbe) consul and secretary to the legation in Tōkyō. In addition to an English translation of the *Nihon shoki* (720; tr *Nihongi*, 1896), an early chronicle of Japanese history, he was the author of such works as *A History of Japanese Literature* (1899) and *Shinto* (1905) as well as the first English-language grammar of spoken and written Japanese. He also made a comparative study of Japanese and the Indo-European languages.

astronomical observatories   天文台

(*temmondai*). There are three kinds of astronomical observatories and observation facilities in Japan: those belonging to national universities, those belonging to institutes for scientific research, and those belonging to amateur astronomers. Major astronomical observatories staffed by full-time research workers are the NATIONAL ASTRONOMICAL OBSERVATORY, the Kwasan (Kasan) Astronomical Observatory, and the MIZUSAWA ASTROGEODYNAMICS OBSERVATORY. There are also full-time research workers at the Geographical Survey Institute of the Ministry of Construction (the government agency in charge of geodetic survey astronomy for national land surveying), the Hydrographic Department of the Maritime Safety Agency, and the Ministry of Transport (the editor and publisher of the Japanese ephemeris), but their objectives are the work assigned to their agencies rather than the study of astronomy. The National Astronomical Observatory (established in 1878 as an adjunct of Tōkyō University, with its present headquarters in the city of Mitaka, Tōkyō Prefecture) is the largest in Japan; it has five observatories with research departments covering nearly all fields of astronomy except surface observation of the moon and planets and routine tracking observation of latitude. The main observatory of the Kwasan Astronomical Observatory (belonging to Kyōto University) is the Hida Observatory in Gifu Prefecture, where the surface and atmosphere of the moon and planets are studied. The Mizusawa Astrogeodynamics Observatory, located at 39° 08′ north latitude in the city of Mizusawa, Iwate Prefecture, established in 1899, has a department to observe the polar motion of the earth

and a department to study geophysics. The International Latitude Observation Project Center was once in this observatory, and the International Polar Motion Observation Project Center has been there since 1962. Most Japanese private astronomical observatories were established by amateur astronomers for their own use; these have become well known for the discovery of many new comets. See also ASTRONOMY.

astronomy   天文学

(*temmongaku*). It was not until the early Meiji period (1868–1912) that astronomy as a branch of science became established in Japan. Prior to that, astronomy was valued chiefly for its use in chronological reckoning (see CALENDAR, DATES, AND TIME). With the Meiji Restoration of 1868 the government began to promote the study of Western astronomy, and today Japanese astronomers are active in celestial physics and radio astronomy as well as classical astronomy.

History of Astronomical Studies in Japan—The Meiji government in the late 19th century encouraged practical astronomical studies, such as those concerned with geodetic surveys and navigation. In 1878 the Ministry of Education established an observatory at Tōkyō University as an educational facility; it also carried out astronomical and weather observations. In 1888 these facilities were integrated with Tōkyō University to form the Tōkyō Astronomical Observatory (now the NATIONAL ASTRONOMICAL OBSERVATORY), the only astronomical observatory in Japan at the time.

It was not until after the removal of the Tōkyō Astronomical Observatory to Mitaka on the outskirts of the city in 1924 that astronomical projects began to be carried out actively. In 1927–30 eight asteroids were discovered by Oikawa Okurō (1896–1970) and others as the result of observations with a 20-centimeter (8-in) telescope. Japanese achievements in position astronomy include the discoveries of the paths of asteroids by Hirayama Kiyotsugu (1874–1943) and the studies of the movements of artificial satellites by Kozai Yoshihide (b 1928).

The International Latitude Observatory at Mizusawa (see MIZUSAWA ASTROGEODYNAMICS OBSERVATORY) was established in 1899 and an International Time Station in Mitaka in 1923. These facilities were instrumental in the discovery by KIMURA HISASHI (1870–1943) of the Z-term in latitude variation and in Miyachi Masashi's (1902–86) detections of latitude variation.

Recent Developments—Celestial physics has been an active field of study in Western Europe and the United States since the 1930s, but the absence of large telescopes long hindered Japanese astronomers in pursuing the basic observational studies fundamental to work in this area. The Okayama Astrophysical Observatory, equipped with a 188-centimeter (74-in) reflecting telescope, was established in 1960, and since then studies have advanced greatly. Yamashita Yasumasa (b 1931) and others have published a standard spectral atlas of fixed stars based on observations made with this Okayama telescope; this atlas is highly rated as a basic reference tool.

Since radio astronomy principally developed after World War II, Japanese astronomers were able to participate actively in its establishment as a field of study. One important contribution of Japanese astronomy has been in pioneering electromagnetic radiation observations in the millimeter-wavelength

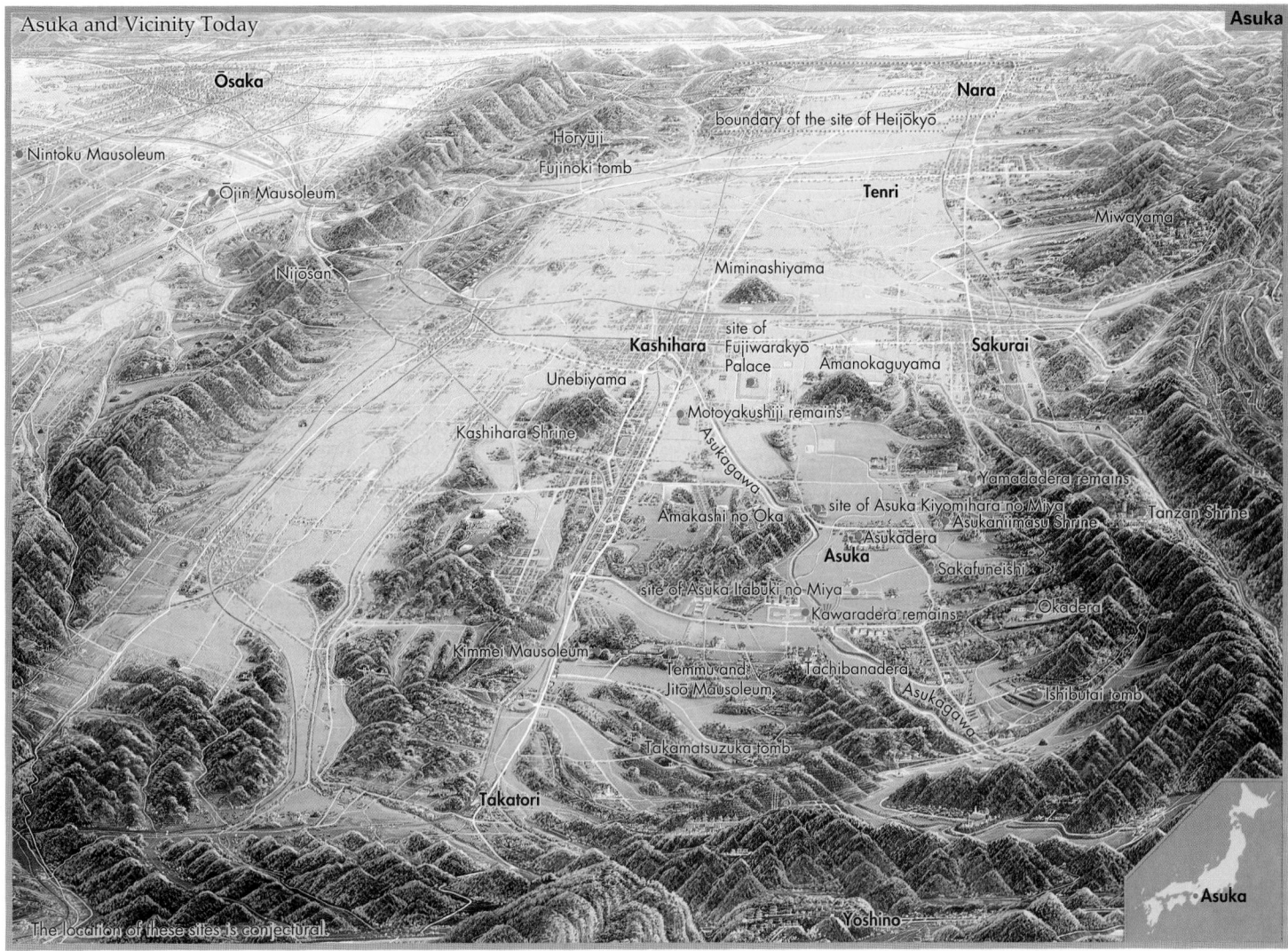

Asuka and Vicinity Today

The location of these sites is conjectural.

range. In 1987, for example, staff members at the Nobeyama Radio Observatory were the first to observe protostar nebulas using a 45-meter (147.6-ft) diameter millimeter-wavelength telescope.

To counter a lack of facilities and limited opportunities for young researchers, efforts have been made to arouse public interest by means of scholarly gatherings such as the international symposium on celestial mechanics that was held in Tōkyō in 1978 in honor of HAGIWARA YŪSUKE. Sponsored by the International Astronomical Union, this symposium gave worldwide recognition to Japanese contributions to astronomy. The Astronomical Society of Japan publishes the results of the research of its members in the English-language *Publications of the Astronomical Society of Japan* six times a year.

Asuka   飛鳥

Name for the region around the present-day village of Asuka, Nara Prefecture; the political and cultural center of Japan during the 6th and 7th centuries before the establishment of the capital at HEIJŌKYŌ in 710. From about 400 the Asuka region was settled largely by branches of the AYA FAMILY, immigrants from Korea. The residences of most Japanese sovereigns before the 8th century—including Emperor JIMMU's legendary Kashihara Palace, the palace ASUKA KIYOMIHARA NO MIYA, and the capital FUJIWARAKYŌ—were either in Asuka or close by. Many of the events described in the chronicle NIHON SHOKI (720) took place in the area.

Except for foundation stones, none of the original palace or temple buildings remains. The Asuka Daibutsu, a bronze image of the Buddha incorporating parts of one cast in 606, is housed in an Edo-period (1600–1868) building on the site of the ancient temple ASUKADERA. Asuka came to public attention in 1972 with the discovery of unusual paintings on the walls and ceiling of a stone burial vault excavated at the TAKAMATSUZUKA TOMB.

Asuka   明日香[村]

Village in northern Nara Prefecture, central Honshū. Now a quiet rural village, during the 7th century Asuka was the site of several imperial palaces (see ASUKA PERIOD). Asuka was designated a special historical area under a law protecting ancient capitals (Koto Hozon Hō). The ISHIBUTAI TOMB, the TAKAMATSUZUKA TOMB, and the temples ASUKADERA and Tachibanadera attract many visitors. Pop: 7,363.

Asuka culture   飛鳥文化

(Asuka *bunka*). The culture that developed in Japan early in the Asuka period (593–710) over a term of years centered on the reign of Empress SUIKO (r 593–628). Beginning in the mid-6th century, numerous embassies arrived from PAEKCHE on the Korean peninsula, bringing with them various Buddhist ritual objects and sutra texts; among members of these embassies were scholars of the Confucian classics, of medicine, and of calendar making, as well as priests, sculptors of Buddhist images, and builders of Buddhist temples. Asuka culture is the product of the incipient assimilation of this largely Chinese cultural assemblage. During this period the first histories of Japan (TENNŌKI AND KOKKI) were compiled in Chinese by Prince SHŌTOKU, no less than 40 Buddhist temples were constructed throughout the country, and works of Buddhist art were produced that show the strong influence of various cultural spheres in China during the period known as the Southern and Northern Dynasties (386–589). The Buddhist images fashioned by KURATSUKURI NO TORI and members of his school display the stylistic influence of the sculpture of the Chinese Northern Wei dynasty (386–535). Examples of pictorial art of the time are the paintings decorating the panels of the household votive shrine known as Tamamushi Shrine (see PAINTING). The era of Asuka culture was followed in the late Asuka period by HAKUHŌ CULTURE. See also BUDDHIST ART.

Asukadera   飛鳥寺

Also known as Moto Gangōji, Hōkōji, and Angoin. The first full-fledged temple complex built in Japan, erected soon after 588. A small sanctuary (called Angoin) still remains on the original site, located in the ASUKA district on the southeast edge of the Yamato plain about 24 kilometers (15 mi) from Nara. The early history of Asukadera is documented in the 8th-century chronicles NIHON SHOKI and *Shoku nihongi* and in its own temple records. Its founding patron was SOGA NO UMAKO, chief minister to the throne and head of the powerful SOGA FAMILY, which had championed the Buddhist faith throughout the 6th century. Umako was closely associated with Prince SHŌTOKU. The only remaining artistic relic of the temple is a bronze statue 2.75 meters (9 ft) high of the Buddha, known as the Asuka Daibutsu. It incorporates fragments from a statue completed in 606 and described in the *Nihon shoki.* See also BUDDHIST ARCHITECTURE.

Asukagawa 飛鳥川

River in the Nara Basin, Nara Prefecture, central Honshū, originating in the Ryūmon Mountains and emptying into the river Yamatogawa. It flows through such historic sites as the village of Asuka and the city of Kashihara. It is referred to in ancient poems, including the 8th-century anthology *Man'yōshū.* Length: 23 km (14 mi).

Asukai Masaari 飛鳥井雅有

(1241–1301). Courtier, WAKA poet, and scholar. Grandson of ASUKAI MASATSUNE (1170–1221), who established the family tradition of expertise in classical poetry and in the court game of kickball (KEMARI). A partisan of the innovative Kyōgoku poetic faction, Masaari had 68 poems included in imperial anthologies, beginning with the *Shoku kokinshū* (1265, Collection from Ancient and Modern Times, Continued). His personal collection, which he entitled *Rinjoshū* (Collection of Poems as Ugly as the Jealous Woman Next Door), contains more than 2,600 poems. He was also the author of a half dozen autobiographical works, including lyrical diaries and accounts of his travels to Kamakura. Masaari was noted as a student of the KOKINSHŪ and as an authority on the *Genji monogatari* (TALE OF GENJI).

Asukai Masatsune 飛鳥井雅経

(1170–1221). Progenitor of the Asukai branch of the Fujiwara family, courtier, WAKA poet, and expert in the courtly game of kickball (KEMARI). Masatsune studied classical poetry with the great Shunzei (FUJIWARA NO TOSHINARI) and was an associate of Shunzei's son Teika (FUJIWARA NO SADAIE). Masatsune was one of the compilers of the eighth imperial anthology, the SHIN KOKINSHŪ (ca 1205, New Collection from Ancient and Modern Times), which contains 22 of his poems.

Asuka Kiyomihara Code
飛鳥浄御原律令

(Asuka Kiyomihara Ritsuryō). Earliest law code of Japan to be divided into criminal laws (*ritsu*) and administrative regulations (*ryō*). Begun in 681, in the reign of Emperor TEMMU, it was promulgated in 689 under Temmu's widow and successor, Empress JITŌ. It is named for the ASUKA KIYOMIHARA NO MIYA, the imperial residence from 672 to 694. The administrative section is lost; much of the criminal section can be deduced from the NIHON SHOKI (720) and other sources. It was the model for the TAIHŌ CODE, which superseded it in 702. See also RITSURYŌ SYSTEM.

Asuka Kiyomihara no Miya
飛鳥浄御原宮

(Asuka Kiyomihara Palace). Residence of Emperor TEMMU and Empress JITŌ from 672 to 694. It is thought to have been located in the present-day village of Asuka, Nara Prefecture. The NIHON SHOKI (720) mentions a palace complex with a hall of state (DAIGOKUDEN) and administrative offices. Archaeological findings suggest that it had an elaborate drainage system and unusually shaped stone fountains. A semiurban capital district (*kyō*) grew up around the palace, and the new Capital Office (Kyōshiki) was established to govern it. After Temmu's death in 686, his widow

and successor, Empress Jitō, ruled from Asuka Kiyomihara no Miya for eight years before moving the capital in 694 to nearby FUJIWARAKYŌ.

Asuka period 飛鳥時代

(593–710; Asuka *jidai*). Period in the history of Japan dated from 593, the year in which Empress SUIKO (r 593–628) was crowned and took up residence in the Toyura Palace in Asuka, Yamato Province (now Nara Prefecture). Because written materials become more numerous from this time, the Asuka period is usually considered to coincide with the beginning of the historic age in Japan. The period also includes the decade after 645 when Emperor KŌTOKU (r 645–654) removed the capital to Naniwa (now the city of Ōsaka) and issued the edicts of the TAIKA REFORM, and the interval commencing in 694 when Empress JITŌ (r 686–697) entered FUJIWARAKYŌ and ending in 710 when the capital was shifted to HEIJŌKYŌ, marking the beginning of the NARA PERIOD (710–794).

Buddhism and the Ascendancy of the Soga Family—Asuka, a narrow area in the southeastern corner of the Nara Basin behind which rise the Yoshino Mountains, was the territory of the SOGA FAMILY, whose leaders possessed the title *omi* and served the YAMATO COURT in the ministerial capacity of financial administrators and diplomats, and who were instrumental in introducing continental culture, in particular Buddhism, to Japan. As the leading *omi*, the Soga also held the right to provide consorts and wives to the imperial line. This right was later granted to the MONONOBE FAMILY and the Nakatomi family, both of which held the title *muraji* and which were, respectively, professional soldiers and proprietors of Shintō religious affairs. Fraternal succession to the throne was common, and was initially determined by consensus of heads of the leading families (*uji*). See UJI-KABANE SYSTEM.

The issue of the acceptance of Buddhism, reported in the historical chronicle NIHON SHOKI to have been introduced in 552, became closely linked to rivalry between the Soga family on one side and the Mononobe and the Nakatomi on the other, over control of the process of kingmaking and the administration of court affairs. Buddhist ritual paraphernalia was brought from the continent by an embassy from the Korean kingdom of PAEKCHE that had come to seek military aid in its struggle against SILLA, another Korean kingdom. In addition to being a highly developed religion whose deities might be invoked to protect the nation, Buddhism held the potential of offering a broad range of cultural contributions, such as literacy, craftsmanship, and advanced forms of architecture. At the request of the emperor, but against the strong opposition of the Mononobe and Nakatomi, Soga no Iname (d 570) agreed to worship the Buddhist ritual objects. Following the death of Emperor Yōmei (r 585–587) rumor spread of a conspiracy by MONONOBE NO MORIYA to install a successor, and in 587 the Soga, led by SOGA NO UMAKO and joined by many other major *uji*, attacked Moriya in his home, destroying him and his family and with them the chief opposition to Soga dominance at court and the acceptance of Buddhism.

Early Temples and the Cultural Role of Prince Shōtoku—In 588, according to the *Nihon shoki*, Soga no Umako initiated construction of Asukadera, the first full-fledged *garan*, or temple compound, in Japan. In 593, upon acceding to the throne, Empress Suiko

declared her acceptance of Buddhism and encouraged the building of temples. In the same year, again according to the *Nihon shoki*, Prince SHŌTOKU ordered the construction of SHITENNŌJI. In 605 Shōtoku, who in 593 had been appointed regent and crown prince to Suiko, took up residence in Ikaruga, an alluvial terrace in the northwest of the Nara Basin, and at about this time built the temple Ikarugadera in fulfillment of the professed desire of his father, Emperor Yōmei. It is recorded that with the aid of Korean tutors Shōtoku studied Buddhist scriptures, on some of which he gave lectures and wrote detailed exegeses (SANGYŌ GISHO). He is also credited with writing the now lost national histories TENNŌKI AND KOKKI. In 604, he issued the SEVENTEEN-ARTICLE CONSTITUTION and established the court ranks, KAN'I JŪNIKAI, which was the first step in the process of replacing the *uji-kabane* system of hereditary titles assumed by leaders of *uji* with one based upon the merit of personal service to the sovereign.

The temples built at the direction of Shōtoku, including Shitennōji and Ikarugadera, were laid out according to a plan current in Paekche. A rectangular *garan*, or inner precinct—enclosed by a roofed corridor and entered from the south through the *chūmon*, or middle gate—contains in a line on the long north–south axis a PAGODA (*tō*), a main hall (*kondō*, literally, "golden hall"), and, in some cases, a lecture hall (*kōdō*), the front of which was flush with the corridor marking the north perimeter of the precinct. Destroyed by fire in 670, Ikarugadera was rebuilt toward the end of the century and renamed Hōryū Gakumonji (Hōryū Temple of Learning; now called HŌRYŪJI), following the practice of using sinicized names established by Emperor TEMMU (r 672–686) in 679. The new ground plan displays native innovation in the positioning of the pagoda and main hall. The long sides of the rectangular inner precinct run east to west, and a north–south line from the middle gate passes between the pagoda on the west side of the compound and the main hall on the east side.

The *Nihon shoki* reports that in 594, in the wake of Suiko's public promotion of Buddhism, the *omi* and *muraji*, who were the leading nobles at court, were vying with one another in the erection of temples. A census in 624 lists 46 temples attended by 816 monks and 569 nuns. There is mention in 680 of "the 24 temples of the capital" and in 690 of "the Seven Temples," at which resided 3,363 monks, or an average of 480 at large temples. The construction of YAKUSHIJI was ordered in 680 by Emperor Temmu when his consort, who later reigned as Empress Jitō, fell ill. Its monumental gilt bronze triad of the Buddha of healing, Yakushi (Skt: Bhaiṣajyaguru), and the bodhisattvas of the sun, Nikkō (Skt: Sūryaprabha), and the moon, Gakkō (Skt: Candraprabha), were installed in 696. The inner precinct is rectangular with the main hall at its center and two pagodas, one disposed to the east and one to the west. See also BUDDHIST ARCHITECTURE.

Imperial Palaces—It is thought that it was not until the Taika Reform of 645 and the introduction of Chinese-style palace design that emperors lived in residences substantially different from those of the leaders of powerful *uji*. Excavations at the site of the palace of Emperor Kōtoku, built between 645 and 653 in the capital city Naniwakyō, clearly show that it followed the Chinese model. There was a large compound (*chō-*

dōin) containing the Eight Ministries and behind it a smaller one, entered through a massive gate, that contained the quarters of the emperor. Similarly, reference in the annals to the great gates, gardens, hall of state (DAIGOKUDEN), ministry buildings, and imperial residence, and to the ceremonial events conducted at the emperor's court, indicate that ASUKA KIYOMIHARA NO MIYA, constructed in 672 by Emperor Temmu, also introduced many features of Chinese palace design. However, it has not been determined where in the Asuka area the palace was situated, precluding verification by archaeological study. It was the custom during much of the Asuka period for each ruler to build one or more palaces, a practice that inhibited the development of a stable political order. Fujiwara no Miya, occupied by Empress Jitō from 694 and until 710 by her successors, MOMMU (r 697–707) and Gemmei (r 707–715), was the first multigenerational palace. It was situated in the northern part of the planned city Fujiwarakyō and was closely modeled, as was the grid layout of the city itself, on the Chinese pattern.

The Taika Reform——Following the deaths of Prince Shōtoku in 622 and Soga no Umako in 626, manipulation by Soga family leaders in succession struggles became increasingly high-handed. Umako's son, Soga no Emishi (d 645), intervened to force the accession of Emperor Jomei (r 629–641) over more logical candidates. In 643, the second year of the reign of Empress Kōgyoku (r 642–645; as SAIMEI she reigned again from 655 to 661), SOGA NO IRUKA, Emishi's son, schemed to have Jomei's prince, Furuhito no Ōe, ascend the throne, and toward this end he forced the suicide of Prince YAMASHIRO NO ŌE, Shōtoku's eldest son and the leading candidate to succeed. In 645 Nakatomi no Kamatari (later FUJIWARA NO KAMATARI) and Prince Naka no Ōe, brother of Furuhito no Ōe and emperor as TENJI from 661 to 672, played leading roles in a coup in which Soga no Iruka was assassinated, followed by the suicide of Emishi. The court was removed from Soga territory to Naniwa, where its structure and functions were fully reorganized. Four edicts issued in 646 laid the basis for an ongoing process of reform and are termed, in the narrow sense, the Taika Reform. They dealt with land control and government structure and included limitations on the size of burial mounds (KOFUN). The implementation of these edicts required the definition of land boundaries (see JŌRI SYSTEM), a major system of roads, formation of local offices, a census and the levying of taxes (see SO, YŌ, AND CHŌ), allotment of land to families and individuals responsible for cultivation (see HANDEN SHŪJU SYSTEM), and the standardization of village size. By 649, eight state ministries, after the Chinese model, presided over by ministers, and a new system of 19 ranks for the nobility had been established.

The Reigns of Emperors Tenji and Temmu——Domestic security in the wake of the Taika reforms was threatened by Silla, which was poised to conquer the entire Korean peninsula, so that the pace of reform slowed considerably after 650. An army was dispatched to the peninsula to defend Paekche against Silla and its powerful ally Tang (T'ang) dynasty (618–907) China. Empress Saimei went to Kyūshū to direct military operations but died there in 661, and during the reign of the succeeding emperor Tenji Japan was defeated in a decisive naval engagement with the Tang in 663 and Paekche was vanquished (see HAKUSUKINOE, BATTLE OF). Hasty

measures were taken to fortify north Kyūshū, but the Tang fleet was withdrawn.

Emperor Tenji expired in 672 and his son ascended the throne as Emperor Kōbun. In the same year, however, Kōbun was defeated in battle (see JINSHIN DISTURBANCE) by Tenji's brother, who, as Emperor Temmu, made further reforms in the system of hiring provincial and central government bureaucrats, established in 684 a new system of eight court ranks (YAKUSA NO KABANE) under which the former high titles *omi* and *muraji* were displaced toward the bottom, and initiated the compilation of legal statutes that were distributed in 689 as the ASUKA KIYOMIHARA CODE. The Asuka Kiyomihara Code was the first Japanese legal code that was divided into criminal laws (*ritsu*) and administrative regulations (*ryō*), and it was the basis for the more comprehensive TAIHŌ CODE of 701. See also ŌMI CODE.

Culture——Although the Chinese system of writing was in use in Japan in the 6th century, the oldest extant inscriptions are on halos of Buddhist images of the early 7th century and on *mokkan* (wooden tallies used for recording the receipt of goods) excavated from Asuka no Itabuki Palace, which was occupied around the mid-7th century by the empress who reigned as Kōgyoku and Saimei. Paekche sent specialists in a number of fields, such as priests and diviners, temple builders, bronze casters, and roof tile makers; it also introduced to Japan the Confu-

cian classics, continental music and dance, and Chinese court ceremonies. Calendar makers arrived in 602 and by the 8th century the Chinese practice of using era names (*nengō*) was fully established.

Reading and writing in Chinese spread among the aristocracy and it is recorded in the introduction to the KAIFŪSŌ (751), an anthology of Chinese poetry by Japanese, that Chinese verse was being written at the court of Emperor Tenji in the mid-7th century. The use of Chinese characters to denote Japanese words or syllables, the method employed to write the mid-8th-century anthology of Japanese poetry MAN'YŌSHŪ, seems to have developed by the 7th century; it was by this means that the great early poets of the native tradition, such as KAKINOMOTO NO HITOMARO and NUKATA NO ŌKIMI, recorded their verses.

Almost all of the works of art that remain from the Asuka period are related to Buddhist worship. The Shaka (Sākyamuni) Triad (623) at Hōryūji by KURATSUKURI NO TORI, a work that is strongly influenced by Northern Wei (386–535) sculptural style, is the earliest piece of Buddhist statuary that can be positively dated. Another important piece from about the same period is the seated bodhisattva at CHŪGŪJI. An important example of painting of the 7th century is the Tamamushi Shrine, on whose panels are depicted scenes

Atami The bright lights of hundreds of hotels and spas illuminate the sea and mountains surrounding the city of Atami, a hot-spring resort since the 8th century.

from the previous lives of the Buddha and other Buddhist scenes.

Asukata Ichio
飛鳥田一雄

(1915–90). Politician; chairman of the JAPAN SOCIALIST PARTY (1977–83). He was born in Yokohama and graduated in 1937 from Meiji University Law School. In December 1945 he helped to reorganize the Japan Socialist Party. After serving in the Kanagawa Prefectural Assembly, he was elected in 1953 to the House of Representatives, where for 10 years he effectively opposed the government on defense and diplomatic issues. Elected mayor of Yokohama in 1963, the following year he formed the National Association of Progressive Mayors. As chairman of the Japan Socialist Party, he sought to unite its various factions and cooperate with other opposition parties against the ruling Liberal Democratic Party. Asukata resigned as party chairman in 1983; ISHIBASHI MASASHI succeeded him.

Atagawa Hot Spring
熱川温泉

(Atagawa Onsen). Common-salt spring in the town of Higashi Izu, Izu Peninsula, eastern Shizuoka Prefecture, central Honshū. Located in a scenic area, it is a popular tourist spot featuring the Atagawa Tropical and Alligator Garden. Water temperature 32°–100°C (90°–212°F).

Atago Shrine
愛宕神社

(Atago Jinja). Shintō shrine in Ukyō Ward, Kyōto, on the mountain ATAGOYAMA. It is now divided into two shrines. The main shrine (hongū) is dedicated to Izanami no Mikoto, who was mother of the fire god; Wakumusubi no Kami, a deity of agriculture; and three other deities. The subsidiary shrine (wakamiya) is dedicated to the fire god, Kagutsuchi no Mikoto, and two other deities. The Shintō deities of the Atago Shrine were thought to protect the capital, prevent fires, and look after the well-being of warriors. Pilgrims climb the mountain on 31 July to buy talismans for protection from house fires. The annual festival is held on 28 September.

Atagoyama
愛宕山

Mountain to the northwest of the city of Kyōto; one of the Tamba mountains. The ATAGO SHRINE is located at its summit. Height: 924 m (3,031 ft).

Ataka
安宅

NŌ play. Attributed to KANZE NOBUMITSU. It is classified as a yobamme-mono ("part-four play"). MINAMOTO NO YOSHITSUNE (the kokata or child character), who has quarreled with his elder brother MINAMOTO NO YORITOMO, is fleeing north in disguise to the Ōshū Fujiwara family stronghold at Hiraizumi. At the government barrier station at Ataka in Kaga Province, he and his followers must deceive the guard (the waki or subordinate

character) in order to proceed. Yoshitsune's loyal retainer BENKEI (the shite or main character) picks up a handscroll the disguised warriors have with them, claiming that it is a kanjinchō (document authorizing solicitation of religious donations) issued by the great Nara temple TŌDAIJI and reads it aloud to intimidate the guard, whom he also threatens with physical force. Very much aware of the travelers' identities but impressed by Benkei's loyalty, the guard permits the group to continue north. See also KANJINCHŌ.

Atami
熱海［市］

City in eastern Shizuoka Prefecture, central Honshū, on the Izu Peninsula. Overlooking Sagami Bay and surrounded by mountains on three sides, it is noted for its mild climate and numerous hot springs. Atami developed as a resort town in the 8th century. The construction of the Tanna Tunnel in 1934 and the Tōkaidō Shinkansen (the super-speed railway) in 1964 has made it one of the most frequented resorts in Japan. A part of FUJI-HAKONE-IZU NATIONAL PARK, Atami has easy access to JIKKOKU PASS, the island of HATSU-SHIMA, and the Nishikigaura coast. There is a plum festival in January, a fireworks display in early August, and in the fall a festival honoring author OZAKI KŌYŌ, whose novel Konjiki yasha (1897–1903; tr The Golden Demon, 1905) is partially set here. Pop: 47,291.

Atōda Takashi
阿刀田高

(1935–). Short-story writer. Born in Tōkyō. Graduate of Waseda University. He received the Award of the Mystery Writers' Association of Japan in 1979 for Raihōsha (The Caller). A master of high-spirited, yet polished, short stories, Atōda won the Naoki Prize for Naporeon kyō (1979; tr Napoleon Crazy and Other Stories, 1986). His other works include the short-story collections Yumehandan (1983, Dream Judgment) and Atama wa bōshi no tame ja nai (1988, The Head Was Not Made for Wearing Hats).

atomic bomb
原子爆弾

(genshi bakudan). The first atomic bomb to be used against human targets was dropped at 8:15 AM, 6 August 1945, on Hiroshima, Japan, a city of approximately 350,000 people. Three days later a second bomb was dropped at 11:02 AM over Nagasaki, population 270,000.

Historical Background—In 1939, fearing Nazi Germany might develop an atomic bomb, Albert Einstein urged President Franklin Delano ROOSEVELT to initiate an American atomic weapons program. Finally launched in 1942, after the United States had entered World War II, the Manhattan Project eventually engaged 125,000 people to produce fissionable uranium 235 and plutonium 239; it also mobilized thousands of scientists at Los Alamos, New Mexico, to produce the bomb itself.

Although historians are still debating whether the use of the first atomic bombs against Japan resulted from a series of specific decisions or from the project's momentum and the pressures of war, the first documented discussion of targets suggests that the Japanese fleet in the harbor of Truk, one of the Caroline Islands, was under consideration as of 1943. On 31 May 1945 the Interim Committee, set up to advise the new president, Harry S. TRUMAN, on atomic policy, concluded that the target should be within Japan, that the bomb should be used without specific warning, and that "we should seek to

make a profound psychological impression." It was further suggested that the most desirable target would be "a vital war plant employing a large number of workers and closely surrounded by workers' houses" and that the bomb should be used on an area relatively undamaged by conventional bombing. On 13 June the targets of Kokura, Niigata, and Hiroshima were chosen; Nagasaki was added later.

By this time there were signs that Japan was seeking to end the war, although the Allies largely discounted these. A cable from the Japanese Foreign Ministry communicated to the Soviet Union the emperor's desire to end the war swiftly. Joseph Stalin relayed this message to Truman at the Potsdam Conference, unaware that it had already been intercepted and decoded by the United States. Truman by this time also knew of the success of the first atomic bomb test conducted at Alamogordo, New Mexico, on 16 July. The POTSDAM DECLARATION, calling for Japan's unconditional surrender, was issued 26 July. Some in the US government believed that if assurances were included in the declaration that the Allies were willing to permit retention of the emperor system, Japan would probably be persuaded to surrender. The declaration, however, contained no mention of this.

By early August the two bombs thus far produced were in the South Pacific and assembled. The decision was made to drop one over Hiroshima on the first clear day, which turned out to be 6 August. The second bombing, scheduled for 11 August, was moved up to the 9th, in view of the weather forecast. Nagasaki was substituted for Kokura. The bomb dropped on Hiroshima was 3.0 meters (9.8 ft) long and 0.7 meters (2.3 ft) in diameter, weighing 4.0 metric tons (4.4 short tons). Only 1.0 kilogram (2.2 lb) of the 10.0–30.0 kilograms (22.0–66.0 lb) of uranium 235 used actually fissioned, producing the trinitrotoluene (TNT) equivalent of 13 kilotons of explosive power. The Nagasaki bomb, both larger (1.5 meters [4.9 ft] in diameter and 4.5 metric tons [5.0 short tons]) and longer (3.5 meters [11.5 ft]), used plutonium 239 to produce an explosive power equal to 22 kilotons of TNT. Despite the greater power of its bomb, Nagasaki sustained less damage than Hiroshima because of differences in terrain and the location of the hypocenter (the point on the ground above which the bomb detonated).

In each city the bomb detonated 500–600 meters (1,640–1,970 ft) above the ground. The explosion created a massive fireball, with the temperature near the point of explosion (epicenter) reaching as high as several million degrees centigrade (in contrast to several thousand with a conventional bomb). A mushroom-shaped cloud was observed rising after the explosion. Approximately 35 percent of the total energy generated by the bomb was transmitted as heat rays (thermal radiation), 50 percent in the form of blast (expansion of air), and 15 percent as radiation.

Immediate Effects of the Atomic Bombs—The temperature at the hypocenter was estimated at 3,000°–4,000°C (5,400°–7,200°F). An iron bar melts at half that temperature. Those exposed to heat rays within 1.0 kilometer (0.6 mi) of the hypocenter died within a week, their skin and internal organs ruptured by the intense heat. People as far away as 3.5 kilometers (2.2 mi) suffered skin burns. Spontaneous combustion and charring of buildings, railroad ties, fences, and other materials occurred within a 3.0-kilometer (1.9-mi) radius from the hypocenter.

As air surrounding the epicenter rapidly expanded, shock waves at or above the speed of sound were followed by a subsonic flow of air. Theoretical calculations show that a height of 600 meters, approximately where both bombs exploded, maximizes the destructive power of the blast through the Mach effect, the turbulent intensification that occurs when shock waves reverberating from the ground collide with oncoming waves. Within 2.0 kilometers (1.2 mi) of the hypocenter, all wooden structures were obliterated; concrete buildings generally withstood the pressure, although they were damaged. People near the hypocenter were blown into the air, whether inside or outside buildings.

Fire storms caused by thermal radiation and secondary sources ravaged both cities, lasting several hours in Hiroshima and burning every combustible object within a 2.0-kilometer radius. In Hiroshima 70,000 of 76,000 buildings near the hypocenter were destroyed beyond use; in Nagasaki approximately 18,000 of 49,000 were unsalvageable. Because of its hilly terrain, Nagasaki did not suffer as intense a fire storm. Moisture condensing on rising ash and dust later came down as "black rain" in both cities.

A lethal dose of radiation is considered to be 700 rads; a semilethal dose is 400 rads, and half of those who receive it will die. Those within 1.0 kilometer of the hypocenter in Hiroshima and 1.2 kilometers (0.7 mi) in Nagasaki received at least a semilethal dose. Approximately 20 percent of the total deaths are attributed to initial exposure to gamma rays and neutrons emitted within one minute of the explosion, but those who entered the cities within 100 hours after the bombings also received a considerable dose of residual radiation.

Aftereffects of the Atomic Bombs— According to a 1977 estimate some 130,000–140,000 people died in Hiroshima and 60,000–70,000 died in Nagasaki by the end of 1945 (there is, however, quite a range of estimates; for example, see ATOMIC-BOMB-RELATED DISEASE). In both cities the death rate within 1.0 kilometer was close to 100 percent, decreasing to 50 percent between 1.0 and 1.5 kilometers. Among total related deaths by the end of 1945, 60 percent were from burns caused by thermal radiation and fire, 20 percent from blast injuries, and 20 percent from radiation. The death rate of 50 percent of the population in both cities by 1950 was much higher than the rate in even the heaviest conventional bombings, which ran around 17 percent.

The effects of atomic bombs on humans are usually divided into acute effects (those that developed by the end of 1945) and delayed effects. Although acute effects were caused by the synergy of heat, blast, and radiation, delayed effects were often due to radiation alone. Those who received heavy doses of radiation, even though their burns or other injuries were not so severe as to cause death within the first week, developed such symptoms as weakness, nausea, vomiting, diarrhea, bloody vomit, bloody stools, and bloody urine. Most of these people died within 10 days of the bombing. Those who survived later developed other symptoms, such as hair loss, hemorrhage, declining white-cell and platelet counts, and oral and pharyngeal lesions.

Although most hibakusha (atomic bomb survivors, including those who entered the

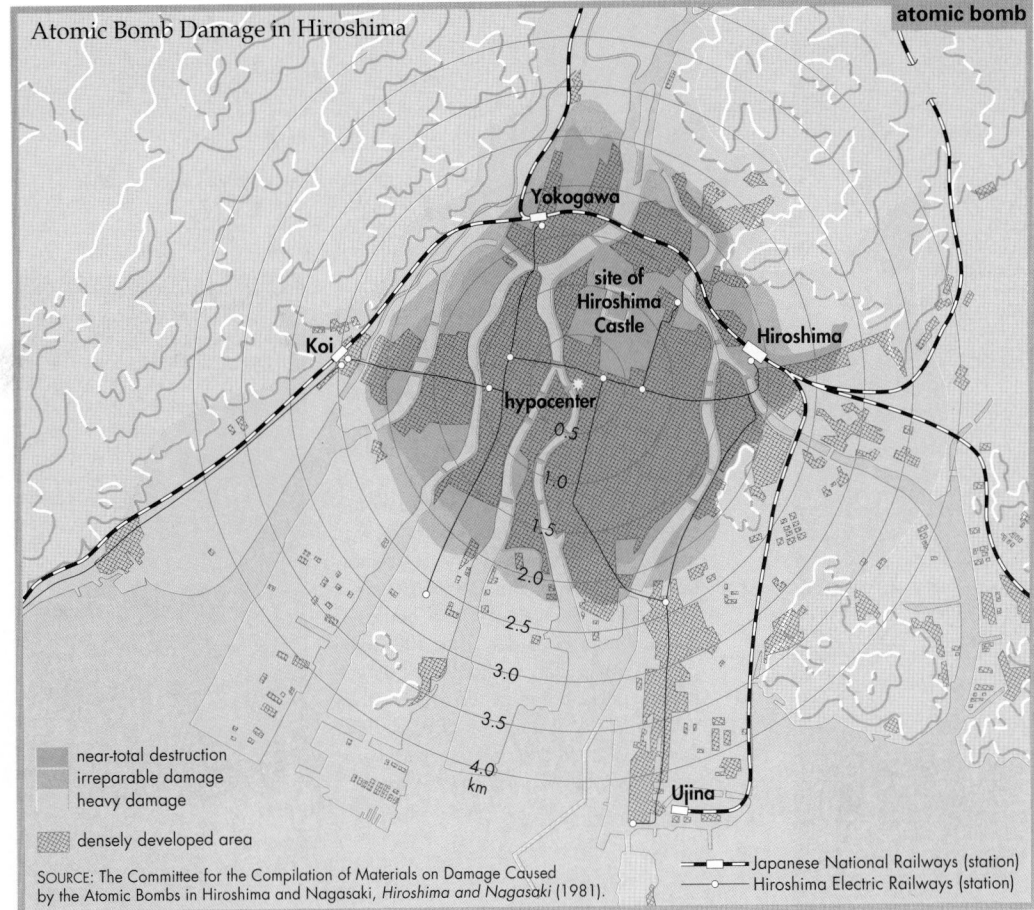

Atomic Bomb Damage in Hiroshima

near-total destruction
irreparable damage
heavy damage

densely developed area

SOURCE: The Committee for the Compilation of Materials on Damage Caused by the Atomic Bombs in Hiroshima and Nagasaki, *Hiroshima and Nagasaki* (1981).

Japanese National Railways (station)
Hiroshima Electric Railways (station)

affected areas soon after the bombings) who lived through the acute stage seemed to regain health, delayed effects gradually appeared. After the burns from thermal radiation healed, there remained protuberant keloid scars on over half the burn victims. The incidence of cataracts was high, showing a definite correlation with radiation dosage. A decrease in the production and count of white and red blood cells and platelets still persisted among some hibakusha even 10 years afterward. Leukemia and multiple myeloma, cancers of the blood, both remain higher among hibakusha than among the general population. Leukemia is also observed among those who entered either city immediately after the explosion. The incidence of malignant tumors among hibakusha increased around 1960, with cancers of the thyroid, breast, lungs, and salivary gland correlating with radiation received.

Development problems occurred among those exposed to the blast while young or *in utero*, since the actively dividing cells of the young are more sensitive to radiation. Height and weight of young hibakusha were significantly less than those of comparable groups in the general population. Delayed growth and congenital malformations such as microcephaly (abnormally small head, accompanied by mental retardation in severe cases) appeared among the several thousand children exposed *in utero* to radiation at Hiroshima and Nagasaki. No definite research has yet demonstrated, however, that the unexposed offspring of hibakusha are suffering from any genetic changes.

Hibakusha have also suffered psychological problems. After the explosion they were "immersed in death," watching families, friends, and colleagues lying dead around them or hearing their pleas for help. Their ability to survive emotional collapse was due to the mechanism of "psychic numbing." As the delayed effects of radiation began to appear, hibakusha realized that

theirs was a "permanent encounter with death."

Because normal support structures within the family and community were destroyed, it was even more difficult for survivors to cope. More than half of all families lost their main breadwinner, thousands of children were orphaned, and rates of unemployment, job change, and absence from work were higher for hibakusha than for others. Poor health and poverty have plagued the survivors, and the numerous social, economic, physical, and emotional problems that afflict them intensify with age. Non-Japanese hibakusha (including the nearly 40,000 Koreans affected by the two bombs) and the approximately 1,000 hibakusha now living in the United States have fared even worse, usually because their countries have no special provisions for dealing with atomic bomb victims.

Postwar Developments— In the immediate postwar years it was difficult for hibakusha to learn what had happened to them or to receive specialized medical care. The War Victim Relief Law of 1942 was administered by the Japanese military until early October 1945, after which victims received treatment only at their own expense. In September 1945 the Allied forces in Japan issued a press code effectively banning release of any information on the atomic bomb; they also restricted Japanese research on the bombs' effects. In early 1947 the United States established the Atomic Bomb Casualty Commission (ABCC), whose studies produced much of the available information on the bombs' effects. But, as a research organ, the ABCC only tested hibakusha; it did not offer medical treatment. Not until 1957, when Japan passed the Law for Health Protection and Medical Care for Atomic Bomb Explosion Sufferers (known as the A-Bomb Medi-

Continued on page 78 ➤

A Tragic End to a Tragic War

The United States exploded the first atomic bomb in a test at Alamogordo, New Mexico, on 16 July 1945. Immediately thereafter the heavy cruiser *Indianapolis* left San Francisco with the components of a second atomic device in its hold. On 25 July, the day before the Potsdam Declaration was issued, US president Harry S. Truman authorized use of the weapon against Japan. Acting Chief of Staff Thomas T. Handy issued the order: "The 509 Composite Group, 20th Air Force, will deliver its first special bomb as soon as weather will permit visual bombing after about 3 August 1945 on one of the targets: Hiroshima, Kokura, Niigata, and Nagasaki."

Hiroshima

At 1:45 AM (Japan time) on 6 August 1945 the B-29 bomber *Enola Gay* took off from Tinian in the Mariana Islands. It carried a uranium-235 atomic bomb. Weather observation planes had departed for Hiroshima, Kokura, and Nagasaki an hour earlier. The primary target, Hiroshima, was then being fortified by the Japanese as a stronghold against the Ameri-

The watch Futagawa Kengo wore as he crossed Kannon Bridge, 1.6 kilometers from ground zero, at the moment the bomb exploded over Hiroshima. He died 16 days later.

Victims gathered at Miyuki Bridge roughly three hours after the Hiroshima blast. Some of the people at left have already died. Miyuki Bridge was 2.2 kilometers from the hypocenter.

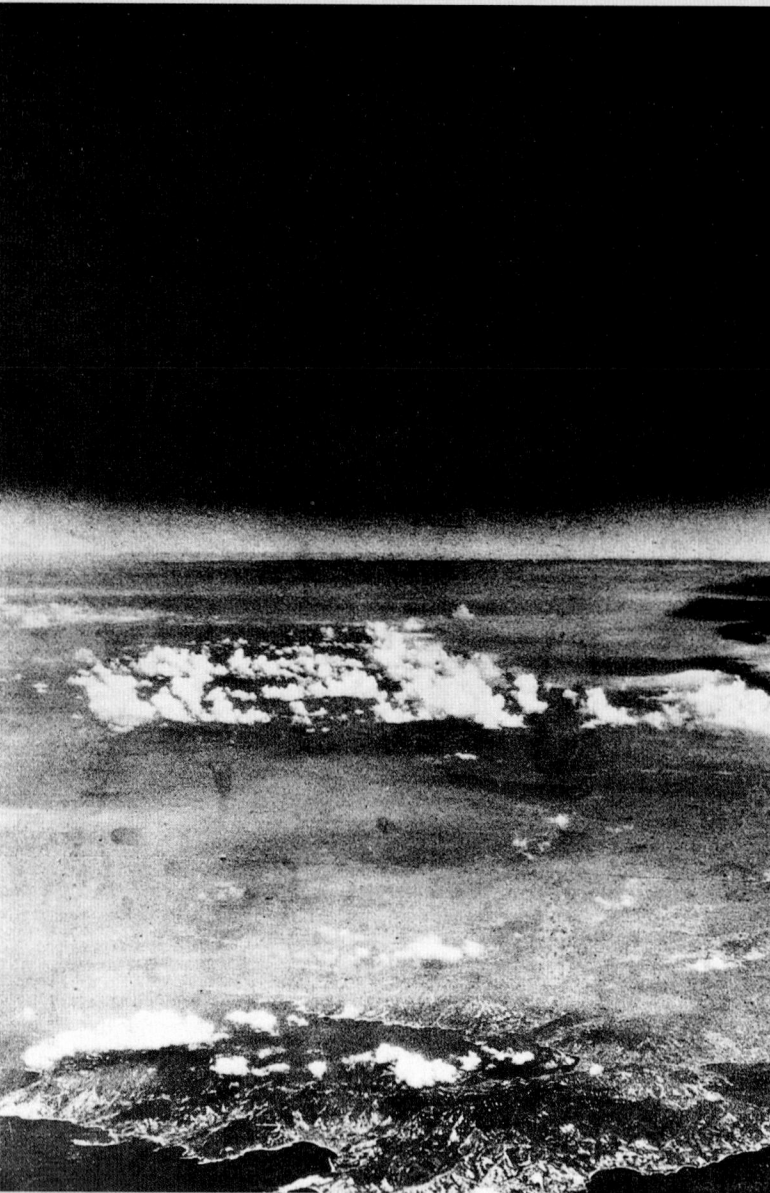

76

can invasion they expected. Crews of men, women, and students were at work dismantling and clearing away buildings and houses to create firebreaks. Above them the skies were clear. At roughly 7:30 AM an observation plane sent a coded signal to the *Enola Gay*, then 45 minutes away, that it should proceed to Hiroshima and drop the bomb.

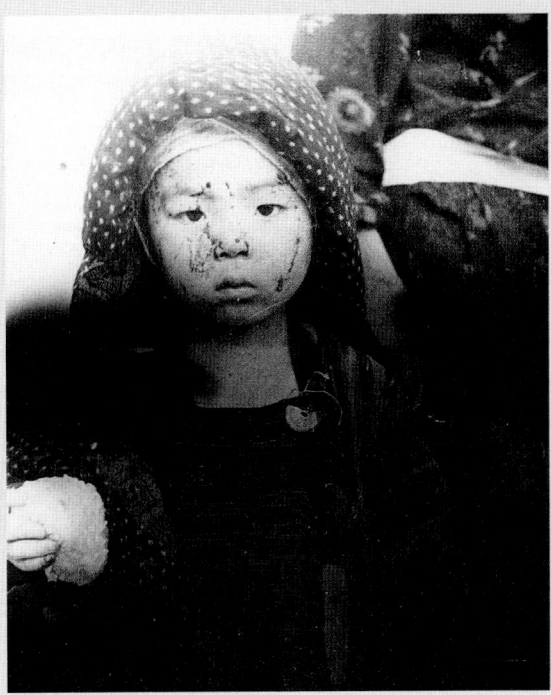

▶ **A boy holds a rice ball** given out by an emergency kitchen on 10 August, the day after Nagasaki was hit.

◀ **Hiroshima around one hour after the bomb exploded,** as photographed from a US plane. What is left of the city lies beneath the mushroom cloud. Observers on the ground reported that at times the darker portions of the cloud gave off a pink or orange glow. (Photo from US Armed Forces Institute of Pathology.)

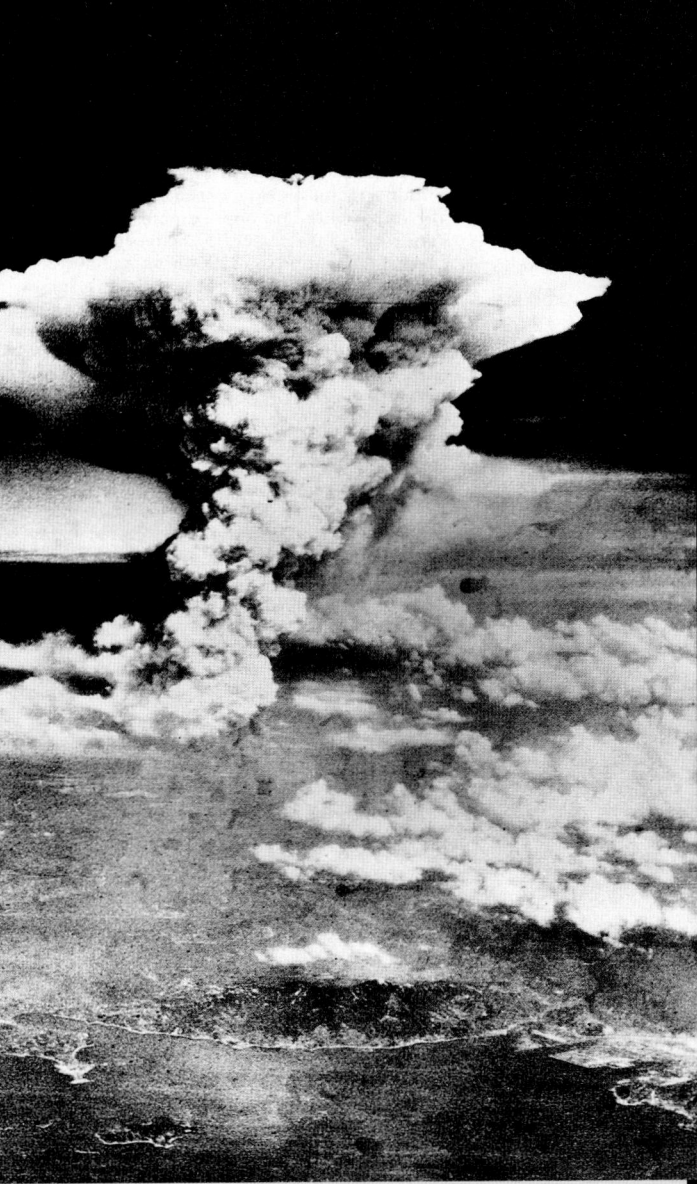

▶ **The Romanesque Urakami Cathedral,** which took 20 years to build and was once the grandest in Asia, stands in ruins. It was located in the Urakami district of Nagasaki.

▼ **The Hiroshima Prefecture Industrial Promotion Hall,** at left center, has been preserved as shown in this October 1945 photograph and is known as the Atomic Bomb Dome. The hypocenter of the blast was 160 meters southeast of the building at an altitude of 580 meters.

Nagasaki

On 9 August a second atomic bomb was dropped. The earlier bomb had reduced Hiroshima to a plain of rubble in an instant; the plutonium-239 device dropped on Nagasaki was almost twice as powerful. The objective of the bomb run was the heavily built-up Urakami Valley. The nearly four kilometers of homes, schools, churches, and factories along its length were entirely destroyed by the shock wave and ensuing fires. Fire-fighting and rescue efforts proved hopeless, and survivors were left to wander aimlessly. Six days later Japan surrendered.

Clinical Symptoms of Radiation Injuries

Degree of severity[1]	First week	Second week	Third week	Approximate mortality and time of death in weeks
Very severe (Group I)	Nausea and vomiting ■ Fever, apathy, delirium, diarrhea ■ Lesions[2] ■ Leukopenia ■	Fever ■ Emaciation Leukopenia ■ Anemia Hemorrhagic diathesis Epilation ■		100% First or second
Severe (Group II)	Nausea and vomiting ■ Anorexia Fatigue	Fever ■ Leukopenia Anemia	Anorexia, emaciation, fever, diarrhea, epilation ■ Oropharyngeal lesions ■ Hemorrhagic diathesis ■ Leukopenia ■ Anemia	50% Third to sixth
Moderately severe (Group III)	Gastrointestinal syndrome[3] ■	Leukopenia ■	Anorexia, emaciation, fever, diarrhea, epilation ■ Oropharyngeal lesions ■ Hemorrhagic diathesis ■ Leukopenia ■ Anemia	Less than 10% Sixth or later
Mild (Group IV)	Gastrointestinal syndrome	Leukopenia ■	Fever ■ Epilation Oropharyngeal lesions ■ Hemorrhagic diathesis ■ Leukopenia ■	None

■ ■ ■ rate the symptoms in order of increasing severity.

[1] These descriptive terms were used by the US-Japan Joint Commission, appointed in October 1945 by the United States National Academy of Sciences and the Science Council of Japan to carry out long-term research on radiation effects.
[2] These lesions (ulcerations) occurred on all mucous membrane surfaces but were more prevalent in lymphoid areas than elsewhere. The tonsils, pharynx, larynx, nasal passages, and tongue were frequently involved.
[3] Gastrointestinal syndrome includes nausea, vomiting, anorexia, and diarrhea.
NOTE: This classification is presented only as an orientation; there was undoubtedly overlap between categories.
SOURCE: T. Ohkita, "Acute Effects," Journal of Radiation Research, Supplement (1975).

cal Law), were *hibakusha* extended free medical examinations and care for injuries or sickness due to the atomic bombs. Approximately 360,000 people now hold *hibakusha* certificates enabling them to receive benefits under this law.

In the SAN FRANCISCO PEACE TREATY, which formally ended the war, the Japanese government renounced its right to claim war damages against the United States. It was later made clear that this included the right of *hibakusha* to claim compensation. In 1963 the Tōkyō District Court ruled that since a group of *hibakusha* who had sued the government had no right of claim against the United States under either domestic or international law, they could not juridically lay the obligation on Japan. At the same time, the court recognized that the atomic bombings of Hiroshima and Nagasaki were violations of international laws of war, and also ruled that the issue of compensation from the Japanese government originates in its responsibility for the war's outbreak. Five years later the Hibakusha Special Welfare Law was enacted to aid victims through special financial allowances. By 1976 approximately one-third of those who had been issued *hibakusha* certificates received some aid under the law.

The governments of Hiroshima and Nagasaki, with help from nonprofit organizations, citizens' groups, doctors, and others, have taken the lead in establishing A-bomb hospitals, nursing homes, recreational facilities, and special agencies for the *hibakusha*. The two cities have held memorial services for victims every year since 1946, and both are active in promoting world peace. Religious organizations have also been active, setting up orphanages and workshops to help *hibakusha* deal with their suffering. The primary aid for survivors, however, has come from among themselves. After postwar economic conditions improved and the peace treaty brought an end to press restraints, *hibakusha* in both cities formed self-help organizations to improve their economic, social, and medical situations. In 1956 the Japan Confederation of A- and H-Bomb Sufferers Organizations (Nihon Gensuibaku Higaisha Dantai Kyōgikai, or Hidankyō) was formed to unify the objectives of various *hibakusha* groups. By the late 1950s the larger antinuclear PEACE MOVEMENT subsumed *hibakusha* efforts. As of the early 1990s, Hidankyō's goal was the enactment of a national compensation law for *hibakusha*, based on the responsibility of the Japanese government for the outbreak of war. Hidankyō believes that such a law would not only help *hibakusha* but would also solidify the Japanese commitment to peace embodied in the CONSTITUTION OF JAPAN. 🔗 76–77

atomic-bomb-related disease

原爆症

(*gembakushō*). Direct atomic bomb injuries include those caused by the mechanical, thermal, and radiation effects of a nuclear explosion; victims of the atomic blasts in Hiroshima and Nagasaki in 1945 suffered such injuries. Radioactive fallout of fission products causes injuries even to people far from the site, as in the Bikini atoll test explosion in 1954.

The number of deaths in Hiroshima by November 1945 due to the atomic bomb is estimated by a report dated 1951 to have been about 64,600; the corresponding figure for Nagasaki is estimated by a similar report dated 1956 to have been about 39,000. (There are various other estimates; for example, see ATOMIC BOMB.) The actual number of dead is considered much larger because these statistics do not include military personnel. In 1947 the Atomic Bomb Casualty Commission (ABCC) was organized and administered with the cooperation of the Japan National Institute of Health. In April 1975, the ABCC evolved into the Radiation Effects Research Foundation (RERF), in which Japan and the United States both participated.

Tsuzuki Masao (1892–1961), a doctor who studied the clinical course of Hiroshima and Nagasaki bomb injuries, divided the course into four periods: first (early) period, within two weeks of the explosion; second (middle) period, third to eighth week; third (late) period, third to fourth month; and fourth (last) period, long term. In the first period, almost 100 percent of the population within a radius of 500 meters (1,640 ft) from the hypocenter and approximately 80 percent within 1,000 meters (3,280 ft) died from blast and radiation injuries, burns, and other traumas. Symptoms in other victims included systemic emaciation, anxiety, fever, vomiting, and such hemorrhagic manifestations as mucosal bleeding, hemoptysis, hematemesis, and melena. Epilation and cutaneous hemorrhage were observed in the second period. About half the deaths occurred during the first week, three-fourths by the end of the second week, and the remaining one-fourth during the second period; that is, the victims who were fated to die did so within two months after exposure. In and after the third period, injuries stabilized or improved to some degree.

Mechanical Injuries—Glass fragments, beams, and roof tiles blown off collapsing buildings caused most mechanical injuries. Even people as far away as 5,000 meters (16,400 ft) from the hypocenter suffered mechanical injuries. Severe injuries such as fractures were infrequent, possibly because many crippled victims burned to death. The most common injuries were contusions and lacerations. The body areas most commonly affected were the head, face, neck, and upper limbs. Some injuries were complicated by burns and radiation problems. Of the mechanically injured, 50 percent healed within 4 weeks and 90 percent within 20 weeks, although some victims still have glass fragments embedded in their bodies today.

Burns—The majority of burns were flash burns. The temperature of the hypocenter is estimated to have reached 3,000° to 4,000°C (5,400° to 7,200°F). Burn injuries occurred within 0.3 seconds of the explosion. In Hiroshima flash burns were observed among people within a radius of approximately 4.5 kilometers (2.8 mi). The widespread fires caused another type of injury, fire burns. Half the fire burns suppurated. Fifty percent of the flash burns healed by the 4th week, 90 percent by the 18th week, and 95 percent by the 23rd week after the explosion. Burns were observed among approximately 90 percent of the people in Hiroshima who were unshielded and within 4.0 kilometers (2.5 mi) of the hypocenter, and among 78 percent of the comparable population in Nagasaki.

Radiation Injuries—The effects of ionizing radiation are the chief characteristics of atomic bomb injuries. The severity of radiation injuries depends on the exposure dose. Exposure doses resulting from residual radioactivity are estimated at approximately 80 rads at the hypocenter in Hiroshima and 50 rads in Nagasaki. Acute symptoms among victims surviving three weeks or more after the explosion included vomiting, fever, epilation, purpura, and oropharyngeal ulceration, all of which varied according to exposure. An ABCC survey showed that acute

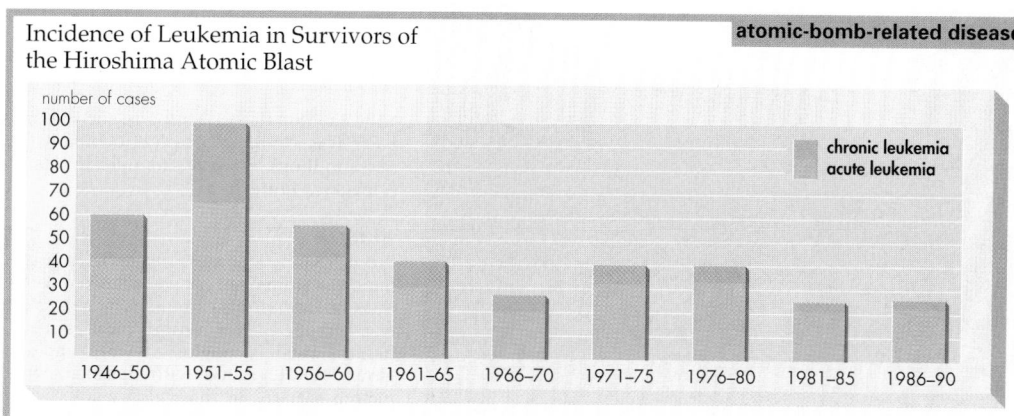

Incidence of Leukemia in Survivors of the Hiroshima Atomic Blast

number of cases

chronic leukemia
acute leukemia

1946–50 1951–55 1956–60 1961–65 1966–70 1971–75 1976–80 1981–85 1986–90

NOTE: These statistics include new cases reported yearly involving survivors who were within 2,000 meters of the hypocenter of the explosion. While accurate contemporary records of survivors are not available, a 1975 survey recorded 36,114 survivors, and a 1989 survey recorded 28,163 survivors. In 1990, an average of 4.37 cases of leukemia of all types were reported for every 100,000 persons in Japan.
SOURCE: Kamata Nanao, Research Institute for Nuclear Medicine and Biology, Hiroshima University.

symptoms occurred in 5 to 10 percent of survivors exposed to doses of 50 rads and in 50 to 80 percent of those who received approximately 300 rads.

Late-effects studies made so far have been largely epidemiological. The incidence of leukemia, in particular, began to increase about three years after exposure to the bomb, reached a peak in 1951, and gradually decreased thereafter. Nevertheless, the present level of incidence is higher than usual. The incidence of acute leukemia among survivors who were under 16 years of age at the time of exposure increased during the first 10 years but has decreased since 1960. Chronic leukemia has been high among survivors who were 30 years of age and over. In general, the incidence of chronic myeloid leukemia has been higher than normal, especially among Hiroshima survivors. The incidence of leukemia rises with an increase in exposure dose, and there has been a difference between the survivors in Hiroshima and those in Nagasaki, probably because the two cities had different patterns of radiation. The incidence of leukemia is high among victims exposed to doses of 20 rads or higher in Hiroshima and 100 rads or higher in Nagasaki. No increase in the incidence of leukemia has been observed among children exposed to the bomb *in utero* or whose parents were irradiated.

Other forms of cancer are also found among survivors. A 1960 report revealed that thyroid carcinoma was more frequent among those exposed to higher doses of radiation. The incidence of thyroid carcinoma among those so exposed was 6 to 9 times higher than usual for women and 2 to 3 times higher for men. The risk of breast cancer in females exposed to doses of 200 rads or higher has been 3.6 times higher than usual. The rate of mortality from lung cancer during the period 1950–70 among bomb survivors exposed to doses of 200 rads or higher was 1.5 times greater than usual. In addition, approximately 2.5 percent of the survivors who were within 1.0 kilometer (0.6 mi) of the hypocenter developed cataracts, the first proven late effect of the bomb.

In Hiroshima retarded body weight and height was observed among survivors who were under 7 years of age at the time of the bombing, but no apparent lag appeared among survivors 12 years of age or older. Young adults exposed to estimated doses of 100 rads or higher were 3 to 5 centimeters (1.2 to 2.0 in) shorter and 3 to 4 kilograms (6.6 to 8.8 lb) lighter than normal. Retarded mental capacity was found in about half of the 60 microcephalic children whose mothers had been exposed to high doses of radiation.

According to a Radiation Effects Research Foundation investigation, malignant lymphoma, stomach cancer, salivary gland tumors, and hematologic disorders other than leukemia were more prevalent among bomb victims. Lymphocyte cultures have revealed that the frequency of chromosome aberrations among bomb survivors is higher than usual and proportional to exposure doses. As yet, the effects of these aberrations on future health is unknown.

Bikini Radiation Injuries—Radioactive fallout produced by a US thermonuclear test in the Pacific Bikini atoll at about 3:50 AM (JST) on 1 March 1954 inflicted radiation injuries on 23 Japanese fishermen, 239 Marshall Islanders, and 28 Americans, who were all at a great distance from the test site. The Japanese exposed to the fallout, the crew of the *Lucky Dragon V* (see LUCKY DRAGON INCI-

DENT), were males aged between 18 and 39. The initial general symptoms appearing in the crew included fatigue, nausea, vomiting, and anorexia. Conjunctivitis was observed in all cases. Leukopenia, thrombopenia, and moderate or mild anemia also occurred. A few cases also showed mild hemorrhagic tendencies. These findings correlated with the condition of the crew's bone marrow. The affected bone marrow ran a course from aplasia to hypoplasia to partial recovery to normalization. As the bone marrow recovered, peripheral blood-cell counts approached normal levels. A temporary decrease in the number of spermatozoa was found, but signs of recovery appeared two years after exposure, and there was no permanent exposure-related sterility. The main site of injury was the exposed areas of the skin. Work clothes, gloves, and shoes played an unexpected role in preventing the crew from beta-ray exposure.

Atomic Energy Commission
原子力委員会

(Genshiryoku Iinkai). Prime minister's advisory commission that oversees the research, development, and use of nuclear power in Japan. Founded in 1956. The committee consists of five members and is headed by the director of the Science and Technology Agency. The commission publishes the *Genshiryoku hakusho* (White Paper on Nuclear Energy) annually.

atomic energy, laws concerning
原子力関係法

(*genshiryoku kankei hō*). A special characteristic of Japanese laws concerning atomic energy is that, because of the RENUNCIATION OF WAR clause (art. 9) contained in the 1947 constitution, the laws limit the uses of atomic energy to peaceful purposes. The centerpiece of nuclear energy legislation is the Basic Law concerning Atomic Energy (Genshiryoku Kihon Hō, 1955), which contains the three principles that nuclear research, development, and utilization will be for peaceful purposes only; that there will be full public disclosure; and that administration will be autonomous and democratic.

The peaceful uses of nuclear energy are broadly classified into use as a source of power and use of radioactive isotopes. The basic laws and regulations relating to the use of nuclear energy regulate nuclear materials and reactors, prevention of radiation and radiation sickness, and liability for damages caused by nuclear energy.

Atomic Energy Research Institute, Japan
日本原子力研究所

(Nihon Genshiryoku Kenkyūjo). Government research corporation founded in 1956

to promote the research, development, and utilization of atomic energy. Its activities include the basic and applied study of atomic energy, research in such areas as high-temperature gas-cooled nuclear reactors and nuclear fusion, the training of researchers, and the production and distribution of radioactive isotopes. It maintains research facilities at the Tōkai Research Laboratory (Ibaraki Prefecture), the Takasaki Radiation Chemistry Research Laboratory (Gumma Prefecture), the Ōarai Research Laboratory (Ibaraki Prefecture), and the Radio Isotope Center (Tōkyō).

atomic weapons, movement to ban
原水爆禁止運動

(*gensuibaku kinshi undō*). With the US nuclear attacks on Hiroshima and Nagasaki in early August 1945, during the final days of World War II, Japan became the only country to experience atomic devastation. However, the anti-nuclear-weapons movement did not congeal into a force of national significance until the mid-1950s because of difficult living conditions immediately after the war and the restrictions imposed by the Allied OCCUPATION. Testing by the United States of a hydrogen bomb on Bikini Island in 1954 provided the catalyst. A Japanese fishing vessel called the *Lucky Dragon V* (see LUCKY DRAGON INCIDENT) happened to wander into the radioactive radius just after the blast. Several of the ship's crewmen fell ill, one dying from exposure to the radioactive fallout. The incident caused an uproar in Japan. A signature-collecting campaign was begun in May 1954 to protest nuclear tests and call for the abolition of all nuclear bombs, and more than 30 million signatures were eventually gathered.

In September 1955 the Gensuibaku Kinshi Nihon Kyōgikai (Japan Council against Atomic and Hydrogen Bombs; commonly called Gensuikyō) was founded, seeking to abrogate the UNITED STATES–JAPAN SECURITY TREATIES as part of its efforts to eliminate all nuclear arms. Gensuikyō had broad support from the citizenry, but when the JAPAN COMMUNIST PARTY and its supporters gained a dominant influence within the organization, rival factions broke off and formed their own groups. In 1961 the Democratic Socialist Party and the Liberal Democratic Party formed the Kakuheiki Kinshi Heiwa Kensetsu Kokumin Kaigi (National Council for Peace and against Nuclear Weapons; also called Kakukin Kaigi). In 1965 the Japan Socialist Party formed the Gensuibaku Kinshi Nihon Kokumin Kaigi (Japan Congress against Atomic and Hydrogen Bombs; also called Gensuikin).

Atsuta Shrine This Shintō shrine has enjoyed the patronage of the imperial court since the 9th century. Here, priests perform an annual ritual, held on 11 January, to dispel evil and bring good fortune.

Atsumi Kiyoshi A 1970 film poster of the actor in the role that made him famous: Tora san, the plainspoken hero of the film series *Otoko wa tsurai yo* (It's Tough Being a Man).

Organizational fragmentation diminished the effectiveness of the movement, but, at the time of the United Nations Second Special Session on Disarmament (SSD II) in 1982, the SSD II Japanese Liaison Committee for Nuclear and General Disarmament, representing a cooperation of several groups, mounted another signature campaign. Other groups initiated their own campaigns, and a total of 82 million signatures were carried to United Nations headquarters in New York.

Atomi Kakei   跡見花蹊

(1840–1926). Educator and painter; founder of Atomi Gakuen, now a private women's educational institution consisting of a middle school, a junior college, and a university. Born in Ōsaka, the daughter of a poet; original name Atomi Takino. In her mid-teens she went to Kyōto to study traditional poetry and the painting of the MARUYAMA-SHIJŌ SCHOOL. After operating private schools in both Ōsaka and Kyōto, she went to Tōkyō and in 1875 started the private school that came to be known officially as Atomi Gakuen.

Atsugi   厚木[市]

City in central Kanagawa Prefecture, central Honshū. Situated on the river SAGAMIGAWA, Atsugi developed as a port and one of the post-station towns in the Edo period (1600–1868). A commuter suburb of Tōkyō, it produces automobile components, electrical appliances, and rubber goods. Fishing for *ayu* (sweetfish) on the Sagamigawa is a popular pastime; the Ayu Festival is held in August. Pop: 197,283.

Atsugi Nylon Industrial Co, Ltd   厚木ナイロン工業[株]

(Atsugi Nairon Kōgyō). One of Japan's leading manufacturers of seamless stockings and tights. Incorporated in 1947. The company is also engaged in manufacturing panty hose, socks, foundation garments, and lingerie. The firm has a production joint venture in Korea and a sales organization in Hong Kong. Sales for the fiscal year ending November 1991 totaled ¥52.6 billion (US $402.4 million), and capitalization stood at ¥48.2 billion (US $368.9 million) in the same year. Corporate headquarters are in the city of Ebina, Kanagawa Prefecture.

Atsugi Unisia Corporation   [株]アツギユニシア

(Atsugi Yunishia). Automobile parts maker affiliated with the NISSAN MOTOR CO, LTD. Incorporated in 1956 as a result of the separation of the Atsugi plant from its parent company, Nissan Motor. It manufactures propeller shafts, clutches, pistons, and suspension parts. It has incorporated production plants in Taiwan and Mexico. Sales for the fiscal year ending February 1991 totaled ¥170.3 billion (US $1.3 billion), and the company was capitalized at ¥11.0 billion (US $84.3 million). Headquarters are in Atsugi, Kanagawa Prefecture.

atsuita   厚板

A type of heavy brocade (NISHIKI). Originally imported from China, it was named after the thick boards (*atsuita*) around which the cloth was wrapped. The most typical is a six-harness twill of unglossed warp and unglossed weft ground with optional, weft-picture patterns in thick glossy silk.

For male characters in the NŌ theater, *atsuita* often functions as a small-sleeved undergarment over which a cloak such as the *happi*, *mizugoromo*, or *sobatsugi* is worn. For old men's roles, *atsuita* costumes have stripes or checks without pictorial designs. For warrior costumes, short, design-float stitches compose triangles, hexagons, or lattice patterns. Supernatural-being roles use bold designs with strong color contrast. Garments with long float stitches forming a surface design over the geometric ground designs are known as *atsuita kara-ori* and may be worn draped as a cloak over broad divided skirts (*hangiri*).

Atsumi Kiyoshi   渥美清

(1928–). Comic actor. Real name Tadokoro Yasuo. Born in Tōkyō. In the early 1950s he began working as a comedian in the Asakusa amusement district of Tōkyō. In the late 1950s he began to appear on television. He made his film debut in 1958. With the phenomenal success of the series *Otoko wa tsurai yo* (It's Tough Being a Man), which was created by YAMADA YŌJI in 1969 and included 43 films as of 1991, he became familiar to the public under his character's name, TORA SAN. He also appeared in Nomura Yoshitarō's *Haikei tennō heika sama* (1963, Greetings, Mr. Emperor) and HANI SUSUMU's *Buwana Toshi no uta* (1965, Bwana Toshi).

Atsumi Peninsula   渥美半島

(Atsumi Hantō). Located in southern Aichi Prefecture, central Honshū. Bounded on the north by Atsumi Bay and on the south by the Enshū Sea, this long narrow stretch of land extends about 10 km (6 mi) east to west. Iragomisaki, a cape at its southwestern tip, is noted for its spectacular rock formations and lovely beach, and portions of the coastline are included in the Mikawa Bay Quasi-National Park. Area: 200 sq km (77 sq mi).

Atsumori   敦盛

NŌ play by ZEAMI. Classified as a *nibammemono* ("part-two play"), it is based on a story from the HEIKE MONOGATARI. A former warrior, KUMAGAI NAOZANE (the *waki* or subordinate character), visits Ichinotani, site of the battle where he slew TAIRA NO ATSUMORI. Kumagai's part in young Atsumori's death had moved him to enter a Buddhist order, taking the priestly name Renshō, and he comes to Ichinotani to pray for the repose of Atsumori's spirit. A flute is heard, and the grounds keepers who tend the battle site appear. One of them is an incarnation of Atsumori (the *maejite* or main character at the beginning of a play); the rest function as the *tsure* or "companion" characters. Renshō chants prayers for Atsumori's spirit throughout the night, and Atsumori's ghost (the *nochijite* or main character at the end of a play) appears before him. The angry ghost dances a reenactment of the decline of the Taira clan and Atsumori's death. About to attack its former enemy, the ghost refrains when it realizes the contrite Renshō is praying on its behalf. Beseeching him to continue, the ghost vanishes.

Atsuta Shrine   熱田神宮

(Atsuta Jingū). Shintō shrine in Atsuta Ward, Nagoya, Aichi Prefecture, which purportedly enshrines the sacred sword known as the Kusanagi no Tsurugi ("grass-cutting sword"), one of the three IMPERIAL REGALIA. According to tradition, the shrine was built by the consort of the legendary hero Prince YAMATOTAKERU, whose life was miraculously saved by this sword during his campaign to bring eastern Japan under imperial rule. Atsuta Shrine enjoyed the patronage of the imperial court from the 9th century and that of the Muromachi and Tokugawa shogunates from the 15th century. The annual festival date is 5 June.

attachment   差押え

(*sashiosae*). Compulsory procedure provided by civil courts to prevent persons from disposing of their assets or the legal rights to such assets by physical or legal means. Attachments under the Law of Civil Execution are most typically a part of compulsory civil enforcement proceedings. As the first step in obtaining satisfactions of monetary claims under private law, the code forbids the debtor from disposing of his or her assets or from exercising his or her legal rights regarding such assets and requires such assets to be preserved. For attachment to be permitted, there must be a judgment for payment, a provisional order for payment, an instrument of execution, or some other proof of debt authorizing the attachment.

In general, all the property of the debtor at the time of the attachment may be levied upon, but there are some exceptions. These include things that cannot be transferred because of their intrinsic nature (personal rights) or because of legal prohibitions (opium, counterfeit money) and things that are exempted from attachment for various other reasons (necessities for daily living of the debtor and his or her family). Attachment is also permitted under the National Tax Collection Law as a stage in the collection of unpaid taxes, and under the Code of Criminal Procedure for the seizure of material evidence or other objects. See also ADMINISTRATIVE LAW.

Attu   アッツ島

(Attsutō). The westernmost of the American Aleutian Islands; scene during World War II of the first "total sacrifice" (*gyokusai*) by Japanese forces. Having seized Attu on 7 June 1942, some 2,500 troops reportedly fought to the last man before 12,000 American troops retook the island on 30 May 1943. In fact, the Americans took 29 prisoners.

audiovisual education   視聴覚教育

(*shichōkaku kyōiku*). Since the end of World War II, audiovisual education has been fully developed and widely used in Japan. Educational silent films were frequently used in classrooms in the 1920s, and in 1933 the publicly operated Japan Broadcasting Corporation (see NHK) started radio broadcasts for school use. After World War II, audiovisual education was given an enormous boost with the introduction of the theories of the Americans C. F. Hoban and E. Dale and the US Occupation authorities' encouragement of using films in classrooms.

Recently, there has been growing interest in the educational potential of television, audio and video tapes, and other electronic media. Audiovisual media are used mostly in elementary schools; EDUCATIONAL BROADCAST-ING has become very popular, with television programs produced by NHK being shown in virtually all elementary schools.

auditing standards 監査基準

(*kansa kijun*). Current Japanese auditing standards were established in 1956 as a tentative statement of the Council of Business Accounting of the Ministry of Finance, although they have been subjected to several revisions since then. Japanese auditing standards are divided into three sections. Section 1 includes general standards covering the auditor's professional competence as well as fairness, due care, and other ethical questions; summaries of sections 2 and 3 are also included. Section 2 includes fieldwork standards covering the scope of the auditor's responsibility and the application of audit sampling techniques. Section 3 includes reporting standards covering the content of the auditor's report.

August First declaration 八・一宣言

(Hachiichi *sengen*). Joint appeal issued by the Chinese Communist Party and the Chinese Soviet Government calling for a united front of all Chinese to oppose Japan's incursions in North China. Issued on 1 August 1935, the declaration proposed that the Communist Party and the ruling Nationalist Party end their civil war and unite in resistance against Japanese aggression. On the same day the Comintern issued its own appeal for a Chinese united front. The Nationalist government rejected all appeals to cooperate with communists until the XI'AN (SIAN) INCIDENT of December 1936, when its leader, Chiang Kai-shek, was forced to accept the principle of a united front.

Aung San アウンサン

(1915–47). Burmese political leader. A prominent nationalist in the years before World War II, he organized the Burma Independence Army with Japanese assistance in 1942 (see MINAMI KIKAN) and later became minister of defense in BA MAW's wartime regime. He was soon disillusioned by Japan's occupation policies and helped to form the Anti-Fascist People's Freedom League, which rose against the Japanese early in 1945. Upon his return from independence talks in London in 1947, he was assassinated at the instigation of a political rival. See also BURMA AND JAPAN.

Australia and Japan
オーストラリアと日本

(Ōsutoraria *to* Nihon). The relationship between Australia and Japan has become of considerable international importance because of the rapid development of trade between the two countries in the 1960s and 1970s and its continued expansion in the 1980s and 1990s. The two economies have become highly complementary, Australia supplying Japan principally with minerals and agricultural products, and Japan supplying Australia largely with manufactured items. This economic relationship in turn has led to a developing political relationship of great significance in the western Pacific region.

From the late 1950s onward, the discovery and exploitation of vast mineral wealth in Australia coincided with the extremely rapid development of the manufacturing industry in Japan, and this coincidence created opportunities for economic exchange that both countries were quick to seize. By the late 1970s Japan was by far the largest market for Australia's exports and was exceeded only marginally by the United States as the largest source of Australian imports. In the overall trading picture of Japan, Australia loomed less large, although it was a key source of certain vital resources, notably iron ore, coal, alumina, bauxite, and wool. The balance of trade was consistently in Australia's favor.

Historical Background——Contacts between Australia and Japan date to shortly before the Meiji Restoration (1868). The first Japanese actually to settle in Australia, a circus proprietor, arrived in Queensland in 1871. By the time the Australian federation was formed in 1901, there were more than 3,000 Japanese residents, but the Immigration Restriction Act of 1902, which provided for a dictation test "in a European language," effectively prevented further entry of more than a very few Japanese on short-term visits. See AUSTRALIAN IMMIGRATION POLICY AND JAPAN.

Before World War II, Britain was by far Australia's largest trading partner. By the mid-1930s, however, a healthy 13 percent of Australia's exports went to Japan, which had become Australia's second-largest export market. This market was curtailed in 1936 by the so-called trade-diversion episode. A rapid increase in imports of Japanese textiles at the expense of textile imports from Britain led to British pressure upon Australia to reduce Japanese imports. In May 1936 Australia unilaterally imposed new and high tariffs on Japanese textiles, which in turn led to discriminatory treatment by Japan against imports from Australia. After it became clear that both sides were being seriously harmed by these policies, it was agreed in 1937 to relax them. In December 1940 Tōkyō became the second capital (Washington was the first) where Australia set up a legation independent of the British diplomatic establishment.

During World War II, Australian territory was directly threatened by the Japanese armed forces. A planned invasion, however, was not carried out. Politically the most important consequence of the war from the Australian point of view was that the United States replaced the United Kingdom as the principal guarantor of Australian security.

Postwar Development——Immediately after the war the general Australian attitude toward Japan remained extremely hostile. The Australian Labor government believed that the emperor should be tried as a war criminal and strong measures taken to prevent the revival of Japanese industry. William MacMahon BALL, the Australian who was the British Commonwealth member of the ALLIED COUNCIL FOR JAPAN in 1946 and 1947, was frequently at loggerheads with General Douglas MACARTHUR concerning basic policy for Japan. The Australian government sought a significant role in the postwar administration of Japan, but though Australia provided the largest contingent in the BRITISH COMMONWEALTH OCCUPATION FORCE, centered on Kure, near Hiroshima, and was represented on the Allied Council for Japan and the FAR EASTERN COMMISSION, the role that Australia was allowed to play was far smaller than that initially envisaged. See OCCUPATION.

The government of Robert Menzies, which came to power in December 1949, pressed for restrictions on Japanese rearmament to be written into the peace treaty but

was forced to back down in the face of lack of support from most of the other Allied powers. The ANZUS Pact—signed by Australia, New Zealand, and the United States at the same time as the peace treaty with Japan—served to reassure an Australian government that was becoming more concerned about the possibilities of communist, rather than Japanese, aggression. The Australian Labor Party and sections of the trade union movement, however, maintained their suspicions of Japan well into the 1950s.

The Growth of Trade——The Agreement on Commerce between Australia and Japan—signed in 1957, renewed in 1960, and amended in 1963—was a turning point in relations between the two countries and laid the groundwork for a trade boom of major proportions. The agreement guaranteed both sides most-favored-nation status in respect to tariffs, while also providing that there should be no discrimination in respect to trade between them unless discriminatory measures were applied equally to all third countries.

The Relationship in the 1970s and 1980s——By the early 1970s, although Japan and Australia had become major trading partners, comparatively few efforts had been made to foster mutual understanding, and so a series of measures to remedy the situation was undertaken by both nations. The Australia, Japan, and Western Pacific Economic Relations Research Project, a continuing program funded by the Australian and Japanese governments, was inaugurated in 1972 in Canberra and Tōkyō. In April 1976 it brought together the results of three years of research in a report that stressed the complementarity of the two economies and pointed out the beneficial "interdependence" of the trade and investment relationship between them. A cultural agreement between Australia and Japan, resulting from Australian government initiatives, was signed in Canberra in 1974.

The report of an Australian government committee chaired by Sir John CRAWFORD, which concluded that it was desirable to go beyond the cultural agreement if relations between Australia and Japan were to be deepened, led the government to establish the Australia-Japan Foundation in 1976. The foundation has its headquarters in Sydney and works to promote a closer relationship and greater understanding and interchange between Australia and Japan. It opened an office in Tōkyō in 1980. It was estimated that in 1988 some 40,000 Australian schoolchildren were studying the Japanese language in elementary and secondary schools throughout the country, while most universities and some colleges of advanced education taught Japanese studies, including the language. The Basic Treaty of Friendship and Cooperation between Japan and Australia was also signed in 1976. It provides each country with what is, in effect, most-favored-nation treatment.

The liberalization of Australia's immigration policy in the early 1970s removed the last vestiges of discrimination on grounds of race from official policy on entry and stay. Since immigration had long been a difficult issue in Australia-Japan relations, the effective demise of the "White Australia" policy naturally contributed to a better understanding between the two countries.

Economic relations between Australia and Japan also changed in the 1970s and

81

Australia and Japan

automotive industry
A Nissan Motor Co assembly line. Welding robots appear on both sides of a partially completed car. Robots are now used extensively in the Japanese automobile industry.

1980s. The oil crisis of 1973 had a major impact on the nature of Australian exports to Japan. In the wake of the crisis, the emphasis formerly placed by the Japanese economy on heavy industry gradually shifted to high-technology precision machinery and electrical and electronic appliances; coal to supply thermal power plants and industrial products, such as partially processed aluminum, replaced iron ore as major exports to Japan. In 1990 Australian exports to Japan totaled US $12.4 billion and imports from Japan US $6.9 billion, making Japan Australia's largest export trade partner and its second largest import trade partner.

In 1980, during a state visit to Australia, Japanese prime minister ŌHIRA MASAYOSHI proposed the concept of economic cooperation among countries of the Pacific Rim, and in September of that year the Pacific Economic Cooperation Conference (PECC) was established. In 1989, on the initiative of Prime Minister Robert Hawke, the first Asia-Pacific Economic Cooperation (APEC) Ministerial Meeting was held in Canberra and attended by representatives of a number of Pacific Rim countries, including Japan.

In recent years the number of Japanese tourists visiting Australia has increased dramatically, as has Japanese investment in Australian real estate. The latter phenomenon has drawn considerable criticism, particularly in Queensland, where numerous Japanese resort-development projects have been initiated. In 1988 direct Japanese investment in Australia was US $4.3 billion, a sum more than three times that of the previous year. The greater economic roles being played by Japan and Australia in the western Pacific economy suggest that Japan and Australia will need to keep their political and economic relationship under constant review.

Australian immigration policy and Japan
オーストラリアの移民政策と日本
(Ōsutoraria *no imin seisaku to* Nihon). At the time of Australian federation in 1901, more than 3,000 Japanese were resident in Australia. An abrupt halt was brought to further Japanese immigration into Australia by the Immigration Restriction Act of February 1902. The act made immigration dependent on passing a dictation test in a European language (not necessarily English), and this provision was used to exclude completely any further immigrants from Japan. Feelings of racial superiority mingled with fears of being swamped by other races to produce the policy that came to be known as "White Australia."

By the 1930s the Japanese population in Australia had declined, and after the Allied victory in World War II, practically all the Japanese-born residents were deported to Japan. From 1947 a vigorous program of attracting immigrants from European countries was begun. At the same time, Australian servicemen in the Occupation of Japan who had married Japanese women were not allowed to bring them back to Australia, a prohibition that was lifted only in 1952. In 1956 Asians married to Australians, or those who had resided in Australia for 15 years, became eligible for naturalization. The dictation test was formally abolished in 1958. In 1966 the period required for a non-European to become naturalized was reduced to 5 years, and indefinite stay was permitted for non-Europeans deemed to have skills needed but not available in Australia, although a judgment about assimilability was required for such applicants. Finally, in 1973, a policy was adopted of nondiscrimination on grounds of race, color, or nationality in the selection of immigrants.

Austria and Japan
オーストリアと日本
(Ōsutoria *to* Nihon). Official contacts between Austria and Japan began when a mission of the Austro-Hungarian Empire visited Japan in October 1869 and signed a treaty of amity, commerce, and navigation. Ties were quick to develop between the two nations. Japan was invited to participate in the World Exhibition held in Vienna in 1873, providing the first official opportunity to introduce Japan's culture and economy overseas. The IWAKURA MISSION, touring the advanced nations of the time, stopped in Vienna during the same year. In 1893 Crown Prince Franz Ferdinand spent four weeks in Japan during a world tour. By 1900 Austria was already an important trading partner of Japan, direct shipping lines having been established between Trieste and Yokohama.

In the cultural sphere, Austrian interest in Japan had already developed before the beginning of the Meiji period (1868–1912). August Pfizmaier (1808–87), a linguist at the University of Vienna, became in 1847 the first scholar to indicate the relationship between Japanese and Altaic languages and was also the first translator of a Japanese novel into a Western language (RYŪTEI TANEHIKO's *Ukiyogata rokumai byōbu* [1821; tr *Sechs Wandschirme in Gestalten der Vergänglichen Welt*, 1847]). In the Meiji period academic research concerning things Japanese, especially in the natural science field, and scientific exchange played an important role in Austrian-Japanese relations. Austria sent researchers to investigate sericulture techniques in Japan, while the Japanese invited Amerigo Hoffmann (1875–1945) to assist them with problems caused by mountain torrents and forest erosion. His work during the years from 1904 through 1909 is known in Japan to this day.

Heinrich von Siebold (1852–1908), the younger son of the German physician Philipp Franz von SIEBOLD, worked as an interpreter and joined the staff of the Austro-Hungarian mission in 1872. He was greatly interested in anthropology and traveled to Hokkaidō with another Austrian active in Meiji Japan, geographer Gustav von Kreitner (1848–93). Siebold's writings on the Ainu culture of Hokkaidō were the first detailed descriptions in a European language, and his collections of cultural artifacts became the basis for the Japanese collection of the Anthropological Museum (Museum für Völkerkunde) in Vienna.

ITŌ HIROBUMI, who had visited Vienna as a member of the Iwakura Mission, returned there in 1882 to meet and consult with Lorenz von STEIN, a German expert on constitutional law at the University of Vienna. Stein's advice to Itō and his group greatly influenced the process of drawing up the 1889 CONSTITUTION OF THE EMPIRE OF JAPAN. Another early connection between the two countries was skiing, which was introduced to Japan by Austrian military officer Theodor von Lerch in 1910 or 1911 and soon became a popular sport.

In the period between the two world wars, Baron Mitsui Takaharu (1900–1983) established the Japanese-Austrian Society (1935), and the University of Vienna established the Institute for Japanese Studies in 1937. Cultural and academic relations were strong, but the two countries had no shared political concerns of note.

Following World War II, diplomatic relations were restored on 29 December 1953, and Austria opened a legation in Tōkyō in April 1955. Its embassy was established in 1957. In 1959 Chancellor Julius Raab became the first European premier to visit Japan after the war.

Today trade and cultural relations continue to prosper. Cultural exchange is particularly active in the field of music, with some 40 visits to Japan each year by Austrian orchestras or musicians. While Japan is Austria's third largest trading partner, the balance of trade is in Japan's favor. In 1990 Japanese imports from Austria totaled US $705.3 million, while exports from Japan were US $1.6 billion. The main Japanese exports are automobiles, machinery, and electronic goods. Imports from Austria include automobile parts, rubber products such as tires, and sporting goods, especially skiing equipment, which has a 25 percent share of the Japanese market. Since the late 1980s

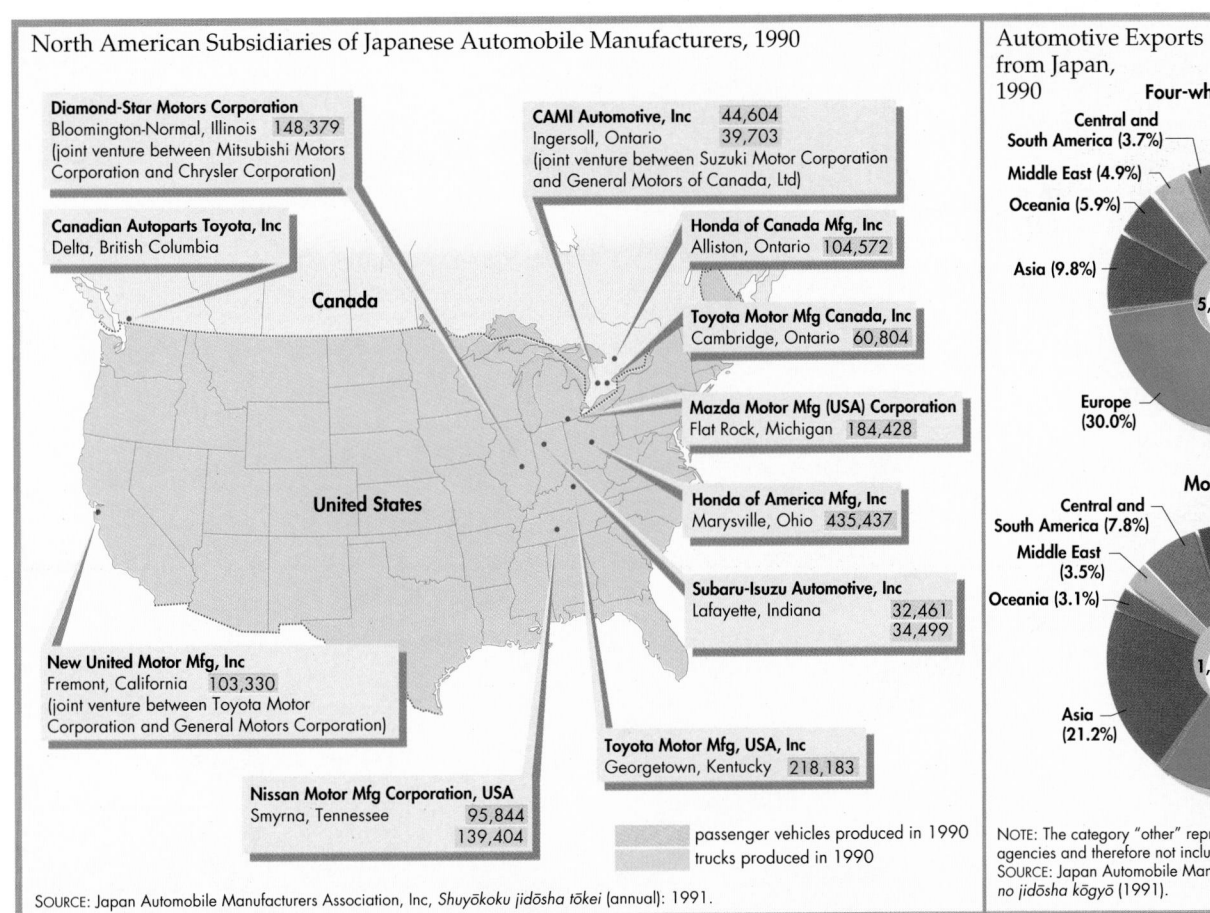

North American Subsidiaries of Japanese Automobile Manufacturers, 1990

Diamond-Star Motors Corporation
Bloomington-Normal, Illinois 148,379
(joint venture between Mitsubishi Motors Corporation and Chrysler Corporation)

Canadian Autoparts Toyota, Inc
Delta, British Columbia

CAMI Automotive, Inc 44,604
Ingersoll, Ontario 39,703
(joint venture between Suzuki Motor Corporation and General Motors of Canada, Ltd)

Honda of Canada Mfg, Inc
Alliston, Ontario 104,572

Toyota Motor Mfg Canada, Inc
Cambridge, Ontario 60,804

Mazda Motor Mfg (USA) Corporation
Flat Rock, Michigan 184,428

Honda of America Mfg, Inc
Marysville, Ohio 435,437

Subaru-Isuzu Automotive, Inc
Lafayette, Indiana 32,461
34,499

New United Motor Mfg, Inc
Fremont, California 103,330
(joint venture between Toyota Motor Corporation and General Motors Corporation)

Toyota Motor Mfg, USA, Inc
Georgetown, Kentucky 218,183

Nissan Motor Mfg Corporation, USA
Smyrna, Tennessee 95,844
139,404

Canada

United States

☐ passenger vehicles produced in 1990
☐ trucks produced in 1990

SOURCE: Japan Automobile Manufacturers Association, Inc, *Shuyōkoku jidōsha tōkei* (annual): 1991.

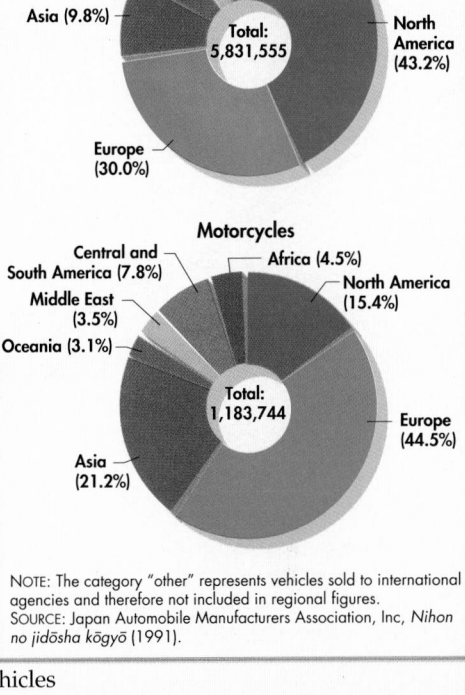

Automotive Exports from Japan, 1990

Four-wheeled vehicles

Central and South America (3.7%)
Middle East (4.9%)
Oceania (5.9%)
Asia (9.8%)
Africa (2.2%)
other (0.3%)
North America (43.2%)
Europe (30.0%)
Total: 5,831,555

Motorcycles

Central and South America (7.8%)
Middle East (3.5%)
Oceania (3.1%)
Asia (21.2%)
Africa (4.5%)
North America (15.4%)
Europe (44.5%)
Total: 1,183,744

NOTE: The category "other" represents vehicles sold to international agencies and therefore not included in regional figures.
SOURCE: Japan Automobile Manufacturers Association, Inc, *Nihon no jidōsha kōgyō* (1991).

Austria has made a particular effort to attract Japanese investment, and as of 1989 some 31 Japanese companies had set up operations in Austria. An aviation treaty was signed in March 1989, and the first direct flight from Tōkyō to Vienna was inaugurated in July of that year. In October 1989 Chancellor Franz Vranitsky visited Japan, and Foreign Minister Nakayama Tarō (b 1924) went to Austria in December of the same year to discuss conditions in Eastern Europe. It is expected that Japanese business interest in Austria will grow considerably as the country once again takes up its pivotal position in a Europe that is no longer divided.

Automobile Liability Security Law
自動車損害賠償保障法

(Jidōsha Songai Baishō Hoshō Hō). Law enacted in 1955 to guarantee compensation for victims of automobile accidents. Heavy liability for damages is imposed on the person who is in control of the automobile (usually its owner or someone with authority to drive it). In order to obtain compensation for damages under the Civil Code, the victim must establish that the party causing the injury was negligent (Civil Code, art. 709). However, in the case of automobile accidents, this special statute has shifted the burden to the person in control of the automobile. He will not be able to escape liability for damages unless he can prove that (1) there was no negligence on his part or on the part of the driver; (2) there was negligence on the part of the victim or some third party; and (3) there was no structural defect or functional disorder in the automobile.

The law establishes a system of compulsory liability insurance so that even if the party inflicting the injury is without financial resources, the victim is assured of receiving compensation. The law also establishes a governmental system to guarantee compensation, whereby the government indemnifies victims of hit-and-run accidents and acci-

Japan's Production and Export of Four-Wheeled Vehicles

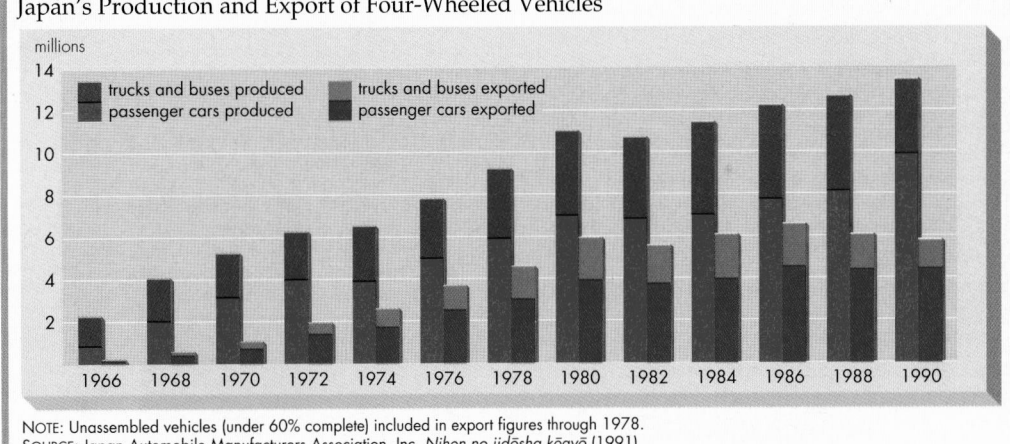

millions

☐ trucks and buses produced ☐ trucks and buses exported
☐ passenger cars produced ☐ passenger cars exported

1966 1968 1970 1972 1974 1976 1978 1980 1982 1984 1986 1988 1990

NOTE: Unassembled vehicles (under 60% complete) included in export figures through 1978.
SOURCE: Japan Automobile Manufacturers Association, Inc, *Nihon no jidōsha kōgyō* (1991).

dents caused by vehicles that are not covered by mandatory liability insurance.

automotive industry
自動車産業

(*jidōsha sangyō*). The Japanese automotive industry got its start in 1902 with the production of a small, low-power (12-hp) trial vehicle by two independent makers. Trial models by many other makers followed, but domestic makes, produced in small quantity, could not compete with the imported cars (mostly from the United States) that flooded Japan just after the Tōkyō Earthquake of 1923. Ford and General Motors, with their superior production techniques, marketing, and service systems, established subsidiary companies in Japan in 1925–26 and started assembling trucks and passenger cars from imported parts. Soon after, foreign automobiles completely took over the Japanese market. There were some 16,000 imported cars in Japan by 1929, and it was not until 1933 that annual domestic automobile production surpassed 1,000 vehicles.

Before and during World War II, the Japa-

nese automotive industry, under government direction, concentrated on producing trucks for the military. Such early manufacturers as NISSAN MOTOR CO, LTD; TOYOTA MOTOR CORPORATION; and later the forerunner of ISUZU MOTORS, LTD, were licensed under the Automotive Manufacturing Industries Law (Jidōsha Seizō Jigyō Hō) of 1935. This act was aimed at protecting and promoting domestic automobile production by providing tax breaks for domestic manufacturers and by imposing restrictions on (and in 1940 eliminating altogether) the activities of foreign automobile makers. MITSUBISHI HEAVY INDUSTRIES, LTD, and HINO MOTORS, LTD, were also involved in wartime production. After the war, Occupation authorities allowed Japanese manufacturers to continue some production, mostly of trucks, but total production in 1946 was only 20,000 vehicles. Passenger car production began again in 1952, with most of the demand for passenger cars coming from

Continued on page 86 ▶

Shifting into Overdrive: A Postwar Chronicle of the Japanese Auto Industry

1940

1945 Automotive industry shut down by Occupation authorities.

1947 Production of 300 vehicles permitted by Occupation authorities.

1947 Nissan produces the Datsun DA; Toyota produces the Toyota SA.

1950

◄ **1952** Company tie-ups between Nissan and Austin, Hino and Renault, and Isuzu and Hillman enable Japanese firms to study foreign production technology. Pictured is Nissan's first Austin model.

1955 Toyota unveils its Toyopet Crown and Nissan its Datsun 110—the first two postwar autos built in volume. Demand, however, remains highest for taxis.

▲ **1954** First Tōkyō Motor Show, held at Hibiya Park.

In the aftermath of World War II, Japan's car manufacturers faced numerous obstacles in their struggle to make the Japanese auto industry a viable one. With the economy in ruins, many people in governmental and financial circles argued that it would be cheaper to buy cars from the United States than to manufacture them at home; some said Japan didn't need to make automobiles at all.

Judged by even the most modest standards, the nation's prewar domestic auto production had been surprisingly limited and sporadic. Although the first Japanese-built passenger vehicle—a steam-powered bus—appeared in 1904 and minor successes at building gasoline-powered cars came during the 1910s, the biggest advance occurred in 1931 when the precursor of today's Nissan Motor Co, Ltd, produced the first Datsun passenger car. Still, the future automotive giant made only 800 of these small cars per month during the peak years of 1937–38.

What saved Japan's automotive industry after the war was a call to supply and service vehicles used by United Nations forces enmeshed in a new conflict: the Korean War (1950–53). Restrictions on foreign car imports between the mid-1950s and early 1960s, prompted by Japan's foreign currency shortage, also gave domestic makers some needed impetus. In addition, Prime Minister Ikeda Hayato's bold plan to double incomes over the next decade, announced in 1960, led to a boost in demand for private cars, signaling the end of an era dominated by taxis, hired cars, and other fleet vehicles.

Since demand until then had been primarily for such hired vehicles, Japanese cars were tougher, heavier, and not as spirited in performance as private cars needed to be. However, after Japan's first international grand prix races in 1963 and the 1965 opening of its first superhighway, domestic manufacturers began to concentrate on enhancing performance and creature comforts. In later years, the industry's advanced production technology and innovative use of electronics allowed it to overcome several formidable challenges—capital liberalization, imposition of the world's strictest exhaust emission controls, and the oil crises of the 1970s—while building its current international reputation for quality and design excellence.

Takashima Shizuo

1960

1964 Honda enters the international F1 Grand Prix racing scene.

▲ **1961** Following the Ministry of International Trade and Industry's recommendation to produce a "people's car," Toyota unveils the Publica.

1963 Honda brings out a small sports car, the Honda Sport S500.

1963 The country's first international grand prix races, held at Suzuka Circuit, prompt Japanese automakers to redouble their research and development efforts.

► **1965** Honda's first F1 win—the Mexican Grand Prix. Shown here are winning driver Richie Ginther (left) and team leader Nakamura Yoshio (right).

1970

1970 Photochemical smog becomes a major problem in Tōkyō.

1971 Capital ties are established between Mitsubishi and Chrysler and Isuzu and General Motors.

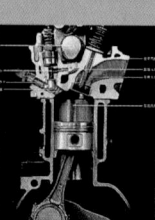

◄ **1971** Honda develops the low-emission CVCC (Compound Vortex Controlled Combustion) engine to comply with US antipollution legislation embodied in the Muskie Act. The picture shows the engine's block.

1973 The first major oil crisis forces gas stations to close on Sundays.

◄ **1980** Japanese carmakers voluntarily restrict exports to the United States, no doubt partly inspired by demonstrations such as this one by laid-off American autoworkers in Detroit.

1980 Japanese production figures surpass those of the United States, making Japan the world's top auto-producing nation.

► **1982** Local production of the Honda Accord begins in Ohio. This car was the first off the line.

1990 Sales of luxury foreign import cars take off; Mercedes-Benz models prove particularly popular.

▼ **1990** Mitsubishi brings out the latest model of its off-road four-wheel-drive Pajero, sparking a buying boom of such vehicles.

▲ **1990** Honda begins volume production of the world's first luxury sports car with an all-aluminum body, the Honda NSX.

▲ **1991** Research into using alternative energy sources such as hydrogen, electricity, solar cells, and methanol to run vehicles intensifies. Pictured is Toyota's solar-cell car, the RaRa II.

▲ 1957 Prince brings out the Skyline, and Toyota introduces the Corona; shown here is a page from the Skyline catalog.

▶ 1958 Fuji Heavy Industries produces the Subaru 360, proving the viability of light, inexpensive passenger cars that perform well.

▶ 1957 Two Toyota Crowns (one being off-loaded here) become the first Japanese cars exported to the United States after the war.

1958 A Nissan Datsun comes in first in its class at an Australian road race.

1959 Nissan's new Bluebird passenger car achieves phenomenal sales.

1965 The opening of Japan's first superhighway, the Meishin Expressway, spurs Japanese carmakers to produce higher-performance cars.

1966 Two new models, the Nissan Sunny and the Toyota Corolla, herald the one-car-family era.

1966 Nissan and Prince merge in anticipation of the imminent liberalization of capital, which will expose Japanese industry to outside investment.

1966 Fuji Heavy Industries brings out a small front-wheel-drive car, the Subaru 1000.

1967 Honda withdraws from F1 Grand Prix racing.

▲ 1967 Toyota unveils its first high-performance sports car, the 2000GT, pricing it at a heady ¥2.38 million (US $7,000–$8,000 abroad).

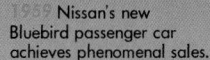

◀ 1967 Tōyō Kōgyō (later renamed Mazda) produces the Cosmo Sports, the world's first successful rotary-engine vehicle. Pictured is the car's engine block.

▶ 1967 The number of cars in Japan surpasses 10 million; traffic congestion becomes an increasingly familiar problem.

▲ 1968 The first environmental protection regulations are instituted, aimed at cutting noise pollution and exhaust emissions. A surge in vehicle mishaps leads to tightened road safety laws; here some whiplash victims receive treatment.

1974 Isuzu and General Motors announce their jointly developed Gemini model.

1975 The Toyota Corolla becomes the world's best-selling car.

1976 The first regular Japanese F1 Grand Prix event opens at the Fuji Speedway.

1978 Japan's exhaust emission controls become the world's toughest.

1978 Import tariffs on foreign cars are abolished.

1979 Exports of Toyota automobiles pass the 10-million mark.

1980

1983 Honda returns to F1 Grand Prix racing.

1984 US production of the Nissan Sunny (sold as the Sentra) and the Toyota Corolla (concurrently marketed as the Chevrolet Nova) begins.

1986 Nissan opens its first factory in the United Kingdom.

▶ 1987 Nissan brings out the limited-production Pao, which boasts a deliberately nostalgic design and is sold at premium prices.

1988 The first batch of US-produced Honda Accords is exported to Japan.

1990

▶ 1991 A lack of space and rapidly rising land prices in urban areas put the squeeze on car owners, leading to creative solutions such as this vertical parking setup designed for private residences.

▲ 1991 Car manufacturers adapt satellite technology for on-board electronic navigation systems.

▶ 1991 Mazda becomes the first Japanese team to win the Le Mans 24-hour race.

▲ 1991 Technology on display at the 29th Tōkyō Motor Show attracts the world's attention.

aviation Kawasaki Heavy Industries was the primary contractor in the development of the T-4 jet trainer used by the Air Self Defense Force.

the taxi business. It was around this time that major domestic auto manufacturers began competing for technical agreements with European manufacturers to improve manufacturing technology, leading to such affiliations as Nissan-Austin, Hino-Renault, and Isuzu-Hillman. These ties were temporary and limited to the transfer of technology for small passenger cars. Also from around this time, the government, led by the MINISTRY OF INTERNATIONAL TRADE AND INDUSTRY (MITI), began its support and protection of the domestic auto industry. MITI ensured favorable allocations of foreign currency for the acquisition of new technology, restricted vehicle imports and foreign investment, and helped the development of the auto parts industry.

After 1960 the domestic production of passenger cars increased at an unprecedented rate. Companies that began manufacturing passenger cars around this time included the Tōyō Kōgyō Co, Ltd (now MAZDA MOTOR CORPORATION); FUJI HEAVY INDUSTRIES, LTD; DAIHATSU MOTOR CO, LTD; and HONDA MOTOR CO, LTD. Many large new factories were built, the parts industry was integrated and concentrated (facilitating the development of an organized subcontracting system), and nationwide sales networks were strengthened.

After 1965, some key mergers and formations of automotive business groups occurred. Toyota forged agreements with Hino and Daihatsu and created its own group. Nissan absorbed Prince Motor, Ltd, in 1966 and established a tie with Fuji Heavy Industries, forming the Nissan group. Other automobile manufacturers began seeking ties with foreign manufacturers. Mitsubishi established capital and operational ties with Chrysler Corporation in 1969; this was followed by a capital tie between Isuzu and General Motors in 1971, and sales and operational ties between Tōyō Kōgyō and Ford Motor Company the same year.

Around 1968 Toyota and Nissan increased their exports of automobiles and light trucks. By 1975 they were joined by Honda and other Japanese manufacturers. In the wake of the oil crisis of the 1970s, demand in the American automobile market shifted from the large, high-powered, gas-guzzling models to the smaller, more fuel-efficient makes for which Japanese manufacturers were known, bringing their share of the North American automobile market to 23 percent by the late 1970s. Pressure from American domestic manufacturers led to VOLUNTARY EXPORT RESTRICTIONS on Japanese auto manufacturers. After 1985, increasing US-Japan trade friction and a drop in export profits led more and more Japanese auto manufacturers to set up production plants in Canada and the United States. As of 1990,

eight Japanese auto companies had established 11 plants (3 of which are joint ventures) in North America, with total annual output approaching 1,600,000 vehicles; in Europe, Japan's second largest automotive export market, Japanese automobile assembly plants had also started production (in the United Kingdom); and in Southeast Asia, Japanese manufacturers were either cooperating with domestic automobile producers or setting up multinational diversified assembly operations. Japanese parts suppliers followed the major auto manufacturers abroad, expanding their overseas production capacity and building up technology transfer and cooperation networks. In 1990 the Japanese automobile industry produced 13,486,796 vehicles, of which 5,831,555 were exported.

☎ *84–85*

avatar   化身・権化

(*keshin; gonge*). The visible or even incarnate form taken by a supernatural being in order to manifest itself in the human world. In Buddhism the bodhisattva KANNON (Skt: Avalokiteśvara) is the most celebrated avatar, assuming, according to the LOTUS SUTRA, 33 transformations in order to succor suffering sentient beings. With the Shintō KAMI, the idea of the divinity itself assuming animal or bird form should be distinguished from the apparition of a messenger or servant. The *keshin* forms assumed by the YAMA NO KAMI are especially numerous and diverse. The principal shapes in which he appears are (a) a woman, either old and ugly or young and beautiful; (b) a snake or dragon; (c) a pair of deities, male and female, often with red faces; (d) a four-legged animal such as a deer or bear; (e) a TENGU; and (f) an ONI. For the doctrine that the Shintō *kami* are *keshin* of certain Buddhist divinities, see HONJI SUIJAKU.

aviation   航空

(*kōkū*). The first real progress in the field of aviation in Japan came after World War I. Before that, there had been complete dependence upon importation of aviation equipment. Japan soon began to design its own aircraft, featuring many original characteristics, particularly in military planes. After World War II, aviation facilities and technology were converted to peacetime purposes, and the industry is now up to world standards.

The first airplane flights in Japan were made on 19 December 1910 at Yoyogi drill ground in Tōkyō. Other efforts followed, but aviation technology was still considerably behind that of the advanced nations of Europe and the United States. When the Japanese army and navy established air units, they imported equipment from France, Germany, the United States, and the United Kingdom and produced planes under international licensing agreements at military arsenals. After World War I broke out, planes were developed at a rapid pace in Europe, but Japan, although participating in the war, was far removed from the main battlefields in Europe and fell even further behind aviation technology.

While Japanese manufacturers were engaged in the production of aircraft under international license, they succeeded in developing their own designs, and in the late 1920s domestic production of military airplanes began with planes such as the Mitsubishi shipboard attack plane Model 13 (1924) and the Kawasaki reconnaissance plane Model 88 (1928), which were adopted as

standard types. These models still displayed the overwhelming influence of foreign engineers and techniques. Around 1935 Japanese aeronautical technology began to produce solely Japanese-made planes with features not to be found in European and American aircraft. Japanese-made planes dating from this period were chiefly warplanes, but some outstanding civilian planes were also produced.

While the European and American air forces preferred heavy fighter planes with relatively high-wing loading capacities and high-horsepower engines, capable of striking one blow and making a high-speed escape, the Japanese military rated more highly light varieties of fighter planes with low-wing loading capacities, easy maneuverability in circular flight, and the capability of sharp turns. In the first half of World War II, these flight characteristics contributed appreciably to the early air war victories scored by Japan's army and navy. The representative Japanese fighters were the navy's Model 96 (Mitsubishi, 1936), Model Zero (commonly called Zerosen or ZERO FIGHTER; Mitsubishi, 1940), and *Shiden*-modified (Kawanishi, 1944) and the army's Model 97 (Nakajima, 1937), HAYABUSA (Nakajima, 1941), and *Hayate* (Nakajima, 1944). Long-distance high-speed reconnaissance planes, called command reconnaissance airplanes by the army, were a type unique to Japan. Japan did not build any large strategic bombers such as the B-17 and B-29 of the United States.

With defeat in 1945, Japan was completely prohibited from the production and use of airplanes, and all facilities for aviation research and the production of aircraft were either dismantled or converted to other purposes. This proscription lasted until April 1952, when Japanese aviation activities were resumed with the conclusion of the SAN FRANCISCO PEACE TREATY. In the seven years of Japanese aviation industry inactivity, the world switched from propeller to jet planes and aircraft construction changed greatly in all areas, including performance, structure, and equipment. The Japanese aircraft industry rapidly absorbed the new technology after 1952, however, and in January 1956 a Lockheed T-33A jet trainer, manufactured by Kawasaki Aircraft Co under license, made the first flight of a postwar Japanese-made jet plane. The first purely domestic airplane was the T1 jet trainer developed and built by FUJI HEAVY INDUSTRIES, LTD; the prototype made its first flight in January 1958 (see also YS-11). In later years KAWASAKI HEAVY INDUSTRIES, LTD, and MITSUBISHI HEAVY INDUSTRIES, LTD, developed a variety of military planes used by the SELF DEFENSE FORCES. The success of these companies demonstrates that the Japanese aircraft industry possesses the ability to design and build all types of planes independently, including supersonic-class jets.

Until 1977 nearly 90 percent of the postwar gross sales of the Japanese aircraft industry was accounted for by the demand for national defense, a strikingly high dependence on military demand in comparison with other countries. This imbalance has been redressed to some extent by the civil demand for the Boeing 767, which Fuji Heavy Industries, Kawasaki Heavy Industries, and Mitsubishi Heavy Industries began building in 1978 in the joint-development YX project with Boeing Aircraft. The 767 entered service in 1982, and production is continuing.

awabi→abalones

Awa Dance 阿波踊

(Awa *odori*). Variation of the Bon dance (BON ODORI) traditionally performed in and around the city of Tokushima (in Tokushima Prefecture, formerly known as Awa Province) from 12 August to 15 August during observance of the BON FESTIVAL. Groups of men and women parade, dancing and singing the song "Yoshikono-bushi" to the accompaniment of *shamisen* (lutes), flutes, and drums. The dance is also known as the "Fool's Dance" (Ahō *odori*) because of the song's refrain, "You're a fool (*ahō*) whether you dance or not, so you might as well dance." It is said to have originated when Hachisuka Iemasa (1558–1639) built a castle in Tokushima and provided *sake* (rice wine) for the townspeople, who became drunk and began to dance.

Awajishima 淡路島

Island in the eastern Inland Sea, southeast of Hyōgo Prefecture, central Honshū; part of Hyōgo Prefecture; the largest island in the Inland Sea. A rough triangle in shape, it is surrounded by Ōsaka Bay on the east, the Harima Sea on the west, and the Kii Channel on the south. It has little level land but no high mountains. The climate is mild with relatively little precipitation. Agricultural products include flowers, loquats, mandarin oranges (*mikan*), and onions; beef and dairy cattle are raised. Awajishima is also a tourist spot with such attractions as the temple ruins of the Awaji Kokubunji and the whirlpools at Naruto. Awaji dolls are a special product. Awajishima is the midpoint on the series of bridges connecting Honshū and Shikoku, which were opened in 1985. The major city is Sumoto. Area: 593 sq km (229 sq mi); pop: 166,218.

Awa maru 阿波丸

Japanese passenger-cargo ship with over 2,000 people aboard that was sunk in the Formosa Strait by a US submarine on 1 April 1945 while proceeding under a World War II safe-conduct agreement with the United States. The United States accepted liability, but settlement was postponed until 1949. Japan waived all claims arising from the incident "in appreciation of the assistance . . . received during the post-surrender period from the Government of the United States of America." At the same time Japan recognized in a separate understanding that the OCCUPATION costs and loans, as well as credits extended by the United States, were valid debts owed by Japan.

Awano Seiho 阿波野青畝

(1899–1992). HAIKU poet. Real name Hashimoto Toshio. Born in Nara Prefecture. A major disciple of TAKAHAMA KYOSHI, the leader of the influential coterie associated with the haiku magazine HOTOTOGISU. His haiku, while generally faithful to the spare realism of the *Hototogisu* style, are infused with humanity and humor; collections include *Manryō* (1931), *Teihon Seiho kushū* (1947), and *Kōshien* (1972).

Awara 芦原[町]

Town in northern Fukui Prefecture, central Honshū. Awara is noted primarily for its hot springs, discovered in 1883. Such areas as TŌJIMBŌ and Lake Kitagata also attract visitors. Pop: 14,120.

aware→mono no aware

Awasaka Tsumao 泡坂妻夫

(1933–). Writer. Real name Atsukawa Masao. Born in Tōkyō; graduate of Kudan High School. Awasaka is known for his mystery novels, which include *Midare karakuri* (1977, Disordered Devices) and *Orizuru* (1988, Origami Crane). In recent years he has turned his hand to mainstream fiction, winning the Naoki Prize in 1990 for *Kagekikyō* (The Bellflower Crest), a novel which draws on the author's experience as a designer of traditional family crests.

Awashima 粟島

Island, formed by three mountains joined by sandbars, in the eastern Inland Sea. One of the Shiwaku Islands, it is administratively part of Kagawa Prefecture, Shikoku. The island is famous for its associations with the legend of URASHIMA TARŌ. Area: 4 sq km (1.5 sq mi).

Awa Shrine 安房神社

(Awa Jinja). Shintō shrine in the city of Tateyama, Chiba Prefecture; dedicated to Ame no Futotama no Mikoto, the divine ancestor of the IMBE FAMILY of ritualists. Tradition has it that the Awa Shrine was built during the reign of the legendary first emperor, Jimmu. Today it is associated with fertility of the soil. The annual shrine festival is celebrated on 10 August.

Awataguchi Yoshimitsu 粟田口吉光

(fl 13th century). Swordsmith from Yamashiro (now part of Kyōto Prefecture); member of the Awataguchi (the armorers' district of Kyōto) school of sword making. With Masamune of Sagami (now part of Kanagawa Prefecture) and Yoshihiro of Etchū (now Toyama Prefecture), he was regarded as one of the three great swordsmiths of his time. He was particularly known for his short swords.

Awazu Hot Spring 粟津温泉

(Awazu Onsen). Located in the city of Komatsu, Ishikawa Prefecture, central Honshū. A saline and sulfur hot spring; temperature of 50°–60°C (122°–140°F). Said to have been discovered in the early Heian period (794–1185), it is the oldest hot spring in the Hokuriku region.

Ayabe 綾部[市]

City in central Kyōto Prefecture. Ayabe derives its name from work groups (BE) of natu-

ralized Chinese and Korean immigrants (see AYA FAMILY) who settled in the area in the 400s and engaged in weaving. During the Edo period (1600–1868) it served as a castle town for the Kuki family. In modern times the city's tradition as a textile and sericulture center has been revived; it is the home base of GUNZE, LTD. Pop: 40,595.

Aya family 漢氏

(Ayashi). A large and influential group of immigrants (KIKAJIN) and their descendants in ancient Japan. Not strictly a "family," most prominent among them were the Yamato no Aya, who settled in Yamato Province (now Nara Prefecture), especially in the ASUKA region. The original group probably arrived in Japan around 400, led by Achi no Omi, who, according to the genealogy of the SAKANOUE FAMILY (a branch line), fled with his own and seven other families from the Korean peninsula. Other immigrants (often called *ayahito*) from Korea settled in Japan at Achi no Omi's behest. Immigrants in the 5th and 6th centuries were commonly called *imaki no* (newly arrived) *ayahito*. These immigrants may, as Achi no Omi's progeny later claimed, have descended from Chinese who had earlier settled in Korea. The branches of the Yamato no Aya became closely allied with the SOGA FAMILY in the mid-7th century, and many of its members were prominent in court and military affairs, as well as the support of Buddhism. They tended to gravitate to the region of the capital and were less geographically scattered than the HATA FAMILY, also from Korea.

ayame→irises

Aya no tsuzumi 綾鼓

(The Damask Drum). NŌ play. Author unknown. It is classified as a *yobamme-mono* ("part-four play"). An aging yard sweeper (the *maejite* or main character at the beginning of a play) of humble station falls in love with a beautiful court lady (the *tsure* or "companion" character). Resolving to convince him of his folly, she orders one of her retainers (the *waki* or subordinate character) to fashion a drum out of damask cloth. She has the drum presented to the old man and promises that if he can make it sound, she will consent to meet him. The old man beats frantically upon it, but the drum remains silent. In despair he drowns himself in a pond in the lady's garden. Later his ghost

Awa Dance This traditional dance of late summer, performed during the Bon Festival, is also known as the "Fool's Dance," from the comic song that accompanies it.

Aya no tsuzumi In a scene from this Nō play, the ghost of a dead servant rises from a pond to reproach the unattainable court lady whose love he had once hoped to win.

azaleas
1 The *satsuki* is an evergreen late-blooming species of azalea. Pictured at the Ninomaru Garden of the Imperial Palace in Tōkyō.
2 Many varieties of azalea have been developed from the *renge tsutsuji* (pictured), a wild azalea that is generally found at altitudes of over 1,000 meters.

(the *nochijite* or main character at the end of the play) rises out of the water, angrily reprimands the lady, and sinks once more beneath the surface.

Ayase 綾瀬[市]

City in central Kanagawa Prefecture, central Honshū. After World War II, Ayase, with neighboring Yamato, became the site of a US Air Force base. Long a rice-producing area, it is being rapidly urbanized as a residential and industrial center. Pig breeding and market gardening are the main agricultural occupations. Pop: 77,926.

Ayrton, William Edward
エイヤトン, W. E.

(1847–1908). British electrical engineer who contributed significantly to the development of electrical engineering in Japan. In 1873 he accepted an invitation from the Japanese government to teach physics and electrical engineering at Kōbu Daigakkō (Engineering College; now part of Tōkyō University), where he remained until 1879. He is credited with introducing arc lighting to Japan in 1878.

ayu 鮎

(sweetfish). *Plecoglossus altivelis*. Important Japanese freshwater fish of the family Plecoglossidae, order Salmoniformes, class Osteichthyes. It is usually less than 20 centimeters (8 in) long and has an adipose fin. Spawned in rivers late in autumn, it descends to the sea and swims upstream early in spring. As fry it feeds on microscopic animals but later on plankton and, as an adult, on diatomic algae, which it scrapes from rocks on river bottoms with its saw-shaped teeth. Taking advantage of its habit of trying to expel intruders from its territory, a special fishing method called *tomozuri* (decoy fishing) is often employed. Cormorants are also used to catch *ayu* (see CORMORANT FISHING). Aquiculture is also practiced. *Ayu* are eaten broiled with salt, fried, or

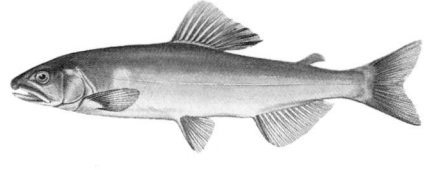

ayu The natural population of sweetfish has declined due to river pollution, though they are now raised artificially in many areas.

as *ayuzushi* (raw *ayu* with vinegared rice).

The sweetfish appears as a good omen in ancient chronicles. It has been a highly valued fish throughout Japanese history, and today is popular as a sport fish.

Ayukawa Nobuo 鮎川信夫

(1920–86). Poet and literary critic. Real name Kamimura Ryūichi. Born in Tōkyō; studied at Waseda University before withdrawing to serve in Japan's armed forces. In 1939 he helped found the poetry magazine ARECHI, which was influential in the 1940s. A central figure of the Arechi coterie, he made a significant contribution to the development of postwar Japanese poetry. He was also an active polemicist who insisted on the poet's social and political responsibility. His works include a critique of modern Japanese poetry, *Gendaishi to wa nani ka* (1949–50), and *Ayukawa Nobuo shishū* (1955), a collection of postwar poems.

Azabu 麻布

District in the central part of Minato Ward, Tōkyō. During the Edo period (1600–1868) there were many *samurai* residences here. Today there are a number of embassies, including those of France and Germany, and high-income private residences. The TŌKYŌ METROPOLITAN CENTRAL LIBRARY is situated here on the grounds of the Arisugawa no Miya Memorial Park.

azaleas 躑躅・皐月

(*tsutsuji; satsuki*). *Tsutsuji* is the most general term in Japanese for evergreen and deciduous azaleas. One evergreen late-blossoming species called *satsuki* (*R. indicum*) is distinguished from other azaleas, though it is also referred to as *satsuki tsutsuji*. Azaleas have been cultivated in Japan since the Kamakura period (1185–1333), particularly during the Edo period (1600–1868).

Species of Tsutsuji—The *yama tsutsuji* (*Rhododendron kaempferi*) is a half-evergreen shrub that grows in hilly areas throughout Japan. Its flowers, which can be scarlet, white, pinkish purple, single, or double, appear in May or June against the new leaves. The *mochi tsutsuji* (*R. macrosepalum*) is an evergreen shrub with hairy leaves and branchlets that grows in hilly areas of central and western Honshū and is also cultivated in gardens. In the spring, light reddish purple flowers open in a rounded cluster. The *miyama kirishima* (*R. kiushianum*) is an evergreen shrub that grows in mountainous areas of Kyūshū. It

has small leaves and small magenta or reddish flowers. The *renge tsutsuji* (*R. japonicum*), a deciduous shrub, is generally found in clusters at altitudes of over 1,000 meters (about 3,300 ft). The flowers are usually orange red, but scarlet or yellow types also occur.

The Satsuki—The *satsuki* or *satsuki tsutsuji* is an evergreen shrub found growing wild on rocks along rivers in Kyūshū, Shikoku, and western Honshū. It is also cultivated in gardens. It grows to a height of 15–90 centimeters (6–35 in) and resembles the *yama tsutsuji* but has thicker and glossier leaves. Its reddish purple flowers (3–5 cm [1–2 in] across) have dark reddish purple blotches on the upper side of the petals. Many varieties have been developed, including both white-flowered and double-flowered types. There are now more than 500 varieties of *satsuki*, many potted or cultivated as *bonsai*. *Satsuki*'s popularity continues to increase.

azami → thistles

Azuchi 安土[町]

Town in central Shiga Prefecture, central Honshū, on the eastern shore of Lake Biwa. Its chief occupation is farming. Sites of historical interest include the ruins of AZUCHI CASTLE, built by ODA NOBUNAGA in the 16th century; Kannonji Castle, stronghold of the Sasaki family; and the temple Kuwanomidera, where the priest Jōe, the son of FUJIWARA NO KAMATARI, is said to have planted mulberry seeds he brought from Tang (T'ang) China. Pop: 11,664.

Azuchi Castle 安土城

(Azuchijō). Castle built in Azuchi (in what is now Shiga Prefecture) by the late-16th-century military hegemon ODA NOBUNAGA to defend Kyōto and to consolidate his control over the country. Construction began in 1576 and took three years to complete. Built on Azuchiyama, a mountain bordering Lake Biwa, its fortifications stretched to the top of the mountain. Azuchi Castle was regarded as the model castle of the age because of its magnificent seven-story donjon (*tenshukaku*). The layout and building formation represented a transition between the mountain castle and the plains castle. The inner keep had an irregular octagonal base above which alternating square and octagonal levels were erected. The inner chambers were decorated with wall paintings by KANŌ EITOKU. The castle was destroyed shortly after Nobunaga's death in 1582.

Azuchi-Momoyama period 安土桃山時代

(1568–1600; Azuchi-Momoyama *jidai*). During the Azuchi-Momoyama period, a short but spectacular epoch, Japanese society and culture underwent the transition from the medieval to the early modern era. The political order was transformed, and there was an unprecedented efflorescence of the arts. The activities of European traders and Catholic missionaries in Japan, no less than Japanese ventures overseas, gave the period a cosmopolitan flavor rare in the country's premodern history.

Azuchi-Momoyama witnessed Japan's unification after a century of civil war, the Sengoku period (1467–1568). The country was reunited by three hegemons, ODA NOBUNAGA (1534–82), TOYOTOMI HIDEYOSHI (1537–98), and TOKUGAWA IEYASU (1543–

1616). The first of these "Three Heroes" founded, and the second developed, the so-called Shokuhō regime, which reconstituted Japan's body politic. The third, Ieyasu, won the hegemony at the Battle of SEKIGAHARA in 1600 and three years later established the Tokugawa shogunate (1603–1867), thereby starting a new regime and a new epoch, the Edo period (1600–1868). Institutional historians accordingly set the dates of the Azuchi-Momoyama period from 1568, the year of Nobunaga's emergence as a power in national politics, to 1600, the year of Ieyasu's great victory. The epoch's radiance continued after those events, however, and its terminal date is advanced into the Kan'ei year period (1624–44) by cultural historians focusing on artists such as HON'AMI KŌETSU and Tawaraya SŌTATSU, whose work brought the aesthetic traditions of the Azuchi-Momoyama period to a brilliant culmination.

The period is named after the sites of two castles, Nobunaga's palatial fortress at Azuchi to the east of Kyōto and Hideyoshi's headquarters at Momoyama in Fushimi to the immediate south of Kyōto. Indeed, castles are the best symbols of this age. They were meant not only for military defense but for the glorification of their builders. They glittered with gold and dazzled the viewer with refined luxury, displaying the lords' wealth and overwhelming the vassals with a pictorial profusion of emblems of authority.

Institutional Developments of the Period—The central governmental system that developed in Japan during the Azuchi-Momoyama period is called the Shokuhō regime after alternative readings of the initial characters of its founders' names, Oda and Toyotomi. Oda Nobunaga and Toyotomi Hideyoshi not only reunified Japan militarily; they devised new measures to regulate society on a nationwide basis.

Nobunaga's march on Kyōto in 1568 initiated the regime. His ostensible purpose was to install the "legitimate" claimant, ASHIKAGA YOSHIAKI, in the Muromachi shogunate, but restoration of legitimacy in the old governing order was not Nobunaga's true objective. Instead, he wanted to enhance his own prestige and power by playing the lead role on the central stage of politics. From the beginning, Nobunaga sought to dominate Yoshiaki and dictated policy to the shogunate. Far from subordinating himself to his protégé, Nobunaga posited a supervening polity, the tenka or "realm," a commonweal over which he himself presided.

Nobunaga did not remain unchallenged; throughout his career, formidable enemies confronted him. The most prominent of these were the daimyō ASAI NAGAMASA of northern Ōmi Province (now Shiga Prefecture) and ASAKURA YOSHIKAGE of Echizen (now part of Fukui Prefecture); the pontiff of the Buddhist "religious monarchy" of the HONGANJI, Kennyo Kōsa (1543–92); and the great eastern house of Takeda, rulers of Kai (now Yamanashi Prefecture) and its neighboring provinces. Of all these major powers of the Sengoku period, none proved a match for Nobunaga in the end.

Their early successes, however, in 1573 enticed the shōgun Yoshiaki into opening hostilities against Nobunaga. The hegemon responded by burning the greater part of Kyōto, the national capital, but the shōgun remained belligerent. In August 1573 Nobunaga drove Yoshiaki from Kyōto. Yoshiaki would refuse to abdicate until 1588, and the Muromachi shogunate therefore re-tained a shadowy legal identity; as a functioning political entity, however, it was finished. The regime of unification led by Nobunaga had replaced it at the central fulcrum of politics.

In that same year of 1573, Nobunaga crushed Asakura Yoshikage and Asai Nagamasa. At the crucial encounter of NAGA-SHINO in 1575, his modern musketry tactics swept the medieval chivalry of TAKEDA KA-TSUYORI from the battlefield. Also in 1575, Nobunaga conquered Echizen Province from the armed adherents (IKKŌ IKKI) of the Honganji. In 1580, the Honganji itself surrendered and its provincial domain in Kaga (now part of Ishikawa Prefecture) was conquered. In 1582, Nobunaga destroyed Katsuyori and distributed the Takeda domains among his own victorious generals.

As Nobunaga's power and stature increased, his military command structure turned into a public administration with the potential for national governance. Nobunaga achieved mastery over his "realm" by ruthlessly eliminating his daimyō opponents and the armed leagues (ikki) of the populace. He maintained it by a new type of command relationship with his vassals, demanding total respect and obedience from them "for the sake of the realm" and binding them with formal regulations even as he assigned them their domains. He moved them and their subordinate samurai from one fief to another at will and disenfeoffed those he found lacking in fighting zeal and organizational talent. In order to bring the indigenous gentry of conquered areas to heel, Nobunaga's regime set about destroying their forts and instituted provincewide land surveys (KENCHI). In 1575–76, the regime followed up the conquest of Echizen by conducting a SWORD HUNT (katanagari; confiscation of weapons from the populace) in that province, ordering peasants to confine themselves to agriculture, and prohibiting them from changing their status. These measures represented an early attempt at the separation of the military from the farming class (heinō bunri), later identified as one of the Shokuhō regime's cardinal policies. Villagers in Echizen were moreover forced to abjure their allegiance to the Honganji and affiliate themselves with temples approved by the regime, foreshadowing the religious inquisition (SHŪMON ARATAME) of the Edo period.

When Nobunaga was killed in the HONNŌJI INCIDENT of 1582, the "realm" governed by his regime covered no less than 30 of Japan's 68 provinces. Central Japan had been reunited under one political authority. Great areas of the country, however, remained unsubdued. The task of national unification was far from over.

That task was completed by Nobunaga's erstwhile subordinate Toyotomi Hideyoshi. Hideyoshi did not inherit Nobunaga's base of power effortlessly. First he destroyed Nobunaga's assassin, AKECHI MITSUHIDE, at the Battle of YAMAZAKI, a mere 11 days after the Honnōji Incident. The next year, Hideyoshi defeated SHIBATA KATSUIE, the ruler of Echizen and Kaga, at the Battle of SHIZUGATAKE. By 1583, Hideyoshi had reached an accommodation with Mōri Terumoto (1553–1625), the lord of vast territories in westernmost Honshū. Early in 1585, Tokugawa Ieyasu too agreed to subordinate himself to Hideyoshi, after fighting him to a standoff in the KOMAKI NAGAKUTE CAMPAIGN the previous year. In 1585, Hideyoshi conquered Shikoku; in 1587, he overran Kyūshū, bringing the Shimazu to heel. Three years later, he led the armies of his vassal daimyō against the Hōjō of Odawara and subjugated the Kantō region.

The northern provinces Mutsu and Dewa remained an arena of internecine struggle. Immediately after the surrender of the Hōjō in August 1590, Hideyoshi sent armies under his principal generals to sweep this giant region; by the end of October 1591, after a second campaign, they had wiped out all traces of resistance. When he finally subjugated Mutsu and Dewa, Hideyoshi could for the first time truly claim that he had extended his regime nationwide.

The local barons of Mutsu and Dewa whom Hideyoshi confirmed in their domains were ordered to observe three conditions: to send their wives and children to reside in Kyōto, Hideyoshi's capital (a measure prefiguring the SANKIN KŌTAI system of the Edo period); to destroy all forts in their territories save for the lord's residential castle and to have their retainers' wives and children move to the castle town (jōka machi); and to undertake a cadastral survey (kenchi) of their fiefs. These conditions ensured that the provincial lords would be integrated into Hideyoshi's national regime. Insofar as Hideyoshi recognized their autonomous existence, petty barons who had never been secure in their possessions were transformed into daimyō with full authority over their vassals and the populace of their domains. The price they paid was the surrender of their independence to him. Removed from the countryside to the castle town, the military men were destined to turn into a class of bureaucratic administrators.

The samurai were not the only social group given a new identity by the Shokuhō regime. Hideyoshi's national sword-hunt decree of 1588 disarmed the countrymen, thereby in effect eliminating the village samurai (jizamurai) stratum that had been so turbulent in the Sengoku period and setting the distinction between samurai and farmer. In 1591, Hideyoshi prohibited the change of status among samurai, farmer, and merchant, thereby laying the foundation for the class system of the Edo period.

By the time of Hideyoshi's death in 1598, the great wave of cadastral surveys ordained by him had covered the entire country. All the arable land was measured and assessed by these surveys; its putative agricultural yield was entered on cadastral registers (kenchichō) prepared village by village for submission to Hideyoshi and his daimyō vassals. Being listed in these registers gave the villagers an unprecedented security of tenure, which served as an incentive to increase production. A uniform system of taxation had replaced the multiple accretion of taxes and dues characteristic of the medieval shōen form of landholding.

The Oda-Toyotomi regime displaced the long-established medieval political order, but it lacked its own, clearly formulated justification in political theory. Nobunaga had not been granted the time to develop an ideology for his own political creation, the tenka. The parvenu Hideyoshi sought to mystify his obscure origins, to aristocratize himself, and to bind the daimyō to allegiance by identifying himself with the ideal model of political authority in Japanese history, the imperial institution. No matter how powerful he became, he could not hope to obtain the throne himself, but he drew his

Azuchi-Momoyama period

1 Depicted in this early-Edo-period screen painting is the 1584 Komaki Nagakute Campaign fought between Tokugawa Ieyasu and Toyotomi Hideyoshi, part of the struggle for political unification that transformed Japan during this period.

2 Beginning in the late 16th century, Spanish and Portuguese trading vessels increasingly called on Japanese ports. The foreign visitors inspired a genre of art depicting their manners and customs, represented here by an early-Edo-period folding screen.

legitimation from the use of the traditional symbols of authority associated with it. These included most prominently the lofty aristocratic offices of *kampaku* (imperial regent), with which he had the emperor invest him in 1585, and of *dajō daijin* (grand minister of state), which he obtained in January 1587.

Hideyoshi failed, however, to safeguard the perpetuity of his house and his regime. Upon his death, the regime was rent by the competing ambitions of his vassals, among whom Tokugawa Ieyasu proved to be the most powerful. After the great succession struggle, the Shokuhō regime was followed in 1603 by the Tokugawa shogunate, which built upon the framework of its policies. In order to safeguard its own perpetuity, however, the shogunate in 1614 attacked Hideyoshi's son and heir, Hideyori (1593–1615), in his stronghold, Ōsaka Castle, and the next year succeeded in destroying the Toyotomi family.

The Culture of the Period—Opulence and ostentation coexisted with restraint and studied rusticity in the epoch's dominant modes of artistic expression. The greatest symbol of Azuchi-Momoyama is the castle—a representation of power, built on a grand scale, decorated lavishly, and meant to overawe the viewer. A nearly coequal symbol is the teahouse—an evocation of aestheticism, content with a space nine feet square, eschewing ornamental decor, and designed to permit the visitor to withdraw into solitude from the world of affairs.

Nothing illustrates the ambivalence of Azuchi-Momoyama culture better than Hideyoshi's "Mountain Village Tearoom," a small rustic hut he had built within the precincts of Ōsaka Castle, and his portable "Golden Tearoom," in which every conceivable surface was gilded and almost all the utensils were golden. The interior decorator, SEN NO RIKYŪ, a rich merchant often described as the very incarnation of the ideals of *wabicha* ("poverty tea"; a type of tea ceremony supposedly governed by restraint), served the powerful aspirant to cultural accomplishment, Hideyoshi, as his tea master in both these contradictory settings.

The decorative arts flourished in Azuchi-Momoyama. The period's most important artistic commissions were large scale wall paintings and paintings on folding screens (*byōbu*) produced for the new warrior aristocracy's residences or the religious shrines they patronized. Richly colored and gilded decorative paintings (*kimpekiga*) are the period's representative works of art. Their grand conception and sumptuous execution distinguish the newly blossoming Azuchi-Momoyama culture from the previously dominant aesthetic heritage of the Higashiyama epoch (1449–90), which was characterized by monochromatic restraint.

The most renowned master of the grandiose Azuchi-Momoyama style of painting was KANŌ EITOKU, who decorated several palatial residences, including Hideyoshi's Ōsaka Castle and his Jurakudai in Kyōto. He made his career, however, with the magnificent project he undertook for Nobunaga in the donjon of Azuchi Castle. In this great

tower, the axial edifice of Nobunaga's "realm," Eitoku's art was made to reinforce Nobunaga's statecraft: the lavish decorative program bore a clear political message, made explicit by the edifying themes of the paintings and emphasized by the abundance of gold in their execution. None of these paintings survived when Azuchi Castle was burned after Nobunaga's assassination, however, and few of Eitoku's works remain in existence.

Of the Azuchi-Momoyama period's major painters, only UNKOKU TŌGAN remained essentially a conservative, rarely infusing color into his work and dealing with his traditional topics in a severe style. Eitoku's other great contemporaries, KAIHŌ YŪSHŌ and HASEGAWA TŌHAKU, who were specialists in ink painting, adapted themselves more readily to the tastes of the times and produced undoubted masterpieces in rich, gilded polychrome.

Another type of versatility was that displayed by Hon'ami Kōetsu, an accomplished calligrapher, potter, and designer of elegant colored paper (*shikishi*) and lacquer ware. Kōetsu's social position in the high bourgeoisie, no less than his reputation as a creative connoisseur of the arts, enabled him to associate with some of the period's most powerful personages, including Hideyoshi and Ieyasu. In addition, he was on close terms with important members of the Kyōto aristocracy and shared their interest in reviving the classical culture associated with the golden age of the imperial court in the Heian period (794–1185). In his art, Kōetsu accordingly referred consciously to Heian tastes, seeking to evoke the effect of courtliness (*miyabi*), which was that period's prime aesthetic category.

Kōetsu's approach to art expressed itself perfectly in the luxury editions of Japanese classical literature which he began to publish in the first decade of the 17th century at Saga to the northwest of Kyōto. Kōetsu also collaborated with Tawaraya Sōtatsu in a set of handscrolls of Japanese court poetry (*waka*), another extraordinary example of artistic integration. The classical texts appear in masterful calligraphy on paper decorated in gold and silver wash with motifs derived from the YAMATO-E tradition of Japanese painting; those motifs, familiar since the Heian period, were transformed by Kōetsu and Sōtatsu into stylized if not archetypal patterns, resulting in one of the most elegant products not only of their own epoch but of all of Japanese art history. Sōtatsu was expert at ink painting in the Chinese manner as well. His multiple accomplishment crowns the art history of the Azuchi-Momoyama period.

In the history of literature, Azuchi-Momoyama cannot boast a similar richness. The most important classical and medieval genres, including WAKA and linked verse (RENGA), continued throughout the period, but their vital force was expiring, while new traditions, such as JŌRURI and KABUKI drama, were barely beginning.

Some of the most interesting literary works to appear during the Azuchi-Momoyama period were produced for the Christian mission and printed by the JESUIT MISSION PRESS. It is doubtful, however, that these books reached a substantial audience before the Tokugawa shogunate in 1614 initiated the nationwide persecution of Christianity, which put a stop to the activities of the mission press and thereby ended a cosmopolitan trend in Japanese literature before it had really had a chance to start.

The International Dimension of the Period—The pronounced international flavor of Azuchi-Momoyama was brought about largely by the novel presence of European traders and Catholic missionaries. For the first time, Japan came directly in contact with European civilization, and Europe, through the missionaries' widely published reports, was made familiar with events in Japan in great and dramatic detail.

A full view of this relatively cosmopolitan epoch takes in portions of the Sengoku and Edo periods and spans the years from 1543, when the first recorded Portuguese traders arrived in Japan, to 1639, when the Tokugawa shogunate's final NATIONAL SECLUSION (Sakoku) directive put an end to the Portuguese trade and proscribed all Japanese traffic with Catholic lands. A closer but narrower view extends from 1563—the year when the Kyūshū baron ŌMURA SUMITADA, seeking to cement his ties with the Portuguese traders, accepted baptism from the Jesuit missionaries whom they supported, thus becoming the first of the CHRISTIAN DAIMYŌ—to 1597, when the TWENTY-SIX MARTYRS of Japan were crucified on Hideyoshi's orders in the first bloody persecution of Christianity.

To be sure, the period's international history is not circumscribed solely by the compass of the Portuguese merchants and the Catholic priests who came to Japan. The war that Toyotomi Hideyoshi fought in Korea between 1592 and 1598, a brutal but unsuccessful aggression, is an inexpungible part of that history. Its most distinctive element, however, was contributed by the commercial and religious activities of the Europeans and the growth of a substantial body of Japanese believers in Christianity, who numbered as many as 300,000 in the first decade of the 17th century.

Between 1543 and 1639 the history of Japanese initiatives toward foreign lands described a full circle, from strictly defined and limited contacts to booming expansiveness, and back again to rigidly limited contacts. The tributary relationship with Ming China, established in the form of the so-called TALLY TRADE in the first years of the 15th century, continued until the return of the last official mission in 1549, coincidentally the year when the first Christian missionary, the Jesuit Francis XAVIER, landed in Japan. Although pirates (WAKŌ) and illicit traders remained ac-

tive even after that date, maintaining a flow of contraband between Japan and China, and although commercial intercourse continued with the Ryūkyū Islands and with Korea, in the 1550s Portuguese traders became the most important source of overseas products, and they maintained that role throughout the Azuchi-Momoyama period. The end of the 16th century, however, saw the beginning of an extraordinary burst of Japanese activities directed toward mainland East Asia and the littoral of the South China Sea. The 1590s witnessed Hideyoshi's abortive military adventure in Korea, which began with bombastic plans to conquer and divide up not only that country but also Ming China, and which ended, after much of Korea was devastated, with the ignominious withdrawal of the beleaguered Japanese troops upon Hideyoshi's death. Japanese ambitions for overseas ventures were thereupon redirected into a more peaceful channel with the systematization of the VERMILION SEAL SHIP TRADE (*shuinsen bōeki*) under Tokugawa Ieyasu in the first years of the 17th century.

As the Azuchi-Momoyama epoch blended with the Edo period, Spanish, Dutch, and English merchants had joined the Portuguese in Japan, and Japanese traders were ranging as far as Indochina, Siam, and the Spice Islands in search of profits. In the 1620s and 1630s, however, the Tokugawa shogunate applied ever stricter controls both on foreigners resident in Japan and on Japanese voyaging abroad. From 1639, Japan maintained only a highly restricted form of diplomatic and commercial relations with a few foreign nations, namely the Koreans, the Chinese, and the Protestant Dutch. Merchants from Catholic countries were excluded under the laws of National Seclusion, and Christianity was proscribed as the "pernicious doctrine" (*jahō*).

The receptivity to contacts with Europeans and the encouragement of Christian missions that had been characteristic of Japan during most of the Azuchi-Momoyama period were replaced at the Edo period's beginning by the execration of everything Christian and by suspiciousness toward Europeans as the potential bearers of the Christian contagion. Azuchi-Momoyama, an extroverted period of history, was followed by a long era of introversion.

Azuchi Shūron　　　　安土宗論

(Azuchi Disputation). A formal doctrinal debate between representatives of two Buddhist sects, the JŌDO SECT (or Pure Land sect) and the NICHIREN SECT (or Lotus sect), held on 21 June 1579 at the behest of the hegemon ODA NOBUNAGA in his castle town of Azuchi. Nobunaga, concerned about the Nichiren sect's general intransigence, combative missionary methods, and growing popularity in Azuchi, ordered the debate after Nichiren zealots disrupted a Jōdo sermon. The Nichiren partisans were declared the losers of the contest, and three of their principals were executed on the hegemon's orders. Threatened with a general persecution, the main temples of the Nichiren sect acknowledged defeat, swore to abandon their habitual intolerance of other sects, and paid a heavy fine to Nobunaga. In his management of this dispute Nobunaga showed once again that his unification regime meant to exercise firm control over religious organizations.

azuki　　　　小豆

Phaseolus angularis. Also known as adzuki. A bean plant of the family Leguminosae,

which was introduced from China early in Japan's history and is still widely cultivated. It grows to about 60 centimeters (24 in), with pods containing 8 to 10 beans each. In Japan the red, cylindrical bean is boiled with rice on special occasions, red being considered an auspicious color (see SEKIHAN). It is also used for traditional Japanese confections, such as *yōkan* (sweet jelly), *shiruko* (sweetened *azuki* bean soup with rice cakes), and *amanattō* (sugared *azuki* beans), which account for 75 percent of total consumption. In 1990 domestic production was 117,900 metric tons (129,700 short tons).

azuki The red beans of this plant are cooked with rice as a treat for festive occasions.

Azuma kagami　　　　吾妻鏡

(Mirror of Eastern Japan). A historical account of the KAMAKURA SHOGUNATE. Its 52 chapters cover the 86 years from 1180, the beginning of the TAIRA-MINAMOTO WAR, to 1266. Scholars generally attribute authorship to shogunate scribes and archivists, whose names are unknown. Apart from a few letters and documents, the work is in an awkward form of Chinese, the language of the official imperial histories.

The text is arranged in chronological order, as if the accounts had been written and entered as events occurred. Actually, the work was compiled between 1266 and 1301. The compilers relied heavily on a variety of contemporary, unofficial materials, including the records of military families and religious institutions, diaries and travel accounts of court nobles, and war romances such as the HEIKE MONOGATARI and the GEMPEI SEISUIKI.

The *Azuma kagami* is a valuable source of information on the political history of the Kamakura period (1185–1333) and on early warrior society. The dozen or so extant editions of the work include the Hōjō edition, which became famous when TOKUGAWA IEYASU, the founder of the Tokugawa shogunate (1603–1867), used it as a manual of government.

Azuma Ryōtarō　　　　東竜太郎

(1893–1983). Educator; sports administrator; governor of Tōkyō (1959–67). He was born in Ōsaka. A Tōkyō University graduate, he became a professor of medicine there in 1934. Azuma was a pioneer in the field of sports medicine in Japan and also served as president of several sports organizations, including the JAPAN AMATEUR SPORTS ASSOCIATION. In 1950 he became the first Japanese to serve on the International Olympic Committee. While governor of Tōkyō he sponsored the 1964 TŌKYŌ OLYMPIC GAMES.

Azumasan　　　　吾妻山

Volcanic mountain group on the border of Fukushima and Yamagata prefectures; highest peak Nishi Azumasan (2,035 m; 6,676 ft). Located within the Bandai-Asahi National Park, almost all these mountains are covered with virgin forests.

Azumidaira → Matsumoto Basin

Azusagawa　　　　梓川

River in central Nagano Prefecture, central Honshū. It originates at Yarigatake, the second highest peak in the Hida Mountains, flows through the valley of KAMIKŌCHI, and joins the Naraigawa near the city of Matsumoto, where the river's name changes to Saigawa. The land along this river forms part of the Chūbu Sangaku National Park. Length: 77 km (48 mi).

Baba Akiko 馬場あき子

(1928–). TANKA poet. Real name Iwata Akiko. Born in Tōkyō; graduate of Shōwa Women's University. Her love of NŌ drama and knowledge of the Japanese classics give her works a style that is at once powerful and refined. Her poetry collections include *Hayabue* (1955), *Hikashō* (1972), and *Ōka denshō* (1977). Baba has also published a number of outstanding critiques of classical literature, including *Shikishi Naishinnō* (1969, Princess Shikishi) and *Oni no kenkyū* (1971).

Baba Keiji 馬場敬治

(1897–1961). Scholar of business administration. Born in Ōsaka Prefecture, Baba graduated from Tōkyō University and in 1931 became a professor there. His initial research was in industrial economics. In the 1930s, however, influenced by German managerial economics, he came to believe that the core of modern management lay in organizational theory. After World War II, Baba introduced to Japan the theories of American scholars C. I. Barnard and H. A. Simon, whose influence is reflected in Baba's last work, *Keieigaku to ningen soshiki no mondai* (1954, Management and Human Organizational Problems). Baba's many writings are credited with having helped modernize the postwar Japanese management system.

Baba Kochō 馬場孤蝶

(1869–1940). Essayist and translator. Real name Baba Katsuya. Born in what is now Kōchi Prefecture; younger brother of BABA TATSUI. Graduate of Meiji Gakuin, Tōkyō. He joined the Bungakukai literary group in 1893. His best essays were reminiscences of writers of the late Meiji period (1868–1912). He translated works by Daudet, Gorky, Tolstoy, and others and taught European languages at Keiō University.

Baba Tatsui 馬場辰猪

(1850–88). Political thinker active in the FREEDOM AND PEOPLE'S RIGHTS MOVEMENT of the 1870s and 1880s. The son of a retainer of the *daimyō* of the Tosa domain (now Kōchi Prefecture), Baba studied English at FUKUZAWA YUKICHI's Keiō Gijuku (now Keiō University) and made two trips to England during the 1870s to study Western law and politics. On his return to Japan in 1878 Baba became involved with the people's rights movement; he befriended its leaders, ITAGAKI TAISUKE and GOTŌ SHŌJIRŌ, and with NAKAE CHŌMIN quickly established himself as one of the theoreticians of the movement. In 1881 Baba helped organize Japan's first national political party, the JIYŪTŌ. He often criticized the Meiji leaders, and in 1885 he was arrested for antigovernment activities. After his release in 1886 he left Japan for political exile in the United States. There he wrote a long essay in English, *The Political Condition of Japan, Showing the Despotism and Incompetency of the Cabinet and the Aims of the Popular Parties* (1888). He died in Philadelphia.

Baba Tsunego 馬場恒吾

(1875–1956). Journalist. Born in Okayama Prefecture. Baba left Waseda University before graduating and became an employee of the English-language newspaper the JAPAN TIMES. He later went to the United States and established the *Oriental Economic Review* in 1909. In 1912 the review was discontinued, and Baba returned to the *Japan Times.* He also worked for the KOKUMIN SHIMBUN and wrote many articles expounding liberalism. From 1945 to 1951 he was president of the YOMIURI SHIMBUN.

Bacon, Alice Mabel ベーコン, A. M.

(1858–1918). American teacher of English and a writer on women and life in Japan during the Meiji period (1868–1912). Born in New Haven, Connecticut. In 1871 the Japanese government sent five young girls with the IWAKURA MISSION to be educated in the United States. Bacon's family sponsored Yamakawa Sutematsu. Another student, TSUDA UMEKO, also became a close friend. Bacon visited Japan in 1888 and 1900 at their invitation. Bacon taught English on her first trip, and on her second trip she assisted Tsuda in founding an advanced English-language school for women, later known as Tsuda Eigakujuku (now Tsuda College). She also taught at the Tōkyō Women's Higher Normal School (now Ochanomizu Women's University) and wrote several books on Japanese life and folktales, including *Japanese Girls and Women* (1891; revised and enlarged, 1902).

badger → tanuki

badminton バドミントン

(*badominton*). Although badminton was played in Japan in the 1930s, it did not become widely popular until after World War II. In 1946 the Nippon Badminton Association was set up, and All-Japan Championship matches were held starting the next year. Today the number of players registered in the Nippon Badminton Association is about 100,000. The number of regular players in the country in the mid-1980s was estimated to be five million.

Baibunsha 売文社

("Writing for Sale Association"). Organization founded in Tōkyō by SAKAI TOSHIHIKO in 1910 in response to government persecution of socialists following the arrest of KŌTOKU SHŪSUI and others in an alleged plot against the emperor's life (see HIGH TREASON INCIDENT OF 1910). The Baibunsha provided employment opportunities, such as copywriting, translation, editing, and other literary services, for many blacklisted socialists—including ARAHATA KANSON, ŌSUGI SAKAE, YAMAKAWA HITOSHI, and TAKABATAKE MOTOYUKI—and became a political club. In 1919 the association broke up because of ideological disagreements. Takabatake revived it briefly to publish his magazine *Kokka shakai shugi* (National Socialism).

bail 保釈

(*hoshaku*). In Japan, as a general rule, a court must grant bail if a defendant so requests, except in the case of serious felonies and other exceptional cases as provided by law; this is called "bail as of right." Bail is set and posted at an amount sufficient to ensure the defendant's appearance. In addition to cash, bail may also be posted in the form of valuable securities or a letter of guarantee from a third party. Release of a suspect on bail at the preinformation stage is not currently permitted in Japan, but there is some support for amending this rule to allow bail in such cases as well. There are no bondsmen in Japan. There is also a system of suspending execution of detention, which is similar to the bail system, whereby the defendant is released in the custody of relatives or a custodial organization of some sort. This sys-

tem of nonmonetary conditional release has its origins in the legal systems of East Asia. Its use is limited mainly to emergency situations.

baishin 陪臣

Secondary (*bai*) vassal (*shin*); the vassal of a vassal; also called *matamono*. During the Edo period (1600–1868), for example, the vassals of DAIMYŌ and HATAMOTO were *baishin* of the SHŌGUN, and the vassals of a daimyō's vassal were *baishin* of that daimyō. Most daimyō of the Edo period had two or three *baishin* for every 100 *koku* (see KOKUDAKA) of rice they received as income from their domains. Regardless of the size of their stipends, the vassals of a daimyō remained *baishin* of the shōgun, in contrast to direct shogunal vassals (*jikisan*).

Baishōron 梅松論

(The Plum and Pine Discourse). Historical discourse or treatise (*shiron*) in two volumes (or scrolls) probably written between 1352 and 1387 and of unknown authorship. In it an aged monk recounts the development of the role of the SHŌGUN and the history of the Kamakura shogunate (1192–1333). He also explains the discourse's name: the prosperity of the shōgun will unfold like plum blossoms, and the longevity of the shogunate will be like the pine. The *Baishōron*'s characteristics classify it as a GUNKI MONOGATARI (war chronicle), and it is clearly related to variants of the TAIHEIKI. The version of the *Baishōron* best known until recently is contained in the "Kassembu" (Battle Section) of GUNSHO RUIJŪ, an Edo-period (1600–1868) compendium of classical writing.

Bakan Sensō → Shimonoseki
Bombardment

bakemono 化け物

Any of various monsters, apparitions, or goblins; preternatural beings in general. *Bakemono* (sometimes called *obake*) are generically termed *yōkai*, as distinguished from GHOSTS or *yūrei*, which typically appear in their original human form. *Yōkai*, by contrast, may appear in various nonhuman forms, including sounds, fire, or wind, and usually manifest themselves at dusk in a specific place (e.g., a mountain, roadside, body of water, or room). TENGU, YAMAMBA, HITOTSUME KOZŌ, and KAPPA are just a few of the types of *bakemono*, which number more than 500.

Bakin 馬琴

(1767–1848). Also known as Takizawa Bakin and Kyokutei Bakin. Scholar, novelist, critic, diarist, and HAIKU poet. Real name Takizawa Okikuni. Born in Edo (now Tōkyō), he wrote KUSAZŌSHI ("chapbooks") and YOMIHON ("reading books"), two popular genres of Edo-period (1600–1868) prose fiction, and is most famous for his historical romance NANSŌ SATOMI HAKKENDEN (1814–42, Satomi and the Eight "Dogs").

Life—Bakin was the fifth son of a low-ranking *samurai*. Misery, suffering, and the death of family members filled his youth. After a period of drifting, he gave up his samurai status in 1789 and lived as a townsman, depending almost entirely on writing for his livelihood. In 1793 he married Aida Hyaku, a widow three years his senior who was the owner of a shop in the Iidamachi district of Edo. She bore him two daughters and a son, Sōhaku (1797–1835), who was

sickly. Although Bakin himself had irrevocably forsaken his samurai status, he tried his utmost to preserve samurai privileges for Sōhaku and to secure for him the best education possible. Sōhaku's early death meant continued hardship for Bakin as family head. Aside from his writing activities, Bakin's major goal was the restoration of the family's fortunes. While composing the celebrated romance *Hakkenden* he lost his eyesight; the work was completed with the aid of his daughter-in-law in 1841.

Works—Bakin's career as an author may be divided into three periods. For more than a decade (1790–1802) after becoming a pupil of popular contemporary writer SANTŌ KYŌDEN, he wrote mostly *kusazōshi*. Later, after journeying to Nagoya, Kyōto, and Ōsaka, he turned his efforts to *yomihon* and *zuihitsu* (miscellaneous essays) during the years 1803–13, becoming the leading author in Edo. From the time he began publishing *Hakkenden* in periodic installments in 1814 until the end of his life, he devoted himself to long romances, scholarship, correspondence, and his diary.

Bakin is best remembered for his *yomihon*, of which he published more than 30 titles. Next to his masterpiece, *Hakkenden*, his most widely read work is CHINSETSU YUMIHARIZUKI (1807–11, Crescent Moon: The Adventures of Tametomo), an adventure tale about a historical 12th-century bowman of legendary skill who strives to restore his family's fortune. Loyalty, filial piety, and the restoration of samurai families like his own were his main themes. His special interest in Chinese and Buddhist philosophy was tempered by a belief in the efficacy of the Japanese gods and a concern for language and style. Underlying his writings is a deeply moral sensibility, seasoned by compassion and a belief in human dignity.

Among his nonfiction writings, his diary is a rich source for information on everyday life in early-19th-century Edo. His autobiographical works *Aga hotoke no ki* (1822, The Lineage of Our House) and *Nochi no tame no ki* (1835, For the Sake of Survival) are important sources for social history. Among his achievements, Bakin is remembered as a pioneering critic of the novel and a historian of developments in Edo-period prose fiction. In *Kinsei mono no hon: Edo sakusha burui* (1834, Edo Authors: The Categories of the Modern Novel) he categorizes 17th- to 19th-century literature into two broad divisions: an early period centered in the Kyōto-Ōsaka area and a later one concentrated in Edo; scholars still accept this view. Bakin remains one of the giants of Japanese literature.

bakufu → shogunate

bakuhan system 幕藩体制

(*bakuhan taisei;* literally, shogunate [*baku,* from *bakufu*] and domain [*han*] system). The term currently used by most Japanese historians to describe the government, economy, and society of the Edo period (1600–1868).

Samurai and Government—The SAMURAI were the ruling class of the *bakuhan* system. Most of them had been transformed from part-time to full-time soldiers, trained and equipped for war but for little else. By the beginning of the 17th century they were a self-perpetuating elite, who saw the rest of society as inferior. During the next hundred years they were brought in from the countryside to specified quarters in the CASTLE TOWNS. Once there, drawing salaries instead of controlling their own fiefs, they no longer had any independence.

There was no significant mobilization of troops in Japan between 1638 (the year of the SHIMABARA UPRISING) and 1853 (when Commodore PERRY's ships sailed into Edo Bay [now Tōkyō Bay]), so the members of this ruling class, while they maintained their military trappings (see BUSHIDŌ), were very much more sedentary government servants than warriors. It was a numerous class, representing at its peak as many as 2 million samurai and their families, some 7 percent of the total population.

The entire samurai hierarchy was organized along feudal lines, with ties of vassalage linking every man to his lord and, ultimately, to the shōgun, who stood above them all (see TOKUGAWA SHOGUNATE). Above him, of course, was the emperor, but he had no contact with samurai beyond delegating responsibility to their nominal leader, the shōgun. Under the shōgun were two groups of vassals. The first, some 260 in number, were the DAIMYŌ, to whom he entrusted most of the task of provincial administration. They were nominally his vassals, divided into categories of SHIMPAN, FUDAI, and TOZAMA, but many, regardless of their classification, ruled their domains as independent princes. The SANKIN KŌTAI system, which forced them up to Edo (now Tōkyō) each alternate year, obliged them to recognize the shogunate's authority, but otherwise little was required of them. The real Tokugawa vassals were the HATAMOTO ("bannermen") and GOKENIN ("housemen") who made up the Tokugawa *kashindan*, or vassal band. Under them, and also under the various daimyō, came the bulk of the samurai class, who

Baba Tsunego This journalist wrote numerous articles in support of party politics and the parliamentary system. He served as president of the newspaper *Yomiuri shimbun* from 1945 to 1951.

Japan's International Balance of Payments

	1980	1981	1982	1983	1984	1985	1986	1987	1988	1989	1990
					(in millions of US dollars)						
Current account balance	10,746	4,770	6,850	20,799	35,003	49,169	85,845	87,015	79,631	57,157	35,761
Merchandise trade balance	2,125	19,967	18,079	31,454	44,257	55,986	92,827	96,386	95,012	76,917	63,528
Trade balance in invisibles	11,343	13,573	9,848	9,106	7,747	5,165	4,932	5,702	11,263	15,526	22,292
Unilateral transfer balance	1,528	1,624	1,381	1,549	1,507	1,652	2,050	3,669	4,118	4,234	5,475
Capital account balance	5,465	7,407	16,548	17,677	53,946	65,478	133,070	112,667	111,409	68,435	22,118
Balance of long-term capital	2,324	9,672	14,969	17,700	49,651	64,542	131,461	136,532	130,930	89,246	43,586
Balance of short-term capital	3,141	2,265	1,579	23	4,295	936	1,609	23,865	19,521	20,811	21,468
Errors and omissions	3,115	493	4,727	2,055	3,743	3,991	2,458	3,893	2,796	22,008	20,877
Overall balance	8,396	2,144	4,971	5,177	15,200	12,318	44,767	29,545	28,982	33,286	7,234

NOTE: Figures in red are deficits; figures in bold are totals.
SOURCE: Ministry of Finance, *Zaisei kin'yū tōkei geppō* (monthly): August 1991.

were Tokugawa rear-vassals (BAISHIN)—that is, men who had sworn allegiance to others in turn pledged to the Tokugawa.

Farmers and Taxes—It was important to the shogunate and domain governments that agricultural productivity be concentrated in the hands of small farmers so that the government's share of productivity would be maximized. KENCHI (cadastral surveys) assessed the likely yields (KOKUDAKA) of paddies and fields and made each farmer personally responsible for paying taxes on the land ascribed to him. The TAHATA EITAI BAIBAI KINSHI REI of 1643 restrained them from selling their land. Similarly, to ensure a stable agricultural class and therefore a stable tax base, each domainal government forbade its farmers either from taking up other occupations or from moving to any other area.

Townsmen and Commerce—Specialist craftsmen played a vital role in their society but were assigned the third position on the social scale, below samurai and farmer. On the fourth and lowest position of accepted society were the merchants and those employed by them. Since specialist craftsmen, merchants, and those employed by them lived in cities and towns, they were all officially classified together under the title CHŌ-NIN (townsmen). The merchants of the *baku-han* system worked within the confines of an almost totally self-contained economy. Despite the constraints of the shogunate's NATIONAL SECLUSION policy, which cut Japan off from foreign trade, the merchants managed very well under the system.

Rural Development—The *bakuhan* system survived for the better part of 300 years without overt challenge. However, the official ideal of an orderly society in which samurai, farmers, and townsmen applied themselves diligently to their appointed roles, had begun to crumble within a hundred years of the system's foundation.

It was in the villages that the most ominous cracks appeared. Scholars have estimated that, in the course of the 17th century, Japan's agricultural productivity grew by as much as 50 percent, partly because of extensive land reclamation and partly through more intensive use of land already under cultivation. Increased productivity and the failure of governments to survey reclaimed dry fields or to rigorously resurvey paddies left an agricultural surplus in the hands of the farmers. Many farmers aban-

doned subsistence farming for cash crops.

Some farmers became rich. Others failed, borrowed money, and fell into debt, from which not many could escape. Despite the general prohibition, the sale of land became common and with it the appearance of landless agricultural laborers (MIZUNOMI-BYAKUSHŌ). By the end of the *bakuhan* system, as many as half the farmers in Japan spent all or part of their time working the land of wealthy landowners (*oyakata*). Many more moved to find employment in towns and cities. In general, the countryside of the late *bakuhan* system was very much more prosperous than it had once been, although the prosperity was unequally distributed.

Urban Development—In the 17th century it seemed that cooperation between business and government would be to their mutual benefit, as illustrated by the granting of monopoly status to TOIYA (wholesale dealers) and KABUNAKAMA (merchant associations) toward the end of the century. Because of the National Seclusion policy (which precluded participation in any overseas trading ventures), there was no feasible alternative to close contact with central and domainal governments. At its best, such contact gave protection from competition and an assured income; all too often, however, it was accompanied by pressures for loans from merchants to the major political powers. The issue of price control, particularly on rice (a major source of tax income), was the source of considerable anxiety to the shogunate and domains from the 18th century onward. The 18th and 19th centuries saw both wild fluctuations in the price of rice and fairly constant rises in prices for other commodities.

In the early 19th century the rural agricultural surplus and the varieties of village commerce and manufacturing resulting from it attracted population away from the towns and cities, many of which began to decline. As they declined, so too did the fortunes of established merchants, but the governments of the *bakuhan* system were now powerless to help them.

Developments in Government—Village administration became less responsive to direction from a distant officialdom, resulting in a fall in government revenues and the growth of rural commerce. Also, since samurai were paid in rice and were denied any share in increased agricultural productivity, they became completely vulnerable to market fluctuations, making them easy prey for moneylenders and their daimyō, who often

borrowed money from their own samurai but rarely repaid it. Economic problems, therefore, did much to destroy the morale of the samurai class and much, too, to limit their effective response to military crisis when it eventually came.

As the 19th century wore on, it became increasingly clear that the *bakuhan* system was under severe stress. Disturbances in town and country were both more frequent and larger in scale; samurai were restive and critical of their superiors; the shogunate and domain governments, all financially troubled, were coming to mistrust each other and had begun to move outside the political conventions. In the mid-19th century, Japan seemed to be on the threshold of some major change. In the 1850s the question of institutional change was overtaken by the challenge of the Western powers and their pressure to open Japan to diplomacy and trade; Japan could no longer face its internal problems in isolation. This combination of internal and external strains finally led to the destruction of the Tokugawa shogunate and the disintegration of the *bakuhan* system as a whole.

balance of payments　　国際収支

(*kokusai shūshi*). A statistical record of all economic transactions between residents of the reporting country and residents of all other countries. By defining certain categories in the balance-of-payments accounts, economists attempt to evaluate various analytical and policy issues raised by the evolution of international transactions.

Merchandise Trade Balance—Defined as the difference between exports and imports, this is one of the most frequently used measures of a country's balance-of-payments performance. Japan ran a deficit in merchandise trade in the early postwar years through the mid-1950s, a time when the national economy underwent gradual recovery. In the 10 years that followed, through the mid-1960s, Japan's merchandise TRADE BALANCE fluctuated between deficit and surplus as the economy went through periods of overheating, followed by tight economic policies (see BUSINESS CYCLES). By the mid-1960s Japan had increased its international competitiveness to the point where it began consistently to run a surplus in its merchandise trade balance, though the margin declined during the OIL CRISIS OF 1973 and the similar crisis in 1979. The merchandise trade surplus expanded rapidly in the 1980s, reaching its peak in 1987. The surplus began to decrease in 1988 as a result of expanding domestic demand and the yen's appreciation following the PLAZA ACCORD of September 1985. In 1990 Japan's total trade surplus was US $63.5 billion calculated on a customs clearance basis. This included a surplus of US $38.0 billion with the United States, US $18.5 billion with the European Community, and US $28.1 billion with the developing economies of East and Southeast Asia.

Trade Balance in Invisibles—Invisible items include expenditures and receipts for transportation, insurance, business travel and tourism, investment income, interest on loans, foreign military forces, and diplomatic bodies. Data on Japanese transactions in invisibles since 1961, the earliest statistics available, show a consistent trend toward larger and larger deficits. A number of factors account for the deficits. First, Japan's net asset position in the postwar years was quite low, and it took a long time to build up foreign assets to the point where earnings on those assets had a perceptible impact on the net invisibles account. Second, because of the nature of Japan's imports, many of which are raw materials, transportation payments tend to be high. Third, the Japanese enthusiasm for travel abroad has not been matched by foreign tourism in Japan. Fourth, for years Japan has acquired a wide range of foreign technology via licensing arrangements with foreign firms. In the second half of the 1980s, Japan's deficit in invisible trade increased rapidly because of the rise in the yen's value and increases in overseas tourism. Japan's deficit in unilateral transfers, sometimes considered part of invisible trade, also grew quickly during this period because of increases in official development assistance (ODA).

Current Account Balance—This balance is another indicator of a country's balance-of-payments performance. It combines net merchandise trade, transfer payments, and net invisibles. Japan's current account fluctuated between deficit and surplus in the mid-1950s and mid-1960s, reflecting general movement of the business cycle. It has since maintained a consistent current account surplus except for a few years of deficit caused by the two oil crises of the 1970s. In the first half of the 1980s the current account surplus grew due to a drop in oil prices and to increases in exports caused by the low value of the yen. However, after peaking as a percentage of the gross national product (GNP) at 4.3 percent in 1986 and peaking in absolute terms at US $87 billion in 1987, it has since fallen substantially. The fall can be attributed to several factors, including a sharp increase in the value of the yen following the September 1985 Plaza Accord and a gradual reduction of the official discount rate and increase in public investment that were designed to spur domestic demand. In 1990 the current account surplus was US $35.8 billion, or 1.2 percent of the GNP.

Capital Account Balance—This is a measure of the net flow of capital into and out of the country. Japan's capital account has been very small relative to other payments accounts over the years because the country needed all the domestic capital available for investments at home, and because the government had a policy of tightly controlling the types and amounts of FOREIGN INVESTMENT IN JAPAN. Policies were substantially relaxed in the late 1970s and capital inflows and outflows have increased substantially. Major increases in OVERSEAS DIRECT INVESTMENT and Japanese holdings of foreign bonds in recent years have led to large deficits in the capital balance. See also ECONOMY, CONTEMPORARY; FOREIGN TRADE, GOVERNMENT POLICY ON.

Ball, William MacMahon

ボール, W. M.

(1901–86). British Commonwealth member of the ALLIED COUNCIL FOR JAPAN in 1946–47 during the Allied OCCUPATION of Japan (1945–52). Born in Casterton, Victoria, Australia, Ball was head of the Department of Political Science at the University of Melbourne from 1932 until 1968. As a representative of Australia, New Zealand, India, and the United Kingdom on the Allied Council, he was critical of many aspects of American Occupation policy. He believed that the Occupation's democratization policies were generally not thorough enough and that retention of the emperor posed considerable risks. He felt that the only important area where the council was allowed to have significant impact on

SCAP (Supreme Commander for the Allied Powers) policy was land reform, where Ball's own 10-point program was partially incorporated. See also AUSTRALIA AND JAPAN.

Bälz, Erwin von

ベルツ, E.

(1849–1913). German physician; resident of Japan 1876–1905. A graduate of the University of Leipzig, Bälz practiced there before going to Japan. As physician-in-waiting to the imperial household and professor at Tōkyō University Medical School, he came to know Meiji Restoration leaders such as ITŌ HIROBUMI and YAMAGATA ARITOMO. His diary *Das Leben eines deutschen Arztes im erwachenden Japan* (1931; tr *Awakening Japan: The Diary of a German Doctor,* 1932) is an insightful account of Japan during an era of great change.

Ba Maw

バモー

(1893–1977). Burmese statesman who became head of state during the Japanese occupation of Burma in World War II. He was educated at Rangoon College, Calcutta University, Cambridge University, and Bordeaux University (in France). Ba Maw became the first prime minister of Burma after its administrative separation from India in 1937, but he resigned in 1939 to join the radical nationalists working to attain Burmese independence. Arrested and imprisoned by the British colonial government in 1940, he escaped in 1942 and, when Burma's independence was proclaimed by Japan on 1 August 1943, became head of state and prime minister. After the war he was imprisoned by the Allies in Japan from December 1945 to July 1946. See also BURMA AND JAPAN.

bamboo

竹・笹

(*take; sasa*). Perennial plants of the family Gramineae that grow wild throughout Japan and are also cultivated for their many uses (see BAMBOO WARE). Some 400–500 species (of over 1,000 species worldwide) are found in the subtropical and temperate zones of Japan.

The Japanese divide bamboo into the taller, economically more important species, known as *take*, and the shorter *sasa*, which are generally no more than 1–2 meters (3–7 ft) in height. There is no strict taxonomic distinction between *take* and *sasa*, although the stem of the *take* discards its sheath as it grows and that of the *sasa* does not. The majority of species found in Japan are *sasa*, which rarely flower. When they do, all the plants in a given area flower together and then usually die. *Take* species bloom only once in 10–40 years.

The *mōsōchiku* (*Phyllostachys* var. *heterocycla pubescens*), originally from China, branches extensively and has small leaves. The hollow woody stems, or culms, grow to 20 centimeters (8 in) in diameter and 20 meters (40 ft) in height. Its shoots (*takenoko*) are edible; the culms are used in handiwork. The *madake* (*P. bambusoides*) is similar to the *mōsōchiku* but has somewhat larger leaves and reaches about 10 centimeters (4 in) in diameter and 20 meters (66 ft) in height. Its sturdy, pliant culm is used for poles and for making the SHAKUHACHI (flute). The shoots are edible. Another variety, the *hoteichiku* (*P. bambusoides* var. *aurea*), grows wild in groves in Kyūshū. It reaches a height of 5–10 meters (16–33 ft) and is used for walking sticks and fishing poles. The thin-leaved *hachiku* (*P. nigra* var. *henonis*) grows to 10 meters (35 ft). A related variety, the ornamental *kurochiku* (*P. nigra*), has a blackish culm. The

chimakizasa (*S. paniculata*) has large, broad leaves, which are used to wrap confections and rice dumplings (*chimaki*).

bamboo ware

竹細工

(*take-zaiku*). Objects made from this strong, flexible, giant grass are common in Japan and vary widely from purely utilitarian, everyday articles to highly prized, decorative, and artistic craft products. Tradition has it that bamboo-weaving techniques were first introduced from China and Korea in the 1st century AD. The oldest bamboo objects existing in Japan are in the SHŌSŌIN in Nara and date from the 8th century. The finest of these artifacts are the vases used in *ikebana* (FLOWER ARRANGEMENT) and known as *hanaike*. Bamboo flower baskets called *hanakago* are also highly regarded. It remains a favorite material for MUSICAL INSTRUMENTS, notably flutes such as SHAKUHACHI and SHŌ. Important tea-ceremony utensils made of bamboo are the tea whisk, or *chasen*, and the tea scoop, or *chashaku*.

Among the most delightful and uniquely Japanese creations are bamboo bird and insect cages. Children's toys, such as tops, kites, and whistles, are often made of bamboo. Bamboo is also used to make many traditional objects of daily use, such as baskets

bamboo
1 A grove of *mōsōchiku* bamboo in Nishiyama, a hilly region west of Kyōto. The grove is one of the most extensive in Japan.
2 The leaves of the diminutive species *kumazasa* (*Sasa albomarginata*), edged with white in winter, are used to decorate platters of food.
3 The species *chishimazasa* (*S. kurilensis*), shown here in flower, is found in mountainous areas.

bamboo ware

Bamboo ware includes objects for everyday use as well as decorative works.

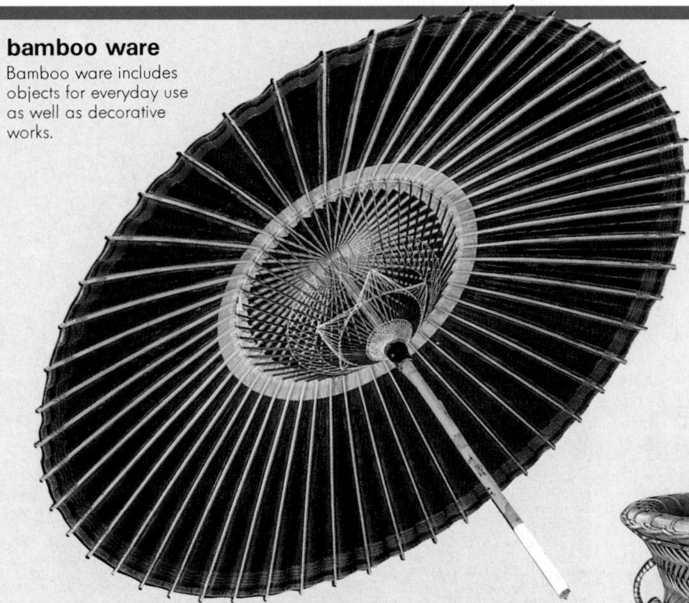

Bamboo umbrellas are made of oiled paper over a bamboo frame. Rare today, they were common before the metal-frame umbrella was introduced.

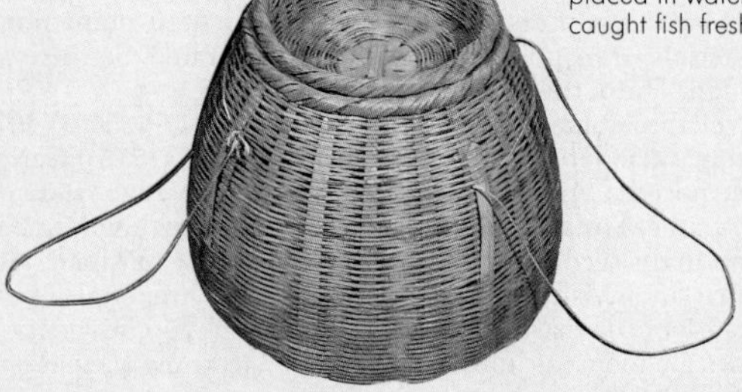

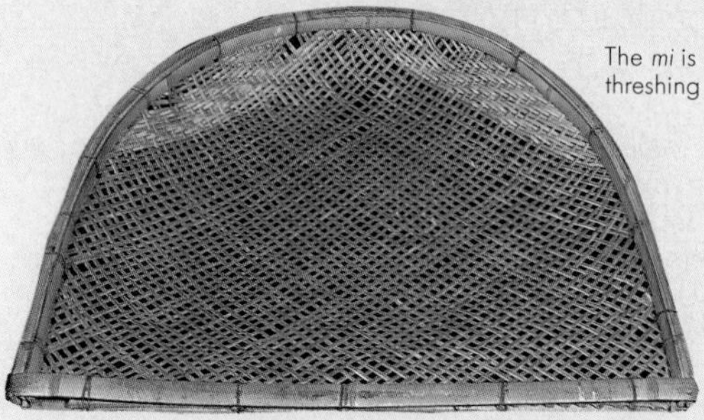

The *mi* is used for threshing and sorting.

The *biku*, or fish creel, is placed in water to keep caught fish fresh.

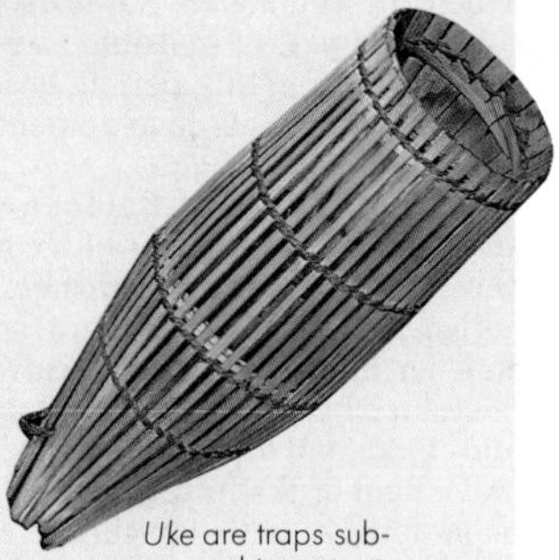

Uke are traps submerged in water to catch fish or eels. The fish swim into the larger end but are prevented from escaping.

Simple bamboo flower vessels like this one (shown enlarged) are widely used in the tea ceremony and for flower arrangement.

and chopsticks, and furniture, such as tables and chairs.

Bancroft, Edgar Addison

バンクロフト, E. A.

(1857–1925). US lawyer and diplomat. Born in Illinois. Bancroft practiced law in Chicago. Appointed ambassador to Japan in 1924, he arrived in Japan a few months after the passage of the US Immigration Act of 1924, a measure used to bar Japanese from immigrating to the United States (see UNITED STATES IMMIGRATION ACTS OF 1924, 1952, AND 1965). During his brief tenure (he died after barely eight months of service), he did much to alleviate the anti-American sentiments caused by the act. The Japanese government honored him with an elaborate funeral and had his body transported in a battleship to San Francisco.

Bandai-Asahi National Park

磐梯朝日国立公園

(Bandai-Asahi Kokuritsu Kōen). Situated in northern Honshū, in Fukushima, Yamagata, and Niigata prefectures. The park is characterized by volcanoes, lakes, gorges, ravines, and dense forests, sheltering numerous species of wildlife. In the north the ASAHI MOUNTAINS are noted for their sheer granite slopes and are the habitat of the Japanese serow (KAMOSHIKA), Japanese bear, and flying squirrel. North of these mountains are the Three Mountains of Dewa, sacred to the SHUGENDŌ sect: GASSAN, YUDONOSAN, and HAGUROSAN.

South of the Asahi Mountains are the Iide Mountains, with forests of Japanese beech trees (*buna*). Still further south lies the volcano BANDAISAN, which erupted in 1888, causing the formation of several lakes on its northern slopes. Its dense forests of birch and larch make it an important sanctuary for birds. On the southern slopes of Bandaisan is Lake INAWASHIRO. Area: 1,870 sq km (712 sq mi).

Bandai Atami Hot Spring

磐梯熱海温泉

(Bandai Atami Onsen). Located in the city of Kōriyama, Fukushima Prefecture, central Honshū. A simple thermal and hydrogen sulfide spring; maximum water temperature 54°C (129°F). Starting point for sight-seeing in the highlands known as BANDAI AZUMA KŌGEN.

Bandai Azuma Kōgen   磐梯吾妻高原

Name given to two highlands in northern Fukushima Prefecture, northern Honshū; part of BANDAI-ASAHI NATIONAL PARK. Bandai Kōgen, which was formed by mudflow from a volcanic eruption in 1888, is located on the northern slope of the mountain BANDAISAN (1,819 m; 5,968 ft); it is virgin forestland. Azuma Kōgen, located west of the Nishi Azuma Volcanic Zone, is virgin forestland dotted with moors.

Ban Dainagon emaki   伴大納言絵巻

(Scroll of the Courtier Ban Dainagon). Also known as *Ban Dainagon ekotoba*. Late-12th-century EMAKIMONO (illustrated handscroll). The earliest surviving *emaki* depicting a historical incident, it comprises a set of three scrolls, now in the Idemitsu Art Gallery in Tōkyō. The story is based on an event in the year 866, when the Ōtemmon, the gate in-

Bandai-Asahi National Park Many species of wildlife thrive in the wide variety of natural habitats contained in this park.
1 *Left to right:* the mountains Yudonosan, Ubagadake, and Gassan.
2 The water of Akanuma, a swampy pond in the crater basin of Bandaisan, is rich in iron and minerals.

side the imperial compound in Kyōto, burned mysteriously (see ŌTEMMON CONSPIRACY). Tomo no Yoshio, or Ban Dainagon, the undersecretary of state, accused his political rival Minamoto no Makoto, the minister of the left (*sadaijin*), of arson. Eventually it was revealed that Yoshio and his son had set the fire, and they and other members of their family were exiled. The tale as depicted in the *emaki* appears in a number of contemporary manuscripts, including the UJI SHŪI MONOGATARI, where the truth is accidentally revealed by the children of servants.

The *Ban Dainagon emaki* has traditionally been attributed to Tokiwa Mitsunaga. The calligraphy of the text has been variously attributed to Fujiwara no Masatsune (1170–1221) and Fujiwara no Norinaga (fl late 12th century).

Bandaisan 磐梯山

Volcano north of the Inawashiro Basin, northern Fukushima Prefecture, northern Honshū. During an eruption in 1888 lava dammed the Nagasegawa river system to form the lakes Hibara, Onogawa, and Akimoto and the swamp called GOSHIKINUMA. There are several hot springs. It is part of Bandai-Asahi National Park. Height: 1,819 m (5,968 ft).

Bandō Tamasaburō V 坂東玉三郎5世

(1950–). KABUKI actor. As the pupil of Morita Kan'ya XIV (1907–75; see MORITA KAN'YA), he made his stage debut at the age of seven, after which Kan'ya adopted him. He took the name Tamasaburō V in 1964. His reputation as an unusually beautiful ONNAGATA (specialist in female roles) grew quickly in the latter half of the 1960s; he became the most popular *onnagata* in kabuki from the 1970s. In 1983 he danced *Sagi musume* (The Heron Maiden) at the Metropolitan Opera in New York as one of the artists from around the world invited to perform in honor of its 100th anniversary. He has also acted extensively in the SHIMPA genre and Western-style drama.

Bandō Tsumasaburō 阪東妻三郎

(1901–53). Film actor. Real name Tamura Denkichi; better known as Bantsuma. Born in Tōkyō. In 1923 he joined the movie production company founded by MAKINO SHŌZŌ. After his film debut in 1923, he starred in a number of movies and was known for his sweeping swordplay. In 1925 he established an independent company, called Bandō Tsumasaburō Productions, and set up his own studio in Kyōto in 1926. However, in the era of the talkies Bantsuma's high, wispy voice disappointed his fans; his popularity waned, and in 1936 his company folded. He later took voice lessons and performed remarkably in films such as the 1943 version of INAGAKI HIROSHI's *Muhō Matsu no isshō* (The Life of Matsu the Untamed).

Bandung Conference→ Afro-Asian Conferences

Bangladesh and Japan バングラデシュと日本

(Banguradeshu *to* Nihon). Bangladesh and Japan established official relations in February 1972, soon after the former gained its independence from Pakistan in 1971. Since then there have been many exchanges on the official level. Economic relations have also grown steadily, particularly in the areas

of trade and economic assistance. In 1990 Bangladesh exported US $70.8 million to Japan, while importing US $376.2 million. The large trade imbalance exists mainly because Japan's exports have consisted of steel, machinery, and vehicles, while its imports have been virtually limited to just two products: jute and prawns. Since 1985 Bangladesh has been the fifth largest recipient of Japanese official development assistance (ODA) and the number one recipient of aid in grant form. In 1988 it received a total of US $341.9 million in ODA from Japan, of which US $133.7 million was in the form of grants. Direct Japanese investment in Bangladesh has been rare, with only three Japanese companies operating there in 1988. In addition to diplomatic and economic relations, the two countries signed a new cultural accord in 1982. Since the late 1980s there has been a growing influx, at times illegal, of laborers from Bangladesh to Japan.

banishment 追放

(*tsuihō*). In premodern Japan banishment was a penal sentence that expelled a criminal indefinitely from a designated area. Banishment first appeared as a penal category in the Kamakura period (1185–1333) and was most widely used in the Edo period (1600–1868). It was discontinued after the Meiji Restoration in 1868. See also PENAL SYSTEM.

bankata 番方

(guards). A term used in the Edo period (1600–1868) to denote *samurai* fighting units, as distinct from samurai administrative units, called *yakukata*. More specifically, it referred to select units whose members were bannermen (HATAMOTO) and housemen (GOKENIN) of the shōgun and whose principal duty was to guard him. The guards were called *banshū* or *banshi*.

Bankei Yōtaku 盤珪永琢

(1622–93). Also known as Bankei Eitaku. Buddhist monk of the RINZAI SECT. Born in what is now the city of Himeji in Hyōgo Prefecture. In 1638 he became a monk under Umpo of the temple Zuiōji in Akō and received the name Yōtaku. Bankei was widely influential; his disciples were said to number some 50,000. He traveled throughout Japan

and founded the temples Ryūmonji, Nyohōji, and Kōrinji. In his teachings he emphasized the Unborn Buddha Mind (Fushōzen). He rejected the use of KŌAN and always preached to his audience in simple, ordinary language.

banking system 銀行制度

(*ginkō seido*). The banking system in Japan is the nation's most important means of channeling individual savings into investment by firms. Banking is more important in Japan than in most industrialized nations because a larger share of savings is held in banks and because corporations have traditionally depended more on borrowing than on stock sales for capital.

The central characteristic of the Japanese banking system is the importance of the large commercial banks. The system is also characterized by the large number of specialized financial services offered by institutions

Japan's Financial Institutions

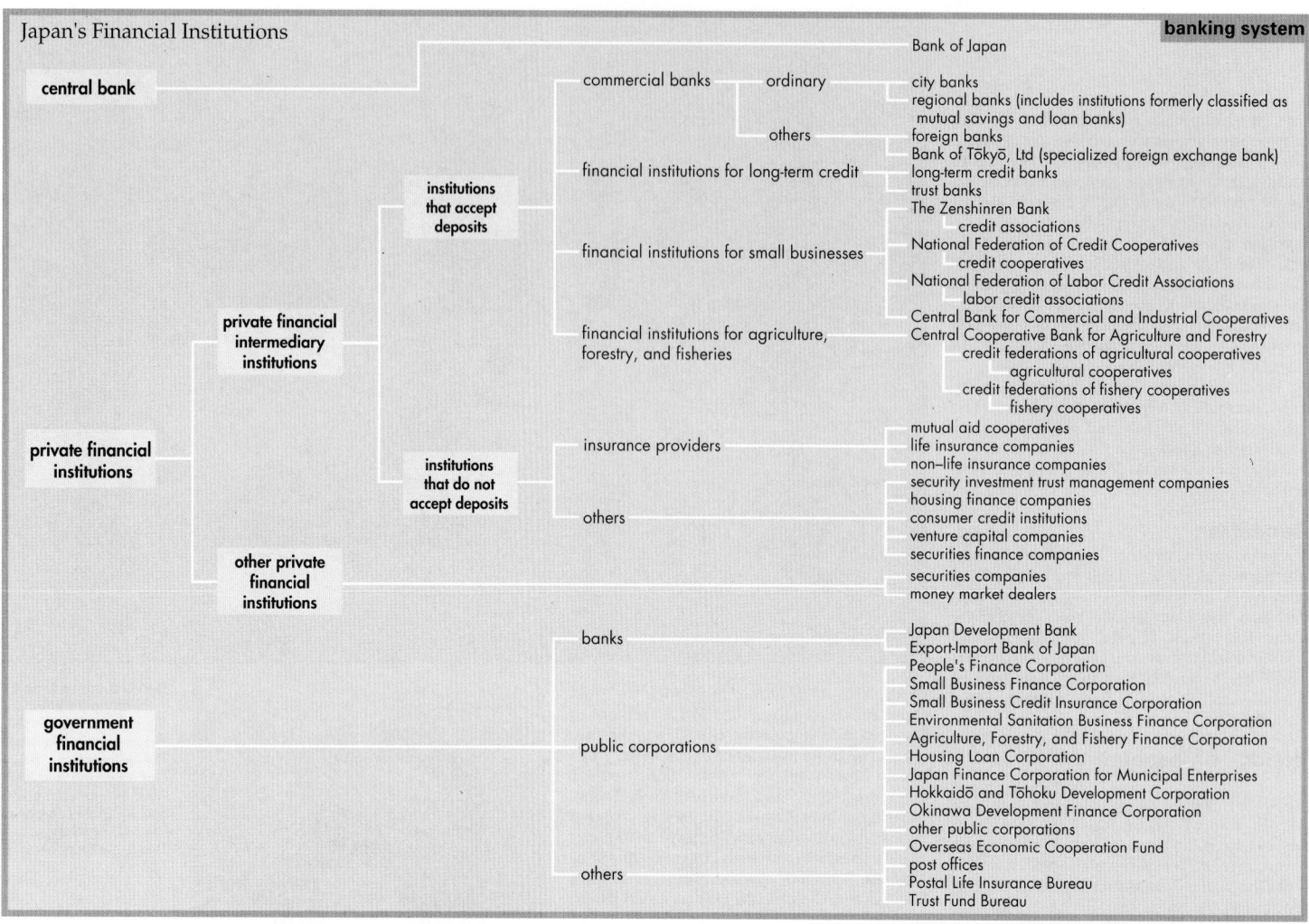

central bank — Bank of Japan

private financial institutions

- private financial intermediary institutions
  - institutions that accept deposits
    - commercial banks
      - ordinary
        - city banks
        - regional banks (includes institutions formerly classified as mutual savings and loan banks)
      - others
        - foreign banks
        - Bank of Tōkyō, Ltd (specialized foreign exchange bank)
    - financial institutions for long-term credit
      - long-term credit banks
      - trust banks
    - financial institutions for small businesses
      - The Zenshinren Bank
        - credit associations
      - National Federation of Credit Cooperatives
        - credit cooperatives
      - National Federation of Labor Credit Associations
        - labor credit associations
      - Central Bank for Commercial and Industrial Cooperatives
    - financial institutions for agriculture, forestry, and fisheries
      - Central Cooperative Bank for Agriculture and Forestry
        - credit federations of agricultural cooperatives
          - agricultural cooperatives
        - credit federations of fishery cooperatives
          - fishery cooperatives
  - institutions that do not accept deposits
    - insurance providers
      - mutual aid cooperatives
      - life insurance companies
      - non-life insurance companies
    - others
      - security investment trust management companies
      - housing finance companies
      - consumer credit institutions
      - venture capital companies
      - securities finance companies
- other private financial institutions
  - securities companies
  - money market dealers

government financial institutions

- banks
  - Japan Development Bank
  - Export-Import Bank of Japan
- public corporations
  - People's Finance Corporation
  - Small Business Finance Corporation
  - Small Business Credit Insurance Corporation
  - Environmental Sanitation Business Finance Corporation
  - Agriculture, Forestry, and Fishery Finance Corporation
  - Housing Loan Corporation
  - Japan Finance Corporation for Municipal Enterprises
  - Hokkaidō and Tōhoku Development Corporation
  - Okinawa Development Finance Corporation
  - other public corporations
- others
  - Overseas Economic Cooperation Fund
  - post offices
  - Postal Life Insurance Bureau
  - Trust Fund Bureau

such as long-term credit banks and trust banks, and by the separation of commercial banking from stock and other securities transactions.

The early 1990s, however, will probably see a major restructuring of the banking system. DEREGULATION is expected to allow commercial banks, long-term credit banks, and trust banks to enter each other's business fields. Lowering of the barriers between the banking and securities industries is also predicted to occur (see SECURITIES EXCHANGE LAW, ARTICLE 65).

Present Banking System——The BANK OF JAPAN is the central bank. It issues currency, acts as a lender of last resort, and serves as the bank for the government. It implements MONETARY POLICY, including changes in the official discount rate, open market operations, and changes in reserve requirements.

Ordinary commercial banks rely on savings deposits for lending capital; they provide commercial as well as industrial funds and engage in both short-term commercial banking and long-term financing. Japanese commercial banks are often closely aligned with specific enterprises or enterprise groups (see KEIRETSU), which rely on their affiliated banks for the greater part of their borrowing. Commercial banks fall into two categories: city banks (toshi ginkō) and regional banks (chihō ginkō). City banks are generally based in large cities, primarily Tōkyō, but operate nationwide; they are the giants of Japanese banking. At the end of 1990, 7 of the world's top 10 banks, in terms of deposits held, were Japanese city banks. The Bank of Tōkyō is traditionally counted as one of the city banks, although legally it is a specialized foreign exchange bank. Regional banks op-

erate primarily in limited local districts, where their clients are mostly local enterprises.

Long-term credit banks (chōki shin'yō ginkō) were established on the basis of the Long-Term Credit Bank Law of 1952 with the intention of ensuring a steady flow of long-term loans for capital investment, which ordinary banks were unable to provide. Three such banks operate today: the INDUSTRIAL BANK OF JAPAN, LTD; the LONG-TERM CREDIT BANK OF JAPAN, LTD; and the NIPPON CREDIT BANK, LTD. The services of the long-term credit banks differ from those of commercial banks in that they are able to issue bank debentures. They are, however, allowed to accept deposits only from certain types of customers, and there are limitations on the short-term loans they can offer.

Trust banks (shintaku ginkō) operate in accordance with the Bank Law, just as commercial banks do. However, they differ from commercial banks in that they engage in both banking and trust transactions as well as serving as savings institutions for the general public. Since the law requires the separation of trust transactions from commercial banking, trust banks manage trust accounts and bank accounts separately. Approval for foreign banks to operate in the Japanese trust market was included in the May 1985 report of the US-Japan Yen-Dollar Committee.

Mutual savings and loan banks (sōgo ginkō), credit associations (shin'yō kinko), and credit cooperatives (shin'yō kumiai) are financial institutions for small businesses. A 1988 revision of the Bank Law transformed the 68 mutual savings and loan banks into regional banks. Credit associations and cooperatives are financial institutions originally organized as COOPERATIVE ASSOCIATIONS,

but they are usually allowed to accept deposits from and make small loans to nonmembers.

AGRICULTURAL COOPERATIVE ASSOCIATIONS (nōkyō) in the farming, fishing, and forestry industries serve as sources of financing for their members. The central banking institution for financing the agricultural, forestry, and fisheries cooperatives is the NŌRIN CHŪKIN BANK.

Various government-run financial institutions also exist to supplement the activities of the private financial institutions. These include the EXPORT-IMPORT BANK OF JAPAN, the JAPAN DEVELOPMENT BANK, the SMALL BUSINESS FINANCE CORPORATION, and the GOVERNMENT HOUSING LOAN CORPORATION. Japan's POSTAL SAVINGS SYSTEM is also an important depository of savings.

Changes in the Japanese Banking System——The Japanese financial system was well suited to meet the vigorous demand for capital, mainly from the private sector, that was necessary to sustain the high growth of the post–World War II economy. For example, loans and discounts from banks and other financial institutions provided more than 90 percent of the total net supply of industrial funds in 1965, at the height of the growth period. The city banks, whose large enterprise clients demanded particularly sizable amounts of capital, depended in turn on funds borrowed from smaller banks, credit institutions, agricultural cooperatives, and the central bank.

During the mid-1970s, however, the growth of the Japanese economy stabilized at a moderate level, and the corporate demand for funds eased. Companies were then able to free themselves somewhat from their dependence on the banks by raising their own funds through corporate bond and stock issues in the capital markets. The use of foreign capital markets by Japanese companies also increased, thus promoting the internationalization of Japanese finance (see FOREIGN EXCHANGE CONTROLS). The government's budget deficit in the 1970s prompted it to issue a large volume of public bonds, which in turn led to a large expansion of the bond-trading market.

In the 1980s the decline in the dependence of major Japanese companies on the commercial banks for funds has led those banks to target smaller businesses and retail banking customers, market segments they had neglected in the past.

As mentioned earlier, deregulation promises to restructure Japan's banking system completely in the 1990s. In June 1991 the Ministry of Finance's FINANCIAL SYSTEM RESEARCH COUNCIL recommended that different types of banks (commercial banks, trust banks, and long-term credit banks), as well as securities firms, be allowed to set up subsidiaries in each other's business fields, or, in some cases, to compete directly by offering comparable financial products and services. Restrictions will probably be put on some new activities, however, in order to protect smaller institutions from direct competition with the powerful city banks.

Bank of Japan　　　日本銀行

(Nippon Ginkō). The central bank of Japan. It is the only note-issuing bank in the country and functions as the lender of last resort to the banking system and as the treasurer of the government.

The Bank of Japan was established in 1882. Its primary objective was to halt the inflation of the early years of the Meiji period (1868–1912). The inflation was mainly due to the overissue of nonconvertible bank notes by NATIONAL BANKS and of paper money by the government. MATSUKATA MASAYOSHI, who became finance minister in October 1881, felt it imperative to replace nonconvertible with convertible money and to establish a central bank.

The role played by the Bank of Japan during the last century has been quite significant. Its chief contributions have been providing adequate bank reserves so commercial banks could fund industrial development and stabilizing funds markets during economic crises. A major responsibility of the Bank of Japan is to avoid inflation and thus maintain the value of the YEN. To do this, it uses such monetary policy measures as changes in lending rates, open market operations, and changes in reserve requirements. Direct credit expansion controls (known as *madoguchi shidō* or "window guidance") have supplemented these instruments. The Bank of Japan also acquired a new, important role in the floating exchange rate system that began in the 1970s: it smoothed the foreign exchange market when currency value fluctuations were erratic. These policy measures have been executed not only from a domestic standpoint, but also under the framework of international policy coordination, especially since the PLAZA ACCORD of 1985. Total assets in 1991 were ¥43.1 trillion (US $320.5 billion). Its head office is in Tōkyō, and it has 33 domestic branches, 12 domestic offices, and 6 overseas offices.

Bank of Japan Building
日本銀行本店ビル

(Nippon Ginkō Honten Biru). Representative work of Meiji-period (1868–1912) Western-style architecture; located in Chūo

Ward, Tōkyō. It was designed by TATSUNO KINGO. Construction began in 1890 and was completed in 1896. The building occupies the southwest corner of the Bank of Japan's home office complex in Nihombashi. The bank is an imposing three-story brick construction faced with stone, with another floor below ground and steel girders for beams and trusses. It is Renaissance in design but has massive columns recalling the baroque. It demonstrates how quickly Japanese architects mastered Western building styles and techniques.

Bank of Korea→Chōsen Ginkō

Bank of Taiwan→Taiwan Ginkō

Bank of Tōkyō, Ltd
[株]東京銀行

(Tōkyō Ginkō). Japan's only specialized foreign exchange bank, so designated by the Foreign Exchange Bank Law of 1954. Incorporated in 1946 as the successor to the YOKOHAMA SPECIE BANK (Yokohama Shōkin Ginkō). While the number of its domestic branches has been limited by law, the size of its overseas network is comparable to that of the world's other leading international banks. The bank has 35 branches, 14 sub-branches, 26 representative offices, and 28 affiliated banks in 42 foreign countries. Of the bank's total of 17,000 employees (including those at subsidiaries and affiliated institutions), 12,000 are non-Japanese working in overseas offices. Ever since the initial overseas economic expansion of Japanese enterprises in the 1950s, and particularly with the intensified internationalization of Japan's economy in recent years, the bank's activities have increased rapidly in both domestic and overseas markets. For the fiscal year ending March 1991 the bank's total assets were ¥31.2 trillion (US $227.4 billion), and deposits were ¥21.0 trillion (US $153.1 billion). The bank was capitalized at ¥241.9 billion (US $1.8 billion) in the same year. Headquarters are in Tōkyō.

Bank of Yokohama, Ltd
[株]横浜銀行

(Yokohama Ginkō). Regional bank based in Kanagawa Prefecture. Incorporated in 1920. It is the leading bank of the 130 regional banks in Japan. In March 1988 the bank had a total of 195 domestic branches, located mainly in Yokohama, Tōkyō, and nearby areas. Overseas it has five branches, three subsidiaries, and four representative offices. The bank's correspondent network covers 98 countries. The bank's total assets were ¥13.5 trillion (US $98.4 billion), deposits were ¥10.2 trillion (US $74.3 billion), and capitalization stood at ¥134.0 billion (US $976.7 million) at the end of March 1991. Headquarters are in Yokohama.

Banko ware　　　万古焼

(*banko-yaki*). Decorated pottery now made principally in and around Yokkaichi, Mie Prefecture. First made in the late 18th century by a local merchant, Nunami Rōzan (1718–77), who established kilns near Kuwana in Ise and later in Edo (now Tōkyō). Old Banko and Edo Banko included tea-ceremony wares, dishes, bowls, *sake* bottles, candlesticks, incense burners and containers, and, most notably, tall Chinese Ming-style ewers with gracefully curved handles and spouts. Covered with a pale yellow, milky glaze, these products were popular for their exotic three-color designs mostly of red, green, and blue or purple, including

Bank of Japan Building This representative work of Meiji-period architecture (center) is the home of Japan's central bank. One of the newer buildings in the bank's headquarters appears at left.

some calico-print motifs. Rōzan's Kuwana kilns were revived in the 1830s, mainly for production of *sencha* tea-ceremony wares.

bankruptcy　　　破産

(*hasan*). In Japan, after a business enterprise has been declared bankrupt under the provisions of the BANKRUPTCY LAW (Hasan Hō) of 1922 (arts. 126, 127, and 132), several alternatives are available. One is to apply for protection under the CORPORATE REORGANIZATION LAW (Kaisha Kōsei Hō). Protection is granted upon presentation of a plan for reconstruction that has been agreed on by management, the labor union, and the supporting financial institutions. Plans often call for changes in management and adding representatives of financial institutions. If no plan for successful reconstruction can be created, the company's assets are sold. The proceeds from the sale are distributed to creditors based upon seniority of debt. Any remaining amount is then distributed to shareholders.

Bankruptcy Law　　　破産法

(Hasan Hō). Law of 1922 providing for judicial proceedings to liquidate the assets of an insolvent debtor and also for proceedings to financially rehabilitate the bankrupt. All kinds of debtors, including nonmerchants and corporations, are subject to such a proceeding, which can begin voluntarily upon a debtor's own application or involuntarily upon an application by a creditor. When the court deems the debtor bankrupt, it appoints an administrator who takes over the assets of the debtor. The administrator has the power to void fraudulent or preferential transfers made by the debtor. Secured creditors are not affected, but unsecured creditors must file their claims with the court in order to obtain dividends from the assets. Certain unsecured creditors enjoy priority over others. See also CORPORATE REORGANIZATION LAW.

Ban Nobutomo　　　伴信友

(1773–1846). KOKUGAKU (National Learning) scholar. The fourth son of Yamagishi Koretomo, a *samurai* of the Obama domain in Wakasa Province (now part of Fukui Prefecture), he was adopted at age 13 by Ban Nobumasa, a samurai of the same domain. For several years Nobutomo served his domain in Kyōto and in Edo (now Tōkyō). In 1801 Nobutomo became an adherent of the philosophical school of MOTOORI NORINAGA, studying with MOTOORI ŌHIRA, Norinaga's adopted son. A prolific author, he is particularly noted for his historical works and his philological studies of such classics as the NIHON SHOKI (720, Chronicle of Japan).

Bansha no Goku　　　蛮社の獄

(Imprisonment of the Companions of Barbarian Studies). A campaign of repression by the Tokugawa shogunate (1603–1867) against WATANABE KAZAN, TAKANO CHŌEI, KOSEKI

banzai This gesture, originally a prayer for the emperor's long life and for national prosperity, has become a way of expressing group emotion on various occasions. Here, *sumō* wrestler Chiyonofuji holds a trophy after his first tournament win, while supporters shout "*banzai*" and raise their hands.

bashaku During the Muromachi period the standard load for one packhorse was three bags of rice. Detail from a pair of six-panel folding screens by Kanō Eitoku titled *Scenes in and around Kyōto*. 1574. City of Yonezawa, Yamagata Prefecture.

SAN'EI, and other scholars of Rangaku (Dutch Learning, or the study of Western science and culture through Dutch; see WESTERN LEARNING) in the late 1830s. Kazan, Chōei, and San'ei were members of an informal study group, the SHŌSHIKAI, which discussed Western ideas and their practical application. The group was also known as Bansha, an abbreviation of Bangaku Shachū, or the "Companions of Barbarian Studies." They wrote tracts advocating Western Learning and criticizing the NATIONAL SECLUSION policy. Twenty-six of the scholars were arrested on charges that included criticism of shogunate policies and insurrection. Chōei and Kazan were convicted of criticizing the government. Kazan was sentenced to house arrest and Chōei to life imprisonment, but both eventually committed suicide. The shogunate's action severely curtailed the open pursuit of Western Learning.

Bansho Shirabesho 蕃書調所

(Institute for the Investigation of Barbarian Books). Japan's first central institution for the translation, study, and teaching of Western languages and scientific and technical subjects. It was a precursor of Tōkyō University. After the visits of Commodore Matthew PERRY in 1853–54, the Tokugawa shogunate (1603–1867) installed its translators of Western books and its collection of Western materials in a new and separate school designed specifically to train experts on Western subjects and handle diplomatic contacts and correspondence. Opening as the Yōgakusho (Institute for Western Learning) in Edo (now Tōkyō) in 1855, it was renamed Bansho Shirabesho and moved to new quarters in 1856. Dutch, the original language of translation, was joined by English, French, and German. The staff of over 50 included such leading scholars of WESTERN

LEARNING as KANDA TAKAHIRA, KATŌ HIROYUKI, NISHI AMANE, and TSUDA MAMICHI.

After several expansions and changes of name and location, the institute (then called Tōkyō Kaisei Gakkō) merged with Tōkyō Igakkō (Tōkyō Medical School) to form Tōkyō University in 1877.

Banshun 晩春

(Late Spring). Film (1949) directed by OZU YASUJIRŌ. Starring HARA SETSUKO and RYŪ CHISHŪ, this masterpiece of domestic drama tenderly depicts the affection between a young woman about to exceed marriageable age, and her father. As her father worries about her fate, she holds back, unwilling to marry and leave him alone. It was with this film that Ozu first assembled the team who would work on his later films—scenarist NODA KŌGO and stars Ryū and Hara.

Banshū Plain → Himeji Plain

Ban'yū Pharmaceutical Co, Ltd
万有製薬［株］

(Ban'yū Seiyaku). Manufacturer of prescription and nonprescription drugs. Incorporated in 1917. Since 1984 the company has been a subsidiary of Merck & Co, Inc, an international research-oriented pharmaceutical company based in the United States. Sales for the fiscal year ending March 1991 totaled ¥100.3 billion (US $731.0 million), of which 80 percent constituted products such as nervous system agents, circulatory agents, antibiotics, and adrenal cortex hormones. The company was capitalized at ¥44.4 billion (US $323.6 million) in the same year. Headquarters are in Tōkyō.

banzai 万歳

The Japanese equivalent of the English "three cheers." Used at celebratory parties and welcoming or farewell banquets to express common congratulations, encouragement, or exhortation. The participants shout the word *banzai* (literally, "ten thousand years") three times in unison, raising their hands in the air each time.

The word *banzai*, which is of Chinese origin, was in use in Japan from around the 8th century in the sense of "long life" to express respect for the emperor (it was then pronounced *banzei*). It went out of use for a long period, to be revived after the Meiji Restoration of 1868. It was only then that it became a triple cheer, in obvious imitation of the Western custom.

Baptist Church バプテスト派教会

(Baputesutoha Kyōkai). The first American Baptist missionary, Jonathan Goble (1827–98), arrived in Japan in 1860, when Christianity was still proscribed. In 1872 Nathan Brown (1807–86) joined him, and in 1876 the first Baptist church was built in Tōkyō. In 1884 the church established a theological school in Tōkyō, which expanded to become Kantō Gakuin University in 1949. In 1916 the Southern Baptist Mission built in Fukuoka a school that became Seinan Gakuin University in 1949. In 1989 the Nihon Baputesuto Remmei (Japan Baptist Convention), affiliated with the Southern Baptist Mission, claimed 29,223 members with 216 churches, whereas the Nihon Baputesuto Dōmei (Japan Baptist Union), affiliated with northern Baptist denominations in the United States, claimed 4,683 members with 54 churches. The remaining Baptist denominations together claimed over 3,000 adherents.

Bar Association → Japan Federation of Bar Associations

barley → wheat and barley

baseball 野球

(*yakyū*). Baseball is the most popular team sport in Japan. The game was first played in Japan in 1873 at Kaisei Gakkō (now Tōkyō University) under the instruction of an American, Horace Wilson. The first Japanese baseball team was organized around 1880, and several college teams were soon formed in Tōkyō. Baseball clubs were formed in middle schools throughout the country around 1900. Baseball became Japan's major school sport, with interscholastic competitions leading the way (see also HIGH SCHOOL BASEBALL). Other amateur teams also compete in regular leagues and tournaments, of which the Intercity Baseball Championship Tournament and the Japan Amateur Baseball Championship Tournament are the most important. All amateur activity, including school baseball, is supervised by the Japan Amateur Baseball Federation.

The first professional team, the Dai Nihon Baseball Club, was organized in 1934, and by 1936 seven professional teams had been formed. The current two-league system, consisting of the Central League and the Pacific League, was set up in 1950. Each league has six teams, all of which are owned and sponsored by large corporations. See also BASEBALL, PROFESSIONAL.

In 1919 a special form of the game using a hollow rubber ball was invented by Suzuka Sakae for young players. The ball is softer and less dangerous, and the rest of the equipment is simpler and cheaper. The rubber ball was taken up by adult players as well and contributed greatly to the popularization of baseball in Japan.

baseball, professional プロ野球

(*puro yakyū*). The first professional baseball team was organized in Japan in 1934, when the mass media entrepreneur and politician SHŌRIKI MATSUTARŌ formed the core of the team that is known today as the Yomiuri Giants. Six additional teams had been established by 1936, when the first professional baseball league was organized. Since 1950 there have been two professional leagues: the Central League and the Pacific League. In 1993 the following teams constituted the Central League: the Yomiuri Giants, the Chūnichi Dragons, the Hanshin Tigers, the Hiroshima Tōyō Carp, the Yakult Swallows, and the Yokohama BayStars. In the same year, the Pacific League comprised the following teams: the Kintetsu Buffaloes, the Seibu Lions, the Fukuoka Daiei Hawks, the Nippon-Ham Fighters, the Orix BlueWave, and the Chiba Lotte Marines. Each team plays the five other teams in its league 26 times each season for a total of 130 games. The teams with the highest winning percentage in each league face each other in the Japan Series to decide that year's championship team. Approximately 20 million fans attend baseball games annually in Japan, and millions more watch it on television, making baseball one of the nation's most popular professional sports.

BASF Japan, Ltd
ビーエーエスエフジャパン［株］

(Bī Ē Esu Efu Japan). Chemical company. Incorporated in 1949 as a subsidiary of the German chemical company BASF Aktiengesellschaft. Sales for the fiscal year ending December 1990 totaled ¥72.0 billion (US $539.1 million), of which chemical products accounted for 25 percent; dyestuffs and synthetic chemicals, 29 percent; plastics, 30 percent; and other products, 16 percent. The company was capitalized at ¥10.4 billion (US $77.9 million) in the same year. Headquarters are in Tōkyō.

bashaku   馬借

(packhorsemen teams). Laborers who transported goods from rural areas to the cities. They first appeared in the Heian period (794–1185) to meet the increasing dependence of Kyōto on goods from outlying regions. By the late Kamakura period (1185–1333) they had a virtual monopoly on overland shipment. Many were farmers who worked during the slack season. *Bashaku* were concentrated in the POST-STATION TOWNS. Generally employed by forwarding agents or horse breeders, they were in some cases controlled by local warlords (SHUGO DAIMYŌ). *Bashaku* eventually gained control of their own enterprises. By the middle years of the Muromachi period (1333–1568) they formed associations that played a role in popular uprisings of the 15th century (see BASHAKU IKKI). In the Edo period (1600–1868) *bashaku* organized themselves into guilds (ZA), and many became rich wholesale merchants in the cities.

bashaku ikki   馬借一揆

(packhorsemen's uprisings). Uprisings in the Muromachi period (1333–1568) led by the packhorsemen (BASHAKU) who monopolized the transport of goods to the cities. They were particularly powerful in the provinces that supplied Kyōto and Nara. The *bashaku* staged uprisings in 1418 and 1426 to protest a decline in the price of rice. Because of close contact with villages along their routes, *bashaku* soon allied with farmers and led a major uprising in the area between Ōmi (now Shiga Prefecture) and Kyōto in 1428 to demand cancellation of cultivators' debts. They played a central role in other agrarian disturbances (TSUCHI IKKI) thereafter.

Bashō   芭蕉

(1644–94). Full name Matsuo Bashō. Poet, essayist, and writer of travel sketches in the early Edo period (1600–1868) who helped perfect the art of *haikai* (see HAIKU) and HAIBUN in the formative years of these genres. He was called Kinsaku in childhood, Matsuo Munefusa after coming of age. The name Bashō ("banana plant") is a sobriquet he adopted around 1681 after moving into a hut with a banana plant alongside.

Early Years——Bashō was born at or near Ueno in Iga Province (now part of Mie Prefecture). He began to write poetry in *haikai* form using the name Sōbō. His earliest surviving poems, dating from 1662, are characterized by elegant humor and clever allusions to Heian-period (794–1185) classics and the NŌ drama. In 1666 Bashō began traveling around the Kyōto area, learning about the fashionable life of the capital. In 1672 he compiled a book of *haikai* matched in contest, *Kai ōi* (Covering Shells), in which he served as judge and commentator.

Settlement in Edo——In 1672 Bashō moved to Edo (now Tōkyō) and gradually established himself as a teacher of *haikai*. Under the new sobriquet Tōsei he wrote poems characterized by wordplay and earthy humor. When he alluded to the clas-

sics, he often parodied or ridiculed them. This style was popular in Edo, and his students steadily increased in number. In 1680 he published *Tōsei montei dokugin nijikkasen* (Best Poems of Tōsei's 20 Disciples). Later that year he settled in a small hut in the Fukagawa district of Edo and shortly afterward began calling himself Bashō. Despite his increasing fame and material well-being, Bashō was apparently not at peace with himself and he began to practice Zen. His poems in *Minashiguri* (Empty Chestnuts), an anthology of verse that he and his disciples published in 1683, suggest his spiritual ambivalence and an experimental disposition. The urge to break down convention and avoid staleness soon took on a more physical form, that of traveling, through which he hoped to attain spiritual and poetic discipline.

Westward Journeys——In the fall of 1684 Bashō traveled west along the Pacific coastline and arrived at his native town of Ueno about a month later. From there he visited Nagoya, where he led a team of poets in composing five volumes of linked verse collectively known as *Fuyu no hi* (1684, The Winter Sun). He also visited Nara, Ōgaki, and Kyōto, before returning to Edo the following summer. This journey resulted in Bashō's journal *Nozarashi kikō* (1685; tr *The Records of a Weather-Exposed Skeleton*, 1966).

In the fall of 1687 he traveled to Kashima, a scenic town northeast of Edo, to see the harvest moon. The trip resulted in a short travel sketch, *Kashima kikō* (1687; tr *A Visit to Kashima Shrine*, 1966). The sketch shows Bashō unmistakably awakening to the value of FŪRYŪ, an aesthetic ideal cherished by eremitic artists since medieval times. Shortly after his visit to Kashima, Bashō set out on another long journey westward. The trip, which lasted 10 months, resulted in two more poetic diaries: *Oi no kobumi* (1690–91; tr *The Records of a Travel-Worn Satchel*, 1966) and *Sarashina kikō* (1688; tr *A Visit to Sarashina Village*, 1966).

Journey to the North——Bashō next undertook a long journey to the most underdeveloped part of Japan, the northern area of Honshū. Leaving Edo in the late spring of 1689, he traveled some 1,500 miles (2,400 km) in 156 days. It was probably then that he evolved his famous poetic principle known as SABI, a dialectic synthesis of gorgeous and lonely beauty. He transformed his experience into OKU NO HOSOMICHI (1694; tr *The Narrow Road to the Deep North*, 1966), one of the high points in the history of the Japanese poetic diary.

Last Years——Bashō spent the next two years in and around Kyōto. He wrote an excellent *haibun*, *Genjūan no ki* (1690; tr *Prose Poem on the Unreal Dwelling*, 1955). This essay and the haiku and linked verse he wrote at this time were later collected in SARUMINO (1691; tr *Monkey's Raincoat*, 1973). His last major work was *Saga nikki* (1691; tr *The Saga Diary*, 1971–72).

Bashō returned to Edo in the winter of 1691. He became increasingly depressed but eventually overcame the problem by striving for what he called *karumi* ("lightness"). This ideal, reflected in an anthology called *Sumidawara* (A Sack of Charcoal), which his students published in 1694, envisioned a life of spiritual detachment while being physically bound to the world. Bashō set out on his last westward journey in the summer of 1694. He contracted a stomach ailment in Ōsaka and died there on 28 November 1694.

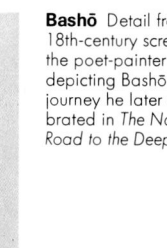

Bashō Detail from an 18th-century screen by the poet-painter Buson depicting Bashō on the journey he later celebrated in *The Narrow Road to the Deep North.*

Reputation and Influence——Bashō is said to have had more than 2,000 students at the time of his death. If this number is debatable, there is no doubt about his high reputation among contemporary and later poets. In the sense that he elevated haiku into a mature art form, he was the founder of the genre they all looked up to. Also, since his poetry went through various phases, he was able to appeal to poets of widely different temperaments. In the 20th century Bashō's influence has reached outside *haikai* circles: some consider Bashō a Wordsworthian figure who sought a mystic union with nature; to others Bashō seems almost a precursor of French symbolism; to modern novelists such as AKUTAGAWA RYŪNOSUKE (1892–1927), Bashō appeared to be a humanist for whom the highest good was poetry. With the increasing interest in haiku outside Japan, his reputation has become international.

Bassui Tokushō   抜隊得勝

(1327–87). Also known as Battai Tokushō. Zen monk of the RINZAI SECT. Born in Nakamura, Sagami Province (now part of Kanagawa Prefecture). Tokushō studied with Kohō Kakumyō (1271–1361), JAKUSHITSU GENKŌ (1290–1367), and others. Tokushō's rigorous spiritual discipline attracted many followers, and a collection of his instructions was published as *Wadei gassui shū* (1386).

Bataan   バターン半島

(Batān Hantō). Mountainous, thickly jungled peninsula to the west of Manila Bay on Luzon Island in the Philippines, which gained notoriety during World War II as the site of the Bataan "death march." In May 1942 about 75,000 Allied captives, 12,000 of them Americans, were forced to march from Mariveles, at the tip of the peninsula, to Camp O'Donnell, some 96 kilometers (about 60 mi) away. General Homma Masaharu (1887–1946), the commanding officer, had made inadequate arrangements for food and medical care. Thousands died on the march, and many more perished at the camp in the ensuing three months.

Batchelor, John   バチェラー, J.

(1854–1944). Anglican missionary; born in Sussex, England. Originally stationed in Hong Kong but forced for reasons of health to live in a colder climate, he went to Hakodate in 1877 to preach among the Japanese on the northern island of Hokkaidō. However, he found it more urgent to work among the AINU, the native inhabitants of the island, and in 1879 was granted permission to do so. He lived among the Ainu people, built schools, and provided medical care. Batchelor spent

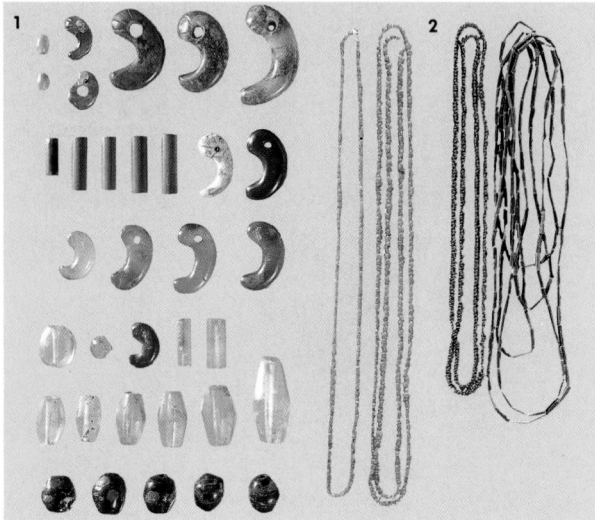

ancient beads

1 Many types of beads were used by the ancient Japanese for ritual and ornamental purposes. Shown here are comma-shaped beads (*magatama*); cylindrical beads (*kudatama*); diamond-shaped, faceted beads (*kirikodama*); and roundish, composite beads (*tombodama*). Kofun period. Kyōto University.

2 Blue-glass bead necklaces dating from the Late Yayoi period. Saga Prefectural Museum.

more than 60 years in Hokkaidō until the beginning of World War II, which forced him to return to England. He also studied Ainu culture and language. His best-known work was *An Ainu English Japanese Dictionary* (1889).

bateren バテレン

Japanese approximation of the Western word "padre"; used to designate Christian priests, especially Jesuits, during the "Christian Century" (1549–1650) and Edo period (1600–1868). Originally *bateren* was a standard neutral appellation. Later the term assumed a distinctly sinister connotation in the popular literature of the KIRISHITAN MONOGATARI genre, which portrayed the grotesque Urugan Bateren (Padre Organtino), Furaten Bateren (the *fratres* or brothers of the mendicant orders under a collective pseudonym), and other *bateren* as evil magicians and agents of a Christian conspiracy intent on subverting and seizing Japan. The subcategory *korobi bateren* refers to apostate priests, such as the Jesuits Christovão Ferreira (Sawano Chūan) and Giuseppe Chiara (Okamoto San'emon), whom the Tokugawa shogunate (1603–1867) used in its anti-Christian inquisition.

bath 風呂

(*furo*). The typical Japanese bath consists of a tub deep enough for the bather to immerse the body up to the neck when sitting. Water is piped into the tub from a water heater or heated in the tub by a gas burner at one end. There is a drain in the floor of the bathroom, and the bather washes and rinses the body completely before entering the tub to soak, thus keeping the bathwater as clean as possible for other bathers, who usually use the same water throughout the day.

As early as the Nara period (710–794), large temples such as TŌDAIJI and HŌRYŪJI provided a kind of public steam bath. Public baths were maintained by temples and by the wealthy for the poor and unfortunate until the Muromachi period (1333–1568). Bathing places for the general public became popular after the first commercial bath was constructed in Edo (now Tōkyō) in 1591. By the time of the Meiji Restoration (1868), there were 600 public baths (*sentō*) in Tōkyō. Not just for bathing, these became social haunts where bathers could spend leisurely hours playing games and eating. In the pleasure districts certain types of public bathing facilities for men provided female attendants called *yuna*, who not only washed the customers' backs while massaging them with their fingertips but also served tea and

provided erotic pleasures on the second floor. The government banned these brothel-bathhouses in 1657, but legitimate public baths flourished afterward.

Modern public baths (still called *sentō*) now have separate entrances, dressing rooms, and bathing rooms for men and women. Plastic stools and basins are provided for the use of customers, who sit in rows before sets of hot- and cold-water faucets where they wash before entering one of the large tubs to soak. However, because people increasingly have baths in their own homes, many *sentō* are going out of business. In 1964 there were 23,016 public baths in Japan, but in 1991 there were only 9,704.

Modern-day baths in the home are in small rooms, usually separate from the toilet. The room is usually tiled. Although traditionally made of wood, tile, or, more rarely, metal, tubs are now often made of polypropylene reinforced with fiberglass. On CHILDREN'S DAY (5 May) many people still put the fragrant leaves of the SHŌBU plant in the bathwater. Several customs of the *furo* have entered other aspects of Japanese life. For example, the square cloth known as *furoshiki* ("bath spread"), used since the Edo period (1600–1868) to carry toilet articles into the *sentō* and to stand on while dressing, is now a common article used to wrap gifts or to carry many other items.

➡ 104–105

bats 蝙蝠

(*kōmori*). In Japanese, *kōmori* is the general name for flying mammals of the order Chiroptera, which is divided into suborders Microchiroptera and Megachiroptera. The former, which includes in it the families Rhinolophidae and Vespertilionidae, is distributed throughout the four main islands of Japan; the latter is represented only by the *ōkōmori* (flying fox; genus *Pteropus*), which inhabits warm regions such as the OGASAWARA ISLANDS and the RYŪKYŪ ISLANDS.

The most common bat throughout Japan is the *abura kōmori* (Japanese pipistrelle; *Pipistrellus abramus*), which lives near human dwellings. The *kikugashira kōmori* (*Rhinolophus ferrumequinum*), *usagi kōmori* (*Plecotus auritus*), and *yama kōmori* (*Nyctalus lasiopterus*) are often found in caves and dark crevices of forest trees. The number of individuals of all these species has been sharply reduced in recent years. The shape of the common Japanese folding fan is said to have been suggested by the bat's wing, and the Japanese once called Western-style umbrellas *kōmorigasa* ("bat umbrellas") by association with the shape.

batsu 閥

A traditional type of clique or faction that is still found in modern Japan. Although factionalism in various forms has been evident in Japanese society for centuries, the word *batsu* became common only during and after the rapid Westernization in the Meiji period (1868–1912) as a convenient term for referring to factionalism based on surviving traditional social and political patterns.

A *batsu* consists of a group of persons with common ties based on institution, geographic region, family, or connection to the same person, who form an in-group, as, for example, in industry, government, a political party, or an educational institution. A *batsu* is basically hierarchical and paternalistic and frequently controls hiring, promoting, and the granting of political and business favors. Members of a *batsu* carry an

obligation (*giri;* see GIRI AND NINJŌ) to help each other and to repay their debt (ON) to their superiors, particularly to the group leader, who not only exercises paternalistic benevolence but also claims loyalty from subordinates. This pseudo familial or OYABUN-KOBUN ("parent-child") relationship is accompanied by a hierarchical structure of authority deriving from length of service (see SEMPAI-KŌHAI).

Particular types of *batsu* may be distinguished by different prefixes, as in GAKUBATSU (school clique) or, in pre–World War II days, GUMBATSU (military clique). *Batsu* are usually found in professions requiring training, such as teaching, medicine, business management, civil service, and politics.

One of the oldest kinds of *batsu* is KEIBATSU, a clique formed through marriage alliances and having some political or economic power. After the Meiji Restoration (1868), men from the former domains (*han*) of Satsuma, Chōshū, Tosa, and Hizen (now the prefectures of Kagoshima, Yamaguchi, Kōchi, and Saga, respectively) came to dominate the government and military through domain-based cliques called HAMBATSU. ZAIBATSU (financial cliques) are the financial-business-industrial conglomerates that emerged in the late 19th and early 20th centuries. *Gakubatsu* are cliques based on the college or university from which one has graduated. A particularly modern incidence of *batsu* is found in political parties and trade unions in which factions (HABATSU) vie for leadership. See also GROUPS.

be 部

Hereditary occupational groups that supplied labor, goods, and other economic services to the YAMATO COURT and to powerful lineage groups (UJI) from the 5th to the 7th century. Until the influx of immigrants from Korea (KIKAJIN) during the 5th and 6th centuries, low-ranking court officials called *tomo* had served the Yamato ruler. The arrival of the *kikajin* was associated with the reorganization of the *tomo* to allow for greater diversification of functions. It was from this time that *tomo* began to be known as *be*. At the head of each *be* was a leader called the TOMO NO MIYATSUKO, who supervised the workers, and the system as a whole was under the general supervision of the court administrators *omi* and *muraji*, who were also leaders of the chief lineage groups. As the *be* system developed, agricultural *be* came to form the chief economic resource of the imperial family (see KOSHIRO AND NASHIRO) and the powerful lineage-group chieftains—*omi*, *muraji*, and *tomo no miyatsuko* (*kakibe*). The *be* system represents the sociopolitical structure of the primitive Japanese state: at the apex was the Yamato sovereign, who had secured the allegiance of powerful *uji* chieftains; below these chieftains were the numerous *be*; at the bottom were the NUHI, or slaves. After the TAIKA REFORM of 645 a more centralized form of state organization was established.

beads, ancient 玉

(*tama*). Beads were used in the prehistoric and protohistoric periods as body ornaments, decorations, and ritual objects. Following the introduction of Buddhism in the 6th century, the practice of decorating the body ceased, and beads were used through the succeeding periods mainly in the BUDDHIST ROSARY. (Modern bead necklaces are commonly worn with Western clothing but never with *kimono*.)

The most significant Japanese bead is the *magatama* (curved jewel); a set of these was included as one of the three IMPERIAL REGALIA as early as the 6th century. Developing from irregularly shaped, perforated jade pebbles as found in the Middle Jōmon period (ca 3500 BC–ca 2500 BC; also dated as ca 3500 BC–ca 2000 BC), the *magatama* became standardized as comma-shaped in the ensuing Yayoi period (ca 300 BC–ca AD 300). In the Kofun period (ca 300–710), green *magatama* of jadite or chalcedony were important marks of status. *Magatama* are often discovered in the Kofun-period mounded tombs (KOFUN) or tunnel tombs (YOKOANA).

A variety of other beads were used in protohistoric ornamentation. Round types included stone beads like those found in Jōmon SHELL MOUNDS and the KAMEGAOKA SITE; shell and blue-glass beads, whose production techniques were developed in the Yayoi period; and silver, gilt-bronze, and multicolored glass beads of the Kofun period. In the Late Kofun period, shapes and materials proliferated; faceted beads (*kirikodama*), jujube-shaped beads (*natsumedama*), flat beads (*hiradama*), cylindrical beads (*kudatama*), and three-peaked beads (*miwadama*) were created in serpentine, rock crystal, amber, agate, jasper, jadite, lignite, and chalcedony. Bead-making sites of the Jōmon, Yayoi, and Kofun periods are known from gemstone sources in Shiga, Ishikawa, Toyama, Kanagawa, Chiba, Ibaraki, and Shimane prefectures.

beanbag   御手玉

(*otedama*). Japanese beanbags are made of colorful scraps of cloth and usually are filled with red *azuki* beans or rice. They are round and small enough to fit into the palm of a child's hand; some have bells attached. The beanbag game, traditionally played by girls, uses a set of five, seven, or nine beanbags. The complexity of the game ranges from simply juggling to performing various maneuvers with one or more of the other bags while one bag is in midair. An ancient game originally played with pebbles, it assumed its present form around the 17th century.

bean paste → miso

Beard, Charles Austin   ビアード, C. A.

(1874–1948). American historian and political scientist. Born in Indiana. He earned his doctorate at Columbia University, joining its faculty in 1904. In 1922 he was invited by GOTŌ SHIMPEI (then mayor of Tōkyō) to conduct a study of Tōkyō's municipal government. As a result of his visit he published *The Administration and Politics of Tōkyō* (1923). Just after the great TŌKYŌ EARTHQUAKE OF 1923, he returned to Japan and advised on the work of reconstruction.

bears   熊

(*kuma*). In Japanese, *kuma* is the general name for mammals of the family Ursidae. Two species are found in Japan: the *higuma* (brown bear; *Ursus arctos*) of Hokkaidō and the *tsukinowaguma* (Asiatic black bear; *Selenarctos thibetanus*) of Honshū, Shikoku, and Kyūshū. The *higuma* is the largest carnivorous animal in Japan, with a length of about 2 meters (6.5 ft) and a weight of about 400 kilograms (880 lb). It is comparatively common in woods near rivers or streams up to an elevation of 1,700 meters (5,600 ft).

The *tsukinowaguma* is of medium size, with a length of about 1.4 meters (5 ft) and

beanbag Made with cloth scraps and *azuki* beans, these small beanbags are used in a juggling game traditionally played by girls.

a weight of about 200 kilograms (440 lb). Its body is black, with a white crescent mark on the chest. It is fairly numerous in woods in central and northern Honshū.

Most Japanese regard the *tsukinowaguma* as an attractive or good-natured mountain creature; it appears only rarely as a dreadful beast in folk traditions and tales. The *higuma* is extremely important in the legends and traditional lifestyle of the AINU people of Hokkaidō.

bedding   寝具

(*shingu*). Traditional Japanese bedding consists primarily of FUTON, padded mattresses and quilts pliable enough to be spread on the floor at night for sleeping and then folded and stored out of sight during the day. In traditional houses a room could thus serve multiple purposes. Although Western beds and bedding, as well as bedrooms, have gained in popularity, traditional bedding is still widely used. Besides *futon*, other articles of bedding include PILLOWS (*makura*), sheetlike covers for quilts (*shikifu*), robelike sleeved quilts (*kaimaki*) for winter use, and lightweight quilts and mosquito nets (*kaya*) for the summer.

The use of cotton quilting for bedding is said to have originated around the mid-16th century. Prior to that the ruling nobility and *samurai* slept on thick woven rush matting such as *tatami* or *goza*, and the common people used straw mats or simply loose straw. People covered themselves with *fusuma*, coverlets that had sleeves and neckbands like *kimono*.

Mosquito nets have been in use from ancient times, and were widely used by all classes from the beginning of the Edo period (1600–1868). The nets are large enough to accommodate several sleepers and are suspended by cords attached to hooks in the four corners of the room. With the increased use of window and door screens, however, nets have almost disappeared from urban areas.

bees and wasps   蜂

(*hachi*). In Japanese, *hachi* is the common name for members of the order Hymenoptera other than ants. More than 100,000 species are known worldwide, and several thousand species are thought to live in Japan. The main species are *habachi* (sawflies), the larvae of which feed on leaves; *kibachi* (horntails), which eat wood; *himebachi* (ichneumons), *komayubachi* (braconids), and *kobachi* (chalcids), which are parasites; *tamabachi* (gall wasps), which cause galls; *bekkōbachi* (spider wasps) and *jigabachi* (sand wasps), which prey on spiders and other insects; *hanabachi* (bees), which gather pollen and nectar; *suzumebachi* (hornets); and *mitsubachi* (honey bees), which live in colonies.

The first recorded appearance of bees in Japanese mythology is in the account in the KOJIKI (712) in which the deity ŌKUNINUSHI NO MIKOTO is put in a chamber full of bees. It is thought that the technique of beekeeping

bears The Asiatic black bear is known in Japan as the *tsukinowaguma* ("moon-circle bear"), a name derived from the white crescent marking on its chest.

was introduced to Japan from Korea in the 7th century. The ENGI SHIKI (927) records that beekeeping had spread throughout the country by the early Heian period (794–1185) when only the powerful and rich used honey. In the Edo period (1600–1868) beekeeping became widespread.

Beheiren → Peace for Vietnam Committee

beigoma   貝独楽

A kind of small top (*koma*); corruption of the word *baigoma* (shell top); originally made by filling a spiral seashell with sand and lead. It is also called *muchigoma*, or "whip top," and is spun with a whipcord. Early in the 20th century *beigoma* made of cast metal were popular children's toys. See also TOPS.

Belgium and Japan   ベルギーと日本

(*Berugī to* Nihon). Diplomatic relations between Belgium and Japan began with the signing of a treaty of amity, commerce, and navigation in 1866. Relations were severed during World War II, but resumed in April 1952 when the SAN FRANCISCO PEACE TREATY went into effect. Japan signed a treaty of

Continued on page 106 →

beigoma These small "fighting tops" (metal type pictured) are used in a game where contestants compete to knock each other's tops off a mat.

The Pleasures of the Bath

Although today's public baths are no longer the great gathering places they once were, they still provide an opportunity for friends, family, and even business associates to get together and relax.

In ancient creation myths, Japanese gods were said to have bathed during and after their labors of producing the universe. Notions of ritual purification and personal cleanliness have been reinforced throughout Japanese history by Shintō religious traditions. While in the West cleanliness has come to be considered "next to godliness" in relatively recent times, in Japan cleanliness and godliness have always been associated.

The Japanese are perhaps unequaled in the degree to which they have celebrated the practice of bathing. While not unique in this—the Romans, after all, are known for their great public baths, the Scandinavians their saunas, and the Turks their steam baths—few cultures have lavished as much attention on bathing customs and accoutrements as the Japanese.

Blessed with numerous geothermal springs and an abundance of fresh water, the volcanic archipelago of Japan has always made cleanliness a simple and economical matter. The hot water that bubbles up limitlessly from the earth has soothed tired muscles and cleansed worn bodies and spirits throughout history. Communal bathhouses were a central fea-

ture of Buddhist temples from about the 7th century on. In more recent eras, large urban bathhouses served as centers of community interaction. Bathhouses were to Japanese cities what the central plaza, town green, and local tavern were to European and American communities: a spot where friends or citizens could gather to exchange news or gossip. Japanese bathhouses provided an atmosphere of relaxation and a "democratic" release from the hierarchical distinctions so rigidly observed in other social contexts. After all, how strictly can class distinctions be observed when everyone is nude?

Although most modern Japanese homes and apartments are equipped with private baths, the Japanese people have not forgotten the benefits of group bathing. An outing with friends or colleagues to a hot-spring resort remains a favorite pastime, and some city dwellers prefer nightly visits to a public bathhouse in the neighborhood to a solitary bath at home.

Rare is the Japanese who does not bathe at least once a day. Unlike the quick, efficient shower that is the usual form of bathing for most Americans and Europeans, Japanese bathing practice still calls for total immersion in a tub of water—as hot as the bather can bear. It should be noted that Japanese bathrooms are exclusively used for bathing. In the English language, the word "bathroom" has come to include the

Since most homes and apartments now have their own baths, public baths are slowly disappearing from Japan's cities. Mt. Fuji is a favorite motif for murals in public baths.

It is easy to forget the problems and pressures of working life when relaxing in an outdoor bath such as this one at Nakabusa Hot Spring in Nagano Prefecture.

A visitor to Iya Hot Spring in Tokushima Prefecture is massaged by a waterfall of hot water.

toilet, but in Japan toilet and bath are kept separate.

Whether at home, a public bathhouse, or a hot-spring resort, etiquette requires that bathers first wash outside the tub, carefully rinsing away all soap and grime. They should be completely clean before settling in for a deep relaxing soak.

The finest tubs in Japan are constructed of soft woods. *Hinoki* (Japanese cypress) and *maki* (Chinese black pine) are considered best. Wooden tubs are carefully crafted to be leakproof and to swell with wetness and contract with dryness without cracking. But fine woods have become scarce in Japan and are extremely expensive; no less rare are the skilled craftsmen able to build such tubs. Consequently, wooden tubs are rapidly becoming a luxury reserved for the wealthy. Far more common today are mass-produced tubs of molded plastic, fiberglass, or enameled steel. Functional, easy to clean, and comparatively inexpensive, they have made the convenience of a private bath available to virtually every Japanese home. Lost, however, is the extraordinarily sensual pleasure afforded by a soak in an old-fashioned wooden tub.

Public Bathhouses

Until recent years, public bathhouses (*sentō*) could be found every few blocks in all Japanese cities. Today, however, many bathhouses have had to close their doors, and those that remain are struggling for survival. Bathhouses are privately owned, but since they provide a valuable service to the community, the costs of construction, fuel, and maintenance are subsidized by public funds.

Urban bathhouses are divided into male and female sections. Bathers pay a fee upon entering (currently ¥330 for adults in the Tōkyō area; about US $2.50), check their shoes in a locker, and proceed to a large antechamber where they undress, placing their clothing in a basket or locker provided for this purpose. The dressing room opens directly onto a large tiled room with one or more deep pool-like tubs. Along the walls are showers and faucets with hot and cold water. The walls may be elaborately decorated with large murals depicting famous scenic spots like Mt. Fuji, the Alps, or the Bay of Naples.

The sunken pools are heated to various temperatures, and the water is constantly replenished from a tap or fountain. Each pool is large enough to accommodate up to 10 bathers, and since all of them have washed outside the tub and never carry soap into it, the communal water usually remains clean until the bathhouse closes at 11 PM. Then the pool is drained and scrubbed in preparation for the next day, when the bathhouse opens for business at 4 PM.

In an effort to attract customers, many public bathhouses have taken to installing various amusements and innovative features. Saunas, steam rooms, and whirlpool baths have become commonplace, as have massage rooms, health bars, and video games.

Hot-Spring Resorts

Hot springs, known as *onsen*, can be found throughout Japan. Legend has it that many hot springs were "created" by the 9th-century Buddhist sage Kūkai, who in the course of his pilgrimages around the country would often strike his staff on a rock, causing an endless stream of hot water to flow forth.

Many hot springs were discovered by hunters tracking their prey into the mountains. Wild monkeys were frequently found to bathe in warm springs, and wounded animals entered the hot mineral waters to heal their injuries. New hot springs are occasionally discovered deep in the mountains by hikers or cross-country skiers and are added to the thousands that have already been developed as resorts listed in travel guides.

Today a visit to a hot spring may be anything from a simple family outing to an organized trip by a club or group of friends or co-workers, who spend a weekend together bathing, eating, drinking, and relaxing. Large hot-spring resorts like Noboribetsu in Hokkaidō, Atami near Tōkyō, and Beppu in Kyūshū rival Las Vegas or Atlantic City in the lavishness and variety of the entertainment they offer. Hundreds of other smaller *onsen* towns—Naruko, Minakami, Kusatsu, Hakone, Shimoda, Kinosaki, Tamatsukuri, and Ibusuki, to name only a few—are likewise devoted to the pleasures of hot-spring bathing. The festive atmosphere of such places is heightened by throngs of high-spirited hotel guests strolling about from baths to bars in colorful *yukata* robes provided by the hotels.

The public baths of resort hotels (nowadays usually segregated into men's and women's facilities) often occupy the finest spot in the hotel and command sweeping views from wide glass windows. A popular phenomenon has been the development of "jungle baths." These are generally huge greenhouselike structures built on the roofs of high-rise hotels or in their gardens. They are densely filled with tropical plants that flourish in the steamy atmosphere rising from the pools. The hedonistic spirit of the *onsen* visitor demands a wide variety of baths in which to immerse the body. Surrounding the clean pools of natural hot water may be smaller milk baths, wine baths, murky sulfurous baths, mud baths, hot sand baths, even baths of heated coffee grounds!

One of the greatest pleasures of many *onsen* is the *roten-buro*, or "open-air bath." These may be small natural pools in scenic locations or huge man-made enclosures where bathers can soak comfortably outdoors, even in the dead of winter when the pool is surrounded by snowdrifts. Such baths can be found everywhere, but are particularly popular at ski resorts, where a soak in deep hot water removes all the aches of an overly strenuous day on the slopes.

It has been said that the bath is one of Japan's secrets for survival in the modern age. A soothing balm that eases the tensions of daily life, the bath makes it possible—at least for one long, luxurious moment—to feel completely carefree.

Peter Grilli

The partition separating the men and women in this rustic bath at Nakabusa Hot Spring does not stop the flow of jokes and banter.

It is not uncommon for Japanese families to bathe together on occasion. Here a young father spends bath time at home with his sons.

bentō
1 This elaborate lunch in an elegant lacquered box is packed for a picnic or other outing. The items include *makizushi* (rolled *sushi*), omelet, assorted vegetables, and *sake* to drink.
2 The *makunouchi bentō* (entr'acte box lunch), not confined to theaters, is the most typical type of Japanese box lunch.
3 One example of the elaborate box lunches that Japanese mothers sometimes make for their children. This one includes a "bear" hamburger, apple and carrot slices, and spaghetti salad.

Ruth Fulton Benedict This American cultural anthropologist is the author of the classic study of Japanese society, *The Chrysanthemum and the Sword.*

commerce with Belgium, the Netherlands, and Luxembourg in 1960.

Japan's exports to Belgium considerably exceed its imports, and the issue of the trade imbalance has been a continuing concern. During a visit to Japan in 1978, Prime Minister Leo Tindemans asked the Japanese government to address the problem, and in 1979 a Japanese delegation for the promotion of imports concluded agreements in Belgium to purchase goods valued at US $96.3 million. Belgium has become a center of operations from which Japanese businesses have expanded their role in the economy of Europe; in 1989, 162 Japanese trading companies and banks maintained offices there. In 1990 Japan's exports to Belgium, chiefly automobiles and communications equipment, totaled US $3.9 billion, and its imports, mainly diamonds and chemical products, totaled US $1.6 billion. During a visit to Belgium in January 1990, Prime Minister KAIFU TOSHIKI agreed with the Belgian government that trade between the two nations should expand in a balanced manner.

bells → suzu

Benedict, Ruth Fulton
ベネディクト, R. F.

(1887–1948). US cultural anthropologist; author of *The Chrysanthemum and the Sword* (1946), a classic study of Japanese society. Born in New York City. A graduate of Vassar College, she received her doctorate in anthropology in 1923 from Columbia University and taught there until her death. Benedict's work on Japan began during World War II in the Office of War Information in Washington, DC, where she helped to pioneer the study of national character and to develop techniques for cultural research at a distance by integrating published materials with interview data. Never having visited Japan or studied its language, Benedict relied on English sources and contemporary Japanese films (including propaganda films) as well as the diaries of several captured Japanese soldiers. In addition, many Japanese residents of the United States were interviewed at length. *The Chrysanthemum*

and the Sword (tr into Japanese as *Kiku to katana*, 1949) has been widely read in Japan as well as in the West. Although later scholars have criticized it on some points, there is general agreement that Benedict's research represents the first significant study of Japanese society by a non-Japanese cultural anthropologist.

benibana
紅花

(safflower). *Carthamus tinctorius.* Annual herb of the family Compositae, primarily cultivated in Yamagata Prefecture. The stem is 0.6–1.0 meter (2.0–3.3 ft) long. In early summer thistlelike, bright yellow flowers appear at the shoot tip; these gradually turn a deep red yellow. The reddish pigment obtained from the flower was used in the past as a textile dye and as an ingredient in cosmetics and medicines. Safflower oil is used in cooking and as an ingredient in margarine, soap, and paint.

Benkei
弁慶

(?–1189). Also called Musashibō Benkei. Legendary warrior-monk; loyal retainer of MINAMOTO NO YOSHITSUNE. Although a historical figure named Benkei is briefly mentioned in the AZUMA KAGAMI (ca 1266–1301, Mirror of Eastern Japan), the only detailed accounts of his life are apocryphal. According to these, Benkei was a man of extraordinary cunning, strength, and martial skill. Benkei accompanied Yoshitsune through all the campaigns of the TAIRA-MINAMOTO WAR (1180–85). After the war, MINAMOTO NO YORITOMO turned against his brother Yoshitsune, who fled with Benkei. When Yoshitsune was surrounded, it was Benkei, fighting alone to the death, who bought time for Yoshitsune to commit an honorable suicide. Benkei's loyalty and courage are depicted in several Nō and *kabuki* plays.

benshi
弁士

Live performer who accompanied all showings of domestic and foreign silent motion pictures in Japan from the late 1890s until the advent of talking pictures. Also known as *katsuben.* The *benshi* sat by the side of the screen in full view of the audience and interpreted a film by providing full dialogue, exposition, and general commentary in addition to reading the subtitles aloud. The origins of the *benshi* are found in traditional storytellers who performed with narrative paintings, in chanters who accompanied classic drama and puppet theater (BUNRAKU), and in the early international practice of showing motion pictures with live lecturers present to explain the contents.

These "poets of the darkness" wrote their own personal interpretations of films and usually performed with piano, violin, cornet, drums, and *shamisen* accompaniment. Frequently the *benshi* was a greater box office attraction than the movie and its stars.

Bentenjima
弁天島

Group of seven islands in the southern part of Lake Hamana, southwestern Shizuoka Prefecture, central Honshū. A shrine dedicated to Benten (Benzaiten, goddess of good fortune) dates from the Edo period (1600–1868). Six of the islands are the result of extensive land reclamation. A hot spring has been developed, and the area is popular for fishing, shellfish digging, and swimming.

bentō
弁当

(box lunch). In premodern Japan box lunches, usually consisting of dried rice,

rice balls (NIGIRIMESHI), or sweet potatoes, wrapped in a leaf or in the sheath of a bamboo shoot, were eaten chiefly by travelers and people who worked outdoors. In the Edo period (1600–1868) elaborate meals were prepared and carried in tiered lacquer boxes (JŪBAKO) on outings. *Bentō* sold at theaters to be eaten during intermission were called *makunouchi bentō* ("entr'acte box lunches"), the prototype of today's *shidashi bentō*, which are usually ordered in quantity and delivered by the restaurant that prepares them. Since the middle of the Meiji period (1868–1912) *bentō* known as EKIBEN ("station box lunches") have been sold at railway stations. In recent years there has been a proliferation of shops that specialize in take-out *bentō*.

Benzaiten → Seven Deities of Good Fortune

Beppu
別府[市]

City in central Ōita Prefecture, Kyūshū, on BEPPU BAY. Beppu has long been famous for its hot springs (some 3,000). To accommodate its visitors (12 million annually) Beppu affords many hotels, Japanese-style inns, restaurants, and recreational facilities. Nearby are the scenic lake Shidakako and Kijima Highland, both easily accessible by the Yamanami Highway. The Medical Institute of Bioregulation, run by Kyūshū University, and the Geophysical Research Station, operated by Kyōto University, are also located here. Pop: 130,334.

Beppu Bay
別府湾

(Beppu Wan). Inlet of the southwestern part of the Inland Sea between the Kunisaki and Saganoseki peninsulas, central Ōita Prefecture, Kyūshū. Connected with the Pacific Ocean through the Bungo Channel. The port of Beppu is a major center of maritime transportation. Marine catches include sardines and prawns. An industrial area is located on the southern coast of the bay. Also near the bay is Beppu Hot Spring.

Berry, John Cutting
ベリー, J. C.

(1847–1936). American medical missionary and educator in Japan from 1872 to 1893. Berry graduated from Jefferson Medical College, Philadelphia, in 1871. In 1872 he accepted an appointment from the Protestant American Board of Commissioners for Foreign Missions as its first medical missionary to Kōbe, and he became director of the Hyōgo Prefectural Hospital the following year. Moving to Okayama in 1879, he headed its new prefectural hospital. In 1885 he became first director of what is now Dōshisha University's Medical School Hospital in Kyōto, later adding the first nurses' training school. Berry was also an advocate of prison reform.

Bertin, Louis-Emile
ベルタン, L.-E.

(1840–1924). French naval engineer and architect who contributed to the development of the Japanese navy. Bertin was educated at the Paris Ecole Polytechnique and quickly won international recognition as a naval architect. Hired by the Japanese government as a special adviser, he spent the years from 1886 to 1890 training Japanese engineers and naval architects, designing warships, and supervising the construction of warships and naval facilities. After his return to France, he served in a number of important posts in naval architecture and construction.

Besshi Copper Mine labor disputes 別子銅山争議

(Besshi Dōzan *sōgi*). Strikes in 1907 and 1925–26 at the Sumitomo Company's Besshi Copper Mine in Ehime Prefecture. The first strike took place in June 1907. When riots broke out, the army was called in to restore order. The company rehired all but 96 of the some 1,000 strikers, but 30 of the leaders were convicted on criminal charges. The second dispute lasted from December 1925 to February 1926. It began as a strike by the local branch of the SŌDŌMEI (Japan Federation of Labor). When the company fired 172 strikers, they sabotaged the mine's generating plant, and Sōdōmei members attacked the Sumitomo family residence in Ōsaka. The strike ended in failure, and its ringleaders were dismissed.

Best Denki Co, Ltd ［株］ベスト電器

(Besuto Denki). Retailer of consumer electric and electronics products. Founded in 1956 as a small television shop by Kitada Mitsuo, the present chairman. In Japan it has 113 stores of its own and 291 franchise stores. It also has franchise operations in Southeast Asia and the United States through a joint venture. For the fiscal year ending February 1991, annual sales were ¥205.7 billion (US $1.6 billion), and capitalization stood at ¥20.1 billion (US $154.0 million). Headquarters are in the city of Fukuoka, Fukuoka Prefecture.

Betsugen Enshi 別源円旨

(1294–1364). Sōtō Zen monk important in the history of GOZAN LITERATURE (Chinese learning in medieval Japanese Zen monasteries). Born in Echizen Province (now part of Fukui Prefecture), Betsugen studied in China (1320–29), returning with SESSON YŪBAI. His poems are collected in two anthologies: the *Nan'yūshū* (those written in China) and the *Tōkishū* (those written after his return).

Betsuyaku Minoru 別役実

(1937–). Playwright. Born in Manchuria. Attended Waseda University. Betsuyaku first attracted public attention with *Zō* (1962, Elephant), which dealt with the inner torment of atomic bomb victims. He received the Kishida Drama Prize for *Matchi-uri no shōjo* (1966, The Little Match Girl) and *Akai tori no iru fūkei* (1967, Landscape with Red Bird). Inspired by the theater of the absurd of Samuel Beckett and others, Betsuyaku examines through his works the anxiety and loneliness of people in the modern world and constructs a pure, abstract poetic space using a refined variant of everyday language and material from fairy tales. Other works include *Fushigi no kuni no Arisu* (1969, Alice in Wonderland).

Bibai 美唄［市］

City in west-central Hokkaidō, on the Ishikari Plain. At one time Bibai was a flourishing coal-mining center, but now all the mines are closed. Beds, plastic goods, and chemicals are produced. It is also a rice market center. Pop: 35,176.

Bible, translations of 聖書の翻訳

(*seisho no hon'yaku*). The Bible was first introduced to Japan in 1549 when Francis XAVIER arrived at Kagoshima with a manuscript translation he had made of the Gospel according to Matthew. In the late 16th and early 17th centuries, Jesuit missionaries made several attempts to translate the Bible, but no copy of any of these early translations is known to exist. The oldest extant Japanese version of any portion of the Bible was a translation of the Gospel according to John and the Epistles of John, done by the Prussian missionary, Karl F. A. Gützlaff (1803–51) and published in Singapore in 1837.

Between 1874 and 1880, a committee of Japanese and Western translators, representing six Protestant denominations and headed by the Presbyterian missionary James Curtis HEPBURN, translated the entire New Testament. A second committee, also headed by Hepburn, completed a version of the Old Testament in 1888, thus making the whole Bible available in Japanese for the first time. The rapid development of biblical scholarship soon rendered the New Testament translation obsolete, and a revised version was produced between 1910 and 1917. Together with the 1888 version of the Old Testament, this became the standard Protestant Bible in Japan for nearly half a century.

Roman Catholic translations of portions of the gospels were published in the 1890s, and a complete New Testament, which became the standard Catholic version, appeared in 1910. The Holy Orthodox Church had published a translation of the New Testament in 1901. Japanese biblical scholars also published a number of individual partial translations; the first full translation of the New Testament solely by a Japanese scholar was published in 1928 by Nagai Naoji (1864–1945).

After World War II, changes in the Japanese language led to an urgent need for a Bible in the colloquial language. (All previous versions had been in classical Japanese.) A new translation was produced by the Japan Bible Society between 1951 and 1955 that was used officially by most of the Protestant churches. A colloquial New Testament produced by Catholic translators in 1953 was followed by the entire Bible in 1964, with later revisions. A joint Catholic-Protestant translation (including the Apocrypha) was conceived in 1966 and published by the Japan Bible Society in 1987 as *Seisho: Shin kyōdōyaku* (New Japanese Common Bible Translation).

bibliography 書誌学

(*shoshigaku*). Modern academic discipline devoted to the scientific study of books. The foundations of modern bibliographical studies in Japan were laid around 1800. The discipline as it has evolved and developed over the past two centuries has emphasized three major areas: historical bibliography, the study of manuscripts predating 1600 and printed books published before 1640; textual bibliography, the analysis of external and internal characteristics of extant works and a study of the transmission of their various texts; and descriptive bibliography, which applies the findings of the first two areas in the compilation of indexes, annotated catalogs, and other reference guides. A 20th-century survey of all important public and private libraries revealed the existence of some 500,000 books written or edited by Japanese prior to the year 1867. It is this vast mass of indigenous premodern textual material that is the chief concern of the discipline of *shoshigaku*.

The books that predate 1867 may be broadly divided into two groups: manuscripts and printed editions. Printed books are further subdivided according to whether they were reproduced by block or movable type. Although printing began about the year 1000, for nearly five centuries it was largely restricted to Buddhist scripture and works in Chinese, and the great majority of native works are known only through their laboriously copied manuscripts, many of which exist in numerous variants. A principal task of the bibliographer is to undertake textual analysis and criticism of the various texts of a given work, historically order them, and define their relationships. Only then might it be possible to recover the shape and character of the original and to determine its authorship, the age in which it was written, and the method of transmission.

The first groundwork in the area of modern textual bibliography was laid in the latter half of the 17th century by the Buddhist monk KEICHŪ and continued through the mid-19th century at the hands of such renowned Edo-period (1600–1868) scholars as KADA NO AZUMAMARO, KAMO NO MABUCHI, MOTOORI NORINAGA, HANAWA HOKIICHI, KONDŌ JŪZŌ, and YASHIRO HIROKATA. Enormous strides were made in this native tradition of textual criticism, but it suffered a temporary setback following the Meiji Restoration of 1868 when Western influence flooded into Japan, sweeping aside everything that seemed of the past. In the 1880s the Western, especially English, science of bibliography was introduced to the Japanese scholarly world, but, with its emphasis on printed books and incunabula, seemingly little of it was relevant to the Japanese situation, in which manuscripts commanded an overwhelming numerical superiority, and its influence was felt only in the more practical area of library science.

Beppu Steam rises from the thousands of hot springs in the city of Beppu. Together the springs release 68,000 liters of water per minute.

benibana The safflower's bright yellow flower appears in early summer.

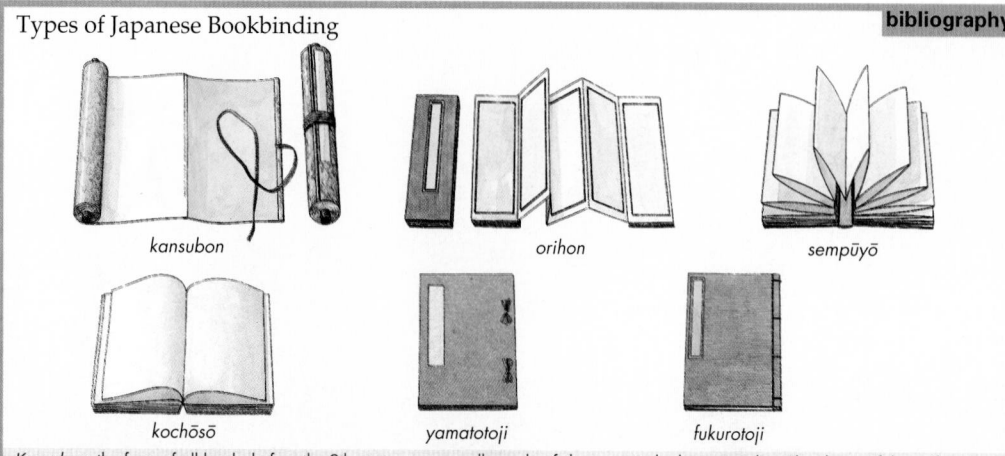

Types of Japanese Bookbinding

kansubon   orihon   sempūyō

kochōsō   yamatotoji   fukurotoji

Kansubon, the form of all books before the 9th century, are scrolls made of sheets pasted edge over edge. The sheets of the orihon, an improvement on the kansubon, are folded accordion-style with heavy paper attached to the front and back. Books in the sempūyō format, a binding that appeared in the 11th century, are folded like orihon and then reinforced on the front, back, and along the spine. The kochōsō style, developed in the 12th century, binds individual folded sheets rather than joining them into a single length. In the yamatotoji format, several signatures are bound together with string at the folded edge. The fukurotoji method, in which folded sheets are individually bound together at the cut edge, came into wide use in the 14th century.

bibliography These Edo-period calendars demonstrate a wide variety of printing formats. *Clockwise from above left:* folding calendar made in Ise; scroll calendar from Kyōto; covered and spine-bound calendar made in Edo (now Tōkyō); pocket calendar for travelers.

Interest in the Japanese classics was revived in the early 20th century when a group of scholars at Tōkyō University came under the influence of the German science of philology and established a new discipline that they called *bunkengaku* (textual studies). In many respects this represented a revival of the textual-criticism approach of the late Edo period, systematized and fortified with theory and methodological discipline. The greatest achievements of modern textual criticism have been in literature, resulting in restored texts for a number of classics such as the TOSA NIKKI and SARASHINA NIKKI and collated editions of all the other masterpieces of the Japanese literary tradition. Less has been accomplished in the field of history, where a traditional emphasis on primary sources has diverted most scholarly attention to the separate but related field of DIPLOMATICS. One exception was the work of the historian KUROITA KATSUMI (1874–1946), who prepared collated texts of the most basic and important historical writings of the pre-Meiji period.

In the field of descriptive bibliography, enumerative and descriptive lists of books appeared as early as the Nara period (710–794), but unfortunately most of these early works have been lost. A number of Heian-period (794–1185) catalogs have been preserved, but the oldest extant catalog of native Japanese books (as opposed to works written in Chinese) is the HONCHŌ SHOJAKU MOKUROKU, compiled in the Kamakura period (1185–1333).

Bibliographic cataloging increased during the Edo period, when lists appeared in rapid succession. Many of the Edo-period catalogs were annotated, beginning with the *Nihon shojaku kō* (1667) of HAYASHI GAHŌ, a list of native works with brief descriptions. The *Gunsho ichiran*, a classified catalog of Japanese books published in 1802, was a

major achievement in this genre.

During the revival of bibliographic activity at the beginning of the 20th century, Samura Hachirō (1865–1915) compiled a valuable annotated catalog of 15,000 Japanese books selected from the Imperial Library; it was supplemented in 1904 with an additional 10,000 titles. In 1939 the publisher IWANAMI SHIGEO initiated a project to edit and publish a more accurate and inclusive catalog of Japanese books dating from the earliest times to 1867. Involving the cooperation of numerous scholars and a nationwide "census" of books that revealed the existence of more than half a million titles, the *Kokusho sōmokuroku* was finally published in 9 volumes between 1963 and 1976. Another enormous bibliography, the *Gunsho kaidai*, was published in 30 volumes between 1962 and 1967, describing in detail the more than 3,000 works contained in the GUNSHO RUIJŪ, a classified collection of Japanese classics completed in the early 19th century. These two monuments of modern descriptive bibliography stand at the head of a host of other specialized catalogs and indexes covering nearly all categories of books and all branches of learning. See also HISTORIOGRAPHY; LIBRARIES; PRINTING, PREMODERN.

bicycle racing → keirin

Bigelow, William Sturgis

ビゲロー, W. S.

(1850–1926). American physician, devoted student of Japanese culture, and discerning early collector of Japanese art (with his friends Edward S. MORSE and Ernest F. FENOLLOSA). Born to a family of prominent Boston physicians, he graduated from Harvard College (1871) and Harvard Medical School (1874). He later gave up medicine and left Boston in 1882 to accompany Morse on the latter's third trip to Japan. Bigelow settled happily into a six-year residence in Tōkyō and Nikkō, traveling widely, collecting art, and studying Buddhism. While in Japan Bigelow gave financial help to OKAKURA KAKUZŌ in setting up the JAPAN FINE ARTS ACADEMY (Nihon Bijutsuin). Bigelow served as a trustee of the Boston Museum of Fine Arts until his death. He donated more than 40,000 paintings, prints, and other art objects to it.

Bigot, Georges

ビゴー, G.

(1860–1927). French illustrator and topical cartoonist. Born in Paris, he studied painting at the Ecole des Beaux-Arts. In 1882 he went to Japan, where he studied Japanese art and taught painting at the Army Academy. He

also worked as an illustrator for the Japanese newspapers YŪBIN HŌCHI SHIMBUN and *Kaishin shimbun* and started his own cartoon magazine, *Tobae* (1887–90), for his satirical caricatures. While in Japan, he illustrated a number of books and worked as a foreign correspondent for French newspapers. He returned to France in 1899.

Bihoro

美幌[町]

Town on the river Abashirigawa in northeastern Hokkaidō. Bihoro is a distribution center for agricultural and forestry products and serves as the gateway to Akan National Park. Beans, potatoes, and sugar beets are the principal crops; dairy farming and food processing are also of importance. Pop: 25,680.

bimbōgami

貧乏神

Type of deity said to bring poverty. Traditionally believed to reside in the home. *Bimbōgami* are exorcised in a rite called *kamiokuri* ("sending off the gods"). Belief in the *bimbōgami*, first mentioned in the literature of the Edo period (1600–1868), is a phenomenon of city life. The *bimbōgami* is commonly portrayed as a thin, pale figure with a tattered fan. Figuratively, the term refers to a person who is constantly indigent and unlucky.

bingata → Okinawan textiles

Bingo Sea

備後灘

(Bingo Nada). Central part of the Inland Sea located off southeastern Hiroshima Prefecture, western Honshū. Bounded by the Shiwaku Islands on the east and the Geiyo Islands on the west. Sea bream, squid, and Spanish mackerel are caught here. Depth: 15–30 m (49–98 ft).

biography and biographical fiction

伝記文学

(*denki bungaku*). The earliest extant Japanese biographies appeared in the 8th century. *Kaden* (2 vols, Family Records) chronicles the lives of the political figures FUJIWARA NO KAMATARI and his son Fujiwara no Takechimaro (680–737), and JŌGŪ SHŌTOKU HŌŌTEI SETSU is a record of the life of Prince SHŌTOKU. Until the close of the Muromachi period (1333–1568), however, the most common subjects of biographies and anthologies of biographical accounts were Buddhist priests. Referred to as *kōsōden* (biographies of venerable priests), these works were, like other early biographies, customarily written in Chinese. A notable example of this genre is GENKŌ SHAKUSHO (1322) by KOKAN SHIREN.

In the Edo period (1600–1868) the development of a commercial publishing industry and a general increase in literacy contributed to the popularization of romanticized biographies of the 16th-century national unifiers ODA NOBUNAGA (*Shinchō kōki*, 1600) and TOYOTOMI HIDEYOSHI (*Taikōki*, 1625; see GUNDAN). Another popular work was KINSEI KIJIN DEN (1790, Tales of Unusual Men of Our Day) by Ban Kōkei (1733–1806).

The sweeping introduction of Western culture during the Meiji period (1868–1912) had a strong impact on Japanese biographical literature. The journalist and nationalist political critic TOKUTOMI SOHŌ wrote a biography of YOSHIDA SHŌIN (*Yoshida Shōin*, 1893), an ideologue of the SONNŌ JŌI (Revere the Emperor, Expel the Barbarians) movement of the late Edo period, in which he succeeded in dramatizing Yoshida's activities against a historical background contemporary to his subject. The character study of the founder of the Kamakura shogunate (1192–1333), MINAMOTO NO YORITOMO, drawn by KŌDA ROHAN in *Yoritomo* (1908), is richly detailed and deeply humanist, and YAMAJI AIZAN's biography of the 14th-century warrior chieftain ASHIKAGA TAKAUJI (*Ashikaga Takauji*, 1909) displays considerable psychological insight.

During the Taishō period (1912–26) MORI ŌGAI wrote the magisterial biographical studies of little-known historical figures that distinguished the final period of his literary career. *Shibue Chūsai* (1916), considered by some to be one of Ōgai's most powerful works, records the life of Shibue Dōjun, a mid-19th-century physician and antiquarian. The account by KOMIYA TOYOTAKA of his mentor NATSUME SŌSEKI (*Natsume Sōseki*, 1938) is one of the most celebrated of Japanese literary biographies. *Roka Tokutomi Kenjirō* (3 vols, 1872–74) by NAKANO YOSHIO, a study of the novelist and eccentric TOKUTOMI ROKA, and KOBAYASHI HIDEO's account of the life of the Edo-period scholar of the Japanese classics MOTOORI NORINAGA (*Motoori Norinaga*, 1965–76) are also regarded as prominent examples of this genre. AGAWA HIROYUKI's *Yamamoto Isoroku* (1964–65; tr *The Reluctant Admiral: Yamamoto and the Imperial Navy*, 1980), a biography of the man who proposed the surprise attack on Pearl Harbor, also won critical acclaim, as have two recent works, HONDA SHŪGO's critical biography of the writer SHIGA NAOYA (*Shiga Naoya*, 1990) and ŌBA MINAKO's life of the educator TSUDA UMEKO (*Tsuda Umeko*, 1990).

biology 生物学

(*seibutsugaku*). Biological study in Japan has progressed rapidly since 1877, when it was added to the curriculum of Tōkyō University, and today ranks among the world's most advanced. Primate research, in particular, has been attracting widespread attention.

Medical and premodern descriptive pharmacognostic studies were brought to Japan from China in ancient times. European-style biology was first introduced to Japan by scholars of Dutch Learning (see WESTERN LEARNING) in the Edo period (1600–1868). After the Meiji Restoration of 1868, Japanese scholars began a systematic introduction of European biology. The first professors of biology at Tōkyō University were Edward S. MORSE and YATABE RYŌKICHI. In the beginning, Japanese students of modern biological studies went to study in England and the United States, but later Germany became Japan's focal point for biological studies. ISHIKAWA CHIYOMATSU, Morse's assistant at Tōkyō University, studied in Germany, after which he returned to Japan to teach. Toward the end of the Meiji period (1868–1912), Japanese biological studies advanced from the imitation of Western studies to more original research, as in the field of plant taxonomy by researchers such as MAKINO TOMITARŌ. Original research in genetics also began early. Two important figures in this field were KIHARA HITOSHI and TOYAMA KAMETARŌ.

The fields of physiology and biochemistry came into their own in Japan during the Taishō period (1912–26) and especially during the early Shōwa period (1926–89). Medical researchers were the most active in these fields. The moving force in Tōkyō University's biology department was SHIBATA KEITA.

After a hiatus during World War II, research resumed with such original work as a study of Japanese MONKEYS (*nihonzaru*) conducted under the leadership of IMANISHI KINJI of Kyōto University. Other notable figures of the postwar period include KATŌ GEN'ICHI, known for his research in nerve physiology, and YAMAGIWA KATSUSABURŌ, who succeeded in artificially producing cancer cells. Since 1980 Japan has become a world leader in molecular biology. Traditional principles of fermentation science, upon which some modern molecular biology research is based, have helped Japan advance to the forefront of the field. In 1987 TONEGAWA SUSUMU was awarded the Nobel Prize for his research in molecular biology.

biotechnology バイオテクノロジー

(*baiotekunorojī*). At the start of the biotechnology boom in Japan in 1981, Japanese researchers relied on cooperation with European and American ventures for basic research technology and for information in such fields as genetic engineering and monoclonal antibodies. Since that time the Japanese have developed considerable expertise in biotechnology. One reason for Japan's rapid advancement in this field is the country's long experience in fermentation technology, which plays a significant role in biotechnology. The *sake, miso,* and soy sauce industries have accumulated a broad knowledge of fermentation and the breeding and stocking of the microorganisms necessary for it, enabling Japanese companies to virtually monopolize the manufacturing of amino acids by the fermentation method.

From about 1986 efforts were concentrated on developing biotechnology as an industry in Japan, making use especially of recombinant DNA and cell fusion techniques, and in 1990 there were more than 200 Japanese companies in the field. However, business ventures that focus strictly on biotechnology, as do many US firms, are rare in Japan. Instead, research and development tends to be done by established firms. Biotechnology research is especially active in the medical (both therapeutic and diagnostic), pharmaceutical, and chemical fields, notably in the production of insulin, growth hormones, interleukins, and interferons, but research is also done by firms involved in food processing, agricultural chemicals, livestock, bioelectronics, and research equipment.

The Japanese government has also taken an interest in biotechnology and considers it to be a major element in the next, increasingly knowledge-intensive phase of Japanese industrial development (see ECONOMIC PLANNING). The Ministry of International Trade and Industry (MITI) and various other ministries play major roles in biotechnology research, and the Ministry of Construction, the Ministry of Labor, and the Environment Agency appropriate funds for biotechnological development in their budgets. In 1989 Japanese investment in biotechnology totaled ¥117 billion (US $850 million), and MITI predicts that by the year 2000 total investment will reach ¥5 trillion (US $35 billion).

Biratori 平取〔町〕

Also called Hiratori. Town on the middle reaches of the river Sarugawa in southern Hokkaidō. Many AINU settlements are located in Biratori, which is the cultural center for the Hidaka Ainu. Rice cultivation, dairy farming, and forestry thrive here, and the town is a commercial center for agriculture and forestry products. Pop: 7,352.

bird-and-flower painting 花鳥画

(*kachōga*). One of three broad categories of East Asian art, the other two being *jimbutsuga* (figure painting) and SANSUIGA (landscape painting). Flowers and birds were first treated as an independent subject for painting in China but did not appear in Japanese art until the Muromachi period (1333–1568), when Japanese Zen priest-painters rendered ink monochromes of bamboo and plum or reeds and geese modeled after Chinese scholar paintings of the Song (Sung; 960–1279) and Yuan (Yüan; 1279–1368) dynasties. In the 15th century, professional artists in Japan began to paint delicate birds and elegant flowers in the naturalistic polychrome style that had reached its maturity in the 12th-century Chinese Imperial Painting Academy.

Japanese artists of the late 15th and 16th centuries established *kachōga* repertoires that set the style throughout the Edo period (1600–1868). SESSHŪ TŌYŌ, KANŌ MOTONOBU, KANŌ EITOKU, Tawaraya SŌTATSU, KANŌ TAN'YŪ, Ogata KŌRIN, and MARUYAMA ŌKYO made significant contributions to *kachōga* during this time.

Bird, Isabella Lucy バード, I. L.

(1831–1904). British traveler and writer whose many books on exotic and remote areas won wide popularity in the English-speaking world during the late 19th century. In 1878, with one attendant, she undertook a 2,300-kilometer (1,400-mi) horseback trip through northern Honshū into Hokkaidō, which she described in *Unbeaten Tracks in Japan* (1880; tr *Nihon okuchi kikō*, 1973). Bird gave an honest, graphic picture of Meiji-period (1868–1912) Japan. She preferred the undeveloped countryside to Tōkyō, which she considered an ugly blend of East and West.

birds 鳥類

(*chōrui*). There is no endemic genus among the 490 bird species found in Hokkaidō and Honshū. The only genera endemic to Japan are those represented by the *meguro* (Bonin honeyeater; *Apalopteron familiare*) and the extinct Ogasawara *mashiko* (Bonin grosbeak; *Chaunoproctus ferreorostris*) of the Ogasawara Islands and the *noguchigera* (Pryer's woodpecker) of Okinawa, all of which are native to islands far from the Asian continent.

Mainland Species—The four truly endemic mainland species are the *yamadori* (copper pheasant), the black *karasubato* (Japanese wood pigeon; *Columba janthina*), the red-cheeked *aogera* (Japanese green woodpecker), and the black-backed *seguro sekirei* (Japanese wagtail). The KOMADORI ("horse bird"; Japanese robin) and the *nojiko* (Japanese yellow bunting; *Emberiza sulphurata*) breed only in Japan and can be classified endemic, but they migrate to warmer climes in winter.

Outer-Island Species—Endemic species of the outer islands include the *akakokko* (Izu Island thrush) in the Izu Islands and Yakushima; the rufous *akahige* (Liukiu robin; *Erithacus komadori*) in the Ryūkyū Islands; the chestnut and blue *rurikakesu* (Lidth's jay; *Garrulus lidthi*) and the Amami *yamashigi* (Amami woodcock; *Scolopax mira*) in Amami Ōshima; the Ryūkyū *karasubato* (Liukiu wood pigeon; *Columba jouyi*) in Okinawa and neighboring islands; the elu-

biwa A performance of Nishiki biwa, a subschool of the popular Satsuma style, on a five-stringed version of this instrument.

sive Miyako *shōbin* (Miyako kingfisher; *Halcyon miyakoensis*) in Miyakojima; and the flightless rail, Yambaru *kuina* (*Rallus okinawae*), an inhabitant of the dense brushlands of northern Okinawa.

Seabirds——Among seabirds seldom seen outside Japan are the very rare *ahōdori* (short-tailed albatross; *Diomedea albatrus*) found in Torishima and the Senkaku Islands; the *umineko* (black-tailed gull), which breeds in Hokkaidō and Honshū; and the *kammuri umisuzume* (Japanese auk; *Synthliboramphus wumizusume*), which breeds in the mainland and the Izu Islands.

Nonendemic Species——Japan's common, nonendemic birds include the *tanchō* (Japanese crane), which breeds in Hokkaidō; the *oshidori* (mandarin duck); the *karugamo* (spotbill duck), found year round throughout Japan; the *sashiba* (gray-faced buzzard eagle), which breeds in the mainland; the mountain-dwelling *kumataka* (Hodgson's hawk eagle), a mainland inhabitant used for hawking; the giant *shimafukurō* (fish owl; *Ketupa blakistoni*) in Hokkaidō; the *kijibato* (eastern turtledove; *Streptopelia orientalis*) and the *hiyodori* (brown-eared bulbul; *Hypsipetes amaurotis*), found all over Japan; the sweet-voiced *uguisu* (BUSH WARBLER); the lemon-breasted *kibitaki* (narcissus flycatcher; *Ficedula narcissina*); the long-tailed *sankōchō* (black paradise flycatcher; *Terpsiphone atrocaudata*); the trainable *yamagara* (varied tit; *Parus varius*); and the nectar-sucking *mejiro* (Japanese white-eye; *Zosterops japonica*).

Other birds worthy of mention are the

rare *toki* (Japanese crested ibis; *Nipponia nippon*), the *onaga* (azure-winged magpie; *Cyanopica cyana*), the giant *ōwashi* (Steller's sea eagle; *Haliaeëtus pelagicus*), the *umiu* (Temminck's cormorant; *Phalacrocorax filamentosus*), several species of *hototogisu* (see CUCKOOS), the *akashōbin* (ruddy kingfisher; *Halcyon coromanda*), the *raichō* (PTARMIGAN), the high-mountain-dwelling *iwahibari* (alpine accentor; *Prunella collaris*), and the *kiji* (common pheasant).

See also the following articles: CHICKEN, JAPANESE; CRANES; CROWS; GEESE; GULLS; HAWKS AND EAGLES; HERONS; KITE, BLACK; LARKS; OWLS; PHEASANTS; PLOVERS; RAILS; REED WARBLERS; SHRIKES; SPARROWS; SWALLOWS; THRUSHES; WAGTAILS; WILD DUCKS; WOODPECKERS.

bird sanctuaries バード・サンクチュアリ

(*bādo sankuchuari*). A number of bird sanctuaries have been established in Japan as a result of advocacy by wildlife preservation groups. The first such area was established in 1981 on the shores of Lake Utonai near the city of Tomakomai in Hokkaidō as a result of independent efforts by the WILD BIRD SOCIETY OF JAPAN. In 1987 the society established the Tsurui-Itō Tanchō Sanctuary in the Kushiro area of Hokkaidō for the protection of Japanese cranes (*tanchō*). In 1991 there were about 500 cranes at the sanctuary. By 1990, eight more bird sanctuaries had been established in Japan.

bird watching バードウォッチング

(*bādo uotchingu*). Bird watching as an organized activity in Japan began when a Buddhist priest of the Tendai sect, Nakanishi Godō (1895–1984), founded the WILD BIRD SOCIETY OF JAPAN in 1934. Critical of the popular practice of keeping caged birds, Nakanishi based his society on the traditional Asian view that nature should be appreciated in its pristine state. Most of today's roughly 200,000 bird watchers are city dwellers who enjoy forays into nature areas for health and recreation. There are about 550 species of wild birds in Japan. See also BIRDS.

Birōjima 枇榔島

Island in Shibushi Bay, off the eastern coast of Ōsumi Peninsula, Kagoshima Prefecture, Kyūshū. The island is part of the Nichinan Coast Quasi-National Park; it is covered with subtropical plants that are protected as Special Natural Monuments by the government. Fountain palm trees (*birō*) are especially plentiful. Area: 0.2 sq km (0.08 sq mi).

Biruma no tategoto ビルマの竪琴

(The Harp of Burma). Film released in 1956, directed by ICHIKAWA KON, starring MIKUNI RENTARŌ and Yasui Shōji (b 1928). The film, based on a novel by Takeyama Michio (1903–84), opens in Burma during the last stages of World War II. After the Japanese army is routed from Burma, one soldier chooses to stay behind and becomes a Buddhist priest in order to bury the corpses of his fallen comrades and pray for their souls. Director Ichikawa did a remake of his own film in 1985, starring Nakai Kiichi (b 1961) and Ishizaka Kōji (b 1941).

Bisai 尾西[市]

City in northwestern Aichi Prefecture, central Honshū, on the river Kisogawa. Bisai developed as a post-station town on the highway Mino Kaidō. During the Edo period (1600–1868) it produced cotton textiles, but it has since shifted to woolens. Pop: 55,880.

bitasen 鐚銭

1. Debased copper coins, privately minted and widely circulated from the 16th century; their lead content was sometimes as much as one-half. Also called *bita kinsen*. The rate of exchange between *bitasen* and coins of better quality varied according to locality. As a *daimyō*, TOKUGAWA IEYASU in 1570 established in the Kantō region an exchange rate of one EIRAKUSEN (an imported Chinese coin) to four *bitasen*. In 1604, a year after coming to power as shōgun, he imposed this exchange rate throughout Japan as part of his attempt to regulate the national currency. See also ERIZENI.

2. Iron and brass coins produced in the 18th century by the Tokugawa shogunate.

Bitō Nishū 尾藤二洲

(1747–1813). Confucian scholar of the Edo period (1600–1868). Also known as Bitō Jishū. Born in Iyo Province (now Ehime Prefecture). A student of Katayama Hokkai (1723–90), he was at first associated with the Ancient Learning (KOGAKU) school of Confucianism, but later became a champion of the Zhu Xi (Chu Hsi; J: Shushi) school of Neo-Confucianism (see SHUSHIGAKU). When in 1790 the shogunate issued its Kansei Prohibition of Heterodoxy (Kansei Igaku no Kin), one of the KANSEI REFORMS, Bitō was made a professor at the national academy, SHŌHEIKŌ.

biwa 琵琶

Short-necked plucked lute derived from the Chinese *piba* (*p'i-pa*). Already in use for Nara-period (710–794) court music, the *biwa* was also used in Kyūshū from at least the 8th century for the *mōsō biwa* (blind monks' lute) style of music; by the 9th century a version of it had reached Kyōto and was associated with the TENDAI SECT of Buddhism.

In court music the *biwa* plays simple figures to accompany the melody instruments of the GAGAKU ensemble. In the 13th and 14th centuries a new kind of *biwa* music developed, the HEIKYOKU, to accompany episodes from secular military romances. The 16th century saw the development of the most popular of all *biwa* music, the Satsuma *biwa* style. The *gaku biwa* of court music is a large instrument played with the neck held horizontally and with a comparatively small plectrum. In later styles a bigger plectrum was used, but the *biwa* was smaller and was played in a more or less vertical position. *Biwa* of the various styles and schools differ in the number of their frets, which varies from four to six, and in the number of strings, which ranges from three to five, four being the usual number. A variety of tunings, finger techniques, and notation systems are also found. The instrument usually plays stereotyped melodic phrases in alternation with the chant. The chant texts are usually in a conventional 7–5 syllabic meter. See also BIWA HŌSHI.

biwa hōshi 琵琶法師

(literally, "lute priest"). Itinerant performers, usually blind, who chanted works of vocal literature to the accompaniment of a BIWA (lute). *Biwa hōshi* shaved their heads and dressed as traveling priests but were not formally ordained. Their origins are obscure, but itinerant Buddhist lay-priest entertainers were also known in China and India, and the tradition possibly entered Japan with the spread of Buddhism. A 10th-century poem by Taira no Kanemori (d 990) makes the first recorded use of the term *biwa hōshi.* Early *biwa hōshi* probably recited a variety of short tales, including accounts of the great battles of the TAIRA-MINAMOTO WAR (1180–85), but by far the most important work in the repertoire from the 13th century on was the HEIKE MONOGATARI (ca 1220; tr *The Tale of the Heike,* 1988). Akashi Kakuichi (d 1371), the most famous *biwa hōshi,* dictated a revised recitation version of the *Heike monogatari,* which has become the popular standard text. Only a very few performers today maintain something of the musical traditions of the *biwa hōshi.* See also HEIKYOKU.

Biwako Canal　　琵琶湖疏水

(Biwako Sosui). Canal in Shiga and Kyōto prefectures, central Honshū, extending from Ōtsu on Lake Biwa to Kyōto and joining the river Ujigawa at Fushimi. The water from Lake Biwa is used for drinking, irrigation, power generation, and industrial purposes. Work on the first part of the canal was completed in 1890. The second part, from Ōtsu to Keage, was completed in 1912. Length: 25 km (15 mi).

Biwa, Lake　　琵琶湖

(Biwako). In central Shiga Prefecture, central Honshū. Japan's largest freshwater lake, it is divided into the North Lake and the South Lake. The average depth of the former is more than 50 m (164 ft), while that of the latter is less than 5 m (16 ft). Known as the location of the eight scenic spots of Ōmi (see ŌMI HAKKEI), the lake has been designated a quasi-national park, and has long been used as a main artery of transportation to provinces in the north. The Great Bridge of Lake Biwa, a toll bridge that connects Ōtsu with Moriyama, was completed in 1964. Lake water is used for irrigation, drinking, and industry, providing water to the Kyōto-Ōsaka-Kōbe area. Sweetfish, trout, carp, crucian carp, and roach are found in the lake. Freshwater pearl culture is also carried out. Area: 672 sq km (259 sq mi); circumference: 277 km (172 mi); deepest point: 104 m (341 ft); altitude: 85 m (279 ft).

Bizen　　備前[市]

City in southeastern Okayama Prefecture, on the Inland Sea. Bizen produces about 30 percent of Japan's refractory bricks. The Imbe district is the center for the production of BIZEN WARE. The Shizutani Gakkō, a school established by IKEDA MITSUMASA, the *daimyō* of Okayama, to educate the children in his domain, is now an educational center for young adults. Pop: 31,148.

Bizen ware　　備前焼

(*bizen-yaki*). Unglazed stoneware made in Okayama Prefecture (formerly Bizen Province) from at least the Kamakura period (1185–1333) to the present. Typical wares have a vitrified body with surfaces of glossy gold, matte orange, iridescent blue-green, or rough, charcoal-like patches that are all produced by sustained, high-temperature firings. Fiery red-glaze streaks are produced where straw wrapped around the pots has burned off. Bizen-ware specialties include storage vessels, mortars, vases, and *sake* bottles.

Early Bizen ware consisted primarily of storage vessels and mortars. TEA CEREMONY ware began to be produced in the late 1400s and early 1500s. The Azuchi-Momoyama period (1568–1600) was Bizen's golden age. Vigorously shaped ware with rich gold, red,

brown, and black surfaces, crisscrossed with rhythmic slashes of a bamboo knife, was made to suit the taste of tea masters SEN NO RIKYŪ and FURUTA ORIBE. Edo-period (1600–1868) wares had thinner walls and were shinier and more decorative.

Approximately 200 potters work at Bizen today, in traditional as well as innovative styles. The potter KANESHIGE TŌYŌ (1896–1967) was recognized as one of the LIVING NATIONAL TREASURES in 1956, as was Fujiwara Kei (1900–1983) in 1970.

Black Dragon Society→Amur River Society

Black, John Reddie　　ブラック, J. R.

(1827–80). Newspaper editor and publisher active in Japan in the early Meiji period (1868–1912). Born in Scotland. Initially a British naval officer, he later became a trader in Australia, during which time he visited Japan and decided to remain. He found work as editor in chief of the JAPAN HERALD, an English-language newspaper, and in 1867 commenced publication of his own English-language paper, the *Japan Gazette.* In 1872 he started the daily Japanese-language newspaper *Nisshin shinjishi.* Barred from newspaper work after 1876 by the Japanese and British governments because of his provocative stance toward the former, he spent his last years writing *Young Japan* (1880), a firsthand account of early Meiji society and politics.

Bloch, Bernard　　ブロック, B.

(1907–65). American theoretical linguist whose work on Japanese in the 1940s resulted in a new and original analysis of the spoken language. Born in New York City and educated at the University of Kansas and Brown University, Bloch began his research on Japanese during World War II, first briefly at Brown University, and then at Yale, where he remained as professor of linguistics until his death. Recognized as a preeminent theoretician by his colleagues in the field, he served as editor of *Language* for 26 years. His interest in both the analysis and teaching of spoken Japanese marked a striking departure from traditional approaches, which tended to stress only the written language. His major achievements in Japanese are con-

tained in two works: *Bernard Bloch on Japanese* (1969), a collection of previously published linguistic papers, and *Spoken Japanese* (1945), a two-volume textbook for Americans, coauthored with Eleanor Harz Jorden.

"Blood Debt" Incident
シンガポール血債問題

(Shingapōru Kessai Mondai). Controversy that developed from the discovery in February 1962 of mass graves of Chinese believed to have been massacred in Singapore and Malaya by Japanese soldiers during the period of occupation by Japan (1942–45). The chambers of commerce of both Southeast Asian countries, representing Chinese citizens, demanded "blood debt" reparations from the Japanese government. The incident became an important issue in the then-proposed Singapore-Malaya merger. Singaporean political parties opposing the merger seized the opportunity to embarrass Singapore's Prime Minister Lee Kuan Yew (b 1923), who had been committed to the merger and was anxious to get Japanese technical and economic assistance.

In October 1966 the Japanese government agreed to grant Singapore ¥2.94 billion (US $8.20 million) and in May 1967 it agreed to grant Malaysia ¥2.94 billion in ships and other capital goods. The "Blood Debt" Incident was settled officially on 7 May 1968 with an exchange of protocols between Japan and the other two countries.

"blood tax" riots→ketsuzei ikki

Board of Audit　　会計検査院

(Kaikei Kensa In). Independent department of the executive branch of the national government in charge of auditing government accounts. The board was established in 1947 to comply with article 90 of the constitution, which requires that the results of an audit be submitted annually by the cabinet to the Diet. The board's auditors regularly monitor the flow of incoming and outgoing money for government ministries, agencies, and public corporations. The auditors have the right to inform concerned authorities and request appropriate action if they discover any mismanagement or misuse of government

Lake Biwa An aerial view, looking northward, of Japan's largest freshwater lake.

Bizen ware The cylindrical shape of this flower vase was common in Bizen ware. 1557. Private collection.

111

Board of Audit

funds. The board consists of the Audit Commission and the General Executive Bureau and is headed by three auditors appointed by the cabinet with the Diet's consent.

board of directors 取締役会

(*torishimariyaku kai*). Organ of joint-stock companies composed of individuals (the law stipulates a minimum of three) selected by the stockholders to determine company policies and supervise operations, except for matters delegated by the COMMERCIAL CODE or the articles of incorporation to the authority of the STOCKHOLDERS' GENERAL MEETING.

Day-to-day management and representation of the company are left to the representative director (*daihyō torishimariyaku*), who is selected by the board of directors. Under express provisions of the Commercial Code, the board of directors has the authority to decide such matters as the convocation of the stockholders' general meeting, the establishment of branch operations, the selection and dismissal of managers, the selection of the representative director, the issuance of new stock, and the issuance of company bonds.

Bōchō kaiten shi 防長回天史

History of the activities of the powerful Chōshū domain (now Yamaguchi Prefecture) during the critical last years of the Edo period (1600–1868) and the early years of the Meiji period (1868–1912). Compiled by SUEMATSU KENCHŌ in 12 volumes in 1920, it emphasizes the role the domain played in the MEIJI RESTORATION.

bodhisattva 菩薩

(J: *bosatsu*). In the Mahāyāna Buddhist tradition, which prevails in Japan, a being of great spiritual attainment who is destined for Buddhahood but has vowed not to become a Buddha until all other beings have been helped to attain this state. The bodhisattva is ranked just below a Buddha and is a pivotal concept in the Mahāyāna tradition, which emphasizes the possibility of all beings attaining Buddhahood. In popular belief, the bodhisattva is viewed as a divine being with boundless compassion who intercedes on behalf of living creatures in distress. The most popular bodhisattvas in Japan are KANNON (Skt: Avalokiteśvara), whose special attribute is compassion; JIZŌ

(Skt: Kṣitigarbha), the protector of children; Fugen (Skt: Samantabhadra) and Monju (Skt: Mañjuśrī), both associated with wisdom; and MIROKU (Skt: Maitreya), who will be the next major Buddha to appear in the world.

Bōeichō→Defense Agency

Bōei Daigakkō→National Defense Academy

Bōei hakusho→Defense White Paper

Bohai (Po-hai) 渤海

(J: Bokkai; Kor: Parhae). A kingdom in southeastern Manchuria and northeastern Korea from 713 to 926 that maintained diplomatic and trading relations with Japan. In 696 remnants of the defeated Korean state of KOGURYŎ fled the territory in which the Chinese Tang (T'ang) dynasty (618–907) had forced them to settle, and two years later declared themselves an independent nation. The Chinese eventually recognized the new kingdom, giving it the name Bohai in 713. Records are scanty, and little is known of Bohai's history beyond the names of its 15 kings.

In 727, when its relations with China were temporarily strained, Bohai sent its first official embassy to Japan, seeking a military alliance. No alliance was concluded, but friendly relations between the two countries continued for 200 years. Numerous missions from Bohai were accompanied by extensive trade and cultural exchange. They were important for the introduction of Chinese culture to Japan. With the collapse of the Tang dynasty, Manchuria fell into chaos. In 926 the proto-Mongolian Khitan people conquered Bohai and incorporated it into their empire.

Boissonade de Fontarabie, Gustave Emile ボアソナード, G. E.

(1829–1910). French legal scholar who was one of many foreign legal scholars employed by the Japanese government in the Meiji period (1868–1912). After receiving his doctorate in law from the University of Paris, he taught at the University of Grenoble. He went to Japan in 1873 at the invitation of the Ministry of Justice and remained until 1895. He served as an adviser to the government and as an instructor in the Law School of the Ministry of Justice. He also made a major contribution to the compilation of legal codes such as the Penal Code and the CIVIL

CODE. His knowledge of international public law, as seen in both the disposition of the TAIWAN EXPEDITION OF 1874 and his opposition to any precipitous revision of the so-called Unequal Treaties (especially as proposed by Foreign Minister INOUE KAORU; see also UNEQUAL TREATIES, REVISION OF), had a great influence on Japan's foreign relations.

Bokutō kidan 濹東綺譚

(tr *A Strange Tale from East of the River*, 1958). Novel written in 1937 by NAGAI KAFŪ (1879–1959); often praised as his finest work. The story is narrated by Ōe Tadasu, an aging writer who frequents Tōkyō's Tamanoi pleasure district east of the river Sumidagawa to gather material for a novel, excerpts of which appear in the story. Ōe, devoted to the vanishing culture of Edo (as Tōkyō was called before the Meiji Restoration of 1868), finds himself drawn to the area with its dark alleys, river air, quiet nights, and Oyuki, a prostitute whose manner evokes the past. There Ōe escapes the unsettling world beyond the Tamanoi borders where sounds of radios, phonographs, and automobiles assault his ears. Kafū pays particular attention to the seasons—most of this work takes place in the hottest part of summer, creating an indolent atmosphere appropriate to the derelict Tamanoi quarter. The affair between Ōe and the prostitute ends without flourish: as the season turns from summer to autumn, Ōe and Oyuki drift apart, each unaware of the other's life outside the district.

bombori→lanterns

bone articles 骨角器

(*kokkakuki*). Tools and decorative items made from the bones, antlers, teeth, tusks, and claws of animals. These were most commonly used by the hunting and gathering societies of the Jōmon period (ca 10,000 BC–ca 300 BC) and the OKHOTSK CULTURE, although they are also found among Yayoi-period (ca 300 BC–ca AD 300) and Kofun-period (ca 300–710) remains.

Bone articles are found preserved in SHELL MOUNDS of the Earliest Jōmon phases. Middle Jōmon tools include barbed harpoon heads, fishhooks, and pronged fishing spears. Items of the Latest Jōmon phases include arrowheads, reinforcements for the notched ends of arrow shafts and bows, ornaments, and revolving harpoon heads. Among the artifacts of the Okhotsk culture in Hokkaidō are hair and ear ornaments, needles, and sickle hafts. The most common bone articles of the proto-historic period are knife hilts, some elaborately carved and painted with CHOKKOMON designs.

bōnenkai 忘年会

("forget-the-year parties"). Type of Japanese-style banquet (ENKAI) held annually in December to give people an opportunity to forget the trials and tribulations of the past year. *Bōnenkai* are most commonly held by companies, in which case a separate party is usually organized for each section, but many other groups in Japanese society hold *bōnenkai* as well, including, in recent years, students and housewives.

Bon Festival 盂蘭盆会

(Urabon'e). Buddhist observance honoring the spirits of ancestors; traditionally observed from 13 to 15 July (August in some areas). Also called Urabon or Obon. The festival is known to have been observed in China by the early 6th century and in Japan since its first recorded occurrence in 657.

Typically at Bon, a "spirit altar" (*shōryōdana*) is set up in front of the BUTSUDAN (Buddhist family altar) to welcome the ancestors' souls; then a priest is requested to come and read a sutra (*tanagyō*). Among the traditional preparations for the ancestors' return are the cleaning of grave sites and preparing a path from them to the house and the provision of straw horses or oxen for the ancestors' transportation. The welcoming fire (*mukaebi*), built on the 13th, and the send-off fire (*okuribi*), built on the 16th, are intended to illuminate the path.

Bon and the NEW YEAR are the two high points of the Japanese festival calendar, and thematically they bear a close resemblance. On both occasions, custom strongly urges all members of a family, no matter how scattered, to gather together to honor their ancestors. Certain observances associated with Bon—the TANABATA FESTIVAL, the BON ODORI, the NEBUTA FESTIVAL, DAIMONJI OKURIBI, and lantern floating (TŌRŌ NAGASHI)—have become tourist attractions.

Bonin Islands → Ogasawara Islands

bonito 鰹

(*katsuo*). A pelagic migratory fish of the family Scombridae, order Perciformes, class Osteichthyes. It reaches 1 meter (3 ft) in length. Distributed in warm seas throughout the world, it is caught by pole fishing and round haul nets. In spring it comes to Japan from the south, swims north as far as the offing of the Tōhoku region, and returns south in autumn. Bonito may be eaten as *sashimi* (sliced raw fish), *tataki* (briefly cooked, the inside remaining raw), *nitsuke* (stewed and seasoned), *katsuobushi* (dried), and *namaribushi* (steamed). It is also canned. The guts are made into *shiokara* (salted fish guts).

In the Edo period (1600–1868) bonito became a favored fish of the common people. The season's first bonito (*hatsugatsuo*) was particularly prized; it is celebrated in a famous *haiku* by the poet Yamaguchi Sodō (1642–1716), "Green leaves to see, the cuckoo to hear, and the early bonito to taste" (*Me ni wa aoba / Yama hototogisu / Hatsugatsuo*).

bonkei and bonseki 盆景と盆石

(*bonkei to bonseki*). Two types of miniature landscape garden (HAKONIWA) arranged either on a flat tray (*bon*) or in a shallow bowl, and conveying strong seasonal associations. *Bonkei* recreate a realistic world in miniature using tiny grasses, trees, moss, stones, and

ceramic objects. *Bonseki* are miniature landscapes composed entirely of sand and stone. The practice of making landscapes in miniature seems to have first appeared in Japan in the Muromachi period (1333–1568). During the Edo period (1600–1868) a number of miniature-landscape schools appeared, each with its own techniques and rules. Among them, the *bonseki* schools of Hosokawa, Sekishū, and Enzan are still active. The Japan Bonkei Association has 16 member schools. See also BONSAI.

Bon odori 盆踊

(Bon dances). Dances performed annually in either mid-July or mid-August, as part of the BON FESTIVAL celebrations to welcome the ancestor spirits on their annual return to the world of the living and to bid them farewell at their departure. Evolving out of NEMBUTSU ODORI, the popular Buddhist chants and folk dances of the late Heian (794–1185) and Kamakura (1185–1333) periods, the Bon *odori* was first mentioned in late-15th-century literature. By the Edo period (1600–1868) it was a widespread national custom characterized by considerable local variation. While in many rural areas the Bon *odori* today retains some of its original religious significance, in the cities it has been greatly secularized. The Bon *odori* is usually performed by large groups of men, women, and children to the accompaniment of music and song. Costumes vary, but loose, cotton summer *kimono* (YUKATA) and straw hats are popular attire. The dancers often move in circles around the musicians or around a temporary platform (*yagura*) set up in a broad, open space.

Bō no Tsu 坊津

Small fishing port in southwestern Kagoshima Prefecture, Kyūshū. It was a flourishing seaport and religious center in the Nara period (710–794). During the Muromachi period (1333–1568), as the seat of the SHIMAZU FAMILY, Bō no Tsu became a major entrepôt of the trade with Ming China and the Ryūkyūs. With Hakata (see HAKATA MERCHANTS) and ANOTSU, it was one of Japan's three principal ports.

bonsai 盆栽

(literally, "tray planting"). The art of dwarfing trees or plants by growing and training them in containers according to prescribed techniques. The word *bonsai* also refers to the miniature potted trees themselves. Bonsai, which first appeared in China more than 1,000 years ago, was introduced to Japan in the Kamakura period (1185–1333) on the wave of cultural borrowings that included Zen Buddhism. In Japan the art was refined to an extent unapproached in China.

Bonsai can be developed from seeds or cuttings, from young trees, or from naturally occurring stunted trees transplanted into containers. Most bonsai range in height from 5 centimeters (2 in) to 1 meter (approximately 3 ft). Bonsai are kept small and trained by pruning branches and roots, by periodic repotting, by pinching off new growth, and by wiring the branches and trunk so that they grow into the desired shape.

Grown in special containers, bonsai are usually kept outdoors, although they are often displayed on special occasions in the *tokonoma*, the alcove in traditional Japanese rooms designed for the display of artistic objects. An unglazed, dark-colored container is usually chosen for a classic bonsai

Bon odori Participants dance around a temporary platform known as a *yagura* during a Bon odori in Shinjuku Ward, Tōkyō.

bonkei and bonseki
A *bonkei* miniature landscape. The art of creating miniature landscapes and rock gardens (*bonseki*) dates from before the 17th century.

or to impart a look of age, but glazed containers are often used for flowering trees. As a rule, oval containers complement deciduous trees; rectangular ones, evergreens.

Growing Bonsai—Given proper care, bonsai can live for hundreds of years, with prized specimens being passed from generation to generation, admired for their age, and revered as a reminder of those who have cared for them over the centuries. Venerable bonsai are generally more respected than young ones, but age is not essential. It is more important that the tree produce the artistic effect desired, that it be in proper proportion to the appropriate container, and that it be in good health. The two basic styles of bonsai are the classic (*koten*) and the informal or comic (*bunjin*). In the former, the trunk of the tree is wider at the base and tapers off toward the top; it is just the opposite in the *bunjin*, a style more difficult to master.

Bonsai are ordinary trees or plants, not special hybrid dwarfs. Small-leaved varieties are most suitable. In Japan varieties of pine, bamboo, and plum are most often used. The artist never merely duplicates nature but rather expresses a personal aesthetic or sensibility by manipulating it. The miniaturized tree may suggest a scene from nature, a family grouping, a scene from a play, or a foolish or even grotesque character. But in all cases the bonsai must look natural and never show the intervention of human hands.

Major Styles—The major styles of bonsai include the upright style; the slanting style; the cascading style, in which the tree is trained to hang over the container's side; the weeping-cascade style; the twisting-trunk style, in which the tree is gnarled and driftwood is sometimes incorporated; the twin-trunk style, in which a single trunk, bifurcat-

Continued on page 116➤

113
bonsai

Bonsai: A Timeless Tradition

*To the Japanese, who have been cultivating bonsai for centuries,
these miniature trees symbolize continuity, rebirth, and immortality.*

A 100-year-old five-needle pine. 61 cm.

The art of *bonsai* can be characterized as the technique of "shrinking" trees to amazingly small dimensions. The dwarf trees flourish in pots measuring barely 30 centimeters (12 in) across. Their leaves are a vibrant green, and they bear no signs of having been cut, bent, wired, and trained or of having been given such minuscule quantities of water, sunlight, and nutrients that in several decades they grow only 50 centimeters (20 in). Although many people claim that the asymmetrical, knotted, and twisted trunks—which may even have part of their heartwood exposed—are a testimony to the torture undergone by the trees, bonsai enthusiasts contend that these very features symbolize qualities that the Japanese have always held dear; namely, the ability to withstand difficulties in order to maintain continuity and preserve tradition. Bonsai trees celebrate the ever-renewing life force, and anyone looking at a bonsai will notice that the misshapen trunk presents a striking contrast to the vital greenness of the leaves.

Trees usually favored for bonsai are evergreens such as pine, cypress, and cedar and deciduous trees such as cherry, maple, zelkova, and beech. Typical heights of bonsai in competitions are 65 centimeters (26 in) for pines, 50 centimeters (20 in) for zelkovas, 37 centimeters (15 in) for beeches, and 17 centimeters (7 in) for maples. In the *kengai* (cascading) style of bonsai, in which the tree is trained to imitate its natural cousin clinging precariously to a cliff, a pine may measure as little as 9 centimeters (3.5 in).

Just as trees of the same species reach different heights in the wild, bonsai also vary in size according to the preferences of their cultivators. Thus it is impossible to give absolute figures for ideal heights, but, as a guideline, a zelkova or beech, which in its natural state can grow to 30 meters (98 ft) and have a diameter of 2 meters (7 ft), can be reduced to one-sixtieth or one-eightieth that size. The five-needle pine, a favorite among bonsai cultivators, rarely exceeds 20 meters (66 ft) in height and can be reduced to one-thirtieth of that.

A Long History | Believed to have originated in China more than a thousand years ago, miniature plants are still cultivated there, as well as in Vietnam and Thailand. Wall paintings found in a Chinese imperial tomb in Shanxi Province reveal that as early as the 8th century miniature gardens arranged in ceramic trays were exchanged as gifts among the aristocracy.

According to Professor Rolf Stein of the Collège de France, this tradition made its way to Japan via the Korean peninsula. However, Japanese bonsai enthusiasts do not regard the Chinese versions as bonsai, but rather as *bonkei* (miniature landscapes). The practice of taking a single tree and nurturing it—sometimes for generations—developed only in Japan. Another characteristic of the Japanese tradition was that bonsai appealed to all classes of people, not just the wealthy. Thus, like many cultural imports, the art of bonsai was developed, refined, and appreciated to a greater extent in Japan than elsewhere.

Bonsai attracted a particularly wide following in the late Edo period (1600–1868), in the early Meiji period (1868–1912), and between 1926 and 1940. Although not as popular today as it once was, bonsai still has the power to move the Japanese spirit and provides a welcome respite from the burdens of daily life.

Bonsai does not require much space. The trees can be grown easily on small balconies of apartment buildings or in narrow alleys between densely packed houses. For much of the year a bonsai is kept outdoors, but on special occasions it is often placed in the *tokonoma* (alcoves) and hallways of traditional-style houses.

A 100-year-old Japanese plum tree. 74 cm.

This *umemodoki* or holly tree was transplanted to this pot 60 years ago. 69 cm.

Beyond Space and Time

In growing bonsai one is creating a microcosm of nature. To an enthusiast, one bonsai may conjure an image of a solitary fruit tree basking in the evening sun of late autumn in a corner of a farmyard. Another bonsai may evoke a stately old tree atop a remote cliff. The tree's crown appears sculpted by the wind, its moss-covered trunk contorted, its exposed roots gripping the earth as it struggles for survival in the impoverished soil. Pebbles placed near the edge of the ceramic pot suggest waves rolling in from the open sea.

To call bonsai cultivators artists is no exaggeration, for that is what they ultimately become as they try to maintain the shape of their trees. In designing a microcosm, they are able to sublimate the natural human desire for complete control and mastery of one's environment, which is impossible to achieve in the real world. This attracts people to bonsai and may be the reason they devote themselves to it with such fervor.

The bonsai has been revered as a symbol of timelessness and continuity, and some carefully tended trees have survived for hundreds of years. One of the most famous is a five-needle pine that was first owned by Tokugawa Iemitsu, the third Tokugawa shōgun, in the 17th century.

Evergreens are the most popular trees cultivated by bonsai growers. The pine, which symbolizes eternity to the Japanese, is especially popular—particularly the five-needle variety.

The tendency of the Japanese to favor trees that evoke eternity is epitomized in the appreciation of tree trunks. Gnarled, moss-covered trunks not only symbolize perpetuity but also hold the promise of rebirth. Thus pine and juniper trunks with peeling bark, exposed heartwood, or even deep cavities are highly valued. Likewise, when a piece of trunk or branch withers and turns bone white, it is called *jin*, which is written with the Chinese character for deity.

Deciduous trees are somewhat less popular than evergreens because they denote the passage of seasons. Within this group fall *himeringo* (crab apple), *mamekaki* (a variety of persimmon), pomegranate, and ginkgo, which are all valued for their fruit. Plum and cherry trees are appreciated for their blossoms. Among deciduous trees, fruit trees are preferred over flowering trees because fruit remains on trees longer than flowers, and thus one is less conscious of the passage of time.

A Demanding Hobby

Cultivating bonsai is time-consuming indeed, and mastering just the basics requires 5 to 10 years. If miniature trains, planes, or ships took that long to assemble, they would surely be abandoned by hobbyists before completion. Bonsai enthusiasts, however, become more deeply engrossed the more time they spend on their trees. Their patience is inexhaustible as they tackle each task, and most of their concerns are unfathomable to outsiders. As a bonsai changes its shape ever so slowly, the cultivator must make sure it receives just the right amount of sunlight, water, and fertilizer—not too much or too little. Exactly the right time must be chosen for such tasks as root trimming, repotting, cutting the branches, and exposing the tree to the sun.

The precept that "it takes three years to master the art of watering" is indicative of the infinite patience required for such a simple task. The time-consuming aspect of bonsai would seem to preclude its being a suitable hobby for elderly people. After all, why would those in their twilight years adopt a hobby that takes so much time to master? Yet bonsai is quite popular among senior citizens. The reason lies in the symbolic connection between bonsai and immortality—a tree cultivated by an older person can be passed down, along with the memory of that person, through the generations.

Ikei Nozomu

The white, withered sections of this juniper's trunk testify to its great age—200 to 300 years. Height 58 cm.

The same *umemodoki* tree after its leaves have fallen.

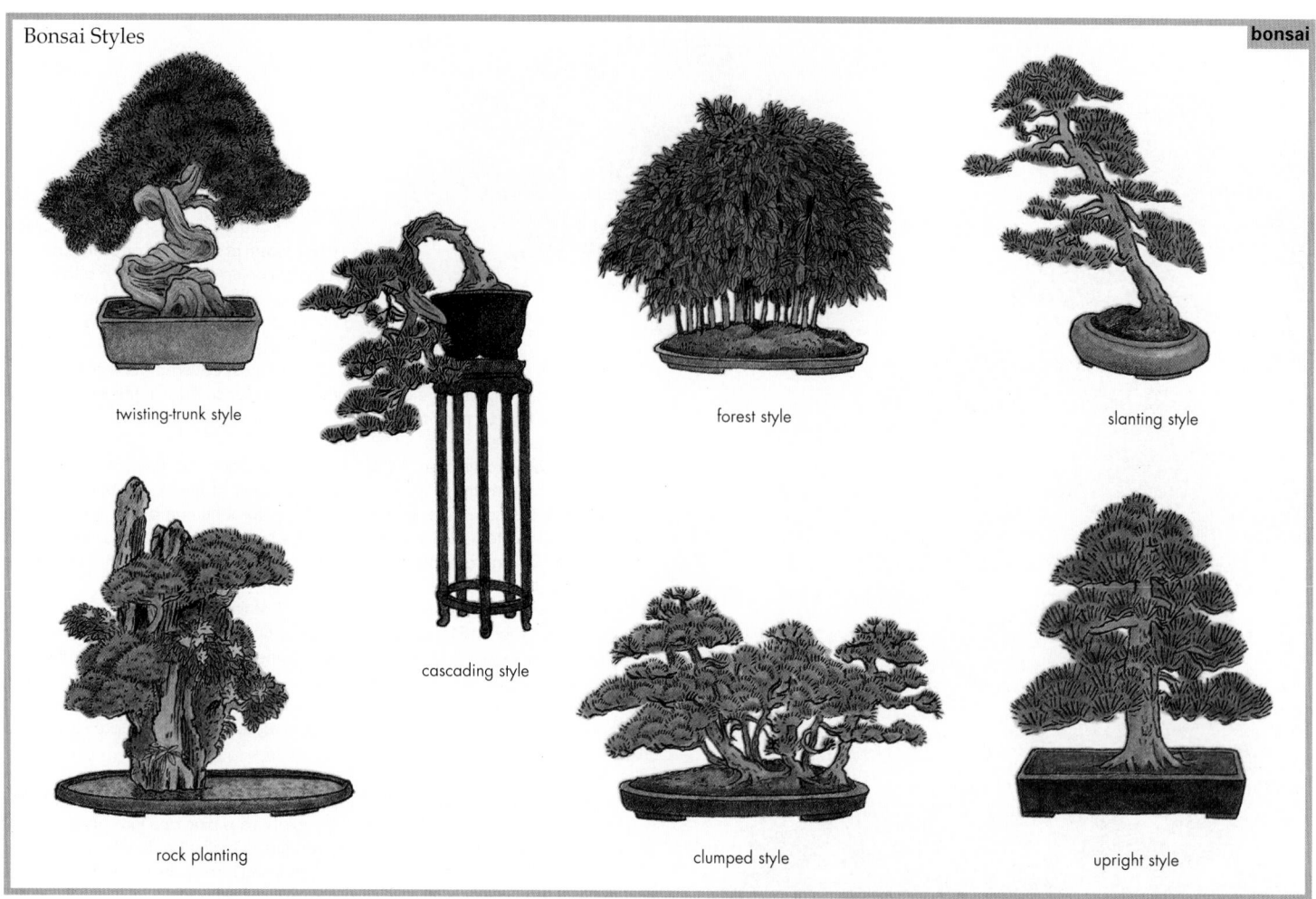

twisting-trunk style

cascading style

forest style

slanting style

rock planting

clumped style

upright style

ing near the soil line, splits to suggest a pair; the clumped style, in which suckers are encouraged to grow so as to form "separate" trees representing a family or group; the forest style, using trees of various sizes planted in a single container; and rock planting, in which the tree grows so as to straddle the rock, with roots exposed at the sides. In an alternate style of rock planting, the tree emerges from a crack in a tall rock set in a shallow container.

Aesthetics and Philosophy——The bonsai with its container and soil, physically independent of the earth since its roots are not planted in it, is a separate entity, complete in itself, yet part of nature. This is what is meant by the expression "heaven and earth in one container." A bonsai tree should always be positioned off-center in its container, for not only is asymmetry vital to the visual effect, but the center point is symbolically where heaven and earth meet, and nothing should occupy this place. Another aesthetic principle is the triangular pattern necessary for visual balance and for expression of the relationship shared by a universal principle (life-giving energy or deity), the artist, and the tree itself. Tradition holds that three basic virtues are necessary to create a bonsai: *shin-zen-bi* (truth, goodness, and beauty). *114–115*

bonus 賞与

(*shōyo*). A sum of money specially given an employee in addition to regular monthly pay. It may amount to several months' pay and is usually given twice a year (June and December). Originally meant as an incentive, bonuses were given in appreciation for the employees' contribution to business performance. Over the years, however, this

practice has become so widely established in Japan that it has become a part of the wage. Where the work force is unionized, the amount of the bonus is often negotiated through collective bargaining. Because the amount varies greatly according to the business performance of individual corporations, the level of wages in Japan can change in relation to business fluctuations. The average bonus paid by Japanese industries as a whole was ¥528,000 (US $4,275) for the winter of 1988, equivalent to 1.7 times the average monthly wage, and ¥476,200 (US $3,311) for the summer of 1989, equivalent to 1.5 times the average monthly wage. Bonuses are also paid to government employees and to employees of public corporations, based on the average bonus amount for private enterprise.

In principle the bonus system applies only to regular, full-time employees and not to temporary workers, though they often receive small sums of bonus money. This distinction is a major factor contributing to the difference in wages between regular and temporary workers. Generally bonus money is used to maintain living standards and may be spent for durable consumer goods, house payments, educational expenses, or retirement savings.

book and magazine distributors
出版取次業

(*shuppan toritsugigyō*). Over 70 percent of all publications in Japan reach the reading public by way of bookstores and the distributors who supply them. Books and magazines are distributed in two ways: on consignment, which permits the return of unsold books, or by order, which does not. New publications are distributed largely on consignment. Publication distributors first appeared in Japan in the 1880s. Under controls during

World War II, all distributors in the country were integrated into one corporation, the Nihon Shuppan Haikyū Kabushiki Gaisha. This corporation disbanded in 1949 and reorganized into what are now the two largest distribution firms in Japan, Tōhan Corporation and Nippon Shuppan Hambai Co, Ltd (Nippan); together they control 70 percent of all publication distribution. Major distributors have gained a voice in the planning of mass publications by providing capital to publishers.

book illustration 挿絵

(*sashi-e*). Book illustration has a long history in Japan, extending back to the 8th century. Two of the earliest forms of book illustration were the illustrated Buddhist sutras of the Nara period (710–794), such as the *E inga kyō*, and the picture scrolls (EMAKIMONO) of the late Heian period (794–1185) through the Kamakura period (1185–1333), such as the GENJI MONOGATARI EMAKI and the *Kitano tenjin engi*. In the Edo period (1600–1868), illustrated reading material was published in large quantities. One well-known example is Ihara SAIKAKU's *Kōshoku ichidai otoko* (The Life of an Amorous Man), whose illustrations were done by Hishikawa MORONOBU, an early UKIYO-E artist. From the middle to the end of the Edo period, illustrated storybooks with a picture on each page—the genres known as *akahon, aohon, kurohon*, and *kibyōshi* (see KUSAZŌSHI)—became popular. Prominent designers were Suzuki HARUNOBU, TORII KIYONAGA, Kitagawa UTAMARO, UTAGAWA TOYOKUNI, UTAGAWA KUNISADA, Katsushika HOKUSAI, and Andō HIROSHIGE.

Modern printing techniques were introduced into Japan in the Meiji period (1868–1912) and were used in reproducing illustrations in newspapers, magazines, and works of literature. When the KEN'YŪSHA group of authors was formed, their works were illustrated by new artists such as Tomioka Eisen (1864–1905) and Takeuchi Keishū (1863–1943) rather than by *ukiyo-e* designers. Other artists of this period include KABURAGI KIYOKATA, Kajita Hanko (1870–1917), and TAKEHISA YUMEJI.

From the Taishō period (1912–26) into the Shōwa period (1926–89), acclaimed illustrators were Ishii Tsuruzō (1887–1973), the first artist to use Conté crayon in illustration; Kimura Shōhachi (1893–1959); and Iwata Sentarō (1901–74), who excelled in the portrayal of women. During the first decade of the Shōwa period, which is known as the golden age of modern illustration, the detailed, graphic pen-and-ink illustrations of Kabashima Katsuichi (1888–1965) and the work of Itō Hikozō (b 1904) captured the imagination of the young. Since World War II, well-known book illustrators have been Sugimoto Kenkichi (b 1905), Miyata Shigeo (1900–1971), Ikuzawa Rō (1906–84), and Kazama Kan (b 1919). In recent years the word *irasuto* (from the English "illustration") has largely replaced the term *sashi-e*.

Booth, Eugene Samuel   ブース, E. S.

(1850–1931). American missionary. Graduate of Rutgers College and Rutgers Theological Seminary. He went to Japan in 1879 as a missionary of the Reformed Church and founded a boys' school in Nagasaki in 1880. Principal of Ferris Seminary in Yokohama from 1882 to 1922, he also participated in planning the Tōkyō Women's Christian University (Tōkyō Joshi Daigaku). Booth returned to the United States in 1922.

bosatsu ⟶ bodhisattva

Bose, Rash Behari   ボース, R. B.

(1886–1945). Indian revolutionary committed to independence for his nation; he spent the years from 1915 to 1945 in Japan. The son of a minor Bengali bureaucrat, Bose masterminded a bomb plot against the viceroy of India (1912) and an intended bombing in Lahore (1913). The latter was discovered by the British authorities, and Bose finally fled to Japan in 1915. With the help of such radical Japanese pan-Asianists as TŌYAMA MITSURU and UCHIDA RYŌHEI, Bose eluded the police and went into hiding. He remained in hiding until his naturalization as a Japanese citizen in 1923, whereupon he began to agitate openly for Indian independence. In 1924 he founded the Indian Independence League. The arrival in Tōkyō of the charismatic Subhas Chandra BOSE in 1943, however, removed Rash Behari Bose from the leadership of the league. Moreover, because of his Japanese citizenship, wife, and son (who was in the Japanese army), he was not completely trusted by his fellow Indians. See also INDIAN NATIONAL ARMY.

Bose, Subhas Chandra   ボース, S. C.

(1897–1945). Prominent Indian nationalist leader and organizer of an anti-British movement outside India during World War II. Born in Orissa, Bose studied at the University of Calcutta and at Cambridge. In 1921 he joined the Congress Party, hoping to gain a majority for his radical alternative to the nonviolent program of Mahatma Gandhi. In January 1938 he succeeded Jawaharlal Nehru as president of the Indian National Congress, but he resigned in April 1939 because of Gandhi's disapproval. Bose welcomed World War II as an opportunity for India to

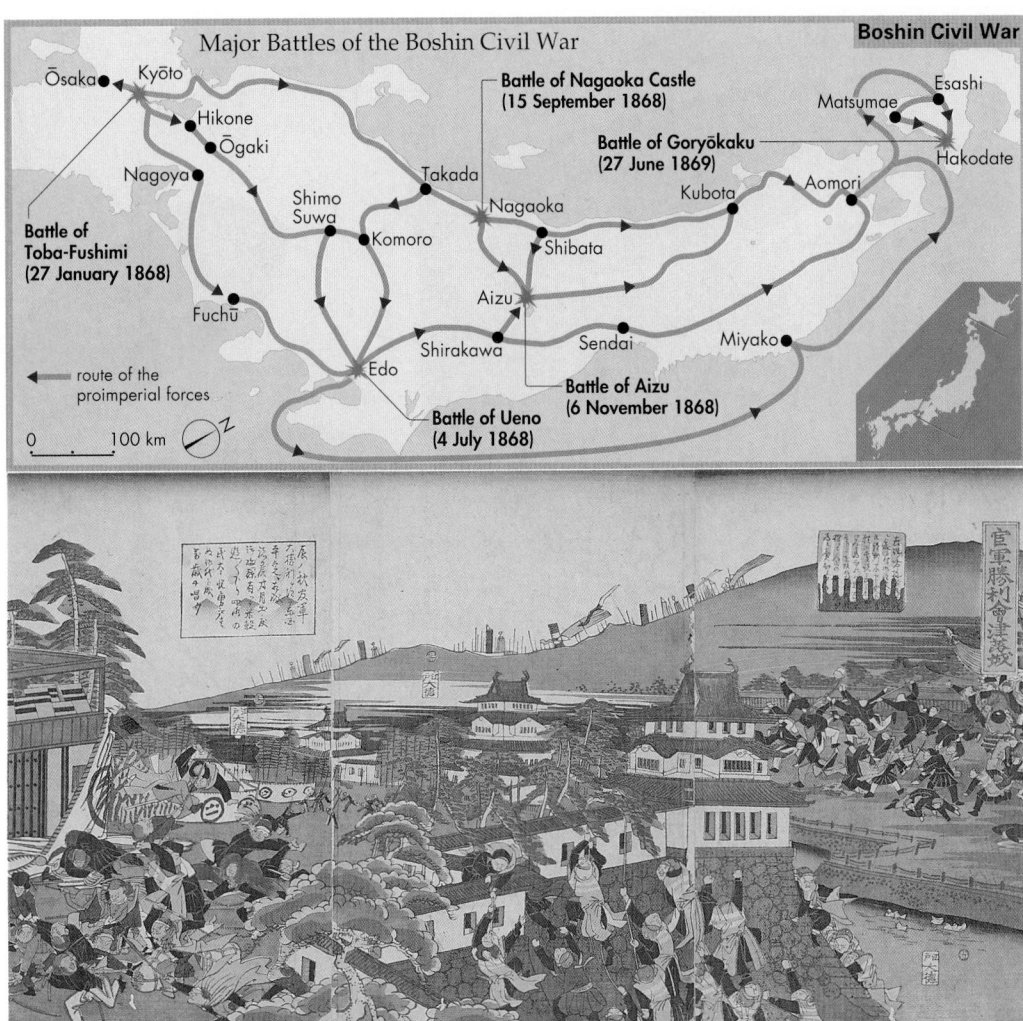

Major Battles of the Boshin Civil War

Battle of Nagaoka Castle (15 September 1868)

Battle of Goryōkaku (27 June 1869)

Battle of Toba-Fushimi (27 January 1868)

Battle of Ueno (4 July 1868)

Battle of Aizu (6 November 1868)

⟵ route of the proimperial forces

0   100 km

Ōsaka · Kyōto · Hikone · Ōgaki · Nagoya · Shimo Suwa · Komoro · Takada · Nagaoka · Shibata · Aizu · Shirakawa · Edo · Fuchū · Sendai · Miyako · Kubota · Aomori · Matsumae · Esashi · Hakodate

free itself. Arrested for anti-British activities in 1940, he escaped to Berlin in 1941 and arrived in Tōkyō in 1943. On 21 October 1943 he proclaimed the PROVISIONAL GOVERNMENT OF FREE INDIA, which was recognized by Japan and other Axis countries. He assumed command of the Japanese-backed INDIAN NATIONAL ARMY and of the Indian Independence League, but after the INA's defeat during the IMPHAL CAMPAIGN, an abortive Japanese attempt to penetrate India from Burma, it ceased to be an effective fighting force. Bose reportedly died in 1945 following an air crash, at a time when his standing in India was at its zenith.

Boshin Civil War   戊辰戦争

(Boshin Sensō). Series of battles that led to the overthrow of the Tokugawa shogunate and the restoration of imperial rule. It began with the Battle of TOBA-FUSHIMI on 27 January 1868 (a year designated *boshin* in the sexagenary cycle) and ended with the Battle of GORYŌKAKU on 27 June 1869.

By 1867 it was clear that the shogunate could not hold out against the proimperial (SONNŌ JŌI) forces led by the Chōshū and Satsuma domains (now Yamaguchi and Kagoshima prefectures, respectively). The shōgun TOKUGAWA YOSHINOBU agreed in November 1867 to accept a compromise solution (see KŌGI SEITAI RON), but by that time Satsuma and Chōshū had decided to overthrow the shogunate by force, and on 3 January 1868 their troops seized the imperial palace in Kyōto and proclaimed an "imperial restoration" (ŌSEI FUKKO).

Yoshinobu withdrew to Ōsaka Castle, but many shogunal vassals were unwilling to surrender to imperial troops, who defeated them easily at Toba and Fushimi. Yoshinobu

then moved to Edo (now Tōkyō). Imperial armies commanded by Prince ARISUGAWA advanced toward Edo, but under an agreement reached by SAIGŌ TAKAMORI of Satsuma and the shogunal retainer KATSU KAISHŪ, the city surrendered peaceably. Yoshinobu was then ordered into domiciliary confinement in Mito (now part of Ibaraki Prefecture), but pro-Tokugawa forces (see SHŌGITAI) continued to resist the troops of ŌMURA MASUJIRŌ and were crushed. Domains in northern Honshū formed a league (ŌUETSU REPPAN DŌMEI) that surrendered on 6 November after the Battle of Aizu (see BYAKKOTAI). The final center of resistance was Ezo (now Hokkaidō), where ENOMOTO TAKEAKI finally surrendered in June 1869. With the conclusion of hostilities, the entire country came under the control of the new "imperial" government. See also MEIJI RESTORATION.

Boshin Shōsho   戊申詔書

Imperial rescript issued by Emperor MEIJI on 13 October 1908; named for *boshin*, the designation in the sexagenary cycle for the year corresponding to 1908. Conservative elements had been alarmed following the Russo-Japanese War (1904–05) by the growth of liberal thought emphasizing individualism and political freedom, by the socialist movement, and by the popular predilection for luxury. They convinced the second KATSURA TARŌ cabinet to have a rescript issued exhorting the people to correct these excesses. This edict, together with the IMPERIAL RESCRIPT ON EDUCATION of 1890, was the official guideline for the nation's morals and ethics until the end of World War II.

Boshin Civil War In October and November 1868 imperial forces clashed with the army of the Ōuetsu Reppan Dōmei, an alliance of pro-Tokugawa domains, in the Battle of Aizu. The battle ended when, as depicted in this *ukiyo-e* print, Wakamatsu Castle fell to the imperial army.

This 18th-century writing box decorated with mother-of-pearl inlay and designs in *maki-e* (a technique employing gold or silver powder and liquid lacquer) was made by Kōrin and is a National Treasure.

Waves and plovers decorate the cover of this writing box, an example of Kagawa lacquer ware.

This letter box (*fubako*), used for storing rolled documents, is decorated with lacquer and images of wild geese and plovers.

Trays and boxes of various sizes for carrying food and *sake* are fitted into the outer frame of this red lacquer picnic set.

An Edo-period (1600–1868) writing box decorated with lacquer and gold *maki-e*.

Bōsō Peninsula　　房総半島

(Bōsō Hantō). Located in Chiba Prefecture, central Honshū, bounded on the east by the Pacific Ocean and on the west by Tōkyō Bay and the Sagami Sea. It is hilly with many beaches to the south. The peninsula contains part of the rapidly growing KEIYŌ INDUSTRIAL REGION. There are also extensive floriculture and truck and dairy farming. Southern Bōsō Quasi-National Park is situated along the southern coast, and Suigō-Tsukuba Quasi-National Park is located in the north. The area of the peninsula is about 5,034 sq km (1,943 sq mi).

botan→peonies

botanical gardens　　植物園

(*shokubutsuen*). In 1991 there were 116 major botanical gardens in Japan. The KOISHIKAWA BOTANIC GARDEN, belonging to Tōkyō University, was the first to be established, in 1877. In 1884 a second botanical garden, the HOKKAIDŌ UNIVERSITY BOTANIC GARDEN, was established. Nonuniversity botanical gardens, such as the JINDAI BOTANICAL PARK, have been established by the Ministry of Health and Welfare, pharmaceutical companies, local governments, and private concerns, each with different aims, such as research, education, and business. After World War II, many leisure-resort botanical gardens, in which tropical plants were grown using heat from hot springs, were set up. Among specialty gardens are the Izu Cactus Park (Shizuoka Prefecture), the Fuji Bamboo Botanical Garden (Shizuoka Pre-

fecture), and a type called a Man'yō botanical garden, where only plants mentioned in the 8th-century poetry anthology MAN'YŌSHŪ are cultivated. In 1983 the TSUKUBA BOTANICAL GARDEN was opened. It contains special exhibits that represent the ecosystem of Japan in precise detail.

Bousquet, Georges Hilaire
　　　　　　　　　　　　ブスケ, G. H.

(1845?–?). French legal adviser to the Meiji government, one of the many FOREIGN EMPLOYEES OF THE MEIJI PERIOD. Bousquet was working as a lawyer for the Court of Appeals in Paris when the Meiji government in 1872 invited him to help with the translation and interpretation of the Napoleonic code. During his four years in Japan, together with Gustave Emile BOISSONADE DE FONTARABIE, he taught law at the Meihōryō (later the Law School of the Ministry of Justice) and assisted in the drafting of the CIVIL CODE and other legislation. He also served informally as a consultant to the Ministry of Justice and wrote the book *Le Japon de Nos Jours* (1877). (Bousquet is often confused with another Frenchman, the military adviser Albert Charles DU BOUSQUET, 1837–82.)

bowing　　御辞儀

(*ojigi*). The bow is the traditional form of salutation in Japan. It accompanies and reinforces (or sometimes replaces) spoken expressions of greeting, thanks, apology, and request, among others. A formal bow is properly made by inclining the body at an angle of about 30 degrees while bringing the hands, palms down, to the knees (the hands may also be left at the sides). In less formal circumstances one inclines the body less. Generally speaking, juniors in age or status are expected to bow slightly lower than their seniors. Bows may be performed while standing (*ritsurei*) or, indoors on *tatami*, kneeling (*zarei*).

Boxer Rebellion　　義和団の乱

(J: Giwadan no Ran; also known as Hokushin Jihen). Xenophobic uprising by peasants in

North China in 1900. The "Boxers" (Ch: Yihe quan or I-ho ch'üan) were members of secret societies affiliated with a heterodox Buddhist sect known as the White Lotus. Loosely organized and led, they practiced boxing, magic, and martial arts and claimed to be invulnerable to weapons. Initially the Boxers' targets were Chinese Christians, foreign missionaries, and even the alien Manchu rulers of the Qing (Ch'ing) dynasty (1644–1912), though by 1899 the Manchu court had managed to convert them into an instrument in its own efforts to drive out Western influence. With the court's backing their numbers increased, and the movement spread throughout North China.

In June 1900 the court allowed the Boxers to enter Beijing (Peking). Thousands of them swarmed into the capital, burning and pillaging. They killed a senior member of the Japanese legation and the German minister and laid siege to the British legation. The uprising was quelled by a foreign expeditionary force from eight nations whose numbers eventually reached 45,000 troops, about half of whom were Japanese. The Manchu court then sued for peace and on 7 September 1901 signed the Boxer Protocol. Responsible persons were severely punished (a number of high officials were executed), apology missions sent to Japan and Germany, foreign legations given the right to self-protection by their own troops, and China agreed to pay an indemnity of $333 million.

The aftereffects of the Boxer Rebellion were far-reaching. Russia refused to withdraw its troops from Manchuria after the disturbance, which led to the RUSSO-JAPANESE WAR of 1904–05. The Manchu court was thoroughly discredited and would be overthrown a decade later, while the huge Boxer indemnity impeded Chinese efforts at reform and modernization.

boxes　　箱

(*hako*). Japanese boxes are made from a variety of materials and have long been prized for their aesthetic as well as their utilitarian value. The earliest boxes appeared during the Nara period (710–794) and examples may be found among the treasures of the SHŌSŌIN art repository in Nara. Boxes are most commonly made from wood and often are decorated with lacquer (see LACQUER WARE). The general term applied to boxes in Japan is *hako* or, when combined with another character, *bako*, as in *bentōbako* (lunch box), HARIBAKO (sewing box), *hōjubako* (jewel box), and *suzuribako* (writing box). The size and design of these boxes vary greatly, from *kōgō*, just a few centimeters square, to large boxes as long as 50 centimeters (20 in). Their shapes also vary greatly. The most uniquely Japanese box form is the INRŌ, a small container for medicine, drugs, or a seal, which consists of several sections held together by a cord.

Other important box types include *bunko* (for manuscripts), *chabako* (for tea), *kagamibako* (for mirrors), *kutsubako* (for shoes), *fudebako* (for pencils and pens), *kōbako* (for incense), *kushibako* (for combs), *obibako* (for obi), *hashibako* (for chopsticks), *suebako* (for priestly robes), *tantōbako* (for swords), *tebako* (for toiletries), *jūbako* (stacked boxes for food), and *sageju* or *sagejūbako* (a set of tiered boxes for holding food or *sake* bottles and cups).

Boy Scouts　　　　　　ボーイスカウト

(Bōi Sukauto). Boy Scout activities in Japan began in Tōkyō in 1915. In 1922 the national organization known as the Boy Scouts of Nippon was formally established. It was disbanded during World War II but resumed activities again after the war. During Boy Scout Week in May, many social-service projects are conducted throughout Japan. In 1989 there were 3,719 Boy Scout groups, with 286,260 members.

bracelets, ancient　　　　　　釧

(*kushiro*). Common body ornaments of the prehistoric and protohistoric periods. After the adoption of Buddhism in the 6th century, body ornamentation gradually ceased, and bracelets were not worn again until the modern influx of Western culture.

Bracelets of the Early Jōmon period (ca 5000 BC–ca 3500 BC) were fashioned by opening a hole in the *akagai* or *sarubō* types of bivalve ark shells. In the Yayoi period (ca 300 BC–ca AD 300) bracelets began to be made of spiral shells and of bronze. Shell and bronze bracelets continued into the Kofun period (ca 300–710) along with new, exquisitely fashioned stone bracelets of jasper or green tuff. Hoe-shaped bracelets (*kuwagataishi*) were stone imitations of Yayoi-period conch-shell bracelets. Wheel-shaped bracelets (*sharinseki*) were stone imitations of limpet shell (*kasagai*) bracelets. These stone bracelets—some decorated with CHOKKOMON designs—are thought to have been treasures rather than everyday items, and they are often discovered as funerary goods in the Kofun-period tomb mounds (see KOFUN) of western Japan. See also EAR ORNAMENTS, ANCIENT; BEADS, ANCIENT.

brain death　　　　　　脳死

(*nōshi*). In Japan, controversy still surrounds the definition of brain death, a concept that allows a person to be declared dead when the overall brain functions stop, even if the heart is still beating. Brain death has an important bearing on organ transplants, since brain-dead patients are potential donors of hearts, lungs, livers, kidneys, and other organs necessary for the survival of the recipients. In 1985 a medical advisory committee on brain death presented Japan's Ministry of Health and Welfare with new guidelines including five necessary conditions that must be evident before a person can be diagnosed as brain dead. They are deep coma, disappearance of spontaneous respiration, fixation of pupils, disappearance of brain stem response, and a period of six hours after the first four conditions have been established, during which it is confirmed that there has been no change in the patient's condition. In

1991 the Provisional Committee for Study on Brain Death and Organ Transplant reaffirmed the 1985 brain death standards. Though in 1991 a consensus had not yet been reached, most Japanese hospitals followed the 1985 standard in pronouncing patients brain dead.

Brandt, Max August Scipio von　　ブラント, M. A. S.

(1835–1920). German diplomat who went to Japan in 1862 as aide to Friedrich Albert EULENBURG, the Prussian delegate sent to conclude the Prusso-Japanese Treaty of 1861. Brandt was appointed the first Prussian consul general in Japan in 1862 and wrote *Dreiunddreissig Jahre in Ost-Asien* (1901, Thirty-Three Years in East Asia).

Brazil and Japan　　　　ブラジルと日本

(Burajiru *to* Nihon). Diplomatic relations between Japan and Brazil were established on 5 November 1895, when a treaty of amity, commerce, and navigation was signed in Paris. Early relations were dominated by the issue of Japanese immigration. In 1891 an emigration office was set up in the Japanese Ministry of Foreign Affairs. For Japan, emigration was a potential solution to the problem of overpopulation, while for Brazil the new immigrants were a source of nuch-needed agricultural labor. However, it was not until June 1908 that the first 781 Japanese immigrants to Brazil landed at Santos. By 1914 about 10,000 Japanese had arrived in Brazil. The total number of Japanese immigrants ultimately reached 190,000 in the period before World War II. See also BRAZIL, JAPANESE IMMIGRANTS IN.

Pre–World War II Commerce—The arrival of the first Japanese immigrants in Brazil was followed by the opening of stores selling Japanese goods. The trade between Japan and Brazil through these merchants amounted in 1913 to £35,933 in imports from Japan, including such items as ceramics, celluloid, toys, toothbrushes, fans, and buttons, while Brazilian exports of rock crystal and coffee to Japan totaled £2,931.

Toward the end of World War I, when imports from Europe were disrupted, Brazil increased its imports from Japan, especially of metal products and sundry goods. When European countries recovered from the war, however, Japanese steel products and machinery could not compete with European products.

In 1935 Japan sent a trade mission to Brazil that led to a great expansion of trade between 1936 and 1941. The chief export from Brazil was cotton. Brazilian exports to Japan jumped from £158,098 in 1935 to £1,683,106 in 1936 and £2,122,106 in 1937, accounting for 5 percent of Brazil's total exports, and continued at this level until World War II. In February 1942 the Brazilian government ordered the freezing of Japanese assets in Brazil, and, in July, Japanese diplomats in Brazil returned to Japan.

Post–World War II Relations and Japanese Investments—In 1949 a Japanese trade mission visited Brazil and reached an agreement covering US $35 million of foreign trade payments. In December 1950 diplomatic ties between the two countries were restored, and in 1952 Brazil approved the entry of 9,000 Japanese families as immigrants. In the late 1950s the Brazilian government adopted a policy of attracting foreign capital and promoting rapid industrial development. Along with European and American corporations, Japanese companies began to

make small-scale investments in Brazil. Early Japanese investments were in the cotton-spinning, automobile, glass, and food sectors. The Japanese company Ishikawajima Heavy Industries Company, Ltd, opened a dockyard in Brazil in 1959. Usiminas Steel, a large-scale joint project of the governments of Japan and Brazil, was established in 1958 and opened in 1961.

In 1961 Brazilian exchange was decontrolled, triggering massive imports of machinery by Japanese companies in Brazil and increasing Brazilian imports from Japan. In that year Brazil's exports to Japan reached US $73 million. Bilateral trade declined thereafter, averaging US $40 million per year between 1962 and 1967. As political and economic conditions in Brazil improved in the late 1960s and early 1970s, however, many more Japanese industries entered Brazil. Two major Japanese trade missions visited Brazil in the early 1970s, and in 1972 the Japan Industrial Fair, sponsored by JETRO, was held in São Paulo. Over 150 Japanese companies opened branches in Brazil between 1968 and 1973. Trade increased rapidly, reaching US $2.1 billion in 1974. Imports from Japan totaled US $1.4 billion, while the remaining US $670.0 million represented Brazilian exports to Japan.

In the late 1970s the focus of the Japan-Brazil economic relationship shifted to large-scale economic cooperative projects based on agreements between the two governments. Among these was a project for developing 50,000 hectares (123,500 acres) of agricultural land in Cerrado.

The progress of closer economic ties was hindered by the Brazilian debt crisis, which began around 1982. Imports to Brazil from Japan dropped sharply, falling from US $1.0 billion in 1982 to US $738.0 million in 1983. Total trade volume recovered thereafter; in 1990 exports to Japan totaled US $3.2 billion and imports from Japan stood at US $1.2 billion.

Prospects for future Japanese investment in Brazil depend largely on Brazil's handling of its debt problem. While in 1988 Japan's total direct investment (largely private) in Brazil stood at US $2.9 billion, Japanese new business investment in Brazil in 1989 was only US $55.7 million.

In the mid-1980s Brazilians of Japanese descent began coming to Japan to look for work, and by 1989 their number was estimated at 40,000 to 50,000. In the same year there were close to 300 Brazilians studying at Japanese institutions of higher education, placing Brazil second among non-Asian countries in terms of number of students in

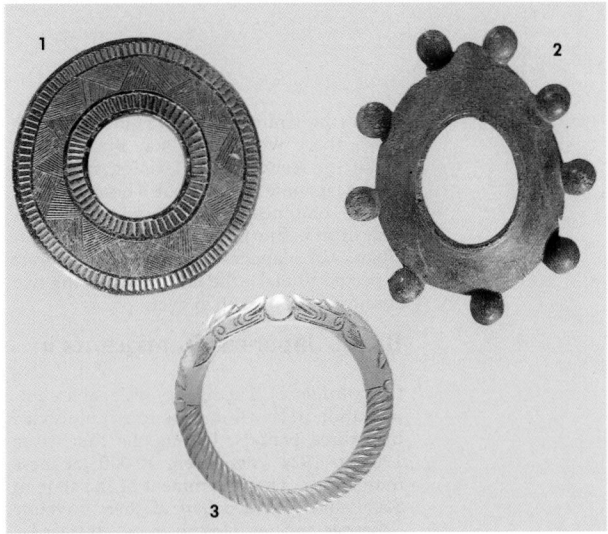

ancient bracelets
1 Middle-Kofun-period stone bracelet from the Nanamawarizuka tomb, Chiba, Chiba Prefecture. Diameter 17 cm. Chiba City Education Committee.
2 Middle-Kofun-period bronze bracelet from the Wadayama tomb clusters, Nomi district, Ishikawa Prefecture. Diameter 18 cm. Kyōto National Museum.
3 Late-Kofun-period stone bracelet from the Hondani tomb clusters, Fukuyama, Hiroshima Prefecture. Diameter 8 cm. Private collection.

Japan (the United States was first). Also in 1989, there were some 400 Brazilians in Japan for technological training sponsored by the Japanese government. These developments, combined with the hundreds of Japanese firms in Brazil and the over 500,000 Brazilians of Japanese descent there, are expected to make the link between the two countries stronger than ever.

Brazil, Japanese immigrants in
ブラジル移民

(Burajiru *imin*). The history of Japanese immigration in Brazil may be roughly divided into three periods. During the first, from 1908 to 1924, there were 40,000 Japanese immigrants. The government of the state of São Paulo provided half of their traveling expenses and received them as contract laborers (*colono*) on coffee plantations. The second period, from 1925 to 1941, the peak period of Japanese immigration, recorded 150,000 immigrants to Brazil. Most of them, like their predecessors, were contract laborers on coffee plantations, but some settled as independent farmers. The third, or postwar, period began in 1953, and by 1989 some 54,000 additional Japanese had relocated to Brazil. After Japan entered its period of high economic growth in the 1960s, however, the number of immigrants decreased to fewer than 100 per year.

Agricultural Areas—The Japanese made a noteworthy contribution to Brazil's agricultural development, and agricultural activity also formed the basis for later Japanese entry into commerce and industry. At the outset Japanese merchants dealing in farm tools and fertilizer found customers chiefly among Japanese farmers, while Japanese manufacturers in rural towns began by processing agricultural products or making farm equipment. The contributions made by Japanese immigrants in agriculture took three main forms, of which the first was the introduction and improvement of foreign plants. Japanese immigrants brought with them numerous plants, ranging from fruit trees to vegetables and ornamentals. The second important Japanese contribution was the introduction of new agricultural techniques, such as the Japanese style of intensive farming on a small unit of land. The third major contribution was the foundation by Japanese immigrants of several large-scale cooperative associations, such as the Cotia Industrial Cooperative, the Sul Brasil Agricultural Cooperative, and the São Paulo Central Association. Established to help Japanese to purchase production equipment and to merchandise their produce, they have grown remarkably, and today they rank among the leading agricultural organizations of Brazil.

Urban Areas—After Japan's defeat in World War II, many immigrants suffered an identity crisis, emerging with a new view of themselves as Japanese Brazilians rather than as Japanese. Many sold their farms and moved to São Paulo, where they ran small businesses, in order to give their children access to higher education. Today Japanese Brazilians employed in tertiary industries, such as commerce, services, communications, and public service, now outnumber those in agriculture.

Another notable change is the increasing frequency of marriage with non-Japanese Brazilians. Until the 1950s, ethnic purism prevailed among Japanese immigrants, and

young Japanese who sought to marry Brazilians met with strong objections from their parents. In the 1960s, however, parents grew more lenient, and today intermarriage has become common. See also BRAZIL AND JAPAN.

brewing
醸造

(*jōzō*). Method of preparing beverages and other foods by fermenting, boiling, steeping, or infusing. The Japanese have traditionally brewed such products as SAKE, MISO, SOY SAUCE, and vinegar. The extensive use of *kōji* (rice, beans, or barley fermented with *Aspergillus* fungi) is characteristic of Japanese brewing. *Kōji* is used as the enzyme for breaking down starch in *sake* brewing (corresponding to malt in beer making); it also supplies the decomposition enzyme for protein in brewing *miso* and soy sauce.

Sake is a liquor made from nonglutinous steamed rice. The *kōji* is made by adding a fungus of the *Aspergillus oryzae-flavus* group to a portion of the steamed rice. Separately, a seed mash (*moto*) is made by leaving another quantity of steamed rice to ferment, producing a large amount of the *sake* yeast. A mixture of steamed rice, *kōji*, and water, totaling 15 times the volume of the seed mash, is added in three stages over 4 days. The fermentation of the main mash (*moromi*) is complete in about 20 days. The fermented mash is filtered, and the raw *sake* is further clarified and then heated 60°–63°C (140°–145° F) for several minutes in order to pasteurize the *sake* and destroy the remaining ferment. It is then left to mature in a cool, dark storage area.

Miso is a traditional Japanese seasoning that is made by fermenting steamed soybeans mixed with rice *kōji* or malt *kōji* and salt. Soy sauce is a liquid seasoning made by fermenting the *kōji* of soybeans and wheat with a solution of salt; it has a distinct aroma and flavor. The final product is made by pressing the fermented mash (*moromi*), heating the raw soy sauce to pasteurize it and solidify the integrated protein, and clarifying the liquid by removing the dregs.

bridges
橋

(*hashi*). According to early chronicles, Japan's first bridge was built in the 4th century across the inlet Ikai no Tsu in what is now Ōsaka Prefecture. In 612 technology

bridges

A number of ancient bridges survive, while recent bridges employ state-of-the-art technology.

▶ Kazurabashi, a suspension bridge made of vines, spans the Iyadani Gorge in Tokushima Prefecture.

for the construction of bridges was introduced from Paekche on the Korean peninsula. Typical premodern Japanese bridges had timber abutments and piers supporting plank walkways. They were built until the mid-19th century and may be seen in the woodblock prints of HOKUSAI. Extant examples of other types of premodern bridges are Kintaikyō (1673), a series of five timber arches on stone piers extending across the river Nishikigawa at Iwakuni, Yamaguchi Prefecture; Saruhashi, a timber bridge across a narrow gorge in Ōtsuki, Yamanashi Prefecture, whose longitudinal beams are supported by bracket-complex abutments jutting toward each other from either side of the gorge; and Kazurabashi, a suspension bridge made of vines in the village of Nishiiyayama, Tokushima Prefecture. In the Kyūshū area there are over 40 stone arch bridges, the oldest of which, Meganebashi (1634), is in Nagasaki. A double-arch stone bridge, it is said to have been built by the Chinese monk Ruding (Ju-ting).

During the Meiji period (1868–1912) Western bridge-building methods were introduced and the first iron bridge, Kurogane-bashi, was built in Nagasaki with the aid of Western technicians in 1868. The first iron truss bridge designed by a Japanese and built with girders manufactured in Japan was Danjōbashi (1878) in Tōkyō. The first steel bridge was built in 1888 and the first reinforced-concrete bridge in 1903. Following the TŌKYŌ EARTHQUAKE OF 1923 three bridges, introducing innovative native design features, were constructed across the river Sumidagawa. Major bridges built in the post–World War II period include the Saikai Bridge (1955, steel arch), the Kammon Bridge (1973, suspension), and the Minato Bridge (1974, cantilever). Technological advances achieved in the construction of these and other bridges have been applied to the design of the HONSHŪ-SHIKOKU BRIDGES (anticipated date of completion 1998), a system of 17 island-hopping bridges that will connect three points on the island of Honshū with three points on the island of Shikoku. Part of the system, which links Kojima in Okayama Prefecture with Sakaide in Kagawa Prefecture, was opened to automobile and rail traffic in 1988. See also TŌKYŌ BAY BRIDGE AND TUNNEL.

◄ Dating from 1673, Kintaikyō consists of a series of five timber arches across the river Nishikigawa at Iwakuni in Yamaguchi Prefecture.

► A reconstruction of a 13th-century wooden bridge supported by a series of horizontal beams, Saruhashi spans a deep, narrow gorge in Ōtsuki, Yamanashi Prefecture.

▼ A double-arch stone bridge in Nagasaki called Meganebashi ("Spectacles Bridge") was constructed in 1634.

▲ The Yokohama Bay Bridge, an 860-meter cable-stayed bridge, became a major tourist attraction when it opened in 1989.

Bridgestone Corporation

[株]ブリヂストン

(Burijisuton). One of the world's leading manufacturers of tires and other rubber products. Incorporated in Kurume, Fukuoka Prefecture, in 1931 by ISHIBASHI SHŌJIRŌ. To complement its commanding share of the tire market in Japan, Bridgestone increased its global presence in May 1988 by merging with Firestone Tire & Rubber Co. Together with associated companies, Bridgestone manufactures tires on six continents. Other products include rubber and nonrubber items for industry and sporting goods. Annual sales for the fiscal year ending December 1990 totaled ¥724.3 billion (US $5.4 billion), of which tires and tubes accounted for 76 percent and nontire products 24 percent. In the same year exports were 30 percent of sales, and the company was capitalized at ¥74.2 billion (US $555.6 million). Headquarters are in Tōkyō.

Bridgestone Museum of Art

ブリヂストン美術館

(Burijisuton Bijutsukan). Museum in Chūō Ward, Tōkyō. Established in 1952 by ISHIBASHI SHŌJIRŌ, the founder of the BRIDGESTONE CORPORATION. Paintings by European impressionists and by modern Western-style Japanese artists predominate among the more than 1,000 items in the collection, which includes works by Corot, Manet, Gauguin, and van Gogh. Japanese artists represented include ASAI CHŪ, KURODA SEIKI, AOKI SHIGERU, and FUJITA TSUGUHARU. The collection also includes sculptures by Rodin and Emile Bourdelle.

Brinkley, Frank

ブリンクリー, F.

(1841–1912). Anglo-Irish journalist. Owner and editor of the Tōkyō English-language newspaper the Japan Mail from 1881 and a Tōkyō-based correspondent for the Times of London, notably during the RUSSO-JAPANESE WAR of 1904–05. Born in Ireland, Brinkley arrived in Japan as a Royal Artillery officer of the British legation in 1867. In 1871 he resigned his commission to become a military instructor for the new Meiji government. He later taught mathematics at the national Engineering College (Kōbu Daigakkō), later part of Tōkyō University, until

he joined the Japan Mail. He wrote Japan: Its History, Arts, and Literature (1901) and compiled a Japanese-English Dictionary (1896).

British Commonwealth Occupation Force

イギリス連邦占領軍

(BCOF; J: Igirisu Rempō Senryōgun). Air, sea, and land forces drawn from Great Britain, Australia, New Zealand, and India; stationed in Japan during the Allied OCCUPATION (1945–52). The BCOF was never large, numbering about 39,000 troops in mid-1946. It generally operated in the Chūgoku region (western Honshū) and on the island of Shikoku. The Australian role in the BCOF was considerable, since the commander in chief was an Australian who had direct access to the supreme commander for the Allied powers (SCAP). See also AUSTRALIA AND JAPAN.

broadcasting

放送

(hōsō). Broadcasting is defined in Japan's BROADCASTING LAW (Hōsō Hō, 1950) and Radio Law (Dempa Hō, 1950) as "wireless communication intended for direct reception by the general public." Radio and television broadcasts transmitted by coaxial cable for direct public reception are sometimes included in the term "broadcasting," but legally they are differentiated from wireless broadcasting.

History of Broadcasting in Japan— From the time of the Meiji Restoration in 1868 the government sought to control public communications. However, the Communications Ministry (Teishinshō; now the Ministry of Posts and Telecommunications) did not place radio broadcasting under its direct jurisdiction; instead, under a Teishinshō ordinance of 20 December 1923, broadcasting stations were defined as nonprofit, private organizations that were to function as corporate juristic persons (shadan hōjin). Private management was such in name only, however, because the Teishinshō ordinance placed strict limitations on the ownership of private radio equipment for broadcast purposes. In actuality, the establishment of juristic persons gave the government almost complete control of broadcasting stations. On 20 August 1926 the Communications Ministry established the Nippon Hōsō Kyōkai (NHK; Japan Broadcasting Corporation).

NHK monopolized the country's broadcasting industry until after World War II. As with its predecessors, NHK was placed under the strict supervision of the Communications Ministry.

After World War II the Occupation authorities abolished all legislation suppressing freedom of speech and the press in an effort to further Japan's democratization. NHK complied by eliminating all provisions in its articles of association granting authority to the government. When the Broadcasting Law came into effect in June 1950, NHK was reorganized, and a new corporation was formed. This law also paved the way for private commercial broadcast stations. In April 1950 preliminary licenses were issued to a total of 16 private broadcast stations in 14 districts of the country. Despite early pessimism about their commercial viability, these ventures soon showed large profits. The way was opened for television broadcasting with the granting of a preliminary license to NIPPON TELEVISION NETWORK CORPORATION (NTV) on 31 July 1952. The first actual telecast in Japan was made by NHK's Tōkyō station on 1 February 1953.

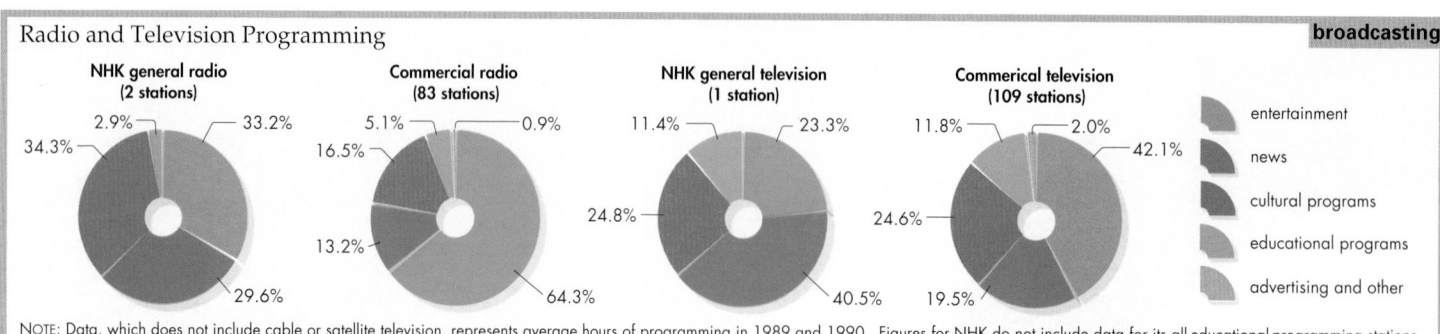

Radio and Television Programming

NHK general radio
(2 stations)

2.9% — 33.2%
34.3%
29.6%

Commercial radio
(83 stations)

5.1% — 0.9%
16.5%
13.2%
64.3%

NHK general television
(1 station)

11.4% — 23.3%
24.8%
40.5%

Commerical television
(109 stations)

11.8% — 2.0%
42.1%
24.6%
19.5%

- entertainment
- news
- cultural programs
- educational programs
- advertising and other

NOTE: Data, which does not include cable or satellite television, represents average hours of programming in 1989 and 1990. Figures for NHK do not include data for its all-educational-programming stations.
SOURCES: NHK and the National Association of Commercial Broadcasters in Japan.

Present-Day Broadcasting in Japan
Japan's broadcasting system consists of two types of broadcast enterprise: NHK, which is a government-sponsored venture, and the various commercial companies. As a special corporation, NHK is neither a state-operated enterprise nor a public corporation. However, unlike the private companies, NHK's activities are subject to restrictions by the government and the Diet. The Management Commission makes major decisions regarding NHK, including the content of programs, and is a governing organ with the authority to appoint the president and other high officials of NHK. The members of the Management Commission are appointed by the prime minister after obtaining the approval of the Diet.

Programming. The Broadcasting Law stipulates the types of programs to be broadcast domestically. NHK is required to (1) broadcast high-quality programs that will both satisfy the demands of the public and elevate the country's cultural level, (2) broadcast local as well as national programs, and (3) contribute to the preservation of traditional culture and foster and publicize modern cultural events. Programs shown by both NHK and private commercial broadcasting firms are required by the Broadcasting Law to (1) guard against disturbing public peace and order and damaging morals, (2) maintain political impartiality, (3) include truthful news broadcasts, and (4) present all sides of complex issues and maintain a balance among educational, cultural, news, and entertainment programs.

Networks. NHK operates a nationwide broadcasting network. Private broadcasting stations licensed in their respective local regions also have their own networks. As of 1992, commercial television broadcasting consisted of five networks centered on the following key stations: TŌKYŌ BROADCASTING SYSTEM, INC (TBS) (28 stations), Nippon Television Network Corporation (30 stations), FUJI TELECASTING CO, LTD (27 stations), ASAHI NATIONAL BROADCASTING CO, LTD (22 stations), and TELEVISION TŌKYŌ CHANNEL 12, LTD (5 stations). At the center of each of these networks is a news network. General programming other than news is also distributed through these networks. In 1992 there were 115 commercial television stations, 47 commercial AM radio stations, 39 FM stations, and 1 shortwave station.

There are two major commercial radio broadcasting networks: the Japan Radio Network and the Nippon Radio Network, both established in 1965. Commercial FM broadcasting is dominated by the Japan FM Broadcasting Association, which operates a nationwide network with FM Tōkyō as its key station.

Financing. The ordinary operating revenues of NHK are obtained from viewer fees, government subsidies for NHK's international broadcasts, and miscellaneous reve-

nues from other sources, with some 98 percent of the entire revenue represented by viewer fees. The distribution of television sets, however, has almost reached the saturation point, so that it is difficult to foresee any large increase in revenue from future fees. (Radio fees were abolished in 1968.)

Private television broadcasting companies are showing large profits with the tremendous increase in revenue from television advertising. Advertisement expenditures paid to television firms exceeded those paid to newspapers in 1975, and television has been the top advertising medium ever since.

Television viewing. In 1990, 33.5 million households were paying reception fees to NHK. Television sets are owned by practically all Japanese families, and according to a recent survey television ownership now averages two sets per household.

New media. New broadcast technology made possible the introduction of multiplex sound broadcasting in 1978 for stereo and bilingual programming and also text multiplex broadcasting for captioned news and other programs. HIGH-DEFINITION TELEVISION (HDTV) and extended definition television (EDTV) technologies have been developed to improve picture quality. Videocassette recorder ownership expanded rapidly beginning in the mid-1980s, reaching a total of 66.8 percent of the population by 1990. In 1984 NHK began direct satellite broadcasting, and in 1989 the launch of a communications satellite made possible the establishment of a commercial network combining satellite and cable transmission. CABLE TELEVISION has also begun to make significant inroads into urban areas. Japanese television programs are also broadcast directly to the United States and other countries via satellite.

broadcasting, commercial
商業放送

(*shōgyō hōsō*). Japanese commercial broadcasting, as distinguished from public broadcasting (see NHK), dates from 1 September 1951, when the first privately owned radio stations went on the air in Nagoya and Ōsaka; commercial television followed on 28 August 1953. Beginning about 1960 radio fell on difficult times because of the rise in popularity of television. To win back their audience, radio stations changed their format, incorporating live programs that ran for several hours, celebrity shows, late-night broadcasts, and traffic reports, and began making a comeback in the late 1960s. Commercial FM broadcasts began in 1969.

Commercial television stations were allowed to open throughout Japan in 1957. Coverage of spectacular events such as the Crown Prince's wedding in 1959 and the Tōkyō Olympic Games in 1964 served to increase the number of television owners. Technological developments such as color programming and satellite-relay broadcasts paved the way for further growth of the television industry. By 1975 the amount of

money spent on television advertising had surpassed that for newspaper advertising, and television became the top advertising medium.

In 1990 there were 83 radio stations (47 AM, 35 FM, 1 shortwave) and 109 television stations (48 VHF and 61 UHF) licensed for commercial broadcasting. Advertising revenue for 1988 amounted to ¥187.9 billion (US $1.5 billion) for radio and ¥1.3 trillion (US $10.3 billion) for television. There were some 28,000 people employed in commercial broadcasting. NHK, by comparison, had 15,000 employees.

Commercial radio and television networks operate as cooperatives under the leadership of certain key stations. Among AM radio networks are the Japan Radio Network (JRN), led by TŌKYŌ BROADCASTING SYSTEM, INC (TBS), and the National Radio Network (NRN), with NIPPON CULTURAL BROADCASTING, INC, and NIPPON BROADCASTING SYSTEM, INC, as key stations. Television networks include the Japan News Network (JNN), again led by TBS; the Nippon News Network (NNN), led by Nippon Television; the All Nippon News Network, led by ASAHI NATIONAL BROADCASTING CO, LTD; and the Fuji News Network (FNN), led by FUJI TELECASTING CO, LTD.

Daily television viewing time for the average Japanese amounts to about three hours per day, demonstrating that television has indeed become an indispensable entertainment medium for the Japanese public. The prime viewing hours between 7:00 and 10:00 PM, when advertising is most effective, are referred to as the "golden hours," and during these hours there is fierce competition among stations for viewers. In 1978 Japan led the world in developing multiplex television sound broadcasts, which made possible stereo and bilingual broadcasts.

Broadcasting Law
放送法

(Hōsō Hō). Law defining the principles for regulation of broadcasting; passed in 1950 together with a law regulating the use of radio waves (Dempa Hō) and a law establishing a commission to supervise that use (Dempa Kanri Iinkai Setchi Hō). Known as the "Three Radio Wave Laws" (Dempa Sampō), they were part of the move away from government interference with the media that occurred after World War II. The Broadcasting Law ensured the broadcast media's independence while requiring that they maintain political neutrality. It also defined the purpose, management, and organization of the Japan Broadcasting Corporation (see NHK).

broadcasts, late-night
深夜放送

(*shin'ya hōsō*). Late-night radio broadcasting in Japan began around 1960 and has become an important part of the country's youth and automobile subcultures. Almost all commercial AM radio stations in Japan, particularly the large stations in cities such as Tōkyō and Ōsaka, offer after-midnight

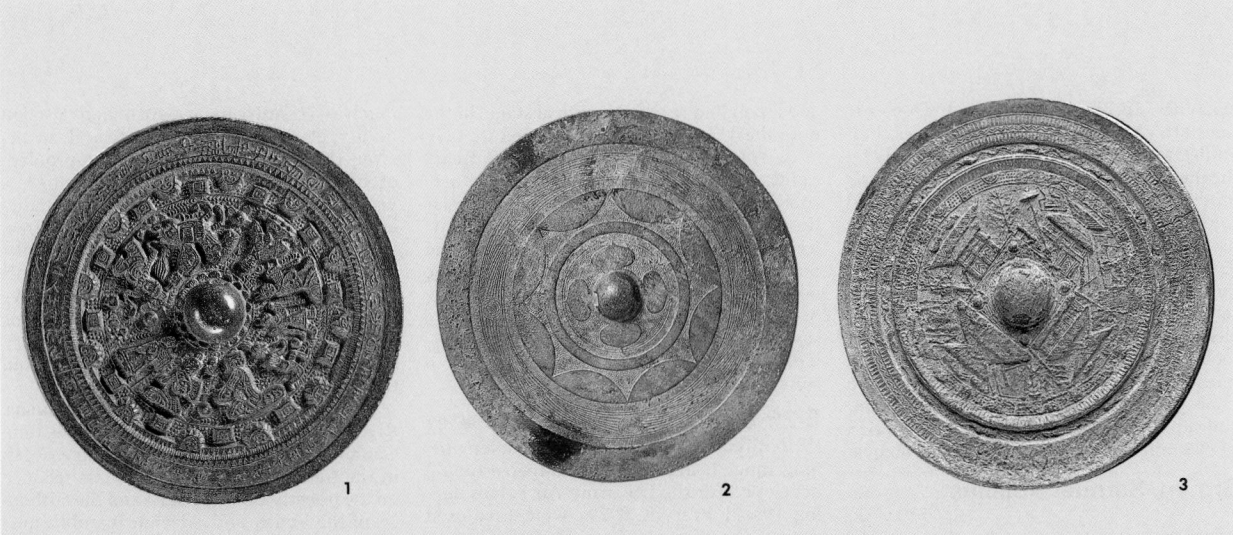

bronze mirrors
1 A "gods and beasts" mirror unearthed in the town of Suda, Wakayama Prefecture. Bronze. Diameter 20 cm. Suda Hachiman Shrine. National Treasure.
2 A "flower petals" mirror excavated from the Ōtsuka tomb in Nara Prefecture. This popular motif was based on Chinese models. Bronze. Diameter 40 cm. Imperial Household Agency.
3 A mirror with architectural motifs excavated from the Samida Takarazuka tomb in Nara Prefecture. Bronze. Diameter 23 cm. Imperial Household Agency.

broadcasts. Programs are mainly directed either at young people or at drivers. Youth programming responds to events in the daily lives of the young audience, who can call in or fax their requests for songs or for advice on personal problems. Japanese and Western pop and rock favorites are played. Programs for late-night drivers tend to have women disc jockeys who act as radio companions for the drivers. Program format includes reading fan mail, playing request numbers (mostly Japanese popular music), and giving periodic traffic reports.

Late-night television broadcasting began in 1965 with such pioneer programs as "11 PM." During the 1970s energy conservation considerations forced stations to impose temporary self-restrictions on broadcasting hours, but in the 1980s stations gradually expanded their late-night broadcasting hours. Twenty-four-hour broadcasting began in the Kantō region in 1987.

brocade → nishiki

bronze age
青銅器時代

(*seidōki jidai*). The YAYOI PERIOD (ca 300 BC–ca AD 300) is sometimes referred to as Japan's bronze age, although it has few of the features associated with Near Eastern or Chinese bronze-age civilizations. Both bronze- and iron-working, along with other Chinese and Korean ideas, entered Japan during the Yayoi period. See also DŌTAKU; BRONZE WEAPONS; BRONZE MIRRORS.

bronze mirrors
青銅鏡

(*seidōkyō*). In ancient Japan, bronze mirrors were more treasures or ritual implements than utilitarian items. They were also important symbols of political authority, as attested by the inclusion of a bronze mirror (the Yata no Kagami) among the three IMPERIAL REGALIA. Cast as round disks, the bronze mirrors of ancient China and Japan have one perfectly smooth side for reflection purposes; the back is decorated and has a perforated knob in the center through which a cord can be passed. Bronze mirrors were first brought from China to Japan in the Yayoi period (ca 300 BC–ca AD 300). In the 3rd and 4th centuries the Japanese began producing them.

Initially the Japanese imitated such Chinese motifs as "flower petals" and "gods and beasts." Motifs peculiar to Japan, such as geometric CHOKKOMON and FERN FROND DESIGN or village scenes, came to be applied to native products of the 5th and 6th centuries, and by the Heian period (794–1185) the style of Japanese bronze mirrors (*wakyō*) had become

quite distinct. With such native motifs as autumn grasses, flowing water, and flowers and birds, the elegant Heian-period mirrors were very thin and had small unadorned cord knobs. In the Kamakura period (1185–1333) mirrors were more substantial and motifs changed to realistic scenes. In the succeeding Muromachi period (1333–1568), auspicious motifs such as the pine, bamboo, and plum pattern or the crane and turtle pattern became very popular. Near the end of this period, handled mirrors were made and became extremely popular during the Edo period (1600–1868). Bronze mirrors fell into disuse after Japanese production of glass mirrors began in the late 19th century.

bronze weapons
青銅武器

(*seidō buki*). Weapons made of bronze (*seidō* or *dō*) were used in Japan mainly during the Yayoi period (ca 300 BC–ca AD 300). These included *dōken* (bronze swords), *dōhoko* (bronze spearheads), and *dōka* (bronze halberd heads). The bronze weapons appearing at the end of the Early Yayoi period were imported, but from the late Middle Yayoi period (ca 100 BC–ca AD 100) through the Late Yayoi period (ca 100–ca 300), bronze weapons were produced and used in western Japan, centering on northern Kyūshū.

Bronze weapons originated in China and were introduced into northern Kyūshū from the Korean peninsula. The first metal-age product in Japan, these Korean-made bronze weapons were placed as auxiliary burial articles in burial jars. Bronze weapons do not appear to have been used for their original purpose in Japan: none of the bronze weapons found in burial jars show damage through use in battle. The fact that bronze weapons have also been found buried in clusters in pits dug on hills or other high places has led archaeologists to conclude that they served both as symbols of power and as ritual objects.

Swords—The double-edged swords were piercing rather than cutting weapons. A center shaft protruded at the base and fit into a hilt. Bronze swords can be classified into four types according to shape: (1) The narrow-blade sword (*hosogata dōken*) is a narrow sword with sharp edges on both sides. The cross section of the body of the sword is diamond-shaped. (2) The medium-narrow sword (*nakaboso dōken*), although similar in form to the narrow-blade sword, is longer. The blade has also become flatter. (3) The medium-breadth sword (*nakahiro dōken*), a longer and larger version of the medium-narrow sword, is characterized by a spoon-shaped widening of the blade toward the base. (4) The flat-blade sword (*hiragata*

dōken) has quite a wide body and almost straight edges, with the point tending to be rounded. The shaping of the blade toward the base has disappeared, and instead two thornlike protrusions are found roughly one-third the length of the blade from the base. Flat-blade swords with patterns on the blade have also been discovered.

Spearheads—A piercing weapon; the lower part of the spearhead forms a tapered socket in which a handle was inserted, and a metal loop was attached to the side of this socket. Like bronze swords, bronze spearheads can also be classified into four types according to shape: (1) The narrow-blade spearhead (*hosogata dōhoko*) narrows to a point in an elongated triangular shape. (2) The medium-narrow spearhead (*nakaboso dōhoko*) has straight-running edges and a rounded point. (3) The medium-breadth spearhead (*nakahiro dōhoko*) has a lengthened and flattened body, and in some cases no hole has been incised in the loop on the socket. (4) The broad-blade spearhead (*hirogata dōhoko*) has a very flat body, and the loop on the socket is also flattened with the hole completely gone.

Halberd Heads—Similar in form to spearheads but slanting to one side rather than rising straight from their base, halberd heads were attached to long shafts, forming an acute angle to the shaft because of their tilted shape. Two holes for tightening it in its hilt are at the base of the halberd head. The bronze halberd heads also fall into four types according to the width of the blade. There is also an Ōsaka Bay–type halberd head labeled according to its regional distribution. See also YAYOI CULTURE.

Brooke, John Mercer
ブルック, J. M.

(1826–1906). American naval officer and scientist. Born in Florida; graduate of the United States Naval Academy (1847). The inventor of a deep-sea sounding apparatus, in 1858 he was commissioned to map the topography of the North Pacific sea floor. The following summer his schooner, the *Fenimore Cooper*, was wrecked in Japanese waters. In 1860 he and his men assisted the Japanese crew of the KANRIN MARU, the first Japanese ship to cross the Pacific (see also UNITED STATES, MISSION OF 1860 TO).

Brother Industries, Ltd
ブラザー工業[株]

(Burazā Kōgyō). Company engaged in the manufacture of sewing machines, household electrical appliances, machine tools, office machines, knitting machines, and business

bronze weapons
1 A narrow-blade spearhead of unknown date from the Ukikunden site in Saga Prefecture. Kyōto University.
2 A Middle-Yayoi-period narrow-blade sword from the Yoshitake-Takagi site in Fukuoka Prefecture. Agency of Cultural Affairs.
3 A Late-Yayoi-period flat-blade sword from Yugasan in Okayama Prefecture. Private collection.
4 A Middle-Yayoi-period halberd head from the Yoshitake-Takagi site. Agency of Cultural Affairs.

123

Buddha tiles These fragments of a clay tile depicting the Buddha were found at the site of the temple Tengeji in Mie Prefecture. 7th century. Original size 22 × 14 cm. Nara National Museum.

machines. Incorporated in 1934. Domestic sales are carried out by Brother Sales, Ltd, while overseas sales are conducted chiefly by Brother International Co. The company's products are exported to more than 100 countries throughout the world. Sales for the fiscal year ending November 1990 totaled ¥166.0 billion (US $1.3 billion), of which business machines constituted 42 percent; sewing machines, 35 percent; household electrical appliances, 6 percent; machine tools, 8 percent; knitting machines, 3 percent; and other products, 6 percent. In the same year the export ratio was 65 percent, and capitalization stood at ¥18.7 billion (US $144.9 million). Headquarters are in Nagoya.

Brown, Samuel Robbins
ブラウン, S. R.

(1810–80). American educator and missionary. Born in East Windsor, Connecticut, Brown graduated from Yale University in 1832. He served as a missionary in China (1839–47) and then in US ministries. In 1859 he was sent to Kanagawa (now part of Yokohama) by the Dutch Reformed Mission, becoming one of the first missionaries to enter Japan since the 17th century. For the next 20 years Brown served as an influential teacher and missionary. He was a founder and early president of the Asiatic Society of Japan. He translated portions of the New Testament into Japanese.

Brunton, Richard Henry
ブラントン, R. H.

(1841–1901). Scottish engineer employed in Japan from 1868 to 1876. British envoy Sir Harry PARKES insisted that Japan fulfill its treaty obligations (see ANSEI COMMERCIAL TREATIES) by making its ports and waters safe for navigation. Thereupon, the Japanese government engaged the Edinburgh firm of D. and T. Stevenson to chart Japan's waters for the first time and, in particular, to build lighthouses. Brunton headed this project. He greatly extended the work already begun by French engineer François VERNY by erecting 34 lighthouses and by charting the Inland Sea and approaches to the major ports. He is best known for the construction of the stone lighthouse at Mikomotojima, a rocky ledge off Shimoda.

Brussels Conference
ブリュッセル会議

(Buryusseru Kaigi). International conference held from 3 to 15 November 1937 as a consequence of the China Incident, which had occurred in July (see SINO-JAPANESE WAR OF 1937–1945). The United States attempted to force Japan into a settlement by pointing out that Japan's attack violated the Nine-Power Treaty, signed at the WASHINGTON CONFERENCE in 1922 by Great Britain, the United States, France, Italy, Belgium, the Netherlands, China, Japan, and Portugal. The Brussels Conference was convened with eight of the nine signatories, along with the Soviet Union, taking part. Japan refused to attend. The conference achieved no concrete results. The Japanese government's refusal to discuss the attack on China indicated its disregard of foreign opinion.

Bryan note
ブライアン・ノート

(Buraian *nōto*). Document communicated by US Secretary of State William Jennings Bryan (1860–1925) to the Japanese government on 13 March 1915, when negotiations on the TWENTY-ONE DEMANDS between China

and Japan had reached a critical stage. In the note the US government reviewed its OPEN DOOR POLICY in China, affirmed US treaty rights, and acknowledged that Japan's "territorial contiguity" created "special relations" between Japan and the Chinese territories of Mongolia, Manchuria, and Shandong (Shantung). In conclusion, the note expressed Washington's deep concern over Japanese encroachment on Chinese sovereignty. Together with strongly anti-Japanese world opinion, the note helped to soften Japan's demands on China.

B-29 bomber
B29爆撃機

(Bī-Nijūku *bakugekiki*). A four-engine, long-range heavy bomber ("Superfortress") developed for the US Army Air Forces during World War II. B-29s were first used against Japan on 16 June 1944. From November 1944, B-29 raids over Japan were frequent, and these bombings spread terror throughout Japan. In the 10 March 1945 raid more than 250 B-29s dropped some 2,000 tons of incendiary bombs over Tōkyō, destroying the heart of the city and killing or wounding 185,000 civilians. On 6 August 1945 the B-29 *Enola Gay* dropped an ATOMIC BOMB over Hiroshima; three days later another B-29 dropped a second atomic bomb at Nagasaki. Japan initiated peace negotiations the next day.

Buddha
仏陀

(J: Budda). In Buddhism an epithet applied to one who has attained enlightenment, i.e., perfect insight into the nature of the world and the beings that inhabit it. A Buddha is regarded as the embodiment of both wisdom and compassion. In the Theravāda Buddhism of Southeast Asia only one Buddha is recognized, namely, Gautama, also known as Śākyamuni (J: Shaka), the historical founder of Buddhism, who lived in India in the 4th or 5th century BC. According to the Mahāyāna tradition, the type of Buddhism practiced in Japan, China, and Korea, Śākyamuni is but one of countless Buddhas presently active. Although all Buddhas are equal in their wisdom and merit, they differ with respect to the specific vows they make before achieving Buddhahood. The most popular Buddhas in Japan are Shaka, who is particularly venerated in the TENDAI SECT, the NICHIREN SECT, and ZEN; AMIDA (Skt: Amitābha), who is the object of devotion in the Pure Land sects (JŌDO SECT, JŌDO SHIN SECT, and JI SECT); and DAINICHI (Skt: Mahāvairocana), who is the central divinity in the SHINGON SECT as well as in the esoteric branch of the Tendai sect. See also BUDDHISM; BUDDHIST ART; BUDDHIST SCULPTURE.

Buddha tiles
塼仏

(*sembutsu*). Unglazed, baked clay tiles with mold-impressed Buddhist images such as the AMIDA trinity, bodhisattvas, and RAKAN; produced in Japan beginning in the late 7th century under the influence of Chinese Tang (T'ang) dynasty (618–907) Buddhism. They were embedded in the walls of temples and used as objects of worship. The Nara-period (710–794) tiles from the temples Tachibanadera and Okadera are noted for their lifelike realism. See also BUDDHIST SCULPTURE.

Buddhism
仏教

(J: Bukkyō). According to tradition, the founder of Buddhism, Gautama Siddhārtha, was born about 446 BC as the first son of King Śuddhodana of the Śākya clan at the castle Kapilavastu, located in the center of the clan's domain in what is now Nepal. Some scholars, however, place the birthdate as

much as a century earlier. Although raised in luxury, at age 29 he left home to seek an answer, through renunciation, to the problem of human existence. After completing six years of asceticism, he experienced enlightenment at Buddhagayā beneath the bo tree, becoming the Buddha ("one who has awakened to the truth"). Thereafter, until his death at Kuśinagara at the age of 80, he traveled throughout central India sharing his wisdom. He became known by the honorary name Śākyamuni (the sage or holy one from the Śākya [J: Shaka] clan).

Early Buddhism —— In the central Ganges River Basin and eastern India at the time Gautama lived, affluence had led to a decay in the traditional caste system, less reliance on the priestly Brahmin class and the authority of the Vedas, and a decline in public morality. Philosophers became involved in endless metaphysical discussions of problems that had no solutions, but Gautama asserted that such metaphysical questions were meaningless. Buddhism attempted to point to and teach dharma, the "true eternal law" or "perennial norm" that would be valid for humanity for all ages. Buddhist doctrine is not specific, established dogma, but a practical wisdom or ethic that promises us the ideal state of humanity.

In Gautama's view, life is suffering (Skt: *duḥkha*), in the face of which man is helpless. We experience suffering because everything is the result of ever-changing, interrelated conditions and causes; human existence is always in flux and in transience (Skt: *anitya*; J: MUJŌ). Therefore, it is impossible to claim anything as belonging to oneself, or to assert that there is a self (Skt: *ātman*). By denying the existence of *ātman*, Buddhists also rejected the dichotomy between the subjective and objective worlds. Our perplexing and painful existence stems from various causes, and if those causes are extinguished, the confusion and suffering will also dissolve. In Japanese this chain of causality is called *engi* (dependent origination; Skt: *pratītyasamutpāda*).

Those who wish to be free from suffering must come to a clear understanding (enlightenment) concerning suffering, impermanence, nonself (Skt: *anātman*), and reality. To attain true knowledge (Skt: *prajñā*), all lust and attachment—the root of illusion—must be extinguished. In order to achieve this, one must undergo spiritual discipline, abide by the precepts, and practice meditation. Only then will one be able to free oneself from myriad restrictions and attain that freedom called *nirvāṇa* (J: *nehan*). The two extremes of hedonism and self-mortification are rejected; the Middle Way of no suffering and no pleasure is to be taken. Buddhism also emphasized compassion, teaching that it should be extended to all sentient beings.

Upon attaining enlightenment, the Buddha gathered around him a group of disciples; this community adopted the organizational principles of the *saṃgha*, which generally referred to a confederate form of government or a guild. The religious *saṃgha* was composed of both mendicant monks and lay believers, male and female. The mendicants were expected to be celibate and to refrain from secular occupations and economic transactions.

Later, rules for the religious life were stipulated: 250 precepts for males (*bhikṣu*; J: *biku*) and 500 for females (*bhikṣuṇī*; J: *bikuni*). Lay believers were instructed to maintain a good household, engage in proper work, strive to help others, and secure honor and fortune through diligent effort so that, upon death, they would be reborn in heaven. Five precepts are particularly emphasized: (1) do not kill; (2) do not steal; (3) do not act immorally; (4) do not lie; (5) do not drink liquor. Sorcery, magic, and divination were strictly forbidden, and believers were told to reject the authority of the Vedas and to eschew ceremonies involving sacrifice. While monks and nuns sought the ultimate goal of *nirvāṇa*, the laity aimed at a better rebirth.

The mendicant was enjoined to advocate the equality of all people and to reject the socially discriminatory caste system. Within the religious community (*saṃgha*), which included outcastes as well as members of the educated castes, the monk's rank was determined according to the length of time of spiritual discipline since entering the order. The *saṃgha* received financial support from wealthy merchants, who also believed in abolishing the Brahmanical caste system.

The literature of early Buddhism exists in Pāli texts and in Chinese translations, as well as fragmentarily in Sanskrit. Pāli is thought to have been originally a branch of the ancient Magadha tongue, in which Gautama spoke, and to have evolved into a language of the scripture. Pāli scripture has survived in what is now Sri Lanka, Burma, Thailand, Cambodia, and Laos, among other places. It is composed of three main sections (the Tripiṭaka; see DAIZŌKYŌ): *vinaya*, the rules and their explanations regarding discipline for monks and practitioners; *sūtra*, records of sermons by Gautama as well as his dialogues with his disciples; and *abhidharma*, commentaries and treatises regarding the sutra section.

Spread of Buddhism——In the 3rd century BC, under King Aśoka, India was united as one country. Aśoka supported the Buddhists, and Buddhism spread throughout the country. Around that time Buddhists split into two groups: the conservative elders (Theravādin), whose purpose was to maintain traditional rules; and others, who called for various changes within the religious order. By the 1st century BC there were as many as 20 factions. These groups tended to be self-righteous and aloof from the needs of the common people and in time came to be called the "lesser vehicle" (Hīnayāna; J: Shōjō) by their opponents.

Mahāyāna ("greater vehicle"; J: Daijō) Buddhism developed among the common people. Mahāyānists believed in a series of Buddhas (apart from the historical Buddha)—Buddhas from the cosmic past and also Buddhas-to-be, or bodhisattvas (J: *bosatsu*)—who had deferred their own salvation until the salvation of all mankind. Mahāyāna stressed that the path of the bodhisattva was open to both monks and laity. Several Mahāyāna texts were compiled. First to appear were the *Prajñāpāramitā* sutras (J: *Hannyakyō*), which taught that all things are empty (Skt: *śūnya*; J: *kū*). These were followed by the *Vimalakīrti-nirdeśa-sūtra* (J: *Yuimakyō*) and the *Śrīmālādevī-siṃhanāda-sūtra* (J: *Shōmankyō*), which propagated lay Buddhism; the *Avataṃsaka-sūtra* (J: *Kegonkyō*), which taught the altruistic way of the bodhisattva and idealism; the Pure Land sutras, which advocated belief in the Buddha Amitābha (J: AMIDA); and the LOTUS SUTRA (*Saddharma-puṇḍarīka-sūtra*; J: *Hokkekyō* or *Hokekyō*). The latter taught that various Buddhist practices would lead practitioners to perfection and that ultimately there is one eternal Buddha.

Two major philosophical schools also arose in the Mahāyāna branch during this period. The Mādhyamika school (J: Chūganha), founded by Nāgārjuna (J: Ryūju; ca 150–ca 250), emphasized *śūnyatā* (emptiness). The second school, Yogācāra (J: Yugagyōha), brought to doctrinal completion by Vasubandhu (J: Seshin; 4th century), taught that the basis of our existence is a spiritual principle, *ālayavijñāna*, from which all things become manifest.

In 320 the Gupta dynasty was established. Buddhists developed the esoteric teachings of tantrism, known as Vajrayāna or Mantrayāna (J: Mikkyō), which incorporated elements of Brahmanism and folk religion. Esoteric Buddhism, however, tended to be absorbed by Hinduism. At the beginning of the 12th century, when India was conquered by Muslims, many Buddhist monasteries were destroyed, and Buddhism all but disappeared from India.

The Diffusion of Buddhism in Asia——King Aśoka had sent out numerous Buddhist missionaries. A branch of Theravādin Buddhism was transferred to Ceylon (now Sri Lanka) and then to Burma, Thailand, Cambodia, and other Southeast Asian lands. The Buddhist tradition in these areas is generally called "Southern Buddhism."

In the Kashmir and Gandhara regions in northwest India, the Theravādin lineage, especially the Sarvāstivādin teachings (J: Setsu Issai Ubu), was popular. Later, Mahāyāna Buddhism became prevalent and from here spread throughout the western region. In Nepal as well, Mahāyāna Buddhism, especially the esoteric branch, was disseminated.

From the 8th century, Mahāyāna Buddhism, predominantly esoteric Buddhism, was transmitted to Tibet and, upon fusion with indigenous folk beliefs, developed into what is popularly known as Lamaism. In Lamaism, or Tibetan Buddhism, some lamas ("superior ones") were worshiped as incarnations (*tulkus*) of their predecessors. Lamaism eventually spread even throughout Mongolia and the Rehe (Jehol) region of northeastern China.

Buddhism was introduced to China in the 1st and 2nd centuries. Buddhist literature was subsequently translated into Chinese from Sanskrit (or its vernacular) originals. The Buddhism that came to flourish in China was chiefly Mahāyāna and reflected the influence of Taoism and Confucianism. Among the more important Chinese schools are the Pure Land (Ch: Jingtu or Ching-t'u; J: Jōdo), Chan (Ch'an; J: Zen), Tiantai (T'ient'ai; J: Tendai), and Zhenyan (Chen-yen; J: Shingon), all of which were transmitted to Japan.

Chinese Buddhism had been, at the beginning, a religion mostly of immigrants from India and Central Asia. But from the late 3rd century it spread among the native Chinese population. Buddhism was gradually modified to conform to the Chinese way of thinking: it became less speculative and more concrete; direct and intuitive expression came to be favored over abstract doctrine; and, in keeping with Confucian ethics and the tendency to focus on man and life in the everyday world, stress was placed on one's relation to others, in the family and in hierarchical society.

Buddhism in Japan——According to one of Japan's earliest chronicles, the NIHON SHOKI (720), Buddhism was officially introduced into Japan from Korea in 552, when the king of PAEKCHE sent a mission to the emperor of Japan bearing presents including "an image

of Śākyamuni in gold and copper" and "a number of sutras." However, current scholarship favors another traditional date for this event, 538.

The SOGA FAMILY argued that Japan should accept Buddhism. Others, particularly the MONONOBE FAMILY and the Nakatomi family, claimed that the native gods would be offended by the respect shown to a foreign deity. Buddhism was publicly accepted after the Soga family's political and military defeat of the Mononobe and became prominent in the 7th-century reign of the empress SUIKO. Her regent, the devout Prince SHŌTOKU, is considered the real founder and first great patron of Buddhism in Japan. He established a number of important monasteries, among them HŌRYŪJI and SHITENNŌJI.

Studies of Buddhist teachings began in earnest as six prominent schools were introduced from China during the 7th and the early 8th centuries. These were the RITSU SECT, the KUSHA SCHOOL, the JŌJITSU SCHOOL, the SANRON SCHOOL, the HOSSŌ SECT, and the KEGON SECT. In the Nara period (710–794), especially under the aegis of Emperor SHŌMU, Buddhism was promoted as the state religion. Official provincial monasteries (KOKUBUNJI) were established in each province. At TŌDAIJI, the head monastery, an enormous image of the Buddha (see DAIBUTSU) was erected.

Early in the Heian period (794–1185), the TENDAI SECT and SHINGON SECT were introduced to Japan. They received support principally from the ruling aristocratic class. At the beginning of the Kamakura period (1185–1333), ZEN Buddhism was introduced from China and was especially favored by the dominant military class. The popular sects of NICHIREN and PURE LAND BUDDHISM emerged around the same time.

Under the Tokugawa shogunate (1603–1867), Buddhism and its network of temples were used to eradicate Christianity (see SHŪMON ARATAME), but Buddhism also came under the strict regulatory power of the shogunate. While sectarian divisions that had been established in previous times continued, there were also modernizing tendencies, such as SUZUKI SHŌSAN's (1579–1655) occupational ethics and the popularization of Zen by Shidō Bunan (1603–76), BANKEI YŌTAKU (1622–93), and HAKUIN (1685–1769). Another sign was the movement to return to the true meaning of Buddhism as revealed in the original Sanskrit texts, led by Fujaku (1707–81), Kaijō (1750–1805), and JIUN ONKŌ (1718–1804). After the Meiji Restoration (1868), the government sought to establish SHINTŌ as the national religion, and many Buddhist temples were disestablished (see HAIBUTSU KISHAKU). Since then, Buddhist organizations have survived by adjusting to the developments of the modern age.

After World War II, many religious groups among the so-called *shinko shūkyō* (NEW RELIGIONS) were organized as lay Buddhist movements. Several of the largest of these groups (SŌKA GAKKAI, RISSHŌ KŌSEIKAI, REIYŪKAI, Myōchikai, etc) draw upon Nichiren's teachings and the Lotus Sutra.

Several characteristic tendencies can be seen in the history of Japanese Buddhism: (1) an emphasis on the importance of human institutions; (2) a nonrational, symbolic orientation; (3) an acceptance of the phenomenal world; (4) an openness to accommodation with ancient shamanistic practices and Shintō; and (5) the development of lay leadership.

▶ Bird's-eye view of the western part of the late-7th-century temple Hōryūji, with the enclosed West Precinct (Saiin) at the center. The main hall, visible to the right of the five-storied pagoda, is the oldest wooden structure in the world. Nara Prefecture.

▼ Fan raftering is visible in the roof of the delicate relic hall of Engakuji in Kamakura, Kanagawa Prefecture.

Ground Plans of 6th- to 8th-Century Temples

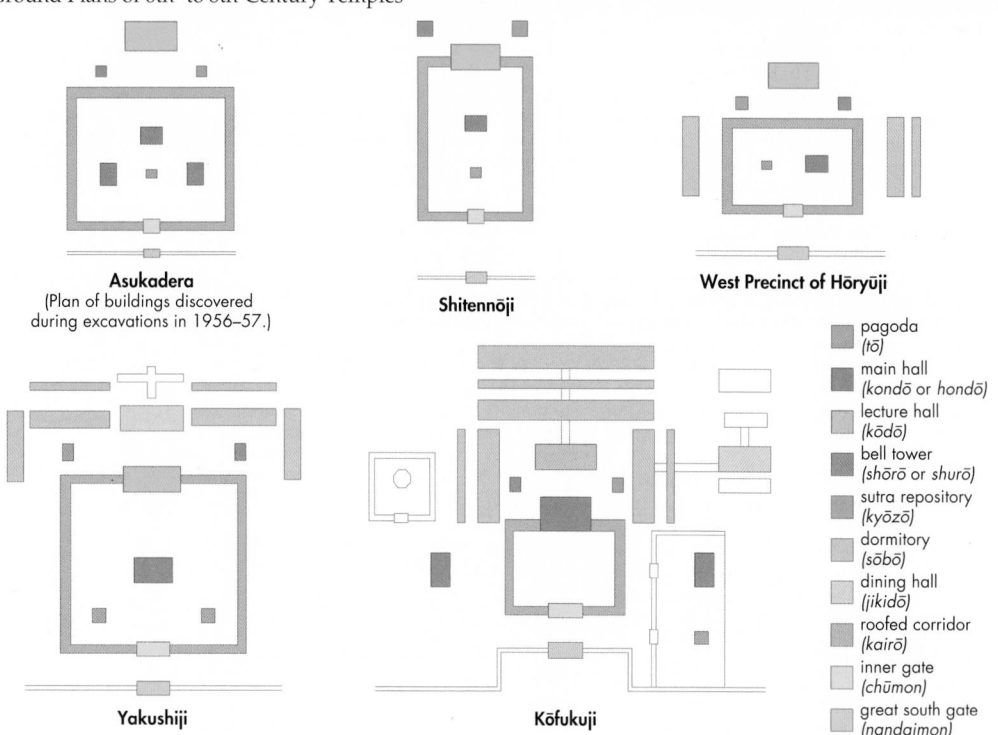

Asukadera
(Plan of buildings discovered during excavations in 1956–57.)

Shitennōji

West Precinct of Hōryūji

Yakushiji

Kōfukuji

- ■ pagoda *(tō)*
- ■ main hall *(kondō or hondō)*
- ■ lecture hall *(kōdō)*
- ■ bell tower *(shōrō or shurō)*
- ■ sutra repository *(kyōzō)*
- ■ dormitory *(sōbō)*
- ■ dining hall *(jikidō)*
- ■ roofed corridor *(kairō)*
- ■ inner gate *(chūmon)*
- ■ great south gate *(nandaimon)*

Statistically, Japan is a country of Buddhists. More than 85 percent of the population professes the Buddhist faith. Buddhism in Japan maintains some 75,000 temples with nearly 200,000 priests.

Buddhist architecture 寺院建築

(*jiin kenchiku*). Major style of religious architecture in Japan that originated in Chinese and Korean structural forms. The term is used to describe systems of buildings within temple compounds that, taken together, constitute great architectural ensembles of BUDDHIST ART. A temple was a place dedicated to worship of the Buddha. It also functioned as a place where monks or nuns lived, underwent religious training, and studied sutras, and for each of these pur-

poses a building was erected. A temple was also a place where lay worshipers gathered, and facilities for this function were also important.

Principal Temple Halls—By the 8th century a complex of temple buildings consisted of seven basic structures (*shichidō garan*): (1) the PAGODA (*tō*); (2) the main hall (*kondō*); (3) the lecture hall (*kōdō*); (4) the bell tower (*shōrō*; also called *shurō*); (5) the sutra repository (*kyōzō*); (6) the dormitory (*sōbō*); and (7) the dining hall (*jikidō*). The most important of these structures were the main hall, the lecture hall, and the multistoried pagoda, where sacred relics, believed to be pieces of the historical Buddha's remains, were enshrined.

In temple compounds of the Asuka (593–710) and Nara (710–794) periods, there was a rectangular inner precinct surrounded by a

roofed corridor (*kairō*) and entered by a gate called the *chūmon*. Within were the main hall and pagoda; the lecture hall was located outside the precinct behind the rear corridor. As styles changed, however, the lecture hall was connected to the rear corridor. The temple compound itself was enclosed by earthen walls (*tsuijibei*) with gates on each side. The names of the gates derived from the directions in which they faced—for example, *nandaimon*, or "great south gate," and *tōdaimon*, or "great east gate." The great south gate was the main gate, and in early times it was located very close to the larger inner gate (*chūmon*), but by the Nara period it had come to rival the inner gate in size. The other outer gates, although called *daimon*, or "great gates," were not particularly large. Temples of the TENDAI SECT and SHINGON SECT were generally erected on mountainous sites, and in this case gates were situated according to the contours of the terrain. The inner gate was regarded as next in importance to the main hall and pagoda. The most common type of gate was the two-storied *rōmon*. In temples of the Zen sect the inner gate was called the *sammon*, from which a series of corridors connecting at right angles extended to the *butsuden*, or Buddha hall, the Zen equivalent of the *kondō*. No examples of the early *kairō* corridors survive, and the practice of building them was not observed by sects of Buddhism that flourished in the medieval period (mid-12th–16th centuries).

In the Asuka and Nara periods the main hall, which housed the principal object of worship, was called the *kondō* (literally, "golden hall"), but in the Heian period (794–1185) the custom of referring to it as the *hondō*, or "main hall," arose. Surviving examples of *kondō* include the main hall in the West Precinct (Saiin) of HŌRYŪJI and the main hall at TŌSHŌDAIJI. The lecture hall, customarily referred to as the *kōdō*, was the place where monks assembled for instruction, study, or ritual and was usually the largest structure in early temples. Surviving examples of the Asuka and Nara periods are the lecture hall in the East Precinct (Tōin) of Hōryūji and the one at Tōshōdaiji. At Zen temples the lecture hall is called the *hattō* (also pronounced *hōdō*; literally, "dharma hall").

◄Built in 1397, the main hall of Kakurinji typifies late medieval eclecticism, which blended delicate *wayō* architecture with later, more imposing styles. Hyōgo Prefecture.

▼The great south gate of the temple Tōdaiji was probably originally built in the mid-8th century in the *wayō* style. The present gate, in the "great Buddha" style, is a reconstruction of 1199. Nara Prefecture.

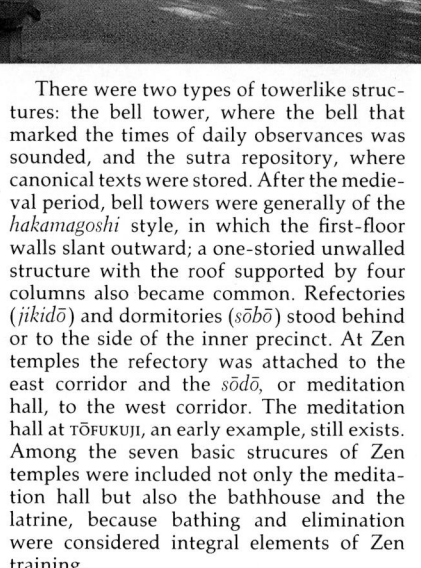

◄The main hall of the temple Saimyōji is a rare surviving example of the *wayō* style, the prevailing mode of Buddhist architecture until the 12th century. Shiga Prefecture.

There were two types of towerlike structures: the bell tower, where the bell that marked the times of daily observances was sounded, and the sutra repository, where canonical texts were stored. After the medieval period, bell towers were generally of the *hakamagoshi* style, in which the first-floor walls slant outward; a one-storied unwalled structure with the roof supported by four columns also became common. Refectories (*jikidō*) and dormitories (*sōbō*) stood behind or to the side of the inner precinct. At Zen temples the refectory was attached to the east corridor and the *sōdō*, or meditation hall, to the west corridor. The meditation hall at TŌFUKUJI, an early example, still exists. Among the seven basic strucures of Zen temples were included not only the meditation hall but also the bathhouse and the latrine, because bathing and elimination were considered integral elements of Zen training.

When Buddhism was first introduced into Japan, sacred relics were the chief objects of worship, and the pagoda was at the center of the compound. Excavations at the original site of ASUKADERA, the oldest full-fledged Buddhist temple in Japan—construction was begun in 588—reveal that a pagoda was at the center of the temple precinct and that on both sides and to the rear there were main halls. At SHITENNŌJI (ca 593) the single main hall is situated behind the pagoda. These arrangements indicate that the pagoda was considered the most important building. However, at Kawaradera (ca mid-7th century; see KAWARADERA REMAINS) and at Hōryūji (7th century) the pagoda is off center and stands side by side with a main hall. At YAKUSHIJI (late 7th century) the main hall is the central structure of the inner precinct and a pair of pagodas function chiefly as decorative features. The 8th-century temples TŌDAIJI and DAIANJI also had two pagodas, but they were situated outside the inner precinct, as were the single pagodas at KŌFUKUJI and Tōshōdaiji. These changes reflect a gradual transformation in the emphasis placed on the relics of the Buddha as well as the introduction of new architectural styles.

Among other buildings in temple compounds is the *azekura*, which is constructed, in log-cabin style, with interlocking horizontal members that are triangular in section. Built largely during the Asuka and Nara periods to serve as sutra or treasure repositories, *azekura* survive at Tōdaiji and Tōshōdaiji. Although in principle monks lived in groups, Tendai and Shingon monks of aristocratic origin often established separate quarters called *shiin.* Similarly, among Zen monks the practice arose of establishing separate quarters (*tatchū*) in order to tend the grave of a renowned priest. Eventually, many *shiin* and *tatchū* were built about the perimeters of the main temples of these sects. Other buildings were erected to fulfill functions peculiar to individual sects, such

as the *kanchōdō* of esoteric Buddhism for performing ceremonies related to the assumpton of priestly rank; still others were devoted to worship of specific deities, such as the *amidadō* (Amida hall), which developed during the Heian period (794–1185) along with the rise of Pure Land Buddhism.

Styles of Buddhist Architecture——The Asuka style of temple architecture was derived from 5th- and 6th-century Chinese architecture and was followed by the Tang (T'ang) style, which predominated in the Tempyō era (729–749; see TEMPYŌ CULTURE). This simple style, marked by broad proportions and little decoration, is called the *wayō*, or Japanese mode, to distinguish it from the *daibutsuyō* (great Buddha mode) and the Zen style, or *karayō* (Chinese mode), which were introduced during the Kamakura period (1185–1333). The great Buddha mode,

which is also referred to as *tenjikuyō*, is notable for its integration of southern Chinese architectural features with the traditional style and is exemplified by the *nandaimon* (great south gate) of Tōdaiji designed by Chōgen (1121–1206). *Karayō*, on the other hand, arose from the attempt to build in Japan temples that were exactly like the Zen temples of southern China. *Karayō* structures were smaller and daintier than *wayō* buildings, and much more complex in detail. Fan raftering curved prominently upward, and there were paneled doors, arched windows (*katō mado*), and many decorative nosings and sculptures. Masonry flooring (*ishidatami*) was employed instead of the traditional raised wooden floor. The most significant of surviving examples of *karayō* is

Left: **Fugen Bosatsu** The bodhisattva Fugen (Skt: Samantabhadra) appears to sincere believers in the Lotus Sutra and offers them divine protection. 12th century. Colors on silk. 159 × 75 cm. Tōkyō National Museum. National Treasure.
Middle: **Portrait of Kichijōten** A Buddhist deity of Indian origin, Kichijōten bears a magical jewel in her left hand. 8th century. Colors and gold on hemp. 53 × 32 cm. Yakushiji, Nara Prefecture. National Treasure.
Right: **The Guze Kannon** This gilt camphor wood image of the bodhisattva Kannon is carved in the style of the sculptor Kuratsukuri no Tori. Hōryūji, Nara Prefecture. 7th century. Height of body 179 cm. National Treasure.

the *shariden* (relic hall) of ENGAKUJI in Kamakura. The eclectic mode (*setchūyō*), an intermingling of *wayō* style with great Buddha and Zen styles, soon arose, and by the Muromachi period (1333–1568) pure *wayō* construction became increasingly rare.

Buddhist art　　仏教美術

(Bukkyō *bijutsu*). Like Japanese BUDDHISM itself, Japanese Buddhist art was a national variant of an international tradition. In Japan the Buddhist art forms that were periodically introduced from China and Korea were tempered in the crucible of local custom and usage, to yield a rich tradition of religious art and architecture.

The Buddhist Mainstream—Buddhism was formally transmitted to Japan from China and Korea in the 6th century. The forms of Buddhism and Buddhist art that first arrived in Japan were chiefly those of the Mahāyāna (J: Daijō Bukkyō) tradition, a theistic and catholic system of belief that stressed universal salvation and that was to remain the underlying framework of most sects of Buddhist belief and practice in Japan through the modern era.

From its inception Buddhism in Japan engaged the concern and patronage of ruling interests and became virtually a state creed. Temples and monastic compounds usually consisted of at least seven typical structures, including a *tō* (pagoda), a main hall called the *kondō* ("golden hall"), a lecture hall called the *kōdō*, and a *kyōzō* or sutra repository. They were built as the seats of Buddhist worship and instruction. In the first wave of such construction, numerous temples were erected from the late 6th to the early 7th century in what is now the Kyōto-Ōsaka region, most notably ASUKADERA, SHITENNŌJI, and HŌRYŪJI. After HEIJŌKYŌ (Nara) was designated the national capital in 710, a new wave of temple construction in the early 8th century produced the great Nara-period (710–794) metropolitan monasteries, among them KŌFUKUJI, DAIANJI, and YAKUSHIJI.

A tremendous amount of Buddhist art was commissioned for the halls and chapels of these temple complexes. Paintings and sculptures representing various Buddhas, bodhisattvas, and guardian deities were the icons to which worship and ritual were directed. Important examples of such early artworks are the 7th-century gilt-bronze Shaka Triad (Shaka [Skt: Śākyamuni] flanked by two bodhisattvas) and Yakushi (Skt: Bhaiṣajyaguru), attributed to KURATSUKURI NO TORI, at Hōryūji; the 8th-century gilt-bronze Yakushi Triad at Yakushiji; and the 8th-century clay Niō (Skt: Vajradhara; Benevolent Kings) at Hōryūji. Realistic portraits of famous monks, such as the 8th-century lacquer sculpture of GANJIN at Tōshōdaiji, were also enshrined at temples. A corollary art form, that of the illustrated handscroll (EMAKIMONO), was developed for Buddhist narrative instruction. The oldest in this genre is the 8th-century biography of Shaka called the *E inga kyō* (Illustrated Sutra of Cause and Effect).

The construction of TŌDAIJI from 747 marked the apex of classical Buddhist art and architecture in Japan. The temple's *honzon*, or principal object of worship, is a colossal gilt-bronze image—measuring some 15 meters (49 ft) in height—of the cosmic Buddha called Birushana (Skt: Vairocana; see DAINICHI). A technical feat, this giant sculpture—called the Nara Daibutsu ("Great Buddha of Nara"; see DAIBUTSU)—came to symbolize the power, wealth, and intrusiveness of state-sanctioned Buddhism.

Esoteric Buddhism—In part as a reaction to the state Buddhism symbolized by Tōdaiji and the Nara Daibutsu, a new regime moved the capital to HEIANKYŌ (now Kyōto) in 794. Largely coincidental with this move was the emergence into prominence of *mikkyō*, "the secret teachings," a system of esoteric Buddhist belief and practice (see ESOTERIC BUDDHISM) that was to be articulated in the SHINGON SECT and the TENDAI SECT.

The Buddha Dainichi (Skt: Mahāvairocana), a cosmic force that was already evident in Buddhist ideology by the time of the Nara Daibutsu, became the organizing principle of esoteric Buddhism and the focus of worship. Esotericism also involved a vastly enhanced pantheon of deities, many culled from non-Buddhist traditions, and an increased emphasis on elaborate ritual as a means of harnessing the power inherent in this pantheon.

Perhaps the most characteristic art form of esotericism is the MANDALA, a schematic depiction of the cosmos and its various gods that is used as the focus of meditation and ritual. Key to Shingon and Tendai practice were the paired mandalas of the Diamond or Thunderbolt Realm (KONGŌKAI) and the Matrix or Womb Realm (TAIZŌKAI), together referred to as the RYŌBU MANDARA or "Two Mandalas." An important early example of this format is the 9th-century *Takao mandara* (Takao Mandala) at JINGOJI.

Unlike the metropolitan temples of the 8th century, Shingon and Tendai temples as a whole were constructed away from centers of urban concentration, usually in a mountain setting. For example, ENRYAKUJI, seat of the Tendai sect, was built on the slopes of Mt. Hiei (Hieizan), and KONGŌBUJI on Mt. Kōya (Kōyasan) became the headquarters of the Shingon sect. In both cases buildings were distributed in an irregular fashion over a hilly, forested terrain.

The paintings and sculptures that filled these buildings, in keeping with their function as iconic representations of esoteric deities, displayed an aesthetic and stylistic tenor appropriate to the mystery of ritual and meditation at a remote temple. An important example of this tendency is seen in the 9th-century set of five statues of the Bodhisattvas of the Void (Go Dai Kokūzō Bosatsu), each in painted wood, at Jingoji. Also coincidental with the development of esotericism was a trend in sculpture toward the carving of votive statues out of single blocks of wood, their surfaces left unadorned with paint or lacquer in deference to the inherent sanctity of the sacred tree (*shimboku*). The principal examples of this "plain wood" style are the Yakushi figures at GANGŌJI

The Buddha Amida Gilt-wood statue sculpted by Jōchō. Both the canopy and the statue are National Treasures. 1053. Byōdōin, Kyōto Prefecture. Height 284 cm.

(early 9th century) and at Jingoji (ca 783).

Pure Land Buddhism—Even though esotericism remained a major element in Japanese religious life, by the close of the 10th century it had begun to give way as a system of popular belief to Pure Land faith and practice. In the Pure Land tradition worship focused on the Buddha Amida (Skt: Amitābha) and on rebirth in his Western Paradise, or Pure Land, called Gokuraku (Skt: Sukhāvatī). Artworks were essential to Pure Land doctrine and its next-world emphasis on rebirth and salvation: as guides in meditational practices directed at visualizing Amida in his paradise, as markers of the "awesome splendor" (*shōgon*) of the Buddha, and as a means of accumulating religious merit. Indeed, the 11th and 12th centuries saw a dramatic increase in the production of Buddhist art and architecture.

A celebrated example of Pure Land art and aesthetics is the *amidadō* (Amida hall), now called the Phoenix Hall (Hōōdō), at BYŌDŌIN in Uji, which was constructed in 1053 by

FUJIWARA NO YORIMICHI (992–1074), who, with his father, FUJIWARA NO MICHINAGA (966–1028), was one of the great patrons of Pure Land Buddhism and art. Like other temples of its day, which were much influenced by descriptions in Pure Land scripture of Amida's palatial residence, Byōdōin was at the same time a detached residence in the SHINDEN-ZUKURI mode, where Yorimichi might live as well as pray.

Enshrined at Byōdōin's Phoenix Hall is a gilt-wood sculpture of Amida by the artist JŌCHŌ (d 1057), who in this work and others like it set a technical and stylistic standard that would remain in place through the 13th century. On the walls of the Phoenix Hall is a series of paintings depicting the various degrees of rebirth in Amida's paradise; these are attributed to the artist TAKUMA TAMENARI (fl mid-11th century), a member of a family dynasty of Buddhist artists believed to be the forerunners of the TAKUMA SCHOOL.

One of the principal treatises of Japanese Pure Land Buddhism—one that had a major

impact on art production—was a work by the Tendai monk GENSHIN (Eshin Sōzu; 942–1017) called *ŌJŌYŌSHŪ* (985, The Essentials of Pure Land Rebirth), in which was set forth an exhaustive account of Amida's nine sectors of paradise and the nine degrees of rebirth (*kubon ōjō*) therein. This stimulated development of the *kutai amidadō* (nine-image Amida hall), also called *kutaidō* (nine-image hall), in which nine monumental figures of Amida were enshrined. An example of this format is seen at JŌRURIJI, a temple built in the 11th century.

In painting, a key Pure Land genre was the so-called RAIGŌZU, in which Amida and his heavenly entourage are shown arriving to welcome and guide the dying to paradise. Like the opulent *amidadō* built at Byōdōin and other temples, as well as the parallel development of the *kutaidō* architectural format, the *raigōzu* genre was heavily influenced by Genshin's work. An important

Buddhist art

▶ **Stork Room** The elaborate ceiling designs, intricately carved transoms, and painted walls and doors of this reception hall at the temple Nishi Honganji in Kyōto make this a splendid example of *shoin-zukuri*-style architecture. 17th century.

▼ **Rock and Sand Garden** The Zen-influenced garden pictured here was constructed in 1939 at the Kōmyōin, a subsidiary temple of the temple Tōfukuji, Kyōto.

▲ **Entrance to Shinjuan** The pattern of the stepping-stones in the entryway to the temple Shinjuan, a subsidiary temple of Daitokuji in Kyōto, is said to echo the layout of the rock and sand garden within the temple courtyard.

▼ **Catching a Catfish with a Gourd** Detail of a painting by the monk-painter Josetsu. Ca 1413. Ink and pale colors on paper. 112 × 76 cm. Myōshinji, Kyōto. National Treasure.

example of an early *raigō* painting is the mid-12th-century triptych *Amida shōju raigōzu* (Descent of Amida and the Heavenly Multitude), now preserved on Mt. Kōya but originally enshrined at Enryakuji on Mt. Hiei.

In *Ōjōyōshū* Genshin did not limit his discussion to paradise; the first part of this treatise provides a horrific vision of the six realms of existence (*rokudō*), and especially various hells, as a means to awakening faith and penitence. This, too, was reflected in contemporary Pure Land painting, particularly in the *emakimono* format; by the 12th century an imagery of hell and karmic retribution was fully developed. Celebrated examples of this genre are the *Gaki-zōshi* (Scrolls of Hungry Ghosts) and JIGOKU-ZŌSHI (Scrolls of Hells). Another *emakimono* genre, that of temple histories (*engi*) and biographies of saints and monks, was also developed. An example of this popular genre is SHIGISAN ENGI EMAKI (The Legends of Mt. Shigi).

Zen Buddhism—In the 13th century the ZEN (Ch: Chan or Ch'an) sect, disseminated by Japanese and Chinese monks, took hold among the ruling military elites and introduced new currents in art. Zen monasteries, such as KENCHŌJI and ENGAKUJI, emerged as both seats of religious discourse and centers for the secular cultural activities for which the Zen monks became increasingly known: literary studies, poetry, painting, and calligraphy.

Zen temples were strongly continental in flavor and differed significantly from the architectural models used in other sects. Layout, nomenclature, furnishings, and even structural details were derived from the Buddhist architecture of south central China. The typical Zen monastic compound, especially the semiautonomous subtemple known as *tatchū*, usually incorporated a carefully composed small garden. In keeping with the austerity of Zen taste, some of these gardens, in a format called "rock and sand garden" (*karesansui*), were landscaped without the standard pond or stream; the flow of water was evoked through the raking of smooth sand and gravel.

Paintings in a variety of genres figured in Zen ritual and monastic life. The public ceremonial halls of Zen temples enshrined depictions of the deities, great monks, and great events significant to Zen tradition, such as the portrayal of the death of Śākyamuni (*nehanzu*) painted by MINCHŌ for Kyōto's TŌFUKUJI in 1408. The private halls and quarters at a Zen compound accommodated a more informal imagery, such as painted portraits of patriarchs of the sect (see CHINSŌ).

A category of painting that was particularly favored in Zen circles was the *dō-shakuga*, a picture of a Taoist or Buddhist subject that was rendered with innovative handling of brush and ink and employed simplified motifs. A prominent *dōshakuga* subject was the White-Robed Kannon (Byakue Kannon), as seen in *Kannon enkaku zu* (Kannon with Monkey and Crane) by MOKKEI (Ch: Muqi or Mu-ch'i; fl 13th century) at DAITOKUJI in Kyōto. Included in *dōshakuga* imagery were depictions (called *zenkizu*; "scenes of Zen") of quasi-legendary and eccentric figures exemplifying Zen ideals. An important example of this genre is *Eka dampi zu* (Huike Cuts Off His Arm), painted by SESSHŪ TŌYŌ in 1496 and now housed at Sainenji, Aichi Prefecture. Sesshū shows the second Chan patriarch, Huike (Hui-k'o; J: Eka), proffering his severed right arm to Bodhidharma.

Another means for expression of Zen ideals through painting was the calligraphic exercise called *bokuseki* ("ink traces"). A distinguished monk would write, often in a bold and assertive style, an evocative phrase for the edification of a disciple or visitor, and the product would be cherished for its artistic value and for its historical associations.

The impact of Zen aesthetics and doctrine

was by no means limited to the monastic compound. The development of a pure landscape painting genre in Japan (see SANSUIGA), as well as the emergence of a mature *suibokuga* (INK PAINTING) tradition, owes much to the influence of Zen and Zen monk-painters.

Buddhism under the Tokugawa Shogunate—The spread of Neo-Confucian orthodoxy in China and Korea also affected Japan, where the unifying ideology of the Tokugawa shogunate (1603–1867) and its widespread educational system constituted an official state Confucianism (see SHU-SHIGAKU). As Buddhism lost its centrality to politics and culture, Buddhist art gave way to secular forms, although Buddhist values remained visible in much of Japanese taste and aesthetics.

The arts, however, were not entirely devoid of Buddhist genres. While not organized into a formal school, the tradition of the Zen monk–amateur painter flourished to the end of the 19th century and has recently been given the name ZENGA, "Zen painting." Important painters in this genre were the monks HAKUIN Ekaku (1686–1769) and SENGAI GIBON (1750–1837). In sculpture, a handful of eccentric artists produced roughly carved, highly personal interpretations in wood of various Buddhist icons. Among these innovative artists were ENKŪ (ca 1632–95) and Mokujiki Gogyō (1718–1810; see MOKUJIKI). See also BUDDHIST SCULPTURE; PAINTING; BUDDHIST ARCHITECTURE; TEMPLES; SHINTŌ ART.

Buddhist iconography 仏教図像

(Bukkyō *zuzō*). In Japanese BUDDHISM, Buddhist deities are divided into four principal groups: NYORAI (Skt: *tathāgata*), *bosatsu* (Skt: BODHISATTVA), TEMBU (Skt: *deva*), and MYŌŌ (Skt: *vidyārāja*). Each group has a specific vocabulary of costume, stance, and symbolic gesture (Skt: *mudrā*) represented in paintings and sculpture, and individual deities within each group have additional identifying attributes.

A *nyorai* is a Buddha and is generally shown in plain monk's raiment, without decoration. Among the *nyorai* are AMIDA (Skt: Amitābha), the Buddha of light; Yakushi (Skt: Bhaiṣajyaguru), the Buddha of healing; and Shaka (Skt: Śākyamuni), the historical Buddha. DAINICHI (Skt: Mahāvairocana), the cosmic Buddha, an exception to the rule, is depicted in princely costume of the type worn by a bodhisattva.

Bodhisattvas are compassionate beings who have postponed their own enlightenment in order to save others. Generally a bodhisattva is shown dressed in clothing that might be worn by a prince: elaborate robes, accessories such as a sash and scarf, and jewelry, which often includes a crown. Among the bodhisattvas frequently encountered in art are KANNON (Skt: Avalokiteśvara), who represents compassion; Monju (Skt: Mañjuśrī), who represents wisdom; and Fugen (Skt: Samantabhadra), who represents praxis. MIROKU (Skt: Maitreya), the Buddha of the future, is usually depicted as a bodhisattva. The bodhisattva JIZŌ (Skt: Kṣitigarbha), however, is usually shown in the robes of a monk.

Buddhas and bodhisattvas are often presented in triad form, with a Buddha flanked to the right and left by a bodhisattva. In a Shaka triad, Shaka is flanked by Fugen and Monju. In a Yakushi triad, the attendant bodhisattvas are Nikkō (Skt: Sūryaprabha) and Gakkō (Skt: Candraprabha). Kannon and Seishi (Skt: Mahāsthāmaprāpta) flank

Amida in an Amida triad.

Tembu are deities introduced into the Buddhist pantheon from non-Buddhist religious traditions, most importantly those of pre-Buddhist India. Most gods in this class are guardian deities, usually depicted in warrior dress, with weapons in their hands. Among the guardian deities most often encountered in art are the Twelve Guardian Generals (Jūni Shinshō), the Benevolent Kings (Niō; also called Kongō Rikishi), and the Four Heavenly Kings (Shitennō).

Myōō, warlike deities representing the luminescent wisdom of the Buddha, were introduced into the Japanese Buddhist pantheon with the arrival of ESOTERIC BUDDHISM in the 9th century. The most widely encountered *myōō* are the Go Dai Myōō or "Five Wisdom Kings": Fudō (Skt: Acalanā-

tha); Gōzanze (Skt: Trailokyavijaya); Gundari (Skt: Kuṇḍalī); Daiitoku (Skt: Yamāntaka); and Kongōyasha (Skt: Vajrayakṣa).

Exhaustive iconographic reference works explaining the purpose and the meaning associated with each deity in Japanese Buddhism were compiled as early as the 10th century by esoteric Buddhist monks and were relied upon to elucidate Buddhist theology. KAKUZENSHŌ (1176–1218) is one such compendium. See also BUDDHIST ART; BUDDHIST SCULPTURE. ☎ 132–133

Buddhist rites 仏教儀式

(Bukkyō *gishiki*). Many Buddhist sects in Japan possess their own distinctive rites.
Continued on page 134➡

The Four Principal Types of Buddhist Deities

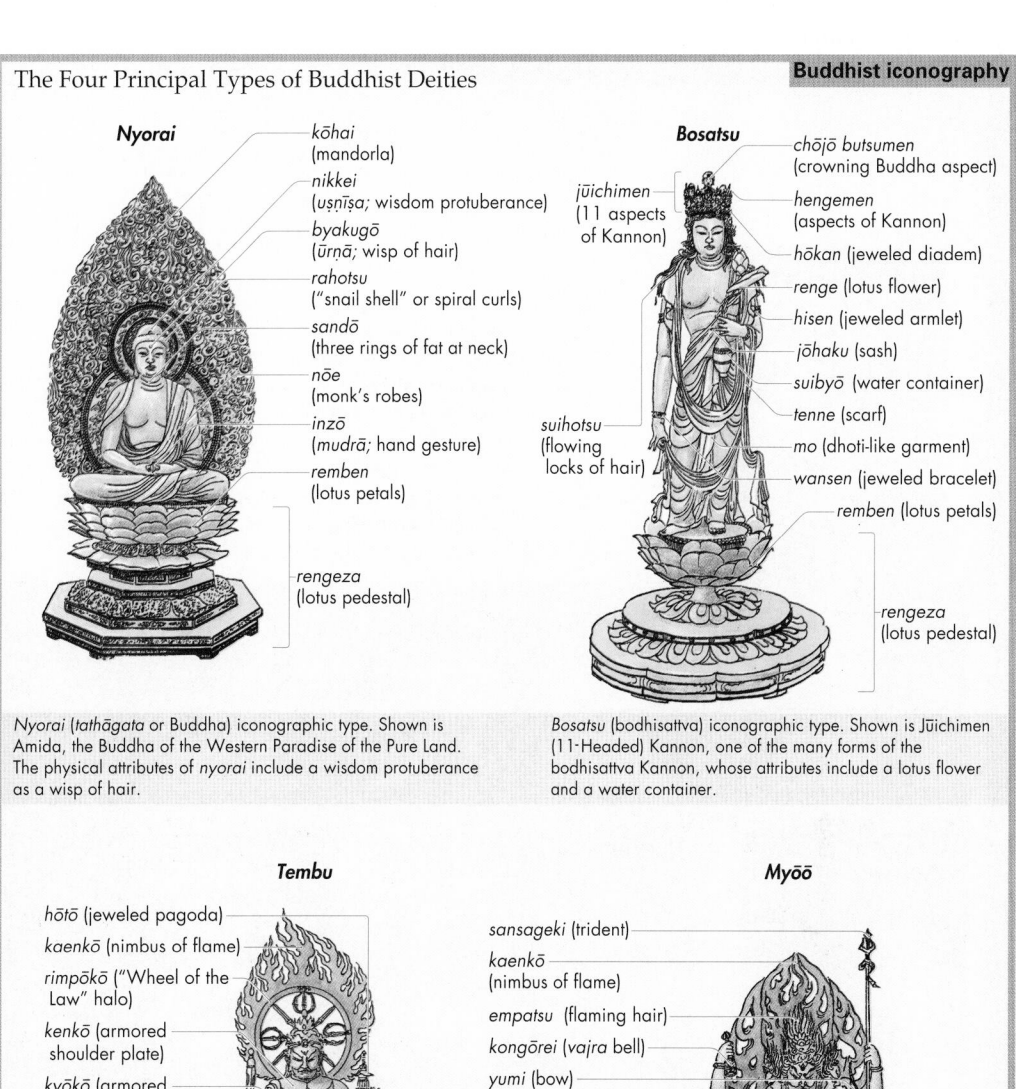

Nyorai
- kōhai (mandorla)
- nikkei (uṣṇīṣa; wisdom protuberance)
- byakugō (ūrṇā; wisp of hair)
- rahotsu ("snail shell" or spiral curls)
- sandō (three rings of fat at neck)
- nōe (monk's robes)
- inzō (mudrā; hand gesture)
- remben (lotus petals)
- rengeza (lotus pedestal)

Nyorai (*tathāgata* or Buddha) iconographic type. Shown is Amida, the Buddha of the Western Paradise of the Pure Land. The physical attributes of *nyorai* include a wisdom protuberance as a wisp of hair.

Bosatsu
- chōjō butsumen (crowning Buddha aspect)
- hengemen (aspects of Kannon)
- jūichimen (11 aspects of Kannon)
- hōkan (jeweled diadem)
- renge (lotus flower)
- hisen (jeweled armlet)
- jōhaku (sash)
- suibyō (water container)
- suihotsu (flowing locks of hair)
- tenne (scarf)
- mo (dhoti-like garment)
- wansen (jeweled bracelet)
- remben (lotus petals)
- rengeza (lotus pedestal)

Bosatsu (bodhisattva) iconographic type. Shown is Jūichimen (11-Headed) Kannon, one of the many forms of the bodhisattva Kannon, whose attributes include a lotus flower and a water container.

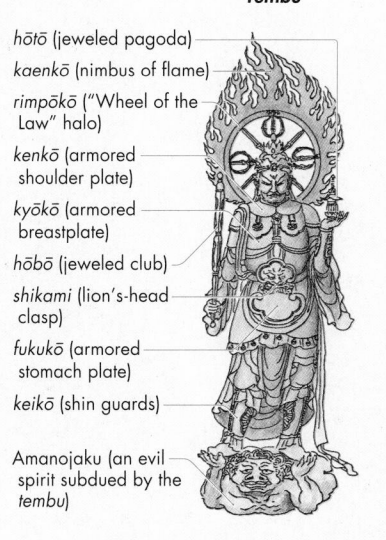

Tembu
- hōtō (jeweled pagoda)
- kaenkō (nimbus of flame)
- rimpōkō ("Wheel of the Law" halo)
- kenkō (armored shoulder plate)
- kyōkō (armored breastplate)
- hōbō (jeweled club)
- shikami (lion's-head clasp)
- fukukō (armored stomach plate)
- keikō (shin guards)
- Amanojaku (an evil spirit subdued by the tembu)

Tembu (*deva* or heavenly beings) iconographic type. Shown is Bishamonten, one of the Four Heavenly Kings, whose attributes include a jeweled pagoda and a jeweled club.

Myōō
- sansageki (trident)
- kaenkō (nimbus of flame)
- empatsu (flaming hair)
- kongōrei (vajra bell)
- yumi (bow)
- inzō (mudrā; hand gesture)
- hōken (jeweled sword)
- ya (arrow)
- shikami (lion's-head clasp)
- kohikun (tiger-skin girdle)
- saku (lasso)
- Daijizaiten (Siva, god of destruction)
- Umahi (Siva's queen)
- sokusen (anklet)
- iwaza (rocklike base)

Myōō (*vidyārāja* or kings of light or wisdom) iconographic type. Shown is Gōzanze, whose attributes include a trident, *vajra* bell, bow, arrow, jeweled sword, and lasso.

Kōmokuten

The Universe Reflected in Buddhist Iconography

The lecture hall (*kōdō*) of the temple Tōji in Kyōto contains 21 sculptures that together form a three-dimensional cosmological mandala. Mandalas in the form of paintings or sculptures portray the relationships between the deities in the Buddhist pantheon, whose traits are revealed by their costumes, stances, and symbolic gestures. The Shingon sect, introduced to Japan by Kūkai (774–835), sees mandalas as crucial for transmitting esoteric doctrine. This one, designed by Kūkai himself, is an exceptionally complete presentation of the four principal groups of deities: Buddhas, bodhisattvas, wisdom kings, and heavenly beings. The mandala embodies the spiritual order in tangible form. Placed facing outward near the southernmost entrance to the ancient capital, it serves the dual purpose of instructing onlookers and guarding the state against disasters.

The five Buddhas (*nyorai*) are placed at the center

Five Myōō

Taishakuten

Zōchōten

How the Twenty-One Sculptures Are Arranged

Kōmokuten
Daiitoku Kongōyasha
Taishakuten Fudō
Gundari Gōzanze
Zōchōten **The Five Myōō**

Fukūjōju Ashuku
Dainichi
Muryōju Hōshō
The Five Nyorai

Tamonten
Kongōgō Kongōsatta
Kongōharamitsu Bonten
Kongōhō Kongōhō
Jikokuten
The Five Bosatsu

Tamonten

Bonten

of the hall with the five bodhisattvas (*bosatsu*) to their east and the five kings of wisdom (*myōō*) to their west, all facing south. The heavenly beings (*tembu*) are situated at the eastern and western ends of the hall. They include the figures at the four corners of the hall, known as the Four Heavenly Kings (Shitennō), and the representations of Brahma (Bonten) and Indra (Taishakuten), east center and west center, respectively. Dainichi, surrounded by the four other Buddhas, forms the focal point of the mandala. Source of the Buddhist law and of all creation, his high abstract realm manifests itself both as the compassionate bodhisattvas in the east who enlighten mankind and as the wrathful wisdom kings in the west who chastise human willfulness and obduracy. The six heavenly beings guard the Buddhist law. Overall, the group of sculptures at Tōji is a portrait of the cosmos according to esoteric Buddhism.

Five Nyorai

Five Bosatsu

The Five Nyorai. As the foundation of cosmic consciousness, the central figure of Dainichi embodies the Five Great Elements (earth, water, fire, wind, and emptiness), the Five Directions (east, west, north, south, and center), and the Five Wisdoms. The four other Buddhas who surround Dainichi represent the essence of Buddhist law and truth. From left in the photograph they are Muryōju, Fukūjōju, Ashuku, and Hōshō.

The Five Bosatsu. Buddhist compassion is exemplified by the five bodhisattvas who remain in this world to teach others how to attain enlightenment. Arranged around the central figure of Kon-

gōharamitsu are, from left, Kongōhō, Kongōgō, Kongōsatta, and Kongōhō. (Although two bodhisattvas have names pronounced Kongōhō, the names are written with different Chinese characters.)

The Five Myōō. Poised around Fudō Myōō (the Immovable One), four more wisdom kings embody the wrathful aspect of Dainichi Nyorai. From left: Gundari, with snakes entwined around his arms and legs; the six-headed, six-armed, six-legged, centipedelike Daiitoku seated on the back of an ox; the three-headed, six-armed Kongōyasha; and the three-headed, eight-armed

Gōzanze trampling underfoot the god Siva and Siva's queen. Representation of the Five Wisdom Kings as a sculptural group as at Tōji had no precedent in Japan. Fudō Myōō has been one of the most widely portrayed figures in Buddhist iconography.

The Six Tembu. The heavenly beings include Bonten and Taishakuten and the Four Heavenly Kings (Zōchōten, Kōmokuten, Tamonten—also known as Bishamonten—and Jikokuten), who stand at the corners of the mandala. The six are the faithful servants and guardians of Buddhist law.

Jikokuten

Buddhist ritual implements *Vajra* (J: kongōshō), stylized thunderbolts that symbolize the delusion-destroying power of wisdom, are often paired with bells in esoteric Buddhism. Pictured is a set of Buddhist ritual implements from the 13th century. Gilt bronze. Itsukushima Shrine, Hiroshima Prefecture.

Buddhist sculpture

Korean immigrant sculptors in Japan carved this image of the bodhisattva Miroku. 7th century. Height of body 84 cm. Kōryūji, Kyōto. National Treasure.

The rites can be divided into those that religious practitioners perform among themselves and those conducted on behalf of the laity. The first category includes rites conducted to develop personal religious faith, such as offerings and daily recitation of sutras or mantras; and rites centering on devotion toward Buddhas, patriarchs, and sect founders. The latter include the services for Shaka Kōtan'e (Buddha's birthday) on 8 April and Nehan'e (feast of the Buddha's entry into nirvana) on 15 February, as well as memorial services conducted for the founders of particular sects, such as Daishikō on 23 November (for the founders of the SHINGON SECT and the TENDAI SECT) and Hōonkō (for SHINRAN, the founder of the JŌDO SHIN SECT) on 28 November in the temple Higashi Honganji and 16 January in Nishi Honganji.

Rites conducted for the laity may be subdivided into rites beseeching the protection of Buddhas, bodhisattvas, and heavenly beings for the sake of national security or the good fortune of groups or individuals and rites for the deceased (see ANCESTOR WORSHIP). Since the Edo period (1600–1868) the majority of temples in Japan have emphasized funeral and memorial services, providing the bereaved with a measure of comfort, which the Shintō religious tradition, due to its treatment of death as defilement, did not.

Annual rites include Shushōe, rites carried out at the New Year, including supplications for peace for the nation and prosperity for the people; Nehan'e, rites performed on 15 February in commemoration of the Buddha's death and entry into parinirvana or complete extinction; and Higan'e, rites conducted on the three days before and after the spring and autumn equinoxes. The original purpose of Higan'e was attaining the Way of the Buddha; the word HIGAN means the other shore or the Pure Land, and PILGRIMAGES and the recitation of the NEMBUTSU were major features. Activities on Higan today, however, tend to center on visits to the graves of departed family members to conduct memorial services. Shushōe and Higan'e are Buddhist rites unique to Japan. Shaka Kōtan'e, or Busshōe (Buddha's birthday), is also known as Kambutsue (rite of bathing the Buddha) and popularly as Hana Matsuri (Flower Festival); the main practice of this occasion (8 April) consists of sprinkling a figure of the infant Buddha with sweet tea. During Urabon'e (Skt: Ullambana), conducted 13–16 July (15–16 August in some localities), the souls of deceased family members are believed to return to the home, and family

Buddhist rosary A Buddhist rosary is used during prayer to keep count in reciting the name of the Buddha. Pictured is a rosary made of quartz crystals.

members perform rites to greet them (see BON FESTIVAL). Jōdōe (feast commemorating the attainment of Buddhahood) ceremonies take place on 8 December, the day when Śākyamuni is said to have attained perfect enlightenment.

Occasional rites include Tokudoshiki, the ordination ceremony in which a lay person has his or her head shaved, receives the Buddhist habit and precepts, and becomes a monk or nun; Goma (burning; Skt: Homa), a ceremony practiced in ESOTERIC BUDDHISM; and Kanjō (Skt: Abhiṣeka), an esoteric rite of the Shingon sect, representing the transmission of the secret truth and the conferral of status.

Buddhist ritual implements 仏具

(butsugu). Buddhist implements and instruments reflect the ancient Indian origins of many Buddhist articles, their long historical development, and the diversity of usage among the various Buddhist traditions. Common to Buddhist traditions are basic items such as the monk's robes (kesa), the almsbowl (hachi), and the religious wanderer's water jug (byō or suibyō; Skt: kuṇḍikā), which came to be used for the ceremonial sprinkling of water for symbolic purification. Together with a basin and

towel stand, the jug was part of a lustration set (fusatsu yōgu) for a monthly rite of repentance and purification.

Simple ceremonies of reverence employ three elements: incense, light, and flowers. In Japan this practice is reflected in the basic altar set (mitsugusoku), which consists of three items: a censer for burning incense (kōro), a candlestick (shokudai), and a flower vase (kebyō). The oldest examples found in Japan are from about the 6th or 7th century.

Reliquaries (shari yōgu) serve to house a bone (Skt: śarīra) or relic symbolic of the historical Buddha. This common Buddhist heritage has been diversified by different traditions such as NARA BUDDHISM and exoteric Tendai, esoteric Buddhism, Pure Land, and Zen.

Exoteric Buddhism—A large bell (bonshō) made of cast iron or bronze is struck to announce the time of the ceremony. Monks then enter the main hall of the temple, where a shumidan (a square platform with low railings mounted on a multistepped base, often decorated with Buddhist motifs) occupies the central area.

Two small altar tables (wakizukue), placed before an image, hold offerings and ritual implements and flank the celebrant's low, square seat (raiban). Exquisitely crafted

boxes (*kyōbako*) of lacquered wood or metal
are used for the storage of sutras.

The monk celebrant may carry a staff of
office that may be the *shakujō*, a walking
stick with clanking metal rings; the *shubi*, an
oblong, fan-shaped brush; or a short staff
(*nyoi*) with a stylized cloud-shape on one
end. Musical instruments, such as a gong or
the *nyō*, a castanet-like rattle on a handle,
mark the hours for monastic discipline or
punctuate ceremonies.

Esoteric Buddhism—Shingon and Tendai esotericism continued to use exoteric
Buddhist implements, with enlarged or specifically esoteric interpretations, and added
complex elaborations of its own. The esoteric
altar is a MANDALA, a circular or square diagram that symbolically represents the Buddhist universe. The *vajra* (J: *kongōshō*; a short
bronze baton with symmetrical prongs) is
used as a symbol for the Buddha, karma, or
wisdom. Bells (*kongōrei*) are also important.

The complex esoteric rituals involve various other articles, placed in significant order
with *vajra*, bells, and *cakra* (J: *rimbō*; an ancient Indian wheel-symbol) on the altar. For
incense rituals the Shingon sect uses a lotus
flower altar (*kegyōdan*), consisting of a
square platform with a double row of lotus
petals around the base as its great altar and
an altar with legs curved like an elephant's
tusks. Esoteric Tendai tradition uses a plain
boxlike table altar for both purposes.

Pure Land Buddhism—Objects especially characteristic of Pure Land Buddhism
include the *nenju* (rosary) for marking off
recitations of the mantra, and various
rhythm instruments, such as gongs and the
mokugyo, a fish- or dragon-shaped drum of
hollow wood.

Zen—Zen usage has favored other types
of gongs, drums, and bells, including the
umban, a suspended gong in the shape of a
stylized cloud. A censer with eight legs is
unique to Zen Buddhism. The Zen monk's
staff varies from the *shujō* (a long walking
stick) to the *hossu* (a short staff with a tail-
like brush) or the short *kyōsaku* used to
awaken the drowsy meditator or to communicate a nonverbal experience of enlightenment.

Buddhist rosary 数珠

(*juzu*). Circular string of small beads used to
keep count in reciting the name of Buddha
(see NEMBUTSU). Held in the hand or worn
around the neck, the *juzu* is a symbol of the
Buddhist believer, especially the adherent of
the JŌDO SECT (Pure Land sect). There are
usually 108 beads symbolizing the 108 evil
passions of humankind that must be subdued. The beads are commonly made of
nuts from the bo (pipal) tree, quartz crystals,
or sandalwood.

Buddhist sculpture 仏教彫刻

(Bukkyō *chōkoku*). Buddhist sculpture was
introduced to Japan from China and Korea,
and from the 6th through the 8th century
Japanese Buddhist sculpture closely followed continental prototypes. A more native style did not evolve until the 9th century.

Most early sculpture was rendered in gilt
bronze (see KONDŌ BUTSU) or wood. Continental models provided the stylistic framework
for much of the sculpture produced for
Asuka-period (593–710) temples. Important
examples of early Buddhist sculpture include the gilt-bronze Shaka Triad (the Buddha Shaka [Skt: Śākyamuni] flanked by two
bodhisattvas) in the main hall at the temple
HŌRYŪJI near Nara, dated 623 and attributed
to the sculptor Tori Busshi (KURATSUKURI NO
TORI); the wood Guze Kannon in the Dream
Hall (Yumedono) at Hōryūji; and the wood
statue of the bodhisattva MIROKU (Skt: Maitreya), probably a Korean work, at KŌRYŪJI in
Kyōto. An important collection of early gilt-
bronze statuary is the celebrated "48 Buddhas" group (SHIJŪHATTAI BUTSU).

After the capital at HEIJŌKYŌ (present-day
Nara) was built and occupied in 710, inaugurating the Nara period (710–794), much
sculpture was commissioned for the various
temples being constructed in and around the
new city. Although bronze remained an important medium, more works were rendered
in clay (*sozō*) and in two "dry" lacquer techniques (*kanshitsuzō*): hollow lacquer and
wood-core lacquer. In addition to sculptures
in the round, numerous relief plaques in clay

(*sembutsu;* see BUDDHA TILES) and in bronze
repoussé (OSHIDASHIBUTSU) were used for
iconic representations.

Important works of the 8th century preserved in the Nara region include the gilt-
bronze Yakushi Triad (the Buddha Yakushi
[Skt: Bhaiṣajyaguru] flanked by two bodhisattvas) and Shō Kannon (Skt: Ārya
Avalokiteśvara) at YAKUSHIJI; the hollow-lacquer Rushana (Skt: Vairocana) at TŌSHŌDAIJI;
and the hollow-lacquer portrait of the monk
GANJIN (Ch: Jianzhen or Chien-chen), also at
Tōshōdaiji. The construction of TŌDAIJI initiated another wave of sculpture commissions,
with a government-sponsored workshop,
headed by the artist KUNINAKA NO MURAJI
KIMIMARO, assigned to sculpture production.
The principal Tōdaiji project was the development of the colossal gilt-bronze Rushana
that became known as the Great Buddha of
Nara (Nara Daibutsu; see DAIBUTSU), a sculpture some 16 meters (53 ft) in height. As
other halls at Tōdaiji were completed, more
sculptures were produced for them, largely
in clay and in lacquer: Tōdaiji's *hokkedō* (hall
for meditations on the Lotus Sutra) contains
an important group of such 8th-century
sculptures, among them the guardian deity
called Shikkongōshin.

By the end of the 8th century, with the
move of the capital from Nara to HEIANKYŌ
(present-day Kyōto) and the start of the
Heian period (794–1185), wood had emerged
as the favored medium for sculpture and was
to remain so through the modern era. At first
most sculptures were carved from one large
block of wood, in a technique called single-
woodblock construction (*ichiboku-zukuri*),
but by the 11th century, as demand for
sculpture increased, joinery (joined-wood-
block construction; *yosegi-zukuri*) was the
preferred—and more efficient—method.

The Heian period saw the emergence of
Buddhist monk-sculptors, called *busshi*, and
sculptor lineages as an artistic and economic
force in Kyōto and Nara. Through the 10th
century, most sculptors had remained in residence at major temples such as ENRYAKUJI or
TŌJI in Kyōto. However, starting with the

Buddhist sculpture

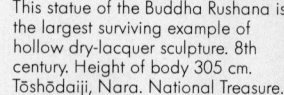

A group of gilt-bronze figurines showing the miraculous birth of the historical Buddha from the sleeve of Queen Māyā (second from left). Shijūhattai Butsu ("48 Buddhas") collection. Early 7th century. Height of Queen Māyā 17 cm. Tōkyō National Museum.

This statue of the Buddha Rushana is the largest surviving example of hollow dry-lacquer sculpture. 8th century. Height of body 305 cm. Tōshōdaiji, Nara. National Treasure.

A pair of Benevolent King (Niō) statues, produced at the workshop of Unkei and Kaikei, stand guard at the south gate of the temple Tōdaiji in Nara. 1203. Joined woodblock construction. Color on wood. Heights 836 cm (left), 842 cm (right). National Treasure.

The Edo-period sculptor Mokujiki Gogyō carved this beaming self-portrait when he was 83 years old. 1801. Wood. Height of body 76 cm. Japan Folk-Craft Museum, Tōkyō.

11th-century artist JŌCHŌ, whose patrons were FUJIWARA NO MICHINAGA and FUJIWARA NO YORIMICHI, sculptors became largely independent of temples, although an important lineage remained at KŌFUKUJI in Nara. See EN SCHOOL; IN SCHOOL.

Important works of the early Heian period include the 9th-century wood sculpture of Yakushi at JINGOJI in Kyōto and the group of 9th-century wood sculptures, arranged in the form of a MANDALA, in the kōdō (lecture hall) at Tōji. The Jingoji sculpture is also notable because it displays the interest in plain, unadorned wood shared by many sculptors in the esoteric Buddhist tradition (see ESOTERIC BUDDHISM). One of the most influential late-Heian works is the gilt-wood sculpture of the Buddha AMIDA (Skt: Amitābha) in the amidadō (Amida hall), or Phoenix Hall, at BYŌDŌIN near Kyōto. Completed by Jōchō in 1053, it is one of the earliest extant works in the full-blown joinery method and established a technical and stylistic standard that sculptors honored through the 13th century.

The KEI SCHOOL, a 12th-century lineage of sculptors located at Kōfukuji but closely associated with the Kyōto-based In and En schools, produced key artists, among them UNKEI and KAIKEI, who would define sculpture in the Kamakura period (1185–1333). Wood

remained the favored medium and joinery the technique, but, in contrast to the Heian tendency to gild statuary, Kamakura-period sculptors also showed much interest in paint as a finish for sculptures. Kaikei's 13th-century figure of the bodhisattva JIZŌ (Skt: Kṣitigarbha), originally at Tōdaiji, is an example of this tendency. In addition, the eyes of the sculpture have been inlaid with crystal in the "jewel eyes" (gyokugan) technique, which was developed late in the 12th century and became a standard feature in the increasingly "realistic" forms of Kamakura-period sculpture.

Sculpture after the Kamakura period tended to become increasingly standardized, with sculptors producing works largely limited to conventional modes based on the Jōchō or Unkei-Kaikei models. Two celebrated exceptions were the Edo-period (1600–1868) artists Mokujiki Gogyō (see MOKUJIKI) and ENKŪ. See also BUDDHIST ICONOGRAPHY.

budget, national　　　予算

(yosan). The general account budget of the national government's revenues and expenditures is usually regarded as the most important of all government budgets. In addition to this budget, there are also individual budgets for a group of special accounts created to implement government policies. Thirty-eight special accounts were operative in 1991.

Social Security——Various outlays for public assistance programs, social welfare programs, social insurance programs, public health services, and unemployment measures are included in this category. Public assistance provides support to individuals who are unable to meet the cost of living. This assistance includes livelihood aid, educational aid, medical aid, housing aid, vocational aid, maternity aid, and funeral aid. The national government provides 75 percent of this assistance and local governments 25 percent. Social welfare programs are intended to support those people who find it difficult to support themselves and for whom care is necessary, such as children, the aged, and the physically and mentally disabled.

Social insurance can be classified into MEDICAL AND HEALTH INSURANCE, PENSIONS, and unemployment insurance. The health insurance system consists of employee insurance and national health insurance. Employee insurance covers persons employed by firms, while national health insurance covers the self-employed and those without employment. The pension system, similarly, has two classes. National pension insurance provides basic, mandatory coverage for all citizens, while other programs provide additional benefits for private- and public-sector employees. Pensions are paid on the basis of old age, disability, and the death of the insured. Part of the health-insurance and pension systems are administered by the national government, while other programs are administered by local governments. While these programs depend mainly on contributions made by employers and employees, subsidies from the general account are also substantial. Measures to combat tuberculosis, poliomyelitis, and other communicable diseases; cancer; and mental illness are carried out by the public health service (see PUBLIC HEALTH). To cope with unemployment, there are unemployment insurance, unemployment relief works, and special measures to promote employment. See also SOCIAL WELFARE.

General Account Budget, Fiscal 1991

Revenues	Amount (in billions of yen)	Percentage	US dollar value (in billions)
Tax and stamp receipts	61,772.0	87.8	
Monopoly profit	8.6	0.0	
Receipts from government enterprises and properties	19.0	0.0	
Receipts from the sale of government properties	127.2	0.2	
Miscellaneous receipts	2,976.1	4.2	
Public bonds	5,343.0	7.6	
Carried-over surplus	101.4	0.1	
Total	**70,347.4**	**100.0**	**513.1**

Expenditures	Amount (in billions of yen)	Percentage	US dollar value (in billions)
Social security			
Public assistance (aid to needy)	1,074.1		
Social welfare (aid to those incapable of self-support)	2,591.6		
Social insurance (including unemployment insurance)	7,599.6		
Public health service	608.6		
Measures for the unemployed (retraining programs; unemployment relief work projects)	338.4		
Total	12,212.2	17.4	89.1
Education and science			
National government's share of expenses for compulsory education	2,638.2		
Transfers to the National Schools Special Account	1,265.9		
Promotion of science and technology	507.4		
Public school facilities	248.6		
School education assistance (subsidies for school lunches, textbooks, etc)	647.6		
Loan scholarships	86.7		
Total	5,394.4	7.7	39.3
National debt	16,036.0	22.8	117.0
Pensions			
Pensions for civil servants	104.7		
Pensions for veterans and war-bereaved families of soldiers	1,560.8		
Administrative expenses	8.1		
Aid to war-bereaved families of the unrepatriated	134.7		
Total	1,808.4	2.6	13.2
Local allocation tax	15,974.9	22.7	116.5
National defense	4,386.0	6.2	32.0
Public works			
Erosion and flood control	1,146.9		
Road improvement	1,900.0		
Harbors, fishing ports, and airports	544.9		
Housing	808.4		
Public service facilities	1,034.5		
Improvement of conditions for agricultural production	909.8		
Forest roads and water for industrial use	165.8		
Contingency	11.2		
Disaster reconstruction	68.2		
Total	6,589.7	9.4	48.1
Economic cooperation (promotion of foreign trade and economic aid to developing countries)	845.9	1.2	6.2
Measures for small businesses	195.0	0.3	1.4
Measures for energy	592.1	0.8	4.3
Foodstuff control	373.2	0.5	2.7
Transfers to the Industrial Investment Special Account	1,300.0	1.8	9.5
Miscellaneous	4,354.6	6.2	31.8
Contingency for salary increments	135.0	0.2	1.0
Contingency	150.0	0.2	1.1
Grand Total	**70,347.4**	**100.0**	**513.1**

NOTE: Budget estimates are for fiscal year 1991 (1 April 1991–31 March 1992). Totals have been converted into US dollars at the average April 1991 rate of $1.00=¥137.1. Figures may not add up to totals because of rounding.
SOURCE: Ministry of Finance, *Zaisei kin'yū tōkei geppō* (monthly): April 1991.

Public Works—One of the features of Japanese public expenditure is a relatively high level of government investment. The main emphasis since the late 1960s has been on public works aimed at increasing social overhead capital, the development of which had been neglected in comparison with private capital stocks during the rapid growth of the private economy. Social capital includes erosion and flood-control projects; road construction; port, harbor, and airport facilities; housing; public service facilities; improvement of conditions for agricultural production; forest roads; and water supply for industrial use. Of these, the heaviest investment is in road construction, which is managed primarily through the Road Improvement Special Account. The expenditures in this special account consist of expenses for projects under the direct control of the national government, subsidies to local governments, and investments in public expressway corporations. The main sources of revenue for these expenditures are transfers from the general account. The gasoline tax revenue is earmarked for road con-struction and transferred to the special account. See also ROADS; EXPRESSWAYS.

Education—Schools for compulsory education (elementary schools, middle schools, and schools for the blind and the deaf) are operated by local authorities; the national government is required by law to provide one-half of the teachers' salaries in these schools. Other government outlays are expenses for public school facilities, school education assistance, transfers to the National Schools Special Account, loans to students, and the promotion of science and technology by encouraging research and development activities at both governmental and private facilities. The revenue and expenditures of national universities and hospitals attached to national schools are managed through the National Schools Special Account. The expenditures are financed by transfers from the general account and other revenue sources such as tuition fees and hospital revenue.

Transfers to the Foodstuff Control Special Account—The FOODSTUFF CONTROL SPECIAL ACCOUNT was originally created to stabilize the prices of agricultural products by controlling the purchase and sale of rice, wheat, barley, and other commodities. However, sale prices of domestic rice and some other crops are not high enough to cover the government's purchase price and overhead expenses. As a result, a large deficit has developed in this special account, and funds are transferred from the general account each year to cover the deficit. In fiscal 1991, ¥210 billion (US $1.5 billion) was appropriated for this purpose.

Economic Cooperation—In fiscal 1991 the government expenditure for economic cooperation was estimated at ¥846 billion (US $6.2 billion). Government economic assistance to developing countries has increased rapidly.

Local Allocation Tax—This expenditure—which equals 30 percent of income, corporation, liquor, and consumption taxes—is distributed by the national government to assist local governments through a special account for allotment of the local allocation tax and transferred tax. Local gov-

Special accounts for government enterprises	(in billions of yen)
Registration	136.1
Mint Bureau	35.9
Printing Bureau	87.4
National property special consolidation fund	227.4
National Forest Service	789.3
Specific land improvement	479.8
Alcohol monopoly	31.4
Patents	62.5
Harbor improvement	430.6
Airport improvement	471.4
Postal services	6,465.1
Postal saving	13,484.2
Road improvement	3,493.2
Flood control	1,474.1

Special accounts for management	(in billions of yen)
Foreign exchange fund	1,642.8
National schools	2,092.8
National hospitals	894.7
Foodstuff control	4,932.0
Special measures for establishment of farms	32.3
Motorcar inspection and registration	39.8

Special accounts for insurance	(in billions of yen)
Earthquake reinsurance	27.1
Welfare insurance	38,767.5
Seamen's insurance	106.6
National pensions	15,738.3
Agricultural mutual aid reinsurance	124.8
Forest insurance	5.6
Fishing boat reinsurance and fishery mutual aid reinsurance	37.9
Export insurance	1,124.4
Automobile accident compensation reinsurance	720.2
Post office life insurance and postal annuity	6,762.6
Laborers' accident insurance	7,574.0

Special accounts for public investment and loans	(in billions of yen)
Trust Fund Bureau	16,094.8
Industrial investment	1,371.8
Financing for urban development	128.5

Special accounts to consolidate funds	(in billions of yen)
Promotion of electric power resources development	388.6
Allotment of local allocation tax and transferred tax	18,285.4
National debt consolidation fund	44,593.6
Coal and petroleum and alternative energy sources programs	625.0

Total	189,779.2
Total in billions of US dollars	1,384.2

NOTE: Budget estimates are for fiscal year 1991 (1 April 1991–31 March 1992). The total has been converted into US dollars at the average April 1991 rate of $1.00=¥137.1. Figures do not add up to total because of rounding.
SOURCE: Ministry of Finance, *Zaisei kin'yū tōkei geppō* (monthly): April 1991.

ernments can use these grants at their discretion. The national government allocates these grants according to the financial needs of each local government in order to adjust inequality in their revenues. See also FINANCE, LOCAL GOVERNMENT; FISCAL SYSTEM.

bugaku → gagaku

bugei jūhappan 武芸十八般

(the eighteen martial arts). Military techniques considered essential in training SAMURAI in the Edo period (1600–1868). Archery (KYŪDŌ), spear and sword fighting (*yari* and KENDŌ), and HORSEMANSHIP (*bajutsu*) were the principal skills. In most versions of the list the others were: *yawara* (present-day JŪDŌ); swimming (*suieijutsu*); sword drawing (IAI); dagger throwing (*shuriken*); needle spitting (*fukumibari*); spying (NINJUTSU); gunnery (*hōjutsu*); use of the short sword (*tantō*), the NAGINATA (halberd), the KUSARIGAMA (chained sickle), and the staff (*bōjutsu*); and restraining techniques with the JITTE (truncheon), the *mojiri* (a staff with many barbs on one end), and rope (*torite*).

bugyō 奉行

(commissioners). Administrative officials of premodern Japan. The term originally meant "to carry out orders received from a superior." During the Heian period (794–1185) *bugyō* were appointed on a temporary basis to perform ceremonies at the imperial court. MINAMOTO NO YORITOMO, the founder of the Kamakura shogunate (1192–1333), appointed *bugyō* more formally to oversee such administrative functions as the judiciary, shogunal household affairs, temples and shrines, and civil engineering projects. Under the Muromachi shogunate (1338–1573) *bugyō* continued to supervise administrative and judicial affairs. The national unifier TOYOTOMI HIDEYOSHI had a board of Five Commissioners (Gobugyō) to assist him in implementing policies and appointed lesser-ranking *bugyō* to carry out special projects such as land surveys and road construction. When civil and judicial administration was rationalized under the Tokugawa shogunate (1603–1867), *bugyō* became middle-ranking administrators with well-defined duties. Most famous were the commissioners of temples and shrines (JISHA BUGYŌ), the Edo city commissioners (EDO MACHI BUGYŌ), and the commissioners of finance (KANJŌ BUGYŌ). After the Meiji Restoration of 1868 the title was no longer used. See also SAMBUGYŌ; GAIKOKU BUGYŌ.

Building Research Institute 建築研究所

(Kenchiku Kenkyūjo). National institute for research on building technology. Located in the city of Tsukuba, Ibaraki Prefecture, the institute was founded in 1946 to research building construction and disaster prevention techniques suited to Japan's geological and climatic conditions. The institute also engages in city planning.

bukan 武鑑

Registers containing information on *daimyō* and *hatamoto* (direct shogunate vassals) published during the Edo period (1600–1868). A daimyō was listed with his domain (*han*), assessed land value (*kokudaka*), and such information as office, castle, genealogy, and term of attendance in Edo (now Tōkyō). A *hatamoto* was listed with his fief (*chigyō*) and official rank. The first of these registers, the *Chitai fukenki*, appeared in the Kan'ei era (1624–44). In Edo the *Shōtoku bukan*, which first appeared in 1716, was published annually until the end of the Edo period, as was Kyōto's *Taisei bukan*, which first appeared during the Gembun era (1736–41). Invaluable as a source of information on the changing status of daimyō and *hatamoto*, various *bukan* were assembled in 1935 and 1936 in the 13-volume *Daibukan* by Hashimoto Hiroshi.

buke densō 武家伝奏

(court liaison officers). Imperial officers who transmitted messages between court officials and the shogunate in the Muromachi (1333–1568) and Edo (1600–1868) periods; first established at the time of the KEMMU RESTORATION (1333). During the Edo period the title was normally held by two court nobles whose appointment was subject to shogunal approval. At times they exercised considerable influence as political mediators and negotiators.

bukehō 武家法

(warrior class law). Regulations and laws (*hō*) applied to the warrior class (*buke*). Unlike laws for court nobles (*kugehō*) and laws governing land rights (*honjohō*)—both of which developed from the RITSURYŌ SYSTEM—*bukehō* was originally customary law based on the family system and the hierarchy of the military class. With the consolidation of WARRIOR GOVERNMENT after the 12th century, it gradually became the paramount law of the land. *Bukehō* was first codified by the KAMAKURA SHOGUNATE (1192–1333) in the GOSEIBAI SHIKIMOKU (1232). This code was inherited, with modifications (see KEMMU SHIKIMOKU), by the Muromachi shogunate (1338–1573). During the Sengoku period (1467–1568) it served as the basis for domainal codes (BUNKOKUHŌ). By the 15th century *bukehō* had begun to include regulations binding the common people. Under the Tokugawa shogunate (1603–1867) extensive regulations for farmers and townspeople appeared in such shogunal codes as BUKE SHOHATTO (1615, Laws for the Military Houses). *Bukehō* disappeared at the time of the Meiji Restoration (1868).

buke seiji → warrior government

Buke Shohatto 武家諸法度

(Laws for the Military Houses). Codes of conduct issued by the TOKUGAWA SHOGUNATE

(1603–1867) to strengthen control over the *daimyō* (domainal lords). After establishing hegemony over his rivals in 1600, TOKUGAWA IEYASU sought to strengthen his control through numerous regulations. Both Ieyasu's emphasis on formulating codes and the specific contents of the 13 articles of his Buke Shohatto reflected his belief that it was important to define relationships clearly, to assure all honest people a proper social place, and, once the great pattern of society had been properly arranged, to prevent any disruption of that order. Compiled mainly by the Zen monk SŪDEN, the Confucian scholar HAYASHI RAZAN, and scholars from the major Zen temples (GOZAN) of Kyōto, the Buke Shohatto were issued by Ieyasu's successor, TOKUGAWA HIDETADA, after the defeat of TOYOTOMI HIDEYORI in 1615. The codes were later revised and expanded, but the hortatory and prohibitory nature of the guidelines remained unaltered.

The importance of the Buke Shohatto was more symbolic than administrative, and it was increasingly ignored during the second half of the Edo period (1600–1868). By then, however, its basic prohibitions had long since been internalized by the daimyō and even incorporated into their own domainal codes. Moreover, the actual administration of justice rested not on these guidelines but on an extensive corpus of specific laws and precedents (*osadamegaki* and OFUREGAKI), which were compiled and updated periodically throughout the period.

Bukōzan 武甲山

Mountain south of Chichibu, western Saitama Prefecture, central Honshū. Formed almost entirely of limestone, its shape has been destroyed by quarrying. Height: 1,295 m (4,249 ft).

bullfighting 闘牛

(*tōgyū*; also known as *ushizumō* and *tsukiai*). A Japanese rural sport at least 300 years old that is still practiced in several traditional bullfighting towns. Unlike Spanish bullfighting, *tōgyū* pits bull against bull. Standing nearby, handlers called *seko* hold the heads of the bulls down in optimum attack position while delivering a steady and lively stream of directive encouragements. Bloodshed is rare, and losers live to fight another day. A match ends when one bull is driven to its knees or turns and runs.

bullying いじめ

(*ijime*). Bullying among schoolchildren became a serious social problem in Japan in the 1970s and 1980s. In a survey conducted by the Tōkyō Metropolitan Board of Education, bullying is defined as "behavior directed against someone weaker than oneself; objectionable behavior in which physical or psychological attacks are carried out repeatedly, causing deep suffering to the victim." The spread of bullying among schoolchildren was seen as one symptom—along with SCHOOL VIOLENCE, refusal to attend school (see SCHOOL ALLERGY), and other misconduct—of a so-called blight affecting the Japanese educational system. Since 1986 the incidence of bullying has decreased, but the problem has shifted from physical violence to verbal abuse and the practice of ostracizing unpopular students. There has been no clear explanation for the frequent occurrence of bullying. According to one theory, urbanization had led to a decrease in the amount of open space for children to play in; as a result, children were being deprived of

bullfighting Also known as "bull sumō," Japanese bullfighting is rich with pageantry and language similar to that of *sumō* wrestling.

the opportunity to play together in groups and hence of an outlet needed for healthy emotional development.

Bumbuku chagama 分福茶釜

(The Miraculous Teakettle). Folktale of an animal repaying human kindness. A poor man saves a TANUKI (raccoon dog, a badgerlike creature), which, in gratitude, changes itself into a teakettle so that the man can sell it to a temple. Hurt by the fire, or polished too hard, the kettle returns to its original form and runs back to the man. The *tanuki* then transforms itself into a girl and is sold as a prostitute, and so on, each time fleeing back to the man and making him richer. The story is found throughout Japan in many variations, often retold as the history of a particular teakettle treasured by a temple or family. *Bumbuku* is an onomatopoeia for the sputtering of a teakettle.

Bummei ittōki 文明一統記

(On the Unity of Learning and Culture). A one-volume handbook on statecraft, characterized by moral idealism, written by ICHIJŌ KANEYOSHI in the middle of the Bummei era (1469–87). It was written at the request of shōgun Ashikaga Yoshihisa (1465–89; r 1474–89) for his own moral and political guidance.

bummei kaika → Meiji Enlightenment

Bummeiron no gairyaku 文明論之概略

(Outline of a Theory of Civilization). A work of political philosophy published in 1875 by FUKUZAWA YUKICHI, advocating emulation of Western spirit as a means to modernization. The book was Fukuzawa's most sustained philosophical contribution to the encouragement of Westernization, overshadowing his best sellers GAKUMON NO SUSUME and SEIYŌ JIJŌ.

bun 分

A position and set of duties assigned to each member of society in relation to other members thereof. The closest English equivalent is "status" or "role." The term is used either as an independent noun, as in *bun o wakimaeru* ("know one's place"), or as part of a compound noun like *mibun* ("one's social standing").

The concept of *bun* has been important in Japanese society especially since the Edo period (1600–1868), when each person was assigned to a well-defined position in the feudal hierarchy. During the Muromachi period (1333–1568), upward social mobility had been possible, but the Tokugawa rulers froze the social hierarchy, and movement between social classes became virtually impossible. This Tokugawa practice seems to have been responsible for making the Japanese highly status-conscious concerning family background and occupation. Even today, when social mobility is common and most Japanese consider themselves part of a homogeneous middle class, a person's status will in the end be determined by such factors as his family background, education, occupation, age, and sex.

buna 樸

(beech). *Fagus crenata*. A deciduous tree of the family Fagaceae that grows wild in mountainous regions throughout Japan. The *buna* is typical of the various deciduous species that grow in Japan's temperate zone. The tree is about 30 meters (98.4 ft) high and may grow to a diameter of more than 1.5

meters (4.9 ft). Its main trunk grows upright and its bark is smooth and gray. The leaves are ovately elliptical and alternate. The pale yellowish green unisexual flowers bloom in May. The nuts are conical with three ridges and ripen in October. Because of its fine texture the wood of the *buna* is an excellent material for furniture, crossties, and matchsticks. The bark is used to make dyes.

bunchi seigen rei 分地制限令

(laws restricting the partitioning of farmlands). Enacted by the Tokugawa shogunate during the Edo period (1600–1868). Along with the TAHATA EITAI BAIBAI KINSHI REI (Prohibition Against Permanent Alienation of Farmlands) of 1643, these were the most fundamental land laws of the shogunate. *Bunchi* is the practice whereby farmers divided their landholdings among their heirs. Since unrestricted *bunchi* would result in a continual subdivision of farmlands, making it difficult for farmers to make a living and for the government to collect taxes, the shogunate periodically issued *bunchi seigen rei* from 1673 on. Only village heads owning lands with yields of more than 20 *koku* (1 *koku* = about 180 liters or 5 US bushels) of rice and other farmers owning lands with yields of more than 10 *koku* were allowed to partition their holdings. In 1713 partitioning was permitted to village heads and other farmers having lands of one *chō* (1 *chō* = about 1 hectare or 2.5 acres) or more in area or with yields of more than 10 *koku*. The *dai*-

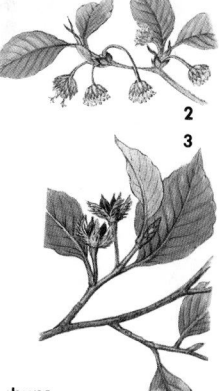

buna
1 A grove of beech trees in May on a patchy field of snow in northern Honshū.
2 A flowering branch with female (far left) and male flowers.
3 Beech nuts ripen in October.

Bungakuza A 1983 performance of this theater company's hit "A Woman's Life." Actress Sugimura Haruko, for whom the play was originally written in 1945, is pictured with Kitamura Kazuo.

myō also enacted similar laws in their domains. This law was apparently abolished in 1872.

Bunchō → Tani Bunchō

Bungakukai 文学界

(The Literary World). 1. Small coterie monthly (January 1893–January 1898) of vast literary influence, considered to have founded the turn-of-the-century romantic literary movement. Members included KITAMURA TŌKOKU, SHIMAZAKI TŌSON, and UEDA BIN and, later, HIGUCHI ICHIYŌ, TAYAMA KATAI, and YANAGITA KUNIO. Tōkoku's poetry and criticism were the journal's central feature until his death in 1894; Ichiyō's stories and Tōson's poems are considered to represent *Bungakukai*'s subsequent evolution. 2. Coterie journal. Japan's leading coterie journal for its first 10 years, it developed into a major commercial literary monthly after World War II. Publication began in October 1933, and, except for a few brief periods in its history, it has been published by BUNGEI SHUNJŪ, LTD. Original members were KOBAYASHI HIDEO, KAWABATA YASUNARI, UNO KŌJI, HIROTSU KAZUO, HAYASHI FUSAO, TAKEDA RINTARŌ, and Fukada Kyūya (1903–71); later members included YOKOMITSU RIICHI, IBUSE MASUJI, KAWAKAMI TETSUTARŌ, HORI TATSUO, ŌOKA SHŌHEI, ABE TOMOJI, SHIMAKI KENSAKU, and FUNAHASHI SEIICHI. After 1947 new members included NIWA FUMIO, ISHIKAWA TATSUZŌ, DAZAI OSAMU, and SAKAGUCHI ANGO. Among contemporary novelists it has published YOSHIYUKI JUNNOSUKE, KOJIMA NOBUO, ENDŌ SHŪSAKU, ŌE KENZABURŌ, and ISHIHARA SHINTARŌ.

Bungakuza 文学座

Theater company founded in Tōkyō in 1937 by the playwrights KISHIDA KUNIO, KUBOTA MANTARŌ, and SHISHI BUNROKU. The Bungakuza was exceptional among theater troupes of the 1930s and 1940s in that it escaped official suppression and remained active throughout the war; this was due to the group's announced intention of providing "lighthearted entertainment," a message that government censors interpreted to mean nonleftist activity. After the war, under the leadership of the actress SUGIMURA HARUKO and the director Inui Ichirō (b 1916), the Bungakuza produced such hits as *Onna no isshō* (1945; tr *A Woman's Life*, 1961–62) and *A Streetcar Named Desire*. The Bungakuza continues to be active as one of Japan's major theater groups.

Bungei 文芸

(The Literary Arts). 1. Popular literary monthly magazine established at the beginning of the so-called period of literary revival that followed the suppression of the PROLETARIAN LITERATURE MOVEMENT. *Bungei* was first published by Kaizōsha from No-

vember 1933 to July 1944, with such contributors as ISHIZAKA YŌJIRŌ, DAZAI OSAMU, OKAMOTO KANOKO, HAYASHI FUMIKO, TAKAMI JUN, NAKANO SHIGEHARU, ODA SAKUNOSUKE, KUBOKAWA TSURUJIRŌ, KAMEI KATSUICHIRŌ, HAYASHI FUSAO, UNO KŌJI, and MIYAMOTO YURIKO. When Kaizōsha was closed by the authorities in 1944, *Bungei*'s name was transferred to Kawade Shobō by the Japan Publishers' Association.

2. Leading literary magazine published since November 1944 by Kawade Shobō. Among its early contributors were SATŌ HARUO, KAWABATA YASUNARI, DAZAI OSAMU, IBUSE MASUJI, and MISHIMA YUKIO. From about 1950 *Bungei* introduced such men of letters as NOMA HIROSHI, NAKAMURA SHIN'ICHIRŌ, and NAKAMURA MITSUO. Publication ceased in 1957. It was revived in 1962 and has continued to publish original works and criticism of wide-ranging interest in the field of contemporary literature. Notable contributors have included TAKAHASHI KAZUMI, ISHIHARA SHINTARŌ, MITA MASAHIRO, and KARA JŪRŌ.

Bungei jidai 文芸時代

(Literary Age). Literary magazine published from October 1924 to May 1927. Members of this small coterie monthly included YOKOMITSU RIICHI, KAWABATA YASUNARI, KON TŌKŌ, and KATAOKA TEPPEI. Opposed to the so-called Japanese NATURALISM, its members disclaimed any thought of starting a literary movement, yet were credited with having created the neoimpressionist or SHINKANKAKU SCHOOL. *Bungei jidai* published little of lasting literary value, but it was highly significant because it offered an alternative to the growing PROLETARIAN LITERATURE MOVEMENT.

Bungei kurabu 文芸倶楽部

(Literary Club). First mass-market literary magazine in Japan; published by HAKUBUNKAN, a leading Tōkyō publishing house, from January 1895 to January 1933. *Bungei kurabu* showed the strong influence of the KEN'YŪSHA coterie of writers. Among its numerous early contributors were KAWAKAMI BIZAN, HIROTSU RYŪRŌ, KOSUGI TENGAI, IZUMI KYŌKA, and HIGUCHI ICHIYŌ. It also welcomed contributions of poetry and prose from readers. It was, together with SHINSHŌSETSU, the leading fiction magazine of the period. Later it put out special editions on popular oral storytelling traditions such as KŌDAN and RAKUGO and by 1907 had become transformed into a popular entertainment magazine. After an attempt to repeat earlier successes by capitalizing on the growing popularity of mystery and detective stories by writers such as EDOGAWA RAMPO, it eventually ceased publication.

Bungei sensen 文芸戦線

(Literary Battlefront). Important leftist literary monthly published from June 1924 to July 1932, first by Bungei Sensen Sha and later by the Labor-Farmer Artists League (Rōnō Geijutsuka Remmei). *Bungei sensen* became a prime force in the PROLETARIAN LITERATURE MOVEMENT. Succeeding TANE MAKU HITO, the *Bungei sensen* group originally included Komaki Ōmi (1894–1978), AONO SUEKICHI, MAEDAKŌ HIROICHIRŌ, and HIRABAYASHI HATSUNOSUKE, who were later joined by HAYAMA YOSHIKI, HAYASHI FUSAO, KUROSHIMA DENJI, KURAHARA KOREHITO, HIRABAYASHI TAIKO, and others. In June 1927, 16 *Bungei sensen* adherents withdrew from the Nihon Puroretaria Geijutsu Remmei (Japan Proletarian Arts League). Among these

16, Aono, Hayama, Hayashi, Maedakō, Kurahara, and others immediately formed the Labor-Farmer Artists League and made *Bungei sensen* its organ. Later that same year this group split; some members withdrew to form the Zen'ei Geijutsuka Dōmei (Avant-Garde Artists Union). The remaining members used *Bungei sensen* to voice their criticism of the Zen Nihon Musansha Geijutsu Remmei (All-Japan Proletarian Art League; better known by the acronym NAPF, from its Esperanto name, and its organ SENKI. *Bungei sensen* played a crucial role in the history of proletarian literature and introduced many new writers; its peak circulation was 20,000.

Bungei shunjū 文芸春秋

Major general-interest monthly magazine, founded by KIKUCHI KAN in 1923 as a literary journal. Members of its managing coterie included YOKOMITSU RIICHI and AKUTAGAWA RYŪNOSUKE. In 1926 *Bungei shunjū* shifted to a general-interest format, although it still retained a strong literary flavor. Since 1935 it has announced the winners of the prestigious AKUTAGAWA PRIZE. It was also the first magazine to publish transcripts of roundtable discussions (*zadankai*), now a popular format in Japanese journalism. It pioneered investigative reporting in Japan in the 1960s and early 1970s. It has launched the careers of many reporters since the initiation of the prize for nonfiction writing named for ŌYA SŌICHI. Circulation was 750,000 in 1990.

Bungei Shunjū, Ltd [株]文芸春秋

(Bungei Shunjū). Publishing house begun by the writer KIKUCHI KAN in January 1923 with the publication of BUNGEI SHUNJŪ, a primarily literary magazine. In 1935 he set up the prestigious AKUTAGAWA PRIZE and NAOKI PRIZE in honor of the writers AKUTAGAWA RYŪNOSUKE and NAOKI SANJŪGO. Since World War II, the company has expanded its publishing activities; besides *Bungei shunjū* it also publishes *Shūkan bunshun* (Weekly Bunshun), *Shokun!* (Friends!), and the Bunshun Bunko series of literary works.

Bungo Channel 豊後水道

(Bungo Suidō). Between western Shikoku and eastern Kyūshū, connecting the Inland Sea with the Pacific Ocean. The climate is hot and humid; subtropical plants grow on the islands in the channel. Fish are plentiful. Length: 50 km (31 mi); width: 35 km (22 mi); deepest point: 418 m (1,371 ft).

Bungo Takada 豊後高田[市]

City in northern Ōita Prefecture, Kyūshū, on the Kunisaki Peninsula. It is the political and economic center of the peninsular area. Principal products are rice, mandarin oranges, and vegetables. The temples Fukiji and Maki no Ōdō house Buddhist images that date to the Heian period (794–1185). Pop: 20,086.

bunjinga 文人画

(literati painting; Ch: *wenrenhua* or *wen-jenhua*). Also known as *nanga*, or "Southern painting." School of Japanese painting of the 18th and 19th centuries based in theory on the Chinese tradition of the scholar-amateur artist (*wenren* or *wen-jen*; J: *bunjin*). The artists had in common an admiration for Chinese culture, particularly the literati painting of the Yuan (Yüan), Ming, and Qing (Ch'ing) dynasties (13th–20th centuries). By the 18th century Chinese studies had gained considerable prestige in Japan, and, though the shogunate severely limited foreign trade, some Chinese paintings came to Japan through the port of Nagasaki. (Such foreign influences gave rise to the so-called NAGASAKI SCHOOL.)

In China, the literati style comprised landscape painting by scholar-gentlemen—proficient in the skills of calligraphy, poetry, and painting—who disdained any display of virtuoso brushwork as characteristic of the purely technical proficiency of academic painting. The subtlety of line of their works could not, however, be faithfully reproduced in the woodblock-print reproductions in books, which were the major source of influence upon Japanese *bunjin* artists. From the start the latter's work had a remarkably eclectic and distinctively Japanese character. The Japanese *bunjin* understood the literati tradition as a rejection of academic styles, specifically the officially recognized styles of the KANŌ SCHOOL and the TOSA SCHOOL. However, they emulated not only Chinese literati painting but also Chinese academic painting and a variety of indigenous art trends, especially that of the RIMPA decorative tradition of the 17th to 19th centuries. The Japanese *bunjin* generally concentrated on traditional Chinese themes such as landscapes, birds and flowers, and the "Four Gentlemen" (SHI-KUNSHI: plum, orchid, chrysanthemum, and bamboo). Compositions were created with layers of brush strokes, and ink tones applied in a wide variety of combinations and patterns. Inscriptions were an important element of many works.

The first generation of Japanese *bunjin* consisted of GION NANKAI, SAKAKI HYAKUSEN, and YANAGISAWA KIEN. The second generation of *bunjin* painters included IKE NO TAIGA; his wife, IKE NO GYOKURAN; and his disciples TOTOKI BAIGAI, Kimura Kenkadō (1736–1802), Kuwayama Gyokushū (1743–99), and Noro Kaiseki (1747–1828).

Taiga's close contemporary was the acclaimed *bunjin* artist and *haikai* (see HAIKU) poet Yosa BUSON. Buson's followers KI BAITEI and the MARUYAMA-SHIJŌ SCHOOL artist MATSUMURA GOSHUN also became well-known *bunjin* artists. YOKOI KINKOKU also demonstrated in his dramatic style a special appreciation of Buson. Succeeding generations of *bunjinga* artists included Kyōto-based painters URAGAMI GYOKUDŌ, AOKI MOKUBEI, OKADA BEISANJIN and his son OKADA HANKŌ, URAGAMI SHUNKIN, YAMAMOTO BAIITSU, TANO-MURA CHIKUDEN, NAKABAYASHI CHIKUTŌ, and RAI SAN'YŌ.

Works by the two leading Edo (now Tōkyō) *bunjin* artists of the late 18th and the early 19th centuries, TANI BUNCHŌ and WATANABE KAZAN, display influences from Western styles, Japanese styles, and the Chinese BIRD-AND-FLOWER PAINTING manner of SHEN NANPIN (Shen Nan-p'in). The Kyōto artist TOMIOKA TESSAI, who died in 1924, is sometimes hailed as the last member of the *bunjinga* school.

Bunka and Bunsei eras

文化文政時代

(Bunka Bunsei *jidai*). Strictly, the years 1804–18 (Bunka era) and 1818–31 (Bunsei era); more broadly, the long rule (1787–1837) of the shōgun TOKUGAWA IENARI as well as the years when Ienari ruled as retired shōgun (ŌGOSHO) until his death in 1841. The Bunka and Bunsei eras were a time of political stability and economic prosperity, but signs of the catastrophe that was to overtake the Tokugawa shogunate (1603–1867) from the 1830s onward were already apparent.

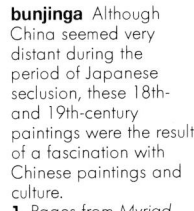

Despite the KANSEI REFORMS (1787–93), shogunal mismanagement of the economy hastened the breakdown of the BAKUHAN SYSTEM. Although rural prosperity remained generally high, peasant uprisings (HYAKUSHŌ IKKI) and urban riots (UCHIKOWASHI) became more frequent. The intrusion of foreign ships into Japanese waters threatened the policy of NATIONAL SECLUSION.

This period is remembered as one of cultural and artistic brilliance. The culture of the townsmen (*chōnin bunka*) had been centered in the Kyōto-Ōsaka region; during this time it was focused in Edo (now Tōkyō). Novels, plays, *ukiyo-e* prints, and *haiku* all flourished. The coming of foreign ships brought about a renewed interest in WESTERN LEARNING, particularly in natural history, economics, and medicine. Knowledge of the outside world resulted in criticism of the shogunate's isolationist policies. As the weaknesses of the Tokugawa shogunate were laid bare, there was also an upsurge in classical Japanese learning (KOKUGAKU, or National Learning).

Bunka Fashion College

文化服装学院

(Bunka Fukusō Gakuin). Private coeducational fashion training school in Shibuya Ward, Tōkyō. Established in 1919 by Namiki Isaburō as a small academy of dressmaking, it later expanded and was given its current name in 1936. Bunka Fashion College has four courses of instruction: general fashion, fashion technology, fashion buying and merchandising, and fashion craft. Of the 6,024 students enrolled in Bunka Fashion College in 1988, 273 were from overseas. The well-known designers TAKADA KENZŌ, YAMAMOTO YŌJI, and KOSHINO JUNKO are among the school's alumni.

Bunka Kunshō→Order of Culture

Bunka no Hi→holidays, national

Bunka shūreishū
文華秀麗集

Early-Heian-period (794–1185) imperial anthology of classical Chinese poetry (*kanshi*); compiled in 818 by FUJIWARA NO FUYUTSUGU and others. It contains some 140 poems in the Chinese *shi* (*shih*) form arranged topically according to the classification scheme found in the *Wen xuan* (*Wen hsüan*; J: *Monzen*), a 6th-century Chinese anthology of poetry and prose.

bunke→honke and bunke

bunjinga Although China seemed very distant during the period of Japanese seclusion, these 18th- and 19th-century paintings were the result of a fascination with Chinese paintings and culture.
1 Pages from *Myriad Subjects in Single Strokes*, a sketchbook by Watanabe Kazan. 1818. Light colors on paper. 27 × 36 cm. Tahara Museum, Aichi Prefecture.
2 Yosa Buson's *Pleasure of Autumn* from *Jūben jūgi* (The Ten Conveniences and Ten Pleasures) by Ike no Taiga and Buson. 1771. Colors and ink on paper. 18 × 18 cm. Kawabata Yasunari Kinen Kai, Kanagawa Prefecture. National Treasure.

bunkobon→paperback books

bunkokuhō
分国法

(domanial codes). The laws (*hō*) by which SENGOKU DAIMYŌ of the Sengoku period (1467–1568) controlled their territories (*bunkoku*). Also known as Sengoku *kahō* (Sengoku house laws). These were often extensions of old family laws (KAKUN) but were also strongly influenced by the laws of the shogunate, particularly by the GOSEIBAI SHIKIMOKU (1232) drawn up by the Kamakura shogunate (1192–1333).

The most important regulations concerned the control of vassals. The lord reserved the right to interfere with a vassal's succession to an estate or family name and also to approve his marriage or decision to take holy orders. There were also restrictions on travel and prohibitions concerning the transmission of messages to other domains. Equally stringent regulations applied to commoners, who were forbidden to cultivate lands in secret or to move or run away.

Some representative domanial codes are the ŌUCHIKE KABEGAKI (1459–95) of the Ōuchi family, the Imagawa Kana Mokuroku

► The largeness of scale that is sometimes achieved in *bunraku* performances is best exemplified by this scene from the tragedy *Imoseyama onna teikin* (1771), which is reminiscent of *Romeo and Juliet*. At the center of the stage runs a river separating the two enemy houses. The chanter at the left provides the voices for the girl's house at left; the chanter at right, for the boy's. National Bunraku Theater, Ōsaka.

▲ In the eighth act of *Keisei Awa no Naruto* (1768), a mother (right) recognizes a chance visitor (left) as her long-lost daughter but is forced by circumstances to send her away without revealing their true relationship.

► The third act of *Ichinotani futaba gunki* (1751). The principal operator wears special elevated clogs.

▲ In the final scene of *Datemusume koi no higanoko* (1773), the heroine rushes out on a snowy night to save her lover.

(1526), the SHINGEN KAHŌ (1547; 1554) of Takeda Shingen, the YOSHIHARU SHIKIMOKU (1567), and the YŪKIKE HATTO (1556) of Yūki Masakatsu. Many of these were incorporated in laws of the Tokugawa shogunate (1603–1867). See also BUKEHŌ.

Bunkyō Ward　　　　　文京区

(Bunkyō Ku). One of the 23 wards of Tōkyō. On the eastern edge of the Musashino Plateau. A residential area with many schools and universities, including Tōkyō University, as well as printing and publishing firms. Popular sights include the Kōrakuen Garden, Rikugien Garden, and Koishikawa Botanic Garden. Pop: 181,269.

bunraku　　　　　文楽

The professional puppet theater of Japan. Like the KABUKI theater, *bunraku* is an enduring form of art developed by city-dwelling commoners of the Edo period (1600–1868).

The term bunraku is of relatively recent origin. Of the many puppet theaters of the Edo period, only that known as Bunraku-za, organized in the early 19th century by Uemura Banrakuken in Ōsaka, survived commercially in modern Japan, and bunraku came to mean "professional puppet theater." The more precise term, *ayatsuri jōruri*, denotes the component elements of the theater: *ayatsuri* means "puppetry," and *jōruri* refers to the dramatic text and the art of chanting it. Historically, it was the fortuitous joining of two independent art forms, puppetry and *jōruri*, that gave birth to bunraku.

Conventions of the Theater—The bunraku theater presents dramas both serious and entertaining, as well as beautifully choreographed dances, for an audience primarily of adults with cultivated sensibilities. The performance is a composite of four elements: the puppets, which are approximately one-half to two-thirds life size; the movement given to the puppets by their operators; the vocal delivery by the *tayū* (chanter); and the rhythmical musical accompaniment provided by the player of the three-stringed SHAMISEN. To add to the complexity of the performance, each puppet portraying a major character is operated jointly by three men.

Bunraku puppets are not operated by strings. With his left arm and hand the *omozukai* (principal operator) supports the puppet and manipulates the mechanisms that control the movable eyelids, eyeballs, eyebrows, and mouth; with his right hand he operates the puppet's right arm. The *hidarizukai* (first assistant) functions solely

to operate the puppet's left arm, and the *ashizukai* (second assistant) operates the puppet's legs. Most female puppets do not have legs, for Japanese women generally wore flowing robes of ankle length or longer, which concealed the lower body. The movements of a female puppet's legs are simulated through manipulating and shaping the lower part of the *kimono.* In the play *Sonezaki shinjū* (1703; tr *The Love Suicides at Sonezaki,* 1961), however, a turn in the plot hinges on the hero's caressing the heroine's foot, which the audience must see. In this instance, a reproduction of a foot is held so as to protrude from the hem of her kimono.

The puppeteers are usually dressed in black robes of coarse weave; the assistants wear black hoods over their heads to become "invisible" in the audience's eyes. Although the *omozukai* may be similarly hooded— usually in scenes that require the utmost delicacy in the expression of emotions—he is most often seen full face by the audience, for he is a celebrity in the theatrical world. At times bedecked in a robe of lustrous white silk and ceremonial vest of brilliant hue, he becomes an important part of the total visual spectacle.

A single *tayū* speaks on behalf of all puppets on the stage—men, women, and children—and so his voice must cover an extremely broad range, from a raspy bass to a silky falsetto. Several *tayū* may perform simultaneously, as in the spectacular opening scene of the best known of all bunraku plays, *Kanadehon chūshingura* (1748; tr *Chūshingura: The Treasury of Loyal Retainers,* 1971). Pageantry is, in the main, a borrowing from the kabuki theater.

A distinguishing aural feature of bunraku is the melodious, deep-toned thrumming of the solo *shamisen,* which contrasts with the lively, high-pitched tone of the tenor *shamisen* of the kabuki theater. In kabuki, an ensemble of 10 or more *shamisen* may play in unison or heterophonically in extravaganzas. In bunraku, the exceptional use of a *shamisen* ensemble may occur when a kabuki spectacle is adapted for performance in the puppet theater.

In bunraku, the puppets' movements must be synchronized with the *tayū*'s chanting and the *shamisen* accompaniment. Seldom is there visual contact between the puppeteers onstage and the *tayū* and *shamisen* player, who face the audience from the *yuka,* an elevated platform projecting from the stage. The *shamisen* player, by his strumming, normally dictates the pace of the narrative and the timing of the action.

Early History——The earliest extant written reference to puppetry in Japan dates from the 11th century. Doubtless even earlier, itinerant hunters and their women earned money by entertaining in the cities, the men

presenting episodic plays with small puppets that they operated with their hands and the women working as prostitutes (see PUPPET THEATER). Eventually a large number settled in Sanjō on the island of Awaji (Awajishima), which became known as the birthplace of professional puppetry.

During the 15th and 16th centuries, blind bards (BIWA HŌSHI) garbed in Buddhist robes were chanting historic episodes described in the *Heike monogatari* (13th century; tr *The Tale of the Heike,* 1975, 1988). These bards accompanied themselves on the BIWA (lute), an instrument that had originated in Persia. Other entertainers chanted tales taken from the *Gikeiki* (15th century; tr *Yoshitsune,* 1966) and the *Soga monogatari* (15th century; tr *The Tale of the Soga Brothers,* 1987).

The chanting style of medieval narratives changed remarkably in the 16th century with the evolution of a style of chanting called *jōruri.* Also around that time the *shamisen* was imported into Japan from Okinawa and came to be preferred over the lute by chanters of *jōruri.* Shamisen players composed new melodies that, in turn, influenced the style of *jōruri* chanting. This collaboration was the beginning of bunraku, which caught the fancy of the townspeople—commoners who were low on the social ladder but who came gradually to dominate the economy, art, and material culture of the new era. With little access to the NŌ drama, by then largely restricted to *samurai* and others of the upper class, the townspeople welcomed the colorful, quick-paced, lively spectacle of the new popular theater— first kabuki, and then bunraku.

Stages of Development——By the mid-17th century the puppet theater was flourishing in Ōsaka and Kyōto, where puppeteers and chanters of *jōruri* were reaching new heights of artistry. Bunraku became the rage in 1685, when the *tayū* TAKEMOTO GIDAYŪ I of Ōsaka garnered accolades for the virile beauty of his chanting style. It was his collaboration, however, with the greatest playwright of the Edo period, CHIKAMATSU MONZAEMON, that led to the transformation of bunraku from popular entertainment to artistic theater.

Chikamatsu employed the imagery, diction, and literary techniques of classical prose, drama, and poetry in writing plays that focused on both historical and contemporary subjects and that emphasized prevalent codes of morality and ethics as thematic material. The success of his *Love Suicides at Sonezaki* in 1703 started a vogue for dramas treating love affairs between merchants and prostitutes. In most of these the tragedy results from the inability of a pair of lovers to resolve the conflict between accepted social codes and their own emotions.

Originally in bunraku, only the puppets

were seen by the audience; all performers were hidden from view by a curtain stretched across the stage. The puppets were held aloft and operated by hands thrust up through the skirt. When *Love Suicides at Sonezaki* was presented, the puppeteer operated the doll of the heroine in front of the curtain. His good looks are said to have contributed to the success of this daring experiment, which gave rise to the tradition of including the doll operators in the visual aspect of bunraku. In 1705 Takemoto Gidayū chanted one act of a new play in full view of the audience; this marked the beginning of the tradition of including the *tayū* and the *shamisen* player in the total visual spectacle of the theater.

Many of the techniques used in bunraku today were developed after Chikamatsu's death. In 1727 puppets acquired movable eyelids and mouths and prehensile hands. In 1728 the *tayū* and *shamisen* player were elevated from a position below stage center to the *yuka.* The puppet operated by three men was introduced in 1734, and by 1736 puppets could roll their eyes and move their eyebrows. Set designs and stage mechanisms became far more elaborate.

These innovations enabled bunraku to compete successfully with kabuki, which enjoyed a surge in popularity with its host of talented actors and repertory of delightful plays (many of them borrowed from bunraku). Kabuki actors were influenced by the style of the bunraku *tayū* and even imitated the stylized gestures of the puppets. If a certain innovation in a kabuki production delighted its audience, the bunraku producers would incorporate it into their own productions.

The Final Stage——Gradually overshadowed by kabuki, bunraku went into a decline after the mid-18th century even though its performers attained new heights of artistry and skill. With the Japanese welcoming Western forms of theatrical art and developing their own "modern" theater, bunraku fared poorly in the competition to attract audiences. After Japan's defeat in World War II, bunraku languished as many Japanese turned away from the traditional aspects of their own culture, and in the early 1960s it tottered on the verge of commercial extinction. It has survived largely with government support and the establishment of the NATIONAL THEATER in Tōkyō and the NATIONAL BUNRAKU THEATER in Ōsaka. Because of the meagerness of the rewards, few youngsters are willing to endure the many years of training needed to acquire the skills of a professional. Traditionally, a puppeteer must spend 10 years operating the legs and 10
Continued on page 146➤

1 In front of Ohatsu, Tokubei (center) demands that Kuheiji return his money. Instead, Kuheiji accuses Tokubei of fraud, and he and his friends beat the hapless young man.

2 Ohatsu spots Tokubei, his face covered by a wicker hat, and slips out to embrace him while trying to remain out of sight of the people of Temma House.

5 Having slipped out of Temma House undetected, the distraught young lovers bid life a tearful farewell on Umeda Bridge.

The Love Suicides at Sonezaki

Based on an actual incident that occurred in 1703, *The Love Suicides at Sonezaki* won Chikamatsu Monzaemon his reputation as a playwright. First performed in Ōsaka at the theater Takemotoza a month after the tragedy, it revived the theater's fortunes and, unfortunately, apparently also inspired a rash of actual suicides.

The three-act play tells the story of Tokubei, the nephew of a soy sauce merchant, and his beloved, the prostitute Ohatsu. In the first scene, a despondent Tokubei chances upon Ohatsu at the Ikudama Shrine. Tokubei has been thrown out of his uncle's household after refusing to marry his aunt's niece. Worse yet, his longtime friend Kuheiji has swindled him out of dowry money obtained from Tokubei's uncle that was meant to set him up in business. Humiliated, the youth resolves to prove his innocence by killing himself.

That evening Tokubei visits Temma House, the brothel where Ohatsu works. Ohatsu conceals him under her *kimono* until he can slip under the porch unseen. Kuheiji and his cronies arrive soon after. While Ohatsu speaks to them with open contempt, she and Tokubei convey solely by touch—an ankle drawn across the throat, a caress of the knees—their mutual love and determination to commit suicide. Later, when all at Temma House are asleep, the lovers slip away.

In the final scene, the two express their poignant farewells to the world they will soon leave. Making their way to Sonezaki Wood, they bind themselves together with Ohatsu's kimono sash and commit suicide.

Fujita Hiroshi

3 With Tokubei concealed under her kimono, Ohatsu pours scorn on the startled Kuheiji.

4 Ohatsu assures Tokubei of her resolve to die with him by touching his throat with her ankle.

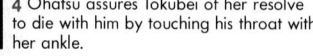

6 The couple express their love for one another as they head toward Sonezaki Wood, where they have decided to die. Such a journey scene, called a *michiyuki*, is a cherished lyrical interlude in many *kabuki* and *bunraku* plays.

Farewell to this world, and to the night farewell.
We who walk the road to death, to what should we be likened?
To the frost by the road that leads to the graveyard,
Vanishing with each step we take ahead:
How sad is this dream of a dream!

From *Four Major Plays of Chikamatsu*, translated by Donald Keene, 1961,
© Columbia University Press, New York. Reprinted with the permission of the publisher.

7 At Sonezaki Wood, the doomed lovers pray that they will be reunited as spirits.

8 So as not to present an unsightly spectacle after death, the pair use Ohatsu's sash to tie themselves together.

9 In the climactic scene, Tokubei prepares to stab Ohatsu in the throat. After she dies, he turns the blade on himself.

bunraku *Bunraku* puppet heads are divided into types based on age, sex, and temperament.
1 A *musume*, or unmarried young woman type.
2 This warrior-type puppet head, known as Bunshichi, is named after the role in which it was first used.
3 Shiratayū, a lively old man from the country, with bushy eyebrows and chubby cheeks.
4 A female clown type.

years the left arm before he may become a principal operator. Bunraku may enjoy a mild revival because of a new appreciation of tradition among younger Japanese, but its future is uncertain.   ☎ 144–145

Bunroku Keichō no Eki → invasions of Korea in 1592 and 1597

Bunten   文展

Abbreviation of Mombushō Bijutsu Tenrankai (Ministry of Education Fine Arts Exhibition). Annual exhibition begun in 1907 under official government sponsorship. The Ministry of Education appointed a group of established artists to the Bijutsu Shinsa Iinkai (Fine Arts Screening Committee) to select works of art for its official exhibition. The Bunten was thereafter held each year until 1918. In 1919 the committee was disbanded because of growing discord between artists of traditional and Western styles. Several successor organizations followed, and since 1958 the exhibitions, now called Nitten (abbreviation of Nihon Bijutsu Tenrankai, or Japan Art Exhibition), have been run by a separate corporation formed for the purpose, Nitten, Inc.

burakumin   部落民

Japan's largest minority group. The *burakumin* have the same racial, cultural, and national origins as their fellow Japanese. As a people physically not distinguishable from other Japanese, they intermingle with the rest of the populace, but when identified as

burakumin, they are subject to prejudice and discrimination. Oppression against the ancestors of this group began hundreds of years ago when the group in power adopted a social stratification system to protect its own status and class. Indignities persist because the *burakumin* continue to be labeled and regarded as somehow hereditarily different from the majority.

Recent government surveys indicate that 1.2 million *burakumin* live in 4,603 communities throughout the country. However, these figures underestimate the true *burakumin* population; in reality there are about 3 million *burakumin* living in some 6,000 communities. This number represents over 2 percent of the Japanese population.

History of Discrimination—It is not clearly known when and why this group became differentiated from the rest of Japanese society. When the coexistence of Buddhism and indigenous Shintō came about in the early Heian period (794–1185), the Shintō association of pollution with death was linked with the Buddhist teaching against the killing of animals. Those who were engaged in work dealing with the dead and the slaughtering of animals were considered polluted, and this defilement was thought to be contagious. Thus, not only was contact with people engaged in such occupations shunned, but there also emerged a pattern of residential segregation. Early references to the *eta* ("pollution abundant") as *toji* ("butchers") and *kawaramono* ("riverbank dwellers") are found in written sources published in the Kamakura period (1185–1333). It was during the Edo period (1600–1868)

that discrimination was formalized and legalized through the warrior-farmer-artisan-merchant-*eta-hinin* (shi-nō-kō-shō-eta-hinin) hierarchical status system.

The label HININ (nonhuman) was first used in the Nara period (710–794) to refer to a person taking part in a treasonous plot against the emperor. Persons who became beggars and vagrants were also called *hinin*. During the early feudal period, actors (*maimai*), SARUGAKU performers, and fabric dyers (*aoya*) were designated as *eta-hinin*, although the two outcaste groups remained separate endogamous groups. In the Edo period the *hinin* made a living mainly in entertainment, the guarding of criminals, and begging, while the *eta* had a virtual monopoly in occupations associated with animal processing and the production of leather goods.

The central and local governments of the Edo period had numerous regulations that rigidly controlled the occupation, residence, marriage, style of dress, and social behavior of the outcastes. They were permitted to work in only those occupations thought to be polluting, demanding, or undesirable. They disposed of the dead, tended graves, guarded tombs, swept streets, and collected garbage. They worked as butchers, tanners, and leather craftsmen. Their residence was limited to designated hamlets (*buraku*; hence the term *burakumin*).

In 1871 the new Meiji government issued an edict legally abolishing the derogatory names of *eta* and *hinin* and stipulating that they be treated as "new common people" (*shin heimin*). No follow-through measures were provided to implement their emancipation, however, and they continued to be relegated to "unclean" work while at the same time losing their monopoly on the more lucrative leather-crafts industry. The emancipation edict had little effect on the Japanese people in general and only worsened economic conditions for the *burakumin*. The *koseki* (household register) system, as well as the existence of special hamlets, made the *burakumin*, now officially known as new commoners, liable to ready identification.

One response to continued discrimination was the organization in 1902 of the Bisaku Heiminkai (Bisaku Common People's Association) by young men from a town in Okayama Prefecture. Similar associations were established in many other localities with the objective of urging *burakumin* to better themselves socially, economically, and educationally so that they would be accepted into the mainstream society. However, such organizations had little effect in altering the deeply embedded discriminatory attitude of the majority of the people toward the *burakumin*.

In 1922 the Suiheisha (Levelers or Equalizers) movement was founded. The tactic changed from self-improvement to thorough denunciation (*tetteiteki kyūdan*); those who discriminated were to be forced to apologize. Following a hiatus during World War II, the fight against discrimination was reactivated when former leaders of the Suiheisha established the Buraku Kaihō Zenkoku Iinkai (All-Japan Committee for Buraku Liberation). In 1955 its name was changed to Buraku Kaihō Dōmei (Buraku Liberation League). The group, now reorganized, worked toward the goal of equality made explicit in the new postwar constitution. It continued to challenge discrimination on the individual level and increased activities on the societal level.

In response to the movement the national government established a Special Integration Policy Deliberation Committee in 1960. After several years of investigation and deliberation, the first specific policy for improving the lot of the *burakumin* was implemented by the government; the enabling law took effect in 1969, with funding to cover a 10-year period.

The main objectives of the integration law were to improve living conditions for the *burakumin* and to eradicate discrimination. Although there has been some improvement in *buraku* living conditions, particularly in housing, neither of the goals of the legislation has been achieved adequately. A number of examples show that considerable economic and social discrimination against the *burakumin* persists in Japan.

One of the better-known incidents is the 1964 Sayama case, in which the police searched a *buraku* village in an attempt to solve a murder case. The police arrested a young *burakumin*, Ishikawa Kazuo, on unrelated charges and, after a month-long detention period, eventually forced him to make a false confession. After Ishikawa was convicted of the murder based on this coerced confession, some 4.6 million people signed a petition attesting to his innocence. This show of public support did not influence the Supreme Court, however, which in 1977 refused to examine new evidence or to grant a request for a retrial. The court is now reviewing a second appeal. The trial and subsequent court rulings have become a symbol of discrimination against all of the *burakumin.*

Status of Burakumin Today—In 1990, some 7 percent of *burakumin* were receiving PUBLIC ASSISTANCE—a figure six times the national average—and unemployment among *burakumin* continued to run at a much higher rate than that prevalent among the general population. Among the most clearcut examples of discrimination in the workplace are the so-called *buraku* lists (*chimei sōkan*), which are compiled by detective agencies for the purpose of making the identification of people of *buraku* origins easier. Over 200 corporations in Japan are reported to have purchased these lists and to have used them to exclude job applicants of *buraku* origins. As a result of strong denunciation by *buraku* representatives, many corporations have established orientation programs on *buraku* problems within their companies. Nevertheless, it remains unclear how many such lists have been compiled and sold and the extent to which data on the *burakumin* still circulate; recent reports indicate that *buraku* lists have been distributed even through computer networks. In addition, some companies, although smaller in number, still openly acknowledge that they will not hire *burakumin.*

Discrimination also persists in many aspects of social life. Parents routinely hire detectives to investigate the background of their children's prospective marriage partners. It is not uncommon for a pending marriage between a *burakumin* and a person of non-*buraku* origin to be broken up because of strong objections by the latter's family. A number of such incidents have led to suicides by one or both of the young people involved. In recent years there has been an apparent increase in the number of incidents of harassment against *burakumin*. But as there is no law in Japan prohibiting incitement to discrimination, there are no effective measures to cope with such incidents.

In response, the Buraku Liberation League has campaigned for the enactment of the Fundamental Law on Buraku Liberation and continues to press for drastic improvements in the social and economic status of the *burakumin* and for the eradication of prejudicial attitudes still prevalent among the general population. The league also has taken the lead in the formation of a new international organization, the International Movement Against All Forms of Discrimination and Racism. This organization, established on 25 January 1988, includes organizations and individuals from all over the world that are committed to the elimination of discrimination.

bureaucracy　　　　　　　　官僚制

(*kanryōsei*). Japanese public bureaucracy comprises a national government bureaucracy, various local government bureaucracies, and the bureaucracies of public and semipublic corporations.

During the Meiji period (1868–1912) creation of a cabinet system and promulgation of Imperial Ordinance No. 37 (1887) and the CONSTITUTION OF THE EMPIRE OF JAPAN (1889) established the outlines of a national bureaucracy modeled on that of Prussia. Architects of the Meiji regime viewed a powerful parliament, local autonomy, and party government as threats to national cohesion and the development of urban-based industrialization. To protect public administration from the perceived dangers of localism and politics civil servants were selected through competitive examinations. Civil service became a lifetime career, with service being to emperor and nation rather than to domain or class. Virtually essential to a high-level bureaucratic career was graduation from an elite state university, such as Tōkyō or Kyōto University, with these two schools providing the vast majority of senior civil servants. Emphasis on education helped develop a truly meritocratic civil service.

Government and bureaucracy were intimately linked: 36 percent of pre–World War II cabinet ministers were former bureaucrats. In 1899, the government also secured amendment of the Civil Service Appointment Ordinance to restrict severely the scope of appointments that elected politicians could make within the bureaucracy. Top positions in the ministries were reallocated following displacement of the party in power, but this usually involved replacing one career civil servant with another deemed more favorable to the new ruling party.

Under the Meiji regime, each minister was appointed by—and directly responsible to—the emperor. Collective cabinet responsibility was further diminished by the emperor's right of supreme command (*tō-suiken*), which meant that the emperor, rather than the prime minister or any other civilian authority, had control over the military. This resulted in two national bureaucracies, one civil, the other military, with the latter manipulating its privileged access to control cabinet composition and government policy making.

Although every law required the consent of the IMPERIAL DIET, few originated there. Most were drafted within agencies of the bureaucracy and then presented for ratification. An IMPERIAL ORDINANCE, while technically issued by the emperor, provided extralegislative means for direct bureaucratic control over much public policy making.

During the Allied OCCUPATION of Japan (1945–52), proscription of the military and

significant change to the constitutional powers of the emperor, DIET, and local governments bore upon both national and local bureaucracies. Under the new CONSTITUTION OF JAPAN (1947), bureaucrats were responsible to the PRIME MINISTER AND CABINET rather than to the emperor. Most PUBLIC EMPLOYEES were also prohibited from striking or even engaging in collective bargaining.

The National Government Organization Law of 1948, still the basic outline for the country's civil service, provides for four types of administrative organs: ministries, offices on the ministerial level, agencies, and commissions. The first two are the primary administrative organs of national government. The latter two oversee areas of administration different from the main work of a ministry or involving overlap, or potential conflict, with other ministries. Unable to submit proposed legislation or cabinet orders directly to the Diet, or to issue ministerial orders, these hold less formal power than the ministries.

As of 1992, there were 12 main ministries (*shō*) in the Japanese government, each headed by a minister (*daijin*) who is almost invariably a member of parliament. Each minister is assisted by one or two parliamentary vice-ministers (*seimu jikan*), usually members of parliament who serve as liaison between their ministry and the Diet. Career civil servants constitute the remainder of the ministry and are headed by an administrative vice-minister (*jimu jikan*) who oversees all administrative matters within the ministry. Each ministry is typically divided into 6 to 12 functional bureaus (*kyoku*), headed by bureau chiefs (*kyokuchō*), plus a secretariat (*kambō*) responsible for ministerial records, statistics, personnel, public relations, and financial accounts. Bureaus may be subdivided into several departments (*bu*), or directly into sections (*ka*), the basic working units of the ministry. Most ministries also include auxiliary organs, and many oversee detached agencies or commissions. Each ministry has advisory committees (*shingikai*) composed of representatives of private interest groups and individual experts to provide advice on matters under ministry jurisdiction.

The PRIME MINISTER'S OFFICE is responsible for the overall coordination of government policies. Under the Prime Minister's Office is the MANAGEMENT AND COORDINATION AGENCY, which provides overall coordination of government departments, overseeing such operations as administrative inspection, personnel, and government pensions.

LOCAL GOVERNMENT is a two-tiered system comprising 47 larger units, known as prefectures, and their approximately 3,250 cities and smaller units, known collectively as municipalities. Almost all of the more than 3 million local public officials are local civil service personnel, appointed and paid by local public bodies.

In principle, local government entities are autonomously governed and administratively independent of the national government. In fact, a good deal of national governmental work is often delegated to local government agencies, and their actions are often directly overseen by the central government. Relying heavily on central financing, local government accounts for about two-thirds of total government disbursements, yet collects only about one-third of the nation's tax receipts.

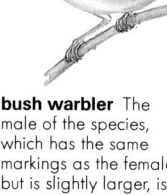

bush warbler The male of the species, which has the same markings as the female but is slightly larger, is noted for the song it sings during the spring mating season.

There are approximately 100 public corporations in Japan, each legally independent but supervised by a national government agency and subject to Diet budgetary control. Performing wide-ranging functions in such diverse fields as transportation, public broadcasting, cultural exchange, energy development, etc, these public corporations employ some 620,000 individuals. About half of their top officials are retired senior civil servants.

Taken together, national government, local government, and public corporations have about 5 million full-time employees. Although this number constitutes a nearly 10-fold increase over the size of Japan's wartime bureaucracy, it is still significantly lower than those for most other industrialized countries.

National civil service is overseen by the Management and Coordination Agency, which handles organizational issues, and the National Personnel Authority (NPA), responsible for enforcement of the National Civil Service Law. Entrance and promotion are based primarily on written and oral examinations administered by the NPA. Although theoretically any Japanese citizen is eligible, a narrow and homogeneous group dominates the ranks of successful applicants. Education still plays the main role, with graduates of Tōkyō and Kyōto universities predominating.

Once appointed to a post, an individual typically remains with the same agency throughout his career. Advancement is primarily a function of seniority: members of an entering class move upward as a cluster through a variety of positions within an agency. The most senior positions are held for only two or three years before early retirement at age 51 to 55. With government pensions low, most retired bureaucrats find second careers, often in private industry or public corporations overseen by the agencies for which they worked (see AMAKUDARI). A small proportion go on to politics, customarily with the ruling LIBERAL DEMOCRATIC PARTY (LDP). Their influence, locally and nationally, is considerable: approximately 20 percent of Japan's postwar cabinet ministers have been former bureaucrats, and the prime ministership has been held by more ex–civil servants than professional politicians.

Because service in a single ministry is the rule and lateral entry rare, loyalty to one's agency or section runs deep, often exaggerating bureaucratic tendencies toward tunnel vision and compartmentalization. Even sections within the same agency frequently resist cooperation, each seeking to maximize its sphere of influence. Some coordination is achieved through an informal weekly conference of administrative vice-ministers. Interministry teams are also established ad hoc to analyze and make policy recommendations on short-term problems.

The technical expertise of Japan's bureaucrats allows them to exercise substantial power in public policy formulation: approximately 90 percent of all legislation passed by the Diet since 1955 was drafted within the bureaucracy. Individual agencies have the power to issue ministerial ordinances (*shōrei*), and the cabinet can issue a CABINET ORDER (*seirei*), both of which supplement but can also bypass the legislative process. Although advisory commissions theoretically provide agencies with outside expertise, the ministerial staff defines the problem being investigated, oversees the investigation, and generally writes up the final report. "Retired" agency personnel who go on to second careers outside the bureaucracy perpetuate its influence: rarely are links to the former home agency severed; instead, they are used to facilitate coordination with private sector groups, and even committees of the LDP.

In contrast to the intimacy between the top levels of the bureaucracy and the Japanese political and economic establishment, the lower levels have been highly unionized since the Occupation. Although largely denied the right to strike, public employees once played a key role in the spring wage offensive (SHUNTŌ). However, the public sector unions were weakened by the PRIVATIZATION of leading public corporations. The public sector unions are now associated with RENGŌ.

Efforts to improve efficiency by reducing the size and complexity of the national bureaucracy (see SECOND PROVISIONAL COMMISSION FOR ADMINISTRATIVE REFORM) have enabled Japan, alone among the major industrialized countries, to stabilize the size of its national civil service. On the other hand, local bureaucracies have grown rapidly, and the trend in recent years has been to reassign centralized functions of national government to local levels of administration.

buri → yellowtail

Burma and Japan   ビルマと日本

(Biruma *to* Nihon). Relations between Japan and Burma (from 1988, Myanmar) barely existed before World War II, since Burma was a British colony. The total number of Japanese in Burma in 1911 was only 442, and no Japanese diplomatic representatives were posted to Burma prior to 1940. Actual relations between the two countries began when Japanese Imperial Army forces entered Burma in late 1941, occupying the whole area of the country by May 1942. Simultaneously the Burma Independence Army, formed around a cadre of 30 young Burmese nationalists, began operations under the leadership of the MINAMI KIKAN, a Japanese military intelligence organization. The Japanese government granted Burma independence in August 1943, proclaiming BA MAW head of state. It was, however, a sham, as Burma continued to be under Japanese military occupation. AUNG SAN, minister of defense, together with other political leaders, organized a resistance movement against Japan in July 1944. Attacks against Japanese forces began throughout the country in March 1945.

Burma achieved full independence from Britain in January 1948. A peace treaty and a reparations agreement were concluded between Burma and Japan in November 1954. Japan's reparations payments to Burma, totaling US $200 million, began in 1955. An additional reparations program totaling more than US $140 million was launched in 1965. Since 1975 Japan has provided economic assistance in such areas as food production, debt relief, and the improvement of public services and facilities.

The commercial relationship between the two countries has long been an unequal one. Between 1982 and 1990, imports from Burma accounted for only 0.02–0.03 percent of Japan's total imports. In contrast, over 30 percent of Burma's imports originated in Japan. From 1984 to 1988, Japan provided US $325 million to Burma as grants-in-aid. During that same period, Japanese loans totaled US $600 million. Burma's economic dependence on Japan was exacerbated by the rapid deterioration of Burma's national economy after 1962, when General Ne Win seized power and placed all economic enterprises under military control.

bushi → samurai

bushidan   武士団

Independent warrior bands or leagues of the 10th–16th centuries. As the authority of the central government declined in the latter part of the Heian period (794–1185), militant local landholders and members of branches of the nobility that had been sent to the provinces largely took control of provincial governments (*kokuga*) and private estates (SHŌEN) and formed military bands out of related and dependent families. These groups, which came to be called *bushidan*, appeared in all parts of Japan, but the largest and most powerful—especially those of the MIURA FAMILY and the HATAKEYAMA FAMILY— were located in the Kantō region. As the powerful regional hegemons known as the SHUGO DAIMYŌ and SENGOKU DAIMYŌ rose to dominance and began to establish their own vassal systems, the ties that bound the *bushidan* weakened and these groups gradually disappeared. See also SAMURAI.

bushidō   武士道

(literally, "the Way [*dō*] of the warrior [*bushi*]"). A term that came into common use during the Edo period (1600–1868) to designate the ethical code of the ruling *samurai* class. *Bushidō* involved not only martial spirit and skill with weapons, but also absolute loyalty to one's lord, a strong sense of personal honor, devotion to duty, and the courage, if required, to sacrifice one's life in battle or in ritual suicide.

Although *bushidō* assumed its mature form as a deliberately articulated ethical system and martial cult only in the 17th and 18th centuries, the warrior class had dominated the political life of Japan from the establishment of the Kamakura shogunate by MINAMOTO NO YORITOMO in the late 12th century. Earlier, warrior bands held together by kinship bonds, regional ties, and fierce personal loyalty to their leaders had become active in the provinces from about the 10th century with the erosion of central imperial authority.

Early Warrior Society and Bushidō— The key to understanding the Japanese warrior ethic prior to the Edo period lies in an understanding of the medieval lord-retainer nexus involving favor from the lord and service from the retainer. Although a distinct *bushi* ethic based on absolute loyalty was taking shape, many warriors gave only qualified allegiance to their nominal overlords, saw the relationship in economic and contractual terms, and vigorously pursued their own self-interest. The strength of the bond varied with prevailing personal, local, and historical circumstances. The volatility of *bushi* loyalty patterns was both cause and effect of the phenomenon of "the lower overturning the upper" (GEKOKUJŌ), which was a prominent feature of medieval Japan.

Transition to Tokugawa Bushidō— MIYAMOTO MUSASHI's *Gorin no sho* (ca 1643; tr *The Book of Five Rings*, 1974), a treatise on strategy and the art of war, emphasized the application of military strategy to gain glory for the samurai and his lord as the true dis-

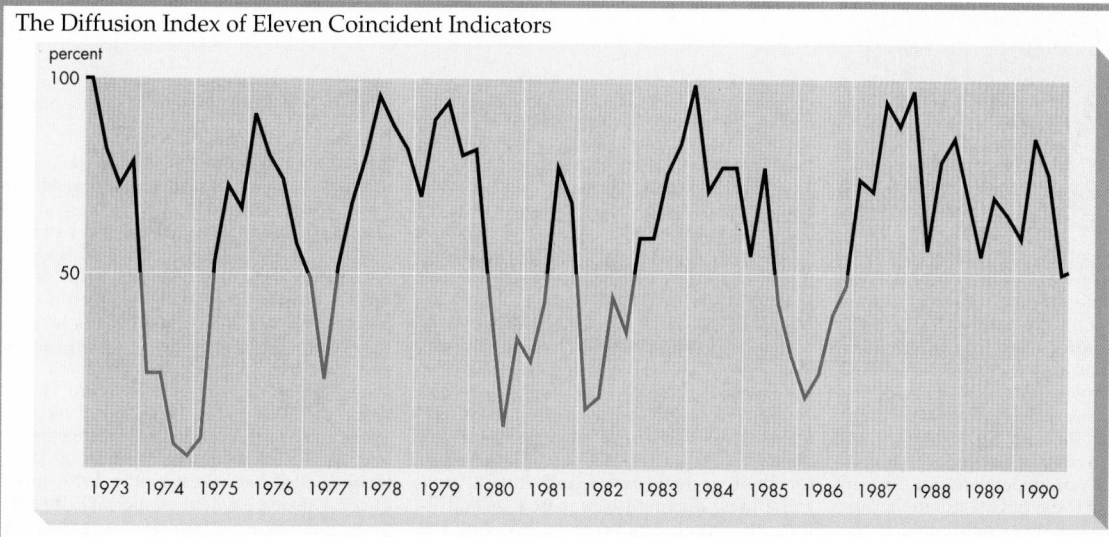

The Diffusion Index of Eleven Coincident Indicators

percent

100

50

1973 1974 1975 1976 1977 1978 1979 1980 1981 1982 1983 1984 1985 1986 1987 1988 1989 1990

The eleven coincident indicators are
- index of industrial production (mining and manufacturing)
- index of consumption of raw materials (manufacturing)
- electric power consumption (total)
- index of the capacity utilization ratio (manufacturing)
- index of labor input (manufacturing)
- index of producers' shipments of capital goods (excluding transport equipment)
- sales at department stores
- index of sales in the wholesale trade
- net profits (all industries)
- index of sales in small and medium-sized enterprises (manufacturing)
- ratio of job offers to applicants (excluding new graduates)

NOTE: This type of diffusion index is widely used in Japanese publications as a measure of business conditions in Japan. Figures exceeding 50 percent represent an economic upturn; figures below 50 percent indicate a downturn. Quarterly averages of monthly index values are plotted on the second month of each quarter.
SOURCE: Economic Planning Agency, *Annual Report on Business Cycle Indicators: 1991.*

tinction of a warrior. But even then military adventuring was being sharply curtailed, as warriors were gathered in castle towns. Cut off from direct control of land and peasants, reduced to fixed stipends in an age of rising costs, and with opportunities for advancement through warfare restricted under the NATIONAL SECLUSION policy and the enforced peace under the Tokugawa shogunate (1603–1867), samurai became increasingly dependent on the shogunate or their domainal governments for survival. The samurai were gradually converted from fighting men into a ruling elite whose time was taken up in the administration of their domains, or in the ceremonial requirements of alternate-year attendance (SANKIN KŌTAI) at the shogunal capital of Edo (now Tōkyō).

It was in the relatively stable social and intellectual climate of Tokugawa Japan that *bushidō,* as the ethical system and martial cult of a "tamed" samurai class, came to fruition. The idealized medieval tradition of absolute loyalty and willingness to die for one's lord survived, but was now overlaid with Confucian ethics. The underlying native tradition found its most eloquent expression in Yamamoto Tsunetomo's *bushidō* classic HAGAKURE (1716). According to the *Hagakure,* the samurai ideal and essence of *bushidō* are expressed in self-effacing service to one's lord.

The samurai scholar and military strategist YAMAGA SOKŌ stressed that samurai, to justify their existence in Tokugawa society, where they had neither to fight nor to contribute to production, had a duty to devote themselves to moral and political leadership. They were to embody both Confucian and feudal virtues and realize in practice the Way of moral virtue in the exercise of government.

This composite of indigenous and Confucianized *bushidō* regulated much of the ethical behavior and intellectual inquiry of the samurai class in the Edo period. The emphasis on action, purity of motivation, loyal service, and political and intellectual leadership inherent in *bushidō* helps to explain why the samurai class could serve as the moving force of the movement that led to the MEIJI RESTORATION (1868), then go on to destroy the feudal system of which they had been the apex, and ultimately play an influential role in the modernization of Japan.

The Legacy of Bushidō — Although the Meiji Restoration and the dismantling of the Tokugawa feudal structure involved the ab-

olition of the samurai class, it did not mean the end of *bushidō* as a compelling emotive force. Although *bushidō* was temporarily submerged in the early Meiji surge of modernization and Westernization, from the mid-1880s, and especially after the Sino-Japanese War (1894–95), it found new expressions in patriotism and devotion to the emperor. It was also later interpreted by UCHIMURA KANZŌ as loyalty to Christ, and by NITOBE INAZŌ in his *Bushido: The Soul of Japan* (1899) as all that was most admirable in Japanese tradition and society.

The more martial aspects of *bushidō* came into vogue in the militarist 1930s, but again fell into disfavor in the aftermath of World War II. Most Japanese then disowned *bushidō* as incompatible with their postwar democratic society, although the tradition still exerts considerable fascination. One Japanese who sought to reinstate *bushidō* in postwar Japanese society was the novelist MISHIMA YUKIO. For Mishima, *bushidō* was to be the means of assuring a return to national pride and cleansing the corruption of modern Japanese society. He was attracted by the *Hagakure* and fascinated by the sword and the cult of death in *bushidō,* a fascination that culminated in his death by ritual suicide (HARAKIRI) in November 1970.

bush warbler 鶯

(*uguisu*). *Cettia diphone.* A member of the family of small birds called Muscicapidae that is known for its beautiful song. The male and female are olive-brown in color, with a white eye ring and long tail. Its total length is about 15 centimeters (6 in). Feeding on insects, it breeds throughout Japan in mountainous areas. Between April and August it builds ball-shaped nests in dwarf bamboo thickets, where the female lays four to six reddish brown eggs. In autumn and winter, bush warblers move down to the plains. Besides Japan, their range includes northeastern China, Korea, Sakhalin, and the Philippines. See also REED WARBLERS.

The Japanese people have long loved the plaintive, whistling song of the *uguisu,* which they pronounce as *hōhokekyo;* to them it signifies good luck and rejoicing. In particular, Japanese writers and artists have prized the combination of "warblers and plum blossoms." The bird appears frequently in Japanese poetry and art as a motif paired with bamboo, willows, cherry trees, or pine. These birds have been raised as pets since at least the 16th century.

business cards → name cards

business cycles 景気変動

(*keiki hendō*). Just after World War II, cycles of prosperity and recession in Japan were closely related to government policies. During the Allied OCCUPATION of 1945–52, the PRIORITY PRODUCTION PROGRAM of inflationary financing of reconstruction through the Reconstruction Finance Bank and price differential subsidies contributed to the economic recovery from the war, while the deflationary DODGE LINE was held responsible for the recession that followed. In the early 1950s the expansion of exports and the large expenditures by the American military in Japan and Korea led to the Korean War Boom (peak in June 1951) and the Post-Korean War Boom (peak in June 1954). Increase in private plant and equipment investment was a major force in the Jimmu Boom (peak in June 1957), the IWATO BOOM (peak in December 1961), and the short-lived Olympic Boom (peak in October 1964). The end of each of these booms was effected by tight monetary and fiscal policies introduced by the government to deal with unfavorable developments in Japan's BALANCE OF PAYMENTS. The subsequent recession of 1965 was the most severe to that time.

Private plant and equipment investment was again the leading force in the 57-month IZANAGI BOOM (peak in July 1970), although American military expenditures related to the Vietnam War also stimulated growth. The boom ended when the government adopted restrictive policies to combat wholesale price inflation. Government policies to counteract the deflationary impact of yen revaluation were associated with the Postrevaluation Boom (peak in November 1973), while the recession that followed, the deepest of all postwar recessions, was related to higher oil prices (see OIL CRISIS OF 1973), which applied a deflationary shock to the economy. Although booms since the mid-1970s have tended to average about 24 months, in early 1991 the HEISEI BOOM ended after more than 50 months of expansion.

The Japanese cyclical business fluctuations of the late 1970s, the 1980s, and the early 1990s have been less pronounced than those of previous decades. One of the chief reasons for this change is the lessening im-

Buson Detail from Buson's *Landscapes of Mt. Gabi*, a handscroll portraying a Chinese mountain. Ca 1778–83. Light colors on paper. 29 × 240 cm. Private collection.

portance of agriculture and manufacturing in Japan and the growing importance of the service sector. Wide-ranging business fluctuations are common to economies heavily dependent on manufacturing, because changes in inventory and import/export levels influence company profitability. Service industry businesses, which sell assistance and expertise rather than tangible products, do not maintain inventories in the traditional sense and are not dependent on foreign trade. The rise of the service sector in the Japanese economy has thus contributed to the leveling out of Japanese business cycles. The ECONOMIC PLANNING AGENCY compiles and analyzes data on the cycles of prosperity and recession in Japan. See also ECONOMIC PLANNING.

Buson　蕪村

(1716–84). Leading *haikai* (see HAIKU) poet of the late 18th century and, with BASHŌ (1644–94) and ISSA (1763–1827), one of the great names in haiku. Also known as Yosa Buson or Taniguchi Buson. Also a distinguished BUNJINGA painter, he perfected the *haiga* ("haiku sketch") as a branch of Japanese pictorial art. His best-known painting disciple, MATSUMURA GOSHUN, also known as Gekkei, founded the Shijō school.

Early Career—Born near Ōsaka, as a youth Buson went to Edo (now Tōkyō). For five years (1737–42) he belonged to a *haikai* linked-verse circle (see RENGA) over which Hayano Hajin (1676–1742) presided. Here he learned the traditions of the Bashō school *haikai* as transmitted by HATTORI RANSETSU and TAKARAI KIKAKU. After Hajin's death Buson spent much time around Yūki, north of Edo, where he painted, practiced *haikai*, and wrote *Hokuju Rōsen o itamu* (1745, Elegy to Hokuju Rōsen), the first of his innovative poems that foreshadow modern free verse. Buson also visited places in northeastern Japan famed in Bashō's poetic diary, OKU NO HOSOMICHI (1694; tr *The Narrow Road to the Deep North*, 1966).

Buson settled in Kyōto in the late 1750s. He was active in Mochizuki Sōoku's (1688–1766) poetry circle and was also actively painting in the Chinese-inspired *bunjinga* style. By practicing both poetry and painting, he aspired to the ideals of the *bunjin* (Ch: *wen-ren* or *wen-jen*; literati) of China. One of Buson's commissions involved collaborating with IKE NO TAIGA on a landscape series based on Chinese poems, *Jūben jūgi*

butsudan A cabinet-style *butsudan* housing a Buddhist image and the family ancestral mortuary tablets.

(1771, Ten Conveniences and Ten Pleasures), now a National Treasure. In 1770 he took the name Yahantei (Midnight Hermitage) for his studio. In painting, his best-known name is probably Shunsei (Spring Star).

Master of Poetry and Painting—Buson found his distinct voice partly from association with two dissimilar poets, TAN TAIGI and Kuroyanagi Shōha (d 1772), both of whom helped him develop his spontaneous and sensual style. Following their passing, Buson emerged as the central figure of a *haikai* revival known as the "Return to Bashō" movement. In 1776 his own poetry group built a clubhouse, the Bashōan (Bashō Hut), for their regular *haikai* and linked-verse gatherings. Buson also prepared several illustrated scrolls and screens, including the text of *Oku no hosomichi*, which helped canonize Bashō as a grand saint of poetry. Although Buson sought to emulate Bashō, his own poetry is much more subjective in its pursuit of romantic lyricism, delicate sensitivity, and mood.

bussangaku　物産学

Term used in the late Edo period (1600–1868) to refer to the study of local products, whether natural, processed, or manufactured. *Bussangaku* was encouraged in the 18th and 19th centuries throughout Japan to increase production of cash crops and to develop markets for specialized products as a means of augmenting domainal revenues (see KOKUSAN KAISHO). *Bussangaku* initially focused on the collection and classification of specimens but eventually led to scientific experiments and technological innovations.

bussho　仏所

Workshop where Buddhist sculptures were carved or, by extension, a group of sculptors of the same school. During the Nara period (710–794) *bussho* were established on temple construction sites, but by the mid-Heian period (794–1185) leaders of each school had workshops at their homes. In the Kamakura period (1185–1333) *bussho* developed into guild-like organizations (see ZA). The Shichijō *bussho* of the KEI SCHOOL, the Sanjō *bussho* of the EN SCHOOL, and the Shichijō-Ōmiya *bussho* of the IN SCHOOL are well known. Many such *bussho* existed during the Muromachi period (1333–1568), but most had disappeared by the Edo period (1600–1868).

bussokuseki　仏足石

("stone footprints of the Buddha"). Representations of the Buddha's footprints carved in stone, showing the "wheel of a thousand spokes" (*sempukurin*), which symbolizes the dharma, or Buddhist law, believed to have been miraculously imprinted on the soles of the Buddha's feet as one of the 32 mystic signs attesting to his Buddhahood. These representations of the Buddha's footprints on stone were among the first Buddhist icons. The oldest extant *bussokuseki* in Japan is preserved in the temple YAKUSHIJI in Nara and was carved in 753. The footprints are incised on the flat top of a small breccia pillar. Next to the pillar is a slate stele (height: 193.9 cm or 76.3 in; width: 48.5 cm or 19.1 in) of a similar date on which are inscribed 21 ancient Japanese Buddhist poems attributed to the empress KŌMYŌ. These poems of 38 syllables have come to be called *bussokuseki no uta;* they resemble WAKA but have an extra 7-syllable line at the end.

butō　舞踏

Japanese avant-garde dance form. *Butō* is an original Japanese dance form that differs from both the traditional Japanese dance and such Western forms as the ballet or modern dance. The founder of *butō* is said to be HIJIKATA TATSUMI (1928–86), who developed a unique form that he called *ankoku butō* in the late 1950s, seeking his inspiration from bodily attitudes and gestures associated with Japanese folk practices. Another important early *butō* figure is ŌNO KAZUO (b 1906). In the 1970s, Kasai Akira (b 1943) and Maro Akaji (b 1943) were particularly active. The latter, who founded a troupe called DAI RAKUDAKAN in 1972, introduced a strong element of spectacle into the performances. *Butō*, which was regarded as having spiritual associations with the traditional Japanese dramatic and dance form NŌ, attracted much attention in the United States and Europe. In the 1980s the most active troupe was SANKAI JUKU, which was founded in 1975 by Amagatsu Ushio (b 1949), who had been a member of Dai Rakudakan. The performers of this troupe, their heads shaved, their bodies painted white, created a sensation with their performances in various countries around the world.

butsudan　仏壇

Small cabinet or niche containing an image of Buddha flanked by the family ancestral mortuary tablets (*ihai*). Along with the *kamidana* (Shintō family altar), the *butsudan* is a sacred place in many households. Originally, the term meant a platform in a Buddhist hall where images were placed. The small cabinet-form *butsudan* became common when the Tokugawa shogunate (1603–1867) required each household to register with a temple of a Buddhist sect (see SHŪMON ARATAME). Buddhism by then had a firm place in the traditional ANCESTOR WORSHIP of each household. The image placed inside the *butsudan* may be a statue or a picture of Buddha, and the cabinet may be placed in a special room. Offerings of food, flowers, and incense are made regularly upon the *butsudan*, and Buddhist scriptures are read in front of it. See also SHINTŌ FAMILY ALTARS.

butsumetsu → rokuyō

Butsurui shōko　物類称呼

A dictionary of Japanese dialects of the late Edo period (1600–1868). It was written by the *haiku* poet Koshigaya Gozan (also known as Aida Gozan; 1717–87) and published in 1775 in five volumes. The work contains approximately 550 entries with 4,000 annotated dialectical words. One of the few works on dialects of this time, it is a valuable source on the Japanese language in the Edo period.

butterflies　蝶

(*chō*). Diurnal insects belonging to the order Lepidoptera. About 20,000 species are known worldwide, of which 300 species of nine families are recorded in Japan.

Family Papilionidae: 22 species, including the *gifuchō* (*Luehdorfia japonica*) and *jakō ageha* (*Byasa alcinous*), which are endemic to Japan; the *hime gifuchō* (*L. puziloi*); the *usuba shiro chō* (*Parnassius glacialis*); 7 species of the genus *Papilio*, the larvae of which feed on citrus trees; and 2 species of the genus *Graphium* (*G. doson* and *G. sarpedon*) found abundantly in southern Asia.

Family Pieridae: 30 species, including spe-

The Graceful Image of the Butterfly

With its beautiful wings and graceful flight, the butterfly has long been a popular symbol in Japan, featured in the family crests of warrior clans and inscribed on their helmets. Perhaps because its metamorphosis suggests a change from one spiritual state to another, the butterfly has been endowed with mystical significance. In Buddhist lore, the sudden appearance of a cloud of butterflies might signal a spirit's presence or portend the death of an ill person. These delicate, ephemeral creatures are also regarded as symbols of a conventional notion of femininity, especially in poetry, and can often be seen adorning *kimono* and various decorative objects. Some of the many butterfly species that inhabit Japan are shown below.

Ōmurasaki, of the family Nymphalidae.

Monkichō, of the family Pieridae.

Daimyō seseri, of the family Hesperiidae.

Sujigurokaba madara, of the family Danaidae.

Komurasaki, of the family Nymphalidae.

Tenguchō, of the family Libytheidae.

Agehachō, of the family Papilionidae.

The Kochō (Dance of the Butterfly), performed by four children in costumes fitted with elaborate butterfly wings, was once a great favorite at the imperial court.

Butterfly wings worn for the *Kochō.*

A decorative plate from the Edo period (1600–1868). The butterfly's symmetrical form has made it a common design motif for a variety of goods.

This Nō costume from the Edo period is decorated with a butterfly motif. The butterflies, one of which is shown enlarged (above right), are embroidered with gold, silver, black, and red thread.

Byōdōin Dedicated to the Buddha Amida, this building at the temple Byōdōin is popularly known as the Phoenix Hall because of the symmetrical wings of its ground plan and the bronze birds that ornament its roof. Completed in 1053, it is a National Treasure.

cies of the genera *Anthocharis, Leptidea, Aporia,* and *Gonepteryx,* distributed in East Asia and the Palaearctic region; and genera *Hebomoia, Eurema,* and *Catopsilia,* distributed widely in the tropics.

Family Nymphalidae: 68 species—about one-third of which are the so-called fritillaries—including the genera *Argynnis, Argyronome,* and *Melitaea.* This family includes the Asama *ichimonji* (*Ladoga glorifica*), the only endemic species; the *ichimonji chō* (*L. camilla*); the *ōmurasaki* (*Sasakia charonda*), the best-known Japanese species; and the *komurasaki* (*Apatura ilia*), the *kujaku chō* (*Inachis io*), the *kiberi tateha* (*Nymphalis antiopa*), and the *hiodoshi chō* (*N. xanthomelas*), which are also distributed widely in Europe.

Family Satyridae: 30 species, including the *takane hikage* (*Oeneis asamana*), the Daisetsu *takane hikage* (*O. daisetsuzana*), the *satoki madara hikage* (*Neope goschkevitschii*), and 3 species of the genus *Ypthima,* which are endemic to Okinawa; and the genera *Erebia, Coenonympha,* and *Lasiommata,* which are found largely in northern Japan.

Family Danaidae: 24 species, including the *asagi madara* (*Parantica sita*). Species other than this can be found in the islands in southern Japan.

Family Libytheidae: 2 species.

Family Curetidae: 1 species.

Family Lycaenidae: 81 species, including about 20 species of the group once called the *zephyrus,* which is distributed throughout East Asia; and the *urakin shijimi* (*Ussuriana stygiana*), the Fuji *midori shijimi* (*Quercusia fujisana*), and the *benimon karasu shijimi* (*Strymonidia iyonis*), which are endemic.

Family Hesperiidae: 38 species with thick bodies, including the Ogasawara *seseri* (*Parnara ogasawarensis*) and the Asahina *kimadara seseri* (*Ochlodes asahinai*), which are endemic to the Ogasawara and Ishigaki islands respectively; and the *kochabane seseri* (*Thoressa varia*), which is found only on the main islands of Japan.

A government proscription against a sect of Taoism that venerated the larva of the swallowtail butterfly may have been the rea-

son that no mention of butterflies is found in the 8th-century poetry anthology *Man'yōshū.* By the mid-Heian period (794–1185) the butterfly had come to be regarded as "something lovable," as SEI SHŌNAGON fondly describes it in her *Makura no sōshi* (ca 996). From the Muromachi period (1333–1568) the butterfly became a popular decorative motif. ☎ 151

buyaku 夫役

Corvée labor. Under the RITSURYŌ SYSTEM of government established in the 7th century, labor services required by the authorities were called YŌEKI. The term *fueki* (or *bueki*) referred to both corvée labor and miscellaneous taxes paid with goods. These terms fell into disuse toward the end of the Heian period (794–1185) and were replaced by *buyaku.*

Under the SHŌEN (estate) system, from the 8th to the 15th century, taxes were classified into the rice tax (*shotō;* later NENGU) and KUJI, a tax paid in labor or miscellaneous products. At first *buyaku* meant mainly agricultural labor, but soon the term was applied to reclamation and irrigation, repair of roads and buildings, the transportation of tax rice, and military duties (GUN'YAKU). These services were requisitioned by estate proprietors (*ryōshu*) and the JITŌ (shogunate-appointed land stewards) and later by the SHUGO (military governors) and by SENGOKU DAIMYŌ. During the Edo period (1600–1868), cash payments replaced most labor requirements (see KUNIYAKU), although some services were retained, such as the maintenance of post stations (SUKEGŌ).

buyō→dance, traditional

Buzen 豊前〔市〕

City in eastern Fukuoka Prefecture, Kyūshū, on the Suō Sea. Buzen produces rice, vegetables, and lumber. Thermal power plants and metalwork factories are located in the coastal industrial area. Many of its residents commute to the city of KITA KYŪSHŪ. Pop: 31,089.

Byakkotai 白虎隊

(White Tiger Brigade). A corps of a few hundred youths, organized in March 1868 by the

pro-Tokugawa Aizu domain (now part of Fukushima Prefecture) to resist the forces of the imperial restoration in the BOSHIN CIVIL WAR. The Byakkotai was decimated by an imperial army in the Battle of Tonokuchihara (part of a longer conflict known as the Battle of Aizu, which had begun in the late summer) on 8 October 1868. Twenty survivors made their way back to Wakamatsu Castle, the Aizu stronghold, but seeing it in flames and believing their cause to be lost, they committed suicide on a nearby mountain, Iimoriyama. The group became a popular symbol of loyalty, determination, and courage.

byōbu→screen and wall painting

Byōbugaura 屏風ヶ浦

Coastal area south of the city of Chōshi, northeastern Chiba Prefecture, central Honshū. The Shimōsa Plateau juts out into the Pacific Ocean with cliffs approximately 60 m (195 ft) high for a distance of 10 km (6 mi) in the form of a folding screen (*byōbu*). It forms part of the Suigō-Tsukuba Quasi-National Park.

Byōdōin 平等院

A temple founded in the 11th century at Uji, southeast of Kyōto. Originally a large compound of buildings, its chief relic today is the *amidadō,* popularly known as the Hōōdō (Phoenix Hall). A hall dedicated to the Buddha AMIDA (Skt: Amitābha), this is one of the finest examples of the aristocratic art and architecture of the late Heian period (794–1185). It was originally built as a model of Amida's heavenly palace in the Pure Land (see PURE LAND BUDDHISM) and was affiliated with the TENDAI SECT. It has also been associated with the JŌDO SECT since the late 17th century but no longer serves in the performance of regular Buddhist ceremonies.

In 998 FUJIWARA NO MICHINAGA restored a rural villa on the Uji River, where he retired to practice Buddhist meditation and austerities. This villa was converted into a temple in 1052 by his son FUJIWARA NO YORIMICHI. In 1053 the *amidadō* was completed.

In the Kamakura period (1185–1333), a *kannondō* (Kannon hall) was built to enshrine a Heian-period 11-headed statue of the bodhisattva KANNON (Skt: Avalokiteśvara). Both hall and image are still extant.

The Phoenix Hall has often been damaged and restored. Attached high on the inner wall around the main image are 52 small wooden images of bodhisattvas. The majority of these are as old as the hall itself. On the inside of the doors and walls of the hall were painted scenes depicting various aspects of Amida's powers of salvation. These paintings have been attributed to the artist TAKUMA TAMENARI.

Dominating the interior of the hall is the large statue of Amida, a National Treasure. It is the only extant work known to have been carved by JŌCHŌ.

Although today the principle deity (*honzon*) of the temple is Amida, the *honzon* was Dainichi Nyorai (see DAINICHI) until 1336, when a fire destroyed all but the Phoenix Hall and the Kannon hall.

Cabin Co, Ltd　　　　　　［株］キャビン

(Kyabin). Retail chain operator, mainly handling women's casual wear. Incorporated in 1971. Cabin has developed its own brands, especially in women's wear. It is affiliated with La Boutique de Marie Claire, a French company, for sales of designer household goods under its license, and it has also established ties with a Taiwanese manufacturer. Sales for the fiscal year ending February 1991 totaled ¥57.5 billion (US $440.7 million), and capitalization stood at ¥15.2 billion (US $116.5 million). Headquarters are in Tōkyō.

cabinet → prime minister and cabinet

Cabinet Library　　　　　　　内閣文庫

(Naikaku Bunko). Part of the NATIONAL ARCHIVES, located in Kitanomaru Park, Chiyoda Ward, Tōkyō. With about 530,000 volumes, the library, which was established in 1884, is one of the largest branches of the NATIONAL DIET LIBRARY. Important items in the library include the Momijiyama Bunko of TOKUGAWA IEYASU, the collection of the SHŌHEIKŌ (the Confucian college of the Tokugawa shogunate), and books assembled by the Wagaku Kōdansho (the research bureau founded by HANAWA HOKIICHI).

cabinet order　　　　　　　　政令

(seirei). Within the class of laws promulgated by administrative agencies and called orders (meirei), those promulgated by the cabinet are called cabinet orders. Cabinet orders rank above ministerial orders (shōrei), which are promulgated by individual ministers.

Under the 1889 constitution, the cabinet could deviate from the will of the IMPERIAL DIET and issue independent orders necessary to preserve public order or to advance the welfare of the people, as well as emergency orders having the same effect as statutes (HŌRITSU) to respond to a crisis. Under the present CONSTITUTION OF JAPAN, however, the Diet is the sole legislative body, and these types of orders are no longer permitted. The cabinet or a minister may issue only executive orders (shikkō meirei), establishing regulations for the implementation of statutes, and delegated orders (inin meirei), determining matters delegated by statute. No penalties may be established without a specific statutory delegation.

cable audio broadcasting　　有線放送

(yūsen hōsō). Wire-relayed broadcasts started in Japan in 1932 when the Ministry of Communications (Teishinshō) and NHK (Japan Broadcasting Corporation) built an experimental facility to receive radio transmissions at one place and retransmit them to homes by means of cable. Community reception facilities spread to many areas during World War II and were used for emergency communications such as air-raid warnings. After the war cable audio broadcasting spread rapidly in areas where radio reception was poor, such as Hokkaidō and southern Kyūshū.

In the 1960s cable audio broadcasting facilities offering various types of music were established in cities; they are widely used, particularly by drinking establishments, to provide background music. Today companies offering this service have a total of some 100,000 subscribers. See also CABLE TELEVISION.

cable television　　　　　ケーブルテレビ

(kēburu terebi). Also known as CATV (Community Antenna Television). CATV was started in 1954 by the Japan Broadcasting Corporation (NHK), originally to serve areas that had difficulty picking up regular television signals. By the end of the 1960s, CATV was used to serve city areas where tall buildings hampered reception. The first CATV system in Japan was put into operation in Ikaho, Gumma Prefecture. Since then cable television has experienced considerable growth. The most remarkable development of CATV has been in the area of independent television broadcasting. However, because of high costs, the success of these independent, cable-broadcast ventures has been uneven. In 1973 a law was passed that set strict regulations on licensing and reporting, further hindering the free development of independent broadcasting. As of 1989, 18.6 percent of the households with televisions were served by CATV.

Cabral, Francisco　　　　　カブラル, F.

(1528?–1609). Portuguese Jesuit priest who served as the Superior of the Christian Mission in Japan, 1570–81. Born in the Azores, he left for India in 1550 and entered the Society of Jesus there. Arriving in Japan in 1570, he insisted that Japanese Christians should adapt themselves to the language and culture of European missionaries rather than the reverse and placed tight restrictions on the admission of Japanese into the Society of Jesus. These strictures clashed with the more liberal views of the Jesuit visitor Alessandro VALIGNANO. Cabral left Japan in 1583 and died in Goa.

Cachon, Mermet de　　　　カション, M.

(1828–70). French Catholic priest and missionary in Japan. Cachon played an important role in politics and diplomacy in the last years of the Tokugawa shogunate (1603–1867). A member of the French Société des Missions Etrangères (Society for Foreign Missions), Cachon came to Okinawa in 1855. After serving as interpreter for the first French embassy to Japan in 1858, he went to Hakodate, where he spent several years in missionary and teaching activities. He left Japan in 1863 but returned the following year with Léon ROCHES, then French minister to Japan. As Roches's interpreter, adviser, and representative, Cachon had a crucial role in the development of a special relationship between France and the Tokugawa regime. After his return to France in 1866 he published a French-English-Japanese dictionary.

Cai E (Ts'ai O)　　　　　　　蔡鍔

(1882–1916; J: Sai Gaku). A brilliant military and political figure in early republican China. Born in Hunan, Cai E participated in the short-lived radical reform movement there in the late 1890s. After the movement's collapse he followed LIANG QICHAO (Liang Ch'i-ch'ao) to Japan, where he studied at the Army Academy in Tōkyō. Returning to China, he played a prominent role in overthrowing Qing (Ch'ing) authority in Yunnan and subsequently led the movement to rescue the Chinese republic from the imperial pretensions of YUAN SHIKAI (Yüan Shih-k'ai).

Cairo Declaration　　　　　カイロ宣言

(Kairo Sengen). First public outline of the Allies' post–World War II plans for territories occupied by Japan. Leaders of the forces

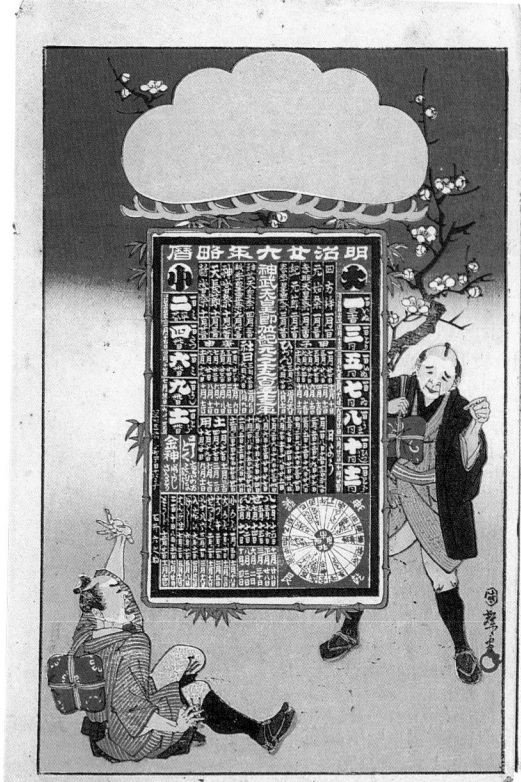

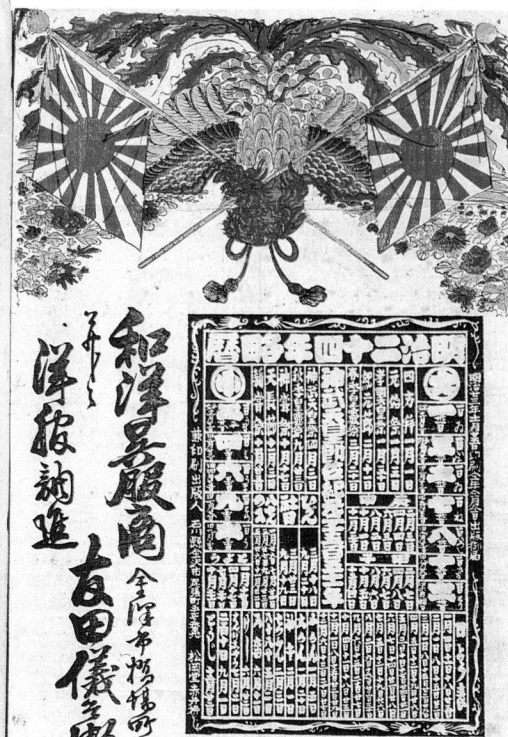

fighting Japan met in Cairo in November 1943. US President Franklin D. Roosevelt, British Prime Minister Winston Churchill, and Chinese Generalissimo Chiang Kai-shek issued the Cairo Declaration, which also demanded the unconditional surrender of Japan. Disclaiming any interest in territorial expansion themselves, the Allies agreed that Japan should be stripped of all conquests made since 1914, which included Japan's island possessions in the Pacific as well as parts of China such as Taiwan, Manchuria, and the Pescadores. They also agreed that Korea, a Japanese colony since 1910, should be given independence. See also YALTA CONFERENCE; POTSDAM DECLARATION.

calendar, dates, and time 暦

(*koyomi*). Since 1 January 1873 the Japanese have used the Gregorian calendar. Except for the practice of numbering years serially from the year in which a reigning emperor ascended the throne, the Japanese method for designating dates does not differ from the Western. Before 1873, however, the official, or civil, Japanese calendar was a lunar calendar.

The essential differences between the Japanese lunar calendar and the Western solar calendar were reflected in a close correspondence between civil and natural months under the lunar system, with a less exact correspondence between civil and natural years than with the solar calendar. In order to assure a rough correspondence between months of the civil year and seasons of the natural year, a 13th month was added (intercalated) to the lunar calendar in some years.

The Old Solar Calendar——Although the Japanese civil calendar was a lunar calendar, farmers needed a calendar that would tell them the best times for planting and harvests, activities that followed the seasons of the natural year. Ancient Chinese astronomers provided a solar calendar that was both simple and accurate and that became an unofficial calendar for Japanese farmers. The nomenclature of this old solar calendar is still in common use among Japanese, and some of its devices must be understood for the bearing they had on the operation of the lunar civil calendar.

The natural year was measured by reference to the period between two successive occurrences of the winter solstice. In fact the winter solstice was not taken as the beginning of the solar year; it was the midpoint of the first of 12 divisions (called *setsu*) of the year. Each *setsu* was of absolutely equal duration; that is, each contained a fractional number of days—about 30.44. The beginning of a *setsu* was known as *sekki*, and the midpoint of a *setsu* was known as *chūki*. As the winter solstice marked the first *chūki* of the solar year, the first *sekki*, which began the year, occurred about 15 days earlier, approximately 7 December in the Gregorian calendar. Each *sekki* and *chūki* had its own name, often highly expressive of weather or agricultural phenomena. These 24 points (Nijūshisekki) in the old solar calendar correspond very closely to dates of the Gregorian calendar.

The Old Lunar Calendar——A date in the Japanese lunar calendar conveys three pieces of information: the year, the month, and the day of the month. There are four different methods for specifying a year of the old civil calendar. (1) One method used the name of a calendrical era (NENGŌ) and the number of a year within the era. (2) Another used the sexagenary cycle. (3) For dates in early Japanese history, a year was identified by its number in the reign of an emperor. (4) Dates were sometimes shown as part of a continuing era dated from 660 BC, the legendary date of the founding of the Japanese imperial dynasty.

Nengō——The use of relatively brief calendrical eras known as *nengō* was an imitation of Chinese practice, adopted in Japan in AD 645. The first Japanese era name, commemorating the revolutionary political changes of that year, was Taika, or Great Reform. Except for a brief lapse in the late 7th century, *nengō* have been in continuous use ever since.

Customarily a new era was declared by the imperial court within a year or two after the accession of a new emperor. In addition, at two points in each sexagenary cycle, the 1st year and the 58th (which were thought to be auspicious), a new era was usually proclaimed.

Premodern *nengō* are not reign names. Only after 1868 did the Japanese adopt the practice of including the entire reign of an emperor in one era. Meiji, the era proclaimed in that year, continued until the death of the reigning sovereign in 1912.

The Sexagenary Cycle——In addition to cardinal numerals, the Chinese and Japanese employ two sets of terms for purposes of enumeration (see JIKKAN JŪNISHI). One set contains 10 terms known as *jikkan* (the 10 stems). The other contains 12 terms called *jūnishi* (the 12 branches).

Since ancient times, East Asian peoples have used these two sets of terms to enumerate years (and other units) of their civil calendars. When both series are used together they form a greater cycle of 60 combinations, as 60 is the least common multiple of 10 and 12. The 1st combination in the sexagenary cycle is formed of the 1st stem and the 1st branch, followed by the 2nd stem and the 2nd branch, and so on. The 11th combination consists of the 1st stem and the 11th branch, the 12th the 2nd stem and 12th branch, and the 13th the 3rd stem and 1st branch. Each of the 10 stems corresponds to a certain final digit in the number of a Christian-era year.

The Japanese "Imperial Era"——The method of counting years from the legendary founding of Japan in 660 BC was begun in the early Meiji period (1868–1912) and commonly used until the end of World War II, when it was abandoned. The word *kigen* (the beginning of the dynasty) or *kōki* (imperial era) is sometimes prefixed to such dates to differentiate them from years of the Christian era.

Reign Years——For dates of the 7th century and earlier, when official *nengō* did not exist, years may be designated by number within the reign of an emperor. In this case the official posthumous name of the emperor is used, and it is usually followed by the word *tennō* (sovereign) to distinguish the designation from a true *nengō*. This system appears similar to that for assigning *nengō* today. However, it differs in one important respect. The "first year" of a reign is taken, for calendrical purposes, to be the first full calendar year after the emperor's accession, rather than the year in which the accession took place, as with *nengō* today.

Months——All civil months (except the first, which was usually known as Shōgatsu) were designated by number or, if intercalary,

The Twenty-Four Points (Sekki and Chūki) of the Old Solar Calendar

Gregorian calendar	Old solar calendar	Name of sekki or chūki		Meaning	Associations
4 February	1 January	Risshun	立春	Beginning of spring	Old solar "New Year"
18 or 19 February		Usui	雨水	"Rainwater"	Snow melting to rain
5 or 6 March	1 February	Keichitsu	啓蟄	"End of insect hibernation"	Warmer weather; emergence of insects
20 or 21 March		Shumbun	春分	Vernal equinox	
4 or 5 April	1 March	Seimei	清明	"Pure and clear"	Southeasterly winds and pleasant weather
20 or 21 April		Kokuu	穀雨	"Grain rains"	Germination of grains in spring rains
5 or 6 May	1 April	Rikka	立夏	Beginning of summer	
21 May		Shōman	小満	"The lesser ripening"	Growth of all things
5 or 6 June	1 May	Bōshu	芒種	"Grain beards and seeds"	Transplanting of rice
21 or 22 June		Geshi	夏至	Summer solstice	
7 or 8 July	1 June	Shōsho	小暑	"The lesser heat"	Increase in summer heat
22 or 23 July		Taisho	大暑	"The greater heat"	Maximum summer heat
7 or 8 August	1 July	Risshū	立秋	Beginning of autumn	
23 or 24 August		Shosho	処暑	"Manageable heat"	Autumn winds and lessening of heat
7 or 8 September	1 August	Hakuro	白露	"White dew"	Autumn weather; migration of birds
23 September		Shūbun	秋分	Autumnal equinox	
8 or 9 October	1 September	Kanro	寒露	"Cold dew"	Turning of leaves; height of autumn
23 or 24 October		Sōkō	霜降	"Frost falls"	First frost; end of autumn
7 or 8 November	1 October	Rittō	立冬	Beginning of winter	
22 or 23 November		Shōsetsu	小雪	"The lesser snow"	Light snowfall
7 or 8 December	1 November	Taisetsu	大雪	"The greater snow"	Heavy snowfall; winter weather
21 or 22 December		Tōji	冬至	Winter solstice	
5 or 6 January	1 December	Shōkan	小寒	"The lesser cold"	Increase in cold weather
20 or 21 January		Daikan	大寒	"The greater cold"	Maximum winter cold

spring summer autumn winter *sekki* *chūki*

by the character *jun* or *uruu* plus the name of the preceding month. Terms of the sexagenary cycle could theoretically be applied to months but almost never were in practice.

In addition to their formal Sino-Japanese names (Shōgatsu or Ichigatsu, Nigatsu, Sangatsu, etc), the months had informal or poetic ones of native Japanese origin. The following are the informal or poetic names for the months in the old Japanese calendar. There are various theories regarding their origins and etymologies; the most commonly accepted folk versions of their meanings are given below. (1) Mutsuki: the month of affection—when family and friends join to celebrate the New Year. (2) Kisaragi: the month of putting on more clothes against the cold. (3) Yayoi: the month of renewed growth. (4) Uzuki: the month in which the deutzia blooms. (5) Satsuki: the month of planting rice shoots. (6) Minazuki: the waterless month. (7) Fuzuki or Fumizuki: the month in which the rice ears swell; the month of writing poetry. (8) Hazuki: the month of (falling) leaves. (9) Nagatsuki: the month of long nights. (10) Kannazuki: the godless month—when legend has it that the gods leave their homes all over Japan to assemble at the Great Shrine of Izumo. (11) Shimotsuki: the month of frost. (12) Shiwasu: the month of busy priests—who run about attending to religious services as the year draws to an end. These names are rarely used as parts of full dates.

Times of Day—Until the Meiji period, when the Western system for telling time came into general use, the Japanese described times of day in two different ways. One of these made use of the 12 branches of the sexagenary system. The period from sunset to sunrise was divided into six equal parts, and the period from sunrise to sunset also into six equal parts, but not necessarily of the same duration as the other six. Sometimes a cyclical sign might be used for the beginning of a period, rather than its whole duration. The other system divided the day into the same 12 parts but assigned numbers to them. See also PERIODIZATION; SHIBUKAWA SHUNKAI; TAKAHASHI YOSHITOKI.

calligraphy 書道

(*shodō;* the Way of writing). In Japan, as in other countries in the Chinese cultural sphere, calligraphy is considered one of the fine arts. In China, the birthplace of the East Asian tradition of calligraphy, the three disciplines—poetry, calligraphy, and painting—were considered the proper attainments of every cultured person, and excellence in writing thought to be a manifestation of the practitioner's character. The respect accorded to calligraphy in Japan is essentially an extension of its status in China.

The history of Japanese calligraphy begins with the introduction into Japan of the Chinese writing system in about the 5th century AD. Initially the Japanese wrote in Chinese, but they soon began using Chinese characters, or KANJI, in new ways to suit the requirements of their native language. The poetry anthology MAN'YŌSHŪ (mid-8th century), for example, was written using Chinese characters to convey either Japanese words or syllables. The latter phonetic method of writing is now known as *man'yōgana.* This practice ultimately led to the creation in the early 9th century of Japanese syllabaries, or KANA, that were used either alone or in combination with Chinese characters. The Japanese *kana* script was in

wide use in the 10th century and emerged as a major calligraphic form after the 11th century. Nevertheless, for a long time the Chinese language retained its status as the literary language of the elite, and to varying degrees it was favored in later periods as well (see POETRY AND PROSE IN CHINESE).

Scripts—Various types of Chinese-character scripts, or SHOTAI, representing the historical development of writing in China, are practiced. *Tensho,* or archaic script, is traditionally used for carving official SEALS. *Reisho,* or clerical script, was once used for official documents. These are very ancient Chinese scripts and did not come into extensive use in Japan until the Edo period (1600–1868), when Chinese historical studies received much attention. More common is *kaisho,* or block-style script, perhaps the most popular style since the characters are easily recognizable. *Gyōsho,* or "running-style" script, is created by a faster movement of the brush and some consequent abbreviation of the character. This script is frequently used for informal writing. *Sōsho,* or "grass-writing," is a true cursive style that abbreviates and links parts of a character, resulting in fluid and curvilinear writing. In *sōsho* writing, variations in the size of different characters may occur in the flow of a column, and some characters may be joined to the next, creating rhythmic and artistic forms.

Implements—Compared to writing styles, calligraphy implements have changed very little since the early days of the art. There are two basic kinds of brush: *futofude* (thick brush) and *hosofude* (slender brush); the former is generally used for the main body of a text, and the latter for inscriptions and signature at the end of a work, or for small-character calligraphy or fine cursive writing. *Sumi,* or Chinese ink, is usually

The Premodern Time System

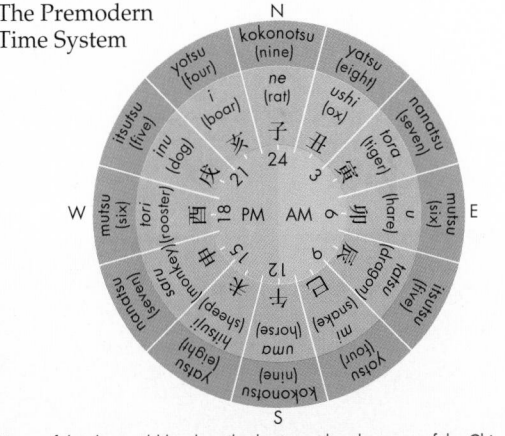

Hours of the day could be described using either the terms of the Chinese sexagenary cycle (the 12 branches) or numbers. *Ne* (rat) corresponds roughly to the period between 11:00 P.M. and 1:00 A.M. The "hour of the rat" might also be referred to as the *kokonotsu-doki* or the "ninth hour." Additional terms distinguishing daytime and nighttime hours were used in combination with the numbers. The 12 branches were also used to indicate direction.

made of soot from burned wood or oil mixed with fishbone or hide glue and dried into a stick. To make liquid ink the stick is rubbed on an inkstone, or *suzuri,* that has an indentation at one end to hold water that gradually darkens as the stick is rubbed. The *suiteki,* or small water dropper, which is either ceramic or metal, completes the basic paraphernalia. When not in use, writing equipment is kept in a box called a *suzuribako,* which is usually lacquer ware and often elaborately decorated.

Early History—The earliest Japanese writing in Chinese is found in INSCRIPTIONS in stone or metal, and among the oldest of these are the cast or incised inscriptions on a

calligraphy

Poems of the 8th- to 9th-century poet Ki no Tsurayuki are shown in this detail from the 12th-century *Anthologies of the Thirty-Six Poetic Geniuses.* National Treasure.

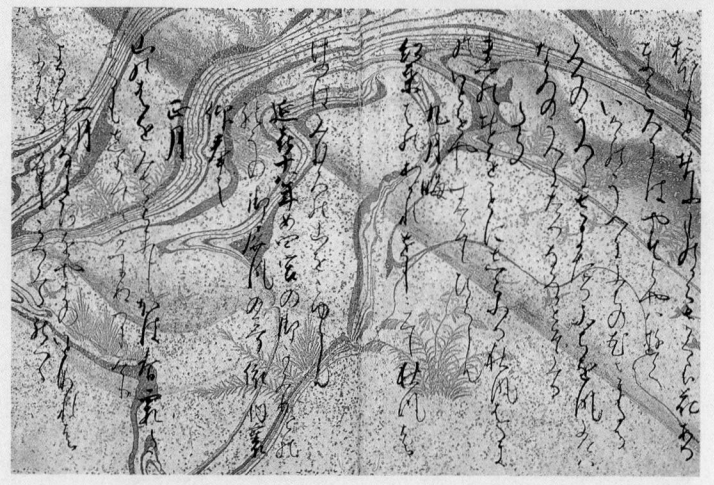

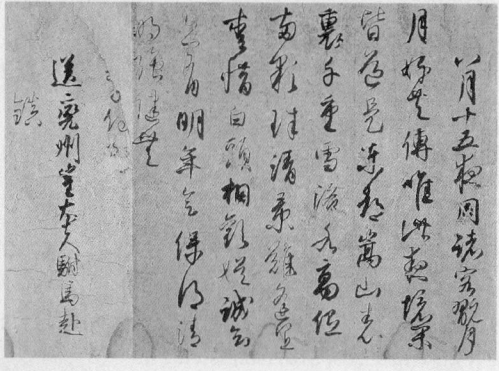

A poem by mid-Heian-period calligraphy master Fujiwara no Sukemasa in his own hand. National Treasure.

A surviving portion of an early-9th-century holograph commentary by the monk Kūkai on the Buddhist sutra *Kongō hannyakyō.* National Treasure.

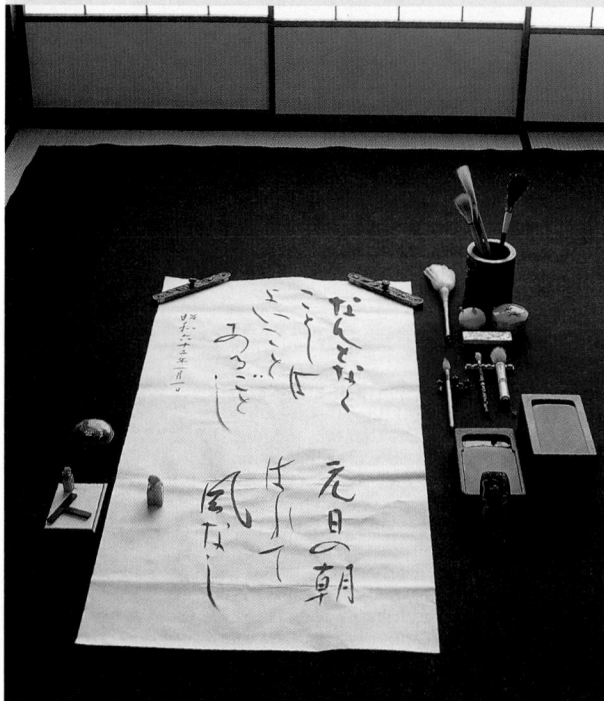

Here, brushes, inkstones, and other calligraphy implements are carefully laid out for the first writing of the New Year (*kakizome*), customarily done on 2 January.

who introduced the calligraphic style of Yan Zhenqing (Yen Chen-ch'ing; 709–785), then popular in metropolitan Tang China, and promoted an awareness of calligraphy as an aesthetic form. Kūkai and his contemporaries, Emperor SAGA (786–842) and the courtier TACHIBANA NO HAYANARI (d 842), were known to later generations as the Sampitsu (the "Three Brushes").

A major transformation in calligraphy from a rigid emulation of Chinese styles to creative assimilation occurred in the 10th and 11th centuries. This was the time of the Sanseki (Three [Brush] Traces): ONO NO TŌFŪ (894–966), FUJIWARA NO SUKEMASA (944–998), and FUJIWARA NO YUKINARI (or Fujiwara no Kōzei; 972–1028). Yukinari is known for various transcriptions of Chinese poems, yet no example of *kana* in his hand remains. Nevertheless, the 11th-century transcripts of KOKINSHŪ poems called *kōyagire* (Mt. Kōya fragments) are generally regarded as classic examples of the tradition of Yukinari-style *kana* calligraphy. This was the standard followed by courtier-calligraphers into the Kamakura period (1185–1333), when it became known as the Sesonji-school style, after a temple associated with Yukinari. To describe this style of calligraphy, which resulted from the assimilation of Chinese models, the term *wayō* (Japanese mode) is often used. A variant *wayō* style, which became known as the Hosshōji school, was established by Fujiwara no Moromichi (1062–99) and his grandson Tadamichi (1097–1164).

Kamakura and Muromachi (1333–1568) Periods——The continued transmission of the orthodox Sesonji-school calligraphy resulted in increasing mannerism. However, Son'en (1298–1356), the sixth prince of Emperor FUSHIMI (1265–1317)—himself an enthusiastic follower of the Yukinari style—revitalized the tradition by creating a style of calligraphy that came to be known as the Shōren'in-school style. Another important development was the appearance of strongly personalized styles, most notably those of the poet-calligraphers FUJIWARA NO TOSHINARI (1114–1204) and his son FUJIWARA NO SADAIE (1162–1241).

Chinese Song (Sung; 960–1279) calligraphy had a great impact on Japanese practitioners, especially through Zen monks. EISAI (1141–1215) and DŌGEN (1200–1253) returned from pilgrimages to China in the late 12th and early 13th centuries, respectively, and their surviving calligraphic works reflect the influence of the Southern Song revival of Northern Song calligraphy, a trend embodied in the works of Su Shi (Su Shih; 1036–1101) and Huang Tingjian (Huang T'ing-chien; 1045–1105). Huang Tingjian, in particular, was eagerly emulated by the monks of the GOZAN Zen temples, such as KOKAN SHIREN (1278–1346), who mastered both the semicursive *gyōsho* and cursive *sōsho* modes. No calligrapher, however, was so artistically aware of the expressive potential of Song calligraphy as SŌHŌ MYŌCHŌ (1282–1337). His powerful style follows in the Song tradition, particularly that of Huang Tingjian, without being overly imitative. Lanqi Daolong (Lan-ch'i Tao-lung; J: RANKEI DŌRYŪ; 1213–78), one of a number of Chinese monks who came to Japan, wrote in the style of the Song calligrapher Zhang Jizhi (Chang Chi-chih; 1186–1266), best known for his regular script.

Works of calligraphy by Zen monks came to be known as *bokuseki* ("ink traces") and

bronze mirror excavated in Wakayama Prefecture and a bronze sword recently unearthed at the INARIYAMA TOMB in Saitama Prefecture.

With the introduction of Buddhism and Confucianism to Japan around the 6th century, numerous examples of Chinese writing entered Japan, mostly sutras and Buddhist commentaries written in brush and ink on paper in varied script styles. The earliest extant handwritten text by a Japanese is thought to be the *Commentary on the Lotus Sutra* (see SANGYŌ GISHO), which is purported to have been written by Prince SHŌTOKU (574–622). It is written in a typical clerical-cursive style that was current in China from the late 4th century to the late 6th century.

From the late 7th century through the 8th century, early Tang (T'ang; 618–907) dynasty calligraphic styles were rapidly mastered in Japan, notably through increased sutra-copying activities that began in earnest with the establishment of the Shakyōjo, or Sutra-Copying Bureau, in the capital city of Nara. An important example of Nara-period calligraphy is the inventory of items offered to the temple TŌDAIJI. Written by Empress KŌMYŌ (701–760), it has been preserved, along with many of the articles that it documents, at the SHŌSŌIN imperial storehouse.

Heian Period (794–1185)——An early influence upon the development of Japanese calligraphy was the monk KŪKAI (774–835),

camellias
1 Considered sacred, the *tsubaki* is often planted in temple and shrine gardens.
2 The *yabutsubaki* species is the parent stock of most Japanese horticultural varieties of camellia.

were prized by monastic communities, which treated them as icons symbolizing spiritual transmission from master to master. Particularly noted for their calligraphy were the Zen monks MUSŌ SOSEKI (1275–1351), Kokan Shiren, SESSON YŪBAI (1290–1346), TESSHŪ TOKUSAI (fl 1342–66), and ZEKKAI CHŪSHIN (1336–1405). The two-volume *Bokuseki soshi den* (1805) contains texts of 119 Chinese and 104 Japanese Zen calligraphers.

The traditional Sesonji and Shōren'in schools of *wayō* calligraphy, which developed along family lines, reached the point of stagnation in the 16th century. However, their broad influence resulted in their application to all kinds of formats: official documents, letters, commercial inventories, and signs. The Shōren'in school became popularly known as *oieryū*, or "honorable family school."

Azuchi-Momoyama (1568–1600) and Edo (1600–1868) Periods—Three creative calligraphers who brought new life to the *wayō* mode were HON'AMI KŌETSU (1558–1637), the aristocrat KONOE NOBUTADA (1565–1614), and the monk of the esoteric Shingon sect of Buddhism, SHŌKADŌ SHŌJŌ (1584–1659). Kōetsu incorporated into Shōren'in-style *kana* the cursive style of Zhang Jizhi. Nobutada's style, although said to have derived from the Shōren'in tradition, is highly individualized, bold, and vigorous. Shōkadō Shōjō, who also arose from the Shōren'in tradition, developed an eclectic *kana* style influenced by the calligraphy of Kūkai and Fujiwara no Yukinari.

The establishment in 1661, largely by Chinese monks, of the ŌBAKU SECT of Zen in Uji, south of Kyōto, contributed to an influx of Ming-dynasty (1368–1644) styles of calligraphy. They were enthusiastically received by Japanese men of letters, who created a new orthodoxy called *karayō* (Chinese mode), which eventually overshadowed the *wayō* tradition. HOSOI KŌTAKU (1658–1735), RAI SAN'YŌ (1781–1832), and SAKUMA SHŌZAN (1811–64) are among the more famous calligraphers who wrote in this mode, which was greatly favored by literati scholars and artists (see BUNJINGA) throughout the Edo period.

Contemporary Calligraphy—In the modern era, calligraphy has continued to thrive, and it is represented, along with painting and sculpture, at the government-sponsored annual Nitten exhibitions. In post–World War II Japan, avant-garde calligraphy (*zen'ei shodō*) was born—a genre in itself. This recent trend in calligraphy asserts new artistic forms of pure abstraction, coming close to some aspects of 20th-century Western pictorial art and deviating sharply from the traditional script styles and emulative aspects of the age-old art of calligraphy. 📞 *158–159*

Calpis Food Industry Co, Ltd
カルピス食品工業[株]

(Karupisu Shokuhin Kōgyō). Manufacturer of soft drinks and dairy products. Incorporated in 1948. The company is known for its main product, Calpis (Calpico in overseas markets), a soft drink made from skimmed milk by a lactic acid bacterial fermentation process that was invented around 1919 by Mishima Kaiun, the company's founder. Sales for 1990 totaled ¥68.5 billion (US $512.9 million), and the company was capitalized at ¥13.1 billion (US $98.1 million) in the same year. Headquarters are in Tōkyō.

Calsonic Corporation カルソニック[株]

(Karusonikku). Manufacturer of heat-related automobile parts, including radiators, car heaters, air conditioners, oil coolers, and mufflers. Incorporated in 1938. A consolidated subsidiary of NISSAN MOTOR CO, LTD, Calsonic has production and sales subsidiaries and representative offices in the United States, Europe, Australia, and Southeast Asia and distributes comprehensive lines of components to local automakers. For the fiscal year ending March 1991, sales totaled ¥208.5 billion (US $1.5 billion) and capitalization stood at ¥9.4 billion (US $68.5 million). Headquarters are in Tōkyō.

Cambodia and Japan
カンボジアと日本

(Kambojia to Nihon). The first known contact between Cambodia and Japan was during the 16th and 17th centuries, when trade was begun and residential quarters for Japanese merchants (NIHOMMACHI) were established in Cambodian port towns. Contact between the two countries remained at a low level until 1940, when Japan intervened in the Thai-Indochinese border dispute and forced the French (who at the time ruled all of Indochina as a colony) to accept Thai claims on the western provinces of Cambodia and Laos. In July 1941 Japan and the Vichy government of France reached an agreement on the joint defense of Indochina, and Japanese troops were stationed in Cambodian territory. In March 1945 the Japanese army ousted the French administration from Indochina and had King Norodom Sihanouk declare Cambodia's independence. Japanese patronage of Cambodia ended in August 1945 with Japan's defeat in World War II.

After the conclusion of the SAN FRANCISCO PEACE TREATY in 1951, diplomatic relations were resumed between Japan and Cambodia. In 1955 Norodom Sihanouk visited Japan and signed a friendship treaty. In 1970 General Lon Nol deposed Sihanouk, and Japan officially recognized the new government. Economic relations between Japan and Lon Nol's Cambodia did not develop smoothly, however, since Cambodia was engaged in an intense civil war.

After Phnom Penh fell to the Khmer Rouge in April 1975, Japan recognized the new Pol Pot government. When open conflict broke out between Cambodia and Vietnam and between China and Vietnam in early 1979, Japan joined with China and the Association of Southeast Asian Nations (ASEAN) in support of anti-Vietnamese forces in Cambodia and did not recognize the Vietnamese-backed Heng Samrin government. Japan also began providing substantial amounts of aid to Cambodian refugees in Thai territory. In 1989 Japan was a participant in the international meetings on Cambodia held in Paris, and in 1990 it sponsored a conference in Tōkyō that was attended by the leaders of the four factions contending for power in Cambodia.

camellias 椿

(*tsubaki*). Evergreen trees of the tea family (Theaceae), genus *Camellia*, indigenous throughout Japan except to Hokkaidō. They are also widely grown as ornamentals. Two species are native to Japan: the *yabutsubaki* (*Camellia japonica*) and the *yukitsubaki* (*C. rusticana* or *C. japonica* var. *decumbens*). From these two, many horticultural varieties have been developed (about 200 horticultural varieties were recorded in Japan by 1695). The flowers of horticultural varieties range in color from white to pink, dark red, and streaked types.

The *yabutsubaki*, also known as *yamatsubaki*, grows on hills and in thickets along the coasts of Honshū, Shikoku, and Kyūshū. It reaches more than 10 meters (33 ft) in height. The bark is grayish white; its thick, glossy alternate leaves are oval and pointed at both ends. It blossoms in November in warm areas and in early spring in colder areas. The single, usually red, flowers have five petals that merge into a cylinder at the base, where abundant nectar attracts small birds for pollination.

The *yukitsubaki* is a shrub that grows 1–2 meters (3–7 ft) high in regions of deep snow along the coast of the Sea of Japan in northern Honshū. In late spring the *yukitsubaki* produces mostly red flowers with deep yellow stamen filaments. A double-flowered variety is also cultivated.

Camellia wood is hard and has long been used for making implements. The oil pressed from the round seeds of the camellia was prized for cooking and as hair oil. Today ornamental varieties are planted in shady areas and used as windbreaks. Varieties with small leaves are used in BONSAI, and some types are popular in early spring flower arrangements. See also SAZANKA.

Bold Strokes: The Modern Rebirth of Calligraphy

Prior to the modern era, two writing traditions dominated the realm of Japanese calligraphy. One genre focused on Chinese ideograms (*kanji*), while the other involved writing in Japanese phonetic symbols (*kana*). When Japan's long seclusion ended in the late 19th century, renewed contact with China led to a modern rebirth of the art as enthusiastic Japanese calligraphers regained access to the vast and valuable resources of classical Chinese calligraphy. Japanese seal engravers, for instance, inspired by seals carved by their Chinese peers, crafted superb works that reinvigorated the genre. By World War II, seal engraving was viewed as a 20th-century art form in its own right, and seals were often displayed alongside examples of *kana* and *kanji* at exhibitions.

The postwar period—marked by heightened interest in exhibitions, a relatively liberal social atmosphere, and a more Westernized lifestyle—injected new energy into calligraphy. One offshoot, oversized *kana* symbols, had great impact when displayed in spacious modern exhibition halls. Other subgenres, known collectively as contemporary calligraphy, include a minimalist style called *shōjisū sho*, which involves limited numbers of characters; so-called avant-garde works, in which characters are often abstracted; and calligraphic transcriptions of passages from modern Japanese literature. While calligraphy remains rooted in a rich and venerable tradition, new forms and styles are emerging to expand its boundaries.

Sugawara Norio

Nishikawa Yasushi received the Art Academy prize at the 10th Nitten exhibition for the 1953 work at left (two panels, 128 × 28 cm each), rendered with a power and weight that recalls the calligraphic style of the Chinese literati painters of the Qing dynasty. In contrast, Aoyama San'u strives for a more emotive effect in the 1977 work below. 108 × 103 cm.

Kanji

The mystique of ancient Chinese characters and the interest they inspired in the roots of calligraphy are strongly reflected in the works of Nishikawa Yasushi, whose strong hand and balanced sense of composition produced calligraphy that was eventually recognized as a distinct style. His disciple Aoyama San'u further refined Nishikawa's approach.

Although well versed in the Chinese tradition, Suzuki Suiken looked to ancient Japanese models for inspiration. His singular style, built around gracefully flowing lines, captured the lyric nature of the native aesthetic.

Suzuki Suiken used the rounded sweep of his brush to imbue the characters with something of his own towering spirit. 1953. 36 × 139 cm.

Seal Carving

The seals that calligraphers and artists use to sign their works feature archaic forms of Chinese characters. In the modern era, renewed contact between Japan and China exposed Japanese calligraphers to examples of early Chinese writing that sparked renewed Japanese interest in carving seals. Nakamura Rantai I and Kawai Senro, for example, went to China and collected innovative seals from the late Qing dynasty (1644–1912) that bore the influences of archaic characters; their own works subsequently infused new energy into the genre. Kawai, whose seals display both scholarship and exquisite craftsmanship, exerted a strong influence over seal carvers and calligraphers like Nishikawa Yasushi. The following generation of carvers was led by a Kawai disciple, Yamada Shōhei, and Nakamura Rantai II, among others.

Kawai Senro's work reflects his deep knowledge of calligraphy. At far left, the simplicity and sharpness of line displayed in an early-1930s work convey the clarity of Kawai's vision. 1.6 × 1.6 cm. Skillful carving accentuates the inherent interest of the letter forms in the seal impression at left by Yamada Shōhei. 1960. 3.4 × 3.4 cm.

The fluid shapes of the *kana* in this 1968 piece by Hibino Gohō reflect his utter control of the brush—a sureness of stroke he gained from writing oversized characters. 17 × 17 cm.

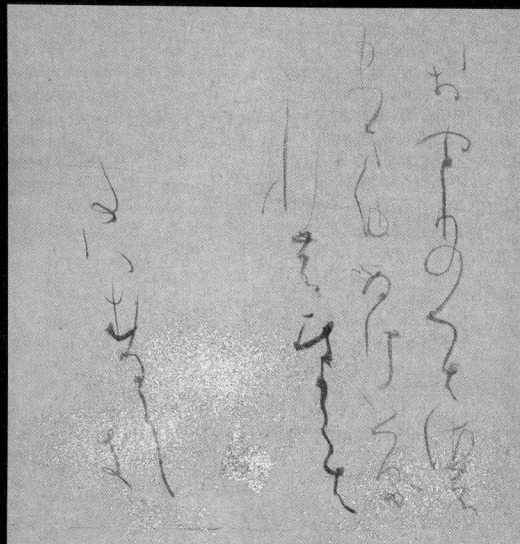

Kana

While still firmly linked to works done as far back as the Heian period (794–1185), *kana* calligraphy underwent some changes during the post–World War II era. Hibino Gohō, along with others such as Andō Seikū and Miyamoto Chikukei, devised oversized *kana* calligraphy, including some works as tall as a human being. Hibino later reverted to standard-sized *kana* and produced a number of fine pieces before formulating a distinctive style of "detached" *kana*, dispensing with the customary connection between characters. This was his response to the quandary facing *kana* calligraphers: how to exploit the classical tradition without being shackled by its conventions.

This 1956 piece by Inoue Yūichi was featured in Herbert Read's *A Concise History of Modern Painting*. The thick brushstrokes, endowed with the force of life, are a distinctive feature of Inoue's art. The movement coming off the top and bottom of the paper stimulates the viewer's imagination. 187 × 176 cm.

The novel composition and powerful form of this work by Teshima Yūkei, which won a prize at the art exhibition held at the Brussels World Fair in 1958, embody the freshness of the artist's insight. 1955. 69 × 140 cm.

Minimalism

In this style, called *shōjisū sho*, the number of characters is limited to keep the primary focus on their meaning. Teshima Yūkei displayed a groundbreaking four-character work at the 1949 Nitten exhibition that shaped characters in novel ways to express what they meant and instilled in them some of the literally pictographic quality of Chinese ideograms at their most primitive. Teshima's career might be summarized as an effort to merge calligraphy with the plastic arts while simultaneously avoiding repetition of past styles.

Literary Transcriptions

This subgenre's practitioners draw material from modern literature, bringing the works they create—and calligraphy itself—closer to the general public. Conceived by Kaneko Ōtei, the movement gained strength after World War II with the addition of new members like Iijima Shunkei, Shinoda Tōkō, and Aoki Kōryū. In their drive to popularize calligraphy, these individuals overcame the formalistic challenge of combining rigid, highly structured Chinese characters with *kana*'s curved, elegant lines.

Kaneko Ōtei's 1986 transcription of a prose poem by Inoue Yasushi is mounted on an eight-panel folding screen. The calligraphic style is clear and easy to read, and a taut balance is maintained between the *kanji* and *kana* characters. 138 × 416 cm.

Avant-Garde

Postwar practitioners Ueda Sōkyū and Uno Sesson held that calligraphy expressed an interior vision. They worked to develop a calligraphy unfettered by symbols and refused to distinguish between forms that represented characters and those that did not. Employing a line tempered by calligraphic technique, they crafted works that share features with abstract art. Inoue Yūichi has also been praised in the West for pieces considered in the tradition of contemporary painting. By challenging the notion that calligraphy is confined to the writing of letters, the avant-garde continues to test the supposed separation between calligraphy and modern art.

camphor tree The *kusunoki* produces panicles of small white flowers in late spring. The tree is a source of camphor, which has long been used for incense and as a medicine.

camera industry カメラ産業

(*kamera sangyō*). The first commercially produced camera in Japan was the Cherry, put on sale by Konishi Honten (forerunner of the KONICA CORPORATION) in 1903. A dryplate box camera aimed at the amateur market, it was heavily dependent on technology pioneered by European and American manufacturers. Japanese camera production grew slowly in the following decades, and even in 1930 total output stood at a mere 36,700 units.

The real boom in the Japanese camera industry came after World War II. Optical manufacturers, which had been geared to military production, turned to production of cameras. Major camera companies such as NIKON CORPORATION and CANON, INC, established their position in the market during the postwar years. Growing domestic demand fueled production, which passed the 1 million unit mark in 1955. By 1962 Japan had replaced West Germany as the world's largest camera manufacturer, producing 2.9 million units in that year. In the 1970s innovations in optics and electronics made possible quantum leaps in camera performance—the first autofocus system for a popular-priced camera made its debut in 1977. By 1990 domestic camera production reached more than 16.9 million units, and if production by overseas subsidiaries is added, total output for the industry stood at nearly 30 million units. Japan now accounts for 80 percent of global production of 35-millimeter single-lens reflex cameras. 🖝 161

camphor tree 樟

(*kusunoki;* also known as *kusu*). *Cinnamomum camphora.* An evergreen tree of the family Lauraceae that grows wild in warm regions of western Honshū and in Shikoku and Kyūshū. *Kusunoki* grow up to 20 meters (65 ft) in height, with a trunk diameter of up to 2 meters (6.5 ft); gigantic specimens close to 1,000 years old are known. The leaves are alternate, ovate, leathery, and glossy. Spring-blooming panicles of small white flowers later turn yellowish, and the globular fruit turns black when ripe. The wood of the *kusunoki* is used for ornamental woodwork, carvings, musical instruments, furniture, and shipbuilding. The *kusunoki* is a major source of camphor and camphor oil.

Canada and Japan カナダと日本

(Kanada *to* Nihon). The first contact between Japan and Canada took place during the Meiji period (1868–1912), when two Canadian Methodist missionaries, George Cochran (1835–1901) and Davidson McDonald (1836–1905), landed at Yokohama in 1873. Cochran was instrumental in the conversion of prominent Meiji leaders; McDonald, a doctor, contributed to the development of modern medicine in Japan. By the turn of the century, many Methodist missionaries had come to Japan from Canada and converted thousands of Japanese.

Nagano Manzō (1855–1924) became the first Japanese immigrant to Canada in 1877. Envisioning North America as the promised land, many Japanese thereafter immigrated to Canada, which needed cheap labor to develop its west coast. As the Japanese and Chinese population increased, however, anti-Asian sentiment grew, culminating in the Vancouver riot of 1907, which destroyed Japanese and Chinese settlements. After this incident, the Japanese government regulated the number of immigrants to Canada in accordance with the Lemieux Agreement (1908). Nevertheless, immigration continued to be a sore point in Japan-Canada relations, the issue having become increasingly complicated with the 1902 signing of the ANGLO-JAPANESE ALLIANCE. To avoid being caught between Japan and Britain in regard to the immigration problem, Canada took the initiative in bringing about the abrogation of the alliance at the WASHINGTON CONFERENCE OF 1921–22.

In 1929 Canada established a legation in Tōkyō. Trade with Japan was the major reason for this Canadian move. A Japanese legation had been established in Canada in 1928, and even after Japanese aggression in Chinese territory, beginning with the MANCHURIAN INCIDENT of 1931, Canada tried to maintain friendly relations with Japan. Prime Minister W. L. Mackenzie King (1874–1950) believed that it was in Canada's interest to avoid entanglement in power struggles between major nations in the international community. Japan's attack on Pearl Harbor in 1941, however, led to a rupture in diplomatic relations between the two countries.

Canadian policy toward Japan after the war had three major aims: to ensure that Japan would never again threaten world peace and Canada's security, to democratize Japan, and to help Japan's economic rehabilitation with an eye to future trade with Japan. In line with these principles, Canada played a mediating role among the Allied powers during the Allied OCCUPATION of Japan (1945–52).

When the San Francisco Peace Treaty came into effect in 1952, Japan and Canada resumed diplomatic relations; in June of that year their legations were raised to the status of embassies. Japan's primary goal after defeat was to recover full membership in the community of nations. Canada supported Japan by taking the initiative for Japanese membership in the General Agreement on Tariffs and Trade (GATT) in 1955, the United Nations in 1956, and the Organization for Economic Cooperation and Development (OECD) in 1963. Japan also looked to Canada for its abundant natural resources and by 1972 had passed Britain to become the second most important customer (after the United States) for Canada's exports.

Although trade has been the most vital concern for both countries, the bilateral relationship has been strengthened in other areas as well. In 1976 the Cultural Agreement between the two nations was signed, together with the "Framework Agreement for Economic Cooperation between Japan and Canada." The Japanese Association for Canadian Studies was founded the following year. Japanese immigrants are now welcomed by Canada: since 1966 the Canadian government has operated a special visa office in Tōkyō to encourage qualified Japanese to immigrate to Canada.

In the area of trade, relations between Japan and Canada have grown increasingly close. In 1990 Japan's imports from Canada totaled US $8.4 billion and its exports to Canada US $6.7 billion, making Japan Canada's second largest trading partner next to the United States in both imports and exports. The chief product that Japan exports to Canada is automobiles, and its most important imports are coal, lumber, and wood pulp. Canada is at present seeking the expansion of its exports of high-technology and other industrial products to Japan.

In the period 1987–89 direct Japanese investment in Canada amounted to US $2.6 billion, which represents 57.5 percent of total investments between 1951 and 1989. Nevertheless, Japan's share of total foreign investment in Canada is less than 2 percent. Canada has requested that Japan increase its investment to a tenth of the US investment share of 41.4 percent.

Canada, Japanese immigrants in カナダ移民

(Kanada *imin*). The first Japanese settler in Canada is believed to have arrived in 1877. There was sparse but steady migration after that with a heavy, yet transitory, migration in the last years of the 1890s, when perhaps 12,000 immigrants came. The 1901 census found fewer than 5,000 Japanese in Canada, most of them in British Columbia. The 1941 census showed only 23,000, of whom about 60 percent were native-born Canadians; some 96 percent of all Japanese Canadians lived in British Columbia. At this time, Japanese immigrants accounted for only 2–3 percent of British Columbia's population, but they were particularly important in fishing and agriculture.

By the 1890s, western Canada had a full-blown anti-Oriental tradition and "YELLOW PERIL" phobia. Canada, however, was inhibited by the ANGLO-JAPANESE ALLIANCE (1902–23), which meant that it was impossible for Canada to pass the same kind of discriminatory legislation against Japanese immigrants that it had against earlier Chinese immigrants. Executive agreements between Canada and Japan kept immigration at a trickle after 1919. Canadian law allowed Japanese immigrants to become naturalized citizens and, by 1941, 64 percent of the Japanese-born aliens in Canada had become Canadian citizens. But in British Columbia, where almost all of the Canadian Japanese lived, the right to vote was denied them.

Only five days after President Franklin D. Roosevelt signed an executive order that enabled the US Army to evacuate West Coast Japanese Americans, Canadian prime minister William Lyon Mackenzie King issued a similar order (24 February 1942) which gave his government control over the movements of all persons of Japanese origin in certain "protected areas" including the 100-mile-wide strip along the Pacific Coast. Japanese were forced to abandon most of their property. The Canadian government forced men

The Evolution of the Japanese Camera

By 1903 Japanese imitations of Western box cameras were being produced to meet the needs of non-professionals, but imported lenses and shutter mechanisms made them expensive. As manufacturers in Japan began making these components themselves in the early Shōwa period (1926–89), the size and cost of cameras began to shrink, eventually

bringing them into reach for the average family. Booming economic growth after the mid-1950s led camera manufacturers eager for market share to diversify and customize their product lines. After racing to develop the optimum single-lens reflex (SLR) camera for professionals and camera buffs, they went on to create compact cameras, half-frame

cameras, and disposable cameras that even children could handle. Today, thanks to decades of trial and error in market research and sales analysis, features like built-in, metered strobes are commonplace, and options such as automatic focus, exposure, and dating are taken for granted.

Shibata Takao

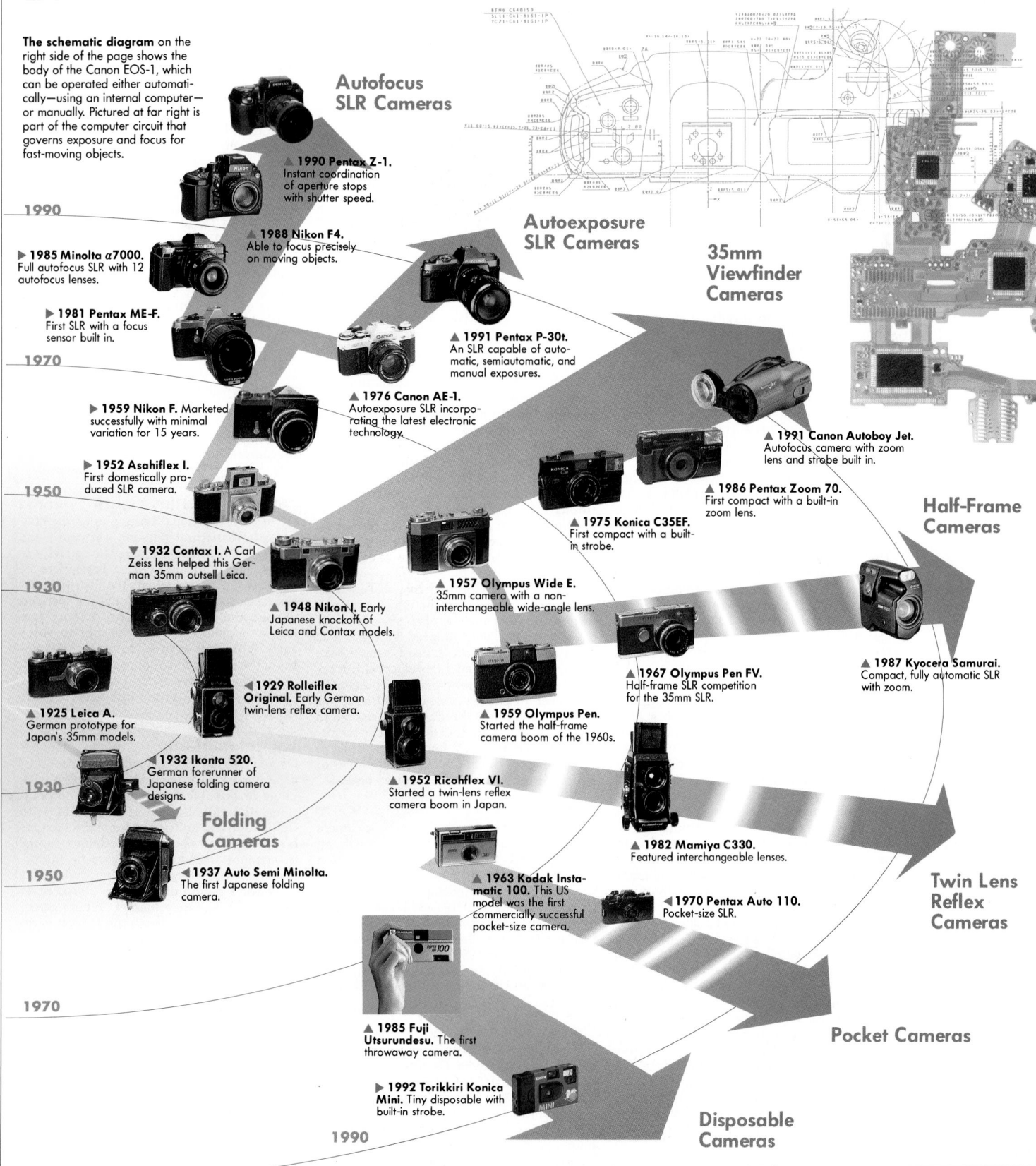

The schematic diagram on the right side of the page shows the body of the Canon EOS-1, which can be operated either automatically—using an internal computer—or manually. Pictured at far right is part of the computer circuit that governs exposure and focus for fast-moving objects.

Autofocus SLR Cameras

1990 Pentax Z-1. Instant coordination of aperture stops with shutter speed.

1988 Nikon F4. Able to focus precisely on moving objects.

1985 Minolta α7000. Full autofocus SLR with 12 autofocus lenses.

1981 Pentax ME-F. First SLR with a focus sensor built in.

1959 Nikon F. Marketed successfully with minimal variation for 15 years.

1952 Asahiflex I. First domestically produced SLR camera.

1932 Contax I. A Carl Zeiss lens helped this German 35mm outsell Leica.

1948 Nikon I. Early Japanese knockoff of Leica and Contax models.

1925 Leica A. German prototype for Japan's 35mm models.

1929 Rolleiflex Original. Early German twin-lens reflex camera.

1932 Ikonta 520. German forerunner of Japanese folding camera designs.

Folding Cameras

1937 Auto Semi Minolta. The first Japanese folding camera.

1952 Ricohflex VI. Started a twin-lens reflex camera boom in Japan.

1963 Kodak Instamatic 100. This US model was the first commercially successful pocket-size camera.

1985 Fuji Utsurundesu. The first throwaway camera.

1992 Torikkiri Konica Mini. Tiny disposable with built-in strobe.

Autoexposure SLR Cameras

1991 Pentax P-30t. An SLR capable of automatic, semiautomatic, and manual exposures.

1976 Canon AE-1. Autoexposure SLR incorporating the latest electronic technology.

35mm Viewfinder Cameras

1991 Canon Autoboy Jet. Autofocus camera with zoom lens and strobe built in.

1986 Pentax Zoom 70. First compact with a built-in zoom lens.

1975 Konica C35EF. First compact with a built-in strobe.

1957 Olympus Wide E. 35mm camera with a non-interchangeable wide-angle lens.

1967 Olympus Pen FV. Half-frame SLR competition for the 35mm SLR.

1959 Olympus Pen. Started the half-frame camera boom of the 1960s.

1982 Mamiya C330. Featured interchangeable lenses.

1970 Pentax Auto 110. Pocket-size SLR.

Half-Frame Cameras

1987 Kyocera Samurai. Compact, fully automatic SLR with zoom.

Twin Lens Reflex Cameras

Pocket Cameras

Disposable Cameras

161

Cancer Mortality Rates in Japan

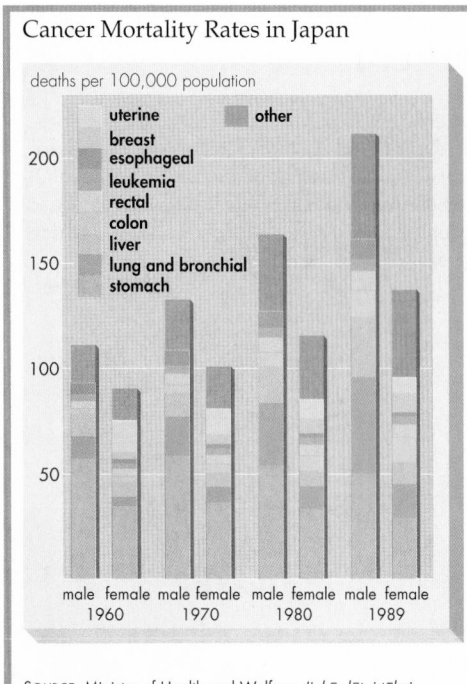

deaths per 100,000 population

uterine | other
breast
esophageal
leukemia
rectal
colon
liver
lung and bronchial
stomach

male female | male female | male female | male female
1960 | 1970 | 1980 | 1989

SOURCE: Ministry of Health and Welfare, *Jinkō dōtai tōkei* (annual): 1991.

International Cancer Mortality Rates

Type of cancer	Japan, 1989		United States, 1988		France, 1988	
	Male	Female	Male	Female	Male	Female
(deaths per 100,000 population)						
Stomach	50.3	28.8	6.8	4.4	15.8	10.5
Lung and Bronchial	43.0	15.4	73.5	35.9	67.6	9.6
Liver	21.1	6.6	2.0	0.8	8.8	1.8
Colon	12.1	11.8	19.6	19.6	20.4	19.7
Rectal	8.9	5.9	3.4	2.9	8.5	6.5
Leukemia	5.6	3.8	8.1	6.2	8.9	7.3
Esophageal	9.6	2.0	5.8	1.9	15.9	2.2
Breast	—	9.2	—	33.5	—	34.8
Uterine	—	4.5	—	4.7	—	8.5
Other	60.8	49.1	96.3	70.1	159.7	86.5

NOTE: Rates for Japan in the graph and table differ because the Japanese Ministry of Health and Welfare and the World Health Organization define some types of cancer differently.
SOURCE: World Health Organization, *World Health Statistics Annual*: 1991.

of Japanese origin to stay in isolated "road camps" and kept women and children in remote rural villages called "interior housing centres." Many of the restrictions on Japanese Canadians were kept in force after the war; many displaced Japanese were not allowed to return to coastal British Columbia until after 1 April 1949. The Japanese Canadian population declined between 1941 and 1951 from 23,149 to 21,663.

In a country that now embraces multiculturalism as an official policy, Japanese Canadian citizens enjoy full rights. According to Canadian government statistics, Japanese immigrants to Canada between 1946 and 1975 totaled 9,239. From 1971 to 1975, immigrants from Japan to Canada averaged 780 per year. The Japanese Canadian population has resumed its slow growth—the 1986 survey found more than 41,000—with Ontario and British Columbia the major areas of the Japanese Canadian population.

cancer   癌

(*gan*). In 1981 cancer became the foremost killer in Japan, claiming even more lives than cerebral apoplexy, which had previously been the most common cause of death in the country. Cancer was responsible for 217,367 deaths in 1990, or 26.5 percent of all the deaths in the nation that year. Gastric cancer claimed the most lives of both sexes in Japan, although it was declining due to medical advances, changes in eating habits, and more accessible and frequent health examinations, among other factors. The numbers of deaths due to cancers of the lung, liver, colon, and rectum, however, were increasing. It has been noted that, while the number of deaths due to colon cancer is low in Japan compared to Europe and North America, it has risen considerably as the Japanese diet has become more Westernized. Fewer women were dying of uterine cancer, but deaths caused by breast cancer were increasing in number.

As of 1991, there was still no definitive method of preventing or curing all forms of cancer, so the most urgent task was to develop a means of detecting and treating the disease as early as possible. According to the Law concerning Health and Medical Services

for the Aged (effective 1983), each municipality was required to offer annual examinations for gastric and uterine cancer to persons 40 years of age or older. Many municipalities were also offering annual examinations for lung and breast cancer, and some offered the examinations to all people 30 years of age or older. X-ray computerized-tomography scanner and ultrasonic diagnostic devices were obtaining excellent results in detecting cancer deep within the body. Good progress was also being made in cancer research through the application of laser beams, the development of nuclear magnetic resonance devices, and diagnostic studies using monoclonal antibodies, which recognize only cancerous cells.

The national Comprehensive Ten-Year Strategy for Cancer Control, which gave priority to subjects such as oncogenes (cancer-causing genes), was adopted in 1983. The main results of the project so far have been the discovery of a genetic predisposition toward stomach and lung cancers and confirmation of the effectiveness of heat therapy as a form of treatment. Invitations are issued to foreign scholars in the field of cancer research to join the study, and the program also promotes the education and employment of young cancer researchers. See also DISEASES.

Canon, Inc   キヤノン[株]

(Kyanon). One of the world's leading camera manufacturers. Founded in 1937 by Mitarai Takeshi (1901–84), a medical doctor. Canon is also a major producer of office products in the information, telecommunications, and computer fields and of advanced electro-optical products for industrial, medical, and broadcasting use. Sales for the fiscal year ending December 1990 totaled ¥931.3 billion (US $7.0 billion), and capitalization stood at ¥82.1 billion (US $614.8 million) in the same year. Headquarters are in Tōkyō.

Canon Sales Co, Inc   キヤノン販売[株]

(Kyanon Hambai). Sole distributor in Japan of all Canon products. Incorporated in 1968 as a marketing arm of CANON, INC. Recently Canon Sales began to handle some non-Canon products. Sales for fiscal 1990 totaled ¥456.1 billion (US $3.4 billion), of which photo products accounted for 12 percent; business machines, 44 percent; electronic

equipment, 12 percent; system equipment, 21 percent; and optical products, 11 percent. The company was capitalized at ¥40.2 billion (US $301.0 million) in the same year. Headquarters are in Tōkyō.

Cao Rulin (Ts'ao Ju-lin)   曹汝霖

(1876–1966; J: Sō Jorin). Japanese-educated Chinese politician; leader of pro-Japanese politicians in early republican China. Cao is best known as an important target of the May 1919 student demonstrations (see MAY FOURTH MOVEMENT). He studied at Chūō University in Tōkyō. In 1915, as vice-minister of foreign affairs, he negotiated with the Japanese over the TWENTY-ONE DEMANDS. From 1916 to 1919 he associated himself with the government of DUAN QIRUI (Tuan Ch'i-jui), which was maintained through dubious dealings with the Japanese, notably the NISHIHARA LOANS. When it became known that he had been involved in the agreements confirming Japanese succession to German rights in Shandong (Shantung), student demonstrators burned his house in Beijing (Peking) on 4 May 1919. He resigned from the government a month later. Cao left China in 1949, living first in Japan and later in the United States.

capacity to act   行為能力

(*kōi nōryoku*). Legal term. The capacity to perform a valid JURISTIC ACT autonomously. Japanese judicial decisions and legal theory protect infants, mentally ill persons, and others who do not have the mental capacity to comprehend the consequences of their acts. See also PERSON WITHOUT CAPACITY.

capacity to enjoy rights   権利能力

(*kenri nōryoku*). Legal term. Under the CIVIL CODE, both natural persons (*shizenjin*) and juristic persons (HŌJIN) have the capacity to enjoy legal rights and duties. Foreigners are an exception in some instances (see FOREIGNERS, LEGAL STATUS OF). All natural persons possess the capacity equally. A fetus does not, as a rule, have the capacity to enjoy such rights, but in order to protect the unborn, the Civil Code does recognize, retroactively upon its live birth, a fetus's capacity to enjoy rights in certain instances. See also CAPACITY TO ACT.

capital markets   資本市場

(*shihon shijō*). The principal functions of capital markets are to make available a wide range of possible investments for corporations, individuals, or other entities with funds to invest and at the same time to give borrowers sources of funds to finance capital investment and long-term working capital. A market where lending and borrowing take place for a period of less than a year is referred to as a money market. Where agreements extend over a year, the market is referred to as a capital market.

Backed by the substantial savings of Japanese households and other sources of funds, Japan's capital markets have expanded rapidly in size and importance within the international financial system. Japan's principal capital markets are the bond market and the stock market. Hedging of investments in these markets is carried out in the bond futures market and the stock index futures market.

Japan's bond market has grown to become one of the largest in the world in terms of bonds outstanding and level of transactions. The market is dominated, however, by government bond issues, which accounted for ¥153.5 trillion (US $1.2 trillion) of the total ¥246.2 trillion (US $2.0 trillion) in bonds (excluding convertible bonds) outstanding in June 1988. The next largest category of bonds outstanding was bank debentures, which are issued primarily by long-term credit banks to finance the long-term capital and working capital requirements of private companies. Corporate bonds accounted for only ¥9.1 trillion (US $72.9 billion), and yen-denominated bonds issued by foreign borrowers accounted for only ¥4.8 trillion (US $38.5 billion).

Because of intense trading activity of banks and other institutional investors, transactions in the bond market have risen to one of the highest levels in the world, ¥5,544.4 trillion (US $38.3 trillion) in 1987 and slightly less in 1988. Since the opening of a bond futures market in 1985, transactions in this market have also risen to exceptionally high levels by international standards as investors have made full use of the futures markets to hedge their bond investments.

Types of bonds that private companies can issue in the Tōkyō bond market are straight and convertible bonds and bonds with warrants. Although the market has undergone considerable liberalization, one of the pending issues, which will probably be addressed more positively in the early 1990s, is to achieve greater flexibility for issuers in timing and terms. A major step has already been taken in the introduction of a bond rating system, which replaced the former system of setting bond terms and conditions based mainly on corporate size. This system is paving the way for the issue of uncollateralized bonds by a wider range of companies.

Japan's stock markets have grown to become the world's largest in terms of market value and are comparable to the United States in trading volume. For example, in 1987, according to data from the Japan Securities Dealers Association, the total value of stocks listed on Japan's major exchanges (dominated by the TŌKYŌ STOCK EXCHANGE) was the equivalent of $2.9 trillion, compared with $2.1 trillion for the United States and $664.0 billion for the United Kingdom. Similarly, trading volume of equities in 1987 amounted to $1.7 trillion versus $1.8 trillion for the United States and $272.8 billion for the United Kingdom.

Important trends in recent years have included the simplification of listing requirements for both Japanese and foreign companies. This has brought an increase in the number of companies listing their shares for trading and making initial public offerings. Relaxation of listing conditions has also resulted in expansion of listings by venture businesses on the over-the-counter exchange. Listings of foreign corporations in Tōkyō have also been sharply increasing, rising from less than 20 in the early 1980s to nearly 120 in the late 1980s. Although further deregulation is required, Japan's capital market (centered in Tōkyō) is already one of the world's three largest, along with New York's and London's. See also CORPORATE FINANCE; BANKING SYSTEM.

capital punishment 死刑

(*shikei*). Public debate in Japan concerning the retention or abolition of capital punishment has continued since the Meiji period (1868–1912), but as of 1990 no legislative action had been taken by the Diet to abolish the death penalty. In the courts the number of cases in which the death penalty is handed down has declined steadily. In addition, in most cases where persons have received the death sentence the execution of the sentence is usually greatly delayed by repeated appeals for a retrial or reduction in sentence.

Under the present criminal code, crimes for which capital punishment may be prescribed include sedition, foreign insurrection, arson, high-explosive bombing, murder, and homicide associated with such crimes as derailment of trains, poisoning of water supplies, and armed robbery. Among these the only crime that carries a mandatory death sentence is participation in armed foreign intervention in Japan (*gaikan yūchizai*) under the category of foreign insurrection. For all other crimes listed above, penal servitude for life or specific prison terms can also be handed out.

capital structure 資本構成

(*shihon kōsei*). The ratio of a corporation's shareholders' equity to its liabilities. The higher the ratio of capital to liabilities, the more flexibility in financial payments, the less need to borrow, and the greater the financial stability. Capital ratios in postwar Japan have generally been lower than in the United States or Europe because (1) Japan's financial system was structured to provide funds primarily through commercial and long-term credit banks; (2) tax provisions permitted deduction of interest as an expense, while dividends had to be disbursed from after-tax income; and (3) equity shares during most of the postwar period were issued at a fixed, par value, generally well below market value. Since about 1980, additions to retained earnings along with rising profitability, issuance of stock at or near market value, and issuance of large volumes of convertible bonds and bonds with warrants in Japan and in overseas capital markets have brought a marked improvement in the capital structure of leading corporations. See also CORPORATE FINANCE.

Capron, Horace ケプロン, H.

(1804–85). Commissioner of agriculture for the United States (1867–71) and agricultural adviser to the Japanese government (1871–75). Born in Attleboro, Massachusetts. He went to Japan in 1871 as an adviser to the Hokkaidō Colonization Office (KAITAKUSHI), which was in charge of Hokkaidō's development and settlement. There he introduced large-scale farming with American agricultural methods, implements, seeds, and livestock.

Caraway, Paul Wyatt
キャラウェー, P. W.

(1905–85). US Army lieutenant general who was from 1961 to 1964 high commissioner of the United States Civil Administration of the RYŪKYŪ ISLANDS and commander of the US Army forces there. He preserved US rights and resisted steps toward autonomy for the Ryūkyū Islands at a time when President John F. Kennedy and Prime Minister IKEDA HAYATO had agreed on further joint efforts to improve the well-being of the Ryukyuan people. See also OKINAWA.

carbon fiber 炭素繊維

(*tanso sen'i*). The Japanese firms of TŌRAY INDUSTRIES, INC; Mitsubishi Rayon Co, Ltd; and TŌHŌ RAYON CO, LTD, were the world's leading manufacturers of carbon fiber in 1991. Carbon fiber is a typical reinforced fiber. One type of carbon fiber results from the calcina-

tion of acrylic fiber in a closed nitrogen environment. Another is made from pitch derived from natural fossil fuels. The former is called polyacrylonitrile carbon fiber, while the latter is known as pitch carbon fiber. Tōray Industries and Tōhō Rayon are known as manufacturers of polyacrylonitrile carbon fiber. Two large Japanese manufacturers of pitch carbon fiber are MITSUBISHI KASEI CORPORATION and TEIJIN, LTD. Carbon fiber has been widely used in aerospace and automobile manufacturing, as well as for the shafts of golf clubs and for fishing rods.

carp 鯉

(*koi*). *Cyprinus carpio*. Freshwater fish of the family Cyprinidae, order Cypriniformes, class Osteichthyes. Distributed in the temperate and subtropical zones of Asia and Europe, it sometimes grows to over 1 meter (3 ft). It is an important food fish in Japan; in addition to the edible carp, there are specially bred ornamental varieties. One of these, the *nishikigoi* (also known as *irogoi* and *hanagoi*), originally bred in Niigata Prefecture, is world famous. There are over 20 types of *nishikigoi*, and expensive specimens are displayed at annual fairs.

The Japanese have long praised the *koi* as the "king of river fish" in contrast to the *tai* (sea bream), the "king of sea fish." With the "king of birds," the crane, these are said to constitute the "three ultimates in food." This threesome is considered highly auspicious. On CHILDREN'S DAY most families with boys set up carp streamers as symbols of strength and perseverance.

carpenters' tools 大工道具

(*daiku dōgu*). Prototypes of many of the basic tools used by Japanese carpenters came from the Asian continent between the late Yayoi period (ca 300 BC–ca AD 300), when iron implements were first introduced into Japan, and the Nara period (710–794). Indigenous refinement of these primary hand tools and the development of related tools with highly specialized functions kept pace with the evolution of traditional Japanese architecture.

In cutting, framing, and joining timbers, usually from the soft, straight-grained wood

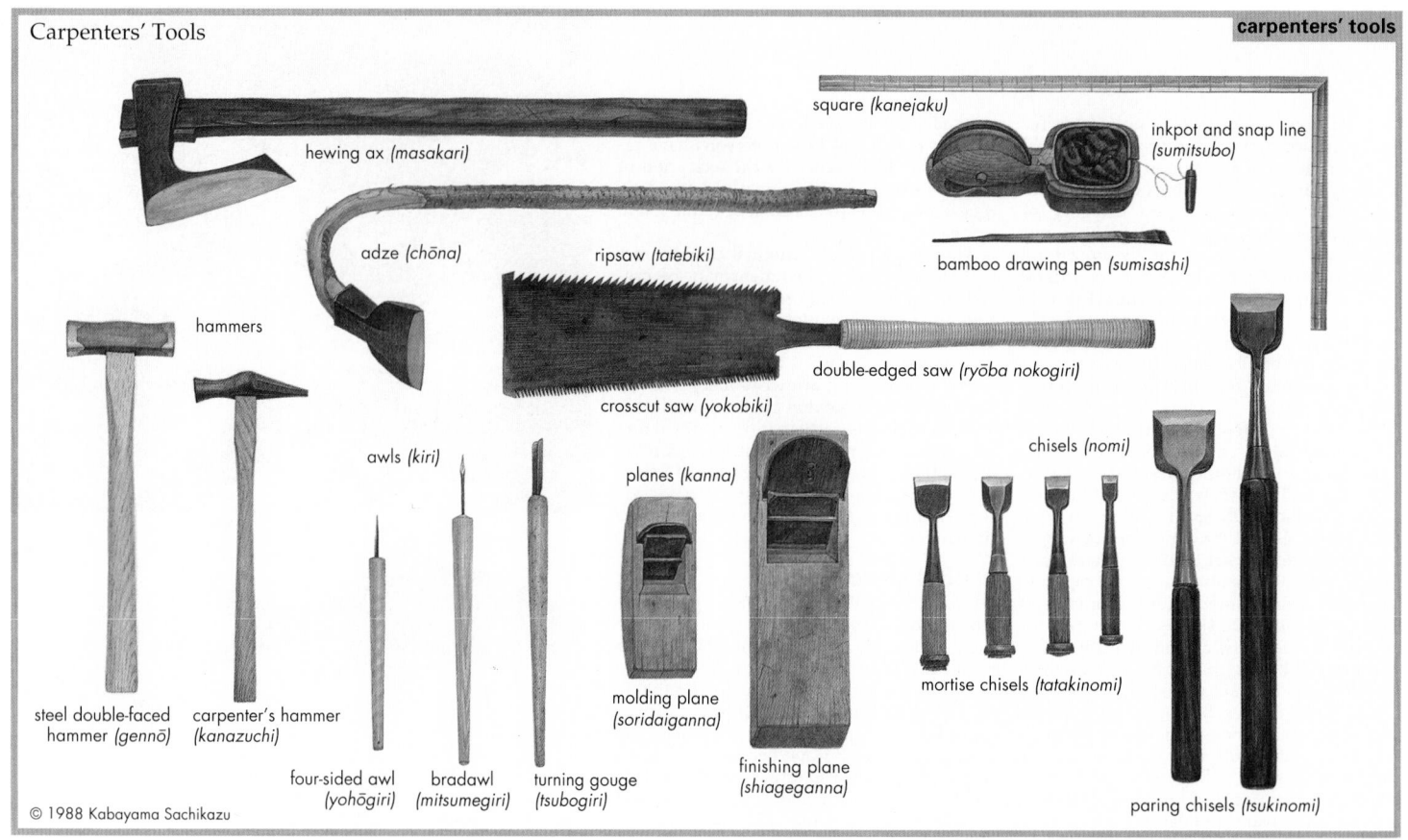

square (kanejaku)

inkpot and snap line (sumitsubo)

hewing ax (masakari)

adze (chōna)

ripsaw (tatebiki)

bamboo drawing pen (sumisashi)

crosscut saw (yokobiki)

double-edged saw (ryōba nokogiri)

hammers

awls (kiri)

planes (kanna)

chisels (nomi)

mortise chisels (tatakinomi)

steel double-faced hammer (gennō)

carpenter's hammer (kanazuchi)

four-sided awl (yohōgiri)

bradawl (mitsumegiri)

turning gouge (tsubogiri)

molding plane (soridaiganna)

finishing plane (shiageganna)

paring chisels (tsukinomi)

© 1988 Kabayama Sachikazu

of conifers such as cedar and cypress, the Japanese carpenter employs tools like the following: saws (nokogiri), planes (kanna), chisels (nomi), awls (kiri), hammers (kanazuchi or gennō), axes (ono), adzes (chōna), squares (kanejaku), and an inkpot-and-snap-line set (sumitsubo) used like a chalk line.

There are two types of hand saws: ripsaws (tatebiki) for cutting with the grain and crosscut saws (yokobiki) for cutting against the grain. Crosscut saws have been found in tombs of the Kofun period (ca 300–710). The teeth have three edges, are beveled, and are set to avoid binding. Ripsaws were not employed until the 15th century. Until then wedges were used to split wood along the grain. The teeth of ripsaws have two edges and are set but not beveled.

The standard plane, a rectangular block of oak wood with a blade inserted in an angled slot, was not introduced until the Muromachi period (1333–1568). Previously wood surfaces were first dressed with an adze. Ridges were then smoothed with a yariganna, a long-hafted tool with a blade shaped much like that of a spear, and a finish was given by rubbing with the dried stems of the scouring rush (tokusa).

Chisels are of two varieties: tatakinomi, used with a hammer to cut mortises, and tsukinomi, manipulated with the hands to smooth sides of mortises or to dress the ends of channels inaccessible to planes. Primitive chisels have been found in Kofun-period burial mounds. The basic set of tatakinomi consists of nine chisels with cutting edges increasing in width in 3-millimeter (0.12-in) increments.

Since World War II, with the advent of modern construction techniques, electric tools have largely replaced traditional hand tools. In 1943, prior to the proliferation of power tools, a survey found that the customary complement of tools used by Japanese carpenters consisted of 179 items. This comparatively large number is attributable to a special need for precision in Japanese construction since few nails are used.

cartels   カルテル

(karuteru). Agreements or associations between companies for the purpose of controlling the market. Cartels are, in principle, prohibited in Japan by the ANTIMONOPOLY LAW (1947). However, if approval is given by the Fair Trade Commission, later revisions to the Antimonopoly Law permit the formation of cartels when necessary for trade reasons, for depressed industries, or for industries requiring rationalization. The purpose of the Law on Extraordinary Measures for Stabilization of Specific Depressed Industries (1978) and its successor, the Temporary Measures Law for the Structural Adjustment of Specific Industries (1983), was to provide relief to structurally depressed industries in the period of low growth following the oil crisis of 1973. In the latter law, joint action for the disposition of excess capacity was permitted in 26 different depressed industries, including aluminum refining and petrochemicals. This law was repealed in March 1988, although several cartel laws such as the Law concerning the Organization of Small and Medium-Sized Enterprises are still in full force. A number of foreign countries have criticized these remaining laws as excessive protection of domestic industries.

Cary, Otis   ケーリ, O.

(1851–1932). American Congregational missionary; professor of homiletics and practical sociology at Dōshisha Theological Seminary from 1892 to 1918. Born in Foxboro, Massachusetts, he attended Amherst College (where he became acquainted with NIIJIMA JŌ, who was later to found Dōshisha; see DŌSHISHA UNIVERSITY) and Andover Theological Seminary. After his ordination in 1877 he was assigned to mission work in Japan. The governor of Okayama invited Cary, his wife, and three other missionaries to be the prefecture's first Western residents. He wrote and

(with collaboration) translated Christian manuals and tracts into Japanese. Cary also wrote Japan and Its Regeneration (1899) and A History of Christianity in Japan (1909).

Casio Computer Co, Ltd
カシオ計算機[株]

(Kashio Keisanki). Manufacturer and distributor of electronic instruments. Incorporated in 1957. It is one of the largest makers of electronic calculators in the world. It is also a leader in the production of digital watches and has entered the field of electronic musical instruments and office computers. Casio's products are sold in over 140 countries. Sales for the fiscal year ending March 1991 totaled ¥281.2 billion (US $2.0 billion); exports made up 59 percent of sales. In 1991 the company's capitalization stood at ¥36.2 billion (US $183.1 million). Headquarters are in Tōkyō.

castles   城

(shiro). Japanese castles were originally military fortifications designed to provide protection against enemy attack. With the rise of FEUDALISM, however, they became distinctive architectural forms serving as both palatial residence and seat of military and political power of feudal barons.

Ancient Fortifications——Three types of fortification have been identified as existing in ancient Japan. These are the grid-pattern city (tojō), the mountain fortress (yamajiro), and the palisade (ki).

The grid-pattern city. This Chinese city-type inspired the building in Japan of similar grid-pattern cities, beginning with the ancient imperial capitals of FUJIWARAKYŌ and NANIWAKYŌ and culminating in HEIJŌKYŌ (now Nara) and HEIANKYŌ (now Kyōto). The grid-pattern city in Japan was more of a government and political center than a truly defensive facility. The Japanese grid-pattern city wall was a slight earthen embankment less than 3 meters (10 ft) in height and affording little real protection; the wall eventually disappeared altogether.

Gujō Hachiman Castle was originally a mountain fortress dating from the 16th century. The present structure, built in 1933, incorporates features of several other types of castles. Gifu Prefecture.

The mountain fortress. Ruins of ancient mountain fortresses have been found distributed in an area centered in northern Kyūshū. Rows of stones known as KŌGOISHI, once thought to be connected to some sort of ancient religious ritual, have also been identified as remains of ancient mountain fortresses. The remains known as MIZUKI also reveal an ancient defense facility, whose long earthworks and moat were constructed at a point where mountains came together and closed off a plain.

The palisade. Unlike mountain fortresses, palisades were semipermanent fortifications, built on plains or plateaus. Many palisades were constructed in northeastern Honshū between the 7th and 9th centuries for defense against the aboriginal EZO tribesmen and for administration of the surrounding countryside. See also SAKU.

Medieval Castles—Internal wars were frequent in Japan during the medieval period (mid-12th–16th centuries). From the period of the Northern and Southern Courts (1337–92) to the Sengoku period (1467–1568), territorial warlords repeatedly fought each other, and castles were constructed throughout the country. Their forms varied, but many were small, semipermanent fortifications built at the tip of steep mountain ridges. To prevent enemy approach, two or three lines of advance fortifications were built. Along the ridge line a trench was dug, the peak and mountainside were terraced, and palisades were erected around the perimeter. Stone walls were uncommon, and, since these facilities were used only in times of war, they were not built to last.

By the Sengoku period, constant warfare made it necessary to build more permanent structures. Military chieftains built fortifications similar to their own residences, with the addition of raised watchtowers on the roof. This was the beginning of castle architecture in Japan. Most castles of the medieval period were of the mountain castle type and were used only in times of war. Ordinarily the warrior chieftain lived in a fortified residence located on a plain or low plateau. This was the origin of the plain castle (*hirajiro*) and the so-called hill-on-the-plain castle (*hirayamajiro*). An example of the *hirajiro* is EDO CASTLE in Tōkyō. The *hirayamajiro* was generally sited on a low-lying plateau set in a plain.

Azuchi-Momoyama and Edo Period Castles—There was great development in the building of castles during the Azuchi-Momoyama period (1568–1600), and the castle became a complex of many structures. With the reorganization of the feudal system by the Tokugawa shogunate (1603–1867), the *daimyō* built castles in the center of their domains, and the *hirayamajiro* thus became the standard type. The castle included the residences of the castle lord and his chief retainers. Located as it was, near a plain, the feudal castle now required additional fortifications. Stone walls developed, moats (*hori*) were dug, and earthworks were added. Around these castles developed CASTLE TOWNS (*jōka machi*). The castle became not just a defensive facility but the administrative and economic center of its region.

The military hegemons ODA NOBUNAGA and TOYOTOMI HIDEYOSHI were responsible for major developments in castle architecture. Between 1576 and 1579 Nobunaga constructed the central part of an enormous castle project at Azuchi in what is now Shiga Prefecture. AZUCHI CASTLE was destroyed after

Continued on page 168 ►

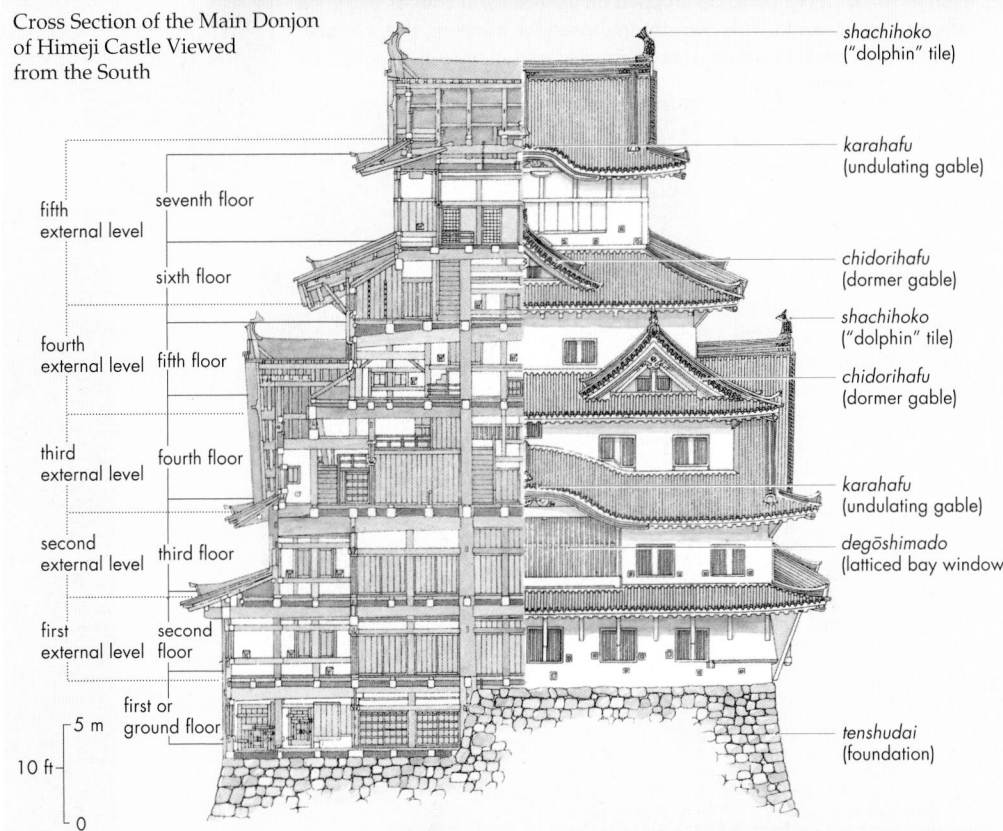

Cross Section of the Main Donjon of Himeji Castle Viewed from the South

shachihoko ("dolphin" tile)

karahafu (undulating gable)

chidorihafu (dormer gable)

shachihoko ("dolphin" tile)

chidorihafu (dormer gable)

karahafu (undulating gable)

degōshimado (latticed bay window)

tenshudai (foundation)

fifth external level — seventh floor

sixth floor

fourth external level — fifth floor

third external level — fourth floor

second external level — third floor

first external level — second floor

first or ground floor

5 m

10 ft

0

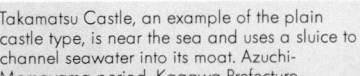

Takamatsu Castle, an example of the plain castle type, is near the sea and uses a sluice to channel seawater into its moat. Azuchi-Momoyama period. Kagawa Prefecture.

Built in the early Edo period on a small hill near Lake Biwa, Hikone Castle is an example of the hill-on-the-plain style. Shiga Prefecture. National Treasure.

The Castle as Labyrinth

Japanese castle architecture united an elegant sense of design with a deadly military function. A renowned example is Himeji Castle in the city of Himeji, Hyōgo Prefecture, also known as White Egret (Shirasagi) Castle for its soaring white walls.

The castle was built in the mid-14th century, improved by Toyotomi Hideyoshi in the 1580s, and brought to its present form by the *daimyō* Ikeda Terumasa in 1609. It was designed to impress the populace through its immense size and beauty, while confronting an attacking force with an intricate array of deceptive defenses. The moats, outer walls, and watchtowers constituted the first layer of protection. Once beyond these, attackers plunged into forking, labyrinthine passageways intended to confine and confuse, while hidden defenders peppered them with musket and longbow fire. At the end of this maze stood the four linked donjons, with their firing ports and chutes through which stones could be dropped on the enemy. In case of siege, the donjons had access to wells and storage space for weapons, rice, and salt.

Completed near the end of Japan's greatest period of castle building (ca 1568–1615), Himeji Castle epitomized military architecture; however, it was never actually assaulted during the more than two centuries of peace that followed the establishment of the Tokugawa regime (1603–1867). Like many other Japanese castles, this ultimate fortress functioned primarily as an administrative center and symbol of the lord's might.

The route to the Ha Gate (see diagram). The loopholes in the plastered wall at right allowed defenders to fire down into the secondary enclosure. Enemy troops entering this narrow corridor could be fired on from above the stone wall at left.

The fourth floor of the main donjon. The platforms above the small staircases were firing positions for archers and musketeers, as was the alcove set beneath the overhanging roof gables.

The Ni Gate passageway (see diagram). Defenders in the room above this passageway could remove hidden panels and thrust downward with spears. The approaches to the donjons led through a series of such fortified gates, which forced the enemy into more and more confined spaces.

The tortuous design of this route, one of several leading from the Caltrop Gate to the main donjon, was intended to slow and bewilder the enemy with switchbacks and sudden descents.

① Hishi no Mon (Caltrop Gate)
② I no Mon (I Gate)
③ Ro no Mon (Ro Gate)
④ Ha no Mon (Ha Gate)
⑤ Ni no Mon (Ni Gate)
⑥ Ho no Mon (Ho Gate)
⑦ Sangokubori (Three-Province Moat)

⑧ *tenshu* (donjons)
  (a) *daitenshu* (main donjon)
  (b) (c) (d) *shōtenshu* (minor donjons)
⑨ *hommaru* (main enclosure)
⑩ *ninomaru* (secondary enclosure)
⑪ *sannomaru* (tertiary enclosure)
⑫ *nishinomaru* (western enclosure)

0   50m
100ft

N

The donjons (tenshu) of Himeji Castle are shown here from a different angle than in the diagram of the entire castle on the facing page. (They can be found in the upper right corner of the diagram.) This group, the largest of its kind in Japan, consists of a main donjon linked by passageways to three minor ones.

castle towns This Edo-period folding screen is decorated with a detailed map of the castle town of Takamatsu. The castle (bottom center) is protected by three moats.

the death of Oda Nobunaga in 1582. It established a tradition of large-scale, sumptuous castles that was continued in FUSHIMI CASTLE (1594) and ŌSAKA CASTLE (1583), both built by Hideyoshi and no longer extant. After the Battle of Sekigahara (1600) through the Keichō era (1596–1615), there was a surge of castle construction by daimyō throughout the country. Many of these survive today or did until World War II.

By 1615 the Tokugawa shogunate, seeking to secure complete control over the country, ordered that there could be only one castle to each domain. Each daimyō was permitted to maintain only his main castle. The art of castle architecture went into a gradual decline during the Edo period (1600–1868).

Castle-Building Techniques and Design——The most important step in building a castle was the site planning (*nawabari*), in which the building's outline was fixed on the prospective site by stretching ropes. Ideally, a castle was composed of a main compound or ward (*hommaru*) centered around the donjon or main tower (*tenshu* or *tenshukaku*) surrounded by or connected with minor compounds or enclosures. There were different architectural types of donjon: the single type; the compound type, where a minor keep projected from a side of the main donjon; the linked type, where the main tower and a minor keep were connected by a passageway; and the group type, where the major donjon was joined by passageways to several "minor donjons" (*shōtenshu*). The most important feature of castle architecture from the late Muromachi period (1333–1568) through the Edo period,

the donjon originated in the watchtower built atop a warrior's residence. There were several entrances to the castle, but the important ones were called the *ōte* and *karamete*. The former was the main entrance and the latter the rear entrance. In case the castle was overrun, the *karamete* could be used as an avenue of escape. A moat (*hori*) or system of moats, ponds, waterways, and trenches surrounded the castle, and natural features of the land were also employed in its fortifications. In order to reach the donjon it was necessary to traverse a mazelike route.

Stone foundation walls (*ishigaki*) were built vertically in earlier times on sites with foundation soil, but where the ground was not stable, walls with a concave profile came to be used both for structural and decorative reasons. The principal construction material of a castle was wood. The early donjon had exposed wood members such as columns, horizontal members, and eaves, but at the height of the castle-building era most surfaces came to be plastered for the sake of increased protection against firearms. Arrows could be shot through rectangular openings in the walls, and muskets fired through round, triangular, or square openings. All such loopholes were known as *sama* or *hazama*. Both the inner ward and the outer enclosures were reinforced with small towers (*yagura*), one- to three-storied structures similar in design to the donjon. The entrances to various parts of the castle were sometimes fortified with *masugata* (bastions laid out so as to form a rectangular courtyard), from which flanking fire could be directed upon assailants and in which defenders could group for a sudden sally. So-called mounted exits (*umadashi*) were earthworks constructed in front of the main gateways

(*koguchi*) to mask the egress of mounted soldiers from the castle. Two gates peculiar to castle architecture were the *kōraimon* and the *yaguramon*. The *kōraimon* was one bay wide, with support posts on either side; it had a main roof over the two supporting pillars and auxiliary roofs projecting from them. The *yaguramon* was a two-storied gatehouse whose first level served as an entranceway while the second, from which it took its name, was a magazine (*yagura*; literally, "store for arrows"; the same word is used for the small towers of the castle).

☎ 166–167

castle towns 城下町

(*jōka machi*). The administrative center of a *daimyō* domain and the characteristic form of Japanese city from the mid-16th century until the Meiji Restoration of 1868. The antecedents of *jōka machi* can be traced to the turbulent 14th and 15th centuries, when local magnates built wooden fortresses, often situated on bluffs and protected by walls or moats, to secure control over surrounding territories. Full-fledged urban communities emerged in the 16th century with the enforced resettlement of *samurai* around their lord's castle and the joining of market (see MARKET TOWNS) and castle in a single location.

Initially, castle towns were small, consisting of the castle complex and surrounding dwellings. They increasingly mirrored in their imposing city plans the growing authority of the daimyō. The relatively few daimyō who survived the internecine warfare of the 16th century converted their cities from defensive outposts to administrative and commercial headquarters for mobilizing the area's resources. After the advent of

Tokugawa rule in 1600, separate branch-castle settlements were abolished by the rule "one domain, one castle." The number of *jōka machi* stabilized at between 200 and 250. The authorities' preoccupation with social distinctions is seen in the segregation of elite residences, the correspondence of a lot's size and proximity to the castle with its samurai resident's rank, and the designation of urban commoners' (CHŌNIN) wards. These highly ordered features of the castle town began to disappear abruptly after the abolition of the feudal domains in 1871 (see PREFECTURAL SYSTEM, ESTABLISHMENT OF).

The castle towns monopolized local and regional military and administrative functions and prevailed in commerce and crafts as well. Almost all of the large population concentrations occurred in *jōka machi*, which generally contained about one-tenth of a domain's population, including all or most of the samurai. By the early 18th century most *jōka machi* had reached their peak populations, as opposed to some smaller, local centers less encumbered by monopolies and duties, which continued to grow.

catfishes 鯰

(*namazu*). Freshwater fish of the family Siluridae, order Siluriformes, class Osteichthyes. The name *namazu* is used to denote the three catfish species found in Japan, or more specifically *Parasilurus asotus*, the most common species. Two other species are indigenous to Lake Biwa; the larger of these, the Biwako *ōnamazu* (*P. biwaensis*), grows to 70 centimeters (28 in). The common *namazu*, found in Japan and the east coastal regions of the Asian continent, grows to 50 to 60 centimeters (20–24 in). It lives on the muddy bottoms of streams, especially where water weeds flourish. *Kabayaki* (charcoal broiling and flavoring with soy sauce) and *tempura* (deep frying) are the customary ways to prepare *namazu*.

Japanese legend has it that earthquakes are caused by the shaking of a giant *namazu* living under the ground. In the late Edo period (1600–1868) the *namazu* was thought capable of predicting earthquakes.

Catholic Church → Christianity

Catholic missionaries カトリック宣教師

(Katorikku *senkyōshi*). Catholic missionaries first came to Japan in 1549, when Francis XAVIER arrived in southern Kyūshū. Converts are said to have reached 300,000 by the end of the century, but under a series of edicts issued by the Tokugawa shogunate (1603–1867) in the early 17th century, Christianity was proscribed, foreigners were forbidden to enter the country, and the church was all but extinguished (see ANTI-CHRISTIAN EDICTS). From this time, the so-called KAKURE KIRISHITAN ("hidden Christians") secretly practiced their religion for over two centuries. See CHRISTIANITY.

Catholic missionary activity was resumed in 1859. The anti-Christian edicts were formally abolished in 1873 by the new Meiji government, making it possible for missionary work to begin on a freer basis. The Dominicans arrived in 1904 and the Jesuits in 1907. By 1941, 16 men's and 13 women's missionary groups were at work. In 1940 all non-Japanese bishops were replaced by Japanese. Today the foreign missionary personnel amounts to 948 priests, 105 brothers, and 525 sisters, representing 49 men's and 114 women's religious groups (1990).

Educational institutions and schools were founded by sisters, brothers, and priests from the early Meiji period (1868–1912). Missionaries have distinguished themselves through their scholarship in linguistics, historical studies, religion, philosophy, and the arts. A number of Catholic missionary professors have taught at Japanese universities. Missionaries have translated both the Old and the New Testaments into Japanese and have published a Catholic encyclopedia, *Katorikku daijiten* (5 vols, 1940–60). Charitable and social welfare institutions also have been an important part of missionary work.

With regard to the contemplative life, the first Trappist (Cistercian) monastery was started in 1896; a second monastery was founded in 1927. The Trappist Sisters founded a convent in 1898, and three more followed in 1933 and 1954. Other contemplative orders in Japan are the Carmelite Sisters, the Dominican Sisters, the Poor Clares, the Sisters of the Precious Blood, the Sisters of the Most Holy Redeemer, and the Passionist Sisters.

cats 猫

(*neko*). The domestic cat (*Felis catus*) was introduced to Japan from Korea and China in ancient times. Although cats were probably rare and highly prized until the 10th century, they appear to have become common by the 12th century. As a rule systematic breeding has not been practiced in Japan, but the variety known as the Japanese cat (Nihon *neko*) has been described since ancient times as a white short-haired cat with black and brown spots and a round face. Cats with long tails were once favored, but from the late Edo period (1600–1868) those with stubby tails became popular.

According to a 1990 survey, 26 percent of those who had pets in Japan had cats, a considerable increase over the 3 to 5 percent figure derived from a 1976 study.

There are many stories in Japanese literature relating to cats. An observant, if cynical, cat was made the narrator of *Wagahai wa neko de aru* (1905; tr *I Am a Cat*, 1961) by NATSUME SŌSEKI. There is a folk belief that when killed cats avenge themselves, and a whole subgenre of stories about "monster cats" (*bakeneko*) has sprung up. The MANEKI-NEKO, a cat figurine with one of its forepaws raised as if to beckon, is believed to draw customers to a shop and bring riches to the owner.

cattle 牛

(*ushi*). Japanese cattle are believed to have been bred from cattle introduced to Japan from Korea in the Yayoi period (ca 300 BC–ca AD 300). Until the end of the 19th century they were used mainly for draft purposes, since eating animal flesh was prohibited by Buddhism. Most of the cattle now being bred in Japan are of native stock crossed with such European breeds as Shorthorn and Brown Swiss. Dairy cattle are primarily Holstein and Jersey, and beef cattle are Shorthorn. The Tajima *ushi*, raised in the Tajima district of Hyōgo Prefecture, are especially famous as beef cattle. Their meat is marbled generously (this is called *shimofuri*) and is particularly favored by the Japanese. Efforts have been made to preserve the Mishima *ushi*, the only pure Japanese cattle, which are indigenous to the Mishima district of the city of Hagi, Yamaguchi Prefecture, by prohibiting interbreeding. A small number of water buffaloes are raised in Okinawa Prefecture.

The bullfights at Tokunoshima in Kagoshima Prefecture and Uwajima in Ehime Prefecture are well known. In Japanese BULLFIGHTING (*tōgyū*), the contest, however, is not between bull and matador, but between two bulls, the loser being the animal that flees.

These three kittens display the basic markings of the variety of cat known as Nihon *neko*, or Japanese cat.

From its perch behind the counter, a cat coolly surveys the goings-on in a candy shop.

Tortoiseshell tomcats, which are rare, have long been prized by sailors in Japan as protection against shipwreck. The stubby tail is typical of Japanese cats.

Cats Enjoying the Evening Cool, one of a number of whimsical woodblock prints featuring cats by Utagawa Kuniyoshi.

CD-ROM

シーディー・ロム

(compact disc read-only memory; J: *shīdīromu*). CD-ROM is a form of read-only memory (ROM) in which data is stored electronically on an optical disc. A single 12-centimeter (5-in) diameter disc can store up to 600 megabytes of data—the equivalent storage capacity of more than 400 high-density floppy discs—in digital format. CD-ROM is the predominant form of optical information storage in computing because of its capacity to store large quantities of information economically with little or no distortion of data. In Japan, CD-ROM is used to distribute reference materials such as dictionaries, telephone directories, and records of legal proceedings and patent specifications in a format known as electronic publishing. For example, one of Japan's most widely used contemporary lexicographical dictionaries and concise encyclopedias, *Kōjien*, is now sold in CD-ROM format as well as a one-volume hardcover edition. In 1990 Sony Corporation began marketing a portable electronic device that accesses materials published electronically on 8-centimeter (3-in) CD-ROM discs. Many publishing companies have marketed "electronic books" in CD-ROM format in response to this new technology.

Cécile Co, Ltd

[株]セシール

(Seshīru). Apparel maker that sells its goods through a catalog-shopping system. Established in 1972. Many of its products are produced in cooperation with major overseas apparel manufacturers in Korea, Taiwan, China, Thailand, Indonesia, and Hong Kong. For the fiscal year ending March 1990, sales totaled ¥150.9 billion (US $981.1 million) and capitalization stood at ¥5.1 billion (US $33.2 million). Headquarters are in Takamatsu, Kagawa Prefecture.

cedar, Japanese → sugi

censorship

検閲

(*ken'etsu*). Government censorship in Japan from the beginning of the Edo period (1600–1868) until the end of World War II was aimed at the suppression of antigovernment and anti-imperial ideas and activities, as well as Christian thought in the Edo period and socialism in the 20th century. Explicit sexual material was also censored. Since World War II, obscenity laws and prior restraint of materials injurious to the reputations of others have constituted the only official restrictions on freedom of expression; the 1947 CONSTITUTION OF JAPAN explicitly states that "no censorship shall be maintained" (art. 21, para. 2).

Edo Period—Censorship during the Edo period was primarily directed at Christianity, writings critical of the shōgun TOKUGAWA IEYASU and the Tokugawa family, criticism of the shogunal government and of the official ideology (Neo-Confucianism; see SHUSHIGAKU), and explicit sexual materials. Christian writings were first censored after the religion was banned in Japan in 1613. A ban on all Western books, mitigated somewhat in 1720 to allow import of scientific works, was in large part responsible for the lag in development of natural science in modern Japan.

The first official prohibitions of publications were established in 1723 by ŌOKA TADASUKE, the Edo (now Tōkyō) town magistrate (EDO MACHI BUGYŌ). He issued two decrees, the Yomiuri Kinrei (Prohibition of Broadsides) and the Shuppan Rei (Publication Decree). The latter decree prohibited the following publications: all new interpretations of Confucianism, Buddhism, Shintō, medicine, and poetry; erotic books; genealogies; and books about the Tokugawa family. Authors and publishers were also required to identify themselves in all publications. The censorship of publications was delegated to a committee of eight officials selected from the Shomotsuya Nakama, an officially recognized association of book dealers. Aside from the decade 1841–51, when such merchants' associations were banned, this group exercised self-censorship of publishing until 1868.

During the KANSEI REFORMS (1787–93) restrictions on political writing and obscenity were tightened. In 1790 a new edict required prepublication permission for books and the form of popular fiction known as KUSAZŌSHI.

In 1841 censorship authority for religious texts and poetry was turned over to the Yushima Seidō, the shogunal institute for Confucian studies, while municipal authorities took control of popular history and popular literature. Censorship authority was returned to the publishers' association in 1851.

Meiji Period (1868–1912)—After the Meiji Restoration of 1868, the emperor, his sanctity, and the imperial system replaced the shōgun as the focus of protection. Socialism and communism, rather than Christianity and anti-Confucian scholasticism, came to be seen as subversive ideologies. Control of erotic literature continued unchanged. In 1869 the first ordinance concerning publishing control was promulgated: the PUBLICATION ORDINANCE OF 1869 (Shuppan Jōrei). The ordinance banned certain subjects and had pre- and postpublication requirements. A government office to examine publications was established, and the publishers' association dissolved around 1875. In 1870 the publishing control office was incorporated into the DAJŌKAN government system under various bureaus. All censorship and publication control was placed under the jurisdiction of the Naimushō (HOME MINISTRY) in 1875.

Newspapers fell under a separate system of censorship, which began shortly after the first modern newspapers appeared in the 1860s. The Shimbunshi Inkō Jōmoku (Ordinance regarding Newspaper Publication) of 1869 was the first modern newspaper law.

In response to the upsurge of political activity in the 1870s (see FREEDOM AND PEOPLE'S RIGHTS MOVEMENT), the government promulgated a succession of new laws limiting freedom of speech: the LIBEL LAW OF 1875 (Zamboritsu), the PRESS ORDINANCE OF 1875 (Shimbunshi Jōrei), a revised Publication Ordinance, and Publication Ordinance Penalties (Shuppan Jōrei Bassoku). The Shimbunshi Jōrei was so severe that it was often referred to as the "newspaper abolition law." The Shuppan Jōrei was revised in 1887 to include the provisions of the Libel Law and the Shimbunshi Jōrei; the revision also added the crime of obscenity and placed penalties for this on the author, in contrast to the newspaper laws, which held the publishing company liable. The Shimbunshi Jōrei was amended in 1887 to prohibit the sale of foreign-language newspapers that carried objectionable material.

The government utilized prepublication censorship under imperial authorization during periods of crisis, such as the Sino-Japanese War of 1894–95 and the Russo-Japanese War of 1904–05, and a censorship agency was installed in the ARMY MINISTRY (Rikugunshō). The Shuppan Jōrei was replaced by the PUBLICATION LAW OF 1893 (Shuppan Hō), establishing the system of publication control that was maintained until the end of World War II. The Shimbunshi Jōrei was replaced by the PRESS LAW OF 1909 (Shimbunshi Hō); it was made to conform with the Publication Law, and detailed punitive provisions were added. The law remained in effect until after World War II.

Taishō Period (1912–1926)—This was a period of great social ferment, and the government was heavy-handed in its attempts to prevent the spread of democratic and socialist opposition. Immediately after Japan entered World War I in 1914, the military ministries announced the implementation of prior censorship and issued standards for newspaper articles. The PEACE PRESERVATION LAW OF 1925 (Chian Iji Hō) systematized the repression of both socialism and the movement for Korean independence. It was later expanded to include religious groups and intellectuals; in 1928 the death penalty was added for certain violations of the law. An ideological prosecution system (*shisō kenji*) was established, and a SPECIAL HIGHER POLICE force (Tokubetsu Kōtō Keisatsu) began to deal with ideological offenses throughout Japan.

Early Shōwa Years (1926–1936)—The first decade of the Shōwa period (1926–89) saw the suppression of political and social movements. In 1924 the Publication Department (Toshoka) of the Home Ministry had been divided into three sections: censorship, general affairs, and investigation. Systematic censorship was thus created, and a policy of thorough control was enacted. With the increase in publications advocating war after 1934, the army, navy, foreign, and home ministries required publishers to attend regular advisory sessions. The Publication Law was revised to include harsher penalties and incorporate recordings under its provisions. All censorship came under the jurisdiction of the Home Ministry. In 1936 an information and propaganda committee was formed within the cabinet.

The War Period (1937–1945)—Between 1937 and 1945 the Japanese war effort dominated politics, and censorship formed one part of an extensive thought control system. The Publication Law was greatly expanded in 1937. The Publications Control Committee (Shuppambutsu Tōsei Iinkai) was created to regulate publications. In 1940 the cabinet's Information Department (Jōhōbu) was elevated in status to become the Information Bureau (Jōhōkyoku), which consolidated the functions of the information departments of the military ministries, the Foreign Ministry, and the Criminal Affairs Bureau of the Home Ministry. The bureau had direct control over all news, advertising, and culture.

The 1941 revision of the NATIONAL MOBILIZATION LAW (Kokka Sōdōin Hō), passed in preparation for World War II, totally eliminated freedom of the press. All periodicals except general-interest magazines were ordered to merge; 572 literary, women's, music, art, and photography magazines were consolidated into 174. The Temporary Mail Control Ordinance (Rinji Yūbimbutsu Torishimari Rei) was also issued, giving censors the authority to open and censor mail leaving and entering Japan. Senders were required to print their addresses clearly on all mail. In 1942, after the war began, newspapers were ordered to merge or cease publication, and their number was reduced by almost 95 percent, to 54. As government repression grew harsher, the Nihon Shuppankai (Japan Publishers Association) cooperated by conducting investigations within the industry. Books were first submitted in outline, then the manuscript and printer's proofs were handed over to the association for censorship. The government took over the distribution of paper, releasing supplies only for the publication of matters relating to national policy.

In 1944 the publishers' association also took over the censorship of periodicals and the merger of magazines. Only 34 magazines were left in operation. In 1945 newspapers were limited to one per prefecture. Under orders from the Information Bureau, the publishers' association tightened censorship and further restricted the allocation of paper supplies.

The Postwar Period (from 1945)— During the post–World War II Allied OCCUPATION, the instruments for suppressing the freedom of speech—the publication and newspaper laws—were abolished, but new controls were exercised under the Occupation Press Code and by the office of the supreme commander for the Allied powers (SCAP). The control of obscenity remained under the Japanese police jurisdiction. In 1946 the Home Ministry eliminated all censorship procedures and thus formally put an end to the Japanese prewar system of publication control. Article 21 of the 1947 CONSTITUTION OF JAPAN guaranteed the freedom of speech.

Despite the relaxation of Occupation censorship, restrictions were placed on Japanese publications about China and the Soviet Union as cold-war hostilities intensified in 1949. The CIVIL INFORMATION AND EDUCATION SECTION OF SCAP acquired the power to ban translations by requiring that all works that fell under international copyright law be granted permission prior to publication. In 1952 the Occupation came to an end, and the Press Code was lifted; the same year, however, the SUBVERSIVE ACTIVITIES PREVENTION LAW (Hakai Katsudō Bōshi Hō) was passed, and the PUBLIC SECURITY INVESTIGATION AGENCY (Kōan Chōsa Chō) began its operations.

Since that time, obscenity has been the primary target of publication controls under article 175 of the Penal Code. Imported publications, films, pictures, and photographs are covered by customs laws, and customs authorities are given the authority to delete or confiscate obscene materials.

The right of the government to conduct such activities has been contested. In 1984, however, the Supreme Court of Japan ruled that the screening of imported books and magazines by customs authorities did not constitute censorship. Various media, with an eye toward avoiding prosecution, have developed systems of self-censorship that enforce the vague government standards; serious questions can be raised as to whether this is an effective way to defend freedom of expression.

The prior restraint of publications considered injurious to others has been another significant area of controversy. Again the Supreme Court has ruled in favor of restraints on the freedom of speech; prior restraint of a publication has been found justified in cases where it is reasonable to expect that the publication will cause irrevocable damage to the plaintiff's reputation. The government has engaged in prosecutions over invasion of privacy, and legal action under the privacy and libel laws has been considered by the Imperial Household Agency to discourage publications that show disrespect for the imperial family. Another form of publication control has been the government system of authorizing textbooks for use in public schools (see IENAGA TEXTBOOK REVIEW CASE).

census 国勢調査

(*kokusei chōsa*). In Japan, the census was first conducted in 1920 and has been conducted every 5 years since then. A formal census is carried out every 10 years, while midway through the period a simplified census is taken. (Because of the confusion at the end of World War II, no census was taken in 1945, although there was a provisional census in 1947.)

At present the national censuses are conducted in accord with the Statistics Law, issued and instituted in 1947. The agency for their execution is the Statistics Bureau of the Management and Coordination Agency which, with the assistance of prefectural governors, conducts censuses through reliance on city, ward, town, and village mayors. The main purpose of the census is to determine the permanent population as of midnight on 30 September/1 October. Specific items in the census include the number of family members, sex, age group, nationality, and employment or schooling. There are also varying additional items that are deemed to be of importance at the time of each census.

Results of the census are indispensable for the maintenance of population statistics. Figures announced each year projecting population growth are later revised by working back from the latest census to the previous one. Life expectancy tables are formulated according to results obtained from the national census, and census information concerning the family is used as a statistical basis for sample surveys related to the family. Results of the census are of great importance to the fulfillment of every function of government. For example, the number of Diet members is determined by reference to the most recent national census.

Central Alps → Kiso Mountains

Central Council for Education 中央教育審議会

(Chūō Kyōiku Shingikai or Chūkyōshin). One of the advisory councils for the minister of education; established in 1952. The council studies, reviews, and makes recommendations about fundamental policies related to education, culture, and the arts and sciences. It is composed of a maximum of 20 persons who are appointed for two-year terms by the minister of education with the approval of the cabinet.

The council resulted from a reorganization of the EDUCATION REFORM COUNCIL, which was created in 1946 to study and review educational reform. Until 1955 the council focused on compulsory education, the maintenance of the political neutrality of teachers, and improvements in the textbook compilation system. Up to 1965 the council made reports related to improving the junior college system, promoting science and technical education, and encouraging the expansion of scholarships and aid. In 1984, with the organization of the PROVISIONAL COUNCIL ON EDUCATIONAL REFORM, the council temporarily ceased activities. It was reconvened in 1989 and in 1990 issued reports on LIFELONG LEARNING and high school education.

Central Glass Co, Ltd セントラル硝子[株]

(Sentoraru Garasu). Chemical company engaged in the production and sale of glass, chemical products, and fertilizer. Incorporated in 1936. The company took its current name in 1963. It started production of ammonium chloride for fertilizer in 1953 and sheet glass in 1958. It has a joint-venture manufacturing subsidiary and a sales firm in Thailand. Annual sales for the fiscal year ending March 1991 totaled ¥173.1 billion (US $1.3 billion), of which glass products made up 65 percent; chemical products, 25 percent; and fertilizer, 10 percent. In the same year the export ratio was 4 percent, and the firm was capitalized at ¥17.9 billion (US $130.5 million). Headquarters are in Tōkyō.

Central Japan Railway Co 東海旅客鉄道[株]

(Tōkai Ryokaku Tetsudō). One of Japan's six regional passenger railway companies (see JR). Operates the Tōkaidō SHINKANSEN line between Tōkyō and Ōsaka and provides a range of other transportation and related services throughout its operating area. The Central Japan Railway Co was established as part of the privatization of the JAPANESE NATIONAL RAILWAYS (JNR) in 1987. The company's operating area encompasses the central portion of Honshū; its 13 lines extend a total of approximately 2,000 kilometers (1,242 mi). Company plans call for the development of a train that will travel at speeds of nearly 500 kilometers (310 mi) per hour between Ōsaka and Tōkyō. It has overseas offices in London, Los Angeles, and Sydney. Sales for the fiscal year ending May 1990 totaled ¥1.0 trillion (US $6.6 billion), and capitalization stood at ¥112.0 billion (US $731.6 million). Headquarters are in Ōsaka and Nagoya.

Central Labor Relations Commission 中央労働委員会

(Chūō Rōdō Iinkai; abbreviated as Chūrōi). A labor relations commission composed of 39 members, appointed by the minister of labor from the labor, management, and public sectors. The commission's chairman is chosen from the public sector. It is an external ministerial bureau of the Ministry of Labor. The main duties and powers of the commission are as follows. First, during labor strikes and other forms of dispute, it provides conciliation, mediation, arbitration, and emergency adjustment services. It has superior jurisdiction over matters that involve important problems for two or more prefectures or the whole country. Second, it screens the qualifications of labor unions, approves the expanded application of labor agreements, and adjudicates unfair labor practices. In adjudicating unfair labor practices, the commission has the power to review and overrule orders of the local labor relations commissions. Third, the commission establishes its own regulations and procedures for such matters as the investigation of unfair labor practices. See also MINISTRY OF LABOR.

ceramics 陶磁器

(*tōjiki*). Ceramics in Japan has a long history, stretching over 12,000 years. The Japanese archipelago is abundantly supplied with the raw material for ceramics, and an appreciation for clay and its multitude of possible

Continued on page 174 ▶

Japanese Pottery: Grasping the Natural

The Japanese affection for ceramic ware extends beyond shape, design, and color to include touch. Japanese teabowls, for example, are made without handles, meant to be cradled in the palm. Accompanying this emphasis on the tactile is a passionate regard for the clay itself and for the art of firing. And, contrary to traditional Western notions of quality, incidental imperfections—cracked, uneven glazing, marks left by the potter's tools and hands, lumpy, irregular shapes—are cherished because they lend the look of nature to what is man-made.

Kilns were built wherever fine-quality clay was found, and all of the traditional pottery styles mirror local conditions and history. Arita ware, for example, shows the contributions of potters from China and Korea in its elaborate decoration. Bizen pottery's rustic quality echoes the simple lifestyle of the farmers who used it, and Raku ware, from Kyōto, suggests the serenity of the tea ceremony by its poise.

This portable sake container from the 19th century is typical of the Tsuboya style—simple, sturdy, glazed primarily in brown, and bearing an inlaid design.

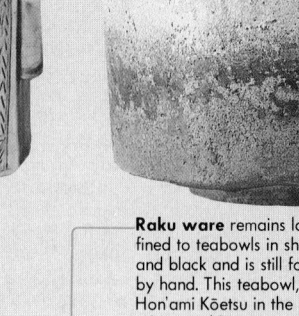

Raku ware remains largely confined to teabowls in shades of red and black and is still formed solely by hand. This teabowl, crafted by Hon'ami Kōetsu in the 17th century, is a National Treasure.

Hagi ware is prized for its rustic simplicity and its ability to retain heat. Because of these qualities, Hagi vessels such as this 17th-century teabowl have long been part of the tea ceremony.

Fashioned from a white clay, Shigaraki pottery turns russet and gains rivulets of natural ash glaze when fired unglazed at high temperatures. The storage vessel shown here dates back to the Muromachi period (1333–1568).

This Karatsu-style water jar, fired in the 17th century, was employed in the tea ceremony. The simple design of reeds was created by using an iron-oxide underglaze overlaid with a greenish feldspathic glaze.

Fukuoka

9
8
7 6
4
3
5
10
2
1

Nabeshima serving plate, Edo period (1600–1868).

Kakiemon and Nabeshima are among several styles of porcelain made in Saga Prefecture's Arita region that are collectively referred to as Arita ware. Kakiemon pieces are known for their almost transparent mat glaze and finely drawn, realistic designs; Nabeshima ware is recognized for its red, yellow, and bluish green overglaze enamels.

Kakiemon vase, Edo period.

Unglazed stoneware cast in a bold and forceful idiom, Bizen pottery is made from plastic rice-paddy clay and is known for its sturdiness. The spouted water jug shown here was made in the 16th century.

Tamba ware presents a pleasing blend of somber earth tones—light brown, russet, and black—and refined shapes, as in this Kamakura-period (1185–1333) storage vessel.

The potters of Iga are renowned for their vases and tea ceremony implements, many of which, like this water jar from the late 16th century, have twisted shapes.

This Tokoname plate, fired in 1969, bears a characteristic ash glaze of deep olive and the reddish brown produced by the naturally high iron content of the clay in the area.

Major Ceramic Styles and Production Centers by Prefecture

1 **Tsuboya** Okinawa	16 **Kyōto** Kyōto	31 **Kutani** Ishikawa
2 **Satsuma** Kagoshima	17 **Raku** Kyōto	32 **Suzu** Ishikawa
3 **Arita** Saga	18 **Shigaraki** Shiga	33 **Kamei** Saitama
4 **Karatsu** Saga/Nagasaki	19 **Iga** Mie	34 **Kanai** Gumma
5 **Onta** Ōita	20 **Banko** Mie	35 **Kasama** Ibaraki
6 **Koishiwara** Fukuoka	21 **Tokoname** Aichi	36 **Mashiko** Tochigi
7 **Takatori** Fukuoka	22 **Atsumi** Aichi	37 **Sōma** Fukushima
8 **Agano** Fukuoka	23 **Kosai** Shizuoka	38 **Iizaka** Fukushima
9 **Hagi** Yamaguchi	24 **Sanage** Aichi	39 **Aizu Hongō** Fukushima
10 **Tobe** Ehime	25 **Seto** Aichi	40 **Sasagami** Niigata
11 **Sue** Kagawa	26 **Mino** Gifu	41 **Hirashimizu** Yamagata
12 **Kameyama** Okayama	27 **Kaneyama** Gifu	42 **Tōkita** Miyagi
13 **Bizen** Okayama	28 **Nakatsugawa** Gifu	43 **Tsutsumi** Miyagi
14 **Tamba** Hyōgo	29 **Echizen** Fukui	44 **Takōda** Miyagi
15 **Suemura** Ōsaka	30 **Kaga** Ishikawa	45 **Shinanoura** Miyagi

▲ Inactive premodern kilns

■ Active premodern kilns

● Modern kilns

Often graced with a few brush-strokes that represent the stalks of flowers and grasses, Mashiko ware is sturdy everyday pottery. It has a relaxed, earthy look exemplified by this 20th-century serving dish by Hamada Shōji.

Characterized by elaborate designs and rich hues, Kutani ceramics take their thematic cues from Tang-dynasty (618–907) Chinese models, as seen in this large 17th-century serving dish.

Mino ware refers to several ceramic styles, including *kiseto*, *setoguro*, Shino, and Oribe. These four, considered among the more notable styles of the Azuchi-Momoyama period (1568–1600), exhibit a boldness that sometimes approaches the eccentric.

Kiseto bowl. Late 16th century.

Setoguro teabowl. Late 16th century.

Oribe serving dish. Late 16th century.

Shino teabowl. National Treasure. Late 16th century.

173

uses has been a steady force in Japanese culture for millennia.

The Japanese islands contain all the major types of materials that fall into the classification of clay. These range from primary clay, lying deep in the mountains close to its parent igneous rock, to broad beds of secondary clay mixed with sand and organic material along riverbanks and valley floors. Many secondary, or transported, clays are easily accessible and require only bonfire temperatures (600°–900°C or 1,112°–1,652°F) to harden into the soft, porous, red ceramic substance called earthenware. Primary clay must be mined, processed, and fired in a kiln in order to reach a temperature high enough (1,000°C or 1,832°F) to turn it into a hard, nonporous material colored beige, gray, or white and termed pottery, stoneware, or porcelain depending upon its hardness and purity. The pure white clay called kaolin is the material for porcelain, turning glasslike and translucent when fired. Related feldspars are required for making glassy coatings, or glazes, on high-fired wares.

In the development of ceramic materials, China was the great innovator, and all of Japan's advanced technology came directly or indirectly from there; more often than not, China also set the style. Yet also typical of Japan's attitude toward ceramics was the fact that, while newer wares representing advanced technology might be accorded a position of highest status, they by no means obliterated existing wares and techniques, which for the most part continued unaffected. As a result, Japanese ceramics became steadily richer in variety, and the ceramic articles produced in Japan today cover the full range from earthenware directly descended from neolithic precedents to the most demanding Chinese-style glazed wares.

Early Earthenware—It seems to have been almost 12,000 years ago that people in Japan began to use sedimentary clay to form vessels. JŌMON POTTERY, characterized by its "cord-impressed" patterns, dates from as early as 10,000 BC. Its earliest forms resemble deep cylindrical baskets with pointed bottoms.

Early vessels served all storing, soaking, and boiling purposes, but, by the middle of the Jōmon period (ca 10,000 BC–ca 300 BC), potters in the area corresponding to modern Nagano Prefecture—which contains the largest concentration of Jōmon sites—had developed the full range of basic pottery shapes. These potters also created the most dramatically ornamented Jōmon pottery, with heavy rims convoluted, asymmetrical, and embellished with added coils, animal forms, and faces. Such pots, as well as the small clay figurines called dogū, raise the question of the relationship of pottery, especially earthenware, to religious ritual.

With the introduction of rice cultivation to Japan in the succeeding Yayoi period (ca 300 BC–ca AD 300), the heavy, elaborate Jōmon style gave way to the smooth, thin, symmetrical, minimally ornamented Yayoi style. The change reflected a shift of habitation centers from highlands to river deltas where rice was grown: whereas Jōmon clay is usually stiff, requiring considerable temper, and too coarse to take a fine finish, pots of the Yayoi period are formed from the plastic, fine-grained clay found in such deltas. Whereas ceramics in the Jōmon period seems to have been the primary form of artistic expression, Yayoi culture had access to other materials introduced from the continent—

most significantly bronze—and this is reflected in the pottery. Certain design elements in Yayoi pots, such as raised horizontal ridges, suggest the aesthetic influence of cast metal. See also YAYOI POTTERY.

Sue and Haji Wares—During the Kofun period (ca 300–710) influences from the Korean peninsula wrought radical changes in Japanese culture and technology. By the mid-5th century a method of making high-fired stoneware ceramics known as SUE WARE had been introduced and was rapidly developed by Korean craftsmen residing in what are now the Nara and Ōsaka regions, eventually superseding earthenware in production and status. Sue vessels, produced in through-draft or tunnel kilns (anagama), were of superior quality for storing liquids.

Earthenware, however, now known as HAJI WARE, remained indispensable for cooking purposes and also for ritual. Pottery grave goods, such as portable clay stoves and tall flanged pots, were placed in the conspicuous aboveground tombs (KOFUN) after which the period is named, and by the 6th century elaborate grave offerings of metal weapons and armor had been replaced with pottery replicas. Clay cylinders, or HANIWA, were arranged around raised tomb mounds; eventually these cylinders were rendered as figurines and placed atop the tombs.

Early High-Fired Pottery and Glazed Ceramics—Sue ware, the high-status gray stoneware introduced during the Kofun period, at first borrowed its shapes and techniques from earthenware prototypes, especially for ritual pottery. Complex vessels were assembled from coiled and wheel-thrown elements. However, new shapes arriving from Tang (T'ang; 618–907) China required predominant use of the wheel, which was also essential for increased production. By the Nara period (710–794) another continental ceramic technology had been introduced: intentional glazing of high-fired wares.

Early sue ware was blackened by smoking at the end of firing to make it waterproof. Ash glazing on the upper surface of some sue wares was the result of wood ash accidentally settling on the pot during firing. In the late 7th and early 8th centuries, intentional glazing was introduced from Tang China and developed in two forms: polychrome lead-based glaze on refined earthenware, and feldspathic ash glaze applied to high-fired pottery.

Production of lead-glazed wares began at kilns in or around the modern city of Nara. Plain green-glazed pieces were being made by the late 7th century, and polychrome glazes were added by the early 8th century. These early Nara wares, produced under government control, include three-color wares—usually green, white, and yellowish brown—called sansai tōki; two-color wares—usually green and white—called nisai tōki; and green-glazed wares called ryokuyū tōki. From the 9th century until the demise of lead-glazed ware at the end of the 12th century, the glaze reverted to plain green in imitation of the imported Chinese ceramics bearing the iron-tinted greenish ash glaze known as celadon.

Actual duplication of the celadon technology occurred with the development at the SANAGE kilns (in the vicinity of modern Nagoya) of a feldspathic glaze applied to a high-fired gray or white body. Sanage had begun as a sue-ware center, but the fortuitous availability of white clay made it a natural locale for the development of ash-glaze techniques, in which wood ash was sprin-

kled thinly over the shoulders of vessels prior to firing. Sanage received direct support from the Heian court, its most eager customer, and it remained the major center of ceramic production through the Heian period (794–1185). The ash-glazed Sanage wares were a ready and popular substitute for the highly prized Chinese celadons imported from the continent. Production expanded rapidly, and, with each wave of celadon imports, new shapes and decorative techniques—such as incising, use of underglaze iron paint, and reticulating—were introduced.

By the end of the 12th century, however, most central Sanage kilns were making only the unglazed, popular tablewares called YAMACHAWAN. The disappearance of ash glaze at Sanage is believed to have resulted from a division of labor among kilns. A movement from eastern Sanage toward better sources of white, kaolin-like clay led to the establishment of a new center for glazed ware in Seto (see SETO WARE).

Medieval Ceramics—Under the patronage of the Kamakura shogunate (1192–1333) and Zen temples, Seto began by copying newly introduced Southern Song (Sung; 1127–1279) Chinese forms—four-eared jars, flasks, ewers—with amber or green ash glaze applied over carved, stamped, or sprigged designs. By the 14th century Seto had also perfected use of the iron-brown temmoku glaze inspired by brown-glazed teabowls brought back from China.

Seto kilns reached their peak in the mid-15th century, but their development was cut short by the outbreak of the ŌNIN WAR (1467–77). The center for glazed wares shifted to Mino (now part of Gifu Prefecture), which had also produced first sue, then Sanage-type, and finally Seto-type glazed wares (see MINO WARE). At the beginning of the 16th century a change occurred in the kiln, as the through-draft or tunnel kiln introduced with sue ware was replaced by the larger, more reliable ōgama ("great kiln"). Efforts to imitate porcelains from Ming (1368–1644) China led to the development of the opaque, white feldspathic glaze with underglaze iron decoration that became popular as Shino ware late in the century.

Although glazed as well as unglazed wares continued to be produced at Seto, Mino, and other medieval kilns, from the 12th through the 16th century the principal Japanese ceramic product was a sturdy, unglazed stoneware, called yakishime or sekki, that was made in a limited set of shapes primarily for utilitarian storage. The most important kilns to produce this type of stoneware were those at Tokoname (see TOKONAME WARE) in Owari (now part of Aichi Prefecture). Potters used the clay without alteration, employing simple coiling and scraping construction methods. Tokoname potters probably also spread the medieval kiln (a variation of the tunnel kiln but at a steeper angle and with a flame-diverting pillar behind the firebox) and encouraged the shift from reduction to oxidation firing. The Tokoname kilns were part of the so-called Owari kiln group, which also included Seto and Sanage and which manufactured a full range of ceramics for its clients.

The archaeologist Narasaki Shōichi has identified six types of high-firing ceramic production during the medieval period: (1) Seto and Mino, whose glazed wares carried on the ash-glazing tradition of the Heian period; (2) the kilns in the former ash-glazed-ware center of Sanage; (3) the kilns of the Sanage lineage that turned to production of large stoneware vessels (such as Toko-name ware, Atsumi ware, Kosai ware, and others); (4) the kilns that produced *sue* ware in the Heian period but that, under the influence of Tokoname, turned to production of medieval stonewares (such as ECHIZEN WARE); (5) the kilns that employed *sue* firing techniques at first but changed, by the early 13th century, from reduction to oxidation firing (producing such wares as SHIGARAKI WARE, IGA WARE, TAMBA WARE, and BIZEN WARE); and (6) the *sue*-derived kilns that continued to produce reduced black ware (such as Suzu ware, Kameyama ware, and others).

With the growing commercial significance of ceramics in the Muromachi period (1333–1568), when unglazed stonewares in particular emerged as valuable sources of cash income, potters became more professional as output increased. Beginning with tea jars, everyday wares began to be glazed, resulting in further improvements in kiln structure. Mino potters were most influential in dispersing glazing technology to stoneware kilns.

Nevertheless, the same kilns that were striving to develop glazes were also influenced by the interest of the tea masters in unglazed pieces (particularly in ceramics imported from Southeast Asia, known as *nam-ban* ware) for use as TEA CEREMONY vessels. This interest reflected an increasing appreciation of simplicity and rusticity, aesthetic values that came to a peak in the tea ceremony school founded by SEN NO RIKYŪ (1522–91). Bizen produced the outstanding early pieces in this mode. Around 1600 the conscious manipulation at the Iga kilns of the features of unglazed medieval stonewares, including "natural" ash glaze, represented the epitome of the artificial naturalism espoused by many tea ceremony adherents.

Edo-Period Ceramics——The Edo period (1600–1868) saw a continuation of innovative stylistic and technological developments in stonewares and in glazed and unglazed ceramics—fueled not only by the aesthetic tastes of tea masters but also by the by-now-enormous commercial market for pottery. Innovations involved not only the popular decorated wares, such as Shino ware, Oribe ware, and KARATSU WARE, but also the more austere wares, such as RAKU WARE, Iga ware, and Bizen ware, which underwent more subtle changes in form and design.

Japan's INVASIONS OF KOREA IN 1592 AND 1597 gave military leaders the opportunity to bring Korean potters, with their superior skills of throwing and glazing, to Japan to work in their domains. The introduction from Korea of the *noborigama* ("climbing kiln") revolutionized the firing of stonewares and made possible the successful firing of porcelain after suitable clays were discovered in the Arita area of northern Kyūshū by Korean potters (see RI SAMPEI) in the early 17th century.

The desire to make porcelain had been stirred by imported Ming porcelains, and Chinese ware had provided the earliest models, but by the mid-17th century a second crucial influence was added in the form of the European market. The Dutch East India Company not only placed enormous orders but also provided explicit models. Special preference was accorded an Arita-produced decorated ware called KAKIEMON WARE, which was characterized by application of polychrome enamels and underglaze cobalt to a milk-white porcelain body. The second half of the 17th century saw

the full flowering of such decorated wares. Colorful Imari ware (see ARITA WARE) and Kakiemon ware were shipped to Europe from Kyūshū in great quantities; the finer Kakiemon and NABESHIMA WARE porcelains were reserved for local rulers. In Kyōto, a popular form of decorated earthenware or stoneware known as *kyō-yaki* (see KYŌTO CERAMICS) was developed by such potter-decorators as NONOMURA NINSEI (fl mid-17th century) and Ogata KENZAN (1666–1743). Only isolated ventures, such as Himetani ware and KUTANI WARE, attempted the production of porcelain in competition with the dominant kilns in Arita.

With the exception of a few inspired wares such as BANKO WARE of Ise Province (now part of Mie Prefecture), ceramic production through the 18th century was mostly time-proven utilitarian wares. As the 18th century drew to a close, new kiln sites began to be opened throughout the country, and a resurgence of activity took place in and around the old kiln centers. In the early 19th century OKUDA EISEN (1753–1811), NIN'AMI DŌHACHI (1783–1855), and AOKI MOKUBEI (1767–1833) led the way to a colorful new aesthetic in Japanese ceramic art, making use of overglaze enamel decoration owing much to the painters and potters of the RIMPA style as well as to Chinese ceramic models.

Modern Ceramics——The opening of Japan to the West brought new opportunities for ceramics export and the development of porcelain centers at Kyōto and Yokohama. Through the work of the German technician Gottfried WAGENER (1831–92) in Arita, Kyōto, and Tōkyō, and through Japanese participation in international expositions in Europe and the United States, Western ceramic technology and taste were introduced. Major ceramic centers opened training laboratories and began the process of transforming the workshop into the factory.

Contemporary Japanese ceramics may be said to have begun shortly after 1900 with the emergence of the "studio potter" with an individual name and style. Although precedents for the artist-potter reached back in Kyōto as far as the Raku family, Nonomura Ninsei, or Ogata Kenzan, most traditional potters were anonymous artisans following precedents. The studio potter of the 20th century came to ceramics by choice rather than by birth, and the typical eclectic style was based on a strong knowledge of Japanese ceramic history. ITAYA HAZAN (1872–1963), for example, was trained as a sculptor, and KITAŌJI ROSANJIN (1883–1959) began making pottery to supply his own gourmet restaurant.

From 1926, the FOLK CRAFTS movement led by YANAGI MUNEYOSHI (1889–1961) began to foster interest in the aesthetic value of traditional craftwork and skillfully made simple objects of daily use—among them ceramics. The potters KAWAI KANJIRŌ (1890–1966) and HAMADA SHŌJI (1894–1978) participated in this movement, and it was through the latter, who established his workshop in MASHIKO, that the town became famous as a center of folk-style pottery. See also MASHIKO WARE.

The first BUNTEN (Ministry of Education Fine Arts Exhibition) to include ceramics was held in 1927, and the postwar designation of LIVING NATIONAL TREASURES influenced the emergence of individual potters at traditional ceramic centers and fostered public awareness of local clays and techniques. The potters awarded the title of Living National Treasure include ARAKAWA TOYOZŌ (1894–1985) for Shino and Black Seto wares,

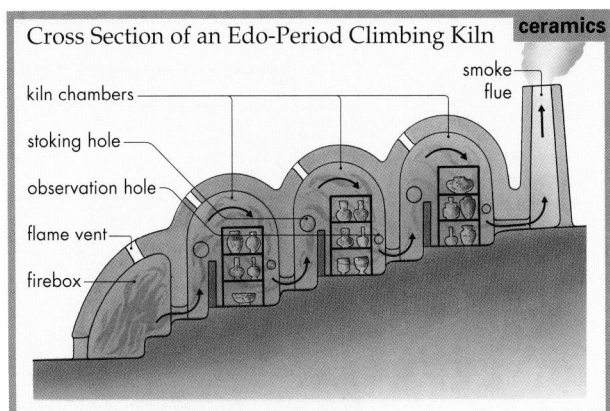

Cross Section of an Edo-Period Climbing Kiln — ceramics

kiln chambers
stoking hole
observation hole
flame vent
firebox
smoke flue

This type of through-draft kiln was fired to temperatures as high as 1,300° to 1,400°C. When heat within the chambers successively reached desired levels, the stoking holes were unplugged in turn and fuel added. The arrows indicate the direction of heat flow.

Fujiwara Kei (1899–1983) for Bizen ware, Hamada Shōji for trailed glazes, Imaizumi Imaemon XIII (b 1926) for Nabeshima ware, ISHIGURO MUNEMARO (1893–1968) for iron glaze, KANESHIGE TŌYŌ (1896–1967) for Bizen ware, KATŌ HAJIME (1900–1968) for overglaze-enamel porcelain, Kinjō Jirō (b 1912) for Ryūkyū ware, Kondō Yūzō (1902–85) for underglaze cobalt, MIWA KYŪWA (or Kyūsetsu X; 1895–1981) for HAGI WARE, Nakazato Muan (1895–1985) for Karatsu ware, Sakaida Kakiemon XIII (1906–82) for KAKIEMON WARE, and TOMIMOTO KENKICHI (1886–1963) for overglaze-enamel porcelain. The more recent designation of Traditional Handcraft Products (Dentōteki Kōgeihin) has provided government support for the continuation of traditional skills at ceramic centers. ☎ 172–173

Cerqueira, Luis de   セルケイラ, L.

(1552–1614). Second and last Catholic bishop to work in Japan during the early period of CHRISTIANITY. Born in Vila de Alvito, Portugal, he entered the Society of Jesus in 1566 and was consecrated bishop in 1593. He arrived in Nagasaki in 1598 to succeed the expelled Bishop Pedro Martins (1542–98). Cerqueira ordained the first Japanese priests in 1601 and established a diocesan clergy. His term of office was marked by the controversy between the JESUITS and friars and by the increasing anti-Christian hostility of the Japanese authorities. He died in Nagasaki.

certified public accountants
公認会計士

(*kōnin kaikeishi*). Responsibilities of certified public accountants in Japan include the audit and certification of financial reports as required by the Commercial Code (Shō Hō) and Securities Exchange Law (Shōken Torihiki Hō), preparation of financial reports, investigation and design of accounting systems, and consultation on financial matters. To become a certified public accountant one must pass a government-sponsored, three-stage examination, and one's name must be registered. Auditors may establish their own corporations to strengthen their position with respect to the companies they audit. In April 1990, there were 8,662 certified public accountants in Japan.

chadō→tea ceremony

Chaguchagu Umakko
ちゃぐちゃぐ馬子

Horse festival held on 15 June (formerly the 5th day of the 5th month of the lunar calendar); the one at the Komagata Shrine (formerly Sōzen Shrine) in the village of Takizawa in Iwate Prefecture attracts many

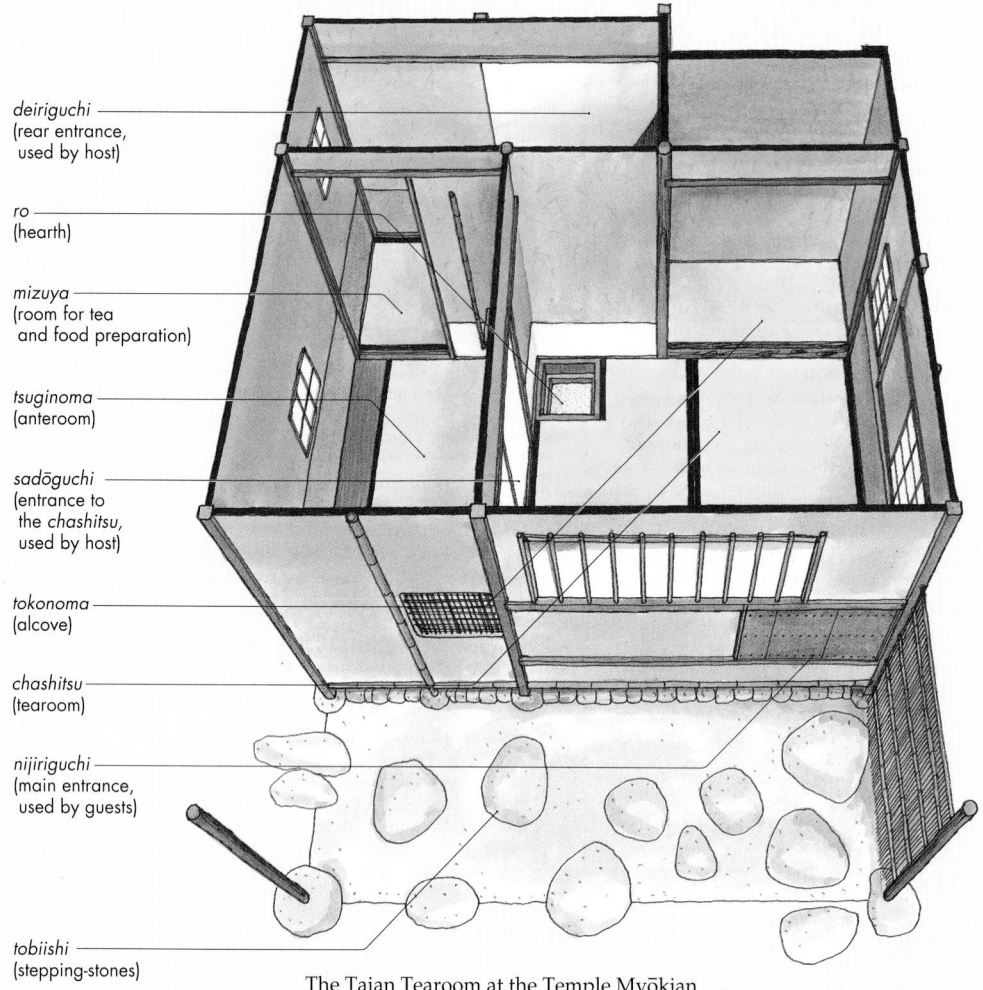

deiriguchi
(rear entrance,
used by host)

ro
(hearth)

mizuya
(room for tea
and food preparation)

tsuginoma
(anteroom)

sadōguchi
(entrance to
the chashitsu,
used by host)

tokonoma
(alcove)

chashitsu
(tearoom)

nijiriguchi
(main entrance,
used by guests)

tobiishi
(stepping-stones)

The Taian Tearoom at the Temple Myōkian

briefly controlled maritime traffic between
Silla, China, and Japan in the early 9th century. As a youth Chang had seen Koreans
sold into slavery by Chinese pirates. The
Silla king appointed Chang to police sea
trade, hoping to end this practice. Exploiting
his assignment, Chang developed considerable power and disrupted the exchange of
goods and ideas between China and Japan;
this was a significant factor in reducing Chinese influence on Japan in the Heian period
(794–1185). Chang provided transportation
and aid for the monk ENNIN on the latter's trip
to China in 838. Chang amassed great wealth
and influence in Silla politics before being assassinated in 841 or 846.

Chang Tso-lin → Zhang Zuolin
(Chang Tso-lin)

Chang Tzu-p'ing → Zhang Ziping
(Chang Tzu-p'ing)

Chanoine, Charles Sulpice Jules
シャノワーヌ, C. S. J.

(1835–1915). French army officer and military adviser to Japan. A graduate of the St.
Cyr Military Academy, Chanoine served for
two years as chief of the French forces in
China. He was selected to head the 15-man
mission of instructors requested by the
Tokugawa shogunate through Léon ROCHES,
the French minister in Japan. Arriving in
Japan in 1867, Chanoine began training Japanese troops and presented to shōgun
TOKUGAWA YOSHINOBU a program to reorganize
and modernize the shogunate army. The
mission's efforts met with only limited success before the MEIJI RESTORATION of 1868, although the French-trained shogunal troops
proved their mettle in battle. Chanoine returned to France in 1869.

chanoyu → tea ceremony

charcoal making
炭焼

(*sumiyaki*). Charcoal has been used in Japan
since the ancient past in the smelting and
casting of metals. In the Edo period (1600–
1868), the demand for charcoal increased
rapidly with the spread of HIBACHI braziers
and KOTATSU heaters. With the switch to
modern heating, the use of the *hibachi* has
declined, and charcoal making has greatly
diminished. In many places in western Japan
it is believed that the method for making
charcoal was first taught by the priest KŪKAI

---

tourists. The surrounding area, a part of the
former Nambu domain, has long been
known for its fine horses, called *nambu-goma*.
Boys and girls in festive attire mount decorated horses, which are led to the shrine,
where respects are paid to the tutelary god
of horses. Votive plaques with pictures of
horses (EMA) as well as prayers are offered. A
procession to the city of Morioka follows.
The bells on the horses are said to make the
sound *chagu chagu*.

chakaiseki → tea ceremony

chambara
ちゃんばら

SAMURAI sword fights, especially in films and
plays. The term originates in the onomatopoeia "*chan-chan-bara-bara*," an approxi-

Chaguchagu Umakko
This ritual procession of
decorated horses from
the Komagata Shrine to
the city of Morioka,
Iwate Prefecture, is part
of a well-known version
of this early summer
horse festival.

mation of the dramatic, staccato rhythm of
the background music played for silent
films. *Chambara* films flourished during the
silent era and continued to be popular after
talking pictures were introduced.

Chamberlain, Basil Hall
チェンバレン, B. H.

(1850–1935). One of the foremost Western
interpreters of things Japanese. Born of a distinguished family in Southampton, England,
on 18 October 1850. Educated in Europe and
England. His father intended him to be a
banker, but at age 18 he became ill. His physician recommended travel, and Chamberlain landed in Japan on 29 May 1873.

He taught at the imperial naval school in
Tōkyō from 1874 to 1882. His most important position, however, was as professor of
Japanese at Tōkyō University beginning in
1886. It was here that he gained his reputation as a student of Japanese language and
literature. His many works include the first
translation of the KOJIKI into English (1906),
A Handbook of Colloquial Japanese (1888),
Things Japanese (1890), and *A Practical Guide
to the Study of Japanese Writing* (1905). With
W. B. Mason he wrote *A Handbook for Travelers in Japan* (1891), which went through
numerous editions. He retired to Geneva,
Switzerland, in 1911.

Chang Hsüeh-liang → Zhang
Xueliang (Chang Hsüeh-liang)

Chang-ku-feng Incident → Zhang-
gufeng (Chang-ku-feng) Incident

Chang Po-go
張宝高

(?–841 or 846; J: Chō Hōkō). Adventurer of
the ancient Korean kingdom of SILLA who

Stepping-stones mark a path through the garden at one of the Ura Senke tearooms in Kyōto.

(774–835). There are several superstitions and taboos about charcoal making. For example, charcoal makers were often required to lead an ascetic life, and women were forbidden at the charcoal huts.

Charter Oath 五力条の御誓文
(Gokajō no Goseimon; literally, Imperial Oath of Five Articles). A statement of national policy pledged by Emperor MEIJI to his imperial ancestors. It was read aloud on 6 April 1868 by the deputy chief executive (fukusōsai) SANJŌ SANETOMI in the presence of the emperor and more than 400 officials in the Shishinden (the main ceremonial hall) in the Kyōto Imperial Palace. The oath reads: "(1) An assembly shall be widely convoked, and all measures shall be decided by open discussion. (2) High and low shall be of one mind, and the national economy and finances shall be greatly strengthened. (3) Civil and military officials together, and the common people as well, shall all achieve their aspirations, and thus the people's minds shall not be made weary. (4) Evil practices of the past shall be abandoned, and actions shall be based on international usage. (5) Knowledge shall be sought all over the world, and the foundations of imperial rule shall be strengthened." It was reissued verbatim on 1 January 1946 in the name of Emperor SHŌWA (Hirohito). The five articles of the oath's first draft were composed by a junior councillor (san'yo), YURI KIMIMASA, in January 1868 and revised by another junior councillor, FUKUOKA TAKACHIKA, probably in early February. Although later idealized as a far-sighted statement, the oath was primarily a short-term tactic of the Meiji government to stabilize its new rule.

chashitsu 茶室
(literally, "tearoom"). A space for performing the TEA CEREMONY. The term chashitsu generally refers to a separate building, often with a garden surrounding it, but can also refer to a room where the tea ceremony is performed within a larger building. Styles of chashitsu vary but construction consistently incorporates wooden posts and floors raised off the ground; sand-finished, mortared walls over bamboo lattice; windows that may reveal the inner lattice; wooden sheet and bamboo ceilings; papered window panels (SHŌJI); and sliding doors (fusuma). The roof may be thatched, shingled, or now oc-

casionally tiled. Whereas the main entrance (nijiriguchi) is only about 60–70 centimeters (27.5–31.5 in) high, so that the guests have to crouch and crawl through, the host's entrance (sadōguchi) is of normal height. The tearoom is typically 4½ TATAMI mats (7.29 sq m; 78.44 sq ft) in area and has a TOKONOMA (alcove) on the north wall toward the east. In the tokonoma a hanging scroll may be displayed along with other objects. Chashitsu that have been designated National Treasures include the Taian (built by SEN NO RIKYŪ) in the town of Ōyamazaki, Kyōto Prefecture, and the Joan (built by ODA URAKU), now in Inuyama, Aichi Prefecture.
👁 178–179

chawan 茶碗
Ceramic bowls in which rice or tea is served. The word chawan (literally, "teabowl") originally referred to bowls used in the TEA CEREMONY; it is now also the general term for rice bowls (meshi-jawan) and teacups without handles (yunomi-jawan). In the typical Japanese household each person has a rice bowl and teacup reserved for his or her exclusive use. As it is customary in Japan to hold the rice bowl in one hand as one eats, the bowl is normally of a standard shape and weight, making it easy to pick up and hold. Teacups are of a wide variety of shapes and sizes, some with lids.

Chaya Shirojirō 茶屋四郎次郎
The name of successive heads of the Chaya family, a wealthy merchant house of the Azuchi-Momoyama (1568–1600) and Edo (1600–1868) periods. The family's prosperity is linked to the ties that Shirojirō I (Kiyonobu; 1545?–96) established with TOKUGAWA IEYASU, whom he aided in escaping to safety from the Kyōto area after the HONNŌJI INCIDENT of 1582. During the hegemony of TOYOTOMI HIDEYOSHI, he maintained confidential contacts with the imperial court on Ieyasu's behalf and was the intendant (DAIKAN) of Tokugawa holdings in Ōmi Province (now Shiga Prefecture). He acted as Ieyasu's quartermaster in the ODAWARA CAMPAIGN of 1590 and in the same year assisted in the city planning of Edo (now Tōkyō), Ieyasu's new capital. Shirojirō II (Kiyotada; 1582–1603) was at Ieyasu's side at the Battle of SEKIGAHARA (1600); after the victory, Ieyasu appointed him head townsman (sō machigashira) in Kyōto. Shirojirō III (Kiyotsugu; 1584–1622) was active in Nagasaki as Ieyasu's agent in the regulated silk trade (ITOWAPPU) with the Portuguese. The Chaya sent abroad at least 11 "vermilion seal ships" (shuinsen; see VERMILION SEAL SHIP TRADE). The family received trading privileges from the shogunate which they held throughout the Edo period.

chazuke 茶漬け
A simple Japanese dish made by pouring hot green tea or hot water over a bowl of rice that has been topped with any of a variety of ingredients, including pickled plum (UMEBOSHI), salted cod roe (tarako), salted salmon, or TSUKUDANI (delicacies simmered in soy sauce). Cold or hot water was poured over rice as early as the Heian period (794–1185), but it was not until the popularization of green tea during the Edo period (1600–1868) that pouring hot tea on rice became a common practice.

chemical industry 化学工業
(kagaku kōgyō). The Japanese chemical industry was created in the 1870s, when the

chazuke Shown here is tai chazuke, in which the rice is topped with raw sea bream and garnished with slivers of seaweed (nori) and a dollop of green horseradish (wasabi).

government imported technologies for the production of glass, inorganic chemicals, cement, and other products from Europe and the United States. The electrochemical industry was developed during the early 1900s, utilizing the surplus power generated by hydroelectric plants. In the 1930s coal came into increasing use as a power source as a result of the rising cost of electricity and the government policy of fostering coal mining. On the eve of World War II, production in the chemical fertilizer, rayon, and soda industries had reached international levels.

After the war, the first industry to recover was chemical fertilizers, because of the urgent need to increase food production. In the late 1950s, the Japanese PETROCHEMICAL INDUSTRY made its debut, spurred by two major factors. First, the conversion of energy production from hydroelectric and coal to oil resulted in a surplus of naphtha (a product of oil refining and an important material for petrochemical production). Second, the enactment of the Foreign Investment Law facilitated the introduction of foreign technology. The petrochemical industry grew rapidly and was able to reduce manufacturing costs through expansion in the scale of production. The Japanese chemical industry accounted for 7.4 percent (¥22.1 trillion; US $160.5 billion) of the nation's industrial output in 1989, a full 42 percent of the industry's output being in petrochemicals. The fine chemicals sector (pharmaceuticals and cosmetics) has been steadily expanding since the mid-1980s. In the late 1980s the industry was investing heavily in the research and development of new materials and biotechnology products, spending ¥687.4 billion (US $4.1 billion) in 1987. New materials are being used in consumer goods, construction, and electronics, and biotechnology applications have begun in such fields as medical products and horticulture.

charcoal making
A charcoal-making plant in the town of Kodama, Saitama Prefecture. White smoke can be seen rising from the clay kiln at the start of the charcoal-making process, in which wood is charred by gradually raising it to a temperature of 380°C then leaving it to cool for three to four days.

Stepping-stones traverse the *roji*, the garden which separates the teahouse from the world. Guests stop at a stone basin called a *tsukubai* to purify their hands and mouth with water before entering.

The Joan teahouse has been moved three times and is now in the garden Urakuen in the city of Inuyama, Aichi Prefecture. It has been designated a National Treasure.

The Japanese Teahouse and the Aesthetics of Wabi

The nijiriguchi, the tiny entry to the teahouse used by guests, is only 60 centimeters square. Whatever their worldly status, all must bend low when entering to practice the tea ceremony.

The custom of drinking tea for alertness during Buddhist meditation reached Japan in the 8th century. By the late 15th century, Japanese aristocrats had transformed the ritual for serving this stimulant into an excuse for showing off gorgeous tea vessels to guests in sumptuous pavilions. Murata Shukō, a priest and tea master to the shōgun Ashikaga Yoshimasa, led a backlash against these fancy trappings. Believing that tea was best savored in a small, unadorned space, Shukō designed a teahouse with the scale and furnishings of a peasant's cottage. Its tearoom, containing only $4\frac{1}{2}$ *tatami* mats (2.7 meters square), is a pure, plain rejection of material opulence. Shukō believed that in a life purged of excess a higher beauty is revealed. This moral and aesthetic concept that poverty and austerity are best, that less is more, is known as *wabi*. Shukō, and tea masters Takeno Jōō and Sen no Rikyū after him, made the tea ceremony a vehicle to express and refine *wabi*. For *samurai*, trained to bear spartan rigors, its appeal was powerful.

The teahouses Rikyū designed in the 16th century are even smaller and more spartan than Shukō's. Reached by rough stone paths, they are huts secluded from the world by gardens. In their tiny alcoves, or *tokonoma*, flowers or calligraphy are displayed.

The teahouse shown here, called Joan, was built in 1618 by Oda Uraku, brother to the mid-16th-century hegemon Oda Nobunaga and disciple of Sen no Rikyū. Uraku's devotion to *wabi* is seen in its plain plaster walls supported by rough-hewn posts and papered along the bottom with old calendars.

The tea ceremony is conducted in a space of less than 9 square meters. A sunken hearth for boiling water flanks a log pillar.

Light diffused by paper windows reveals the powerful lines and plain materials dictated by the *wabi* aesthetic. In the far corner is the *tokonoma* for displaying flowers and calligraphy.

A wooden nameplate hung beneath the ridgepole is inscribed with Chinese characters reading "Joan." Uraku was a Christian convert, and the teahouse name is derived from his baptismal name, João.

The round lattice window in the wall facing the tiny entry was created by leaving this circular portion of the wall's wattled framework unplastered.

Photographs by Sasaki Hikaru

flowering cherry

1 The *somei yoshino* is one of the most common varieties of cherry and is especially popular in Tōkyō. It blooms in early April.
2 The *gyoikō*, a horticultural strain of the flowering cherry, is noted for its unusual yellow-green blossoms.
3 The *ōshimazakura* grows wild in temperate coastal regions and is also cultivated. Its leaves are pickled in salt and used in Japanese confections.
4 The *yamazakura* grows wild in mountainous areas south of central Honshū and is distinguished from the similar *somei yoshino* by its lack of leaf and stem hairs.

chemistry 化学

(*kagaku*). Modern chemical research in Japan began with foreign professors who were invited to teach in Japan by the Meiji government (see FOREIGN EMPLOYEES OF THE MEIJI PERIOD) and with young Japanese scholars selected from the Kaisei Gakkō (forerunner of Tōkyō University) for study in Europe and the United States. NAGAI NAGAYOSHI, who studied at the University of Berlin, went on to discover ephedrine and established the science of organic chemistry in Japan. ASAHINA YASUHIKO was chief among Nagai's students in this field. TAKAMINE JŌKICHI, a graduate of the Kōbu Daigakkō (later the engineering department of Tōkyō University) who studied in England and Scotland, made notable contributions to Japan's chemical industry. He succeeded in the production of the enzyme preparation known as Taka-Diastase and the crystallization of adrenaline.

Development of facilities for chemical research included the founding in 1917 of the INSTITUTE OF PHYSICAL AND CHEMICAL RESEARCH. At this institute and others, Japanese chemists have registered outstanding achievements in the fields of complex chemistry, geochemistry, analytical chemistry, physical chemistry, and organic chemistry. Since the 1950s, when a strong petrochemical industry emerged, significant advances have been made in plastics and other chemical products, leading to exports of chemical technology through patent transfers and reciprocal agreements.

The number of active research chemists, both academic and industrial, has grown from a few thousand in 1910 to some 40,000 today. Some of the most notable achievements include MIZUSHIMA SAN'ICHIRŌ's work in 1925 on molecular polarization, Kita Gen'itsu (1883–1952) and SAKURADA ICHIRŌ's study of plastics and synthetic rubber, the extraction of the substance later known as vitamin B₁ by SUZUKI UMETARŌ in 1910, and FUKUI KEN'ICHI's "frontier orbital theory" of chemical reactions, for which he received the Nobel Prize in 1981. See also CHEMICAL INDUSTRY; PETROCHEMICAL INDUSTRY.

Chemulp'o, Treaty of 済物浦条約

(Saimoppo Jōyaku). An agreement between Korea and Japan, signed on 30 August 1882, that resolved tensions resulting from the IMO MUTINY in Korea in July. Korea agreed to pay an indemnity and the costs of stationing and maintaining a Japanese legation guard in Seoul and to punish those responsible for the mutiny. The treaty was undermined by the KAPSIN POLITICAL COUP in 1884. See also KOREA AND JAPAN.

Cheng Ch'eng-kung → Zheng

Chenggong (Cheng Ch'eng-kung)

Cheng Hsiao-hsü → Zheng Xiaoxu

(Cheng Hsiao-hsü)

Chen Shunchen → Chin Shunshin

Chen Tianhua (Ch'en T'ien-hua) 陳天華

(1875–1905; J: Chin Tenka). Chinese revolutionary. A native of Hunan Province, Chen went to Tōkyō on a government scholarship and there joined the rapidly growing contingent of Chinese revolutionary activists. Returning to China in 1904, he participated with HUANG XING (Huang Hsing) and others in an abortive revolutionary plot. Escaping arrest after the uprising, Chen again went to Japan. In July and August 1905 he played a leading role in establishing the Tongmeng Hui (T'ung-meng Hui; United League), China's first national republican revolutionary society. In December 1905 Chen committed suicide, an act intended to shock Chinese students in Japan into a disciplined devotion to their country's salvation.

Ch'en T'ien-hua → Chen Tianhua

(Ch'en T'ien-hua)

cherry blossom viewing → hanami

cherry, flowering 桜

(*sakura*). *Prunus* spp. Any of a number of deciduous trees of the family Rosaceae that grow wild in mountainous areas throughout Japan and are also widely cultivated. The word *sakura* is generally used for those species of cherry appreciated for the beauty of their blossoms rather than those grown for their fruit. The wood is used for fine furniture, carving, and woodblock printing. The *sakura* is mentioned frequently in Japanese literature, both ancient and modern; traditional Japanese values of purity and simplicity are thought to be reflected in the form and color of its blossoms. Since it flowers very briefly and then scatters, the cherry blossom has also become a symbol of the Japanese appreciation of ephemeral beauty.

Cherry-blossom-viewing parties (see HANAMI) were popular among the Japanese nobility in ancient times, and by the early 17th century the custom had spread to the common people. Picnicking and drinking *sake* with family, friends, and co-workers beneath flowering cherry trees remains a popular rite of springtime in contemporary Japan.

There are now about 300 varieties of *sakura*. The following are three species admired in Japan:

The *somei yoshino* (*P. yedoensis*) is planted in parks and along riverbanks. This relatively short-lived variety matures in about 20 years, reaching a height of about 7 meters (23 ft), and bears large, pink, single-petaled flowers.

The *yamazakura* (*P. jamazakura*) grows wild in mountainous areas south from central Honshū and has long been cultivated. It reaches a height of 20 to 25 meters (66 to 82 ft). Its oblong leaves have toothed edges and its flowers are pink or nearly white.

The *shidarezakura* (*P. itosakura*) has long been planted in temple gardens. It reaches a height of some 20 meters (66 ft). Its thicker branches spread horizontally and its longer, slender branches hang down vertically. Its blossoms are usually single and pinkish white, but are occasionally double or red.

Japanese *sakura* are said to have first been imported to the United States in 1862. In 1909 Tōkyō presented Washington, DC, with a goodwill gift of over 2,000 *sakura* of 11 varieties. ☎ *182–183*

chestnut 栗

(*kuri*). *Castanea crenata*. The Japanese chestnut tree is distributed from Hokkaidō to Kyūshū, but few chestnuts are harvested for eating in Hokkaidō or northern Honshū. The large fruits are suitable for cooking and are made into candied chestnuts, sweet jelly (*yōkan*), and sweet caramelized chestnuts. As it is hard to remove the pellicle of the Japanese chestnut, Chinese chestnuts are imported in quantity. The rot-resistant wood is used for house foundations and for furniture. Chestnuts other than *C. crenata* are not grown in Japan because of the large amount of rainfall.

Chiang Kai-shek 蔣介石

(1887–1975; J: Shō Kaiseki). Chinese head of state, military commander, and party leader. A native of Zhejiang (Chekiang) Province, Chiang entered the Baoding (Paoting) Military Academy in 1907. From 1908 to 1910 he attended the Shimbu Gakkō, a military school in Tōkyō. Chiang joined the revolutionary United League (Tongmeng Hui or T'ung-meng Hui) in Japan and returned to China during the revolution of 1911. After YUAN SHIKAI (Yüan Shih-k'ai) took power in 1912, Chiang returned to Japan. In 1913 he was briefly in China for the abortive revolution against Yuan. In late 1915 he returned to China and spent the next two years in Shanghai. In 1918 Chiang joined SUN YAT-SEN in Guangzhou (Canton) and became a member of Sun's Nationalist Party, the Guomindang (Kuomintang; KMT). He went to Moscow in 1923 to study the Red Army. While hostile to the communist goal of social revolution, he was influenced by the Leninist theory of imperialism and Soviet organizational techniques. After his return to China he founded the Huangpu (Whampoa) Military Academy and created a KMT party army.

Sun died in 1925, and Chiang gradually became the most powerful KMT leader. By 1928 a national government was established in Nanjing (Nanking) with Chiang at its head. Chiang's government faced two major challenges: Japan and the Chinese communists. Regarding the communists as the greater threat, Chiang resolved to crush them before resisting Japan. This policy was unpopular, and late in 1936 he was compelled to abandon it in favor of resistance against Japan (see XI'AN [SIAN] INCIDENT). Full-scale fighting broke out in 1937 (see SINO-JAPANESE WAR OF 1937–1945; WORLD WAR II), forcing Chiang's government inland to Chongqing (Chungking) for the rest of World War II.

The civil war between the KMT and the communists started in 1946, and in 1949 Chiang and his government fled to Taiwan. Chiang led the KMT government until his death.

Chian Iji Hō→Peace Preservation Law of 1925

Chian Keisatsu Hō→Public Order and Police Law of 1900

Chiao-chou concession→Jiaozhou (Kiaochow) concession

Chiba   千葉[市]

City in northwestern Chiba Prefecture; capital of Chiba Prefecture; about 34 km (21 mi) southeast of Tōkyō on Tōkyō Bay. Under the control of the Chiba family from the 12th to the 15th centuries, it developed as a prosperous castle town, and during the Edo period (1600–1868) was a post-station town serving several highways. With the opening of a railway line in the late 19th century it became the prefecture's political, economic, and cultural center. During World War II, Chiba was a military base. The site of a large-scale postwar reclamation project, the city became part of the KEIYŌ INDUSTRIAL REGION, with large steel mills and thermal power plants. The port of Chiba handles one of the largest import-export volumes in Japan. Many housing complexes have been built on the reclaimed land, causing an increase in population. Pop: 829,455.

Chiba Bank, Ltd   [株]千葉銀行

(Chiba Ginkō). One of the largest regional banks in Japan. Incorporated in 1943. It has 165 domestic offices, branches in New York and Hong Kong, and a representative office in London. Its total assets for the fiscal year ending March 1991 reached ¥9.0 trillion (US $65.6 billion), and the bank was capitalized at ¥106.8 billion (US $778.4 million). Headquarters are in the city of Chiba, Chiba Prefecture.

Chiba-Kaihin New Town
千葉海浜ニュータウン

(Chiba-Kaihin Nyū Taun). Planned residential and business community being constructed on reclaimed land on the shore of Tōkyō Bay in the city of Chiba, Chiba Prefecture. The prefectural government is the chief sponsor of the project. Area: 12.7 sq km (4.9 sq mi). Projected pop: 160,000.

Chiba New Town   千葉ニュータウン

(Chiba Nyū Taun). Planned residential community in northwestern Chiba Prefecture, central Honshū. Chiba Prefecture is the chief sponsor of the development, which is in-

tended as housing for Tōkyō commuters. Area: 29.1 sq km (11.2 sq mi). Projected pop: 180,000.

Chiba Prefecture   千葉県

(Chiba Ken). Located in central Honshū and bordered by Ibaraki Prefecture to the north, the Pacific Ocean to the east and south, and Tōkyō Bay, Tōkyō, and Saitama Prefecture to the west. Composed of an extension of the KANTŌ PLAIN in the north and hilly BŌSŌ PENINSULA to the south. The rivers TONEGAWA and EDOGAWA form Chiba's northern and western borders, respectively. Its population is mainly concentrated in the northwestern part, which has become a residential and industrial satellite of the Tōkyō-Yokohama urban belt.

Under the ancient provincial system (KOKUGUN SYSTEM) it was divided into the three provinces of Shimōsa, Kazusa, and Awa. It was incorporated into the modern prefectural system in 1875.

Its mild climate and relatively level terrain are suited for truck farming, rice production, and dairy farming. Commercial fishing in Tōkyō Bay, once important, has become impossible because of industrial pollution. Traditional industries such as soy-sauce manufacture and weaving were prominent before World War II. Petrochemical, electrical, steel, shipbuilding, and other companies are located in the northwestern section. The NEW TŌKYŌ INTERNATIONAL AIRPORT in Narita is Japan's major center for international air transport.

Chiba is an important recreation area, with numerous beaches providing fine ocean bathing, especially the KUJŪKURIHAMA area on the Pacific Coast. TŌKYŌ DISNEYLAND opened in 1983. The temple Shinshōji at Narita attracts over a million pilgrims and visitors to the prefecture annually. There are also two quasi-national parks, Suigō-Tsukuba in the north and Southern Bōsō, a seacoast area, in the south. Area: 5,150 sq km (1,988 sq mi); pop: 5,555,429; capital: CHIBA. Other major cities include FUNABASHI, ICHIKAWA, MATSUDO, and CHŌSHI.

Chiba University   千葉大学

(Chiba Daigaku). National coeducational university; main campus located in the city of Chiba, Chiba Prefecture. It was founded in 1949 with the merger of existing institutions of higher education in Chiba Prefecture. It has departments of science, education, letters, law and economics, medicine, pharmacology, nursing, engineering, and horticulture. Enrollment in 1989 was 11,550.

Chi-Ch'a Autonomous Political Council→Ji-Cha (Chi-Ch'a) Autonomous Political Council

Chichibu   秩父[市]

City in western Saitama Prefecture, central Honshū. A commercial and silk-producing center since the Edo period (1600–1868), Chichibu has a thriving cement industry. An all-night festival held at the Chichibu Shrine each December attracts many visitors. Pop: 60,915.

Chichibu Basin   秩父盆地

(Chichibu Bonchi). In the Chichibu Mountains, western Saitama Prefecture, central Honshū. This rectangular fault basin, consisting of the floodplain of the upper reaches of the river Arakawa, has ravines with exposed crystalline schists. Limestone is quarried at the mountain Bukōzan, and the numerous mulberry orchards contribute to the

area's flourishing sericulture. Chichibu is the major city. Area: approximately 100 sq km (40 sq mi).

Chichibu Cement Co, Ltd
秩父セメント[株]

(Chichibu Semento). Producer of cement. Incorporated in 1923. The company provides technical advice to numerous countries, including China, Taiwan, Greece, Peru, and Saudi Arabia. Sales for the fiscal year ending March 1991 totaled ¥81.1 billion (US $591.1 million), and the company was capitalized at ¥5.6 billion (US $40.8 million) in the same year. Headquarters are in Tōkyō.

Chichibu Incident   秩父事件

(Chichibu Jiken). A peasant uprising in the Chichibu region of Saitama Prefecture from 31 October to 10 November 1884. One of the so-called gekka (gekika) jiken, "incidents of intensified violence," of the second decade of the Meiji period (1868–1912) in which peasants of the Kantō region of eastern Honshū, led by members of the FREEDOM AND PEOPLE'S RIGHTS MOVEMENT, rebelled against the government. In Chichibu the rebels were mostly peasants impoverished by deflationary policies implemented in the early 1880s by Finance Minister MATSUKATA MASAYOSHI. Triggered by creditors' refusal to allow a moratorium on repayment of loans, more than 6,000 peasants marched on government offices and loan sharks' shops, fighting against police and army troops. By 10 November the rebellion had been suppressed by regiments from the Tōkyō military garrison, and some 3,000 peasants had been arrested. While most of these escaped with fines, some received prison sentences of five to eight years. The seven leaders were tried (two in absentia) and sentenced to death. In February 1885, less than three months after they were arrested, five were hanged. See also KOMMINTŌ.

Chichibu, Prince   秩父宮雍仁親王

(1902–53; Chichibu no Miya Yasuhito Shinnō). Imperial prince. Second son of Emperor TAISHŌ; brother of Emperor SHŌWA (Hirohito). After studying at Oxford University, Prince Chichibu attended the Army Staff College. Upon graduation he was assigned to regimental posts and to General Staff Headquarters. During the 1930s it was rumored that he was sympathetic to the KŌDŌHA, the extremist right-wing faction in the army. After World War II, he served as head of several athletic organizations.

Chichibu-Tama National Park
秩父多摩国立公園

(Chichibu-Tama Kokuritsu Kōen). Situated in the KANTŌ MOUNTAINS, it is the national park closest to Tōkyō, stretching west from the boundary of Tōkyō Prefecture into Saitama, Nagano, and Yamanashi prefectures. The eastern region of the park, known as OKU TAMA, is dominated by the peaks Kumotoriyama and Mitakesan. The western region of the park, known as OKU CHICHIBU, is dominated by the peaks KIMPUSAN, Kokushigatake, and KOBUSHIGADAKE. From these mountains flow two major rivers, TAMAGAWA and ARAKAWA.

Two famous shrines here are Mitake Shrine at the summit of Mitakesan and Mitsumine Shrine on top of MITSUMINESAN. The gorge SHŌSENKYŌ, in the southwest, is cele-

Continued on page 184►

Chiba Prefecture
Location and Prefectural Crest

Shidarezakura (weeping cherry), an especially durable species that often lives for several hundred years.

A sword guard with an open-worked cherry-blossom design.

Fleeting Emblem of Spring

The arrival of spring in Japan is heralded by a wave of cherry blossoms that begins in Kyūshū around the end of March and, as warm weather spreads northward, reaches Tōkyō in early April and Hokkaidō in mid-May. The weather bureau issues forecasts on when the trees will blossom in each region, and the press chronicles the entire process from first flowering to full bloom.

Cherry blossom time coincides with the beginning of the Japanese school year, and the sight of trees in bloom often brings back memories of the first day of school. Blossom-viewing picnics, exuberant affairs often complete with portable *karaoke* equipment, are a ritual of the season. Nighttime blossom-viewing is regularly enlivened by quantities of beer and *sake* in city parks where spotlights shine through the trees, illuminating the pale flowers against the darkness.

The Japanese have long been moved by the brief existence of the cherry blossom, which culminates in a great scattering of petals. Over the centuries they have expressed their affection for this flower in a variety of ways. Today's raucous drinking parties beneath the trees are a far cry from the poetry and songs of the past, but the sentiment of appreciation remains the same. After only a matter of days, even before they fade, the blossoms begin to fall. The slightest breeze produces a shower of petals—a reminder of the fleeting nature of beauty.

Flower-viewing was a common subject for woodblock prints during the 18th and 19th centuries, when such outings gained popularity among townspeople of the great cities. In Edo (now Tōkyō) cherry trees were planted in numerous locations, including scenic Asukayama, shown in this triptych.

A cloud of petals wafts away from a *yamazakura* (mountain cherry), a variety distinguished by the simultaneous appearance of leaves and blossoms.

A black lacquer comb with a gold cherry-blossom motif.

This Edo-period hair ornament depicts, in gold and silver with coral beads, a butterfly alighting on cherry blossoms.

A lacquered Edo-period writing-equipment box elaborately decorated with a "flower blizzard" motif in inlaid mother-of-pearl.

This kimono is decorated with a pattern showing rafts floating along a stream scattered with cherry blossoms.

A white-blossomed *shidarezakura* contrasts with the azure sky.

Petals float in the pale light of a string of lanterns.

183

Chichibu-Tama National Park This large mountainous park is relatively easy to reach from Tōkyō.
1 The gorge Shōsenkyō features dramatic granite cliffs.
2 Another gorge, Nakatsukyō, is famous for spectacular fall foliage.

brated for its scenic beauty. Among other tourist attractions are cherry blossoms in the Lake Oku Tama region, abundant wildlife, Japanese hemlock (*kometsuga*) forests, and the stalactites in a Nippara cave (see NIPPARA SHŌNYŪDŌ). Area: 1,216 sq km (469 sq mi).

Chichijima 父島

Also known as Peel Island. Island in the Pacific Ocean, 1,000 km (621 mi) south of Tōkyō. It is the largest island and the political and economic center of the OGASAWARA ISLANDS; administratively part of Tōkyō Prefecture. It is composed largely of hilly land and valleys with tropical plants. It was first settled by European and Hawaiian whalers in 1830, but Japanese emigrants to the island increased after 1876. An important Japanese navy base during World War II, Chichijima was occupied by the United States after the war but reverted to Japan in 1968. It is part of Ogasawara National Park. Area: 24.0 sq km (9.3 sq mi).

chicken, Japanese 鶏

(*niwatori*). *Gallus gallus domesticus.* The term "Japanese chicken" denotes both indigenous strains of domestic fowl and those developed in Japan in premodern times; it does not include modern commercial breeds developed through crossbreeding with Western strains. The majority of the approximately 30 breeds of Japanese chickens are not raised for their meat or eggs but are kept by fanciers as pets. Seventeen of these breeds have been designated as protected animals by the Japanese government. The following are some of the better-known breeds:

The *jidori* is an indigenous, primitive breed that closely resembles the red jungle fowl of Southeast Asia. It has a red body with black tail and a predominantly black breast. As a basic strain, it has contributed to the formation of many other Japanese breeds.

The *shōkoku* was introduced to Japan from China during the Heian period (794–1185). Its feather coloring is silvery, golden, or white. It has an elegant posture and a longish, flowing tail. It was used in cockfights in ancient times and was kept in shrines as a sacred bird. Like the *jidori*, the *shōkoku* is a basic strain used in breeding.

The *onagadori* (or *chōbikei*) is a striking, long-tailed breed developed in Tosa (now Kōchi Prefecture), Shikoku, during the Edo period (1600–1868). Its coloring is silvery, white, or brown. The cock's colorful tail feathers grow longer every year without molting, sometimes reaching 8 meters (26 ft) or more. In order to protect their tails, *onagadori* are kept in special elevated cages. The breed is known in the West as the Yokohama.

The *chabo* is believed to have been imported from the Champa region of Indochina sometime during the Edo period. It is an extremely small bantam with short legs and a large head. The best known of the many varieties of *chabo* is the *katsura chabo*. The breed is also popular among fanciers in the West.

The *shamo* originated from a game breed of Southeast Asia and was later improved in Japan. The breed was used in COCKFIGHTING. Its meat is of excellent quality.

The *ukokkei* is thought to have been derived from a mutant type brought into Japan during the Edo period, probably from China, and later developed as a breed. Peculiarities of the *ukokkei* include its plumage, which resembles silky hair, and its skin, flesh, and bones, all of which are darkly pigmented. It has a feather-crowned head, hairy legs, and five-toed feet.

The chicken appears to have played a prominent role in ancient Japanese culture. Chickens are represented in HANIWA pottery figures from the Kofun period (ca 300–710) and are also mentioned in Japanese mythology. They were used for food, despite Buddhist injunctions against eating animal flesh, and their meat and eggs were used for some medicinal purposes. Chickens were also at the root of various folk beliefs and their cries were thought to be effective in driving away evil spirits associated with darkness. During the Heian period the court used them to know the time and held annual ceremonial cockfights; the sport was also popular among commoners. In later periods certain decorative breeds of chicken were the subjects of paintings and woodblock prints. After Japan opened its doors to the West in the 19th century, farmers who kept chickens for practical purposes abandoned the native breeds for more productive Western strains.

chidori → plovers

Chifuren 地婦連

(abbreviation of Zenkoku Chiiki Fujin Dantai Renraku Kyōgi Kai; National Federation of Regional Women's Organizations). Chifuren was founded in 1952 by YAMATAKA SHIGERI to elevate the status of women, reform home and social life, and promote social welfare. It has a membership of around 6 million. The organization is especially active in the CONSUMER MOVEMENT.

Chigasaki 茅ヶ崎[市]

City in southern Kanagawa Prefecture, central Honshū, at the mouth of the river Sagamigawa. Since the opening of a station on the Tōkaidō main rail line here in 1898, Chigasaki has become a residential area with numerous villas and beach resorts. It is becoming a suburb of the Tōkyō-Yokohama district, with industries. Pop: 201,675.

chigo 稚児

Children attendants in temples and in warrior and noble households. Today the word *chigo* refers to parish children, usually from three to twelve years old, who dress in traditional attire and parade at shrine and temple festivals. *Chigo* are often chosen to offer sacred wine, perform dances, and be archers at ceremonies that accompany Shintō observances. In the past children were considered uncontaminated by the world, and young boys performed special functions at Shintō and Buddhist ceremonies. At some festivals, a young boy was chosen as a representative (*tōya*) of the parishioners to ride on a horse and was expected to fall asleep when the gods possessed him. (Young boys who served as *chigo* at Buddhist temples in premodern Japan were often the partners for homosexual monks. In the Meiji period [1868–1912] *chigo* referred to a male student who was the object of an older male student's affection. See also HOMOSEXUALITY.)

chigyō 知行

(usufruct, proprietorship). The exercise of rights to land. As the RITSURYŌ SYSTEM of centralized administration broke down in the 10th century, it was replaced by the *bunkoku* or CHIGYŌKOKU system, whereby the imperial house, court nobility, and religious institutions were granted administrative rights and powers of taxation in designated provinces. Proprietors remained in the capital, delegating their functions to tax managers (ZURYŌ). Under the growing private-estate (SHŌEN) system of proprietorship, *chigyō* came to mean the actual exercise of rights to the land, as opposed to *shiki*, the possession of those rights. During the Kamakura period (1185–1333) legitimate rights that had not been exercised for 20 years were forfeited, while the shogunate gave official recognition (ANDO) to *tōchigyō* (de facto rights) that had been exercised for 20 years. By the middle of the Muromachi period (1333–1568), when *shōen* had become virtually the private domains of the military governors (SHUGO) appointed by the shogunate, *chigyō* meant simply overlordship of territory. The territorial lords, now called SHUGO DAIMYŌ, allotted land to their retainers (*chigyōnin*), who reciprocated with military service (*chigyōyaku*). In the Edo period (1600–1868) *chigyō* referred to the retainer's right to tax and administer his fief and to the rice stipends (also called KURAMAI) issued to retainers without land.

chigyōkoku 知行国

(proprietary province). A province (*koku*) whose usufruct (CHIGYŌ) was assigned to an individual or a temple. From the late 10th century retired emperors (see INSEI) and imperial kinsmen received allotment provinces (*bunkoku*); later such *chigyōkoku* were assigned to courtiers and religious institutions as well and were a great source of income and patronage. The proprietors appointed tax managers (ZURYŌ) for their holdings, which were administered in much the same way as private estates (SHŌEN). Originally assigned for four-year terms, these proprietorships became hereditary. At the beginning of the Kamakura period (1185–1333), the shōguns and their vassals became proprietors, and by the 13th century two-thirds of the provinces were hereditary *chigyōkoku*. *Chigyōkoku* disappeared in the 15th century, when the provinces came under the control of regional lords (SENGOKU DAIMYŌ).

chijimi 縮み

General name for crepe fabrics. The first large-scale production of silk crepe was at Akashi (in what is now Hyōgo Prefecture) during the early Edo period (1600–1868). Echigo Province (now Niigata Prefecture) and Awa Province (now Tokushima Prefecture) also became noted in the Edo period for their crepe fabrics. Crepe fabric may be made from cotton, linen, silk, or synthetic fibers; silk crepe is often called CHIRIMEN. Cotton and linen crepe are very absorbent and cool to wear and are still used for traditional Japanese summer clothing and for undergarments.

Chijiwa Miguel 千々石ミゲル

(ca 1570–?). One of four young envoys sent by the CHRISTIAN DAIMYŌ of Kyūshū on the MISSION TO EUROPE OF 1582. Born Chijiwa Seizaemon and baptized Miguel, he was a kinsman of the *daimyō* ARIMA HARUNOBU and ŌMURA SUMITADA, sponsors of the mission. The mission returned to Japan in 1590 after visiting Spain, Portugal, and Italy. Chijiwa entered the Society of Jesus in 1591 but later left. His subsequent career is unknown.

Chikamatsu Hanji 近松半二

(1725–83). Generally regarded as the last major playwright of the BUNRAKU puppet theater. Born in Ōsaka. His father, Confucian scholar Hozumi Ikan (1692–1769), was a close acquaintance and admirer of the playwright CHIKAMATSU MONZAEMON. Taking the name of Chikamatsu, Hanji began writing for the Takemotoza theater in the early 1750s. After long years as an apprentice staff writer under the tutelage of Takeda Izumo III (see TAKEDA IZUMO), he became head playwright. Hanji waged a desperate struggle against the rising popularity of the KABUKI theater, trying to emulate kabuki by employing elaborate and colorful stage settings, emphasizing spoken dialogue, and reducing the length of chanted narrative. In addition to *Imoseyama onna teikin* (1771, An Example of Noble Womanhood), his major plays (written in collaboration with others) include *Ōshū adachigahara* (1762, Sodehagi's Petition to the Gods), *Ōmi Genji senjin yakata* (1769, Moritsuna's Camp), and *Igagoe dōchū sugoroku* (1783, The Vendetta at Iga). In all, he wrote 57 plays.

Chikamatsu Monzaemon 近松門左衛門

(1653–1724). Edo-period (1600–1868) playwright, especially for the puppet theater called BUNRAKU or *ningyō jōruri* and also for the KABUKI theater. Generally considered Japan's greatest dramatist. His pen name was Chikamatsu Monzaemon, or simply

Japanese chicken
1 A diminutive chicken, the *chabo* has short legs and a large head. Plumage colors vary widely.
2 The *onagadori*, or long-tailed fowl, is a decorative breed of chicken. The cock's tail feathers do not molt and can grow to more than 8 meters in length.
3 The *shamo*, raised for cockfighting, was developed during the Edo period from a strain imported from Thailand.
4 The *minohiki* is a decorative breed whose neck and tail feathers are said to resemble a straw raincoat (*mino*).

Chikamatsu, and his family name was Sugimori, boyhood name Jirōkichi, and adult given name Nobumori. He belonged to a *samurai* family from the province of Echizen (now part of Fukui Prefecture).

The first puppet drama definitely attributable to him is *Yotsugi Soga* (1683, The Soga Heir). Two years later he started to write for the JŌRURI chanter TAKEMOTO GIDAYŪ I. The year 1684 saw his first kabuki play, and by 1693 he had turned almost entirely to writing for this live theater. In 1703, however, the interrupted connection with Gidayū was resumed, and from 1705 until his death he maintained his position as writer for the Takemotoza, Gidayū's puppet theater.

Puppet Plays——Chikamatsu wrote scripts for the chanter who delivered the words of puppet plays while accompanied by a SHAMISEN player. This material formed a complete narrative with scene settings and comments incorporated into the text, which could be read like a novel. Nearly 100 such puppet plays were written by him, and he probably collaborated in the writing of several more in his early days.

These early plays contain many elements of the war chronicles from which they were derived. In *Yotsugi Soga* the plot involves the efforts of two brothers to avenge a slight upon their masters, the Soga brothers, after the deaths of the latter in connection with the famous Soga vendetta (see SOGA MONOGATARI). New elements include the parts played by the two courtesan mistresses of the Soga brothers, who travel to tell the dead heroes' mother of her sons' fate. The *michiyuki* or poetic-journey theme concerns the pitiful destiny of prostitutes and the impossibility of lasting relationships with those they love.

This is the first appearance of a theme that runs through much of Chikamatsu's work: the high-principled mistress. It is continued in his next important play, *Shusse Kagekiyo* (1686, Kagekiyo Victorious). The play shows a realistic conflict of emotions and is generally classified as "new *jōruri*," although such elements as the hero's colossal strength

and his miraculous survival clearly link it with "old *jōruri*."

In the next two decades Chikamatsu devoted most of his attention to the live kabuki theater. He nevertheless wrote about 20 puppet plays, typical historical pieces (*jidaimono*); only in 1703, when he once again concentrated on writing for Gidayū, did he discover a new vein that would make the "new *jōruri*" a reality, the *sewa-mono*, or drama of contemporary life. Following a precedent of the novelist Ihara SAIKAKU (1642–93) of basing stories on actual incidents, Chikamatsu turned the love suicides

chigo This modern-day *chigo*, a parish child in traditional attire, helps celebrate the Gion Festival at the Yasaka Shrine in Kyōto.

Chikamatsu Monzaemon The *bunraku* and *kabuki* playwright in the latter part of his life, pictured in a modern copy of an 18th-century hanging scroll.

of Tokubei, a shop clerk, and Ohatsu, a prostitute, into the play SONEZAKI SHINJŪ (1703; tr *The Love Suicides at Sonezaki*, 1961). The play was a great success, and Chikamatsu went on to write over 11 such love-suicide dramas during his career. Chikamatsu's successful portrayals caused such an increase in the frequency of these suicides that the authorities made them a crime, decreeing a surviving partner guilty of murder and exhibiting the corpses of the lovers like those of common criminals.

The conflicts of duty and human affection (GIRI AND NINJŌ) that beset Chikamatsu's domestic dramas moved audiences to tears and became the most characteristic theme of the puppet theater. From 1703 until his death Chikamatsu composed 50 or more historical dramas for the puppet theater. One of them, KOKUSEN'YA KASSEN (1715; tr *The Battles of Coxinga*, 1951), ran for 17 months, an unprecedented phenomenon, and is sometimes regarded as his most successful work.

Kabuki Works——For about 10 years until 1705 Chikamatsu served as staff writer with the kabuki theater of SAKATA TŌJŪRŌ I, a famous player of lovers' roles, in Kyōto. Inferior to that of the actor, Chikamatsu's function consisted of suggesting a plot and then supplying appropriate dialogue in sessions where all could join in with their ideas. He was involved in about 30 kabuki plays. There has been much speculation about why he switched from *jōruri* to kabuki and back. An early dissatisfaction with puppets and a belief that live actors were more effective may have been replaced by discontent at the inferior position of the kabuki writer.

Literary Stature——With Matsuo BASHŌ (1644–94) and Ihara Saikaku, Chikamatsu forms the trio of outstanding authors of the brilliant late-17th-century period. His puppet plays were works of outstanding genius, establishing the tradition upon which bunraku was to develop into the world's most advanced puppet theater. Nowadays seldom given in their original form, Chikamatsu's plays were skillfully adapted by such writers as CHIKAMATSU HANJI (1725–83). Later developments and refinements in the puppet theater have led to the virtual disappearance of lesser authors such as KI NO KAION (1663–1742), but Chikamatsu's ability to make his portrayals of characters overcome all the difficulties of the form for which he was writing has ensured his continued reputation.

Chikamatsu Shūkō 近松秋江

(1876–1944). Novelist. Real name Tokuda Kōji. Born in Okayama Prefecture; graduate of Tōkyō Semmon Gakkō (now Waseda University). His first wife, despairing over the poverty and misery of their life together, left him; Chikamatsu recounted the loneliness and pain caused by this experience in *Wakaretaru tsuma ni okuru tegami* (1910). Other autobiographical novels (see I-NOVEL) are *Giwaku* (1913) and *Kurokami* (1922), which established him as a prominent writer of the naturalist school. He remarried in 1922, and novels such as *Ko no ai no tame ni* (1924) reflected a calmer personal life and a profound love for his children.

chikkyo → heimon

Chikubashō 竹馬抄

(literally, The Bamboo Stilt Anthology). Muromachi-period (1333–1568) book of moral instruction for *samurai*. Completed in 1383 by Shiba Yoshimasa (1350–1410), a deputy shōgun (KANREI) of the Ashikaga shogunate, it details samurai rules of behavior and stresses the importance of cultivating both the martial and the classical arts.

Chikubushima 竹生島

Island about 2 km (1 mi) off the north shore of Lake Biwa, Shiga Prefecture, central Honshū. Composed of granite but covered with green foliage, this island forms one of the so-called Eight Views of Lake Biwa (Biwako Hakkei). It is the site of the Tsukubusuma Shrine and the temple Hōgonji. Area: 0.14 sq km (0.05 sq mi).

Chikugo 筑後[市]

City in southern Fukuoka Prefecture, Kyūshū. Formerly a post-station and market town. Machinery and textiles are major industries. The cultivation of rice, grapes, pears, and rush for making *tatami* mats are other principal activities. With the neighboring city of KURUME, the area is known for its ikat dyed cloth (KASURI). The Funagoya Hot Spring nearby is noted for its camphor trees. Pop: 43,835.

Chikugogawa 筑後川

The longest river in Kyūshū; in Ōita, Kumamoto, Fukuoka, and Saga prefectures. The Kusugawa, which originates in the mountain Kujūsan, and the Ōyamagawa, which originates in the mountain Asosan, converge in the Hita Basin to become the Mikumagawa. It flows into the Tsukushi Plain to become the Chikugogawa, which empties into the Ariake Sea. Forestry thrives on its upper reaches, and fertile grain fields are located along the middle and lower reaches. Twenty electric power plants and the industrial city of Kurume are located on the river. The water is utilized for irrigation. Precipitation on the upper reaches averages 2,000 mm (80 in) annually. Length: 143 km (89 mi); area of drainage basin: 2,860 sq km (1,104 sq mi).

Chikuhō Coalfield 筑豊炭田

(Chikuhō Tanden). Located in northeastern Fukuoka Prefecture, northern Kyūshū; situated on the river Ongagawa. Its development began in 1877, and at its peak in 1940, coal output totaled 20.8 million metric tons (22.8 million short tons). The coal produced here provided the fuel base for development of the KITA KYŪSHŪ INDUSTRIAL ZONE. Production began to decline in the late 1950s; by 1986 all the mines in the field had suspended or ceased their operations.

Chikumagawa 千曲川

River in northeastern Nagano Prefecture, central Honshū, originating at the mountain Kobushigatake in the Kantō Mountains. After flowing through the basins of Saku, Ueda, Nagano, and Iiyama, it enters Niigata Prefecture to become the SHINANOGAWA. Length: 214 km (133 mi).

Chikuma Shobō Publishing Co, Ltd [株]筑摩書房

(Chikuma Shobō). Publishing house. Founded in 1940 by Furuta Akira, in cooperation with the writer USUI YOSHIMI. In 1946 it first published the intellectual monthly TEMBŌ (Outlook). In 1953 Usui planned and edited the first publication of *Gendai Nihon bungaku zenshū* (Collected Works of Modern Japanese Literature). This successful undertaking comprised 56 volumes and was later increased to 99 volumes, providing a model for later collections of literature by Japanese authors. In 1978 the company went bankrupt, but it soon reentered the publishing business.

Chikura 千倉[町]

Town in southern Chiba Prefecture, central Honshū, on the southeastern tip of the BŌSŌ PENINSULA. Chief industries are fishing and greenhouse cultivation of flowers and vegetables. Tourist attractions include swimming beaches and hot springs. Pop: 14,403.

Chikushino 筑紫野[市]

City in west-central Fukuoka Prefecture, Kyūshū. Formerly a post-station town, it was a market town on the road to DAZAIFU, the government outpost in Kyūshū in ancient times. It is now a satellite city of FUKUOKA. It is known for rice, mandarin oranges, tea, and vegetables. The Gorōyama tomb and the remains of the Kii fortress nearby are tourist attractions. Pop: 70,303.

childhood and child rearing 子供としつけ

(*kodomo to shitsuke*). Japanese infants and small children are accorded a level of parental (mostly maternal) nurturance and indulgence not usually found in the West. A relatively high degree of dependence is fostered early on via almost constant physical and emotional contact between mother and child. Discipline is lenient until children enter school, at which time a more severe regime is imposed.

Physical and Emotional Closeness—— Japanese mothers tend to hold their babies more and talk to them less than Western mothers. Infants and small children often bathe with their parents and may also sleep with them. Children up to age four or five are treated quite permissively and are practically never left alone; babysitters, other than a grandparent or close relative, are virtually unknown in Japan.

The Japanese mother tends to view her baby as an extension of herself, blurring the psychological boundaries between parent and child. She looks to her offspring for companionship and entertainment, and, as they mature, her prestige and virtue are judged by their achievements. Children develop a high level of psychic dependence (see AMAE) on their mothers, which manifests itself later in life as a strong need for the warmth and approval of the group. Psychologists and teachers have voiced concern over this level of dependence and the resulting lack of autonomy and self-reliance seen in many Japanese children. Maternal overprotection, they argue, renders these children incapable of making their own judgments and decisions.

A Japanese father's relationship to his children depends largely upon the nature of his job. A white-collar worker in a major city may seldom be home during a young child's waking hours; typically he sees his children mostly during weekends and leaves them exclusively in their mother's care. Other fathers tend to have more extensive contact with their children, and some younger urban fathers are taking a more active role in daily child care.

Shitsuke and Contemporary Child Rearing——Modern Japanese child-rearing techniques are grounded in the traditional concept of *shitsuke*, the training and disciplining of children by teaching them appropriate behavior in daily life and by educating them in manners and etiquette. The original meaning of the word was the development of an adequately trained member of the community (or group). The term is not limited to technical training; it includes the teaching of values, beliefs, and manners commonly accepted and approved by the community. Essentially the method is to let children and youths learn by imitating their teachers, who then patiently correct their pupils' mistakes.

The majority of modern Japanese parents hold to this traditional ethic; positive methods of obtaining compliance are extensively used and praise is frequent. Parents tend to feel that the best instruction is provided through setting a proper example. Although adults rarely chastise young children or express disapproval (especially in public), negative mechanisms for ensuring compliance do exist, most of them based on the fear of being ostracized from one's group. Among these are threats that the child might be abandoned or taken away by some strange person or creature, attempts at shaming the child by pointing out the effect his behavior will have on himself and his family, and admonitions that "people will laugh at you," which are particularly effective when combined with parental disapproval.——

Parents as Disciplinarians——In contemporary Japan, particularly in urban areas, the mother acts as the disciplinarian, often completely replacing her husband as the authority figure. Faced with disobedience, a mother may resort to what Freud called "moral masochism"—hurting oneself to generate guilt in another person as a control mechanism. Antisocial behavior, failure, and laziness are all seen as injuring parents and thus produce guilt; a Japanese mother will not verbalize her suffering so much as live it out before her children's eyes while criticizing herself for their failings. Her quiet suffering is extremely effective in inducing guilt, the expiation of which motivates the child to achieve. As the child matures, the father may play a more important role as disciplinarian, but he joins his wife in doing this, rather than taking over her role. The traditional images of the stern, authoritarian father and the protective mother are no longer the reality in many Japanese homes.

Ceremonies of Childhood——A number of traditional rituals are still performed by many families at regular intervals after the birth of a child. The naming ceremony takes place between the 3rd and 14th day (see SHICHIYA); a visit to a tutelary shrine is made on the 32nd or 33rd day (see MIYAMAIRI); the "first eating ceremony" takes place on the 100th day; and SHICHIGOSAN, or ceremonial visits to a shrine, are made at ages three, five, and seven. Also common is the annual observance of the DOLL FESTIVAL, a celebration for girls, and CHILDREN'S DAY, which is chiefly for boys.

Children's Day こどもの日

(Kodomo no Hi). Festival held on 5 May; one of five traditional celebrations (see SEKKU). Traditionally known as the Tango Festival (Tango no Sekku) or Iris Festival (Shōbu no Sekku), the fifth day of the fifth month has been observed since ancient times. This became a festival for boys corresponding to the DOLL FESTIVAL for girls on the third day of the third month. In 1948, 5 May was designated a national holiday and renamed Children's Day; however, it is still observed in most families in the traditional way as a festival for boys.

It is customary on this day for families

with male children to fly carp (a symbol of success) streamers (koinobori) outside the house, display warrior dolls (mushaningyō) inside, and eat chimaki (rice cakes wrapped in cogon grass or bamboo leaves) and kashiwamochi (rice cakes filled with sweet bean paste and wrapped in oak leaves). In China it was customary on this day to hang mugwort (J: yomogi) from the eaves of the roof in order to repel disease. Since irises (shōbu; correctly, sweet flag) were also believed to repel evil spirits, the Japanese developed the practice of hanging a combination of iris and mugwort.

children's literature 児童文学

(jidō bungaku). Before the Meiji period (1868–1912), children's literary entertainment consisted mainly of folktales (MUKASHIBANASHI) and fairy tales (OTOGI-ZŌSHI); HAKUBUNKAN's 1891 publication of IWAYA SAZANAMI's Koganemaru marked the start of the modern genre. Dissatisfied by the obvious didacticism in Iwaya's children's magazine Shōnen sekai, OGAWA MIMEI wrote Akai fune (1910, Red Boat), a collection of children's stories showing a high degree of creativity and artistic refinement. In 1918 SUZUKI MIEKICHI began publishing the magazine AKAI TORI; presenting stories rich in artistic value and written with careful attention to juvenile sensibility, it had the backing of educators and intellectuals, and its contributors included AKUTAGAWA RYŪNOSUKE, TSUBOTA JŌJI, Niimi Nankichi (1913–43), and ARISHIMA TAKEO, as well as KITAHARA HAKUSHŪ and SAIJŌ YASO.

Akai tori's success spawned other magazines such as Otogi no sekai (1919–22) and Kin no fune (1919–22). These were gradually overshadowed by more varied and commercially oriented magazines, such as the immensely popular SHŌNEN KURABU; contributors to this last included novelists of POPULAR FICTION such as YOSHIKAWA EIJI, OSARAGI JIRŌ, and EDOGAWA RAMPO. It carried historical romances, adventure and detective stories, tales of exploration and warfare, and humorous stories.

Later influences on children's literature included the PROLETARIAN LITERATURE MOVEMENT of the late 1920s and a pacifist and humanist orientation soon after World War II. Of note were Takeyama Michio's (1903–84) Biruma no tategoto (1947–48; tr The Harp of Burma, 1966), Ishii Momoko's (b 1907) Non chan kumo ni noru (1947, Non chan Rides on a Cloud), and TSUBOI SAKAE's Nijūshi no hitomi (1952; tr Twenty-Four Eyes, 1957). Other works of the postwar period are Tatsu no ko Tarō (1960; tr Tarō, the Dragon Boy, 1967) by MATSUTANI MIYOKO and Daremo shiranai chiisana kuni (1959; tr A Little Country No One Knows, 1988) by Satō Satoru (b 1928). There are abundant translations of children's literature from other countries. Japanese illustrators of children's books, such as ANNO MITSUMASA, have also gained international recognition.

children's songs 童謡

(dōyō). Children's songs in Japan fall roughly into three categories: warabe uta, traditional songs children sing at play; dōyō, songs written for children by poets and musicians; and shōka, songs composed for classroom use. Warabe uta include counting songs, teasing songs, parodies, tongue-twisters, and the like. Dōyō were first written in the Taishō period (1912–26), when there was a conscious movement to compose songs of high artistic quality for children.

Such poets as KITAHARA HAKUSHŪ, SAIJŌ YASO, and NOGUCHI UJŌ collaborated with such composers as YAMADA KŌSAKU, NAKAYAMA SHIMPEI, Hirota Ryūtarō (1892–1952), and Motoori Nagayo (1885–1945) to produce many songs of enduring value before the movement lost momentum in the late 1930s.

With the establishment of universal education in 1872, shōka became part of the primary school curriculum. The words to these songs tended to be serious and didactic, stressing loyalty to the emperor or praising the beauties of nature and the Japanese spirit, and have little, if any, meaning for children of today.

child welfare 児童福祉

(jidō fukushi). Japan's system of comprehensive child welfare originated with the CHILD WELFARE LAW (Jidō Fukushi Hō), which was enacted in 1947. Before World War II, child welfare in Japan was limited to the institutionalization of orphans and impoverished children and the protection of child laborers and low-income mothers and children. Today child-counseling centers, which numbered 171 in 1990, are the focus of child welfare activities in Japan. Services provided by these centers include counseling for delinquent children, arranging for the admission of children into child welfare institutions and foster homes, and advising parents regarding discipline and a variety of issues related to child rearing. Prenatal and infant care is provided, using a system based on the keeping of a mother and child "health log" (see MATERNITY PASSBOOK); medical checkups are performed at regular intervals and guidance is offered. Children who are without guardians or whose guardians are unable to give them adequate care are referred to foster homes or child welfare institutions. Financial assistance in the form of loans is provided to fatherless families. Local children's centers, equipped with libraries, playrooms, and other facilities, provide a nurturing setting for children's activities. The children's allowance system, which was introduced in 1971, distributes a monthly allowance to children up to three years of age in families with incomes below a specified ceiling. From January 1992 the monthly allowance per child in families with up to two children was ¥5,000 (US $40); in families with more than two children it was ¥10,000 (US $80).

The percentage of the Japanese population under age 14 has decreased with the decline in the nation's birth rate. In addition, the increased number of nuclear families has reduced the size of the average household, which consisted of 3.05 persons in 1990. With the projection of further reductions in average household size, it is evident that the home will play a decreased role in child raising. The rising divorce rate and increase in the number of working women have meant major changes in the lives of children as well. Numerically speaking, there are sufficient day-care centers in Japan, but there are calls for the day-care system to be more responsive to the varied needs of today's society, such as the need for more day care at night and during extended daytime hours as well as for day care for children with special needs.

Child Welfare Law 児童福祉法

(Jidō Fukushi Hō). Law requiring national and local government bodies to ensure the proper health care of all children. The law was enacted in 1947 as a substitute for the Youth Education Law (1933) and the Child Abuse Prevention Law (1933), which were directed at the protection and education of problem children. It specifically guarantees the right to live (SEIZONKEN) of all children (CONSTITUTION OF JAPAN, art. 25).

The national government, prefectures, cities, towns, and villages are each required to establish child welfare councils, which investigate and survey matters regarding the mentally infirm, nursing and expectant mothers, and children and report their opinions to the appropriate institutions. The prefectures are required to establish child consultation centers staffed by qualified child welfare officials. Children's committees must be maintained in the wards of the cities, towns, and villages. The law also provides education for institutionalized children and sets standards for such institutions as homes for orphans, nursing clinics, maternity hospitals, and child health facilities.

Chile and Japan チリと日本

(Chiri to Nihon). Formal relations between Chile and Japan started with the signing of a treaty of amity and commerce in 1906. Unlike neighboring countries such as Argentina and Peru, Chile did not become a major destination for Japanese emigrants, although some Japanese settled in Chile via Peru in the 1910s. Diplomatic relations were severed during World War II but restored in 1952 by the San Francisco Peace Treaty. Economic contacts increased, first in trade and recently in investment. The balance of trade has been consistently in Chile's favor because of Japan's large demand for Chilean minerals and foodstuffs. Copper has been Chile's major export. Japanese goods sold to Chile are predominantly machinery and tools. In 1990 Japan exported goods worth US $483 million to Chile, of which machinery and tools constituted 80.1 percent. Its imports from Chile reached more than US $1.6 billion, and copper and ore accounted for 47.3 percent of this figure. Investment in Chile by Japanese companies increased greatly in 1988. The number of Japanese-affiliated companies increased from 28 in

1987 to 33 in 1988. They operate primarily in the manufacturing and fishing industries.

Chimmoku 沈黙

(1966; tr Silence, 1969). Novel by ENDŌ SHŪSAKU (b 1923) depicting the persecution of Christians in late-17th-century Japan (see CHRISTIANITY). Rodrigues, a young Portuguese priest, goes into hiding in a village near Nagasaki but is betrayed by a Judas-like figure named Kichijirō and taken prisoner. The title of the work refers to the silence Rodrigues feels is the only response of God to the cruel tortures being suffered by his Japanese disciples in their martyrdom. To save them from this fate Rodrigues recants his own faith, but at that moment hears the compassionate voice of Christ. God, as portrayed by Endō, is not harsh and judgmental, but a loving being who understands and comforts the weak. The author uses the theme of renunciation to confront the central issues of the Christian faith.

chin → Japanese spaniel

China and Japan 中国と日本

(Chūgoku to Nihon). For Japan, China was for more than two millennia a wellspring of advanced civilization and institutional and technological progress. Although by the 9th century Japan had succeeded in developing a distinct civilization out of elements of Chinese culture transformed by the native genius, until the 19th century it was continually reshaped by the introduction of Chinese influences. The consequence has been a tension between the awareness of a cultural debt to China and the assertion of a native cultural tradition.

The Early Period—The Japanese language, like the Altaic tongues of north Asia, is agglutinative and thus linguistically distinct from the isolating Sino-Tibetan tongues, and it is likely that the dominant ethnic strains that mingled to form the Japanese people came from northern Asia. However, it was from China, directly or via the Korean peninsula, that Japan derived its knowledge of wet-rice agriculture, bronze, and iron, the distinctive features of the YAYOI CULTURE that prevailed from about 300 BC to about AD 300.

The earliest references to contacts between the Japanese archipelago and China are found in entries in Chinese dynastic chronicles dating from the 1st century AD that mention a people of the eastern seas called Wo (J: WA). The Chinese history Song shu (Sung shu; History of the Liu-Song [Liu-Sung] Dynasty [420–479]) mentions some nine Japanese embassies to China between 413 and 478 and gives accounts of the FIVE KINGS OF WA, who brought tribute and petitioned the court to be confirmed in kingdoms in the southern part of the Korean peninsula. It is clear that during the 5th century western Japan, probably YAMATO, was in constant contact with southern China, participated in the Chinese tribute system, and sought Chinese acquiescence in Japanese activities on the Korean peninsula. Among Korean and Chinese immigrants to Japan (see KIKAJIN) were scribes, potters, weavers, and metalworkers, who imparted, besides technical skills, knowledge of Chinese writing, political administration, CONFUCIANISM, and BUDDHISM.

In the 6th century, the Yamato court was bitterly divided between rival lineage groups (UJI). The victory of the pro-Buddhist and reform-minded SOGA FAMILY in 587 led to

state patronage of Buddhism and a period of some 300 years during which the political structure and aristocratic culture of Japan was reshaped on the models of Sui (589–618) and Tang (T'ang; 618–907) dynasty China. Prince SHŌTOKU (574–622) and SOGA NO UMAKO (d 626) pressed ahead with reforms, adopting the Chinese calendar (see CALENDAR, DATES, AND TIME), instituting a revised system of Chinese court ranks (see KAN'I JŪNIKAI), and promulgating the SEVENTEEN-ARTICLE CONSTITUTION, which reflects the influence of Confucian and Legalist principles.

At least four embassies were dispatched to China between 600 and 614 (see SUI AND TANG [T'ANG] CHINA, EMBASSIES TO). Monks and scholars who had accompanied them contributed to the TAIKA REFORM of 645, which laid the ground for the adoption of Chinese administrative and penal institutions during the ensuing century (see RITSURYŌ SYSTEM). In 710 the capital city HEIJŌKYŌ (now Nara), modeled on the Tang capital Chang'an (Ch'ang-an), was founded. Chinese-style architecture, sculpture, painting, and music were introduced; Buddhist monasteries proliferated; and the Japanese court elite devoted themselves to the study of the Chinese classics. Eloquent testimony of the pervasive influence of Chinese culture on 7th- and 8th-century Japan is provided by the remains of grid-patterned fields (see JŌRI SYSTEM) in western and central Japan, the treasures of temples such as HŌRYŪJI and TŌDAIJI, relics from China and from the SILK ROAD in the SHŌSŌIN storehouse, Japan's earliest histories (see RIKKOKUSHI), which were written in Chinese, and the KAIFŪSŌ (751), a collection of Chinese poetry written by Japanese.

In 794, the court was removed to HEIANKYŌ (now Kyōto), a large new city also modeled on Chang'an. The monk SAICHŌ introduced from China practices and teachings of the Tiantai (T'ien-t'ai) sect (see TENDAI SECT) of Buddhism, and KŪKAI learned in China the esoteric Indian teachings that are an essential element of the doctrine of the SHINGON SECT. Native SHINTŌ beliefs came under the strong influence of Buddhist theology, but were never displaced.

A true Chinese meritocracy did not develop in Japan; the government drew its officials from the hereditary court nobility. Similarly, nationalization of agricultural land was honored in the breach, and by the close of the 9th century Japanese political institutions had largely departed from the Chinese model. Although court officials continued to write their documents and diaries in Chinese and to delight in Chinese verse, the great age of classical Japanese literature, written with the KANA syllabary derived from Chinese characters, was about to begin. Reports of dynastic decline and disorder in Tang China contributed to the suspension of an embassy to the continent in 894, and there were no more during the Heian period (794–1185).

Medieval Period (mid-12th–16th centuries)—The HŌJŌ FAMILY, regents of the KAMAKURA SHOGUNATE (1192–1333), were eager to maintain trade with Southern Song (Sung) dynasty (1127–1279) China. Swords and gold were exchanged for silk, art objects, and copper cash (SŌSEN), the latter stimulating commercial growth. Chan (Ch'an; J: ZEN) Buddhism found favor in warrior society, and Zen temples became outposts of Chinese culture, introducing Song-style CALLIGRAPHY, INK PAINTING, PORTRAIT PAINTING, Neo-Confucian ideas of social and political order, and the TEA CERE-

MONY (see also GOZAN LITERATURE). By the late 13th century, however, Mongol domination of China had not only brought an end to amicable relations but led to two MONGOL INVASIONS OF JAPAN.

The Muromachi shogunate (1338–1573) adopted a generally positive policy toward relations with China. The powerful third shōgun, ASHIKAGA YOSHIMITSU, won the trust of Ming-dynasty (1368–1644) emperors by curbing the pirates (WAKŌ), chiefly Japanese, who infested the coastal waters of East Asia. Yoshimitsu entered into a nominal tribute relation with China and was permitted to engage in the lucrative TALLY TRADE (see also KITAYAMA CULTURE). The fourth shōgun, Ashikaga Yoshimochi (1386–1428), considered the relationship demeaning and refused to deal with the Ming, but the missions were reinstated by ASHIKAGA YOSHINORI in order to bring relief to increasingly straitened shogunal finances. The tally trade ended in the mid-16th century, but the Chinese models—in architecture, interior and garden design, aesthetics, painting, and calligraphy—that were transmitted through Zen monasteries stimulated the creative talents of such men as the Nō dramatist ZEAMI and the painter SESSHŪ TŌYŌ (see also HIGASHIYAMA CULTURE).

The Edo Period (1600–1868)——Relations between Japan and China in the premodern era reached their lowest ebb due to TOYOTOMI HIDEYOSHI'S INVASIONS OF KOREA IN 1592 AND 1597, but TOKUGAWA IEYASU, who achieved military supremacy following Hideyoshi's death, succeeded in establishing the VERMILION SEAL SHIP TRADE with Chinese merchants who were willing to flout their government's embargo in order to gain access to Japanese silver. In 1639 Ieyasu ushered in two centuries of NATIONAL SECLUSION during which Japan's contacts with the outside world were limited to the Dutch and Chinese, who shared the NAGASAKI TRADE, and to periodic embassies from Korea. In contrast to the dozen Dutch trading vessels that might dock at Nagasaki each year, between 30 and 115 Chinese merchant junks arrived. To limit the outflow of silver, the number of Chinese vessels was later restricted, and Chinese residents were confined to one quarter of the city.

Although Japanese scholars were denied the opportunity to visit China, Chinese learning still exerted a powerful influence. The Neo-Confucian philosophy (SHUSHIGAKU) of Zhu Xi (Chu Hsi; 1130–1200) was adopted as the ideological buttress of the social order prescribed by the Tokugawa shogunate, at the pinnacle of which was the warrior class (see SHI-NŌ-KŌ-SHŌ). Other sources of Chinese influence were medical texts, agricultural manuals, herbals, and treatises on astronomy and technology. Motifs from Ming and Qing (Ch'ing; 1644–1912) dynasty stories found their way into Tokugawa literature, while themes from Chinese art emerged in Japanese woodblock prints.

In the 18th century scholarly investigation of the ancient literary classics of Japan led to a new appreciation of native culture and the Shintō tradition and to serious questioning of Chinese intellectual authority. MOTOORI NORINAGA and other scholars of the discipline known as KOKUGAKU (National Learning) argued that the purely emotional perceptions manifested in ancient Japanese myths and literature offered a truer understanding of the human condition than Chinese Confucian moralizing and rationalization. By the mid-19th century, with China's

weakness exposed in the Opium War (1840–42) and Japan itself under pressure from the West, Chinese learning seemed irrelevant to many.

The Meiji Period (1868–1912)——Among the first actions of the Meiji leaders in 1868 was the dispatch of an envoy to China to announce the inauguration of the new imperial government and request treaty relations. The 1871 treaty of friendship between the two governments instituted diplomatic representation, low tariff rates, and extraterritorial privileges for citizens of both countries. It was the first time in history that China and Japan formally accepted each other as equals.

Almost at once, however, a crisis developed due to Japanese designs on the RYŪKYŪ ISLANDS, a traditional tributary kingdom of China, and on TAIWAN. Having laid claim to sovereignty over the Ryūkyūs, the Japanese government used this as a lever to force its claims on Taiwan. The murders of some Ryukyuan and Japanese fishermen provided a pretext for the Meiji government to launch the punitive TAIWAN EXPEDITION OF 1874. In settlement the Qing government paid a large indemnity and recognized Japanese claims over the Ryūkyū Islands (see RYŪKYŪ KIZOKU MONDAI). Differences between the two countries over Korea had graver consequences. To the Qing government Korea was an important tributary, but some in Japan viewed it as a staging area for Japanese continental expansion (see SEIKANRON). For 20 years China and Japan vied to gain ascendancy, and in 1894 the SINO-JAPANESE WAR OF 1894–1895 broke out between Japanese and Chinese troops dispatched to quell the TONGHAK REBELLION. Pursuant to the Treaty of SHIMONOSEKI (1895), the Qing government recognized the independence of Korea, paid an indemnity of 200 million taels, ceded the Liaodong (Liaotung) Peninsula and Taiwan to Japan, and granted Japan privileges in China that were enjoyed by the Western powers. Some of the fruits of victory were snatched from the Japanese by the TRIPARTITE INTERVENTION of Russia, France, and Germany, which forced the return of the Liaodong Peninsula to China.

The Chinese Revolution of 1911 and Its Aftermath——The Chinese Revolution was triggered by a military uprising in Central China. Japan came to the aid of the beleaguered Qing monarchy, but when the Yangzi (Yangtze) Valley area, a sphere of British influence, fell to the rebels, Britain supported establishment of a republic under YUAN SHIKAI (Yüan Shih-k'ai). SUN YAT-SEN became provisional president of the revolutionary government in Nanjing (Nanking) in January 1912, but when the last Qing emperor, Xuantong (Hsüan-t'ung; see PUYI [P'u-i]), abdicated, Sun was succeeded by Yuan.

Although he had managed to stabilize his government with a substantial REORGANIZATION LOAN from Japan, Britain, France, Russia, and Germany, Yuan faced a second revolution in mid-1913. When their coup against Yuan failed, Sun, HUANG XING (Huang Hsing), and other leaders fled to Japan, where they founded the China Revolutionary Party with Sun Yat-sen as its head. Following the outbreak of World War I in 1914, European involvement in China weakened, and Japan rushed to fill the vacuum, declaring war on Germany and seizing the German JIAOZHOU (KIAOCHOW) CONCESSION on the Shandong (Shantung) Peninsula. In early 1915, Japan presented the TWENTY-ONE DEMANDS to the Yuan government, requiring that China rec-

ognize its right to German interests in Shandong and extend Japan's lease on PORT ARTHUR and Dalian (Ta-lien; J: Dairen) on the Liaodong Peninsula, both of which were spoils of the RUSSO-JAPANESE WAR of 1904–05. Most infamous of the demands was article 5, which stipulated that China employ Japanese advisers, purchase Japanese weapons and munitions, and permit joint policing of certain areas. Japan withdrew article 5 under pressure of foreign opinion and a Chinese boycott, but forced China to agree to its other demands. A power vacuum following the death of Yuan in 1916 was filled by DUAN QIRUI (Tuan Ch'i-jui), who was supported by the Japanese, and to whom, at the expense of Chinese interests, the TERAUCHI MASATAKE cabinet gave strong financial support (see NISHIHARA LOANS).

This series of affronts to Chinese national integrity inflicted by the Japanese contributed to the eruption of the MAY FOURTH MOVEMENT, the ostensible purpose of which was to protest the refusal of the Western powers at the Paris Peace Conference to restore the Jiaozhou concession to China. The movement began on 4 May 1919, when some 4,000 student demonstrators in Beijing (Peking) stormed the residence of pro-Japanese transportation minister CAO RULIN (Ts'ao Ju-lin). Arrests by martial police prompted demonstrations across China, forcing the government to dismiss Cao and other pro-Japanese officials. China never signed the Treaty of VERSAILLES, which was concluded at the Paris Peace Conference and ended World War I. At the WASHINGTON CONFERENCE (late 1921 to early 1922), the Western powers reformulated their colonial policies, and in the NINE-POWER TREATY, of which Japan was a signatory, they supported development of a stable, unified Chinese government.

Chinese anti-imperialist sentiment continued to run strong with boycotts of Japanese goods and demands for the abrogation of all of China's unequal treaties with foreign countries. In the spring of 1925, Chinese workers at Japanese spinning mills in Shanghai and Qingdao (Tsingtao) went on strike. Both strikes were suppressed, but in Shanghai many demonstrating workers were killed or wounded by International Settlement police under the command of the British (see MAY 30TH INCIDENT). Anti-Japanese and anti-British general strikes brought the economy of the settlement to a virtual halt, and it was only in September that order was restored by the Manchuria-based warlord ZHANG ZUOLIN (Chang Tso-lin).

The Manchurian Incident and the Sino-Japanese War of 1937–1945——In July 1926 CHIANG KAI-SHEK, commander of the National Revolutionary Army, initiated the Northern Expedition, an attempt to bring all of China under Nationalist control. On 18 April 1927 the National Government of the Republic of China was established in Nanjing, and on 9 June 1928 Chiang's army occupied Beijing. Zhang Zuolin, the most powerful of the northern warlords, had withdrawn his forces to Manchuria, where on 4 June he was killed in a train explosion masterminded by an officer of the Japanese GUANDONG (KWANTUNG) ARMY. Zhang's son and successor, ZHANG XUELIANG (Chang Hsüeh-liang), reached a compromise with the Nationalists, and the Nationalist flag was flown over Manchuria. Britain, the United States, and several other powers recognized China's right to tariff autonomy and established diplomatic relations with the Nationalist government.

The Treaty of PORTSMOUTH, concluding the Russo-Japanese War of 1904–05, had given to Japan the Russian concession on the Liaodong Peninsula and the SOUTH MANCHURIA RAILWAY, which the Japanese used to extend their control over Manchuria and to exploit its rich natural resources. However, the Chinese began to develop the port of Huludao (Hulutao) on the mainland side of the Gulf of Liaodong and built competing railways that undercut Japanese profits; in 1931 the South Manchuria Railway was for the first time in deficit.

The interests of Japan in Manchuria were threatened on the one hand by competition from the Nationalists and on the other by the growing power of the Soviet Union to the north, and in September 1931 officers of the Japanese Guandong Army, who were anxious to tighten the Japanese hold on Manchuria, blew up a section of the South Manchuria Railway north of Mukden (now Shenyang), blaming it on the Chinese (see MANCHURIAN INCIDENT). Japanese troops occupied Mukden, Changchun, and Andong (Antung), and units of the Japanese Korean Army crossed the Yalu River into China. The League of Nations passed a resolution demanding that the Guandong Army return to its former position, but the Guandong Army leaders were convinced that Japan should set up independent governments in Manchuria and Mongolia and stepped up military operations. The United States replied with its NONRECOGNITION POLICY, and Chiang Kai-shek launched a nationwide boycott of Japanese goods. Nevertheless, in March 1932 the puppet state of MANCHUKUO was established with Puyi, the former Qing emperor, as its nominal ruler. In October 1932 the LYTTON COMMISSION recommended to the League of Nations that Manchuria be placed under international control, and in March 1933 Japan announced its resignation from that organization (see LEAGUE OF NATIONS AND JAPAN).

In May 1933 the Japanese invaded Hebei (Hopeh) Province and threatened Beijing and Tianjin (Tientsin). Chiang, who desired to eliminate the Chinese Communist Party and its forces before dealing with the Japanese, concluded the TANGGU (TANGKU) TRUCE, under which the Japanese agreed to withdraw their troops north of the Great Wall. The HE-UMEZU (HO-UMEZU) AGREEMENT and the DOIHARA-QIN (DOIHARA-CH'IN) AGREEMENT of June 1935 resulted in the weakening of the Nationalist government's influence in Hebei and Qahar (Chahar) provinces, and in November the puppet EAST HEBEI (HOPEH) ANTI-COMMUNIST AUTONOMOUS GOVERNMENT was established. The Chinese Communist Party had previously issued its AUGUST FIRST DECLARATION, which called for a united front against Japan, and on 9 December outraged Chinese students mounted an anti-Japanese demonstration that grew into the DECEMBER NINTH MOVEMENT, which also called for the subordination of domestic rivalries to united resistance to Japanese aggression. On 12 December 1936 Chiang Kai-shek was taken captive by Zhang Xueliang, who demanded the suspension of civil war and release of anti-Japanese leaders (see XI'AN [SIAN] INCIDENT). But the communists mediated for Chiang's release, and in September 1937 the Nationalist government announced that a coalition with the communists had been formed to resist Japan (see SECOND UNITED FRONT).

Japan, however, had already committed itself to all-out war. An exchange of fire between Japanese and Chinese troops near Beijing on 7 July (see MARCO POLO BRIDGE INCIDENT) and the shooting of a Japanese naval officer in August in Shanghai were the proximate causes of the SINO-JAPANESE WAR OF 1937–1945. Japanese forces occupied Nanjing, the Nationalist capital, on 13 December (see NANJING [NANKING] MASSACRE). On 16 January 1938 the KONOE FUMIMARO cabinet announced that Japan would no longer negotiate with the Nationalist government and that it intended to set up its own regimes in occupied China. In March 1940 the Japanese-controlled REORGANIZED NATIONAL GOVERNMENT OF THE REPUBLIC OF CHINA was established in Nanjing. Although Japan held the principal cities of China and occupied areas along important rail lines, its control was always threatened from the rear by Nationalist and Chinese communist armies.

On 8 December 1941 Japan declared war on the United States and its allies, and on the following day the Nationalist government issued a formal declaration of war on Japan. The fact that for four years 1 million Japanese soldiers were engaged on the Chinese mainland proved of great aid to the Allies. In 1945, with the US Air Force in command of the skies over China, the Nationalist and communist armies took the offensive, forcing Japanese troops to withdraw to the outskirts of major cities. On 8 August 1945, the Soviet Union declared war on Japan, and its troops poured into Manchuria. Following Japan's surrender on 14 August, the Nationalist government commanded Japanese forces in China to defend major Chinese cities against communist troops, whose numbers had increased from 30,000 or 40,000 in 1937 to some 3 million in 1945, and to return them to Nationalist control. The Japanese complied with these terms and on 9 September General Okamura Yasuji (1884–1966), commander of Japanese expeditionary forces in China, surrendered to HE YINGQIN (Ho Ying-ch'in), the supreme commander of the Chinese Nationalist Army. In its eight-year war with China, Japan had suffered some 1.3 million dead and wounded, and the Chinese, not including countless civilian casualties, 3.1 million.

Postwar Relations—Full-scale civil war broke out between the Nationalist and communist armies in July 1947, and by May 1949 the communists had occupied Shanghai, Nanjing, and Beijing. The People's Republic of China (PRC) was established in Beijing on 1 October, and the Nationalist government fled to Taiwan, where it maintained an independent government.

In early 1950 the PRC concluded a 30-year treaty with the Soviet Union pledging mutual assistance if either was attacked by Japan or its allies. Within months the KOREAN WAR broke out, and Chinese forces joined the fighting on the side of North Korea. China was declared an aggressor by the United Nations and, together with Taiwan, was excluded from signing in September 1951 the SAN FRANCISCO PEACE TREATY, which formally ended the war against Japan. The same day Japan concluded a security treaty with the United States (see UNITED STATES–JAPAN SECURITY TREATIES) and signed a separate peace treaty with the Taiwan government, thus recognizing it as the government of China.

Despite the rupture of formal diplomatic relations between Japan and mainland China, a private trade agreement between the two nations was concluded in 1952. In

1957, however, Prime Minister KISHI NOBUSUKE endorsed Chiang Kai-shek's announced intention to reconquer the mainland, and relations between Japan and the PRC worsened. A fourth private trade agreement between the two countries was concluded in March 1958, but diplomatic privileges and the right to raise their national flag were denied to members of the trade mission. Three months later a Japanese youth hauled down the PRC national flag at a Chinese postage stamp fair in Nagasaki, and, angered by Prime Minister Kishi's mild response, China broke off all negotiations, including those on the repatriation of Japanese nationals (see NAGASAKI FLAG INCIDENT).

In October 1962 Takasaki Tatsunosuke, a member of Japan's ruling Liberal Democratic Party, visited Beijing and concluded a five-year trade agreement with LIAO CHENGZHI (Liao Ch'eng-chih). Japan's moves to improve relations with mainland China met with the disapproval of the Nationalist government on Taiwan. In August 1963 the Nationalist government recalled its ambassador to Japan to protest loans by the EXPORT-IMPORT BANK OF JAPAN to finance a synthetic fiber plant in China, but a new envoy was sent to Tōkyō when former prime minister YOSHIDA SHIGERU agreed on behalf of the Japanese government to cancel the loan. Prime Minister SATŌ EISAKU's meeting with Chiang Kai-shek in Taiwan in September 1967 and the SATŌ-NIXON COMMUNIQUÉ of 1969, in which reference was made to the concern of the United States and Japan for the security of Taiwan, incurred the anger of China.

In 1971 the PRC was formally admitted to the United Nations, and the following February President Richard Nixon of the United States visited Beijing. On 29 September 1972 Prime Minister TANAKA KAKUEI announced in Beijing that Japan recognized the People's Republic of China as the legal government of China, of which Taiwan was an integral part, and Foreign Minister ŌHIRA MASAYOSHI later issued a statement annulling the 1951 peace treaty with Taiwan. Diplomatic relations between Japan and Taiwan were severed, and in early 1973 the PRC and Japan exchanged ambassadors. Subsequently agreements on trade, air, navigation, fishery, and other matters were concluded between the two countries. Formal negotiations on a peace treaty were initiated in January 1975, but negotiations proved difficult: the Chinese insisted that the term "antihegemony" be inserted in the text of the peace treaty, while the Japanese, worried lest any implied negative reference to the Soviet Union harm their relations with that country, opposed its inclusion. The CHINA-JAPAN PEACE AND FRIENDSHIP TREATY was finally signed on 12 August 1978. Article 2 of the treaty stipulates that neither nation will seek hegemony in any part of the world and article 4 that the treaty does not affect the position of either nation in its relations with third parties, thus permitting the agreement to coexist with the current US-Japan security treaty.

In December 1978 China instituted an economic policy that was not rigidly based on communist ideology. The Japanese government supported this change, and during a visit to Beijing in December 1979 Prime Minister Ōhira Masayoshi promised the first yen loan (1979–84; ¥330.9 billion [US $1.4 billion in 1984 dollars]) to China. In May 1980 Chinese prime minister Hua Guofeng (Hua Kuo-feng) visited Japan and in December China and Japan held their first minister-level conference. In March 1984 Japanese prime minister NAKASONE YASUHIRO agreed in Beijing to the second yen loan (1984–89; ¥540.0 billion [US $3.9 billion in 1989 dollars]) to China.

Friendly relations between the two countries have occasionally been strained. Controversies developed over Japanese government approval of history textbooks in 1982 (publishers were required to weaken descriptions of Japan's invasion of China in the 1930s) and over official visits by Japanese prime ministers to the YASUKUNI SHRINE (seen by some as a symbol of Japanese militarism in the 1930s and 1940s). Following the suppression of the massive demonstration in Tiananmen (T'ien-an-men) Square in Beijing in June 1989, Japanese economic assistance to China was put in abeyance, but in November 1990 payments began on the third yen loan (estimated total, ¥810.0 billion [US $6.3 billion in 1988 dollars]).

Since 1972 there have been great increases in programs for cultural exchange. The number of Chinese students and researchers in Japan grew rapidly, doubling between 1980 and 1985, and doubling again by 1988, when there were 15,642 students and researchers at Japanese universities (the total includes Taiwanese and represents 53.7 percent of all foreign students and researchers in Japan). In addition, 35,388 Chinese students were studying at such Japanese educational institutions as language, computer, and beauty schools.

In 1972 Japan's total import-export trade with China was US $1.1 billion, but by 1978 Japan's exports had jumped to US $3.1 billion and its imports to US $2.0 billion. In 1990, on the basis of total imports and exports, China was Japan's sixth largest trade partner, in that year Japan's exports totaled US $6.1 billion and its imports US $12.1 billion. Since the resumption of diplomatic relations, contact between Japan and China has grown increasingly close; however, there remain a number of issues of considerable gravity, such as the status of Taiwan, the mutual threat posed by the military capabilities of China and Japan, and the relations of China with Russia and with the United States.

Taiwan and Japan—Following the severance of diplomatic relations, contact between Japan and Taiwan has continued on the private level through such organizations as the Japan-Taiwan Interchange Association and the Association of East Asian Relations. Economic relations between Japan and Taiwan, however, have continued to expand, and, on the basis of total imports and exports, Taiwan was Japan's fourth largest trade partner in 1990. Japan's exports to Taiwan in that year totaled US $15.4 billion and its imports US $8.5 billion. According to Taiwanese figures Japanese investment in Taiwan in 1988 and 1989 led that of all other nations; and in 1989 Japanese investment was US $640 million, chiefly in the electric and electronic appliance industries and the hotel and other service industries. In 1989 some 500,000 Taiwanese visited Japan and over 1 million Japanese went to Taiwan.

chinaberry 栴檀

(*sendan*). *Melia azedarach* var. *japonica*. A deciduous tree of the family Meliaceae that grows wild on hills and coastal areas of Shikoku and Kyūshū and is also planted in house gardens. It reaches a height of more than 7 meters (23 ft). The compound leaves consist of pointed, oval leaflets growing al-

ternately in twos or threes. In May and June flower stalks produce clusters (panicles) of light purple or white flowers. Known as *kurenshi*, the yellowish, elliptical fruits (drupes) were used for medicinal purposes.

In ancient times this tree was called *ouchi*, while the word *sendan* referred to the sandalwood (*Santalum album*), now called *byakudan*.

China, economic relations with 日中経済関係

(Nitchū *keizai kankei*). The economic relationship between the People's Republic of China and Japan has grown significantly since the normalization of diplomatic relations in 1972. Total bilateral trade stood at US $1.1 billion in 1972, expanded to US $5.0 billion in 1978, and reached US $18.2 billion in 1990. Economic ties in the areas of direct investment and economic cooperation have also deepened. The growth of bilateral economic relations has been based on complementary need: China is rich in natural resources and has an extensive domestic market, while Japan is able to provide advanced technology and investment capital.

The domestic political situation in China has influenced the health of bilateral economic ties. In particular, the political turmoil following the death of Mao Zedong (Mao Tse-tung) and the downfall of the Gang of Four in the mid-1970s dampened the growth of the economic relationship. However, the program of political and economic modernization pursued by Deng Xiaoping (Teng Hsiao-p'ing) since 1978 paved the way for the rapid expansion of economic ties. In the future as well, domestic political developments in China will continue to affect the China-Japan economic relationship.

A number of bilateral agreements and treaties form the framework underlying the economic relationship between the two countries. The restoration of diplomatic relations in the China-Japan Joint Communiqué of September 1972 resulted in the signing of a general trade agreement in January 1974, which was soon followed by separate agreements on aviation, marine transport, and fisheries. At the same time that the two nations concluded the China-Japan Peace and Friendship Treaty in 1978, they also signed the China-Japan Long-Term Trade Agreement.

Japan-China Trade—Japan's 1990 trade with China represented 3.5 percent of Japan's total trade in that year. Exports to China were valued at US $6.1 billion and imports at US $12.1 billion. China is Japan's 12th largest export market and is the 4th largest supplier of imports entering the Japanese market. In 1988 China ranked as Japan's 5th largest trading partner. By 1990, however, it had dropped to 6th place, primarily because of the effects of the Tiananmen (T'ien-an-men) Square Incident and stronger import restrictions in China. Japan is China's second largest overall trading partner, trailing only Hong Kong. Japan had run a trade surplus with China since 1984, but this turned into a surplus in China's favor in 1988–90.

Japan's principal exports to China in 1990 fall under the category of machinery and transport equipment, which includes televisions, videocassette recorders, and automobiles. This category accounted for 46.2 percent of Japan's total export volume to China. Other major export items were steel (17.3 percent of total exports) and chemical products (12.3 percent). Japan's principal import

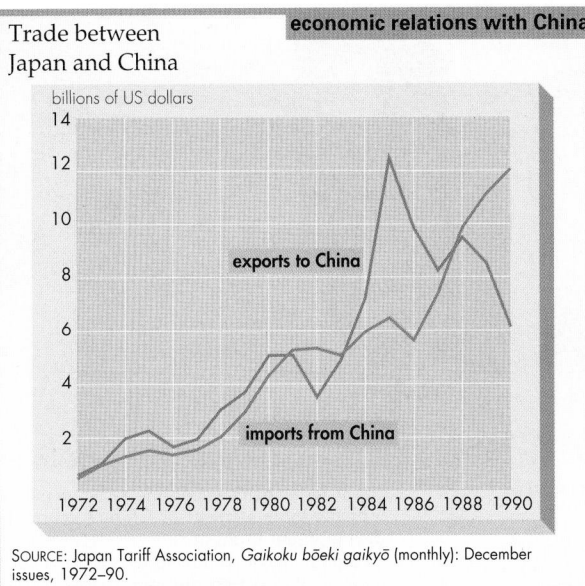

economic relations with China

Trade between Japan and China

billions of US dollars

exports to China

imports from China

1972 1974 1976 1978 1980 1982 1984 1986 1988 1990

SOURCE: Japan Tariff Association, *Gaikoku bōeki gaikyō* (monthly): December issues, 1972–90.

items from China in 1990 were textile products (accounting for 26.5 percent of total import volume from China), crude oil and other fuel resources (24.2 percent), and food and fishery products (16.1 percent).

China's industrialization has progressed rapidly as a result of the establishment of several special economic zones along its coasts in the 1980s. Accordingly, the share of manufactured goods in China's total exports has grown to a considerable level. In 1990, the share of raw materials in Japanese imports from China declined, and the share of manufactured goods, especially machinery, increased.

Japanese Investments in China—From fiscal year 1979 to 1988, Japan's total OVERSEAS DIRECT INVESTMENT in China totaled US $2.8 billion, accounting for only 1.0 percent of Japan's total overseas direct investment. However, in 1988 Japan surpassed the United States to become the second largest investor in China, ranking behind Hong Kong–Macao. Japanese direct investment is increasingly centered on manufacturing, as companies move to take advantage of low labor costs. Some Japanese enterprises have relocated production facilities from Taiwan and South Korea to China, and this appears to be an increasing trend. Interest in direct investment in China on the part of Japanese investors is expected to increase as a result of the China-Japan Investment Protection Agreement of August 1988, guaranteeing Japanese nationals and firms within China the same legal rights that are granted to indigenous people and firms.

Development Assistance to China—Japan's announcement of its first offer of YEN CREDIT to China during Prime Minister Ōhira Masayoshi's visit there in 1979 marked a new development in Sino-Japanese economic cooperation. China's response to Japan's offer resulted in a rapid rise in China's use of yen credits, to ¥855.0 billion (US $6.7 billion). In 1990 China was the second largest recipient of Japan's official development assistance (ODA), receiving US $723.0 million of the total worldwide Japanese disbursements of US $9.2 billion. In 1990 the aggregate assistance given to China by all developed countries that are members of the Organization for Economic Cooperation and Development's Development Assistance Committee (DAC) totaled US $1.4 billion. Japan's contribution of US $723.0 million constituted 51.0 percent of the total assistance to China from DAC member

chinaberry The flowers of this tree bloom from May through June in loose clusters 8–13 cm long.

chindon'ya Once a common sight in urban areas, these street performers are now becoming increasingly rare.

countries. Japan's economic assistance is an indispensable element of China's economic development program.

Japan provided low-interest, long-term yen credits on two different occasions between fiscal years 1979 and 1989 to help finance 20 infrastructure projects in China. These included railways, fisheries, and water-resource development projects. During Prime Minister Takeshita Noboru's visit to China in August 1988, Japan announced a third yen credit, totaling ¥810.0 billion (US $6.3 billion), to be administered over a six-year period beginning in fiscal year 1990. Most of Japan's economic cooperation with China takes the form of yen credits, but grants and technical cooperation projects also play a significant, although smaller, role.

China-Japan Joint Communiqué of 1972 日中共同声明

(Nitchū Kyōdō Seimei). Communiqué, issued 29 September 1972, providing for normalization of relations between China and Japan and determining the basic objectives that should govern relations between the two countries. The preamble includes the statement that "Japan is keenly conscious of its responsibility for the serious damage inflicted in the past on the Chinese people through war and deeply reproaches itself." Nine articles follow that accordingly provide for (1) termination of the "abnormal state of affairs" between the two countries; (2) the Japanese government's recognition of the government of the People's Republic of China as "the sole legal government of China"; (3) the Japanese government's "full understanding of and respect for the position" of the Chinese government with regard to Taiwan, namely that it is "an inalienable part" of the territory of the People's Republic of China; (4) establishment of diplomatic relations as of 29 September 1972; (5) renunciation by the Chinese government of war reparations from Japan; (6) establishment of friendly relations based on five principles of peaceful coexistence; (7) the two countries' common opposition to hegemony; (8) negotiations for the conclusion of a treaty of peace and friendship; and (9) negotiations for the conclusion of commercial agreements.

China-Japan Peace and Friendship Treaty 日中平和友好条約

(Nitchū Heiwa Yūkō Jōyaku). When the governments of Japan and the People's Republic of China normalized relations by a joint communiqué of 29 September 1972, they agreed to enter into negotiations for the purpose of concluding a treaty of peace and friendship. Negotiations started in November 1974 but were not concluded until 12

August 1978, when the treaty was finally signed in Beijing (Peking). One particularly controversial issue had been Chinese insistence on, and Japanese resistance to, a clause providing that neither country would seek hegemony in the Asia-Pacific region or elsewhere and that they both opposed efforts by any other country to do so. As signed the treaty included a balancing clause stipulating that the treaty would not affect either country's relations with a third country. The treaty is not a treaty of peace in the technical sense, which puts an end to the legal state of war, but a treaty for the consolidation and development of relations of peace and friendship. The successful conclusion of the treaty can be regarded as the completion of the political process of normalizing and consolidating relations between Japan and the People's Republic of China.

chindai 鎮台

(army camps). Temporary organs for military administration established in February 1868, immediately after the Meiji Restoration; they were abolished later in the year. *Chindai* also refers to headquarters for local army commands established in 1871. In 1888 the *chindai* were reorganized and renamed *shidan* (divisions). See also IMPERIAL JAPANESE ARMY.

chindon'ya ちんどん屋

Street entertainers employed to advertise the opening of new stores, sales, plays, and other events. They once paraded boisterously through the city streets, dressed in gaudy costumes, carrying placards or sandwich boards, distributing leaflets, and playing a variety of musical instruments—gongs, drums, SHAMISEN, and clarinets. In the Meiji (1868–1912) and Taishō (1912–26) periods they were more frequently known as *tōzaiya* or *hiromeya;* in the Shōwa period (1926–89) they came to be called *chindon'ya* (from *chin* and *don,* the sounds made by their gongs and drums). Until fairly recently they were a familiar part of the urban scene in Japan; now their numbers are in decline.

Chinese characters → kanji

Chinese Eastern Railway 東清鉄道

(Tōshin Tetsudō; also known in Japan as Tōshi Tetsudō and Hokuman Tetsudō). In 1896 Russia gained permission from China to extend the Trans-Siberian Railroad through China directly across northern Manchuria to Vladivostok. That rail line, the Chinese Eastern Railway (CER), provided opportunities for the Russians to exploit northern Manchuria economically, to interfere in Chinese politics, and to bring military power swiftly to bear in the Far East. In 1898 Russia exacted Chinese consent to build another line from PORT ARTHUR north to the CER; this later became known as the SOUTH MANCHURIA RAILWAY (SMR). These railways formed a framework over which Russian influence spread rapidly through Manchuria. After the Japanese victory in the RUSSO-JAPANESE WAR of 1904–05, Russia ceded the SMR to Japan.

After the Japanese conquest of Manchuria (see MANCHURIAN INCIDENT) in 1931, the Soviet Union realized that the CER was surrounded by Japanese-controlled territory and, in case of war, could easily be seized by the Japanese. Accordingly, negotiations were concluded in March 1935 with an agreement whereby the Soviets sold the CER to the Jap-

anese puppet state of Manchukuo. Soon afterward it was placed under the control of the South Manchuria Railway Company.

Chinjufu 鎮守府

(Headquarters for Pacification and Defense). Military headquarters established during the Nara period (710–794) in northern Honshū to subjugate the EZO tribes. The Chinjufu was commanded by a *chinjufu shōgun* ("chinjufu general"). First located at TAGAJŌ (now in Miyagi Prefecture), the base was moved to IZAWAJŌ (now in Iwate Prefecture) after the conquest of the Ezo by SAKANOUE NO TAMURAMARO in 802. By the mid-11th century, local warrior families, such as the Kiyohara family and the ŌSHŪ FUJIWARA FAMILY, took over the base. It was temporarily revived during the KEMMU RESTORATION (1333–36). From the Meiji period (1868–1912) to the end of World War II, the term *chinjufu* was applied by the government to certain important naval bases, notably those at Yokosuka (Kanagawa Prefecture), Kure (Hiroshima Prefecture), Sasebo (Nagasaki Prefecture), and Maizuru (Kyōto Prefecture).

chinju no kami 鎮守の神

(literally, "pacifying guardian god"). Also called *chinjugami.* The tutelary deity of a given locale. While the *chinju no kami* is technically distinct from the UJIGAMI (clan deity) and UBUSUNAGAMI (deity of one's birthplace), in popular practice these categories of deities are now often indistinguishable. The *chinju no kami* was often officially recognized as a regional deity by local lords and landholders, who contributed to the support of its shrine. The term *chinju no kami* has also been applied, in its specific sense of "guardian deity," to the gods who protect the grounds of a temple, a castle, or a private residence.

Chino 茅野[市]

City in central Nagano Prefecture, central Honshū, on the slopes of the mountain YATSUGATAKE. Chino's cold and dry winters make it ideal for processing agar-agar (*kanten*); lettuce and celery are grown here in the summer. Since World War II, electronics and precision-instruments industries have developed. Tourist attractions include the highland called TATESHINA KŌGEN. Pop: 50,064.

Chinon Industries, Inc チノン[株]

(Chinon). Company engaged in manufacture and sale of 35mm cameras, video camera lenses, and information equipment. Incorporated in 1948. The firm has substantially increased its production of information equipment, particularly floppy disk drives and printers. Chinon also supplies 35mm cameras to Eastman Kodak. Kodak Japan is now the largest shareholder of Chinon Industries. Sales for the fiscal year ending March 1991 totaled ¥55.4 billion (US $403.8 million), and capitalization stood at ¥6.9 billion (US $50.3 million). Headquarters are in Suwa, Nagano Prefecture.

Chinsetsu yumiharizuki 椿説弓張月

(Crescent Moon: The Adventures of Tametomo). A 5-section, 29-volume YOMIHON by Kyokutei BAKIN (1767–1848); published 1807–11. A heroic adventure tale, *Chinsetsu yumiharizuki* describes the life of the legendary 12th-century archer MINAMOTO NO TAMETOMO and his exploits after being exiled to Ōshima Island off the Izu Peninsula. Tametomo makes his way to the Ryūkyū Islands (now Okinawa Prefecture), where he assists the heiress to the throne, quells uprisings, and restores peace to the Ryūkyū kingdom. *Chinsetsu yumiharizuki* is patterned on Chinese novels in its careful rendering of both historical fact and contemporary manners. The first of Bakin's epic history tales, its grand design and flights of fantasy make this one of Bakin's most impressive works.

Chin Shunshin　陳舜臣

(1924– ; Ch: Chen Shunchen or Ch'en Shun-ch'en). Novelist. Born in Hyōgo Prefecture. Graduated from Ōsaka University of Foreign Studies. Of Chinese descent, Chin retains Taiwanese citizenship. He received the Edogawa Rampo Prize for *Karekusa no ne* (1961, Roots of Dried Grass), a mystery about the murder of a Chinese loan shark, and the Naoki Prize for *Seigyoku shishi kōro* (1968, Sapphire Lion Incense Burner). He has written many historical novels, as well as travel pieces and essays, about China. Other works include a 3-volume epic novel, *Ahen sensō* (1967, The Opium War), and the 15-volume *Chūgoku no rekishi* (1980–83, The History of China).

chinsō　頂相

Also pronounced *chinzō* or *chōsō*. Painted portraits and sculptures of Zen priests. *Chinsō* were popular in China from the time of the Song (Sung) dynasty (960–1279). The practice of making *chinsō* was transmitted to Japan during the Kamakura period (1185–1333), and many were produced at that time and during the Muromachi period (1333–1568). *Chinsō* tended to be extremely realistic likenesses, and also conveyed a sense of the subject's character and spirit. A priest would often have his disciples paint a *chinsō* of him as evidence of their training and then award it to them. *Chinsō* in sculpture form were usually created after the priest's death.

Chion'in　知恩院

Head temple of the JŌDO SECT of Buddhism, located in Higashiyama Ward, Kyōto. The precincts of the Chion'in include the site where HŌNEN, the founder of the Jōdo sect, settled after leaving the mountain HIEIZAN in 1175 to proclaim his new Pure Land teachings and the site where he later died after returning from exile. The original temple, honoring Hōnen, was built in 1234 by his disciple Genchi (1183–1238). The temple was destroyed several times, including during the ŌNIN WAR (1467–77), which ravaged Kyōto, but was restored each time. In 1523 the temple became the head temple of the Jōdo sect. Destroyed by fire in 1633, the temple was rebuilt by the third Tokugawa shōgun, Iemitsu (1604–51); this is the complex that stands today. In 1607 Chion'in was designated a *monzekidera*, a temple whose abbot must be chosen from the imperial family or the aristocracy.

The colossal two-story ceremonial gate at the entrance to the temple complex is the largest surviving structure of its kind in Japan. Among the temple's many art treasures are an early-14th-century scroll depicting Hōnen's life, a RAIGŌZU depicting the Buddha AMIDA and accompanying bodhisattvas descending to receive the faithful, and sliding doors painted with landscapes that have been attributed to the KANŌ SCHOOL artists of the early Edo period (1600–1868).

Chiossone, Edoardo　キヨソーネ, E.

(1832–98). Italian artist and copperplate engraver employed by the Japanese govern-

ment from 1875 to 1891. He designed Japan's first modern paper money and trained Japanese in all phases of currency production. Outstanding examples of Chiossone's work were the first and second government issues made in Japan (1878 and 1881) and the first and second Bank of Japan notes (1884 and 1888). His work blended Eastern and Western motifs, reinforced the image of the Meiji government, and set a high aesthetic standard for Japanese paper currency. He also produced drawings and etchings of notable figures in contemporary government and social circles, including Emperor Meiji and Empress Shōken.

Chiran　知覧[町]

Town in southwestern Kagoshima Prefecture, Kyūshū. Chiran is noted for its tea and tobacco. *Samurai* homes and gardens dating from the Edo period (1600–1868) can still be seen. An air base constructed here during World War II served as a base for KAMIKAZE suicide missions; a memorial honors the pilots. Pop: 14,599.

chirimen　縮緬

(silk crepe). It is believed that the technique for making silk crepe was brought to Japan from China in the late 16th century. Some varieties of *chirimen* are known by the way the crimping in the fabric is produced. Other varieties, such as Tango *chirimen* (Kyōto Prefecture), are known according to their production area. *Chirimen* is still widely used for high-quality traditional clothing (KIMONO, *haori*, and OBI) and accessories. See also CHIJIMI.

Chiryū　知立[市]

City in central Aichi Prefecture, central Honshū, near NAGOYA. It was a post-station town on the TŌKAIDŌ during the Edo period (1600–1868). Textile mills and sewing-machine plants are located here. Pop: 54,059.

Chishakuin　智積院

Head temple of the Chizan branch of the SHINGON SECT of Buddhism, located in Higashiyama Ward, Kyōto. It was originally built in the 14th century as part of the Dai Dembōin temple complex in Negoro, Wakayama Prefecture. Toyotomi Hideyoshi (1537–98), in a campaign to gain control over the country, burned down the temples at Negoro in 1585. Gen'yū (1529–1605), who was then abbot, fled to Kyōto, where he propagated the Shingi (New) Shingon doctrines. Chishakuin was reestablished in 1600, and in 1872 the government designated it and HASEDERA as the two head temples of the Shingi branch of the Shingon sect. In 1900 Chishakuin established itself as the head temple of the Chizan branch. It is famous for its gardens and paintings, which date from the late 16th century.

Chishima Islands → Kuril Islands

Chishimakan Incident　千島艦事件

(Chishimakan Jiken). International incident arising from the 1892 collision of the Japanese torpedo gunboat *Chishima* and the British steamship *Ravenna* of the Peninsular and Oriental Navigation Co. After the *Chishima* sank Japan sought ¥850,000 in damages. The P&O eventually agreed to a settlement of only £10,000 (about ¥91,000), thereby heightening Japanese sentiment for treaty revision (see UNEQUAL TREATIES, REVISION OF).

Chion'in The grounds of the head temple of the Jōdo sect of Buddhism. The double-roofed structure at center is the Amida hall.

Chishima Volcanic Zone　千島火山帯

(Chishima Kazantai). Volcanic zone extending about 1,400 km (870 mi) from central Hokkaidō to the Kamchatka Peninsula. It includes the KURIL ISLANDS (Chishima Islands). There are numerous active volcanoes, some of which have heights exceeding 1,000 m (3,280 ft). Major peaks include Oakandake, Meakandake, Tokachidake, and Asahidake (2,290 m; 7,513 ft), which is Hokkaidō's highest. There are many calderas and caldera lakes.

Chiso Kaisei → Land Tax Reform of 1873–1881

Chisso Corporation　チッソ[株]

(Chisso). Manufacturer of chemical products, including synthetic resins, synthetic fibers, fine chemicals, organic chemicals, and chemical fertilizers. Incorporated in 1950. The serious mercury poisoning of hundreds of residents of the city of Minamata in Kumamoto Prefecture was caused by effluents from the Chisso acetaldehyde factory in that city. The poisoning first appeared in the mid-1950s. The company was found guilty of negligence by the Kumamoto District Court in 1973 (see POLLUTION-RELATED DISEASES). Compensation paid to victims between 1973 and 1990 totaled ¥91.5 billion (US $665.5 million). Sales for the fiscal year ending March 1991 totaled ¥159.2 billion (US $1.2 billion), and capitalization was ¥7.8 billion (US $56.9 million). Headquarters are in Tōkyō.

Chita　知多[市]

City in Aichi Prefecture, central Honshū, on the west coast of the Chita Peninsula. The city has long been famous for its Chita cotton. Seaweed (*nori*) is cultivated on the coast. More recently, a thermoelectric plant and oil refineries have been constructed. Pop: 75,433.

Chita Peninsula　知多半島

(Chita Hantō). Located in western Aichi Prefecture, central Honshū. It divides the bays of Ise and Mikawa. Horticulture and dairy farming have flourished since the construction of the AICHI CANAL. The area near the city of Nagoya is being industrialized and transformed into a residential area. The southern part of the peninsula is part of Mikawa Bay Quasi-National Park. Area: 355 sq km (137 sq mi).

chiteki shoyū ken → intellectual property

Chitose　千歳[市]

City in southwestern Hokkaidō on the river Chitosegawa. It was first settled in 1869; one of East Asia's largest salmon and trout hatcheries is located here. A naval airfield built

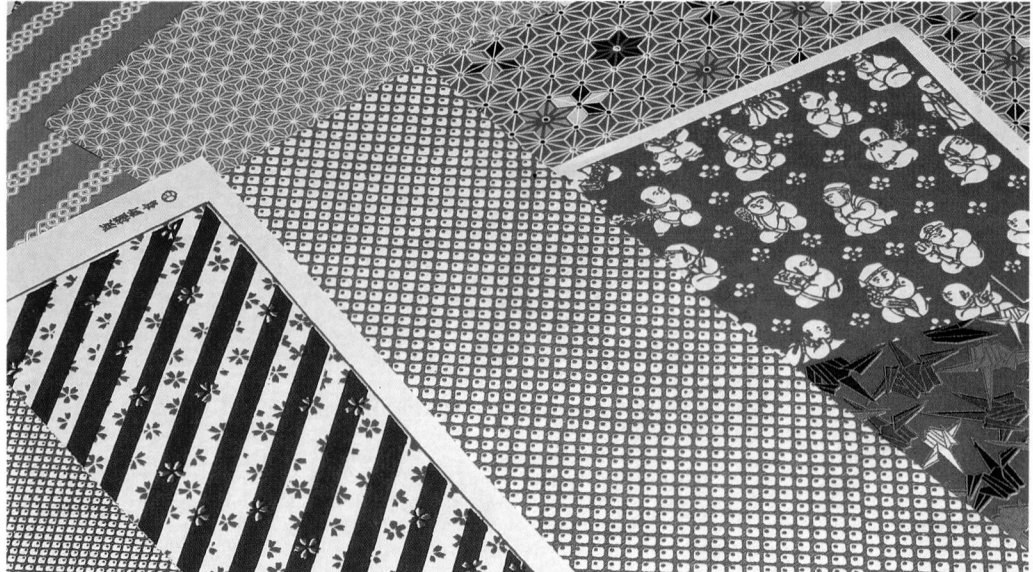

chiyogami A display of some of the many colorful patterns that decorate this type of paper, which is often used for such handicrafts as origami and paper doll construction.

before World War II is now the largest airport in Hokkaidō. Principal industries are food processing, nonferrous metals, furniture, and dairy farming. The city is part of Shikotsu-Tōya National Park. Pop: 78,946.

chitsuroku shobun 秩禄処分

Measures (*shobun*) adopted by the government in the 1870s to abolish the hereditary stipends (*chitsuroku*) granted to the nobility and members of the *samurai* class immediately after the Meiji Restoration of 1868. In 1869 the court aristocracy and former *daimyō* had been classified as *kazoku* (see PEERAGE), while the former samurai were divided into SHIZOKU or *sotsu;* these status distinctions became the basis for computing the stipends to be paid to members of these groups.

By 1871, however, the government began to reconsider the whole stipend system. The cost of rice stipends alone constituted 30 percent of total government expenses and was diverting essential resources from other crucial tasks such as the development of a modern army and navy. As a result, the government began to tax the stipends in 1873, and in 1876 decreed that all stipends be converted into government bonds called KINROKU KŌSAI that would not be redeemable for a five-year period. These measures were a blow to the former samurai and, together with the loss of other feudal privileges, led to a wave of samurai revolts culminating in the SATSUMA REBELLION of 1877. By 1880 more

Chiyonofuji Using strength and brilliant technique to make up for his relatively small size, Chiyonofuji, nicknamed "The Wolf," dominated *sumō* in the 1980s.

than half of the poorer samurai had sold off their bonds; the nobility and former daimyō fared better, many using the bonds as investment capital in the newly formed national bank system (see NATIONAL BANKS).

Chiyoda Corporation 千代田化工建設[株]

(Chiyoda Kakō Kensetsu). Plant engineering firm. Incorporated in 1948. Chiyoda Corporation (formerly Chiyoda Chemical Engineering Construction Co, Ltd) has played a major role in the development of Japan's oil, gas, and other processing industries. The company is involved in some 500 plant engineering projects, including over 100 in 35 foreign countries. Chiyoda has also used its engineering skills and technologies to diversify into other industries. Sales for the fiscal year ending September 1990 totaled ¥212.1 billion (US $1.5 billion), and capitalization stood at ¥14.8 billion (US $106.5 million). Headquarters are in Tōkyō.

Chiyoda Mutual Life Insurance Co 千代田生命保険[相]

(Chiyoda Seimei Hoken). One of the "Big Eight" life insurance companies in Japan. Incorporated in 1904. Chiyoda Life participates in a worldwide network with Norwich Union Insurance Group in England, Prudential Insurance Group and CNA Insurance Group in the United States, and Winterthur Insurance Group in Switzerland. Assets for the fiscal year ending March 1991 totaled ¥5.2 trillion (US $38.0 billion). Premiums reached ¥1.0 trillion (US $7.3 billion) in the same year. Headquarters are in Tōkyō.

Chiyoda Ward 千代田区

(Chiyoda Ku). One of the 23 wards of Tōkyō. The city's, and Japan's, economic and political center. Site of the Imperial Palace, the Diet building, various ministries, and judicial organs. The population is the smallest among the wards. Government offices are located in the Nagatachō and KASUMIGASEKI districts, business offices in the MARUNOUCHI and ŌTEMACHI districts. A number of universities and many bookstores are located in the KANDA district, while the AKIHABARA district is noted for its wholesale and discount electrical appliance stores. Pop: 39,472.

chiyogami 千代紙

A type of Japanese paper decorated with brightly colored, woodblock-printed patterns. Used today for a variety of handicrafts, such as covering small boxes and making *kimono* for paper dolls, *chiyogami* was first produced by UKIYO-E artists in the late 18th

century. The word is a combination of *chiyo* (literally, "a thousand generations") and *kami* (*gami*), or paper, and has auspicious connotations similar to those evoked by the pine, bamboo, and plum-blossom motifs with which it is often printed. See also WASHI.

Chiyonofuji 千代の富士

(1955–). SUMŌ wrestler; 58th grand *sumō* champion (*yokozuna*). Real name Akimoto Mitsugu. Born in Hokkaidō. A member of the Kokonoe stable, he fought his first match in 1970, achieved top-division (*makuuchi*) status in 1975, and became *yokozuna* in 1981. In 1990 he won his 31st *sumō* tournament championship, bringing him just short of the record of 32 championships established by TAIHŌ. In 1991 he established a new record of 1,045 wins before announcing his retirement. In 1992 he became head of the Kokonoe stable and took the name Kokonoe Oyakata.

chlorella クロレラ

(*kurorera*). *Chlorella* spp. General term for species of green algae of the division Chlorophyta, family Chlorellaceae, genus *Chlorella*. Chlorella are very common in freshwater areas and often turn the water green. They are easily produced in pure cultures and have long been used in research on photosynthesis. Chlorella have also been promoted as a food supplement since 1948, because they are particularly rich in protein and vitamins. In Japan species suitable for consumption are cultivated indoors by being shifted into consecutively larger containers and are finally placed outdoors in a large round culture reservoir under natural light until their full nutritive value is reached. Outdoor culture reservoirs are best located in subtropical areas because the most suitable temperature for growth is approximately 25°–30°C (77°–86°F). Chlorella are currently sold in pill form as a food supplement, and they are also used as a food in space travel.

chōchin → lanterns

Chōdensu → Minchō

Chōfu 調布[市]

City in Tōkyō Prefecture. A post-station town in the Edo period (1600–1868), it is now a residential suburb, with electrical equipment and food-processing factories, and is an important transportation center. The Chōfu Airfield is northwest of the city. Well-known tourist spots are the Jindai Botanical Park and the temple Jindaiji. Pop: 197,677.

Chōfu 長府

District in the eastern part of the city of Shimonoseki, Yamaguchi Prefecture, western Honshū. Once the capital of Nagato Province, in the Edo period (1600–1868) it became a castle town of the MŌRI FAMILY. It is now a residential area undergoing rapid industrialization. Chōfu is part of the Kita Kyūshū Industrial Zone.

Chōgo Sonshiji → Shigisanji

Chōheirei → Conscription Ordinance of 1873

Chōjirō 長次郎

(1516–92). Kyōto potter; generally acknowledged originator of RAKU WARE. Chōjirō began his career as a tilemaker. He soon attracted the attention of the tea master SEN NO

RIKYŪ (1522–91) and under his guidance began making Raku ware for the tea ceremony. Chōjirō's bowls are soft-bodied, low-fired, and shaped by hand. Many of his tea-bowls, either black, red, or white Raku, have survived, and several are designated as Important Cultural Properties. These bowls, which may actually include some by his assistants, are simple and unpretentious in design and shape, possessing a raw yet inviting tactile quality.

Chōjū giga　　　　　　鳥獣戯画

(Scrolls of Frolicking Animals). Also called *Chōjū jimbutsu giga* (Scrolls of Frolicking Animals and Humans). Group of ink paintings on scrolls (EMAKIMONO) and a few detached segments mainly depicting various animals, some behaving as if they were human. Dating from the Heian (794–1185) and Kamakura (1185–1333) periods, the principal surviving scrolls of the *Chōjū giga* are the four in the KŌZANJI, a temple in the northwestern section of Kyōto. In addition, there are several important detached segments that must once have been attached to the Kōzanji scrolls. Unlike other surviving scroll paintings from the Heian and Kamakura periods, the *Chōjū giga* scrolls contain no text.

Scroll A of the Kōzanji scrolls is the most famous and consists entirely of animals burlesquing the activities of monks and laymen. Scroll B consists of animals disporting themselves in a more or less continuous landscape. Both of the foregoing are considered to be works of the late Heian period. Scroll C, which is inscribed with the date 1253, begins with a sequence of games and contests between monks and laymen and ends with a sequence of competing animals. Scroll D, also thought to be of the 13th century, depicts human clerics engaged in rituals and amusements.

Traditionally, the paintings of the *Chōjū giga* were attributed to TOBA SŌJŌ (1053–1140). Recent studies have suggested, however, that even within Kōzanji scroll A, more than one artist might have been involved. The use only of ink and the fluid lines of these scrolls prefigure the rise of ink monochrome as a major mode of Buddhist painting. See also INK PAINTING; HAKUBYŌGA.

chōka　　　　　　長歌

("long poem"). Also called *nagauta*. A WAKA verse form consisting of any number of alternating 5- and 7-syllable lines ending with an extra 7-syllable line. Distinguished from the 31-syllable TANKA ("short poem"). The *chōka* was often followed by one or more 31-syllable envoys in *tanka* form, called *hanka* or *kaeshiuta*, that summarized or elaborated on its theme. The form flourished in the late 7th and early 8th centuries and was perfected by KAKINOMOTO NO HITOMARO. The MAN'YŌSHŪ (ca 759), the oldest extant Japanese poetry anthology, contains 265 *chōka*.

Chōkaisan　　　　　　鳥海山

Composite volcano in the Chōkai Volcanic Zone. Also known as Dewa Fuji or Akita Fuji. It is on the border between Akita and Yamagata prefectures, northern Honshū. The highest of the several peaks on the crater rim is Shinzan. The lake Torinoumi is also on the rim. The central peak of Chōkai Quasi-National Park, Chōkaisan erupted in 1974 for the first time in 153 years. Ōmonoimi Shrine is on its summit. Height: 2,236 m (7,336 ft).

Chōkai Volcanic Zone　　　鳥海火山帯

(Chōkai Kazantai). Volcanic zone extending along the Sea of Japan coast from southwestern Hokkaidō to Niigata Prefecture, Honshū. The zone centers on the highest peak, CHŌKAISAN (2,236 m; 7,336 ft), and is dominated by the DEWA MOUNTAINS. IWAKISAN is another important peak. Parts of the Chōkai Volcanic Zone are included in Oga and Chōkai quasi-national parks.

Chōkei, Emperor　　　　　長慶天皇

(1343–94; Chōkei Tennō). The 98th sovereign (*tennō*) in the traditional count (which includes several legendary emperors); reigned 1368–83. He was the eldest son and successor of Go-Murakami (1328–68; r 1339–68), second emperor of the Southern Court (1337–92; see NORTHERN AND SOUTHERN COURTS). Because the Southern Court was hard pressed by the forces of the Northern Court and the Muromachi shogunate (1338–1573), Chōkei was forced to change residence frequently during his 14-year reign, staying in temples designated as "temporary palaces." In 1383 he abdicated in favor of his brother GO-KAMEYAMA. Chōkei wrote *Sengenshō*, a commentary on the TALE OF GENJI. Documentation on his reign is scanty, and he was not placed on the official list of emperors until 1926.

chokkomon　　　　　　直弧文

("straight-curved pattern"). A form of decoration of obscure origin and uncertain meaning found on Kofun-period (ca 300–710) objects of the 4th to the 6th centuries. The pattern is generally composed of crossing diagonal lines imposed over fragmented arcs of circles; it is found painted or incised on shell bracelets, bone sword guards, stone headrests, and HANIWA funerary sculptures and cast on BRONZE MIRRORS. On a larger scale it may be carved or painted on stone coffins, walls, or other parts of the ORNAMENTED TOMBS found in western Japan. The *chokkomon* design has been variously explained as a skeuomorph, a plaited rope, a device to bind the spirit to the tomb chamber, a pattern to placate the spirit of the dead, or as simple cosmic symbolism.

Chōkōdō ryō　　　　　　長講堂領

(domains of the Chōkōdō). The Chōkōdō was a chapel built in 1185 by retired emperor GO-SHIRAKAWA to which he commended numerous estates (SHŌEN). The holdings amounted to over 180 proprietorships in 42 provinces, yielding an enormous income. After the division of the imperial house into the Daikakuji line and the Jimyōin line, the domains became the principal economic asset of the latter. During the period of the NORTHERN AND SOUTHERN COURTS (1337–92) these domains were largely appropriated by provincial warriors. The domains were completely dispersed in the ŌNIN WAR (1467–77).

Chōkokuji → Hasedera

chokurei → imperial ordinance

chokusenshū → imperial anthologies

Chōkyōsai Eiri　　　　　鳥橋斎栄里

(fl late 18th century). UKIYO-E artist. Also known as Hosoda Eiri. Specialized in portraits of contemporary beauties (*bijinga*); influenced by the style of Kitagawa UTAMARO. Eiri, along with Hosoda Eishō, is one of the best-known disciples of HOSODA EISHI. There is some question concerning the identity of Chōkyōsai Eiri; he is considered by some to be the same person as Rekisentei Eiri or Shikyūsai Eiri, but others maintain that these are all different people.

Chōmonkyō　　　　　　長門峡

Gorge on the middle reaches of the river ABUGAWA, Yamaguchi Prefecture, western Honshū. This quartz porphyry gorge abounds in sheer cliffs, deep ravines, gigantic rocks, and waterfalls. Part of the Chōmonkyō Prefectural Natural Park, it attracts numerous tourists in the *ayu* (sweetfish) fishing season and in autumn when the leaves turn crimson. Yunose Hot Spring is located here. Length: 12 km (7.5 mi).

chōnaikai　　　　　　町内会

A type of neighborhood association. Also called *chōkai* or *jichikai*. *Chōnaikai* are quasi-governmental organizations that have limited responsibility for local administration

Chōjū giga Detail from scroll A, the most famous of this set of four scrolls containing satirical drawings of animals and human beings. Attributed to the Tendai monk Toba Sōjō. 12th century. Ink on paper. Entire scroll 31 × 1,148 cm. Kōzanji, Kyōto. National Treasure.

chokkomon The back of this 4th-century bronze mirror, found at the Shin'yama tomb in the town of Kōryō, Nara Prefecture, is decorated with the enigmatic *chokkomon* design. Diameter 28 cm. Imperial Household Agency.

chōnin Japanese cities experienced enormous growth beginning in the late 16th century. *Chōnin* such as merchants, financiers, artisans, and laborers populated these centers of feudal administration.
1 A detail from the 1805 scroll *Illustrations of Chōnin Life* portrays an *izakaya*, an eating and drinking establishment.
2 A detail from the same scroll shows a stand selling grilled eel.

and coordinate numerous local activities in urban neighborhoods of up to several hundred households. Modern *chōnaikai* descend from local administrative systems, highly developed during the Edo period (1600–1868), that held local residents communally responsible for collecting taxes, maintaining order, and enforcing orthodox behavior. After the Meiji Restoration (1868) these local groups lost legal standing, but in the 1920s they reappeared in many urban neighborhoods.

In 1940 *chōnaikai* became legally mandatory in all cities and were responsible for rationing, civil defense, and stifling dissent. Because they were closely linked to the war effort and presumably antidemocratic, Occupation authorities abolished *chōnaikai* after World War II. Partially resurrected in the early 1950s, *chōnaikai* are now nominally independent voluntary associations, but most still maintain close ties with local governments. *Chōnaikai* also play an important role in social life, providing a vehicle for informal social ties among neighbors. One of their most important symbolic activities is organizing local festivals (*matsuri*). See also GONINGUMI; LOCAL GOVERNMENT; NEIGHBORHOOD ASSOCIATIONS.

Chongqing (Chungking) government 重慶政府

(Jūkei *seifu*). The Guomindang (Kuomintang; KMT; Nationalist Party) government of China during the period of the SINO-JAPANESE WAR OF 1937–1945 after its move from Nanjing (Nanking) to Chongqing in the southwestern province of Sichuan (Szechwan). In December 1937 the Chinese capital at Nanjing fell to the Japanese. The Guomindang government fled west to Hankou (Hankow), Hubei (Hupeh) Province. When the Japanese took the latter city in October 1938, the Guomindang moved further west to Chongqing, where it continued its resis-

tance to the Japanese in an uneasy alliance with the Chinese Communist Party. It returned to Nanjing in the spring of 1946.

chōnin 町人

(townsmen). The inhabitants—other than nobles, *samurai*, and priests—of urban administrative districts or *chō* (*machi*) in premodern times, especially in the Edo period (1600–1868). In a more restricted sense it is sometimes used to describe commoners owning real property in, and participating in the administration of, such urban districts. Although some were wealthy financiers and wholesale merchants, the vast majority of *chōnin* were poor artisans, peddlers, and day laborers. Under the Tokugawa system of social classes—*shi* (samurai), *nō* (farmers), *kō* (artisans), and *shō* (merchants)—*chōnin* were either artisans or merchants, but the term is basically a classification of townsmen for administrative purposes rather than on simply geographical or occupational lines (see SHI-NŌ-KŌ-SHŌ).

Chōnin first became important as an object of urban administration around 1600. They were always subordinate to the samurai authorities. Guilds, groups, and other associations of townsmen existed for control purposes rather than for self-government. Typically the premodern Japanese city grew up around a castle, which formed the center of feudal administration, and the function of *chōnin* was to serve the needs of that administration and of the samurai who staffed it. Official policy was that they should be confined to that role, but once a city reached a certain size, further growth largely served the needs of the *chōnin* themselves.

Early History—The term *chōnin* (*machibito, machiudo*) originated in Kyōto during the late Heian period (794–1185), where the smallest geographic unit or block was known as a *chō*. Merchants in towns such as Kyōto became the first *chōnin*, but it was not until the unification of the country under ODA NOBUNAGA and TOYOTOMI HIDEYOSHI in the late 16th century and the urbanization of the samurai class that large cities grew up around the castles to serve the needs of the military leaders. *Chōnin* as an administrative class first became established under the Tokugawa shogunate (1603–1867) in the early 17th century in Kyōto, Ōsaka, and Edo (now Tōkyō), and later in the larger CASTLE TOWNS and major ports.

Emergence of the Chōnin Class—Kyōto had long been the seat of the imperial court and an established financial and handicraft center. Its *chōnin* were financial agents and quartermasters for leading military figures. After the Tokugawa shogunate destroyed the remnants of the Toyotomi faction in 1615, Ōsaka became the center into which western Japan's rice revenues flowed, and by the late 17th century its merchants and financiers became the channel through which the shogunate sought to control the national economy. Edo, the seat of the shogunate, was a city of samurai, large numbers of whom were required to reside there under the SANKIN KŌTAI (alternate attendance) system. Edo's *chōnin* community grew from the construction workers and small shopkeepers who served the samurai.

Kyōto, perhaps because it had the longest experience of *chōnin*, provided the model, and codes issued there by ITAKURA KATSUSHIGE from 1603 to 1619 formed the basis for much of Tokugawa legislation concerning city administration. The codes gave the *chō*-

nin an identity defined by sumptuary regulations and special systems of administrative control. These controls were administered in detail both by geographic units (*chō*) and, perhaps more importantly, through occupational groups (see also MACHI YAKUNIN; MACHIBURE).

Further Development of Chōnin—As the Japanese economy and interregional trade developed toward the end of the 17th century, urban communities became not simply providers for the needs of the ruling class but also a major source of demand on their own account. Edo's population, for example, reached 1 million by 1720, as *chōnin* came from other towns to settle there. Official attempts to control trade in the interests of shogunal policy took the form of encouraging or even requiring the formation of associations of merchants (*nakama*, KABUNAKAMA) and artisans, which received some privileges in return for being amenable to official direction, and led to the founding in the late 17th century of wholesale merchant guilds (TOIYA) in Ōsaka and Edo.

Strata of Chōnin—The few great financiers and wholesale merchants of Ōsaka and Edo were the leaders of the *chōnin* community, but at the other end of the scale was a much larger number of poor peddlers and laborers. In between were smaller wholesalers, retailers and stallholders, building contractors, master craftsmen, independent tradesmen, and their employees and apprentices, as well as contract and casual laborers, workers in the pleasure quarters, and those in the restaurant and lodging businesses. The urban poor, of which there were 200,000 in Edo in 1832, were a potential source of unrest, and in times of famine or high prices, rioting became a serious problem. Measures such as the return of certain residents to their villages (HITOGAESHI) proved effective only in the maintenance of order and did not reduce the urban population.

Daily Life—The wealthy *chōnin* of Kyōto, Edo, Ōsaka, and Nagasaki lived a strictly regulated life devoted to business and the maintenance of their credit and reputations. Most of the larger establishments codified rules of both business and private conduct for themselves and their employees. Despite the economic power that their wealth gave them, *chōnin* were always strictly subject to the samurai authorities. Regulations, tradition, and etiquette were punctiliously observed. Although their style of life was regulated by sumptuary laws and conspicuous extravagance was liable to bring summary punishment, rich *chōnin*, such as KINOKUNIYA BUNZAEMON, lived a luxurious life. So too did the Edo FUDASASHI (financiers of the direct retainers of the shogunate), but for most *chōnin* in Edo life was a constant struggle to survive. Nevertheless, city life was in many ways preferable to life in the poorer villages. *Chōnin* were virtually free of tax obligations. There was usually some work available, and, although wages were low, by working hard even poor *chōnin* could usually eat rice every day. Moreover, life in the city was socially much freer and more mobile than in the village and offered much more in the way of entertainment for those who could afford it. By talent, hard work, or good fortune *chōnin* could rise in the world and make a name for themselves. Thus, although city life lacked the security of life in the villages, *chōnin* were proud of their independence and self-reliance.

Chōnin Culture — Much of the art, literature, music, and drama of the Edo period is associated particularly with *chōnin,* including the KABUKI theater and the music of the SHAMISEN. After the MEIJI RESTORATION of 1868 *chōnin* disappeared as an administrative class, but they continued to play an important economic role, stubbornly maintaining their SHITAMACHI culture against official efforts to impose samurai norms. In the post–World War II period, however, both *chōnin* and samurai ethics became so attenuated as to be scarcely recognizable.

chōnindō 町人道

("Way of the merchant," as distinguished from BUSHIDŌ, "Way of the warrior"). Term used in the Meiji period (1868–1912) to designate the behavioral and ethical code of the townsmen (CHŌNIN) or merchant class during the Edo period (1600–1868). It affirmed the pursuit of profit through the exercise of business acumen and frugality and advocated respect for propriety and fulfillment of social and familial obligations as the prerequisites of financial success. In the 18th century quasi-religious schools of popular philosophy such as Sekimon Shingaku (see SHINGAKU) developed such codes of behavior to foster a sense of pride in the merchant class. See also CHŌNIN KŌKEN ROKU.

Chōnin kōken roku 町人考見録

Set of instructions completed by Mitsui Takafusa (1684–1748) in 1728 to explain the MITSUI house laws to his descendants and to ensure the family's continued prosperity, using the experiences of Kyōto merchant houses as examples. It is an invaluable source of information on the behavior of merchants during the late 17th and early 18th centuries.

chopsticks 箸

(*hashi*). All Japanese dishes are eaten with *hashi;* in the case of soups, the solid ingredients are eaten with *hashi* and the stock sipped directly from the soup bowl. *Hashi* are commonly made of light but strong wood, such as cypress or willow, and then lacquered; they are also made of bamboo or, increasingly, of plastic. It is customary in the Japanese household for each person to have a pair of *hashi* reserved for his or her exclusive use. Disposable plain-wood chopsticks (*waribashi*), which the diner splits apart before using, are common in restaurants. Long chopsticks made of bamboo and used for cooking are called *saibashi.* Long metal chopsticks with wooden handles are used for deep-frying. When not in use during a meal, *hashi* are rested upon small ceramic, wooden, or glass stands called *hashioki.*

Chōri Co, Ltd 蝶理[株]

(Chōri). General trading firm specializing in textiles, chemical products, machinery, and other commodities. Established in 1861. Overseas it has a total of 36 offices and 22 joint ventures for the import and export of textiles and chemical products. Sales for the fiscal year ending March 1991 totaled ¥718.0 billion (US $5.2 billion), 66 percent of which was textiles. In the same year the firm was capitalized at ¥9.1 billion (US $66.3 million). Headquarters are in Ōsaka and Tōkyō.

chōsan 逃散

(literally, "flight"). Abandonment of land by tenant farmers in order to avoid payment of taxes (NENGU) and compulsory labor service (BUYAKU). The term came into use late in the Heian period (794–1185). Peasants usually

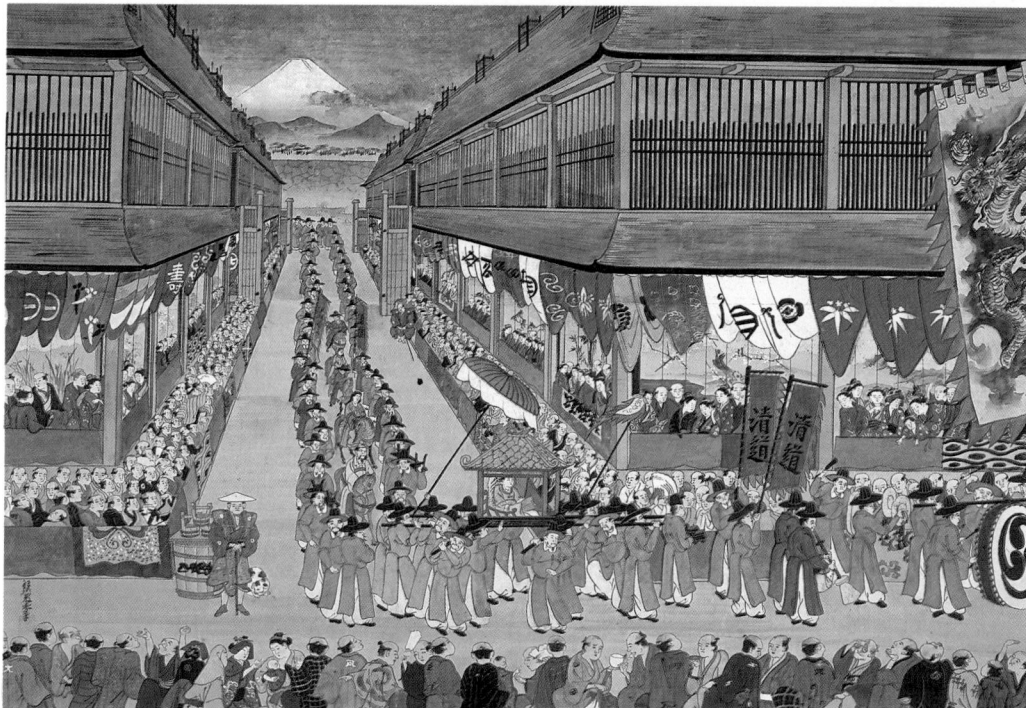

fled to neighboring estates (SHŌEN) or became vagrants. In the Kamakura period (1185–1333) tenants often defected en masse to demand lighter tax and labor burdens or to protest the corrupt practices of *shōen* officials. Typically they would hide in the mountains while negotiations took place and afterward return to the land. Early in the Muromachi period (1333–1568) these protests developed into shows of force (GŌSO) and violent uprisings (IKKI), and, from the Sengoku period (1467–1568) onward, growing numbers of peasants abandoned their land entirely and moved to the cities. During the Edo period (1600–1868) peasants continued to abscond in order to force better conditions.

Chōsei 長勢

(1010–91). Heian-period (794–1185) Buddhist sculptor; leading disciple of the well-known sculptor JŌCHŌ. Founder of the Sanjō BUSSHO (workshop), which came to be known as the EN SCHOOL of Buddhist sculpture. In 1065 he was awarded the Buddhist rank of *hokkyō* in appreciation of the statues he made for the Kyōto temple Hōjōji. He attained the rank of *hōgen* in 1070 and *hōin,* the highest Buddhist rank, in 1077. Among his surviving works are the bodhisattvas Nikkō (Skt: Sūryaprabha) and Gakkō (Skt: Candraprabha) and the Twelve Divine Generals (J: Jūni Shinshō) at the temple Kōryūji in Kyōto.

chōsen 庁宣

(provincial governor's decree). Official documents regarding local affairs; issued from around the mid-Heian period (794–1185) through the 14th century. Many were sent to local subordinates by provincial governors (KOKUSHI) or by top officials of the government headquarters in Kyūshū (DAZAIFU), who often administered their provinces from Kyōto rather than moving to their assignments. The format of the *chōsen* followed the style of KUDASHIBUMI.

Chōsen Ginkō 朝鮮銀行

(Bank of Korea). The central bank of Korea during the period of Japanese colonial control (1910–45). Established by the Japanese in 1909 as the Kankoku Ginkō, the bank took the place of the Japanese Daiichi Kokuritsu Ginkō (First National Bank), which had established a Korean branch in 1878 and had

operated as the central bank of Korea after the conclusion of the Russo-Japanese War of 1904–05. The bank was reorganized in 1911 after the annexation of Korea by Japan, and the name was changed to Chōsen Ginkō to reflect the Japanese colonial name for Korea. The bank's stock was owned by private Japanese banks and corporations, but its board of governors was appointed by the Japanese government. The bank issued the Korean currency, controlled domestic prices, and serviced international trade through branches in Manchuria, the major ports of China and Japan, London, and New York. The bank was dissolved by order of the Allied forces at the end of World War II.

Chōsen Kaikyō → Korea Strait

Chōsen tsūshinshi 朝鮮通信使

Delegations from the Korean YI DYNASTY to the TOKUGAWA SHOGUNATE during the Edo period (1600–1868). Relations between Japan and Korea, broken off with the INVASIONS OF KOREA IN 1592 AND 1597, were resumed after the establishment of the Tokugawa shogunate. The first envoy, accompanied by 467 attendants, came to Edo (now Tōkyō) in 1607 to congratulate TOKUGAWA HIDETADA, who had become shōgun two years earlier. Twelve delegations were sent in all, usually for auspicious occasions such as the succession of a new shōgun; the last was in 1811. The Korean visits had a special significance for Japan during this period of NATIONAL SECLUSION.

Chōshi 銚子[市]

City in northeastern Chiba Prefecture, central Honshū, at the mouth of the river TONEGAWA. A major fishing port, with the largest catch of sardines, bonito, and tuna in the prefecture, Chōshi has numerous factories that process marine products. Soy sauce is another important industry. Pop: 85,138.

Chōshū domain 長州藩

(Chōshū *han*). Also known as Hagi domain. Edo-period (1600–1868) domain that extended over all of SUŌ PROVINCE and Nagato Province; present-day Yamaguchi Prefecture. It was granted to Mōri Terumoto (1553–1625; see MŌRI FAMILY), who, having sided with TOKUGAWA IEYASU after the Battle

Chōsen tsūshinshi
This mid-18th-century woodblock print shows one of these Korean delegations touring the city of Edo (now Tōkyō).

chopsticks Japanese chopsticks are usually made of wood, bamboo, or plastic and are often lacquered or decorated.

of SEKIGAHARA (1600), received the status of TOZAMA (outside vassal). The domain played a central role in the movement culminating in the MEIJI RESTORATION of 1868, producing such leaders as YOSHIDA SHŌIN, TAKASUGI SHINSAKU, and KIDO TAKAYOSHI. OMOTEDAKA (estimated annual production of rice): 369,000 KOKU (1 *koku* = 180 liters or 5 US bushels).

Chōshū Expeditions 長州征伐

(Chōshū Seibatsu). Two punitive expeditions (1864 and 1866) by the Tokugawa shogunate against the Chōshū domain (now Yamaguchi Prefecture). In 1864 Chōshū activists attempted to regain control of Kyōto, which they had lost during the COUP D'ETAT OF 30 SEPTEMBER 1863, but failed (see HAMAGURI GOMON INCIDENT). The shogunate was given a mandate to punish them, thus precipitating the first Chōshū expedition.

Chōshū, now controlled by a conservative clique, accepted mild terms of surrender, and the shogunate withdrew its forces, assured that Chōshū posed no further threat to its national policies. In 1865, however, difficulties with the shogunate arose after radicals, led by TAKASUGI SHINSAKU, again took control of Chōshū. In 1866 shōgun TOKUGAWA IEMOCHI led a second expedition. This time, however, not only did several domains refuse to supply troops, but Chōshū had won the support of Satsuma (see SATSUMA-CHŌSHŪ ALLIANCE). The shogunal campaign went badly, and Iemochi's death in the fall of 1866 was used as a pretext to withdraw forces. The second campaign's failure severely damaged the shogunate's prestige and contributed greatly to its downfall in November 1867.

Chōsokabe family 長宗我部氏

(Chōsokabeshi; also known as Chōsogabeshi). Warlords of Tosa Province (now Kōchi Prefecture), Shikoku, and later *daimyō* there in the Sengoku period (1467–1568). Said to be descended from the HATA FAMILY, the Chōsokabe fought under the HOSOKAWA FAMILY during the wars of the period of the Northern and Southern Courts (1337–92) and became a leading family of Tosa. After a brief interruption of the male line at the beginning of the 16th century, the family rose again under Chōsokabe Kunichika (1502–60). His son CHŌSOKABE MOTOCHIKA brought all of Shikoku under his sway, but he was defeated by TOYOTOMI HIDEYOSHI in 1585 and his domain reduced to Tosa alone. His domainal legal code (see CHŌSOKABE MOTOCHIKA, 100-ARTICLE CODE OF) is a model of its kind. His son Morichika (1575–1615) sided with the losing Toyotomi faction in the Battle of SEKIGAHARA (1600), and his domain was confiscated. When Morichika was executed by the Tokugawa after the final assault on Ōsaka Castle in 1615 (see ŌSAKA CASTLE, SIEGES OF), the Chōsokabe were completely destroyed.

Chōsokabe Motochika 長宗我部元親

(1538–99). SENGOKU DAIMYŌ of Tosa Province (now Kōchi Prefecture) in Shikoku. After Motochika became head of the CHŌSOKABE FAMILY in 1560, he eliminated his rivals, expelled the provincial governor, and took full control of Tosa in 1575. By 1583 he had conquered all of Shikoku. In 1585 he was defeated by forces sent by TOYOTOMI HIDEYOSHI and was left with Tosa Province alone. Motochika then retired except for temporary service under Hideyoshi in Kyūshū in 1597 and in the INVASIONS OF KOREA IN 1592 AND 1597.

He is remembered for his survey of Tosa in 1587 (the registers are in the Kōchi Prefectural Library) and his domainal legal code of 1597 (see CHŌSOKABE MOTOCHIKA, 100-ARTICLE CODE OF).

Chōsokabe Motochika, 100-Article Code of 長宗我部元親百箇条

(Chōsokabe Motochika Hyakkajō, or Chōsokabe Okitegaki). Domainal laws (BUNKOKUHŌ) issued by CHŌSOKABE MOTOCHIKA, *daimyō* of Tosa domain (now Kōchi Prefecture), and his son Morichika (1575–1615) in 1597. Applicable to both his retainers and the domain's general population, they governed litigation, tax payments, inheritance, and relations between *samurai* and other classes.

chōson gappei→towns and villages, consolidation of

Chou En-lai→Zhou Enlai (Chou En-lai)

Chou Hung-ch'ing Incident→Zhou Hongqing (Chou Hung-ch'ing) Incident

Chou Tso-jen→Zhou Zuoren (Chou Tso-jen)

Chōya gunsai 朝野群載

A collection of official and unofficial writings of the Heian period (794–1185) compiled by the scholar-official Miyoshi Tameyasu (1049–1139), this anthology was intended as a reference for officials drafting state documents. Modeled on earlier literary collections, its first 3 fascicles were devoted to poetic works. The remaining 27 fascicles, 9 of which are now lost, presented a meticulously classified collection of official documents with occasional comments on proper bureaucratic procedure and documentary style. Although over 80 percent of the datable items are from the period 1067–1132, the earliest item dates from 737. Tameyasu attempted to provide samples of all forms of documents used in the central government of his day; his work is the principal source on documentary procedure of the early period of rule by retired emperors (INSEI). The author included documents of historical value and preserved information on relations between Japan and Song (Sung) dynasty (960–1279) China, the epidemic of 737, the incursion of Jurchen pirates (TOI) into northern Kyūshū (1019), and the activities of MINAMOTO NO YOSHIIE in the EARLIER NINE YEARS' WAR (1051–62).

Christian art, 16th and 17th centuries→namban art

Christian Churches, Japan Association of 日本キリスト教連合会

(Nihon Kirisutokyō Rengōkai). An association of all Japanese Christian church bodies, made up of 35 Christian denominations and 29 independent church bodies. It was established in 1946 for the purpose of maintaining communication among churches and guarding freedom of religion in Japan. It is affiliated with the JAPAN RELIGIOUS LEAGUE.

Christian daimyō キリシタン大名

(*kirishitan daimyō*). Regional rulers (see DAIMYŌ) of the late Sengoku period (1467–1568) and the Azuchi-Momoyama period (1568–1600) who were baptized Christians. Included under this loosely applied term are some of the epoch's greatest names, such as

ŌTOMO SŌRIN (Dom Francisco), as well as a number of petty barons. The "Christian daimyō" actively assisted the Jesuit missionaries in the conversion of their territories, sometimes through force, intimidation, and the destruction of native religious symbols and institutions. However, they were severely tested by the national unifier TOYOTOMI HIDEYOSHI, who restricted the practice of Christianity in 1587, and they disappeared when the Tokugawa regime in 1612 began persecuting the religion (see ANTI-CHRISTIAN EDICTS).

Their motives for conversion varied, as did the measure of their devotion and constancy. ŌMURA SUMITADA (Dom Bartolomeu), lord of the Sonogi region of Hizen Province (now part of Nagasaki Prefecture) was attracted to baptism in 1563 by the Jesuits' promise to ensure that Portuguese trading ships would call at harbors in his domain. He even ceded the area of Nagasaki to the Jesuits in 1580. Ōtomo Sōrin of Bungo Province (now part of Ōita Prefecture) was the leading power of Kyūshū when he was baptized in 1578 after 27 years of friendship with Jesuit missionaries. He remained faithful throughout the nine years of defeat and calamity that followed.

Some daimyō were drawn to Christianity by the model of a valued friend, and their example in turn influenced others. For instance, TAKAYAMA UKON (Dom Justo; baptized in 1564) influenced GAMŌ UJISATO (Dom Leão) to become a Christian, and Ujisato helped Ukon to persuade KURODA YOSHITAKA (Dom Simeão).

However, the "Christian daimyō" never formed a united front, and the Jesuits' faith in their allegiance was misplaced. By and large, they pursued their own interests before those of their church. They were daimyō first, and Christians second. The notable exception was Takayama Ukon, whose life was marked by an extraordinary devotion to his Christian faith. At the outset of the general persecution of Christianity in 1614, he was expelled from Japan by the Tokugawa regime and died the next year in exile in Manila. See also CHRISTIANITY.

Christianity キリスト教

(Kirisutokyō). Christianity was introduced into Japan in the middle of the 16th century. The religion was generally tolerated until the beginning of the 17th century, but the Tokugawa shogunate (1603–1867) eventually proscribed it and persecuted its adherents. When relations with the West were restored in the middle of the 19th century, Christianity was reintroduced and has continued to exist in Japan with varying fortunes.

Introduction to Japan—Portuguese traders first reached Japan in 1543, to be followed by the Jesuit missionary Francis XAVIER, who arrived in 1549 with two companions. Xavier's preaching met with some success, although his efforts were hampered by the language barrier. Reinforcements arrived to continue his work and were in general well received by local rulers, who often associated them with the lucrative Portuguese trade. Activity was concentrated in Kyūshū, especially Nagasaki, although Christian communities were also established in Honshū. In 1563 ŌMURA SUMITADA became the first *daimyō* to receive baptism, and by 1579 no fewer than six daimyō had been converted. By that time the number of Christians was estimated at about 100,000, but this figure includes those converts who embraced the faith at the behest of their Christian lords. In 1579 the Jesuit Alessandro VALIGNANO arrived to conduct the first of three inspection tours of the mission. When he left in 1582, he was accompanied by four boys who formed an embassy to Rome on behalf of the Christian daimyō of Kyūshū (see MISSION TO EUROPE OF 1582).

By this time Christianity had attracted the attention of national figures. The national unifier ODA NOBUNAGA favored the missionaries and granted them generous concessions. His successor, TOYOTOMI HIDEYOSHI, continued this policy until 1587, when, on realizing the extent of Christian influence in Kyūshū, he abruptly ordered missionaries to leave the country. His edict was neither obeyed nor enforced, but it marked the end of the initial favorable reception. The Jesuits were eventually joined by Spanish friars; while the new influx added impetus to evangelization, national rivalries gave rise to unseemly quarrels among the religious orders.

Martyrdoms—In 1596 the Spanish ship *San Felipe* foundered off Shikoku and the Japanese confiscated its rich cargo. A controversy among Japanese, Jesuits, and friars resulted; Hideyoshi once more turned anti-Christian and condemned to death the Franciscans and their parishioners in Kyōto. Twenty-six Christians—both foreigners and Japanese—were crucified at Nagasaki in 1597 (see TWENTY-SIX MARTYRS). No further hostile action was taken, and missionary work continued unobtrusively. By this time the Church had reached its greatest expansion, with the number of Christians being estimated at about 300,000. TOKUGAWA IEYASU, who became the de facto ruler in 1600, was at first willing to tolerate the missionaries' presence for the sake of the profitable Portuguese trade, but the arrival of Protestant Dutch and English merchants allowed him to act more freely against the Catholic missionaries. As the final showdown between Ieyasu and TOYOTOMI HIDEYORI, son of the late Hideyoshi, approached, Ieyasu turned against the Church, knowing that his rival commanded considerable support in western Japan, where Christian influence was strongest. Ieyasu was victorious, and in 1614 the Tokugawa shogunate ordered missionaries to leave the country; most of them departed, but some 40, including a few Japanese priests, remained to continue their work under cover.

Persecution and Suppression— Within a few years organized persecution commenced. In 1622, 51 Christians were executed at Nagasaki, and two years later 50 were burned alive in Edo (now Tōkyō). A total of 3,000 believers are estimated to have been martyred; this figure does not include the many who died as a result of sufferings in prison or in exile. In 1633 some 30 missionaries were executed, and by 1637 only 5 were left at liberty. The SHIMABARA UPRISING of 1637–38 prompted the government to sever contacts with the West, except for some merchants of the Dutch East India Company, confined to DEJIMA. Subsequent missionary attempts to enter and work in the country were unsuccessful.

The Japanese are noted for their religious tolerance, and the persecution was occasioned by social and political rather than purely religious factors. Christian exclusivism, with its unwillingness to tolerate other religions, aroused resentment in some circles. Missionaries were regarded as a potential fifth column preparing the way for Iberian colonialism. More significantly, the shogun-

ate was on the alert for any coalition of disaffected elements that might threaten its hegemony, and Christianity was viewed as a possible catalyst. Finally, Christian insistence on the primacy of the individual's conscience was regarded as subversive in a society that attached overwhelming importance to unconditional obedience to superiors.

Reintroduction—Japan's period of isolation ended in the mid-19th century, when Westerners were again allowed to enter the country. In 1859 a Catholic priest took up an appointment as interpreter for the French consulate in Edo, and in the same year representatives of three Protestant churches reached Japan. Ostensibly these ministers came to serve foreign residents, but their true aim was to begin direct work among the Japanese.

Kakure Kirishitan. In 1865 a group of people at Nagasaki publicly identified themselves as Christians. Soon various communities of KAKURE KIRISHITAN, or "hidden Christians," were discovered in the region. Located in remote areas where government surveillance was at its weakest, these communities had preserved their religion in secret for more than two centuries. Of approximately 60,000 Kakure Kirishitan discovered at that time, only about half chose to return to the reintroduced church. The anti-Christian laws were still in effect, and many of the discovered Christians were jailed or exiled to other parts of the country (see PERSECUTIONS AT URAKAMI). It was only in 1873 that the Meiji government withdrew religious sanctions, although freedom of religion was not specifically granted. Even the 1889 CONSTITUTION OF THE EMPIRE OF JAPAN guaranteed only qualified religious freedom "within limits not prejudicial to peace and not antagonistic to [believers'] duties as citizens."

Catholic. Catholic activity was entrusted to the Paris Foreign Mission Society until the beginning of the 20th century. A steady if unspectacular expansion took place, and by 1937 the Catholic population was reported as 118,000, with a preponderance of the faithful living in the Nagasaki region. A network of schools, mostly run by religious orders, was established throughout the country. In 1913 SOPHIA UNIVERSITY (Jōchi Daigaku) was founded in Tōkyō; the Sacred Heart College, founded in 1915, was reorganized as a women's university (UNIVERSITY OF THE SACRED HEART) in 1948; in the following year NANZAN UNIVERSITY was founded in Nagoya.

Orthodox. In 1872 Ioann Kasatkin, better known as Father NIKOLAI, established a branch of the Russian Orthodox Church (see HOLY ORTHODOX CHURCH) in Tōkyō. He consecrated an Orthodox cathedral in Kanda, Tōkyō, in 1891, and the church still remains a landmark in the capital. Nikolai died in 1912, at which time there were about 30,000 Orthodox believers in Japan. By 1931 membership had grown to 40,000, but in recent years the numbers have declined.

Protestant. In the first decade after missionary activity resumed in Japan, the Protestant church was represented there by four denominations (Anglican-Episcopal, Presbyterian, Dutch Reformed, and American Baptist Free Mission Society), joined later by representatives of other churches. From the beginning, importance was attached to education as a means of spreading the Christian message. Dōshisha English School (now DOSHISHA UNIVERSITY) was founded in Kyōto in 1875, and Aoyama Gakuin (now

Christianity This memorial in Nagasaki marks the site where 26 Japanese and foreign Christians were crucified in 1597 by order of Toyotomi Hideyoshi.

AOYAMA GAKUIN UNIVERSITY) and St. Paul's School (now RIKKYŌ UNIVERSITY) in Tōkyō in 1874. In 1953 INTERNATIONAL CHRISTIAN UNIVERSITY (Kokusai Kirisutokyō Daigaku) was founded in Tōkyō. The Protestant contribution to the development of women's education is also noteworthy.

Uchimura Kanzō. Missionary teachers in the Meiji period (1868–1912) were often regarded as representatives of a superior civilization, and Christianity was popularly identified with the West. This tendency was opposed by UCHIMURA KANZŌ, the founder of MUKYŌKAI or Nonchurch Christianity. In his later years Uchimura refused to be identified with any particular church, insisting on the need for a "Japanese Christianity" untainted by Western influence. Some of the issues raised by Uchimura have yet to be satisfactorily settled by the churches.

Social Activity—At the beginning of the 20th century Christians made a notable contribution to the foundation of the socialist and trade union movements in an effort to solve the grave social problems caused by rapid industrialization. Many of the founding members of the Social Democratic Party (Shakai Minshutō; 1901) were active Christians. A Christian, SUZUKI BUNJI, founded the YŪAIKAI or Friendship Association, in 1912; this later developed into the Nihon Rōdō Sōdōmei, or Japan Federation of Labor. The Nihon Nōmin Kumiai (Japan Farmers' Union) was founded in 1922 by two Christian socialists. Despite this contribution at the time of their foundation, many of these movements were later split by disputes and much of the initial Christian influence was weakened or lost.

The churches have also sponsored a variety of social and medical projects, such as hospitals, sanatoriums, leprosariums, and orphanages; the popular image of Christianity is often associated with such work.

War and Recovery—The growing spirit of nationalism in the 1930s raised problems of conscience for Christians, especially when the authorities urged attendance at Shintō shrines as "a civil manifestation of loyalty." Foreign missionaries of all churches were interned or repatriated at the outbreak of World War II or at best allowed limited freedom. In 1941 government pressure led to the formation of the Nihon Kirisuto Kyōdan, or UNITED CHURCH OF CHRIST IN JAPAN, a union of some 30 Protestant churches. After the war some churches withdrew from the union, but it is still regarded as the most influential Protestant body today.

The immediate postwar period witnessed a revival of Christian activity. The social upheaval and disillusionment caused by the nation's defeat prompted many Japanese to turn to Christianity to find some meaning in

Chūbu Sangaku National Park The Tateyama mountain group seen from Kurobe-daira on the northwestern shores of Lake Kurobe. A ropeway has made the mountains more accessible to visitors.

their lives. However, this period, coinciding approximately with the Allied OCCUPATION of 1945–52, was brief, and the disorganization of the churches at the time prevented their taking full advantage of the opportunity.

Christianity Today— At present Christianity in Japan is characterized by unobtrusive activity, with emphasis still placed on education as a means of spreading the gospel message. In recent years there has been a growing ecumenical spirit between the Protestant and Catholic churches, although contacts at the grass-roots level are often still tenuous. Discussions have been held between Christian and Buddhist scholars to reach a better mutual understanding and appreciation of the two religions. In 1990, Christians numbered some 1,075,000, or less than 1 percent of the population. There were 436,000 Catholics with some 800 parishes in 16 dioceses, while Protestants numbered 639,000 with nearly 7,000 churches.

Conclusion—In popular estimation Christianity is still regarded as a "foreign" creed, preaching admirable ideals but unsuitable for ordinary Japanese. Because of its "foreign" nature, the religion has been persecuted when demands for national identity were strong; it has been widely accepted during periods of social instability (the 16th century, the early Meiji period, and the immediate postwar period), but once social equilibrium was restored interest rapidly waned. Apart from the Nagasaki region, Christianity has yet to make any appreciable impact on rural communities; it draws its strength from the urban, professional classes.

Various aspects of Christian teaching differ fundamentally from the more traditional patterns of Japanese thought and outlook—for example, monotheism versus traditional polytheism; the concept of a transcendent God versus the immanent Japanese deities; an individual ethic versus a group-oriented ethic. It is doubtful whether organized Christianity can accommodate itself to traditional thought in Japan as much as Buddhism (also an "imported" religion) has done, but there still remains much scope for expressing Christian thought in a more Japanese form.

Christmas　　　　　　クリスマス

(Kurisumasu). Christmas was first celebrated in Japan as a religious observance in the mid-16th century by the converts of Spanish and Portuguese missionaries (see CHRISTIANITY). It was only in the early Meiji period (1868–1912) that Christmas was observed on a

larger scale, but even then it was mainly confined to churches and schools sponsored by foreign missionaries. From the early 20th century the Japanese began to adopt the custom of exchanging presents. From the early 1930s, department stores began holding Christmas sales, which conveniently coincided with distribution of the year-end wage bonus and the custom of presenting SEIBO (year-end presents). Christmas Day is not a holiday in Japan, although many people go to Western-style parties on Christmas Eve, friends and family members may exchange gifts, and parents sometimes give their children "decoration cakes" sold in bakeries and department stores. Except among Christians, the observance of Christmas in Japan is wholly secular in nature.

Chrysanthemum and the Sword→Benedict, Ruth Fulton

Chrysanthemum Festival　菊の節句

(Kiku no Sekku). Also called Chōyō no Sekku. Festival held on the ninth day of the ninth month in the old lunar calendar; now the least celebrated of the five SEKKU or seasonal celebrations. In China this day was called Chungyang (Ch'ong-yang; J: Chōyō) and was known for the custom of drinking chrysanthemum wine (kikuzake). In Japan it became an official event in the Heian period (794–1185); in the Edo period (1600–1868) the custom of holding elaborate chrysanthemum exhibits was begun. Because the ninth month of the lunar calendar fell at the time of the rice harvest, the festival was closely associated with harvest rites in rural villages.

chrysanthemums　　　　　　　菊

(kiku). Chrysanthemum morifolium. The chrysanthemum, a perennial flowering herb of the family Compositae, has been cultivated in Japan since ancient times and is celebrated as a plant representative of autumn. Its woody stem reaches a height of about 1 meter (3 ft) and its leaves are alternate and petioled. In autumn the stem branches out and each branchlet grows a flower head. Autumn chrysanthemums are classified by flower head size as ōgiku (large), chūgiku (medium), or kogiku (small). Varieties that bloom in spring (harugiku), summer (natsugiku), winter (kangiku), and throughout the year (shikizaki) have been developed, and there is also an edible variety known as shokuyōgiku.

Chrysanthemums were introduced to Japan from China in the 5th century for medicinal purposes. Ornamental varieties were introduced late in the 8th century. The Japanese nobility of the Heian period (794–1185) cultivated chrysanthemums, and the celebration of the CHRYSANTHEMUM FESTIVAL (now rarely observed) dates from this period. Chrysanthemums became popular among the common people in the Edo period (1600–1868), during which time many varieties were developed and growing techniques were perfected. The chrysanthemum has long been considered a noble flower, and the crest of the imperial household is a stylized representation of a chrysanthemum blossom.　　　　🌸 201

Chūbu Electric Power Co, Inc
中部電力［株］

(Chūbu Denryoku). Supplier of electricity to the prefectures of Aichi, Gifu, Mie, Nagano, and Shizuoka (west of the Fuji River) in cen-

tral Japan. Incorporated in 1951. The company ranks third among Japan's nine electric power companies. The company's total generating capacity in 1990 was 21 million kilowatts, of which 72 percent was furnished by thermoelectric plants, 16 percent by hydroelectric plants, and 12 percent by nuclear power plants. Plans call for diversifying fuel sources, with an emphasis on nuclear power and coal. In the fiscal year ending March 1991 the company sold 99.8 billion kilowatt-hours, total revenue was ¥1.8 trillion (US $13.1 billion), and capitalization stood at ¥369.6 billion (US $2.7 billion). Headquarters are in Nagoya, Aichi Prefecture.

Chūbu-Nippon Broadcasting Co, Ltd (CBC)　　中部日本放送［株］

(Chūbu-Nippon Hōsō). A commercial radio and television broadcasting station based in the city of Nagoya and serving the three surrounding prefectures of Aichi, Gifu, and Mie. It was established in 1950, at the same time as the MAINICHI BROADCASTING SYSTEM, INC (MBS), in Ōsaka, as one of the first commercial radio stations in Japan. Original backing came from the Chūnichi shimbun, a local daily newspaper, and financial interests in the greater Nagoya area. It began operating a television station in 1956 and went on to become an influential Chūbu (central Honshū) region broadcasting enterprise. As one of the key affiliate stations of the Japan News Network (JNN), a group of 25 commercial stations centered on TŌKYŌ BROADCASTING SYSTEM, INC (TBS), it also televises a wide variety of dramatic and educational programs to a national viewing audience.

Chūbu region　　　　　　中部地方

(Chūbu chihō). Encompassing Niigata, Toyama, Ishikawa, Fukui, Yamanashi, Nagano, Gifu, Shizuoka, and Aichi prefectures in central Honshū. Geographically divided into three districts: the HOKURIKU REGION on the Sea of Japan side, the Central Highlands (or Tōsan), and the TŌKAI REGION on the Pacific seaboard. The principal city of the region is NAGOYA. The region, largely mountainous, is dominated by the JAPANESE ALPS and contains numerous volcanoes including Mt. Fuji (Fujisan). Some of Japan's longest rivers, the Shinanogawa, Kisogawa, and Tenryūgawa, flow through the region. The Niigata Plain along the Sea of Japan is one of the largest rice-producing areas in Japan, and the Nōbi Plain on the Pacific coast is the most densely populated and highly industrialized area in this region. Numerous inland basins have very cold winters. The Pacific side is generally mild, and the Sea of Japan side has long snowy winters.

The Chūbu region includes three industrial areas (the Chūkyō Industrial Zone and the Tōkai and Hokuriku industrial regions). Agricultural products include rice, tea, mandarin oranges, strawberries, grapes, peaches, and apples. Fishing is important all along its coast. Area: 66,777 sq km (25,783 sq mi); pop: 21,020,562.

Chūbu Sangaku National Park
中部山岳国立公園

(Chūbu Sangaku Kokuritsu Kōen). Situated in central Honshū, in Nagano, Niigata, Toyama, and Gifu prefectures, this rugged region is dominated by the HIDA MOUNTAINS, also known as the Northern Alps, with peaks averaging 3,000 m (9,840 ft). Towering escarpments, ravines, and gorges have made this the foremost hiking and climbing area in

Flower of Autumn

The delicate simplicity of the chrysanthemum perfectly embodies the traditional Japanese concept of beauty. Its subtle charms have made this flower a favorite among the plants that adorn Japanese gardens, and its tidy blossoms are a cherished symbol of autumn. Long associated with nobility, chrysanthemums are invariably on display at ceremonial events in Japan. The cultivation of chrysanthemums first gained popularity as an elegant hobby during the Edo period (1600–1868) and still remains a beloved pastime, with exhibitions held every autumn. But these flowers are not merely treasured for their beauty—growers in northeastern Japan cultivate smaller varieties whose petals, served boiled and vinegared, are an autumn delicacy.

Kogiku (small chrysanthemums), often used in *bonsai* or displayed freshly cut.

Futokuda, a chrysanthemum grown mainly for formal exhibitions.

Ōzukami, a lushly colored chrysanthemum featured prominently in flower shows.

Kudamono, the subtlest and most elegant of the larger varieties of the chrysanthemum, much beloved by gardeners.

Kengai (cascade chrysanthemums), often grown and shaped for competitions.

Ornamental detail on a Chinese-style gate at the Ninomaru Palace in Kyōto's Nijō Castle. The use of stylized gold chrysanthemums indicates the noble standing of the castle's original occupants.

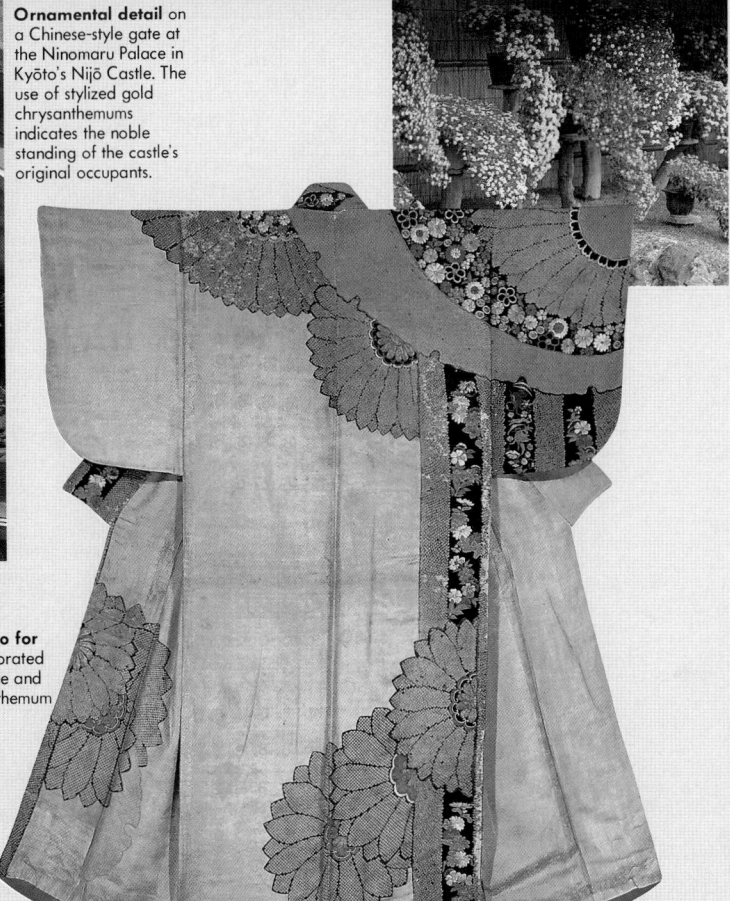

A silk kimono for autumn, decorated with both large and small chrysanthemum patterns.

An autumn-flower motif adorning a lacquered incense box from the Muromachi period (1333–1568).

Chūgūji This convent-temple's main icon, the Asuka-period lacquer-on-wood image of the bodhisattva Miroku, shown here, has been designated a National Treasure.

Japan. In the center of the park rises the mountain group known as TATEYAMA. Together the group is considered one of Japan's three sacred mountains (with FUJISAN and HAKUSAN). To its north lie the peaks SHIROUMADAKE and KASHIMA YARIGATAKE. South of Tateyama are YAKUSHIDAKE; YARIGATAKE; HOTAKADAKE, the third highest mountain in Japan; and NORIKURADAKE. The forests consist mainly of Japanese beech (*buna*), Japanese oak (*nara*), and evergreen conifers. The rivers AZUSAGAWA and KUROBEGAWA cut deep canyons through the forests. The gorge KUROBE KYŌKOKU, which terminates at the KUROBE DAM, has spectacular fall foliage. There are numerous hot-spring resorts. Area: 1,743 sq km (673 sq mi).

Chūchō jijitsu   中朝事実

(True Facts of the Central Realm). Historical work in two volumes written in 1669 by the Confucian scholar YAMAGA SOKŌ. Sokō claimed that in its history and natural features Japan was in no way inferior to China and that Japan, not China, was the true Middle Kingdom, or central realm.

Chūdenkō Corporation   ［株］中電工

(Chūdenkō). Company engaged in planning, designing, and construction for electrical work, electrical and optical communication systems, and mechanical and plumbing work. Incorporated in 1944, it is affiliated with Chūgoku Electric Power Co, Inc. Sales for the fiscal year ending March 1991 totaled ¥160.2 billion (US $1.2 billion), and the company was capitalized at ¥2.6 billion (US $19.0 million) in the same year. Headquarters are in Hiroshima.

Chūgai Pharmaceutical Co, Ltd   中外製薬［株］

(Chūgai Seiyaku). Manufacturer of prescription, over-the-counter, and diagnostic drugs; agrochemicals; and food products. Founded in 1925. Chūgai is a fully integrated, research-oriented company, emphasizing the research and development of biotechnological products. Its anti-ulcerant, Sucralfate, is marketed worldwide. Sales for the fiscal year ending December 1990 totaled ¥125.5 billion (US $939.7 million), and capi-

talization stood at ¥21.0 billion (US $157.2 million). Headquarters are in Tōkyō.

Chūgan Engetsu   中巌円月

(1300–1375). Zen monk of the Rinzai sect and poet associated with GOZAN LITERATURE (Chinese learning in medieval Japanese Zen monasteries). Born in Kamakura, Chūgan studied in China from 1325 to 1332. His poems are collected in the anthology *Tōkai ichiō shū.* He wrote the *Nihonsho,* a history of Japan which argued that the Japanese imperial house was descended from the Chinese Duke of Chou (Zhou); the work was suppressed by imperial order.

chūgen   中元

Custom of giving gifts at midsummer, particularly at the time of the Buddhist BON FESTIVAL (all souls' day festival); also the gifts themselves. Traditionally, offerings to the souls of deceased family members made during Bon, in the seventh month of the lunar calendar, were distributed to relatives and others so as to share symbolically divine qualities among mortals. This custom has become secularized in recent years, so that even though gifts are given in coincidence with the Bon Festival, they are no longer offerings to the souls of the deceased but are purchased at a store and delivered directly to a family. *Chūgen* gifts, as is the case with year-end (SEIBO) gifts, are never given within a family but are customarily presented to one's social superior, such as a teacher of traditional arts, and not to those below one's own status. See also GIFT GIVING.

chūgen   中間

A type of low-ranking retainer in the service of a warrior; popularly known as *orisuke.* The term, in use from the 13th century through the Edo period (1600–1868), literally means "middle space," indicating that such men were ranked between the lowliest SAMURAI or footsoldiers (ASHIGARU) and menials (*komono* or *kobito*). In the Tokugawa bureaucracy, about 550 *chūgen* were divided into three groups and placed under the charge of the junior councillors (WAKADO-SHIYORI); they guarded gates or served as standard-bearers. DAIMYŌ had similar low-ranking retainers in their domainal governments.

Chūgoku Electric Power Co, Inc   中国電力［株］

(Chūgoku Denryoku). Company supplying electricity to the prefectures of Hiroshima, Okayama, Tottori, Shimane, and Yamaguchi in western Honshū. Incorporated in 1951. Because the CHŪGOKU REGION has few sites suitable for hydroelectric generation, the company has relied mainly on thermoelectric generation. Since 1974 the company has been expanding its Shimane nuclear power plant. The company's total generating capacity in 1990 was 9.2 million kilowatts, of which 69 percent was furnished by thermoelectric plants, 11 percent by hydroelectric plants, and 20 percent by nuclear power plants. In the fiscal year ending March 1991 annual revenue totaled ¥897.5 billion (US $6.5 billion), and the company was capitalized at ¥183.1 billion (US $1.3 billion). Headquarters are in Hiroshima.

Chūgoku Mountains   中国山地

(Chūgoku Sanchi). Mountain range extending east to west through the Chūgoku region, western Honshū. It forms the watershed between the north and south portions of west-

ern Honshū, i.e., the San'in and San'yō regions. There are numerous peaks in the 1,000 m (3,300 ft) range, including SAMBESAN (1,126 m; 3,694 ft), DŌGOYAMA (1,269 m; 4,163 ft), and KAMMURIYAMA (1,339 m; 4,393 ft).

Chūgoku region   中国地方

(Chūgoku *chihō*). Encompasses the entire western tip of Honshū, comprising Hiroshima, Okayama, Shimane, Tottori, and Yamaguchi prefectures. With the Chūgoku Mountains as the dividing line, the Inland Sea side is called the San'yō region and the Sea of Japan side, the San'in region. It is a mountainous region with many small basins and coastal plains. The most heavily populated areas are along the Inland Sea coast, around the cities of HIROSHIMA (the principal city), KURASHIKI, and OKAYAMA. The Inland Sea coast is a major area of industry and commerce. The Okayama Plain and the coastal plains along the Sea of Japan are important areas for the production of rice. The warm, dry climate of the Inland Sea coast is also ideal for citrus fruits and grapes. The waters off the coast were once among Japan's richest fishing grounds, but catches have declined because of industrial pollution. Area: 31,790 sq km (12,274 sq mi); pop: 7,745,085.

Chūgoku zanryū koji →displaced Japanese war orphans in China

chūgū   中宮

(empress, consort). In the Heian period (794–1185), a title for a principal wife of an emperor; similar to the title KŌGŌ. Fujiwara no Onshi (885–954), wife of Emperor DAIGO, was the first of several empresses to be designated *chūgū* instead of the customary *kōgō.* When Emperor ICHIJŌ was forced in 1000 to take FUJIWARA NO MICHINAGA's daughter Shōshi (JŌTŌ MON'IN) as his second empress (the first was FUJIWARA NO TEISHI), she was designated *chūgū,* the senior lady retaining the title *kōgō.* The same practice was followed later whenever an emperor had two empresses. Later the titles came to be used interchangeably.

Chūgūji   中宮寺

Convent-temple affiliated first with the HOSSŌ SECT, later with the SHINGON SECT, and, since World War II, with the Shōtoku sect of Buddhism. Also known as Ikaruga convent, Chūgūji, located east of the temple HŌRYŪJI in the town of Ikaruga, Nara Prefecture, was moved 500 meters (985 ft) west of its original site during the late 16th century when it became part of Hōryūji. Tradition has it that Chūgūji was once a palace built in 596 by Prince SHŌTOKU for his mother. Temple tradition holds that in her honor he had an image made of Nyoirin KANNON as the main icon. However, the extant image, designated a National Treasure, has been identified as the bodhisattva MIROKU and dated as having been made during the Asuka period (593–710). Another National Treasure of Chūgūji consists of portions of two embroidered tapestries known as the *Tenjukoku mandara* (Tenjukoku Mandala).

Chu Hsi school →Shushigaku

Chūjitsuya Co, Ltd   ［株］忠実屋

(Chūjitsuya). Supermarket chain operator with 77 stores in the Tōkyō metropolitan area. Founded in 1933; incorporated in 1951. The company has a joint venture in Malaysia, named Chūjitsu Superstore Sdn

Bhd. Sales for the fiscal year ending February 1991 totaled ¥315.4 billion (US $2.4 billion), and capitalization stood at ¥12.3 billion (US $94.3 million) in the same year. Headquarters are in Tōkyō.

chūkan shōsetsu 中間小説

("midway" or "middlebrow" fiction). Term referring to a type of novel or short story standing midway between "serious" and "popular" literature and incorporating some of the qualities of both. It has been said that the term was first used in the early post–World War II period by HAYASHI FUSAO to describe the fiction that was appearing in newly published popular magazines such as *Bessatsu bungei shunjū* (1946), *Nihon shōsetsu* (1947), and *Shōsetsu shinchō* (1947) by writers who included ISHIZAKA YŌJIRŌ, FUNAHASHI SEIICHI, INOUE YASUSHI, and TAMURA TAIJIRŌ.

As time went on, the term tended more and more to mean the application of some of the techniques of the serious novel to material that was increasingly common and sensational. But from the late 1950s, literature followed the general trend toward mass production and mass consumption, and the level of literary interest went steadily down. What would once have been referred to as *chūkan shōsetsu* seemed almost to have become, in an essentially middlebrow culture, a kind of "high-class" popular literature. See also FŪZOKU SHŌSETSU; POPULAR FICTION.

Chūkyō Industrial Zone 中京工業地帯

(Chūkyō Kōgyō Chitai). Centered on the city of Nagoya. Japan's third largest industrial zone, it extends east to Toyohashi in Aichi Prefecture, north to southern Gifu Prefecture, and west to northern Mie Prefecture. The major industries are chemical fibers in the cities of Gifu and Okazaki, automobiles in Toyota, petroleum refining and petrochemicals in Yokkaichi, and steel and machinery in Nagoya.

chūma 中馬

(packhorse service). Commodity transportation service of the Edo period (1600–1868). This carrying trade originated in the 17th century in mountainous Shinano Province (now Nagano Prefecture), where farmers hired out their workhorses as pack animals. During the 18th century it expanded, coming into increasing competition with the services of the licensed forwarding agents (TOIYA) on the major roads. In response to the lawsuits of the latter, the Tokugawa shogunate in 1764 regulated but did not abolish the *chūma*.

Chungking government → Chongqing (Chungking) government

Chūnichi shimbun 中日新聞

A leading daily newspaper of central Japan, published in the city of Nagoya. The paper was launched in 1942 when two prominent Nagoya dailies, the *Shin Aichi* and the *Nagoya shimbun*, merged to form the *Chūbu Nippon shimbun*. In 1965 its name was changed to *Chūnichi shimbun*. The paper is managed by the Chūnichi Shimbunsha, which publishes two other papers, the *Hokuriku chūnichi shimbun* (in Kanazawa) and the *Tōkyō shimbun*. Circulation was 2.3 million in 1990.

Chūō kōron 中央公論

(The Central Review). An important monthly general-interest magazine. It was originally launched in 1887 as the *Hanseikai*

zasshi, a small coterie magazine of a Kyōto student group known as the Hanseikai, which was devoted to character building and abstinence from alcohol. The magazine moved to Tōkyō in 1896, and in 1899 the name was changed to *Chūō kōron*. It became more of a literary journal as time went by. TAKITA CHOIN joined the magazine as editor and expanded it into a general-interest magazine that included articles on politics, literature, education, religion, and economics. In the early decades of the 20th century it provided writers like TANIZAKI JUN'ICHIRŌ, SHIGA NAOYA, and AKUTAGAWA RYŪNOSUKE with a forum for their writing and helped launch their careers. YOSHINO SAKUZŌ and ŌYAMA IKUO, two champions of TAISHŌ DEMOCRACY, exerted considerable influence on political opinion through their contributions to the magazine. Toward the end of World War II, it was suppressed by the Japanese military authorities. Publication resumed in 1946, and *Chūō kōron* continues to be an influential journal of opinion and current affairs.

Chūō Kōron Sha, Inc ［株］中央公論社

(Chūō Kōron Sha). Publishing house. Started by a study group at the Buddhist temple Nishi Honganji in Kyōto in 1887 in order to publish the magazine *Hanseikai zasshi* (Magazine of the Self-Examination Society). The publishing house moved to Tōkyō in 1896, and in 1899 the title of the magazine was changed to CHŪŌ KŌRON (The Central Review). During World War II, the firm was suppressed by the government because of its liberal stance and was finally ordered to close down in 1944. After the war, *Chūō kōron* was revived. Other periodicals published by the company include the women's magazine FUJIN KŌRON, the fashion magazine *Mari Kurēru* (Marie Claire), and the cooking magazine *Kurashi no sekkei* (Life Design).

Chūō Kyōiku Shingikai → Central Council for Education

Chūō University 中央大学

(Chūō Daigaku). Private, coeducational university located in the city of Hachiōji, Tōkyō Prefecture. Its predecessor was the Igirisu Hōritsu Gakkō (the English Law School), founded in 1885. The school developed with an emphasis on the study of British and American jurisprudence. In 1903 it became Tōkyō Hōgakuin Daigaku (Tōkyō College of Law) and in 1905 took its present name. It maintains faculties of law, economics, commerce, literature, and science and engineering. Night courses are offered in all departments, and it has affiliated high schools. Enrollment in 1989 was 29,851.

Chūō Ward 中央区

(Chūō Ku). One of the 23 wards of Tōkyō. Located at the mouth of the River Sumida (Sumidagawa), it is a commercial and economic center with many textile and paper wholesale dealers. The NIHOMBASHI district is a banking and shopping area, while the GINZA district is a thriving shopping and amusement center. A central wholesale fish market is located in the Tsukiji district. The Kabutochō district, home of the TŌKYŌ STOCK EXCHANGE, is called the Wall Street of Japan. Pop: 68,041.

Chūritsu Rōren 中立労連

(abbreviation of Chūritsu Rōdō Kumiai Renraku Kaigi; Federation of Independent Unions). Federation formed in 1956 by 13 labor unions (with 750,000 members) not affiliated with any national labor organiza-

tion. In 1987 Chūritsu Rōren dissolved and became part of RENGŌ (Japanese Trade Union Confederation). Since many of its unions were in growth industries, it had great influence on nationwide wage bargaining patterns. Chūritsu Rōren took a moderate political stance and advocated the unification of a labor front based on private-sector workers, a position that resembled that of Dōmei (Japanese Confederation of Labor). In 1987, with 10 affiliated organizations comprising 1,599,000 individual members, Chūritsu Rōren was the third largest of Japan's labor federations. It was a driving force in forming Rengō. See also LABOR UNIONS.

Chūseikai 中正会

(Upright Party). Political party formed in the Diet in December 1913 by 21 members of the Ekirakukai and 16 members of the Seiyū Kurabu (a faction of the RIKKEN SEIYŪKAI). Founded by OZAKI YUKIO, HANAI TAKUZŌ, and several other critics of the oligarchs (*genrō*) with the aid of the Kokumintō (National Party) and the RIKKEN DŌSHIKAI. With the establishment of the TERAUCHI MASATAKE cabinet in October 1916, almost all members of the Chūseikai were absorbed into the KENSEIKAI, and the party disbanded.

chū senkyoku sei 中選挙区制

(medium-sized constituency system). Common term for the electoral districting system for the lower house of the DIET that was established in 1925 and continues in revised form down to the present. It operates on the principle of dividing each Japanese prefecture into a number of separate electoral districts, each of which sends between three and five representatives to the lower house. These districts are termed "medium-sized" in contrast to both the earlier "large constituency" system in which each prefecture composed a single multimember district, and to the "small" or single-member constituency system found in various other countries with parliamentary systems. See ELECTIONS.

Chūsonji 中尊寺

Head temple of the TENDAI SECT of Buddhism in the Tōhoku (northern Honshū) area; located in the town of HIRAIZUMI in Iwate Prefecture. There is a tradition that the Buddhist priest ENNIN (794–864) founded the temple. According to temple inscriptions, Chūsonji was rebuilt by Fujiwara no Kiyohira (1056–1128), in honor of emperors Horikawa and TOBA and to console the souls of warriors killed during the EARLIER NINE YEARS' WAR (1051–62) and the LATER THREE YEARS' WAR (1083–87). Construction was begun in 1105, and the temple was dedicated in 1126.

The original complex contained an esoteric pagoda (*tahōtō*) as well as several Amida halls (*amidadō*)—notably the Daichōjuin (Great Hall of Longevity) and the Konjikidō (Golden-Colored Hall)—a sutra repository (*kyōzō*), a bell tower, a great gate, and other buildings. The finished complex had over 40 temples and shrines, as well as over 300 cells for priests. The prestige of the temple began to decline at the end of the 12th century, and a fire in 1337 destroyed many buildings. Some were rebuilt by the DATE FAMILY in the 17th century. Today only two buildings in the temple precincts remain from the Fujiwara era: the Golden-Colored Hall, which preserves a number of national treasures, and the sutra repository. — *See photo, next page.*

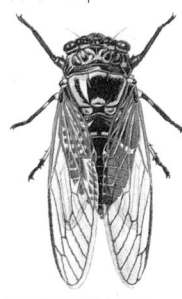

Chūsonji The interior of the Konjikidō (Golden-Colored Hall). The central dais, inlaid with mother-of-pearl and precious stones, contains the mummy of Fujiwara no Kiyohira, who rebuilt the temple in 1124. Gold leaf covers the ceiling and floor of this National Treasure.

cicadas The *kumazemi*, which grows to as much as 7 cm in length, is the largest of the more than 30 species of cicada found in Japan.

Chūyūki 中右記

Also called *Munetada Kō ki*, or *Gurin*. Diary of the Heian-period (794–1185) courtier Fujiwara no Munetada (1062–1141). The diary, over 100 volumes of which are still extant, covers the years 1087–1138. It contains a wealth of information on political, economic, social, and religious affairs in the early years of rule by retired emperors (INSEI).

Chūzan'ō 中山王

(King of Chūzan). Title of kings in the Ryū-kyū Islands from the 14th century until the establishment of Okinawa Prefecture in 1879. In the mid-14th century three kingdoms (Hokuzan, Chūzan, and Nanzan) emerged on the island of Okinawa. Their rulers entered into tributary relations with China's Ming dynasty (1368–1644) and received the titles Hokuzan'ō, Chūzan'ō, and Nanzan'ō respectively. In 1429 King Shō Hashi (1372–1439) of Chūzan united the three kingdoms. The title became synonymous with that of king of the Ryūkyūs. Many literary works on Okinawa refer to it as Chūzan. See also OKINAWA.

Chūzenji, Lake 中禅寺湖

(Chūzenjiko). Also called Lake Chūgūji and Lake Sachinoumi. Lake in the city of Nikkō, northwestern Tochigi Prefecture, central Honshū, located under the southern slope of the mountain NANTAISAN. The waters of the lake flow eastward to become the KEGON FALLS. It is part of Nikkō National Park. Area: 11.5 sq km (4.4 sq mi); circumference: 24 km (15 mi); depth: 163 m (535 ft); altitude: 1,269 m (4,163 ft).

cicadas 蟬

(*semi*). In Japanese, *semi* is the common name for insects of the order Hemiptera, family Cicadidae. About 1,500 species of these insects are known in the world, of which 35 live in Japan. Japanese cicadas are 1–7 centimeters (0.4–2.8 in) in length; the largest is the *kumazemi* (*Cryptotympana facialis*). The larval period is from two to six years. Adults feed on sap from trees, with some species, such as the *aburazemi* (*Graptopsaltria nigrofuscata*), sucking juice from fruits, and others, such as the *iwasaki kusazemi* (*Mogannia iwasakii*), sucking sap from grass.

In the Japanese poetry of the Nara (710–794) and Heian (794–1185) periods, the cicada appears as an insect of autumn and a symbol of solitude and melancholy, probably because of the influence of Chinese literature. And even though in the HAIKU of the Edo period (1600–1868) it was a symbol of the thriving life of full summer, there was a lingering hint of the fleetingness of life. It is as a summer insect that most Japanese now think of the cicada.

citizens' movements 市民運動

(*shimin undō*). A term that originally referred to nationwide campaigns of the 1950s and early 1960s in which ordinary citizens (*shimin*) temporarily joined left-wing student, labor, and socialist organizations to oppose the ruling conservative party's decisions on specific social and political issues (see also STUDENT MOVEMENT). The most notable instances were the movements to ban atomic weapons (see ATOMIC WEAPONS, MOVEMENT TO BAN), terminate the UNITED STATES–JAPAN SECURITY TREATIES, and end the Vietnam War (see PEACE MOVEMENT). From the mid-1960s the term *shimin undō* came to refer to local protests by groups of ordinary citizens against industrial pollution and environmental destruction caused by economic development.

In the mid-1960s the Japanese public, which a decade earlier had been willing to overlook such side effects of industrial development as the introduction of toxic chemicals into the environment and general environmental pollution, moved to protest against an array of "public hazards" (*kōgai*). The genesis of much of this opposition lay in the "victims' movements" (*higaisha undō*) organized by several groups of farmers, fishermen, and their families who suffered physical harm from POLLUTION-RELATED DISEASES. These groups soon attracted the attention and interest of doctors, lawyers, scientists, professors, students, journalists, and others with the resources and willingness to aid them through political action. Activist lawyers, many of them affiliated with left-wing labor and political organizations, provided the legal expertise needed to file suit for damages. By 1973 all of these suits had ended with landmark judgments in the plaintiffs' favor, and by about the same time antipollution and antidevelopment protest had achieved the force and character of a general social movement.

Between 1967 and 1973 constant media coverage of the victims' legal proceedings won them considerable public sympathy and stimulated intense concern about all types of pollution, arousing citizens to organize local movements to prevent pollution hazards from reaching lethal proportions elsewhere. Housewives, for example, already organized to protest prices, product quality, and other CONSUMER MOVEMENT issues, formed special groups to attack such urban problems as traffic, smog, and refuse disposal.

The local movements of the 1960s and early 1970s took pride in their independence and grass roots character. The typical citizens' movement styled itself as a nonpartisan, nonideological coalition organized to protest a specific pollution or development project. It tended to rely on existing organizations to arouse local interests in its goals, but it usually created a council to transcend established political and cultural divisions within the community.

After the mid-1970s the issues addressed

by citizens' movements began to extend beyond local concerns about pollution and land development to encompass broader issues of global environmental concern. The 1979 accident at the nuclear plant at Three Mile Island in the United States aroused concern over the use of nuclear power in Japan, and opposition picked up after the Tsuruga radiation leakage incident in 1981. After the 1986 accident at the nuclear power plant at Chernobyl in the Soviet Union, Japanese antinuclear movements became even more intense. In 1988 residents of the Noto Peninsula, Ishikawa Prefecture, filed suit to prevent the construction of a nuclear power plant there. The following year citizens of the village of Rokkasho, Aomori Prefecture, recalled their mayor, who favored constructing a nuclear-power-related facility in the area, and elected a mayor who supported a freeze on planning for the facility.

The environment remained a key concern of citizens' movements through the 1970s and 1980s. The most widely publicized environmental action of this period was opposition to the construction of an airport in ISHIGAKIJIMA, Okinawa Prefecture. When plans for the airport were announced in 1979 it was discovered that its construction would destroy valuable species of coral. Japanese environmental activists immediately began protests to halt construction of the airport. They received support from overseas environmental groups, which recommended that the airport developers reconsider their plans. In 1989, after protracted protests and much publicity, Okinawa Prefecture finally decided to cancel construction at the original site and began searching for a new location for the airport.

The 1980s also saw a resurgence of the citizens' movement against nuclear weapons in Japan. The movement dates from the atomic bombings of Hiroshima and Nagasaki in 1945 and has wide public support. It became more active during the nuclear weapons buildup by the United States and the Soviet Union in the early 1980s and was fueled by the mass protests in Europe that followed the deployment of cruise missiles there in 1982 and 1983.

As citizens' movements grew more conscious of global concerns in the 1970s and 1980s their organization began to change. Permanent organizations were set up in place of previous localized, temporary organizational structures. Permanent headquarters and staffs were formed, together with networks for exchanging information with domestic and foreign groups holding similar objectives. The tactics used by the groups also changed. In contrast to the earlier "victims' movements," which gained prominence by demanding legal compensation for victims of industrial pollution and development, later movements were of the "preventive" type and employed such methods as environmental impact assessment to prevent pollution and environmental disruption. In the late 1980s a number of participants in citizens' movements were elected to public office, at both the local and national levels. Japanese citizens' movements have come to play an important role in the resolution of environmental and other issues and have gained considerable influence with government, business, and the mass media.

Citizen Watch Co, Ltd

シチズン時計[株]

(Shichizun Tokei). Japan's largest wristwatch maker. Citizen Watch was incorporated in 1930 to manufacture wristwatches domestically; it now also produces lens shutters, electronic equipment, and machine tools. The company concluded a business tie-up with Bulova Watch Co of the United States in 1960, thus entering the overseas market. Citizen has sales companies in the United States and Germany, as well as watch manufacturing companies in South Korea, Taiwan, Hong Kong, and Mexico, and it also produces watches for China on a consignment basis. Total sales for the fiscal year ending March 1991 were ¥247.8 billion (US $1.8 billion), with an export ratio of 64 percent. The company was capitalized at ¥25.7 billion (US $187.3 million) in the same year. Headquarters are in Tōkyō.

C. Itoh & Co, Ltd → Itōchū Corporation

Civil Code   民法

(Mimpō). The first project to construct a civil code in Japan was headed by G. E. BOISSONADE DE FONTARABIE, who used the French Civil Code as a model; the code was promulgated in 1890 and is referred to as the "Old Civil Code." This version faced strong opposition, however, and did not go into effect in 1893 as the legislation required, because it was felt that it would vitiate the Japanese people's traditional concepts of obligations and responsibilities. A new committee to examine legal codes was established, with HOZUMI NOBUSHIGE, TOMII MASAAKI, and UME KENJIRŌ as members. They also were influenced by the French Civil Code but took as their model the first draft of the German Civil Code, which had just been made public.

Among the five chapters that compose the Civil Code in effect to this day, the first three were promulgated in 1896 and consist of General Provisions, followed by RIGHTS IN REM and Obligations, or property law. Domestic Relations and Inheritance, or family law, followed in 1898.

The code, being a product of modern liberalism, is founded on the principles of freedom and equality, and acknowledges absolute private PROPERTY RIGHTS and FREEDOM OF CONTRACT. However, as Japanese capitalism developed, issues emerged that could not be resolved under the principles of the code, resulting in increasing inequalities. After World War I, problems in areas such as housing and the increasing size of enterprises developed to the point that the code's provisions for rental relations and labor-management relations, respectively, were rendered inadequate. Consequently, legislation such as the Leased Land Law, the Leased House Law, and the Labor Standards Law was enacted. In the area of mortgages, the code was again insufficient, and the Law for the Hypothecization of Factory Property (1905), the Trust Law (1922), and the Enterprise Security Law (1958) were thus enacted. See also LEASED LAND RIGHTS; LEASED HOUSE RIGHTS.

Family law was formed around the household system of premodern times. However, the post–World War II CONSTITUTION OF JAPAN took the concepts of respect for the individual and the basic equality of the sexes as primary tenets, and major amendments to the inheritance and domestic relations chapters thus became necessary. The old household system was abolished. Two new influential provisions established that private rights defer to the public good and recognized the equality of men and women. During the 1970s, a reexamination of the property system for married couples and the inheritance law system was conducted by the Ministry of Justice, and the inheritance system was amended effective at the beginning of 1981. See also INHERITANCE LAW; MARRIAGE LAW; OBLIGATION; PARENT AND CHILD, LEGAL DEFINITION OF.

Civil Code controversy   民法典論争

(Mimpōten ronsō). Dispute among legal specialists from 1889 to 1892 over the nation's first modern code of private law. Promulgated in 1890, the "Old Civil Code" (Kyū Mimpō) had not been implemented because of strong criticism from some legal experts, and in 1898 it was replaced by the "New Civil Code" (Shin Mimpō). The controversy centered on the French style and inspiration of the code, most of its critics having been trained in English law and most of its supporters in French law. Since the Penal Code, in force since 1882, was closely patterned after French law, enforcement of the Civil Code would give men trained in French law an enormous advantage in bar and civil service examinations.

From 1870 on, various agencies had worked on drafts of a civil code. A French legal adviser, G.E. BOISSONADE DE FONTARABIE, was put in charge in 1880 and completed most of a five-book code patterned after the French Civil Code by 1886. The remaining sections, dealing with inheritance and family law, were drafted in 1887 by two French-trained Japanese, Isobe Shirō (1851–1923) and Kumano Toshizō (1854–99). In 1888 the Ministry of Justice revised the Isobe-Kumano draft to give support to the *samurai* family tradition of an authoritarian headship and primogeniture.

Meanwhile, the German legal adviser K. F. Hermann ROESLER had drafted the Commercial Code. Despite public controversy, both codes were promulgated in 1890. As soon as the first Diet convened, a two-year postponement of the Commercial Code was voted by large majorities in both houses of the Diet. Encouraged by this action, a member of the "postponement faction" (enkiha), HOZUMI YATSUKA, published an article entitled "Mimpō idete chūkō horobu" (If the Civil Code Comes in, Loyalty and Filial Piety Will Go) in the journal of Tōkyō Hōgakuin, a law school (now Chūō University) that taught only English law. This was, in fact, a gross misrepresentation of the sections of the code dealing with family and inheritance as they stood after revision. A rival private law

Lake Chūzenji
A wintertime view of the lake, with the mountain Nantaisan in the background. Hotels and vacation homes ring the lake.

school, Meiji Hōritsu Gakkō (now Meiji University), which taught French law, was the stronghold of the "quick enforcement faction" (dankōha).

In 1892 the Diet passed a law postponing the Civil Code (and a large part of the Commercial Code) until the end of 1896. The government reluctantly appointed a Codes Investigating Committee (Hōten Chōsakai), among whose members the postponers were in the ascendant, and wholesale revision of the Civil Code became inevitable. The "New Civil Code," completed in 1898 after a second postponement, was closer to German law than to French, both in structure and in content.

civilian control of the military
文民統制

(bummin tōsei). Because of Japan's bitter experience with militarism in the past, the 1947 CONSTITUTION OF JAPAN stipulated in article 66 that the prime minister and cabinet ministers had to be civilians. In creating the SELF DEFENSE FORCES, a provision was made that its head, the director-general of the Defense Agency, would be responsible to the prime minister. The SECURITY COUNCIL plays an important role in ensuring civilian control over the military.

Civil Information and Education Section of SCAP
民間情報教育局

(Minkan Jōhō Kyōiku Kyoku). Abbreviated as CIE; an organization under SCAP (Supreme Commander for the Allied Powers) in charge of overseeing education in occupied Japan from September 1945 until April 1952. Its goal was to increase democracy and remove militaristic and ultranationalistic influences in the educational system. See also EDUCATIONAL REFORMS OF 1947.

civil liberties, protection of
人権擁護

(jinken yōgo). The modern Western idea of fundamental human rights was first introduced to Japan in the latter half of the 19th century. But it was only after World War II that Japan established constitutional guarantees of civil liberties. Although the 1889 CONSTITUTION OF THE EMPIRE OF JAPAN guaranteed a number of rights and freedoms in chapter II, they were all subject to restriction by the national Diet and, ultimately, to imperial prerogative. Under the constitution of 1889, there was no JUDICIAL REVIEW of legislation, and, with the rise of militarism in the second quarter of the 20th century, a series of laws was enacted that limited free exercise of basic democratic rights. See also PEACE PRESERVATION LAW OF 1925.

The 1947 CONSTITUTION OF JAPAN, on the other hand, was created as the supreme law of the land by express declaration that "no law . . . or other act of government . . . contrary to the provisions hereof, shall have legal force or validity" (art. 98). Furthermore, it vested in the Supreme Court as the court of last resort the "power to determine the constitutionality of any law . . ." (art. 81), and thus made the judiciary a major safeguard of civil liberties.

Chapter III of the constitution enumerates a variety of rights and freedoms, including freedom of expression, freedom of assembly and association, and freedom of religious faith, as well as universal suffrage, equal protection under the law, the rights of the ac-

cused, and many socioeconomic rights. Consequent to this constitutional entrenchment of a bill of rights, many prewar statutory provisions were either abolished or revised. The most important of all was a total reconstruction of the CRIMINAL PROCEDURE. The old inquisitorial system was replaced by an accusatorial system modeled on that prevailing in the United States, and the 1948 Code of Criminal Procedure established new rules of evidence and other procedural safeguards that implemented the constitutional rights of suspects and accused persons. Unfortunately, however, these constitutional and statutory rights have often been ignored by law enforcement agencies. This was particularly the case during the period of transition from the old to the new constitution.

Other problem areas in civil liberties include prejudice and discrimination against women, mentally and physically handicapped persons, BURAKUMIN (a group of people whose ancestors were considered to be outcastes), Koreans and Chinese who were born in Japan, and FOREIGN WORKERS without proper working visas.

In order to promote the protection of civil liberties, the Civil Liberties Bureau (Jinken Yōgokyoku) was established as an organ of the MINISTRY OF JUSTICE with power, under the Civil Liberties Commissioners Law of 1949, to appoint up to 20,000 citizens to deal with local problems. As of 1 January 1991 there were 13,072 civil liberties commissioners.

The Lawyers' Law (Bengoshi Hō) of 1949 makes it the duty of every lawyer to protect human rights, and the educational system accords great importance to the teaching of civil liberties.

Civil Procedure, Code of
民事訴訟法

(Minji Soshō Hō). Body of law by which disputes between private individuals are received and processed through the Japanese courts. The resulting final judgment embodies the parties' substantive rights and duties, which may then be enforced by state powers of execution. There are thus two distinct phases: the procedures for trial resulting in a judgment and the provisions for enforcement of the judgment. The prejudgment and judgment procedures are contained in the Code of Civil Procedure, but the provisions for enforcement of judgments were taken out of the code and enacted in the new Civil Execution Law (Minji Shikkō Hō, Law No. 4, 1979), effective 1980.

Civil procedure applies only to adjudication of disputes between private individuals or entities. Civil procedure is thus distinguished from CRIMINAL PROCEDURE and from ADMINISTRATIVE LITIGATION.

Historical Background—The mature system of Japanese civil procedure centers on the Code of Civil Procedure (hereafter CCP), first enacted in 1891. It was at that time a Western importation, highly innovative in the Japanese context, as was justiciable law (or lawyers' law) in general.

Just after World War II, the CCP was amended, but in contrast to the Code of Criminal Procedure (entirely rewritten, mainly to safeguard rights of the accused; see CRIMINAL LAW), the amendments to the CCP were limited to the following important points, suggesting some US influence: responsibility for examining witnesses and producing other evidence was shifted from the court to the parties, and new Rules of Civil Procedure were issued under the new rule-making powers of the Supreme Court to

implement the changes in the procedure for examining witnesses.

Format of the Code—As procedural law, the CCP exists to enforce rights accorded by the substantive law in the CIVIL CODE, the COMMERCIAL CODE, and a host of other statutes.

The overall framework of the code is Germanic; it is divided into nine major parts. Part I is entitled General Provisions (Sōsoku). It provides rules for relations between courts, capacity and joinder of parties, representatives, court costs, and general rules. Part II is entitled Proceedings at First Instance (Dai isshin no soshō tetsuzuki) and includes the rules for evidence. Part III is entitled Appeals (Jōso). Part IV is entitled Retrial (Saishin). It provides for extraordinary retrial of suits for limited, specific reasons. Part V is entitled Dunning Procedure (Tokusoku tetsuzuki; sometimes translated as Summary Procedure). These rules provide for an abbreviated trial in summary courts on certain legal instruments or fungible or money claims.

Part V-II, added in 1964, is entitled Special Provisions concerning Litigation of Bills and Checks (Tegata soshō oyobi kogitte soshō ni kansuru tokusoku). It provides for suits on bills and checks in the summary court or, if the amount sought comes to the jurisdictional amount of ¥300,000, in the district court. Part VI (1979) is entitled Confirmation of Judgments and Suspension of Execution (Hanketsu no kakutei oyobi shikkō teishi). Part VII is entitled Public Peremptory Notice Procedure (Kōji saikoku tetsuzuki; alternative translation, General Pressing Notice) and deals with certain instances specially covered by substantive laws. Finally, Part VIII, entitled Arbitration Procedure (Chūsai tetsuzuki), covers rules by which the courts enforce in certain instances arbitral contracts and awards.

civil procedure, international
国際民事訴訟法

(kokusai minji soshō hō). A field of law concerned with the process of civil suits involving foreign countries. Since the end of World War II, international civil suits have been on the rise in Japan, stirring debate over such issues as legal jurisdiction. Other issues currently being studied include the status of foreigners in litigation, notification and examination of evidence according to the principles of INTERNATIONAL LEGAL COOPERATION, recognition and execution of foreign judicial decisions, international competitive jurisdiction, and arbitration. Although there is no single code governing international civil procedure in Japan, there are a number of discrete rules of international civil procedure found within the Code of Civil Procedure itself (art. 51, concerning the disposing capacity in the lawsuits of aliens; art. 175, concerning overseas servicing; and art. 200, concerning the efficacy of foreign judgments), as well as a law established on the basis of an international convention (the Law for the Execution of the Convention Relating to Civil Procedure). Areas where rules are not delineated are decided by judicial precedent.

Clarion Co, Ltd
クラリオン[株]

(Kurarion). Manufacturer of car audio systems, supplied primarily to the NISSAN MOTOR CO, LTD. Incorporated in 1940. In 1976 it began successful sales of KARAOKE (prerecorded background music systems) throughout Japan. Clarion supplies car audio systems to more than 20 domestic and overseas auto firms. The company manufactures car audio systems abroad in plants in the United States, England, France, Mexico, Malaysia, and Taiwan. Sales for the fiscal year ending September 1990 totaled ¥148.6 billion (US $1.1 billion), and capitalization stood at ¥18.3 billion (US $131.7 million) in the same year. Headquarters are in Tōkyō.

Clark, Edward Warren

クラーク, E. W.

(1849–1907). American educator and Episcopalian minister. Attended Rutgers College. In 1871 he became the first foreign teacher at the Denshūjo, a leading center of Western studies in Shizuoka. There he taught science, English, and (unofficially) the Bible until 1873, when he was invited to Tōkyō to teach chemistry at the Kaisei Gakkō, a predecessor of Tōkyō University. He returned to the United States in 1875.

Clark, William Smith

クラーク, W. S.

(1826–86). US educator, scientist, and entrepreneur who became one of the more famous advisers to the Japanese government during the 1870s phase of modernization. Born in Ashfield, Massachusetts, he graduated from Amherst College in 1848. His interest in science resulted in his study at Georgia Augusta University in Göttingen, Germany. After receiving his doctorate in 1852, he joined the faculty at Amherst, remaining there until 1867, except for a brief service in the Civil War. In 1867 he became the first active president of Massachusetts Agricultural College (MAC).

In 1876 he was engaged for one year (on leave from MAC) by the Japanese government to serve as the vice-president of a projected agricultural college in Sapporo, Hokkaidō. He presided over the opening of Sapporo Agricultural College (SAC; now part of HOKKAIDŌ UNIVERSITY), planned and developed the curriculum, directed a building program, and taught. He also served as technical adviser on agricultural matters to the agency responsible for the development of Hokkaidō. He is credited with having said to his students, "Boys, be ambitious!"—a phrase still familiar to almost all Japanese.

classical Japanese

古語

(kogo). The literary languages of premodern Japan, especially that of the poetry and prose of the Heian period (794–1185), upon which subsequent developments in literary Japanese were based. Although this early form of literary language corresponded closely to the spoken language of the time, by the Edo period (1600–1868) the two were widely divergent, and in the Meiji period (1868–1912) a movement arose to develop a literary form based on the grammatical and lexical usages of modern spoken Japanese (see GEMBUN ITCHI). Now little used, except in the composition of poetry (see TANKA), classical Japanese is nevertheless taught in high schools and universities for the study of premodern literature and other writings.

Classical Japanese refers, first and foremost, to the high-classical literary style of the 9th, 10th, and 11th centuries and, specifically, to the language employed in works of fiction, such as the *Genji monogatari* (early 11th century, TALE OF GENJI); anthologies of poetry, such as the KOKINSHŪ (905); diaries, such as TOSA NIKKI (935); and collections of essays, such as MAKURA NO SŌSHI (ca 1000).

These Japanese writings (wabun), many of which are attributed to women, are distinguished from other, chiefly nonliterary, works that were written in Chinese (KAMBUN) by men. The vocabulary employed in vernacular works of the early and mid-Heian period consists almost entirely of native Japanese words, supplemented by a limited number of words of Chinese origin. The works are written in the *hiragana* phonetic script (see KANA), with Chinese characters (KANJI) introduced only rarely. The uniformity of language in passages of narrative and dialogue indicates that there were no striking differences between the written and spoken languages of the time.

Toward the close of the Heian period, however, literary Japanese began to undergo a change due to the influence of Chinese. The practice had developed early in the period of supplying interlinear notations and Japanese grammatical particles and verb inflections to passages of Chinese, enabling them to be read as a hybrid variety of Japanese. A consequence was the development of a literary style (wakan konkō bun) that retained fundamental elements of the classical lexicon and grammar but that also employed a large number of Chinese loanwords. *Wakan konkō bun* was used in early medieval period (mid-12th–16th centuries) works, such as the war tale HEIKE MONOGATARI, the collection of essays HŌJŌKI (1212), and the travel diary KAIDŌKI (ca 1223), and its basic characteristics remained unchanged into the Meiji period.

During the early Edo period only well-educated women continued to write in the pure high-classical prose style, which by then was quite different from the colloquial language; however, in the 18th century scholars of National Learning (KOKUGAKU) began to study the tradition of native Japanese poetry and to use the classical language in their writings. The growing disparity between the largely static classical grammar employed in literary language of the standard *wakan konkō bun* style and the constantly evolving grammar of colloquial speech led to the use of the spoken language in literary works in which dialogue played an important role, such as the fiction of Ihara SAIKAKU, the domestic dramas of CHIKAMATSU MONZAEMON, and the fictional genres SHARE-BON and NINJŌBON. Following the Meiji Restoration (1868) a movement arose for the establishment of colloquial Japanese as the standard literary language. Although the first novel written wholly in the colloquial style, *Ukigumo* by FUTABATEI SHIMEI, appeared between 1887 and 1889, it was not until the Taishō period (1912–26) that the use of classical grammar and phrasing in prose literary works was completely abandoned. For a description of other types of literary language, see HENTAI KAMBUN; SŌRŌBUN.

Claudel, Paul Louis Charles

クローデル, P. L. C.

(1868–1955). French diplomat, poet, and playwright. After a distinguished 30-year career in the French diplomatic corps, he served as French ambassador in Tōkyō from December 1921 to February 1927. During his term, he sought to strengthen cultural relations between the two nations and worked to establish the Maison Franco-Japonaise. Claudel won the goodwill of the Japanese through his aid efforts following the disastrous TŌKYŌ EARTHQUAKE OF 1923. His lectures

and writings on Japan were collected in *L'Oiseau noir dans le soleil levant* (1928, Black Bird in the Rising Sun). One of his greatest plays, *Le Soulier de satin* (1927, The Satin Slipper), was completed during his stay in Tōkyō. In 1927 he was assigned to Washington, where he played a crucial role in negotiating the KELLOGG-BRIAND PACT.

Clean Government Party→

Kōmeitō

climate

気候

(kikō). As a nation straddling a number of climatic zones from north to south and subject to the atmospheric influence of both the Eurasian continent to the west and the Pacific Ocean to the east, Japan is characterized by a wide diversity of climates, dramatic changes in weather, and clearly differentiated seasons. Although the total land area of the nation is only some 377,000 square kilometers (146,000 sq mi), the islands stretch from about latitude 20°N at the southernmost point of Japan, the island of OKINOTORISHIMA (700 km [435 mi] southwest of the IŌ ISLANDS), to about latitude 45°30′N at the northernmost point of HOKKAIDŌ, roughly the distance between Florida's southern tip and the Canadian border. Hence, the difference between the climate of Japan's southern and northern extremes is great. Hokkaidō lies in the subarctic zone; central Japan (Honshū, Shikoku, and Kyūshū), in the temperate zone; and the southern islands, in the subtropical zone.

A second major influence on the climate of Japan is the archipelago's location in the temperate monsoon zone of East Asia. The monsoons of this region are seasonal winds that flow eastward off the continent in winter and northward from the South Pacific in the summer. Japan's seasons are largely determined by these winds and the shifts in weather caused by the transition between the winter and summer wind patterns. Japan also has mountainous terrain running through the center of its main islands. Land to the leeward of these mountain ranges is shielded from the full impact of the monsoon winds: heavy snows, brought by the winter winds, fall on the Sea of Japan coast, which faces northwest, but not on the Pacific coast; conversely, summer typhoons often strike the southeast coast but not the Sea of Japan coast.

Complex local variations in Japan's climate are introduced by radical variations in geomorphology, which appear as soaring mountains, small basins, deep valleys, and narrow plains areas. Japan's weather is also moderated by a warm ocean current, the KUROSHIO, which flows along the Pacific coast. These factors combine to create widely varied seasons, dramatic changes in weather, and diversity of climate.

Seasons in Japan— *Winter* (fuyu). The monsoon that brings winter to Japan develops as a series of anticyclones over Siberia in late November. It continues through the end of February, when the Siberian high recedes. The air that breaks out as the winter monsoon is part of a continental polar air mass that originates within the Siberian high. This air mass begins dry and highly stable, but as it approaches the Sea of Japan it accumulates heat from the lower strata of the atmosphere and becomes increasingly unstable. At the same time it also picks up

William Smith Clark
One of the many foreign advisers employed by the Japanese government during the early Meiji period (1868–1912), Clark played a key role in the establishment of Sapporo Agricultural College in Hokkaidō.

Annual Japanese Climatic Cycle

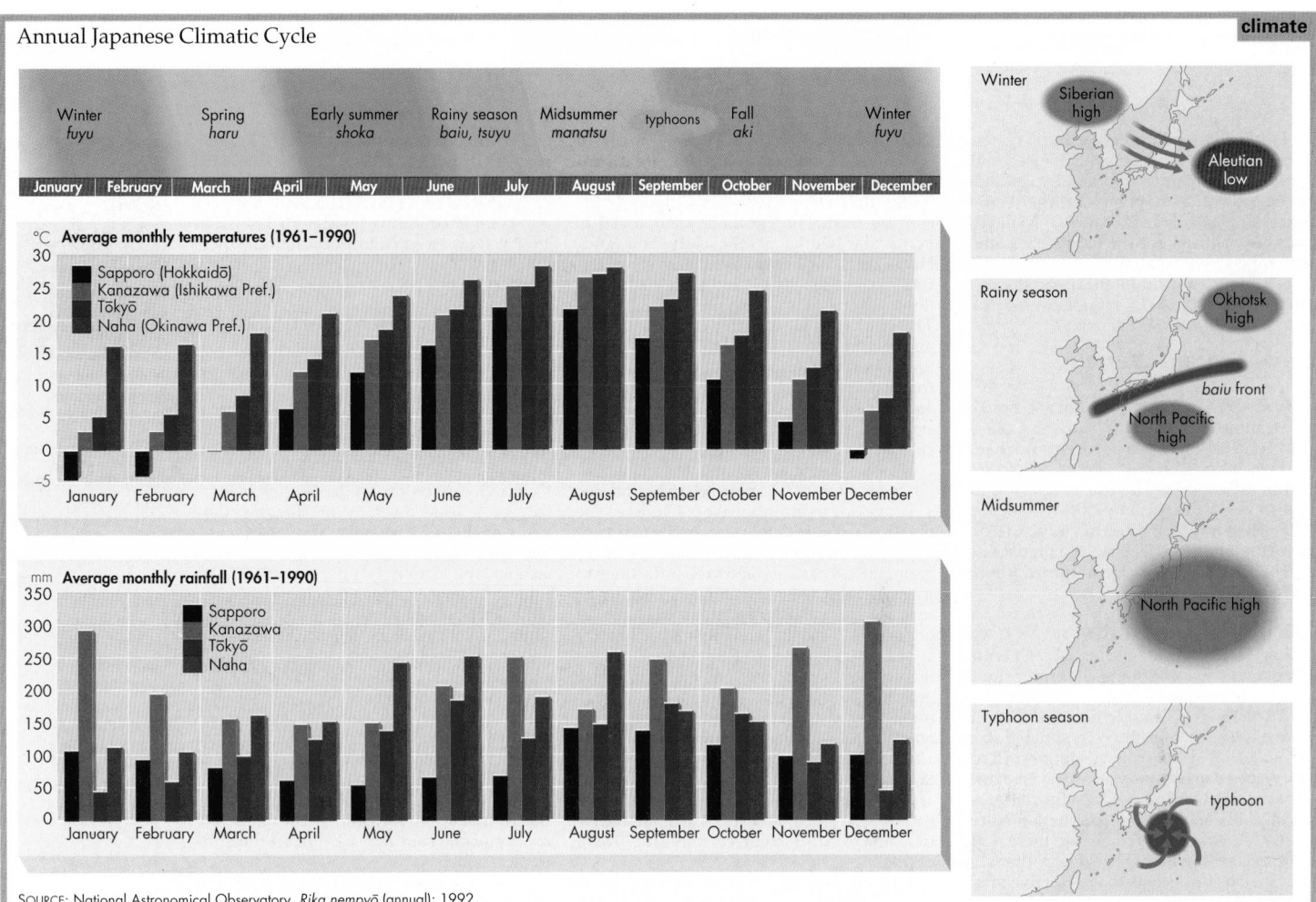

| Winter fuyu | Spring haru | Early summer shoka | Rainy season baiu, tsuyu | Midsummer manatsu | typhoons | Fall aki | Winter fuyu |

| January | February | March | April | May | June | July | August | September | October | November | December |

°C Average monthly temperatures (1961–1990)
- Sapporo (Hokkaidō)
- Kanazawa (Ishikawa Pref.)
- Tōkyō
- Naha (Okinawa Pref.)

mm Average monthly rainfall (1961–1990)
- Sapporo
- Kanazawa
- Tōkyō
- Naha

Winter — Siberian high, Aleutian low

Rainy season — Okhotsk high, baiu front, North Pacific high

Midsummer — North Pacific high

Typhoon season — typhoon

SOURCE: National Astronomical Observatory, *Rika nempyō* (annual): 1992.

water vapor from the ocean. A characteristic cloud layer develops by the time the air mass reaches the central eastern sections of the Sea of Japan. When this air mass reaches the northern slopes of the Japanese archipelago, it ascends sharply, develops a thick layer of clouds, and drops a heavy snowfall. This mountainous region is called the "snow country," or *yukiguni*. Having dropped heavy snows on the windward side of Japan, the air mass is extremely dry by the time it passes over the mountain range of central Japan to the leeward side. Clouds disappear, and the sky remains clear for most of the winter. Snow and rain occasionally fall on the Pacific Ocean side of Japan during the winter, but this precipitation is due to extratropical cyclones originating in the East China Sea.

Spring (haru). As the temperature on the Asian mainland rises, the strength of both the Siberian high and the associated monsoons weakens, signaling the end of winter and the beginning of spring. A series of fast-traveling anticyclones that pass over Japan within a period of several days and frontal zones alternate. The temperature in all regions rises.

Early summer (shoka). Together with the weakening of the Siberian high, the domain of the continental frigid air mass shrinks back toward the mainland gradually and is replaced by a continental tropical air mass that advances toward the Japanese archipelago from the Yangzi (Yangtze) River basin. The atmosphere becomes very dry, and an extended period of ideal springtime weather called *satsukibare* begins. The temperature rises sharply, and in early June there may even be days as hot as those of

late summer. However, early summer does not pass directly into a hot summer season but is rather followed by the *baiu* season (rainy season; also called *tsuyu*), which affects all regions of Japan except Hokkaidō.

The baiu *season.* Beginning generally after the first week of June, the Sea of Okhotsk maritime air mass, a blocking anticyclone that forms in the Sea of Okhotsk, moves toward Japan from the northeast. At the same time, in the southern seas off Japan, the North Pacific high gradually increases in strength and creates the tropical Bonin air mass, which also blows toward the Japanese archipelago. These two air masses meet when they reach Japan, resulting in a polar front, the *baiu* front, which stretches east to west across the islands. The two air masses reach an equilibrium, which is perpetuated by the general circulation pattern of the air, and the *baiu* front moves slowly over Japan. A thick layer of clouds and heavy rains develops along this front, and the stormy weather is aggravated by the frequent emergence of extratropical cyclones. The combination of these conditions gives rise to a rainy season of considerable length.

Midsummer (manatsu). Midsummer commences as the Bonin air mass begins to dominate the entire archipelago. Throughout summer, air pressure continues to be high in the south and low in the north. However, since the difference between these two atmospheric areas is relatively small, the summer monsoon winds are much weaker than winter's. Furthermore, the Bonin air mass is much more stable than the Siberian air mass of winter. For these reasons, the Pacific slope, which is on the windward side of the summer monsoons, is not subject to long periods of bad weather. Although thunderstorms sometimes develop, summer is typi-

cally a period of uninterrupted clear, hot weather. Midsummer is a short, dry season, which comes to an end as TYPHOONS approach in late summer.

Fall (aki). When August ends, as the North Pacific high recedes gradually to the south, the force of the Bonin air mass begins to weaken, and a new season develops with continental frigid air masses becoming dominant. The cold air front, which remains north of Japan through spring and summer, begins moving southward in September. This move results in another rainy period, the *shūrin* season. In mid-October Japan is often traversed by migratory anticyclones and by oblong high-pressure zones extending from east to west. This season is characterized by clear autumnal weather with comparatively light and pleasant winds. At the end of November, fall ends and winter begins with the appearance of the monsoons.

Land Utilization and the Climate

Cultivation of rice. Annual cultivation of rice takes place in almost all parts of the country. In northeastern Japan, where the winter is very cold and snowy, rice crops are planted only once a year, while in southwestern Japan two crops can be planted.

Agriculture in warm districts. Since intensive cultivation of arable land has long been widespread in Japan, dry-field farming, which takes advantage of climatic conditions, developed quite early. The Pacific coast region, which experiences warm winter temperatures, provides a typical example of the forced raising of vegetables, flowers, fruits, and other crops out of season. The increased availability of hothouses has resulted in the rapid spread of raising crops out of season to districts subject to cold winter temperatures.

This *dai-dokei* ("table clock"), with its lid at right, served as both alarm clock and calendar.

This *mannen-dokei* ("thousand-year clock") has six different faces, showing Western time, traditional Japanese time, the phases of the moon, etc.

The *yagura-dokei* ("turret clock") was modeled after the Western lantern clock.

clocks and watches

These Edo-period *wadokei*, mechanical clocks based on Western clocks brought to Japan in the 16th century, were adapted for use with the traditional Japanese timekeeping system.

A clock mounted in an *inrō*, a small container traditionally suspended by a cord from the sash of a man's *kimono*.

This *taiko-dokei* ("drum clock") chimes to indicate the hour.

Agriculture in highland areas. The volcanic slopes, high-mountain plateaus, and other sections in the high altitudes of central Japan have become major locations for dry-field farming in recent years. Since harvest-time comes earlier here than in the lowlands, the early shipping of off-season vegetable produce—especially cabbage, Chinese cabbage, and lettuce—guarantees advantageous selling prices on the city markets.

Crop damage due to weather. In years when the strength of the Sea of Okhotsk maritime air mass persists over an unusually long period and causes an abnormally long *baiu* season, midsummer fails to appear at all, and instead a period of continually low temperatures and little sunshine, known as a "cool summer" (*reika*), ensues. Such cool summers cause crop failures and food shortages. Northern Japan, especially along the Pacific slopes, is most vulnerable to the intrusion of the Sea of Okhotsk air mass and has often experienced food shortages due to cool summers.

Drought. Midsummer is typically a time of uninterrupted dry and clear weather. Therefore, the annual *baiu* season is essential to ensure an ample supply of water. However, in years when the *baiu* season is short because the front is weak, fails to develop, or passes unusually quickly over Japan, there is a serious danger of drought.

Floods. With the exception of the winter snows on the Sea of Japan coast, all precipitation is brought by such phenomena as typhoons, extratropical cyclones, or storm fronts. Heavy rainfalls occur frequently, but extremely heavy downpours of more than 100 millimeters (4 in) in a day are confined to certain especially rainy regions.

The foehn phenomenon. In the early spring when the cyclones develop rapidly over the Sea of Japan, the foehn phenomenon (in which a warm, dry, erratic wind is deflected down the side of a mountain) frequently occurs in the region facing the Sea of Japan. As a result of the strong effects of the foehn in this region, large fires are a serious danger.

clocks and watches 時計

(*tokei*). The earliest reference to a timepiece in Japan appears in the historical chronicle *Nihon shoki* (720), which mentions a water clock constructed in the year 670. The date of its first use corresponds to 10 June in the modern calendar and is commemorated in Japan as Toki no Kinembi (Time Day).

The Edo period (1600–1868) saw the invention of *wadokei*, mechanical clocks based on imported foreign models but adapted to register the hours of the traditional Japanese system of timekeeping (see CALENDAR, DATES, AND TIME). The vagueness of this system, combined with technical problems in manu-

facturing parts, such as mainsprings, limited the utility of *wadokei* as timepieces, and greater energy was expended on their decoration and embellishment than on their accuracy.

In 1873, soon after the Meiji Restoration (1868), Japan converted to the Western-style calendar and time system, spurring a new concern with accuracy in timekeeping. Initially, however, timepieces were chiefly imported, and it was not until the 1920s that exports exceeded imports. Even then, however, the quality of Japanese manufacture was below that of foreign competitors in Switzerland and the United States.

In the 1950s the Japanese clock and watch industry made rapid advances in both technology and production levels. Seikō timepieces (see SEIKŌ CORPORATION) that were officially adopted for use at the 1964 Tōkyō Olympics were the first Japanese chronometers employed in the Olympic Games.

Japanese clock and watch manufacturers were quick to realize the potential of electronics. In 1969 they marketed the first quartz crystal watch, improving accuracy to ±0.3 seconds per day versus the ±20 seconds per day of existing mechanical watches. Capital investment and technical innovation in electronics led to the mass production of inexpensive, compact, high-performance quartz watches by 1975. In 1971 quartz watches represented only 0.02 percent of Japanese production; by 1980 this figure had grown to 61.2 percent.

With this rapid growth in production, quartz soon came to dominate watchmaking technology worldwide. In response to the increasing diversity of consumer demand, the Japanese watch industry is now concentrating on development of multipurpose high-value-added products, among them a quartz watch with a self-winding power source that will eliminate the need for batteries. See also PRECISION MACHINERY INDUSTRY.

cloisonné 七宝

(*shippō;* literally, "seven precious stones"). A type of enameling in which artistic designs are created by applying enamel glass to metal. Thin metal strips or wires are attached to a metal base, producing cells into which enamels of different colors are poured. After firing, the resulting surface is

smoothed by grinding and polishing. Alternately cells can be carved out of solid metal in a technique known as *champlevé*, hammered out of sheet metal in *repoussé*, or cast. The earliest example of enameling in Japan is a small hexagonal plaque with amber and white enamels in a floral pattern attributed to the Asuka period (593–710).

The Hōōdō (Phoenix Hall; dedicated in 1053) of the temple Byōdōin has door fittings with *champlevé*-enameled designs, and Ashikaga Yoshimasa's (1436–90) Higashiyama retreat (GINKAKUJI) is extensively decorated with cloisonné. However, it was not until the 17th century that cloisonné became widely used in Japan. Cloisonné was used for architectural embellishments (e.g., doorpulls and nail covers), fittings of swords and of chests, holders for writing brushes, and water droppers for preparing ink. Hirata Dōnin (also known as Hirata Hikoshirō; 1591–1646) is credited with the fittings (dated 1634) at the TŌSHŌGŪ mausoleum at Nikkō, and Kachō (dates unknown) is thought to have made the exquisite doorpulls at the KATSURA DETACHED PALACE. The period from the mid-17th through the 18th century was a golden age for the artistic creation of enameled objects. After the early 18th century there was a gradual decline in artistic quality that was not reversed until the 1830s when Kaji Tsunekichi (1803–83) developed new techniques based on a study of European enameled wares. Around 1875 the German Gottfried WAGENER introduced modern European enameling methods, which eventually led to the mass export production of cloisonné objects. In the 1880s Namikawa Sōsuke (1847–1910) succeeded

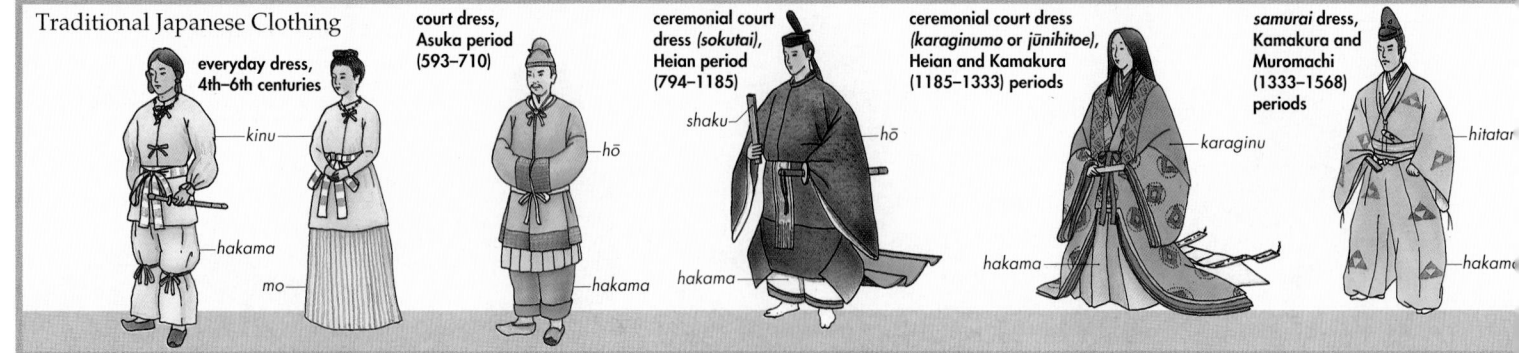

everyday dress,
4th–6th centuries

— kinu

— hakama

— mo

court dress,
Asuka period
(593–710)

— hō

— hakama

ceremonial court
dress (sokutai),
Heian period
(794–1185)

shaku —

— hō

hakama —

ceremonial court dress
(karaginumo or jūnihitoe),
Heian and Kamakura
(1185–1333) periods

— hō

hakama —

samurai dress,
Kamakura and
Muromachi
(1333–1568)
periods

— karaginu

— hitatar

hakama —

— hakame

in developing a technique called *musen shippō* (lineless *shippō*), in which the enamels are not separated by metal lines. At the same time Namikawa Yasuyuki (1845–1927) distinguished himself in the traditional *yūsen shippō* (*shippō* with lines) in which the enamels are separated by cloisons, reproducing classic Japanese paintings in a naturalistic style.

cloister government→insei

clothing
衣服

(*ifuku*). Clothing in Japan is broadly categorized as either *wafuku* (Japanese style) or *yōfuku* (Western style). KIMONO is the modern designation for the traditional Japanese robelike garment that is worn belted at the waist, but this garment was historically called a *kosode* ("kimono" can also mean traditional dress in general). The history of Japanese clothing is in large part the history of the evolutior f the *kosode* and the Japanization of imported styles and TEXTILES.

Ancient Clothing (to AD 794)—The type of clothing worn during the Jōmon period (ca 10,000 BC–ca 300 BC) is unknown, although jewelry from that period has been found. People probably used fur and bark to cover themselves. With the Yayoi period (ca 300 BC–ca AD 300) came the rise of SERICULTURE (silkworm breeding) and weaving techniques. The Chinese chronicle WEI ZHI (*Wei chih*) describes the early Japanese as wearing sheets of cloth woven from flax or silk. The HANIWA clay figurines from 4th- and 5th-century tombs show men in *kinu*, long, belted upper garments, with straight sleeves

cloisonné A cloisonné fitting from a lacquer box, showing a hollyhock and arabesque pattern. Cloisonné came into widespread use in the mid-17th century, when this piece was created. 13 × 11 cm. Tōshōgū, Nikkō.

tied at the wrists and elbows. As a lower garment men wore HAKAMA, loose trousers tied below the knees. Women wore *kinu*, similar to the men's, and pleated wrap-skirts (*mo*). The material was generally vegetable fiber, such as *asa* (bast fiber), although aristocrats sometimes wore silk.

Influenced by the importation of Buddhism and the Chinese government system, Prince SHŌTOKU (574–622) followed the practice of the Sui court (589–618), establishing rules of dress for aristocrats and court officials. Figures depicted in paintings and embroideries wear long, loose clothing that shows the influence of Han-dynasty (25–220) fashion. The TAIHŌ CODE (701) and YŌRŌ CODE (718; effective 757) reformed clothing styles, following the system used in Tang (T'ang) China (618–907). Garments were divided into three categories: ceremonial dress, court dress, and working clothes.

Heian Period (794–1185)—As Japan drew away from continental influence, clothing became simpler in cut but more elaborate in layers. For formal occasions the male aristocrat's layered outfit (*sokutai*) included loose trousers stiffened by divided skirts (*ōguchi*), worn underneath, and many layers of long, loose upper garments (*hō*). For less formal court wear and in leisure, men wore the *hō* over *sashinuki* (laced pantaloons secured at the ankle), with *ōguchi* underneath. For everyday wear courtiers replaced the *hō* with the shorter *nōshi* mantles. When hunting, they wore *kariginu*, bast-fiber mantles with loose sleeves that could be laced tight at the wrist. This later became the formal dress of warrior leaders.

The formal costume of the Heian lady-in-waiting was the *karaginumo*, often referred to after the 16th century as the 12-layered garment (JŪNIHITOE). Its most important element was the *uchiki*, the layers of lined robes (5, 10, or more) also called *kasane-uchiki* or *kasane* (layers). Great consideration was given to the combination of colors in the layers of *uchiki*. Each layer was longer than the one over it, so that the edge of each color showed, creating a striking effect. For everyday occasions women wore a simplified version (*kouchiki*) or else a loose upper garment with trousers. For travel the head was covered either by a straw hat (*ichimegasa*) with a veil made of strips of cloth (*mushitare-ginu*) or by an unlined garment (*kinukazuki*). Ordinary women wore simpler clothes, including short, sleeveless robes (*tenashi*).

Kamakura (1185–1333) and Muromachi (1333–1568) Periods—With the establishment of the Kamakura shogunate and the decline of the prestige of the imperial court, stiffened military garments replaced luxurious silk. The highest officials wore the formal *sokutai* of the Heian period, but the informal hunting jacket (*kariginu*) became the standard uniform of the *samurai*, along with a stiffened cloak (*suikan*). For everyday wear the upper garment (*hitatare*) had a broad collar that crossed in front of the

body. The *hitatare* was tucked into the trousers, rather than belted over them.

At the beginning of the Kamakura period, women wore a combination of *uchiki* robes and *hakama* skirt-trousers as the formal outfit. Later these were replaced by the small-sleeved undergarment, the *kosode*, worn with *hakama*. In the Muromachi period an extra jacket (*uchikake* or *kaidori*) was worn over the *kosode* to complete the formal dress; today it is part of the bridal outfit.

Azuchi-Momoyama Period (1568–1600)—In the late 16th century the powerful generals ODA NOBUNAGA and TOYOTOMI HIDEYOSHI, great patrons of the arts, encouraged a wave of bold, decorative brilliance. This found echoes in clothing, which grew more sumptuous. New contact with the West through the Portuguese and trade with China influenced styles as well. The samurai continued to wear matched upper and lower garments (*kamishimo*). The upper garment was sleeveless. Gradually the material was made stiffer and the shoulders more flared; together with trailing pleated trousers (*nagabakama*), this continued as formal wear for samurai throughout the Edo period.

Edo Period (1600–1868)—During the 250 peaceful years of Tokugawa government, the wealthy merchant community (CHŌNIN) supported new forms of artistic expression. The KABUKI theater and the entertainment quarters led fashion. The *kosode*, the basic garment for both men and women, was more brilliantly decorated after the development of YŪZEN dyeing and TIE-DYEING patterns. In the late Edo period the lavishness of the bourgeoisie was curtailed by government regulations restricting the types, colors, and materials of clothing worn by commoners. These regulations led people to cultivate a new, more subtle sense of beauty (see IKI AND SUI). Plain overall patterns, such as stripes, checks, and dots (KOMON) in quiet colors, were balanced by elaborate HAIRSTYLES and exquisite accessories.

During the Edo period the OBI, the long sash worn with the *kosode*, changed from a narrow band to a stiff belt, approximately 30 centimeters (1 ft) wide and 4 meters (13 ft) long. Decorated with rich embroidery or woven, raised designs, it was tied in a variety of decorative ways, either in front or in back of the body. Over the *kosode* the Edo man often wore a HAORI jacket, a loose garment with a straight collar. The Tokugawa shogunate reformed clothing regulations for the military class toward the close of the period. The standard uniform became a *kosode*, ankle-length *hakama*, and *haori*. A number of early-Edo-period fashions reflected Portuguese influence. From the Portuguese large cape came the *kappa* raincoat. The *juban* kimono, worn under the *kosode*, derived its name from the Portuguese word for underwear: *gibão*.

Modern Developments—After the Meiji Restoration of 1868 the Japanese slowly changed over to Western clothing.

winter court dress, Muromachi and Azuchi-Momoyama (1568–1600) periods

uchikake or kaidori

samurai court dress, Azuchi-Momoyama and Edo (1600–1868) periods

kataginu

hakama

everyday dress of samurai, Edo period

obi

kosode

formal dress of married women, Edo period

haori

obi

everyday dress, Meiji (1868–1912) and early Taishō (1912–26) periods

kosode

haori

hakama

student dress, Meiji and early Taishō periods

kimono

hakama

The process began with a government decree that civil servants, such as soldiers, police, and postmen, should wear Western dress. Soon students were also wearing Western uniforms. By World War I, almost all men dressed in trousers, shirts, and jackets.

Women were generally slower in adopting Western styles. The aristocracy, however, sported imported Western gowns and accessories at the European-style balls held at the ROKUMEIKAN from 1883 to 1889, and after World War I professional and educated women began to adopt Western clothing as their daily wear. It was not until after World War II that the habit of wearing Western clothing became the norm for all classes. Today most Japanese women wear their traditional kimono only on special occasions, such as festivals and weddings. Men wear traditional clothing even more rarely. The cotton summer kimono or YUKATA is worn by both men and women at resorts and summer festivals. ☎ 212–213

coal 石炭

(*sekitan*). The coal industry was slow to develop in Japan and had its real beginning after the Meiji Restoration (1868). It grew rapidly with the introduction of Western mining techniques and prospered during the period before and after World War I. As the major source of energy for Japan, coal was highly exploited during World War II and the postwar reconstruction period. During the 1960s, coal was replaced by petroleum, and production was reduced. In recent years large amounts of coal have been imported.

Coal is said to have been discovered in Japan in Miike, Kyūshū, in 1469, but was not commonly used as fuel until the late 19th century, when it began to be employed to power steamships and locomotives. The Meiji government took over the operation of the TAKASHIMA COAL MINE and the MIIKE COAL MINES and introduced Western mining techniques, though mining was still done with chisels and picks. From 1880 to 1900, capital became increasingly concentrated and smaller mines were merged. The Takashima and Miike mines were sold to MITSUBISHI and MITSUI, respectively.

During the first quarter of the 20th century, mining was modernized by the introduction of electric machinery. In 1929 the worldwide economic depression spurred efforts to rationalize the coal-mining industry with the formation of production cartels. After 1931 enlarged munitions production raised the demand for coal, and the Coal Mining Department was established in 1939 within the Ministry of Commerce and Industry to administer production.

After World War II, increased coal production was adopted as a high-priority policy (see PRIORITY PRODUCTION PROGRAM). From 1955 onward, however, coal use declined as Japan increased its reliance on imported oil. This led to a policy of reducing production by closing unprofitable mines (see MIIKE STRIKE). The decline was reversed after the OIL

CRISIS OF 1973. Coal was reconsidered as a major source of energy, and both domestic output and imports increased. In 1988 annual coal production was 11.2 million metric tons (12.4 million short tons). Coal imports in the same year totaled 101.2 million metric tons (111.3 million short tons). Researchers are now studying ways to gasify and liquefy coal.

Coca-Cola (Japan) Co, Ltd

日本コカ・コーラ[株]

(Nihon Koka-Kōra). Wholly owned subsidiary of Coca-Cola Export Corporation of the United States. Incorporated in 1957. Coca-Cola (Japan) produces Coca-Cola concentrate and beverage bases and supplies 17 independent, locally owned bottlers across Japan. Coca-Cola has a 60 percent share of the carbonated soft drink market in Japan, and its noncarbonated products have nearly a 40 percent share. In the fiscal year ending December 1990, sales totaled ¥47.3 billion (US $354.2 million) and capitalization stood at ¥3.6 billion (US $27.0 million). Headquarters are in Tōkyō.

cockfighting 闘鶏

(*tōkei*). Also known as *tori-awase*. Cockfighting was introduced to Japan from China early in the 8th century. In the Nara (710–794) and Heian (794–1185) periods it became a popular amusement among the nobility. By the Kamakura period (1185–1333) cockfighting matches were held each March and became an occasion for gambling. Although officially banned in 1873, cockfighting continues sporadically in local areas. In Japanese cockfighting, cocks are led to a dirt ring surrounded by a barrier of straw matting. When one bird refuses to fight or is ejected from the ring three times, he is declared the loser.

Cocks, Richard コックス, R.

(1566–1624). Manager of the English East India Company's trading post in Japan during its 10-year existence, 1613–23. The East India Company set up a trading post, or "factory," in the port town of Hirado (now part of Nagasaki Prefecture, Kyūshū) under the supervision of Cocks. The manager made two visits to Edo (now Tōkyō), during the first of which, in 1616, he was received by the shōgun TOKUGAWA HIDETADA. As the Japanese government increasingly curtailed English trading privileges following the death of TOKUGAWA IEYASU in 1616, the fortunes of the trading post, which had never prospered, further declined. In 1623 the post was closed down by the East India Company, and Cocks and his staff were recalled in disgrace, leaving behind considerable debts owed to the company. Cocks died at sea on 27 March 1624 while returning to England.

Cocks's chief claim to fame rests on his incomplete diary, which runs from June 1615–January 1619, and again from December 1620–March 1622; this account is supplemented by a score of lengthy letters. The

diary is a rich source of information about daily life in Hirado, business transactions, and visits to temples and monuments.

coeducation 男女共学

(*danjo kyōgaku*). In Japan, Confucian morality long advocated educating male and female students separately. Compulsory primary education was made coeducational under the EDUCATION ORDER OF 1872 and extended throughout the entire school system in the EDUCATIONAL REFORMS OF 1947. In practice, however, many private schools continue to be for boys or girls only.

coffeehouses 喫茶店

(*kissaten*). Establishments that serve coffee, tea, and other beverages and snacks. Japan's first modern coffeehouse, the Kahii Sakan, opened its doors in 1888 in the Ueno district of Tōkyō. In addition to serving coffee, it provided magazines and board games for customer use. Soon after, similar establishments began springing up around the Ginza area. After World War II "specialty" coffeehouses, establishments that play a particular type of music (such as jazz or classical) or are designed with some special theme in mind, became popular. Today coffeehouses can be found all over Japan, especially in urban areas. Certain coffeehouses have breakfast and lunch menus and are more like American-style coffee shops. Although a cup of coffee can be expensive, ranging from ¥300 to ¥500 (US $2.35–$3.90), customers are permitted to stay as long as they like and are not required to order anything else. Coffeehouses are popular places for meeting with business associates or, informally, with friends.

collective bargaining right

団体交渉権

(*dantai kōshōken*). One of the three FUNDAMENTAL LABOR RIGHTS guaranteed by article 28 of the 1947 CONSTITUTION OF JAPAN. The Labor Union Law (Rōdō Kumiai Hō) also provides that an employer's refusal to bargain without a justifiable reason is an unfair labor practice, and a labor relations commission may order the employer to bargain. Japanese law thus guarantees the right to engage in collective bargaining as a right separate and independent from the RIGHT TO ORGANIZE LABOR UNIONS and the RIGHT TO STRIKE. In Japan a number of labor unions may coexist within a single enterprise, where each possesses an equal right to bargain. See LABOR LAWS; UNFAIR LABOR PRACTICES; LABOR RELATIONS COMMISSIONS.

collective labor agreements

労働協約

(*rōdō kyōyaku*). In Japan the overwhelming majority of collective agreements, those reached by collective rather than individual bargaining, are concluded between com-

Continued on page 214—

Japanese Clothing: A Lively Pastiche

On the streets of Japan's cities, men and women sport a panoply of styles. The international recognition accorded Japan's top fashion designers, coupled with a relatively affluent economy at home, have sparked an interest in fashion among Japanese consumers. In fact, Japan has become one of the world's major retail markets for designer wear—both domestic and imported. The Japanese appetite for designer merchandise is legendary, and Gucci handbags, Louis Vuitton luggage, and Hermès scarves are popular commodities. So too are the fashions of Western couturiers, from Giorgio Armani and Ralph Lauren to Agnès b. and Donna Karan.

Western-style apparel was first introduced to Japan during the Meiji period (1868–1912), when the country ended its long isolation and began to open up to American and European cultural influences. While many men quickly adopted Western clothing, it was not until after World War II that large numbers of Japanese women abandoned *kimono* in favor of the more practical styles worn by Westerners. Nowadays, most women don kimono only on special occasions, and men do so even less frequently.

The luxurious fabrics and sophisticated motifs used for kimono continue to inspire some of Japan's leading couturiers, while others are striking out in new directions. Drawing upon a rich textile heritage, designers like Mori Hanae, Takada Kenzō, Miyake Issei, Yamamoto Kansai, Kawakubo Rei, and Yamamoto Yōji are able to infuse their fashions with a distinctly Japanese flavor.

But fashionable clothing is by no means the rule in Japan. For millions of people—schoolchildren, office workers, department store employees, taxi drivers, and businessmen—daily attire is a uniform of one sort or another. Together with their stylishly clad compatriots, these people in regulation attire contribute to the lively pastiche that characterizes contemporary Japanese dress. The photographs shown here provide a sample of what people in Japan were wearing in 1992.

combs
1 This comb and hairpin set is painted in black lacquer and decorated with a *maki-e* and mother-of-pearl design.
2 The manner in which traditional combs and hairpins were used can be seen in this Edo-period woodblock print by Kitagawa Utamaro.

pany unions and their individual companies. The Trade Union Law of 1949 gives binding legal force to collective agreements that stipulate better working conditions than those in individual employment contracts (see LABOR LAWS). The law also extends to all workers in an establishment any collective agreement that already applies to three-fourths or more of its workers. The labor minister or a prefectural governor may declare that an agreement accepted by a majority of the workers in a particular occupation in a locality holds for all other workers there in that occupation, when either party to such an agreement requests such an extension. See also EMPLOYMENT CONTRACTS.

colonialism 植民地政策

(*shokuminchi seisaku*). Japan was the only non-Western colonial power in the world until it was stripped of all its colonial possessions in 1945 as a result of defeat in World War II. At the time its colonies included Korea, TAIWAN, the southern half of Karafuto (the Japanese name for the island of SAKHALIN), the GUANDONG (KWANTUNG) TERRITORY (Japan's territory on the Liaodong [Liaotung] Peninsula in southern Manchuria), and the Pacific Islands, totaling some 298,454 square kilometers (115,233 sq mi), or more than three-quarters the area of Japan.

Korea was the most important colony in size, geographic proximity, and historical ties. Its colonial experience was unique in two ways. First, it was annexed in 1910 as a result not of military conquest but of a treaty

agreement (see KOREA, ANNEXATION OF). The Japanese government pledged, however half-heartedly, to provide "equal treatment" for Koreans. Accordingly, an unusually large number of Koreans were employed in the colonial government at all levels, even the police force. Second, the Koreans possessed a cultural identity fostered by more than 2,000 years of history as an independent nation, and once the country was annexed, a strong nationalist movement emerged with open demands for restoration of independence.

Taiwan, Japan's first colony, acquired in 1895 following the Sino-Japanese War (see SHIMONOSEKI, TREATY OF), served as a training ground for numerous colonial officials whose experience later proved valuable in the administration of other colonies. Programs successfully implemented in Taiwan, such as land survey, population census, and government monopolies, set precedents for other colonies. More important, the island was the most profitable colony within the Japanese empire. Like Korea, it shipped half its annual rice harvest to Japan. Taiwan's sugar industry enabled Japan to become the fourth largest cane sugar producer in the world, and it attracted an enormous amount of private Japanese investment capital.

The southern half of Karafuto was acquired in 1905 following the Russo-Japanese War (see PORTSMOUTH, TREATY OF). Unlike Korea and Taiwan, it was a settlement colony, virtually all of whose inhabitants were Japanese (there were also more than 21,000 Koreans). As a settlement colony, Karafuto was in many respects more integrated with Japan than were the other colonies, and in 1943 it was made part of Japan proper.

When Japan defeated Russia in 1905, the lease of the Guandong Territory was transferred from Russia to Japan, together with the right to control the SOUTH MANCHURIA RAILWAY. Its colonial government was entrusted with the administration of the railway, paving the way for the penetration of the Japanese GUANDONG (KWANTUNG) ARMY deep into the heartland of Manchuria.

The Pacific Islands consisted of most of what is known as Micronesia. Shortly after the outbreak of World War I in 1914, the islands, which had been purchased by Germany, were seized by the Japanese navy. In 1919 the League of Nations awarded Japan the mandate to rule them. The native population was small, maintaining a steady level of about 50,000 throughout the 30 years of Japanese rule; they were rapidly outnumbered by Japanese settlers, most of them from Okinawa, who numbered 84,000 in 1942.

Japan's intention was to convert the colonies into defense outposts of the empire as well as springboards for expansion. This goal was achieved in both China and the Pacific. Earlier, Japan had aspired to become a world power equal in prestige with the Western nations. Now, as a colonial power, Japan had achieved that goal as well.

There was an effort to make the colonies absorb some of Japan's excess population, but the results were mixed. Colonization was successful in southern Karafuto and to a lesser degree in the Pacific Islands; in Korea, Taiwan, and the Guandong Territory, which were already heavily populated, it failed. Japanese residents in the latter colonies were mostly officials, business employees, and their families, whose presence frequently caused friction with the native population. Despite repeated efforts and generous subsidies, the three colonies did not attract a significant number of agricultural settlers. There were more Korean laborers who migrated to Japan than Japanese who settled in Korea.

Japan hoped to develop an integrated economy in which it would provide the colonies with capital and technology in return for supplies of foodstuffs, raw materials, and lucrative opportunities for investment. All available economic data clearly indicate that Japan succeeded in interlocking the economies of the five colonies with its own.

It must be emphasized that economic development was carried out with the welfare of Japan, not of the colonies, in mind and that it was often achieved at great expense to the native populations.

Colonization Office → Kaitakushi

Combined Fleet, Imperial Japanese Navy 連合艦隊

(Rengō Kantai). The Combined Fleet's origins can be traced to the founding of the standing fleet in 1889. It was composed of various units, including battleships, cruisers, aircraft carriers, destroyers, submarines, and airplanes. During World War II, the Combined Fleet lost its power and initiative as a result of defeats at the Battle of MIDWAY and in the Solomons Campaign in 1942.

combs 櫛

(*kushi*). Traditional Japanese combs, in addition to being functional, were often products of fine craftsmanship. By the medieval period (mid-12th–16th centuries) gold-lacquered and mother-of-pearl inlaid wooden combs were being made. In the Edo period (1600–1868), as the variety of HAIRSTYLES increased, ornamental combs were manufactured in many designs, differing according to the wearer's social class or age. Materials such as wood, bamboo, tortoiseshell, ivory, and metal were used. During the Meiji period (1868–1912) the spread of occidental hairstyles diminished the demand for traditional combs.

comic magazines 漫画雑誌

(*manga zasshi*). The flourishing of a "comic culture" is one of the significant features of mass culture in present-day Japan. Comic magazines fall into four categories: boys' comics (*shōnen manga*), girls' comics (*shōjo manga*), youth comics (*seinen manga*), and adult comics (*seijin manga*). Comic magazines are published weekly, biweekly, and monthly.

Boys' and girls' comics average around 400 pages, and a given issue usually contains some 15 serialized stories. Especially popular serials may continue for 10 years. Total combined circulation of the major weekly boys' comic magazines is about 10 million, and it is estimated that two-thirds of all boys aged 5 to 18 read these magazines on a regular basis. More than one-sixth of Japanese girls in the same age group are regular readers of girls' comics. Youth and adult comics average about 250 pages and contain about 10 serialized "story cartoons" and 5 "nonsense cartoons" in each issue. Including the so-called vulgar (*zokuaku*) comics, 40 to 50 different youth and adult comic magazines are published.

The popularity of comic magazines began in 1959 with the publication of *Shōnen sandē* and *Shōnen magajin.* Other children's comics appeared in rapid succession, and a large number of talented cartoonists emerged to meet the demand. Youth and adult comics eventually attracted the former readers of these children's comics, and the popularity of the genre expanded greatly. Since 1985 educational comics for adults have become popular. The content of these comics ranges from history to cooking instruction to how to conduct oneself on business occasions. See also MAGAZINES. ▶▶216–217

coming-of-age ceremonies→
gempuku

Comintern 1927 Thesis
コミンテルン27年テーゼ

(Kominterun Nijūshichinen Tēze). Resolution concerning the status of the communist movement in Japan adopted on 15 July 1927 in Moscow by the presidium of the Communist International (Comintern). Among the Japanese representatives invited to discussions of the resolution were TOKUDA KYŪICHI, WATANABE MASANOSUKE, and FUKUMOTO KAZUO. The thesis was subsequently adopted by the JAPAN COMMUNIST PARTY (JCP) as its first formal platform. Noting the threat posed by Japanese imperialism, the thesis prescribed a two-stage process: an initial bourgeois democratic revolution that would quickly develop into a socialist revolution. Though not as thoroughgoing as the COMINTERN 1932 THESIS, it was important in providing the JCP with a basic political strategy.

Comintern 1932 Thesis
コミンテルン32年テーゼ

(Kominterun Sanjūninen Tēze). Policy statement concerning the Japanese communist movement issued in May 1932 by the executive committee of the Communist International (Comintern). The thesis was based on a report by O. V. Kuusinen (1881–1964) criticizing the Trotskyist content of the 1931 draft thesis of the JAPAN COMMUNIST PARTY (JCP), which declared that the inevitable revolution would be a single-step proletarian revolution broadly embracing a simultaneous bourgeois revolution. The 1932 Thesis reverted to the policy of the COMINTERN 1927 THESIS by prescribing a two-stage process through which bourgeois democratic revolution would lead to general socialist revolution. The more exhaustive 1932 Thesis also emphasized the importance of agrarian revolution and outlined the unique significance of the emperor system in its relationship with monopolistic capitalism and a semifeudal system of land tenure. Consequently, the thesis regarded the overthrow of the emperor system as the first task of the revolution. The thesis formed the basis of subsequent JCP policy and influenced intellectuals outside the party as well.

Commercial Code   商法

(Shōhō). The legal framework that defines the nature and operation of commercial entities and the essential features of commercial relationships in Japan. The Commercial Code establishes rules for the regulation of all commercial activities and is central to the operation of the Japanese economy, underlying all domestic and international economic activities.

The Development of a Commercial Code—The commercial law system since the Meiji Restoration (1868) has been subject to three major formative influences: Japan's own traditional legal system and, more particularly, the commercial system of the late Edo period (1600–1868); the influence of Western ideas throughout the Meiji period (1868–1912); and the particular influence of

the United States in the period after 1945. By the end of the Edo period, Japan had developed a sophisticated commercial system that provided a basis for rapid economic development in the late 19th century. The concepts of group organizations were highly developed in the guilds (ZA), principles governing the sale and distribution of goods were quite sophisticated, and a system of credit had long operated. The draftsmen of the new commercial law system chose to look outside Japan, especially to German law, for their inspiration.

After several initial drafts, a revised code was adopted in 1899, which dealt with general concepts, corporations, commercial transactions, bills of exchange and checks (this section was later deleted), and maritime law. During the OCCUPATION period (1945–52), significant amendments were made to the corporations section of the Commercial Code, particularly to strengthen the powers of the shareholders, and new laws to regulate unfair business practices, monopolistic practices, and dealings in corporate securities were introduced, based upon US regulatory systems. There have been no fundamental changes to the Commercial Code since 1951, although there were important amendments to details in 1955, 1966, 1974, and 1981.

The Commercial Code and Other Commercial Laws—Apart from the Commercial Code there are other important sources of commercial law. CUSTOMARY LAW, special legislation, and case law all play important roles. The Commercial Code preserved the possibility of incorporating Edo-period commercial customs into the new system. Article 1 of the code prescribes that, where there is no specific provision in the Commercial Code covering a particular problem, resort may be made to customary law, and if customary law provides no answer, then an answer may be sought in the CIVIL CODE. The Civil Code sets out the general framework for the law of CONTRACTS, TORTS, and PROPERTY RIGHTS, all of which are of great importance to the operation of the commercial law system. The importance of judicial decisions in Japan must not be underestimated. The courts appear to play a more important role in developing law in Japan than in some other civil law countries. There are also cases where the courts have developed principles that are not covered by legislation.

The Commercial Code establishes three types of commercial entity: the LIMITED PARTNERSHIP COMPANY, the UNLIMITED PARTNERSHIP COMPANY, and, most important, the JOINT-STOCK COMPANY. The Limited Liability Company Law, adopted in 1938, provides a fourth commercial entity.

Since it is often remarked that Japanese do not seem to rely on formal written contracts in their commercial transactions, it is important to note that, so long as the basic prerequisites for a contractual relationship do exist, the Commercial Code and the Civil Code provide quite specific answers to most problems that may arise during the course of the contract.

commercial paper   手形・小切手

(tegata; kogitte). The Japanese Bills and Notes Law (Tegata Hō) and Checks Law (Kogitte Hō), both in effect since 1934, are based upon the international Convention providing a Uniform Law for Bills of Exchange and Promissory Notes of 1930 and the Convention providing a Uniform Law for Checks of 1931. The Bills and Notes Law primarily governs bills and notes of ex-

change, with many of its provisions applying to promissory notes. A large portion of the bills and notes used within Japan are promissory notes. Since 1966, bills and notes that are to be paid at a bank must be printed on a standard form issued by the Federation of Bankers Associations of Japan (Zenkoku Ginkō Kyōkai Rengō Kai).

A severe sanction called a trade suspension disposition (torihiki teishi shobun) is imposed by clearinghouses on the guarantor of a bill of exchange or the drawer of a promissory note that has not been paid at maturity at the bank where payment is due. Clearinghouses and participatory banks have a duty not to advance credit or allow checking transactions to a person who has twice dishonored a bill or note within a six-month period. This suspension, under clearinghouse rules rather than the law, lasts two years. As a result, a person who has been subject to a trade suspension disposition cannot obtain credit or a checking account at any bank whatsoever. This disposition system poses problems because it imposes extremely harsh sanctions on merchants. However, in view of the bad effects of delinquent bills or notes on the entire economy, case precedent has upheld the legality of this sanction. This system also applies to drawers of checks.

Commission on the Constitution
憲法調査会

(Kempō Chōsakai). Commission created by an act of the Diet in 1956 to investigate the origins, operation, and possible amendment of the 1947 CONSTITUTION OF JAPAN. It was made up of Diet members and scholars and was chaired by TAKAYANAGI KENZŌ. The socialists boycotted the group on the grounds that the conservative majority was biased in favor of amendment. The proceedings and reports of the commission generated a massive quantity of factual data and a great variety of opinions. A majority of the members believed that the postwar constitution imposed on Japan by the Allied OCCUPATION authorities should be altered to make the emperor head of state and to explicitly permit defensive armament. In 1965 the commission disbanded after submitting to the Diet an inconclusive report detailing the opinions of both supporters and opponents of constitutional reform. As of 1990 no changes had been made in the basic law. See also CONSTITUTIONAL PROBLEMS STUDY GROUP; CONSTITUTION, DISPUTE OVER REVISION OF.

Committee of Seven to Appeal for World Peace
世界平和アピール七人委員会

(Sekai Heiwa Apīru Shichinin Iinkai). Committee of seven prominent Japanese; founded in 1955 to campaign for world peace. The committee has advocated the banning of nuclear weapons and the establishment of a world federation of nations. Its first members were its organizer, SHIMONAKA YASABURŌ, former president of Heibonsha, Ltd, Publishers, and six other scholars and social leaders: former Minister of Education MAEDA TAMON; the physicists YUKAWA HIDEKI and KAYA SEIJI; the president of the Japan YWCA, UEMURA TAMAKI; the president of Japan Women's University, Jōdai Tano (1886–1982); and the feminist HIRATSUKA RAICHŌ. Any vacancy in the committee caused by a member's death is filled by a new person selected by the remaining members.

The Manga Kingdom

In a nation that prides itself as one of the world's most literate, an estimated one-third of all published material is comics.

One of the most striking features of modern Japan is its enormous appetite for *manga*, or comics. In no other country have comic books and magazines become so popular or developed into such a huge industry. Japan today, as the local media are fond of noting, is the comics capital of the world.

Manga are sold in bookstores, magazine kiosks, and vending machines; they are read not only in homes, but in beauty parlors, coffee shops, schools, offices, and commuter trains. Their readers range in age from 5 to 50. Although comic magazines are targeted at specific audiences, it is not uncommon for men to read manga designed for women, for women to read manga for men, and for children to read nearly anything they please. Manga sales exceed ¥515 billion (US $3.8 billion) per year, but that is only the tip of the iceberg, for the comics industry in Japan has become the engine that drives a powerful money-making machine.

Manga stories are typically serialized in magazines. If they catch on with the public, they are compiled and published as paperback or even hardback books. The most popular stories are turned into animated television series and/or movies. The characters are then licensed for merchandise, and their likeness appears on everything from toys and clothes to bicycles and stationery. The stories may also inspire radio shows, musicals, live action films, novels, and record albums. The popularity of Japanese manga continues unabated in large part because of its symbiotic, rather than competitive, relationship with television.

Format The format of comic pages, which is essentially the same throughout the world, follows the American convention of sequential illustrated panels with "speech balloons." But the term "comic book" has different meanings. In the United States, "comic books" normally are not books but slim magazines of 30 or so color pages with one main story and several advertisements. They are the descendants of newspaper comic strips, which were first compiled and issued in magazine format early in this century.

In Japan, manga have evolved in quite a different direction. Since the 1930s thick comic magazines have contained not one serialized story but many, the most popular of which are later compiled into book form. Today that trend continues, only on a larger scale. There are two types of comic magazines: those having approximately 200 pages held together with staples, and those having an even greater number of pages held together with an adhesive binding. A single magazine may contain up to 20 stories. Although a few of the initial pages may be printed in full color, most are in monochrome. Sometimes the first story is printed with an overlay of red or blue to give an illusion of color. Unlike American comic books, which are savored, collected, and often preserved as a future investment, most Japanese manga are thrown away after a single reading, and their paper is recycled again and again. The paperback and hardback books, which contain the collected stories printed on better paper, are usually kept.

In the United States, comic books are generally issued monthly, but in Japan the most popular magazines are issued weekly and have astronomical circulations. *Shōnen jampu* (Boys' Jump), the most popular weekly for boys, is about 400 pages long, retails for ¥200 ($1.60), and regularly sells over 5.3 million copies. As with American cars of the 1960s, size itself has become a selling point. One monthly for girls, *Būke* (Bouquet), regularly exceeds 600 pages in length.

When stories from the magazines are compiled into paperback books, they are issued as a series, with each volume containing more than 200 pages. In any given month, as many as 350 such titles may be published. Some series, such as Yaguchi Takao's *Tsurikichi Sampei* (Fishing-Crazy Sampei), consist of up to 67 volumes. In paperback, a single story can generate sales of more than 50 million copies over the years.

Sex and Violence Many foreigners are struck by the level of scatology, eroticism, and violence in Japanese comic magazines. Historically, manga are direct descendants of the woodblock picture books of the late 18th and 19th centuries, which scandalized authorities of the day. Japanese artists have often used eroticism and violence over the years as a way of tweaking the noses of the establishment.

To North Americans raised on comic books that have been heavily regulated by the Comics Code Authority since the early 1950s and accustomed to thinking of comics as lighthearted entertainment for children and adolescents, Japanese manga are a shock. There are restrictions on their content, but most consist of vaguely defined editorial policies that try to take into account the tastes of the readers. Manga are, nonetheless, covered by the same obscenity laws that apply to other media. In some regards these laws are stricter than in many Western industrialized nations. (As a matter of convention, pubic hair and adult genitalia cannot be depicted in films or printed materials in Japan.) But with changing social mores and greater concentration by authorities on the video market, a huge genre of erotic manga has developed. Irresponsible artists and editors have used gratuitous violence and twisted sexuality to enhance sales of their product.

Manga for men, in particular, contain a distressing level of violence against women. In the early 1980s there was also a thriving genre of what are called *rorikon*, or "Lolita-complex" stories, even in mainstream magazines for boys. These stories depicted naked prepubescent girls in relationships with older men who used them as surrogates for adult women. Technically, artists remained within the bounds of the

© Ōtomo Katsuhiro, Nagayasu Takumi, KODANSHA

© Kawaguchi Kaiji, KODANSHA

© Tezuka Production Co., Ltd.

© Takahashi Rumiko, Shogakukan

© Newsweek Japan

law, which restricts only the depiction of adult genitalia. But the end product had far more disturbing overtones than if the artists had simply chosen to create traditional erotic art.

Beginning in 1990, a backlash against the most offensive manga finally occurred. Several artists, publishers, and distributors of extreme material were arrested in nationwide crackdowns by law enforcement officials. A wave of reflection and introspection swept the industry, extending beyond issues of sex and violence to depictions of minorities. The result was a taming of some of the excesses.

Creative Strides

Despite the pressures of weekly publication and widespread commercialism within the industry, a number of manga artists have managed to extend the boundaries of their medium through the creative use of graphics and the development of imaginative themes. In the monthlies and in avant-garde publications, artists vie with each other for technical excellence. Some are seriously trying to create a new visual literature. It is not uncommon for the best manga books to be displayed on bookshelves with the best novels and even for their creators to win prestigious awards. If there is any irony in this, it is that most major publishers of literature in Japan, such as Kōdansha, Ltd, today effectively subsidize literary works with the profits made from sales of manga magazines and books.

Manga stories are just as diverse as stories in any other medium, and themes run the gamut from adventure tales, mysteries, and romances to science fiction and the occult. In contrast to the heroes of mainstream American comic books, who still tend to be superheroes, most manga heroes are mortals. Romances for girls and women, which have virtually disappeared from the American comic book scene,

sell extremely well in Japan. The characters in them often look Western, even if they are really Japanese. They have long-legged, lanky physiques, saucer-shaped eyes and, on color covers, what sometimes appears to be blond hair. Sports stories for both sexes, again a virtually extinct genre in the United States, are also immensely popular. In addition to tales of *sumō, jūdō, karate,* and *kendō* (Japanese fencing), there are hundreds of stories of golf, surfing, skiing, soccer, and volleyball, but the most popular theme of all is baseball. Besides sports, stories of gambling—particularly Mah-Jongg—are certainly unique to Japan. More than a dozen manga magazines are devoted to Mah-Jongg stories.

The most influential pioneer in the creative development of manga was Tezuka Osamu (1926–89). After World War II he demonstrated that many cinematic techniques in animation and live action films, such as pans, dissolves, and montages, could be incorporated into comics and that by reducing the number of words in a story and expanding the number of pages he could create a new type of visual narrative. The result was the "story manga," often thousands of pages long, that is now so popular in Japan. Tezuka used this format to create works such as *Hi no tori* (1954–88, Firebird; known in English as *Phoenix 2772*), *Adorufu ni tsugu* (Tell Adolph), and *Budda* (Buddha), stories that rival the world's best literature in their portrayal of the human condition.

Today, as manga become more and more integrated into society and as their readers steadily mature, artists and publishers are exploring new ways to use the manga format. One result has been an explosion of educational nonfiction manga for both children and adults. These information manga use an entertaining, accessible package to reach their readers. The trend was legitimized in 1986, when the *Nihon keizai shimbun,* the Japanese equivalent of *The Wall Street Journal,* published a hardcover manga book by Ishinomori Shōtarō. Titled *Manga Nihon keizai nyūmon* (An Introduction to the Japanese Economy), it was a reworking of a serious economics book that had been published several years earlier. *Manga Nihon keizai nyūmon*

did so well (selling nearly half a million copies in a year) that it was translated into English and distributed in the United States under the title *Japan Inc.* It also spawned a host of imitators. Today regular bookstores carry manga versions of everything from analyses of the stock market to explanations of proper business etiquette.

Manga's Influence Abroad

Given the size of the Japanese comics industry, it is not surprising that manga have had considerable influence overseas. Both pirated and legitimate translated versions of Japanese comics have appeared in other Asian nations for more than a decade. In Europe, manga have been given a boost by the popularity of Japanese animation, and several translated and redrawn editions of comic stories have appeared. In the United States, readers were slow to appreciate Japanese manga, but there are now fan clubs of manga and of Japanese animation in most major cities. Since the mid-1980s, a number of US comics publishers have issued translated Japanese manga, an example being Marvel's colorized version of Ōtomo Katsuhiro's science fiction tale *Akira.*

The United States invented the modern comic book and has had an enormous influence on the development of manga in Japan. But now manga are playing an important role in revitalizing the industry in America.

Like their Japanese counterparts, US comic book publishers have begun compiling paperback versions of popular works. And many of the best American artists, like Frank Miller, have been strongly influenced by the more visually oriented page layouts and storytelling techniques of Japanese artists. Some Americans like Ben Dunn, author of *Ninja High School,* emulate manga art styles in their work, drawing characters with large dreamy eyes.

Manga, as an immediate, accessible form of visual communication, are more than just another export from Japan. They are an important element in the cross-fertilization taking place between the popular cultures of both nations.

Frederik L. Schodt

© Ōyama Akira, KODANSHA

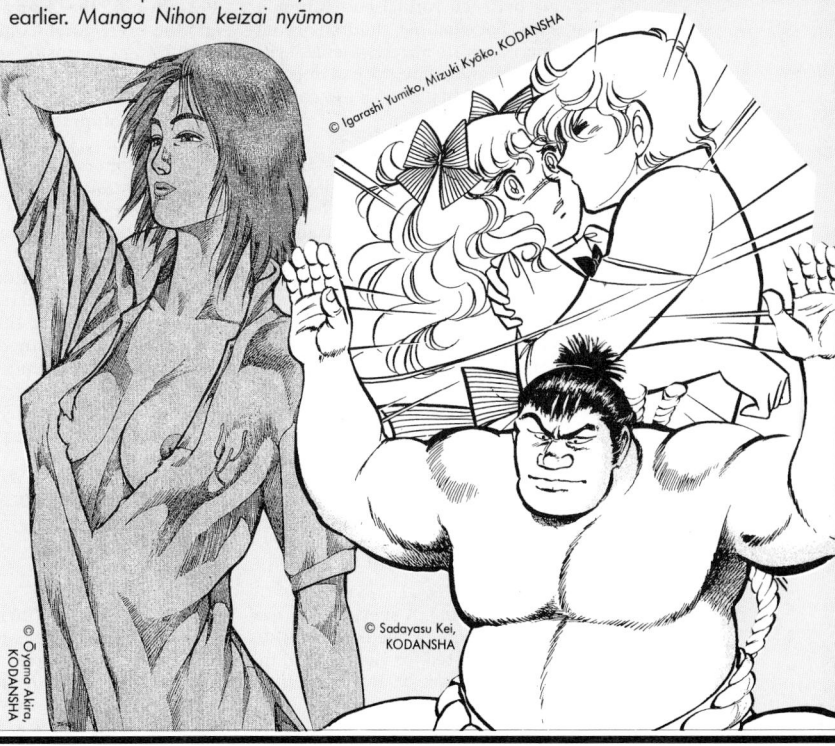

© Igarashi Yumiko, Mizuki Kyōko, KODANSHA

© Sadayasu Kei, KODANSHA

Committee on Foreign Exchange and Other Transactions

外国為替等審議会

(Gaikoku Kawaseto Shingikai). Advisory body established by the MINISTRY OF FINANCE in December 1980 that investigates and reviews key aspects of direct investment by foreign companies in Japan and contracts between Japanese and foreign companies for the introduction of foreign technology into Japan. It also reviews such general foreign-currency-exchange matters as international financial transactions. The committee reports to the minister of finance and the minister of international trade and industry. It consists of 15 members who are nominated for a term of two years by the minister of finance.

commoners → heimin

common-law marriage

内縁

(naien). Common-law marriage, cohabitation of a man and a woman but lacking legal sanction, is not unusual in Japan. A marriage is not valid under Japanese law until it is formally registered with the proper public authority. In the past, couples often neglected to register simply because they were unfamiliar with the registration requirement. Furthermore, especially in rural areas, it was fairly common not to register a marriage until after a "trial period," often lasting until the birth of the couple's first child. The law has gradually come to recognize certain features of common-law marriage as legally binding and has provided a certain measure of legal protection.

Persons who, without a valid reason, unilaterally break off a common-law marriage relationship have an obligation to compensate the other party for tangible and intangible damages. There are, in addition, precedents where the distribution of property is sometimes made as in a divorce. A common-law wife is entitled to survivors' benefits paid to families of males injured in accidents that are work related. There are, however, distinctions between formal and common-law marriages. For example, children of common-law marriages are not considered legitimate, and a common-law spouse does not have inheritance rights. See also MARRIAGE.

Communications Research Laboratory

通信総合研究所

(Tsūshin Sōgō Kenkyūjo). Laboratory adjunct of the Ministry of Posts and Telecommunications concerned with data transmission. Established in 1952 as the Radio Research Laboratory (Dempa Kenkyūjo), the laboratory adopted its present name in 1988. It is located in the city of Koganei, Tōkyō Prefecture. The laboratory conducts a broad range of research covering the fundamentals and applications of communications, data, and electromagnetic propagation, as well as human and biological information sciences, communication in manned space exploration, materials science and quantum devices, and terrestrial and extraterrestrial environmental sciences.

communists, public trial of (1931–1932)

「共産党事件」公判

(Kyōsantō Jiken kōhan). A special open trial of some 300 members of the JAPAN COMMUNIST PARTY (JCP) arrested for violations of the PEACE PRESERVATION LAW OF 1925 in nation-wide roundups of thousands of suspects conducted on 15 March 1928 and 16 April 1929 (see MARCH 15TH INCIDENT; APRIL 16TH INCIDENT).

The special open trial at the Tōkyō District Court (108 sessions from 25 June 1931 to 2 July 1932, with sentencing on 29 October) was carefully staged by the Ministry of Justice to expose the inner workings of the Communist Party and reveal its nature and tactics. It marked the beginning of a system that emphasized TENKŌ (recantation of communist ideology coupled with rehabilitation) and was designed to reform communists and other "thought criminals" and reintegrate them into society. All defendants at the trial were found guilty and given stiff prison sentences, but those who later recanted had their penalties reduced.

community centers

公民館

(kōminkan). Multipurpose community facilities built and operated by cities, towns, and villages. After World War II, the Ministry of Education introduced the community center concept to Japan as part of its community education (shakai kyōiku; literally, "social education") revitalization program, which aimed in part at encouraging the democratic rebuilding of communities. Community centers offer various educational, technical, recreational, and cultural programs for the layperson. They conduct special lecture series and sponsor a variety of demonstrations, technical courses, and physical-education and recreational activities as well. Each community center is staffed by a full-time director and several assistants. Advisory boards are set up to help the center director. As of 1990 there were 17,347 kōminkan in Japan. See also COMMUNITY EDUCATION.

Community Chest

共同募金

(Kyōdō Bokin). Organization of citizens and private social welfare groups to raise funds for the benefit of the less fortunate. The first attempts to organize a community chest in Japan occurred in Nagasaki Prefecture in 1921. In 1947 the Central Community Chest and the Prefectural Community Chest were organized as means of securing financial resources for voluntary social-welfare services badly in need of reconstruction.

The Community Chest conducts an annual fund drive, giving red-feather pins (akai hane) to donors. In 1987 total donations to the Community Chest drive totaled over ¥23 billion (US $159 million). Of this amount, the largest share came from door-to-door solicitation (43.5 percent), followed by corporate contributions. These donations are shared by organizations and individuals engaged in providing services to the needy. Other funds are obtained through the sale of special donation-included postcards for exchanging New Year's greetings and through the large-scale, annual year-end fund drive sponsored by Japan's public broadcasting corporation (NHK).

community education

社会教育

(shakai kyōiku; literally, "social education"). The term "community education" is defined by the Community Education Law (Shakai Kyōiku Hō) of 1949 as "organized educational activities . . . (including physical and recreational activities) other than those provided in school courses."

After World War II, the first of the UNITED STATES EDUCATION MISSIONS TO JAPAN issued a report on adult education that emphasized the importance of establishing LIBRARIES and MUSEUMS, making school facilities available for use by the public, and encouraging group discussions. In response, the Community Education Law of 1949, the Library Law (Toshokan Hō) of 1950, and the Museum Law (Hakubutsukan Hō) of 1951 were enacted, along with various measures encouraging the people to create active and autonomous community education programs. Major developments included the establishment of kōminkan (COMMUNITY CENTERS) as comprehensive facilities for community education, the organization of parent-teacher associations (PTAs) in each school, and the promotion of independent study group activities in communities and workplaces. Community use of school facilities for extension classes and lectures was also encouraged. After the enactment in 1953 of the Law for Promotion of Youth Classes (Seinen Gakkyū Shinkō Hō), classes providing general education, information, and training in vocational and homemaking skills to working young people became widespread.

By 1980 an increase in the number of people of retirement age, combined with an increased emphasis on leisure time due to a higher standard of living, had increased the number of people who were eager to study. Responding to this demand, the government made the promotion of LIFELONG LEARNING a national priority; local governmental bodies also involved themselves in the planning and development of community education. As of 1987, Japan's community-education facilities included 17,440 community centers, 1,801 libraries, 737 museums, 1,053 youth centers, and 34,409 physical-education and recreation facilities. Lectures and classes targeted, among others, women, youth, and the elderly.

Community education in Japan is offered not only by such public facilities as community centers but also by MISCELLANEOUS SCHOOLS and CULTURE CENTERS operating in the private sector. While most courses offered by the government are free or quite inexpensive, the commercially offered courses far outstrip their public counterparts in diversity, quality, and number of participants. Furthermore, universities in Japan have recently begun to follow the American pattern of offering extension courses and night classes leading to bachelor and postgraduate degrees. Many Japanese also study languages, humanities, and science through UNIVERSITY OF THE AIR broadcasts and the educational channel of NHK. Corporations also offer seminars and on-the-job training to help employees cope with rapid technological change.

commuting

通勤

(tsūkin). Commuting to work (tsūkin) and commuting to school (tsūgaku) are daily problems faced by Japanese workers and students as a result of industrialization and urbanization. Residential districts have spread away from the inner city to outlying suburbs, and since transportation facilities and road maintenance and expansion have not kept up with demand, public transportation is often severely overcrowded. According to a 1990 survey conducted by NHK (Japan Broadcasting Corporation), the average daily time used in commuting to work was 1 hour and 5 minutes. More time is required in larger urban areas. Average weekday commuting time in the Tōkyō area is 1 hour and 19 minutes, and in the Ōsaka area 1 hour and 9 minutes. Transportation fares are largely paid by employers; companies with 1,000 or more employees pay 97.7 percent of their employees' commuting expenses, and even small businesses with 30 to 99 employees pay 90.1 percent.

company housing　社宅

(*shataku*). A form of employee benefit in which Japanese companies acquire housing facilities and make them available to their employees at a reduced rent. The practice of providing housing began in the early period of Japanese modernization, when it was necessary to bring farm workers from rural areas to the factories and also when mining operations were set up in remote locations. At that time it was also a way of attracting unmarried workers at low wages. Most of these recruits were in their early teens, and, notably in textiles and other light industries, many were young girls. In the 1920s and 1930s, when the practice of long-term employment of regular workers within individual firms was widely adopted, it became common for companies to relocate white-collar employees, especially professionals, in order to meet company needs, and company housing was provided to facilitate the process.

After World War II, because of the national shortage of housing, company housing was needed both to attract new employees and to provide a minimum standard of living. In the high-growth period of the 1960s, large numbers of dormitories for unmarried workers were constructed throughout the country in order to recruit young employees. Later, companies began to shift to a "single-family-home policy," providing financial support for buying land and building houses. Beginning in the late 1980s, steep increases in the price of land made the single-family-home policy financially impractical. As a result, there is again a growing need for company housing for married workers. At the same time, it is becoming increasingly difficult to hire new employees. High-quality dormitories for unmarried workers and company housing for married employees are becoming a requirement for attracting new college graduates.

Comprehensive National Land Development Plan　全国総合開発計画

(Zenkoku Sōgō Kaihatsu Keikaku). A national plan for regional development adopted in October 1962 in conformity with the National Land Development Law (Kokudo Sōgō Kaihatsu Hō) of 1950. Its purpose was to alleviate urgent demographic problems centering on the overpopulation and excessive industrialization in certain urban areas, as well as on the underpopulation of others. The plan established developmental strategies for congested regions, auxiliary regions surrounding congested areas, and undeveloped regions. However, the rapid expansion of the Japanese economy in the 1960s exceeded the plan's expectations, resulting in a continuing deterioration of the urban environment and a population loss in rural areas. The plan was expanded in 1969 and revised further in 1972, 1977, and, most recently, 1987, when the FOURTH COMPREHENSIVE NATIONAL LAND DEVELOPMENT PLAN was created. See also POPULATION REDISTRIBUTION.

compromise　→ wakai

comptroller　監査役

(*kansayaku*). Position in a business corporation held by the person who oversees the

corporation's business and accounts. The duties of the comptroller are to collect from directors reports on the corporation's business operations and to investigate the operations and property of the corporation; to collect from subsidiary corporations reports on their business operations and to investigate their business and property; to participate in meetings of the BOARD OF DIRECTORS; to enjoin illegal acts by directors; to investigate, inspect, and report on documents presented to the shareholders' meeting; and to bring actions and claims under the corporation law. The comptroller also owes his corporation the duty of exercising the care of a conscientious administrator (*zenryō na kanrisha no chūi gimu*).

compulsory education　義務教育

(*gimu kyōiku*). The system of compulsory education in Japan was established by the EDUCATION ORDER OF 1872 and the Elementary School Order of 1886. The orders originally prescribed a period of four years; this was extended to six years in 1907. Since the end of World War II, compulsory education has been provided for and regulated by the CONSTITUTION OF JAPAN and the Fundamental Law of Education. The prescribed period is nine years.

computer industry　コンピューター産業

(*kompyūtā sangyō*). Japan has the second largest data-processing industry in the world after that of the United States, with large-scale subsectors producing mainframe computers, minicomputers, peripheral equipment, and software. The Japanese market is the largest computer market in the world outside the United States, and accounts for about 20 percent of all computer sales worldwide. In 1989 the Japanese computer industry controlled 60 percent of the domestic mainframe market and 70 percent of the domestic market for office computer equipment. Total domestic production in 1990 reached ¥5.81 trillion (US $40.1 billion), and exports amounted to about ¥1.7 trillion (US $11.7 billion). In 1989 FUJITSŪ, LTD, and IBM JAPAN, LTD, each held 25 percent of the domestic mainframe market, followed by HITACHI, LTD (18 percent) and NIPPON ELECTRIC CO, LTD (NEC; 17 percent). Fujitsū topped the office computer equipment market (26 percent), closely followed by NEC (25 percent); TŌSHIBA CORPORATION held a 10 percent share.

The market for PERSONAL COMPUTERS was dominated by NEC's 50 percent share. Manufacture and sales of personal computers are particularly vigorous; over 2.9 million units were produced in 1989, and the market was valued at ¥798.9 billion (US $6.9 billion). On the technical front, research and development programs are currently under way for fifth-generation computer systems, and the results are widely expected to determine the direction that the next generation of computers will take.

History—Although Ōsaka University launched Japan's first computer development program in 1947, the nation's first electronic digital computer was not constructed until 1956, 10 years after Sperry Rand developed the first electronic computer in the United States. Following the first exports of US computers to Japan in 1954, the MINISTRY OF INTERNATIONAL TRADE AND INDUSTRY (MITI) organized the Research Committee on the Computer to coordinate computer industry development, but the committee's initial budget was low; computers did not attain ur-

commuting
1 Morning rush hour at Tōkyō Station. As workers move far from central Tōkyō in search of affordable housing, the number who must commute long distances is increasing.
2 A railway employee packs passengers into a crowded Tōkyō commuter train at the height of the rush hour.

gent priority in Japanese INDUSTRIAL POLICY until the mid-1960s.

The major role of foreign-affiliated firms in the Japanese computer industry dates from 1960 when IBM was granted permission to manufacture in Japan in return for licensing basic patents to all interested Japanese manufacturers; 13 Japanese companies immediately entered cross-licensing agreements with IBM. Between 1961 and 1964 RCA, TRW, Honeywell, and General Electric, in addition to IBM and Sperry Rand, all entered technical assistance agreements with Japanese makers.

The Japanese government's vigorous promotion of the computer industry dates from 1964. In that year IBM introduced its System 360, representing the third generation of computers, which graphically demonstrated to Japanese political and business circles the strategic potential of computers. Interest was also stimulated by two other events of 1964: the success of the IBM System 360 at the Tōkyō Olympic Games and the purchase of the largest French computer manufacturer by the US firm General Electric. Japan, with its computer production of less than US $100 million, distributed among seven small domestic firms plus IBM, looked vulnerable. Computers came to be seen in Japan as a strategic industry whose fate held profound implications for Japan's future.

To achieve rapid advancement in domestic computer technologies, MITI launched several national priority projects. The FONTAC project (1962–64), undertaken by Fujitsū, OKI ELECTRIC INDUSTRY CO, LTD, and NEC—the FONTAC acronym is derived from the names of the companies involved—was the first prototype manufacturing project of a general-purpose large-scale computer system in Japan. Another project, aimed at prototype manufacture of a super-high-performance computer system, was undertaken from 1966 to 1972. This was the result of the Electronics Industry Deliberation Council Report of 1966, prepared under the aegis of MITI and often called the most important document in the industry's history. As a result of the commercial agreements with US firms and the success of these vigorously coordinated domestic projects, the Japanese computer industry made rapid strides in the late 1960s. Epitomizing the new priority given to computers, government RESEARCH AND DEVELOPMENT (R&D) subsidies by 1967 were four times 1960 levels.

In the early 1970s, prior to liberalizing the Japanese computer market and opening it to foreign imports, a process that was com-

computer industry
At this trade show held in 1991 in Tōkyō, 90 personal computers were connected in a local area network (LAN) to enable visitors to try out new software products.

pleted by 1975, MITI organized the six mainframe makers into three specialized R&D groups with the aim of developing a computer to match IBM's 370 series; the groups were provided with government R&D subsidies amounting to 50 percent (US $195.9 million) of the expenses incurred. When IBM brought out its fourth-generation computer utilizing VLSI (very large scale integration) technology, MITI responded by organizing another "national project": two new cooperative research groups consisting of Fujitsū, Hitachi, and MITSUBISHI ELECTRIC CORPORATION in one group, and NEC and Tōshiba in the other. The project was so successful that by the late 1970s Fujitsū and Hitachi were selling computers to their US and European rivals. By the early 1980s the Japanese computer industry had in many respects closed the 10-year gap in hardware sophistication that had existed in relation to IBM in the 1950s, although its software remained inferior in most applications. IBM, which still dominates the computer market worldwide, was in Japan by the early 1990s no more than one among several major manufacturers; in 1990 it had to yield its leading position in the mainframe market to Fujitsū.

Structure of the Industry — In contrast to US and European patterns, there are virtually no specialized major computer makers in Japan, and none at all with a background in business machines. Except for Fujitsū, there is not a single major Japanese computer maker for which computers provide over 35 percent of total sales. Three of the six major producers, Fujitsū, NEC, and Oki, are telecommunications firms that diversified into

computers. The other three computer firms, Hitachi, Mitsubishi Electric, and Tōshiba, are general electronics firms that diversified into computers in the early 1960s.

The unusual composition of sales at Japanese computer companies makes them extremely flexible in the corporate strategy they may pursue toward the industry's development. It also reduces the pressure they feel to push development aggressively. This weak sense of immediacy is compounded by the weakness of vested interests supporting computers in the political world and business leadership. As a new industry not employing large numbers of workers, nor assuming a major presence in any domestic locality, nor having retired executives in key positions in the business world, it has had relatively little influence with either the ruling Liberal Democratic Party or KEIDANREN (Federation of Economic Organizations). For structural reasons, then, it has been the bureaucracy, especially MITI, that has been the constant initiator of policy on computers, rather than individual firms, as has been the case with other industries. MITI has frequently taken the initiative at key stages in the development of the computer industry by providing strategic direction and by organizing and subsidizing industry research groups.

The character of Japanese government R&D assistance to computers has been somewhat different historically from that of the United States. US manufacturers receive aid in connection with projects designed primarily for governmental end-use, especially in the defense and aerospace sectors. Japanese makers receive aid, often in the form of direct subsidies, for commercial R&D, although the amounts are relatively modest by international standards.

A further crucial factor greatly contributed to the development and competitiveness of the Japanese computer industry. During the so-called calculator war that began in the mid-1960s, a furiously competitive process of cost cutting and progressive miniaturization brought down the price of calculators from ¥400,000 (US $1,100) in the mid-1960s to ¥10,000 (US $37) in 1973. By the 1980s calculators were selling for a mere ¥1,000 (US $4), 1/400th of their original mid-1960s price. In the same 20-year period calculators were reduced from the size of television sets to that of credit cards. It was this ferocious competition among the leading manufacturers that enabled them to develop the kind of high-quality, low-cost mass-production manufacturing techniques that served them so well when they moved into the computer market.

conciliation   調停
(*chōtei*). A procedure in Japanese law by which the parties to a civil dispute resolve their differences through mutual agreement before a conciliation committee established by the court. If conciliation is effected, the agreement has the same validity as a final judgment by a court. There are two types: civil conciliation and family affairs conciliation. Civil conciliation is optional, but a suit or trial of a family affairs case cannot begin until conciliation measures have been exhausted. A conciliation committee is composed of a judge and two private citizens. See DISPUTE RESOLUTION SYSTEMS OTHER THAN LITIGATION.

In labor law, conciliation is called *assen* and is conducted by conciliators appointed by LABOR RELATIONS COMMISSIONS. *Assen*

(sometimes translated as "good offices") is the least formal of the standard LABOR DISPUTE RESOLUTION PROCEDURES.

Concordia Society   協和会
(Kyōwakai). An organization for mass political mobilization in Manchuria after its occupation by the Japanese GUANDONG (KWANTUNG) ARMY in the MANCHURIAN INCIDENT of September 1931. Founded by Japanese civilian residents of Manchuria, or MANCHUKUO, as the puppet state created by the Guandong Army was called, the association endeavored to gather support among the other resident ethnic groups for a permanent Japanese presence there by espousing pan-Asian doctrines of racial harmony (*minzoku kyōwa*).

Although the Kyōwakai was originally intended by its founders to be a single mass political party by which Manchukuo would be governed after separation from China, it never achieved this status. It was preempted as an administrative organ by a regular Manchukuo government structure, containing hundreds of Japanese bureaucrats freshly arrived from the homeland, that conformed closely to guidelines set by the Guandong Army staff. From 1937 to 1945 the Kyōwakai became virtually an arm of the Manchukuo government, launching many social, economic, and political mobilization programs. The association expanded to reach 3.5 million members before the end of the war.

Conder, Josiah   コンドル, J.
(1852–1920). British architect, urban planner, and teacher. Born in London. A graduate of the Royal British Institute of Architects, Conder came to Japan in 1877. He served concurrently as a professor of architecture at the government's Kōbu Daigakkō (later part of Tōkyō University) and as a consultant for the Ministry of Engineering. His pupils, such as TATSUNO KINGO, formed the first generation of Western-style architects in Japan and laid the foundation for its modern architectural development. Between 1878 and 1907 Conder designed over 50 major buildings in Tōkyō that served both as practical models and as symbols of the Westernizing Meiji state. They include the Tōkyō Imperial Museum (1881), the ROKUMEIKAN pleasure palace (1883), Nikolai Cathedral (1891), and the Navy Ministry building (1895). He also designed residences for prominent Meiji officials and for the Mitsubishi Co's Iwasaki family. Conder's buildings were often part of urban development plans such as Mitsubishi's buildup of the Marunouchi district of Tōkyō, Japan's first large-scale private development. His designs characteristically featured red brick with white stone trim. Conder published a number of books, including *Landscape Gardening in Japan* (1893).

confections, traditional   和菓子
(*wagashi*). The development of what are now considered "traditional" Japanese confections was affected by a series of stimuli from abroad, beginning in the Nara period (710–794) with the introduction of Chinese confections by Japanese scholars studying in China, then the spread of Zen Buddhism (also from the continent, where *wagashi* were an integral part of the priests' vegetarian diet) during the Kamakura period (1185–1333), and later by such *namban-gashi* ("southern barbarian" confections) as KASUTERA, brought to Japan by Portuguese missionaries during the Muromachi period (1333–1568).

Josiah Conder The Nikolai Cathedral (1891), one of the many buildings in Tōkyō that this British architect and teacher designed while employed by the Japanese government.

traditional confections

Japanese confections are made with ingredients and aromas that complement the astringent taste of green tea.

▶ Awa okoshi (left), made from millet, and okoshi (right), made from puffed rice.

▶ Karintō, deep-fried dough coated with melted brown sugar, became popular in Edo (now Tōkyō) in the 1830s.

Moist confections (below) enjoyed during the tea ceremony come in shapes and colors appropriate to the season.

▼ The semimoist confection monaka originally consisted only of dry wafers, but bean paste was later introduced.

▲ This assortment of confections typically served during a tea ceremony includes the dry confection known as rakugan and semimoist sweets as well.

▼ Dorayaki ("gong cakes") are named for their resemblance to the musical instrument.

A "plum" within a plum-colored wrapper, folded in the manner of a traditional love letter, is a popular springtime confection.

Gelatin representing a rolled-up bamboo blind evokes coolness on a hot summer day.

A "maple leaf" with shading from yellow to red is a confection for an autumn tea ceremony.

A pale-pink "flower petal," folded over a slice of sweetened gobō (burdock root), is served in winter.

The popularization of the TEA CEREMONY during the Edo period (1600–1868), especially in the Genroku era (1688–1704), saw a dramatic increase in wagashi varieties, many of which have remained unchanged into the present. Around this time the first stores specializing in confections (kashiya) began to appear in Edo (now Tōkyō), in Ōsaka, and particularly in Kyōto, where confections called kyōgashi were developed as religious offerings and to be presented to the imperial household.

In the Edo period an expanding network of castle towns, temple towns, and transportation routes brought with it the development of regional varieties of wagashi Throughout Japan there emerged wagashi made from local products, their forms reflecting the history and traditions of each locality.

Among the defining characteristics of wagashi are their distinctive ingredients. The principal ingredient is an, a sweet paste made of red azuki beans or white bush beans, sugar, and water, which was first developed in the Kamakura period. Wheat and rice flours are also used, but dairy products and vegetable oils are not. Instead, sparing use is made of such ingredients as walnuts, peanuts, or sesame seeds, which have their own natural oils. Artificial flavoring is not added, and even natural flavorings with strong aromas are avoided. Another characteristic is the way seasonal change is incorporated in the shapes and colors of wagashi, as well as in the names chosen for each variety. For instance, sakuramochi ("cherry" confections) are the color of cherry blossoms (white or light pink) and are wrapped in pickled cherry leaves. Until recently, many varieties were available only during specific seasons.

Wagashi can be roughly divided into three categories: namagashi (moist confections), han-namagashi (semimoist confections), and higashi (dry confections).

Namagashi include MANJŪ, YŌKAN, DAIFUKU, DANGO, and OHAGI. Han-namagashi, also called yakigashi (grilled confections), include chatsū (made from a green tea and flour dough filled with black sesame–flavored an and lightly grilled), dorayaki (bean paste sandwiched between flour pancakes), kasutera, and monaka (an encased in waferlike rice cakes). Higashi include rakugan (a sugar and flour mixture pressed into various shapes), okoshi (dry cakes made of puffed rice and starch syrup), and karintō (logs of dough deep-fried until crisp and coated with melted brown sugar).

Although some wagashi are associated specifically with the tea ceremony, other varieties are widely enjoyed with Japanese tea on less formal occasions.

confession　　　　　　　　自白

(jihaku). In criminal cases in Japan, confession, as the statement of a person with firsthand experience of a crime, has been traditionally treated as an important form of evidence. The use of torture was permitted to obtain confessions up to the early Meiji period (1868–1912) because the defendant could not be found guilty without a confession. With the establishment of a modern legal system, confessions came to be treated equally with other forms of evidence. After World War II, strict evidentiary controls were imposed through the new constitution and Penal Code. When a confession has been obtained by force, torture, or intimidation, or after an unduly long period of detention, in sum, if there is any doubt as to its voluntary nature, it is not admissible as evidence. Where a confession is the only incriminatory evidence against the defendant, a verdict of guilty cannot be made.

In civil cases, confession consists of the acknowledgment of the truth of assertions made by the accuser that are unfavorable to the accused. Findings based on evidence are unnecessary if a judicial confession is ob-

tained, and the court must take the confession as the basis for its decision. Once a confession is made, it cannot be withdrawn, and it binds the confessing party on appeal as well. Where a party does not clearly dispute his or her opponent's allegations, he or she is deemed to have made a "constructive confession."

conflict resolution　　　紛争解決

(funsō kaiketsu). Conflict resolution is usually translated into Japanese as funsō kaiketsu ("conflict settlement") or funsō shūketsu ("conflict termination"), although funsō shori ("conflict management") may be preferred, since in Japan conflict is usually channeled and controlled rather than actually eliminated. It is not uncommon for individuals with deeply conflicting interests to be bound together in intimate, emotionally charged social relationships in which conflict is carefully avoided or obscured. Conversely, persons with fewer apparent conflicts of interest may engage in bitter, nearly uncontrollable conflict. Internal sources of conflict in Japan can be understood as the interaction between conflicts of interest and the institutions that have been developed to manage or control them.

Conflict-Resolution Processes—Regardless of the source or scale of conflict, the experience of direct, face-to-face confrontation between individuals is regarded as extremely unpleasant. By contrast, expressing direct conflict in a large solidarity group is less traumatic and may even occasionally be a satisfying experience. A major technique for anticipating and preventing conflict in Japan is the extensive use of prior consultation, or NEMAWASHI (literally, "binding the roots"). Well before any decisions are made or meetings called to discuss solutions to a problem, all involved parties are consulted individually about the matter. Nemawashi is a delicate combination of salesmanship, vote-counting, fact-finding, problem-solving, and horse-trading. Skill in conducting *nemawashi*, an essential quality of leadership in Japan, requires sensitivity, patience, and flexibility. A closely related technique is the use of go-betweens, typically when the parties are not yet in a direct personal relationship, as in the case of marriage arrangements or business contracts between independent firms.

Institutionalized Conflict-Resolution Procedures—Several different types of conflict-resolution procedures have been developed in Japan to handle situations of recurrent conflict. The most general is consensus decision making, a method that encourages the suppression and avoidance of conflict. The rules require that all decisions be made with the agreement of all participants; until everyone consents, no decision has been reached. In order to achieve a consensus, the participants must search for common ground and work to meet the objections of any individual who is reluctant to consent. At the same time, each participant is placed under increasing pressure to accept the growing consensus, regardless of private objections. Consensus decision making is the routine procedure for most decision-making bodies, with the notable exception of the Diet, which uses Western-style parliamentary procedure and individual votes.

A variant of consensus decision making, the so-called RINGI SYSTEM, is used by bureaucratic organizations for administrative decisions that are made by different units and levels over a period of time, rather than in a joint meeting. A written document (*ringisho*) containing a proposal is circulated in a fixed order to all units and individuals who should participate in accepting it. After internal discussion, the head of each unit signifies agreement by affixing his personal stamp to the document. The document may be delayed temporarily, and the stamp may be placed upside down to indicate some reservations, but eventually it must be approved. As the document moves upward in the bureaucracy, it acquires the force of a growing consensus, although the person ultimately in charge has the formal authority not to act on the proposal.

Consensus decision making and the *ringi* system are procedures for making a decision within a single group or organization. Failure to achieve consensus is a sign of conflict so deep that it threatens the survival of the group, since there are no established procedures for this contingency.

The essentially VERTICAL SOCIETY of Japan leaves horizontal relations weak and can make it difficult for equal but separate units of a bureaucratic organization or independent organizations to work together. One common procedure is to create a joint consultative body containing representatives of the units involved, but such bodies are not always effective.

Still another institution for conflict resolution is the use of third-party bodies, such as the courts, to help resolve conflicts between individuals or groups. Japanese courts rely extensively on mediation and conciliation procedures and favor settlements that avoid polarization of the conflicting parties or clear establishment of a guilty and an innocent party (see DISPUTE RESOLUTION SYSTEMS OTHER THAN LITIGATION). Despite this, some scholars have shown that Japanese tend to

avoid use of the legal system to settle private disputes precisely because of its polarizing, conflict-laden character.

Just as the formal institution of consensus decision making relies heavily on the informal practice of *nemawashi* for its success, so are the formal legal processes of conflict resolution supported by informal means of achieving out-of-court settlements. Professional specialists in achieving such settlements are called *jidan'ya* (compromise-brokers). It has been pointed out that the interplay between the formal (*tatemae*) or "front-stage" (*omote*) procedures and rituals and the informal (*honne*) or "back-stage" (*ura*) negotiations is essential to successful conflict resolutions (see TATEMAE AND HONNE).

Ritualization of Conflict—Confrontation rituals are sometimes staged by organized groups to permit anger and frustration to be vented and in some cases to set the stage publicly for serious private negotiations. The annual spring labor offensive, or SHUNTŌ, is a relatively controlled confrontation ritual through which unions demonstrate their power with a brief strike before settling down to negotiations. Quite different from confrontation rituals are conflict-resolution rituals symbolizing the formal end of a conflict. Conflict-resolution rituals all involve some form of apology, which requires acceptance of responsibility for the conflict and signals a willingness to end it. See also COLLECTIVE BARGAINING RIGHT; LABOR DISPUTE RESOLUTION PROCEDURES.

Confucianism 儒教

(Jukyō). Tradition of Chinese origin said to have been known in Japan since the 5th century. Confucianism has religious aspects but is mainly a philosophical, ethical, and political teaching. In Japan it assumed particular importance during the 6th to 9th centuries and from the Edo period (1600–1868) through the early Shōwa period (1926–89).

Confucius and the Tradition in Ancient China—Confucianism owes its basic orientation largely to Kong Qiu (K'ung Ch'iu), a teacher and philosopher of the Zhou (Chou) dynasty (1027 BC–256 BC). Confucius, as he is known in the West, wished to restore the hierarchical but harmonious feudal society he believed to have existed at the beginning of the Zhou dynasty. This concern gave the tradition a generally conservative orientation, an element of protest against contemporary society, and an intense interest in political power and office. Confucius believed that the ideal social order should be achieved not by the enforcement of law but by the moral example of those in authority. Rulers should delegate power to officials chosen solely on the basis of their moral and intellectual capacities. The source of each individual's morality lay in filial piety, a child's respect for and obedience to its parents (in practice mainly to the father, for the tradition concerned itself rather little with women). Confucius taught further that men should study and cultivate themselves to become "superior men" (*zhunzi* or *chun-tzu*; J: *kunshi*). This ideal, held to be an end in itself, was characterized by knowledge of classical songs, ritual, and music and by such virtues as loyalty, uprightness, and moderation. Most important, however, was *ren* (*jen*; J: *jin*), a kind of benevolence or altruism. The humanism that these concerns suggest was reflected in Confucius's lack of interest in metaphysical or religious questions and in the rational temper of his thought.

Confucius called himself "a transmitter,

not a creator," and did not write original works. Tradition, however, ascribes to him the editing of the following texts: *Yi jing* (*I ching*; Book of Changes), basically a manual of divination; *Shu jing* (*Shu ching*; Book of Documents), a collection of historical works; *Shi jing* (*Shih ching*; Book of Songs), an anthology of early song texts; *Li* (Ritual), a ritual text no longer extant; and *Chun qiu* (*Ch'un ch'iu*; Spring and Autumn Annals), a brief history of Confucius's own state of Lu. With these were later grouped the *Lun yu* (*Lun yü*; Analects), a collection of sayings by Confucius and his disciples; the *Xiao jing* (*Hsiao ching*; Classic of Filial Piety); and a number of commentaries and ritual compendia including the influential *Li ji* (*Li chi*; Record of Ritual). These texts constituted the Confucian canon, and their study was a basic commitment of Confucians in all times and places.

After his death, followers of Confucius suffered persecution under the despotic Qin (Ch'in) dynasty (221 BC–206 BC). Under the succeeding Han dynasty (206 BC–AD 220) Confucianism entered its long ascendancy in China. The principle of Confucian meritocracy was institutionalized in 124 BC when a state college staffed by doctors of the Confucian classics and a system of written examinations for appointment to the state bureaucracy were established. During the Han, Confucius himself became the object of a state cult of sacrifices and worship. At the same time, a detailed cosmology was developed according to which the universe was seen as an organic structure under the control of Heaven and composed of the two forces of *yin* (negative) and *yang* (positive) and the five elements. Man, particularly the ruler, played a pivotal role as mediator between Heaven and the natural order. It was the ruler's function to instruct his subjects to conform to Confucian precepts; according to his success or failure, Heaven responded with auspicious events, portents, or visitations. This system gave rise to a school of divination and a body of literature that dealt with directional taboos and calendrical superstitions. Known as *yinyang dao* (*yin-yang tao*; J: OMMYŌDŌ), this system was only tenuously Confucian and indeed contrary to the rational spirit of Confucius's teaching, yet it exercised great influence on the lives of the Chinese and later of the Japanese.

Confucianism in Ancient Japan—Confucianism was transmitted to the kingdoms of Korea during the course of the 4th century. Tradition claims that from there it was introduced to Japan with the arrival from the Korean state of PAEKCHE (J: Kudara) in 404 and 405, respectively, of the Korean scholars who are known in Japan as Achiki and WANI. The increasing centralization of Japanese society from the late 6th century created a climate particularly favorable to Confucianism. From the reign of the empress Suiko (r 593–628), the tradition is closely linked with the development of the Japanese state. It was not, however, its exclusive official ideology, for the Japanese court, like its Chinese model, remained ideologically pluralist.

The opening of diplomatic relations with the Chinese Sui dynasty (589–618) and its successor the Tang (T'ang) dynasty (618–907) created a more direct path for the transmission of Confucianism to Japan. From 608, students were included in the Japanese missions to China, and men such as MINABUCHI NO SHŌAN (fl early 7th century) and the scholar-monk SŌMIN (d 653), who spent many years in China, spread Confucian ideas on their return. Some were closely involved in the TAIKA REFORM of the second half of the 7th century, and there is little doubt that their Confucian ideas played an important role in this sustained attempt by the Japanese court to emulate the style and institutions of the centralized bureaucracy of Tang China. To the extent that the latter was a Confucian state, therefore, the conduct and institutions of government in Japan now also assumed a Confucian coloring. Although the Tang Confucian state ritual program was apparently not adopted in full, Japanese emperors assumed the Confucian stance of moral responsibility for the welfare of their subjects, enjoined Confucian values on their officials, and issued decrees proclaiming the importance of ritual propriety for the maintenance of social order. The RITSURYŌ SYSTEM of administration (the word *ritsuryō* refers to penal and administrative codes) established during this period also shows Confucian influence in its underlying assumption that government is moral in purpose. Still, the *ritsuryō* lawmakers appear to have balked at the full-scale Confucianization of Japanese society, and there were several departures from the Chinese model.

The most conspicuous and sustained Confucian influence in ancient Japan was in the field of state-sponsored education. Here the Japanese attempted to reproduce the Chinese system of metropolitan and provincial schools and state examinations designed to provide Confucian-educated personnel for the bureaucracy. As established under the *ritsuryō* codes, the DAIGAKURYŌ, a university, was a department of the Shikibushō (Ministry of Ceremonial). Its academic staff included one doctor and two assistant doctors of the Confucian classics. The curriculum was devoted to these classics and followed the Tang model. Students selected texts for study from a list of seven classics with prescribed commentaries by Han or post-Han Chinese scholars. In addition, all studied the *Analects* and the *Classic of Filial Piety*. Study appears to have been rigidly formalized and to have stressed memorization. Outside the capital, *kokugaku* (provincial schools) modeled on the metropolitan university were officially prescribed for each province. The curriculum probably resembled that of the university. Graduates could proceed to the university for further study or take the state examinations for admission to court rank and office in the Ministry of Ceremonial.

Such, in outline, were the institutions of Confucian learning prescribed under the early-8th-century codes. Had they functioned ideally, they might have made Confucian learning the basic qualification for bureaucratic office and realized the principle of Confucian meritocracy. From the beginning, however, there were serious obstacles. First, it was a long time before the university or the provincial schools even began to approach their prescribed strength. Second, the restricted social basis for admission effectively excluded a truly meritocratic standard of recruitment to the bureaucracy through the system. Confucian education, therefore, did not become in Japan, as it did in Tang China, an important path to highest office. The university functioned instead to train middle- and lower-ranking officials whom birth normally denied high rank and office. Finally, in Japanese society at large, Confucianism never seriously challenged Buddhism as the dominant religious or intellectual persuasion. It was mainly to Buddhism that the Nara government looked for ideological support, and even officers of the Confucian Daigakuryō seem to have embraced it as their private faith.

By the early 10th century, the general decay of the *ritsuryō* system was well advanced. Confucianism, as yet shallowly rooted in Japan, rapidly declined into a remote and formal pursuit. The meritocratic ideal of Confucian education was undermined by the growth within the university of semiprivate halls (*bessō*) devoted to the interests of particular families, such as the KANGAKUIN of the Fujiwara family. Hereditary occupation of academic office became established, and, from the 11th century, university posts were virtually monopolized by a few court families. Moreover, Buddhism increasingly penetrated the university. The standard of examination, believed hitherto to have been high, also declined. Examination questions were leaked, and, from the 11th century, many students passed merely on the recommendation of an unqualified dignitary.

Confucianism in Medieval China: The Neo-Confucian Revival—The state-sponsored Confucianism of the Tang dynasty and of ancient Japan had tended to stress the institutional and ritual aspects of the tradition. During the Song (Sung) dynasty (960–1279) in China, however, Confucianism underwent a revival and development known as Neo-Confucianism, and it was in this form that it was destined to become most widely studied in Japan from the 13th or 14th century. There were two main schools of Neo-Confucianism. The more important is known as the Cheng-Zhu (Ch'eng-Chu) school. In Japanese it is usually referred to as SHUSHIGAKU (the Zhu Xi school). This was a dualistic system of thought centered on the concepts of "principle" (*li*; J: *ri*) and "ether" or "material force" (*qi* or *ch'i*; J: *ki*). Principle was the organizing, rationally accessible category that governed the properties of things and the course of events. It was permanent, good, and unchanging and was endowed in man as his nature. This nature, however, could be obscured by the quality of the material force, the physical component of man's makeup and of the world. It was man's task to purify his *qi* by a number of techniques, including objective study of principle itself and subjective introspection. Zhu Xi Neo-Confucianism was admirably suited to a conservative order and was established as the official orthodoxy in China, having become the basis for the civil service examinations by 1314.

The second school of Neo-Confucianism reached maturity only in the Ming dynasty (1368–1644). It is usually known in Japan as the Yangming (J: Yōmei) school (see YŌMEIGAKU) after the cognomen of its leading thinker, Wang Yangming (1472–1529). Wang deplored what he considered the unpractical and academic emphasis of the Zhu Xi system. He reformulated Neo-Confucian doctrine as a monistic idealism in which the mind contained all things and was itself principle (*li*). Wang thus rejected the objective study of principle and substituted subjective intuition as the standard of moral action. Wang's system, because of its activism, subjectivity, and concern with internal motivation rather than adherence to external norms, held a potential appeal for those dissatisfied with the status quo, especially in times of rapid change.

Confucianism in Medieval Japan— The date of the arrival of Neo-Confucian doctrines in Japan is uncertain, but it was in the Zen Buddhist community (see GOZAN) rather than among the traditional Kyōto court Confucian families that they first took root. Zen monks saw in Neo-Confucianism a useful secular complement to their own religious teachings, of particular value in their relations with political leaders. This eclecticism set the tone for the Confucianism of the Kamakura (1185–1333) and Muromachi (1333–1568) periods, and there came into being a type of Buddhist-Confucian monk known as a *jusō*. The first century of the Muromachi period saw a continuation of the activity of *jusō* and the subordination of Confucianism to Buddhism. At the same time, syncretism between Neo-Confucianism and Shintō was also explored by such scholars as ICHIJŌ KANEYOSHI and YOSHIDA KANETOMO, who founded schools of thought that survived into the Edo period.

The Edo Period: Official Patronage and Education—The establishment of the Tokugawa peace made the world-denying assumptions of Buddhism less attractive and heightened interest in questions of society and of government. Confucianism was equipped to meet this concern at many levels. Its ideal society was in many respects congruent with the feudal order of Tokugawa Japan. *Samurai*, whom peace caused increasingly to assume the role of bureaucrats, could derive a moral raison d'être from the gentlemen-officials of the Confucian ideal. Increased wealth, leisure, and use of printing made the tradition ever more widely accessible. Japanese Confucian scholarship and thought achieved genuine creativity, and the Edo period became the golden age of the tradition in Japan.

Confucianism was accorded official recognition under the third Tokugawa shōgun, Iemitsu (r 1623–51), and its position was further improved under the fifth shōgun, Tsunayoshi (r 1680–1709), himself a keen student of the tradition. During the reigns of the next two shōguns, however, Confucian influence was exercised less on an institutional basis than through the personal efforts of the scholar ARAI HAKUSEKI. The eighth shōgun, Yoshimune (r 1716–45), encouraged diffusion of Confucian teachings among the non-samurai urban population. He also employed Confucian advisers such as MURO KYŪSŌ and the brilliant OGYŪ SORAI.

Shogunate patronage of Neo-Confucianism underwent an important development during the period of the KANSEI REFORMS (1787–93). Ideological uniformity was imposed in 1790 by prohibiting all but Cheng-Zhu teachings (the so-called Kansei prohibition on heterodoxy). An official college known as the Shōheizaka Gakumonjo (see SHŌHEIKŌ), designed to train shogunal administrators, was founded a few years later. Examinations based on a Cheng-Zhu syllabus were now conducted every three years (from 1818 every five years). For the first time since the failure of the ancient Daigakuryō, Confucian learning could be considered a formal preparation for government service. In the late Edo period the shogunate also established special schools for commoners in shogunal lands and supported lectures by representatives of popular religious movements, such as SHINGAKU, which had a strong Confucian component.

The most conspicuous Confucian institutions of the Edo period were the official domain schools (HANKŌ). The majority of the staff of the domain schools were Confucian scholars, and the curriculum placed great weight on the study of Confucian texts. Samurai who did not attend domain schools might go to private institutions, often run by a single Confucian scholar who usually employed the Confucian classics as his texts. By 1870 there were some 1,400 such schools in Japan. The non-samurai social classes were less well provided with the opportunity for Confucian study. Some 17 domains, however, are known to have admitted commoners into their schools. Moreover, Confucian ethics, particularly filial piety, were an element in TERAKOYA (village school) education, whose main purpose was the inculcation of basic literacy among commoners. It has been estimated that, by 1868, some 43 percent of boys and 10 percent of girls attended some form of school. All of these would probably have been exposed at least to the main Confucian ethical concepts.

The effect of this wide diffusion of Confucian teaching is difficult to gauge. It is clear, however, that there were important limitations to the penetration of Confucianism in Tokugawa Japan, when compared with Buddhism or Shintō. Religious practices remained largely Buddhist or Shintō, and the number of Buddhist publications greatly outnumbered the Confucian. Furthermore, the basic structure of Japanese society was not radically modified by Confucianism. Confucian meritocracy made undramatic progress against the predominantly hereditary occupation system. The samurai were not dissuaded from their martial values by Confucian civilian ideals, and the Japanese kinship system remained to a large extent unaltered by Confucian norms. The native system of ethical values, too, although many of its concepts assumed Confucian names, retained much of its indigenous character. However, the conservative, hierarchical, and harmonistic emphases of Confucianism certainly exerted an integrating and stabilizing influence at many levels and in many areas of Edo-period life, especially in the intellectual life of the period.

Edo-Period Confucian Thought — Traditional accounts divide Tokugawa Confucianism into four phases, in each of which a seminal thinker developed or reinterpreted the ideas of a particular school of thought. The first phase spanned the 17th century, but its ideas also found adherents throughout the remainder of the period. Its dominating assumption was that the Neo-Confucianism of the Song and Ming dynasties was broadly congruent with the realities of Japanese society. Two important schools emerged in the Cheng-Zhu tradition. The Kyōgakuha school, founded by FUJIWARA SEIKA and whose most prominent scholar was HAYASHI RAZAN, developed under Razan the medieval tradition of syncretism between Neo-Confucianism and Shintō. The Kimon Gakuha (Yamazaki school), founded by YAMAZAKI ANSAI, emphasized a "reverence" (TSUTSU-SHIMI), and its insistence on the loyalty owed by subjects to their ruler was to exert influence on the imperial loyalists of the MEIJI RESTORATION of 1868. The first important exponent of the doctrines of Wang Yangming was NAKAE TŌJU. His most influential disciple was KUMAZAWA BANZAN, whose rational and humanitarian views on administrative and economic issues laid the foundation for much of the Confucian social and economic thought of the Edo period.

The second phase began in the mid-17th century, when thinkers began to find an incongruity between their own experience and sense of the needs of contemporary society and what they felt to be the static, contemplative emphasis of Neo-Confucianism. These men rejected much of the Neo-Confucian system of metaphysics and self-cultivation and advocated a return to what they held to be pristine Confucianism. They are often grouped together under the name of Kogakuha (School of Ancient Learning; see KOGAKU). The earliest major figure in this tradition is YAMAGA SOKŌ, who advocated regulation of society less by self-cultivation in the manner of orthodox Neo-Confucianism than by the external restraints of rituals and codes of conduct. His detailed prescriptions for samurai became known as BUSHIDŌ (the Way of the warrior). Another critic of Neo-Confucianism was ITŌ JINSAI, who taught a practical ethics based on benevolence, loyalty, and faithfulness. His rejection of Neo-Confucianism was consolidated and given a political thrust by Ogyū Sorai, who urged rigorous philological study of the classics to enable an adaptation of the institutions created by the ancient sage-kings of China to the ordering of contemporary society.

The third phase of Tokugawa Confucian thought, which spanned the 18th century and beyond, was complex and even confused. Several trends can be identified. A tendency toward rationality and empiricism is seen in a number of thinkers, mainly in the Cheng-Zhu tradition, such as KAIBARA EKIKEN. In response to the sectarian spirit occasioned by Sorai's attack on the Cheng-Zhu system, the SETCHŪGAKUHA (Eclectic school) drew on Chinese exegetical studies and the philological approach of Sorai. Arising from the Kansei prohibition on heterodoxy of 1790, the Cheng-Zhu school underwent a revival and came to form the conceptual basis for early Japanese attempts to understand Western science. Yet another trend was the reformulation of Confucian doctrines syncretically with Shintō and Buddhism. The popular Shingaku (Heart Learning) movement founded by ISHIDA BAIGAN in the early 18th century exemplifies this development, and it gained many adherents among townsmen. Its rural counterpart, the Hōtoku (Repayment of Virtue) movement led by the peasant teacher NINOMIYA SONTOKU, flourished in the 19th century.

The final phase of Edo Confucian thought coincided with the quickening of intellectual life that took place against the background of the challenge of the West and the decline of shogunal power. One theme was an increased, if largely private, interest in the teachings of Wang Yangming, whose combination of activism and subjectivity was attractive in a time of intellectual and political turbulence. The most conspicuous trend, however, was the reemergence, with an intensified element of national feeling, of the ancient synthesis of Confucianism, Shintō, and imperial ideology. The chief origin of this trend was among the MITO SCHOOL, which compiled the DAI NIHON SHI (1657–1906, History of Great Japan), whose emphasis on loyalty, particularly toward the emperor, attained prominence in the first half of the 19th century. Similar loyalist and nationalist feeling was expressed in *Nihon gaishi* (ca 1836, Unofficial History of Japan) by the Confucian historian RAI SAN'YŌ. Such proimperial and antiforeign rhetoric was widely influential and inspired imperial restoration activists such as YOSHIDA SHŌIN. Not all Confucian thinkers of the time, however, accepted the antiforeign views that were inspired by the Mito school. Men such as SAKUMA SHŌZAN, a military scientist and Cheng-Zhu thinker, and YOKOI SHŌNAN tried to assimilate the implications of Western science and civilization within a Confucian metaphysical framework.

Confucianism in Modern Times — From one point of view the Meiji Restoration of 1868 and the establishment of the new bureaucratic state may be interpreted as a long-delayed realization of Confucian meritocracy. For many Japanese, however, the opening of Japan to massive Western influence must have shattered the cogency and integrity of the traditional Confucian world view. After a brief initial period during which the restorationists attempted to model the Japanese state on the Confucian-inspired institutions of the early 8th century, a reaction took place. The shogunal college and most of the domain schools were refounded as Western-style institutions or abolished within a few years of the Restoration. Confucianism, however, had by now become so well established that its influence was likely to persist, even if only in fragmented form. That it reasserted itself so soon was in no small degree due to the influence on the Meiji emperor (r 1867–1912) of his Confucian preceptor MOTODA NAGAZANE and to the advocacy of the philosopher and educator NISHIMURA SHIGEKI, who attempted a synthesis of Confucian metaphysics with Western thought. The culmination of their efforts, the influential IMPERIAL RESCRIPT ON EDUCATION of 1890, expressed a combination of Shintō tradition concerning the imperial dynasty with a Confucian view of the duties of his subjects. In this way, the survival into modern times of the Mito fusion of Confucian ethics with national tradition was secured.

The deterioration of both the domestic and the international situations by the early 1930s provided a receptive atmosphere for this synthesis of nationalism with Confucianism. From about 1933, Confucian ideas were seen as a means for achieving the ideological mobilization of the nation, and the promotion of Confucianism was an essential feature of both domestic and foreign policy. The most notable example of this was the KOKUTAI NO HONGI (Cardinal Principles of the National Polity of Japan) of 1937, which presents the emperor as a ruler in the Confucian style and enjoins loyalty, filial piety, harmony, and diligent industry upon the Japanese people.

Following defeat in World War II, however, the Japanese once more turned their backs on their Confucian heritage. In recent years, however, there have been signs of a modest revival of interest. Popular studies of the Confucian classics continue to be published, and the *Analects* are still quoted in speeches on such occasions as graduation days. Although echoes of prewar Confucianism may still occasionally be heard, this new interest in the tradition seems usually to be free of explicitly nationalist sentiments.

conjuring　奇術

(*kijutsu*). Japanese conjuring has been greatly influenced by its Chinese origins. During the Nara period (710–794), the variety show was imported from China, along with illusions such as the "Hindu mango tree" trick, in which a tree appeared to grow from a seed. There are records indicating that street artists who performed magic and acrobatics existed in Japan during the Muromachi period (1333–1568), but the details of their repertoires are sketchy. Conjuring emerged as an independent art form in Japan in the early Edo period (1600–1868). Magic tricks came to be called *tejina*, or "sleight of hand," and professional magicians performed *karakuri*, or tricks that relied on mechanical devices. Among these early professional magicians were Shioya Chōjirō, who was known for an illusion in which he appeared to swallow a horse; Satake Sentarō, who extricated himself from caldrons and trunks; and Yanagawa Itchōsai, who performed an illusion in which paper butterflies appeared to come alive. In the late 17th century, books revealing the secrets of magic tricks were published in large numbers. These instruction books explained how to produce an unending flow of water from a bottle, how to change a bamboo leaf into a fish, how to breathe air into a piece of white paper to change it into an egg, and other such tricks.

In the Meiji period (1868–1912) various illusions and techniques of magic were introduced to Japan from the West. Among these was an illusion known as "the Sphinx," in which a severed head appeared to speak. One of Japan's most famous magicians during the Meiji period was Shōkyokusai Ten'ichi (1853–1912), who was best known for his "thumb tie" trick, in which he tied the ends of a piece of string to his thumbs and then passed the string intact through a rod. After Ten'ichi's death his student Shōkyokusai Tenkatsu (1886–1944) assumed the leadership of his troupe. Tenkatsu, a woman, was celebrated throughout Japan as "the queen of magic" during the Taishō (1912–26) and early Shōwa (1926–89) periods.

In post–World War II Japan, the spread of television and the performances of various Western magicians contributed to an increasing interest in magic. The best-known magicians of this time were Hikita Tenkō (1934–79), who first achieved fame with his televised escape feats, and Adachi Ryūkō (1896–1982), who combined magic with storytelling.

Magicians practicing in Japan today include Shimada Haruo, famous for his "dragon illusion"; a pair of comic magicians who call themselves the Napoleons; and Mr. Maric (b 1949), a "psychic illusionist."

consanguinity　　　　　親族

(*shinzoku*). A legal relationship between persons arising as a result of blood or marital ties. The Japanese Civil Code establishes provisions concerning three types of such relations: (1) a blood relation within the sixth degree of kinship; (2) spouse; and (3) a marriage relation within the third degree of kinship (art. 725). In addition to these three classifications, there are four generally recognized means of categorizing consanguinity: direct line (*chokkei*; including ancestors and descendants), collateral line (*bōkei*; parallel descendants from the same ancestor), ascendants (*sonzoku*; persons of preceding generations), and descendants (*hizoku*; persons of succeeding generations).

Certain relationships of consanguinity give rise to obligations for support (Civil Code, arts. 877–881) and rights of inheritance (Civil Code, arts. 887–890). Marriage between persons of close consanguineous relationship is prohibited (Civil Code, art. 734).

Conscription Ordinance of 1873　　　　　徴兵令

(Chōheirei). Law making military service compulsory for all males, enacted in January and effective from April 1873. Successive peasant uprisings and rebellions by discontented *samurai* (see SHIZOKU) after the MEIJI RESTORATION of 1868 had shown that military forces from the southwestern domains of Satsuma (now Kagoshima Prefecture) and Chōshū (now Yamaguchi Prefecture), upon which the new government relied, were not enough, and arguments were made for an army under direct government control. Opinions were divided as to whether service should be voluntary or compulsory, but ŌMURA MASUJIRŌ and YAMAGATA ARITOMO of Chōshū forced the adoption of a conscription system, citing the fact that such systems had been adopted by advanced nations of Western Europe and had proved both militarily and financially advantageous. Also cited was the success of the "irregular militia" (KIHEITAI) made up of all classes of society in Chōshū.

Under the ordinance all males who reached 20 years of age were required to serve for 3 years. Numerous exceptions were made, however, for several categories of people, including those who paid proxy money. The government's successful suppression of the SATSUMA REBELLION (1877), a large-scale revolt by former samurai of that domain, proved the value of conscription, and steps were then taken to make it universal. Following extensive revisions in April 1927, the Conscription Ordinance was replaced by the Military Service Law (Heieki Hō). This was abolished in November 1945 during the OCCUPATION of Japan.

conservation　　　　　自然保護

(*shizen hogo*). Conservation as a conscious movement aimed toward the protection of nature so as to ensure adequate supplies of natural resources and provide a wholesome environment for future generations is relatively new in Japan. The beginnings of Japan's modern conservation movement lay, for the most part, in the Meiji period (1868–1912). MIYOSHI MANABU, a professor of botany at Tōkyō University who was impressed with the conservation efforts he had witnessed in Germany, began a campaign early in the 20th century to awaken public opinion to the need for implementing conservation programs in Japan. From this came Japan's first conservation law, enacted in 1919, and the National Parks Law of 1931.

Early movements concentrated mainly on the protection of rare natural phenomena or places prized for their historical import or exceptional scenic beauty. Conservation movements in the truly contemporary sense of the term actually began in the 1950s, when Japanese post–World War II industrial development began to affect the environment profoundly (see COMPREHENSIVE NATIONAL LAND DEVELOPMENT PLAN; CULTURAL PROPERTIES LAW). The 1960s were a period of rapid economic development in Japan. Under the Comprehensive National Land Development Plan, land development programs were instituted in many parts of Japan (see LAND RECLAMATION). Following the reclamation of shoreline lands and the erection of giant oil-refining complexes, however, residents in the areas affected rose in protest. This swelled the ranks of the conservation movement (see CITIZENS' MOVEMENTS).

This movement continued into the 1970s,

when pollution and environmental destruction in Japan became ever more visible. Damage attributed to photochemical smog became a serious public issue in 1970; this prompted the unification of 77 of the nation's conservation groups under the umbrella of the Japan Union of Nature Conservation in 1971. During that same year the government established the ENVIRONMENT AGENCY. At the time of its inception, the agency took a positive stance toward promoting conservation and betterment of the environment. In 1972 the Diet passed the Nature Conservation Law. The oil crisis of 1973 resulted in a setback in land development plans. This might have seemed welcome to the conservation movement; however, in some sectors of society and in the Environment Agency itself, restrictions on development and environmental pollution tended to slacken in order to provide relief from the economic recession brought on by the oil crisis. This led to confrontations between the Environment Agency and citizens' groups behind the conservation movement. Japan's official nature conservation policy in 1990 was based on two pieces of legislation, the Nature Conservation Law and the POLLUTION COUNTERMEASURES BASIC LAW. A concern of the government has been the need to improve the assessment of the extent of environmental damage. Since the abandonment of attempts to get an Environmental Impact Assessment Bill through the Diet in 1984, such assessment has been left to the discretion of government agencies. Local authorities have responded to this situation by following the lead set by the city of Kawasaki in Kanagawa Prefecture, which in 1976 passed its own environmental impact assessment ordinance. By 1990, 27 local authorities had instituted similar ordinances. Citizens' nature conservation movements resulted in the founding of the Japanese Union of National Trust Movements in 1983; some 60 trust groups were active in 1991. See also ENVIRONMENTAL QUALITY; NATURAL MONUMENTS AND PROTECTED SPECIES; WILD BIRD SOCIETY OF JAPAN; BIRD SANCTUARIES; RED DATA BOOK.

▶▶ 226–227

conservatives and reformists　　　　　保守と革新

(*hoshu to kakushin*). The terms conservative (*hoshu*) and reformist (*kakushin*) are commonly used to refer to the two major political blocs that have emerged in Japanese domestic politics in the post–World War II era. This division became clearly established in 1955 when the two main conservative parties merged to form the LIBERAL DEMOCRATIC PARTY (LDP), while at the same time the reformist forces coalesced around a newly unified JAPAN SOCIALIST PARTY (JSP) and its occasional ally, the JAPAN COMMUNIST PARTY (JCP). In other words, the label conservative usually denotes the LDP, which has been the party in power since 1955, while reformist is a term used to describe the various opposition forces arrayed against it. (See POLITICAL PARTIES.)

One of the principal areas of conflict between conservative and reformist camps has been Japanese foreign policy. The conservatives have historically advocated the strengthening of Japan's ties with the United States and Western Europe, while the reformists have stressed a neutralist, antiwar stance and the fostering of amicable relations

Continued on page 228▶

From Sea Ice to Coral

A conservationist and writer celebrates Japan's natural wonders and deplores the nation's shortcomings in environmental planning and protection.

Japanese people frequently ask me why I like Japan so much. There is no easy answer, but often I reply, "What other island nation has sea ice in the north and coral in the south?" The river that flows outside my study window is of crystal-pure water; trout and char swim in it. Beyond is a dormant volcano, clothed in forest, twice as high as any mountain in Wales, the land of my birth, and wild bears live there. A few days ago I stayed on a small island near the mysterious, mountainous island of Iriomotejima deep in the south of Japan. I saw a young humpback whale, fruit bats, jet-black butterflies on scarlet hibiscus. I dived in the coral. Only a week before that I had been filming at early morning temperatures of –30°C (–22°F) in Hokkaidō. Japan never fails to amaze me.

Near the end of the Edo period (1600–1868), Edo, soon to be renamed Tōkyō, was the most important city in Japan and the biggest in the world. When Commodore Matthew Perry and his "black ships" sailed into Edo Bay (now Tōkyō Bay) in 1853, determined to force the country to open to the West, Japan was already a highly civilized, intensely organized nation, one that would not take long to leapfrog into the industrial age. Yet, partly because of official land-management policies and partly because of the absence of modern heavy industries, the state of its natural ecosystems, fauna, and flora was far superior to that of the European countries of the time. Britain, for example, was being ravaged by the industrial revolution, with many of its major species of wild animals long since exterminated and vast tracts of woodland replaced by farmland and sheep pastures.

How has Japan's natural environment fared during the century and a half since Commodore Perry's entrance?

On first coming to Japan in 1962, I had the typical Westerner's ignorance of what Japan was really like. Although I was prepared for the size and bustle of Tōkyō and for the hard training at the martial arts *dōjō*, I knew little of Japan's natural world beyond the existence of snowcapped Mt. Fuji, cherry trees, wind-bent pines, and, of course, the famous frog that plopped into the pond in Bashō's *haiku*.

My first glimpse of the richness and nearness of the country's natural resources came on a crowded Tōkyō street within days of my arrival. I paused at an open-fronted fish shop and stared at the great variety of fish and crustaceans on display. Many I knew from Wales—herring, sardines, mackerel, cod, flounder, eels, and such—but others I had never seen before, except perhaps in an aquarium. What especially interested me was that several of the fish were lying on slabs or in boxes of ice with gills still moving.

Nowadays I use the fish market at Tsukiji in Tōkyō, the world's largest, to demonstrate to guests the astounding variety of Japan's coastal resources. A glance at a good map will show you how long and complicated the coastline is, with thousands of islands. Before the country started to tamper with, landfill, tetrapod, and concrete the coast, the range of coastal environments was vast indeed.

Japan's mountainous character gave it thousands of fast-flowing, oxygen-rich rivers that merged and spread out into broad estuaries. Several species of salmon, char, and trout thrived. The plentiful lakes, too, had all manner of freshwater creatures, and many supported productive, sustainable fisheries. In smaller watercourses and in ditches around rice-paddy fields there were tasty loach, and there were edible water snails in the paddy mud. It was customary, before the introduction of pesticides, to raise and fatten carp in paddies, too.

The Mountains | When I started to escape the bustle of Tōkyō by hiking in the mountains, the profusion of nature excited me. Within just a couple of hours by train I could be in densely forested hills with clean, swift streams. Hiking up from little valley hamlets I could be in the domain of the wild boar, bear, and deer, as well as such creatures as the hare, fox, and badger and many others that I had not encountered before.

Venturing further, I went west to Nagano Prefecture, where I now make my home. On one three-day trip I walked in a forest of virgin beech, with trees so large that it took three of us linking hands to encompass the trunks. These primeval forests were far more extensive than the remnants I had known in Britain, and, as Japan had never been scoured by the glaciers of the ice ages, there were far more species of plants, insects, birds, and other animals. At that time, the early 1960s, 67 percent of Japan was covered with forest, despite considerable logging. Although that figure included plantations for the cultivation of single species of conifers, there still was lots of wild mixed forest.

Mountain trails were well marked, and fellow hikers and climbers, as well as the local people, were always kind and informative, so it was no problem to take trips alone. I enjoyed companionship but preferred to take time along the way to stop and look. Mountain villages, which had long relied on and maintained balance with their environment, were fascinating. Mountain people are generally most hospitable, and I was able to attend wedding feasts, traditional masked dances performed to drive out demons, and lion dances. I sat many a night over *sake*, talking with foresters, farmers, and even *matagi*, traditional hunters of bear.

While staying at *minshuku* lodges I was treated to a profusion of specialties—wild mountain vegetables and roots, all kinds of mushrooms, trout, char, pheasant, hare, duck, and even bear and *tanuki* (raccoon dog) stews. Here in Nagano some people (myself included) still enjoy the larvae of ground wasps, hornets, and a type of wood beetle, as well as grasshoppers and other insects that have contributed protein to the human diet since prehistoric times. City-bred Japanese will smugly tell you that the Japanese were never hunters, but that certainly isn't true of mountain folk, who have long followed the practice of hunting and trapping for fur and food. Indeed, wild duck is traditionally served at the emperor's table.

Flora and Fauna | Even today, the variety of Japanese species remains astounding. My life in Nagano—where in the early 1980s I managed to buy more than 30 acres of mixed woodland and meadow—allows me to study this abundance intimately. This land, recently increased to 45 acres, had been cut over and neglected. The oldest tree was perhaps a mere 60 years old, the growth was crowded and strangled by vines, and the streams were clogged with debris.

My intention is to spend the rest of my life nurturing, protecting, and improving these woods. I now employ a full-time forester and assistant, and after just a few years I am delighted by the vigor with

The ancient Jōmon cedar tree on the island of Yakushima.

which the woods are responding, with more birds, more wild mushrooms, more insects. The small black bears of the region (called *tsukinowaguma*, or "mooncircle bears," for their white chest marking) even come down from the mountain adjoining my land and feed on the wild grapes and cherries. Recently we found a rare Japanese dormouse too. Most of Nagano is snow country, and when the snows come we can find tracks of hare, squirrel, fox, raccoon dog, weasel, and marten. On those white pages, a new story each day.

We have macaques, some of which like to relax in hot-spring pools. South of my home are wild boar, deer, and serow and also such animals as the masked palm civet (a silly name for it in English, as there are no palms in this area). Small mammals include 2 species of flying squirrels, 3 of moles, 10 of bats, 10 of rats, mice, and voles, as well as 3 of shrews. Reptiles are also numerous, with 12 species of frogs and toads, 2 of small land turtles, 2 of lizards, a black and red newt, and 3 species of salamanders. And all of this in just one part of Japan with a fairly severe winter climate. In Britain we had only 2 kinds of true snakes; in Nagano alone I know of 7.

In Hokkaidō, in the north of Japan, there is a brown bear, very big, while at the southern end of the archipelago, on the island of Iriomotejima, you can find a rare wildcat. Many other kinds of creatures and plants thrive in the south, varying often from island to island. There are small deer, fruit bats, deadly *habu* snakes, and giant freshwater eels. There are tropical seas and jungle. Yakushima, an island south of Kyūshū, contains the biggest cedars in the world, with many aged thousands of years; one, the famous Jōmon cedar (pictured below and on opposite page), some experts have argued to be more than 7,000 years old.

Government Policy

I could tell more of the natural wonders of Japan—the 500 or so species of birds, the incredible number of flowers, the four-foot-long giant salamander I once saw in a park in Tōkyō—but nowadays I would be painting too pretty a picture. The bitter truth is that since the end of World War II, as the nation dragged itself out of the ashes to become a major world power, Japan has achieved its monumental economic success at the expense of its natural resources and beauty. In the postwar period more harm has been inflicted on nature than ever occurred during the war, much of it utterly senseless destruction on a huge scale. Worse still, the government often seems to ignore, or even aggravate, the situation. This aspect of "the Japanese miracle" is particularly evident with regard to wildlife and marine conservation as they have been adversely affected by forestry and resort development.

To give a local example, in April 1981, together with a party of local hunters, I climbed part of Mt. Iizuna, close by my land. That day we saw 4 bears and tracked a total of 7. When I went alone the next year that whole part of the mountain, formerly a lovely area of virgin hardwoods many hundreds of years old, had been razed, with just a few trees left on the ridges. Eventually it was replanted with larches and cedars. In one year, 13 bears, including females with cubs, were killed in that area on "pest extermination permits." Even as I check this manuscript, hunters are going out on another such permit to try to kill 5 more bears. The mountains are being so thoroughly cleared of mixed deciduous forest that there is little left for the bears to eat. They are forced to come down to raid fields and beehives, thus coming to be considered pests. Even bears that do not raid are liable to be taken, out of season, on these permits, and females with cubs are blasted at short range in their lairs. This is the case all over the country where bears still manage to survive, and I believe that the government does nothing to correct the situation.

Japan's strict game laws and hunting seasons go largely unenforced. Even a large national park like Shiretoko in Hokkaidō has but one ranger, sometimes two, and they stay mostly at their desks. In comparison, when I was a game warden in Ethiopia my staff included a well-trained assistant, 20 armed rangers, and a Peace Corps volunteer.

The few rangers there are come straight out of college with little or no field training, and they are usually posted to a park for a mere two years before being moved elsewhere. In the 11 years that I have lived on the edge of Jōshin'etsu National Park, in which I frequently roam, I have never seen a ranger nor even tracks of one. Over this period the single ranger stationed there has been changed six times.

Forestry at Fault

The Forestry Agency has a history of self-serving activity. At the end of World War II, Japan badly needed to rebuild its cities. Forests were severely cut, and the Forestry Agency budget was made independent of the rest of the government. It made its money from the sale of timber. At first, with a great reserve of natural forests, the agency waxed strong. In the 1950s it implemented a policy of planting single species of conifers and encouraged private owners to do the same. Because many areas were not suited for this, just a small percentage of those planted trees are now ready to harvest, not nearly enough to support the salaries and upkeep of the agency. As long as I have lived here the agency has been cutting deep into the national parks' remaining virgin forest. The cutting not only ignores conservation policies, it also increases the danger of avalanche and landslide.

My forester, who formerly worked for the government, related an incident in

The bark of the Jōmon cedar. This magnificent tree, thought to be more than 7,000 years old, is a testament to the strength of nature.

which he was ordered to cut down a valley full of deciduous hardwoods, many over 400 years old. He told his supervisor that they would not be able to extract the logs, but the supervisor said that the area had been designated for cutting, and so he should cut. The whole valley was felled, then the trees just left there. Despite a lot of citizen protest, such mistaken practices are followed all over the country.

New laws intended to facilitate the creation of resorts, chiefly golf courses and ski slopes, have caused accelerated development with ecologically horrifying results. Uncontrolled use of pesticides and herbicides kills all nearby streams and pollutes water sources, while regulations are either inadequate or ignored.

In the past there were restrictions on cutting ancient forests at high altitudes, which in my area meant above 1,500 meters (4,921 ft), in some areas 1,800 meters (5,905 ft). I believed that to be woefully high even then, but the resort development laws have swept aside even those limitations. Furthermore, possibly because of global warming, the snow season seems to be shortening, so ski-slope developers want to cut even higher. They are also targeting north-facing slopes, vital denning areas for bears, where trees grow slowly and snow lasts longer. Then the resort operators scatter chemicals on the snow to retard melting, which of course eventually pollutes water sources.

Opportunity for mutual profit encourages collusion among local contractors, developers large and small, and the government. And so the developers leap at a savage rate from one towering, forested slope to the next.

Nature's Future?

During my service on an advisory panel for the Japanese government's Environment Agency, I found that most of the members were keen to do something to achieve better conservation policies. Unfortunately, the panel spent far too much time worrying about the wording of reports instead of tackling real problems. Moreover, the director of the agency was changed three times within a year, much to the frustration of the panel. One director had tried hard to be effective, demanding a review of the heavily protested damming of the Nagaragawa, the last wild river, while the next stated that he would do nothing about it. As for the budget allotted to the environment, it is pitiful and fails to grow along with the country's economic might.

Japan's part in the destruction of tropical forests in other countries, to satisfy its own lumber-hungry construction industry, is well known, but given the government's record in domestic forestry this is hardly surprising. The official Japanese stance on marine conservation and fishing is also disturbing, but here the issues are more complex. I believe that whalers are not taking any species of protected whales, only those that are plentiful and increasing, such as minke whales. Also, the various foods taken from whales are traditional to the tables of many of Japan's coastal areas. On the issue of dolphins, however, I cannot support what is being done by Japan, even though dolphins too have customarily been eaten in some areas. The modern dolphin hunt is excessive and uncontrolled, with the price of the meat and the demand for it very much on the rise due to the ban on whaling.

The future outlook on the environment, though, is positive because the Japanese citizenry—probably the most educated and literate in the world, enjoying full freedom of speech—is becoming active in trying to improve environmental policy. In the government, too, there are some aware, intelligent people who are motivated to address the issues.

Judging from the hundreds of letters I receive from readers of my books, I can say with confidence that Japanese people of all ages and walks of life are part of the worldwide trend to give environmental issues top priority. Eventually Japan will move seriously to improve the environment, and I predict that the move will be more powerful than might now be imagined.

C. W. Nicol

Photographs by Yamashita Hiroaki

with the socialist countries. The two groups have clashed over such specific issues as the presence of American bases in Japan, the Vietnam War, and the UNITED STATES–JAPAN SECURITY TREATIES, as well as the constitutionality of Japan's SELF DEFENSE FORCES in light of the RENUNCIATION OF WAR clause contained in article 9 of Japan's postwar constitution.

In recent years, major changes in the structure of international politics resulting from the collapse of communist governments in the former Soviet Union and Eastern Europe, as well as the emergence of domestic centrist parties such as the KŌMEITŌ (Clean Government Party) and DEMOCRATIC SOCIALIST PARTY, have begun to blur the distinction between conservative and reformist camps and to modify the framework of Japanese politics that was established in the mid-1950s.

consolidated financial statements
連結財務諸表

(*renketsu zaimu shohyō*). In recent decades an intensification of economic competition among Japanese corporations has resulted in the increasing prevalence of enterprise groups (see KEIRETSU) as a means of securing profits, spreading risks, and stabilizing management. Consolidated financial statements are formulated and made public in order to disclose the operating results and financial condition of these groups. Japan's consolidated financial statement system was initiated in April 1977. The consolidated financial statement consists of a consolidated balance sheet, a consolidated income statement, and a consolidated statement of retained earnings. These statements are prepared through a procedure that combines the individual financial statements of the parent company and all of its subsidiaries. The objectives of the consolidated financial statement are to prevent such cosmetic practices as forced sales to subsidiaries and to provide for accurate disclosure of the actual financial condition of a group of companies.

Consolidated financial statements are not covered by Japan's Commercial Code. Their use as attachments to the annual securities report and the securities registration statement is significantly different from standard practices in the United States and Europe.

constitutional litigation
憲法訴訟

(*kempō soshō*). Article 81 of the 1947 CONSTITUTION OF JAPAN confers upon the SUPREME COURT and all lower courts the power to determine the constitutionality of laws, orders, regulations, and official acts (see JUDICIAL REVIEW). Constitutional issues are decided by the courts only after first being raised in criminal, civil, or administrative cases. The scope of constitutional litigation has at times been limited when the Supreme Court has determined that an issue is highly political in nature. In such cases, the Supreme Court has deemed it more appropriate for the issue to be resolved by popular suffrage or other political means rather than judicial review.

Constitutional Problems Study Group
憲法問題研究会

(Kempō Mondai Kenkyūkai). A private organization of liberal scholars of law and politics. It was founded in 1958 by MIYAZAWA TOSHIYOSHI and ŌUCHI HYŌE to counter the influence of the government's COMMISSION ON THE CONSTITUTION, which was seen as favoring

a conservative revision of the postwar constitution. The threat of revision having receded, the group disbanded in 1976. See also CONSTITUTION, DISPUTE OVER REVISION OF.

constitution, dispute over revision of
憲法改正問題

(*kempō kaisei mondai*). Debate, continuing since the early 1950s, between opponents and supporters of the 1947 CONSTITUTION OF JAPAN, which was enacted under the Allied OCCUPATION (1945–52). Advocates of revision have contended that the present constitution is not an ideal one because it was "imposed" by an army of occupation and does not reflect the history, tradition, and customs of the Japanese people. Those opposed to revision argue that the constitution has served as the foundation for a new Japanese democracy that has been welcomed by the people. The main issues argued in the debate have been the future of the renunciation of war stipulated by article 9 and proposals to strengthen the status and authority of the emperor while weakening those of the Diet. The COMMISSION ON THE CONSTITUTION found no serious defects in the constitution, and possible revision has not been a major issue since the mid-1960s.

Constitution of 1868 → Seitaisho

Constitution of Japan
日本国憲法

(Nihonkoku Kempō). The Constitution of Japan, successor to the CONSTITUTION OF THE EMPIRE OF JAPAN (1889; also known as the Meiji Constitution), became effective on 3 May 1947. It is notable for its declaration that sovereignty resides with the people, its assertion of fundamental human rights, and its renunciation of war and arms. A thoroughly democratic document, it reflected the policies of the Allied OCCUPATION and was largely modeled after the British and American constitutions. It revolutionized the political system, which under the Meiji Constitution had been based on the principle that sovereignty resided with the emperor. The constitution incorporates a democratic quest for social justice.

Enactment—The Japanese surrender in WORLD WAR II took the form of acceptance of the terms of the Potsdam Declaration, which called for the removal of obstacles to democratic tendencies and the establishment of a peace-loving government in accordance with the freely expressed will of the Japanese people. In October 1945 Prime Minister SHIDEHARA KIJŪRŌ appointed MATSUMOTO JŌJI to head a committee to investigate the question of constitutional revision. The following February the staff of US General Douglas MACARTHUR, the supreme commander for the Allied powers (SCAP), became convinced that the Matsumoto committee was incapable of adequately democratizing the constitution and that the Far Eastern Commission (representing the Allied powers) might soon intervene in the matter. MacArthur directed his Government Section to formulate a model constitution for Japan. The Government Section's hastily drafted constitution was based in part on a policy paper of the American State-War-Navy Coordinating Committee (SWNCC). On 13 February 1946 Government Section officials delivered their draft to the Japanese cabinet and said that the adoption of its basic principles would help to protect the imperial throne and to hasten the end of the Allied Occupation.

After difficult negotiations the SCAP and Japanese officials agreed on a draft constitu-

tion based on the SCAP model. The only major concession to Japanese views was that the Diet (parliament) be bicameral rather than unicameral. On 6 March 1946 the Shidehara cabinet published the text as its own handiwork, although it differed radically from the previously published proposals of the Matsumoto committee.

To ensure legal continuity with the imperial constitution, the proposed new constitution was passed in the form of a constitutional amendment almost unanimously by both houses of the Imperial Diet, and on 3 November 1946 it was promulgated by the emperor, to become effective 3 May 1947.

Provisions—The new Constitution of Japan declares that the emperor shall be "the symbol of the State and of the unity of the people, deriving his position from the will of the people with whom resides sovereign power." All acts of the emperor in matters of state now require the advice and approval of the cabinet, and the emperor has no "powers related to government." The emperor appoints as prime minister the person selected by the Diet and appoints as chief judge of the Supreme Court the appointee of the cabinet.

The new constitution enumerates the rights and duties of the people, such as freedom of speech. Unlike the Meiji Constitution, it does not make their exercise subject to "the limits of law." Discrimination "in political, economic or social relations because of race, creed, sex, social status or family origin" is forbidden. The people have the right to maintain "minimum standards of wholesome and cultured living," and the state is expected to promote social welfare and public health. The right to own property is declared inviolable. The most famous provision of the constitution is article 9, which states that the Japanese people "forever renounce war" and that "land, sea, and air forces . . . will never be maintained."

If the lower house passes a resolution of no confidence in the cabinet, the cabinet must resign or the lower house must be dissolved within 10 days. Thus the new constitution established the parliamentary-cabinet system of democracy, similar to that of Great Britain. The two houses of the Diet designate the prime minister, but if the two houses are unable to agree, the choice of the House of Representatives (lower house) prevails. The defeat of a bill by the House of Councillors (upper house) may be overridden by a two-thirds majority vote of the lower house, except that a lower-house simple majority may prevail where the budget, a treaty, or the designation of the prime minister is involved.

The Japanese Supreme Court has explicit authority to determine the constitutionality of legislation and government acts. The Japanese system is unitary rather than federal: local governments may exercise legislative and other authority in matters of local concern only insofar as such exercise does not contradict statutes passed by the Diet.

The New Constitution in Practice—Shortly before and after the new constitution became effective, the Diet passed 45 laws to implement its provisions. This legislation included the new Imperial Household Law, the Cabinet Law, the Diet Law, the Local Autonomy Law, electoral laws, and amendments to the CIVIL CODE and the Code of Civil Procedure.

Since the Occupation ended in 1952, the government has interpreted the constitution to mean that it may dissolve the House of Representatives without having to wait for a vote of no confidence. The government, which has been dominated by the conservatives, has dissolved the lower house at times advantageous to the conservatives. Since the governing conservatives appoint Supreme Court justices and have usually held majorities in both houses, they have been able to dominate the system.

Over the years, the constitutionality of the SELF DEFENSE FORCES has been frequently challenged in the courts, but the Supreme Court has avoided ruling definitively on this issue. Although conservatives have advocated amendments that would clarify the right to maintain military forces and enhance the status of the emperor, the Japanese people have thus far not altered a word of their democratic constitution.

THE CONSTITUTION OF JAPAN, 1946

Promulgated on November 3, 1946; Put into effect on May 3, 1947

We, the Japanese people, acting through our duly elected representatives in the National Diet, determined that we shall secure for ourselves and our posterity the fruits of peaceful cooperation with all nations and the blessings of liberty throughout this land, and resolved that never again shall we be visited with the horrors of war through the action of government, do proclaim that sovereign power resides with the people and do firmly establish this Constitution. Government is a sacred trust of the people, the authority for which is derived from the people, the powers of which are exercised by the representatives of the people, and the benefits of which are enjoyed by the people. This is a universal principle of mankind upon which this Constitution is founded. We reject and revoke all constitutions, laws, ordinances, and rescripts in conflict herewith.

We, the Japanese people, desire peace for all time and are deeply conscious of the high ideals controlling human relationship, and we have determined to preserve our security and existence, trusting in the justice and faith of the peace-loving peoples of the world. We desire to occupy an honored place in an international society striving for the preservation of peace, and the banishment of tyranny and slavery, oppression and intolerance for all time from the earth. We recognize that all peoples of the world have the right to live in peace, free from fear and want.

We believe that no nation is responsible to itself alone, but that laws of political morality are universal; and that obedience to such laws is incumbent upon all nations who would sustain their own sovereignty and justify their sovereign relationship with other nations.

We, the Japanese people, pledge our national honor to accomplish these high ideals and purposes with all our resources.

CHAPTER I. THE EMPEROR

Article 1. The Emperor shall be the symbol of the State and of the unity of the people, deriving his position from the will of the people with whom resides sovereign power.

Article 2. The Imperial Throne shall be dynastic and succeeded to in accordance with the Imperial House Law passed by the Diet.

Article 3. The advice and approval of the Cabinet shall be required for all acts of the Emperor in matters of state, and the Cabinet shall be responsible therefor.

Article 4. The Emperor shall perform only such acts in matters of state as are provided for in this Constitution and he shall not have powers related to government.

(2) The Emperor may delegate the performance of his acts in matters of state as may be provided by law.

Article 5. When, in accordance with the Imperial House Law, a Regency is established, the Regent shall perform his acts in matters of state in the Emperor's name. In this case, paragraph one of the preceding article will be applicable.

Article 6. The Emperor shall appoint the Prime Minister as designated by the Diet.

(2) The Emperor shall appoint the Chief Judge of the Supreme Court as designated by the Cabinet.

Article 7. The Emperor, with the advice and approval of the Cabinet, shall perform the following acts in matters of state on behalf of the people:

(i) Promulgation of amendments of the constitution, laws, cabinet orders and treaties;

(ii) Convocation of the Diet;

(iii) Dissolution of the House of Representatives;

(iv) Proclamation of general election of members of the Diet;

(v) Attestation of the appointment and dismissal of Ministers of State and other officials as provided for by law, and of full powers and credentials of Ambassadors and Ministers;

(vi) Attestation of general and special amnesty, commutation of punishment, reprieve, and restoration of rights;

(vii) Awarding of honors;

(viii) Attestation of instruments of ratification and other diplomatic documents as provided for by law;

(ix) Receiving foreign ambassadors and ministers;

(x) Performance of ceremonial functions.

Article 8. No property can be given to, or received by, the Imperial House, nor can any gifts be made therefrom, without the authorization of the Diet.

CHAPTER II. RENUNCIATION OF WAR

Article 9. Aspiring sincerely to an international peace based on justice and order, the Japanese people forever renounce war as a sovereign right of the nation and the threat or use of force as a means of settling international disputes.

(2) In order to accomplish the aim of the preceding paragraph, land, sea, and air forces, as well as other war potential, will never be maintained. The right of belligerency of the state will not be recognized.

CHAPTER III. RIGHTS AND DUTIES OF THE PEOPLE

Article 10. The conditions necessary for being a Japanese national shall be determined by law.

Article 11. The people shall not be prevented from enjoying any of the fundamental human rights. These fundamental human rights guaranteed to the people by this Constitution shall be conferred upon the people of this and future generations as eternal and inviolate rights.

Article 12. The freedoms and rights guaranteed to the people by this Constitution shall be maintained by the constant endeavor of the people, who shall refrain from any abuse of these freedoms and rights and shall always be responsible for utilizing them for the public welfare.

Article 13. All of the people shall be respected as individuals. Their right to life, liberty, and the pursuit of happiness shall, to the extent that it does not interfere with the public welfare, be the supreme consideration in legislation and in other governmental affairs.

Article 14. All of the people are equal under the law and there shall be no discrimination in political, economic or social relations because of race, creed, sex, social status or family origin.

(2) Peers and peerage shall not be recognized.

(3) No privilege shall accompany any award of honor, decoration or any distinction, nor shall any such award be valid beyond the lifetime of the individual who now holds or hereafter may receive it.

Article 15. The people have the inalienable right to choose their public officials and to dismiss them.

(2) All public officials are servants of the whole community and not of any group thereof.

(3) Universal adult suffrage is guaranteed with regard to the election of public officials.

(4) In all elections, secrecy of the ballot shall not be violated. A voter shall not be answerable, publicly or privately, for the choice he has made.

Article 16. Every person shall have the right of peaceful petition for the redress of damage, for the removal of public officials, for the enactment, repeal or amendment of laws, ordinances or regulations and for other matters, nor shall any person be in any way discriminated against for sponsoring such a petition.

Article 17. Every person may sue for redress as provided by law from the State or a public entity, in case he has suffered damage through illegal act of any public official.

Article 18. No person shall be held in bondage of any kind. Involuntary servitude, except as punishment for crime, is prohibited.

Article 19. Freedom of thought and conscience shall not be violated.

Article 20. Freedom of religion is guaranteed to all. No religious organization shall receive any privileges from the State nor exercise any political authority.

(2) No person shall be compelled to take part in any religious acts, celebration, rite or practice.

(3) The State and its organs shall refrain from religious education or any other religious activity.

Article 21. Freedom of assembly and association as well as speech, press and all other forms of expression are guaranteed.

(2) No censorship shall be maintained, nor shall the secrecy of any means of communication be violated.

Article 22. Every person shall have freedom to choose and change his residence and to choose his occupation to the extent that it does not interfere with the public welfare.

(2) Freedom of all persons to move to a foreign country and to divest themselves of their nationality shall be inviolate.

Article 23. Academic freedom is guaranteed.

Article 24. Marriage shall be based only on the mutual consent of both sexes and it shall be maintained through mutual cooperation with the equal rights of husband and wife as a basis.

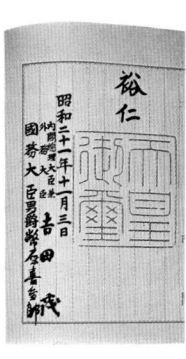

Constitution of Japan
The official manuscript of the constitution, promulgated on 3 November 1946, is preserved in the National Archives. The page shown here bears the imperial seal and signature and the signatures of Prime Minister Yoshida Shigeru and Minister of State Shidehara Kijūrō.

(2) With regard to choice of spouse, property rights, inheritance, choice of domicile, divorce and other matters pertaining to marriage and the family, laws shall be enacted from the standpoint of individual dignity and the essential equality of the sexes.

Article 25. All people shall have the right to maintain the minimum standards of wholesome and cultured living.

(2) In all spheres of life, the State shall use its endeavors for the promotion and extension of social welfare and security, and of public health.

Article 26. All people shall have the right to receive an equal education correspondent to their ability, as provided by law.

(2) All people shall be obligated to have all boys and girls under their protection receive ordinary educations as provided for by law. Such compulsory education shall be free.

Article 27. All people shall have the right and the obligation to work.

(2) Standards for wages, hours, rest and other working conditions shall be fixed by law.

(3) Children shall not be exploited.

Article 28. The right of workers to organize and to bargain and act collectively is guaranteed.

Article 29. The right to own or to hold property is inviolable.

(2) Property rights shall be defined by law, in conformity with the public welfare.

(3) Private property may be taken for public use upon just compensation therefor.

Article 30. The people shall be liable to taxations as provided by law.

Article 31. No person shall be deprived of life or liberty, nor shall any other criminal penalty be imposed, except according to procedure established by law.

Article 32. No person shall be denied the right of access to the courts.

Article 33. No person shall be apprehended except upon warrant issued by a competent judicial officer which specifies the offense with which the person is charged, unless he is apprehended, the offense being committed.

Article 34. No person shall be arrested or detained without being at once informed of the charges against him or without the immediate privilege of counsel; nor shall he be detained without adequate cause; and upon demand of any person such cause must be immediately shown in open court in his presence and the presence of his counsel.

Article 35. The right of all persons to be secure in their homes, papers and effects against entries, searches and seizures shall not be impaired except upon warrant issued for adequate cause and particularly describing the place to be searched and things to be seized, or except as provided by Article 33.

(2) Each search or seizure shall be made upon separate warrant issued by a competent judicial officer.

Article 36. The infliction of torture by any public officer and cruel punishments are absolutely forbidden.

Article 37. In all criminal cases the accused shall enjoy the right to a speedy and public trial by an impartial tribunal.

(2) He shall be permitted full opportunity to examine all witnesses, and he shall have the right of compulsory process for obtaining witnesses on his behalf at public expense.

(3) At all times the accused shall have the assistance of competent counsel who shall, if the accused is unable to secure the same by his own efforts, be assigned to his use by the State.

Article 38. No person shall be compelled to testify against himself.

(2) Confession made under compulsion, torture or threat, or after prolonged arrest or detention shall not be admitted in evidence.

(3) No person shall be convicted or punished in cases where the only proof against him is his own confession.

Article 39. No person shall be held criminally liable for an act which was lawful at the time it was committed, or of which he has been acquitted, nor shall he be placed in double jeopardy.

Article 40. Any person, in case he is acquitted after he has been arrested or detained, may sue the State for redress as provided by law.

CHAPTER IV. THE DIET

Article 41. The Diet shall be the highest organ of state power, and shall be the sole law-making organ of the State.

Article 42. The Diet shall consist of two Houses, namely the House of Representatives and the House of Councillors.

Article 43. Both Houses shall consist of elected members, representative of all the people.

(2) The number of members of each House shall be fixed by law.

Article 44. The qualifications of members of both Houses and their electors shall be fixed by law. However, there shall be no discrimination because of race, creed, sex, social status, family origin, education, property or income.

Article 45. The term of office of members of the House of Representatives shall be four years. However, the term shall be terminated before the full term is up in case the House of Representatives is dissolved.

Article 46. The term of office of members of the House of Councillors shall be six years, and election for half the members shall take place every three years.

Article 47. Electoral districts, method of voting and other matters pertaining to the method of election of members of both Houses shall be fixed by law.

Article 48. No person shall be permitted to be a member of both Houses simultaneously.

Article 49. Members of both Houses shall receive appropriate annual payment from the national treasury in accordance with law.

Article 50. Except in cases provided by law, members of both Houses shall be exempt from apprehension while the Diet is in session, and any members apprehended before the opening of the session shall be freed during the term of the session upon demand of the House.

Article 51. Members of both Houses shall not be held liable outside the House for speeches, debates or votes cast inside the House.

Article 52. An ordinary session of the Diet shall be convoked once per year.

Article 53. The Cabinet may determine to convoke extraordinary sessions of the Diet. When a quarter or more of the total members of either House makes the demand, the Cabinet must determine on such convocation.

Article 54. When the House of Representatives is dissolved, there must be a general election of members of the House of Representatives within forty (40) days from the date of dissolution, and the Diet must be convoked within thirty (30) days from the date of election.

(2) When the House of Representatives is dissolved, the House of Councillors is closed at the same time. However, the Cabinet may in time of national emergency convoke the House of Councillors in emergency session.

(3) Measures taken at such session as mentioned in the proviso of the preceding paragraph shall be provisional and shall become null and void unless agreed to by the House of Representatives within a period of ten (10) days after the opening of the next session of the Diet.

Article 55. Each House shall judge disputes related to qualifications of its members. However, in order to deny a seat to any member, it is necessary to pass a resolution by a majority of two-thirds or more of the members present.

Article 56. Business cannot be transacted in either House unless one-third or more of total membership is present.

(2) All matters shall be decided, in each House, by a majority of those present, except as elsewhere provided in the Constitution, and in case of a tie, the presiding officer shall decide the issue.

Article 57. Deliberation in each House shall be public. However, a secret meeting may be held where a majority of two-thirds or more of those members present passes a resolution therefor.

(2) Each House shall keep a record of proceedings. This record shall be published and given general circulation, excepting such parts of proceedings of secret session as may be deemed to require secrecy.

(3) Upon demand of one-fifth or more of the members present, votes of the members on any matter shall be recorded in the minutes.

Article 58. Each House shall select its own president and other officials.

(2) Each House shall establish its rules pertaining to meetings, proceedings and internal discipline, and may punish members for disorderly conduct. However, in order to expel a member, a majority of two-thirds or more of those members present must pass a resolution thereon.

Article 59. A bill becomes a law on passage by both Houses, except as otherwise provided by the Constitution.

(2) A bill which is passed by the House of Representatives, and upon which the House of Councillors makes a decision different from that of the House of Representatives, becomes a law when passed a second time by the House of Representatives by a majority of two-thirds or more of the members present.

(3) The provision of the preceding paragraph does not preclude the House of Representatives from calling for the meeting of a joint committee of both Houses, provided for by law.

(4) Failure by the House of Councillors to take final action within sixty (60) days after receipt of a bill passed by the House of Representatives, time in recess excepted, may be determined by the House of Representatives to constitute a rejection of the said bill by the House of Councillors.

Article 60. The Budget must first be submitted to the House of Representatives.

(2) Upon consideration of the budget, when the House of Councillors makes a deci-

sion different from that of the House of Representatives, and when no agreement can be reached even through a joint committee of both Houses, provided for by law, or in the case of failure by the House of Councillors to take final action within thirty (30) days, the period of recess excluded, after the receipt of the budget passed by the House of Representatives, the decision of the House of Representatives shall be the decision of the Diet.

Article 61. The second paragraph of the preceding article applies also to the Diet approval required for the conclusion of treaties.

Article 62. Each House may conduct investigations in relation to government, and may demand the presence and testimony of witnesses, and the production of records.

Article 63. The Prime Minister and other Ministers of State may, at any time, appear in either House for the purpose of speaking on bills, regardless of whether they are members of the House or not. They must appear when their presence is required in order to give answers or explanations.

Article 64. The Diet shall set up an impeachment court from among the members of both Houses for the purpose of trying those judges against whom removal proceedings have been instituted.

(2) Matters relating to impeachment shall be provided by law.

CHAPTER V. THE CABINET

Article 65. Executive power shall be vested in the Cabinet.

Article 66. The Cabinet shall consist of the Prime Minister, who shall be its head, and other Ministers of State, as provided for by law.

(2) The Prime Minister and other Ministers of State must be civilians.

(3) The Cabinet, in the exercise of executive power, shall be collectively responsible to the Diet.

Article 67. The Prime Minister shall be designated from among the members of the Diet by a resolution of the Diet. This designation shall precede all other business.

(2) If the House of Representatives and the House of Councillors disagrees and if no agreement can be reached even through a joint committee of both Houses, provided for by law, or the House of Councillors fails to make designation within ten (10) days, exclusive of the period of recess, after the House of Representatives has made designation, the decision of the House of Representatives shall be the decision of the Diet.

Article 68. The Prime Minister shall appoint the Ministers of State. However, a majority of their number must be chosen from among the members of the Diet.

(2) The Prime Minister may remove the Ministers of State as he chooses.

Article 69. If the House of Representatives passes a non-confidence resolution, or rejects a confidence resolution, the Cabinet shall resign en masse, unless the House of Representatives is dissolved within ten (10) days.

Article 70. When there is a vacancy in the post of Prime Minister, or upon the first convocation of the Diet after a general election of members of the House of Representatives, the Cabinet shall resign en masse.

Article 71. In the cases mentioned in the two preceding articles, the Cabinet shall continue its functions until the time when a new Prime Minister is appointed.

Article 72. The Prime Minister, representing the Cabinet, submits bills, reports on general national affairs and foreign relations to the Diet and exercises control and supervision over various administrative branches.

Article 73. The Cabinet, in addition to other general administrative functions, shall perform the following functions:

(i) Administer the law faithfully; conduct affairs of state;

(ii) Manage foreign affairs;

(iii) Conclude treaties. However, it shall obtain prior or, depending on circumstances, subsequent approval of the Diet;

(iv) Administer the civil service, in accordance with standards established by law;

(v) Prepare the budget, and present it to the Diet;

(vi) Enact cabinet orders in order to execute the provisions of this Constitution and of the law. However, it cannot include penal provisions in such cabinet orders unless authorized by such law.

(vii) Decide on general amnesty, special amnesty, commutation of punishment, reprieve, and restoration of rights.

Article 74. All laws and cabinet orders shall be signed by the competent Minister of State and countersigned by the Prime Minister.

Article 75. The Ministers of State, during their tenure of office, shall not be subject to legal action without the consent of the Prime Minister. However, the right to take that action is not impaired hereby.

CHAPTER VI. JUDICIARY

Article 76. The whole judicial power is vested in a Supreme Court and in such inferior courts as are established by law.

(2) No extraordinary tribunal shall be established, nor shall any organ or agency of the Executive be given final judicial power.

(3) All judges shall be independent in the exercise of their conscience and shall be bound only by this Constitution and the laws.

Article 77. The Supreme Court is vested with the rule-making power under which it determines the rules of procedure and of practice, and of matters relating to attorneys, the internal discipline of the courts and the administration of judicial affairs.

(2) Public procurators shall be subject to the rule-making power of the Supreme Court.

(3) The Supreme Court may delegate the power to make rules for inferior courts to such courts.

Article 78. Judges shall not be removed except by public impeachment unless judicially declared mentally or physically incompetent to perform official duties. No disciplinary action against judges shall be administered by any executive organ or agency.

Article 79. The Supreme Court shall consist of a Chief Judge and such number of judges as may be determined by law; all such judges excepting the Chief Judge shall be appointed by the Cabinet.

(2) The appointment of the judges of the Supreme Court shall be reviewed by the people at the first general election of members of the House of Representatives following their appointment, and shall be reviewed again at the first general election of members of the House of Representatives after a lapse of ten (10) years, and in the same manner thereafter.

(3) In cases mentioned in the foregoing paragraph, when the majority of the voters favors the dismissal of a judge, he shall be dismissed.

(4) Matters pertaining to review shall be prescribed by law.

(5) The judges of the Supreme Court shall be retired upon the attainment of the age as fixed by law.

(6) All such judges shall receive, at regular stated intervals, adequate compensation which shall not be decreased during their terms of office.

Article 80. The judges of the inferior courts shall be appointed by the cabinet from a list of persons nominated by the Supreme Court. All such judges shall hold office for a term of ten (10) years with privilege of reappointment, provided that they shall be retired upon the attainment of the age as fixed by law.

(2) The judges of the inferior courts shall receive, at regular stated intervals, adequate compensation which shall not be decreased during their terms of office.

Article 81. The Supreme Court is the court of last resort with power to determine the constitutionality of any law, order, regulation or official act.

Article 82. Trials shall be conducted and judgment declared publicly.

(2) Where a court unanimously determines publicity to be dangerous to public order or morals, a trial may be conducted privately, but trials of political offenses, offenses involving the press or cases wherein the rights of people as guaranteed in Chapter III of this Constitution are in question shall always be conducted publicly.

CHAPTER VII. FINANCE

Article 83. The power to administer national finances shall be exercised as the Diet shall determine.

Article 84. No new taxes shall be imposed or existing ones modified except by law or under such conditions as law may prescribe.

Article 85. No money shall be expended, nor shall the State obligate itself, except as authorized by the Diet.

Article 86. The Cabinet shall prepare and submit to the Diet for its consideration and decision a budget for each fiscal year.

Article 87. In order to provide for unforeseen deficiencies in the budget, a reserve fund may be authorized by the Diet to be expended upon the responsibility of the Cabinet.

(2) The Cabinet must get subsequent approval of the Diet for all payments from the reserve fund.

Article 88. All property of the Imperial Household shall belong to the State. All expenses of the Imperial Household shall be appropriated by the Diet in the budget.

Article 89. No public money or other property shall be expended or appropriated for the use, benefit or maintenance of any religious institution or association, or for any charitable, educational or benevolent enterprises not under the control of public authority.

Article 90. Final accounts of the expenditures and revenues of the State shall be audited annually by a Board of Audit and submitted by the Cabinet to the Diet, together with the statement of audit, during the fiscal year immediately following the period covered.

(2) The organization and competency of

the Board of Audit shall be determined by law.

Article 91. At regular intervals and at least annually the Cabinet shall report to the Diet and the people on the state of national finances.

CHAPTER VIII. LOCAL SELF-GOVERNMENT

Article 92. Regulations concerning organization and operations of local public entities shall be fixed by law in accordance with the principle of local autonomy.

Article 93. The local public entities shall establish assemblies as their deliberative organs, in accordance with law.

(2) The chief executive officers of all local public entities, the members of their assemblies, and such other local officials as may be determined by law shall be elected by direct popular vote within their several communities.

Article 94. Local public entities shall have the right to manage their property, affairs and administration and to enact their own regulations within law.

Article 95. A special law, applicable only to one local public entity, cannot be enacted by the Diet without the consent of the majority of the voters of the local public entity concerned, obtained in accordance with law.

CHAPTER IX. AMENDMENTS

Article 96. Amendments to this Constitution shall be initiated by the Diet, through a concurring vote of two-thirds or more of all the members of each House and shall thereupon be submitted to the people for ratification, which shall require the affirmative vote of a majority of all votes cast thereon, at a special referendum or at such election as the Diet shall specify.

(2) Amendments when so ratified shall immediately be promulgated by the Emperor in the name of the people, as an integral part of this Constitution.

CHAPTER X. SUPREME LAW

Article 97. The fundamental human rights by this Constitution guaranteed to the people of Japan are fruits of the age-old struggle of man to be free; they have survived the many exacting tests for durability and are conferred upon this and future generations in trust, to be held for all time inviolate.

Article 98. This Constitution shall be the supreme law of the nation and no law, ordinance, imperial rescript or other act of government, or part thereof, contrary to the provisions hereof, shall have legal force or validity.

(2) The treaties concluded by Japan and established laws of nations shall be faithfully observed.

Article 99. The Emperor or the Regent as well as Ministers of State, members of the Diet, judges, and all other public officials have the obligation to respect and uphold this Constitution.

CHAPTER XI. SUPPLEMENTARY PROVISIONS

Article 100. This Constitution shall be enforced as from the day when the period of six months will have elapsed counting from the day of its promulgation.

(2) The enactment of laws necessary for the enforcement of this Constitution, the election of members of the House of Councillors and the procedure for the convocation of the Diet and other preparatory procedures for the enforcement of this Constitution may be executed before the day prescribed in the preceding paragraph.

Article 101. If the House of Councillors is not constituted before the effective date of this Constitution, the House of Representatives shall function as the Diet until such time as the House of Councillors shall be constituted.

Article 102. The term of office for half the members of the House of Councillors serving in the first term under this Constitution shall be three years. Members falling under this category shall be determined in accordance with law.

Article 103. The Ministers of State, members of the House of Representatives, and judges in office on the effective date of this Constitution, and all other public officials, who occupy positions corresponding to such positions as are recognized by this Constitution shall not forfeit their positions automatically on account of the enforcement of this Constitution unless otherwise specified by law. When, however, successors are elected or appointed under the provisions of this Constitution, they shall forfeit their positions as a matter of course.

Constitution of the Empire of Japan 大日本帝国憲法

(Dai Nippon Teikoku Kempō). Also known as the Meiji Kempō or Meiji Constitution. The constitution of Japan in effect from 29 November 1890 to 2 May 1947; replaced by the present CONSTITUTION OF JAPAN on 3 May 1947. The idea of formulating a written constitution incorporating Western principles of parliamentary government had been advocated since the early Meiji period (1868–1912) both within and outside government circles. There was heated debate between advocates of gradualism within the Meiji oligarchy (see GENRŌ) and FREEDOM AND PEOPLE'S RIGHTS MOVEMENT activists who demanded the immediate convocation of an elected assembly and the promulgation of a constitution.

Drafting the Constitution—On 21 October 1881 a special government bureau was established to act as a consultative body on the formulation of the constitution, with ITŌ HIROBUMI as chairman. In 1882 Itō led a mission to Europe to observe and study different constitutional systems, particularly that of imperial Germany. The advice of German legal scholars, such as Rudolf von GNEIST and Lorenz von STEIN, had a decisive impact on the framing of the Meiji Constitution.

The central problem confronting those drafting the document, Itō Hirobumi, INOUE KOWASHI, ITŌ MIYOJI, KANEKO KENTARŌ, and legal advisers Hermann ROESLER and Albert MOSSE, was how to resolve the contradiction between the principle of imperial sovereignty and the principle of constitutional, that is, limited, government. From 1886 to 1888, in an atmosphere of utmost secrecy, many drafts were prepared, discussed, and revised. The final draft was submitted to the emperor in April 1888, and the Constitution of the Empire of Japan was promulgated on 11 February 1889.

Role of the Emperor—Article 1 stated that "the Empire of Japan shall be reigned over and governed by a line of Emperors unbroken for ages eternal," and sovereign power was clearly vested in the person of the emperor. In following articles he was given the sole right to declare war, make peace, and conclude treaties; to exercise supreme command over the army and navy; to dissolve the lower house of the Diet; and to issue imperial ordinances in the place of laws when the Diet was not in session.

Yet the second part of article 4 stated that the emperor's rights of sovereignty were to be exercised "according to the provisions of the present Constitution." The emperor's judgments and even his commands had no legal force in themselves: "All Laws, Imperial Ordinances, and Imperial Rescripts of whatever kind, that relate to the affairs of the State, require the countersignature of a Minister of State" (art. 55). This meant essentially that the emperor could take no action without the advice and consent of his cabinet ministers. In turn, the ministers of state were held responsible to the emperor, and to him alone, rather than to the people and the Diet—a concept known as "TRANSCENDENTAL" CABINETS.

Constitutional Government—Despite its absolutist tendencies, the constitution established clear limits to the sovereign rights of the emperor and the power of the executive. The judiciary was made independent of executive interference, and the Diet was given authority to initiate legislation, approve all laws, and approve the budget. In addition, the rights of the people were guaranteed by constitutional provisions regarding the right of habeas corpus, the right to a fair trial, inviolability of home and property, and freedom of religion, speech, and assembly, although all of these rights could be abridged through laws enacted by the Diet.

The Meiji Constitution was an ambivalent and ambiguous charter, poised between the two contradictory principles of imperial sovereignty and parliamentary government. It was left to the leaders of the government and of the political parties in the Diet to develop either the authoritarian or the liberal potential of the constitution. Much of the constitutional and, indeed, the larger political history of Japan in the first half of the 20th century consisted of a struggle over how this fundamental question was to be resolved.

CONSTITUTION OF THE EMPIRE OF JAPAN, 1889

Imperial Oath Sworn in the Sanctuary in the Imperial Palace (Tsuge-bumi)

We, the Successor to the prosperous Throne of Our Predecessors, do humbly and solemnly swear to the Imperial Founder of Our House and to Our other Imperial Ancestors that, in pursuance of a great policy coextensive with the Heavens and with the Earth, We shall maintain and secure from decline the ancient form of government.

In consideration of the progressive tendency of the course of human affairs and in parallel with the advance of civilization, We deem it expedient, in order to give clearness and distinctness to the instructions bequeathed by the Imperial Founder of Our House and by Our other Imperial Ancestors, to establish fundamental laws formulated into express provisions of law, so that, on the one hand, Our Imperial posterity may possess an express guide for the course they are to follow, and that, on the other, Our subjects shall thereby be enabled to enjoy a wider range of action in giving Us their support, and that the observance of Our laws shall continue to the remotest ages of time. We will thereby to give greater firmness to the stability of Our country and to promote the welfare of all the people within the boundaries of Our dominions; and We now establish the Imperial House Law and the

Constitution. These Laws come to only an exposition of grand precepts for the conduct of the government, bequeathed by the Imperial Founder of Our House and by Our other Imperial Ancestors. That we have been so fortunate in Our reign, in keeping with the tendency of the times, as to accomplish this work, We owe to the glorious Spirits of the Imperial Founder of Our House and of Our other Imperial Ancestors.

We now reverently make Our prayer to Them and to Our Illustrious Father, and implore the help of Their Sacred Spirits, and make to Them solemn oath never at this time nor in the future to fail to be an example to Our subjects in the observance of the Laws hereby established.

May the heavenly Spirits witness this Our solemn Oath.

Imperial Rescript on the Promulgation of the Constitution

Whereas We make it the joy and glory of Our heart to behold the prosperity of Our country, and the welfare of Our subjects, We do hereby, in virtue of the supreme power We inherit from Our Imperial Ancestors, promulgate the present immutable fundamental law, for the sake of Our present subjects and their descendants.

The Imperial Founder of Our House and Our other Imperial Ancestors, by the help and support of the forefathers of Our subjects, laid the foundation of Our Empire upon a basis, which is to last forever. That this brilliant achievement embellishes the annals of Our country, is due to the glorious virtues of Our Sacred Imperial Ancestors, and to the loyalty and bravery of Our subjects, their love of their country and their public spirits. Considering that Our subjects are the descendants of the loyal and good subjects of Our Imperial Ancestors, We doubt not but that Our subjects will be guided by Our views, and will sympathize with all Our endeavors, and that, harmoniously cooperating together, they will share with Us Our hope of making manifest the glory of Our country, both at home and abroad, and of securing forever the stability of the work bequeathed to Us by Our Imperial Ancestors.

Preamble [or Edict] (Jōyu)

Having, by virtue of the glories of Our Ancestors, ascended the Throne of a lineal succession unbroken for ages eternal; desiring to promote the welfare of, and to give development to the moral and intellectual faculties of Our beloved subjects, the very same that have been favored with the benevolent care and affectionate vigilance of Our Ancestors; and hoping to maintain the prosperity of the State, in concert with Our people and with their support, We hereby promulgate, in pursuance of Our Imperial Rescript of the 12th day of the 10th month of the 14th year of Meiji, a fundamental law of the State, to exhibit the principles, by which We are guided in Our conduct, and to point out to what Our descendants and Our subjects and their descendants are forever to conform.

The right of sovereignty of the State, We have inherited from Our Ancestors, and We shall bequeath them to Our descendants. Neither We nor they shall in the future fail to wield them, in accordance with the provisions of the Constitution hereby granted.

We now declare to respect and protect the security of the rights and of the property of Our people, and to secure to them the complete enjoyment of the same, within the ex-

tent of the provisions of the present Constitution and of the law.

The Imperial Diet shall first be convoked for the 23rd year of Meiji and the time of its opening shall be the date, when the present Constitution comes into force.

When in the future it may become necessary to amend any of the provisions of the present Constitution, We or Our successors shall assume the initiative right, and submit a project for the same to the Imperial Diet. The Imperial Diet shall pass its vote upon it, according to the conditions imposed by the present Constitution, and in no otherwise shall Our descendants or Our subjects be permitted to attempt any alteration thereof.

Our Ministers of State, on Our behalf, shall be held responsible for the carrying out of the present Constitution, and Our present and future subjects shall forever assume the duty of allegiance to the present Constitution.

CHAPTER I. THE EMPEROR

Article 1. The Empire of Japan shall be reigned over and governed by a line of Emperors unbroken for ages eternal.

Article 2. The Imperial Throne shall be succeeded to by Imperial male descendants, according to the provisions of the Imperial House Law.

Article 3. The Emperor is sacred and inviolable.

Article 4. The Emperor is the head of the Empire, combining in Himself the rights of sovereignty, and exercises them, according to the provisions of the present Constitution.

Article 5. The Emperor exercises the legislative power with the consent of the Imperial Diet.

Article 6. The Emperor gives sanction to laws, and orders them to be promulgated and executed.

Article 7. The Emperor convokes the Imperial Diet, opens, closes, and prorogues it, and dissolves the House of Representatives.

Article 8. The Emperor, in consequence of an urgent necessity to maintain public safety or to avert public calamities, issues, when the Imperial Diet is not sitting, Imperial Ordinances in the place of law.

(2) Such Imperial Ordinances are to be laid before the Imperial Diet at its next session, and when the Diet does not approve the said Ordinances, the Government shall declare them to be invalid for the future.

Article 9. The Emperor issues or causes to be issued, the Ordinances necessary for the carrying out of the laws, or for the maintenance of the public peace and order, and for the promotion of the welfare of the subjects. But no Ordinance shall in any way alter any of the existing laws.

Article 10. The Emperor determines the organization of the different branches of the administration, and salaries of all civil and military officers, and appoints and dismisses the same. Exceptions especially provided for in the present Constitution or in other laws, shall be in accordance with the respective provisions (bearing thereon).

Article 11. The Emperor has the supreme command of the Army and Navy.

Article 12. The Emperor determines the organization and peace standing of the Army and Navy.

Article 13. The Emperor declares war, makes peace, and concludes treaties.

Article 14. The Emperor declares a state of siege.

(2) The conditions and effects of a state of siege shall be determined by law.

Article 15. The Emperor confers titles of nobility, rank, orders and other marks of honor.

Article 16. The Emperor orders amnesty, pardon, commutation of punishments and rehabilitation.

Article 17. A Regency shall be instituted in conformity with the provisions of the Imperial House Law.

(2) The Regent shall exercise the powers appertaining to the Emperor in His name.

CHAPTER II. RIGHTS AND DUTIES OF SUBJECTS

Article 18. The conditions necessary for being a Japanese subject shall be determined by law.

Article 19. Japanese subjects may, according to qualifications determined in laws or ordinances, be appointed to civil or military or any other public offices equally.

Article 20. Japanese subjects are amenable to service in the Army and Navy, according to the provisions of law.

Article 21. Japanese subjects are amenable to the duty of paying taxes, according to the provisions of law.

Article 22. Japanese subjects shall have the liberty of abode and of changing the same within the limits of the law.

Article 23. No Japanese subject shall be arrested, detained, tried or punished, unless according to law.

Article 24. No Japanese subject shall be deprived of his right of being tried by the judges determined by law.

Article 25. Except in the cases provided for in the law, the house of no Japanese subject shall be entered or searched without his consent.

Article 26. Except in the cases mentioned in the law, the secrecy of the letters of every Japanese subject shall remain inviolate.

Article 27. The right of property of every Japanese subject shall remain inviolate.

(2) Measures necessary to be taken for the public benefit shall be provided for by law.

Article 28. Japanese subjects shall, within limits not prejudicial to peace and order, and not antagonistic to their duties as subjects, enjoy freedom of religious belief.

Article 29. Japanese subjects shall, within the limits of law, enjoy the liberty of speech, writing, publication, public meetings and associations.

Article 30. Japanese subjects may present petitions, by observing the proper forms of respect, and by complying with the rules specially provided for the same.

Article 31. The provisions contained in the present Chapter shall not affect the exercises of the powers appertaining to the Emperor, in times of war or in cases of a national emergency.

Article 32. Each and every one of the provisions contained in the preceding Articles of the present Chapter, that are not in conflict with the laws or the rules and discipline of the Army and Navy, shall apply to the officers and men of the Army and of the Navy.

CHAPTER III. THE IMPERIAL DIET

Article 33. The Imperial Diet shall consist of two Houses, a House of Peers and a House of Representatives.

Article 34. The House of Peers shall, in accordance with the Ordinance concerning the House of Peers, be composed of the members of the Imperial Family, of the orders of nobility, and of those who have been nominated thereto by the Emperor.

Article 35. The House of Representatives shall be composed of Members elected by the people, according to the provisions of the Law of Election.

Article 36. No one can at one and the same time be a Member of both Houses.

Article 37. Every law requires the consent of the Imperial Diet.

Article 38. Both Houses shall vote upon projects of law submitted to it by the Government, and may respectively initiate projects of law.

Article 39. A Bill, which has been rejected by either the one or the other of the two Houses, shall not be brought in again during the same session.

Article 40. Both Houses can make representations to the Government, as to laws or upon any other subject. When, however, such representations are not accepted, they cannot be made a second time during the same session.

Article 41. The Imperial Diet shall be convoked every year.

Article 42. A session of the Imperial Diet shall last during three months. In case of necessity, the duration of a session may be prolonged by the Imperial Order.

Article 43. When urgent necessity arises, an extraordinary session may be convoked in addition to the ordinary one.

(2) The duration of an extraordinary session shall be determined by Imperial Order.

Article 44. The opening, closing, prolongation of session and prorogation of the Imperial Diet, shall be effected simultaneously for both Houses.

(2) In case the House of Representatives has been ordered to dissolve, the House of Peers shall at the same time be prorogued.

Article 45. When the House of Representatives has been ordered to dissolve, Members shall be caused by Imperial Order to be newly elected, and the new House be convoked within five months from the day of dissolution.

Article 46. No debate can be opened and no vote can be taken in either House of the Imperial Diet, unless not less than one-third of the whole number of Members thereof is present.

Article 47. Votes shall be taken in both Houses by absolute majority. In the case of a tie vote, the President shall have the casting vote.

Article 48. The deliberations of both Houses shall be held in public. The deliberations may, however, upon demand of the Government or by resolution of the House, be held in secret sitting.

Article 49. Both Houses of the Imperial Diet may respectively present addresses to the Emperor.

Article 50. Both Houses may receive petitions presented by subjects.

Article 51. Both Houses may enact, besides what is provided for in the present Constitution and in the Law of the Houses, rules necessary for the management of their internal affairs.

Article 52. No member of either House shall be held responsible outside the respective Houses, for any opinion uttered or for any vote given in the House. When, however, a Member himself has given publicity to his opinions by public speech, by documents in print or in writing, or by any other similar means, he shall, in the matter, be amenable to the general law.

Article 53. The Members of both Houses shall, during the session, be free from arrest, unless with the consent of the House, except in cases of flagrant delicts, or of offenses connected with a state of internal commotion or with a foreign trouble.

Article 54. The Ministers of State and the Delegates of the Government may, at any time, take seats and speak in either House.

Article 55. The respective Ministers of State shall give their advice to the Emperor, and be responsible for it.

(2) All Laws, Imperial Ordinances, and Imperial Rescripts of whatever kind, that relate to the affairs of the State, require the countersignature of a Minister of State.

Article 56. The Privy Councillors shall, in accordance with the provisions for the organization of the Privy Council, deliberate upon important matters of State, when they have been consulted by the Emperor.

Article 57. The Judicature shall be exercised by the Courts of Law according to law, in the name of the Emperor.

(2) The organization of the Courts of Law shall be determined by the law.

Article 58. The judges shall be appointed from among those, who possess proper qualifications according to law.

(2) No judge shall be deprived of his position, unless by way of criminal sentence or disciplinary punishment.

(3) Rules for disciplinary punishment shall be determined by law.

Article 59. Trials and judgments of a Court shall be conducted publicly. When, however, there exists any fear, that such publicity may be prejudicial to peace and order, or to the maintenance of public morality, the public trial may be suspended by provisions of law or by the decision of the Court of Law.

Article 60. All matters, that fall within the competency of a special Court, shall be specially provided for by law.

Article 61. No suit at law, which relates to rights alleged to have been infringed by the illegal measures of the administrative authorities, and which shall come within the competency of the Court of Administrative Litigation specially established by law, shall be taken cognizance of by a Court of Law.

Article 62. The imposition of a new tax or the modification of the rates (of an existing one) shall be determined by law.

(2) However, all such administrative fees or other revenue having the nature of compensation shall not fall within the category of the above clause.

(3) The raising of national loans and the contracting of other liabilities to the charge of the National Treasury, except those that are provided in the Budget, shall require the consent of the Imperial Diet.

Article 63. The taxes levied at present shall, in so far as they are not remodelled by a new law, be collected according to the old system.

Article 64. The expenditure and revenue of the State require the consent of the Imperial Diet by means of an annual Budget.

(2) Any and all expenditures overpassing the appropriations set forth in the Titles and Paragraphs of the Budget, or that are not provided for in the Budget, shall subsequently require the approbations of the Imperial Diet.

Article 65. The Budget shall be first laid before the House of Representatives.

Article 66. The expenditures of the Imperial House shall be defrayed every year out of the National Treasury, according to the present fixed amount for the same, and shall not require the consent thereto of the Imperial Diet, except in case an increase thereof is found necessary.

Article 67. Those already fixed expenditures based by the Constitution upon the powers appertaining to the Emperor, and such expenditures as may have arisen by the effect of law, or that appertain to the legal obligations of the Government, shall be neither rejected nor reduced by the Imperial Diet, without the concurrence of the Government.

Article 68. In order to meet special requirements, the Government may ask the consent of the Imperial Diet to a certain amount as a Continuing Expenditure Fund, for a previously fixed number of years.

Article 69. In order to supply deficiencies, which are unavoidable, in the Budget, and to meet requirements unprovided for in the same, a Reserve Fund shall be provided in the Budget.

Article 70. When the Imperial Diet cannot be convoked, owing to the external or internal condition of the country, in case of urgent need for the maintenance of public safety, the Government may take all necessary financial measures, by means of an Imperial Ordinance.

(2) In the case mentioned in the preceding clause, the matter shall be submitted to the Imperial Diet at its next session, and its approbation shall be obtained thereto.

Article 71. When the Imperial Diet has not voted on the Budget, or when the Budget has not been brought into actual existence, the Government shall carry out the Budget of the preceding year.

Article 72. The final account of the expenditures and revenues of the State shall be verified and confirmed by the Board of Audit, and it shall be submitted by the Government to the Imperial Diet, together with the report of verification of the said Board.

(2) The organization and competency of the Board of Audit shall be determined by law separately.

Article 73. When it has become necessary in future to amend the provisions of the present Constitution, a project to the effect shall be submitted to the Imperial Diet by Imperial Order.

(2) In the above case, neither House can open the debate, unless not less than two-thirds of the whole number of Members are present, and no amendment can be passed, unless a majority of not less than two-thirds of the Members present is obtained.

Article 74. No modification of the Imperial House Law shall be required to be submitted to the deliberation of the Imperial Diet.

(2) No provision of the present Constitution can be modified by the Imperial House Law.

Article 75. No modification can be introduced into the Constitution, or into the

Imperial House Law, during the time of a Regency.

Article 76. Existing legal enactments, such as laws, regulations, Ordinances, or by whatever names they may be called, shall, so far as they do not conflict with the present Constitution, continue in force.

(2) All existing contracts or orders, that entail obligations upon the Government, and that are connected with expenditure, shall come within the scope of Article 67.

(The above is the semi-official translation, which appeared in H. Itō, *Commentaries on the Constitution of the Empire of Japan,* tr M. Itō, 1889.)

construction industry 建設業

(*kensetsugyō*). Japan has the world's largest construction market, with 1988 domestic construction investment estimated at ¥67.1 trillion (US $523.6 billion), or 17.4 percent of the gross national product. This construction investment was 40 percent civil engineering works and 60 percent (building) construction works; 36 percent of the total investment went to public works. Nationally there are some 510,000 construction companies, and the approximately 5.8 million construction industry workers represent 9.7 percent of all workers. In recent years, however, the industry has suffered from a serious shortage of workers.

In 1983 overseas construction orders exceeded ¥1.0 trillion (US $4.2 billion); this figure had not increased noticeably by 1989 due to the increase in the value of the yen. Although orders have increased from the industrialized countries, primarily the United States, 87 percent of the orders received from the United States are development investments and factory construction projects for Japanese companies operating there. Foreign construction companies have encountered difficulty in breaking into the Japanese domestic market, but extended negotiations have produced some results: by 1989, 21 foreign companies from the United States, Korea, and France had received construction licenses.

construction machinery industry 建設機械産業

(*kensetsu kikai sangyō*). After experiencing rapid expansion during Japan's high economic growth period in the 1960s, with production increasing from ¥115.0 billion (US $800.0 million) in 1965 to ¥1.2 trillion (US $8.6 billion) in 1980, the Japanese construction machinery industry has showed little change in the 1980s and early 1990s. Of the more than 90 domestic manufacturers, the top 5 hold about 80 percent of the market.

As a result of the shift since 1975 in the nature of projects requiring construction equipment from basic industrial facilities to residential facilities, the importance of hydraulic excavators and crawler loaders has increased. Exports dropped after a 1985 peak of ¥600.0 billion (US $4.3 billion) with an export ratio of 53 percent. Influenced by policies designed to increase domestic demand, 1990 production was ¥1.8 trillion (US $12.8 billion), of which exports were about 30 percent.

consumer movement 消費者運動

(*shōhisha undō*). Blanket term applied to a broad range of activities on the part of organizations seeking to mobilize consumer power to resist harmful business practices. Relatively unnoticed for many years, the consumer movement catapulted to national attention in the late 1960s and early 1970s as a result of several widely publicized consumer group campaigns and has become identified as part of a general upsurge of citizen activism known as CITIZENS' MOVEMENTS (*shimin undō*).

History—In the first years after World War II, a consumer movement centered around women's groups, and labor-affiliated CONSUMERS' COOPERATIVES sprang up in response to the scarcities of a war-devastated economy. Both served as mutual aid societies, while the women's groups, the most prominent of which was the Japan Housewives Association (SHUFUREN), also carried on campaigns against rampant black-market profiteering and fraudulent merchandising. At times these groups were aided and encouraged by the Occupation authorities (see SCAP) and the Japanese government, which hoped to use them to help curb illegal and undesirable business activities.

The 1960s brought a shift in focus toward comparative product testing, consumer information, and consumer education. This led to the creation of a new product-testing and consumer-education organization, the Japan Consumers Association (Nihon Shōhisha Kyōkai), sponsored jointly by business, government, and several women's groups. By the mid-1970s the consumer movement had a complex organizational structure. At the neighborhood and community levels, the organizational base of the majority of groups could be traced to women's groups (*fujinkai*). At the other end of the organizational spectrum were groups that focused primarily on national policy. Most prominent of these were Shufuren, whose operations have over the years acquired a high degree of sophistication and professionalism; the Consumers Union of Japan (Nihon Shōhisha Remmei), a leading practitioner of Ralph Nader–style tactics in Japan; the Japan Cooperative Consumers Union (Nihon Seikatsu Kyōdō Kumiai Rengōkai), closely associated with the left wing of the labor movement and, with Shufuren, a leading consumer interest advocate since the 1950s; and the National Federation of Regional Women's Organizations (CHIFUREN), an umbrella organization for neighborhood *fujinkai*, with a membership of over 6 million women.

Recent Developments—In the 1980s the consumer movement diversified to incorporate the issues of health, safety, and environment. Demands for higher standards of food safety arose from concerns about the potential danger to consumers from antibiotics administered to livestock, chemicals applied to foreign agricultural products during transportation to Japan, and radiation contamination of imported food caused by the Chernobyl nuclear accident. The environmental protection movement seized on issues relating to consumption and waste disposal, such as the use of synthetic detergents, nuclear power, and chlorofluorocarbons (CFCs).

consumer protection laws 消費者保護法

(*shōhisha hogo hō*). Body of national laws, administrative regulations, and local ordinances providing for administrative or judicial intervention in order to protect consumers directly or indirectly. Until the late 1960s little attention was given to legislation designed primarily to protect consumers. The passage of the Basic Law for Consumer Protection (Shōhisha Hogo Kihon Hō) in 1968 was the first effort to organize various regulatory statutes into a comprehensive scheme aimed directly at consumer protection. Although the broad policy goals of the Basic Law remain unfulfilled, new legislative activity on both the national and local levels has given consumer protection more coherence and force than was previously the case. The Basic Law did not, however, affect the private laws governing consumer problems or alter the essentially bureaucratic and regulatory nature of Japanese consumer protection.

The ANTIMONOPOLY LAW of 1947, the INSTALLMENT SALES LAW of 1961, and the Household Products Quality Indication Standard Law of 1962 were the major laws aimed at consumer protection in the pre–Basic Law era. Within several years after the enactment of the Basic Law, approximately 30 statutes were passed by the Diet. Among them were the revision of the Local Autonomy Law in 1969, which clarified the responsibility and authority of local government in consumer protection, the Agricultural Products Quality Indication Law of 1970, the Travel Agencies Law of 1971, and the Consumer Products Safety Law of 1973. Since 1974, a number of municipalities have passed local ordinances to enforce their consumer protection policies.

The Basic Law calls for measures to be taken to consolidate and reform consumer protection laws, to ensure consumer safety, to guarantee proper measurement techniques in consumer transactions, to guarantee proper representation of product specifications and content, to assure fair and free competition, to promote consumer information and education and establish a system to reflect consumer opinion in national policy, to provide for the testing and inspection of consumer products and the publication of those results when necessary, and to provide for appropriate and prompt resolution of consumer disputes.

The Basic Law appears to establish a strong national policy in favor of consumer protection. Like other basic laws, however, it is abstract and general, and each of its provisions requires a separate specific statute to give it substantive content. By itself it gives consumers no new legal rights, against either business or government, nor does it create substantive legal duties within the national or local administration. It has thus been criticized for being nothing more than a political ploy to appease consumers. It has also been criticized for its requirement that whatever action the government or consumers take to promote consumer protection should "conform to" the needs of economic development.

Coordination and reform of the national and local administration of consumer protection laws have been carried out by the establishment of the Consumer Protection Conference in 1968 within the Prime Minister's Office. The conference determines national policy, which is then carried out by the various ministries and agencies having jurisdiction over the specific statutes involved. See also CONSUMER MOVEMENT.

consumers 消費者

(*shōhisha*). Numbering over 123 million in 1990, Japan's population provides the motive force for one of the largest, most rapidly changing, and most affluent consumer markets in the world.

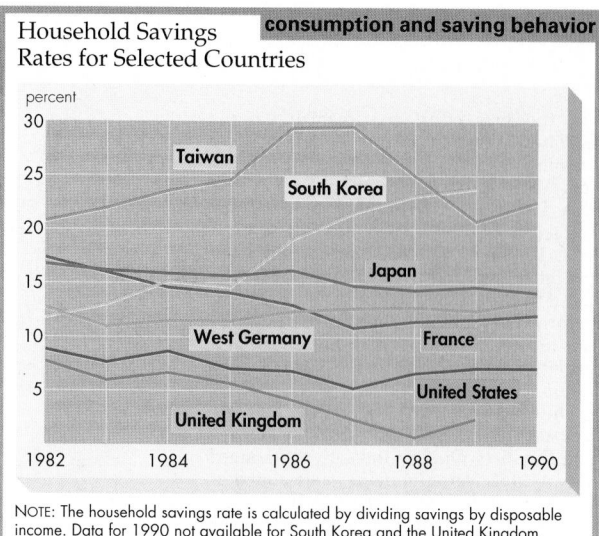

Household Savings Rates for Selected Countries

consumption and saving behavior

NOTE: The household savings rate is calculated by dividing savings by disposable income. Data for 1990 not available for South Korea and the United Kingdom.
SOURCE: Bank of Japan, *Kokusai hikaku tōkei* (annual): 1991.

Population and Income—The number of consumers, which in broadest terms is identical with the population, exceeded 100 million in the late 1960s and is expected to rise to 128 million by the year 2000. The number of households was slightly more than 36 million in the 1980 census and 41 million in the 1990 census; this number is expected to rise to 45 million by 2000.

Incomes have continued to expand steadily along with economic growth. Individual household income in 1990 was computed by the Statistics Bureau of the Management and Coordination Agency at ¥521,800 (US $3,600) per month in 1990, or nearly ¥6.3 million (US $43,200) annually. In terms of purchasing power in Japan, conversion to dollars is somewhat misleading since, according to a number of surveys, prices in Japan for many consumer goods exceed those overseas. Nevertheless conversion to dollars is meaningful in determining the international purchasing power of Japanese consumers; that is, their ability to buy services such as overseas travel and, potentially, more imports from other nations.

By most social statistics, Japan ranks with Western nations in wealth and consumption. For example, in terms of gross national product and total consumer spending Japan ranks second to the United States. In recent years, depending on the fluctuations in the yen-dollar exchange rate, Japan's GNP per capita has sometimes exceeded that of the United States. Indicators of material welfare, including ownership of consumer durables, place Japan's standard of living at or above that of most industrialized nations. The primary constraints on the standard of living of the Japanese consumer are limitations on space and the high costs of land and housing.

Trends in Expenditures—Some of the important features and trends in major categories are as follows:

Food. Japanese households spent ¥79,000 (US $550) monthly for food in 1990, about 1.2 times the level for 1980. Food consumption has continued to undergo steady Westernization, but the traditional framework of a rice-centered diet remains, along with a relatively high level of consumption of fish, a lower consumption of meat (especially beef) when compared to other industrialized nations, and a lower consumption of dairy products. While the traditional dietary framework has remained, there has been rapid growth in some areas, including soft drinks and fast foods.

Apparel. Monthly spending on clothing and footwear by the average household amounted to ¥23,000 (US $160) in 1990, 1.3 times the level for 1980. The market for apparel is predominantly oriented toward Western-style clothing, although women still prefer traditional Japanese *kimono* for such special occasions as weddings and New Year's. Japan's apparel market and fashion industry has become very sophisticated over the past two decades, leading to a rise in imports, the manufacturing of foreign designs on a licensed basis in Japan, and the diversified development of the fashion industry in Japan.

Housing. Approximately 70 percent of households own their own homes in Japan—a relatively high figure—and owning a home and upgrading its size and quality are important goals. Buying real estate in major urban areas has become almost prohibitively expensive, however. In 1990 to purchase 40–50 square meters (430–538 sq ft) of living space cost Japanese 12–15 times their annual income, whereas Americans had to pay 5–9 times their income to purchase the same area, and Germans paid only 3–4 times.

Education and leisure. The average household spent ¥16,800 (US $115) monthly for education in 1990. Total monthly expenditures for education, cultural services, and entertainment amounted to ¥48,600 (US $335), about 1.6 times the level of 1980. This increase reflects the growing interest in continuing education and the increase in leisure time. The nature of these expenditures differs widely by income level, age, and sex. Women in their mid-forties or older tend to prefer traditional pursuits such as flower arranging and tea ceremony, but younger women tend to favor sports and travel. Participation in sports tends to rise significantly with income level, while watching television is a nearly universal leisure activity. One of the fastest-growing leisure activities in recent years has been overseas travel, as airfares have been reduced and Japanese consumers have begun to realize what their incomes will buy overseas. In 1987 the Japanese government set a goal of having 10 million Japanese nationals travel overseas by 1991. But growth thereafter was so rapid that overseas travelers topped 11 million in 1990.

Savings and consumer credit. A key distinguishing feature of Japanese consumers is the high percentage of disposable income they save. Japan's household savings rate has been about 16 percent in recent years, which compares to about 6 percent in the United States, 12 percent in France, and 5 percent in the United Kingdom. According to a Bank of Japan survey, the average salaried worker household had ¥11.8 million (US $81,500) in savings in 1990, or about 1.9 times annual income. Although consumers are becoming more sensitive to interest rates, they still show a strong preference for putting their monetary assets into bank accounts. There is, however, a strong trend toward more investments in investment trusts or mutual funds. Although restricted in the 1950s and 1960s, consumer credit is now readily available from banks and other sources for qualified borrowers. With the increase in land and stock prices since the mid-1980s banking institutions have become much more aggressive in seeking out high-net-worth individuals and providing them with home equity and other loans.

Market segments and trends. Along with affluence, consumption patterns in Japan have become much more diverse. Sharp differences are now evident in the way various age groups spend their incomes. Although members of the population 30 years of age and under account for slightly more than 40 percent of the population and set many of the directions of the market, Japan's population is also aging very rapidly, and by the early 21st century Japan will have the largest percentage of persons over 60 among the industrialized nations. The so-called silver market, named for the gray hair of the older generation, is thus becoming increasingly important for many industries, including leisure, pharmaceuticals, and medical services.

Also important are the gift market and the growing segmentation of the consumer market by type of retail outlet. Japan has two gift-giving seasons, one in summer and the other at year end. In addition, gifts are considered an important part of etiquette during social visits and a number of other occasions. Also, as retailing has developed with growth in large chain outlets, many neighborhood stores have remained in operation to suit the preferences of housewives for shopping near their homes, and differentiation of lines of goods by type of outlet has become increasingly important. See also STANDARD OF LIVING; CONSUMPTION AND SAVING BEHAVIOR.

Consumer's Cooperative Kōbe

生活協同組合コープこうべ

(Seikatsu Kyōdō Kumiai Kōpu Kōbe). Largest consumers' cooperative society in Japan. Founded in 1921. It has some one million members, most of whom reside in Hyōgo Prefecture. In addition to the sale of food, housewares, and clothing, the society is engaged in cultural and welfare activities. For the fiscal year ending March 1990, sales totaled ¥297.6 billion (US $1.9 billion), and capitalization stood at ¥22.0 billion (US $143.7 million). Headquarters are in Kōbe.

consumers' cooperatives 生協

(*seikyō*). Also called *shōhi seikatsu kyōdō kumiai*. The first modern consumers' cooperative in Japan was the Kyōritsu Shōsha, organized in 1879, which dealt chiefly in rice, soybean paste (*miso*), and fuel. In 1900 the Industrial Association Law (Sangyō Kumiai Hō) was enacted, and under its provisions cooperative purchasing societies such as the Nada Purchasing Society and the Kōbe Consumers' Cooperative were founded; this law was replaced in 1948 by the Consumers' Cooperative Law (Shōhi Seikatsu Kyōdō Kumiai Hō). In 1951 the Japanese Consumers' Co-operative Union was founded to support the activities of consumers' organizations. By the 1970s these organizations were involved in virtually every aspect of members' material lives, including not only the sale of commodities for household consumption but also the provision of various types of insurance and of housing, bathing, dining, and medical facilities. In 1990 the Japanese Consumers' Co-operative Union had 674 member organizations with a total membership of 14.1 million. In the same year, consumers' cooperatives received ¥2.5 trillion (US $18.3 billion) from the sale of commodities and services and held a 2.5 percent share of the retail market.

consumption and saving behavior

貯蓄と消費

(*chochiku to shōhi*). The ratio of saving to income among Japanese households has declined in recent years but remains high. Average household savings in 1990 stood at ¥11,810,000 (US $81,600), or 1.9 times average annual income. The average household savings portfolio for 1990 shows the Japanese preference for low-risk saving methods over speculative investments: 46.5 percent of savings (¥5,490,000; US $37,900) was in bank and other savings deposits, and 21.2 percent (¥2,500,000; US $17,300) was in life and nonlife insurance policies. Stocks and bonds accounted for 16.2 percent (¥1,910,000; US $13,200) of savings, and other speculative investments made up the remaining 16.1 percent. The main saving objectives of the Japanese—providing for illness and accident (74.3 percent) and for old age (52.4 percent)—point to a lack of adequate SOCIAL WELFARE programs in Japan as a significant factor behind the high rate of saving.

In 1990 the percentage of income remaining after expenditures (the "propensity to save") reached 24.7 percent (16.9 percent if only savings and insurance premiums are considered). In the same year the average amount saved monthly by the household of a male office worker (SARARĪMAN) was ¥108,900 (US $750), 70.6 percent of which represented a net increase in such financial assets as savings deposits, insurance, stocks, and bonds; 22.4 percent, a net decrease in liabilities through housing loan or other credit repayments; and the remaining 7.0 percent, a net increase in nonfinancial assets.

Savings can be broadly divided into fixed saving (including loan repayments and insurance premiums), which is characterized by regular required payments, and discretionary saving, such as savings deposits and asset purchases. In recent years increases in fixed saving have pushed up saving propensity and held down consumption. Whether or not the Japanese saving ratio will decline in the long term largely depends on developments in the social welfare system and housing market. It seems likely that the rapid rise in the number of elderly living off their savings will depress the national average saving rate.

According to Management and Coordination Agency statistics, the monthly expenditures of a male office worker's household in 1990 were ¥331,600 (US $2,290). Of the 10 major expenditure categories listed by the agency, "other expenses" at ¥90,600 (US $630), or 27.3 percent, was the largest. This category includes entertainment and other miscellaneous expenses that have increased significantly with improvements in the STANDARD OF LIVING. Food, the next largest category at ¥79,000 (US $550), or 24.1 percent, continued its post–World War II decline as a percentage of total expenditures. The relative weight of Japanese expenditures on consumer durables—5.1 percent for educational and recreational products, such as televisions and videocassette recorders, and 4.0 percent for furniture and household appliances, including refrigerators and air conditioners—remains fairly low. Spending has shifted from categories such as food to expenditures on transportation, communications, entertainment, and other leisure-related activities. Although the ratio of total expenditures to disposable income has actually declined slightly from 75.7 percent in 1974 to 75.3 percent in 1990, many people are concerned about what they see as increasingly extravagant Japanese lifestyles based on excessive consumption.

Average Household Savings in Japan, Based on a 1990 Survey

Category	Average savings (in millions of yen)	Average savings (in US dollars)	Bank savings accounts	Postal savings accounts	Insurance	Securities	Others
			(in percentages)				
Overall	11.81	81,600	33.9	12.6	21.2	16.2	16.1
Employment of household head:							
Agriculture, forestry, and fisheries	11.45	79,100	42.0	14.2	23.1	5.8	14.9
Self-employed	12.85	88,700	36.8	11.4	25.8	15.6	10.4
Office worker	9.55	66,000	31.1	13.1	20.2	17.2	18.4
Blue-collar	7.03	48,600	36.0	14.5	25.2	8.5	15.8
Manager	16.16	111,600	30.0	9.7	19.9	22.2	18.2
Freelance	16.10	111,200	30.2	12.0	21.6	17.2	19.0
Others	14.86	102,600	33.0	14.9	15.2	17.8	19.1
No reply	10.45	72,200	54.4	11.7	12.7	10.6	10.6
Household income level:							
Less than ¥2 million	4.08	28,200	37.3	18.9	16.7	7.1	20.0
¥2 to 3 million	8.20	56,600	40.0	16.5	16.6	12.7	14.2
¥3 to 4 million	7.27	50,200	28.9	16.2	23.4	16.1	15.4
¥4 to 5 million	8.70	60,100	37.2	15.4	21.5	12.2	13.7
¥5 to 7 million	11.38	78,600	34.9	12.4	22.8	14.0	15.9
¥7 million and above	18.25	126,000	32.2	10.1	21.0	19.7	17.0
No reply	10.49	72,400	35.7	15.7	17.0	13.1	18.5
Age of household head:							
Twenties	4.13	28,500	27.8	10.7	26.9	6.3	28.3
Thirties	6.45	44,500	35.8	12.9	25.0	11.6	14.7
Forties	9.67	66,800	33.8	11.9	24.2	14.3	15.8
Fifties	14.36	99,200	33.2	11.3	21.3	18.2	16.0
Sixties	17.52	121,000	32.6	13.4	18.8	17.8	17.4
Seventies	16.69	115,300	38.5	16.3	14.1	16.4	14.7
Home ownership:							
Homeowner	13.75	95,000	33.7	12.4	20.7	17.1	16.1
Nonhomeowner	7.74	53,500	33.9	13.0	23.0	13.2	16.9

NOTE: Data based on replies to a survey of 6,000 households. Yen figures have been converted into US dollars at the average 1990 rate of $1.00=¥144.79. The savings category of "securities" includes bonds, stocks, and trusts; "others" includes trust cash funds, loan funds, postal pensions, reserve pensions, workers' property accumulation savings, and other financial products.
SOURCE: The Central Council for Savings Information, *Chochiku ni kansuru yoron chōsa* (annual): 1990.

consumption tax   消費税

(*shōhizei*). A value-added tax introduced in April of 1989 as part of a national tax reform package designed to decrease government dependence on income TAXES and stabilize revenue sources in anticipation of the aging of Japanese society. For consumers, the tax is equivalent to a general sales tax of 3 percent. In the case of business enterprises, a uniform tax of 3 percent is applied only to the difference between sales and purchases (i.e., value added) in order to avoid multiple taxation. The tax applies to all transactions except those involving education, medicine and welfare, and other specified exemptions. Exceptions include an exemption for businesses with annual taxable revenues not exceeding ¥30 million (US $217,000). Objections from consumer groups and opposition parties within the Diet made the tax one of the most contentious issues of the late 1980s.

contracts   契約

(*keiyaku*). There are two discrete aspects to contracts in Japan. The first is the formal legal principles that govern the formation and parameters of contracts. The second is the role and use of contracts in the Japanese setting.

Governing Principles—The law on contracts in Japan is fundamentally identical to German law. Despite important differences in code and statutory provisions, the infusion of German civil law theory during the first quarter of the 20th century recast Japanese civil law into an almost exclusively German mold. The primary source of contract law is the CIVIL CODE as construed by court decisions and scholars. As general law, the code articulates the concepts and principles that underlie all private law in Japan. Book I, on General Principles (*sōsoku*), sets out the primary concepts that govern, unless otherwise provided, all other areas of private law (TORTS, obligations, contracts, unjust enrichment, management of affairs without mandate, family law, and inheritance). The conceptual linchpin of the code is the notion of the JURISTIC ACT (*hōritsu kōi*; German: *Rechtsgeschäft*; French: *acte juridique*). A juristic act may be formed by a unilateral declaration of intention (as in the case of testamentary will) but more typically by two or more mutual declarations of intention. The prototypical juristic act is thus the "obligation" (*saiken*), covered in Book III, and the prototypical obligation is the contract (*keiyaku*). Chapter 2 of Book III similarly contains general provisions for all contracts as well as provisions for 13 particular types of contract. These are gifts (*zōyo*), articles 549–554; sales (*baibai*), articles 555–585; exchange (*kōkan*), article 586; loans for consumption (*shōhi taishaku*), articles 587–592; loans for use (*shiyō taishaku*), articles 593–600; leases (*chintaishaku*), articles 601–

622; service or employment (*koyō*), articles 623–631; contracts for work (*ukeoi*), articles 632–642; mandates (*inin*), articles 643–656; deposits (*kitaku*), articles 657–666; Civil Code partnerships or associations (*kumiai*), articles 667–688; life annuities (*shūshin teikikin*), articles 689–694; and Civil Code compromises (*wakai*), articles 695–696. As a general rule the provisions on obligations including contracts are not mandatory and therefore can be varied by contract. Also, the overriding principle of freedom of contract gives substantial emphasis to party autonomy, the right of private parties to create rights and duties at variance with the code's provisions.

Organization Guide—Many of the basic concepts of Japanese contract law are what might be called organizing principles without decisional importance. For example, in theory all contracts can be classified as either consensual (*dakusei*) or real (*yōbutsu*), depending on whether the contract is formed by mutual assent or delivery; gratuitous (*mushō*) or onerous (*yūshō*), depending on whether there is an exchange of economic benefits of equal value; and one-sided (*hemmu*) or two-sided (*sōmu*), depending on whether the duties to be performed are perceived to be of equal value. Under the code, loans for consumption and deposit are real contracts in that they do not become effective until delivery of the money to be lent or the thing to be deposited. Nonetheless, purely executory loan and deposit agreements are valid and enforceable under general contract principles.

Other conceptual dichotomies in Japanese contract law have more decisional consequence. For instance, the distinction of whether the object of a sales contract is specific (*tokuteibutsu*) or nonspecific (*futokuteibutsu*) determines under the code (arts. 534, 535, 401[2]) at what point the risk of loss shifts from the seller to the buyer. Of course, the parties can allocate the risk differently by agreement.

Although in most instances, albeit by separate routes, the actual results in specific cases under Japanese law will approximate the results reached under the law in most common law jurisdictions, there are critical differences. First, there is no consideration requirement in Japanese law. Thus an executory gift or one-sided commitment is valid and enforceable. Nor is there any writing requirement except for executory gifts (art. 550). Consequently, there is no parole evidence role or statute of frauds. Also, there is no strict tender rule in the law of sales; substantial performance satisfies the obligation in all cases. Japanese law maintains a strict approach to privity of contract, limiting, therefore, manufacturer liability for defective products. There is no distinction between equitable and legal remedies, and specific performance is the usual remedy. In practice, however, difficulties in enforcement make damages the more common form of relief. Finally, Japanese courts have been quite strict in enforcing contractual commitments despite unforeseen supervening events even though acknowledging the validity of a changed-circumstances excuse under the good faith doctrine of article 1 of the code.

Role and Use of Contracts—Paralleling the lack of inhibiting formation requirements and coincident limitations on effective enforcement is the tendency of Japanese parties to view formal contract writings less as legal documents than as descriptive guidelines detailing a course of expected performance. Contractual provisions dealing with the legal rights and duties of the parties will be typically quite brief, often with critical issues left to settlement by consultation. Yet there may be quite detailed technical provisions. There is also widespread use of standardized form agreements often drafted by trade associations or other groups. In many instances, these will include broad, overreaching provisions, but they are in fact seldom if ever enforced.

When disputes do arise, there appears to be a strong tendency to avoid reliance on the written contractual commitment as the basis for resolution. Rather the parties are more likely to reach accommodations in ways other than litigation. See also CIVIL PROCEDURE, CODE OF; DISPUTE RESOLUTION SYSTEMS OTHER THAN LITIGATION.

"Control" faction→Tōseiha

cooking, Japanese   日本料理

(Nihon *ryōri*). There are three fundamental types of traditional full-course Japanese cuisine: HONZEN RYŌRI, an assembly of dishes served on legged trays at formal banquets; *chakaiseki ryōri*, a series of dishes sometimes served before the TEA CEREMONY; and KAISEKI RYŌRI, a series of dishes for parties, often served at restaurants specializing in Japanese cuisine (*ryōtei*). Other types are OSECHI RYŌRI, dishes traditionally served on important holidays such as New Year's, and SHŌJIN RYŌRI, Buddhist vegetarian dishes.

The main ingredients in Japanese cooking are seafood, vegetables, and rice. The consumption of raw seafood has long been a distinguishing feature of native cuisine, and its preparation requires that fish be very fresh and that it be skillfully cut with a very sharp knife (*hōchō*). Because of the abundance of foods supplied by the seas surrounding Japan and the influence of Buddhism, which militated against the killing of animals, Japanese cooking formerly made little use of the flesh of animals and fowl, dairy products, and oils and fat. Principal seasonings are fermented products of soybeans, such as SOY SAUCE (*shōyu*) and MISO (soybean paste), or of rice, such as SAKE, vinegar, and MIRIN (sweet *sake*). *Mirin* has a smoother sweetness than sugar and is used in small amounts to enhance the taste of soy sauce and *miso*, as well as to mitigate the acidity of vinegar. To preserve the natural flavors of ingredients, strong spices are avoided in favor of milder HERBS AND SPICES, such as *kinome* (aromatic sprigs of the tree known as *sanshō*), *yuzu* (citron), *wasabi* (Japanese horseradish), GINGER, *myōga* (a plant of the same genus as ginger), and dried and ground *sanshō* seeds.

In preparing foods for serving one arranges them in a manner that harmonizes colors and textures, on plates or in bowls that accord with the season of the year; for example, glass and bamboo are considered appropriate for summer. Dishes of contrasting shapes, sizes, and patterns are used during the course of a meal to achieve an aesthetic balance between food and receptacle that pleases the eye and stimulates the appetite.

Another characteristic of Japanese cooking is the tendency to assimilate foreign recipes. The process of selection and rejection of ingredients has been applied to such an extent that one may speak of Japanese-style Western or Chinese cooking. See also FOOD AND EATING.

The basis of all Japanese cooking is stock (*dashi*), the standard form of which is made with the type of seaweed known as sea tangle (KOMBU) and dried bonito-fillet (KATSUOBUSHI) shavings. As both of these materials have distinct flavors, it is important when making *dashi* not to leave them in the pot too long. First, about 30 grams (1 oz) of tangle are placed in 1 liter (a little more than 1 quart) of water and brought to a boil over a medium flame. The tangle is removed just before the pot starts to boil and a small amount of water and about 30 grams (1 oz) of bonito shavings are added. When the pot reaches a boil, the flame is turned off and the foamy substance that has formed on the surface skimmed off. After the bonito shavings sink to the bottom, the contents of the pot are then poured through cheesecloth. Among other types are stocks made from fish or chicken bones, dried sardines (*niboshi*), or tangle and dried mushrooms. Instant stock in powdered form is now widely used.

The categories into which all Japanese cooking falls are described below. Each Japanese term that appears in subheadings not only expresses the method of cooking but also denotes the dish itself.

Shirumono—*Shirumono* (soups) can be roughly divided into two types, *sumashijiru* and *misoshiru* (see MISO SOUP). Ingredients may include white-fleshed fish, prawns, shellfish, *tōfu*, fowl, seaweed, and seasonal vegetables; one or two ingredients that accord with the remainder of the menu are selected from among these. To add more zest and aroma, *yuzu*, *kinome*, *sanshō*, ginger, or *mitsuba* (a trifoliolate herb of the same genus as honewort) may be added.

For *sumashijiru*, or clear soup, *dashi*, to which salt and soy sauce have been added, is customarily used. Ingredients to be added to the soup should be cut and warmed in a separate stock. If the ingredients are *tai* (red snapper) or *hamaguri* (a type of clam), from which a good flavor can be obtained, stock is made with the clams or with the bones of the *tai* and a pinch of salt. The ingredients are arranged in a bowl that has been warmed beforehand, hot stock is poured over them, and the aromatic substance is added last.

Yakimono—The principal ingredients of *yakimono* (grilled foods) are fish, shellfish, meat, and vegetables. Foods are pierced with a skewer or placed on a wire net and grilled over an open fire. One may also make *yakimono* using an iron skillet or oven broiler. The basic type of *yakimono* is *shioyaki*, in which salt is sprinkled over the food before grilling. The distinctive flavor of fish is best enjoyed in this way. For *tsukeyaki* the food is first marinated for about an hour in *awase-jōyu*, a mixture of soy sauce and *sake* or *mirin*. TERIYAKI is a *yakimono* prepared with a stronger-flavored *awase-jōyu*. For *misozukeyaki*, the food is marinated in *miso* flavored with *sake* or *mirin*. In arranging a grilled whole fish on a plate, the head of the fish is positioned to the left with the belly facing the diner.

Nimono—*Nimono* are stewed dishes seasoned with salt, soy sauce, *sake*, *mirin*, sugar, vinegar, or other condiments. The most common *nimono* is *nitsuke*—fish or shellfish cooked briefly in a relatively thick mixture of *sake*, soy sauce, *mirin*, and sugar. In the case of the white-fleshed fish *tai* and *buri* (yellowtail), the fillets are removed and used for *sashimi* or *yakimono* and the head and backbone chopped in pieces, washed in hot water, and cooked with a relatively light mixture of water, *sake*, *mirin*, and soy sauce until the juice is almost entirely absorbed. Bluefish, such as mackerel, sardines, and saurel, are first cooked in a mixture of water, *sake*, and *mirin*. *Miso* that has been diluted with a ladleful of the broth (*nijiru*) is then added to mask the strong flavor of the fish. This is called *misoni*. *Mizoreni* is a method of preparation in which bluefish is cooked in seasoned *dashi* with a generous amount of grated white radish. In making *nimono* it is important to use heavy covered pots so that the heat and the *nijiru* spread evenly.

Agemono—*Agemono*, or deep-fried foods, are of three basic types. *Suage*, in which foods are fried without a coating of flour or batter, is appropriate for freshwater fish, eggplant, green peppers, and other vegetables whose color and shape can be utilized to good effect. *Karaage* frying, in which food is first dredged in flour or arrowroot starch, preserves the natural water content of the food and crispens the outer surface. In *tatsutaage*, a variant of *karaage*, pieces of chicken are marinated in a mixture of *sake*, soy sauce, and sugar, lightly covered with arrowroot starch, and deep-fried. TEMPURA belongs to a third type of *agemono*, in which foods are coated with batter.

For *agemono* a heavy pot with a wide bottom is used. Vegetable oil is poured into the pot to a depth twice the thickness of the foods to be fried, and heated to a temperature of 160° to 180°C (320° to 360°F). To keep the oil at a constant temperature, it is important that the foods not cover more than a third of the surface area of the oil. See also TONKATSU.

Mushimono—*Mushimono* are steamed foods. With this method, natural flavors do not escape and the taste is very light. Foods may be sprinkled with salt and steamed (*shiomushi*) or sprinkled with salt and *sake* (*sakamushi*). The latter method is particularly appropriate for clams or abalone. *Mushimono* are served with seasoned *dashi* thickened with arrowroot starch and sprinkled with grated ginger, *yuzu* rind, or chopped scallion. The foundation of *chawan mushi* is a mixture of beaten eggs and lukewarm *dashi* (about three times the volume of the eggs). Ingredients such as shrimp, mushrooms, and chicken are placed in individual bowls. The egg mixture is poured in and the bowls covered and steamed over medium heat.

Sunomono and Aemono—*Sunomono* are vinegared fish or vegetables; *aemono* are fish or vegetables with a dressing, the basic ingredient of which is ground sesame seed, *miso*, or mashed *tōfu*. Fish and shellfish are sometimes broiled or steamed, or they may be sliced, sprinkled with salt, and marinated in vinegar or sea-tangle stock. Vegetables are either blanched, rubbed with salt, boiled, or steamed. Excess water should be eliminated. Of the two main types of vinaigrette for *sunomono*, *nihaizu* is a combination of vinegar, soy sauce, and *dashi*. *Sambaizu* is *nihaizu* to which a small amount of sugar is added. Grated horseradish, ginger, or white radish, or the juice of citrus fruits, may also be added. To the basic ingredient of dressings for *aemono*, soy sauce, vinegar, *mirin*, sugar, and *dashi*—and sometimes hot mustard and *kinome*—are added. Both *sunomono* and *aemono* should be prepared immediately before being served. Garnishes of aromatic vegetables should also be added. These two dishes are not main courses but are served in small quantities at the end of a meal, between courses, or as appetizers when drinking *sake*.

Yosemono and Nerimono—*Yosemono* are molded dishes made with agar-agar or gelatin. Foods such as rock trout, flounder, and chicken that have a relatively high gelatin content are used. *Nerimono* are foods that have been mashed into a paste. For one such dish, fish or shellfish is chopped into small pieces and mashed in a mortar with a pinch of salt. The paste is mixed with beaten eggs, grated *yamanoimo* (a type of yam), and *dashi* and divided into portions for boiling, deep-frying, or steaming. It is eaten with soy sauce and grated ginger. Both *yosemono* and *nerimono* should be served in small portions.

Gohammono—*Gohammono* are dishes consisting of rice combined with other ingredients. *Takikomigohan* is made by cooking rice and another ingredient—in spring, green peas or pieces of bamboo shoot; in autumn, *matsutake* mushrooms or chestnuts—in seasoned water or *dashi*. *Gomokumeshi* (also known as *kayakugohan*) is prepared by adding finely diced chicken, carrot, fried *tōfu*, *shiitake* mushroom, and burdock to rice and cooking it in *dashi* seasoned with soy sauce, *sake*, and sugar. *Domburimono* are dishes in which cooked rice is placed in a bowl (*domburi*) that is larger than the usual rice bowl and then topped with various prepared ingredients (see OYAKO DOMBURI; KATSUDON; TENDON). See also KARĒ RAISU; ZŌSUI; SEKIHAN; CHAZUKE; NIGIRIMESHI.

Menrui—*Menrui* is a category of dishes, served hot or cold, whose chief ingredient is noodles. The most common types of noodles are UDON, SŌMEN, and SOBA. The first two are made with wheat flour, and *soba* with buckwheat flour. *Sōmen* is always dried; *soba* and *udon* may be either fresh or dried.

Nabemono—*Nabemono* are dishes cooked in a pot of simmering broth at the table. Ingredients are arranged on platters so that each person may cook what he or she likes. The chief types of *nabemono* are *mizutaki*, *yudōfu*, *udonsuki*, *kanisuki*, *dotenabe*, SHABUSHABU, and SUKIYAKI. *Mizutaki* is prepared by cooking fillets of white-fleshed fish with vegetables, *tōfu*, and *harusame* (thin potato-starch noodles) in a pot of *kombu* stock, or chicken and vegetables in chicken broth. Grated white radish, red pepper, and chopped onion are used as condiments, and the food is dipped in *ponzu*, a sauce made from citron and soy sauce. *Yudōfu* is prepared by simmering cubes of *tōfu* in *kombu* stock. It is eaten with the same sauce and condiments as *mizutaki*. *Udonsuki* is prepared by cooking *udon* noodles, various vegetables, shrimp, shellfish, *yuba* (the dried skim of boiled *tōfu* milk), and *fu* (a light cake made of wheat gluten) in a thin *dashi*. *Kanisuki* is made with crab. To make *dotenabe*, *miso* is spread on the inside of the pot before adding *dashi*. The *miso* gradually dissolves and flavors oysters and vegetables. See also SUSHI; SASHIMI: PICKLES. ☎ 240-245

cooperative associations   協同組合

(*kyōdō kumiai*). Business organizations of small, independent producers or consumers seeking, through cooperative efforts, the benefits of large-scale management. They are distinguished from stock corporations and other juristic persons. Prior to World War II, there existed cooperative associations in which membership was required by the state. Since the war, only voluntary organizations have been allowed. Separate laws regulate cooperatives in the following four areas: AGRICULTURAL COOPERATIVE ASSO-

CIATIONS, marine products cooperative associations, medium and small enterprise cooperatives, and CONSUMERS' COOPERATIVES. Cooperative associations must meet requirements established by the ANTIMONOPOLY LAW.

Copyright Law   著作権法

(*Chosakuken Hō*). The Copyright Law of 1970, currently in force, is entirely new legislation that supersedes the Copyright Law of 1899. The current law protects the copyright and moral rights of authors, as well as the so-called neighboring rights of performers, producers of phonograms, broadcasting organizations, and cable-diffusion organizations.

A "work of authorship" (*chosakubutsu*) is defined as a "production in which thoughts or emotions are expressed in a creative way and which falls in the literary, scientific, artistic or musical domain" (art. 2[1] i). The law lists as examples nine categories of works of authorship entitled to copyright protection: (1) novels, dramas, theses, lectures, and other literary works; (2) musical works; (3) choreographic works and pantomimes; (4) paintings, woodcut prints, engravings, sculptures, and other works of art; (5) architectural works; (6) maps, as well as plans, charts, models, and other figurative works of a scientific nature; (7) cinematographic works; (8) photographic works; and (9) program works (art. 10[1]). Compilations (*henshūbutsu*) are protected if there exists some creativity in the selection or arrangement of the materials (art. 12[1]). Data bases (*dētabēsu*) are also protected as works of authorship if they possess creativity in the selection or systematic organization of those pieces of information that constitute the data bases (art. 12-2[1]).

Copyright (*chosakuken*) consists of the following exclusive rights: the right to reproduce a work (art. 21); the right to perform a work (art. 22); the right to broadcast a work or transmit it by cable (art. 23); the right to recite a work (art. 24); the right to exhibit a work (art. 25); the right to present publicly and distribute a cinematographic work (art. 26); the right to rent copies of a work (art. 26-2); and the right to translate or adapt a work, that is, the right to create a derivative work (art. 27). Copyright accrues at the moment of the creation of a work and subsists for the life of the author and 50 years after his or her death. In addition to copyright, an author is entitled to protection of his or her moral rights (*chosakusha jinkakuken*), that is, the right to make a work public (*kōhyōken;* art. 18), the right to claim authorship or paternity right (*shimei hyōjiken;* art. 19), and the right to the integrity of the work (*dōitsusei hojiken;* art. 20). An author's moral rights are exclusively personal and terminate on his or her death.

The neighboring rights (*chosaku rinsetsuken*) of performers, producers of phonograms, broadcasting organizations, and cable-diffusion organizations accrue from the moment of performance, first fixation of sound, first broadcast, or first cable diffusion and subsist for 50 years.

Japan is a signatory to the following international conventions: the Paris Act of 1971 of the Berne Convention for the Protection of Literary and Artistic Works; the Convention Establishing the World Intellectual Property Organization; the Paris Revision of

Continued on page 246➤

Savoring the Seasons in Japanese Cuisine

Stimulating all five senses with ingredients that evoke the season is the goal of Japanese cooking. A meal should delight the taste buds with a full range of flavors, the nose with its fragrant aromas, and the eyes with its appearance. Its texture in contact with the teeth or tongue should give tactile pleasure, and the conversation it inspires should please the ears. When a balance has been struck among all these elements in a dining experience that perfectly reflects the season, the Japanese ideal has been achieved.

How a meal looks receives as much attention as how it tastes. Throughout the year, cooks coordinate the forms and colors of foods and table settings with the unique spirit of each season. Proper selection and preparation of ingredients is vital, but the display of the meal on the table must also evoke sensations that seem perfect for that time of the year.

Japanese cooks began to stress seasonal themes over 400 years ago when the tea master Sen no Rikyū (1522–91) incorporated banquets called *chakaiseki* into the tea ceremony. His suggestion that "everything should seem as cool as possible in the summer and as warm as possible in the winter" demonstrates how the essence of the season can be communicated to the senses by means of a thoughtfully prepared meal. This emphasis on savoring the moment continues to influence Japanese cooking today.

Spring

After the passing of winter, the Japanese celebrate the arrival of spring with meals that evoke the spirit of the season. Sheltered by the branches of a flowering cherry tree, participants in an outdoor tea ceremony such as that pictured above may partake of a variety of seasonal delicacies including boiled bamboo shoots, dandelion leaves, and *warabi* sprouts. The mood of spring may be further enhanced by the presentation of the food, which is often molded in the shape of cherry or plum blossoms or garnished with sprays of fragrant wildflowers.

An autumn harvest. This wicker tray holds an elaborate assortment of autumn fare that includes *matsutake* mushrooms, cuttlefish, sandfish, and stuffed citrons (*yuzu*), all of which are to be grilled on the charcoal brazier, upper right.

Summer

Dining over or near water is one way to attain the cal-culated coolness sought in summer dining. Serving simple, lightly flavored fare chilled with ice on glass hollowware is another. As the humidity mounts, it has long been the practice to prepare rich foods, such as broiled eel, to help prevent loss of vigor.

Autumn

A box lunch packed with seasonal specialties and a flask of heated *sake* make the perfect repast for an autumn afternoon. Meals can be imbued with the splendor of fall in a variety of ways. The dishes may be decorated with motifs that feature the harvest moon or falling leaves, and the images of autumn plants and flowers might adorn the lacquer ware on which the food is served. A meal thus presented can be a rather poignant event—a tribute to the passing glory of autumn.

Winter

A rustic mountain cottage surrounded by snow is an ideal setting for a winter feast—a steaming pot of veg-etables and meat cooked slowly over a traditional wood-burning hearth. In ordinary homes as well, hearty one-pot meals are a winter favorite. The New Year's observance, howev-er, calls for its own very spe-cial cuisine.

Spring

The Doll Festival Feast

Ceremonial meals connected with spring holidays include the Doll Festival Feast prepared on 3 March in the homes of young girls. The *hamaguri* clam, symbolizing chastity and a happy marriage match, is the key ingredient in a meal which represents the warm wishes of a girl's parents that she mature into healthy womanhood and achieve a happy marriage. The banquet is laid out before a display of splendidly costumed dolls depicting the emperor and empress and their courtiers.

Clamshells in a basket hold *sushi* rice topped with thin strips of seasoned egg, left, and finely ground fish, right. Sprigs of *sanshō* garnish both. The oblong dish contains the shellfish *akagai*; the small dish holds shoots of field horsetail (*tsukushi*) and leaf buds of the Japanese angelica tree (*taranoki*).

Shapes of the Season

Pressing rice into a mold (*mossō*) so it will take the form of a seasonal symbol is a long-standing Japanese custom. Rice dishes and *sushi* that evoke a season by their color and fragrance may reinforce this effect by their pleasing shapes. The spring symbols used include butterflies and plum or cherry blossoms.

The Scent of Spring

The key ingredients of some dishes are prized for their fragrance: rape flowers, chrysanthemum leaves, or sprigs of the *sanshō* tree. When the lid is removed from a bowl of soup made from these greens and flowers, scents that evoke all the freshness of spring fill the air.

The hand-pressed sushi above features vinegared slices of *sayori*, a fish eaten in spring, laid out like flower petals. The *sushi* balls topped in red tuna and white sea bream, above right, suggest round clusters of blossoms. At right, rice is mixed with and shaped like cherry blossoms.

A bowl of clear broth or *sumashi*, inset at upper right, contains seaweed, chrysanthemum leaves, and a clamshell stuffed with clams and white fish meat that have been ground and steamed. The *sumashi* shown in the larger photo contains the head of a sea bream and thin slices of *udo* stalk. Sprigs of *sanshō* provide fragrance.

Summer

Looking Cool

To make a meal seem cooler, cooks can take advantage of the fresh look of plain wooden tubs, wetted green bamboo trays, translucent porcelain, glassware, or blocks of ice. Serving up cold, lightly flavored fare on dishes that exude coolness is the essence of summer hospitality.

The basketlike bowl has a silver frame, but the bowl itself is glass. Inside are *ayu* or sweetfish, *kawaebi* (oriental river prawn), and slices of pickled *shirouri* melon. Below, a plain wooden bucket contains *hiyashi sōmen* (thin wheat noodles on ice) for two. The form suggests a stream flowing over rocks. A bowl of soy-based dipping sauce has been provided for each diner, into which grated ginger root and chopped chives from the condiment dish will be mixed.

Rich Foods on Hot Days

In the *Man'yōshū*, an 8th-century anthology of Japanese verse, the poet Ōtomo no Yakamochi advises dining on *unagi*, or eel, to avoid getting rundown when summer turns hot and humid. Fortifying meals of *unagi* and *tempura* (batter-fried fish, shellfish, or vegetables) are still eaten in this season.

Charcoal-broiled eel flavored with *teriyaki* sauce sits atop rice in the bowl at the top of the page; the dish is called *unadon*. At right is *tempura*: batter-fried shrimp, abalone, and vegetables usually dipped in a sauce seasoned with grated radish.

A Floating Feast

To refined, worldly men in the Edo period (1600–1868), summer fun meant savoring the cool of the evening aboard a boat while eating, singing, and dancing. One wealthy merchant, Kinokuniya Bunzaemon, is said to have tossed gold-lacquered *sake* cups over the waves like so many flower petals. Here, a meal set out on a strip of bamboo husk shaped like a boat and painted gold—with cups alongside—recalls the splendors enjoyed by those who "lived it up on boats" (*funaasobi*) in the past.

The cargo of this "boat" includes, from the rear of the boat, conger eel (*anago*) wrapped in rolls of fried egg; soybean pods; skewered slices of cucumber, boiled shrimp, and squid; sardinelike *ayu*; and *tōfu* rolls flanked by octopus and molded rice. Complementing these delicacies is a bowl of broth with loach (*dojō*) set in a cake of unsweetened custard.

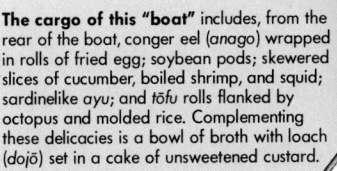

Autumn

Hors d'oeuvres for moon viewing. The yolk of a quail's egg in soy-flavored aspic on the tray suggests the full moon. At left, chrysanthemums add color and flavor to a portion of sea bream. The tray's design features autumn plants like eulalia grass.

A Meal for Moon Viewing

Greeted with offerings of seasonal delicacies and symbols, the harvest moon in September casts a special glow on what was traditionally an evening spent composing poetry in praise of its beauty. Moon viewing has been treated as a major seasonal rite since at least the Nara period (710–794). At feasts marking this ritual, the decorative motifs of the serving dishes and the ways in which foods are presented emphasize lunar and harvest themes.

Blessings of the Mountains

Among the "blessings of the mountains" (*yama no sachi*), as foods produced inland are called, the autumn favorite is the *matsutake* mushroom. To make the most of this scarce item's short-lived peak of freshness, cooks have developed numerous mushroom dishes, including mushroom rice and *dobin mushi* (mushroom broth steamed in a teapot, or *dobin*). Charcoal-broiling is another way to preserve or enhance the aroma for which the *matsutake* is prized. The tastiest ones come from Kyōto and Gifu prefectures.

An assortment of mushrooms, extreme left photo, will be heated on a charcoal brazier until the aroma fully emerges. The juice of *sudachi* citruses is squeezed over the mushrooms just before serving. The mushroom rice set out on a bamboo husk, upper right photo, was created by cooking rice and *matsutake* mushrooms in a *kombu* (kelp) stock. To make *dobin mushi*, lower right photo, shoots of *mizuna* (a potherb mustard) and *matsutake* were steamed in a flavorful broth seasoned with *yuzu* (citrons).

Dressing Fall Dishes in Fall Colors

The dishes and containers in which Japanese cuisine is served are regarded as an integral part of the meal itself, its "garment." Just as a *kimono* enhances the beauty of the person who wears it, seasonally inspired serving vessels make food more attractive and may even seem to augment the flavor. Serving autumn fare in scooped-out persimmon skins or dishes shaped like fall flowers, for example, reinforces the seasonal motif and makes the meal more aesthetically pleasing.

Fall specialties on dishes shaped like the Chinese bellflower, which blooms in autumn. At left, slices of dried persimmon and grated radish mixed in citrus juice are served in a persimmon skin. Above are brine-cooked chestnuts.

Steaming Hot Dishes for Cold Nights

On chilly winter evenings, food that warms the body to the core is best. *Nabemono* are one-pot dishes cooked at the table in their own simmering broth. In addition to imparting the requisite heat, *nabemono* can also generate a warm sense of companionship among people dining together out of the communal pot. *Sukiyaki*, a popular *nabemono* dish, is made by cooking meat, *tōfu*, vegetables, and broth in a large skillet or pot. Also popular in winter are *mushimono*, or steamed foods. *Chawan mushi*, a custard made by steaming egg and broth in a *chawan*, or teacup, is typical.

Cuts of globefish, or *fugu*, simmered with *tōfu* and vegetables in a *dashi* broth in an earthenware pot (right), are then dipped in *ponzu*, a citrus-and-soy sauce, and eaten hot; this *nabemono* dish is called *fuguchiri*.

Winter

To make kabura mushi (right), conger eel (*anago*), gingko nuts, grated turnips, and egg whites are mixed together, steamed, and then topped with a thick broth and a pinch of *wasabi* horseradish. Shown below the *kabura mushi* are steamed rolls of *yuba*, a *tōfu* by-product, filled with *matsubagani* ("pine needle" crab) and the parsleylike herb *mitsuba*. They are served piping hot with a soy-based sauce.

A hagoita paddle used to play *hanetsuki*, a New Year's game for girls that resembles badminton, furnishes the setting for these delicacies to be consumed with New Year's *sake*. Their forms suggest seasonal symbols. The leaf cluster at left, for example, depicts the shuttle used with the paddle. Also included are seasonal specialties such as *kazunoko* (herring roe) and black beans. Below, the traditional New Year's soup, *zōni*, features a round *mochi* (rice cake) set atop strips of *daikon* radish and carrot supported by a taro root cut in the shape of a tortoiseshell.

Courting Good Fortune at New Year's

Cooks preparing New Year's banquets try to incorporate as many symbols of good fortune into the meal and its settings as they can. Pine and bamboo, which stay green through the winter, are matched with plum, the first tree to flower in spring; cranes and turtles together symbolize longevity. Pairing red and white is also thought to be auspicious. Diners consuming dishes that feature these symbols from Chinese and Japanese mythology believe they are improving their prospects in the coming year. New Year's fare, called *osechi ryōri*, is prepared and arranged with this purpose in mind.

cormorant fishing
On the river Nagaragawa in Gifu Prefecture, fishermen set out at night with lighted torches and cormorants. The birds are trained to catch fish attracted by the torchlight.

► Continued from page 239

1971 of the Universal Copyright Convention; the Convention of the Protection of Producers of Phonograms against Unauthorized Duplication of Their Phonograms; and the International Convention for the Protection of Performers, Producers of Phonograms, and Broadcasting Organizations.

cormorant fishing　　鵜飼い

(*ukai*). Traditional method of catching small river fish by manipulating a trained cormorant. The lower part of each cormorant's neck is collared to prevent the bird from swallowing its catch. The practice has a long history and is described in records attributed to the 7th and 8th centuries.

Particularly renowned is the annual cormorant fishing on the river Nagaragawa, Gifu Prefecture, which has taken place for more than a millennium. From May to October small wooden boats work the river while drifting downstream, each with as many as a dozen cormorants on hand ropes about 3.3 meters (10 ft) long. When the bird surfaces with a fish, the fisherman hauls in the rope and, after having the bird disgorge its catch, lets out the line so it can dive again into the water in quest of another prey. This method of catching fish is far less efficient than angling or netting, but cormorant fishing prospers as a tourist industry, attracting sightseers.

corporate culture　　企業文化

(*kigyō bunka*). The unique style and policies of a company. Despite their individual differences, Japanese corporate cultures tend to share certain basic understandings and managerial ideologies that differ from those of European and American corporations, including conceptions of such crucial matters as profits, dividends, contractual obligations, and company personnel practices. These features reflect the values and characteristics of Japan's social and economic systems.

Background—Many businessmen of the Meiji period (1868–1912) gained skills and confidence through study visits abroad, and many of the early factories were initially organized with the aid of foreign technicians (see FOREIGN EMPLOYEES OF THE MEIJI PERIOD). But in almost all instances foreign influence became but a part of larger and more complex developments, in which the legacies of premodern Japan and particular processes and markets played significant roles. Two sources of indigenous organizational influence were the official HAN (domain) and Tokugawa shogunate bureaucracies (see BAKUHAN SYSTEM) and the successful merchant houses (*shōka*). The supreme ideal of serving political authority and thus society was espoused by merchants as well as bureaucrats. Merchant houses developed from a family business core and grew typically by the addition first of relatives and then of young apprentices.

Confucian thought—with its conception of the social order as one of many parts working together for the common good, its acceptance of hierarchy, and its emphasis on social identity—was easily adapted as an ideology for modern organizations. The close-knit agricultural hamlet (*buraku*) and the work-oriented forms of the patron-client (OYABUN-KOBUN) relationship are two elemental social institutions influencing Japanese corporate consciousness.

Typical Corporate Ideology—The contemporary Japanese company generally possesses an official company ideology expressed in the company song, in essays by company elders, in catechismlike lists of primary goals and values, and in annual celebrations and public events. Each company's leader seeks to create a distinct ideology and company spirit; yet in fact company ideologies vary little. They portray the company as a big family, or in terms that underline common interest, comradeship, and long-term relationships. Harmony, cooperation, and hard work will bring prosperity and growth despite what is portrayed as a fiercely competitive and changing environment. Thanks to permanent employment, those who build success are also the ones to benefit, at least within the span of their careers. They are also building a better future for younger generations of company members, just as they are the beneficiaries of the accomplishments of previous generations. The company is clearly the highest priority, and the morality of membership is judged in terms of loyal service to the company.

It is also common for company ideologies to contain lofty pronouncements stressing that business success must be honestly won with the best interests of society in mind. The company's work is seen as contributing to the glory and prosperity of Japan. Company ideologies of this type encourage a Confucian rather than a utilitarian sense of productive organization in Japan. The money, the people, the company's history, and the results of business are all seen as merged into one organic social entity.

Socialization and Reinforcement— Japanese have little trouble accepting that companies will try to mold their members to fit a particular ethos and style. The worker's character, attitudes, and values are properly subjects of company concern. Therefore, new employees usually undergo intensive CORPORATE EDUCATION AND TRAINING PROGRAMS.

Training, like the many activities publicizing the ideology of the company, represents a conscious effort on the part of management to reinforce corporate culture. Most employees display a general acceptance of such a corporate culture, as evidenced by their participation in informal company-sponsored activities. Relations within small work groups are expected to be personal, warm, and actively developed outside working hours. Relations between superiors and subordinates also echo basic values found in official ideology. The ideal boss is one who will aid subordinates in personal problems, give advice, and enter into a close association. In many respects the ideal model here is the good father or elder brother.

A confirmation of the general relevance of corporate culture is the predictability of employee dissatisfaction should such an ideology not be projected and reinforced by trained behavior. A prime example is the simple matter of morning greetings among workers. Typically company policy calls for a brief ceremony to begin the day in each office or workshop and, however routine and seemingly mundane it may become, its absence can create difficulties.

One of the most characteristic qualities of Japanese corporate culture, in fact, is the degree to which it is managed. Japanese of all ages and stations in life tend to defer to the group, particularly its leaders. Due to the general absence of strong personal religious beliefs and concomitant ideological commitment, the governance of daily social conduct has typically become a matter of rather particularistic group and institutional norms. Japanese companies fulfill this role through the sponsorship of their own lively subculture. See also PATERNALISM; EMPLOYMENT SYSTEM, MODERN; MANAGEMENT.

corporate decision making
意思決定

(*ishi kettei*). The RINGI SYSTEM, a process of decision making through the use of circular letters, is known as a decision-making system unique to Japanese enterprises. More formal decisions, however, often are made in a meeting of directors, managing directors, or representative directors in which the chairman or chief executive officer (CEO) takes the lead, as is the case in other countries. Top management decides fundamental managerial policy and the means of coping with important issues; proposals for and research on actual measures to be followed are assigned to each responsible division. Middle management takes a leading part in planning a measure, and after informal negotiations with other related departments the plan is formally presented in the form of a *ringisho*, a letter bearing the proposal that is circulated among the various departments of the organization. Since information is reported to the top level, the upper management, including the CEO, is well acquainted with the plan when it is finally submitted at a board of directors' meeting. Consequently the support of the plan in such a meeting is, in principle, unanimous.

As a company increases in size and the business diversifies, decision-making authority is passed down to each responsible division. Some examples of the resulting structures are the headquarters system (Sumitomo Bank, Ltd), divisional organization (Matsushita Electric Co, Ltd), and the divided-company system (Saison group). There are a number of cases in which divided companies are allowed to offer their shares to the public. Even in these cases, however, at the very least fundamental plans for the corporate group and decisions on important matters are made at meetings of the parent company's top-level management. In addition the CEO of the parent company controls the whole group by retaining control over important personnel appointments and budget allocations to each division or subsidiary. In Japan it is the company's main bank, its principal customer, and its employees' union, rather than its stockholders, that exercise outside influence on the decision-making process.　　▶▶*248–249*

corporate education and training programs　　企業内教育訓練

(*kigyōnai kyōiku kunren*). Education and training programs provided by companies for their employees. Corporate education and training programs in modern Japan began with the Meiji period (1868–1912) apprentice system. From the Taishō period (1912–26) up to World War II, major companies carried out extensive training programs for technical and craft skills. However, it was not until the middle of the Shōwa period (1926–89), after the war, that the education and training programs were expanded to include all employees and used to support the growing lifetime employment system.

The era of postwar education and training development can be divided into three periods. In the first period, from 1945 to 1955, American-style management training was extensively carried out during the OCCUPATION under the direction of American civilian personnel as one measure for promoting the recovery of Japanese industry. The following fixed-format training programs were common: CCS (civil communication section) lectures for upper management, MTP (management training programs) for middle management, and TWI (training within industry) programs in the factory for first-line supervisors. These programs were taught by trainers who were qualified in standardized content and instruction methods. Also in this period the concept of quality control was introduced to Japan by the American W. Edwards Deming (b 1900) in 1950. Later, Japanese companies further developed the concept in the form of what became known as QC CIRCLES (quality control circles) in which groups of employees were encouraged to work together to devise new ways of improving the quality of their work.

The second period, from 1955 to about 1970, was one in which Japanese companies adapted the ideas introduced during the Occupation to the social and cultural realities of Japanese business life. People gradually became dissatisfied with fixed-format programs after they had been in operation for some time, because they were based too much on theory and principles. A more practical training program using the case method began to be introduced. At the same time, various companies, especially the major ones, began to create their own education and training programs. Organized and planned programs were established for each function and level, and overall education and training promotion systems were created. Lively experimentation took place in an effort to go beyond standard training with regard to both content and method. Research into the company's own management problems and study of changes in the management environment were added to the curriculum. Such attitude-enhancing training methods as role playing, sensitivity training, business games, and group discussion were implemented.

Beginning in the late 1960s, management by objectives was used by many companies to cultivate the abilities of staff members. To set and achieve objectives effectively, managers must be able to identify and solve problems and to motivate their subordinates; extensive training in these areas was therefore carried out. To parallel this, organizational development training was used to promote the ability to achieve objectives by changing the organizational climate itself. Because the liberalization of trade and foreign exchange further stimulated the need to increase company competitiveness, management techniques were introduced, and education and training provided, in such areas as creativity development, value and system engineering, and project management.

The third period began during the time of low economic growth in the mid-1970s and includes the later period of rapid development of internationalization and information systems. Education and training programs designed to increase management effectiveness have been developed, emphasizing innovation in production control, development of office automation, and increased efficiency in research and development, engineering, and sales departments. From the beginning of this period, the importance of the activities of small groups, exemplified by QC circles, has expanded within the overall organization. Taking place inside these groups, in addition to education and training, is mutual and reciprocal learning that is closely integrated with the work itself. Also, a wide range of developments have occurred in education and training programs in an effort to meet company needs in areas such as manager training for business diversification and strategic planning and training for job changes. A new issue currently being addressed is the need for diverse education and training plans to support the career development of each employee.

corporate finance   企業金融

(*kigyō kin'yū*). During most of the post–World War II period, Japan's major corporations depended principally on bank borrowing to finance their growth. In recent years, however, as industries have matured and many Japanese companies have emerged as major international enterprises, profitability has risen, and companies have turned to a broader range of financing options, including the issue of equity and equity-linked bonds.

Until the 1980s, the high dependency on bank borrowings of Japanese corporations was reflected in typical debt-to-equity ratios of 4 to 1, which compared at that time with ratios of 1 to 1 in the United States and 2 to 1 in Europe. Consequently, Japanese firms were less dependent on the issue of stocks and bonds to provide funds. As a result, the ratio of shareholders' equity to total assets was the lowest among the major industrialized nations—about 16 to 18 percent in the mid-1970s, compared with about 30 percent for European corporations and 40 to 50 percent for US corporations.

However, the creditworthiness of Japanese companies may be considerably understated by the application of financial criteria typically used in the United States and Europe. Analysts in Japan have thus taken into account other considerations. For example, because Japan's postwar financial system was structured to emphasize the channeling of savings through the BANKING SYSTEM to finance industrial development, a close relationship with a main bank was an important criterion in evaluating corporate financial strength. In addition, tax provisions permitted companies to set aside tax-exempt reserves. Adjusting for these reserves generally improved the financial ratios of Japanese companies. Finally, since corporations were not required to restate the value of securities and real estate at market prices, many corporations' assets were substantially undervalued. With these adjustments taken into account, the creditworthiness of Japanese companies is usually substantially higher.

During the 1980s, financial ratios of Japanese companies rose even more, due to a combination of higher profitability following the adjustment to the upward revaluation of the yen in the mid-1980s and increased issues of equity, convertible bonds, and bonds with warrants both in Japan and in overseas CAPITAL MARKETS. For example, the ratio of shareholders' equity to total assets for principal enterprises surveyed by the Bank of Japan had risen to more than 25 percent by 1988. For manufacturing alone, this ratio has exceeded 33 percent. Also, the ratio of cash and deposits to borrowings has risen significantly, and some companies have shifted their attention to more active management of their assets to improve their profitability.

corporate history   企業の歴史

(*kigyō no rekishi*). An analysis of the development of business. The present article deals with the modernization of Japanese business from the Meiji period (1868–1912) to the eve of World War II. For aspects of postwar development, see CORPORATE CULTURE; EMPLOYMENT SYSTEM, MODERN; MANAGEMENT; SMALL AND MEDIUM ENTERPRISES.

The Legacy of the Edo-Period Merchants—It was principally due to the activities of the merchants of the Edo period (1600–1868) that the use of money spread throughout Japan and resulted in an increasingly unified market. Ōsaka became the commercial and financial center of the country. The city merchants, operating under a monopolistic guild system, developed highly advanced trading and financial techniques. Central to the organization and conduct of commerce was the concept of the household (IE), composed of the owner-family and all those employed by it, who, in exchange for absolute loyalty, were guaranteed permanent employment. Within the household each member had his place in a strictly ordered hierarchical system.

The Leaders of the Meiji Government as Modernizers—The leaders of the MEIJI RESTORATION of 1868 undertook sweeping military and economic development. They superimposed selected Western-style institutions on traditional Japanese society. Class privileges and class restrictions were abolished, and former *samurai* were helped toward gainful employment (see SHIZOKU); merchant guilds were prohibited; freedoms of enterprise and migration were proclaimed. In 1871 a unified currency, based on the YEN, was established. The land tax became payable in cash to the central government (see LAND TAX REFORM OF 1873–1881). The Ministry of Public Works (Kōbushō), established in 1870, planned the importation of technology and the promotion of industry; within a few years it employed more than 500 foreign experts as technicians and instructors. See FOREIGN EMPLOYEES OF THE MEIJI PERIOD.

After 1884, most government enterprises were sold to private entrepreneurs (see KAN'EI JIGYŌ HARAISAGE). The best-known and most innovative of the older merchant houses were MITSUI and SUMITOMO. Among the successful upstarts were the founders of ZAIBATSU, such as YASUDA ZENJIRŌ, ASANO SŌICHIRŌ, and ŌKURA KIHACHIRŌ. Among former samurai–administrators were IWASAKI YATARŌ, the founder of MITSUBISHI; SHIBUSAWA EIICHI; and GODAI TOMOATSU. Western-style businesses, notably factories and banks, were hailed as part of the new era of "Civilization and Enlightenment" (see MEIJI ENLIGHTENMENT). The government, however, saw modern business primarily in terms of strengthening the state

Continued on page 250➤

Negotiating with the Japanese

In a business culture where personal ties are more binding than contracts, foreigners often find themselves at a loss.

Compared to previous decades, the 1990s have seen an enormous increase in corporate negotiations involving Japanese and non-Japanese. This represents more than just a quantitative leap: the business locales have become more diverse and the types of interactions more varied. Japanese personnel are working abroad in unprecedented numbers, especially as expatriate managers negotiating with local businesses. A greater number of Japanese are also employed by foreign companies, both in Japan and overseas, and are negotiating on their behalf. Although many of these dealings are one-time negotiations, leading to agreements on things like joint ventures, scientific cooperation, or procurement, there has also been a significant increase in ongoing service relationships between foreign supplier companies and their Japanese customers. Such account-service relationships are distinctive because the non-Japanese supplier/seller has to negotiate with his customers, not once, but repeatedly over time.

Contrasting Business Cultures

The Japanese business culture is not conducive to negotiation per se because negotiation connotes confrontation—a disagreeable notion to the Japanese. Their instinct is for agreements worked out behind the scenes, with an emphasis on harmony and long-term interest. Even in everyday life in Japan, there is little experience of bargaining to buy household goods or of using arguments in a debating fashion to win points. Whereas foreign, especially American, negotiators may develop strategic maneuvers as a matter of course in their prenegotiation planning, this is unusual for the Japanese. They prefer to involve the people on the other side, listen to their views, and, when no strongly dissenting views remain, arrive at a decision. Sometimes the decision just seems to "happen."

Here is one common illustration of the kind of confusion and misunderstanding that can result from contrasting business cultures. Suppose you are visiting a Japanese company to make a presentation. You deliver your presentation with skill and confidence, making eloquent arguments that underscore the obvious benefits of what you are proposing. The information you have put forth and the assertions you have made about quality control, delivery, etc, are then questioned by a number of people. Many of the same questions are asked over and over again, and there is a skeptical edge to some of them. Thinking that you effectively answered every question put to you by your Japanese audience, you come away feeling that the order is close to being in the bag. But as the weeks pass, the Japanese side gives no signal about its real intentions, however much you inquire. If there is feedback from them, it is at best ambiguous. As time goes by, you pass through stages of declining confidence, disbelief, anger, resentment, and, if the order still hasn't arrived, finally resignation.

Let us now return to the meeting situation and look at it from a different point of view. Although you thought your presentation was professional and convincing, some of your Japanese counterparts may not have perceived it the same way.

Indeed, to the Japanese it is not skill in argumentation or the ability to overcome objections with verbal flair that makes for a good negotiator. The common Western ideal of a persuasive communicator making reasoned, enthusiastic appeals is not attractive to most Japanese. Instead, the Japanese try to influence others and achieve their goals by subtle, indirect suggestion.

As is now well known, most Japanese companies prefer to make decisions by consensus. In a process often described as "bottom up," a proposal for a new business transaction typically begins at the middle-management level and then must obtain the approval of all relevant sections and departments within the company before making its way to top management for final approval. Getting the consensus of so many people is a time-consuming process. If different departments, factions, or interests persist in raising objections along the way, there will be no decision until those objections are resolved.

So when all the dealings with you are finished, the individual members of the Japanese team most likely will have no idea whether or not they as a group are going to decide in favor of your project. No matter how financially attractive your specific Japanese audience may have found your proposal, they face the formidable task of bringing around others in the company, whom you may never have met, to agree to the deal.

Building Relationships

If rational appeals alone do not work, what can? Without a doubt, building a strong personal, trusting relationship with your Japanese client is the most important and effective way to succeed. Many salespeople, for example, manage to promote their wares in Japan without making a sales pitch. There is a saying among pharmaceutical salespeople: "Many doctors will buy my products as long as I never mention them." In place of the sales pitch, these sales representatives offer personal attention and service. Instead of calls that focus on hard data about new drugs, many spend time playing golf with their client, entertaining him, and even taking his wife out shopping.

Once personal trust is established, cooperation increases, and more can be accomplished. If a difference arises between a Japanese supplier and his longtime Japanese client, their negotiation is likely to be friendly, cooperative, and quick to be resolved, since they know each other and both want the relationship to continue. On the other hand, if a Japanese commodity buyer is visiting a foreign country to make a one-time purchase from people he has never dealt with before and may never deal with again, he may opt for a more cautious, distant approach to bargaining that is preeminently tactical.

Using a Middleman

The emphasis on trust and personal relationships in business explains why attempts to contact the Japanese without prior introduction or appointment do not work. In fact, it is always wiser in Japan to make no approach at all until you find a reputable middleman who can speak on your behalf and point out your strengths and interests. This middleman may be an organization such as a bank or trading company, a buyer from or supplier to the target company, or the like. The middleman can also be used during negotiations to provide hard-to-acquire information about the other side or to help resolve problems or conflicts. If persistent problems arise with midlevel managers on the Japanese team, a Western decision-maker may be impatient to bypass them and talk to the top man, who usually does not take part in negotiations until a decision is imminent. The appropriate way to accomplish this is, again, through a middleman rather than direct contact. In this manner, the middleman plays a vital role in smoothing out difficulties and maintaining harmony.

The Role of Socializing

The emphasis the Japanese place on cultivating close ties is often evident from a Westerner's first encounter with his or her Japanese counterparts. The Japanese often open initial meetings with lengthy speeches on the company's history and achievements, expressions of goodwill, and hopes for the future. This is followed by cordial discussion of common interests and international ties, as well as positive comments on hospitality previously received. Through this sort of conversation, the Japanese show how much it means to them to establish a good rapport that will enable both sides to work together harmoniously.

The desire to forge a strong, friendly connection with business partners is shown in the importance the Japanese place on entertaining or socializing with clients. Indeed, as the experience of the pharmaceutical salespeople indicates, regular socializing with a Japanese client can be more effective than any sales pitch. Yet, for all its alleged importance, to many Westerners what happens during an entertainment session with Japanese businessmen can seem trivial if not bizarre.

The Japanese like to throw off ceremony when entertaining a client. A foreigner might be taken, for example, to a *karaoke* club, in which patrons go up on stage and sing popular songs. Talent is not a prerequisite for performance. In fact, it is considered a bit rude to decline the microphone, no matter how flat your voice. After singing and drinking together, the Japanese and the foreigner have begun to see each other in human terms.

This type of behavior demonstrates the desire of the Japanese to forge strong emotional ties with the people they do business with. Revealing one's true personality to another is rare in the intensely formal business society of Japan and therefore especially valued.

These encounters can also be advantageous in other ways. The Japanese show a fine delicacy in raising issues in informal settings that might otherwise prove embarrassing. Requests for price reductions, discussion of proposed initiatives, and notification of events (personnel changes, new business activities) are often conveyed in informal get-togethers, where some Japanese feel more comfortable broaching sensitive issues.

If you do have such informal discussions, be sure to report them in detail to your fellow team members, since even seemingly casual questions may reveal what the Japanese consider important. This also means that you must be careful about what you reveal in these chats. The Japanese are information-hungry and ask many questions, even in informal junior-level meetings. Some questions may be part of the process of building trust and dependency, while others may be aimed at gathering information about your position.

In the course of a negotiation I was involved with many years ago, a junior member on our side inadvertently disclosed some confidential information to two of our Japanese counterparts over dinner, with the result that they were able to gain a clear picture of our position. Since that time, I have always emphasized the need for discretion in these informal discussions, which, if conducted carelessly, can end up hurting your bargaining position.

Attitude toward Contracts

One of the least understood and most exasperating aspects of Japanese business culture is the attitude toward contracts. The relative indifference of the Japanese on this score stems from a widespread belief that if two parties trust each other, money and other details need not be set out in writing. Accordingly, in many domestic Japanese business relationships, written agreements are not used. Million-dollar transactions have been conducted based on no more than oral agreements. If a

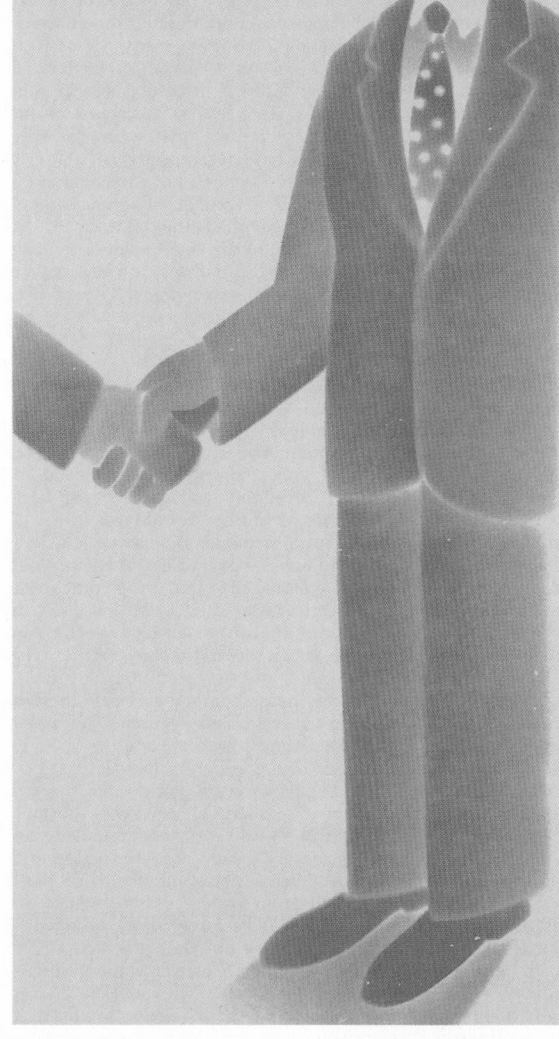

snowstorm keeps moviegoers away from theaters, for instance, theater owners may ask film companies for a cancellation of the movie lease—and get it, with cash gifts to the affected theaters, too. And one of Japan's foremost oil refineries does not demand written contracts, simply because its customers dislike such documents.

In Japan, contracts serve more as a formal acknowledgment of the general relationship being forged than as an exhaustive list of legally binding clauses and commitments. Thus, when contracts are drafted in Japan their contents are generally vague, with few clauses and only the most important elements of the agreement included. Moreover, many Japanese assume that the rights and duties stipulated in the contract are provisional and tentative rather than absolute. Instead of trying to spell out all possible contingencies and provisions for enforcement in rigid terms, they prefer to handle problems as they arise, recognizing the doctrine of "changed circumstances" (*jijō henkō*). In practice, this means that the specific items of a contract can be open to renegotiation, even immediately after signing, if circumstances change.

Working as a consultant in Japan, I myself have encountered this plea based on "changed circumstances." I once entered into an agreement with a Japanese consultant on a project for a large foreign company. We agreed to share profits on a 50-50 basis after expenses had been paid. As part of his "expenses," however, my Japanese colleague arbitrarily deducted 20 percent of the total fee as his "overhead and tax provision." After I persistently questioned his rationale for this, he finally revealed what was probably his real thinking from the start.

"You know, March san," he said, "business has been very slow for me this year. I have two offices to keep up. I doubt if I can survive."

Faced with what would only escalate into deeper melodrama, I decided to help him out by reducing my share of the profits by 10 percent. No doubt, by Western standards, I acted foolishly or overgenerously, for I had right and the law squarely on my side. On the practical side, however, even if I had decided to sue, it would have taken years to get to court, and the outcome would have been uncertain. More importantly, if I had tried to shame my associate or exert pressure on him in some way in front of business society (that is, the circle of our common professional acquaintances), in the end I, not he, would have suffered, since most Japanese would be shocked at any attempt to use force instead of a mutually conciliatory approach.

As my Japanese friends always say, "Don't try to use power plays; negotiate amicably with the client." This advice has served me well in facing many business problems in Japan. Following the ways of Japanese businessmen, I have learned to be generous when others are in trouble, or claim they are, and to take modest losses to maintain harmony.

It may be comforting for Western businesspeople to know that a small but growing number of Japanese, especially in large trading companies and multinationals, are rejecting these traditional attitudes and adopting a more legalistic approach to business dealings. Yet the fact remains that many Japanese still enter into contracts with non-Japanese assuming they will be able to alter specific clauses if circumstances change. Except perhaps for complex contracts such as financial arrangements or construction projects, Westerners would do well to expect continuous renegotiation and adjustment of contracts with the Japanese.

In summary, ongoing personal relationships, not written contracts, serve as the mainstay of business deals in Japan. Effective management of the human element is thus essential in establishing and maintaining a successful business relationship.

Robert M. March

rather than in terms of satisfying consumer demands.

The Growth of Modern Business (1868–1937)—The overall growth of modern business passed through four major stages in Japan. There was a pioneering period from 1868 to 1884, when sound financial conditions were restored after the government initiated deflationary policies in 1881 (see MATSUKATA FISCAL POLICY). Many firms collapsed during the period of deflation. They had started without solid foundations, because of government policies encouraging business and an expanding economy. The second period, from 1884 to 1919, was one of accelerated growth that was stimulated by Japan's policy of imperial expansion, notably after the SINO-JAPANESE WAR OF 1894–1895 and the RUSSO-JAPANESE WAR of 1904–05. The latter gave a particular impetus to the ship-building industry and to heavy industry in general. Newly acquired colonies provided additional markets. Industrial paid-up capital tripled during World War I, when the Asian market was left totally open to Japanese trade. Worldwide economic dislocation following World War I led to the prolonged depression that was the major feature of the third period, which ended in 1931. There were waves of bankruptcies, mass unemployment, and a growing concentration of capital in the hands of the *zaibatsu*. After 1931, the fourth period saw a reflation under the influence of war preparations. The yen was devalued against the United States dollar. Exports were strongly promoted, and the economy reflated toward full employment.

Modern banks were, after many false starts, successfully launched in 1876 in the form of NATIONAL BANKS. The BANK OF JAPAN, established in 1882, acted as the central bank, and a few government-run banks granted long-term loans for the promotion of foreign trade, industry, and agriculture. The main weakness of Japan's new banking system was the large number of small banks that were closely tied to individual firms by continued extension of large loans. In periods of crisis, many such banks failed, and this in turn led to a heavy concentration of banking capital. Between 1926 and 1929 the number of banks decreased from 1,417 to 897, and, by 1935, 40 percent of all deposits were held by the "Big Five" (Dai-Ichi, Mitsui, Mitsubishi, YASUDA [now FUJI BANK, LTD], and Sumitomo).

During the 1920s and 1930s GENERAL TRADING COMPANIES, notably those of the *zaibatsu*, played the key role in expanding Japan's international trade. The ŌSAKA SPINNING MILL, built in 1882, stimulated a building boom of large mills (see TEXTILE INDUSTRY). The Mitsubishi, Kawasaki, Ishikawajima, and Hitachi shipyards grew and integrated vertically into large industrial enterprises that produced heavy machinery, railway engines and coaches, electric cables, and other heavy iron and steel products as well (see also SHIPBUILDING INDUSTRY). Shipping received some subsidy and encouragement but was left to private initiative. NIPPON YŪSEN KAISHA (controlled by Mitsubishi), Ōsaka Shōsen, and Tōyō Kisen emerged as the three major shipping companies.

By 1886 a total of 32 railway companies had come into existence, and by 1905, 67 percent of some 7,800 kilometers (4,846 mi) of railway lines were operated by private companies. Nationalization of all but 9 percent of the lines was carried out in 1906–07

(see RAILWAYS). Sumitomo, Mitsui, Mitsubishi, and FURUKAWA had operated mines since the 1870s; MINING became one of the main sources of profit for all four of these *zaibatsu*.

Forms of Business—The JOINT-STOCK COMPANY (*kabushiki kaisha*) received strong backing from the government. The Commercial Code of 1901 distinguished three types of company: LIMITED LIABILITY COMPANY (*yūgen kaisha*), LIMITED PARTNERSHIP COMPANY (*gōshi kaisha*), and UNLIMITED PARTNERSHIP COMPANY (*gōmei kaisha*). The *zaibatsu* HOLDING COMPANIES controlled the expanding network of financial and industrial companies through a system of direct and interlocking stockholdings and through the appointment of loyal top managers, who were given almost unlimited authority.

There were four main reasons for the growth of Japan's *zaibatsu*. First, they had large initial capital resources born of previous business. Second, the holding-company system itself gave them ready access to financial resources (banks), raw materials (mines), and direct lines of foreign trade. Third, they were led by decisive and able individuals who were outstanding entrepreneurs and who actively and systematically sought out and secured new managerial talent. Fourth, they were family-based organizations that applied the concept of the household (*ie*) to the new business environment. They delegated decision making but demanded the unswerving loyalty of their managers and employees.

corporate recruitment 採用

(*saiyō*). Among large Japanese corporations the general employment pattern is long-term employment for both workers and management. This has allowed firms to plan for their projected employment needs and hire on a highly systematic basis. Large companies recruit new employees (the company's future managers) almost exclusively from the finest universities—it is extremely rare for a manager to join a top company in midcareer. The graduates are hired on the assumption that they will be with the same company until they retire, are given on-the-job-training, and are promoted within the company. Most companies begin holding company information seminars for undergraduates about eight months to one year before college graduation in March; official hiring begins after graduation and employment begins in April. However, the labor shortage of recent years has compelled some companies to "decide" on students unofficially well before the students have actually graduated from college. This practice has been officially discouraged by universities and the Ministry of Labor, but many companies continue to recruit undergraduates secretly.

Small and medium-sized companies are generally more flexible in hiring executive staff and may hire people who have had prior work experience. The main reason for this is that almost all of the most promising new graduates are quickly snatched up by the large companies in March. Recently, more companies of all sizes have been filling white-collar positions at nonstandard times and through nontraditional means, such as headhunters. Also, growing numbers of workers are now leaving their jobs of their own accord and looking for better opportunities at other companies. These changes reflect the increasing mobility in the Japanese labor market.

Corporate Reorganization Law 会社更生法

(Kaisha Kōsei Hō). Law concerning the judicial proceeding for the financial rehabilitation of a stock corporation. It was promulgated in 1952 and extensively amended in 1967. The institution was derived from chapter 10 of the American Bankruptcy Act (pre-1978 amendment) and built upon the framework of the BANKRUPTCY LAW (Hasan Hō) of 1922, which had been largely derived from the German Bankruptcy Law of 1877. The practice is not available to small and privately owned companies, which must resort to composition under the Composition Law (Wagi Hō) of 1922 or adjustment under the COMMERCIAL CODE.

corporate stock 株式

(*kabushiki*). Ownership shares in a corporation that are a claim on its earnings and assets and permit the owner to exercise certain voting rights. Stocks in Japan are currently issued at or near the prevailing market value of outstanding shares or at a par value of ¥50 or ¥500 (US $0.33 or $3.30 at an exchange rate of ¥150 to US $1) for newly formed corporations. Issuance of shares in rights offerings to existing shareholders at well below market value has become much less common as issuance of new stocks along with the exercise of warrants to purchase new shares has become common for large corporations. Stockholders are entitled to dividend payments, provided certain before-tax profitability conditions are satisfied and the payments are approved by the board of directors. These dividend payments are still often calculated as a percentage of the par value. Another means of rewarding stockholders is through free distributions of shares to stockholders of record. Legal regulations governing the issuance of stock include the Securities and Exchange Law and the Commercial Code. See also STOCK EXCHANGES; CAPITAL MARKETS.

corporations 企業

(*kigyō*). Japan has more than 1.3 million legally constituted corporations. As in other developed economies, however, there is considerable concentration of economic power in a small number of corporations. Of the 1,267,642 corporations existing at the time of the 1986 census, only 297 had more than 5,000 employees. These 297 companies, which represented 0.02 percent of all Japanese corporations, accounted for nearly 14 percent of all regular employees. Another indication of the number of major corporations is that 1,627 firms are listed on the Tōkyō Stock Exchange.

Financial Characteristics—The huge capital requirements of many corporations during the period of rapid ecoonomic growth, which began in the 1950s, led to the dependence on debt financing that has characterized modern Japanese corporations. Since Japan's CAPITAL MARKETS were still undeveloped at that time, companies were forced to rely on the banks for financing. Banks were then able to exert considerable influence over management decisions, while holders of common shares exerted little control over CORPORATE DECISION MAKING. Because banks, in turn, were fully loaned and had to rely on the BANK OF JAPAN, the country's central bank, for additional funds, the government was able to exercise a major influence on important corporate decisions using direct credit expansion controls known as

Japan's Corporations by Company Type and Size

Corporation size	All types		Joint-stock companies		Limited liability companies		Other companies¹	
By number of employees	Enterprises	Employees	Enterprises	Employees	Enterprises	Employees	Enterprises	Employees
0–4 persons	629,773	2,758,287	255,241	1,171,836	354,732	1,507,601	19,800	78,850
5–9	274,505	2,583,323	146,544	1,404,045	121,739	1,122,580	6,222	56,698
10–19	175,009	3,024,417	113,035	1,987,411	58,592	979,797	3,382	57,209
20–29	64,400	1,845,802	47,589	1,375,150	15,746	440,604	1,065	30,048
30–49	52,496	2,316,794	42,637	1,897,023	9,087	386,794	772	32,977
50–99	38,570	2,982,213	34,351	2,673,750	3,800	277,746	419	30,717
100–299	24,504	4,314,877	23,598	4,171,461	823	130,120	83	13,296
300–999	6,468	3,445,989	6,428	3,429,655	31	12,135	9	4,199
1,000–1,999	1,033	1,505,727	1,032	1,504,014	—	—	1	1,713
2,000–4,999	587	1,853,032	585	1,845,383	—	—	2	7,649
Over 5,000	297	4,275,681	282	3,787,403	—	—	15	488,278
By amount of capitalization (in yen)								
Less than 1 million	176,857	1,162,308	39,823	276,966	122,854	690,900	14,180	194,442
1 to less than 2 million	244,354	2,116,702	91,499	812,816	146,135	1,047,675	6,720	256,211
2 to less than 5 million	359,560	3,668,779	174,077	2,040,810	179,841	1,566,971	5,642	60,998
5 to less than 10 million	234,512	3,553,527	146,587	2,514,166	84,907	991,264	3,018	48,097
10 to less than 30 million	176,465	5,198,695	147,123	4,670,467	27,493	483,027	1,849	45,201
30 to less than 50 million	38,074	2,420,740	35,306	2,353,506	2,507	58,191	261	9,043
50 to less than 100 million	20,575	2,226,444	19,800	2,206,883	695	16,903	80	2,658
100 million to less than 1 billion	14,428	3,874,999	14,297	3,862,174	116	2,423	15	10,402
1 to less than 5 billion	1,949	1,968,220	1,945	1,948,079	2	23	2	20,118
Over 5 billion	868	4,715,728	865	4,561,264	—	—	3	154,464
All corporations	1,267,642	30,906,142	671,322	25,247,131	564,550	4,857,377	31,770	801,634

Corporate Headquarters in Japan's Eight Largest Metropolitan Areas

Metropolitan area	Total of all company types	Percentage of all companies	Joint-stock companies		Limited liability companies		Other companies¹	
			Enterprises	Percentage*	Enterprises	Percentage*	Enterprises	Percentage*
Tōkyō/Kawasaki/Yokohama	423,651	33.4	220,086	32.8	197,437	35.0	6,128	19.3
Ōsaka/Kyōto/Kōbe	167,213	13.2	131,006	19.5	34,603	6.1	1,604	5.0
Nagoya	86,605	6.8	51,434	7.7	27,166	4.8	8,005	25.2
Kita Kyūshū/Fukuoka	38,568	3.0	19,928	3.0	17,718	3.1	922	2.9
Sapporo	25,798	2.0	16,022	2.4	9,705	1.7	71	0.2
Hiroshima	19,590	1.5	10,651	1.6	8,898	1.6	41	0.1
Sendai	17,338	1.4	8,920	1.3	7,979	1.4	439	1.4
Okayama	15,625	1.2	7,437	1.1	8,111	1.4	77	0.2
All 8 metropolitan areas	794,388	62.7	465,484	69.3	311,617	55.2	17,287	54.4

¹Includes limited and unlimited partnership companies and mutual insurance companies.
*Percentage of the national total of that type of company.

NOTE: All data is as of 1 July 1986. Public corporations are not included.
Percentages may not add up to totals due to rounding.
SOURCE: Management and Coordination Agency, *Jigyōsho tōkei chōsa hōkoku* (1986).

madoguchi shidō (literally, "window guidance").

In the 1980s, however, development of the capital markets and substantial liquidity in the total economy led to a reduction in dependence on debt financing and a corresponding reduction in the use of this type of government influence. See also ADMINISTRATIVE GUIDANCE; BANKING SYSTEM; CORPORATE FINANCE.

Enterprise Groups and Subsidiaries— Following World War II, the *zaibatsu* (financial and industrial combines) were dissolved by OCCUPATION fiat (see ZAIBATSU DISSOLUTION). Many groups later recombined, however, because of traditional ties and an urgent need for the capital that could be obtained from the banks and trust companies of the group. Although mutual shareholding reinforces the connections, there is no central ownership, and group coordination is much looser than in prewar *zaibatsu*. See KEIRETSU.

Of more importance to the operations of the corporation than its connections with other large companies is the pattern of subsidiaries and subcontracting firms that has developed. A close relationship exists between the size of a firm and the level of compensation: the smaller firm not only pays substantially lower wages, but also provides a much smaller package of benefits (see DUAL STRUCTURE). This means that there is a considerable economic advantage to using the smaller firm as a supplier, especially of those components or subassemblies that require less-skilled labor. The subsidiary or subcontractor relationship also gives the parent company flexibility in scheduling and allows cyclic downturns in demand to be displaced onto the smaller firms. Another useful function of the subsidiary is as a repository for employees, especially executives, who no longer have a role in the parent corporation.

Employment Practices—The prototypical pattern of Japanese employment has as its basis a mutual commitment by the corporation and the employee. The corporation undertakes to retain each person that it selects until retirement, despite later temptations to terminate employment. Employees undertake to remain in the employ of the corporation once they make their choice, however attractive alternative positions might appear. Large corporations recruit employees directly from school, and hiring is not for a particular skill or job. In fact, neither party knows what the particular job of a successful candidate will be, and each assumes that over time the individual will fill a range of positions. The employment commitment is for the career, and compensation thus follows a quite explicit career pattern. Noncash benefits play an important part. Compensation is based on seniority, with rank, performance, and other special conditions as additional considerations.

The effect of this pattern—and the expectation of the pattern—is to establish an unusual identity between the interests of the individual employee, at whatever level in the corporation, and the interests of the corporation itself. The employee's security and assurance of continued improvement in income depend directly on the success of the firm. Midcareer moves from one Japanese firm to another for more money or responsibility are relatively rare. Since most LABOR UNIONS are organized on a companywide basis, they tend to reinforce rather than dilute employee identification with the company (see LABOR).

It should be noted that this employment pattern applies only to regular, and not to temporary, employees. Changes in the pattern are occurring, but only slowly. Regular female employees are still sometimes expected—though not required—to leave the firm on marriage. Some companies have tried to shift the emphasis from seniority to performance when determining promotions and raises, but results have been mixed. Hiring of experienced personnel by foreign companies in Japan has opened up a limited number of opportunities for career changes. See also EMPLOYMENT SYSTEM, MODERN.

Future Issues—With the increasing integration of much of the world economy, two issues have moved to a prominent position in the concerns of the Japanese corporation. The first is the need for innovative RESEARCH AND DEVELOPMENT, a need that became evident in the late 1970s following recovery from the oil crisis. Funding of research in Japan is almost entirely by the corporation, in contrast to the economies of the West, where government plays a much larger role. As Japanese corporations have caught up to and even surpassed their Western counterparts in the area of technical expertise, there has been less and less chance to purchase or license technology from abroad. Corporate research funding has massively increased, along with a need to address organizational issues to allow for flexible use of younger researchers and for career paths more suited to research careers than the traditional ones.

The second major issue is the need to move toward a global organizational structure. Many of Japan's most important corporations need to establish worldwide positions in technology and manufacturing as well as trade. Direct investments in Asia to secure lower factory costs are now being exceeded by investments in North America and Europe to secure market positions. These extensions abroad of the Japanese corporation raise questions about the integration of non-Japanese nationals into the organization, about dealing with very different approaches to unionization, about the political consequences of the acquisition of substantial foreign assets by Japanese corporations, and about the development of worldwide product and personnel management systems—questions that the Japanese corporation is only beginning to address. No doubt the requirement to become multinational will in turn affect the nature of the Japanese corporation at home as well.

corporations, establishment of
会社の設立

(*kaisha no setsuritsu*). In Japan the various types of business corporation, such as UNLIMITED PARTNERSHIP COMPANY (*gōmei kaisha*), LIMITED PARTNERSHIP COMPANY (*gōshi kaisha*), JOINT-STOCK COMPANY (*kabushiki kaisha*), and LIMITED LIABILITY COMPANY (*yūgen kaisha*), are profit-making associations with the status of juristic persons (HŌJIN). A company is established when a group of individuals who have joined together for the common purpose of making profits has acquired the status of a juristic person as specified under provisions set forth in the CIVIL CODE and the COMMERCIAL CODE.

The procedure for establishing a company is (1) drafting of articles of association; (2) determination of the identity of the members of the association (investors or stockholders); (3) establishment of offices to engage in company activities, i.e., appointment of directors and comptrollers (*kansayaku*); (4) application for registration of the association's establishment and filing of the articles of association at the appropriate administrative office in the ward of the company's head office; and (5) recording the establishment of the association. The procedure for establishment differs according to the type of company. The greatest difference is between the establishment of a joint-stock company and that of an unlimited partnership company. In an unlimited partnership company, the articles of association are drafted jointly by all those who will become members of the company. In the case of a joint-stock company, the articles of association are drafted by "promoters" (*hokkinin*) and the shareholders are not named in the articles of association.

correspondence courses
通信教育

(*tsūshin kyōiku*). Academic and nonacademic courses for which instruction is offered through the mail, on radio, or on television. The practice was begun in Japan in 1886 by WASEDA UNIVERSITY. These courses generally fall into two categories: regular school courses, through which credits and a diploma can be earned, and community education courses (*shakai kyōiku*; literally, "social education"), which are usually vocational, cultural, or hobby courses for adults.

In recent years, due to a rise in the number of children with SCHOOL ALLERGY and people with an interest in lifelong learning, enrollment in correspondence courses has increased. In 1989 approximately 164,000 students took these courses, some 151,000 of whom were registered in correspondence courses offered by 13 private junior colleges and 13 universities, including the UNIVERSITY OF THE AIR (Hōsō Daigaku).

Community education courses include bookkeeping, stenography, amateur radio, drafting, child care, painting, and calligraphy. In 1988, 179 courses of 44 institutions were sanctioned by the Ministry of Education and there were 194,773 subscribers to these courses.

cosmetics
化粧

(*keshō*). The manufacture and use of face powder, rouge, eyebrow paint, and other cosmetics was imported to Japan as early as the 6th century from Korea and China. In early times cosmetics were used only by participants in religious ceremonies and festivals, but the practice gradually spread among the court aristocracy as a means of enhancing one's beauty, and in the Heian period (794–1185) men as well as women used cosmetics. During the Edo period (1600–1868) the vogue was usually set by KABUKI actors, courtesans, and GEISHA through UKIYO-E prints and popular literature, and by beauticians who helped set fashions. After the Meiji Restoration of 1868 gradual Westernization in clothing and makeup occurred. Blackening of the teeth (OHAGURO) gradually became obsolete. Today traditional makeup is used mainly by kabuki actors, geisha, and *maiko* (young apprentice geisha).

Oshiroi. White face powder; originally made from white soil and rice flour. In the 7th century the manufacture of *keifun* (mercury chloride) and *empaku* (white lead) was imported from China. In the 1870s the toxic quality of lead was recognized, and a lead-free facial powder began to be domestically produced. Today makeup foundation has completely replaced the traditional white powder.

Beni. Rouge. In the early 7th century safflower (*benibana*), which had come from Egypt via India, Central Asia, China, and Korea, was introduced into Japan, and an extract was used as rouge. Rouge was applied mainly to the lips; at the end of the 18th century *sasabeni*, an iridescent greenish rouge, commonly applied to the lower lip, became the vogue. In the late Meiji period (1868–1912) Western rouge, similar to the present-day lipstick, was adopted.

Mayuzumi. Eyebrow paint. Black soil and ashes were used in ancient times, followed by lampblack and soot from burned ears of Indian rice. From Heian times the practice of shaving the eyebrows developed, along with tooth blackening, to indicate that a girl had come of age. *Okimayu*, shaving the eyebrows and drawing new ones, was practiced particularly among the upper classes. The custom whereby the average woman shaved her eyebrows after marriage and delivery of a child continued through the end of the 19th century.

To maintain a beautiful complexion the woman of the past used a *nukabukuro*, a small bag of rice bran, to wash her face and body when taking a bath. The juice of gourds (*hechima*) and cucumbers was used as a face lotion. Other types of cosmetics, such as perfumes and facial packs, were also available, in much the same variety as they are today. See also HAIRSTYLES.

Cosmo Oil Co, Ltd
コスモ石油[株]

(Kosumo Sekiyu). Oil refining and sales company. Established in 1986 through a merger of Daikyō Oil and Maruzen Oil. The company has an integrated oil industry operation extending from oil procurement to sales. It has its own oil research institution for the development of high technology. Cosmo has subsidiaries in Abu Dhabi (United Arab Emirates), Al Mubarraz (Saudi Arabia), Singapore, and New York and representative offices in London and Abu Dhabi. Sales for the fiscal year ending March 1991 totaled ¥1.7 trillion (US $12.4 billion). Capitalization stood at ¥28.3 billion (US $206.3 million) in the same year. Headquarters are in Tōkyō.

Council on the National Language
国語審議会

(Kokugo Shingikai). Organ of the Ministry of Education that advises the government on matters pertaining to the improvement, teaching, and romanization of the Japanese language. It was established in 1934. Reorganized in 1949, it merged with a survey council on romanization in 1950. Since the end of World War II, it has promoted various language reforms involving the *tōyō kanji* (Chinese characters in daily use) and JŌYŌ KANJI (Chinese characters for common use), current usage of KANA (the Japanese syllabary), and romanized spelling of Japanese.

counters
助数詞

(*josūshi*). Also called numeral classifiers, numerary adjuncts, etc. Forms that are added to numerals in the Japanese language to indicate the class of the thing that is being counted. These forms are similar to such English forms as "sheets" (of paper) or "head" (of cattle) in that they classify things into groups sharing some characteristic, but the number of classifications and classifiers in Japanese is much greater. Examples are -*nin* (persons) as in *onna sannin* (three women); -*hon* (cylindrical objects) as in *empitsu nihon* (two pencils); and -*mai* (thin, flat objects) as in *kami ichimai* (one sheet of paper). These counters are usually used—as in the examples given—with numerals of Chinese origin; however, in certain cases native Japanese numerals can be substituted.

Coup d'Etat of 30 September 1863
文久三年八月十八日の政変

(Bunkyū Sannen Hachigatsu Jūhachinichi no Seihen). Incident of 30 September 1863 in which anti-Western, antishogunate activists (mostly low-ranking *samurai*) from the Chōshū domain (now Yamaguchi Prefecture) were driven from Kyōto by the more moderate forces of the Satsuma (now Kagoshima Prefecture) and the Aizu (now part of Fukushima Prefecture) domains. In 1862 Chōshū persuaded the emperor KŌMEI to demand the expulsion of all foreigners on 25 June 1863. Only Chōshū carried out the order, firing on Western ships near its shores. Such an extreme antiforeign stance alarmed moderate samurai and led to the coup on 30 September. Court nobles identified with the extremists fled to Chōshū (see SHICHIKYŌ OCHI). The court then came under the influence of Satsuma, which sought reconciliation with the shogunate (see MOVEMENT FOR UNION OF COURT AND SHOGUNATE).

court-appointed attorneys
国選弁護人

(*kokusen bengonin*). Legal counsel assigned by the court under article 37, paragraph 3, of the CONSTITUTION OF JAPAN. The Code of CRIMINAL PROCEDURE requires the court, upon demand, to appoint legal counsel for a defendant who, because of poverty or other cause, cannot obtain legal counsel himself. The accused cannot dismiss a court-appointed attorney.

court nobles → kuge

court ranks 位階

(*ikai*). Also called *kurai* or *i* (literally, "sitting place"). Refers to a system of ranks granted to aristocratic male and female subjects, establishing their positions among the nobility and their eligibility for appointment to government office. It also refers to a system of ranks granted to members of the imperial family determining their positions among the royalty.

Origins—A system of court rank called the KAN'I JŪNIKAI (12 grades of cap rank) was instituted in 604 to take precedence over the UJI-KABANE SYSTEM, which had defined the status at court of chiefs of corporate groups of households (UJI) through reference to the hereditary titles (KABANE) of their lineages. Enacted by Prince Shōtoku (574–622), in principle the new system established bureaucratic expedience and imperial appointment as conditions for the granting of rank. The *kan'i jūnikai* was a series of six basic ranks, each of which was divided into greater (*dai*) and lesser degrees (*shō*), forming 12 grades that were signified by caps of darker and lighter shades of six colors ranging from purple (the highest) to black. In 647, adjunct to the TAIKA REFORM (645), a new set of 13 grades of rank was established. In 649 an additional 6 grades were added. The system was further expanded to 26 grades in 664, and for the first time members of the royal family who were not children or siblings of emperors were accorded rank in a separate system. In 686 the system was thoroughly revised; although it remained a series of six ranks, each was divided into eight degrees for a total of 48 grades.

Taihō Code System—In 702, as part of the TAIHŌ CODE, court ranks were again wholly revised. The system then created remained substantially unchanged until the Meiji period (1868–1912). It was patterned after that of the Chinese Tang (T'ang; 618–907) dynasty; however, unlike its model, grants of rank preceded rather than derived from awards of public office and were primarily determined by birth. The code provided for three classes of rank: one for princes and princesses, another for the remaining royalty, and a third for noble subjects. The rank system for subjects consisted of eight numbered ranks (first rank being the highest) and an additional rank that was termed "initial" (*soi*). Before assuming their positions, holders of the highest offices in the government bureaucracy (a group known as KUGYŌ) had usually received one of the highest three ranks, each of which was divided into senior and junior degrees. The fourth through the eighth ranks were each divided into junior (*ju*) and senior (*shō*), which were further subdivided into upper (*jō*) and lower (*ge*); the initial rank was divided into greater (*dai*) and lesser (*shō*), which were also subdivided into upper and lower. There was thus a total of 30 grades of subject rank. With few exceptions all of the holders of the first three ranks and many of the fourth and fifth rank holders were permitted to attend the emperor during audiences at the Tenjō no Ma (Courtiers' Hall) and were thus termed TEN-JŌBITO. The number of *tenjōbito* numbered from 30 to as many as 100. None of the holders of the sixth through the initial ranks except sixth-rank officials of the KURŌDO-DOKORO (Bureau of Archivists) were allowed audience and, consequently, were referred to as JIGE ("groundlings"). Appointments to the lowest 20 grades of subject

ranks, senior fifth-rank upper (*shōgoi no jō*) to lesser initial-rank lower (*shōsoi no ge*), were further qualified as *nai-i* (inner rank) and *ge-i* (outer rank).

Revisions—In 1869, following the Meiji Restoration, the number of grades of rank was reduced from 30 to 20 and in 1887 further cut back to 16. After 1889 royalty was no longer ranked. A cabinet decision of 3 May 1946 ruled that thenceforth only posthumous grants of rank (*ikai*) and DECORATIONS for achievement (*kunshō*) would be made. In 1963 awards to living persons were restored in the case of decorations. See also PEERAGE.

Cowra Prisoner-of-War Outbreak
カウラ捕虜暴動

(Kaura Horyo Bōdō). A major escape attempt in 1944 by Japanese prisoners of war in Australia. Over 900 prisoners of war in a camp at Cowra, a country town some 320 kilometers (200 mi) west of Sydney, attempted a mass breakout at about 2:00 AM on 5 August 1944. Many Japanese prisoners were killed; others committed suicide. Those who escaped either committed suicide or were recaptured. In all about 234 Japanese were killed and about 103 were wounded. Four Australians were killed and 3 wounded. The incident is commemorated by a Japanese war cemetery on the outskirts of Cowra.

Coxinga → Zheng Chenggong (Cheng Ch'eng-kung)

crabs 蟹

(*kani*). In Japanese, *kani* is the common name for arthropods of the order Decapoda, tribe Brachyura. Most Japanese crabs are marine, living from coastal to deep-sea areas; a few are half-terrestrial, living in river mouths and other freshwater areas. Only the *sawagani* (river crab; *Potamon dehaani*) is a true freshwater species. Over 4,500 species of crabs have been identified worldwide; among the many species in the waters around Japan are the *benkeigani* (*Sesarma intermedia*), the *kegani* (*Erimacrus isenbeckii*), and the *takaashigani* (giant spider crab; *Macrocheira kaempferi*), the world's largest arthropod.

Because crabs frequently shed their shells and regenerate limbs, in premodern Japan they were revered as beings symbolizing the life force and regeneration. Some types of crabs whose shells bear a pattern resembling a human face were thought to be inhabited by ghosts; the *heikegani* (*Dorippe japonica*)

mentioned in Lafcadio HEARN's book *Kottō* is an example of this belief.

crafts → folk crafts

cram schools 予備校

(*yobikō*). Schools whose primary purpose is preparing students to pass the highly competitive ENTRANCE EXAMINATIONS of Japanese universities. Most cram school enrollees are recent high school graduates who are seeking admission to colleges and universities and who failed in their first sitting for the entrance examination. In 1989 there were 165 *yobikō* in Japan with a combined enrollment of about 205,510.

In recent years competition among those hoping to pass college entrance examinations has been increasing, and large numbers of students commute to cram school while still in high school. There is currently a trend toward the development of cram school networks centered on the three largest *yobikō*. Since there is no effective nationwide institution in Japan charged with college and university entrance requirements and standards, the information regarding university entrance examinations provided by the major *yobikō* is indispensable not only to their enrolled students but to all prospective test takers. See also JUKU.

cranes 鶴

(*tsuru*). In Japanese, *tsuru* is the common name for large wading birds of the family Gruidae, distinguished by their long necks and legs. Seven species have been sighted in Japan. The *nabezuru* (hooded crane; *Grus monacha*) and *manazuru* (white-naped crane; *G. vipio*) breed in eastern Siberia and regularly winter by the thousands in the city of Izumi, Kagoshima Prefecture, sometimes accompanied by one or two *kurozuru* (common crane; *G. grus*), *kanadazuru* (sandhill crane; *G. canadensis*), *sodegurozuru* (Siberian white crane; *G. leucogeranus*), and *anehazuru* (demoiselle crane; *Anthropoides virgo*). About 100 *nabezuru* also come annually to Yashiro in Yamaguchi Prefecture. About 350 *tanchō* (Japanese crane; *G. japonensis*) are found in the marshlands of eastern Hokkaidō. The crane's call is a vibrant trumpet note.

Cranes, particularly the *tanchō*, have long been regarded as auspicious birds and as a popular symbol of longevity. The expres-

crabs Some 1,000 recorded species of crab live in the waters of Japan, ranging in size from the giant spider crab to the tiny *kagizume pinno*, a parasite on bivalve clams.

1 *Tarabagani* (*Paralithodes camtschaticus*).
2 *Benkeigani*.
3 *Hanasakigani* (*Paralithodes brevipes*).
4 *Heikegani*.
5 River crab.
6 *Akategani* (*Sesarma haematocheir*).
7 *Kagizume pinno* (*Pinnotheres pholadis*).
8 *Iwagani* (*Pachygrapsus crassipes*).
9 *Kegani*.
10 Giant spider crab.

cranes
1 Japanese cranes (*tanchō*) perform a mating dance at Kushiro Marsh in Hokkaidō. A protected species in Japan, this rare crane breeds only in Siberia and Hokkaidō.
2 An adult and a juvenile hooded crane (*nabezuru*) search for food in a rice field. Measuring 100 cm from head to tail, these cranes breed in Siberia but winter in Yamaguchi and Kagoshima prefectures.

sion "voice of the crane" is used to describe a decision from on high breaking a deadlock. The crane is also a popular decorative motif.

Crawford, Sir John Grenfell

クローフォード, J. G.

(1910–84). Australian economist who played an important role in the development of economic relations between Australia and Japan after World War II. After occupying several senior posts in the Australian public service, he joined the Australian National University in 1960 as professor of economics and director of its School of Pacific Studies; he became chancellor of the university in 1976. In 1957 he played a key role in the negotiation of the Agreement on Commerce between Australia and Japan while serving as secretary of the Australian Commonwealth Department of Trade. He also headed the Australia-Japan Research Centre.

cremation 火葬

(*kasō*). Although cremation is by far the most common mortuary practice in Japan today, in prehistoric times coffin or noncremation burial was the prevalent form of interment for all classes of society (see JAR BURIALS; DOLMEN BURIALS; HŌKEI SHŪKŌBO). The first record of cremation comes from documents describing the funeral of the Buddhist monk Dōshō (629–700). Cremation was practiced in Buddhist funeral rites

crests
1 A cloak said to have been worn by Date Masamune, *daimyō* of the Sendai domain in the early Edo period. The elaborate crest of two sparrows encircled by bamboo is the symbol of the Date family.
2 The Tokugawa family crest as it appears on a roof tile at the temple Kongōshōji in Ise, Mie Prefecture, built in 1609.

based on the doctrine of the transmigration of souls (RINNE), which holds that a corpse must be disposed of quickly so that the deceased can be reborn. As Buddhism became established during the Nara period (710–794), cremation gradually spread from the Buddhist priesthood to the imperial family and nobility.

With the continued popularization of Buddhism throughout the Kamakura (1185–1333) and Muromachi (1333–1568) periods, cremation became a practice of the masses. By the Edo period (1600–1868), however, the growing influence of Confucian ideology led to a tendency to avoid cremation, and in certain areas the practice of coffin burial was reinstated. In the Meiji period (1868–1912) cremation was prohibited between 1873 and 1875 during the upsurge of anti-Buddhist sentiment that accompanied the early Meiji government's efforts to encourage Shintō (see HAIBUTSU KISHAKU), but it once again became a common practice after the government directed that fatalities from contagious disease be cremated to halt the spread of epidemics. Crematoriums were constructed in numerous towns and villages, and, as a result, ordinances in many regions and municipalities came to prohibit coffin burial.

According to a 1989 Ministry of Health and Welfare survey, 96 percent of Japanese burials involve cremation. Most modern crematoriums use gas or oil furnaces that cremate the body in about an hour. The remains are then presented to family members and funeral participants. Regional variations exist but the general practice is for several bones to be passed by chopsticks from one funeral participant to another and then placed in a mortuary urn (*kotsutsubo*). After a set period of time the urn is deposited in a grave or tomb (see also FUNERALS). In addition to religious custom, sanitary concerns and scarcity of burial space, especially in Japan's larger cities, are major factors contributing to the continued prevalence of cremation over other forms of burial.

crests 紋

(*mon*; also called *monshō*). Symbols or designs adopted as insignia by individuals, families, or other groups and applied to banners or armor for identification in battle, or to clothing or possessions for decoration; sometimes applied also to commercial goods as trademarks. The heraldic emblems of Japan are simpler and aesthetically finer than the escutcheons of European blazonry. Unlike coats of arms, they occupy an esteemed place among the graphic arts of their country, and their symbolic connotations are generally appreciated throughout the society. Many of the most popular motifs first appeared in Japan simply as patterns (*moyō, yūsoku mon'yō*) on the costumes and para-

phernalia of the court aristocracy of the Nara (710–794) and Heian (794–1185) periods. Family crests (*kamon*) were a product of the wars that ushered in the warrior class and the feudal era in the late 12th century.

From the 14th to late 16th centuries, warrior families proliferated, formed branches, suffered schisms, and rose and fell by the sword; in the process both the number and variety of family crests and the conventions governing their use multiplied. Crests became items of political and social exchange, to bestow upon inferiors, share with equals, appropriate from fallen foes, even steal from obscure genealogies. The great houses frequently accumulated and used 10 or more different crests.

The first practical illustrated text devoted to the family crests of the warriors appears to have been sponsored by the Muromachi shogunate (1338–1573) during the early 16th century and contained 255 crests in all. During the Tokugawa shogunate (1603–1867) the ruling elite became fixed and settled enough to permit the regular publication of books of heraldry (*bukan*). Peace allowed the regularization of crests but also fostered their further elaboration, popularization, and dandification. As civilian display replaced practical battlefield use, the warriors' crests became both more ornamental and more symmetrical. It became common at this time to enclose the basic design within a circular border and to display the crest in relatively small size, from 2 to 4 centimeters (0.8 in to 1.6 in) in, in the three or five prescribed places on regular garments. Crests came into use by courtesans, KABUKI actors, commoners, tradesmen, and others. As crests were used decoratively and commercially, purists lamented these trends, but eventually the situation came full cycle and crests were viewed again as the purely aesthetic patterns from which the earliest crests had been derived in the Heian period. During the Edo period (1600–1868) and later, designers' catalogs known as *monchō* or *monkan* were published, containing thousands of variations of the basic design motifs, usually in white on a black background.

The long evolution of Japanese crests essentially ceased with the end of the feudal era. There is no single definitive collection of Japanese crests in general or of family crests in particular. The total number of design variations is probably between 4,000 and 5,000, and the number of different subjects depicted is approximately 250. By far the most popular general category is that of plants, flowers, and trees. Also depicted are tools, implements, and other man-made objects; birds, insects, and animals; heavenly bodies and geographical features; abstract patterns and designs; and ideographs and symbols. The conventional basic categories are crests that commemorate a specific honor or act of valor; martial motifs (sometimes metaphorical); superstitious and auspicious crests; crests with religious associations; denotative crests, in which the family surname is directly or obliquely conveyed; and preeminently decorative motifs, in which the

A Wealth of Japanese Family Crests

Like the heraldic devices of Europe, Japanese family crests developed as the battlefield insignia of feudal nobles and warriors during the 12th century. Over time they were adopted and altered by institutions, businesses, and the common people. The subdued, monochromatic crests draw from a number of simple motifs—mostly animals and insects, natural phenomena, abstract designs, symbols and ideographs, man-made objects, and plants. They range from quite literal depictions—an anchor or a fan, for instance—to highly stylized ones, such as Mt. Fuji in the mist. Crests are still a valued part of Japan's aesthetic wealth, and virtually every Japanese family has one, although most now display these elegant symbols only during formal occasions.

Abstract Designs

 Three linked circles
 Three-diamond triangle
 Square

 Four squares with eyes
 Three left-facing "commas"
 Nine stars
 Four adjacent diamonds

 Three linked tortoise shells
 Linked mountains
 Small tortoise shell over large one
Two lines encircled

Man-Made Objects

 Pouch with drawstring
 Four-sickle wheel
 Six-arrow wheel

 Anchor
 Chinese fan
 Five-slatted fan
Crossed candles in bold circle

Modified Written Characters

 "Good fortune" in diamond shape

 "Tree"
 "Happiness" encircled

In the *kabuki* drama *Shibaraku* (One Moment), which the legendary Ichikawa Danjūrō I (1660–1704) wrote and starred in, Danjūrō wore a robe displaying his family's *mimasu* (three "nested" measuring boxes) crest. Other acting families still need the Ichikawa clan's approval to stage *Shibaraku*, and the robe worn by Danjūrō's character must bear his crest. Danjūrō XII (b 1946) is shown here in the role.

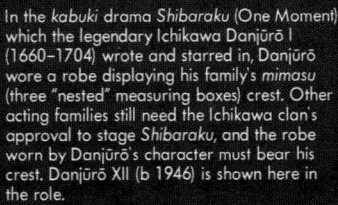

Natural Phenomena

 Moon and flowing water
 Lightning bolts
 Mist

 Mt. Fuji in mist
 Star and crescent moon
 Ocean waves encircled
Facing waves

Plants

 16-petal chrysanthemum
 "Five-seven-five" paulownia blooms
 Three *aoi* leaves encircled

 Crossed *daikon* radishes
 Paired Japanese ginger shoots
 Three-chrysanthemum wheel
 Five dwarf bamboo leaves

 Takasago pine
Pine needles in diamond shape
Plum blossom, side view
 Hanging wisteria

Animals and Insects

 "Knotted" goose

 Plover encircled
 Rabbit facing front

 Circular descending crane
 Swallowtail butterfly

beauty of the subject and design is most important.

Most crests depict a single motif, although combinations are not uncommon. The crests are almost always rendered monochromatically, but the coloring may vary in accordance with the setting. During the Edo period, crests were altered by the addition of standard elements, alteration of the style of drawing or angle of depiction, synthesis of motifs, and combinations of subjects in a dozen or more conventional ways.

☎ 255

crickets 蟋蟀

(*kōrogi*). In Japanese, *kōrogi* is the common name of insects of the order Orthoptera, family Gryllidae, subfamily Gryllinae. Many species are autumnal chirping insects. About 40 species are found in Japan, including the *emma kōrogi* (*Teleogryllus emma*), the *okame kōrogi* (*Loxoblemmus arietulus*), and the *tsuzuresase kōrogi* (*Scapsipedus aspersus*).

Altogether seven poems on the *kōrogi* are found in the 8th-century anthology MAN'YŌSHŪ, although it is believed that the word *kōrogi* in these poems was used as a general term for insects that chirp. In Japanese literature crickets have been associated with the arrival of autumn. During the Edo period (1600–1868) vendors sold crickets in bamboo cages, although in fact the insects sold were more often than not *kantan* (*Oecanthus longicaudus*), *matsumushi* (*Xenogryllus marmoratus*), *suzumushi* (*Homoeogryllus japonicus*), or *kutsuwamushi* (*Mecopoda nipponensis*).

crime 犯罪

(*hanzai*). The Japanese Penal Code of 1907 defines and prescribes the kinds and ranges of punishment for most conventional crimes (see CRIMINAL LAW). In addition, there are many statutes containing penal provisions. Some deal with specific aspects of criminality not adequately covered by the Penal Code, such as corrupt practices in elections, aircraft hijacking, endangering of air flights, use of explosives and incendiary devices, aggravated forms of violent conduct, taking hostages, air and water pollution, and trafficking in and abuse of dangerous drugs. Other statutes, far greater in number, generally penalize the so-called regulatory offenses. No legal distinction is made between felonies, misdemeanors, and violations.

Crime Statistics—In 1990 there were 2,217,559 offenses as defined in the Penal Code and 99,127 violations of other penal statutes. A substantial number of Penal Code offenses (580,931 or 26 percent) were cases of negligent homicide or bodily injury sustained in traffic accidents. Such negligent offenses cannot be viewed as conventional crimes. Thus, Penal Code offenses exclusive of traffic negligence (nontraffic Penal Code offenses) should be used to index crimes for chronological and international comparison.

The number of nontraffic Penal Code offenses on police records decreased from 1,599,968 in 1948 to 1,190,549 in 1973 but again increased to 1,636,628 in 1990. The number of offenses per 100,000 population in these three years was 2,000, 1,091, and 1,323, respectively. The increase since 1973 is accounted for by a significant rise in property offenses. The incidence of violent offenses has steadily decreased since 1964.

A comparison of crime statistics between 1973 and 1982 in the United States, England and Wales, the Federal Republic of Germany, France, and Japan clearly shows that the crime rate in Japan remained quite low, in sharp contrast to the steep rise in criminal behavior in the other four areas. However, international comparisons of crime rates based on statistical data must be viewed with circumspection, since the definition of crime and the manner of gathering statistics differ considerably from country to country.

Areas of Concern—While the general crime situation in Japan has been relatively stable, there are several specific areas of crime that worry the general public and criminal justice agencies. These include juvenile delinquency (see JUVENILE CRIME), organized crime (see YAKUZA), terrorist activities of extremist groups (see RED ARMY FACTION), abuse of amphetamines (see DRUG ABUSE), and white-collar crimes, including corrupt political practices.

Social Factors in Crime—The homogeneity of Japanese society seems to generate relatively little internal conflict. Informal social control through such traditional institutions as family, school, and local community still functions with reasonable effectiveness. Also, small groups of people working together in the same place or sharing common interests similarly contribute to the socialization of their members. Individual members have a strong sense of loyalty to the whole group and consciously avoid behavior offensive to other group members. Such group tendencies among the Japanese act as a model of the behavior in large organizations and in the nation as a whole. Modernization and increasing individual freedom do not seem to have caused any significant change in the group-oriented attitudes of the Japanese. A group-centered orientation, however, becomes a menace to society when the group has antisocial goals. Organized criminal groups as well as the extremist political bodies represent an exaggerated and pathological form of the group-centeredness that characterizes the Japanese in general.

The reasonable efficiency and fairness of law enforcement and criminal justice administration may also have contributed to the successful control of crime. Guns and other lethal weapons are effectively controlled, and the rate of crime clearance is relatively high. In a majority of cases, criminal proceedings are concluded in a short period of time. Institutionalization of offenders is avoided to a great extent by the extensive use of suspended prosecution, fines, and suspended sentences. Sentences are generally moderate and fair. Serious efforts to rehabilitate offenders are undertaken in institutions and the community with the assistance of many volunteers. The centralized operation of all the agencies involved in the administration of justice, from the police and prosecution to the judiciary and corrections, has improved the system considerably. See also CRIMINAL PROCEDURE; CRIMINOLOGY; PENAL SYSTEM; POLICE SYSTEM.

crime victims, compensation for 犯罪被害者補償

(*hanzai higaisha hoshō*). System of government payments to compensate for damage caused by crime, started in Japan in 1981. During the 1960s and 1970s, as many foreign countries instituted such a system, interest increased in Japan as well. The Law for the Payment of Compensation to Crime Victims (Hanzai Higaisha Tō Kyūfukin Shikyū Hō) was enacted after a government feasibility study. Under the law, prefectural public safety commissions will hear cases presented by the crime victims or their families (if the victim is deceased) and determine the amount of compensation.

Criminal Compensation Law 刑事補償法

(Keiji Hoshō Hō). A 1950 law providing for compensation by the state to persons who have been imprisoned and subsequently found not guilty. The constitution provides in article 40 that "any person, in case he is acquitted after he has been arrested or detained, may sue the State for redress as provided by law," thus making criminal compensation an obligation of the state.

There are strict requirements that must be met, and a court can decline to make a full award if it finds that the principal deliberately invited internment or if he or she is declared not guilty of only part of multiple criminal violations. The amount of compensation is determined by the court after taking into consideration such factors as the kinds and length of confinement, the losses of assets the principal suffered, mental suffering or bodily injury, or intent or negligence on the part of the police, the prosecutor, or the court. The amount of compensation for a death sentence is defined as the amount of losses to assets suffered as a result of the principal's death (the amount proved) plus ¥25 million. Fines and surcharges are returned with 5 percent per annum interest.

criminal investigation 捜査

(*sōsa*). Criminal investigations in Japan are chiefly conducted by the police and PUBLIC PROSECUTORS. There are other officials that have extraordinary investigatory powers in specific areas, such as narcotics control officers and officers in the Self Defense Forces. The police department is the major investigatory agency; the public prosecutor acts mainly in cases involving public officials or complicated economic or white-collar crimes. However, because it is the public prosecutor's function to determine whether to prosecute, investigations are organized so that at the final stages, the responsibility for the case lies chiefly in the prosecutor's hands. Techniques of crime investigation used in Japan are much the same as in other modern nations.

The suspect is assured the right to meet privately with an attorney. Only a small number of suspects are actually arrested; in the majority of cases, requests for voluntary appearance are employed. Emphasis is placed on interrogation of the suspect while in physical detention. A meticulous written statement of evidence may be prepared, leading to an indictment (see CONFESSION). A large proportion of indictments end in conviction.

criminal law 刑法

(*keihō*). Legislation defining crimes and offenses and the sanctions attached to them. The basic legislation is the Penal Code (Keihō; Law No. 45, 1907, as amended), but special crimes are distributed throughout compiled legislation (*Roppō zensho*).

History—Before the Meiji Restoration of 1868, crimes and transgressions against the moral order were commingled. Codes enacted in 1873 and 1880 were based on the Chinese and French penal codes, respectively, but the present 1907 code was modeled on the German code of the time. Only a few amendments were mandated by the 1947 CONSTITUTION OF JAPAN. Article 14 of the constitution, requiring equality of all persons under the law, impelled repeal of special provisions protecting imperial family members and their property and punishing adulterous wives and their paramours. That provision also served as a basis for the invalidation of a penal code provision—article 200, which provided more severe punishment for PARENTICIDE than for ordinary homicide. Ascendancy, however, was accepted as a basis for aggravating punishment for assaultive crimes (Penal Code, arts. 205, 218). The renunciation of the war provision (Const., art. 9) also led to changes in crimes against the state and contraction of jurisdiction affecting acts done outside Japan.

The code applies to all crimes committed on Japanese territory or aboard a Japanese vessel or aircraft outside Japan (art. 1). There are provisions for crimes that are committed outside Japan by Japanese citizens and aliens. See also PRIVATE INTERNATIONAL LAW.

Unlike Anglo-American law, Japanese law has no crime of conspiracy or felony-murder (circumstances of homicide are taken into account in determining sanctions). There is no burglary. Intrusion into a habitation (fuhō shinnyū; arts. 130, 132) is prohibited, and crimes committed within a structure are conceptually connected (kenrenhan; art. 54) and control punishment if they are of graver weight than the intrusion itself. ABORTION (datai) is punished (arts. 212–216), but therapeutic abortion is little affected because of the independent EUGENIC PROTECTION LAW (Yūsei Hogo Hō; Law No. 156, 1948, as amended).

General Doctrines—The principle that a prohibitory norm must exist before an act can be prosecuted or punished (nullum crimen, nulla poena, sine lege; J: zaikei hōteishugi; cf. Anglo-American prohibitions against ex post facto legislation and bills of attainder), also known as the principle of legality, has been recognized in Japanese law since the legislative revision of 1880. Japanese criminal law also recognizes that there must be a concurrence of prohibited activity or inactivity and subjective responsibility or culpability (mens rea; J: sekinin). Prohibited conduct is defined through code articles describing specific crimes. Generally, however, a special provision is required before acts done without criminal intent, purpose, or knowledge can be punished (Penal Code, art. 38[1]). The latter includes intentional conduct done with knowledge of likely harm (dolus eventualis). Accordingly, culpability based on negligence (kashitsu) requires special mention. This is found in the code contexts of negligent burning (arts. 116, 117–2), use of explosives (arts. 117, 117–2), flooding (art. 122), endangering traffic (art. 129), and infliction of bodily injury (arts. 209, 211) and death (arts. 210, 211) and in the ROAD TRAFFIC LAW (Dōro Kōtsū Hō; Law No. 105, 1960, as amended; art. 121). There are many regulative statutes bearing vicarious punishment provisions (ryōbatsu kitei), under which owners or employers, whether natural persons (shizenjin) or juristic persons (hōjin), are punishable for conduct of employees unless they establish due care in hiring or supervising such employees. See also EMPLOYERS' LIABILITY.

At times, punishment is not imposed despite harm and culpability:

Immaturity. Those under 14 years are not punishable under the code (art. 41); instead, they are adjudicated under the JUVENILE LAW (Shōnen Hō; Law No. 168, 1948, as amended).

Impaired mental condition. If a person's loss of mental capacity (shinshin sōshitsu) does not comport with legal culpability, punishment should not be imposed (Penal Code, art. 39[1]). Mental illness impairing but not destroying mental ability (shinshin kōjaku) may be used by a court to mitigate penalties (art. 39[2]).

Intoxication. No special code provisions govern physical or mental condition impaired through use of alcohol or psychotropic substances. A court, however, may consider the fact of intoxication in determining whether a defendant committed charged acts with requisite culpability (art. 38[1]); impaired mental condition also may arise from this source (art. 39[2]).

Mistake. Erroneous fact assumptions negating criminal intent or knowledge render offenders nonpunishable (art. 38[1]) but essentially form the basis for punishable negligence. Ignorance about criminal law (art. 38[3]), including gravity of criminality (art. 38[2]), does not eliminate criminal responsibility but may, depending on circumstances, justify a reduction in punishment.

Necessity. Persons forced to protect themselves or others against imminent unlawful acts are not punishable; if they act to an excessive degree in responding, punishment may be reduced or remitted (art. 36).

Self-denunciation. Once a crime has been committed, a change of heart or remorse does not erase it. However, offenders who identify themselves to authorities or complainants before they are detected can receive reduction in punishment (art. 42).

Those who actively join in the commission of a crime are coprincipals (kyōdō seihan) and incur full punishment (art. 60). An abettor (kyōsahan) who successfully solicits a crime also is punishable with the same penalty as principals (arts. 60, 61). Those who aid the commission of a crime (or solicit others who aid) are punishable as accessories (jūhan) even though they do not qualify as coprincipals (art. 62). Penalties for accessories are reduced (art. 63) according to a statutory formula (art. 68).

Japanese criminal procedure does not differentiate between adjudication of guilt and assessment of punishment. Japanese criminal law includes three primary classes of punishment: death (shikei) by hanging; incarceration, which often includes forced labor; and pecuniary sanctions. PARDON (onsha) is constitutionally a function of the cabinet (Const., art. 73[7]). See also CRIME; CRIMINAL PROCEDURE; PENAL SYSTEM.

criminal procedure 刑事訴訟

(keiji soshō). Law governing the administrative and judicial resolution of criminal charges. The legal sources of criminal procedure are the constitution, the Code of Criminal Procedure, and the Criminal Procedure Rules.

History—No formal procedural law existed in Japan until after the Meiji Restoration (1868); all procedures were informal and administrative in character. In 1880 and 1890 codes adapted from French models were instituted. They were supplanted in 1923 by a German-inspired code, replaced in turn by the present 1948 code.

Basic Characteristics—Japanese procedure is adversary: constitutionally independent judges preside over proceedings in which public prosecutors and defense attorneys function as equal adversaries.

Criminal Investigation—Police officers must obtain a judicially approved warrant

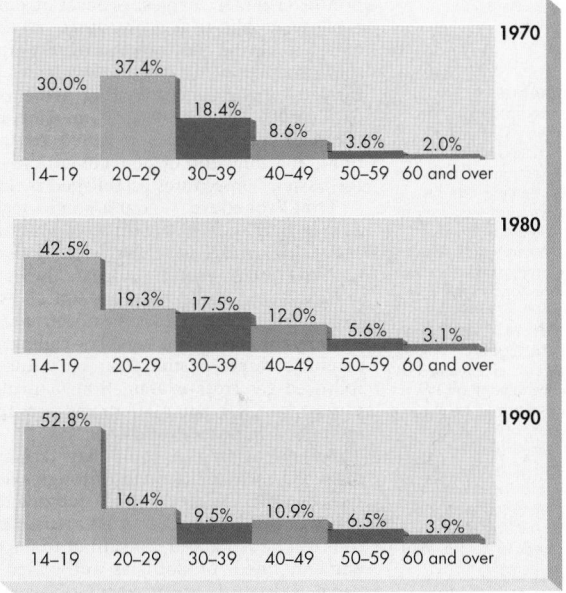

Type of crime	Offenses	Arrests	Arrest percentage
Theft	1,444,067	537,300	37.2
Fraud	50,919	48,926	96.1
Embezzlement	40,401	40,219	99.5
Vandalism	22,824	3,619	15.9
Infliction of bodily injury	19,436	17,294	89.0
Intrusion into a habitation	11,603	4,177	36.0
Forgery	11,517	11,247	97.7
Extortion	10,093	7,332	72.6
Assault	7,362	6,302	85.6
Sexual assault and child molestation	2,730	1,929	70.7
Robbery	1,653	1,272	77.0
Rape	1,548	1,274	82.3
Arson	1,491	1,229	82.4
Receiving stolen goods	1,437	1,436	99.9
Gambling	1,413	1,413	100.0
Murder	1,238	1,197	96.7
Other	6,896	6,427	93.2
Total all types	**1,636,628**	**692,593**	**42.3**

Criminal Offenses and Arrests in Japan by Type, 1990

NOTE: Traffic offenses and offenses by minors under age 14 are not included.
SOURCE: Ministry of Justice, *Hanzai hakusho* (annual): 1991.

Criminal Offenses by Age Group

1970
30.0% (14–19) | 37.4% (20–29) | 18.4% (30–39) | 8.6% (40–49) | 3.6% (50–59) | 2.0% (60 and over)

1980
42.5% (14–19) | 19.3% (20–29) | 17.5% (30–39) | 12.0% (40–49) | 5.6% (50–59) | 3.1% (60 and over)

1990
52.8% (14–19) | 16.4% (20–29) | 9.5% (30–39) | 10.9% (40–49) | 6.5% (50–59) | 3.9% (60 and over)

NOTE: Traffic offenses and offenses by minors under age 14 are not included.
SOURCE: Ministry of Justice, *Hanzai hakusho* (annual): 1991.

Criminal Offenses in Japan, 1946–1990

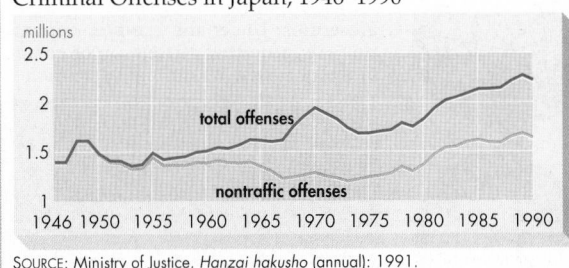

total offenses
nontraffic offenses

SOURCE: Ministry of Justice, *Hanzai hakusho* (annual): 1991.

before making any arrest, search, or seizure, unless they must act urgently to apprehend flagrant offenders or meet other emergencies. A compelled CONFESSION is inadmissible as evidence. See CRIMINAL INVESTIGATION.

Detention—Arrested persons can be held by police no more than 48 hours without judicial authorization and then must be transferred to a public prosecutor, who has a maximum of another 24 hours within which to request a detention order or release the

cuckoos The *hototogisu* (little cuckoo) dwells in forested mountain areas and feeds on tree-crawling insects. Male and female have the same markings.

suspect. No one can be detained without adequate cause. Suspects can be detained no more than 20 days for ordinary crimes and 25 days for exceptional crimes, such as sedition; accused persons may be detained until grounds for detention disappear, an adjudication is entered, or BAIL is granted.

Institution of Charges—Only public prosecutors may submit accusatory instruments to a court; victims and other officials cannot do so, although in specified instances they can file complaints or accusations with public prosecutors. Dissatisfied victims, complainants, or accusers can seek administrative review by PROSECUTION REVIEW COMMISSIONS.

Constitutional Rights of Accused Persons—The constitution guarantees to accused persons the rights of prompt adjudication of criminal charges, counsel at public expense, public trial proceedings, physical presence during trial proceedings, compulsory production of favorable witnesses, refusal to provide incriminating evidentiary data (RIGHT TO REMAIN SILENT), an impartial tribunal, freedom from repeated prosecutions, and infliction of punishment only on the basis of procedures established by law.

Trial Procedure—Trial is conducted by a three-judge collegial court in serious cases and a single judge in others. Most trials extend over many months or years. Juries are not used, and guilty pleas are not allowed. Testimony by WITNESSES is the norm, as regulated by the LAW OF EVIDENCE. The calling side conducts direct examination of witnesses followed by cross-examination, a mandatory prosecution summation, and perhaps a voluntary defense summation.

Adjudication—A court may terminate cases on procedural grounds through a decision or order or may enter a judgment of guilty or not guilty. Convicted accused persons can be sentenced to death or to imprisonment, fined, or both, as authorized by penal legislation; enforcement of sentence can be suspended in delineated instances, and accused persons can be placed under probationary supervision. Enforcement of all forms of punishment is overseen by a public prosecutor. Under the CRIMINAL COMPENSATION LAW, acquitted persons can be compensated for custodial arrest and detention.

Appeal—High courts sit in panels of three judges. Both a public prosecutor and an accused person may appeal to a high court. Accused persons are compensated if a government appeal fails.

The SUPREME COURT has discretion to review high court adjudications concerning constitutional issues, conflicts with earlier Supreme Court or GREAT COURT OF CASSATION precedents, or important legal questions requiring resolution. See also CRIME; CRIMINAL LAW.

Extraordinary Proceedings—Reopening of proceedings may be sought in a court that entered an original adjudication, based on newly discovered evidence indicating innocence or mitigated criminality, proof of forged or perjured evidentiary data at the original proceeding, or proof that an official participant in earlier proceedings has been convicted of misconduct. Reopening may be requested by a public prosecutor, a convicted person, or a legal representative of the convicted. The second extraordinary appeal is brought by the prosecutor-general in the Supreme Court, asserting that the trial or adjudication violated legal rules. An original adjudication may be overturned only if it was unfavorable to an accused person; errors benefiting the defense can be noted, but the original adjudication of acquittal cannot be disturbed.

criminology　犯罪学

(*hanzaigaku*). The discipline of criminology began to develop in Japan in the mid-19th century, when studies were made of European criminal justice systems. In the late 1880s, Japanese criminology came under the influence of German criminology, which formed the basis for the current Penal Code of 1907. Beginning around 1910, the disciplines of medical science, psychology, psychiatry, and sociology were applied to the field of crime studies. From this time on, there was a special interest in the area of juvenile and female crime in Japan.

An area of special excellence in Japanese criminology is the administration of PRISONS and other correctional institutions, particularly in the area of sanitation. This reflects the early efforts of John Cutting BERRY, a physician and missionary who came to Japan in 1872.

The JUVENILE LAW was promulgated in 1948 and became effective in 1949. It requires the consultation of experts in medicine, psychology, sociology, and education in determining the proper treatment of juvenile crime. Interest in criminology continues to be strong. See also CRIME; CRIMINAL LAW.

crows　烏

(*karasu*). In Japanese, *karasu* is the general name for birds of the genus *Corvus*. Their bodies are entirely black and range in length from roughly 33 to 60 centimeters (1–2 ft). Two species, the *hashibuto-garasu* (jungle crow; *C. macrorhynchos*) and the *hashiboso-garasu* (carrion crow; *C. corone*) are permanent residents in Japan. Migratory species wintering in Japan include the *watari-garasu* (raven; *C. corax*) in northern Hokkaidō and the *miyama-garasu* (rook; *C. frugilegus*) and *kokumaru-garasu* (jackdaw; *C. monedula*) in northern Kyūshū.

The Japanese have long considered the crow a messenger of the gods. At the ATSUTA SHRINE (in the city of Nagoya) and Taga Shrine (in Shiga Prefecture) ceremonies are held in which crows are given offerings of rice cakes.

crucian carp　鮒

(*funa*). *Carassius* spp. Freshwater fish of species and subspecies belonging to the genus *Carassius* of the family Cyprinidae, order Cypriniformes, class Osteichthyes. Among the most common freshwater fishes in Japan, they are also among the most popular for angling. The *kimbuna* (also known as *kintarō;* 16 cm [6 in] long) is the most commonly caught; the *gengorō-buna* (also known as *herabuna;* 40 cm [16 in]) is harder to catch. The *gimbuna* (also known as *mabuna;* up to 30 cm [12 in]) is an important edible fish.

Funa no tsutsumiyaki, a dish of *funa* stuffed with five ingredients including sea tangle, steamed chestnuts, and walnuts, seasoned with *sake* and salt, and then roasted, was served at the imperial court and later at banquets for warlords. Today Japanese anglers go out in large numbers for *kambuna* ("midwinter crucians") in January and February, as *funa* is fat and tasty at this time. *Funa* dishes include *funazushi* (*funa* with vinegared rice) and *funa no kanroni*, *funa* cooked in a sweetened soy sauce and served at New Year's.

CSK Corporation　[株]シーエスケイ

(Shī Esu Kei). Computer software development company, offering computer services such as systems development, facilities management and data entry, computer sales and leasing, systems integration, and education. Incorporated in 1968. The company concentrates on high-technology fields such as software and robots and provides a full spectrum of integrated information services. It has developed new technologies in areas such as artificial intelligence and networking. One of CSK's affiliates is in the computer game industry. Sales for the fiscal year ending September 1991 totaled ¥90.1 billion (US $669.5 million), and capitalization was ¥45.0 billion (US $334.4 million). Headquarters are in Tōkyō.

cuckoos　杜鵑

(*hototogisu*). Birds of the family Cuculidae. Several species are found in Japan, but the *hototogisu* (little cuckoo; *Cuculus poliocephalus*) is by far the best known. The *hototogisu* is about 28 centimeters (11 in) long, with a comparatively lengthy tail and wings. The back and breast are gray and the belly white with black horizontal stripes. It arrives in Japan around May and stays in the broad-leaved forests of mountainous regions through the summer. It is a parasitic breeder, leaving its eggs mainly in the nests of the bush warbler (*uguisu*). Other members of the family Cuculidae that breed in Japan are the *kakkō* (Japanese cuckoo; *C. canorus telephonus*), the *tsutsudori* (Himalayan cuckoo; *C. saturatus*), and the *jūichi* (hawk cuckoo; *C. fugax*).

The clear, gentle call of the *hototogisu* is one of the most appreciated of Japan's bird songs and has inspired Japanese poets from the days of the 8th-century MAN'YŌSHŪ to the present as a symbol of early summer.

cucurbits　瓜類

(*urirui*). Vegetables and fruits belonging to the gourd family (Cucurbitaceae). Cucumbers, squashes, and melons are grown extensively in Japan. Cultivated in small quantities are the bottle gourd (*yūgao*), wax gourd (*tōgan*), dishcloth gourd (*hechima*), balsam pear (*tsurureishi*), and chayote (*hayatouri*).

The cucumber (*kyūri*) is one of the most popular vegetables in Japan. It is slimmer

cucurbits

1 The hardy squash known as *kabocha*, introduced to Japan by the Portuguese in the 16th century, can be grown in a wide range of climates.
2 The variety of watermelon most common in Japan today was developed in Nara Prefecture in the 1880s.
3 The *yūgao*, or bottle gourd, is chiefly used as an ingredient in *sushi*. It is also prized for the beauty of its night-blooming flowers.
4 This slim, rough-skinned Japanese variety of cucumber has been cultivated in hotbeds since the early 19th century.

than foreign varieties, has a rough skin, and grows to about 15–20 centimeters (6–8 in) in length. Cucumbers are used mainly in salads or in Japanese-style PICKLES (tsukemono).

Squashes (kabocha) grown in Japan include the Nihon kabocha (Cucurbita moschata), an acorn-type squash introduced to Japan in early times, and European pumpkins (C. maxima), which have become popular in recent years; although several varieties of both kinds are extensively cultivated, demand for them has been decreasing. They are usually eaten boiled.

Smooth-skinned Asian melons and hybrids of foreign species are cultivated both outdoors and in greenhouses. Shirouri, one of the smooth-skinned varieties, is grown for pickling. The watermelon (suika) is a popular summer fruit cultivated throughout the country. The bottle gourd is used mainly as kampyō, an ingredient in SUSHI; its flesh is peeled in ribbonlike strips and dried. The wax gourd is grown in the summer and eaten cooked.

Cultural Properties Law
文化財保護法

(Bunkazai Hogo Hō; literally, "Law for the Protection of Cultural Properties"). Promulgated in 1950 to broaden the preservation of cultural properties, it consolidated several existing laws. The law divides cultural properties into five groups: (1) Buildings, paintings, sculptures, books, and archaeological and historical materials; when designated for protection, these become Important Cultural Properties, including the category of NATIONAL TREASURES. (2) Forms of theater, music, and applied arts; when designated for preservation, these become Important Intangible Cultural Properties, and their practitioners are included in the category of LIVING NATIONAL TREASURES. (3) Folk traditions, folk crafts, traditional clothing, utensils, and furniture; when designated for protection, these become Important Intangible Folk-Cultural Properties. (4) SHELL MOUNDS, tomb mounds (KOFUN), castles, palaces, archaeological sites, gardens, bridges, gorges, beaches, and mountains as well as animals, plants, and natural resources; when designated these are termed Historic Sites, Places of Scenic Beauty, and Natural Monuments. (5) Groups of historic buildings or structures having high historical, artistic, or academic value; these are called HISTORIC PRESERVATION DISTRICTS if designated for preservation. The designation of cultural properties is made by the Ministry of Education. The restriction on alteration, which prevents uncontrolled changes in historic sites or preservation districts, is enforced by the head of the Agency for Cultural Affairs.

culture centers
カルチャーセンター

(karuchā sentā). English words used in Japan as a general term for commercially operated adult-education centers offering courses on a wide variety of subjects for a fee. Culture centers first became popular in the late 1970s. Many such centers are operated by newspaper companies, department stores, and broadcasting companies. Culture centers offer a rich variety of courses, including such subjects as languages, art, traditional Japanese accomplishments, sports, musical instruments, personal computers, and word processing. The Asahi Culture Centers, the largest chain of such centers in the Tōkyō metropolitan area, are operated by the newspaper Asahi shimbun. The largest of Asahi's three Tōkyō centers offers 1,300 classes in 560 subjects (counting different levels of the same subject) to some 65,000 students, about 75 percent of whom are women.

cumulative guidance record
指導要録

(shidō yōroku). An official record compiled for each pupil in primary, middle, and high school. It is consulted when students take entrance examinations for higher schools, change schools, require academic guidance, or begin employment. Its form and content are determined by the Ministry of Education, which requires schools to keep the record and to retain it for 20 years. Known until 1949 as gakusekibo (pupil record), the record lists a student's full name, date of birth, address, dates of enrollment and graduation, attendance record, scholastic achievement, attitude and personality, and physical condition. See also REPORT CARDS.

Cuong De
クオン・デ

(1882–1951). Vietnamese prince who was prominent in the Vietnamese nationalist movement against French colonial rule in the early 20th century and who spent many years in exile in Japan. Appointed by Vietnamese nationalist leader PHAN BOI CHAU in 1904 to head the Vietnam Duy Tan Hoi (Vietnam Reformation Society), he studied at a government military school in Tōkyō in 1906 and then at a private preparatory school until he was expelled from Japan in 1909. Cuong De became the president of the Vietnam Quang Phuc Hoi (Vietnam Restoration Society), established at Guangzhou (Canton) by Phan Boi Chau in 1912, but returned to Japan in 1915. As the Pacific War approached, he founded the Phuc Quoc Dong Minh Hoi (National Revival Association) and helped the Japanese set up in Taiwan a Vietnamese-language propaganda broadcasting team. He also organized a Vietnamese military group in Guangzhou that started an abortive insurrection in Vietnam in 1940. He faded from the political scene after the war and died in Japan.

Currency Museum
貨幣博物館

(Kahei Hakubutsukan). Museum established by the Bank of Japan in 1985 in Chūō Ward, Tōkyō. Japanese currency, arranged chronologically from ancient to modern, is on display, shown in relation to the development of other world currencies. Exhibits include the WADŌ KAIHŌ, Japan's oldest coin; HANSATSU, the paper money issued by Japanese feudal lords for use in their domains; the Tenshō ōban, a large gold coin minted in the latter part of the 16th century; and the Keichō koban, a gold coin in circulation during the Edo period (1600–1868).

customary law
慣習法

(kanshūhō). One of the unwritten sources of Japanese law. Custom becomes a legally enforceable norm when the fact that it has social support is judicially recognized. In general, customary law is considered supplementary to written law and is applied only when there is no appropriate statutory provision. Thus, article 2 of the Law on the Applicability of Laws (see HŌREI) asserts the general principle that custom not in contradiction to public order or opposed to accepted morality shall have effect equal to that of an applicable statutory provision or shall serve as a rule of law in the absence of such a provision. In the field of commercial law, commercial custom prevails over provisions of the CIVIL CODE (art. 1 of the COMMERCIAL CODE). There is, however, no equivalent of English criminal common law in Japan; article 31 of the constitution prohibits the imposition of criminal penalties except through procedures established by legislation.

cycling
サイクリング

(saikuringu). Cycling as a leisure sport became quite popular in Japan beginning in the mid-1950s. There are now cycling routes or courses throughout Japan. Facilities such as hostels for cyclists (called "cycling terminals") and recreation centers ("cycling parks") are widely available. The Japan Cycling Association, founded in 1964, maintains branch offices in every prefecture in Japan and as of 1989 had nearly 120,000 members. The nationwide and regional cycling rallies it sponsors attract cyclists from throughout the world.

cypresses
檜

(hinoki). Chamaecyparis obtusa. Evergreen trees that are among Japan's most important sources of lumber. A member of the family Cypressaceae, the cypress's height averages 30–40 meters (100–130 ft) and its diameter 0.8–1.5 meters (2.6–5.0 ft). The bark is reddish brown and splits vertically before splintering and falling off. The branches are slender and extend horizontally. The leaves are deep green scales. The flowers are monoecious and, after blooming, form cones. Cypresses grow on three of Japan's main islands (Honshū, Shikoku, and Kyūshū) and have been cultivated since ancient times. The Kiso and Yoshino areas of central Honshū are particularly well known for their cypress forests.

In ancient times fire was produced by rubbing together sticks of cypress; hence the origin of the name hinoki ("tree of fire"). The delicate quality, medium hardness, fine luster, fragrance, and durability of cypress make it the most desirable lumber in Japan. It is used in the construction of Shintō shrines, Buddhist temples, and other buildings. Cypress is also used in ornamental woodworking. Splintered cypress wood is made into water-resistant rope for anchors and rafts, cypress bark is used for roofing, and the oil from cypress leaves is used in perfumes and solvents.

A number of ornamental varieties have been developed. The chabohiba (C. obtusa var. breviramea) is a spire-shaped variety with short branches growing in clusters. The kujakuhiba (C. obtusa var. filicoides) has small, clustered branches that droop somewhat and give the appearance of being a single branch. The suiryūhiba (C. obtusa var. pendula) has long, drooping branches. The hōōhiba (C. obtusa var. ericoides) has branches that extend straight out; the tree is pyramidal in shape.

cypresses Cypress wood has long been used in the construction of temples, shrines, and other buildings. Nagano Prefecture is well known for its cypress trees (photo at top).

Daianji　大安寺

A ranking temple of the SHINGON SECT of Buddhism, located in the city of Nara, Nara Prefecture; an early SANRON SCHOOL center. Originally established in 617 as a monastery by Prince SHŌTOKU at Kumagori, it was converted into a great temple by Emperor Jomei (r 629–641) in 639. The temple became the palace chapel, a position it held for the next 100 years. In 673 Emperor TEMMU moved the temple to Takaichi in Asuka and rebuilt it as the Takechi no Ōdera. It was renamed Daikan Daiji (The Great Temple of the Great Palace) in 677. In 710, with the establishment of the new capital of HEIJŌKYŌ (now the city of Nara), the temple was installed on a new site as the palace chapel. Some buildings were finished by 718, and many magnificent structures were added as the temple prospered. The temple was renamed Daianji (Temple of Great Peace), probably in 729. Fires, earthquakes, and typhoons destroyed most of the buildings by the 18th century. Portions of the temple were rebuilt in the early part of the 20th century.

Daibon Sankajō　大犯三箇条

(Three Regulations for Great Crimes). A term used to define jurisdiction of the officials known as SHUGO (constables; later military governors) under the Kamakura shogunate (1192–1333). Originally *shugo* were responsible for mustering troops for guard duty in Kyōto and were given jurisdiction over two major crimes: murder and rebellion. These three responsibilities were formalized in the GOSEIBAI SHIKIMOKU code of 1232. The term continued to be used into the Muromachi period (1333–1568).

Daibosatsu Pass　大菩薩峠

(Daibosatsu Tōge). Located in the Daibosatsu Mountains, east of the city of Enzan, northeastern Yamanashi Prefecture, central Honshū. The highway Kōshū Urakaidō runs through the pass to connect the Kōfu Basin with the upper reaches of the river Tamagawa. It is famous as the setting of NAKAZATO KAIZAN's novel *Daibosatsu Tōge*. Numerous hikers climb the pass from the Tōkyō-Yokohama district. It lies within the Chichibu-Tama National Park. Height: 1,897 m (6,224 ft).

Daibosatsu Tōge　大菩薩峠

(Great Bodhisattva Pass). Multivolume novel by NAKAZATO KAIZAN (1885–1944); originally published 1913–41. The protagonist is the master swordsman Tsukue Ryūnosuke, who travels throughout the tumultuous Japan of the 1850s and 1860s offering his talents as a sword-for-hire. The plot is episodic, depicting the nihilistic Ryūnosuke's various encounters with a wide cast of characters whose empty lives embody the author's deeply ingrained fatalism based on the Buddhist concept of karma. The work was left unfinished at Nakazato's death. Considered by many to be the most successful work of POPULAR FICTION in Japan, *Daibosatsu Tōge* has had a significant influence on later works of the genre. A partial translation of the novel into English, *Great Boddhisattva Pass*, was published in 1929.

daibutsu　大仏

(great Buddha; i.e., great Buddhist statue). Technically *daibutsu* are statues of Buddhas and bodhisattvas that reach or exceed a height known as *jōroku* (i.e., 1 *jō* 6 *shaku*, an old measure equaling 4.9 m or 16.1 ft). This measure was believed to be the actual height of the Buddha, more than twice the height of an ordinary human. The earliest extant fragments of a *daibutsu* are those from an image cast in 606 by the master KURATSUKURI NO TORI and later incorporated in the so-called Asuka Daibutsu at the temple ASUKADERA in what is now Nara Prefecture. The most famous early *daibutsu* is the gilt-bronze image of Buddha Vairocana (J: Birushana; see DAINICHI) at the temple TŌDAIJI in Nara (known as the Nara Daibutsu). It was twice badly damaged and the only original parts of the current statue are fragments of the lotus-petal throne. The seated bronze image of the Buddha Amitābha (AMIDA) at the temple Kōtokuin in Kamakura, known as the Kamakura (or Hase) Daibutsu, dates from the mid-13th century. This 11.4 meter (37.4 ft) high *daibutsu* has been in the open since the temple building that housed it was lost in 1495.

Daicel Chemical Industries, Ltd　ダイセル化学工業[株]

(Daiseru Kagaku Kōgyō). Company engaged in the manufacture of cellulose derivatives, organic chemicals, plastics, films for packaging, and propellants such as gun powder. Incorporated in 1919. Daicel is the largest domestic producer of cellulose acetate, acetate tow for cigarette filters, and acetic acid and its derivatives. It has offices in New York, Los Angeles, and Düsseldorf. Sales for the fiscal year ending March 1991 totaled ¥168.2 billion (US $1.2 billion), with exports constituting 17 percent; the company was capitalized at ¥36.2 billion (US $263.8 million). Headquarters are in the city of Sakai, Ōsaka Prefecture.

Daidō Danketsu Movement　大同団結運動

(Daidō Danketsu Undō). Political movement led by members of the FREEDOM AND PEOPLE'S RIGHTS MOVEMENT between 1886 and 1890; it sought to reorganize members of the former political parties in preparation for the new parliamentary system promised by 1890. The movement was launched in October 1886, when HOSHI TŌRU asked former JIYŪTŌ party members to cast aside their petty differences and unite for a larger common purpose (*daidō danketsu*). At a second meeting in May 1887, it became clear that former Jiyūtō politicians, led by ITAGAKI TAISUKE and GOTŌ SHŌJIRŌ, were planning to organize a new political party.

In October some 70 former political party members formed the "1887 Club" (Teigai Kurabu) and made concrete plans for the formation of a new political party. The government retaliated with the repressive PEACE PRESERVATION LAW OF 1887 (Hoan Jōrei). In March 1889 Gotō accepted a post in the KURODA KIYOTAKA cabinet, which weakened the Daidō Danketsu Movement considerably, but the movement did prepare the way for party politics under the 1889 Meiji Constitution.

daidōgei　→ street entertainment

Daidōji Yūzan　大道寺友山

(1639–1730). Military strategist of the Edo period (1600–1868); also known as Daidōji Shigesuke. A native of Yamashiro Province (now part of Kyōto Prefecture), he went to Edo (now Tōkyō) to study military strategy under Hōjō Ujinaga (1609–70). His book *Budō shoshin shū* (Introduction to the Way of the Warrior) is a study of classical BUSHIDŌ.

Daidō Life Foundation

大同生命国際文化基金

(Daidō Seimei Kokusai Bunka Kikin). A foundation established in 1985 by the Daidō Mutual Life Insurance Co. It sponsors prizes for Japanese research into cultures around the world. It also translates into Japanese and publishes books on modern Asian art and culture, and translates into Asian languages and publishes works of Japanese literature. A related program provides financial support for foreign students in Japan. In 1990 total assets were ¥1.2 billion (US $8.3 million). Headquarters are in the city of Suita, Ōsaka Prefecture.

Daidō Steel Co, Ltd

大同特殊鋼[株]

(Daidō Tokushukō). Manufacturer of specialty steel, cast steel, forged steel, industrial furnaces and machinery, titanium, and magnetic products. Incorporated in 1950. Some 60 percent of its products are manufactured for automobile makers, primarily NISSAN MOTOR CO, LTD. Sales for the fiscal year ending March 1991 totaled ¥326.0 billion (US $2.4 billion), of which sales of specialty steel made up 65 percent; forged steel products, 15 percent; industrial furnaces and machinery, 8 percent; and others, 12 percent. In the same year the company was capitalized at ¥35.9 billion (US $261.7 million). Headquarters are in Nagoya.

Daiei Co, Ltd

大映[株]

(Daiei). Motion picture company. Established in 1942. The company is well known for its production of such post–World War II masterpieces as *Rashōmon* (1950) by KUROSAWA AKIRA and *Jigokumon* (1953, Gate of Hell) by KINUGASA TEINOSUKE. The company's business failed in 1971 but since has been reestablished. In 1988 the company produced *Tonkō* (Dunhuang or Tun-huang) and won various prizes including the Japan Oscar. For the fiscal year ending August 1990, sales totaled ¥4.9 billion (US $35.7 million) and capitalization stood at ¥200.0 million (US $1.5 million). Headquarters are in Tōkyō.

Daiei, Inc

[株]ダイエー

(Daie). Japan's largest chain of supermarkets, ranking first in annual retail sales. Incorporated in 1957 by NAKAUCHI ISAO. Daiei, based in the Kansai area around Ōsaka, operates 191 stores throughout Japan. The company also operates department stores and is involved in hotel and restaurant operations, financial services, and real-estate development. Among its overseas tie-ups is a link with the French department store Au Printemps S.A. Sales for the fiscal year ending February 1990 totaled ¥1.8 trillion (US $12.4 billion), and capitalization stood at ¥35.7 billion (US $245.3 million). Headquarters are in Ōsaka and Tōkyō.

daifuku

大福

Confection consisting of sweetened bean paste (*an*) wrapped in a skin of steamed and pounded glutinous rice (MOCHI). *Daifuku*, which have been eaten in Japan since the Edo period (1600–1868), belong to the category of sweets known as *mochigashi*.

Daigakuryō

大学寮

(often translated as "The University"). A Confucian training institution for government administrators established in the 7th century during the reign of Emperor TENJI. It was reorganized under the TAIHŌ CODE of 701

and further expanded in the Heian period (794–1185). Located in Kyōto, the Daigakuryō was placed under the jurisdiction of the Shikibushō (Ministry of Ceremonial) and modeled after Chinese institutions that aimed to teach politics and morality. The school was open to sons of the higher nobility—i.e., fifth rank and above—and, upon application, to those of certain lower-ranking nobles and provincial officials (see COURT RANKS). These students entered the school at 13 to 16 years of age. Those who finished the prescribed course were required to pass an examination given by the Shikibushō and were given offices according to their performance.

Daigenkai

大言海

A dictionary of the Japanese language, containing roughly 100,000 words. The *Daigenkai* was published from 1932 through 1935 in four volumes, with an index volume published in 1937; revised editions in one volume were issued in 1956 and 1982. Edited by ŌTSUKI FUMIHIKO, the *Daigenkai* is an enlarged version of his earlier effort, the *Genkai* (1889–91). The *Daigenkai* long ranked with the DAI NIHON KOKUGO JITEN as a modern dictionary of the Japanese language, and these two works exercised a considerable influence on later DICTIONARIES.

Daigo

大子[町]

Town in northern Ibaraki Prefecture, central Honshū. Daigo is noted for its production of tea and for *mitsumata* and *kōzo* trees, used for making Japanese paper (WASHI). Several hot springs in the town have been designated, along with the FUKURODA FALLS, part of the Oku Kuji Prefectural Natural Park. Pop: 27,067.

Daigo, Emperor

醍醐天皇

(885–930; Daigo Tennō). The 60th sovereign (*tennō*) of Japan in the traditional count (which includes several legendary emperors); reigned 897–930. Eldest son of Emperor UDA. Like his father, Daigo attempted to rule without a Fujiwara regent (see REGENCY GOVERNMENT), but rivalry between his chief ministers Fujiwara no Tokihira (871–909) and SUGAWARA NO MICHIZANE brought a resurgence of Fujiwara power. Daigo's reign saw the last revival of the RITSURYŌ SYSTEM, and

later generations considered the Engi era (901–923) a golden age of government and culture (see ENGI TENRYAKU NO CHI). Daigo's Engi Reform of 902, which attempted to reinstate central control and limit private estates (*shōen*), was not effective. The ENGI SHIKI (Procedures of the Engi Era), the history *Nihon sandai jitsuroku* (see RIKKOKUSHI), and the poetic anthology KOKINSHŪ were completed during his reign.

Daigo fukuryū maru Jiken→

Lucky Dragon Incident

Daigoji

醍醐寺

Head temple of the Daigo branch of the SHINGON SECT of Buddhism; located in Fushimi Ward, Kyōto. A sprawling monastic complex of numerous temples and halls, Daigoji is comprised of separate upper and lower precincts. In 874 the monk Shōbō (832–909) constructed a hermitage on the mountain Kasatoriyama, which became known as Kami (Upper) Daigo. Daigoji was formally founded two years later, with the installation of a pair of images of two avatars of KANNON (Skt: Avalokiteśvara), Juntei (Skt: Cundī) and Nyoirin (Skt: Cintāmaṇicakra), in two newly constructed worship halls, each named for the image it housed. In 907 the emperor DAIGO visited, beginning a long period of close association between Daigoji and members of the imperial family.

A five-story pagoda built in 952 is the oldest surviving structure at Daigoji and has been designated a National Treasure. Numerous other buildings were constructed between 1068 and 1129 under the patronage of the retired emperor SHIRAKAWA, when the monastery experienced its golden age.

daibutsu When this image, popularly known as the Great Buddha of Nara, was completed in 752 it was the largest and most splendid in Japan. The present image has undergone several major restorations. Gilt bronze. Height 15 meters. Tōdaiji, Nara Prefecture.

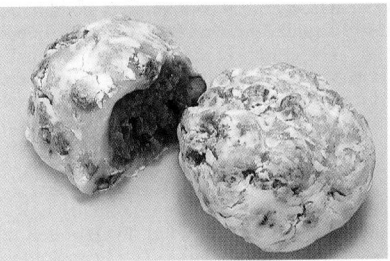

daifuku This type of sweet is made from steamed glutinous rice dough wrapped around red bean paste. In the example shown here, beans are incorporated into the dough.

Daigoji Built in 952, the five-story pagoda of this temple has been designated a National Treasure. Temple patron Toyotomi Hideyoshi ordered many cherry trees transplanted here, and Daigoji is now famous for its cherry blossoms.

Among those added was the Sambōin, the principal monastery of the lower precinct, founded in 1115 by the priest Shōkaku (1057–1129). The Sambōin was the head temple of the Tōzan branch of the SHUGENDŌ sect of mountain ascetics (YAMABUSHI) throughout the Edo period (1600–1868).

Although most of the temple buildings were destroyed by fire in the Ōnin War (1467–77), another patron, TOYOTOMI HIDEYOSHI, rebuilt many of the halls in the late 16th century; most of the present buildings date from this period. The complex houses numerous National Treasures of architecture, sculpture, painting, and calligraphy, as well as many Important Cultural Properties.

Daigoji Treasure House
醍醐寺宝聚院霊宝館

(Daigoji Hōjuin Reihōkan). Located at the temple DAIGOJI to the south of the city of Kyōto. A splendid collection, opened in 1935, of paintings, calligraphy, sculpture, lacquer ware, metalwork, and temple documents of importance for the study of Japanese art from the Nara (710–794) through the Kamakura (1185–1333) periods and from the early 17th century. Among the items are a section of the illustrated sutra *Kako genzai inga kyō* (Nara period), a number of iconographic drawings by Shinkai (late 13th century), painted wooden panels from the five-story pagoda of the early Heian period (794–1185), a sutra in KŪKAI's handwriting, screen paintings by SŌTATSU, and sculpture of the Heian and Kamakura periods. The treasure house is open each spring and autumn.

Daigokuden
大極殿

The Great Hall of State (literally, Hall of the Great Ultimate) in the imperial residences of ancient Japan; ideally located at the north of the palace's official compound (Chōdōin) as its principal edifice and the seat of the sovereign. The chronicle NIHON SHOKI (720) mentions several buildings named Daigokuden. The earliest Daigokuden whose existence and name are verified by archaeology as well as written sources include those of FUJIWARA-KYŌ, the capital from 694 to 710; HEIJŌKYŌ (Nara), dating from ca 724; and NAGAOKAKYŌ, the seat of government from 784. The Daigokuden of HEIANKYŌ (Kyōto), inaugurated in 796, is the most famous. The Daigokuden

was intended to be where the sovereign held regular state councils, but as early as the 9th century it was reserved for the most important ceremonies. The Shishinden, located in the residential compound (DAIRI) of the palace, took its place as the council hall.

Daihatsu Motor Co, Ltd
ダイハツ工業[株]

(Daihatsu Kōgyō). Company producing small-size passenger cars and trucks. Established in 1907. A member of the Toyota group, it has a wide variety of products, including the passenger cars Applause, Charade, Mira, Leeza, Rugger, and Delta-wide and the trucks Hijet and Delta. Daihatsu exports its vehicles to over 120 countries. Sales for the fiscal year ending in March 1991 totaled ¥787.5 billion (US $5.7 billion), and the company was capitalized at ¥28.1 billion (US $204.8 million). Headquarters are in Ikeda, Ōsaka Prefecture.

Daihon'ei
大本営

(Imperial General Headquarters). Before Japan's defeat in World War II, the nation's highest military council. It was under the direct command of the emperor and composed of military officers. It was established three times, during the SINO-JAPANESE WAR OF 1894–1895, the RUSSO-JAPANESE WAR OF 1904–05, and WORLD WAR II. During World War II, prime ministers and cabinet ministers did not have the right to attend its deliberations.

Daiichi Chūō Kisen Kaisha
第一中央汽船[株]

(Daiichi Chūō Kisen). Company operating tramp steamers. Incorporated in 1960, it is an affiliate of the MITSUI O.S.K. LINES, LTD. Its ships transport cargo exclusively for Sumitomo-affiliated companies. Since 1970 the company has also operated oil tankers. It has affiliated firms in New York and London. The company has six ships totaling 950,213 deadweight tons. Sales for the fiscal year ending March 1991 totaled ¥68.5 billion (US $499.2 million), and the company was capitalized at ¥12.4 billion (US $90.4 million) in the same year. Headquarters are in Tōkyō.

Dai-Ichi Kangyō Bank, Ltd
[株]第一勧業銀行

(Dai-Ichi Kangyō Ginkō). Japan's largest commercial bank. Created through the merger of Dai-Ichi Bank, Ltd, and Nippon Kangyō Bank, Ltd, in 1971. Dai-Ichi Bank was established in 1873 as Japan's first state bank and became a commercial bank in 1896. Dai-Ichi Kangyō Bank is the largest single source of yen-denominated funding and a key presence in international financial and capital markets. In Japan, the bank has a vast network of 367 branch offices providing services to more than 756,000 customers. It has 63 overseas offices in 28 countries. In March 1991, the bank had assets of ¥62.6 trillion (US $456.3 billion) and deposits of ¥47.3 trillion (US $344.8 billion); capitalization was ¥457.9 billion (US $3.3 billion) in the same year. Headquarters are in Tōkyō.

Dai-Ichi Mutual Life Insurance Co
第一生命保険[相]

(Dai-Ichi Seimei Hoken). The first life insurance company in Japan; ranked second among Japanese life insurance companies in the total amount of policies in force. Incorporated in 1902. The company has 96 branches, 105 district offices, and 1,843 unit offices in Japan. International activities include participation in a worldwide network

for pooling group insurance for multinational corporations, reinsurance treaties with various foreign insurers, and active overseas investment programs in the form of loans, stock purchases, and real estate. In March 1991 total assets were ¥19.2 trillion (US $140.0 billion), with premium income totaling ¥3.7 trillion (US $27.0 billion) in the same year. Headquarters are in Tōkyō.

Daiichi Pharmaceutical Co, Ltd
第一製薬[株]

(Daiichi Seiyaku). Pharmaceutical manufacturer concentrating on the production of ethical drugs. Incorporated in 1918. The company is a leading manufacturer of both cardiovascular and respiratory drugs. Sales for the fiscal year ending March 1991 totaled ¥178.0 billion (US $1.3 billion), and capitalization stood at ¥22.7 billion (US $145.4 million). Headquarters are in Tōkyō.

Dai Jitao (Tai Chi-t'ao)
戴季陶

(1891–1949; J: Tai Kitō). Chinese journalist and personal secretary to SUN YAT-SEN; counseled conciliation instead of resistance to Japan's military incursions in China in the 1930s. After studying law at Nihon University in Tōkyō from 1906 to 1909, Dai joined Sun's United League (Tongmeng Hui; T'ung-meng Hui) in 1911, becoming his personal secretary in 1912. He followed Sun to Japan after the latter's failure to unseat the president of the republic, YUAN SHIKAI (Yüan Shih-k'ai). After Sun's return to China in 1916 Dai made informal diplomatic trips to Tōkyō. Following Sun's death in 1925, Dai wrote two books on Sun's ideas that provided the ideological basis for the purge of communists from the Guomindang (Kuomintang; Nationalist Party). In February 1927 Dai led a mission to Tōkyō to enlist Japanese sympathy for the Guomindang's Northern Expedition to unify China. After the MANCHURIAN INCIDENT in September 1931 Dai advocated negotiating with Japan and avoiding war.

Daijōin jisha zōji ki
大乗院寺社雑事記

(Records of Miscellaneous Matters concerning the Monastery and the Shrine, Written at the Daijōin). An important collection of documents of the Muromachi period (1333–1568). The Daijōin, established in 1087, became in medieval times (mid-12th–16th centuries), together with the Ichijōin, one of the two principal *monzeki* (family-controlled temples) of the KŌFUKUJI, the great FUJIWARA FAMILY monastery in Nara. *Daijōin jisha zōji ki* comprises the diaries of three major priests of the temple—Jinson (1430–1508), Seikaku (d 1494), and Kyōjin (d 1526)—as well as other documents, providing a wealth of political, economic, social, and cultural information for the years 1450–1527.

Daijōsai
大嘗祭

(Great Food Offering Ritual). Also known as the Ōnie no Matsuri. Dating at least to the late 7th century, it is performed by a new emperor in the autumn of the year of his formal enthronement, replacing the NIINAMESAI (Festival for the New Tasting), or annual imperial harvest festival. In modern times, the Daijōsai has been held in the year following the previous emperor's death. It is the third of the three ceremonies marking the enthronement, the other two being the *senso*, or proclamation made before the palace shrines immediately after the death of an emperor announcing that an heir has suc-

The Daijōsai compound constructed on the grounds of the Imperial Palace for Emperor Akihito's observance of the ceremony in 1990.

Daijōsai

The last of the three ceremonies that mark the enthronement of a new emperor, this ritual offering of food is performed in the autumn of the year of formal enthronement.

Emperor Akihito conducting the Daijōsai. After offering specially prepared food to the Shintō gods the emperor engages in a ceremony of spiritual communion called naorai.

The nighttime observance of Daijōsai gives the ceremony a mystical air. Here, Empress Michiko, dressed in white at far left, proceeds along a section of the Daijōsai compound.

ceeded him, and the *sokui no rei,* or formal enthronement ceremony traditionally held within the Imperial Palace shortly before the Daijōsai.

An outline of the Daijōsai is given in the TAIHŌ CODE (701), and more detailed procedures are preserved in the ENGI SHIKI (927, Procedures of the Engi Era). The Daijōsai fell out of practice in the mid-15th century and was revived in the late 17th. The procedures were revised after the MEIJI RESTORATION (1868). In 1909 a law prescribing the procedures of the enthronement ceremonies (Tōkyokurei) was issued, and the Daijōsai for both Emperor TAISHŌ and Emperor SHŌWA (Hirohito) was performed according to this law. In the new IMPERIAL HOUSEHOLD LAW issued in 1947 there was no stipulation for the Daijōsai, and the Tōkyokurei with its detailed procedural prescriptions was nullified, but centuries of custom and precedent continue to serve as a guide for the conduct of the ritual.

As soon as the date for the Daijōsai has been determined, a formal announcement is made at the palace shrines, the Grand Shrine of Ise, and a number of imperial tombs. An ancient technique of divination is used to select two consecrated paddy fields, one to the east and one to the west of Kyōto, to grow the ceremonial rice. The two rice fields correspond to the Yuki and Suki halls, temporary unpainted wood structures erected in an area of the Imperial Palace grounds designated as the Daijōsai compound, where the rice will be offered. The rice is cultivated with elaborate ritual procedures and then borne by imperial messengers to the Daijōsai compound. Before the Daijōsai takes place, purification rituals (see HARAE) are performed by the emperor and other participants. Following a solemn procession to the Yuki Hall in the evening, the emperor offers a range of specially prepared foods to AMATERASU ŌMIKAMI (the sun goddess) and the deities of heaven and earth (*tenjin chigi*); the emperor himself then partakes of steamed rice, millet, and sacred rice wine (*miki*), by means of which he enters into spiritual communion with the gods (see NAORAI). The ceremony is repeated in the Suki Hall later in the night. Imperial banquets are held in the days following.

Following the death of Emperor Shōwa in 1989, the Daijōsai for Emperor AKIHITO was held in the Imperial Palace in Tōkyō on the night of 22 November 1990. The ceremony was surrounded by a debate on the imperial system and the constitutionality of the use of public funds for the ceremony. Threats of terrorism based on opposition to the imperial system led to the preparations' being conducted in great secrecy and to stringent security measures at the time of the ceremony.

Daikakuji 大覚寺

Main temple and headquarters of the Daikakuji branch of the Shingon sect. Located in Ukyō Ward, Kyōto. The temple grounds were originally the site of the detached palace of Emperor SAGA (r 809–823), who received the teachings of the founder of the Shingon sect KŪKAI. In 876 Emperor Seiwa (r 858–876) proclaimed the former palace a Buddhist temple. From the time of the third abbot, Jōshō (911–983), the temple was for 280 years under the control of abbots of Ichijōin, a subtemple of KŌFUKUJI, and fell into decline. However, in the Kamakura period the temple was particularly esteemed by the emperors Go-Saga (r 1242–46) and Kameyama (r 1260–74). In 1308 the retired emperor Go-Uda (r 1274–87) took Buddhist orders and made Daikakuji his palace. In the Muromachi period (1333–1568), the temple was patronized by the Ashikaga family, but it again declined in the late Edo period (1600–1868). The hall known as the Shinden has wall paintings by KANŌ SANRAKU and KANŌ TAN'YŪ, and in the *hondō* (main hall) there is a fine Kongō Yasha (Skt: Varjrayakṣa; dated 1176) by MYŌEN.

daikan 代官

(intendants). Local administrators of premodern Japan. Early in the medieval period (mid-12th–16th centuries) *daikan* were men sent either temporarily or permanently to different parts of the country by the shogunate or by estate (SHŌEN) proprietors to act as their local representatives. By the 16th century the term was applied to persons entrusted by military lords with the civil administration of their domains. Under the Tokugawa shogunate (1603–1867) *daikan* became a formal, permanent office of local government. Although *daikan* were appointed by both the shōguns and the *daimyō,* the term referred particularly to the low-ranking Tokugawa vassals who managed many of the direct holdings (TENRYŌ) of the shogunate. By the turn of the 18th century, there were about 50 *daikan,* most of them senior Tokugawa vassals (HATAMOTO) chosen from among the commissioners of finance (KANJŌ BUGYŌ). They supervised police and judicial matters, promoted agriculture, pro-

tected natural resources, guided the people morally, and, above all, collected taxes. After the shogunate's fall at the time of the Meiji Restoration of 1868, the office of *daikan* was abolished.

Dai kanwa jiten 大漢和辞典

Chinese-Japanese character dictionary compiled by MOROHASHI TETSUJI; 12 volumes with index, published 1955–60. The largest of its kind, the work lists 50,000 head entries and 520,000 compounds. An abridged edition was published in 1966–68 and a revised version in 1989–90. See also DICTIONARIES.

Daiken Trade & Industry Co, Ltd 大建工業（株）

(Daiken Kōgyō). Company engaged in the manufacture and sale of construction and industrial materials. Incorporated in 1945. It exports its products to Asia, the Middle East, Europe, and the United States. It has also branched out into the housing industry through Daiken Home Co, its subsidiary firm. Sales for the fiscal year ending March 1991 totaled ¥184.7 billion (US $1.3 billion), and the company was capitalized at ¥13.1 billion (US $95.5 million) in the same year. Headquarters are in Ōsaka.

Daikin Industries, Ltd ダイキン工業（株）

(Daikin Kōgyō). Company engaged principally in the manufacture of large-size airconditioning equipment for office use; also produces oil-pressure gauges and chemical products. A member of the Sumitomo group of companies, Daikin was incorporated in 1934. Its research and development programs include cryogenics, computer graphics, and robotics. It has overseas subsidiaries in Belgium, Australia, and Singapore. Sales for the fiscal year ending March 1991 totaled ¥344.1 billion (US $2.5 billion), and the company was capitalized at ¥27.7 billion (US $201.9 million). Headquarters are in Ōsaka.

Daikō Advertising, Inc （株）大広

(Daikō). Advertising and marketing agency. Incorporated in 1944. It is engaged in the planning, marketing, and production of ad-

Daimonji Okuribi This late-summer event in Kyōto, held at the end of the Bon Festival, is known for its huge mountainside bonfire in the shape of the character *dai* ("great").

vertisements and advertising campaigns. Sales for the fiscal year ending March 1991 totaled ¥174.5 billion (US $1.3 billion), and capitalization in the same year stood at ¥1.9 billion (US $13.9 million). Headquarters are in Ōsaka.

Daikokuten 大黒天

The god of wealth. Also known as Daikoku or as Mahakara, from the Sanskrit Mahākāla. In India, Mahākāla was a god who fought the forces of evil. He was believed to be especially devoted to the Three Treasures (J: Sambō; Buddha, the Law, and the Priesthood). He is said to have been introduced to Japan by the priest SAICHŌ, who subsequently dedicated a shrine to him at Mt. Hiei outside Kyōto. Since Daikokuten's name is homophonous with an alternate reading of the ideograms for ŌKUNINUSHI NO MIKOTO, a god of the Shintō pantheon, the two have become confused. Daikokuten came to be regarded, along with EBISU, as one of the most important of the so-called SEVEN DEITIES OF GOOD FORTUNE (Shichifukujin). With Ebisu, he is venerated as the tutelary deity of the kitchen. Daikokuten is usually represented as wearing a black hat with a round crown, holding a wish-granting mallet in his right hand, and carrying a big bag slung over his left shoulder.

Daikokuya Kōdayū 大黒屋光太夫

(1751–1828). Japanese seaman who spent several years in Russia during the period of NATIONAL SECLUSION. A native of Ise Province (now part of Mie Prefecture), Kōdayū was captain of the ship *Shinshō maru* when it was blown off course in 1783 and cast up on Amchitka Island in the Aleutians. Kōdayū traveled to St. Petersburg for an audience with Catherine II. He returned to Japan in 1792 with the Russian envoy Adam LAXMAN. For his violation of the Tokugawa shogunate's seclusion policy he was sentenced to house arrest for life in Edo (now Tōkyō). Kōdayū's information on the outside world was compiled by shogunate scholars, including KATSURAGAWA HOSHŪ, in *Hokusa bunryaku* (1794).

daikon → radishes

Daikuhara Gintarō 大工原銀太郎

(1868–1934). Agrochemist and educator. Born in what is now Nagano Prefecture. After graduating from Tōkyō University, he entered the Agricultural Experiment Station of the Ministry of Agriculture and Commerce, where he did outstanding studies on the analysis, improvement, and distribution of acid soils in Japan. Called Daikuhara acidity, the measuring method and unit he invented to determine the acidity of soil with potassium chloride was utilized widely.

Successively president of Kyūshū University and of Dōshisha University in his later years, he was well known as an educator. He was the author of *Dojōgaku kōgi* (1920, Lectures in Soil Science).

Daikyō, Inc ［株]大京

(Daikyō). Real estate company engaged in construction of condominiums and office buildings and in property development projects. Incorporated in 1964. Daikyō has long been Japan's leading builder of condominiums. Its overseas operations began in 1972 with the establishment of Daikyō Australia Pty, Ltd, through which Daikyō has provided consulting services for several major property development projects, hotels, and leisure facilities in Australia and New Zealand. Sales for the fiscal year ending March 1991 totaled ¥705.9 billion (US $5.1 billion), and capitalization stood at ¥70.1 billion (US $510.9 million). Headquarters are in Tōkyō.

Daimaru, Inc ［株]大丸

(Daimaru). Department store company based in the Kansai region. The Daimaru organization includes supermarkets, specialty stores, and related trading, marketing, and manufacturing enterprises. Established as a clothing store in Kyōto in 1717. It has 7 department stores in Japan under its direct management, 10 affiliated department stores, and a group of department stores handling Daimaru's original brand goods throughout the country. It established a store in Hong Kong in 1960 and since then has expanded its operations to Thailand, France, and Singapore. Sales for the fiscal year ending February 1991 totaled ¥606.6 billion (US $4.6 billion), of which clothing accounted for 36 percent; foodstuffs, 17 percent; household goods, 15 percent; sundries, 14 percent; and other products, 18 percent. The company was capitalized at ¥20.3 billion (US $155.6 million) in the same year. Headquarters are in Ōsaka.

Daimonji Okuribi 大文字送り火

Also called Daimonji Yaki. An event held annually on 16 August, which features an enormous bonfire on the side of the mountain DAIMONJIYAMA on the eastern edge of Kyōto. After sunset pine branches, laid out in the shape of the Chinese character *dai* (meaning "great"), are set on fire. Within minutes on other mountains surrounding the city, four other fires are lit in the shape of a smaller *dai*, a boat, the characters for the word *myōhō* (referring to Buddha's law), and a *torii* (Shintō gateway). Daimonji Yaki is the most famous of the *okuribi* bonfires lit in many regions to bid farewell to the souls of ancestors at the end of the BON FESTIVAL.

Daimonjiyama 大文字山

Hill in the eastern section of Kyōto. It is famous for its fire-lighting ceremony (DAIMONJI OKURIBI) held annually on 16 August, the day of the BON FESTIVAL, to send off the souls of the deceased. Height: 466 m (1,529 ft).

daimyō 大名

A generic term applied to the largest of the landholding military lords in premodern Japan. In the term, *dai* means large and *myō* stands for *myōden* (literally, "name land"), meaning private land. Lesser holders of name land were sometimes referred to as *shōmyō*. The term appears in 11th-century documents in reference to civil as well as military landholders, but by the end of the

16th century it came to be exclusively attached to military lords whose lands produced not less than 10,000 *koku* (1 *koku* = 180 liters or 5 US bushels) of grain per year.

Early History——The Japanese military aristocracy (*buke* or SAMURAI) had a lengthy history going back to the mid-Heian period (794–1185). With the establishment of the KAMAKURA SHOGUNATE (1192–1333), provincial military houses acquired titles such as JITŌ (land steward) or SHUGO (military governor) from the shōgun. As leaders among the local military aristocracy obtained proprietary rights over increasing amounts of land and attracted increasing numbers of military followers, they emerged as daimyō in the literal sense of the term. The widespread fighting and general political instability that marked the years between the fall of the Kamakura authority in 1333 and the stabilization of the MUROMACHI SHOGUNATE (1338–1573) in 1392 saw a number of military families establish themselves as dominant figures in the provinces.

Under the Muromachi shogunate, *shugo* were given jurisdiction over one or more provinces, although often they held little of the land in the province to which they were assigned, and might have their primary holdings in another province. The *shugo* were able to exploit certain traditional provincewide taxation rights. They also settled land disputes and divided the spoils after military actions. As the *shugo* added to their holdings and converted an increasing number of local gentry into their direct vassals, they became provincial magnates in their own right and emerged as what modern historians have called SHUGO DAIMYŌ. Such were the 15th-century HOSOKAWA, UESUGI, TAKEDA, TOKI, SHIBA, Isshiki, KYŌGOKU, YAMANA, HATAKEYAMA, ŌUCHI, ŌTOMO, and SHIMAZU families.

With the ŌNIN WAR (1467–77) the stability of the shōgun/*shugo* relationship was broken. Most *shugo daimyō* of this period were destroyed and were supplanted by what historians have called SENGOKU DAIMYŌ. These new daimyō built their domains by accretion through military action, so that all land within them was held either directly or in fief by pledged vassals. Although their holdings might be smaller than those of the *shugo*, the land was held more securely.

Sengoku daimyō built CASTLE TOWNS in their domains from which they could control their vassals—themselves for the most part petty castle holders—and the villages that served as their land base. They issued their own laws (BUNKOKUHŌ). The most powerful of the Sengoku daimyō claimed the right of local governance based on having demonstrated their right to rule by their ability to bring law and order to the domains. Such were the Later Hōjō (see HŌJŌ FAMILY), Takeda, Uesugi, IMAGAWA, ASAI, Ukita, CHŌSOKABE, MŌRI, Ōtomo, RYŪZŌJI, and Shimazu families.

It was upon this condition of extreme territorial decentralization that military unification was imposed, first by ODA NOBUNAGA and then by TOYOTOMI HIDEYOSHI. Under Nobunaga and Hideyoshi the daimyō extended their capacity to govern their domains at the same time that they were forced to yield some of their autonomy to the national hegemon.

Daimyō and the Bakuhan System——It remained for TOKUGAWA IEYASU to institutionalize what historians have called the BAKUHAN SYSTEM of government, one that rested on a strong national authority (the shogunate or *bakufu*) set above the daimyō domains

Patterns of Land Administration under the Tokugawa Shogunate, ca 1644

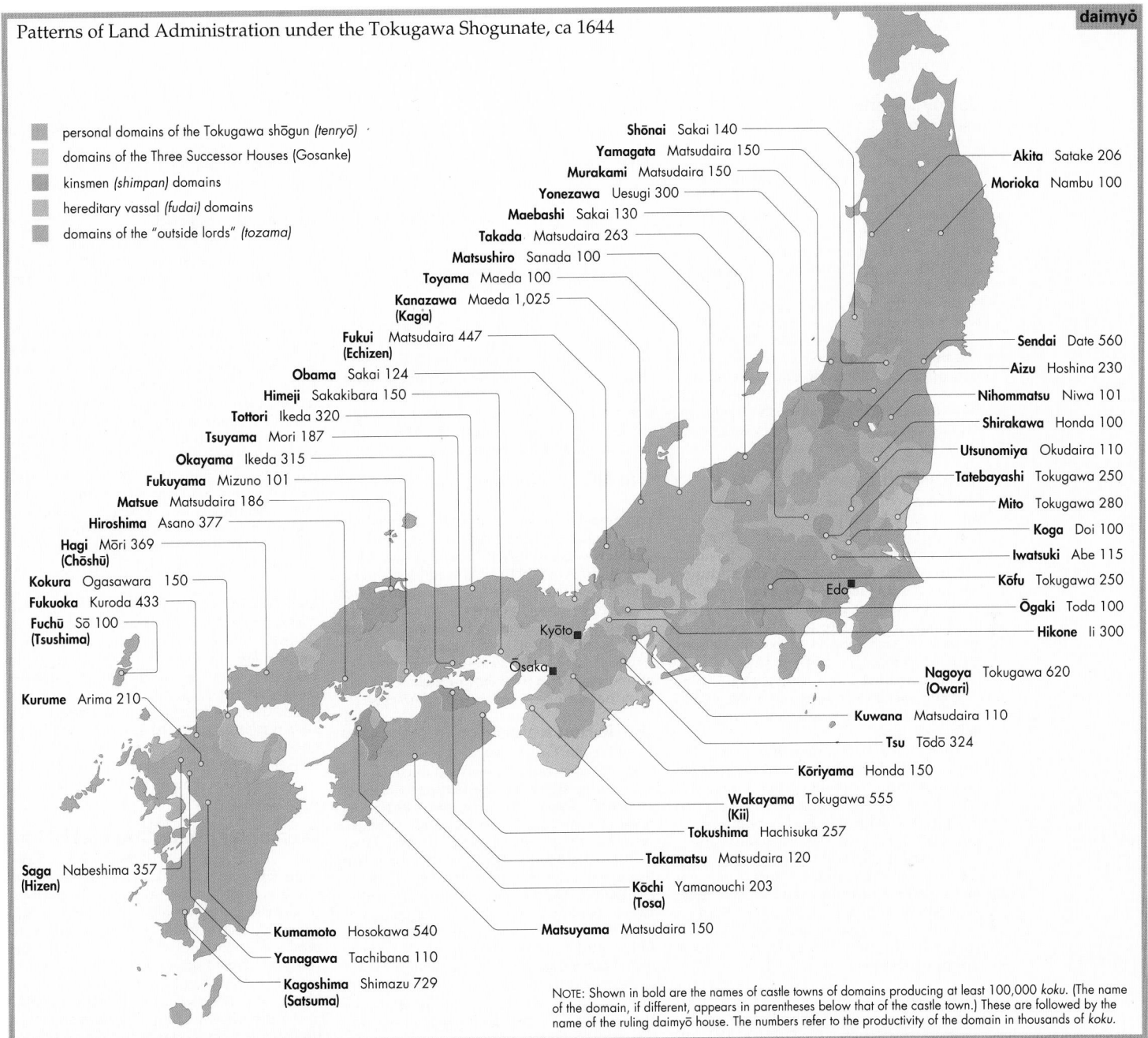

- ▨ personal domains of the Tokugawa shōgun (tenryō)
- ▨ domains of the Three Successor Houses (Gosanke)
- ▨ kinsmen (shimpan) domains
- ▨ hereditary vassal (fudai) domains
- ▨ domains of the "outside lords" (tozama)

Shōnai Sakai 140
Yamagata Matsudaira 150
Murakami Matsudaira 150
Yonezawa Uesugi 300
Maebashi Sakai 130
Takada Matsudaira 263
Matsushiro Sanada 100
Toyama Maeda 100
Kanazawa (Kaga) Maeda 1,025
Fukui (Echizen) Matsudaira 447
Obama Sakai 124
Himeji Sakakibara 150
Tottori Ikeda 320
Tsuyama Mori 187
Okayama Ikeda 315
Fukuyama Mizuno 101
Matsue Matsudaira 186
Hiroshima Asano 377
Hagi (Chōshū) Mōri 369
Kokura Ogasawara 150
Fukuoka Kuroda 433
Fuchū (Tsushima) Sō 100
Kurume Arima 210
Saga (Hizen) Nabeshima 357
Kumamoto Hosokawa 540
Yanagawa Tachibana 110
Kagoshima (Satsuma) Shimazu 729

Akita Satake 206
Morioka Nambu 100
Sendai Date 560
Aizu Hoshina 230
Nihommatsu Niwa 101
Shirakawa Honda 100
Utsunomiya Okudaira 110
Tatebayashi Tokugawa 250
Mito Tokugawa 280
Koga Doi 100
Iwatsuki Abe 115
Kōfu Tokugawa 250
Ōgaki Toda 100
Hikone Ii 300
Nagoya (Owari) Tokugawa 620
Kuwana Matsudaira 110
Tsu Tōdō 324
Kōriyama Honda 150
Wakayama (Kii) Tokugawa 555
Tokushima Hachisuka 257
Takamatsu Matsudaira 120
Kōchi (Tosa) Yamanouchi 203
Matsuyama Matsudaira 150

Edo ■ Kyōto ■ Ōsaka ■

NOTE: Shown in bold are the names of castle towns of domains producing at least 100,000 koku. (The name of the domain, if different, appears in parentheses below that of the castle town.) These are followed by the name of the ruling daimyō house. The numbers refer to the productivity of the domain in thousands of koku.

(han). Under the TOKUGAWA SHOGUNATE (1603–1867) both the national powers of the hegemon (now the shōgun) and the local powers of the daimyō were further extended. The status and form of the daimyō domain within the *bakuhan* system continued to evolve and did not reach full development until the early years of the 18th century. It is at that point that historians apply the term *kinsei* (early modern) to the daimyō domain. As the final product in the evolution of the daimyō system of local rule, the *kinsei* daimyō domain differed from its predecessors in being much more systematically centralized and responsive to the daimyō's authority.

Daimyō of the Edo period (1600–1868) were classified by size, resources, and the history of their relationship to the shogunal house as kinsmen (SHIMPAN), hereditary vassals (FUDAI), or allies called "outside lords" (TOZAMA). All daimyō were sworn vassals of the shōgun, from whom they received their patents of investiture to their domain.

The daimyō under the *bakuhan* system were granted certain rights of autonomy, but there were also limitations on their freedom. Daimyō were given free administration of their domains, including rights of taxation, law enforcement, criminal justice, and the maintenance of a domain army. In return they recognized certain responsibilities: absolute loyalty to the shōgun, adherence to the shōgun's basic laws, the provision of military services on demand, the fulfillment of periodic demands by the shōgun for assistance in the construction of castles and other public works, and above all the peaceful administration of the domain.

All daimyō came under the provisions of the Laws for the Military Houses (BUKE SHO-HATTO), issued first by Ieyasu in 1615 and subsequently revised several times. The code eventually included provisions against the practice of Christianity and the building of ocean-going vessels, and the requirement of SANKIN KŌTAI (alternate year or half-year attendance at the shōgun's court in Edo [now Tōkyō]). Although the *sankin kōtai* made for a uniform and cosmopolitan way of life among the daimyō, the cost of maintaining two residences and of traveling in state became a heavy drain on daimyō finances, a situation the shogunate encouraged.

Decline—The story of the daimyō under the *bakuhan* system and the conditions cre-

ated by the Tokugawa Great Peace is one of early institutional consolidation leading to eventual political and economic weakness. During the first century of the Edo period the daimyō moved rapidly to consolidate their bureaucratic control over their domains, but after 1800 they were plagued by social and economic problems. The shogunate and most daimyō were seriously in debt, and countermeasures often brought daimyō and shogunate interests into conflict.

As political activists emerged among the samurai retinues of the larger domains, they proceeded to use their daimyō as figureheads to work for the destruction of the shogunate and the creation of a national state structure. In 1868 once the "return to imperial government" (MEIJI RESTORATION) was promulgated, the daimyō and their domains were quickly discarded. In 1871 they were replaced with a system of 75 prefectures governed by officials appointed by the central government (see PREFECTURAL SYSTEM, ESTABLISHMENT OF). The former daimyō became a pensioned nobility residing in Tōkyō.

daimyō loans　　　　　　大名貸

(*daimyōgashi*). Cash loans by wealthy merchants to DAIMYŌ (domainal lords) during the Edo period (1600–1868). Because of frequent requisitions by the shogunate and the expense of living in Edo (now Tōkyō) in alternate years (see SANKIN KŌTAI), many of the daimyō experienced financial difficulties throughout the period, especially after the mid-17th century. Since daimyō sometimes reneged on their loans, bankrupting their creditors, the merchants protected themselves by demanding security and charging extremely high interest rates. The interest was usually collected in rice, the staple crop and principal source of domainal income. These merchants, known as KAKEYA and *kuramoto*, came to control much of domainal finance as debts increased. See also KŌNOIKE FAMILY; KURAYASHIKI; RYŌGAESHŌ.

daimyō processions　　　　大名行列

(*daimyō gyōretsu*). The long train or procession of vassals and servants that accompanied daimyō on their annual or biannual journeys to attend the Tokugawa shōgun at Edo (now Tōkyō; see SANKIN KŌTAI) during the Edo period (1600–1868). The size of the entourage was a mark of daimyō status, but the shogunate tried to limit the number of persons in each retinue by issuing specific regulations fixing numbers in proportion to official domainal size (OMOTEDAKA). During the 17th and early 18th centuries the processions of major daimyō numbered in the thousands.

The procession consisted of units of pikemen, mounted and unmounted swordsmen, banner carriers, KARŌ and other domain officials with some of their own vassals and servants, the daimyō in his palanquin (KAGO) surrounded by a variety of personal attendants, extra palanquin carriers (*rokushaku*), porters, and then rearguard units of samurai and servants. The routes and timing of these processions were carefully systematized. A network of inns developed on the major highways to accommodate these large groups of travelers.

Dainichi　　　　　　　大日

(literally, "Great Sun"; Skt: Mahāvairocana; also known in Japanese as Dainichi Nyorai). The Dharmakāya or Cosmic Buddha; the focus of devotion in ESOTERIC BUDDHISM. Dainichi is a further development of the Buddha Vairocana (J: Birushana Butsu). Esoteric Buddhist teachings (*mikkyō*) are taken to be the teaching of Dainichi. He is the principle, or the essence, of the universe and all phenomena are embraced in him; Dainichi is thus the Buddha of beginningless and endless ultimate reality. The realms KONGŌKAI (Diamond or Thunderbolt Realm; Skt: Vajradhātu) and TAIZŌKAI (Womb or Matrix Realm; Skt: Garbhadhātu) manifest the dual aspects of Dainichi. The first symbolizes the manifestation of his wisdom, and the second represents the world of his eternal and all-embracing enlightenment.

Dai Nihon chimei jisho
　　　　　　　　　大日本地名辞書

A geographical dictionary of place names written by the polymath YOSHIDA TŌGO. Started in 1895, it was published between 1900 and 1907. It is made up of 11 volumes with some 40,000 entries. One of the unique features of the work is that Yoshida drew extensively on ancient documents for his entries on towns, villages, cities, famous shrines and temples, and historical sites.

Dai Nihon enkai yochi zenzu
　　　　　　　　大日本沿海輿地全図

A collection of 225 maps by INŌ TADATAKA covering all of Japan and based on an actual survey of its coasts. Generally known as "the Inō maps." From 1800 to 1816 Inō surveyed almost all of Japan's seacoasts and inland areas, making the first maps of the entire country. After Inō's death, TAKAHASHI KAGEYASU collected the maps and completed them in 1821. The maps are the first in Japan to record longitude and latitude and also list in detail names of domains, shogunal land, temples, shrines, towns, and villages. They are valued for their aesthetic quality as well as their accuracy and until the 1880s were used as models for mapmaking.

Dai Nihon kokugo jiten
　　　　　　　　　大日本国語辞典

Japanese-language dictionary compiled by UEDA KAZUTOSHI and Matsui Kanji (1863–1945). It was published in four volumes between 1915 and 1919, followed by a single-volume edition in 1952. Containing over 200,000 entries, it became the standard work for editors of later dictionaries. Though often compared to DAIGENKAI, it is distinguished by its cautious treatment of etymologies and its policy of including only information of unquestioned accuracy.

Dai Nihon komonjo　　　大日本古文書

(Archives of Great Japan). A vast compilation of historical documents published as a continuing series by the HISTORIOGRAPHICAL INSTITUTE, TŌKYŌ UNIVERSITY, since 1901. The first of its three parts, *hennen monjo* (annals), consists of chronologically edited documents from 685 to 780, most of which had been preserved in the SHŌSŌIN repository at the temple Tōdaiji. The second part, *iewake monjo*, contains various historical materials kept by *daimyō* and other families, monasteries, and temples. The third part, *bakumatsu gaikoku kankei monjo*, is a collection of chronologically compiled documents from 1853 to 1860, relating to the diplomacy of the last days of the Tokugawa shogunate. See also DAI NIHON SHIRYŌ.

Dai Nihon shi　　　　　　大日本史

(History of Great Japan). A history of Japan compiled at the behest of TOKUGAWA MITSUKUNI, *daimyō* of the Mito domain (now part of Ibaraki Prefecture). The 397-volume work was begun in 1657 and completed in 1906. Written in classical Chinese (*kambun*) and following the format of the official Chinese histories, it covers the years from the accession of JIMMU, Japan's legendary first emperor, to the reign (1382–1412) of Emperor GO-KOMATSU. The work is divided into four sections: the *hongi* (basic annals) describe imperial careers; the *retsuden* (biographies) contain the lives of court ministers, shogunate officials, and other eminent people; the *shi* (treatises) contain information on Shintō, the KOKUGUN SYSTEM, rites and ceremonies, and punishments; and the *hyō* (tables) list civil and military ranks and offices. Great care was taken in the selection, verification, and documentation of sources, setting an unprecedentedly high standard for historical compilation.

Mitsukuni's primary purpose in commissioning the history was to define the correct relationship between ruler and subject from a Neo-Confucian point of view (see SHUSHIGAKU). The work reinterpreted the status of important historical rulers and gave moral force to the proimperial movement at the end of the Edo period (1600–1868) that led to the MEIJI RESTORATION. See also MITO SCHOOL.

Dai Nihon shiryō　　　　大日本史料

(Historical Materials of Great Japan). Monumental collection of source materials on Japanese history in the process of being compiled at the HISTORIOGRAPHICAL INSTITUTE, TŌKYŌ UNIVERSITY. By March 1989, 319 volumes of these materials had been published, the first of which appeared in 1901. The work is intended to provide a thorough and comprehensive chronological documentation of the events of Japanese history from 887, the last year covered by the ancient RIKKOKUSHI (Six National Histories), to the Meiji Restoration of 1868. Each section begins with a brief summary of an event, followed by the annotated texts of pertinent documents. Marginal notes supply the gist of important documents, access to which is further facilitated by a summary index, *Shiryō sōran* (17 vols, 1923–63).

Dai Nippon Fujinkai　　　大日本婦人会

(Great Japan Women's Society). National organization designed to mobilize all women to support Japan's war effort. It was formed in 1942 through the government-sponsored merger of three existing women's associations: the DAI NIPPON KOKUBŌ FUJINKAI, the AIKOKU FUJINKAI, and the Dai Nippon Rengō Fujinkai. It promoted patriotism, aid for soldiers and their families, and the collection of scrap materials. The group dissolved as the war ended.

Dainippon Ink & Chemicals, Inc
　　　　　　　大日本インキ化学工業[株]

(Dainippon Inki Kagaku Kōgyō). Chemical manufacturer producing ink, resins, plastics, construction materials, machinery, and chemical, petrochemical, and biochemical products. Incorporated in 1937. In 1952 the company joined with Reichhold Chemicals, Inc, of the United States to form a joint affiliate, and the two firms merged in 1962 under the current name. The company has a total of 146 overseas subsidiaries in 35 countries. Sales for the fiscal year ending March 1991 totaled ¥505.2 billion (US $3.7 billion), of which resins accounted for 27 percent; ink, 26 percent; chemicals, 14 percent; and other products, 33 percent. The company was capitalized at ¥80.8 billion (US $588.9 million) in the same year. Headquarters are in Tōkyō.

Dai Nippon Kokubō Fujinkai
　　　　　　　　大日本国防婦人会

(National Defense Women's Association). Patriotic women's organization. Formed in 1932, soon after the 1931 beginning of the MANCHURIAN INCIDENT, it was reorganized in 1934 with the merger of related groups. Its main activities were sending off soldiers to the front, tending the wounded, and aiding families of war dead. Led by Mutō Nobuko, its governing board consisted of wives of military officers; its membership was more open than that of the more elite AIKOKU FUJINKAI. Between 1934 and 1941 it grew to 10 million members. In 1942 the government merged it with the Aikoku Fujinkai and other women's groups to form the DAI NIPPON FUJINKAI in an attempt to mobilize women for Japan's war effort.

Dai Nippon Kokusuikai 大日本国粋会

(Great Japan National Essence Society). A major pre–World War II right-wing organization formed in 1919 by Nishimura Isaburō with the support of TOKONAMI TAKEJIRŌ, then the home minister. Apprehensive of political liberalism (see TAISHŌ DEMOCRACY), the society followed an emperor-centered philosophy and advocated "proper guidance of public thought" (i.e., opposition to socialism) and "reconciliation of labor and management." Through SUZUKI KISABURŌ, who became its head in 1926, the society had ties with the ruling political party, the Rikken Seiyūkai. The society's members frequently resorted to violence, as in the 1924 Nara clash with members of the Suiheisha, a national group that sought to abolish discrimination against outcastes. The Kokusuikai, with a membership of 600,000, was dissolved at the end of World War II. See also RIGHT WING.

Dainippon Pharmaceutical Co, Ltd
大日本製薬［株］

(Dainippon Seiyaku). Pharmaceutical manufacturer of chemotherapeutic, circulatory, and nervous system agents. Incorporated in 1897. The firm distributes antifungal agents in 14 countries. Sales for fiscal year ending March 1991 totaled ¥105.2 billion (US $766.8 million). The company was capitalized at ¥13.4 billion (US $97.7 million) in the same year. Headquarters are in Ōsaka.

Dai Nippon Printing Co, Ltd
大日本印刷［株］

(Dai Nippon Insatsu). Known internationally by its abbreviation DNP, Dai Nippon Printing is the largest comprehensive printing company in the world. The company was founded in 1876 as Shūeisha. Dai Nippon's range of printed products includes publications (books and magazines), sales promotion materials (product catalogs, posters, etc), packaging (paper, film, plastic, and other materials), interior decorating materials (designs printed on metal, wood, etc), and business forms and securities. It also produces such precision electronic components as shadow masks for color television tubes and photo masks for integrated circuits. The company has a nationwide network of sales organizations and 70 affiliates. Overseas it has subsidiaries in Hong Kong, Singapore, Jakarta, New York, Sydney, Düsseldorf, and London. Sales in the fiscal year ending March 1991 totaled ¥1.0 trillion (US $7.3 billion). The company was capitalized at ¥104.6 billion (US $762.4 million) in the same year. Headquarters are in Tōkyō.

Dai Nippon Rengō Seinendan
大日本連合青年団

(Federation of Youth Groups of Japan). National organization for young men established in April 1925. Like the AIKOKU FUJINKAI (Patriotic Women's Association) and the IMPERIAL MILITARY RESERVISTS' ASSOCIATION, youth associations were an outgrowth of the nationalism that swept Japan after the RUSSO-JAPANESE WAR of 1904–05. In 1925 various youth groups united as the Dai Nippon Rengō Seinendan. In 1941 it was merged with other youth groups to form the Dai Nippon Seishōnendan (Youth and Children's Group of Japan).

Dainippon Screen Mfg Co, Ltd
大日本スクリーン製造［株］

(Dainippon Sukurīn Seizō). Precision machinery maker specializing in image re-production equipment. Incorporated in 1943. The company's products include electronic color scanners, semiconductor-manufacturing equipment, metal meshes for electron tubes, and shadow masks for cathode-ray tubes. The firm has overseas subsidiaries in the United States and Europe and offices in Hong Kong, Singapore, China, and Australia. Sales for the fiscal year ending March 1991 totaled ¥139.6 billion (US $1.0 billion), and capitalization stood at ¥27.4 billion (US $199.7 million). Headquarters are in Kyōto.

Dai Nippon Teikoku 大日本帝国

(Empire of Great Japan). The official name of Japan as prescribed by the CONSTITUTION OF THE EMPIRE OF JAPAN (1889). For diplomatic purposes the designation Nipponkoku (Country of Japan) was used as well. On 18 April 1936 the Ministry of Foreign Affairs announced that henceforth Japan would be called Dai Nippon Teikoku in international agreements, diplomatic credentials, and the like and that the emperor would be referred to as *tennō* ("heavenly sovereign") rather than *kōtei* ("emperor"). Since World War II, the name Dai Nippon Teikoku, with its imperialist overtones, has been completely abandoned, and Nipponkoku (or, more commonly, Nihonkoku) is generally used.

Dai Nippon Teikoku Kempō→
Constitution of the Empire of Japan

Dai Nippon Toryō Co, Ltd
大日本塗料［株］

(Dai Nippon Toryō). Paint manufacturer, producing various industrial paints and lead oxides; incorporated in 1929. Sales for the fiscal year ending March 1991 totaled ¥63.7 billion (US $464.3 million), of which paints accounted for 91 percent, lead chemical products 4 percent, and other products 5 percent. The company was capitalized at ¥6.1 billion (US $44.5 million) in the same year. Headquarters are in Ōsaka.

Daiō Paper Corporation
大王製紙［株］

(Daiō Seishi). Paper and pulp manufacturer. Incorporated in 1943. Sales for the fiscal year ending March 1991 totaled ¥275.4 billion (US $2.0 billion), of which newsprint accounted for 27 percent; printing paper, 34 percent; wrapping paper, 11 percent; sanitary paper, 12 percent; and other products, 16 percent. The company was capitalized at ¥18.3 billion (US $133.4 million) in the same year. Headquarters are in Tōkyō.

Daiōzaki 大王崎
Cape on southeastern Shima Peninsula, Mie Prefecture, central Honshū; part of Ise-Shima National Park. Sea cliffs and rocky reefs characterize its coast. The port of Nagiri is located in the area.

Dai Rakudakan 大駱駝艦
BUTŌ (avant-garde dance) troupe founded in 1972 under the leadership of Maro Akaji (b 1943). Dai Rakudakan took the principles of *butō* as laid down by HIJIKATA TATSUMI—the purposeful degradation of the human image to lower forms of existence, the use of inherited folk styles of movement—and introduced a strong element of spectacle into *butō* performance. Dai Rakudakan spawned a number of other *butō* groups, such as SANKAI JUKU, Sebi, Byakkosha, and Dance Love Machine.

dairi 内裏
(inner palace). In premodern times, the area inside the palace grounds within which the emperor resided. Also called *kinri* or *kinchū*. Usually comprised of a set of buildings—the Shishinden, or main ceremonial hall, where the emperor conducted affairs of state; the Seiryōden, his living quarters; and the Jōneiden, the principal residence of the emperor's consorts and ladies-in-waiting—which were linked into a rectilinear compound connected by corridors and galleries. Surrounding the *dairi* were the palace grounds, referred to as the *daidairi*, in which the buildings containing the principal government offices and ministries were located. Palace complexes employing this basic arrangement were built at several different sites, including FUJIWARAKYŌ and HEIJŌKYŌ, before the imperial capital finally settled at HEIANKYŌ (now Kyōto). The *dairi* of the Heian Palace was destroyed by fire several times in the course of the Heian period (794–1185), forcing the emperors to use the mansions of high-ranking court nobles as temporary residences (known as the *satodairi*). By the end of the Heian period, residence in one or another of these *satodairi* had become the norm, and the *dairi* itself was used only for ceremonial purposes. In the Kamakura period (1185–1333), the *dairi* of the Heian Palace burned once again; it was not rebuilt. A mansion known as the Tsuchimikado Higashi no Tōindono, one of many *satodairi* employed by the emperors, eventually became established as a permanent *dairi* during the Northern and Southern Courts period (1337–92) and is the predecessor of the present KYŌTO IMPERIAL PALACE (Kyōto Gosho). This site was the residence of the emperors until the imperial family moved to Tōkyō in 1869 following the Meiji Restoration of 1868.

dairi 代理
(agency). In Japanese law, a system whereby one person (the agent) performs a JURISTIC ACT or acts in the name of a second person (the principal) and the effect of these acts is attributed directly to the principal (CIVIL CODE, art. 99). Agency is not recognized, however, with regard to juristic acts such as marriage that require that the principal form the requisite intent.

Voluntary agency (*nini dairi*) is created by a grant of agency (*dairiken juyo*) from the principal to the agent and is based on contractual relations. Statutory agency (*hōtei dairi*) is created by law in cases where the agency is not or cannot be based on the intent of the principal. Such agency can be based on the parent-child relationship (parental authority; guardianship) or be created by the appointment of a steward over an absentee's property or of an administrator or executor.

Daisen 大山
Double conical stratovolcano in western Tottori Prefecture, western Honshū; the highest peak in the Daisen Volcanic Mountain Group. Also called the Mt. Fuji of Hōki after the name of a former province. It is the habitat of birds and animals belonging to both the frigid and temperate zones. Daisenji, a temple of the Tendai sect of Buddhism, is located here. Daisen is at the center of the Daisen-Oki National Park. Height: 1,729 m (5,673 ft).

Daisen-Oki National Park

1 A view of the rugged coastline of Nishinoshima, the westernmost of the Oki Islands, which served as a place of exile for two emperors.

2 An autumn view of the richly forested peaks of Daisen. The remains of an 8th-century Buddhist temple are located on this conical volcano's lower slopes.

Daisen-Oki National Park

大山隠岐国立公園

(Daisen-Oki Kokuritsu Kōen). Situated in western Honshū, in Shimane, Tottori, and Okayama prefectures. The focus of the park is DAISEN, a conical volcano in the east with forests of maple, Japanese oak (*nara*), Japanese beech (*buna*), red pine (*akamatsu*), and a species of dwarf creeping yew (*daisen kyaraboku*). Stretching south from the volcano is HIRUZEN KŌGEN, a highland with peaks over 1,000 m (3,300 ft). In the west is the extinct volcano SAMBESAN. To the north between Sambesan and Daisen is the hilly SHIMANE PENINSULA, lying parallel to the Honshū coast and joined to it on the west by the IZUMO PLAIN, near Japan's oldest Shintō shrine, the IZUMO SHRINE. The peninsula's western tip, HINOMISAKI, is famed for the Hinomisaki Shrine and for its beautiful stretch of coast, rivaled only by that of the eastern tip, MIHONOSEKI, the location of the Miho Shrine. The OKI ISLANDS lie 46 km (29 mi) north of the peninsula. Area: 319 sq km (123 sq mi).

Daisetsuzan

大雪山

Also called Taisetsuzan. A group of volcanic mountains in central Hokkaidō. More than 10 of the volcanoes exceed 2,000 m (6,560 ft). Between the mountains are crater lakes and swamps. The foothills have hot springs and base camps for mountain climbing. Daisetsuzan forms the center of Daisetsuzan National Park. The highest peak in Hokkaidō, Asahidake (2,290 m; 7,513 ft), is located here.

Daisetsuzan National Park

大雪山国立公園

(Daisetsuzan Kokuritsu Kōen). Japan's largest national park, situated in central Hokkaidō amid dense mountains, gorges, rivers, and waterfalls. DAISETSUZAN is a group of volcanoes, most of which exceed 2,000 m (6,560 ft), including Hokkaidō's highest peak, Asahidake (2,290 m; 7,513 ft), in the north. TOKACHIDAKE, an active volcano, lies in the southwest, and ISHIKARIDAKE in the east. The river ISHIKARIGAWA flows through the gorge SŌUNKYŌ, and the river Chūbetsugawa through the gorge TENNINKYŌ. On the southern edge of the park are Lake Nukabira and Lake Shikaribetsu. The forests consist mainly of Yeddo spruce (*ezomatsu*) and Sakhalin fir (*todomatsu*); the park is renowned for its vast alpine meadows. The Asiatic pika, or mouse hare (*nakiusagi*), is found in the region. There are a number of hot-spring resorts. Area: 2,309 sq km (892 sq mi).

Daishin'in → Great Court of Cassation

Daishōwa Paper Mfg Co, Ltd

大昭和製紙[株]

(Daishōwa Seishi). Manufacturer of paper products. It controls a large share of the Japanese market for newsprint, kraft paper, printing paper, and paperboard. Daishōwa was incorporated in 1938 in Shizuoka Prefecture with the merger of five paper manufacturers. In addition to its five domestic pulp, paper, and paperboard mills, the company has been actively expanding its overseas operations in Canada, the United States, and Australia. The company's overseas offices coordinate the purchase of wood chips and wood pulp for consumption at its mills in Japan. Sales for the fiscal year ending March 1991 were ¥353.6 billion (US $2.6 billion). The company was capitalized at ¥26.5 billion (US $193.1 million) in the same year. Headquarters are in Fuji, Shizuoka Prefecture.

Daitō

大東[市]

City 11 km (7 mi) east of the city of Ōsaka. A residential suburb, one of its attractions is the temple Jigenji, popularly known as the Nozaki Kannon. Pop: 126,460.

Dai Tōa Kyōeiken → Greater East Asia Coprosperity Sphere

Daito Gyorui Co, Ltd

大都魚類[株]

(Daito Gyorui). Wholesaler of marine products. Incorporated in 1947. Sales for the fiscal year ending March 1991 totaled ¥207.7 billion (US $1.5 billion), of which frozen fish accounted for 54 percent; fresh fish, 29 percent; and salted and dried fish, 17 percent. The company was capitalized at ¥1.4 billion (US $10.2 million) in the same year. Headquarters are in Tōkyō.

Daitōjuku

大東塾

("Great East Academy"). An ultranationalist organization founded by Kageyama Masaharu (1910–79) in April 1939. Kageyama had joined the rightist group Dai Nihon Seisantō (Japan Production Party), and in 1933 he was arrested in the SHIMPEITAI INCIDENT. After his release Kageyama founded the Daitōjuku school for the study of Shintō and NIHON SHUGI (Japanism). During World War II, the school incurred government opprobrium for its criticism of wartime leaders such as TŌJŌ HIDEKI. On 25 August 1945, 10 days after the defeat of Japan, Kageyama's father Shōhei and 13 other members of the Daitōjuku committed suicide by *harakiri*. The Daitōjuku was reorganized in April 1954 by Kageyama. See also RIGHT WING.

Daitokuji

大徳寺

Head temple of the Daitokuji branch of the RINZAI SECT, located in the Murasakino section of the city of Kyōto. The temple was originally a small monastery built by the ZEN priest SŌHŌ MYŌCHŌ in 1315. In 1325, at the request of the retired emperor Hanazono (1297–1348; r 1308–18), the monastery was converted into a supplication hall for the imperial court. It is said that in 1333 Daitokuji was ranked among the GOZAN (the Five Temples; the ranking system of the most important Zen temples) by Emperor GO-DAIGO, but when the shōgun ASHIKAGA YOSHIMITSU announced a new ranking of the Gozan in 1386, Daitokuji was omitted.

A fire in 1453 destroyed most of the temple buildings. They were reconstructed, but another fire during the ŌNIN WAR (1467–77) ravaged the complex once more. In 1474 IKKYŪ Sōjun was designated by Emperor Go-Tsuchimikado (r 1464–1500) as the head priest of Daitokuji. With the help of merchants of the city of SAKAI in what is now Ōsaka Prefecture, he contributed greatly to its rehabilitation. In 1582 TOYOTOMI HIDEYOSHI buried his predecessor ODA NOBUNAGA at Daitokuji; he also contributed land and built the Sōken'in Hall. Daitokuji was soon fully restored, as several other *daimyō* built temples on its grounds. SEN NO RIKYŪ and KOBORI ENSHŪ also contributed to the cultural development of Daitokuji at this time by building tearooms and tea gardens.

During the Edo period (1600–1868), the temple prospered from its estates. One of the best known of Daitokuji's head priests during the Edo period was TAKUAN SŌHŌ. After the Meiji Restoration (1868) the temple declined; in 1876 it became an independent temple of the Daitokuji branch of the Rinzai Zen sect.

Within Daitokuji there were originally 24 subsidiary temples (*tatchū*); the number increased to about 60 during the Edo period, but today only about 20 remain. The *tatchū* Daisen'in is known for its garden, which features beautiful stones donated by ASHIKAGA YOSHIMASA, as well as for the magnificent wall paintings within the *tatchū*, ascribed to KANŌ MOTONOBU. The South Garden of the *tatchū* Ryūgen'in is said to hold the grave of MURASAKI SHIKIBU, the author of the TALE OF GENJI. The *tatchū* Jukōin is noted for its famous examples of BIRD-AND-FLOWER PAINTING, attributed to KANŌ EITOKU. There are many other important works of art at Daitokuji, among them a painting of KANNON by the Chinese painter Muqi (Mu-ch'i; J:

MOKKEI, 13th century) and a painting of a dragon done by KANŌ TAN'YŪ on the ceiling of the dharma hall (*hōdō*).

Dai-Tōkyō Fire & Marine Insurance Co, Ltd

大東京火災海上保険［株］

(Dai Tōkyō Kasai Kaijō Hoken). Insurance company, incorporated in 1918; assumed its current name in 1949. The firm has overseas subsidiaries in London, New York, Dover (England), and Luxembourg; underwriting agencies in Rotterdam and Athens; and liaison offices in London and New York. Total assets for the fiscal year ending March 1991 reached ¥1.4 trillion (US $10.2 billion). Net premiums for the same year were ¥358.3 billion (US $2.6 billion), and the company was capitalized at ¥57.1 billion (US $416.2 million). Headquarters are in Tōkyō.

Daiwa Bank, Ltd

［株］大和銀行

(Daiwa Ginkō). Major Japanese city bank (*toshi ginkō*). Incorporated in 1918. Daiwa had its origins in the Ōsaka Nomura Bank, the securities division of which became independent in 1925 as NOMURA SECURITIES CO, LTD. Daiwa is the only city bank that deals in both commercial and trust banking (excluding loan trusts). The bank is the top pension-fund manager in Japan, with over ¥4.3 trillion (US $28.3 billion) under management, and is also involved in real estate. Daiwa maintains offices in New York, London, Chicago, Los Angeles, Frankfurt, Hong Kong, Singapore, and Seoul. As of March 1990 assets totaled ¥17.9 trillion (US $117.9 billion), deposits totaled ¥13.6 trillion (US $88.8 billion), and capitalization stood at ¥169.0 billion (US $1.1 billion). Headquarters are in Ōsaka.

Daiwabō Co, Ltd

大和紡績［株］

(Daiwa Bōseki). Company engaged in the manufacture of cotton yarn and cloth, as well as chemical and synthetic fiber and fabrics. Incorporated in 1941. The firm operates joint-venture spinning companies in Indonesia and Brazil. Sales for the fiscal year ending March 1991 totaled ¥75.5 billion (US

$550.3 million), with an export ratio of 4.0 percent. The company was capitalized at ¥18.2 billion (US $132.7 million) in the same year. Headquarters are in Ōsaka.

Daiwa Can Co, Ltd

大和製罐［株］

(Daiwa Seikan). Manufacturer of coffee cans, aerosol cans, plastic containers, and various types of packaging materials. Incorporated in 1950. Part of the Nippon Steel group. The company has furnished can-manufacturing technology to a number of overseas licensees. It maintains eight plants throughout Japan. Sales for the fiscal year ending March 1990 totaled ¥290.3 billion (US $1.9 billion), and capitalization stood at ¥2.4 billion (US $15.7 million). Headquarters are in Tōkyō.

Daiwa House Industry Co, Ltd

大和ハウス工業［株］

(Daiwa Hausu Kōgyō). Manufacturer of steel-reinforced, prefabricated houses. Incorporated in 1947. The company initially erected temporary buildings, but beginning with the production of prefabricated houses, it moved into the housing and land development industries. During the 1970s the company established itself as a major developer of suburban residential complexes, resort facilities, and hotels throughout Japan. The company procures construction materials and machinery through subsidiary firms. Daiwa House has subsidiaries in the United States, Australia, and China. Annual sales for the fiscal year ending March 1991 were ¥802.1 billion (US $5.8 billion), and capitali-

zation stood at ¥73.7 billion (US $537.2 million). Headquarters are in Ōsaka.

Daiwa Securities Co, Ltd

大和証券［株］

(Daiwa Shōken). One of the "Big Four" Japanese securities firms. It was founded in 1902 as a bill broker and incorporated under its present name in 1943. The company engages in underwriting, brokerage, and trading. In 1977 it issued the first Euroyen bonds through the European Investment Bank. Backed by a network of 122 domestic and 30 overseas offices, Daiwa provides a full spectrum of securities, international banking, and other financial services to clients around the world. Revenues for the fiscal year end-

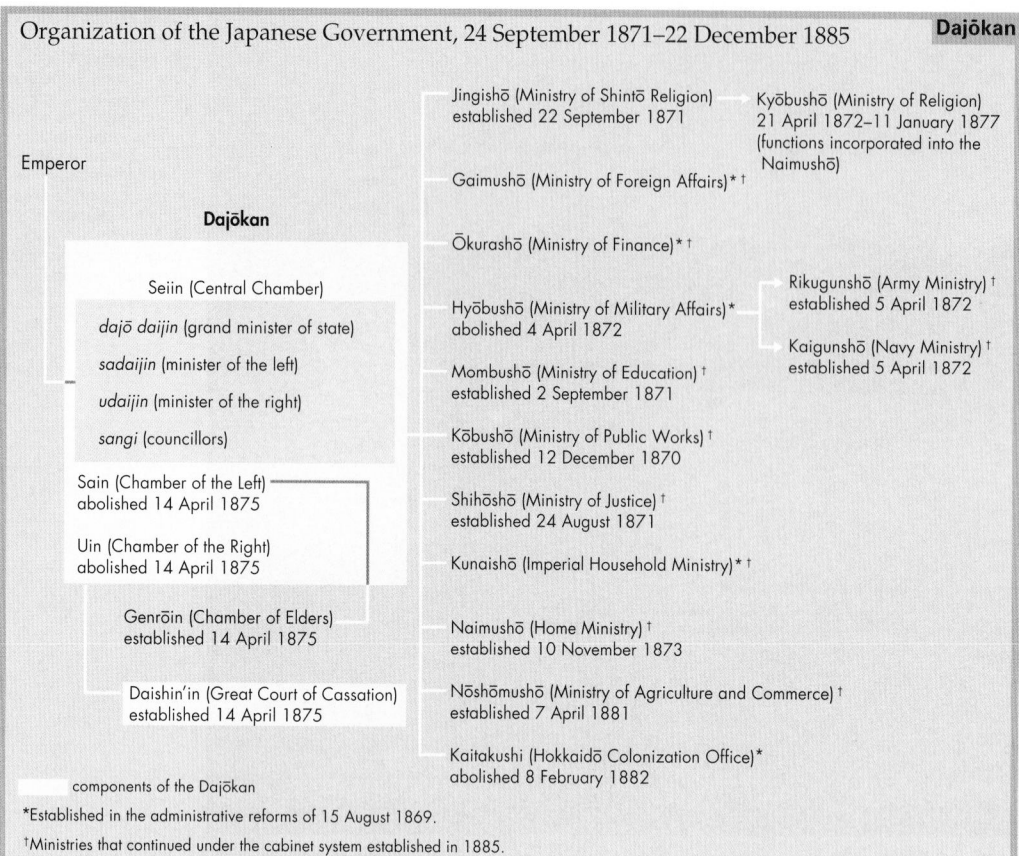

Emperor

Dajōkan

Seiin (Central Chamber)

dajō daijin (grand minister of state)

sadaijin (minister of the left)

udaijin (minister of the right)

sangi (councillors)

Sain (Chamber of the Left)
abolished 14 April 1875

Uin (Chamber of the Right)
abolished 14 April 1875

Genrōin (Chamber of Elders)
established 14 April 1875

Daishin'in (Great Court of Cassation)
established 14 April 1875

Jingishō (Ministry of Shintō Religion)
established 22 September 1871

Kyōbushō (Ministry of Religion)
21 April 1872–11 January 1877
(functions incorporated into the
Naimushō)

Gaimushō (Ministry of Foreign Affairs)* †

Ōkurashō (Ministry of Finance)* †

Hyōbushō (Ministry of Military Affairs)*
abolished 4 April 1872

Rikugunshō (Army Ministry) †
established 5 April 1872

Kaigunshō (Navy Ministry) †
established 5 April 1872

Mombushō (Ministry of Education) †
established 2 September 1871

Kōbushō (Ministry of Public Works) †
established 12 December 1870

Shihōshō (Ministry of Justice) †
established 24 August 1871

Kunaishō (Imperial Household Ministry)* †

Naimushō (Home Ministry) †
established 10 November 1873

Nōshōmushō (Ministry of Agriculture and Commerce) †
established 7 April 1881

Kaitakushi (Hokkaidō Colonization Office)*
abolished 8 February 1882

☐ components of the Dajōkan

*Established in the administrative reforms of 15 August 1869.

†Ministries that continued under the cabinet system established in 1885.

---

ing March 1991 totaled ¥977.4 billion (US $3.5 billion). The company was capitalized at ¥136.9 billion (US $997.8 million) in the same year. Headquarters are in Tōkyō.

Daizōkyō   大蔵経

(Ch: Dacang jing [Ta-ts'ang ching]; "Tripitaka" or "Great Scripture of the Three Baskets"). Also called Issaikyō, "All the Scriptures." The Buddhist canon. Traditionally the Buddhist canon is divided into three sections, or "baskets" (Skt: *tripiṭaka;* J: *sanzō*): sutras (Skt: *sūtra;* J: *kyō*), rules of conduct for monks and nuns (Skt: *vinaya;* J: *ritsu*), and commentaries and other treatises on doctrine (Skt: *abhidharma;* J: *ron*). There are Pali, Chinese, Tibetan, Mongolian, and Japanese editions. The *Taishō shinshū Daizōkyō,* called the Taishō Edition of the Tripitaka (*Taishō Daizōkyō*), was published in Japan from 1924 to 1934. It is the largest edition of the Buddhist canon published to date. Numbering 100 volumes, it contains the Chinese canon, texts written by Japanese monks, scriptures from the caves at Dunhuang (Tun-huang), and iconographies.

Dajōkan   太政官

(Grand Council of State). Also known as Daijōkan or Ōimatsurigoto no Tsukasa. The central administrative organ in the RITSURYŌ SYSTEM of government established in the late 7th and early 8th centuries; also, during the Meiji period (1868–1912), the collective name for the Japanese government between 1868 and 1885. As prescribed by the TAIHŌ CODE (completed 701; effective 702) and the YŌRŌ CODE (effective 757), the Dajōkan was divided into three sections: a policy-making section composed of the *dajō daijin* (grand minister of state), the *sadaijin* (minister of the left), the *udaijin* (minister of the right), and the *dainagon* (great counselors); an administrative section composed of the *sabenkan* (controllers of the left) and *ubenkan* (controllers of the right); and the emperor's

secretariat composed of the *shōnagon* (lesser counselors) and the *geki* (secretaries). The term Dajōkan was normally used in reference to the policy-making section alone. The Jingikan (Office of Shintō Worship), which was in charge of such state festivals as the DAIJŌSAI and the *ōharae* purification rituals (see HARAE), often appears as parallel and equal to the Dajōkan in organizational charts; in fact, it was administered by the policy-making section of the Dajōkan.

The Dajōkan system was modeled on the administrative system of the Tang (T'ang) dynasty (618–907) of China. The Japanese Dajōkan, however, was more powerful than any individual Chinese governmental organ. It could issue orders independently of the emperor, and imperial edicts were either accompanied by written orders (KAMPU) from the Dajōkan or excerpted and incorporated into the Dajōkan's orders. Thus, the Dajōkan (staffed by members of powerful noble families) could limit the emperor's political power.

With the weakening of the *ritsuryō* bureaucratic system early in the Heian period (794–1185), the *kurōdo* (archivists; see KURŌDO-DOKORO) and *benkan* (controllers) gradually took over the functions of the Dajōkan. In 857 the long-vacant post of *dajō daijin* was given to FUJIWARA NO YOSHIFUSA, and as the Fujiwara REGENCY GOVERNMENT came to dominate state affairs, the Dajōkan lost its significance. During the period of warrior rule, from the Kamakura (1185–1333) through the Edo (1600–1868) period, the Dajōkan survived as a part of the vestigial imperial government.

The Early Meiji Dajōkan—The MEIJI RESTORATION of 1868 was ostensibly a return to the political system of the Nara and early Heian periods in which the emperor was the actual, not just titular, ruler. Accordingly, after briefly experimenting with the SANSHOKU system of government, Dajōkan and other ancient terms for government offices were adopted. However, in keeping with the principles in the so-called Constitution of

1868 (SEITAISHO), several attempts were made in the next few years to divide the government into legislative, executive, and judiciary branches along Western lines.

By 1875 the Meiji government had taken the form it was to retain, with minor modifications, for the next decade. The government was still collectively known as the Dajōkan. It was headed by the *dajō daijin* (grand minister of state, or "president"), who was assisted by the *sadaijin* and *udaijin* (ministers of the left and right, or "vice-presidents"). Under their chairmanship the councillors (SANGI), who served concurrently as heads of ministries, met daily to discuss and decide important matters. Decisions were submitted by the presidents to the emperor for approval and then issued as decrees or orders of the Dajōkan.

The result was quite an efficient form of government, since the men who made the decisions in council could immediately implement them in their own ministries. On the other hand, the narrow monopoly of power by 10 or so *sangi,* serving concurrently as ministry heads, aroused considerable envy and suspicion. The failure of the government to fulfill its promise of 1868 to decide all matters by public deliberation led to growing popular agitation from 1875 to 1885 (see FREEDOM AND PEOPLE'S RIGHTS MOVEMENT). In response the government established the GENRŌIN (Chamber of Elders, or "Senate") to review major items of legislation and the Daishin'in (GREAT COURT OF CASSATION) to adjudicate important legal appeals. In December 1885 the Dajōkan was abolished and replaced by the cabinet (*naikaku*) system of government.

Dajōkan satsu   太政官札

The first national paper currency in Japan, issued by the Grand Council of State (DAJŌKAN) in July 1868, immediately following the MEIJI RESTORATION (1868). Proposed by YURI KIMIMASA, the Dajōkan *satsu* (also called *kinsatsu*) appeared in five denominations, and bills with a face value of 48 million *ryō* (US $48 million at the then prevailing exchange rate) were in circulation by 1869. However, acceptance of the bills was slow, and their purchasing power dropped by as much as 20 percent. In 1872 the government issued new bills, and by 1879 the old bills had been withdrawn from circulation.

Dake Hot Spring   岳温泉

(Dake Onsen). Located on the eastern slope of Adatarayama, central Fukushima Prefecture, northern Honshū. An acidic vitriol spring; water temperature 65°C (149°F). A quiet mountain spa at an altitude of 540 m (1,772 ft), it has been designated as a National Health Resort Hot Spring. Climbs up ADATARASAN start here.

damages, compensation for
損害賠償

(*songai baishō*). Compensation in kind or specie for injury to a victim in order that the victim be made whole, i.e., restored to his or her pre-injury status. The right to demand compensation for injury arises when one has been injured by another's failure to perform an obligatory duty or commission of a tort.

With regard to compensation for damage resulting from another's default of an obligatory duty, the CIVIL CODE provides: "Absent an expression of intent to the contrary, the amount of compensation [for damage] shall be determined in specie." This provision is applied *mutatis mutandis* to compensation for damage arising from torts. For example, a medical malpractice suit can be pursued either on a theory that the defendant has failed to perform an obligatory duty or on a tort theory. The two differ in such matters as who bears the burden of proof of negligence (the obligor bears the burden in the former case) and the relevant statute of limitations (it is 10 years in the former case and 3 years in the latter). Judicial precedent holds that either theory may be pursued, i.e., whichever is to the plaintiff's advantage.

Dampatsurei 断髪令

Also known as Sampatsu Dattō Rei. Government ordinance of September 1871 encouraging the common people and former *samurai* (SHIZOKU) to cut the topknot (*chommage*; see HAIRSTYLES) and discard their swords. With the issuance of the HAITOREI ordinance in 1876, former samurai were forbidden to wear swords except on ceremonial occasions.

dams ダム

(*damu*). Dams were used in Japan from ancient times for small-scale farm irrigation, but not until the 20th century did dams for hydroelectric power become important.

History—By around 700 many earthen dams had been constructed in the Kinki region for water reservoirs to be used in connection with paddy rice cultivation. Following the construction of the dam on MANNŌ POND by the monk KŪKAI during the Heian period (794–1185), many more small-scale earthen irrigation dams were built. This pattern of construction remained unchanged until the Meiji period (1868–1912), during which construction technology for concrete dams was imported from the West and dam building in Japan gained impetus from the increased water needs of developing industries. The first concrete dam in Japan was the Nunobiki Dam, a 33.3-meter (109-ft) high gravity dam completed in 1900 on the river Ikutagawa. The dam is still in use. The continued development of dam construction was aimed almost solely at the harnessing of hydroelectric power, and from the 1920s to the early 1940s electric power generation from dams experienced unprecedented growth.

Postwar Dam Construction—After World War II, preparations were made to begin construction of the hydroelectric dam projects abandoned during the war. The completion in 1961 of Japan's highest gravity dam, the OKU TADAMI DAM (157 m; 515 ft), was followed by a succession of dams over 100 meters (328 ft) high. The first Japanese dam in the 150-meter class, the SAKUMA DAM (155.5 m; 510 ft), was completed in 1956. Advances in civil engineering and construction techniques have been applied to rock-fill earthen dams that use several layers of stones, such as the Takase Dam (176 m; 577 ft), completed in 1981. The low cost and high earthquake resistance of this type of dam have contributed to its continued importance. In 1990 there were 2,471 dams over 15 meters (49 ft) high in Japan. Some 1,475 of these were irrigation dams; multipurpose dams (436) and hydroelectric power dams (369) formed the second and third largest categories.

dance, traditional 舞踊

(*buyō*). The general Japanese word for dance is *buyō*, a term written with two Chinese characters: *mai* (also pronounced *bu*), which denotes ancient and medieval dance (until

ca 1600), and *odori* (also pronounced *yō*), which denotes the dances of the Edo period (1600–1868). Thus *mai* implies mainly court dance and upper-class theater dance, while *odori* comprises above all the popular and KABUKI dance forms developed in Edo (now Tōkyō). There is also a great variety of folk and popular regional dances. The tremendous diversity of Japanese traditional dances makes it hard to characterize them simply; however, most are "close dances" with smooth, earthbound movements of lower legs, arms, and head, and they are appreciated more for their aesthetic than for their symbolic meaning. The simplest gestures have to be performed with attention to subtle aesthetic ideals, such as MA, the observed and felt interval between two dance movements or poses.

Origins to the End of the Kamakura Period (1333)—The KOJIKI (712, Records of Ancient Matters), an early historical chronicle, describes a dance performed by the goddess Ame no Uzume to entice the sun goddess AMATERASU ŌMIKAMI out of hiding in the Rock Cave of Heaven. This is the legendary origin of KAGURA, the oldest Japanese dance form. From *kagura*, originally a ritual dance performed by a shamanic priestess, descended all the Shintō shrine dances of later times. Its influence may also be seen in theater dance, particularly that of kabuki.

GIGAKU, a masked religious mime introduced to Japan from the Asian mainland in the early 7th century, was the first foreign music and dance form to take root in Japan. *Gigaku* included a two-man lion dance (SHISHI-MAI), ancestor of all later Japanese lion dances. In the 7th and 8th centuries various other forms of music (called GAGAKU) and dance (called *bugaku*) were introduced at the Japanese court, mainly from Korea and China. Ancient native Japanese dances such as *yamato-mai*, *azuma-asobi*, and GOSE-CHI NO MAI were also classified as *bugaku*. The dancers in *bugaku* usually wear masks, except in the Japanese forms, as well as elaborate and richly colored costumes. Generally the dancers are male, and at least four are needed to perform a dance. *Bugaku* spread to outlying shrines and monasteries and was performed along with local *kagura* and Buddhist ceremonies. It has survived to the present day.

Two other imports from China in the 8th century were *tōka* or "stamping songs," a type of New Year's ritual, and *sangaku*, an acrobatic or circus display modeled on the Chinese *sanyue* (*san-yüeh*). Both were performed at the court. *Sangaku* contributed both to later *gagaku* and to the medieval SARUGAKU and DENGAKU. *Dengaku* was originally a fertility ritual performed in the fields and survives today in the rice-planting songs and dances (*taue odori*) of the Japanese countryside. It later evolved into the street dances that were popular in 16th- and 17th-century Kyōto. From the early 14th century onward there was also a dramatized version, *dengaku* Nō.

One other entertainment was ENNEN, which was associated with Buddhist monas-

teries in the Kamakura (1185–1333) and Muromachi (1333–1568) periods. It was apparently a type of dance-drama, with the dance element uppermost. The repertoire included *chigo-mai* (boys' dances), SHIRABYŌSHI (a court dance-song for young women), and *furyū* (a court dance in the form of a dialogue between the emperor and his minister; several other dance forms were also called FURYŪ). In the Edo period *ennen* virtually disappeared, and it survives today only at certain monasteries and shrines in northern Japan.

Nō and Other Dance Forms of the Medieval Period—In the Kamakura period the most important new form in the performing arts was NŌ drama, which developed out of *sarugaku*. The *sarugaku* performers KAN'AMI Kiyotsugu and his son ZEAMI Motokiyo created a new type of theater, which incorporated elements from both *sarugaku* and *dengaku* and was imbued with a serious Buddhist tone. It emphasized music and dance, particularly through insertion of the *kuse-mai* dance, which had a strong, idiosyncratic rhythm and chantlike melodies. The structure and movements of the *kuse-mai* dance were apparently related to those of *shirabyōshi*. It was gradually changed, but something of its original character may be preserved in the intonation of Nō chant, in the *hiranori* metrical pattern (three syllables chanted to two rhythmic beats), and in the so-called *nidan-guse* sections of certain plays.

Within the structure of a Nō play certain sections are the occasion for a dance. The general name for these is *maigoto*, which constitute one class of *hayashigoto*, pure instrumental music. Dance movements are composed of many *kata* (forms), which vary from school to school. From the actor's point of view no firm distinction can be made between dance and other movements on stage. *Maigoto* proper tend to occur at the climax of a play. Nō dance, like all Nō movements, is controlled and deliberate.

Though it had popular roots Nō became an upper-class entertainment, as did the accompanying KYŌGEN farces. Dance in *kyōgen* is known as *komai* and is said to date from 1349. *Komai* are independent short dances that may be inserted in any *kyōgen*; their *kata* are more realistic than those of Nō.

Another medieval dance form was KŌWAKA-MAI. It evolved from the 15th through the 18th century into a simple narrative dance performed by three men to texts taken from the military romances (GUNKI MONOGATARI) and originally accompanied by two hourglass drums (TSUZUMI) and a flute. Other popular dance forms were *hayashi-mai*, a general name for a variety of folk and festival dances; NEMBUTSU ODORI, a Buddhist in-

dams

1 Rock-fill earthen dams, such as the Miboro Dam in Gifu Prefecture (pictured), are especially suited to earthquake-prone Japan.
2 At 186 meters, the Kurobe Dam in Toyama Prefecture is the highest arch-type dam in Japan.

traditional dance

Japanese dance has taken many forms throughout its history: it has been a celebration of the cycles of agriculture, an expression of religious faith, and a profession requiring years of training. All of these things are reflected in the traditional dances that survive today.

▼ The *kabuki* play *Yoshitsune sembon-zakura* (1747, The Thousand Cherry Trees of Yoshitsune) is well known for its dance scenes.

▲ Kyōto *geisha* and *maiko* (geisha-in-training) perform each spring in the Miyako Odori, a gala dance festival that has been held yearly since 1872.

◀ Bon *odori* dances such as this one held in Tōkyō evolved out of medieval Buddhist chants and folk dances. Today they are performed each summer as entertainment.

cantation dance that influenced many later forms, including BON ODORI (the Bon Festival dance); and *furyū*.

Kabuki and Other Urban Dances of the Edo Period—The earliest dances of kabuki, as performed by female troupes in Kyōto in the early 17th century, were adapted from *nembutsu odori* and from a type of *furyū* called *yayako odori* (or *kaka odori*). *Wakashu kabuki* (young men's kabuki) came into prominence after *onna kabuki* (women's kabuki) was banned in 1629. *Wakashu kabuki* also incorporated *hōka* (acrobatics and juggling) and *kyōgen komai*. *Yarō kabuki*, the adult male troupes that took the place of *wakashu kabuki* in 1652, inherited these elements of *kyōgen* and popular entertainment and gradually added to them stories and techniques taken directly from Nō, from the BUNRAKU puppet theater of the late 17th and 18th centuries, from folk dance, and from other sources. All these are reflected in the immense repertoire of kabuki dance (*kabuki odori*), which today basically preserves a 19th-century art form. However, many plays are no longer performed in their entirety, and it has always been common for dance episodes to be staged as independent units.

Kabuki's movement shows principally the influence of *kyōgen*, bunraku, and folk dance. In contrast to Nō, kabuki dances reflect a taste for gaudy, spectacular, and sensational effects. Two early styles were *tanzen* and *roppō*, used from the late 17th century for boisterous male entrances. The term *shosagoto* (dance style) came to be used for the dances of female impersonators. *Shosagoto* became the most important kind of kabuki dance, differentiated mainly according to the various types of music that accompany it: the lyrical NAGAUTA or more narrative types such as TOKIWAZU-BUSHI, *tomimoto-bushi*, and KIYOMOTO-BUSHI.

Outside the kabuki theater there were many other dance forms, especially in Edo. Older dances, such as the *harugoma* New Year's dance, continued, and the courtesans of the Yoshiwara pleasure quarters and the GEISHA developed their own dances, such as the *niwaka* dance of the Yoshiwara.

Developments since the Meiji Restoration—After 1868 many more Nō dances and themes were introduced into kabuki. More significant was the new dance-drama advanced by TSUBOUCHI SHŌYŌ, which drew on many native traditions but also introduced Western instruments. The dancer Fujikage Shizue (1880–1966) was the leader of the "New Dance" (*shimbuyō*) movement, which gave women the freedom to perform kabuki dances, if not in kabuki itself, at least in dance recitals. This movement also led to a proliferation of dance schools within the old *ryūgi* (school) system, so that today there are some 168, and most of their pupils are women. The leading schools include Fujimaryū, founded by Fujima Kambei (d 1769); Nishikawaryū, founded by Nishikawa Senzō I (d 1756); Hanayagiryū, a Nishikawa offshoot founded in 1849; and Wakayagiryū, started in 1893, a Hanayagi offshoot. Thus, within a traditional framework, Japanese dance continues to flourish, and regional folk dance also remains strong.

danchi   団地

Generic term for housing developments composed of groups of apartment buildings, townhouses, or individual detached units. Depending on its size, a *danchi* may also contain additional facilities such as community centers, parks, clinics, schools, stores, post office branches, and local government offices.

In Japan, land has always been at a pre-

mium, with 73 percent of total land area unsuitable for housing construction. Urbanization and rapid economic growth have also increased the demand for convenient, affordable housing. *Danchi* have proven to be an effective response to this set of conditions.

The first *danchi* built in Japan was an apartment complex in the Daikan'yama district of Tōkyō (see DŌJUNKAI APARTMENTS), constructed as part of the recovery efforts after the TŌKYŌ EARTHQUAKE OF 1923. After World War II, multistory apartment blocks of reinforced concrete were built in large numbers by local government bodies to relieve the housing shortage in major urban areas. In 1955, the Japan Housing Corporation (since 1981 the HOUSING AND URBAN DEVELOPMENT CORPORATION) was created and commenced the development of *danchi* integrating high-rise apartment blocks and various support facilities into large-scale residential complexes. Beginning in the 1960s, local governments and public corporations took the concept of the *danchi* one step further, initiating construction of planned cities on the outskirts of existing urban agglomerations (see TAMA NEW TOWN; SENRI NEW TOWN). Rising land prices in recent years have encouraged this trend toward large-scale development.

Danchi Service Co, Ltd
[株]団地サービス

(Danchi Sābisu). Apartment-complex management and maintenance company. Incorporated in 1961. The firm has 800,000 units under its management throughout Japan, including houses constructed by the HOUSING AND URBAN DEVELOPMENT CORPORATION. For the fiscal year ending March 1990, sales totaled ¥128.7 billion (US $840.7 million) and capitalization stood at ¥360.0 million (US $2.4 million). Headquarters are in Tōkyō.

Dandō Shigemitsu   団藤重光

(1913–). Scholar of criminal law and legal theory. Born in Yamaguchi Prefecture. Dandō graduated from Tōkyō University in 1935 and was a professor there from 1947 to 1974. He served as a justice of the Supreme Court from 1974 to 1983. As a legal scholar, Dandō played a crucial role in the establishment and development of criminal law studies in post–World War II Japan. His publications include *Keihō kōyō: Sōron* (rev ed, 1979, Principles of Criminal Law: Outline), *Keihō kōyō: Kakuron* (rev ed, 1972, Principles of Criminal Law: Analyses), and *Shin keiji soshō hō kōyō* (7th ed, 1972; 6th ed, 1964, tr *Japanese Law of Criminal Procedure*, 1965).

dango   団子

Confection made of dough, consisting mainly of rice flour, that is kneaded and shaped into small balls, which are steamed or boiled. The balls are then given any of a variety of coatings, such as sweet bean paste (*an*) or soybean flour (*kinako*), or they are dipped in soy sauce and grilled, often on bamboo skewers. *Dango* have long been eaten in Japan, often on the occasion of seasonal observances, such as cherry-blossom or moon viewing, and following Buddhist rituals.

dangō 談合

Literally translated, *dangō* means "consultation" or "conference," but it has strong overtones of consultation for the purpose of collusion prior to submitting bids for projects. Especially in industries such as construction, where there is a strong "live and let live" mentality, the practice is often for industry participants to consult among themselves before making bids for large construction projects. Thus, prior to the submitting of bids, construction companies will essentially decide which company should be the low bidder on a particular contract based upon an ongoing series of negotiations and established relationships. *Dangō* is believed to be most common in bidding for public or semipublic projects. For private-sector projects there is usually a more stringent set of bidding criteria. See also CONSTRUCTION INDUSTRY.

Dangyokei 断魚渓

Gorge on the middle reaches of the river Nigorigawa (tributary of the Gōnokawa), central Shimane Prefecture, western Honshū. The river has carved through veins of rhyolite, creating waterfalls, pools, and shoals for approximately 4 km (2.5 mi).

Dan Ikuma 團伊玖磨

(1924–). Composer-conductor, especially well known for his operas and songs. Grandson of the famous businessman DAN TAKUMA. Born in Tōkyō to a family of scholars, Dan was exposed to Western music from childhood and began composing at an early age. After graduating from Tōkyō School of Music (now Tōkyō University of Fine Arts and Music) in 1945, he won recognition as a composer in 1950 with his Symphony no. 1 in A. Being a Japanese composer writing Western-style music has been a continual challenge for him—one he successfully met in his first and perhaps most popular opera, *Yūzuru* (The Twilight Crane). With a libretto by KINOSHITA JUNJI based on a Japanese folktale, this opera was an attempt to synthesize the essence of traditional Japanese theatrical arts with Western opera. Dan's works include five operas, five symphonies, a variety of orchestral and chamber music, many songs, and choral works. He is also well known as an essayist.

danka 檀家

A term derived from *dan* (a transliteration of the Sanskrit *dānapati*, meaning a lay believer who gives donations to a monk or the Buddhist community) and *ka* (Japanese for "house"). A *danka* indicates a family that requests a particular Buddhist temple to conduct all its funeral, memorial, and other services in exchange for which it offers remuneration and partial provision for the upkeep of the temple. The Tokugawa shogunate (1603–1867) institutionalized this practice by creating a nationwide *danka* system (see TERAUKE).

dankai no sedai 団塊の世代

(baby boomers; literally, "the clumped generation"). Phrase coined by the writer SAKAIYA TAICHI in his 1980 novel of the same title to refer to the generation of Japanese born in the late 1940s, during the explosive rise in the birth rate that followed the end of World War II. In the years 1947–49 recorded births topped 2.6 million annually—in comparison, the birth rate in recent years has stabilized at about 1.5 million.

The *dankai no sedai*, which constituted about 8.9 percent of Japan's total population in 1990, forms the backbone of contemporary Japanese society. Although the baby boomers faced intense competition for entrance to schools at all levels and an equally fierce struggle after graduation for jobs and career advancement within Japan's traditional seniority-oriented employment system, they have also been consistently wooed by manufacturers and distributors as the arbiters of Japan's consumer culture.

Dan Kazuo 檀一雄

(1912–76). Novelist. Born in Yamanashi Prefecture; graduate of Tōkyō University. He became a follower of the novelist SATŌ HARUO and later associated with DAZAI OSAMU and others. He made his debut with *Hanagatami* (1937), a collection of stories, and won critical praise with two novels about the tragic death of his wife, Ritsuko: *Ritsuko, sono ai* (1950) and *Ritsuko, sono shi* (1950). In 1951 he was awarded the Naoki Literary Prize for *Shinsetsu Ishikawa Goemon* (1950–51). Other works include *Yūhi to kenjū* (1955–56) and *Kataku no hito* (1955–75).

Dannoura 壇ノ浦

Coastal area. Eastern part of the city of Shimonoseki, Yamaguchi Prefecture, western Honshū. This area was the site of the Battle of DANNOURA (1185), in which the Taira family was defeated. Akama Shrine and Hinoyama Park are tourist attractions here.

Dannoura, Battle of 壇ノ浦の戦い

(Dannoura no Tatakai). Naval engagement in the Shimonoseki Strait on 25 April 1185. The conclusive battle of the TAIRA-MINAMOTO WAR, ending in the destruction of the Taira and the rise of the Minamoto to national hegemony. Forces under the command of MINAMOTO NO YOSHITSUNE cornered the Taira fleet at the westernmost exit from the Inland Sea and annihilated it in a half day's combat. The defeated admiral TAIRA NO TOMOMORI drowned himself; the seven-year-old emperor ANTOKU, grandson of TAIRA NO KIYOMORI, was also drowned—a tragic scene memorialized in the 13th-century military romance HEIKE MONOGATARI. Kiyomori's heir, TAIRA NO MUNEMORI, was captured by the Minamoto and executed three months later. The victory cleared the way for MINAMOTO NO YORITOMO to consolidate his regime and establish the KAMAKURA SHOGUNATE in 1192.

Danrin, Empress 檀林皇后

(786–850; Danrin Kōgō). Nonreigning empress (*kōgō*); consort of Emperor SAGA. Her personal name was Tachibana no Kachiko. She was interested in Zen Buddhism and sent the monk Egaku to China to invite the priest Gikū (Ch: Yikong or I-k'ung) to Japan. Gikū gave the first Zen lectures in Japan at Danrinji temple. The temple had been built by the empress, and her name was derived from it. With her brother Tachibana no Ujikimi, she also built the Gakukan'in, a school for family members.

Danrin school 談林派

(Danrinha). A school of *haikai* (see HAIKU) that arose as a radical revolt against the conservatism of the predominant Teimon

school led by MATSUNAGA TEITOKU and that held the stage between 1673 and 1683. Its leader was NISHIYAMA SŌIN (1605–82), a renowned RENGA master and *haikai* poet, but it was his disciples who earned it an avantgarde reputation. This group's style was demonstrated in the *Ikutama manku*, a sequence of 10,000 verses composed by Ihara SAIKAKU and others in 1673. It was not long before the BASHŌ style of *haikai* took the reins from Danrin, but Bashō readily acknowledged the liberating influence of Sōin and the Danrin school.

danseigo → masculine language

Dan Takuma 団琢磨

(1858–1932). Businessman. Born in what is now Fukuoka Prefecture. In 1871 Dan accompanied the IWAKURA MISSION to the United States, graduating from the Massachusetts Institute of Technology in 1878 with a degree in mining engineering. He taught briefly at Tōkyō University and joined the Ministry of Public Works (Kōbushō) as an engineer at the government-owned MIIKE COAL MINES in Fukuoka Prefecture. He joined the MITSUI company after its acquisition of the mines in 1888. In 1914 he was appointed managing director of the Mitsui holding company, Mitsui Gōmei Kaisha, becoming head of all Mitsui operations. An active leader in Japanese and foreign industry and business, he was strongly antilabor and mounted a successful campaign in 1929 to defeat the labor-union bill proposed by the HAMAGUCHI OSACHI cabinet. Dan was assassinated by an ultranationalist in the LEAGUE OF BLOOD INCIDENT of 1932.

Dantani Corporation 段谷産業[株]

(Dantani Sangyō). Comprehensive housing materials manufacturer. Incorporated in 1934. The company has 7 factories and 40 branch offices across Japan. Besides marketing a full line of housing materials, it is engaged in housing construction. The company also imports and markets foreign-made (mainly Southeast Asian) wood products in Japan. Sales for the fiscal year ending November 1990 were ¥94.2 billion (US $729.8 million), with capitalization at ¥3.9 billion (US $30.2 million). Headquarters are in Kita Kyūshū, Fukuoka Prefecture.

daruma 達磨

Dolls representing the Indian priest Bodhidharma (J: Bodai Daruma or Daruma), the founder of ZEN Buddhism in China, who is said to have lost the use of his arms and legs after spending nine years meditating in a cave. Available in different sizes, the dolls are usually made of papier-mâché on a bamboo frame and consist of a bright red, rounded amalgam of head and body with two large spaces for eyes. They are used as charms for the fulfillment of some special wish, such as a plentiful harvest or successful election to public office; the custom is for the purchaser to paint in one eye, place the *daruma* in the family shrine, and paint in the other eye when the wish is fulfilled.

Prototypes of these dolls, called *okiagari koboshi* ("the little priest who stands up")

Dan Kazuo This novelist posthumously received two literary awards for his final work, *Kataku no hito* (1955–75).

273
daruma

daruma

1 The custom of using *daruma* dolls as wish-fulfillment charms developed in the silk-producing areas of the Kantō region and is now common throughout Japan.
2 A Muromachi-period (1333–1568) hanging scroll depicts the legend that the Indian priest Bodhidharma (J: Daruma) journeyed from India to China on a reed leaf.
3 A *daruma* fair is held each January at Darumadera, a temple in Takasaki, Gumma Prefecture.

because they return to an upright position when tipped over, were popular during the 16th century. The present form of the doll dates from the Edo period (1600–1868), when it was regarded as a talisman for protection against smallpox.

Daruma are often sold in special "daruma fairs" (*darumaichi*), generally held in eastern Japan from the end of the year to the early spring. Makers are located throughout the Kantō area, especially in Gumma Prefecture.

dashi 山車

Tall, elaborately decorated floats towed by parishioners in shrine festivals; in western Japan they are also called *yama*, *hoko*, or *danjiri*. The *dashi* originally seems to have been in the shape of a pole decorated at the top, symbolizing the divine presence. During the Heian period (794–1185) people began displaying various decorative objects in festival processions, and, as is typified in the huge floats used in the GION FESTIVAL, *dashi* became

dashi These large, ornately decorated floats are among the highlights of many shrine festivals.

Date Masamune Detail of a 17th-century portrait of Masamune, *daimyō* of the huge Sendai domain. A skilled warrior, Masamune was also proficient in Nō drama, calligraphy, and the art of incense.

the center of attraction for many festivals. See also MIKOSHI.

DAT → digital audiotape

data base services データベース

(*dētabēsu*). Computer data base services in Japan are a recent development compared to those of other advanced industrialized nations, having been in operation only since the 1970s. Their market scale is still relatively modest. According to a survey by the MINISTRY OF INTERNATIONAL TRADE AND INDUSTRY (MITI), in 1989 there were 2,128 commercial data bases in the country. Sales amounted to ¥157.6 billion (US $1.1 billion), which was 3.6 percent of overall sales in the information services industry. However, sales for 1989 had increased by 48 percent over the previous year, indicating a rapid rate of growth. There were 211 firms participating in data base services in 1989, and the survey showed that the number of users, mainly in research and business, was increasing yearly; of the businesses surveyed, 68 percent used data bases. The yearly usage fee by large enterprises reached an average of more than ¥46.4 million (US $337,000). However, most of the domestic data bases procured their data from European and American sources; independently produced Japanese data bases amounted to less than 31 percent. Japanese data base services are improving in quality and capacity, however, and are becoming more readily available overseas. Japanese commercial data bases include JOIS of the Japan Information Center of Science and Technology (JICST) and NEEDS of the Nihon Keizai Shimbun, Inc.

Date 伊達[市]

City in southwestern Hokkaidō on Uchiura Bay. It was settled in 1870 by a branch of the DATE FAMILY. Agricultural products include potatoes, asparagus, beets, and flax. Marine products are salmon, trout, sea urchin, oysters, and kelp. Date also produces lumber and agricultural machinery. Its Zenkōji is the oldest temple in Hokkaidō. Pop: 34,507.

Date family 伊達氏

(Dateshi). Family of provincial military leaders (later *daimyō*) from the Kamakura period (1185–1333) through the Edo period (1600–1868). Based in the Isa district of Hitachi Province (now Ibaraki Prefecture), founder Isa Tomomune assisted MINAMOTO NO YORITOMO in his battle for power in 1189 and was rewarded with the Date district (now

Fukushima Prefecture) of Mutsu Province in northern Honshū, whence the family took its name. During the period of the NORTHERN AND SOUTHERN COURTS (1337–92), the Date fought for the Southern Court, but submitted to the Muromachi shogunate (1338–1573) in the early 1400s, becoming SENGOKU DAIMYŌ by the 1500s. Their domainal legal code, the JINKAISHŪ, was drawn up by Date Tanemune (1488–1565) in 1536. DATE MASAMUNE (1567–1636) greatly increased the family holdings while serving under TOYOTOMI HIDEYOSHI. However, he fought for TOKUGAWA IEYASU at the Battle of SEKIGAHARA, and for his efforts he was rewarded with the Sendai domain (now Miyagi Prefecture). In addition to Sendai, which had substantial income, branches of the Date controlled the Yoshida and Uwajima domains in Iyo Province (now Ehime Prefecture). In the mid-1600s, the Date of the Sendai domain were divided by a family succession struggle (see DATE SŌDŌ).

Date Masamune 伊達政宗

(1567–1636). Warrior of the Azuchi-Momoyama (1568–1600) and early Edo (1600–1868) periods. Eldest son of Date Terumune (1544–85), lord of Yonezawa Castle (in what is now Yamagata Prefecture). He was known by the nickname Dokuganryū ("One-Eyed Dragon") because he had lost sight in one eye as a child. Succeeding to the headship of the family at 17, he extended his sway over more than 30 districts (*gun*) in the provinces of Mutsu (now Fukushima, Miyagi, Iwate, and Aomori prefectures) and Dewa (now Yamagata and Akita prefectures). In 1589 Date defeated the Ashina family and moved his base to a castle in Aizu in what is now Fukushima Prefecture. The following year he was obliged to yield the castle to TOYOTOMI HIDEYOSHI. Later he was given another castle by Hideyoshi for his role in suppressing peasant uprisings. In the Battle of SEKIGAHARA he fought on the side of TOKUGAWA IEYASU, and for his efforts he was rewarded with the enormous Sendai domain. While ruling with an iron hand as *daimyō*, Date built up the castle town of Sendai, promoted land reclamation, and started a salt industry. Originally interested in Christianity and the West, he abandoned this stance after the shogunate proscribed Christianity and limited foreign contacts.

Date Sōdō 伊達騒動

(Date Family Disturbance). A family succession struggle (OIE SŌDŌ) of the 1660s and early

1670s between members of the DATE FAMILY, lords of the Sendai domain (now Miyagi Prefecture). In 1660 the Tokugawa shogunate, charging the *daimyō* Date Tsunamune (1640–1711) with immoral conduct, placed him under house arrest and designated his infant son Tsunamura (1659–1719) as heir. Real power, however, rested with Date Munekatsu (1621–79), Tsunamune's uncle. In 1666 an attendant died immediately after test-tasting the boy Tsunamura's meal, and rumor linked Munekatsu with this poisoning. Late in 1670 Munekatsu's poor handling of domainal affairs was reported to the shogunate by a Date family member. A few months later, at the home of shogunate great elder (*tairō*) SAKAI TADAKIYO, who was about to announce his judgment, the informer was murdered by one of Munekatsu's officials. The assassin was beheaded, and the shogunate soon after sentenced Munekatsu to indefinite detention in the Tosa domain (now Kōchi Prefecture).

day lilies 黄菅

(*kisuge*). *Hemerocallis thunbergii* Baker, the best known of the various native Japanese day lilies, perennial herbs of the family Liliaceae. The *kisuge* (also called *yūsuge*) grows in the highlands of Kyūshū and western and central Honshū. The *kisuge* fields in the Nikkō, Oze, and Asama highlands of central Honshū are particularly well known. The leaves are 40–60 centimeters (16–24 in) long, stiff, and sword-shaped; they grow in two rows. Several lemon-colored, fragrant flowers with petals about 7 centimeters (3 in) long bloom in the summer from a flower stalk (scape). The flowers open in the evening and wither before noon the following day. Similar species growing wild in Japan include the *nokanzō* (*H. longituba*), which has yellowish red flowers; the *yabukanzō* (*H. fulva* var. *kwanso*), which originally came from China and has tawny double flowers; and the *hamakanzō* (*H. littorea*), which grows in coastal areas and has tawny flowers.

Dazaifu 太宰府[市]

City in west-central Fukuoka Prefecture, Kyūshū. Its history dates back to the 7th century, when Dazaifu, the government headquarters in Kyūshū, was established; the city has many historical sites, such as the remains of the main government office. Recently Dazaifu has become a satellite of the city of FUKUOKA. The Dazaifu Temmangū (see DAZAIFU SHRINE) is dedicated to the 9th-century scholar SUGAWARA NO MICHIZANE. Pop: 62,402.

Dazaifu 大宰府

Government headquarters in northern Kyūshū from the late Kofun period (ca 300–710) through the Heian period (794–1185); later a town near modern Fukuoka. From perhaps the 3rd century special officials (later known as *dazai*) were stationed there to regulate contacts with China and Korea. The TAIHO CODE of 701 charged Dazaifu with the administration of the Kyūshū provinces, in addition to earlier diplomatic and defense responsibilities. Thus Dazaifu occupied a uniquely important place in early Japan's system of local government and was an exception to the rule that the court directly administered the provinces. During the 8th and 9th centuries this flourishing city was known as the "distant capital."

From the 9th century, assignment to Dazaifu became a form of exile for out-of-favor officials. The most famous exile was

SUGAWARA NO MICHIZANE, who died there in 903. Although official contacts with China ceased in the 9th century, Dazaifu remained a center for foreign commerce. During the Kamakura period (1185–1333) the office survived in name only, but the town prospered. It was the castle town (*jōka machi*) of the SHŌNI FAMILY and a center for Japan's defense against the MONGOL INVASIONS OF JAPAN in the 13th century. During the 16th century Dazaifu lost its political importance, but the shrine dedicated to Michizane continued to thrive, and the present town grew up around it (see DAZAIFU SHRINE).

Dazaifu Shrine 太宰府天満宮

(Dazaifu Temmangū). Shintō shrine in the town of Dazaifu, Fukuoka Prefecture, Kyūshū; dedicated to the spirit of the slandered scholar and statesman SUGAWARA NO MICHIZANE, who died in exile at Dazaifu in 903. A shrine was built by imperial command in 919, and Michizane became the patron of scholarship and calligraphy. The present main shrine building dates from 1591. The annual festival is held on 25 September. A service called Usokae, to which people bring a bird-shaped amulet (*uso*) and walk in a circle around a tree, exchanging their *uso* with those of others in the hope of acquiring a special *uso* of good luck carried secretly by shrine officials, is performed on 7 January. On the same date there is a spectacular ritual of exorcism (*tsuina;* see SETSUBUN) known as Onisube. See also TEMMANGŪ; KITANO SHRINE.

Dazai Osamu 太宰治

(1909–48). Writer, chiefly of short stories and novelettes; the laureate of the bleak, chaotic years immediately following Japan's defeat in World War II. Real name Tsushima Shūji. The son of a wealthy landlord, he was born in northern Honshū. Since his father, a member of the House of Peers (Kizokuin), was often away from home, and his mother was chronically ill (after giving birth to 11 children), he was brought up almost entirely by servants. After a lonely childhood, he was sent to Aomori for middle school and then to Hirosaki for higher school. During this time, he edited and contributed works to student publications, while paying regular visits to red-light districts. He also came under the influence of left-wing activists, which resulted in 1929 in his first suicide attempt, presumably from guilt for having been born into the wrong class. In 1930 he matriculated into the French department of Tōkyō University, but he dropped out after five years. His half-hearted involvement in underground causes lasted for two more years, until he was forced to "convert" (see TENKŌ) as the authorities tightened the measures for suppression. He made a second suicide attempt while an undergraduate. A young *geisha* he had known in Aomori joined him in Tōkyō and, facing family disapproval, he tried to drown himself—with a different girl, a Ginza barmaid he scarcely knew. She succeeded; he failed. Eventually he and the hometown geisha came to live together.

Writing Career—In 1933 he adopted the pen name of Dazai Osamu. Beginning to think seriously of a writing career, he sought out the tutelage of the established writer IBUSE MASUJI, through whose aid his publications increased and his reputation grew. In a third attempt at suicide in 1935, he tried to hang himself because of his failure to obtain a job in a newspaper company.

He soon became addicted to morphine and had to be sent away for treatment. Dur-

ing his hospital stay, he learned that his Aomori geisha had had an affair. Disillusioned by the inconstancy of pure love, Dazai decided once again to take his life—in a joint effort with the girl. Both failed, and they separated. Throughout these failure-laden years, he persevered in his writing. As the threat of war intensified, his turmoil subsided, especially after his marriage to a middle-school teacher in 1939, and it was during this period of stability that he published the short story "Hashire Merosu" (1940; tr "Run, Melos," 1988).

During World War II, Dazai continued writing, and in the immediate postwar period he became a celebrity. In 1947 he was asked by a perfect stranger to help her become the mother of his child; he obliged. Soon thereafter, he also entered into a relationship with another woman, a war widow and writer-hairdresser. Disregarding the decline in his health brought on by tuberculosis, he threw away all he had earned on drinks for himself and for numerous friends. As his tuberculosis worsened, he struggled to complete several major works, such as SHAYŌ (1947; tr *The Setting Sun*, 1956), "Biyon no tsuma" (1947; tr "Villon's Wife," 1955), and NINGEN SHIKKAKU (1948; tr *No Longer Human*, 1958). In the spring of 1948 he was in the process of writing a novelette to be serialized in the newspaper *Asahi shimbun* with the title of "Gutto bai" (Good-bye) when he leapt into a rain-swollen stream near his home—with the writer-hairdresser mistress—at last fulfilling his longtime goal of ending the life he found too perplexing. The bodies of Dazai and his third death-mate were discovered on 19 June, his 39th birthday.

Works—The single most important feature of his works is their "first person" quality. All his stories are autobiographical in some way. His favorite modes were the diary, essaylike reportage, letter, or soliloquy. His reinterpretations of old works such as *Hamlet* (*Shin Hamuretto*, 1941) and well-known nursery tales (*Otogi-zōshi*, 1945) are examples of more objective works.

His works display the paradox between honesty and fiction inherent in the form of the *watakushi shōsetsu* (I-NOVEL), the orthodoxy of modern Japanese fiction. Dazai's readers know that they are treated, in any new story, to a grandstand view of a new performance in his ongoing circus of life. His style sensitively shifts and fluctuates from pathos to humor, from melodrama to comedy, from the ponderous to the light. His vocabulary deftly responds to altering needs and adjusts itself to formality and colloquialism, exoticism and slang, foreign words and baby talk. Dazai's works survive because he never abandoned his love of language.

Dazai Shundai 太宰春台

(1680–1747). Confucian scholar of the Edo period (1600–1868). His given name was Jun.

Dazaifu Shrine The main building of this shrine (pictured) is dedicated to the spirit of the scholar and statesman Sugawara no Michizane, who died in exile in Dazaifu in 903.

day lilies This variety of day lily, the *kisuge*, has yellow flowers that open at night.

Dazai Osamu This author drew heavily on the I-novel tradition; his fiction is distinguished by dexterous shifts in tone from pathos to humor, from the ponderous to the light.

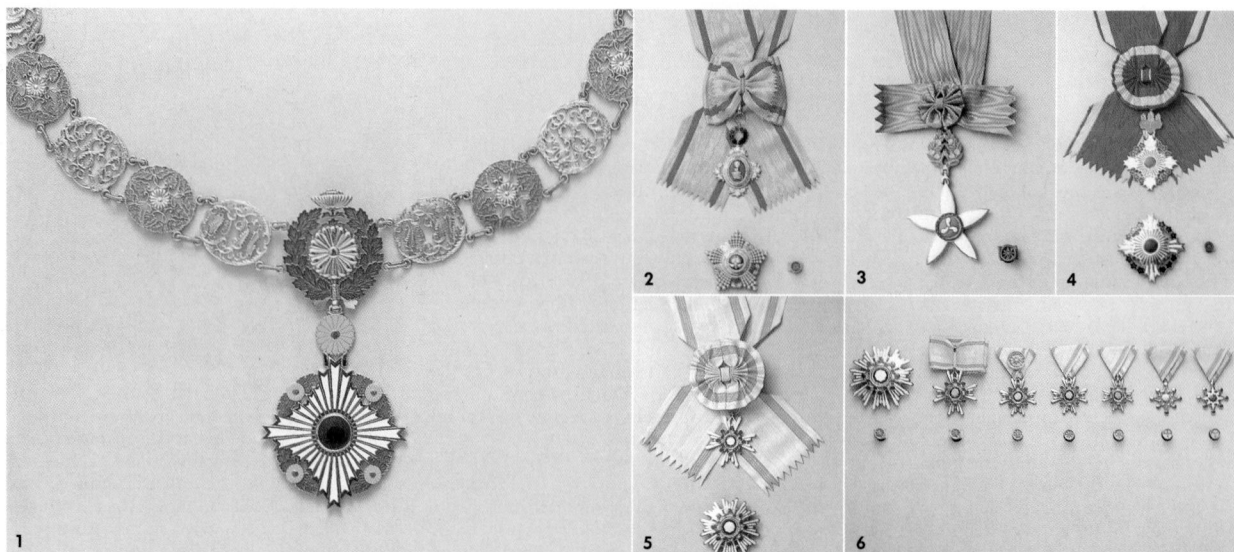

decorations Official decorations are awarded by the government to honor those whose work has especially benefited the Japanese nation.
1 Collar of the Supreme Order of the Chrysanthemum, the highest degree of honor awarded to men.
2 Grand Cordon of the Order of the Precious Crown, for women.
3 Order of Culture, conferred on both men and women in recognition of outstanding accomplishments in the arts and sciences.
4 Grand Cordon of the Order of the Rising Sun, Paulownia Flowers, for men.
5 Grand Cordon of the Order of the Sacred Treasure (first rank), for men and women.
6 The second through eighth ranks of the Order of the Sacred Treasure, from left, in descending order of rank.

Born in Iida in Shinano Province (now Nagano Prefecture), as a child Shundai accompanied his father to Edo (now Tōkyō). At the age of 15 he entered the service of Matsudaira Tadanori, the *daimyō* of the Izushi domain (in what is now Hyōgo Prefecture). When Shundai withdrew from service at the age of 21, he incurred the displeasure of domainal authorities and spent the following years studying in the Kyōto-Ōsaka area. He returned to Edo 11 years later and became a student of OGYŪ SORAI. Shundai and HATTORI NANKAKU were considered two of Sorai's most brilliant students. Shundai excelled in the field of political economy. In his *Keizairoku* (1729, Discussions of Economics) he emphasized the importance of economic affairs in both public and private life.

DC Card Co, Ltd   ディーシーカード[株]

(Dīshī Kādo). Credit card company. Incorporated in 1967. DC Card Co has cooperative agreements with Master Card and Visa International. DC Card members numbered 8.7 million as of March 1991. For the fiscal year ending March 1991, sales totaled ¥896.7 billion (US $6.5 billion) and capitalization stood at ¥2.5 billion (US $18.2 million). Headquarters are in Tōkyō.

debenture   社債

(*shasai*). Certificate of indebtedness issued by private companies to raise long-term funds for capital investment and working capital. In a broad sense, debentures issued by Japan's long-term credit banks and certain other banks also come under this classification. Funds raised by issuance of bank debentures are used by the issuing institutions for long-term lending. Creditworthiness of corporate debentures is rated by several private agencies in Japan and by US or European rating agencies for overseas debenture issues. Corporate debentures are underwritten by securities companies, then sold to individual or institutional investors. After being issued, they can be freely traded in the secondary market. All nonbank debentures had to be secured by collateral until 1979; since then, the MINISTRY OF FINANCE has stipulated a minimum bond rating for debentures issued without collateral. Bank debentures are issued in maturities from one to five years. See also CORPORATE STOCK; CAPITAL MARKETS.

December Ninth Movement   十二・九運動

(Jūnikyū Undō). Chinese patriotic movement named for a massive demonstration organized by university students in Beijing (Peking) on 9 December 1935 in response to Japanese threats to the territorial integrity of North China. The demonstration marked the beginning of a broad movement among intellectuals and members of the middle class for the subordination of domestic rivalries to a united national resistance against Japan. The Japanese had been agitating for the separation of North China by engineering a series of incidents and exerting diplomatic pressure. This aggressive diplomacy included the HE-UMEZU (HO-UMEZU) AGREEMENT and the DOIHARA-QIN (DOIHARA-CH'IN) AGREEMENT of June to remove Guomindang (Kuomintang; Nationalist Party) influence from Hebei (Hopeh) and Qahar (Chahar) provinces; the October announcement of Japanese Prime Minister HIROTA KŌKI that envisioned a Japan-Manchukuo-China anti-Communist alliance; and the establishment in November of the EAST HEBEI (HOPEH) ANTI-COMMUNIST AUTONOMOUS GOVERNMENT in northern Hebei.

Students in Beijing organized demonstrations and strikes that soon spread to other cities. When factions developed in Beijing, leadership of the movement passed to Shanghai, where the NATIONAL SALVATION ASSOCIATION was formed in June 1936.

The movement was one of the factors that finally forced CHIANG KAI-SHEK, the Guomindang leader, to abandon his efforts to appease the Japanese.

decorations   勲章

(*kunshō*). The Japanese system of awarding official decorations was established by the 54th proclamation of the Great Council of State (Dajōkan) in 1875. Besides the Supreme Order of the Chrysanthemum (Daikun'i Kikkashō) as the highest degree of honor for men, the Order of the Rising Sun (Kyokujitsushō) also for men, the Order of the Precious Crown (Hōkanshō) for women, and the Order of the Sacred Treasure (Zuihōshō) for both men and women were also established. These decorations were ranked from the first class to the eighth class according to different degrees of meritorious service. In 1890 the Order of the Golden Kites (Kinshi Kunshō) was established to honor members of the armed forces, but this was abolished under the new constitution in 1947. An addition in 1937 was the ORDER OF CULTURE (Bunka Kunshō) to honor those in the sciences and the arts. Since 1964 it has been customary for decorations to be awarded twice a year, in the spring and the fall. The emperor bestows these decorations based upon the recommendations of the cabinet.

deer, Japanese   鹿

(*shika*). Also known as sika deer. *Cervus nippon*, a deer of small to medium size with four-tined antlers that is distributed over East Asia. Its head and body measure about 1.4 meters (4.5 ft) in length, and it weighs about 40–80 kilograms (85–180 lb). Chestnut in color, it invariably has white spots in summer; a long mane grows on the upper surface of the buck's neck in winter. In Japan it is distributed throughout Hokkaidō, Honshū, Shikoku, and Kyūshū, but the population has been reduced greatly by hunting. It is now generally found only in limited reservations such as Nara Park in Nara Prefecture and Kinkazan in Miyagi Prefecture. Most of the year the males and females remain in separate herds and graze in open grasslands in the morning and evening, emerging from their resting places in the woods. The mating season runs from early October through the end of December, and a single offspring is born annually after a gestation period of seven to eight months.

Japanese deer
1 A sika buck depicted in the autumn mating season, when the membrane, known as "velvet," that covers his antlers is lost.
2 Roe and fawn in summer show seasonal coloring of mottled white on the chest and belly.

The sika deer has been introduced as a game animal to various places in the world, including the United Kingdom, New Zealand, and North America. The antlers are used for a variety of handicrafts and ornaments.

Defense Agency 防衛庁

(Bōeichō). Cabinet-level agency of the national government responsible for the direction and administration of Japan's defense. Created in June 1954, it administers the ground, maritime, and air SELF DEFENSE FORCES (SDF), formulates strategy for the defense of Japan, and coordinates defense intelligence and security operations. It also prepares Japan's defense budget, orders the manufacture and purchase of military equipment, and administers military bases. The agency's director-general, a civilian who serves as both a minister of state and a member of the SECURITY COUNCIL, presides over the SDF under the supervision of the prime minister. In this manner, strict civilian control is maintained over the SDF, whose existence has been criticized by some Japanese as a violation of the 1947 constitution's RENUNCIATION OF WAR provision.

The Defense Agency operates the NATIONAL INSTITUTE FOR DEFENSE STUDIES, the NATIONAL DEFENSE ACADEMY, the National Defense Medical College, and the Technical Research and Development Institute. The Defense Facilities Administration Agency is attached to the Defense Agency.

Defense Buildup Programs 防衛力整備計画

(Bōeiryoku Seibi Keikaku). A series of programs begun in 1958 to build up Japan's defensive capabilities systematically. The first program was implemented during 1958–60, the second during 1962–66, the third during 1967–71, and the fourth during 1972–76. Each plan was generated by the DEFENSE AGENCY and reviewed and approved by the National Defense Council (now the SECURITY COUNCIL) and the cabinet. The plans served as the basis for annual government budget requests for defense funding. See also NATIONAL DEFENSE PROGRAM OUTLINE.

defense industry 防衛産業

(bōei sangyō). In 1988 defense-related production in Japan accounted for only 0.38 percent of the gross national product (GNP), while government spending on defense accounted for 6.5 percent of the national budget.

Of total military purchases in 1987, aircraft accounted for 34 percent; firearms and ammunition, 22 percent; communications equipment, 19 percent; ships, 9 percent; fuel, 3 percent; and vehicles, 2 percent. In terms of contracts, in 1987 MITSUBISHI HEAVY INDUSTRIES, LTD, handled 21 percent of total defense production; KAWASAKI HEAVY INDUSTRIES, LTD, 14 percent; MITSUBISHI ELECTRIC CORPORATION, 7 percent; TOSHIBA CORPORATION, 6 percent; and NEC CORPORATION, 5 percent.

The Japanese defense industry produces extremely sophisticated military equipment, and in 1990 over 90 percent of military supplies were procured domestically, but some technology is still imported from the United States. In 1988 Japan and the United States agreed to codevelop Japan's new-generation fighter plane, the FS-X. See also ARMS EXPORT, THREE PRINCIPLES OF.

Defense White Paper 防衛白書

(Bōei hakusho). Official report of the DEFENSE AGENCY, analyzing the international military

situation and elaborating Japan's defense policies and posture. First published in 1970 and irregularly thereafter. Published annually since 1976. The 1988 white paper encouraged cooperation between the United States and Japan in defense matters; the 1990 version removed references contained in earlier versions to the "Soviet potential threat." See also NATIONAL DEFENSE.

Deguchi Nao 出口ナオ

(1837–1918). Prophetess and founder of the ŌMOTO movement. Born in Fukuchiyama, Tamba Province (now part of Kyōto Prefecture). Married in 1855, Nao was widowed in 1887 and supported her eight children by menial work. In 1892 Nao began to claim that the god Ushitora no Konjin spoke to her and she decided to serve as the god's vessel. Although she had little education, her writings (called ofudesaki) became the core of Ōmoto teachings. These held that the god would reappear, heralding an age of peace. They were also sharply critical of the imperialist establishment and the concept of STATE SHINTŌ. In 1898 Nao met Ueda Kisaburō (later DEGUCHI ONISABURŌ), who proved an able interpreter of her message and an outstanding organizer of the religious movement centering on Nao. He married Nao's daughter Sumi (1883–1952) and became the leader of the Ōmoto movement.

Deguchi Onisaburō 出口王仁三郎

(1871–1948). Leader of the ŌMOTO religious movement. Born Ueda Kisaburō in Anao (now in the city of Kameoka), Kyōto Prefecture. In 1898 he underwent an intense religious experience that led him to become a Shintō preacher. That same year he met the prophet DEGUCHI NAO and soon joined her religious group, later marrying her daughter Sumi. Knowledgeable about Shintō practices, Onisaburō was able to articulate Nao's revelations in terms that appealed to those uneasy with Japan's swift industrialization. The movement, eventually named Ōmoto, expanded rapidly under his guidance, but it came into conflict with official STATE SHINTŌ and was brutally suppressed in 1921. In 1935 the police arrested Onisaburō and many members in an attempt to eradicate the movement. After World War II, Onisaburō worked to restore the Ōmoto organization. Onisaburō published 81 volumes of Reikai monogatari (1921–27, 1934–35), an account of his spiritual odyssey.

Dejima 出島

Also called Deshima. Artificial island constructed in Nagasaki Harbor by the Tokugawa shogunate (1603–1867) between 1634 and 1636. Its 1.31 hectares (3.24 acres) comprised the only place in Japan where Westerners, first the Portuguese and then the Dutch, were allowed to reside from the 1630s to 1856 (see NATIONAL SECLUSION).

After Dejima's construction with funds from 25 wealthy Japanese traders, the shogunate transferred to the island all Portuguese residing in Japan. Then, particularly after the SHIMABARA UPRISING, the Portuguese were forced to leave Dejima and move with their Japanese wives and children to Macao. In 1641 the shogunate moved all the Dutch, by then the only Westerners permitted to trade with Japan, to Dejima. From then until the United States–Japan Treaty of Peace and Amity in 1854 (see KANAGAWA TREATY), Dejima was the sole conduit for commercial and cultural exchange between Japan and the West (see DUTCH TRADE). During the recon-

struction of Nagasaki Harbor in the Meiji period (1868–1912), Dejima was connected to the city by landfill. In 1957 the city restored the former Dejima warehouse as a historical monument. See also NETHERLANDS AND JAPAN.

Dejima This detail from a late-17th-century folding screen depicts the artificial island of Dejima, the only place of residence allowed to Westerners during the more than two centuries of national seclusion.

dekasegi→ temporary workers

delegation of power to legislate 委任立法

(inin rippō). Assignment of legislative functions to organs other than the national DIET. The power to legislate has been delegated to the SUPREME COURT in matters related to judicial procedures. The cabinet, the ministers of each ministry, and other administrative officials are entrusted with legislative functions in regard to other matters. Legislative functions delegated by law to administrative organs are known as "administrative legislation." Legal norms enacted through administrative legislation are generally called orders (meirei). The delegation of legislative power is elaborated in individual laws. Almost every law is supplemented by administrative legislation as stipulated in numerous provisions.

De Long, Charles Egbert デ・ロング, C. E.

(1832–76). US envoy to Japan from 1869 to 1873. He also represented the Kingdom of Hawaii in Japan. On behalf of the United States, he recognized Japan's claim to the Ryūkyū and Ogasawara islands. In 1871, together with Robert W. IRWIN, he represented the Hawaiian government in negotiating a treaty of friendship and commerce between Hawaii and Japan. In 1872 he advised Japan to enter into arbitration with Peru over the MARIA LUZ INCIDENT.

demae 出前

Home delivery of prepared food from restaurants. Sushi shops and noodle shops commonly offer this service, as do a few larger restaurants. Customers give their orders by phone and pay for their meals when delivered. There is no service charge. After eating, dishes are put outside and the deliv-

Deguchi Onisaburō The activities of this charismatic religious leader were forcibly suppressed by the government in 1921 and again in 1935.

denden taiko Toy drums like this one are often used to pacify and amuse young children.

ery person returns to collect them. Recently, establishments that offer such foods as pizza and hors d'oeuvres by delivery only have appeared.

demetaka 出目高

Also pronounced *demedaka*. Surplus tax revenues obtained by raising the tax rate, changing the method of assessment, or debasing coinage. The term was frequently used in connection with official land surveys (KENCHI), particularly during the Edo period (1600–1868). The *demetaka* was the amount by which the new tax assessment of a given plot of land exceeded the old.

democracy 民主主義

(*minshu shugi*). Japan has a functioning democratic system, that is, a system in which sovereignty resides in the people, who exercise it through elected representatives and who are guaranteed the civil liberties essential to its exercise. The present PO-LITICAL SYSTEM is in part a result of reforms introduced into Japan by the United States during the Allied OCCUPATION (1945–52) and is embodied in the CONSTITUTION OF JAPAN, which became effective in May 1947.

History—Japan's democratic tradition stretches back to the early Meiji period (1868–1912). Although there was little discussion of democratic ideals and institutions at the time of the MEIJI RESTORATION of 1868, in the 1870s dissatisfied former *samurai* and landowners who were not represented in the new government launched a movement for representative institutions, or "popular rights" (see FREEDOM AND PEOPLE'S RIGHTS MOVEMENT). Led by such people as ITAGAKI TAISUKE, they formed several POLITICAL PAR-TIES in the 1870s and 1880s. Ideologically, Itagaki and his followers were influenced by the ideals of French radicalism, while ŌKUMA SHIGENOBU, founder of the RIKKEN KAISHINTŌ, based his platform on the ideas of English liberalism and parliamentary goverment.

In 1889 the Japanese government adopted a constitution that permitted a weak House of Representatives and a limited franchise (see CONSTITUTION OF THE EMPIRE OF JAPAN). Po-litical parties gradually became accepted in government after the first party cabinet was formed in 1898, reaching a peak of power and public respect during the Taishō period (1912–26; see TAISHŌ DEMOCRACY).

The end of World War I, with the apparent victory of democracy in the West and of Marxism in Russia, coupled with a postwar recession in Japan, stimulated a movement for social, economic, and political reform in Japan among many students, writers, intellectuals, journalists, politicians, and labor leaders. They called for reforms ranging from the introduction of socialism and Marxism and the formation of LABOR UNIONS to the development of true liberal democracy. The SŌDŌMEI (Japan Federation of Labor) was formed in 1919 and a communist and several socialist parties were formed in the 1920s.

The Japanese government responded to demands for reform with a series of both conciliatory and repressive acts. Some progressive factory and labor laws were adopted and the Universal Manhood Suffrage Law (see UNIVERSAL MANHOOD SUFFRAGE MOVEMENT) was passed in May 1925, but these acts were coupled with the repressive PEACE PRESERVA-TION LAW OF 1925 and a series of police raids that destroyed many left-wing groups or drove them underground by the early 1930s.

Liberal democracy as it existed in Japan was suppressed in the 1930s as the military came to dominate government. From 1930 on army and navy officers involved themselves in a series of incidents that indicated the degree to which the military was able to act freely of civilian restraint. Key events included the MANCHURIAN INCIDENT in 1931 and the assassination of Prime Minister INUKAI TSUYOSHI in 1932 (see MAY 15TH INCIDENT), and a full-fledged military insurrection in 1936 (see FEBRUARY 26TH INCIDENT). Political parties lost their power and prestige and the military held sway over Japan politically, economically, and socially until the end of World War II. See also MILITARISM.

Postwar Development—Japan's present democratic system centers on the primary authority of a bicameral DIET (parliament) of representatives elected by the people. Executive power is exercised by a prime minister (chosen by the Diet) and by a cabinet he appoints (see PRIME MINISTER AND CABINET). Judicial power resides in the Supreme Court and lower courts (see JUDICIAL SYSTEM). Popular control over LOCAL GOVERNMENT is exercised through a system of local and prefectural assemblies and executives elected by the people. A system of checks and balances distributes power among the executive, legislative, and judicial branches and assures the people of a voice in government. The present constitution guarantees fundamental civil rights and liberties, including freedom of expression, assembly, press, scholarship, and association, as well as rights of habeas corpus, education, work, health, property, political participation (including voting, petitioning, recall, and referendum), and judicial relief. Democratic institutions have had broad public support in Japan since the end of World War II and most Japanese have made full use of their freedoms and rights.

However, public confidence in democracy has been severely tested in postwar Japan. A series of scandals in the 1970s and 1980s, including the LOCKHEED SCANDAL, the Nisshō-Iwai Incident, the RECRUIT SCANDAL, and other corrupt practices (see POLITICAL CORRUPTION) have occasioned a certain amount of disillusionment and discontent with the actual workings of Japan's political system.

The infrequency with which elected legislative bodies initiate legislation has also been a problem. Representation rarely means the introduction of bills, since at all levels of government most bills are introduced by the executive after limited consultation with parties and interest groups (see PRESSURE GROUPS). On the local level such bills are rarely debated and are generally passed with little opposition. This procedure is democratic in that there is an interpellation of the executive during each legislative session at which problems and conflicts needing resolution are raised for consideration. Citizen groups' petitions are also directed to the executive, usually through a legislator. However, the subsequent process of negotiating a consensus occurs behind closed doors, and even the legislative committee "hearings" (where bills are rarely discussed or amended) are not really open either to the public or to interest groups, although the press is usually in attendance. A predictable consequence of this situation has been a general loss of public confidence in government and increasing feelings of apathy and detachment from the political process. That politicians have sensed this trend and begun to respond to public demands for more thor-

oughly democratic practices was evidenced in the early 1990s, as plans began to take shape for the first significant reform in the system of election districting since 1945. See also ELECTIONS.

Democratic Socialist Party 民社党

(DSP; J: Minshatō). One of the major "middle-of-the-road" parties in Japanese politics. Founded on 24 January 1960 as the Minshu Shakaitō through secession from the JAPAN SOCIALIST PARTY (JSP), its name was changed in 1970 to Minshatō. Because of its pivotal role as an opposition party that cooperates on a wide range of issues with the ruling LIB-ERAL DEMOCRATIC PARTY (LDP), the DSP has, since the early 1970s, assumed substantially greater influence in the Japanese political system than its numerical Diet strength would suggest.

The DSP's party chairmen have included NISHIO SUEHIRO (1960–67), KASUGA IKKŌ (1971–77), and SASAKI RYŌSAKU (1977–85). In 1990 it was chaired by ŌUCHI KEIGO.

The primary political support of the Democratic Socialist Party comes from the labor unions of some of Japan's major corporations and from small businesses, particularly small-scale manufacturers. The DSP conceives of itself as being a "people's," rather than a "class," party, open to all willing to embrace the ideals of democratic socialism. The party's major formal policy goal is the attainment of a welfare state in Japan through major expansion of social welfare benefits and an intensification of antiunemployment measures.

demons—→oni

denden taiko でんでん太鼓

Also called *denden-daiko*. A children's toy consisting of a small drum, usually made of paper, attached to a handle, and with bells hanging from strings on both sides. When one shakes the handle the bells strike the surface of the drum, making the *denden* sound from which the name derives. It was particularly popular in the 17th century. Its shape is modeled after the *furitsuzumi*, a type of TSUZUMI drum used in *bugaku* (see GAGAKU).

Den'enchōfu 田園調布

Planned residential community on the northwestern edge of Ōta Ward, Tōkyō. Den'enchōfu was laid out in 1918 by SHI-BUSAWA EIICHI on the model of an English garden city. A series of concentric streets connect avenues that radiate from the Tōkyū Railway's Den'enchōfu Station. A tomb mound (KOFUN) known as Kamedayama is located here.

dengaku 田楽

Term used in a wide sense by contemporary scholars to refer to a variety of performing arts centering upon the production of rice. Used in a more traditional sense, the term refers to a specific type of performance, the *dengaku* dance, which was popular among the newly important military class in the Kamakura period (1185–1333). These were geometrically choreographed dances to the music of the flute, drum, and *sasara* (wooden pieces threaded together to produce a cracking sound when snapped). These dances were an important item in the repertories of certain groups of performers that were accordingly called *dengaku* troupes. The repertory of the *dengaku*, which also included acrobatics and other performances, is often mentioned along with the repertory of troupes known for another type of performance, SARUGAKU, as one of the antecedents of the classical NŌ drama. Today examples of the *dengaku* dance in the narrow sense can be seen performed as part of festivals and ceremonies at various shrines and temples in the Japanese countryside.

The *dengaku* dance itself is only one of many types of music, dance, recitation, and imitative and masked events associated with agriculture. The creation of new performance types continued even into the Edo period (1600–1868), and today there is a strong living tradition of these preserved in a multitude of festivals related to agriculture. It is to this wider tradition that the term *dengaku* as used by modern scholars refers. See also DANCE, TRADITIONAL.

Den Hideo 田英夫

(1923–). Politician. Born in Tōkyō. Graduate of Tōkyō University. Den joined the JAPAN SOCIALIST PARTY in 1970 and was elected to the House of Councillors in 1971. He left the Japan Socialist Party in 1977 and the following year participated with EDA SATSUKI and others in the founding of the UNITED SOCIAL DEMOCRATIC PARTY. Den functioned as the party's leader from its founding until 1985, when he was succeeded by Eda.

Denison, Henry Willard

デニソン, H. W.

(1846–1914). US legal adviser to the Japanese Ministry of Foreign Affairs, 1880–1914, and one of the Japanese government's longest-term FOREIGN EMPLOYEES OF THE MEIJI PERIOD. His expertise and discretion became invaluable as Japan sought to revise the so-called Unequal Treaties with Western nations, advance its position in Asia, and establish itself as a world power (see UNEQUAL TREATIES, REVISION OF).

Born in Guildhall, Vermont, and educated in law at Columbia College (now George Washington University) in Washington, DC, Denison joined the US consulate in Yokohama, where he remained until 1878. In 1880 he was engaged by Foreign Minister INOUE KAORU and for the next 34 years Denison served as aide to each foreign minister. He was influential in the negotiations that led to the ANGLO-JAPANESE COMMERCIAL TREATY OF 1894; relations with Russia before and after the RUSSO-JAPANESE WAR (1904–05); and planning the ANGLO-JAPANESE ALLIANCE (1902) and its subsequent revisions in 1905 and 1911. Denison remained an American citizen, but Japan named him one of its representatives at the Hague Court of International Justice and awarded him high imperial honors, including the Order of the Rising Sun.

Denki Kagaku Kōgyō KK 電気化学工業[株]

(Denki Kagaku Kōgyō). Also known as Denka. Comprehensive chemical company. Incorporated in 1915 as a producer of carbide products. It now manufactures more than 100 different products, including plastics, synthetic rubber, organic chemicals, fertilizers, and cement. In recent years, the company has developed many specialty items, notably magnetic disks and other new ceramics-based products, using its wide-ranging technologies both in organic and inorganic chemistry. In the fiscal year ending March 1991, sales totaled ¥221.8 billion (US $1.6 billion) and capitalization stood at ¥35.3 billion (US $257.3 million). Headquarters are in Tōkyō.

Denki Rōren 電機労連

(abbreviation of Zen Nihon Denki Kiki Rōdō Kumiai Rengōkai; All-Japan Federation of Electrical Machine Workers' Unions). A national federation of electrical machine workers' unions. Membership totaled 669,000 in 1989. Denki Rōren was formed in 1953 by the merger of the Tōkyō Shibaura Electric Co employees' union and a federation of unions from heavy and light electrical machinery enterprises. As the core organization of CHŪRITSU RŌREN (Federation of Independent Unions), Denki Rōren subsequently took the initiative in 1964 of founding the IMF-JC (International Metal Workers' Federation–Japanese Committee; see KINZOKU RŌKYŌ). Denki Rōren's quick development reflected the rapid growth of the electrical machinery industry.

Denmark and Japan デンマークと日本

(Demmāku *to* Nihon). Diplomatic relations between Denmark and Japan began with the conclusion of a treaty of commerce and navigation in 1912. Although relations were severed during World War II, Denmark later returned all Japanese assets seized during the war.

Emperor SHŌWA visited Copenhagen in 1971. In 1975 Foreign Minister K. B. Andersen came to Tōkyō, where an office was later opened by the Danish Chamber of Commerce to handle the sale of Danish products. In the 1980s visits were exchanged by the prime ministers, foreign ministers, and royalty of the two countries.

As of 1990 the trade balance between Denmark and Japan had for four years been in favor of Denmark. In 1990 Japan's exports to Denmark, chiefly automobiles, transport equipment, and electric and electronics products, totaled US $969 million; imports, mainly cheese, pork, and pharmaceuticals, totaled $1.1 billion.

Denny's Japan Co, Ltd

[株]デニーズジャパン

(Denīzu Japan). Restaurant chain operator with 353 coffee shop–style restaurants located mainly in the Tōkyō, Ōsaka, and Nagoya areas. Incorporated in 1973; a member of the Itō-Yōkadō group. In 1984 Denny's Japan agreed to acquire from Denny's, Inc, of the United States all rights within Japan to the Denny's name. The company is rapidly expanding its network of franchised chain stores. Sales for the fiscal year ending February 1991 totaled ¥79.2 billion (US $607.0 million), and capitalization stood at ¥7.1 billion (US $54.4 million). Headquarters are in Tōkyō.

Dentsū, Inc [株]電通

(Dentsū). Japan's largest advertising agency. It was founded in 1901 by MITSUNAGA HOSHIRŌ as Nihon Kōkoku Kabushiki Kaisha, an advertising company; in the same year, Mitsunaga also founded the Dempō Tsūshinsha, a telegraph company and news agency. The two companies were merged in 1907 as the Nihon Dempō Tsūshinsha, which was called Dentsū for short. The company performed both advertising and telecommunication functions until the news agency was merged with the Shimbun Rengōsha to become DŌMEI TSŪSHINSHA in 1936. The advertising agency officially changed its name to Dentsū in 1955. Dentsū conducts marketing and media surveys, monitors the effectiveness of its advertising, plans and produces

commercials, and provides public relations services. The accounts of most large Japanese companies are handled by Dentsū. The company also has invested heavily in television companies, where it controls seats on the boards of directors and exercises considerable power. Corporate headquarters are in Tōkyō. Sales for the fiscal year 1991 were ¥1.3 trillion (US $9.4 billion); capitalization stood at ¥4.6 billion (US $33.6 million).

deregulation 規制緩和

(*kisei kanwa*). A term often used to refer to the process of easing or abolishing government regulations pertaining to various aspects of Japanese society and economy from the early 1950s to the present; sometimes referred to as liberalization.

Like many other countries, prior to the 1980s Japan had extensive government regulation of private sector activities in industries and areas that were regarded as serving the public interest or having an important impact on the public welfare. Some of the areas that were, or still are, subject to extensive supervision and regulation include banking, securities, and other financial activities; foreign trade and foreign exchange; telecommunications; transportation; construction and land use; and pharmaceuticals.

The trend in Japan since the 1950s has been toward gradual deregulation in many areas, often as a result of pressure from Japan's trading partners, notably the United States. One of the first examples came in the mid-1960s, when Japan achieved the status of an article 8 nation under the rules of the International Monetary Fund (IMF) and made partial relaxations of restrictions on foreign trade and foreign exchange (see TRADE LIBERALIZATION). Similarly, Japan's quotas and TARIFFS on manufactured and other goods were lowered progressively, especially as do-

dengaku

1 A *dengaku* performance recorded on a panel of the 16th-century screen *Tsukinami fūzoku zu* (Genre Scenes of the Twelve Months). Musicians play while farmers transplant rice. 2 This performance of *dengaku* is part of a festival held in the Nishiure district of the town of Misakubo, Shizuoka Prefecture.

Dewa Sanzan Shrines
The main hall (pictured) serves as a common oratory for the three Dewa shrines.

mestic industries became internationally competitive.

The most prominent examples of deregulation, however, came in the 1980s during the prime ministership of NAKASONE YASUHIRO. Two major factors combined to bring about the deregulatory measures of this period. First, the Japanese government wanted to free itself from the huge burden of public debt (see GOVERNMENT BONDS FOR DEFICIT FINANCING), which had built up in the 1970s, by privatizing major government enterprises, notably the JAPANESE NATIONAL RAILWAYS (JNR). Second, the perceived failure of Keynesian economic policies to deal with the economic slump of the late 1970s led to an upsurge of opinion in various Western nations that government regulation of the economy and society should be eased or removed in order to unleash private initiative and revivify the economy. Such calls for "small-scale cheap government" also found an echo in Japan.

For these reasons the government proceeded to relax restrictions on construction in the early 1980s, paving the way for the boom in urban renewal and redevelopment of waterfront areas in Tōkyō and other major cities in the late 1980s. This in turn contributed to Japan's recovery from recession following the upward revaluation of the yen in the mid-1980s (see PLAZA ACCORD) and also to the long economic uptrend into the early 1990s that was led by domestic demand (see also DOMESTIC DEMAND, EXPANSION OF; HEISEI BOOM).

Major deregulatory steps included the privatization in 1985 of the government enterprises JAPAN TOBACCO, INC, and NTT (NIPPON TELEGRAPH AND TELEPHONE CORPORATION). The following year the government proceeded to open up the telecommunications industry to entry by competitive firms, thus ending the monopoly of Nippon Telegraph and Telephone Corporation on domestic telecommunications services, and that of KOKUSAI DENSHIN DENWA CO, LTD (International Telegram and Telephone Co, Ltd; KDD), on international telecommunications services. The entry of competitor companies into these areas resulted in marked reductions in charges to customers and stimulated both NTT and KDD to become more customer and market oriented.

The most significant and controversial privatization was that of the Japanese National Railways in 1987. This huge organization was split into seven regional companies (see JR). The enormous JNR debts have been shelved, and plans call for repaying a substantial portion through the development of former JNR land and through the sale of stocks held by the government in the JR companies when these companies eventually list on the stock exchanges.

Deregulatory measures stimulated by external pressure have included the deregulation of bank deposit interest rates that began in the late 1970s and that was accelerated by agreements at the United States–Japan Yen-Dollar Committee in the mid-1960s. Similarly, relaxation of restrictions on setting up large retail stores was in part due to the urging of US representatives in the STRUCTURAL IMPEDIMENTS INITIATIVE TALKS (SII). See also UNITED STATES, ECONOMIC RELATIONS WITH.

de Rijke, Johannes   デ・レーケ, J.

(1842–?). Dutch engineer and technical adviser to the Japanese government. In 1873 de Rijke accepted an invitation from the Japanese government to train engineers. He spent 28 years in Japan, concerned chiefly with the building of dams and the lining of riverbeds with rocks for channel control; many of his engineering techniques are still in use in Japan. He also laid down guidelines for the construction of the Tōkyō sewer system. He returned to the Netherlands in 1901.

de Sade case   サド裁判

(Sado *saiban*). The major Japanese Supreme Court obscenity decision (1969) after the LADY CHATTERLEY'S LOVER CASE (1957). In 1959 and 1960 an abridged translation of the Marquis Donatien de Sade's *L'Histoire de Juliette; ou, Les Prosperités du vice* (Japanese title: *Akutoku no sakae*) was published in two volumes, of which *The Travels of Juliette* (*Jurietto no henreki*) became the object of prosecution. The translator, SHIBUSAWA TATSUHIKO, and the publisher, Ishii Kyōji, were indicted for the sale and possession for sale of obscene literature under article 175 of the Penal Code. On 16 October 1962 the Tōkyō District Court acquitted the accused on grounds that the brutality and ugliness of de Sade's work militated against "wanton appeal to sexual passion," a requirement for a finding of obscenity. The Tōkyō High Court (21 November 1963) disagreed on that point and found both guilty; the Supreme Court (G. B., 15 October 1969; 23 Keishū [no. 10] 1239 [1969]) quashed their appeal by an eight-to-five decision. See also OBSCENITY.

Descente, Ltd   [株]デサント

(Desanto). Manufacturer and seller of sportswear and sole distributor of Munsingwear in Japan. Incorporated in 1949; assumed its present name in 1961. The company has its own research laboratory and supports a foundation for sports science. Technical and design tie-ups have been made with foreign companies, including Alfred Dunhill, Andre Courrèges, Chloe, Cerruti, and Adidas. Descente acquired trademark rights from Munsingwear of the United States for use in Japan and some Southeast Asian countries. Products are exported to the United States and Europe. Sales for the fiscal year ending March 1991 totaled ¥79.9 billion (US $582.4 million), and capitalization stood at ¥3.8 billion (US $27.7 million) in the same year. Headquarters are in Ōsaka.

design in textiles   染織のデザイン

(*senshoku no dezain*). Throughout Japan's history traditional techniques of textile design have generally involved dyeing and weaving. There are very few clues about the types of clothing worn in Japan before the 5th century, but it appears that by the mid-3rd century dyes of various colors were being used on natural, plain white fabrics made of such bast fibers as ASA. Other evidence indicates the early use of striped cloth (*shizuri*), cloth with a cross-thread design (*kamuhata*, an early form of KASURI), and cloth dyed with indigo (*aozuri*).

With the introduction of more advanced weaving techniques from China came the production of brocade (NISHIKI) and twill (*aya*). Since clothing regulations, modeled after Chinese examples, stipulated the color of formal clothing to be worn by officials of various ranks, dyeing techniques must have been advanced enough to permit gradations of color. Extant fabrics from this period include dyed material, woven material, and embroidered and woven belts. The designs on the fabrics include symmetrical designs, a crossed or entangled ribbon design (*tasuki mon*), and vertical or horizontal striped and medallion designs.

Heian (794–1185) and Kamakura (1185–1333) Periods—Special clothing fabrics were required for imperial court rituals and ceremonies and to distinguish among the different ranks of court officials. While *kōkechi* dyeing (see TIE-DYEING) became the most popular method among commoners, aristocrats wore more than two layers of KIMONO made of single-color fabric. Thus the choice of colors for the fabric and its lining (*awase irome*) and the color combination of the warp and woof (*ori irome*) became important aesthetic concerns. During the Kamakura period, color combinations were used in the *odoshi* (braid) of *samurai* armor. A wide variety of designs were created in the *odoshi* by weaving in colorful strings or dyed leather strips.

Later Developments—A new type of imported fabric called MEIBUTSUGIRE greatly influenced textile design of the Muromachi (1333–1568) and Azuchi-Momoyama (1568–1600) periods. The most typical examples of textile design during these two periods are found in NŌ costumes. In everyday wear the layered kimono was replaced by the single, simple one-piece style of kimono with shorter sleeves called *kosode*, the prototype of the modern kimono.

The kimono underwent several design and fabric changes during the Edo period (1600–1868). Painted designs in the form of sketches were fashionable, and by the mid-Edo period a new dye-resist technique called *yūzen-zome* (see YŪZEN) was developed. Decorative motifs came from many sources. After the center of culture shifted from Kyōto to Edo (now Tōkyō), a new aesthetic called *iki* (see IKI AND SUI) developed among wealthy townspeople, and sober colors such as dark blue, gray, or brown became popular. Various kinds of stripes or crisscross stripes were fashionable. It was also fashionable among the wealthy townspeople of the period to add sophisticated designs to parts of a kimono that were not visible, such as the lining or openings of sleeves. See also CLOTHING; DYES AND DYE COLORS; TEXTILES.

Design Law   意匠法

(Ishō Hō). The Design Law of 1959 protects designs (*ishō*) by registration at the Patent Office. Design is defined as "the shape, pattern, or color, or combination of these, of an article which through the sense of sight arouses an aesthetic sensation" (art. 2[1]). To be registrable a design must be novel and nonobvious (art. 3). Registration confers on the registrant an exclusive right to work (*jisshi*; i.e., to execute) his or her registered design in business (art. 20).

Deusu   デウス

Religious term derived from the Latin word *Deus*, meaning "God," and used by the early (16th century) Christian missionaries working in Japan. The Buddhist name Dainichi (Skt: Mahāvairocana) had first been employed but was soon superseded by Deusu so as to distinguish clearly the Christian concept of the deity from the Buddhist one. For the same reason, other Western theological terms were assimilated into Japanese; e.g., *sakuramento* (sacrament), *anima* (soul), and *eukarisuchiya* (Eucharist). Today the Japanese word *kami* is used for the Christian God. See also CHRISTIANITY.

Dewa Mountains 出羽山地

(Dewa Sanchi). A series of interconnected mountain ranges in Aomori, Akita, and Yamagata prefectures, northern Honshū. The mountains run north to south, parallel to the Ōu Mountains. The Dewa Mountains are known for Japanese cedar and cypress. Gold, silver, and copper deposits are also found here.

Dewa Sanzan 出羽三山

A group of three mountains in central Yamagata Prefecture, northern Honshū: GASSAN (1,984 m; 6,509 ft), YUDONOSAN (1,504 m; 4,934 ft), and HAGUROSAN (414 m; 1,358 ft). It is a center of worship for the religious sect SHUGENDŌ and part of Bandai-Asahi National Park.

Dewa Sanzan Shrines 出羽三山神社

(Dewa Sanzan Jinja). A group of three Shintō shrines—the Gassan Jinja, Ideha Jinja (also called Dewa Jinja), and Yudonosan Jinja—in Yamagata Prefecture. The shrines are situated on the Three Mountains of Dewa or Dewa Sanzan (Gassan, Hagurosan, and Yudonosan, respectively), part of the Dewa Mountains. The Gassan Jinja is dedicated to the moon deity Tsukiyomi no Mikoto. The Yudonosan Jinja, which is sacred to the mountain deity Ōyamatsumi no Kami, is unusual in that its object of worship is not housed in a shrine building but rather is an exposed sacred rock from which issues a hot spring. The Ideha Jinja enshrines a local deity called Ideha no Kami. The deities of the three Dewa shrines were considered Japanese incarnations (*suijaku*) of Buddhist deities. The complex is one of the major centers for SHUGENDŌ, a Buddhist-Shintō syncretic mountain cult. A common oratory for all three shrines is at the foot of Hagurosan, where festivals are held. The annual festival is held on 15 July. See also HONJI SUIJAKU.

dharma 法

(J: *hō*). An Indian term with various meanings such as law, custom, prescribed conduct, duty, justice, and good works. Dharma is used by Buddhists primarily in two senses, the first being the more common: (1) the teachings of the Buddha, i.e., Buddhism, and (2) the various elements that combine to make up the physical world as well as the body and mind of the sentient being, i.e, any living creature. The KUSHA SCHOOL recognizes 75 such dharmas, and the HOSSŌ SECT 100 dharmas.

dialects 方言

(*hōgen*). Japanese dialects are regionally distinct forms of the Japanese language. They evolved from a common ancient language into separate localized speech forms because geographical or social distance allowed linguistic changes to develop independently.

Dialect Divisions—The main dialect divisions include:

Kyūshū dialects. Kagoshima has a transi-

tional dialect between the dialects of Honshū and the RYŪKYŪ DIALECTS. This transitional dialect is marked most notably by the frequent glottal stop that replaces a final consonant/vowel syllable, e.g., *jet'* (standard Japanese *eki*, station). The west coast of Kyūshū is distinguished by its adjectival ending *-ka* in place of the *-i* of other dialects, e.g., *akaka* (standard Japanese *akai*, red; cf the Okinawan usage *akasan*).

Honshū dialects. These are divided into western (Kansai) and eastern (Kantō) by all scholars, but the boundary line chosen by most runs either east or west of Gifu Prefecture and the city of Nagoya. The western Honshū group, which includes Shikoku, is often divided into two groups, Okayama-Hiroshima and Ōsaka-Kyōto. The former has an accent system similar to the Tōkyō system (see ACCENT IN THE JAPANESE LANGUAGE), while sharing common grammatical traits with the Ōsaka-Kyōto group. The eastern Honshū group is dominated by the Tōkyō dialect, from which most people further distinguish the northeastern (Tōhoku) dialect group because of the latter's peculiar treatment of the vowels *-i-* and *-u-* when combined with the sibilants *z* and *j*. Although Old Japanese distinguished the four syllables *zu, dzu, ji,* and *dzi*, only a limited area in Kyūshū and southern Shikoku has kept the distinction. In some parts of northeastern Kyūshū one still finds three of the four preserved: *dzu, ji,* and *dzi*. Most of Japan, like the Tōkyō or standard dialect, now has only the two: *zu* and *ji*. The northeastern Honshū dialects have pushed the process still further and have only *zu* for all four syllables (hence their nickname: *zūzūben* or *zūzū* dialects).

Even the nonspecialist in Japan becomes strongly aware of dialectal characteristics that separate the eastern and western parts of Honshū. These characteristics generally are related to grammatical structure. Because of compulsory education, the Tōkyō or standard dialect is understood virtually everywhere.

Social Dialects—The most important varieties of social language are treated under other entries (see FEMININE LANGUAGE; MASCULINE LANGUAGE; NYŌBŌ KOTOBA; TABOO EXPRESSIONS). A few other varieties have become obsolete, including a special language called *kuruwa kotoba* that once flourished in the Yoshiwara pleasure quarter of Edo (now Tōkyō) and fell into disuse in the Meiji period (1868–1912); court language (*kyūteigo*); and expressions peculiar to the military.

Diamond Lease Co, Ltd

ダイヤモンドリース[株]

(Daiyamondo Rīsu). Comprehensive leasing firm affiliated with the Mitsubishi group of companies. Incorporated in 1971. It has 12 branches and 7 offices. Sales for the fiscal year ending March 1991 totaled ¥286.6 billion (US $2.1 billion), of which leasing accounted for 70 percent; installment credits, 21 percent; and other revenues, 9 percent. The company was capitalized at ¥6.9 billion (US $50.3 million) in the same year. Headquarters are in Tōkyō.

dictionaries 辞書

(*jisho*). Japan had no indigenous writing system when the influence of foreign culture, especially that of China, first began to be felt in the 7th century. The earliest written documents in Japan were mainly Buddhist writings and scriptures in Chinese and are believed to have been imported by way

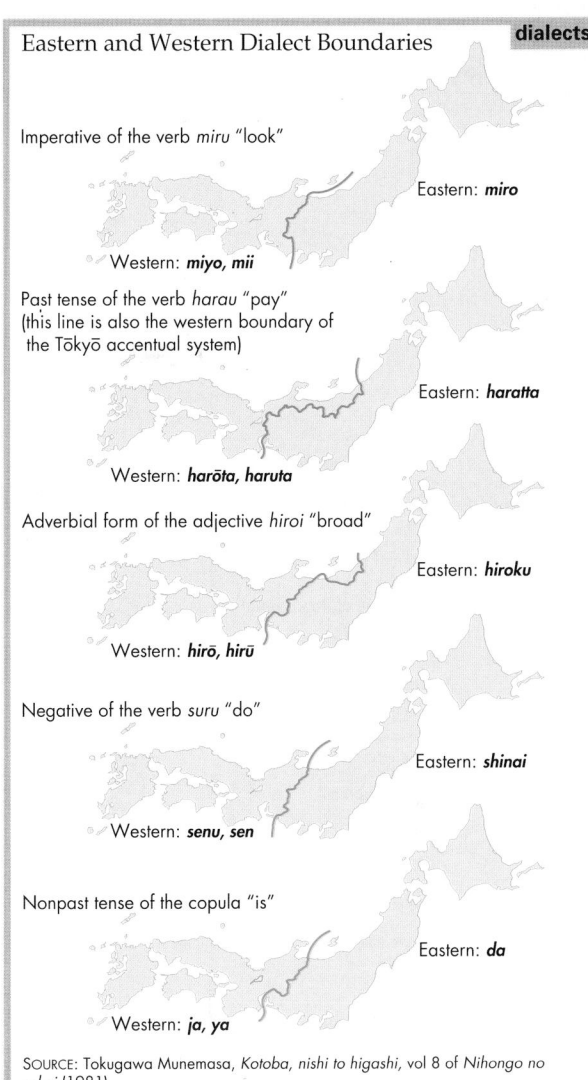

Eastern and Western Dialect Boundaries — dialects

Imperative of the verb *miru* "look"
Eastern: *miro*
Western: *miyo, mii*

Past tense of the verb *harau* "pay" (this line is also the western boundary of the Tōkyō accentual system)
Eastern: *haratta*
Western: *harōta, haruta*

Adverbial form of the adjective *hiroi* "broad"
Eastern: *hiroku*
Western: *hirō, hirū*

Negative of the verb *suru* "do"
Eastern: *shinai*
Western: *senu, sen*

Nonpast tense of the copula "is"
Eastern: *da*
Western: *ja, ya*

SOURCE: Tokugawa Munemasa, *Kotoba, nishi to higashi*, vol 8 of *Nihongo no sekai* (1981).

of Korea in the early 7th century.

The Japanese need for dictionaries in learning to read and write Chinese was first met by importing Chinese-Chinese dictionaries, such as the *Shuowen* (*Shuo-wen*), *Erya* (*Erh-ya*), and *Yunpian* (*Yün-p'ien*). Gradually, however, the Japanese began to undertake dictionary compilation themselves. Dictionaries in Japan traditionally have been classified as follows: *kanwa jiten*, Chinese-Japanese character dictionaries; *kokugo jiten*, dictionaries of indigenous Japanese words; and *semmongo jiten*, dictionaries of specialized or technical terms. However, the boundaries between these categories are not always clear; *kokugo jiten*, for example, often include Chinese or other loanwords as well as words that might easily be treated as technical or specialized terms.

Kanwa Jiten—The first Chinese character dictionary produced in Japan was the SHINSEN JIKYŌ, compiled by a Buddhist monk probably between 898 and 901. Following the *Shinsen jikyō*, numerous *kanwa jiten* appeared. Among those produced from the Heian period (794–1185) through the Edo period (1600–1868), four were outstanding: *Tenrei banshō meigi* (early 9th century) by the Buddhist monk KŪKAI, RUIJU MYŌGI SHŌ (early 12th century), and *Jikyō* and *Wagokuhen* (dates and compilers unknown).

Two important factors in the development of the Japanese dictionary were the importation of Western-language dictionaries in the late Edo period—whose influence resulted, for example, in the appending of in-

Legislative Flow in the Diet

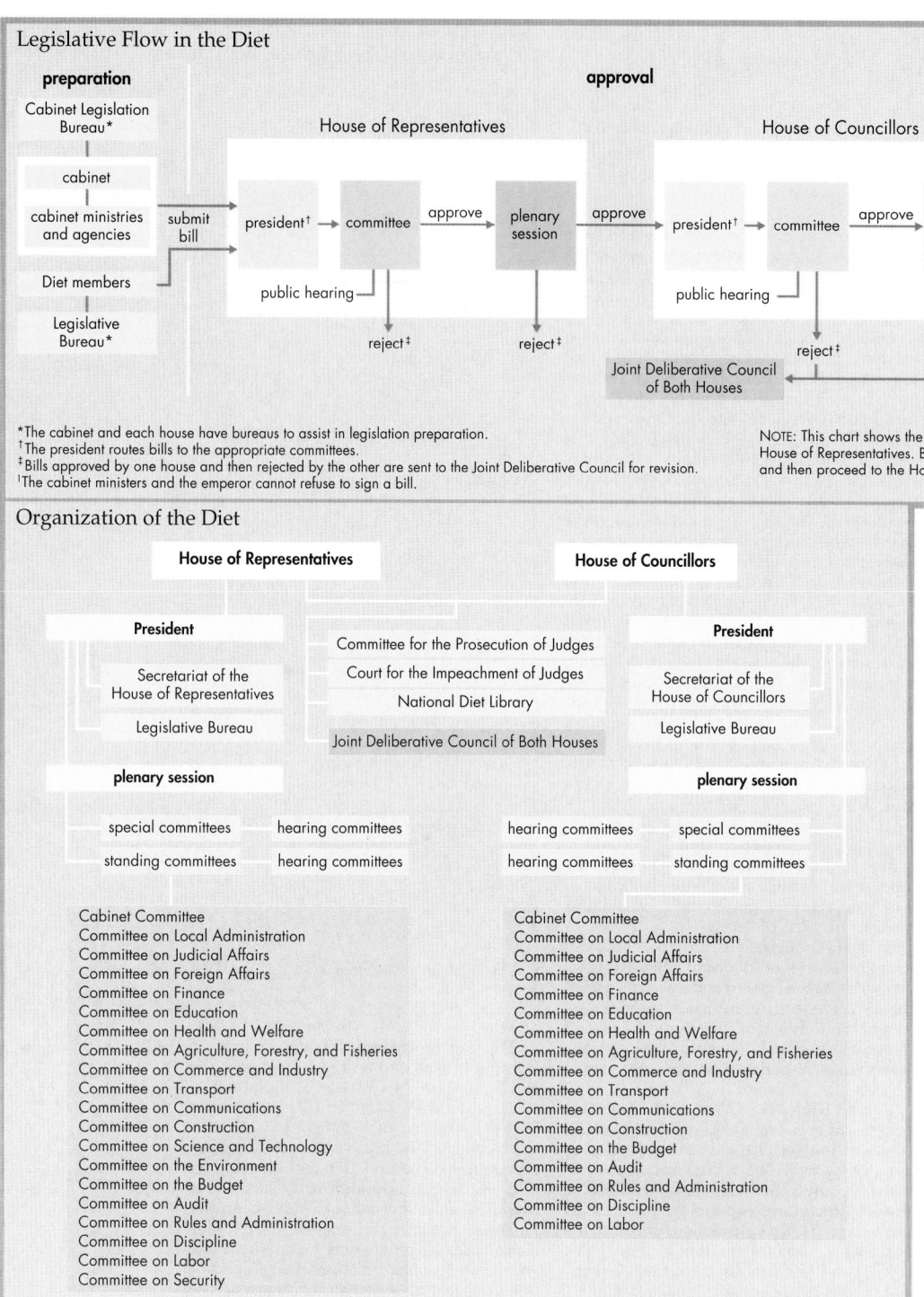

*The cabinet and each house have bureaus to assist in legislation preparation.
†The president routes bills to the appropriate committees.
‡Bills approved by one house and then rejected by the other are sent to the Joint Deliberative Council for revision.
¹The cabinet ministers and the emperor cannot refuse to sign a bill.

NOTE: This chart shows the legislative enactment process for bills introduced in the House of Representatives. Bills may also be initiated in the House of Councillors and then proceed to the House of Representatives.

dexes to the bodies of *kanwa jiten*—and the system of compulsory education adopted in the early Meiji period (1868–1912), which contributed to the mass production of all types of dictionaries in Japan. Of the numerous *kanwa jiten* published for general use, the following gained a particularly wide circulation: *Kanwa daijiten* (1903), jointly compiled by SHIGENO YASUTSUGU, Mishima Takashi, and Hattori Unokichi (1867–1939), and *Daijiten* (1917), by UEDA KAZUTOSHI. The most comprehensive of the modern *kanwa jiten* is the *Dai kanwa jiten*, compiled by MOROHASHI TETSUJI and published in 1955–60.

Kokugo Jiten—The creation of a Japanese writing system (based on the two phonetic syllabaries, *katakana* and *hiragana;* see KANA) resulted in a need for dictionaries that included indigenous Japanese words as well as borrowed words. One of the earliest ex-

tant *kokugo jiten* is the IROHA JIRUI SHŌ, compiled by Tachibana no Tadakane between 1174 and 1181. It is a prototype of similar dictionaries in use today. Unlike the *kanwa jiten,* its entries are arranged according to sound rather than Chinese character. Recently compiled *kokugo jiten* are generally arranged according to the standard *gojūon* (50-sound) system (see GOJŪON ZU).

Notable examples of the many *kokugo jiten* produced from the late Muromachi period (1333–1568) to the late Edo period include SETSUYŌSHŪ; WAKUN NO SHIORI; GAGEN SHŪRAN; and RIGEN SHŪRAN. Among those widely used in the Meiji and Taishō (1912–26) periods are *Kotoba no sono* (1885); *Kotoba no hayashi* (1888); *Genkai* (1889–91; a later edition of this is the revised and expanded DAIGENKAI); NIHON DAIJISHO (1892–93); *Kotoba no izumi* (1898); and *Jirin* (1907).

There are currently hundreds of different *kokugo jiten* in print. One of the largest and

most comprehensive is the 20-volume NIHON KOKUGO DAIJITEN completed by Shōgakukan Publishing Co, Ltd, in 1976. One of the most widely used contemporary *kokugo jiten* is the *Kōjien* (1955), essentially a lexicographical dictionary and a concise encyclopedia.

Semmongo Jiten—Although the *semmongo jiten* developed as a genre only after 1945, there were already more than 2,000 dictionaries of this type available by the late 1980s. Some are clearly lexical dictionaries and others are closer to encyclopedias. There is great diversity in the way entries are arranged, and they cover a wide range of subjects. There are dictionaries that deal exclusively with recently coined words, slang, trade terms, place and personal names, recently introduced loanwords, acronyms, sports and leisure activities, and so on. Field-specific dictionaries exist for such subjects as mathematics, physics, chemistry, computer science, linguistics, Japanese literature, world literature, music, history, geography, medicine, social work, transportation, architecture, communication, law, economics, management, business, education, the performing arts, and movies.

Diet   国会

(Kokkai). The legislative branch of the Japanese government. According to the CONSTITUTION OF JAPAN, the Diet is "the highest organ of state power" and the "sole law-making organ of the State." The Diet consists of two chambers: the HOUSE OF REPRESENTATIVES (Shūgiin), or lower house, and the HOUSE OF COUNCILLORS (Sangiin), or upper house. All Diet members are selected in popular elections.

History—The Japanese Diet is the oldest national assembly in Asia. The IMPERIAL DIET (Teikoku Gikai), the direct predecessor of the present Diet, was established in 1890 through provisions in the CONSTITUTION OF THE EMPIRE OF JAPAN (1889) and consisted of a House of Peers (Kizokuin) and a House of Representatives. Constitutionally, the Imperial Diet was weak, primarily because the power of legislation was vested in the emperor and because the cabinet was responsible to the emperor rather than to the Diet. Furthermore, the House of Peers, which consisted of imperial princes, the hereditary peerage, imperial nominees, and certain of the nation's highest taxpayers, was given equal power with the elected House of Representatives. Initially, the House of Representatives reflected the opinions of a highly restricted segment of the public, representing only the 1.5 percent of the population who paid an annual tax of ¥15.0 or more. Not until the passage of the Universal Manhood

Suffrage Law in 1925 did all male citizens over the age of 25 obtain the right to vote and thus the possibility of influencing their legislative representatives. See UNIVERSAL MANHOOD SUFFRAGE MOVEMENT.

Especially during the Taishō period (1912–26), substantial changes occurred in Japan's body politic, including its national assembly: Sovereignty might be constitutionally vested in the emperor, but legislative power was exercised by him and his advisers with the consent of the Diet. Members formally organized themselves into parliamentary parties and articulated alternative policies that were covered by the newspapers and thus helped shape public attitudes. This in turn influenced, to some degree at least, the civilian and military bureaucrats. See TAISHŌ DEMOCRACY; POLITICAL PARTIES.

Possibly the best indication of the Diet's growing powers in the 1920s was the energy that its opponents devoted to circumscribing them. Members were accused (sometimes correctly) of being the corrupt handmaidens of vested corporate interests, incapable of protecting the "national polity" (KOKUTAI). Terrorist groups plotted assassinations, some of which were successful. By the end of the 1930s, parliamentarianism was a flame that flickered uncertainly. Parliamentary parties were forced into the IMPERIAL RULE ASSISTANCE ASSOCIATION in order to better serve the interests of the nation's predominantly military rulers. The Diet became a rubber stamp, but those in power did not take the final step of abolishing it altogether.

The transformation of the Imperial Diet into the present Diet was set forth initially in the postwar constitution (effective in May 1947). Unlike the previous constitution, the new constitution gave supreme legislative power to the Diet and made it the most important organ of the government.

Organization—Bicameralism was retained at the insistence of Japanese authorities, who feared that a single chamber might be captured by a radical majority. However, the hereditary and appointive House of Peers was replaced by the elected House of Councillors, which consists of 252 members who serve six-year terms. The prime minister and a majority of his cabinet ministers were required to be members of the Diet and, "in the exercise of executive power, shall be collectively responsible to the Diet"; this is in direct contrast to the relationship that had prevailed under the Meiji Constitution. A revolution in constitutional doctrine had taken place: the entire membership of the Diet would be publicly elected, and the cabinet, in which executive authority was vested, would be responsible to the Diet. The doctrine of parliamentary supremacy had supplanted that of imperial prerogative.

At the same time, the new constitution altered the relationship between the two chambers. The House of Representatives and the House of Councillors share legislative power: "A bill becomes a law on passage by both Houses . . . ." However, the 512 representatives, whose term of office is four years unless the house is dissolved, have authority in three important areas. First, in the designation of the prime minister, if there is disagreement between the two chambers, "the decision of the House of Representatives shall be the decision of the Diet." Second, the national budget must first be submitted to the House of Representatives. Furthermore, if the two houses fail to reach agreement on the budget, and if joint committees fail to resolve the matter or no decision is made by the House of Councillors within 30 days, the will of the lower house prevails, regardless of inaction or contrary action by the upper house (see BUDGET, NATIONAL). Third, while international treaties may first be introduced for approval in either chamber, the decision of the lower house prevails over a contrary judgment by the upper house if joint committees fail to resolve the matter or no decision is made by the House of Councillors within 30 days. Also, in all fields of legislation, the House of Representatives can override the House of Councillors by a two-thirds vote. Thus the Diet is bicameral, but the House of Representatives is predominant in certain crucial spheres. Finally, like the old constitution, the Occupation-sponsored organic law is silent on the subject of political parties.

Enhancing the position of the Diet, especially that of the House of Representatives, by constitutional edict constituted only the first step in reorganizing the national legislature. Of equal importance was revising the Imperial Law of the Houses, which governed its internal operations. The new Diet Law (Kokkaihō) and the Rules of the House of Representatives and House of Councillors (Shūgiin Kisoku and Sangiin Kisoku) were passed between April and June 1947, some six weeks prior to the formal adoption of the new constitution. The Diet Law and the Rules of the respective houses have been amended in the intervening years but not in a fashion to undermine fundamentally the broad principles of the legislation adopted in 1947.

The Workings of the Diet—If an item of legislative business is not controversial, the system usually works smoothly. Legislation is drafted by government bureaucrats in the various ministries. Then it follows a process leading to final approval that is carefully programmed by the majority party, with the tacit concurrence of the opposition parties. In contrast, parliamentary procedures have been subjected to almost unbearable strain whenever the Diet has become the battleground for the resolution of social conflict. For the governing majority party, highest priority must be accorded to maintenance of intraparty consensus on the substance of the proposed legislation as well as on the parliamentary tactics to be employed. For the opposition-party representatives and councillors, the harsh reality of their minority status involves serious tactical problems. They recognize that, barring a split in the majority party, their chances of prevailing against the governing party's overwhelming power are virtually nil.

The Diet is a legislative institution, but it is also a representative assembly. To be sure, the electoral system has been criticized as not being entirely fair. First, rural voters, a declining percentage of the public, are overrepresented (see REAPPORTIONMENT ISSUE). Second, campaigning is becoming increasingly expensive, giving an advantage to the wealthy and those with close ties to corporate interests. Third, certain social groups hold a disproportionate share of seats. Fourth, because members must spend an inordinate amount of time performing "errand-boy" functions for their constituents, they have too little energy to devote themselves to being their nation's supreme legislators.

It is important to note, however, that, despite its problems, the Diet has become the principal training ground for Japan's supreme political leaders: the prime minister and his cabinet ministers. A lengthy career in the Diet has become an absolute prerequisite to high political office. See also PRIME MINISTER AND CABINET.

Diet member legislation 議員立法

(*giin rippō*). General term for bills proposed by DIET members and for such bills when enacted into law. It also includes committee bills proposed by committees and submitted under the name of the chairperson. The constitution does not specify who may propose bills to the Diet, but it is commonly recognized that the cabinet (see PRIME MINISTER AND CABINET) and individual Diet members have the right to propose bills. As in the English parliamentary system, most of the bills proposed to the Diet are offered by the cabinet.

Until 1955, a single Diet member could propose a piece of legislation, but at present a limitation on such proposals requires 20 or

Diet
1 Completed in 1936, the Diet Building has an exterior of domestic granite and covers an area of 12,400 square meters. Shown here are the building's main entrance and central tower.
2 Statues of several Meiji-period (1868–1912) statesmen stand in the Diet Building's central entrance hall.
3 Members meet in the main chamber of the House of Representatives. The speaker of the house sits at the raised dais behind the central podium.

more members of the House of Representatives or 10 or more members of the House of Councillors to propose a bill, or, if the bill accompanies a budget, 50 or more representatives or 20 or more councillors.

Diet, members of　国会議員

(*kokkai giin*). The term *kokkai giin* encompasses both members of Japan's HOUSE OF REPRESENTATIVES and members of its HOUSE OF COUNCILLORS. Candidates for the House of Representatives must be at least 25 years of age, and candidates for the House of Councillors must be at least 30. Except when caught in the act of committing a crime, members of the Diet may not be arrested while the Diet is in session without the consent of the members of the house to which they belong. Members are also granted other rights, such as the right not be held liable outside the Diet for their statements and votes within it. Traditionally many members of the Japanese Diet have been former bureaucrats, labor union leaders, and secretaries to Diet members; in recent years, there has come into existence a new generation of members, which consists of the children of former members. See also DIET; ELECTIONS.

digital audiotape　デジタルオーディオテープ

(DAT; J: *dejitaru ōdiotēpu*). A technology that records audio signals by converting the signals into bits of digital information and transferring the information to magnetic (cassette) tape; the digitally encoded audio signals are converted to an analog state for playback. The sound quality is virtually the same as that of a compact disc (CD). Japanese electronics manufacturers began marketing DAT recorders in 1987, and by 1990 about 150,000 DAT units were being sold per year in Japan. Sales in the United States, however, were blocked from the beginning by such organizations as the International Federation of the Phonographic Industry (IFPI) and the Recording Industry Association of America (RIAA), which feared that the recording capability of DAT would wipe out the CD market and rob artists of the royalties they would receive from the sale of CDs. After a prolonged struggle Japanese manufacturers changed DAT specifications to limit digital copying of commercial recordings to a single generation. Following acceptance of the practice by IFPI and RIAA, production under the revised specifications was scheduled to begin after 1991. In Japan in 1991 portable DAT units (without copy limitations) were selling for less than ¥100,000 (US $690).

Digital Equipment Corporation Japan　日本ディジタルイクイップメント[株]

(Nihon Dijitaru Ikuippumento). Vendor and assembler of computer systems for Digital Equipment Corporation (DEC) of the United States. Incorporated in 1982 as DEC's Japanese subsidiary. It has 18 branches and 30 service centers in Japan. For the fiscal year ending June 1990, sales totaled ¥128.8 billion (US $837.6 million) and capitalization stood at ¥4.8 billion (US $31.2 million). Headquarters are in Tōkyō.

Diners Club of Japan, Inc　[株]日本ダイナースクラブ

(Nihon Daināsu Kurabu). Credit card company. Incorporated in 1960 as the first credit card company in Japan. The firm was founded by FUJI BANK, LTD; JAPAN TRAVEL BU-REAU, INC; and Diners Club (USA). The company offers its members various services in fields such as mail-order sales, travel, real estate, and insurance. For the fiscal year ending March 1990, sales totaled ¥259.2 billion (US $1.7 billion) and capitalization stood at ¥100.0 million (US $653,000). Headquarters are in Tōkyō.

Ding Ruchang (Ting Ju-ch'ang)　丁汝昌

(?–1895; J: Tei Joshō). Chinese admiral who built up China's first modern navy in the late 19th century, only to have it defeated in the SINO-JAPANESE WAR OF 1894–1895. Although outwardly modernized, the Chinese navy was poorly prepared for combat. After being defeated by the Japanese navy in a 17 September 1894 battle off the mouth of the YALU RIVER, the Chinese navy ultimately fled to Weihaiwei, Shandong (Shantung). In February 1895 the Japanese captured the hills above Weihaiwei and forced the surrender of Admiral Ding. Ding refused an offer for refuge in Japan and committed suicide.

Diplomatic Bluebook　外交青書

(*Gaikō seisho*). Report on Japan's diplomatic activities published annually since 1957 by the Ministry of Foreign Affairs. Formal title *Waga gaikō no kinkyō* (Japan's Diplomatic Activities). The bluebook begins with an overview of the international situation and a statement of Japan's basic foreign policy objectives; this is followed by sections providing more detailed treatment of specific issues and initiatives and reports on the status of Japan's relations with individual countries and regions. The bluebook has been published in English translation since 1987.

Diplomatic Record Office, Ministry of Foreign Affairs
外務省外交史料館

(Gaimushō Gaikō Shiryōkan). The office founded by the Ministry of Foreign Affairs in 1971 to collect, organize, compile, and preserve diplomatic records. Located in Minato Ward, Tōkyō, the office maintains a reading room and exhibits that are open to the public. The archives have approximately 48,000 volumes of diplomatic records from 1869 to 1945; the *Tsūshin zenran* (319 vols) and *Zoku tsūshin zenran* (1,784 vols), which record diplomatic affairs during the period 1859–1868; some 600 treaty-related documents; and approximately 1,100 official and personal letters and notes of state leaders. In 1991 the office compiled the 171st volume of *Nihon gaikō bunsho* (Documents on Japanese Foreign Policy).

diplomatics　古文書学

(*komonjo gaku*). Diplomatics is a field of scholarship concerned with the physical features and interpretation of a wide variety of historical documents. It developed in Europe in the 17th century and was introduced in Japan at the end of the 19th century. An indispensable ancillary discipline of historiography, diplomatics covers a wide area, ranging from methodology for the decipherment and criticism of texts to investigation of the authorship of documents and study of their relationship to historical events. *Komonjo* (literally, "old documents") are defined as written instruments that convey the will of one person to another and include such materials as imperial edicts, shogunal orders, private contracts, and personal letters, but not other primary sources such as annals and diaries. The writing material, documentary form, style of language, orthography, calligraphy, the use of a seal (*in*) or monogram (*kaō*), and the manner of dating documents vary widely with each historical period.

Characteristics of Documents——Although during the 7th and 8th centuries wooden tablets (MOKKAN) were also used, the chief writing material of documents was paper (see WASHI). Before the mid-12th century *tategami*, a single sheet of unfolded paper with writing on one side, was the only form in which documents were written; thereafter *tategami* was used mainly for court documents and private legal instruments. From the mid-12th century to the 16th century *origami*, a single sheet of paper folded in half horizontally with writing on both outer surfaces, was preferred by members of the military class, and it was used for shogunal documents of the Kamakura (1185–1333) and Muromachi (1333–1568) periods and for most private documents. *Kirigami*, a half sheet of paper or a piece cut to fit a message, appeared in the 14th century and was widely used, along with *origami*, in the Edo period (1600–1868).

Both Chinese characters (KANJI) and the Japanese syllabary (KANA) were used in documents; characters, however, were often abridged, altered, or substituted for each other, and *kana* usage was not standardized. The Chinese characters in almost all formal documents connected with the RITSURYŌ SYSTEM, which was instituted beginning in the 7th century, were written in *kaisho* ("square-character") CALLIGRAPHY. Most private documents, as well as public documents after the late 10th century, were in *gyōsho* ("running-hand") or the radically cursive *sōsho* ("grass") calligraphy. As styles of calligraphy and conventions of usage differed according to social class and historical period, their study is an essential adjunct of diplomatics.

The vast majority of documents before the 10th century were written in classical Chinese (KAMBUN). However, certain imperial proclamations (SEMMYŌ), chiefly of 8th-century provenance and of which few survive, were written in Japanese, using Chinese characters both in their semantic senses to indicate Japanese words and as phonetic markers to represent Japanese syllables. From the 10th century the Chinese used in documents was increasingly corrupted by the introduction of Japanese usages (see HENTAI KAMBUN), and by the Sengoku period (1467–1568) there had developed from it a hybrid style of literary Japanese (see SŌRŌBUN). In addition to these basic linguistic complexities, interpretation of *komonjo* is further complicated by the use of TABOO EXPRESSIONS (for example the substitution of the character for "joy" in place of that for "illness") and the occurrence in provincial documents of dialect.

From the mid-Heian period (794–1185) onward there were two main types of public documents. KUDASHIBUMI were issued as a direct command, with the name of the issuing authority at the beginning, followed by the name of the recipient, and at the end the signature of the agent responsible for the document. *Migyōsho* came from the hand of an attendant who relayed in letter form a message from a higher authority—emperor, regent, or shōgun—whose identity remained undisclosed; the text preceded all else and the name of the recipient appeared at the end. Once a scholar has identified the signature (or, from the 10th century, the *kaō*, or monogram) of the nominal issuing agent of

Treatment Rates for Major Ailments

	1955	1960	1965	1970	1975	1980	1984	1990
				(per 100,000 population)				
Tuberculosis	452	358	301	192	116	56	38	27
Infectious diseases (excluding tuberculosis)	359	436	336	313	270	213	135	131
Cancer	36	55	63	86	95	130	161	218
Diabetes	6	13	34	64	87	103	119	161
Mental disorders	67	113	207	247	269	290	315	367
Heart disease	55	83	156	222	263	272	246	259
High blood pressure	61	130	244	343	475	473	548	554
Cerebral hemorrhages, infarctions, and thromboses	15	28	69	118	158	221	226	305
Respiratory ailments	320	532	730	1,078	1,067	978	873	809
Digestive tract ailments	684	1,157	1,444	1,688	1,535	1,545	1,284	1,331

SOURCE: Ministry of Health and Welfare, Kōsei hakusho (annual): 1992.

such a document, he must then determine the actual author. In the case of private documents, such as letters, the person whose signature or *kaō* appears under the date is normally the author. The recipient is relatively easy to identify in the case of documents sent from superiors to inferiors, but not in the case of documents sent from inferiors to superiors, since these were often addressed to attendants of the intended receiver. When the recipient of a document was the emperor or shōgun, the space where the addressee's name would normally have been written was left blank.

Opening and closing remarks in the main text of public documents, though formulaic, differed considerably depending on the gravity of the contents, providing scholars with a clear indication of a document's relative importance. With the exception of legal and judicial documents, it was common to write the entire message on a single sheet of paper, resorting to margins and interlinear space when necessary. The date of a document usually followed the main text, but only on public documents was it customary to record the date in full.

Evolution of Historical Documents— Approximately 30,000 wooden tablets from the 7th and 8th centuries have been discovered. The oldest extant paper documents date from 702, and 8th-century documents number around 15,000, most of them preserved at the SHŌSŌIN storehouse. Although a number of Heian-period diaries written by court nobles have been preserved, only some 10,000 *komonjo* of the period are extant. Edicts issued by the *ritsuryō* government to its subordinate offices were known as KAMPU; however, changes in the institutional apparatus of the imperial government in the 9th century, such as the establishment of an executive chancellery (KURŌDO-DOKORO), were accompanied by a change in documentary form. When the Fujiwara family rose to the imperial regency in the 10th century, more changes occurred, culminating in the appearance of *kudashibumi* and *migyōsho*.

Nearly half a million documents survive from the Kamakura and Muromachi periods. During the early Kamakura period, not only commands related to the administration of government but also all matters concerning vassals, such as their investiture or confirmation in domainal lands and appointment to office, were conveyed by *kudashibumi*; *migyōsho* were used in transmitting the shogunate's instructions or official messages to its deputies (TANDAI). When the HŌJŌ FAMILY became the de facto rulers of the Kamakura shogunate, the *gechijō*, a condensed form of *migyōsho* and *kudashibumi*, developed.

During the Muromachi period *migyōsho* were the primary instrument for the transmission of shogunal orders. Powerful shogunal vassals, who had been made provincial governors (SHUGO) and who developed from around the end of the 14th cen-

tury into largely independent regional rulers (SHUGO DAIMYŌ), issued orders and sanctions that were in many respects similar to those of the shogunate. In the late 15th century SENGOKU DAIMYŌ, who had largely displaced the *shugo* daimyō, issued *imbanjō*, documents in letter form with personal SEALS affixed in lieu of a monogram. The imperial court issued a fairly large number of documents, but these are of less interest as historical sources because of the court's weakened authority. Documents of religious institutions, rich in quantity and variety, are important because the most powerful, such as the temples TŌDAIJI and ENRYAKUJI, constituted an independent political force. Documents written by commoners appeared for the first time during the Muromachi period. These included petitions by peasants requesting reduction of taxes, contracts between neighboring villages governing water use, and regulations established by villagers for their own observance.

There is an abundance of surviving documents from the Azuchi-Momoyama (1568–1600) and Edo periods; those related to local administration alone are estimated at well over 50 million. SHUINJŌ, documents impressed with the shōgun's seal, were used to issue the basic codes governing the activities of religious institutions, the imperial court, and domainal lords (daimyō), while *hammotsu*, which bore the shōgun's monogram, were used from TOKUGAWA IEMITSU's time for directives issued to the imperial court and powerful daimyō. *Rōjū hōsho* were orders emanating from or issued in the name of the shōgun by senior councillors (RŌJŪ); *tasshi* and *fure* were orders issued by the *rōjū* to their retainers and to commoners or by government bureaucrats to their subordinates. Daimyō and their administrations issued similar documents for the management of domainal affairs. In addition, an immense number of private documents—genealogical records, promissory notes and agreements, real estate contracts, and letters—shed light on such activities as farming, fishing, handicrafts, transportation, commerce, and finance. See also DAI NIHON KOMONJO.

direct demand 直接請求

(*chokusetsu seikyū*). A system of direct participation in government by local inhabitants, designed to make up for the shortcomings of representative democracy in local administration. The Local Autonomy Law (Chihō Jichi Hō) of 1947 provides for the following types of direct demands: (1) enactment, revision, or repeal of ordinances; (2) auditing of the affairs of a local public body or those that come under the authority of the executive organ of a local public body; (3) dismissal of the assembly of a local public body; (4) dismissal of a local public body assemblyman; (5) dismissal of the head of a local public body; and (6) dismissal of a vice-governor or deputy official of a local public body, the official in overall

charge of revenue and expenditures or a revenue official, or a member of the election administration commission, auditing commission, or public safety commission.

diseases 病気

(*byōki*). The disease incidence rate of the Japanese was 6,768 per 100,000 inhabitants in 1990. Disorders of the digestive tract accounted for 20.8 percent of the total; disorders of the circulatory system, 17.4 percent; respiratory tract disorders, 12.6 percent; osteomuscular disorders, 10.6 percent; nervous and sensory system disorders, 7.9 percent; mental disorders, 5.7 percent; metabolic and nutritional disorders, 3.7 percent; cancers, 3.4 percent; dermatologic disorders, 3.2 percent; urogenital disorders, 3.0 percent; and infectious and parasitic diseases, 2.5 percent. In 1960 digestive tract disorders ranked first, followed by respiratory tract disorders, infectious and parasitic diseases, and circulatory system disorders. The most distinctive change over the next 30 years was a marked reduction in the incidence of infectious and parasitic diseases.

Infectious Diseases—Contagious diseases have declined in Japan as a result of improvements in living conditions, progress in medical science, and the widespread dissemination of knowledge concerning sanitation. Cholera, smallpox, the plague, yellow fever, relapsing fever, and rabies are hardly ever found. Typhoid fever, diphtheria, malaria, and poliomyelitis have also markedly decreased. However, there has been only a slight decline in the number of cases of dysentery, scarlet fever, Japanese encephalitis, measles, tetanus, and influenza.

Parasitic Diseases—Japan has long had a reputation of being a country with many parasitic diseases such as *Schistosoma japonicum*, scrub typhus, Japanese river fever, lung fluke, oriental liver fluke, and filariasis, but it is now quite unusual to find patients suffering from these diseases.

Neoplasm—Malignant neoplasm (CANCER) constitutes a particularly important problem in Japan and ranks as the leading cause of death (26.5 percent of all deaths in 1990). The number of deaths due to cancer has risen steadily; in 1990 stomach cancer ranked first among all cancers as a cause of death in both males and females. Next came lung, liver, and pancreatic cancer. Esophageal cancer and rectal cancer ranked fifth and sixth, respectively, in males. Breast cancer ranked fifth in females, followed by cancer of the uterus. Japan and France had the highest rates of liver cancer of all the industrially developed countries in 1968, and the Japanese rate has tended to rise gradually. In the Japanese, liver cancer often occurs in association with liver cirrhosis, a combination thought to be accountable for the poor record of success in surgical removal.

285

Disorders of the Respiratory Tract—

Tuberculosis, once the number-one killer in Japan, began to decrease in the mid-1930s, and by 1990 it had dropped sharply to 3.0 deaths in 100,000 (3,664 deaths in total). It has recently become more prevalent in the upper age range, as is the case in Western countries. There were once many hospitals and sanatoriums specializing in tuberculosis in Japan, but these have gradually been converted into hospitals specializing in thoracic disorders (mainly lung cancer) or in geriatric diseases.

Disorders of the Circulatory System—

While cerebral apoplexy was the leading cause of death in the late 1970s, its place was taken in the late 1980s by cancer and heart disease. Cerebral hemorrhage remains more common than cerebral infarction, although occurrences of the latter have been increasing since the late 1950s. This is probably due to an important rise in cerebral arteriosclerosis as one of the causative factors of infarction. Ischemic heart diseases increased fivefold as a cause of death during the years between 1955 and 1990. Intake of salt is much greater among the Japanese than among Westerners, which may partly account for the high incidence of hypertension. Stress is also considered an important factor in the fluctuation of blood lipids.

Common among the Japanese is the aortitis syndrome (often called Takayasu disease), an inflammatory disease particular to the aorta and the main adjacent arteries. As it is accompanied by an inability to palpate the radial artery, it is also called the "pulseless" disease. It is common among Asians 15–25 years old, and is five to seven times more common in females than in males.

Disorders of the Digestive Tract—

In Japan the most common cancer of the digestive tract is stomach cancer. Viral hepatitis, occurring after blood transfusion, was a social problem until Ōkōchi Kazuo (b 1928) clarified the connection between hepatitis and the Au-antigen, which was discovered by Baruch S. Blumberg in 1964. This led to the study of the Hb-antigen.

Blood Disorders—

Aplastic anemia is a common blood disease in Japan. Hemoglobinopathies are also common in Japan. The death rate from leukemia in Japan ranks 30th in the world. Acute myelogenous leukemia is the most common type in Japan.

Nervous Disorders—

SMON (subacute myelo-opticoneuropathy) affects the spinal cord, the peripheral nerves, and the optical nerves and is usually preceded by abdominal pain and diarrhea. It was found to be caused by chinoform, a drug used to combat amoebic dysentery. New outbreaks of SMON DISEASE virtually ceased in 1970 when chinoform was banned. Multiple sclerosis did not exist among the Japanese before World War II, but it has become fairly common in the postwar period.

Allergic Disorders—

Asthma is increasing in Japan. It is sometimes caused by allergic reaction to foods but in many cases is the result of air pollution.

Collagen Disease—

Behçet disease is a systemic inflammatory disorder. There were some 12,000 cases in Japan in 1990, probably the highest incidence in the world. Viral etiology is suspected, but causative linkages have not yet been established.

Poisoning—

"Minamata disease" became famous as the name for organic mercury poisoning after a large number of people from the city of Minamata were poisoned by eating fish and shellfish contaminated by methyl mercury. Mercury poisoning causes numbness of hands and feet, an unstable walk, narrowing of the visual field, deafness, and paralysis. Agricultural chemical poisoning began to appear in the 1950s, and the number of cases reached 1,564 in 1964; however, this problem has decreased as a result of the development of exotoxins and government control over agricultural chemicals. Globefish (*fugu*) poisoning results in severe paralysis of the respiratory muscles and is caused by a neurotoxin contained in the liver and ovaries of the fish, which is eaten as a delicacy in Japan. The government strictly controls the preparation of globefish, but poisoning still occurs occasionally. See also POLLUTION-RELATED DISEASES; AIDS.

dismissal of employees　　解雇

(*kaiko*). Under the Japanese CIVIL CODE, an employer can terminate without cause an employment contract that bears no terms of duration, so long as two weeks' advance notice is given (art. 627[1]). Nevertheless, to protect workers the Labor Standards Law (1947) sets various restrictions upon employers. In cases where employees suffer labor-related injuries, for example, employers cannot dismiss them until 30 days have elapsed following recuperation (art. 19). Dismissal is also prohibited during maternity leave and for a period of 30 days after childbirth (art. 19).

In principle the Labor Standards Law requires a minimum of 30 days' advance notice or severance pay equivalent to 30 days of labor or more. While the provisions of the older Civil Code remain on the books with respect to dismissal of employees, in practice those of the Labor Standards Law usually govern most cases of dismissals which are brought before the courts. Employers may dismiss employees without prior notice in cases of natural disaster or employee misconduct (art. 20). However, even in these cases employers are required to obtain approval from one of the LABOR STANDARDS INSPECTION OFFICES. Employees are protected from discrimination based on citizenship, beliefs, social position, or, in the case of female workers, marital or maternal status. Workers who have informed the authorities of an employer's violations of the Labor Standards Law, or who are engaged in legitimate union activities, are also protected (see LABOR LAWS).

Japan's present labor laws were instituted by the Allied OCCUPATION authorities after 1945 as part of a wholesale program of legal reform regarding the status of workers, and they have remained the basis of government labor policy to the present. However, although employees' rights are guaranteed in Japan by laws similar in principle to those existing in other industrial democracies, the manner in which employees are dismissed in Japan differs considerably from that of other countries. Since lifetime employment has been, and to a lesser extent still is, a common practice, it is difficult for a company to dismiss its regular employees prior to a fixed retirement age. Therefore, when adverse business conditions require management to reduce the labor force, part-time workers are in most cases the first to be discharged. If this proves insufficient to meet the situation, management will order some full-time employees to stay home until they are recalled. Commonly called *ichiji kaiko*, or "temporary discharge," this practice is a rough equivalent of the layoff system that is common in the United States. But unlike its US counterpart, *ichiji kaiko* does not end the employment relationship, and employers are required to pay their discharged workers a minimum of 60 percent of their full salaries during their suspension period (art. 26).

It is only when this too fails to solve the overemployment problem that companies start dismissing their regular employees. The first step commonly taken at this stage is to offer an open invitation for voluntary retirement with increased severance pay. The next step, if necessary, is the so-called *kata tataki*, or "tap on the shoulder": managers discreetly urge certain elderly or female employees to leave the firm. Because of its opaque nature, this practice often results in disputes over the "voluntariness" of retirement. Compulsory dismissal comes last. Normally employees above a certain age are targeted as a group, and the naming of individuals is avoided as much as possible. In practice, however, there are many instances where companies are accused of deliberately and selectively discharging union activists.

displaced Japanese war orphans in China　　中国残留孤児

(Chūgoku *zanryū koji*). At the end of World War II, a number of Japanese children who were orphaned or separated from their families, ranging from infants to 10-year-olds, were left behind in China, particularly Northeast China—then known as Manchuria. After normalization of diplomatic relations between Japan and China in 1972, many of these Japanese orphans began to search for the surviving members of their families in Japan. In 1981 the Japanese government began a program of inviting the orphans to visit Japan and carry on their search there. As of 1988, 1,588 people had visited Japan for that purpose, and 582 of them had established their identities as a result of the visit. The total number of orphans who asked the Japanese government for aid in establishing their identities was 2,181. Of these, 1,174 succeeded in establishing their identities, and 728 returned to live in Japan.

dispute resolution systems other than litigation　　裁判によらない紛争処理

(*saiban ni yoranai funsō shori*). Several methods are used extensively in Japan to settle disputes without resort to a formal lawsuit (*soshō*). Some of these nonlitigious methods, such as private negotiations between disputants (see JIDAN), have deep roots in Japanese social traditions; others are modern legal innovations (see LAW, ATTITUDES TOWARD). These latter types include CONCILIATION (*chōtei*), compromise (WAKAI), and ARBITRATION (*chūsai*).

Historical Background—

When discussing Japanese legal topics, it is essential to understand that the Japanese, like most people, prefer to avoid litigation; they have been successful in avoiding it because they have such efficient social alternatives. Justiciable law (or professional lawyers' law) was largely alien to Japanese culture prior to the Meiji Restoration (1868) and is not so widely resorted to in Japan today as it is in most Western nations. Part of Japan's comparatively high degree of success in settling disputes without lawsuits may be attributable to a long-standing bias of officialdom in favor of authority and against litigation. Some see the shallow penetration of justiciable law into Japanese society as a result of the

Examples of Distribution Systems in Japan

Home electronics products

NOTE: With most of its products flowing from the manufacturer's sales company to affiliated retail outlets and large discount stores, the home electronics products industry has one of the shortest, most direct distribution systems in Japan.

Farm produce

NOTE: The majority of farm produce still follows a complicated system of distribution channels, flowing through multiple levels of wholesalers and brokers before reaching the local retailer and the consumer. Alternative channels exist, such as direct distributors linking producer and consumer, but they only handle a relatively small volume of goods.

national emphasis on harmony of feeling or emotion to control human relations. Important also is the traditional Japanese delegation of dispute resolution functions to the family, village, or other intimate social groups (see IE; FAMILY; MURA).

Purely Social Methods of Dispute Resolution ── During the Tokugawa shogunate (1603–1867), traditional conciliation (naisai or atsukai, also sometimes translated "mediation") was highly developed in the towns and villages, using persons of status. Modern practice also confers a large role on informal conciliators such as superiors in the place of work, school, or neighborhood. With an enviable position of trust within his neighborhood, the Japanese policeman is often looked to for all sorts of counseling. Larger police stations have facilities assigned exclusively for this purpose with an experienced older officer in charge. Many municipalities have similar facilities manned by volunteers.

In domestic relations, the go-between (NAKŌDO) is used in arranged marriages, which still persist in various forms. In case of marital trouble, the go-between is available and consulted to smooth things over. Even if divorce is unavoidable, the law (Civil Code, art. 763) permits, and most Japanese spouses have for years resorted to, voluntary divorce agreements (kyōgi rikon), often mediated by go-betweens and thus outside the courts (see DIVORCE). Such divorces are effective when registered with the local government office in charge of household registers.

In workplaces (business or governmental bureaus) or neighborhoods, informal groupings of persons usually exist, held together by personal allegiance to the same prestige figure (oyabun) or by common university, village, or other ties (see OYABUN-KOBUN). Oyabun settle quarrels between members of their groups and negotiate differences between groups.

For disputes in the modern public law field (between a citizen and a government office or bureaucrats), the Japanese use of informal procedures and volunteer go-betweens is particularly instructive. Suits against the government are scarce in the Japanese courts. One reason lies in the traditional attitude of respect for officials (kanson mimpi), due particularly to the general incapacity of the citizenry to sue officials before the new constitution of 1947. Another reason is the official habit, even now, of "guiding" the citizenry by informal per-

suasion instead of resorting to the formal legal system. This broad usage is subsumed under the term ADMINISTRATIVE GUIDANCE (gyōsei shidō). It has manifold forms and procedures, all informal and vague, rendering legal suits in opposition ineffectual.

Another reason for the infrequency of litigation against the government is the extensive and effective network of volunteers organized throughout the country, under the supervision of the MANAGEMENT AND COORDINATION AGENCY (Sōmuchō) in the Prime Minister's Office. In 1955 the agency, then called the Cabinet Administrative Management Office, began to offer, informally, the "good offices" of its Administrative Inspection Bureau (Gyōsei Kansatsu Kyoku) to hear individual complaints. This practice proved so successful that the agency's enabling act was legally amended in 1960 to authorize this work in offices of every prefecture in the country. Later, a network of volunteers (local administrative counselors) was organized to reach every locality and to receive complaints, to try to adjust them, and, after screening them, to send those with merit to the bureau. See also ADMINISTRATIVE LITIGATION.

Worth mentioning also is the separate work of the Civil Liberties Bureau (Jinken Yōgo Kyoku) of the Ministry of Justice with its 50 local officers and 273 branches staffed by more than 13,000 volunteer civil liberties commissioners. The work is legally limited to complaints alleging civil liberties violations, but in practice this mandate is broadly construed.

Nonlitigious Dispute Resolution in Court ── The three main types of legal procedure in the settling of disputes with the aid of the courts but without filing a lawsuit are conciliation, compromise, and arbitration.

Conciliation (chōtei). Since 1951 formal conciliation, previously administered under separate piecemeal statutes beginning in the 1920s, has been codified in Japan by the Civil Conciliation Law (Minji Chōtei Hō) and administered by the summary courts and district courts and occasionally even by the high courts. Since 1974 conciliation committees, composed of laymen plus a judge, have been appointed by the SUPREME COURT to serve in each of the 452 summary courts and 50 district courts. The committees are assigned disputes and conduct meetings at the court with the concerned parties to negotiate settlements. Prior to filing suit in the 50 family courts in certain

family disputes, as prescribed by the Domestic Affairs Adjustment Law (Kaji Shimpan Hō, 1948), the parties must first attempt conciliation by law committees. Since 1974 traffic and pollution matters have been brought into the conciliation process by special provisions.

Arbitration (chūsai). Arbitration is alien to the Japanese tradition. It does not take place in court. As elsewhere in the world, arbitration is a voluntary process but in a limited sense: the parties relinquish both the right to sue and the right to reject the decision (award), which once made is binding without further consent. Also, both the contract to arbitrate and the award may be enforced by the court.

The Code of Civil Procedure (Minji Soshō Hō, 1891; see CIVIL PROCEDURE, CODE OF) defines the scope of arbitrable contracts that the courts will enforce. It provides also for the dismissal of suits filed in violation of arbitral agreements and for the recognition and enforcement of awards when rendered.

In practice, international arbitration in Japan is promoted by a private organization, the Japan Commercial Arbitration Association (JCAA; Kokusai Shōji Chūsai Kyōkai). Because of the prevalence of prior conciliation settlements before arbitration begins, few cases (annually about a dozen out of over 1,000 brought to the JCAA) are actually arbitrated to an award.

Compromise (wakai). The Civil Code (art. 695) recognizes compromise as a type of enforceable contract in Japanese law. Compromises by the parties to a dispute outside court are also enforceable. Also, in special procedures for the summary courts (Code of Civil Procedure, art. 356), the parties may come before the judge to attempt a compromise even before filing a suit. If these efforts fail, the parties may proceed to trial as if the suit had been filed. Since 1960 compromise methods have disposed of 25 to 30 percent of all cases filed in courts of first instance. See also JUDICIAL SYSTEM; LABOR DISPUTE RESOLUTION PROCEDURES; LEGAL SYSTEM.

distribution system　流通制度

(ryūtsū seido). Multilayered system of wholesalers in Japan, which distributes consumer and industrial products from manufacturers to retailers or end users. The history of commerce in the United States and Western Europe has involved a gradually

Divorce Rates for Selected Countries

divorces per 1,000 population

NOTE: Data is not available for Italy until 1971, when divorce became legal.
SOURCES: United Nations, *Demographic Yearbook* (annual): various years; Health and Welfare Statistics Association, *Jinkō dōtai tōkei* (annual): various years.

declining role for intermediary wholesalers, while manufacturers and retailers have grown in size. Although a similar trend has been evident in Japan, concentration in retailing has still not reached a level comparable to that in the United States. Wholesalers continue to play a number of important roles since companies approaching a new market for the first time have comparatively high entry costs. This situation is compounded by Japanese business practices, which usually dictate a longer period of "courtship" before business relationships can be established.

One of the principal factors affecting the development of the distribution system has been the unusually large number of small retailers in Japan compared with the numbers in other industrialized countries. This system is supported by a number of economic factors, including the preference of housewives for shopping in their neighborhoods (especially for everyday goods such as fresh foods), the inconvenience and cost of using automobiles in crowded urban areas, the absence of inexpensive land sites in suburban areas to build large shopping centers, and the Japanese preference for the convenience and service that small neighborhood stores can provide.

Although change is apparent in the retailing sector, as evidenced by gradual concentration along with the growth of larger chain supermarkets, the bulk of Japanese retailing remains highly fragmented. This means that the requirements of small retailers for finance, inventory, frequent deliveries, and collection of accounts must be satisfied. Wholesalers have traditionally performed this role and still are best positioned to support the small retail sector. For example, because of the small size of the typical retail outlet, the wholesaler is called on to hold much of its inventory and to provide frequent deliveries. In addition, the small size of the average retailer and the closely related practice of selling the majority of products on consignment are factors that increase the risk of transactions with the retail sector. The wholesaler is generally in a better position to deal with small retail stores and can spread the cost of doing so over a range of products.

Despite the factors supporting the complex structure of Japan's distribution system, there is evidence that gradual change is taking place, with concentration in the retail sector bringing pressures on the wholesaling

sector. This has resulted in shorter and simpler distribution channels for many products. Greater concentration of sales of certain products in supermarkets has increased the potential for more direct distribution of both domestically manufactured and imported products. However, without changes in regulations that restrict establishment of large retail stores and other incentives for concentration in retailing, the pace of change is likely to remain very slow. See also RETAIL INDUSTRY; LARGE-SCALE RETAIL STORES LAW.

Divers, Edward   ダイバーズ, E.

(1837–1912). British chemist and a founder of inorganic chemistry in Japan. Born in London, he graduated from the Royal College of Physicians. In 1854 he became an assistant professor at Queen's College, Dublin. He returned to England in 1866. He taught at Japan's Kōgakuryō (later the Kōbu Daigakkō), the Imperial College of Engineering, from 1873 until 1886. Divers was then transferred to Rika Daigaku (College of Science), where he was professor of chemistry. Before his return to England in 1899, the Japanese government awarded him the Order of the Rising Sun and the Order of the Sacred Treasure and made him professor emeritus, a rare honor for a foreigner. On his return to London, he was named a fellow of the Royal Society.

dividends   配当

(*haitō*). Payments to the owners of equity shares of a corporation, made annually or semiannually in Japan. Japanese corporations tend to maintain stable dividends, even when profitability declines, in part because of the high percentage of ownership by financial institutions. Dividends are still frequently expressed as a percentage of the par value of the stock, which is usually well below market value. Corporations tend not to raise dividends as earnings increase; rather, free stock shares are distributed, which results in higher rates of total dividend payment.

divination   占い

(*uranai*). The term divination comprises the various methods used to communicate with a supernatural being or to interpret cosmic forces in order to obtain answers to questions insoluble by ordinary human faculties. In Japan a number of such methods, termed *uranai*, have been employed since early times, of which the following five are the most important:

1. *Futomani*, or divination by interpreting patterns of cracks made on a deer's shoulder blade when heated, is thought to have been brought to Japan from the Asian continent. It is mentioned in the 3rd-century Chinese chronicle WEI ZHI (*Wei chih*) and in the 8th-century chronicle KOJIKI.

2. *Kiboku*, or divination by interpreting cracks on an incised and heated turtle shell, is believed to have been imported from China about AD 200. From the mid-7th century until 1868, *kiboku* was used in the Jingikan (Office of Shintō Worship).

3. Communion with the gods through dreams for divinatory purposes was practiced in shrines and temples during the Heian (794–1185) through Muromachi (1333–1568) periods. The pilgrim journeyed to a holy spot to solicit the answer to a problem from the presiding god or bodhisattva in a dream. The oracular answers were often delivered in the form of WAKA (31-syllable poems).

4. Divination by means of a shamanistic medium was once in widespread use in village rituals termed *takusen matsuri*. Now virtually extinct, these rites are still practiced by certain KŌ (pilgrimage groups) and involve an ascetic (*gyōja*) or YAMABUSHI who summons the KAMI (deity) into the medium's body for questioning.

5. Divination by the *Yi jing* (*I ching*; J: *Ekikyō*), employing the traditional Chinese method with yarrow stalks, is widely used in both shrines and temples by professional diviners.

divorce   離婚

(*rikon*). Divorces in Japan are regulated by provisions of the Civil Code, the Domestic Relations Adjudication Law, and other related laws. There are four general categories of divorce: divorce by agreement, divorce by arbitration, divorce by decree of a family court, and divorce by judicial decision. All but the first are known as court divorces.

Divorce by agreement. A husband and wife can divorce by mutual agreement, regardless of cause.

Divorce by arbitration. A husband or wife desiring a divorce can request arbitration by a family court.

Divorce by decree of a family court. If arbitration fails, the family court has the power to render a judgment of divorce. If either party objects, the proposed judgment is nullified.

Divorce by judicial decision. If the parties are unable to conclude a divorce by agreement, arbitration, or decree of a family court, either spouse can appeal for a divorce by the decision of a district court. The Civil Code specifies five grounds for divorce: (1) infidelity on the part of either spouse; (2) malicious abandonment, including any failure to fulfill the duties of cohabitation, mutual cooperation, and assistance without justifiable cause; (3) uncertainty about whether or not a spouse is alive, if it continues for more than three years from a spouse's last communication, regardless of cause; (4) incurable mental illness; and (5) a general category, which includes such matters as maltreatment or cruelty, severe insult or contempt, incompatibility, and loss of love between the spouses.

The courts have previously refused to recognize demands for divorce from the spouse at fault, but the Supreme Court reversed this position in a 1987 decision. However, the court attached the provision that the divorce must not cause the other party to suffer undue social, emotional, or economic duress.

General terms. When a marriage is dissolved by divorce, all rights and obligations between the two parties created through marriage are terminated, and the legal relationship between each party and the spouse's family is ended.

Custody of children. In cases where the marriage has produced offspring, a divorce by agreement may not be granted unless the spouses agree on who will maintain parental authority over the children. It is not necessary that one parent retain parental authority over all children. In cases of court divorce, the court decides who shall exercise parental authority.

Disposition of property. Financial affairs conducted jointly by husband and wife are terminated by divorce; therefore, common property obtained through the cooperation of the husband and wife while married must be liquidated. Allocation of responsibility for the future living expenses of the spouse with weaker earning power as well as the possible obligation of the spouse at fault to pay damages to the other are also included in this disposition of property.

The total number of divorces in Japan in 1990 was 157,608 (95,937 in 1970). The average length of marriage at the time of divorce was 9.6 years (1970: 6.8 years), and some 62.7 percent (1970: 59.1 percent) of those who divorced had children.

dōbōshū   同朋衆

Attendants to the shōgun during the Muromachi period (1333–1568), many of whom possessed artistic and technical skills. Use of the title *ami* was customarily granted to members of the *dōbōshū*; among the more prominent recipients of the designation were the Nō actors and dramatists KAN'AMI and ZEAMI. The title first appears in records compiled during the rule of the third shōgun, ASHIKAGA YOSHIMITSU (r 1369–95). Although the suffix *ami* derives from Amida, the Buddha of the Western Pure Land, the practice of attaching it to the names of *dōbōshū* appears to have been largely unrelated to religious belief. By the time of the eighth shōgun, ASHIKAGA YOSHIMASA (r 1449–74), the functions of *dōbōshū* as practitioners of the fine and dramatic arts, connoisseurs and administrators attached to the shogunal treasure house, and personal attendants to the shōgun had become clearly defined, and, though initially of very low social status, they had won acclaim for their technical and artistic achievements.

Dodge line   ドッジ・ライン

(Dojji *rain*). Also called Dodge plan. The popular name for a series of financial measures designed to control the inflation that gripped Japan during the years immediately following World War II. Its ultimate goal was to promote Japanese economic recovery and self-sufficiency. The major points of the Dodge line were to balance the consolidated national budget; to establish the US Aid Counterpart Fund, consisting of the proceeds from the sale of US aid goods in Japan; to terminate the lending activities of the RECONSTRUCTION FINANCE BANK; to establish a foreign exchange rate of 360 yen per US dollar; to return international trade to private channels; and to decrease the scope of government intervention in the private economy.

Under the Dodge line, consumer prices fell gradually until the beginning of the Korean War, when they began to rise again. The overall rate of inflation, however, was close to zero for the period of the program. The stabilization measures also caused a minor recession, exacerbating the problems of unemployment and creating some social unrest.

The man after whom the plan was named, Detroit banker Joseph Morrell Dodge (1890–1964), served from 1949 to 1952 as General Douglas MACARTHUR's financial adviser during the Allied Occupation. The Japanese government decorated him with the Grand Cordon Order of the Rising Sun.

Doeff, Hendrik   ズーフ, H.

(1777–1835). Director of the Dutch Factory on the island of DEJIMA in Nagasaki Harbor from 1803 to 1817. He first arrived in Nagasaki in 1799 and, after a brief trip to Batavia (now Jakarta) the following year, served as secretary to the director at Dejima. Doeff became director in 1803; he made three ceremonial visits to the shōgun (see EDO SAMPU). Doeff sided with the shogunate and staunchly defended the Dutch post during the PHAETON INCIDENT (1808). He again defended Dejima when Thomas S. Raffles (1781–1826), the British lieutenant governor of Java, attempted to capture Dejima in 1813. Under Doeff's guidance a Dutch-Japanese dictionary was compiled. Known as *Dōyaku Haruma* (also referred to as *Nagasaki Haruma*, in distinction to the earlier *Edo Haruma*) it was published in 1833 (see HARUMA WAGE). Upon returning to Holland in 1819 he wrote his memoirs, *Herinneringen uit Japan* (1833). See also WESTERN LEARNING.

Dōgashima   堂ヶ島

Scenic area on the west coast of the Izu Peninsula, central Honshū; a part of the town of Nishi Izu, Shizuoka Prefecture. Dōgashima is noted for its hot springs, grotesquely shaped rock islets, and the cave Tensōdō.

Dōgen   道元

(1200–1253). Also known as Dōgen Kigen or Kigen Dōgen. Founder in 1227 of the SŌTŌ SECT of ZEN Buddhism and of the monastery EIHEIJI in Echizen Province (now part of Fukui Prefecture). He wrote SHŌBŌ GENZŌ (1231–53, Treasury of the True Dharma Eye), a classic of Buddhist literature. Born in Kyōto, Dōgen entered the monastic life at Yokawa on Mt. Hiei (Hieizan; see ENRYAKUJI) in 1213, where he studied TENDAI SECT esotericism and received ordination. In about 1214 Dōgen was referred to Myōan EISAI, founder of the Japanese RINZAI SECT of Zen Buddhism. Dōgen entered Eisai's temple KENNINJI in about 1217 and studied the Rinzai tradition under Myōzen (1184–1225), Eisai's disciple.

Still feeling spiritually unfulfilled, in 1223 Dōgen went to Mingzhou (Mingchou) in what is now Zhejiang (Chechiang) Province, China. After studying at the monastery Jingdesi (Ching-te-ssu) on Mt. Tiantong (T'ient'ung), Dōgen made a pilgrimage to various monasteries in Zhejiang. Learning that the Sōtō Zen master Zhangweng Rujing (Changweng Ju-ching; J: Chōō Nyojō; 1163–1228) had become head of the monastery on Mt. Tiantong, Dōgen returned in June 1225 and became his student. Within two months, Dōgen made a breakthrough to enlightenment. Rujing recognized his spiritual progress and in 1227 presented Dōgen with a certificate declaring him his successor in the tradition of Sōtō Zen.

Upon his return to Japan Dōgen initially resided at Kenninji and wrote *Fukan zazengi* (1227, A Universal Promotion of Zazen Principles). Dōgen's single-minded advocacy of Zen provoked the animosity of monks at the Tendai centers on Mt. Hiei and at Kenninji, and in 1230 he moved to An'yōin, a temple in Fukakusa (now part of the city of Kyōto). There he wrote "Bendōwa" (1231, Discourse on the Practice of the Way), the earliest of the essays in *Shōbō genzō*.

In 1233 Dōgen moved to a nearby temple, Kannon Dōriin, which was expanded in 1236 with the erection of a monk's hall (*sōdō*), the center of Zen monastic life. Renamed Kōshō Hōrinji, it became the first full-fledged Sōtō Zen monastery in Japan. During this period Dōgen wrote 44 chapters of *Shōbō genzō*, wherein he asserts that enlightenment is accessible to any person through reliance solely on meditation in the Lotus position (*shikan taza*).

Sometime in 1242–43, Dōgen submitted a memorial, *Gokoku shōbōgi* (Significance of

the True Dharma for the Protection of the Nation), to the imperial court on behalf of the legitimacy of his approach to Zen; however, the Tendai Buddhists at Mt. Hiei were incensed and drove him from Kōshō Hōrinji. In 1243 Dōgen moved his headquarters to Echizen Province, where he wrote 29 more chapters of *Shōbō genzō*, in which he claimed that the catholicity of the Buddha dharma embraces and transcends all sectarian divisions, rejecting even the designations "Zen sect" and "Sōtō Zen." In 1244 Dōgen founded Daibutsuji, two years later renamed Eiheiji, on a mountain that came to be known as Mt. Kichijō. He died in the autumn of 1253 in Kyōto.

dogfighting   闘犬

(*tōken*). A sport, long popular for gambling in Japan. Dogfighting is still held in a few places, the most famous being Kōchi Prefecture, but gambling on dogfights is now illegal. The famous TOSA DOG of Kōchi, which is used for dogfighting, is the hybrid of a native Japanese dog bred with several Western breeds.

dog, Japanese   日本犬

(*nihonken* or *nipponken*). *Canis familiaris*, L., var. *japonicus*. Also called Nihon *inu* or Nippon *inu*. General term for varieties of the indigenous dog of Japan, usually excluding such relatively new breeds as the *chin* (JAPANESE SPANIEL) and the Tosa *inu* (Japanese fighting dog; see TOSA DOG), which were developed during the Edo (1600–1868) and Meiji (1868–1912) periods, respectively, as well as the Karafuto *inu* (Sakhalin dog), a breed derived from a different strain of northern sled dog, which is found in a small population in Hokkaidō.

There are various types of indigenous Japanese dogs, categorized by size, function, and locality. Their common characteristic is that of a primitive canine type, with small pricked ears and curled or upright bushy tails. Their eyes are rather small and triangular, with a slant set. The Japanese dog is typically a one-man dog, very faithful and obedient to one master.

From the Meiji period onward, Japanese dogs were mixed with foreign breeds and thus were in danger of extinction as pure types. The Society for the Preservation of the Japanese Dog (Nihonken Hozonkai) was organized in 1928 to save, standardize, and protect pure-blooded breeds. Around that time, several surviving indigenous breeds won official recognition from the government under the Law for the Protection of Notable Natural Objects (Tennen Kinembutsu Hogo Hō). Until World War II, Japanese native dogs were not commonly known in the West. The large-sized breed (Akita) was recognized by the British Kennel Club in 1954 and by the American Kennel Club in 1956; the standard for the breed was established in both countries.

Japanese dog

▶ Once used by the Ainu people to hunt bear, the Hokkaidō *inu* reaches a height of some 50 cm and may have a coat of russet, fawn, black, or brindle.

▼ With a shoulder height of some 65 cm, the Akita *inu* is the largest among Japanese dogs. Its coat may be white, russet, or black, and mottled or brindled.

▼ The Kishū *inu* has a height of about 50 cm and is used in hunting deer and boar. Its coloring ranges from white and pale fawn to russet and black.

▶ The *shiba inu* is the smallest among Japanese dogs, reaching around 38 cm at the shoulder. It may be russet, brown, or white.

◀ With a black or russet brindle coat and about 45 cm tall, the Kai *inu* was long used for hunting small game.

Today the Japanese dog is classified for convenience into three categories: large, medium, and small types. Each has its respective standard.

Large type (*ōgata*). The Akita *inu*. Also once called Ōdate *inu*. A very large, magnificent dog. Height at the shoulder is approximately 65 centimeters (26 in); weight, 35–55 kilograms (75–120 lb). Coloring is varied; temperament is dignified and calm. The breed won the status of a government-protected animal in 1931, and the breed standard was established to restore the original character of the dog. However, the present-day Akita is different from the original local hunting dog, its progenitor, and may be considered a fairly recent breed. It is used as a guard dog, no longer for big game hunting.

Medium type (*chūgata*). The medium-sized native dogs are still commonly named after localities: e.g., the Hokkaidō *inu* (*ainuken*), Kai *inu*, Kishū *inu*, and Shikoku *inu*. Many of the historically known local breeds have become extinct. Some of these dogs are also classified according to their use: *shishi inu* (boar-hunting dog), *shika inu* (deer-hunting dog), *matagi inu* (Tōhoku hunter's dog), and so on. They retain the primitive, well-balanced, and muscular body conformation; height is about 50 centimeters (20 in), weight about 20 kilograms (44 lb). They are courageous and capable hunters, used for big game, such as bear, boar, and deer. In 1934 several of the regional types were designated as protected animals.

Small type (*kogata*). Also called *shiba inu*. These small dogs are found mainly in mountainous areas, especially in the Chūbu and Chūgoku districts. They have been used for small game, such as hare, raccoon dog (*tanuki*), fox, weasel, or birds. The small Japanese dog was officially recognized as a government-protected animal in 1936.

Religious and magical beliefs in Japan include religious rituals focusing on a dog or wolf spirit. Since the wolf in Japan has often

been confused with the feral dog (*yama inu*), the cult object alternated between wolf and dog. The worship of these animals found a place in agricultural society, as dog-wolf spirits fused with the familiar spirit of *yama no kami*, or "mountain god," who protected crops from wild beasts. Dogs and wolves are also featured in supernatural tales, in which they sometimes have a ghostlike mysterious power.

Dōgo   島後
Volcanic island in the Sea of Japan off the coast of western Honshū; part of Shimane Prefecture. The largest of the OKI ISLANDS. The opening of an airport has enhanced Dōgo's tourism industry. The island is part of Daisen-Oki National Park. Area: 243 sq km (93.8 sq mi).

Dōgo Hot Spring   道後温泉
(Dōgo Onsen). Located in the eastern part of the city of Matsuyama, western Ehime Prefecture, Shikoku. A simple alkaline spring; water temperature 42°–50°C (108°–122°F). Numerous inns and souvenir shops are located around public-operated hot-spring bathhouses. One of Japan's oldest spas, it is mentioned in many literary works, including Natsume Sōseki's novel *Botchan* (1906).

Dōgoyama   道後山
Mountain on the border between Tottori and Hiroshima prefectures, western Honshū. Cattle graze on its summit. It is part of the Hiba-Dōgo-Taishaku Quasi-National Park. Height: 1,271 m (4,170 ft).

dogū→Jōmon figurines

Dohi Keizō   土肥慶蔵
(1866–1931). Dermatologist and venereologist. Born in Echizen Province (now part of Fukui Prefecture). Graduate of Tōkyō University. After his return from further studies in Europe, he taught at Tōkyō University, lecturing on cutaneous diseases and syphilis. He became president of the Cutaneous Disease Society (now the Japanese Dermatological Association) in 1900 and started its journal. Dohi also established the Japan Venereal

Disease Preventive Association in 1905. He contributed greatly to the establishment of dermatology in Japan by reporting on new cutaneous diseases and developing new therapies.

dohyō   土俵
Ring used in SUMŌ wrestling. The *dohyō* is a 54-centimeter (21-in) high, 5.7-meter (18.7-ft) square mound of special clay packed hard and sprinkled with sand. The borders of this mound are defined by the tops of 32 straw bags filled with earth and pebbles and sunk in the clay during construction. Another 20 straw bags are similarly sunk in the mound to form a circle 4.6 meters (14.9 ft) in diameter. In the middle of the circle are two white lines about 0.9 meter (3.0 ft) long, which face each other about 0.7 meter (2.3 ft) apart. These are the *shikirisen* (literally, "dividing lines"), at which the two wrestlers position themselves for the *tachiai* (initial charge) that begins their bout. Over the *dohyō* hangs a roof (*yakata*) designed in a Shintō style of architecture called *shimmei-zukuri*. From each of the four corners of the *yakata* hangs a giant tassle representing one of the seasons—green for spring, red for summer, white for autumn, black for winter.

Doi Bansui   土井晩翠
(1871–1952). Also known as Tsuchii Bansui. Poet and scholar of English literature. Real name Tsuchii Rinkichi. Born in Sendai (Miyagi Prefecture); graduate of Tōkyō University. His romantic poems on historical themes, written in a style with classical Chinese overtones, are often compared with those of his contemporary, SHIMAZAKI TŌSON. He is best remembered for his poem "Kōjō no tsuki" (The Moon over the Ruined Castle), made famous by composer TAKI RENTARŌ, who set it to music. His major publications include *Tenchi ujō* (1899), a collection of poems, and a translation of Homer's *Iliad*. He was awarded the Order of Culture in 1950.

Doihara-Ch'in Agreement→
Doihara-Qin (Doihara-Ch'in) Agreement

Doihara Kenji 土肥原賢二

(1883–1948). Army general. Also known as Dohihara Kenji. Born in Okayama Prefecture. He graduated from the Army Academy in 1904 and the Army War College in 1912. After serving in China for nearly 15 years, in 1931 he became director of the Military Intelligence Bureau in Mukden (now Shenyang), Manchuria. After the military occupation of Manchuria by Japanese forces (see MANCHURIAN INCIDENT), he became mayor of Mukden. In 1935 he concluded the DOIHARA-QIN (DOIHARA-CH'IN) AGREEMENT, under which Chinese Nationalist troops withdrew from Qahar (Chahar) Province in North China. During World War II, he served as area army commander and became inspector general of military education in 1945. Convicted as a class A war criminal by the Allies after the war, he was executed on 23 December 1948 (see WAR CRIMES TRIALS).

Doihara-Qin (Doihara-Ch'in) Agreement 土肥原・秦協定

(Doihara-Shin Kyōtei). Pact concluded on 23 June 1935 between DOIHARA KENJI, an officer of Japan's GUANDONG (KWANTUNG) ARMY in Manchuria, and General Qin Dechun (Ch'in Te-ch'un; 1893–1963) of the Qahar (Chahar) provincial government. It provided for the political and military withdrawal of the Guomindang (Kuomintang; Nationalist Party) government from Qahar Province. With the HE-UMEZU (HO-UMEZU) AGREEMENT of 10 June 1935, which had made similar provisions for the province of Hebei (Hopeh), the Doihara-Qin Agreement was a first step by the Japanese military in China toward the establishment of a puppet administration that would be favorable toward Japanese interests in North China and Manchuria. The agreements aroused Chinese patriotic sentiments that culminated in the anti-Japanese DECEMBER NINTH MOVEMENT in Beijing (Peking) at the end of 1935.

Doi Takako 土井たか子

(1928–). Politician. Born in Hyōgo Prefecture. Doi graduated from Dōshisha University. In 1969 she won a seat in the House of Representatives, running as the JAPAN SOCIALIST PARTY (JSP) candidate from Hyōgo Prefecture. Within the party she was active as a specialist in social, international, and defense issues. From 1983 she served as vice chairperson under ISHIBASHI MASASHI, and in 1986 she became the 10th chairperson of the party, stepping down in 1991. She was the first woman in the history of Japanese politics to become a party chairperson. In July 1989, under her leadership, the JSP in concert with other opposition parties won an upset victory in the elections for the House of Councillors, breaking the long-standing LIBERAL DEMOCRATIC PARTY majority in the upper house.

Doi Tatsuo 土井辰雄

(1892–1970). Sixth Catholic archbishop of Tōkyō and the first Japanese to be raised to the rank of cardinal. Born in Sendai, Miyagi Prefecture. After studying in Rome he was ordained in 1921. Having gained wide experience in pastoral work, he was appointed the first Japanese archbishop of Tōkyō in 1938. He was made cardinal by John XXIII in 1960 and took part in the Second Vatican Council (1962–65). Under his direction the modern Catholic Cathedral in Bunkyō Ward, Tōkyō, was completed in 1964.

Doi Toshikatsu 土井利勝

(1573–1644). Senior councillor (*rōjū*) and great elder (*tairō*) under TOKUGAWA HIDETADA (1579–1632) and TOKUGAWA IEMITSU (1604–51), the second and third rulers of the TOKUGAWA SHOGUNATE (1603–1867). When Hidetada was born in 1579, his father, TOKUGAWA IEYASU (1543–1616), placed the six-year-old Toshikatsu in Hidetada's service. Although officially the son of Mizuno Nobumoto, and later adopted by Doi Toshimasa, Toshikatsu was rumored to have been fathered by Ieyasu. Toshikatsu was one of Hidetada's close advisers in Edo (now Tōkyō) during the years Hidetada and Ieyasu ruled jointly (1605–16), and he rose to senior councillor in 1610. From then until 1632 Toshikatsu was one of the most powerful men in the government. His influence waned after Hidetada's death, however; his promotion to *tairō* in 1638 was an honorary one, representing his removal from actual power. At his death Toshikatsu was the *daimyō* of a 160,000-*koku* (see KOKUDAKA) domain at Koga in Shimōsa (now part of Ibaraki Prefecture).

Dōjima Rice Market 堂島米市場

(Dōjima Kome Ichiba). Wholesale rice market west of Ōsaka Castle on a slender island between the Shijimi and Dōjima rivers; established in 1697. The Yodoya merchant house was the first dominant firm there, but after its dissolution in 1705 there was a period of marketing disorder. During the 1720s merchants from Edo (now Tōkyō) took over much of the business. Ōsaka merchants objected, and in 1730 merchants from Ōsaka were licensed to handle the Dōjima rice brokerage business. Money changers (RYŌGAE-SHŌ) and warehouse (KURAYASHIKI) operators set up establishments on the island, which became a major mercantile area.

Following the collapse of the Tokugawa shogunate and the formation of the Meiji government in 1868, the Dōjima Rice Market was reorganized and a new marketing system, called the Ōsaka Dōjima Komeshō Kaisho, was established. In 1893 this system was renamed the Ōsaka Dōjima Beikoku Torihikisho (Dōjima Rice Marketplace). In 1939 it was absorbed by the government-sponsored Nihon Beikoku Kabushiki Kaisha (Japan Rice Co, Ltd).

dojōsukui 泥鰌掬い

Comic dance of the city of Yasugi, Shimane Prefecture, performed to the accompaniment of the folk song "Yasugi-bushi." With *kimono* tucked up and a towel wrapped about his face, the dancer mimes the successful scooping up (*sukui*) of a loach (*dojō;* a carplike fish) with a shallow basket. It is thought that the dance's movements originally derived from the sifting (*sukui*) of soil (*dojō*) to obtain iron.

Dōjunkai apartments 同潤会アパート

(Dōjunkai *apāto*). Public apartments built by Dōjunkai, a nonprofit government foundation set up in 1924 to rebuild the areas hardest hit by the TŌKYŌ EARTHQUAKE OF 1923. The Dōjunkai apartments were Japan's first Western-style public apartments. By 1941, when its operations were taken over by the government-run Jūtaku Eidan, Dōjunkai had built a total of 12,000 dwelling units. Such Dōjunkai projects as the Aoyama Apartments and the Daikan'yama Apartments were modeled on Western concepts of collective housing planning and construction, incorporating flush toilets and other Western amenities new to Japan. These and other Dōjunkai projects strongly influenced subsequent apartment-building construction in Japan. See also HOUSING, MODERN.

Dōkai Bay 洞海湾

(Dōkai Wan). Inlet of the Genkai Sea. Off the city of Kita Kyūshū, Fukuoka Prefecture, Kyūshū. With steel mills, chemical plants, and other heavy industry, the area is a nucleus of the Kita Kyūshū Industrial Zone. Wakato Bridge spans the mouth of the bay.

Dōkō Toshio 土光敏夫

(1896–1988). Businessman. Born in Okayama Prefecture, he graduated from Tōkyō Technical Higher School (now Tōkyō Institute of Technology) in 1920. In 1950 he became president of Ishikawajima Heavy Industries, assuming the presidency of the newly merged ISHIKAWAJIMA-HARIMA HEAVY INDUSTRIES CO, LTD, in 1960. At the request of ISHIZAKA TAIZŌ, Dōkō became president of the faltering TOSHIBA CORPORATION and in eight years revived worker and management morale and led the company to prosperity. After he became president of the KEIDANREN (Federation of Economic Organizations) in 1974, he successfully opposed a revision of the ANTIMONOPOLY LAW. He fought against exploitation of the Keidanren for political fund-raising by the Liberal Democratic Party and arranged for a provisional prohibition of political contributions by public utility companies. Dōkō resigned as Keidanren's president in 1980. In 1981 he became chairman of the Committee on Administrative Reform, serving until 1983. In that year Dōkō became chairman of the Council for the Promotion of Administrative Reform—a watchdog organization monitoring the progress of administrative reform programs—remaining in the post until 1986.

Dōkyō 道鏡

(?–772). Buddhist priest of the HOSSŌ SECT who acquired great political power through

dojōsukui This comic dance suggests both the scooping of *dojō* (loach) from the water and the sifting of sand, also called *dojō*, for iron ore. A five-yen coin under the performer's nose emphasizes the comic nature of the *dojōsukui*.

Dōkō Toshio This businessman's long list of achievements includes the rebuilding of the Tōshiba Corporation during the 1960s.

Dōjunkai apartments Dōjunkai public apartments, such as these in Kudan, Chiyoda Ward, in central Tōkyō, were Japan's first Western-style public housing.

Doll Festival The formal display of dolls became the focus of this festival during the early Edo period. **1** Emperor and empress, attendants, and miniature household goods are arranged hierarchically on a tiered stand. **2** Young girls in *kimono* celebrate the festival with a special meal in front of a display stand.

his association with Empress KŌKEN. After the unsuccessful revolt of FUJIWARA NO NAKAMARO in 764, Kōken, who had abdicated in 758, reascended the throne as Empress Shōtoku; Dōkyō became head of both the secular bureaucracy and the ecclesiastical establishment, receiving the title *dajō daijin zenji* ("priestly grand minister of state"). In 769 a plot to have Dōkyō succeed Shōtoku as sovereign was foiled by WAKE NO KIYO-MARO and other court officials. Dōkyō continued to live in nearby Kawachi Province (now part of Ōsaka Prefecture), but when Shōtoku died in 770 he was banished to Shimotsuke Province (now Tochigi Prefecture). The Dōkyō affair may be one of the reasons the capital was moved from Nara, where the influence of the monasteries had become oppressive, to Kyōto.

Doll Festival 雛祭

(Hina Matsuri). Festival for girls held on 3 March. Tiered platforms for *hina ningyō* (*hina* dolls, a set of dolls representing emperor, empress, attendants, and musicians in ancient court dress) are set up in the home, and the family celebrates with a meal, eating *hishimochi* (diamond-shaped rice cakes) and drinking *shirozake* (made with rice malt and *sake*). Also called Jōshi no Sekku, Momo no

dolmen burials The Satotabaru site in the town of Tabira, Nagasaki Prefecture, is an example of the southern type of dolmen burial, dating from the Early Yayoi period (ca 300 BC–ca 100 BC). The capstone is 193 cm in diameter.

Sekku (Peach Festival), and Sangatsu Sekku (Third Month Festival). See also SEKKU.

The modern Doll Festival derives from several different customs. One is a Chinese purificatory rite that was held along a river early in the third lunar month. During the Heian period (794–1185) courtiers called in diviners on the third day of the third month to exorcise their impurities, transferring them to paper images (see KATASHIRO), which were thrown into the river or ocean. The *hina* dolls of the modern festival are thought to be a combination of the *katashiro* and the paper *hina* dolls with which Heian-period girls played. The practice of displaying dolls dates from the early Edo period (1600–1868). See DOLLS.

dolls 人形

(*ningyō;* archaic pronunciation of the same Chinese characters: *hitogata,* literally "human form"). Japanese decorative and folk-art dolls trace their origin back to prehistoric examples thought to have had religious or magical significance. The earliest findings are clay and stone figurines of the Jōmon period (ca 10,000–ca 300 BC; see JŌMON FIGURINES). In the Kofun period (ca 300–710), HANIWA (larger human figures, as well as animal and architectural forms constructed of hollow clay) encircled the tomb mounds of the ruling class.

Nara through Azuchi-Momoyama Periods (710–1600)—Dolls apparently served many functions in premodern times. Effigies called *hitogata* or KATASHIRO (or in certain cases *nademono*) were used as scapegoats to remove defilement, absorb malevolent influences, or prevent disease. An ancient folk belief held that dolls or effigies possessed souls of their own, a theme explored in PUP-PET THEATER. Folk traditions also associate dolls and effigies with sympathetic magic.

Small wooden figures excavated at Nara from the ruins of HEIJŌKYŌ (the capital from 710 to 784) point to the use of dolls as playthings, as does the literature of the Heian period. During this period hand-operated puppets (*ayatsuri ningyō*), the forerunners of the marionettes of the BUNRAKU puppet theater, were used by itinerant performers (*kairaishi* or *kugutsushi*). Dolls also played specific roles in Shintō-related court ceremonies. During the Kamakura period (1185–1333) dolls served didactic functions in moralistic dioramas set up by Buddhist monks along the roadsides.

Edo Period (1600–1868)—Dollmaking flourished in the Edo period. In a custom that continues today in annual shrine celebrations, dolls were drawn through the streets atop tall, two-wheeled carts (DASHI). The DOLL FESTIVAL (Hina Matsuri), celebrated by young girls on the third day of the third month, included a formalized display of dolls as the focal point of individual household festivities. The CHILDREN'S DAY festival now celebrated on 5 May also includes a display of dolls (*gogatsu ningyō*).

Within every region unique varieties of doll charms were available only at local temples and shrines. They were known collectively as *tsuchiningyō* (earthen or clay dolls).

Some new types of dolls appreciated primarily for their aesthetic value were *gosho ningyō, ishō ningyō, kimekomi ningyō,* and Saga *ningyō*. The most characteristic *gosho ningyō* (palace dolls) are chubby, nude infant boys with exaggeratedly large, childish heads. *Ishō ningyō* (costume dolls) are elegantly coiffured and costumed in expensive brocades. *Kimekomi ningyō* (also known as

Kamo *ningyō* after the Kamo Shrines in Kyōto) are made with a wooden base to which silk brocade and crepe cloth are glued to create the illusion of thick clothing. Saga *ningyō* favor Buddhist subjects and have costumes painted in brilliant textile patterns.

The Edo period saw the rapid development of mechanical dolls or automatons (*karakuri ningyō*). Children's dolls such as the *mitsuore ningyō* (triple-jointed dolls) benefited from technical advancements. *Mitsuore ningyō* were often modeled after real people and were sold with elaborate wardrobes. More often children received *hadaka ningyō* (naked dolls), often of the *mitsuore* type, for which they had to design and sew little costumes. The *anesama ningyō* (elder sister dolls), complex constructions of colored paper with folded paper *kimono,* also became popular. KOKESHI, the limbless wooden dolls of northeastern Japan, which are classified today as folk art, were originally children's toys. Toward the end of the Edo period, realistic life-size dolls known as *ikiningyō* (live dolls) were made for public display. With costumes made of live flowers, *kikuningyō* (chrysanthemum dolls) appeared in the early 19th century and are still displayed at flower exhibits.

Meiji Period (1868–1912) to the Present—Japanese versions of Western-style dolls appeared on the domestic market in the Meiji period. By 1936 dollmaking had gradually achieved the status of an officially recognized art. Since 1955 five doll masters have been designated Intangible Cultural Properties (*mukei bunkazai;* popularly called LIVING NATIONAL TREASURES or *ningen kokuhō*): HIRATA GŌYŌ, HORI RYŪJO, KAGOSHIMA JUZŌ, Noguchi Sonoo (b 1907), and Ichihashi Toshiko (b 1907). 🔾 293

dolmen burials 支石墓

(*shisekibo*). Either of two types of prehistoric graves—northern and southern—dating from the end of the neolithic period and found on the Shandong (Shantung) Peninsula of northeastern China, the Korean peninsula, and northern Kyūshū. The southern type can be seen from the middle of the Korean peninsula southward and consists of a large rock supported above ground by several small stones. In Japan the ground below may house one or many burials in either jars or cist graves. The northern type consists of three or four large flat rocks arranged to form the walls of a squarish chamber in the ground and then covered with a large ceiling rock. See also FLEXED BURIALS; HŌKEI SHŪKŌBO; JAR BURIALS.

dolphins → whales

domain schools → hankō

Dōmei Tsūshinsha 同盟通信社

(Dōmei News Agency). Sole news agency in operation in Japan during World War II. Established in 1936 as an amalgamation of the news sections of two major news agencies of the day, the Shimbun Rengōsha (Associated Press) and the Nihon Dempō Tsūshinsha (Japan Telegraphic News Agency; see DENTSŪ, INC). Dōmei issued news that followed government policy lines and collated and analyzed information to be passed on to government offices and the armed forces. It also engaged in propaganda activities directed at foreign countries. It was disbanded in 1945 and replaced by the KYŌDO NEWS SERVICE and the JIJI PRESS.

A Japanese Doll Collection

Dolls (*ningyō*) have been part of Japanese culture since prehistoric times, but it was in the Edo period (1600–1868) that dollmaking began to thrive. Innovative techniques produced new varieties of decorative dolls, while advances in technology led to the rapid development of mechanical dolls, considered marvelous achievements at the time. By the early Shōwa period (1926–89), the public's fancy had been captured by the virtuosity of master dollmakers like Hirata Gōyō, Hori Ryūjo, and Kagoshima Juzō, all three of whom were later designated Living National Treasures. Their creations and those of others have come to be regarded as authentic works of art—dolls that express the unique insights of their makers.

Kamibina (paper dolls) like this pair were once displayed in Japanese homes to commemorate the Doll Festival on 3 March, an occasion traditionally devoted to girls.

Kimekomi ningyō ("grooved" dolls) are made from pieces of carved willow wood fitted with well-placed grooves into which the edges of pieces of cloth are tucked, giving their costumes a very natural look. The first such dolls were fashioned from spare wood and fabric remnants at the Kamo Shrines in Kyōto in the 1730s.

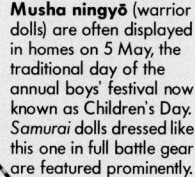

Musha ningyō (warrior dolls) are often displayed in homes on 5 May, the traditional day of the annual boys' festival now known as Children's Day. *Samurai* dolls dressed like this one in full battle gear are featured prominently.

Ishō ningyō (costume dolls), as the name suggests, are primarily intended as showpieces for the elaborate garments with which they are outfitted. The body of such a doll, hidden under its finery, is usually little more than a stick of wood wrapped in straw.

Gosho ningyō (palace dolls), so called because they were once dispensed as gifts at the old Kyōto imperial palace, are made of wood coated lightly with plaster of Paris. The predominant motif—adorable, fat-cheeked baby boys—is a large part of their appeal.

Ichimatsu ningyō, reportedly named for their resemblance to the 18th-century *kabuki* actor Sanogawa Ichimatsu, were originally made of molded sawdust. They were once given to girls as toys but are now most often seen in decorative displays.

Hakata ningyō were first produced at the beginning of the 17th century in Hakata, now part of the city of Fukuoka. Made of clay, these dolls are known for their realistic details.

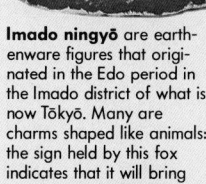

Imado ningyō are earthenware figures that originated in the Edo period in the Imado district of what is now Tōkyō. Many are charms shaped like animals: the sign held by this fox indicates that it will bring romance to the lovelorn.

Kagoshima Juzō, working mainly with paper, imbued his creations with a lyrical quality. This doll, entitled *Winds of Asuka*, is fashioned from *washi*, or handmade paper.

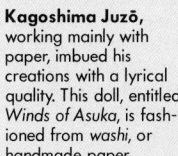

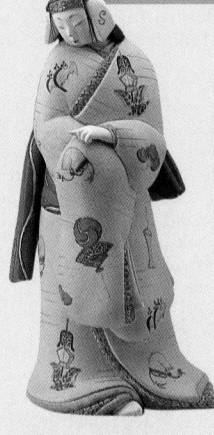

Hirata Gōyō created this doll, entitled *A Good Day*, in 1959. Hirata's dolls are distinguished by their gracefully shaped limbs and often have a vaguely erotic appeal.

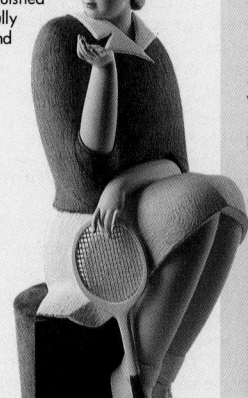

Hori Ryūjo is known for costumed dolls that exhibit a mystical charm—this one is called *Bashful*. Her subjects range from contemporary women to aristocratic ladies of ancient China.

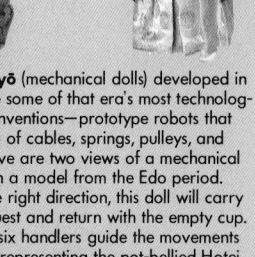

The karakuri ningyō (mechanical dolls) developed in the Edo period were some of that era's most technologically sophisticated inventions—prototype robots that moved with the help of cables, springs, pulleys, and wooden gears. Above are two views of a mechanical tea bearer based on a model from the Edo period. When pointed in the right direction, this doll will carry a cup of tea to a guest and return with the empty cup. In the photo below, six handlers guide the movements of a *karakuri* figure representing the pot-bellied Hotei, one of the Seven Deities of Good Fortune, atop a festival float in Takayama, Gifu Prefecture.

Domon Ken Titled *Out-of-Work Father and Child*, this photograph from the 1950s exemplifies Domon's belief that photography should concern itself with social issues.

domestic demand, expansion of　内需拡大

(*naiju kakudai*). Strong foreign demand for Japanese products has contributed greatly to postwar economic development but has also led to massive trade surpluses and trade frictions with foreign economic partners. In an effort to reduce Japan's trade surpluses, the government since 1985 has tried to make economic growth more dependent on domestic demand. The so-called MAEKAWA REPORT in 1986 called for the stimulation of the domestic economy through government spending on public works, increased deregulation, measures to promote imports, and efforts to stimulate private consumption. In May 1987 the budget called for government expenditures totaling ¥6 trillion (US $41.5 billion), including ¥5 trillion (US $34.5 billion) for public works and a tax reduction of ¥1 trillion (US $7.0 billion). This stimulation of domestic demand accounted for a 6.8 percent rise in the nation's gross national product (GNP) in 1988. In contrast, foreign demand declined by 1.7 percent, resulting in an overall GNP growth rate of 5.1 percent. In 1989 domestic demand increased by a further 5.7 percent while foreign demand fell 0.7 percent, giving a GNP growth rate of 5.0 percent. Japan's economic growth for 1988 and 1989 was thus attributable to domestic demand. However, the balance of trade remains strongly in Japan's favor (over US $90 billion annually), and policy measures to further increase domestic demand are likely to continue.

Dominicans　ドミニコ会士

(Dominikokaishi). Dominican friars conducted missionary work in Japan in the early 17th century but were exiled or executed during the anti-Christian persecution in the early Edo period (1600–1868). The first friars arrived in 1602 and labored mostly in Kyūshū. Although the number of friars in Japan was relatively small, no fewer than 32 were martyred during the persecution, the last friar being executed in 1637. They returned in the 20th century, and as of 1990 there were 67 Dominican friars in Japan, engaged mostly in parish work. See also CHRISTIANITY.

Domon Ken　土門拳

(1909–90). Photographer. Noted for his advocacy of social criticism in photography, he was an extremely influential figure in Japanese photography after World War II. Born in Yamagata Prefecture, Domon attended Nihon University but withdrew before graduating. In 1933 he began studying photography under Miyauchi Kōtarō. From 1935 to 1939 he worked as a member of Nihon Kōbō, a group of photographers led by NATORI YŌNOSUKE. After World War II, Domon became a free-lancer. His best-known collections include *Hiroshima* (1958), *Chikuhō no kodomotachi* (1960, Children of Chikuhō), and *Koji junrei* (5 vols, 1963–75, A Pilgrimage to Old Temples). In 1983 the Domon Ken Museum of Photography was opened in his home town of Sakata in Yamagata Prefecture.

Dōmoto Inshō　堂本印象

(1891–1975). Japanese-style painter. Real name Dōmoto Sannosuke. Born and lived in Kyōto. He worked in traditional Japanese styles (NIHONGA) and avant-garde Western styles. Dōmoto studied painting at Kyōto Shiritsu Kaiga Semmon Gakkō (now Kyōto City University of Arts) and later with Nishiyama Suishō (1879–1958). He won the Teikoku Bijutsuin (Imperial Fine Arts Academy) prize in 1925. An artist for the imperial household (*teishitsu gigeiin*) and a member of the JAPAN ART ACADEMY (Nihon Geijutsuin), he was awarded the Order of Culture in 1961. In 1966 he designed the Dōmoto Art Museum in Kyōto to exhibit his paintings. He executed wall paintings for several Buddhist temples, including Shitennōji in Ōsaka.

Donchō　曇徴

(fl early 7th century; Kor: Tamjing). Korean Buddhist monk of the KOGURYŎ kingdom (37–668) who came to Japan in 610. According to the NIHON SHOKI (720), he was a scholar and artist who introduced techniques for making paper, black ink (*sumi*), and watercolor paints into Japan. He is said to have built Japan's first water-powered mill.

Donker Curtius, Jan Hendrik　ドンケル・クルチウス, J. H.

(1813–79). Dutch diplomat. In 1852 he was appointed chief merchant (*kapitan*) of the DUTCH FACTORY at DEJIMA; in 1855 his title was changed to the more prestigious Netherlands government commissioner. Donker Curtius arranged for the Dutch government to present the Japanese government with a steamship and advised the Japanese to request a detachment of Dutch officers to instruct them in naval training. Diplomatic re-

Japanese dormouse The nocturnal *yamane* sleeps during the day in abandoned birds' nests or tree hollows dressed with bark and moss.

lations between Japan and Holland were strengthened as a result of Donker Curtius's strategic dealings, and in 1856 he concluded the Dutch-Japanese Treaty of Amity, a draft of which had been rejected in 1852.

donsu　緞子

(damask). Originating in the Middle East and China, it is said that the technique for weaving damask was brought to Japan by a Chinese craftsman in the late 16th century. The art was then transmitted to the Nishijin weaving district of Kyōto. Heavy-quality *donsu* may be used for making OBI (sashes worn with traditional Japanese KIMONO); lighter *donsu* is used for bedding and cushions.

Door-to-Door Sales Law　訪問販売法

(Hōmon Hambai Hō). In Japan door-to-door sales are regulated by the 1976 Law concerning Door-to-Door Sales and Other Sales (Hōmon Hambai Tō ni kansuru Hōritsu). Under this law a door-to-door sale involves the sale of certain products (designated by cabinet ordinance) at a place other than the merchant's place of business, sales agency, or other place designated by order of the Ministry of International Trade and Industry (MITI). This law was enacted in response to a growing number of complaints from consumers about heavy-handed or fraudulent door-to-door sales practices. It guarantees a seven-day cooling-off period and limits the amount of compensation for damages. The law also applies to mail-order sales and multilevel marketing systems. See also INSTALLMENT SALES LAW.

dormouse, Japanese　山鼠

(*yamane*). *Glirulus japonicus*. A small rodent of the family Gliridae that is native to Japan. It is found in Honshū, Shikoku, and Kyūshū. It resembles the common dormouse of Europe, with a head and body of about 7 centimeters (3 in) and a tail of about 5 centimeters (2 in). A dark brown stripe runs along the back; the body is buff-colored. Dormice usually live in mountainous wooded areas at an elevation of 800 to 2,000 meters (2,600–6,600 ft) and spend much of their time in trees. Their food includes seeds, fruits, and insects; they sometimes eat baby birds. Dormice hibernate from December through March and breed twice a year, with litters of three to seven young.

doro-e　泥絵

Pictures painted with colorants (*doro enogu*) made from mixtures of pigment, water, and the calcareous powder obtained from fired seashells. Such coloring matter was used to paint votive pictures (EMA), graphic signboards, and stage settings from the late Edo period (1600–1868).

Doro Hatchō → Dorokyō

Dorokyō　瀞峡

Gorge on the upper reaches of the river Kitayamagawa (a tributary of the river Kumanogawa), Kii Peninsula, central Honshū. Divided into three distinct sections (Doro Hatchō, Kami Doro, and Oku Doro), the gorge is noted for towering rocky cliffs, extensive rapids, and masses of azaleas and rhododendrons blooming on the cliffs in early summer. Located within Yoshino-Kumano National Park. Length: Doro Hatchō (1.3 km; 0.8 mi); Kami Doro (2.1 km; 1.3 mi); Oku Doro (20 km; 12 mi).

Dōsen 道璿

(702–760; Ch: Daoxuan or Tao-hsüan). Chinese monk said to have first transmitted the precepts (Skt: *vinaya*) and teachings of the KEGON SECT of Buddhism to Japan. Accompanied by the Indian monk Bodhisena (J: Bodaisenna) and the Champa (now part of Vietnam) monk Fozhe (Fo-che; J: Buttetsu), Dōsen arrived in Japan in 736 and participated in the ceremony of enshrinement there for the newly installed image of the Great Buddha. He took up residence at the Nara temple Daianji, later moving to the temple TŌDAIJI. Dōsen taught the Japanese monk Gyōhyō (724–797), who became the teacher of the priest SAICHŌ. Dōsen had an important influence on early-Nara-period (710–794) Buddhism.

Dōshisha University 同志社大学

(Dōshisha Daigaku). Dōshisha (literally, "one purpose institution"), one of Japan's oldest private educational institutions, includes Dōshisha University with six faculties (theology, letters, law, economics, commerce, and engineering), a women's college, a two-year women's junior college, four senior and four junior high schools, and a kindergarten. Founded in Kyōto in 1875 by NIIJIMA JŌ and Jerome D. Davis, Congregational missionary, with eight students, the institution now spreads over four campuses and enrolls some 28,000 students. Dōshisha was the first university to admit women. It maintains close ties with Amherst College. University enrollment was 20,259 in 1989.

The year after its founding Dōshisha's emphasis on Christian precepts attracted the "Kumamoto Band," the group of students who had studied with Captain Leroy Lansing JANES in Kumamoto, including Tokutomi Iichirō (later TOKUTOMI SOHŌ) and Kenjirō (later TOKUTOMI ROKA), UKITA KAZUTAMI, YAMAMURO GUMPEI, ABE ISOO, KOZAKI HIROMICHI, and EBINA DANJŌ.

Dōshō 道昭

(629–700). Founder of the HOSSŌ SECT (Ch: the Faxiang, or Fa-hsiang, school) of Buddhism in Japan. Born in Kawachi (now part of Ōsaka Prefecture). After taking Buddhist orders he traveled to China where he studied with the great master Xuanzang (Hsüan-tsang; J: Genjō), a 7th-century Chinese pilgrim-priest. After his stay in China, commonly said to have lasted from 653 to 660 or 661, Dōshō returned to Japan and first introduced Hossō teachings at ASUKADERA, a monastery in Asuka (near Nara). Later he traveled widely throughout the country undertaking various social welfare projects such as bridge-building and construction of irrigation systems. Dōshō's disciples included the monk GYŌGI, who carried on his master's work in the field of social welfare.

dōshū 堂衆

Lower-ranking Buddhist monks of ancient and medieval times; alternate terms include *geshū* and *gyōnin*. Usually descendants of temple slaves (*nuhi*) and ranked lower than *gakuryo* (scholar-priests), they performed services such as maintaining buildings and fighting fires. During the Heian period (794–1185), armed *dōshū* served major temples such as ENRYAKUJI in the Nara-Kyōto area (see WARRIOR-MONKS).

dosō 土倉

Pawnbrokers and usurers of the late Kamakura period (1185–1333) and the Muromachi period (1333–1568). Also called *tokura*. The term literally means "earthen warehouse," referring to the solid godowns where pawnbrokers stored pledged goods; by the 14th century it had replaced the earlier term for loan agent, KASHIAGE. A pawnbrokers' council (*dosō yoriaishū*) existed in Kyōto as early as 1278; by 1316, at least 335 *dosō* establishments were active in that city, 280 of them being JINNIN of the Hie Shrine or otherwise affiliated with Enryakuji, the great monastery of the Buddhist Tendai sect on Mt. Hiei (Hieizan) northeast of Kyōto. *Dosō* were protected under article 6 of the fundamental law of the Muromachi shogunate, the KEMMU SHIKIMOKU of 1336, because the shogunate lacked a secure landed base for its finances and increasingly depended for support on special imposts (*kurayaku*) levied on the *dosō*. *Dosō* accumulated capital, largely through rice hoarding and price manipulation, and hence came under attack from rural leagues (TSUCHI IKKI). After the assassination of the shōgun ASHIKAGA YOSHINORI in 1441, their warehouses were repeatedly pillaged by peasant forces. That *dosō* were active in provincial regions as well as in Kyōto is evident from domainal law codes of 16th-century *daimyō* (BUNKOKUHŌ), such as the IMAGAWA KANA MOKUROKU.

dōsojin 道祖神

Guardian deity of roads and village boundaries, worshiped in the form of stone images along the roadside. Also known as *sae no kami* (or *sai no kami*), an ancient designation that suggests the function of "obstructing" or "keeping out" (*sae*) evil spirits. The *dōsojin* is often identified with the god Sarudahiko, who guided NINIGI NO MIKOTO, the supposed ancestor of the imperial line, on his descent to earth. The object of worship takes various physical forms. Today *dōsojin* function also as gods of marriage, birth, and other areas of concern.

The *dōsojin* are widely celebrated throughout Japan on the occasion of the burning of the New Year's ornaments on 14 and 15 January (the practice called *dondo*). Children in some regions go door-to-door to solicit *mochi* (rice cakes) or other offerings "for the *dōsojin*"; in a specially constructed hut called a *dondo-goya* or *tori-goya*, they eat the *mochi* and sing songs.

dōtaku 銅鐸

Native bronze bells of the Yayoi period (ca 300 BC–ca AD 300). Over 400 of these bells, ranging from 10 to 130 centimeters (4 to 51 in) in height, have been discovered in Japan, usually singly or in pairs. Up to 14 bells have been unearthed together, and some are found with BRONZE MIRRORS or BRONZE WEAPONS. The bells have elongated bodies and are oval in cross section and open at one end. Semicircular handles are cast at the top, and most bells have flanges at the side seams. Some of the bells are thought to have been musical instruments, but others seem to have been ceremonial implements. Early bells had clappers, which rang against a raised band inside the mouth of the bell. Changes in the form of this band suggest that the nature of the bells evolved gradually from a functional into a ceremonial item.

The designs cast onto the surfaces of the bronze bells fall into three major categories: horizontal banded designs, square block patterns, and flowing water designs. Others are illustrated with a FERN FROND DESIGN or figures of people and animals. One bell from Kagawa Prefecture depicts scenes of hunting, pounding rice, and a raised storehouse; another from Hyōgo Prefecture also shows hunting scenes. — See photos, next page.

Dōwa Mining Co, Ltd 同和鉱業[株]

(Dōwa Kōgyō). Company engaged in the mining and refining of nonferrous metals. Originally known as Fujita-Gumi, the company was founded by Fujita Denzaburō when he bought the government-owned Kosaka Mine in Akita Prefecture in 1884. The present name of the company was assumed in 1945. After World War II, Dōwa continued to explore for new veins in existing mines; it has developed into a refining firm that uses a high percentage of ore derived from its own mines. It operates joint copper-mining ventures in Canada and Indonesia. Sales for the fiscal year ending March 1991 totaled ¥203.2 billion (US $1.5 billion), and capitalization stood at ¥22.2 bil-

dōsojin Originally worshiped as the protectors of village boundaries, these deities are depicted in various forms—as inscribed stelae, phallic stones, or human figurines. The stone shown here, which depicts a male and female deity in an intimate pose, is a typical example of the "paired *dōsojin*." Village of Azusagawa, Nagano Prefecture.

dōtaku

Elaborately decorated ceremonial bronze bells more than 1,600 years old have been discovered in various places in Japan. The three major types of decoration identified include a square block pattern, horizontal banded designs, and flowing water designs.

◄The flowing water design is highly stylized. Yao, Ōsaka Prefecture. Middle Yayoi period. Height 45 cm. Tōkyō National Museum.

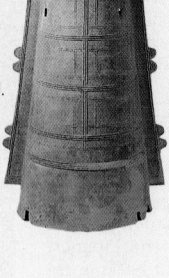

◄Bell with a large handle and flanges, decorated with a square block pattern. Habikino, Ōsaka Prefecture. Late Yayoi period. Height 89 cm. Agency for Cultural Affairs.

◄Bell with square block pattern. Kōbe, Hyōgo Prefecture. Middle Yayoi period. Height 64 cm. Kōbe City Museum. National Treasure.

◄Two figures pounding grain on a bell with a square block pattern. Kōbe, Hyōgo Prefecture. Middle Yayoi period. Kōbe City Museum. National Treasure.

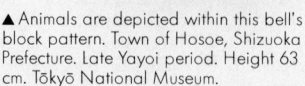

▲ Animals are depicted within this bell's block pattern. Town of Hosoe, Shizuoka Prefecture. Late Yayoi period. Height 63 cm. Tōkyō National Museum.

lion (US $161.8 million). Headquarters are in Tōkyō.

doyō   土用

Strictly speaking, the term *doyō* refers to the 18 days that precede the beginning of each of the four seasons as defined by Japan's old solar calendar (see CALENDAR, DATES, AND TIME); however, it is the 18 days before the beginning of autumn (*risshū*) that are most commonly referred to by this term. Because it is usually quite hot during this period, which corresponds to late July and early August in the modern calendar, there are many Japanese customs that call for particular attention to be paid to one's health at this time. One such custom still widely practiced in Japan is the eating of eel for its high protein content on the day traditionally held to be the hottest.

dōyō ⟶ children's songs

Dōzen   島前

A subgroup of the OKI ISLANDS in the Sea of Japan off the coast of western Honshū; part of Shimane Prefecture. Nishinoshima, Nakanoshima, and Chiburishima are Dōzen's main islands. Small-scale agriculture and fishing are the principal activities, although fish cultivation and tourism are becoming increasingly important. Dōzen is part of Daisen-Oki National Park. Area: 104 sq km (40 sq mi).

Draft Law to Control Radical Social Movements

過激社会運動取締法案

(Kageki Shakai Undō Torishimari Hōan). A proposed antiradical law introduced in the Diet in early 1922 but not enacted. The bill was one government response to the rise of leftist radicalism after World War I. Justice officials of the TAKAHASHI KOREKIYO cabinet, led by HIRANUMA KIICHIRŌ and SUZUKI KISABURŌ, presented the government's case to a committee of the House of Peers beginning 21 February 1922. The bill passed the House of Peers, but the cabinet decided not to try to push it through the House of Representatives for fear of jeopardizing more pressing legislation.

dragonflies   蜻蛉

(*tombo*). Insects of the order Odonata. About 190 species, divided into three suborders, have been identified in Japan.

Suborder Zygoptera (damselflies). The fore- and hind-wings are of the same shape and possess feeble powers of flight. Species of the genera *Mnais* and *Calopteryx* are quite large, but others are generally small. There are about 50 species of 26 genera in Japan, of which several are endemic. These include the *hanadaka tombo* (*Rhinocypha ogasawarensis*), the *togeotombo* (*Rhipidolestes aculeata*), the Ryūkyū *rurimon tombo* (*Coeliccia ryukyuensis*), and the Ogasawara *itotombo* (*Boninagrion ezoin*).

Suborder Anisoptera. These are powerful fliers with wings wider than those of the Zygoptera. The group includes large species such as the *oniyamma* (*Anotogaster sieboldii*) and genera such as *Boyeria* and *Anax*, but most are of medium size. There are about 135 species of 54 genera in Japan, of which about 50 species are endemic, including about 20 species of genus *Gomphus* and its allied genera.

Suborder Anisozygoptera. The wings resemble those of suborder Zygoptera and the body that of suborder Anisoptera. This is a primitive group that flourished from the Mesozoic to the Cenozoic eras. The only surviving species are the *mukashitombo* (*Epiophlebia superstes*) of Japan and another species of the Himalaya area.

The dragonfly was believed to be the spirit of the rice plant and a harbinger of rich harvests. It may have been used as a symbol of the power of the 8th-century Yamato court. Dragonflies often appear in Japanese poetry and are beloved by Japanese children.

drama, modern   近現代の演劇

(*kingendai no engeki*). "Modern drama" here refers to drama written and performed since the Meiji Restoration of 1868. In the modern period, the NŌ and BUNRAKU theaters have almost exclusively performed plays written before 1868, and they will therefore not be considered here. The major part of KABUKI's repertory has similarly been premodern, but many new plays for kabuki have been written over the past century.

The development of modern theater in Japan was subject to the twin stimuli of a reaction against an orthodoxy perceived as stultifying, as in kabuki, and imported Western drama and dramaturgy. SHIMPA, which developed in the 1890s, was a genre similar to kabuki in its acting methods; *shimpa*, however, utilized actresses (kabuki was all male) and was more open to outside influence in all aspects of its performance. SHINGEKI, a movement that began at the turn of the 20th century, was also created in reaction to kabuki and its highly commercial character, but was stimulated by Ibsen, Shakespeare, and other (mainly naturalist and romantic) playwrights. From around 1910 to the late 1960s the main genres of modern Japanese theater were kabuki, *shimpa*, and *shingeki;* these three genres are broadly categorized as presentational, semirepresentational, and naturalistic, respectively. The performance style of SHIN-KOKUGEKI, a drama troupe formed in the second decade of the 20th century, occupied a position somewhere between *shimpa* and *shingeki. Shōgyō engeki* ("commercial theater"), a catchall category, corresponded roughly to the more popular productions on Broadway and in the West End. *Shingeki* itself became an orthodoxy in the eyes of aspiring young actors in the 1960s. In reaction to this new orthodoxy emerged the SHŌGEKIJŌ UNDŌ, a movement also known as *angura geki* ("underground theater"). Lack of inhibition and restraint, which was the movement's hallmark, accelerated its development to the point where, in contrast to *shingeki*'s slow progress to maturity over about five decades, the *shōgekijō undō* had reached its fourth generation by the late 1980s.

The Beginning of Modern Japanese Drama—After the Meiji Restoration the initial momentum for change in theater came from a kabuki actor, Ichikawa Danjūrō IX (1838–1903; see ICHIKAWA DANJŪRŌ), who tried to encourage historical verisimilitude in kabuki by promoting *katsureki-mono* ("living history" plays), and from a playwright, Kawatake MOKUAMI, who wrote such plays for him. Parallel to this in the new field of drama theory, TSUBOUCHI SHŌYŌ urged psychological realism in his *Shōsetsu shinzui* (1885–86, The Essence of the Novel). The novelist MORI ŌGAI, who disagreed with those who thought reform should begin in the physical theater, argued authoritatively for a drama that should first of all have literary merit. After an important debate between Ōgai and Shōyō on the place of idealism in literary works, drama's right to be considered an essential part of a new Japanese literature was generally recognized.

Shōyō always tried to match theory with practice. In his critical work *Waga kuni no shigeki* (1893–94, Japan's Historical Drama), there was a general move toward emphasis on characterization rather than situation, and his play *Kiri hitoha* (1894–95, Paulownia Leaf) is typical of this trend. OKAMOTO KIDŌ, collaborating closely with a kabuki actor as had been the pattern in kabuki playwriting since the 17th century, wrote *Shuzenji monogatari* (1911; tr *The Mask Maker*, 1928). MAYAMA SEIKA, after writing mainly for *shimpa*, teamed up with the same actor, Ichikawa Sadanji II (1880–1940), in the mid-1920s and wrote many historical dramas combining historical accuracy, realistic dialogue, and modern characterization. Mayama is most famous for his dramatization of the FORTY-SEVEN RŌNIN INCIDENT, entitled *Genroku chūshingura* (1934–41). During the late 1920s and 1930s the writer HASEGAWA SHIN generated a vogue in *matatabi-mono*, a literary (and later cinematic) genre portraying the world of gamblers and gangsters, and was a great box-office success.

Shingeki and Other Forms—The *shingeki* movement started in earnest around 1910, when the theater groups Jiyū Gekijō (Free Theater), led by Sadanji II and OSANAI KAORU, and Bungei Kyōkai (Literary Society), led by Shōyō and SHIMAMURA HŌGETSU, offered different solutions to the problem of confronting kabuki in the modern theater. Bungei Kyōkai used amateur actors; Jiyū Gekijō used kabuki actors, who were expected to retrain in modern acting techniques. Neither group succeeded technically but they provided a stimulus to a new generation of playwrights. Japanese naturalism, which was heavily influenced by the works of Ibsen, reached its peak in Nakamura Kichizō's (1877–1941) *Kamisori* (1914; tr *The Razor*, 1923), the story of a murder in a barber shop. Other playwrights preferred European romantic and symbolist models. Mori Ōgai wrote the tragic romance *Ikutagawa* (River Ikuta) in 1910, while KINOSHITA MOKUTARŌ's *Nambanji monzen* (1909, Before the Gate of the Namban Temple) has a strong symbolist undercurrent.

By the end of the second decade of the 20th century, drama had become voluminous and varied. It was characterized by spectacular theatrical successes and lifeless literary exercises. Perhaps because the concept of the playwright as an artist in his own right was still new in Japan, all novelists were assumed to be good playwrights and seemed to wish to try their hands at playwriting. Such *Lese-drama* (the German term was used) contributed little overall to Japan's modern theater. By contrast the box-office

hits of the period have been frequently performed since. Very popular at the time was *Sono imōto* (1915; tr *The Sister*, 1936), by the leader of the SHIRAKABA SCHOOL literary group, MUSHANOKŌJI SANEATSU. The play depicts a war-blinded painter and his self-sacrificing sister. Also popular were KURATA HYAKUZŌ's *Shukke to sono deshi* (1917; tr *The Priest and His Disciples*, 1922), a play about SHINRAN, the founder of the Jōdo Shin sect of Buddhism; and KIKUCHI KAN's *Chichi kaeru* (1917; tr *The Father Returns*, 1925), the story of the return, rejection, and final forgiving of a prodigal father.

The opening in 1924 of the Tsukiji Shōgekijō (Tsukiji Little Theater), the first theater in Japan built specifically for the staging of modern drama, marked a watershed year for *shingeki*. The mid-1920s also saw the rise of Marxist drama, which by the end of the decade had become dominant in *shingeki* and even extended its influence into the commercial theater. Expressionism, represented by Akita Ujaku's (1883–1962) *Gaikotsu no butō* (1924, The Dance of the Skeletons), was followed by proletarian realism. FUJIMORI SEIKICHI took the *shingeki* and commercial theater worlds by storm with his *Nani ga kanojo o sō saseta ka* (1927, What Made Her Do It?), about a girl whose suffering at the hands of "respectable" society leads her to burn down the orphanage she lives in. MURAYAMA TOMOYOSHI's *Bōryokudan ki* (1929, Record of a Gang of Thugs) was another landmark in proletarian drama. Proletarian realism was followed in the 1930s by socialist realism, with such plays as KUBO SAKAE's *Kazan-baichi* (1937; tr *Land of Volcanic Ash*, 1986) and HISAITA EIJIRŌ's *Hokutō no kaze* (1937, The Northeast Wind) portraying large social issues in a realistic way that was not necessarily revolutionary.

During the same period some playwrights turned away from left-wing drama. MIYOSHI JŪRŌ wrote *Bui* (1940, Lifebuoy), which was based on his wife's struggle with tuberculosis. Other playwrights had never accepted left-wing drama. KUBOTA MANTARŌ's *Ōdera gakkō* (1927, Ōdera School) portrays a school headmaster unable to comprehend the societal changes leaving him behind. KISHIDA KUNIO was uncompromising in his insistence that the quality of stage language was the key to new drama. He produced a series of finely detailed and delicately wrought plays, notably *Chiroru no aki* (1924; tr *Autumn in the Tyrol*, 1968) and *Ushiyama Hoteru* (1929, Hotel Ushiyama).

During World War II, theatrical experimentation of any kind was virtually impossible. Left-wing drama was officially banned, and the heavy hand of government censorship extended to any production that could be construed as not supporting the war effort.

Theater after World War II—The removal of restrictions after the war released pent-up dramatic energies, producing a flowering of theater during the next two decades. MORIMOTO KAORU's *Onna no isshō*

(1945; tr *A Woman's Life*, 1961–62) became one of Japanese commercial theater's greatest modern successes. Three *shingeki* companies, GEKIDAN HAIYŪZA, GEKIDAN MINGEI, and BUNGAKUZA, dominated modern theater during these years. Playwrights active before the war continued to write, and new playwrights emerged. KINOSHITA JUNJI, who delighted *shingeki* and kabuki audiences with such folktale plays as *Yūzuru* (1949; tr *Twilight Crane*, 1956), also probed modern Japanese history through his dramas about 20th-century intellectuals. In *Shigosen no matsuri* (1978, The Dirge of the Meridian) he combined choral speaking and historical realism in a re-creation of the fall of the Taira, a medieval Japanese warrior family. The novelist MISHIMA YUKIO dissected the psychology of his characters in his very successful rewriting of selected Nō plays. TANAKA CHIKAO, the novelist ABE KŌBŌ, and the scholar YAMAZAKI MASAKAZU have all, as playwrights, made important contributions to the self-confidence and stability that *shingeki* has achieved.

Shingeki's very stability provoked an angry reaction from young actors and playwrights during the 1960s. This backlash, strengthened by widespread political discontent in Japan over the UNITED STATES–JAPAN SECURITY TREATIES in 1960, gave birth to the "underground" theater movement known as *shōgekijō undō*. The movement's first generation of writers, which included BETSUYAKU MINORU, KARA JŪRŌ, SUZUKI TADASHI, and TERAYAMA SHŪJI, shocked audiences with their total disregard for *shingeki* theatrical conventions. The theater they created recognized no barriers of logic, genre, or morality. The second generation of playwrights, whose best-known figures were TSUKA KŌHEI, Yamazaki Tetsu (b 1946), and Takeuchi Jūichirō (b 1947), reduced the jumbled images

dragonflies
1 The 10 species of *kawatombo* ("river dragonfly") are relatively large (50–60 mm in length), with metallic-colored bodies and varying wing colors.
2 The *gin'yamma* (left), 70 mm in length, and *oniyamma*, 95–100 mm in length, are among the largest Japanese dragonflies.
3 The *akiakane*, also known as *akatombo*, "red dragonfly," is the subject of a favorite Japanese song.
4 The *mukashitombo* ("ancient dragonfly") is one of only two surviving species of dragonflies that can be traced back more than 100 million years.

modern drama
A scene from the theatrical troupe Yume no Yūminsha's 1990 production of *Hanshin* (Demigod), starring troupe leader Noda Hideki (center). The play was based on a comic book by Hagio Moto.

and elements of the early underground movement and concentrated more on single, often disturbing, social themes. Important playwrights of the third generation included NODA HIDEKI and Watanabe Eriko (b 1955). Their dramas have a complex, Chinese-box-like configuration, often containing a number of plays within the play. A similar technique is employed by fourth-generation playwrights such as Kawamura Takeshi (b 1959) and Kōkami Shōji (b 1958).

A noteworthy tendency in the Japanese theatrical world in the 1980s was the great popularity of American and British musicals. In addition to revivals of older Broadway hits, such as *Fiddler on the Roof,* many new musicals, such as *Cats* and *Les Misérables,* were being performed in Japanese-language versions. Especially active in the production of foreign musicals was ASARI KEITA's theatrical company, GEKIDAN SHIKI.

drivers' licenses　　　運転免許

(*unten menkyo*). Licenses required by the ROAD TRAFFIC LAW of 1960 for all operators of motor vehicles. They are of two kinds, Class I for drivers of private vehicles and Class II for drivers of commercial passenger-carrying vehicles (taxis and buses), and must be renewed every three years. Anyone 18 years of age (20 for trucks over 5 tons and noncommercial buses, 16 for motorcycles) may obtain a Class I driver's license by passing an examination given by the Public Safety Commission in the prefecture where he or she lives. Applicants for a Class II license and for a Class I license permitting operation of trucks over 11 tons must be 21 years old. The examination is in three parts: a test for vision, color blindness, and hearing; a road test of driving skills; and a written test on traffic regulations. Anyone certified by an accredited driving school is exempt from the road test, and nearly all applicants today are certified this way. The possessor of a foreign driver's license is exempt from the road test and the written test. A foreign national who holds an international driver's license may drive in Japan for one year after arrival without applying for a Japanese license.

drug abuse　　　薬物の濫用

(*yakubutsu no ran'yō*). Drugs of an addictive and narcotic nature (*mayaku*), the use of which is strictly controlled in Japan, are divided into three categories. The first category includes four kinds of drugs covered by the Narcotics Control Law (Mayaku Torishimari Hō) enacted in 1953 (revised in 1963): drugs extracted from the opium poppy (such as morphine, heroin, and codeine), drugs extracted from the coca plant (such as cocaine), synthetic drugs, and psychotomimetic drugs or hallucinogens (such as LSD). The second category comprises marijuana and opium, which are controlled by the Hemp Control Act (Taima Torishimari Hō) enacted in 1948 and the Opium Control Act (Ahen Torishimari Hō) enacted in 1954, respectively. The third category is made up of stimulant drugs (such as amphetamines) regulated by the Stimulant Drugs Control Act (Kakuseizai Torishimari Hō) enacted in 1951.

The rates of drug addiction and drug-related offenses are much smaller in Japan than in many other countries. Prior to 1945 Japan had no drug abuse problem worth mentioning. The first period of widespread indiscriminate drug use, which began among the young and involved trafficking in stimulants and narcotics, came immediately after World War II and spread in the late 1940s and early 1950s. Heroin was the predominant narcotic during the late 1950s and into the 1960s. This was followed by a crackdown in the late 1960s as stiffer drug control laws were established. Marijuana use spread in the 1970s but the number of marijuana-related offenses was low thereafter. Abuse of stimulant drugs was on the rise from 1970 onward. Although stimulant drug offenses have recently decreased (16,866 arrests in 1989), they still represent over 90 percent of all drug offenses. Arrests for the possession of cocaine are rare in Japan (113 arrests and 69 kilograms [152 pounds] seized in 1990).

drugs　　　薬

(*kusuri*). The traditional medicine of Chinese origin known as *kampō* was the predominant form of medicine practiced in Japan until the late 19th century. Western-style medicine was introduced to Japan in the 16th century, but it was not until the Meiji period (1868–1912), when the government actively promoted the adoption of Western medicine, that Western drugs came into wide use.

After the Meiji Restoration of 1868, Western drugs were imported to Japan in increasing quantities. Quality standards and analytical techniques were also introduced, and the government issued the first PHARMACOPOEIA OF JAPAN in 1886. The profession of pharmacy also became established. However, many Japanese physicians, in accordance with ancient *kampō* precepts, continued to prescribe, prepare (in the case of traditional medicines), and dispense medicines themselves. Even today, the division of responsibilities between physician and pharmacist is not as clear as in some other countries.

Before World War I almost all modern drugs used in Japan were imported, especially from Germany. When imports were interrupted by the war, the domestic drug industry advanced rapidly in both scale and quality. Shortages of materials and destruction of factories during World War II, however, dealt a crushing blow to the Japanese drug industry. It gradually resumed its activities after the war.

The standards of approval for drug manufacture were toughened in 1967. As a result, the number of drug manufacture approvals sharply decreased after 1968. In 1991 there were about 30,000 drugs on the Japanese market; about 14,000 of these were ethical (prescription) drugs and about 16,000 were over-the-counter drugs.

Since 1956 it has been national policy to separate the responsibilities of physician and pharmacist concerning the dispensing of drugs, but in 1988 only 10 percent of prescriptions were filled by pharmacists. The reason is that, under the present system, the income of doctors increases in proportion to their willingness to dispense drugs to their patients. Added to this is a tendency among some Japanese patients to depend excessively upon drugs for medical treatment. The routine use of such health aids as vitamins and "stamina" pills and drinks is an example of the Japanese penchant for drugs. In 1989 Japanese spent a total of over ¥19.7 trillion (US $143.0 billion) on medical treatment, of which payments for drugs accounted for some 31 percent.

In 1989 drug production in Japan was valued at ¥5.5 trillion (US $39.8 billion), of which ethical drugs made up 85 percent and over-the-counter drugs 15 percent. The total number of pharmaceutical companies was about 2,000, the 20 largest companies accounting for about 21 percent of total production. Cardiovascular drugs ranked first among drugs produced, accounting for 14.0 percent of total drug production, followed by antibiotics, 13.2 percent; central nervous system drugs, 10.2 percent; gastrointestinal drugs, 9.5 percent; and metabolism agents, 7.9 percent.

DRUG ABUSE is not as widespread in Japan as it is in such countries as the United States. However, the number of known violations of the law concerning drugs in Japan jumped from 8,422 cases in 1975 to 29,765 cases in 1990, and drug abuse is now seen as a growing social problem. See also PHARMACEUTICAL INDUSTRY; MEDICINE, TRADITIONAL.

dual structure　　　二重構造

(*nijū kōzō*). Concept used to delineate a particular type of economic and industrial structure and defined by the Marxist economist and statistician ARISAWA HIROMI (1896–1988) in 1957 as "a structure in which corporations seek to maximize their capital accumulation by utilizing small and medium enterprises which themselves are only able to subsist on a basis of low wages and unstable employment." In the Japanese context the concept points up the difference between large corporations on the one hand—where practices such as lifetime employment, the seniority wage system (*nenkō joretsu*) with its bonuses and allowances, and company-based unions ensure stable employment, highly defined status relationships, and relatively high wage levels (see EMPLOYMENT SYSTEM, MODERN)—and, on the other hand, small and medium enterprises—where such practices are much reduced or nonexistent and where, as a result, wage levels are lower and job mobility greater. Such smaller companies therefore tend to employ more women, FOREIGN WORKERS, and part-time workers.

The dual structure concept came to be applied particularly to the Japanese economy prior to the high-growth period of the 1950s, before almost full employment narrowed wage differentials between employees in large corporations and those in smaller enterprises. In the 1980s, however, wage differentials between large corporations and smaller companies tended to widen again as the corporations' size and higher capital/labor ratios enabled them to attract employees in a shrinking labor market with higher wages and benefits, while smaller companies were forced to rely more on women and unskilled foreign workers. Moreover, there has been no significant lessening of the relationships of dependency upon the business of a single large corporation in which many small subcontractors and component suppliers find themselves. The Japanese economy thus seems likely to continue to be characterized by the dual structure concept. See also INCOME DISTRIBUTION.

Duan Qirui (Tuan Ch'i-jui)　　　段祺瑞

(1865–1936; J: Dan Kizui). Warlord who dominated Beijing (Peking) politics from 1916 to 1920; provisional chief executive of the Chinese Republic from November 1924 to April 1926. A top-ranked graduate of the Beiyang (Peiyang) Military Academy in 1887, Duan studied artillery engineering in Germany. After his return to China, he became the trusted lieutenant of YUAN SHIKAI (Yüan Shih-k'ai) and leader of the central government after Yuan's death in June 1916. Between 1916 and 1918 he was premier three times. At the expense of Chinese national interests, Duan obtained extensive financial aid from Japan through the NISHIHARA LOANS. Duan's government was extremely unpopular, largely due to the Sino-Japanese joint military agreements signed in May 1918, which provoked antigovernment demonstrations, resulting in the MAY FOURTH MOVEMENT the following year. Despite Japanese support of his Anhui (Anhwei) faction, Duan was defeated in a week-long war with Anhui's rival, the Zhili (Chihli) faction, in July 1920. He returned to power as chief executive of the provisional government in 1924 but was forced to resign in 1926. After the Japanese occupation of Manchuria in 1931, CHIANG KAI-SHEK, fearing that the Japanese might persuade Duan to set up a puppet government in North China, invited him to reside in Shanghai, where Duan died in 1936.

Du Bousquet, Albert Charles

デュ・ブスケ, A. C.

(1837–82). French military officer influential in building the modern Japanese army early in the Meiji period (1868–1912); born in Belgium of French parents. After service as an infantry officer in China and in France, he went to Japan in February 1867 with other French advisers at the invitation of the shogunate. When the shogunate collapsed in the MEIJI RESTORATION of 1868, Du Bousquet remained in Tōkyō as an interpreter for the French legation and played an active role in diplomatic relations between France and Japan. In 1870 he became a military adviser to the Ministry of Military Affairs (Hyōbushō). In 1871 he was employed by the legislative Chamber of the Left (Sain; see DAJŌKAN) and from 1874 to 1877 worked for the Chamber of Elders (GENRŌIN). He submitted numerous recommendations on military organization, most of which were adopted. After leaving the Japanese government's employ, Du Bousquet returned to the French legation in 1880 and was made consul. He died in Tōkyō. See also IMPERIAL JAPANESE ARMY.

Dulles, John Foster

ダレス, J. F.

(1888–1959). US lawyer and negotiator of the 1951 peace and security treaties with Japan and US secretary of state from 1953 to 1959. Born in Washington, DC, he was the grandson of John Foster and the nephew of Robert LANSING, both former secretaries of state. He graduated from Princeton University in 1908, studied at the Sorbonne, graduated from George Washington Law School in 1911, and entered law practice in New York. He served in the US Army in World War I as a captain on the War Industries Board and attended the Versailles Peace Conference as a US reparations expert. In 1945 he was senior adviser to the US delegation to the San Francisco Conference, which established the United Nations. On 6 April 1950 he was appointed by President Truman as foreign policy adviser to the secretary of state, and on 18 May 1950 he was assigned to negotiate a peace treaty with Japan. The treaty was signed in San Francisco on 8 September 1951 by 49 nations, including Japan (see SAN FRANCISCO PEACE TREATY). That same afternoon the United States and Japan signed the United States–Japan Security Treaty (see UNITED STATES–JAPAN SECURITY TREATIES).

Dulles succeeded in restoring Japan to a place of respect and importance in the community of nations. An ardent anticommunist, Dulles advocated liberation as opposed to containment, and brinkmanship and massive retaliation as opposed to neutralism. However, as secretary of state from 1953 to 1959 he worked to prevent serious military conflict.

Du Pont Japan, Ltd

デュポン ジャパン リミテッド[株]

(Dyupon Japan Rimiteddo). Manufacturer, exporter, importer, and marketer of chemical-related products. Incorporated in 1983. A wholly owned subsidiary of the American company E. I. du Pont de Nemours & Co, Ltd. Du Pont Japan's main products include engineering plastics, industrial and apparel-use fiber, organic and other chemicals, electronics materials, printing and industrial films, pharmaceuticals, and a wide array of household products. The company has made technological advances in specialty polymers, biotechnology, and other fields. It is involved in joint ventures with such Japanese firms as Tōray and Mitsui. Sales in 1991 totaled ¥102.6 billion (US $800.9 million), and capitalization stood at ¥29.1 billion (US $227.0 million). Headquarters are in Tōkyō.

D'urban, Inc

[株]ダーバン

(Dāban). Manufacturer and distributor of men's ready-made apparel. Incorporated in 1970 as a joint investment of RENOWN, INC, and four other companies. For the fiscal year ending December 1990, sales totaled ¥70.9 billion (US $516.8 million) and capitalization stood at ¥8.4 billion (US $61.2 million). Headquarters are in Tōkyō.

Duskin Co, Ltd

[株]ダスキン

(Dasukin). One of Japan's largest franchising companies. Incorporated in 1963. Franchised businesses include dust control, food services, and management services. Duskin is Japan's largest dust control company, and its Mister Donut food service franchise and its housecleaning business also hold dominant market shares. Sales for the fiscal year ending March 1991 totaled ¥137.0 billion (US $998.5 million), and capitalization stood at ¥2.3 billion (US $16.8 million). Headquarters are in Ōsaka.

Dutch Factory

オランダ商館

(Oranda Shōkan). A trading post of the Dutch East India Company. Founded in Hirado in 1609, it was moved to DEJIMA, a small island in Nagasaki Harbor, in 1641, under the terms of the Tokugawa shogunate's (1603–1867) policy of NATIONAL SECLUSION. Because of the seclusion policy, the Dutch company, together with the Chinese, was able to monopolize foreign trade with Japan, bringing in mainly raw silk and sugar and taking out gold, silver, and copper. The small Dutch trading post was not only an important base of foreign trade but also the only window through which Western culture could be introduced to Japan. Among the employees of the company were many who contributed to the development of WESTERN LEARNING in Japan, including Hendrik DOEFF, Philipp F. von SIEBOLD, and Carl P. THUNBERG. The trading house became the Dutch consulate in 1860. See also NAGASAKI TRADE.

Dutch Learning → Western Learning

Dutch trade

オランダ貿易

(Oranda bōeki). Trade conducted between Japan and Holland from the early 17th century through the period of NATIONAL SECLUSION, until the OPENING OF JAPAN in the 1850s. As the only Europeans allowed in Japan, the Dutch became the chief source of Japanese knowledge of European civilization and stimulated the WESTERN LEARNING movement.

In April 1600 the LIEFDE, a ship sent to East Asia by a Rotterdam trading company, ran ashore in Bungo Province (now Ōita Prefecture). The future shōgun TOKUGAWA IEYASU granted an audience to William ADAMS, the English navigator of the ship, and expressed his wish to open trade with Holland. In 1609 the Dutch East India Company sent two merchant ships to Japan. They obtained a SHUINJŌ license permitting them to trade within Japan and established a trading house at HIRADO in Kyūshū.

As a result of the ordinance of 1614 proscribing Christianity, from 1616 foreign trade was limited to the two ports of Hirado and Nagasaki. After the SHIMABARA UPRISING by Christian rebels in 1639, the Dutch trading house was moved to the island of DEJIMA (Deshima) in Nagasaki Harbor in 1641 (see NAGASAKI TRADE). According to the SHŌTOKU NAGASAKI SHINREI regulations of 1715, Dutch trade was limited annually to two ships. However, with their network of trading houses throughout Southeast Asia, the Dutch were able to bring in highly profitable merchandise, such as raw silk, silk textiles, medicine, and books. They exported silver, copper, camphor, and lacquer ware. More than 600 Dutch ships visited Japan during the period of National Seclusion, after which Dutch trade declined in the face of competition.

dyes and dye colors

染色

(senshoku). A refined dye technology was developed quite early in Japan. A description of the Japanese in the late-3rd-century Chinese chronicle WEI ZHI (Wei chih) mentions the dye plants INDIGO (ai) for blue and madder (akane) for red. By the 6th century a variety of dyes and dye techniques had been imported from the Asian continent. Also adopted was an elaborate color-ranking system correlating court rank with the right to wear garments of specific shades of color dyed with specific plants. Detailed recipes for these colors are to be found in the ENGI SHIKI (927). Mordants (substances used to fix the colors) were limited to ash-lye and iron.

The multilayered JŪNIHITOE costume of aristocratic women in the Heian period (794–1185) used color for its main design effect. Kamakura-period (1185–1333) armor was made of stencil-dyed leather and small metal plates held together by repeated rows of silk braids, often organized in large pattern blocks of color. New dye materials and mordants were imported from China and Southeast Asia during the Muromachi period (1333–1568). Colors were more complex, reflecting the aesthetic values of wabi and sabi, associated with the TEA CEREMONY.

In the Edo period (1600–1868) the newly prosperous merchant class employed new dye techniques and a variety of mordants to produce imitations of purple and red from commonly available dye materials. Today there is an upsurge of interest in natural dyes. See also SANKECHI; TIE-DYEING; WAX-RESIST DYEING.

eagles ➞ hawks and eagles

Earlier Nine Years' War 前九年の役
(Zenkunen no Eki). Military campaign waged intermittently by the imperial court against the Abe family of Mutsu Province (now Aomori, Iwate, Miyagi, and Fukushima prefectures) between 1051 and 1062. (Only nine of those years saw fighting, and the war is termed "earlier" to distinguish it from the LATER THREE YEARS' WAR, which broke out in the same region some 20 years afterward.) When ABE NO YORITOKI invaded neighboring areas and refused to forward tax revenues, the court dispatched Minamoto no Yoriyoshi (988–1075) and his son MINAMOTO NO YOSHIIE to subdue him. After Yoritoki was killed in 1057, the fighting continued under his sons ABE NO SADATŌ and ABE NO MUNETŌ, until, aided by the Kiyohara family of Dewa Province (now Akita and Yamagata prefectures), the court armies crushed the Abe. The victory is celebrated in the late-11th-century war chronicle *Mutsu waki* and illustrated in the 14th-century scroll *Zenkunen kassen emaki*, preserved in the Tōkyō National Museum.

early Japanese song 古代歌謡
(*kodai kayō*). The term *kodai kayō* refers primarily to songs and ballads recorded in the earliest Japanese written sources, such as the chronicles KOJIKI (712, Record of Ancient Matters) and NIHON SHOKI (720, Chronicles of Japan) and the verse anthology MAN'YŌSHŪ (mid-8th century). However, since the activities of courtly society did not change quickly in Japan, many songs that came after these earliest sources are best understood as outgrowths of earlier songs. Thus, the Heian-period (794–1185) *kagura* songs (KAGURA UTA) and SAIBARA songs are included in the category of *kodai kayō*.

Early Sources——Allowing for the several songs that appear in both the *Kojiki* and *Nihon shoki*, there are about 190 unique song texts in the chronicles. Nothing is known about the music they were sung to, but the prose narrative in which they are embedded states that they were sung by the legendary figures whose deeds the chronicles supposedly relate. The songs are of two chief types: a group of older, unaltered, often ceremonial texts that were fitted into various tales, and a group of later songs that seem to have been specially composed or reworked to bring lyrics or dramatic highlights to certain episodes.

In the *Man'yōshū* we have to deduce, from their content or the circumstances in which they were apparently composed—the banquet table, for example—which poems might have been sung. Some may rather have been chanted. Some also appear in the *Kojiki*, where they are described as songs.

Additional 8th-century sources include the FUDOKI, provincial gazetteers, altogether containing some 20 songs, a few of which may reflect the practice of song in the countryside; the *Shoku nihongi* (Continuation of the Chronicles of Japan); the NIHON RYŌIKI, Japan's oldest collection of Buddhist miracle tales; and a stone that has 21 religious songs—called "The Buddha's-Footprint-Stone Songs"—carved into it.

Heian Sources——There are five main collections of song compiled in the early 10th century that often incorporated much older material. The *kagura* songs, the largest group, first became important at the rituals and festivities surrounding the investiture of a new emperor. Many *kagura* songs deal with natural images, particularly the leafy decorated branches used in the ceremony. It has been argued that *kagura* songs may have been used originally as word magic—for example, singing to the emperor about the branches gave him some of their vital power. The *kagura* ceremony is still held at the Imperial Palace, and detailed information exists about its instrumentation and how it should be carried out.

Many of the 61 extant *saibara* songs, which date from the 9th century, sound like folk songs, as do the 8 Azuma *asobi uta* (Songs for Music of the Eastlands) and the 53 *fuzoku uta* (Songs from the Countryside). These songs were sung by the Heian upper class at such occasions as banquets and shrine festivals, their sentimental themes striking Heian aristocrats as primitive and quaint. Their popularity helps explain why, 200 years later, as many as 43 *saibara* songs were quoted in the TALE OF GENJI.

The fifth collection, the *Kinkafu* (Scores for Koto Songs), is a late-10th-century manuscript of 22 songs once part of the repertory of court musicians. The *Kinkafu* gives first a plain, unadorned version of a song, then a performance text showing instructions for voice and *koto*. It is an important indication of the singing and instrumental styles of the time of its compilation and perhaps earlier.

Song Use——The songs mentioned above were the property of court aristocrats and those who served them. They were used for enjoyment, worked into romantic and historical settings as in the chronicles, or put to serious use at formal ceremonies. It is possible that they were also made part of musical performances that were staged by professional servant-performers (see KATARIBE).

There appears to have been a good deal of consistency between court and countryside in how songs were used. In texts of folk songs recorded in the last century it is possible to discern the same kind of word magic once lavished on a monarch blessing a pair of newlyweds or the owner of a new house. Some songs at drinking parties are similar to those sung by *Kojiki* characters or found among banquet poems in the *Man'yōshū*. Indeed, we may assume not only that farmers of the *Kojiki* age sang much the same kinds of songs but also that some of the songs of the imperial court had in fact derived from an ancient song tradition rooted in village life. The UTAGAKI, or song festival, for example, where songs could be exchanged between courting men and women, was one rural custom with considerable effect on the poetic tradition.

early literature 上代の文学
(*jōdai no bungaku*). The oldest extant texts in the canon of Japanese literature; the term customarily includes a wide variety of materials, some of which were composed in the preliterate past and orally transmitted to later redactors. Thus, although the term refers chiefly to the major texts of the Nara period (710–794), such as the KOJIKI (712, Records of Ancient Matters), the NIHON SHOKI (720, Chronicle of Japan), and the MAN'YŌSHŪ (late 8th century, Collection of Ten Thousand Leaves or Collection for Ten Thousand Generations), it must also comprehend not only now-lost early written records but oral traditions that extend back to the 5th century and beyond. The existence of previous records is borne out, for example, by the practice in the *Nihon shoki*

of prefacing each among a series of variant versions of a narrative with the phrase "according to another text . . ."

Sources—The overall aim of the two historical chronicles, *Kojiki* and *Nihon shoki*, appears to have been to verify the divine authority of the Yamato line of kings from the time of their ancestral gods, who created and pacified the islands of Japan, through the age of legendary monarchs, who are described as having extended their rule throughout the land, to the historical period of emperors and empresses, who maintained relations with the countries of the Korean peninsula and China and began the task of establishing a centralized government after the Chinese model.

In telling this story the *Kojiki* and *Nihon shoki* draw upon a wide range of older materials: Chinese literature and history, myths and legends, genealogies of the imperial line and of other major lineage groups, and brief stories of romance and intrigue. For all the political coloration of these works, many of the myths and legends appear to be rooted in the oral traditions of an agrarian peasant culture. Inserted into varied and episodic prose matrices, we find songs and poems—calls to battle, magical incantations accompanying court ritual, scraps of reworked folk song—as well as a style of dramatic lyricism highlighting many otherwise bare narratives.

The most important among other early literary works was the *Man'yōshū*, the oldest extant collection of Japanese verse, which contains some 4,500 poems, many of them from the 7th century. Supplementary sources include the FUDOKI, geographical reference books compiled by provincial officials beginning in 713, in which were recorded natural and agricultural resources and traditional lore and accounts of the etymologies of place names; the KAIFŪSŌ (751, Verses in Memory of Poets Past), the earliest anthology of poetry in Chinese by Japanese poets and a precursor of Chinese poetry anthologies that proliferated in Japan in the early 9th century; and the KOGO SHŪI (Collected Remnants of Ancient Stories), submitted to the throne in 807, which gives interesting variants, related by Imbe no Hironari, of *Kojiki* and *Nihon shoki* myths. Also of note is the *Kinkafu* (ca 810, Scores for *Koto* Songs), a valuable source of information on the manner in which some of the songs of the *Kojiki* and the *Nihon shoki* were performed at court.

Transmission and Redaction—Behind much of the material in the *Kojiki* and *Nihon shoki* lie oral traditions of song and verse, myth and legend, with origins in the era when wet-rice agriculture and its accompanying culture became established in Japan; the roots of these traditions reach back and intertwine with the traditions of Korea, South China, and Southeast Asia, and even, in some instances, with those of the distant cultures of Polynesia. For upwards of a millennium narratives were passed down by unknown bards from generation to generation; however, by the 7th century there appear to have developed occupational groups attached to the Yamato court and to powerful families (UJI) that were responsible for the recitation and transmission of oral culture. Although modern scholars are not certain of the nature of these groups, or KATARIBE, nor have even found mention of the term until sources of the Heian period (794–1185), there is reference in records of the 7th century to various persons who have the

element *katari* (reciter; reciting) in the titles granted them by the court, and, in the time of Emperor TEMMU (r 672–686), to fishermen reciters' groups (*amagataribe*) that sang songs at court in praise of the emperor. The relation of these reciters to the *Kojiki* is, however, by no means clear.

In the preface to the *Kojiki* it is stated that the records kept by the various powerful lineage groups were fraught with errors and that, in order to rectify these, Temmu commanded one Hieda no Are to memorize accounts recorded in certain texts; in the reign of Empress Gemmei (r 707–715), Hieda no Are recited these to Ō NO YASUMARO, who compiled the *Kojiki.* Although oral narration was apparently still considered an important means of cultural transmission, it is clear that by the late 7th century there had come into existence an assortment of written records that were the primary sources from which the *Kojiki* was created.

Accounts in the *Kojiki* and *Nihon shoki* claim that as early as the 3rd century Korean scribes as well as scholars learned in the Confucian classics crossed the Korea Strait to Japan. Certainly from the 4th and 5th centuries, Japanese monarchs had need not only of record keepers but also of scribes who could handle diplomatic correspondence with the Korean kingdoms and China. Chinese and Japanese are fundamentally unrelated languages, and it was a formidable task for native students to learn to read Chinese, much less compose in it. Yet well before the Nara period some among them had not only a degree of mastery over literary Chinese but had begun to bend and shape its writing system into a tool for recording their own language. The prose of the *Kojiki*, though written with Chinese characters, is essentially a sinicized form of Japanese and makes little sense to anyone attempting to read it as Chinese. Some Chinese characters were used for their semantic value, so that a certain graph would be read using the Japanese word for the thing that it represented (rather like reading the figure 5 as "five," rather than *cinq*); others were used not for their inherent meaning, but for their

phonetic value to represent a particular Japanese syllable.

The prose of the *Nihon shoki* is much closer to classical Chinese; however, in the case of song and explicatory notes appended to myths and legends, Chinese characters are used to express Japanese semantic and sound values. The poems of the *Man'yōshū* are also written with a complex mixture of Chinese characters representing Japanese words. The phonetic component of this system of writing, which was also used in the *Kojiki*, has come to be known as *man'yōgana* (see KANA), the precursor of the Japanese phonetic syllabary.

Despite the use of a foreign system of writing and the pervasive political preoccupations brought to bear on both works, comparison of the *Nihon shoki* and the *Kojiki*—in particular their accounts of the folk hero YAMATOTAKERU—shows that the *Kojiki* has preserved through the medium of *man'yōgana* elements of an ancient tradition of oral cultural transmission.

ear ornaments, ancient　耳飾り

(*mimikazari*). Stone earrings and clay earplugs were already in use in the Jōmon period (ca 10,000 BC–ca 300 BC) of Japanese prehistory. The former were used throughout Japan from Early to Final Jōmon; these C-shaped, flattened rings were slipped through a hole in the earlobe and worn with the slit facing down. Earplugs were popular from Middle to Final Jōmon and are found most often in eastern Japan. Some are elaborate examples of fired-clay openwork designs. The custom of inserting ornaments into the earlobe did not survive into the succeeding Yayoi period (ca 300 BC–ca AD 300).

In the Kofun period (ca 300–710) simple rings made of gold, silver, gilt bronze, or iron were popularly worn clamped onto the ears of both males and females, as seen on the HANIWA funerary sculptures of the Kantō region. The nobility wore earrings with fine gold pendants attached. These have been discovered in mounded tombs (KOFUN) such

Earlier Nine Years' War This scene from a 14th-century handscroll depicts Minamoto no Yoriyoshi, leader of the victorious army, and several of his generals.

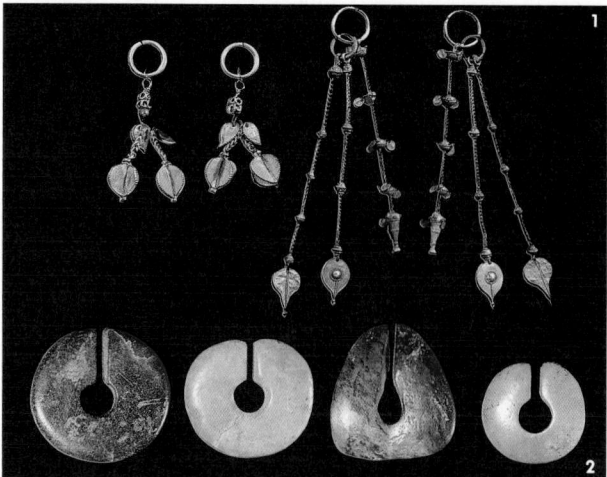

as the ŌZUKA TOMB and the ETA FUNAYAMA TOMB. The custom of wearing ear ornaments disappeared after the 7th century in Japan.

Earthquake Research Institute, Tōkyō University 東京大学地震研究所

(Tōkyō Daigaku Jishin Kenkyūjo). Institute conducting basic research in the earth sciences in order to discover more effective ways to predict earthquakes. Founded in 1925 in Tōkyō, the institute has 15 seismological observatories throughout Japan.

earthquakes 地震

(*jishin*). Earthquakes are a frequent phenomenon in Japan; nearly 10 percent of the energy released worldwide by earthquakes each year is concentrated in and around the Japanese islands. In the last century Japan has experienced 23 destructive earthquakes with measured or estimated magnitudes of 6 or higher on the scale used by the Meteorological Agency of Japan. This scale, in use since 1949, roughly approximates the better-known Richter scale used in the West. Both scales measure the magnitude of an earthquake by the energy released from its epicenter, but the Richter scale is based on measurements of vertical movement, whereas the Japanese scale measures horizontal movement.

The most famous earthquake in Japan was the great TŌKYŌ EARTHQUAKE OF 1923, which was later assigned a magnitude of 7.9 on the Japanese scale. Centered near metropolitan Tōkyō and Yokohama, the nation's most densely populated area, the quake resulted in more than 100,000 deaths and billions of dollars in property loss. In Tōkyō alone it took the lives of more than 60,000 people, of whom more than 50,000 died in quake-related fires that raged out of control.

Causes and Distribution of Earthquakes in Japan — The Tōkyō earthquake was caused by movement along a fault, that is, a fracture in the earth's crust. The upper layer of the fault zone shifted about 6 meters (20 ft) east and about 3 meters (10 ft) south with respect to the lower layer. The surface of the earth moved upward and toward the Pacific Ocean. This same type of movement is seen in virtually every earthquake that occurs along the Pacific coast of Japan.

Earthquakes tend to recur periodically, the interval between occurrences varying with locale. In the southern Kantō region, the interval is approximately every 100 years on the Pacific side; in the inland section of southwestern Japan, recurrence is estimated at 1,000 years. Seismologist Kawasumi Hiroshi (1907–72) estimated that the mean time between major earthquakes in the southern Kantō region is 69 years. There are also "swarms," sustained periods of numerous small quakes. The longest recorded swarm took place in the mid-1960s at Matsushiro in Nagano Prefecture.

Earthquake activity in Japan is accompanied by various forms of crustal distortion and fault displacement depending on the geographic and geologic area involved. For example, the tips of such peninsulas as the Bōsō, Miura, and Kii, all of which jut out into the Pacific Ocean, slowly sink into the ocean at the rate of 1 centimeter (0.4 in) a year. If this depression were to continue for 100 years, it would amount to 1 meter (3.3 ft), but a major earthquake would then lift the tip to compensate instantly for the accumulated depression. On the other hand, earthquakes occurring in southwestern Japan west of the FOSSA MAGNA are created by sudden movements of the earth along an existing fault zone, and unlike earthquakes on the Pacific coast, these quakes are not preceded by crustal movement. The Fossa Magna, a fault zone of the left-slip type, extends roughly north and south; the Median Tectonic Line, running from central Honshū to Kyūshū, is a fault zone of the right-slip type, extending roughly east and west. Quakes in the inland area of southwestern Japan occur along this pair of zones.

The crustal distortion accompanying Pacific coast quakes is caused by mantle convection, the flow of heat within the earth. In the southeastern Pacific Ocean there is a ridge, the Southeast Pacific Rise, toward which mantle convection surges from the earth's core; mantle convection then moves horizontally toward Japan before creeping downward again to the core. When continental plates collide, they fold the thick continental crust upward into mountain ranges; but beneath the oceans, where the crust is much thinner, a collision causes one plate to subduct, or dive under the other, and become absorbed in the underlying mantle. The involvement of peninsula tips in this movement causes their slow depression between earthquakes, the rate of depression being equal to the speed of mantle convection. The sudden upheaval of a peninsula's tip in an earthquake is due to "elastic rebound," the theory of which helps explain the periodicity of earthquakes.

Pacific coastal areas are gradually compressed by mantle convection in the intervals between earthquakes, and in a large earthquake they rebound toward the Pacific. Accordingly, the greater the accumulation of pressure from the Pacific Ocean, the greater the probability that an earthquake will occur in the region. Significant horizontal movements in several areas along the Pacific coast of Japan within the last 70 years suggest that a major one is imminent.

Earthquake Prediction — Since 1965, funds have been allocated for research on earthquake prediction, most of it centering on characteristic crustal distortions. In 1969 the METEOROLOGICAL AGENCY, the GEOGRAPHIC SURVEY INSTITUTE, and several national universities formed the Coordinating Committee for Earthquake Prediction to pool the results of their research; the committee meets once every three months. It was decided to conduct surveys over the entire area of Japan and to repeat measurements of geologic changes at short intervals by means of leveling and triangulation in comparatively small areas of the country deemed important, such as the southern Kantō area and the Tōkai region (Shizuoka and Aichi prefectures). Distortion and faulting also have been monitored continuously, using sensitive instruments such as the tiltmeter and extensometer. The occurrence of earthquakes is closely related to the motion of a fault zone, and it is therefore necessary to investigate active faults and active foldings and keep them under continuous observation. Since it is known that microelastic impact waves are generated in considerable numbers before rock fractures under the accumulation of strain, which is thought to resemble foreshock activity preceding large earthquakes, rock-breaking tests are being conducted to see if there is a correlation. The flow of heat that is transmitted from the core of the earth to the surface is closely related to crustal phenomena; further, terrestrial magnetism and earth current are said to change in relation to a large earthquake. Therefore, the measurement of mantle heat flow and investigations of terrestrial magnetism and earth current are being conducted to determine if there is some connection that will contribute to earthquake prediction.

Three factors—when, where, and how severe—are essential to earthquake prediction. Although quakes do occur periodically and are accompanied by characteristic crustal movements, the difficulties of predicting precisely when a quake will strike are not likely to be solved soon, and the likelihood of a quake's occurrence will continue to be based on statistical probability.

Most of the enormous damage accompanying large earthquakes comes from fire following building collapse, and also from the effects of TSUNAMI. Earthquakes are particularly destructive in Japan because closely packed structures, usually of wood, make for inadequate firebreaks, while the popularity of small space heaters fueled by gas or kerosene increases the chance of fire. The key to preventing earthquake damage is preparedness along with a system of building regulations designed to make utility lines and construction resistant to earthquakes and fire. See also EARTH SCIENCES; LARGE-SCALE EARTHQUAKE COUNTERMEASURES LAW.

earth sciences 地球科学

(*chikyū kagaku*). The earth sciences were introduced into Japan by European scientists in the early Meiji period (1868–1912), and Japan's frequent earthquakes fueled the rapid development of seismology and geology in particular. Seismology was introduced by John MILNE of England and James Alfred EWING of Scotland. Their lectures on engineering and studies of seismographic equipment gave impetus to the Japanese efforts that followed. In 1892 the Committee for Earthquake Disaster Prevention (Shinsai Yobō Chōsakai) was established. ŌMORI FUSAKICHI (1870–1948) and Imamura Akitsune (1870–1948), professors of seismology at Tōkyō University, were two of the scientists active on the committee, which became Japan's most important organization for the study of seismology and geophysics. In 1925 the committee became the Earthquake Research Institute of Tōkyō University. As a result of Imamura's work in predicting the TŌKYŌ EARTHQUAKE OF 1923 and the 1946 Nankaidō Earthquake, a national earthquake forecast program was started in 1965. See also EARTHQUAKES.

Geology in Japan began with Edmund NAUMANN, a German scientist who came to Japan in 1875 and later served as professor of geology at Tōkyō University. Naumann divided Japan into northeastern and southwestern areas separated by the FOSSA MAGNA fault line. HARADA TOYOKICHI, also a professor at Tōkyō University, was one of the first Japanese geologists.

earthworms 蚯蚓

(*mimizu*). In Japanese, *mimizu* is the common name for segmented worms of the phylum Annelida, class Oligochaeta. The largest species in Japan is the *hattamimizu* (*Drawida hattamimizu*) of northern Honshū, which reaches a length of about 60 centimeters (24 in). Next in size is the *shīboruto mimizu* (*Pheretima sieboldi*), which inhabits mountainous areas southward from central Japan and grows to about 45 centimeters (18 in). The *futsūmimizu* (*P. communissima*), reaching about 20 centimeters (8 in), and *shima-mimizu* (*Eisenia foetida*), reaching about 10 centimeters (4 in), are found throughout Japan and are used for fishing bait. Other small species, such as the *itomimizu* (*Tubifex hattai*) and *yurimimizu* (*Limnodrilus socialis*), are used as food for aquarium fishes. Unusual species include the *hotarumimizu* (*Microscolex phosphoreus*), which becomes luminous when aroused and lives in various places throughout the country.

The early Japanese used dried earthworms as a fever remedy. The folk belief that earthworms chirp was prevalent for a long time in Japan and appears in both *haiku* poetry and folktales.

East Asia cultural sphere
東アジア文化圏

(Higashi Ajia *bunkaken*). The countries of East Asia—China, Korea, Japan, and Vietnam—all traditionally shared certain distinct cultural features, including the use of Chinese characters (KANJI), the governmental and family practice of CONFUCIANISM, belief in BUDDHISM, and institutions shaped by a *ritsuryō* (Ch: *lüling*) legal and administrative system (see RITSURYŌ SYSTEM). In this sense the countries of East Asia can be said to constitute an East Asian cultural sphere.

Because this common cultural heritage originated in China, the formation of the East Asian cultural sphere is quite naturally explained in terms of the dissemination of Chinese culture. This spread of Chinese culture, however, was not a spontaneous process; it derived in large part from the Chinese court's creation of a system of international relations, with itself at the center. Eager to receive legitimation from the dominant power in the known world, the leaders of the various national groupings around China sought titles of office or nobility from the Chinese emperor. Through exchanges of embassies and through conferrals of titles on the rulers of the Korean states KOGURYŌ, PAEK-CHE, and SILLA in the 3rd through 6th centuries and on the rulers of independent Vietnam in the 10th century, the Chinese court established a system of tributary relations. Although Japanese rulers did not receive formal titles from the Sui (589–618) and Tang (T'ang; 618–907) dynasties, they received and sent many embassies and thus participated in the system (see SUI AND TANG [T'ANG] CHINA, EMBASSIES TO). In all these countries, relations with China led to the adoption of the Chinese writing system, Confucianism, Buddhism, and administrative practice.

This East Asia cultural sphere was profoundly affected by changes in China, such as the downfall of the Tang dynasty in 907 and the collapse of Chinese hegemony in East Asia under Western attack in the 1800s. The ensuing influx of Western culture

had a marked effect, transforming the East Asia cultural sphere into a variant of a modern shared world civilization.

East China Sea 東シナ海

(Higashi Shinakai). Sea surrounded by the Chinese mainland, the Nansei Islands, and Taiwan. The gross area is 1,240,000 square kilometers (about 480,000 sq mi); the maximum depth is 2,719 meters (about 8,920 ft); and the greater part of the Chinese side forms a continental shelf with a depth of 200 meters (660 ft) or less. It is a good fishing ground for croakers, cuttlefish, and cutlass fish and is heavily fished by Japanese fleets.

Eastern European nations and Japan 東欧諸国と日本

(Tōō *shokoku to* Nihon). During the Meiji period (1868–1912), Japan's attention was mainly focused on Western Europe since it was the Western colonial powers that affected Japanese interests most directly, while Eastern European interest in Japan was first aroused by the latter's victory in the RUSSO-JAPANESE WAR of 1904–05. By the 1920s Japan's attention had begun to turn toward Eastern Europe as well, due to such factors as the region's proximity to the newly established, avowedly revolutionary Soviet Union, with which Japan was on uneasy terms; the politics and diplomacy of the Balkan states, which had been a major factor in the outbreak of World War I; and the consequences of land reforms in Eastern Europe after the war. Following Japan's invasion of Manchuria in 1931 and its adoption of an openly anti-Soviet strategy, Japan sought contacts in Eastern Europe, both to determine Eastern European responses to Japan's actions and to gather intelligence concerning the Soviet Union. Japan's first overseas cultural exchange was with an Eastern European country, Hungary, in the form of the Japan-Hungary Cultural Agreement, concluded in November 1938.

After World War II, Japanese Marxists introduced and translated works from a number of socialist states in Eastern Europe. However, the Japanese interpretation of the socialist structure of these countries tended to be dogmatic, sometimes disregarding historical realities. Although Yugoslav opposition to the Soviet Union after 1948 drew considerable attention in Japan, it was not until after the 1956 disturbances in Poland and Hungary that Japanese Marxists, and Japanese academics and social and political commentators in general, began to adopt a more independent and critical perspective on Eastern European socialism. This change in outlook was reinforced by the ideological differences between the Soviet Union and the People's Republic of China and by the Soviet invasion of Czechoslovakia in 1968.

In the 1970s academic studies of Eastern European society and culture expanded dramatically, but, in the worsening East-West climate of the early 1980s, Japan's trade and economic relations with Eastern Europe declined. In 1988 trade with the region represented a mere 0.3 percent of total Japanese trade. With the improvement of East-West relations in the late 1980s, the breakup of the Soviet Union in 1991, and the move to unify the European market in the 1990s, Japanese business began to show greater interest in the region; however, given the unstable political and economic conditions in the area, the Japanese private sector required government backing for its participation in economic reconstruction projects in Eastern

Europe. For their part, the Eastern Europeans looked increasingly to Japan since they were well aware that, along with Germany, Japan was one major creditor nation that was able to provide the enormous funds through both direct and indirect investment that were needed if they were to reconstruct their economies.

East Hebei (Hopeh) Anticommunist Autonomous Government 冀東防共自治政府

(Ch: Jidong Fanggong Zizhi Zhengfu or Chi-tung Fang-kung Tzu-chih Cheng-fu; J: Kitō Bōkyō Jichi Seifu). Puppet regime representing Japanese ambitions to link North China more closely with the newly created Japanese puppet state of MANCHUKUO and with Japan. Created late in 1935, the East Hebei regime embraced 22 counties of North China that had been demilitarized under the TANGGU (TANGKU) TRUCE of 1933 and purged of Nationalist influence under the terms of the HE-UMEZU (HO-UMEZU) AGREEMENT of 1935. The pro-Japanese East Hebei regime was an affront to Chinese Nationalist aspirations to unify China and was a key factor leading to the SINO-JAPANESE WAR OF 1937-1945. In 1938 the East Hebei regime was absorbed by the PROVISIONAL GOVERNMENT OF THE REPUBLIC OF CHINA, a puppet government established by Japan.

East Japan Railway Co 東日本旅客鉄道[株]

(Higashi Nihon Ryokaku Tetsudō). The largest of Japan's six regional passenger-railway companies. Operates passenger lines in the Kantō region and northern Honshū. Established in 1987 as part of the privatization of the JAPANESE NATIONAL RAILWAYS. The company operates the Tōhoku and Jōetsu Shinkansen lines, providing service between Tōkyō and the cities of Morioka and Niigata, respectively. It also provides a variety of services related to travel, warehousing, advertising, insurance, and information processing. Operating revenues for the fiscal year ending March 1990 totaled ¥1.7 trillion (US $11.3 billion), while capitalization stood at ¥200.0 billion (US $1.3 billion). Headquarters are in Tōkyō.

Ebara Corporation [株]荏原製作所

(Ebara Seisakusho). Enterprise engaged in the manufacture and sale of pumps, fans, compressors, and refrigeration equipment. Incorporated in 1920. The company started by developing applications of INOKUCHI ARIYA's theory of centrifugal pumps; it now provides engineering services and equipment for environmental protection facilities, chemical plants, and nuclear power stations. The company has 53 affiliates or subsidiaries, 11 of which are incorporated outside Japan. Net sales for the fiscal year ending March 1991 totaled ¥230.0 billion (US $1.8 billion), with an export ratio of 7 percent; capitalization stood at ¥25.3 billion (US $184.4 million). Headquarters are in Tōkyō.

Ebashi Setsurō 江橋節郎

(1922–). Pharmacologist. Born in Tōkyō. Graduate of Tōkyō University. He contributed to the science of muscle physiology through his research on muscular contraction mechanisms and the role played in them by calcium, the endoplasmic reticulum, and the protein troponin. Ebashi became a professor at Tōkyō University in 1959. He is known for applied research, especially in di-

Ebino Kōgen Steam rises in the distance from some of the many hot springs in this highland region, and spikes of white eulalia decorate the autumnal fields.

agnostic methods for muscular dystrophy. In 1985 he became the director of the National Institute for Physiological Research. He was awarded the Order of Culture in 1975.

Ebetsu 江別[市]

City to the west of Sapporo in Hokkaidō. Located on the Ishikari Plain, at the confluence of the rivers Ishikarigawa and Ebetsugawa, Ebetsu was settled in 1878 by 12 farmer-militia families (TONDENHEI) from Iwate Prefecture. There is a thriving dairy industry, as well as paper, brick, and metal industries. It has become a residential satellite city of Sapporo. Pop: 97,201.

ebi→shrimps, prawns, and lobsters

Ebina 海老名[市]

City in central Kanagawa Prefecture, central Honshū, on the river Sagamigawa. Ebina has more than 150 factories producing metallic products, machinery, and electrical appliances. The city is also a bedroom suburb of Tōkyō and Yokohama. The remains of an 8th-century provincial temple (KOKUBUNJI) are here. Pop: 105,822.

Ebina Danjō 海老名弾正

(1856–1937). Christian leader and educator. Born in Chikugo Province (now part of Fukuoka Prefecture); attended Kumamoto Yōgakkō, a local school for Western studies. There he came under the influence of Leroy L. JANES and was baptized. Together with other newly baptized students, he formed what came to be known as the Kumamoto Band. Upon graduating from the Dōshisha (now Dōshisha University) in Kyōto, Ebina became pastor of Annaka Church in Gumma Prefecture. He also engaged in missionary work in Kōbe, Kumamoto, and Kyōto. From 1897 to 1920 he served as the pastor of Hongō Church in Tōkyō; his oratorical skills and liberal theology won many converts.

ebine 蝦根

(orchid). *Calanthe discolor.* Perennial herb of the family Orchidaceae cultivated as a garden plant. Also grows wild in mountain forests throughout Japan. Its leaves are pointed, about 20 centimeters (8 in) long, dark purple, and hairy underneath. In spring each plant produces about 10 blossoms with purple brown outer perianths and white to light purple inner perianths and lip.

Plants of the genus *Calanthe* grow mainly in the tropics of Asia, and about 150 species are known. Other species found growing wild in Japan include the yellow-flowered *kiebine* (*C. sieboldii*) and white-flowered *kirishima ebine* (*C. aristulifera*) of Kyūshū; the *natsuebine* (*C. reflexa*), growing in warm places westward from central Honshū; and the *sarumen ebine* (*C. tricarinata*), growing in beech forests on mountains throughout Japan.

During the Edo period (1600–1868) these

ebine The rhizome of this perennial herb, which is a member of the orchid family, is used in a folk remedy for tonsillitis.

various species were crossbred, producing many new varieties. After the Meiji period (1868–1912) cultivation of the *ebine* declined, but it is now being rediscovered.

Ebino えびの[市]

City in southwestern Miyazaki Prefecture, Kyūshū. Ebino is mainly known for its rice, tobacco, melons, *shiitake* (mushrooms), and lumber. The highlands of Ebino Kōgen to the south form part of the Kirishima-Yaku National Park. Pop: 26,825.

Ebino Kōgen えびの高原

Highland in southwestern Miyazaki Prefecture, Kyūshū. Surrounded by the peaks Koshikidake, Shiratoriyama, and Karakunidake; strewn with lakes and hot springs. Popular with campers and hikers, it is part of Kirishima-Yaku National Park. Elevation: approximately 1,200 m (3,900 ft).

Ebisu 恵比須

One of the SEVEN DEITIES OF GOOD FORTUNE (Shichifukujin); venerated throughout Japan as the tutelary deity of one's occupation. In some communities Ebisu is regarded specifically as the god of fishing, farming, and commerce and as the tutelary deity of the house. The name Ebisu means "foreigner" or "barbarian" and reflects the belief in deities who have come from afar (MAREBITO). He is also identified variously as Kotoshironushi no Kami, the son of the god ŌKUNINUSHI NO MIKOTO. The feast of Ebisu is celebrated in January or October, depending on the area. In farming communities Ebisu is worshiped along with DAIKOKUTEN in the kitchen. Ebisu is usually represented as wearing a *kimono*, a divided skirt (*hakama*), and a tall cap folded in the middle (*kazaori eboshi*), holding a fishing rod in his right hand and carrying a sea bream (a symbol of good luck) under his left arm.

Eboshidake 烏帽子岳

Mountain located in the HIDA MOUNTAINS on the border of Nagano and Toyama prefectures, central Honshū. The mountain's name derives from the granite at the summit, which is in the shape of a type of traditional Japanese aristocratic headgear called an *eboshi*. Height: 2,627 m (8,619 ft).

ebusshi 絵仏師

Artists who specialized in religious painting, as distinguished from *eshi*, or secular artists. The term *ebusshi* first appeared in documents of the late Heian period (794–1185) and does not include the Zen painter-priests of later periods. Originally, *ebusshi* seem to have been independent of the religious institutions of their day. But schools of *ebusshi* had developed by the end of the 12th century, and several of the major schools became affiliated with offices of painting (EDOKORO) at important temples and shrines in Nara and Kyōto. Examples are the KOSE SCHOOL at the temple KŌFUKUJI in Nara and the TAKUMA SCHOOL at KŌZANJI and JINGOJI in Kyōto.

Echigo Komagatake→Komagatake

Echigo Mountains 越後山脈

(Echigo Sammyaku). Mountain range running north to south, parallel to the Sea of Japan in Niigata, Yamagata, Gumma, and Fukushima prefectures, central northern Honshū. The range includes the Asahi, Iide, and Jōetsu mountains. The highest peak is Dainichidake (2,128 m; 6,982 ft) in the Iide

Mountains. There are plentiful water resources and many dams and hydroelectric power stations.

Echigo Plain→Niigata Plain

Echigo Province 越後国

(Echigo no Kuni). Present-day Niigata Prefecture, excluding the island of Sado. Established in the early 8th century when Koshi Province was divided into Echizen, Etchū, and Echigo provinces. The outposts NUTARI NO KI and IWAFUNE NO KI were built here to station troops for the control of aboriginal EZO tribesmen. Noted for its production of rice, cloth, and petroleum, the province was ruled by the UESUGI FAMILY from the mid-12th to the 16th century. In the Edo period (1600–1868) it was divided into a number of domains.

Echigo Yuzawa Hot Spring 越後湯沢温泉

(Echigo Yuzawa Onsen). Located in the town of Yuzawa, southern Niigata Prefecture, central Honshū. A common salt spring; water temperature 30°–85°C (86°–185°F). It is well known as the setting for KAWABATA YASUNARI's novel *Yukiguni* (tr *Snow Country*, 1956).

Echizemmisaki 越前岬

Cape on the Echizen Coast, northwestern Fukui Prefecture, central Honshū; part of Echizen-Kaga Coast Quasi-National Park. A marine terrace 100 m (328 ft) long is the site of a lighthouse. The cape is noted for its sea-eroded cliffs with oddly shaped rocks and tunnels.

Echizen ware 越前焼

(*echizen-yaki*). Ceramics produced in Echizen Province (now part of Fukui Prefecture) from the late Heian period (794–1185) to the present. Early dated pieces include a jar dated 1323. Echizen kilns produced wares mainly for domestic use, including mortars or storage jars of various kinds. The stony clays that are used often fire a dark reddish brown as a result of high iron content. Pieces are unglazed, but liberal amounts of green or brown natural glaze often accent the asymmetrical, rugged shapes.

Ceramic production declined from the Meiji period (1868–1912), and only six kilns were operating by 1965. In 1970 a potters' village was established at the village of Miyazaki to revitalize Echizen wares. A variety of work is made for the tourist and gift industries and for the TEA CEREMONY, rather than for functional domestic needs.

economic agencies 経済官庁

(*keizai kanchō*). Government ministries and agencies concerned with economic policies, in particular, the MINISTRY OF FINANCE, the MINISTRY OF INTERNATIONAL TRADE AND INDUSTRY (MITI), and the ECONOMIC PLANNING AGENCY (EPA). The Ministry of Finance helps prepare the national budget and revisions to the tax system and also provides supervision and guidance to banks and securities companies. MITI supervises individual industries and is responsible for the formulation and enforcement of international trade policies. It influences the industrial world through its ADMINISTRATIVE GUIDANCE powers. The EPA coordinates economic policies and prepares long-term economic plans, annual economic forecasts (in conjunction with the national budget), and the WHITE PAPER ON THE ECONOMY.

Economic Growth Rates, 1886–1991

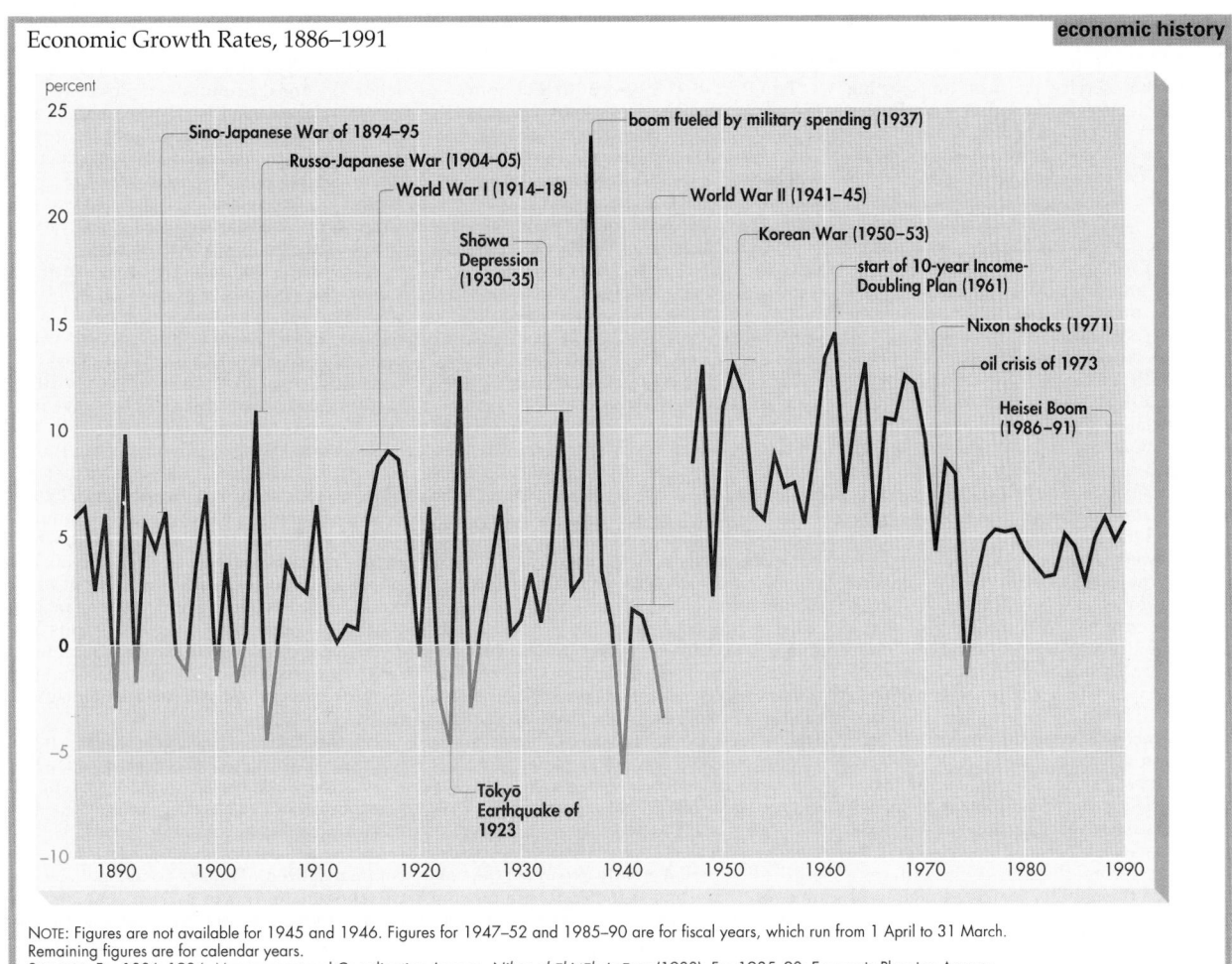

NOTE: Figures are not available for 1945 and 1946. Figures for 1947–52 and 1985–90 are for fiscal years, which run from 1 April to 31 March. Remaining figures are for calendar years.
SOURCES: For 1886–1984: Management and Coordination Agency, *Nihon chōki tōkei sōran* (1988). For 1985–90: Economic Planning Agency, *Keizai hakusho* (annual): 1990 and 1991.

Since the Japanese government often manipulates public works expenditures as a way to control business fluctuations, the MINISTRY OF CONSTRUCTION and the MINISTRY OF TRANSPORT also have important economic roles. The MINISTRY OF FOREIGN AFFAIRS, MITI, the EPA, and the Ministry of Finance divide the responsibility for overseas economic aid.

economic history 日本経済史

(Nihon *keizaishi*). This article treats Japan's economic history from premodern times to the 1960s. Subsequent economic developments are described in ECONOMY, CONTEMPORARY.

PREMODERN ECONOMY (TO 1868)

The economic history of Japan includes the history of agriculture, trade, handicraft production, finance, and transportation, as well as the policies developed to direct economic activity, to control resources and land, and to utilize manpower.

Economic History before 1600—
JŌMON CULTURE, which flourished from around 10,000 BC to around 300 BC, provides the first evidence of economic activity. Early Jōmon people formed a hunting and gathering society that left behind SHELL MOUNDS containing pottery, tools, and other artifacts. Agriculture entered Japan in the 3rd century BC, and a new culture emerged, YAYOI CULTURE, marking a transition to a settled agricultural society.

Around AD 250 a powerful elite group, known for its construction of great tomb mounds (KOFUN), appeared within Yayoi so-

ciety. Iron was in wider use for weapons, and artifacts suggest an emergent ruling elite with an advanced material culture. Social differentiation was first visible during the KOFUN PERIOD (ca 300–710). The ruling clans (UJI) controlled support groups (BE or *tomo*) composed of craftsmen, warriors, ceremonial personnel, or cultivators. Manpower, rather than land, was the index of wealth and determined the relative strength of the *uji*. By the mid-5th century the Yamato *uji*, forerunner of the imperial house, which claimed descent from the sun goddess, was dominant in western Japan. The emergent YAMATO COURT, centered in the Yamato Basin, showed evidence of barter and foreign trade.

The ritsuryō system. The 6th and 7th centuries saw new tensions in Yamato society as the SOGA FAMILY attempted to usurp political leadership. The coup in 645 against the Soga family, which resulted in the TAIKA REFORM, however, reasserted the authority of the sovereign. A new RITSURYŌ SYSTEM of government, modeled after that of Tang (T'ang) China (618–907), was eventually developed. The state took title to all agricultural land. An elaborate system of land management (the HANDEN SHŪJU SYSTEM) rationalized field boundaries and assigned rights to income and cultivation. Land replaced manpower as the index of wealth and power.

In 723 the government offered tenure for three generations to those who reclaimed lands (see SANZE ISSHIN NO HŌ). In 743 this was extended to perpetual tenure rights as an in-

centive for land reclamation (see KONDEN EISEI SHIZAI HŌ). These policies undermined state control over agricultural land and contributed to the eventual breakdown of the *handen shūju* system. Economic expansion in the 8th century is indicated by the issuance of coins by the central government in 708 (see WADŌ KAIHŌ). Japan was not yet a monetary society, and coins circulated largely in the Kinai or capital region. Official missions to and from China encouraged the growth of foreign trade. See SUI AND TANG (T'ANG) CHINA, EMBASSIES TO.

Shōen. Private control of land spread in response to government efforts to increase the amount of land under cultivation. Limits were set by rank, but many elite houses and major shrines and temples exceeded their allotments and reclaimed vast tracts of land for private use. While these lands were subject to taxes (see SO, YŌ, AND CHŌ), permanent tenure was the first step toward the creation of private landed estates (SHŌEN), in which the proprietor assumed the duties of governance. By the 12th century 5,000 *shōen* existed, comprising most of the agricultural land in Japan. A hierarchy of proprietors guaranteed rights to income and cultivation in exchange for services rendered.

Monetary economy. Foreign trade increased in the Heian period (794–1185), and, until it was restricted after 1254 at the request of the Chinese authorities, Song (Sung) dynasty (960–1279) copper coins (SŌSEN) circulated widely in Japan and brought great profits to their importers. The use of coins for transactions became more common during the 13th century. The required labor service (KUJI) of transporting *shōen* tax goods was burdensome, and these goods were increasingly sold at local markets for cash. Members of the SAMURAI (warrior) class were increasingly dependent on cash in the Kamakura period (1185–1333), obtaining cash loans from moneylenders (*kariage* or KASHIAGE). MARKET TOWNS appeared in the Kamakura period. Retail shops emerged, and wholesalers (TOIMARU), who began as merchant-officials charged with marketing and storing *shōen* tax goods, appeared to supply them with goods.

The 14th century saw the diffusion of intensive cultivation methods in agriculture. Commercial agricultural expansion resulted in more monetary transactions in the 14th and 15th centuries, especially in the economically advanced Kinai region and in commercial centers such as Kyōto. As commerce and the monetary economy grew, the *sake* brewers (SAKAYA) and pawnbrokers (DOSŌ) became tax collectors for the shogunate and provincial warlords (SHUGO DAIMYŌ). They loaned funds to both daimyō and the urban nobility and amassed great economic power. By the time of the ŌNIN WAR (1467–77), wealthy urban residents (MACHISHŪ) administered much of Kyōto, and their authority increased as the power of the MUROMACHI SHOGUNATE declined.

Autonomous domains. The Ōnin War destroyed the *shōen* system and the authority of the Muromachi shogunate. *Shugo daimyō* were replaced by local military leaders (SENGOKU DAIMYŌ), and the wars of the 16th century tested their ability to defend their local authority. Sengoku daimyō domains were autonomous and independent of central sources of authority. The Sengoku daimyō instituted a new tax system that replaced *shōen* revenues. All taxing authority was in the hands of the daimyō, and local and absentee power holders were eliminated.

Urbanization. The 16th century was a period of major URBANIZATION. Trade and handicraft production were concentrated in the CASTLE TOWNS (*jōka machi*) of the daimyō. Samurai were assembled in the castle towns, leaving village administration in the hands of the farmers. The castle towns became political, economic, and transportation centers of the domains. Daimyō eliminated trade barriers and broke up the monopolistic powers of the guilds (see RAKUICHI AND RAKUZA), which encouraged trade expansion and accelerated commercial activity. In the 1540s European traders entered Japanese waters bringing new commodities such as European luxury goods and firearms (see FIREARMS, INTRODUCTION OF).

Unification. The political unification of Japan under ODA NOBUNAGA and TOYOTOMI HIDEYOSHI in the late 16th century altered many economic relationships. Under Nobunaga many toll barriers (SEKISHO) were eliminated, merchants and artisans were concentrated in castle towns, and many guilds were abolished. Nobunaga surveyed all land under his control and replaced the *kandaka* system of taxes computed in cash with the KOKUDAKA system, in which productivity was measured in rice as the tax base (see also KENCHI). After Nobunaga's death in 1582, unification of the country in 1590 enabled Hideyoshi to extend Nobunaga's policies to the entire country. A four-class system (SHI-NŌ-KŌ-SHŌ) was implemented, with warriors, farmers, artisans, and merchants as the major divisions of society.

Edo-Period (1600–1868) Economy— Following the death of Hideyoshi in 1598, TOKUGAWA IEYASU emerged as the most powerful warlord in the country. In 1603 his rule was legitimized as the TOKUGAWA SHOGUNATE. The shogunate was headquartered in Edo (now Tōkyō), which soon developed into the largest city in Japan. In order to secure the political subservience of the other daimyō, the Tokugawa instituted the SANKIN KŌTAI system, whereby daimyō were required to spend alternate years in Edo in attendance upon the shogun. This political measure was to have profound economic effects. Edo became the center of a new economic network as all kinds of commodities were shipped to the city for consumption by the daimyō, their samurai retainers, and the artisans, merchants, and service personnel who attended them. By the mid-18th century, Edo had a population of over 1 million. Ōsaka, with its easy access to waterborne transport, became the primary commodity market and processing center in the central Kinai region. Daimyō from western Japan shipped tax rice to Ōsaka for sale to obtain the cash necessary to support their Edo residences and their travels to and from the capital. Ōsaka merchants hired by the daimyō as warehouse managers (*kuramoto*) or account agents (KAKEYA) provided the cash required to support domain expenses in Edo. In time they also provided the daimyō with long-term credit as well.

Commercial expansion. Urbanization during the Edo period greatly expanded the volume of trade and handicraft production. Population growth continued from the early 17th through the mid-18th century, when growth leveled off. Demands for food, textiles, utensils, housing, and other essentials led to a rapid expansion in commercial activity. This in turn required increases in the volume of currency and banking facilities. The Ōsaka money changers (RYŌGAESHO) organized an official association, and, by 1670, 10 moneylenders supervised financial activity in the city. Bills of exchange and certificates of deposit circulated like paper money within and between cities, contributing to expanded commercial relations, and daimyō domains issued paper currency (HANSATSU) for circulation within domain boundaries.

Foreign trade. Foreign trade during the Edo period was subject to new controls imposed by the shogunate. After rapid expansion of overseas trade by Japanese, Chinese, Korean, and European merchants during the 16th century, the shogunate in the early 17th century excluded Portuguese and Spanish merchants, prohibited foreign voyages by Japanese, and concentrated foreign trade in Nagasaki (see NATIONAL SECLUSION). There was trade with Korea through the daimyō of Tsushima, and the Satsuma domain (*han*) also traded with the Ryūkyū Islands (see RYŪKYŪ TRADE), but all other trade was monopolized by the shogunate at Nagasaki (see NAGASAKI TRADE). There was limited trade with Holland, Dutch traders being confined to the island of DEJIMA in Nagasaki Harbor. See DUTCH TRADE.

Employment options. New professions developed in the cities, and employment opportunities increased. Enterprise size ranged from large merchant houses such as the MITSUI and the SUMITOMO, with hundreds of employees and family members, to small retail or craft shops. A wide range of artisans and entertainers made urban life possible and attractive, and many village residents derived their incomes exclusively from wage labor or nonagricultural employment. As commercial agricultural production and part-time employment spread, it was only in remote areas that trade and craft production were clearly separated from farming. This separation of economic roles, which was the foundation of the Edo-period class system, increasingly became a legal fiction.

Until the boom in castle-town construction in the late 16th century, there had been few large towns outside the Kyōto-Ōsaka region, but by the mid-18th century the urbanized population had increased to over 10 percent. Urban life, however, proved difficult for the daimyō and samurai as revenues and incomes failed to keep pace with the costs of city existence. Daimyō were forced to borrow from their retainers, further reducing samurai disposable income. The incomes of both the daimyō and the samurai were based on land taxes paid in kind, while their expenditures were in cash. As tax receipts proved inadequate, the best sources of credit were the merchants who managed their rice warehouses. Merchants thus became major creditors to daimyō and samurai. The loans carried high interest rates, and the level of daimyō and samurai indebtedness rose annually.

By the mid-19th century Japan, which had entered the Edo period as an agrarian society, had a highly integrated system of transportation and a well-developed handicraft industry and commodity markets; the economy had become highly monetized and commercialized. The economic policies of the shogunate, however, were out of step with economic realities. Neither the shogun nor the daimyō effectively taxed commercial wealth. Land taxes no longer supported the needs of the shogunate or the domain governments. Currency debasement, forced loans, debt abrogations, and temporary levies helped defray immediate crises, but no long-term solutions to the impoverishment of the daimyō and samurai existed. The stage was set for dramatic changes; a new unforeseen economic reality—the demand of foreigners for trade—would totally transform the social and economic order of Tokugawa Japan, forcibly thrusting it into a growing world economy.

EARLY MODERN ECONOMY (1868–1945)

At the time of the MEIJI RESTORATION (1868), a number of conditions that had coalesced over time during the Edo period provided a favorable base for industrialization. Among these were the growth of a large educated population with relatively well-established habits and traditions of discipline, diligence, and group solidarity; a surplus of labor in the agricultural sector; a highly monetized economy controlled by a wealthy and capable merchant class; and the large samurai class, capable of filling leadership and administrative positions.

The opening of Japanese ports to foreign trade in 1859 (see OPENING OF JAPAN) exposed the still-underdeveloped economy to the threat of colonial domination and to the advanced industrial technology and modern political and economic systems of the West. In an effort to avoid the fate of colonialization and economic domination by Western powers that had befallen much of Asia in the 19th century, the Meiji-period (1868–1912) government imposed a number of controls on the economic activities of foreigners in

Japan, including travel restrictions and bans on land ownership.

Industrialization and Economic Modernization — In addition to enacting measures to block inroads of foreign capital, the Meiji government also promoted the rapid development of Japanese industry. Much of the socioeconomic system of the Edo period, including the complex *shi-nō-kō-shō* class system and the commercial KABUNAKAMA or guild system, was dismantled. The SEKISHO (barrier stations) were abolished, and various other restrictions on transportation and communication were lifted. In 1872 the government annulled the TAHATA EITAI BAIBAI KINSHI REI, an ordinance issued by the Tokugawa shogunate in 1643 forbidding the sale and purchase of land; the Bunshi Seigen Rei of 1713, which restricted the partitioning of farmlands, was rescinded; land ownership rights for farmers were established; and restrictions on the planting of crops other than rice were abolished. These reforms led to the modernization of agricultural management. The government also implemented the LAND TAX REFORM OF 1873–1881, under which land taxes, which had been paid chiefly in rice since the early Edo period, were made payable in currency and set at a fixed amount. In 1876 the stipends of former samurai (SHIZOKU) were converted into government bonds and hereditary pensions were paid off on a sliding scale (see CHITSUROKU SHOBUN). With these measures the samurai were deprived of the final vestiges of their long-standing economic privileges.

In an effort to promote the development of modern industry, the Meiji government first abolished the old, complex currency system and established a new, unified national currency system with decimal denominations and standardized units (see YEN). It also introduced new systems of banking and company organization. The banking system was modeled on the US system of national banks, and in 1882 a central bank, the BANK OF JAPAN, was founded.

Private Sector Development Efforts — The private sector played a key role in the modernization of the economy. Private sector leadership was provided in part by a group of individual entrepreneurs. Among these were a number of members of such privileged and wealthy merchant families from the Edo period as the Mitsui and the Sumitomo. Most entrepreneurs, however, came from the ranks of the former samurai, peasant, or merchant classes and became modern businessmen amid the turmoil of the early Meiji period.

The Development of the Factors of Production — The maturation of such factors of production as capital, labor, and technology was also essential to the modernization of the economy. Large amounts of capital accumulated in the hands of merchants and landowners in the late Edo and early Meiji periods. This capital was invested in new companies and business ventures, primarily in factories, machinery, and other fixed assets. A large surplus of workers developed during the depression that accompanied the unification of the currency system from 1881 to 1885 (see MATSUKATA FISCAL POLICY). The price of agricultural products fell throughout this period, while land taxes remained high, causing many farmers to lose their land through bankruptcy. These farmers and members of poor farm families provided a portion of the industrial labor force; low-ranking former samurai and small businessmen also experienced a high rate of bankruptcy during this period, and many then became workers.

Growth Industries — The centerpiece of Japan's expanding industrial development was the TEXTILE INDUSTRY, particularly cotton spinning and silk reeling. Textiles constituted more than half of Japanese imports between 1868 and 1882, and the Meiji government strongly promoted the modernization of this industry in order to reduce dependence on imports, employing foreign technicians to supply technical know-how and assistance (see FOREIGN EMPLOYEES OF THE MEIJI PERIOD). In 1897 cotton yarn exports exceeded imports for the first time. By 1918 six giant spinning firms had been formed: Tōyō Spinning (now TŌYŌBŌ CO, LTD), Dai Nippon Spinning (now UNITIKA, LTD), Kanegafuchi Spinning (now KANEBŌ, LTD), Fujigasu Spinning (now FUJI SPINNING CO, LTD), Nisshin Spinning Co, Ltd (now NISSHINBŌ INDUSTRIES, INC), and Ōsaka United Spinning Co.

The first major production facility in the IRON AND STEEL INDUSTRY, the Tanaka Ironworks in Kamaishi, Iwate Prefecture, began operations around 1890. The government-run YAWATA IRON AND STEEL WORKS began operation in 1901 and became Japan's leading ironworks after the Russo-Japanese War of 1904–05. The SHIPBUILDING INDUSTRY grew rapidly at the turn of the century, fostered by supportive government policies and the efforts of such firms as Mitsubishi Shipbuilding (now MITSUBISHI HEAVY INDUSTRIES, LTD), Kawasaki Shipyard Co (now KAWASAKI HEAVY INDUSTRIES, LTD), and Ōsaka Iron.

During the period from 1887 to 1919, regular banks replaced the national banks, and a number of special banks were established after 1897, including the Nippon Kangyō Bank (now DAI-ICHI KANGYŌ BANK, LTD); the INDUSTRIAL BANK OF JAPAN, LTD; the Bank of Taiwan (TAIWAN GINKŌ); and the Bank of Korea (CHŌSEN GINKŌ). Bank deposits increased, and, with the cancellation of excess loans, five giant banking concerns had come to dominate by 1917: the Dai-Ichi Bank; the Mitsui Bank (now SAKURA BANK, LTD); the MITSUBISHI BANK, LTD; the SUMITOMO BANK, LTD; and the Yasuda Bank (now FUJI BANK, LTD).

The Problems of Growth — Although Japan's modern economy continued its striking growth between 1886 and 1919, this rapid growth in the industrial sector resulted in troublesome developments in other sectors of the economy. One of these was the sluggish development of agriculture, which continued to be characterized by a premodern tenancy system, based on heavy in-kind land rents and small farms averaging less than 1 hectare (2.47 acres). In commerce and industry, alongside the emerging large modern enterprises, numerous small enterprises and cottage industries continued to exist. (This DUAL STRUCTURE has continued to be a central feature of the Japanese economy.) Despite the modernization of important industries, the income level of the common people remained low.

In Europe and the United States, as industrialization spread, so too did the socialist and labor movements. In Japan this was not the case, as the government noted the effects of such movements abroad and took active steps to suppress them at home. The PUBLIC ORDER AND POLICE LAW OF 1900 (Chian Keisatsu Hō) was largely effective in suppressing organized union activity by government surveillance before World War I. Its replacement, the PEACE PRESERVATION LAW OF 1925 (Chian Iji Hō), which was directed against communists and anarchists, prevented the more radical elements within the labor movement· from organizing any sustained challenge to the practices of industrialists in the interwar years.

Economic growth came to a halt in 1920, when the Japanese economy fell into a severe depression following its rapid expansion during World War I. A tolerable recovery had been achieved when, on 1 September 1923, a massive earthquake struck the greater Tōkyō region (see TŌKYŌ EARTHQUAKE OF 1923). In 1927 an unprecedented financial crisis occurred when a number of important banks failed (see FINANCIAL CRISIS OF 1927). Then in 1930–31 the Japanese economy was engulfed by the worldwide depression that followed the 1929 crash of the US stock market; the serious SHŌWA DEPRESSION ensued. Despite these setbacks, productivity continued to increase as a result of technological progress and the rationalization of industry.

Throughout this period of crisis, bankruptcies of small and medium-sized enterprises were common in mining and manufacturing as well as transportation, trade, and finance. There was also a push for the concentration of capital, resulting in a striking growth in the power of the industrial and financial combines known as ZAIBATSU. The Mitsui, Mitsubishi, Sumitomo, and Yasuda *zaibatsu* developed into conglomerates between 1909 and 1920, and in the following decade they expanded their affiliated enterprises and established positions of firm dominance over the Japanese economy. After 1930 a number of new *zaibatsu* emerged, all of which were smaller in scale than the long-established giants.

As a result of the decline in agricultural prices, the farm economy also suffered. During the depression the household accounts of independent farmers, as well as those of tenant farmers and part-owner farmers, ran into debt. Tenant farmers especially suffered from extreme poverty; TENANT FARMER DISPUTES increased in number, and there was an overall growth in social unrest. Against this background the MANCHURIAN INCIDENT occurred in September 1931, and the government soon embarked on a program of increasing military expenditures. Military demand contributed to the recovery of strategic industries, employment, and the farm economy.

On the other hand, the Manchurian Incident was the first in a series of Sino-Japanese conflicts leading to the outbreak of the SINO-JAPANESE WAR OF 1937–1945 and then Japan's ultimately disastrous engagement in World War II in 1941. Throughout the war the government increased military spending, strengthened its control over the economy and the labor force, and promoted the development of strategic industries. Arms production continued to increase until early 1944, but production in important machine-manufacturing industries dropped, especially after 1943, until it collapsed entirely under aerial bombardment in 1944 and 1945. The wartime economy itself collapsed with Japan's surrender on 15 August 1945. Basic industries such as iron and steel, electric power, and machinery managed to preserve a fairly high percentage of their capacity, but the consumption-related industries had declined to a fraction of their prewar output. Overall production at the end of 1945 was only one-sixth of prewar (1935–37 average) levels. At the war's end more than 25 percent of Japan's physical capital stock and 45 percent of the prewar empire had been lost.

OCCUPATION AND RECOVERY
(1945–1960s)
The Allied OCCUPATION of Japan lasted 80 months, from 14 August 1945, when Japan accepted the POTSDAM DECLARATION, to 28 April 1952. It is often divided into four periods: reform (August 1945–February 1947), reverse course (February 1947–December 1948), Dodge Line (December 1948–June 1950), and Korean War (June 1950–April 1952). It was a time of economic and political reform, as well as recovery from the physical destruction and economic exhaustion of World War II.

Background of the Policymakers— The US Occupation forces were ill prepared to deal with Japan's economic problems. Most of its civilian and military personnel were temporary employees, with little prior training or interest in things Japanese. One group saw the Japanese as backward "Asiatics" in need of the charity and enlightenment of the West; another saw the country as capable of high productivity and economic advance if it was freed from the "exploitation" of the *zaibatsu*, large landlords, and the government bureaucracy.

On the Japanese side, official thinking in general had not dared to face the possibilities of surrender and occupation. One important exception existed: an obscure group of bureaucrats, technocrats, and academicians—the Ministry of Foreign Affairs Special Survey Committee—had been meeting at great personal risk under the ministry's protection during the last days of the war. This group began planning a new postwar Japan based on modern large-scale industry and agriculture, to be led by private firms in conjunction with the government in what was later called "indicative planning" (see ECONOMIC PLANNING).

The Reform Period—While economic recovery was left largely in Japanese hands, the activities of SCAP (the Occupation authorities) during 1945–47 were concentrated upon a series of reforms often combined under the title "economic democratization." The most important of these reforms concerned agriculture (the LAND REFORMS OF 1946, encouragement of AGRICULTURAL COOPERATIVE ASSOCIATIONS, and RICE PRICE CONTROLS), LABOR (legalization of trade unions and collective bargaining, and enforcement of labor standards), and industry (passage of an ANTI-MONOPOLY LAW, ZAIBATSU DISSOLUTION, and deconcentration of economic power).

Economic aid. As a simple matter of avoiding famine, massive aid was essential to Japan, with the United States the almost exclusive source. The aid program included a wide range of industrial raw materials and paid for more than half of Japan's total imports through 1949.

Economic purge. Although the OCCUPATION PURGE was directed primarily at political and military leaders of the Japanese war effort, an "economic purge" was extended to cover industrial, commercial, and financial leaders judged to have cooperated actively with the Japanese military. Many of those purged, however, continued to direct their enterprises unofficially as "advisers." The effect of the purge on economic recovery was questionable, and over 200,000 of those purged were later officially depurged by appeals boards and administrative action.

Inflation and inflation control. Because Japan supported the Occupation and financed its political and economic reforms largely by printing new money, the country experienced accelerating inflation in 1945–49. An initial Occupation effort to check this inflation in February 1946 took the form of an abortive "new yen" currency reform. All pre-1946 currency was invalidated, with new notes issued yen-for-yen but only for limited amounts. Both demand and savings deposits were also frozen. However, budgetary deficits of the Japanese government and credit creation by the BANK OF JAPAN continued to be financed by an excessive printing of currency and expansion of bank credit.

Two important agencies of economic recovery and expansion were set up by the Japanese in late 1946, after the failure of the "new yen" experiment. These were the Keizai Antei Hombu, or ECONOMIC STABILIZATION BOARD (ESB), and the Fukkō Kin'yū Kinko, or RECONSTRUCTION FINANCE BANK (RFB). The ESB was the precursor of the present ECONOMIC PLANNING AGENCY, or Keizai Kikaku Chō. New RFB loans were suspended in 1949 and the bank itself was disbanded three years later, but similar development banks and long-term credit banks were established by the Japanese after the Occupation (see BANKING SYSTEM). The ESB planned and supervised, under limited SCAP guidance, a revived system of price controls and rationing. The ESB also subsidized increased production, usually from existing capital facilities, and provided short-term working capital loans for meeting payrolls or covering short-term losses. The RFB made longer-term loans to public and private institutions to increase their productive capacities. A characteristic of Japanese planning was to select particular industries as keys to the next stage of economic expansion, and to concentrate assistance on such industries with little regard for short-term market forces. Priorities shifted from coal and food in 1946 to iron, steel, and fertilizer production in 1948 (see PRIORITY PRODUCTION PROGRAM).

The Reverse Course Period—The reverse course (*gyaku kōsu*) may be dated from 1 February 1947, the scheduled date for a general strike by a united front of government workers' unions. SCAP decided to forbid the strike (see GENERAL STRIKE OF 1947), and a pattern of hostility between SCAP and the Japanese Left crystallized and continued for the remainder of the Occupation. Whereas SCAP had been antimilitarist, antinationalist, and antifascist before February 1947, anticommunism and antiunionism came to overshadow these earlier ideologies after that date (see RED PURGE). In November 1948 SCAP enunciated a three-point wage control program as a major step in inflation control, replacing free collective bargaining altogether.

With partial revival of Japanese production by 1948, international trade became increasingly important, but SCAP's approach to trade remained centralized and authoritarian. All commercial imports required licensed approval by the Japanese authorities (supervised by SCAP). Government approval (with SCAP supervision) was also required for exports, to avoid a drain of essential goods. Only in 1948 did SCAP begin to permit the entry, and then the permanent residence, of foreign private traders.

The Dodge Line Period—In the fall of 1948 Detroit banker Joseph M. Dodge was appointed a special adviser to SCAP on eco-

nomic matters. The measures undertaken during this period were known collectively as the DODGE LINE. Under the Dodge program, the price control system, production subsidies (as well as the public corporations [*kōdan*] that administered them), and the RFB loans were terminated. Dodge advocated free-market economics, balanced budgets, lower taxes, stabilization of the exchange value of the yen (at ¥360 to the US dollar), and strict regulation of the money supply. His drastic anti-inflationary measures, combined with a recession in world markets for Japanese exports, falling domestic black-market prices, and the effects of the sterling devaluation of 1949, brought on a severe decline in aggregate demand; the results were business failures and unemployment. By the spring of 1950 the short-term outlook for the Japanese economy was bleak, and SCAP and the Japanese authorities were deadlocked in disagreement as to the way forward.

The Korean War Period—The outbreak of the Korean War caught both SCAP and the Japanese authorities by surprise. After the war began on 25 June 1950 during the negotiation of the SAN FRANCISCO PEACE TREATY (signed in September 1951), and with the approaching end of the Occupation, the economic policy of both SCAP and the Japanese government floated with the political and military tides. The semimilitary economy that Japan almost immediately became was dominated by TOKUJU (*tokushu juyō*; special procurement demand) for the United Nations forces in Korea; the Japanese economy thus returned to full capacity, boom conditions, inflation, and high growth, both nominal and real. The money supply was freed from its Dodge line fetters. As for the Dodge line as a whole, three main pillars remained in place: an annually balanced budget, a stable yen-dollar exchange rate, and the dissolution of the price-control and rationing machinery. American aid was ended once and for all.

Recovery and Growth—The balance of power among workers, farmers, managers, and owners of capital that had been brought about by Occupation policies was a boost to economic reconstruction and recovery. War procurements during the Korean conflict and a general expansion of world trade enabled Japan to earn the foreign exchange to pay for the imports so essential for growth, surmounting severe constraints. The Japanese rate of growth in the 1950s and 1960s was without historical precedent and came to be called an "economic miracle." Japan was the second largest borrower from the World Bank in the late 1950s, and it was classified as a less-developed nation in the early 1960s. Yet by 1964 it was recognized as one of the advanced industrial nations, and by 1968 it had surpassed West Germany to become the world's second largest market economy. Few in the early 1950s would have anticipated this success. Although postwar Japan had a well-educated labor force and experienced managers, most of its trading partners (but not the United States) were already imposing severe restrictions on Japanese exports. Business optimism, however, began to emerge as the economy moved beyond postwar recovery. Actual performance exceeded expectations, and the rates of growth and labor productivity accelerated. The average annual growth of the gross national product (GNP) rose, despite occasional slowdowns, from 7.1 percent between 1952 and 1957 to 9.8 percent between 1957 and 1962. Prime Minister

IKEDA HAYATO proposed a 10-year INCOME-DOUBLING PLAN in 1960, only to see income double in 7 years. The size of the emerging Japanese economy in the 1960s and its concentration on exports and GNP growth provoked international complaints and retaliation (even from the United States), which played a major part in shaping Japan's economic policies and performance in the 1970s and 1980s. For an analysis of Japan's economy from the 1970s to the present, see ECONOMY, CONTEMPORARY.

economic independence　経済自立

(keizai jiritsu). Term used for a goal of government ECONOMIC PLANNING in the early 1950s, when the Japanese economy was still dependent on the aid and assistance of foreign countries, particularly the United States, despite gaining independence from the Allied OCCUPATION. Economic self-sufficiency, free from special military procurements or foreign economic aid, was achieved during the 1952–55 period. Major economic changes during this period included progress in modernizing the facilities of such basic industries as steel and electric power, expansion of the domestic consumer-goods market, introduction of technologies from abroad and improvement in the balance of international payments, and government assistance in the modernization of plants and equipment. Loans from the JAPAN DEVELOPMENT BANK and tax measures such as a special depreciation system promoted capital accumulation and the modernization of plant and equipment, laying the foundation for the stage of high economic growth that followed.

economic planning　経済計画

(keizai keikaku). Japan has never carried out central planning as practiced by socialist countries and many developing nations, in which the state tends to exercise direct control over the allocation of resources. Japanese economic planning is closer to what is known as indicative planning, in which most enterprises are privately owned and in which the government acts indirectly to influence resource allocation through various inducements. The government's ECONOMIC PLANNING AGENCY has at regular intervals published documents setting forth macroeconomic and social goals for the nation for the next decade or half-decade. These documents are commonly known as "visions" of Japan's future industrial structure and role in the world economy; they have enabled the government to channel resources to key sectors, where development has then had the greatest stimulative impact on the rest of the economy. The enunciation of these "visions" and the securing of industry's adherence to them has been termed ADMINISTRATIVE GUIDANCE (gyōsei shidō).

The role and ultimate effects of this type of indicative planning are difficult to evaluate. On the one hand, some view Japanese indicative planning as playing a vital role in the country's post–World War II economic development. They observe that the effectiveness of Japanese economic planning was at its height during the two decades following the war, when the private sector was considerably dependent on public sector resources. In the 1950s, for example, the government decided to stress the development of the heavy and chemical industries and took a leading role in the development of the IRON AND STEEL INDUSTRY by ensuring adequate financing for the industry from government banks and other sources, lowering interest rates to the steel companies, granting preferential tariff rates for imports of capital equipment, and guiding the rationalization of the steel industry itself. All this was done as part of a planned shift in the nation's INDUSTRIAL STRUCTURE toward heavy industry. However, other observers attribute less importance to government planning, particularly in more recent decades. They maintain that economic planning can be likened to economic forecasting.

Economic planning is carried out by the Economic Planning Agency (EPA), which is responsible for overall planning, in conjunction with other governmental organizations. Of these other organizations, the MINISTRY OF INTERNATIONAL TRADE AND INDUSTRY (MITI) is by far the most important. Since the EPA has virtually no enforcement powers of its own, its principal impact is in shaping a national consensus concerning the direction of the economy. In contrast, although MITI's planning is limited for the most part to industry, its powers to license new plant construction, provide subsidies, and control competition enable it to have considerable influence on enterprise decision making. MITI is divided into numerous bureaus that deal with specific industries, and a few general bureaus that provide a broader policy vision. The INDUSTRIAL STRUCTURE COUNCIL, which advises the minister of MITI, takes the lead in long-range planning. The time frames of the plans vary. Although they used to cover a range of between 5 and 10 years, 5 years and under has become the norm more recently. There have been 12 such plans to date, beginning with the Five-Year Plan for Economic Self-Sufficiency of 1955. The most famous plan is the INCOME-DOUBLING PLAN, developed under Prime Minister IKEDA HAYATO in 1960.

Japanese economic plans generally define the principal objectives of economic policy for each plan period and the measures necessary for realizing these objectives. They also forecast changes in the industrial structure and other likely changes in regional economic situations. They set forth the government's macroeconomic projections for gross national product (GNP), consumption, investment, price trends, unemployment rates, government transfer payments, and government expenditures. They may also specify goals regarding inflation, the environment, or housing construction. Until the New Economic and Social Seven-Year Plan of 1979, public sector planning was also part of economic planning. While the heavy and chemical industries were seen in the 1950s and 1960s as the locomotives of the economy, which would enable Japan to become a major exporter of manufactured goods, in the 1970s and 1980s the goal was for Japan to

Major Economic Plans, 1955–1992

Name of plan and date published	Plan period (fiscal years)	Projected and (actual) economic growth rates	Objectives
Five-Year Plan for Economic Self-Sufficiency, December 1955	1956–60	4.9% (8.8%)	Self-sufficiency of the economy; full employment.
New Long-Range Economic Plan, December 1957	1958–62	6.5% (9.7%)	Maximization of growth; improvement of national quality of life; full employment.
National Income-Doubling Plan, December 1960	1961–70	7.8% (10.0%)	Doubling of the real national income.
Medium-Term Economic Plan, January 1965	1964–68	8.1% (10.1%)	Rectification of economic imbalances.
Economic and Social Development Plan, March 1967	1967–71	8.2% (9.8%)	Balanced and steady economic development.
New Economic and Social Development Plan, May 1970	1970–75	10.6% (5.1%)	Creation of a better society through balanced economic growth.
Basic Economic and Social Plan, February 1973	1973–77	9.4% (3.5%)	Promotion of national welfare and international cooperation.
Economic Plan for the Second Half of the 1970s, May 1976	1976–80	6.0% (4.5%)	Enrichment of national life; stable development of the economy.
New Economic and Social Seven-Year Plan, August 1979	1979–85	5.7% (3.9%)	Stable growth pattern; enrichment of national life; contribution to the international economic community.
Outlook and Guidelines for the Economy and Society in the 1980s, August 1983	1983–90	4.0% (4.5%)	Peaceful and stable international relations; vital and prosperous society and economy; secure and rich national life.
Economic Management Within a Global Context, May 1988	1988–92	3.75%	Rectification of trade and other imbalances; contribution to the world; balanced development of a regional economy; realization of a richer national life.
Lifestyle Superpower Five-Year Plan, June 1992	1992–96	3.5%	Creation of a "lifestyle superpower" that coexists in a global community; reduction of work hours; affordable homes; improvement of rush hour conditions.

SOURCE: Economic Planning Agency.

become a "knowledge-intensive" society focusing on high-technology fields such as computers, optical fibers, lasers, robots, and biotechnology. Such high-technology industries thus moved to the fore in the 1970s and 1980s on a planned basis. A particularly vivid example of this process was the speed with which Japanese manufacturing industry moved over to computer-assisted control and robotics in the late 1970s—the so-called mechatronics movement. This was one of the results of the unusually strong measures taken by MITI to promote the development of the computer industry with the aim of surpassing the industries of the other nations in terms of processing speed and scope. In 1979, however, MITI felt that software (operations systems) was still lagging, and in order to catch up with IBM it set up a five-year, US $319 million research and development program, with the cost to be split equally between private firms and the government.

The prospects for Japanese economic planning in the future are not clear. Today, even socialist nations have given up strict economic planning and are aiming more for economic management based on the price mechanism. Many of the advanced industrial countries are further beset with mounting fiscal deficits, making an active role for the state more difficult. In addition, frequent external shocks, such as oil crises and major exchange rate fluctuations, make accurate planning more difficult than before. The Nakasone cabinet's plan for the years 1983–90, for example, was rendered ineffective by the rise in the value of the yen after September 1985 (see PLAZA ACCORD). On the other hand, even in a country like the United States, where economic planning has always been viewed with some suspicion, there have been growing calls for a more active industrial policy. In Japan, the long-term goal of terminating the issuance of GOVERNMENT BONDS FOR DEFICIT FINANCING was achieved in fiscal 1990, possibly paving the way for a more active role for fiscal policy in the future.

Economic Planning Agency
経済企画庁

(EPA; J: Keizai Kikaku Chō). Cabinet-level government agency attached to the PRIME MINISTER'S OFFICE and responsible for creating nonbinding, indicative economic plans for the nation. Established in its present form in 1955, the EPA had such predecessors as the Economic Deliberation Agency and the ECONOMIC STABILIZATION BOARD, as well as pre–World War II planning groups. The EPA is a relatively small advisory organ of several hundred economic and statistical experts. Its main tasks in recent years have been formulating long-term and annual economic plans, establishing government policies concerning prices, recommending policies that involve two or more administrative organs, and measuring Japan's overall socioeconomic strength and foreign economic trends. The actual implementation of government economic and welfare policies is exclusively in the hands of the ministries of finance, international trade and industry, and health and welfare.

The EPA prepares and publishes annually the WHITE PAPER ON THE ECONOMY (since 1947) and the WHITE PAPER ON THE NATIONAL LIFE (since 1956). As of 1990 it had written 11 major economic plans, the most famous of which was the INCOME-DOUBLING PLAN, approved by the cabinet on 27 December 1960. The actual responsibility for recommending plans to the cabinet is vested in the Economic Council, a prestigious civilian deliberative council (shingikai) attached to the EPA. The EPA is careful to distinguish its activities from economic planning as done in state-controlled command economies. The functions of economic planning in Japan are (1) to clarify the impact of future governmental economic policies; (2) to identify problems and propose remedies by predicting future socioeconomic development; (3) to offer to private enterprises and households guidelines on the optimal course of future economic and social development; and (4) to attempt to coordinate the interests of various social classes and groups in Japanese society.

Economic Stabilization Board
経済安定本部

(Keizai Antei Hombu). Powerful economic agency established in August 1946 to overcome the immediate post–World War II economic crisis by supervising the enforcement of controls over prices, transportation, and finance and by preparing the government budget for public works projects. In March 1947, under the direction of SCAP (the headquarters of the Allied Occupation of Japan), it became an agency to carry out all the planning activities that had been handled by various economic ministries. In June 1947 the board published an eight-item emergency economic program that included the securing of food, the restoring of order in the distribution of commodities, and the revising of the price-wage system. In July 1947 it published the first government WHITE PAPER ON THE ECONOMY. The board was disbanded in July 1952 at the end of the immediate postwar economic crisis. It was replaced by the Economic Deliberations Agency, later renamed the ECONOMIC PLANNING AGENCY.

economy, contemporary
現代日本経済

(gendai Nihon keizai). The Japanese economy is the second largest market economy in the world, with an aggregate output of ¥391 trillion (US $3.0 trillion) in 1990. Per capita income was ¥3.18 million (US $24,400), higher than that of the United States at $20,985. Once corrections are made for the high cost of housing and various goods, however, calculations by the Organization for Economic Cooperation and Development (OECD) show that Japan's effective per capita consumption was 72 percent of the US level in 1987, on a par with the wealthier countries of Western Europe. With its large volume of exports (US $280 billion in 1990) and large, though now declining, trade surpluses (US $64 billion in 1990, including a US $38 billion bilateral surplus with the United States), Japan is unquestionably one of the triumvirate of world economic powers, alongside the United States and the European Community. (For an analysis of Japan's economy from premodern times to the 1960s, see ECONOMIC HISTORY.)

At the end of the Allied OCCUPATION in 1952, however, Japan ranked as a less-developed country, with per capita consumption a mere one-fifth that of the United States. During the period 1953–73, the economy grew with unprecedented rapidity (average growth was 8.0% per annum overall and 10.6% during the 1960s) and Japan became the first less-developed country in the postwar era to graduate to developed status.

During the 1970s and 1980s, the growth rate slowed to 4.4 percent. Nevertheless, in the 1980s Japan performed better than either the United States or Europe in terms of UNEMPLOYMENT, growth, and inflation.

The structure and institutions of Japan's market-based economy have much in common with those of Western industrial nations. Japan and the Western countries will also face many similar challenges in the 1990s and beyond, such as providing for a rapidly AGING POPULATION, managing deregulation of the financial sector, and adapting to rapidly increasing labor costs. At the same time, various elements specific to Japan have contributed to its superior economic performance, such as high personal savings rates. Japan also faces some unique challenges, such as providing better housing and physical infrastructure in the face of extraordinary real estate costs and improving the distribution of goods to lower their cost to final consumers.

The High-Growth Era — Because of Japan's rapid growth between 1953 and 1973, real output per person in 1970 was 2.5 times higher than in 1960. By 1968 Japan had surpassed West Germany to become the world's second largest market economy. Real Japanese consumption was 32 percent that of the United States in 1960, about the same relative status as in 1936; by 1970, it had risen to 52 percent of the United States level. This rapid growth resulted in significant changes to Japan's INDUSTRIAL STRUCTURE. First, production shifted from a heavy reliance on AGRICULTURE and light manufacturing to a focus on heavy industry and, increasingly, services. In 1954, when recovery from World War II was largely complete, the primary sector (agriculture, fisheries, and mining) still accounted for 24.5 percent of output and 37.9 percent of the labor force; in contrast, manufacturing (the secondary sector) accounted for only 23.8 percent of output and 19.5 percent of employment. By 1970, agriculture and mining had fallen to 8.3 percent of output and 17.8 percent of the labor force, while manufacturing had risen to 30.2 percent of output and 27.0 percent of employment. In 1985, 9 percent of the labor force was in primary sector occupations, 33 percent in secondary, and 58 percent in tertiary. URBANIZATION also progressed rapidly, with the proportion of people living in cities escalating from 38 to 72 percent of the population between 1950 and 1970.

Until 1952 economic policy was dictated by the Occupation. Reforms in 1949 under the SHOUP MISSION and DODGE LINE put in place the postwar tax system, balanced the government budget, normalized the financial system, and brought Japan into the world trade system at a fixed exchange rate of ¥360 per US dollar. These reforms cured the postwar hyperinflation but at the cost of a sharp recession. While profits generated by the large number of special orders (TOKUJU) for goods and services in Japan to support United Nations forces during the KOREAN WAR helped end the recession, the economy continued to be buffeted by BUSINESS CYCLES with alternating periods of prosperity and recession.

The first major expansion—the IWATO BOOM (1959–61, average growth 12.2%), spurred by Prime Minister IKEDA HAYATO's 1960 INCOME-DOUBLING PLAN—touched off an investment spree. Growth reached 14.5 percent in 1961, but as in the 1950s this led to increased imports, and the government was forced to slow growth during 1962 because

contemporary economy

▼ Businesspeople hurry to work in the Marunouchi district of Tōkyō, where many of Japan's major corporations have their headquarters.

The Japanese Economy from 1955 to 1990

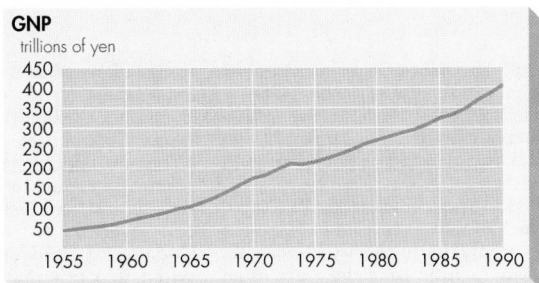

GNP
trillions of yen

NOTE: All GNP statistics used represent real GNP, which is the nominal GNP adjusted for inflation.
SOURCES: Economic Planning Agency, *Kokumin keizai keisan hōkoku* (1985); Bank of Japan, *Kokusai hikaku tōkei* (annual): 1992.

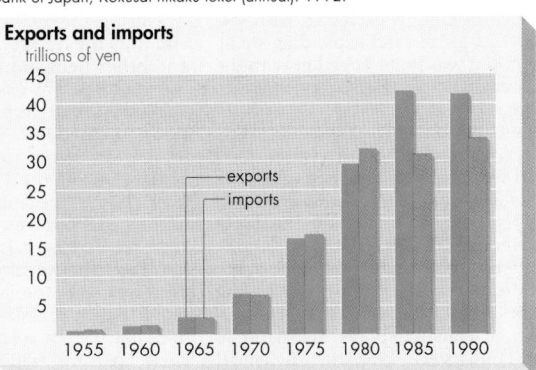

Exports and imports
trillions of yen

SOURCE: Management and Coordination Agency, *Nihon tōkei nenkan* (annual): 1991.

◄A morning assembly of workers is a monthly event at this factory of the Kyōcera Corporation.

▲ Headquarters of the Ministry of International Trade and Industry (MITI), the government ministry responsible for guiding Japan's trade and industrial policy.

Five Industrial Economies Compared, 1990

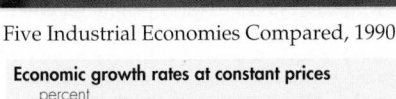

Economic growth rates at constant prices
percent

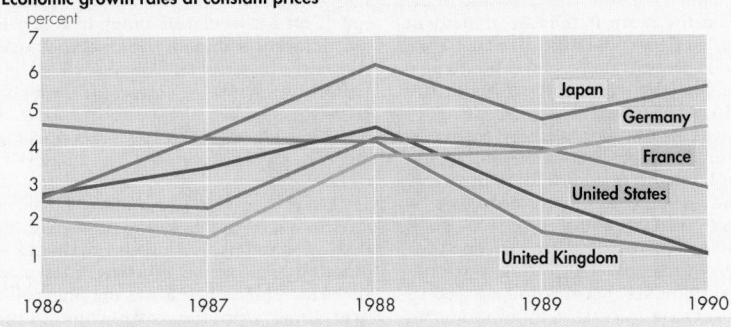

Japan
Germany
France
United States
United Kingdom

SOURCE: Bank of Japan, *Kokusai hikaku tōkei* (annual): 1991.

GNP
trillions of US dollars

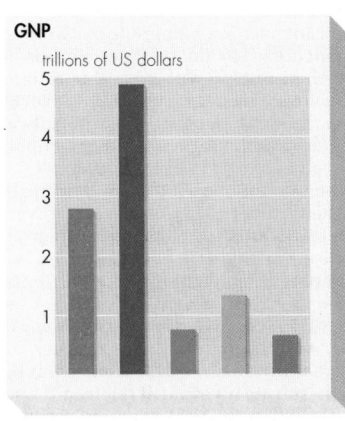

SOURCE: Bank of Japan, *Kokusai hikaku tōkei* (annual): 1992.

Per capita GNP
thousands of US dollars

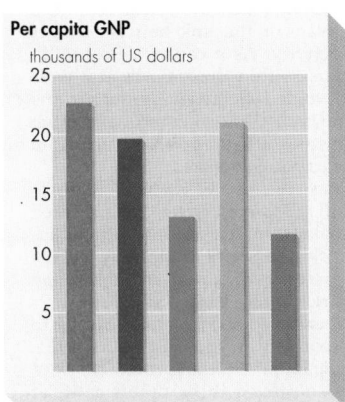

SOURCES: Bank of Japan, *Kokusai hikaku tōkei* (annual): 1992; United Nations, *Monthly Bulletin of Statistics*: December 1991.

Budget deficit as a percentage of GNP
percent

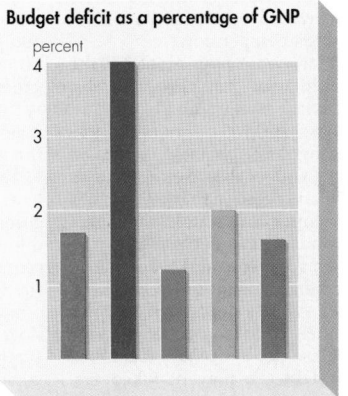

SOURCE: Bank of Japan, *Kokusai hikaku tōkei* (annual): 1992.

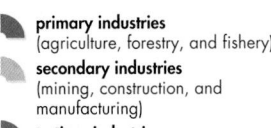

Japan ■ United States ■ United Kingdom ■ Germany ■ France

Japan's employment structure

1955
38.0% / 37.6% / 24.4%

1960
41.8% / 30.2% / 28.0%

1965
44.6% / 23.5% / 31.9%

1970
47.4% / 17.4% / 35.2%

1975
52.0% / 12.7% / 35.3%

1980
54.7% / 10.4% / 34.9%

1985
56.8% / 8.8% / 34.4%

1990
59.0% / 7.3% / 33.7%

■ **primary industries**
(agriculture, forestry, and fishery)
■ **secondary industries**
(mining, construction, and manufacturing)
■ **tertiary industries**
(utilities, wholesale and retail sales, financial and other business services, transportation, and social services)

SOURCE: Management and Coordination Agency, *Nihon tōkei nenkan* (annual): 1991.

of the resulting balance-of-payments crisis. Further expansions occurred in 1963–64 (average growth 11.8%), 1967–70 (the IZANAGI BOOM, average growth 11.2%) and 1972–73 (the Tanaka expansion, average growth 8.9%).

Many factors contributed to rapid growth, including the shift in employment from low-productivity primary sector pursuits to manufacturing and the entry of an increasingly skilled and better-educated postwar-baby-boom generation into the labor force. In addition, macroeconomic policies were conducive to growth, the international environment was blessed with stable commodity prices and expanding trade, and investment was high. Together with the introduction of better technology, productivity increased rapidly.

The contribution of government INDUSTRIAL POLICY to economic growth is less clear, and on net was probably not large. The government was heavily interventionist during the early years of the Occupation, but direct controls were eased after 1949 and largely eliminated by 1955. Industrial policy was implemented via indirect controls, requiring licenses for imports and technology transfer. Japan became a member of the International Monetary Fund (IMF) in 1952 and the General Agreement on Tariffs and Trade (GATT) in 1955. Around 1960, Japan committed itself to TRADE LIBERALIZATION by seeking IMF article 8 status and deciding to join the OECD, both of which were realized in 1964. TARIFFS and quantitative controls on most goods were removed by 1970, and, with the exception of agriculture and some high-technology products, most nontariff barriers were eliminated by the 1980s. Nevertheless, the overall bias was for a greater degree of protection of domestic producers than in the United States (see RESIDUAL IMPORT RESTRICTIONS).

Indirect government assistance also came in the form of tax breaks, treasury investment and loans (ZAISEI TŌYŪSHI), and the MINISTRY OF INTERNATIONAL TRADE AND INDUSTRY's policy of ADMINISTRATIVE GUIDANCE. An important example is the Machinery Industries Promotion Law of 1956, which supported the MACHINE TOOL INDUSTRY as well as automotive parts and other metalworking sectors. Ultimately, most industries obtained some government favors, and it is unclear that any industry was effectively promoted relative to its rivals. However, domestic policies did result in a minimal presence by foreign firms in most sectors, and permitted some industries to survive that would otherwise have succumbed to foreign competition.

Financial assets were wiped out by the 1945–49 hyperinflation, but from the 1950s the BANKING SYSTEM was gradually rebuilt, largely along pre–World War II lines. In 1949 the stock exchange was reopened, but it did not develop into a major source of new funds until the 1980s, and a bond market was not allowed to develop. Banks sought customers in emerging industries, encouraging the entry of new firms into the market and hence the presence of vigorous interfirm competition. CORPORATE FINANCE depended on bank financing as the major source of outside funds, giving rise to a CAPITAL STRUCTURE dominated by debt. To prevent takeovers, enterprise groups, or KEIRETSU, actively sought cross-shareholdings with a variety of firms, including major financial institutions (banks in Japan are permitted to purchase up

to 5% of the shares of a client firm). SMALL AND MEDIUM ENTERPRISES remained relatively important during this period, employing nearly three-quarters of the labor force. However, unlike the larger enterprise groups, small and medium-sized firms were tied to local banks, employed less-skilled or older workers (or temporary and female workers), and paid lower wages. In manufacturing, they often functioned as subcontractors (shitauke) to larger firms (see DUAL STRUCTURE). Overall, there was vigorous competition within the developing Japanese economy.

During the 1950s the major exporters—and thus the leading firms—were in TEXTILES and other light industries, whose products were marketed by GENERAL TRADING COMPANIES (sōgō shōsha); government promotion, however, focused on heavy manufacturing located in major coastal industrial complexes. During the 1960s the IRON AND STEEL INDUSTRY and the SHIPBUILDING INDUSTRY came to the fore, followed by the CHEMICAL INDUSTRY and in the early 1970s the electronics industry; the AUTOMOTIVE INDUSTRY rose to prominence in the late 1970s. Exports were important, especially for textiles and shipbuilding, which were aided by a rapid increase in world trade throughout the 1960s.

But growth was fueled above all by investment based on increased consumer spending. As incomes grew, consumption shifted from basic products such as radios, fans, and scooters to more expensive and luxurious items such as color televisions, air conditioners, and cars. In the case of manufacturing, a mature industrial base made it feasible to purchase new machinery and to concentrate on improving managerial performance. New machinery meant new technology, which meant lower costs and higher profits. Furthermore, in the case of many industries, no firm could afford to lag behind its rivals in installing new equipment. Growth fueled investment, which in turn fueled further growth.

To facilitate the adoption of new technology, after 1955 large firms adopted the modern employment system and trained their "lifetime" employees in new skills (see EMPLOYMENT SYSTEM, MODERN). LABOR UNIONS based on an enterprise rather than an industry or a craft cooperated in this, since new skills led to higher incomes and assured future jobs. LABOR DISPUTES were of minor importance after 1960, and annual contract negotiations occurring during the spring wage offensive (SHUNTŌ) helped to keep workers aware of the link between wages and productivity. As a consequence, inflationary hikes within the WAGE SYSTEM were generally avoided. Because of enterprise rivalry, the pay of workers in steel and other major industries did not diverge much from the manufacturing average.

Rapid growth was not without its problems. Until the late 1960s, Japan faced chronic balance-of-payments difficulties, due variously to surging imports when the economy grew too fast, or poor exports when foreign markets were in recession. The government therefore used MONETARY POLICY to slow the economy in 1953–54, 1957, 1961, 1963, and again in 1967. INFLATION AND PRICE STABILITY also proved to be problematic, at least comparatively: during the 1960s, consumer prices rose at an average annual rate of 5.8 percent in Japan, versus 2.7 percent in the United States. The spread of pollution and POLLUTION-RELATED DISEASES went unchecked until the late 1960s, when abysmal air qual-

ity in Tōkyō and multiple fatalities from mercury and cadmium poisoning prompted more stringent pollution control laws. Government provision for SOCIAL WELFARE also lagged; only from about 1970 did social security coverage become universal, so until then workers had to rely entirely upon private savings. Only in the late 1980s did corporate and national PENSIONS reach a level sufficient to help the average retiree. On the other hand, INCOME DISTRIBUTION remained remarkably even; no underclass emerged.

Toward a Mature Economy: 1973–1990—By 1973, many of the factors that supported rapid growth lost their strength. First, Japanese industry had caught up with the best practices abroad; improving productivity required more resources than in the past. This in turn lowered the profitability of new investment, which fell to a permanently lower level after 1974. By 1973, the growth of the now urban and better-educated labor force had peaked. Finally, the international environment became less favorable, due mainly to the revaluation of the yen and trade friction with the United States. The JAPAN–UNITED STATES TEXTILE TALKS of 1969, the NIXON SHOCKS of 1971, a worldwide commodity price boom that culminated in the quadrupling of oil prices during the OIL CRISIS OF 1973, and the movement of the yen to a floating rate in 1973 all worked to slow growth.

Domestic macroeconomic policy was also less conductive to growth. The government made a major policy blunder in 1971–72, when it permitted exporters to convert their dollars to yen, which rapidly increased the money supply. This was magnified by Prime Minister TANAKA KAKUEI's plan to rebuild the Japanese archipelago (NIHON RETTŌ KAIZŌ RON), which interacted with easy money and rising international commodity prices to touch off a speculative binge in real estate and domestic commodity markets. Japan was thus already suffering from double-digit inflation by October 1973, when the first oil crisis touched off sharp price increases and hoarding. During 1974, consumer prices rose an average of 23 percent, the highest rate since 1948.

It took several years to adjust to this new environment, but between 1975 and 1990 there was relatively stable growth and low inflation. This trend, however, masks considerable shifts in macroeconomic policies over time, with the government running large deficits in the late 1970s and then increasing TAXES and reining in expenditures to run balanced budgets from the mid-1980s. Significant microeconomic reforms were also implemented. The financial system was liberalized, beginning with an easing of international capital controls in 1971–73; several government monopolies, including railways and telecommunications systems, underwent PRIVATIZATION in the late 1980s.

Macroeconomic Changes—Even before the October 1973 oil crisis, the government had started to slow the economy in response to rising inflation; combined with the impact of a quadrupling of oil prices, gross national product (GNP) fell 1.4 percent in 1974, the first actual decline since the 1950s. More significant, the oil shock and recession lowered expectations of future growth: private investment fell from 31 percent of GNP in 1973–74 to under 25 percent of GNP from 1977 on. Growth slowed from the 10 percent level to an average of 3.6 percent during 1974–79 and 4.4 percent during 1980–90. Consumer prices stabilized after 1975, and Japan experienced comparatively low inflation following the second oil crisis in 1978. Furthermore, unemployment never surpassed 3 percent.

The decline in investment by 6 percent of GNP after 1973 threatened the economy with recession, particularly since consumption failed to increase and savings remained high. Tax cuts in 1974, 1975, and 1977, however, served to stimulate the economy, while increases in central government expenditures continued at a steady pace. The central government budget deficit ballooned to 6.1 percent of GNP in 1979, which kept the economy out of recession. The overall government deficit, however, peaked in 1978 at 5.5 percent of GNP, as local and provincial surpluses partially offset the central government deficit. See also BUDGET, NATIONAL; FINANCE, LOCAL GOVERNMENT; GOVERNMENT BONDS FOR DEFICIT FINANCING.

The deficit was held in check from 1979; in addition, monetary policy turned restrictive, with the BANK OF JAPAN raising the discount rate in stages from 4.25 percent to 9 percent. Indeed, continued concerns about large deficits led to a succession of tight budgets throughout the 1980s, though tax increases were held in abeyance until 1987 and 1988. The primary exceptions granted in the tight budgets in the 1980s were for social security, NATIONAL DEFENSE, and FOREIGN AID. By 1985 the consolidated government deficit shrank to 0.8 percent of GNP, and turned into a surplus from 1987. Again, a decline in fiscal stimulus by 6 percent of GNP might be expected to drag the economy into a recession. This time shifts in international trade offset the decline in domestic demand. The TRADE BALANCE remained relatively stable during the 1970s, and in 1980 actually showed a slight deficit. But by 1985, the current account surplus in Japan's BALANCE OF PAYMENTS reached 3.7 percent of GNP. While the economy was weak in 1981–83, exports increased sharply during 1983–85, due in part to the strengthening of the US dollar.

After the 1985 PLAZA ACCORD, the yen rose sharply in value, reaching ¥120 to the US dollar in 1988, twice its average 1984 value and three times its 1971 value. As a result, after 1986 the trade surplus gradually shrank. But this time around, domestic demand increased to pick up the slack in the HEISEI BOOM. Monetary policy was eased four times during 1986, as the Bank of Japan lowered the discount rate from 5.0 percent to 2.5 percent, the lowest level since World War II. Consumption began increasing in 1986, and investment took over during 1987–90; in fact, corporate investment rose to 19.6 percent of GNP in 1988 and 21.7 percent in 1989, far above the 15.3–17.5 percent that had prevailed during 1980–87, and exceeding total investment in plant and equipment in 1989 for the entire United States in both percentage and value. While consumer and producer prices were restrained, the price of land and stocks exploded during 1987–89. By 1989 growth was deemed too strong, and from May 1989 through fall 1990 the Bank of Japan increased its discount rate five times in an attempt to keep inflation low. This had an immediate impact on stock prices, but did not significantly slow growth.

International and Domestic Capital Markets—The revaluing of the yen in 1971 and its change to a floating currency in 1973 both reflected and helped stimulate changes in domestic CAPITAL MARKETS. A second major impetus was the dramatic slowdown in investment after 1973, combined with increased government borrowing. The govern-

ment had been committed to the eventual LIBERALIZATION OF CAPITAL INVESTMENT; in any event, increased trade surpluses in the late 1960s made it impossible for the government to buy up all the dollars earned by exporters. But once flows were liberalized in 1970, it proved no longer possible to peg the yen, nor could major firms be prevented from building up holdings of foreign assets or borrowing overseas.

By the late 1970s, this hole in the dike made it hard for the MINISTRY OF FINANCE and Bank of Japan to maintain tight control on domestic interest rates. In addition, the slowdown in investment decreased the borrowing needs of large firms; in the early 1980s the city banks thus began strenuous efforts to diversify their lending activities to include small business. Increased government borrowing, which sought to place a tremendous volume of low-interest-rate bonds with financial institutions, eventually led to an open domestic bond market. As the initial government bonds approached maturity in the 1980s, competition for attractive market rates of interest encouraged the development of mutual funds and certificates of deposit. This resulted in the effective liberalization of interest rates by the early 1990s.

From 1976 LIFE INSURANCE companies were permitted to hold foreign assets, and they and trust banks have been provided with greater flexibility to respond to a rapidly changing environment. Similarly, broadranging proposals to lower the barriers between securities firms and banks are now under consideration. Finally, investors have proved eager to diversify their portfolios internationally. This was one reason that the yen was not even stronger during the mid-1980s (which in turn made it easier for Japan to export). But it also means that the Tōkyō capital market is now linked to those in New York and London, so that Japanese interest rates are sensitive to—and in turn affect—those of the United States and Europe.

Financial liberalization has meant opportunities for profits, but has also permitted and even encouraged adventuresome behavior. The loose-money policies of the Bank of Japan from 1986 accentuated this tendency, fueling a boom on the STOCK MARKET. With higher stock prices, new equity issues skyrocketed to ¥16.8 trillion (US $116 billion) in 1987 and ¥24.8 trillion (US $177 billion) in 1989, becoming a significant source of finance for corporations for the first time since the crash of the Tōkyō market in 1961. Banks found a new outlet for funds in real estate development. In turn, corporations attempted to maximize the productivity of their assets using real estate holdings as collateral for stock market speculation in a method referred to as ZAITECH ("financial technology"). Since banks in Japan—unlike those in the United States and Great Britain, but like those in Germany—are permitted to hold stock in client firms, high stock prices increased banks' equity, permitting them to increase lending. In the ensuing speculative binge (1986–89), land prices doubled and the Tōkyō Nikkei stock market index rose 2.7 times.

Japan tightened monetary policy beginning in May 1989, and higher interest rates touched off a collapse of stock prices. By the end of 1990, the Tōkyō stock market had fallen 38 percent from its peak, wiping out ¥300 trillion (US $2.3 trillion) in value in the space of a few months. Several major firms declared bankruptcy in 1990, while the decline in the stock market decreased the eq-

uity of banks. It appears likely that several major financial institutions will run into severe difficulties during the 1990s, particularly if land prices in turn decline. The most visible changes to date are the mergers of the Mitsui and Taiyō Kōbe banks, and of the Saitama and Kyōwa banks. The Sumitomo Bank, a 1980s highflier, reshuffled management in 1990 as it sought to deal with scandal and bad loans. A major stock market scandal concerning the payment of compensation for market losses to brokerages' large customers garnered headlines in 1991.

Japan's International Role—Investment abroad, together with trade flows, is shifting Japan's international economic role. First, Japan is now either the number one or number two trading partner for the other countries of the Pacific Rim, including the United States. At the same time, manufactured products constituted over 50 percent of Japanese imports in 1990. Japan is thus a significant market for manufacturers in East and Southeast Asia, including textiles and low-end consumer electronics.

Alongside direct trade flows, Japanese national saving has continued to outstrip domestic borrowing needs, leading to the conspicuous presence of Japan as a major source of portfolio investment in the United States and elsewhere. In the first six months of 1989, for example, Japanese investors purchased US $39.1 billion of US Treasury and other foreign bonds; more visible were purchases of real estate and companies, notably Rockefeller Center, CBS Records, and Columbia Pictures Entertainment. Equally important has been OVERSEAS DIRECT INVESTMENT in manufacturing, tied to protectionist threats or (given the volatility of exchange rates) the need to produce in major markets rather than export to them. Japanese firms now operate 11 automotive assembly plants in North America and account for 20 percent of passenger car production there. Direct investment in Europe has also increased, in anticipation of the 1992 economic unification, while investment in Thailand helped produce a boom there during 1989–90. Finally, in 1990 the Japanese budget for foreign aid surpassed that of the United States; Japan is the largest donor in Asia, both directly and through the ASIAN DEVELOPMENT BANK and other multilateral agencies.

One result of this heightened presence has been trade friction, accentuated by the concentration of much of Japan's exports within a narrow range of goods, such as automobiles. In addition, Japan is strong in certain high-technology products that are perceived in the United States and Europe as critical for strategic reasons. The United States, for example, has been instrumental in the implementation of protectionist measures such as VOLUNTARY EXPORT RESTRICTIONS and orderly marketing arrangements within the Japanese steel, machine tool, automobile, and semiconductor industries. At the same time, the United States has also pushed for more open Japanese markets in high-technology products (satellites and supercomputers), lumber, agriculture, and financial services. These efforts were systematized during the mid-1980s in the bilateral MOSS TALKS, followed in 1989–90 by the STRUCTURAL IMPEDIMENTS INITIATIVE TALKS. Europe has taken a similarly restrictive stance against many Japanese products.

Other Issues—It is not clear what international role Japan will play with its new-

313

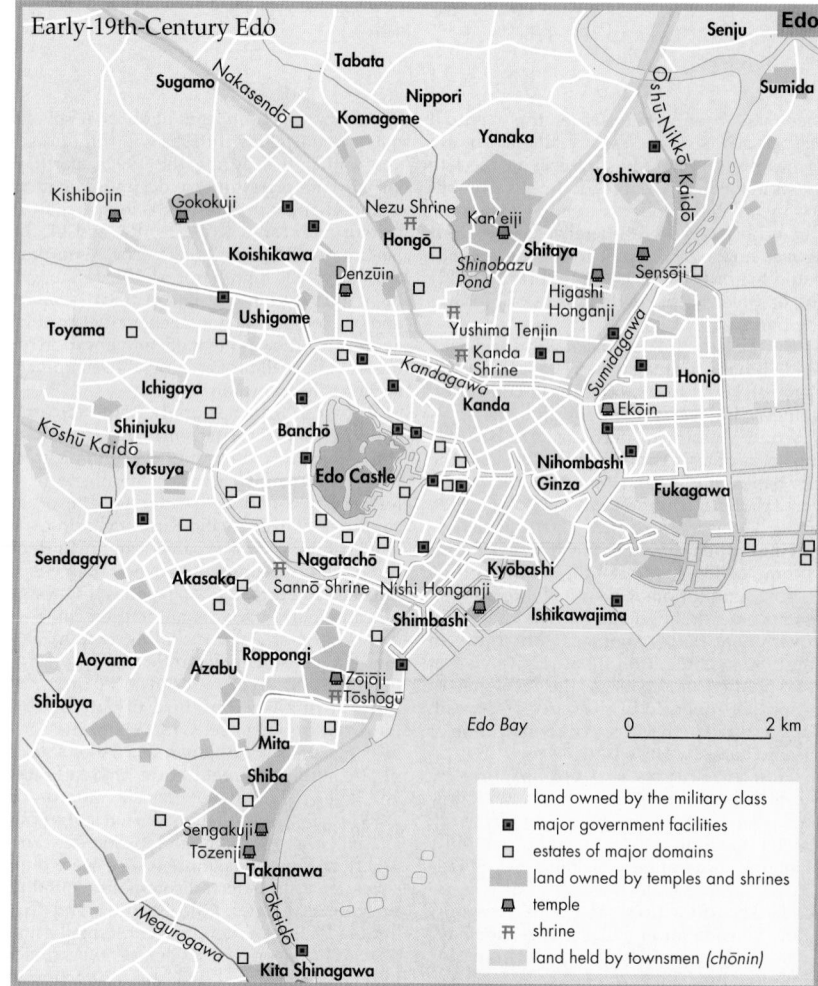

Early-19th-Century Edo

Edo

Senju
Sumida
Tabata
Sugamo
Nakasendō
Nippori
Komagome
Yanaka
Kishibojin
Gokokuji
Nezu Shrine
Yoshiwara
Hongō
Koishikawa
Kan'eiji
Shitaya
Denzūin
Shinobazu Pond
Sensōji
Higashi Honganji
Ushigome
Yushima Tenjin
Toyama
Kanda Shrine
Honjo
Ichigaya
Kandagawa
Kanda
Shinjuku
Bancho
Ekōin
Kōshū Kaidō
Yotsuya
Edo Castle
Nihombashi
Ginza
Sendagaya
Fukagawa
Akasaka
Nagatachō
Kyōbashi
Sannō Shrine
Nishi Honganji
Shimbashi
Ishikawajima
Aoyama
Roppongi
Azabu
Zōjōji
Shibuya
Tōshōgu
Mita
Edo Bay
0   2 km
Shiba
Sengakuji
Tōzenji
Takanawa
Megurogawa
Tōkaidō
Kita Shinagawa

land owned by the military class
major government facilities
estates of major domains
land owned by temples and shrines
temple
shrine
land held by townsmen (chōnin)

found economic strength; coping with financial deregulation and the domestic aspects of prosperity will offer added challenges. One need is to adjust to declining industries while fostering growth industries. As wages rose and the yen strengthened, manufacturing-labor costs in dollar terms more than doubled during 1985–90, and rose 14-fold during 1970–90; firms that exported, or faced potential import competition, have thus had to either increase labor productivity or exit. One response during the 1970s was the development of MANAGEMENT innovations such as the KAMBAN SYSTEM and advanced QUALITY CONTROL procedures. Meanwhile, government attention turned to the high-technology industry and SERVICE INDUSTRIES, viewed as growth sectors appropriate for a costly, educated work force. Not surprisingly, given these challenges, RESEARCH AND DEVELOPMENT expenditures have grown faster than the overall economy, reaching ¥10.6 trillion (US $76 billion) in fiscal year 1988. Most R&D was privately funded and concentrated on new product and process development (63% of R&D); government support was largely restricted to basic research (13% of R&D) and applied research (24%). Government industrial policy since the early 1970s has focused on areas such as semiconductors and computers. By US standards, however, the share of government funding (20%) is small, particularly in industries such as aircraft, software, and pharmaceuticals.

A second challenge is the growing dissatisfaction with the high price of housing and retail products among Japanese consumers. Land prices in Tōkyō are currently so inflated that average residents have little hope of owning their own homes. The recent boom in foreign travel has served only to heighten consumer awareness of the high price of retail goods. In response, proposals to reform the RETAIL INDUSTRY, such as revision of the LARGE-SCALE RETAIL STORES LAW, are under consideration. However, attempts to make housing affordable are more problematic. Lowering the price of real estate would threaten the financial security of those with land, and because land accounts for about two-thirds of Japan's NATIONAL WEALTH, a large drop in real estate values could also threaten the health of the entire financial system. See CONSUMPTION AND SAVING BEHAVIOR; HOUSING PROBLEMS; LAND PROBLEM.

Another set of issues lies in the problems raised by Japan's rapidly aging population. Projections show no growth in the labor force after 1996, while 14 percent of the population will be over age 65 (nearly double the US proportion, though similar to that in Germany and Scandinavia). This shift in labor supply will be exacerbated by the reduction in hours worked by the average employee as Japan moves toward a five-day workweek. By 2020 there will be only three workers for each retiree, and supporting such a large nonproductive population will entail a massive transfer of resources. Before the end of this century, the elderly will begin to draw on their savings, while the government will have to raise additional revenue to finance the social security and NATIONAL HEALTH INSURANCE systems.

At present Japanese taxes are about 29 percent of GNP, the same as in the United States but otherwise by far the lowest rate among the OECD countries. However, any increase in taxes is likely to be met with opposition because the system is already perceived as being unfair. Under the current system, WITHHOLDING TAX is deducted directly from employees' earned income. Nearly 20 percent of Japanese work in a family enterprise or are self-employed and can easily evade this direct tax, while workers who receive a salary are forced to bear its full burden. Tax reform efforts in the 1980s closed a few loopholes, but new ones were opened: the 1989 CONSUMPTION TAX provides extremely generous exemptions for small business. Tax increases and benefit reductions for the elderly cannot help but be politically divisive.

Future Growth——Japanese firms are perceived as the world leaders in a range of industries, such as automobiles, laptop computers, and semiconductor memory chips. Furthermore, Japanese industry is now playing a greater role in developing and applying state-of-the-art technologies in areas ranging from precision machinery to robotics and new materials. In 1987 Japanese firms accounted for 18 percent of all US patent applications, and in the early 1990s Japan will become a net technology exporter. This symbolizes the potential for high-productivity manufacturing to compensate for increasingly scarce and expensive labor and to meet the demands of a more prosperous (and elderly) populace. Japan provides an example of rapid growth that many less-developed countries hope to emulate, and, despite problems that have come to the fore in recent years, the economy continues to have many strengths.

Eda Saburō

江田三郎

(1907–77). Politician. Born in Okayama Prefecture; studied at Tōkyō Commercial College (now Hitotsubashi University) but left school to participate in leftist farmers' movements. Twice jailed in the 1930s for his political activities, he went to China in 1943, where he worked for the Japanese-dominated North China Political Council in Beiping (Peiping; now Beijing or Peking). After his return in 1946 he joined the Japan Socialist Party (JSP) and in 1950 was elected to the House of Councillors. During the 1960s he served several terms as secretary-general of the party and attempted to institute a controversial program that called for worker participation within the existing capitalist system as a way of realizing the socialist revolution.

Eda Satsuki

江田五月

(1941–). Politician and member of the House of Representatives since 1983. Born in Okayama Prefecture. Graduated from Tōkyō University in 1966. In May 1977 he became chairman of the Socialist Citizens' League (SCL; Shakai Shimin Rengō). After his election to the House of Councillors in July 1977, he dissolved the SCL and worked to form the UNITED SOCIAL DEMOCRATIC PARTY (Shakai Minshu Rengō) in 1978. In 1985 Eda succeeded DEN HIDEO as the party's leader.

Edo

江戸

(literally, "Rivergate"). Old name for the city of TŌKYŌ, in use from 1180 to 1868. Situated on Edo Bay (now Tōkyō Bay) on the eastern coast of central Honshū, Edo commanded the water and land transportation routes across much of central and northeastern Japan. As one of the newly planned CASTLE TOWNS (jōka machi) at the end of the 16th century, it developed into a major administrative center. A decade later, following its selection as the seat of the TOKUGAWA SHOGUNATE (1603–1867), Edo developed into the premier city of Japan. When the imperial

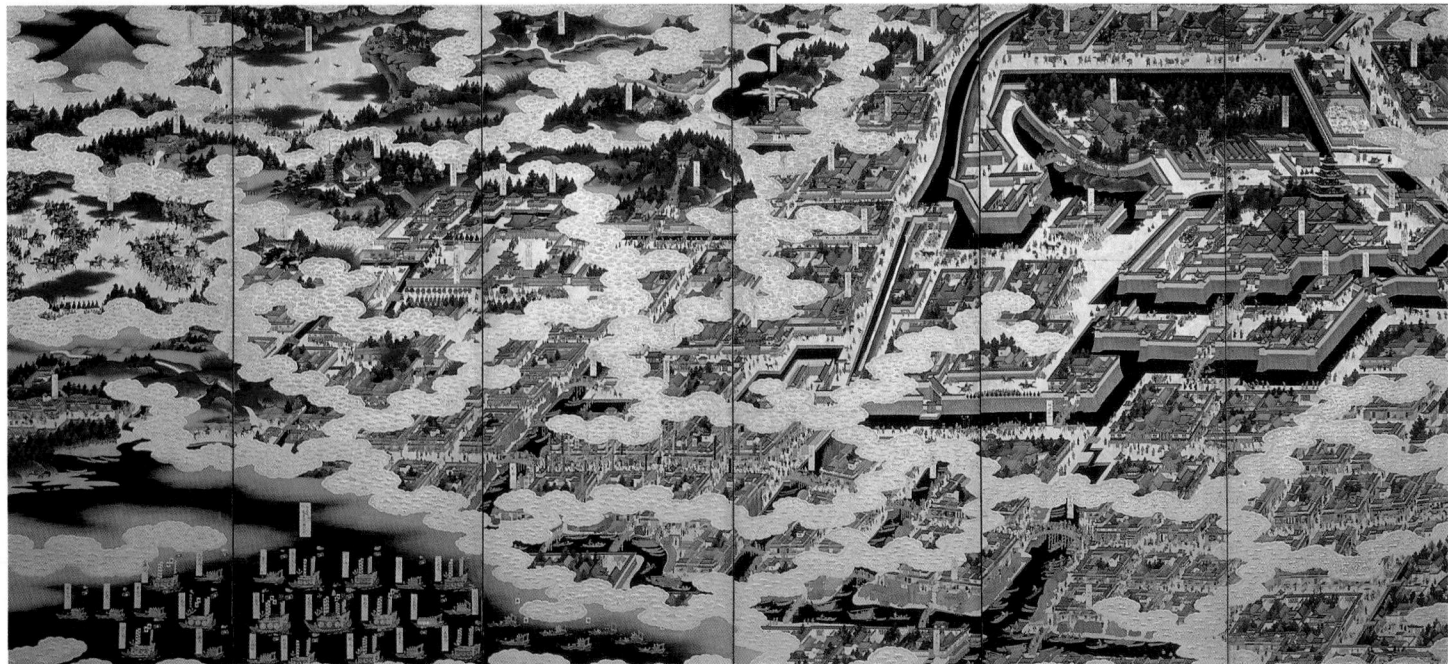

court moved from Kyōto to Edo after the Meiji Restoration of 1868, Edo became symbolically as well as administratively preeminent and was renamed Tōkyō ("Eastern Capital"). Historians later adopted the term EDO PERIOD to designate the years 1600 to 1868.

Development——Built up in the 1590s by TOKUGAWA IEYASU, a powerful *daimyō* who became Japan's military ruler (SHŌGUN) in 1603, Edo was first and foremost a *samurai* city—a residential center for the elite administrative and military personnel of the shōgun and his daimyō. Samurai from central Japan were ordered to move east with their lords and reside within the precincts of the new capital. The construction and reconstruction of majestic EDO CASTLE, the relocation of temples and shrines, and the large-scale building of samurai residential quarters lured townsmen (CHŌNIN) in large numbers. Corvée labor and taxes in kind supported this frenzied development.

During the 18th and 19th centuries the city's population was almost evenly divided between samurai and *chōnin* households; among the *chōnin*, merchants, artisans, and hired laborers predominated. The SANKIN KŌTAI system of obligatory alternate-year residence in Edo for daimyō and their samurai maintained the high proportion of elite residents. The shogunate levied charges upon daimyō for major construction projects, and intense competition and emulation among the daimyō themselves resulted in lavish expenditures. The high cost of living prompted daimyō to raise taxes in their domains on a regular basis. Commerce expanded enormously to meet the city's growing needs and demands. By 1720 it had added at least 1 million to its tiny population of the 1590s. Recent estimates put the total figure during the second half of the Edo period at 1.1 or 1.2 million. Edo's growth set the pace for an unparalleled four- or fivefold jump in the nation's population over roughly the same 130 years.

Land Use——During the second half of the Edo period, Edo occupied 52–65 square kilometers (20–25 sq mi) and was divided into three separate administrative jurisdictions: the samurai residential area, the mixed commercial and residential area densely settled by *chōnin*, and the more spacious precincts of temples and shrines at the city's periphery. Edo Castle formed the nucleus of the approximately two-thirds of the city allotted to daimyō and direct vassal (*gokenin* and *hatamoto*) residences. Location, lot size, and site characteristics all reflected the occupant's feudal rank and need for protection against potential adversaries.

Chōnin areas were clustered near Edo Bay and extended out along rivers and the roads radiating from Nihombashi, the commercial center. This portion of the city comprised some 1,700 wards (*chō*), neighborhoods that originally were often identified with a particular product or service. Little open space existed, even in the inner areas of *chō;* population density far exceeded 100,000 inhabitants per square mile. Shinjuku, Shinagawa, and Senju flourished at the city's outskirts as post-station towns serving the needs of travelers and providing entertainment for Edo residents, along with the downtown entertainment district of YOSHIWARA.

The City's Influence——Over time the demographic balance in Edo shifted from migrants (who worked as *chōnin* or as servants to the samurai) to permanent residents, from samurai to *chōnin*, and from privileged merchants (GOYŌ SHŌNIN) to more recently developed commercial interests. Edo acted as a powerful force in generating changes that swept Japan. Alternate-year residence there broadened the horizons of many samurai. The great cost of living in Edo prompted daimyō to increase the productivity of their domains. Unprecedented levels of consumption attracted goods from throughout Japan. Finally, diverse opportunities for employment—as servants of samurai, as shopkeepers or entertainers, as hired laborers or apprentices in nascent industries such as publishing that served the whole country—lured migrants from near and far. As a city with over 1 million inhabitants, including a disproportionate share of the elite, Edo possibly exerted a greater influence on Japanese society than any other city in premodern times.

Edo Castle   江戸城

(Edojō). Also known as Chiyodajō. Situated in Chiyoda Ward, Tōkyō. Built between 1603 and 1651, Edo Castle was for over two centuries the headquarters of the Tokugawa shogunate (1603–1867). After the Meiji Restoration of 1868 the area encompassed by its inner moat became the IMPERIAL PALACE (Kōkyo). Set off by broad moats and towering stone walls from the frenetic activity of

the modern city, it survives today as a serene island of spacious gardens and woods.

In 1590 TOKUGAWA IEYASU was designated lord of the entire Kantō Plain by the national hegemon TOYOTOMI HIDEYOSHI. At the time, Edo (now Tōkyō) was a coastal village, near which stood a small, dilapidated castle built by ŌTA DŌKAN in 1457. Making Edo their headquarters, Ieyasu and his successors set about constructing a castle that became the seat of shogunal rule in 1603. It served as the shōgun's residence, the center of his administrative bureaucracy, and the site of state receptions for *daimyō* making the formal visits stipulated by the SANKIN KŌTAI regulations for alternate-year attendance in Edo.

When completed, Edo Castle was the largest in the world, its outer defensive perimeter (*gaikaku*) some 16 kilometers (10 mi) in length. The inner defensive perimeter (*naikaku*), consisting of some 6.4 kilometers (4 mi) of moats and walls, encircled what is now the Imperial Palace grounds.

The heart of the castle was the main enclosure (*hommaru*), most of which was occupied by a rambling set of buildings that served as both the shogunal residence and the headquarters of his government and bureaucracy. The shōgun's personal chambers occupied the core of the castle buildings, the area called the Nakaoku (Middle Interior). Directly to its north was the ŌOKU, or Great Interior, where his womenfolk lived in a vast labyrinth of rooms and corridors. To the south was the Omote (Exterior) with its official offices and reception halls. Adjacent to the main enclosure was the western en-

Edo Castle
1 This mid-17th-century screen painting shows Edo Castle and its surroundings before the 1657 fire that destroyed the central keep (far right panel).
2 The Nakanomon, shown here in a 19th-century photograph, was one of several gates leading to the castle's inner compound.

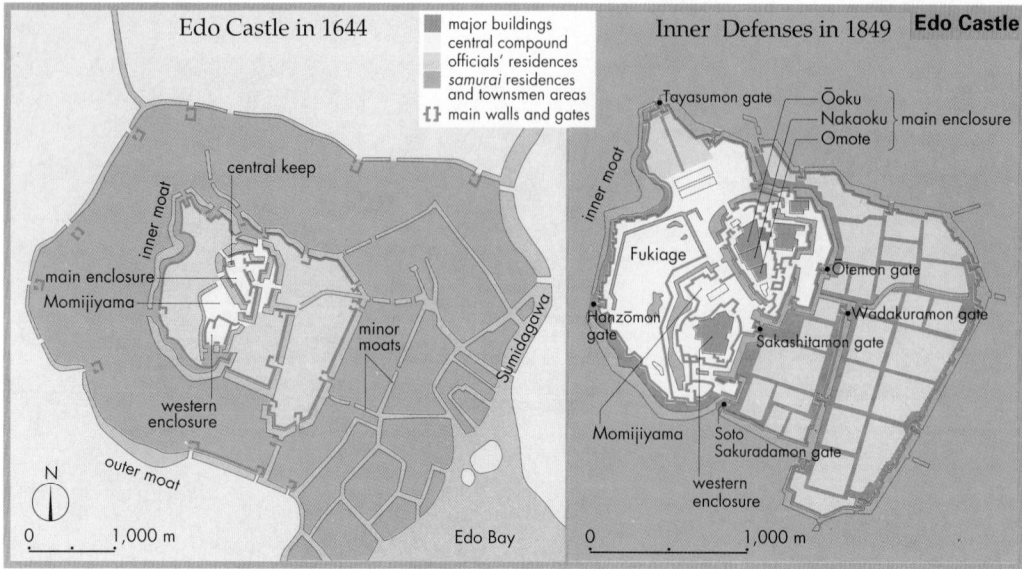

Edo Castle in 1644

■ major buildings
☐ central compound
☐ officials' residences
☐ *samurai residences and townsmen areas*
Ⅱ main walls and gates

central keep

inner moat

main enclosure
Momijiyama

minor moats

western enclosure

outer moat

Sumidagawa

N

0   1,000 m

Inner Defenses in 1849   **Edo Castle**

Tayasumon gate

Ōoku
Nakaoku — main enclosure
Omote

inner moat

Fukiage

Ōtemon gate

Hanzōmon gate

Wadakuramon gate

Sakashitamon gate

Momijiyama

Soto Sakuradamon gate

western enclosure

Edo Bay

0   1,000 m

closure (*nishinomaru*), which usually served as the residence of the heir apparent; the Momijiyama sector, with its shrines to former shōguns; Fukiage, an area of woods, walks, and gardens; and, in the lower-lying plain to the east, an area occupied by the residences of shogunal officials.

During the 1860s a series of disastrous fires destroyed the main building complexes of the castle; when Emperor Meiji located his capital in Edo in 1868, he inherited little more than a gutted shell. Most of the buildings on the grounds of the present Imperial Palace are of recent construction; only the moats and massive stonework of the perimeter remain as testament to the shogunal past. See also CASTLES.

Edogawa   江戸川

River in Chiba and Tōkyō prefectures, central Honshū. Originally the lower course of the river TONEGAWA before the main course of the Tonegawa was changed in 1654 to prevent floods and to secure water for irrigation. The Edogawa separates from the Tonegawa in Chiba Prefecture and flows south along the border of Chiba and Tōkyō prefectures into Tōkyō Bay. Length: 60 km (37 mi).

Edogawa Rampo   江戸川乱歩

(1894–1965). The first modern mystery writer in Japan. Real name Hirai Tarō. Born in Nabari, Mie Prefecture; graduate of Waseda University. His pen name, Edogawa Rampo, is based on the Japanese pronunciation of Edgar Allan Poe. Rampo contributed much to the establishment of the mystery novel in Japan. He is noted for his critical studies of the genre as well as for his encouragement of young mystery writers. As a boy Rampo pored over the translations of KUROIWA RUIKŌ, the pioneer translator of Western detective stories. At college he was an avid reader of foreign detective stories. After graduation he changed jobs more than a dozen times. His "Nisen dōka" (Two-Sen Copper Coin), written when he was unemployed, was published in the detective story magazine *Shin seinen* in 1923; it brought him immediate attention.

After this first work Rampo published "Shinri shiken" (1925; tr "The Psychological Test," 1956) and "Yaneura no samposha" (1925, The Attic Stroller) and became the leading mystery writer in the country. As an outgrowth of his works, the writing of detective stories and novels became firmly established in the Japanese literary world.

Edogawa Rampo The pen name of the father of Japanese mystery fiction is a complex pun: it translates as "strolling by the river Edogawa" and is also based on the Japanese pronunciation of "Edgar Allan Poe."

Rampo's *Injū* (1928, Dark Beasts) is one of his best-known works because of its out-of-this-world atmosphere and its ingenious plot.

Following his success in mystery and detective stories, Rampo switched to the writing of full-length thrillers after 1929, beginning with *Kumootoko* (1929–30, Spider Man) and *Ōgon kamen* (1930–31, Golden Mask). These works appealed greatly to the general public; however, their emphasis on the erotic and grotesque created some unfavorable response. He also continued writing detective fiction such as the popular *Kaijin nijūmensō* (1936, The Man with Twenty Faces). During World War II, the government suppressed detective stories, claiming they ran counter to state policies, so Rampo wrote scientific stories, changing his pen name to Komatsu Ryūnosuke.

After the war Rampo concentrated all his energy on the revival of detective stories. In 1947 he organized the Detective Story Writers Club and became its first president. His prewar collection of commentaries, *Oni no kotoba* (1936, Demon's Words), was followed after World War II by another collection, *Gen'eijō* (1951, Imaginary Castle), which won the Japan Detective Story Writers Club Prize in 1952. His autobiographical *Tantei shōsetsu yonjūnen* (1961, Forty Years of Detective Story Writing) described the development of the detective novel. In 1954 he established the Edogawa Rampo Prize. See also MYSTERY STORIES.

Edogawa Ward   江戸川区

(Edogawa Ku). One of 23 wards of Tōkyō. On Tōkyō Bay, bordering Chiba Prefecture, between the rivers Edogawa and Arakawa. Formerly known for its flourishing goldfish cultivation and large farming population, the ward has become increasingly industrialized and residential. Pop: 565,939.

edokoro   絵所

(office of painting). Organization staffed principally by professional artists; attached to an institution such as the imperial court, the shogunate, or an important temple or shrine and charged with providing artistic services. *Edokoro* were extant in Japan from the Heian period (794–1185) through the Edo period (1600–1868). The oldest and most long-lived of the *edokoro* was the Kyū-tei Edokoro (Imperial Court Office of Painting), which was founded in the late 9th century and abolished in 1868. Of particular importance to the development of both religious and secular art in Japan were the *edokoro* established in many major temples

and shrines in Nara and Kyōto in the late 11th–early 12th centuries.

Edo literature   江戸時代の文学

(Edo *jidai no bungaku*). Literature of the Edo period (1600–1868); also known as Tokugawa literature. The term "Edo literature" is somewhat misleading because much of the literature emanated from Kyōto and Ōsaka. Japanese literary historians usually use the term *kinsei bungaku* (early modern literature).

The period was one of general peace and isolation and was characterized by the broadening of cultural activity from the aristocratic, warrior, and priestly classes to the merchants and townsfolk (see CHŌNIN) and by the development of commercial printing and publication of fiction and poetry, a popular theater using live actors and puppets, and popular art in the form of woodblock prints, all of which reached a public greater than ever before.

Pre-Genroku Literature—The GENROKU ERA (1688–1704) saw a flowering of artistic production in Japan, and the years 1600–1687 can be seen as a preparation for this. Printing spread from religious texts to general books and illustrations, encouraging an interest in old literature, and commercial printing started in 1609 (see PRINTING, PRE-MODERN). Reading and participation in literature thus changed from an elitist to a popular pursuit. Literary production during this period was still generally restricted to the Kyōto-Ōsaka area, for the Tokugawa capital, Edo (now Tōkyō), was as yet too new to support a culture of its own.

Prose fiction of the pre-Genroku period was influenced by OTOGI-ZŌSHI, miscellaneous tales originating in the Muromachi period (1333–1568), and by works printed by the Jesuit priests at Nagasaki (see JESUIT MISSION PRESS). The prose fiction of this period is given the general designation KANA-ZŌSHI, meaning books written in KANA, the Japanese syllabary. These works vary widely in terms of subject matter; one important category is the *hyōbanki*, or critical appraisals of KABUKI actors and prostitutes. The best known *kana-zōshi* author is ASAI RYŌI (d 1691), considered the first professional prose writer in Japan.

During this period, kabuki and the puppet theater (see JŌRURI; BUNRAKU), the two characteristic forms of Edo-period drama, originated in Kyōto. Though influenced by the medieval dance and drama forms NŌ and KŌWAKA-MAI, the official entertainment of the aristocratic warrior class, both kabuki and the puppet theater were basically popular dramatic forms. During this formative period, the puppet theater had more literary sophistication than kabuki, and the plays of the puppet theater were printed and widely read.

The other great literary category of the early period, *haikai* (later known as HAIKU), developed from RENGA or "linked verse." *Haikai* took the first 17 syllables of a *renga* chain and created a new verse form. The enormous popularity of *haikai* led to its division during this period into a number of schools, most notably the traditionalist Teimon school, named after MATSUNAGA TEITOKU (1571–1653), and the witty DANRIN SCHOOL, led by NISHIYAMA SŌIN (1605–82).

Genroku Literature—The Genroku era in literature is dominated by three great figures: the poet Matsuo BASHŌ (1644–94), the prose writer Ihara SAIKAKU (1642–93), and the dramatist CHIKAMATSU MONZAEMON (1653–1724). This period saw great flourishing of all the arts, and the townsfolk of Edo, Kyōto, and Ōsaka began to rival the warriors as patrons of the arts. One reason for this efflorescence was the increased prosperity among merchants arising from the stability of Tokugawa rule. Another was the availability of talent from the *samurai* previously confined to military and administrative duties, but now seeking to earn a living as RŌNIN (masterless samurai).

The most famous of Edo-period *haikai* poets, Bashō brought the *haikai* verse form to a previously unreached level of sophistication with his poignant and deceptively simple style, which shows the influence of both the Japanese and Chinese classics, as well as of Zen Buddhism. He is especially well known for his travel diaries, which mix prose and poetry. After his death, Bashō's methods were carried on by his pupils, among them TAKARAI KIKAKU (1661–1707) and MUKAI KYORAI (1651–1704).

Saikaku gained early fame as a *haikai* poet. In 1682 he published KŌSHOKU ICHIDAI OTOKO (tr *The Life of an Amorous Man*, 1964); this became the first work of a new genre of fiction, UKIYO-ZŌSHI (books of the floating world), which was to replace *kana-zōshi*. Saikaku's works, characterized by his cynical, vivid style, portray not only the floating world of love, but also the life of the samurai and merchant classes.

In 1686, Chikamatsu wrote the *jōruri* play *Shusse Kagekiyo* (Kagekiyo Victorious), considered the first of the "new *jōruri*" because of its innovative style. After 1686, Chikamatsu's name began to appear as author on puppet-play books, an indication of the improved status of playwrights. Chikamatsu also wrote kabuki plays, but he is best known for puppet plays, in particular his double-suicide plays depicting the conflict between GIRI AND NINJŌ ("loyalty and human affection"). In the year that Chikamatsu wrote *Sonezaki shinjū* (1703; tr *The Love Suicides at Sonezaki*, 1961), a noteworthy rival appeared in the form of the *jōruri* playwright KI NO KAION (1663–1742).

Post-Genroku Literature—The early peak of literary production ended with the deaths of the three great figures, Bashō, Saikaku, and Chikamatsu. During the later period (1705–1868), the center of literary production shifted from the Kyōto-Ōsaka region to Edo. Literature during this period was subject to repression by the Tokugawa government.

Poetry. At this time, Yosa BUSON (1716–84) achieved excellence and originality as a painter as well as a *haikai* poet. After him, the tendency was toward a romantic and even sentimental style, best represented by the third of the great *haikai* writers of the period, Kobayashi ISSA (1763–1827). Although the popularity of the *haikai* form did not completely eclipse the traditional 31-syllable WAKA, during this period much *waka* composition was inspired by an interest in the Japanese past, closely related to the KOKUGAKU (National Learning) movement. From about 1800 a reform movement sought to make everyday contemporary life a fit subject for *waka* poetry; it included poets such as KAGAWA KAGEKI (1768–1843), the priest RYŌKAN (1758–1831), and TACHIBANA AKEMI (1812–68). Two comic verse forms in which many writers also composed were the 17-syllable SENRYŪ and the 31-syllable KYŌKA. While *senryū* are typically witty sketches of everyday life, *kyōka* are much more intellectual and are often parodies of classical verse.

Prose fiction. Prose fiction after that of the 17th-century master Saikaku is best considered in terms of genres rather than authors. Narrative prose fiction from the mid-Edo period onward is known collectively as GESAKU (literally, "playful works"), reflecting the primarily entertaining nature of this literature.

After Saikaku, the *ukiyo-zōshi* form was dominated by the writer NISHIZAWA IPPŪ (1665–1731) and by the Kyōto bookseller-publisher Hachimonjiya (see HACHIMONJIYA-BON). Hachimonjiya employed the writer EJIMA KISEKI (1666–1735), who developed the form called *katagi-mono* (character sketch). KIBYŌSHI and GŌKAN, two genres of *gesaku*, are in the tradition known as KUSAZŌSHI, which were fundamentally picture books with a minimum of continuous text. *Kibyōshi* take their subject matter from contemporary life, and the style is racy and colloquial. SANTŌ KYŌDEN (1761–1816) is counted as one of the masters of this genre. *Gōkan*, or "collected volumes," are long novels consisting of many *kibyōshi*-sized volumes. The outstanding author in this genre is RYŪTEI TANEHIKO (1783–1842).

In the YOMIHON (literally, "books for reading"), unlike *kusazōshi*, the illustrations are subordinate to the text. The first important writer of *yomihon* was UEDA AKINARI (1734–1809), whose tales of the supernatural are recognized as *yomihon* masterpieces. Santō Kyōden and Takizawa (or Kyokutei) BAKIN (1767–1848) wrote *yomihon* strongly influenced by Chinese popular novels. Produced contemporaneously with *kibyōshi* and *yomihon* in the late 18th century, SHAREBON focused mainly on the pleasure quarters and are characteristically written in an elegant, clever style. Santō Kyōden was a master of this genre, but his works got him into trouble with the Edo reformist MATSUDAIRA SADANOBU (1759–1829), and he was forced to abandon *sharebon* for other genres.

KOKKEIBON literally means "humorous book." Works in this genre are characterized not only by their humor but also by the unrelenting accuracy of their depiction of contemporary life. The best-known writers in this genre are JIPPENSHA IKKU (1765–1831) and SHIKITEI SAMBA (1776–1822). NINJŌBON, or "human affection books," depict the life of the pleasure quarters in a sentimental and compassionate yet realistic style. The recognized master of this genre is TAMENAGA SHUNSUI (1789–1843).

Drama. The puppet theater plays of this period were most typically long, involved dramas with many subplots, often written by committees of writers. These plays include *Kanadehon chūshingura* (1748; tr *Chūshingura: The Treasury of Loyal Retainers*, 1971), based on the FORTY-SEVEN RŌNIN INCIDENT. Well-known playwrights of this period include Takeda Izumo II (1691–1756; see TAKEDA IZUMO) and NAMIKI SŌSUKE (1695–1751?), both of whom collaborated with Miyoshi Shōraku (1696?–1772?) to write *Chūshingura*, and CHIKAMATSU HANJI (1725–83). After 1765, the puppet theater went into serious decline and was overshadowed by the growing popularity of *kabuki*, which, during this period, was characterized by the absorption of the repertory, music, and acting techniques of the declining puppet theater, and by the rise of such playwrights of considerable literary achievement as TSURUYA NAMBOKU (1755–1829) and Kawatake MOKUAMI (1816–93).

Didactic writing. Not all Edo literature was written for the entertainment of the merchant class. There was also considerable writing about Confucianism and about Neo-Confucianism, the official philosophy of the Tokugawa rulers, by such men as ARAI HAKUSEKI (1657–1725) and OGYŪ SORAI (1666–1728). Such Confucianist scholars were also characteristically experts on Chinese matters in general. Another example of didactic writing is that of the scholars of the Kokugaku school, most notably KAMO NO MABUCHI (1697–1769) and MOTOORI NORINAGA (1730–1801). The latter greatly influenced the native tradition of literary criticism with his studies of the Japanese classics.

After the Edo period came to an end in 1868, a few authors, such as KANAGAKI ROBUN (1829–94), continued to write popular works in the distinctive *gesaku* style, but for the most part there was a clean break with the past, with the dominant influences on writing now coming from the West. From the Meiji period (1868–1912), literature of the Edo period was held in low esteem by scholars, but it has been favorably reassessed since World War II.

Edo machi bugyō　　　江戸町奉行

(Edo city commissioners). Usually referred to by the general term MACHI BUGYŌ. Important officials of the Tokugawa shogunate (1603–1867), responsible for maintaining order in the city of Edo (now Tōkyō). During most of the Edo period (1600–1868) two middle-ranking Tokugawa vassals (HATA-MOTO) held the position, alternating duty from month to month. At his office (*machi bugyōsho*) the commissioner on duty had a small supporting staff and a police patrol of some 120 YORIKI AND DŌSHIN armed with swords and pikes. With these token forces the commissioners were charged with keeping the peace among a city population of about half a million commoners. They also enforced city building regulations and supervised the city civil administrators, city prisons, public relief agencies, religious establishments, and firefighting organizations (HIKESHI). Some Edo city commissioners, notably ŌOKA TADASUKE and TŌYAMA KINSHIRŌ, were among the most able officials in Tokugawa Japan.

Edo period　　　江戸時代

(1600–1868; Edo *jidai*). The Edo period, also called the Tokugawa period, is often dated from 1603, when TOKUGAWA IEYASU received the title of SHŌGUN and established the TOKUGAWA SHOGUNATE in the town of Edo (now Tōkyō), until 1867, when the last Tokugawa shōgun resigned. It is alternatively dated from 1600, when Ieyasu defeated his principal rivals in the Battle of SEKIGAHARA, to 1868, the year of the MEIJI RESTORATION. This encyclopedia has adopted the latter dates. See PERIODIZATION.

One of the major epochs of Japanese history, the Edo period is distinguished by the fact that for more than two centuries (from 1638 to 1864) Japan enjoyed freedom from warfare at home and abroad. Despite authoritarian administration and a policy of NATIONAL SECLUSION, Japan experienced significant political, social, economic, and cultural change during this period.

The Edo period witnessed the stabilization of the system of local rule by military lords (DAIMYŌ) under strong shogunal authority, vested in this case in the Tokugawa family. A self-conscious ruling class of SAMURAI monopolized all functions of government

Edo period A set of Edo-period folding screens depicts the procession of the Maeda *daimyō* as he fulfills the obligation—imposed on all *daimyō* by the shogunate—to move to the capital city of Edo in alternate years. The expense of this repeated change of residence became a major drain on domainal resources.

above the level of village and town. Under them, the Tokugawa shogunate defined separate classes of commoners, the farmer (HYAKUSHŌ) and the townsman (CHŌNIN) being the most important. Since almost the entire samurai class left the countryside to reside in the castle towns of their *daimyō* lords, they stimulated a rapid and widespread growth of cities.

Establishment of the Tokugawa Power Structure Tokugawa Ieyasu received the title of shōgun from the emperor in 1603, three years after achieving military supremacy over all the *daimyō* of Japan in the decisive Battle of Sekigahara. The political system created by Ieyasu is now generally referred to as the BAKUHAN SYSTEM, under which government functioned through two political mechanisms: the *bakufu* or SHOGUNATE and the HAN or *daimyō* domain. Ieyasu had achieved his hegemony as the head of a coalition of vassals and allied *daimyō*. He did not eliminate the *daimyō*; instead he used the *daimyō* system, seeking only to establish a favorable balance of power under his own authority.

Ieyasu set out some of his loyal retainers as *daimyō*, creating a class known as FUDAI (hereditary vassals), a group that eventually numbered 145 houses. A second category of *daimyō* were the SHIMPAN (collateral or cadet *daimyō*), made up of lineages related to the Tokugawa house, of whom 23 eventually survived. The remaining *daimyō* were men who had either survived Sekigahara by joining the Tokugawa side before the battle or who had been spared extinction by Ieyasu despite having fought on the losing side. These *daimyō*, known as TOZAMA (outside lords), numbered some 98 at the end of the 18th century. The Tokugawa house itself constituted a major power bloc. Of Japan's estimated total of 30 million *koku* of land (see KOKUDAKA), the shōgun directly held granary lands (known as TENRYŌ) assessed at some 4 million *koku*, while another 3 million *koku* were held by the shōgun's enfeoffed HATAMOTO (bannermen). The balance of power as measured in landholdings was thus weighted in favor of Tokugawa interests.

Legitimation of the Tokugawa Regime: The Authority Structure Tokugawa Ieyasu used the office of shōgun as his prime means of legitimation. In theory the shōgun was the delegate of the emperor, and Ieyasu fully exploited the symbolism of imperial appointment. At the same time, he and his successors made every effort to limit the emperor's political influence. The court nobility

(*kuge*) were physically confined to the palace enclosure (*gyoen*) in Kyōto, watched over by the shōgun's deputy (KYŌTO SHOSHIDAI) and his garrison at Nijō Castle, and placed under the restraints of a set of regulations known as the KINCHŪ NARABI NI KUGE SHOHATTO (Laws Governing the Imperial Court and Nobility). This document excluded the emperor from participation in affairs of state and made his awarding of court honors to the military aristocracy subject to shogunal approval.

As chief of the military estate, the Tokugawa shōgun exercised broad national authority, regulating affairs among the *daimyō* and religious bodies and setting national military and fiscal policy. In foreign affairs, too, the shōgun assumed the rights to negotiate with other states, stamp out Christianity, control trade, and restrict travel by Japanese. The most important of the shōgun's powers was that of ultimate proprietorship of the country's land. The shōgun held suzerainty over the *daimyō*, who were his sworn vassals and held their domains as grants from him. See KAIEKI.

The shōgun's most effective control device was the SANKIN KŌTAI, or alternate attendance requirement. From the 1630s this practice obliged all *daimyō* and their families to establish residences near Edo Castle and pay regular homage to the shōgun. Most *daimyō* were permitted to return home in alternate years, leaving their wives, children, and ranking officials in Edo as hostages. The *sankin kōtai* system continually affirmed the political centrality of Edo.

The shōgun rarely interfered directly in the internal affairs of the domains, giving the *daimyō* considerable freedom in their administration. However, he did insist upon strict conformity to certain basic policies and regulations. This was made clear in the BUKE SHOHATTO, as amended in 1635, which stated that "throughout the country all matters are to be carried out in accordance with the laws of Edo." The shōgun did not regularly tax the *daimyō*, but the *daimyō* were obliged to keep their domains in order, provide military support, and contribute funds, manpower, and materials for the maintenance of shogunal castles, imperial palaces, and public works.

The shōgun exercised the right to regulate religious bodies as well. In earlier centuries Buddhist communities had played a large role in the political and economic life of the country, but the late-16th-century hegemons ODA NOBUNAGA and TOYOTOMI HIDEYOSHI had succeeded in destroying the political and military power of these religious groups. Under the Tokugawa, religious bodies were

reduced in landholdings and the priesthood strictly regulated through numerous edicts. Nonetheless, the Buddhist establishment continued to prosper during the Edo period, in part because of the service it performed for the shogunate in the eradication of Christianity (see SHŪMON ARATAME; TERAUKE).

The Bakuhan System: Central and Local Administration The administrative map of Japan during the Edo period was extremely complex. To start with, lands under direct control of the Tokugawa house were distributed unevenly throughout Japan. Then there were some 270 *daimyō* jurisdictions, plus the holdings of the 5,000 bannermen, the imperial court, and numerous temples and shrines. Yet all of this somehow was pulled together under the shōgun's overlordship.

The organs of shogunal administration (*bakufu*) emerged from the government that Ieyasu had established when he was still a *daimyō* in the Kantō region. Consequently, even after Tokugawa authority extended over the entire country, office in the *bakufu* was entrusted only to the hereditary-vassal (*fudai*) class of *daimyō*, bannermen, and lesser shogunal retainers (GOKENIN).

The shōgun worked through two boards of retainers. A group of five or six senior councillors (RŌJŪ) appointed from among mid-ranking *fudai* *daimyō* made up a high administrative council with authority over matters of nationwide scope. A second board, consisting of three to five junior councillors (WAKADOSHIYORI), had charge of the shogunate's internal affairs.

The most important functional officers of the shogunate were placed under the senior councillors. These included the commissioners of major cities (MACHI BUGYŌ), the commissioners of finance (KANJŌ BUGYŌ), the keeper (JŌDAI) of Ōsaka Castle, the Kyōto deputy (Kyōto *shoshidai*), the inspectors general (ŌMETSUKE), and lesser officers. All were either *fudai* *daimyō* or bannermen.

Villages functioned as basic units of rural control and taxation. They were composed of taxpaying farmers (*hyakushō*) and their tenants and dependent workers. It was left to the *hyakushō* to maintain village self-management. Each village had its headman (*nanushi* or SHŌYA), assistant headman (*kumigashira*), and *hyakushō* representative (*hyakushōdai*). Village families were obliged to form into neighborhood groups (GONINGUMI), which promoted mutual assistance and responsibility. In both the shogunal and *daimyō* domains, government above the level of headman was monopolized by the samurai class. The headman enforced the

numerous restrictions on the farmers and mediated between villagers and superior authority.

The Bakuhan System: Social Structure and Class Policy—The early Tokugawa shōguns inherited a society that already had begun to differentiate into separate functional classes. Most notable was the sharply defined separation of the warrior elite from the farming class—a phenomenon referred to as *heinō bunri.* The land surveys carried out by Hideyoshi consolidated this separation of the samurai and farmer classes by creating cadastral registers (*kenchichō*) in each village (see KENCHI). Samurai were defined as persons enrolled on the daimyō or shogunal retainer rosters, while *hyakushō* were those listed on the *kenchichō.* Use of the *kokudaka* system also meant that samurai not only were detached from the land but could be paid from the lord's storehouse without reference to any specific fief.

Hideyoshi's domestic measures thus brought into being a new samurai class, urban in residence and bureaucratic in function; a class that neither owned agricultural land nor had the legal right to acquire land by purchase. The daimyō had the right to tax their domains, but held them not as private owners but as delegates of the shōgun. Their powers were political, not proprietary. By the same token, the *hyakushō,* by being recorded in the cadastral register, were made more secure in their occupancy of the lands on which they paid taxes.

Class separation took a major step forward under Hideyoshi. The SWORD HUNT order of 1588 aimed at disarming the rural populace, thereby giving samurai a monopoly in arms-bearing. Thereafter samurai assumed as a badge of class distinction the wearing of two swords, long and short. Hideyoshi's edict of 1591 prohibiting changes in status among samurai, farmers, and merchants, although hard to enforce, furthered the codification of the class structure.

Tokugawa legislation refined this class structure by adopting for official purposes a four-class concept that had originated in China (see SHI-NŌ-KŌ-SHŌ). These classes, in order of importance, were warriors (*samurai*), farmers (*nōmin*), artisans (*kōnin*), and merchants (*shōnin*). In actual practice, since artisans and merchants tended to congregate in the cities, they generally were lumped together under the term *chōnin* (townspeople). Functionally, therefore, Edo society is better conceived of as having had three main classes. In addition, Tokugawa law recognized a number of other social groups, such

as the court aristocracy (*kuge*), priests and nuns (*sō* and *ni*), and outcasts (*eta*—later called BURAKUMIN—and HININ). Each class or group was given a separate identity under law and was treated differently with respect to land rights, tax burden, criminal procedure, and political authority.

The legal separation of classes gave rise to quite different expectations and styles of life for each segment of society. Most samurai lived in towns, within the walled and moated enclosures surrounding their lords' castles, and were restricted to military and civil-bureaucratic service. *Chōnin* were confined to certain sections of town and were expected to provide services for the samurai while maintaining a posture befitting their low status. Farmers by definition lived in villages where they were admonished to work hard and live frugally. Much Tokugawa law dealt with externals—the regulation of housing, clothing, food, and conduct appropriate to each class or group.

Tokugawa law relied heavily on the social concepts of Confucianism. At the start of the Edo period, shōgun and daimyō faced acute problems of social engineering—in legitimizing their rule and in institutionalizing their social controls. Confucianism, with its heavy emphasis on ethical principles and social harmony, proved relevant to their needs. The official reliance on Confucianism was symbolized by the employment of HAYASHI RAZAN as Confucian adviser to the shōgun in 1607. The basic moral concepts advocated by Confucianism—LOYALTY (*chū*) and FILIAL PIETY (*kō*)—were conservative and supportive of the existing social and political order.

Restriction of Foreign Contact—The basic rationale of the *bakuhan* system did not lead necessarily to the adoption of a policy of National Seclusion (Sakoku). But that policy, once adopted, had a profound effect on life in Edo Japan. Ieyasu had tried to develop Edo as a port for trade with the Dutch and English. The failure of this effort, together with a growing suspicion that Christianity was politically dangerous to his regime, prompted him to issue his first anti-Christian edict in 1612. His two immediate successors, TOKUGAWA HIDETADA (r 1605–23) and TOKUGAWA IEMITSU (r 1623–51), intensified this policy, and the SHIMABARA UPRISING of 1637–38 pushed the shogunate to its most extreme anti-Christian measures. From the 1630s the shogunate introduced the *terauke* (temple register) and *shūmon aratame* (religious investigation) requirements. All Japanese families had to register at a local temple (*dannadera*) and give evidence

annually that they were not contaminated by Christianity.

Meanwhile, regulation of foreign trade moved in parallel. Efforts were made to convert the trade with Korea into a tributary relationship, using the SŌ FAMILY (daimyō of Tsushima) as intermediaries. The same was attempted with respect to the Ryūkyūs, using the SHIMAZU FAMILY (daimyō of Satsuma). At Nagasaki, which served as the official Tokugawa door to the outside world, elaborate restrictions were placed on trade and foreign contact. In 1635 Japanese nationals were forbidden to travel abroad or return home from overseas (see KAIGAI TOKŌ KINSHI REI). In 1639 Portuguese ships were excluded from Japanese ports, and only the Dutch and Chinese were allowed to trade at Nagasaki. Trade volume stabilized, but dropped sharply from late in the century, giving Japan minimal contact with the outside world until the 19th century.

Evolution of the Bakuhan State—The pattern of Japanese society and culture under Tokugawa rule retained its general contours from the 17th century until the mid-19th century. But isolation and domestic tranquility did not bring social and political change to a standstill.

The first three shōguns perfected the control mechanisms and the administrative machinery of their regimes and made strenuous efforts to increase the balance of power in favor of the shogunate. However, in 1651 Iemitsu was succeeded by his son TOKUGAWA IETSUNA (r 1651–80), a fragile youth of 10. Under him, policy largely was made by the senior councillors, resulting in a style of shogunal rule that reflected the interests of the *fudai* daimyō more than the central interests of the shōgun.

The fifth shōgun, TOKUGAWA TSUNAYOSHI (r 1680–1709), was both colorful and controversial. A mature man when he became shōgun, he put his personal imprint on shogunate policy from the start, in part by relying heavily on his private officials to circumvent the senior councillors. Tsunayoshi's reliance on his favorite, YANAGISAWA YOSHIYASU, set an example of rule through the grand chamberlain (SOBAYŌNIN). Tsunayoshi's two successors, TOKUGAWA IENOBU (r 1709–12) and Tokugawa Ietsugu (r 1713–16), stayed for a total of only seven years in office. Their years were marked by the influence of the remarkable ARAI HAKUSEKI, Confucian scholar and personal adviser to both shōguns.

In 1716 the main (Hidetada) line of the Tokugawa house failed, so that the eighth shōgun had to be found in one of the collateral houses. The choice fell on TOKUGAWA YO-SHIMUNE (r 1716–45), daimyō of Kii. Mature and experienced, Yoshimune embarked on a strenuous program of bureaucratic and financial reforms. Known as the KYŌHŌ RE-FORMS, these were the first of three major reform attempts made during the period. The main ingredients of these reforms were agrarianism, hard money, fiscal retrenchment, protection of indebted samurai, sumptuary regulation, and control of the commercial economy.

Yoshimune's son and grandson, the shōguns TOKUGAWA IESHIGE (r 1745–60) and Ieharu (r 1760–86), are said to have been manipulated by favorites: Ieshige by Ōoka Tadamitsu (1709–60) and Ieharu by TANUMA OKITSUGU. Both of these officials rose to power from low status; Tanuma in particular has gone down in history as an extreme example of the corrupt favorite. He was driven from office in 1786.

The country faced many critical domestic problems by the 1780s. Rural unrest was widespread, many samurai were in debt, and the shogunate and most daimyō were in financial trouble. Between 1782 and 1787, crop failures caused famine conditions in much of Japan (see TEMMEI FAMINE). Edo was shaken by urban riots, the largest lasting for three days, and Tanuma was an easy scapegoat. The new shōgun, TOKUGAWA IENARI (r 1787–1837), being a minor, was placed under the guidance of a new chief shogunate officer, MATSUDAIRA SADANOBU, who immediately moved to eliminate the influence of Tanuma in government. Sadanobu is credited with carrying out the second of the conservative reform programs, the KANSEI REFORMS. His slogan "back to Yoshimune" is indicative of the general thrust of his policies. The results were no more positive or long-lasting than those of the Kyōhō era had been.

Up to the 1790s the shogunate's problems had been mainly domestic, but by the beginning of the 19th century, with the appearance of Russian and British ships in Japanese waters, Japan faced an external threat as well. In the following decades the shogunate was caught in a double crisis, domestic and foreign. In the 1830s the regime experienced one of its worst famines and in 1837 an attempted rebellion in Ōsaka led by ŌSHIO HEIHACHIRŌ (a minor Tokugawa official) shook shogunate officialdom.

In 1841, upon the death of Ienari, MIZUNO TADAKUNI, chief of the senior councillors, initiated the TEMPŌ REFORMS, the last and most drastic of the three reforms. Mizuno's program was intended to improve the economic and political positions of the shogunate, but he managed to antagonize a wide array of people and was soon forced to resign. His successor as head of the senior councillors, ABE MASAHIRO, rescinded most of his initiatives.

It was Abe, however, who had to face the crisis created by Commodore Matthew PERRY in 1853. Finding himself in an impossible situation, Abe did two things that signaled the end of Tokugawa power. By soliciting all daimyō, including *tozama*, for opinions on how to handle the American request for the opening of Japanese ports, he abandoned the shogunal prerogative of determining foreign policy unilaterally. By encouraging daimyō to build up their own coastal defenses, he weakened the shōgun's power to control their military strength. With the end

of Japan's isolation and the advance of military technology, the shogunate lost its ability to assert national authority, ultimately bringing the Tokugawa regime to an end.

Economic and Cultural Developments of the Period——The Japan "opened" by Perry was vastly different from the Japan that had "closed its doors" in 1639. The greatest achievement of the Tokugawa shogunate was surely the long period of peace and stability it gave to Japan. As a result, the country had prospered both economically and culturally. Along with an increase in population, there is evidence of a general improvement in housing, food, clothing, and education over most of the Edo period.

The most dramatic change to affect Edo society was without question the spread of city life. With the appearance in the mid-16th century of the unified daimyō domains and the movement of the samurai off the land, regional CASTLE TOWNS sprang up rapidly throughout Japan. Each daimyō built at the center of his domain a castle headquarters in which he housed his samurai retainers, necessitating the assembling of service groups, merchants, carpenters, artisans, and the like to meet the needs of the assembled samurai. By the end of the 18th century, Edo, the greatest of the castle towns, had nearly 1 million in population, while Ōsaka and Kyōto each had some 300,000 inhabitants.

The samurai, who by tradition considered themselves rural aristocrats, made the transition from military duty to civil-bureaucratic service, becoming literate, cultured, and urbanized. Stress was placed on spiritual training and the cultivation of BUSHIDŌ, or the Way of the samurai. However, it was in the field of secular scholarship that the samurai of the Edo period made their truly original contribution. The main body of such scholarship was rooted in the Confucian tradition. The turn toward Neo-Confucianism and the concurrent rejection of Buddhism began following the establishment of the Tokugawa shogunate. The precedent set by the Tokugawa shōguns in adding the office of Confucian adviser (*jusha*) to the official bureaucracy and in funding schools, such as the one established by Hayashi Razan in 1630 (forerunner of the SHŌHEIKŌ), was soon followed by the daimyō.

In the early years, Confucian-based scholarship tended to be derivative, as scholars such as Hayashi Razan sought to assimilate the Confucian tradition to conditions in Japan (see SHUSHIGAKU). One product of this effort was the formulation of the principles of *bushidō* as pioneered by YAMAGA SOKŌ. As the Edo period advanced, scholars were at work in many domains compiling domainal histories and making collections of laws and precedents. They also pioneered in the recovery of ancient Japanese texts such as the KOJIKI, MAN'YŌSHŪ, and TALE OF GENJI.

The maturation of urbanized samurai life was accompanied by the rise of an urbanized commercial and service class, the *chōnin*. Confucian theory and Tokugawa law did not serve this class well. For while the *chōnin* were absolutely essential to the samurai in their urban environment, and although many became wealthy by serving the samurai, government policy operated on the premise that merchants were at the bottom of the social scale. The merchant class was denied access to foreign markets and subject to all manner of domestic controls. The small amount of trade permitted at Nagasaki

was handled as a shogunal monopoly, and daimyō commonly used domainal monopoly organizations (HAN'EI SEMBAI) to sell special local products. Merchants were protected as merchants, to be sure, particularly after 1721 when merchant guilds and monopoly associations (*kabunakama*) were permitted. Also, because they lacked political influence, they were largely left alone, free to accumulate wealth.

Commercial wealth and a growing *chōnin* population gave rise to a bourgeois society with its own cultural style. The *chōnin* had their merchant princes in the great shogunal cities of Edo, Ōsaka, and Kyōto, and to a lesser degree in the provincial castle towns. The greatest of the merchant houses, the MITSUI, SUMITOMO, and Kōnoike (see KŌNOIKE FAMILY), continued into modern times.

The main elements of the emerging bourgeois culture (*chōnin bunka*) were brought to their first flowering in Kyōto and Ōsaka during the GENROKU ERA (1688–1704). Such were the JŌRURI (puppet) and KABUKI plays of CHIKAMATSU MONZAEMON, the popular short stories of Ihara SAIKAKU, the woodblock prints of Hishikawa MORONOBU, and the poetic essays and *haiku* of Matsuo BASHŌ. In following decades urban culture continued to develop, and fiction, poetry, drama, and the pictorial arts enjoyed a new burst of vitality in the early 19th century.

The special cultural life of the cities did not extend directly to rural areas. Yet village life did not remain unchanged during the Edo period. From the beginning of this period, agriculture received the particular attention of samurai government. The emphasis was at first on increased production of rice, but eventually such commercial crops as cotton, silk, tobacco, tea, and sugar were stressed.

Commercialization of the rural economy exerted more fundamental, although less visible, influences on village social structure. In the early Edo period, village life generally was dominated by large *hyakushō* families whose extended kinship organization included hereditarily subservient, or servant, households. These dependent family members did much of the work on the main family's large landholdings. More and more, however, large families broke up into smaller units in which the smaller independent families cultivated their own fields while also working portions of other holdings as tenants. The basis of intravillage relations shifted from kinship to economic ties.

Intellectual Ferment and the Sense of Crisis——By the late Edo period a perceptible sense of unease characterized the national mood, the result of a growing realization that the country faced deep social and economic problems as well as new challenges from abroad. Unease did not translate into a widespread feeling of crisis until well into the 19th century, but it did stimulate social and intellectual movements, all of which responded in one way or another to these new problems.

The main line of Confucian influence on education and political-economic thought remained largely scholastic and conservative. However, scholars such as DAZAI SHUN-DAI struggled with questions of government efficiency and how to select officials for merit in a system based on heredity.

Despite the National Seclusion policy, knowledge of Western scholarship and scientific inquiry managed to filter into Japan, particularly after 1720 when Yo-

The Triumph of Merchant Culture

The sustained peace of the Edo period (1600–1868) fostered the growth of a money economy in which urban merchants prospered. Empowered by wealth, they sidestepped the official class system to become

the heroes and consumers of a vigorous, new form of popular culture that celebrated worldly pleasures and rejected the austere warrior code. Although the *samurai* dismissed them as dandies and upstarts, the

merchants were often refined in their pursuit of sensuality and at their best achieved a balance between earthiness and delicacy that makes the popular art created by and for them seem fresh even today.

Samurai and commoner rub elbows at Nihombashi, site of the Edo branch of Echigoya Dry Goods. Residents of Edo liked its fair prices and cash-only policy, and it grew to become the Mitsukoshi Department Store. In the early 19th century, vertically striped *kimono* like the one at center were in vogue. Ca 1820. Woodblock print.

Prostitutes of the Yoshiwara brothel district of Edo hail prospective customers. This was an era in which *iki* (urbane sophistication in manner and dress) mattered most, and prostitutes were pacesetters. This 1804 woodblock print is by Utamaro.

A scene at a post-station town shows travelers on the highway Tōkaidō. Commerce by land and sea linked Edo to the rest of Japan. Ca 1840. Detail from a woodblock print.

The 600 public baths in Edo as of 1800 were social centers for commoners where brawls sometimes broke out. By a 1791 order of the shogunate, men and women bathed in separate facilities. 1868. Woodblock print.

Sumō tournaments were well attended by commoners. The sport was one of many forms of entertainment which flourished under their patronage. 1853. Detail from a woodblock print.

shimune lifted the ban on the importation of foreign books and made it possible for persons other than official interpreters to learn Dutch. By the early 19th century, Dutch studies (Rangaku) or Western studies (Yōgaku) had become fairly widespread and their utility sufficiently recognized so that a number of daimyō began to train specialists in Western medicine and other practical sciences (see WESTERN LEARNING). The shogunate, recognizing the importance of keeping abreast of developments in the West, established in 1811 a center for the translation of Western books. But on the whole, specialists in Western studies in Japan did not become a political force agitating for the eventual reopening of their country to foreign intercourse.

After 1800 many Japanese of all walks of life were attracted to an emerging school of National Learning (KOKUGAKU) that rejected Confucianism and Buddhism as foreign, corruptive influences. This interest in Japanese tradition took on both nationalistic and religious dimensions, especially in the work of HIRATA ATSUTANE, who called for a return to Shintō tradition and asserted Japan's innate superiority to China for having retained an "unbroken line of deified sovereigns." Members of the MITO SCHOOL, such as AIZAWA SEISHISAI, went even further in their rejection of "foreign beliefs" and in their insistence upon Japan's superiority as a "land of the gods (kami)." Revival of the ideological features of Shintō provided many Japanese with a sense of cultural security in their moment of crisis. It laid the basis for the powerful conservative reaction to the foreign threat under the slogan Revere the Emperor, Expel the Barbarians (SONNŌ JŌI).

Bakumatsu: The End of the Tokugawa Regime⸺Between 1853 and 1860, the shogunate, unable to resist foreign pressures, abandoned its traditional policy and opened a number of ports to foreign ships. In 1858, by signing trade agreements (ANSEI COMMERCIAL TREATIES) with the foreign powers despite imperial disapproval, it resigned itself to free foreign intercourse. But the country was not ready to go along. The assassination in 1860 of II NAOSUKE, the shogunate's strongman, brought this phase to an end. There followed an effort to create a coalition government in which the shogunate and daimyō would work together with court nobles under the emperor, who would serve as the symbol of national unity. In a final effort at conciliation, the last shōgun, TOKUGAWA YOSHINOBU (r 1867), offered to resign in late 1867 to make way for a coalition government. See TAISEI HŌKAN.

Already, however, an anti-Tokugawa movement was gathering momentum. The two large tozama domains of Satsuma and Chōshū were drawn into alliance by young activist samurai and allied with key figures at the imperial court. In January 1868 this group captured the emperor and declared in his name a restoration of imperial rule (ŌSEI FUKKO). The shōgun had been outmaneuvered. Tokugawa forces made an attempt to resist this turn of events, but troops from the domains of Satsuma, Chōshū, and Tosa proclaimed themselves an imperial army and routed the Tokugawa forces near Kyōto. The former shōgun was declared a rebel and his lands confiscated. Within a year the new government and the emperor had moved into Edo, where in quick succession the main pillars of the bakuhan system

were pulled down. In 1871 the daimyō domain system was converted into a centralized prefecture system. In 1872, with the declaration of class equality, the samurai class was abolished. In 1873 the kokudaka system of land registration and taxation was converted to a modern property tax system. Between 1853 and 1873 a revolution had taken place. See MEIJI RESTORATION.

☎ 321

Edo sampu   江戸参府

(journeys to the capital at Edo). Journeys made by the overseer (opperhoofd) of the DUTCH FACTORY in Nagasaki and his party to the shogunal capital of Edo (now Tōkyō). The Netherlands East India Company and its successors, from 1639 to 1854 the only Europeans permitted to trade in Japan, maintained a trading post in Hirado from 1609 to 1641 and on the island of DEJIMA in Nagasaki Harbor thereafter. The overseer and his party were required to pay their respects to the shōgun at Edo, generally once each year (once every four years after 1790). They were received in audience by the shōgun and had their trading rights reconfirmed, while at the same time promising to observe Japanese laws. From the Japanese point of view, the granting of audience was a signal honor to the foreigners. Since, however, the Dutch were required to make obeisances before the shōgun and frequently to sing, dance, and otherwise entertain him, descriptions of these audiences by other Europeans brought ridicule on the Dutch in Europe. The most widely read of such accounts were those by Engelbert KAEMPFER, a German physician who joined the overseer's party in 1691 and 1692.

educational broadcasting 教育放送

(kyōiku hōsō). Radio and television broadcasts presenting educational programming of a broadly cultural nature. There are two types: programs intended for in-school use and programs designed for the community at large. These educational programs are aired by Nippon Hōsō Kyōkai (NHK; Japan Broadcasting Corporation), the public network, and by various commercial stations.

Educational radio broadcasting for schools originated in Ōsaka in 1933 and expanded into a national network in 1935. Educational television was initiated in 1953. Programs are drawn up according to school grade level. In 1989 there were 98 weekly series being broadcast that covered practically all subjects taught in school, ranging from science, social studies, and foreign languages to music. The broadcasts are used by 97 percent of Japanese elementary schools and 60 percent of middle schools; most schools also have videotape systems so that the programming can be used when appropriate in the daily schedule. Lecture programs that cover skills and hobbies are also broadcast. See also UNIVERSITY OF THE AIR; AUDIOVISUAL EDUCATION.

educational counseling 教育相談

(kyōiku sōdan). Educational counseling in Japan is usually conducted outside the school system or informally by teachers in the schools. Educational counselors are not licensed or required to have formal qualifications. Japanese educational counseling originated in 1915 with an office established by the Nihon Jidō Gakkai (Societas Paedagogica Japonica). For the first time, counseling was available for problems concerning education, nurturing, and vocational selection for all children, including those

with special needs. In 1936 the first counseling facility affiliated with a university was established within the education department of the Tōkyō University of Science and Literature (now Tsukuba University). Psychologist Tanaka Kan'ichi (1882–1962) was its director.

After World War II, child counseling offices were established in every prefecture under the provisions of the CHILD WELFARE LAW of 1947 (effective 1948). Offices run by prefectural boards of education conduct counseling training for teachers, undertake research on educational counseling, and provide counseling services for the public.

educational expenses 教育費

(kyōikuhi). The School Education Law (Gakkō Kyōiku Hō) of 1947 guarantees free primary and middle school education to all Japanese citizens. However, within the public school system each family must pay supplementary expenses, which may include kindergarten and high school tuition, field trips, supplies, transportation to and from school, school lunches, extracurricular lessons at JUKU (private tutoring schools) and CRAM SCHOOLS, and private lessons in calligraphy, piano, etc.

The total cost per child for a family in 1987 averaged out to ¥179,723 (US $1,242) for public kindergarten and ¥339,767 (US $2,349) for private kindergarten (attended by 76 percent). In the public schools the average per student was ¥184,000 (US $1,275) for elementary school and ¥225,407 (US $1,558) for middle school. Costs in public high schools averaged ¥294,471 (US $2,035) and in private high schools ¥605,481 (US $4,186). Of the 94.3 percent of middle school graduates who went on to high school, 72 percent attended public schools.

Since academic records have a strong influence on social status (see GAKUREKI SHAKAI), parents spare no expense to prepare a child for the ENTRANCE EXAMINATIONS for high school and college. The pressure to send students in the last year of middle or high school to juku or cram schools is acute. Although Japan's consumer price index for 1987 rose only 0.1 percent over the previous year, educational expenses increased by 2.9–4.5 percent, saddling parents of competing children with a great burden, exacerbated by the fact that scholarship grants are rare and educational loans are small and difficult to obtain.

educational reforms of 1947
  教育改革（1947年）

(Kyōiku Kaikaku). The reform of the Japanese school system, educational administration, school curriculum, and course content was a high priority of the post–World War II Allied OCCUPATION, as part of the effort to "democratize" Japan. The first reform, initiated in late 1945, was intended to end the teaching of ultranationalism and militarism, as well as the teaching of SHŪSHIN (moral education). In March 1946 the first of two UNITED STATES EDUCATION MISSIONS TO JAPAN arrived and recommended further reforms.

Working with the Japanese EDUCATION REFORM COUNCIL, the headquarters of the supreme commander for the Allied powers (SCAP) formed these recommendations into the Fundamental Law of Education (Kyōiku Kihon Hō; see EDUCATION, FUNDAMENTAL LAW OF) and the SCHOOL EDUCATION LAW (Gakkō Kyōiku Hō), both of which were enacted in 1947. The Fundamental Law, popularly referred to as the "education constitution," stated the basic aims of the educational system: contributing to the peace and welfare of humanity, the full development of personality, and the creation of a love for truth and justice among students. The law also contained a commitment to academic freedom, equal opportunity, and coeducation. The School Education Law outlined the new system of six-year elementary schools, three-year middle schools, three-year high schools, and four-year universities. Compulsory education was extended from six to nine years, and provision was made for the education of the handicapped. Before the war, standardized textbooks developed by the government had been used. The new system provided for private publication of textbooks with limited government review.

These reforms were first revised in 1956 when the conservative government reasserted control over appointments to local school boards. Government review of textbook content became more strict (see IENAGA TEXTBOOK REVIEW CASE). Efforts were made to curb the political activities of the leftist NIKKYŌSO (Japan Teachers Union), and MORAL EDUCATION was reintroduced into the curriculum, although it no longer stresses loyalty to the emperor. On the whole, the postwar reforms have been retained, and the Japanese educational system remains strongly democratic and relatively free of government direction.

Educational Research, National Institute for　国立教育研究所

(Kokuritsu Kyōiku Kenkyūjo). Located in Meguro Ward, Tōkyō. Established in 1949 under the direct control of the Ministry of Education, the institute, which consists of nine departments, carries out a wide range of studies. Its library has a collection of 90,000 textbooks. The external service department is responsible for coordinating the work of both public and private education research institutes in Japan and for cooperating with the research and training activities of other Asian member-nations of UNESCO. It employed 93 researchers as of 1989.

educational technology　教育工学

(kyōiku kōgaku). Audiovisual and broadcast education in Japan began in the 1930s and became widespread in the post–World War II period. Since 1972 many facilities for research in the use of electronic technology in education have been established at teacher training centers throughout the country, but the growth of the field has been hampered by a lack of coordination among audiovisual education, hardware engineering, programmed and computer-assisted instruction (CAI), and behavioral science. During the 1980s interest in the use of computers for educational purposes increased, and as of 1989 computers had been introduced in 94 percent of public high schools, 36 percent of public middle schools, and 14 percent of public elementary schools. The Ministry of Education encourages research into computer applications in actual teaching situations.

education at home　家庭教育

(katei kyōiku). Various factors have led to changes in the education of children within the home since World War II. Prewar Japanese society was centered on the IE, or household, and, under this extended family system, the principal disciplinarian was the father. Typically three generations lived together, and, when the father was absent, his role was assumed by the grandparents. Education in the home was either moral, infusing a sense of one's social position (mibun), or practical, in the handing down of family customs or trades.

After World War II, the new CONSTITUTION OF JAPAN was adopted, and the CIVIL CODE was revised. The ie was abolished as a legal entity, and this has led to the rise of the nuclear family and the loss of the father's authority. Grandparents no longer play a major role in child rearing, and consequently the mother has become increasingly central. The absence of the father, usually due to long working hours, and the societal emphasis on educational background have combined to produce the phenomenon of the kyōiku mama ("educational mother"), who is oversolicitous of her children's education but does not discipline them strictly. These trends have contributed to the growing demand for a reexamination of education within the family.

education for children of returnees　帰国子女教育

(kikoku shijo kyōiku). The rapid growth of Japan's economy since the 1960s has brought about an increase in the transfer of personnel to positions overseas. A growing number of Japanese children raised and educated abroad must enter, or reenter, the highly competitive Japanese school system upon their return. In 1989 in Japan there were approximately 9,200 children of returnees requiring compulsory education (i.e., children 6 to 15 years old). About 80 percent of these students attended Japanese schools on a regular or part-time basis while abroad. See SCHOOLS FOR JAPANESE CHILDREN ABROAD.

Public elementary and middle schools do not require returning students to take entrance exams, but most children who have acquired part of their education overseas (except those who have studied at overseas Japanese schools) need extra courses of study, especially in reading and writing Japanese. A number of schools provide special review course work or classes.

High schools require entrance examinations of students who have studied overseas, but many of these schools give special consideration to returning students regarding entrance requirements and subjects of examination. Several high schools have been established especially for returning students.

Universities consider students who have graduated from high schools abroad (including those who have obtained International Baccalaureates) separately from the regular pool of applicants. Foreign-educated students are given special consideration regarding entrance examination qualifications, and some university admissions departments also consider the results of overseas tests of scholastic ability, such as the Scholastic Aptitude Test (SAT) in the United States.

Education, Fundamental Law of　教育基本法

(Kyōiku Kihon Hō). Law designating the fundamental objectives and mission of education in order to establish a democratic and peaceful nation, as called for in the postwar CONSTITUTION OF JAPAN. Put into effect in 1947, it replaced the IMPERIAL RESCRIPT ON EDUCATION issued by Emperor Meiji in 1890 and became the basis of all subsequent educational laws and ordinances.

The Fundamental Law of Education is made up of a preamble and 11 articles. The preamble states that the general objective of education is to foster a respect for truth and peace rather than to train people as loyal subjects of the state. The articles are statements of fundamental educational tenets, specifically the aims and principles of education, equal opportunity in education, compulsory education, coeducation, school education, community education (shakai kyōiku), political education, religious education, and school administration. The 11th article provides for the enactment of further laws to carry out these ideals.

education, history of　教育史

(kyōikushi). Education in the sense of reading and writing began in Japan after the introduction of the Chinese writing system in the 6th century or before. The aristocracy was educated in Confucian thought and Buddhism in the Nara (710–794) and Heian (794–1185) periods. Buddhist priests were the first teachers in ancient Japan, and temples became centers of learning. The first official school for the training of government officials was established by the TAIHŌ CODE in 701. Education spread to the military class during the Kamakura period (1185–1333); at the same time, through the growth of popular forms of Buddhism, the peasantry was also increasingly exposed to education. During the Edo period (1600–1868) Neo-Confucian thought was adopted as official ideology. Both the shogunal and domainal governments established schools during the Edo period; the official systems were supplemented by private schools at shrines and temples. Education was widely diffused by the time of the Meiji Restoration of 1868.

Nationalism and the drive toward modernization were strong influences on education during the late 19th century. The nationalist influence was predominant after Japan militarized in the 1930s, while the post–World War II period brought decentralization and new democratic influences to education. The postwar system provides nine years of compulsory schooling, and high school education is also nearly universal. Some 40 percent of Japanese students continue their education in universities. The schools are administered by local and regional autonomous bodies under the broad supervision of the Ministry of Education. Education plays a critical role in preparing students for employment, and career opportunities are determined largely according to school performance.

EDUCATION BEFORE 1600

Prior to the introduction of written language to Japan, education was carried out primarily through an oral tradition of stories concerning history and customs. The introduction of writing to Japan necessitated a more conscious and systematic form of education.

Ancient Japan—Education in ancient Japan was fostered by the imperial family. Prince SHŌTOKU (574–622) adopted the doctrines of Mahāyāna Buddhism and constructed HŌRYŪJI, a temple in Nara, as a place of learning. The emperor SHŌMU (701–756; r 724–749) constructed temples in each province (see KOKUBUNJI); monks were sent to these temples by the government as instructors. Of particular importance in the ancient period was the education of clergy, who were among the leaders of society.

The role of priests in spreading education among the masses during the Nara and Heian periods was considerable. GYŌGI (668–749) built places of training (*dōjō*) in the various regions he visited. Other priests, including KŪYA (903–972) and RYŌNIN (1073–1132), continued this tradition of teaching.

With the establishment of the Chinese-inspired RITSURYŌ SYSTEM of centralized government in the late 7th century, the nobility emerged as the most influential class in Japan. Under the Taihō Code (701) two types of schools were established for the nobility: the DAIGAKURYŌ, to educate the children of the nobility in the capital, and the *kokugaku*, to educate the children of the provincial nobility.

Medieval Education—Political power shifted to the provincial military class with the establishment of the KAMAKURA SHOGUNATE in 1192. *Samurai* during this period drew up KAKUN (house laws) to educate their children and ensure family solidarity. These house laws covered all aspects of warrior life, including relations between lord and vassal, inheritance and succession, and proper treatment of retainers.

The Christian missionaries who came to Japan in the 16th century founded schools where both general and vocational education were conducted. By this time the Daigakuryō had declined, and the provincial *kokugaku* had disappeared entirely. The most representative educational institution of this period was the ASHIKAGA GAKKŌ. The school flourished during the late 1500s, when enrollment reached 3,000, and continued to operate until 1872. Also during this period the foundation was laid for the TERAKOYA, the popular schools of the Edo period.

EDO-PERIOD EDUCATION

The civilizing effect of two and a half centuries of peace and modest economic growth during the Edo period was nowhere more apparent than in the field of formal education. At the beginning of the period literacy was very much a minority accomplishment. Tutors, mostly priests, could be found for the children of noble families, but there were virtually no schools. Such literature as was produced circulated chiefly in manuscript form.

The contrast at the end of the period was great. Large schools formally organized by the domainal authorities (see HANKŌ) gave a graded instruction in the Chinese classics to almost every samurai child in the land, and local *terakoya* taught Japanese reading and writing to villagers as well as townsmen. Other private schools and academics called SHIJUKU provided more advanced instruction in a variety of disciplines and schools of thought to both samurai and commoners. Books abounded. The political and economic systems depended on written communication. Japan had almost certainly reached the 40 percent literacy threshold that some consider a prerequisite for modern growth.

The parallel with the pattern of European education before the rise of science and "modern studies" is striking. For the Japanese of the Edo period the Chinese classics, like the Greek and Roman classics for the Elizabethan Englishman, were the repository of wisdom and knowledge. Learning painfully to "construe" these classics was the central business of the Edo domain schools.

There was, however, an important difference between them. In Europe, religion and morality were predominantly the province of a separately institutionalized and powerful church. In Japan, the more weakly organized Buddhist temples yielded authority in the moral sphere to the new Confucian schools. The school during the Edo period thus came to combine the functions shared in Western society between school and church, with continuing consequences for the educational system of modern Japan.

Confucian Scholarship and School Formation—The establishment of Confucian scholarship as a separate branch of learning, and of the role of the Confucian scholar–governmental adviser–teacher as a distinct profession, was the work of a number of distinguished men of the 17th century: FUJIWARA SEIKA, HAYASHI RAZAN, MATSUNAGA SEKIGO, KINOSHITA JUN'AN, and ITŌ JINSAI. Fujiwara was the first to cut himself off from his temple roots and to declare himself an adherent of the philosophy and ethic of Confucianism as something incompatible with, and indeed opposed to, Buddhism, not just as part of an undifferentiated "scholarship in the Chinese language." See also CONFUCIANISM; for Neo-Confucianism in Japan, see SHUSHIGAKU.

By the end of the 17th century the idea was generally established that every self-respecting *daimyō*'s band of retainers should include a *jusha* (Confucian adviser) to advise on tricky questions of historical precedent or political morality, to tutor the daimyō's heir, and, occasionally perhaps, to give a formal lecture. Some daimyō gave financial assistance to help transform the band of disciples who gathered at the feet of any scholar into the framework of a formal school. Some 20 domains, mostly among the largest ones, had founded schools by 1703. The number was over 200 by 1865. At the end of the Edo period only the smaller domains still let their samurai educate their children in private schools.

Heterodoxy and New Orthodoxy—An emphasis on moral virtue developed, becoming the dominant but by no means the only strand of Confucian thought or of educational philosophy in the Edo period. The leader of a reaction against this trend away from mastery of ancient Chinese texts and commentaries was OGYŪ SORAI (1666–1728). He not only rejected the scriptural authority that was accorded the Song (Sung) Neo-Confucianists but went further and rejected the entire Neo-Confucian notion that the purpose of study was the moral cultivation of the individual. He took the Legalist view that one kept men in order not by winning over their individual hearts and minds to virtue but by establishing institutions that channel their self-interest in socially beneficial directions. Scholarship was the rigorous, intellectual study of such institutions in their varying historical forms. But in addition to that practical purpose it was also an end-in-itself pursuit of intellectual and literary excellence. In the eyes of the Neo-Confucian moralists, these were unworthy pursuits. See also KOGAKU.

For over half a century the followers of Sorai coexisted with the Neo-Confucianists. Some domain schools were firmly in the hands of one faction or the other. Others managed to contain both in an uneasy atmosphere of mutual recrimination and rivalry until MATSUDAIRA SADANOBU's (1759–1829) famous Ban on Heterodox Learning (Kansei Igaku no Kin) of 1790. This edict was specifically an instruction to the shogunate's own

school (the SHŌHEIKŌ), but it had a much wider effect. Henceforth, it ruled, the teachings of Zhu Xi's (Chu Hsi) Neo-Confucian school should be adhered to. The ban was part of Matsudaira's plan to revitalize the Hayashi school, which he expected to play an important role in his attempts to reform the shogunate after the laxity and corruption of the previous TANUMA OKITSUGU (1719–88) regime (see also KANSEI REFORMS). As other domains followed suit, the "Sorai school" practically disappeared as an identifiable group, but the new orthodoxy was in fact a relatively tolerant and eclectic one that had room for political economy and for literary pursuits as well as for moral improvement.

Other Edo-Period Schools—There were two other forms of education that warranted separate institutions. The first was Japanese studies. Half a dozen domains, those most influenced by the National Learning (KOKUGAKU) school, had established schools of national studies by the end of the period, and another 10 did so in the first years of the Meiji government. The other much more consequential innovation of the 19th century was the establishment of schools that specialized in Dutch, later Western, studies. From the first sustained spurt of interest in Dutch science—particularly medical science—in the 1770s until the mid-1850s, these exotic studies were largely carried on by individual doctors and low-ranking samurai. It was not until the 1850s that official patronage began in earnest. A number of special schools for Western studies were begun in that decade, notably the shogunate's BANSHO SHIRABESHO, which was conceived first as a translation bureau for "barbarian books" but rapidly developed into a flourishing school that admitted pupils from all over Japan. See WESTERN LEARNING.

Parallel to these developments was the laying of foundations for mass literacy by the simple private reading-and-writing schools that helped prepare the way for Japan's transition to an industrial society. Widespread schooling also reinforced the general idea of self-improvement, the belief that by study (later, by absorbing the knowledge and techniques of the West) one could enhance one's productiveness, one's ability to understand and control one's environment, and one's position in society.

Convinced that knowledge would enhance the strength and solidarity of the nation, the Meiji government decreed an entirely new educational system based upon imported models. With the possible exception of some small parts of TŌKYŌ UNIVERSITY, none of Japan's great schools and colleges can trace direct links of institutional continuity back to the schools of the Edo period.

MODERN EDUCATION

The history of education in Japan since the Meiji Restoration (1868) can be divided into the following five periods: the period of establishment (1868–85), when the initial framework for a modern educational system was created; the period of consolidation (1886–1916), when various school orders were issued and a systematic educational structure was established; the period of expansion (1917–36), based upon the recommendations of the Extraordinary Council on Education (RINJI KYŌIKU KAIGI; 1917–19); the wartime period (1937–45) of militaristic education; and the present period (from 1945), which was ushered in by educational reforms during the Allied Occupation.

Modern education in Japan has been characterized by the following general features: an important role played by nationalism in the development of the educational system, the emergence of academic credentials as the key determinant of employment and social status, persistently strong foreign influences, and the continuing existence of contending schools of thought within the educational establishment.

The Period of Establishment (1868–1885)—The EDUCATION ORDER OF 1872 (Gakusei) established the foundation for a modern public education system, but the initial plan was too ambitious and was thus revised in 1879 and 1880. The revised orders called for strong central control. Many Edo-period schools were incorporated into the new educational system. *Terakoya* and *shijuku*, schools for the common people, became primary schools; the shogunate-controlled, elite school called Kaiseijo developed into a university that later became Tōkyō University, while many domain schools became public middle schools, which eventually developed into universities. Most of the schools of Western Learning developed into private SEMMON GAKKŌ (professional schools). The Meiji government promoted educational reform by establishing new schools while making use of existing schools.

In 1871 the MINISTRY OF EDUCATION was created, and the following year the school system came into being. The school system followed the American model: the three phases of primary school, middle school, and university were created, and practical, utilitarian educational objectives were promoted. On the other hand, the administrative system followed the French: under the strong central control of the Ministry of Education, university, middle-school, and primary-school districts were created. In 1873 TANAKA FUJIMARO, the vice-minister of education, was made responsible for establishing the school system. With the aid of David MURRAY, an American adviser, he trained capable officials, began teacher education in NORMAL SCHOOLS (*shihan gakkō*), and established the first Western-style university—Tōkyō University.

The educational reform effort was overambitious and soon ran into opposition. The EDUCATION ORDER OF 1879 (Kyōikurei) decreased central control, abolished the school district system, and reduced the period of compulsory attendance. The following year the Revised Education Order (Kaisei Kyōiku Rei, 1880) strengthened central control. A significant development was the 1879 issuance of the Kyōgaku Taishi (Outline of Learning; see MOTODA NAGAZANE), which emphasized Confucian values of humanity, justice, loyalty, and filial piety. This served as a guide for conservative reform. Education in SHŪSHIN ("moral" training) took on new importance. The utmost priority came to be placed on nationalistic moral education. This formed the basis for national educational policy until the end of World War II. See also IMPERIAL RESCRIPT ON EDUCATION.

The Period of Consolidation (1886–1916)—In 1885 the cabinet system was created, and MORI ARINORI became the first minister of education. He created a unified educational framework and, together with INOUE KOWASHI, gradually established the basis of the school system of the following periods. In 1886 he issued in quick succession the Elementary School Order, the Middle School Order, the Imperial University Order, and the Normal School Order. The

IMPERIAL UNIVERSITIES (Tōkyō University was the only such institution until 1897) were intended to be the institutions that would create capable leaders who would absorb advanced Western Learning necessary for the modernization of the nation. Middle schools (especially the higher middle schools that became HIGHER SCHOOLS in 1894) were designed to prepare students for the Imperial University. Elementary schools were considered as training centers for loyal subjects of the emperor.

In these ways a comprehensive school system was established for the purpose of modernization on one hand and the spiritual unification of the people on the other. Later, the development of industry after the Sino-Japanese War (1894–95), the demand for industrial education, and popular demand for higher-level education increased. Inoue Kowashi, who became minister of education after Mori, established systems of vocational and girls' schools. In this period a variety of private *semmon gakkō* (later to become universities) was also established. In 1898 the attendance rate for compulsory education reached 69 percent. Compulsory education was extended to six years in 1907.

Period of Expansion (1917–1936)—Stimulated by the Russo-Japanese War and World War I, capitalism developed rapidly in Japan. The Russian Revolution and worldwide demands for democracy exerted an influence on Japanese politics and education. In 1917 the government created the RINJI KYŌIKU KAIGI (Extraordinary Council on Education). Before it was abolished in 1919, the council issued several reports that formed the basis for the expansion of the education system over the next decade or so. The influence of the council was most important in the area of higher education. Until 1918 universities had been limited to the imperial universities, but the reforms contained in the University Order of 1918 extended recognition to colleges and private universities. In accordance with this order many national, public, and private *semmon gakkō* were raised to the status of university.

During this period, new currents of thought entered Japan, including the advocacy of socialism, communism, anarchism, liberalism, and democracy. Within the educational world, the New Education Movement (see SHIN KYŌIKU UNDŌ), child-centered pedagogy, the organization of the teachers' union, and student movements arose in opposition to nationalistic education. These trends intensified in the late 1920s with the deepening of economic crisis and political confrontation. The government responded with political repression and attempted to counteract the influence of leftist ideology by promoting the so-called Japanese spirit.

The Wartime Period (1937–1945)—After the Manchurian Incident of 1931, educational policy soon became ultranationalistic; after the beginning of the Sino-Japanese War of 1937–45, it became militaristic. Elementary schools were changed to KOKUMIN GAKKŌ (national people's schools), which were to train subjects for the empire, and SEINEN GAKKŌ (youth schools, primarily for vocational education) became obligatory for graduates of elementary schools. Normal schools were raised in status to *semmon gakkō*. After Japan entered World War II, militaristic education became even stronger. In order to enhance nationalistic indoctrination, textbooks, such as the KOKUTAI NO HONGI (Cardinal Principles of the National Entity

of Japan), were compiled for use in the schools, and control over learning, education, and thought was strengthened.

Educational Reforms after World War II (1945–)—After defeat in 1945 Japan was placed under the Occupation of the Allied forces until the San Francisco Peace Treaty of 1952. Reports of the UNITED STATES EDUCATION MISSIONS TO JAPAN, which came to Japan in 1946 and 1950, became the blueprints for educational reform (see EDUCATIONAL REFORMS OF 1947). The reforms were conducted by the EDUCATION REFORM COUNCIL (Kyōiku Sasshin Iinkai), consisting of Japanese civilians, under the leadership and advice of the CIE (CIVIL INFORMATION AND EDUCATION SECTION OF SCAP). The core of the reform was the Fundamental Law of Education (1947; see EDUCATION, FUNDAMENTAL LAW OF), which took the place of the Imperial Rescript on Education as the basic philosophy of education. The new law stated the goal of education as the development of people healthy in spirit and body, who are filled with an independent spirit, respect the value of individuals, and love truth and justice. Based on this law, the SCHOOL EDUCATION LAW OF 1947 was promulgated in the same year, and a new school system was established. The essential elements of the new system were the replacement of the existing dual-track (popular and elite) system with a single-track 6–3–3–4 system (six years of elementary school, three years of middle school, three years of high school, and four years of university), compulsory education in elementary and middle schools, the establishment of the principle of COEDUCATION, and the creation of the board of education system. These reforms completely altered education in Japan. There have been calls for further educational reforms in response to the social and economic changes that have occurred in Japan since the late 1940s, and in 1976 the CENTRAL COUNCIL FOR EDUCATION (Chūō Kyōiku Shingikai) began an investigation of the possible need for such reforms. In 1984 the Nakasone cabinet established its own advisory council, the PROVISIONAL COUNCIL ON EDUCATIONAL REFORM (Rinji Kyōiku Shingikai; also called Rinkyōshin), which presented a final report in 1987.

education law 教育法

(*kyōiku hō*). The legal framework for education in Japan follows the pattern in other centralized, unitary systems. The educational system is controlled nationally by the MINISTRY OF EDUCATION, which exercises supervisory and budgetary control pursuant to a variety of national statutes dealing with education. Any legislation and the administration of public education in Japan are subject to the provisions of the 1947 CONSTITUTION OF JAPAN, which includes express guarantees of ACADEMIC FREEDOM (art. 23); EQUAL OPPORTUNITY IN EDUCATION (art. 26, para. 1); free, COMPULSORY EDUCATION (art. 26, para. 2); and separation of religion and the state (art. 20). The constitution also expressly prohibits use of public funds for the "use, benefit or maintenance" of any religious institution as well as any educational enterprise "not under the control of public authority" (art. 89).

The Fundamental Law of Education (Kyōiku Kihon Hō, Law No. 25, 1947) is considered, along with the constitution, to provide the basic policies governing Japan's educational system. The structure of Japan's

eggplant Eggplants have been cultivated in Japan for more than a thousand years and come in many varieties. **1** The *kinchakunasu* is one of several round varieties. **2** The oblong *mizunasu*. **3** The slender Sendai *naganasu*. **4** A ripening·eggplant.

6–3–3–4 system (six years of elementary school, three years of middle school, three years of high school, and four years of university) is established under the School Education Law (Gakkō Kyōiku Hō) of 1947.

Education Order of 1872 学制

(Gakusei). The government order that established Japan's first consolidated, modern school system. The basic aims of the order are clearly expressed in the ŌSEIDASARESHO, an accompanying proclamation that was meant to explain the theories of modern education to the Japanese public: education is the principal means of advancement in life; the function of schools is to produce independent, moral, and patriotic individuals; schooling must be made available to all; and all Japanese must study practical arts and sciences that will benefit society and help build a modern state.

By 1875 some 25,000 elementary schools for compulsory education had been established. Most of them, however, were merely reorganized village schools (TERAKOYA), and educational expenses were borne by the students' families. Popular resentment was stirred as the government attempted to force the people to adopt a system of education that was uncongenial to their habits of thought and potentially subversive to their way of life. The government was forced to adopt a more flexible system, embodied in the EDUCATION ORDER OF 1879.

Education Order of 1879 教育令

(Kyōikurei). Government order concerning Japan's educational system; a revision of the EDUCATION ORDER OF 1872. The order of 1879 relaxed the compulsory education regulations and decentralized the educational system by abolishing the school districts and allowing localities to establish schools and set educational policies in accord with their own varying needs. The Education Order of 1879 was extensively revised in 1880 and 1885 and finally superseded by the SCHOOL ORDERS OF 1886.

Education Reform Council 教育刷新委員会

(Kyōiku Sasshin Iinkai). Established in August 1946 as an advisory body to the prime minister. It was essentially a reorganization of the Japanese committee that had been set up in 1946 to cooperate with the first of the UNITED STATES EDUCATION MISSIONS TO JAPAN. The proposals it made to the Japanese government included the outline for the Fundamental Law of Education (see EDUCATION, FUNDAMENTAL LAW OF) and for the 6–3–3 school system (six years of elementary school, three years of middle school, three years of high school). In 1952 it became the CENTRAL COUNCIL FOR EDUCATION under the Ministry of Education.

education-related businesses 教育産業

(kyōiku sangyō). As a result of the tremendous importance attached to education and academic affiliation in Japanese society (see GAKUREKI SHAKAI), large numbers of education-related businesses have developed. These include suppliers of textbooks, computers, and educational software as well as schools offering instruction in traditional arts and hobbies. The fastest-growing sector, however, is the "examination business," which includes JUKU (private tutoring schools), CRAM SCHOOLS (yobikō), and firms that offer trial entrance examinations and sell magazines and other publications directed at the examinee and his or her family. These businesses have grown especially rapidly since the 1960s, when the ENTRANCE EXAMINATIONS for the most prestigious schools became increasingly competitive.

Shorter working hours and a growing emphasis on LIFELONG LEARNING have boosted the popularity of other education-related businesses, such as CULTURE CENTERS and CORRESPONDENCE COURSES. Continued high growth for all forms of education-related business is anticipated.

education system reforms 教育制度の改革

(kyōiku seido no kaikaku). The Japanese education system has undergone numerous reforms since modern education was introduced soon after the Meiji Restoration (1868). These reforms have led to changes in the political content of education as well as in the structure and scope of the system. The most recent reform took place during the post–World War II OCCUPATION and laid the basis for the present educational system.

The MINISTRY OF EDUCATION was established in 1871, and the EDUCATION ORDER OF 1872 set up an education system patterned after European and American models. The IMPERIAL RESCRIPT ON EDUCATION (1890) stressed loyalty to the nation and a Confucian-oriented ethical education. In the first half of the 1890s, in the wake of rapid industrial progress, vocational schools and professional schools (SEMMON GAKKŌ) were established for graduates of elementary schools. Secondary schools for girls were set up after 1899.

Elementary school education spread rapidly during the first decade of the 20th century, and the duration of compulsory education was increased to six years. The government also strengthened national controls over content and reinforced the teaching of ethics. The RINJI KYŌIKU KAIGI (Extraordinary Council on Education), formed in 1917, introduced several new measures, including an increase in government subsidies for elementary (compulsory) education and the recognition of colleges and universities outside the imperial university system. It also proposed emphasizing military training at school to promote the concept of national polity (KOKUTAI). SEINEN GAKKŌ, which mixed vocational and military education, were made compulsory for elementary school graduates in 1939, and in 1941 the elementary school system was reorganized under the name KOKUMIN GAKKŌ (national people's schools). After World War II, the EDUCATIONAL REFORMS OF 1947 resulted from the advice of the first of the UNITED STATES EDUCATION MISSIONS TO JAPAN and from the Japanese EDUCATION REFORM COUNCIL. Militaristic education was abolished and an emphasis on peace and democracy was introduced. The complicated, multitrack, prewar system was replaced by a unified system with a six-year elementary school, three-year middle school, three-year high school, and four-year university. The first nine years of the system were made compulsory. Coeducation and equal opportunity in education were promoted. Curriculum was developed under SCHOOL COURSE GUIDELINES of the Ministry of Education. Since 1952 all education policies have been developed by the CENTRAL COUNCIL FOR EDUCATION (Chūō Kyōiku Shingikai), an advisory council attached to the Ministry of Education.

eejanaika ええじゃないか

(literally, "Why not, it's okay!"). Phrase chanted by participants in a massive outbreak in late 1867 of dancing and rejoicing that approached mass hysteria. The outbreak began in Mikawa Province (now part of Aichi Prefecture) when rumors circulated that amulets (GOFU) from ISE SHRINE were falling from the skies over Mikawa. Economically pressed and confused by the political turmoil of the era, the common people interpreted this prodigy as an omen of good times to come. Young and old, male and female alike donned extravagant attire and danced wildly through the streets, or sometimes entered the houses of the well-to-do and helped themselves to food and drink, chanting "eejanaika." The phenomenon quickly spread east to Nagoya, Yokohama, and the shogunal capital of Edo (now Tōkyō). It has been seen as a variant form of OKAGE MAIRI, the traditional mass pilgrimages to Ise. More recently, scholars have interpreted the eejanaika outbreak as a reaction to oppression and anxiety and linked it to other contemporary manifestations of peasant unrest, such as the YONAOSHI REBELLIONS. The fall of the amulets has frequently been explained as the work of antishogunal activists plotting to destabilize the Tokugawa regime by creating social disorder, but no hard evidence has been discovered to substantiate this idea.

eel, Japanese 鰻

(unagi). Anguilla japonica. Freshwater fish of the family Anguillidae, order Anguilliformes, class Osteichthyes. It resembles the eels of North America, which belong to the same genus. Adult unagi normally range from 40 to 50 centimeters (16–20 in) in length, though they sometimes grow to over 60 centimeters (24 in). It is believed to lay its eggs in the sea east of Okinawa and Taiwan. The unagi is generally regarded as a freshwater fish, as the fry born in the sea go upstream and live there for many years. Unagi are actively bred in freshwater ponds in Japan, as natural eels are now very scarce.

Unagi seems to have been considered a nourishing or medicinal food since ancient times. Kabayaki (charcoal broiled and flavored with teriyaki sauce) is the usual method of preparation. The centuries-old custom of eating eel at the height of summer (doyō unagi) survives in modern Japan.

Efu 衛府

Office of the Imperial Guard, established under the TAIHŌ CODE of 701 and modeled on its counterpart in Tang (T'ang) China. Responsible for protecting the imperial family and policing the palace grounds, it initially comprised five sections, later expanded to eight and stabilized at six in 811. The six were the Saemonfu and the Uemonfu (Headquarters of the Gate Guards of the Left and of the Right, respectively); the Sahyōefu and the Uhyōefu (Headquarters of the Military Guards of the Left and of the Right, respectively); and the Sakonoefu and the Ukonoefu (Headquarters of the Inner Palace Guards of the Left and of the Right, respectively). The latter two were divisions of the Konoefu (Headquarters of the Inner Palace Guards). The Efu also patrolled the capital, but in the Heian period (794–1185) this was done by the KEBIISHI (imperial police).

Egami Namio → horse-rider theory

Egawa Tarōzaemon　江川太郎左衛門

(1801–55). Also known as Egawa Hidetatsu or Egawa Tan'an. Pioneering authority on Western military science and industrial technology. Born in Nirayama, Izu Province (now part of Shizuoka Prefecture). From 1841 he studied Western gunnery under TAKASHIMA SHŪHAN, becoming a teacher in Edo (now Tōkyō). SAKUMA SHŌZAN, KAWAJI TOSHIAKIRA, HASHIMOTO SANAI, and KIDO TAKAYOSHI studied under him. In 1842–57 he built an experimental reverberatory furnace (HANSHARO) that became the basis for a huge facility at Nirayama for manufacturing heavy artillery and other munitions. In 1853, the year of Commodore Matthew C. PERRY's arrival, Egawa was assigned to strengthen the defenses of Edo Bay.

eggplant　茄子

(nasu). Solanum melongena. A perennial plant of the family Solanaceae that has long been an important summer vegetable in Japan. It was introduced to Japan in about the 8th century from China. A number of varieties have been developed, all of which are smaller than most Western varieties. Eggplants are pickled in rice-bran paste (see PICKLES); they are also boiled, fried, or grilled. They are produced abundantly during the hot season, which lasts from June to September, and are grown during cooler seasons in greenhouses.

ego　自我

(jiga). According to the structure of self, as formulated by the American philosopher George H. Mead (1863–1931), the Japanese awareness of self can be said to consist of a weak sense of the self-as-subject ("I" or shuga) and a strong sense of the self-as-object ("me" or kyakuga). From early on the Japanese developed a collective, communal lifestyle. The cultural characteristic born of such a collective lifestyle is conformity. Instead of asserting his or her individuality, a Japanese prefers to accept the consensus of the collective whole. Because he or she dislikes being outside the collective whole and derives a psychic satisfaction from being bound emotionally to the group, the "me" under the influence of others and society tends to dominate over the individualistic "I," and even the "I" is concerned with how he or she is perceived by others. The Japanese is, in the American sociologist David Riesman's terms, "other-directed" rather than "inner-directed." The "I" of the Japanese is the "I" of a communal identity.

egonoki　エゴノキ

(Japanese snowbell). Styrax japonica. Also known as chishanoki. Deciduous tree of the storax family (Styracaceae); found in mountainous regions throughout Japan as well as

in Korea and northern China. The egonoki grows to about 3–5 meters (10–16 ft) and has purplish brown bark and numerous branches with alternate, pointed, ovate leaves. Downward-facing clusters of white flowers open in early summer. The skin of the grayish white globular fruit is poisonous when immature, and country children throw the crushed skins into streams to paralyze and catch fish. The high-quality wood is used for alcove posts, carvings, pieces for SHŌGI (Japanese chess), KOKESHI dolls, and the ribs of umbrellas. A similar species, the hakuumboku (S. obassia), with longer, fragrant clusters of flowers, is also found throughout Japan.

egōshū　会合衆

(city elders). Governing body of semiautonomous towns in the late Muromachi (1333–1568) and Azuchi-Momoyama (1568–1600) periods. Composed of merchants, it was responsible for administering local markets and communities and for paying taxes to feudal proprietors. As towns prospered, the townsmen grew more independent, appropriating greater administrative and judicial powers, sometimes taking responsibility for military defense. The egōshū came to wield substantial local power, most notably in SAKAI, now part of Ōsaka Prefecture, and Ōminato, now part of the city of Ise, Mie Prefecture.

Egypt and Japan　エジプトと日本

(Ejiputo to Nihon). The opening of the Suez Canal in 1869 made Egypt the corridor to Europe for Japan. In 1896 the Nippon Yūsen Shipping Line initiated operations on routes between Europe and Japan via Egypt, a service that continued until World War II. Emperor SHŌWA (Hirohito), then prince regent, visited Egypt in 1921. A Japanese consulate general was opened in Alexandria in 1925 for the purpose of developing trade relations with the Arab nations. In 1930 an interim trade agreement was concluded with Egypt, and in 1936 a Japanese legation was established in Cairo.

As a result of World War II and the ensuing Allied OCCUPATION of Japan, diplomatic relations between Japan and Egypt were suspended from 1941 to 1953. In 1957, a cultural exchange agreement was signed by the two countries. Japan's diplomatic and foreign-aid policies vis-à-vis Arab nations assumed a higher profile in the 1970s, and relations have grown closer. In 1988 Egypt received from Japan US $172.9 million in foreign aid, the largest sum granted to a nation outside Asia. Japan's exports to Egypt in 1990 totaled US $526 million and its imports US $119 million.

Ehime Prefecture　愛媛県

(Ehime Ken). Located in northwestern Shikoku and bounded by the INLAND SEA to the north and west, Kagawa and Tokushima prefectures to the east, and Kōchi Prefecture to the south. The terrain is predominantly mountainous, and ISHIZUCHISAN (1,982 m or 6,503 ft) in the northern part of the prefecture is the highest mountain in western Japan. There are various small plains along the Inland Sea coast and in river valleys. The southern part of the coastline is highly irregular and dotted with numerous small islands. The climate is generally warm, particularly in the southern section, but the Inland Sea coast and inland mountain areas tend to be somewhat cooler and drier.

The area boasts a long history and is mentioned in various early writings and legends. Under the ancient provincial system (KOKU-GUN SYSTEM) it was known as Iyo Province. It was incorporated into the modern prefectural system in 1873.

The warm climate is suitable for fruit cultivation, and the prefecture leads the nation in this category, especially in the production of mandarin oranges and other citrus fruits. The fishing industry has declined, being partially replaced by pearl cultivation, seaweed (nori) cultivation, fishing for shellfish, and related processing industries. The northeastern coastal belt from IYO MISHIMA to IMABARI has developed various modern industries that include metals, chemicals, textiles, petroleum refining, and paper. The development of the central and southern portions of the prefecture has been hampered by mountainous terrain and remoteness from major population and commercial centers.

Major tourist attractions include DŌGO HOT SPRING and parts of the northern coastline that belong to the INLAND SEA NATIONAL PARK. The Ishizuchisan region, part of Ishizuchi Quasi-National Park, attracts hikers and sightseers. Area: 5,672 sq km (2,189 sq mi); pop: 1,515,025; capital: MATSUYAMA. Other major cities include NIIHAMA, SAIJŌ, YAWATAHAMA, and UWAJIMA.

Eichelberger, Robert Lawrence

アイケルバーガー, R. L.

(1886–1961). US general and senior field commander in the southwestern Pacific during World War II and second-ranking officer in the OCCUPATION forces in Japan from 1945 to 1948. Born in Urbana, Ohio, and a graduate of West Point, he served with the American Expeditionary Force in Siberia from 1918 to 1920, working closely with the Japanese forces (see SIBERIAN INTERVENTION). In 1942 he served under General Douglas MACARTHUR in the southwestern Pacific region, where he led US and Australian forces to their first important land victory over the Japanese at Buna in New Guinea in late 1942. He led the newly organized Eighth Army in the Philippines campaign in 1944. After the war, he commanded Occupation ground forces in Japan. He was the author of Our Jungle Road to Tokyo (1950).

eidaka　永高

Assessment of land tax in terms of cash value, specifically EIRAKUSEN coins, rather than actual volume of agricultural yield (KOKUDAKA). Eidaka was a particular form of KANDAKA, the generic term for tax assessment in monetary units. The eidaka system was used in the Kantō area during the 16th century, especially in the domain of the Later Hōjō family (see HŌJŌ FAMILY). During the early 17th century the tax system was more completely regularized on the kokudaka basis, and the eidaka system fell into disuse, especially with the proscription of eirakusen in 1609.

Eifuku Mon'in　永福門院

(1271–1342). Empress and classical (WAKA) poet. Daughter of the courtier Saionji Sanekane, in 1288 she was presented to Emperor Fushimi (1265–1317; r 1287–98) and appointed empress (chūgū). She assumed the name and title Eifuku Mon'in when she became a former empress on Fushimi's abdication in 1298. She is perhaps the foremost woman poet and patron of the innovative

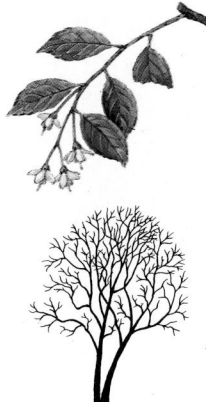

egonoki The fruit of the Japanese snowbell reaches maturity from August to September. The skin, poisonous when immature, contains a substance used as a detergent.

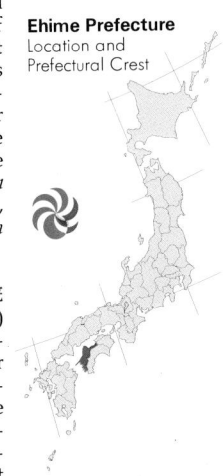

Ehime Prefecture Location and Prefectural Crest

Kyōgoku poetic faction, and her verse is representative of the Kyōgoku style. Her predominantly descriptive seasonal poems display a keen observation of nature in flux; her poems on love and other human affairs tend to be abstract, analytical, and psychologically complex. Some 150 of her poems are included in IMPERIAL ANTHOLOGIES, the bulk of them in the GYOKUYŌ WAKASHŪ (ca 1313, Collection of Jeweled Leaves) and FŪGA WAKASHŪ (ca 1349, Collection of Elegance), the imperial collections compiled and edited by her poetic school.

Eiga monogatari　　栄花物語

(tr *A Tale of Flowering Fortunes*, 1980). Historical tale of the 11th century. The first 30 chapters are often attributed to AKAZOME EMON, and the last 10 to Idewa no Ben. The tale covers the approximately 200 years from the reign of Emperor UDA (r 887–897) to that of Emperor Horikawa (r 1087–1107). The first part focuses on the life of FUJIWARA NO MICHINAGA at the pinnacle of his political glory (*eiga*), while the shorter second part, following Michinaga's death, describes the life of aristocrats at court. It is the first historical work written in the KANA syllabary. It is also the first of the *rekishi monogatari* genre, which are fictionalized or embellished accounts of historical events and figures. In the elegance of its prose style, in its narrative structure, and in its glorification of one individual, *Eiga* reveals closer affinities with the TALE OF GENJI than with its predecessor, the RIKKOKUSHI (Six National Histories).

Eight Views of Ōmi → Ōmi Hakkei

Eiheiji　　永平寺

Temple founded by DŌGEN in 1243 in Echizen Province (now part of Fukui Prefecture) to train monks in the tradition of the SŌTŌ SECT

of ZEN Buddhism. Mounting opposition from the orthodox TENDAI SECT Buddhist establishment and his own resolve to follow the injunction of his Chinese master Tiantong Rujing (T'ien-t'ung Ju-ching) to establish a monastery in the mountains away from secular concerns led Dōgen to choose Echizen as the site for the temple. The monastery, completed in 1244, was first called Daibutsuji. Two years later it was renamed Eiheiji. Eiheiji went into decline from the late 14th century and was extensively damaged by fire in 1473, but it gradually rose to eminence again as the center of Sōtō Zen from the late 16th century. Eiheiji continues to be a major Zen institution known for its rigorous monastic discipline.

Eiko and Koma　　エイコとコマ

(Eiko *to* Koma). Modern dance team; real names Otake Eiko (b 1952) and Otake Takashi (b 1948). The two met and married while studying in Japan under BUTŌ (avant-garde dance) masters HIJIKATA TATSUMI and ŌNO KAZUO. In 1972 they moved to West Germany, and in 1976 settled in New York, which continues to be their base of operations. They collaborate on every aspect of their duet performances, from choreography to staging and design. Having attained a prominent position in the avant-garde dance community overseas with performances at venues such as the Brooklyn Academy of Music's Next Wave Festival, they gave their first performance in Japan in 1989.

eikosaku　　永小作

(permanent tenancy). Form of land tenancy of the Edo period (1600–1868), also known as *eitai azukari*, *eitaisaku*, and *seshū kosaku*. In contrast to regular tenancy, under *eikosaku* tenants were given long-term rights to cultivate the land and were even able to transfer their rights. When the landlord changed, they maintained their rights with the new landlord. They paid taxes directly to the government. Their tenancy fee was low. *Eikosaku* tenancies were fewer in number than regular tenancies but were still fairly widespread throughout the country.

In many cases *eikosaku* rights were offered by landlords as a means of encouraging farmers to develop new croplands. According to Tokugawa shogunate laws, when a regular tenancy had continued for over 20 years, it was to be considered authorized as an *eikosaku*. In the Meiji period (1868–1912), the government restricted the *eikosaku* practice.

Eiraku Hozen　　永楽保全

(1795–1854). Kyōto ceramist. He turned to ceramics at age 20 or 21. He imitated the Chinese ceramics of the Ming dynasty (1368–1644), particularly in his designs using reds and golds. The colors of his glazes greatly in-

fluenced later KYŌTO CERAMICS. At various times he used the names Eiraku and Konan Hozen on his wares.

eirakusen　　永楽銭

Also known as Eiraku *tsūhō*. Chinese copper coins of the Yongle (Yung-lo; J: Eiraku) era (1403–24) of the Ming dynasty. First imported by the retired shōgun ASHIKAGA YOSHIMITSU (1358–1408) and circulated widely in Japan, especially in the Kantō region, where they were used as the basis for assessing the land tax (see EIDAKA). *Eirakusen* were coveted because their copper content was considerably higher than BITASEN, coins privately minted within Japan. In 1609 the Tokugawa shogunate (1603–1867) prohibited the use of *eirakusen*, but they remained in general circulation until the mid-17th century. See also ERIZENI.

Eirin → Motion Picture Code Committee

Eisai　　栄西

(1141–1215). Myōan Eisai, or Yōsai, founder of the RINZAI SECT of Zen Buddhism in Japan. According to the GENKŌ SHAKUSHO (1322), Eisai's father was the chief priest of the Kibitsu Shrine in Bitchū Province (now part of Okayama Prefecture). Eisai began his study of Buddhist teachings at the age of 7. At 13 he took the preliminary Buddhist precepts at ENRYAKUJI, a major TENDAI SECT temple near Kyōto, and became a monk in that monastery.

Eisai became increasingly disillusioned with the laxity of monastic discipline in the Enryakuji community. In 1168 he set out on a pilgrimage to Song (Sung) China. During his five months in China Eisai visited Tendai (Ch: Tiantai or T'ien-t'ai) monastic sites and gathered Tendai texts. In 1187 he made a second journey to China, studying Zen under the Rinzai (Ch: Linji or Lin-chi) master Xu'an Huaichang (Hsü-an Huai-ch'ang). Under Xu'an's guidance Eisai combined meditation and KŌAN study with the study of esoteric practices and the precepts (*kairitsu*) of monastic life. Upon his return to Japan in 1191, Eisai began to advocate the Chinese Zen teachings in Kyūshū and in Kyōto, quickly arousing the anger of the Enryakuji monks and their supporters at court. To defend himself against charges of heresy, Eisai wrote *Shukke taikō* (1192, Essentials of the Monastic Life) and *Kōzen gokoku ron* (1198, The Propagation of Zen for the Protection of the Nation). Eisai's apologia did little to mollify his enemies in the capital, and in 1199 he traveled to Kamakura to seek the patronage of the newly established Kamakura shogunate (1192–1333). He was warmly received by HŌJŌ MASAKO, the widow of the shogunal founder MINAMOTO NO YORITOMO, and her son, the shōgun MINAMOTO NO YORIIE. In 1202 he was made founder-abbot of a new monastery called KENNINJI, where he taught a combination of Zen, Tendai, and esoteric Buddhism.

Eisai Co, Ltd　　エーザイ[株]

(Ēzai). Research-oriented pharmaceutical company particularly well known for its medicines for cardiovascular diseases. Incorporated in 1941. It is currently diversifying into a number of health care–related fields and expanding its international operations by founding subsidiaries in the United States, Europe, and Southeast Asia. Sales for the fiscal year ending March 1991 totaled ¥205.5 billion (US $1.5 billion), and the company was capitalized at ¥22.8 billion (US $166.2 million). Headquarters are in Tōkyō.

Eisei Bunko Museum 永青文庫

(Eisei Bunko). Museum in Bunkyō Ward, Tōkyō. Founded in 1950, it houses art objects acquired by the HOSOKAWA FAMILY. The collection spans more than 700 years and contains approximately 112,000 pieces, including letters by ODA NOBUNAGA and TOKUGAWA IEYASU, calligraphy, Japanese and Chinese paintings, Buddhist images, lacquer ware, and armor. A Chinese metalwork mirror and a saddle with mother-of-pearl inlay are among the eight National Treasures held by the museum.

eiten 栄典

("honors"). Special recognition bestowed by the nation on those who have made meritorious or distinguished contributions to society. The modern system of honors, established in 1881, included the bestowal by the emperor of special decorations and special ranks in the peerage. Awards were made for outstanding contributions in government, politics, and military affairs. In 1937 the ORDER OF CULTURE was created for achievements in science, literature, art, music, and the theater.

The 1947 constitution eliminates the peerage. Moreover, article 9 (see RENUNCIATION OF WAR) eliminates the award of honors for military achievements. In addition to a small number of annual cultural awards, a much larger number of MEDALS OF HONOR is awarded in the fields of lifesaving, virtuous conduct (such as filial piety), business and industry, academic and artistic achievement, social welfare, and philanthropy. Honors are awarded by the emperor with the advice and approval of the cabinet.

Eitoku→Kanō Eitoku

Eizon 叡尊

(1201–90). Also known as Eison. Buddhist monk and founder of the Kamakura-period (1185–1333) movement to revive and popularize Buddhist moral precepts (later to become the Shingon Ritsu sect). Born in Yamato Province (now Nara Prefecture), Eizon lost his mother at the age of 7 and spent the rest of his childhood at the temple DAIGOJI in Kyōto. At age 17 he was ordained a priest. He later entered the temple TŌDAIJI in Nara, where he helped to make the Buddhist precepts more accessible to all.

Eizon served the destitute and established wildlife sanctuaries, yet he is perhaps most famous for his purported role in helping drive the invading Mongols to their defeat (see MONGOL INVASIONS OF JAPAN). In 1281 Emperor GO-UDA ordered Eizon to pray for divine aid against the Mongols, and the storm that destroyed the invading fleet (see KAMIKAZE) was believed to be the answer to his prayers.

Ejima Incident 絵島事件

(Ejima Jiken). A scandal that involved Ejima (1681–1741), a lady-in-waiting in the domestic quarters (ŌOKU) of the shogunal household, and Ikushima Shingorō (1671–1743), a kabuki actor. In 1714 Ejima was introduced to Ikushima after a visit to a shrine. Despite strict prohibitions against consorting with entertainers, she met him secretly. The two were discovered; Ejima was exiled to Takatō in Shinano Province (now Nagano Prefecture) and Ikushima to the island of Miyakejima. In an effort to improve the reputation of the Ōoku, which at the time was notorious for its moral laxity, the shogunate punished more than 1,000 people. The incident has been treated in kabuki and other forms of popular literature.

Ejima Kiseki 江島其磧

(1666–1735). A writer of UKIYO-ZŌSHI of the mid-Edo period (1600–1868). Real name Murase Gonnojō; also known as Ichirōemon. The son of a Kyōto cake shop owner, Kiseki turned to writing after having dissipated his family's fortune. His first literary effort was a JŌRURI play written for Matsumoto Jidayū (fl ca 1680). Soon afterward he became affiliated with the publisher Hachimonjiya Jishō (d 1745) and wrote a series of books evaluating contemporary actors, beginning with *Yakusha kuchijamisen* (1699, The Actor's Oral Shamisen), and ukiyo-zōshi, beginning with *Keisei irojamisen* (1701, The Courtesan's Sensual Shamisen) and culminating in *Keisei kintanki* (1711, The Courtesan's Forbidden Short Temper). All were published under Jishō's name. Kiseki then established his own publishing house. He developed the new genre of "character sketches" (katagi-mono), such as *Seken musuko katagi* (1715, Characters of Worldly Young Men), for which he is best remembered. In 1718 he resumed his association with Jishō.

ekiben 駅弁

Boxed meals sold at train stations and in many trains. *Eki* means station and *ben* is the abbreviation of *bentō* (box lunch). It is said that the first *ekiben* were served at the Utsunomiya station in Tochigi Prefecture in 1885. These first meals were very simple: rice balls and TAKUAN-ZUKE (radish pickles) wrapped in bamboo sheaths. Today the containers are usually paper or plastic. The meals now include rice and several small portions of food, such as TERIYAKI, KAMABOKO (fish-paste cakes), ham, omelets, sweet beans, and fish or vegetables simmered in soy sauce. Western-style sandwiches and other foods are also widely sold. In recent years, *ekiben* featuring special local foods such as eel and squid have increased in popularity.

ekiden kyōsō 駅伝競走

Long-distance relay race in which the distance to be run is divided into sections and a cloth sash is passed among the runners on a team and worn by each member as they run their section. The word *ekiden* derives from the names of two ancient Japanese relay systems of transportation using horses. The average number of team members ranges from 5 to 10. The distance run per section by men ranges from 5 to 20 kilometers (3–12 mi); women runners run from 2 to 10 kilometers (1–6 mi) per section. The first *ekiden kyōsō* was run in 1917 between Kyōto and Tōkyō. Today a wide variety of *ekiden kyōsō* are held in Japan, one of the oldest of which is the Tōkyō–Hakone Ōfuku Daigaku Ekiden, a competition for male college students. There are also international competitions to which foreign teams are invited.

ekisei 駅制

(post-station system). Also known as *eki-densei*. A network of facilities providing food, lodging, and horses along main thoroughfares. Provisions for post stations (*shukueki*) were made as early as 646 in the TAIKA REFORM. Similar facilities were provided for in the TAIHŌ CODE (701) and the YŌRŌ CODE (effective 757). Traveling officials were supplied with the number of men and horses designated on their government-issued *ekirei* (bells that functioned as proof of identity) and *dempu* (tickets). *Ekiko* (grooms) took care of horses and equipment and carried baggage. One of them, the *eki-chō*, assumed general responsibility. With the ENGI SHIKI statutes in 927, post stations came under the supervision of provincial governors and district (*gun*) officials. The system disintegrated with the collapse of central authority in the mid-Heian period (794–1185) but was revived in 1185 by MINAMOTO NO YORITOMO, who established the HIKYAKU postal relay system. TOKUGAWA IEYASU, founder of the Tokugawa shogunate (1603–1867), further refined the system, especially on the five major highways (the GOKAIDŌ). See also POST-STATION TOWNS.

ekisha 易者

Originally, the name given to fortune-tellers employing the Chinese classic of divination, the *Yijing* (*I ching*; J: *Ekikyō*). The traditional method of interpretation is based on 8 symbols called trigrams which are paired in various combinations to select texts for consultation. The pattern of the trigrams and their pairings is determined with the aid of 50 bamboo sticks (*zeichiku*) and 6 wooden divining blocks (*sangi*) manipulated by the diviner. This form of divination flourished in Japan in the Edo period (1600–1868), when it was both the subject of serious research by scholars and practiced by popular fortune-tellers. Today, the term *ekisha* is applied more broadly to refer to all types of diviners, including practitioners of PALMISTRY and PHYSIOGNOMY. Street-corner diviners conducting business from behind a small table by the light of a paper lantern are still a familiar part of the nocturnal landscape.

ekiden kyōsō An exhausted runner passes the cloth sash to her teammate on the final leg of the 1989 Yokohama International Women's Ekiden.

ekiben
1 A box lunch from Odawara Station in Kanagawa Prefecture.
2 A double-decker box lunch from Kobuchizawa Station in Yamanashi Prefecture.

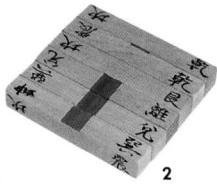

ekisha
1 Here an *ekisha* manipulates bamboo sticks called *zeichiku*.
2 Wooden blocks called *sangi* are laid out according to the results given by the *zeichiku*. The red face of the block indicates *yin*, the other face, *yang*.

elections Surrounded by supporters and passersby, a candidate for the House of Representatives (wearing sash) is introduced by the chairman of his party.

elderly workers 高齢労働者

(*kōrei rōdōsha*). The percentage of people age 65 and above relative to the total Japanese population is expected to reach 15.6 percent, a level similar to that of the West, by the end of the 20th century. A distinctive feature of the elderly population in Japan is the high proportion of those who are employed. In the 1960s some 18–22 percent of elderly women and over 55 percent of elderly men were employed, while in the United States, the United Kingdom, and France annual median figures were 10–11 percent for women and 21–28 percent for men. Since then, with the decrease in the proportion of elderly workers employed in agriculture and forestry and the increase in the numbers of industrial employees retiring at 60, the total percentage of elderly workers has shown a marked decline. However, it is still high (about 35 percent) in comparison with levels of 15–20 percent in the United States and the United Kingdom. Of Japanese men between the ages of 60 and 64, 70 percent are still engaged in some kind of work, and the question of government and company policies for elderly workers is becoming one of paramount importance.

Ordinarily, the retirement age is set by companies at 60, and elderly workers must seek new employment if they wish to continue working, but opportunities are few; half of the unemployed population in Japan is over 40. Over half the elderly workers who manage to become reemployed find jobs in unskilled areas such as security, shops, other service occupations, or simple physical labor. Many work in small companies as day laborers or part-timers, and, for most, reemployment means a considerable drop in working conditions. With the aim of maintaining standards of working conditions for elderly workers, the government is taking increasing responsibility for dealing with the problems of an aging work force.

elections 選挙制度

(*senkyo seido*). Japan has had a national election system since the promulgation of the CONSTITUTION OF THE EMPIRE OF JAPAN on 11 February 1889. The extension of the franchise, limited at first to a small proportion of the adult male population, took place gradually, culminating in the adoption of universal suffrage shortly after the end of World War II.

The Prewar System—The first national election for the HOUSE OF REPRESENTATIVES took place in 1890, but the right to vote was restricted to males who paid annual taxes of ¥15 or more. Over the next three and a half decades the number of enfranchised voters grew from fewer than 500,000 to about 3 million. The Universal Manhood Suffrage Law of 1925 expanded the electorate to

about 12 million by granting the vote to all male citizens 25 years of age or older (see UNIVERSAL MANHOOD SUFFRAGE MOVEMENT), though women were not enfranchised until December 1945.

Before 1945 there were fewer opportunities in general for popular participation in Japanese government, and many executive and legislative positions were appointive. In the IMPERIAL DIET, members of the House of Representatives were elected, but seats in the HOUSE OF PEERS were either appointive or hereditary. LOCAL GOVERNMENT was directly subordinate to the central government, whose authority was exercised through the HOME MINISTRY. Local and prefectural assemblies were popularly elected, but prefectural governors were appointed by the national government. City mayors were appointed by prefectural governors from a list of names submitted by city assemblies. Headmen and mayors of villages and towns were elected by their respective local assemblies.

Current Practices—The election system was given its present form by the Public Office Election Law of April 1950, which embodies some of the provisions of existing laws—prewar and postwar—as well as those of the postwar CONSTITUTION OF JAPAN. All Japanese citizens are eligible to vote if they have reached the age of 20 and have met a three-month residency requirement (for voting in local elections). Candidates for political office must meet the stated age requirement for each office. Members of the House of Representatives and of prefectural and local assemblies must be at least 25 years old. Members of the HOUSE OF COUNCILLORS and prefectural governors must be at least 30.

Japan has had a comprehensive election system incorporating all levels of government since the end of World War II. Under current election laws, members of all legislative bodies, including both houses of the DIET and prefectural, city, town, and village assemblies, are selected by popular vote. Political executives, including prefectural governors and mayors or other chief officials of local governments, are also chosen in popular elections. The prime minister, who is elected by the Diet, is the only political executive not chosen by direct popular vote. Today elections for half of the 252 members of the House of Councillors are held every three years in a combination of nationwide and prefectural districts. In the House of Representatives, 512 members are elected for four-year terms, typically in elections held irregularly after the dissolution of the House by the emperor at the request of the prime minister. Elections are held every four years for most prefectural and local executive offices and assemblies, although some local executives and assemblies are elected at other times because of special local circumstances.

The two national legislative bodies have traditionally been elected in multimember districts, but the size of these districts has varied over time. At present, 511 of the 512 members of the House of Representatives and about a quarter of the 252 members of the House of Councillors are elected in multimember constituencies. Unlike European practice, in elections to the House of Representatives there is no proportional formula for allocating seats in multimember districts according to the party's share of the vote. Rather, winners are selected from among the top vote-getters in each constituency, with each enfranchised citizen having one nontransferable vote. In 1983, however,

a proportional representation system was introduced in elections for the 100 seats in the House of Councillors that are elected on a nationwide basis.

In an effort to achieve representational parity among districts for the House of Representatives, the number of Diet seats allocated to each constituency is decided on the basis of population. In the wake of the rapid population growth in Japan's cities and suburbs after 1950, the number of seats allocated to certain urban and suburban constituencies was split and new constituencies were formed. This resulted in an overall growth of the House from 466 seats in 1946 to 512 seats in 1986. Still, considerable underrepresentation of urban districts has continued into the 1990s. In the summer of 1991 the number of people represented by a single Diet member in the most heavily populated (urban) district was still more than three times as great as the number represented by a single Diet member in the least populous (rural) district (see REAPPORTIONMENT ISSUE).

The medium-sized constituency system (CHŪ SENKYOKU SEI), in which each district sends between three and five representatives to the lower house, has been frequently criticized since the 1970s as the breeding ground for the kind of POLITICAL CORRUPTION manifested in both the LOCKHEED SCANDAL and the RECRUIT SCANDAL. In response to public outcry over the continued existence of "money politics" and the lack of policy-oriented politics, serious deliberation over reform measures that would introduce proportional representation and smaller election districts into elections for the House of Representatives began in the early 1990s. The proposed reforms, originally introduced by the LIBERAL DEMOCRATIC PARTY (LDP), affect many Diet members directly, and opposition to them has been intense.

Administration—Japan's electoral system is overseen by election administration committees within each administrative division of the country, i.e., prefectures, cities, towns, and villages. Administrators in local-government election sections or bureaus assist the election committees in carrying out the day-to-day tasks of managing the system. Election-system administrators in the MINISTRY OF HOME AFFAIRS regulate the system as a whole and collect various statistics on elections and electoral practices.

Laws specifying acceptable campaign practices are extremely detailed and strict in Japan. The period within which public campaigns can be conducted, campaign funding and expenditures, and such matters as the number of posters permitted, size of media advertisements, and many other aspects of campaigning are precisely spelled out. Such practices as sponsorship of parties for constituents, door-to-door visits to solicit voter support, and gift-giving by candidates and their supporters are prohibited. At the time of each national election several hundred to several thousand election violations are reported.

Because multimember constituencies are the rule in Japan's national elections and many districts contain more seats than parties, competition for seats within the major parties, particularly the LDP, is often fierce. Competition encourages independence on the part of individual candidates, who in many cases run more as factional than party candidates. Because of this, many citizens report that they base their voting choices as much on the nature of the individual candidate as they do on his or her official party affiliation.

electric power 電力

(denryoku). Electric power was introduced to Japan in the form of thermal power in 1887; hydroelectric power followed in 1890. From 1887 to 1911, thermal power predominated. Demand for electricity, used primarily to replace gas and kerosene lighting, was mostly limited to cities. But most hydroelectric power plants were located far from cities, and power transmission voltage was low, so that electricity could be transmitted only over short distances, making hydroelectric power unsuitable for city use. Private hydroelectric generating units were used at mines and other places far from cities. Hydroelectric power became more important than thermal power after 1912 and continued to predominate during an almost 50-year period that spanned the two world wars. Early in this period most hydroelectric power was generated by harnessing the natural flow of rivers. In the 1920s, electric utilities began selling surplus electricity inexpensively, encouraging the expansion of electrochemical and other industries. As the great demand for electricity continued, thermal power generating capacity was increased and became almost as important as hydroelectric power.

During the reconstruction period that followed World War II, development of new power generating sites, both thermal and hydroelectric, rapidly increased through the importation of advanced foreign technology. Heavy equipment and large dam power plants began to be used in the development of hydroelectric power to decrease dependence on the natural flow of rivers. In spite of these innovations, thermal power generating facilities took on more importance because construction of hydroelectric generating facilities required a good deal of time and capital—scarce resources in postwar Japan.

After 1960, a period of high economic growth in Japan, iron and steel, chemical, machinery, and other heavy industries expanded rapidly. With the resulting rise in individual incomes, electric appliances became common household items and demand for electricity rose accordingly. As electric generating capacity increased, thermal power continued to gain in importance. Japan's first nuclear power plant for commercial use began operating in July 1966, and after the 1973 oil shock there was an upsurge in the development of nuclear power and a decline in the percentage of electricity generated by thermal power. As of December 1989, 37 nuclear reactors were in operation with a total output of approximately 187.9 billion kilowatt hours. The construction of 17 new reactors is planned as part of the government's program to reduce the nation's dependence on imported energy supplies and develop a stable multiple-energy-supply policy capable of meeting Japan's growing energy requirements. In 1989 total generating capacity amounted to 791.2 billion kilowatt hours, of which oil-fired power stations supplied 32.0 percent; nuclear power plants, 23.1 percent; liquefied natural gas (LNG), 18.7 percent; hydroelectric power plants, 11.3 percent; coal, 14.7 percent; and alternative energy sources such as geothermal power, 0.2 percent. See also ENERGY SOURCES.

Recently nonindustrial use of electricity has increased and the load factor (average amount of electricity generated in proportion to the maximum amount of electricity

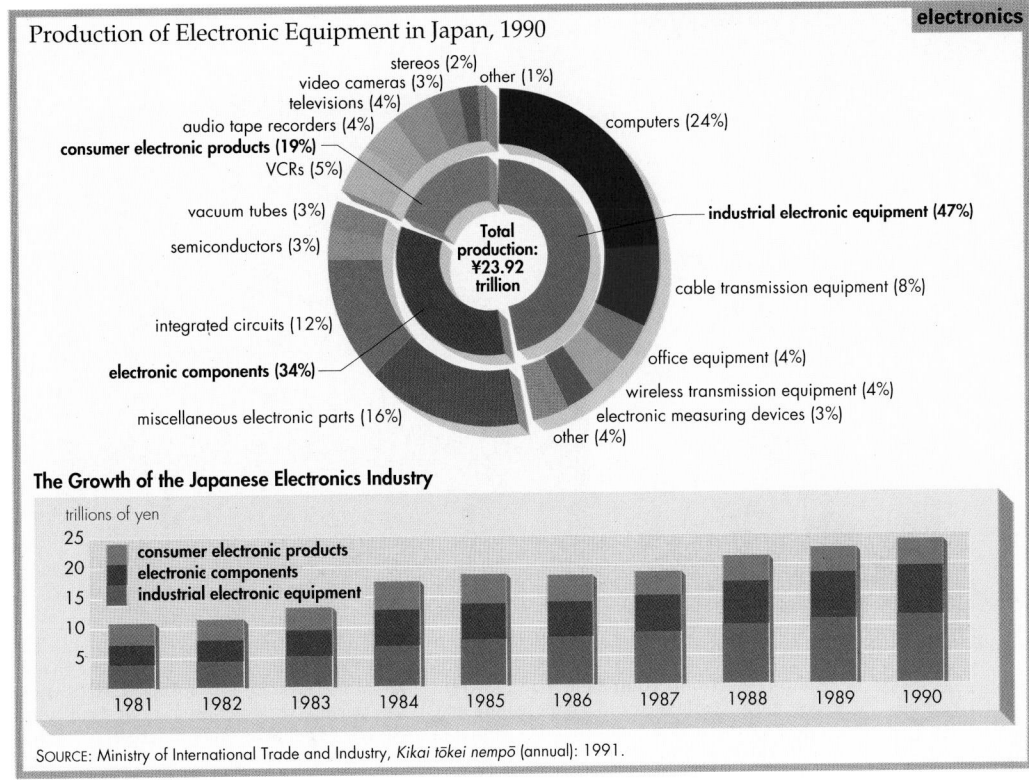

Production of Electronic Equipment in Japan, 1990

Total production: ¥23.92 trillion

stereos (2%)
video cameras (3%)
televisions (4%)
audio tape recorders (4%)
consumer electronic products (19%)
VCRs (5%)
vacuum tubes (3%)
semiconductors (3%)
integrated circuits (12%)
electronic components (34%)
miscellaneous electronic parts (16%)
other (4%)
other (1%)
computers (24%)
industrial electronic equipment (47%)
cable transmission equipment (8%)
office equipment (4%)
wireless transmission equipment (4%)
electronic measuring devices (3%)

The Growth of the Japanese Electronics Industry

trillions of yen

consumer electronic products
electronic components
industrial electronic equipment

25
20
15
10
5

1981 1982 1983 1984 1985 1986 1987 1988 1989 1990

SOURCE: Ministry of International Trade and Industry, *Kikai tōkei nempō* (annual): 1991.

generated) has declined. To avoid air pollution, there has been an increased use of low-sulfur crude oil, liquefied natural gas, and naphtha. However, COAL is used in order to encourage and protect domestic coal production as a result of political rather than energy considerations.

In Japan maximum transmission voltage has been 500 kilovolts since 1974 because of the increase in the number of nuclear and other generating facilities built far from cities. Increasingly, safer underground transmission lines have replaced overhead power lines close to urban areas. Installing an overhead alternating-current transmission line between Honshū and Hokkaidō proved infeasible, so an undersea direct current cable, completed in 1979, has been used instead.

Electric Power Development Co, Ltd 電源開発[株]

(Dengen Kaihatsu). Company constructing electric power facilities, such as hydroelectric, thermal, and geothermal power plants, as well as main transmission lines, which it sells to private electric power companies. The Electric Power Development Co was incorporated in 1952 based on the Law for the Acceleration of Electric Power Development (Dengen Kaihatsu Sokushin Hō). The company owns and operates 60 power plants with a total capacity of 12,240 megawatts. It was engaged in 223 overseas technical cooperation projects in 37 countries as of the end of March 1991. It also receives foreign trainees and dispatches technologists abroad. Annual sales for the fiscal year ending March 1991 totaled ¥340.9 billion (US $2.5 billion), and the company was capitalized at ¥70.6 billion (US $514.6 million). Headquarters are in Tōkyō.

Electric Power Industry, Central Research Institute of the
電力中央研究所

(Denryoku Chūō Kenkyūjo). An institute conducting research into economic and technical problems related to the electric power industry. Established as a joint corporation in 1951 by Japan's nine biggest electric power companies. Its main office is located in Tōkyō, with seven other research institutes and laboratories located in the Kantō region.

electronics エレクトロニクス

(erekutoronikusu). The Japanese electronics industry is one of the largest and most advanced in the world and stands at the center of the nation's economy. The industry experienced especially rapid development in the post–World War II period, growing on the foundation of consumer electronics. High-technology products such as computers and semiconductors became a focus of the industry in the 1970s, signaling a shift in emphasis from consumer to commercial and industrial equipment. In 1990 the total domestic output of the Japanese electronics industry, including semiconductor production, was valued at ¥23.9 trillion (US $165.2 billion), of which household items such as VIDEOCASSETTE RECORDERS and televisions accounted for 19 percent; industrial electronic equipment, 47 percent; and electronic components, 34 percent.

The latest devices invented overseas, such as telephones, wireless communications equipment, and vacuum tubes, as well as information, were transmitted to Japan in the course of the Meiji period (1868–1912). During the Russo-Japanese War (1904–05) the Japanese navy used crystal detectors for wireless communications. Radio broadcasting commenced in Japan in 1925, five years after it did in the United States, and this is generally acknowledged to be the starting point of modern electronics engineering in Japan.

The Yagi-Uda antenna, which is the antenna most widely used in the world for VHF television reception, was invented in 1926 by YAGI HIDETSUGU and Uda Shintarō (1896–1976) of Tōhoku University. The first successful all-electronic image reproduction with the cathode-ray tube, which made possible the subsequent growth of television broadcasting, was announced in 1926 by TAKAYANAGI KENJIRŌ. During 1928, a split-anode type of magnetron known as the Ōsaka tube was invented by a group from Ōsaka University led by OKABE KINJIRŌ.

331

ema
1 These small *ema*, or *koema*, have been offered up as petitions to a shrine's deities for assistance in the achievement of some objective. **2** One meter in width, this *ema* is of the large type known as *ōema*. It depicts a horse and groom and was dedicated in 1643 to Iino Hachiman Shrine in Iwaki, Fukushima Prefecture.

Directly prior to World War II, the output of electrical machinery and apparatus, including electronic equipment, had grown to become a sizable sector in Japanese industry. Most of the leading makers were affiliated with ZAIBATSU industrial conglomerates and began as subsidiaries of giant shipbuilding and mining companies. Many factories were converted to munitions plants during World War II, and, as contacts with overseas technology were cut off, electronics inevitably stagnated. However, research efforts contributed to the postwar development of television and microwave networks.

Major companies were swept up in the postwar ZAIBATSU DISSOLUTION. Moreover, as interchange with overseas technology had been suspended for a long time, the backward state of most Japanese makers was readily apparent. With the outbreak of the Korean War in 1950, however, restrictions imposed by the OCCUPATION forces were gradually lifted, and the electronics industry rapidly recovered in the context of the TOKUJU (war procurement) economic boom.

The effects on electronics of the authorization of private radio broadcasting in 1951 and of the inauguration of television broadcasting in 1953 were complex, but the invention of the transistor in 1948 in the United States had even greater impact. Electronics underwent explosive development in the 10 years after the SONY CORPORATION produced the world's first transistor radio in 1955, and the position of electronics in industrial and academic circles grew in importance. During this period the industry showed a consistent annual growth rate of 20 percent. Under the government's research subsidy policy, basic research in materials science and circuit techniques was stepped up at university and government laboratories. Such efforts contributed not only to technological progress but also to developing capable personnel.

In order to protect and encourage Japan's electronics industry, the government restricted direct investment of foreign capital and worked out special tax measures aimed at stimulating investment. For the purpose of improving the efficiency of nationwide technological development, the MINISTRY OF INTERNATIONAL TRADE AND INDUSTRY (MITI) encouraged the establishment of industry promotion associations and research and development projects in official, private, and academic circles. As a result of such efforts, Japan's electronics industry had achieved in-

ternational competitiveness by 1965. The field was led by three major electric manufacturers (HITACHI, LTD; TŌSHIBA CORPORATION; MITSUBISHI ELECTRIC CORPORATION), four home electric appliance manufacturers (MATSUSHITA ELECTRIC INDUSTRIAL CO, LTD; SAN'YŌ ELECTRIC CO, LTD; Sony Corporation; SHARP CORPORATION), and three telecommunications equipment makers (NEC CORPORATION; FUJITSU, LTD; OKI ELECTRIC INDUSTRY CO, LTD).

In the 1970s the pace of the industry's development was extremely rapid, and the industry gradually changed its emphasis from consumer products to industrial equipment. Output in 1978 was more than six times the 1966 level, and quality and productivity were greatly improved, considerably enhancing the competitive position of Japan's electronics industry in international markets.

Industry has since made use of high-level technology to promote the development of industrial equipment that is comparatively immune to fluctuations in business conditions. In industrial electronics Japan is advanced in such areas as digital computers, high-data-rate microwave communications systems, optical fiber communications systems, numerically controlled machine tools, and robots. Production of semiconductors improved rapidly as a result of intense investment in equipment and technology, and by the mid-1980s Japanese companies had become the world's leading suppliers of semiconductors (see SEMICONDUCTOR INDUSTRY). The VLSI Technology Research Association, set up jointly by the leading companies under the guidance of MITI, played a critical role in this advance. The technological revolution in the semiconductor industry in the 1980s led to a rapid increase in the quality and functional capacities of the products of the Japanese electronics industry. Industrial electronics, telecommunications equipment, and COMPUTERS have become the industry's main products, but international markets for sophisticated consumer electronics products such as videocassette recorders and compact disc players are also dominated by Japanese companies. Today, the electronics industry is one of the three major machinery industries in Japan.

Electrotechnical Laboratory
電子技術総合研究所
(Denshi Gijutsu Sōgō Kenkyūjo). Laboratory attached to the Agency of Industrial Science and Technology, Ministry of International Trade and Industry (MITI). Located in

the city of Tsukuba, Ibaraki Prefecture, it was established in 1891. Its duty is to test, research, and maintain the standard units in the areas of electric technology, electronic technology, and basic science. Its publications are *Denshi gijutsu sōgō kenkyūjo kenkyū hōkoku* (Research Report of the Electrotechnical Laboratory) and *Denshi gijutsu sōgō kenkyūjo ihō* (Bulletin of the Electrotechnical Laboratory).

elementary education
初等教育
(*shotō kyōiku*). The Japanese term *shotō kyōiku* refers both to optional kindergarten (*yōchien*) programs and to the compulsory six years of study at ELEMENTARY SCHOOLS (*shōgakkō*). From the Meiji period (1868–1912), compulsory elementary education was provided on a universal basis. In 1886 a two-level structure was created, with a four-year compulsory primary level (extended to six years in 1907) plus four years of SECONDARY EDUCATION. Today's system, reorganized under the EDUCATIONAL REFORMS OF 1947, provides six years of primary education starting at age six. The responsibility for establishing and maintaining schools is borne by municipalities. The curriculum consists of the Japanese language, social studies, arithmetic, the natural sciences, music, arts and crafts, physical education, and home economics, as well as MORAL EDUCATION and extracurricular activities. Teaching objectives, subject content, hours of instruction, and a number of other aspects of school administration are stipulated by the MINISTRY OF EDUCATION.

elementary schools
小学校
(*shōgakkō*). Japanese elementary schools offer the first six years of the nine-year course of education that is compulsory in Japan. Pupils are enrolled at age six and normally attend a public school in the area in which they live. Private elementary schools exist, but 99 percent of Japanese elementary school pupils were enrolled in public schools in 1990. Classes are coeducational and made up of pupils of the same age. The standard class size is 45 or below. A single teacher is assigned to each class and responsible for instruction in all subjects, except in the upper elementary grades, in which subjects such as music, drawing, and manual arts are taught by special instructors. All pupils are required to follow the same SCHOOL CURRICULUM. The school year, which begins in April and ends in March, is divided into three terms; the students receive REPORT CARDS at the end of each trimester.

Eliot, Charles Norton Edgcumbe
エリオット, C. N. E.
(1862–1931). British diplomat and scholar. Born in Sibford Gower, England. After graduating from Oxford University, Eliot served in various diplomatic positions abroad. He retired from the foreign service in 1904, but in 1918 he was posted to Omsk in connection with the Allied SIBERIAN INTERVENTION. In 1919 he was appointed ambassador to Japan; in this capacity he opposed the termination of the ANGLO-JAPANESE ALLIANCE. His publications include *Letters from the Far East* (1907) and *Japanese Buddhism* (1935).

Elisséeff, Serge
エリセーエフ, S.
(1889–1975). Scholar of Japanese studies. Born in St. Petersburg, Russia. Elisséeff went to the University of Berlin, where he studied Japanese and Chinese from 1907 to 1908, and then enrolled at Tōkyō University. The first

Westerner to be accepted as a regular student by the university, he specialized in Japanese literature.

In 1914 Elisséeff enrolled in the University of St. Petersburg. Upon receiving his doctorate in 1916, he was appointed lecturer in the Japanese language. He left Russia in 1920, eventually settling in Paris and becoming a professor at the Ecole des Hautes Etudes of the Sorbonne.

In 1932 Elisséeff accepted an invitation from Harvard University to teach in its Department of Far Eastern Languages. Two years later he was appointed chairman of the department and director of the Harvard-Yenching Institute. He founded the *Harvard Journal of Asiatic Studies* in 1936. With Edwin O. REISCHAUER he wrote *Elementary Japanese for College Students* (1944), which for many years was the standard textbook.

Elizabeth Saunders Home

エリザベスサンダースホーム

(Erizabesu Sandāsu Hōmu). Orphanage and foundling home established in 1948 by SAWADA MIKI for abandoned children of racially mixed parentage (*konketsuji*). The home, named after the first contributor and located in the town of Ōiso, Kanagawa Prefecture, has endeavored to provide shelter and training for these children. During the 1970s the Saunders Home shifted its supportive efforts toward helping racially mixed young people to obtain Japanese citizenship and to be more successfully assimilated into Japanese society. Now the home also serves as an orphanage for children from broken families.

ema

絵馬

(alternate pronunciations: *ima, emma, euma*). Traditional generic term for pictorial votive offerings. The custom of dedicating votive objects to the deities of revered natural features and places, as well as to shrines and temples, has an enduring history in Japanese religious life and may be traced back to early animistic practices. Over the centuries the main artistic expression of this custom has been the production of *ema*, paintings characteristically executed on flat wooden surfaces. The term *ema* has its origin in ancient ritual, as is apparent from its two character-components: *e* (picture or pictorial representation) and *ma* (horse), a combination that indicates that these votive pictures evolved as modest substitutes for the live horses traditionally installed in prestigious Shintō shrines.

Although some *ema* may be dated as early as the 8th century, the earliest preserved *ema* that can be reliably dated go back only to the end the 14th century. By the mid-Muromachi period (1333–1568), two interrelated but categorically distinct lines are apparent in the evolution of *ema*. One continues the earlier popular religious tradition of works of small size (known as *koema*, or small *ema*) offered by members of the general populace, either in fulfillment of a vow or as an entreaty to a deity for help in achieving an objective or rectifying some unfortunate condition.

Ema belonging to the second line (known as *ōema*, or big *ema*) are characteristically large in dimension and are usually displayed in conspicuous locations in temples or shrines, often in a separate structure specially erected for this purpose called an *emadō*. Among extant pieces there are many that are carefully signed and dated, not only by aspiring lesser-known men but also by some of the most prominent names in later Japanese painting, among them KANŌ MOTONOBU, KANŌ SANRAKU, and KANŌ TAN'YŪ (Kanō school); IKE NO TAIGA and TANI BUNCHŌ (*bunjinga* school); AŌDŌ DENZEN and SHIBA KŌKAN ("Dutch" school); Kō Sūkoku (1737–1811) and HANABUSA ITCHŌ (Hanabusa School); TORII KIYONOBU I, TORII KIYONOBU II, TORII KIYONAGA, KATSUKAWA SHUNSHŌ, HOKUSAI, UTAGAWA TOYOKUNI, and UTAGAWA KUNIYOSHI (*ukiyo-e* school); MARUYAMA ŌKYO, MORI SOSEN, and MATSUMURA KEIBUN (Maruyama-Shijō school); and independents such as Nagasawa ROSETSU and SOGA SHŌHAKU.

emakimono

絵巻物

(literally, "rolled object with pictures"). Long, horizontal handscroll, unrolled from right to left, containing illustrations that tell a story, often with accompanying text. The format, recognized as one of the high points of painting in the native Japanese style (see YAMATO-E), flourished during the Heian

period (794–1185) and Kamakura period (1185–1333).

Format—Handscrolls consist of numerous pieces of paper or silk joined horizontally and rolled around a cylinder or *jiku*. The dimensions of scrolls may vary greatly. The number of rolls making up an *emaki* set may vary from 1 or 2 to as many as 48.

History—The handscroll was in common use in China by the 1st century and was introduced into Japan in the 6th or 7th century along with Buddhism. The earliest extant *emakimono* in Japan is the *Kako genzai inga kyō emaki* (Illustrated Sutra of Past and Present Cause and Effect), popularly known as the *E inga kyō*. The work presents the life of the historical Buddha, Shaka (Skt: Sākyamuni).

The most detailed information about the types of handscrolls that were made by the

preaching. The 12th-century JIGOKU-ZŌSHI (Scrolls of Hells) is perhaps the foremost Japanese example of this type of *emaki*.

The classic 12th-century example of the *setsuwa emaki*, or folktale scroll, is the SHIGISAN ENGI EMAKI (The Legends of Mt. Shigi). The late-12th-century BAN DAINAGON EMAKI (Scroll of the Courtier Ban Dainagon) bears stylistic resemblances to the *Shigisan* scrolls.

The CHŌJŪ GIGA (Scrolls of Frolicking Animals and Humans) dates from the late 12th and 13th centuries. In the early Kamakura period, many new themes appeared in addition to the already familiar romances, collections of poetry, and religious and secular folktales: tales of battle such as the HEIJI MONOGATARI EMAKI (Tale of Heiji Scroll); biographies of priests—for example, the *Ippen Shōnin eden* (Pictorial Biography of the Monk Ippen); and diaries, including the *Murasaki Shikibu nikki emaki* (Diary of Lady Murasaki Scroll).

In later centuries *emakimono* declined in quality as monochrome INK PAINTING became more popular. However, the TOSA SCHOOL of painters continued working in the indigenous Japanese painting style from about the 15th to the 19th century, and a few fine examples of *emakimono* exist from the Edo period (1600–1868).

Embree, John Fee   エンブリー, J. F.

(1908–50). US anthropologist. Born in New Haven, Connecticut; educated at the universities of Hawaii, Toronto, and Chicago. From 1935 to 1936 he conducted fieldwork in the village of Sue, Kuma District, Kumamoto Prefecture. His *Suye Mura: A Japanese Village* (1939) was a pioneering work in cultural anthropological studies of Japanese villages. Embree also did research on societies in Thailand and other Southeast Asian countries.

embroidery   刺繍

(*shishū*). The oldest extant example of Japanese embroidery is the *Tenjukoku mandara shūchō*, a Buddhist MANDALA dating from the Asuka period (593–710). It belongs to the *shūbutsu* tradition of Chinese Buddhist embroidery. Even though trade with China lapsed, Japanese embroidery techniques later became more intricate and were applied to *kimono* and accessories. By the 15th century, after trade between Japan and China was reestablished, Chinese techniques exerted a strong influence on Japanese embroidery. The late Muromachi period (1333–1568) to the early Azuchi-Momoyama period (1568–1600) saw the development of the TSUJIGAHANA technique, a combination of tie-dyeing and embroidery used to produce sumptuous silk garments. In the Edo period (1600–1868) embroidery was increasingly used in combination with dyed cloth. Before the Meiji period (1868–1912) the word for embroidery was *sashi* or *nui* (literally, "sewing"). The word *shishū* was first used during the Meiji period and now generally refers to Western-style embroidery, while the term Nihon *shishū* ("Japanese embroidery") refers to traditional embroidery.

emigration   移民

(*imin*). Emigration has never been a major social trend in Japan. If emigration between 1850 and 1950 is expressed as a percentage of population increase, the emigration rates of such countries as England (74%) and Italy (47%) far exceed Japan's (1%). The major destinations of Japanese emigrants have

been the United States, Brazil, Canada, Argentina, and Peru; in none of these countries do people of Japanese ancestry exceed 1 percent of the population. Japanese emigration began relatively late and fluctuated markedly as domestic conditions, government emigration policy, and the receptivity of destinations changed.

Early Emigration—As part of Japan's NATIONAL SECLUSION policy, in 1635 the Tokugawa shogunate forbade the return of Japanese from trading settlements abroad; the fate of these first, involuntary emigrants is unknown. Thereafter all exit from Japan was forbidden until 1866.

In the Meiji period (1868–1912) the Japanese government discouraged emigration until the deflationary policy of the 1880s created such severe agrarian distress that the government turned to emigration as a form of relief. Officially supervised emigration to Hawaii began under a treaty between the Hawaiian and Japanese governments in 1885, and by 1893 some 30,000 emigrants had entered Hawaii to work on its sugarcane plantations. In 1891 an Emigration Bureau was established. The Emigrant Protection Law was promulgated in 1896. From 1893 on, contract labor began emigrating to Australia, Fiji, Guadeloupe, Canada, Mexico, and Peru, largely to work in mining and in sugarcane cultivation.

The Growth of Exclusionism—No sooner did the mechanisms for emigration become regularized than the countries that had been the major destinations of Japanese emigrants began to close their doors. Australia forbade Japanese immigration in 1898; Canada set limits in 1908; and, in accordance with the so-called GENTLEMEN'S AGREEMENT of 1907–08, the Japanese government allowed only those Japanese with close relatives already living in the United States to migrate there. The United States unilaterally ended Japanese immigration in 1924. Central and South America (particularly Brazil) became alternate destinations, but in Brazil exclusionist sentiment against Japanese immigrants also developed.

Japanese expansion into continental Asia in the 1930s opened another avenue for emigration as a way to ease agrarian population pressure in Japan. However, Japanese emigration to Manchuria after 1931 and to Japanese-occupied China after 1937 was predominantly from the urban-based social and economic elite, whose chief function was to establish and maintain political and economic infrastructures in order to exploit the resources of those areas. In Manchuria in 1939 only 10.3 percent of civilian Japanese were engaged in agriculture; in occupied China in 1940, only 1.0 percent.

Postwar Emigration—During the postwar Allied Occupation, not only were Japanese not permitted to emigrate, but more than 3.1 million Japanese civilians and 3.0 million military personnel were repatriated from former colonies and occupied territories in Asia and the Pacific, placing additional strain on the war-ravaged resources of Japan. Emigration resumed in 1952, primarily to North and South America.

Postwar emigration reached its peak in the late 1950s; thereafter Japan's rapid economic growth and the resulting domestic demand for labor reduced emigration dramatically. As in the prewar period, postwar emigration has been the greatest from southern Japan, particularly from Kyūshū and Okinawa.

Although emigration has had little effect

embroidery

1 The *Tenjukoku mandara shūchō*, the oldest surviving work of Japanese embroidery. Made in 622 at the time of Prince Shōtoku's death, the piece was later extensively reworked. The prince is depicted in a heavenly paradise. Chūgūji, Nara. National Treasure.
2 A silk *kimono* embroidered with wisteria flowers. Early 18th century. Tōkyō National Museum.

early 11th century comes from the "E-awase" (Picture Contest) chapter of the TALE OF GENJI (*Genji monogatari*), a novel written by MURASAKI SHIKIBU around the year 1000. The novel describes handscrolls executed by professional artists, most of whom worked for the imperial court. An illustrated handscroll of the *Tale of Genji*, known as the GENJI MONOGATARI EMAKI, was produced in the early 12th century. The fragments that remain constitute the most complex and accomplished of the illustrated romances in *emakimono* format. Among the other notable illustrated romances in the so-called courtly style is the 12th-century NEZAME MONOGATARI EMAKI (Tale of Nezame Scroll).

In later centuries, *emaki* carried religious messages and were used as visual aids in

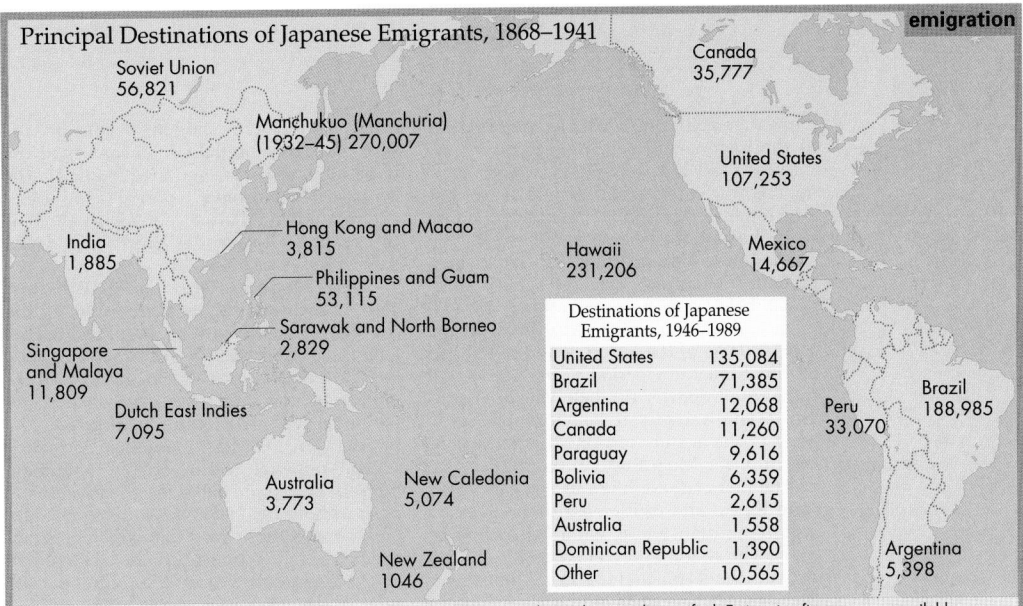

Principal Destinations of Japanese Emigrants, 1868–1941

Canada 35,777
Soviet Union 56,821
Manchukuo (Manchuria) (1932–45) 270,007
United States 107,253
India 1,885
Hong Kong and Macao 3,815
Hawaii 231,206
Mexico 14,667
Philippines and Guam 53,115
Singapore and Malaya 11,809
Sarawak and North Borneo 2,829
Dutch East Indies 7,095
Australia 3,773
New Caledonia 5,074
New Zealand 1046
Peru 33,070
Brazil 188,985
Argentina 5,398

Destinations of Japanese Emigrants, 1946–1989	
United States	135,084
Brazil	71,385
Argentina	12,068
Canada	11,260
Paraguay	9,616
Bolivia	6,359
Peru	2,615
Australia	1,558
Dominican Republic	1,390
Other	10,565

NOTE: Countries listed are those with more than 1,000 Japanese emigrants during the periods specified. Emigration figures are unavailable on a country-by-country basis for Europe, Africa, and western Asia. During the period 1868–1941, there were 7,980 emigrants to destinations other than those shown. Of these, 7,159 left Japan in the years 1899–1901. Figures given here may differ from those appearing elsewhere in this encyclopedia, which are based on different sources.
SOURCES: Ministry of Foreign Affairs, *Waga kokumin no kaigai hatten* (1971); Japan International Cooperation Agency, *Kaigai ijū tōkei* (1990).

on Japanese population pressure, Japanese emigrants have made notable contributions to the countries of destination, despite the obstacles imposed by anti-Japanese reactions and measures such as the relocation programs during World War II, when Japanese nationals and citizens of Japanese descent in North and South America were dispossessed and imprisoned in internment camps (see JAPANESE AMERICANS, WARTIME RELOCATION OF). In general, the prewar generation of Japanese emigrants tried to maintain their own language, culture, and community patterns. Second- and third-generation descendants of emigrants have tended to acculturate, adopting the native languages, religions, and, to a certain extent, lifestyles in South and North America. See also BRAZIL, JAPANESE IMMIGRANTS IN; CANADA, JAPANESE IMMIGRANTS IN; JAPANESE AMERICANS IN HAWAII; JAPANESE AMERICANS.

emigration and immigration control　　　　　　出入国管理

(*shutsunyūkoku kanri*). Immigration into and emigration from Japan are both regulated by the Immigration Control Order (Shutsunyūkoku Kanri Rei) of 1951 (originally a government order, but a law after 1952). In regard to foreigners' entry into Japan, it states that no alien shall enter Japan without a valid passport or crewman's pocket ledger (art. 3). The Ministry of Justice grants visas, often renewable, of no more than three years' duration; only those in special categories such as diplomats and government officials may receive longer visas. Permanent residence is rarely granted. Entry is denied to aliens judged unsuitable by the authorities, and certain undesirable aliens may be deported. All Japanese nationals may emigrate from Japan to any other country except North Korea. Japanese nationals with a known police record have difficulty obtaining a passport. See also FOREIGNERS, LEGAL STATUS OF; FOREIGNERS IN JAPAN; NATURALIZATION.

Emi no Oshikatsu →Fujiwara no Nakamaro

Emishi →Ezo

Emma　　　　　　閻魔

(Skt: Yama). Ruler of the world of demons who confronts the dead with a record of their actions and determines their just rewards and punishments. He is a god of ancient origins, depicted in the oldest Indian religious work, the *Rig Veda*. Absorbed into Buddhism, he was popularly worshiped as the lord of the netherworld who judges human beings at the time of their death. In China fantastic imageries of Emma and his court were created under Taoist influence, and it is in this form that Emma is known and worshiped in Japan. See also HELL; AFTERLIFE.

emperor　　　　　　天皇

(*tennō*; literally, "heavenly sovereign"). The title *tennō* was first assumed by Japanese rulers in the 6th or 7th century and has been used by all subsequent Japanese sovereigns.

Japan's imperial institution, the oldest hereditary monarchy in the world, was already in existence when Japan emerged into recorded history and has since been perpetuated in a male line of descent (though there have been female *tennō*). Although the emperor has almost always been regarded as at least the titular head of the national government, the most striking feature of the

office through most of Japanese history has been the tendency to emphasize instead the emperor's role as chief priest or shaman in the indigenous Japanese religion, SHINTŌ, and to delegate most of the effective powers of government to others.

From Early Historical Times to the Mid-12th Century — The emperor figures centrally in a mythology preserved in its earliest extant form in the historical chronicles KOJIKI (712) and NIHON SHOKI (720). According to this, the sun goddess AMATERASU ŌMIKAMI, chief divinity of the Shintō pantheon, bequeathed to her grandson Ninigi no Mikoto a mirror, jewels, and a sword (see IMPERIAL REGALIA), which he in turn passed on to his descendants, the emperors of Japan, the first of whom was the emperor JIMMU.

The emperor was thought to possess magical powers to propitiate or intercede with divinities. His sacerdotal acts were considered of great importance to the well-being of the state, but because of the awe surrounding his person, it was also considered inappropriate for the emperor to concern himself with the secular business of government. That business, including both the making and execution of policies, belonged to ministers serving the emperor, and there was a tendency from very early historical times for those ministers to form political dynasties of their own (see SOGA FAMILY; ŌTOMO FAMILY; MONONOBE FAMILY).

The only extended period of Japanese history in which the emperor combined the roles of both high priest and functioning head of government in any real sense was from the reign of TENJI, in the latter half of the 7th century, through the reign of KAMMU at the end of the 8th century and the beginning of the 9th. It was Tenji who, in the TAIKA REFORM of 645, made the first major attempt to bring the powerful provincial clans (UJI) under the control of a strong central regime.

This period of direct imperial rule was characterized by the effort to establish a centralized bureaucratic state in Japan patterned on the example offered by Tang (T'ang) dynasty China. The key instrument in this process was the adoption of law codes, known collectively as the RITSURYŌ SYSTEM, that established an elaborate hierarchy of offices headed by the emperor and prescribed the procedures of governmental administration at both national and provincial levels.

However, the 9th century saw several institutional developments that were to undermine drastically the effective political power of the imperial institution. The first was the creation by Emperor SAGA of several new offices outside the *ritsuryō* structure (see RYŌGE NO KAN), including the important private secretariat known as the KURŌDO-DOKORO. This effort to personalize imperial rule by freeing it from the entrenched bureaucracy backfired, beginning a process in which the emperor was increasingly isolated from the machinery of government.

This tendency was exacerbated by the creation or revival of two other extrabureaucratic posts to which the emperor delegated the authority he had formerly wielded personally: SESSHŌ (regent for an emperor still in his minority) and KAMPAKU (regent for an adult emperor). From the late 9th century onward, both posts were dominated by members of the powerful FUJIWARA FAMILY, who, while making no claim to the emperor's title or ritual role, ruled in his name (see REGENCY GOVERNMENT).

The last century of the Heian period (794–1185) saw a waning of the power of the

Emma The lord of hell is pictured in this 13th-century painting with his court attendants and demon assistants; the sinners upon whom he passes judgment will be forced to view their transgressions in a mirror (foreground).

Fujiwara regents and a brief return of power to the imperial house. The leading figures through most of this period, however, were not reigning emperors but retired sovereigns who retained headship of the imperial house after abdication (see INSEI).

Medieval Period (mid-12th–16th centuries) — Three more families, again nonimperial, held sway over the national government and the imperial institution from the closing years of the Heian period to the end of the Kamakura period (1185–1333). All three rose to power through control of provincial land and private military forces, ushering in the age of warrior rule that was to last until the Meiji Restoration of 1868.

The first of these, the TAIRA FAMILY, ruled from Kyōto and legitimated themselves by occupying high offices within the imperial court. The second, the MINAMOTO FAMILY, destroyed the Taira in 1185 in a bloody war they waged from their base at Kamakura in eastern Japan (see TAIRA-MINAMOTO WAR). Remaining there after their victory, they established a wholly new pattern of national government, the KAMAKURA SHOGUNATE. The emperor remained in Kyōto and continued to preside over the imperial government and bureaucracy, but these institutions were now reduced to almost complete impotence, real power and authority devolving on the shogunate. Imperial legitimation for this situation took the form of a commission from the emperor naming the head of the Minamoto family to the office of *seii tai shōgun*, or "barbarian-subduing generalissimo" (see SHŌGUN), and thus by implication granting him absolute authority over territories and population beyond the reach of the much reduced imperial power.

The third family to dominate the national government in this period was the HŌJŌ FAMILY, whose members ruled from 1203 as shogunal regents (SHIKKEN). This initiated a complex and many-tiered delegation of power that has few parallels in world history. The emperor in Kyōto reigned, but the head of the imperial family was a retired sovereign, and the imperial government was controlled by a Fujiwara regent. The effective national government was, however, in Kamakura, nominally headed by a shōgun, but in fact controlled by the Hōjō regent. To complicate matters further, from the mid-13th century the shogunate began to interfere actively in the imperial succession, creating schisms within the imperial house that further decreased its power.

A clean sweep of this meaningless institutional complexity was undertaken by Emperor GO-DAIGO, who abolished the office of retired sovereign and then, in 1333, made war on the Hōjō, destroying the Kamakura shogunate. In the meantime, the Fujiwara regency had fallen vacant, leaving Go-Daigo as head of a reinvigorated imperial government (see KEMMU RESTORATION). This revival of imperial authority was, however, pathetically brief. In 1336 ASHIKAGA TAKAUJI, Go-Daigo's chief military commander, turned against the emperor, deposed him, and set up in his place a puppet from a different branch of the imperial house. The latter then appointed Takauji shōgun, initiating the 250-year MUROMACHI SHOGUNATE.

Go-Daigo fled to the mountains of Yoshino, where he established a rival court that maintained a precarious existence until 1392, when the rivalry between the NORTHERN AND SOUTHERN COURTS was finally resolved by the third Muromachi shōgun, ASHIKAGA YOSHIMITSU. The material circumstances of the imperial house reached their nadir in the course of the Muromachi period (1333–1568) and the Imperial Palace, along with much of the rest of Kyōto, was destroyed in the disastrous ŌNIN WAR (1466–77).

Early Modern Period (mid-16th–mid-19th centuries) — The restoration of the court's fortunes awaited the reunification of Japan, accomplished between 1568 and 1603 by three men—ODA NOBUNAGA, TOYOTOMI HIDEYOSHI, and TOKUGAWA IEYASU—each of whom derived sanction for his rule from the imperial institution. Nobunaga acquired several imperial court titles to legitimate himself; Hideyoshi had himself named to the posts of *kampaku* and grand minister of state (*dajō daijin*); and Ieyasu followed long precedent in having himself named shōgun in 1603, commencing more than 250 years of rule by the TOKUGAWA SHOGUNATE.

The shogunate devoted great attention to the maintenance and control of the imperial institution. The Imperial Palace was restored to its former grandeur, and residences were provided for the entire court nobility (*kuge*). Income from designated lands was earmarked for the imperial treasury. Yet at the same time rigorous restraints were imposed on the freedom of the imperial family and court nobility, codified in the regulations known as the KINCHŪ NARABI NI KUGE SHO-HATTO (1615).

The imperial court in Kyōto had little if any influence on practical state affairs, but the emperor continued to perform certain functions important to the shogunate. The chief of these was the drafting of a document at the beginning of every shogunal reign formally investing the new shōgun in his office. The public acts of the court consisted wholly of the performance of rituals associated variously with Shintō, with Buddhism, or with Confucianism.

Quite apart from this, however, the imperial institution came to play a new symbolic role in Japanese political thought, figuring centrally in a rearticulated national mythology constructed in the course of the Edo period (1600–1868) by writers and thinkers known as *kinnōka*, or "imperial loyalists," who drew their ideas chiefly from various modifications of Confucian theory (see MITO SCHOOL) or from the indigenous intellectual tradition of KOKUGAKU (National Learning). Although the "loyalists" of the 17th and 18th centuries did not in any practical sense call for a restoration of political power to the imperial throne, their stress on the centrality of the imperial house within the Japanese polity proved to be an explosive concept in the mid-19th century, when it combined with the crisis touched off by Western pressure to "open" Japan to foreign trade and diplomacy. The result was a political movement aimed at fending off the foreign threat, abolishing the shogunate, and replacing it with a new national government under direct imperial rule (see SONNŌ JŌI). Within 15 years of Commodore Matthew C. PERRY's arrival in Japan in 1853, this upsurge of imperial loyalism proved a key factor in the toppling of the Tokugawa regime and the initiation of the MEIJI RESTORATION of 1868.

Modern Period (1868–1945) — The leaders of Meiji Japan engaged in 20 years of pragmatic political experimentation before arriving at a redefinition of the imperial institution that embodied their sometimes contradictory goals of modernization and stability. With the proclamation of the CONSTITUTION OF THE EMPIRE OF JAPAN on 11 February 1889, the emperor became a constitutional monarch. Yet at the same time, he also became the fount of all political authority and the focus of loyalty for all Japanese subjects in a centralized and unitary state that was to exercise greater political power than any previous form of government in Japan's history.

According to the constitution, the emperor was "sacred and inviolable," and sovereignty rested with him as the head of the Japanese empire. He commanded the armed forces, declared war, made peace, and concluded treaties; he had emergency powers to maintain public order and declare a state of siege. He determined the organization of the civil and military administration and appointed all officials, civil and military. Moreover, even the legislative power was nominally vested in the emperor, though he was constrained to exercise it with the consent of the IMPERIAL DIET. All laws required the emperor's sanction and enforcement.

The native Japanese cult of Shintō was restructured and officially established under the authority of the Home Ministry and the court. Shintō rites conducted by the emperor were made highly visible to the public to confirm his role as the central manifestation of Japan's unique culture and spirituality.

Paradoxically, however, the supreme authority accorded the emperor in the constitution, and the other efforts made to bolster his centrality to the Japanese polity, were not accompanied by real political power. In fact, the system was designed instead to preserve the emperor's political immunity while he served as the sacrosanct basis for rule by others—namely, the ministers of state and the chiefs of the armed forces. The emperor's primary political role from 1889 to 1947 was to ratify the policies and personnel decisions reached by his government leaders and to put the seal of the imperial will on political decisions they had forged—not to actually make decisions or dictate policy himself.

Contemporary Monarchy (1945–) — Japan's defeat in World War II and the subsequent Allied OCCUPATION wrought momentous changes in the imperial institution and its place in Japanese politics and society. In the early years after the surrender the issue of imperial responsibility for the war was a subject of heated debate, with a significant body of opinion both at home and abroad calling for outright abolition of the "emperor system." A more moderate approach prevailed, however, and the 1947 CONSTITUTION OF JAPAN retained the emperor, though in a drastically altered relation to the state. Drafted under the "guidance" of the Occupation, the new constitution abolished imperial sovereignty and made the emperor "the symbol of the State and of the unity of the people, deriving his position from the will of the people with whom resides sovereign power." He was to have no political powers. All acts by the emperor in matters of state were reduced to merely formal and ceremonial functions, requiring the advice and approval of the cabinet. The autonomous Imperial Household Ministry was demoted to the status of an agency of the Prime Minister's Office (see IMPERIAL HOUSEHOLD AGENCY), the peerage was eliminated, Shintō was disestablished and demythologized, and Emperor SHŌWA (Hirohito) himself declared on New Year's Day 1946 that he was "not divine" (see EMPEROR, RENUNCIATION OF DIVINITY BY). Thus the prewar Japanese state with

Emperors and Reigning Empresses

Number in traditional count	Sovereign	Birth and death dates	Reign dates	Year of enthronement	Number in traditional count	Sovereign	Birth and death dates	Reign dates	Year of enthronement
1	Jimmu				66	Ichijō	980–1011	986–1011	
2	Suizei				67	Sanjō	976–1017	1011–1016	
3	Annei				68	Go-Ichijō	1008–1036	1016–1036	
4	Itoku				69	Go-Suzaku	1009–1045	1036–1045	
5	Kōshō				70	Go-Reizei	1025–1068	1045–1068	
6	Kōan				71	Go-Sanjō	1034–1073	1068–1073	
7	Kōrei				72	Shirakawa	1053–1129	1073–1087	
8	Kōgen	legendary emperors			73	Horikawa	1079–1107	1087–1107	
9	Kaika				74	Toba	1103–1156	1107–1123	1108
10	Sujin				75	Sutoku	1119–1164	1123–1142	
11	Suinin				76	Konoe	1139–1155	1142–1155	
12	Keikō				77	Go-Shirakawa	1127–1192	1155–1158	
13	Seimu				78	Nijō	1143–1165	1158–1165	1159
14	Chūai				79	Rokujō	1164–1176	1165–1168	
15	Ōjin	late 4th to early 5th century			80	Takakura	1161–1181	1168–1180	
16	Nintoku				81	Antoku[3]	1178–1185	1180–1185	
17	Richū	first half of the 5th century			82	Go-Toba	1180–1239	1183–1198	1184
18	Hanzei				83	Tsuchimikado	1195–1231	1198–1210	
19	Ingyō	mid-5th century			84	Juntoku	1197–1242	1210–1221	1211
20	Ankō				85	Chūkyō	1218–1234	1221	
21	Yūryaku				86	Go-Horikawa	1212–1234	1221–1232	1222
22	Seinei				87	Shijō	1231–1242	1232–1242	1233
23	Kenzō	latter half of the 5th century			88	Go-Saga	1220–1272	1242–1246	
24	Ninken				89	Go-Fukakusa	1243–1304	1246–1260	
25	Buretsu				90	Kameyama	1249–1305	1260–1274	
26	Keitai				91	Go-Uda	1267–1324	1274–1287	
27	Ankan	first half of the 6th century			92	Fushimi	1265–1317	1287–1298	1288
28	Senka				93	Go-Fushimi	1288–1336	1298–1301	
29	Kimmei	509–571	531 or 539 to 571		94	Go-Nijō	1285–1308	1301–1308	
30	Bidatsu	538–585	572–585		95	Hanazono	1297–1348	1308–1318	
31	Yōmei	?–587	585–587		96	Go-Daigo	1288–1339	1318–1339	
32	Sushun	?–592	587–592		97	Go-Murakami	1328–1368	1339–1368	
33	Suiko	554–628	593–628		98	Chōkei	1343–1394	1368–1383	
34	Jomei	593–641	629–641		99	Go-Kameyama	?–1424	1383–1392	
35	Kōgyoku[1]	594–661	642–645		N1	Kōgon	1313–1364	1331–1333	1332
36	Kōtoku	597–654	645–654		N2	Kōmyō	1322–1380	1336–1348	1338
37	Saimei	594–661	655–661		N3	Sukō	1334–1398	1348–1351	1350
38	Tenji	626–672	661–672	668	N4	Go-Kōgon	1338–1374	1351–1371	1354
39	Kōbun	648–672	672		N5	Go-En'yū	1359–1393	1371–1382	1375
40	Temmu	?–686	672–686	673	100	Go-Komatsu[4]	1377–1433	1382–1412	1392
41	Jitō	645–703	686–697	690	101	Shōkō	1401–1428	1412–1428	1415
42	Mommu	683–707	697–707		102	Go-Hanazono	1419–1471	1428–1464	1430
43	Gemmei	661–721	707–715		103	Go-Tsuchimikado	1442–1500	1464–1500	1466
44	Genshō	680–748	715–724		104	Go-Kashiwabara	1464–1526	1500–1526	1521
45	Shōmu	701–756	724–749		105	Go-Nara	1497–1557	1526–1557	1536
46	Kōken[2]	718–770	749–758		106	Ōgimachi	1517–1593	1557–1586	1560
47	Junnin	733–765	758–764		107	Go-Yōzei	1572–1617	1586–1611	1587
48	Shōtoku	718–770	764–770		108	Go-Mizunoo	1596–1680	1611–1629	
49	Kōnin	709–782	770–781		109	Meishō	1624–1696	1629–1643	1630
50	Kammu	737–806	781–806		110	Go-Kōmyō	1633–1654	1643–1654	
51	Heizei	774–824	806–809		111	Gosai	1637–1685	1655–1663	1656
52	Saga	786–842	809–823		112	Reigen	1654–1732	1663–1687	
53	Junna	786–840	823–833		113	Higashiyama	1675–1710	1687–1709	
54	Nimmyō	810–850	833–850		114	Nakamikado	1702–1737	1709–1735	1710
55	Montoku	827–858	850–858		115	Sakuramachi	1720–1750	1735–1747	
56	Seiwa	850–881	858–876		116	Momozono	1741–1762	1747–1762	
57	Yōzei	869–949	876–884	877	117	Go-Sakuramachi	1740–1813	1762–1771	1763
58	Kōkō	830–887	884–887		118	Go-Momozono	1758–1779	1771–1779	
59	Uda	867–931	887–897		119	Kōkaku	1771–1840	1780–1817	
60	Daigo	885–930	897–930		120	Ninkō	1800–1846	1817–1846	
61	Suzaku	923–952	930–946		121	Kōmei	1831–1867	1846–1867	1847
62	Murakami	926–967	946–967		122	Meiji	1852–1912	1867–1912	1868
63	Reizei	950–1011	967–969		123	Taishō	1879–1926	1912–1926	1915
64	En'yū	959–991	969–984		124	Shōwa	1901–1989	1926–1989	1928
65	Kazan	968–1008	984–986		125	Akihito	1933–	1989–	1990

▬ The first 14 sovereigns are considered legendary rather than historical by modern scholars; traditional reign numbers are given here for convenience because they are still often used. The traditional reign dates given in the chronicle *Nihon shoki* for these sovereigns and for sovereigns 15 through 28 are rejected as impossibly early; however, the latter (15–28) are accepted as historical figures. The approximate dates given here for sovereigns 15 through 28 are based on recent archaeological evidence and on citations in Chinese and Korean sources.

▬ Indicates empress.

▬ The year of formal enthronement is given when later than the first year of actual reign.

▬ Emperors of the Northern Court (N) during the period of the Northern and Southern Courts.

[1] Kōgyoku (35) later reigned as Saimei (37).
[2] Kōken (46) later reigned as Shōtoku (48).
[3] During the last phase of the Taira-Minamoto War, Antoku (81) fled the capital with the Taira and Go-Toba (82) was installed as rival emperor by the Minamoto; their reign dates thus overlap.
[4] Sixth emperor of the Northern Court from 1382; sole emperor from 1392.
NOTE: The life and reign dates in this table have been carefully corrected for discrepancies between the Japanese lunar and Western solar calendars. In some instances they may differ from the tables in standard Japanese reference works, where the calendar conversion is often approximate. The reign dates of Suiko, for example, are often given as 592–628.

emperor Standing on the dais-of-state (*takamikura*) at rear right, Emperor Akihito receives a congratulatory message from then prime minister Kaifu Toshiki during the formal enthronement ceremonies in November 1990.

its theory of imperial prerogative was thoroughly dismantled.

Along with these fundamental changes in the legal and institutional relationship of the emperor to the political system, efforts were made to "democratize" and "popularize" the imperial institution, presenting the imperial family as the nation's first family, united with the people in warmth and affection. No longer was the emperor to be surrounded by an aura of sanctity, elevated in transcendence above his people—who were now no longer subjects, but citizens. As a symbol the "new" emperor was to mirror a modern, democratic, and middle-class Japan.

Doubts about the imperial institution have remained. A small but vocal minority of Japanese believe that the emperor, by his very nature as a hereditary monarch, contradicts democracy, while others believe that a resurgence of Japanese fascism or absolutism is possible so long as the imperial institution is permitted to exist. But the vast majority of Japanese citizens favor the status quo. This was confirmed when, in January 1989, Emperor AKIHITO became the first emperor to succeed to the throne under the present constitution. The death of his father, Emperor Shōwa, and the ceremonies surrounding Akihito's enthronement sparked a renewed examination of Japan's imperial system and its legacy, but at the time of his accession Emperor Akihito, in a statement that was very well received by the Japanese public, explicitly affirmed his commitment to the symbolic role assigned him by the constitution. Despite dissenting voices, it seems clear that the consensus in Japan continues to support the retention of the imperial house, within a carefully defined legal framework, as a visible manifestation of Japan's links with its past and an assurance of continuity for its future.

emperor-as-organ theory→tennō kikan setsu

emperor, renunciation of divinity by   天皇人間宣言

(*tennō ningen sengen*). A statement in the New Year's rescript of 1 January 1946 in which Emperor SHŌWA (Hirohito) explicitly denied his own divinity. It read in part, "The ties between Us and Our people have always stood upon mutual trust and affection. They do not depend upon mere legends and myths. They are not predicated on the false conception that the Emperor is divine and that the Japanese people are superior to other races and fated to rule the world." The statement is said to have stemmed from the emperor's own desires; however, Prime Minister SHIDEHARA KIJŪRŌ's hand is evident in the rescript's final English version. The language of the Japanese text departs from

the formal court style for the first time, by the emperor's own direction. Well-received abroad and by General Douglas MACARTHUR, head of the OCCUPATION forces, the statement may have been a factor in saving the imperial institution.

employees' health insurance   健康保険

(*kenkō hoken*). Major component of Japan's MEDICAL AND HEALTH INSURANCE system, providing health insurance for private-sector employees and their dependents. The first such plan was instituted in 1927 in accordance with the Health Insurance Law of 1922 and mainly provided coverage for factory workers and miners. After World War II the system was expanded to include all private-sector-company employees and their families. There are now two categories of employees' health insurance: plans managed by incorporated health societies within large companies and plans managed by the government for small or medium-sized companies. Employees' health insurance is financed by contributions from employers and employees proportionate to the employee's salary (in government-managed plans the split is 50-50 but may be less for the employee in health-society-managed plans) and by subsidies from the national treasury. The insurance covers 90 percent of medical costs incurred by principals insured and 80 percent of medical costs incurred by dependents. As of 1989 there were 65.8 million people enrolled in employees' health insurance plans.

Employees' Pension Insurance   厚生年金保険

(*Kōsei Nenkin Hoken*). One of Japan's public pension programs. Established in 1942 as Laborers' Pension Insurance (*Rōdōsha Nenkin Hoken*), the program was given its present name in 1944. Since the reform of the pension system in 1986, the Employees' Pension Insurance program has provided benefits to enrolled private-sector employees, who also receive the basic benefits provided to all Japanese by the NATIONAL PENSION. As of 1989, 28.77 million workers were enrolled in the Employees' Pension Insurance program, representing 44.3 percent of the total number enrolled in Japan's public pension system.

The costs of the program are met entirely by private contributions divided equally between employers and employees. The size of each employee's contribution is determined as a fixed percentage of his or her basic salary (12.4% for males and 11.6% for females). Persons who have contributed to the Employees' Pension Insurance Fund for at least 20 years are eligible to receive benefits. In March 1989 the average monthly employee's pension (including the portion provided by the National Pension) was ¥132,000 (US $1,013), which is 42.1 percent of the average monthly wage earned in Japan. Pension benefits are automatically adjusted in accordance with changes in the consumer price index. See PENSIONS.

employers' liability   使用者責任

(*shiyōsha sekinin*). Legal term referring to the liability that an employer bears for damages caused by an employee who commits a tort, as stipulated by article 715 of the Civil Code. Unlike vicarious liability in Anglo-American law, employers' liability in Japan is construed as liability based on the negligence of the employer; that is, the employer is not liable for the torts of an employee if

the employer can prove that he has exercised sufficient care in assigning and supervising the employee's work. In practice, however, courts almost never exempt an employer from liability, so that in effect employers' liability functions like liability without fault.

A necessary condition for employers' liability is that the tort of the employee must have been committed "in the execution of his work." Judgment is to be made on the basis of whether the act has the objective appearance of being done in the execution of business, regardless of the actual intentions or motives of the employee.

employment contracts   労働契約

(*rōdō keiyaku*). Agreements reached by individual bargaining, as contrasted with COLLECTIVE LABOR AGREEMENTS reached by collective bargaining between trade unions and employers. In practice, usually there is only an oral agreement or a document unilaterally prepared by the management. Because the terms and conditions of employment have already been prescribed either by collective agreements or by the WORK REGULATIONS of the company, the employment contract simply formalizes the acceptance by the worker of management's offer.

The Labor Standards Law of 1947 prohibits employment contracts of longer than one year in order to protect workers from too long-binding a contract (see LABOR LAWS). It requires the employer to clarify the working conditions to the employees before concluding the contract; if the conditions prove other than specified, the worker can cancel the contract. Minors under 15 cannot be employed, except for those older than 12 in some primary and tertiary industries and those under 12 in the theater and cinema.

employment, forms of   雇用形態

(*koyō keitai*). There are three principal forms of employment in Japanese industry: permanent, temporary, and subcontract. Permanent employees account for the main body of a firm's labor force and are hired as regular employees on a long-term basis. Such employees are recruited at regular intervals, according to the company's long-range plans, with the expectation that they will eventually rise through company ranks to hold administrative or supervisory positions. Regular employees are usually selected from recent secondary school and university graduates. Employment experience in another company is not highly valued; workers with experience in numerous companies are generally regarded as lacking in seriousness and cooperative spirit. The wages of regular employees are increased gradually through annual raises and promotions. Through the company welfare system regular employees also receive a number of benefits. Except in cases of grave infraction of company regulations or a permanent reduction in company operations, it is very unusual for regular employees to be discharged before reaching the retirement age set by the company.

Temporary employees are hired to respond to fluctuations in labor demand arising from variations in business volume; they are also hired to take advantage of low-cost labor. These workers are hired for a set period, after which their employment is terminated unless their contract is extended. They are less eligible for company benefits.

Workers employed by subcontractors are called *shagaikō* (noncompany workers) when they are sent to work for the parent company. They may work at special tasks that the company's own workers cannot perform or may be brought in as part of planned increases in the work force. The *shagaikō* serve the same purpose as temporary employees but are employed indirectly through subcontractors. See also LABOR MARKET; LABOR MOBILITY.

Employment Measures Law
雇用対策法

(Koyō Taisaku Hō). Law establishing a basic employment policy for Japan. Enacted in 1966, it has as its objective the stabilization of employment, the elevation of the worker's position in society, the development of the national economy, and the achievement of full employment, via the promotion of a balance in the quality and volume of demand for workers. Provisions for the employment of middle-aged and elderly workers were added in 1973. The law provides a basic framework for government activities in employment guidance, placement, and training; assistance for workers who change jobs or who are transferred; employment security for elderly workers; and measures promoting reform of the employment structure. Some benefits are provided to individuals for training or job searches.

Employment Promotion Corporation
雇用促進事業団

(Koyō Sokushin Jigyōdan). Public corporation founded in July 1961 to promote employment and to improve workers' welfare. In its early days it was concerned with assisting miners with reemployment problems, providing skills retraining, lending money for moving expenses, and finding accommodations for workers who were relocating. Later, as the problem of unemployment receded, the corporation turned to the task of improving workers' welfare. It established the National Institute of Employment and Vocational Research and the Institute of Vocational Training in order to develop skills and maintain the health of the LABOR MARKET.

Employment Security Law of 1947
職業安定法

(Shokugyō Antei Hō). Law enacted in 1947 to give unemployed workers employment opportunities suited to their abilities, to supply labor needed by manufacturing and other industries, to provide employment security, and to contribute to economic prosperity. The law was intended to establish a modern system of employment safeguards and to prohibit the exploitative labor supply and recruitment practices of the pre–World War II era.

The law regulates the job placement and counseling services offered by employment security organs and the job placement, labor recruitment, and labor supply activities undertaken by other persons or organizations. PUBLIC EMPLOYMENT SECURITY OFFICES are the front-line agencies that perform the functions prescribed by the law. Laborers may not be forced to take a job, nor may anyone be subject to unfavorable treatment because of race, nationality, sex, religion, social position, past employment, or union membership. See also EMPLOYMENT SYSTEM, MODERN.

employment structure
就業構造

(shūgyō kōzō). Japanese labor statistics define the potential labor force as all those age 15 and over, and this population of productive age, as it is known, is further divided into the working and nonworking populations.

The working population is divided into employed and unemployed labor force participants, and those employed are classified into three groups: the self-employed, family workers, and employees. Of the total Japanese population of 123,612,000, the potential labor force in 1990 was 100,890,000 (81.6 percent of the total population). The actual working population amounted to 63,840,000 (63.3 percent of the potential labor force). The ratio of the labor force relative to the total population is continuing to fall because of the increasing numbers of students going on to higher education. The 1990 unemployment figure was 1,340,000 (2.1 percent of the actual working population).

In the same year the 48,350,000 employees made up 75.7 percent of the working population. The self-employed numbered 8,780,000 and family workers 5,170,000 (some 200,000 workers were not classified). These figures reveal a marked drop in the number of self-employed and family workers compared to 1957, when the percentage of employees in those categories combined was 48.0 percent. This drop is accounted for by the fall in the number of jobs in agriculture and small trading concerns and the rapid expansion of corporate businesses.

The 1990 figures for the industrial sector distribution of workers were as follows: primary sector, 4,510,000 (7.3 percent); secondary sector, 20,990,000 (33.7 percent); and tertiary sector, 36,690,000 (59.0 percent). The 1965 percentages were 23.5 percent, 31.9 percent, and 44.6 percent, respectively, thus showing a marked decline in the primary sector and expansion in the tertiary sector. The falling figures for the secondary sector in recent years also point to the softening of the economy as it shifts toward service and distribution industries.

Women currently make up 40.6 percent of the working population, a figure that is continuing to rise. The rate of increase in the number of housewives working part-time is particularly high and shows that more and more housewives are taking on jobs in addition to running their households. See also UNEMPLOYMENT.

employment system, modern
近代の雇用制度

(kindai no koyō seido). The employment system in the post–World War II period has been based on three essential institutions: lifetime employment (shūshin koyō), the SENIORITY SYSTEM (nenkō joretsu), and enterprise unionism (see LABOR UNIONS).

Lifetime Employment—In the characteristic Japanese employment system, companies recruit workers immediately upon graduation from a school or university, and these workers continue in the same company until retirement. In Japan this is considered to be the ideal employment relationship, but it is mostly limited to larger firms.

Regular employees can expect to be employed until retirement unless they violate any of the rules of employment in a way that calls for dismissal. Such cases are rare. When business is depressed and there is a need to reduce staff, regular employees are dismissed only as a last resort. In return for this security of employment, employees are expected to accept transfers to other departments or to subsidiary companies when business is bad and to respond positively by working overtime when the company is doing well. As long as employees maintain such a commitment, it is commonly understood to be the

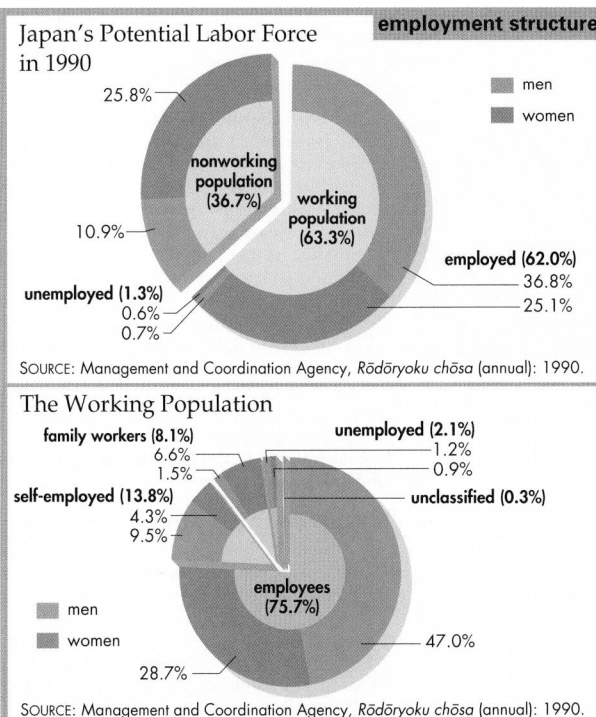

Japan's Potential Labor Force in 1990 — employment structure

men / women

nonworking population (36.7%) 25.8% / 10.9%

working population (63.3%)

employed (62.0%) 36.8% / 25.1%

unemployed (1.3%) 0.6% / 0.7%

SOURCE: Management and Coordination Agency, *Rōdōryoku chōsa* (annual): 1990.

The Working Population

family workers (8.1%) 6.6% / 1.5%

unemployed (2.1%) 1.2% / 0.9%

self-employed (13.8%) 4.3% / 9.5%

unclassified (0.3%)

employees (75.7%) 47.0% / 28.7%

men / women

SOURCE: Management and Coordination Agency, *Rōdōryoku chōsa* (annual): 1990.

employer's responsibility to maintain stability of employment.

Seniority System—This system bases an employee's rank, salary, and qualifications within an enterprise on the length of service in that company. Wage increases and promotions are highly dependent on the employee's school background, sex, and type of work. This system can be traced to a period of serious labor shortages during World War I when the Yokosuka Naval Shipyard adopted it as a means of securing enough technical and skilled workers, although its essential features of respect for age, sex, and school affiliation are all deeply rooted in Japanese traditions.

Enterprise Unionism—The third basic feature of the Japanese employment system is the prevalence of enterprise unions. This form of unionism, instituted after World War II, supplanted earlier efforts to establish craft and industrial unions because of the following factors: (1) strong paternalism among postwar employers of all sizes and types; (2) a wide variety of working conditions, which prevented the development of a unitary wage structure based on technical qualifications and competence; and (3) the interest of union members in secure jobs and income, owing to the inadequacy of government social security. These factors led Japanese union members to prefer to bargain with management at the level of the individual enterprise. Paternalistic management and enterprise unionism have both supported lifetime employment and promoted labor-management harmony.

Temporary Employees—The system that is considered characteristic of Japanese employment is dependent on a variety of temporary employees. Because the number of regular workers is limited, companies take on temporary workers for a fixed period in response to business upturns. If the situation deteriorates, the companies simply release the temporary workers. In addition to temporary employees who work the same hours as regular employees, there are part-time workers, students, and those on loan from employment agencies, who work a limited number of hours only. When regular employees reach retirement age, some are re-

Enchi Fumiko This writer is best known for her novels and short stories exploring modern female psychology and sexuality.

tained with the special status of "nonregular staff" (*shokutaku*), but they are regarded as temporary employees. There is a strict demarcation between regular and temporary employees in terms of working conditions, job status, wages, and benefits.

Smaller firms operate welfare systems similar to those in large companies, but in many small companies working conditions do not improve with increasing length of service. As a result, labor mobility among small firms is high, many workers are hired in midcareer, and there is no clear distinction between regular and temporary employees. Lifetime employment, therefore, is a system operating mainly in large private companies and the public sector.

employment system, premodern
前近代の雇用制度

(*zenkindai no koyō seido*). The primary forms of employment in premodern Japan were vassalage, indentured service, and day labor. Employment was characterized by paternalistic relationships, although in the late premodern era something akin to the modern contractual relationship began to emerge, especially within the growing commercial sector.

Employment before 1600—The earliest records of formal employment relationships are found in the law codes of the RITSURYŌ SYSTEM, first promulgated in the mid-7th century. The codes authorized government offices and agencies to recruit laborers forcibly and pay them fixed wages (*kōchoku*) for their services. This was called *kyōko*, or forced employment. Employment based on the agreement of both parties was called *wako*, or peaceful employment, and the laborers were paid according to prevailing rates. During the early feudal era there were *genin* (household slaves), who were permanent employees. During the Muromachi period (1333–1568), indentured employment began to develop.

Employment during the Edo Period—Employment relationships became widespread late in the Edo period (1600–1868). Employees in this period were called *hōkōnin*. *Hōkōnin* fell roughly into three categories: FUDAI (hereditary vassals), *nenki* (indentured servants), and *hiyō* (day laborers).

Fudai originally was a term denoting the relationship between master and follower in the *samurai* hierarchy. The *fudai* spent their whole lives at the house of their masters, much like slaves, and their descendants did the same. One became a *fudai* by birth, by selling oneself into vassalage, or by being turned over to a master by an impoverished family in order to reduce the number of mouths to feed.

Nenki hōkōnin were hired for a certain number of years and paid wages for their services. Among these indentured servants were the *shichiken hōkōnin*, who paid interest on loans by working for the persons from whom they had borrowed money, and the *ikeshi hōkōnin*, who repaid debts by physical labor. From the 18th century, the *hiwake* (also *hiwari*) *hōkōnin* worked for a certain number of days a month on a one-year contract.

Hiyō were hired on a daily basis and paid daily wages. The practice of day labor was concentrated in cities where there was extensive construction of castles. In farming villages, *hiyō* assumed importance after the mid-17th century. In addition to these principal forms of employment, there was a special category called *tsutome hōkō* involving prostitutes.

With the decline of the *fudai*, some *nōson hōkōnin* (farm employees) went to cities, while those who remained in the villages, freed from their vassalage, continued to serve their former masters in paternalistic relationships termed *oyakata-kokata* (master-servant; see OYABUN–KOBUN) and OYAKATA AND HIKAN (master and extrafamilial vassal). The employment system in large merchant houses developed in the early Edo period and later influenced modern Japanese enterprise management methods. Prospective employees of large houses were limited to members of a *bekke* (branch family), natives of the same province as the master of the store, or the second or third sons of a man who had sufficient assets to repay debts that his son might incur during employment. Women were not allowed to attain managerial posts. Newly employed boys were known as *detchi* (apprentices) or *kozō* (errand boys) and worked at menial tasks. At about 20 years of age, they were promoted to clerk positions—first to *tedai*, then *bantō* (a popular term for *shihainin*, or manager). The *detchi* and *kozō* received only clothing and a small amount of pocket money, while those in positions of *tedai* or higher were paid wages. When they fulfilled their *nenki* contract without mishap, employees were given a separation allowance and the right to use the name of the master's store (*yagō*). As indicated by the term *noren wake* (literally, "to divide the shop curtain"), they continued the relationship of *honke* and *bekke* (principal and branch house). See also HONKE AND BUNKE.

empon
円本

("one-yen book"). Inexpensive books published in collections or series during the 1920s in an effort to revive the moribund Japanese publishing business; so called because a book of up to 500–600 pages sold for one yen. The practice was initiated by the publisher Kaizōsha, which launched a series on contemporary Japanese literature in 1926; Shinchōsha soon joined in with a series on world literature. Other publishers followed suit, and the eventual glut on the market led to the demise of the *empon* around 1930. However, these books greatly contributed to the expansion of the publishing industry and an increase in readership.

emptiness
空

(J: *kū*; Skt: *śūnyatā*). Buddhist term that indicates the elimination of cognition, based on conceptualization and verbal expression, of objects as substantial reality. The achievement of this state is not a total negation of existence, nor is it an affirmation of nihilism.

Nāgārjuna (fl ca 200), an Indian Buddhist of the Mahāyāna tradition, elucidated the idea of emptiness in works such as *Mādhyamika-śāstra* (Treatise on the Middle Way). He states that all things are dependent on causes and conditions for their existence (this is the meaning of "interdependent origin"; J: *engi*) and do not exist by themselves; they are devoid of substantial reality and are empty. Perception based upon conceptualization and verbal expression grasps all things as fixed entities and attributes substantial reality to them. It is because all things are assumed to exist through such ordinary perception that human attachments, passions, suffering, and illusions come into being. To eliminate them and reach enlightenment, it is necessary to realize that "all is empty" (*śūnya*). When this occurs the original form of all things is grasped. This standpoint of emptiness transcends distinctions of affirmation and negation, existence and nonexistence, which necessarily accompany ordinary cognition. In the sense that it is a position of practical reason that transcends both contrary and contradictory concepts, it is called the Middle Way.

The philosophy of emptiness decisively influenced all of later Mahāyāna Buddhism, transcending sectarian lines. However, the emphasis in Japan has not been on Buddhism's theoretical side, as was the case in Indian Buddhism, but on its intuitive and emotional aspect, taking the form of the awareness of impermanence (*mujōkan*). See also MUJŌ.

Ena
恵那[市]

City in southeastern Gifu Prefecture, central Honshū. Ena developed as a post-station town on the highway Nakasendō during the Edo period (1600–1868). Its paper and pulp industry has thrived since early times. In recent years, watch and precision-instrument industries have become firmly established. It is the site of ENAKYŌ, a gorge noted for its grotesquely shaped rocks. Pop: 35,025.

Enakyō
恵那峡

Gorge on the middle reaches of the river Kisogawa, southeastern Gifu Prefecture, central Honshū. It is famous for its natural scenery, which includes fantastically shaped rocks and weather-beaten cliffs. Ōi Dam, Japan's first hydroelectric dam, is here. Enakyō is located within Enakyō Prefectural Natural Park. Length: approximately 12 km (7.5 mi).

Enasan
恵那山

Mountain in the southern Kiso Mountains on the border between Nagano and Gifu prefectures, central Honshū. It is composed mostly of granite. The summit is the site of the Ena Shrine. Height: 2,191 m (7,188 ft).

Enchi Fumiko
円地文子

(1905–86). Author and playwright. Real name Enchi Fumi. Born in Tōkyō. As the daughter of philologist and classicist UEDA KAZUTOSHI (Enchi was her married name), she grew up with a deep familiarity with the Japanese classics. In the late 1920s she wrote several plays that displayed her proletarian sympathies. From the late 1940s Enchi published many novels and short stories exploring female psychology and sexuality, among them "Himojii tsukihi" (1953, Days of Hunger), *Yō* (1956; tr *Enchantress*, 1958), and ONNAZAKA (1949–57; tr *The Waiting Years*, 1971), as well as works that deal with ancient Japan, such as *Namamiko monogatari* (1959–61) and her 1972–73 translation into modern Japanese of the *Genji monogatari* (TALE OF GENJI). She received the Order of Culture in 1985.

Enchin
円珍

(814–891). Tendai priest under whose leadership esoteric Buddhist teachings gained their greatest influence upon the Japanese TENDAI SECT. Born in Sanuki Province (now Kagawa Prefecture). He became a monk at the temple ENRYAKUJI on Mt. Hiei (Hieizan). After five years in China (853–858) studying Tendai and esoteric Buddhism, he returned to Mt. Hiei and restored the temple Onjōji (also known as MIIDERA) in neighboring Ōmi Province (now Shiga Prefecture). Continuing the tendency initiated by his predecessor ENNIN toward extensive incorporation of esoteric elements into the Tendai sect, Enchin declared esoteric teachings based on the Mahāvairocana sutra to be superior to Tendai teachings based on the LOTUS SUTRA. Because of intense rivalry with the followers of Ennin, Enchin's successors were driven from Mt. Hiei and moved to Onjōji. The rivalry between Enchin's line, Jimon, and Ennin's, Sammon, often erupted into violence.

endangered species 絶滅危惧種

(*zetsumetsu kigushu*). In recent times, Japan's once varied and abundant wildlife has become progressively depleted. Many plants and animals are facing extinction due to habitat destruction brought about by deforestation and the development of river and seaside areas. Beginning in 1986 the ENVIRONMENT AGENCY conducted a survey of animal species in need of emergency protection; the report designated 136 species of mammals in need of such protection and pronounced 5 species, including the Nihon ōkami (Japanese wolf; *Canis lupus hodophilax*), already extinct. Listed as being on the verge of extinction were the Nihon kawauso (Japanese river otter; *Lutra nippon*), Tsushima *yamaneko* (Tsushima cat; *Felis euptilura*), and Iriomote *yamaneko* (Iriomote cat; *Mayailurus iriomotensis*). An independent study of Japanese flora, conducted by the Nature Conservation Society of Japan, revealed that 35 types of plants have become extinct and that 147 species are in danger of extinction.

enden 塩田

(salt fields). Seaside areas in which seawater was collected and prepared for the extraction of salt by partially evaporating it with the heat of the sun. Sand with large quantities of adhering salt was gathered and seawater poured over it to dissolve the salt; after partial evaporation by the sun, the resulting concentrated salt water was boiled down to produce edible salt. Originating in the Nara period (710–794), *enden* were an important source of salt in Japan for many centuries because Japan does not produce any rock salt. Moreover, its heavy rainfall and high humidity prohibit the production of salt by conducting seawater into pools for complete solar evaporation.

The earliest salt field technique was the *agehama* system, in which a shallow clay reservoir was constructed beside the sea to collect salt by evaporating seawater. More efficient solar evaporation systems evolved: the *irihama* system in the Edo period (1600–1868) and the *ryūka* system after World War II. In recent years, however, salt field techniques have been rendered obsolete by the development of ion-exchange membrane technology, permitting the production of pure and highly concentrated salt water that is efficiently evaporated in vacuum equipment.

Endō Shūsaku 遠藤周作

(1923–). Popular Catholic novelist and playwright; humorist. Born in Tōkyō, Endō lived in China as a child, returning to Japan with his mother in 1933 after his parents' divorce. A Catholic aunt persuaded him to be baptized at the age of 11. Pleurisy kept Endō from combat in World War II, and he subsequently suffered from serious respiratory ailments. Many of his works are set in hospi-

▲ A distant relative of the carp, the Miyako *tanago* is found only in fresh waters in the Kantō region.

tals, where physical impairment often symbolizes spiritual deformity. Endō, who majored in French literature at Keiō University, went to France in 1950, the first Japanese to study abroad since the war. He spent two and a half years at the University of Lyons, studying Mauriac, Bernanos, and other French Catholic writers.

Soon after his return to Japan, Endō began writing fiction. *Shiroi hito* (1955, White Man), which received the Akutagawa Prize, and *Kiiroi hito* (1955, Yellow Man) contrast Western and Japanese attitudes toward Christianity, sin, and guilt. In his *Umi to dokuyaku* (1957; tr *The Sea and Poison*, 1972), Endō lashes out at the lack of moral conscience that allowed Japanese doctors during the war to vivisect a captured American pilot. In the powerful CHIMMOKU (1966; tr *Silence*, 1969), a study of the persecution of 17th-century Japanese Christians, Endō resolved his conflict as a Japanese embracing a foreign religion by creating a compassionate Christ to whom he believes his countrymen can relate. This image is fleshed out in *Shikai no hotori* (1973, By the Dead Sea) and *Iesu no shōgai* (1973; tr *A Life of Jesus*, 1978). Endō's Noma Literary Prize–winning *Samurai* (1980; tr *The Samurai*, 1982) is both a historical novel describing the 1614 trade embassy to Mexico and Europe and a self-styled I-NOVEL tracing the arduous spiritual journey a Japanese makes to Christianity.

In addition to comic novels like *Taihen dā* (1969, Good Grief!), Endō sprinkles basically serious works like *Obakasan* (1959; tr *Wonderful Fool*, 1974), *Watashi ga suteta onna* (1963, The Girl I Left Behind), and *Kuchibue o fuku toki* (1974; tr *When I Whistle*, 1979) with a unique and affecting humor. During his career he has also edited MITA BUNGAKU, a prestigious literary journal, and has been active in a number of literary organizations. His body of work, as well as his frequent appearances in the mass media, have made him Japan's most admired and widely read Christian writer.

Endō Yukio 遠藤幸雄

(1937–). Gymnast. Born in Akita Prefecture; graduate of Tōkyō University of Education; professor of gymnastics at Nihon University. As captain of the gymnastics team, Endō led Japan to a team championship at the 1960 (Rome), 1964 (Tōkyō), and 1968 (Mexico City) Olympic Games. He won a total of five gold medals.

energy sources エネルギー資源

(*enerugī shigen*). Japan's energy options are seriously limited by its lack of domestic energy sources coupled with the huge energy demands of its industries. Japan's dependence on imports for its energy supply rose from 43.4 percent in 1960 to 84.4 percent in 1970 and then stabilized at about 91 percent in the 1980s.

Oil — From 1965 to 1974 the rapid growth of the Japanese economy led to a 10.2 percent

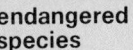

◀ The nocturnal Amami woodcock (Amami *yamashigi*) is found on the island of Amami Ōshima, on the main island of Okinawa, and on neighboring islands.

▼ The Iriomote cat is found only on the island of Iriomotejima in the Ryūkyū chain. An estimated 40 to 100 of the cats remain.

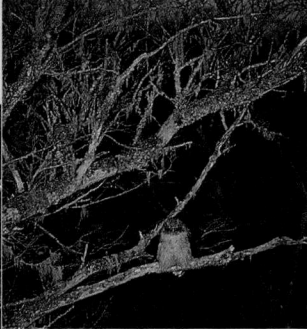

▲ Blakiston's fish owl (*shimafukurō*), once common in Hokkaidō, is today found only in a few isolated locations. It is estimated that just 80 to 100 of these birds survive.

average annual increase in energy demand, more than twice the world average of 4.8 percent. During the same period there was a shift from coal to oil as an energy source because of the depletion of domestic coal mines and the relative efficiency of oil; as a result the increased energy demand had to be met almost entirely by imported oil.

The fourfold increase in oil prices brought on by the OIL CRISIS OF 1973 led to profound changes in Japanese energy policy. In 1973 Japan was importing 99 percent of its crude oil, and the imported oil represented 77 percent of the total energy supply. Eighty-five percent of the imported oil originated in the Middle East and northern Africa. Because of its overdependence on imported oil, the impact of the "oil shock," as it was commonly called, was felt even more strongly in Japan than in many other countries. It affected all sectors of the economy, causing aggravated inflation, prolonged recession, rising unemployment, and business failures. Facing the threat of disruption in the oil supply, the government announced an oil emergency policy in November 1973 aimed at reducing dependence on oil, increasing geographical diversification of oil sources, and conserving energy. At the same time a new policy more sympathetic toward Arab countries was also announced, with a view to improving Japan's relationship with key oil-producing nations.

Although Japan remains heavily dependent on imported oil, as a result of conservation efforts and development of alternative energy sources oil's share of the country's total energy supply dropped to 58.3 percent by 1990. Japan continues to be vulnerable to events in the Middle East, however, as 71.5 percent of its imported oil came from that region in the same year.

Coal — Coal provided 16.6 percent of Japan's energy in 1990. Coal mining is a declining industry in Japan, and, even with maximum effort and government support, domestic production can at best be maintained at the 1989 level of some 10 million

Endō Shūsaku
Japan's most widely read Christian author, Endō is perhaps best known in the West for his powerful historical novel *Chimmoku* (1966, Silence).

341

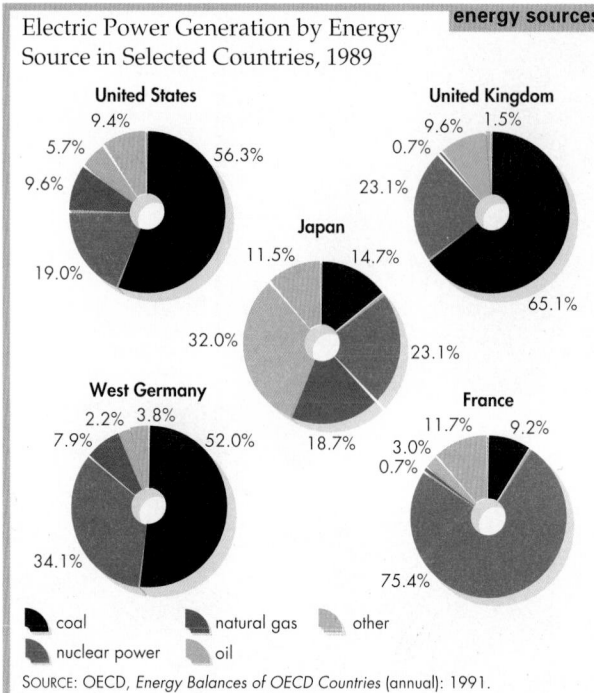

Electric Power Generation by Energy Source in Selected Countries, 1989

United States
9.4%
5.7%
9.6%
56.3%
19.0%

United Kingdom
9.6% 1.5%
0.7%
23.1%
65.1%

Japan
11.5% 14.7%
32.0%
23.1%

West Germany
2.2% 3.8%
7.9%
52.0%
34.1%

France
11.7% 9.2%
18.7%
3.0%
0.7%
75.4%

■ coal ▨ natural gas ▨ other
▨ nuclear power ▨ oil

SOURCE: OECD, *Energy Balances of OECD Countries* (annual): 1991.

Energy Consumption in Japan by Source

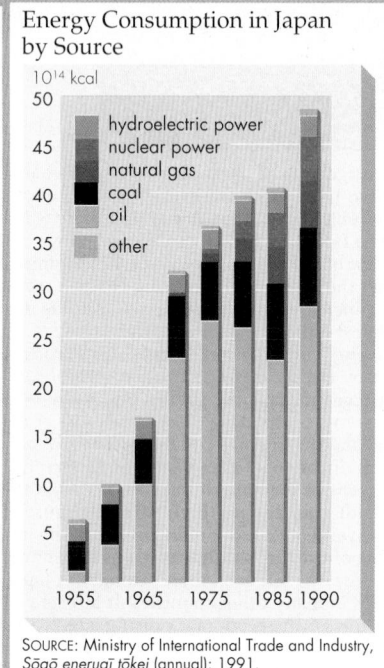

10¹⁴ kcal

hydroelectric power
nuclear power
natural gas
coal
oil
other

1955 1965 1975 1985 1990

SOURCE: Ministry of International Trade and Industry, *Sōgō enerugī tōkei* (annual): 1991.

metric tons (11 million short tons) per year, owing to depletion of resources, higher costs, and the scarcity of skilled mine workers. Thus, any increase in demand must be met by imports, which stood at some 102 million metric tons (112 million short tons) in 1989. Difficulties with the use of coal as an energy source include its relative cost inefficiency and environmental problems, primarily air pollution. A major technical breakthrough, such as gasification or liquefaction, may be necessary in order to achieve a significant shift to coal. Such a shift could face supply problems as well; plentiful world coal reserves exist but Japan may not be able to gain access to them.

Natural Gas——The share of natural gas in Japan's total energy supply was 10.1 percent in 1990. The domestic production of natural gas, like that of oil, is very limited, and if natural gas is to play a significant role in the future as an alternative energy source it will have to be in the form of imports of

liquefied natural gas (LNG). In 1990 Japan imported 36 million metric tons (40 million short tons) of LNG, more than double LNG imports for 1980. Liquefied gas has various advantages as an energy source, including cleanness and convenience. Its areas of production are more evenly distributed around the world than is the case with oil, and it also offers more security of supply through long-term contracts with producing countries.

Nuclear Energy——In Japan, because of its lack of domestic energy resources, nuclear energy has received the highest priority in the search for alternatives to oil. Japan's first nuclear power plant was built in 1963. In 1990 Japan had 39 nuclear reactors totaling 31.5 million kilowatts of capacity in commercial operation—the fourth largest capacity in the world after the United States, France, and the USSR. These reactors provided 9.4 percent of Japan's total energy supply in 1990. Fourteen additional reactors that are either under construction or in the planning stages will have a combined capacity of 14.9 million kilowatts. As in other countries, the antinuclear movement, with its concerns over the location, safety, and waste products of nuclear power plants, has many supporters in Japan. As a result, despite the government's continued commitment to nuclear power development, the industry may not be able to go forward as rapidly as planned.

Other Energy Sources and Conservation——Hydroelectric power accounted for 4.2 percent of the total energy supply in 1990. New energy sources such as geothermal energy, solar power, and wind hold promise for the future, but, while they may be technically feasible and research is proceeding, they are not yet economically practical. These new energy sources provided only 1.4 percent of the total power supply in 1990.

Energy conservation constitutes one of the pillars of Japan's energy policy and many efforts are being made to increase efficiency in energy use. However, great conservation efforts have already been made in industry, which is the major energy-consuming sector in Japan, and most industries will find it extremely difficult to raise efficiency further. Per capita energy consumption in Japan in 1989 was at the relatively low level of about 3.3 metric tons (3.6 short tons) oil equivalent, as against 7.8 metric tons (8.6 short tons) oil equivalent in the United States, which alone indicates that there is limited potential for major benefits from conservation in the future.

Engakuji 円覚寺

Head temple of the Engakuji branch of the RINZAI SECT of Buddhism; located in the city of Kamakura, Kanagawa Prefecture. Engakuji was founded in 1282 by HŌJŌ TOKI-MUNE, the eighth regent of the Kamakura shogunate (1192–1333), as a residence for the Chinese Zen master Mugaku Sogen (Ch: Wuxue Zuyuan or Wu-hsüeh Tsu-yüan; 1226–86), who became its first abbot. In 1283 Engakuji was designated a *kiganjo*, or temple at which prayers were to be offered regularly for the shogunate's prosperity. In 1386 it was ranked second among the five leading Zen monasteries (GOZAN) in Kamakura. Throughout its history Engakuji suffered repeatedly from disastrous fires. The temple was extensively damaged in the Tōkyō Earthquake of 1923, which also struck Kamakura, but was fully restored. The relic hall (*shariden*), a National Treasure, dates from the 15th century.

Engaru 遠軽[町]

Town on the middle reaches of the river Yūbetsugawa in northeastern Hokkaidō; an important transportation point. In 1897 farmers from Akita, Yamagata, and Niigata prefectures began settling here. Dairy farming and forestry both thrive in Engaru. Pop: 19,441.

engi 縁起

(Skt: *pratītya-samutpāda;* "interdependent origination"). Key Buddhist thesis that holds that all things exist through the harmonious interaction of causes (Skt: *hetu;* J: *in*) and conditions (Skt: *pratyaya;* J: *en*). The Pāli Theravāda texts set forth the 12-fold chain of interdependent origination to explain human existence; the scholastic *Abhidharmakośa-bhāṣya* established the theory of six causes and four conditions to explain all existence; the *Mādhyamika-śāstra* defined interdependent origination as EMPTINESS (Skt: *śūnyatā;* J: *kū*). In common Japanese usage *engi* has come to mean (1) the origin of some event or thing, (2) omens or portents, and (3) legends surrounding the founding of a shrine or temple (*jisha engi*).

Engi Kyaku——➤Engi Shiki

Engi Shiki 延喜式

(Procedures of the Engi Era). A collection of 50 books or fascicles (*kan*) of early-10th-century supplementary governmental regulations. These regulations were issued as *kyaku* (penal procedures) and *shiki* (administrative and ceremonial procedures) to implement the laws of the late 7th and early 8th centuries (see RITSURYŌ SYSTEM). The Engi Shiki was compiled by order of Emperor DAIGO between 905 (Engi 5) and 927. Its first 10 books give details for the conduct of festivals and ceremonies under the Jingikan (Office of Shintō Worship). The 11th book deals with procedures for the DAJŌKAN (Grand Council of State); it is followed by 39 books on the eight ministries and other bureaus and offices of government.

The first compilation of *kyaku* and *shiki* was completed in the Kōnin era (810–824) and the next in the Jōgan era (859–877). The Engi Shiki is the third such compilation. The corresponding set of penal procedures, the Engi Kyaku, was compiled between 905 and 907. The Engi Shiki is a sacred book of the Shintō religion and guides its practice even today.

Engi Tenryaku no Chi 延喜・天暦の治

("the Rule of Engi and Tenryaku"). A reference to the Engi (901–923) and Tenryaku (947–957) eras and, by extension, to the entire first half of the 10th century. It is often referred to as a golden period when the emperors resumed an active role in government affairs, strove to check the proliferation of private landed estates (SHŌEN), codified the laws (see ENGI SHIKI), and ordered the compilation of histories (see RIKKOKUSHI) and poetic anthologies (see KOKINSHŪ). In fact, however, it was also the time of the rebellions of FUJIWARA NO SUMITOMO and TAIRA NO MASAKADO and the decline of the RITSURYŌ SYSTEM of central administration.

English language training 英語教育

(*eigo kyōiku*). English is the most widely studied foreign language in Japan. During the Meiji period (1868–1912), the study of

English was considered essential for importing the Western technology necessary for modernization. Language training was based on reading ability and not on conversation. In the Taishō period (1912–26), under the guidance of the English educator Harold E. Palmer, the oral method of teaching was introduced, but large class sizes and the lack of competent teachers prevented its adoption.

Because the written ENTRANCE EXAMINATIONS for universities and high schools test for English ability, grammar and reading comprehension are stressed in the English classes offered by most high schools and middle schools. However, there is a growing awareness that neglecting speaking and listening during the first six years of English language training leads to problems. The SCHOOL COURSE GUIDELINES for 1989 (to be introduced in 1992) stress spoken communication, and the Ministry of Education has brought in native English speakers as assistant teachers of middle and high school English classes. In 1990 there were 2,146 such assistant teachers invited to Japan. Most universities require students to study two foreign languages, including English.

English conversation schools, courses on television and on radio, and company-run classes for employees offer further training in English. In 1988, some 2,361,982 people took the Test in Practical English Proficiency (offered by the Ministry of Education since 1963).

engo 縁語

("associated words"). A rhetorical device, employed mainly in the forms of classic poetry known as WAKA and RENGA, that relies on a particular word's relation to a preceding word or words in a poem to evoke additional meanings through homonymic or other associations. Used in conjunction with the rhetorical devices of MAKURA KOTOBA ("pillow words"), JOKOTOBA (semimetaphorical "prefaces"), and KAKEKOTOBA ("pivot words"), *engo* first appeared in the 10th-century poetry anthology KOKINSHŪ (Collection from Ancient and Modern Times).

Eniwa 恵庭[市]

City in southwest Hokkaidō on the southern fringe of the Ishikari Plain. Settled in 1871 by farmers from Ōsaka, its principal industries are forestry and dairy farming. More recently several machine factories and food-processing mills have been established. Pop: 55,615.

Eniwa case 恵庭事件

(Eniwa *jiken*). Legal case concerning the constitutionality of the Japanese SELF DEFENSE FORCES. In 1962 Nozaki Takemi and Nozaki Miharu, two brothers who owned a dairy farm in Eniwa, Hokkaidō, cut the telephone wires of the local Self Defense Forces' training ground. According to the brothers their action was a protest against the noise of military exercises that had been reducing the milk yield and reproductive rate of their cows. They were charged with violation of the Self Defense Forces Law. The case stimulated much debate over whether the law violated article 9 of the 1947 constitution, in which Japan had renounced war as a sovereign right. Many constitutional scholars supported the brothers, but the Sapporo District Court dismissed the case on the grounds that telephone wires could not be considered weaponry, thereby avoiding a decision on the constitutional issue.

See also NATIONAL POLICE RESERVE CASE; SUNAGAWA CASE; NAGANUMA CASE.

Enjōji Jirō 円城寺次郎

(1907–   ). Journalist and businessman; president (1968–76) and chairman (1976–80) of the company Nihon Keizai Shimbun Sha, which publishes the newspaper NIHON KEIZAI SHIMBUN. Born in Chiba Prefecture. After graduating from Waseda University in 1933, Enjōji joined the staff of the *Chūgai shōgyō shimpō* (predecessor of *Nihon keizai shimbun*). Under his direction the Nihon Keizai Shimbun Sha established two new newspapers, the *Nikkei ryūtsū shimbun* and the *Nikkei sangyō shimbun*, and set up an online news and information service called the Nikkei Economic Electronic Data Bank System (NEEDS).

enka →ryūkōka

enkai 宴会

Japanese-style banquet usually held in a *tatami*-floored room (*zashiki*). Originally court ceremonial parties held at specific times of the year, *enkai* were later adopted by the general populace for the celebration of important occasions such as New Year parties (*shinnenkai*) and year-end parties (BŌNENKAI). The year-end parties (*bōnen* means "to forget the year") in late December offer an opportunity to forget the trials and misfortunes of the past year as well as to welcome the New Year in a cheerful mood. Year-end parties usually take the form of drinking parties among close friends or coworkers.

Enkai are also held on various other occasions. When someone leaves on a long trip, to study abroad, or for a new work assignment, farewell parties (*sōbetsukai*) are held. Welcome parties (*kangeikai*) are held for new members of a club or new employees at a company. When there are changes in personnel at workplaces, both the employee leaving and the newcomer are guests of honor at a "hello–good-bye party" (*kansōgeikai*).

enkiridera →kakekomidera

Enkū 円空

(ca 1632–95). An itinerant Buddhist priest-sculptor known for his prolific production of Buddhist images. Born in Mino Province (now Gifu Prefecture). As a YAMABUSHI priest of the TENDAI SECT of Buddhism, he traveled

Engakuji The relic hall (pictured) of this temple dates from the 15th century and is the oldest representative example of the Chinese-style (*karayō*) architecture seen in Zen temples in Japan. National Treasure.

Enkū Single-block carving of Aizen Myōō, a fierce minor deity. 17th century. Height 68 cm. Takayama Museum of Local History, Gifu Prefecture.

ennen These ritual performances, which combine drama, dance, and song, are an antecedent of the Nō drama. Pictured is the ennen held annually on 20 January at the temple Mōtsuji, Iwate Prefecture.

ennichi In modern times these feast days have lost most of their religious meaning but retain a festival atmosphere. Pictured here are stalls selling snacks and toys along a street in Tōkyō.

Enomoto Ken'ichi This singing comedian was an early proponent of Western popular music in Japan, including jazz in the 1930s and boogie-woogie and mambo after World War II.

through remote villages and mountain hamlets throughout central Japan up to Hokkaidō. In his youth Enkū made a vow to carve 120,000 Buddhist images. Whether or not he fulfilled this promise is not known, but today nearly 7,000 Enkū carvings have been discovered in temples, private homes, and roadside shrines. It was only after World War II that the aesthetic worth of Enkū's sculptures was recognized. The single-block sculptures of Enkū, roughly cut, seemingly unfinished, and disarmingly simple, are distinctive. The great speed with which he worked enhanced the strength and originality of his style. He chose his subjects to suit the material, often employing the natural grain and shape of the split cedar log as an integral part of the design.

enkyoku 宴曲

("banquet songs"). Also known as *sōka*. Narrative lyric current in the Kamakura (1185–1333) and Muromachi (1333–1568) periods; form of entertainment at banquets held by nobles and warriors. In meter (alternating lines of five and seven syllables) and expression *enkyoku* somewhat resemble the songs (UTAI) of NŌ drama. The narratives were sung to the beating of a fan and some-

times to the accompaniment of the *shakuhachi* (bamboo flute). The priest Myōkū (13th century) is acknowledged as the principal composer-author of *enkyoku* as well as the compiler of most of the extant *enkyoku* collections. (The texts of about 170 *enkyoku* are known today.) Altogether, more than 30 authors of *enkyoku* have been identified. By the Edo period (1600–1868), the *enkyoku* was extinct as a performing art; it influenced KOUTA, the genre that superseded it.

ennen 延年

(literally, "long life"). Composite performance, consisting of plays, dances, and songs, presented at the close of religious ceremonies at Buddhist temples of the Kamakura (1185–1333) and Muromachi (1333–1568) periods. Considered an antecedent of the classical NŌ drama, *ennen* are still performed at a number of temples. The earliest record of the term in the context of drama occurs in an 11th-century diary in reference to a performance at a banquet attended by aristocrats. By the 14th century, however, *ennen* had become established as a genre of performances that appear to have been influenced by court dances accompanied by music (GAGAKU) and humorous short dramas called SARUGAKU and that were acted by monks skilled in the dramatic arts (*yūsō*)

and boys who served at temples (CHIGO). The oldest fully representative extant texts are from performances given between 1518 and 1585.

Originally independent dramatic items that were introduced into the repertory include *kaikō*, *tōben*, *furyū*, and *renji*. *Kaikō* is a preliminary utterance prior to a performance. It is composed of two parts, an introduction in Chinese and a humorous passage using puns and verbal dexterity. *Tōben* is a dialogue based on the humorous section of *kaikō*. *Furyū* (derived from the folk performance FURYŪ) is a dialogue drama performed by richly costumed actors and closing with a dance accompanied by music and song. *Renji* is a dialogue performance interspersed with song; it does not include dance.

Enni 円爾

(1202–80). Zen monk of the RINZAI SECT of Buddhism and the reputed founder of the Kyōto temple TŌFUKUJI. Also known as Enni Bennen; given the posthumous title Shōichi Kokushi. Born in Suruga Province (now part of Shizuoka Prefecture). After first studying Tendai Buddhism, he turned to the study of Zen and traveled to China in 1235, where he studied for six years. After returning to Japan he became the first abbot of Tōfukuji and worked to spread Rinzai Zen through his numerous associations with the imperial family and the court aristocracy. It was through his efforts that Rinzai Zen Buddhism became firmly established in Kyōto.

ennichi 縁日

(feast day). Day held to have a special connection (*en*) with certain Shintō or Buddhist deities. It was believed that those who participated in religious services on such a day would receive special divine favors or acquire merit. The custom of observing the 18th day of the month as the *ennichi* of KANNON or the 24th as that of JIZŌ are some of the earliest established examples. These feast days tended to attract a large number of believers and led to the setting up of booths, fairs, and periodic markets. *Ennichi* became increasingly secularized from the 15th century; sources from the Edo period (1600–1868) describe *ennichi* as drawing crowds of fun-loving townspeople. Today, *ennichi* have been largely emptied of their religious meaning, with temple compounds and the immediate neighborhood resembling a vast fairground.

Ennin 円仁

(794–864). Buddhist priest of the Japanese TENDAI SECT. Born in Shimotsuke Province (now Tochigi Prefecture), he became a disciple of SAICHŌ at the temple ENRYAKUJI on Mt. Hiei (Hieizan) in 809. After studying esoteric and Tendai Buddhism in China (838–847) he returned to Mt. Hiei to propagate esoteric doctrines, which within several years came to dominate the Tendai sect. Furthermore, he established *nembutsu-zammai* (NEMBUTSU meditational exercises) based on the musical *nembutsu* then current at the celebrated Chinese Buddhist center on Mt. Wutai (Wu-tai) in Shanxi (Shanhsi) Province; this is the seed that, on flourishing, made Mt. Hiei the center of PURE LAND BUDDHISM later in the Heian period (794–1185). In 854 Ennin was appointed the third chief abbot of the Tendai sect. He was given the posthumous title Jikaku Daishi. Ennin and his diary (*Nittō guhō junrei kōki*) are the subject of a book by Edwin O. Reischauer, *Ennin's Travels in T'ang China* (1955).

En no Gyōja 役行者

Semilegendary sorcerer of the late 7th century. Also known as En no Ozunu. He practiced asceticism on Mt. Katsuragi in Yamato (now Nara Prefecture). Karakuni no Muraji Hirotari, an envious follower, made false charges that led to En no Gyōja's exile to the island of Ōshima in Izu in 699. According to legend, En no Gyōja would bind with a spell spirits and demons (see ONI) who refused to do his bidding. He is said to have ordered spirits to make a rock bridge from Mt. Katsuragi to Kimbusen (see KIMPUSENJI). He is considered the founder of SHUGENDŌ, a Buddhistic tradition based on religious asceticism, and is venerated as En no Gyōja or Jimben Dai Bosatsu (Miraculous Great Bodhisattva).

Enomoto Ken'ichi 榎本健一

(1904–70). Singing comedian. Best known by his stage name, Enoken. At age 17 he began his show-business career in his hometown of Tōkyō. By the time he established his own Enoken Troupe in 1932, he was a top star who had created a uniquely cosmopolitan Tōkyō style of comedy. Beginning in 1935 Enoken alternated his frequent stage appearances with starring roles in Japan's first film musicals, directed by his long time collaborator YAMAMOTO KAJIRŌ. Many of Enoken's stage and film vehicles were parodies of period pieces with familiar heroes, which he alternated with comedies about contemporary life in Tōkyō and occasional appearances in experimental stage productions. As the nation's most popular entertainer between 1935 and 1955, Enoken was the major force in the postwar comedy revival, starring in film, television, radio, and stage performances. Enoken's archetypal character was the clever, pathetic little man—small in physical and social status—who explodes in revolt against the frustrations of everyday life.

Enomoto Takeaki 榎本武揚

(1836–1908). Naval officer, diplomat, and statesman who served the Tokugawa shogunate and subsequently the Meiji government. Born in Edo (now Tōkyō). In 1858 Enomoto became a teacher at the shogunate's naval school in Edo. From 1862 until 1866 he studied law, military science, and mechanics in Holland. Influential in naval affairs after his return, Enomoto rose to become vice commander-in-chief of the navy.

In October 1868, some eight months after the MEIJI RESTORATION had ended shogunal rule, Enomoto escaped from Edo with eight warships and a small army of Tokugawa supporters and headed for Ezo (now Hokkaidō). Late that year he declared Ezo an independent republic. Imperial forces under KURODA KIYOTAKA landed in Ezo in 1869 and after heavy fighting (see GORYŌKAKU, BATTLE OF) Enomoto surrendered. He was imprisoned but received a special pardon in 1872. In 1874 Enomoto became vice admiral and was appointed envoy extraordinary and minister plenipotentiary to Russia. Enomoto concluded the Treaty of ST. PETERSBURG with Russia on 7 May 1875, according to which Japan abandoned all claims to Sakhalin in exchange for the central and northern Kuril Islands.

Enomoto was appointed navy minister in 1880. In 1882 he became minister to China and assisted the oligarch ITŌ HIROBUMI in concluding the 1885 Treaty of Tianjin (see TIAN-JIN [TIENTSIN] CONVENTION). Enomoto held a series of cabinet posts after 1885: communications, education, foreign affairs, and agriculture and commerce. In 1887 he was made a viscount and in 1890 he was named adviser to the Privy Council. In 1897 he resigned as minister of agriculture and commerce in protest against the ASHIO COPPER MINE INCIDENT.

Enoshima 江の島

Island in Sagami Bay, south of the city of Fujisawa, southern Kanagawa Prefecture, central Honshū. It is connected with Katase on the mainland by a sandbar and two bridges. Located near the city of Kamakura and only one hour by train from Tōkyō, Enoshima is a popular tourist spot. Enoshima Shrine has been a popular place of worship since the Kamakura period (1185–1333). Area: 0.2 sq km (0.08 sq mi).

Enryakuji 延暦寺

Head temple of the TENDAI SECT of Buddhism; located on HIEIZAN, a mountain on the outskirts of Kyōto. Hieizan has been a center for religious practices since the Heian period (794–1185). The founders of new sects during both the Kamakura (1185–1333) and Muromachi (1333–1568) periods were, almost without exception, originally trained at Hieizan. They included RYŌNIN, founder of the YŪZŪ NEMBUTSU SECT; HŌNEN of the JŌDO SECT; SHINRAN of the JŌDO SHIN SECT; EISAI, who introduced the RINZAI SECT to Japan; DŌGEN who did the same for the SŌTŌ SECT; and NICHIREN, founder of the NICHIREN SECT.

In 788 SAICHŌ erected a temple that was named Enryakuji by Emperor SAGA in 823. By the end of the 9th century, under the third abbot, ENNIN, and the fifth, ENCHIN, Enryakuji flourished as the center of the esoteric teachings of the Tendai sect (taimitsu). By the time of RYŌGEN, its 18th abbot, in the 10th century, a conflict arose between the sammon, or "mountain faction," based at Enryakuji and the jimon, or "temple faction," based at MIIDERA, which led to a period of armed struggle lasting from 993 through the 15th century involving thousands of WARRIOR-MONKS (sōhei). ODA NOBUNAGA viewed Enryakuji as a threat to his campaign to unify the country and in 1571 destroyed much of the complex. Many new buildings were added later. Among them the Kompon Chūdō (1642), the third largest wooden structure in Japan, has been designated a National Treasure.

Enoshima A small island linked to the mainland by a narrow sandbar and bridges, Enoshima is visible in the center of this evening view of Mt. Fuji and Sagami Bay.

Enryakuji, burning of 延暦寺焼打ち

(Enryakuji yakiuchi). An action undertaken by the hegemon ODA NOBUNAGA on 30 September 1571 resulting in the destruction of the vast monastery complex ENRYAKUJI on Mt. Hiei (Hieizan) to the northeast of Kyōto. Enryakuji, as the Japanese headquarters of the TENDAI SECT, represented the quintessence of traditional Buddhism's entrenched power. From the standpoint of Nobunaga, its destruction was a necessary strike at an enemy: Enryakuji, which had military forces at its disposal and occupied a strategic position commanding the approaches to Kyōto from Echizen and northern Ōmi provinces (now parts of Fukui and Shiga prefectures), was at least a covert participant in a coalition of religious and secular lords who planned to destroy the emergent hegemon, and it had in 1570 given shelter to some of their troops. The burning of the Enryakuji was not the temple's end; it was restored under the patronage of Nobunaga's successors, but it never again wielded secular power.

enryo 遠慮

(reserve, constraint). A cardinal principle of personal conduct in Japan. Though a difficult word to translate, it can be illustrated. When a guest unwittingly stays at someone's home until mealtime and the host invites him to a meal, the guest declines out of enryo, but the host insists, saying, "Please, enryo is unnecessary!" The guest may or may not accept the invitation, depending upon how much enryo he decides to maintain vis-à-vis the host. Again, one may keep silent among certain people or keep one's distance toward a specific person out of enryo. If one speaks without reserve in a given circle or helps himself uninvited to another person's material possessions, he may be blamed for not having enryo. Without enryo, one imposes too much of one's needs and demands upon others. With too much enryo, one can never become close to others. Enryo is least expected between parents and children, and then between other close kin and friends. According to the psychologist Doi Takeo (b 1920), enryo is least needed where AMAE (dependency need) is most gratified. Neither is enryo expected between total strangers. It is expected between those who are neither

entrance examinations Triumph and tragedy prevail at Tōkyō University as applicants check entrance examination results, posted at left. In the foreground, university rugby club members recruit successful examinees.

close relatives nor total strangers. As a counterbalance to *amae*, it prevents people from imposing on or presuming too much of one another. A considerable degree of social tact is required to maintain an appropriate balance between *enryo* and *amae* in Japanese interpersonal relationships.

En school 円派

(Empa). Group of sculptors of Buddhist images active in the late Heian period (794–1185). It originated in the Sanjō workshop (BUSSHO) established by CHŌSEI, a disciple of the famed sculptor JŌCHŌ. Since many sculptors in this group include *"en"* in their names they became known to later generations as the En school. During the late Heian period the group was active in Kyōto along with the rival IN SCHOOL. En-school sculpture played a leading role in Buddhist sculpture. MYŌEN (d 1199) was one of the last major En-school sculptors.

Enshū Sea 遠州灘

(Enshū Nada). Also called the Tōtōmi Sea (Tōtōmi Nada) or the Tenryū Sea (Tenryū Nada). Part of the Pacific Ocean off western Shizuoka and Aichi prefectures, central Honshū. Extending from the western end of the Atsumi Peninsula to the cape Omaezaki, it has been regarded as dangerous since ancient times because of its heavy seas. Bonito and tuna are caught here.

ensoku 遠足

One-day field trips taken by classes of kindergarten, elementary, or middle school students under the guidance of their teachers. Classified as one of the GAKKŌ GYŌJI (school events), *ensoku* are usually taken twice annually, once each in spring and autumn. Activities and locales for these trips are chosen to provide healthy recreation (such as hiking trips to the seaside or mountains) or opportunities to experience and observe the adult world (such as tours of factories or newspaper publishers).

Ensuikō Sugar Refining Co, Ltd 塩水港精糖[株]

(Ensuikō Seitō). Sugar refining company. Incorporated in 1950. The company, a subsidiary of Taiyō Fishery Co, Ltd, has two affiliates, Taiheiyō Sugar Refining and Daishin Sugar Refining. For the fiscal year ending March 1991, sales totaled ¥28.4 billion (US $207.0 million) and capitalization stood at ¥1.8 billion (US $13.1 million). Headquarters are in Yokohama.

Entairyaku 園太暦

Abbreviation of *Nakazono taishōkoku ryakki* (Diary of the Great Minister Nakazono),

diary of the courtier Tōin Kinkata (1291–1360; religious title, Nakazono), grand minister of state (*dajō daijin*) in both the NORTHERN AND SOUTHERN COURTS. The diary describes political and social conditions during that tumultuous period. Only one of more than 120 scrolls survives complete, covering the year 1311. Summaries of entries for 1343–60 were made in the 15th and 16th centuries.

enterprise groups → keiretsu

Enterprise Incident エンタープライズ事件

(*Entāpuraizu* Jiken). Mass demonstrations in Tōkyō, Sasebo, and other cities, preceding the visit to Japan in January 1968 of the American aircraft carrier *Enterprise* and two escort ships. Though some of the demonstrations were violent, only minor incidents took place during the carrier's five-day visit to Sasebo beginning 19 January. The *Enterprise* was the first nuclear-powered surface warship to enter Japan, although for four years US nuclear-powered submarines had been visiting Japan. The carrier was engaged in combat off the coast of Vietnam and was widely thought to be carrying nuclear weapons, stirring Japanese fears of involvement in the Vietnam War and of violations of Japan's antinuclear policy. Smaller nuclear-powered warships of the US Navy entered Japanese ports regularly after the *Enterprise* visit. For several years the Japanese public continued to be greatly concerned over the reported danger of radioactive effects caused by these vessels. See also HIKAKU SANGENSOKU.

enterprise unions → labor unions

entō 遠島

(literally, "remote island"). Also known as *shimanagashi*. A punishment of exile to a remote island and total confiscation of property; next to execution, it was considered the most severe punishment, and any attempt to escape was punishable by death. In the Edo period (1600–1868) *entō* was the punishment for gambling, manslaughter, statutory rape, and breaking priestly vows of chastity (*nyobon*). Although *entō* was in principle for life, pardons were occasionally granted. Following the Meiji Restoration (1868), *entō* was discontinued. See also PENAL SYSTEM.

entrance examinations 入学試験

(*nyūgaku shiken*). Entrance examinations are given great weight in Japan's educational system. Although nursery, primary, and middle schools also conduct such tests, Japanese society attaches the most importance to entrance exams for public and private high schools and universities.

High school is attended by 94 percent of middle school graduates in Japan, so the function of high school entrance tests is not to weed out unqualified applicants, but to determine which school a student may attend. Private high schools design their own tests and conduct applicant interviews to select students, while public high school entrance standards are determined by the local school system. Generally, achievement test results in five categories (English, mathematics, Japanese, social studies, and science) are evaluated, along with the student's junior high school records, to rank applicants.

Objective achievement-test performance is the key factor in university applicant selection, but certain universities or depart-

ments may include essay-writing tests (usually on contemporary social issues), or performance tests for applicants in music or physical education, in their evaluation process. Private universities also prepare their own examinations in certain subjects. All national and other public universities (and a few private ones) require prospective applicants to take the UNIVERSITY ENTRANCE EXAMINATION CENTER TESTS—a series of standardized multiple-choice examinations measuring competence in the Japanese language, social studies, mathematics, science, and foreign languages. Based on the results, students may then make a more informed choice as to which schools to apply to. Ultimately, admission is based on the combined results of the general test plus the independent examination offered by the university in question. Entrance examinations for both high schools and universities are administered each year during the period from January through March. Students may apply to more than one high school or university and to more than one department within a university.

The Japanese entrance examination system does not establish in advance a target score that, if achieved, assures admission; those applying at the same time compete for a limited number of openings. In Japanese society it is generally accepted that the school (particularly, the university) one attends will decisively influence the course of one's life and career (see GAKUREKI SHAKAI). Entrance tests are therefore regarded as major events in determining one's fate, and the battle to qualify for the best schools is waged with fierce intensity. The competition perceptibly heightened in the 1960s and is seen as having assumed excessive proportions in the 1980s. This has not only led to enormous prosperity for the operators of JUKU and CRAM SCHOOLS and other principals of the so-called examination industry, but is also thought to have helped precipitate many education-related problems. These include increasing juvenile delinquency, apathy on the part of students not targeted as high achievers, and SCHOOL ALLERGY, a phenomenon whereby some students are unable to attend school for emotional reasons.

Entsuba Katsuzō 円鍔勝三

(1905–). Sculptor. Real name Entsuba Katsuji. Born in Hiroshima Prefecture. A graduate of Japan Art College (Nihon Bijutsu Gakkō), he studied under the sculptor SAWADA SEIKŌ. Characterized by a bright lyricism, his works were awarded special honors at the Nitten (Japan Art Exhibition) and Bunten (Ministry of Education Fine Arts Exhibition). He was chief director of the Japan Sculpture Association (Nihon Chōkokukai) and received the Order of Culture in 1988.

Environment Agency 環境庁

(Kankyōchō). Government agency attached to the Prime Minister's Office responsible for environmental conservation and pollution control. Established in 1971, the agency, with a director-general of cabinet rank, is charged with the implementation of antipollution laws, the planning and coordination of governmental pollution-related activities, the establishment of environmental quality standards and emission standards for specific pollutants, the compilation of statistics and related data on pollution, and the administration of education and training programs in pollution control.

environmental law 環境法

(*kankyō hō*). Laws aimed at the prevention and control of pollution, the preservation of nature, and the resolution of disputes arising from pollution. Starting in the 1950s and reaching its peak in the 1960s, rapid industrial growth concentrated in a relatively small area combined with governmental indifference resulted in a series of pollution disasters, the best known of which is the incident of mercury poisoning known as Minamata disease (see POLLUTION-RELATED DISEASES). Undoubtedly because of the trauma of such disasters, Japanese environmental law is most highly developed in those areas directly concerning public health.

The Statutory Framework of Environmental Policy——The fundamental law establishing the principles and objectives of environmental policy and providing the legal mechanism for their implementation is the POLLUTION COUNTERMEASURES BASIC LAW (Kōgai Taisaku Kihon Hō). Enacted in 1967 and then significantly strengthened in 1970, it follows the pattern set by other "basic laws" (*kihon hō*), broadly setting forth the relative priorities of pollution abatement policy, the administrative structure and methods for its implementation, and the respective responsibilities of all the parties involved in pollution. Although the Basic Law has no specific legally binding provisions, it anticipated and made possible the specific legislation that followed. Priority is given to health protection by article 1 of the law. Subsequent legislation directly addresses the conservation of nature for its own sake, but it consists of relatively weak and peripheral statutes.

Aside from setting broad objectives, the law also outlines the measures to be taken to attain them and delineates generally governmental and private areas of responsibility. Private enterprises are urged to take measures to prevent pollution and are obligated to bear "all or part of the necessary cost" of their own antipollution measures and of those taken by the state to control pollution arising from that enterprise's activities.

In terms of the state's responsibilities, the Basic Law sets forth a blueprint for legislative and administrative action, most of which has been vigorously implemented. Besides the abstract injunction to "establish fundamental and comprehensive policies" for environmental pollution control, the state must establish environmental quality standards for air, water, noise, and soil; develop a system of monitoring and surveillance of environmental conditions; and disseminate information about pollution. Although the Basic Law called for the consideration of environmental problems in regional planning, the government has not followed through on this particular aspect of the law.

As a response to the failure of the Pollution Countermeasures Basic Law to commit the government to the preservation of the natural environment per se, environmentalists have developed the concept of an ENVIRONMENTAL RIGHT. Based on the constitutional guarantees of a full and cultured life, the environmental right would require a court to enjoin any public or private act that threatened to harm the environment. However, the future of Japanese environmental law is much more likely to be found in the gradual loosening of administrative and tort doctrines to permit greater use of injunctive re-

lief against those responsible for pollution. See also ENVIRONMENTAL QUALITY.

environmental quality 環境問題

(*kankyō mondai*). Environmental pollution in Japan has accompanied industrialization since the Meiji period (1868–1912). Among the earliest cases were the copper poisoning caused by drainage from the Ashio Copper Mine in Tochigi Prefecture, beginning as early as 1878 (see ASHIO COPPER MINE INCIDENT), and the air pollution created by the Besshi Mine Field in Shikoku, first noticed in 1893. The subsequent development of the textile and paper and pulp industries led to water pollution, and the use of coal as the major fuel for industry in general contributed to widespread but still localized air pollution. In the period of rapid growth following World War II, however, the isolated cases coalesced into a national crisis, with Japan becoming one of the most polluted countries in the world.

Public and private concern with environmental protection has gone through a series of distinct stages in Japan. At first there was widespread ignorance on the part of the public and apathy on the part of the government, which was loath to permit anything that might interfere with the rapid economic growth of the postwar period. Thus, although the pollution-related Minamata disease (see POLLUTION-RELATED DISEASES) was first reported in May 1956, it was found to have existed since 1953. The existence of the disease had been concealed and patients secretly hospitalized in municipal isolation wards for fear this "weird" disease was contagious. Although a Kumamoto University research team identified mercury from the CHISSO CORPORATION plant as the cause of the disease in 1959, the government (MINISTRY OF HEALTH AND WELFARE) did not officially recognize this as the cause until 1968. By the late 1960s, however, the degradation of the environment had deeply struck the national consciousness, and a series of strict environmental protection measures were taken.

These were quite successful in some areas, most notably in the removal of toxic substances from the water and the reduction of sulfur oxides in the air, measures that helped to dull the public's sense of urgency. At the same time other concerns came increasingly to the fore, especially such economic issues as inflation, unemployment, the sharp increase in oil prices following the oil crisis of 1973, the decline of industries such as shipbuilding and textiles, the prolonged slump in others such as steel, and the ending of the period of rapid growth. Under these conditions, public pressures for a clean environment became subdued and the government weakened its standards. Thus, whereas in May 1973 the ENVIRONMENT AGENCY set a maximum permissible level for nitrogen oxides (a major contributor to photochemical smog) of 0.02 ppm (parts per million), the world's strictest standard, met in only 16.5 percent of the places monitored in 1976, it agreed in June 1978 to a request by the MINISTRY OF INTERNATIONAL TRADE AND INDUSTRY (MITI) and business circles to relax the standard to 0.06 ppm in cities and 0.04 ppm elsewhere. By the late 1970s, then, the urgency with which Japan, prodded by public sentiment, had responded to environmental problems a decade earlier was lost. Still, much of the struggle against pollution had already been institutionalized, and further moderate improvement seemed in store, although the long-range outlook remained uncertain.

1878	Drainage from the Ashio Copper Mine, Tochigi Prefecture, contaminates nearby rivers.
1893	Air pollution from the Besshi Mine Field, Ehime Prefecture, is first noticed.
1953	Minamata disease appears in Kumamoto Prefecture.
1955	First public reports of *itai-itai* disease, previously diagnosed by a doctor in Toyama Prefecture.
1963	Marked increase in the number of cases of asthma in Yokkaichi, Mie Prefecture, is first connected to air pollution from an industrial complex.
1964	Minamata disease appears in Niigata Prefecture.
1967	Pollution Countermeasures Basic Law is passed.
1968	Air Pollution Control Law is passed.
1970	Photochemical smog appears in Tōkyō.
1971	Environment Agency is established.
1972	Nature Conservation Law is passed.
1974	National Institute for Environmental Study is established.
1980	Research begins on acid rain.
1983	Dioxin is found in emissions from trash incineration.
1988	Ozonosphere Protection Law is passed, with provisions to reduce the use of chlorofluorocarbons.
1989	Air Pollution Control Law is amended to control the use of asbestos.

In four major lawsuits regarding pollution-related diseases, the right of the victims to compensation was established. The decisions in cases involving *itai-itai* disease (1971), Niigata Minamata disease (1971), Yokkaichi asthma (1972), and Kumamoto Minamata disease (1973) eased the burden of proof on the victims. These decisions made it possible to demonstrate the cause-effect relations by using epidemiological evidence rather than by showing such relations in each individual instance of the disease, and they clarified the responsibility of the companies to ensure that their activities were nonpolluting and to prevent pollution from actually taking place.

Water pollutants are divided into two broad categories: those that affect human health directly (cyanides, alkyl mercury, organic phosphorous, cadmium, lead, sexivalent chrome, arsenic, and total mercury) and those that affect the living environment (including biochemical oxygen demand and chemical oxygen demand). Efforts to limit noxious substances in the first category have been much more successful than efforts to limit the organic pollution of the second category. Four major factors have especially contributed to the emergence in Japan of water-pollution problems: rapid industrialization, rapid urbanization, the lag in constructing such social overhead capital facilities as sewage systems, and the fact that water pollution in Japan emerged from a public policy that heavily favored economic growth over public health and a clean environment. The lag in the construction of sewage systems was thus just one part of a systematic policy outlook.

As a consequence of the increased concern with pollution problems since the late 1960s, there has been an overall improvement in water quality, but the progress has been uneven. Strict emission controls on waste industrial waters have reduced cases of toxic-substance pollution to a very small number. On the other hand, rivers—especially medium-sized and smaller rivers—and coastal waters within metropolitan districts continue to suffer considerable pollution from organic substances. The problem is even more severe in bays, inland seas, lakes, and other water areas with a somewhat "walled-in" character, including Tōkyō, Ise, and Ōsaka bays and Lakes Biwa, Kasumigaura, and Suwa. In these areas there is relatively little "transfusion" of water, so the enormous amounts of nutritive salts of nitrogen and phosphorus poured into them lead to a multiplication of plankton or algae and eutrophication.

Another water-pollution problem, one whose dimensions are still not clear, is that of thermal pollution. As an increasing number of power plants are being built on an ever-larger scale, their heating of surrounding waters poses a threat to marine life and the fishing industry, which has already been severely affected by water pollution. Although heavy-metal pollution is no longer a serious problem in most of Japan's coastal waters, the ports, harbors, and their surrounding coastal waters remain highly polluted; in addition to household and industrial wastes discharged directly or via rivers, oil dumped by ships, often deliberately, is a significant source of maritime pollution. Among the maritime areas, the INLAND SEA is especially polluted.

A number of measures have been taken to improve the quality of the water in Japan. These include the setting of national standards for toxic substances and of variable standards for the living environment (depending on the use and type of water area) and the establishing of strict effluent controls and of a comprehensive surveillance and monitoring system. Also, many laws fixing responsibility for pollution damages have been passed, court decisions favorable to victims have reinforced these, and projects to improve sewers have extended sewer service to a greater proportion of the population.

Japan's efforts to control air pollution have also met with mixed results. For certain pollutants, sharp decreases in concentration have been recorded, while in other cases concentrations remain high. The greatest success has been attained in limiting pollution by sulfur oxides and carbon monoxide. The relatively successful control of sulfur oxides reflects a long-term commitment on the part of the government to reduce their concentrations.

In the case of nitrogen oxides, emission standards were not adopted until August 1973, and the overall relaxation of standards in 1978 suggested that the delay in significantly reducing nitrogen oxide concentrations in the air could be prolonged indefinitely. Photochemical smog, to which nitrogen oxides are a principal contributor, first appeared in Tōkyō in July 1970; since then it has appeared regularly in different parts of Japan.

Besides water and air pollution, the Japanese government recognizes and has taken measures to cope with a variety of other forms of pollution or environmental disruption, including noise, vibration, waste disposal, ground subsidence, offensive odors, soil pollution, and pollution by agricultural chemicals. The number of complaints about noise received by government officials each year is greater than for any other type of pollution. The greatest number of complaints concerns noise from factories, but construction, traffic, airport, and railroad (especially the high-speed SHINKANSEN line) noise have all generated a considerable number of complaints.

In response to the sharp deterioration in the natural environment caused by the postwar period of rapid economic growth, the Nature Conservation Law was passed in 1972 to serve as the basis for all legal measures to protect the natural environment. To protect nature and promote recreation, an extensive system of national parks, quasinational parks, and prefectural natural parks was established. In urban areas, the government has sought to expand city park areas.

Environmental deterioration has led to sharp decreases in the number of such birds as hawks and owls, while various species, including the Japanese crested ibis, the stork, and the red-crested crane, have become threatened with extinction (see RED DATA BOOK). Since 1972, however, the observed number of migratory birds—ducks, swans, and geese—has generally been increasing, suggesting that environmental protection measures are bringing favorable results.

The POLLUTION COUNTERMEASURES BASIC LAW was passed in 1967 in response to accelerated environmental deterioration brought on by rapid economic growth. It sought to create common principles and policies for pollution control in all government agencies, which previously had carried out their antipollution efforts for the most part independently of each other, and to promote an integrated effort to clean up the environment. The Basic Law targets air pollution, water contamination, noise, vibration, ground subsidence, and offensive odors and indicates the responsibilities of the central government, local governments, and business firms with regard to controlling these. In addition, the Basic Law laid the framework for establishing environmental quality standards, drafting pollution-control programs, and aiding victims of diseases caused by pollution.

Although antipollution policies are mainly national, much of the enforcement is done at a prefectural or municipal level. Moreover, to facilitate taking into account specific local conditions, the designation and classification of pollution or environmental protection zones are often done by local governments, which are also empowered to adopt standards stricter than national ones if they feel that local conditions require such action. In the 1970s Japan adopted the Polluter Pays Principle, according to which polluting enterprises had to accept financial responsibility for damages they inflicted on the community. Even so, the tolerable limits remained high for many substances, and it became clear that, when environmental goals conflicted with "stable" growth, the latter would prevail.

By the 1980s the public outcry over pollution that characterized the two preceding decades had subsided, though many problems still remained. Moreover, new environmental issues, such as groundwater contamination by organic solvents in the effluence from semiconductor factories, the pollution of rivers and streams by agricultural chemicals used to maintain the grounds of golf courses, and ACID RAIN, have aroused concern. The swift growth of Japan's economy has also been accompanied by large-scale land development, and the attendant damage to the natural environment has spurred increasing attention to CONSERVATION issues.

In the late 1980s a growing body of scientific evidence suggested that the ozone layer of the atmosphere is being destroyed by chlorofluorocarbons and that an increase in carbon dioxide in the atmosphere is causing a general rise in world temperatures. Concern over these findings in Japan, which produces 10 percent of the annual world supply of chlorofluorocarbons, led to the passing of the Ozonosphere Protection Law of 1988. The Japanese government has declared that the chief object of its environmental policy in the 1990s is to make contributions toward the improvement of the global environment. See also INDUSTRIAL WASTE; MINING POLLUTION.

environmental right 環境権

(*kankyōken*). A constitutional right advocated by Japanese environmentalists that would protect the natural environment from deterioration. First proposed in 1970, the environmental right theory has gained significant popular support and is often cited by plaintiffs in environmental litigation, although it has not been explicitly recognized by the courts. See also ENVIRONMENTAL LAW.

enza 縁坐

A kind of collective responsibility according to which the family of a criminal was subject to the same penalty as the criminal. Under the TAIHŌ CODE (701) *enza* was applied mainly in cases of treason or rebellion, the miscreant and his sons or brothers being stripped of office or exiled. Later, in the Muromachi period (1333–1568), it was invoked for a wider variety of crimes, including murder. During the Edo period (1600–1868) the application of *enza* to commoners was generally restricted to cases of patricide or murder of a superior; for *samurai*, it was more broadly and frequently invoked. *Enza* continued to be practiced until 1882.

Enzan 塩山[市]

City in northeastern Yamanashi Prefecture, central Honshū. It is a distribution center for lumber and stone material. Agricultural products are grapes and peaches. The graves of TAKEDA SHINGEN and YANAGISAWA YOSHIYASU are located at the temple Erinji. The city is the gateway to the CHICHIBU-TAMA NATIONAL PARK. Enzan Hot Spring has been known for its curative waters since the 14th century. Pop: 26,551.

Equal Employment Opportunity Law for Men and Women
男女雇用機会均等法

(Danjo Koyō Kikai Kintō Hō). Law designed to eliminate discrimination against women in the workplace. The law was passed in May 1985 (effective in April 1986) to enable ratification of the United Nations Convention for Eliminating All Forms of Discrimination against Women, which Japan had signed in 1980.

The chief provisions of the law are these: (1) employers must provide equal opportunities to women in recruiting, hiring, transfer of work assignment or place, and promotion; (2) employers must not discriminate between men and women with regard to education and training, benefits, retirement age, resignation, or dismissal; (3) employers are required to establish bureaus to handle grievances related to equal employment opportunity policies and to work with women to resolve them; (4) an equal opportunity mediation commission must be established in each prefectural Women's and Young Workers' Office to settle disputes.

On passage of the Equal Employment Opportunity Law for Men and Women, the Labor Standards Law of 1947 was revised to relax restrictions on overtime and holiday work by women and to abolish restrictions on night work by women managers and professionals.

equality of the sexes under the law 両性の平等

(*ryōsei no byōdō*). Prior to 1945 women's civil rights were restricted, and women were not treated equally with men under family, labor, or property law. The postwar CONSTITUTION OF JAPAN, which came into effect in 1947, guaranteed the equality of the sexes (art. 14). Under Japan's revised CIVIL CODE women were recognized as legal persons capable of holding property and entering into legal agreements. Husband and wife became equal partners in marriage and shared equal responsibility for and authority over their children (see also DIVORCE). The INHERITANCE LAW was also revised to afford women the same rights as men.

An impediment to the achievement of absolute equality, however, was the fact that article 14 of the constitution could be interpreted as permitting different treatment of men and women when there are reasonable grounds for doing so. Hence, welfare programs and labor legislation applying only to women were upheld as constitutional, as were certain restrictions on working conditions that in effect deprived women of employment opportunities (see WOMEN WORKERS, PROTECTIVE LEGISLATION FOR). Although the Labor Standards Law of 1947 specifically provided for equal wages for men and women, this provision was not strictly enforced. It was the custom among privately owned companies to ask female workers to retire after marriage, until 1967, when the Supreme Court held this practice to be illegal. Instances of such treatment are now rare.

In 1981 the Supreme Court ruled in a case involving the auto industry that a five-year difference in the retirement ages for male and female workers was a violation of constitutionally mandated public policy (see also DISMISSAL OF EMPLOYEES). In 1985 the Diet passed the EQUAL EMPLOYMENT OPPORTUNITY LAW FOR MEN AND WOMEN, which eliminated any legal sanction for restrictions on the rights of women in the workplace. Despite such advances, women in Japan still face various forms and degrees of discrimination in their daily lives (see WOMEN IN JAPAN, HISTORY OF).

equality under the law 法の下の平等

(*hō no moto no byōdō*). Fundamental constitutional principle that takes as its basis a philosophy of individualism in which all individuals have equal value as human beings. Article 14 of the CONSTITUTION OF JAPAN states that "all of the people are equal under the law and there shall be no discrimination in political, economic or social relations because of race, creed, sex, social status or family origin" (para. 1). Accordingly, the article rejects the aristocratic system (para. 2) and recognizes no privilege to accompany any award of honors (para. 3). Furthermore, in addition to guaranteeing universal adult suffrage (art. 15, para. 3), the constitution prohibits any discrimination in setting qualifications for members of both houses of the Diet and their electors (art. 44). It also guarantees sexual equality (art. 24) and

equal opportunity for education (art. 26). All of these stipulations are based upon the principle of equality under the law.

The constitutional principle of equality under the law has been interpreted by the Supreme Court as a prohibition of unjustifiable discrimination, rather than as a guarantee of absolute equality. Judgment on what is unjustifiable discrimination under the constitution may depend upon the special nature of the case, the background of the times, and social and political conditions.

equal opportunity in education 教育の機会均等

(*kyōiku no kikai kintō*). The right of all Japanese, regardless of race, sex, creed, wealth, or social status, to receive an equal education correspondent with their ability is guaranteed by article 26 of the 1947 constitution and article 3 of the Kyōiku Kihon Hō (see EDUCATION, FUNDAMENTAL LAW OF). The principle was set forth in the EDUCATION ORDER OF 1872, but discrimination persisted until after World War II. With the enactment of the Fundamental Law in 1947 all such inequalities were to be swept away, although full equality in higher education has yet to be realized in practice.

era names → nengō

Erimomisaki 襟裳岬

Cape in southern Hokkaidō. Located at the southern tip of the Hidaka Mountains, the cape ends in a towering cliff rising 60 m (197 ft) above the Pacific Ocean. The meeting of cold and warm currents here results in dense summer fog.

erizeni 撰銭

("selecting of coins"). Also known as *erisen* or *sensen*. The practice of appraising coins according to their quality or condition. Beginning in the late Heian period (794–1185), Chinese Song (Sung) dynasty (960–1279) coins (SŌSEN) were introduced to Japan, and by the second half of the 15th century a variety of coins of different copper content were in circulation. Most better-quality coins, such as EIRAKUSEN and KŌBUSEN, were imported from China; poorer quality coins (BITASEN) were usually minted privately in China or Japan. Refusal to accept coins at face value became pronounced after the ŌNIN WAR (1467–77), and many regional DAIMYŌ and powerful temples prohibited *erizeni*, declaring all coins except *bitasen* to be of equal value. The MUROMACHI SHOGUNATE (1338–1573) issued ineffective edicts forbidding *erizeni*. *Erizeni* ended in the Edo period (1600–1868), when the Tokugawa shogunate succeeded in strictly controlling the minting and circulation of coins.

Eroshenko, Vasilii Iakovlevich エロシェンコ, V. I.

(1890–1952). Russian poet, author of children's books, and internationalist. Born in the village of Obukhovka near Kursk, Eroshenko lost his sight at the age of four. A graduate of Moscow's School for the Blind, he went to Japan in 1914 to attend the Tōkyō School for the Blind. He produced popular children's stories dictated in Esperanto and published in Japanese. Eroshenko was expelled from Japan in 1921 for his socialist sympathies. He then taught at Beijing (Peking) University. Returning to the USSR in 1924, Eroshenko taught at Moscow's Communist University of Toilers of the East until

1927. He remained active in the Esperanto movement until his death.

erotic art → shunga

Esaki Reona 江崎玲於奈

(1925–). Physicist known for the semiconductor diode that bears his name. Born in Ōsaka Prefecture, he graduated from Tōkyō University in 1947. He entered Tōkyō Tsūshin Kōgyō Co, Ltd (now SONY CORPORATION), in 1956, and there discovered the tunneling effects in high-concentration p-n junctions, the phenomenon on which his diode was based. This Esaki diode, also called the tunnel diode, with its unique operating characteristics and excellent high-frequency performance, has revolutionized circuit design in the areas of frequency generation, amplification, and switching at ultrahigh frequencies. Esaki moved to the United States in 1960 to join the Watson Laboratories of the International Business Machines Corporation (IBM). In 1973 he won the Nobel Prize in physics, and in 1974 he received the Order of Culture. Esaki became president of Tsukuba University in 1992.

Esaki Reona Recipient of the Nobel Prize for physics in 1973, Esaki became president of Tsukuba University in 1992.

Esashi 江刺[市]

City in southern Iwate Prefecture, northern Honshū. Esashi developed as a trading post for boats on the river KITAKAMIGAWA, but farming is now its main industry. Horses and cattle are raised at the base of the Kitakami Mountains. Pop: 34,434.

Esashi 江差[町]

Port town on the west coast of the Oshima Peninsula in southwestern Hokkaidō. Herring fishing flourished here until the early 20th century. Today salmon and squid fishing and rice and potato farming are the principal economic activities. Pop: 12,234.

eschatology 終末観

(*shūmatsukan*). There is no clear concept of eschatology in the Japanese SHINTŌ tradition. The clearest expression of eschatological thought in Japan is found in the Buddhist concept of *mappō*, or "the latter days of the law," a degenerate age in which the teachings of the Buddha are in decline and people fail to reach enlightenment through their own efforts. Beginning in the late Heian period (794–1185) there was a pervasive sense that Japanese society had entered the age of *mappō*, and a succession of great Buddhist masters such as HŌNEN, SHINRAN, and NICHIREN encouraged their followers to rely on the saving grace of Buddhas such as AMIDA or upon the recitation of certain scriptures such as the LOTUS SUTRA (see TARIKI). Some also believed that the bodhisattva Maitreya (MIROKU), the future Buddha, would come and save those not already saved by the historical Buddha, Gautama. This belief was taken up by later religious leaders including DEGUCHI NAO of the ŌMOTO sect. Drawing on a completely different tradition, Japanese Christians such as UCHIMURA KANZŌ and Nakada Jūji (1870–1939) promoted a movement centered upon awaiting the Second Coming of Christ.

esoteric Buddhism 密教

(*mikkyō*; literally, "the secret teachings"). Also known as *himitsu* Bukkyō, or "secret Buddhism." A special tradition within Buddhism stemming from the belief that the most profound doctrines of Buddhism are to

Etō Jun This noted literary critic and author is also known for his frank criticism of Japanese politics and the postwar intellectual community.

be kept secret, not expounded publicly. The word "secret" also refers to the mystical character of these teachings. Although the origins of this school can be traced back to the early days of Buddhism, the 7th-century Indian monk Nāgārjuna (J: Ryūmyō) is traditionally known as its founder. This school gives the name Mahāvairocana (J: DAINICHI) to the most fundamental Buddha, the principle or essence of all things, whose teachings are said to be expounded by *mikkyō*.

Mikkyō was brought from China to Japan by KŪKAI, whose teachings form the basis of the SHINGON SECT. The esoteric teachings of this particular sect received the name Tōmitsu (Eastern *mikkyō*) to distinguish them from those of the TENDAI SECT, transmitted by SAICHŌ, which go under the name Taimitsu (*mikkyō* of the Tendai sect).

Esperanto エスペラント

(Esuperanto). In Japan the biologist OKA ASAJIRŌ was promoting the cause of the universal language Esperanto as early as 1891. The Japan Esperanto Association (later renamed the Japan Esperanto Institute) was formed in 1906; a dictionary was published the same year. There are an estimated 10,000 speakers and users of Esperanto in Japan.

Esso Sekiyu KK エッソ石油[株]

(Esso Sekiyu). Importer and seller of petroleum products. Incorporated as a Japanese company in 1961. A wholly owned subsidiary of the American company Exxon Corporation. Esso Sekiyu is descended from the Standard Vacuum Oil Co's Japan division, established in 1933. In 1961 that company was divided into Esso Standard Oil Co and the company that would become MOBIL SEKIYU KK. In 1982 Esso Standard was renamed Esso Sekiyu KK. The company maintains 18 branch offices throughout Japan, along with 14 storage tank sites and 1 liquefied petroleum gas (LPG) terminal. Annual sales for the fiscal year ending December 1991 totaled ¥629 billion (US $4.9 billion), and capitalization stood at ¥20 billion (US $156.1 million). Headquarters are in Tōkyō.

Eta Funayama tomb 江田船山古墳

(Eta Funayama *kofun*). A mid-5th-century mounded tomb (KOFUN) located in Eta, Kikusui Chō, Kumamoto Prefecture. In 1873 a crown and other courtly items were recovered from the stone coffin buried in the center of the tomb's rear mound. The most important item was an iron sword with an inscription inlaid in silver on its blade. The illegibility of many of the characters has led to conflicting opinions about the meaning of the inscription and the date of the sword's manufacture. Scholars once thought that one set of characters should be read Tajihi no Mizuha Wake and that it thus referred to the Yamato ruler posthumously known as Emperor Hanzei (first half of the 5th century). However, since the discovery in 1978 of similar inscriptions on a sword from the INARIYAMA TOMB and the identification of some characters with an alternative name (Waka Takeru) for Emperor Yūryaku (latter half of the 5th century), a growing number of scholars believe that the Eta Funayama sword, too, should be read Waka Takeru and identified with Yūryaku.

Etajima 江田島[町]

Town on the island of Etajima off the coast of Hiroshima Prefecture. Well known from 1888 as the location of the NAVAL ACADEMY, it is now the home of a Maritime Self Defense Force training school. The area produces cabbages, tomatoes, mandarin oranges, and navel oranges. Oysters and seaweed are also cultivated. Many residents commute to the cities of Kure and Hiroshima. Pop: 15,110.

ethics, East and West
東洋と西洋の倫理学

(Tōyō *to* Seiyō *no rinrigaku*). In the East (meaning chiefly the Chinese cultural sphere, which includes Japan) ethics is the study of intersubjectivity—the study of the community—while in the West it emerges as the study of individuality or subjectivity, thus giving rise to different perceptions on ethical thinking.

The contrast can be observed, for example, in the concept of social responsibility. The English word "responsibility" was not used in the sense of moral accountability for one's actions until the late 18th century, but from the time of ancient Rome there has existed the concept of person (*persona*) as the subject of action. Thus there was the ontological idea that all human beings were equal as persons before God.

In the Far East, the concept of responsibility already existed in the classic period, but the individual was inseparable from his status in the community. Each individual had a responsibility toward heaven and the community, and virtue lay in carrying out this responsibility. This concept made its appearance in medieval Japan under the form of the Japanese term *giri*. The superiority of *giri* (community responsibility) as opposed to *ninjō* (personal emotions) formed the theme of much of the literature of the Edo period (1600–1868). (See GIRI AND NINJŌ.) The idea of suicide as the highest form of taking responsibility demonstrates that there was no concept of an ontological *persona* forming the nucleus of historical existence.

In ancient Japan the KOJIKI, the NIHON SHOKI, the SEMMYŌ (imperial proclamations), and the NORITO (ritual Shintō prayers) all cited a clear, pure, and upright heart (*akaki, kiyoki, naoki kokoro*) as ideal. The white clothes worn at Shintō shrines attest to the importance placed on purity. The ENGI SHIKI, a code of practices dating from 927, contains the ritual prayers known as *Minazuki no tsugomori no ōharae*, by which all sins (TSUMI) are said to be blown away with the wind and carried to the bottom of the ocean. This is an approach to sin in which the concept of individual conscience is lacking. This, however, does not mean that the ancient Japanese lacked ethical ideas. A beautiful heart was one filled with the love to care for and nurture all things. This spirit is at the very core of Japanese ethical concepts, no matter what form they take. SUGAWARA NO MICHIZANE, the poet-scholar of the Heian period (794–1185), left a poem that captures this spirit: "If my heart but follow the Way, the gods will watch over me though I neglect to pray to them." As this verse suggests, the Japanese were moving toward an internalized nonreligious ethic with sincerity (see MAKOTO) as its axis. See also MORALITY.

etiquette 礼儀作法

(*reigi sahō*). "Etiquette" refers to conventional rules of behavior concerning interpersonal relationships. It differs from morality or ethics in that it concerns specific rules as applied to concrete situations rather than generalities and states requirements of outward conduct rather than inner beliefs or convictions. This distinction is important, because although at one level of consciousness Japanese recognize that etiquette and morality should go hand in hand, they also recognize that in reality the two may be discrepant.

Formalized Ideal and Real Behavior—When a person bows deeply to a social superior, he or she is supposedly showing respect toward the latter. But both parties know that a deep bow is required even if the former does not respect the latter and that outward behavior can be empty of meaning.

Westerners tend to make personal comfort or their own notions of right and wrong the primary guide for conduct. When faced with a situation that may require conduct and speech that imply contradictory moral stances, Japanese do not feel an inconsistency in moral principle, because moral values are understood to be situation-specific. Therefore, Japanese tend to place greater emphasis on the rules of etiquette in everyday life than do Westerners.

Since Japanese society is based on the notion that one's existence is dependent upon those around one, it is essential to maintain smoothly operating human relations. Society thus demands the suppression of any antagonistic feelings one may have toward another and requires an outward behavior that reflects social harmony. This dichotomy is expressed in the Japanese concept of *tatemae*, or pro forma aspects of social relationships, versus *honne*, or one's inner feelings and intentions (see TATEMAE AND HONNE). The two are not expected to coincide in all cases, but socially proper conduct always takes precedence. Accordingly, Japanese strive to be aware of a possible discrepancy between outward conduct and true feeling and must be able to guess the latter, while interacting as if there were no discrepancy. This is often easier said than done—a reason why intermediaries are so often used in sensitive negotiations.

Although the discrepancy between expected conduct and inner feelings exists in all societies, in Japan it is openly condoned as natural. As a corollary to this, the rules of etiquette are more fully elaborated, and the social expectation to learn and conform to rules of etiquette is very strong.

Social Organization—By specifying rules of behavior appropriate for each status, etiquette helps to define social organization. Japanese etiquette specifies, for example, that the younger show deference to the older, and the female toward the male. The level of formality in speech is one of the more obvious ways in which status difference is manifested. The Japanese language is equipped with an elaborate set of expressions indicating different degrees of respect (see HONORIFIC LANGUAGE). Characteristically, Japanese wear clothes, such as uniforms, that readily manifest their social status, allowing others to interact with them in a socially appropriate manner. Seating arrangement is another way of defining status: those of higher social status are seated at a more honored place, closest to the TOKONOMA (decorative alcove) in a Japanese-style living room.

Status difference may be underlined by deprecating oneself or extolling the other person. It is customary to praise another's house, clothes, and so forth even beyond what is truthful, to create a cognitive reality that, false though it may be, helps participants interact without friction.

Japanese rules of etiquette not only are concerned with how to please and comfort others but are closely related to aesthetics as well. In serving meals, the dishes used and the arrangement of the food must display visual beauty. The manners of walking and of opening and shutting a sliding door emphasize gracefulness of movement. One of the reasons why etiquette assumes such importance in Japan is that it affords the opportunity for aesthetic gratification in everyday life. See also REI.

eto → jikkan jūnishi

Etō Jun 江藤淳

(1933–). Literary critic. Real name Egashira Atsuo. Born in Tōkyō; graduate of Keiō University and professor at the Tōkyō Institute of Technology. Etō made his debut with *Natsume Sōseki ron* (1955), a critique of the Meiji-period (1868–1912) novelist NATSUME SŌSEKI. His *Sakka wa kōdō suru* (1959) argues that a writer's style is inseparably related to his behavior. *Kobayashi Hideo* (1962) is a study of the well-known literary critic. Later Etō published *Ichizoku saikai* (1967–72), in which he seeks his own roots and those of his homeland. Other works include *Seijuku to sōshitsu: Haha no hōkai* (1967) and *Sōseki to sono jidai* (1970). He is outspoken about the present state of politics in Japan and is known for his conservative critique of the postwar intellectual community. He has also written a historical novel, *Umi wa yomigaeru* (5 vols, 1976–83).

Etorofu 択捉

Also known as Iturup. Volcanic island between the Okhotsk Sea and the Pacific Ocean; southwest of the KURIL ISLANDS. The northern tip of Etorofu Island is the northernmost point in Japan at latitude 45° 33' north. The Japanese fleet that attacked Pearl Harbor sailed from Hitokappu Bay on the Pacific coast. At the end of World War II, Etorofu was occupied by the Soviet Union; in early 1992 it was still occupied by the Russian Federation (see TERRITORY OF JAPAN). Area: 3,139 sq km (1,212 sq mi).

Etō Shimpei 江藤新平

(1834–74). Politician known chiefly for his leadership of the unsuccessful SAGA REBELLION against the Meiji government in 1874. Born into a *samurai* family in the Saga domain (now Saga Prefecture). When the BOSHIN CIVIL WAR broke out, Etō was made military superintendent (*gunkan*) in the imperial army. After the MEIJI RESTORATION of 1868 he was appointed to several government posts, including minister of justice (*shihōkyō*) in 1872. He effected numerous legal reforms, including the drafting of the penal code KAITEI RITSUREI. The following year he became a councillor (SANGI) in the Dajōkan. He resigned in 1873 after a proposal by SAIGŌ TAKAMORI to send a military expedition to Korea was rebuffed (see SEIKANRON). Etō returned home to Saga to join others discontented with the loss of the former privileges of the samurai class. This group formed Japan's first nascent political party, the AIKOKU KŌTŌ (Public Party of Patriots) in Tōkyō. Etō was also one of the signers of the Tosa Memorial of January 1874 (Minsen Giin Setsuritsu Kempakusho), which criticized the government and called for the election of a national legislature. After the memorial's rejection he finally resorted to armed force against the government, collecting money and some 3,000 followers for an uprising. After the insurgents attacked a bank in Saga, government forces suppressed

the rebellion, and Etō was captured and executed.

Eugenic Protection Law 優生保護法

(Yūsei Hogo Hō). Law aimed at the protection of the life and health of mothers and at preventing the birth of deformed children. The law was enacted in 1948 as a replacement for the National Eugenic Law (1940). Its main provisions are as follows. Surgery may be performed to sterilize a woman when the woman, her spouse, or a family member within the fourth degree of kinship has a serious genetic disease, and there is a fear that pregnancy or childbirth will endanger her life. The operation requires the consent of the woman as well as of her spouse. Such surgery is performed after the investigation and review of a prefectural Eugenic Protection Council. An abortion may be performed if the woman, her spouse, or a relative of the fourth degree of kinship has a hereditarily transmitted malady; if the subject or her spouse has leprosy; if the health of the mother is in serious danger; if the pregnancy has resulted from rape; if the fetus is not viable outside the mother. The consent of the woman and of her spouse is necessary. The implementation and guidance of birth control are limited to doctors, nurses, and midwives. Persons other than doctors allowed to work in this area must be designated by the prefectural government. In prefectures and towns that establish health centers, Eugenic Protection Counseling Offices provide marriage counseling and information about birth control methods. Despite its legitimate purpose, the Eugenic Protection Law is often criticized for its discriminatory effects against the handicapped.

Eulenburg, Friedrich Albrecht
オイレンブルク, F. A.

(1815–81). Prussian statesman who opened German relations with Japan. A career diplomat, in 1859 he was made both minister-plenipotentiary and commander of Prussia's Far Eastern Expedition. He arrived in Japan in 1860 and early the following year concluded a treaty of friendship and commerce with the Tokugawa shogunate (1603–1867). He negotiated a similar treaty with China. He then served in the Prussian government for 15 years. His book *Ostasien 1860–62* was important in introducing Japan to European readers.

European Community, economic relations with 日本EC経済関係

(Nihon Ī Shī keizai kankei). Japan's economic relationship with the European Community (EC) is on a considerably smaller scale than its economic ties to the United States. However, both Japan and the EC nations anticipate that their trade and investment ties will grow as Europe moves to unify its market in the 1990s.

The EC is currently the third largest trading area for Japan, ranking behind the United States and Southeast Asia. However, annual trade between Japan and the EC (US $88.5 billion in 1990) is about 60 percent of the total annual US-Japanese trade (US $142.7 billion in 1990). In 1990, 18.7 percent of Japan's exports went to the EC while 14.9 percent of its imports originated from the EC. In the same year, Japan purchased only 6.6 percent of all exports leaving the EC (excluding trade among EC members) while providing 9.1 percent of total imports entering the EC. Japan's principal exports to the EC consisted of electrical and electronic con-

economic relations with the European Community
Trade between Japan and the European Community

billions of US dollars

exports to the European Community

imports from the European Community

1980 1982 1984 1986 1988 1990

SOURCE: Japan Tariff Association, *Gaikoku bōeki gaikyō* (monthly): December issues, 1979–90.

sumer goods, machinery, and transportation equipment, led by automobiles and business-related equipment (computers, photocopy machines etc). Such products accounted for 80.8 percent of Japan's total exports to the EC. Japan's primary imports from the EC include electrical and electronic goods, machinery, chemical products, textiles, and foodstuffs. Consistent Japanese trade surpluses with the EC and the concentration of exports in a small number of products have resulted in various trade disputes. However, in the late 1980s and early 1990s the gradually rising level of imports from the EC, combined with the revitalization of the EC economies, has helped the two sides to avoid some of the serious trade frictions that have developed between Japan and the United States.

Nevertheless, with the buildup to the unification of the EC market in the 1990s, EC reaction to Japanese investment was by no means uniform. Some countries, notably the United Kingdom and the Benelux countries, broadly welcomed it, while others, such as France and Italy, were more wary and even at times critical. Japan's cumulative direct investments in Europe (including European countries that are not EC members) amounted to US $59.3 billion as of fiscal year 1990. This accounted for 19.1 percent of Japan's total direct investments. The United Kingdom was host to the largest portion of these investments (US $22.6 billion), followed by the Netherlands (US $12.8 billion) and Luxembourg (US $5.6 billion). In particular, Japanese manufacturing firms increased their investments significantly in anticipation of the unification of the EC market. As of May 1989 there were 403 cases of Japanese investment, resulting in the employment of approximately 108,000 workers. In addition, Japanese banks and securities companies are in the process of increasing their presence in the EC, prompting demands from the EC that its financial firms be granted similar access to the Japanese market.

Interest in the Japanese market among EC members is also growing, so it is clear that both Japan and the EC have come to recognize the mutual importance of their economic relationship. Furthermore, there is a growing need for cooperation from Japan and the EC to ensure the health of the global economy, such as the efforts by the Group of

Etō Shimpei A highly placed member of the early Meiji government, Etō fell out with other government leaders, resigned, and was later executed for his role in the abortive Saga Rebellion of 1874.

Expo '70 At the first World's Fair held in Asia, Taiyō no tō (Sun Tower), a work by Okamoto Tarō, stood in the center of the Ōsaka exposition grounds.

Expo '85 A nighttime view of this international exposition, which attracted some 20 million visitors.

Expo '90 A night view of the six-month-long flower and gardening exposition that was held in Ōsaka in 1990. Japanese businesses and the government sponsored more than 30 pavilions throughout the site.

Seven (see G5, G7) to stabilize exchange rates and to increase economic policy coordination. Two bodies, the EC-Japan Ministerial Conference (set up in November 1983) and the EC-Japan High-Level Conference (set up in May 1973), have been established so that the two sides can discuss bilateral and global issues.

euthanasia   安楽死

(*anrakushi*). An act of euthanasia constitutes murder in Japan unless the specific conditions of a special legally defined situation are met (Penal Code, arts. 199, 202).

In a well-known 1962 case of euthanasia, the Nagoya High Court convicted a man of murdering his father, rejecting the defense that the father had requested that he be killed because of his unbearable, incurable suffering after a cerebral hemorrhage. The court ruled that taking a person's life was justifiable as an act of euthanasia under certain specified conditions, but that the requirements had not been fulfilled in this particular case.

Dying with Dignity (Songenshi)— In recent years, new problems relating to euthanasia have emerged as a result of the development of medical technology. Many patients with brain damage or other irreparable physical problems continue to survive with severe brain dysfunction in an unconscious state by means of life-supporting medical treatment. Whether an act or omission, such as terminating or withholding this life-supporting treatment, constitutes an act of euthanasia is a difficult question. Such an act or omission is not covered by the conventional concept of euthanasia.

evil   悪

(*aku*). The Japanese understanding of good and evil is somewhat different than that found in the West. In the earliest mythic sources, the adjectives good (*yoshi*) and evil (*ashi*) were associated with an opposition between the beautiful, pure, and ordered and the ugly, unpure, and disordered. All evil was theoretically capable of being purified and transformed. The Japanese understanding of evil in the ethical and legalistic sense seems to have been formulated under the influence of Confucianism and Buddhism between the mid-5th and mid-6th centuries and was institutionalized in the RITSURYŌ SYSTEM in the 7th century. See also HARAE; KEGARE; TSUMI.

Ewing, James Alfred   ユーイング, J. A.

(1855–1935). British engineer and physicist. One of the FOREIGN EMPLOYEES OF THE MEIJI PERIOD (1868–1912). Born in Scotland. Graduate of the University of Edinburgh. Ewing

Expo '75 Visitors to the 1975 World's Fair held in Okinawa lining up to see the Aquapolis, a marine city.

entered Japan in 1878 and taught mechanical engineering at Tōkyō University. He erected an earthquake observatory on the university grounds, invented a seismometer, and conducted the first seismological research in Japan. He returned to Britain in 1883.

examination hell   試験地獄

(*shiken jigoku*). *Shiken jigoku* is a phrase coined by the Japanese mass media to refer to the trials faced by Japanese students in the highly competitive race to pass the ENTRANCE EXAMINATIONS required for admission to the more prestigious schools and universities. Competition is fueled by the belief that all future success is contingent on academic attainment and affiliations. Sensationalized tales of suicides by despondent applicants or of the trauma suffered by children studying late into the night at JUKU (private tutoring schools) are a staple of the Japanese press, and some observers feel that the entire "examination hell" phenomenon may be largely a product of media exaggeration.

execution of judgment→kyōsei shikkō

existentialism   実存主義

(*jitsuzon shugi*). Existentialism, in the sense of a philosophical style that stresses the priority of the individual in determining the nature of his existence in the face of collectivization and systematization, is primarily associated with European thinkers such as Karl Jaspers, Martin Heidegger, and Jean-Paul Sartre. European existentialism was introduced to Japan prior to World War II and had an important impact on Japanese thought and literature both before and after the war. The ground for this had been prepared, however, by an indigenous existentialist tradition rooted in ZEN. Sources for this Japanese form of existentialism may be traced to DŌGEN's concept of *jizai* (freedom, lack of restriction), MOTOORI NORINAGA's concept of *mono no aware* ("the pathos of things"), and the poetry of BASHŌ. OKAKURA KAKUZŌ, author of *The Book of Tea* (1906), was one of the first modern Japanese thinkers to draw on this tradition, and the thought of NISHIDA KITARŌ, especially his concept of pure experience, also has deep affinities with it. In this sense it is possible to acknowledge an existentialism native to Japan that would later interact with philosophical influences from Europe.

exorcism   憑物落とし

(*tsukimono otoshi*). The various methods whereby a malignant spiritual entity is driven out of the body of a person whom it is possessing. In Japan the entities believed capable of possessing a human being and thereby causing sickness or madness of various kinds are (1) a *kami* (Shintō deity) enraged by neglect or sacrilege; (2) a discontented ancestral spirit, angered by neglect by its descendants of the proper cult attention required by the dead; and (3) a witch animal, such as a fox, a snake, or, in the Shikoku area, a dog (*inugami*).

The process whereby these entities are persuaded to leave the bodies of their victims requires first a competent exorcist. Such a person is usually a YAMABUSHI or a Buddhist priest of the Shingon, Tendai, Nichiren, or occasionally the Zen sect. The techniques he may employ for communicating with the entity include (1) recitation of a holy and potent text such as the Lotus Sutra or a mantra (the sound alone of such a text is sometimes sufficient to effect a cure); (2) a ritual such as the Hikime no Hō of the SHUGENDŌ; and (3) methods whereby the possessing entity is forced to speak, to name itself, to state its grievance, and to agree to terms whereby it will leave its victim. Such methods fall into two groups: (1) The entity is forced to leave its victim and enter the body of a medium, usually a woman or a small child, through whose mouth it is persuaded to answer the questions of the exorcist. (2) The entity is forced to speak through the mouth of the possessed, who is meanwhile reduced to a state of dissociation through long repetition of a sacred formula such as the *daimoku* (holy invocation) of the Nichiren sect. Descriptions of exorcism can be found throughout Heian-period (794–1185) literature, particularly SEI SHŌNAGON's *Makura no sōshi* (Pillow Book) and the diary of MURASAKI SHIKIBU.

expense accounts 交際費

(*kōsaihi*). Funds used by corporations to entertain clients and guests. Beginning in the 1970s the Japanese government sharply curtailed the amount that companies can deduct as entertainment expenses. As of 1990, all such expenses, except for companies with capital of less than ¥50 million (US $333,000), have been disallowed. In computing taxes, corporations must therefore add back such expenses to taxable income and absorb these costs of doing business.

Prior to the sharp change in tax policy, deductible amounts were very liberal, and special deductions were allowed for entertaining foreign buyers. This special provision was created to help encourage exports from Japan but was subsequently eliminated. As a result of relatively liberal provisions for entertainment in the past, a subculture characterized by conspicuous entertainment consumption (*shayōzoku*) grew up. Despite the curtailment of favorable tax treatment, entertainment expenses have still remained at a high level and continue to support a highly developed restaurant and bar industry in Japanese cities of any significant size. The combination of less favorable tax treatment and somewhat stronger emphasis on spending time with one's family among younger people has slowed the growth of conspicuous spending on entertainment, but businessmen in their mid-forties and older still have a fondness for an occasional night on the town with customers. See also SETTAI.

Export-Import Bank of Japan
日本輸出入銀行

(Nihon Yushutsunyū Ginkō). Also known as EXIM Japan. Government-funded financial institution. Established in 1950. It provides a wide range of financial services to Japanese industry in order to supplement medium- and long-term financing offered by private financial institutions for international activities. Credit facilities of EXIM Japan fall into four categories: export credit, import credit, overseas investment credit, and funds recycled to developing countries. EXIM Japan also is authorized to guarantee the obligations of borrowers. It established equity investment operations in 1989. As of the end of March 1990, the bank's total assets were ¥5.9 trillion (US $38.5 billion), outstanding loans were ¥5.7 trillion (US $37.2 billion), and capitalization stood at ¥967.3 billion (US $6.3 billion). Headquarters are in Tōkyō.

Expo '70 日本万国博覧会

(1970 Japan World Exposition; J: Nihon Bankoku Hakurankai). World's Fair held in Ōsaka in 1970, the first in an Asian country. The theme was "Progress and Harmony of Mankind." Its special features were exhibitions about space technology. The exhibition of a stone from the moon and an Apollo spacecraft was one of the most popular attractions. A monorail, a moving sidewalk, electric cars, information outputs from electronic computers for visitors' use, and systematic control of traffic were all introduced at this World's Fair. Approximately ¥120.0 billion (US $330.0 million) was invested, and 77 countries participated in the fair, which was visited by 64 million people.

Expo '75 沖縄国際海洋博覧会

(1975 Okinawa International Ocean Exposition; J: Okinawa Kokusai Kaiyō Hakurankai). World's Fair held in the town of Motobu, Okinawa Prefecture, from July 1975 to January 1976. The exposition, the first international exhibition to focus on the subject of the ocean, attracted the participation of 36 countries. The exhibition site covered 1,000 square kilometers (386 square miles), and the total investment, including related public works projects, was ¥300 billion (US $1 billion). Visitors to the exhibition numbered 3.48 million. Since the close of the exhibition, the site has been used as the Okinawa Old Battlefield National Park.

Expo '85 国際科学技術博覧会

(1985 Tsukuba International Science and Technology Exposition; J: Kokusai Kagaku Gijutsu Hakurankai). World's Fair held in the city of Tsukuba, Ibaraki Prefecture, from 16 March to 16 September 1985. The theme was "Dwellings and Surroundings—Science and Technology for Man at Home." Forty-eight countries, 37 international organizations, 27 domestic enterprises, and 1 Japanese prefecture (Ibaraki) participated. Exhibits included mammoth high-fidelity screens, stereographic images, and robots that played the piano, painted visitors' portraits, and performed other feats. The exposition drew more than 20 million visitors.

Expo '90 国際花と緑の博覧会

(1990 Ōsaka International Garden and Greenery Exposition; J: Kokusai Hana to Midori no Hakurankai). A flower and gardening exposition held on the Tsurumi Green in Ōsaka from 1 April to 30 September 1990; the fourth international exposition held in Japan. Under the theme "The Symbiosis of Man and Nature," Expo '90 brought together representatives from 80 countries as well as a number of private commercial exhibitors. A state-of-the-art greenhouse held some of the 2 million plants on display, with a total of about 1,200 varieties represented. Over 23 million people attended Expo '90.

expressways 高速道路

(*kōsoku dōro*). Construction of expressways in Japan began in the 1960s. Intercity expressways are designed for a maximum speed of 120 kilometers (75 mi) per hour, although legal speed limits are usually lower. These four-lane, limited-access, divided highways have a 3.6-meter (11.8-ft) lane width.

Since the opening in 1965 of the Meishin Expressway between Nagoya and Kōbe, the first part of the expressway system, 4,869 kilometers (3,025 mi) had been completed by March 1991, and construction of the projected 11,520-kilometer (7,157-mi) network is expected to be finished early in the 21st century. Because of the nature of the terrain and the high concentration of housing, cultivated land, and factories along the routes, the cost of highway construction has been high in Japan relative to that in other countries, and expressway tolls are also proportionately high. However, expressways are used extensively; in fiscal 1990 average daily traffic between Tōkyō and Komaki in Aichi Prefecture was 366,917 automobiles. Of the total traffic in that year, 75 percent consisted of passenger cars and 25 percent of other vehicles. Expressways are congested during morning and evening rush hours and often during nonpeak hours. Measures are being taken to protect residents along routes against highway noise and exhaust fumes. Expressways are administered by the JAPAN HIGHWAY PUBLIC CORPORATION. See also ROADS. ►*See maps, next page.*

extradition 犯罪人引渡し

(*hanzainin hikiwatashi*). The Fugitive Criminal Extradition Law (Tōbō Hanzainin Hikiwatashi Hō) of 1953 stipulates the conditions and procedures for extradition of a criminal from Japan at the request of a foreign country. Article 2 of the law establishes categories of criminals who are not to be extradited, such as political criminals. Extradition is not obligatory under international law, and without a formal treaty it is left to the discretion of the country to which the request is made. At present Japan's only formal extradition treaty is the Japan–United States Extradition Treaty, first concluded in

Japan's Expressway System in 1991

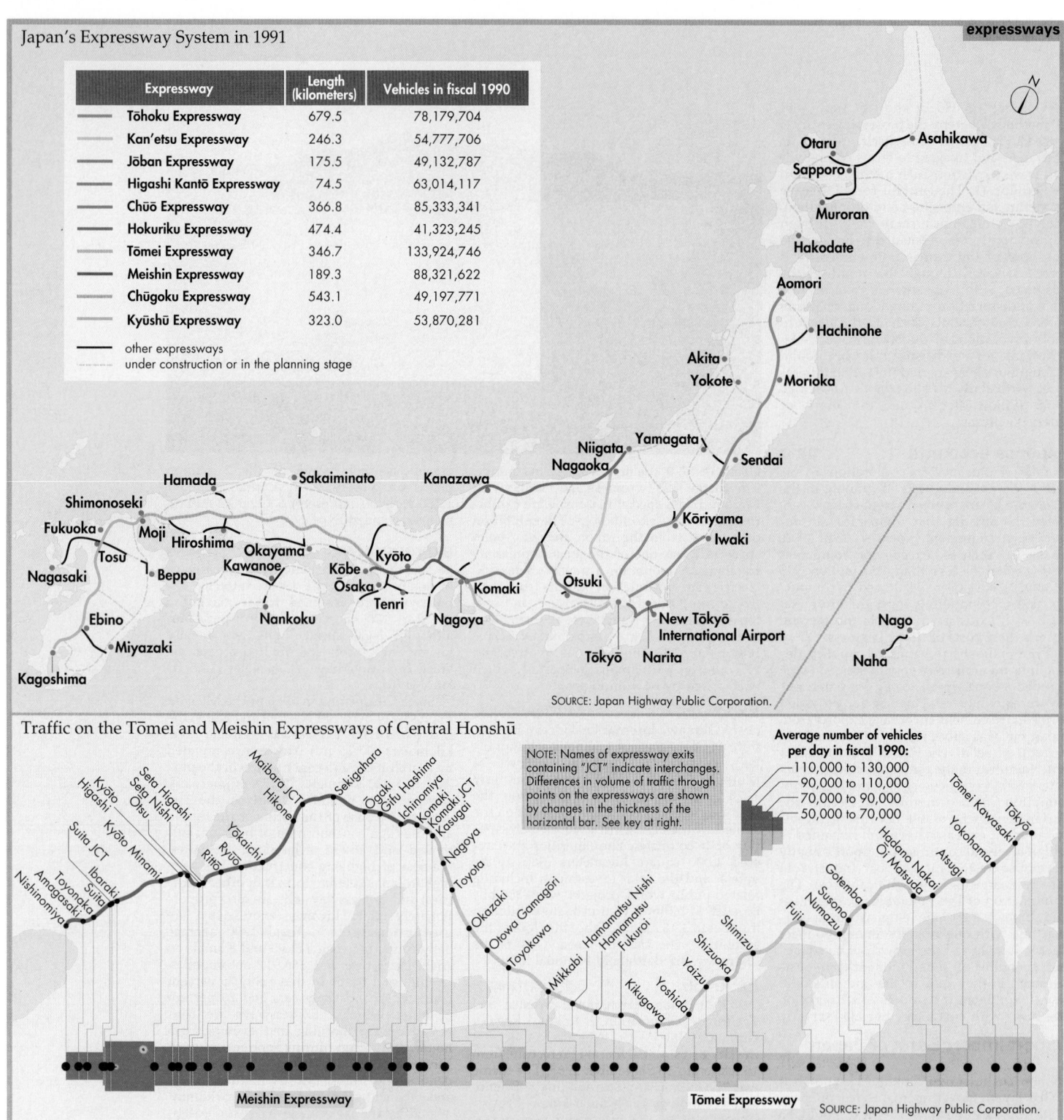

Expressway	Length (kilometers)	Vehicles in fiscal 1990
Tōhoku Expressway	679.5	78,179,704
Kan'etsu Expressway	246.3	54,777,706
Jōban Expressway	175.5	49,132,787
Higashi Kantō Expressway	74.5	63,014,117
Chūō Expressway	366.8	85,333,341
Hokuriku Expressway	474.4	41,323,245
Tōmei Expressway	346.7	133,924,746
Meishin Expressway	189.3	88,321,622
Chūgoku Expressway	543.1	49,197,771
Kyūshū Expressway	323.0	53,870,281

other expressways
under construction or in the planning stage

SOURCE: Japan Highway Public Corporation.

Traffic on the Tōmei and Meishin Expressways of Central Honshū

NOTE: Names of expressway exits containing "JCT" indicate interchanges. Differences in volume of traffic through points on the expressways are shown by changes in the thickness of the horizontal bar. See key at right.

Average number of vehicles per day in fiscal 1990:
110,000 to 130,000
90,000 to 110,000
70,000 to 90,000
50,000 to 70,000

Meishin Expressway

Tōmei Expressway

SOURCE: Japan Highway Public Corporation.

1886 with revisions taking effect in 1980. The treaty does not require that Japan deliver up its own citizens for extradition, but stipulates that Japan and the United States may extradite a national "in situations where it is deemed proper" (art. 5).

In the case of countries not maintaining treaties with Japan there are no statutory provisions concerning extradition, and Japanese requests for extradition are usually made through diplomatic channels. See also INTERNATIONAL LEGAL COOPERATION.

Ezaki Glico Co, Ltd   江崎グリコ[株]

(Ezaki Guriko). General confectionery company engaged in the manufacture and sale of candies, chocolates, snack foods, ice cream, and other items. Founded by Ezaki Riichi (1882–1980) in 1922. It has expanded its business by developing distinctive sales promotions and by mass-marketing a limited number of product lines. Foreign affiliates include Thai Glico Co, Ltd, and Glico American Co, Ltd. Sales for the fiscal year ending March 1991 totaled ¥139.6 billion (US $1.0 billion). The company was capitalized at ¥6.5 billion (US $47.4 million) in the same year. Headquarters are in Ōsaka.

Ezo   蝦夷

Name used until the late 19th century for (1) the aboriginal inhabitants of northern Japan and (2) the area comprising Hokkaidō, Sakhalin, the Kuril Islands, and Kamchatka. The term originally referred to tribal peoples who had once inhabited the entire Japanese archipelago but had retreated northward by the 8th century under military pressure from the Yamato state. The Chinese characters used to write their name have been read variously as Ezo, Ebisu, and Emishi. From the 14th and 15th centuries the name Ezo denoted the proto-Caucasoid aborigines of Hokkaidō, now known as AINU. Scholars disagree on whether the ancient Ezo were ancestors of the Ainu, unpacified Japanese, or people of some as yet unidentified provenance. As a geographical name Ezo (or Ezochi) was applied before and during the Edo period (1600–1868) to the lands north of Honshū. Carrying connotations of "northern" and "barbarian," Ezo had no fixed location. After the Meiji government coined the name Hokkaidō in 1869, the name Ezo gradually fell into disuse.

F

Fabian
ハビアン

(1565?–after 1620). Signatures include Fucan Fabian and Fukansai Habian; also known as Unguio Fåbian. Japanese author, apologist, and apostate of the Jesuit mission. A native of Kyōto, he evidently spent his early years in a Zen monastery but was converted to Christianity around 1583. Admitted into the Society of Jesus as a lay brother (*irmão*) in 1586, he was given theological and humanistic training. By 1590 he was teaching Japanese in the Jesuit *collegio* of Amakusa, where he compiled the first of his major works, a romanized version of the great 13th-century classic HEIKE MONOGATARI (The Tale of the Heike), published in 1592.

Assigned to the Kyōto mission by 1603, Fabian achieved notoriety as a preacher and disputator. He wrote an argumentative defense of Christianity, *Myōtei mondō* (1605, The Myōtei Dialogue). Around 1608 he abandoned the Jesuits, ostensibly because of their failure to promote him to the priesthood but possibly because of an affair with a woman. By 1618 he was actively engaged in the persecution of Jesuits in Nagasaki. In 1620 he wrote his most famous work, the bitterly denunciatory *Ha Daiusu* (Deus Destroyed), in effect a refutation of the *Myōtei mondō*, and a tract upon which much of the anti-Christian polemic of the Edo period (1600–1868) is founded.

factions→batsu

Factory Law of 1911
工場法

(Kōjō Hō). The first Japanese legislation to protect labor in private industry. Enacted on 29 March 1911 and enforced from 1 September 1916, the law established a minimum age of 12 for child labor, limited working hours to 12 per day, outlawed night labor for women and children under 16, and established guidelines for workers' accident compensation. Special regulations regarding mine work were also put into effect in 1916. The Factory Law was passed during the second cabinet of KATSURA TARŌ as a palliative for the harsh suppression of the leftist movement that followed the HIGH TREASON INCIDENT OF 1910. The Factory Law was weaker than similar legislation in Europe. It was binding only on factories with 15 or more employees, and in those workshops the minimum working age was lower than in Europe. Furthermore, many provisions had loopholes. Work hours and job safety regulations were similarly loose. Enforcement of the law was rare. The legislation was strengthened marginally in 1923 and eventually absorbed into the Labor Standards Law of 1947. Job safety regulations were incorporated into the Workmen's Compensation Law of 1947. See also LABOR LAWS.

Fair Trade Commission→Antimonopoly Law

falconry
鷹狩

(*takagari*). The technique of hunting with hawks or falcons. It is thought to have been adopted from China in the 4th century. Mention of hunting excursions with hawks or falcons appears in the KOJIKI (712). In the Heian period (794–1185) falconry was practiced by emperors and their courtiers. In the Kamakura period (1185–1333) *samurai* established schools for the transmission of differing traditions. In the Edo period (1600–1868) falconry was officially patronized by the shogunate, and the position of master falconer (*takajō*) was established in the government bureaucracy. Today falconry has all but died out but is practiced in ceremonial form in Yamagata and Akita prefectures. See also HAWKS AND EAGLES.

family
家族

(*kazoku*). The most common Japanese terms for family are IE, *kazoku*, and *setai*; although these words are often used interchangeably today, in the past they had different meanings. *Ie* (often translated as "household") has come to be used by scholars for Japan's traditional type of family, especially as it existed during the Edo period (1600–1868); it means a united or corporate group of people who share residence and economic and social life and who regard themselves as a continuing unit of kin. The term *kazoku* appears to be more recent than *ie*. When used distinctively, it means a corporate domestic group consisting only of genetic and affinal kin or in-laws. *Setai* denotes a residential group or household, regardless of the relationships of its members, although these are most commonly kin. Neither *kazoku* nor *setai* carries the connotation of continuity of the term *ie*.

The Traditional Family—The family was organized as a hierarchy with the male household head at the apex, theoretically in a position of absolute authority over others. Until after World War II, this authority was supported by law. The authority of the wife of the family head related to domestic matters. Seniority in age conferred prestige, but sex and specific position of authority strongly affected status. A retired household head was respected but had little or no authority. Generally, when the head retired, his eldest son succeeded him, remaining with his parents after marriage and maintaining the continuity of the family line. The future household head held a status much superior to that of his younger siblings; however, an eldest son who showed no promise of becoming an effective family head might be replaced by a younger son or an outsider (see ADOPTION). Likewise, a bride, who traditionally held the lowest status in the family, might also be divorced if she failed to please her in-laws or produce a child.

Authority meant responsibility as well as privilege. The family head was responsible for the economic welfare and also the deportment of other members. He exercised control over family property and the conduct of farming or other occupations, and he was also responsible for the welfare of deceased ancestors, seeing that proper ceremonies were conducted in their honor.

Functions of the family. The welfare of the family ideally took precedence over the needs of any individual member, and identity with the group was emphasized. Confucian views on relations between husband and wife and between parent and child were explicitly taught. Religion, whether SHINTŌ or BUDDHISM, with its emphasis on reverence for ancestors, also gave support to the traditional family organization. The functions of the family related to almost every aspect of life, including psychological well-being. Close emotional bonds have continued to characterize the Japanese family and Japanese society in general.

The Contemporary Family—The typical Japanese family today is a nuclear family, with a mother, father, and two children, in a two- or three-bedroom apartment or house

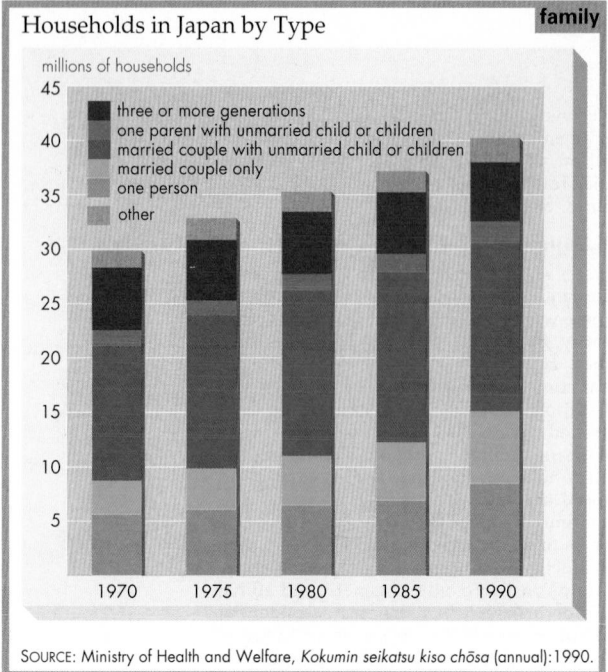

Households in Japan by Type

millions of households

- ■ three or more generations
- ■ one parent with unmarried child or children
- ■ married couple with unmarried child or children
- ■ married couple only
- ■ one person
- ▦ other

SOURCE: Ministry of Health and Welfare, *Kokumin seikatsu kiso chōsa* (annual):1990.

---

in an urban area. Most typically, the father commutes by train to his job in the city, while the wife cares for the children and the house, creating a nurturing environment for the whole family.

Western culture and values have had a large influence, inspiring postwar legal reforms and general social change. The ancient distinctions between eldest and younger sons, and between sons and daughters, have decreased, although they have not disappeared. Eldest sons are no longer universally expected to live with and take care of their parents, and daughters-in-law have been freed from the absolute authority of their mothers-in-law. Women, less restricted to the home, are freer to pursue education, jobs, and hobbies, and to initiate DIVORCE.

Despite such rapid change, however, the Japanese family is characterized by stability and continuity. Growing individualism still gives way to the needs of the group, and roles within the family remain clearly differentiated. Mate selection is still a family matter for many young people. The divorce rate remains low compared to that of the United States. Children still feel an indebtedness (ON) to their parents and care for them in their old age.

As a result of Japan's postwar prosperity, almost all families consider themselves middle class and, in fact, the urban middle-class family is the dominant type and model for all Japan. Middle-class ideals and standards of living have penetrated rural areas as well. Notable variations on this model exist among families where husbands and wives work together in a family business, or in farm families where the husband is employed in an outside job while his wife and possibly his parents maintain the farm.

Marriage planning. Decisions about MARRIAGE are largely cooperative decisions shared by parents and children. Often families will be involved in an ongoing discussion of the kind of spouse most suitable for a child and later of the pros and cons of all prospects. Typically a family looks for a mate with a similar or better economic, social, and educational background and a compatible personality.

The Japanese distinguish between the more traditional arranged marriage (MIAI) and the more Western-style love marriage

(*ren'ai kekkon*). In a *miai,* the young couple are introduced after both families tentatively approve the match (see NAKŌDO). In a *ren'ai kekkon,* the young couple meet each other on their own, for instance, at school or work. But even in the latter case, the families' approval is important. If the family strongly disapproves, the couple may well decide against marriage, recognizing the interdependence of family members. After marriage, in case of health, financial, or emotional problems, the goodwill and help of their families are likely to be needed.

Both men and women often live with their parents until they marry, because of strong family ties as well as the high cost of housing. Since young Japanese marry primarily to start a family, they do not marry until they are economically and socially prepared to do so. In 1991 the average age at marriage was 25.9 years for women, 28.4 for men. The first baby often arrives about a year after the wedding. In 1990 households with children had an average of 1.81 children.

Husband-wife relationships. In contrast to the past, today a woman's relationship with her husband is much more important than her relationship with any of his relatives. Most young people, influenced by the West, want to have a more companionable and romantic marriage than their parents had. Nevertheless, after a year or two of marriage, most couples settle into a pattern of separate social worlds and a clear-cut division of labor. The husband's life is absorbed in his company; he works long hours and socializes with his work group. The wife becomes absorbed in her mothering role as soon as she becomes pregnant. Her social life revolves around her children but may include female relatives and friends.

The husband nominally heads the family and bears clear responsibility for financial support. However, far from being a strong authority figure, he is more likely to let his wife take effective charge of everything concerning the house and children. Though the custom is on the decline, the husband often turns his salary over to his wife, and she controls the finances, including the allocation of her husband's spending money. See HOUSE-WIVES.

Though some couples are quite close and companionable, emotional intimacy is less important than in the West. Fulfillment of one's duties as a parent takes precedence over affective needs. The continuity of the family is thought to be more important than marital gratification. Accordingly the divorce rate in Japan has remained rather low (around 1.3 per 1,000 persons in 1990), although the number fluctuates slightly.

Child rearing and education. Not only is the rearing and education of children the responsibility of the mother, but it is a task that does not allow for substitutes. Motherhood and the careful nurturing of children are valued as supremely important in Japan. Mother and child are usually inseparable when the child is young, and even in later years the mother-child relationship continues to be the strongest and closest within the family. See CHILDHOOD AND CHILD REARING.

In order to assure a child's success in the Japan of today, whether the child is a boy or a girl, the mother must spend much time and thought on education. Often from the time her children enter the fourth grade in elementary school, she arranges for tutors or after-school study in JUKU to prepare the child for middle-school, high-school, and the all-important college ENTRANCE EXAMINA-

TIONS. Though Japanese complain about the examination system and often make fun of the so-called education mother (*kyōiku mama*) who single-mindedly drives her children toward educational achievement, most middle-class mothers feel they have no choice but to be one.

Attitudes toward working women. Economic growth has produced an increase in the number of women in the work force, especially the number of older married women. In 1990, 50.1 percent of women of working age were in the labor force, and 64.9 percent of all women working were married. Women want to work for a variety of reasons such as to increase the family's ability to pay for better housing, children's education, or personal luxuries. Some better-educated women want to work in order to pursue careers of their own. Nonetheless, the ideal for most women seems to remain that of life at home with the children.

Strong moral feelings seem to be involved in attitudes toward working women. A woman receives social approval if she is clearly working for the welfare of the family. However, the woman who works for her own interests is likely to be considered selfish, or at least insufficiently devoted to her family. The use of day-care centers or baby-sitters is still controversial because of the strong feeling that children should be cared for by their own mothers. See WOMEN IN THE LABOR FORCE.

Grandparents. Filial piety is no longer the cornerstone of Japanese morality. Still, most Japanese consider it "natural" to take care of their parents in their old age. There are a few NURSING HOMES, but most middle-class adults would consider it shameful to allow their parents to live in one. Elderly parents ideally live with or near one grown child, and while there remains some tendency to choose an elder son, many parents now prefer to live with a daughter, since mother-in-law problems are avoided. After a man's RETIREMENT, his world and his wife's world come together. Some wives, however, complain that they can never really retire, for they always have to take care of their husbands. Men who have been devoted to their companies all their lives may feel lost when separated from the company. Mothers may experience the loneliness of the "empty nest" after their children grow up and leave home. However, for some elderly couples the later years are often a pleasant time for enjoying hobbies and grandchildren without the responsibilities of the working years.

family court　　　　家庭裁判所

(*katei saibansho*). Court of the first instance having general jurisdiction over domestic and juvenile cases. The family court corresponds in level to the district court (*chihō saibansho;* see JUDICIAL SYSTEM). The present family court system was established in January 1949.

The ordinary administrative business of the court is the responsibility of the chief judge (although important matters are decided by a judges' conference). The principal officials of the court are judges, family court probation officers, and court clerks.

Domestic Cases—There are two separate procedures for domestic cases before the family court: the determination procedure and the conciliation procedure. Domestic cases are grouped into two categories: (1) declaration of incompetence, declaration of absence, permission to adopt a minor, declaration depriving a parent of his parental rights,

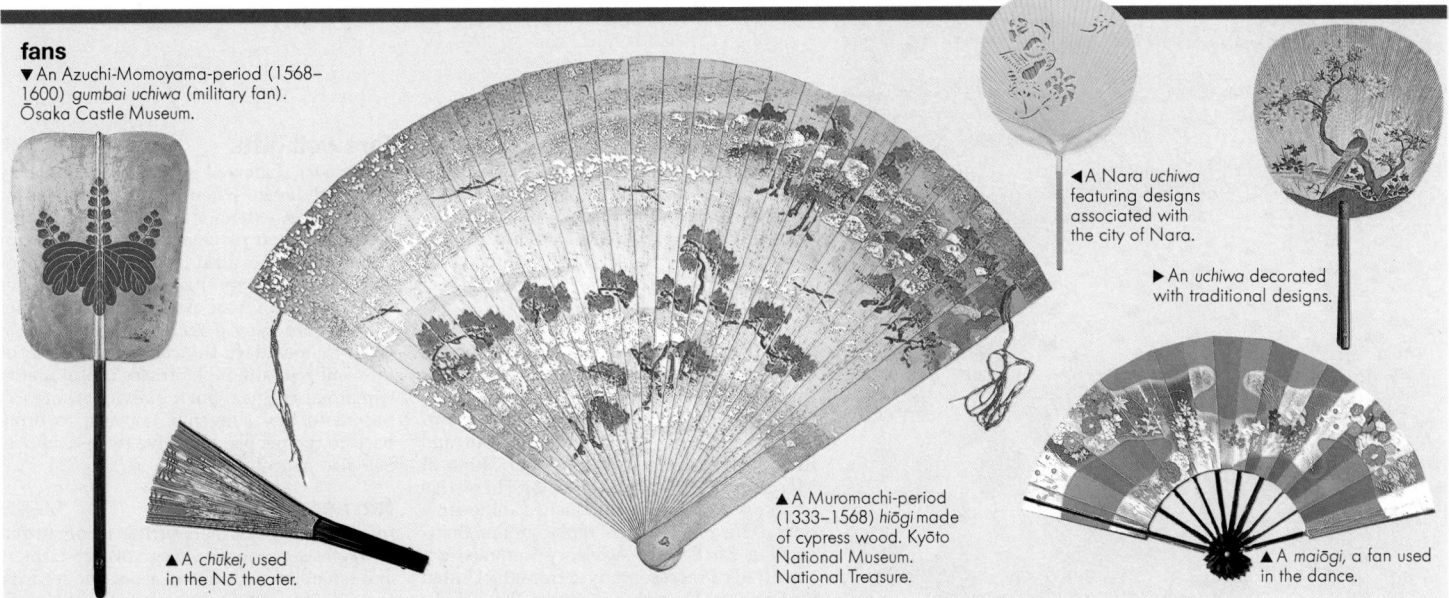

fans

▼ An Azuchi-Momoyama-period (1568–1600) *gunbai uchiwa* (military fan). Ōsaka Castle Museum.

▲ A *chūkei*, used in the Nō theater.

▲ A Muromachi-period (1333–1568) *hiōgi* made of cypress wood. Kyōto National Museum. National Treasure.

◄ A Nara *uchiwa* featuring designs associated with the city of Nara.

► An *uchiwa* decorated with traditional designs.

▲ A *maiōgi*, a fan used in the dance.

and so on; and (2) divorce, distribution of property upon divorce, awarding of parental rights after divorce and subsequent changes thereof, order of support, the dissolution of an adoptive relationship, distribution of a decedent's estate, and so on. The cases in the first group must be handled solely by the determination procedure, and the cases in the second group may be handled by either determination or the conciliation procedure. If conciliation fails, these cases must be decided through ordinary litigation.

Juvenile Cases—Juvenile cases are provided for in the Juvenile Law. A juvenile is defined as any person under 20 years of age. Criminal acts by a person under 14 are not punishable under the Penal Code. Article 3 of the Juvenile Law gives the family court jurisdiction over juveniles. In most cases, a police investigation precedes a family court procedure, after which the case must be sent to the family court, either directly or through the public prosecutor. The family court may, when it is necessary to conduct a hearing, order the placement of the juvenile under the care of a family court probation officer or the commitment of the juvenile to a reformatory (see JUVENILE REFORMATORIES AND CLASSIFICATION CENTERS). After hearing the case, the family court makes one of the following determinations: (1) determination not to order an educative measure; (2) determination to order an educative measure such as placement of the juvenile under the probationary supervision of the Probation Parole Supervision Office or commitment of the juvenile to a reform and training school; or (3) determination to send the case to a public prosecutor.

FamilyMart Co, Ltd

[株]ファミリーマート

(Famirīmāto). One of Japan's largest convenience chain store operators, with franchised chain stores located mainly in the Tōkyō metropolitan area. In 1978 FamilyMart began business as a retail sales division of Seiyū Stores, Ltd; it became an independent firm in 1981. FamilyMart founded its first overseas franchising affiliate, Taiwan FamilyMart Co, Ltd, in 1988. Sales for the fiscal year ending February 1991 totaled ¥323.5 billion (US $2.4 billion), and capitalization stood at ¥13.2 billion (US $96.2 million) in the same year. Headquarters are in Tōkyō.

family planning

家族計画

(kazoku keikaku). The concept of limiting births for economic reasons has existed in

Japan at least since the Edo period (1600–1868). Despite peace and economic growth the Edo-period population stabilized at around 26 million—a fact attributable largely to family planning practices. The principal methods were abortion (*oroshi*) or infanticide (*mabiki;* literally, "thinning out") performed by the mother herself, a midwife (*samba*), or a practitioner of Chinese medicine (*kampōi*).

The Family Planning Movement—After the Meiji Restoration of 1868, new laws banned both infanticide and abortion, since the Western economic principles then in favor stressed the creation of a large industrial labor force. Thus rapid economic growth, a rising birthrate, and improved public health measures boosted Japan's population to over 55 million by 1920.

With the economic depression after World War I, efforts to advocate birth control developed. These efforts were initially led by the physician Majima Kan (1893–1969). In the late 1920s the cause was taken up by the women's movement, whose leaders appealed for protection of women's health and a more liberal sexual morality. In 1922 the general-interest magazine *Kaizō* invited family planning advocate Margaret SANGER to visit Japan. Although the government confiscated pamphlets encouraging sympathy for her cause and prohibited her from lecturing in public, she succeeded in heightening interest in birth control (see KATŌ SHIZUE). Under the slogan *umeyo fuyaseyo* (Bear Children, Swell the Population), prewar militarist governments made population growth an official policy. Following the outbreak of the SINO-JAPANESE WAR OF 1937–1945, laws against birth control were rigidly enforced, and the movement remained suppressed until the end of World War II.

After the war 5 million people were repatriated from occupied areas and former overseas territories. The population was also swelled by a postwar baby boom. The population increase, the diminished size of Japan's territory, the devastation of industries, and underproduction in rural areas led to an acute lack of food and housing. In response there was a much greater interest in birth control. Japan's birthrate began to fall, mainly because of abortions, which were legalized in 1948 (see EUGENIC PROTECTION LAW).

Contraceptive Methods—Gradually, contraceptive practices became widespread as the government began to encourage family planning through legislation and numerous programs. Public health nurses (*hokenfu*)

and midwives (*josampu*) were given instruction and then licensed to sell condoms and spermicides. As of 1990, the most commonly reported contraceptive method was the condom (73.9 percent), followed by the rhythm method (15.3 percent); there were a small number of diaphragm users (0.3 percent). The rhythm method is based largely on research by the physician OGINO KYŪSAKU, so it is popularly known in Japan as the Ogino method.

Although an IUD was developed in Japan as early as 1930, at that time contraception was not encouraged, and it was not until 1974 that the government sanctioned its distribution. Oral contraceptives ("the pill") remain controversial in Japan, as conservatives see a danger of moral corruption if such a convenient and effective contraceptive were widely available. Reported side effects have strengthened the government's refusal to approve the sale of the pill for contraceptive purposes, and it is sold only as a treatment for menstrual problems.

Abortion—Use of the Ogino method, even in combination with the condom, entails a high number of unwanted pregnancies, leading to a large number of abortions. The annual number of reported abortions, which were legalized in 1948, reached a peak of 1,170,143 in 1955 and declined to the present figure of about 500,000 per year, although, as this number represents only those abortions that are reported, the actual number may be much higher. There seems to be very little tendency to use female sterilization to prevent pregnancy.

The Role of Government and Other Organizations—Founded in 1954, the Japan Family Planning Federation (Nihon Kazoku Keikaku Remmei) coordinates the various Japanese organizations concerned with family planning. Another group, the Japan Family Planning Association (Nihon Kazoku Keikaku Kyōkai), distributes information and contraceptives and in 1978 founded the Family Planning Research Institute.

family registers → household registers

fans

うちわ・扇

(uchiwa; ōgi). Traditional accessories carried by both men and women. The first fans are believed to have been introduced to Japan from China during the Nara period (710–794). Called *uchiwa* in Japanese, these early

farming techniques
1 Soilless agriculture allows year-round cultivation of many crops. At this hydroponic greenhouse in Shiga Prefecture, the aquatic herb *mitsuba* (hornwort) is grown.
2 This experimental robotic harvester is an example of the new technologies being developed.

fans were stiff and flat. The folding fans known as *ōgi* are a Japanese invention, originating early in the Heian period (794–1185).

Frames of *uchiwa* are usually made of bamboo; the number of ribs may vary from 3 to 25. The frame is covered with paper that is usually decorated with painted or printed designs or calligraphy. *Uchiwa* are used for ceremonial as well as for purely utilitarian or decorative purposes. Commanders in battle carried *gumbai uchiwa*, stiff iron fans decorated with symbolic designs or family crests.

Ōgi were traditionally used to indicate a person's rank, status, and profession; the iron-ribbed *ōgi* used by *samurai* were known as *jinsen*, while *hiōgi* were folding fans employed at court. *Maiōgi* are used in dance, *chūkei* in the Nō theater, and Rikyū *ōgi*, named after the noted tea master SEN NO RIKYŪ (1522–91), in the tea ceremony.

Fanuc, Ltd   ファナック[株]

(Fanakku). Firm engaged in the manufacture and sale of computer numerical control (CNC) systems, industrial robots, plastic injection molding machines, and laser oscillators. Incorporated in 1972. The company is the world's largest manufacturer of CNCs and industrial robots. It has concentrated its highly automated factories, research laboratories, and headquarters at the foot of Mt. Fuji. To foster internationalization, GM Fanuc Robotics Corporation was jointly established by General Motors and Fanuc to manufacture industrial robots, and GE Fanuc Automation Corporation was jointly established by General Electric and Fanuc to produce factory automation systems. Sales for the fiscal year ending March 1991 totaled ¥184.6 billion (US $1.3 billion), and capitalization stood at ¥68.1 billion (US $496.4 million). Headquarters are in the village of Oshino, Yamanashi Prefecture.

Far East Command
アメリカ極東軍司令部

(FEC; J: Amerika Kyokutōgun Shireibu). The US military headquarters in the western Pacific after World War II. The Far East Command was part of the combined General Headquarters (GHQ) that carried out both the responsibilities for the Occupation of Japan of the supreme commander for the Allied powers (SCAP) and US military responsibili-

ties throughout the Far East as the FEC. Some staff sections served both SCAP and the FEC, and other sections served only one. General Douglas MACARTHUR, and later General Matthew RIDGWAY, served both as supreme commander for the Allied powers and as commander-in-chief, Far East Command.

Far Eastern Commission
極東委員会

(FEC; J: Kyokutō Iinkai). Inter-Allied body responsible for the formulation of policy for the OCCUPATION of Japan (1945–52). The FEC was established by the foreign ministers of the United States, the United Kingdom, and the USSR, with the concurrence of China, at Moscow on 27 December 1945. The ALLIED COUNCIL FOR JAPAN was established at the same time. The FEC, which replaced the then-existing Far Eastern Advisory Commission, consisted of representatives from the United States, the United Kingdom, the USSR, China, France, the Netherlands, Canada, Australia, New Zealand, India, and the Philippines. Burma and Pakistan subsequently became members. The FEC's functions were to formulate policies for the fulfillment by Japan of the surrender terms of the POTSDAM DECLARATION and to review directives or actions by the supreme commander for the Allied powers (SCAP) in Japan. The FEC met regularly in Washington from early 1946 until September 1951, when the SAN FRANCISCO PEACE TREATY with Japan was signed. Its importance declined after 1948, however, as US policy began to emphasize economic development over the implementation of surrender terms.

Far Eastern Conference →Tōhō Kaigi

Far Eastern Republic   極東共和国

(Kyokutō Kyōwakoku). Temporary buffer state in the territory east of Lake Baikal fostered by Russia in April 1920 in order to avoid a full-scale confrontation with Japan, which, along with other Allied nations, had dispatched large forces to Siberia in 1918 in the wake of the Bolshevik Revolution (see SIBERIAN INTERVENTION). Although the United States, Great Britain, and France had withdrawn their troops by 1920, Japanese forces remained. Since Tōkyō was not prepared to deal with a communist regime, the formation of an ostensibly independent republic made possible discussion between the two countries. Once the Japanese troops had been withdrawn from the Maritime Province in 1922, the Far Eastern Republic was incorporated into what was then called the Russian Soviet Federated Socialist Republic.

Far East Network   エフイーエヌ

(FEN; J: Efu Ī Enu). US Armed Forces radio and television broadcast network serving American military personnel in the Far East; it includes AM, FM, and SW radio, as well as VHF television stations and cable television and radio services. Programming mainly consists of news, music, and variety shows.

FEN began operating in 1945 when US Occupation forces in Japan started making radio broadcasts to transmit information and instructions to US military personnel, utilizing the facilities of Nippon Hōsō Kyōkai (NHK; Japan Broadcasting Corporation). Currently the Air Force Pacific Broadcasting Squadron administers and manages FEN. The United States–Japan Security Treaty stipulates that the Radio Law (Dempa Hō) not be applied to the Far East Network.

farewell gifts   餞別

(*sembetsu*). Farewell gifts are customarily given in Japan when a person moves or leaves on an extended trip. A student going to another part of Japan to enter college or going abroad to study, a person leaving for employment in another city, or a company employee taking an assignment in another country are typical recipients of *sembetsu*. Cash is nowadays the commonest form of farewell gift, although articles useful on the trip are also given. Such individuals are expected to buy souvenirs (MIYAGE) to bring back to the people who gave them *sembetsu*. See also GIFT GIVING.

farmers' movement   農民運動

(*nōmin undō*). Term referring to organized struggles by poor Japanese owner-farmers and tenants for social and economic security from the late 19th century to World War II. Matsukata Masayoshi's (1835–1924) deflationary policies (see MATSUKATA FISCAL POLICY) resulted in steep rural depression and large-scale riots in the early 1880s, most notably the CHICHIBU INCIDENT in 1884. Farm productivity stagnated after World War I, by which time half of all cultivated land was held in tenancy. Farmers increasingly sought security in unions during the 1920s. In 1922 the Nihon Nōmin Kumiai (Japan Farmers' Union) was formed to bargain collectively for permanent rent reductions and cultivation rights. In the severe farm depression of the 1930s, landlord-tenant disputes became increasingly frequent.

The farmers' movement was primarily an indecisive struggle against landowners, commercialization, urbanization, and the breakup of village solidarity. The movement neither showed much strength at the polls nor persuaded the government to intercede actively on behalf of tenants until wartime mobilization drastically revised landlord-tenant relationships after the outbreak of war with China in 1937. This process of land reform was continued after World War II by the Japanese government in cooperation with the Occupation authorities. See LAND REFORMS OF 1946.

farming techniques   農業技術

(*nōgyō gijutsu*). Farming techniques in Japan have shown a wide range of responses to varying conditions in each region of the country and in different historical periods.

Rice Planting—Weather conditions in July and August are critical to the growth of rice plants, particularly because of their effects on the duration of sunshine and atmospheric and water temperatures. For this reason rice planting techniques differ considerably from region to region in Japan. In Hokkaidō and Tōhoku (northern Honshū), the coldest regions, protected rice nurseries and growth control techniques are utilized to keep the average temperature above 17°C (63°F) during the plant's panicle formation stage and to maintain a temperature of 10°C (50°F) when the plants ripen. In the warm and humid areas of southwestern Japan, where the water temperature in the paddy fields sometimes rises to 30°–40°C (86°–104°F) in summer, special strains of rice with high levels of thermosensitivity are grown, and the harvest is finished by mid-August. In more temperate regions, double-cropping of rice plants is practiced.

Dry Field Farming—Since the Edo period (1600–1868), landowners have placed special emphasis on rice growing in their efforts to improve farmland and develop better varieties of plants. Dry field farming techniques, therefore, were less advanced than their paddy field counterparts, except for some industrial crops. Since 1959 the development of dry field farming technology has received a new impetus from the government's farming promotion policy. Dry field farming has attained fairly high levels of productivity through such practices as crop rotation, double-cropping, and triple-cropping.

Animal Husbandry—Animal husbandry in Japan once depended heavily on stall feeding rather than grazing because of the country's limited amount of open space and heavy precipitation. After World War II, however, increased demand for dairy products and the widespread use of agricultural machinery radically changed the nature of Japan's livestock industry. Dairy cattle, beef cattle, pigs, and chickens are bred on a massive scale. Breeding of hardy and highly productive varieties and strains suitable for mass production is being conducted, and many techniques, including sperm freezing, artificial insemination, and embryo transfer, are being developed and put to use, while qualitative improvement of domestic animals is being promoted through genetic research.

Horticulture—It was only in the Meiji period (1868–1912) that large-scale commercial cultivation of fruit trees and vegetables was begun. Horticulture grew rapidly with the help of plant strains introduced from foreign countries. Recent improved techniques in fruit growth control have led to reductions in production costs and work hours. Ripening-period controlling agents, crop-thinning agents, and coating agents are being developed and utilized. To make agricultural work easier, dwarf fruit trees are grown, and development of grafting stocks and better pruning techniques has been promoted. Mechanization of fruit tree cultivation is also under way. Disease-resistant and highly productive hybrid varieties of many fruits and vegetables are grown to ensure a steady year-round supply of produce.

New Varieties—In the Edo period, plant breeding was carried out close to the place of cultivation, and varieties with outstanding qualities were selected and improved by diligent farmers. In the Meiji period, introduction and trial cultivation of high-quality plants originating in Western countries were encouraged by the government in the course of its agricultural promotion program. As cross-breeding techniques based on the principles of genetics were introduced in the Taishō period (1912–26), propagation and widespread distribution of imported plants and their varieties by the pure-line selection process was replaced by improvement of varieties by cross-breeding. At present, breeding projects are conducted for a very wide range of plants, domestic animals, and silkworms. The main characteristics sought are higher yield, disease resistance, insect resistance, and longer storage life; widely used breeding methods include hybridization, mutation breeding by radiation, and breeding by tissue culture and by utilization of haploids or polyploids.

Agricultural Implements—The principal agricultural implements in premodern Japan were cultivating tools that employed human or animal power. Remarkable progress in agricultural implements was made after World War I, as internal combustion engines and electric engines were introduced and power equipment for processing

came into use. Since World War II, the use of mechanized agricultural equipment, especially for rice planting, has become general. Agricultural implements now widely used include power tillers, tractors, mechanical sprayers and sprinklers, power reapers, threshers, combines, dryers, hullers, pumping and draining machines, milkers, and many others. Another innovation, the development of controlled-environment farming using hothouses and cloches, has made year-round cultivation of many crops possible.

Fertilizers—In premodern Japan, various types of animal and plant manures were used as fertilizers. As the nation's plant improvement activities were directed toward development of varieties that would respond well to fertilizers, and as cultivation methods emphasized dense planting practices with heavy doses of fertilizers, the traditional manures were largely replaced by chemical fertilizers. At present nitrogenous, phosphatic, and potash fertilizers and mixed fertilizers of such trace elements as magnesium, manganese, molybdenum, boron, and zinc are produced and applied in large quantities.

Agricultural Chemicals—As a result of dense-planting practices with heavy applications of fertilizers and year-round cultivation in greenhouses and other structures, the use of chemical crop protection and of growth-controlling agents has grown markedly. New distribution techniques, including aerial spraying, have been perfected, enabling farmers to cover large areas in very limited time. As the use of agricultural chemicals has increased, examination of their toxicity and residual effects on human bodies has become a standard practice.

Plant Diseases and Insect Pests—The wide range of climate zones in Japan causes the appearance of plant diseases and insect pests on crops to differ in different regions. The national and prefectural governments are constantly engaged in detecting early danger signals; they issue warnings of disease outbreaks and insect infestations as well as periodic reports on blight and insect conditions. Preventive measures taken by farmers on the basis of these warnings and reports include cultivation-related methods (use of blight-resistant varieties, crop rotation, and fallow periods; suspension of cultivation during blight-prone periods; and rationalization of fertilizer application), ecological prevention (eradication of bacilli and extermination of intermediate hosts), physical prevention (disinfection of soil and protection of seeds), and chemical prevention (disinfection of soil and seedlings; use of insecticides, fungicides, and so forth). In recent years biological prevention methods have been stressed to minimize pollution by agricultural chemicals.

fashion design   ファッションデザイン

(*fasshon dezain*). The Japanese began wearing Western-style clothing during the Meiji period (1868–1912). Although men were quick to adopt such Western fashions as suits, Japanese women did not shift to Western-style clothing in appreciable numbers until after World War II. Likewise, fashion design in the Western sense and the design profession itself did not become well established in Japan until after the war.

Among designers influential in establishing postwar Japanese fashion were Sugino Yoshiko (1892–1978), a founder of the SUGINO COLLEGE OF DRESSMAKING; Tanaka Chiyo (b 1906); and Kuwasawa Yōko (1910–

77), all of whom taught Western apparel making before the war. The Nippon Designers' Club was formed in 1948 and the Nippon Fashion Editors' Club in 1952, marking improved organization in the Japanese fashion industry. The 1953 Christian Dior showing, which was held in Japan, spurred the Japanese fashion world toward Paris haute couture.

The 1960s saw the flowering of fashion design in Japan, as the population gradually grew more fashion-conscious. The decade nurtured such leading Japanese designers as TAKADA KENZŌ, KOSHINO JUNKO, and MATSUDA MITSUHIRO, all of whom graduated from the BUNKA FASHION COLLEGE in 1961. MIYAKE ISSEI gained attention at this time while still a student at Tama Art University. It was also during the 1960s that world attention focused on the originality of Japanese designers. MORI HANAE unveiled her first overseas collection in New York in 1965. Her successful evening dresses, featuring a Japanese motif, utilized traditional YŪZEN textile dyeing. Takada Kenzō opened his own shop in Paris in 1970, gathering a clientele impressed with his exotic "Asian" sense and youthful designs. Miyake Issei exhibited his first overseas collection in New York in 1971. His fashions downplay gender differences and express an art in which clothing goes beyond fashionable attire and becomes a medium for expressing the personality. YAMAMOTO KANSAI's very successful 1971 London showing had a "Japanesque" theme that included *kabuki* music. His designs are in a pop vein, with touches of Japanese folklore and kitsch.

In the early 1980s YAMAMOTO YŌJI and KAWAKUBO REI went beyond established concepts of apparel making and womanly beauty with an anti-haute-couture approach, often described as "fake poverty" or "the post-apocalyptic look," that strongly influenced the fashion world. In 1985 the Tōkyō Council of Fashion Designers began holding the fashion shows known as the TŌKYŌ COLLECTIONS twice a year. The shows have been instrumental in placing Tōkyō alongside Paris, London, Milan, and New York as a generator of high fashion.

Faulds, Henry   フォールズ, H.

(1843–1930). Scottish medical missionary and amateur scientist. He lived in Japan from 1874 to 1886 helping to establish education for the blind. His studies on fingerprints led scientists to conclude that each individual's were unique. Born in Ayrshire, Faulds attended medical school in Glasgow and went to Tōkyō in 1874 to establish a hospital for the United Presbyterian Church of Scotland. In 1875 he helped found the Rakuzenkai, Japan's first society for the blind, and in 1880 a school for the blind called the Kummōin.

February 26th Incident   二・二六事件

(Niniroku Jiken). A military rebellion in Tōkyō, 26–29 February 1936, in which several political figures were killed and the center of the capital was seized in an attempted coup d'état. The rebellion was swiftly suppressed, and its leaders were sentenced to death and executed.

In the early hours of 26 February 1936 about 1,400 troops led by junior army officers seized the central part of Tōkyō and shot to death Finance Minister TAKAHASHI KOREKIYO, Lord Keeper of the Privy Seal SAITŌ MAKOTO, and Inspector General of Military Education General WATANABE JŌTARŌ. They

February 26th Incident This abortive military revolt in 1936 stunned the Japanese public and ironically resulted in even greater intrusions by the military into the political arena.
1 The Tōkyō garrison advancing on the rebel-held Diet Building.
2 One of the rebel officers addressing troops occupying the prime minister's official residence.
3 Early in the morning of 27 February, martial law was declared in Tōkyō. The martial law headquarters, in Kudan, Chiyoda Ward, is pictured here.

also attacked the residences of Prime Minister OKADA KEISUKE, Grand Chamberlain SUZUKI KANTARŌ, and former Lord Keeper MAKINO NOBUAKI. Okada escaped death when the rebels mistakenly killed his brother-in-law. Suzuki was severely wounded. Makino managed to flee. Five policemen were also killed. The rebels' attempt to seal off the Imperial Palace failed when the guards resisted.

The rebel leaders, all of them junior officers or discharged junior officers, approached Army Minister Kawashima Yoshiyuki (1878–1945) and demanded that a new cabinet, headed by a general sympathetic to their cause, be set up to carry out reforms. Eager to avoid a civil war in the capital, military authorities were reluctant to use force against the rebels. Some high-ranking officers supported the rebels' cause and urged compliance with their demands. The army minister authorized a statement supporting their aims, and the Tōkyō garrison recognized the rebel forces as acting on its behalf to maintain law and order. But there was strong opposition to the rebels in the general staffs of the army and the navy, which dispatched warships to Tōkyō Bay. The rebels' staunchest opponent was Emperor Shōwa (Hirohito), in whose name they claimed to act and to whom they declared absolute loyalty. The emperor was outraged over the killing of his close advisers and refused to give in to the rebels' demands.

On 27 February martial law was proclaimed in Tōkyō and reinforcements were called in. On 28 February the emperor signed an imperial command ordering the martial law headquarters (formerly the Tōkyō garrison) to evict the rebels from their positions. On 29 February the army launched a psychological campaign aimed at persuading the common soldiers under the rebels' command to abandon their posts. The exhausted officers did not deter their men, and by noon of that day most of the troops had returned to their barracks.

Two rebels committed suicide, but the other leaders of the rebellion were court-martialed by a secret tribunal and 19 of them —including the radical right-wing thinker KITA IKKI and his disciple NISHIDA MITSUGI, who had acted as the rebels' ideological mentors—were executed. Seventy others were imprisoned. Most of the common soldiers were not prosecuted. Martial law in Tōkyō was lifted on 18 July 1936.

The military took advantage of the incident to increase its power and political influence and to obtain bigger budgets. The

HIROTA KŌKI cabinet, which was installed in March 1936, tightened censorship and carried out policies favorable to the army. This laid the groundwork for the SINO-JAPANESE WAR OF 1937–1945, which broke out the following year. The February 26th Incident was thus an important landmark in the ascent of the military to a position of dominant political power in Japan in the late 1930s.

The incident has frequently been used as a subject for books and films. Two well-known novels based on it are *Kizoku no kaidan* (1959, The Steps of the Aristocrats) by TAKEDA TAIJUN and *Gekiryū* (1959–63, Turbulent Waves) by TAKAMI JUN.

Federation of Economic Organizations→Keidanren

feminine language   女性語

(*joseigo*). A variety of Japanese, called *joseigo* or *onnakotoba*, that is typically used by females as a reflection of their femininity. The existence of clearly marked, gender-differentiated language styles is a frequently mentioned characteristic of Japanese.

Among upper-class women of Japan, a special style of language evolved that became associated with their special position in society. The earliest reference to the existence of distinctions between male and female language occurs in an early-11th-century collection of essays, *Makura no sōshi* (The Pillow Book), by the female author SEI SHŌNAGON. As Japanese society became more feudalistic, the distinctive position of women became more sharply defined. The Muromachi period (1333–1568) marked the beginning of the development of NYŌBŌ KOTOBA, a variety of women's language distinguished by its special vocabulary.

Feminine language can be described in terms of features that occur almost exclusively in the language of females and features that are, in a given context, more typical of the language of females. Aside from the high pitch, distinctive voice quality, and particular sentence-final intonations that are associated with the speech of Japanese females, and aside from the vocabulary associated with topics predominantly of interest to females, feminine features include lexical items, such as: (1) the self-reference terms *atashi* and *atakushi*, as less formal equivalents of *watakushi* (I); (2) the sentence particle *wa* in sentence-final position with rising intonation—or prefinal before *yo* or *ne* (*nē*)—indicating gentle assurance; (3) sentence-final *koto* occurring in exclamations, for example: *Kirei da koto* (How pretty it is!); (4) particular interjections, for exam-

ple: *Ara, mā, uwā* (indicating surprise).

Most commonly, feminine language is characterized by certain features that occur in a particular context or with a marked frequency. The most striking example is the feature of politeness. Given the socialization process, which trains Japanese women to be polite and subservient to men, it follows that the honorific and formal varieties of Japanese language are used more frequently by women. This does not mean that the forms themselves are feminine, but rather that their frequent use and their occurrence in certain social situations are typical of female usage. Thus, a polite form that would be used by a man only when talking to a person of extremely high position might be used by a woman in talking to a casual acquaintance.

Some patterns, which traditionally have been cited as features of the language of females, are more accurately described as feminine-oriented features in that they are indications of gentleness used predominantly by females but also used by males in certain situations, as when addressing women and children. The linguistic signal of such forms is not femaleness but rather gentleness, nonassertiveness, and empathy.

Research—Considering the frequently cited distinctiveness of Japanese feminine language, comprehensive empirical research on the current state of the language has been limited. There is a tendency to confuse gentle language with female language, with the distinction between the two rarely made. See also MASCULINE LANGUAGE.

FEN→Far East Network

Fenollosa, Ernest Francisco
フェノロサ, E. F.

(1853–1908). American educator and student of Asian fine arts who brought an appreciation of traditional Japanese art to the West. He also contributed to the reassessment of

Ernest Francisco Fenollosa An American educator, Fenollosa was instrumental in awakening interest in traditional Japanese art, both in Japan and abroad.

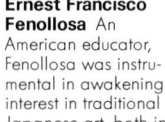

Japanese art within Japan and played a major role in the early efforts to preserve Japan's artistic treasures. A native of Salem, Massachusetts, Fenollosa studied philosophy and sociology at Harvard University. In 1878 Fenollosa went to Tōkyō University to teach philosophy and political economy (1878–80) and philosophy and logic (1880–86). Among his students were such distinguished men as INOUE TETSUJIRŌ, Ariga Nagao (1860–1921), MIYAKE SETSUREI, TSUBOUCHI SHŌYŌ, HOZUMI YATSUKA, KANAI NOBURU, TAKADA SANAE, INOUE ENRYŌ, KANŌ JIGORŌ, and Wadagaki Kenzō (1860–1919).

Fenollosa is best known for his work in preserving and exhibiting traditional Japanese art. He not only patronized traditional artists such as KANŌ HŌGAI and HASHIMOTO GAHŌ but also worked ceaselessly to convince the Japanese that their art was worth preserving. He saved many pieces from destruction and acquired an outstanding private collection, now at the Boston Museum of Fine Arts. A rough draft of his major work, *Epochs of Chinese and Japanese Art*, was published in 1912. His other works include *The Masters of Ukiyoe* (1896), and two works on the Nō theater, published posthumously from his notes and manuscripts by Ezra Pound, who served as his literary executor.

fern frond design 蕨手文

(*warabidemon*). A curved-line motif ending in a tight spiral resembling a newly unfolding fern frond; used singly or in pairs back to back on artifacts of the Yayoi (ca 300 BC–ca AD 300) and Kofun (ca 300–710) periods, especially on Yayoi pottery, bronze bells (DŌTAKU), bronze weapons, BRONZE MIRRORS, HANIWA (funerary sculptures), and in the painted decorations of ORNAMENTED TOMBS.

ferns 羊歯

(*shida*). Plants of the division Pteridophyta, especially of the order Filicales. Since the islands of Japan cover several distinct climatic regions ranging from the cool temperate zone of Hokkaidō to the subtropical zone of the Ryūkyūs, the country is host to over 700 species of ferns. Most of these are found southward from the Bōsō Peninsula (Chiba Prefecture) of Honshū, where the average annual temperature is 16°C (60°F) or higher.

Ferns appeal to the austere Japanese taste embodied in aesthetic concepts such as WABI and SABI. Several species, including the *benishida* (*Dryopteris erythrosora*), the *nankai itachishida* (*D. varia*), the *inode* (*Polystichum polyblepharum*), and the *kusasotetsu* (*Matteuccia struthiopteris*), are frequently grown in Japanese gardens, and small ferns, such as the *nokishinobu* (*Lepisorus thunbergianus*), are cultivated as BONSAI. The *urajiro* (*Gleichenia japonica*) is a symbol of long life, and its fronds are used in New Year decorations. Shoots of WARABI (*Pteridium aquilinum*) and *zemmai* (*Osmunda japonica*) are prized by Japanese gourmets.

Fesca, Max フェスカ, M.

(1846–1917). German agriculturist and agrochemist; regarded as a pioneer in the modernization of Japanese agriculture. Upon invitation from the Japanese government, he traveled to Japan in 1882 and engaged in soil surveys at the Geological Research Institute of the Ministry of Agriculture and Commerce. He also taught agriculture at Komaba Agricultural School (now part of Tōkyō University). Fighting against traditional RŌNŌ agricultural methods, he made recommendations about the improvement of farm implements, adoption of deep-tillage methods, crop-rotation systems, and the use of domestic animals. He returned to Germany and was a professor at Berlin Agricultural College.

festivals 祭

(*matsuri*). Japanese festivals, holidays, and other ceremonial occasions fall into two main categories: *matsuri* (festivals) and NENCHŪ GYŌJI (annual events; also pronounced *nenjū gyōji*). *Matsuri* are essentially native Japanese festivals of Shintō origin, held annually on established dates. *Nenchū gyōji* is a larger category of annual and seasonal observances, many of which are of Chinese or Buddhist origin. *Nenchū gyōji* are arranged seasonally to form an annual calendar of events. *Matsuri* are often included in this calendar, and there is some overlapping between the two categories. See also HOLIDAYS, NATIONAL.

Matsuri are chiefly of sacred origin, related (at least originally) to the cultivation of rice and the spiritual well-being of local communities. They derive ultimately from ancient Shintō rites for the propitiation of the gods and the spirits of the dead, and for the fulfillment of the agricultural round. Some of these Shintō rites were incorporated, along with Buddhist and Confucian rites and ceremonies imported from China, into the imperial calendar of annual observances (*nenchū gyōji*).

The word *matsuri* includes the rites and festivals practiced in both FOLK SHINTŌ and institutionalized Shintō. A *matsuri* is basically a symbolic act whereby participants enter a state of active communication with the gods (KAMI); it is accompanied by communion among participants in the form of feast and festival. In a broad sense, *matsuri* may also include festivals in which the playful element and commercial interests have all but obliterated the original sacramental context.

There are several types of Shintō *matsuri* in Japan: *matsuri* of supplication to the gods (as for a successful harvest), others of thanksgiving, and still others to drive away pestilence and natural disasters. There are solemn *matsuri* and boisterous occasions featuring games and entertainment. Elaborate festivals flourish in the big cities and small-scale ones in more personal settings or in small communities. Some *matsuri* are performed in a very traditional way, and some have been considerably adapted to modern times.

The *matsuri* have two major aspects. The first is communion between gods and people. This comprises purificatory rites (*monoimi*), offerings, and communal banquets between gods and humans (NAORAI). The offerings, in particular, have been important from ancient times. The second aspect of *matsuri* is communion among people. Many Japanese festivals feature a parade of MIKOSHI (portable shrines) and contests or games that provide opportunities for community members to play together and match skills. The strictures of everyday life are relaxed, and the atmosphere is one of spiritual renewal.

Hare and Ke — The Japanese have a concept of two dimensions of life, *hare* and *ke*. *Hare* correlates with the out of the ordinary, *ke* with the routine, and this duality extends over time, space, and things. Shintō shrines have special festival days set aside for *matsuri*; these, as well as such occasions as New Year's Day, the Bon Festival, birthdays, and weddings, are termed *hare*. *Hare* and *ke* thus resemble the idea of the sacred contrasting with the profane, but it is perhaps more accurate to define them in terms of special and everyday (see SACRED, THE).

The Matsuri and the Seasons — *Matsuri* are in origin and tradition closely related to rice-centered agriculture, especially the growing cycle of rice. Among annual rites, spring and autumn *matsuri* are the most important. The spring festivals invoke a rich harvest or celebrate an anticipated good harvest; the autumn festivals are held in thanksgiving for a plentiful harvest.

Besides spring and autumn fêtes, there are summer festivals (*natsu matsuri*) and winter festivals (*fuyu matsuri*). In farming areas the summer *matsuri* have the role of driving away natural disasters that might threaten the crops. In the cities, especially since the medieval period (mid-12th–16th centuries), the role of such festivals has been to ward off plague and pestilence (see NAGOSHI). The winter *matsuri*, held between the harvest and spring seeding, have elements of both the autumn and spring *matsuri*. Thus, Japanese *matsuri* are synchronized with seasonal changes and are classified according to the four seasons.

Essentials of the Matsuri — *Monoimi, or purificatory asceticism.* In the center of the Shimane Peninsula on the coast of the Sea of Japan is the Sada Shrine. Each year at the end of September the shrine celebrates the Gozakae Matsuri (literally, "seat-changing rite"). In a midnight ceremony Shintō priests change the seat on which the god is to sit. Priests participating in these rites must confine themselves to the shrine for a week of purificatory asceticism prior to the rite. *Monoimi* serves as the symbolic gate by which the participants in a festival leave the everyday world (*ke*) to enter into the special realm (*hare*) of the *matsuri*. The purification rites have been greatly simplified in recent years. In premodern Japan, however, people were not allowed to participate in the *matsuri* unless they had undergone this purification process.

Offerings. Another essential element of the *matsuri* is the offerings made to the gods. Typical items include regular and glutinous (*mochi*) rice, *sake* (rice wine), seaweed, vegetables, and fruits. In Japan there are no sacrifices of living creatures during *matsuri*, nor is there any offering of broken bread.

Communion. The *naorai*, in which participants in the *matsuri* partake of the food offerings at the place of celebration together with the gods, is another essential element of the *matsuri*. In recent years the word *naorai* has also come to include the eating of offerings at a place separate from the *matsuri* site after the festival has ended, but this is essentially a banquet and not a true *naorai*.

In addition to these three elements of *matsuri*, there are a number of other items. Trees and branches are sometimes used to delineate the *matsuri* site; the evergreen SAKAKI is particularly favored. This custom derives from the belief that the gods will use these markers in order to descend to the site of the festival.

Also important are the special events that take place on the day of the *matsuri*. Japanese festivals often feature tug-of-war contests (*tsunahiki*), horse races, and boat races. The special ceremonial dancing known as *kagura* also retains significance in the *matsuri*. In

Continued on page 366 ►

fern frond design The designs on a bronze bell of the Middle Yayoi period. Kōbe City Museum. National Treasure.

A Calendar of Japanese Festivals

January—Wakakusayama Turf Burning

February—Kamakura Festival

March—Omizutori

April—Takayama Festival

May—Hakata Dontaku

	DATE	EVENT	LOCATION	DESCRIPTION
January	7	**Dazaifu Usokae**	Dazaifu Shrine, Dazaifu, Fukuoka Prefecture	• Participants exchange bullfinch-shaped amulets at random in the hope of acquiring special good-luck amulets circulated by disguised shrine officials.
	9–11	**Tōka Ebisu**	Imamiya Ebisu Shrine, Ōsaka	• Prayers are offered to Ebisu, one of the Seven Deities of Good Fortune. Shrine visitors take home branches hung with coins or other valuable objects as good-luck charms.
	14–15	**Niino Snow Festival**	Izu Shrine, Anan, Nagano Prefecture	• A ceremony in which snow, thought to bring about a bumper crop for the coming year, is offered to the gods.
	15	**Wakakusayama Turf Burning**	Nara, Nara Prefecture	• Participants costumed as warrior monks burn the turf on the hillside at Wakakusayama at twilight. This event is believed to have originated in a boundary dispute between the temples Tōdaiji and Kōfukuji.
	20	**Mōtsuji Madarajin Festival**	Mōtsuji, Hiraizumi, Iwate Prefecture	• Rituals of song, dance, and drama (*ennen*) are performed following ceremonies to honor Madarajin, the temple's guardian deity.
February	early February	**Sapporo Snow Festival**	Sapporo, Hokkaidō	• A tourist-oriented spectacle featuring large, elaborate ice and snow sculptures.
	15–16	**Kamakura Festival**	Yokote, Akita Prefecture	• Children build small snow huts (*kamakura*) containing ceremonial altars dedicated to the Shintō water gods (*suijin*).
	17–20	**Hachinohe Emburi**	Hachinohe, Aomori Prefecture	• Residents honor Inari (the deity associated with the rice harvest) with dances that mime the planting of rice. The *emburi* is a type of agricultural tool.
March	12–13	**Omizutori**	Tōdaiji, Nara, Nara Prefecture	• A ceremony symbolizing the arrival of spring in which torches scatter purifying sparks over participants, and monks draw water from a nearby well to offer to the bodhisattva Kannon.
	13	**Kasuga Festival**	Kasuga Shrine, Nara, Nara Prefecture	• A series of rites, said to be unchanged since the 9th century. Of note is the *yamato-mai*, a ritual dance performed by 10 men.
April	14–15	**Takayama Festival**	Hie Shrine, Takayama, Gifu Prefecture	• In honor of the shrine deities, 12 high-wheeled floats are paraded through the city streets.
May	early May	**Ombashira Festival**	Suwa Shrine, Suwa, Nagano Prefecture	• A ceremony held every sixth year in which tall fir trees are cut down and used to replace four posts at each of the shrine's two main buildings.
	3–4	**Hakata Dontaku**	Fukuoka, Fukuoka Prefecture	• Local citizens dressed as the Seven Deities of Good Fortune parade through the streets accompanied by colorful floats.
	3–5	**Hamamatsu Festival**	Hamamatsu, Shizuoka Prefecture	• A kite-flying competition is followed by a procession of shrine floats.
	15 May, alternate years	**Kanda Festival**	Kanda Shrine, Tōkyō	• About 200 portable shrines are paraded in honor of the deities of the Kanda Shrine.
	15	**Aoi Festival**	Kamo Shrines, Kyōto	• Participants, costumed as Heian-period court nobles, wear headgear decorated with leaves of the *futaba aoi* plant; the leaves are believed to help ward off thunder.
	third weekend	**Sanja Festival**	Asakusa Shrine, Tōkyō	• High points of the festival include a procession of about 100 portable shrines and numerous *geisha*.

June—Saikusa Festival

July—Sōma Nomaoi Festival

August—Kantō

September—Tsurugaoka Hachimangū Yabusame

October—Kurama Torch Festival

November—Karatsu Kunchi

December—Okera Festival

Month	Date	Festival	Location	Description
June	first Sunday	**Mibu no Hanadaue**	Chiyoda, Hiroshima Prefecture	• Farmers transplant rice while singing traditional songs and beating drums to welcome the god of the rice paddies to the fields.
	7–16, alternate years	**Sannō Festival**	Hie Shrine, Tōkyō	• Portable shrines are paraded to honor the shrine deities. The festival alternates with the Kanda Festival.
	17	**Saikusa Festival**	Isakawa Shrine, Nara, Nara Prefecture	• Shrine maidens, holding lilies and dressed in white *kimono* with red skirts, dance in honor of the shrine deity.
July	17	**Gion Festival**	Yasaka Shrine, Kyōto	• The monthlong festival reaches its height on 17 July with a parade of floats bearing musicians or figures of historical and mythical personages.
	23–25	**Sōma Nomaoi Festival**	Ōta, Nakamura, and Odaka shrines, Fukushima Prefecture	• Horsemen, dressed as feudal warriors, engage in horse races, a parade of horses, a competition for shrine flags, and other events.
	24–25	**Tenjin Festival**	Temmangū, Ōsaka	• A procession of ornately decorated boats—some carrying portable shrines—on the river Ōkawa in honor of Temma Tenjin, the shrine's deity.
	last Sunday	**Peiron Boat Race**	Nagasaki, Nagasaki Prefecture	• Teams of 36 men (including coxswain, drummer, and gong beater) race long, narrow boats to the cheers of the crowd.
August	1–7	**Nebuta Festival**	Aomori and Hirosaki, Aomori Prefecture	• Large floats are paraded though the city in the evening, with townspeople singing and dancing to musical accompaniment.
	4–7	**Kantō**	Akita, Akita Prefecture	• Nighttime parade-competitions in which young men balance long bamboo poles hung with tiers of lanterns.
	12–15	**Awa Dance**	Tokushima, Tokushima Prefecture	• A variation of the Bon dance in which groups of men and women parade, dancing and singing, along the main streets of Tokushima.
September	16	**Tsurugaoka Hachimangū Yabusame**	Tsurugaoka Hachiman Shrine, Kamakura, Kanagawa Prefecture	• Horsemen dressed in the hunting costume of feudal warriors compete in a contest of traditional mounted archery.
October	7–9	**Nagasaki Suwa Festival (Okunchi)**	Suwa Shrine, Nagasaki, Nagasaki Prefecture	• Main events include a parade of umbrella-topped floats whirled in circles by groups of young men, as well as a Chinese-style dragon dance.
	22	**Kurama Torch Festival**	Yuki Shrine, Kyōto	• Two portable shrines are paraded by torchlight through a crowd of festival participants. Large torches are carried about the shrine grounds until dawn.
November	2–4	**Karatsu Kunchi (Karatsu Festival)**	Karatsu Shrine, Karatsu, Saga Prefecture	• Beautifully lacquered floats representing *samurai* helmets and such animals as lions and dragons are carried through the town in this 400-year-old festival.
	2 or 3 days at 12-day intervals	**Tori no Ichi**	Ōtori shrines throughout Japan	• Vendors lining the streets in front of Ōtori shrines sell such charms as *kumade* (rakes, to "rake in" fortune) decorated with imitation gold coins.
December	3	**Chichibu Festival**	Chichibu Shrine, Chichibu, Saitama Prefecture	• An event known for its fireworks display and parade of floats bearing musicians and singers.
	17	**Kasuga Wakamiya Grand Festival**	Kasuga Wakamiya Shrine, Nara, Nara Prefecture	• Dressed as ancient courtiers and feudal warriors, participants hold a procession in honor of the shrine deity.
	31	**Okera Festival**	Yasaka Shrine, Kyōto	• A sacred fire of the medicinal herb *okera* is lit on New Year's Eve, and through the early hours of 1 January visitors can take home some of the fire kindled on lengths of special rope. Used to cook the first meal of the year, the sacred fire is believed to prevent illness.

Nebuta Festival: The Magic of the Matsuri

A workman puts the finishing touches on a huge paper figure in the photo above. The larger *nebuta* may be as much as nine meters wide and five meters tall.

A young dancer, above right, has her costume adjusted by her mother, who sports a straw hat adorned with flowers. Anyone wearing festival attire may participate in the Nebuta Matsuri.

Of the thousands of annual festivals (*matsuri*) observed throughout Japan, few can match the Nebuta Festival held in the city of Aomori for sheer grandeur. Every year during the first week of August, the capital city of Aomori Prefecture comes alive in a wild display of color, light, music, and motion. The activity centers on nightly processions of giant floats, which are carried or wheeled through the streets of the city in the company of thousands of singing, dancing citizens clad in traditional festival attire. Arrayed atop these floats are huge, luminous paper effigies—*nebuta*—portraying famous warriors, characters from *kabuki* plays, and other celebrated personages. The sight of these huge spectral figures riding through the night, throngs of revelers swarming around them, is unforgettable.

Like most *matsuri*, the Nebuta Festival began as a ritual linked to the cultivation of rice—an occasion for communicating with the gods and communing with one's fellow celebrants. The origins of this festival can be traced to an ancient rite in which townspeople sought to purify themselves by casting away paper images and other objects, symbolically driving away fatigue, bad weather, and all that might interfere with a successful autumn harvest. Even today, amid all the merrymaking of the Nebuta Matsuri, vestiges of the festival's ritual origins remain: on the final night of the festival, the *nebuta* are put on boats and carried out to sea.

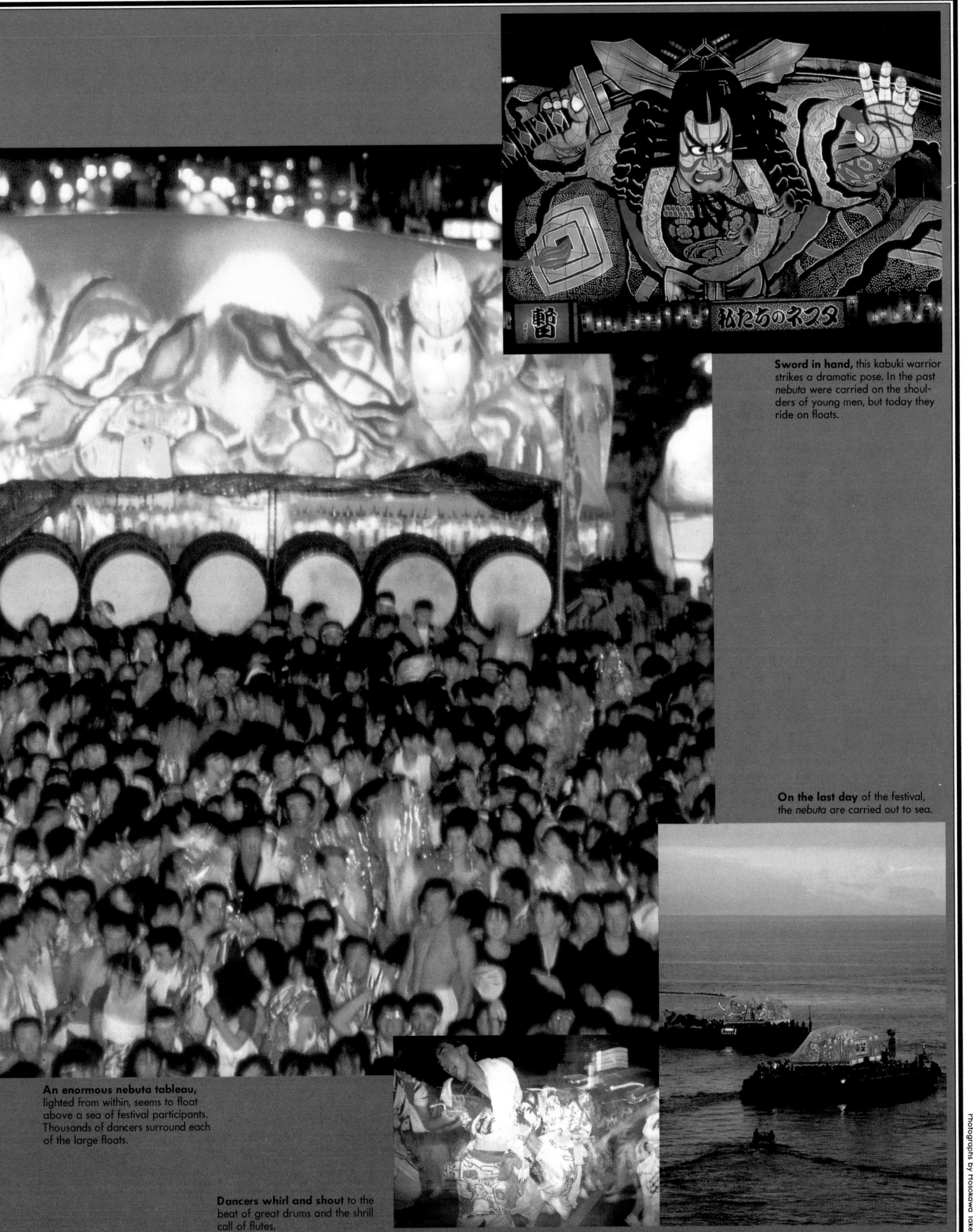

Sword in hand, this kabuki warrior strikes a dramatic pose. In the past *nebuta* were carried on the shoulders of young men, but today they ride on floats.

On the last day of the festival, the *nebuta* are carried out to sea.

An enormous nebuta tableau, lighted from within, seems to float above a sea of festival participants. Thousands of dancers surround each of the large floats.

Dancers whirl and shout to the beat of great drums and the shrill call of flutes.

← Continued from page 361

modern times these events have become mere entertainment for the audience. In former times, however, these contests, races, and dances were employed along with oracles as a means of summoning the divine will.

The Matsuri and the Group—The *matsuri* presupposes the existence of a definite group of people to act it out. Generally speaking, in both the cities and villages of Japan every local community has a shrine that is its religious symbol. The members of a community, and thus of a certain shrine, are known as *ujiko*, and they in turn refer to their shrine as the *ujigami*.

Most *matsuri* are conducted by a ceremonial organization consisting of Shintō priests and a small group of laymen selected from the *ujiko* community. Rites centering on a communion between gods and humans are usually the domain of the Shintō priest. Some *matsuri* are carried out by a special organization called the *miyaza*. Membership is limited to particular family lines, and a special established process is required for entry. The person selected from the *miyaza* to preside over the *matsuri* for the year is called the *tōya*. The *tōya* must undertake the same austerities and purification rites as the Shintō priest in order to represent the people during religious rites.

Village and City Festivals—Although village festivals and city festivals resemble each other in several ways because they developed from the same origin, there are differences: village festivals tend to center on agricultural rites in the spring and autumn, and city festivals occur mostly in the summer; village festivals emphasize a man-god communion, and the city festivals stress human camaraderie. The most famous of all summer festivals is Kyōto's GION FESTIVAL.

The Matsuri and Modern Society—After World War II, Japan underwent rapid changes in population distribution and the structure of traditional communities. These changes had direct and indirect effects on the *matsuri*. Although many of the traditional patterns are still evident on closer scrutiny, human interaction has become the framework of new events, showing a move from the closed and vertical order of communion between man and god to the more open and horizontal order of interpersonal relationship. See also AGRICULTURAL RITES.

☎ 362–365

feudalism 封建制度

(*hōken seido*). Various aspects of the social and political organization of premodern Japan bore a marked resemblance to feudalism as it appeared in medieval Europe. However, there is disagreement among scholars as to whether the term feudalism can be applied to Japan. The Japanese term *hōken seido* (feudal system) comes from the Chinese *fengjian* (*feng-chien*), the word for the decentralized political system that prevailed in China during the Zhou (Chou) period (1027 BC–256 BC). Japanese scholars of the Edo period (1600–1868) described their own political system as *hōken*, and they contrasted it with the centralized *gunken* (from the Chinese *jun xian* or *chün-hsien*; literally, "province-district") system of imperial China. During the Meiji period (1868–1912) Japanese historians began to use the term *hōken seido* as a translation for "feudalism" (Eng), *féodalité* (Fr), or *Lehnwesen* (Ger). By the 1920s the broad Marxist usage of "feudalism"—as a general stage of socioeconomic development through which societies pass on their way from ancient "slave society" to modern "capitalist society"—had become common. After World War II, the term "feudalistic" (*hōkenteki*) had become vulgarized as a pejorative epithet referring to old-fashioned, conservative, backward, or authoritarian attitudes and behavior.

With the development of modern historiography, the question of feudalism became a central concern of Japanese scholars. ASAKAWA KAN'ICHI, one of the first historians to compare the institutional structures of medieval Japan and Europe, described Japan as feudal, and his lead was followed by other Japanese legal historians. Japanese Marxist historians engaged in a lengthy and heated debate over when "feudalism" began in Japan. Some pointed to the establishment of the SHŌEN system in the late Heian period (794–1185), while others argued that feudalism did not come to full maturity until the establishment of "centralized feudalism" in the Edo period.

Feudalism in Comparative History—While it is unlikely that any definition of feudalism will satisfy everyone, one can build a model based on the example of "high feudalism" found in 11th- and 12th-century Europe. The elements of that model would include an agrarian economy, levels of trade lower than in prefeudal or postfeudal times, a dominant class of armored horse-riding warriors, a network of relationships among the warrior elite based on ties of vassalage and the grant of a landed fief or other benefits by the lord to the vassal, a highly fragmented and undifferentiated political system with weak central authority, and a prevailing elite ethos glorifying the virtues of personal loyalty, servitude, honor, courage, and physical prowess.

It is clear that premodern Japan shared many or all of these characteristics. One can find evidence of a mounted warrior class as far back as the Kofun period (ca 300–710) and the existence of landed fiefs in the mid-9th century. However, the central question is, when did the overall configuration of Japanese society and polity most closely resemble the model? Many would probably agree with the American historian John Whitney Hall that the closest fit is to be found in the early 16th century, a period of "mature feudalism."

Mature Feudalism in Japan—As in Europe, a mature feudal system grew out of evolutionary developments. These stretch back to the establishment of the Kamakura shogunate (1192–1333) in the 12th century, when a landed warrior elite began to encroach on the rights and authority of the Heian aristocracy. The founder of the shogunate, MINAMOTO NO YORITOMO, attempted to build a system of governance on a base of personal vassalage. He granted his vassals (known as *gokenin*; literally, "honorable housemen") land rights on estates (*shōen*) and appointed them as local land stewards (*jitō*) or provincial constables (*shugo*). In many ways the Kamakura system resembled what some Western historians call "Carolingian feudalism," in which Charlemagne's vassals became his officials and his officials became his vassals.

A fully articulated, mature feudal structure did not take shape until the final collapse of central authority in the late 15th century. The ŌNIN WAR in 1467–77 deprived the imperial court and the court aristocracy of their last vestiges of authority and fatally weakened the shogunate. In the wake of the war a more or less constant cycle of local warfare, pitting provincial warrior leaders against one another, continued for nearly a century. Japanese historians usually refer to this century as the "Warring States period" (SENGOKU PERIOD; 1467–1568), a term also applied to the total fragmentation of power in the late Zhou period in China.

The central figure in this mature feudal system was the DAIMYŌ, a local territorial magnate who ruled over a more or less compact feudal domain. At any one time there were several hundred daimyō. The more powerful held sway over areas as large as or larger than the old imperial provinces, and the weaker controlled smaller domains in inland valleys or on smaller agricultural plains. The boundaries of daimyō domains shifted often in the ebb and flow of warfare, and a daimyō family might lose its local ascendancy in the space of a generation.

The daimyō exercised control within his domain through the power to grant or confirm landholdings. The grant of land resembled the classic European fief. The daimyō might confirm a vassal's right to ancestral lands, or he might assign him new lands, but in either case these rights depended on the sufferance of the daimyō. Vassals were relatively free to dispose of ancestral lands, but they were usually denied or restricted in the right to dispose of land newly granted to them. Since most vassals pledged allegiance to the daimyō in order to protect their fiefs, this restriction did not pose a great problem.

The tie of vassalage between the daimyō and his retainer was usually confirmed by a formal, written oath of allegiance fixed with the vassal's personal seal and sworn before a host of deities. The tie was a contractual one. The vassal was required to render military service to his daimyō in proportion to the size of his fief. A vassal with land worth so many bushels of rice or so many pieces of gold was required in time of war to furnish his daimyō with so many horsemen, so many spearmen, and so on.

Vassalage networks were much simpler than in Europe, where knights often made themselves vassals of several lords at once in order to acquire more fiefs. Since the knight was obliged to render service to all his lords, multiple homage caused difficulty when one of the vassal's lords fought another. This gave rise to the practice of liege vassalage, whereby the knight selected one lord to whom he owed primary vassalage. In Japan the tradition of single allegiance remained strong. Vassals often turned against their daimyō lords, but they did not pledge allegiance to more than one at a time.

Mature feudalism in Japan was different from European high feudalism in other ways. First, daimyō never extracted from their vassals feudal aids or special levies required by European lords for the payment of ransom, for the inheritance of a fief, or for the knighting of the lord's son or the marriage of his daughter. Nor was it possible for vassals to pay scutage, or army aid in lieu of military service. Second, the formal ceremonies for entering into a daimyō's service were far less elaborate than European investiture ceremonies. The lord-vassal relationship in Japan was basically a military and political one, and its goal was to buttress a structure of political authority rather than a structure of social status.

The period of mature feudalism came to an end in Japan for many of the same reasons that it did in Europe. The introduction of firearms into Japan in the 1540s dealt a serious blow to the ascendancy of the horse-riding, armored warrior on the battlefield, and daimyō shifted to the recruitment of peasant armies. As the military service of vassals became less important, the daimyō themselves began to accumulate more power. By the end of the 16th century, the largest daimyō subjected their vassals and peasants to closer and more complex administrative control, and their domains began to resemble integrated local states more than feudal domains.

Centralization and Decline in the Edo Period—The establishment of the TOKUGAWA SHOGUNATE by Tokugawa Ieyasu in 1603 completed a trend toward political reintegration and unification of Japan that had begun in the latter half of the previous century. Even after the founding of the Tokugawa regime, daimyō continued to have considerable local autonomy, but the first century of Tokugawa rule saw a steady decline in their ability and willingness to challenge the authority of the shogunate. As direct vassals of the shōgun they found themselves under increasingly tight central control and supervision and were transformed from rugged provincial military leaders into aristocratic courtiers with diminished political responsibilities.

Moreover, in the course of the 17th century the vassals and subvassals of the daimyō became urbanized, lost their ties to the land and the peasants who worked it, and surrendered the effective autonomy they had enjoyed in the period of mature feudalism. The warrior class was gradually transformed from a fief-holding fighting force into an administrative bureaucracy, and vassalage itself became less contractual and personal, with the pledge of loyalty directed more toward the office of daimyō than the man who occupied it. Finally, the growth of the commercial economy from the middle of the Edo period eroded the dominant social position of the daimyō and warrior class. All of these factors combined to render the feudal elite increasingly anachronistic. When the special privileges of the warrior class were abolished after the MEIJI RESTORATION of 1868, there was only weak and sporadic protest. Some historians regard the reforms after 1868 as the "abolition of feudalism," but the substance of feudalism as an effective system of governance had come to its real end long before this.

fiction, modern　　　　近現代の小説

(*kingendai no shōsetsu*). Modern fiction in Japan has its origins in the Meiji period (1868–1912), when a flood of translations of Western literature collided with a vigorous native tradition of imaginative writing. The GESAKU fiction of the Edo period (1600–1868) continued to have a powerful influence upon the style and content of the early Meiji fiction, and it was in reaction to this influence that TSUBOUCHI SHŌYŌ produced the first critical treatise in Japanese regarding the theory and aims of the modern novel, *Shōsetsu shinzui* (1885–86, The Essence of the Novel).

Fiction had been traditionally regarded as a form of vulgar entertainment, and Tsubouchi, after examining recently imported Western models of writing, sensed the need for a new kind of imaginative writing capable of depicting the realities of modern life and establishing the novel as a serious form of artistic expression. He argued the merits

of realistic fiction as a medium for expressing the perceptions and aspirations of contemporary society, and discussed the need for novelists to create a written language with the vigor and comprehensibility of the spoken language, as well as the versatility and precision essential to a serious literature (see GEMBUN ITCHI).

Relying upon Tsubouchi's theories and personal guidance, FUTABATEI SHIMEI produced what has been called Japan's first modern novel, UKIGUMO (1887–89, Drifting Clouds; tr in *Japan's First Modern Novel: Ukigumo of Futabatei Shimei*, 1967). The plot concerns an unremarkable government clerk whose tenacious adherence to old-fashioned virtues renders him a pathetic figure in the eyes of both his more opportunistic colleagues and his female cousin, who is also his presumed fiancée. What is strikingly fresh about the novel is the colloquial style of the language, Futabatei's conception of his hero's plight within the context of a quickly changing society, and his subtle psychological examination of his protagonist.

For over a decade after *Ukigumo*, few writers shared Futabatei's interest in or understanding of the modern psychological novel. But in the 1890s this quest was continued by several young writers who are usually associated with the romantic movement centering on the famous literary journal BUNGAKUKAI (1893–98, The Literary World). The most impressive work of fiction published in *Bungakukai* was the story TAKEKURABE (1895–96; tr "Growing Up," 1956) by HIGUCHI ICHIYŌ. Ichiyō's language is still heavily classical in diction and imagery, but the content of the story is extraordinarily modern. In this tale of children living in the shadow of the Yoshiwara pleasure quarter, Ichiyō describes the loneliness of adolescence, the confusion that attends a growing awareness of sex, and the callousness of the adult world, which must soon be theirs. The subtlety and seriousness of her handling of youthful psychology betokens something very new in her vision.

But Ichiyō died too young, and her works were too fragile, to have much effect on the general development of modern Japanese fiction. It was another of her colleagues from *Bungakukai*, SHIMAZAKI TŌSON, who set the pattern for one stream of modern writers by moving gradually from romantic poetry to the writing of realistic fiction to assert the authenticity of the individual personality. His first novel, HAKAI (1906; tr *The Broken Commandment*, 1974), relates the story of a BURAKUMIN schoolteacher who hides his origins in the outcaste community until he realizes his only salvation as a human being lies in divulging his secret. In this powerful work, themes of bigotry, guilt, and isolation are treated with a psychological sophistication and social awareness that were new in Japanese literature. Absolutely modern in language as well, *Hakai* is a triumph of the new Japanese realism in its opposition of personal integrity to the values of an entire society and in its insistence that the self is the ultimate standard.

After *Hakai*, however, Tōson followed the direction set by TAYAMA KATAI's confessional novel *Futon* (1907; tr *The Quilt*, 1981) and retreated into his own private world to write in the genre of autobiographical or semiautobiographical novel known as the I-NOVEL. His characters, like Katai's, turn inward, and his novels become records of the survival of the author's identity. Tōson's abandonment of social realism helped to es-

tablish the genre of personal fiction, with its narrow world of limited alternatives, which for years nearly dominated the literary scene.

Thus it was not through Tōson but through NATSUME SŌSEKI that the modern Japanese realistic novel was brought to full maturity. Sōseki wrote a series of novels that are still among the most probing fictional accounts of the vicissitudes of modern middle-class life in Japan. His heroes are usually university-educated men made vulnerable by the new "egoism" and a too-keen perception of their separation from the rest of the world. In KOKORO (1914, The Heart; tr *Kokoro*, 1957), the most popular of his later novels, the hero, lonely and unable to overcome his guilt for having driven a friend to suicide because of their love of the same woman, finally kills himself. Guilt, betrayal, and isolation are for Sōseki the inevitable consequences of the liberation of the self and all the uncertainties that have come with the advent of Western culture. These motifs are also explored in his novels *Mon* (1910, The Gate; tr *Mon*, 1972) and *Kōjin* (1912–13; tr *The Wayfarer*, 1967).

Although there appeared in Sōseki a novelist whose claim to world recognition still seems legitimate, for many Japanese it is MORI ŌGAI who stands as the *the* great modern Japanese writer. Doctor, head of the army medical corps, German scholar, translator, master stylist, critic, historian, and novelist, he was the versatile intellectual par excellence of his time. Ironically, it is his own ambivalence toward fiction—reflecting a persistent suspicion in Japan of the artifice and unreality inherent in the genre—that seems to play a large part in the veneration with which Ōgai is regarded.

Ōgai first won acclaim with three romantic short stories set in Germany, each with a central Japanese character. The most popular, "Maihime" (1890; tr "The Dancing Girl," 1975), deals with the doomed love affair of a young Japanese student in Berlin with a German dancer of humble circumstances. Ōgai's major novels with contemporary settings are not as dramatic as Sōseki's, nor are they as rich in explicit social commentary. Yet in such works as GAN (1911–13; tr *The Wild Geese*, 1959), about a usurer's mistress who falls in love with a student, we find a new complexity in the psychological delineation of the characters. Unlike Sōseki, who continued to the end to employ fiction as a means of articulating the dilemmas of modernity, in his later years Ōgai questioned the very basis of his own fiction, seeking solace from the ambiguities of modern, Westernized experience by immersing himself in the past. His most representative late works are essentially fictionalized studies in history and biography, such as the short story "Sakai jiken" (1914; tr "The Incident at Sakai," 1977) and the meticulously researched life of an Edo-period doctor presented in *Shibue Chūsai* (1916).

AKUTAGAWA RYŪNOSUKE, a younger contemporary of Ōgai's and one of Japan's most famous short-story writers, also sought an outlet for his sly and supple imagination by setting many stories in the past, though without Ōgai's rigorous attention to historical veracity. For Akutagawa, the past offered through its very remoteness a freedom that the present could not. Such stories as RASHŌMON (1915; tr "Rashōmon," 1930), "Jigokuhen" (1918; tr "Hell Screen," 1948), and

"Yabu no naka" (1922; tr "In a Grove," 1952) are brilliantly told, combining psychological subtlety and modern cynicism with a fanciful delight in the grotesque. Toward the end of a meteoric career terminated by his suicide, Akutagawa began to try his hand at autobiographical fiction, notably in the chilling story "Haguruma" (1927; tr "Cogwheel," 1965), which expresses the mental and physical anguish of the final year of his life.

NAGAI KAFŪ was another of the major figures in modern Japanese fiction who reflected the tension between modernity and a yearning for an older Japan. His life as a writer began with travels to America and France and an infatuation with French literature, out of which came two early collections of short stories, *Amerika monogatari* (1908, American Stories) and *Furansu monogatari* (1909, French Stories). He is best known, however, for his elegiac later works—notably BOKUTŌ KIDAN (1937; tr *A Strange Tale from East of the River*, 1958)—depicting the fading demimonde of Tōkyō with a richness of attention to place and mood that has won him a lasting place in literary history.

SHIGA NAOYA, who established his reputation with a body of brilliantly crafted short stories, went on to cap his accomplishments with a single full-length psychological novel, AN'YA KŌRO (1921–37; tr *A Dark Night's Passing*, 1976). He did not share the sense of nostalgia for the premodern culture of Japan seen in such writers as Ōgai or Kafū, but the search for identity in the modern world is still the theme of this masterwork, as the hero, born of an incestuous liaison between his mother and her father-in-law, learns this ugly fact and suddenly finds his sense of self challenged at its very foundations.

Despite its skillful presentation of the fantasies and inner life of its protagonist and its blurring of the lines between conscious and subconscious, dream and reality, Shiga's major work stayed largely within the stylistic conventions of the I-novel genre. It was TANIZAKI JUN'ICHIRŌ who took modern Japanese writing a step further into a realm of pure and playful fictionality. In early novels such as *Chijin no ai* (1924–25; tr *Naomi*, 1985) and *Manji* (1928–30), Tanizaki went far beyond the conventions of earlier realistic fiction. Both works are tales of sexual infidelity, abandon, obsession, and fantasy in which the deceptions engaged in by the characters are metaphors for the deceptiveness of fiction itself. Tanizaki was constantly mindful of the writer's responsibility to entertain, and of the reader's pleasure in being manipulated and deceived. He also possessed a rare capacity to articulate through allegory the cultural confusions of modern Japan. In novels such as *Tade kuu mushi* (1928–29; tr *Some Prefer Nettles*, 1955), Tanizaki sought a sense of continuity amid contemporary uneasiness by turning to the past; his hero, an indecisive, Westernized man living in Ōsaka, his marriage turned loveless, slowly begins to discover beauty in such traditional arts as the puppet theater.

In the work of writers like Tanizaki and Kafū from the late 1920s and 1930s, a lingering aura of tradition still infuses their settings and locales, and a sense of cultural continuity, however tenuous, is still available to them. Japan's plunge into World War II and the shattering defeat that ensued, however, were sufficiently powerful to obliterate such communion with the past. The writer who

most clearly reflected the sense of loss and confusion following the war, both in his writing and his tragic life, was DAZAI OSAMU. Dazai's early work focused upon his own dissipation and debauchery, but the chaos is intensified to the breaking point in SHAYŌ (1947; tr *The Setting Sun*, 1956) and the novel published just before his suicide, NINGEN SHIKKAKU (1948; tr *No Longer Human*, 1958). Individual madness and pain become, in the process, a mirror of the disintegration of the entire social order.

Not every writer after the war accepted Dazai's utterly negative response to the defeat. IBUSE MASUJI was one who clung to a sense of geographical place as a mooring, but his focus was on the struggle to maintain that identification in the face of forces that threaten to obliterate it. This is clear in his finest work, KUROI AME (1965–66; tr *Black Rain*, 1969), about the atomic bombing of Hiroshima. The greatness of the novel, which is narrated through the diaries of ordinary people, lies in its ability to depict all of the horrifying details of the event and yet conclude with an affirmation of humanity.

Not long after the defeat, Tanizaki Jun'ichirō also published his masterpiece, the massive novel SASAMEYUKI (1943–48; tr *The Makioka Sisters*, 1957), serial publication of which had been suppressed during the war. A chronicle of the lives of the daughters of a patrician merchant family in its last stages of decline before the outbreak of the war, it is a beautiful elegy to the final passing of all that remained of an older and more elegant world. It shares with Tanizaki's other works his concern for cultural values and his eagerness to depict both a society and individual characters flickering through a stage of transition.

Writers such as ENCHI FUMIKO also sought to reestablish the severed links with the cultural past by calling upon such classical texts as the TALE OF GENJI and transporting them into a very different modern setting. Her novels ONNAZAKA (1949–57; tr *The Waiting Years*, 1971) and *Onnamen* (1958; tr *Masks*, 1983) describe the continuing struggle of women confined within traditional social roles.

The link between people and place has grown painfully fragile in the fiction of Japan's Nobel laureate, KAWABATA YASUNARI. In novels such as YUKIGUNI (1935–48; tr *Snow Country*, 1956), Kawabata creates enormous distances between his characters, suggesting a dread of intimacy that threatens even the most promising of human relationships. After the war, Kawabata took to writing what he called "elegies to the lost Japan" in such works as *Yama no oto* (1949–54; tr *The Sound of the Mountain*, 1970), in which the aging protagonist, Shingo, unable to endure the frustrating losses that surround him, opens a gulf between himself and his family by retreating into his memories of the irretrievable past.

Yet Japanese writing in the early postwar years could not be characterized solely in terms of the shock and dislocation of defeat. There was, in fact, a vigorous renascence of literary activity after 1945, and a new group of writers who debuted at this time came to be known as the "first generation" of postwar authors. They had been attracted to Marxist philosophy before the war, and returned from the war to assert the need for a type of fiction that would examine all the political, philosophical, and moral aspects of their experience. Implicit in much of their writing was a critique of the values and social

system they felt had led Japan into the conflict. Members of this group include NOMA HIROSHI, whose novel *Shinkū chitai* (1952; tr *Zone of Emptiness*, 1956) depicts the military in wartime as an extension of the oppressive prewar Japanese social order, and ŌOKA SHŌHEI, who in NOBI (1951; tr *Fires on the Plain*, 1957), a novel set in the last days of the fighting in the Philippines, depicts a solitary Japanese soldier who is reduced to the lowest level of humanity by his wartime experiences.

The "second generation" of postwar writers includes ABE KŌBŌ and MISHIMA YUKIO, both of whom debuted in the late 1940s. Abe would eventually create a distinctive type of Kafkaesque existential allegory in novels such as SUNA NO ONNA (1962; tr *The Woman in the Dunes*, 1964), while Mishima attracted an international readership with his opulent aestheticism, his vision of a postwar Japan clinging to external forms but hollow within, and his complex psychological examination of character and motivation in such works as KINKAKUJI (1956; tr *The Temple of the Golden Pavilion*, 1959).

Critics have posited a turning point in the 1950s, after which Japanese fiction can no longer be easily characterized in terms of the early postwar consciousness. Beginning about this time, a revival and restructuring of the I-novel form was achieved by a "third generation" of postwar writers—KOJIMA NOBUO, who examined the collapse of the family system in *Hōyō kazoku* (1965, Embracing Family); YASUOKA SHŌTARŌ, who brought a new sense of ironic perspective to the personal narrative in *Umibe no kōkei* (1959; tr *A View by the Sea*, 1984); and SHIMAO TOSHIO, whose fiction, culminating in *Shi no toge* (1960; tr *The Sting of Death*, 1985), transposes the agony and anxiety of his war experience onto his postwar marital relationship. Also included in this group is ENDŌ SHŪSAKU, a Catholic convert who examines the issues of betrayal, cowardice, and martyrdom in novels such as CHIMMOKU (1966; tr *Silence*, 1969), set during the Christian persecutions of early-17th-century Japan.

From the 1960s onward, writers have sought to synthesize various approaches to fiction or to experiment with new modes of representation. ŌE KENZABURŌ has been a prodigiously inventive force in contemporary fiction, continuously experimenting with form and mode of presentation in dealing with both political and personal issues in such novels as KOJINTEKI NA TAIKEN (1964; tr *A Personal Matter*, 1968) and MAN'EN GANNEN NO FUTTOBŌRU (1967; tr *The Silent Cry*, 1974). KŌNO TAEKO has examined the repressed psychology of women in *Fui no koe* (1968, Sudden Voice) and other works, while TSUSHIMA YŪKO, the daughter of Dazai Osamu, has explored the lives of women who are single parents in *Chōji* (1978; tr *Child of Fortune*, 1983) and many excellent short stories. And finally, the generation raised on the rebellious, rock-and-roll international culture of the last decades has found its voice in writers such as MURAKAMI RYŪ, author of *Kagirinaku tōmei ni chikai burū* (1976; tr *Almost Transparent Blue*, 1977), and MURAKAMI HARUKI, whose *Noruuē no mori* (1987; tr *Norwegian Wood*, 1989) sold more than 3 million copies. In Japan, as in the West, critics have periodically proclaimed the death of fiction and bemoaned the decline in the audience for serious literature, but this news has apparently not reached the Japanese public, which is buying and reading a

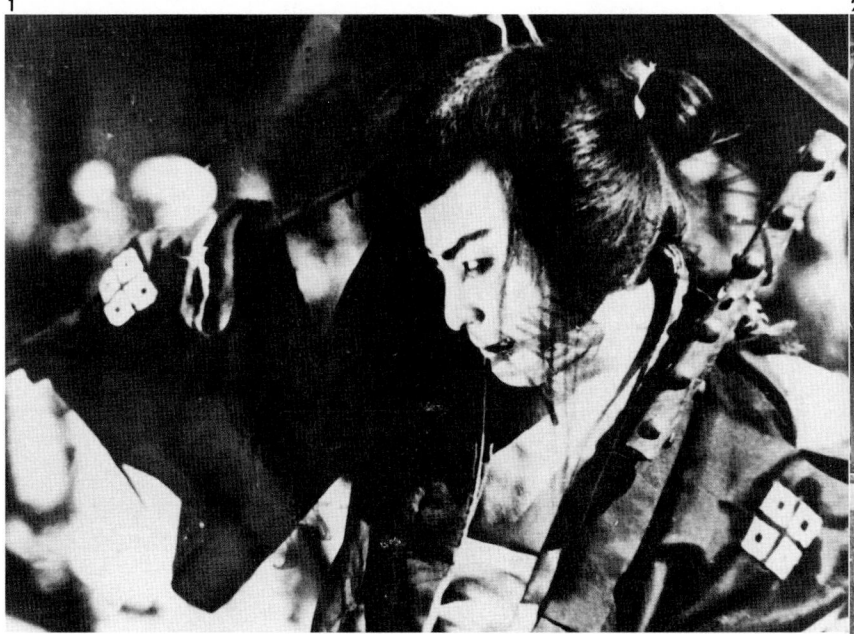

greater number and variety of books than ever before.

fidelity guaranty　　　身元保証

(*mimoto hoshō*). In Japanese law, the duty of a third party (the *hoshōnin* or surety) to pay damages when an employer suffers losses through the acts of an employee; the term is also used to refer to a contract giving rise to such a duty. The Law concerning Fidelity Guaranty (Mimoto Hoshō ni kansuru Hōritsu) of 1933 defines the responsibilities of the surety and the employer as follows: (1) Fidelity guaranty contracts run for three years unless otherwise specified, in which case the maximum period is five years. (2) The employer must notify the surety when there is evidence of the employee's incompetence or lack of faith or when the duties or posting of the employee change in a way that adds to the surety's responsibility. (3) On receiving such notice, the surety may cancel the personal surety contract. (4) In determining damages, the court shall take the entire situation into account, including contributory negligence on the part of the employer.

Fifth-Generation Computer Systems Project

第5世代コンピュータープロジェクト

(Daigo Sedai Kompyūtā Purojekuto). "Next-generation" computer project carried out between 1982 and 1992 by the Institute for New Generation Computer Technology under the guidance of the MINISTRY OF INTERNATIONAL TRADE AND INDUSTRY (MITI). The goal of the project was to develop computer systems characterized by sophisticated artificial-intelligence technology more capable of simulating human thought processes such as inference and problem solving than existing computer systems. The planned computer systems were termed fifth generation because they were intended to supersede the preceding four generations of development in computer component technology from vacuum tubes to very large scale integrated circuitry. Research topics included spoken-language recognition.

A significant achievement of the fifth-generation project in the years 1982–84 was the personal sequential inference (PSI) machine, capable of making logical inferences

from known facts. Between 1985 and 1988, research in parallel processing and knowledge processing led to the development of a multi-PSI system linking 64 processors in a parallel inference machine (PIM) system, and development of a 1,000-processor system had begun by 1991.

Although the fifth-generation computer project officially ended in 1992, research in this area was scheduled to be continued by the Real World Computing Program that had been outlined by MITI in March 1991.

filial piety　　　孝

(*kō;* also known as *kōkō* or *oyakōkō*). The notion that children owe an obligation to their parents to be obedient, to care for them in their old age, and to venerate them after their death was a basic tenet of CONFUCIANISM, which was introduced to Japan from China in the 5th or 6th century. The Chinese Confucians saw filial piety as the cornerstone of the family, and the family in turn as the cornerstone of society. The upper stratum of Japanese society took this notion, along with the notion of loyalty (*chū*), as its primary ideal.

During the Edo period (1600–1868), the concept of filial piety spread through the warrior class. Filial piety was considered closely related to LOYALTY to one's lord. After the Meiji Restoration (1868), filial piety was deliberately propagated among all classes of Japanese and became part of the national ethic. Indeed, it was used by the government to foster the ideals of patriotism and nationhood; loyalty to the emperor, it was argued, was simply filial piety writ large. Since World War II, the inculcation of filial piety has been officially abandoned.

Film Center　　　フィルムセンター

(Firumu Sentā). There are a number of film libraries in Japan; the most important is the Film Center attached to the NATIONAL MUSEUM OF MODERN ART, TŌKYŌ, originally established in 1952. The Film Center's holdings concentrate chiefly on the Japanese film industry; in 1989 the collection consisted of 9,000 Japanese films (1,000 of them feature length) and about 900 foreign films. A new building equipped with two theaters, video booths, a library, and exhibition spaces was under construction in 1991 to house the Film Cen-

ter, and in 1986 a separate Film Center Archive with a storage capacity for 22,000 feature films was created in Kanagawa Prefecture to serve the center's long-term storage needs. The Film Center serves the needs of both film scholars and the general public, providing research materials and assistance as well as offering regular public screenings of films.

film, Japanese　　　日本映画

(Nihon *eiga*). The Japanese first imported motion pictures in 1896. By 1899 they were filming their own. Until the coming of talkies, movies in Japan were accompanied by a BENSHI, a live performer who sat by the side of the screen and orally interpreted the images of the film. Because *benshi* supplied expository connections and full dialogue, the first filmmakers replicated Japanese stage plays and generally ignored film techniques being developed in the West by such film directors as D. W. Griffith (1875–1948).

Early History——MAKINO SHŌZŌ (1878–1929), the father of the Japanese period film, gradually dropped KABUKI elements from his costume dramas to concentrate on stories from juvenile literature and the traditional genre of oral storytelling known as KŌDAN. Films with contemporary stories drew on the SHIMPA theatrical repertoire throughout the early 1900s. After World War I, would-be filmmakers, influenced by the ideals of SHINGEKI ("new theater") and by the flood of movies from abroad, cried for "modernization and realism." They sought naturalistic acting and the casting of actresses instead of traditional ONNAGATA (female impersona-

Continued on page 372➤

Japanese film

1 In Futagawa Buntarō's *Orochi* (1925, Serpent), Bandō Tsumasaburō starred as the archetypal *jidaigeki* (period film) hero: a lonely, alienated *rōnin* (masterless *samurai*).
2 Tasaka Tomotaka's seminal war movie *Gonin no sekkōhei* (1938, Five Scouts) focused on everyday front-line activity rather than patriotic heroics.
3 Gosho Heinosuke's *Madamu to nyōbō* (1931, The Neighbor's Wife and Mine), an early and successful talkie, starred Watanabe Atsushi (center) and Tanaka Kinuyo (right).

Masterpieces of Japanese Cinema

To commemorate the publication of its 1,000th postwar issue in 1989, *Kinema jumpō*, Japan's leading journal of film criticism, polled 86 movie enthusiasts in order to determine the "Ten Best Japanese Films of All Time." The survey participants, who included writers, artists, entertainers, and people in the film industry, responded with an unexpected profusion of suggestions. What emerged was the expanded list presented here—the top 10 (including 2 films that posted identical scores) and 16 others (not numbered here) that finished in the top 20 due to a 7-way tie vote for 20th place.

The release dates shown tell the story of Japan's postwar film industry: the 1950s produced 12 of the films selected, the 1960s only 4, and the 1970s merely a single selection. Japanese cinema found new life in the 1980s, however, and 6 films were chosen from that decade.

1 **Shichinin no samurai** (1954, Seven Samurai); director Kurosawa Akira. In this epic period film, which broke new ground in Japanese filmmaking with its magnificent large-scale battle scenes, an embattled farm village hires a disparate group of seven unemployed samurai to protect it from bandits. The same plot was adapted to the American West in the 1960 American film *The Magnificent Seven*.

5 **Kiga kaikyō** (1964, The Straits of Hunger); Uchida Tomu. A criminal who murdered his confederates in a pawnshop robbery escapes justice for 10 years but is finally caught as a result of a good deed he performed immediately after the crime.

6 **Bakumatsu taiyō den** (1957, A Tale of the Sun Tribe during the Last Days of the Shogunate); Kawashima Yūzō. A comedy about a penniless townsman who lives in a brothel and gets caught up in a plot to overthrow the shogunate.

7 **Saikaku ichidai onna** (1952, shown abroad as *The Life of Oharu*); Mizoguchi Kenji. An aging prostitute who was once a court lady remembers the men who contributed to her fall to the bottom of society.

Jingi naki tatakai (1973–74, Combat without a Code, color); Fukasaku Kinji. A realistic portrayal of conflict in the world of organized crime.

Tengoku to jigoku (1963, shown abroad as *High and Low*); Kurosawa Akira. A thriller about a kidnapping investigation.

Mata au hi made (1950, Until the Day We Meet Again); Imai Tadashi. A tragic wartime love story.

Ninjō kamifūsen (1937, Humanity and Paper Balloons); Yamanaka Sadao. A period film about lower-class city dwellers.

Ningen no jōken (1959–61, The Human Condition); Kobayashi Masaki. The story of a World War II soldier.

Osōshiki (1984, The Funeral, color); Itami Jūzō. This satirical comedy takes aim at the conventional Japanese funeral.

Kaze no tani no Naushika (1984, Nausicaä of the Valley of the Wind, color); Miyazaki Hayao. An adventure-story animation film.

Gojira (1954, Godzilla); Honda Ishirō. A monster is brought to life by radiation from hydrogen-bomb testing.

2 **Tōkyō monogatari** (1953, Tōkyō Story); Ozu Yasujirō. An elderly couple from a small town travel to Tōkyō to visit their children, who find their presence a burden.

The film is a poignant expression of this director's typical concerns: isolation, loneliness, and the unraveling of Japanese family life in postwar society.

3 **Ikiru** (1952, To Live); Kurosawa Akira. After learning that he has but a few months to live, an aging civil servant searches for a way to give his life meaning. He succeeds by pushing plans for a small children's park through the intransigent bureaucracy of which he was so long a part.

4 **Ukigumo** (1955, Floating Clouds); Naruse Mikio. A married man and a young woman meet and fall in love in Southeast Asia during World War II. Their bitter, obsessive affair continues back in Japan as she struggles to survive during the dark postwar years.

8/9 **Ugetsu monogatari** (1953, shown abroad as *Ugetsu*); Mizoguchi Kenji. A 16th-century potter is bewitched by a lovely ghost in a film that borrowed from the Nō theater and was praised for its camera work.

8/9 **Yōjimbō** (1961); Kurosawa Akira. An Edo-period masterless samurai wanders into a town where two rival gangs are fighting for control; playing one side against the other, he saves the town from both.

10 **Nijūshi no hitomi** (1954, Twenty-Four Eyes); Kinoshita Keisuke. On a small Inland Sea island a young teacher and her 12 pupils endure the hardships of the 1930s and 1940s.

Rashōmon (1950); Kurosawa Akira. This period film about the nature of truth won the 1951 Venice Film Festival Grand Prix.

Chigoineruwaizen (1980, Zigeunerweisen, color); Suzuki Seijun. Fantasy and reality blur in this nostalgic look at prewar Japan.

Kazoku gēmu (1983, The Family Game, color); Morita Yoshimitsu. A comedy about modern Japanese family life.

Nihon no yoru to kiri (1960, Night and Fog in Japan, color); Ōshima Nagisa. A critical view of the Japanese left wing.

Doro no kawa (1981, Muddy River); Oguri Kōhei. The story of a childhood friendship.

Banshun (1949, Late Spring); Ozu Yasujirō. A quiet tale of the love between a father and daughter.

Muhō Matsu no isshō (1943, Rickshaw Man); Inagaki Hiroshi. An allegorical portrait of a humble but likable rickshaw puller.

Yuki yukite, shingun (1987, shown abroad as *The Emperor's Naked Army Marches On*, color); Hara Kazuo. Documentary about an ex-soldier's postwar crusade.

tors), subject matter that stretched beyond the narrow range of *shimpa* and kabuki plays, and the adoption of expressive techniques seen in foreign films.

Film critic Kaeriyama Norimasa (1893–1964) was among the first to experiment with Western editing techniques, complex stories, and actresses, in *Sei no kagayaki* (1919, The Glow of Life). At Nikkatsu (see NIKKATSU CORPORATION), the first major film company, Tanaka Eizō (1886–1968) introduced new techniques and content with *Ikeru shikabane* (1918, The Living Corpse). Shōchiku (see SHŌCHIKU CO, LTD), an entertainment conglomerate that controlled first-class live drama, expanded into the movie business in 1920. There MURATA MINORU (1894–1937) and OSANAI KAORU (1881–1928) made *Rojō no reikon* (1921, Souls on the Road), which critics since have called equal to any contemporary foreign work.

The First Jidaigeki and Gendaigeki—

The early 1920s marked the emergence of JIDAIGEKI, the genre that encompasses all films set before the Meiji period (1868–1912). In 1924 Makino Shōzō collaborated with the SHINKOKUGEKI drama troupe in a movie version of its swashbuckling hit *Kunisada Chūji*. The head of Shinkokugeki, SAWADA SHŌJIRŌ (1892–1929), had earlier developed *chambara* (spectacular sword-fighting scenes) as the basis for his popular theater. The plays staged by Sawada were derived, in part, from the *taishū bungaku* (popular literature) movement that had originated a decade earlier in the sword-fighter novels of NAKAZATO KAIZAN (1885–1944). *Jidaigeki* subsequently evolved over 60 years through a symbiotic relationship among literary, theater, and film works focused on swords and solitary heroes.

The men who defined the *jidaigeki* genre were directors ITŌ DAISUKE (1898–1981), Makino's son MAKINO MASAHIRO (b 1908), and Futagawa Buntarō (1899–1966) and scenarist Susukita Rokuhei (1899–1960). They created the archetypical *jidaigeki* hero: an alienated, imperfect human—almost always a mid-19th-century *rōnin* (masterless samurai) or a sword-fighting, common gambler—caught in conflict between his obligations (*giri*) and his personal feelings (*ninjō*). During the 1920s their movies brought quick fame to an array of sword-fighting stars led by BANDŌ TSUMASABURŌ (1901–53) and ŌKŌCHI DENJIRŌ (1878–1962), who dominated the *jidaigeki* genre for three decades.

Gendaigeki, the other genre of the post-1920 Japanese cinema, encompasses all stories with modern settings. Until 1926 the only *gendaigeki* that outdrew *jidaigeki* at the box office were either adventure stories patterned after foreign serials or sentimental love stories based on popular songs. Meanwhile, former Hollywood actor Abe Yutaka (1895–1977) led an "Americanism" school with his "smart, modern, speedy" comedies. MIZOGUCHI KENJI (1898–1956), the most eclectic of early *gendaigeki* directors, drew on sources ranging from the German film *The Cabinet of Dr. Caligari* to traditional *shimpa* drama. The most substantial experimental efforts—suggestive but not imitative of the avant-garde of Europe—were KINUGASA TEINOSUKE's (1896–1982) *Kurutta ippeiji* (1926, A Page Out of Order; shown abroad as *A Page of Madness*) and his *jidaigeki* film *Jūjiro* (1928, Crossroads). SHIMAZU YASUJIRŌ (1897–1945) introduced white-collar workers as a prime *gendaigeki* subject in such

family-centered comedies as *Nichiyōbi* (1924, Sunday). GOSHO HEINOSUKE's (1902–81) *Mura no hanayome* (1928, The Village Bride) and Ushihara Kiyohiko's (1897–1985) *Kare to Tōkyō* (1928, He and Tōkyō) established another *gendaigeki* focus: strong women and weak men caught in familial conflict.

The Late 1920s and Early 1930s—

The economic depression that hit Japan before 1929 engendered left-wing tendencies in literature (see PROLETARIAN LITERATURE MOVEMENT), *shingeki*, and films. Nihilistic, egocentric swordsmen became fighting protectors of the downtrodden in *jidaigeki*. Modern heroes and heroines opposed the oppressive system in *gendaigeki* such as UCHIDA TOMU's (1898–1970) *Ikeru ningyō* (1929, A Living Doll) and Mizoguchi's *Tokai kōkyōgaku* (1929, Metropolitan Symphony). After the invasion of Manchuria in 1931, more stringent government censorship ended these mildly radical efforts. The cutting edge of *jidaigeki* moved to satire and comedy after ITAMI MANSAKU's (1900–1946) *Kokushi musō* (1932, Peerless Patriot). The most important new direction for *jidaigeki* was initiated by YAMANAKA SADAO (1909–38) and INAGAKI HIROSHI (1905–80), who brought the slice-of-life, lower-class urban milieu of many *gendaigeki* to the period film. In *gendaigeki*, Shimazu, with his *Tonari no Yae-chan* (1934, Our Neighbor Miss Yae), turned toward stories focused on the small joys and passive endurance of the world. The works of OZU YASUJIRŌ (1903–63) best reflected the continuing development of the *shōshimin geki*, "dramas about the petite bourgeoisie." For three years in a row, critics chose his stories of imperfect fathers—UMARETE WA MITA KEREDO (1932, I Was Born, But . . .), *Dekigokoro* (1933, Passing Fancy), and *Ukigusa monogatari* (1934, A Story of Floating Weeds)—as the best pictures of their respective years.

The Talkies—

Gosho's family comedy *Madamu to nyōbo* (The Neighbor's Wife and Mine) was Japan's first technically successful talkie as well as the critical and popular success of 1931. Although talkies strained the capital resources of the industry (and drove the live *benshi* out of movie theaters), the innovation did not displace established film talent as it did abroad. Not until 1934–35 did talkies constitute more than half of all Japanese feature production.

In 1936 Mizoguchi became the pioneering exponent of a new "talkie realism" with *Gion no shimai* (Sisters of the Gion) and NANIWA EREJI (Ōsaka Elegy), which combined *shimpa* motifs (such as the exploited woman) with precise local color. At Nikkatsu, Uchida Tomu abandoned his satirical *jidaigeki* to concentrate on gritty *gendaigeki* about society's victims in *Jinsei gekijō* (1936, Theater of Life; based on a novel by OZAKI SHIRŌ [1898–1964]) and in his semidocumentary about peasant life, *Tsuchi* (1939, Earth; based on a novel by NAGATSUKA TAKASHI [1879–1915]). Contemporary novels were the prime sources for many films in the late 1930s. TOYODA SHIRŌ (1906–77) led a "pure literature" film movement with adaptations of ISHIZAKA YŌJIRŌ's (1900–1986) *Wakai hito* (1937, Young People) and Ogawa Masako's *Kojima no haru* (1940, Spring on a Small Island). Upon its establishment in 1937, Tōhō (see TŌHŌ CO, LTD), a consolidation of smaller studios, became an instant rival to the two old majors, Nikkatsu and Shōchiku. Seeking urban appeal, Tōhō developed musicals and comedies under the leadership of directors YAMAMOTO KAJIRŌ (1902–73)

and Saitō Torajirō (1905–82).

The bulk of *jidaigeki* continued to be nihilistic *chambara* adventures. Several small studios survived throughout the 1930s by turning out cheap, silent *jidaigeki* for the surviving *benshi* market. Although feature production had risen to a steady average of 650 per year by the mid-1920s, the average annual output stabilized at 550 throughout the 1930s. Under wartime restraints this number suddenly decreased to 232 in 1941 and fell to 26 in 1945.

Censorship, the War, and the Postwar Era—

Film censorship was consolidated under the control of the national Police Bureau (Keihokyoku) of the Home Ministry in 1925 and gradually tightened during the 1930s. In 1939 the Home Ministry ordered filmmakers to follow its list of essential "national policy" subjects, which accented patriotic home life and sacrifice for the nation. Despite strong official encouragement, fewer than one-fifth of all wartime features complied with government guidelines. Fewer than 2 percent of all films produced between the 1937 start of war in China and the 1945 surrender of Japan were stories about the military. TASAKA TOMOTAKA (1902–74) made the seminal war pictures GONIN NO SEKKŌHEI (1938, Five Scouts) and *Tsuchi to heitai* (1939, Mud and Soldiers). Subsequent war movies tended to be biographical in structure like YOSHIMURA KŌZABURŌ's (b 1911) *Nishizumi senshachō den* (1940, The Story of Tank Commander Nishizumi) or episodic sketches of men of all ranks engaged in specific campaigns as in Yamamoto Kajirō's *Hawai–Marē oki kaisen* (1942, The War at Sea from Hawaii to Malaya).

The American OCCUPATION abolished Home Ministry censorship and set up its own office to supervise film content. The Americans banned most presurrender films. They also opposed production of *jidaigeki* with *chambara* scenes because of the genre's alleged feudal outlook and encouraged democratic and modern subjects. *Jidaigeki* swords soon turned into pistols in detective and gangster *gendaigeki* action films. In 1949 Occupation authorities eased their controls in return for the industry's establishment of a self-regulatory body, the MOTION PICTURE CODE COMMITTEE (Eirin), which administered a production code patterned after Hollywood's. Japanese cinema was without official, formal censorship and within a year sword fighting was back.

After disrupting production for two years, striking union militants occupied the Tōhō studios in 1948. Japanese police, aided by American tanks, quickly quashed the strike. Activists quit Tōhō and began to make a scattering of low-budget, independent features that had a defiant leftist sensibility long missing from the Japanese cinema. In 1947, during the union turmoil, a large anticommunist faction left the parent Tōhō company to establish SHIN TŌHŌ as the fourth major studio of the postwar period. (The two major studios in the late 1930s were Shōchiku and the parent Tōhō company. In 1942, the government had engineered the amalgamation of the faltering Nikkatsu company with two lesser studios to create the third major studio, Daiei [see DAIEI CO, LTD].) Two small postwar studios combined in 1951 to produce the fifth major studio, Tōei (see TŌEI CO, LTD). A new Nikkatsu production company, with no connection to Daiei, became the sixth major studio in 1953. The six major studios controlled the industry through a cartel-like hold on film distribu-

Japanese film

A selection of film posters from the past few decades.

Kurosawa Akira's classic *Shichinin no samurai* (1954, Seven Samurai) is considered by many to be one of the finest Japanese films ever made.

Directed by Masuda Toshio, the popular action film *Sabita naifu* (1958, The Rusty Knife) starred Ishihara Yūjirō.

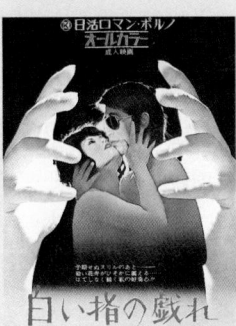

Murakawa Tōru's *Shiroi yubi no tawamure* (1972, White Fingers of Ecstasy) was a Nikkatsu Corp. film in the *roman poruno* ("romantic pornography") genre.

Suna no onna (1964, Woman in the Dunes), directed by Teshigahara Hiroshi, was based on the novel by Abe Kōbō.

Nishikawa Katsumi's *Izu no odoriko* (1974, The Izu Dancer) was the sixth film based on the Kawabata Yasunari story.

Yamashita Kōsaku's *Hibotan bakuto* (1968, The Scarlet Peony Gambler) began a gangster film series of the same name.

Fantasy and realism were combined in *Chigoineruwaizen* (1980, Zigeunerweisen), Suzuki Seijun's nostalgic look at prewar Japan.

tion and exhibition. The number of movie theaters reached an all-time high of 7,457 in 1960. This was 8.8 times as many as when the war ended. Two men whose directing careers had begun during the war came to the forefront during the early Occupation era: KUROSAWA AKIRA (b 1910) and KINOSHITA KEISUKE (b 1912). Along with two other directors of their generation, IMAI TADASHI (b 1912) and Yoshimura Kōzaburō, they dominated the 1947–50 period with films about postwar life.

The 1950s—The decade of the 1950s, apart from being the most prosperous in the history of the Japanese cinema, is considered by many to be its creative Golden Age. Five times during this decade critics voted a film by Imai the best of the year, a streak that began with *Mata au hi made* (1950, Until the Day We Meet Again). When Kurosawa's innovative *jidaigeki* RASHŌMON (1950) won the top prize at the Venice Film Festival in 1951, it opened the Japanese cinema to international audiences. Kurosawa's cosmopolitan style alternated between such social issue–oriented *gendaigeki* as IKIRU (1952, To Live) and such seminal *jidaigeki* epics as *Shichinin no samurai* (1954, SEVEN SAMURAI).

Kurosawa's rival for international attention, Mizoguchi, abandoned his early postwar love stories to refashion the period film with such exquisite works as *Saikaku ichidai onna* (1952, The Life of a Woman by Saikaku; shown abroad as *The Life of Oharu*) and UGETSU MONOGATARI (1953, Ugetsu). Starting with BANSHUN (1949, Late Spring), Ozu Yasujirō and his scenarist NODA KŌGO (1893–1968) concentrated on the emotional complexities of middle-class family life, while NARUSE MIKIO (1905–69) and Gosho Heinosuke continued the prewar *shōshimin geki* tradition. Naruse later turned to a new major interest: portraits of women fighting the domination of men in such films as UKIGUMO (1955, Floating Clouds). Gosho's major work was *Entotsu no mieru basho* (1953, Where Chimneys Are Seen).

Throughout the 1950s the war remained an obsession. Treatment of it took four distinct directions. The cruelty of military life was revealed in ICHIKAWA KON's (b 1915) BIRUMA NO TATEGOTO (1956, Harp of Burma) and *Nobi* (1959, Fire on the Plains), YAMAMOTO SATSUO's (b 1910) *Shinkū chitai* (1952, Vacuum Zone), and KOBAYASHI MASAKI's (b 1916) six-part (often shown in three parts) NINGEN NO JŌKEN (1959–61, The Human Condition). These and many other postwar films were based on major works of contemporary fiction. A second direction explored the effects of the war on the home front. Ōba Hideo's (b 1910) three-part tragic wartime romance, KIMI NO NA WA (1953–54, What's Your Name?), was seen by one-third of the population, influenced popular song and fashion for more than a year, and was imitated relentlessly. Kinoshita Keisuke's NIJŪSHI NO HITOMI (1954, Twenty-Four Eyes), about a rural schoolteacher and her pupils during the militaristic 1930s and 1940s, became the definitive expression of Japanese sentimentality on film. Other directions for films about war were hagiographies of military leaders set against epic battle sequences and nostalgic comedies about life in the imperial military. Muckraking exposés of contemporary life flourished for several years after the Occupation ended. Among these were Imai's revelations of injustice in the legal system in MAHIRU NO ANKOKU (1956, Darkness at Noon), Kobayashi's disclosure of criminal activity around US military bases in *Kuroi kawa* (1957, Black River), and MASUMURA YASUZŌ's (b 1924) denunciation of corruption in the business world in *Kyojin to gangu* (1958, Titans and Toys).

Comedy grew in sophistication. Shibuya Minoru (1907–80) perfected the well-wrought farce in *Honjitsu kyūshin* (1952, Clinic Closed Today), Kawashima Yūzō (1918–63) created the definitive postwar *jidaigeki* comedy in *Bakumatsu taiyō den* (1957, A Tale of the Sun during the Last Days of the Shogunate), and Ichikawa pio-

neered black humor in *Kagi* (1959, The Key; shown abroad as *Odd Obsession*). The new Tōei company captured a large new audience for *jidaigeki* by creating young *chambara* stars, and it also backed *jidaigeki* old masters: Itō, Uchida, and Makino Masahiro. Tōhō and Daiei countered Tōei with their own brands of *jidaigeki* program pictures, while they supported new directions for period films by Kurosawa, Mizoguchi, and Inagaki. To strengthen its principal market among urban, middle-class audiences, Tōhō made pop musicals and dozens of comedies about middle-aged white-collar workers. In 1954 Tōhō created Japan's first film monster in GODZILLA (*Gojira*). A horde of Tōhō and Daiei monsters followed for two decades. Kinoshita's *Karumen kokyō ni kaeru* (Carmen Comes Home) inaugurated a decade of technical innovation in 1951 with the first Japanese color feature. Three years later Kinugasa's *Jigokumon* (1953, Gate of Hell) won the highest international acclaim for innovative use of color. Anamorphic widescreen features appeared in 1957, but it took more than seven years for the new frame dimensions to become standard in Japan. In the late 1950s, a new short-lived genre, *taiyōzoku* (sun tribe) films, so called after a group of young people portrayed in the best-selling novel *Taiyō no kisetsu* (1955, Season of the Sun; tr *Season of Violence*, 1966) by ISHIHARA SHINTARŌ (b 1932), exploited the hedonism of affluent postwar youth. This accelerated interest in movie sex and violence.

Television and a New Wave—In 1958, five years after television broadcasting had begun, there were 1.6 million television sets throughout the country. By 1969 there were 21.9 million sets, a figure almost equal to the number of households. Attendance at the movies fell from the all-time high of 1.1 billion in 1958 to 300 million in 1968. The Shin Tōhō studios went bankrupt in 1961. Half of

373

film, Japanese

Local Government Budgets for Fiscal 1989 — local government finance

Revenues and Expenses	All local governments	Prefectures	Tōkyō's 23 wards	Large cities	Other cities	Towns and villages
	(in percentages)					
Revenues						
Local taxes	42.6	40.9	36.3	48.0	47.8	22.8
Local equalization grants*	18.0	18.2	27.8	7.2	10.6	35.9
Treasury grants	13.8	17.4	6.7	10.3	9.3	6.5
Prefectural grants	—	—	3.0	1.4	4.1	7.6
Municipal bonds	7.5	7.3	2.2	7.9	7.1	7.9
Rents, fees, and charges	2.5	2.3	1.5	3.4	2.3	1.9
Miscellaneous	15.6	13.9	22.5	21.8	18.8	17.4
Expenses						
Local assemblies and general administration	13.4	9.5	20.7	11.0	16.2	22.6
Social welfare	10.6	6.0	28.9	16.7	16.9	9.7
Public works	22.6	21.5	18.7	31.5	23.1	14.7
Education	21.0	25.0	19.7	12.0	15.3	15.0
Public loans	8.7	7.7	4.4	9.8	8.6	10.2
Miscellaneous	23.7	30.3	7.6	19.0	19.9	27.8

Duplicate accounts (amounts counted as revenues or expenses by more than one entity) have been subtracted.

Figures for the Tōkyō Metropolitan Government are included.

Sapporo, Sendai, Yokohama, Kawasaki, Nagoya, Kyōto, Ōsaka, Kōbe, Hiroshima, Kita Kyūshū, and Fukuoka.

*In the case of wards, financial adjustment grants (*zaisei chōsei kōfukin*).

NOTE: The fiscal year runs from 1 April to 31 March.

SOURCE: Ministry of Home Affairs, *Chihō zaisei tōkei nempō* (annual): 1991.

---

the movie theaters in the country closed during the 1960s.

In 1958 Masumura Yasuzō called for the destruction of the established Japanese cinema and soon was joined by other young directors. ŌSHIMA NAGISA (b 1932) demanded an end to lyricism, heaviness, naturalism, MONO NO AWARE, and the omnipotent conventions of the international cinema of realism. Ōshima and two tradition-breaking fellow directors at Shōchiku, SHINODA MASAHIRO (b 1931) and Yoshida Yoshishige (b 1933), were dubbed the "Shōchiku Nūberu Bāgu" (*nouvelle vague*, or new wave). Ōshima's Brechtian *Kōshikei* (1968, Death by Hanging) and *Shinjuku dorobō nikki* (1969, Diary of a Shinjuku Thief) established him as the principal new talent of the cosmopolitan 1960s. IMAMURA SHŌHEI (b 1926) rivaled Ōshima with a call to destroy the illusionistic pretensions of fiction and documentary films. Imamura searched for clues to Japanese national identity in the pseudobiography *Nippon konchūki* (1963, Story of a Japanese Insect; shown abroad as *The Insect Woman*) and the modern primitive myth *Kamigami no fukaki yokubō* (1968, The Profound Desire of the Gods; shown abroad as *Kuragejima: Tales from a Southern Island*). Other new talents who began to work during this period were HANI SUSUMU (b 1928), one of the pioneer cinema verité documentary makers, and TESHIGAHARA HIROSHI (b 1927), who took a distinctive symbolic approach in his early features such as *Suna no onna* (1964, Woman in the Dunes).

For the first time the Japanese cinema dealt with the prejudice, oppression, and poverty faced by Koreans living in Japan and by the indigenous BURAKUMIN through films by Ōshima, Ichikawa, Imamura, Urayama Kirio (b 1930), and KUMAI KEI (b 1930). Meanwhile, the assembly lines of Tōei, Daiei, and Nikkatsu produced the *gendaigeki* genres that dominated the 1960s: gangster, punk, motorcycle-gang, truck-driver, and police-action stories. Tōhō continued with its house specialties: white-collar and city-life comedies. Shōchiku's pictures held on to the studio's old standards: "women's melodramas" and *hōmu dorama* ("home drama"). The latter is a postwar genre that presents the commonplace lives of middle-class families. It became the primary form of serial drama on television.

In *jidaigeki*, major directors looked occasionally to the classical theater. Kurosawa adapted elements from the NŌ theater to his syncretic version of *Macbeth, Kumonosujō* (1957, Throne of Blood). Uchida Tomu in *Naniwa no koi no monogatari* (1959, Naniwa Love Story) and Shinoda Masahiro in *Shinjū Ten no Amijima* (1969, Love Suicide at Amijima; Double Suicide) used plays by CHIKAMATSU MONZAEMON (1653–1724) and borrowed respectively from kabuki and BUNRAKU drama. In 1963 Tōei originated a new direction for ultraviolent *chambara*: the *yakuza* (gangster) genre. The plots of these films were invariably formalistic variations of intricate *giri-ninjō* sword-fighting dramas, portraying a righteous gangster amid low-life corruption in prewar Japan. The immediate popularity of Tōei *yakuza* pictures soon wiped out *jidaigeki* as the main arena for *chambara*.

Coupled with the relentless drop in movie attendance and a relaxation of obscenity laws, the *pinku* (pink) movie appeared. Pink movies, usually made by small companies, are very low budget, one-hour-long, minimally narrative soft-core pornography. Although the sexual explicitness of these movies—particularly their sadomasochism—increased over the years, they never crossed over into hard-core pornography (which remained prohibited as of 1991). Admissions continued to decline. Daiei went bankrupt, Nikkatsu halted regular production, and the three remaining major studios underwent extensive reorganization. Nikkatsu soon resumed production by concentrating on low-cost ROMAN PORUNO ("romantic pornography"). Between 1956 and 1972 the number of features made annually in Japan averaged 450. After 1977 production stabilized at about 340 features per year, of which 75 percent were pink movies, *roman poruno*, and other soft-core pornography.

Since the Late 1970s—The three remaining major studios looked to various—and ultimately unsuccessful—alternatives to revive business. One response was the spectacular disaster film, such as Moritani Shirō's (b 1931) *Nihon chimbotsu* (1973, Japan Sinks). Despite the huge success of several big-budget spectacle films, the odds in the shrinking domestic market simply did not favor big money gambles. In 1976 Ichikawa Kon's gothic murder mystery *Inugamike no ichizoku* (The Inugami Family), with its inflated admission charges, became the largest grossing Japanese film of all time.

The dominant director of the 1970s was a major-studio man, YAMADA YŌJI (b 1931) of Shōchiku. Although his principal works were prize-winning portraits of lower-class family life, his overwhelmingly popular success was the TORA SAN series. Beginning in 1969 and continuing for more than two decades, Yamada has written and directed more than 40 films in this series, which fuses the two bedrock motifs of Japanese film: the everyday collective life of a family and the adventures of a lonely wanderer. Films by other key 1970s figures echoed Yamada's concern for local color and realism. In *Shinobugawa* (1972, The Long Darkness) and other pictures, Kumai Kei updated the "woman's melodrama" genre. In lyrical works including *Tsugaru jongara-bushi* (1973, Tsugaru Folk Song), Saitō Kōichi (b 1929) explored the popular search for Japanese national identity with the escape of lovers to the beauties of nature.

From the late 1960s most major directors as well as promising newcomers could not depend on the studios for employment. As independents, they had to raise money bit by bit themselves. After 1985, cash-heavy Japanese companies (including media conglomerates but not the poor movie studios) were backing Broadway shows and Hollywood movies. By the time Sony bought Columbia Pictures in 1989 as an investment in American, not Japanese, filmmaking, Ōshima, Kurosawa, Shinoda, and ITAMI JŪZŌ (b 1933) were looking abroad for production funds.

Comedies dominated Japanese film production in the 1980s, especially Itami's satires TAMPOPO (1985, Dandelion) and *Marusa no onna* (1988, A Taxing Woman). Exceptions are the serious films of OGURI KŌHEI (b 1945), who won the jury prize at the 1990 Cannes Film Festival for *Shi no toge* (1990, The Sting of Death). The youngest generation of directors brought postmodernist sensibilities to comedies and fantasies that had minimal plot and maximal eclectic, erotic, and pictorial elements. With extremely limited resources, they often bypassed what was left of the established film industry to shoot their features in Super 8 and 16mm and exhibit them in rented halls and theaters. By 1990 total annual movie admissions had declined to 143 million in a market now dominated by American blockbusters; the number of theaters decreased to about 1,900, and overall annual feature production dwindled to 239.

☎ 370–371

finance law   財政関係法

(*zaisei kankei hō*). The CONSTITUTION OF JAPAN stipulates the basic principles of Japanese public finance: the assessment of new taxes shall be determined by appropriate laws; the disbursement of national expenditures shall be based on a resolution of the Diet; the budget for every fiscal year must be passed by the Diet; the expenditure of public funds for religious organizations or any organizations not under the control of public authority is prohibited; and the disbursement of revenues must undergo an audit by the Board of Audit.

The principal laws relating to the public finance of the country are as follows:

1. The Finance Law (Zaisei Hō), in addition to establishing the system of the national budget and settlement of accounts, stipulates that annual expenditures must, in principle, be derived from annual revenues of financial sources other than public bonds or borrowed funds; that the national annual fiscal year shall start 1 April of every calendar year and end 31 March of the following year; and that the expenses for every fiscal year must be paid for with that fiscal year's revenues.

2. The Public Accounts Law (Kaikei Hō) mainly establishes strict limits on national

expenditures. This law stipulates the basic provisions of government contracts.

3. Tax laws include the Income Tax Law (Shotokuzei Hō), the Juristic Persons Tax Law (Hōjinzei Hō), the Liquor Tax Law (Shuzei Hō), the National Tax Common Provisions Law (Kokuzei Tsūsoku Hō), and the National Tax Collection Law (Kokuzei Chōshū Hō).

4. The Tax Allocation to Local Governments Law (Chihō Kōfuzei Hō) stipulates a system whereby a fixed ratio of the national tax is allocated to local public bodies.

finance, local government 地方財政

(chihō zaisei). Local government in Japan today operates under a system of local autonomy, wherein each governmental unit has an elected head and assembly and exercises control over a budget. This system contrasts sharply with the situation prior to World War II when, for example, the central government appointed the governor of each prefecture. See also LOCAL GOVERNMENT.

There were a total of 3,292 units of local government in Japan in 1990: 47 prefectures, 11 large cities, 644 smaller cities, 2,001 towns, and 589 villages. In 1989 the combined budgets of all local governments totaled ¥74.6 trillion (US $540 billion), an amount roughly equivalent to the total national budget. The major areas of expenditure were education, public works, and social welfare. The major revenues were local taxes (42.6 percent), treasury grants (13.8 percent), local equalization grants from the national budget to economically weak local governments (18.0 percent), and municipal bonds (7.5 percent).

financial aid for students 奨学金制度

(shōgakukin seido). In Japan, as elsewhere, financial aid is given to promising students in need of financial assistance. However, Japanese financial aid consists primarily of interest-free loans provided by the government and private organizations, according to a student's academic achievement, financial condition, character, and health. In fiscal year 1989 the Nihon Ikueikai (Japan Scholarship Foundation), a government-subsidized foundation established in 1943, provided loans totaling ¥165.7 billion (US $1.2 billion) to 446,626 students throughout the country. Its sources of funds are national bonds and remittances from student loans.

In 1988, 1.9 percent of senior high school students (both public and private), 12.6 percent of university students (both public and private), 33.5 percent of master's course students, and 55.0 percent of doctoral candidates were receiving financial aid. Loan recipients do not have to pay back their loans if they go into teaching or do research for a specified amount of time.

Financial Crisis of 1927 金融恐慌

(Kin'yū Kyōkō). Financial panic in the spring of 1927, during which 37 banks closed and the first WAKATSUKI REIJIRŌ cabinet was forced to resign. After the business boom of 1915–20 and the ensuing slowdown of the economy, many overextended businesses and their banks were saved from bankruptcy only by government-backed relief loans. In particular, the BANK OF JAPAN lent extensively to banks affected by the TŌKYŌ EARTHQUAKE OF 1923 by discounting commercial paper that became known as "earthquake bills" (shinsai tegata). In January 1927 the Japanese government proposed a plan for redemption of the remaining earthquake bills. Rumors

spread that banks in possession of these bills were in danger of collapse, triggering runs on banks. Thirty-seven banks suspended operations, including the Bank of Taiwan (see TAIWAN GINKŌ), which had been lending to the speculative trading firm SUZUKI SHŌTEN. In order to save the bank, the Wakatsuki cabinet tried to have an emergency decree (kinkyū chokurei) issued to allow the Bank of Japan to extend relief loans. This motion was denied by the Privy Council, and the cabinet resigned. The succeeding TANAKA GIICHI cabinet managed to control the panic by taking a number of forceful steps, including a three-week bank moratorium and the issuance of central bank loans amounting to ¥2 billion. Because of this crisis many small local banks failed and the five great ZAIBATSU banks gained domination over the financial community.

Financial System Research Council 金融制度調査会

(Kin'yū Seido Chōsakai). Council advising the minister of finance and formulating long-term financial policy. It was set up on a permanent basis in 1956 and is made up of 20 members, including individuals prominent in finance and industry and scholars familiar with the financial system. Recent topics taken up by the council include recommendations on reform of the financial system, specifically regarding the reduction of regulatory barriers among different types of financial institutions and the introduction of new financial markets in Japan, such as the financial futures market.

Firearms and Sword Possession Control Law 銃砲刀剣類所持等取締法

(Jūhō Tōken Rui Shoji Tō Torishimari Hō). The law regulating the possession and use of firearms, bladed weapons (those having a blade 15 cm [6 in] long or more and switchblade knives having a blade 5.5 cm [2.2 in] long or more), and other similar objects. Since the Meiji period (1868–1912) the Japanese government has restricted the carrying of swords and has had a licensing system for the possession of firearms. By order of the Occupation authorities, a Firearms, Etc, Possession Prohibition Order was enacted in 1946. In 1950 this order was superseded by the Firearms and Sword Possession Control Order. The 1958 Firearms and Sword Possession Control Law was patterned after this order and has since been revised several times, giving Japan the world's strictest legislation for controlling firearms and swords.

The possession of firearms or swords is prohibited except in specific cases (for example, the possession of pistols by policemen on duty). Possession for hunting, international competition, or other purposes is permitted only to licensed persons, and the licensing criteria are severe.

firearms, introduction of 鉄砲伝来

(teppō denrai). Firearms were introduced to Japan by Portuguese castaways on the island of Tanegashima, off Kyūshū, in 1543. The Japanese may have had some basic knowledge of explosive weapons before the Portuguese arrived, but the introduction of European firearms marked the beginning of widespread use of such weapons.

Portuguese harquebuses greatly impressed the daimyō TANEGASHIMA TOKITAKA, who ordered his craftsmen to duplicate them. Many Japanese warlords hastened to master the techniques for producing them. As early as 1549 ODA NOBUNAGA bought 500 matchlocks from gunsmiths in Kunitomo in

fire defense system
1 A fully equipped Japanese firefighter in gear that includes gas mask and flame-resistant clothing.
2 Firefighters demonstrate a high-tech mobile fire detection robot equipped with heat sensors, video camera, and robotic arm for handling hazardous materials.

Ōmi (now Shiga Prefecture) and established a firearms brigade in his army. In the 1550s TAKEDA SHINGEN, lord of the province of Kai (now Yamanashi Prefecture), also organized a firearms unit.

By the late 16th century firearms (teppō) had become the most important offensive weapon; perhaps a third of the daimyō armies of the 1570s carried guns. Oda Nobunaga used his firearms units to advantage in the Battle of ANEGAWA in 1570 and in the Battle of NAGASHINO in 1575. TOYOTOMI HIDEYOSHI also supplied his troops with firearms, which he used during his campaigns against the Shimazu family of Kyūshū in 1586 and against the Later Hōjō family in the ODAWARA CAMPAIGN in 1590.

The spread of firearms helped to stimulate industrial and commercial activities by creating an increased demand for muskets, ammunition, and other matériel. Also, the popularization of firearms, together with the establishment of an armed infantry, largely recruited from the peasantry, promoted social mobility. See also HINAWAJŪ.

fire defense system 消防

(shōbō). The first government fire defense system in Japan was established by the Tokugawa shogunate in 1629. This system was known as daimyō hikeshi. There were two more kinds of HIKESHI in the Edo period (1600–1868): the jōbikeshi, organized from among the bannermen (hatamoto) in 1650, and the machi hikeshi, made up of commoners, organized in 1718. After the Meiji Restoration in 1868, the daimyō hikeshi and jōbikeshi were disbanded and the machi hikeshi was reorganized into shōbōgumi (firefighting companies). In 1881 these shōbōgumi were placed under Tōkyō's Metropolitan Police Office.

With the promulgation of the Law of Fire Defense Organization (Shōbō Soshiki Hō) in 1948, fire-fighting operations were removed

traditional firemen's uniforms While not typical, this uniform is an example of the decorative ones worn by some high-ranking members of the fire brigades maintained by *daimyō* of the Edo period.

from the police force, and independent city, town, and village fire departments were established. Aside from the central districts of large cities, there were few high-rise buildings in Japan before World War II, and almost all buildings were wooden. However, with the improvement of architectural techniques after the war, skyscrapers could be erected even in earthquake-prone Japan. There has also been a striking increase in ferroconcrete and steel-frame buildings. Thus the need for hook-and-ladder trucks has sharply increased. Accompanying the development of oil refining and the petrochemical industry has been an increasing number of giant petrochemical complexes with an ever-increasing danger of large-scale conflagration.

According to the Law of Fire Defense Organization, the responsibility and cost of fire fighting lie with the municipalities. All cities and large towns have a fire department and fire station staffed with professional fire fighters, but smaller municipalities have relied on volunteer fire brigades. Towns and villages have increasingly cooperated with fire departments of neighboring cities, and some towns and villages have banded together to form local or regional fire-fighting associations. Since 1965, designated municipalities have been required by government order to maintain both fire departments and fire stations. In each of the urban and rural prefectures is located a fire defense school, where professional fire fighters and fire brigade members are trained. The prefectures also oversee the fire defense operations of the municipalities.

Nationally, the Fire Defense Agency is an external organ of the Ministry of Home Affairs; it guides fire defense in the municipalities and also drafts fire standards and ordinances. The affiliated Fire Defense Research Institute and Fire Defense College conduct research into fire defense techniques and provide higher education. Fire defense operations can be roughly divided into preservation of order at the outbreak of fire or other disaster, fire prevention, and rescue and ambulance operations.

fireflies 蛍

(*hotaru*). In Japanese, *hotaru* is the common name for members of the family Lampyridae in the order Coleoptera. Japanese *hotaru* are small to medium in size (5–20 mm; 0.2–0.8 in). The back is flat or convex with luminous species having convex backs. The larvae, usually terrestrial, feed on shelled mollusks such as snails, but the *genji-botaru* (*Luciola cruciata*) and *heike-botaru* (*L. lateralis*) are aquatic as larvae and feed on the shellfish called *kawanina* (*Semisulcospira bensoni*). About 2,000 species of fireflies are known in the world, of which some 25–30 species, including 10 luminous, are found in Japan. Representative are the *hime-botaru* (*Hotaria parvula*), the *mune kuriiro-botaru* (*Cyphonocerus ruficollis*), and the *akimado-botaru* (*Pyrocoelia rufa*).

The *hotaru* has long been associated in Japan with the Chinese legend of a poor scholar who, unable to afford lamp oil, studied by the glow of fireflies. In numerous poems in the 8th-century anthology *Man'yō-shū*, the *hotaru* is a metaphor for passionate love. According to a folk belief, the spirit of a living person or the ghost of the dead assumes the shape of the *hotaru*. FIREFLY VIEWING was popular during the Edo period (1600–1868).

firefly viewing 蛍狩

(*hotarugari*). The pastime of watching the flickering lights of fireflies on summer nights. These insects have long drawn attention in Japan because their lights were thought to symbolize the souls of the dead; they have been celebrated in verse since the 8th-century poetry collection MAN'YŌSHŪ. Firefly viewing was mainly enjoyed by the aristocracy during the Heian period (794–1185) but spread among the common people during the Edo period (1600–1868). Since the number of fireflies in Japan today has decreased because of pollution and agricultural chemicals, fireflies are raised for hotels and large restaurants, which sponsor firefly displays to attract guests.

firemen's uniforms, traditional 火事装束

(*kaji shōzoku*). Uniforms worn by fire fighters during the Edo period (1600–1868). In Edo (now Tōkyō) each neighborhood had its own fire brigade (*machi hikeshi*) and each of the resident *daimyō* lords had a fire brigade (*daimyō hikeshi*). Each of these brigades was identified by its particular outfit. The basic uniform of the daimyō fire brigade consisted of a *kaji-baori*, a damask-lined short coat of wool or leather appliquéd with distinctive white wool CRESTS (*mon*); an undervest called a *muneate;* a belt; and a helmet. Men of high rank also wore *nobakama*, long pleated trousers of damask with black velvet cuffs. The town fire fighters were organized into groups (*kumi*), each with its own crest and standard (*matoi*); they wore, instead of a *haori* (a loose jacket), a *hanten* (a one-layer, quilted cotton jacket) and a hood (*zukin*) of leather or quilted cotton. See also HIKESHI.

fireworks 花火

(*hanabi*). Fireworks, along with firearms, were introduced to Japan by the Portuguese at the end of the 16th century. The first recorded fireworks display was held by shōgun TOKUGAWA IEYASU in 1613. Eventually fireworks were adopted by the common people for their own amusement. Commercial fireworks manufacturers appeared, and specialty shops, such as the Tamaya and Kagiya in Tōkyō, became widely known. Occasionally fireworks displays were prohibited because of the danger of fire. With improved manufacturing techniques, innovative Japanese projectile types and set pieces were constructed. The summer fireworks on the banks of the Sumida River (Sumidagawa) in Tōkyō have been famous since they were first staged in 1733. Toy fireworks originated in the 18th century. Many varieties, including sparklers and "mouse" fireworks that dart about on the ground before they expire with a bang, are popular diversions for children on summer evenings.

fiscal system 財政制度

(*zaisei seido*). The fiscal system of Japan, in its broader sense, includes not only the accounts of the national government but also those of local governments and various government-affiliated agencies. The accounts of the national government are divided into the general account and special accounts, with the former regarded as the most important element of the Japanese fiscal system. Thus the term "budget" usually refers to the general account budget (see BUDGET, NATIONAL).

National tax revenue belongs to the general account, with the exception of a small portion of tax revenues that belongs directly to special accounts. Tax and stamp revenues constituted 84 percent of the total revenue in fiscal year (FY) 1989 (i.e., from 1 April 1989 to 31 March 1990). Until the early 1970s, public bond policy was restricted to construction bonds. Since 1975, however, huge bond issues (deficit-financing bonds) have been necessary to meet the budget deficit. The ratio of bond revenue to total general account revenue was 11.8 percent in FY 1989. Other revenue was composed of profits from government monopoly and other enterprises, receipts from the sale of government properties, miscellaneous receipts, and the carried-over surplus. See TAXES.

The special accounts are established by law when the government carries out specific projects or when it becomes necessary to administer revenue and expenditures separately from the general revenue and expenditures. In FY 1989 there were 38 special accounts, each with its own specific revenue sources, such as transfers from the general account, receipts from enterprises administered under the special accounts, and social insurance contributions. The revenue of some special accounts includes borrowing.

Government-affiliated agencies have separate legal status from government departments in order to ensure efficient management. They include the GOVERNMENT HOUSING LOAN CORPORATION, the JAPAN DEVELOPMENT BANK, and the EXPORT-IMPORT BANK OF JAPAN. The budgets of government-affiliated agencies must be approved by the Diet.

fish and shellfish farming 養殖・栽培漁業

(*yōshoku; saibai gyogyō*). The artificial cultivation of marine products (also called aquiculture) plays an important role in the Japanese fishing industry. Japan has long been engaged in the farming of freshwater fish, NORI (a type of seaweed), and oysters. In recent years the farming of such choice fish as yellowtail, red sea bream, and prawns has proliferated. In addition, in order to increase coastal fishing catches, a large number of fish and shellfish farming centers have been established along Japan's shores. At these centers, selected species of fish and shellfish are artificially bred and raised to a certain size, then released to the sea to grow to sizes fit for harvesting.

Freshwater Fish Culture——Carp were raised in Japan from early times, but organized carp farming did not begin until 1623. There is little space in Japan for developing large-scale freshwater fish farming. The climate, however, ranges from near subarctic to semitropical, and intensive farming of a variety of species of both cold and warm water fish has developed through the use of sophisticated fish culture techniques.

Species that have been successfully farmed in Japan include tilapia. Following the introduction of *Tilapia mossambica* in 1954, experimental farming of a total of eight strains of tilapia was attempted, and the results showed that *T. nirotica* was best suited to the Japanese climate.

Saltwater Fish Culture——*Nori* and oyster farming are said to have started in Japan about 300 years ago. However, it was only in 1957 that saltwater fish (yellowtail) farming was started in earnest. Saltwater farming is also applied to shrimp, lobsters, prawns, octopuses, oysters, scallops, and seaweed (*nori, wakame,* and kelp).

Methods of Culture——Methods of culture are divided into lake, river, pond (flowing water and stationary water types), paddy-field, reservoir, canal, and shallow saltwater cultures. Methods are also classified by type of facility as follows: fish preserve, net-enclosure, embankment, pond, reservoir, and raft cultures.

Depending on the species raised, seeds are either bred artificially or taken from among seeds naturally grown. Typically, seeds are bred artificially and raised in a protected or controlled environment to commercial sizes, then shipped to the farms. The method in which artificially bred seeds are raised to egg-bearing sizes and then harvested after bearing the eggs is called full-cycle culture.

In the case of freshwater fish, composite feed is used, while fish meat is used for feeding saltwater fish (except sea bream). Ingredients for composite feed are adjusted to the nutrition requirements of different species. Oil additives are sometimes used to increase the nutritional value of the feed, and the pellets contain many pores to help them float. Such abundant and inexpensive fish as sardines, mackerel, and saury pike are used as feed, either fresh or frozen. Oxygen consumption by fish varies from one species to another, and even differs among the same species depending on such factors as the size of the fish. Oxygen is supplied by exchanging the water in the fish farm, so it is necessary to maintain the fish population at a level compatible with the water-exchanging capacity of the farm. Unlike livestock, fish are difficult to observe at close range, and the raising of fish requires minute care.

Fish Farming——The term "fish farming" refers to an operation in which fish seeds are produced in large quantity, released in a protected sea environment for growth, and harvested when grown to a commercial size. Techniques for mass-producing seeds for fish farming have many elements in common with those employed for fish culture, and the techniques have been developed in tandem. Fish farming owes its recent rapid development to the growing importance of coastal fishing and was made possible by the development of techniques for mass-producing seeds. Fish farming also requires the devel-

opment of techniques for the initial raising of fish and their release into the natural environment. These techniques are designed to protect the seeds from being preyed upon by other fish and to prevent natural attrition by helping them develop resistance to the rigors of the natural environment.

Fish farming is carried out through public projects of the central and prefectural governments. The first fish-farming center was established by the government in 1962 in the Inland Sea. Since 1973, a number of similar centers have been established by prefectural governments with subsidies from the central government. Fish and shellfish now being raised, including those in the experimental stage, cover about 100 species, including yellowtail, harvest fish, flounder, horse mackerel, hardtail, Spanish mackerel, grouper, rockfish, rock trout, black porgy, flatfish, king crab, northern sea shrimp, and cuttlefish. See also SEAWEED CULTIVATION.

fishery agreements　　漁業条約

(*gyogyō jōyaku*). Japan is a participant in a diverse set of international agreements relating to fishing and marine resources. These agreements can be divided into two principal categories: multilateral conventions structured to ensure the conservation and rational use of the biological resources of the world's resources, and bilateral fisheries agreements designed to establish and maintain mutually recognized coastal fishing areas.

Japan is a signatory of at least 11 multilateral agreements and a member of the international commissions established through them to monitor and regulate the use of marine resources in the areas concerned. Some, such as the International Convention for the Regulation of Whaling, are global in scope; others are regional, such as the International Convention for the High Seas Fisheries of

the North Pacific Ocean and the Indian Ocean Fisheries Commission.

A broad set of international standards regarding fishing practices was established in a group of four conventions adopted by the First United Nations Conference on the Law of the Sea in 1958. However, in ensuing years the content of these agreements was eroded by a number of separate developments, such as the unilateral adoption by individual countries of exclusive fishing zones wider than three nautical miles offshore. In response, the United Nations held two more conferences on the law of the sea, and in 1982 a new Convention on the Law of the Sea was adopted. Although it was still not in force in 1990, a number of the provisions of this convention were being observed as customary international practice.

One such provision stipulates that maritime nations may expand the designation of their territorial waters to as much as 12 nautical miles offshore and may establish an exclusive economic zone (the area in which they exercise sovereign rights over natural resources) to a distance of 200 nautical miles. By 1990, 104 countries had adopted 200-mile zones.

As a country engaged in deep-sea fishing off the coasts of numerous countries, Japan has been party to a variety of bilateral fishery agreements. The present agreements, which are based on recognition of the 200-mile zone, set the conditions under which fishing in the zone is to be conducted, including the number of boats permitted, the allocation of the catch, and the fees to be paid for fishing rights in the zone. These conditions are subject to annual renegotiation. As of 1990, Japan had concluded bilateral fisheries agreements with the United States, the Soviet Union, Canada, France, Portugal, Mo-

fireworks Now staged every year on the last Saturday in July, the summer fireworks display on the river Sumidagawa in Tōkyō has delighted viewers ever since it was first held in 1733.

fishing

1 This pay fishpond in Shinjuku Ward, Tōkyō, is regularly stocked with fish.
2 *Ayu* fishing in the river Okitsugawa, Shizuoka Prefecture. These fishermen are using a type of feather jig known as a *kebari*; no other bait is used.

Japan's Seafood Production

Type of production	1960	1965	1970	1975	1980	1985	1990
			(in thousands of metric tons)				
Open-sea fishing	1,410	1,733	3,429	3,168	2,167	2,111	1,496
Offshore fishing[1]	2,515	2,788	3,279	4,469	5,705	6,498	6,081
Coastal fishing[2]	1,893	1,861	1,889	1,935	2,037	2,268	1,992
Marine aquiculture	285	380	549	773	992	1,088	1,273
Inland fishing and aquiculture	90	146	168	199	221	206	209
Total	6,193	6,908	9,315	10,545	11,122	12,171	11,052

[1]Boats weighing 10 tons or more.
[2]Boats weighing less than 10 tons.
NOTE: Figures may not add up to totals due to rounding.
SOURCE: Ministry of Agriculture, Forestry, and Fisheries, *Gyogyō yōshokugyō seisan tōkei nempō* (annual): 1991.

rocco, South Africa, Australia, New Zealand, North and South Korea, China, and various island countries in the Pacific.

fishery zone 漁業専管水域

(*gyogyō senkan suiiki*). Also called fishing zone. An area in which a coastal state can exercise its powers, so far as fishing is concerned, in the same manner as within its TERRITORIAL WATERS. Japan established an exclusive fishery zone extending to 200 miles (320 km) with the passage of the Law on Provisional Measures relating to the Fisheries Zone (Law No. 31 of 2 May 1977). See also FISHERY AGREEMENTS.

fishes 魚類

(*gyorui*). There are about 3,000 species of freshwater and seawater fishes in and around the Japanese islands. Important freshwater fish include the river-dwelling AYU (sweetfish); the *iwana* (charr; *Salvelinus pluvius*), of mountain streams; the *moroko* (*Gnathopogon elongatus*), of rivers on plains; the *wakasagi* (*Hypomesus olidus*), of lakes and swamps; the *koi* (CARP), distributed intermittently in Europe and East Asia; the *funa* (CRUCIAN CARP), found throughout the world; the *medaka* (Japanese killifish; *Oryzias latipes*); and the *dojō* (loach; *Misgurnus anguillicaudatus*). More than 10 species of the beautiful *tanago* (bitterling; *Acheilognathus moriokae*) inhabit rivers and swamps in northern Japan and lay eggs in the gills of such shellfish as the *karasugai* (*Cristaria plicata*); many of these are endangered endemic species, such as the *miyako tanago* (*Tanakia tanago*) in rivers on the Kantō Plain. The *mahaze* (goby) is found along the coast from Hokkaidō down to Kyūshū, and the *tobihaze* (mudskipper; *Periophthalmus cantonensis*) is found in the western part of Tōkyō Bay and along the coasts of South Asia, Australia, and Africa.

In southern Japan, brightly colored coral fish such as the *chōchōuo* (butterfly fish; *Chaetodon collare*) and the *tsubameuo* (*Platax pinnatus*) are found. In the Ryūkyū Islands there is an even wider variety of coral fish, including the *kumanomi* (anemone fish; *Amphiprion bicinctus*), demoiselles such as the *suzumedai* (*Chromis notatus*), parrot fish such as the *hibudai* (*Scarus ghobban*), and beautiful wrasses such as the *hiregurobera* (*Ledidaplois hirsutus*). Also here is the huge *nishikiebi* (spiny lobster; *Panulirus ornatus*), up to 55 centimeters (22 in) long. In the Inland Sea lives the *namekujiuo* (lancelet; *Branchiostoma belcherii*). Rare species live in the deep waters of Sagami Bay and Suruga Bay, including the *mitsukurizame* (Japanese goblin shark; *Scapanorhynchus owstoni*), found

elsewhere only in the sea south of Australia and off the coast of Portugal, and the *rabuka* (frilled shark; *Chlamydoselachus anguineus*), found elsewhere only off Norway, northwestern Africa, and California.

See also ANGLERFISHES; BONITO; CATFISHES; EEL, JAPANESE; GLOBEFISHES; GOBIES; GOLDFISH; HERRING; MACKEREL; SALMONS; SAMMA; SARDINES; SEA BREAM; TUNA; WHITEBAIT; YELLOWTAIL.

fishing 釣

(*tsuri*). Fishing has played an important part in Japan's food production since early times, but fishing as a leisure activity did not start until the Edo period (1600–1868). Contemporary Japanese sportfishing methods and equipment are very similar to those of the United States and Europe. The traditional method used to catch the aggressive *ayu* (sweetfish), however, is peculiar to Japan. A live *ayu* is attached to a line and set in the water. Its swimming movements attract other *ayu*, making it possible to snag them with a bare hook. In another method of fishing in Japan, popular since the 1930s both for eating and for sport, customers pay a fee to fish in an artificial pond or dammed-off section of a stream stocked with a particular variety of fish, such as *herabuna* (crucian carp) or rainbow trout. Each prefecture in Japan has its own laws regarding fishing seasons, restrictions, creel limits, and conservation. See also CORMORANT FISHING; FISHING INDUSTRY.

fishing industry 漁業

(*gyogyō*). The modern Japanese fishing industry operates boats worldwide, though the principal Japanese fisheries are in the North Pacific, including the Bering Sea and the Sea of Okhotsk. Industry production for 1989—12.0 million metric tons (13.2 million short tons) of fish and other seafood—was the second largest in the world after China's and amounted to 11.5 percent of total world seafood production. Japanese fishing industry production was 11.1 million metric tons (12.2 million short tons) in 1990.

Traditional Japanese Fishing—Although modern commercial fishing methods are responsible for the bulk of Japan's fish production, traditional techniques are still in use. Angling, with pole and line or with hand line, and traditional spearfishing are common. Japanese fishers also use setnets, or stationary nets, driving fish into the nets by such methods as beating the water's surface with poles. Long "fish corrals," up to 1,000 meters (3,281 ft) in length and made of bamboo or net hurdles, are used in lakes, and weirs are built into streams to catch river fish. The Japanese catch octopuses in ceramic or concrete pots suspended from lines (a traditional method also used in Southeast Asian and Mediterranean countries). Japanese divers (see AMA) collect abalone, oysters, and sea plants, as well as pearls. CORMORANT FISHING, an ancient technique for catching river fish,

has survived to the present day as a tourist attraction.

The State of the Industry—In 1990 there were 185,000 fishing concerns in Japan, of which 67 percent were family-run operations using boats of less than 10 tons, and 24 percent were family-run aquiculture firms, including SEAWEED CULTIVATION and FISH AND SHELLFISH FARMING businesses. Large and medium-sized fishing companies made up the remaining 9 percent. All large Japanese fishing companies (except for setnet fisheries) are licensed by the national or prefectural governments.

Some 370,000 people were employed in the Japanese fishing industry in 1990, with about 81 percent of the workers employed in the coastal fishing sector. Because of the low salaries and the hard, dirty work involved, the outflow of young workers to other industries has gradually increased in recent years. In 1990 some 3.2 percent of fishing industry workers, mostly from the coastal fishing labor force, left the industry, further contributing to the rising average age of its labor force.

Modern Commercial Fishing—The Japanese fishing industry has adopted a host of new fishing devices and techniques to reduce operating hours and compensate for the shrinking labor force. Highly automated fishing vessels are now common, and various types of ultrasonic devices that monitor the movement of fish around boats, warn of fish entering a net, and provide information on the condition of the net are widely used. Remote-control meters show the height of a net in relation to fish movements, allowing a boat to adjust its speed accordingly, and seine net depth meters are widely used to help boats place nets in the path of oncoming fish.

In 1990 the total catch from coastal fisheries was slightly under 2.0 million metric tons (2.2 million short tons). Although the coastal fishing catch has been dropping since the early 1980s, the shortfall has been made up by aquiculture harvests, which amounted to nearly 1.3 million metric tons (1.4 million short tons) of products in 1990. Seaweed cultivation accounted for 44 percent of this figure; shellfish, nearly 34 percent; and fish and crustacean farming, nearly 22 percent. The refinement of breeding techniques for salmon, sea bream, and abalone in recent years has boosted the importance of aquiculture in the fishing industry.

Offshore fishing within about 20 kilometers (12 mi) of shore is carried out by boats of more than 10 tons using purse seines, trawls, drift nets, and hook and line. Most fish caught offshore are migrating species, so catches vary widely from year to year. In 1990 the offshore catch totaled approximately 6.1 million metric tons (6.7 million short tons), of which sardines and mackerel accounted for over 72 percent.

Open-sea (pelagic) fishing, conducted with large factory ships equipped with freez-

ing and processing equipment, also uses such methods as purse seining, trawling, and drift netting, along with longline angling. Annual catches were large throughout the late 1960s and early 1970s: in 1973, Japanese boats took 4.5 million metric tons (5.0 million short tons) of fish from waters within 200 miles of the coasts of such countries as the United States, the Soviet Union, and Canada.

Around the mid-1970s, however, the industry initiated self-imposed restrictions on the size of open-sea catches in anticipation of changes in international fishing zones. In 1976 the United States adopted a 200-mile fishery zone, as did Canada, the Soviet Union, and various European countries (see FISHERY AGREEMENTS; FISHERY ZONE). This put many fishing grounds off limits to Japanese boats, compelling the Japanese government to negotiate with various countries for open-sea quotas approaching previous catches. The negotiations were largely unsuccessful, and efforts to develop previously unused fishing grounds ended in failure. The government launched a long-term program to increase the amount of fish and sea life in Japan's own 200-mile fishing zone, which included improving the environment of coastal fishing areas and releasing fingerlings, but in the meantime increasing demand for fish, combined with shrinking catches, boosted Japan's imports of marine products. By 1990 Japan's open-sea catch had fallen to 1.5 million metric tons (1.7 million short tons), and imports of marine products had soared to 2.5 million metric tons (2.8 million short tons), making Japan the world's leading importer of marine products. 👁 380–381

Five Kings of Wa 倭の五王

(Wa no Goō). Five rulers of the kingdom of WA (the Chinese name for ancient Japan) during the 5th century who are named in the *Song (Sung) shu* (History of the Liu-Song Dynasty [420–479]), the *Nan Qi (Ch'i) shu* (History of the Southern Qi Dynasty [479–502]), the *Liang shu* (History of the Liang Dynasty [502–557]), and other Chinese histories of the Six Dynasties period (220–589). In Japanese pronunciation, the names of the kings are San, Chin, Sei, Kō, and Bu.

There are some discrepancies between the *Song shu* and the *Liang shu* regarding the lineage of the five kings, but San and Chin are described as brothers, as are Kō and Bu. This is consonant with the genealogy given in the NIHON SHOKI (720), which indicates that at least three emperors between ŌJIN (late 4th to early 5th century) and Yūryaku (latter half of the 5th century) were succeeded by male siblings.

Since the early Japanese chronicles offer little solid evidence for the historicity of these 5th-century rulers, the Chinese records provide valuable corroboration. These records also provide information on the nature of the YAMATO COURT and on diplomatic relations in East Asia during the 5th century.

flags and banners 旗と幟

(*hata to nobori*). The first flag in Japan is said to have been presented in the 3rd century by the Chinese Wei dynasty (220–265). It was a yellow flag hung from the head of a spear as a symbol of imperial authority. Through the Heian period (794–1185) flags called *ban* were flown at imperial palaces. They were used later mainly as military emblems; the white flag of the MINAMOTO FAMILY and the red flag of the TAIRA FAMILY are famous examples. Each military family came to have its own flag with a distinctive color and emblem.

Banners called *nobori* were used on the battlefield to identify groups of warriors. These long, rectangular banners were hung vertically from a crosspiece at the top of a pole and were attached to the pole on one side by loops. These banners commonly showed identifying marks or names. Since the Edo period (1600–1868) *nobori* have been flown on CHILDREN'S DAY and are often used to mark the location of theaters, shops, temples, shrines, and SUMŌ matches.

flexed burials 屈葬

(*kussō*). A prehistoric burial practice that involved bending the arms and legs of the body before interment. Flexed burials were used most widely in Japan in the Jōmon period (ca 10,000 BC–ca 300 BC), and the method was gradually abandoned in the Yayoi period (ca 300 BC–ca AD 300). It has not yet been explained why bodies of the dead were flexed rather than buried in a straight position, but one explanation is that Jōmon peoples may have believed it prevented the spirit of the dead from leaving the body and moving about. Also, some of the flexed burials of the Jōmon period have stones placed on top of them, possibly for the same reason. See also DOLMEN BURIALS; HŌKEI SHŪKŌBO; JAR BURIALS.

flexible manufacturing system フレキシブル生産システム

(FMS; J: *furekishiburu seisan shisutemu*). An automated manufacturing system designed to produce a variety of products in small quantities with maximum efficiency. Originating in the United States and first employed by Japanese industries in the early 1980s, the flexible manufacturing system is supported by hardware such as numerically controlled machine tools, industrial robots, and computerized control systems. FMS was taken up with particular rapidity by the Japanese automobile-manufacturing industry. The full automation of small-scale batch production and the resultant improvements in quality and delivery time greatly boosted the international competitiveness of Japanese companies. A combination of office automation, computer-aided design (CAD), and computer-aided manufacturing (CAM), FMS results in an almost completely automated factory. The most noted FMS facility in Japan is the FANUC, LTD, plant at the base of Mt. Fuji, where robots are used to build robots.

flower arrangement 生け花

(*ikebana*; literally, "flowers kept alive"). Also called *kadō*, or the Way of flowers. Japanese flower arrangement had its origin in early Buddhist flower offerings and developed into a distinctive art form from the 15th century, with many styles and schools. The attention given to the choice of plant material and container, the placement of the branches, and the relationship of the branches to the container and surrounding space distinguished this art from purely decorative uses of flowers.

Traditional Ikebana—Buddhist ritual flower offerings (*kuge*) were introduced to Japan from China early in the 7th century by ONO NO IMOKO, from whom the IKENOBŌ school of arranging claims descent. The important "three-element" (*mitsugusoku*) offering placed in front of a Buddhist image consisted of an incense burner flanked by a candlestick and a vase of flowers. These flower offerings were arranged with the main stem approximately one and a half times the height of the container and set vertically at its center; two additional stems

Continued on page 382➤

Blessed with a large catch, fishing vessels returning to port fly colorful flags to thank the Shintō deities and to request their aid again next time out.

Japan's coastal waters are worked by smaller fishing vessels 10 to 100 tons in size. This one is unloading a full haul of sardines. (*iwashi*).

Fishermen scatter bait to lure their intended catch, in this case bonito (*katsuo*).

Harvesting the Bounty of the Sea

For thousands of years the sea has been an essential source of sustenance for the Japanese. Fish and shellfish have long been the primary source of animal protein in the Japanese diet, and as a nation Japan is still among the world's largest consumers of marine products. This insatiable demand long ago gave birth to what is now a world-class fishing industry, one that embraces both traditional methods and sophisticated technology. Although Japanese deep-sea fishing fleets roam the world's oceans, most of the nation's annual catch, which includes artificially raised marine life, is brought in by smaller vessels that fish Japan's coastal waters. On ships such as these, one can sometimes still see fishermen plying their trade with poles and line or even spearfishing. For the most part, however, the Japanese fishing industry relies on modern methods and equipment. The availability of laborsaving technology has, in fact, become more important than ever in recent years as a means of coping with the industry's shrinking labor pool. The abundance of jobs in other fields, particularly white-collar positions, has reduced the potential work force, and in many villages, even where fishing has always been the primary means of livelihood, young men no longer follow their fathers down to the sea.

This large trawler works the waters off the coast of Madagascar. Equipped with onboard refrigeration and processing facilities, larger ships can rove the open seas for months at a time.

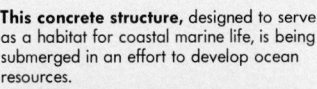

Japan's crab-fishing grounds are gradually being depleted despite attempts to conserve stock.

Chōshi Harbor in Chiba Prefecture is one of Japan's biggest fishing ports.

The artificial breeding of yellowtail (*buri*) and sea bream (*tai*) helps satisfy Japan's growing demand for these fish.

Kombu, a variety of seaweed used extensively in Japanese cooking, is harvested by hand. More than 95 percent of the *kombu* consumed in Japan comes from Hokkaidō.

A wholesale fish market receives the day's catch once it has been unloaded in the harbor. The fish will be sold later at auction.

Damming a river to catch *ayu* (sweetfish) as they return to spawn in autumn is an ancient fishing technique still in use.

Tuna from the Pacific, Indian, and Atlantic oceans, frozen on board the ship for the long trip back to Japan, are about to be sold at the Chōshi fish market.

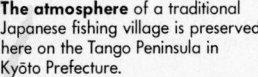

The atmosphere of a traditional Japanese fishing village is preserved here on the Tango Peninsula in Kyōto Prefecture.

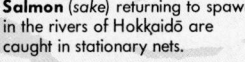

Salmon (*sake*) returning to spawn in the rivers of Hokkaidō are caught in stationary nets.

381

flower arrangement
1 Guests are greeted by a large arrangement of cherry blossoms and pine branches in this home's vestibule.
2 An avant-garde arrangement of bamboo by Teshigahara Hiroshi, the third head of the Sōgetsu school of modern flower arranging.

were placed symmetrically to the left and right.

Aside from religious offerings, there is no record of any systematized form of flower arrangement in Japan prior to the late 15th century. From the *mitsugusoku* tradition developed the style known as *rikka* ("standing flowers"), a more sophisticated arrangement that sought to reflect the majesty of nature and from which all later schools of Japanese flower arrangement derive. The *rikka* style is said to have its origins in Kyōto in 1462 with an innovative arrangement by Senkei of the Ikenobō school. The style of arrangement derived from Sengyō was asymmetrically global, with complex symbolism from Buddhist cosmology attached to each of seven branches. These branches represented seven natural scenic features: (1) *ryō*, a peak, below which is (2) *gaku*, a hill, down which (3) *rō*, the waterfall, cascades, reaching (4) *shi*, a town, where people gather by the flowing water, and (5) *hi*, a valley to the rear of the mountain. The entire scene is divided into (6) *yō*, the sunlit or positive side, corresponding to the Chinese *yang*, and (7) *in*, the shaded side facing the earth, or the negative side, corresponding to *yin.*

During the 16th and 17th centuries, although the Ikenobō school predominated, various schools of *rikka* rose and flourished under the patronage of the aristocracy.

The present-day *rikka* style, which originated in the late 18th century, uses nine branches, which emerge from a central radius three-dimensionally: (1) The *shin* (truth) branch is most important and is centered in the arrangement. Its height ranges from three to five times that of the container; all the other branches conform to it following a set pattern of proportions. Curved or straight, the *shin* branch determines the style of the whole arrangement.

(2) The *soe* (supporting) branch is designed to aid and amplify the *shin*. Usually of a contrasting material, the *soe* gives the arrangement breadth, while the *shin* provides height. (3) The *uke* (receiving) branch is placed low on the negative side of the *shin*. (4) The *shōshin* (true *shin*) branch is straight and at the center of the arrangement, connoting peace of mind. (5) The *mikoshi* (overhanging) branch arises from the rear of the *shōshin* and conveys distance, looking down on the entire arrangement like a faraway mountain. (6) The *hikae* (moderating) branch is opposite the *uke* and of the same length, providing breadth and depth. (7) The *nagashi* (flowing) branch conveys a sense of flow, as of water; its point of origin must be hidden while its tip is emphasized. (8) The *dō* (body) branch hides the meeting points of the other branches, and (9) the *maeoki* (anterior), the ninth and final branch, is placed last and in the forefront to give the arrangement depth.

In the late 16th century, a new form of flower arrangement called *nageire* ("to throw or fling into") emerged for use in the TEA CEREMONY. An austere and simple form was required for *chabana*, a general term for flower arrangements used in the tea ceremony, rather than the increasingly elaborate *rikka* styles. SEN NO RIKYŪ (1522–91) is regarded as the founder of both the ritualistic tea ceremony and the accompanying *nageire* style of flower arrangement, in which a single vase might hold only one flower disposed with deceptively simple elegance.

The late 17th century saw the emergence of a thriving merchant class and a shift away from aristocratic and priestly forms of flower arrangement. A growing demand for simplification of the increasingly contrived *rikka* styles gave rise to a new form of arrangement called *shōka* or *seika* (living flowers), basically consisting of three main branches arranged in an asymmetrical triangle. Whereas *rikka* expressed the majesty of nature by symbolic representation of a landscape, the ideal in *shōka* was to convey the plant's essence. *Shōka* combined the dignity of *rikka* with the simplicity of *nageire*, and by the end of the 18th century it had be-

come the most popular style. Diverse angles of placement and varying lengths of branches define the styles of the various schools of *shōka*. Early in the 19th century, the three main branches used in *shōka* became commonly known as *ten* (heaven), *chi* (earth), and *jin* (man). The height of the *jin* varies, but the *ten* is two-thirds as high as the *jin*, while the *chi* is one-third as high. Each proportionate level has its own group of supporting branches. Traditional *shōka* used one or two varieties of material, but modern *shōka* commonly uses three. A distinctive feature of all traditional styles, however, is the *mizugiwa* (water's edge), a critical area where the plant material, devoid of foliage, rises about 10 centimeters (4 in) above the mouth of the container as a single unit.

Modern Ikebana——After the Meiji Restoration of 1868, traditional Japanese arts, including *ikebana*, were temporarily overwhelmed by enthusiasm for Western culture. In the late 19th century, however, there was a revival of *ikebana* when Ohara Unshin (1861–1914), founder of the OHARA SCHOOL, introduced his *moribana* (piled-up flowers) style. Based on the classic principles of the three-branch design, *moribana* stressed color and natural plant growth, utilizing low arrangements that sometimes nearly touched the sides of shallow, wide-mouthed containers. It was probably designed to employ newly introduced Western flowering plants.

The new freedom in arranging that began with *moribana* was expanded in the modern *jiyūka* (free-style flowers). The free-style flower movement began around 1921 in reaction against the restrictiveness of traditional styles and the increasing formality of *moribana*. In the free-style movement the strictly artistic aspects of flower arrangement were emphasized.

In the late Taishō (1912–26) and early Shōwa (1926–89) periods, the foundations of modern *ikebana* were laid in the work of Ohara Kōun (1880–1938) and Adachi Chōka (1887–1969), among others. Up until about 1930, *ikebana* was taught exclusively by private instructors in upper-class homes, but now masters began to concentrate on developing *ikebana* schools that could attract large numbers of students from all social classes. They emphasized three-dimensional arrangements that were loosely derived from the traditional triangle pattern of the *ten-chi-jin* (heaven-earth-man) form of *shōka.*

In the postwar era, avant-garde *ikebana* (*zen'eibana*), spearheaded by SŌGETSU SCHOOL founder Teshigahara Sōfū (1900–1979), Ohara Hōun (b 1908), and Nakayama Bumpo (1899–1986), revolutionized the materials considered acceptable. These artists used not only live flowers and grasses but also plastic, plaster, and steel to express surrealistic and abstract concepts in their arrangements.

Today, there are approximately 3,000 *ikebana* schools in Japan, with 15 million to 20 million students, mostly women between the ages of 18 and 26. The most popular styles are the Ikenobō, Ohara, and Sōgetsu, each of which attracts some 3 million students. Still practiced are *rikka* and *shōka,* as well as more modern styles.

Before World War II, foreign interest in, and knowledge of, *ikebana* was scant. After the war, however, *ikebana* became popular with the wives of Allied military officers stationed in Japan, and many returned home as certified teachers, bringing the influence of *ikebana* to untold numbers of students abroad. Ikebana International, founded in Tōkyō in 1956 by Ellen Gordon Allen (1898–1972), encourages the teaching of *ikebana* as an art form throughout the world. Overseas expansion of *ikebana* schools, which began seriously in the 1960s, continues today. ☎ 384–385

flying squirrels　　　　　鼯鼠

(*musasabi; momonga*). The principal flying squirrel species in Japan is the relatively large *musasabi* (*Petaurista leucogenys*) of Honshū, Shikoku, and Kyūshū. It is also native to Korea and China. Its head and body measure about 40 centimeters (16 in) long and the tail about 36 centimeters (14 in). Its color ranges from gray to blackish brown on the back, with striking white spots on the cheeks and a white underbelly. It is common in forested areas up to an elevation of 2,000 meters (6,600 ft) and often lives in tall trees near human dwellings. An annual litter of two is born in spring or summer. The *musasabi* glides from tree to tree for an average span of 30 meters (100 ft) and a maximum of 180 meters (590 ft). It feeds on plants. The other flying squirrel found in Japan is the smaller *momonga* (Eurasian flying squirrel; *Pteromys momonga*).

Musasabi was often used as a nickname for burglars because of the way the animal glides nimbly and silently through the air. It is also claimed to be the true identity of the TENGU (long-nosed goblins) said to live in the mountains.

folk crafts　　　　　　　民芸

(*mingei*). The term *mingei* refers to objects handcrafted for daily use, as well as to the movement begun by YANAGI MUNEYOSHI (1889–1961), who coined the term in 1926. Yanagi himself preferred to translate *mingei* as "folk crafts," which emphasizes the utilitarian aspect, rather than "folk arts," although both terms have been used.

The Folk Craft Movement——Collecting examples of folk crafts from the Korean Yi dynasty (1392–1910) led Yanagi to realize that the most beautiful objects were the products not of individual artists but of the collective genius of the Korean people. He

concluded that the approach of modern European art history, which emphasized the creativity of individual artists, was inadequate in understanding *mingei.*

Instead, Yanagi turned his attention to the work of a Japanese priest, Mokujiki Gogyō (1718–1810; see MOKUJIKI), who had carved tens of thousands of rough Buddhist images while traveling throughout Japan. To Yanagi these figures, created in response to the hopes and aspirations of the masses, were more beautiful than the Buddhist images by famous sculptors displayed by great temples. Around this time Yanagi also discovered TAMBA WARE, with its rich patterns of glaze formed during firing from wood ash randomly falling and fusing with the ceramic surface. Reflecting on this process, he concluded that beauty was not the result of any conscious intent but was born of chance and the cumulative skill of generations of unknown artists. Yanagi saw this process as akin to the Buddhist concept of TARIKI, the attainment of salvation not through one's own merits but through complete reliance on the Buddha's mercy.

Based on these theories Yanagi coined the term *mingei* to differentiate between *bijutsu,* or fine art, which he saw as created for aesthetic appreciation alone, and *kōgei,* or utilitarian craftwork made for practical use. Yanagi saw *kōgei* as a broader term than *mingei: kōgei* included objects made by machine and by individual artists, as well as "aristocratic" works. But he also claimed that the best of *kōgei* belonged to the category of *mingei.* According to Yanagi, the character of *kōgei* was defined, first, by *yō* (use or function): *kōgei* objects must be simple and sturdy to function effectively. Second, *kōgei* objects must be produced on a large scale at low prices. Third, the beauty of authentic *kōgei* is created by anonymous laborers who have honed their skill by turning out large numbers of articles without thought of self-expression. Fourth, handcrafted *kōgei* objects are superior to those made by machine.

Yanagi's aesthetics of folk crafts attracted the British potter Bernard LEACH (1887–1979), as well as the potters TOMIMOTO KENKICHI (1886–1963), HAMADA SHŌJI (1894–1978), and KAWAI KANJIRŌ (1890–1966). These four men led the Japanese *mingei* movement, though artists from other fields subsequently participated, such as SERIZAWA KEISUKE (1895–1984), a master dye artist; Tonomura Kichinosuke (b 1898) and Yanagi Yoshitaka (b 1911), master weavers; Kuroda Tatsuaki (1904–82), a master woodworker; and MUNAKATA SHIKŌ (1903–75), a woodblock print master.

The *mingei* movement had three objectives: the collection and display of folk crafts, a thorough survey and study of *mingei* in Japan, and financial assistance to declining *mingei* arts along with the organization of craftsmen to engage in the production and sale of authentic *mingei* articles. The first objective was realized with the establishment of the JAPAN FOLK-CRAFT MUSEUM in Tōkyō in 1936. Surveys of folk crafts in Hokkaidō and Taiwan during World War II resulted in Yanagi's posthumously published *Teshigoto no Nihon* (1972, Handcrafts in Japan), and periodicals devoted to crafts helped disseminate the ideals of the *mingei* movement in Japan. With the third objective, however, the *mingei* movement was less successful.

The significance of the *mingei* movement may be seen in its antimodern tendencies,

flying squirrels The *musasabi* uses its long tail for stability when gliding. It is nocturnal, feeding in treetops on nuts, berries, and leaves.

Buddhist influences, and emphasis on regional and ethnic culture. Adherents of the *mingei* movement revered products that expressed regional and ethnic distinctions and claimed that the Japanese central government was ruining local culture and encouraging its absorption by a uniform society.

History of Japanese Folk Crafts——Tracing the history of folk crafts following the canons laid down by Yanagi is difficult because so few examples survive. Some scholars consider the earthenware of the Jōmon (ca 10,000 BC–ca 300 BC) and Yayoi (ca 300 BC–ca AD 300) periods to be the first folk art in Japan. The "six old kilns" (*roku koyō*) were established in Echizen, Shigaraki, Seto, Tokoname, Tamba, and Bizen during the Heian period (794–1185), each producing pottery with distinct local characteristics. However, pottery then was considered precious and rare. Most of what is today considered *mingei* survives from the Muromachi period (1333–1568). This is doubtless partly because the traditional Japanese style of living, as presently understood, became widely established at that time: the SHOINZUKURI type of architecture was perfected, and techniques for making lacquer ware (see NEGORO-NURI; KAMAKURA-BORI) and pottery were highly developed. This, along with increased production, led to wider distribution of articles. The popularization of the TEA CEREMONY from the Muromachi period through the Azuchi-Momoyama period (1568–1600) was another important factor. Local pottery and textile producers flourished in the latter half of the Edo period (1600–1868). Many examples from this period can still be found, and they set the standards of beauty in Japanese folk crafts. By the early 20th century, however, with the introduction of synthetics and increasing reliance on machinery, folk crafts began to decline. Folk crafts in Yanagi's sense of the term have nearly become extinct in Japan.

However, folk traditions in a broader sense are thriving. Under the CULTURAL PROPERTIES LAW of 1950 the concept of cultural assets (*bunkazai*) was revised and broadened, encouraging governmental participation in the preservation of folk knowledge, folk performing arts, games, and folk utensils (MINGU) used for making clothing, food, and shelter and in trade or communal life.

Classification of Folk Crafts——Folk crafts are generally classified in the categories of ceramics; wood and bamboo articles; metal and leather objects; dyeing and weaving; paper; and painting, sculpture, and calligraphy.

Continued on page 386 ➡

The Hidden Structure of Ikebana

In contrast to the typically rigid symmetry of a Western-style flower arrangement, an *ikebana* composition appears refreshingly uncontrived. Indeed, at its core are only three stems, cut at differing lengths and positioned at seemingly random angles.

Yet the apparent simplicity of ikebana belies a sophisticated set of principles that unify the asymmetrical parts into a balanced and harmonious composition. The Sōgetsu school, one of the largest schools of ikebana in Japan, has devised a series of elementary patterns, or *kakei*, based on these principles.

The two introduced here, the Basic Upright and Basic Slanting, are the foundation for all *kakei* styles. Each *kakei* is composed from three main stems known as the *shushi*. The longest stem, the *shin*, determines the line of the composition; the next longest, the *soe*, supports the *shin*, while the shortest, the *hikae*, counterbalances the others to unify the arrangement. Supplementary stems, or *jūshi*, complement these main stems and give balance and fullness to the overall composition.
Fukushima Kōka

Moribana and Nageire

Ikebana can be roughly classified by the type of vase used for the arrangement. Ikebana in shallow containers are known as *moribana*, while those in tall vases are called *nageire*. For *moribana*, stems and branches are inserted into a spiked metal holder called a *kenzan*. *Nageire* are secured by manipulating the plant material itself, sometimes using props or supports fashioned out of branches.

A Few Fundamentals

An arrangement is first conceptualized by drawing linear diagrams, or *kakeizu*, which illustrate the basic formation of the primary stems. Two *kakeizu* are usually drawn: one for the frontal view of the arrangement and the other for the overhead view (see combined example, above right). Primary stems are represented by symbols: O for the *shin*, □ for the *soe*, and △ for the *hikae*. According to the degree system used in these *kakeizu*, any line perpendicular to the surface of the water is 0°.

Determining Stem Lengths——To determine the appropriate lengths for the main stems, you must first measure the size of the vase:

Vase Size = Diameter or Diagonal Length of Mouth of Vase + Height of Vase

Measure the stem lengths using these ratios:

$$Shin = 1\tfrac{1}{2}\ Vase\ Size \qquad Soe = \tfrac{3}{4}\ Shin$$
$$Hikae = \tfrac{1}{2}\ to\ \tfrac{3}{4}\ Soe$$

Basic Ikebana Techniques——To better preserve the plant material, submerge stems and branches in water and snip off 2–3 cm from the ends before you begin arranging.

Use a bending technique to accentuate or straighten the natural curves of a stem or branch: for branches, hold both hands closely around the point to be bent and slowly apply pressure; for flowers and grasses, add a slight twist.

Lesson I: Moribana Basic Upright Style

The foundation for all *kakei* variants, the Basic Upright Style is characterized by the strong, masculine line formed by the upright *shin*.

Materials——Branches and flowers (one variety of each), a shallow vase or similar container, a *kenzan*, or spiked holder (available at florists), a pair of garden clippers or ikebana scissors.

1 Look carefully at the *kakeizu* and, keeping in mind the desired lines for this style, select appropriate materials for the three main stems. It is advisable for the beginner to choose branches for the *shin* and *soe* and a flower for the *hikae*. (For the pictured arrangement, mountain ash branches were used for the *shin* and *soe* and a dahlia for the *hikae*.) Trim off any excess leaves or twigs that disrupt the line of the stem or branch.

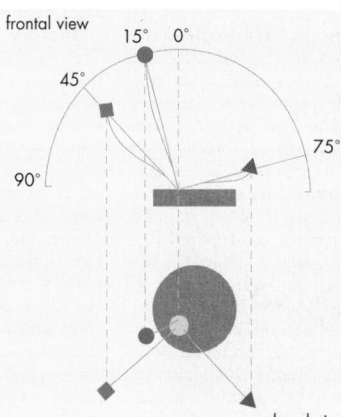

◀ *Kakeizu* combining frontal view (top) with overhead view (bottom). Position of *kenzan* is indicated in yellow. Symbols for the three branches are as explained above.

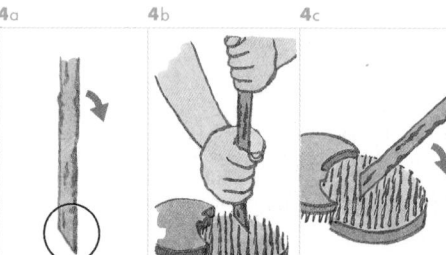

4a　4b　4c

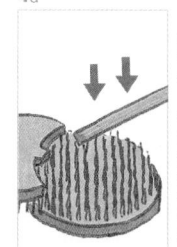

4d

2 Measure the appropriate lengths for the stems according to your vase size.

3 Place the *kenzan* in the container as shown in the *kakeizu* and fill with just enough water to cover the *kenzan*.

4 Cut and affix each branch and stem onto the *kenzan* in the order of *shin*, *soe*, and *hikae* as follows:
For branches: Determine which side of the branch will incline when fixed on the *kenzan*. Place the branch firmly between the scissor blades and cut the end at a slant, leaving more bark on the side that will incline (4a). Holding the branch securely with both hands, insert it between the needles of the *kenzan* and slant it to the opposite side of the cut (4b–4c).

For flowers and grasses: Cut the stem straight across with the tips of the blades and press it against the needles of the *kenzan* at the proper angle (4d).
For each stem, refer to the *kakeizu* to determine its correct position and proper degree of inclination. Take special care to adjust the space between the *hikae* and the *soe*. Too much space will dissipate the tension that holds the composition together, while too little space will constrict the arrangement.

5 Add *jūshi* to the areas around the main stems, keeping in mind that *jūshi* should always be shorter than the stems they support. Special attention should be given to filling out the area in the rear; only a few judiciously placed stems and branches are needed to give the arrangement volume and depth, as shown at right.

6 Carefully examine your completed arrangement, making sure that all the stems are in proportion to each other. Trim off any excess leaves or twigs that disrupt the overall balance of the composition.

5

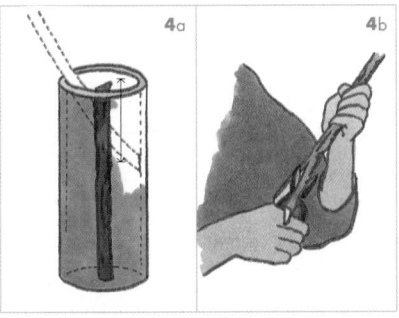

Lesson II: Nageire Basic Slanting Style

The *shin* and *soe* switch places to form this graceful variant of the Basic Upright Style.

Materials—Branches and flowers (one variety of each), a tall vase or similar container, one thick branch to use as a prop, a pair of garden clippers or ikebana scissors.

1 Examine the *kakeizu* below (vase is indicated in gray). Select the appropriate materials for the *shushi*—again it is best to use branches for the *shin* and *soe* and a flower for the *hikae*. Find a branch with a gently curved shape to set off the graceful lines of this style. (In the pictured arrangement, branches of the Japanese beautyberry were used for the *shin* and *soe* and a prairie gentian for the *hikae*.)

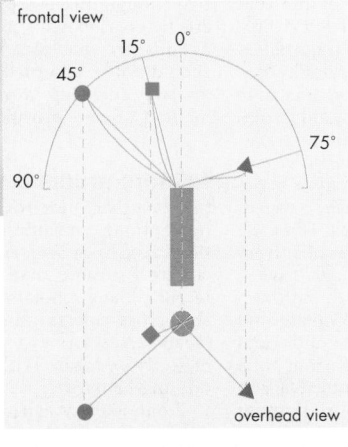

frontal view

overhead view

2 Using your vase size, measure the proper length for the *shin* and mark this spot with your finger. Before cutting, you must also add the portion that will go inside the vase as follows:
Holding the marked spot at the mouth of the vase, incline *shin* to the proper angle (45°). With your other hand mark the point where the end of the branch will touch the inner wall of the vase (2a). Cut the branch at this point at a slant that corresponds to the inner wall of the vase (2b).

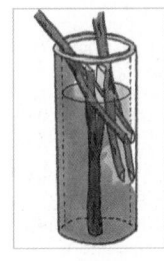

2a

3 Use a sturdy, straight branch for the prop. Cut it straight across at both ends so that it can stand upright in the vase at a height slightly shorter than the mouth of the vase.

2b

4a   4b

4 Determine where the *shin* will intersect the prop when placed inside the vase at the appropriate angle (4a). With scissor blades pointing directly toward the branch end, carefully split the prop in half, cutting until just beyond this intersection point (4b).

5 Split the *shin* in the same manner, cutting lengthwise until just beyond the intersection point formed with the prop. Make sure the fork opens up in a way that allows the *shin* to face the right direction when interlocked with the prop.

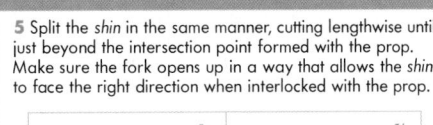

6a   6b

6 Fasten the *shin* onto the prop and insert the fixture into the vase (6a). The *shin* should rest against the mouth of the vase with its end touching the inner wall, while the prop should stand firmly on the bottom of the vase (6b). If the *shin* does not rest properly against the mouth of the vase, use the bending technique to correct its shape.

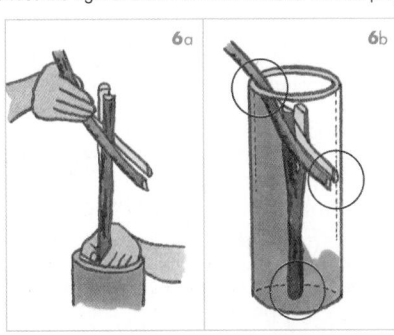

7 Select and measure the *soe*. As for the *shin*, look carefully at the *kakeizu* and estimate how the *soe* should rest inside the vase, then cut the end at the proper slant. Split its base in half and interlock with either the *shin* or the prop.

7

Reversed Arrangements

Depending on where you place your ikebana, inclining the stems in the opposite direction may give your arrangement better balance with its particular *kūkan*, or the "space" surrounding it. To arrange the *kakei* in their reversed styles, simply trace the *kakeizu* on transparent paper, turn it over, and arrange accordingly.

Free-style Ikebana

Once you have mastered the basics, develop your own ikebana style. Analyze the essential features of your materials—the colors, the line of each stem and branch, the masses formed by leaves or blossoms—and think of a way to rearrange these natural features into a fresh, original composition. Then make a freehand sketch of your ideas and arrange accordingly. But don't follow your diagram too rigidly. In free-style ikebana, always let your own aesthetic sense be your final guide.

This festive free-style arrangement was made from poinsettia, trifoliate orange, and artificial holly.

8 Select and measure the *hikae*, compensating for the portion inside the vase. Trim off all leaves from the part that will go inside the vase. Unlike branches, flowers and grasses are inserted directly into the container without splitting. Cut the stem of the *hikae* at a slant and fasten it by inserting it among the interlocked branches, adjusting so that it rests at the proper (75°) angle.

9 Add *jūshi* to complete the arrangement.

10 Stand back and observe your composition. Trim off any entangled leaves or branches. Check the area in the rear, as shown below. If this space is left unfilled, the whole arrangement will lose its strength.

10

Photos and illustrations © Sogetsukai Foundation

385

With regard to the first category, the kilns of Okinawa produce various types of ceramics called TSUBOYA WARE. In Kyūshū, such ceramics as KARATSU WARE, AGANO WARE, and TAKATORI WARE are produced by techniques learned from Korean potters. Imari ware (see ARITA WARE) is also famous for its excellent quality. Other superior ceramics are Futakawa ware (Fukuoka Prefecture), KOISHIWARA WARE, and ONTA WARE. Kilns are also located in Naeshirogawa (Kagoshima Prefecture) and Yatsushiro (Kumamoto Prefecture). In the Shikoku region, the only well-known ceramic ware is Tobe ware (Ehime Prefecture). In the Chūgoku region, some of the most ancient Japanese kilns are found in Fushina (Shimane Prefecture), Ushinoto (Tottori Prefecture), and Bizen (eastern part of Okayama Prefecture; see BIZEN WARE). The Kinki region is noted for Tamba ware, KYŌTO CERAMICS, SHIGARAKI WARE, and IGA WARE. The Chūbu region, largest of Japan's ceramics centers, is famous for SETO WARE and MINO WARE. The Kantō region produced unglazed pottery such as *imado-yaki*. The center of the folk crafts movement is Mashiko (Tochigi Prefecture; see MASHIKO WARE). Much pottery is also produced in the Tōhoku region.

Wood and bamboo craftworks include lacquer work inlaid with gold from Okinawa; dolls from Hakata (Fukuoka Prefecture); lacquer ware and *ikkambari uchiwa* (fans made by painting lacquer over a paper frame) from Shikoku; *yanagi-gōri* (wicker trunks made of willow branches) from the San'in region; *funadansu* (ship trunks) from Niigata Prefecture used on ships (KAISEN) traveling between Ōsaka and northern Japan during the Edo period; Wakasa and Wajima lacquer ware from Fukui and Ishikawa prefecture; woodcrafts from Hida (Gifu Prefecture) and Matsumoto (Nagano Prefecture); birch, bamboo, and other woodcrafts, including KAGO, JIZAIKAGI, MAGEMONO, and *kabazaiku* (birch woodcrafts), from the Hokuriku region; lacquer ware such as *aizu-nuri* (Fukushima Prefecture), *shunkei-nuri* (Akita Prefecture), and *tsugaru-nuri* (Aomori Prefecture); and Ainu woodcrafts from Hokkaidō.

Metalwork includes *kiseru* (smoking pipes), made by town craftsmen in various regions of Japan; tableware made in Tsubame City (Niigata Prefecture); hardware and carpentry tools from Miki (Hyōgo Prefecture); razors and other cutting instruments from Seki (Gifu Prefecture); metal fittings made in Sendai (Miyagi Prefecture); and iron pots and kettles produced throughout Japan.

Textiles include *bingata* and *bashō* cloth from Okinawa (see OKINAWAN TEXTILES); Satsuma *jōfu* (linen cloth) from Kagoshima Prefecture; *kurume-gasuri* (Kurume ikat cloth) from Fukuoka Prefecture and *iyo-gasuri* (Iyo ikat cloth) from Ehime Prefecture; INDIGO (*ai*) from Tokushima Prefecture, which was once valued throughout the country as *awa-ai*, a natural dye; cotton cloth from Tamba (Hyōgo and Kyōto prefectures); *saki-ori* (woven from strips made from old clothes) from the Hokuriku and Tōhoku regions; *habutae* silk from Fukui Prefecture and CHIJIMI from Niigata Prefecture; *mikawa momen* from Aichi Prefecture and *kaiki* from Yamanashi Prefecture; silk weaving from the Kantō region at Kiryū (Gumma Prefecture), Ashikaga (Tochigi Prefecture), and Hachiōji (Tōkyō Prefecture); *kogin* from the Tsugaru region; *hi-*

shizashi, distinguished by their embroidered patterns in white cotton thread, from Aomori and Iwate prefectures; and SASHIKO (quiltings) made by the Ainu in Hokkaidō.

Washi (Japanese paper), once produced throughout the country, is now rarely used in everyday life. Japanese papers still produced today are *tosa-gami* from Kōchi Prefecture and Sekishū *hanshi* and *izumo-gami* from Shimane Prefecture. *Washi* made in Kyōto and Nara has been famous for centuries. Dyed pattern paper is still produced in Mie Prefecture. Echizen *hōsho* and *torinoko-gami* from Fukui Prefecture are well known, as is *yao* paper made in Toyama Prefecture. Surviving *washi* products include KITES from Nagasaki Prefecture and *shibuuchiwa* (fans) from Kutami in Kumamoto Prefecture.

Numerous types of paintings and religious sculptures are considered representative of Japanese folk crafts, although in these categories there are different opinions about what is and what is not folk craft. (According to Yanagi's somewhat personal and subjective criteria, ŌTSU-E are included among folk arts whereas UKIYO-E are not.) Present designations of what can be considered *mingei* should not be accepted as final, since scholars may develop a more comprehensive method of categorization in the future.

☞ 388–389

folk studies 民俗学

(*minzokugaku*, not to be confused with a homophone meaning ethnology). Antiquarians have been examining Japan's folk culture for more than a century, but only recently have scholars applied comparative and cross-cultural methodologies. Today Japanese folklore is a well-established field of study in Japan, with several universities offering courses.

From as early as the 8th century, gazetteers such as the FUDOKI were compiled, and anthologies of folktales such as the 12th-century KONJAKU MONOGATARI and the 13th-century UJI SHŪI MONOGATARI were widely read, but it was only in the 18th century that this vast body of folk traditions and crafts came under scrutiny by Japanese scholars. Two studious exponents were SUGAE MASUMI and Kitagawa Morisada (b 1810), the author of MORISADA MANKŌ. It was not, however, until the start of the Meiji period (1868–1912) and the introduction of Western scholarship (including European anthropology) that Japanese scholars became aware of their folk culture as an object worthy of study. The English term folklore was first introduced to Japan by the English literature scholar UEDA BIN.

The first folklore surveys in Japan were carried out under the leadership of the Anthropological Society of Nippon (established in 1884). The development of folklore studies as a discipline began with YANAGITA KUNIO, a government official whose travels in Japan gave him time to develop a fieldwork approach and made him particularly interested in the oral narrative tradition. In 1934, having established methodological guidelines and trained young folklorists, Yanagita used his 100-item *Folklore Handbook* to conduct nationwide surveys of farming and fishing villages. Folklorists trained in the 1930s became the nucleus of the Japan Folklore Institute (1947–57).

Following Yanagita's death, folklore studies underwent a period of questioning and methodological self-criticism. Yanagita's focus on cognitive and expressive folklore had neglected the study of material cul-

ture and paid only minor attention to the literary side of ancient records. YANAGI MUNEYOSHI redressed this imbalance through his study of examples of folk architecture, folk arts, and crafts that he collected. Yanagi, who is often associated with the *mingei* (folk crafts) movement in Japan, was instrumental in founding a number of folk art museums. A different but related approach was developed by Kon Wajirō (1888–1973), who collected the everyday objects found in urban life.

Much more in keeping with traditional Japanese scholarly approaches, the literary-philological folklore approach is best illustrated by the career of ORIKUCHI SHINOBU. Like Yanagi, Orikuchi worked closely with Yanagita Kunio during the 1930s. Later, however, he established a folklore group at Kokugakuin University and issued his own folklore journal. Although productive, Orikuchi's application of folklore techniques to the written sources of ancient Japanese is generally considered outside the realm of folklore proper.

Given the overlap in research objects, folklore scholars have found it difficult to defend their area of interest from encroachment by the more established fields of anthropology, sociology, and history. Moreover, folklore studies have not enjoyed the financial benefits of the more institutionalized social sciences. Whether such studies can thrive as an independent field of study, as in the United States, or will be subsumed under older disciplines, as in other countries, remains uncertain at this point.

folk performing arts 民俗芸能

(*minzoku geinō*). Also called *kyōdo geinō* or *minkan geinō*. *Minzoku geinō* is a technical term used by Japanese scholars of the performing arts to refer to an extremely diverse range of Japanese folk performance types, which can be classified into several subgroups. The term is much more specific in reference than its English equivalent. The most basic types include performances connected with Shintō or Buddhist rites, with aspects of rice agriculture, and with the exorcism of malevolent spirits, as well as folk versions of courtly or city stage performing arts, such as NŌ, KABUKI, and the traditional puppet theater (BUNRAKU). This diversity is made even richer by historical and geographical factors. Aspects of performing arts from the Edo period (1600–1868), the Muromachi period (1333–1568), the Kamakura period (1185–1333), and in a few cases even earlier historical periods have been retained extensively within the active repertories of what is performed today at festivals and other observances, largely in the countryside. Of the huge number of performances of this sort found throughout Japan, including Okinawa, most did not originate where they are performed at present but were brought into these areas, where in time they became acclimatized as an integral part of the annual local tradition.

Within such a diverse body of material it is difficult to enumerate common characteristics. Most *minzoku geinō* regularly occur as part of observances held annually or at other fixed intervals. Patrons, audiences, and performers are regularly local inhabitants, and the latter do not usually earn their livelihood from performance. Most Japanese folk performances are related to agriculture, to a multitude of folk beliefs that have been a part of the life of the people from time immemorial, and, of course, to the seasons.

folk performing arts

▼ Children's *kabuki* being performed on a stage built atop a festival float in the city of Tonami, Toyama Prefecture, where children's *kabuki* has been performed since the late 18th century.

◀ Edo *daikagura*. This *kagura*-type folk performing art is performed by two dancers, with one manipulating the lion-head mask.

▲ The Kuromaru *odori*, a *furyū*-type folk performing art, is performed in the city of Ōmura, Nagasaki Prefecture. The drummer carries a display made from 81 bamboo poles on his back.

Agriculture, primarily rice growing, was the major occupation of the Japanese over many centuries, so it is natural that many folk performance events have had and still retain an intimate connection with farming in spite of the rapid industrialization of Japan. Beliefs have undergone a change in the 20th century, and it is difficult to measure accurately the degree to which they remain alive as a prerequisite for the continuation of folk performances into the future. It is possible that folk beliefs are being replaced by such new incentives as the recognition of festivals as part of the national cultural heritage, their usefulness for tourist or commercial benefit, or simply the pride a village takes in the arts of its ancestors (this last, of course, was a factor in transmission at an earlier time as well). But surely beliefs such as that in the efficacy of ritual purification and procession have been a major factor both in determining the original nature of performances and in guaranteeing a degree of preservation. Purification can be a part of the Japanese experience of the seasons, since it is a way of preparing for the arrival of the New Year gods. It can be part of a festival (a preliminary observance by means of song or dance, for example), which is also an invocation of the gods. The procession is a means of invoking the gods at the beginning of a festival or sending them away at its end. Invocation by means of procession might involve large floats carried through a teeming mass of people lining city streets, a cortege of strangely costumed figures from myth and history, or the single line of lofty banners and streamers carried through a summer field.

The Honda Classification——The seasonal sense is such a pervasive part of Japanese folk beliefs, religious feeling, personal lives, and festival activities that it is only natural that the seasons have served as a setting for Japanese folk performances as well. Some scholars have suggested that the four

seasons are the only natural way of grouping so large and disparate a body of material. The classification of folk performance types devised by Honda Yasuji (b 1906) is, however, the one most commonly accepted. In performance, individual items find themselves not in isolation but within a larger entity, the festival, and beyond that the religious and the everyday life of the people. Useful insights into these larger entities would come from an approach to folk performance types through religious studies, anthropology, or sociology. But the truly proper supplement to Honda's classification is the uniquely Japanese method of folklore studies (*minzokugaku*) developed by YANAGITA KUNIO and ORIKUCHI SHINOBU. Also noteworthy are the recent efforts of Ikeda Yasaburō (1914–82) to conceptualize a theory for the entire range of the performing arts of Japan, as arising from deep-seated folk beliefs and practice.

The three primary categories of *minzoku geinō* in Honda's system are KAGURA (a large body of performances related to Shintō festivals and ceremonies, either of the imperial court or of individual shrines), DENGAKU (various types of performance centered on the growing of rice), and FURYŪ (a category of performance in which a malevolent or harmful spirit is invoked and then disposed of). Honda's approach to these categories is based on the impulses that he sees as having given birth to each. Thus for him *kagura* is an event performed for the prolongation or revitalization of human life, *dengaku* is performed as a prayer for an abundance of the food (rice primarily) that nourishes life, and *furyū* is performed to avert pestilence and disease that threaten life. *Minzoku geinō* events that fall outside these three primary categories were assigned by Honda to two other categories: arts related to the storytelling tradition and arts that either came to Japan from abroad or contain an element imported from abroad.

The latter is a miscellaneous grouping

rather than one whose logic is immediately apparent; however, it is important, for it includes *minzoku geinō* versions of GIGAKU, *bugaku* (see GAGAKU), SARUGAKU, ENNEN, Nō, puppet theater, and kabuki. It is indisputable that the survival in countryside performances of elements of Japan's classical theaters provided much of the original enthusiasm for the early studies of *minzoku geinō*. In some cases what survives in this way reflects a state before Nō, kabuki, and the puppet theater became the classical arts known today; in others it simply reflects a somewhat later phase in their long development. In either case these folk performances continue to add much to an understanding of the major dramatic arts of Japan.

folk religion   民間信仰

(*minkan shinkō*). Beliefs, customs, and rituals that are held, practiced, and transmitted by the people or "folk" outside organized religion. Formally, folk religion is easily distinguishable from the highly organized religions in that it knows no founder, may be transmitted orally rather than by written traditions and formal liturgies, and may be carried out by the people, separate from any specific ecclesiastical institution. However, in practice folk religion cannot always be easily separated from Shintō and Buddhism for it has assimilated and preserved many practices of these established religions.

There is no single "orthodox" folk religion for the Japanese people. Practices are known by their concrete names, such as "greeting the New Year" or "holding the rice-transplanting ceremony." Folk religion has varied considerably among different regions and occupations. Some elements have been nearly universal but with local variations. It is still possible, however, to see gen-

Continued on page 390➤

Yanagi Muneyoshi and the Discovery of Japanese Folk Crafts

Yanagi Muneyoshi, a leading spokesman of the Japanese folk-craft movement, believed that handcrafted objects could possess artistic merit even if they were functional and had been turned out in quantity for daily use. Yanagi was attracted to the uncontrived beauty of objects produced by craftsmen who viewed their work not in terms of self-expression but matter-of-factly, as a job. To stimulate public appreciation of Japan's long tradition of anonymous craftsmanship, Yanagi and others opened the Japan Folk-Craft Museum in 1936. Its holdings range from lacquer ware and fabrics to woodwork and pottery. Works like the 12 examples shown here communicate a great deal about life as it was actually lived in the places where they were used.

Chests (tansu) were fashioned by hakoya, or box makers, and often made in two stackable sections. Joiners and metalworkers also played roles in tansu production. Stained and polished hardwoods or a strong, light wood like paulownia were used for the frame, drawers, sliding doors, and double doors. To these were fitted metal hinges, handles, locks, and embellishments. 19th century. Zelkova wood. 94 x 70 x 36 cm.

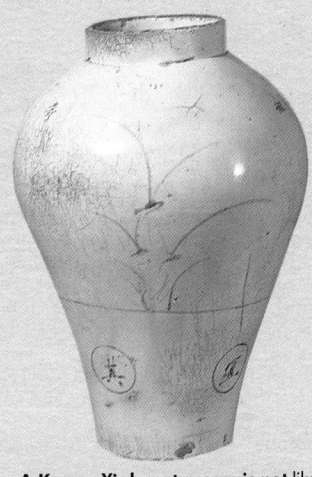

A Korean Yi-dynasty ceramic pot like this one opened Yanagi's eyes to the beauty of folk crafts. Such pots were turned out in large numbers for use in ordinary homes during the Yi dynasty (1392–1910), when Korean crafts flourished. A mastery of design, evident here in the graceful lines, pale white glaze, and simple indigo figures, was typically displayed. 18th century. Height 39 cm.

Women wore kazuki robes loosely around their bodies and draped them over their heads when going out. To create the design, a dye-resistant paste was stenciled on the cloth or applied freehand before dyeing. This style of garment originated in the Kyōto area. Later, craftsmen in more far-flung regions produced some superb designs. This example is from Yamagata Prefecture. 18th century. Resist-dyed hemp. Length 155 cm.

Japanese homes were lit by candles and oil lamps in the pre-electric era. This candlestand features a pair of tweezers for trimming wicks, suspended from a hook, and a compartment for spare wicks. 19th century. Brass. Height 29 cm.

Japanese lacquer ware is known worldwide; in English, to "japan" something once meant to coat it with varnish. Durable and resistant to moisture, lacquer ware was the predominant form of Japanese hollowware until the 18th century. To create this "Hidehira bowl," thin gold leaf was applied over wet lacquer. 17th century. Diameter 13 cm.

This kettle's flared base complements the flowing curves of the spout and handles, but it also enhances heat absorption. Incorporating functional innovations into a pleasing and harmonious design is the mark of the expert craftsman. Today's top industrial designers carry on the tradition. 19th century. Brass. Height 29 cm.

Bamboo is strong, light, and flexible. Many varieties grow in Japan, where craftsmen have used bamboo in handcrafting a wide range of products, including baskets, boxes, utensils, and tools. Woven-bamboo hampers (kōri) like this one were used to store clothes. 19th century. 22 x 40 x 33 cm.

Storage jars like this one were first produced by kilns at Tamba early in the Kamakura period (1185–1333). Tea-ceremony connoisseurs prized Tamba ware, but kilns also turned out simpler work for poorer customers with a rustic grace all its own, "the beauty of poverty," as Yanagi called it. Wood ash settling on this jar made the glaze green. Muromachi period (1333–1568). Stoneware. Height 42 cm.

Cloth cutouts were sewn onto this Ainu robe and elaborated with embroidery to create the design. The Ainu people of northern Japan sometimes used Japanese and even European fabrics for the appliqué figures. Bold, powerful compositions typify Ainu design. 19th century. Elm-bark fiber cloth and cotton appliqué. Length 118 cm.

This carp-shaped crosspiece forms part of an adjustable pot-hanging system suspended from a rafter over an open hearth (irori). Crosspieces in the form of creatures associated with water were employed as talismans against fire. 19th century. Zelkova wood. Length 36 cm.

A spouted vessel from the Nishishimmachi kiln in Fukuoka Prefecture. Its lipped neck makes this large vessel easy to pick up and pour from any direction. Craft artists, devoted to making their products functional, developed many practical innovations. 19th century. Stoneware with iron glaze and green drip overglaze. Height 28 cm.

Stencil-dyed bingata is the most colorful of Okinawa's local textiles. Yanagi felt the stylized beauty of the plants, animals, and natural scenery depicted in bingata "surpasses nature itself." The motifs of this kimono design are birds, stream, and chrysanthemums. 19th century. Cotton. Length 140 cm.

eral patterns of folk religion throughout much of Japanese history that have helped define the overall world view of the Japanese people and given meaning and order to their lives. Two of the most important patterns are the round of seasonal customs and rituals related to the LIFE CYCLE. Nearly all Japanese people have participated in some or most of these customs.

One distinctive feature of the Japanese religious year is that much of it is dominated by folk customs observed and transmitted outside established religions. The most important seasonal celebration is the NEW YEAR. While one of the most conspicuous of New Year's customs is the practice of visiting Shintō shrines and Buddhist temples, many important customs are observed in the home. The household is thoroughly cleaned to drive out impurities of the old year, and the entrance is decorated with a straw rope (SHIMENAWA) to indicate a purified or sacred place; pine decorations at the gate also indicate the renewal of life at New Year's. On New Year's Day special ritual significance is attached to the *first* occurrence of an activity for that year, such as the first dream or first calligraphy. Also important is the observance in late summer for the spirits of the dead, the BON FESTIVAL, marked by elaborate family celebrations and special dances (BON ODORI).

Although Japan formally adopted the Western calendar in the Meiji period (1868–1912), people retain observances of the complex Chinese calendar, especially when choosing a propitious day (and avoiding an unlucky one) for a wedding or funeral. Many of the reasons for these particular days' being lucky and unlucky are based on Chinese customs long forgotten, but the days are common knowledge (see CALENDAR, DATES, AND TIME). The five central Chinese-inspired festivals celebrated in Japan are known as Gosekku (see SEKKU; Jinjitsu no Sekku), 3 March (DOLL FESTIVAL), 5 May (Boys' Day; modern CHILDREN'S DAY), 7 July (TANABATA FESTIVAL), and 9 September (CHRYSANTHEMUM FESTIVAL).

Another major pattern of Japanese folk religion is the traditional round of rituals that follow the individual from the cradle to the grave. There are special religious observances for the pregnant woman, birth, early childhood, marriage, and death. Marriage was usually performed in the house, and many of the important customs surrounding death were performed by the family and neighbors of the deceased.

Patterns of seasonal and life-cycle rituals helped orient the traditional Japanese in their passage through time. Families and villages maintained their sense of belonging in the world by marking the regularly recurring seasonal rituals, and the individual marked his or her progress in life by observing the successive life-cycle rites.

Folk Religion in the Modern World— Much of traditional folk religion lives on in modern Japan, although many folk customs have become severely attenuated and others have passed out of existence. Perhaps the best example of the perseverance of folk religion in contemporary Japan is the presence of many folk religious beliefs within the NEW RELIGIONS (shinkō shūkyō), religious movements that have become conspicuous in number and membership since the early 19th century. See also SEKKU; FOLK SHINTŌ.

Folk Shintō 民俗神道

(Minzoku Shintō). A loose category adopted after 1945 by historians of Japanese religion to describe that aspect of SHINTŌ that centers around the traditional local religious practices of the village or of the individual household, as opposed to those rites and rituals organized and promoted by the state. Folk Shintō's relatively simple festivals celebrate local deities toward whom members of the community have strong feelings of kinship. Folk Shintō has no conscious religious ideology and no founder or hereditary succession.

There are three dimensions to Folk Shintō: communal, domestic, and cult. On the communal level it focuses on the village shrine (sonsha) and the "unranked shrine" (mukakusha). The shrines in these two categories are usually dedicated to regional deities (ubusunagami; popularly called ujigami), i.e., local tutelary deities. The festivals at these shrines are generally conducted by village residents organized in a hereditary shrine association known as a *miyaza* (shrine guild). On the domestic level Folk Shintō is represented by the SHINTŌ FAMILY ALTARS (kamidana) found in most households. Farming families also often erect an outdoor miniature shrine (hokora) at the northwest corner of the paddy field for the worship of a *yashikigami*, i.e., a deity of special relation to an individual household. On the cult level Folk Shintō is manifested in the voluntary religious association (kō), which comprises believers in a particular deity or religious practice and is organized along either geographical or occupational lines for the purpose of periodic group worship or pilgrimages. See also SECT SHINTŌ; SHRINE SHINTŌ; STATE SHINTŌ.

folk song 民謡

(min'yō). Although it renders an old Chinese term, in current usage the Japanese word min'yō is a translation of the English term "folk song" with all that is connoted by this ambiguous foreign concept. However, there is no doubt that an identifiable body of song exists in Japan that may conveniently be called min'yō, even if some categories might also be treated as classical, as theater, or as urban popular music (see RYŪKOKA).

According to Uehara Rokushirō (1848–1913), there were two scales in Japanese music of the Edo period (1600–1868): the *in* scale, with a flattened second and sixth, and the *yō* scale, with a major second and sixth. Uehara claimed that the *in* scale was that of urban music, and the *yō* scale that of peasant music, although in folk music both are found. In recent years Koizumi Fumio (1927–83) has proposed a more sophisticated structure based on conjunct and disjunct tetrachords. These tetrachords are constructed from nuclear tones (kakuon), with four possible intermediate tones. The choice of intermediate tone depends on the type of music, but all four possibilities are found in various kinds of Japanese folk song.

The meter of Japanese folk song is usually duple or quadruple, but the total rhythmic effect is frequently subtle, even when the beat is strongly emphasized, and some tunes use a compound meter with a loping three-beat rhythm. Japanese folk songs are generally strophic and often have repeated refrains, typically using nonsense syllables (hayashi kotoba). Many dialect expressions are found, and the pronunciation of words (especially in northern Honshū and in the extreme south) tends to follow local usage.

Types of min'yō include religious songs, occupational songs, songs for various kinds of social gatherings, and CHILDREN'S SONGS. The themes of the texts are the usual ones of folk song—love, food, nature—but there are no long ballads or epics such as we encounter in many other countries, since their place is filled by other genres of music: HEIKYOKU and other types of BIWA song; GIDAYŪ-BUSHI; NAGAUTA; TOKIWAZU-BUSHI and other types of theater music. For instrumental accompaniment folk songs use the SHAMISEN, a TAIKO or a waisted drum, a shrill transverse flute (shinobue), and sometimes an end-blown flute (SHAKUHACHI).

Regional and Historical Characteristics—Japanese folk songs are difficult to classify according to region since, as in other settled countries, well-loved songs have traveled throughout the land, and accordingly in different places there are many different versions of the same song. Nevertheless it is often possible to identify the origin of a particular song: for example, the *jinku*, a song-type that originally mimicked the speech of courtesans from Echigo but has now lost its regional affiliations, and the *oiwake*, a type of travelers' song that moved from Shinano to Echigo and spawned a whole family of other songs.

It is also possible to consider min'yō historically and to identify some types that are no longer extant. The oldest anthology of Japanese verse, the MAN'YŌSHŪ, contains many anonymous poems that can fairly be called folk songs. There are numerous literary references to folk song from the TOSA NIKKI of KI NO TSURAYUKI onward, and many old song collections consist of or include folk songs. Among these may be mentioned the *Kinkafu* (981), the RYŌJIN HISHŌ (1169), the KANGINSHŪ (1518), and the undated *Tauezōshi*, a collection of medieval rice-planting songs.

Folk song has influenced other kinds of Japanese music: imayō, the popular court songs of the Heian period (794–1185); sōga, the banquet songs of the Kamakura period (1185–1333); the entertainment music (SŌKYOKU, KOUTA, etc) and theater music (gidayū-bushi, nagauta, etc) of the Edo period; and the popular music of the last hundred years. Most of the folk songs preserved in present-day practice date from the Edo period or later. See also FOLK PERFORMING ARTS.

folktales 民話

(minwa). Narrative literature of the people, handed down orally from generation to generation. Some tales can be traced back even before writing was introduced to Japan. The term *mukashi-banashi* (tale of yore) is assigned by Japanese folklorists to denote the "folktale" as against the *densetsu* or "legend"; the latter is defined as a marvelous incident that is believed by the folk to have actually happened.

Written History—Outside of the oral tradition, there is rich documentation of folk material throughout the ages. The 8th century saw the first written records of the imperial history with the KOJIKI and NIHON SHOKI, which contain many tale motifs. The NIHON RYŌIKI, KONJAKU MONOGATARI, and UJI SHŪI MONOGATARI of the following centuries are collections of traditional narratives, Buddhist and secular, totaling well over 1,000 in number. Also, the classic dramas of the 15th century, the NŌ and KYŌGEN, as well as KABUKI, which originated in the early 17th century, are examples of how dramatists based their plots and themes on folk material, resulting in the preservation of tale motifs today.

Collecting Folktales—Systematic collecting of folktales was started in the 1930s, following the precepts of a list of 100 major story types devised by YANAGITA KUNIO, who wrote *Mukashi-banashi saishū techō* (1936, Manual for Collecting Folktales). During the period 1935–37 *Mukashi-banashi kenkyū* was published monthly, providing space for local collectors' reports. The journal featured articles on folk literature in general and introduced Western theories and methodology for folktale study. Several other folklore journals that contained regional tales and legends were also published at that time. Tale collections of particular localities—usually of an island or a county, or the repertory of a single informant—have appeared to date in single-volume form and in series. Tale collecting is becoming popular as both a student project and a senior citizen activity.

The first attempt to tabulate the collected material in classified order was *Nippon mukashi-banashi meii* (1948, A List of Japanese Folktales). Listing the outlines of various tale types in one volume, it is useful as a handbook for tale collecting. In 1958 the original classification system of Yanagita was expanded sevenfold by Seki Keigo (b 1899) in a classified anthology of 8,600 folktale synopses entitled *Nippon mukashi-banashi shūsei*, published in six volumes.

Type and Motif—*A Type and Motif Index of Japanese Folk Literature* (1971) by Hiroko Ikeda presents the body of Japanese folk literature, oral and written, in the Aarne-Thompson tale-type classification system, together with motif analyses. Certain types that appear in Europe as folktales are found in Japan as myths, legends, and other forms of literature. Antti Aarne (1867–1925) and Stith Thomson (1885–1976) were originators of the concepts of "type" and "motif," respectively. These concepts provide the basis for the systematic classification of folk literatures applied internationally, thus laying a foundation for comparative and other literary studies.

Diffusion Routes to Japan—In compiling her *Index*, Ikeda was able to perceive various dissemination routes of tale types, which reached Japan from many directions and at different times, group by group. In prehistoric times Japan seems to have had closer contact with the Eurasian continent than is commonly thought. It was an era of dynamic migration from east to west along many routes. One that intimately concerns Japan was the circumpolar route that eventually populated the Americas. Situated adjacent to this route, Japan shares many cultural features with the races along this grand migration route, including the Fox-Bear Cycle, which originated and still thrives in northern Europe.

The warm tides washing the shores of Japan suggest another far-reaching route of diffusion. Because many Japanese myths and legends correspond to those of ancient Greece, there is a strong possibility of an overseas route that connected the two areas by way of ports of call dotting the southern fringe of the Eurasian continent. Analogues in Japan of marine animal fables such as "The Bridge of Crocodiles" and "The Monkey Who Left His Liver at Home" are found in the *Panchatantra* of India and *Kalila wa Dimna* of Persia, present-day Iran. Wolfram Eberhard (1909–89) long maintained that strikingly close analogues exist in the tales of Turkey and southern China.

Again there are Japanese tales and legends that are shared by cultures on the perimeter of the Pacific Ocean. This circumpacific diffusion route follows the Japan Current, which circulates clockwise about the Pacific, north from Taiwan along the east coast of Japan, then across to the western shores of North and South America, and returns west through the Southern Pacific Ocean. The story of a child born of a dead mother in her grave, "The Monkey's Hand Caught in a Clam," and "Recovering the Lost Fishhook" are examples of types and motifs that have widespread distribution along the path of the Japan Current.

With the advent of the YAYOI PERIOD (ca 300 BC–ca AD 300), an entirely new sort of culture complex came into Japan from the southern part of Korea. A considerable number of migrants arrived with the technology of rice cultivation, weaving, the use of iron tools, bronze weapons, dolmens, pot coffins, and the making of Yayoi pottery. Yayoi culture flourished in northern Kyūshū for some time and then spread eastward. From about the 3rd to the 5th centuries, the present emperor's ancestors consolidated their power in central Honshū. The *Kojiki* and *Nihon shoki* trace the imperial family history back to the mythical era and incorporate many preexistent tale motifs.

With the introduction of writing and Buddhism to Japan, first from Korea and then directly from China, Japanese folk literature gained yet another overland route to sources in Central Asia and down to India through Tibet. Tales recorded in the *Nihon ryōiki* and *Konjaku monogatari* belong to this group.

Well-known folktales of Japan include "Peach Boy" (MOMOTARŌ), "The Wen Removed" (KOBUTORI JIJII), "The Tongue-Cut Sparrow" (SHITAKIRI SUZUME), and "Kachikachi Mountain" (KACHIKACHI YAMA). Standardization of the repertory and form of tales is chiefly the result of compulsory schooling since the 1870s, when government-compiled textbooks were used uniformly throughout Japan. The textbook adapted several popular folktales from chapbooks for children published during the Edo period (1600–1868). See also HANASAKA JIJII; SARUKANI KASSEN; BUMBUKU CHAGAMA; GHOSTS; HAGOROMO LEGEND; HITOBASHIRA; KAPPA; KASA JIZŌ; KINTARŌ; MIRUNA NO ZASHIKI; OBASUTE; OCHIUDO LEGENDS; ŌTOSHI NO KYAKU; SEVEN DEITIES OF GOOD FORTUNE; SUMIYAKI CHŌJA; TANUKI; TSURU NYŌBŌ; URIKO-HIME; WARASHIBE CHŌJA; YAMAMBA; YUKI ONNA; YURIWAKA LEGEND.

Fontanesi, Antonio   フォンタネージ, A.

(1818–82). Italian painter, known in the West for romantic landscapes in the style of the French Barbizon school; noted in Japan for being the first to introduce the materials, techniques, and theory of Western oil painting. He influenced the first generation of late-19th-century Western-style (YŌGA) painters, including ASAI CHŪ, Koyama Shōtarō (1857–1916), Goseda Yoshimatsu (1855–1915), Matsuoka Hisashi (1862–1944), Nakamaru Seijūrō (1841–96), and YAMAMOTO HŌSUI.

Fontanesi was born in Reggio d'Emilia and educated in its academy. He was professor of landscape painting at the Turin Academy of Art from 1869 to 1876. In 1876 Fontanesi joined his countrymen Vincenzo RAGUSA and Giovanni Cappelletti as foreign instructors hired by the Japanese government for its new Technical Fine Arts School (Kōbu Bijutsu Gakkō) in Tōkyō. Importing

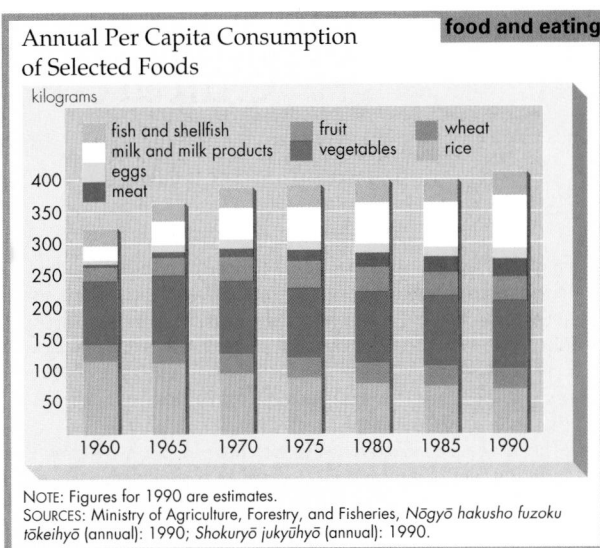

Annual Per Capita Consumption of Selected Foods

NOTE: Figures for 1990 are estimates.
SOURCES: Ministry of Agriculture, Forestry, and Fisheries, *Nōgyō hakusho fuzoku tōkeihyō* (annual): 1990; *Shokuryō jukyūhyō* (annual): 1990.

Western materials, Fontanesi introduced his students to charcoal, crayons, and oil; he also introduced sketching from life, plaster models, and nature and taught perspective, anatomy, and Western art theory. Serious illness in 1878 forced Fontanesi to return to Turin, where he resumed teaching.

food additives   食品添加物

(*shokuhin tenkabutsu*). The Food Sanitation Act (Shokuhin Eisei Hō, 1947) defines food additives broadly as any artificial substance added to or otherwise mixed in with food at any stage of its manufacture, including substances introduced for the preservation of food. In 1991 there were 349 of these artificial, or chemically synthesized, substances officially approved as food additives. By law, artificial food additives must be listed on a product's packaging. Natural substances added to foods—that is, substances extracted from natural sources—are generally not subject to government requirements for testing before approval. Since 1989, however, the government has made mandatory the package listing of some 1,000 natural food additives. Food products manufactured outside Japan must also conform to regulations regarding artificial additives and package listing.

food and eating   日本人の食生活

(*nihonjin no shokuseikatsu*). The distinguishing features of the food eaten by Japanese people today can be traced back to the prehistoric era. Prior to the introduction of rice cultivation in the Yayoi period (ca 300 BC–ca AD 300), the Japanese fished along the coastline or hunted inland in the mountainous areas that make up the greater part of their island country. The basic characteristics of Japanese cooking were determined by the types of food available, in particular the abundant fish and other marine food, remains of which have been uncovered in Jōmon-period (ca 10,000 BC–ca 300 BC) archaeological sites (see SHELL MOUNDS). This protein source was later supplemented by rice, for which the climate and soil of Japan are eminently suited. Japanese cooking henceforth evolved around rice, while other foods were consumed as side dishes. This pattern, firmly established early in the dietary life of the Japanese, is still prevalent today.

The wide-scale importation of Chinese culture from the 7th to the 9th century influenced Japanese ways of growing and cooking food. The introduction of Buddhism
Continued on page 394

Culture and Cuisine

Japan's eagerness to embrace and assimilate various aspects of
Western culture is nowhere more apparent than on its dining tables.

In recent years Japan's traditional cuisine has attained international recognition for its use of fresh seasonal ingredients, its subtle, understated flavorings, and the intricate care with which dishes are presented. Today most of the world's major cities boast at least one Japanese restaurant, and words such as *tōfu*, *tempura*, *sushi*, and *miso* have entered the gastronomic lexicons of people on six continents.

The process of discovery has not been a one-way street: Japan has embarked on a full-fledged love affair with foreign, especially Western, tastes. The perception that the daily diet of people in Tōkyō or Ōsaka consists exclusively of raw fish, fermented soybeans, and *kaiseki* (Japanese haute cuisine) is as outmoded as the stereotype that Japanese women always wear *kimono*. A cursory glance through the food floors of any department store will reveal a cornucopia of Western fare.

Yet only three decades ago imported foods were considered exotic. Now they have been adopted as a chic fashion statement that is an accepted element of the modern Japanese lifestyle. Over the past 30 years, consumption of rice, the staple grain, has declined by 40 percent. Consumption of *miso* (fermented soybean paste)—once an essential source of protein—has also fallen about 40 percent over the same period. The demand for fish has been decreasing, while the demand for meat has been booming, especially since the market for imported beef was liberalized in 1991.

How, then, has this shift in food sensibilities come about? Japan's traditional diet—which evolved during two and a half centuries of national isolation under the Tokugawa shogunate (1603–1867)—first came under assault from foreign influences during the heady days of Emperor Meiji in the late 19th century. The taboo on meat eating, stemming from the Buddhist tradition, eroded rapidly. Western customs gained credence, at least among the sophisticated urban elite, and the nation seized upon a host of new culinary delights. *Sukiyaki, tonkatsu* (deep-fried breaded pork cutlets), cheese, chocolate, and coffee made their appearance at this time, although they did not all win immediate acceptance without modification.

The second assault from overseas occurred after Japan's defeat in World War II. As the nation struggled to recover from the privations of war and the years of austerity that followed, the beacon of American strength and prosperity beckoned. Milk, bread, and meat became the staples of postwar nutritionists and were promptly included in elementary school lunch programs, instilling in youngsters a taste for these "wonder foods." When this generation came of age in the early 1970s, Japan's first fast-food hamburger restaurant opened in Tōkyō's fashionable Ginza district. Burger, fried chicken, and pizza outlets are now common throughout Japan.

New trends first take root in cities. The rural population, the blue-collar communities, and the older generation tend to be more conservative toward change. Yet no part of Japan remains untouched by the rapid influx of coffee shops, supermarkets, and soft-drink vending machines.

Eating at Home

The key to a nation's eating habits is the first meal of the day. The traditional Japanese breakfast, like lunch and dinner, is constructed of the basic building blocks of rice, fish, *miso* soup, seaweed, and pickled vegetables, accompanied by green tea. But today in cities and suburban areas, breakfast is just as likely to consist of toast, eggs, cereal, and coffee (milk or juice for children). Salaried workers,

who frequently commute two hours to work each day, have little time for more than a cup or can of coffee or a vitamin-enriched drink.

It is still customary in Japan for housewives to do their food shopping daily, buying only what is needed for a single day. One of the benefits of frequent, small-scale marketing is that the groceries do not tie up storage space in the typically cramped Japanese home. Fish, meat, *tōfu*, and seasonal produce are all available from neighborhood stores, which besides providing food also form the social focus of each community.

The preference for daily shopping and for fresh ingredients means there is less demand for frozen and microwave food products in Japan than in Europe and North America. But the demand for convenience foods is rapidly rising as more married women return to work after their children are in school. Quick and easy-to-prepare foods are also popular among young

singles living on their own.

Mini-supermarkets and 24-hour convenience stores, which now flourish even in smaller rural communities, offer a wide range of precooked meals. The Japanese answer to the invasion of American fast foods is the take-out store specializing in simple, Japanese-style box lunches (*bentō*) of freshly cooked rice with a few side dishes such as fish, meat, vegetables, and pickles. This type of establishment has become so popular that one chain alone operates 2,000 franchise stores nationwide.

For those still living in traditional three-generation households, dinner, the main meal of the day, can be surprisingly elaborate. Though rarely of the complexity of a formal meal in a high-class restaurant, it may consist of several courses: a couple of appetizers to accompany the beer or *sake*; some fish or meat dishes; and a dish or two of vegetables and seaweed. All this will invariably be accompanied by the obligatory rice, *miso* soup, and pickles.

Variations in the menu are largely dictated by the seasons. In winter, hearty one-pot fish, meat, and vegetable stews (*nabemono*) are cooked over a movable gas ring set in the middle of the table. Spring is celebrated by the inclusion of young bamboo shoots and tender wild greens. The heat of summer is offset by chilled *tōfu* or cold *sōmen* noodles or sustaining foods like charcoal-broiled eel or chicken. Autumn brings newly harvested rice and freshly picked mushrooms—of which the most prized is the incomparable *matsutake*.

Although Japanese housewives are expected to be competent in all aspects of their national (or, at least, regional) cuisine, some dishes are rarely prepared at home. *Sushi*, for example, is generally ordered from a nearby restaurant and delivered, since the skills of making the vinegared rice and choosing the freshest fish are considered the province of the professional. *Tempura*, also, is a dish often left to the experts; many housewives find the effort involved in deep-frying too bothersome.

In today's nuclear family, traditional eating patterns are not as carefully observed. Dinner is frequently a two-tiered event—the children eat with their mothers, and their fathers, who return home from work late, eat afterward. Children's favorite dishes, such as *karē raisu* (curry with rice), instant *rāmen* noodles, hamburgers, and spaghetti, tend to be those popularized in school lunch programs or in television programs.

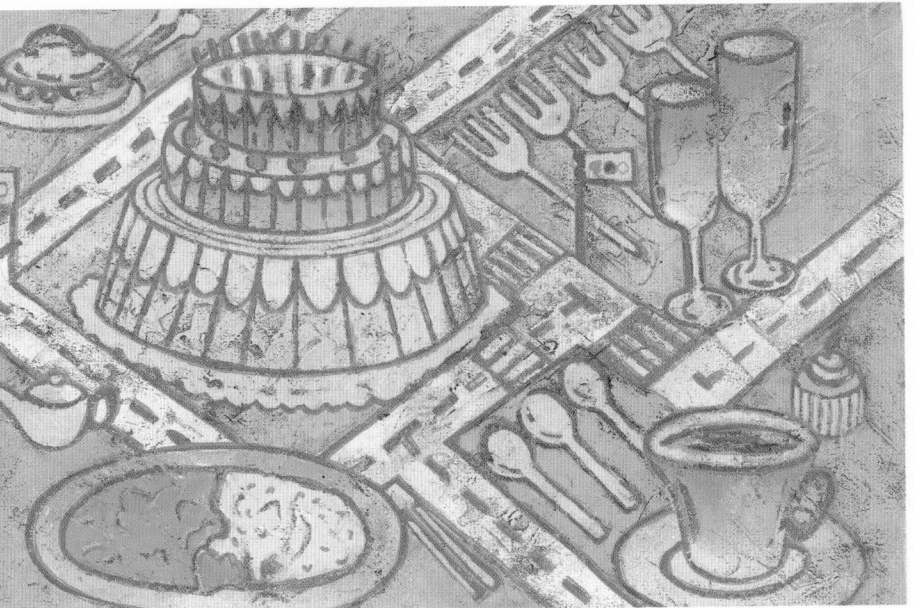

Dining Out | The only opportunity for many families to eat together is on weekends. The recent gourmet boom, fueled by magazine articles, television programs, and comic books, has prompted some men to try their skills at cooking on their days off. But dining out on weekends is a popular pastime. A new type of restaurant that caters to families has opened. Chain restaurants such as Skylark and the American Denny's offer a wide selection of both Japanese and American dishes and provide a children's menu, all at budget prices.

Eating out has always been part of Japanese life. Mobile food stalls (*yatai*) used to be as much a feature of cities in Japan as they still are in other parts of Asia. These have not entirely vanished, and as evening falls, food stalls serving *yakitori* (kebabs of broiled chicken), *oden* stew, or *rāmen* noodles appear on street corners, particularly near subway or railway stations.

A nation as constantly on the move as Japan requires portable sustenance. Box lunches sold at railway stations (*ekiben*) offer a variety of regional and seasonal specialties, which are packed in attractive containers. These compact meals are served to almost a million travelers a day. Although dining adds to the pleasure of long-distance train travel, it is considered ill-mannered to eat on local trains or buses or while walking down the street.

Lunchtime—especially in central Tōkyō where the daytime population almost doubles—is an exercise of considerable logistical proportions. Several million office workers demand to be fed within the space of a single hour. The custom of carrying a box lunch prepared at home is now quite rare, except among schoolchildren and blue-collar workers. In larger companies, cafeterias provide low-cost meals, and desk-bound employees can have simple meals delivered to the office through a service known as *demae*, offered by many *sushi* and noodle shops. But the vast majority of office workers flock outside to eat meals that can be ordered and consumed quickly.

Popular foods are noodles (*soba, udon*, or Chinese-style *rāmen*), *domburimono* (a large bowl of hot rice topped with foods such as *tempura*, broiled eel, or breaded pork cutlets), and the ubiquitous Chinese stir-fries. Most restaurants provide a lunchtime set menu, whether of Japanese or Western fare.

The frenzied feeding at lunchtime gives way to a more relaxed pace in the evening, although the Japanese seem to approach their play as energetically as their work. Nighttime carousing is often done under the guise of entertaining business clients and solidifying relationships, and the evening invariably centers around liquid sustenance. Beer has long been the lubrication of choice, far outpacing traditional brews of *sake* and *shōchū* (distilled spirits). Recent reductions in import tariffs have boosted the demand for imported liquors—scotch for businessmen, bourbon for the fashion-conscious young.

Unlike Japanese restaurants abroad, which serve a selection of dishes, most restaurants in Japan specialize in a single discipline such as *shabushabu, sukiyaki, tempura*, or *yakitori*. Such restaurants can be found throughout any Japanese city, catering to all budgets, from the cheap-and-cheerful to the designer palaces of conspicuous consumption. Business executives on expense accounts often opt for lavish hotel restaurants or Japanese restaurants that offer choice meals in private dining rooms. For captains of industry and senior politicians there are the more exclusive *ryōtei*, where the subtlety of the *kaiseki* cuisine is matched by the refinement of the surroundings.

New Trends | A sign of the times can be seen in the proliferation of ethnic restaurants. The younger generation likes to go to the fashionable neighborhoods of large cities to sup on Italian, French, Indian, or Thai delicacies. Most of these diners are couples—a phenomenon never before seen in a country where the sexes have by custom led separate lives, both before and after marriage.

The most obvious change associated with the postwar diet of the Japanese is in the national physique, and today's teenagers stand head and shoulders above their grandparents. But obesity and the so-called civilized diseases are also increasing commensurately. While doctors used to caution people about having too much salt in their diets—believed to be the cause of Japan's high incidence of stomach cancer—they are now putting up flags about excessive cholesterol and fat consumption. Heart disease has become a major cause of death, and cancer of the lungs and intestinal tract is on the rise.

There is a certain irony to the fact that while the rest of the world has come to recognize the attributes of the Japanese diet, the Japanese themselves are now suffering the ill effects of the Western diet. Nutritional concerns—imported along with hamburgers and fried chicken—have sparked a new era of health awareness, however, and an appreciation of the traditional Japanese way of eating.

R. C. F. Swinnerton

food and eating In order to obtain the freshest ingredients for their meals, many Japanese do their grocery shopping on a daily basis, patronizing small neighborhood vendors like the ones pictured here.

earlier in the 6th century led to the avoidance, at least publicly, of eating the flesh of animals and fowl. The establishment of warrior rule in the 12th century brought about a change in eating habits, with the frugal meals of the warrior replacing the more formal Chinese-influenced meals of the court aristocracy. The vegetarian cooking (SHŌJIN RYŌRI) of the Zen Buddhist sect also influenced the diet of the Japanese. By the 15th century many of the foods eaten by Japanese today had already made their debut, notably, *shōyu* (SOY SAUCE), MISO (bean paste), TŌFU (bean curd), and other products made from soybeans. At the same time, HONZEN RYŌRI, a style of banquet cooking derived from the cuisine of the court aristocracy, was gradually refined and conventionalized.

One may say that Japanese cooking reached its final form in the Edo period (1600–1868), when Chinese and Korean influences, and even some Western influence—mainly from the Spanish, the Portuguese, and the Dutch—had been fully assimilated. Worthy of particular mention is the full development of the meal served during the TEA CEREMONY (*chakaiseki ryōri*), which had appeared in the Azuchi-Momoyama period (1568–1600) and which adopted the formalities of *honzen ryōri* and the spirit and frugality of Zen. A later development, KAISEKI RYŌRI, adopted some of the cooking techniques of *honzen ryōri* and *chakaiseki ryōri* but emphasized the taste of the food rather than the ritual involved in presentation. It should be remembered that the elaborate meals and food preparation now considered characteristic of Japanese cooking were accessible only to the ruling classes. The dietary habits of the common folk were rarely recorded; their meals were simple, and many lived on a subsistence level or nearly starved in times of famine.

The custom of eating three meals per day began in the mid-Edo period. In premodern times it had been customary to eat twice a day, once at 10 AM and again at about 5 PM, although farmers and others who engaged in physical labor ate three or, when especially active, four meals daily.

The influx of Western civilization after the Meiji Restoration (1868) had an enormous influence on the dietary life of the Japanese people. Superstitions and taboos concerning food began to fade, and the eating of flesh and fowl once again became acceptable. Western foods that gradually became popular included the Irish potato, tomato, onion, cabbage, asparagus, and celery. Demand for

pork, chicken, and eggs increased. Various types of oil, butter, milk, cheese, and other dairy products were incorporated, and Western dishes modified to suit the taste of the Japanese, resulting in such dishes as TONKATSU, or pork cutlets, and *korokke*, or potato croquettes.

The dietary habits of the Japanese underwent an even more substantial change after World War II. The popularization of frozen and instant foods is an outstanding example. And yet at the same time there has been a reaction, a movement to reevaluate Japanese cooking as a cuisine using natural foods. Today, rice remains the primary staple (the word for boiled rice, MESHI or *gohan*, can also mean "meal"), although barley and millet (sometimes boiled together with rice), noodles, and bread are also considered staple foods. As a rule staple foods are unseasoned, whereas side dishes (*sōzai*), including vegetables, fish, and meat, are usually served seasoned. Side dishes served with *sake* and other drinks are called *sakana* (not to be mistaken for fish, also called *sakana*). They are essentially the same as the side dishes eaten in a regular menu.

In traditional Japanese cooking, emphasis is placed on preserving the innate flavor and texture of the ingredients. Complicated cooking procedures are avoided, and the principal concern is the arrangement and display of food in an attractive manner. Japanese cooking relies heavily on *shōyu* (soy sauce) and *miso*, both made from soybeans (see also MISO SOUP). The history of *miso* is long, but *shōyu* did not come into general use until the beginning of the 17th century. *Sake* and MIRIN (a sweet *sake*) are also used for marinating and flavoring. Worcestershire sauce, adapted to fit Japanese tastes, has been in use since the late 19th century. Some traditional Japanese spices are *wasabi* (Japanese horseradish), *sanshō* (Japanese pepper), GINGER, Indian mustard, *yuzu* (citron), WELSH ONION (*negi*), and, less frequently, *tōgarashi* (cayenne pepper; see also HERBS AND SPICES). Stock (dashi) is made from KATSUOBUSHI (dried bonito), KOMBU (kelp), or *niboshi* (boiled and dried baby sardines). This stock is used not only for flavoring foods but also as a soup base. Instant powdered soup stock is now commonly used in Japanese households.

Although Japan suffered from serious food shortages during and after World War II, by the 1990s the country had reached what some have called "the Age of Gluttony," with the majority of the population exceeding medically determined daily caloric requirements. More important, the pro-

portion of calorie intake attributable to fats has increased as the taste for Western foods has grown. Various government health campaigns are now urging people to examine their eating habits and consider the health benefits of the traditional low-fat diet centering on rice, fish, and vegetables.

▶▶ 392–393

food processing industry　食品工業

(*shokuhin kōgyō*). The Japan food processing industry's 1987 production was ¥28.0 trillion (US $193.0 billion), or 11.0 percent of all manufactured goods. The 1,650,000 industry employees represent 11.3 percent of all manufacturing sector employees. The food processing industry relies heavily on smaller companies, with approximately 60.0 percent of all production handled by firms with from 20 to 299 employees. Another significant aspect of the industry is its low capital-labor ratio and labor-intensive character. In 1987 there was ¥6.34 million (US $43,800) in tangible fixed assets per food processing industry employee, compared to ¥7.4 million (US $51,200) for the manufacturing sector as a whole. The growing sophistication and affluence of the Japanese consumer has increased demand for health and natural foods and led to diversification of the food products and package sizes available.

Food Sanitation Law　食品衛生法

(Shokuhin Eisei Hō). Law enacted in 1947 to regulate the sanitation of foodstuffs. The law specifically regulates the following areas: foodstuffs (all food and drink, with the exception of prescription and nonprescription drugs); food additives; implements used to produce, process, transport, or display foods and additives; containers and packages of foodstuffs and additives; and cleaning agents for toys, vegetables, fruits, and eating and drinking utensils.

Food and additives or implements, containers, and packages must be labeled according to prescribed standards. False or deceptive advertisements or statements about foods or additives are prohibited.

Those desiring to operate any of 34 types of food and drinking establishments stipulated by cabinet order must receive permission from the prefectural governor. See also FOOD PROCESSING INDUSTRY.

food service industry　外食産業

(*gaishoku sangyō*). In addition to such eating and drinking establishments as coffee shops, bars, noodle shops, and restaurants, the Japanese food service industry also includes chain facilities that offer meals or take-out services. The market reached ¥23 trillion (US $179.5 billion) in 1988 and represented 10 percent of all personal consumption expenditures. The increase in leisure time and the decrease in time spent on housework by women have contributed to a dramatic expansion in this market. The number of chain restaurants, in particular, has increased in recent years, and their low prices and consistent quality, made possible by centralized preparation and distribution, have led to increased sales.

As a result of capital liberalization and the simplification of the Foreign Investment Law, many new joint-venture companies have been established. These companies include Japan Kentucky Fried Chicken (Mitsubishi Corporation), established 1970; McDonald's Co (Japan), Ltd (Fujita Shōten and Fujita Den), established 1971; and Denny's Japan Co, Ltd (Itō-Yōkadō Co, Ltd), established 1973. Domestic chain restaurant companies include SKYLARK CO, LTD (a chain of American-style family restaurants); Kozō-zushi Hombu Co, Ltd (take-out *sushi*); and Lotteria Co, Ltd (a fast-food chain).

Foodstuff Control Special Account　食糧管理特別会計

(Shokuryō Kanri Tokubetsu Kaikei). The government account for the purchase, sale, and storage of foodstuffs, primarily rice. It was established in 1921 to stabilize the price of rice, which had been fluctuating violently—soaring during World War I (resulting in the RICE RIOTS OF 1918) and plummeting in the postwar depression. Under the current system, the government is committed to purchase an unlimited amount of rice at specified prices. Japan's rice production, however, has increased dramatically as a result of improved agricultural methods, while consumption has declined steadily since 1963 because of changing dietary habits. The accumulation of surplus rice in recent years has led to large deficits in the account, amounting to ¥1.2 trillion (US $9.2 billion) in 1989 and requiring the transfer of funds from the government's general account. In response, the government has tried to encourage a reduction in rice production but has met with little success due to political pressure from farmers and farm organizations. See also RICE PRICE CONTROLS.

foodstuff control system　食糧管理制度

(*shokuryō kanri seido*; abbreviated *shokkan seido*). System by which the national government controls the production and price of rice and wheat according to the Foodstuff Control Law (1942) to assure an adequate food supply for the population. Each farmer produces rice according to the government's estimates of supply and demand. The government buys the rice at a specified price (the "producer rice price") and sells it to distributors licensed by the prefectural government at another specified price (the "government sale price"), which is lower than the total government costs (the producer rice price plus government management costs). The difference between total government costs and the government sale price is called the "backspread" (*gyakuzaya*) in buying and selling, and the total backspread cost constitutes the major part of the deficit in the FOODSTUFF CONTROL SPECIAL ACCOUNT. Since producer prices are higher than they would be if there were a natural balance of supply and demand, more rice is produced than is consumed. A government policy of regulating production through reduction of rice-growing acreage and subsidized crop-conversion programs is thus in effect. See also RICE.

food supply　食糧需給

(*shokuryō jukyū*). Japan has experienced a progressive deterioration in its food self-sufficiency in the years since the end of World War II. This is the result of a number of factors, including the emphasis in economic policy on industrial growth at the expense of agriculture, the dramatic shift in the population from the countryside to the cities, and the increase in the population and its caloric consumption. While the future supply of food from Japan's major import sources (the United States, Canada, and Australia) appears assured, sudden shifts in agricultural policy, lengthy dockworker strikes, or crop-damaging weather in those countries could cause serious shortages.

These possibilities have made the issue of food supply a matter of continuing political concern and debate.

Japan's food self-sufficiency is among the lowest of the industrialized nations. According to government figures, overall self-sufficiency declined from 93 percent in 1960 to 70 percent in 1988. Domestic production provided only 17 percent of Japan's wheat and 6 percent of its soybeans in 1988. Although meat and milk have largely been supplied by domestic producers, their production is highly dependent on foreign sources of animal feed. The self-sufficiency rate for animal feed dropped from 63 percent in 1960 to 26 percent in 1988. Considered on an original calorie basis (in which livestock calories are expressed in terms of the original calories in the feed eaten by the animals) Japan's overall food self-sufficiency rate appears even lower, 52 percent in 1985, compared to 127 percent for the United States, 77 percent for the United Kingdom, and 65 percent for Switzerland.

One important product in which Japan is self-sufficient is RICE, which constitutes a central part of the Japanese diet. Because of its low rate of overall food self-sufficiency, Japan has, at the 1990 GATT (General Agreement on Tariffs and Trade) meetings and elsewhere, opposed liberalization of its rice market as a threat to its food security. See also RICE PRICE CONTROLS; AGRICULTURE.

footgear, traditional　履物

(*hakimono*). According to the 3rd-century Chinese chronicle WEI ZHI (Wei chih), all Japanese of that time went barefoot. Archaeological evidence, however, indicates that some sort of footgear was worn at least as early as the Kofun period (ca 300–710). The cultural influence of China on Japan during the Nara (710–794) and Heian (794–1185) periods fueled the development of ZŌRI, flat thonged sandals made of straw or leather, and GETA, wooden clogs. Most Japanese of the Kamakura (1185–1333) and Muromachi (1333–1568) periods wore *zōri* or, when making long journeys on foot, WARAJI (rough straw sandals). The *samurai* class favored *ashinaka*, *zōri*-like footgear designed for fighting. *Geta* became popular among city dwellers during the Edo period (1600–1868). Specialized traditional footgear included KANJIKI ("cleats"), WARAGUTSU (woven reed snowboots), and TAGETA ("rice-paddy geta"). Western footgear gained initial acceptance during the Meiji period (1868–1912) and became the norm after World War II. Today *zōri* are worn only on special occasions as part of a formal KIMONO ensemble, and *geta* are worn almost exclusively with traditional casual clothing such as the YUKATA. Many carpenters and laborers, however, still regularly wear *jikatabi*, split-toed rubber-soled canvas boots.

foreign aid　海外援助

(*kaigai enjo*). In Japan the term "foreign aid" is synonymous with Japan's official development assistance (ODA), which includes grants-in-aid, technical assistance, loan aid, and financial support contributed to international organizations engaged in development and relief work. The term "economic cooperation" (*keizai kyōryoku*) covers a wider range of activities that include foreign aid, other official flows such as government support for export credits, and private flows such as private export credits, direct investment, and grants by private voluntary organizations.

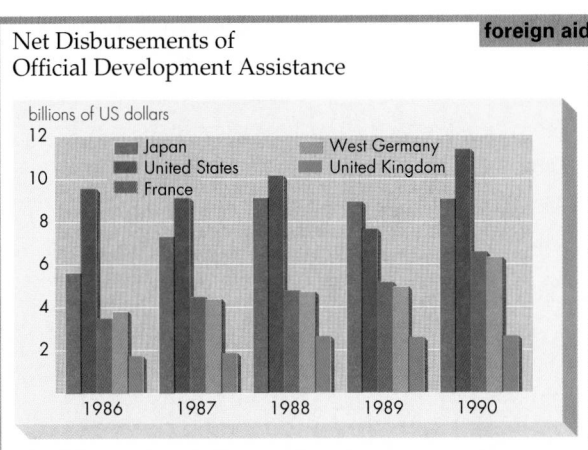

Net Disbursements of Official Development Assistance

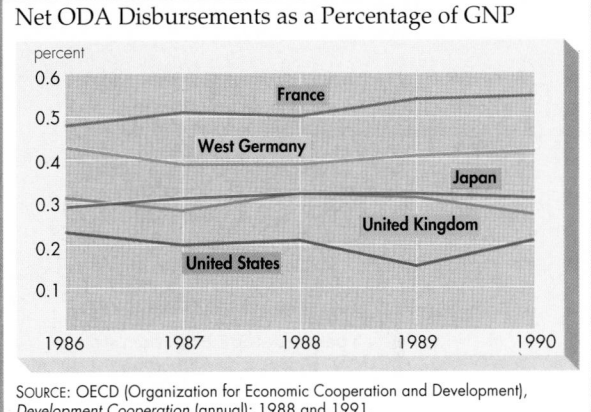

Net ODA Disbursements as a Percentage of GNP

SOURCE: OECD (Organization for Economic Cooperation and Development), *Development Cooperation* (annual): 1988 and 1991.

With an outlay of US $9.22 billion in foreign aid in 1990, Japan became the world's second largest aid donor, as measured by the disbursement of official development assistance by the industrial countries represented in the Development Assistance Committee (DAC) of the Organization for Economic Cooperation and Development (OECD). However, measured as a percentage of gross national product (GNP), at 0.31 percent Japanese aid ranked 12th among DAC nations and was slightly less than the DAC average of 0.35 percent. Japanese aid in 1990 was 16.7 percent of the total disbursed by all DAC nations.

In 1990, 59.3 percent of Japanese official development assistance went to Asia, 11.4 percent to Africa, 10.2 percent to the Middle East, and 8.1 percent to Central and South America. Between 1987 and 1990 Indonesia was the largest single aid recipient at 12.5 percent, followed by China, 10.4 percent; the Philippines, 9.3 percent; Thailand, 6.0 percent; and Bangladesh, 5.4 percent.

Aid Administration——The administration of official Japanese aid programs and policies rests with a number of government ministries and agencies, in particular the MINISTRY OF FOREIGN AFFAIRS, the MINISTRY OF FINANCE, the MINISTRY OF INTERNATIONAL TRADE AND INDUSTRY (MITI), and the ECONOMIC PLANNING AGENCY. They are backed up by three government-funded institutions, the OVERSEAS ECONOMIC COOPERATION FUND, the EXPORT-IMPORT BANK OF JAPAN, and the JAPAN INTERNATIONAL COOPERATION AGENCY, which respectively oversee the disbursement of soft loans, export credits, and technical assistance and grant aid. There is no central aid agency as in some other donor countries, and the administration of aid policy has always been characterized by differences in approach among the main ministries and by disagreement over how aid policy can help Japan fulfill its international duties.

Foreign Currency Reserves in Selected Countries

billions of US dollars

Japan

West Germany

United States

France

Italy

United Kingdom

1970　1975　1980　1985　1990

SOURCE: Bank of Japan, *Kokusai hikaku tōkei* (annual): 1981, 1986, 1991.

foreign employees of the Meiji period
Foreign experts played an important role in the modernization of Japan during the Meiji period. Pictured in this 1871 photograph are (from left) James R. Clark, Horace Capron, Thomas Antisell, A. G. Warfield, and Stuart Eldridge, all of whom helped with the settling of Hokkaidō.

Changes in Aid Policy—Japanese foreign aid following World War II began in the 1950s in the form of reparations payments to Burma, the Philippines, Indonesia, and Vietnam and grants resembling reparations to several other Asian nations, including South Korea (the Republic of Korea; see REPARATIONS FOR SOUTHEAST ASIA). This was followed by a period in the 1960s when strong export expansion was a principal interest in foreign aid programs. In the late 1960s and early 1970s the provision of aid and investment aimed at securing agricultural and raw material supplies, called "development import" (*kaihatsu yunyū*) assistance, became a dominant emphasis.

The marked contrast between the stances taken by Japan at the First United Nations Conference on Trade and Development (UNCTAD I), held in Geneva in 1964, and the fifth conference (UNCTAD V), held in Manila in 1979, illustrates clearly the significant change in the Japanese approach to economic cooperation with developing countries as a focus in foreign economic policy. The former meeting saw Japan, preoccupied with its own program of heavy industrialization and economic relations with the advanced powers, adopting a very negative attitude toward development assistance and the developing countries' case for preferred access to export markets in developed countries. By the time of the 1979 meeting, however, development issues were at the forefront of Japan's foreign policy interests; Japan had become the fourth or fifth largest aid donor, with ODA spending of about US

$2.6 billion. In 1978 Prime Minister FUKUDA TAKEO had responded to continuing criticism of Japan's efforts by promising to double the disbursement of Japan's official development assistance within three years. Between 1977 and 1990 annual ODA spending increased over sixfold to reach US $9.2 billion.

In 1988 the government set the medium-term target for official development assistance for the period 1988–92 at over US $50 billion, more than double the disbursements for the 1983–87 period. The government has emphasized that a priority will be increasing the ODA grant aid component in accordance with the international view that grants ought to be the principal form of aid, and also in response to requests from poorer countries that are in urgent need of this form of aid. Grant aid—funds provided without the need for repayment—should be distinguished from the grant element (GE) of official development assistance, which is an index of the financial terms of aid rendered. The grant element of a commercial loan (with interest rate above 10 percent) is zero percent, and as the terms (interest rate, repayment period, grace period) are relaxed, the GE figure rises, reaching 100 percent in the case of a grant. The grant aid share of Japan's total official development assistance, which was only 43.2 percent in 1988–89, was the lowest among the 18 DAC countries; and at 77.6 percent, Japan's grant element was also the lowest among DAC member states during that period. It is these two figures, for grant aid share and grant element, that the government has committed itself to increase.

The government has also sought to broaden the geographical scope of Japanese aid, which has tended to be concentrated on Asia; accordingly, Africa's share of total bilateral official development assistance consistently increased during the 1980s (though its share dropped slightly in 1990). It is also intended to increase aid significantly to Central America and the South Pacific, which have traditionally received very little Japanese aid. In response to Japan's increasing worldwide economic impact in the 1980s, the government has gradually moved beyond narrow economic objectives in an effort to shoulder greater responsibility in the international economy. See also YEN CREDIT.

foreign attorneys　外国弁護士

(*gaikoku bengoshi*). Foreign attorneys are permitted to practice law in Japan as "attorneys of foreign law." In order to adjudicate more comprehensively cases which relate both to Japan and a foreign country and in response to complaints from various countries that the Japanese legal profession was closed to foreigners, a law came into effect on 1 April 1987 enabling attorneys qualified to practice law in a foreign country to open an office in Japan upon obtaining permission from the minister of justice and registering with the JAPAN FEDERATION OF BAR ASSOCIATIONS. The following are among the many regulations that apply to attorneys of foreign law: (1) practice is limited to attorneys from nations where Japanese attorneys are permitted to practice; (2) they must submit to the rules and supervision of the Japan Federation of Bar Associations; (3) their practice is limited to the law of the country of their qualification and to the law of other foreign countries designated by the minister of justice; and (4) foreign attorneys are prohibited from forming partnerships with Japanese attorneys. As of April 1991, 80 foreign

attorneys were registered to practice in Japan.

foreign banks in Japan　在日外国銀行

(*zainichi gaikoku ginkō*). With the liberalization and internationalization of Japanese finance, there has been a substantial increase in the number of foreign banks operating in Japan. Most begin by opening branches, while others establish themselves in Japan by setting up overseas affiliates. All are referred to as foreign banks in Japan. At the end of 1989 there were 82 foreign banks with 119 branches, as well as 9 foreign trust banks. Once a foreign bank has obtained a license from the minister of finance, it is officially allowed to provide the same services as any Japanese bank. Many foreign banks in Japan now specialize in wholesale banking, but there are also moves to develop retail banking.

foreign concessions, 19th century
→kyoryūchi

foreign currency reserves
外貨準備高

(*gaika jumbidaka*). Gold and foreign currency held by the government and the BANK OF JAPAN for use in making payments in foreign countries. Until the mid-1970s there had been a continuous foreign currency shortage. For the next ten years or so Japan's foreign currency reserves rose gradually, then began to increase drastically in 1986 as a result of the large-scale dollar purchases made by Japan's monetary authorities in response to the drop in the value of the dollar that followed the PLAZA ACCORD in September 1985. In the late 1980s Japan's foreign currency reserves were the largest in the world, but as a result of large-scale selling of dollars following the strengthening of the dollar relative to the yen in 1989, these reserves have been steadily decreasing.

foreign employees of the Meiji period　御雇外国人

(*oyatoi gaikokujin;* literally, "hired foreigners"). The several thousand foreign teachers, technologists, and advisers who were hired by the Japanese government in the Meiji period (1868–1912) to provide expertise in the wide range of fields in which it was felt that the West excelled. The primary function of the foreign employees was to assist Japan in its quest for modernity and equality with Western nations.

In April 1868 the young Emperor Meiji promulgated the CHARTER OATH, calling upon the people to eschew old-fashioned ways and insisting that "knowledge shall be sought throughout the world." In response, increasing numbers of Japanese students were sent abroad to study, and foreigners were brought to Japan by the Meiji government to teach such subjects as military science, engineering, foreign affairs, agriculture, surveying, and medicine. These *oyatoi gaikokujin*, together with the many foreigners in private Japanese employ, played a significant role in the rapid transformation of Japan from feudal backwardness into a world power in little more than a generation.

The years following the Meiji Restoration of 1868 saw a quickening of the process of absorbing Western ideas, methods, and materials. Japan paid the entire cost of hiring and transporting several thousand foreigners to Japan. The foreigners were given no real policy-making authority. Their job was to implement policy decisions already made

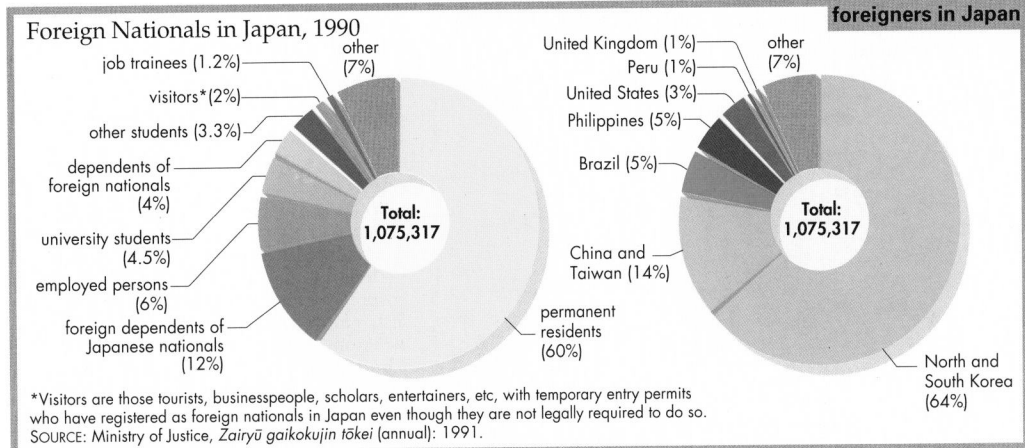

Foreign Nationals in Japan, 1990

job trainees (1.2%)
visitors* (2%)
other students (3.3%)
dependents of foreign nationals (4%)
university students (4.5%)
employed persons (6%)
foreign dependents of Japanese nationals (12%)
other (7%)
permanent residents (60%)

Total: 1,075,317

United Kingdom (1%)
Peru (1%)
United States (3%)
Philippines (5%)
Brazil (5%)
other (7%)
China and Taiwan (14%)
North and South Korea (64%)

Total: 1,075,317

*Visitors are those tourists, businesspeople, scholars, entertainers, etc, with temporary entry permits who have registered as foreign nationals in Japan even though they are not legally required to do so.
SOURCE: Ministry of Justice, *Zairyū gaikokujin tōkei* (annual): 1991.

and to train Japanese to take over their functions. The term *oyatoi gaikokujin* itself reflected the prevailing Japanese attitude, as did its shortened form *yatoi*, or "hired hand," both of which carried a pejorative flavor.

Most of the foreigners were paid very well and, indeed, often handsomely. It has been estimated that fully three-fourths of all *oyatoi gaikokujin* received salaries equal to those of Japanese officials in the first and second levels of the bureaucratic hierarchy.

More than two dozen nations have been identified as providing *oyatoi gaikokujin* to the Japanese government, but most of the foreigners were English, German, French, and American. Teachers and engineers made up a majority. Foreign employees who played a significant role in Japan's modernization included Guido VERBECK, K.F. Hermann ROESLER, Ernest FENOLLOSA, Captain Frank BRINKLEY, Gustave BOISSONADE DE FONTARABIE, Edward S. MORSE, Henry DENISON, Horace CAPRON, Basil Hall CHAMBERLAIN, Edoardo CHIOSSONE, William Smith CLARK, David MURRAY, and Richard H. BRUNTON.

foreigners in Japan 在日外国人

(*zainichi gaikokujin*). The number of foreign nationals resident in Japan steadily increased throughout the 1980s to 1,075,317 in 1990—a 26.4 percent increase over 1985. This figure includes only foreigners registered in accordance with the Alien Registration Law; tourists in Japan for less than 90 days, children under the age of two months, and members of foreign diplomatic services are not included, except for the small number who register without being required to do so. The largest national group represented, accounting for 64 percent of the total, is composed of North and South Koreans (687,940), followed by citizens of China and Taiwan (150,339), Brazil (56,429), the Philippines (49,092), and the United States (38,364). Whereas the number of other foreign nationals resident in Japan has continued to grow, the population of North and South Korean nationals has actually decreased slightly as a result of the amendment of Japan's Nationality Law in 1985, which made more Korean residents of mixed parentage eligible to become Japanese citizens.

Since the implementation of the revised Immigration Control Law in 1990, regulations governing employment of foreigners have been more strictly enforced; however, the revised law also makes foreign nationals of Japanese descent eligible for permanent resident status, and their numbers have suddenly increased. For example, the number of Brazilians of Japanese descent resident in Japan increased almost 29 times between 1985 and 1990.

Fifty-five percent of all foreigners in Japan live in the four prefectures of Tōkyō, Ōsaka, Hyōgo, and Aichi, with the highest concentration in Tōkyō, where there are 213,056 foreign nationals. Of registered aliens in Japan, 60.0 percent were permanent residents in 1989; the rest were in the country as temporary residents pursuing a variety of activities, drawn to Japan by increasing foreign direct investment, by employment opportunities offered by the growing demand of Japanese firms for FOREIGN WORKERS, and by the chance to study in Japan (see FOREIGN STUDENTS IN JAPAN). The influx of workers from South America, South and Southeast Asia, and the Middle East—a significant number of whom are employed illegally—has become a much-discussed trend.

The number of international marriages increased 3.5 times between 1965 and 1985. From 1975 onward, the number of marriages involving Japanese men and foreign women—many from China, Korea, or the Philippines—surpassed the number of Japanese women marrying foreign men.

A number of Japanese local government organizations have begun to implement new services to respond to the needs of foreign residents, such as the publication of information pamphlets in English, Chinese, and Portuguese and the assignment of English-speaking personnel to provide assistance (the Tōkyō Metropolitan Government has staffers fluent in English, Chinese, and French). Since many foreign nationals of Japanese descent bring their families with them to Japan, special courses are being set up in elementary schools in areas where their numbers are especially concentrated. See also KOREANS IN JAPAN; ALIEN REGISTRATION.

foreigners, legal status of 外国人の法的地位

(*gaikokujin no hōteki chii*). The legal status of foreigners in Japan is principally regulated by the Alien Registration Law (Gaikokujin Tōroku Hō) of 1952, as amended. Under the law, *gaikokujin* (foreigner or alien) refers to all persons without Japanese citizenship. Persons holding citizenship in both Japan and another country are regarded as Japanese citizens unless they explicitly waive their Japanese citizenship. The legal status of aliens in Japan is essentially the same as that of the Japanese: they are under Japanese sovereignty and must obey Japanese law. Under public law, aliens do not have the right to participate in Japan's political process, but they generally have the same tax obligations as Japanese citizens. Their entry into and departure from Japan are legally regulated, and aliens residing in Japan for more than one year must obtain certificates of ALIEN REGISTRATION. In private law, equal rights are provided for both Japanese and aliens, though there are certain important restrictions applicable only to the latter. Aliens are denied the right to own shipping companies and mines, and their right to own land and to demand compensation for damages from the state or public bodies is limited. Special restrictions also exist on their right to acquire patents, trademarks, and copyrights. See also FOREIGNERS IN JAPAN.

Foreign Exchange and Foreign Trade Control Law 外国為替及び外国貿易管理法

(FECL; J: Gaikoku Kawase oyobi Gaikoku Bōeki Kanri Hō). The basic law concerning trade and foreign exchange, its purpose is to normalize trade and maintain the balance of international payments. It was enacted in 1949 with the resumption of private trade

following World War II and was substantially amended in 1979. In Japan, the law is often called the Foreign Exchange Law (Gaikoku Kawase Hō; abbreviated as Gaitame Hō).

The 1949 law was based on the principle of allowing freer trade than the prewar Foreign Exchange Law (1933), but a high level of governmental control was maintained. This control has since been relaxed, most significantly in 1979 with liberalizing amendments. Changes brought about by the 1979 amendments include the following: whereas payments involving foreign parties, and the acquisition or transfer of foreign bonds, securities, or real property had previously been prohibited in principle except for special exceptions, such transactions are now freely allowed in principle with restrictions in special cases. Also, the Foreign Investment Law of 1950 (Gaishi ni kansuru Hōritsu; see FOREIGN EXCHANGE CONTROLS) was abolished, and the regulation of foreign capital transactions was placed under the Foreign Exchange Law. Under the 1979 law, exchange controls on payments and financial transactions may be instituted only when there is a recognized need—for instance, to maintain the BALANCE OF PAYMENTS.

Trade controls are as follows: under export control regulations, the government can impose an obligation to obtain approval for exports in order to maintain the balance of payments. Exporters are obliged to collect payments for exports, and the shipment of goods can be halted in cases of emergency. Import control regulations authorize the imposition of an import approval system if it is necessary to maintain the healthy development of the national economy. Import quotas are retained on some items, and prior authorization is required for imports from designated areas. See also FOREIGN INVESTMENT IN JAPAN.

foreign exchange controls 外国為替管理

(*gaikoku kawase kan'ri*). Legal and extralegal arrangements concerning the use of national and foreign currencies and other means of financing exports, imports, and foreign investments. Before 1930 no extensive control of foreign exchange transactions existed in Japan and relatively free trade prevailed. A system of controls came into being during the 1930s and formed an integral part of the overall war-oriented economy, which involved comprehensive control of production, distribution, and foreign trade. In post–World War II Japan, the system evolved until 1978 around two related laws: the FOREIGN EXCHANGE AND FOREIGN TRADE CONTROL LAW (FECL) and the Foreign Investment Law (FIL), enacted in 1949 and 1950, respec-

397

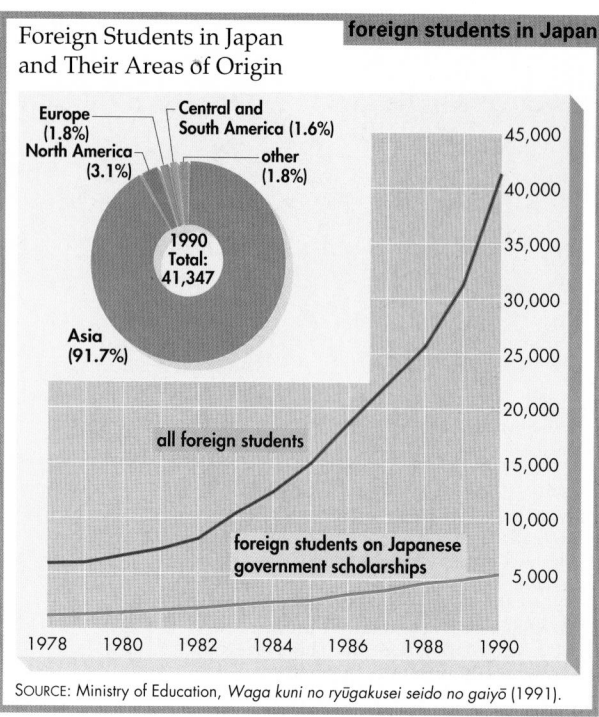

Foreign Students in Japan and Their Areas of Origin

Europe (1.8%)
North America (3.1%)
Central and South America (1.6%)
other (1.8%)

1990 Total: 41,347

Asia (91.7%)

all foreign students

foreign students on Japanese government scholarships

1978 1980 1982 1984 1986 1988 1990

SOURCE: Ministry of Education, *Waga kuni no ryūgakusei seido no gaiyō* (1991).

tively. These laws provided the legal framework through which the Japanese government regulated the kind and extent of foreign goods, capital, and technology entering Japan with the objective of protecting and promoting domestic industries. Many postwar laws pertaining to regulation of foreign trade find their prototypes among the laws promulgated for similar objectives dating back to the 1930s, including the FECL, which had its origin in the prewar Foreign Exchange Control Law of 1933. Both before and after the war, the nation needed to rapidly accelerate domestic production. The rationale for control was that the Japanese economy was so vulnerable that without control and regulation the nation would be unable to maintain its BALANCE OF PAYMENTS equilibrium.

In recent years, however, Japan has been the object of increasing criticism from abroad for its controls on foreign exchange. The speed of deregulation—the easing of import restrictions and the relaxation of control over capital transactions—has been judged too slow relative to what is expected of Japan as a member of the community of advanced nations. In 1977 and 1978 the government responded by significantly liberalizing foreign exchange transactions and procedures for settlement methods, remittances, foreign currency deposits, hedging operations, transactions in gold and real estate, outward and inward direct investments, and introduction of foreign technologies. It went on to make amendments to the FECL in 1979 that abolished the FIL and placed the regulation of foreign capital transactions under the FECL. By the end of 1980 the legal situation had been changed so that exchange transactions would henceforth be governed by general principles of freedom and access rather than by principles of prohibition and restriction. Restrictions were to be allowed only under special circumstances, such as during wild fluctuations of exchange rates or during major disturbances in the equilibrium of the international balance of payments. As a result, long-term capital outflows from Japan increased from about US $10 billion in 1981 to US $86 billion in 1986. In 1985 Japan surpassed the Organization of Petroleum Exporting Countries (OPEC) to become the world's leading creditor.

In 1984 Japan responded to further American pressure for liberalization of its financial markets by abolishing the principle of actual demand in forward foreign exchange transactions and by lifting restrictions on contract periods. Limits on the acquisition of specified corporate stocks by foreign investors were also removed, and Japan agreed to remove restrictions on Euro-yen bonds and banking. Considerably fuller foreign participation in Japanese financial markets was guaranteed by deregulatory measures taken between 1985 and 1987 in line with the US-Japan Yen-Dollar Committee report of 1984 (see YEN). As a result of all the changes introduced, especially since 1979, Japan's foreign exchange practices now accord much more with those prevailing in other developed nations, and Tōkyō is on a par with New York and London as an international financial center.

foreign investment in Japan
在日外資

(*zainichi gaishi*). Foreign investment in Japan includes whole and part ownership of companies or subsidiaries, the establishment of branch offices, capital ownership in Japanese firms, joint ventures, and technical and financial assistance agreements.

Early History—After the Meiji Restoration of 1868, both the government and newly formed enterprises sought technical assistance from overseas. Direct ties with foreign firms were perceived at the time as expedient vehicles for obtaining technology, access to foreign markets, capital, and expertise in factory management.

Through technical tie-ups and the large-scale recruitment of American and European engineers and technicians, various industrial technologies were brought into Japan. Out of fear of foreign domination, however, Japan resisted the introduction of direct subsidiaries. When the Japanese had acquired the expertise or technology they desired, the foreign instructors were sent home. See FOREIGN EMPLOYEES OF THE MEIJI PERIOD.

From the Sino-Japanese War of 1894–95 until the outbreak of World War I, emerging Japanese firms in the heavy manufacturing and chemical industries sought selective but more direct tie-ups with leading American and European manufacturing firms. Whereas in the previous period it had been sufficient to learn how to operate imported machinery, these firms now required closer access to proprietary technologies held by the Western industrial firms. At this juncture, American and European firms began to extend specialized technical assistance to Japanese firms through technical licensing agreements. This was sometimes done in exchange for part ownership of the Japanese licensee's voting capital. General Electric of the United States and the predecessor of TŌSHIBA CORPORATION entered into such a relationship for manufacturing light bulbs, and Tōshiba was subsequently granted exclusive access to General Electric's technological developments. Nippon Electric Co was established as a joint venture with International Telephone and Telegraph of the United States, and Mitsubishi Electric Co obtained technical assistance from Westinghouse Electric International of the United States.

Postwar Foreign Investment—Following the formal close in 1952 of the Allied Occupation of Japan, the Japanese government implemented a system of indicative ECONOMIC PLANNING that guided the pace and direction of the nation's growth. A key element in this planned growth was the control of foreign investment. Outright foreign operations by wholly owned or majority-owned subsidiaries were initially prohibited and only gradually decontrolled, and Japanese financial borrowing from foreign firms was restricted and carefully screened. The only permissible form of foreign investment was the technical licensing agreement, and even these agreements were carefully screened by the government.

Until the early 1960s, Japan remained relatively unattractive and somewhat mysterious to potential investors. Very few foreign firms foresaw Japan's rapid industrial recovery from the devastation of World War II. Rather than setting up shop in Japan, many foreign firms chose simply to sell their standard technologies to the Japanese. Foreign firms that did attempt to open their own factories in Japan faced a choice of being shut out of the market or earning only incremental returns through the licensing of their technologies.

Japan's practice of freely engaging in international trade and investment while exercising strict control of such activities at home did not last long. As exports of manufactured goods increased, foreign pressure mounted for Japan to open its markets to foreign goods and services. After 1960 Japan began to liberalize imports by lifting such nontariff barriers as quotas and cumbersome import restrictions. The first industries to be opened to foreign investment were those unlikely to attract foreign capital—soy-sauce brewing is a typical example.

After 1968, however, Japan expanded the number of industries in which foreign firms were permitted to establish subsidiaries. Foreign investment increased gradually throughout the 1970s and 1980s, but in the early 1990s entry into the Japanese market was still seen as a difficult process by many foreign companies. Some of the most common reasons given were the complicated Japanese distribution system, exclusionary tactics among affiliated Japanese companies, and the difficulty of finding qualified Japanese executives willing to work at a foreign company.

That it is possible, however, for a foreign company to establish profitable operations in Japan is evidenced by such success stories as IBM Japan, Ltd; Coca-Cola (Japan) Co, Ltd; and Procter & Gamble Co. IBM, which first entered the Japanese market in 1937, held the top share of the Japanese business computer market in the early 1990s. Coca-Cola, which entered Japan with the US Occupation forces just after World War II, now has about a 50 percent share of the Japanese market for soft drinks. Procter & Gamble is also considered a market leader.

In 1990 the country-by-country breakdown of 2,884 foreign companies operating in Japan was as follows: the United States, 46.8 percent; Germany, 11.4 percent; Great Britain, 10.2 percent; France, 6.7 percent; Switzerland, 6.0 percent; Asian countries, 4.8 percent; other countries, 14.1 percent. Of these companies, 1,379 were 100 percent foreign owned (i.e., the percentage of foreign capital was 100 percent); 489 were between 50 and 100 percent foreign owned; 614 were 50 percent foreign owned; and 402 were less than 50 percent foreign owned.

▶▶ 400–401

Foreign Investment Law→
foreign exchange controls

foreign law, study of 外国法の研究

(gaikokuhō no kenkyū). The modernization of Japan beginning in the mid-19th century was a Westernization process, and thus the incorporation of Western legal systems occurred as a matter of course. Incorporation, however, does not mean mere transplantation or translation of one legal system into another culture. Sensible adaptation requires analysis of the structure and implications of foreign legal ideas, as well as their origins, purposes, and effects. Therefore, many scholars in Japan tried to comprehend Western legal ideas that were based on individual rights and to assess the possibility of their acceptance in their own collectivity-oriented culture. The natural first step was to translate Western laws into Japanese. Transplanted into Japan in this manner were French laws in the years 1868–80, German laws during the period 1880–1945 (i.e., from the time when the Meiji Constitution, constructed on a German model, was being enacted until the end of World War II), and American laws during the post–World War II Occupation period (1945–52) and after.

Eminent foreign scholars in each of these fields taught at universities and participated in legal reform activities, including, during the Meiji period (1868–1912), Gustave Emile BOISSONADE DE FONTARABIE and K. F. H. ROESLER. Among Japan's leading prewar specialists in foreign law were HOZUMI NOBUSHIGE and TAKAYANAGI KENZŌ (English law), UME KENJIRŌ and SUGIYAMA NAOJIRŌ (French law), and OKANO KEIJIRŌ and MATSUMOTO JŌJI (German law). After World War II, the study of foreign law became more methodical, reflective, and comprehensive. Many active learned societies were established, of which the largest is the Hikakuhō Gakkai (Comparative Law Association).

foreign policy → international relations, history of

foreign students in Japan
外国人留学生

(gaikokujin ryūgakusei). The first foreign students to study in Japan were the 13 dispatched by China after the Sino-Japanese War of 1894–95. In 1949 the Japanese government began granting scholarships to students from Asian countries. In 1954 Japanese government scholarships for foreign students (the so-called Mombushō scholarships) were established. By 1990 approximately 38,000 foreign students from more than 100 countries had studied in Japan under these scholarships. At present Japan accepts foreign students in two categories—those receiving Japanese government scholarships and those receiving government or private support from their own countries (the latter category includes exchange students in reciprocal programs). Students receiving Japanese government scholarships are themselves divided into two categories: research students, who pursue graduate-level studies, and undergraduate students, who enroll in university departments, technical colleges, or special training schools. Government scholarship students in fiscal 1990 numbered 4,961, of whom more than 90 percent were Asians. Students not on Japanese government scholarships numbered 36,386 in 1990, most of them specializing in social sciences and the humanities.

Since 1980 the total number of foreign students in Japan has grown each year, increasing from 6,572 in 1980 to 41,347 in 1990.

However, these figures are still small when compared with the 343,780 foreign students in the United States in 1985; with West Germany's 79,354 in 1985; and with France's 133,848 in 1984. Hoping to admit 100,000 foreign students into Japan by the year 2000, the Ministry of Education is increasing the number of Japanese government scholarship recipients.

foreign trade
貿易

(bōeki). Narrowly defined, foreign trade refers to the import of goods and services into Japan and the export of goods and services from Japan to other countries. However, in the sense of international commerce, it can be considered to include financial or capital flows as well.

The Opening of Japan—Japan's modern foreign trade officially began in 1859. The Tokugawa shogunate (1603–1867) at Edo (now Tōkyō) until then had maintained a policy of NATIONAL SECLUSION. However, with the signing of the HARRIS TREATY (United States–Japan Treaty of Amity and Commerce) in July 1858, Japan opened its doors to Western commerce. At the outset the most important Japanese export was raw silk. High-quality Japanese raw silk was welcomed in the European market as an alternative to raw silk from China. Other exports were primarily raw material goods, semimanufactures, and foodstuffs; these included tea, copper ware, marine products, medicine, oil, and lacquer ware. Key imports were cotton thread, cotton and wool textiles, ironware, sugar, medicinal herbs, military ships, and guns. Approximately 80 percent of Japan's trade was with the United Kingdom, the next largest trading partners being the United States and the Netherlands. There was also a relatively small amount of trade with France and Russia.

In the four to five years after trading began, Japan maintained a continual surplus balance of trade, and domestic prices soared because of the large volume of goods flowing out of the country. However, because Japan lowered import tariffs after the signing of the Tariff Convention of 1866, imports of manufactured goods increased, and Japan entered a period of deficit trade balances. Trade treaties concluded during this period did not recognize Japan's right to set its own customs duties, and Japan did not obtain tariff autonomy until 1911 (see UNEQUAL TREATIES, REVISION OF).

From the Meiji Restoration (1868) to World War I—After the MEIJI RESTORATION, Japanese foreign trade, including both exports and imports, increased dramatically every year. As part of its efforts to increase production and modernize Japanese industry, the government actively worked to further foreign trade and, beginning with a display of goods at the 1873 Vienna International Exposition, promoted overseas such products as raw silk, tea, hemp, tobacco, camphor, and soy. Considering individual products, raw silk's percentage of total exports gradually declined from the level of more than 70 percent in 1863. Manufactured goods such as matches, silk products, cotton thread, and cotton textiles began to be exported around 1890. Initially, 80 percent of imports consisted of cotton and wool textiles, metal, and ships. Cotton thread imports largely replaced those of cotton and wool textiles by 1900. After 1900, raw cotton imports replaced cotton thread, iron became the primary metal import, and ship imports were supplanted by various types of machinery.

The Senshū Kaisha (a trading company and predecessor of MITSUI & CO, LTD) was formed in 1874 by INOUE KAORU. However, in the early Meiji period (1868–1912) almost all commercial trading rights were held by foreign merchants, primarily English traders. According to an 1877 study, 94 percent of all exports were handled by foreign firms.

Japan's trade volume, which in 1870 had been less than ¥30 million (US $84,000), exceeded ¥500 million (US $1.4 million) by World War I. During the 47 years from 1868 to 1915, there were only 12 years in which

Continued on page 402 ►

Japan's Exports to and Imports from Major Trading Partners, 1970–1990   foreign trade

Country	1970 Exports	1970 Imports	1975 Exports	1975 Imports	1980 Exports	1980 Imports	1985 Exports	1985 Imports	1990 Exports	1990 Imports
	(in millions of US dollars)									
United States	5,939.8	5,559.6	11,148.6	11,608.1	31,367.3	24,408.0	65,277.6	25,793.0	90,322.4	52,368.6
West Germany	550.2	617.0	1,660.7	1,139.0	5,756.4	2,500.8	6,937.8	2,928.0	17,782.0	11,487.1
South Korea	818.2	229.0	2,247.7	1,308.0	5,368.3	2,996.3	7,097.2	4,091.9	17,457.2	11,706.7
United Kingdom	479.9	395.2	1,473.2	810.5	3,781.9	1,954.4	4,722.8	1,816.8	10,786.1	5,238.7
Australia	589.0	1,597.7	1,738.9	4,156.1	3,388.9	6,981.6	5,379.0	7,452.2	6,900.3	12,368.8
Canada	563.3	928.6	1,150.8	2,498.8	2,436.6	4,724.2	4,520.2	4,772.9	6,726.5	8,392.2
China	568.9	253.8	2,258.6	1,531.1	5,078.3	4,323.4	12,477.4	6,482.7	6,129.5	12,053.5
France	127.3	186.4	699.2	500.8	2,021.2	1,295.6	2,083.1	1,323.7	6,127.8	7,589.6
Italy	192.1	134.4	333.6	365.2	955.3	938.5	1,116.7	1,049.8	3,408.6	5,008.2
Soviet Union	340.9	481.0	1,626.2	1,169.6	2,778.2	1,859.9	2,750.6	1,429.3	2,562.8	3,351.0

NOTE: Exports are calculated on a free on board (FOB) basis, and imports are calculated on a cost, insurance, and freight (CIF) basis.
SOURCE: Japan Tariff Association, Gaikoku bōeki gaikyō (monthly): December issues, 1970, 1975, 1980, 1985, 1990.

Foreign Trade Per Capita and Degree of Dependency on Foreign Trade, 1990

Country	Foreign trade per capita[1] Exports (in US dollars)[3]	Foreign trade per capita[1] Imports (in US dollars)[4]	Dependency on foreign trade[2] Exports (in percentages)	Dependency on foreign trade[2] Imports (in percentages)
Hong Kong	14,264	14,318	115.1	115.6
Switzerland	9,592	10,478	27.1	29.6
Netherlands	8,888	8,503	47.0	45.0
United States	1,583	2,075	7.1	9.4
Canada	5,022	4,762	22.8	22.0
France	3,857	4,174	18.2	19.7
United Kingdom	3,237	3,895	18.8	22.8
Italy	2,962	3,164	15.7	16.8
Japan	2,331	1,907	9.7	7.9
West Germany	6,774	5,723	27.2	22.9
South Korea	1,533	1,643	26.8	28.8

[1]Calculated by dividing trade values by 1989 estimated population.
[2]Calculated by dividing trade values by GDP for Hong Kong, by GNP for others.
[3]Calculated on a free on board (FOB) basis, except for US exports, which are calculated on a free alongside ship (FAS) basis.
[4]Calculated on the basis of cost, insurance, and freight (CIF).
SOURCE: Bank of Japan, Kokusai hikaku tōkei (annual): 1991 and 1992.

Breaking into the Japanese Market: Foreign Companies and Products in Japan

Despite ongoing complaints about Japan's restrictive trade policies and byzantine distribution system, a growing number of American and European businesses are taking root in foreign soil.

One of the most puzzling misconceptions the world has about Japan is that the Japanese have a strong cultural bias against foreign products. What makes the persistence of this myth particularly odd is that it is disproved by simple statistics. Between 1985 and 1990, for example, Japan's imports of consumer goods nearly tripled. By the beginning of the 1990s, the Japanese were spending as much per capita on American merchandise as Americans were spending per capita on Japanese merchandise.

Statistics alone cannot convey the prestige associated with foreign products. For an affluent Japanese male, nothing establishes the aura of success more than driving a BMW or a Mercedes. The upmarket man is likely to have his own bottle of Scotch whisky on reserve at his favorite bar, and, if he smokes, his brand will almost certainly be a foreign one such as Lark or Marlboro.

Supplying those near and dear to him with comparable indulgences is also a point of pride for the successful Japanese male. For cosmetics, his wife may favor the Clinique line; for handbags and leather accessories, Gucci; and when she sets off on a trip abroad, it will be with Louis Vuitton luggage.

The children of chic parents, naturally, have the best—clothes by Italy's Bennetton and toys by the Japanese subsidiary of Denmark's Lego. Even the family pets may contribute to the national import bill. A beloved cat or dog may feast on one of the carefully formulated pet foods produced by subsidiaries of America's Mars Company.

Although the buying habits of prosperous Japanese are significant, of even greater importance is the degree to which foreign goods or products made in Japan by foreign-owned companies have become part of everyday life for middle-class Japanese. Chances are three out of four, for instance, that a Japanese "salaryman" will begin his day by shaving with an American-made razor blade (unless he happens to use an electric razor). For breakfast, a typical young Japanese couple might have a cup of Maxim's instant coffee, toast, and perhaps a bit of fruit from one of the Tupperware food storage containers in the refrigerator. And if the baby needs changing, there's a good chance the parents will reach for a box of Pampers, which were the first disposable diapers sold in Japan and which, despite substantial domestic competition, still remain one of the three most popular brands.

A casual stroll through any Japanese city will reveal the wide range of foreign companies and products that have taken root. McDonald's is the country's biggest food service operation and is so much a part of the national scene that Japanese children have been known to express surprise at the discovery there are McDonald's in America too. But if McDonald's outlets are the most ubiquitous, other American food chains—Kentucky Fried Chicken, Domino's Pizza, and Dunkin' Donuts, to name a few—are familiar sights as well. At every turn one's eye falls on the advertisements and vending machines of giant

Coca-Cola Japan, whose products, some of which were developed exclusively for the Japanese market, account for half of all carbonated beverages sold in the country.

For the American tourist with a sweet tooth, Japan's streets and shops offer a wide variety of familiar temptations: M & M's candies, Nestlés' chocolate bars, Dentyne and Chiclets chewing gum, Häagen Dazs and Baskin-Robbins ice cream, Chips Ahoy, and David's Cookies. Supermarket shelves display processed foods galore by Nestlé (which in 1988 did some $4 billion worth of business in Japan), as well as an ever-growing array of other foreign products ranging from Knorr's soups to Ritz crackers. Drugstores dispense remedies produced by foreign pharmaceutical firms including Merck, Warner-Lambert, Bayer, Geigy, and Smith Kline. And it is not surprising to find Kodak film on sale alongside knicknacks decorated with likenesses of Mickey Mouse, Goofy, or Donald Duck.

Impressive as these examples are, they do not begin to tell the full story of foreign penetration of the Japanese market. They do not reflect the success enjoyed by the Japanese subsidiaries of American and European companies whose business lies wholly or largely outside the consumer products field. Here the prototype is IBM Japan which, despite enormous gains made by its Japanese competitors, remains a powerhouse in Japan's computer industry. IBM Japan may owe some of its success to having been first in its field. No such advantage was enjoyed, however, by a far smaller American-owned computer maker, Nihon Digital Equipment, which in the latter half of the 1980s began to achieve rapid growth in the same crowded business.

A strong foreign presence can be felt not only in Japan's computer industry, but in a number of other highly competitive nonconsumer businesses as well. Foreign subsidiaries or joint ventures between foreign and Japanese firms have become major—indeed sometimes dominant—players. Among these: Fuji Xerox in copiers, America's DuPont and Britain's ICI in chemicals, Weyerhaeuser in forest products, Johnson Wax in industrial maintenance products, Yamatake-Honeywell in automatic controls, and Yokogawa–Hewlett-Packard in instrumentation.

When one considers this catalog of success stories, the question that inevitably comes to mind is: Why do people believe that it is almost impossible for a foreign business to make a go of it in Japan?

Part of the answer lies in the fact that for the first 20 years or so after the end of World War II, Japan's government did undeniably maintain formidable barriers to foreign penetration of its markets. But even since those barriers began to fall, a large percentage of the foreign firms seeking to do business in Japan have been unsuccessful and have pulled out in defeat. According to one authority on the subject, as of the late 1980s, a small American firm seeking to win a foothold in Japan had less than a 50–50 chance of succeeding. While the success ratio was

far better for foreign firms with large resources and a strong domestic base, it was not promising enough to attract many expansion-minded companies.

Long-Term Commitment | The main reason so many foreign firms have failed in Japan is that they try to break into the Japanese market without taking the trouble to study its special characteristics. Yet those characteristics are not difficult to identify, and much can be learned from a careful look at the experiences of the hundreds of American and European companies whose goods or services have won acceptance in Japan.

Perhaps the single most important thing such companies have in common is patience and the readiness to underwrite a long-term commitment. In Japan quick payouts are usually not forthcoming. In fact, turning a large profit right from the start may even be a harbinger of trouble to come—as American microchip manufacturers are now painfully aware. The introduction of a highly profitable new product in Japan is virtually certain to attract local competitors. By pursuing longer-range strategies aimed primarily at building market share, the local competitors may ultimately outstrip the pioneering foreign firm.

Almost without exception, foreign companies that have won the confidence of the Japanese business community and the Japanese consumer have done so by forswearing quick profitability and making it clear that they are in Japan to stay. Thus, BMW, which as of 1991 was exporting well over twice as many cars to Japan as General Motors, Ford, and Chrysler combined, achieved that status by doing something that Detroit's Big Three flatly refused to do—invest a great deal of time, energy, and money in the establishment of its own dealer networks and service facilities. By Japanese standards, the four or five years that it took the German auto company to win a solid foothold in Japan's luxury car market was little more than the blink of an eye.

Another successful company that took the long view is Seibu Allstate Life Insurance (now Saison Life Insurance), a joint venture of Sears Roebuck and one of Japan's leading merchandising firms. Despite the marketing expertise and prestige of the parent organizations, the company did not reach the cumulative break-even point for 10 years.

Besides reflecting the necessity for patience, the Seibu–Sears Roebuck alliance exemplifies another principle that has guided the activities of most successful foreign firms. That is, in Japan long-term relationships, both corporate and personal, count for a great deal more than they normally do in American or European business. Frequent changes in suppliers, distributors, or joint-venture partners are seen as evidence of irresponsibility. So foreign companies that take pains to choose associates they are prepared to stick with are those that most rapidly win acceptance by Japan's economic establishment.

Choosing the right associates at the start has other advantages. On the most obvious level, entering into a partnership with a Japanese company usually gives a foreign firm much easier access to local capital as well as to potential customers. When Heublein, an American company, and the Mitsubishi Corporation jointly launched Kentucky Fried Chicken Japan, they put up only $100,000 apiece in paid-in capital. But on the strength of the Mitsubishi connection, the management of the joint venture was able to borrow many millions in working capital.

Similarly, by the early 1990s, the Ford Motor Company was able to acquire a large lead over General Motors and Chrysler in Japanese sales by drawing on manufacturing and marketing opportunities stemming from its 25-percent interest in Japan's Mazda.

As useful as joint ventures or interlocking ownerships can be, other forms of association with Japanese companies have sometimes served foreign outfits just as well or better. As one American with long experience in Japan has observed, "In this country, your de facto partners can be more important to you than your legal ones." Executives of Warner-Lambert agree. They maintain that the dominance of Schick razor blades in Japan was largely a result of the shrewd marketing tactics and clout of the Seikō Corporation, the company that has served as Schick's Japanese distributor since the 1950s.

An even more ingenious use of de facto partners established the American Family Assurance Company of Columbus, Georgia, as Japan's biggest underwriter of cancer insurance. Instead of using individual agents, the company decided to sell its policies through the corporate agencies that are set up by many large Japanese firms to handle employee benefits.

Another reason for American Family's success was that its Japanese operation was run almost entirely by Japanese executives, including a former official of the Ministry of Finance, the agency that oversees insurance operations in Japan. Reliance upon Japanese executives is characteristic of the majority of well-established foreign subsidiaries. Obviously, the fewer American and European faces in the offices of a foreign company, the less alien its image will seem. The advantages of hiring a former senior official of the government are no less obvious. In the 1980s Texas Instruments succeeded in hiring a former high-level official of the powerful Ministry of International Trade and Industry to run its Japanese subsidiary.

Another practice of successful foreign firms is to recruit new university graduates from topflight schools. Every Tōkyō, Kyōto, or Waseda University graduate hired increases a company's chances of winning a sympathetic hearing in Japanese government circles in years to come. The reason for this is that prestigious universities produce a sizable percentage of Japan's future bureaucrats and politicians, and the lifelong bond between college classmates in Japan remains strong.

Product Modification, Quality, and Innovation

Another advantage of hiring Japanese executives is that they are likely to have a better sense than foreigners of whether it is necessary to adjust a product to suit Japanese tastes and lifestyles. This, of course, is an important issue for companies doing business in Japan, and one for which there is no single recommended approach.

A great many foreign products, ranging from Mark Cross pens to Kodak's disposable cameras, have done extremely well in Japan with no significant modifications. There are also products whose appeal depends on their very "foreignness," such as imported luxury automobiles. While right-hand drive is standard on cars in Japan, many people opt for the more inconvenient but "exotic" left-hand drive that is considered fashionable.

To assume that a Western product must always be redesigned to succeed in Japan is foolish. The only thing that is even more foolish is to make the opposite assumption—that because a product sells well in Europe or America it will necessarily sell well in Japan in the identical form. Many products have caught on with the Japanese because they have been subtly reformulated to suit Japanese tastes. Kodak, for example, alters the color balance of the amateur film it sells in Japan to produce snapshots with "beefy flesh tones," a reddish tint that American camera buffs dislike but that the Japanese favor. And at the request of Japanese consumers, who like their sweets less sweet than Americans, Nabisco is marketing an Oreo cookie without the sugar cream center. According to Nabisco's Japanese partner, Yamazaki-Nabisco, "Petit Oreos Non Cream" have been selling at a brisk rate.

Whether or not product redesign proves necessary, every foreign company must adapt to Japanese standards of quality and service—which are generally higher than those in the West. The response to Japanese quality requirements, in fact, constitutes the most significant difference between foreign ventures that prosper in Japan and those that fail. Nowhere has this fact been more dramatically demonstrated than in the paper industry.

For two decades or more, a number of American and Canadian papermakers complained that major segments of the Japanese market were effectively closed to them. However, while others were crying foul, Weyerhaeuser was quietly enlisting Japan's Jūjō Paper as a minority partner in a newsprint venture. Weyerhaeuser invested hundreds of millions of dollars and five years of effort in the project. Besides building new plants capable of producing newsprint that met the exacting standards of Japanese newspapers, the company had to create its own shipping subsidiary in order to assure Japanese customers of unfailing on-time delivery. It also had to equip its vessels with specially designed loading and humidity-control devices to prevent damage to the paper in transit. In achieving standards that other North American producers had dismissed as unrealistic, Weyerhaeuser earned a double payoff. It not only built a flourishing newsprint business in Japan but found that American customers were willing to pay a premium for its higher-quality product as well.

Along with dedication to quality, foreign firms must have the ability to mobilize quickly in response to changes in the marketplace. Because competition in Japan is keener perhaps than anywhere in the world, products are brought to market and evolve there much more rapidly than in Europe or the United States. Generalizations about Japan's economic behavior that may well be true today can easily prove outmoded tomorrow.

Future Prospects

For many years, conventional wisdom had it that the greatest barrier to foreign penetration of the Japanese market lay in the country's distribution system. Though complexities and inefficiencies in distribution still abounded in the early 1990s, they were being steadily mitigated by such developments as the advent of shopping malls, the easing of legal obstacles to the establishment of large retail stores, the growing success of catalog sales operations, and the spread of discounting into product areas where it was hitherto unknown.

The highly publicized joint venture between Toys 'R' Us and McDonald's Japan, which was designed to capitalize on the twin addictions of youthful Japanese to fast food and fanciful playthings, represented an innovation in retailing. Instead of the traditional partnership between a foreign firm and a Japanese firm, it was an alliance between two US companies, both of which were known for their distinctly American styles and images. It would be hard to conceive of a better example of the significant headway foreign enterprises have made—and continue to make—in the Japanese market.

Robert C. Christopher

Illustration by Takeshima Kōji

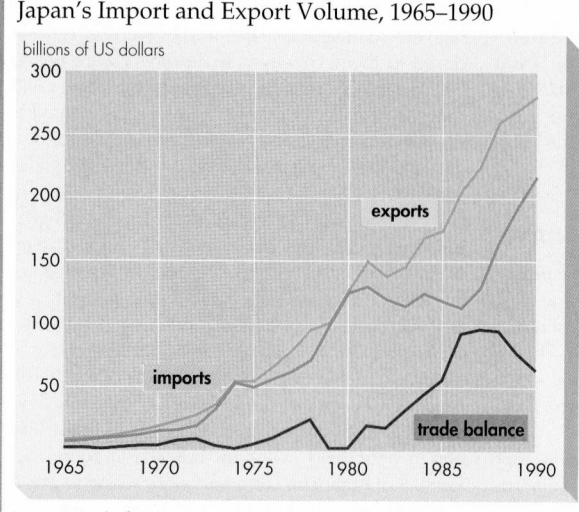

Japan's Import and Export Volume, 1965–1990

billions of US dollars

SOURCES: Bank of Japan, *Hompō keizai tōkei* (annual): 1967; *Keizai tōkei nempō* (annual): 1976 and 1991.

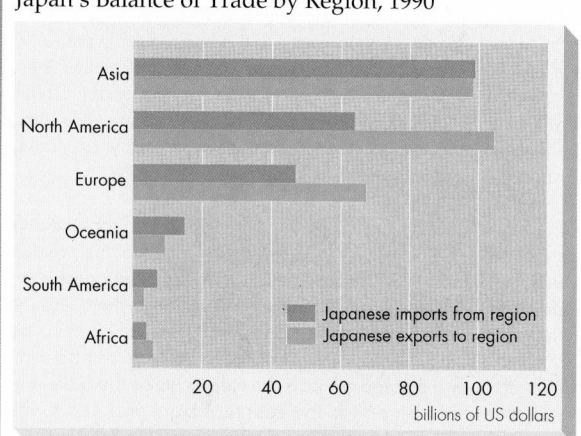

Japan's Balance of Trade by Region, 1990

Japanese imports from region
Japanese exports to region

billions of US dollars

NOTE: All of the Soviet Union is included in the statistics for Europe.
SOURCE: Japan Tariff Association, *Gaikoku bōeki gaikyō* (annual): 1991.

Japanese Imports by Type, 1960–1990

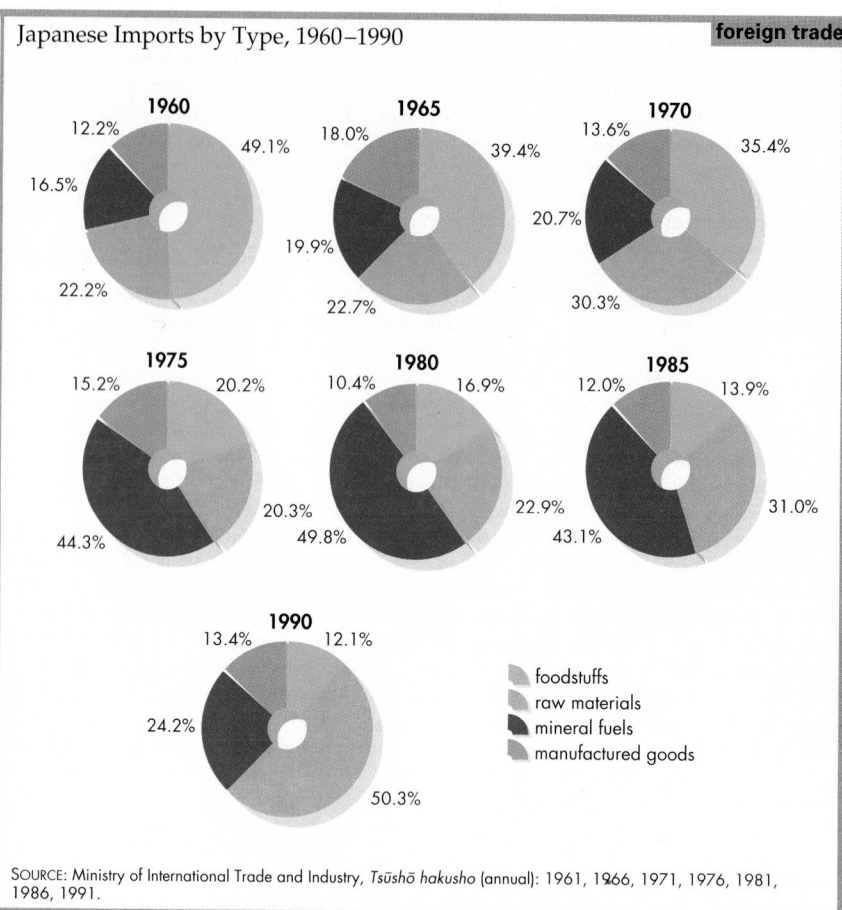

foodstuffs
raw materials
mineral fuels
manufactured goods

SOURCE: Ministry of International Trade and Industry, *Tsūshō hakusho* (annual): 1961, 1966, 1971, 1976, 1981, 1986, 1991.

Japan had a surplus balance of trade.

From World War I Prosperity to a Wartime Trading System——World War I provided the opportunity for a major increase in export business. The war caused a sharp decrease in exports of European and US products and an increase in demand for Japanese products, particularly in Southeast Asian markets. There was also an increase in exports of military supplies to the countries at war, especially Russia. Japanese cotton textiles, knitted goods, machinery, copper, iron, and metal products replaced European and US goods in the international market. As a result, the structure of Japanese exports changed, with a decrease in the percentage of raw materials and semimanufactures and an increase in the percentage of finished goods. Compared to prewar statistics, Japan's exports doubled by 1916, and in 1918, the last year of the war, exports were three times prewar levels. The cumulative trade surplus during the four years of the war was ¥1.4 billion (US $3.9 million).

After the war, conditions were favorable for exports both to countries such as the United States, which had benefited economically from the war, and to Western European countries, where the recovery of production capacity was delayed. However, because of an increase in Japan's domestic demand, the foreign trade balance changed from a surplus to a deficit. The worldwide Great Depression, which began with the New York stock market crash of 1929, dealt a serious blow to Japan's foreign trade. The

adverse effect was heightened by a steep increase in the value of Japanese currency resulting from Japan's ill-timed and temporary return to the gold standard in January 1930. Japan's 1930 exports declined 31.6 percent compared to the previous year, and 1931 exports declined another 46.6 percent compared to 1930. Because of the drastic reduction in buying power and the fall in prices, import levels also dropped severely. Imports in 1930 declined 30.2 percent compared to the previous year, and 1931 imports declined 40.3 percent compared to 1930. See SHŌWA DEPRESSION.

Following the MANCHURIAN INCIDENT (1931) Japan adopted foreign trade and exchange controls in the course of organizing its war economy. The Great Depression increased the development of trading blocs within the world trading system, and the 1930s were marked by a great expansion in the importance of Japan's trade with its colonies. With the outbreak of the SINO-JAPANESE WAR OF 1937–1945, Japan's foreign trade began increasingly to take on a wartime character. Imports became a means of obtaining military materials and the basic necessities for living. Exports were promoted in order to acquire the foreign currency needed for imports.

Japanese trade controls were imposed progressively following the 1937 conflict with China that launched the Pacific War. In 1940, the Tripartite Pact including Japan, Germany, and Italy was formalized. In 1941, with the issuance of the Trade Control Order, Japan began a program of general mobilization. Consequently, Japan became heavily dependent on trade within the "yen bloc," which included its colonies, and trade with countries outside this bloc was cut drastically. Japan had a trade surplus with respect to yen bloc countries and a large trade deficit with other countries.

Foreign Trade after World War II——Immediately following World War II, a lack of natural resources and destruction of pro-

duction facilities caused a continuing foreign trade deficit in Japan. The country also suffered from a chronic lack of foreign currency. Beginning in the high-growth period of the late 1950s and early 1960s, export power increased significantly because of dramatic advances in manufacturing production capacity and technology. As a result, Japan's trade balance began to show a surplus starting in the second half of the 1960s. Export volume increased consistently through the 1970s and 1980s, although oil crises in 1973 and 1979 (see OIL CRISIS OF 1973) caused a temporary balance-of-trade deficit. In the second half of the 1980s, Japan's trade surplus soared, reaching a peak of US $96.4 billion in 1987, then fluctuated (see TRADE BALANCE).

Postwar Exports——Although textiles had previously accounted for more than 50 percent of Japanese exports, in the 1950s their relative importance declined with the increase in exports of heavy-industry products. In the 1960s, Japan's average dollar-base export increase of 18.4 percent per year was 2.3 times the overall rate of increase in world trade. The makeup of Japan's exports continued to shift to the heavy-industry fields of steel, machinery, and chemical products and away from textiles and light-industry products. In the 1970s, the importance of industrial raw materials exports such as chemicals and steel dropped, and exports of machinery and electronics jumped as increasing emphasis was placed on high-value-added products. As a result, the focus of trade friction shifted from textiles and steel to products such as color televisions and automobiles. In the 1980s, exports of advanced-technology-intensive products including computers, semiconductors, videocassette recorders, machine tools, and facsimile machines continued to increase sharply, and trade friction over these products began to occur. Developing nations continue to be important destinations for Japanese exports, primarily countries in

Southeast Asia that are closely linked to Japan geographically and historically. In the 1980s, one-third of all exports went to the United States.

Postwar Imports——In the period immediately following World War II, raw fuels and textile raw materials made up the bulk of the imports. The relative importance of textile raw material imports decreased and that of mineral fuels and metal raw materials increased, along with the drop in the price of oil and development of Japanese heavy industry. Crude oil remained at less than 20 percent of Japan's total imports until the beginning of the 1970s. As a result of the 1973 and 1979 oil crises, crude oil prices soared and prices of other mineral fuels also increased. In 1980 mineral fuels were approximately 50 percent of total imports. By 1990, however, mineral fuels had fallen to 24.2 percent of imports due to lower oil prices and the successful energy-conservation efforts of Japanese industry. During the same period imports of manufactured goods increased, and in 1990 they constituted more than 50 percent of Japan's imports.

Prior to the oil crisis of 1973, approximately one-third of Japan's imports came from the United States, approximately one-sixth from Southeast Asia, and only about one-eighth from the Middle and Near East. Following the oil crisis, the Middle and Near East, which supply 70 percent of Japan's imported oil, provided nearly 30 percent of total imports, and the US share fell to less than 20 percent. When the price of crude oil fell in the 1980s, the percentage of imports coming from the Middle and Near East dropped. At the same time, imports of manufactured goods from Europe, the United States, and the developing countries of Asia increased.

foreign trade, government policy on 貿易政策

(*bōeki seisaku*). Japan's modern trade policy began in the Meiji period (1868–1912), and its first major objective was the achievement of parity with the West. Until the end of the Unequal Treaties, TARIFFS and trade were in the hands of the Western powers, so the Japanese government was limited in the measures it could take to improve the nation's trade position (see UNEQUAL TREATIES, REVISION OF). The government promoted industrialization and economic development through subsidies, loans, and technical assistance. This necessitated the import of equipment, ships, steel, and other commodities that Japan itself did not make and that had to be paid for by exports. Thus evolved what has remained a fundamental part of Japan's trade policy: Japan exports in order to import, and exports and imports reflect the economy's competitive development.

After 1899 tariff protection of specific industries was undertaken. At the same time, tariffs on raw materials were kept low, increasing the effective protection and further stimulating manufacturing. Protection of the home market was extended to colonies and the occupied territories. Exports of heavy industrial products to these areas rose throughout the 1920s and 1930s, while food and raw materials represented most imports (see also COLONIALISM). The need to secure raw material and markets in a hostile and depressed international trading environment led to efforts to form the so-called GREATER EAST ASIA COPROSPERITY SPHERE in the years immediately preceding World War II.

Following the war there was an immedi-ate need to resuscitate the economy, especially trade. Since Japan had a shortage of land and raw materials but a large labor force, an economic revival could be accomplished only by promoting manufacturing and manufactured exports. Specific trade-related measures included quotas on imports of critical raw materials like coal, oil, wool, cotton, and chemicals. Priorities for imports were set by the government in conjunction with business. There were protective tariffs on manufactured goods, while raw materials were allowed in essentially duty-free. Specific assistance was given or removed as industries developed or gained strength. Thus steel was given priority first, then automobiles in the 1950s, and computers in the 1960s and 1970s. Industries with either export potential or strategic economic importance were favored, and the government encouraged exports via special tax and credit incentives.

Since trade trends are a reflection of the economy, fundamental economic policies have had as much of an impact on trade as trade-specific policies. The government's push to industrialize placed a premium on investment and growth. Financial resources were channeled through the city banks, the government development banks, the tax structure, and the government's expenditure patterns to such areas as steel, chemicals, shipping, and shipbuilding. The primary architect of the plan was the Heavy Industry Bureau of the MINISTRY OF INTERNATIONAL TRADE AND INDUSTRY (MITI), along with the MINISTRY OF FINANCE. The focus on growth and industrialization in turn led to rapid increases in manufacturing investment and productivity, which enhanced Japanese competitiveness.

Import liberalization continued slowly through the 1960s and 1970s as Japan's industrial strength and export surplus developed further. After 1968 particularly, Japan's export surplus developed rapidly due to the Vietnam War, rising US inflation, and Japan's improving productivity. In turn, external pressures, especially from the United States, for real and substantive liberalization increased markedly. But the government still did not embrace full liberalization quickly, not yet really appreciating Japan's international competitiveness or the nation's growing structural trade surplus.

Beginning in the 1980s the major trade issue has been the growing trade surplus, and Japan's current trade policies are thus increasingly oriented toward encouraging imports while keeping the volume of exports down. This has created the need for major institutional reversals, which have been difficult to achieve. Liberalization of agricultural imports, particularly rice, continued to be a politically sensitive issue, since a large portion of the governing Liberal Democratic Party's support remains in agriculture. Some obvious policy steps have been taken to encourage imports, including unilateral tariff cuts, removal of import restrictions, reform of the system for standards certification, import promotion campaigns, and increased government spending to stimulate domestic demand. In addition, there have been periodic VOLUNTARY EXPORT RESTRICTIONS on items such as automobiles to specific markets, primarily the United States and the European Community. Foreign production by Japanese firms as a substitute for exports has been facilitated by credit availability, tax benefits, and exchange control liberalization.

Much remains to be done to change in-grained procedures. Many of the gains in import liberalization have come only as a result of direct foreign pressure. For example, the United States Omnibus Trade and Competitiveness Act of 1988 led to the United States–Japan Structural Impediments Initiative talks in 1989, in which the Japanese government agreed to work toward removing structural obstacles to imports, such as the complexities of Japan's distribution system. See also FOREIGN TRADE.

foreign workers 外国人労働者

(*gaikokujin rōdōsha*). Paid employment of workers who are citizens of foreign countries is strictly regulated by the Immigration Control Law, which was extensively revised in 1989; the revisions were implemented in 1990. Except for special groups, including spouses of Japanese nationals and people of Japanese descent, permission to work is granted to foreigners only in 28 skilled employment categories such as education, communications, medicine, finance, and computer software design. In principle, manual workers are not allowed entry, and students from overseas who work part-time are also subject to restrictions.

The majority of illegal foreign workers in the early 1980s were women who had entered the country with tourist visas and worked in bars and entertainment districts. However, the economic boom of the late 1980s led to severe shortages of labor, especially in the construction and service industries, and the appreciation in the value of the yen in recent years has attracted a large influx of male foreign workers, mostly from Asian countries such as the Philippines, China, Pakistan, Bangladesh, and Iran. In recent years Japanese have shown a marked lack of interest in so-called "3K" jobs (those that are *kitsui, kitanai, kiken;* "difficult, dirty, dangerous"), and there has been a significant increase in the number of construction and small engineering firms that are prepared to employ foreign manual laborers illegally.

While the 1989 revision of the Immigration Control Law increased opportunities for skilled professionals to work in Japan, it also strengthened the restrictions on entry of unskilled workers and established penalties for employers who hire illegal foreign workers. Severe labor shortages are likely to continue, however, and the number of companies hiring foreigners of Japanese descent has increased since the 1989 revision of the Immigration Control Law extended the right of long-term residence to descendants of Japanese emigrants and removed restrictions on their ability to work in Japan. Due to high inflation in Brazil, many Brazilians of Japanese descent have sought to take advantage of this change in the law; twice as many were working in Japan in 1990 as in the previous year.

forestry 林業

(*ringyō*). About 70 percent of Japan's total area is wooded. Forests play a particularly important role in land conservation in Japan, as steep mountain ranges run along the midline of the islands from north to south and the rivers are short and torrential. Japan is a great consumer of wood as well as the world's greatest importer of logs and wood chips (accounting for about 20 percent of the world's wood trade). It is also notable for its exceptionally high proportion of planted

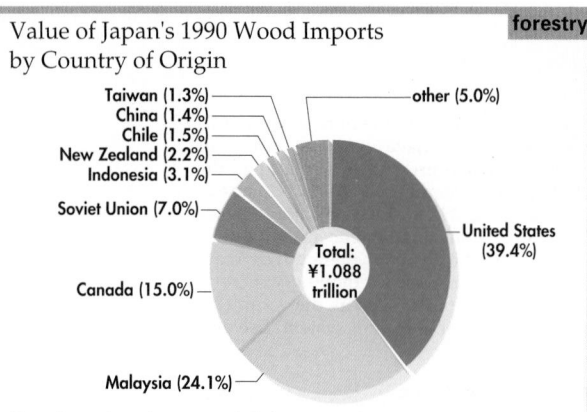

Value of Japan's 1990 Wood Imports by Country of Origin

forestry

- Taiwan (1.3%)
- China (1.4%)
- Chile (1.5%)
- New Zealand (2.2%)
- Indonesia (3.1%)
- Soviet Union (7.0%)
- Canada (15.0%)
- Malaysia (24.1%)
- other (5.0%)
- United States (39.4%)

Total: ¥1.088 trillion

NOTE: Figures for pulp are not included.
SOURCE: Japan Tariff Association, *Gaikoku bōeki gaikyō* (monthly): December 1990.

Consumption of Domestic and Imported Wood

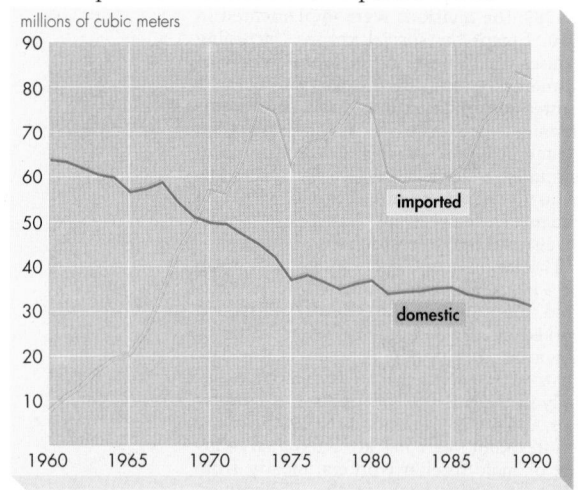

millions of cubic meters

imported

domestic

90
80
70
60
50
40
30
20
10

1960 1965 1970 1975 1980 1985 1990

NOTE: Processed materials have been calculated in terms of their log equivalents.
SOURCE: Forestry Agency, *Mokuzai jukyū hyō* (annual): 1990.

forestry
1 Lumberyards at Shin Kiba in Kōtō Ward, Tōkyō. The location on Tōkyō Bay facilitates the processing of imported lumber.
2 *Hinoki* (cypress) harvesting in the Kiso region of Nagano Prefecture. A high-quality wood, cypress is in great demand.

forests, which occupy about 40 percent of the nation's total forest area.

Forest Conditions in Japan—A great variety of trees rich in regional differences grow in Japan because of the marked temperature differences from north to south and a high level of humidity brought about by warm ocean currents. Trees can be classified as evergreen broad-leaved types such as CA-MELLIAS and *kusunoki* (CAMPHOR TREE), deciduous broad-leaved types such as *buna* (beech) and *tochinoki* (HORSE CHESTNUT, JAPANESE), and conifers such as SUGI (cedar) and *hinoki* (see CYPRESSES). Of the total forest area of about 24.7 million hectares (61.0 million acres), about 9.9 million hectares (24.5 million acres) support planted forests consisting mainly of cedar, cypress, and PINES.

Forestry Operations—In the 18th century, exploitive forestry aiming at simply gathering wood from natural forests was replaced by sustained-yield forestry with artificial planting and cultivation of trees. After the Meiji Restoration of 1868 forestland was divided into privately owned and government-owned areas. National forests account for about 7.3 million hectares (18.0 million acres) of the total wooded area of Japan, private forests for 14.0 million hectares (34.6 million acres), and forests owned by local governments for the remainder. Private forests occupy 56 percent of Japan's entire forest area and are owned by individuals, companies, associations, shrines, and temples. The continued migration of young farm workers to urban areas and factories has greatly reduced the number of forestry workers, resulting in the predominance of elderly workers.

History of Wood Utilization—Wood has been used for construction and fuel in Japan since early times, but the use of lumber for construction increased rapidly starting in the 8th century as wooden palaces and temples such as TŌDAIJI and TŌJI were built. The city of Kyōto became Japan's center of wood consumption, with such products as lumber, charcoal, and firewood brought from all over the country.

With the flourishing of urban culture in the Edo period (1600–1868), there was an increasing demand for wood products for furniture, building, and fuel. Starting in the late 18th century, regional lumber markets developed along the lower reaches of the large rivers; these markets continued to grow in the 19th century. With the modernization of the Japanese economy following the Meiji Restoration, the demand for wood grew rapidly. Following the TŌKYŌ EARTHQUAKE OF 1923, imports, particularly from the United States, became an important factor in Japan's wood supply.

After World War II, the need for building materials escalated, as did the demand for such wood products as paper pulp and plywood, and investment in the forestry industry greatly expanded. However, as demand for wood continued to increase, domestic production was on the decline. The artificial forests planted after the war were not fully mature, forestry routes were inadequately developed, and there was a shortage of young workers. Finally, in recent years emphasis has been increasingly placed on forests as places of recreation and as natural environments in need of conservation. Thus Japan has had to rely more and more on outside sources of wood. In 1990 Japan's total wood consumption was 113 million cubic meters (4.0 billion cu ft), of which only 28 percent was domestically produced. Lumber made up 48 percent of the total, pulp and wood chips 37 percent, and plywood 13 percent.

Forty-Seven Rōnin Incident The masterless *samurai* who avenged their lord are depicted storming the residence of Kira Yoshinaka in this pictorial votive offering dating from 1715.

Forty-Seven Rōnin Incident

赤穂事件

(Akō Jiken; literally, Akō Incident). The revenge of the 47 RŌNIN (masterless *samurai*) is one of the most celebrated examples of loyalty and warrior ethics in Japanese history; the incident has become the subject of innumerable plays and stories. Although it is remembered by the Japanese each year on 14 December, the incident actually occurred in the early morning hours of 31 January 1703 (Genroku 15.12.15). A band of former retainers of Asano Naganori (1665–1701), the late lord of Akō, raided the heavily guarded residence of KIRA YOSHINAKA, a direct retainer of the Tokugawa shōgun, and assassinated him, thus avenging the wrong they believed had been done their lord.

It was customary during the Edo period (1600–1868) for the imperial court in Kyōto to send envoys bearing New Year's greetings to the shōgun in Edo (now Tōkyō). In 1701 Asano was asked to serve as a shogunal representative to receive the envoys. The shōgun's chief of protocol was Kira, who, it is believed, treated Asano superciliously and failed to advise him properly on unfamiliar points of protocol. On the third day of the reception, Asano, provoked by Kira's arrogance, drew his sword and attacked him in the shogunal castle. Because the act of drawing a sword in Edo Castle was illegal, Asano was ordered to commit suicide, and his domain in the province of Harima (now part of Hyōgo Prefecture) was confiscated by the shogunate.

Forty-seven Akō warriors vowed to avenge their lord's death. Almost two years later, 46 samurai charged into the Kira mansion and killed Kira. Of the original 47 Akō warriors, one dropped out just before the raid; nevertheless, they have always been known as the "47 *rōnin*" (Shijūshichishi).

The warriors then marched to Sengakuji, the temple where Asano was buried, and presented Kira's head to their lord's grave.

The Akō warriors' action posed a dilemma for the shogunal government. They had violated the public law by resorting to violence as a group, but they had also faithfully lived up to the cardinal duty of the samurai: absolute loyalty to their lord. But from the shogunate's standpoint, their action went beyond vengeance. It had been carried out by a large group of warriors in the shōgun's capital city and involved a case that the shōgun himself had adjudicated. In effect, the shogunate's decision in the affair, as well as its ultimate authority, had been challenged. As punishment, the 46 samurai, ranging in age from 15 to 77, were ordered to commit suicide, which they did in March 1703. They were buried near their master's grave at Sengakuji. The warriors' action won them popular acclaim, and they were immediately regarded as heroes. The most famous play—and the model for all subsequent plays on this incident—was *Kanadehon chūshingura* (1748; tr *Chūshingura: The Treasury of Loyal Retainers*, 1971) by Takeda Izumo II (see TAKEDA IZUMO) and others.

Fossa Magna フォッサマグナ

(Fossa Maguna). Large depressed land zone extending from north to south over the center of Honshū, the main island of Japan. It effectively divides Japan geologically into a northeastern and a southwestern sector. It was named by the German geologist Edmund NAUMANN. The western boundary of this zone is the Itoigawa-Shizuoka Tectonic Line (a fault line extending from Itoigawa, Niigata Prefecture, on the Sea of Japan to the city of Shizuoka on the Pacific coast, via Lake Suwa). The eastern boundary is formed by the mountains on the western border of the Kantō region (east central Honshū). This zone consists of sedimentary, volcanic, and pyroclastic rock and is covered by volcanoes of the Quaternary period. Its formation is believed to have occurred before or during the Miocene period.

fossils 化石

(*kaseki*). Not until the early Meiji period (1868–1912) did paleontology as a branch of science become established in Japan. The first scientific study of Japanese fossils was an article published in a German magazine in 1877, dealing with Jurassic plants that had been collected by a German geographer, Johannes Justus Rein (1843–1918), in Ishikawa Prefecture in 1874. At the end of the 19th century Japanese paleontology came into its own, and Japan is now a leader in fossil studies among Asian nations.

The oldest known fossils in Japan date from the Ordovician period. Marine fossils predominate throughout the Paleozoic and Mesozoic eras. The percentage of fossilized land plants and animals begins to increase among fossils of the Cenozoic era.

Paleozoic fossils. Fossil assemblages from the Ordovician period to the late Carboniferous period (the Viséan epoch) differ considerably from those recorded for the rest of the Paleozoic era ending with the Permian period. The first part is characterized by the dominance of reef forms consisting mainly of tabulate corals and stromatoporoids. To these are added trilobites, brachiopods, and radiolarians. In the Devonian beds, fossil brachiopods, including *Cyrtospirifer*, have been discovered in large numbers, as well as a fossil flora consisting of *Leptophloeum* and

other vascular plants.

From the Viséan epoch on, sedimentary facies were differentiated into clastic and thick limestone beds. Fossils are abundant in the calcareous facies, including many fusulines, corals, bryozoans, brachiopods, and calcareous algae, plus a few goniatites and trilobites. The abundant fusulines include *Fusulinella, Parafusulina, Neoschwagerina, Verbeekina, Yabeina,* and others. The chronology of the Late Carboniferous and Permian periods in the northwest Pacific region is based on the evolution of these genera. Corals are represented by simple corals indigenous to East Asia, such as *Dibunophyllum* and *Kueichouphyllum,* and colonial coral, such as *Lonsdaleia.* On the other hand, fossils are comparatively scarce in clastic sediments where only pelecypods, brachiopods, and conodonts are found preserved. In a few areas of northeastern Japan, Permian plant assemblages consisting of *Sphenophyllum* and *Taeniopteris,* which are closely related to flora of the Asian continent, have been discovered.

Mesozoic fossils. The Mesozoic era in Japan was a period of mountain building, causing remarkable diversification in faunas and floras. In the Triassic period marine beds still prevailed, and pelecypods and ammonites are the main fossil groups. Pelecypods were particularly common; for example, *Eumorphotis, Myophoria, Halobia,* and *Monotis (Entomonotis).* These are used as index fossils in biochronological zonation. Ammonites have been found in comparatively small numbers and in poorly preserved condition, but most representative index fossils of the Alpine Triassic, such as *Glyptophiceras, Subcolumbites, Hollandites,* and *Protrachyceras,* have been identified. Recently fossil conodonts have been found in considerable numbers in beds that had hitherto been thought to be unfossiliferous Paleozoic. These fossils are providing invaluable basic information to the study of the Triassic. Fossil vertebrates from this period are extremely rare in Japan, but *Utatsusaurus,* a marine reptile belonging to the order Ichthyopterygia, has been found in the Kitakami Mountains. Fossil land plants are

known from the Middle and Late Triassic, representing the so-called Dipteridacean flora. These flourished from the Late Triassic to the Early Jurassic all over Japan.

Characteristics of the Jurassic fossils resemble those of the Triassic. Pelecypods and ammonites are dominant, followed by belemnites, corals, stromatoporoids, calcareous algae, radiolarians, and echinoderms. Fossil vertebrates are very rare. Only the cranial bones of the ichthyosaur are known. Fossil plants are comparatively numerous; ferns, Cycadophyta, and Ginkgoales range from Upper Jurassic to Upper Cretaceous.

During the Cretaceous period many of the major islands of Japan were born. The most abundant fossils are pelecypods and ammonites. The Late Cretaceous ammonites from Hokkaidō are particularly rich and well preserved. Biochronology founded on the ammonites is one of the standards for the Pacific region. *Nipponites,* well known for their complicated whorls, were originally discovered in Hokkaidō. Marine pelecypods are also quite numerous. *Inoceramus,* among others, are known from all stages of the Cretaceous system. Freshwater pelecypod fossils of such genera as *Plicatounia, Nakamuranaia,* and *Trigonioides* are found in newly risen land areas. Other fossil invertebrates of the Cretaceous age are belemnites, gastropods, echinoderms, crinoids, and estherians. Foraminifers are also discovered in small

fossils
1 A Late Cretaceous ammonite, *Anagaudryceras limatum,* found in Hokkaidō.
2 Teeth and other fossils of extinct Pleistocene elephants have been discovered in many regions of Japan. These *Palaeoloxodon* teeth were found in Hokkaidō.
3 Fossil fragments of *Plesiosauria,* a species of extinct reptile, were found in Late Cretaceous beds in Fukushima Prefecture.
4 A reconstruction of the skeleton of the same reptile.

Fossa Magna

The Fossa Magna Land Zone

Itoigawa
Fossa Magna land zone
Shiojiri
Nirasaki
Shizuoka

— Itoigawa-Shizuoka Tectonic Line

foxes Foxes often appear in Japanese myth and legend as creatures capable of bewitching people. The fox is found throughout Japan, occasionally near human habitation, and feeds on rats and mice, rabbits, birds, and even insects.

quantity. Vertebrate fossils are few in individuals but numerous in species. Jawed fishes (Teleostei) and reptiles (such as chelonians, pterodactyls, ichthyosaurs, and plesiosaurs) are found. Plant fossils are also fairly common. Flowering plants, or angiosperms, are recorded from Late Cretaceous deposits.

Cenozoic fossils. There was a remarkable difference in geologic environment between the Paleogene and Neogene epochs in Japan. In the Paleogene epoch Japan was almost completely converted into land. As a result marine sediments exist only to a limited extent in northern Kyūshū, along the southwestern Pacific coast, and in Hokkaidō. Marine fossil occurrences are consequently also limited. Such foraminifers as *Nummulites* and *Discocyclina*, pelecypods, and gastropods appear only in small numbers. In the nonmarine sequence coal-bearing formations are introduced. Flora indicative of a warm and humid climate, characterized by *Woodwardia*, *Sabalites*, and *Musophyllum*, have been found in these formations.

In the Neogene epoch a new island arc was formed along the line linking the Kuril Islands, northeastern Japan, Izu, and the Ogasawara Islands. In the greater part of this arc localized marine sedimentary basins were formed. Fossil faunas and floras also tended to be localized. The molluscan fauna, consisting mainly of pelecypods and gastropods, is the most characteristic fossil group of this period. These faunas tend to be divided into the northern (Sea of Japan) type and southern (Pacific Ocean) type. Smaller foraminifers are also very abundant and, together with mollusks, furnish the basis for biochronological classification of the Neogene. Fossils of nearly all other invertebrates are also known, as well as a small number of vertebrate fossils. Fishes, reptiles (especially chelonians), and mammals are reported. *Desmostylus*, a strange amphibious form related both to elephants and sea cows, is worthy of special mention. Most plant fossils are of broad-leaved trees characteristic of temperate to subtropical zones. With the approach of the Quaternary period, plants suggesting cold climates increase in quantity.

Even in the Quaternary period crustal movements continued in the Japanese islands. The distribution of Quaternary fossils is therefore remarkably localized. Since the Pleistocene epoch the alternation of hot and cold climates has been clearly reflected in fossil assemblages. Because of the lowering of the sea level during glacial periods, the Japanese islands were connected with the Asian continent, which permitted free passage of large mammals. Examples of extinct Pleistocene elephants include fossils of *Gomphotherium*, *Stegotrebelodon* (*Parastegodon*), *Palaeoloxodon*, and *Mammuthus* (*Archidiskodon*). Such large mammals as *Rhinoceros*, *Leptobison*, and *Sinomegaceroides* are also reported. Small fossil mammals have been unearthed in large numbers from cave deposits, as have human fossils. The oldest known human fossil found in Japan is the left hipbone of the *Nipponanthropus* (probably *Homo erectus*) from a bed believed to be Early Pleistocene. Most human fossils, however, are of *Homo sapiens.*

In 1935 the Palaeontological Society of Japan was founded as a branch of the Geological Society of Japan (it became independent of the Geological Society in 1957). In 1990 the Palaeontological Society had nearly 800 members. Since 1951 it has issued the quarterly magazine *Nihon koseibutsu gakkai hōkoku kiji* (Transactions and Proceedings of the Palaeontological Society of Japan).

Four Books and Five Classics 四書五経

(Shisho Gokyō). Two sets of Chinese classic texts of Confucianism. The Four Books (Ch: Si Shu or Ssu Shu; J: Shisho) consist of *The Great Learning* (Ch: *Daxue* or *Ta hsüeh;* J: *Daigaku*), *The Doctrine of the Mean* (Ch: *Zhongyong* or *Chung yung;* J: *Chūyō*), *The Analects* (Ch: *Lun yu* or *Lun yü;* J: *Rongo*), and *Mencius* (Ch: *Mengzi* or *Meng-tzu;* J: *Mōshi*). The Five Classics (Ch: Wu Jing or Wu Ching; J: Gokyō) consist of *The Book of Changes* (Ch: *Yi jing* or *I ching;* J: *Ekikyō*), *The Book of Documents* (Ch: *Shu jing* or *Shu ching;* J: *Shokyō*), *The Book of Odes* (Ch: *Shi jing* or *Shih ching;* J: *Shikyō*), *The Book of Rites* (Ch: *Li ji* or *Li chi;* J: *Raiki*), and *The Spring and Autumn Annals* (Ch: *Chun qiu* or *Ch'un ch'iu;* J: *Shunjū*). Of the Four Books, *The Great Learning* and *The Doctrine of the Mean* are sections from *The Book of Rites*, one of the Five Classics.

The Five Classics were the basic texts of Confucianism in China for many centuries until the time of the Neo-Confucian philosopher Zhu Xi (Chu Hsi; 1130–1200), in whose philosophy the Four Books assumed central importance (see SHUSHIGAKU). It became customary to start one's studies with the Four Books and then proceed to the Five Classics. These texts had been introduced to Japan by the mid-13th century, but it was in the Edo period (1600–1868) that they became especially important. See also CONFUCIANISM.

442nd Regimental Combat Team 第442部隊

(Dai Yonhyakuyonjūni Butai). The most highly decorated US World War II combat unit, composed solely of *nisei* (second-generation JAPANESE AMERICANS). It included the 442nd Infantry Regiment, the 522nd Field Artillery Battalion, and the 232nd Engineer Combat Company, all of whom fought in France and Italy. The Japanese Americans who joined the unit saw it as a means to strongly assert their patriotism and to dispel the widespread false impression that they were second-class citizens who could not be trusted in the US war effort. During 225 days of combat, over 10,000 men passed through the ranks of the 442nd Regimental Combat Team. Several hundred were killed, and 1,700 were maimed or critically wounded. By the end of the war, the soldiers accumulated 18,143 medals for valor, including 1 Medal of Honor, 52 Distinguished Service Crosses, 1 Distinguished Service Medal, 560 Silver Stars plus 28 Oak Leaf Clusters, 4,000 Bronze Stars with 1,200 Oak Leaf Clusters, and 9,486 Purple Hearts. The unit's famous motto, "Go for Broke," was an expression of its intense patriotic spirit and desire for honor on the battlefield.

Four-Power Treaty 四ヵ国条約

(Yonkakoku Jōyaku). One of the agreements reached at the WASHINGTON CONFERENCE of 1921–22; signed by France, Great Britain, the United States, and Japan on 13 December 1921. To maintain the status quo in the Pacific, all agreed to respect one another's Pacific territorial possessions, to consult jointly if their rights were threatened, and to terminate the ANGLO-JAPANESE ALLIANCE of 1902, which the United States considered too exclusive.

Fourth Comprehensive National Land Development Plan

第四次全国総合開発計画

(Daiyoji Zenkoku Sōgō Kaihatsu Keikaku; abbreviated as Yonzensō). Japan's fourth COMPREHENSIVE NATIONAL LAND DEVELOPMENT PLAN was drawn up in 1986 by the NATIONAL LAND AGENCY as a national land plan that would take Japan into the 21st century. The plan covers the 15 years from 1986 to 2000 and extends the concept of "Established Zones for Habitation" (a government plan to encourage population growth and development in certain regions) featured in the 1972 Third Plan. Other goals of the fourth plan include social and economic planning in anticipation of the further aging of the Japanese population, increased regional autonomy with emphasis on the role of the core cities of Japan's various regions, the construction of a high-speed transportation network, the establishment of a communications network capable of handling a large volume of information of many types, and a wider distribution (away from Tōkyō) of gateway cities to the outside world. A final overall goal of the plan is to achieve a balance between regional autonomy and regional cooperation with the central government.

foxes 狐

(kitsune). Two subspecies of the Eurasian red fox (*Vulpes vulpes*) of the family Canidae are found in Japan: the *kitakitsune* (*V. vulpes schrencki*) of Hokkaidō and the *hondokitsune* (*V. vulpes japonica*) of Honshū, Shikoku, and Kyūshū. The *hondokitsune* has a head and body length of about 70 centimeters (28 in) and a tail length of about 40 centimeters (16 in); the *kitakitsune* is slightly larger. Both have brown fur. Common carnivores, foxes live in both plains and mountainous districts and often near villages. The female usually bears four or five cubs in the spring.

Since ancient times the Japanese have thought foxes had spiritual power and were capable of bewitching people. Foxes are also thought to be messengers of INARI, the deity of cereals. The story of a fox marrying a man by assuming the shape of a woman is found in many folktales, and tales of foxes bewitching people have survived into the 20th century.

France and Japan フランスと日本

(Furansu to Nihon). The first contact between Japan and France was in 1585 when a Christian mission dispatched to Rome by three Japanese CHRISTIAN DAIMYŌ met the papal nuncio of King Henry III of France. Soon after the beginning of the 17th century, another Christian delegation, which was led by HASEKURA TSUNENAGA and sought trade contacts in Mexico and Europe, visited France. The first French visitor to Japan was the Dominican friar Guillaume Courtet (1589–1637), who came to Japan with a Spanish mission in 1637, despite the repression directed against Christianity and the prohibition of residency and trade to all foreigners except the Dutch and the Chinese under the NATIONAL SECLUSION policy of the Tokugawa shogunate (1603–1867). During that period Japanese craft works became extremely popular in Europe, stimulating French interest in Japan. Although there was intransigent opposition by the shogunate and the Dutch, the idea of trade with Japan remained an alluring goal to the French.

The Tokugawa shogunate opened the country in 1854, and France, following the United States, Great Britain, the Netherlands, and Russia, in 1858 concluded a treaty of friendship and trade (see ANSEI COMMERCIAL TREATIES) with Japan. This was the first official treaty between the two countries. In the tumultuous last days of the shogunate, in order to oppose the British who favored the anti-Tokugawa forces of the Satsuma and Chōshū domains (now Kagoshima and Yamaguchi prefectures) and to ensure a place for French industry in Japan's developing economy, French consul general Léon ROCHES backed the Tokugawa government. Roches initially arranged for military assistance by sending the first French military mission, which helped the shogunate in building the Yokosuka arsenal and the Yokohama foundry. On the economic level, Roches sought favorable treatment for French imports by establishing a Franco-Japanese trade society.

After its establishment in 1868 the Meiji government protested France's continued support for the anti-imperial forces during the BOSHIN CIVIL WAR accompanying the restoration of imperial rule. When the Meiji government began to concentrate on industrialization, which required foreign assistance, particularly from France, relations between the two nations rapidly improved. French aid played an important role as the new government launched its modernization drive, providing technical expertise and advice in many fields, ranging from military affairs to law, economics, and culture.

Against the background of growing ties with the West, as exemplified by the ANGLO-JAPANESE ALLIANCE of 1902, Japan emerged as a major Asian power with its victory in the RUSSO-JAPANESE WAR of 1904–05. France arranged for a loan to help Japan repay funds borrowed from Britain and the United States to cover the costs of the war with Russia. The FRANCO-JAPANESE AGREEMENT OF 1907 contained a secret clause that recognized the two nations' sovereignty over their respective possessions in Asia, and a period of diplomatic and economic cooperation between the two nations ensued. The Banque Franco-Japonaise was opened in 1912. Japan's interest in preserving the status quo in Asia against the incursions of the Germans led it to join the Allied forces with the outbreak of World War I in 1914.

Financial, economic, and cultural cooperation between France and Japan continued after World War I. The Maison Franco-Japonaise, a prominent institution of cultural exchange, was established in Tōkyō in 1924. During the 1920s and 1930s, however, French and Japanese interests in Asia began to diverge. Increasing tension over commercial negotiations between Japan and French-

ruled Indochina resulted in a gradual deterioration of relations between the two countries.

Japan's intentions for Indochina became clear soon after the beginning of the SINO-JAPANESE WAR OF 1937–1945, when the Japanese asked the French to cease selling arms to the Chinese forces of Chiang Kai-shek and then in 1939 occupied the island of Hainan. By 1940 the Vichy government of France, unable to provide effective resistance to Japanese forces threatening northern French Indochina, entered into negotiations with Japan and agreed to allow Japanese forces to enter that region after September 1940. Indochina was made an autonomous province of the Japanese empire in August 1944 and was annexed by Japan on 9 March 1945. Although the Vichy government maintained relations with Japan throughout the war, even with the Japanese in Indochina, the Free French government declared war with Japan on 8 December 1941.

After World War II, when the SAN FRANCISCO PEACE TREATY between Japan and the Allied powers went into effect in April 1952, ties between Japan and France were formally resumed, and in May 1953 a bilateral cultural agreement was concluded.

Since the war there has been regular high-level contact between the two nations, particularly at the annual summit talks of the major industrial nations, at OECD (Organization for International Cooperation and Development) meetings in Paris, and at other international conferences. During the visit of Prime Minister IKEDA HAYATO to France in November 1962, arrangements were made for regular conferences between the two countries, and annual cabinet-level meetings have been held since Prime Minister Georges Pompidou's visit to Japan in April 1964. During Prime Minister SUZUKI ZENKŌ's visit to France in 1981, an organization that aims to strengthen economic ties between the two countries, Le Comité des Sages Franco-Japonais, was formed.

The Mitterrand government, established in 1981, indicated its interest in cooperation with Japan in the political realm, but economic issues have continued to overshadow other aspects of the bilateral relationship. Since the 1970s the trade imbalance in particular has been the subject of chronic controversy, and the French have grown increasingly wary of Japanese economic expansion into their country. By the early 1980s France had imposed import restrictions on automobiles, televisions, and eight other items.

Disagreement over trade issues extends even to the trade figures themselves; the Japanese and the French use radically different methods for calculating the balance of trade. According to French figures, exports from Japan to France for 1990 totaled US $9.3 billion and imports to Japan from France stood at US $4.0 billion, resulting in a French trade deficit with Japan of US $5.3 billion. The Japanese calculations record a 1990 trade deficit with France of US $1.5 billion. Based on the 1990 Japanese figures, Japanese exports to France consist primarily of electronic equipment and other machine-industry products; major imports to Japan from France are art objects (37.2 percent), chemicals (12.8 percent), alcoholic beverages (10.3 percent), and textiles (4.8 percent). (Japanese statistics treat the import of a work by a French artist as an import from France, regardless of what nation it was imported from.)

The problem of rectifying the trade imbalance notwithstanding, the French have

welcomed Japanese business investment in their country. Japanese direct investment in France has increased rapidly, reaching 168 cases for a total of US $1.136 billion for 1989.

France Bed Co, Ltd　フランスベッド[株]

(Furansu Beddo). The largest bed manufacturer in Japan. Incorporated in 1946 as a maker of car seats, it started manufacturing beds in 1956. The company has diversified into the manufacture of down quilts, furniture, and bedding. Innerspring beds are still its core business, backed up by advanced technology introduced from various sources, including Leggett & Platt of the United States, and Slumberland of the United Kingdom. Sales for the fiscal year ending March 1991 totaled ¥80.9 billion (US $589.7 million), and capitalization was ¥5.5 billion (US $40.1 million). Corporate headquarters are in Tōkyō.

Franciscans　フランシスコ会士

(Furanshisukokaishi). The Franciscan friars first arrived in Japan in the 16th century, were exiled or executed during the anti-Christian persecution in the early Edo period (1600–1868), and returned to Japan in the 20th century. In the earlier period, the first Franciscan arrived in Japan in 1582 and the last in 1632; a total of 60 friars labored in the country, 29 of whom were martyred in the persecution. As of 1990 there were 195 Franciscan friars in Japan, engaged mostly in parish and educational work. See also CHRISTIANITY.

Franco-Japanese Agreement of 1907　日仏協約

(Nichifutsu Kyōyaku). Treaty concerned with mutual interests in China and French Indochina; signed on 10 June 1907 in Paris. The signing of this treaty was a stimulus to the conclusion of a similar Russo-Japanese agreement that followed on 30 July (see RUSSO-JAPANESE AGREEMENTS OF 1907–1916). With these treaties, Japan was drawn closer to the Triple Entente in its growing confrontation with Germany. France and Japan declared their support for the OPEN DOOR POLICY and for the independence and territorial integrity of China. They promised to respect the status quo in Asia, to honor each other's rights and territorial possessions there, and to maintain the security and stability of Chinese territory in which each had special interests.

Freedom and People's Rights Movement　自由民権運動

(Jiyū Minken Undō). Also called the Popular Rights Movement. A nationwide political movement of the early Meiji period (1868–1912) involving loosely allied dissident groups composed of former samurai (shizoku) and commoners (heimin) whose primary goal was to reform the new Meiji government along Western democratic lines.

Background—The movement began with the breakup into factions of the Grand Council of State (DAJŌKAN) in October 1873 over the issue of Japan's policy toward Korea. It was from the membership of the losing faction in the Korean debate (SEIKAN-RON) that the leadership of the Popular Rights Movement was drawn.

The origins of the Korean debate can be traced back to the MEIJI RESTORATION of 1868. At that time leadership of the anti-Tokugawa forces was dominated by a number of younger samurai from the domains of Chōshū (now Yamaguchi Prefecture) and Satsuma (now Kagoshima Prefecture), in particular, Chōshū loyalists YAMAGATA ARITOMO and ITŌ HIROBUMI and Satsuma strongmen SAIGŌ TAKAMORI and ŌKUBO TOSHIMICHI. Of lesser importance in the overthrow of the Tokugawa regime were samurai from the domains of Saga (also called Hizen; now Saga Prefecture) and Tosa (now Kōchi Prefecture), the more noteworthy being ŌKUMA SHIGENOBU and ETŌ SHIMPEI of Saga and ITAGAKI TAISUKE and GOTŌ SHŌJIRŌ of Tosa.

Except for the Satsuma general Saigō Takamori, the Chōshū-Satsuma faction's oligarchs were in favor of a nonexpansionist, hands-off-Korea foreign policy, arguing that military involvement in Korea would only divert the nation's scarce resources from the more important task of internal development. On the other side of the debate, apart from Ōkuma Shigenobu, who sided with the Chōshū-Satsuma faction, the oligarchs from Saga and Tosa contended that, by going to war with Korea, Japan could enhance its national prestige and at the same time restore a sense of pride to the increasingly disaffected former samurai class. When the Dajōkan ruled in favor of the Chōshū-Satsuma faction, Itagaki, Etō, Gotō, and others from Saga and Tosa, along with Saigō, resigned from the government.

Early Organization of the Popular Rights Movement — The losers in the Korean debate thereafter adopted different tactics in trying to regain what political power they had lost in 1873. Etō Shimpei in 1874 and Saigō Takamori in 1877 reluctantly opted for armed revolt, leading uprisings of former samurai from their respective domains, but both rebellions were quashed by the new conscript armies led by Satsuma and Chōshū generals (see SAGA REBELLION; SATSUMA REBELLION).

Itagaki Taisuke and Gotō Shōjirō organized local political societies that tapped the forces of social discontent by advocating a liberal ideology of power-sharing diametrically opposed to the Satsuma-Chōshū practice of rule by a few. This strategy gradually developed into a political movement of national proportions—the Popular Rights Movement.

In its first five years of existence, the Popular Rights Movement's political societies, largely Itagaki's creations, were based in Tosa and composed of former samurai like himself. One of the first such organizations, the AIKOKU KŌTŌ (Public Party of Patriots), was founded by Itagaki and several other former samurai on 12 January 1874. Its guiding philosophy was the doctrine of natural rights and its primary political goal was popular representation in government. On 17 January it submitted to the government the Tosa Memorial, which called for the establishment of a representative national assembly. Despite the egalitarian ethos that underlies the doctrine of natural rights, this society, like many others that succeeded it, was notably elitist. Itagaki made clear that by "popular representation" he meant a government chosen by a highly exclusive franchise limited to former samurai, wealthy merchants, and landlords. This emphasis on rule by an elite has prompted many scholars to dub the early phase of the Popular Rights Movement as *jōryū minken* or *shizoku minken* (upper-class or former-samurai popular rights).

Another example of Itagaki's elitist orientation is the RISSHISHA (Self-Help Society), which he founded in his native Tosa domain (from 1872 called Kōchi Prefecture) in April 1874. During the late 1870s young former samurai from around the nation attended the Risshisha "school" and then returned to their own prefectures to set up political societies modeled after the Tosa parent organization.

On 22 February 1875 Itagaki's Risshisha invited leading samurai political activists to convene in Ōsaka for the purpose of creating a national popular rights organization that would henceforth coordinate antigovernment activities. The AIKOKUSHA (Society of Patriots) was the product, though in effect it was stillborn, for, even as the meeting was being held, oligarchs Ōkubo Toshimichi and Itō Hirobumi were convincing Itagaki in the ŌSAKA CONFERENCE OF 1875 to rejoin the government. Once Itagaki had done so, the leaderless Aikokusha dissolved. Itagaki's rapproachment with the Meiji oligarchs was brief; he resigned from the government on 27 October 1875. During Itagaki's tenure in government, the Risshisha remained active and its leadership shifted to more democratic-minded men such as KATAOKA KENKICHI and UEKI EMORI, who began establishing links with popular rights organizations in other prefectures.

Growth of Local Popular Rights Societies — A movement to reestablish the Aikokusha began in April 1878 and culminated in a general convention in September that year and a second national meeting in March 1879, at which 18 prefectures were represented by 21 regional political societies. By 1880 as many as 150 local societies existed. Chief among the aims of these societies was the "establishment of a national assembly" (*kokkai kaisetsu*)—that is, a parliament that would require a measure of government accountability to an as yet unspecified electorate.

The extent to which the popular rights societies were mobilizing support for a national parliament was indicated by the 96,900 people whom 114 delegates to the LEAGUE FOR ESTABLISHING A NATIONAL ASSEMBLY (Kokkai Kisei Dōmei) claimed to represent in a March 1880 meeting. By the second meeting of the league in November 1880, 64 delegates were speaking for about 130,000 members of various local popular rights societies, and a growing percentage of the league's national representatives now came from the commoner (*heimin*) as opposed to the former-samurai stratum of society.

The Rise of the Parties — In October 1881 Ōkuma Shigenobu resigned from the government over the issue of establishing a constitutional government; the day after his resignation it was announced that a national assembly would be convened nine years thereafter. The local political societies served as the raw material out of which Japan's first national political party, the Jiyūtō, was formed on 29 October (see POLITICAL CRISIS OF 1881). A few months later Ōkuma and his followers formed the RIKKEN KAISHINTŌ (Constitutional Reform Party; commonly called Kaishintō).

Eclipse of the Popular Rights Movement — Between 1882 and late 1884, as the rural economy faltered under the impact of the government's deflation policy, certain incidents occurred in the more commercialized areas of Fukushima, Gumma, Ibaraki, Saitama, and a few other prefectures. Though the incidents differed in size, tactics,

and degrees of violence, they were more or less organized around Jiyūtō's leaders. The Meiji government reacted violently toward the various popular rights incidents. Military and police force against the rebels resulted in the imprisonment of hundreds of leaders and the execution of a few. Repressive legislation followed, placing severe limits on speech, publication, association, and assembly. Hobbled by the authorities, embarrassed by the rebellions, and afflicted by internal discord between reformers and rebels, the Jiyūtō voted for dissolution on 29 October 1884. Ōkuma's Kaishintō effectively followed suit two months later.

Under Gotō Shōjirō's leadership there was an attempt in the late 1880s to reunite the disparate elements of the movement into the DAIDŌ DANKETSU MOVEMENT (Movement for a Union of Like Thinkers). Even this attempt was effectively short-circuited by the PEACE PRESERVATION LAW OF 1887 (Hoan Jōrei), which forced the political opposition into internal exile.

The promulgation of the CONSTITUTION OF THE EMPIRE OF JAPAN in 1889 sounded the death knell for the Popular Rights Movement. Though many of the democratic ideals that had informed the movement since the late 1870s lived on and found eloquent spokesmen in the socialist and labor organizers of the early 20th century, the movement itself was laid firmly to rest as its once notable leaders—Itagaki, Ōkuma, Gotō, and others—joined the government in constitutional Japan.

freedom of assembly 集会の自由

(*shūkai no jiyū*). Civil right guaranteed by the 1947 CONSTITUTION OF JAPAN. Article 21, paragraph 1, of the constitution states that "freedom of assembly and association as well as speech, press and all other forms of expression are guaranteed." As generally construed, freedom of assembly means freedom to hold a meeting at a specific place as well as freedom to conduct any other type of demonstration in which people gather, such as public parades. Freedom of assembly is regulated by prefectural public safety ordinances (KŌAN JŌREI). *Kōan jōrei* vary in content, and most ordinances are concerned only with demonstrations on public roads, but some control indoor assemblies as well. Many ordinances have established a permit system. Since each prefectural public safety commission has some discretionary power in issuing a permit, the constitutionality of *kōan jōrei* has become a controversial issue. Not all local governments have adopted *kōan jōrei*, and local governments without *kōan jōrei* regulate public demonstrations and the like by means of a national traffic regulation code. See also TŌKYŌ ORDINANCE DECISION.

freedom of association 結社の自由

(*kessha no jiyū*). Freedom to form an association is guaranteed by article 21 of the 1947 CONSTITUTION OF JAPAN. The right of workers to organize is independently protected by article 28 of the constitution. In prewar Japan the PUBLIC ORDER AND POLICE LAW OF 1900 (Chian Keisatsu Hō) extensively controlled people's freedom of association, but it was abolished after the war. At present, only the financial activities of political parties are monitored by the Political Fund Regulations Law. Freedom of assembly is now a reasonably well-enforced right, and the only curtailment is the SUBVERSIVE ACTIVITIES PREVENTION LAW (commonly known as Habō Hō) of

1952. The Public Safety Examination Commission (Kōan Shinsa Iinkai) may restrict those activities of an association that the commission finds "subversive" through its investigations. Since no association has ever been designated subversive, the constitutionality of the law remains undetermined.

freedom of contract 契約自由の原則

(*keiyaku jiyū no gensoku*). Principle of private law holding that contractual relationships should be determined by the free will of the parties involved, including the freedom to choose the other party and to determine the form and content of CONTRACTS. In Japan as elsewhere, this freedom has been restricted by legislation intended to protect weaker parties, such as consumers, who are often at a disadvantage in negotiating contracts.

freedom of information system 情報公開制度

(*jōhō kōkai seido*). Demand for the establishment of a legal framework to ensure freedom of information in Japan gained momentum after the LOCKHEED SCANDAL came to light in 1976. Advocates of this system called for legal recognition of the right of the public and mass media to demand access to information possessed by government agencies and of the government's duty to make such information available. In a 1978 decision involving the leaking of a Foreign Ministry telegram, the Japanese Supreme Court lent support to this position, declaring the public's right to know—to demand and receive free access to information—to be the fundamental basis of the constitutional right to freedom of expression.

The first concrete step toward the establishment of a freedom of information system came in 1982 with a local ordinance established in the town of Kanayama in Yamagata Prefecture. This was followed in 1983 with a freedom of information ordinance enacted in Kanagawa Prefecture that became a model for the rest of the country. By the end of the 1980s, 157 prefectural and local governments had established ordinances and regulations concerning freedom of access to information. The creation of a freedom of information system at the national level has been extensively debated, and the issue was raised in the report submitted by the Second Provisional Commission for Administrative Reform, but as of 1991 specific legislation for this purpose had not yet been initiated.

freedom of religious faith 信教の自由

(*shinkyō no jiyū*). Article 20, paragraph 1, of the CONSTITUTION OF JAPAN guarantees freedom of religion to every person. Considered to be a part of freedom of thought and conscience (art. 19), freedom of religion is understood to include freedom to believe or not to believe in a religion, freedom to alter one's religion, and freedom to keep silent about one's religion. It is also construed to imply freedom of religious activity; that is, freedom to worship, to hold religious assemblies and form religious associations, and to propagate religions. Moreover, the constitution clearly stipulates the principle of separation of state and religion (art. 20, para. 3). Although religious freedom was guaranteed in the pre–World War II constitution (art. 28), the government developed a form of national religion now called STATE SHINTŌ. The provisions for the separation of state and religion in the present constitution are aimed at preventing this kind of government encroachment on religious belief.

freedom of speech 言論の自由

(*genron no jiyū*). Fundamental civil right guaranteed by the CONSTITUTION OF JAPAN. Freedom of speech refers narrowly to oral expression, but it is usually used synonymously with freedom of expression (*hyōgen no jiyū*) to connote the "Freedom of . . . speech, press and all other forms of expression" (Constitution, art. 21, para. 1). At present, publishing, broadcasting, and motion pictures have become the most effective means of expressing ideas, and FREEDOM OF THE PRESS has accordingly become the core of freedom of speech.

The present constitution makes especially clear the prohibition on censorship by means of prior restraint, which poses the greatest threat to freedom of speech. The freedom to gather information has been recognized as a corollary of freedom of expression, and the courts have ruled that it is protected by the guarantee of freedom of speech. Laws prohibiting libel and slander, the invasion of privacy, and OBSCENITY have been ruled constitutional. See also CENSORSHIP.

freedom of speech, regulation of 言論統制

(*genron tōsei*). When publishing became widespread in Japan after the beginning of the Edo period (1600–1868), the shogunate began strict regulation of publications. In 1684 an order was issued forbidding the publication of the broadsheet publications called *yomiuri* (later called KAWARABAN) and of books treating questions of the day. Regulations became stricter with the passage of time. However, by the end of the shogunate, publications on current topics and every sort of illegal publication were increasing, and the system of publication controls gradually collapsed.

Government Limitations—Strict control of publications was reimposed during the Meiji (1868–1912) and Taishō (1912–26) periods. The first systematic legislation was the Shimbunshi Inkō Jōrei (Newspaper Publishing Ordinance) and the Shuppan Jōrei (see PUBLICATION ORDINANCE OF 1869). As the expression of political dissent grew in the 1870s, the government enacted the Shimbunshi Jōmoku (1873; Newspaper Stipulations) and the Shimbunshi Jōrei (see PRESS ORDINANCE OF 1875). In 1883 a revision of the 1875 Press Ordinance added even stricter controls.

One characteristic of the newspaper laws in Japan was that the home minister, who had jurisdiction over publication control, was given wide discretionary powers and was able to seize or prohibit the publication of a specified edition of a newspaper or a magazine or to suspend its publication for a set period of time. The Press Ordinance was replaced by the PRESS LAW OF 1909 (Shimbunshi Hō), which remained the basic law for the control of speech until Japan's defeat in World War II in 1945.

When radio broadcasting in Japan started in 1925, the government instituted prebroadcast censorship of scripts and established a system of surveillance that included the means to cut off the power supply to the microphones at any time. This censorship in effect brought about state-run broadcasting. During the 1930s and World War II, laws regulating the mass media were enacted one after another, and government control of the media became even more severe. The establishment of the Cabinet Information Bureau (Naikaku Jōhō Kyoku) in 1940 unified and centralized the government's censorship and propaganda activities.

Postwar Freedoms—After the war, OCCUPATION authorities ordered the repeal of government censorship and issued regulations to guarantee freedom of speech. At the same time they strictly forbade any criticism of Occupation policies, issuing the Press Code and Radio Code for Japan, and introduced their own censorship system. Occupation controls on the Japanese media came to an end in 1952 when the SAN FRANCISCO PEACE TREATY restored Japan's sovereignty. Legislation with provisions that restrain speech in post-Occupation Japan include the BROADCASTING LAW (Hōsō Hō; 1950), the SUBVERSIVE ACTIVITIES PREVENTION LAW (Hakai Katsudō Bōshi Hō; 1952), and the Defense Secrets Protection Law (Himitsu Hogo Hō; 1954), which supplements the UNITED STATES–JAPAN SECURITY TREATIES. At present there are no newspaper, publishing, or film laws in existence in Japan. The sole mass media law, the Broadcasting Law, contains nothing more than a declaration of program standards. OBSCENITY, libel and slander, and privacy legislation are the only other areas where freedom of speech is restricted. See also CENSORSHIP.

freedom of the press 出版・報道の自由

(*shuppan, hōdō no jiyū*). Under the 1889 Meiji Constitution and other laws, the Japanese media were severely restricted before World War II. After the war, Japanese media came under the protection of article 21 of the 1947 constitution, which guarantees "[freedom of] assembly and association as well as speech, press and all other forms of expression" and prohibits censorship. The lese majesty provision of criminal law and crimes concerning the disclosure of military secrets were also abolished as unconstitutional. In defamation cases, the principle of truth was adopted, and special treatment was accorded crime reports and criticisms of public officials. However, the act of soliciting the disclosure of secrets from public officials is prohibited by the Public Employee Law. Regulations also exist to control violations of reputation and privacy, and others prohibit the use of obscene expressions (see OBSCENITY). In addition to these general restrictions, the BROADCASTING LAW of 1950 regulates broadcasting on such matters as the principle of political impartiality. See also CENSORSHIP; HAKATA STATION FILM CASE.

Free Thai Movement 自由タイ運動

(FTM; J: Jiyū Tai Undō). Anti-Japanese resistance movement of the Thai people during World War II. Organized in the United States in 1942 by SENI PRAMOT (then Thai ambassador to the United States), it soon had branches in Great Britain and Thailand as well. In the fall of 1943, FTM forces from the United States stationed in southern China, and members of the British branch in India, infiltrated Thailand and joined domestic forces. An anti-Japanese military uprising was planned by PRIDI PHANOMYONG, leader of the domestic FTM, but it had not yet materialized when Japan surrendered in August 1945. The FTM was dissolved in October 1945. See also THAILAND AND JAPAN.

freight transportation 運送業

(*unsōgyō*). Shipping and trucking are Japan's most important means of domestic freight transportation, accounting for 50.0 percent

frogs
1 The *amagaeru*, a tree frog, is common in lowlands throughout Japan. Adults measure up to 4 cm in length.
2 The *hikigaeru* (common toad) can be found throughout Japan, excluding Hokkaidō. Adults are 10 to 14 cm long.
3 The *tonosamagaeru* is found in much of Japan, inhabiting wet areas. Males and females are different colors. Adults reach about 7 cm in length.

and 45.0 percent, respectively, of the nation's freight traffic in 1987. In contrast, railways, once major freight carriers, accounted for a mere 4.6 percent, while the share of air transportation was only 0.1 percent. In 1988 domestic transportation totaled 489.2 billion ton-kilometers (300.0 billion ton-miles). Shipments of large-volume items such as coal and grain are on the decline, while demand for a wide variety of relatively small-volume items has increased rapidly in recent years. To cope with this crucial change, giant line-haul trucking firms specializing in the transportation of small cargoes have steadily built up nationwide computerized distribution networks, established numerous distribution centers at strategic points, and introduced automatic cargo-sorting machines and automated multilevel warehouses. These moves, together with the initiation of parcel delivery systems for the general public and other services, have contributed to the swift growth of the freight transportation industry. By linking their nationwide distribution centers with on-line communication systems, freight transportation companies have built information networks and initiated new services such as bill collection, inventory management, and the gathering of client data. Japanese freight transportation companies also are entering the field of international distribution services and are building global networks through tie-ups with overseas corporations.

fringed pink The wildflower *kawara nadeshiko* is found in mountain meadows and along streams. The delicate flowers bloom in summer and early fall.

fringed pink 河原撫子

(*kawara nadeshiko*). *Dianthus superbus*. Also known in Japanese as Yamato *nadeshiko* or *nadeshiko*. Perennial herb of the family Caryophyllaceae that grows wild in fields and mountains throughout Japan and is one of the traditional seven flowers of autumn (*aki no nanakusa*). It grows to 50–60 centimeters (20–24 in), with opposite, lanceolate leaves and pink, five-petaled flowers (3–4 cm [1.0–5 in] across) that bloom all summer. Related Japanese wildflowers include the *takane nadeshiko* (*D. superbus* var. *monticola*), which grows high in the mountains and the *miyama* (or *shinano*) *nadeshiko* (*D. barbatus* var. *shinanensis*), a relative of the sweet William, which grows in the mountains of central Honshū. "Yamato *nadeshiko*" is some-

times used as a metaphor for Japanese womanhood.

Fröbel, Friedrich Wilhelm August

フレーベル, F. W. A.

(1782–1852). German educator; founder of the kindergarten. In his major work, *Die Menschenerziehung* (1826, Human Education), he expounded a developmental pedagogy based on the premise that the child is fundamentally good by nature. He created teaching materials that were intended to foster creativity by developing an awareness of the universal gift of life. Fröbel's pedagogy was first introduced to Japan by Clara Matsuno (d 1941), a German-born teacher at Japan's first kindergarten, founded in 1876 in affiliation with Tōkyō Women's Normal School (now Ochanomizu Women's University). His pedagogy has had a profound influence on early childhood education in Japan.

frogs 蛙

(*kaeru*). In Japanese, *kaeru* is the general name for amphibians belonging to the order Anura, class Amphibia. Twenty-seven species of six families, including the families Bufonidae, Hylidae, and Ranidae, inhabit Japan. Most common is the *hikigaeru* (common toad; *Bufo bufo*), which stays away from water except when laying eggs and is found from mountainous districts to urban areas, as is the tree-dwelling *amagaeru* (*Hyla arborea*). The *tonosamagaeru* (*Rana nigromaculata*) and *darumagaeru* (*R. brevipoda*) inhabit paddy fields, ponds, and swamps in great numbers. The *ushigaeru* (bullfrog; *R. catesbeiana*), a North American species, was introduced to Japan in 1919 as an edible frog.

The croaking of the frog appeals to the Japanese sense of season and has been much admired since early times. The end of winter is signaled by the frog's mating call, heard from the still chilly ponds and swamps. The Nihon *akagaeru* (*R. japonica*) has been used as a medication and food, and the *yama akagaeru* (*R. ornativentris*) was relished as a delicacy. The *hikigaeru* was believed to cause a lunar eclipse by swallowing the moon.

Frois, Luis フロイス, L

(1532–97). A Jesuit missionary noted for his reports on contemporary events. Born in Lisbon, Frois arrived in Japan in 1563. With the exception of two years in Macao, he spent the rest of his life in Japan and died in Nagasaki. In the course of his long career Frois met leading figures of the day. A keen observer and a meticulous recorder, he assembled and sent back to Europe detailed annual reports of missionary activity. He also composed a valuable account of the Christian church in Japan from 1549 to 1593, the *Historia de Japam*, as well as treatises on Japanese customs, Hideyoshi's Korean campaign, and the downfall of TOYOTOMI HIDETSUGU.

fuchi 扶持

(literally, "support"). Also called *fuchimai* (support rice). A type of salary for SAMURAI paid in rice or its money equivalent during the Edo period (1600–1868). When samurai society became more urbanized and the number of samurai who received rice stipends (KURAMAI) increased, *fuchi* became a basic form of salary for low-ranking samurai. *Fuchi* payment was also made to higher-ranking vassals and samurai, many of whom had fixed incomes based on the size of their

fiefs. This payment, called *kafuchi* (additional support), was a supplementary allowance for those assigned to important offices or duties. Not infrequently, *fuchi* was also extended to deserving farmers, important merchants, and even mistresses of shōguns or *daimyō*. See also KIRIMAI.

Fuchū 府中[市]

City in central Tōkyō Prefecture, situated on the northern bank of the river Tamagawa. Its importance dates from the 7th century, when it became the capital of Musashi Province (now Saitama, Tōkyō, and part of Kanagawa prefectures). The production of electrical appliances, machinery, and foodstuffs has replaced agriculture as its main occupation. A growing residential suburb of Tōkyō, it is noted for its racetracks, the largest in Japan, and the Ōkunitama Shrine. Pop: 209,396.

Fuchū 府中[市]

City in eastern Hiroshima Prefecture, western Honshū, on the river Ashidagawa. A provincial capital in ancient times, Fuchū has traditionally been known for its furniture, *kasuri* cloth, and *miso* (bean paste). Other industries include ironwork, machinery, and clothing. Pop: 45,739.

fudai 譜代

(literally, "successive generations"). Hereditary vassals or servants. A term used from the Heian period (794–1185) onward to denote one whose family stood in hereditary subordination to another family. Thus a *fudai* peasant family would provide a well-to-do landholding family with agricultural and domestic services from generation to generation. See also OYAKATA AND HIKAN; NAGO.

The term took on particular importance during the Edo period (1600–1868), when hereditary vassal families who served a powerful *samurai* family were known as *fudai* to distinguish them from TOZAMA (outside vassals) who had only recently entered into service. The Tokugawa shogunate designated about 150 families who had served the Tokugawa family before the Battle of SEKIGAHARA (1600) and had then been raised to DAIMYŌ status as *fudai daimyō*. Although *fudai* daimyō had smaller domains than *tozama* daimyō (some 80 families who had acquired daimyō status under ODA NOBUNAGA or TOYOTOMI HIDEYOSHI and who had later sworn allegiance to the Tokugawa), they held powerful hereditary posts in the shogunate.

fudasashi 札差

Also called *kurayado*. Merchants who, probably from the 1640s, acted as financiers and rice dealers for the *hatamoto* (bannermen) and other direct retainers of the Tokugawa shogunate (1603–1867) who received salaries in rice (*kuramai*); they also lent money at interest. For most of the 18th century they were a major influence in the Edo (now Tōkyō) rice and money markets. Their wealth, extravagance, and power were notorious. They were dealt a heavy blow by the KANSEI REFORMS (1787–93) and the TEMPŌ REFORMS (1841–43); they were finally wiped out in the MEIJI RESTORATION (1868).

The *fudasashi* became a KABUNAKAMA (monopolistic trade association) in 1724. In 1777 the groups were reorganized and placed under the overall direction of the Edo city commissioners (EDO MACHI BUGYŌ). The *fudasashi* received commissions for collecting or selling rice for shogunal retainers, but their chief profits came from an interest of 15 percent, later reduced to 12 percent, on advances against future crops. In addition, they controlled bidding for government rice and made large profits on its later resale. Their wealth enabled them to maintain an extravagant lifestyle. Monopolistic organizations were abolished in the Tempō Reforms, and, though the monopoly rights of the *fudasashi* were restored in 1851, they never recovered financially. When, with the Meiji Restoration, *kuramai* stipends were terminated without compensation for outstanding loans, the *fudasashi* lost their wealth and livelihood.

fudoki 風土記

Collections of 8th-century reports on the natural resources, geophysical conditions, and oral traditions of each of approximately 60 Japanese provinces. The only *fudoki* of any substantial length that have survived are the reports from the provinces of Bungo (now part of Ōita Prefecture), Harima (now part of Hyōgo Prefecture), Hitachi (now part of Ibaraki Prefecture), Hizen (now Saga and Nagasaki prefectures), and Izumo (now Shimane Prefecture), and only the last-named retains its original form. The reports from other provinces remain only in some 100 fragments known as *fudoki itsubun* ("once scattered and lost *fudoki*"). All of these documents are customarily referred to as *kofudoki* (old *fudoki*) in order to differentiate them from similarly titled later works such as *Shimpen Musashi fudoki kō* (1828, A New Draft of Musashi Fudoki) and *Kii zoku fudoki* (1839, The Second Series of Kii Fudoki). Today the term *fudoki* is used to indicate general works describing customs, culture, and economic life in local regions.

In 713 the central government ordered the governors of each province to submit in writing surveys of products, animals, plants, and land conditions; etymologies of place names; and oral traditions. It is assumed that the surveys were to be used for taxation and security purposes, while the etymologies and oral traditions were for the forthcoming compilation of the NIHON SHOKI (720). Local governments kept copies or original drafts of these reports. In 925 the central government requested the provincial governments to resubmit these antiquated documents, and some of the information thus assembled for the second time found its way into the ENGI SHIKI. Possible prototypes of favorite Japanese tales such as URASHIMA TARŌ and the HAGOROMO LEGEND are found in some of the *fudoki itsubun*.

Fudō Myōō →myōō

Fuefukigawa 笛吹川

River in Yamanashi Prefecture, central Honshū, originating in the Kantō Mountains and joining the river KAMANASHIGAWA in the Kōfu Basin to form the FUJIKAWA. Known as a "wild" river, the Fuefukigawa has caused much flooding. Length: 55 km (34 mi).

Fūgai Ekun 風外慧薫

(1568–1654). Zen monk of the Sōtō sect and painter. After taking the tonsure as a youth in his native Kōzuke (now Gumma Prefecture), he served in the temple Jōganji in Sagami (now part of Kanagawa Prefecture). In his later years he became a wandering monk, refusing honors or official positions and lived for a time in caves, for which habit he received the name Ana Fūgai (Cave Fūgai). His paintings date from the later period of his life and are all individualistic ink studies of Zen-related subjects. He most often chose to depict Hotei (Ch: Budai or Putai), the happy-go-lucky monk, or Daruma (Bodhidharma), the first patriarch of Zen.

Fūga wakashū 風雅和歌集

(Collection of Elegance). A 20-volume, 2,211-verse anthology of WAKA (traditional Japanese poetry) collected during the Northern and Southern Courts era (1337–92); compiled around 1349. The 17th of the IMPERIAL ANTHOLOGIES, it was supervised by the retired emperor Hanazono (1297–1348; r 1308–18), but the poems were assembled by his nephew, the retired emperor KŌGON (1313–64; r 1331–33) with assistance from Ōgimachi Kinkage (1297–1360), Reizei Tamehide (1300?–1372), and Fujiwara no Tamemoto (dates unknown). It is the second and last imperial anthology of the Kyōgoku poets, the first having been the GYOKUYŌ WAKASHŪ (ca 1312, Collection of Jeweled Leaves) edited by KYŌGOKU TAMEKANE. The Kyōgoku aesthetic is set forth by Hanazono in two prefaces, written in KANA and KAMBUN respectively. Poets featured include the compilers of the collection as well Emperor FUSHIMI, EIFUKU MON'IN, and others associated with the Kyōgoku school.

fugu →globefishes

Fuji 富士[市]

City in eastern Shizuoka Prefecture, central Honshū. At the southern base of Mt. Fuji (FUJISAN), facing Suruga Bay, Fuji was formed by the merger of two towns in 1966. It has paper and pulp, chemical fiber, film, and pharmaceutical industries. Pop: 222,490.

fuji →wisteria, Japanese

Fujian (Fukien) People's Government 福建人民政府

(J: Fukken Jimmin Seifu). Opposition government established in China's Fujian Province in November 1933 by rebel members of the Guomindang (Kuomintang; Nationalist Party) who objected to the Guomindang's authoritarian government and its conciliatory policy toward Japanese aggression in China. The rebel government called for a democratic national government and a strong resistance to Japan's invasion. To its surprise, support for these policies did not materialize. The Chinese Communist Party, with whom the rebels had formed an agreement, refused to aid the revolt, and by mid-January 1934 the Fujian government had collapsed. National unity against Japan would begin in China only after the XI'AN (SIAN) INCIDENT in 1936.

Fuji Bank, Ltd [株]富士銀行

(Fuji Ginkō). One of Japan's city banks. Founded in 1864, when YASUDA ZENJIRŌ started a money-exchange business that became the Yasuda Bank in 1880. It subsequently absorbed numerous small and medium-size banks to become the largest bank in Japan in deposits. In 1948 it became the Fuji Bank.

It initiated overseas activities with the establishment of branches in London in 1952 and in New York in 1956 and has since added 14 more branches and 23 representative offices throughout the world. The bank also has an extensive network of overseas subsidiaries and affiliates that provides services ranging from commercial and investment banking to factoring, leasing, securities-related business, and mergers and acquisitions advisory services. The Fuji Bank is one of the central enterprises of the Fuyō group. At the end of March 1991 total assets were ¥59.2 trillion (US $431.5 billion), deposits were ¥41.8 trillion (US $304.7 billion), and capitalization stood at ¥421.8 billion (US $3.1 billion). Corporate headquarters are in Tōkyō.

Fujieda 藤枝[市]

City in south-central Shizuoka Prefecture, central Honshū. Fujieda developed as a castle town and post-station town during the Edo period (1600–1868). Now a distribution center for tea, *shiitake* mushrooms, and mandarin oranges, it also has synthetic resin and pharmaceutical industries. Attractions include Rengeji Pond and Shida Hot Spring. Pop: 119,815.

Fujieda Shizuo 藤枝静男

(1907–93). Novelist and physician. Real name Katsumi Jirō. Born in Shizuoka Prefecture; graduate of Chiba Medical College (now a part of Chiba University). He combined his medical practice with writing. His writings follow the autobiographical tradition of the *watakushi shōsetsu* (see I-NOVEL). His principal works include *Iperitto-gan* (1949), *Inu no chi* (1956), *Kyōto Tsuda Sanzō* (1961), *Kūki atama* (1967), and *Kanashii dake* (1979).

Fuji Electric Co, Ltd 富士電機[株]

(Fuji Denki). Manufacturer of heavy electric machinery and electronic components. Incorporated in 1923. Its telecommunications division, which became independent in 1935, was the forerunner of FUJITSŪ, LTD. The company manufactures hydroelectric and thermal power generation equipment, industrial measuring devices, transistors, integrated circuits, peripheral equipment for computers, photoconductive drums for photocopy machines, and related products. Sales for the fiscal year ending March 1991 totaled ¥592.0 billion (US $4.3 billion), with heavy electric machinery constituting 36 percent; distribution and control equipment, 21 percent; measuring instruments, 12 percent; electronic devices, 15 percent; and specialty electric appliances and vending machines, 16 percent. The company was capitalized at ¥46.8 billion (US $341.1 million) in the same year. Headquarters are in Tōkyō.

Fuji Fire & Marine Insurance Co, Ltd 富士火災海上保険[株]

(Fuji Kasai Kaijō Hoken). Nonlife insurance company. Incorporated in 1918. The company issues all classes of nonlife insurance and is known for its direct writing system and maturity-refund-type insurance for fire and personal accident. It has two wholly owned subsidiaries overseas—American Fuji Fire and Marine Insurance Co in Chicago and Fuji Fire and Marine Insurance Co, Ltd, in London. Representative offices are located in London, Chicago, New York, Los Angeles, Singapore, Hong Kong, Bangkok, and Düsseldorf. For the fiscal year ending March 1991, total assets reached ¥1.1 trillion (US $8.0 billion), and the overall net premium income was ¥306.7 billion (US $2.2 billion). Capitalization was ¥22.8 billion (US $166.2 million) in the same year. Headquarters are in Ōsaka.

Fuji-Hakone-Izu National Park This park's wide range of attractions includes Mt. Fuji, a scenic coastline, and popular hot-spring resorts.
1 Viewed from the Izu Peninsula across Suruga Bay, Mt. Fuji seems to rise directly from the water.
2 Tall cedars nearly 300 years old line a rare remaining segment of the Hakone Road, which forms a part of the Tōkaidō, the major thoroughfare from Edo (now Tōkyō) to Kyōto during the Edo period (1600–1868).

Fuji Five Lakes 富士五湖

(Fuji Goko). Five lakes on the northern slopes of Mt. Fuji (FUJISAN), southeastern Yamanashi Prefecture, central Honshū. The group is composed, from the east, of Lake YAMANAKA (Yamanakako), Lake KAWAGUCHI (Kawaguchiko), Lake Sai (Saiko), Lake Shōji (Shōjiko), and Lake Motosu (Motosuko). Created when lava flows from eruptions of Fujisan dammed valleys of the Misaka Mountains, the lakes were later filled with rainwater and underground water. The largest is Lake Yamanaka (6.4 sq km; 2.5 sq mi); the smallest is Lake Shōji (0.7 sq km; 0.3 sq mi). The deepest is Lake Motosu (122 m; 400 ft); the shallowest is Lake Yamanaka (13 m; 43 ft). Lake Yamanaka is at the highest altitude (981 m; 3,218 ft); Lake Kawaguchi is at the lowest (831 m; 2,726 ft).

Fujigawa, Battle of 富士川の戦い

(Fujigawa no Tatakai). The first major victory of MINAMOTO NO YORITOMO in the TAIRA-MINAMOTO WAR (1180–85). Yoritomo rose against the Taira on 8 September 1180. He was badly defeated on 15 September 1180 in the Battle of Ishibashiyama and retreated to Awa Province (now part of Chiba Prefecture) to regroup. In November he led his troops into Suruga Province (now part of Shizuoka Prefecture), where a Taira army was encamped on the western bank of the river Fujigawa. According to the chronicle AZUMA KAGAMI (compiled in the late 13th century), a small band of Yoritomo's men attempted a night crossing and startled a flock of geese. The Taira forces panicked and fled, giving Yoritomo the victory without a fight

Fujiko Fujio Obake no Kyūtarō, the cartoon ghost that launched the career of "Fujiko Fujio," the name under which a pair of cartoonists produced some of Japan's most popular children's entertainment.

and enabling him to consolidate his power in eastern Japan.

Fuji-Hakone-Izu National Park
富士箱根伊豆国立公園

(Fuji-Hakone-Izu Kokuritsu Kōen). Situated in Tōkyō, Yamanashi, Kanagawa, and Shizuoka prefectures. The park also includes the IZU ISLANDS. The varied topography of the park's four sections features Mt. Fuji (FUJISAN), lakes, hot-spring resorts, subtropical volcanic islands, and a long stretch of coast. The volcanic cone of Japan's highest mountain, Mt. Fuji (3,776 m; 12,388 ft), sweeps up directly from the sea about 100 km (62 mi) west of Tōkyō. The surrounding hills, wooded with pines and firs, have five major lakes (FUJI FIVE LAKES). Southeast of Mt. Fuji, the wooded volcanic Hakone region, famed for its hot-spring resorts, is dominated by the peak Komagatake and the large caldera lake ASHINOKO. South of the Hakone region lies the scenic IZU PENINSULA, together with the mountain group AMAGISAN and YUGASHIMA HOT SPRING. On the east coast are many hot springs, such as those at Atami and Itō.

Proximity to Tōkyō, the spectacular views around Mt. Fuji, the hot-spring resorts and forests of Hakone, and the bathing beaches of the Izu Peninsula have made the park Japan's most popular vacation and resort area. Area: 1,227 sq km (474 sq mi).

Fuji Heavy Industries, Ltd
富士重工業[株]

(Fuji Jūkōgyō). Manufacturer of automobiles, buses, and airplanes. It is a major producer of small automobiles in Japan, and its products are well known abroad under the brand name Subaru. Its predecessor was the Airplane Research Institute, founded in 1917 by NAKAJIMA CHIKUHEI. This firm was divided into several separate companies after World War II, but in 1955 they were reunited to form the present company. Its aircraft division now produces light aircraft for military and civilian use. The company has sales subsidiaries in the United States and Belgium. Sales for the fiscal year ending March 1991 totaled ¥755.8 billion (US $5.5 billion), with an export ratio of 38 percent. The company was capitalized at ¥80.7 billion (US $588.2 million) in the same year. Headquarters are in Tōkyō.

Fujiidera 藤井寺[市]

City in southeastern Ōsaka Prefecture, central Honshū. The site of the provincial capital of Kawachi Province in ancient times, it is now a residential suburb of Ōsaka. Principal products include fruits and other agricultural produce. It is the site of several imperial

burial mounds (KOFUN) as well as the temples Fujiidera and Dōmyōji. Pop: 65,922.

Fujii Heigo 藤井丙午

(1906–80). Businessman and politician. Born in Gifu Prefecture. Graduate of Waseda University. Fujii joined NIPPON STEEL CORPORATION in 1937 as secretary to President Hirao Hachisaburō (1866–1945). After World War II, when the company was divided into two separate firms, Yawata Steel and Fuji Steel, Fujii stayed with the former and became vice-president in 1962. He concurrently served as a member of the National Public Safety Commission and vice-chairman of the Japan Committee for Economic Development. When Yawata Steel and Fuji Steel merged in 1970 to once again form Nippon Steel, he became vice-president. In 1974 he was elected to the House of Councillors.

Fujii Kenjirō 藤井健次郎

(1866–1952). Cytologist. Born in Kanazawa (now in Ishikawa Prefecture). Graduate of Tōkyō University. He went to Europe to study plant morphology and cytology under the German scholar Eduard Strasburger (1844–1912). He became a professor at Tōkyō University in 1911 and contributed to the first lectures on genetics given there in 1918. He founded the international periodical *Cytologia* in 1929 and worked to raise the field of cytology in Japan to an international level. He received the Order of Culture in 1950.

Fujikawa 富士川

River in Yamanashi and Shizuoka prefectures, in central Honshū, originating in the northern Akaishi Mountains and the Kantō Mountains and flowing into Suruga Bay. The rivers KAMANASHIGAWA and FUEFUKIGAWA converge in the Kōfu Basin at Kajikazawa to form the Fujikawa. The water is used for industry, electric power generation, and irrigation. Length: 128 km (80 mi); area of drainage basin: 3,990 sq km (1,540 sq mi).

Fujikawa Yū 富士川游

(1865–1940). Medical historian. Born in Aki Province (now Hiroshima Prefecture). Graduate of Hiroshima Igakkō. He studied in Germany for two years. Fujikawa was the first to write a systematic account of Japanese medical history. Among his major works is *Nihon igaku shi* (1904), translated into English as *Japanese Medicine* (1934).

Fujiko Fujio 藤子不二雄

Pen name used for joint projects by the cartoonists Fujimoto Hiroshi (b 1933) and Abiko Motoo (b 1934), both of whom were born in Toyama Prefecture. The pair first achieved fame with their children's comic *Obake no Kyūtarō*, which appeared in the children's comic magazine *Shōnen sandē* in 1964. That comic was followed by a succession of extremely popular serialized comics for children including *Ninja Hattori kun*, *Pāman*, and *Doraemon*. Many of the duo's hit comics were made into animated television programs and motion pictures, which have enjoyed similar popularity. Fujiko Fujio's works epitomize the Japanese children's comic. In 1989 the two artists began working independently.

Fuji Kōsan Co, Ltd 富士興産[株]

(Fuji Kōsan). Company engaged in the manufacture and sale of petroleum products. Incorporated in 1949. Fuji Kōsan is a wholly independent refining company producing

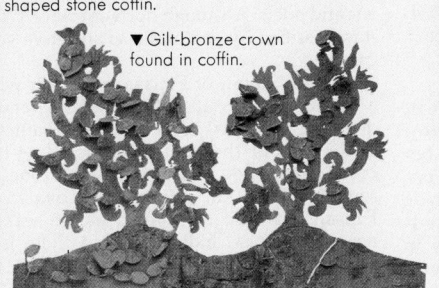

Fujinoki tomb

This late-6th-century round tomb mound in the town of Ikaruga, Nara Prefecture, is believed to be an imperial burial site.

► The interior of the stone coffin.

◄ Corridor-type stone chamber containing a house-shaped stone coffin.

► Gilt-bronze crown found in coffin.

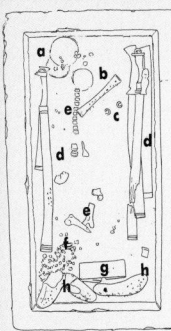

▲ Main objects in coffin: **a** bronze mirrors; **b** gilt-bronze cylindrical object; **c** earrings; **d** swords; **e** human bones; **f** gilt-bronze crown; **g** bronze belt; **h** gilt-bronze shoes.

lubricating oil, heavy oil, liquefied petroleum gas, and other products. Sales for the fiscal year ending March 1991 totaled ¥143.5 billion (US $1.0 billion). The company was capitalized at ¥4.0 billion (US $29.1 million) in the same year. Headquarters are in Tōkyō.

Fujikura, Ltd   [株]フジクラ

(Fujikura Densen). Company engaged in the manufacture and sale of electric wire and cable and accessory products, as well as the design and construction of related projects. Incorporated in 1885. Fujikura is the fourth largest electric wire producer in Japan. The company has also entered the optical systems field and is engaging in research and development for optical fibers. It has 26 overseas subsidiaries in Singapore, Malaysia, Thailand, Korea, Taiwan, the United States, Brazil, the United Kingdom, the Netherlands, and Saudi Arabia. Annual sales for 1991 totaled ¥254.4 billion (US $1.9 billion), and the company was capitalized at ¥30.9 billion (US $225.2 million). Headquarters are in Tōkyō.

Fujima Kanjūrō VI   藤間勘十郎6世

(1900–1990). Head of the Fujima school of the Japanese-style dance and kabuki-dance choreographer. Real name Fujima Hideo. Born in Tōkyō. Fujima originally took the professional name of Onoe Umeo, but he was later adopted into the Fujima family, and in 1927 he became Fujima Kanjūrō VI. The same year he was made a choreographer for the Kabukiza after designing dances for the KABUKI actor Onoe Kikugorō VI (1885–1949). He is highly regarded both for his delicate yet highly orthodox choreography for classical dance pieces and for his novel designs for modern-style pieces. He is also known as a master of *suodori*, dances performed without costume or masks. He was designated as a Living National Treasure in 1960. In 1963 he received the Japan Art Academy Prize for his choreography for *Makurajishi*, and in 1967 he became a member of the academy. In 1982 he was awarded the Order of Culture. At his retirement in 1990 he conferred the name Fujima Kanjūrō on his daughter and took the name Fujima Kanso II.

Fujimi   富士見[市]

City in southern Saitama Prefecture, central Honshū, about 27 km (17 mi) northwest of Tōkyō. An agricultural area in the past, it is now a residential suburb of Tōkyō. Pop: 94,864.

Fujimori Seikichi   藤森成吉

(1892–1977). Novelist and playwright. Born in Nagano Prefecture. While a student at Tōkyō University he gained recognition with the novel *Nami* (1914; reissued as *Wakaki hi no nayami*, 1920). After teaching for a brief period he devoted himself to writing full time; he also became involved in the proletarian and labor movements. In 1926 he published his first celebrated play, *Haritsuke Mozaemon*, followed by *Gisei* (1926) and *Nani ga kanojo o sō saseta ka* (1927). Like many other proletarian writers in the early 1930s, he was forced by the government to undergo "conversion" (TENKŌ). Subsequently he confined his writing to nonpolitical biographical and historical fiction. After World War II, he joined the Japan Communist Party and was a leader of the leftist group Shin Nihon Bungakukai (see SHIN NIHON BUNGAKU). Other works include *Watanabe Kazan* (1935) and *Kanashiki ai* (1955).

Fuji, Mt. → Fujisan

Fujin kōron   婦人公論

(Women's Review). Women's magazine, started in 1916 by the publishing company CHŪŌ KŌRON SHA, INC. Unlike most other women's magazines at that time, *Fujin kōron* focused on intellectual, progressive subjects such as equal rights for women. After World War II, it had a leading role in spreading "democratic" concepts about women. Since 1958 its image has been adapted to appeal to a wider audience.

Fujin no tomo   婦人之友

(Woman's Friend). The oldest women's magazine in Japan. Founded by HANI MOTOKO and her husband Hani Yoshikazu (1880–1955) in 1903. Originally entitled *Katei no tomo* (Friend of the Home), it changed to its present title in 1908. Hani Motoko's intention was to create a magazine for the enlightenment of the middle-class housewife, and each issue contained her ideas, based on a Christian view of society, for the improvement of women's lives. *Fujin no tomo* differed from other women's magazines in that, besides offering practical suggestions for improvements in areas of home economics and health, it gave advice on possibilities for changes in family relationships and the lives of working women. In 1930 the publishers of *Fujin no tomo* founded a national organization for women, Tomo no Kai, in order to promote further the views of the magazine.

Fujino Chūjirō   藤野忠次郎

(1901–85). Businessman; chairman of MITSUBISHI CORPORATION (1974–80). Born in Saitama Prefecture. After graduating from Tōkyō University in 1925, Fujino joined Mitsubishi Corporation. By reunifying that company and several other Mitsubishi companies that had been broken up in the ZAIBATSU DISSOLUTION program instituted by the Occupation, he helped forge a new Mitsubishi Corporation in 1954 and became its president in 1966. He served as representative manager (1974–79) of the "Friday Association," a group of the heads of 27 Mitsubishi companies. He also served as vice-chairman of the Tōkyō Chamber of Commerce and Industry (1969–81).

Fujinoki tomb   藤ノ木古墳

(Fujinoki *kofun*). A round tomb mound dating from the latter half of the 6th century; located in the town of Ikaruga, Nara Prefecture. The tomb has a diameter of about 48 meters (158 ft) and a height of about 7.5 meters (25 ft). It was excavated in three stages from 1985 to 1988, principally by the Nara Prefectural Kashihara Archaeological Institute. The first excavation, of its corridor-type stone chamber, led to the discovery of a house-shaped stone coffin painted cinnabar red, three sets of horse trappings, and various earthenware objects. The outstanding metalworking techniques evident on the horse trappings led experts to conclude that they may have been imported from China to Korea. The coffin was opened during the third stage of excavation. Two skeletons were found inside, one of which was identified as that of a male in his twenties. Other items discovered in the coffin included a crown, shoes, and a cylindrical object, all fashioned of gilt-bronze; a bronze belt; four mirrors; earrings and beads; and five large swords. Archaeologists believe that the people buried in the Fujinoki tomb were members of the imperial family. As one of the few tombs of this kind never plundered by thieves, it is an invaluable source of information regarding ancient Japanese culture and relations with continental Asia.

Fujinomiya   富士宮[市]

City in eastern Shizuoka Prefecture, central Honshū, at the southwestern base of Mt. Fuji (FUJISAN). Fujinomiya developed around the SENGEN SHRINE and as a base camp for Mt. Fuji. Paper, spinning, and chemical industries flourish. A part of the FUJI-HAKONE-IZU NATIONAL PARK, its tourist attractions are the Asagiri Highland, SHIRAITO FALLS, and Inokashira Park. Taisekiji, the main temple of the Nichiren Shōshū sect, is located on the outskirts. Pop: 117,092.

Fuji Oil Co, Ltd   不二製油[株]

(Fuji Seiyu). Maker of edible oils. Incorporated in 1950. The largest producer of palm and coconut oil in Japan, it also produces cocoa butter and soybean-protein food materials for manufacturers of processed food. Sales for the fiscal year ending March 1991 totaled ¥81.0 billion (US $590.4 million), and the company was capitalized at ¥13.2 billion (US $96.2 million). Headquarters are in Ōsaka.

Fuji Oil Co, Ltd 富士石油[株]

(Fuji Sekiyu). Company engaged in petroleum refining. Incorporated in 1964. It belongs to the Kyōdo Sekiyu group and is engaged in international and domestic trade and storage of crude oil and petroleum products. It operates the Sodegaura refinery in Chiba Prefecture. Sales for the fiscal year ending March 1990 totaled ¥256.6 billion (US $1.7 billion), and capitalization stood at ¥10.0 billion (US $65.0 million). Headquarters are in Tōkyō.

Fujioka 藤岡[市]

City in southern Gumma Prefecture, central Honshū. Fujioka developed as a market town and post-station town in the Edo period (1600–1868). Known for its sericulture and *kawara* (roof tiles), it now has automobile and electrical-goods industries also. A kiln site where ancient tomb figurines (HANIWA) are said to have been fired and several ancient tomb mounds (KOFUN) are here. Pop: 60,981.

Fujioka Sakutarō 藤岡作太郎

(1870–1910). Pen name Tōho. Scholar of Japanese literature; noted for his incisive critical eye and elegant prose style. Born in Kanazawa, Ishikawa Prefecture. Graduate of Tōkyō University, where he was later a professor. His works include *Kinsei kaiga shi* (1903), a history of the arts in the Edo period (1600–1868), and *Kokubungaku zenshi: Heianchō hen* (1905), a pioneering study of Heian-period (794–1185) literature.

Fuji Photo Film Co, Ltd 富士写真フイルム[株]

(Fuji Shashin Fuirumu). Japan's largest producer of photosensitive material. It was incorporated in 1934 when the photo film division of Dai-Nippon Celluloid Co (now DAICEL CHEMICAL INDUSTRIES, LTD) became independent. It expanded into the camera field in 1948. In 1960 it began production of magnetic tape and in recent years has initiated production of such diverse products as photosensitive material for medical and printing purposes, noncarbon paper, and video tapes. In 1962 it established FUJI XEROX CO, LTD, jointly with Rank Xerox of Great Britain. It has 17 overseas subsidiaries in 10 countries and offices in 5 other countries. Sales for the fiscal year ending October 1990 totaled ¥860.9 billion (US $6.6 billion), of which consumer photographic products constituted 46 percent; commercial products, 44 percent; and magnetic products, 10 percent. The overseas sales ratio was 31 percent, and the company was capitalized at ¥37.4 billion (US $288.3 million) in the same year. Headquarters are in Tōkyō and Minami Ashigara, Kanagawa Prefecture.

Fujisan 富士山

(Mt. Fuji; commonly known overseas, but not in Japan, as Fujiyama). The highest mountain (3,776 m; 12,388 ft) in Japan and the most loved by the Japanese. Located on the border of Shizuoka and Yamanashi prefectures in central Honshū, Fujisan boasts a superb conical form that has become famous throughout the world as a symbol of Japan and has inspired generations of Japanese artists and poets. Although dormant since 1707, it is classified by geologists as an active volcano.

At the summit of Fujisan is a crater with a diameter of about 800 m (2,600 ft) and a depth of about 200 m (660 ft). The diameter at the base of the mountain, including the broad lava fields of the piedmont zone, is roughly 40–50 km (25–30 mi). Lava from Fujisan has been discovered in the seabed near TAGONOURA, indicating that there is a vertical range in the lava distribution of nearly 4,000 m (13,100 ft).

In broad perspective Fujisan is part of the FUJI VOLCANIC ZONE. It lies in the FOSSA MAGNA (Great Fissure Zone), dividing the island of Honshū into southwest Japan and northeast Japan. While Fujisan appears to be a volcano of the simple cone type, it is actually a composite volcano formed by three separate volcanoes known as Komitake, Ko Fuji, and Shin Fuji. Shin Fuji, the most recent of the three, is thought to have begun its activity approximately 10,000 years ago and has continued to erupt intermittently throughout recorded history. Basaltic lava and solid material discharged by Shin Fuji have covered the two older volcanoes, enlarged the piedmont area substantially, and given the mountain its present shape. The timberline is found in the altitude range of 2,400–2,800 m (7,900–9,200 ft); between this line and the peak are naked slopes of lava and lapilli. Fujisan has few alpine plants compared with other mountains exceeding 2,500 meters (8,200 ft) in central Japan.

The area remains largely undeveloped due to its lack of water; it has no constant streams or springs. The only major exception to this pattern is the area around Gotemba in the eastern piedmont where there are springs at an altitude of 600 m (2,000 ft). Rice has been cultivated here since early times, and the construction of villas started in the Meiji period (1868–1912). While water on Fujisan itself is scarce, streams flow through the piedmont and abound in waterfalls cascading down the lava bed, such as Shiraito Falls on the river Shibakawa and Ayutsubo Falls on the Kisegawa. There are also many lava tunnels. These along with the FUJI FIVE LAKES are major tourist attractions. At the summit there is a meteorological observatory where continuous meteorological observations have been carried out since 1939. Fujisan is unusual in that fumarole activity and volcanic earthquakes are completely absent, despite its comparatively recent volcanic activities.

Climbing of Fujisan started as a religious practice. Adherents of Fujikō (see KŌ), a syncretic sect with both Buddhist and Shintō elements, regard the mountain as sacred. Climbers from this group originated the custom of dividing routes to the summit into 10 stations or stages (*gōme*). The Shintō shrine Fujisan Hongū Sengen Jinja, whose main shrine is in the city of Fujinomiya, south of the mountain (see SENGEN SHRINE), also treats Fujisan as sacred. Nowadays many people climb Fujisan for pleasure. It is crowded with tens of thousands of climbers daily during the climbing season, which runs from 1 July to 31 August. Motor roads now run up to the fifth station, from which the summit can be reached in about five hours on foot. ☎ *416–417*

Fujisawa 藤沢[市]

City in central Kanagawa Prefecture, central Honshū. Fujisawa developed during the Edo period (1600–1868) as a post-station town on the highway TŌKAIDŌ and as a temple town around the Yugyōji, the main temple of the JI SECT. Many of its residents commute to Tōkyō and Yokohama. Plants manufacture metallic products, machinery, and foodstuffs. The island of ENOSHIMA and Katase Beach are tourist attractions. Pop: 350,330.

Fujisawa Pharmaceutical Co, Ltd 藤沢薬品工業[株]

(Fujisawa Yakuhin Kōgyō). Pharmaceutical maker focusing on antibiotics. The company dates back to 1894, when Fujisawa Tomokichi opened a pharmaceutical business in Ōsaka. Since then Fujisawa has grown to be one of Japan's foremost manufacturers in this field, devoting over 10 percent of annual revenue to research and development. Fujisawa promotes many overseas activities, including joint ventures and licensing arrangements. Sales for the fiscal year ending March 1991 totaled ¥221.2 billion (US $1.6 billion), of which antibiotics accounted for 28 percent; digestive agents, 20 percent; nervous system agents, 20 percent; circulatory and respiratory agents, 12 percent; and other products, 20 percent. The company was capitalized at ¥16.2 billion (US $124.3 million) in the same year. Headquarters are in Ōsaka and Tōkyō.

Fujisawa Rikitarō 藤沢利喜太郎

(1861–1933). Mathematician. Born in Niigata Prefecture. Graduate of Tōkyō University in 1882. Between 1883 and 1887 Fujisawa studied analysis in England and Germany. Upon returning to Japan in 1887, he assumed the post of professor of mathematics at Tōkyō University. Fujisawa is known for having introduced to Japan the newest mathematics of his time, including statistics. He also introduced the concept of life insurance to Japan and brought back from Germany the seminar style of university instruction. Among the graduates of his seminars were the mathematicians HAYASHI TSURUICHI and TAKAGI TEIJI.

Fujisawa Shūhei 藤沢周平

(1927–). Novelist. Real name Kosuge Tomeji. Born in Yamagata Prefecture. Graduate of Yamagata Normal School. Fujisawa first became known for *Kurai umi* (1971, Dark Sea), the story of an UKIYO-E artist. He received the Naoki Prize for his period novel *Ansatsu no nenrin* (1973, The Annals of Assassination); his works in that genre are especially popular. Other works include *Yōjimbō jitsugetsushō* (1978, A Bodyguard's Story) and *Shiroki kame* (1986, The White Urn).

Fujisawa Takeo 藤沢桓夫

(1904–89). Author. Born in Ōsaka. As a high school student he began to write for little magazines, winning praise from such older writers as KAWABATA YASUNARI. While attending Tōkyō University he began to write "proletarian" short stories, the best known of which is "Kizudarake no uta" (1930). He was a patient in a tuberculosis sanatorium from 1930 to 1933. After his discharge he shifted to popular fiction. His melodramatic novel *Shinsetsu* (1941–42) was made into a film in 1942.

Fujishima Takeji 藤島武二

(1867–1943). Western-style painter. Born in what is now Kagoshima Prefecture, he went to Tōkyō in 1884. The following year he became a pupil of KAWABATA GYOKUSHŌ. Already accomplished in Japanese-style painting, Fujishima switched to Western-style painting in 1890 and studied under Soyama Yukihiko (1859–92), Matsuoka Hisashi, YAMAMOTO HŌSUI, and others. In 1896, when a Western-style painting department was established in the Tōkyō Bijutsu Gakkō (now Tōkyō University of Fine Arts and Music), he was appointed to its faculty. In the same year he participated in the founding of the HAKUBAKAI.

From 1905 to 1910 Fujishima studied in France and Italy. His works came to be characterized by bold brushwork and brilliant colors. In 1910 he was appointed full professor at the Tōkyō Bijutsu Gakkō, where he taught for 30 years. He also exhibited with the BUNTEN, a government-sponsored body. In 1924 he became a member of the Imperial Art Academy. He received the first Order of Culture in 1937.

Fuji Spinning Co, Ltd 富士紡績[株]

(Fuji Bōseki). Textile company producing cotton, wool, and synthetic fibers. Incorporated in 1896. It has a joint enterprise in Thailand. Sales for the fiscal year ending March 1991 totaled ¥86.0 billion (US $626.8 million), of which chemical and synthetic fibers accounted for 29 percent; cotton, 58 percent; and wool and other products, 13 percent. The export ratio was 10.9 percent. The company was capitalized at ¥5.4 billion (US $39.4 million) in the same year. Headquarters are in Tōkyō.

Fuji Sumiko 富司純子

(1945–). Actress. Real name Terashima Junko. Born in Wakayama Prefecture. She gained fame in Tōei's YAKUZA (gangster) films (see TŌEI CO, LTD). She played opposite TAKAKURA KEN and Tsuruta Kōji (1924–87) and became a leading lady. Soon she had major parts in films such as the *Hibotan bakuto* (1968–72, The Scarlet Peony Gambler) series and *Onna toseinin* (1971, Women Yakuza). She charmed her audiences, playing the calm, silent woman who fights with a Japanese sword like a man. After marrying in 1972 she began making television appearances. Long known to her fans as Fuji Junko she took the name Sumiko in 1989 and returned to movie acting.

Fujita Art Museum 藤田美術館

(Fujita Bijutsukan). Located in Ōsaka. Collection, opened in 1954, of Chinese and Japanese painting, calligraphy, sculpture, ceramics, lacquer, textiles, and metalwork and Japanese tea-ceremony objects, all assembled by Baron FUJITA DENZABURŌ and his sons. The Japanese paintings include 13th- and 14th-century scrolls, paintings of the 16 RAKAN (Skt: *arhat*) by TAKUMA EIGA, and the painting *New Moon over the Rustic Gate* (1405) by an unknown artist. The Chinese paintings are attributed to Song (Sung) dynasty (960–1279) artists. The section of Japanese ceramics includes teabowls by CHŌJIRŌ, NONOMURA NINSEI, and Dōnyū and square dishes by KŌRIN and KENZAN.

Fujita Corporation [株]フジタ

(Fujita). Company engaged in construction, public works, and real estate. Founded in 1910 and incorporated as Fujita-Gumi in 1937. The company adopted its present name in 1990. Sales for the fiscal year ending March 1991 totaled ¥744.7 billion (US $5.4 billion), of which construction accounted for 60 percent; civil engineering, 17 percent; and real estate, 23 percent. The company was capitalized at ¥57.7 billion (US $420.6 million) in the same year. Headquarters are in Tōkyō.

Fujita Denzaburō 藤田伝三郎

(1841–1912). Entrepreneur. Born in the Chōshū domain (now Yamaguchi Prefecture). He worked in the family business of manufacturing *sake* and soy sauce but, influenced by the *samurai* TAKASUGI SHINSAKU, he became involved in the antishogunate movement. After the MEIJI RESTORATION (1868) Fujita moved to Ōsaka. During the SATSUMA REBELLION of 1877, he reaped enormous profits from supply contracts with the military. In 1881, together with his brother and Kuhara Shōzaburō (the brother of KUHARA FUSANOSUKE), he founded the Fujita-Gumi (now DŌWA MINING CO, LTD). He was a friend of INOUE KAORU and other members of the Chōshū clique (see HAMBATSU). Fujita was made a baron for organizing the sale of large quantities of government bonds during the Russo-Japanese War (1904–05).

Fujitani Mitsue 富士谷御杖

(1768–1823). WAKA poet and KOKUGAKU (National Learning) scholar of the late Edo period (1600–1868). Born in Kyōto, he was the son of the linguist FUJITANI NARIAKIRA. His analytical approach to the study of classical texts is demonstrated in such works as *Kojiki tomoshibi* (1808), a study of the 8th-century semihistorical chronicle known as the KOJIKI (Records of Ancient Matters), and *Man'yōshū tomoshibi* (1822), a similar study of the 8th-century MAN'YŌSHŪ. He emphasized what he viewed as a uniquely metaphysical quality in these early texts based on the concept of *kotodama* ("word spirit"), as expounded in his *Makoto ben* (ca 1804–48). He was also the author of a detailed study of grammatical particles, the *Haikai te-ni-ha shō* (1807). A selection of his poems was collected in the anthology *Fujitani Mitsue no ushi kabun* (1824).

Fujitani Nariakira 富士谷成章

(1738–79). Literary theorist and grammarian of the Edo period (1600–1868). Born in Kyōto, younger brother of the Confucian scholar and Chinese grammarian Minagawa Kien (1734–1807). His literary theories were developed by his son and successor, FUJITANI MITSUE, and his grammatical theories were developed by members of MOTOORI NORINAGA's school, in particular SUZUKI AKIRA, MOTOORI HARUNIWA, and TŌJŌ GIMON.

Nariakira's most noted contribution to Japanese grammar was his theory of word classes, reminiscent of the parts of speech in traditional European grammar. His terminology was based on a clothing metaphor. The classes were *na* (names), corresponding to nouns; *yosoi* (robes), corresponding to verbs and adjectives; *kazashi* (hairpins), corresponding to adverbs and some conjunctions or interjections; and *ayui* (binding cords), corresponding to prepositions and other conjunctions or interjections. Nariakira's best-known works are the *Kazashishō* (1767) and the *Ayuishō* (1778). Nariakira has some claim to be regarded as the most original of the early Japanese grammarians, although there is a clear influence in his work of traditional Chinese grammar. See JAPANESE LANGUAGE STUDIES, HISTORY OF.

Fujita Tōko 藤田東湖

(1806–55). Leading Confucianist of the MITO SCHOOL. Born in Mito (now in Ibaraki Prefecture), he was the son of FUJITA YŪKOKU, master of the domain's academy, the Shōkōkan. After studying in Edo (now Tōkyō), he served at the Shōkōkan from 1827. In 1829 when a succession dispute divided leaders of the domain, Tōko, along with AIZAWA SEISHISAI and others, campaigned successfully for TOKUGAWA NARIAKI. In 1844, when the shogunate reprimanded Nariaki and placed him under house arrest for his open disagreement with its policies, Tōko too was punished with house arrest. During this period he concentrated on writings such as his KŌDŌKAN KI JUTSUGI, which became a basic book of the Mito school's ideology and called for strengthening the imperial institution and defying the foreign powers (see SONNŌ JŌI). After Nariaki was pardoned in 1849 Tōko enjoyed a great reputation as his adviser and as an exponent of nationalist views.

Fujita Tourist Enterprises Co, Ltd 藤田観光[株]

(Fujita Kankō). Leading operator of hotels and restaurants. Incorporated in 1955. The company operates resort hotels in Japan and Guam as well as an urban business hotel chain. It is also engaged in real estate development and sales of residential housing lots, resort houses, and membership villas. Recently it opened a Japanese-style restaurant, Chinzan-sō, in the United States as a joint investment with YAOHAN JAPAN CORPORATION, and it has been commissioned to operate a hotel in China. Sales for the fiscal year ending December 1991 totaled ¥79.1 billion (US $617.7 million), and capitalization stood at ¥12.1 billion (US $94.3 million). Headquarters are in Tōkyō.

Fujita Tsuguharu 藤田嗣治

(1886–1968). Western-style painter. Also known as Fujita Tsuguji and Léonard Foujita. A native of Tōkyō, he graduated from the Tōkyō Bijutsu Gakkō (now Tōkyō University of Fine Arts and Music) in 1910. Three years later he went to Paris, where he met Picasso, Modigliani, and Soutine. He lived primarily in France but made periodic trips to Japan. Over the next half century he achieved a distinction rivaled by few, if any, Japanese painters of his generation. World War II brought him back to Japan, where he painted battle scenes for the army. In 1949 he left Japan permanently, spending one year in the United States before his return to France. In 1955 he became a French citizen and two years later was awarded the Legion of Honor. His fine detail, delicate line, and effective use of milky white (inspired by *ukiyo-e* prints) won him fame in the West. A convert to Catholicism in 1966, when he was christened Léonard, he designed the stained-glass windows and murals for the chapel of Notre Dame de la Paix in France.

Fujita Yūkoku 藤田幽谷

(1774–1826). Confucian scholar of the MITO SCHOOL. Born in Mito domain (now part of Ibaraki Prefecture). Fujita became a student of Tachihara Suiken (1744–1823), a Confucian scholar who headed SHŌKŌKAN, the office founded by TOKUGAWA MITSUKUNI to compile the DAI NIHON SHI (History of Great Japan). Fujita, though barely 14, was invited to join

Continued on page 418➡

The Faces of Mt. Fuji

Elegantly symmetrical in profile, Japan's most famous peak displays a myriad of shifting aspects depending upon the season, weather, time of day, and viewpoint of the observer. Seen from a distance, Fujisan presents a gently sloping curve. Above the timberline, however, its surface becomes rugged and rock-strewn. Still classed as an active volcano, Fujisan is a living mountain whose character is deeply inscribed in Japanese tradition, from the poetry of the *Man'yōshū* to the woodblock prints of Hokusai. The mountain has also been an object of religious reverence since ancient times.

Unique cloud formations hovering over the 3,776-meter peak of Japan's highest mountain usually herald a change in the weather.

The southwest face in autumn. From the end of a wide vehicular road (foreground), it is about a five-hour hike to the summit. During July and August, the climbing season, some 200,000 people make the trek to the top.

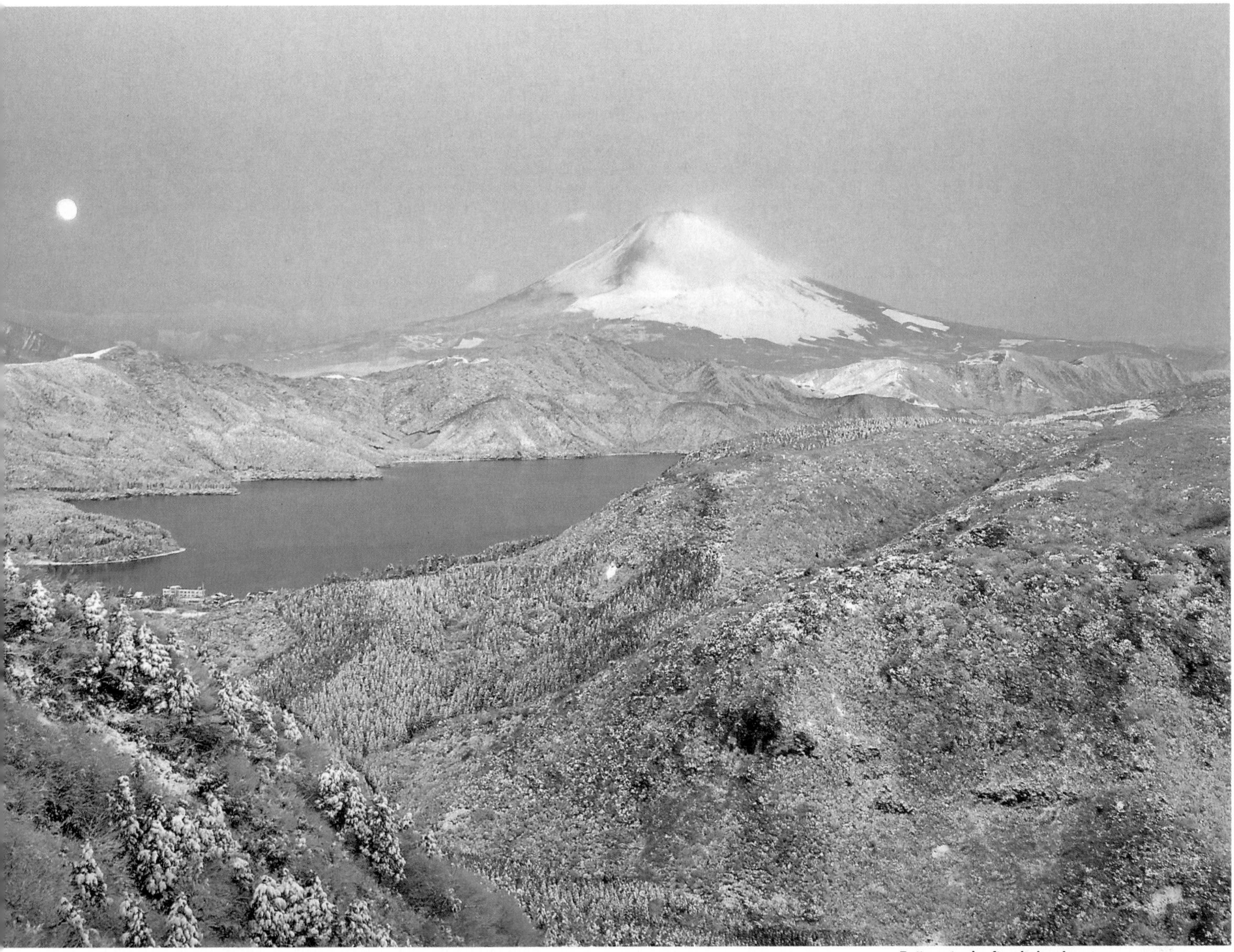

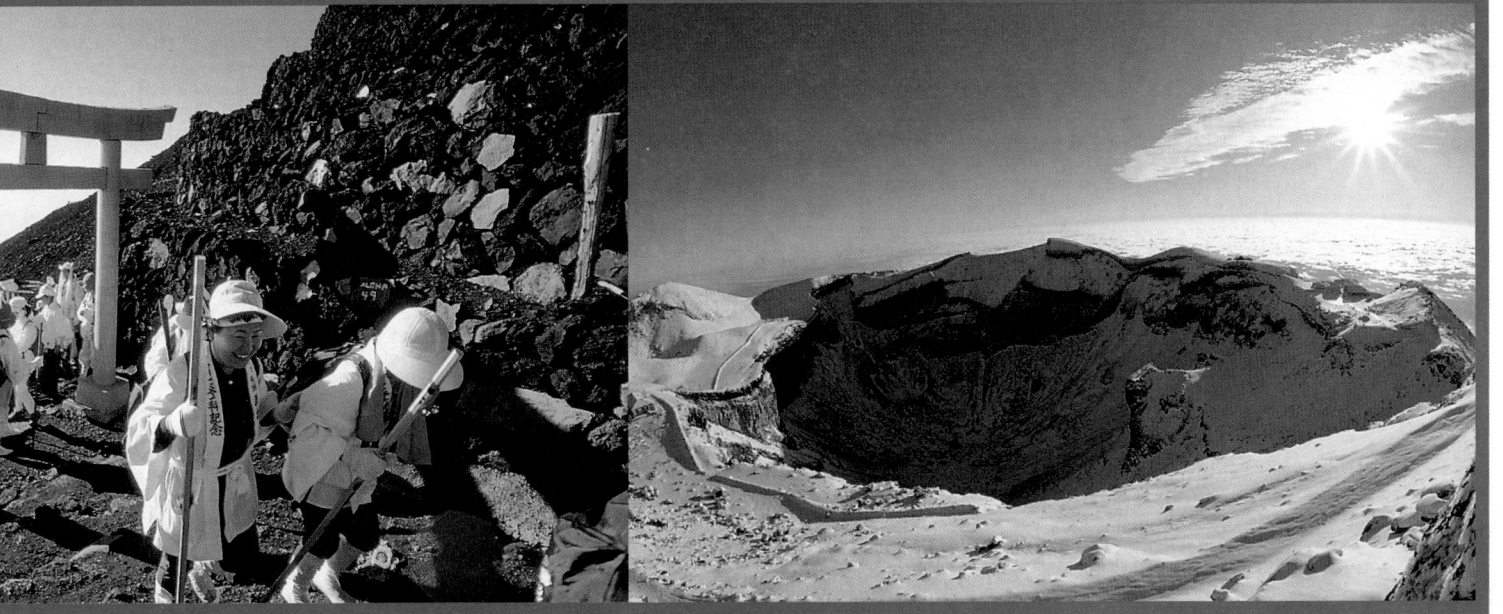

Fujisan in the first light of a winter morning, seen from the foothills surrounding the lake Ashinoko. Newly fallen snow silvers the landscape beneath a full moon.

The ascent of Fujisan can be a profound spiritual experience. This group of pilgrims arrives at a shrine near the 3,500-meter level.

The summit in winter. The crater, 3.5 km in circumference, is rimmed with snow. There is a weather observation station at the highest point of the rim.

Photographs by Ōyama Yukio

the editorial staff of the Shōkōkan and was eventually named its head in 1807. Besides working on the *Dai Nihon shi*, he strove to spread the ideas of the Mito school. Several of his students, including FUJITA TŌKO (his second son) and AIZAWA SEISHISAI, later took up the call for SONNŌ JŌI (Revere the Emperor, Expel the Barbarians) and influenced the movement to overthrow the Tokugawa shogunate.

Fuji Telecasting Co, Ltd

[株]フジテレビジョン

(Fuji Terebijon). Commercial broadcasting company based in Tōkyō and serving the Kantō (eastern Honshū) area. It began operations in 1959 with joint support from a number of firms, including NIPPON CULTURAL BROADCASTING, INC (Bunka Hōsō), NIPPON BROADCASTING SYSTEM, INC (Nippon Hōsō), SANKEI SHIMBUN, a major Tōkyō newspaper company, and several motion picture companies, which together are known today as the Fuji Sankei Communications Group, a conservative journalistic enterprise. Fuji Telecasting is affiliated nationwide with 27 stations (1992), which together compose the Fuji News Network (FNN).

Fujitsū General, Ltd

[株]富士通ゼネラル

(Fujitsū Zeneraru). Company engaged in the production of audiovisual products, satellite broadcast receivers, home electrical appliances, and information equipment. Incorporated in 1936 as the General Corporation, it established a capital tie-up with Fujitsū, Ltd, in 1984, assuming its current name in 1985. It now provides the Fujitsū group with consumer electrical appliances. It has sales companies in eight countries, including the United States. Sales for the fiscal year ending March 1991 totaled ¥152.3 billion (US $16.8 billion), and capitalization stood at ¥15.8 billion (US $115.2 million). Headquarters are in Kawasaki, Kanagawa Prefecture.

Fujitsū, Ltd

富士通[株]

(Fujitsū). Manufacturer and seller of data processing systems, telecommunications systems, and electronic components, including semiconductors. It ranks first in Japan in production of data processing systems and second in sales of telecommunications systems. Established in 1935, Fujitsū traces its origins to the telephone division of FUJI ELECTRIC CO, LTD. After World War II, it advanced into the field of electronics and in 1954 developed and commercialized Japan's first relay computer, the FACOM 100. Fujitsū has a long tradition of depending on its own technology for the design and manufacture of its products. It is active overseas and has operations in more than 100 countries.

Fujitsū's sales for the fiscal year ending March 1991 totaled ¥2.3 trillion (US $16.8 billion), with data processing systems accounting for 72 percent; telecommunications systems, 17 percent; and electronic devices, 11 percent. The company was capitalized at ¥221.6 billion (US $1.6 billion) in the same year. In 1972 Fujitsū established the Japan-America Institute of Management Science (JAIMS) in Honolulu, and the company continues to support this nonprofit institution dedicated to cross-cultural education. Headquarters are in Tōkyō.

Fuji Volcanic Zone

富士火山帯

(Fuji Kazantai). Volcanic zone running south across central Honshū from Yakeyama,

Niigata Prefecture, and extending to the Mariana Islands. It includes the Hakone Mountains, the Izu Peninsula, and the IZU ISLANDS. The major volcanic peaks in the zone are MYŌKŌSAN, YATSUGATAKE, FUJISAN, HAKONEYAMA, MIHARAYAMA, as well as the island of Ōshima. Located in the zone are the two national parks of Jōshin'etsu Kōgen and Fuji-Hakone-Izu.

Fujiwara culture

藤原文化

(Fujiwara *bunka*). The culture of the Fujiwara period, during which the FUJIWARA FAMILY was at the height of its power and influence; the period extended roughly from the late 9th century until the end of the Heian period (794–1185).

With the termination of embassies to China in 894 (see SUI AND TANG [T'ANG] CHINA, EMBASSIES TO) and the fall of BOHAI (Po-hai) and SILLA on the Korean peninsula in the 10th century, official contact with the continent came to a close. What had been imported for the preceding three centuries was now more fully assimilated, leading to a more native style of culture. In Buddhism, the esoteric TENDAI SECT and SHINGON SECT, with their emphasis on philosophy and doctrine, declined, and instead, pietistic teachings like those of the JŌDO SECT spread among the common people. This was reflected in the visual arts, which attempted to portray the Pure Land, or the Buddhist paradise. In architecture the characteristically Japanese SHINDEN-ZUKURI style was created as was the YAMATO-E, or Japanese style of painting, with its spare lines and rich colors. The KANA syllabaries were created and used for literature, particularly in many outstanding literary works written by court women. Another characteristic of this period is the spread of culture from the Kyōto capital to the provinces, as witnessed by the building of the temple CHŪSONJI at HIRAIZUMI in what is now Iwate Prefecture.

Fujiwara family

藤原氏

(Fujiwarashi). Courtier family that exercised great political power during much of the Heian period (794–1185), especially during the period of REGENCY GOVERNMENT in the 10th and 11th centuries. Its domination of the imperial court during this period was so complete and its influence on the culture of the years before and after was so pervasive that the last three centuries of the Heian period are commonly referred to as the Fujiwara period.

Origin——The family was founded in the 7th century by FUJIWARA NO KAMATARI, a member of the influential Nakatomi family. When the authority of the ruling family was threatened by the rival SOGA FAMILY, it was to Kamatari that the imperial prince Naka no Ōe turned for help. Between them they carried out a coup d'état in 645 that saw the elimination of the Soga and the initiation of a series of sweeping changes in government known as the TAIKA REFORM, modeled on Chinese political institutions and intended to strengthen the ruling family and the central government. In 669 the prince, now Emperor TENJI, conferred on Kamatari the new family name of Fujiwara.

Growth of Fujiwara Power——Kamatari's son FUJIWARA NO FUHITO (also known as Fubito; 659–720) gave daughters in marriage to Emperor MOMMU and Emperor SHŌMU, thereby initiating a practice that was to become the keystone of Fujiwara power—its attachment to the imperial family through the marriage of Fujiwara daughters to reign-

ing and future emperors. As maternal grandfathers, uncles, and fathers-in-law of emperors, Fujiwara family heads wielded tremendous influence. Meanwhile, Fuhito's four sons each became the head of a branch family, of which the Hokke, or northern branch, grew to be the most powerful.

In 866 FUJIWARA NO YOSHIFUSA further advanced the family's cause by having himself appointed regent (SESSHŌ) for Emperor Seiwa (850–881; r 858–876), his grandson. It was the first time in Japanese history that someone not of imperial blood had assumed the regency. The Fujiwara had found a way of virtually usurping the throne without occupying it.

The only flaw in the system from the standpoint of the Fujiwara was that the regency had to be vacated when a young emperor came of age. Fujiwara no Mototsune (836–891), Yoshifusa's nephew and adoptive son, established the new post of KAMPAKU in 887 to function as Emperor Kōkō's (830–887; r 884–887) spokesman even though the sovereign was already an adult. Mototsune was challenged by Kōkō's successor, Emperor UDA, and Mototsune's death only four years after Uda's accession gave Uda six years of rule free from Fujiwara interference.

If Uda and his successor, DAIGO, had any illusions about restoring imperial authority over the Fujiwara, these were quickly dispelled by Tokihira (871–909), Mototsune's son, who successfully removed all opposition and reestablished Fujiwara supremacy. Among his victims was the celebrated scholar-statesman SUGAWARA NO MICHIZANE.

The most powerful Fujiwara of them all was FUJIWARA NO MICHINAGA (966–1028), father of four empresses and grandfather of three emperors, who dominated the imperial court for more than 30 years. His rule was marked by a court life whose splendor was unmatched by any before or after him.

Decline of Fujiwara Influence——However, even before Michinaga's time, Fujiwara influence had begun to decline, especially in the provinces. There, the landed gentry, who had commended lands to the Fujiwara in the past, now tended to commend them to the rising military families, thus drastically reducing the economic basis of Fujiwara power (see SHŌEN). Only 40 years after Michinaga's death, the Fujiwara could not prevent GOSANJŌ, who did not have a Fujiwara mother, from ascending the throne. The system of government by a retired emperor (see INSEI), established in 1087, also served as a base for effectively challenging Fujiwara power. Finally, in 1156, in a succession dispute known as the HŌGEN DISTURBANCE, the TAIRA FAMILY (a warrior family) emerged as the country's most powerful family. In 1160, when the Taira defeated a coalition of the Fujiwara and the MINAMOTO FAMILY, the days of Fujiwara power had come to an end (see HEIJI DISTURBANCE). Although certain high offices continued to be filled by scions of the Fujiwara (see GOSEKKE), the family had ceased to be a factor in the politics of the country by the mid-12th century. Several members of the family, however, notably the poets FUJIWARA NO SADAIE, FUJIWARA NO TAMEIE, and FUJIWARA NO TOSHINARI, acted as literary arbiters in later years.

Fujiwara Ginjirō

藤原銀次郎

(1869–1960). Businessman and politician. Born in Nagano Prefecture. Graduate of Keiō Gijuku (now Keiō University). Fujiwara joined Mitsui Bank in 1894 and Mitsui & Co in 1899. In 1911 he moved to ŌJI PAPER CO, LTD,

Genealogy of the Fujiwara Family

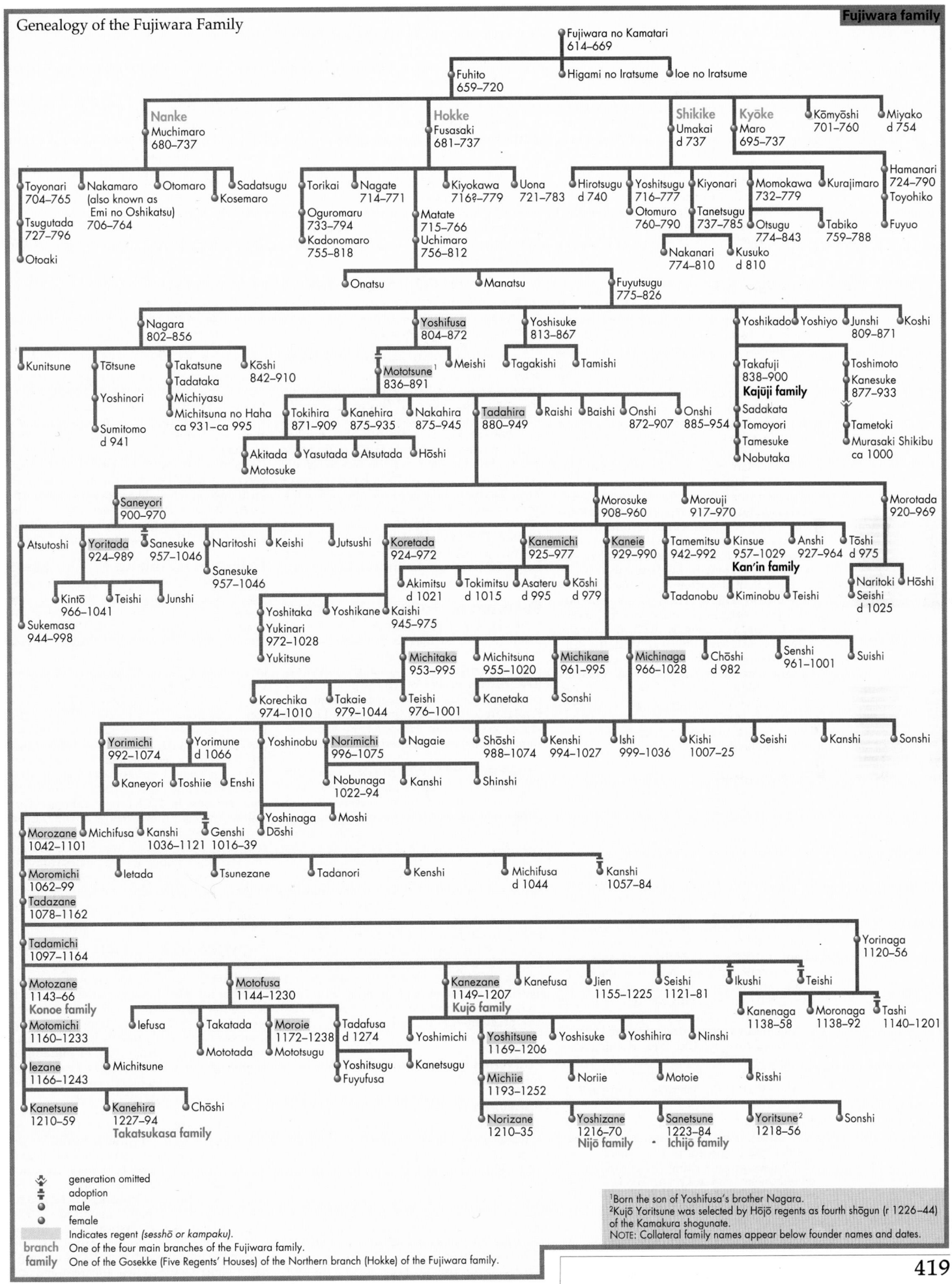

a Mitsui affiliate, where he rehabilitated the company and became its president. He merged the company with Fuji Seishi and Karafuto Kōgyō in 1933, making Ōji the biggest paper company in Japan. After retiring as chairman in 1940 Fujiwara entered politics. He served as commerce and industry minister and munitions minister during World War II. Enthusiastic about education, he established Fujiwara Technological University (now the Engineering Department of Keiō University) in 1939 and the Fujiwara Foundation of Science in 1959.

Fujiwara Kikan 藤原機関

Also known as Efu (F) Kikan. World War II intelligence operation, headed by Major Fujiwara Iwaichi (1908–86), that induced surrendered Indian officers and soldiers to shift their allegiance from the British Army during the Malayan operation in 1941–42. Organized to facilitate the conquest of Malaya by mobilizing anti-British elements, it won over enough Indian officers and soldiers to create, with Captain Mohan SINGH's cooperation, the INDIAN NATIONAL ARMY with 40,000 Indian prisoners of war. In appreciation of the Fujiwara Kikan's rescue and subsequent protection of the sultan of Kedah and his family, the young prince Abdul Rahman (1903–90), who was to become the first Malaysian prime minister (1963–70), volunteered to broadcast a message urging his people to cooperate with the Japanese.

The Kikan also attempted to mobilize the anti-British Young Malay Union but met with little success since its principal members had been arrested by the British shortly after the outbreak of the war. With the British surrender in Singapore in February 1942, the Fujiwara Kikan was dissolved. A new liaison agency, named the Iwakuro Kikan after its chief, Colonel Iwakuro Hideo (1897–1970), was created to coordinate the activities of the Indian National Army and the Japanese military.

Fujiwarakyō 藤原京

The capital of Japan from 694 to 710; located in what is now the city of Kashihara, Nara Prefecture. The three sovereigns JITŌ, MOMMU, and Gemmei (661–721; r 707–715) held court there. The empress Jitō, widow and successor of Emperor TEMMU, devoted several years to the construction of Fujiwarakyō and moved her court there in 694.

Excavations since 1934 have revealed that the central compound, the Chōdōin, was about 230 meters (750 ft) east-to-west by about 320 meters (1,050 ft) north-to-south. More recent diggings show that the entire capital area measured 2,140 meters (7,021 ft) by 3,210 meters (10,531 ft) and that Fujiwarakyō was the first capital in Japan to be laid out in a grid pattern with broad thoroughfares forming the axes. Roofing tiles and some 6,700 inscribed wooden tallies (MOKKAN) have also been unearthed. Records indicate that it was destroyed by fire in 711.

Fujiwara no Akihira 藤原明衡

(989–1066). Late-Heian-period (794–1185) scholar and originator of the Fujiwara style of Chinese prose writing. He compiled and edited the HONCHŌ MONZUI (ca 1060), a collection of 427 Chinese poems written by Japanese during the preceding 200 years. He also edited the MEIGŌ ŌRAI (mid-11th century), a collection of models for letter writing. He

wrote the *Shin sarugō ki*, which described life in Kyōto in the mid-11th century.

Fujiwara no Akisuke 藤原顕輔

(1090–1155). Also called Rokujō no Akisuke. Classical (WAKA) poet and compiler of the sixth imperial anthology of court poetry, the SHIKA WAKASHŪ or *Shikashū* (ca 1151, Collection of Verbal Flowers). About 80 of Akisuke's own poems are preserved in imperial anthologies from the KIN'YŌ WAKASHŪ on. His personal collection, *Akisuke shū*, contains some 145 poems.

Fujiwara no Fuhito 藤原不比等

(659–720). Aristocrat and court official. The second son of FUJIWARA NO KAMATARI, he established the power and prosperity of the FUJIWARA FAMILY. For drawing up the TAIHŌ CODE (701), Fuhito was appointed great counselor (*dainagon*) and later minister of the right (*udaijin*). In 718 he began to compile the YŌRŌ CODE, but died before its completion. Fuhito married his daughters to emperors, one to Emperor MOMMU and another (later known as Empress KŌMYŌ) to Emperor SHŌMU. Fuhito promoted the careers of his sons, Muchimaro (680–737), Fusasaki (681–737), Umakai (d 737), and Maro (695–737), who established the four branches of the family (Nanke, Hokke, Shikike, and Kyōke). Fuhito was posthumously awarded the title grand minister of state (*dajō daijin*). Four of his poems are included in the anthology KAIFŪSŌ.

Fujiwara no Fujifusa 藤原藤房

(1295–?). Court noble. Under Emperor GO-DAIGO he rose to middle counselor (*chūnagon*). In 1331 he participated in Go-Daigo's plan to overthrow the KAMAKURA SHOGUNATE (see GENKŌ INCIDENT). When the plot was discovered, Fujifusa was exiled, returning to Kyōto in 1333 at the time of Go-Daigo's KEMMU RESTORATION. However, he soon became disillusioned and retired.

Fujiwara no Fuyutsugu 藤原冬嗣

(775–826). Court official; son of Fujiwara no Uchimaro (756–812) of the Northern Branch (Hokke) of the FUJIWARA FAMILY. In 810, during the turbulence which led to the KUSUKO INCIDENT, Fuyutsugu was appointed by the emperor SAGA to head the KURŌDO-DOKORO, an informal secretariat created to ensure secrecy in imperial affairs. In 825 he became minister of the left (*sadaijin*). He helped to compile the BUNKA SHŪREISHŪ (818), a collection of poetry in Chinese; and the *Kōnin kyakushiki* (820), a set of legal regulations and precedents. He founded the family school KAN-GAKUIN in 821. He arranged his daughter's marriage to Emperor Nimmyō (810–850; r 833–850) and prepared the way for the future preeminence of the Fujiwara Northern Branch.

Fujiwara no Hidehira → Ōshū

Fujiwara family

Fujiwara no Hidesato 藤原秀郷

(fl early 10th century). Popularly known as Tawara Tōta. Warrior; military official. Hidesato was a descendant of Fujiwara no Uona (721–783) and son of Fujiwara no Murao, an official in Shimotsuke Province (now Tochigi Prefecture) in eastern Japan. Exiled in 916, he was later pardoned and appointed a military constable (*ōryōshi*) in Shimotsuke. He helped put down the rebellion of TAIRA NO MASAKADO in 940 and was rewarded with the post of general of the

Headquarters for Pacification and Defense (CHINJUFU) in the northeast and the governorship of Shimotsuke. The eastern warrior families Shimokōbe, Oyama, and Yūki, among others, were descended from Hidesato, and the ŌSHŪ FUJIWARA FAMILY claimed to be. Hidesato is the hero of a legend in which he kills the giant centipede of Mt. Mikami.

Fujiwara no Hirotsugu, Rebellion of 藤原広嗣の乱

(Fujiwara no Hirotsugu no Ran). Rebellion of 740 led by the court official Fujiwara no Hirotsugu (d 740), head of the Shikike (or Shiki) branch of the FUJIWARA FAMILY. In 738 Hirotsugu was transferred to the post of junior assistant (*shōni*) to the governor-general of Dazaifu, the government headquarters in Kyūshū. Hirotsugu believed that the powerful court figures TACHIBANA NO MOROE, GEMBŌ, and KIBI NO MAKIBI were the cause of this demotion, and in the summer of 740 he addressed a memorial to the throne, urging their removal. When his appeal was ignored, Hirotsugu assembled some 10,000 troops in Kyūshū. They were defeated by imperial forces in a battle near the Itabitsu River. Hirotsugu escaped, but was eventually captured and executed. His death signaled the decline of his branch of the Fujiwara and the emergence of the Nanke or southern branch.

Fujiwara no Ietaka 藤原家隆

(1158–1237). Classical (WAKA) poet. A member of the so-called Mini branch of the Fujiwara family, Ietaka became a pupil of the great FUJIWARA NO TOSHINARI (Fujiwara no Shunzei), by whom he was reared. He was later adopted as a son-in-law by the priest JAKUREN. Older and of more humble origins than his contemporary FUJIWARA NO SADAIE (Fujiwara no Teika), Ietaka rose slowly in the court hierarchy. Next to Teika, he was the most outstanding of the group of younger poets and pupils of Shunzei. From 1186, when he composed a sequence of 100 poems at the request of the priest SAIGYŌ, Ietaka participated in numerous poetic gatherings and competitions. In 1201 former Emperor Go-Toba appointed him a fellow of the Bureau of Poetry (Wakadokoro) and one of the six compilers of the eighth imperial anthology, SHIN KOKINSHŪ. Imperial anthologies from the SENZAI WAKASHŪ on include 282 of Ietaka's poems. His personal collection, *Minishū*, contains the unusually large number of 3,200 poems.

Fujiwara no Kamatari 藤原鎌足

(614–669). Original name Nakatomi no Kamatari. Founder of the FUJIWARA FAMILY. Member of the Nakatomi family, which served the YAMATO COURT and oversaw SHINTŌ worship. In 552 the Nakatomi, with the MONONOBE FAMILY, vigorously but unsuccessfully fought the introduction of Buddhism. Opposing them was the SOGA FAMILY. The Soga forces won, and Buddhism later became virtually the state religion of Japan.

Prince Naka no Ōe, son of Emperor Jomei (593–641; r 629–641), enlisted the help of Kamatari to eliminate the powerful Soga. Legend says that they made their plans in a wisteria arbor (*fujiwara*). In 645 SOGA NO IRUKA was slain, and his father, Soga no Emishi, took his own life. Empress Kōgyoku (SAIMEI), who had been supported by the Soga, was forced to abdicate, and Prince Karu, her younger brother, ascended the throne as Emperor KŌTOKU. Kōtoku designated Naka no Ōe as heir apparent and appointed Kamatari as inner minister (*uchitsuomi* or *naishin;* from 669 called NAIDAIJIN). Kamatari and Naka no Ōe launched the TAIKA REFORM of 645 to strengthen the central government. Naka no Ōe, who ascended the throne as Emperor TENJI in 661 (formally in 668), conferred on Kamatari the new family name Fujiwara.

Fujiwara no Kaneie   藤原兼家

(929–990). Court official of the Heian period (794–1185); younger brother and rival of FUJIWARA NO KANEMICHI. In 969 Emperor Reizei (950–1011; r 967–969) appointed Kaneie middle counselor (*chūnagon*), and he became great counselor (*dainagon*) in 972. After the death of his eldest brother, the imperial regent (SESSHŌ) Fujiwara no Koretada (924–972), the regency passed to Kanemichi. Kanemichi died in 977, after arranging for Kaneie's demotion and the selection of his cousin Fujiwara no Yoritada (924–989) as regent. In 978, however, Kaneie was appointed minister of the right (*udaijin*) and married his daughter Senshi (961–1001) to Emperor En'yū (959–991; r 969–984). When Senshi gave birth to the future emperor ICHIJŌ, Kaneie gained control of the imperial succession. In 986 Kaneie induced his grandnephew Emperor KAZAN to abdicate and installed his own grandson Ichijō on the throne. Kaneie finally became regent, first as *sesshō,* then KAMPAKU. He advanced the careers of his three sons, including FUJIWARA NO MICHINAGA, who succeeded him as regent.

Fujiwara no Kanemichi   藤原兼通

(925–977). Court official of the Heian period (794–1185); second son of Fujiwara no Morosuke (908–960). On the death of his elder brother, the imperial regent (SESSHŌ) Fujiwara no Koretada (924–972), Kanemichi and his younger brother FUJIWARA NO KANEIE vied to succeed him. Kanemichi won the appointment and in 974 became grand minister of state (*dajō daijin*) as well. When he learned on his deathbed that Kaneie aspired to succeed him, Kanemichi arranged for Kaneie's demotion and for his cousin Fujiwara no Yoritada (924–989) to replace him as regent.

Fujiwara no Kanesuke   藤原兼輔

(877–933). Courtier and classical (WAKA) poet, one of the Thirty-Six Poetic Geniuses (SANJŪROKKASEN). Kanesuke had 55 poems included in imperial anthologies beginning with the KOKINSHŪ (905, Collection from Ancient and Modern Times). His personal anthology, *Kanesukeshū,* contains some 125 poems.

Fujiwara no Kanezane → Kujō Kanezane

Fujiwara no Kintō   藤原公任

(966–1041). Classical (WAKA) poet and critic. Son of the chancellor Fujiwara no Yoritada. Kintō belonged to the highest level of the court aristocracy. He figures in the diary of MURASAKI SHIKIBU and in SEI SHŌNAGON's *Makura no sōshi,* as well as in later accounts of the age such as EIGA MONOGATARI, ŌKAGAMI, and KONJAKU MONOGATARI and in the poetic handbooks and tale collections of later periods. Kintō's poetic activities were varied, and his aesthetic standards shaped the tastes of his time. Nearly 100 of his poems were included in imperial anthologies beginning with the SHŪI WAKASHŪ (ca 1005, Collection of Gleanings), of which he was probably the compiler. His personal collection, *Kintōshū,* contains some 385 of his poems. His brief poetic treatise, *Shinsen zuinō* (The Essence of Poetry, Newly Selected), sets forth his poetic ideal of "deep feeling, beauty of effect, and an engaging touch of novelty in conception." Other contributions of Kintō were his *Sanjūrokunin sen* (Selections from Thirty-Six Exemplary Poets) and WAKAN RŌEISHŪ (Collection of Chinese and Japanese Poems for Singing), a collection of 216 Japanese poems and 587 Chinese couplets for singing or chanting to musical accompaniment.

Fujiwara no Kiyohira → Ōshū Fujiwara family

Fujiwara no Kiyokawa   藤原清河

(716?–779?). Court official; fourth son of Fujiwara no Fusasaki (681–737) and grandson of FUJIWARA NO FUHITO. Kiyokawa was an envoy to China in 750 and arrived in 752 at Chang'an (Ch'ang-an), the capital of the Tang (T'ang) dynasty (618–907). His attempts to return to Japan were frustrated by storms, then by the rebellion of An Lushan in 755–757. Offered official employment by the Chinese emperor, he took a Chinese name and, like his compatriot ABE NO NAKAMARO, was promoted to high posts at the Tang court. He died in China.

Fujiwara no Kiyosuke   藤原清輔

(1104–77). Classical scholar and WAKA poet; son of FUJIWARA NO AKISUKE; member of the Rokujō family. Ninety-four of his poems were included in imperial anthologies from the SENZAI WAKASHŪ on. Kiyosuke is chiefly noted as a scholar and critic. His most important extant writings are *Ōgishō* (ca 1140 with later revisions, Notes on Basic Principles) and *Fukuro-zōshi* (ca 1157, Commonplace Book). Such extensive compilations of poetic lore had scarcely existed before Kiyosuke's time, and these and other of his works were much used and quoted by later poets and scholars. Among Kiyosuke's less ambitious works are *Waka shogaku shō* (Notes on Japanese Poetry for Beginners) and *Waka ichiji shō* (Notes on Poetic Diction), both intended as handbooks for aspiring poets. Kiyosuke's dissatisfaction with the brevity of the imperial anthology SHIKA WAKASHŪ, compiled by his father, Akisuke, led him to compile a supplement, *Shoku shikashū* (Shikashū Continued), but the death of former emperor Nijō in 1165 prevented its recognition as an official imperial anthology.

Fujiwara no Korechika   藤原伊周

(974–1010). Son of the imperial regent (KAMPAKU) Fujiwara no Michitaka (953–995), Korechika expected to succeed him. Emperor ICHIJŌ appointed instead Korechika's uncle Michikane (961–995), who died one week later. Korechika was passed over again, in favor of another uncle, FUJIWARA NO MICHINAGA. Accused of various crimes, Korechika was exiled in 996. He returned to court in a general amnesty in 997 but never regained his influence.

Fujiwara no Michinaga   藤原道長

(966–1028). Court official of the Heian period (794–1185). He ruled Japan for 30 years and brought the FUJIWARA FAMILY to the height of its power. His father, FUJIWARA NO KANEIE, rose to be regent (SESSHŌ OR KAMPAKU; see also REGENCY GOVERNMENT) for Emperor ICHIJŌ, Kaneie's grandson. In 995 Michinaga became head of the Fujiwara family and was appointed both minister of the right (*udaijin*)

Fujiwara no Michinaga The most powerful statesman of the Heian period, Michinaga is depicted here in a scene from the 13th-century scroll *Illustrated Diary of Lady Murasaki.*

and examiner of imperial documents (*nairan*). Having caused the banishment of his nephew and chief rival, FUJIWARA NO KORECHIKA, in 996, Michinaga enjoyed uncontested political dominance.

Although he did not formally assume the post of regent (*kampaku*), which his father and brothers had held, Michinaga exercised its powers to the full and maintained absolute control of the throne and the court. Four of his daughters married emperors, two emperors were his nephews, and three were his grandsons. He also allied himself with the Seiwa Genji branch of the MINAMOTO FAMILY. In 1016 Michinaga became regent (*sesshō*) for his grandson Emperor GO-ICHIJŌ. A year later he became grand minister of state and gave the regency to his son FUJIWARA NO YORIMICHI. In 1019 Michinaga retired, became a Buddhist monk, and built the monastery Hōjōji (1022). In retirement he governed through Yorimichi and continued to dictate the imperial succession. His diary is titled MIDŌ KAMPAKU KI.

Fujiwara no Michinori   藤原通憲

(1106–60). Courtier and scholar. Priestly name Shinzei. He was the dominant member of Emperor GO-SHIRAKAWA's entourage after the latter's abdication in 1158. An ally of TAIRA NO KIYOMORI, he also made many enemies, including MINAMOTO NO YOSHITOMO. Michinori died in the HEIJI DISTURBANCE of 1160, which aimed to end his political influence. He compiled the national history HONCHŌ SEIKI.

Fujiwara no Michitoshi   藤原通俊

(1047–99). Classical (WAKA) poet and compiler of the fourth imperial anthology, *Goshūi wakashū* (Go shūishū; 1086, Later Collection of Gleanings). Appointed as compiler by Emperor Shirakawa (r 1073–87) in preference to more senior and established candidates such as MINAMOTO NO TSUNENOBU and ŌE NO MASAFUSA, Michitoshi incurred their displeasure. Tsunenobu impugned Michitoshi's taste in a work entitled *Nan goshūi* (Criticisms of the Go shūishū). Michitoshi replied in defense of his choice of poems for the anthology in *Goshūi mondō* (Dialogue on the Go shūishū). As an anthologist, Michitoshi was relatively conservative, displaying a preference for the witty conceit and courtly elegance that distinguished the three preceding imperial anthologies. He also wrote a Japanese preface to the Go shūi-

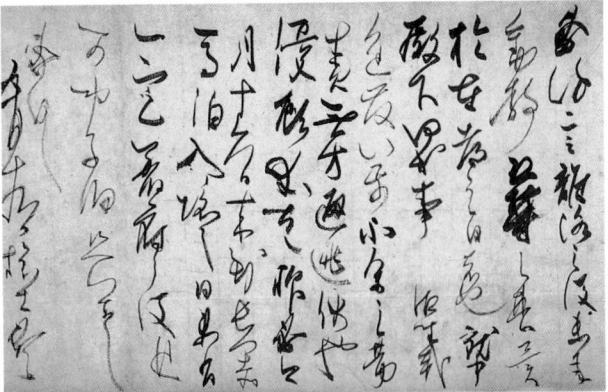

Fujiwara no Suke-masa A letter from the famous calligrapher to his nephew; one of the few extant examples of Sukemasa's work. 991. Hatakeyama Museum, Tōkyō. National Treasure.

shū, the first compiler to do so since Ki no Tsurayuki in the KOKINSHŪ. Michitoshi selected 5 of his own poems for the *Go shūishū*, and 22 others are preserved in imperial anthologies from the KIN'YŌ WAKASHŪ on.

Fujiwara no Michitsuna no Haha 藤原道綱母

(ca 931–ca 995). Poet and diarist of the Heian period (794–1185). Real name unknown. Secondary wife of FUJIWARA NO KANEIE, she is generally referred to as the mother of Fujiwara no Michitsuna (Fujiwara no Michitsuna no Haha). Her diary, KAGERŌ NIKKI (tr *The Gossamer Years*, 1964), records the unhappiness of her marriage; its vivid psychological description is said to have influenced the TALE OF GENJI (*Genji monogatari*). Her poems are included in such anthologies as SHŪI WAKASHŪ.

Fujiwara no Motohira → Ōshū
Fujiwara family

Fujiwara no Mototoshi 藤原基俊

(ca 1056–1142?). Classical (WAKA) poet and scholar. He was a conservative adversary of the more experimental, innovative poet MINAMOTO NO TOSHIYORI. More than 100 of his poems are preserved in imperial anthologies from the KIN'YŌ WAKASHŪ on. Anecdotes about him in medieval handbooks and tale collections emphasize his pride and arrogance, sometimes displayed to his own discomfiture. Mototoshi is remembered as the poetry teacher of FUJIWARA NO TOSHINARI and as the compiler of the *Shinsen rōeishū* (ca 1110), a collection of Chinese and Japanese verse for singing and reciting that was modeled upon the WAKAN RŌEISHŪ compiled by FUJIWARA NO KINTŌ.

Fujiwara no Mototsune → Akō
Incident of 887

Fujiwara no Nakamaro 藤原仲麻呂

(706–764). Also known as Emi no Oshikatsu. Grandson of FUJIWARA NO FUHITO. Courtier of the Nara period (710–794). Nakamaro enjoyed power late in Emperor SHŌMU's reign (724–749) through his aunt, the nonreigning empress KŌMYŌ, and dominated the court after his son-in-law, Emperor Junnin (733–765), succeeded Empress KŌKEN in 758. However, after Empress Kōmyō's death, Nakamaro came into conflict with the retired empress Kōken and her favorite, the priest DŌKYŌ. In 764 he unsuccessfully attempted to seize the government; he and all his family lost their lives. Kōken deposed Junnin and reascended the throne.

Fujiwara no Nobuzane 藤原信実

(ca 1177–ca 1265). WAKA poet and painter, noted for portraiture. The eldest son of FUJIWARA NO TAKANOBU, Nobuzane was the second in a lineage of six successive genera-

tions of painters specializing in a type of realistic portraiture known as *nise-e*. Nobuzane executed paintings at the request of retired Emperor GO-TOBA and, later, retired Emperor Go-Horikawa (1212–34; r 1221–32) and members of the KUJŌ FAMILY of aristocrats.

The most important extant painting attributed to Nobuzane is the portrait of the retired Emperor Go-Toba belonging to the Minase Shrine, located in Mishima, Ōsaka Prefecture. In addition, the paintings of two versions of the SANJŪROKKASEN (Thirty-Six Poetic Geniuses), one formerly in the Satake Collection and one known as the Agedatami version, have been traditionally attributed to Nobuzane. The *Zuishin teiki* scroll of portraits of members of the imperial bodyguard, in the Ōkura Collection, also has been associated with him.

Fujiwara no Sadaie 藤原定家

(1162–1241). Also known as Fujiwara no Teika. Classical (WAKA) poet, critic, editor, and scholar; one of six compilers of the eighth of the IMPERIAL ANTHOLOGIES (*chokusenshū*) of classical Japanese poetry, the SHIN KOKINSHŪ (ca 1205, New Collection from Ancient and Modern Times), and sole compiler of the ninth, *Shin chokusenshū* (1235, New Imperial Collection). He was also referred to as Kyōgoku Chūnagon (Kyōgoku Middle Counselor) and, from 1233 when he took Buddhist orders, as Myōjō.

Life—The last of several sons of the classical poet and critic FUJIWARA NO TOSHINARI, or Fujiwara no Shunzei, he became a favorite of the young former emperor GO-TOBA (r 1183–98). An accomplished poet and the most exalted patron of the age, Go-Toba appointed Teika and 10 others as fellows (*yoriudo*) of the Bureau of Poetry (Wakadokoro), which he established in 1201 to conduct poetry meetings, contests, and other events and to gather materials for a new imperial anthology. Later in the same year, Go-Toba commissioned the *Shin kokinshū*, in many respects the greatest of the 21 imperial anthologies, naming Teika as one of the compilers. Thenceforth for a period of several years Teika ill-humoredly danced attendance upon the capricious ex-sovereign, gaining greatly in poetic authority and prestige.

Teika succeeded to the headship of the Mikohidari family, a branch of the FUJIWARA FAMILY, on Shunzei's death in 1204. As head of the foremost family of court poets, he served as teacher of poetry to a number of important individuals, including the young shōgun MINAMOTO NO SANETOMO, who became Teika's pupil in 1209, and acted as judge of numerous poetry contests (UTA-AWASE). In 1232 Teika was appointed to his highest bureaucratic position, provisional middle counselor (*gon chūnagon*). In the eighth month of the same year, he was granted the highest poetic recognition by receiving a command from Emperor Go-Horikawa (1212–34; r 1221–32) to compile an imperial anthology. The compilation of the anthology, the *Shin chokusenshū*, was interrupted by the death of Go-Horikawa, but it was finally submitted to Emperor Shijō (1231–42; r 1232–42) in 1235. Teika kept a detailed, circumstantial diary. Known as MEIGETSUKI (Journal of the Full Moon), the work covers intermittently the period from 1180 to 1235.

Poetry and Poetic Ideals—In 1216 Teika made a collection of his own poems, entitled *Shūi gusō* (Foolish Verses of the Court Chamberlain), to which he later added *Shūi gusō ingai* (Supplement to *Shūi*

gusō). In later life he made several collections of favorite poems by other poets, chiefly as exemplary verses for emulation by his pupils. The most famous is the HYAKUNIN ISSHU (Single Poems by 100 Poets). Teika's verses were inspired by the practice of early classical poets of the late 9th century, such as the so-called Six Poetic Geniuses (ROKKASEN), as well as by Shunzei's neoclassical prescriptive ideal of "old words, new treatment" and his aesthetic of YŪGEN, or "mystery and depth." However, Teika developed his own ideal of *yōen*, "ethereal beauty"—the evocation of a magical atmosphere of romance, "like a celestial maiden descending to earth on a hazy moonlit night in spring." The rich tonal and symbolic qualities of this verse were often conveyed by allusion and the technique of allusive variation (HONKADORI). From the 1200s, he gradually began to espouse the ideal of "conviction of feeling" (USHIN), an effect of lyric integrity for which he derived inspiration from the more passionate, intense verses of the late-9th-century poets. From his fifties, his style gradually became conventional and less ornate. More than 430 of his poems, out of a canon of some 4,500, are included in successive imperial anthologies beginning with the SENZAI WAKASHŪ (ca 1188, Collection of a Thousand Years).

Teika's critical ideals and standards are expressed explicitly in his written comments for various poetry contests, in his brief but important prefatory essays for both *Eiga taigai* (ca 1222, Essentials of Poetic Composition) and *Kindai shūka* (ca 1209; tr *Superior Poems of Our Time*, 1907), and most extensively in his epistolary treatise, *Maigetsushō* (ca 1219, Monthly Notes).

Fujiwara no Shōshi → Jōtō Mon'in

Fujiwara no Shunzei → Fujiwara no Toshinari

Fujiwara no Sukemasa 藤原佐理

(944–998). Also known as Fujiwara no Sari. Calligrapher and court noble of the mid-Heian period (794–1185). One of the Sanseki (Three Brush Traces), with ONO NO TŌFU and FUJIWARA NO YUKINARI. Sukemasa, whose calligraphy is distinguished by an easy elegance, was particularly influenced by the work of Tōfu and the Chinese calligrapher Wang Xizhi (Wang Hsi-chih; ca 307–365?). Only a few of Sukemasa's works are extant, and none of these are examples of his calligraphy in the KANA syllabary, of which he was said to be a master.

Fujiwara no Sumitomo 藤原純友

(?–941). Provincial official and rebel of the Heian period (794–1185). Dispatched by the court in the early 930s to serve as a minor official in Iyo (now Ehime Prefecture), Sumitomo was ordered in 936 to suppress pirates on the Inland Sea. However, he eventually became their leader. The governor of Iyo adopted a policy of appeasement, and pirate activity abated. In January 940, corresponding with the revolt in the northeast of TAIRA NO MASAKADO, Sumitomo rose against the government. The court attempted to mollify him by awarding him the fifth court rank; however, Sumitomo's band of pirates continued their depredations, ravaging settlements in 11 provinces along the Inland Sea. With the death of Masakado and the end of his revolt in March, the court sent a large fleet under Ono no Yoshifuru (884–968) against the pirates; Sumitomo was defeated at Hakata Bay and fled to Iyo, where he was killed. This rebellion and the revolt led by Taira no Masakado are collectively known as the rebellions of the Jōhei (931–938) and Tengyō (938–947) eras; they were the chief civil disturbances in a period otherwise noted for renewed central authority (see ENGI TENRYAKU NO CHI); nevertheless, they were a clear sign of weakening control over the provinces.

Fujiwara no Tadamichi →Hōgen Disturbance

Fujiwara no Takanobu 藤原隆信

(1142–1205). Courtier, poet, and painter. An accomplished WAKA poet, Takanobu composed verses included in many anthologies. His poems are collected in the *Fujiwara no Takanobu Ason shū*. Takanobu was the first of six generations of portrait painters who established and developed a style of portraiture known as *nise-e*. *Nise-e* portraits incorporate a meticulously detailed and realistic approach to the depiction of individual facial features. Many *nise-e* portraits are on the relatively small scale characteristic of some YAMATO-E figure paintings and illustrations.

The most important surviving paintings attributed to Takanobu are three portraits belonging to the JINGOJI, a Kyōto Buddhist temple. The Jingoji portraits depict MINAMOTO NO YORITOMO, TAIRA NO SHIGEMORI, and Fujiwara no Mitsuyoshi, all prominent nobles of the day. All are large in scale, painted in ink and colors on silk, and mounted as hanging scrolls. Takanobu's son FUJIWARA NO NOBUZANE also became an outstanding painter of *nise-e* portraits. See also PORTRAIT PAINTING.

Fujiwara no Tameie 藤原為家

(1198–1275). Classical (WAKA) poet and son and poetic heir of FUJIWARA NO SADAIE (Teika). Scion of the poetic house established by the great *waka* poet FUJIWARA NO TOSHINARI (Shunzei) and consolidated by Teika. Tameie succeeded to the family headship on his father's death in 1241, becoming by inheritance the acknowledged master and arbiter of Japanese poetry at court. Thereafter Tameie presided as judge at numerous poetry contests (UTA-AWASE) and wrote a poetic treatise known as *Eiga ittei* (The Correct Style of Poetic Composition) or *Yakumo kuden* (Secret Teachings on the Art of the Eightfold Clouds). Tameie was commanded by former emperor GO-SAGA (r 1242–46) to compile the 10th imperial anthology, *Shoku gosenshū* (Later Collection, Continued), completed in 1251, and he collaborated in the compilation of a second imperial anthology, *Shoku kokinshū* (Collection from Ancient and Modern Times Continued), completed in 1265. His personal collection contains over 2,000 poems, 332 of which are included in imperial anthologies beginning with the *Shin chokusenshū*.

Fujiwara no Teika →Fujiwara no Sadaie

Fujiwara no Teishi 藤原定子

(976–1001). Also known as Fujiwara no Sadako. A daughter of the regent Fujiwara no Michitaka (953–995), Teishi became a junior consort (*nyōgo*) of Emperor ICHIJŌ and then empress (CHŪGŪ). When Teishi's uncle FUJIWARA NO MICHINAGA had his daughter Shōshi (988–1074) named *chūgū* in 1000, Teishi received the more prestigious title of

KŌGŌ. This was the first time an emperor had two official empresses. The two empresses were also at the center of a literary rivalry between SEI SHONAGON, who served Teishi, and MURASAKI SHIKIBU, who served Shōshi.

Fujiwara no Toshinari 藤原俊成

(1114–1204). Poet, critic, and arbiter of WAKA; compiler of the seventh of the IMPERIAL ANTHOLOGIES (*chokusenshū*) of classical Japanese poetry, the SENZAI WAKASHŪ (ca 1188, Collection of a Thousand Years). Also known as Fujiwara no Shunzei. Father of the famous FUJIWARA NO SADAIE (Fujiwara no Teika). Shunzei was born into a branch of the Fujiwara clan known as the Mikohidari family and followed a typical court career. He took Buddhist orders in 1177, adopting the priestly name Shakua.

Poetic Career——His reputation as a poet was established by his selection with 13 others as a contributor to the collection known as the "Poetic Sequences of the Kyūan Era" (*Kyūan hyakushu*), commissioned by the ex-emperor SUTOKU in 1150. Overcoming the opposition of competing poetic factions, especially the powerful Rokujō family, he became the foremost judge of poetry contests (UTA-AWASE) and arbiter of classical poetry of his century. In 1183 he was ordered by the ex-emperor GO-SHIRAKAWA to compile the *Senzai wakashū*. Thenceforth he enjoyed a position of unprecedented honor and prestige as the "grand old man" of Japanese poetry.

Poetry——In 1138 Shunzei was accepted as a disciple of the conservative arbiter FUJIWARA NO MOTOTOSHI, then in his eighties. However, he also greatly admired the poetry of Mototoshi's more innovative poetic rival MINAMOTO NO TOSHIYORI, especially his quiet, reflective, descriptive verse. Shunzei's personal collection, *Chōshū eisō* (Poems from the Palace of Long Autumns), contains 652 of his poems in its standard version, including two *chōka* ("long poems") covering the years from his mid-twenties to his late eighties. Several hundred additional poems are scattered among a variety of other sources. Some 430 of his poems, an unusually large number, are included in successive imperial anthologies, beginning with a single one in the sixth, the SHIKA WAKASHŪ (ca 1151–54, Collection of Verbal Flowers).

Poetic Principles——Shunzei's ideals and standards shaped the poetry of the period that culminated in the "Age of the SHIN KOKINSHŪ" (New Collection of Ancient and Modern Times) in the early 13th century. From Buddhism he adapted the practice of meditation, especially the "concentration and insight" (*shikan*) of the TENDAI SECT, applying its disciplinary principles to poetic composition. The single aesthetic ideal most closely associated with Shunzei is that of YŪGEN, "mystery and depth." The most important theme in his poetry is the passage of time, the fragile beauty of a world in which only change is constant. Shunzei also favored the technique of allusive variation, or HONKADORI; that is, weaving words and phrases from a well-known older poem into a new composition. The most important of his critical statements is KORAI FŪTEI SHŌ. By action and personality, Shunzei succeeded in bringing to a deeply divided poetic world a new unity of purpose and practice, preparing the way for the great efflorescence of classical poetry in the late 12th and early 13th centuries.

Fujiwara no Toshinari no Musume 藤原俊成女

(ca 1171–1254; "Fujiwara no Toshinari's Daughter"). Also known as Shunzei no Musume ("Shunzei's Daughter"). Court lady and classical (WAKA) poet. Although called the "daughter" of the great poet and critic Fujiwara no Shunzei (FUJIWARA NO TOSHINARI), she was actually his granddaughter, but was adopted by him at an early age and brought up in his household. In 1202 she was appointed lady-in-waiting to the former emperor GO-TOBA, who had heard of her poetic talents. Ranking as one of the outstanding women poets of her day, Shunzei's daughter participated in numerous poetry contests. Her poetry displays the romantic aura and descriptive symbolism that marked the poetry of Shunzei's son FUJIWARA NO SADAIE (Teika). Some 724 of her poems are preserved in imperial anthologies from the SHIN KOKINSHŪ (29 poems) on, in her personal collection, and in poetic documents and records of poetry contests.

Fujiwara no Yorimichi 藤原頼通

(992–1074). Eldest son of FUJIWARA NO MICHINAGA, Yorimichi ruled Japan for half a century, holding the post of regent (SESSHŌ or KAMPAKU; see also REGENCY GOVERNMENT) for the successive emperors GO-ICHIJŌ, Go-Suzaku (1009–45; r 1036–45), and Go-Reizei (1025–68; r 1045–68), each of whom was either his nephew or son-in-law, or both. Yorimichi lost control of the imperial succession when none of his daughters produced an imperial heir. In 1068 he was obliged to allow the enthronement of Emperor GO-SANJŌ, who was unrelated to the Fujiwara and determined to reassert imperial power. This led to a decline in the Fujiwara fortunes. Yorimichi transferred the post of regent (*kampaku*) to his younger brother Norimichi (996–1075), retired to his villa at Uji, which he had converted into the famous temple BYŌDŌIN in 1052, and became a monk.

Fujiwara no Yorinaga →Hōgen Disturbance

Fujiwara no Yoshifusa 藤原良房

(804–872). Court official of the early Heian period (794–1185). Through a series of marriage alliances he established the FUJIWARA FAMILY's dominance of the central government. His father was FUJIWARA NO FUYUTSUGU, who had earlier gained the confidence of Emperor SAGA, and in 814 Yoshifusa was married to one of Saga's daughters. He then arranged for his younger sister, Junshi, to marry Emperor Nimmyō (810–850; r 833–850), and after the JŌWA CONSPIRACY of 842 he succeeded in having a son from this union named crown prince. When the prince came to the throne as Emperor Montoku (827–858; r 850–858), he was married to Yoshifusa's daughter; their son ascended the throne as Emperor Seiwa in 858. Because of Seiwa's youth, his grandfather Yoshifusa, who was grand minister of state (*dajō daijin*), managed government affairs. In the ŌTEMMON CONSPIRACY of 866 Yoshifusa established himself as regent (SESSHŌ), the first regent not a member of the imperial house. He was able to perpetuate the post in his family, thus establishing the system of REGENCY GOVERNMENT that was dominated for the next 300 years by the Fujiwara family.

Fujiyama Aiichirō
A Liberal Democratic Party Diet member, he worked for the restoration of diplomatic relations between Japan and the People's Republic of China before withdrawing from politics in 1975.

Fujiyama Kambi This comic stage actor was noted for the sense of personal interaction with his audience that he was able to create.

Fukazawa Shichirō
Known for his expressive portrayals of the lives of the poor, this writer drew heavily on elements of Japanese folklore and tradition in his work.

Fujiwara no Yoshitsune 藤原良経

(1169–1206). Also known as Go-Kyōgoku Yoshitsune, Kujō Yoshitsune, and Lord Nakanomikado. Classical (WAKA) poet, courtier, and literary patron. He studied poetry under FUJIWARA NO TOSHINARI (Shunzei), whose style of verse he supported at court. When the retired emperor GO-TOBA established his Bureau of Poetry (Wakadokoro) in 1201, Yoshitsune was appointed head fellow. He wrote the Japanese preface for the eighth imperial anthology, the SHIN KOKINSHŪ (completed 1205), in which 79 of his poems are included. Skilled in the descriptive mode, Yoshitsune wrote poems that are both elegant and evocative, conveying the tone of melancholy (*sabi*) esteemed by the age, while also displaying a "manly vigor" (*masuraoburi*) uniquely his own. His personal collection of Japanese poems, known as *Akishino gessei shū* (ca 1204, Collection of Autumnal Bamboo Grass and Moonlit Radiance), contains more than 1,600 poems, and more than 300 are included in imperial anthologies from the SENZAI WAKASHŪ on.

Fujiwara no Yukinari 藤原行成

(972–1028). High-ranking court noble and calligrapher of the mid-Heian period (794–1185). Also known as Fujiwara no Kōzei. One of the Sanseki (Three Brush Traces), along with ONO NO TŌFŪ and FUJIWARA NO SUKEMASA. Yukinari brought to perfection the classical style of calligraphy known as *jō-daiyō*. His style became the model for the Sesonji school, long considered the authority on Japanese calligraphy. Extant works include his transcriptions of the poetry of the Chinese poet Bo Juyi (Po Chü-i; 772–846) and a diary called GONKI.

Fujiwara Opera 藤原歌劇団

(Fujiwara Kagekidan). Opera company founded by Fujiwara Yoshie (1898–1976) in 1934. The company mounted the first full-scale opera produced in Japan, *La Bohème*, followed by *Carmen* and other, mainly Italian, operas. Since 1939 it has mounted two operas per year at Tōkyō's Kabuki Theater (Kabukiza). In 1952 the group performed *Madame Butterfly* in New York, becoming the first Japanese opera company to perform abroad. After Fujiwara's death in 1976, the company underwent a series of financial and other difficulties, which lasted until 1985, when the opera singer Igarashi Kiyoshi (b 1928) became general director. Since then famous guest artists have frequently performed with the company, and the use of Japanese supertitles for foreign language performances has also helped attract larger audiences.

Fujiwara Seika 藤原惺窩

(1561–1619). Neo-Confucian scholar of the Edo period (1600–1868). Born in Harima (now part of Hyōgo Prefecture) into the noble Reizei branch of the FUJIWARA FAMILY. He became a Zen monk but later left holy orders and turned to Chinese studies and literary pursuits.

Neo-Confucianism had been introduced to Japan by Buddhist monks during the Kamakura period (1185–1333), and in the Muromachi period (1333–1568) it had become mixed with the Buddhist teachings of Zen monks within the GOZAN temple system. Although Seika formally broke with this established tradition, he still preferred

the life of a cultured recluse to the mundane world of government and warrior power. Philosophically, he drew from several traditions: ancient Confucianism, Neo-Confucianism, the teachings of Wang Yangming (see YŌMEIGAKU), and Zen mysticism. Seika's most famous disciple, HAYASHI RAZAN, served under the first four Tokugawa shōguns and in 1630 founded the Hayashi school of Neo-Confucianism (see SHŌHEIKŌ).

Fuji Xerox Co, Ltd 富士ゼロックス[株]

(Fuji Zerokkusu). Company engaged in the manufacture and sale of electronic copying machines, facsimile machines, electronic printers, computer network systems, workstations, and other equipment. Fuji Xerox was established as a joint venture in 1962, with capital furnished by FUJI PHOTO FILM CO, LTD, and Rank Xerox, Ltd, of the United Kingdom, which is a subsidiary of Xerox Corporation of the United States. Fuji Xerox has more than 40 affiliated companies in Japan and Southeast Asia. In recent years, it has been exporting products developed with its own technology to the companies of the Xerox group, of which it is now a prominent member. Sales for the fiscal year ending October 1990 totaled ¥466.0 billion (US $3.6 billion). The company was capitalized at ¥20.0 billion (US $154.2 million) in 1990. Headquarters are in Tōkyō.

Fujiya Co, Ltd [株]不二家

(Fujiya). Confectionery firm producing chocolates and candies. It has been managed by the Fujii family since its establishment in 1938. Fujiya has a nationwide franchise chain of shops and tea parlors and has built numerous restaurants in the suburbs of large cities. It also has concluded tie-ups with the British confectionery company Rowntree Macintosh, Ltd, and with Hershey Foods Corporation of the United States. Sales for the fiscal year ending March 1991 totaled ¥127.4 billion (US $928.6 million), and the company was capitalized at ¥6.3 billion (US $45.9 million). Headquarters are in Tōkyō.

Fujiyama Aiichirō 藤山愛一郎

(1897–1985). Businessman and politician. Born in Tōkyō; the son of FUJIYAMA RAITA, a prominent businessman. After attending Keiō University, he succeeded his father as president of the Dai Nippon Sugar Manufacturing Co, Ltd. He became chairman of the Japan Chamber of Commerce and Industry in 1941. After World War II, Fujiyama was temporarily barred from public office by the OCCUPATION authorities. He served as minister of foreign affairs in the KISHI NOBUSUKE cabinet (1957) and in 1958 was elected to the House of Representatives as a candidate of the Liberal Democratic Party (LDP). In 1964 he was defeated by IKEDA HAYATO in a bid to become president of the LDP. He withdrew from politics in 1975.

Fujiyama Kambi 藤山寛美

(1929–90). Comic actor and producer. Real name Inagaki Kanji. Born in Ōsaka. In 1935 he made his acting debut as a child actor with a SHIMPA troupe in Ōsaka. He later appeared in KABUKI plays and performed with the drama troupe SHINKOKUGEKI. In 1948 he joined the comedy troupe Shōchiku Shinkigeki (Shōchiku New Comedy), formed by Soganoya Jūgo (1891–1974) and SHIBUYA TENGAI. Fujiyama won acclaim for his role as a foolish son in the 1959 television drama *Oyabaka kobaka* (Foolish Parent, Foolish Child). After Shibuya's death Fujiyama as-

sumed the leadership of Shōchiku Shinkigeki and became known for his performances in *ninjō kigeki*, a variety of comic melodrama.

Fujiyama Raita 藤山雷太

(1863–1938). Entrepreneur. Born in what is now Saga Prefecture; graduate of Keiō University. After serving in the Nagasaki Prefectural Assembly, he joined the MITSUI enterprise and under NAKAMIGAWA HIKOJIRŌ helped Mitsui to buy the ŌJI PAPER CO, LTD. He also participated in the founding of the Tōkyō Municipal Tramway Company (Tōkyō Shigai Dentetsu), the Nippon Fire Insurance Company (Nippon Kasai Hoken), and the Teikoku Theater. His greatest success was in reorganizing and expanding the Dai Nippon Sugar Manufacturing Co, Ltd, and in developing sugarcane and pulp industries in Taiwan. In later years he was president of Tōkyō's Chamber of Commerce and Industry. He was the father of politician FUJIYAMA AIICHIRŌ.

Fuji Yoshida 富士吉田[市]

City in southeastern Yamanashi Prefecture, central Honshū, on the highlands of the northern slopes of Mt. Fuji (Fujisan). Fuji Yoshida developed as a Shintō shrine town and as a base camp for pilgrims climbing Mt. Fuji. Silk weaving is a traditional cottage industry. The city is a convenient base for visiting the FUJI FIVE LAKES (Fuji Goko). The Fire Festival at the Fuji Sengen Shrine (26–27 August) is a tourist attraction. Pop: 54,804.

Fuju Fuse sect 不受不施派

(Fuju Fuse *ha*). A branch of the NICHIREN SECT of Buddhism, the Fuju Fuse (literally, "not giving, not receiving") group has been noted for its perseverance in the face of political persecution, maintaining a purist doctrinal position that the believers of the truth of the LOTUS SUTRA, as interpreted by the Nichiren sect's founder-patriarch NICHIREN, should neither receive offerings from nonbelievers nor give them to nonbelievers. Moreover, the group held that the believer should exhort the rule not to commit sacrilege. Toward the close of the 16th century, in the face of collaboration with secular authorities by other Buddhist groups, including the majority of the Nichiren sect, a small group of Nichiren's followers adhered to these doctrines. A leader of the group, NICHIŌ, was exiled by the future shōgun TOKUGAWA IEYASU. The sect was proscribed in 1655, and many members were exiled or put to death throughout the Edo period (1600–1868). The group nonetheless kept alive a clandestine organization until the ban was lifted in 1876. In 1989 it comprised two sects, each with some 30,000 followers.

Fukada Yūsuke 深田祐介

(1931–). Novelist. Born in Tōkyō. Graduate of Waseda University. Fukada's *Shin seiyō jijō* (1975, New Conditions in the West) is based on his experiences living abroad as an airline employee. He received the Naoki Prize for *Ennetsu shōnin* (1980–82, Merchants in the Sweltering Heat), a novel about Japanese traders in the Philippines during and after World War II.

Fukagawa 深川[市]

City in central Hokkaidō on the northern Ishikari Plain. It was settled from 1895 to 1896 by colonist militia (TONDENHEI). Its abundant rice crop is due mainly to the Taishō Canal, which was built in 1916 to channel the waters of the river Ishikarigawa. It is an agricultural region producing such crops as potatoes and apples and has a developed food-processing industry. Pop: 30,671.

Fukagawa Edo Museum
深川江戸資料館

(Fukagawa Edo Shiryōkan). Museum in Kōtō Ward, Tōkyō. Established in 1986, the museum features furnished reproductions of buildings as they appeared in the late Edo period (1600–1868) in the Fukagawa district of Edo (now Tōkyō; see SHITAMACHI). The buildings at the museum, all of which were reproduced using traditional construction methods and materials, include a one-story wood-frame row house, a produce store, warehouses, and a fire tower.

Fukasaku Kinji
深作欣二

(1930–   ). Film director. Born in Ibaraki Prefecture. He attended Nihon University. In 1953 he joined the TŌEI CO, LTD and worked as a scriptwriter and assistant director on numerous low-budget "B" pictures. His training at Tōei guided Fukasaku into the gangster genre, for which he created one of the most popular film series of the 1970s, *Jingi naki tatakai* (Combat without a Code). Fukasaku received high praise for *Gunki hatameku moto ni* (1972, Under the Flag of the Rising Sun), which was called one of the finest antiwar pictures ever made in Japan. Other films include *Kamata kōshinkyoku* (1982, Fall Guy) and *Kataku no hito* (1986, House on Fire), the latter based on a novel by DAN KAZUO.

Fukaya
深谷[市]

City in northern Saitama Prefecture, central Honshū. Fukaya prospered as a market town, post-station town, and marketing center for silk during the Edo period (1600–1868). It was long known for its tiles, bricks, and earthenware pipes; more recently electrical and metal industries have been founded here. Pop: 94,017.

Fukazawa Shichirō
深沢七郎

(1914–87). Author. Born in Yamanashi Prefecture. He was a classical guitarist before publishing his first short story, "Narayamabushi kō" (1956; tr "The Song of Oak Mountain," 1966), a retelling of the ancient OBASUTE legend. It received the Chūō Kōron Literary Prize in the year of its publication. Fukazawa's 1960 satirical short story "Fūryū mutan" scandalized the Japanese right wing with its irreverent treatment of the imperial family and caused the SHIMANAKA INCIDENT, in which the publisher's wife was injured and her housemaid killed. Based largely on folklore, his works vividly portray the lives of the poor and contain an element of anti-intellectualism. Other works include the novel *Fuefukigawa* (1958) and the collections of short stories *Shomin retsuden* (1962–69, Biographies of the People) and *Michinoku no ningyōtachi* (1980, Dolls of Northern Japan).

fuki
蕗

(butterbur). *Petasites japonicus*. Edible perennial herb of the family Compositae, native to mountain areas of Honshū, Shikoku, and Kyūshū. It is also cultivated as a vegetable. The plant spreads by means of rhizomes (underground stems). The round or kidney-shaped, irregularly serrated leaves (about 15–30 cm [6–12 in] across) are connected to the rhizome by long leafstalks. In early spring the *fuki* produces edible shoots called *fukinotō*. Its distinctive flavor is prized in soups and condiments. The leafstalks are also boiled, peeled, and eaten. A larger variety, called *akitabuki*, grows in the cold regions of northern Honshū and Hokkaidō. Its leafstalks measure up to 2 meters (7 ft) in length, and the leaves grow to 1.5 meters (5 ft) in diameter.

Fukiage
吹上[町]

Town in northern Saitama Prefecture, central Honshū. After World War II, factories for *tabi* (traditional Japanese socks) and other clothing were established here, but they have since been replaced by machinery factories. Numerous housing developments have been built. Pop: 26,928.

Fukiagehama
吹上浜

Coastal area in the western part of the Satsuma Peninsula, Kagoshima Prefecture, Kyūshū. Facing the East China Sea, it is noted for its sand dunes and pine trees. Swimming and camping grounds are available. Length: approximately 40 km (25 mi); width of sand dunes: 1–3 km (0.6–2 mi); highest point: 47 m (154 ft).

Fukien People's Government→
Fujian (Fukien) People's Government

Fukiji
富貴寺

Sometimes called Fukidera. Buddhist temple belonging to the Tendai sect; located in the city of Bungo-Takada, Ōita Prefecture, Kyūshū. According to temple records Fukiji was built in 718 by the monk Nimmon. The main hall (*ōdō*) of the temple, which dates from the 12th century, houses a seated image of the Buddha AMIDA and is a good example of the Amida hall (*amidadō*) architecture of the late Heian period (794–1185). One of the oldest wooden structures in Kyūshū, it has been designated a National Treasure.

fukin and fugin
夫金・夫銀

(*fukin to fugin*). Commutation payments in lieu of corvée labor service (BUYAKU) during the Edo period (1600–1868); *fukin* and *fugin* (also read *bukin* and *bugin, kin* meaning gold and *gin* meaning silver) were payments in money, while *fumai* (*bumai*) was payment in rice. The practice was made possible by and also contributed to the growth of a money economy. See also KOKUDAKA; OMOTEDAKA.

fukinuki yatai
吹抜屋台

("houses with blown-off roofs"). Artistic convention associated with pictorial handscrolls of the Heian period (794–1185) and later, whereby the roof of a mansion is "removed," enabling the viewer to look directly into the rooms from above.

fukkisō
富貴草

Pachysandra terminalis. Sometimes called Japanese spurge. Evergreen perennial herb of the box family (Buxaceae) that grows wild in mountain areas of Hokkaidō, Honshū, and Shikoku. It is also cultivated as a garden plant and as a ground cover. The slanting stem (30 cm; 12 in) rises from long underground roots. The *fukkisō* has alternate, thick, oval leaves, dark green on top and with serrated tips. A short flower stalk produces spikes of pale yellow, petalless unisexual flowers through spring and summer. Mutant varieties with speckled leaves appear from time to time.

Fukko Shintō→ Restoration Shintō

Fukiji The main hall (pictured) of this Buddhist temple dates from the 12th century and is one of the oldest wooden structures in Kyūshū. National Treasure.

Fukko Yamato-e school
復古大和絵派

(Fukko Yamato-e Ha). Late-18th-century and early-19th-century movement among Kyōto artists to revitalize classical YAMATO-E, the native tradition of Japanese painting. The movement was led by Tanaka Totsugen (1767–1823), Ukita Ikkei (1795–1859), and REIZEI TAMECHIKA.

fuko
封戸

("vested households"). A form of official income, consisting of tax payments from specific households, received by high-ranking nobles under the RITSURYŌ SYSTEM of government adopted in the late 7th century. There were three kinds: *ifu*, granted on the basis of rank (*i*); *shikifu*, awarded for office (*shiki*); and *kōfu*, awarded for meritorious service (*kō*). A noble was allotted a number of households according to the level of his office and rank and received half (later all) of the rice tax, as well as the miscellaneous and corvée taxes, of those households. *Fuko* quickly disappeared in the mid-Heian period (794–1185) with the rise of private landed estates (SHŌEN). See JIKIFU.

fukoku kyōhei
富国強兵

(literally, "Enrich the Country and Strengthen the Military"). A slogan of ancient Chinese origin used by the Japanese government in the Meiji period (1868–1912) to promote strategic industries and to strengthen Japan vis-à-vis the Western powers. Toward the end of the Edo period (1600–1868) these goals had been openly endorsed by HASHIMOTO SANAI, SAKUMA SHŌZAN, YOKOI SHŌNAN, and others. The leaders of the Meiji government similarly stressed *fukoku kyōhei* because they believed that only a militarily strong Japan could effect the revision of the so-called Unequal Treaties (see UNEQUAL TREATIES, REVISION OF) and withstand the threat of Western imperialism.

The Meiji government instituted the EDUCATION ORDER OF 1872, the CONSCRIPTION ORDINANCE OF 1873, and the LAND TAX REFORM OF 1873–1881; established government-operated factories and the Ministry of Public Works (Kōbushō); and promoted the dissemination of Western thought (*bummei kaika*). The principal thrust of these policies was to enrich the country (*fukoku*) so that it could support a strong military (*kyōhei*). Tremendous amounts of public capital were invested, with leadership centered in the Ministry of Public Works and the HOME MINISTRY. Of importance were the military industries, the transportation and communications industries, the mines, and the spinning and textile industries. The promulgation of the Conscription Ordinance was the beginning of a program of military expansion that came to include aggression on the Asian continent (see MILITARISM).

fuki This perennial herb grows in the wild and is also cultivated as a vegetable. This illustration shows the radial leaves of the *fuki*, the leafstalk with head flower, and the underground stem with thin rhizomes. At right, the young inflorescence, or *fukinotō*.

fukkisō The Japanese spurge grows in shady mountain sites, and its flowers bloom from late spring to early summer.

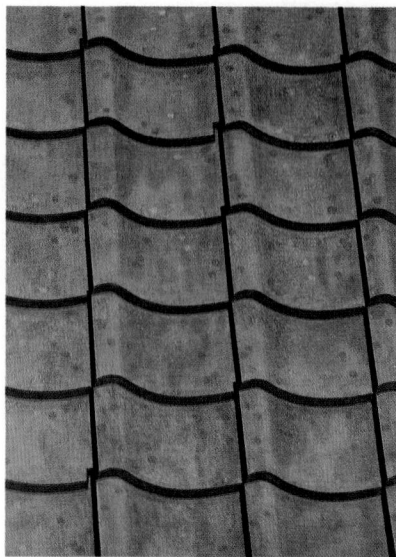

Fukuda Heihachirō
Rain. 1953. Colors on paper. 109 × 87 cm. National Museum of Modern Art, Tōkyō.

Fukui Ken'ichi The chemist in 1981, the year he received the Order of Culture and the Nobel Prize in chemistry.

Fukoku Mutual Life Insurance Co
富国生命保険[相]

(Fukoku Seimei Hoken). Life insurance company specializing in fixed-term life insurance policies. Incorporated in 1923. In the fiscal year ending March 1991 assets totaled ¥2.5 trillion (US $18.2 billion) and the company received total premiums of ¥558 billion (US $4.1 billion). Headquarters are in Tōkyō.

Fukuba Bisei
福羽美静

(1831–1907). Also known as Fukuba Yoshishizu. Scholar of KOKUGAKU, studies emphasizing the classical Japanese tradition. Born in the Tsuwano domain (now part of Shimane Prefecture). Fukuba first studied at the domain school Yōrōkan and later with ŌKUNI TAKAMASA, under whose influence he joined the proimperial anti-Tokugawa cause. After the Meiji Restoration of 1868, he entered the Office of Shintō Worship (Jingikan) and worked to promote SHINTŌ. He was appointed to the GENRŌIN (Chamber of Elders, a proto-senatorial body) in 1881 and later served in the Imperial Household Ministry (Kunaishō) and in the House of Peers.

Fukuba Hayato
福羽逸人

(1856–1921). Horticulturalist and agriculturalist. Native of what is now Shimane Prefecture; adopted son of FUKUBA BISEI. He studied in France and Germany. He is best known for his development of a strain of strawberry that bears his name (Fukuba *ichigo*).

fukubiki
福引

Popular pastime involving the drawing of lots or some similar method to win prizes. In the oldest known form, first recorded in the 8th century, two people pulled at a piece of rice cake (MOCHI) at New Year's and predicted the future according to the results; hence the name, which literally means "pulling or drawing good luck." Peddlers were also known to conduct simple lotteries, and in the early 1900s stores began giving out lottery prizes as a way of attracting customers. The latter practice continues especially during the midsummer and year-end gift-giving seasons.

Fukuchi Gen'ichirō
福地源一郎

(1841–1906). Meiji-period (1868–1912) journalist, essayist, and playwright. Pen name Fukuchi Ōchi. Born the son of a Nagasaki doctor, he studied the Dutch language as a youth. At the age of 18 he went to Edo (now Tōkyō) to study English and later worked as an interpreter and translator for the Tokugawa shogunate (1603–1867). He traveled twice to Europe. In 1868, after the Meiji Restoration, he launched the illustrated newspaper *Kōko shimbun.* Taking a pro-Tokugawa shogunate stance, he later converted to Meiji-government views and from 1874 to 1888 worked as chief editor and president of the newspaper *Tōkyō nichinichi shimbun* (see MAINICHI SHIMBUN).

Fukuchiyama
福知山[市]

City in west-central Kyōto Prefecture, central Honshū, at the confluence of the rivers Yuragawa and Hazegawa. Originally a castle town, it developed as a river port during the Edo period (1600–1868). In the Meiji period (1868–1912) it became an army town, and at present it serves as a base for the Self Defense Forces. Since World War II, it has developed into an industrial center, with textile and machinery factories, and into a distribution center for Tamba beef, which is produced in the nearby Tamba area. Pop: 66,506.

Fukuda Gyōkai
福田行誡

(1806–88). Buddhist monk of the JŌDO SECT and scholar of the early Meiji period (1868–1912) who sought to strengthen the monkhood in the face of anti-Buddhist sentiment. In its early years the policy of the Meiji government was to promote Shintō as the national creed at the expense of Buddhism (see HAIBUTSU KISHAKU). In protest Gyōkai presented a memorial to the government. During his religious career Gyōkai became abbot of the Tōkyō temple Zōjōji; shortly before his death he was appointed abbot of the Kyōto temple CHION'IN and head of the Jōdo sect.

Fukuda Heihachirō
福田平八郎

(1892–1974). Japanese-style (NIHONGA) painter. A native of Ōita Prefecture, he graduated from Kyōto Shiritsu Kaiga Semmon Gakkō (now Kyōto City University of Arts). While influenced to some extent by the RIMPA school, Fukuda maintained a distance from traditional artistic solutions throughout his career. His independence was strengthened and validated by a careful study of nature, carried out in the spirit of scientific inquiry. His solutions to problems of color and form were always based on observation and experience. As a member of the Rikuchōkai artists' group, Fukuda came in close contact with artists working in oils, which acquainted him with the artistic problems involved in the Western medium. His style evolved gradually from a minutely detailed ultrarealism to simplicity and elegance. His themes remained constant: birds, flowers, and plants, especially bamboo, for which he had a special affinity. Among his best-known works are *Shinsetsu* (1945, Newly Fallen Snow) and *Ame* (1953, Rain). He received the Order of Culture in 1961.

Fukuda Hideko
福田英子

(1865–1927). One of the first feminists in Japan; promoter of women's rights and of the socialist and pacifist movements. Also known as Kageyama Hideko. Born in what is now Okayama Prefecture. In 1882 she was inspired by a speech on women's rights given by KISHIDA TOSHIKO and became active in the FREEDOM AND PEOPLE'S RIGHTS MOVEMENT. In 1885 Hideko was implicated in a plan by radical elements of the people's rights movement to aid reform in Korea; she was imprisoned with ŌI KENTARŌ and others (see ŌSAKA INCIDENT). From 1903 to 1909 Fukuda Hideko was involved with the Japanese socialist movement, first as a member of the socialist organization HEIMINSHA and later as an editor of the socialist-feminist periodical SEKAI FUJIN. She was active in the movement to revise the PUBLIC ORDER AND POLICE LAW OF 1900, which discriminated against women. After 1906 Hideko campaigned on behalf of the pollution victims in the ASHIO COPPER MINE INCIDENT. Her writings include her autobiography, *Warawa no hanshōgai* (1904, Half of My Life).

Fukuda Takeo
福田赳夫

(1905–). Politician and bureaucrat; prime minister (1976–78). Born in Gumma Prefecture; graduate of Tōkyō University. A career bureaucrat in the Ministry of Finance, Fukuda served as chief of the Budget Bureau in 1947. He resigned in 1948 when implicated in the SHŌWA DENKŌ SCANDAL. A member of the House of Representatives since 1952, Fukuda served successively as minister of agriculture (in the second KISHI NOBUSUKE cabinet), of finance (first and second SATŌ EISAKU cabinets), and of foreign affairs (third Satō cabinet). In the MIKI TAKEO cabinet he was deputy prime minister and director-general of the Economic Planning Agency. He became president of the LIBERAL DEMOCRATIC PARTY and prime minister in 1976 but was defeated by ŌHIRA MASAYOSHI in the 1978 intraparty vote for party president.

Fukuda Tokuzō
福田徳三

(1874–1930). Economist. Born in Tōkyō. After graduating from Tōkyō Higher Commercial School (now Hitotsubashi University), he studied in Germany under Professor Lujo Brentano. In 1901 he returned, becoming a professor at his alma mater. He favored the classical school of economics as expressed in the work of Alfred Marshall and came to criticize Marxism and the German historical school, both of which he had earlier introduced to Japan. Fukuda was a leading theorist of the TAISHŌ DEMOCRACY movement. With YOSHINO SAKUZŌ, he organized the REIMEIKAI, a group advocating democratic government. His works are collected in *Fukuda Tokuzō keizaigaku zenshū* (1925–27).

Fukuda Tsuneari
福田恆存

(1912–). Dramatist and literary critic. Born in Tōkyō; graduate of Tōkyō University. After working as a high school teacher and editor, Fukuda emerged as one of the foremost critics of postwar Japanese literature. An advocate of the separation of literature and politics, a staunch conservative, and an opponent of the dogmatic leftist stance of many Japanese intellectuals, he is also known for arguing against simplification of the Japanese writing system (see JAPANESE LANGUAGE REFORMS). Noted for satirical plays such as *Kitī taifū* (1950, Typhoon Kitty), he also translated all of Shakespeare's plays into Japanese. Other important works include the plays *Ryū o nadeta otoko* (1952, The Man Who Patted the Dragon), *Akechi Mitsuhide* (1957), and *Sōtō imada shisezu* (1970, The Chief of Staff Still Hasn't Died).

Fukue
福江[市]

City on the island of Fukuejima, one of the Gotō Islands off the coast of Nagasaki Prefecture, Kyūshū. The only sizable city in the Gotō Islands, it is the center of government, culture, and transportation in the area. Agriculture and fishing are the principal industries. Fukue was originally the castle town of the Gotō family; the remains of a 19th-century castle can be seen. Pop: 29,709.

Fukuejima 福江島

Volcanic island in the East China Sea, Nagasaki Prefecture, northwestern Kyūshū. The largest island in the GOTŌ ISLANDS. Principal activities are fishing, agriculture, and cattle raising. Area: 327 sq km (126 sq mi).

Fukuharakyō 福原京

The capital of Japan for six months of the year 1180. The Fukuhara area (now part of Kōbe) was the site of a residential estate of TAIRA NO KIYOMORI, leader of the house of Taira. Kiyomori forced the transfer of the capital from Kyōto to this location early in the summer of 1180, immediately after suppressing the revolt of Prince Mochihito (1151–80) and MINAMOTO NO YORIMASA that foreshadowed the TAIRA-MINAMOTO WAR (1180–85). Kiyomori apparently wanted to have the imperial court in an area totally under his own control. The move met with strong opposition from all quarters; the high courtier KUJŌ KANEZANE denounced it as a "demonic device to destroy the imperial house." In the eastern provinces, moreover, the future shōgun MINAMOTO NO YORITOMO rebelled against the Taira. As a result, Kiyomori moved the court back to Kyōto late in 1180. Ravaged during the Taira-Minamoto War, Fukuhara was awarded to the victorious Yoritomo at the war's conclusion.

Fukui 福井[市]

City in northern Fukui Prefecture, central Honshū; capital of Fukui Prefecture. Fukui developed as a castle town under SHIBATA KATSUIE, who built a castle in 1575. Ravaged twice, in 1945 by Allied bombings and in 1948 by an earthquake, it has been completely rebuilt. Long the center of a weaving industry, the city also produces synthetic fabrics. Machinery and foodstuff industries also flourish. Attractions include the former site of Fukui Castle, Asuwayama Park, the grave of the Edo-period loyalist HASHIMOTO SANAI, and the remains of Ichijōdani, the fortress of the ASAKURA FAMILY. Pop: 252,743.

Fukui Cave 福井洞穴

(Fukui Dōketsu). Archaeological site in Fukui, Yoshii Chō, Nagasaki Prefecture. Seven strata (1, 2, 3, 4, 7, 9, and 15) of the 16 excavated since 1960 indicate human occupation. The STONE TOOLS from stratum 15, dated by radiocarbon to more than 31,900 years ago, are most certainly of human manufacture (see PALEOLITHIC CULTURE). Pottery with strips of clay applied to the surface was excavated from stratum 3. Its radiocarbon date of 12,700 ± 500 years ago is the oldest obtained for pottery in the world. Pottery with small semicircular impressions (tsumegatamon; "fingernail-impressions") was excavated from stratum 2, dated to 12,400 ± 350 years ago, and roulette-stamped ware was found in stratum 1. See JŌMON POTTERY.

Fukui Ken'ichi 福井謙一

(1918–). Chemist. Born in Nara Prefecture, he was a graduate of Kyōto University, where he became professor of physical chemistry. Fukui received the Nobel Prize in chemistry in 1981 for his work applying the theory of quantum mechanics to chemical reactions. His "frontier orbital theory" explains chemical reactions by calculating the shape and density of the outer electron clouds. He was a recipient of the Order of Culture in 1981.

Fukui Plain 福井平野

(Fukui Heiya). Located in northern Fukui Prefecture, central Honshū. With diluvial uplands in the north, this low-lying rice-producing region consists of the floodplain of the river Kuzuryūgawa, with sand dunes bordering the Sea of Japan. The major city is Fukui, which has a thriving synthetic fiber industry. Area: approximately 480 sq km (190 sq mi).

Fukui Prefecture 福井県

(Fukui Ken). Located on the Sea of Japan in central Honshū and bounded by Ishikawa Prefecture on the north, Gifu Prefecture on the east, Shiga and Kyōto prefectures on the south, and the Sea of Japan on the west. It is geographically divided into northern and southern districts. The northern district, which includes most of the land area and population, is largely occupied by mountain ranges interspersed with coastal plains and river valleys. The southern district is a narrow strip of rocky coast along WAKASA BAY, separated from Shiga and Kyōto prefectures to the south by mountain ranges. Major rivers include the KUZURYŪGAWA, Hinogawa, and Asuwagawa. The climate is fairly typical of the Sea of Japan coastline—humid and cloudy with heavy rain and snowfall, particularly in the northern district.

The area contains numerous archaeological sites, indicating early settlement. Under the ancient provincial system (KOKUGUN SYSTEM), it was divided into the provinces of Echizen and Wakasa, with much of the land owned by important temples. It was incorporated into the prefectural system in 1881.

The agricultural sector continues to be strong in Fukui, with rice as the principal crop. Textile mills developed rapidly in the Meiji period (1868–1912), and textiles are still the prefecture's dominant industry, with production centering on synthetic fibers. Chemicals and machines, as well as more traditional products such as lacquer ware and cutlery, are also produced there. Fukui exports over 75 percent of its fishing catch to neighboring prefectures and also provides nuclear energy for the heavily populated KANSAI REGION to the south. The prefecture is well served by major highways and railways; Hokuriku Tunnel, the second longest tunnel in Japan, is located near TSURUGA.

Historically, Fukui Prefecture has long maintained close cultural and economic ties with Kyōto; hence its numerous important temples and works of art. Especially noteworthy is the Zen Buddhist temple of EIHEIJI. Some of the major tourist attractions are the coastal areas that belong to Wakasa Bay and Echizen-Kaga Coast quasi-national parks and part of HAKUSAN NATIONAL PARK. Area: 4,192 sq km (1,619 sq mi); pop: 823,585; capital: FUKUI. Other major cities include TAKEFU, SABAE, and Tsuruga.

fukujusō 福寿草

(adonis). Adonis amurensis. A perennial herb of the family Ranunculaceae that grows wild in deciduous forests from central to northern Japan. The stem grows to a height of 20–30 centimeters (7.9–11.8 in). The leaves are alternate and pinnate. A single golden yellow flower blooms at the tip of the stem between February and March. Since the blooming of the flower coincides with the traditional lunar calendar New Year's celebration, the fukujusō (literally, "happiness forever plant") is considered auspicious. It is also known as the ganjitsusō or "New Year's Day plant."

Fukumoto Kazuo 福本和夫

(1894–1983). Leading theoretician of the JAPAN COMMUNIST PARTY in the 1920s. Born in Tottori Prefecture, he graduated from Tōkyō University in 1920, taught at Matsue Higher School (now part of Shimane University), and in 1922 went to study in Europe and North America. Returning to Japan in 1924, he joined the Communist Party and published in the party journal Marukusu shugi. His criticisms of the established Marxists YAMAKAWA HITOSHI and KAWAKAMI HAJIME won him support among younger Marxists. In April 1925 he helped to reactivate the Japan Communist Party in Tōkyō. In December 1926 he became head of its political section but in July 1927 was forced to resign the position because of Comintern criticism. His stress on attaining ideological purity by purging the party of heterodox Marxist elements—the so-called Fukumotoism—was held responsible for the party's failure to create a mass movement in Japan. He remained a party member until his arrest in June 1928. Sentenced to 10 years' hard labor, he was actually jailed for 14 years. In 1950 he rejoined the party but was expelled in 1958. He later wrote numerous studies of Japanese cultural and economic history.

Fukunaga Takehiko 福永武彦

(1918–79). Novelist and poet. Born in Fukuoka Prefecture. Graduate of Tōkyō University. He was a member of the Matinée Poétique (Matine Poechikku), a group of poets. His novels, poetry, and criticism were strongly influenced by the French symbolists, particularly Baudelaire and Rimbaud. He also wrote mystery novels under the pseudonym Kada Reitarō and science fiction under the name Funada Gaku. He translated several works by Jean-Paul Sartre. His critical biography of Paul Gauguin, Gōgyan no sekai, won the Mainichi Book Award for 1961. Major novels include Fūdo (1957) and Bōkyaku no kawa (1964).

Fukuoka 福岡[市]

Capital of Fukuoka Prefecture; in northwestern Fukuoka Prefecture, northern Kyūshū. Situated on Hakata Bay, its importance as the political, economic, and cultural center of northern Kyūshū dates to the 7th century, when the port of Hakata (now Hakata Ward) was the point of departure for travel to the Chinese continent. DAZAIFU, the government outpost governing the entire Kyūshū area at the time, was also nearby. Hakata reached its height of prosperity during the 15th and 16th

Fukui Prefecture
Location and Prefectural Crest

centuries as a result of trade with Ming dynasty (1368–1644) China. In 1601 a castle was constructed in the western part of Hakata and the area surrounding the castle was named Fukuoka. In 1889 Hakata and the castle town of Fukuoka merged to form the city of Fukuoka.

Principal industries are chemicals, textiles, food processing, electrical equipment, machinery, and printing. It boasts one of the largest marine catches in Japan. The city has long been known for its silk (*hakata-ori*) and dolls (Hakata *ningyō*). Educational institutions include Kyūshū University. Among Fukuoka's attractions are archaeological sites, mounded tombs (KOFUN), remains of fortifications built to ward off the MONGOL INVASIONS OF JAPAN, many famous shrines and temples, and the Hakata Dontaku Festival on 3–4 May. Area: 338 sq km (130 sq mi); pop: 1,237,062.

Fukuoka Art Museum　福岡市美術館

(Fukuoka Shi Bijutsukan). Located in the city of Fukuoka, Fukuoka Prefecture. Opened in 1975. Among the museum's holdings is the collection of the Kuroda family, a *daimyō* family that once ruled the area; that collection includes seals of historical importance (see KAN NO WA NO NA NO KOKUŌ NO IN), weapons, and paintings. The collection of MATSUNAGA YASUZAEMON (which includes works by Ogata KENZAN and NONOMURA NINSEI), Buddhist art from the temple Tōkōin, Japanese-style paintings by TOMITA KEISEN, and works by such pioneers of Western painting in Japan as KURODA SEIKI and AOKI SHIGERU are among the museum's other holdings.

Fukuoka Plain　福岡平野

(Fukuoka Heiya). Alluvial plain in northwestern Fukuoka Prefecture, Kyūshū. The major city is Fukuoka. Primarily a farming area, it has been rapidly urbanized. Area: 250 sq km (100 sq mi).

Fukuoka Prefecture　福岡県

(Fukuoka Ken). Located in northern Kyūshū and bounded by the Hibiki Sea to the north, the INLAND SEA to the east, Ōita Prefecture to the southeast, Kumamoto Prefecture to the south, the Ariake Sea and Saga Prefecture to the southwest, and the Genkai Sea to the northwest. Yamaguchi Prefecture, on the southwestern tip of Honshū, lies just across the Kammon Strait north of the city of KITA KYŪSHŪ. The terrain is dominated by the Tsukushi Mountains, which cut across the middle of the prefecture from southwest to northeast. Flat areas are found in river and mountain valleys, including the broad plains around the river Chikugogawa in the south, the region around the city of FUKUOKA in the west, and the area between the cities of NŌGATA and Kita Kyūshū in the north. The climate is generally warm and mild, with relatively little precipitation in the coastal areas. Cloudy and stormy weather is common in the winter months.

Because of its proximity to the Asian mainland and its strategic location between Kyūshū and Honshū, the Fukuoka area was one of the first areas to display notable cultural development. YAMATAI, the ancient Japanese kingdom referred to in the Chinese chronicle WEI ZHI (*Wei chih*), is believed by some scholars to have been located here, and prehistoric artifacts have been discovered in great quantity. DAZAIFU, the central govern-

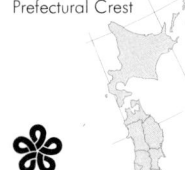

Fukuoka Prefecture
Location and
Prefectural Crest

ment outpost for all of Kyūshū in the protohistoric and ancient periods, was located approximately 15 km (9 mi) south of what is now the city of Fukuoka; it served as the embarkation point for government missions to China. The Fukuoka coast was the scene of the MONGOL INVASIONS OF JAPAN in the 13th century and of a flourishing foreign trade from the 15th to the early 17th century. Under the ancient provincial system (KOKU-GUN SYSTEM) the area was divided into the three provinces of Chikuzen, Chikugo, and Buzen; it received its present form and name under the modern prefectural system in 1876.

Coal in the Chikuhō, Miike, and Kasuya districts provided the basis for the rapid development of heavy industries starting in the late 19th century. The prefecture remained Japan's principal source of coal for several decades in the late 19th and early 20th centuries. Major industries, centered largely around Kita Kyūshū, include steel, food processing, cement, glass, ceramics, and chemicals, although the prefecture's share of the country's total industrial output has declined since World War II because of the decrease in coal deposits. Agriculture (mainly rice, vegetables, fruit, tea, and livestock) is also important. Fishing is carried out in both coastal and deep-sea waters.

Fukuoka's long history and varied coastline constitute major tourist attractions. Part of the Inland Sea National Park is located within the prefecture, as are the quasinational parks Yaba-Hita-Hikosan, Northern Kyūshū, and Genkai. Dazaifu—with its plum blossoms, Temmangū Shrine, and ancient ruins—is also a popular area for sightseeing. The city of Fukuoka, the site of Kyūshū University, is the major educational and cultural center in Kyūshū. Area: 4,963 sq km (1,916 sq mi); pop: 4,811,050; capital: Fukuoka. Other major cities include Kita Kyūshū, KURUME, and ŌMUTA.

Fukuoka Takachika　福岡孝弟

(1835–1919). Statesman. Born in the Tosa domain (now Kōchi Prefecture). In 1867 he and GOTŌ SHŌJIRŌ went to Kyōto and persuaded the shōgun TOKUGAWA YOSHINOBU to return political authority to the emperor (see TAISEI HŌKAN). After the MEIJI RESTORATION (1868), as a *san'yo* (junior councillor) for the new government, Fukuoka helped draft the CHARTER OATH. He was largely responsible for the SEITAISHO, Japan's first "constitution." He later served as minister of education and privy councillor.

Fukuroda Falls　袋田ノ滝

(Fukuroda no Taki). Located on the upper river Kujigawa, northern Ibaraki Prefecture, central Honshū. Water falls in a series of four cascades. The surrounding area is a popular tourist attraction, famous for its beautiful autumn foliage. Fukuroda Hot Spring is nearby. Height: 127 m (417 ft); width: 73 m (240 ft).

Fukuroi　袋井[市]

City in southwestern Shizuoka Prefecture, central Honshū. Fukuroi developed as a post-station town on the highway Tōkaidō during the Edo period (1600–1868). Principal agricultural products are melons and tea. Chemical, musical-instrument, and pharmaceutical industries have flourished here. Pop: 53,180.

Fukushi Kōjirō　福士幸次郎

(1889–1946). Poet. Born in Aomori Prefecture. In 1909 he joined a poetry group, the

Jiyūshi Sha (Free Verse Society). His *Taiyō no ko* (1914, Sun Child) was the first outstanding work of free verse written in the spoken language to be published in Japan. In 1923 he returned to Aomori and became interested in regionalism, attempting to compose poems in dialect. He also made a study of Japanese ethnology, *Gen Nihon kō* (1942).

Fukushima　福島[市]

Capital of Fukushima Prefecture; in northern Fukushima Prefecture, northern Honshū, on the river ABUKUMAGAWA. Fukushima developed as a castle town and a post-station town along the highway Ōshū Kaidō during the 15th century. Principal industries include food processing, electrical appliances, machinery, and agriculture, primarily fruit. It is the site of Fukushima University. Iizaka Hot Spring is in the northern part of the city. Mt. Adatara (Adatarasan), which is nearby, is a part of the BANDAI-ASAHI NATIONAL PARK. Pop: 277,528.

Fukushima Basin　福島盆地

(Fukushima Bonchi). In northern Fukushima Prefecture, northern Honshū. Bounded by the Abukuma and Ōu mountains, the basin consists mainly of the floodplain of the river Abukumagawa and alluvial fans and river terraces below the fault scarp. The area is known for its sericulture, apples, and vegetables. The major city is Fukushima. Area: approximately 700 sq km (270 sq mi).

Fukushima Incident　福島事件

(Fukushima Jiken). The first in a series of popular uprisings occurring 1882–84 connected with the FREEDOM AND PEOPLE'S RIGHTS MOVEMENT. Fukushima Prefecture became a center for the movement after KŌNO HIRONAKA founded the Sekiyōsha political society there in 1875 to expand political consciousness and participation.

In 1882 the government appointed MISHIMA MICHITSUNE as governor of Fukushima. Mishima announced his intention to suppress the people's rights movement, support the local branch of the progovernment RIKKEN TEISEITŌ, and construct new roads. His plans called for doubled local taxes as well as conscripted labor for the roads. He immediately encountered the opposition of the Fukushima Jiyūtō, a local affiliate of the JIYŪTŌ, led by Kōno, who was president of the Fukushima Prefectural Assembly. When local Jiyūtō leaders agitated against "despotic rule," Mishima quickly had them outlawed.

Many peasants refused or were unable to contribute labor for road construction or to pay the high local taxes. Prefectural officials responded by declaring the peasants' property open to public auction. In November 1882 several Jiyūtō leaders were imprisoned for condemning this step. On 28 November, when some 1,000 peasants gathered outside the Kitakata police station to demand their release, violence erupted. Kōno Hironaka and 57 others were charged with treason, but only 6 were found guilty, including Kōno, who was sentenced to seven years imprisonment. The incident became a symbol of popular resistance to despotic rule.

Fukushima Kazuo　福島和夫

(1930–). Composer and musicologist. Born in Tōkyō. An early work, *Ekāgura* (1957), was accepted at the Second International Festival of Contemporary Music at Karuizawa in 1957 and, with the encouragement of composer Igor Stravinsky, performed the following year in Los Angeles.

Since 1964 Fukushima has been a professor at Ueno Gakuen College, Tōkyō, and since 1973 he has been director of the college's Research Archives for Japanese Music. His works include *Chūu* (1959), *Mei* (1962), *Suirin* (1967), and *Kaze no wa* (1968).

Fukushima Masanori　福島正則

(1561–1624). *Daimyō* of the Azuchi-Momoyama period (1568–1600) and early Edo period (1600–1868). Masanori gained fame as one of TOYOTOMI HIDEYOSHI's "Seven Spears" (Shichihon'yari) at the Battle of SHIZUGATAKE in 1583. He participated in Hideyoshi's conquest of Kyūshū in 1587, the ODAWARA CAMPAIGN of 1590, and the first of the INVASIONS OF KOREA IN 1592 AND 1597. In 1595 he was made daimyō of Kiyosu in Owari Province (now part of Aichi Prefecture). In 1600 Masanori became a follower of TOKUGAWA IEYASU, distinguished himself at the Battle of Sekigahara, and was rewarded with a great fief at Hiroshima, but in 1619 his domain was confiscated for his attempt to improve Hiroshima Castle against shogunate orders, and possibly because he was sympathetic to Christians. Masanori was demoted to a much smaller fief, which he held until his death.

Fukushima Prefecture　福島県

(Fukushima Ken). The southernmost prefecture of the Tōhoku region in northern Honshū; bounded by Yamagata and Miyagi prefectures to the north; by the Pacific Ocean to the east; by Ibaraki, Tochigi, and Gumma prefectures to the south; and by Niigata Prefecture to the west. Contains three major mountain ranges, all running in a north-south direction. The ABUKUMA MOUNTAINS separate the Pacific coastal plains from the Fukushima and Kōriyama basins in the center of the prefecture, which in turn are separated from the Aizu district to the west by the ŌU MOUNTAINS. The ECHIGO MOUNTAINS rise in the western part of the prefecture. HIU-CHIGADAKE (2,356 m; 7,730 ft) in southwestern Fukushima is the highest mountain in the Tōhoku region. Principal rivers include the ABUKUMAGAWA, Nippashigawa, and TADA-MIGAWA. Hot summers and cold winters are typical of the entire prefecture. Precipitation is plentiful on the western side of the Ōu Mountains, with heavy winter snowfall, while the eastern areas tend to be drier.

The Fukushima area has long been a major transportation link between northeastern Honshū and the rest of the main island. A part of Mutsu Province under the ancient provincial system (KOKUGUN SYSTEM), it took its present form and name under the modern prefectural system in 1876.

Agriculture is the principal occupation, with approximately half of all acreage devoted to rice production. Other crops include tobacco, cucumbers, tomatoes, peaches, apples, and pears. Ample energy is provided by nuclear power generation. Major industrial products are metal, chemical and machine goods, foodstuffs, and textiles.

Tourist attractions are BANDAI-ASAHI NATIONAL PARK, including Lake Inawashiro, and hot-spring resorts such as Iizaka, Tsuchiyu, Dake, and Kasshi. Area: 13,784 sq km (5,321 sq mi); pop: 2,104,058; capital: FUKUSHIMA. Other major cities include AIZU WAKAMATSU, IWAKI, KŌRIYAMA, and SUKAGAWA.

Fukushima Yasumasa　福島安正

(1852–1919). Army general. Born in Shinano Province (now Nagano Prefecture). He is probably best remembered for his solitary crossing of Siberia on horseback in 1892–93. During the 14-month trip from Berlin to Vladivostok, which made him a national hero, he collected information on Russian military capabilities in the Far East. He served in the SINO-JAPANESE WAR OF 1894–1895, the BOXER REBELLION, and the RUSSO-JAPANESE WAR of 1904–05.

Fukusuke Corporation　福助[株]

(Fukusuke). Manufacturer and wholesaler of clothing and footwear. Incorporated in 1919 as a maker of TABI, a type of traditional Japanese footwear. Fukusuke has cooperative agreements with Pierre Balmain, Christian Dior, and MIYAKE ISSEI (Issey Miyake). For the fiscal year ending March 1991, sales totaled ¥83.1 billion (US $605.7 million) and capitalization stood at ¥3.4 billion (US $24.6 million). Headquarters are in Ōsaka.

fukutoshin → urban subcenters

fuku warai　福笑い

New Year's game for children. A blindfolded player tries to place pieces of paper in the shape of eyebrows, eyes, nose, and mouth within the outline of an *otafuku*, the face of a homely woman with round cheeks and a flat nose. The disorderly placement of the features creates amusing expressions.

Fukuyama　福山[市]

City in southeastern Hiroshima Prefecture, western Honshū, at the mouth of the river Ashidagawa. Developed early on as a port, it became a castle town during the Edo period (1600–1868). Traditionally known for its *tatami* mat coverings and *kasuri* (ikat) cloth, with the opening of factories by NKK Corporation in 1961, it has developed as a heavy industrial city. Tourists are drawn to Fukuyama Castle and the island of Sensuijima. Pop: 365,612.

Fukuzawa Ichirō　福沢一郎

(1898–1992). Western-style painter. Born in Gumma Prefecture. Attended Tōkyō University, then went to France, where he was deeply influenced by the work of Giorgio de Chirico (1888–1978) and Max Ernst (1891–1976). Returning to Japan, he championed avant-garde art rooted in surrealism. He founded the Art Culture Association (Bijutsu Bunka Kyōkai) in 1939. After World War II he traveled in Latin America; his paintings of the people he met there express a great vitality and deep humanism. He received the Order of Culture in 1991.

Fukuzawa Yukichi　福沢諭吉

(1835–1901). Prominent educator, writer, and propagator of Western knowledge during the Meiji period (1868–1912); founder of Keiō Gijuku (now KEIŌ UNIVERSITY), of the newspaper JIJI SHIMPŌ, and of the art of public speaking in Japan. His collected works, written over a period of 30 years, fill 22 large volumes and cover a variety of subjects ranging from philosophy to women's rights.

Born in Ōsaka into the family of an impoverished low-ranking *samurai* of the Nakatsu domain (now part of Ōita Prefecture) in Kyūshū, Fukuzawa from an early age hated what he regarded as the "narrow stiffness" of the feudal domain. To escape from its restrictions, he went to Nagasaki in 1854 to study Western gunnery and to Ōsaka in 1855 to join the Tekijuku, the celebrated school for Dutch studies run by the scholar OGATA KŌAN. There he studied the Dutch language with tireless enthusiasm,

together with any branch of Western science—chemistry, physics, or anatomy—for which there were textbooks in the meager school library.

In 1858 he was summoned to Edo (now Tōkyō) by his domainal authorities to start a school for the study of Dutch. He lost no time in visiting the new foreign trading community in Yokohama, only to discover to his chagrin that the foreign merchants spoke not Dutch, but English, and that he must set to work to learn the latter language. Undaunted, in 1860 he joined the first Japanese mission to America, sailing in the small vessel KANRIN MARU to San Francisco, where the party was lavishly entertained. Two years later he joined the first Japanese mission to Europe, visiting France, England, Holland, Russia, and Portugal, and learning all he could of Western civilization.

The information he collected on this journey later formed the basis of his celebrated work SEIYŌ JIJŌ (Conditions in the West; published in 10 volumes in 1867, 1868, and 1870). This book gave a simple readable account of everyday Western customs and institutions and proved so popular that the sales of volume 1 reached the huge figure of 150,000. Fukuzawa's reputation as an authority on things Western was thenceforth made. It was only after the Meiji Restoration of 1868, however, that he came to realize his mission in life. This was nothing less than to educate his countrymen to an entirely new way of thinking based on the principles of Western civilization. Japan was weak and backward, he decided, because its culture lacked two things possessed by Western nations: science and the spirit of independence. Inculcate these things into the Japanese nation and it would soon grow in power and wealth so as to rival Great Britain and be secure from any threat of Western attack and exploitation.

To the task of enlightening (*keimō*) the Japanese people in this manner Fukuzawa devoted the rest of his life. In his teaching at Keiō Gijuku (already one of the largest schools in the country), through the policy of his newspaper, in his personal life, and above all in his voluminous and lucid writings, he constantly strove to show that traditional Japanese ideas and values were wrong and to replace them with others derived from Western positivism and liberalism. To this end, he defined a new concept of *jitsugaku*, or practical knowledge, and propounded new views of history, ethics, politics, and international relations. He proposed a new scheme of family relationships, championing particularly the cause of women.

fuku warai These children are using the traditional *otafuku* face, but this New Year's game is now sometimes played using the faces of popular cartoon and comic-book characters.

Fukushima Prefecture Location and Prefectural Crest

Fukuzawa Yukichi This journalist and educator was a major force in the introduction of Western thought to Meiji-period Japan.

429

Fukuzawa Yukichi

fumie

1 In this 19th-century painting, a man (at center) treads on one of these Christian images in order to prove that he is not a Christian.
2 This religious icon was confiscated from its Christian owner and mounted on a board for use as a *fumie*.

fundoshi A group of loincloth-clad men gather during the Hakata Gion Yamagasa, a festival in Fukuoka Prefecture. *Fundoshi* are rarely worn today except on ritual occasions.

Fukuzawa never accepted any government post, remaining a private citizen all his life. By the time of his death he was a national figure, with former pupils in all walks of life, and revered as one of the founders of the new Japan. His principal works include GAKUMON NO SUSUME (1872–76; tr *An Encouragement of Learning*, 1969), BUMMEIRON NO GAIRYAKU (1875; tr *An Outline of a Theory of Civilization*, 1973), and his lively autobiography, *Fukuō jiden* (1899; tr *The Autobiography of Yukichi Fukuzawa*, 1972).

Fulbright Commission → Japan– United States Educational Commission

Fulbright, James William
フルブライト, J. W.

(1905–). US politician. Born in Sumner, Missouri. He was elected to the US House of Representatives in 1942 and served in the Senate from 1945 to 1975. He is known as the author of the Fulbright Act of 1946, which established a program of educational exchange between the United States and other countries. In its first 40 years the program sponsored more than 156,000 scholars and professionals from 120 nations. Of this number more than 7,000 Americans and Japanese participated in the Japan Fulbright program. See also JAPAN–UNITED STATES EDUCATIONAL COMMISSION.

fumai → fukin and fugin

fumie
踏絵

(literally, "pictures to step on"). Pictures of Christian figures used during the Edo period

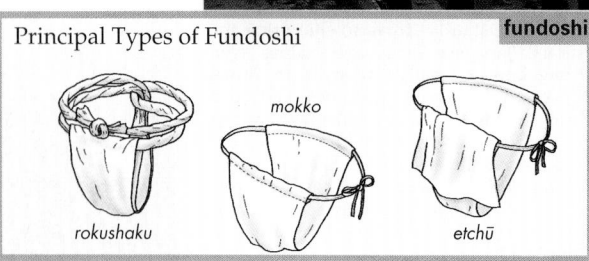

Principal Types of Fundoshi **fundoshi**

rokushaku

mokko

etchū

(1600–1868) to identify adherents of CHRISTIANITY, proscribed in 1613. Suspects were ordered to trample these Christian images underfoot on the assumption that those who refused or hesitated revealed themselves as Christians. The practice was first used in Nagasaki in 1629 or 1626. It later spread to northern Kyūshū, where it was known as *ebumi*. Initially *fumie* were simply crosses or religious pictures, but later, brass crucifixes were cast at Nagasaki and issued to *daimyō* of adjoining domains especially for examining suspects. Official use of *fumie* as an instrument of control continued until 1858. See also SHŪMON ARATAME.

funa → crucian carp

Funabashi
船橋[市]

City in northwestern Chiba Prefecture, on Tōkyō Bay, 20 km (12 mi) east of Tōkyō. Funabashi has been a satellite city of Tōkyō since the late 1920s. The coastal area is part of the KEIYō INDUSTRIAL REGION, with steel, machinery, and food-processing plants. Pop: 533,270.

funadama
船霊

(literally, "spirit of the ship"). Tutelary deity of ships, seamen, and fishermen who ensures safety and a plentiful catch. In a secret ceremony the *shintai*, or physical representation, of the *funadama* is placed in a hole at the base of the mast by the ship's carpenter. The god may be represented by a lock of woman's hair, a pair of dice, a pair of male and female dolls, one or two coins, grain, cosmetics, or even mouse droppings. The ceremony for installing the *shintai* is always performed from the port side because by custom the bodies of those who drown are hauled on board ship from the starboard side. Because of the belief that the *funadama* is a female deity and the superstition against having a lone woman aboard ship, some vessels refrain from enshrining the god's *shintai*. The *funadama* is said to warn of approaching danger or storms by making a chiming sound.

Funahashi Seiichi
舟橋聖一

(1904–76). Novelist and playwright. Born in Tōkyō. Graduate of Tōkyō University. Inspired by such French writers as Gide and Malraux, he participated in the humanist movement associated with the magazine *Kōdō* and in 1934 published the novel *Daibingu* (Diving), which brought him literary recognition. More typical of his work in this period are such conventional novels as *Bokuseki* (1938) and *Shikkaiya Kōkichi* (1945). After World War II, Funahashi became known for erotic novels such as *Yuki fujin ezu* (1948–50) and *Geisha Konatsu* (1952). The novels *Aru onna no enkei* (1963) and *Sukina onna no munekazari* (1967) won, respectively, the Mainichi Book Award and

the Noma Literary Prize. In 1966 he was elected to the Japan Art Academy.

Funai Electric Co, Ltd
船井電機[株]

(Funai Denki). Company engaged in the production and sale of audiovisual equipment, information and communication equipment, household electrical appliances, and hotel-related equipment. Incorporated in 1961. For the fiscal year ending June 1990, sales totaled ¥140.0 billion (US $1.0 billion) and capitalization stood at ¥482.5 million (US $3.5 million). Headquarters are in Daitō, Ōsaka Prefecture.

Funakoshi Gichin
船越義珍

(1868–1957). Popularizer of KARATE in modern Japan and founder of the Shōtōkan Ryū style of *karate*. He was born in Okinawa, where he studied with the man who had developed *karate* in the region, Itosu Ankō (1832–1916). Funakoshi mastered both the Shōrinryū and the Shōreiryū styles and went on to become the president of Okinawa's *karate* club, the Okinawa Shōbukai. In 1922 the Ministry of Education invited him to do a demonstration of *karate* in Tōkyō; knowledge of the art spread throughout Japan thereafter and *karate* clubs were organized at many universities. In 1947 the Japan Karate Association named him the country's top master of *karate*.

fundamental labor rights
労働基本権

(*rōdō kihonken*). Rights of workers to organize, bargain collectively, and engage in concerted action (strikes). These three rights are guaranteed by article 28 of the 1947 CONSTITUTION OF JAPAN. Any law, government action, or private activity that violates these rights is considered illegal and invalid. On the other hand, all three rights are denied to public employees of the police and fire departments, prisons, the Defense Agency, and the Maritime Safety Agency. The rights to strike and bargain collectively are denied to national and local government clerical workers; the right to strike is denied to national and local government nonclerical workers, employees of public enterprises, and workers at local public corporations. See also COLLECTIVE BARGAINING RIGHT; LABOR LAWS; RIGHT TO STRIKE; PUBLIC EMPLOYEES.

fundamental liberties
自由権

(*jiyūken*). General term for those rights that secure personal freedom from interference by governmental authority. The 1947 CONSTITUTION OF JAPAN emphasizes the guarantee of fundamental liberties in detailed provisions. First, it guarantees freedom of intellectual activities, including freedom of thought and conscience (art. 19), FREEDOM OF RELIGIOUS FAITH (art. 20), FREEDOM OF SPEECH, FREEDOM OF THE PRESS, FREEDOM OF ASSEMBLY, and FREEDOM OF ASSOCIATION (art. 21, para. 1), privacy of correspondence (art. 21, para. 2), and ACADEMIC FREEDOM (art. 23). Second, it guarantees the freedom of one's person. Detailed constitutional provisions guarantee due process of law (art. 31), as well as the rights of the accused (arts. 33, 34, and 39), reflecting the influence of the US Constitution. Third, it guarantees freedom of economic activities, including the freedom to move one's residence and to choose one's occupation (art. 22), and it guarantees property rights (art. 2). The right of JUDICIAL REVIEW is recognized so that the constitutionality of laws that might limit fundamental liberties can be determined in a court of law. Finally, fundamental liberties are not limited to those enumerated in the constitution; the right to privacy is an example of such a freedom.

fundoshi 褌

(loincloth). An article of men's clothing consisting of a long strip of cloth fastened around the waist, passed between the legs, and tucked in or tied at the back. Also called *shitaobi*. Judging from clay figurines (HANIWA) of the Kofun period (ca 300–710), *fundoshi* appear to have been in use from the ancient past. At first they were made of linen, but from the Edo period (1600–1868) cotton was more widespread. The upper classes favored loincloths made of silk. The most popular kinds of *fundoshi* were the *rokushaku*, so called because of its length (six [*roku*] *shaku*; about 2.2 m or 7.2 ft) and made of a single piece of cloth; the *etchū fundoshi*, half as long as the *rokushaku*, but with one end of the central cloth section folded over and sewn to accommodate a string waistband; and the *mokko fundoshi*, with both ends of the cloth sewn over the waistband, which is tied at one side. During the Shōwa period (1926–89), *fundoshi* were gradually replaced by Western-style underwear. The *fundoshi* worn by SUMŌ wrestlers, a special version made of heavy silk, are known as *mawashi* or *shimekomi*.

funerals 葬儀

(*sōgi*). About 90 percent of the funerals in Japan are conducted according to Buddhist rites. Upon death the body is washed with hot water (*yukan*), then dressed by family members in white garments (*kyōkatabira*) or in his favorite clothes. More recently it has become the practice for physicians and nurses to cleanse the body and for morticians to dress it. In many cases the entire process of funeral rites is entrusted to a mortuary.

The body is laid out with the head toward the north without a pillow and is covered with a sheet of white cloth. A priest from the Buddhist parish temple recites sutras at the bedside and gives a posthumous Buddhist name (*kaimyō*) to the deceased. The body is then placed in an unpainted wooden coffin. A notice of mourning, written on a piece of white paper with a black frame, is posted on the front door or gate of the house throughout the mourning period (*kichū*). An all-night wake (*tsuya*) or a briefer "half wake" (*hantsuya*) is held. Refreshments are served and mourners present gifts of "incense money" (KŌDEN). The day after the wake the funeral service is held at home, the parish temple, or a funeral hall. There are both Buddhist and Shintō forms of service.

After CREMATION pieces of the bones of the deceased are gathered, placed in a small jar (*kotsutsubo*), and brought home for later burial. Every 7th day until the 49th day, rites are held around the altar where the *kotsutsubo* is kept. The family members of the deceased express their gratitude to mourners by sending acknowledgment notes and return gifts (*kōdengaeshi*) valued at about half of the *kōden*. The *kotsutsubo* is buried at the grave site during this period.

Anniversaries (*hōyō*) are observed in a similar manner on the 1st, 2nd, 6th, 12th, 16th, and 32nd anniversaries in Western reckoning. On the days of the spring and autumn equinox (HIGAN) and during the BON FESTIVAL, the family and relatives visit the grave with offerings.

Funka Bay → Uchiura Bay

Fun'ya no Watamaro 文屋綿麻呂

(765–823). Military leader of the early Heian period (794–1185). He held various court appointments but was imprisoned in 810 for his part in the KUSUKO INCIDENT. Watamaro was pardoned through the intervention of SAKANOUE NO TAMURAMARO and again took service with the court, mostly in campaigns against the EZO, aboriginal inhabitants of northern Japan. He was eventually given the post of *chūnagon* (middle counselor) in 818 as a reward for his services.

Furano 富良野［市］

City in central Hokkaidō. An agricultural and lumber-producing center, its principal products are rice, potatoes, beets, onions, asparagus, and watermelon. Textiles, dairy, and sugar-refining industries are also located here. Pop: 26,665.

Furano Basin 富良野盆地

(Furano Bonchi). In central Hokkaidō. Bounded by the Ishikari and Yūbari mountains, this fault basin consists of the floodplain of the upper river Sorachigawa and low-lying river terraces. Rice and vegetables are cultivated. The major city is Furano. Area: approximately 130 sq km (50 sq mi).

Fūren, Lake 風蓮湖

(Fūrenko). Lagoon in the western part of the city of Nemuro, eastern Hokkaidō. Famous for the white swans that migrate from Siberia and make the lagoon their habitat from the end of October to March. Sandbars mark the division between the eastern side of the lagoon and Nemuro Bay. Area: 60.5 sq km (23.4 sq mi); circumference: 96 km (59.6 mi); depth: 13 m (42.7 ft).

Fūren Shōnyūdō 風連鍾乳洞

Limestone caves in the town of Notsu, southeastern Ōita Prefecture, northeastern Kyūshū. There are two grottoes; the older one is over 420 m (1,400 ft) long. The newer one, situated about 100 m (330 ft) above the older, is about 82 m (270 ft) long. Both contain stalactites and stalagmites.

fūrin → wind-bells

furisode 振袖

A style of women's *kimono* characterized by wide flowing sleeves that, when the arm is extended, hang down further than those on ordinary kimono. The *furisode* with the longest sleeves, which hang down about 105 centimeters (41 in), are called *ōburisode*; those with medium-length sleeves, about 95 centimeters (37 in), are called *chūburisode*; and those with the shortest sleeves, about 85 centimeters (33 in), are called *koburisode*. *Furisode* came into fashion in the mid-Edo period (1600–1868) among the young daughters of wealthy families. Today *furisode* are worn as part of the traditional bridal ensemble and by young unmarried women on special occasions.

Furisode Fire → Meireki Fire

furniture, traditional 伝統家具

(*dentō kagu*). Traditional Japanese furniture includes screens, shelves, cabinets, and tables. The forms are usually simple, with emphasis on verticals and horizontals and box shapes that blend in with the simple lines and post and lintel construction used in traditional Japanese architecture. Wood is the main material used in the making of Japanese furniture, but such materials as ceramics, paper, bamboo, and metal are also employed. Articles may be decorated with beautiful designs in lacquer; the best of them are regarded as major works of art. See MOTHER-OF-PEARL INLAY; LACQUER WARE.

The earliest examples of furniture in Japan date from the Nara period (710–794) and are preserved in the 8th-century storehouse of artistic treasures, the SHŌSŌIN, on the grounds of the temple TŌDAIJI in Nara. Virtually all the types of furniture housed in the Shōsōin are of Chinese origin, and many of the pieces were made in China during the Tang (T'ang) dynasty (618–907). With some changes and modifications, basically the same kinds of interior furnishings have been employed throughout Japanese history, and it is only during the modern period, under the influence of the West, that completely different kinds of furniture have been intro-

Furano Basin Lavender fields in summer, with the Ishikari Mountains in the background.

funerals An altar prepared for a Buddhist funeral service. At center is a photograph of the deceased, before which stands the *ihai*, a small tablet inscribed with a posthumous Buddhist name. Visible among the candleholders and other Buddhist ritual implements are large wooden tablets identifying the donors of flowers.

furoshiki A selection of colorful cotton *furoshiki* tied in various styles.

Furuhashi Hironoshin
This world-record-setting swimmer, known abroad as the "Flying Fish of Fujiyama," helped reawaken Japanese national pride after defeat in World War II.

duced. Some traditional furnishings are still widely used, often in concert with more modern pieces.

Of the furniture once common in Japanese houses, palaces, and temples, the most distinctive is the *byōbu* (screen), used to create privacy, to partition a room, or for purely decorative purposes; many screens are adorned with paintings or calligraphy (see SCREEN AND WALL PAINTING). Since the Japanese traditionally sat on a floor covered with TATAMI mats or on cushions called *zabuton*, serving tables and desks (*chabudai* and *tsukue*) are lower than those in the West. Cabinets, called *kodansu* or *kodana*, have either drawers or open shelves. Cupboards, called *zushi*, either look like Western cupboards or bookcases or take the form of tiered shelves (*tanazushi*). Boxes (*hako*) for such items as writing materials, food, cosmetics, and swords were long in use. Chests or *tansu* range from simple boxes to elaborately decorated chests of drawers. Other traditional pieces of furniture are *hibachi* (charcoal braziers), used for warming the interior of a house, and *ikō*, which serve as clothing stands or towel racks.

furoshiki 風呂敷
A square cloth used for wrapping, storing, and carrying objects. The word *furoshiki* (from *furo*, "bath," and *shiki*, "spread") dates from the early Edo period (1600–1868), when such wrappers came into wide use in public bathhouses for spreading on the floor while undressing and for wrapping bathing articles. *Furoshiki* range in size from 70 to 220 centimeters (27.6 to 86.6 in) square and are made of silk, cotton, synthetic fabrics, or vinyl, in solid colors or patterns. *Furoshiki* are gradually being replaced by modern handbags and shopping bags.

Furugaki Tetsurō 古垣鉄郎
(1900–1987). Journalist and diplomat. Born in Kagoshima Prefecture. He studied at Lyons University in France and worked for the League of Nations in Geneva. Joining the newspaper ASAHI SHIMBUN, he was active as an international journalist and then became chairman of the board of Nippon Hōsō Kyōkai (NHK; Japan Broadcasting Corporation) in

1949. After resigning as NHK chairman in 1956, he was appointed ambassador to France, a post he held for five years.

Furuhashi Hironoshin 古橋広之進
(1928–). Swimmer called the "Flying Fish of Fujiyama." Born in Shizuoka Prefecture. While at Nihon University, he set numerous swimming records. In the late 1940s he broke more than 30 Japanese and world records. In the US Outdoor Men's Swimming Championship in 1949, he set a new world record of 18:19.0 in the 1,500-meter freestyle and won the 400-meter and 800-meter. In 1990 Furuhashi was vice president of the Fédération Internationale de Natation Amateur (FINA), an international swimming association, and professor of physical education at Nihon University. He was named president of the Japan Olympic Committee in May of that year.

Furuhata Tanemoto 古畑種基
(1891–1975). Serologist and specialist in forensic medicine. Born in Mie Prefecture. Graduate of Tōkyō University. Furuhata successively taught at Kanazawa Ika Daigaku (now Kanazawa University), Tōkyō University, and Tōkyō Medical and Dental University. He also performed many postmortem examinations in criminal cases such as the TEIGIN INCIDENT and the SHIMOYAMA INCIDENT. He discovered the Q-type blood group (1934) and investigated the heredity of blood groups. In his last years Furuhata was director of the National Research Institute of Police Science of the National Police Agency. He received the Order of Culture in 1956.

Furuichi Kimitake 古市公威
(1854–1934). Civil engineer. Born in Edo (now Tōkyō), he studied at Tōkyō Kaisei Gakkō (now Tōkyō University) until 1875, when he was selected by the government to study in France. Returning to Japan in 1880, he entered the Ministry of Home Affairs, where he instituted programs for the construction of hydroelectric power plants, tapwater supply networks, river control facilities, and harbors. From 1886 to 1898 he served as the first dean of Tōkyō University's College of Engineering. From 1898 to 1910 he directed the construction of, and managed, high-priority railroads in Korea used by the Japanese troops stationed there. In 1914 he became the first president of Japan's newly formed Civil Engineering Society. During his career, Furuichi served in numerous high posts, including director-general of the Ministry of Communications and director of the INSTITUTE OF PHYSICAL AND CHEMICAL RESEARCH. He was Japan's first doctor of engineering.

Furui Yoshikichi 古井由吉
(1937–). Novelist. Born in Tōkyō. A graduate of Tōkyō University in German literature, he taught German at Kanazawa University and Rikkyō University. In 1970 he resigned his teaching post to become a full-time writer. His short novel *Yōko* (1970) was awarded the Akutagawa Prize in 1970. Through depictions of everyday life he looks at the oddities and inner realms of human existence. Other works include the short story "Tsumagomi" (1970; tr "Wedlock," 1977) and the novels *Kushi no hi* (1974, Fiery Comb) and *Asagao* (1983, Rose of Sharon).

Furukawa 古川[市]
City in northern Miyagi Prefecture, northern Honshū, on the river Eaigawa. Furukawa de-

veloped as a market town and a post-station town during the Edo period (1600–1868). It is now the administrative and commercial center of northern Miyagi. Rice cultivation is carried out on a large scale. Electronics and fodder plants have been constructed recently. Pop: 64,230.

Furukawa 古河
Former *zaibatsu*, or industrial combine. In 1877 FURUKAWA ICHIBEI (1832–1903) purchased the Ashio Copper Mine in Tochigi Prefecture. By 1885 his many mines produced 50 percent of Japan's copper. After Furukawa's death his operations were reorganized into the Furukawa Kōgyō Kaisha in 1905; this later became FURUKAWA CO, LTD. By the end of World War II, the Furukawa *zaibatsu* controlled 84 companies, including Furukawa Electric Co, Ltd, Fuji Electric Co, Ltd, Nippon Light Metal Co, Ltd, and Yokohama Rubber Co, Ltd. Under the Occupation's ZAIBATSU DISSOLUTION order, the Furukawa *zaibatsu* companies became independent, but by the late 1970s they were reorganizing as the Furukawa group.

Furukawa Co, Ltd 古河機械金属[株]
(Furukawa Kikai Kinzoku). Company primarily engaged in the refining of copper and the manufacture of industrial machinery such as construction equipment, rock drills, and belt conveyors. It also produces chemical products and electronic materials. The company was incorporated in 1918 as the mining division of the former Furukawa ZAIBATSU and is a leading member of the Furukawa group, which is active both in Japan and overseas. The company provides technological assistance to numerous foreign countries. Sales for the fiscal year ending March 1991 totaled ¥164.0 billion (US $1.2 billion), with copper accounting for approximately 34 percent; industrial machinery, 51 percent; and other products, 15 percent. The company was capitalized at ¥23.4 billion (US $170.6 million) in the same year. Headquarters are in Tōkyō. See also FURUKAWA ICHIBEI; FURUKAWA ELECTRIC CO, LTD; NIPPON LIGHT METAL CO, LTD; FUJI ELECTRIC CO, LTD; FUJITSŪ, LTD.

Furukawa Electric Co, Ltd
古河電気工業[株]
(Furukawa Denki Kōgyō). Manufacturer of electric wire and cable, rolled copper products, and aluminum products. The company traces its origins to the formation of the Furukawa ZAIBATSU in 1884, when FURUKAWA ICHIBEI succeeded in smelting copper. In 1908 Furukawa Kōgyō, the central member of the Furukawa *zaibatsu*, acquired control of the Yokohama Wire Manufacturing Co, and in 1920 it merged that company with its own Nikkō Copper Works and Honjō plant to create Furukawa Electric. Furukawa Electric has joint-venture companies producing wire and cable in the United States, China, Singapore, Malaysia, Brazil, Indonesia, Thailand, and Saudi Arabia. Sales for the fiscal year ending March 1991 totaled ¥628.9 billion (US $4.6 billion), of which wire and cable accounted for 54 percent; light metals, 21 percent; rolled copper products, 12 percent; and other products, 13 percent. The export ratio was 7 percent, and the company was capitalized at ¥56.6 billion (US $412.5 million) in the same year. Headquarters are in Tōkyō.

Furukawa Ichibei 古河市兵衛
(1832–1903). Mining industry entrepreneur and business leader during the Meiji period (1868–1912). Born in Kyōto. He became a

silk-purchasing agent with ONO-GUMI, a Kyōto-based commercial silk firm. In 1871 Furukawa imported equipment and built Japan's first mechanical silk filature. With the 1874 financial collapse of Ono-Gumi, Furukawa became manager of a mining enterprise operated by the Sōma family in the Tōhoku region. With capital from financier SHIBUSAWA EIICHI, the company grew to include several copper and silver mines. When the Sōma family withdrew its support, Furukawa assumed ownership and expanded the enterprise with continued financial support from Shibusawa, purchasing the Ashio Copper Mine. At its peak, the Furukawa enterprise produced over a third of Japan's copper and included at least 20 major mines, forming the basis of the Furukawa ZAIBATSU. His economic achievements were marred, however, by the discharge of mining waste at the Ashio Copper Mine, which poisoned several hundred people. See ASHIO COPPER MINE INCIDENT.

Furukawa Roppa 古川緑波

(1903–61). Comedian, critic, radio performer, and comedy writer. Born in Tōkyō. His given name was Ikurō. Roppa became a professional film critic at the age of 18 and later was the editor of a popular movie magazine. He joined a musical review in 1932 as a comedian. In the following year, with Watanabe Atsushi (1898–1977) and TOKUGAWA MUSEI, Roppa organized the Warai no Ōkoku (Kingdom of Laughter) troupe, which specialized in contemporary farce and parody. In 1935 he established his own Roppa Troupe. During the decade that followed, Roppa gave frequent stage and film performances.

Roppa had a major success with ENOMOTO KEN'ICHI in KIKUTA KAZUO's 1947 adaptation of the perennial *Hizakurige* (Shank's Mare), but Roppa's subsequent career declined. He was left with supporting roles in film comedies but also found extensive employment in radio with his impersonations of the famous. Throughout his acting career, Roppa continued to work as an entertainment critic and journalist.

Furuno Inosuke 古野伊之助

(1891–1966). Second president of DŌMEI TSŪSHINSHA, Japan's only news agency during World War II. He helped IWANAGA YŪKICHI found the Dōmei Tsūshinsha and became president after Iwanaga's death in 1939. After World War II, he was imprisoned as a class-A war criminal but was released in 1946. He exerted great influence on Japanese journalism as a director of the JIJI PRESS and as the chairman of the administrative committee of Nippon Telegraph and Telephone Public Corporation (Nihon Denshin Denwa Kōsha; now NIPPON TELEGRAPH AND TELEPHONE CORPORATION).

Furusawa Shigeru 古沢滋

(1847–1911). Politician of the Meiji period (1868–1912); also known as Furusawa Uruo. Born in Tosa (now Kōchi Prefecture). After the MEIJI RESTORATION of 1868 he studied in England. Following his return he and ITAGAKI TAISUKE petitioned for the establishment of a popularly elected assembly, spearheading the FREEDOM AND PEOPLE'S RIGHTS MOVEMENT. He participated in the formation of the RISSHISHA (Self-Help Society) and the AIKOKUSHA (Society of Patriots) and served as spokesman for the political party JIYŪTŌ and editor of its newspaper *Jiyū shimbun* and as editor and publisher of the *Ōsaka nippō shimbun.*

He later served in several government ministries and held three prefectural governorships. He was appointed to the House of Peers in 1904.

Furuta Oribe 古田織部

(1544–1615). Warrior and celebrated tea master. Born in Mino Province (now Gifu Prefecture); real name Furuta Shigenari. Originally a retainer of ODA NOBUNAGA and TOYOTOMI HIDEYOSHI, he received from the latter the courtly title of Oribe no Kami and a fief near Kyōto. Oribe fought for TOKUGAWA IEYASU at Sekigahara (see SEKIGAHARA, BATTLE OF) in 1600. But in the 1615 campaign against the Toyotomi family (see ŌSAKA CASTLE, SIEGES OF) he betrayed the Tokugawa cause by conspiring with the Toyotomi forces. He was ordered by Ieyasu to commit suicide.

Oribe became Japan's foremost tea master after the death of his teacher, SEN NO RIKYŪ, and the type of TEA CEREMONY he established is known as Oriberyū. Oribe taught the tea ceremony to the shōgun TOKUGAWA HIDETADA. He preferred a type of ceramics for the tea ceremony that has come to be known as Oribe ware (see MINO WARE). Among his disciples were the tea master KOBORI ENSHŪ and the artist HON'AMI KŌETSU.

Furuyama Komao 古山高麗雄

(1920–). Novelist. Born in Korea; entered the Third Higher School in Kyōto (now Kyōto University) but withdrew in protest against the school's promilitaristic aura. Drafted during World War II, Furuyama served in Southeast Asia and after the war was imprisoned by the French for eight months as a war criminal. He returned to Japan in 1947, worked as an editor, and in 1969 wrote his first short story, "Bochi de." His second short story, "Pureō 8 no yoake" (1970), a wry, humorous account of former Japanese soldiers in a Saigon prison, received the 1970 Akutagawa Prize. Other works include the novels *Chiisana shigaizu* (1972) and *Dansakusen* (1982).

Furuyama Moromasa 古山師政

(fl early 18th century). UKIYO-E artist active in Edo (now Tōkyō) in the first half of the 18th century. He specialized in portraits of famous beauties (*bijinga*) and genre subjects. When he was a pupil of Hishikawa MORONOBU, he used the name Hishikawa Masanori. Later, after Moronobu's death, he studied with his father, the *ukiyo-e* artist Furuyama Moroshige (fl late 17th century). Because Moromasa adopted Western-style perspective in his work and created a new style that signaled the end of the Hishikawa tradition, he is famous as the last of the Hishikawa line. Few of his works are extant.

furyū 風流

Term designating a wide range of traditional types of performances. Despite apparent differences, these share a single element: the use of colorful decorations and music, dance, or song to invoke a baleful or pestilential spirit and later dispose of it where it can do no harm. Initially used in the latter part of the Heian period (794–1185) to refer to the colorful decorations on floats (DASHI) and to the costumes of the people who pulled them during festivals, it subsequently came to refer also to gaudily dressed performers who danced and sang to the accompaniment of flute, drum, and cymbals during festivals.

The GION FESTIVAL, which originated in the Heian period, was conducted in Kyōto in

summer when, following spring flooding, epidemic disease often broke out. It was thought that the baleful gods who visited destruction upon the populace were drawn to the float and costume decorations, which served as a temporary abode (*yorishiro*); the gods could thus be carried out of the city. Yasuraibana, a festival serving the same function that was first performed in the 12th century, centered on a procession of gaily costumed men and women who performed a dance called *furyū odori* to the music of pipes and drums.

Furyū as a type of performing art persists today in a wide variety of regional dance performances and in generalized forms such as SHISHIMAI (lion dance), BON ODORI (Bon dance), and NEMBUTSU ODORI, a development of the Pure Land Buddhist tradition. It has also been suggested that KABUKI dances were initially onstage performances of *furyū odori.* The decorative aspect of *furyū* is reflected in the appellation *furyū* Nō, which is applied to gorgeously staged Nō plays such as MOMIJIGARI and HAGOROMO.

furyū 風流

Sometimes pronounced *furyu;* refers to the refined taste of a cultivated, sophisticated person and to works of art and other things associated with such persons. The word was derived from the Chinese term *fengliu,* which literally meant "good deportment and manner." After reaching Japan around the 8th century, it was employed in a more aesthetic sense, referring to the refined manners of an urbane person and later to all things regarded as elegant, tasteful, or artistic. The term *fūga* is sometimes employed in the same sense as *fūryū,* but, in general, *fūryū* is a more inclusive term, referring not just to poetry but to all the arts.

In the 12th century *fūryū* began to follow two separate lines of semantic evolution. In one, *fūryū* was applied to the more earthy, showy beauty manifest in popular arts (see FOLK PERFORMING ARTS). In the other, men attempted to discover *fūryū* in the beauty of landscape GARDENS, FLOWER ARRANGEMENT, architecture, and Chinese nature poetry. This latter trend gave birth to the TEA CEREMONY in the Muromachi period (1333–1568).

In the Edo period (1600–1868) popular *fūryū* manifested itself in the type of fiction known as UKIYO-ZŌSHI. The second type was seen in *haikai* (see HAIKU) verse, Chinese poetry, and the *nanga* style of painting (see BUNJINGA).

In the modern era KŌDA ROHAN endeavored to achieve a union of love, art, and religion in the name of *fūryū* in the short story "Fūryū-butsu" (1889). In *Kusamakura* (1906; tr *The Three-Cornered World,* 1965) the novelist NATSUME SŌSEKI attempted to revitalize the concept by injecting it with compassion and humanism.

furyū monji 不立文字

(literally, "not standing on words or letters"). A ZEN Buddhist expression warning against relying on words. In Zen belief, enlightenment (*satori*) is attained not through the study of Buddhist texts or other verbal explanations but through direct experience, either in meditation or interaction with spiritual masters. The phrase is often used in conjunction with another expression, *kyōge betsuden,* which states that enlightenment is not reached by way of written doctrinal exegesis.

Furukawa Roppa This popular comic actor and impersonator also worked as an entertainment journalist throughout his stage, film, and radio career.

Fushimi Inari Shrine
The more than 10,000 gates (*torii*) that line the two paths to this Shintō shrine's oratory were built through donations from shrine patrons.

Futabatei Shimei This leading Meiji-period author and translator of Russian literature brought greater realism and a more colloquial style to Japanese fiction.

fuse 布施

(gift or alms; Skt: *dāna*). A Buddhist term that in contemporary Japan normally refers to donations made to a priest or temple in exchange for funeral and memorial services. *Fuse* is associated with the virtue of generosity, which is classified as one of the "six perfections" (*roku haramitsu;* Skt: *ṣaḍ-pāramitā*) of Mahāyāna Buddhism, the dominant form of Buddhism in Japan. According to Buddhist doctrine, *fuse* should not be performed with any expectation of reward.

Fusen Kakutoku Dōmei 婦選獲得同盟

(Women's Suffrage League; called Fujin Sanseiken Kakutoku Kisei Dōmeikai at its founding in 1924; renamed in 1925). Main organization of Japanese women campaigning for the right to vote. The league was especially active in 1924–25, just before the Diet decided to extend suffrage to all adult males (see UNIVERSAL MANHOOD SUFFRAGE MOVEMENT). Starting with a core group of 200 members led by ICHIKAWA FUSAE, KUBUSHIRO OCHIMI, KAWASAKI NATSU, and Kaneko Shigeri (later YAMATAKA SHIGERI), in 1931 it had 1,500 members in 11 branches. Its official magazine was called *Fusen* (Women's Suffrage). The league was dissolved in 1940. See also WOMEN'S SUFFRAGE.

Fuseya Soteki 伏屋素狄

(1747–1811). Scholar of WESTERN LEARNING and the first Japanese to conduct physiological experiments. Popular name Manchō Gonnoshin; pen name Kimpan. Born in Kawachi (now part of Ōsaka Prefecture). Fuseya studied Western Learning with Hashimoto Sōkichi (1763–1836). After reading a Dutch medical book, Fuseya conducted studies on the kidney. In the postscript of his two-volume work, *Oranda iwa* (1803, Story of Dutch Medicine), he described his experiments on the formation of urine in the kidney and his theory of filtration in the kidney.

Fūshi kaden 風姿花伝

(Transmission of the Flower of Acting Style). Also known as *Kadensho*. Treatise on the principles of NŌ drama written ca 1400–1418 by ZEAMI. Composed of a preface and a text categorized into seven parts, it deals with the correct mental attitude of Nō actors; methods of rehearsal and spiritual practice, divided according to the actor's age; nine basic types of roles and the concept of *mono-mane* (imitating); theories, expressed in dialogue form, of aesthetics, acting technique, and performance; the origins of Nō in SARUGAKU; stylistic differences between *sarugaku* and DENGAKU; rules for composition of Nō; and the meaning of *hana* (flower). *Hana*, an aesthetic concept that assumes a central role in this work and in Zeami's subsequent critical writings, represents the beauty created by an actor in performance. Purportedly based on the teachings of his father, KAN'AMI, *Fūshi kaden* is Zeami's first and most important theoretical work.

Fushimi 伏見

Area in the Momoyama Hills overlooking the river Ujigawa in Fushimi Ward, Kyōto. The area became important politically and economically after TOYOTOMI HIDEYOSHI built Fushimi Castle here in the late 16th century; the Battle of TOBA-FUSHIMI was fought here in 1868. Traces of Fushimi's past as a castle town remain to this day, and the area is nationally known for its *sake*-brewing industry, which relies on techniques passed down for generations. The town is also the site of the FUSHIMI INARI SHRINE, dedicated to the deities of agriculture and commerce.

Fushimi Castle 伏見城

(Fushimijō). Castle built as a retirement home by TOYOTOMI HIDEYOSHI in the years 1592–96; situated near the southern end of the Higashiyama ridge above the Uji River in the Momoyama district of Kyōto. Its main ramparts encompassed an area approximately 1 kilometer (0.6 mi) square. Hideyoshi lived in this beautiful castle until his death in 1598. After the Battle of Sekigahara (1600) TOKUGAWA IEYASU made it his residence in the central provinces until ŌSAKA CASTLE came into his hands in 1615. After TOKUGAWA IEMITSU was named shōgun in Fushimi Castle in 1623, the castle was torn down, its treasures, timbers, and other materials being distributed to a number of temples and other castles.

Fushimi, Emperor 伏見天皇

(1265–1317; Fushimi Tennō). The 92nd sovereign (*tennō*) in the traditional count (which includes several legendary emperors); reigned 1287–98. Son of Emperor GO-FUKAKUSA, in 1275 he became crown prince to Emperor GO-UDA, inaugurating a practice of two imperial lines alternating on the throne. Fushimi took personal power only after his father's withdrawal into the priesthood in 1290; he ruled as retired emperor (see INSEI) during the reigns of Go-Fushimi (1288–1336; r 1298–1301) and Hanazono (1297–1348; r 1308–18). Fushimi was an accomplished calligrapher and poet. Parts of his diary, *Fushimi In gyoki*, survive, providing information on court ceremonials (YŪSOKU KOJITSU) and contemporary society.

Fushimi Inari Shrine 伏見稲荷大社

(Fushimi Inari Taisha). Shintō shrine at the foot of Inariyama (Mt. Inari) in Fushimi Ward, Kyōto; dedicated to Uka no Mitama no Kami and four other deities, all of whom are said to be manifestations of INARI, originally the deity of cereals. First built in 711 atop Inariyama, the shrine was moved to its present location following a petition by KŪKAI (774–835), the founder of the Shingon sect of Buddhism, so that its deities might protect TŌJI, a nearby Shingon temple. In time the shrine's deities came to be regarded as deities not only of agriculture but also of commerce and eventually as household deities. The Fushimi Inari is one of the country's most popular shrines and is regarded as the central shrine for the more than 30,000 Inari shrines throughout Japan. The main sanctuary dates from 1499. The shrine's annual festival, the Inari Matsuri, begins on the Sunday nearest to 20 April and ends on 3 May. It is still a popular custom to visit the Fushimi Inari Shrine on the first day of the horse (HATSUUMA), which tradition holds to be the day that Inari was originally enshrined there.

Fussa 福生[市]

City in the west-central part of Tōkyō Prefecture. It borders the city of Tachikawa in the east. Originally a farming village with a thriving sericulture industry, during World War II it developed as a military air base. After the war the base was taken over by OCCUPATION authorities and became known as Yokota Air Base. Today it is a commuter suburb of Tōkyō. Pop: 58,062.

Futaba Corporation 双葉電子工業[株]

(Futaba Denshi Kōgyō). Manufacturer of electronic and mechanical components for industrial use. Incorporated in 1948. The company's best-selling products include vacuum fluorescent displays (VFD), which are used in videocassette recorder control panels and automobile instrument panels, and radio control systems. In cooperation with companies in the United States, Germany, Hong Kong, Taiwan, and Korea, Futaba is developing a worldwide marketing system. Sales for the fiscal year ending March 1991 totaled ¥104.2 billion (US $759.5 million), and capitalization stood at ¥21.3 billion (US $155.2 million). Headquarters are in the city of Mobara, Chiba Prefecture.

Futabatei Shimei 二葉亭四迷

(1864–1909). One of the leading Japanese authors and translators of the late 19th century, who created Japan's first modern novel (UKIGUMO) while still in his early twenties. Real name Hasegawa Tatsunosuke; born in Edo (now Tōkyō). Brilliant, idealistic, and imbued with a passion for his country, Futabatei epitomizes the talented youth who led Japan to a new eminence in the Meiji period (1868–1912). He began *Ukigumo* shortly after leaving the Tōkyō Gaikokugo Gakkō (now Tōkyō University of Foreign Studies), where he had immersed himself in Russian studies from 1881 through 1885. His translations of Russian literature introduced a whole generation to the greatness of 19th-century Russian fiction. To write his novel and to prepare his translations, Futabatei consciously constructed an appropriate language for the literature of contemporary Japan, shearing away the elegances of the classical written language and replacing them with a style known as GEMBUN ITCHI (unification of the spoken and written language).

In January 1886 Futabatei sought the friendship of TSUBOUCHI SHŌYŌ, a successful critic, novelist, and translator of English literature. With Tsubouchi's guidance, Futabatei wrote *Ukigumo* (1887–89, Drifting Clouds; tr in *Japan's First Modern Novel: Ukigumo of Futabatei Shimei*, 1967), a concise, moving work. *Ukigumo* employs with remarkable cogency the theories of art and language Tsubouchi defined in his critical essay *Shōsetsu shinzui* (1885–86, Essence of the Novel). Tsubouchi had called for psychological realism, and in his own novel Futabatei succeeded in creating multifaceted characters of considerable dimension. More important, he created a fully realized alienated hero, the prototype of the immobilized antihero who was to populate so much of 20th-century Japanese fiction.

Futabatei was wretched over his novel, despite a generally favorable critical reaction, and, as the final chapters were appearing in serial form in July 1889, he accepted a post in the office of government publications. Poverty beset his parents, but as a government servant Futabatei was financially secure and felt himself better able to continue his studies. Futabatei believed that to write for money was to violate one's art; he hoped that a regular income from another source would free him to write and publish only what he chose.

From 1896 until his death in 1909, Futabatei published translations of works by Turgenev, Gogol, Tolstoy, Dostoevsky, Chekov, Goncharov, and Gorky. His translations of Turgenev, in particular, greatly inspired the young Japanese naturalists. In the years 1904 to 1909, articles on Japanese and Russian literature and social problems in Japan and abroad, as well as autobiographical essays, appeared.

From October to December 1906, Futabatei published *Sono omokage* (tr *An Adopted Husband*, 1919), a work that brought him renewed critical attention. The central character is an impotent man, intimidated by his wife and mother-in-law and beset by what was rapidly becoming the classic inertia of intellectual heroes. Futabatei's final work of fiction was *Heibon* (tr *Mediocrity*, 1927), a semiautobiographical study published serially from October to December 1907.

Futabatei's personal life was not a happy one. He was married twice, first to a prostitute with whom he led a miserable existence and by whom he had two children. They were divorced in 1896. In 1902 he married a young woman with whom he had been living and who bore him two sons. Futabatei traveled to the Asian mainland for the first time in 1902, where he worked first in Harbin and then in Beijing (Peking). He returned to Tōkyō in 1903. In 1908 he was appointed the Russian correspondent of the newspaper *Asahi shimbun*, but he became ill almost immediately upon arriving in St. Petersburg and died on 10 May 1909 as his ship was crossing the Bay of Bengal on its journey back to Japan.

Futabayama 双葉山

(1912–68). SUMŌ wrestler; 35th grand *sumō* champion (*yokozuna*). Real name Akiyoshi Sadaji. Born in Ōita Prefecture. He entered the Tatsunami stable in 1927 and achieved top-division (*makuuchi*) status by 1932 and champion (*ōzeki*) status in 1937. He was designated a *yokozuna* in May 1937. Futabayama ranks with TAIHŌ as one of *sumō*'s immortals. After achieving *makuuchi* status he placed first in 12 tournaments and was undefeated in 8 of them. He won 80.2 percent of his matches and between 1936 and 1939 won 69 matches in a row, a record that still stands. Retiring in 1945, he was honored with a new name, Tokitsukaze, and in 1957 became chairman of the Japan Sumō Association.

Futaki Kenzō 二木謙三

(1873–1966). Epidemiologist. Born in Akita Prefecture. Graduated from Tōkyō University and studied further in Germany. In 1919 he became director of the Komagome Hospital in Tōkyō (an isolation hospital for contagious diseases) and in 1921 was appointed professor at Tōkyō University, where he also served as director of the Institute for Infectious Diseases. In 1903 he discovered that two bacilli (Komagome A and B, *Shigella flexneri*) other than *Shigella dysenteriae* (discovered by SHIGA KIYOSHI) could cause dysentery. In 1915 he identified *Spirochaeta morsus muris* (later corrected to *Strepto bacillus moniliformis*), which causes rat-bite fever. He received the Order of Culture in 1955.

Futamigaura 二見浦

Coastal area in the northeastern part of the town of Futami, Mie Prefecture, central Honshū; faces Ise Bay. It is famous for two rocks, called Meotoiwa ("Wedded Rocks"), which are joined by Shintō ropes. Futamigaura is part of ISE-SHIMA NATIONAL PARK. Length: approximately 5 km (3 mi).

Futarasan Shrine 二荒山神社

(Futarasan Jinja or Futarayama Jinja). Shintō shrine complex in and around the city of Nikkō, Tochigi Prefecture; dedicated to Ōnamuchi no Mikoto (ŌKUNINUSHI NO MIKOTO) and two lesser deities. The main shrine is located within the city; the "inner shrine" sits atop Mt. Futara (Futarasan, also called Nantaisan); the "middle shrine" is situated on the shores of Lake Chūzenji. Having its origins in the worship of Mt. Futara (see MOUNTAINS, WORSHIP OF), the shrine is believed to have been founded by the monk Shōdo (737–817) in the 8th century and has long been a sacred place of SHUGENDŌ. Its annual festival is held on 17 April.

Futarayama Shrine 二荒山神社

(Futarayama Jinja). Shintō shrine in the city of Utsunomiya, Tochigi Prefecture; dedicated to the spirit of Toyokiirihiko no Mikoto, a prince of the legendary emperor SUJIN. Popularly known as Utsunomiya Daimyōjin, the shrine has been revered by warriors and common people alike. Its annual festival is held on 21 October.

futon 布団

The main component of traditional Japanese BEDDING. A *futon* consists of a *shikibuton* (quiltlike mattress) and a *kakebuton* (thick quilted bedcover), laid out on the floor at night for sleeping and put away in closets each morning. *Futon* originated in the mid-16th century, replacing rush or straw mats, or loose straw, as bedding.

Standard measurements of *shikibuton* are 90 by 195 centimeters (35.4 by 76.8 in) or 100 by 210 centimeters (39.4 by 82.7 in). Cotton wadding is most widely used because of its resilience, retention of heat, and absorption of moisture. *Kakebuton* are 150 by 210 centimeters (59.1 by 82.7 in) or 170 by 210 centimeters (66.9 by 82.7 in). At night *futon* are wrapped in *shikifu*, a practice similar to Western sheeting, and during the day they are aired in the sun. Beautiful and luxurious *futon*, in a matched set of two *kakebuton* and two *shikibuton*, are often given as part of a bride's dowry.

Futsū Senkyo Kisei Dōmeikai 普通選挙期成同盟会

(League to Petition for Universal Suffrage). 1. Group within the TŌYŌ JIYŪTŌ (Oriental Liberal Party), formed in November 1892 by ŌI KENTARŌ, TARUI TŌKICHI, and others, calling for universal manhood suffrage. It was dissolved in 1893 at the same time as the party itself.

2. Organization formed in 1897 by Nakamura Tahachirō (1868–1935) and KINOSHITA NAOE to agitate for universal manhood suffrage. It changed its name to Futsū Senkyo Dōmeikai in 1900. Members included socialists, newspapermen, and liberal politicians such as KATAYAMA SEN, KŌTOKU SHŪSUI, KŌNO HIRONAKA, and KUROIWA RUIKŌ. Following the HIGH TREASON INCIDENT OF 1910, in which Kōtoku and others were arrested and executed, the Dōmeikai was disbanded (1911). It was revived in 1914, 1918, and 1919 but remained powerless. Around 1920 the organization dissolved. See also UNIVERSAL MANHOOD SUFFRAGE MOVEMENT.

Futsū Senkyo Undō →Universal Manhood Suffrage Movement

Futtsu 富津[市]

City in southwestern Chiba Prefecture, central Honshū. Principal products are rice and vegetables. Its northern part has been reclaimed for industry. The coastal area, with swimming beaches, is part of the Minami Bōsō Quasi-National Park. The city is noted for its 56 m (168 ft) high statue of the bodhisattva KANNON. Other tourist attractions are the Kanōzan hill and Takagoyama, the habitat of several hundred wild monkeys. Pop: 54,876.

Fuwa no Seki →sekisho

Fuwa Tetsuzō 不破哲三

(1930–). Politician. Real name Ueda Kenjirō (Fuwa Tetsuzō is a pen name). Born in Tōkyō, he graduated from Tōkyō University in 1953. He was elected to the House of Representatives in 1969 as a JAPAN COMMUNIST PARTY candidate from Tōkyō. In 1970, at the age of 40, he became the youngest member of the party's central leadership and at the same time assumed the office of secretary-general. In 1982 he was elected to succeed MIYAMOTO KENJI (b 1908) as the party chairman. He is known as the party's leading theorist and is the author of many books and articles. His brother, Ueda Kōichirō (b 1927), is also a member of the party leadership.

Fūyō wakashū 風葉和歌集

Twenty-volume collection of WAKA verse gathered from a wide range of works of prose fiction (*monogatari*; see MONOGATARI BUNGAKU) and completed in 1271. Initiated at the behest of Ōmiya In, consort of the emperor GO-SAGA, it is thought to have been compiled by FUJIWARA NO TAMEIE. Only 18 volumes, comprising 1,418 verses, survive. It has a KANA (Japanese-syllabary) preface modeled

Futabayama Considered the greatest *yokozuna* in the history of *sumō*, Futabayama set a record of 69 consecutive match victories.

on that of the KOKINSHŪ. *Waka* from some 200 *monogatari* of the mid-Heian (794–1185) to Kamakura (1185–1333) periods are classified, in the manner of IMPERIAL ANTHOLOGIES, in groupings based on themes such as season, love, parting, and travel. Many of the poems are from UTSUBO MONOGATARI, the TALE OF GENJI, and SAGOROMO MONOGATARI. *Fūyō wakashū* is the only extant collection of *monogatari* verse and is the chief resource for information concerning lost or partial *monogatari* and for insight into contemporary evaluations of individual *monogatari*.

fuyu and funyū   不輸不入

(*fuyu to funyū*). *Fuyu* was the right of tax exemption granted by the court to the holder of an estate (SHŌEN); *funyū* was the right of the holder to prohibit government fiscal officials from entering the estate. Beginning in the 10th century, as new lands were opened up, *shōen* proprietors came into conflict with provincial governors (KOKUSHI), who decided (upon inspection by their agents) which lands would be exempted from taxation. The proprietors appealed to the central government and succeeded in gaining the right to exclude local officials; this right was later extended to police officials (KEBIISHI) as well. These two rights of exemption and exclusion contributed to the growing independence of the *shōen* from government control.

Fuzambō   冨山房

Publishing firm, founded by Sakamoto Kajima (1866–1938). Its publications include *Dai Nihon chimei jiten* (1900–1907), a seven-volume geographical dictionary; *Fuzambō dai eiwa jiten* (1931), an English-Japanese dictionary edited by Ichikawa Sanki (1886–1970) and others; and the two monumental Japanese-language dictionaries DAI NIHON KOKUGO JITEN, in five volumes edited by UEDA KAZUTOSHI and Matsui Kanji (1863–1945), and DAIGENKAI, in five volumes edited by ŌTSUKI FUMIHIKO. The company is also noted for its textbooks and study guides.

fūzokuga   風俗画

(genre painting). Paintings describing the activities and appearances of people in contemporary society. A mode of painting that was produced from the late 16th century to the end of the 17th century, *fūzokuga* reflected a heightened awareness of both the daily involvements and the special pleasures of the secular world. It grew out of native Japanese traditions: YAMATO-E pictures of famous places (*meisho-e*), seasonal paintings (*shiki-e*), and depictions of monthly events (*tsukinami-e*); it was succeeded by UKIYO-E ("pictures of the floating world"), idealizations of beautiful women and portrayals of actors.

Emergence of Fūzokuga—The rudiments of *fūzokuga* were latent in early *yamato-e*. Literary records of wall paintings of the 10th and 11th centuries indicate that vignettes of people on pleasure outings enlivened scenic panoramas, while 12th–14th-century narrative handscrolls include numerous portrayals of the daily activities of noble and commoner alike.

The transition from *yamato-e* to *fūzokuga* occurred in the 16th century and can be seen in the depictions of monthly events (*tsukinami fūzokuga*). But the primary matrix for the transformation was the *rakuchū rakugai zu* (scenes in and around the capital), a theme found in the screen paintings of KANŌ EITOKU, whose attention to human activity heralded the arrival of true genre painting. From its emergence in the 1560s until its displacement in the 1680s, *fūzokuga* falls into three major divisions centering on the eras of Keichō (1596–1615), Kan'ei (1624–44), and Kambun (1661–73).

Keichō Fūzokuga—Early genre painting was nurtured in the capital of Kyōto, commissioned by powerful warriors and courtiers and painted by important KANŌ SCHOOL artists on large-scale folding screens and sliding-door panels intended to evoke environments of relaxed enjoyment of worldly pleasure. Demand for *fūzokuga* increased remarkably after 1600. Lively festivals such as the GION FESTIVAL and the KAMO NO KURABEUMA were popular subjects, as were the vigorous warrior sports of archery, dog chasing, horsemanship, and falconry.

Kan'ei and Kambun Fūzokuga—*Fūzokuga* changed direction about 1620, shifting from the Keichō genre of public festivities painted on large surfaces to the Kan'ei genre of private pastimes depicted on smaller screens suitable for merchants' townhouses. Shops of *machi eshi* (town painters) emerged to supply the market. Especially popular during the Kan'ei era were montages of amusements.

As more attention was given to stylish charm, paintings isolating a single, standing female beauty became popular, and smaller scrolls replaced screens as the favored format. The final phase of Japanese *fūzokuga* is represented by the delicate and romantic Kambun *bijin*, or "beauty of the Kambun era," paintings. As the center of popular culture shifted from Kyōto to Edo (now Tōkyō) during the last quarter of the 17th century, stereotyped expression of *fūzokuga* gave way to the new creations of early *ukiyo-e*.

fūzoku shōsetsu   風俗小説

Fiction depicting contemporary social manners, mores, and conditions. In Japan, where fine distinctions are drawn between literary genres and subgenres, critics have traditionally regarded the *fūzoku shōsetsu* as a form of popular fiction and assigned it a low literary status. The reasons for this are the very commonness of its subject matter and the fact that many *fūzoku shōsetsu* do tend to be superficial descriptions of whatever happens to have caught the public fancy, with little concern for possible philosophical or psychological implications.

The genre has its antecedents in the Edo period (1600–1868), and since then authors have satirized the adoption of Western culture after the Meiji Restoration of 1868 (see KANAGAKI ROBUN), criticized the traditional family system and male-dominated morality in the years following World War I (see KIKUCHI KAN), portrayed urban culture during the 1930s (see KAWAGUCHI MATSUTARŌ), and, after World War II, given greater expression to sexual themes and the portrayal of the Americanization of the Japanese lifestyle (see ISHIZAKA YŌJIRŌ).

Ever since the triumph of Japanese NATURALISM, with its emphasis on the individual, in the late Meiji period (1868–1912), novels of social manners—however much they delighted readers—had been regarded as inferior. In the 1960s, however, writers such as TACHIHARA MASAAKI, ITSUKI HIROYUKI, and TANABE SEIKO began to show the insight and reflection necessary to raise the status of the *fūzoku shōsetsu*. Some critics have begun to urge that the genre be given its due. See also CHŪKAN SHŌSETSU; POPULAR FICTION.

Fuzuki—→calendar, dates, and time

fuzzy engineering   ファジー工学

(*faji kōgaku*). The development or application of computer control technology based on fuzzy logic, a branch of logic that simulates human thought processes, including degrees of uncertainty indicated by terms such as "somewhat" or "quite possibly," in a matter amenable to computer processing. The concept of fuzzy logic was first proposed in the United States in the mid-1960s, and the first practical computer system using fuzzy logic was produced in Denmark in 1980. The first Japanese company to apply fuzzy logic was Fuji Electric Co, Ltd, which marketed a fuzzy logic computer system in 1985 that controlled additives to community water supplies. In 1987 the city of Sendai, Miyagi Prefecture, installed a fuzzy logic system for controlling subway operations. Various other applications followed, and by the late 1980s Japan had become a world leader in fuzzy engineering research. In 1989 the MINISTRY OF INTERNATIONAL TRADE AND INDUSTRY (MITI), in cooperation with 42 private companies, established the Laboratory for International Fuzzy Engineering Research. Fuzzy logic became a buzzword in Japan in the early 1990s through association with the design and marketing of household appliances that were equipped with computer control systems.

gagaku

Although sometimes performed as instrumental concert music, this traditional imperial court music is also played as accompaniment to a form of masked dance called *bugaku*, which features the use of wooden masks such as those pictured here.

▼ An exhibition of *gagaku* and *bugaku* is held every spring and autumn at the Kasuga Shrine in Nara. The spring performance, given on Children's Day, is shown here.

▲ *Kananfu* is a *bugaku* dance created during the Kamakura period. In the scene pictured here, a cook, sneaking a taste, catches a fish bone in his throat.

▶ Two masks from the *tōgaku* repertoire: above right, a late-Heian-period Haremen ("Swollen Face") mask caricatures the bloated features of an old woman; right, the eyes and chin of this 12th-century Ryōō mask are movable, as is the dragon on top.

gagaku   雅楽

Traditional music of the Japanese imperial court. The term derived from the Chinese word *yayue* (*ya-yüeh*), which denotes ancient ritual music played by a large orchestra of stone chimes, bronze bells, flutes, drums, and numerous other instruments. *Gagaku* comprises three main bodies of music: *tōgaku*, music said to be in the style of Tang (T'ang) dynasty (618–907) China; *komagaku*, a music style said to have been introduced from ancient Korea; and, finally, all of the many forms of native Japanese music associated with rituals of the Shintō religion.

Tōgaku makes up the largest part of the repertoire and includes well over 100 compositions. These can be performed as instrumental concert pieces called *kangen* ("winds and strings") or as dance pieces, in which case the performance is referred to as *bugaku* ("dance music"). *Komagaku* includes a smaller number of compositions that are always performed as *bugaku*. The *tōgaku* and *komagaku* repertoires exist in written Japanese notation, a different method of notation being required for each instrument of the ensemble. According to tradition, *tōgaku* is said to include not only compositions from Tang China, but also a number of compositions from India, Southeast Asia, and Central Asia. Today the exact origins of each *tōgaku* composition are not clear, since compositions from many parts of Asia were already combined into the *tōgaku* style at the time of the introduction of this music into Japan from China. Subsequently new compositions in the *tōgaku* style were added by Japanese composers. *Komagaku* is thought to include compositions from each of the three Korean kingdoms of ancient times: Silla, Koguryŏ, and Paekche. Japanese compositions in the *komagaku* genre were even more numerous than in *tōgaku*.

The oldest and most carefully preserved of the various forms of Shintō ritual music and dance used in the imperial court is the KAGURA, formally called *mikagura* (court *kagura*) in order to distinguish it from the various folk forms of Shintō music that are also called *kagura*. Besides the *mikagura*, this group of Shintō ritual songs and dances includes the Yamato *uta*, Azuma *asobi*, and Kume *uta*. The *mikagura* is central to the Shintō ritual style, and the other three forms are in some way modeled on it. Also included in the *gagaku* repertoire are SAIBARA (regional Japanese folk songs reset in an elegant court style), though only a small number of *saibara* compositions continue to be performed by court musicians.

History—During the Nara period (710–794), a great number of styles of music existed, each with its own special musicians, dancers, and types of instruments. In the early Heian period (794–1185), the various styles of foreign music were combined into the *tōgaku* and *komagaku* categories and were performed both by the court nobles and by hereditary guilds of professional musicians. With the fall of the noble classes in the early part of the Kamakura period (1185–1333), the popularity of *gagaku* waned. It was maintained by guilds and the remaining nobles, each in relative isolation from the other. The guild musicians were divided into three groups and were in service in Kyōto, Nara, and Ōsaka.

After the Meiji Restoration of 1868 and the relocation of the Imperial Palace to Tōkyō, the three groups were brought together as the official musicians of the newly established state. The musicians of the present-day Imperial Palace Music Department are still largely the direct descendants of the members of the first musicians' guilds that performed *gagaku* in Japan during the 8th century. They perform all the ritual music and dances required by the court and also give regular public *gagaku* concerts.

Instruments—The instruments used in performances of *gagaku* are Japanese modifications of those used in the Tang court ensembles. The instrumentation is determined by the type of music being performed. A small double-reed pipe similar to an oboe or shawm, called the HICHIRIKI, is used in all the instrumental ensembles. Three different types of flute are used, the *kagurabue* generally for the Shintō rituals, the *komabue* for *komagaku*, and the *ryūteki* or dragon flute for *tōgaku*. In addition to these wind instruments, *tōgaku* uses a small mouth organ of 17 bamboo pipes called the SHŌ, which plays tone clusters of 5 or 6 notes. *Tōgaku* and *komagaku* each use three percussion instruments, two of which are common to both types of music. These are a hanging TAIKO, or large drum, and the *shōko*, a small bronze gong. In *komagaku* there is also a small hourglass drum called *san no tsuzumi*, played with a single stick (see TSUZUMI); the *kakko*, a small drum played with two sticks, is used in *tōgaku*. In Shintō vocal music, the only percussion instrument is a pair of wooden clappers (*shakubyōshi*). Stringed instruments are no longer used in the *tōgaku* dance repertoire or in *komagaku*, but two have been retained in the *kangen*, or chamber music setting of *tōgaku*: the *gakusō*, which is usually called by its common name, KOTO, and the BIWA. Only one stringed instrument, the *wagon*, is used in Shintō music. The repertoire of *gagaku* music is played at tempos that, although varied, seem very slow when compared to Western music or even to other forms of Japanese music.

Gagen shūran　　　　雅言集覧

A classical-Japanese-language dictionary compiled toward the close of the Edo period (1600–1868) by ISHIKAWA MASAMOCHI, a learned KOKUGAKU (National Learning) scholar and KYŌKA ("mad verse") poet. A typical example of an early dictionary, the *Gagen shūran* consists of 50 fascicles in 21 volumes. It mainly contains the vocabulary of Heian-period (794–1185) classical literature arranged in traditional *iroha* alphabet order. It was compiled as a standard reference for use in writing classical-style Japanese and remains valuable for studying ancient Japanese. Publication began in 1826 but was discontinued halfway through; the unpublished remainder has been handed down in manuscript form. Copies presently in circulation are of the enlarged 1887 edition with a supplement by Nakajima Hirotari (1792–1864).

gaikoku bugyō　　　　外国奉行

(commissioner of foreign affairs). A short-lived (1858–68) government post created by the Tokugawa shogunate to oversee diplomatic relations. Forced in 1858 to sign the HARRIS TREATY with the United States, the shogunate replaced its coastal defense officers (*kaibōgakari*), whose duties were mainly military, with the *gaikoku bugyō*, who received diplomatic missions and performed related functions. Initially, five direct shogunal vassals (HATAMOTO) were selected to serve on a rotating basis; later the number varied. The commissioners were responsible to the senior councillors (*rōjū*) and maintained a bureaucratic staff that included translators and other specialists. After 1862 their subordinates also included assistant commissioners of foreign affairs (*gaikoku bugyō nami*). The post was abolished after the fall of the shogunate.

gaikoku hōjin　　　　外国法人

(foreign juristic person). Juristic person (HŌJIN) established under the provisions of the law of a foreign country. Only the existence of states, administrative divisions of states, and trading companies as foreign juristic persons is recognized under the Japanese CIVIL CODE. However, the code does provide that other foreign juristic persons can be recognized, provided that they have been established under the provisions of Japanese laws or treaties. The code also provides that foreign juristic persons enjoy the same rights

as those of the same classes of Japanese juristic persons, provided that they are not rights that aliens, as individuals, cannot enjoy and that there are no provisions to the contrary in laws or treaties (Civil Code, art. 36). In addition to the provisions in the Civil Code, which are basic, the COMMERCIAL CODE contains a chapter relating to foreign companies and their operations in Japan as juristic persons (Commercial Code, Part II, chap. 6).

gaikokujin gakkō　　　　外国人学校

(international schools). Schools for the children of foreign nationals resident in Japan. Established and maintained by foreign nationals, these schools are classified under Japanese law as one of the various types of MISCELLANEOUS SCHOOLS. The St. Maur International School, established in 1872 in Yokohama, was the first school of this type in Japan. It was intended for children from the United States and Europe, as were most of the international schools established before World War II. The majority of the international schools opened since the end of the war are for children of Korean ancestry born in Japan. As of 1989 there were over 142 international schools nationwide.

Gaikokusen Uchiharai Rei

　　　　外国船打払令

(Order for the Repelling of Foreign Ships). Also known as Ikokusen Uchiharai Rei. Order issued in 1825 embodying the policy of the Tokugawa shogunate (1603–1867) toward foreign ships. The shogunate had maintained a NATIONAL SECLUSION policy since 1639, and in 1791 the shogunate issued a new order ruling that whenever a foreign ship drifted ashore or approached the coast, the ship and crew should be detained. In 1806, however, as a result of negotiations with the Russian envoy Nikolai Petrovich REZANOV, the 1791 order was revised to provide that foreign ships entering Japanese waters would be peacefully made to leave and that those that drifted ashore or were damaged would be given provisions and then requested to leave.

At the beginning of the 19th century, English and American whaling ships began to appear in coastal waters. The shogunate issued a new order, the Gaikokusen Uchiharai Rei, prescribing that all foreign ships were to be repelled. The MORRISON INCIDENT, in which an American merchant ship was bombarded under this policy, as well as the news of China's defeat in the Opium War (1839–42), prompted the shogunate to reassess its seclusion policy. In 1842 the shogunate revoked the *uchiharai* order and replaced it with the SHINSUI KYŌYO REI (Order for the Provision of Firewood and Water).

Gaimushō → Ministry of Foreign Affairs

gairaigo → loanwords

Gakken Co, Ltd　　　　[株]学習研究社

(Gakushū Kenkyūsha). One of the largest general and educational publishing companies in Japan. It was established by Furuoka Hideto (b 1908) in April 1946. When its first publication of an educational magazine was rejected by wholesale distributors, Furuoka organized his own sales network and expanded the business. Today, in addition to educational magazines, Gakken publishes many other types of magazines, as well as general books and dictionaries. It also pro-

duces and sells educational films, toys, and other teaching aids. In 1984 the company's stock was listed on the Tōkyō Stock Exchange, First Section.

gakkō gyōji　　　　学校行事

(school events). As defined in the Japanese Ministry of Education's SCHOOL COURSE GUIDELINES, the term *gakkō gyōji* encompasses six types of activities: ceremonies, such as those for school entrance and graduation; arts programs, such as performing arts presentations (GAKUGEIKAI) and film shows; physical education programs, such as athletic meets (UNDŌKAI); one-day field trips (ENSOKU) and trips lasting longer than one day (SHŪGAKU RYOKŌ); activities relating to health and safety, such as fire and earthquake drills; and activities relating to labor and productivity, such as school cleanups, community service projects, and visits to workplaces.

Before World War II, ceremonies were typically held on national holidays, such as National Founding Day, the Emperor's Birthday, and New Year's Day. On the day of the ceremony teachers and students would assemble at the school in accordance with the nationwide practice of paying respect to the imperial portrait and reading the IMPERIAL RESCRIPT ON EDUCATION. These ceremonies were held for the sole purpose of instilling a sense of patriotism and loyalty to the emperor. By the second half of the Meiji period (1868–1912) school events such as *undōkai* and *shūgaku ryokō* had also become well established throughout Japan.

After World War II, in accordance with OCCUPATION directives, imperial portraits were removed and ceremonies for paying respect to the emperor were discontinued. However, entrance and graduation ceremonies, as well as other school events, are still accorded a prominent place in the school curriculum.

Gakkō Kyōiku Hō → School Education Law of 1947

gakubatsu　　　　学閥

(academic cliques or alumni cliques). Mutual support groups formed of graduates of the same school. Most universities and colleges have alumni associations (*dōsōkai*) to which all graduates automatically belong. These associations facilitate the formation of *gakubatsu* within large corporations and government bureaus. When employment openings occur or opportunities for advancement arise, members of the same alumni group will receive preferential treatment.

During the Meiji period (1868–1912) the Japanese government placed great importance on the school system as a modernizing institution. Tōkyō University and a network of higher educational facilities were established to produce high-level bureaucrats and scholars and to develop business, educational, and military leaders. Great numbers of graduates from these institutions took posts in government or large enterprises.

In order to strengthen harmony and cooperation within the group, standards recognized by all members, such as the year of graduation, are applied in making the important distinctions of SEMPAI-KŌHAI (senior-junior), teacher and disciple, and school classmate. The *gakubatsu* also contains elements of GIRI AND NINJŌ relations.

Some have contended that the prevalence of *gakubatsu* has transformed Japanese society into a "credential society" (GAKUREKI

gakkō gyōji

Official school events include several types of activities, including field trips, ceremonies, and athletic meets.

Elementary school students participate in a day-long athletic meet. This is a game of *tama-ire*, in which teams compete to toss as many balls as possible into a basket.

Formally dressed parents accompany their children to a school entrance ceremony in April.

During one-day field trips, students may travel relatively far from their schools to visit important natural, historical, or cultural sites.

Parents, teachers, and students assemble for a photograph following a graduation ceremony.

SHAKAI) where a person's worth is measured by academic degree and school. There are some indications that ability is beginning to take precedence over background in Japanese society, but the *gakubatsu* still exert a powerful influence.

gakugeikai   学芸会

(literally, "school arts convocation"). One of the GAKKŌ GYŌJI (school events) in Japanese elementary schools. Parents and neighbors are invited to a presentation of plays, choruses, and concerts in which students collectively display skills they have acquired in school. These creative productions are intended to nurture skills in both group cooperation and self-directed planning, although teachers do play a supervisory role. Usually held in the fall, *gakugeikai* are classified as one of the "special education activities" in the SCHOOL CURRICULUM.

Gakumon no susume   学問のすゝめ

(An Encouragement of Learning). A series of 17 pamphlets, published 1872–76, intended as an elementary-school text by FUKUZAWA YUKICHI, the preeminent thinker of the MEIJI ENLIGHTENMENT, the movement to modernize Japan on the Western model. The first pamphlet began with Fukuzawa's famous assertion that "heaven never created a man above another man nor a man below another man." Fukuzawa meant that in Meiji society, where hereditary rank no longer prevailed, wealth and honor would result only from individual diligence and study. He argued that Western learning and an independent spirit of rationality were necessary to strengthen Japan against the West. Despite its conservative emphasis, *Gakumon no susume* was banned as a textbook in the early 1880s as part of a government reaction to the FREEDOM

AND PEOPLE'S RIGHTS MOVEMENT and to Western influence in general, and publication ceased after 1890.

Gakuō Zōkyū   岳翁蔵丘

(fl ca 1482–ca 1514). Zen monk-painter identified in a contemporary monk's diary as a disciple of SHŪBUN, the influential master painter of the Zen temple SHŌKOKUJI in Kyōto. Associated with Ise Province (now part of Mie Prefecture), where many of his paintings were preserved, Gakuō was the most faithful follower of Shūbun's style of ink landscape painting. Many later historians confused his paintings with those of his teacher. Although few details are known about Gakuō's life, his paintings, the majority of which are landscapes, survive in relatively large numbers and record his artistic career more completely than those of many of his contemporaries. See INK PAINTING.

gakureki shakai   学歴社会

("credential society"). Term used in Japan from the 1960s to refer to the great emphasis the Japanese place on a person's educational background. In Japan an individual's social and occupational status is generally considered to be determined not only by the level of education completed, but also by the rank and prestige of the particular universities attended. Factors such as class, race, religion, and personal wealth, which are important determinants of social status in other societies, are not quite as significant in Japan because of the country's high level of homogeneity and lack of extreme inequalities in the distribution of wealth. A person's educational career, on the other hand, provides a convenient determinant of status. With a high percentage of students attending institutions of higher learning, the status distinc-

tions among schools have become increasingly pronounced. As a result of this, the competition to gain entrance to the most prestigious schools has intensified markedly. See ENTRANCE EXAMINATIONS; CRAM SCHOOLS.

Gakuren Incident→Kyōto
University Incident

Gakushūin University   学習院大学

(Gakushūin Daigaku). Private university located in Toshima Ward, Tōkyō. Its immediate predecessor was the Gakushūin, a school opened in 1877 in Tōkyō under the auspices of the Kazoku Kaikan (Peers' Hall). The school remained an educational institution mainly for children of the imperial family and the nobility and was known as the Peers' School until after World War II, when the peerage system was abolished. In 1947 it became a private school open to the general public. It maintains faculties of law, economics, letters, and science and has affiliated schools from kindergarten through senior high and a two-year junior college for women. Enrollment was 7,472 in 1989.

Gamagōri   蒲郡[市]

City in southeastern Aichi Prefecture, central Honshū, on Mikawa Bay. Long known for its cotton cloth (Mikawa *momen*) and hemp rope, Gamagōri has a port with facilities for freighters. The city is situated within the Mikawa Bay Quasi-National Park; Miya and Nishiura hot springs and Takeshima, an island connected to the mainland, are favorite tourist sites. Pop: 84,819.

gambaru   頑張る

(to persist, to hang on, to do one's best). An important word in Japanese interpersonal re-

Ganjin This likeness of the blind monk in meditation is thought to have been made shortly before his death in 763. The painted dry-lacquer image is a National Treasure.

sponsor horse, bicycle, powerboat, and motorcycle racing. In 1989 annual proceeds from public gambling reached ¥7 trillion (about US $51 billion).

Betting on animal contests, such as BULL-FIGHTING, DOGFIGHTING, and COCKFIGHTING, once popular in Japan, is now practiced in only a few places. Public gambling and private establishments where one can play *hanafuda*, dice (*saikoro*), MAH-JONGG, or PACHINKO (pinball) are plentiful. Although there are notices prohibiting cash wagering in these establishments, in reality gambling is very common. In spite of the fact that gambling has been prohibited by various laws since the 7th century, gamblers and proprietors of such facilities are rarely prosecuted.

games
遊び

(*asobi*). Since ancient times, the Japanese have engaged in all kinds of games. Matching games or "comparisons" (*awase*) have a long history in Japan: two of the earliest are *e-awase* (picture-comparing contests) and UTA-AWASE (poetry contests). Similar games involve comparing flowers, roots, incense (see INCENSE CEREMONY), birds, insects, and shells (see KAI-AWASE).

Many board games were imported from China. The best known are GO, SHŌGI, and SUGOROKU. A popular children's board game was JŪROKU MUSASHI. WORD GAMES are abundant in Japan because of the great number of homonyms in the language. Matching games using PLAYING CARDS (referred to as *karuta*) are popular today, such as HANAFUDA, HYAKUNIN ISSHU, and IROHA KARUTA.

Important traditional children's games are OHAJIKI; BEANBAG (*otedama*); cat's cradle (*ayatori*); TOPS, including the BEIGOMA; MENKO; hide-and-seek (*kakurembo*); tag (*onigokko*); KAGOME KAGOME; NEKKI; *tōsenkyō* (a game in which players throw folding fans at a target); *takeuma* (STILTS or hobbyhorse); TEMARI (handball); KEN; PAPER BALLOONS (*kami fūsen*); and paper folding (ORIGAMI).

Games particularly associated with New Year's include kite flying (*takoage;* see KITES), the *Hyakunin isshu* card game, FUKU WARAI, and battledore and shuttlecock (see HANE-TSUKI). Recently, VIDEO GAMES are increasingly being played by both adults and children.

Gamō Kumpei
蒲生君平

(1768–1813). Japanese classical scholar of the Edo period (1600–1868). Born into a merchant family in the castle town of Utsunomiya (now in Tochigi Prefecture), he studied the Japanese classics. His association with FUJITA YŪKOKU and other members of the MITO SCHOOL further inspired his interest in history. His studies on the question of the "true relations between sovereign and subject" (*taigi meibun*) awakened in him a deep concern over the decline of the imperial family in power and prestige. In 1796 and 1799 he toured the country inspecting imperial tombs and in 1808 published *Sanryōshi* (History of Imperial Tombs). For his proimperial ideas he is considered a precursor of the movement to overthrow the shogunate and restore direct imperial rule in the late Edo period.

Gamō Ujisato
蒲生氏郷

(1556–95). Christian name, Leão. *Daimyō* of the Azuchi-Momoyama period (1568–1600); son of Gamō Katahide (1534–84), lord of Hino Castle in Ōmi (now Shiga Prefecture). The Gamō sided with ODA NOBUNAGA when he marched on Kyōto in

1568; Ujisato was married to Nobunaga's daughter and served Nobunaga in various campaigns. After Nobunaga's assassination in 1582, Ujisato served TOYOTOMI HIDEYOSHI and distinguished himself in several campaigns, including the sweep through northernmost Honshū in 1591 that completed Hideyoshi's unification of Japan. Ujisato was ultimately awarded fiefs that totaled an assessed yield of 919,320 *koku* (see KOKUDAKA). He thereby became one of Japan's five greatest daimyō. Ujisato fell ill while in Nagoya (now in Saga Prefecture), the Kyūshū headquarters for Hideyoshi's invasions of Korea, and died in Kyōto on his way home; the story that he was poisoned is unfounded. He converted to Christianity in 1585 but lost his zeal after Hideyoshi's ANTI-CHRISTIAN EDICTS in 1587.

Gan
雁

(tr *The Wild Geese*, 1959). Novel by MORI ŌGAI (1862–1922), published 1911–13, that recounts the emotional plight of Otama, a young woman set up as the mistress of an unpleasant moneylender to improve her family's declining fortunes. It seems that Otama may allay the loneliness that accompanies her circumstances by developing a relationship with a medical student, Okada, who often passes her house; but he leaves Tōkyō to pursue studies in Germany before their romance fully develops. Although the narrative is introduced by a friend of Okada's, the point of view gradually shifts to that of Okada, and finally to that of the young woman. A touching account of the birth of modern self-consciousness in a woman, *Gan* is also a historical re-creation of life in Tōkyō at the beginning of the Meiji period (1868–1912). It remains a favorite among Japanese readers today.

Gangōji
元興寺

Also known as Shin Gangōji. Temple of the KEGON SECT of Buddhism; located in the city of Nara. Founded by SOGA NO UMAKO soon after 588, the temple originally was located in Asuka, where it was known by both its formal title Hōkōji and the popular name ASU-KADERA.

When the imperial court moved to Nara (HEIJŌKYŌ) from Asuka, this temple was one of the first to reestablish itself there in 718 and was called Shin (New) Gangōji (the original temple in Asuka then came to be called Moto [Original] Gangōji). Formally classified as a SANRON SCHOOL temple during the Nara period (710–794), Gangōji is mentioned as having played a part in many important state ceremonies of the Nara and Heian (794–1185) periods. Gangōji prospered and was numbered among the so-called Seven Temples of Nara, including TŌDAIJI, KŌFUKUJI, DAIANJI, YAKUSHIJI, SAIDAIJI, and HŌRYŪJI. From the mid-Heian period, however, Gangōji fell into disrepair. Nothing remains now of the original buildings except the stone pagoda base, excavated in modern times after its final destruction by fire in 1859. The main hall and an attached *zenshitsu* (meditation hall), rebuilt in the Kamakura period (1185–1333), remain on the site and have been designated National Treasures.

Ganjin
鑑真

(688–763). Chinese Buddhist monk who introduced the RITSU SECT of Buddhism to Japan and founded the temple TŌSHŌDAIJI in Nara. Ganjin is the Japanese pronunciation of the Chinese name Jianzhen (Chien-chen). Born in Yangzhou (Yang-chou), China. At age 13

lationships. Probably derived from *ga o haru* (to be self-willed), the word originally had the negative connotation of asserting oneself against group decisions and norms. Since the 1930s, however, *gambaru* has become a positive word, commonly used to exhort enthusiasm and hard work, usually toward a group objective. For example, when a village youth leaves for a new job in the city, he promises his friends, parents, and teachers that he will *gambaru.* The implication is that he will try not to disappoint them. The word is also used among members of a group to encourage each other in cooperative activities, often in the imperative form *gambare.*

gambling
賭博

(*tobaku* or *bakuchi*). Today all forms of gambling other than those specifically recognized by law, such as betting on HORSE RACING, bicycle racing (see KEIRIN), or powerboat racing, and certain lotteries (*takarakuji*), are prohibited in Japan.

A board game resembling backgammon called *sugoroku* was imported from China in the 6th century. *Sugoroku* and other dice games, as well as simpler forms of gambling, such as coin-tossing games, gained great popularity. In the 16th century when Europeans began arriving in Japan, *carta*, the Portuguese word for "playing card," was adopted as *karuta*, and card games became popular. Gambling was often prohibited by law, but as each type of game was banned, another replaced it. *Hanakaruta* (now called HANAFUDA) remains the most popular form of card gambling in Japan. See PLAYING CARDS.

From the end of the 18th century professional gamblers called YAKUZA (or *bakuchi uchi* or *bakuto*) provided gambling places, extracting a service fee from the players and offering protection from arrest and harassment. By the early 20th century public (government-sponsored) gambling appeared in the form of national horse racing administered by the government. From about 1950 local governments began to

he became a monk at a local temple and later studied monastic discipline under the famed master Daoan (Tao-an) at the Longxing (Lung-hsing) monastery in Yuezhou (Yüehchou), China. At age 20 he became a Buddhist monk.

In 732 the Japanese government decided to resume dispatching envoys to Tang (T'ang; 618–907) China (see SUI AND TANG CHINA, EMBASSIES TO). It also hoped to invite to Japan Chinese monks who would firmly establish the precepts necessary to regulate monastic life and establish in the capital an authentic ordination platform. In 742 Ganjin accepted the invitation of the Japanese monks Yōei and Fushō. Between 743 and 748 Ganjin made five unsuccessful attempts to reach Japan. In 754 Ganjin, age 66 and totally blind, finally reached the southern shores of Kyūshū. Three months later, in the spring of that year, he arrived in Nara and immediately established an ordination platform at TŌDAIJI. In 759 he established Tōshōdaiji, where he resided; Tōshōdaiji became the headquarters of the Ritsu sect.

Ganjitsu → holidays, national

gankake　　　　　　願掛

Also termed *gandate;* prayers or petitions to a Shintō or Buddhist deity to obtain a specific request. *Gankake* are accompanied by offerings or promises to fulfill certain acts or penances and may be made either by groups or individuals. In the former case *gankake* often involve an entire village or community in prayers for the rain or sun necessary for a good harvest, for protection from the ravages of war or epidemic, or for a villager who is gravely ill. Individual petitions, generally for personal health or marital happiness, may involve the entire family; they have remained the more prevalent form of *gankake* in modern times and are still made at temples or shrines noted for their miraculous powers.

PILGRIMAGES to shrines and temples are considered a form of *gankake.* Offerings made to the deity may include food or goods (e.g., rice cakes, wine, or cloth) or a votive tablet (EMA) inscribed with a picture of an afflicted organ to Yakushi NYORAI, the Buddha of healing. *Ema* inscribed with prayers for success in school and university entrance examinations are probably the most common form of *gankake* in contemporary Japan. The process of *gankake* is concluded by a special visit of thanks to the shrine or temple in question upon fulfillment of the petitioner's request.

Ganku　　　　　　岩駒

(1756?–1839). Painter and founder of the Kishi school of painting. Surname Kishi; given name Koma. Born in Kanazawa (now in Ishikawa Prefecture), which he left in 1780 for Kyōto. A self-taught artist, Ganku seems to have studied KANŌ SCHOOL techniques, and he acknowledged a debt to the Chinese painter SHEN NANPIN (Shen Nan-p'in); the influence of the MARUYAMA-SHIJŌ SCHOOL is also present. Ganku's style, however eclectic and rooted in other schools of painting, is bold and vigorous. In addition to Ganku's son Gantai (1782–1865) and his son-in-law Ganryō (1797–1852), the Kishi-school painters include Renzan (1804–59), Yokoyama Kazan, and Shirai Kayō (fl ca 1840–60).

ga no iwai　　　　　賀の祝い

A Japanese rite of passage celebrated at various ages to pray for long life. Also called *toshiiwai; sanga.* Imported to Japan from China. Originally *ga no iwai* was celebrated once every ten years beginning when one turned 40 according to the traditional Japanese method of calculating age (*kazoedoshi*). *Ga no iwai* dates are always decided on the basis of *kazoedoshi.* Toward the latter part of the Muromachi period (1333–1568), *ga no iwai* came to be celebrated beginning when one turned 61 (see KANREKI) and subsequently at ages 70 (KOKI), 77 (*kiju*), 80 (*sanju*), 88 (*beiju*), 90 (*sotsuju*), and 99 (*hakuju*). In *kazoedoshi,* one is considered to be one year old the year of birth and becomes one year older at the beginning of each subsequent New Year. This calculation results in an age that ranges from one to two years greater than the age as calculated by the usual Western method. The ritual is usually celebrated with relatives and friends on the person's birthday or on Respect-for-the-Aged Day (15 September). The ages at which *ga no iwai* is celebrated can differ according to the area of the country. These ages are closely related to YAKUDOSHI (the ages determined to be critical or unlucky according to Japanese folk belief), and what is considered a *yakudoshi* in one region can be a year for *ga no iwai* in another.

garabō　　　　　　ガラ紡

(*gara* spinning). A process for spinning cotton thread, named for the clattering noise made by water-driven throstles. Invented in 1873 by a Buddhist monk named Gaun Tatchi (1842–1900), it was capable of mass-producing cotton yarn from waste fiber. It spread rapidly throughout the country and played an important part in the early development of Japan's modern spinning industry. With the increased importation of Western machinery after 1900, the *garabō* process virtually disappeared.

gardenia　　　　　　栀子

(*kuchinashi*). *Gardenia jasminoides* f. *grandiflora.* Also known as cape jasmine. The *kuchinashi* is the most common species of gardenia found in Japan. An evergreen shrub of the family Rubiaceae, it reaches a height of about 2 meters (6.6 ft). The leaves are opposite, oblong, and glossy. In summer it produces fragrant white flowers 6–7 centimeters (about 2.5 in) across. The fruit is obovate and turns yellowish red when ripe. The plant grows wild in western Honshū as well as in Shikoku and Kyūshū. It has long been cultivated as a garden plant, and numerous varieties, such as those with variegated leaves or with double flowers, have been developed.

The fruit is a source of yellow dye used in foodstuffs and as a stain for wooden utensils. Tea made of the dried fruit was used to treat jaundice, and a plaster made of the powdered dried fruit was used as a folk remedy for bruises or cuts. Japanese gardenias have been exported and crossed with other species.

gardens　　　　　　庭園

(*teien*). Japanese gardens possess a unique beauty derived from the combination and synthesis of various elements. There is a compositional beauty derived from a blending of natural plantings, sand, water, and rock, made unique by the natural beauty of Japan's landscape, seasonal change, and a symbolic beauty arising from the expression of SHINTŌ beliefs and Buddhist intellectual conventions.

History——It has been said that the use of groupings of rocks is a distinguishing feature of the Japanese garden and provides its basic framework. The ancestors of the modern Japanese referred to places surrounded by natural rock as *amatsu iwasaka* ("heavenly barrier") or *amatsu iwakura* ("heavenly seat"), believing that gods lived there. Dense clusters of trees were also thought to be the dwelling places of gods and were called *himorogi* ("divine hedge"). Moats or streams that enclosed sacred ground were called *mizugaki* ("water fences").

The first gardens amidst the mountains of YAMATO (now Nara Prefecture), where the Japanese state was established during the 6th and 7th centuries, imitated ocean scenes with large ponds rimmed by wild "seashores" and dotted with islands. During this period Buddhism was transmitted to Japan, and immigrants from PAEKCHE on the Korean peninsula contributed continental influences to the Japanese garden. The theme of Shumisen (Skt: Sumeru), one of the Buddhist paradises, was incorporated, and stone fountains and bridges of Chinese origin were added.

In 794 the capital was moved from Nara to Kyōto. Here several rivers converged, and channels were dug to carry water through the city. In order to provide some relief from the summer heat, waterfalls and ponds were fashioned, and narrow streams (*yarimizu*) were made to pass between buildings and flow through the gardens of the SHINDENZUKURI mansions. The ponds were of simple shape yet were large enough for boating, and at their edges, jutting out over the water, were erected fishing pavilions (*tsuridono*) connected by roofed corridors to the other structures of the mansion. The large area between the main buildings and the pond was covered with white sand and used for formal ceremonies.

With the rise of the cult of the Buddha AMIDA in the 10th century, the *shinden* style of garden, modeled on the image of the Pure Land (Jōdo) as described in scripture and religious tracts, was developed. A good example of this is the garden of the BYŌDŌIN, a temple at Uji near Kyōto that was originally the country residence of FUJIWARA NO MICHINAGA. Because of the interest in gardens among aristocrats, there appeared many excellent critical works on the subject, the oldest of which is *Sakuteiki* (Treatise on Garden Making), written by Tachibana no Toshitsuna (1028–94).

From the Kamakura period (1185–1333) priestly garden designers were called "rock-placing monks" (*ishitatesō*), the placement of rocks implying the creation of a garden. The greatest of these *ishitatesō* was MUSŌ SOSEKI. At the temple SAIHŌJI he constructed a garden with 10 views based on the Chinese compositional method known as *shijing* (*shihching*; J: *jukkyō*) or "ten realms."

The Muromachi period (1333–1568) has been called the golden age of Japanese gardens. Skilled groups of craftsmen known as *senzui kawaramono* ("mountain, stream, and riverbed people") were active, and the new *karesansui* ("dry mountain stream") style of garden appeared. Waterless rock and sand

Continued on page 444►

gardenia The *kuchinashi* is the most common Japanese species of gardenia.

441

gardens

Karesansui: Microcosmic Gardens

Landscape by Li Tang. The bold, almost abstract style of 12th-century Chinese ink paintings such as this one exerted a lasting influence on Japanese garden design.

❶ East garden of Daisen'in. The heart of the garden, with stones and trees representing a deep mountain ravine and white gravel forming a frozen impression of a powerful cascade.

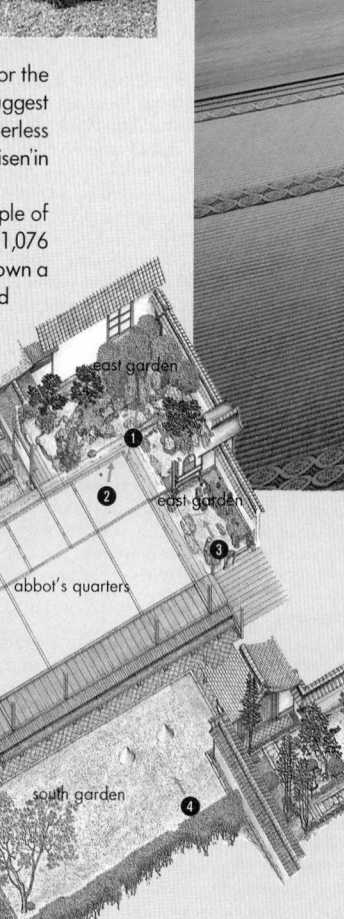

Expanses of sand or fine gravel subtly textured to represent rivers or the sea, a carefully balanced placement of rocks and stones to suggest lonely islands or rugged crags—this is the art of *karesansui*, the waterless rock and sand gardens of Japan, exemplified by the renowned Daisen'in gardens pictured here.

The east garden of the abbot's quarters at the Daisen'in, a subtemple of the temple Daitokuji in Kyōto, occupies only about 100 square meters (1,076 sq ft), but it contains the condensed image of a waterfall cascading down a ravine among towering mountains, broadening into a stately river, and winding its way to the sea.

The antecedents of the style are reflected in the *Sakuteiki*, a late-Heian-period (794–1185) gardening treatise, but it was not until the Muromachi period (1333–1568) that it achieved perfection, notably in the gardens of Zen temples and monasteries. The transcendent quality of the ink paintings of Song-dynasty (960–1279) China was much admired by Japanese Zen monks and served as one source of inspiration for these universes in miniature. The economy of expression found in such paintings is echoed in the dynamic symbolism characteristic of *karesansui*.

east garden

inner garden

east garden

abbot's quarters

south garden

Plan of the Daisen'in garden. The abbot's quarters, at center, surrounded by the east, south, and inner gardens. The east garden is especially prized and has served as a model for many other *karesansui* gardens. The numbered arrows indicate the respective locations from which the accompanying photographs were taken.

② View of the east garden from the abbot's quarters. The two massive upright stones just beyond the corner of the structure are named after the Buddhist divinities Kannon and Fudō. To the right is the configuration representing the waterfall. The stream of gravel passing under the stone bridge below and to the right of the two standing stones suggests a placid river's course.

❸ Katei Bridge. This architectural element, thought to be a later addition to the original design, bisects the longer arm of the east garden; its window frames the stones of the central arrangement. In the foreground, a stone "boat" makes its way downstream.

❹ South garden. The minimalist design of raked white gravel, its twin mounds suggesting islands in a cosmic sea, lends this garden a tranquil atmosphere suited to meditative contemplation.

▶ This *shūyū*-style garden at the temple Saihōji in Kyōto was designed by Zen master Musō Soseki in the early Muromachi period. The famous moss garden gives the temple its popular name, Kokedera (Moss Temple).

▼ The tranquillity and natural beauty of this Kyōto tea garden prepare visitors for participation in the tea ceremony.

▼ The pond of the Heian-period garden at the temple Mōtsuji in Hiraizumi, Iwate Prefecture, in winter. The *funa asobi* style used here was popular for gardens of *shinden-zukuri*-style mansions.

▲ The bridge and pond of the Edo-period *kaiyū*-style garden at Ritsurin Park in Takamatsu, Kagawa Prefecture.

gardens (*karesansui*) arose under the influence of ZEN Buddhist doctrine, *shoin*-style architecture (SHOIN-ZUKURI), and Chinese ink painting, together with potted dwarf trees (BONSAI), and tray landscapes (see BONKEI AND BONSEKI), the ideal being the symbolic expression of the universe within a limited space. Although *karesansui* is a garden form found nowhere else in the world, its development was probably influenced by the methods and perspective employed in the Chinese ink paintings known as *canshan shengshui* (*ts'an-shan sheng-shui;* J: *zanzan jōsui*), landscapes of barren mountains and dry riverbeds.

The TEA CEREMONY (*sadō*) as taught by SEN NO RIKYŪ emphasized a quiescent spirituality. The approach to a teahouse was through a tea garden (*roji* or *chaniwa*), the ideal of which Rikyū sought in the desolate tranquility of a mountain trail. Among the contributions of the tea garden to the contemporary Japanese garden are stepping-stones, stone lanterns, and groves of trees, as well as stone washbasins and simply constructed gazebos for guests being served tea.

During the Edo period (1600–1868) a synthesis of preceding forms took place. The garden of the KATSURA DETACHED PALACE, which achieved considerable renown

through the writings of the German architect Bruno TAUT, is made up of a number of tea gardens. This is an example of the *kaiyū* or "many-pleasure" style, which became fully established in the mid-Edo period. A representative garden designer of this period was KOBORI ENSHŪ, whose work included the gardens of the Sentō Palace in Kyōto.

The Use of Space——Methods of dividing the surface plane of a Japanese garden may be classified into four groups. The *funa asobi* ("pleasure boat") style (centered on an oval-shaped pond where courtiers went boating) was a popular type of garden in the Heian period (794–1185) for mansions on the outskirts of the capital. The *shūyū* ("stroll") style (in which a garden's chief feature is a path leading from vantage point to vantage point from which changing scenes can be viewed) was often employed in gardens of temples and mansions during the Heian, Kamakura, and Muromachi periods. The *kanshō* or *zakan* ("contemplation") style (in which the garden is viewed from within a central structure, emphasis being placed on the creation of a carefully composed scene suggestive of a picture and suitable for long and studied viewing) was designed to be seen from a *shoin*, a room in a type of building constructed in the *shoinzukuri* style. The *kaiyū* ("many-pleasure") style (in which various gardens, usually tea

gardens, were constructed around a central pond, displaying striking changes of scene to viewers) was often employed in the gardens of *daimyō* during both the Azuchi-Momoyama (1568–1600) and Edo (1600–1868) periods. Additionally, gardens may be designed on the basis of adaptations of these four styles.

Methods of Scenic Composition—— There are three basic principles of scenic composition: reduced scale, symbolization, and "borrowed views." Reduction in scale refers particularly to the *kaiyū*-style garden, which brings together in a confined area representations of famous scenes and places of historical interest through miniaturization of natural views of mountains and rivers and, as in tea gardens, the creation, even within a city, of idealized scenes of a mountain village. Methods of symbolization are abstraction, as in the use of white sand to suggest the ocean, and inference, as in a grouping of stones or an island signifying the felicitous crane and tortoise. The term "borrowed view" (*shakkei*) describes the use of background views outside and beyond the garden, such as a mountain, a broad plain, or the sea. The garden is designed in such a way that they become part of the interior scenic composition. For this reason the surrounding view is an important factor in the selection of a garden site.

☎ *442–443*

GARIOA-EROA   ガリオア・エロア資金

(Garioa-Eroa Shikin). Abbreviation for Government and Relief in Occupied Areas—Economic Rehabilitation in Occupied Areas. Two US legislative programs in the post–World War II period (EROA was eventually included in GARIOA) authorizing funds for economic relief and reconstruction in occupied countries. From 1947 to 1951 contributions to Japan under these programs totaled about $2.1 billion. Major items were food, fertilizer, petroleum, medical supplies, and nonindustrial raw materials; some civilian personnel costs were also paid from GARIOA funds. In 1962 the United States and Japan agreed on the figure of $1.8 billion as Japan's total GARIOA debt to the United States for postwar assistance and on the sum of $490 million as the amount Japan would pay in settlement over 15 years. The United States agreed to use $25 million of this money for educational and cultural exchange programs, which included the Fulbright educational exchange and the US-Japan Friendship Commission.

Gassan 月山

Shield volcano in central Yamagata Prefecture, northern Honshū. Gassan is one of the Dewa Sanzan (Three Mountains of Dewa Province), a center for the religious exercises of the SHUGENDŌ sect (see DEWA SANZAN SHRINES). Gassan Shrine is on the summit. Alpine flora abound. There is summer skiing and mountain climbing. Height: 1,984 m (6,509 ft).

gateball ゲートボール

(*gētobōru*). Outdoor game, modeled on croquet, that was developed in Japan shortly after World War II. (The name "gateball" is a Japanese coinage.) Synthetic-resin balls 7.5 centimeters (3 in) in diameter are hit with wooden mallets and driven through a series of three metal gates (arches) to strike a goalpost ("goal pole") in the center of the court. The game is played by two competing five-person teams, each person having one ball. The winner is the first team whose members all reach the goalpost within a 30-minute time limit (or the team that comes the closest to doing so). The game became popular around 1975 as a sport for the elderly and was spread throughout Japan by senior citizens' clubs. Nationwide there are from 4.7 to 6 million players.

gates 門

(*mon*). Gates are a major architectural feature of temples and shrines, palaces, castles, and domestic architecture. Their various forms range from imposing edifices symbolizing sacred or secular authority to simple bamboo or thatch gates of teahouse gardens.

Temple gateways establish hierarchic divisions between different parts of the Buddhist temple and give eloquent testimony to the power and authority of Buddhism in Japan. The *nandaimon*, or "south great gate," is the main exterior gateway of the temple, located on its major north–south axis. The *chūmon*, or "inner gate," provides access to the inner precinct of the temple and is usually aligned with the *nandaimon* on the north–south axis. See also BUDDHIST ARCHITECTURE.

The open TORII gateway is a distinctive feature of native SHINTŌ ARCHITECTURE. It consists primarily of two principal columns and bridging architrave, and its absence of doors symbolizes permanent openness. Placement of *torii* at intervals along the approaches to sacred sites was borrowed from Buddhist practice. Early Shintō shrines, or those preserving ancient forms such as ISE SHRINE, have gates identical to Buddhist temple gateways.

Mansion Gates — Gates are also an important feature of domestic architecture. They were integral to the SHINDEN-ZUKURI mansions of the aristocracy during the Heian period (794–1185). Contemporary picture scrolls (EMAKIMONO) show three common gate types. The *agetsuchimon*, or "raised earth gate," is a simple two-pillared gate set into and supported by the outer wall of the mansion. It is roofed with wooden slats and covered with clay for weatherproofing and decoration. The *munamon*, or "ridged gate," is incorporated into the mansion wall but has a more elaborate gabled roof of wood shingle or tile. The *yotsuashimon*, or "four-legged gate," was usually larger than the *agetsuchimon* and *munamon* and was freestanding by virtue of two pillars at the front and two central pillars bracing the rear. Mansion gateways such as these were important sta-

tus symbols and objects of government regulations, which ensured close correlation between architectural style and the social status of the family for which they were constructed. New gate types developed in response to changing political and social circumstances in the Kamakura period (1185–1333). Gate style became a virtual badge of rank within the *samurai* class.

Castle Gates — Gates were a vital aspect of the fortifications of CASTLES of the Azuchi-Momoyama (1568–1600) and Edo (1600–1868) periods. Gateways were constructed at critical points of entry and had to be defended effectively to maintain the security of the castle. They were often incorporated into ingenious mazelike entrances and cunningly constructed to maximize their defensive advantage. The *masugatamon*, for example, was a commonly used barbican gateway of great size and strength. A small outer gate affords limited access to, and therefore hinders ready escape from, a courtyard surrounded by high walls and a heavily guarded tower gate. Attackers could easily be dealt with in the confined space of the courtyard from the numerous fire positions overlooking it. EDO CASTLE was protected by a ring of these *masugatamon*, which also provided articulate expression of the shogunate's power.

GATT 関税と貿易に関する一般協定

(General Agreement on Tariffs and Trade; J: Gatto; Kanzei to Bōeki ni kansuru Ippan Kyōtei). Set of international agreements established in 1947 to provide a forum for the creation of rules regulating world trade and to reduce worldwide tariff levels. Japan applied to join GATT in 1952. Initially some GATT signatories opposed Japanese membership on the grounds that Japan still maintained substantial tariff barriers and that the export competitiveness of Japanese textiles and other labor-intensive sectors threatened their domestic industries. The United States supported Japan's membership and encouraged approval of its application by offering tariff reductions to those GATT nations that agreed to Japan's entry. After three years of difficult negotiations, Japan gained admittance to GATT in August 1955. At that time 14 member nations invoked the agreement's article 35, which allowed them to withhold most-favored-nation status from new GATT members. In subsequent decades Japan liberalized its trading practices and successfully negotiated an end to the treatment imposed by most of these 14 nations.

Japan originally was allowed to maintain some import restrictions to prevent chronic BALANCE OF PAYMENTS deficits, but by 1963 it was required to fulfill the principles of article 11, which prohibits nations from imposing quantitative import restrictions. As a consequence, the percentage of Japan's imports not covered by any restrictions increased to about 90 percent in 1963, from a level of about 40 percent in 1960.

The Tōkyō Round of multilateral trade negotiations under GATT, held from 1973 to 1979, brought steep reductions in tariff rates, second only to the reductions achieved during the Kennedy Round negotiations a decade earlier. Agreements were also reached on the establishment of codes to regulate eight categories of nontariff barriers, including subsidies and countervailing measures. Another round of GATT negotiations, the Uruguay Round, was proposed to President Ronald Reagan by Prime Minister NAKASONE YASUHIRO at the November 1983 United

gateball The first national gateball competition, held in 1986. This outdoor game was developed in Japan and is a favorite form of exercise for older people.

States–Japan summit. As a result of the multilateral GATT negotiations, separate bilateral agreements, and various initiatives to open markets by the Japanese government, Japan's remaining tariffs and import restrictions are among the lowest maintained by any developed nation.

Gaun nikkenroku 臥雲日件録

Diary of the Zen priest Zuikei Shūhō (1391–1473) of the temple Shōkokuji in Kyōto. Zuikei (pen name Gaun) was a confidant of the shōgun ASHIKAGA YOSHIMASA. The diary covers the years from 1446 to 1473 and is an important source of information on Zen Buddhism. The original text had 74 fascicles, but the work survives only in a partial copy made by Ikō Myōan in 1562.

geese 雁

(*gan* or *kari*). Large water birds of the family Anatidae, measuring 61–87 centimeters (2–3 ft) in length. The bodies of most geese, both male and female, are grayish brown. Nine species have been recorded in Japan, all as winter visitors. They frequent broad paddies and fields, salt marshes, and coastal waters, but in recent years have become rare except in wildlife refuges. Among the geese found in Japan, the *kokugan* (brant; *Branta bernicla*) and *magan* (white-fronted goose; *Anser albifrons*) are also found in both Europe and North America; the *haiirogan* (greylag goose; *A. anser*), *karigane* (lesser white-fronted goose; *A. erythropus*), and *hishikui* (bean goose; *A. fabalis*) are found in Europe; and the *shijūkaragan* (Canada goose; *B. canadensis*), *hakugan* (snow goose; *A. caerulescens*), and *mikadogan* (emperor goose; *A. canagicus*) are found in North America. The only species found in Asia alone is the now rare *sakatsuragan* (swan goose; *A. cygnoides*).

Geese are mentioned in the earliest Japanese chronicles. Their arrival is used in poetry to symbolize the coming of autumn, a convention borrowed from China.

Geiami 芸阿弥

(1431–85). Successor of NŌAMI as DŌBŌSHŪ, the painter-connoisseur-curator of the Ashikaga shōguns' collection. Also known as Shingei. He appears to have worked for the shōguns from at least 1458 on, and like Nōami and his own son and successor SŌAMI, he gave evaluations of paintings and was charged with the care of the collection. Geiami's only fully attested painting, *Viewing a Waterfall* (*Kambakuzu*; in the collection of the NEZU ART MUSEUM), was given to his student Kenkō SHŌKEI when they parted. The landscape mode of Geiami was based on Southern Song (Sung; 1127–1279) academy model styles, notably that of Xia Gui (Hsia

geisha An 1869 woodblock-print triptych depicts three *geisha* practicing on traditional instruments (left panel, *kokyū*; center, *shamisen*; right, *koto*). Such musical accomplishments are an important part of the geisha's repertoire of skills.

Kuei). Moreover his artistic heritage, reflected in works of the Shōkei school in Kamakura, further suggest that he paid little attention to the wash-oriented landscape styles of Muqi (Mu-ch'i; J: MOKKEI) and Yujian (Yü-chien); he does appear, however, to have transmitted, like so many contemporaries, a Muqi-oriented style in figure paintings. See also AMI SCHOOL; INK PAINTING.

Geibikei   猊鼻渓

Gorge in the town of Higashiyama, southern Iwate Prefecture, northern Honshū. Approximately 2 km (1.2 mi) long, it abounds in steep cliffs and strangely shaped rocks on both sides of the river Satetsugawa, a tributary of the Kitakamigawa.

geisha   芸者

Also called *geigi* and *geiko*. Traditional female entertainers who provide singing, dancing, conversation, games, and companionship to customers in certain restaurants. The *geisha* world in general is referred to as the *karyūkai* ("flower and willow world").

The total number of geisha in the 1920s was roughly 80,000. In the late 1980s geisha numbered around 10,000. One reason for their current decline in number is the encroachment by Western-style bar hostesses.

The Profession — The profession of geisha is rather unusual in the Japanese entertainment business because women can make it a lifelong career. Since the premium is on artistic skills and conversational abilities rather than just youth and good looks, geisha may continue to work to an advanced age. If they cease working as geisha, many go into related occupations, such as operating a restaurant, bar, or shop where they can use their geisha background and connections to advantage. Occasionally they become the mistress or even the wife of a customer.

When geisha marry, they leave their profession. While they are working their relations with men may be of several types. It is generally considered desirable to have a patron (*danna*) with whom the geisha is involved emotionally, sexually, and economically. Every geisha also tries to build up a clientele of dependable favorite customers (*gohiiki*).

Before World War II, a geisha generally had to have a patron to help support her, and every geisha apprentice had to undergo the "defloration ceremony" (*mizuage*) with some important customer before she could attain full geisha status. But now it is quite possible to make a living from wages and tips alone, so the matter of whether or not

to accept a man as one's patron can be decided more freely.

Training — No matter where they work, aspiring geisha must take lessons in various traditional arts. Lessons are required in classical dancing, playing the SHAMISEN (a stringed instrument), and several styles of singing.

Traditionally children were often adopted into geisha houses (*okiya*) for training. Such girls (called *shikomi*) were assigned much of the household drudgery as part of their discipline and were treated like maids or servants. Sometimes girls were indentured by their parents, especially in times of famine when a family could not support all its children.

From the ages of about 13 to 18 would-be geisha used to serve as apprentices, generically termed *oshaku* and called *hangyoku* ("half-jewel") in the Kantō area around Tōkyō or *maiko* (dance child) in the Kansai area around Kyōto and Ōsaka. Such apprentices wore a distinctive kimono and hairstyle while they underwent their initial training period. At present the apprentice stage has all but vanished in Tōkyō, while the *maiko* in Kyōto are dwindling. One reason for this is the compulsory education law requiring everyone to complete middle school, with the usual age of graduation at 15. This means a modern-day *maiko* starts out at the age when traditionally she would be getting ready to assume full-fledged geisha status.

Organization — The geisha are divided into discrete groups called *hanamachi* ("flower towns"), each organized around its own registry office (*kemban*). Every geisha must be registered in her particular area and receive her assignments through the *kemban* to attend those establishments that are members of the "restaurant union" (*ryōtei kumiai*) of the area. *Ryōtei* is a generic term for this kind of restaurant, although in Kyōto establishments where geisha entertain are generally called *ochaya*. Meals are brought in to *ochaya* by catering shops called *ryōriya*.

The guest makes arrangements for geisha entertainment through these restaurants and must abide by the rules of the geisha union (*geigi kumiai*) regarding a geisha's times of attendance and fees. The local *kemban* is the central organizing office that coordinates geisha schedules and is also the location of the "three unions" (*sangyō kumiai*) that are the working elements of each *hanamachi*. Along with the restaurant union and geisha union, there is the geisha house union (*geigiya kumiai*) consisting of those establishments with a license (*kamban*).

The geisha fee (called *hanadai*, *senkōdai*,

or *gyokudai*) applies equally to all geisha in a given area. It is referred to in units of "sticks," since the fee was formerly figured by the length of time it took a stick of incense (*senkō*) to burn down. Currently one hour is generally considered to be "one stick."

History — The geisha system emerged around the mid-Edo period (1600–1868). The first geisha were male entertainers (also called HŌKAN or *taikomochi*) and thus the first such women were designated *onna* (female) *geisha*. Gradually such entertaining became a female occupation. By the 1700s the profession of geisha was associated with the government-licensed brothel quarters, or *yūkaku* (see YOSHIWARA). From the end of the Edo period to the present, geisha have had considerable connection with politics, as the teahouses provided convenient gathering places for political meetings. Geisha find it professionally in their interest to be closemouthed about what goes on at these gatherings, but even so, opposition factions seldom patronize the same geisha.

Geiyo Islands   芸与諸島

(Geiyo Shotō). Group of islands in the central Inland Sea, between Hiroshima Prefecture, in southwestern Honshū, and Ehime Prefecture, in Shikoku. The group includes Mukaishima, INNOSHIMA, ŌMISHIMA, and Ikuchishima. They are hilly islands with an average elevation of about 400 m (1,312 ft). Principal activities are the cultivation of citrus fruits and shipbuilding. The islands have many scenic spots as well as historic remains of ancient piracy. In the early 1980s work began on a series of bridges to connect Honshū and Shikoku via the Geiyo Islands.

gejijō   下知状

A form of old document (*komonjo*); also known as *gechijō*. A modification of the KUDASHIBUMI style of document, *gejijō* were used to transmit orders to subordinates. They were named for the concluding words *geji kudan no gotoshi* ("the above is herewith ordered"). During the Kamakura period (1185–1333) *gejijō* were issued by shogunate officials to hand down decisions in lawsuits, confirm landholdings (ANDO), and order prohibitions. *Gejijō* were used less frequently in the Edo period (1600–1868). See also DIPLOMATICS.

Gekidan Haiyūza   劇団俳優座

SHINGEKI theater group. Formed in 1944 by the playwrights Aoyama Sugisaku (1889–1956) and SENDA KOREYA and the actors Ozawa Eitarō (b 1909) and Higashiyama Chieko (1890–1980), the group first performed publicly in 1946. One of postwar Japan's most important *shingeki* ("new theater") groups, the Gekidan Haiyūza stages a wide variety of plays ranging from classic foreign works to new works by Japanese playwrights. Its performances of works by such contemporary playwrights as MAFUNE YUTAKA, TANAKA CHIKAO, and ABE KŌBŌ have been particularly successful, and the group was acclaimed for the introduction of the works of Bertolt Brecht to the Japanese public. NAKADAI TATSUYA is one of the best-known actors to have been a member of the Gekidan Haiyūza; Katō Gō (b 1938) and Kurihara Komaki (b 1945) are among its core members today.

Gekidan Mingei   劇団民芸

(Mingei Repertory Theatre Company). SHINGEKI theater company. The company was first established in Tōkyō in 1947 as the Minshū

Geijitsu Gekijō (People's Art Theatre) by a group including the actors UNO JŪKICHI and TAKIZAWA OSAMU. The company disbanded in 1949 and was re-formed by the same group in 1950 under its present name. The company first produced modern Japanese plays by such authors as KUBO SAKAE and KINOSHITA JUNJI, then expanded its repertoire to include works by Chekhov and Arthur Miller. The death of Uno in 1988 dealt the company a great blow, but the members continue to carry on the tradition of modern realistic theater that he helped establish.

Gekidan Shiki　劇団四季

(Shiki Theatrical Company). Theater company. Founded in 1953 by the director ASARI KEITA in collaboration with the actors Kusaka Takeshi (b 1931) and Fujino Setsuko (1928–86). With the traditional Western theater as their ideal, they began by producing works by Jean Giraudoux and Jean Anouilh. After 1970, the Gekidan Shiki began to produce such Anglo-American musicals as *Jesus Christ Superstar* (1973) and *Cats* (1984), becoming the most popular and the best-attended major theater group in Japan.

gekokujō　下剋上

(literally, "those below overcoming those above"). A term applied to political or social upheaval when persons of inferior status displace their superiors: when vassals usurp the place of their lords or when junior officers reject the authority of their commanders. The term probably first occurs in the GEMPEI SEISUIKI, an anonymous 13th-century military romance. It appears most frequently in the diaries of court nobles and in the military chronicles of the 14th–16th centuries. These times witnessed destruction of the KAMAKURA SHOGUNATE (1333); the failure of Emperor GO-DAIGO to restore imperial rule (1333–38; see KEMMU RESTORATION); the treachery of ASHIKAGA TAKAUJI, who established the MUROMACHI SHOGUNATE (1338); the lengthy war between the NORTHERN AND SOUTHERN COURTS (1337–92); the devastating ŌNIN WAR (1467–77); and the century of warfare among provincial *daimyō* that followed. A passage in the TAIHEIKI, a military romance of the mid-14th century, reads, "Now is a time when vassal kills lord and child kills father. Only naked strength prevails. Indeed it is the extremity of *gekokujō*." Since the medieval period (mid-12th–16th centuries) writers have used the term loosely to describe a variety of situations in which established authority was being challenged from below, such as the coup plots and military insubordination of the 1930s (see FEBRUARY 26TH INCIDENT; MILITARISM).

Gembikei　厳美渓

Gorge in the city of Ichinoseki, southern Iwate Prefecture, northern Honshū. Created when the Iwaigawa, a tributary of the Kitakamigawa, carved through veins of liparite for a distance of about 2 km (1.2 mi). It abounds in waterfalls and strangely shaped rocks.

Gembo　玄昉

(?–746). Buddhist priest and court official of the Nara period (710–794). In 717, with the scholar KIBI NO MAKIBI, he accompanied an embassy to Tang China (see SUI AND TANG [T'ANG] CHINA, EMBASSIES TO), where he studied HOSSŌ SECT doctrines. Gembō returned to Japan in 735. In 737 he was made *sōjō* (primate); he and Kibi no Makibi soon became influential in government under the patronage of Emperor SHŌMU and TACHIBANA NO

Gembudō Eleven meters at its deepest point, this basaltic cave is part of the San'in Coast National Park.

MOROE. In 740 Fujiwara no Hirotsugu rebelled against the government in an attempt to overthrow them (see FUJIWARA NO HIROTSUGU, REBELLION OF); he failed, but Gembō's position was no longer secure. Gembō's influence in Nara declined with the rise to power of FUJIWARA NO NAKAMARO, the favorite of Shōmu's consort, Empress KŌMYŌ. In 745 Nakamaro banished him to Kyūshū, where he died the following year.

Gembudō　玄武洞

Basaltic cave in the city of Toyooka, northern Hyōgo Prefecture, western Honshū, formed by quarrying operations conducted there in premodern times. Located on a mountain slope on the east bank of the river Maruyamagawa, it is composed of hexagonal and other types of columnar joints and has been designated as a natural monument. Gembudō is flanked by similar caves called Seiryūdō and Suzakudō.

gembun itchi　言文一致

(unification of the spoken and written language). Process through which the classical styles of the written language (*bungo*) used in the Meiji period (1868–1912) were replaced by colloquial styles (*kōgo*).The written language of the late Edo period (1600–1868) comprised an almost continuous chain of styles ranging from pure classical Chinese, through its adaptations and mixed forms, to pure classical Japanese. After the Meiji Restoration of 1868 some of these styles continued to be used, but in addition a new modernized classical style, the Classical Standard, evolved from them. Neither the traditional styles nor the Classical Standard were close to spoken Japanese, and they were incomprehensible without concentrated study. At the same time that the Classical Standard emerged, a new style of language, the Colloquial Standard, developed in Tōkyō and penetrated gradually into the domains of the classical styles, and it is this process that has been given the name *gembun itchi.* The term was first used by KANDA TAKAHIRA in 1885. The first great achievement in employing a colloquial style in writing was FUTABATEI SHIMEI's *Ukigumo* (1887–89; tr in *Japan's First Modern Novel: Ukigumo of Futabatei Shimei,* 1967). Other writers followed suit, and by 1908 all novels were in the Colloquial Standard. Primary school textbooks completed the switch by 1903, and the transition of the

newspapers to the Colloquial Standard was completed in the 1920s. The contemporary Colloquial Standard (Standard Japanese) uses basically the same grammar as contemporary spoken Japanese, but many of its written styles are considerably different from the spoken language in their complicated syntax and in their vocabulary.

Gempei no Sōran → Taira-Minamoto War

Gempei seisuiki　源平盛衰記

(The Rise and Fall of the Genji and Heike). Also known as *Gempei jōsuiki.* Military chronicle (GUNKI MONOGATARI) of unknown authorship dating from the late Kamakura period (1185–1333), it recounts the shifting fortunes of the MINAMOTO FAMILY (or Genji) and of the TAIRA FAMILY (or Heike) at the close of the Heian period (794–1185). Generally considered to be a variant of another famous military chronicle, the HEIKE MONOGATARI, it has greater historical detail and breadth than that work, especially in descriptions of the Minamoto. It includes a large number of incidental legends, religious fables, and tales from Chinese antiquity not included in the *Heike monogatari.* The style features a mixture of Japanese and Sino-Japanese vocabulary (*wakan konkōbun*) and seems to have been intended for reading, unlike the *Heike monogátari,* which was generally recited by professional entertainers or bards. See also TAIRA-MINAMOTO WAR.

gempuku　元服

A coming-of-age ceremony, observed from at least the 7th century through the Edo period (1600–1868), in which a boy assumed adult clothing, hairstyle, and name. There was no precise age for the ceremony (in early times it was performed when a boy reached the height of about 136 cm [4.5 ft]), but it generally fell between the ages of 10 and 16, depending on family convenience. After the ceremony the boy was considered eligible to take on adult responsibilities, participate in religious ceremonies, and marry. Among the court nobility the event was known as *kanrei* or "cap ceremony," because it was then that the young man began to wear the kind of cap called a *kammuri* (see HEADGEAR). Girls had a similar ceremony between the ages of 12 and 16.

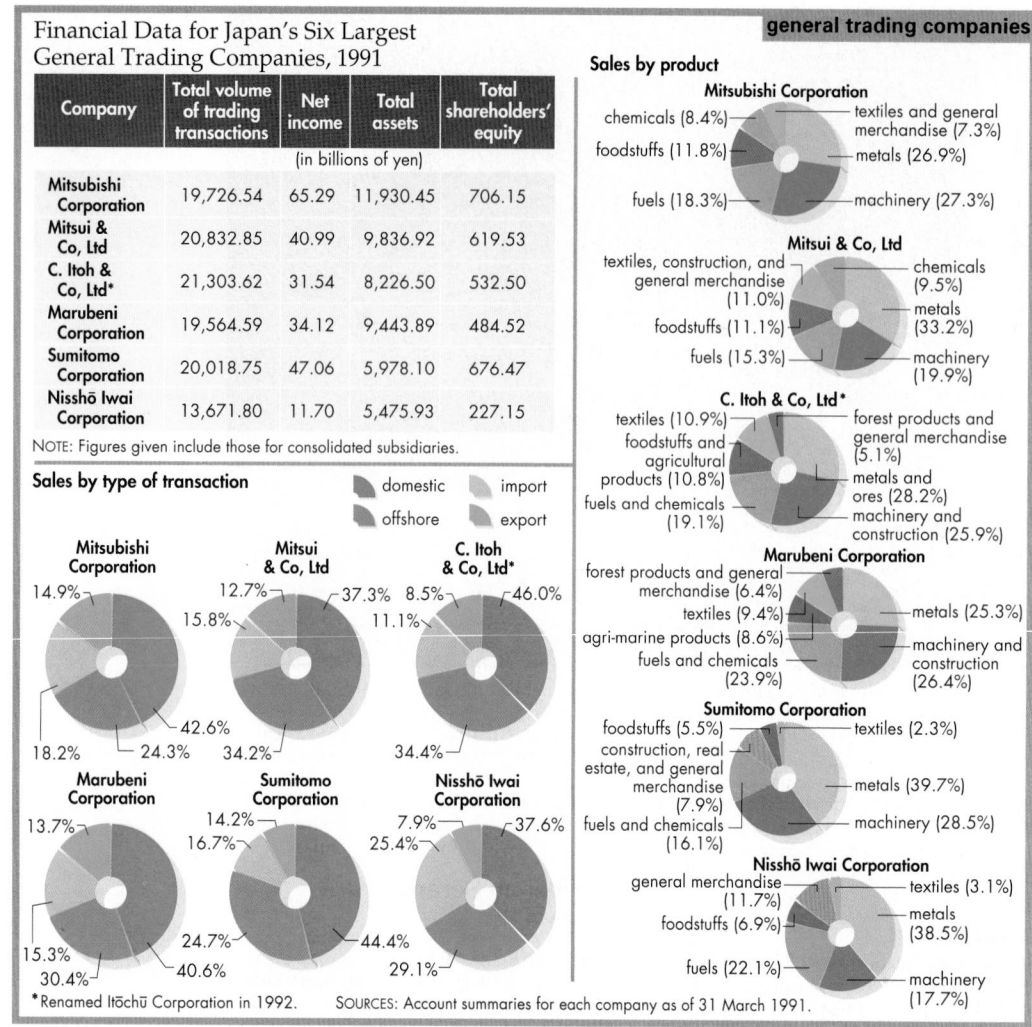

Financial Data for Japan's Six Largest General Trading Companies, 1991

Company	Total volume of trading transactions	Net income	Total assets	Total shareholders' equity
	(in billions of yen)			
Mitsubishi Corporation	19,726.54	65.29	11,930.45	706.15
Mitsui & Co, Ltd	20,832.85	40.99	9,836.92	619.53
C. Itoh & Co, Ltd*	21,303.62	31.54	8,226.50	532.50
Marubeni Corporation	19,564.59	34.12	9,443.89	484.52
Sumitomo Corporation	20,018.75	47.06	5,978.10	676.47
Nisshō Iwai Corporation	13,671.80	11.70	5,475.93	227.15

NOTE: Figures given include those for consolidated subsidiaries.

Sales by type of transaction — domestic, import, offshore, export

Mitsubishi Corporation: 14.9%, 15.8%, 18.2%, 24.3%, 42.6%
Mitsui & Co, Ltd: 12.7%, 37.3%, 34.2%
C. Itoh & Co, Ltd*: 8.5%, 46.0%, 11.1%, 34.4%
Marubeni Corporation: 13.7%, 15.3%, 30.4%, 40.6%, 24.7%
Sumitomo Corporation: 14.2%, 16.7%, 44.4%, 24.7%
Nisshō Iwai Corporation: 7.9%, 37.6%, 25.4%, 29.1%

* Renamed Itōchū Corporation in 1992. SOURCES: Account summaries for each company as of 31 March 1991.

Sales by product

Mitsubishi Corporation: chemicals (8.4%), foodstuffs (11.8%), fuels (18.3%), textiles and general merchandise (7.3%), metals (26.9%), machinery (27.3%)

Mitsui & Co, Ltd: textiles, construction, and general merchandise (11.0%), foodstuffs (11.1%), fuels (15.3%), chemicals (9.5%), metals (33.2%), machinery (19.9%)

C. Itoh & Co, Ltd*: textiles (10.9%), foodstuffs and agricultural products (10.8%), fuels and chemicals (19.1%), forest products and general merchandise (5.1%), metals and ores (28.2%), machinery and construction (25.9%)

Marubeni Corporation: forest products and general merchandise (6.4%), textiles (9.4%), agri-marine products (8.6%), fuels and chemicals (23.9%), metals (25.3%), machinery and construction (26.4%)

Sumitomo Corporation: foodstuffs (5.5%), construction, real estate, and general merchandise (7.9%), fuels and chemicals (16.1%), textiles (2.3%), metals (39.7%), machinery (28.5%)

Nisshō Iwai Corporation: general merchandise (11.7%), foodstuffs (6.9%), fuels (22.1%), textiles (3.1%), metals (38.5%), machinery (17.7%)

Even today, the idea of a formal coming-of-age ceremony survives in the national holiday Coming-of-Age Day (Seijin no Hi). Observed each 15 January, young people who have reached their legal majority (20 years) in the past year are encouraged to visit shrines and attend receptions held by local governments. See also LIFE CYCLE.

Gendaishi techō 現代詩手帖

(Contemporary Poetry Notebook). Monthly poetry journal published since June 1959 by Shichōsha. *Gendaishi techō* plays a key role in fostering contemporary poetry through its efforts to discover new talent while at the same time opening its pages to poets of all ages and styles. In recent years it has invited contributions from writers active in fields other than poetry and poetics.

Genda Minoru 源田実

(1904–89). Naval officer and politician. Born in Hiroshima Prefecture. He graduated from the Naval Academy in 1924. Admiral YAMAMOTO ISOROKU chose him to draft the details of the plan for the attack on PEARL HARBOR. After the war he joined the Air Self Defense Force and was its chief of staff from 1959 to 1962. From 1962 to 1986 he was a member of the House of Councillors.

Gen'e 玄慧

(?–1350). Buddhist priest and Confucian scholar. Gen'e tutored Emperor GO-DAIGO in the Confucian classics and was involved in the KEMMU RESTORATION. ASHIKAGA TAKAUJI, who overthrew Go-Daigo, employed Gen'e to help him formulate the KEMMU SHIKIMOKU, the basic code of the Muromachi shogunate

(1338–1573). TEIKIN ŌRAI, a manual of letter writing, is also attributed to Gen'e.

genealogy 系譜学

(*keifugaku*). Since ancient Japanese society was based on the family or clan (UJI) system and appointment to public office was hereditary, keen interest in genealogy dates from earliest times. In 815 the genealogical records known as SHINSEN SHŌJIROKU were completed, listing more than 1,100 families of the capital region. The Japanese words *keifu* and *keizu* are used interchangeably to mean genealogical records but, strictly speaking, *keizu* are graphic representations of *keifu*, or genealogical relations. The charts known as *kakeizu* usually recorded the line of male descent.

In the Kamakura (1185–1333) and Muromachi (1333–1568) periods lineage and family tradition were closely connected with rights to family landholdings and other property, and many counterfeit genealogies appeared. The SOMPI BUMMYAKU, compiled by Tōin Kinsada (1340–99) and others, is fairly reliable. The principal genealogical works of the Edo period (1600–1868) include the officially sponsored KAN'EI SHOKA KEIZU DEN (1643) and the KANSEI CHŌSHŪ SHOKA FU (1812). These have great historical value, because they were carefully checked by scholars after being presented to the Tokugawa shogunate.

gene banks 遺伝子銀行

(*idenshi ginkō*). Facilities for the collection and storage of plant and animal genes and cell cultures for cytogenetic research and breeding. Research in the field of biotechnology developed rapidly in Japan during the 1980s, and a number of gene banks were established by the Japanese government, in-

dependent regional organizations, and commercial firms. The following three facilities, mutually distinct in function, are the most important Japanese gene banks, supplying materials to a variety of research institutions.

In 1985 the Ministry of Health and Welfare established the Japan Cancer Research Resources Bank in Shinagawa Ward, Tōkyō, under the auspices of the National Institute of Health. The bank's chief role is the collection and storage of DNA clones for cancer research in support of the Comprehensive Ten-Year Strategy for Cancer Control initiated in 1984. The National Center of Genetic Resources was established in 1985 by the Ministry of Agriculture, Forestry, and Fisheries as an organ of the National Institute for Agrobiological Resources, which is located in the city of Tsukuba, Ibaraki Prefecture. The center engages in the collection of seeds, spermatozoa of domestic animals, useful microorganisms, and other biological resources related to agricultural production for purposes such as the improvement of species. In 1987, with the object of developing Japanese biotechnology, the Science and Technology Agency founded the Riken Gene Bank in Tsukuba as a facility attached to the Institute of Physical and Chemical Research. The bank collects and stores DNA clones and cell cultures.

general clause 一般条項

(*ippan jōkō*). A legal term referring to a provision that abstractly and generally determines legal conditions; also called a summary provision. Most such instances arise in private law; examples are provisions that determine public order and good morals (see KŌJO RYŌZOKU), ABUSE OF RIGHT, suitable reasons for cancellation of land leases and house leases (Leased Land Law, art. 4; Leased House Law, art. 1, para. 2), and major reasons making the continuation of a marriage relationship difficult (CIVIL CODE, art. 770). In public law, provisions regarding determinations for which there are no concrete standards are also called general clauses.

General Council of Trade Unions of Japan →Sōhyō

General Sekiyu KK ゼネラル石油[株]

(Zeneraru Sekiyu). Marketer of petroleum products. Incorporated in 1947. Affiliated with Exxon, the company imports, refines, and sells a variety of petroleum products. It has strengthened its affiliation with Esso Sekiyu in both production and distribution of oil products. Sales for the fiscal year ending March 1991 totaled ¥579.5 billion (US $4.2 billion), of which gasoline accounted for 40 percent; naphtha, 12 percent; fuel and crude oil, 23 percent; kerosene and gas oil, 16 percent; and liquefied petroleum gas and other products, 9 percent. The company was capitalized at ¥10.2 billion (US $74.3 million) in the same year. Headquarters are in Tōkyō.

General Strike of 1947 二・一スト

(Niichi Suto; literally, February First Strike). A general strike scheduled for 1 February 1947 but prohibited on 31 January by General Douglas MACARTHUR, supreme commander for the Allied powers. It was the first confrontation between labor and the OCCUPATION, which until then had not only officially encouraged unionization but remained neutral in labor disputes. The strike promised a show of labor unity between government employees and the private sector.

Much, but not all, of the initiative came from communist or procommunist organizers and the radical labor federation SAMBETSU KAIGI. The demands of the strike were both economic and political: higher wages, the guarantee of minimum wages to counter spiraling inflation, and the resignation of the YOSHIDA SHIGERU cabinet and its replacement by a leftist coalition.

In the aftermath of the Occupation ban, labor unity was shattered (it is still a problem today), and the communists lost most of their influence in the labor movement to the more moderate socialists.

general trading companies
総合商社

(*sōgō shōsha*). Large, highly diversified Japanese commercial houses that structure and facilitate the flow of goods, services, and money among client firms, operating both within Japan and globally. Nine firms (MITSUBISHI CORPORATION; MITSUI & CO, LTD; ITŌ-CHŪ CORPORATION; MARUBENI CORPORATION; SUMITOMO CORPORATION; NISSHŌ IWAI CORPORATION; TŌMEN CORPORATION; KANEMATSU CORPORATION; and NICHIMEN CORPORATION) are considered to constitute the ranks of the general trading companies, although some smaller and less diverse trading houses are also sometimes called by the same designation. The total sales of the nine firms equaled almost 29 percent of Japan's gross national product in 1990, and the imports and exports handled by them accounted for about half of the nation's foreign trade.

The *sōgō shōsha* have their roots in the development of industry and foreign trade during the Meiji period (1868–1912). The functions of a *sōgō shōsha* include both financing and conducting trade. A firm may offer its clients a wide assortment of financing—including trade credit, inventory financing, factoring, loan guarantees, and even equity participation—as well as financial services such as foreign-exchange risk management. In Japan, the *sōgō shōsha* are very important sources of funds for business borrowing. They also play an important role in the establishment of large-scale projects by consortia of firms, especially overseas. Each of the six largest *sōgō shōsha* is a member of one of the six major enterprise groups (see KEIRETSU).

The trading firms compete vigorously with each other to maximize trading volume, while cutting their margins typically to 1 or 2 percent. The average pretax profit on sales of the nine firms was 0.33 percent in 1991. Nonetheless, since the firms deal in huge quantities, revenues are substantial. Even more than on price, *sōgō shōsha* compete on service, endeavoring to make themselves into "eyes and ears" for their clients, bringing opportunities to their attention.

Geneva Naval Conference of 1927
ジュネーブ海軍軍縮会議

(Junēbu Kaigun Gunshuku Kaigi). Naval conference held from June to August 1927 in Geneva, Switzerland, and attended by representatives of Great Britain, the United States, and Japan to discuss the limitation of auxiliary ships (cruisers, destroyers, and submarines). This conference followed the WASHINGTON CONFERENCE of 1921–22, which had set limits on the size of each country's fleet of battleships. The discussions were inconclusive, largely because of substantial disagreements among the participating nations, and the issue remained unresolved until the LONDON NAVAL CONFERENCES.

genin
下人

(literally, "inferior people"). A term applied to the lower class from the early Heian period (794–1185) through the Edo period (1600–1868). Initially a general term for people of low class, in late Heian times it came to mean bond servants of proprietary estates (SHŌEN) and religious institutions, as well as of aristocrats, *samurai*, and independent cultivators (MYŌSHU). By the Kamakura period (1185–1333) *genin* supplied a majority of agricultural labor, although it was by no means the only function in which they served. They lived in their masters' households, had no economic rights, marital choice, or freedom of movement, and could be sold, transferred, or bequeathed as property. From the late Muromachi period (1333–1568) onward, *genin* were tenant farmers with rights to the land. By the Edo period, *genin* referred to annually contracted tenant farmers and to servants in general. See also NAGO; FUDAI.

Genji→Minamoto family

Genji Keita
源氏鶏太

(1912–85). Novelist. Real name Tanaka Tomio. Born in Toyama Prefecture. He had been a white-collar worker for more than 15 years when he wrote his first short story, "Tabako musume" (1947, Cigarette Girl). The joys and sorrows of white-collar workers are described with humor and pathos in *Santō jūyaku* (1951–52, A Third-Rate Executive). His "Eigoyasan" (1951; tr "The English Interpreter," 1972) received the Naoki Prize.

Genji monogatari→Tale of Genji

Genji monogatari emaki
源氏物語絵巻

(*Tale of Genji* Scrolls). General term for illustrated handscrolls (EMAKIMONO) portraying scenes from the 11th-century novel TALE OF GENJI (*Genji monogatari*) and accompanied by prose passages. Elaborate and richly colored as a rule, *Genji* illustrations have formed one of the main themes of YAMATO-E (native-style Japanese painting) since the 12th century.

The oldest and finest examples of *Genji* handscrolls now exist only in sections and are found in the Tokugawa Art Museum, Nagoya, and the Gotō Art Museum, Tōkyō, with a few additional fragments in other collections. All date from the early 12th century, slightly more than 100 years after the novel was written. Only 13 of the 54 chapters of the *Tale of Genji* are represented among the 20 surviving illustrations for these handscrolls, 19 of which have prose explanations. The complete set would probably have comprised 10 or 12 scrolls with 80 or 90 illustrations. The paintings are relatively uniform in size: 21 to 22 centimeters (8.3 to 8.7 in) wide and either 39 or 48 centimeters (15.4 or 18.9 in) long.

Elements of Style——Perhaps the most striking peculiarity of the style is that both male and female figures have round, fat-cheeked faces, generally in three-quarter view, with the same highly conventional features: thick eyebrows, eyes that appear at first to be a single line (*hikime*), a simple hook shape for the nose (*kagibana*), and a small red dot for the mouth. A careful com-

Genji monogatari emaki Detail of an illustration from the *Tale of Genji* Scrolls showing an episode in the 36th chapter, "Kashiwagi." Genji (upper left) holds the baby Kaoru, son of Genji's wife and Kashiwagi. 12th century. Colors on paper. Tokugawa Art Museum, Nagoya, Aichi Prefecture. National Treasure.

Genji Keita The world of the white-collar worker inspired many of the tales by this popular novelist who kept his office job for nine years after becoming a successful writer.

parison of the faces shows that, despite their apparent simplicity and lack of individuality, there are differences in facial expression, producing subtle variations in emotional effect.

The interior views utilize a strongly diagonal perspective combined with the FUKINUKI YATAI, or "blown-off roof" technique. In this treatment roofs of buildings are omitted to produce clear overhead views of the inhabitants. An example of this type of composition is the first illustration for the chapter "Kashiwagi," in which the retired emperor visits his daughter, who, having betrayed her husband, Genji, has decided to become a nun. The steep diagonal lines of the architecture, crossed at many different angles by the screens set up around the lady, emphasize the conflicting emotions of the characters.

The single most important factor in the artistic impact of the *Genji monogatari emaki* is the lavish use of thick colors, carefully selected to enhance the mood of each scene. Mineral pigments such as bright red, green, and blue were used together with gold and silver for a gorgeous effect, and the costumes and furnishings were decorated with delicate patterns. Production of the paintings was clearly a group project using an elaborate method of construction referred to in Heian documents as *tsukuri-e*, "manufactured painting." A supervising artist drew outlines in India ink and his assistants painted in the colors.

The accompanying texts are written in a running style on sheets of fine paper made from fibers of the shrub called *gampi* (*Wikstroemia sikokiana*). Each sheet is decorated differently. The decorations of the paper include brown, red, and yellow colors; delicate underpaintings of grasses, flowers, and bamboo; and gold and silver leaf in the form of small squares and triangles, hairlike threads, or tiny dots (*kirihaku, noge*, and *sunago*, respectively).

The Artists — The paintings have been traditionally attributed, at least since the Edo period (1600–1868), to Fujiwara no Takachika (fl mid-12th century) or his father, Takayoshi (1127–74); the calligraphy to Fujiwara no Korefusa (1030–96), JAKUREN, Fujiwara no Masatsune (1170–1221), and Takachika. All of these attributions are plausible, but there is no proof for any of them. Furthermore, it is now clear that the paintings, as well as the calligraphy, are in several distinct hands. A date of circa 1110–20 for the *Genji* scrolls seems likely.

Genkai Sea 玄界灘

(Genkai Nada). Arm of the Sea of Japan off the northern coast of Fukuoka and Saga prefectures, Kyūshū. The East China Sea is on the west, and the Hibiki Sea leads to the Sea of Japan on the east. The Genkai Sea has long been important as a transportation link between Japan and the continent. The Tsushima Current flows through these waters, making them a rich fishing ground. Average depth: 50–60 m (165–200 ft); deepest point: approximately 100 m (330 ft).

Genkō → Mongol invasions of Japan

Genkō Incident 元弘の変

(Genkō no Hen). Civil strife (1331–33) that led to the fall of the KAMAKURA SHOGUNATE. Emperor GO-DAIGO, determined to rule and keep succession in his line, had been enlist-

ing supporters against the HŌJŌ FAMILY regents and the shogunate since his unsuccessful coup of 1324 (see SHŌCHŪ CONSPIRACY). In 1331 he fled to Nara; the shogunate set up Emperor KŌGON of the rival line. Go-Daigo was captured and exiled to the Oki Islands (now part of Shimane Prefecture), but Go-Daigo's son Prince MORINAGA continued resistance with KUSUNOKI MASASHIGE. In 1333 Go-Daigo escaped. ASHIKAGA TAKAUJI, the Kamakura general sent to suppress the rebellion, saw an opportunity to become shōgun himself and changed sides, capturing Kyōto in Go-Daigo's name. Shortly thereafter NITTA YOSHISADA marched on Kamakura and destroyed the Hōjō and the shogunate. Go-Daigo returned to Kyōto to inaugurate the KEMMU RESTORATION (1333–36).

Genkō shakusho 元亨釈書

The earliest comprehensive history of Japanese Buddhism; completed in 1322. The author, KOKAN SHIREN, a founder of GOZAN LITERATURE (Chinese secular learning cultivated in the Zen monasteries), wrote entirely in Chinese following Chinese models. There are three major divisions: biographies (*den*), annals (*hyō*), and essays (*shi*). The first division is by far the largest and also the most widely read; together with portions of the essays, a Japanese rendering of it was printed in 1690 for a popular audience. It recounts the lives of over 400 persons, predominantly monks, but also a few women, pious laymen, and even some native deities who the author believed had shown special favor toward Buddhism.

genre painting → fūzokuga

genrō 元老

(elder statesmen; literally, "the original elders"). The unofficial designation given to the "founding fathers" of the modern state of Japan; in the mid-Meiji period (1868–1912) they became the chief advisers to the emperor with the right to select and recommend prime ministers to the emperor for appointment. The *genrō* undoubtedly originated in the traditional councils of elders (RŌJŪ) so common in the Edo period (1600–1868), but the term seems to have been first used by a newspaper in 1892. The term is often linked with the GENRŌIN, the legislative Chamber of Elders in existence from 1875 to 1890, but the establishment of the *genrō* was not related to that body or its abolition. Experienced leaders were singled out for meritorious service, honored by the emperor as *genkun* (veteran or elder statesmen), and asked to act as imperial advisers. The institution was extraconstitutional and informal. With the exception of SAIONJI KIMMOCHI, the last of the *genrō*, who came from an imperial court family, all the *genrō* were *samurai* of medium or lower rank, four each from Chōshū (now Yamaguchi Prefecture) and Satsuma (now Kagoshima Prefecture), the domains that had played the most prominent roles in the MEIJI RESTORATION of 1868 (see HAMBATSU).

The first two Meiji leaders to be given the title of *genkun*, in 1889, were ITŌ HIROBUMI and KURODA KIYOTAKA. Five others were similarly honored later, constituting the original seven Meiji *genrō*. They were MATSUKATA MASAYOSHI, ŌYAMA IWAO, SAIGŌ TSUGUMICHI, YAMAGATA ARITOMO, and INOUE KAORU. These seven men were the SANGI (imperial councillors) who remained in this office when the title, established in 1869, was abolished in

1885. For most of the years from 1885 to 1900, Chōshū and Satsuma *genrō* alternated as prime minister; Itō was prime minister three times, Yamagata and Matsukata twice, and Kuroda once. Between 1901 and 1913 KATSURA TARŌ and Saionji—the protégés of the most powerful *genrō*, Yamagata and Itō—alternated as prime minister. Katsura and Saionji became *genrō* in 1912, but by then the institution's importance had already begun to decline.

Genrōin 元老院

(Chamber of Elders, or Senate). A quasi-legislative body of the early Meiji period (1868–1912). Established in 1875 as part of an administrative reform of the DAJŌKAN system following the ŌSAKA CONFERENCE OF 1875, the Genrōin replaced the Sain (Chamber of the Left) and was responsible for reviewing legislation, although it had no power to initiate legislation. Its members, theoretically nominated by the emperor, were chosen from the ranks of the peerage, upper-grade bureaucrats, and legal scholars. The ministers of the left (*sadaijin*) and right (*udaijin*) served as chairmen. In 1876 the Genrōin was commissioned to draw up a constitution. The draft, the Nihon Kokken An, completed in 1880, was rejected by the government leaders ITŌ HIROBUMI and IWAKURA TOMOMI as too liberal. The Genrōin was dissolved in 1890 with the formation of the IMPERIAL DIET. Although it was short-lived, the Genrōin represented an early attempt by the Meiji government to establish a separation of powers.

Genroku era 元禄時代

(Genroku *jidai*). Genroku, the era name (NENGŌ) for the years 1688–1704, is commonly used to refer to the entire rule of the fifth Tokugawa shōgun, TOKUGAWA TSUNAYOSHI, from 1680 to 1709. It is sometimes used even more broadly to include the flowering of culture, especially among the townsmen (CHŌNIN), from the middle of the 17th to the middle of the 18th centuries.

During the first half of the 17th century, the TOKUGAWA SHOGUNATE established a strict ordering of all groups in the society. It disciplined the *daimyō* and tightened the class order that separated *samurai*, farmers, and townspeople (see SHI-NŌ-KŌ-SHŌ). By the time of the death of the third shōgun, TOKUGAWA IEMITSU, in 1651, and the succession of his son, TOKUGAWA IETSUNA, the security of the regime had been clearly demonstrated and the policy of strict controls gradually moderated. Education of samurai had been encouraged from the early 17th century to direct them toward peacetime employment in administrative functions rather than in military roles. Samurai thus tended to become more bureaucrats and gentlemen than military men. This trend was given special encouragement by Tsunayoshi, who played the role of Confucian pedant and neglected military skills. He also set an example of extravagance and self-indulgence that reflected the spirit of his prosperous times.

There was also an increase in literacy among merchants, other urban residents, and prosperous farmers. The increase in agricultural productivity and the quickening of commerce in the 17th century were accompanied by the rapid growth of cities, in particular Kyōto, Edo (now Tōkyō), and Ōsaka. As unprecedented affluence came to a larger number of merchants and artisans of the cities, their demand for goods and services stimulated the development of new styles of clothing, entertainment, and arts tailored to their tastes. Unlike the samurai, who were disciplined by an obligation to perform military and administrative service, urban commoners were free to devote themselves to making and spending money. Their pastimes were less restrained and their tastes less informed by tradition. While NŌ was considered the form of drama appropriate to the samurai class, KABUKI and PUPPET THEATER, which developed from the early 17th century, were shaped increasingly to *chōnin* audiences, and the Genroku era is celebrated as the golden age of both types of theater. SAKATA TŌJŪRŌ I and Ichikawa Danjūrō I (see ICHIKAWA DAN-JŪRŌ) established distinctive acting styles, while Japan's most famous playwright, CHIKAMATSU MONZAEMON, wrote for both the kabuki and puppet theaters.

The introduction of improved printing techniques from Korea at the end of the 16th century and the encouragement of education spurred a rapid increase of publication by woodblock printing. In addition to Japanese literary classics and Confucian works, smaller books called KANA-ZŌSHI written in simple language became popular. As the readership became larger and more sophisticated, there appeared more urbane stories about contemporary urban society in illustrated books called UKIYO-ZŌSHI (booklets of the floating world). The most famous writer of such works was Ihara SAIKAKU. The UKIYO-E style of painting and prints frequently depicted leading actors and well-known prostitutes. From the second and third decades of the 18th century color began to be added to *ukiyo-e* prints using additional woodblocks, and the art of the multiple-block Japanese print was born.

During the Genroku era there was also a resurgence of the Tosa style of painting (see TOSA SCHOOL), which then merged with the Chinese-inspired KANŌ SCHOOL to become the RIMPA style of Ogata KŌRIN, with its rich colors, strong patterns, and precise draftsmanship. A similar boldness of design was also found in YŪZEN (textile dyeing) and NISHIJIN-ORI (silk fabrics), in lacquer and metalwork, and in other crafts.

A major development in poetry was the evolution of Matsuo BASHŌ's style of *haikai no renga* (comic linked verse) and HAIKU (17-syllable poem) composition. Bashō expressed a sensitivity to nature and an understanding of human emotions that made him the most celebrated haiku poet.

The decades that bracketed the turn of the century brought a flowering of scholarship to the samurai class, especially in the study of CONFUCIANISM. Scholars of Chinese studies of this time made original contributions in adapting Confucian ideas to Japanese society. These years also saw the beginning of serious scholarship in classical Japanese literature (see KOKUGAKU). The image popularly invoked by the name of Genroku, however, is of a time of prosperity, extravagance, and indulgence, with only the vendetta of the FORTY-SEVEN RŌNIN INCIDENT to remind people of honor, loyalty, and sacrifice.

Gensen 言泉

A dictionary of the Japanese language in five volumes plus index. Edited under the supervision of HAGA YAICHI until his death in 1927 and published 1921–29, it is a revision and enlargement of OCHIAI NAOBUMI's *Kotoba no izumi* (5 vols, 1898–99). It has some 270,000 entries, including not only modern standard Japanese, but also classical Japanese, dialect items, and argot.

Genshin 源信

(942–1017). Scholar monk of the TENDAI SECT of Buddhism. Also known as Eshin Sōzu. Author of the ŌJŌYŌSHŪ (985, Essentials of Pure Land Rebirth) and other works and considered the founder of the Eshin school of Tendai oral transmission. His scholarship had a great influence on the later development of PURE LAND BUDDHISM in Japan.

Genshin was born in Yamato Province (now Nara Prefecture) into a family of provincial gentry named Urabe. It is said that he left home in 950 and entered the Tendai center on Mt. Hiei (HIEIZAN) near Kyōto. He is thought to have been formally received into the Tendai order while in his teens and to have become the disciple of the noted Tendai reformer RYŌGEN (912–985). Genshin first gained fame in 974, when he was appointed to speak in an official debate at one of the Tendai sect's most important ceremonies. He later retired to the Shuryōgon'in, a small, secluded temple, where he devoted himself to scholarship.

Genshin's study of the LOTUS SUTRA convinced him that there must be a way to achieve salvation that was open to all people. His solution was trust in the saving powers of the Buddha AMIDA (Skt: Amitābha). Although none of his artistic works remain, Genshin also gained fame as an artist and sculptor, and he inspired a major style of Buddhist art (RAIGŌZU), in which Amida is depicted welcoming the faithful to the Pure Land.

In Japanese Buddhist circles there has been a long controversy as to whether Genshin was primarily a Tendai or Pure Land thinker, whether his essential message was Tendai enlightenment or Pure Land rebirth. However, for Genshin, Pure Land faith was totally consistent with the Tendai teaching that all beings are destined to ride the "one vehicle" (*ichijō*) to Buddhahood by following seemingly different paths. Pure Land faith was for Genshin one such path, and NEMBUTSU was the fundamental practice for rebirth. Genshin's concept of *nembutsu* was founded on the Tendai scripture *Maka shikan* (Ch: *Mohe zhiguan* or *Mo-ho chih-kuan*) as well as certain Pure Land scriptures, and thus included meditation and contemplation, as well as the invocation of Amida Buddha with the phrase *Namu Amida Butsu;* later ages focused on invocation to the exclusion of the other forms of *nembutsu.* The vivid descriptions of the sufferings of this world and the beatitudes of the Pure Land in his *Ōjōyōshū* have been an enduring inspiration to popular Pure Land faith.

Gensuikin →atomic weapons, movement to ban

Gensuikyō →atomic weapons, movement to ban

gentians 竜胆

(*rindō*). The best known of the various species of the gentian family (Gentianaceae) found in Japan is the *rindō* (*Gentiana scabra* var. *buergeri*), a perennial herb that grows wild in fields and forests of Honshū, Shikoku, and Kyūshū. Its flower has long been a beloved symbol of autumn. It grows to 60 centimeters (24 in), and the stalkless leaves are opposite and lance-shaped. Violet, five-lobed, bell-shaped flowers bloom in autumn. There is also a variety with white flowers, called the *sasarindō.* The roots of the *rindō* are used as a stomach medicine.

The *oyama rindō* (*G. makinoi*) grows wild in alpine areas northward from central Honshū, reaching a height of 20–60 centimeters (8–24 in), with one to seven violet flowers blooming in autumn. Along with the similar species Ezo *rindō* (*G. triflora* var. *japonica*), it is cultivated for cut flowers. The *tōyaku rindō* (*G. algida*), also native to high mountain areas, is 10–25 centimeters (4–10 in) in height and is known as a medicinal herb. The flowers, pale yellow with fine green spots, bloom in summer.

Gentlemen's Agreement 日米紳士協約

(Nichibei Shinshi Kyōyaku). Executive agreement between the United States and Japan in 1907–08 by which the United States limited the number of Japanese immigrants while Japan avoided the embarrassment of having its nationals barred by the act of another government. Its immediate cause was anti-Japanese agitation in California and elsewhere on the US Pacific coast, which, having begun in the early 1890s, became intense in 1905–06 (see SEGREGATION OF JAPANESE SCHOOLCHILDREN IN THE UNITED STATES).

The Gentlemen's Agreement is not a single document; its substance is found in six notes exchanged between the governments in late 1907 and early 1908. Its essence was that Tōkyō agreed not to issue passports valid for the continental United States to laborers, either skilled or unskilled, and that Washington agreed not to object to the issuance of passports to "laborers who have already been in America and to the parents, wives, and children of laborers already resident there." This agreement endured until its unilateral abrogation by the United States in the 1924 immigration act, which, in effect, excluded Japanese.

Intended as a tension-reducing device, the Gentlemen's Agreement did calm tensions for a while. It also unintentionally provided a firm demographic basis for the establishment of second-generation JAPANESE AMERICANS (*nisei*) who, by virtue of their American birth, were citizens. See also UNITED STATES IMMIGRATION ACTS OF 1924, 1952, AND 1965.

Gen'yōsha 玄洋社

(Black Ocean Society). Pioneer ultranationalist group founded in 1881 by Hiraoka Kōtarō (1851–1906), TŌYAMA MITSURU, and other former *samurai* of the Fukuoka domain (now part of Fukuoka Prefecture). They participated in the uprisings of former samurai against the government, but after the government suppressed the SATSUMA REBELLION in 1877, they joined the FREEDOM AND PEOPLE'S RIGHTS MOVEMENT and formed a political organization, the Kōyōsha, to agitate for a national parliament. From 1881 the group argued for Japanese expansion on the Asian mainland; to mark this change of purpose the Kōyōsha was renamed the Gen'yōsha, referring to the Genkai Sea, which separates Japan from Korea.

In 1889 the Gen'yōsha criticized the treaty revision plan of ŌKUMA SHIGENOBU. A society member threw a bomb at Ōkuma, wounding him seriously. The Gen'yōsha also intimidated members of opposition parties and assisted the government in the election interference (see SENKYO KANSHŌ) of 1892. As the SINO-JAPANESE WAR OF 1894–1895 approached, the group engaged in undercover activities in Korea. In the RUSSO-JAPANESE WAR of 1904–05, the Gen'yōsha engaged in covert intelligence-gathering activities. After the

gentians Japanese gentians, popular as potted plants and as cut flowers, have bell-shaped flowers that close at night or on overcast days.

war the Gen'yōsha supported PAN-ASIANISM and cooperated in the annexation of Korea in 1910. It formed the Greater Japan Production Party (Dai Nippon Seisantō) to work against socialism in the labor unions. In its later years the Gen'yōsha produced such important political figures as NAKANO SEIGŌ and HIROTA KŌKI and exerted considerable influence on the politics, diplomacy, and thought of pre–World War II Japan. After World War II, it was disbanded by the OCCUPATION authorities.

Geographical Survey Institute
国土地理院

(Kokudo Chiriin). Government bureau under the Ministry of Construction that conducts geological and topographical surveying and mapmaking. Its major functions involve the collation of geological and topographical data, aerial photographic surveys, the preparation of topographical maps, and the compilation of land utilization maps and tables. It also carries out research in earthquake forecasting and administers examinations for land surveyors. Established in 1888, the parent body of the present organization was part of the land survey section of the General Staff Office of the Japanese Imperial Army. From the end of World War II until 1948, it belonged to the Ministry of Interior, and since then has been under the Ministry of Construction. It was reorganized as the Geographical Survey Institute (GSI) in 1960. Institute headquarters are located in TSUKUBA, and it maintains nine regional survey offices.

geography
地理学

(chirigaku). Descriptive regional geography in Japan dates back to the beginning of the 8th century when regional gazetteers known as FUDOKI were compiled. It was not, however, until after the 17th century that modern geographical concepts emerged. The factors that accelerated the growth of modern geography in Japan were the rational thinking contained in the Zhu Xi (Chu Hsi; see SHUSHIGAKU) and Wang Yangming (see YŌMEIGAKU) schools of Confucianism as well as scientific technology and new knowledge about the world introduced to Japan by Christian missionaries and Dutch traders. Such geographers as NISHIKAWA JOKEN and ARAI HAKUSEKI compiled geographies of Japan and the world. The systematic exploration and surveying of the coastline of Japan by the noted cartographer INŌ TADATAKA culminated in the comprehensive geographic survey DAI NIHON ENKAI YOCHI ZENZU in 1821. Two detailed world maps and geographies compiled during this period were *Shintei bankoku zenzu* (1810) by TAKAHASHI KAGEYASU and *Hakkō tsūshi* (1851) by MITSUKURI GEMPO. Geographies compiled by UCHIMURA KANZŌ, SHIGA SHIGETAKA, and MAKIGUCHI TSUNESABURŌ around the turn of the 20th century played a valuable role in enlightening the people about geography at a time when formal courses in geography were not offered in Japanese universities.

Japanese and world geography are taught for two years in junior high school, and senior high schools offer an elective course that emphasizes anthropogeography. Courses in anthropogeography are generally offered at universities, of which some 75 have independent or semi-independent departments of geography, but only some 20 universities offer graduate study programs.

The oldest geographical society in Japan is the TŌKYŌ GEOGRAPHICAL SOCIETY, established in 1879. The most representative society is the ASSOCIATION OF JAPANESE GEOGRAPHERS (1925). The GEOGRAPHICAL SURVEY INSTITUTE plays an important role in the application of geography and cartography.

Geography in Japan
ジオグラフィーインジャパン

(Jiogurafī in Japan). A collection of academic papers by Japanese geographers in the English language published in 1976 by the ASSOCIATION OF JAPANESE GEOGRAPHERS. Edited by KIUCHI SHINZŌ, this special collection was published in commemoration of the association's 50th anniversary. The papers cover all aspects of geography.

Geological Survey of Japan
地質調査所

(Chishitsu Chōsajo). Government institute that undertakes the drawing of basic geological maps in Japan, as well as the survey and research of Japanese natural resources, geotechnics, and hydraulics. Founded in 1882. Located in the city of Tsukuba, Ibaraki Prefecture. The institute is subordinate to the AGENCY OF INDUSTRIAL SCIENCE AND TECHNOLOGY of the MINISTRY OF INTERNATIONAL TRADE AND INDUSTRY (MITI). It publishes the *Bulletin of the Geological Survey of Japan* (monthly), *Report: Geological Survey of Japan*, and *Geology Monthly*.

Germany and Japan
ドイツと日本

(Doitsu to Nihon). The first well-documented cases of Germans visiting Japan are those of the gunner Hans Wolfgang Braun, who came to Japan in the Dutch service and was ordered in 1639 by the third shōgun, TOKUGAWA IEMITSU, to cast mortars in the Dutch factory at Hirado in what is now Nagasaki Prefecture, and Engelbert KAEMPFER, a physician attached to the Dutch East India Company, who lived in Japan from 1690 to 1692. Philipp Franz von SIEBOLD, another German physician also in the Dutch service, came to Japan in 1823. He traveled throughout the country and taught Western medicine and the Dutch language, playing a major role in introducing Western knowledge to Japan (see WESTERN LEARNING). Siebold later wrote *Nippon, Archiv zur Beschreibung von Japan*, a valuable source of information on 19th-century Japan.

Shortly after the opening of Japan with the arrival of Commodore Matthew PERRY and his US fleet, the first German trader, August Luedorf, arrived in Shimoda in 1855. In 1860 Count Friedrich Albrecht EULENBURG came to Japan as ambassador from Prussia. After four months of difficult negotiations, a treaty of amity and commerce was signed in January 1861; it became effective in January 1864.

During the Meiji period (1868–1912) many Germans came to work in Japan and contributed to the development of Japan's technology and culture (see FOREIGN EMPLOYEES OF THE MEIJI PERIOD). At one period as many as 50 Germans were working as advisers and teachers in Japanese institutions. Among them were the chemist Gottfried WAGENER, the engineer and chemist Rudolf Lehmann (1842–1914), the mining engineer Curt Netto (1847–1909), the agricultural chemist Oskar KELLNER, and the political economist Paul Mayet (1846–1920). Germans perhaps left their most lasting mark on a modernizing Japan in the fields of MEDICINE and law. In

1869 the newly established Meiji government decided that Japanese medicine was to be modeled after that of Germany, and from that time until 1945, after which its influence was largely replaced by that of American medicine, the influence of German medicine was very prominent. Among the distinguished physicians who came to Japan were Leopold Mueller (1824–93), Julius Scriba (1848–1905), and Erwin von BÄLZ, who served for a time as court physician.

The CONSTITUTION OF THE EMPIRE OF JAPAN (1889) was greatly influenced by the thought of two German legal scholars, Rudolf von GNEIST and Lorenz von STEIN, whom the Meiji politician ITŌ HIROBUMI had met in Berlin and Vienna and by whom he had been instructed while on a trip to Europe in 1882 to study European constitutions. Albert MOSSE, Gneist's student, and Hermann ROESLER, another constitutional lawyer, traveled to Japan, where they helped draft the constitution, local government laws, and the COMMERCIAL CODE.

German-Japanese relations in the Meiji period expanded rapidly through growing trade, while another major German influence was that on the Japanese army. Following Prussia's victory over France in the Franco-Prussian War of 1870–71, YAMAGATA ARITOMO worked to bring about the full conversion of the army to the Prussian military system, a process that was implemented after 1884 (see ARMED FORCES, IMPERIAL JAPANESE). German-Japanese cultural relations have also been greatly influenced by several societies, among which the Deutsche Gesellschaft für Natur und Völkerkunde Ostasiens (OAG), founded in 1873, was (and still is) the most active. German Jesuits founded Sophia University in Tōkyō in 1913 with financial aid from Germany.

German-Japanese relations were temporarily interrupted by World War I, when Japan entered the conflict as an ally of Great Britain. Japan seized the German colonial territories of QINGDAO (Tsingtao) on the Chinese mainland and the Mariana, Caroline, and Marshall islands in the Pacific, but German residents in Japan were left unharmed, although merchants were forced to suspend their business activities. After World War I, cultural exchange was strengthened with the establishment of a number of new organizations, the Japan Institut (Berlin, 1926), the Japanisch-Deutsches Kulturinstitut (Tōkyō, 1927), and the Japanisch-Deutsches Forschungsinstitut (Kyōto, 1934).

With the rise of fascism both countries formed closer political ties in the latter half of the 1930s, signing the ANTI-COMINTERN PACT (1936) aimed against the Soviet Union, and the TRIPARTITE PACT (1940) including Italy. It was under the terms of this latter pact that Germany declared war on the United States on 11 December 1941 following Japan's own declaration of war after the attack on Pearl Harbor on 8 December 1941 (Japanese time). Japan obtained little practical military advantage from the pact, as neither of the two European powers was willing to fulfill the close military cooperation called for in the treaty, while Japan declined to assist Germany after 1941 by moving against the Soviet Union.

After their defeat in World War II, Germany and Japan were both occupied, and in 1949 Germany split into two states, the Federal Republic of Germany and the German Democratic Republic. Japan regained full sovereignty with the SAN FRANCISCO PEACE TREATY in 1952. Diplomatic relations were re-

Commonly Used Hand Gestures

money or approval   beckoning   disapproval   fight or bad feelings   angry or jealous woman   self-reference

stored with West Germany in May 1955 and with East Germany as late as May 1973.

Postwar relations have centered on trade. Prior to the reunification of Germany in 1990, West Germany was Japan's largest European Community (EC) trading partner, and Japan was the Federal Republic's most important trading partner in Asia. Since 1970 German-Japanese economic relations have been subject to the joint trading policy of the EC. The first joint German-Japanese conference of economics specialists was held in Bonn in 1975, and talks on economic and trading policies are held regularly.

Negotiations on economic issues have centered on Japan's export drive and the opening of its domestic market. Europe and the United States became increasingly critical of Japan during the 1970s due to the rapid growth of its economy and its increasing exports. France was particularly vocal in its criticism, but West Germany, dedicated to the principle of free trade, adopted a more conciliatory tone. In recent years, nevertheless, German industry and labor unions have begun to take a harder line.

Prior to the establishment of diplomatic relations between Japan and East Germany in 1973, an economic council of representatives of Japanese and East German business was created in January 1971. Treaties to promote cultural exchange and cooperation in science and technology were signed in 1977. Chairman Erich Honecker visited Japan in 1981; on this occasion a trade and navigation treaty was signed. In 1987 NAKASONE YASUHIRO became the first Japanese premier to visit East Germany.

In 1990 imports to Japan from both West and East Germany came to US $11.5 billion. Main import items were chemicals, machinery, and cars. Exports from Japan to the two German states reached US $17.8 billion. The main export articles were electrotechnical equipment of all kinds, cars, bicycles, and precision mechanical products (cameras, watches). West German capital investment in Japan up to 1989 reached nearly US $690 million in value (mainly in banking and the machinery industry) compared with Japanese capital investment in West Germany of just over US $3.4 billion (mainly in the chemical and machinery industries).

German cultural activities in Japan have been supported by a treaty signed on 14 December 1957. The Goethe Institut, with offices in Tōkyō, Ōsaka, and Kyōto, aims at promoting the German language and culture in Japan. A mutual exchange of students and teachers is organized under the Deutscher Akademischer Austauschdienst (DAAD), or German Academic Exchange Service. Scientific exchanges were strengthened by a treaty signed in October 1974 and are also supported by the DAAD and the Humboldt Foundation. Both organizations invite Japanese students and scholars to study at German universities.

In the late 1960s Düsseldorf became the most important center for German-Japanese economic relations, and Japanese organizations such as JETRO (the Japan External Trade Organization) have their main offices here. Japanese cultural activities in Germany center on the Japanisches Kulturinstitut, founded in 1969.

Since the reunification of Germany in October 1990, Japanese business circles have maintained a cautious approach to events, believing the infrastructure of the former East Germany to be too weak to warrant substantial investment. Nevertheless, the reunification of Germany is expected to give strong impetus both to the developing convergence of the European Community economies and to the integration of the economies of Eastern Europe within the capitalist system—processes in which Japan has a keen interest.

Gero   下呂[町]

Town in central Gifu Prefecture, central Honshū, on the river HIDAGAWA. Gero has been famous for more than a thousand years for its hot springs. The river gorge NAKAYAMA SHICHIRI, 28 km (17 mi) in length, is noted for its beauty. The historic houses in the nearby Hida-Takayama region are also tourist attractions. The forestry and lumber industries flourish in the area. Pop: 15,568.

gesaku   戯作

(also pronounced *kisaku, gisaku,* and *kesaku*). The generic term for all popular fiction written between the mid-18th century and the close of the Edo period (1600–1868) and for literature of the early Meiji period (1868–1912) that continued this tradition. The term originally meant "written for fun"; the genre is characterized by the flippant attitude of the author, or *gesakusha,* toward his work and a style combining a facetious tone with elaborate structure.

Gesaku emerged from the stagnation of Tokugawa feudalism. *Bunjin* (dilettantist men of letters), who originally cultivated in their art a lofty style influenced by Chinese scholarship, began from the mid-18th century to write more vulgar literature, particularly fiction, which they kept distinct from their "serious" work.

Later generations viewed HIRAGA GENNAI as the founding father of *gesaku.* His work heralded the golden age of early *gesaku* in the 1770s and 1780s. Besides books classified today as early KOKKEIBON and early YOMIHON, the main *gesaku* genres of this period were KIBYŌSHI and SHAREBON. Representative authors of early *gesaku* include Gennai, ŌTA NAMPO, and SANTŌ KYŌDEN. Early *gesaku* is characterized by wordplay, parody of earlier works, and intricate formal construction at the expense of the story itself. Life in fashionable circles, gossip, and the goings-on at the theater and in the pleasure quarters provide the main subject matter.

A crackdown on various forms of popular culture accompanying the KANSEI REFORMS (1787–93) effectively silenced some writers and served as an admonishment to others to mend their ways. This had a lasting impact on the development of the genre. More significant was the expansion of the reading public. The early *gesaku* dilettantes, who,

except for Kyōden, were members of and wrote for the urban intelligentsia of *samurai* stock, were outstripped by professional writers supplying an anonymous public through booksellers and lending libraries. From about 1800, *kokkeibon,* NINJŌBON, GŌKAN, and *yomihon* gradually crystallized as the main genres of late *gesaku,* represented by the work of JIPPENSHA IKKU, SHIKITEI SAMBA, TAMENAGA SHUNSUI, RYŪTEI TANEHIKO, BAKIN, and Santō Kyōden, who are known collectively as the Gesaku Rokkasen, the Six Poetic Sages of Gesaku. In symbiosis with the performing arts (JŌRURI, KABUKI, RAKUGO, etc) and book illustration, late *gesaku* achieved immense popularity. However, in the wake of the TEMPŌ REFORMS (1841–43), *gesaku* completely lost its vigor and creative force.

After the MEIJI RESTORATION of 1868 some authors, such as the *kokkeibon* writer KANAGAKI ROBUN, began writing for the new popular press and managed to adjust to the new age. The production of *gesaku* proper, however, ceased at the end of the 1880s, although elements of *gesaku* are to be found in the style of TSUBOUCHI SHŌYŌ and FUTABATEI SHIMEI. Despite being almost eradicated, the tradition lives on in commercial literature, popular journalism, and other forms of modern mass culture. Even in "pure literature"—NATSUME SŌSEKI's early works or those of NAGAI KAFŪ—echoes of *gesaku* can be heard. Among contemporary writers, INOUE HISASHI carries on the tradition of hilarious exaggeration and tongue-in-cheek humor native to the *gesaku* tradition.

Gesshō   月照

(1813–58). Buddhist priest associated with the late-Edo-period (1600–1868) movement to overthrow the TOKUGAWA SHOGUNATE and restore imperial rule. Born in Ōsaka. He became friends with activists UMEDA UMPIN and SAIGŌ TAKAMORI. To escape the ANSEI PURGE in 1858, Gesshō and Saigō fled to Satsuma (now Kagoshima Prefecture) but were refused asylum and threw themselves into Kagoshima Bay. Saigō survived, but Gesshō drowned.

gestures   ジェスチャー

(*jesuchā*). The Japanese preference for communication by indirect, nonverbal means is often manifested in the use of gestures. While Americans and other Westerners tend to gesture to emphasize the meaning of what they are saying, Japanese often employ gestures in place of direct spoken expression.

Most Japanese gestures differ considerably from those used in Western countries; others resemble Western gestures but carry entirely different meanings. For example, forming a circle with the thumb and index finger is a reference to money, whereas a clenched fist means tightfisted. The little finger pointed straight up is commonly taken to mean girlfriend or mistress, often with a vulgar connotation, while a raised thumb—the Western signal for approval—means boyfriend or husband. When beckoning to

geta Dating from the Yayoi period (ca 300 BC–ca AD 300), these wooden clogs are still worn in Japan today.
1 *Nurigeta.* Lacquered *geta* for women.
2 *Geta.* The paulownia-wood platforms of this pair of men's clogs are overlaid with a bamboo veneer.
3 A *geta* thong being attached by hand in the Aizu district of Fukushima Prefecture, which is known for the high quality of its paulownia wood.

someone, the arm is extended out and the hand is turned downward (palm in) and fluttered. The right hand waved quickly in front of the face, as if fanning a flame, signifies a negative response. The rapid crossing of the index fingers tells of a fight or bad feelings between two persons. An angry or jealous wife (or girlfriend) is suggested by bringing the hands to the forehead and pointing the forefingers up and outward like horns. Japanese point to their noses when indicating themselves (as in "Who, me?"), rather than to their hearts. And the right hand held stiffly in front of the face with the thumb near the nose is the gesture used to ask indulgence when crossing the path of another or passing between two persons. See also NON-VERBAL COMMUNICATION.

geta 下駄

Outdoor footwear consisting of a thong attached to a wooden platform with two crosswise supports. TAGETA (snowshoelike footwear used for working in paddies) date from the Yayoi period (ca 300 BC–ca AD 300). *Geta* were called *ashida* in the Heian period (794–1185) and *bokuri* in the Muromachi period (1333–1568). The word *geta* came into use during the Edo period (1600–1868). The word *takageta* refers to *geta* with especially high supports. The *geta* platform is usually made of paulownia or cryptomeria wood, the supports (called *ha*, "teeth") of oak or magnolia, and the thong of cloth or leather. *Geta* are still worn today as informal footwear, especially with the unlined *kimono* called *yukata*.

G5, G7 先進国蔵相会議

(Senshinkoku Zōshō Kaigi). G5 is the abbreviation for the Conference of Ministers and Governors of the Group of Five Countries, which is an unofficial international forum composed of the finance ministers and presidents of the central banks of the five main International Monetary Fund (IMF) members (the United States, the United Kingdom, France, Germany, and Japan). In 1986 the G7, or Group of Seven, was formed consisting of G5 member countries plus Italy and Canada. These forums are convened to deal with global economic or financial problems and to promote the international coordination of financial policies. For instance, under the terms of the September 1985 PLAZA ACCORD the G5 agreed to intervene in ex-

change markets to reduce the high value of the dollar, and in 1989 the G7 agreed to intervene for the same purpose. The G5 also conducts multilateral monitoring of economic policies of member nations, using indicators such as growth and inflation rates, current account and trade account balances, and exchange rate values.

ghosts 幽霊

(*yūrei*). The term for ghost in Japanese is *yūrei*, which generally means the spirit or soul of a dead person. In popular parlance, the term *yūrei* is often confused with *yōkai* (see BAKEMONO). A *yūrei* is the departed soul of a person, which appears as a shadowy likeness of the deceased. A *yūrei* is said to have a specific purpose for returning to the world of the living and to reveal itself only to certain persons, most often surviving relatives but occasionally other intimate acquaintances. The spirits of those who died violently or unnaturally are believed to be unable to make their final passage into the world of the dead; they appear before their relatives and acquaintances and express their reluctance to depart this world.

Since the mid-Edo period (1600–1868), in such ghost stories as TŌKAIDŌ YOTSUYA KAIDAN (The Ghost Story of Tōkaidō Yotsuya) and *Botan-dōrō* (Peony Lantern), *yūrei* have been depicted as having disheveled hair, elongated dangling arms, and no legs. See also MONONOKE.

GHQ 連合国最高司令官総司令部

(General Headquarters; J: Rengōkoku Saikō Shireikan Sōshireibu). Term used in post-World War II Japan to refer to the combined Tōkyō headquarters of the supreme commander for the Allied powers (SCAP) and the US FAR EAST COMMAND (FEC). SCAP was responsible for occupied Japan, and FEC for US military forces throughout the Far East.

gidayū-bushi 義太夫節

Type of JŌRURI narrative chant originated by TAKEMOTO GIDAYŪ I (1651–1714) for his Takemotoza, a puppet theater in Ōsaka (founded 1684). His most important collaborator at this theater was the playwright CHIKAMATSU MONZAEMON, and the style and repertoire created by these two men and their successors are partially preserved today by the Bunrakuza theater in Ōsaka. *Gidayū-bushi* also had a profound influence on all later styles of KABUKI music and on regional styles of puppetry and of SHAMISEN chant. *Gidayū-bushi* is powerful, expressive music. The chanting is forceful and declamatory, and the single *shamisen* that accompanies it is a large, deep-toned instrument.

Nothing of Gidayū I's own recitation style has survived directly. In 1703 one of his pupils, Toyotake Wakatayū I (1681–1764), founded a rival theater, the Toyotakeza. This represented what came to be known as the "Eastern" school and used the brighter *yō* scale, as opposed to the "Western" Takemoto school, which used the more astringent *in* scale. After a celebrated performance of *Chūshingura* in 1748, the Eastern and

Western schools began to reconcile their differences, though the two styles of chanting can still be distinguished.

Gidō Shūshin 義堂周信

(1325–88). Zen monk of the Rinzai sect; important figure in GOZAN LITERATURE (Chinese learning in medieval Japanese Zen monasteries). Born in Tosa Province (now Kōchi Prefecture), Gidō was a disciple of MUSŌ SOSEKI. He became a Confucian tutor to the young shōgun ASHIKAGA YOSHIMITSU. Gidō's journal, entitled *Nichiyō kufūshū*, is an invaluable source for the history of this period. Gidō is considered one of the greatest poets of the Gozan monasteries. His poems are collected in *Kūgeshū*.

gift giving 贈答

(*zōtō*). Gift giving in Japan involves elaborate rules and is part of a larger system of social exchange. There are several major gift-giving seasons during the year: the New Year (OTOSHIDAMA given chiefly to children), the end of the year (SEIBO gifts), and the midyear (CHŪGEN gifts). Significant stages in human life such as birth, coming of age (*seijin*), and marriage, as well as funerals and partings (see FAREWELL GIFTS) require gifts. Gifts are given to the sick or victims of fire or other disasters as encouragement (MIMAI); as souvenirs after even the shortest trip (see MIYAGE); and for happy celebrations (see SHŪGI). In recent years it has become common, especially among the young, to exchange gifts at Christmas and on Saint Valentine's Day.

Gifts are often given out of a sense of obligation and usually require a return gift (KAESHI), except in the cases of gifts (such as *seibo* and *chūgen*) given to a superior or to someone to whom one is indebted. When asking for an unusual or substantial favor of a person one does not know, an advance gift (*meishigawari*; literally, "in place of name card"), often of considerable value, is given. Most gifts simultaneously express one's gratitude or respect, serve material ends, and fulfill important social obligations.

Gifu 岐阜[市]

Capital of Gifu Prefecture, central Honshū, on the river NAGARAGAWA. A castle town of the Toki family during the Muromachi period (1333–1568), in the late 1500s it came under the rule of the warlord ODA NOBUNAGA, who changed its name from Inokuchi to Gifu. It prospered during the Edo period (1600–1868) as one of the post-station towns on the highway Nakasendō. Traditionally known for its umbrellas, lanterns, and fans, it now has textile and machinery industries. Tourist attractions are Gifu Castle, the temple Entokuji, and CORMORANT FISHING (*ukai*). Pop: 410,324.

Gifu Prefecture 岐阜県

(Gifu Ken). Located in central Honshū and bounded by Toyama Prefecture to the north, Nagano Prefecture to the east, Aichi and Mie prefectures to the south, and Shiga, Fukui, and Ishikawa prefectures to the west. The terrain is almost totally mountainous, and major ranges include the Hida and Ryōhaku mountain ranges in the north, with some peaks measuring over 3,000 m (9,840 ft) in height. The southern section is composed of lower mountains and the NŌBI PLAIN around the city of GIFU, which is the prefecture's major economic and population center. Major rivers are the KISOGAWA, IBIGAWA, and NAGARAGAWA. The climate is mild in the southern section but cooler in the mountainous north. Precipitation is heavy in both areas. Almost all major cities are located in the south and form an integral part of the CHŪKYŌ INDUSTRIAL ZONE.

Modern Gifu Prefecture was created in 1876 through the merger of Hida and Mino provinces, which correspond roughly to the northern and southern portions of the prefecture. The area has long been of strategic importance as a link between eastern and western Honshū as well as between the Pacific and the Sea of Japan coasts. It was the site of several major battles, including the Battle of SEKIGAHARA (1600), which established the hegemony of the Tokugawa shogunate.

Industrial activity, centered in the south, is led by such manufactures as textiles, clothing, ceramics, transportation equipment, pulp, and paper. Gifu is also a leading producer of lumber.

The mountain scenery and historic villages and towns of the Hida region, notably TAKAYAMA, constitute Gifu's outstanding tourist attractions. CORMORANT FISHING (*ukai*), also a major attraction, is carried out on the Nagaragawa. Part of the CHŪBU SANGAKU NATIONAL PARK is within the prefecture. Other parks include the Hida-Kisogawa Quasi-National Park and the Ibi-Sekigahara-Yorō Quasi-National Park. Area: 10,596 sq km (4,091 sq mi); pop: 2,066,569; capital: Gifu. Other major cities include ŌGAKI, TAJIMI, KAKAMIGAHARA, and Takayama.

gigaku   伎楽

Ancient masked dance drama that flourished in Japan during the Nara period (710–794). Although the performance tradition for this genre died out during the Edo period (1600–1868), there are a number of historical documents as well as artifacts that tell something about *gigaku*. It was said to have been brought to Japan in the early 7th century by a certain Mimashi, a native of Paekche, one of the three kingdoms of Korea, who had learned the dances in the region of Wu in China. From surviving evidence, it appears that *gigaku* may have been a mime performance or a processional combined with dance and music. As such, it may have resembled a mystery play or a masked dance drama. An excellent set of Nara-period MASKS carved of camphor wood is preserved in the SHŌSŌIN repository in Nara. The historical references to *gigaku* indicate that the music for *gigaku* performances made use of singers, an ensemble of flutes, TSUZUMI (hourglass-shaped drums), and cymbals. Examples of the music survive in a manuscript containing notation for the flute, which gives only the basic melodic contour and the placing of the main drum strokes. Since notation for Japanese music of this period seems to have been used primarily as a mnemonic aid, the manuscript tells very little about the manner in which *gigaku* might have actually been performed.

giin rippō → Diet member legislation

Gikeiki   義経記

Popular account of the life of MINAMOTO NO YOSHITSUNE (1159–89); written around 1400 to 1450; translated as *Yoshitsune*, 1966. The anonymous author draws selectively on a large body of popular legends concerning Yoshitsune that developed during the centuries following his death. The author gives little weight to the public career of Yoshitsune as a Minamoto warrior, the image developed in such warrior tales as HEIKE MONOGATARI and GEMPEI SEISUIKI. Similarly, *Gikeiki* largely avoids the more supernatural elements found in other Yoshitsune legends and presents a relatively naturalistic fictional biography of Yoshitsune with sympathetic depiction of his mistress Shizuka and several of his loyal retainers. One of these, Saitō Musashibō BENKEI, emerges as a figure of interest equal to Yoshitsune himself. Particularly in the latter half of the work, Yoshitsune is depicted as a passive character in contrast to the powerfully assertive Benkei, who remains devotedly loyal to Yoshitsune. The narrative tells of the enmity of Yoshitsune's elder half brother MINAMOTO NO YORITOMO, which accounts for Yoshitsune's eventual death and for the popular sympathy toward Yoshitsune that subsequently developed.

giko monogatari   擬古物語

(literally, "tales copied after the old"). Tales of the Kamakura period (1185–1333) imitating Heian-period (794–1185) classical fiction. In a broader sense, the term also includes Edo-period (1600–1868) works such as *Tamakura* (The Pillowing Arm) by the scholar of KOKUGAKU (National Learning) MOTOORI NORINAGA. Written by aristocrats for an aristocratic audience, *giko monogatari* such as *Sumiyoshi monogatari* (The Tale of Sumiyoshi) and *Koke no koromo* (The Moss-Covered Robe) were most strongly influenced by the *Genji monogatari* (TALE OF GENJI) but had a greater sense of Buddhist fatalism. In the Muromachi period (1333–1568) they were superseded by OTOGI-ZŌSHI, brief tales designed to reach a broader readership.

Gila River Relocation Center
    ヒラリバー収容所

(Hira Ribā Shūyōjo). Wartime relocation facility for Japanese Americans from California; located on the Gila River Indian Reservation, Arizona. In operation from 20 July 1942 until 10 November 1945, it held a maximum of 13,348 persons at any one time; a total of 16,655 persons were confined there. It was one of two camps located on Indian reservations. See JAPANESE AMERICANS, WARTIME RELOCATION OF; WAR RELOCATION AUTHORITY.

ginger   生姜

(*shōga*). *Zingiber officinale*. Perennial plant of the family Zingiberaceae, the rhizome of which is used as a food in Japan. It is grated for use as a condiment or thinly sliced and pickled in sweetened vinegar. The latter is the standard garnish for SUSHI. Similarly the young rhizome with a portion of its leaf stalk may be pickled whole in sweetened vinegar; called *fudeshōga*, it is also served as a garnish.

Ginkakuji   銀閣寺

(Temple of the Silver Pavilion). Formally known as Jishōji; considered the epitome of HIGASHIYAMA CULTURE. Temple in Sakyō Ward, Kyōto, belonging to the SHŌKOKUJI branch of the Rinzai sect of Zen Buddhism. The Ginkakuji stands on the site of an abandoned Tendai monastery, the Jōdoji, in a scenic area of Kyōto that was favored by ASHIKAGA YOSHIMASA, the eighth Muromachi shōgun (r 1449–74). The eminent Zen monk Musō Soseki (1275–1351) was designated the honorary first abbot of the temple. Hōsho Shūzai, a tonsured adopted son of Yoshimasa, was chosen as the second (actually the first functioning) abbot. Thereafter most

of the abbots of the Ginkakuji were selected from such aristocratic families as the Konoe.

Influenced by the example of the gilded KINKAKUJI built in 1397, Yoshimasa planned to cover the Kannon Hall with silver leaf but died before this could be done. Although the silver leafing was in fact never accomplished the Kannon Hall is traditionally referred to as the Silver Pavilion (Ginkaku).

The lower of the Ginkaku building's two stories is laid out in *shoin* style (see SHOIN-ZUKURI). The Tōgudō, the only other building in the compound spared from fire, contains altars enshrining images of Amida Buddha. Between the two buildings is a fine garden.

ginkgo   銀杏

(*ichō*). *Ginkgo biloba*. This deciduous tree is the only surviving member of the once widespread family Ginkgoaceae. The ripe seed has a fleshy, foul-smelling outer covering, but its kernel, called *ginnan*, is edible. The gingko grows fast and is resistant to cold weather, fire, diseases, and urban atmo-

Ginza The main street of this Tōkyō district becomes a "pedestrian's paradise" (hokōsha tengoku) on weekends and holidays, when it is closed to vehicular traffic.

spheric conditions; it often is planted as a roadside tree or firebreak. The tree attains a height of up to 30 meters (100 ft) with a diameter of 2 meters (7 ft). The leaves are fan-shaped and turn yellow in the autumn. In April male and female flowers grow on separate trees, and the pollen of the male flowers is carried by the wind to the female flowers. The pollen remains inactive until autumn, when fertilization finally takes place. The fact that the pollen produces motile sperm cells at this time was discovered in 1896 by HIRASE SAKUGORŌ, who also established the ginkgo's taxonomic position as a single-species genus. The genus Ginkgo is said to have thrived worldwide in the prehistoric period. The ginkgo no longer grows wild, but it is cultivated on a large scale mainly in Japan, China, and Korea.

Ginowan　宜野湾［市］

City on the island of Okinawa, Okinawa Prefecture. Ginowan was heavily damaged during World War II, after which half of it was allocated for American military use. The city remains economically dependent on the American military. Pop: 75,905.

Ginza　銀座

Shopping and entertainment district in the southwestern part of Chūō Ward, Tōkyō. It centers on the 1.1-kilometer (0.7-mi) section of the street known as Chūō-Dōri. The name Ginza (literally, "silver mint") refers to a mint for casting silver coins built here in 1612 by the Tokugawa shogunate. The 1872 opening of a railway between the international port of Yokohama and nearby Shim-

Gion Small bars line the alleyways of this popular entertainment area in Kyōto, formerly a government-licensed brothel quarter.

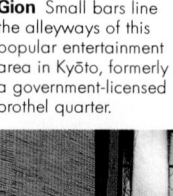

bashi, and the proximity of the Ginza to Tsukiji, where many foreigners resided, led to its swift assimilation of Western culture and its establishment as a fashion center. Today the main street of the Ginza is lined with department stores, expensive shops, and fashionable boutiques; along the back streets are a myriad of restaurants, bars, and coffeehouses.

ginza → kinza, ginza, and zeniza

Ginzan Hot Spring　銀山温泉

(Ginzan Onsen). Located in the city of Obanazawa, northeastern Yamagata Prefecture, northern Honshū. A hydrogen sulfide spring containing salt; water temperature 63°C (145°F). This spa, situated along the Ginzan Gorge east of the city, has been designated as a National Health Resort Hot Spring.

Giōji　祇王寺

Convent in Ukyō Ward, Kyōto; affiliated with the DAIKAKUJI branch of the SHINGON SECT of Buddhism. Giōji's fame is based on the story from the HEIKE MONOGATARI (The Tale of the Heike) of Giō, a great beauty who, after losing the favor of the great Taira family (Heike) chieftain TAIRA NO KIYOMORI, renounced the world at age 21 along with her sister and mother to take up residence here and devote herself to the Buddha AMIDA and rebirth in his Pure Land. The convent, long in a state of disrepair, was rebuilt and given its present name in honor of Giō in 1895. It is now dedicated to the Buddha DAINICHI (Skt: Mahāvairocana).

Gion　祇園

The district surrounding YASAKA SHRINE in Higashiyama Ward, Kyōto. From the early 18th century until the mid-20th century it flourished as an elegant, government-licensed brothel quarter, and remains today a popular entertainment area of bars, GEISHA establishments, and Japanese-style restaurants (ryōtei).

The district has retained much of the atmosphere of the past: the old wooden buildings in the vicinity of the bridge Gion Shimbashi have been designated a national historical preservation district, and geisha provide music and conversation for parties of diners at ryōtei. Each year in April the Miyako Odori festival of traditional dance, lasting several weeks, is held in the Gion district. In July Gion is the site of the GION FESTIVAL, which originated in the early Heian period (794–1185).

Gion Festival　祇園祭

(Gion Matsuri). Gion festivals are conducted throughout Japan, but the best known is that sponsored by the YASAKA SHRINE in Kyōto. The deity honored is Gavagriva (J: Gozu Tennō), a god of good health and the guardian deity of the Jetavana monastery (J: Gion Shōja) in India. The festival is also called Gion Goryōe (goryōe meaning "service for souls"), often abbreviated to Gion'e. It originated in 869 when, to counter an epidemic that was sweeping the city, 66 tall spears (hoko) representing the provinces of Japan were erected and prayers were offered. Discontinued in the confusion following the ŌNIN WAR (1467–77), the festival was revived in the 16th century by an organization of merchants and reached its present form during the Edo period (1600–1868). Conducted throughout the month of July, it reaches its high point on the 17th with a parade of floats (see DASHI). The original hoko (spears) have been replaced by giant, wheeled floats of the same name. Topped by a tall spearlike pole, they carry groups of musicians playing music known as gion-bayashi. The smaller floats, termed yama ("mountains"), bear life-size figures of famous historical or mythical personages. Similar festivals are the Hakata Gion Yamagasa in the city of Fukuoka, the Sannō Festival in Tōkyō, and the Takayama Festival in Gifu Prefecture.

Gion Nankai　祇園南海

(1677–1751). Poet and calligrapher; one of the pioneers of BUNJINGA painting. Real name Gion Yu. The eldest son of a Confucian scholar and physician to the Kii domain (now Wakayama Prefecture). Nankai studied Confucianism and Chinese poetry with the scholar KINOSHITA JUN'AN in Edo (now Tōkyō) and quickly established himself as a Chinese-language poet and a fine calligrapher. From 1697 he served as official Confucian scholar to the Kii domain. After falling into disfavor and being placed under confinement (1700–1710), he again participated in domainal affairs. In 1713 he was appointed a professor at the newly opened domainal school.

Girard case　ジラード事件

(Jirādo jiken). Also called the Sōmagahara Incident. A case involving legal jurisdiction over American military personnel on duty at US bases in post-Occupation Japan. On 30 January 1957 William S. Girard, an American soldier guarding the Sōmagahara rifle range in Gumma Prefecture, shot and killed a Japanese farm woman who was scavenging for empty shell cases on the range. There was great public outcry in Japan, and the United States decided that Girard should be tried under Japanese law, a decision that was ultimately upheld by the US Supreme Court. Girard was found guilty and given a three-year suspended sentence. The Girard case was significant legally in that the highest US court confirmed the validity of criminal jurisdiction arrangements under status-of-forces agreements.

giri and ninjō　義理と人情

(giri to ninjō). Social obligation (giri) and human feelings (ninjō). Giri refers to the obligation to act according to the dictates of society in relation to other persons. It applies, however, only to particular persons with whom one has certain social relations and is therefore a particular rather than a universal norm. Ninjō broadly refers to uni-

gissha Detail from *The Flight to Rokuhara*, an illustrated handscroll (part of the late-13th-century *Heiji monogatari emaki*) showing a *gissha* being used to carry the emperor from Nijō Palace in Kyōto.

versal human feelings of love, affection, pity, sympathy, sorrow, and the like, which one "naturally" feels toward others, as in relations between parent and child or between lovers.

Giri is a norm that obliges the observance of reciprocal relations—to help those who have helped one, to do favors for those from whom one has received favors, and so forth. The concept implies a moral force that compels members of society to engage in socially expected reciprocal activities even when their natural inclination (*ninjō*) may be to do otherwise. To feudal warriors, *giri* referred foremost to their obligation to serve their lord, even at the cost of their lives, and to repay ON (favor) received from the lord. In Japan, to be observant of *giri* is an indication of high moral worth. To neglect the obligation to reciprocate is to lose the trust of others expecting reciprocation and eventually to lose their support.

Generally human feelings do not conflict with social norms, and observance of *giri* does not contradict *ninjō*. However, occasions sometimes arise where one is caught between social obligation and natural inclination. Though *giri* and *ninjō* as terms have outmoded connotations in modern Japan, the concepts are still important in guiding the conduct of the Japanese. Younger Japanese are inclined to value *ninjō* over *giri*, but as they enter the adult world, where human relations depend so much on reciprocal obligations, they learn to conform to social norms and become more observant of *giri* obligations. In neglecting these obligations, a Japanese will find it difficult to get along with others, let alone advance in a career.

Girl Scouts
ガールスカウト

(Gāru Sukauto). The first Girl Scout organization in Japan was formed in 1920. Girl Scout activities were prohibited during World War II but reappeared in 1949 with the formation of the Girl Scouts of Japan. Summer camp activities are held annually, and international exchanges are also conducted. As of 1989 there were 1,646 Girl Scout groups, with a total membership of approximately 95,000.

giseigo → onomatopoeia

Gishi wajinden → Wei zhi (Wei chih)

gissha
牛車

A two-wheeled enclosed carriage drawn by one ox; used by the nobility in the Heian period (794–1185). Although transportation by horseback was common in ancient Japan, horse-drawn vehicles were never used. The average *gissha* could carry four passengers. *Gissha* differed considerably in size, style of construction, and decorative embellishment,

depending on the rank or title of the owner. Strict rules determined which social strata were entitled to use them. There was also a detailed code of etiquette on how one should board or alight from the carriage compartment and how these vehicles should be lined up when in procession or on review. In the Kamakura period (1185–1333) the *gissha* declined in popularity, being replaced by the palanquin (see KOSHI).

gitaigo → onomatopoeia

glass
ガラス

(*garasu*). At first a treasure suitable for the most sacred uses, glass in Japan eventually, under Western influence, became more utilitarian and was appreciated for functionalism as well as beauty. The earliest Japanese words for glass were *hari* (colorless glass) and *ruri* (colored glass). During the Edo period (1600–1868) the terms *bīdoro* and *giyaman* were used. Today glass is known simply as *garasu*.

Yayoi period (ca 300 BC–ca AD 300). The earliest glass pieces, such as the disks with open centers known as *heki* (Ch: *bi* or *pi*), were all found in northern Kyūshū but may have been made in China or from Chinese materials. Glass *magatama* ("curved jewels"; see BEADS, ANCIENT), beads, and several other items from this period have also been found.

Kofun period (ca 300–710). Increasing use of glass and expanding technology mark this period. Glass *magatama* and vast quantities of glass *marudama* (round beads), *kodama* (small beads), *kudatama* (tubular beads), and several natural forms have been excavated from burial mounds of this period. When the color range expanded, drops of molten colored glass or bits of cooled glass were sometimes added to a molten body to make a new form of glass, the *tombodama* (dragonfly bead). Another decorative innovation was the attachment of glass beads by wires. Following the introduction of Buddhism to Japan in 538, glass was used for making reliquaries for Buddhist relics (*shari*).

Nara period (710–794). Glassmaking advanced technologically and artistically. Many Buddhist temples had manufacturing bureaus of their own. Beads continued to have symbolic as well as decorative significance. Bead techniques included casting, coiling, and blowing to produce a variety of forms, often with an added crosswise bore for intricate decorative stringing.

Heian period (794–1185). Glassmaking declined after the demise of imperial and temple manufacturing bureaus, and extant examples from this period are rare, although beads show greater variety. Some have bigger bores, and larger examples appear hollow and fragile.

Medieval period (mid-12th–16th centuries). Glass beads were still cherished, but local glassmaking had clearly declined by the Kamakura period (1185–1333). Except in a few symbolic beads, the use of glass was apparently unknown by the period's end. So forgotten was glass that the first blown-glass vessels brought by traders and Jesuit missionaries in the late 16th century were thought to be made of an entirely new, exotic substance.

Edo period (1600–1868). Glass objects imported from Spain, Portugal, and the Netherlands were used as everyday utensils or ornaments and did not have the symbolic power that had earlier been associated with glass. Japanese artisans in Nagasaki, Satsuma (now Kagoshima Prefecture), and Edo (now Tōkyō) learned the techniques to produce glass themselves. Numerous glass items from the Edo period survive.

Meiji period (1868–1912) to present. Under the impetus of Western influence there were new needs for glass in foreign-style buildings, railroad cars, ships, and street lighting. Imports were initially necessary until the Japanese could master unfamiliar mechanized equipment and techniques. Today industrial glass has advanced substantially; it is generally characterized by high-quality artistic production and good design.

globefishes
河豚

(*fugu*). In Japanese, *fugu* is a general name for fish of the family Tetraodontidae, order Tetraodontiformes, class Osteichthyes. It is also used more broadly to indicate all fish that can swell their bellies or have a solid square shape, and more narrowly as the name of the genus *Fugu* of the family Tetraodontidae living only in waters surrounding Japan. Several species, including the *torafugu* (*Fugu rubripes*), are used for food.

While the *fugu* has long been praised in

glass This boat-shaped cobalt blue bowl is a mid-19th-century example of Satsuma cut glass. Length 18 cm. Suntory Museum of Art, Tōkyō.

go One of Japan's most popular board games, go has numerous professional and amateur ranks. These men are playing at one of the many neighborhood go clubs found throughout the country.

Japan as the most delicious of all fishes, it has also been dreaded, as improper preparation may cause fatal poisoning. The poisonous parts, such as the ovary and the liver, have been identified, and strict supervision by health authorities has decreased the number of accidents. Still, *fugu* caused the death of a famous *kabuki* actor in 1975. Lanterns made of *torafugu* skins, originally children's toys, are sold to tourists as folk art.

Glover, Thomas Blake

グラバー, T. B.

(1838–1911). English trader active in Japan during the last years of the Tokugawa shogunate (1603–1867) and early in the Meiji period (1868–1912). Born in Scotland, he traveled to Shanghai in 1858 and founded the firm of Glover and Co in Nagasaki in 1859. Glover exported gold, silver, and marine products to the West and imported ships and arms. The latter were supplied to the domains of Satsuma (now Kagoshima Prefecture) and Chōshū (now part of Yamaguchi Prefecture), centers of activity against the shogunate.

Beginning in 1868 Glover's company cooperated with the Saga domain (now part of Saga Prefecture) in developing the TAKASHIMA COAL MINE, introducing new types of mining equipment from England. It also participated in the 1868 construction of the Kosuge shipyards, forerunner of the Mitsubishi ship-

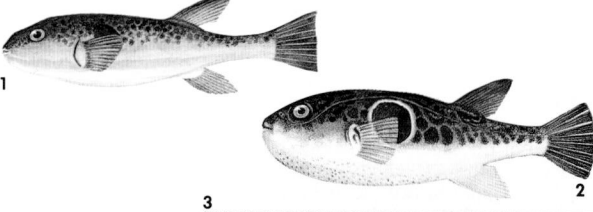

globefishes
1 *Mafugu* (*Fugu porphyreus*) is a popular edible species.
2 *Torafugu* (*Fugu rubripes*) is the species most prized by *fugu* lovers; the raw fillets are often served as *sashimi*, in paper-thin slices.
3 The one-pot dish called *tetchiri* is another of the many ways of preparing *fugu*. *Fugu*, *tōfu*, and vegetables are simmered together and served with a condiment of citrus-flavored soy sauce.

gobies The *mahaze*, found in shallow waters along the coast of Japan and in rivers, is both a common food and an extremely popular sport fish.

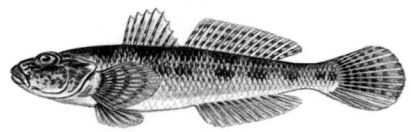

yards. Glover and Co opened offices in Kōbe and Ōsaka but went bankrupt in 1870 when orders for arms were drastically reduced after the Meiji Restoration (1868). Glover himself remained active, and when the Takashima mines became the property of Mitsubishi in 1881, he became an adviser to the company in its dealings with foreigners. In 1908 the Meiji government awarded him the Order of the Rising Sun, second class.

Gneist, Rudolf von

グナイスト, R.

(1816–95). German legal scholar and politician. Law professor at the University of Berlin; representative to the Prussian national assembly (1858–93) and to the German national assembly (1868–84); German supreme court judge from 1875. In 1882, when the Meiji politician ITŌ HIROBUMI and his party traveled to Europe to learn about European constitutions, Gneist instructed them in German constitutional law for six months. The CONSTITUTION OF THE EMPIRE OF JAPAN (1889) reflects Gneist's conservatism in limiting the power of the parliament and strengthening that of the ministers of state. His student Albert MOSSE later came to Japan as legal adviser to the Meiji government.

go

碁

Also called *igo*. A game for two players in which black and white stones are alternately placed at the intersections of lines on a board with the object of capturing the opponent's stones and securing control over open spaces on the board.

Some historical accounts place the origin of *go* in ancient China, while others trace the game to India, where early forms of chess were also played more than 4,000 years ago. Whereas chess spread widely throughout the West and the East (it is called SHŌGI and played by somewhat different rules in Japan), *go* was until recently played only in China (where it is known as *weiqi* or *wei-ch'i*), Korea (*paduk*), and Japan. It is somewhat hard to understand why the game did not spread further in early times, for some have called it the world's most intellectual game, and many aficionados in Japan consider it a true art. Its rules are simple and few, yet the number of possible play sequences is staggering; it is calculated to be 10^{750} or 1 followed by 750 zeros.

Basic Rules—Modern *go* is played on a wooden board, the surface of which is engraved with 19 vertical and 19 horizontal lines, thus producing 361 intersections. Nine of the intersections are specially marked with a small dot and called *hoshi* (star); these serve to orient the players and are also used as positions for handicap stones in official matches.

Only four basic rules are necessary to describe *go*, the second of which contains the central premise of the game: (1) Two players (Black and White) alternate in placing their stones on unoccupied intersections of the board, Black being the first to play. A stone cannot be moved once it is played, except when it is captured. (2) If a stone or a group of stones is completely surrounded by the opponent's stones with no empty points within the surrounding area, it is captured, removed from the board, and retained by the opponent. (3) Each captured stone or

surrounded intersection counts as one point. (In China the stones on the board are also counted.) (4) If a move would result in the reversal of the previous move by the opponent, the player is required to abstain from that move until other plays have been made; this is called *kō* and is meant to prevent stalemates through perpetual repetition.

The game ends when all stones have been placed or the possibilities for gaining territory or capturing the opponent's stones have been exhausted. At this point all captured stones are placed in the opponent's vacant spaces, and the player with the most remaining vacant spaces under his control wins.

History—Legend attributes the invention of *go* to a vassal named Wu in ancient China, perhaps 4,000 years ago, although some accounts state that the game developed in India. From China *go* was brought to Korea and later to Japan by Chinese missionaries in the 5th or 6th century. The oldest *go* board in Japan is displayed at the SHŌSŌIN in Nara, and the game is mentioned in the 11th-century TALE OF GENJI.

Modern *go* history begins in 1612, when the Tokugawa shogunate set up four *go* schools, called HON'IMBŌ, Hayashi, Inoue, and Yasui. Intense competitions were held to determine the best player of the game, who was installed in the position of *godokoro*. Annual official games were held in the presence of the shōgun at his castle in Edo (now Tōkyō); these were called *oshirogo*. Dōsaku, Hon'imbō IV (1645–1702), was the most outstanding player of the early modern period and is referred to as the "saint of *go*."

Professional *go* players met hard times after the MEIJI RESTORATION (1868) when their stipends were discontinued by the government. Top professionals formed a study group called Hōensha in the Meiji period (1868–1912), and the JAPAN GO ASSOCIATION was formed in 1924. At this time Shūsai, Hon'imbō XXI (1874–1940), gave the title Hon'imbō to the association to be awarded in regular competition thereafter. Kitani Minoru (1909–75) and Wu Qingyuan (Wu Ch'ing-yüan; J: Go Seigen; b 1914) invented a new type of *fuseki* (opening theory) in the 1930s. Takagawa Kaku (1915–86) and Sakata Eio (b 1920) were the outstanding players of the post–World War II period. Younger players active in the 1980s included Lin Haifeng (J: Rin Kaihō; b 1942), Ōtake Hideo (b 1942), Katō Masao (b 1947), Ishida Yoshio (b 1948), Takemiya Masaki (b 1951), Kobayashi Kōichi (b 1952), and Cho Chihun (J: Chō Chikun; b 1956).

Professional and International Go—There are millions of *go* fans in Japan but only about 400 professionals. Amateurs are ranked from the ninth *kyū* or degree, the lowest, to the first *kyū*; from there the rankings advance to *shodan* (first grade), with *rokudan* (sixth grade) usually the highest amateur ranking. A small number of *nana-dan* (seventh grade) amateurs are as strong as professionals of the professional first grade (*shodan*); the top of the professional rankings is *kudan* (ninth grade). The ranks are used to decide handicaps for official matches; each rank represents a one-stone handicap for amateurs and a one-third-stone handicap for professionals. Promotions are granted on the basis of official games (*ōteai*). Newspapers sponsor regular competitions under such names as Kisei, Meijin, Hon'imbō, Jūdan, Tengen, and Ōza; professionals make their living through prize money offered in these matches.

Go is slowly but steadily spreading in the Western world. Iwamoto Kaoru (b 1902), a former Hon'imbō, contributed much to the internationalization of the game. The International Go Federation, based in Tōkyō, was organized in 1982. As of 1989 there were go associations in 35 countries, with an estimated combined membership of 13 million.

👁 460–461

gō 郷

(township or village). Unit of local administration from the Nara (710–794) through the Muromachi (1333–1568) periods. The township or village headmen (gōji) became the nucleus of the emergent local landholding class (RYŌSHU). The gō remained as a directly governed local unit until the time of the nationwide land survey (KENCHI) in the 1580s.

gobies 沙魚

(haze). Salt, fresh, or brackish water fish of the family Gobiidae, order Perciformes. Over 200 species are found in Japan; most are small and live along sea or river bottoms. The best known of these is the mahaze (Acanthogobius flavimanus), often simply called haze, an edible species caught in bays and river mouths. It grows to about 25 centimeters (10 in). It is also found in Korea and China. One of the most popular sport fish in Japan, it is used in TEMPURA and other traditional dishes. Haze fishing was a favorite autumn recreation of the people of Edo (now Tōkyō).

Gobō 御坊[市]

City in central Wakayama Prefecture, central Honshū, at the mouth of the river Hidakagawa. Gobō developed as a temple town (MONZEN MACHI) of a branch of the temple NISHI HONGANJI, the headquarters of the Jōdo Shin sect, and as a collection center for lumber transported down the Hidakagawa. Greenhouse cultivation of vegetables is widespread. It is located along the route to the temple Dōjōji, celebrated in NŌ and KABUKI plays. Pop: 29,133.

Gobō no Keiji 五榜の掲示

(Five Public Notices). Ordinances issued by the government immediately following the MEIJI RESTORATION (1868); promulgated together with the CHARTER OATH, which set down the broad outlines of government. The first two notices, besides exhorting the traditional Confucian virtues, prohibited homicide, arson, robbery, formation of factions, and desertion of the home (CHŌSAN) in order to escape taxes. The third proscribed Christianity and other "heterodox" sects; the fourth forbade any injury to foreigners; and the fifth prohibited travel out of Japan. Apart from the fourth, they did not differ from ordinances issued by the Tokugawa shogunate (1603–1867) and were on the whole ignored.

Gobusho 五部書

(The Five Books of Shintō). Also called Shintō gobusho. Forming the basic canon of the Watarai school of Shintō (see WATARAI SHINTŌ), the Gobusho narrate the origin and history of the ISE SHRINE in order to stress its superiority and the divine origin of the imperial family. Scholars now generally agree that the Gobusho were produced around the 13th century by members or associates of the Watarai family, hereditary priests of the Outer Shrine (Gekū) of Ise. The Gobusho borrowed heavily from Buddhism, Taoist philosophy, yin-yang thought, and Confucianism. The texts were regarded as secret,

Godzilla The original Godzilla, made in 1954, was the first Japanese film to score a major box office hit with overseas audiences.

not to be taken beyond the shrine precincts or to be shown to anyone under age 60.

Go-Daigo, Emperor 後醍醐天皇

(1288–1339; Go-Daigo Tennō). The 96th sovereign (tennō) in the traditional count (which includes several legendary emperors); reigned 1318–39. The second son of Emperor GO-UDA, Go-Daigo was responsible for the KEMMU RESTORATION. Undaunted when his plot to overthrow the Kamakura shogunate in 1324 was discovered (see SHŌCHŪ CONSPIRACY), he planned a second attempt, during which he was arrested and banished to the Oki Islands (see GENKŌ INCIDENT). He escaped in 1333 and enlisted military support, most notably that of KUSUNOKI MASASHIGE.

Later that year, ASHIKAGA TAKAUJI, commander of a shogunal army, changed his allegiance and destroyed the shogunate, allowing Go-Daigo to establish personal rule in Kyōto. His rule alienated many of his former supporters, however, and in 1335 Takauji revolted against Go-Daigo and quickly defeated his forces. Takauji placed Emperor Kōmyō (1322–80; r 1336–48) on the throne; Go-Daigo fled to a remote stronghold in the mountains of Yoshino and established the rival Southern Court, precipitating a succession dispute and civil war that lasted until 1392 (see NORTHERN AND SOUTHERN COURTS). Go-Daigo abdicated in 1339 in favor of his son Go-Murakami (1328–68; r 1339–68) and died the following day.

Godai teiō monogatari 五代帝王物語

(Tale of Five Imperial Reigns; also known as Godaiō ki). Historical tale of unknown authorship, probably composed near the end of the Kamakura period (1185–1333). It describes events of the reigns of emperors Go-Horikawa (r 1221–32), Shijō (r 1232–42), GO-SAGA (r 1242–46), GO-FUKAKUSA (r 1246–60), and KAMEYAMA (r 1260–74). It is a valuable source of information on events leading to a schism within the imperial house (see NORTHERN AND SOUTHERN COURTS).

Godai Tomoatsu 五代友厚

(1836–85). Entrepreneur. Born in the Satsuma domain (now Kagoshima Prefecture); studied at the Nagasaki Naval Training Center (KAIGUN DENSHŪJO; 1857–59). After personal involvement in the KAGOSHIMA BOMBARDMENT Godai went to Europe, where he negotiated with the Comte des Cantons de MONTBLANC about joint business ventures. He persuaded Satsuma's daimyō to build steamships, develop the spinning industry, and send promising students abroad. At the same time, Godai used his European contacts to purchase weapons and supplies for the struggle against the TOKUGAWA SHOGUNATE (1603–1867). Soon after the MEIJI RESTORATION (1868) Godai, now a junior councillor (san'yo) and a staff officer of the precursor of the Ministry of Foreign Affairs, used his diplomatic skills in handling several incidents of antiforeign violence on the part of the samurai.

Resigning from government office in 1869, Godai turned his full attention to the economic development of Japan. From his headquarters in Ōsaka, he organized, operated, or promoted no fewer than 10 major companies. His entrepreneurship was distinguished by an emphasis on international trade, the systematic organization of economic plans, and reliance on Western technology and the joint-stock company system of organization.

Godzilla ゴジラ

(Gojira). A 1954 film directed by Honda Ishirō (b 1911). Starring SHIMURA TAKASHI,

Continued on page 462 ➤

Emperor Go-Daigo Early-14th-century portrait of the emperor who attempted the restoration of direct imperial rule in 1333–36.

Go: Battle in Black and White

Considered by some to be the world's foremost intellectual game, go nevertheless has simple rules and strong visual appeal. Good moves are found as much through intuitive pattern recognition as complex tactical reasoning. An interesting feature of the game is that it is constructive rather than destructive: the object is not annihilation but coexistence on advantageous terms. The sample match cited on the facing page took place in the 17th century between rival go masters Dōsaku and Chitetsu. It is a classic example of a well-played game.

James Davies

How to Play

Equipment—Go is played with round, lens-shaped black and white pieces called stones on a board marked with a grid. The standard board has 19 horizontal and 19 vertical lines, but go can be played on a board of any size. The 9-by-9 board is popular for beginners.

Procedure—Starting from an empty board, Black and White take turns placing stones on the intersections of the grid. Black plays first. The object of the game is to gain territory, either by surrounding vacant areas or by surrounding and capturing opponent's stones. The winner is the player with the most territory and prisoners at the end.

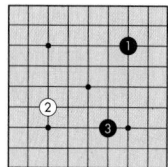

The beginning of a game on a 9-by-9 board.

Capturing—A stone is captured when the opponent occupies all its adjacent points (called liberties). Prisoners are saved for use in counting.

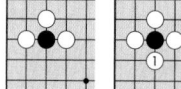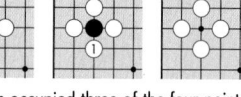

White has occupied three of the four points adjacent to the black stone in the diagram at left. The black stone is in *atari*, meaning that it has only one liberty left. At center, by playing 1, White captures the black stone and removes it from the board as a prisoner. At right is the result.

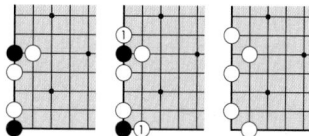

Here is how to capture a stone on the edge or in the corner.

Two or more stones can be captured at once. The opponent must occupy all their liberties, including internal liberties.

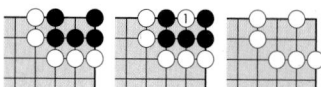

Black is in *atari*, at left, with only one liberty. In the center, White 1 captures five black stones. At right is the result.

Self-Capture—Self-capturing moves are illegal.

For example, White cannot play 1 because then his own stones would have no liberties.

Kō—A *kō* is a position in which one black stone and one white stone could capture and recapture each other endlessly. To keep the game from degenerating, a special rule states that after each capture in a *kō*, the opponent must play elsewhere before recapturing.

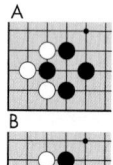

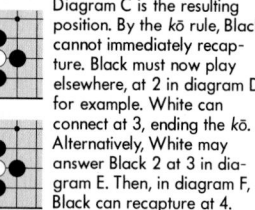

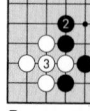

The black stone furthest to the left in diagram A is in *atari* in this example of a *kō* position. In diagram B, White 1 captures one stone. Diagram C is the resulting position. By the *kō* rule, Black cannot immediately recapture. Black must now play elsewhere, at 2 in diagram D, for example. White can connect at 3, ending the *kō*. Alternatively, White may answer Black 2 at 3 in diagram E. Then, in diagram F, Black can recapture at 4. Diagram G is the result, and now White must play elsewhere.

Life, Death, and Seki—One way to defend an attacked group—to keep it "alive"—is to form two independent, internal liberties, called eyes.

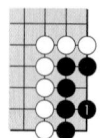

Black 1 makes two eyes. White cannot play above or below 1 (either move would be self-capture), so Black is permanently alive.

Another possible way to live is known as *seki*, which is shown in the following example.

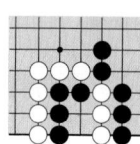

Three white stones and four black stones share two common liberties. If either player occupies one of these liberties, his opponent will capture him by occupying the other. Neither Black nor White can attack, so both are alive.

Isolated groups of stones that cannot live by making two eyes or forming a *seki* are said to be dead. Dead stones do not actually have to be captured during the game. If they are still dead at the end of the game, they are removed as prisoners.

End of Game and Counting—The game is over when both players agree to end it. A player's score is the number of vacant points (territory) he has surrounded minus the number of prisoners he has lost. No points are counted in a *seki*.

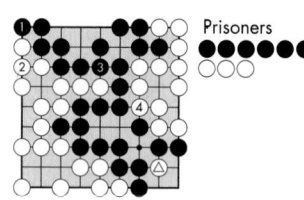

Prisoners

The last few moves of a game on a 9-by-9 board. Black has captured three white prisoners; White has captured seven black prisoners. The white stone marked with a triangle is dead.

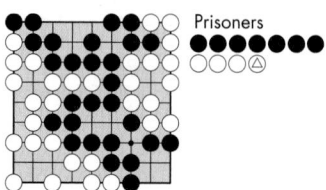

Prisoners

To count the score, first all dead stones are removed as prisoners.

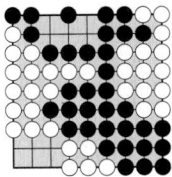

Then the prisoners are replaced on the board to deduct them from the territories. White prisoners are replaced inside white territory, black prisoners inside black territory.

The territories can be rearranged for easy counting. White ends with six points and Black with five, so White wins by one point.

Handicaps—Go has a handicapping system that lets players of different strengths compete on equal terms without distorting the tactics or strategy of the game. Black starts by placing two to nine stones, depending on the size of the handicap, on points marked with dots known as "star points." White makes the next move, after which the players alternate in the usual manner. Another handicapping system adds points called *komi* to one player's final score. In tournaments, $5\frac{1}{2}$ points are often added to White's score to compensate for Black's playing first. This system also prevents draws.

Classic Game: A Saint's Victory

The following game was played in 1676 between Dōsaku, head of the Hon'imbō school of professional go players, and Chitetsu, head of the rival Yasui school. Dōsaku was the founder of modern opening theory and is one of two Japanese players known as "saints of go."

White: Hon'imbō Dōsaku
Black: Yasui Chitetsu
(Black's moves are odd numbers, and White's moves are even numbers.)

Moves 1–100

Black 1–White 16: Sound strategy is to start in the corner areas then develop along the sides. Most early moves are played on the 3rd or 4th line from the edges.

Black 17–27: A standard corner pattern or *jōseki* that is still used in modern games. White 26 captures Black 23.

White 40–50: White begins attacking the black group on the left side.

White 52–56: White defends his own group.

Black 57–67: Refuted by White's next move.

White 68: If Black now tries to escape at A, White can trap him with B.

White 70: White renews his attack.

Black 85: Black recovers from his earlier failure by cutting off White 34 and 36.

White 92–94: Intercepting Black 91, White again threatens the main black group.

Moves 101–200

Black 1–23: White scores a big gain by forcing Black to live in a confined space. The surrounding white wall secures a large territory in the upper left and promises more in the center.

White 28: White completes the enclosure of the center.

Black 29–53: Black promptly invades and manages to rescue the three stones that had been trapped by White 68 in the top diagram. In the process, Black captures a pair of white stones and isolates the white group on the lower side.

Black 59: Black cannot immediately recapture White 58 because of the *kō* rule.

White 62: Necessary to make two eyes.

White 80 (above 58): By connecting here, White eliminates the threat of a *kō* fight.

Moves 201–277

Black 35–49: An intentional sacrifice.

White 50–60: White has to spend three extra moves capturing the sacrificed stones. In the meantime, Black captures a white stone with 57.

White 64 (left of 51: This is not a *kō*, so White can recapture immediately.

White 66–Black 77: A one-point *kō* fight in which Black and White alternately capture at 57 and the point below. Black wins this *kō* and connects with 77.

At the end, it does not matter who occupies A, B, and the point below 9. When the point below 9 is filled in, however, White comes into *atari* and has to connect at 5. Black 35 and the stones marked with triangles are dead and are removed as prisoners.

Result: White wins by 9 points.

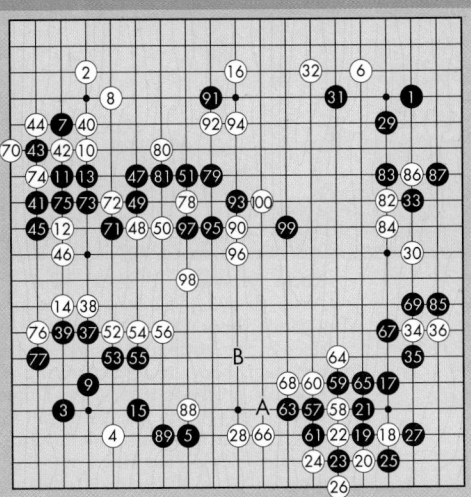

Moves 1–100
62 connects at 23.

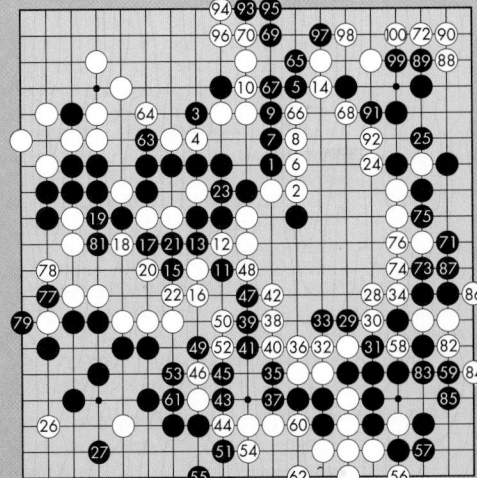

Moves 101–200
80 connects above 58.

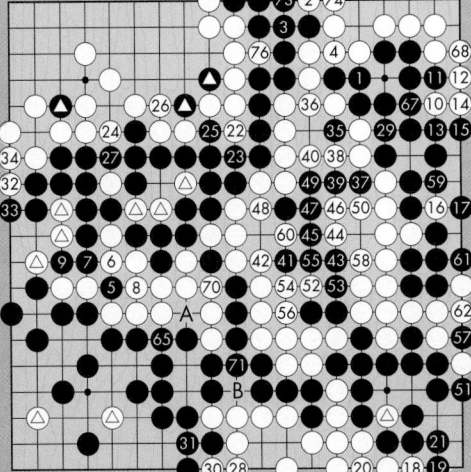

Moves 201–277
63 at 5, captures two white stones.
64 left of 5, recaptures 63.
66 above 51, captures 57.
69 at 57, recaptures 66.
72 above 51, recaptures 69.
75 at 57, recaptures 72.
77 connects above 51.

Go boards like this one are usually made from a solid block of *kaya* wood and have ornately carved legs. Less expensive flat and folding boards are also widely used.

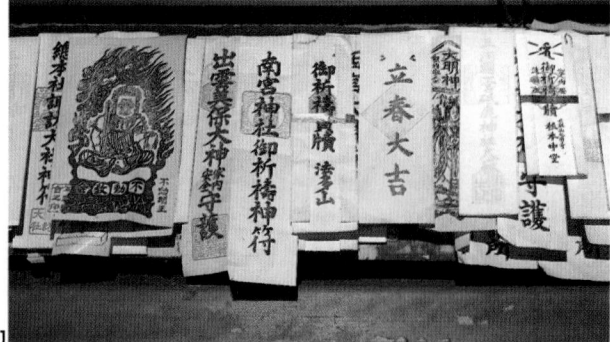

gofu
1 Protective amulets, gathered from temples and shrines around the country, are displayed over a doorway in a private home.
2 Gofu from Shiba Daijingū, a Shintō shrine in Tōkyō. The amulet at left would be placed on a Shintō family altar; the tiny amulet at right would be carried on one's person; the paper behind it is a shrine calendar.

gohei
1 Gohei such as this one are used in rites of purification.
2 A parishioner of the Maegawa Shrine in Fukui Prefecture carries a large gohei in the annual shrine festival.

1

2

Kōchi Momoko (b 1932), and Takarada Akira (b 1934), *Godzilla* is the story of a gigantic dinosaur awakened from his long sleep at the bottom of the South Pacific by hydrogen bomb testing. Arriving in Japan, Godzilla proceeds to destroy Tōkyō. With special effects by TSUBURAYA EIJI, *Godzilla* was Japan's first full-scale science fiction monster movie, inspiring a wave of similar films.

gofu 護符

Protective amulet commonly termed *omamori* or *ofuda*, distributed or sold at Shintō shrines and Buddhist temples and believed to bring good health, household safety, financial success, and so forth. These rectangular slips of paper (or occasionally wood) are generally placed in the *kamidana* (SHINTŌ FAMILY ALTARS), affixed to a doorway, or carried on one's person. They usually bear the name of a deity; those issued by Buddhist temples may also display a Buddhist image. The *gofu* issued by the Mitsumine Shrine in Chichibu (Saitama Prefecture), for example, carries the image of a wolf who is the familiar of the god. It is said to prevent burglary when affixed to doorways and to prevent rat damage if displayed in rooms where silkworms are tended.

Go-Fukakusa, Emperor 後深草天皇

(1243–1304; Go-Fukakusa Tennō). The 89th sovereign (*tennō*) in the traditional count

gōgai Japanese read a gōgai reporting the death of Emperor Shōwa (Hirohito) in 1989.

(which includes several legendary emperors); reigned 1246–60; a son of Emperor GO-SAGA. During Go-Fukakusa's childhood his father continued to rule from retirement (see INSEI) and in 1260 forced Go-Fukakusa to abdicate in favor of his younger son Kameyama, while at the same time making Kameyama's son (later Emperor GO-UDA) crown prince. Go-Fukakusa appealed to the KAMAKURA SHOGUNATE and was able to have his own son, the future emperor FUSHIMI (r 1287–98), named Go-Uda's successor; during his son's reign, Go-Fukakusa finally came to control state affairs. Thereafter, succession to the throne alternated between the senior Jimyōin line (descended from Go-Fukakusa) and the junior Daikakuji line (descended from Kameyama).

gōgai 号外

"Extra" editions put out by newspapers. The first such extra in Japan was a special issue put out by the *Chūgai shimbun* on 5 July 1868 reporting on the Battle of Ueno. From around the time of the Sino-Japanese War of 1894–95, hawkers began selling extra editions in the streets of Tōkyō by ringing bells to attract attention. With radio and television now widespread, only a few newspaper extras appear each year. On 7 January 1989 extra editions were issued on the death of Emperor SHŌWA (Hirohito).

gōgaku 郷学

(literally, "village schools"). Educational institutions set up during the Edo period (1600–1868). Known also as *gōkō*, *gōgakkō*, or *gōgakusho*, many of them lasted until the beginning of the Meiji period (1868–1912), when they were incorporated into the public primary and middle school system under the EDUCATION ORDER OF 1872. *Gōgaku* were mainly of two types. The first, like the *hankō* (domainal schools), was for the education of domainal retainers and their children. The second type was set up and operated by commoners but, unlike the TERAKOYA, received domainal or shogunate guidance. In both cases, the curriculum was centered on reading, writing, and arithmetic. Among the better-known *gōgaku* were the Shizutani Gakkō, founded in 1668 by IKEDA MITSUMASA, the *daimyō* of Okayama, and the KAITOKUDŌ, founded in 1724 by Ōsaka merchants.

Go-Hanazono, Emperor 後花園天皇

(1419–71; Go-Hanazono Tennō). The 102nd sovereign (*tennō*) in the traditional count

(which includes several legendary emperors); reigned 1428–64. Great-grandson of Emperor Sukō (1334–98; r 1348–51) of the Northern Court and eldest son of Prince Fushimi no Miya Sadafusa. In 1428 Emperor Shōkō (1401–28; r 1412–28), who had no heir, became seriously ill. Although the schism between the NORTHERN AND SOUTHERN COURTS had been healed in 1392, the Muromachi shogunate, in order to avoid any possibility of a descendant of the Southern Court succeeding to the throne, arranged for Go-Hanazono to be adopted by the retired emperor GO-KOMATSU (of the Northern Court) and enthroned as emperor. Go-Hanazono relinquished the throne to his son Go-Tsuchimikado (1442–1500; r 1464–1500) in 1464. Go-Hanazono was a patron of the arts and an accomplished poet.

gohei 御幣

Also called *shide*, *nigite*, *nusa*, or *mitegura*. Wand decorated with paper or cloth streamers that is used by shrine priests or MIKO (female attendants at Shintō shrines) in performing Shintō rituals. The streamers, though usually white, are occasionally gold, silver, or of several different colors. Zigzag paper streamers, also called *gohei*, are often attached to the straw ropes (called *shimenawa*) that are used to mark sacred precincts or are affixed, for example, to the ridgepole during a house-raising ceremony (see KENCHIKU GIREI). The *gohei* serves to attract the gods or may be waved as a gesture of purification.

Goichigo Jiken →May 15th Incident

Go-Ichijō, Emperor 後一条天皇

(1008–36; Go-Ichijō Tennō). The 68th sovereign (*tennō*) in the traditional count (which includes several legendary emperors); reigned 1016–36. Son of Emperor ICHIJŌ and JŌTŌ MON'IN, eldest daughter of FUJIWARA NO MICHINAGA. He succeeded Emperor SANJŌ (r 1011–16). The young emperor Go-Ichijō married Michinaga's third daughter, Ishi (999–1036), his aunt. Michinaga dominated the court for most of Go-Ichijō's reign.

Gojō 五条[市]

City in west-central Nara Prefecture, central Honshū, on the river Yoshinogawa. It is a market center for lumber and woodworking; pears and persimmons are cultivated. Gojō was the site of an anti-Tokugawa uprising, the TENCHŪGUMI REBELLION, in 1863. Eizanji, an 8th-century temple associated with the FUJIWARA FAMILY, is in the area. Pop: 34,545.

Gojū no tō 五重塔

(tr *The Five-Storied Pagoda*, 1982). Novella by KŌDA ROHAN (1867–1947); serialized in the magazine *Kokkai* in 1891–92. The main figure, Jūbei, an apprentice carpenter with a reputation for being lazy and dull-witted, is fired with ambition when he learns that a pagoda is to be built on the grounds of a Buddhist temple. He begs to be allowed to build it single-handedly, despite suggestions from the abbot that he and Genta, the accomplished temple craftsman, construct it together. Intent on revealing his buried artistic genius, Jūbei refuses Genta's generous offers of assistance. However, the determined apprentice succeeds in building a magnificent pagoda that survives a violent storm, a dramatic final test for the structure. On the day of its dedication, the abbot climbs to the top of the pagoda and writes the words "Built by Jūbei and achieved by

Genta," honoring Jūbei's artistic talent and Genta's Confucian virtue, the ability to yield. In its passion and grandeur, the novella is representative of Rohan's often lofty style.

gojūon zu　　　　　　　　　五十音図

(literally, "chart of the 50 sounds"). Table of the 50 syllables in the Japanese phonetic writing system (KANA), arranged in intersecting vertical columns (gyō) and horizontal rows (dan) in such a way that each horizontal row brings together all syllables that end in the same vowel and each vertical column brings together all syllables that begin with the same consonant.

The accompanying table shows the syllables in katakana accompanied by roman letters. It reads from left to right; however, in the normal Japanese arrangement the first column, a-i-u-e-o, appears at far right, followed, moving one column to the left, by ka-ki-ku-ke-ko, etc. The syllables チ chi and フ fu belong to the "t" and "h" columns, respectively, but this ceases to be an anomaly when kana or a slightly different system of romanization is used. There are in the "w" column three syllables ヰ i, ヱ e, and ヲ o, represented by distinct kana, and a fourth, エ e in the "y" column, the phonetic values of which, formerly distinguished, have become equivalent to ヰ i, エ e, and オ o of the first, or vowel, column. Although ヲ o remains in use only as a grammatical particle, ヰ i and エ e are no longer recognized in contemporary kana usage (see KANAZUKAI). There are also two syllables, ィ i of the "y" column and ウ u of the "w" column, with phonetic values equivalent to ィ i and ウ u of the first column, for which previous phonetic distinction has not been verified. The "n" in the last column is syllable-final ン n, and was formerly not included in the table.

In the premodern era, the chart of 50 sounds came to be used to explain Japanese grammar, a pedogogical system that in modified form remains in use today. Verbs were classified according to which column of gyō their final syllables fell into, or, in cases where the final syllable is lost in conjugation, the penultimate syllable. Verb conjugations were named according to which column or how many rows or dan were represented in them; examples of the former are kagyō henkaku and ragyō henkaku and of the latter, shimonidan and yodan (see CLASSICAL JAPANESE). The order of syllables in the chart also came to be used—along with the now little-used iroha system (see IROHA POEM)—for classifications and dictionary listings, just as the alphabet is used in the West.

Gokaidō　　　　　　　　　五街道

(The Five Highways). Collective name for a network of centrally administered highways crossing central Japan and converging at Nihombashi in Edo (now Tōkyō), during the Edo period (1600–1868). Radiating like spokes from Edo, these roads were the TŌKAIDŌ, NAKASENDŌ, Kōshū Kaidō, Nikkō Kaidō, and Ōshū Kaidō. Special controls ensured tight regulation of travel along these roadways. POST-STATION TOWNS along the route provided services for travelers.

The Tōkaidō followed the coastline from the post station of Shinagawa to Kyōto. This 500-kilometer (310-mi) road connected the densely populated corridor between Edo and Kyōto. The Nakasendō took a slightly longer and more mountainous inland course to Kyōto. Bisecting these two major highways,

the Kōshū Kaidō wound through the mountains to Kōfu. North of Edo, the Nikkō and Ōshū Kaidō roads followed a common route before branching off, the first terminating at the Tokugawa family shrine at Nikkō, while the Ōshū Kaidō continued north from Utsunomiya to Shirakawa.

The five roads were divided into sections; post stations and nearby villages were assigned responsibility for bridge construction, road maintenance, and tree planting in each section, as well as for regular assessments of men and horses to keep the traffic moving (see SUKEGŌ). Officials checked identifications at a number of barrier stations (SEKISHO). Above all, the Gokaidō were the routes used for the Tokugawa shogunate's SANKIN KŌTAI system requiring residence in Edo, normally in alternate years, of the DAIMYŌ and their large retinues (see DAIMYŌ PROCESSIONS; HONJIN). In addition to the movements of the daimyō, the shogunate could monitor communications and troop movements through its control of the roads. As the core of the road system for official and personal travel, the Gokaidō integrated the Japanese polity.

Gokajō no Goseimon → Charter Oath

Go-Kameyama, Emperor
後亀山天皇

(?–1424; Go-Kameyama Tennō). The 99th sovereign (tennō) in the traditional count (which includes several legendary emperors); reigned 1383–92 as the fourth and last emperor of the Southern Court. With the shōgun ASHIKAGA YOSHIMITSU, in 1392 he effected the reconciliation of the NORTHERN AND SOUTHERN COURTS after 56 years of schism. It was agreed that members of the two rival imperial branches would alternate in occupying the throne, and Go-Kameyama surrendered the imperial regalia to Emperor GO-KOMATSU of the Northern Court. After Yoshimitsu's death (1408), Go-Kameyama in 1410 tried unsuccessfully to revive the Southern Court when it became clear that the Northern Court would not observe the agreement.

gōkan　　　　　　　　　　合巻

(literally, "bound-together volumes"). Format for illustrated fiction that was popular from the first decade of the 19th century; suggests also the kind of fiction usually published in that format. Physically, the gōkan derives from the KIBYŌSHI ("yellow covers"), the dominant medium for illustrated fiction in the late 18th century. Sometime around 1805, publishers began the practice of binding separate fascicles into one or two larger volumes. SHIKITEI SAMBA claimed to have introduced the form with Ikazuchi Tarō gōaku monogatari in 1806, but most scholars now agree that the format came into existence a few years earlier. The appearance of the gōkan coincided with and fostered a new vogue for intricately plotted historical romances and adventures of considerably greater length than previous kibyōshi stories.

From the beginning gōkan showed a strong influence from the KABUKI theater. A great many gōkan borrow their plots explicitly from popular kabuki plays. Many gōkan illustrations were produced by artists of the UTAGAWA SCHOOL of UKIYO-E. SANTŌ KYŌDEN (1761–1816) is credited with popularizing the use of nigao-e, illustrations in which characters in the stories are made to resemble famous actors. RYŪTEI TANEHIKO, who

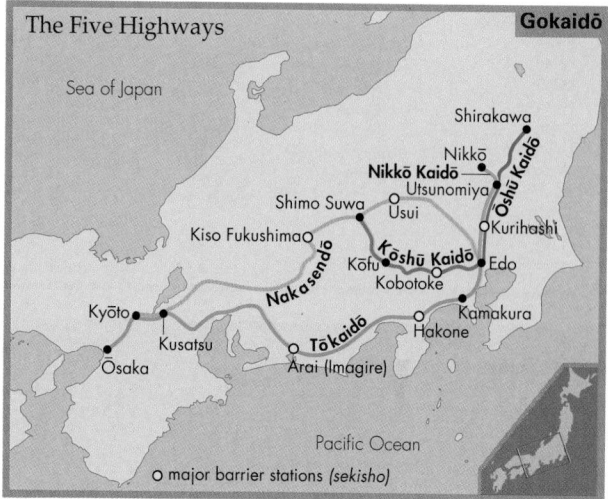

The Five Highways　　Gokaidō

Sea of Japan

Shirakawa
Nikkō
Nikkō Kaidō　Ōshū Kaidō
Shimo Suwa　Utsunomiya
Usui　Kurihashi
Kiso Fukushima
Kōshū Kaidō　Kōfu　Edo
Nakasendō　Kobotoke
Kyōto　　Kamakura
Kusatsu　Hakone
Tōkaidō
Ōsaka　Arai (Imagire)

Pacific Ocean

○ major barrier stations (sekisho)

with Shōhonjitate (1815–31) popularized the use of theatrical conventions in gōkan, is the name most closely identified with the gōkan in its heyday. His Nise Murasaki inaka Genji (The False Murasaki and the Rustic Genji), which appeared between 1829 and 1842, is regarded as the masterpiece of the genre. Gōkan appeared in numbers larger by far than any other fictional form of the late Edo period (1600–1868).

Gokanoshō　　　　　　　　五家荘

Hamlet in the mountain recesses of eastern Kumamoto Prefecture, Kyūshū. According to local tradition Gokanoshō was settled in the 12th century by remnants of the TAIRA FAMILY. Principal products are lumber, rice, wheat, tea, and shiitake (Japanese mushrooms).

Gokasegawa　　　　　　　　五ヶ瀬川

River in northern Miyazaki Prefecture, Kyūshū, originating in the Kyūshū Mountains and flowing east to empty into the Hyūga Sea at the city of Nobeoka. The Takachihokyō, the gorges in its upper reaches, are the supposed site of the legendary descent of the Shintō gods from heaven (see MYTHOLOGY). Length: 106 km (66 mi); area of drainage basin: 1,820 sq km (703 sq mi).

gokasho shōnin　　　　　　五箇所商人

(literally, "merchants of the five places"). Merchants of the Edo period (1600–1868) who monopolized the trade in raw silk imported from China. Merchants from Sakai, Nagasaki, and Kyōto controlled the trade under the ITOWAPPU system, established in 1604. They were joined by merchants from Edo (now Tōkyō) and Ōsaka in 1631 and thereafter called gokasho shōnin. See also SAKAI MERCHANTS; NAGASAKI KAISHO.

The Five Home Provinces and Seven Circuits

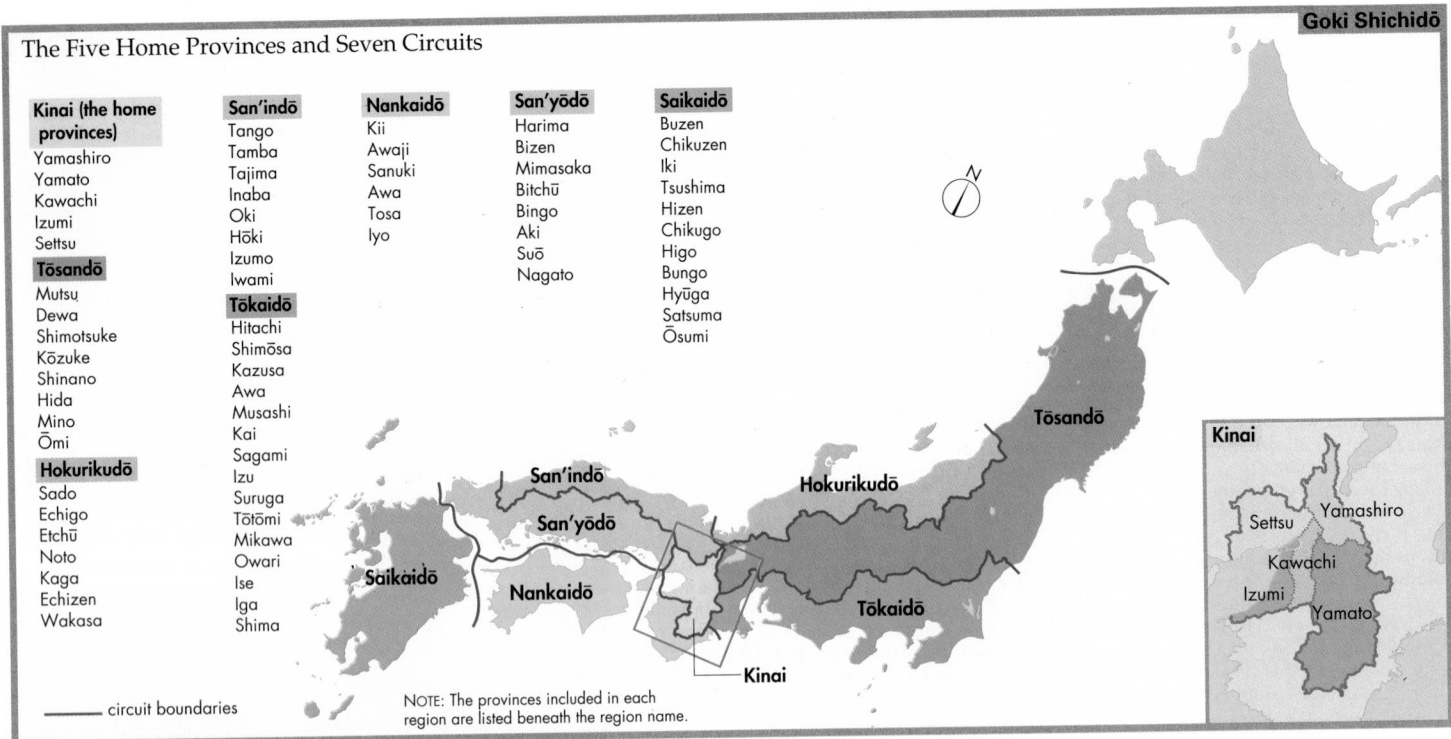

Kinai (the home provinces)	San'indō	Nankaidō	San'yōdō	Saikaidō
Yamashiro	Tango	Kii	Harima	Buzen
Yamato	Tamba	Awaji	Bizen	Chikuzen
Kawachi	Tajima	Sanuki	Mimasaka	Iki
Izumi	Inaba	Awa	Bitchū	Tsushima
Settsu	Oki	Tosa	Bingo	Hizen
	Hōki	Iyo	Aki	Chikugo
Tōsandō	Izumo		Suō	Higo
Mutsu	Iwami		Nagato	Bungo
Dewa				Hyūga
Shimotsuke	**Tōkaidō**			Satsuma
Kōzuke	Hitachi			Ōsumi
Shinano	Shimōsa			
Hida	Kazusa			
Mino	Awa			
Ōmi	Musashi			
	Kai			
Hokurikudō	Sagami			
Sado	Izu			
Echigo	Suruga			
Etchū	Tōtōmi			
Noto	Mikawa			
Kaga	Owari			
Echizen	Ise			
Wakasa	Iga			
	Shima			

—— circuit boundaries

NOTE: The provinces included in each region are listed beneath the region name.

Kinai: Settsu, Yamashiro, Kawachi, Izumi, Yamato

Gokayama *Gasshō-zukuri* farmhouses in the Suganuma section of this Toyama Prefecture hamlet have become an attraction for sightseers.

Gokayama　五箇山

Hamlet in southwestern Toyama Prefecture, central Honshū. Secluded in the mountainous recesses of the upper reaches of the river Shōgawa, Gokayama retained a medieval way of life until comparatively recently. Its old houses, made in the *gasshō-zukuri* style (see MINKA), attract visitors.

gokenin　御家人

(housemen). Direct vassals of the shogunate in the Kamakura (1185–1333) through Edo (1600–1868) periods. With the founding of the Kamakura shogunate some 2,000 warriors of MINAMOTO NO YORITOMO, mostly from eastern Japan, became hereditary vassals of his house. He gave them land grants and appointments as estate stewards (JITŌ) or military governors (SHUGO); in return, *gokenin* fought for the shogunate, served as its guards, and contributed funds to the shōgun. To protect the *gokenin* from financial ruin (many of them had borrowed money at high rates of interest), the shogunate issued edicts of debt cancellation (TOKUSEI) and forbade the mortgage or sale of *gokenin* estates, but this policy failed and *gokenin* discontent with the Kamakura shogunate eventually caused its downfall.

In the Muromachi period (1333–1568),

there were *gokenin* who were direct vassals of the shogunate, called *hōkōshū*, and those under the control of *shugo*, called *jitō gokenin*. During the Edo period, *gokenin* were the lower-ranking direct vassals of the Tokugawa shogunate. By 1800 there were some 20,000 *gokenin*. Their stipends ranged from 260 KOKU (1 *koku* = about 180 liters or 5 US bushels) of rice to a mere 4 RYŌ in cash; most *gokenin*, however, received less than 100 *koku*.

Goken Sampa Naikaku　護憲三派内閣

(literally, "Cabinet of Three Groups Supporting the Constitution"). A coalition cabinet headed by KATŌ TAKAAKI from June 1924 to July 1925. It was a product of the second MOVEMENT TO PROTECT CONSTITUTIONAL GOVERNMENT, in which three major political parties joined forces. They were the KENSEIKAI, led by Katō; the RIKKEN SEIYŪKAI, led by TAKAHASHI KOREKIYO, who became minister of agriculture and commerce; and the KAKUSHIN KURABU, led by INUKAI TSUYOSHI, appointed minister of transportation. Major acts passed under this cabinet in 1925 included the Universal Manhood Suffrage Law, the elimination of four army divisions, the establishment of diplomatic relations with the Soviet Union, and the repressive PEACE PRESERVATION LAW OF 1925 (Chian Iji Hō). In July 1925 internal dissension led the cabinet to resign, and Katō formed a new Kenseikai cabinet the following month.

Gōke shidai　江家次第

Also known as *Gōshidai*. An encyclopedia of court ceremonial completed in 1111 by ŌE NO MASAFUSA. *Gōke* refers to the Ōe family, who had served the court for generations as literary scholars. Masafusa undertook the work at the request of the regent (KAMPAKU) Fujiwara no Moromichi (1062–99). Of 21 original chapters, 19 survive.

Goki Shichidō　五畿七道

(Five Home Provinces and Seven Circuits). A general term for administrative units under the RITSURYŌ SYSTEM of the late 7th century. Goki refers to the five provinces around the old capitals of Nara and Kyōto (see KINAI): Yamato, Yamashiro, Settsu, Kawachi, and Izumi. Shichidō refers to the seven regions or circuits (*dō;* literally, "roads") into which

the remaining 60-or-so provinces were grouped: Tōkaidō, Tōsandō, Hokurikudō, San'indō, San'yōdō, Nankaidō, and Saikaidō.

gokō gomin　五公五民

(literally, "five for the lord; five for the commoner"). A term of the Edo period (1600–1868) indicating that half of a crop was to be paid as tax (*nengu*) to one's lord while half was to be retained by the producer. The term expressed a goal rather than actuality; in practice the percentage of yield paid as tax varied from domain to domain and year to year, rarely exceeding 50 percent and in shogunate domains (*tenryō*) commonly falling into the 30 to 35 percent range. See also JŌMEN.

Gōko Kiyoshi　郷古潔

(1882–1961). Businessman. Born in Iwate Prefecture. After graduating from Tōkyō University in 1908, he joined Mitsubishi Corporation, becoming president of MITSUBISHI HEAVY INDUSTRIES, LTD, in 1941. From 1945 to 1951 he was barred from business activities by order of the Occupation authorities (see OCCUPATION PURGE). After the purge order was rescinded, Gōko became the first Chairman of the Japan Association of Defense Industries (1952–60) and also served as a counselor of the Japan Productivity Center (1956–61).

Gokokuji　護国寺

Large temple in Bunkyō Ward, Tōkyō; center in eastern Japan of the Buzan branch (see HASEDERA) of the SHINGON SECT of Buddhism. The Gokokuji was founded in 1681 by the monk Ryōken (1611–87) at the request of the fifth Tokugawa shōgun, Tsunayoshi (1646–1709), and his mother Keishō In (1627–1705), who together served as its lay patrons. The main hall of the temple, now an Important Cultural Property, was constructed in 1698. Its cemetery contains the graves of more than 40 Confucian scholars of the Edo period (1600–1868). The temple is dedicated to the bodhisattva Nyoirin Kannon.

Go-Komatsu, Emperor　後小松天皇

(1377–1433; Go-Komatsu Tennō). The 100th sovereign (*tennō*) in the traditional count (which includes several legendary emperors); reigned 1382–1412. Eldest son of Emperor Go-En'yū (1359–93; r 1371–82) and a ruler of the Northern Court (see NORTHERN AND SOUTHERN COURTS). In 1392 the schism in the imperial house ended when the Muromachi shogunate persuaded Emperor GO-KAMEYAMA of the Southern Court to abdicate in favor of Go-Komatsu and turn over to him the IMPERIAL REGALIA, but Go-Komatsu remained under the firm control of the shōgun ASHIKAGA YOSHIMITSU. Go-Komatsu abdicated in 1412 and entered the Buddhist priesthood in 1431.

gold beetle　　　黄金虫

(*koganemushi*). *Mimela splendens.* Beetle of the order Coleoptera, family Scarabaeidae, whose distribution ranges over all Japan as well as Korea, Taiwan, China, and India. Its body is oval, usually an iridescent green with a golden sheen, and widest in the posterior section, with a rounded back. About 20 millimeters (0.8 in) long, it appears in June and July and feeds on young leaves of broadleaf trees, such as *kunugi* (a kind of oak) and cherry. The larva is a grub that lives in the soil and feeds on tree roots. The insect takes from one to two years to develop from an egg into an adult.

Golden Week　　　ゴールデンウイーク

(Gōruden Uīku). A week extending from the end of April to the beginning of May during which a number of national holidays occur in Japan. The principal holidays involved are Midori no Hi (Greenery Day), on 29 April, Kempō Kinembi (Constitution Memorial Day), on 3 May, and Kodomo no Hi (CHILDREN'S DAY), on 5 May. In addition, many companies give employees a holiday on May Day, 1 May, and in 1992, 4 May was designated a principal holiday. When this period includes a weekend, the result can be a vacation of as many as ten days. At this time of year people flock to resorts, inns, and hotels and traffic is particularly heavy. The number of Japanese people who travel abroad during Golden Week has increased in recent years.

goldfish　　　金魚

(*kingyo*). *Carassius auratus.* Freshwater fish of the family Cyprinidae, order Cypriniformes, class Osteichthyes. The goldfish is thought to have been artificially bred from the crucian carp in China. At present more than 20 varieties are raised in Japan, some of which were originally imported and others developed domestically.

It is presumed that around the 11th century goldfish breeding was actively conducted in China, and goldfish are thought to have been imported to Japan during the 16th and 17th centuries. Goldfish became widely popular during the Bunka and Bunsei eras (1804–30), when they were frequently kept in garden ponds. Street vendors carrying goldfish in an oval tub first appeared during these years and were common until the outbreak of World War II. Exports to the United States from Japan began in the 1890s, with a large-scale trade starting around 1907, but declined after 1933 when the United States succeeded in mass goldfish breeding.

golf　　　ゴルフ

(*gorufu*). Golf was introduced to Japan by Arthur H. Groom, an English merchant, in the early 20th century. Since World War II, the popularity of golf has increased tremendously, even though golf is one of Japan's most costly sports. Many corporations buy company memberships in golf clubs for en-

goldfish
1 Typically, the head of the *tanchō* is red, while the body is white.
2 The *wakin* is the variety most commonly kept in ponds.
3 The variety called *kurodemekin*, introduced from China, has bulging eyes and a three- or four-sectioned tail.
4 With its striking appearance, the *ranchū* is considered the most magnificent of Japanese goldfish.

tertaining and other business purposes; however, the number of college-student and women golfers is on the increase. As of 1988 the number of professional golfers was well over 2,700, including 300 women. The same year there were approximately 640 golf courses, which were being used by some 12 million golfers.

Golovnin, Vasilii Mikhailovich　　　ゴローニン, V. M.

(1776–1831). Russian naval officer and explorer, famous for an 1816 book translated as *Narrative of My Captivity in Japan, during the Years 1811, 1812, and 1813* (1818). Born into a noble family, Golovnin was orphaned at age nine. In 1788 he entered the Naval School and subsequently was attached to the British navy for three years. Given command of the Russian frigate *Diana*, in 1807 Golovnin was sent on an around-the-world expedition from Kronstadt to Kamchatka and thence to the little-known islands between northeastern Asia and northwestern North America. His account of his capture by the Japanese while he was charting the Kuril (Chishima) Archipelago brought him worldwide fame.

In retaliation for depredations on the Kuril Islands instigated by Nikolai Petrovich REZANOV, Lieutenant Commander Golovnin and several subordinates were lured ashore on Kunashiri Island and taken prisoner in July 1811. Lieutenant Commander Petr Ivanovich Rikord, who had stayed aboard the *Diana*, captured an influential Hokkaidō merchant, TAKATAYA KAHEI, and with his help eventually negotiated the release of the Russians. The memoirs of Golovnin's three-year-long captivity, which were translated and reprinted widely, remained the most significant firsthand portrayal of the Japanese available in Russia until the opening of Japan, if not until the beginning of the 20th century. He later had a distinguished career in the Russian navy.

goma　　　胡麻

(sesame). *Sesamum indicum* L. Annual plant of the sesame family, the seeds of which are used in various forms in Japanese cooking. They are often roasted and sprinkled on white rice or dressed dishes. Various dress-

ings are made by mixing roasted and ground sesame seeds with other condiments such as MISO (to make *goma miso*), vinegar (to make *gomasu*), or SOY SAUCE (to make *goma-jōyu*). *Goma-dōfu*, ground sesame seeds mixed with kudzu flour and molded in squares, is one of the dishes in the group known as SHŌJIN RYŌRI, or Buddhist vegetarian cooking. In the Nara (710–794) and Heian (794–1185) periods, oil extracted from sesame seeds was used as lamp oil; today it is used as a cooking oil and in salad dressings.

gōmei kaisha →unlimited

partnership company

Gomi Yasusuke　　　五味康祐

(1921–80). Author. Born in Ōsaka. Attended Waseda University. In the late 1940s and 1950s he created a fad with his historical fiction about *kengō*, or skilled swordsmen, and contributed to the popularity of stories about *ninja* (see NINJUTSU). He received the Akutagawa Prize in 1953 for his short story "Sōshin" (1952, Oblivion); other works include the novel *Futari no Musashi* (1956–57, The Two Musashis).

Go-Mizunoo, Emperor　　　後水尾天皇

(1596–1680; Go-Mizunoo Tennō). The 108th sovereign (*tennō*) in the traditional count (which includes several legendary emperors); reigned 1611–29. The third son of Emperor Go-Yōzei (r 1586–1611), in 1620 he married TOKUGAWA KAZUKO, daughter of the shōgun TOKUGAWA HIDETADA; she became his official empress in 1624. Unhappy with his forced marriage and other shogunal interference in court affairs (see SHIE INCIDENT), he abdicated in 1629 in favor of his five-year-old daughter Empress Meishō (r 1629–43), the first reigning empress since the 8th century. Go-Mizunoo dominated the court from retirement and for the next 51 years built the SHUGAKUIN DETACHED PALACE in northeastern Kyōto. His WAKA verses are collected under the title *Osōshū* (A Seagull's Nest).

gomoku narabe →renju

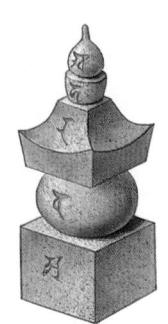

gorintō The five tiers of this type of Buddhist monument represent (from top to bottom) emptiness, wind, fire, water, and earth.

gonaisho　　　　　　御内書

Personal letters from the shōguns used from the mid-1300s through the Edo period (1600–1868) to convey holiday congratulations, messages, and even requests for military aid. Less formal than official orders (KUDASHIBUMI) or "instructions" (migyōsho), they began to replace these forms to transmit shogunal policy during the rule (1369–95) of ASHIKAGA YOSHIMITSU. They were usually dictated but sometimes written by the shōgun himself, and they bore his monogram (KAŌ) or, in the Edo period, his personal seal (inshō).

Goncharov, Ivan Aleksandrovich
ゴンチャロフ, I. A.

(1812–91). Russian novelist whose description of mid-19th-century Japan influenced generations of Russian readers, and whose best-known novel, *Oblomov* (1859), influenced FUTABATEI SHIMEI and other Japanese writers of the Meiji period (1868–1912). Goncharov graduated from Moscow University in 1834. In 1852 he accompanied Admiral Evfimii PUTIATIN on a voyage to Japan. After returning to Russia in 1854 he published his account of the voyage in serial form. In 1858 the series was published in book form as *Fregat Pallada* (tr *The Voyage of the Frigate Pallada*, 1965). Its condescending yet amusing characterization of the Japanese left a lasting imprint on the minds of its readers. Goncharov depicted the Japanese military as the diametric opposite of what Russians would call soldiers. His descriptions of the Japanese as laughable and effeminate contributed to the failure of the Russian government and public to take Japan seriously until the Russo-Japanese war of 1904–05.

Gondō Seikyō　　　　　権藤成卿

(1868–1937). Also known as Gondō Nariaki. Rightist thinker and writer. Born in Fukuoka Prefecture. Gondō became a proponent of Japanese expansion after an extended trip to Korea and China in 1886. He joined the AMUR RIVER SOCIETY as editor of *Tōa geppō* (East Asia Monthly News). In 1902 he moved to Tōkyō, becoming acquainted with KITA IKKI, ŌKAWA SHŪMEI, and other rightist thinkers. He joined the Rōsōkai, a study group concerned with national problems, and in 1920 he founded the Jichi Gakkai (Self-Rule School). A proponent of agrarian nationalism (NŌHON SHUGI), Gondō envisioned a state composed of self-governing village communities directly ruled by the emperor and freed of bureaucracy and monopolistic capitalism. His teachings had great influence on the radical nationalist movements of the early 1930s. He was suspected of involvement in two ultra-right-wing plots of 1932, the LEAGUE OF BLOOD INCIDENT and the MAY 15TH INCIDENT. Gondō's writings include *Kōmin jichi hongi* (1920, Basic Principles of Self-Rule by the Emperor's Subjects) and *Jichi mimpan* (1927, People's Guide to Self-Rule).

gongen → honji suijaku

goningumi　　　　　　五人組

(literally, "five-man groups"). Mutual-responsibility units of local political organization during the Edo period (1600–1868). Promoted by rulers in the early 17th century as a mechanism of social control, they gradually evolved into devices for local self-help and self-governance. The concept, introduced into Japan from China in the 7th century, was later employed by such leaders as TOYOTOMI HIDEYOSHI and TOKUGAWA IEYASU in a number of different forms for civil, government, and military purposes. During the rule (1623–51) of the shōgun TOKUGAWA IEMITSU, *goningumi* became a part of the formally codified local administration in both shogunal and *daimyō* domains.

The "five-man groups" did not consist of five men. Optimally they consisted of five households, but might be composed of one to more than a dozen households. The groups provided members with communal defense against outsiders and an organized system for mutual aid, resolution of internal disputes, and allocation of such tasks as road and waterway maintenance and corvée labor service. They provided rulers with identifiable groups that could be held collectively responsible for tax obligations. The groups also supervised members' behavior and maintained statistics on births, deaths, marriages, and adoptions. Each group had an appointed or elected leader (often called *goningumi-gashira*) who would represent his group's interests in the town or village. The procedures of *goningumi* varied greatly from place to place. Their members assembled periodically in gatherings known as *goningumi yoriai*. Compilations of regulations and prohibitions for daily life (often called *goningumi chō*) helped *goningumi* evolve from instruments of the government into forms of local social organization.

Gonin no sekkōhei　　　五人の斥候兵

(Five Scouts). A 1938 film directed by TASAKA TOMOTAKA, starring Kosugi Isamu (1904–83), Miake Bontarō (b 1906), Izome Shirō (b 1907), Izawa Ichirō (b 1912), and Nagao Toshinosuke (b 1909). It is a war movie, and the plot revolves around a Japanese army detachment stationed on the Chinese front during the Sino-Japanese War. Rather than attempting to fan the flames of patriotism or stir up militarist sentiment, the film concentrates on the affection among comrades-in-arms and the human desire to stay alive at all costs in the midst of the extreme circumstances of a battlefront. It was the first Japanese war film to earn a reputation for artistic merit.

Gonki　　　　　　　　権記

Also called *Yukinari Kyō ki*. Diary of the Heian-period (794–1185) courtier and calligrapher FUJIWARA NO YUKINARI (also known as Fujiwara no Kōzei; 972–1028). Its name derives from one of Yukinari's official posts, *gon dainagon* (provisional great counselor). The diary's 50 chapters cover the years 991–1011 and provide important information on politics and court life under Fujiwara rule.

gōnō　　　　　　　　　豪農

(literally, "rich farmers"). General term for farmers who had extensive landholdings or managed large-scale operations; more particularly, modern historians writing about the late Edo period (1600–1868) and early Meiji period (1868–1912) use it to refer to local farmers and wealthy merchants who acted as the economic and administrative leaders of their communities.

Having participated in domain and shogunate politics as village officials, *gōnō* became even more politically conscious as Japan was swept up in the events that eventually led to the MEIJI RESTORATION (1868).

Many of them took part in the movement to overthrow the Tokugawa shogunate (1603–1867), acting as the leaders of the movement in their villages. Again, after the restoration, as the FREEDOM AND PEOPLE'S RIGHTS MOVEMENT in opposition to the "tyranny" of the new government gained momentum throughout the country, *gōnō* acted as the leaders and representatives of the farming populace. With the LAND TAX REFORM OF 1873–1881 the *gōnō* as a class disintegrated.

Gōnokawa　　　　　　　江川

Also known as Gōgawa and Gōkawa. River in Hiroshima and Shimane prefectures, western Honshū, originating in the Mikasa Pass and flowing through the Chūgoku Mountains to empty into the Sea of Japan at the city of Gōtsu. It is the largest river in western Honshū. The water is used for electric power generation, drinking, and industry by the Inland Sea Industrial Region. Length: 194 km (121 mi); area of drainage basin: 3,870 sq km (1,494 sq mi).

go on　　　　　　　　　呉音

(the Wu pronunciation). One of the several varieties of *on* readings of Chinese characters (KANJI) as used in Japan. *On* readings are Japanese approximations of the way the characters were pronounced in Chinese. *Go on* consist of pronunciations that had been introduced into Japan in the 6th century and before. In the 7th century a new variety of pronunciations called *kan on* (a closer approximation of the Tang [T'ang] dynasty contemporary pronunciations) was introduced. However, *go on* persisted, particularly in words related to Buddhism and also in many common words that had become deeply entrenched in Japanese. Wu (J: Go), originally the name of an ancient kingdom, referred to a region in the lower Yangzi (Yangtze) River area, and perhaps the older Japanese pronunciations came from the Chinese of this area. See ON READINGS.

Gōra Hot Spring　　　　強羅温泉

(Gōra Onsen). Located on the slopes of the mountain Sōunzan in the town of Hakone in Kanagawa Prefecture, central Honshū, it has a simple thermal spring and a saline spring with water temperatures of 30°–94°C (86°–201°F). Gōra Hot Spring is often used as a starting point for sight-seeing in the Hakone area.

gorintō　　　　　　　　五輪塔

(literally, "five-wheel pagoda"). A kind of small stupa that came into use in Japan about the mid-Heian period (794–1185) as a Buddhist memorial, grave marker, or sutra mound monument. Usually constructed of stone, a *gorintō* is composed of five distinct tiers of different shapes, each representing one of the five elements believed in ESOTERIC BUDDHISM to make up the universe. A Sanskrit character is often inscribed on each. See also SUTRA MOUNDS.

gōri system　　　　　　郷里制

(gōrisei). A term referring to the two smallest units—village (gō) and hamlet (ri)—in the four-tier structure of local administration briefly incorporated into the RITSURYŌ SYSTEM in the 8th century. The TAIKA REFORM of 645 had established a three-tier structure—province (kuni), district (gun), and village (ri). The gōri system, initiated in 715, subdivided the smallest unit in order to improve government control and to facilitate tax collection. The former villages (*ri*) were now designated *gō*; each village was to contain two or three new and smaller hamlets (*ri*). Each was to have its own headman. The household system was to be changed as well. *Gō* were to organize extended families or groups of related families, called *gōko*; *ri* were to organize smaller family units, called *bōko*. Because of the social and political instability of the times, the program could not be fully implemented. The attempt was abandoned about 740, and the local administration reverted to the three-tier structure of province, district, and village (the last now being called *gō*).

goroku 語録

("recorded sayings"). Term that strictly speaking refers to records of the oral teachings of masters of the ZEN sect of Buddhism taken down by their disciples but that is also used loosely to refer to collections of the teachings of other religious leaders or tracts written by the teachers themselves. The phrase FURYŪ MONJI ("not standing on words or letters") expresses the Zen idea that enlightenment cannot be communicated by writing or even by words but can only be initiated directly from heart to heart. As a result, Zen masters were not in the habit of putting down their teachings in writing, and *goroku* came into being through the desire of disciples to make records of their masters' words and deeds. The tradition originated in Tang (T'ang) dynasty (618–907) China and was transmitted to Japan, where most examples are from the Kamakura period (1185–1333). Some of the best-known *goroku* include TANNISHŌ by SHINRAN, *Ippen Shōnin goroku* by IPPEN, SHŌBŌ GENZŌ by DŌGEN, and *Minobusan gosho* by NICHIREN (persons cited as authors are the masters whose words are recorded).

goryō 御霊

Also called *onryō*. Malevolent spirits of persons of rank or influence who died unnaturally or in a state of anger or resentment. It was believed that spirits of the dead influenced the living and that the spirits of those who lived extraordinary lives or died unusual deaths were to be particularly feared and placated lest they cause harm. Buddhist monks and ascetics were solicited to perform religious services on behalf of such vengeful spirits, who were sometimes deified to avert their wrath. The *goryō* cult, prominent in the late Nara period (710–794), played a significant role in the court intrigues of the Heian period (794–1185). Feudal warriors also tried to appease the spirits of slain enemies. The festivals or *matsuri* of such deified spirits usually take place in summer (see GION FESTIVAL), while those of traditional deities (KAMI) are observed in spring and autumn.

Goryōkaku, Battle of 五稜郭の戦い

(Goryōkaku no Tatakai). Also known as the Battle of Hakodate. Battle between imperial forces and supporters of the recently overthrown Tokugawa shogunate that marked the end of the BOSHIN CIVIL WAR. In October 1868 shogunate naval commander ENOMOTO TAKEAKI assembled more than 2,000 troops and established his headquarters in a fortress called Goryōkaku at Hakodate in Ezo (now Hokkaidō). An imperial force under KURODA KIYOTAKA began an assault on the city on 20 June 1869 (Meiji 2.5.11) and, on 27 June (5.18), forced the surrender of Goryōkaku.

Go-Saga, Emperor 後嵯峨天皇

(1220–72; Go-Saga Tennō). The 88th sovereign (*tennō*) in the traditional count (which includes several legendary emperors); reigned 1242–46. Son of Emperor TSUCHIMIKADO. His accession set an important precedent, for the KAMAKURA SHOGUNATE intervened in his behalf in determining the succession. Go-Saga abdicated after a reign of only 4 years but dominated the court from retirement for the next 26 years. In 1260 he forced his son and successor Emperor GO-FUKAKUSA to relinquish the throne to Go-Saga's younger son KAMEYAMA. The ensuing rivalry between the two brothers led, by 1287, to the practice of alternating the imperial succession between the senior Jimyōin line (descended from Go-Fukakusa) and the junior Daikakuji line (descended from Kameyama). The anthology *Zoku kokinshū*, sequel to the KOKINSHŪ, was compiled at the order of Go-Saga, himself an accomplished poet.

Go-Sanjō, Emperor 後三条天皇

(1034–73; Go-Sanjō Tennō). The 71st sovereign (*tennō*) in the traditional count (which includes several legendary emperors); reigned 1068–72. Son of Emperor Go-Suzaku (r 1036–45) and Yōmei Mon'in (Princess Teishi), he succeeded his half-brother Emperor Go-Reizei (1025–68; r 1045–68). Because he was not directly related to the Fujiwara regents' house (see REGENCY GOVERNMENT), Go-Sanjō was largely able to restore the authority of the throne. Having surrounded himself with non-Fujiwara officials, he established a manorial Records Office (KIROKU SHŌEN KENKEIJO) to check the proliferation of tax-exempt private estates (SHŌEN). Six months before his death, Go-Sanjō abdicated in favor of his son Emperor SHIRAKAWA and arranged for his two sons by a consort from the MINAMOTO FAMILY to succeed in turn.

Gosanke 御三家

(The Three Successor Houses). The three DAIMYŌ families of the domains of Mito (now part of Ibaraki Prefecture), Owari (now part of Aichi Prefecture), and Kii (now Wakayama Prefecture); the most highly ranked SHIMPAN daimyō and the most honored branches of the Tokugawa family. They traced their ancestry from the three youngest sons of TOKUGAWA IEYASU, the dynastic founder: the Owari branch (with a domain assessed at 619,500 *koku*; see KOKUDAKA) from Yoshinao (1600–1650), the Kii branch (555,000 *koku*) from Yorinobu (1602–71), and the Mito branch (350,000 *koku*) from Yorifusa (1603–61). The Gosanke were expected to support the shōgun against any daimyō challengers and to supply successors in the event that he died without male issue. They were frequently involved in Tokugawa family politics but were also great autonomous lords themselves. See also GOSANKYŌ; TOKUGAWA FAMILY.

Gosankyō 御三卿

("The Three Lords"). The three junior collateral houses of the Tokugawa family. The three senior collateral houses of Owari, Kii, and Mito (see GOSANKE) had been established by TOKUGAWA IEYASU to fill any vacancy in the shogunal succession, but as the blood relationship between the shōgun and the three houses became more distant, it became necessary to look elsewhere for a successor. Three new houses were set up from sons

born to shōguns by secondary wives: the Tayasu from the 8th shōgun TOKUGAWA YOSHIMUNE's second son, Munetake (1715–71), was set up in 1731; the Hitotsubashi from Yoshimune's fourth son, Munetada (1721–65), in 1740; and the Shimizu from the 9th shōgun TOKUGAWA IESHIGE's second son, Shigeyoshi (1745–95), in 1759. The house names were taken from their places of residence. See also TOKUGAWA FAMILY.

Gosannen no Eki →Later Three Years' War

Gose 御所[市]

City in west central Nara Prefecture, central Honshū. Gose was a castle town during the early Edo period (1600–1868). Known for its *yamatogasuri* (ikat weave) and traditional medicines, it now specializes in cotton goods, footwear, and fountain pens. There is a keyhole-shaped tumulus (KOFUN) here. Gose is a part of the Kongō-Ikoma Quasi-National Park. Pop: 36,644.

gosechi no mai 五節の舞

An ancient form of *bugaku* dance (see GAGAKU) performed by women as part of court ceremonies; it is said to have originated in the late 7th century during the reign of Emperor Temmu (r 672–686), having been modeled on dances of Tang (T'ang) dynasty China. During the Nara period (710–794) the dance was customarily performed before the emperor on major holidays and special occasions. But in the Heian period (794–1185) its performance was limited to the feasts known as DAIJŌSAI (Great Food Offering Ritual; an enthronement ceremony) and NIINAMESAI (Festival for the New Tasting; an annual harvest rite). Dancing maidens (five for the former festival and four for the latter) were selected from among the imperial family and nobility. Although the dance was discontinued in the Sengoku period (1467–1568), it was revived at the official enthronement ceremonies of Emperor Taishō (held in 1915), Emperor Shōwa (1928), and Emperor Akihito (1990). It is no longer performed, however, at the annual Niinamesai.

Goseibai Shikimoku 御成敗式目

(The Formulary of Adjudications). Law code established by the KAMAKURA SHOGUNATE (1192–1333) for its vassals (GOKENIN) in 1232 (Jōei 1); also known as Jōei Shikimoku and by several other titles. The Goseibai Shikimoku was the first codification of warrior house law, or BUKEHŌ, which remained dominant in Japan from the 13th through the mid-19th centuries. Originally warrior law was a synthesis of the laws of the imperial government in Kyōto, provincial governments, private estates (SHŌEN), ecclesiastic orders, and other institutions. Warrior law

Gosho Heinosuke
1 Tanaka Kinuyo (left) and Kobayashi Tokuji in a scene from the film *Izu no odoriko* (1933, The Izu Dancer). The earliest of several film treatments of the story by Kawabata Yasunari, Gosho's version is still considered the best.
2 Gosho, who made the first technically successful Japanese sound film, *Madamu to nyōbō* (1931, The Neighbor's Wife and Mine).

was basically pragmatic, dictated by common sense, precedent, and rule by consensus of the shogunate leadership.

The Goseibai Shikimoku owed its birth to the JōKYū DISTURBANCE of 1221. By establishing this code the shogunate aimed to clarify the extent of its newly expanded jurisdiction against that of the Kyōto authorities and to strengthen and formalize its relationship with its own vassals. Supplementary articles (*tsuika*) to the Goseibai Shikimoku were issued from time to time. The subsequent MUROMACHI SHOGUNATE (1338–1573) regarded its own laws as supplements to the Goseibai Shikimoku.

Gō Seinosuke   郷誠之助

(1865–1942). Businessman. Born in what is now Gifu Prefecture. After studying at Dōshisha Eigakkō (now Dōshisha University), he went on to Tōkyō University. In 1884 he went to Germany for further education. On his return he worked for the Ministry of Agriculture and Commerce. He became president of Nippon Un'yu in 1895 and later served as an executive in a variety of large corporations, including Nippon Meriyasu, Iriyama Saitan, and Ōji Paper. Skilled in rebuilding and merging corporations, he played a leading role in pre–World War II business and industrial circles despite his lack of *zaibatsu* affiliations.

Gosekke   五摂家

(Five Regents' Houses). The five major branches of the FUJIWARA FAMILY from which regents (*sesshō* and *kampaku*) and empresses were chosen; specifically the KONOE, KUJŌ, Nijō, Ichijō, and Takatsukasa families, all of which were established early in the Kamakura period (1185–1333). They were all descended from FUJIWARA NO MICHINAGA, of the powerful Northern Branch (Hokke) Fujiwara, and the fifth-generation descendant of Michinaga, Fujiwara no Tadamichi (1097–1164). The first division occurred when Tadamichi's eldest son, Motozane (1143–66), adopted the name Konoe, and his third son, KUJŌ KANEZANE (1149–1207), took the name Kujō. Later, two younger sons of Kanezane's grandson Kujō Michiie (1193–1252) branched off to form the Nijō and Ichijō houses. In 1252 the Takatsukasa house branched off from the Konoe. Such splits were common in other large courtier and warrior families of the time, reflecting a general breakdown of the patrimonial system. See SŌRYŌ SYSTEM.

Gosen   五泉[市]

City in central Niigata Prefecture, central Honshū, on the river Aganogawa. During the 19th century Gosen was noted for its *gosenhira*, a silk fabric used for making the pleated *hakama* skirt. Today it is one of Japan's largest producers of knitted goods. Pop: 39,375.

Gosen wakashū   後撰和歌集

(Later Collection of Japanese Poetry). Commonly abbreviated to *Gosenshū* or *Gosen*. Second of the IMPERIAL ANTHOLOGIES (*chokusenshū*) of classical Japanese poetry. Its compilation was ordered in 951 by Emperor Murakami (926–967; r 946–967) and was carried out by the so-called Five Men of the Pear Chamber (Nashitsubo no Gonin): ŌNAKATOMI NO YOSHINOBU, Kiyohara no Motosuke, MINAMOTO NO SHITAGAU, Ki no Tokibumi, and Sakanoue no Mochiki. It consists of 20 books and contains 1,426 poems in the most authoritative text. The date of completion is unknown but is conjectured as sometime around 955. As its title, "Later Collection," suggests, the anthology stands in the shadow of the KOKINSHū (ca 905, Collection from Ancient and Modern Times), the intent being primarily to provide a supplement to the earlier work rather than a collection of new poetry. Thus, no poems by the compilers are included, and the 219 poets represented belong chiefly to the age of the *Kokinshū*, the late 9th and early 10th centuries.

gōshi   郷士

(rural *samurai*). In the Edo period (1600–1868) the term *gōshi* properly signified low-ranking samurai who lived in the countryside and who supported themselves from holdings they oversaw personally. In this, they were the exception to the efforts by Japan's rulers since the 1590s to separate the warriors from the peasantry and to require samurai to reside in the castle towns of their domains. Relative rank and status varied by region but were uniformly below those of the castle town samurai. *Gōshi* were part of a social structure more commonly found in the less developed TOZAMA ("outer") domains than in the heartland of the Kinai and Kantō plains.

Gōshi could serve both military and administrative functions. In the Satsuma domain (now Kagoshima Prefecture) *gōshi* were in charge of villages and rural towns and served at frontier and highway checkpoints. In the Tosa domain (now Kōchi Prefecture) the rank was used as an incentive to reward reclamation of productive land, offering upward mobility for a rural elite. In its broadest sense the term even extended to include non-samurai village heads who were given permission to assume surnames and carry swords. By the early 19th century this diverse rural elite had developed an awareness of its common interests and social importance. Significant numbers of *gōshi* were active in the politics of the period surrounding the Meiji Restoration of 1868, and it was to these independent, strong-willed "country gentlemen" (*inaka no shinshi*) that TOKUTOMI SOHŌ and others like him looked for leadership in early Meiji Japan.

gōshi kaisha→limited partnership company

Goshikinuma   五色沼

A group of ponds in the Bandai Azuma highland, Fukushima Prefecture, northern Honshū. The name Goshikinuma ("five-colored ponds") refers to the coloration of the waters by minerals and microorganisms.

Go-Shirakawa, Emperor   後白河天皇

(1127–92; Go-Shirakawa Tennō). The 77th sovereign (*tennō*) in the traditional count

(which includes several legendary emperors); reigned 1155–58. After his abdication he controlled affairs for 34 years (see INSEI), which saw the rise and fall of the TAIRA FAMILY and the establishment of the KAMAKURA SHOGUNATE, attempting to maintain imperial power by playing factions against each other. The fourth son of Emperor TOBA, Go-Shirakawa came to the throne with opposition from the retired emperor SUTOKU; this led to the HōGEN DISTURBANCE of 1156. Go-Shirakawa reaffirmed his authority with Taira support. In retirement Go-Shirakawa established numerous imperial estates, most notably the CHŌKŌDŌ RYŌ. In the Shishigatani Conspiracy of 1177 he attempted to dispose of the Taira with the aid of the monk SHUNKAN; in the HEIJI DISTURBANCE of 1160 he exploited the rivalry between the Taira and the MINAMOTO FAMILY, and then turned MINAMOTO NO YORITOMO against his younger brother MINAMOTO NO YOSHITSUNE. He was responsible for the compilation of contemporary songs (*imayō*) called RYŌJIN HISHŌ.

Goshkevich, Iosif Antonovich   ゴシケビッチ, I. A.

(?–1875). Russian linguist and diplomat. He was educated at the seminary in Minsk, Belorussia. After service as an Orthodox missionary in China, he became a member of the Asiatic Department of the Russian Foreign Ministry. From 1852 to 1855 he served as Chinese language interpreter for the Russian expedition to Japan under Vice Admiral Evfimii Vasil'evich PUTIATIN. Tachibana Kōsai (later christened Vladimir Iosifovich Iamatov), a Japanese man smuggled out by the Russians, became Goshkevich's tutor in Japanese, and they compiled a Japanese-Russian dictionary together. Goshkevich returned to Japan in 1858 to serve as Russia's first consular representative.

Goshogawara   五所川原[市]

City in western Aomori Prefecture, northern Honshū. Its principal products are rice and apples. It is also a distribution center for the agricultural produce of the surrounding area. Pop: 47,966.

Gosho Heinosuke   五所平之助

(1902–81). Film director. Noted for his human interest stories of contemporary life. He entered what is now SHŌCHIKU CO, LTD, in 1923. He made the first successful Japanese sound film, *Madamu to nyōbō* (1931, The Neighbor's Wife and Mine). Gosho's films are almost invariably based on contemporary life, taking as their subject events that disrupt ordinary lives. He found humor and pathos in equal measure in these lives and though he tended toward sentimentality, his characters are believable and likable. The most notable technical device he employed is the painstaking editing of hundreds of separate shots to create the proper atmosphere for his story and characters. Among Gosho's finest films are *Entotsu no mieru basho* (1953, Where Chimneys Are Seen), *Ōsaka no yado* (1954, An Inn at Ōsaka), and *Takekurabe* (1955, Growing Up).

Goshun→Matsumura Goshun

gōso   強訴

(forceful appeals). A form of protest made by groups of people to high authorities. During the Heian period (794–1185) deputations of WARRIOR-MONKS (*sōhei*) from the temples ENRYAKUJI and KŌFUKUJI often marched into the capital to protest policy or make demands. They usually bore portable shrines or other sacred objects to intimidate the court. In the Kamakura (1185–1333) and early Muromachi (1333–1568) periods, *gōso* referred to peasant demands that the proprietors of landed estates (SHŌEN) lower land tax (NENGU) and corvée labor (BUYAKU) requirements; with collective absconding (CHŌSAN), it was their principal means of protest. During the Edo period (1600–1868) *gōso* was synonymous with HYAKUSHŌ IKKI, armed uprisings by peasants.

gōson system 郷村制

(*gōsonsei*). A rural community system based on the *gōson*, semiautonomous villages that developed from *sō*, local self-governing bodies dating from the 14th century. These villages served as the basic administrative units of the Tokugawa shogunate's (1603–1867) BAKUHAN SYSTEM (shogunate-domain system).

From the late 13th century to the 14th century great economic and political developments took place in the KINAI, the capital provinces surrounding Kyōto and Nara. With the disintegration of the *myōden* system—the landholding pattern under the *kōryō* (imperial or public domain) and SHŌEN (private estate) systems—class stratification began to develop among the MYŌSHU (local landholders). The more powerful among them created self-governing organizations called *sō*, with GŌ and MURA (villages) as the units of area.

During the Muromachi period (1333–1568) the *sō* came to control many aspects of village life. They organized villagers against exploitation by *shōen* proprietors, SHUGO DAIMYŌ (provincial military lords), and KOKUJIN (local gentry) by resorting to *gōso* (group petitions), CHŌSAN (desertion of farmland), and TSUCHI IKKI (peasant uprisings). In the Sengoku (Warring States) period (1467–1568) the SENGOKU DAIMYŌ ruled their domains through the *gōson* as a unit and accelerated the disintegration of the old estate system.

At the end of the 16th century, by enacting land surveys (KENCHI), *katanagari* (see SWORD HUNT), and laws controlling social classes, the hegemons ODA NOBUNAGA and TOYOTOMI HIDEYOSHI were able to separate the cultivating class from the warrior class. Some local landholders gained *samurai* status, became vassals of the DAIMYŌ, and lived in CASTLE TOWNS. The rest of the farmers were classified into various smaller groupings such as HOMBYAKUSHŌ (propertied farmers), *kobyakushō* (petty farmers), MIZUNOMI-BYAKUSHŌ (landless agricultural laborers), and GENIN (menials; servants). By the method called *muragiri* (village division) village boundaries were redrawn and such administrative divisions as *gō* and *shō*, dating from the *shōen* system, disappeared. The more powerful and established *hombyakushō* became village headmen (called *shōya, nanushi*, or *kimoiri*) and took care of overall village administration. Each *gōson* was assessed a land tax based on estimates of annual rice production (see NENGU). The *hombyakushō* were made collectively responsible for the tax payments, as well as for legal and administrative matters within the village, including maintenance of order and the exercise of commonage and water rights. Thus the village evolved into the new administrative unit of the Tokugawa *bakuhan* system.

The last years of the Tokugawa shogunate

saw many economic and social changes. The *gōson* system itself was shaken, as villages rebelled (see HYAKUSHŌ IKKI) and peasants participated in millenarian movements (YONAOSHI REBELLIONS). However, even after the fall of the Tokugawa shogunate, the new Meiji government retained the *gōson* as an administrative unit. In 1872, to strengthen centralization, the government combined towns and villages. Under the *shisei chōsonsei* (municipal organization system) of 1888–90, a nationwide merger of towns and villages was carried out and the *gōson* system dissolved. See also LOCAL GOVERNMENT.

Gotemba 御殿場[市]

City in northeastern Shizuoka Prefecture, central Honshū. Gotemba developed as a post-station town and as a base camp for Mt. Fuji (FUJISAN). With the opening of the Tōmei Expressway in 1969, automobile-related and acoustic industries have developed. Tourist attractions are the Otome Pass, Komakado Lava Tunnel, and a botanical garden. Pop: 79,557.

Gotō Art Museum 五島美術館

(Gotō Bijutsukan). Located in Tōkyō. Collection of Chinese and Japanese paintings, calligraphy, sutras, and ceramics; Chinese mirrors and early jades; Japanese lacquer, tea-ceremony, and archaeological objects; and a few Korean ceramics built around the private collection of the late GOTŌ KEITA. The museum is perhaps best known for its sections of the GENJI MONOGATARI EMAKI, a well-known picture scroll (EMAKIMONO) of the Heian period (794–1185). It also owns *emakimono* from the Kamakura period (1185–1333), Heian and Kamakura religious paintings and decorated sutras, and examples of RIMPA painting. The Dai Tōkyū Memorial Library of Chinese and Japanese books adjoins the museum.

Go-Toba, Emperor 後鳥羽天皇

(1180–1239; Go-Toba Tennō). The 82nd sovereign (*tennō*) in the traditional count (which includes several legendary emperors); reigned 1183–98. After his death he was first called Kentoku and later Go-Toba. Go-Toba was placed on the throne at the age of three. He remained titular sovereign for 15 years, abdicating at the age of 18, thereafter placing his sons TSUCHIMIKADO (r 1198–1210) and JUNTOKU (r 1210–21) and then Juntoku's son Chūkyō (1218–34; r 1221) in turn upon the throne. Determined to bring down the "illegitimate" Minamoto-Hōjō shogunal regime at Kamakura and restore authority to the Kyōto court, Go-Toba initiated the abortive JŌKYŪ DISTURBANCE in 1221. Go-Toba, with Juntoku and Chūkyō, then went into exile, spending his 18 remaining years on the island of Oki in the Sea of Japan.

Go-Toba is also known as a serious poet of WAKA, or Japanese poetry, an interest he cultivated after his abdication. His teacher was the great Fujiwara no Shunzei (FUJIWARA NO TOSHINARI). In 1201 Go-Toba established the Bureau of Poetry (Wakadokoro), a committee of which compiled the eighth imperial anthology, the SHIN KOKINSHŪ (New Collection from Ancient and Modern Times). The committee did the groundwork, but Go-Toba retained veto power, and his final decisions were often at variance with the wishes of the compilers. The *Shin kokinshū*, which contains 34 of Go-Toba's poems, is a brilliant achievement of a brilliant age of poetry. Go-Toba also wrote a poetic treatise commonly known as *Go-Toba no In gokuden*

(Ex-Emperor Go-Toba's Secret Teachings), one of the important poetic documents of the age.

Gotō Chūgai 後藤宙外

(1866–1938). Author. Real name Gotō Toranosuke. Born in Akita Prefecture; graduate of Tōkyō Semmon Gakkō (now Waseda University). Gotō edited SHINSHŌSETSU, a prominent literary magazine, from 1900 and made it successful with the help of writers belonging to the KEN'YŪSHA (Friends of the Inkstone). He criticized Japanese NATURALISM (*shizen shugi*), which began to flourish at that time. His writings include *Funikudan* (1899), a novel; *Hi shizen shugi* (1908), an essay collection; and *Meiji bundan kaikoroku* (1936), a reminiscence about the Meiji literary establishment.

Gotō Fumio 後藤文夫

(1884–1980). Bureaucrat and politician. Born in Ōita Prefecture; graduate of Tōkyō University. Gotō held positions in the Home Ministry, served as director of administration in the Government-General of Taiwan, and in 1930 was appointed to the House of Peers. A leader of the new bureaucrats (*shinkanryō*) who were sympathetic to the militarists after the MANCHURIAN INCIDENT (1931), he served as minister of agriculture in the SAITŌ MAKOTO cabinet, home minister and acting prime minister in the OKADA KEISUKE cabinet, and minister of state in the TŌJŌ HIDEKI cabinet. Temporarily barred from public office after World War II, he was elected to the House of Councillors in 1953.

Gotō Islands 五島列島

(Gotō Rettō). Group of islands in the East China Sea, west of the Nishi Sonogi Peninsula, Nagasaki Prefecture, Kyūshū; part of Nagasaki Prefecture. The group includes Nakadōrishima, Wakamatsujima, Narushima, Hisakajima, and Fukuejima. Fishing is the chief industry, with abundant catches of horse mackerel, mackerel, and sardines. Sweet potatoes are cultivated on terraced land. Located near the Chinese mainland, the islands have played a historic role as a stopping place for priests and scholars dispatched to China and as a base for pirates. They have been the site of numerous Christian hamlets since the Edo period (1600–1868) and are part of the Saikai National Park. Area: 638 sq km (246 sq mi).

Gotō Katsu 後藤濶

(1863–89). Early spokesman for the Japanese community in Hawaii. Born in what is now Kanagawa Prefecture, he was recruited at the age of 22 for a three-year contract as a sugar plantation laborer in Hawaii. After the expiration of his contract, he opened a general store in Honokaa on the island of Hawaii and served as an interpreter and adviser in the endless plantation labor disputes. During one such dispute he was killed by agents of the planter R. M. Overend.

Gotō Keita 五島慶太

(1882–1959). Entrepreneur. Founder of the TŌKYŪ CORPORATION, a major conglomerate comprising electric railways, tourism, department stores, and real estate. He was born in Nagano Prefecture and graduated from Tōkyō University. After serving in the government (including the Railway Agency) for 10 years, Gotō became successful in railroad construction in the Tōkyō suburbs. He later merged railroad companies in the suburban

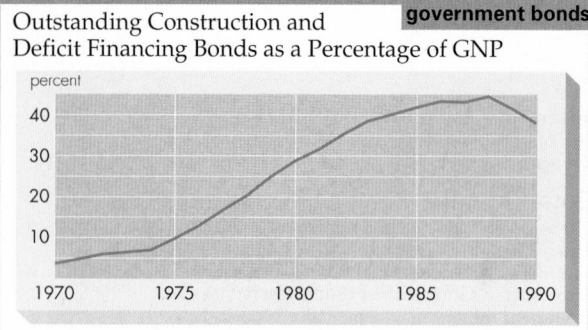

Outstanding Construction and Deficit Financing Bonds as a Percentage of GNP

SOURCE: Ministry of Finance, *Zaisei kin'yū tōkei geppō* (monthly): April 1991.

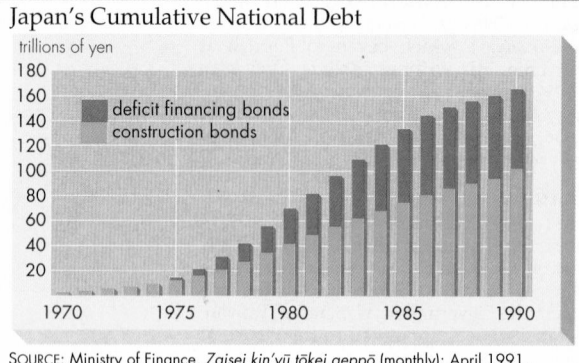

Japan's Cumulative National Debt

trillions of yen

- deficit financing bonds
- construction bonds

SOURCE: Ministry of Finance, *Zaisei kin'yū tōkei geppō* (monthly): April 1991.

Gotō Midori Known internationally as Midori, this young violinist has dazzled audiences with her masterful performances.

Gotō Shimpei This government official of the Meiji and Taishō periods advocated Japanese expansion on the Asian continent and served as a colonial administrator.

Tōkyō area, becoming the most powerful man in the Japanese private railway industry. During World War II, he expanded his business operations into bus transportation, department stores, and motion pictures. When the Excessive Economic Power Decentralization Law was passed after World War II, he was forced to relinquish control of three railroad companies. Although purged by Occupation authorities after the war, Gotō later regained control of many railroad and bus companies in southern Tōkyō. He also made investments in residential development and tourist facilities. Enthusiastic about cultural affairs, he created the network of schools and colleges known as the Gotō Ikūeikai and the GOTŌ ART MUSEUM.

Gotō Konzan 後藤艮山

(1659–1733). Physician of the Edo-period (1600–1868) classicist school (koihō). Also called Gotō Saichirō. Born in Edo (now Tōkyō). Gotō studied medicine on his own after being turned down by koihō teacher NAGOYA GEN'I. Gotō believed the cause of all diseases to be the stagnancy of ki (Ch: qi or ch'i), the vital energy that exists in the universe. He defined health (genki) as that condition in which the body is filled with this energy and advocated that medical treatment be based on junki (correcting the imbalance of ki). He frequently used MOXA TREATMENT and recommended hot-spring therapy and medicines such as dried bear gall.

Gotō Meisei 後藤明生

(1932–). Novelist. Real name Gotō Akimasa. Born in North Korea. Graduate of Waseda University. Gotō writes of people oppressed by the everyday realities of modern life. His *Kakarenai hōkoku* (1971, Unwritten Report) is a stream-of-consciousness account of a man living in a housing development, and *Hasamiuchi* (1973, Attacked from Both Sides) tells the story of a man who tries to confirm his existence by wandering in search of an old overcoat. Other works include *Yoshino-dayū* (1981, The Courtesan Yoshino) and *Kabe no naka* (1986, Within Walls).

Gotō Midori 五嶋みどり

(1971–). Known outside Japan as Midori. Violinist. Born in Ōsaka Prefecture. She began to play the violin at the age of 3 and at 10 moved with her mother to the United States to study at New York's Juilliard School. In the summer of 1986 she appeared with the Boston Symphony at Tanglewood, where she broke the violin strings twice in a single performance, each time astounding the audience and her fellow musicians by continuing flawlessly on a borrowed violin. In 1988 she became the youngest musician ever to receive the Education Minister's Art Encouragement Prize for Young Artists.

Gotō Mitsutsugu 後藤光次

(1571–1625). Metalworker; also known as Gotō Shōzaburō. Said to have been born in Ōmi Province (now Shiga Prefecture). He became a disciple of the master metalworker Gotō Tokujō (1550–1631), who allowed him to adopt the Gotō name. In the mid-1590s TOKUGAWA IEYASU employed Mitsutsugu to mint gold coins (see ŌBAN; KOBAN), and in 1601 he appointed him head of the *kinza*, the official shogunal gold mint (see KINZA, GINZA, AND ZENIZA). Mitsutsugu was instrumental in establishing a standardized national currency and served as an adviser on finance, trade, and diplomacy. His heirs and successors, who retained the name Shōzaburō, served as directors of the *kinza* until its dissolution in 1869. The *ōban* coins minted by the Gotō all bore their family mark.

Gotō Noboru 五島昇

(1916–89). Businessman; leader of the Tōkyū group of companies. Born in Tōkyō. After graduating from Tōkyō University in 1940, Gotō joined Tōshiba Corporation. He later shifted to TŌKYŪ CORPORATION, becoming its president in 1954. As leader of the Tōkyū group he was a skillful manager of department store businesses, hotel operations, and real estate development firms, expanding the enterprise his father, GOTŌ KEITA, had established. As of 1989 the Tōkyū group consisted of 351 companies and 8 corporations with 92,000 employees. Annual sales totaled ¥3.1 trillion (US $23.8 billion). Gotō Noboru also served as chairman of the JAPAN CHAMBER OF COMMERCE AND INDUSTRY (1984–87). He promoted the idea of a pan-Pacific economy and held the office of international chairman of the PACIFIC BASIN ECONOMIC COUNCIL (1978–80).

Gotō Ryūnosuke 後藤隆之助

(1889–1984). Political figure; close adviser to KONOE FUMIMARO, a classmate at Kyōto University who served as prime minister in 1937–39 and 1940–41. Gotō became active in the national Youth Association (Seinendan) and later helped to form the Young Adult Association (Sōnendan) movement to build a broad base for a new political party. In 1933 Gotō created a study group to devise policies for a future Konoe cabinet, this group evolved into the Shōwa Research Association (SHŌWA KENKYŪKAI). In 1940 Gotō's influence was particularly evident during the NEW ORDER MOVEMENT (Shin Taisei Undō), which planned to replace established political parties with a new "national organization." Gotō assumed a top post in the resulting IMPERIAL RULE ASSISTANCE ASSOCIATION (Taisei Yokusankai) in the fall of 1940 but was soon forced to resign because of allegations that he was a communist. After 1945 Gotō was active in the Shōwa Brotherhood (Shōwa Dōjinkai), which promoted public discussion of important issues facing Japan.

Gotō Shimpei 後藤新平

(1857–1929). Administrator and government official of the Meiji (1868–1912) and Taishō (1912–26) periods. Born in the Mizusawa domain (now Iwate Prefecture). Gotō studied medicine at the Sukagawa Igakkō in Fukushima Prefecture and at the Nagoya Medical School. In 1877 Gotō served as a physician for the government during the SATSUMA REBELLION. At age 25 he became president of the Nagoya Medical School. In 1890 Gotō was sent to Germany to study, and upon his return was appointed chief of the medical bureau of the Home Ministry. In 1898 Gotō became civilian governor of Taiwan (under the governor-general). In 1906 he was appointed to the presidency of the newly created SOUTH MANCHURIA RAILWAY. In 1908 Gotō was appointed minister of communications and director-general of the Railway Agency (Tetsudōin) in the second KATSURA TARŌ cabinet. In 1912 Gotō was given the director-generalship of the Colonization Bureau (Takushokukyoku). Following the TAISHŌ POLITICAL CRISIS of 1912–13, he assisted Katsura in organizing a political party, the RIKKEN DŌSHIKAI. In 1916 Gotō was appointed home minister and then in 1918 minister of foreign affairs in the TERAUCHI MASATAKE cabinet. An avid pan-Asianist, Gotō advocated an aggressive and expansionist diplomacy and endorsed Japan's participation in the SIBERIAN INTERVENTION. Gotō, appointed mayor of Tōkyō in 1920 and home minister in 1923, contributed enormously to the reconstruction following the devastating TŌKYŌ EARTHQUAKE OF 1923.

Gotō Shōjirō 後藤象二郎

(1838–97). Politician of the late Edo period (1600–1868) and early Meiji period (1868–1912). Born in the Tosa domain (now Kōchi Prefecture). Under the influence of his fellow Tosa *samurai* SAKAMOTO RYŌMA, Gotō was drawn to the proimperial (SONNŌ JŌI) cause. Through the *daimyō* YAMANOUCHI TOYOSHIGE he called on the shōgun TOKUGAWA YOSHINOBU to return rule peaceably to the emperor (see TAISEI HŌKAN). After the Meiji Restoration (1868) he was appointed to high posts, but in 1873 he resigned in opposition to the government's decision not to invade Korea (see SEIKANRON). Together with ITAGAKI TAISUKE, Gotō formed the AIKOKU KŌTŌ, predecessor of the JIYŪTŌ (Liberal Party). After the ŌSAKA CONFERENCE OF 1875 he became briefly a member of the GENRŌIN (Senate). He managed the TAKASHIMA COAL MINE in Kyūshū for a time, but failing to realize profits, he sold his interests to IWASAKI YATARŌ. In 1881, with Itagaki, he formed the Jiyūtō. In 1887 he organized the DAIDŌ DANKETSU MOVEMENT but left it to join the KURODA KIYOTAKA cabinet as communications minister. He held the same post in the YAMAGATA ARITOMO and MATSUKATA MASAYOSHI cabinets and was named agriculture and commerce minister in the second ITŌ HIROBUMI cabinet, but he resigned when he was implicated in a scandal.

Gotō Shuichi 後藤守一

(1888–1960). Archaeologist. Born in Kanagawa Prefecture. After graduating from Tōkyō Higher Normal School (later Tōkyō University of Education) in 1913, he taught at a middle school in Shizuoka before joining the staff of the Tōkyō Imperial Household Museum (now the Tōkyō National Museum) in 1921. He subsequently became a professor at Meiji University. Gotō had

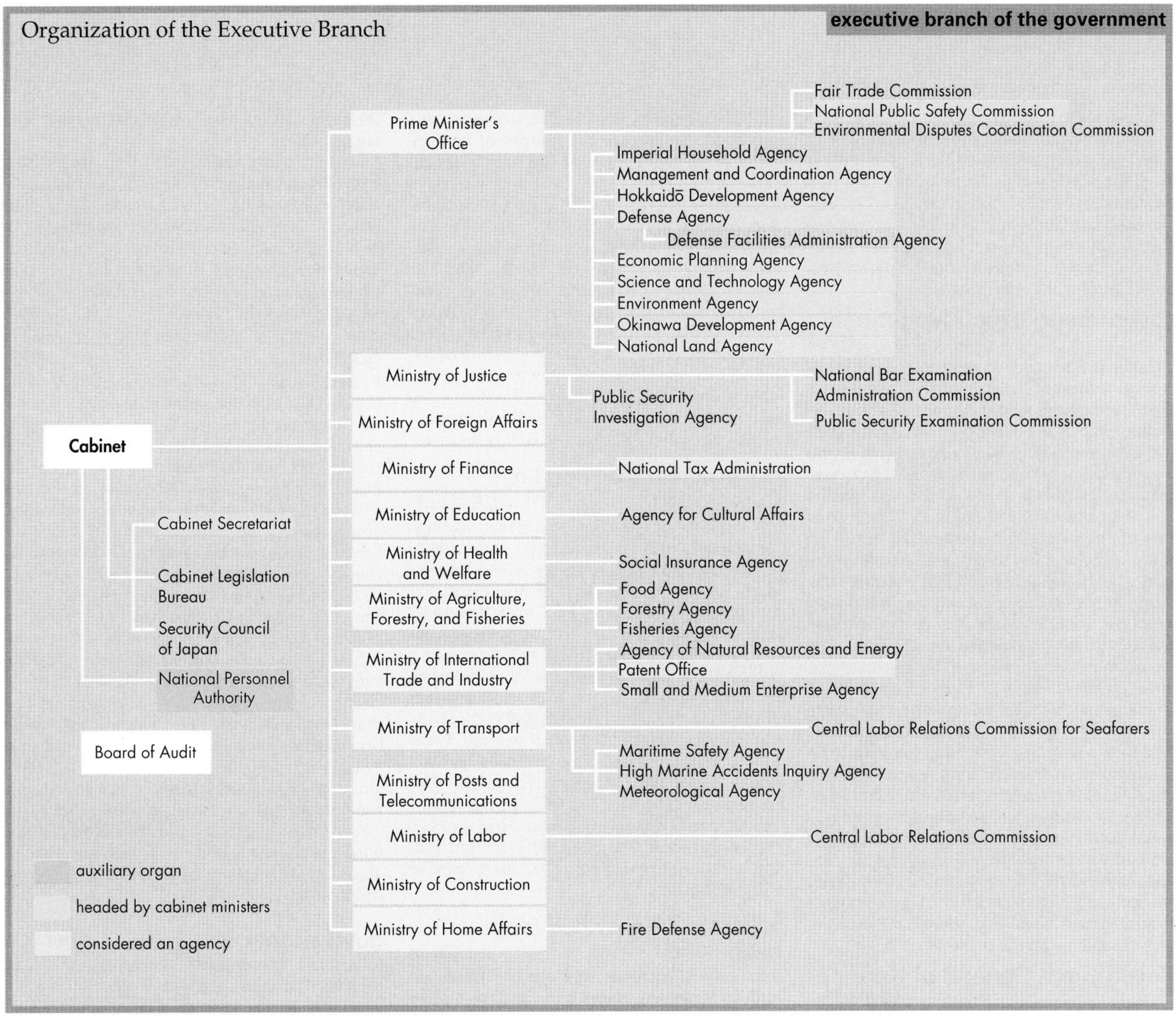

Organization of the Executive Branch

Prime Minister's Office
- Fair Trade Commission
- National Public Safety Commission
- Environmental Disputes Coordination Commission
- Imperial Household Agency
- Management and Coordination Agency
- Hokkaidō Development Agency
- Defense Agency
  - Defense Facilities Administration Agency
- Economic Planning Agency
- Science and Technology Agency
- Environment Agency
- Okinawa Development Agency
- National Land Agency

Cabinet
- Cabinet Secretariat
- Cabinet Legislation Bureau
- Security Council of Japan
- National Personnel Authority
- Board of Audit

Ministry of Justice
- Public Security Investigation Agency
- National Bar Examination Administration Commission
- Public Security Examination Commission

Ministry of Foreign Affairs

Ministry of Finance
- National Tax Administration

Ministry of Education
- Agency for Cultural Affairs

Ministry of Health and Welfare
- Social Insurance Agency

Ministry of Agriculture, Forestry, and Fisheries
- Food Agency
- Forestry Agency
- Fisheries Agency

Ministry of International Trade and Industry
- Agency of Natural Resources and Energy
- Patent Office
- Small and Medium Enterprise Agency

Ministry of Transport
- Central Labor Relations Commission for Seafarers
- Maritime Safety Agency
- High Marine Accidents Inquiry Agency
- Meteorological Agency

Ministry of Posts and Telecommunications

Ministry of Labor
- Central Labor Relations Commission

Ministry of Construction

Ministry of Home Affairs
- Fire Defense Agency

Legend:
- auxiliary organ
- headed by cabinet ministers
- considered an agency

---

broad interests in Japanese prehistory and early history, directing excavations at the TORO SITE and ŌYU STONE CIRCLES. His specialty was the mounded tombs (KOFUN) and culture of the Kofun period (ca 300–710). His major works include *Nihon kōkogaku* (1927, Japanese Archaeology) and *Nihon rekishi kōkogaku* (1937, Japanese Historical Archaeology).

Gotō Yūjō   後藤祐乗

(1440–1512?). Metalworker. Born in the province of Mino (now Gifu Prefecture). A *samurai* serving the Muromachi shogunate (1338–1573), he developed great skill in fashioning sword mountings (KOSHIRAE) and originated the technique of working in high relief. Yūjō's descendants in the service of the Tokugawa shogunate (1603–1867) carried on the Gotō tradition of metalworking until the end of the Edo period (1600–1868).

Gōtsu   江津[市]

City in central Shimane Prefecture, western Honshū, at the mouth of the river Gōnokawa. Gōtsu developed in the Edo period (1600–1868) as a port town on the Sea of Japan. Its main industry is ceramics; pulp and textile industries are also well established. The *tōrō nagashi* (casting lanterns on the water as offerings to the departed), an event held every August during the BON FESTIVAL, is well known. Pop: 27,748.

Go-Uda, Emperor   後宇多天皇

(1267–1324; Go-Uda Tennō). The 91st sovereign (*tennō*) in the traditional count (which includes several legendary emperors); reigned 1274–87. Son and successor of Emperor KAMEYAMA, the founder of the Daikakuji line, he lived in an era of intense rivalry over the succession to the throne. Go-Uda was succeeded on his abdication by the emperors FUSHIMI and Go-Fushimi (1288–1336; r 1298–1301), both of the rival Jimyōin line; he later induced the KAMAKURA SHOGUNATE to recognize officially the tradition of alternating succession from the two lines. He exercised political control from retirement until 1322 during the reigns of his sons, the emperors Go-Nijō (1285–1308; r 1301–08) and GO-DAIGO (r 1318–39).

government bonds   国債

(*kokusai*). The FINANCE LAW (Zaisei Hō), the fundamental law governing the management of public finance in Japan, stipulates that the central government operate on a balanced budget, but it also authorizes the issuance of government bonds (construction bonds) to finance government investment projects. The law provides that these bonds be sold on the open market to banks, corporations, and individuals, but it prohibits their direct sale to the BANK OF JAPAN.

Since 1965, when the government increased its expenditures to provide recession relief and issued bonds to cover the cost, the government has issued bonds each year. During the 1970s, issues of government bonds increased dramatically. In the 1980s a combination of growing government revenues and the government's efforts to reduce its bond issues resulted in a much lower dependency on bonds. In fiscal 1990, government bonds issued amounted to ¥7.3 trillion (US $50.4 billion). The cumulative national debt in fiscal 1990 stood at ¥166.3 trillion (US

$1.1 trillion). See also GOVERNMENT BONDS FOR DEFICIT FINANCING.

government bonds for deficit financing   赤字国債

(*akaji kokusai*). Government bonds issued to make up for revenue shortfalls; distinguished from construction bonds, which are issued to finance public works projects. Deficit financing bonds were issued in 1965 for the first time since the end of World War II and were issued annually from 1975 through 1989. In the original budget for fiscal 1989, the deficit-financing-bond issuance amount was set at ¥1.3 trillion (US $9.5 billion), while all government bonds (including construction bonds) accounted for 2.8 percent of the general account budget revenues in the same fiscal year.

government compensation   国家賠償

(*kokka baishō*). Compensation for damages paid by a government or a public body when it illegally invades the rights of a citizen. This legal responsibility is called both state tort liability and state liability.

According to the Meiji Constitution (1889), under the principle of sovereign immunity the national government would not bear any compensatory responsibility for TORTS. Since 1915, however, it has been recognized that there is government liability for harm resulting from the faulty administration of roads, rivers, harbors, and the like. Moreover, under the CIVIL CODE, government compensatory liability was recognized for

Gotō Shōjirō A member of the early Meiji government, Gotō resigned in 1873 and became active in the movement calling for the establishment of a representative national assembly.

torts caused by the government's operation and administration of profitable enterprises. The 1947 CONSTITUTION OF JAPAN guarantees the right of the people to seek compensation for damages (art. 17). Based upon this principle, the State Compensation Law and various special laws were enacted to define and clarify compensatory liability on the part of national and local governments.

government, executive branch
行政府

(*gyōseifu*). The executive branch of the Japanese government consists of the cabinet and the organizations under its control and jurisdiction: the PRIME MINISTER'S OFFICE (Sōrifu) and 12 ministries, as well as 24 agencies and 7 commissions. According to the 1947 CONSTITUTION OF JAPAN, the executive power is vested in the cabinet (*naikaku*), which consists of the prime minister and 20 ministers of state and is collectively responsible to the DIET, the highest organ of the state. The prime minister (*naikaku sōri daijin*) is designated by the Diet from among its members and nominally appointed by the emperor. He appoints or dismisses the ministers of state (*kokumu daijin*), more than half of whom must be Diet members. The prime minister, representing the cabinet, submits bills to the Diet, supervises and controls the administrative branch, and reports on national and foreign affairs to the Diet. The cabinet is charged with formulation of national policy, preparation of the annual budget, conduct of foreign relations and conclusion of treaties, administration of the civil service, and administration of government programs and laws. See also PRIME MINISTER AND CABINET. — *See chart, previous page.*

Government-General of Korea
朝鮮総督府

(Chōsen Sōtoku Fu). On 30 September 1910, shortly after the annexation of Korea by Japan, the Office of the Resident General in Korea was replaced by the Government-General of Korea. This colonial government, largely controlled by the Japanese military, remained the central organ of Japanese rule until it was abolished on 15 August 1945 in accordance with the terms imposed by the POTSDAM DECLARATION. The head of the colonial administration, the governor-general of Korea, was a Japanese general or admiral appointed by and directly responsible to the emperor. He was in command of the armed forces on the Korean peninsula and had broad powers of control over legislative, judicial, and executive matters. The government-general attempted to assimilate the Korean people into the Japanese empire through indoctrination and a variety of harshly repressive measures. After 1931, the Korean government was used to mobilize Korean resources and labor for the Japanese war effort.

government grants-in-aid
補助金

(*hojokin*). Government subsidies, primarily from the central government of Japan to local governments. In principle, prefectural and municipal governments are totally responsible for the expenses of their administration, but the national government assists in the payment of social welfare, public works projects, disaster relief, and other major government expenses. The assistance comes in the form of treasury grants, which totaled ¥9.8 trillion (US $76.5 billion) in 1988.

Aid is granted on the basis of need and serves to standardize the quality of government services throughout the nation. At the same time, central government assistance has been criticized for leading to excessive dependence and opening the door for national government intervention in local affairs. Inadequate provision of aid has also placed severe constraints on local governments. In addition to aiding local governments, subsidies are extended to individuals and private enterprises that cooperate in national projects. In fiscal 1989 grants totaled ¥15 trillion (US $115 billion), of which some 65 percent was extended to local governments. See also FINANCE, LOCAL GOVERNMENT.

Government Housing Loan Corporation
住宅金融公庫

(Jūtaku Kin'yū Kōko). Government agency, capitalized entirely by national government funds, that provides long-term low-interest loans for the construction of houses. Incorporated in 1950. Some 11.4 million houses were constructed with corporation loans between 1950 and 1990; the loans totaled ¥64.6 trillion (US $444.8 billion). In 1990 loan amounts ranged from ¥4.5 million (US $31,000) to ¥13.0 million (US $89,800), at annual interest rates of 5.5 to 6.7 percent. Over 27.4 percent of Japanese building private homes have used corporation loans. The Government Housing Loan Corporation also makes loans to building contractors. In 1990 the corporation budgeted ¥7.0 trillion (US $48.3 billion) in loans for the construction of 550,000 houses.

government-operated factories, Meiji period
官営工場

(*kan'ei kōjō*). Factories operated by the Japanese government, mainly in the first half of the Meiji period (1868–1912), to import advanced Western technology and facilitate Japan's industrialization. Factories such as the NAGASAKI SHIPYARDS and the SAKAI SPINNING MILL were inherited from the Tokugawa shogunate and various domains. Other enterprises, such as the TOMIOKA SILK-REELING MILL and the SENJU WOOLEN MILL, were set up by the Meiji government. Reflecting the government's SHOKUSAN KŌGYŌ (Increase Production and Promote Industry) policy, the emphasis varied from enhancement of national power, as in the case of strategic industries, to import substitution and promotion of private enterprise, as in the case of the model factories under the Home Ministry and the Hokkaidō Colonization Office (KAITAKUSHI). The majority of the factories proved to be a drain on state finances and were sold off to private interests in the 1880s (see KAN'EI JIGYŌ HARAISAGE; MATSUKATA FISCAL POLICY). The bulk of the strategic industries remained in government hands, to be joined later by the YAWATA IRON AND STEEL WORKS, founded in 1896.

governors and mayors
知事と市町村長

(*chiji to shichōsonchō*). In Japanese, governors of prefectures are called *chiji*, and mayors of cities, towns, and villages are called *shichō*, *chōchō*, and *sonchō*, respectively. As chief executives, these officials initiate local policies, present the budget and draft bills for enactment by the local assemblies, and coordinate and supervise their enforcement by local officials. They represent their local entities in securing subsidies, grants, and loan permits from the national government. As agents of the national or prefectural gov-

ernments, they also carry out certain assigned tasks.

According to the constitution, local chief executives are directly elected. In contrast to the parliamentary type of democracy at the national level, Japan has a presidential system at the local level. However, local chief executives may lose their office by a vote of nonconfidence of their assemblies or by a successful recall.

goyōkin
御用金

Forced loans levied during the Edo period (1600–1868) by the shogunate on GOYŌ SHŌNIN (chartered merchants, i.e., official merchants to the shogunate) and others. The funds were initially used to regulate the price of rice but were later used for repairs to the shogunal castle, coastal defense, and other emergency needs. These periodic demands for cash were not taxes as such and were in theory intended to be returned with interest. The domain governments also issued orders for *goyōkin* from time to time.

The first of some 18 known instances of *goyōkin* was demanded of the fourth SUMITOMO KICHIZAEMON and 33 other merchants in the mid-1700s. The largest demand was made in 1866 to support the second of the shogunate's punitive expeditions against the Chōshū domain (now Yamaguchi Prefecture; see CHŌSHŪ EXPEDITIONS). At the time of the MEIJI RESTORATION (1868) the government levied *goyōkin* to help consolidate its finances, but the following year it abandoned the practice in favor of government bonds.

goyō shōnin
御用商人

(chartered merchants). General term for merchants and traders who were regular purveyors to the Tokugawa shogunate and the *daimyō* domains during the Edo period (1600–1868). Many *goyō shōnin* acted as financial agents for *samurai* officials, whose stipends were paid in rice (KURAMAI) and had to be converted to cash. The merchants profited greatly from the association, although they were periodically obliged to supply large loans (GOYŌKIN) to the government. Because of this mutual dependency, few *goyō shōnin* survived the demise of the shogunate in 1867–68. Notable exceptions included the MITSUI family, who went on to become leading entrepreneurs in the Meiji (1868–1912) and later periods. See also KAKEYA; FUDASASHI.

Gozaishoyama
御在所山

Principal peak of the SUZUKA MOUNTAINS on the border of Mie and Shiga prefectures, central Honshū. Gozaishoyama is composed of granite, and its northern face is suitable for rock climbing. The YUNOYAMA HOT SPRING is located at its eastern foot, and there are lodging and skiing facilities on its summit. Height: 1,212 m (3,976 ft).

Gozan
五山

(The Five Temples; literally, "five mountains," the word mountain being synonymous with temple or monastery). Also pronounced Gosan. A ranking system of officially sponsored Zen Buddhist monasteries organized in the 14th and 15th centuries by the Kamakura (1192–1333) and Muromachi (1338–1573) shogunates.

During the 14th and 15th centuries the major RINZAI SECT Zen monasteries in Kamakura and Kyōto were integrated by the HŌJŌ FAMILY regents and ASHIKAGA FAMILY shōguns into a three-tiered hierarchy of officially sponsored monasteries. This configuration was modeled after the network of official Zen monasteries established in China during the Song (Sung) dynasty (960–1279).

The Gozan system originally included three monasteries in Kyōto and two in Kamakura, but it was soon expanded. In 1380 the Kamakura Gozan were, in order of seniority, KENCHŌJI, ENGAKUJI, Jufukuji, Jōchiji, and Jōmyōji. The corresponding Kyōto monasteries were NANZENJI, TENRYŪJI, KENNINJI, TŌFUKUJI, and Manjuji. In 1386 Nanzenji was raised to a special position at the head of the Gozan in order to allow for the inclusion of the newly built SHŌKOKUJI as the second-ranking Kyōto monastery. The 1386 ranking remained unchanged.

Beneath the 11 full Gozan were the *jissatsu* ("10 temples"), major provincial monasteries. By the 15th century there were 60 of these. On the lowest tier in the system were 230 smaller provincial monasteries known as the *shozan* ("various mountains").

From hesitant beginnings after its formal introduction by the priests EISAI and ENNI in the 12th and 13th centuries, Zen became a vital branch of Japanese Buddhism. The metropolitan Zen monasteries served as conduits through which the cultural interests and values of the Chinese gentry, with whom Chinese Zen monks consorted, poured into Japan. Chinese monks such as ISSAN ICHINEI, who came to Japan in the late 13th century, not only taught Zen meditation and KŌAN study but also lectured on the Chinese classics, poetry, ink painting, calligraphy, and even political thought. Gozan monasteries were centers for the development of the literary and cultural movement known as GOZAN LITERATURE.

Not all medieval Zen monasteries were included in the official Gozan system. The several thousand SŌTŌ SECT temples as well as the Kyōto Rinzai sect monasteries DAITOKUJI and MYŌSHINJI and their branches were excluded. After the ŌNIN WAR (1467–77) the political authority of the Ashikaga and their ability to protect the Gozan declined, and by the end of the century the Gozan had lost most of their landholdings.

Gozan literature   五山文学

(Gozan *bungaku*). Term that, in its broadest sense, refers to the whole tradition of Chinese learning as cultivated in the GOZAN monasteries of Kyōto and Kamakura and in the affiliated smaller monasteries (*jissatsu* and *shozan*) from about the second half of the 13th century through the end of the 17th. The writings of the monks, exclusively in the Chinese language, included religious and secular compositions both in poetry and in prose: diaries, biographies, prefaces, commentaries, congratulatory pieces, treatises of all kinds, records of the teachings of eminent monks, poems, and poetic anthologies. In its narrow sense "Gozan literature" denotes a large body of mostly secular Chinese poetry within this literature.

Historical Background—Almost from the beginning, ZEN teaching used biographies and anecdotes of its patriarchs to provide examples for disciples; Zen monks expressed their spiritual intuition in a kind of verse called *gāthā* (a Sanskrit word; Ch: *ji* or *chi*; J: *ge*). During the Song (Sung; 960–1279) and Yuan (Yüan; 1279–1368) dynasties in China, Zen (Ch: Chan or Ch'an) had a special attraction for members of the educated class; monks were often men who had originally studied for the civil service examination and

retained their interest in secular learning after entering the monastery. Poems in the standard secular verse form, the *shi* (Ch: *shi* or *shih*), and compositions in parallel prose were used in the celebration of religious anniversaries; they were presented to new abbots and to others who retired from their posts. For Japanese Zen monks, Chinese secular learning was a way to gain entrance to the imperial court and the shogunate. Some Gozan monks, such as the renowned MUSŌ SOSEKI, vehemently disapproved of the craze for literature, but in many of the Gozan monasteries, from the 15th century on, such admonitions came to be entirely forgotten. Gozan monks on the whole possessed greater facility in the Chinese language than did the *kambun* and *kanshi* (see POETRY AND PROSE IN CHINESE) writers of earlier times, if only because significant numbers of them had actually lived and studied in China. Authorities agree that the best years of Gozan poetry lie toward the latter part of the 14th century. Its deterioration in the 15th and 16th centuries was accompanied by increasing interest in scholarship, poetic criticism, and composition of parallel prose.

Outstanding Figures—ISSAN ICHINEI (Ch: Yishan Yining or I-shan I-ning; 1247–1317) arrived in Japan from China in 1299. To a far greater extent than any previous Zen master, Issan provided his pupils with secular as well as religious instruction; for this reason he is often described as the founder of Gozan literature. Among the disciples who flocked to him were KOKAN SHIREN and SESSON YŪBAI. Kokan was the author of the monumental GENKŌ SHAKUSHO, the earliest comprehensive history of Japanese Buddhism, composed, according to one account, because of questions put to him by Issan. Other major 14th-century figures are BETSUGEN ENSHI, unusual in that he belonged to a Sōtō rather than a Rinzai lineage, and CHŪGAN ENGETSU. The two poets generally considered the best were both dharma disciples of Musō: GIDŌ SHŪSHIN and ZEKKAI CHŪSHIN. Among the many later Gozan masters were Taihaku Shingen (d 1415), who excelled at parallel prose, and the poet Shinden Seiha (1375–1447).

goze   瞽女

Blind women who traveled about Japan singing and playing the SHAMISEN. First appearing in the 16th century, the *goze* spread throughout Japan during the Edo period (1600–1868). Their numbers have gradually dwindled, and few now remain; the best known are in Jōetsu, Niigata Prefecture.

The *goze* lived in tightly organized groups, each based in a communal house, usually established in a castle town under the protection of the local *daimyō*. In a time when entertainment was scarce in the countryside, they were welcomed warmly. The *goze* played an important part in the spread and development of Japanese folk song. Their repertoire included not only folk and popular ballads but also sequences of song mixed with formalized recitation several hours long, based on Shintō or Buddhist teachings. Wanderers, the handicapped, and performing artists were often thought to have supernatural powers, and many *goze* served as healers and casters of agricultural fertility spells. See also ZATŌ; BIWA HŌSHI.

gozen kaigi   御前会議

(imperial conferences). Conferences on matters of grave national importance convened in the presence of the emperor between 1894 and 1945. These extraconstitutional confer-

gozen kaigi At this imperial conference held on 11 January 1938, Emperor Shōwa presides as officers of the navy (left) and army (right) discuss possibilities for resolving the Sino-Japanese War.

ences usually sought final imperial approval of courses of action already decided upon by the other participants, usually elder statesmen (GENRŌ), the prime minister, cabinet officials, and representatives of the armed forces. The first *gozen kaigi* was convened on the eve of the SINO-JAPANESE WAR OF 1894–1895; others were held to deliberate the TRIPARTITE INTERVENTION of 1895 and the RUSSO-JAPANESE WAR (1904–05). No further conferences took place until 1938, during the SINO-JAPANESE WAR OF 1937–1945. More than a dozen were held thereafter, to deliberate the signing of the TRIPARTITE PACT in 1940, the attack on PEARL HARBOR in 1941, and acceptance of the POTSDAM DECLARATION surrender terms in August 1945. At this last *gozen kaigi*, the emperor, who usually remained silent, broke the deadlock by personally advocating unconditional surrender.

graduate schools   大学院

(*daigakuin*). Japanese graduate schools were reorganized along American lines in 1947. The usual Japanese graduate program is five years, two for the master's degree and three for the doctorate. Exceptions are medical and dental schools, which have a four-year doctoral program only.

The first Japanese graduate school was at Tōkyō University, where postgraduate courses in various faculties were instituted in 1880. Before World War II graduate schools had no exclusive facilities or teaching staff, and the number of students was very small. Even after the war not all universities had graduate programs. Through the 1980s the number of graduate schools and the quality of the programs offered were increased, but in the early 1990s graduate study in Japan still lagged behind that of other advanced countries. In 1990, 61.7 percent of Japan's universities maintained graduate schools. Approximately 6.4 percent of college graduates went on to receive master's degrees; of these, 63.8 percent attended national universities. In all, 45.9 percent of the master's candidates were in engineering. Of master's degree holders, 15.7 percent proceeded into doctoral programs. In 1990 the total number of graduate students was 61,884 in master's and 28,354 in doctoral programs.

graffiti   落書

(*rakugaki*). The word *rakugaki* corresponds closely to the casual use of the English word "graffiti"; *rakusho*, another reading for the same characters, has a broader range of meaning, often with an emphasis on the elements of social and political criticism. In this

article "graffiti" is used in the broadest sense of *rakusho*.

Most Japanese graffiti are anonymous. They are found in every sort of setting from public rest rooms to historical monuments. Graffiti written on paper may be dropped along public roads, thrown into someone's garden, or pasted on walls or gates.

From the mid-13th century through the Muromachi period (1333–1568), there even existed a type of public trial sometimes known as *rakugaki kishō* ("graffiti confession"). People with knowledge of a crime were encouraged to inform on the perpetrator through one of the above-mentioned types of graffiti.

In 1945 an enormous number of early graffiti were discovered on the ceiling boards of the main hall of the 7th-century temple HŌRYŪJI. Later, graffiti from the Tempyō era (729–749) were found in numerous locations. In one corner of a scroll in the SHŌSŌIN is a drawing of a pop-eyed, bearded man with shoulders hunched angrily.

Graffiti criticizing government policies flourished during the rule of TOKUGAWA YOSHIMUNE (r 1716–45). Subsequently, because of their political content, graffiti were banned by the Tokugawa shogunate. Despite repeated warnings against writing them, however, they continued to appear.

In the late Edo period, graffiti became an information conduit, a trend accelerated by the arrival of Commodore Matthew PERRY's ships in 1853. Their informational content increased, but the elements of satire and wordplay waned as graffiti became a deadly serious political weapon. During the Meiji period (1868–1912) the role of graffiti was partly taken over by newspapers, and the appearance of "letters to the editor" columns in the Taishō period (1912–26) further absorbed the functions of graffiti. Japanese student activists of the late 1960s, influenced by the Paris student uprisings, adopted the slogan "white walls belong to me" and conducted what amounted to public trials by criticizing the "establishment" through graffiti.

grain embargo controversy
防穀令事件

(Bōkokurei Jiken; Grain Protection Order Incident). Dispute between Japan and Korea over an embargo on rice and soybeans in 1889. Following the signing of the Treaty of KANGHWA (1876), Japan had increased its political and economic penetration of Korea, still technically a protectorate of China. In 1889, because of a poor harvest, a Korean provincial governor issued an order prohibiting the export of rice and soybeans. Japanese

brokers in Korea, who had cornered the Korean market, demanded that the Japanese government put pressure on the Korean government to revoke the order and give them monetary compensation. The order was rescinded in January of the following year and ¥110,000 was paid to the brokers in 1893. Japan's handling of the incident, which included military threats, strained relations with both Korea and China. See also KOREA AND JAPAN.

grand chamberlain → sobayōnin
Grant, Ulysses Simpson
グラント, U. S.

(1822–85). General and 18th president of the United States. He was born in Ohio and was a graduate of West Point. During the Civil War he commanded the Union Army; he was elected president in 1868. Early in 1872 he greeted the IWAKURA MISSION upon its visit to the United States. During a tour of the world after his retirement, Grant visited Japan in 1879. While there he mediated unsuccessfully between China and Japan to settle the problem of suzerainty over the Ryūkyū Islands. See RYŪKYŪ KIZOKU MONDAI.

grapes
葡萄

(budō). Several species of grape are found growing wild in Japan; the principal cultivated species are the wine grape (*Vitis vinifera*) and the fox grape (*V. labrusca*). The native Kōshū variety of wine grape has been grown in the Kōfu Basin of Yamanashi Prefecture since early times, but Campbell Early and Delaware grapes, which were introduced from the United States in 1872–73, are now the main varieties grown throughout the country. The fox grape is suited to the Japanese climate with its rainy summers, but wine grapes such as Muscat of Alexandria are grown in greenhouses to avoid disease. Wine grape varieties such as Neo Muscat and Kyohō have been especially developed for the Japanese climate and are grown both in fields and under cover. Most of the grapes grown in Japan are consumed as table fruit, but about 10 percent of the harvest, consisting principally of Kōshū and Delaware, is devoted to wine production.

graphic design
グラフィック・デザイン

(gurafikku dezain). Commercial graphic design in Japan dates from at least the mid-Edo period (1600–1868), when color woodblock prints known as *nishiki-e* were used as advertisements for dry goods stores and *kimono* shops. In the late Edo period, as commercial activity increased and a wider range of social classes gained economic power, the use of *nishiki-e* and *hikifuda*, a type of one-page printed handbill advertising store openings and sales of goods, became widespread. The Edo period also saw the introduction of Western printing technology and the spread of BOOK ILLUSTRATION, exemplified by the illustrated books known as KUSAZŌSHI.

After the Meiji Restoration of 1868, influence from the West, especially from Europe, inspired the development of a new style of graphic design that blended elements of Japanese and Western practice. This new style became especially evident in newspaper and magazine advertisements. Later the art nouveau movement in the West directly influenced Japanese design, and from about the early 1900s graphic design in Japan developed in tandem with that of the West. Sugiura Hisui (1876–1965), a poster designer active in this period, is known for his adaptations of the art nouveau and art deco styles.

An organization of commercial designers was established in the 1920s, and Western design trends, such as the constructivist style of the Bauhaus, continued to influence Japanese graphic design. Well-known designers of the 1920s and 1930s include Yamana Ayao (1897–1980), a pioneer in the field, who is known for the posters, packaging, and advertising brochures he designed for the Shiseidō Co, Ltd. Yamana's refined, modernistic designs gave the company a distinctive image that it retains to this day. In magazine design, the 1930s photo magazine *Nippon*, founded by the pioneer photojournalist NATORI YŌNOSUKE, displayed a high level of artistic achievement. Also significant were the World War II propaganda magazine *Front* (1941–45) and its art director, Hara Hiromu (1903–86). Directed at an overseas audience, *Front* displayed Hara's striking sense of visual expression, which was influenced in part by Western cinematic montage techniques. The magazine set the standard for 1940s Japanese editorial design.

Graphic design was dealt an almost fatal blow with Japan's defeat in World War II. However, in the immediate postwar period there were still a number of good commercial design schools and a large number of graphic designers waiting for the opportunity to demonstrate their talents. Foreign influence continued to help shape the Japanese design scene after the war, but the source of the influence shifted away from France and Germany to the United States. After 1945 such American commercial design concepts as the art-director system were introduced to Japan, resulting in heavy American influence on postwar Japanese design, especially in advertising. Typical of this influence is the 1952 Peace cigarettes logo, created by the American designer Raymond Lowey and now recognized as a classic in postwar Japanese design. With the growth of postwar industry and mass media, the level of technical expression in graphic design increased dramatically. The Japan Advertising Arts Club (JAAC), a nationwide organization of commercial designers, began holding regular exhibitions in the early 1950s. The organization (disbanded in 1971) contributed much to the discovery and development of talented young designers.

The 1960s are known as the golden age of poster design in Japan. The designers KAMEKURA YŪSAKU and Katsumi Masaru (1909–83) received high praise for their roles in the visual presentation of the 1964 Tōkyō Olympic Games. Other important Japanese postermakers include YOKOO TADANORI, known for his collage posters; Nagai Kazumasa (b 1929), who is known for his highly abstract, geometric forms and who also designed the 1972 Sapporo Winter Olympics logo; Fukuda Shigeo (b 1932), whose works are infused with unexpected humor and a sense of visual fantasy; Tanaka Ikkō (b 1930), who employed traditional Japanese color and form with techniques of modern design; NAGAOKA SHŪSEI, whose hyper-realistic style has attracted such diverse clients as General Motors and the American band Earth, Wind, and Fire; and Sugiura Kōhei (b 1932), a postermaker and book designer with a unique visual vocabulary. Posters, prominently displayed in Japan's extensive public transportation system, remain a major graphic design medium.

Japanese commercial designers have also shown great creativity in book illustration. With Japan's high-volume publishing business, book illustrators have a ready-made market. In this as in other fields of graphic design, both computer-aided design (CAD) and desktop publishing technologies have shown explosive growth in the late 1980s and early 1990s. The television commercial is another field in which Japanese designers have displayed great originality and in which Japan has received numerous international awards. The Japan Graphic Designers' Association (JAGDA), founded in 1978, is one of the important design associations in Japan. Since 1981 it has published the annual *Graphic Design in Japan*.

☎ 476–477

Great Court of Cassation 大審院

(Daishin'in; sometimes called Taishin'in). The highest judicial tribunal in Japan under the Meiji Constitution of 1889. The leaders of the Meiji Restoration made no distinction between administrative and judicial affairs until April 1875 when, as a result of the Ōsaka Conference, a separate judicial organ was established to act as a final court of appeal for both civil and criminal cases, deal with crimes against the state or the imperial family, and decide cases affecting diplomatic relations. All inferior courts remained under the jurisdiction of the minister of justice, however, as did the administration and personnel of the Great Court of Cassation itself. A truly independent judiciary was not realized in Japan until the creation of the SUPREME COURT after World War II.

Greater East Asia Coprosperity Sphere 大東亜共栄圏

(Dai Tōa Kyōeiken). A slogan used by the Japanese government during World War II to express the idea of a politically and economically integrated Asia free from Western domination and under Japanese leadership, but also used to rationalize Japan's expansionist ambitions on the continent. Initially the sphere consisted of Japan, Japanese-occupied China, MANCHUKUO (Japan's puppet state in Manchuria), French Indochina, and the Dutch East Indies. It later included the Japanese-held islands of the Pacific and all of Southeast Asia.

The New Order in East Asia—The direct predecessor of the Greater East Asia Coprosperity Sphere was the "New Order in East Asia" (Tōa Shinchitsujo) proclaimed by KONOE FUMIMARO's government on 3 November 1938. Although the 16-month-old SINO-JAPANESE WAR OF 1937–1945 had thus far been marked by tactical successes, there were some farsighted statesmen and soldiers who feared that a protracted war would leave the Japanese empire exhausted and vulnerable. There was every reason, then, for the Japanese government to make at least some conciliatory gestures toward China in the hope that the Chinese will to resist would diminish or that a Chinese collaboration movement might emerge and become viable.

It was in this context that Prime Minister Konoe proposed the New Order. He tried to convince China that Japan, far from desiring territory or special privileges in China, looked forward to cooperating with China against both communism and the imperialistic ambitions of the West. Out of this cooperation would emerge the New Order in East Asia reflecting an equal partnership between Japan and China. Though flawed, the New Order was not merely an empty opportunistic slogan; it reflected Japanese—and Chinese—bitterness about the "old order" established in Asia by the Western colonial powers. While CHIANG KAI-SHEK rejected

Konoe's offer, Chiang's longtime rival WANG JINGWEI (Wang Ching-Wei) defected in December 1938 and began negotiating terms that would culminate in March 1940 in the creation of a collaborationist regime, the so-called REORGANIZED NATIONAL GOVERNMENT OF THE REPUBLIC OF CHINA. While the apparent invincibility of the German Reich allowed pro-Axis spokesmen like Foreign Minister MATSUOKA YŌSUKE the opportunity to press for Japan's full-scale participation in the TRIPARTITE PACT signed in September 1940, Japan moved to widen the scope of its own New Order in East Asia. Increasingly the phrase "Greater East Asia" appeared in the rhetoric of those in favor of further expansion.

The Greater East Asia Coprosperity Sphere—For some time one faction of the Japanese expansionist movement had stressed the necessity of a Japanese drive southward to gain control of the resource-rich and strategically important European colonial possessions in Southeast Asia (see SOUTHERN EXPANSION DOCTRINE). In September 1940 Japan made the first move by demanding of French authorities the right to station troops, use airfields, transport supplies, etc, in the northern part of French Indochina; the French had no choice but to yield. In August Matsuoka had proclaimed that the New Order had been expanded into a "Greater East Asia Coprosperity Sphere." In addition to the countries embraced by the New Order (Japan, China, and Manchukuo), he announced that "Greater East Asia" would include French Indochina and the Dutch East Indies. In December 1941 the China war expanded into the Pacific phase of World War II, which was officially designated by Japan as the "Greater East Asia War" (Dai Tōa Sensō) shortly after the Pearl Harbor attack.

In the spring of 1942 the government of Premier TŌJŌ HIDEKI began to make plans for the creation of a Greater East Asia Ministry (Dai Tōa Shō) responsible for coordinating relations between Tōkyō and the various nations and territories of the sphere. The ministry was created on 1 November 1942 but there was little centralized planning or direction of the Coprosperity Sphere in Tōkyō.

In November 1943 the leaders of the five major states participating in the Coprosperity Sphere assembled in Tōkyō for the Greater East Asia Conference (Dai Tōa Kaigi), the only meeting of its kind held during the existence of the Coprosperity Sphere. The leaders attending the Tōkyō conference were Wang Jingwei, representing the Reorganized National Government of the Republic of China; Zhang Zhunghui (Chang Chung-hui), prime minister of Manchukuo; Prince Wan Waithayakon of Thailand (which had formally declared war on the Allies in January 1942); José Paciano LAUREL, president of the Republic of the Philippines (which had been established by Japan just three weeks before the conference met); and BA MAW, the leader of a Burmese regime that had gained its "independence" in August 1943. The conference addressed few substantive issues; it was really an occasion for ringing oratorical pledges of solidarity, condemnation of Western imperialism, and visions of a resurgent Greater East Asia. Whatever the various motivations of the Japanese in setting up the Coprosperity Sphere—in their expansionist policies they were, after all, following Western imperialist models—there are indications that, while deploring the economic rapaciousness of the Japanese authorities and the often brutal and arrogant behavior of the Japanese military, some peo-

grapes
1 The large and juicy Kyohō variety, which ripens between mid-August and mid-September, was developed expressly for the Japanese climate. **2** The Kōshū, the oldest variety cultivated in Japan, ripens between late September and early October.

ple in the states that comprised the Coprosperity Sphere recognized the significance of the catalytic historical role that Japan had played in the process that led to the liberation of the peoples of India and of East Asia from Western colonial rule both during and after World War II.

Green Cross Corporation [株]ミドリ十字

(Midori Jūji). Manufacturer of pharmaceutical products. Incorporated in 1950. The company manufactures and distributes blood derivatives and is diversifying its product line, focusing especially on the field of biotechnology. In 1978 Green Cross set up Alpha Therapeutic Corporation, a wholly owned subsidiary in California, which manufactures and distributes blood derivatives in the United States. Sales for the fiscal year ending December 1990 totaled ¥72.8 billion (US $545.1 million), and capitalization stood at ¥10.7 billion (US $80.1 million). Headquarters are in Ōsaka.

Grew, Joseph Clark グルー, J. C.

(1880–1965). US ambassador to Japan from 1932 until the attack on Pearl Harbor in 1941. Born 27 May 1880 of a wealthy Boston family, he graduated from Harvard College in 1902. He married Alice Perry, Commodore Matthew PERRY's great-grandniece. Entering the diplomatic service in 1904, he served in various posts, including almost 10 years as secretary of the Berlin embassy and as ambassador to Turkey from 1928 to 1932. Grew arrived in Japan toward the end of the MANCHURIAN INCIDENT of 1931–33. He worked to calm Japanese-American relations and hoped to rebuild friendship.

In 1940 Japan's advance into Indochina and alliance with Germany convinced Grew that sterner measures were necessary. As war neared, Grew warned of a possible Japanese surprise attack. After Pearl Harbor he and his staff returned to the United States in exchange for Japanese diplomats. Near the end of the war, as under-secretary of state, Grew advised President Truman to inform the Japanese that after defeat they would be permitted to retain the emperor, recognizing that such an assurance would be critical in a decision to surrender. Although not stated explicitly, the final surrender terms gave the Japanese just enough hope on this crucial issue for them to submit (see POTSDAM DECLARATION).

grievance procedure 苦情処理手続

(kujō shori tetsuzuki). System for resolving alleged violations of employee rights specified in COLLECTIVE LABOR AGREEMENTS. In the United States many union contracts detail
Continued on page 478 ➤

A Century of Japanese Poster Design

Woodblock-print handbills from the Edo period (1600–1868) are the forerunners of the modern Japanese poster. Like the *ukiyo-e* prints from which they borrowed motifs, these handbills—known as *ebira* and *hikifuda*—appealed to the masses of ordinary citizens in major cities. When the new technique of lithography was introduced from the West, Japanese poster designers were influenced in many ways by the lithographs to which they were exposed. Poster portraits of beautiful women, however, remained a staple of the genre and continued to follow the format popularized by traditional Japanese paintings. By the second and third decades of the 20th century, modernist art from the West—particularly the art nouveau and art deco styles—was affecting design-

A: Artist   D: Designer   AD: Art Director   CD: Creative Director   Ph: Photographer   CW: Copywriter

1881 *Hikifuda* (woodblock-print handbill) using a *kabuki* star to promote cosmetics. Artist unknown.

1897 A *kimono* dyer's *hikifuda* employing the popular "money tree" motif to attract good fortune. Artist unknown.

1909 Department-store poster using a traditional beauty to drum up business. A: Okada Saburōsuke.

1911 Poster for the Export Articles Exhibition. A: Kitano Tsunetomi.

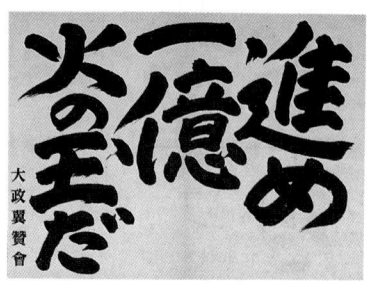

1942 War-effort propaganda exhorting citizens to "Advance/like 100 million/blazing suns." Artist unknown.

1955 Visual pun: a forest depicted by groupings of the character for "tree." D: Yamashiro Ryūichi.

1959 Poster for the Japan Typography Exhibition. D: Hara Hiromu.

1963 Poster for the Tōkyō Olympics. AD: Kamekura Yūsaku. Ph: Hayasaki Osamu.

1976 An exuberant young woman as a department-store symbol. AD: Ishioka Eiko. Ph: Yokosuka Noriaki.

1978 Poster for a stereo system. AD: Hosoya Gan. CD: Akiyama Shō. Original Artwork: Kimura Tsunehisa. CW: Annen Toshihiko. D: Hosokawa Takehisa.

1981 Poster for Nihon *buyō* dance performances sponsored by UCLA. D: Tanaka Ikkō.

1982 Woody Allen promoting the "good life" for a department store. AD: Asaba Katsumi. CW: Itoi Shigesato.

ers in Japan. Many mastered the visual techniques of modern poster art and created designs expressing a greater social awareness. Sugiura Hisui, who with other poster artists formed the Group of Seven (Shichininsha) in 1924, was one of the true originals to emerge out of this creative ferment.

Graphic designers banded together in the years after World War II and used their impact on printed media to profoundly influence the taste and direction of popular culture. After 1960, when Tōkyō hosted the World Design Conference,

graphic designs from Japan began to reach a worldwide audience, and several of its poster makers have developed international reputations. Those working today create their work from a global rather than national perspective and generate much of their visual imagery using electronic technology. Yet the domestic aesthetic tradition often permeates their treatment of color, form, and space, resulting in a distinctively Japanese ambience.

Takami Kenshirō

1914 Department-store poster targeting prosperous female customers. D: Sugiura Hisui.

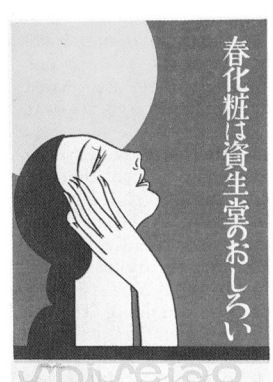

1925 Poster for a cosmetics firm. D: Yabe Renchō.

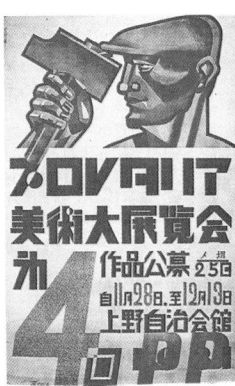

1931 Poster for the Proletarian Art Exhibition. D: Terashima Teishi.

1937 Poster presenting the summer-fabrics line of an apparel manufacturer. D: Okuyama Gihachirō.

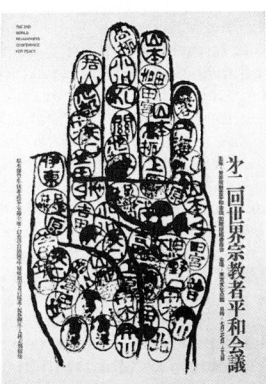

1964 Poster for the International Religious Conference. D: Awazu Kiyoshi.

1965 Poster celebrating the 1st anniversary of a brand of beer. D: Nagai Kazumasa.

1969 Theater bill for a kabuki performance. D: Yokoo Tadanori.

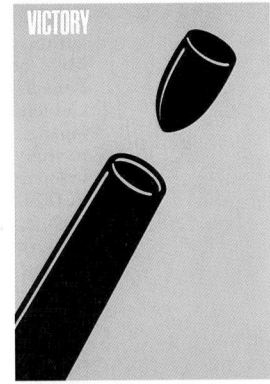

1976 Winner of The 30th Anniversary of Victory in Warsaw Poster Contest. A: Fukuda Shigeo.

1982 Poster announcing a street festival. A: Yumura Teruhiko.

1984 Poster for a graphic design exhibition. D: Sugiura Kōhei and Tanimura Akihiko. A: Watanabe Fujio.

1985 Poster for a printing firm. D: Katsui Mitsuo.

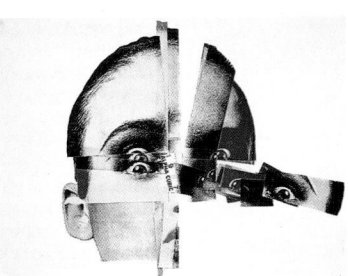

1987 Poster for an apparel manufacturer. D: Saitō Makoto.

the conditions of employment along with a procedure for obtaining relief if an employee feels these conditions are violated. A typical procedure in the United States directs a grievance through a number of stages of negotiations between labor and management representatives, after which it is turned over to a neutral third party for final arbitration.

In Japan, about 50 percent of all labor agreements contain grievance procedures, but their substance and function differ greatly from those in the United States. First, because Japanese labor agreements do not specify the conditions of employment in great detail, grievances are often ill defined. Second, the procedures specify only negotiations between labor and management; thus, an employee is not guaranteed neutral arbitration. Finally, grievance procedures are not widely utilized even where they exist, perhaps because the Japanese do not like to formalize their disputes. Nevertheless, the NATIONAL ENTERPRISE LABOR RELATIONS LAW (Kokuei Kigyō Rōdō Kankei Hō) and the Local Public Enterprise Labor Relations Law (Chihō Kōei Kigyō Rōdō Kankei Hō) provide for the establishment of committees to handle grievance negotiations between labor and management. See also LAW, ATTITUDES TOWARD; LABOR LAWS.

Griffis, William Elliot
グリフィス、W. E.

(1843–1928). US educator, clergyman, and author of numerous books and articles on Meiji-period (1868–1912) Japan. Born in Philadelphia. While a student at Rutgers University (1865–69), Griffis tutored several Japanese students who were among the first to study in the United States. Griffis taught in Japan from 1870 to 1874. Griffis left Japan in 1874 and in 1876 published *The Mikado's Empire*, an early firsthand account of Japan. He wrote 18 books and several hundred articles on Japan and delivered hundreds of public lectures. He was twice the recipient of the Order of the Rising Sun.

group hiring
集団就職

(*shūdan shūshoku*). The practice of hiring middle-school and high-school graduates from rural areas in groups, rather than as individuals. The first instance of group hiring is believed to have been in 1954, when an association of stores in Setagaya Ward in Tōkyō hired a group of middle-school graduates from Niigata Prefecture. Its success is attributed to the employers' provision of good working conditions, including wage regulations and retirement benefits, which had not previously existed in small and medium enterprises.

In the 1960s, a period of rapid economic growth, a severe shortage of labor occurred. From 1963 on, the MINISTRY OF LABOR, metropolitan and prefectural governments, and the JAPAN TRAVEL BUREAU, INC, pooled resources to transport trainloads of high-school graduates to the metropolitan areas. Larger enterprises also went to the countryside to hire young job seekers. In the 1970s the number of young people desiring employment via this system declined annually, and in 1977 the Ministry of Labor suspended its support for the practice.

groups
集団

(*shūdan*). In Japanese society, group consciousness is learned from an early age in the FAMILY, which is the most important primary group for the individual. The family provides the context in which socialization takes place, as well as patterns of interaction that are applied in other, secondary groups such as school and neighborhood cliques, clubs in and out of school, and groups in the workplace. The Japanese are highly rank-conscious, and Japanese groups have fairly clear-cut ranking among members. Each person is linked to a particular individual above him. At the top of the group is one individual to whom all others are related through subordinate linkages (see VERTICAL SOCIETY).

Whatever is imparted or provided by a senior to his subordinate is considered a favor and is in some contexts called ON, an especially profound debt. Whether *on* or not, the favor must be repaid in the form of respect, service, and loyalty to one's superior. The obligation to repay one's debt is often called *giri* (see GIRI AND NINJŌ). The relationship among group members is "functionally diffuse," that is, it is not circumscribed in terms of specific roles, but tends to encompass almost all aspects of one's life.

Dedicated service to one's group comes from self-discipline achieved through a type of character building called *seishin shūyō*. This self-discipline includes deferment of gratification, physical hardship, and the like, in combination with a cognitive orientation that values inner strength and peace through outward physical experience. *Seishin shūyō* is so important that some companies incorporate it into their new-employee orientation programs. One reason given for the success of Japanese companies is the strong link in workers' minds between the company's fate and their own, in contrast to Western workers who are more likely to see their personal interests as being pitted against that of the company.

As a rule, warm, intimate relationships are maintained only among group members, and the group closes its doors to outsiders. A group's internal cohesion is often heightened by recognizing a rival group with which it competes in obtaining certain resources. Branches of a bank, for instance, may be pitted against one another for increasing deposits. Factions (HABATSU) of a political party compete for such political resources as the presidency of the party or ministerial posts.

Guadalcanal
ガダルカナル島

(Gadarukanarutō). A volcanic island in the Solomon Islands, southwestern Pacific Ocean. Occupied early in 1942 by Japanese forces, it was the site of the first Allied invasion (August 1942) to retake Japanese-held territory. After losing more than 17,000 men in heavy combat, the Japanese abandoned it in February 1943.

Guam
グアム島

(Guamutō). An island belonging to the Mariana group in the western Pacific. Now an unincorporated territory of the United States. Guam was discovered by Magellan in 1521; from 1668 it was governed by Spain. Following the Spanish-American War of 1898 it became the property of the United States. The Japanese invaded Guam on 9 December 1941, two days after the attack on PEARL HARBOR. In July 1944 American troops landed, defeating the Japanese in August. Since World War II, Guam has been the site of an American air base and has become a very popular Japanese tourist resort. In January 1972 Yokoi Shōichi (b 1915), a Japanese

Imperial Army sergeant who had not realized that World War II was over, was discovered after remaining in hiding on Guam for 27 years.

Guandong (Kwantung) Army
関東軍

(J: Kantōgun). Unit of the Imperial Japanese Army that was originally assigned to guard areas in southern Manchuria leased by Japan from China after the RUSSO-JAPANESE WAR of 1904–05. In the 1930s it seized all of Manchuria, expanded into Inner Mongolia, and prepared for war against the Soviet Union.

Created on 1 August 1906, the Guandong Army was assigned to defend the Guandong Leased Territory and the railway zone between PORT ARTHUR (Ch: Lüshun; J: Ryojun; now part of Lüda) and Changchun (Ch'angch'un). For over a decade it was administered as a department within the Guandong Government-General, with the governors-general serving concurrently as commanders of the Guandong Army, but on 12 April 1919 the Guandong Government-General was replaced by separate civilian and military administrations, the Guandong Government and the Guandong Army Command, respectively.

Faced with a rising tide of Chinese nationalism and anti-Japanese sentiment in Manchuria during the 1920s, Guandong Army officers came to favor strong measures to protect Japanese interests. Accountable to the emperor through the army high command rather than to civilian authority, a few activist staff officers resorted to unauthorized initiatives, such as the assassination of Manchurian warlord ZHANG ZUOLIN (Chang Tso-lin) on 4 June 1928. On 18 September 1931 Colonels ISHIWARA KANJI and ITAGAKI SEISHIRŌ staged an explosion on the tracks outside of Mukden (now Shenyang) that led to fighting between Guandong Army railway guards and local Chinese forces. Accepted as a fait accompli by the Guandong Army commander, General HONJŌ SHIGERU, the MANCHURIAN INCIDENT (sometimes called the Mukden Incident) precipitated the occupation of all of Manchuria and the creation of the puppet state of MANCHUKUO. The Guandong Army came close to monopolizing political power in Manchuria and wielded strong influence over the SOUTH MANCHURIA RAILWAY Company.

After 1931 Guandong Army strategists regarded the Soviet Union as their chief enemy. As both sides built up their forces, border clashes erupted with increasing frequency and severity. In 1939 the Guandong Army lost close to 18,000 men in a series of battles with the Soviet Red Army at Nomonhan over a disputed section of the Outer Mongolia-Manchukuo border (see NOMONHAN INCIDENT). Tōkyō's 1941 SOUTHERN EXPANSION DOCTRINE left the Guandong Army with a defensive role in Manchuria, but after 1943 its crack units were transferred to Pacific battlegrounds. Within two weeks of a Soviet Red Army strike into Manchuria on 9 August 1945, the Guandong Army lay shattered. Many of its members spent years in Soviet labor camps before being repatriated.

Guandong (Kwantung) Territory
関東州

(J: Kantōshū). A Japanese leasehold from 1905 until 1945, located on the tip of the Liaodong (Liaotung) Peninsula in southern Manchuria. With an area of 3,463 square kilometers (1,337 sq mi), the Guandong Territory comprised land south of a line running along the 39° 20″ north latitude and included the adjacent Changshan Islands, Port Arthur (Ch: Lüshun; J: Ryojun; now part of Lüda) and Dairen (Ch: Dalian or Ta-lien; J: Dairen; Russ: Dalny). The Chinese name Guandong, literally "East of the Pass," traditionally referred to all of Manchuria, i.e., the area east of the Shanhaikwan (Shanhaiguan; "Mountain-Sea Pass"). The Japanese applied the name to their holding on the tip of the Liaodong Peninsula, only a small portion of the area originally encompassed by Guandong.

Japan seized the Liaodong Peninsula during the SINO-JAPANESE WAR OF 1894–1895 and forced China to cede it in the 1895 Treaty of SHIMONOSEKI but was compelled to return it almost immediately under diplomatic pressure (see TRIPARTITE INTERVENTION). In 1898 Russia obtained from China a 25-year lease to Port Arthur and Dairen. Two years later Russia occupied the entire Guandong region during the BOXER REBELLION, only to lose it to Japan during the RUSSO-JAPANESE WAR of 1904–05. The 1905 Treaty of PORTSMOUTH awarded Japan all of Russia's rights to the Guandong region.

To administer the territory the Guandong Government-General (Kantō Totoku Fu) was established in Liaoyang. Moved to Port Arthur in May 1906, it consisted of civil and military departments. Matters of defense fell to the military department, the GUANDONG (KWANTUNG) ARMY. The civil department delegated responsibility for public works, health, and education to the SOUTH MANCHURIA RAILWAY. In May 1915, after Japan presented China with the TWENTY-ONE DEMANDS, the Guandong Territory lease was extended from 25 to 99 years. On 12 April 1919, in order to resolve bureaucratic rivalries arising from the fact that successive governors-general were invariably military officers, the Guandong Government-General was replaced by separate agencies, the Guandong Army Command and the Guandong Government (Kantōchō). After the MANCHURIAN INCIDENT in 1931, the Guandong Army reasserted control over the Guandong Territory. In 1934 the Guandong Government was succeeded by a two-tiered structure. The Guandong District Government (Kantōshū Chō), which handled civil administration, was presided over by the Guandong Bureau (Kantōkyoku), headed by the commander of the Guandong Army. Occupied by Soviet forces in August 1945, the Guandong Territory reverted to China, except for Port Arthur, where the Russians maintained a naval base until 1955.

Guan Yu (Kuan Yü)→Kan U

guardian→kōkennin

Gukanshō
愚管抄

("Notes on Foolish Views"). Secular history of Japan written by the high-ranking Buddhist priest JIEN (1155–1225) just before the JŌKYŪ DISTURBANCE of 1221. The work is colored by Jien's preoccupation with the interdependent functions of three institutions: the imperial household, with which he had close familial ties; the TENDAI SECT of Buddhism, which he had served four times as chief abbot; and the Kujō branch of the Fujiwara family, of which he was probably the most influential member. See KUJŌ FAMILY.

Although the Gukanshō is deeply colored by the author's secular concerns, its main interest lies in its view of history as propelled by divine principles. The book's theological character, in fact, led early readers to call it a "tale of principles" (dōri no monogatari). Jien believed in the existence and power of destructive principles, derived from the ancient Hindu conception of kalpic cycles that were driving secular affairs toward ultimate ruin. He also believed in constructive principles (some Buddhist and some Shintō), which, when followed by enlightened leaders, produced temporary improvement. The primary focus of the Gukanshō is on the possibilities of a better future, when the principle, created by the sun goddess and other ancestral gods, would be realized by which imperial rule would be supported through both aristocratic learning and military might.

gulls
鷗

(kamome). Several species of gulls (medium-sized birds of the family Laridae) are found in Japan. Two of the most common are the umineko (black-tailed gull; Larus crassirostris) and the yurikamome (black-headed gull; L. ridibundus). The word kamome is also used to refer in particular to the mew gull (L. canus), which is distributed throughout northern Eurasia and northwestern North America and comes in great numbers as a winter visitor to Japan. Other gulls found in Japan are the ōseguro kamome (slaty-backed gull; L. schistisagus) and the zuguro kamome (Saunders' gull; L. saundersi). The yurikamome is mentioned as the miyakodori in the 8th-century poetry anthology Man'yōshū.

gumbatsu
軍閥

(military faction). In modern Japanese history this term refers either to the military in general when it vied with nonmilitary factions for control of the government's domestic and foreign policy, or to groups of army or navy officers—linked by common regional origin, social background, or expertise—who competed for control of services policy and of government military and civil policy as a whole. The term first entered common Japanese parlance in the Taishō period (1912–26).

From the establishment of the Imperial Japanese Armed Forces (see ARMED FORCES, IMPERIAL JAPANESE) following the Meiji Restoration of 1868 to their abolition following Japan's defeat in World War II, the army and navy played a crucial role in Japanese politics. Between 1885 and 1945 generals and admirals held 15 of the 30 premierships and 115 of the 404 civilian cabinet portfolios. The military's ability to act as a political faction was based on the common samurai heritage of both civilian and military leaders during the Meiji period (1868–1912) and their concern for the development of national power, the military power and prestige of the armed forces, the broad popular support mobilized through the IMPERIAL MILITARY RESERVISTS' ASSOCIATION and other mass organizations, the independence from civilian control of the Army and Naval General Staff Offices, and the appointment of only active-duty officers to the service ministers' posts in the cabinet (see GUMBU DAIJIN GEN'EKI BUKAN SEI). The political influence of the military increased substantially in the 1930s, reaching its apex in World War II; after Japan's defeat in 1945 it was completely eliminated (see MILITARISM).

Before the Taishō period the dominant factions within the military were the Satsuma faction of the navy and the Chōshū faction of the army (see HAMBATSU). By the Taishō period, however, the Satsuma faction had given way to cliques of NAVAL ACADEMY and Naval Staff College graduates divided

between supporters and opponents of the naval limitation treaties resulting from the WASHINGTON CONFERENCE of 1921–22 and the London Naval Conference of 1930. By 1934 the prolimitation "treaty faction," including such moderate admirals as SAITŌ MAKOTO, OKADA KEISUKE, and TAKARABE TAKESHI, had lost control of naval policy to the "fleet faction," led by Admirals KATŌ HIROHARU and Suetsugu Nobumasa (1880–1944). There was also a clash between an internationalist "administrative group" in the Navy Ministry and a hawkish "command group" in the Naval General Staff and, especially from the mid-1930s, a struggle between a pro-Anglo-American faction and a pro-German faction.

The Chōshū faction controlled the army and exercised a major influence on civil government well into the 1920s through its leader, Field Marshal YAMAGATA ARITOMO. Four of his followers (KATSURA TARŌ, KODAMA GENTARŌ, TERAUCHI MASATAKE, and TANAKA GIICHI) served as army minister between 1898 and 1924, and three of these (Katsura, Terauchi, and Tanaka) served as prime minister between 1901 and 1928. Only after 1912 did graduation from the Army Staff College begin to supplant affiliation with the Chōshū clique as the principal criterion for army leadership positions.

Tanaka Giichi was the last of Yamagata's protégés. UEHARA YŪSAKU, chief of the General Staff Office, and such generals as ARAKI SADAO and MAZAKI JINZABURŌ resisted the continuation of Chōshū power and Tanaka's efforts to appoint UGAKI KAZUSHIGE his successor as army minister in 1924. Although Tanaka eventually pushed this appointment through, his premiership in 1927–28 marked the end of the Chōshū faction's domination of the army.

After 1922 a variety of cliques inside and outside the services claimed to speak for the emperor. This contention led to unrestrained factionalism within the army during the 1930s. Many scholars have viewed this factionalism as a struggle between two primary cliques. The Imperial Way faction (KŌDŌHA) composed of anti-Chōshū generals and young activist officers emphasized the emperor cult and preventive war against the Soviet Union, while the Control faction (TŌSEIHA) composed of strategic planners urged army discipline and rational economic planning before beginning a war. In this view, the Control faction's success in suppressing an attempted Imperial Way faction coup d'état in 1936 (see FEBRUARY 26TH INCIDENT) was a prelude to war with China in 1937 and the United States in 1941. But the complex politics of these and other incidents of the 1930s suggest that an orderly interpretation of the prewar period in terms of factional conflict or the victory of one clique over another is difficult to sustain. What remains incontestable is the impact of the whole military considered as a single faction upon the political life of modern Japan, especially during the years 1937–45, when army and navy officers dominated the government.

gumbu
軍部

(literally, "military component"). Broadly gumbu signifies the pre-1945 military arm of the government and more narrowly the army and navy who, by taking advantage of the right of supreme command (TŌSUIKEN) of the emperor as defined in the 1889 Meiji Constitution, they asserted their independence from the civil government (in this connection, often referred to as the *gyōseibu*, or "administrative component") and increased their political power in the years before World War II. More specifically *gumbu* refers to the military leadership centering on the army and navy general staff headquarters, but also including the two service ministries, military counselors (*gunji sangikan*), and field marshals. See also MILITARISM; GUMBATSU; ARMED FORCES, IMPERIAL JAPANESE.

gumbu daijin gen'eki bukan sei 軍部大臣現役武官制

(active-duty officers as service ministers). Pre–World War II rule whereby only military men on active duty could serve as ministers of the army and navy. It originated in 1871, when the Ministry of Military Affairs (Hyōbushō) required that its head minister hold the rank of major general (or rear admiral) or above, and continued after the creation of separate army and navy ministries in 1872. In order to check the growing power of political parties, the YAMAGATA ARITOMO cabinet in 1900 required that the service ministers be a full general and a full admiral on active duty. In keeping with TAISHŌ DEMOCRACY this provision was abolished by the first YAMAMOTO GONNOHYŌE cabinet in 1913. The rule was revived in 1936 by the HIROTA KŌKI cabinet following the FEBRUARY 26TH INCIDENT, an attempted coup by young army officers. By refusing to nominate service ministers the military often prevented parties from forming cabinets (see GUMBATSU).

Gumma Canal 群馬用水

(Gumma Yōsui). Agricultural canal in south-central Gumma Prefecture, central Honshū, constructed to develop the resources of the river TONEGAWA. Covering 102 sq km (39.4 sq mi), the irrigated area comprises fields on the southern slopes of Akagisan and the eastern slopes of Harunasan.

Gumma Incident 群馬事件

(Gumma Jiken). Riot in May 1884 by indebted farmers in the southern part of Gumma Prefecture; one of several incidents of violence related to the FREEDOM AND PEOPLE'S RIGHTS MOVEMENT. Hard pressed by the deflationary fiscal policy of Finance Minister MATSUKATA MASAYOSHI (see MATSUKATA FISCAL POLICY), farmers rallied under local JIYŪTŌ (Liberal Party) members. Frustrated after unsuccessful attempts to petition the Meiji government for reduction of interest rates, they planned to attack government officials scheduled to attend Emperor Meiji's opening of a new railway station at Takasaki, but the ceremony was postponed. More than 3,000 farmers gathered at the foot of the mountain Myōgisan, attacked the house of a moneylender, and took over a police station. The rioters also planned to attack the garrison at Takasaki, but they were dispersed by police. The leaders were arrested and imprisoned.

Gumma Prefecture
Location and
Prefectural Crest

Gumma Prefecture 群馬県

(Gumma Ken). Located in central Honshū and bounded by Niigata and Fukushima prefectures on the north, Tochigi Prefecture on the east, Saitama Prefecture on the south, and Nagano Prefecture on the west. The terrain is largely mountainous, except for the southeastern corner, which constitutes part of the KANTŌ PLAIN. The TONEGAWA, Japan's second-longest river, originates in the ex-

treme north of the prefecture and flows through it in a southeasterly direction. Most of the major cities are concentrated in the southern plains area. The mountain areas are noted for heavy snowfalls, and the southern plains area has summer thunderstorms and strong, dry winter winds.

The area was settled early on, as evidenced by the IWAJUKU SITE and numerous other archaeological sites. It was known as Kōzuke Province under the ancient provincial system (KOKUGUN SYSTEM). During the medieval period (mid-12th–16th centuries) it was divided among various local warlords; some areas were controlled directly by the Tokugawa shogunate in the Edo period (1600–1868). Gumma took its present form in 1876 after the abolition of feudal domains.

Long a center of raw silk and cereal production, Gumma has recently shifted to vegetable farming to supply the TŌKYŌ market. The textile industry is still dominant in cities such as KIRYŪ, ISESAKI, and TATEBAYASHI, but in recent decades other major cities, notably ŌTA, TAKASAKI, and SHIBUKAWA, have become centers for chemical, electrical, and machine industries, reflecting the northward expansion of the KEIHIN INDUSTRIAL ZONE. Its proximity to Tōkyō and excellent transportation links provide a basis for further expansion.

Although much of Gumma is gradually taking on many of the characteristics of a suburb of Tōkyō, its mountains in the north, including part of NIKKŌ NATIONAL PARK and JŌSHIN'ETSU KŌGEN NATIONAL PARK, continue to be popular with climbers, skiers, and vacationers. Hot-spring resorts such as Minakami, Ikaho, and Kusatsu also attract numerous visitors. Area: 6,356 sq km (2,453 sq mi); pop: 1,966,265; capital: MAEBASHI.

gun → kokugun system

gunchūjō 軍忠状

Reports by warriors in the 14th and 15th centuries recounting successful military exploits; they were submitted after battles to commanders, who endorsed them with their monograms (KAŌ). The reports influenced promotions and land awards and were preserved by the warriors' families. The earliest *gunchūjō* date from the GENKŌ INCIDENT of 1331–33.

gundai 郡代

District deputies or regional intendants in charge of tax collection, census registration, law and order, and other administrative functions. Major provincial officials of the shōguns began to hold this title in the 14th century. Under the TOKUGAWA SHOGUNATE (1603–1867) *gundai* were generally assigned to shogunal land (TENRYŌ) assessed at over 100,000 *koku* (see KOKUDAKA), while the more numerous DAIKAN (intendants) supervised smaller shogunal territories. In 1590 TOKUGAWA IEYASU appointed INA TADATSUGU as his first *gundai* of the Kantō region. In the late Edo period (1600–1868) the number of *gundai* decreased to four, assigned to Kantō, Mino, Hida, and Saigoku. *Daimyō* also appointed *gundai* in their own domains.

gundan 軍談

(war stories). Popular Edo-period (1600–1868) tales about famous battles and the lives of illustrious warrior generals that circulated both as small handwritten books and as oral narratives recited by professional storytellers. They were often embellished accounts of the rise and fall of well-known warrior families—for example, the *Hōjō*

godai ki (incomplete), a history of five generations of HŌJŌ FAMILY rule; the *Shinchō Kō ki* (1600), heroic episodes from the life of ODA NOBUNAGA; and the *Taikōki* (1625), a romanticized retelling of the exploits of TOYOTOMI HIDEYOSHI. The oral form of these stories originated with the professional reciters of the TAIHEIKI, an earlier historical romance. They were adapted for the stage by writers for KABUKI troupes and the JŌRURI puppet theater. In the 18th century Japanese versions of Chinese colloquial martial fiction were popular. In the late Edo period, accounts of happenings in China such as the Opium War (1839–42) and the Taiping (T'ai-p'ing) Rebellion (1850–64) were transformed into *gundan*.

gunji 郡司

Local officials charged with the administration of the *gun* (districts), administrative subdivisions of the *kuni* (provinces) under the RITSURYŌ SYSTEM of government that had evolved after the TAIKA REFORM of 645. They were under the jurisdiction of the KOKUSHI (provincial officials). The four ranks of *gunji* performed functions such as law enforcement and land registration. In contrast with the *kokushi*, who came from the central administration, the *gunji* came from influential local families (KUNI NO MIYATSUKO). They were appointed for life, and the office was virtually hereditary. When local uprisings occurred, the *gunji* often sided with the peasants against the *kokushi*. The post of *gunji* disappeared with the rise of the SHŌEN (private estate) system, and former office-holders became leaders of warrior bands (BUSHIDAN).

Gunji Naritada 郡司成忠

(1860–1924). Also known as Gunji Shigetada. Naval strategist, colonist, adventurer, and entrepreneur in northeast Asia. Born in Edo (now Tōkyō), Gunji graduated from a naval preparatory school in 1879 and reached the rank of first lieutenant by 1890. Gunji regarded the Kuril Islands, which Japan had acquired from Russia in 1875, as vital to national defense and called for their colonization. When the government remained unresponsive, he resigned his naval commission and in 1893 founded the Chishima Hōkō Gikai (Kuril Service Society). In 1896 Gunji established a colony on Shimushu, the Kuril island closest to Kamchatka. In June 1904, during the RUSSO-JAPANESE WAR, he launched an attack on Kamchatka but was captured and imprisoned. In the years following his release, he wrote on naval strategy and headed a fisheries consortium in the Russian Maritime Province. He also undertook a series of confidential government assignments in Siberia until 1920.

Gunjin Chokuyu → Imperial Rescript to Soldiers and Sailors

gunka 軍歌

(war songs). The term *gunka* primarily refers to a genre of Westernized music originating in the late 19th century. The history of Japanese military songs can be traced back to the Kume *uta* supposedly sung by Emperor Jimmu's soldiers in the 7th century BC and still preserved in the court music repertoire, to certain songs in the MAN'YŌSHŪ (completed in 759), and to music for BIWA, including HEIKYOKU. At the Meiji Restoration in 1868 the victorious soldiers sang a marching song in Western style, "Miya san, Miya san," later borrowed by Gilbert and Sullivan for *The Mikado* (1885); this was the first true *gunka*. The Sino-Japanese War (1894–95) and the Russo-Japanese War (1904–05) stimulated the composition of many *gunka*. The most famous is "Gunkan kōshinkyoku" (1900, The Battleship March), a celebration of Japan's new naval might, but almost all the rest have been forgotten. During the 1930s and World War II many more *gunka* were composed.

gunki monogatari　軍記物語

(war tales). Category of prose literature developed in the Kamakura (1185–1333) and Muromachi (1333–1568) periods that deals with warfare, especially the cataclysmic civil wars of 1156–1221 and those that ushered in the Muromachi period.

The story of the political struggles of 1156 and 1159–60, which led to the eclipse of the Fujiwara and subsequent Taira supremacy, is told in the Kamakura-period tales HŌGEN MONOGATARI and HEIJI MONOGATARI (see also HŌGEN DISTURBANCE and HEIJI DISTURBANCE). The story of the Taira leader, Kiyomori, and the TAIRA-MINAMOTO WAR of 1180–85, when the Taira were overthrown by MINAMOTO NO YORITOMO (assisted by his younger brother MINAMOTO NO YOSHITSUNE, the supreme hero figure in Japanese history), forms the subject matter of the 13th-century HEIKE MONOGATARI and the Kamakura-period GEMPEI SEISUIKI. The events of the Jōkyū (or Shōkyū) era (1219–22), when Emperor GO-TOBA attempted to reassert imperial authority against the Hōjō family (see JŌKYŪ DISTURBANCE), figure in *Jōkyūki* (or *Shōkyūki*). The final attempt to reassert imperial authority, by Emperor GO-DAIGO in the first half of the 14th century, and the wars against the ASHIKAGA FAMILY are recounted in TAIHEIKI (14th century). Two other Muromachi war tales center on individual lives—the career of Yoshitsune in GIKEIKI (15th century) and the short lives of the Soga brothers in SOGA MONOGATARI (14th century).

Precedents for war tales were the 10th-century SHŌMONKI and the 11th-century *Mutsu waki*, both in a form of classical Chinese (KAMBUN), and a few tales of warriors in Book 25 of the early 12th-century KONJAKU MONOGATARI. Grammatically simpler than other genres and containing numerous Chinese words, these tales are set down in a vigorous style suited to the portrayal of action and heroic deeds, rather than to the expression of fine shades of feeling. Many characters and events in *gunki* became the stuff of national legend, figuring prominently in numerous NŌ, KABUKI, and JŌRURI dramas, as well as in prose. While national attitudes and ideals of conduct reflected in *gunki* are now regarded as quintessentially Japanese—for example, unflinching bravery and self-sacrificing loyalty—*gunki* may actually have played a role in fostering such concepts.

Gunreibu→Naval General Staff Office

Gunsho ruijū　群書類従

(Classified Collection of Japanese Classics). A monumental collection of Japanese literary classics and historical records. The first series, compiled by HANAWA HOKIICHI (1746–1821), consisting of some 1,270 titles, was completed in 1819; the second, known as *Zoku gunsho ruijū*, comprising 2,103 titles, was completed in 1972. Hanawa classified the materials, which date from the late 9th century to the beginning of the Edo period (1600–1868), into 25 categories.

The project was begun in 1779; the first work printed was the 13th-century text *Ima monogatari*, published in 1786. The *Gunsho ruijū* set the highest standards for bibliographical and philological scholarship, and even today it remains an important reference. The wood blocks used to print the first series—17,244 in all—are preserved at the Onko Gakkai Historical Society. This series has been reissued several times in modern editions.

gun'yaku　軍役

Military levies required of vassals by warrior lords. During the Kamakura period (1185–1333) the shogunate expected vassal family heads (*sōryō*; see SŌRYŌ SYSTEM) to mobilize their kinsmen for military service upon call. By the end of the 16th century a vassal's obligation was determined by the productivity of the lands assigned him in fief (CHIGYŌ) and specified in terms of manpower per *koku* (see KOKUDAKA).

Throughout the Edo period (1600–1868) the Tokugawa shogunate adhered to this policy, issuing *gun'yaku* regulations for all *daimyō* and lesser direct vassals (HATAMOTO and GOKENIN) in 1616, 1633, and 1649. The regulations of 1649 remained unchanged for 200 years, but the shift to a peacetime economy reduced the vassals' ability to meet the requirements, and in 1862 and 1866 the shogunate issued regulations greatly reducing these service requirements. The *gun'yaku* system was abandoned in 1867, and after the MEIJI RESTORATION (1868) the new government adopted the principle of universal military conscription.

Gunze, Ltd　グンゼ[株]

(Gunze). Manufacturer of textile goods, including knitted goods, stockings, and outerwear. Incorporated in 1896 in Kyōto, it soon became a major silk manufacturer. After World War II, with the decline of the silk industry, it switched to the production of synthetic fabrics. It is currently diversifying its lines of business by entering new fields such as machinery for textile production and plastic films and molds. Gunze has many subsidiaries in Japan and affiliates in Korea and Hong Kong. Sales for the fiscal year ending March 1991 totaled approximately ¥180.0 billion (US $1.3 billion), and the company was capitalized at ¥17.3 billion (US $126.1 million) in the same year. Headquarters are in Ōsaka.

Gunzō　群像

Monthly literary magazine founded by Kōdansha, Ltd, in October 1946. *Gunzō* publishes works by established authors of *jumbungaku* ("pure literature") as well as literary criticism. Novels that first appeared in *Gunzō* include TAMURA TAIJIRŌ's *Nikutai no mon* (1947, Gate of Flesh) and TAKEDA TAIJUN's *Fūbaika* (1952, A Flower Pollinated by Wind). Literary critics such as ITŌ SEI and OZAKI KAZUO have contributed articles. In 1958 the Gunzō Literary Prize for New Writers was established. Recipients of the prize include AKIYAMA SHUN and KARATANI KŌJIN, for criticism, and ŌBA MINAKO, LEE HWE-SONG, MURAKAMI RYŪ, and MURAKAMI HARUKI, for fiction.

Guo Moruo (Kuo Mo-jo)　郭沫若

(1892–1978; J: Kaku Matsujaku). Major Chinese writer and historian. Guo Moruo spent some 20 years in Japan as a student and later as a political exile. With YU DAFU (Yü Ta-fu) and ZHANG ZIPING (Chang Tzu-p'ing), he was

a leader of the Creation Society (Chuangzao She or Ch'uang-tsao She), a formative force in modern Chinese literature. Guo was influenced by modern Japanese fiction as well as by Western writers such as Goethe and Whitman.

In 1924 Guo announced his conversion to Marxism, after translating writings of the noted Japanese Marxist KAWAKAMI HAJIME. In 1924 he also wrote the novel for which he is best known in Japan, *Luo ye* (*Lo yeh*; 1933, Fallen Leaves), an autobiographical account of his love affair with Satō Tomiko, whom he married. After the MAY 30TH INCIDENT in 1925 he devoted himself to leftist propaganda work, and in 1927 he joined the Chinese Communist Party. In 1928 he was sent to Japan to escape arrest by the Guomindang (Kuomintang; Nationalist Party). He returned to China in 1937 and participated in the anti-Japanese propaganda effort during the Sino-Japanese War of 1937–45. He remained an important figure in China after the establishment of the People's Republic of China in 1949, holding the positions of chairman of the All-China Federation of Writers and Artists and president of the Chinese Academy of Sciences.

Guo Songling (Kuo Sung-ling)　郭松齡

(1883–1925; J: Kaku Shōrei). A leading commander in the army of ZHANG ZUOLIN (Chang Tso-lin), the Chinese warlord based in Manchuria. Guo revolted against Zhang in 1925 and nearly drove him from power, but the attempt failed when the Japanese GUANDONG (KWANTUNG) ARMY supported Zhang. Guo launched the revolt on 22 November 1925 and during the following two weeks won a series of victories. But Japanese leaders had concluded that Zhang's continued rule in Manchuria served Japan better than would a change to Guo's control, and they therefore gave crucial support to Zhang. Guo's forces were decisively defeated on 23 December. Zhang's men captured Guo and his wife the following day and shot them.

Gusai　救済

(1282?–1376?). Also called Kyūsai. RENGA (linked verse) poet and Buddhist priest. Of humble origins, he was taught linked verse by the master Zenna. In his late fifties he began to emerge as the most important *renga* poet of the age. He became the teacher of such masters as Shūa (dates unknown), ASAYAMA BONTŌ, and NIJŌ YOSHIMOTO. With Yoshimoto he compiled the *Tsukubashū* (Tsukuba Collection), the first anthology of choice *renga* verses, which in 1357 was granted official status equivalent to an imperial anthology of classical poetry. Gusai also aided Yoshimoto in his efforts to codify the rules of linked verse composition.

Gushikawa　具志川[市]

City on the island of Okinawa, Okinawa Prefecture. Long known for its sugarcane. Cattle and hogs have been raised here since World War II. Part of the city has been allocated for US military use. Spinning and paper industries have also been introduced. Pop: 54,018.

gusuku　グスク

Also called *gushiku*. Style of Okinawan castle that prevailed from the 9th to 15th centuries. The word *gusuku* means "castle" or "high place with an enclosure" in the Ryū-

Gunzō Cover of the October 1946 inaugural issue of this monthly literary magazine.

kyū dialect. Although *gusuku* are most commonly seen on the islands of Okinawa Prefecture, they have also been discovered on the island of Amami Ōshima in Kagoshima Prefecture. *Gusuku* usually consisted of an enclosed citadel built on a hill near a village. They are believed to have originally functioned as places of worship or sacred places, but as they evolved during the hundreds of years of their existence their significance is thought to have changed as well. Among surviving *gusuku* are the NAKIJIN CASTLE REMAINS and the SHURI CASTLE REMAINS.

gymnastics 体操

(*taisō*). Western-style gymnastics began officially in Japan in 1878, when the government established a gymnastics institute and invited an instructor from the United States. During the Taishō period (1912–26) Swedish gymnastic exercises were introduced and widely practiced in most schools. There is great public interest in gymnastic exercises, usually calisthenics; NHK (the Japan Broadcasting Corporation) has been broadcasting such exercises since 1928 (see RAJIO TAISŌ). The first Japanese participation in international competition was in the 1932 Los Angeles Olympics. Since World War II, Japan has compiled excellent records in international championships; between 1960 and 1978 the men's team placed first in 10 successive Olympic and International Championship competitions. The governing organization is the Japan Gymnastic Association.

Gyōda 行田[市]

City in northern Saitama Prefecture, central Honshū, between the rivers Tonegawa and Arakawa. It developed as a castle town in the late 15th century. Long known for its TABI (socks worn with *kimono*), Gyōda developed textile and machinery industries after World War II. Pop: 83,181.

Gyōgi 行基

(668–749). Monk of the HOSSŌ SECT of Buddhism (Ch: Faxiang or Fa-hsiang). Also known as Gyōki. Born in Kawachi Province (now part of Ōsaka Prefecture), he studied Hossō teachings at the temple Yakushiji. He devoted himself to the building of temples, particularly the temple TŌDAIJI. He also undertook numerous social welfare projects, such as dam and bridge building. During his later years, the emperor SHŌMU bestowed on him the name Daibosatsu ("Great Bodhisattva") and raised him to the rank of Daisōjō (great bishop or primate). Because of his outstanding virtue, he was often known as Gyōgi Bosatsu (Bodhisattva Gyōgi) and was popularly taken to be a manifestation of Mañjuśrī Bodhisattva. He was long remembered as an ascetic with great charisma, and many temples are attributed to him.

gyōji 行司

The referees in SUMŌ matches who signal when the competition is to begin and who declare the winner. The usual attire of a *gyōji* is a *hitatare*, which is a kimonolike garment similar to that worn by warriors during the Kamakura period (1185–1333). He also wears a tall black lacquered hat (*eboshi*) and holds a warrior's fan (*gumbai*). Like the *sumō* wrestlers themselves, the *gyōji* are ranked. There are eight levels, with *tategyōji* being the highest. Rank is indicated in a variety of ways, including the color of the tassel on the fan and whether footwear is worn.

Gyōki →Gyōgi

Gyokudō →Uragami Gyokudō

Gyokuen Bompō 玉畹梵芳

(1348–ca 1420). Zen monk-scholar who specialized in subdued, monochrome ink paintings of orchids. A poet, calligrapher, and painter as well as a monk, he attained the elevated status of abbot of two major Zen monasteries in Kyōto, first the Kenninji and then the Nanzenji. Bompō's colophons appear on many well-known ink paintings executed by his friends in the Zen cultural milieu in Kyōto. At least 30 of his paintings of orchids, the traditional emblem of moral virtue, are recorded in Japanese and American collections. The compositions generally include long, swaying blades of orchid leaves grouped like a still life with thorns and a sprig of young bamboo, all emerging from the soft folds of a moss-dotted rock. His style has been traced to the work of the mid-14th-century Chinese priest-painter Xuechuang (Hsüeh-ch'uang) and to that of Bompō's older contemporary, the Japanese priest-painter TESSHŪ TOKUSAI.

gyokugan 玉眼

Technique of inlaying crystal balls as eyes in a BUDDHIST SCULPTURE. Pupils were painted directly on the back of the transparent crystals or on a piece of silk attached to them. This produced a more realistic effect than carving and painting eyeballs directly on the sculpture's surface. The technique of *gyokugan*, which goes back to the mid-12th century, reflects the general tendency towards realism in Buddhist sculpture, most notably that of UNKEI. The Amida trinity of the Chōgakuji temple in Nara Prefecture displays an early example of the technique.

Gyokuyō 玉葉

(Leaves of Jade). Also called *Gyokukai* (Sea of Jade). Diary of the court official KUJŌ KANEZANE. Kanezane served as regent (*sesshō* and *kampaku*; see REGENCY GOVERNMENT) in the imperial court and liaison to the KAMAKURA SHOGUNATE (1192–1333). Written in KAMBUN (classical Chinese prose), *Gyokuyō*'s 66 chapters are a valuable source of information on the late 12th century.

Gyokuyō wakashū 玉葉和歌集

(Collection of Jeweled Leaves; abbreviated to *Gyokuyōshū*). The 14th of the IMPERIAL ANTHOLOGIES (*chokusenshū*) of classical Japanese poetry. It was ordered in 1311 by the retired emperor FUSHIMI. Completed between 1312 and 1314, it was compiled by KYŌGOKU TAMEKANE and consists of 20 books containing a total of 2,800 poems. It is the bulkiest of the 21 imperial anthologies. In 1293 Emperor Fushimi commanded Tamekane and several other leading poets to compile a new imperial anthology, but the project dragged on inconclusively and eventually was abandoned. However, when Emperor Hanazono gained the succession in 1308, his father, Fushimi, had a second opportunity to sponsor an anthology. In 1311 he appointed Tamekane as sole compiler over the protests of Tamekane's poetic and political arch rival, NIJŌ TAMEYO. Owing to the domination of court poetry by the conservative Nijō faction, among the last 10 imperial anthologies the dissident Kyōgoku and Reizei factions compiled only 2: the *Gyokuyōshū* and the *Fūgashū* (ca 1346, Collection of Elegance; the 17th). These collections are, therefore,

virtually the sole repositories of what the innovative poets of the age considered their own best work.

Gyōnen 凝然

(1240–1321). Scholar-monk of the KEGON SECT, renowned for his erudition. Born in Iyo Province (now Ehime Prefecture). He was long the abbot of the Kaidan'in of the Nara temple Tōdaiji. His writing, said to include more than 120 works, encompasses the whole range of Buddhist learning. In particular his *Hasshū kōyō* (1268), an outline of the eight sects of Buddhism officially recognized in Japan by the end of the Heian period (794–1185), is considered an excellent introductory textbook to Buddhism.

Gyōsai →Kawanabe Gyōsai

gyōsei shidō →administrative guidance

gyōsei shoshi →administrative scrivener

gyōzui 行水

A term originally applied to ritual bathing by worshipers in streams, pools, or waterfalls in or near a religious precinct. In the Edo period (1600–1868), families who did not have a regular bath chamber would take sponge baths, also called *gyōzui*, using a wooden tub in the yard.

H

habatsu 派閥

(factional clique). A group or faction resulting from a struggle for leadership within a larger group. Although this term is essentially a synonym for the word BATSU, which refers to the cliques found in many large organizations, *habatsu* is most often used to refer to factions within political parties, business corporations, and trade unions. For example, there are several factions within the Liberal Democratic Party (LDP), named for each person who can potentially become prime minister. *Habatsu* generate internal power struggles for the leading position within the organization. Often the struggle hinges on monetary considerations. See also GROUPS.

Habeas Corpus Law 人身保護法

(Jinshin Hogo Hō). Judicial inquiry into lawfulness of physical detention, patterned on Anglo-American habeas corpus. Japan's 1947 constitution (art. 34) prohibits detention without lawful cause and allows detained persons to demand a showing in open court, while represented by counsel, of reasons for detention. Procedure to effectuate the constitutional right is provided by the Habeas Corpus Law of 1948.

Persons in confinement, their counsel, or persons acting on their behalf may apply to a district or high court for an immediate hearing on lawfulness of detention. The legality or constitutionality of court-ordered imprisonment, whether before or after adjudication, may be challenged only through procedures established in the Code of Criminal Procedure. Habeas corpus proceedings must be in open court, and counsel must be supplied for a detained person unable to retain counsel. If lawful grounds for detention exist, the application is denied; if they are wanting, the person is ordered released immediately. Either ruling may be appealed.

Habikino 羽曳野[市]

City in southeastern Ōsaka Prefecture, central Honshū. Situated on a highway that connected the ancient capitals of NANIWAKYŌ and ASUKA, Habikino developed as a market town. There are several imperial tombs, including the ŌJIN MAUSOLEUM, and temples of historical interest. The city is now a residential suburb of Ōsaka. Wine making is the principal industry. The city is part of the Kongō-Ikoma Quasi-National Park. Pop: 115,049.

haboku 破墨

(Ch: *po mo* or *p'o mo;* literally, "break ink"). Technique of INK PAINTING based on vivid tonal contrasts of spontaneously applied ink. Darker washes or lines or dots "break" lighter tonalities of ink or ground to suggest rather than explicate landscape forms, which appear saturated in moist atmosphere.

The first reference to *haboku* in Chinese texts occurs in 847, associating the method with the poet-painter Wang Wei (ca 699–ca 759). Later, a second term pronounced the same (*po mo*), but written with characters meaning "splash ink," described the technique developed by the 9th-century artist Wang Xia (Wang Hsia). The Japanese linked *haboku* almost exclusively with the Yuan (Yüan) dynasty (1279–1368) priest-painter Yujian (Yü-chien). The paintings that they endorsed as his works feature vivid splashes of saturated ink against a background of diluted washes.

From the Yujian prototype, Japanese painters interpreted the *haboku* manner according to their own inclinations. In the late 15th and early 16th centuries, SESSHŪ TŌYŌ and his followers clearly structured these abbreviated motifs. In the late 16th century KAIHŌ YŪSHŌ used this technique. In the 17th century KANŌ TAN'YŪ further economized, reducing forms to spurts of ink.

Habomai Islands 歯舞諸島

(Habomai Shotō). A small group of islands northeast of Nemuro Peninsula, eastern Hokkaidō, including Tarakujima, Shibotsujima, and Suishōjima. The islands were occupied by the Soviet Union at the end of World War II, when the Japanese population was forced to move to the main islands of Japan; in late 1992 they were still occupied by the Russian Federation. See also TERRITORY OF JAPAN. Area: 102 sq km (39 sq mi).

Hachigyaku 八虐

(Eight Outrages). The eight most serious crimes as defined by the TAIHŌ CODE (effective 702) and the YŌRŌ CODE (effective 757). They were (1) rebellion against the emperor, (2) damage of imperial palaces or tombs, (3) treason against the state, (4) murder of one's kin, (5) murder of one's wife or more than three members of any family, (6) theft or damage of imperial or religious property, (7) unfilial acts toward one's parents or senior kin, and (8) murder of one's superior or teacher. These offenses were punishable by death or by various forms of banishment. See also RITSURYŌ SYSTEM.

Hachihachi Kantai 八八艦隊

(Eight Eight Fleet). Name given to a plan for constructing a Japanese fleet that would have eight battleships and eight battlecruisers as its first-line units. It was decided upon as a part of the 1907 Imperial National Defense Policy, which posited the United States as the hypothetical enemy. Because of financial constraints, the plan was initially reduced to eight four and then raised to eight six. Funds for an eight eight fleet were finally approved in 1920 by the HARA TAKASHI cabinet, with completion scheduled for 1927, but the plan was interrupted because of the limits on capital ship tonnage imposed by the WASHINGTON NAVAL TREATY OF 1922. Only four ships were built in accordance with this plan.

Hachijōjima 八丈島

Island approximately 290 km (180 mi) southeast of the Izu Peninsula, central Honshū; one of the IZU ISLANDS. It is part of Tōkyō Prefecture. During the Edo period (1600–1868) it was an island of exile for convicts. Today it is a place of tourism, fishing, and horticulture. The local silk fabric known as *kihachijō* has been designated an Intangible Cultural Property. Hachijōjima is part of Fuji-Hakone-Izu National Park. Area: 69 sq km (27 sq mi).

hachimaki 鉢巻

Thin towel (TENUGUI) or strip of cloth tied around the crown of the head; also, the custom of wearing a *hachimaki*. Originally worn during religious acts, *hachimaki* are still commonly worn by men performing heavy physical labor and for such strenuous activities as carrying MIKOSHI (portable shrines) at festivals. The custom is mentioned in early Chinese accounts of Japan and depicted in the early clay figures known as HANIWA.

hachimaki Originally considered a charm against evil spirits, the *hachimaki* today is worn as a symbol of physical and spiritual determination.

Prior to the Kamakura period (1185–1333) it was called *makkō*.

Hachimaki came to be worn in battle, apparently because they were felt to strengthen the spirit. They were also believed to repel evil spirits; for this reason boys wore *hachimaki* made of iris leaves on Boy's Day (see CHILDREN'S DAY), and sick people or women giving birth often donned *hachimaki*.

Hachiman 八幡

A popular Shintō deity who protects warriors and generally looks after the well-being of the community. Identified as the deified spirit of the legendary emperor Ōjin, he is worshiped as the central deity in a type of shrine known as a Hachimangū, where he is usually flanked by two other deities, Okinagatarashihime no Mikoto (the spirit of Ōjin's mother, the legendary empress Jingū) and Hime Ōkami, Ōjin's deified spouse.

The origins of Hachiman are unknown. The oldest attested reference to the chief Hachiman shrine (USA HACHIMAN SHRINE) occurs in the chronicle *Shoku nihongi* under the year 737. After an oracle declared that Hachiman would provide protection for the construction of the Great Buddha image (DAIBUTSU) in Nara (749), he began to be viewed as a protector of Buddhism and was given the Buddhist title Daibosatsu (Great Bodhisattva). Hachiman's cult became firmly established in Kyōto after the IWASHIMIZU HACHIMAN SHRINE was built there. The main shrine to this deity in eastern Japan is the TSURUGAOKA HACHIMAN SHRINE in Kamakura, established in 1180 by MINAMOTO NO YORITOMO, the founder of the Kamakura shogunate. The

hagi
1 The *yakushimahagi*, admired for its delicate two-colored flowers, is often grown as a potted plant.
2 A deciduous shrub, the *hagi* grows wild throughout Japan.

popularity of the Hachiman cult has grown steadily, as is evidenced by some 25,000 Hachiman shrines throughout Japan today. See also HAKOZAKI SHRINE.

Hachimantai 八幡平

A highland area in the Nasu Volcanic Zone, on the border between Akita and Iwate prefectures, northern Honshū. The area includes the highland called Hachimantai Kōgen and the mountains Yakeyama and Chausudake. Alpine flora, forests, and swamp plants abound. The foothills have numerous hot springs and skiing grounds. It is a principal part of Towada-Hachimantai National Park. Height: 1,614 m (5,295 ft).

hachimonjiya-bon 八文字屋本

Books of the genre UKIYO-ZŌSHI (tales of the floating world) produced in the first half of the 18th century by the Kyōto publisher and bookseller Hachimonjiya Jishō (d 1745). The term is also used to refer to *ukiyo-zōshi*, mainly of the Kyōhō era (1716–36) and later, which are also character studies of denizens of the floating world or tales about courtesans and the disowned sons of wealthy merchants and feudal lords adapted from JŌRURI and KABUKI plays. These works mark a distinct literary-historical period, which is customarily subdivided between works contemporary with the foremost Hachimonjiya writer, EJIMA KISEKI, and those that appeared after his death. Many YOMIHON, more truly novelistic works written in a style partly borrowed from the tradition of the Chinese vernacular novel, adopted the *hachimonjiya-bon* theme of the disowned son.

Hachinohe 八戸[市]

City in southeastern Aomori Prefecture, northern Honshū. Situated on the Pacific Ocean, Hachinohe developed during the Edo period (1600–1868) as a castle town of the Nambu domain. The city is noted for its chemical, paper, and steel industries, as well as for mackerel and cuttlefish fishing and the processing of marine products. The Emburi festival (17–20 February) is held here. Pop: 241,057.

Hachiōji 八王子[市]

City in southwestern Tōkyō Prefecture. It developed during the Edo period (1600–1868) as a post-station town and as a market center for raw silk. Silk products produced in Hachiōji include neckties, mufflers, and *kimono*. The electrical appliance industry is growing in importance. In recent years it has become a residential suburb for commuters to Tōkyō. A number of universities have moved to Hachiōji from central Tōkyō. Pop: 466,347.

Hachirōgata 八郎潟

Also called Kotonoumi. Lagoon in the eastern part of the Oga Peninsula, northwestern Akita Prefecture, northern Honshū. It was the second largest lake in Japan (after Lake Biwa) before land reclamation projects (1957–66) converted practically all the lagoon area into land. It is now one of Akita Prefecture's most important agricultural districts (see ŌGATA), with large-scale group farming utilizing modern machinery. Area of lagoon before land reclamation: about 220 sq km (85 sq mi); current area: 28 sq km (10.8 sq mi); circumference: 36 km (22 mi); depth: 11 m (36 ft).

Hadaka no shima 裸の島

(Naked Island; shown abroad as *The Island*). A 1960 semiautobiographical black-and-

white film written and directed by SHINDŌ KANETO. Toiling for survival with their two sons on a tiny, barren island, a middle-aged farmer (played by Tonoyama Taiji; 1915–89) and his wife (played by OTOWA NOBUKO) experience simple pleasures and great sorrow. With minimal dramatic incident and no dialogue, this elegy to peasant life relies primarily on a highly pictorial style, natural sounds, and background music. In making this film, Shindō pioneered the extremely low budget, independent feature produced communally by a small group. It won first prize at the 1961 Moscow Film Festival.

Hadano 秦野[市]

City in western Kanagawa Prefecture, central Honshū. Once a production center for tobacco and peanuts, it has become a residential district. There is a growing automobile industry. Tourists visit the Tanzawa Mountains and Tsurumaki Hot Spring. Pop: 155,620.

Hagakure 葉隠

("In the Shadow of Leaves"). Properly titled *Hagakure kikigaki* ("Notes of What Was Heard in the Shadow of Leaves"); translated as *Hagakure: The Book of the Samurai* (1979). A manual for SAMURAI consisting of some 1,300 short anecdotes and reflections and completed in 1716. Considered one of the classics on BUSHIDŌ (the Way of the warrior), *Hagakure* is believed to have been dictated by Yamamoto Tsunetomo (1659–1719), a middle-ranking retainer of Nabeshima Mitsushige (1632–1700), *daimyō* of Hizen Province (now Saga Prefecture), to Tashiro Tsuramoto (1678–1748).

The work's often quoted first line, "*Bushidō* is a way of dying," expresses the theme that is elaborated upon throughout the work: only a samurai prepared and willing to die at any moment can devote himself fully to his lord. While *Hagakure* once served as a handbook for young warrior vassals of the Hizen domain, its chief value today is as a source in the history of *bushidō*.

Haga Yaichi 芳賀矢一

(1867–1927). Scholar of Japanese literature. Born in Echizen Province (now Fukui Prefecture). Graduate of Tōkyō University; later a professor there. His works include *Kokubungaku shi jikkō* (1899), a history of Japanese classical literature, and *Kokuminsei juron* (1907), an exploration of the Japanese national character through literary analysis.

Hagerty Incident ハガティー事件

(Hagatī Jiken). Demonstration that took place in Tōkyō on 10 June 1960, when James C. Hagerty, press secretary to US president Eisenhower, arrived to make final preparations for the president's visit. The visit was scheduled to begin on 19 June, the day after the Diet was to complete its approval of the newly revised United States–Japan Security Treaty. The automobile taking Hagerty and two other officials, including US ambassador Douglas MacArthur II, from Haneda Airport to the US Embassy was surrounded by 8,000 to 10,000 demonstrators, mostly labor union members and students who opposed the treaty. After over an hour a US military helicopter was finally able to land, pick up the officials, and take them to downtown Tōkyō. Further demonstrations followed, and on 16 June the Eisenhower visit was canceled. On 23 June Prime Minister KISHI NOBUSUKE announced his decision to resign. The demonstration and subsequent disorders displayed the most serious public opposition to government policy in the postwar period. See also UNITED STATES–JAPAN SECURITY TREATIES.

Hagi 萩[市]

City in northern Yamaguchi Prefecture, western Honshū. Situated on the Sea of Japan, Hagi was the castle town of the MŌRI FAMILY during the Edo period (1600–1868). The city is also known as the birthplace of KIDO TAKAYOSHI, ITŌ HIROBUMI, and other leaders of the MEIJI RESTORATION (1868). Principal products are *natsumikan* (a type of citrus fruit) and marine products. The ruins of Hagi Castle in Shizuki Park, a district containing former *samurai* homes, and the Shōka Sonjuku, a school directed by the proimperial ideologue YOSHIDA SHŌIN, are chief tourist attractions. The production of HAGI WARE dates from the early 1600s. Pop: 50,618.

hagi 萩

(Japanese bush clover). *Lespedeza bicolor* var. *japonica.* Also known as *yamahagi.* Deciduous shrub of the pea family (Leguminosae) growing wild in fields and mountains throughout Japan. It has long been celebrated in Japanese culture as the first of the seven flowers of autumn (*aki no nanakusa*). *Hagi* reaches about 2 meters (7 ft) in height and has many thin branches and compound leaves composed of three wide, oval leaflets. In autumn it produces long, reddish purple flowers in long clusters (racemes) at the tips of its branches.

In early times *hagi* stems and leaves were used to feed livestock, and the stems were also used for fencing, roofing, and rope making. It is said that the ground seeds were mixed with rice gruel, while the leaves were substituted for tea. Other types of *hagi* include the *marubahagi* (*L. cyrtobotrya*), which has round leaves; the *miyaginohagi* (*L. thunbergii*), with drooping branches and elegant flowers; and the *shirahagi* or *shirobanahagi* (*L. japonica*), which has white flowers.

Hagi domain → Chōshū domain

Hagi Rebellion 萩の乱

(Hagi no Ran). Rebellion in October 1876 by former *samurai* at Hagi, Yamaguchi Prefecture. Disturbed by the modernizing policies of the new government and decrees stripping them of traditional privileges (see SHIZOKU), dispossessed samurai rose in arms in several parts of southwestern Japan (see also JIMPŪREN REBELLION and AKIZUKI REBELLION OF 1876). Ex-samurai of the former Chōshū domain (now Yamaguchi Prefecture) led by MAEBARA ISSEI, a onetime official of the Meiji government, planned to attack the prefectural office at Hagi on 26 October, but government troops arrived and soon captured the rebels. Maebara and 8 others were executed; 60 were imprisoned.

Hagiwara Kichitarō 萩原吉太郎

(1902–). Businessman; chairman of Hokkaidō Colliery & Steamship Co (1962–69; 1975–81). Born in Saitama Prefecture. After graduating from Keiō University in 1926, he joined Mitsui Gōmei Kaisha. He moved to Hokkaidō Colliery & Steamship Co in 1940, becoming its president in 1955. From 1970 he promoted the development of new coal mines in Yūbari, Hokkaidō. Assuming responsibility for an underground fire at the coal mine Hokutan Yūbari Shinkō, Hagiwara stepped down as chairman in 1981.

Hagiwara Kyōjirō 萩原恭次郎

(1899–1938). Poet. Born in Gumma Prefecture. With the poets TSUBOI SHIGEJI and Okamoto Jun (1901–78), he founded the anarchist poetry magazine *Aka to kuro* (Red and Black) in 1923. Hagiwara was an early champion of dadaism, futurism, and nihilism. His poem "Mōrokuzukin" (1932, Hood of Senility) deals with the dismal life of a farm village. Major collections are *Shikei senkoku* (1925, Death Sentence) and *Dampen* (1931, Fragments).

Hagiwara Sakutarō 萩原朔太郎

(1886–1942). Poet. Acclaimed for his extraordinarily brilliant free-style poems, Hagiwara is generally considered to have established modern colloquial poetry in Japan. The eldest son of a Maebashi physician in Gumma Prefecture, he wrote TANKA (31-syllable traditional WAKA poetry) against his parents' wishes. Doubtful about a career, he withdrew from two different national higher schools and spent seemingly idle years in Maebashi and Tōkyō writing poetry. In 1913 a leading poet of the day, KITAHARA HAKUSHŪ, published five of Hagiwara's free-style poems in his journal *Zamboa* (Shaddock). Hagiwara met and became friends with MUROO SAISEI through *Zamboa* and collaborated with him in launching a little magazine called *Takujō funsui* (1915, Tabletop Fountain) in which both published their poems.

Hagiwara's first collection of poems, *Tsuki ni hoeru* (1917; tr *Howling at the Moon*, 1978), published with an introduction by Hakushū, marked an epoch in Japanese poetry. He used precise language that appealed to his musical sense and did not use the "symbolism" of Hakushū and other contemporary poets, which, relying on unusual words and expressions in literary language, presented a colorful but ambiguous world. In *Aoneko* (1923; tr *Blue Cat*, 1978) he further displayed his mastery of diction and his deepened skepticism and pessimistic visions of life. The sharp sensuousness of the earlier poems was replaced by a faltering sense of inescapable melancholy, which came to dominate his works.

His critical study *Ren'ai meika shū* (1931, A Collection of Best-Loved Love Poems) showed Hagiwara's appreciation and devotion to classical Japanese poetry, while his *Kyōshū no shijin Yosa Buson* (1936, Nostalgic Poet Yosa Buson) expressed his love for the 18th-century HAIKU poet BUSON, who advocated a return to the poetics of the 17th-century BASHŌ. Hagiwara managed his own journals, cultivated the genre of aphorism, wrote essays on poetic theory, edited works by other poets, and lectured on literature. He taught briefly at Meiji University in Tōkyō. His major work of criticism, *Shi no genri* (1928, Principles of Poetics), detailed his beliefs and practices in poetry. *Shukumei* (1939, Fate) was a collection of his prose poems, one of the earliest of a rather rare genre in the history of Japanese verse.

Hagiwara Yūsuke 萩原雄祐

(1897–1979). Astronomer. Known for his work in celestial mechanics, particularly on the behavior of planets and planetoids. Born in Ōsaka, Hagiwara graduated from Tōkyō University in 1921. He served as professor there from 1935 to 1957 and was also director of Tōkyō Astronomical Observatory (now the National Astronomical Observatory) from 1946 to 1957. He received the Order of

Hagi ware A 17th-century tea ceremony bowl. This type of high-fired ceramics has been produced since the late 1500s. Height 8 cm. Fujita Art Museum, Ōsaka.

Culture in 1954. His publications include *Temmongaku* (1956, Astronomy) and *Celestial Mechanics* (2 vols; 1970, 1972).

Hagi ware 萩焼

(*hagi-yaki*). Glazed, high-fired ceramics made in the castle towns of Hagi (now a city) and Fukawa (now part of the city of Nagato) in Nagato Province (now Yamaguchi Prefecture) from the late 1500s to the present. Although production originally consisted primarily of tableware, *hibachi*, and small storage vessels, Hagi became renowned for TEA CEREMONY wares. Hagi tea bowls are classified by shape, color, surface embellishment, and the number of "nicks" cut in the foot. Typical Hagi-ware decoration includes *hakeme*, or light-colored slip brushed over the surface of the darker clay body; and *mishima*, or slip inlaid in a darker clay. The two basic glazes are "loquat," a thin, yellowish glaze composed of feldspar and mixed hardwood ash, and "straw white," a thin, milky glaze made by adding straw ash, an opacifier, to the loquat glaze. Celadon, red, and brown glazes are also used. Pinkish spots in the glaze, dark blotches under the glaze, and scars left from stacking pots inside the kiln are considered attractive by-products of the firing process. Early Hagi potters were Koreans who came or were brought to Japan around the time of warlord TOYOTOMI HIDEYOSHI's invasions of Korea in 1592 and 1597. Today Hagi has over 100 potters. Hagi-ware collections are on display in three museums in Hagi.

hagoita 羽子板

A wooden paddle used in HANETSUKI, a game played during the New Year's holidays; commonly translated as battledore. Auspicious symbols (such as pine, bamboo, or plum trees) or portraits of beautiful women are portrayed on one or both sides of the paddle. During the Edo period (1600–1868) the decorations on the *hagoita* became increasingly elaborate, the figures (often of popular *kabuki* actors) being made of silk collage. In December *hagoita* fairs (HAGOITA ICHI) are held throughout Japan.

hagoita ichi 羽子板市

A traditional fair at which HAGOITA (decorated battledores or wooden paddles) are

Hagiwara Sakutarō
Author of the free-verse collection *Tsuki ni hoeru* (1917, Howling at the Moon), Hagiwara founded a tradition of modern poetry written in colloquial Japanese.

hagoita ichi A seller of *hagoita* paddles displays his decorated wares near the Asakusa Shrine, Tōkyō, during this annual festival.

sold; held in major cities. In Tōkyō the fair is held toward the end of the year at the Fukagawa Fudō Shrine, the Asakusa Shrine, and various other shrines. Small *hagoita ichi* are also held in the streets. In Kyōto the fair is held in the Shijō and Shin Kyōgoku districts.

Hagoromo 羽衣

(The Feather Robe). Nō play. Author unknown. Classified as a *sambamme-mono* ("part-three play"), it is based on the HAGOROMO LEGEND. One spring morning a fisherman (the *waki* or subordinate character) comes to the pine grove at Miho, a sandbar jutting into Suruga Bay. He hears lovely music and smells perfume in the air. He then finds a robe of feathers (*hagoromo*) hanging from the branch of a nearby pine tree. About to return home with the robe, he is stopped by the sorrowful voice of a heavenly being (the *shite* or main character) who laments that she has lost her feathered costume. Overcome with remorse, the fisherman returns the robe. In gratitude, the spirit dances and, rising upward into the sky, disappears into the morning mist.

Hagoromo legend 羽衣伝説

(Hagoromo *densetsu*; literally, "Feather Robe" legend). Legend found throughout Japan, particularly well known for its adaptation in the Nō play *Hagoromo*. While a celestial nymph (*tennyo*) is bathing in the sea, a man steals her garment made of feathers. She then has no choice but to become his wife and bear his child. Later she recovers her garment and returns to heaven.

Hagurosan 羽黒山

Mountain in northwestern Yamagata Prefecture, northern Honshū. Along with neighboring GASSAN and YUDONOSAN, Hagurosan is one of the Dewa Sanzan (Three Mountains of Dewa Province), a center for religious exercises of the SHUGENDŌ sect. The shrine Ideha Jinja is on the summit. Height: 414 m (1,358 ft).

haibun 俳文

Brief, informal essays, usually light in tone and commonplace in theme, which flourished during the Edo period (1600–1868). The typical *haibun* begins with a short title followed by a prose text and generally ends with a HAIKU that derives from or recapitulates the sense of the prose. Compared to earlier prose genres, *haibun* displayed greater freedom in its use of vocabulary, and its range of subject matter included everyday objects and occurrences that had traditionally been shunned in Japanese literature. Since it is essentially a medium of the haiku poet, *haibun* shares certain haiku characteristics: ellipsis, suggestion, and the use of classical allusion. For the same reason, it also shares with haiku such devices as the associate word (ENGO) and the pun. Despite its commonplace topics, *haibun* was enjoyed by a relatively elite audience because of its pseudoclassical diction, its endless punning, and its many recondite historical and literary allusions.

The first collection of *haibun* is *Takaragura* (1671, A Storehouse of Treasures) by Yamaoka Genrin (1631–72). Roughly during the lifetime of Matsuo BASHŌ (1644–94), *haibun* evolved into a recognized and practiced literary genre, a result both of Bashō's own writing and of his influence on the writing of others. In 1706 the first of the *haibun* an-

thologies was published, the *Fūzoku monzen*, and the anthology continued to be the usual vehicle for the publication of *haibun*. The compiler was Bashō's disciple MORIKAWA KYOROKU (1656–1715). *Haibun* writers of note include Yosa BUSON (1716–84) and YOKOI YAYŪ (1702–83), best remembered for his *Uzuragoromo* (Quail Cloak).

Haibun continued to be written into the Meiji period (1868–1912), but most later works are judged to be mediocre. Today, *haibun* is not written in any significant quantity, although it is still read and remains an object of vigorous scholarship.

haibutsu kishaku 廃仏毀釈

(literally, "abolish the Buddha; destroy Śākyamuni"). Refers to movements to abolish Buddhism beginning in the Tokugawa shogunate (1603–1867) and culminating in the early Meiji period (1868–1912). The policy of the early Meiji government was to promote SHINTŌ as the state religion, and in 1868 the complete removal of Buddhist influence from Shintō shrines was decreed (see SHINTŌ AND BUDDHISM, SEPARATION OF). In some areas this policy encouraged movements to abolish Buddhism, resulting in the destruction of many temples, statues, and implements before the movements declined around 1871.

haihan chiken → prefectural system, establishment of

haikai → haiku

Haikai shichibushu 俳諧七部集

(Seven-Volume Haikai Collection). Compiled by Sakuma Ryūkyo (1686–1748). Popularly known as *Bashō shichibushū*, it brings together, in a chronological arrangement that reflects the development of Matsuo BASHŌ's style of *haikai* (prototype of HAIKU), the seven most representative anthologies of linked verse (*renku*; see RENGA) and haiku (*hokku*) of the Bashō school, namely *Fuyu no hi*, *Haru no hi*, *Arano*, *Hisago*, *Sarumino*, *Sumidawara*, and *Zoku sarumino*.

haiku 俳句

A 17-syllable verse form consisting of three metrical units of 5, 7, and 5 syllables, respectively. One of the most important forms of traditional Japanese poetry, haiku remains popular in modern Japan, and in recent years its popularity has spread to other countries.

Haiku, Hokku, and Haikai — Loose usage by students, translators, and even poets themselves has led to much confusion about the distinction between the three related terms haiku, hokku, and haikai. The term *hokku* literally means "starting verse." A *hokku* was the first or "starting" link of a much longer chain of verses known as a *haikai no renga*, or simply *haikai*, in which alternating sets of 5-7-5 syllables and 7-7 syllables were joined. *Hokku* gradually took on an independent character. Largely through the efforts of MASAOKA SHIKI (1867–1902), this independence was formally established in the 1890s through the creation of the term "haiku." Haiku was a new type of verse, in form quite similar to the traditional *hokku* but different in that it was to be written, read, and understood as an independent poem, complete in itself, rather than as part of a longer chain.

Strictly speaking, then, the history of haiku begins only in the last years of the 19th century. The famous verses of Edo-period (1600–1868) masters such as Matsuo BASHŌ (1644–94), Yosa BUSON (1716–84), and

Kobayashi ISSA (1763–1827) are properly referred to as *hokku* even though they are now generally read as independent haiku.

Development of Haikai — RENGA, or linked verse, which began to be written in the Heian period (794–1185), was originally considered a diversion by which poets could relax from the serious business of composing WAKA poetry. By the time of the *renga* master SŌGI (1421–1502), however, it had become a serious art with complex rules and high aesthetic standards. *Haikai no renga*, or simply *haikai*, was conceived as a lighthearted amusement in which poets could indulge after the solemn refinements of serious *renga*.

When *haikai* began to emerge as a serious poetic genre in the early 16th century, two characteristics distinguished it from serious *renga*: its humorous intent and its free use of *haigon* (colloquialisms, compounds borrowed from Chinese, and other expressions that had previously been banned from the poetic vocabulary). However, the erudite MATSUNAGA TEITOKU (1571–1653) succeeded in establishing a more conservative and formalistic approach to *haikai*. For Teitoku, humor implied a sort of intellectual wit, and the distinction between *haikai* and *renga* lay ultimately only in the use or nonuse of *haigon*. He established strict rules concerning the composition of *haikai* and sought to endow the form with the elegance and aesthetic elevation of *waka* and serious *renga*.

After Teitoku's death his formalistic approach was challenged by the more freewheeling DANRIN SCHOOL of *haikai* led by NISHIYAMA SŌIN (1605–82). Sōin emphasized the comic aspects of *haikai*. Characteristic of the Danrin style of poetry was the practice of *yakazu haikai*, in which a single poet would reel off verse after verse as quickly as possible in a sort of exercise in free association. The most renowned example of this is the legendary performance by Ihara SAIKAKU (1642–93) in 1684 at the Sumiyoshi Shrine in Ōsaka, where he composed 23,500 verses in a single day.

Bashō was not only the greatest of *haikai* poets, he was also primarily responsible for establishing *haikai* as a true art form. Having received instruction in both the Teitoku and Danrin styles of *haikai*, he gradually developed in the late 17th century a new style that, through its artistic sincerity, transcended the conflict between serious *renga* and comic *haikai* and could express humor, humanity, and profound religious insight all within the space of a single *hokku*.

UEJIMA ONITSURA (1661–1738) wrote *haikai* of exceptional quality, and his notion of *makoto* or "sincerity" represents one of the high points of Japanese poetic theory. Other notable poets of the time include KONISHI RAIZAN, IKENISHI GONSUI, and YAMAGUCHI SODŌ. Bashō also had a great number of disciples. Of these, the so-called Ten Philosophers are particularly well known. They are NAITŌ JŌSŌ, MUKAI KYORAI, SUGIYAMA SAMPŪ, MORIKAWA KYOROKU, HATTORI RANSETSU, KAGAMI SHIKŌ, OCHI ETSUJIN, TAKARAI KIKAKU, Shida Yaba (1663–1740), and Tachibana Hokushi (d 1718). NOZAWA BONCHŌ, another of Bashō's disciples, is also worthy of mention.

After Bashō's death many of his disciples set up their own schools of *haikai*. In general these poets sought special effects—with some writing enigmatic, puzzlelike verse and others satisfying themselves with witty wordplay—and at times their *haikai* became virtually indistinguishable from ZAPPAI and

SENRYŪ, popular comic verse forms that had come into vogue in the Genroku period (1688–1704). In the late 18th century, however, there arose a movement of poets who sought to restore high aesthetic standards. The principal figure in this *haikai* reform was the talented painter-poet Buson, and the main cry of the movement was "Return to Bashō!" Buson possessed great imagination and culture and a painter's eye for vivid pictorial scenes. Other important *haikai* poets of the period include TAN TAIGI, KATŌ KYŌTAI, and ŌSHIMA RYŌTA.

The number of composers of *haikai* grew rapidly in the early 19th century. This popularization, however, was accompanied by a general decline in quality. The most notable exceptions were Iwama Otsuni (1756–1823) and Kobayashi Issa. Issa's poems about his poverty and about his love for small animals and insects are particularly memorable, and today he ranks with Bashō and Buson as one of the most beloved *haikai* poets.

Modern Haiku—The history of modern haiku dates from Masaoka Shiki's reform, begun in 1892, which established haiku as a new independent poetic form. It is a history that features constant experimentation and the confluence of various literary trends such as naturalism, romanticism, symbolism, and proletarianism. Basic to the modernization of haiku was Shiki's most important concept, *shasei*, or sketching from life—a term borrowed from the critical vocabulary of Western painting. The magazine that Shiki began in 1897, HOTOTOGISU, became the haiku world's most important publication.

Shiki's reform did not change two traditional elements of haiku: the division of 17 syllables into three groups of 5, 7, and 5 syllables and the inclusion of a seasonal theme. KAWAHIGASHI HEKIGOTŌ, who succeeded his mentor Shiki as haiku editor of the newspaper *Nihon*, carried Shiki's reform further with a proposal that haiku would be truer to reality if there were no center of interest in it. The logical extension of this idea was free-verse haiku, since the traditional patterning was seen as another artificial manipulation of reality. Hekigotō also urged the importance of the poet's first impression, just as it was (*sono mama*), of subjects taken from daily life and of local color to create freshness. Other poets associated with Hekigotō's SHINKEIKŌ HAIKU (New Trend Haiku) movement were Anzai Ōkaishi (1886–1953), ŌSUGA OTSUJI, and OGIWARA SEISENSUI.

Protesting against the prosaic flatness characteristic of much of the works of Hekigotō's school, Seisensui maintained in 1912 that free-verse haiku must also discard the seasonal theme. He held that haiku must capture in its rhythms not the object perceived but the poet's perception. The work of many able poets appeared in his magazine *Sōun*. Notably successful among them were TANEDA SANTŌKA and OZAKI HŌSAI, who both led wandering lives of poverty, like the beggar-priests of the past.

In 1912 TAKAHAMA KYOSHI began in the pages of *Hototogisu* (which he had edited since 1898) his lifelong defense of the traditional 17-syllable form, the seasonal theme, and the descriptive realism of Shiki. He outlined his views in a collection of essays published under the title *Susumubeki haiku no michi* (1915–17, The Path Haiku Ought to Take). The first flowering of the traditional school was in the Taishō period (1912–26) and featured such gifted poets as IIDA

DAKOTSU, KAWABATA BŌSHA, MURAKAMI KIJŌ, and Watanabe Suiha (1882–1946).

By 1920 a second generation of poets clustered about *Hototogisu*, including MIZUHARA SHŪŌSHI, AWANO SEIHO, YAMAGUCHI SEISHI, and TAKANO SUJŪ. The first Shōwa-period (1926–89) poet to break away into subjects previously avoided was HINO SŌJŌ, who wrote verses on romantic and sensuous love. *Hototogisu* continues to represent the central position in haiku to the present day.

Mizuhara Shūōshi broke away from *Hototogisu* in 1931, two years after having assumed the editorship of the magazine *Ashibi*. Shūōshi's talent for making imaginative use of the historical past shines in his collection *Katsushika* (1930). *Ashibi* was an important outlet for such poets as Yamaguchi Seishi, ISHIDA HAKYŌ, and Hashimoto Takako (1899–1963), the foremost woman haiku poet.

In the early Shōwa period the term *shinkō haiku* (new haiku) loosely identified all groups that deviated from the traditional *Hototogisu* school. In addition to the *Ashibi* poets and the modernistic school of Hino Sōjō's magazine *Kikan*, the term also included the proletarian school, headed by Kuribayashi Issekiro (1894–1961), originally of Seisensui's group. Other prominent proletarian poets were Hashimoto Mudō (1903–74), Shimada Seihō (1882–1944), and Yoshioka Zenjidō (1889–1961). Another politicizing group centered around the liberal publication *Kyōdai haiku*, which appeared during the period 1933–40 and accepted both conventional and free-verse haiku.

Joining *Hototogisu* in 1933, NAKAMURA KUSATAO deplored the *shinkō haiku* movement for its emphasis on technique and methodology. By 1939 he was identified along with Ishida Hakyō, KATŌ SHŪSON, Shinohara Bon (1910–75), Ishizuka Tomoji (1906–86), and Nishijima Bakunan (1895–1981) as a member of the Ningen Tankyū Ha ("Humanness" school).

During the military-dominated prewar and World War II period, haiku was controlled by government censorship. The immediate postwar period saw an effort by the leftist union Shin Haikujin Remmei to "break the hold of feudalism in haiku and to expose war collaborators," a pronouncement aimed at *Hototogisu* and other traditional schools. In 1947 many leading poets withdrew from this union. The Modern Haiku Association (Gendai Haiku Kyōkai) was formed in July 1947 to "enhance modern haiku" with the inclusion of all groups from the political left to the literary traditionalists.

The effort to unite all factions was stimulated by a widely discussed 1946 article entitled "Daini geijutsuron" (On a Second-Class Art), in which the critic KUWABARA TAKEO maintained that modern haiku was not a serious literary genre but only a pleasant pastime. A number of efforts to "modernize haiku"—to make it relevant to contemporary experience—were stimulated by the publicity given Kuwabara's article.

One such effort was *Tenrō*, a magazine begun in 1948 under Yamaguchi Seishi's editorship and supported by the prewar liberal Kyōto University haiku association together with some former *Ashibi* poets. *Tenrō* and the prewar *Ashibi*, which continues to appear, are the two most important vehicles of the nontraditional haiku. Other prewar magazines that continue to appear are Ishida Hakyō's *Tsuru* and Katō Shūson's *Kanrai*. Iida Dakotsu's *Ummo* ceased publication in 1992. The extreme haiku fringe of symbolism and surrealism is found in such magazines as *Taiyōkei*, founded in 1946 by Mizutani Saiko (1903–67) and Tomizawa Kakio (1902–62), and *Bara*, started in 1952 by Tomizawa Kakio and Takayanagi Shigenobu (1923–83).

Haiku Abroad—The West's first introduction to haiku came in B. H. Chamberlain's pioneer work, *Japanese Poetry* (1910), in a chapter entitled "Bashō and the Japanese Epigram." William Porter's early anthology of translations was entitled *A Year of Japanese Epigrams* (1911). Haiku was first introduced to France by Paul-Louis Couchoud at the time of the Russo-Japanese War. The title of his introduction to haiku was *Les Epigrammes Lyriques du Japon*. The use of the term "epigram" in these titles is indicative of how haiku was first interpreted abroad.

Ezra Pound quickly noticed and appropriated the haiku technique of cutting up the poem into two independent yet associated images. In France Paul Eluard wrote poems in the haiku style. Haiku has rapidly become naturalized both in Europe and in the United States, and magazines of original haiku are published. Haiku magazines in the United States include *Modern Haiku*, *byways*, *Tweed*, and *New World Haiku*. ▶▶488–489

hairstyles
髪型

(*kamigata*). In Japan, as in other cultures, changes in hairstyles and dress parallel social history. Fashions in Japanese hairstyles reflect the formation of an aristocracy, the rise to power of a warrior class, rigid social stratification under the Tokugawa shogun-

Continued on page 490➤

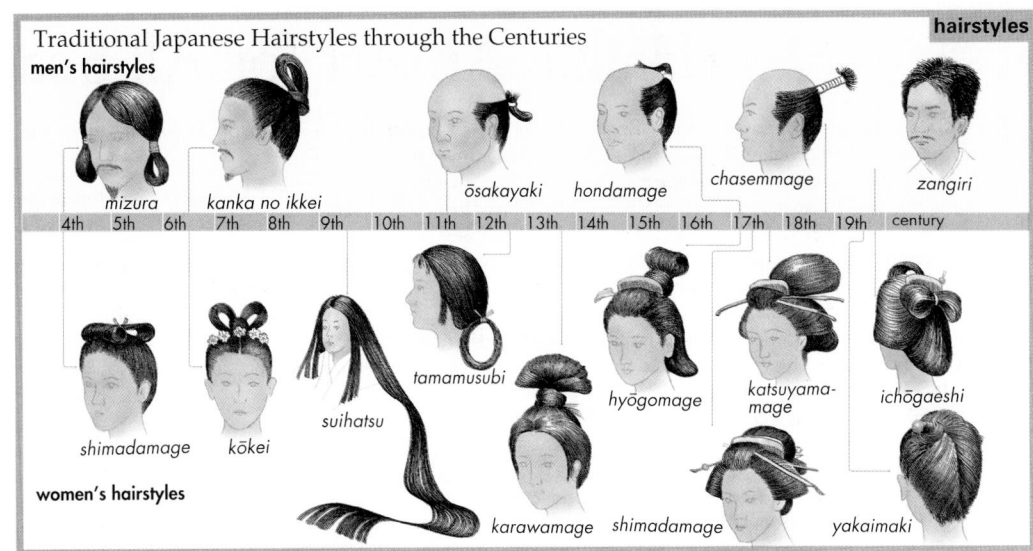

Traditional Japanese Hairstyles through the Centuries

men's hairstyles

mizura — kanka no ikkei — ōsakayaki — hondamage — chasemmage — zangiri

4th 5th 6th 7th 8th 9th 10th 11th 12th 13th 14th 15th 16th 17th 18th 19th century

shimadamage — kōkei — suihatsu — tamamusubi — hyōgomage — katsuyama-mage — ichōgaeshi

women's hairstyles

karawamage — shimadamage — yakaimaki

Haiku: An Art for All Seasons

In 1985 a 12-year-old student of mine, Regina Mylan, came up with the fine definition of *haiku* highlighted below. Haiku is the simplest form of poetry in the world and, in the eyes of many, the deepest. Because of its concise form, it can also be the most taxing. Haiku may be easy to learn, but it is difficult to master. To some it may be a child's game, but to others it is a lifetime discipline.

The creative process of writing haiku involves being moved by an event or object and sharing this experience with others. Haiku is defined as an unrhymed verse, written in 5-7-5 syllabic form, usually in three lines. Its subjects are predominantly nature and life experiences. Because of the phonetic differences between Japanese and English, strict adherence to the 5-7-5 syllabic form is no longer mandatory. Likewise, for aesthetic or experimental purposes, some American poets have adopted a one-line format that has also been used in Japan.

The most famous of haiku poets, Matsuo Bashō (1644–94), once said, "If you want to learn about the pine, go to the pine. If you want to learn about the bamboo, go to the bamboo. When you and the object have become one, your poetry issues of its own accord." Any haiku poet's first exercise must be this simple routine of going to the source.

Bashō was one of the greatest observers of "things" and discoverers of their truths. As the following haiku demonstrates, he was attentive to even the humblest creations of nature.

> Yoku mireba   Looking closely
> nazuna hana saku I find a shepherd's purse blooming
> kakine kana   under the hedge

The process of becoming one with nature by total immersion is at the heart of haiku. To Bashō, nothing was too small or too big. His discerning eye and disciplined mind could penetrate a tiny flower or a vast universe. The next haiku shows the scope of his vision.

> Araumi ya   A surging sea . . .
> Sado ni yokotau   reaching over Sado Isle
> Amanogawa   the Galaxy

Of course, this kind of poetic osmosis is not restricted to haiku alone. Wallace Stevens, William Carlos Williams, and Ezra Pound, for example, also tried to realize the concept of visual immersion in concrete reality. Consider the following lines from Stevens's poem "Thirteen Ways of Looking at a Blackbird":

> Among twenty snowy mountains,
> the only moving thing
> was the eye of the blackbird

Haiku

the deepest feelings

very simple

Rearranged slightly, these lines instantly become a haiku:

> Among snowy mountains
> the only moving thing was . . .
> the eye of the blackbird

With "twenty"—the single logical, Western element in the poem—deleted, the vista of the snowscape opens up in contrast to the minuscule speck of the moving eye of the blackbird.

As Bashō once wrote, "A haiku revealing 70 to 80 percent of its subject is good. Yet, those revealing 50 to 60 percent will never bore us." This is what haiku is all about. Haiku is not what is said but rather what is suggested and evoked. Its power and beauty lie in its ability to capture the essence of something in only a few short lines.

Haiku are known for their subtlety and lack of sentimentality. There is no space for superfluous adjectives. So when you wish to express a sense of solitude, for instance, avoid using obvious adjectives like "lonely" and "desolate." Such sentiments are suggested by juxtaposing images that induce a feeling of solitude. Let us examine another of Bashō's haiku.

> Kono michi ya   Along this way
> yukuhito nashini   goes no traveler . . .
> aki no kure   autumn evening

Here is great loneliness, an almost cosmic solitude. The seasonal phrase *aki no kure*, meaning both "autumn evening" and "the end of autumn," evokes desolation.

Content | Many great haiku poets in Japan spent their lives traveling in search of images, some as beggars, some as sightseers, and others, like Bashō himself, as itinerant haiku masters. He wrote:

> Tabi ni yande   Getting ill on a journey
> yume wa kareno o   my dreams keep running around
> kakemeguru   the withered moor

Some poets never left home, yet they produced rich images from within and around themselves. Masaoka Shiki (1867–1902) was one such poet.

> Nemuran to su   Trying to sleep . . .
> nanji shizukani   please swat the flies
> hae o ute   quietly

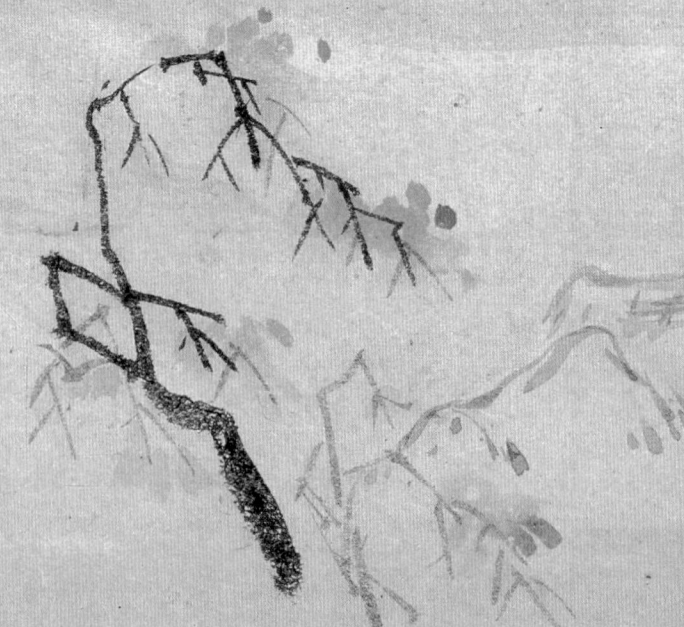

Thus, life presents us with a limitless supply of images that can be rendered into haiku. But how do we capture these images? Like children, we must relearn how to experience the wonders of everyday living. Children have the gift of clairvoyance: their innocent eyes discern nature's truths and those exalted moments of enlightenment. We adults must rediscover the long-forgotten, untapped sources of poetic imagery, both visual and mental, that abound in the here and now.

Form

One of Bashō's most celebrated haiku is:

Furuike ya	Old pond . . .
kawazu tobikomu	a frog jumps in
mizu no oto	water's sound

It is very simple, yet within its spare frame is hidden a profound insight. Unlike Western poetry, which tends to overload each line with information, haiku minimizes content, leaving enough ambiguity for readers to enjoy a lingering poetic evocation. This suggestiveness is known as *yojō*. To give the least information to evoke the most is the way of haiku.

Bashō's haiku is arranged in the standard phonetic notation of three lines, the first of which ends with the word *ya*. This is one example of a *kireji* ("cutting word"), which indicates a pause within a haiku. *Kireji* can also appear at the end of the second line, or in the middle of the second line, thus dividing the haiku into two equal parts. The "old pond" (*furuike*) is set off by the *kireji* "*ya*" and is placed in juxtaposition to "a frog jumps in/water's sound." The sensory and mental images evoked by the old, tranquil pond are contrasted with the vivid image of a leaping frog and the splash it makes. When these images are brought together, they interact, spark, and explode. The immediate effect upon us is sensory. Yet, a moment later it will be mental. This is what I call the haiku moment of illumination—a heightened moment of transcendence.

Season Words

A *kigo*, or "season word," indicates a particular season of the year. For the Japanese, the seasonal word in the preceding haiku, "frog," is a common *kigo* for late spring, when frogs are heard croaking throughout the country. A *kigo* is an essential part of haiku, and it is a convention that even most contemporary haiku in English follow. In whatever part of the world you live, certain seasonal features are unique to the locality. Even in areas without distinct seasons, people's lifestyles are affected by their environment.

The Japanese are fortunate enough to have access to exhaustive compendiums of season words or phrases called *kiyose* or *saijiki*, which list numerous *kigo* according to each of the four seasons, with a supplementary section pertaining to the New Year's holiday. The *kigo* in these five sections are subdivided according to several themes: nature (weather and seasonal effects, astronomy, geology); life and its observances; and living things (plants and animals).

Some *kigo* are universal, but others must be adapted according to the region.

There are *kigo* that have been created for specific uses, especially those in the "life" category. Both in Japan and in the rest of the world, some traditional *kigo* have been rendered obsolete by modern technology. Refrigeration and air-conditioning, for example, have made seasonal fruits, vegetables, and fish—and thus the *kigo* associated with them—available all year round.

In the following haiku, the words in boldface are some examples of modern *kigo*:

Banryoku no	**Myriad greens** . . .
naka ya ako no ha	amid them my baby begins
hae somuru	his teething
	—Nakamura Kusatao

Yukidaruma	A **snowman**
hoshi no oshaberi	stars chattering
pecha kucha to	chattering
	—Matsumoto Takashi

In both Japanese and English haiku today, there are those who want to abolish *kigo* as an essential convention. My feeling is that the haiku moment of illumination comes regardless of the seasonal framework, especially nowadays when we spend much of our lives in controlled environments without direct contact with nature. After all, the most important element in haiku, and in poetry in general, is the depth and intensity of poetic perception.

How to Compose Haiku

- Observe, discover, create, and perfect.
- Open up your five senses, as well as your memory and imagination.
- Above all, open your mind.
- Discover that nature is all around and within you.
- Use *kigo* if appropriate.
- Carry a memo pad to jot down ideas as soon as they occur to you.
- Keep searching for inspiration from the works of haiku masters, old and new.
- Remember there are always better ways of seeing and writing.
- Share your haiku with others and listen to their comments.
- Join haiku circles and classes, and subscribe to haiku magazines.

Things to Beware Of

- Don't use worn-out expressions. Try to come up with original, one-of-a-kind expressions—your own breath, so to speak.
- Don't try to rhyme. Listen to the inner music of the haiku form.
- Don't use adjectives if you can avoid it.
- Don't be readily satisfied with your haiku. Improve it until it is the best it can be.

Soichi Furuta

Detail from *Scenes from a Journey*, a late-17th-century picture scroll painted by the great haiku poet Bashō.

haji ware The pictured examples of this unglazed earthenware were discovered near Nara. Early Kofun period. Height of largest vessel 31 cm. Nara National Cultural Properties Research Institute.

ate (1603–1867), and the modernization of Japan, including Western influences.

The hairstyles of the 4th and 5th centuries can be seen on the HANIWA (clay burial-mound figures) of that era. Men pulled their parted hair into loops over the ears in the *mizura* style, and women looped theirs loosely on top of the head.

The influence of Chinese and Korean cultures from the 5th to the 8th centuries led to styles featuring topknots for both men and women. Hairstyles began to reflect the wearer's age and social rank. The Heian period (794–1185) featured elaborate hairstyles for the aristocracy, but after the 13th century the functional styles of the warrior class (*samurai*) gained ascendancy and spread to the townsmen (CHŌNIN), who were distinguished from the samurai by the shapes of their topknots.

Women generally wore their hair long and straight until the late 16th century, when women of the merchant class began putting their hair up. Women's hairstyles copied men's for a time, but during the Tokugawa shogunate men's hairstyles remained much the same while women's styles became more complex, often incorporating ornaments such as the *kushi* (see COMBS), KANZASHI, and KŌGAI. Women's hairstyles reflected their age, social class, and marital status.

In 1871 a governmental order (DAMPATSUREI) encouraged males to cut off their topknots. Men's hairstyles thereafter were similar to those in the West, and by the Taishō period (1912–26) most young women also wore their hair in Western styles. Traditional Japanese hairstyles are seen today only at NEW YEAR celebrations and on other special occasions. See also CLOTHING; COSMETICS; HEADGEAR.

Haitani Kenjirō　灰谷健次郎

(1934–). Author of children's literature. Born in Hyōgo Prefecture; graduated from Ōsaka Kyōiku University. Haitani's *Usagi no me* (1974, Rabbit's Eyes), the story of an elementary school teacher's relationship with his underprivileged students, was a best seller. His other works include *Taiyō no ko* (1978, Child of the Sun); *Rokubei mattero yo* (1975, Wait Up, Rokubei), a picture book; and *Watashi no deatta kodomotachi* (1981, Children I Have Known).

Haitōrei　廃刀令

Edict prohibiting the wearing of swords issued by the Meiji government in March 1876, not long after the abolition of the *samurai* class (see SHIZOKU). In 1871 the government had discouraged the wearing of topknots (see DAMPATSUREI) to do away with old dress customs related to status. The prohibition of wearing swords, with the universal CONSCRIPTION ORDINANCE OF 1873 and termination of hereditary stipends for samurai (CHITSUROKU SHOBUN), were major causes of discontent among former samurai (see HAGI REBELLION; JIMPŪREN REBELLION; SATSUMA REBELLION).

haji　恥

(shame). In classifying cultures into "guilt cultures" and "shame cultures," the an-

thropologist Ruth BENEDICT described Japanese culture as a typical shame culture. According to her definition, a guilt culture inculcates absolute standards of morality and relies on the development of a personal conscience, while in a shame culture people feel bad only when caught in the act, rather than feeling guilty in an absolute sense. In other words, a shame culture relies on external sanctions for good behavior, not on an internalized conviction of sin.

Benedict's classification of shame and guilt cultures creates an oversimplistic dichotomy, since Western individuals, presumably belonging to a guilt culture, in fact experience shame as well as guilt, and people of so-called shame cultures, including the Japanese, feel guilt as well as shame. In actuality, Japanese culture depends heavily upon individual internalization of behavioral standards, whether exposed to public scrutiny or not. Although there is an expression, *Tabi no haji wa kakisute* (While on a trip shame can be thrown away), and some Japanese tend to act less scrupulously when away from their community, the same notion exists in Western societies as well. A more accurate sense of the Japanese notion of shame is reflected in the expression from the Confucian classic *Zhong yong* (*Chung yung; Doctrine of the Mean*), *Kunshi wa hitori o tsutsushimu* (When alone, the superior man is watchful of himself).

Haji Seiji　土師清二

(1893–1977). Novelist. Real name Akamatsu Shizuta. Born in Okayama Prefecture. After distinguishing himself as a reporter and a literary and drama critic in Ōsaka, Haji established his reputation as an outstanding writer of popular fiction with *Suna-e shibari* (1927, Curse of the Sand Picture), a historical novel about a nihilistic swordsman that was serialized in the newspaper *Asahi shimbun.* He subsequently devoted his energies to serialized fiction. Other works include the novels *Abare noshi* (1951) and *Fūsetsu no hito* (1957–58).

haji ware　土師器

(*hajiki*). A plain, unglazed, reddish earthenware manufactured from the 4th through the 10th centuries. *Haji* ware of the Kofun period (ca 300–710) evolved from the preceding native YAYOI POTTERY, the transition being marked by the gradual disappearance of surface decoration and the standardization of shapes. During the early Kofun period *haji* ware served both ritual and utilitarian functions.

Beginning in the Nara period (710–794) some *haji* vessels were burnished and smoke-blackened and came to be known popularly as *kokushoku doki* ("black-colored pottery"). From this practice developed the *gaki* ("tile vessels"), bowls fired in an atmosphere of reduced oxygen but at low temperatures. The manufacture of *haji* ware as a cohesive tradition came to an end with the development of glazes and the rise of the medieval pottery traditions (see CERAMICS). Little is known of *haji* craft organization, and few kilns or manufacturing sites have been found. It is assumed that the ware was produced in specialized workshops. During the late Kofun period at least some *haji* ware is said to have been produced by BE (production groups) for the exclusive use of the YAMATO COURT.

Haji ware was coil- or ring-built rather than thrown on a potter's wheel; its exterior and often interior surface was finished by

scraping it with a piece of wood. Globular bodies and round bases are characteristic. *Haji* ware forms the basis for dating many archaeological sites.

Hakai　破戒

(tr *The Broken Commandment*, 1974). Novel by SHIMAZAKI TŌSON (1872–1943); published 1906. The protagonist, Segawa Ushimatsu, is an elementary-school teacher whose father has commanded him to keep his BURAKUMIN origins a secret. Segawa does so but hates society for its irrational prejudices and himself for living a lie. In the end, after hearing of the death of a *burakumin* suffrage activist, Inoko Rentarō, whom he had admired, Segawa confesses to his students his own *burakumin* descent and departs for Texas to seek a new life. With its vivid portrayal of the psychology of a young man contending with social prejudice, *Hakai* is widely recognized as one of the earliest examples of NATURALISM.

hakama　袴

Loose trousers tied at the waist with a cord and worn over a *kimono* as part of formal or ceremonial Japanese-style dress. Men's *hakama* underwent a variety of changes over time: the legs were widened, pleats were added at the waist, and they were bound at the ankles with a cord threaded through the hem. During the Heian period (794–1185), court ladies wore loose-fitting crimson *hakama* with their formal court ensemble, or JŪNIHITOE. *Hakama* were worn by the court ladies of the Kamakura (1185–1333) and Muromachi (1333–1568) periods with *kosode* (a type of long-sleeved kimono), although for a time they went out of fashion as formal wear. In the Meiji period (1868–1912), the *kosode* and *hakama* combination was the school uniform for girls. Traditional formal dress for men consists of *hakama* and a jacket known as a HAORI, usually imprinted with the man's family crest. Today *hakama* are often worn by women receiving a degree at university commencement exercises. They are also worn by people engaging in such traditional activities as *kendō* (fencing) and *kyūdō* (archery) and by actors in the Nō theater.

hakase　博士

(doctor or teacher). Official post in the RITSURYŌ SYSTEM of government. The *hakase* instructed and examined students training to be government officials at the DAIGAKURYŌ and those training to be provincial officials at the *kokugaku* (provincial schools). Since the Meiji period (1868–1912) the term has been used to refer to those holding a doctorate, although the pronunciation *hakushi* is more common.

Hakata → Fukuoka

Hakata Dontaku　博多ドンタク

Festival held in the city of Fukuoka in Kyūshū on 3–4 May. It originated as a NEW YEAR celebration of the Muromachi period (1333–1568) in which local citizens dressed up as the SEVEN DEITIES OF GOOD FORTUNE (Shichifukujin) or as CHIGO (child shrine and temple attendants) and performed in the style of the *matsubayashi* processional then popular in Kyōto. Doll-decorated platforms and elaborate floats (DASHI) were added during the Edo period (1600–1868), when the current name was adopted (apparently from the Dutch word *zondag*, "Sunday," which was taken to mean "holiday"). The festival was revived after World War II and amalgamated with the Harbor Festival in May.

Hakata merchants 博多商人

(Hakata *shōnin*). Wealthy merchants of the Muromachi (1333–1568) and early Edo (1600–1868) periods active in Hakata (now part of Fukuoka). Hakata prospered as the principal base for trade with China and Korea. The Koizumi and Sōkin merchant houses of Hakata engaged in the TALLY TRADE with the Ming dynasty (1368–1644) of China during the Muromachi period, and the SHIMAI SŌSHITSU and KAMIYA SŌTAN houses were active in the late 16th century under the patronage of the national unifier TOYOTOMI HIDEYOSHI. These merchants also conducted the affairs of the city. In the early 17th century Hakata lost preeminence in overseas trade to Hirado and Nagasaki; many traders moved to those places and became members of the silk-importing guild (ITOWAPPU).

Hakata Station film case
博多駅フィルム事件

(Hakata Eki *firumu jiken*). Supreme Court case defining protections of and limitations on news-gathering operations of the press. The case involved a January 1968 clash at the Hakata Station in Fukuoka Prefecture, Kyūshū, between local police and student demonstrators opposed to the calling of the nuclear-powered American aircraft carrier USS *Enterprise* at a Japanese port. A request for a quasi-judicial hearing on the grounds of police abuse of authority and brutality was filed. The plaintiffs, the Japan Socialist Party and the National League for the Protection of the Constitution, requested the subpoena as evidence of television film of the incident, and the lower court issued the subpoena. The affected television stations, asserting that the use of film for any purpose other than news reporting jeopardized the freedom to engage in news gathering, refused the court order and filed a special appeal with the Supreme Court. The Supreme Court rejected the appeal on 26 November 1969, ruling that there are limitations on freedom of news gathering when balanced against a constitutional request such as one involving the fair conduct of criminal proceedings. The case was a landmark in the interpretation of the constitution, since it clarified the constitutional guarantee of the right to gather news and established the legal concept of the people's right to know.

Hakkōdasan 八甲田山

Volcano group in the Nasu Volcanic Zone, central Aomori Prefecture, northern Honshū, on the northern fringe of the Ōu Mountains. The highest peak is Ōdake (1,585 m; 5,200 ft). The group is divided into north and south Hakkōdasan, but the north alone is generally referred to as Hakkōdasan. It has numerous hot springs and is a principal part of Towada-Hachimantai National Park.

hakkō ichiu 八紘一宇

(the whole world under one roof; literally, "eight cords, one roof"). Political slogan widely used by the Japanese government from 1940 to the end of World War II. The eight cords indicate the "eight directions" and thus symbolize the world. The phrase was adapted from a quotation in the 8th century chronicle NIHON SHOKI (720) attributed to the legendary first emperor, JIMMU. On 1 August 1940 the second KONOE FUMIMARO cabinet announced a "Fundamental National Policy" that opened with these words: "The basic aim of Japan's national policy lies in the firm establishment of world peace in accordance with the lofty spirit of *hakkō ichiu* in which the country was founded, and in the construction, as the first step, of a new order in Greater East Asia." During Japan's 1941–45 conquest of "Greater East Asia," the slogan *hakkō ichiu* seemed to imply Japanese control (*ichiu*) over the whole world (*hakkō*), rather than universal brotherhood or peace.

Hakodate 函館[市]

City in southwestern Hokkaidō located on the southeastern tip of the Oshima Peninsula, jutting out into the Tsugaru Strait. A flourishing fishing port since 1741, it was one of the first ports opened to foreign trade under the KANAGAWA TREATY (1854). Its harbor is a base for fishing for salmon, trout, and cuttlefish. The processing of seafood and other foodstuffs, shipbuilding, and transport-machinery manufacturing are major industries. Its chief agricultural products are rice, potatoes, and vegetables grown on the Hakodate Plain. The nearby Seikan Tunnel, completed in 1988, provides Hakodate with a rail link to Aomori on Honshū. Tourist attractions include the fort of Goryōkaku, the scene of the last military conflict accompanying the Meiji Restoration (see GORYŌKAKU, BATTLE OF), and a Trappist convent. Pop: 307,249.

Hakodate bugyō 箱館奉行

(commissioner of Hakodate). An office of the Tokugawa shogunate (1603–1867); established in Hakodate in the early 19th century, when government leaders became alarmed at Russian expansionism (see LAXMAN, ADAM ERIKOVICH). In 1799 the shogunate took charge of part of the island of EZO (now Hokkaidō) and dispatched officials, designating them Ezo *bugyō* and later Hakodate *bugyō*, after the port of Hakodate at the southern tip of the island. The shogunate abolished the office in 1821, reestablishing it in 1855 as foreign problems escalated. In its final form the post of commissioner was under the authority of the senior councillors (RŌJŪ) and had an assigned force of 100 patrolmen (YORIKI AND DŌSHIN) and responsibility for administering the entire island.

Hakone 箱根[町]

Town in southwestern Kanagawa Prefecture, central Honshū, located on the lake ASHINOKO. Hakone developed as one of the POST-STATION TOWNS on the TŌKAIDŌ, the major highway during the Edo period (1600–1868). A barrier station, HAKONE NO SEKI, was established here by the Tokugawa shogunate in 1618. The town is the official center of the Fuji-Hakone-Izu National Park, serving as a tourist base for the lake and the mountain HAKONEYAMA. The city affords a magnificent view of Mt. Fuji (Fujisan). There are several hot springs in the area. The remains of the barrier station, the cedar-lined Tōkaidō, a cluster of stone Buddha images, and the HAKONE OPEN-AIR MUSEUM are other attractions. Pop: 19,365.

Hakone Canal 箱根用水

(Hakone Yōsui). Irrigation canal in eastern Shizuoka Prefecture, central Honshū. The water source is the lake Ashinoko. A tunnel bored under the crater of the mountain Hakoneyama carries the water to irrigate approximately 1,000 hectares (2,470 acres) of farmland surrounding the city of Susono.

Construction was completed in 1670. Three small power-generating stations are located on the canal. Length: 7 km (4.3 mi).

Hakone Hot Springs 箱根温泉郷

(Hakone Onsenkyō). Group of hot springs located in the vicinity of the composite volcano HAKONEYAMA and stretching across Kanagawa and Shizuoka prefectures, central Honshū. There are more than 400 hot spring sources here, including simple thermal, common salt, and sulfur. The area is a year-round resort, with historic sites, hiking courses, and museums.

Hakone Museum of Art 箱根美術館

(Hakone Bijutsukan). Located in Hakone, Kanagawa Prefecture; formerly known as the Kyūsei Hakone Art Museum. This museum, opened in 1952, and its sister museum, the MOA MUSEUM OF ART in Atami, belong to the SEKAI KYŪSEI KYŌ (The Religion for the Salvation of the World). The two museums share the collections assembled by OKADA MOKICHI, the late founder of the church. In the larger of two buildings set in a garden, the Hakone Museum of Art exhibits Japanese pottery and porcelains from several eras. The smaller building houses an exhibition of Japanese ceramic techniques.

Hakone no Seki 箱根関

(Hakone Barrier). A checkpoint maintained at the Hakone Pass (now in Kanagawa Prefecture) on the highway TŌKAIDŌ during the Edo period (1600–1868). To secure the de-

Hakodate The mountain Hakodate-yama affords a striking view of the city of Hakodate at dusk. *Right:* Tsugaru Strait; *left:* Hakodate Harbor. Fishing and fish processing are among the city's major industries.

Hakone Pleasure boats on the lake Ashinoko are a popular tourist attraction, offering a view of Mt. Fuji in the distance.

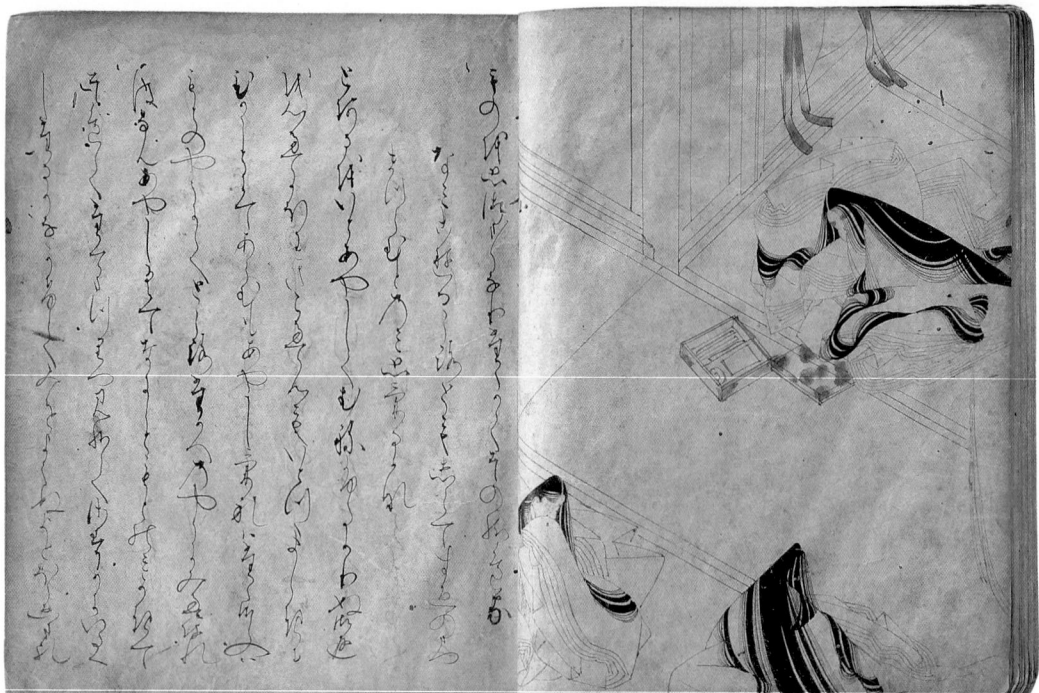

hakubyōga This 13th-century album, with text and illustrations from the "Ukifune" chapter of the *Tale of Genji*, is one of the earliest and best examples of the *hakubyōga* style of ink painting. Ink on paper. 24 × 39 cm. Yamato Bunkakan, Nara.

fense of Edo (now Tōkyō), the Tokugawa shogunate set up a barrier and post station there in 1618. Traffic through this strategic nexus was tightly controlled. Because the wives and daughters of *daimyō* were required under the SANKIN KŌTAI system to remain in Edo, especially stringent checks were made on women. It was removed in 1869, a year after the Meiji Restoration. See also SEKISHO.

Hakone Open-Air Museum
彫刻の森美術館
(Chōkoku no Mori Bijutsukan). Located in Hakone, Kanagawa Prefecture. The museum, established in 1969, owns a collection of 19th-and 20th-century Western and Japanese sculpture, almost all of it shown out-of-doors. The Western section has works by Archipenko, Arp, Bourdelle, Calder, Despiau, Giacometti, Maillol, Marini, Moore, Isamu NOGUCHI, Picasso, and Rodin. One room is devoted to the studies made by Manzu for the doors of St. Peter's in Rome; Emilio Greco's figures are displayed in a garden by themselves. Japanese artists displayed include Amenomiya Jirō (1889–1970), Nakahara Teijirō (1888–1921), OGIWARA MORIE, Shimizu Takashi (1897–1981), TAKAMURA KŌTARŌ, and Tobari Kogan (1882–1927).

Hakone Pass
箱根峠
(Hakone Tōge). Located on the border of southwestern Kanagawa Prefecture and eastern Shizuoka Prefecture, central Honshū. A national highway runs through the pass. Hakone Pass is the area within Fuji-Hakone-Izu National Park from which roads leading to tourist areas such as HAKONE, the lake ASHINOKO, and Izu Peninsula regions branch off. Altitude: 849 m (2,785 ft).

Hakoneyama
箱根山
Composite volcano on the border between Kanagawa and Shizuoka prefectures, central Honshū. The highest peak is Kamiyama (1,438 m; 4,718 ft). Hakoneyama has two crater rims, one old and one new, and seven central domes including Kamiyama and Komagatake (1,350 m; 4,429 ft). The crater lake ASHINOKO is on the southwestern part of the mountain. Hakoneyama is the center of the Hakone area of the Fuji-Hakone-Izu Na-

tional Park. It includes scenic spots and numerous hot-spring spas.

hakoniwa
箱庭
Miniature Japanese gardens created in shallow boxes using sand, stones, ceramic figurines, houses, and bridges, as well as miniature trees (BONSAI) and such plants as azalea, *goyōmatsu* pine, and zelkova. Miniature gardens first became popular during the mid-Edo period (1600–1868). See also BONKEI AND BONSEKI.

Hakozaki Shrine
宮崎宮
(Hakozakigū). Shintō shrine in the Hakozaki section of the city of Fukuoka, Kyūshū; dedicated to Emperor ŌJIN (deified as HACHIMAN) and Empress JINGŪ (both legendary) as well as the deity Tamayorihime no Mikoto. It is one of the great Hachiman shrines of Japan. According to one tradition, it was established in the early 10th century as an offshoot of the USA HACHIMAN SHRINE. Its annual festival is held 12–18 September.

Hakuba
白馬[村]
Village in northwestern Nagano Prefecture, central Honshū, situated on the eastern slopes of SHIROUMADAKE. It is a popular ski resort. Pop: 8,356.

Hakubakai
白馬会
(White Horse Society). Association of Western-style painters and sculptors active in the late Meiji period (1868–1912). It was founded in 1896 when KURODA SEIKI, Kume Keiichirō (1866–1934), and other liberals broke away from the Meiji Bijutsukai (Meiji Fine Arts Society). The association became the leading group in Western-style painting circles, and its position was strengthened by the fact that both Kuroda and Kume were appointed to professorships at the Tōkyō Bijutsu Gakkō (now Tōkyō University of Fine Arts and Music). The Hakubakai sponsored exhibitions, supported research, and trained many young painters before it dissolved in 1910.

Hakubunkan
博文館
Publishing company; one of Japan's largest and most influential publishing houses in the late 19th and early 20th centuries. Founded in 1887 by ŌHASHI SAHEI and his son Ōhashi Shintarō (1863–1944). Hakubunkan published a large number of magazines, totaling

77 by the mid-1920s; among them was TAIYŌ, one of the pivotal literary journals of the period. The firm was dissolved in 1947 and reorganized as Hakubunkan Shinsha in 1950, specializing in diary notebooks. Magazine and book publication was taken over by Hakuyūsha in 1949.

hakubyōga
白描画
("white drawing picture"). Type of monochrome ink line painting often used to illustrate scenes from Japanese courtly romances from the late Heian period (794–1185) onward. Conservative and classical in both subject matter and style, *hakubyōga* make use of light and precise lines in combination with rhythmic patterns of solid black created through the rendering of men's black caps, women's long black hair, interior architectural details, and so on. Occasionally, touches of red or gold pigment are added. Two well-known *hakubyōga* are the 14th-century illustrated scrolls *Toyo no akari emaki* and *Makura no sōshi emaki*. In a broad sense, *hakubyōga* may refer to any ink line painting that does not employ areas of wash; it may also refer to preliminary monochrome underpainting or ink drawings used as models. In this sense, *hakubyōga* can be traced to the 9th century, when Buddhist clergy in Japan copied religious images in simple line drawings (*zuzō*) to serve as iconographic models.

Hakuhō culture
白鳳文化
(Hakuhō *bunka*). The culture of the Hakuhō period, extending from the latter half of the 7th century to the beginning of the 8th century; so called after the Hakuhō era (672–686), an unofficial reign name (*nengō*) associated with Emperor TEMMU (r 672–686). During this time the authority of the emperor was built up under the impetus of the TAIKA REFORM (645). Artistically the period was a continuation of the ASUKA CULTURE but with stronger Tang (T'ang; 618–907) dynasty Chinese influence. The latter half of the period showed the influence of the Gupta court in India transmitted via Tang China. Outstanding examples are the east pagoda of the temple YAKUSHIJI, the statue of the seated Bodhisattva Miroku (Maitreya) at the temple TAIMADERA, and the Amida (Amitābha) Triad, housed in the Lady Tachibana Shrine at HŌRYŪJI. Hakuhō culture was succeeded by TEMPYŌ CULTURE, in which Buddhist art reflecting continental influence reached its peak. See also BUDDHIST ART; PAINTING; BUDDHIST SCULPTURE.

Hakuhōdō, Inc
[株]博報堂
(Hakuhōdō). Advertising firm; Japan's second largest after DENTSŪ, INC. Hakuhōdō was founded in 1895 by SEKI HIRONAO as an agency specializing in advertisements for magazines put out by the HAKUBUNKAN publishing house. Today it controls a major share of advertising in Japanese commercial television, radio, newspapers, and magazines. It is also active in international advertising markets, establishing McCann-Erickson Hakuhōdō in 1960 as a joint venture with the US firm of McCann-Erickson in order to expand and promote its international accounts. Sales for fiscal year ending November 1991 were ¥564.9 billion (US $4.4 billion), and capitalization for the same year was ¥108.0 million (US $832,819). Headquarters are in Tōkyō.

Hakui
羽咋[市]
City in central Ishikawa Prefecture, central Honshū. Hakui has a flourishing silk and rayon fabric industry. Agricultural products

include rice, vegetables, and fruit. Located on the western coast of the Noto Peninsula, it is a part of Noto Peninsula Quasi-National Park. The city has several famous temples and shrines, among them Keta Shrine. Pop: 27,517.

Hakuin 白隠

(1686–1769). Also known as Hakuin Ekaku. RINZAI SECT Zen master, painter, and calligrapher. Born in Hara (in what is now Shizuoka Prefecture). At 15 he entered the ZEN temple of Shōinji in his native village before taking up the life of a wandering monk. He had his first experience of enlightenment at the age of 24, shortly before becoming a pupil of Shōju Rōjin (Dōkyō Etan, 1642–1721). In 1716 he returned to the temple Shōinji in Hara, where he began to instruct a growing number of followers. He reformed the traditions of Zen teachings, insisting that each student must first see into his own nature and then "break his conceptual thought" by meditating upon the paradoxical questions called KŌAN. Most of these *kōan* were taken from early Chinese Zen masters, but Hakuin also used a *kōan* of his own, "What is the sound of one hand clapping?" Hakuin's success in revamping Rinzai training was so decisive that the principles he established are still followed in Rinzai temples. Hakuin produced a voluminous and important body of writing, including sermons, instructional texts, letters, poems, and stories. In his sixties Hakuin turned to brushwork to express his Zen enlightenment. His ink paintings and calligraphy are distinguished by their bold simplicity and wry wit; his powerful portraits of Daruma (Bodhidharma) are especially prized.

hakurai 舶来

("arrived from abroad"). The terms *hakurai* and *hakuraihin* ("imported goods") were used from the Nara period (710–794) to refer to imported goods primarily from China and Korea. With the importation of Western culture after the Meiji Restoration (1868), however, *hakurai* came to mean anything made in Europe or the United States. The Japanese considered these imported products superior to and therefore more prestigious than domestic products, and therefore the word *hakurai* was once synonymous with "good" or "of the highest quality." Today the term has almost disappeared from common use.

Hakusan 白山

Volcano on the border between Ishikawa and Gifu prefectures, central Honshū; the highest peak (2,702 m; 8,865 ft) in the Hakusan Volcanic Zone. Along with FUJISAN (Mt. Fuji) and TATEYAMA, Hakusan is one of the three most popular mountains in Japan as objects of religious worship and for climbing. On the summit are three central domes and seven crater lakes, including Senjagaike. Alpine flora and birds abound. Hakusan is the center of Hakusan National Park.

Hakusan National Park
白山国立公園

(Hakusan Kokuritsu Kōen). Situated in central Honshū, in Toyama, Ishikawa, Fukui, and Gifu prefectures. The park's desolate mountain terrain features numerous lakes, rivers, and spectacular gorges. In the center of the park is HAKUSAN, an extinct volcano. Together with Mt. Fuji (FUJISAN) and TATEYAMA, Hakusan is one of Japan's three sacred mountains. To the north of Hakusan

lie the hot-spring resorts of Chūgū and Iwama, closed during the winter months due to heavy snow. The mountain is open to climbers only in the summer. Hakusan is rich in colorful alpine flora and virgin forests of creeping pine, Japanese beech (*buna*), and Japanese oak (*nara*). It is noted for the 100 or more species of birds, including a rare golden eagle (*inuwashi*). Area: 477 sq km (184 sq mi).

Hakusan Volcanic Zone 白山火山帯

(Hakusan Kazantai). Volcanic zone extending from HAKUSAN, on the border of Ishikawa and Gifu prefectures, central Honshū, to UN-ZENDAKE, Nagasaki Prefecture, northern Kyūshū. The major volcanoes in the zone are Hakusan, DAISEN, SAMBESAN, HIKOSAN, Yufudake, KUJŪSAN, and Unzendake.

Hakusukinoe, Battle of 白村江の戦い

(Hakusukinoe no Tatakai). Naval battle fought in 663 near the mouth of the river Hakusukinoe (or Hakusonkō; Kor: Paekkang, now Kŭm-kang) on the southwestern coast of the Korean peninsula, in which a Tang (T'ang) Chinese naval force destroyed a Japanese expedition sent to restore the kingdom of PAEKCHE. Paekche, with which Japan had had close ties for two centuries, had been occupied in 660 by the Tang in alliance with the kingdom of SILLA. The Paekche king had surrendered and was taken to China, but his son, who was in Japan, had returned to Paekche with a Japanese supporting force in 663. This relief force, under ABE NO HIRAFU, was decisively defeated by the Tang fleet in a naval engagement. As a result, the effort to restore the kingdom of Paekche collapsed, and Japan, convinced of the strength of the Tang and Silla, resolved to strengthen its government administration (see TAIKA REFORM).

Hakutsuru Fine Art Museum
白鶴美術館

(Hakutsuru Bijutsukan). One of Japan's oldest private museums, the Hakutsuru Fine Art Museum was established in the city of Kōbe, Hyōgo Prefecture, in 1934 to house the collection of Kanō Jihei (1862–1951) of the Hakutsuru Sake Brewery. The collection consists mostly of ancient Chinese art such as silver and bronze ware and ceramics, although it also features some Japanese paintings, swords, and lacquer ware. There are some 1,300 works in the entire collection, 2 of which are National Treasures.

Hamada 浜田[市]

City in western Shimane Prefecture, western Honshū. Situated on the Sea of Japan, Hamada developed during the Edo period (1600–1868) as a port and castle town. Today it is the administrative, commercial, and industrial center of the Iwami region of Shimane. An important fishing port, it has a thriving marine-products-processing industry, as well as a growing woodwork industry. The ruins of the 17th-century Hamada Castle may be seen here. Pop: 49,135.

Hamada Hikozō 浜田彦蔵

(1837–97). Also known as Joseph Heco or Amerika Hikozō. The first Japanese person to become an American citizen. Born in Harima (now Hyōgo Prefecture), the son of a ship captain. Hamada and 16 other survivors of an 1850 shipwreck were rescued by the American ship *Oakland*, which arrived in San Francisco in February 1851. The American government was preparing an expedition under Commodore Matthew PERRY to force the OPENING OF JAPAN and arranged to have the 17 castaways sent back with Perry. Upon reaching Hong Kong Hamada was asked to return to the United States. In October 1854 he was baptized a Catholic and was known thereafter as Joseph Heco; he obtained American citizenship in June 1858.

Hamada missed his homeland, however, and obtained ship passage to Japan. En route, in Shanghai in 1858, he met Townsend HARRIS, the first American minister to Japan. Harris appointed Hamada interpreter for the American consulate in Kanagawa.

In 1864 Hamada began publishing *Kaigai shimbun* (Overseas News), the first modern Japanese newspaper, with KISHIDA GINKŌ. During the early years of the Meiji period (1868–1912) he served for a while in the

Hakusan National Park
1 Hakusan ("White Mountain") stands at the center of this national park.
2 One of the mountains in Japan regarded as holy since ancient times, Hakusan is the site of the Shirayama-hime Shrine. Beyond the shrine's *torii*, pictured here, rises the central peak, Gozengamine (elevation 2,702 m).

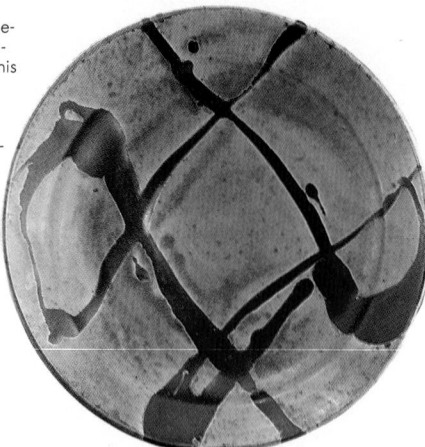

Hamada Shōji A blue-glazed plate with iron-oxide decoration by this famous potter and participant in the Japanese folk-crafts movement. Japan Folk-Craft Museum, Tōkyō.

Ministry of Finance. Hamada wrote two autobiographies, *Hyōryūki* (1863, Record of a Castaway) in Japanese and *The Narrative of a Japanese* (1895) in English.

Hamada Kōsaku   浜田耕作

(1881–1938). Archaeologist. Pen name Hamada Seiryō. Born in Ōsaka, he graduated from Tōkyō University in 1905. He became a lecturer at Kyōto University in 1909. After studying in Europe from 1913 to 1916, he was appointed professor at Kyōto University in 1917, the first in Japan to hold a university chair in archaeology. He served as president of Kyōto University from 1937 until his death.

Hamada introduced scientific methods of archaeology to Japan, and his research group published 14 volumes of research work between 1917 and 1937. In 1925 he formed the Far Eastern Archaeological Society with HARADA YOSHITO of Tōkyō University and Ma Heng of Beijing (Peking) University. Hamada's publications include *Shina komeiki deishō zusetsu* (1927), on Chinese archaeological remains; *Tenshō ken'ō shisetsu ki* (1931), on the MISSION TO EUROPE OF 1582; *Tsūron kōkogaku* (1922), a collection of lectures; and *Kōkogaku nyūmon* (1930), an introductory text.

Hamada Shōji   浜田庄司

(1894–1978). Japan's most renowned potter; a major figure in the Japanese FOLK CRAFTS (*mingei*) movement. Born in Kawasaki, Kanagawa Prefecture, he studied ceramics at Tōkyō Industrial College (now Tōkyō Institute of Technology). He joined fellow potter KAWAI KANJIRŌ as an employee at the Kyōto Ceramic Testing Institute. In 1920 he accompanied Bernard H. LEACH to England, where he helped establish The Leach Pottery. Hamada returned to Japan in 1924 and settled in Mashiko, Tochigi Prefecture. He was designated one of the LIVING NATIONAL TREASURES in 1955 and awarded the Order of Culture in 1968. Hamada used only traditional Mashiko glazes made of local clay, stone, and various types of ash, as well as underglaze pigments, overglaze enamels, and salt glaze. He achieved a great range of effects by free combination of this limited glaze palette.

Hamada Yahyōe   浜田弥兵衛

(fl 1620s). Captain of a trading ship (see VERMILION SEAL SHIP TRADE) sent to Taiwan in 1626 by the Nagasaki merchant SUETSUGU HEIZŌ. When his trading efforts there were thwarted by the Dutch colonists, Yahyōe returned to Taiwan in 1628 with a band of armed men to seek restitution. He held the chief of the Dutch Factory, Pieter Nuijts, at swordpoint until he obtained free passage

home, hostages, and reparations. The Tokugawa shogunate (1603–1867) then undertook reprisals against the Dutch in Japan. The Dutch were forced to surrender Nuijts to the Japanese, and friendly relations were not restored until 1636.

Hama Detached Palace Garden   浜離宮庭園

(Hama Rikyū Teien). Landscape garden at the mouth of the river Sumidagawa in Chūō Ward, Tōkyō. The garden, now a municipal park, was once the site of a villa of the Matsudaira family of Kai Province (now Yamanashi Prefecture) and eventually came into the possession of the imperial household and then the city of Tōkyō. It was opened to the public after World War II. Area: 25 hectares (62 acres).

Hamaguchi Osachi   浜口雄幸

(1870–1931). Also known as Hamaguchi Yūkō. Politician and prime minister (1929–31). Born in Kōchi Prefecture; entered the Ministry of Finance after graduation from Tōkyō University. Elected to the House of Representatives in 1915, Hamaguchi joined the KENSEIKAI party. He served as finance minister in the first and second KATŌ TAKAAKI cabinets (1924, 1925) and as home minister in the WAKATSUKI REIJIRŌ cabinet (1926). In 1927, he became the president of the RIKKEN MINSEITŌ formed by the merger of the Kenseikai and SEIYŪ HONTŌ parties. When the TANAKA GIICHI cabinet (1927–29) collapsed, Hamaguchi became prime minister and formed a Minseitō cabinet. In his efforts to strengthen the national economy, he adopted a policy of austerity while lifting the gold embargo to stimulate exports. In 1930 he pushed through ratification of the treaty resulting from the LONDON NAVAL CONFERENCES. As a result Hamaguchi was accused of having encroached on the emperor's prerogative of supreme command (see TŌSUIKEN). He died in August 1931 from gunshot wounds inflicted by a right-wing youth at Tōkyō Station the previous November.

Hamaguchi Yōzō   浜口陽三

(1909–). Copperplate printmaker. Born in Wakayama Prefecture. Studied at Tōkyō Bijutsu Gakkō (now Tōkyō University of Fine Arts and Music). In 1930 he went to France, returning to Japan in 1939. Having worked in sculpture and oil painting, he devoted himself to copperplate printmaking after World War II. In 1953 he returned to France and from then on exhibited his prints widely, winning many international prizes. He emigrated to the United States in 1981. He is known as a pioneer of the color mezzotint.

Hamaguri Gomon Incident   蛤御門の変

(Hamaguri Gomon no Hen). Also known as the Kimmon or Palace Gate Incident. A military encounter in August 1864 in which forces from the Chōshū domain (now Yamaguchi Prefecture) were prevented from reentering Kyōto.

Nearly a year before, antiforeign, antishogunate Chōshū *samurai* had been expelled from Kyōto in the COUP D'ETAT OF 30 SEPTEMBER 1863. Then, after the IKEDAYA INCIDENT of 1864 in which many Chōshū activists were killed by shogunal agents, a counterattack proposed by MAKI IZUMI and other radicals received official Chōshū approval.

Chōshū squads advanced on Kyōto to de-

mand entry into the city and pardon for pro-Chōshū imperial nobles who had been forced to flee during the September coup. When Maki Izumi and KUSAKA GENZUI, another Chōshū extremist, attempted to force their way into the city on 20 August, they were repelled by troops from the Satsuma (now Kagoshima Prefecture), Aizu (now part of Fukushima Prefecture), and Kuwana (now part of Mie Prefecture) domains. The battle ignited a fire which caused major damage to the city; Kusaka and Maki committed suicide shortly thereafter. Chōshū was immediately declared an "enemy of the court," and the shogunate was ordered by the court to dispatch a punitive force, the first of the CHŌSHŪ EXPEDITIONS.

Hamakita   浜北[市]

City in western Shizuoka Prefecture, central Honshū. Hamakita is the site of numerous automobile and textile plants. Agricultural products include mandarin oranges, saplings, gourds, stud pigs, and chickens. Tourists are drawn to the Prefectural Forest Park. Pop: 81,157.

Hamamatsu   浜松[市]

City in western Shizuoka Prefecture, central Honshū. Situated on the western bank of the river Tenryūgawa. Hamamatsu developed as a castle town and a post-station town on the TŌKAIDŌ, the major highway in premodern times. Today it is best known for its motorcycles and its musical instruments (both YAMAHA CORPORATION and KAWAI MUSICAL INSTRUMENTS MFG CO, LTD, are located here). There is also a cotton textile industry. Melons, tea, and mandarin oranges are grown on the plateau MIKATAHARA; eels and edible seaweed (*nori*) are raised in Lake HAMANA. Attractions include the ruins of Hamamatsu Castle; the site of the Battle of Mikatahara (1572), in which TOKUGAWA IEYASU was defeated by TAKEDA SHINGEN; the IBA SITE; the temple KANZANJI; and the Nakajima sand dunes. Pop: 534,624.

Hamamatsu Chūnagon monogatari   浜松中納言物語

(The Tale of the Hamamatsu Middle Counselor). An 11th-century tale often ascribed to SUGAWARA NO TAKASUE NO MUSUME, the author of the SARASHINA NIKKI. The story concerns the romantic entanglements of the "Hamamatsu Counselor," a Japanese nobleman. While in China visiting a young Chinese prince (actually the reincarnated soul of his father), the counselor has a fateful affair with the prince's mother, a half-Japanese consort of the Chinese emperor. Upon his return to Japan the counselor attempts to serve as guardian for the consort's half sister. The girl, however, is abducted by a philandering prince, and the story ends with the counselor's realization that the child born of this incident is to be none other than the reincarnated soul of the Chinese consort. The extensive use of dreams, karma, and transmigration of souls to control plot and characterization indicates a more intense concern with fantasy and religion than is found in earlier examples of MONOGATARI BUNGAKU (narrative literature).

Hamana, Lake   浜名湖

(Hamanako). In southwestern Shizuoka Prefecture, central Honshū. In 1498 an earthquake broke the sandbars separating the lake from the sea, resulting in seawater's entering the lake. Eel, *suppon* (a type of soft-shelled turtle), oyster, *nori* (a type of seaweed), and prawn culture flourish. The southern bank forms an industrial district, while mandarin oranges and flowers are cultivated on the other banks. Tourist attractions are the island of BENTENJIMA and the hot spring of Kanzanji. Area: 69 sq km (26.6 sq mi); circumference: 141 km (87.6 mi); depth: 16 m (52.5 ft).

Hamao Arata 浜尾新

(1849–1925). Educational administrator and president of Tōkyō University. Hamao was born in Edo (now Tōkyō), the son of a *samurai* retainer of the Toyooka domain (now part of Hyōgo Prefecture). He got his start in educational administration in 1872, when he was employed briefly at the Daigaku Nankō (a forerunner of Tōkyō University). The following year he went to study in the United States. After his return to Japan Hamao served as acting and assistant head of Tōkyō Kaisei Gakkō (successor to Daigaku Nankō) and played a leading role in the consolidation of the newly established Tōkyō University in 1877. In 1880 he joined the Ministry of Education, working for administrative reorganization and systemization of higher education. He became minister of education in 1897. Hamao twice served as president of Tōkyō University (1893–97; 1905–12) and made important contributions to its growth.

Hama Rikyū Teien →Hama
Detached Palace Garden

hamaya and hamayumi 破魔矢と破魔弓

(*hamaya to hamayumi*). Good-luck charms sold at Shintō shrines in early January when Japanese make their first shrine visit of the year (HATSUMŌDE). *Hama* is now written with characters meaning "to repel evil spirits," although it originally meant "target"; *yumi* and *ya* mean "bow" and "arrow" respectively. It is still fairly common for a mother's family to send these two items to her male child on the occasion of his first NEW YEAR or CHILDREN'S DAY festival. Until recently, in certain areas, young boys held archery competitions at New Year's to predict the next fall's harvest.

Hamaya Hiroshi 濱谷浩

(1915–). Photographer. Born in Tōkyō. Hamaya worked for the Oriental Photo Industrial Co, Ltd, and studied under Watanabe Yoshio (b 1907). Around 1940, influenced by folklorists like YANAGITA KUNIO, he began to photograph people participating in folk rites and celebrations. *Ura Nihon* (1957) is a collection of his photographs taken in the area along the Sea of Japan coast.

hamayū 浜木綿

(crinum). *Crinum asiaticum* var. *japonicum*. Also known as *hamaomoto*. Large evergreen perennial herb of the family Amaryllidaceae, found in sandy coastal areas of Okinawa, Kyūshū, Shikoku, and central and western Honshū. The cylindrical stem, which grows to 50 centimeters (20 in), with a circumference of 5–10 centimeters (2–4 in), is actually a false stem made up of multiple layers of fleshy leafstalks. Large green leaves sprout from its tip. In summer, flower stalks about 70 centimeters (30 in) long appear between the leaves, bearing clusters of fragrant white blossoms. The *hamayū* grows only in areas where the mean annual temperature exceeds 15°C (59°F). The northernmost limit

of its range, called the *hamayū* line by botanists, is an important frontier in the distribution of Japanese flora.

hamba seido 飯場制度

(labor-boss system). A system of labor recruitment and management in which a foreman or labor boss, called the *hamba-gashira* or *naya-gashira*, was contracted by a company to hire, supervise, and provide food and lodging for workers. The labor-boss system was characteristic of the Edo period (1600–1868), but survived into Meiji times (1868–1912), particularly in the mining and building industries. The word *hamba* (literally, "a place to eat") generally referred to the lodge where the workers ate and slept while working at a construction or mining site. The system, which was subject to frequent abuses, was outlawed by the Labor Standards Law of 1947 (see LABOR LAWS).

hambatsu 藩閥

(domain clique). A term referring to the close-knit group of men—often referred to as the Meiji oligarchs—who dominated the Japanese government from the beginning of the Meiji period (1868–1912) until the mid-Taishō period (1912–26). These men—among them ŌKUBO TOSHIMICHI, SAIGŌ TAKAMORI, KIDO TAKAYOSHI, ŌKUMA SHIGENOBU, and ETŌ SHIMPEI—came from the domains (HAN) that had played a leading role in the MEIJI RESTORATION of 1868: Satsuma, Chōshū, Tosa, and Hizen (now Kagoshima, Yamaguchi, Kōchi, and Saga prefectures, respectively). Power became increasingly concentrated in the hands of the so-called Satchō (Satsuma and Chōshū) *hambatsu* with the departure of Tosa and Hizen men following the 1873 debate over sending a military expedition to Korea (SEIKANRON) and the expulsion from the government of the Hizen native Ōkuma Shigenobu and his followers in the POLITICAL CRISIS OF 1881. It was from about this time that the term *hambatsu* began to be used as a synonym for the Meiji government; from about 1890, it was used interchangeably with *chōzen naikaku* ("TRANSCENDENTAL" CABINETS), a term that referred to the assertions of the Meiji oligarchs that their policies were of a supraparty nature.

With the exception of Ōkuma and SAIONJI KIMMOCHI, a court noble, every prime minister from 1885 to 1918 was from Satsuma or Chōshū. Members of the Satchō *hambatsu* not only monopolized important government posts but also controlled the army and navy (see GUMBATSU) and extended their influence into the bureaucracy through the appointment and promotion of protégés. After the fourth ITŌ HIROBUMI cabinet (1900–1901), the original *hambatsu* leaders no longer served as prime ministers but continued to exercise political influence as elder statesmen (GENRŌ). The *hambatsu* remained influential through the end of the 19th century. However, the growing influence of political parties eventually weakened, then replaced, the

influence of the *hambatsu*. See also POLITICAL PARTIES.

Hamura 羽村[市]

City in northwestern Tōkyō Prefecture, central Honshū. The Hamura Dam, built in 1654 on the river Tamagawa, is a source of water for metropolitan Tōkyō. Once a farming village, Hamura is now becoming increasingly urbanized and industrialized. Pop: 52,103.

han 藩

(domain). The basic unit of provincial government under the BAKUHAN SYSTEM during the Edo period (1600–1868). Although often translated as "domain" or "*daimyō* domain," the term *han* refers not only to the land entrusted to a DAIMYŌ by the TOKUGAWA SHOGUNATE but also to its military, administrative, and fiscal superstructure. Apparently first used in China during the Zhou (Chou) dynasty (ca 1027 BC–256 BC) to denote the fiefs of feudal magnates, the term came into popular use in Japan only during the 18th century and into official use at the beginning of the Meiji period (1868–1912). Early in the 17th century TOKUGAWA IEYASU acknowledged the existence of 185 *ryōbun* (as domains were then called). Although the number of domains stabilized at around 260 during the 18th century, because of various changes in the location and proprietorship of domains, it is possible to distinguish more than 540 domains (many of which existed only briefly), during the years of Tokugawa rule.

Each domain was assigned directly by the shōgun and was in the charge of a daimyō

hamaya and hamayumi

1 Two New Year visitors to Asakusa Shrine in Tōkyō display their purchases of good-luck *hamaya*.
2 Carpenters often erect a ceremonial Shintō bow and arrow at roof-raisings. The bow and arrow, secured to a temporary structure, is positioned to "shoot down" misfortune from the northeast, an inauspicious direction.

hamayū The fragrant flowers of this evergreen herb bloom in July and August. The plant grows only in the warmer regions of Japan.

The Twelve Suits of the Hanafuda Card Deck

January—pine (matsu) — 20 points | 5 points | 1 point | 1 point
February—plum (ume) — 10 points | 5 points | 1 point | 1 point
March—flowering cherry (sakura) — 20 points | 5 points | 1 point | 1 point
April—wisteria (fuji) — 10 points | 5 points | 1 point | 1 point
May—iris (shōbu) — 10 points | 5 points | 1 point | 1 point
June—tree peony (botan) — 10 points | 5 points | 1 point | 1 point
July—bush clover (hagi) — 10 points | 5 points | 1 point | 1 point
August—pampas grass (susuki) — 20 points | 10 points | 1 point | 1 point
September—chrysanthemum (kiku) — 10 points | 5 points | 1 point | 1 point
October—maple (momiji) — 10 points | 5 points | 1 point | 1 point
November—rain (ame) — 20 points | 10 points | 5 points | 1 point
December—paulownia (kiri) — 20 points | 1 point | 1 point | 1 point

and so, by definition, had an assessed annual productivity of at least 10,000 *koku* of rice (see KOKUDAKA). Each daimyō was expected to meet the expenses of service to the head of the Tokugawa house. The nature of the service differed from period to period, but it always included the obligation of SANKIN KŌTAI, or alternate-year attendance at the shogunal capital, and the maintenance of an army of *samurai* ready to respond when the shōgun required them. The domains varied widely in size, geographical configuration (some consisted of self-contained units, while others consisted of widely scattered pockets of land), productivity, political structure, and degree of political independence. Domains that were large and far from the seat of shogunal government in Edo (now Tōkyō) were more likely to attain significant independence than were smaller domains situated closer to the shogunate. While the domains and loyalties based upon them remained paramount, Japan could not achieve true national unification. That was to require a political and social revolution— the MEIJI RESTORATION—in which both shogunate and domains were destroyed. See PREFECTURAL SYSTEM, ESTABLISHMENT OF.

Hanabusa Itchō　　　英一蝶

(1652–1724). Painter. Real name Taga Shinkō. Born in Kyōto, the son of a physician. At the age of 15 he moved to Edo (now Tōkyō) with his father. He studied HAIKU with Matsuo BASHŌ, calligraphy with Genryū Bunzan, and, purportedly, painting with Kanō Yasunobu (1613–85), eventually establishing himself as a painter. In 1698, for reasons unknown, he was exiled by the shogunate government to Miyakejima, an is-

land south of Edo, where he remained until his pardon in 1709. He returned to Edo, changing his name to Hanabusa Itchō. Many of his paintings, basically of the KANŌ SCHOOL style, are sophisticated depictions of city life.

Hanada Kiyoteru　　　花田清輝

(1909–74). Literary critic, novelist, and playwright. Born in Fukuoka Prefecture; graduated from Kyōto University. During World War II, he published many essays criticizing militarists in the magazine *Bunka soshiki*, which he founded in 1939. After the war he contributed to KINDAI BUNGAKU, a progressive literary magazine. He gained recognition as a critic for his book *Fukkōki no seishin* (1946), a collection of essays on such writers as Dante and Cervantes. He was a Marxist who advocated the dialectical fusion of art and politics and played a leading role in the postwar movement for an integrated audiovisual art form. Most of his writings are in *Hanada Kiyoteru chosakushū* (1963–66).

hanafuda　　　花札

Also known as *hanakaruta* (literally, "flower cards"). A gambling game played with a 48-card deck divided into twelve 4-card suits represented by trees, shrubs, or flowers, each corresponding to a particular month of the year. Each of the 12 suits also has at least 1 card depicting a bird, animal, or stylized figure appropriate to the suit sign; 2 suits have 2 such cards. Three suits have 1 "poem card" showing a red strip of Japanese poem-writing paper (*tanzaku*) on which is written a poem alluding to the month and the floral symbol of the suit; 4 other suits have 1 card with a red *tanzaku* on which no poem is written. In addition, 3 suits have 1 card with a blue *tanzaku*.

Hanafuda evolved from Western-style

playing cards introduced by the Dutch during the Tenshō era (1573–91) and a Heian-period (794–1185) court pastime called *kachō-awase* (literally, "matching birds and flowers"). The object of the game is to collect as many cards as possible by matching suits. All cards have an assigned point value of 20, 10, 5, or 1. However, much of the excitement and fun lies in the many exotic extra-score combinations and the special names and symbolism of the cards themselves. *Hanafuda* is still played and remains more of a backroom gambling game than a family entertainment. See also GAMBLING; PLAYING CARDS.

Hanai Takuzō　　　花井卓蔵

(1868–1931). Attorney and legal scholar. Born in Mihara, Hiroshima Prefecture; adopted as heir to the Hanai family in 1888. He received a law degree from what is now Chūō University and later became president of the Tōkyō Bar Association; earned a doctorate in law (1909); wrote numerous books; taught at Chūō; and served on committees that drafted Criminal Code revisions (1907), the courts-martial law (1921), and the law authorizing trial by jury (1923). He was a defense attorney in many criminal trials; among these were the Viscount Sōma poisoning-and-libel case (1893), the HOSHI TŌRU assassination (1901), the KŌTOKU SHŪSUI high-treason trial (1910), the trials following the RICE RIOTS OF 1918, and several corruption cases including the Siemens naval procurement scandal (1914; see SIEMENS INCIDENT). Hanai was elected to the House of Representatives seven times and led unsuccessful suffrage efforts (see UNIVERSAL MANHOOD SUFFRAGE MOVEMENT). He was an imperially appointed member of the House of Peers from 1922 until his death.

Hanamaki 花巻[市]

City in central Iwate Prefecture, northern Honshū, on the river Kitakamigawa. Hanamaki developed as a castle town and as a post-station town in the Edo period (1600–1868). The town produces electrical appliances, camera lenses, rice, and dairy products. Hot springs and SHISHI ODORI (deer dance) performances attract tourists. Hanamaki is also known as the birthplace of the poet MIYAZAWA KENJI. Pop: 70,514.

Hana Matsuri 花祭

(Flower Festival). The name of several different annual festivals. One is the Buddhist celebration of the birth of Śākyamuni, held on 8 April, in which flowers are used; also called Kambutsue (see BUDDHIST RITES). Another is the folk festival held in the Kita Shitara district of Aichi Prefecture at the end of the year. Various other festivals held during April at Shintō shrines are also referred to as Hana Matsuri.

hanami 花見

(literally, "flower viewing"; generally, cherry-blossom viewing). Excursions and picnics for enjoying flowers, particularly cherry blossoms; one of the most popular events of the spring. In some places flower-viewing parties are held on traditionally fixed dates according to the old lunar calendar. The subject of flower viewing has long held an important place in literature, dance, and the fine arts. In the Heian period (794–1185) flower-viewing parties were popular among the aristocracy, and in the Azuchi-Momoyama period (1568–1600) the practice reached extravagant proportions with the renowned public cherry-blossom–viewing party of the hegemon TOYOTOMI HIDEYOSHI at the temple Daigoji. By the Edo period (1600–1868) the custom had spread to the common people, and today radio and television stations regularly broadcast reports on the blossoming of local cherry trees. Popular viewing spots include YOSHINOYAMA in Nara Prefecture; ARASHIYAMA in Kyōto; and UENO, the river SUMIDAGAWA, KOGANEI, and Asukayama in Tōkyō.

hanamichi 花道

The ramp in a KABUKI theater that extends from stage right through the auditorium to the back of the theater, serving as a secondary stage as well as a means of entry and exit for the performers. Called the *hanamichi* (literally, "flower path") because *hana no yakusha* ("actors in full flower," i.e., stars) achieve their greatest intimacy with the audience from this vantage point. The ramp can represent a corridor, roadway, or path on the way to or from the main stage. With the *jōshikimaku* (main stage curtain) closed, the *hanamichi* can also become the sole staging area for a scene, and for certain plays a second *hanamichi* (extending from stage left, parallel to the first) is added, enabling actors to interact across the auditorium over the heads of the audience.

Hanamori Yasuji 花森安治

(1911–78). Magazine editor. Born in Hyōgo Prefecture, Hanamori graduated from Tōkyō University. In 1940 he took a position with the propaganda division of the Imperial Rule Assistance Association, where one of his responsibilities was writing wartime slogans. In 1946 Hanamori established the Center for Research on Clothing, and in 1948 he founded a household magazine called *Kura-*

Hana Matsuri In a festival at the temple Gokokuji, Tōkyō, a child ladles sweet tea over a statue of the newborn Buddha.

shi no techō. The magazine contributed to Japan's consumer movement with its policy of refusing advertisements and publishing the results of consumer product tests performed in its own laboratory. Hanamori's published works include *Issen gorin no hata* (1971).

Hanamura Nihachirō 花村仁八郎

(1908–). Vice-chairman of KEIDANREN (Japan Federation of Economic Organizations; 1976–88). Born in Fukuoka Prefecture. After graduating from Tōkyō University in 1932, Hanamura joined Jūyō Sangyō Kyōgikai, one of the predecessors of Keidanren, in 1942. He was involved in establishing Keidanren in 1946 and served as its director-general in addition to being vice-chairman. In his unofficial Keidanren role as director of political fund-raising in the business world, he funneled major donations into the Liberal Democratic Party.

Hanaoka Seishū 華岡青洲

(1760–1835). Physician who performed the first surgical operation under general anesthesia. Personal name Furuu; also known as Hanaoka Zuiken. A native of Kii Province (now Wakayama Prefecture), he studied medicine of the classicist school (*koihō*; see MEDICINE, TRADITIONAL) with Yoshimasu Nangai (1745–1813), the son of YOSHIMASU TŌDŌ. He also studied Western surgery under Yamato Kenryū before returning to his native area to practice.

After some 20 years of experimenting Hanaoka succeeded in preparing an anesthetic called *mafutsusan*, a mixture of six crude drugs (including datura and aconite) from the traditional Chinese pharmacopoeia. He used it successfully in a surgical operation for breast cancer in 1805, about 40 years before the first use of ether at Massachusetts General Hospital, Boston, and subsequently used it for other types of operations. His surgical techniques came to be known as the Hanaoka method.

Hanasaka jijii 花咲爺

(The Old Man Who Made the Trees Bloom). Folktale. An honest old man finds gold with the help of his wondrous dog. A greedy old man who lives next door imitates him without success and kills the dog in anger. The good man buries the dog and plants on its grave a tree from which he later makes a mortar. When he pounds rice in the mortar, the rice is immediately transformed into gold pieces, but when the greedy man borrows the mortar, he pounds in vain and burns it. The honest man scatters the ashes on lifeless trees, which burst into bloom. It is believed that the story was originally known in many areas as *Haitori jijii* (The Ash Scatterer) or *Gantori jijii* (The Old Goose Hunter).

Hanasanjin 鼻山人

(1790–1858). Popular writer of the late Edo period (1600–1868). Real name Hosokawa Namijirō; other pen name Tōri Sanjin. A dis-

ciple of SANTŌ KYŌDEN, he produced works in many of the genres of Edo popular literature (see GESAKU). He is often mentioned along with TAMENAGA SHUNSUI as an early writer of the NINJŌBON (a genre of popular fiction). His principal works include *Satokagami* (1822, Mirror of Flowertown), SHAREBON ("witty book"), and *Kuruwa zōdan* (1825, Tales of the Pleasure Districts), a *ninjōbon*.

hanashibon → kobanashi

hanashōbu → irises

Hanawa Hokiichi 塙保己一

(1746–1821). A KOKUGAKU (National Learning) scholar and textual editor of the late Edo period (1600–1868). Born in Musashi Province (now Saitama Prefecture), he was blind from age five. He studied under KAMO NO MABUCHI and other Kokugaku scholars and, relying on his extraordinary memory, mastered the Chinese and Japanese classics. In 1793 he established the Wagaku Kōdansho, a center for the study of Japanese classics. He devoted his life to the editing and publication of classical texts, compiling with YASHIRO HIROKATA the monumental 530-volume GUNSHO RUIJŪ (1779–1819).

Hanayagi Shōtarō 花柳章太郎

(1894–1965). Stage and film actor. ONNAGATA (female impersonator). Real name Aoyama Shōtarō. Born in Tōkyō, he studied acting under KITAMURA ROKURŌ. Hoping to revitalize the SHIMPA school of drama, he participated in the founding of the Shingekiza (New Drama Theater) in 1921 and the theatrical troupe Shōchiku Gekidan in 1927. In 1939 he starred in MIZOGUCHI KENJI's popular *Zangiku monogatari* (The Story of the Last Chrysanthemum), which launched him on a successful movie career.

He was awarded numerous prizes, such as the Japan Art Academy Prize (1954) and the Asahi Bunka Prize (1962). He was designated one of the LIVING NATIONAL TREASURES (1960) and a Contributor to Culture (1964). He also wrote 15 books, among them *Kimono* (1941).

hanami Crowds of picnickers and pedestrians enjoy the springtime cherry blossoms at Ueno Park in Tōkyō.

Hanayagi Shōtarō A noted *shimpa* stage actor who specialized in female roles, Hanayagi was also a successful film actor.

Hanasaka jijii A book illustration for this famous folktale in which an honest old man makes the trees bloom.

hanetsuki Two children enjoying this badmintonlike game, traditionally played at New Year's.

Hani Motoko This journalist became Japan's first woman newspaper reporter in 1897 and with her husband later published the influential women's magazine *Fujin no tomo*.

Hanazono Tennō shinki
花園天皇宸記

Diary of Emperor Hanazono (1297–1348; r 1308–18). The diary covers the years 1310–32 and is an important source for the study of relations between the court and the shogunate at the end of the Kamakura period (1185–1333). Hanazono was of the Jimyōin imperial line but remained aloof from struggles for succession with the rival Daikakuji line. He was a scholar, poet, and Buddhist.

Handa
半田[市]

City in Aichi Prefecture, central Honshū, on the eastern coast of the Chita Peninsula. In the Edo period (1600–1868) it was a prosperous port of call for cargo ships (KAISEN). Today it is the largest producer of vinegar in Japan. Other industries include *sake* and soy-sauce brewing, textiles (the area has long been known for its Chiga *sarashi*, a cotton cloth), steel, rolling stock, and machinery. Horticulture in the hills relies on water from the AICHI CANAL. The temple Jōrakuji has associations with TOKUGAWA IEYASU. Pop: 99,550.

handen shūju system
班田収授法

(*handen shūju no hō*; land allotment system). System for state distribution of land to peasants; instituted in late-7th-century Japan and most widely applied during the 8th century. Every six years local officials granted small parcels of paddy land to all commoners and menials aged six years and older. The subsistence grant enabled the local and central governments to draw frequently on peasant labor services. The *handen shūju* system gradually deteriorated in the late 8th and 9th centuries as a result of growing population pressure on limited land resources and ecclesiastical and aristocratic encroachment on government lands. The system was derived from Chinese models after the JINSHIN DISTURBANCE of 672 and used the existing JŌRI SYSTEM of land division.

The regulations governing the operation of state land distribution can be found in the TAIHŌ CODE of 701 and the YŌRŌ CODE of 718 (effective 757). Provincial officials granted "personal-share land" (KUBUNDEN) to all commoners and menials at the age of six. The basic grant was 2 *tan* (1 *tan* = 0.1 hectare or 0.25 acre) of paddy land for a free male and two-thirds of that amount for a woman. Members of the lowest classes usually received one-third of this amount of land. Everyone who received a *kubunden* grant was responsible for paying a light tax of 1.5 sheaves of rice per *tan*, or about 3 percent of the total annual yield. Recipients were also obliged to contribute labor and military service (see SO, YŌ, AND CHŌ). Permanent transfer of personal-share land was strictly forbidden by law. In the first year of state land

distribution after a recipient's death, the household head returned the vacant parcel of land to state control.

The first step in the complex allocation process was to prepare the HOUSEHOLD REGISTERS with the name, age, sex, and tax status of each individual in every household, followed by consultation between central government and local officials. If there was any personal-share land available after land grants were awarded, the provincial governor (KOKUSHI) was permitted to rent this land to any grantee who wanted it.

The last nationwide state allocation of land took place in 800. Although the imperial court made various attempts at reviving the *handen shūju* system through the reign (897–930) of Emperor DAIGO, the land grant system worked only infrequently and unevenly. See also RITSURYŌ SYSTEM; SHŌEN.

han'ei sembai
藩営専売

(domainal monopolies). Commercial operations managed as monopoly enterprises by domainal (HAN) governments during the Edo period (1600–1868). Domainal monopolies began to appear in the 1760s. Intended to enrich the domainal treasury, they were designed for maximum income and formed in whatever field seemed most advantageous—ranging from silk thread and ceramics to iron, salt, paper, wax, and medicines. In the early monopolies domain officials did little more than supervise existing production. During the 19th century, however, domains established offices (KOKUSAN KAISHO) to exercise direct control of operations, from production to marketing. Growing fear of foreign aggression led several domains to establish defense-related monopolies after the 1840s. Domainal monopolies reflected a realization of the importance of commerce and industry to government finance; this growing awareness of the economic roots of national stability and growth was also evident in the commercial policies of the new government that emerged after the Meiji Restoration of 1868 (see SHOKUSAN KŌGYŌ).

hanetsuki
羽根突き

Traditional girls' game for New Year's played by one or two persons. A wooden paddle called a HAGOITA is used with a shuttlecock (*hane*) made of soapberry seed and feathers. When one person plays, the object of the game is simply to keep the shuttlecock in the air. When two people play, the game resembles badminton without a net. The game has existed since the 15th century and is still played today.

Hani Gorō
羽仁五郎

(1901–83). Historian and critic. Born in Gumma Prefecture; married to Hani Setsuko, daughter of the educator HANI MOTOKO, and adopted into the Hani family. He studied at Tōkyō University and Heidelberg University and taught at Nihon University and Jiyū Gakuen, the school founded by Hani Motoko. In the 1930s he was a prominent contributor to the series NIHON SHIHON SHUGI HATTATSU SHI KŌZA (Studies on the History of the Development of Capitalism in Japan). In 1947 he was elected to the House of Councillors as an independent. His works, especially his study of cities, *Toshi no ronri* (1968), had a profound influence on the radical student movement of the 1960s and 1970s. See also NIHON SHIHON SHUGI RONSŌ.

Hani Motoko
羽仁もと子

(1873–1957). Japan's first female newspaper reporter, publisher of magazines for women

and children, and founder of the private school Jiyū Gakuen. Born in Hachinohe, Aomori Prefecture; original name Matsuoka Moto. Graduate in 1891 of the Tōkyō First Higher Girls' School (Daiichi Kōtō Jogakkō). Baptized a Christian around 1890, she went on to study at Meiji Girls' School (Meiji Jogakkō), where she was influenced by educator IWAMOTO YOSHIHARU and worked for his magazine JOGAKU ZASSHI. She taught for a time in Aomori but then returned to Tōkyō and was employed by the woman doctor YOSHIOKA YAYOI. With Yoshioka's encouragement Motoko secured a position with the newspaper *Hōchi shimbun*. In 1901 she married colleague Hani Yoshikazu (1880–1955), who was to become her partner in journalistic and educational ventures, especially the magazine FUJIN NO TOMO (Woman's Friend). In 1921 Motoko and her husband founded the school Jiyū Gakuen, whose philosophy of liberal education combined both Protestant and Confucian ethics, and she remained associated with it until her death.

Hani Susumu
羽仁進

(1928–). Film director and theorist of the postwar era. Born in Tōkyō; son of the scholar HANI GORŌ. Hani graduated from the Jiyū Gakuen, a progressive school founded by his grandmother, HANI MOTOKO. He directed his first film in 1952. Among his most influential early works are *Kyōshitsu no kodomotachi* (1955, Children in the Classroom) and *E o kaku kodomotachi* (1956, Children Who Draw), which introduced a revolutionary camera technique to documentary filmmaking. Instead of employing the conventional hidden camera, Hani set up his apparatus in the middle of the classroom and allowed the schoolchildren to become accustomed to its presence. This technique probably influenced the documentary-style techniques of the 1960s Japanese New Wave in commercial cinema.

In 1961 Hani's first feature, *Furyō shōnen* (Bad Boys), incorporated his documentary techniques and won the top national awards for the year. In the mid-1960s Hani embarked on unusual and stirring portraits of Japanese abroad in *Buwana Toshi no uta* (1965, Bwana Toshi) and *Andesu no hanayome* (1966, Bride of the Andes). Hani returned to the turmoil of Japanese urban life in 1968 with *Hatsukoi jigoku hen* (Nanami: Inferno of First Love). He continued to use nonactors, natural settings, and contemporary subject matter into the 1970s. In 1980 Hani directed *Afurika monogatari* (1980, Africa Story). Hani is now active in production for television, continuing the themes of conservation and protection of endangered species explored in this film.

haniwa
埴輪

(literally, "clay ring"). A collective term for the unglazed earthenware cylinders and hollow sculptures that decorated the surface of the great mounded tombs (KOFUN) built for the Japanese elite during the 4th to 7th centuries. *Haniwa* sculptures were as tall as 1.5 meters (4.9 ft) and were made in a variety of forms: houses, human figures, animals, and a multitude of military, ceremonial, and household objects. But the basic and most common shape was the simple cylinder, averaging 40–50 centimeters (16–20 in) in diameter and 1 meter (3.3 ft) in height.

Unlike tomb figurines in other parts of the world, *haniwa* were erected on the exterior surface of the tomb mound rather than buried in the chamber with the deceased. Half-

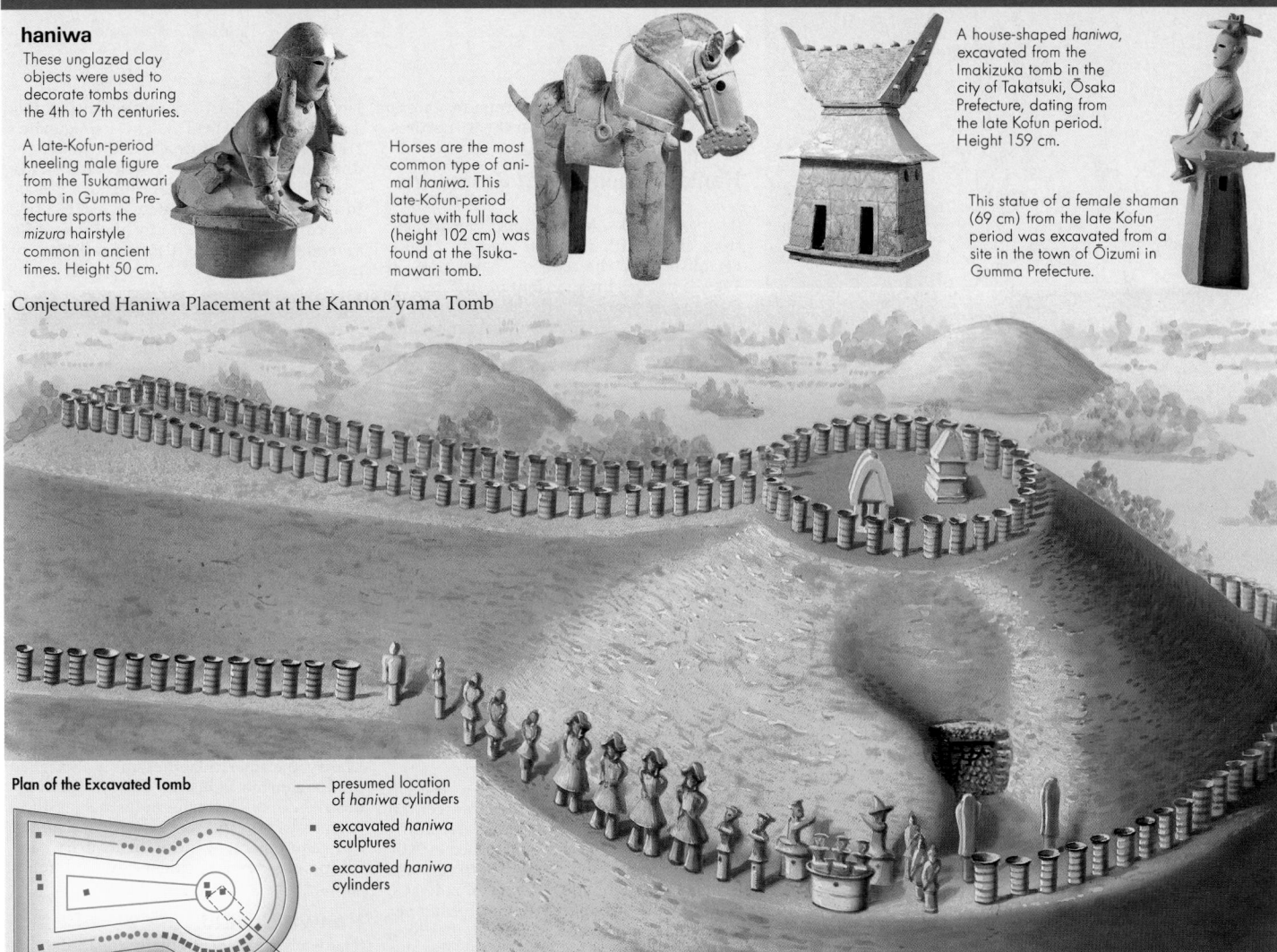

haniwa

These unglazed clay objects were used to decorate tombs during the 4th to 7th centuries.

A late-Kofun-period kneeling male figure from the Tsukamawari tomb in Gumma Prefecture sports the *mizura* hairstyle common in ancient times. Height 50 cm.

Horses are the most common type of animal *haniwa*. This late-Kofun-period statue with full tack (height 102 cm) was found at the Tsukamawari tomb.

A house-shaped *haniwa*, excavated from the Imakizuka tomb in the city of Takatsuki, Ōsaka Prefecture, dating from the late Kofun period. Height 159 cm.

This statue of a female shaman (69 cm) from the late Kofun period was excavated from a site in the town of Ōizumi in Gumma Prefecture.

Conjectured Haniwa Placement at the Kannon'yama Tomb

Plan of the Excavated Tomb

— presumed location of *haniwa* cylinders
■ excavated *haniwa* sculptures
● excavated *haniwa* cylinders
— corridor-type stone chamber

Artist's conception of the 6th-century Kannon'yama tomb in Gumma Prefecture. The diagram at left shows the actual position of *haniwa* on the tomb as excavated and presumed locations of others not discovered.

embedded in the earth for stability, the cylinders stood in rows on or around the mound; they may have been joined together by rope or wooden poles threaded through holes in their upper walls. Standing upright on similarly embedded cylindrical bases, *haniwa* sculptures highlighted the patterns made by the rows of cylinders by occupying the corners or interiors of the rectangles or dotting the tomb mound, which was marked off at the edges by the rows of cylinders.

Archaeologists now recognize two principal patterns of *haniwa* placement on the tombs. The first was prominent during the 4th and 5th centuries and accompanied pit-style graves dug into the summit of the tomb mound. *Haniwa* cylinders and sculptures were grouped in rectangular patterns around the graves. This placement pattern has been found mainly in and around the Kinai (Ōsaka-Kyōto-Nara) region, the center of the early Kofun culture. The second pattern was associated with a corridor-type stone burial chamber that was introduced from the continent in the late 5th or early 6th century, at which time *haniwa* production ceased in the Kinai and blossomed in the Kantō region of eastern Japan. In the second placement pattern, which is mainly known from the Kantō tombs, the cylinders and sculptures are lined up on the slopes of the tomb or outline the contours of the tomb mound. The Kinai ceremonial and military *haniwa* appear to have performed the ritual function of defining the sacred precincts of the burial and providing protection for its

occupant. These *haniwa* are stately in appearance and very large. In contrast, Kantō *haniwa* are lively and expressive, reflecting the frontier blend of military and common folk.

According to a legendary account in the chronicle NIHON SHOKI (720), *haniwa* originated as substitutes for sacrificial victims—attendants of the deceased who were buried alive in the tomb mound. Historians have since recognized this as a fiction; there is no evidence of an ancient practice in Japan of burying sacrificial victims alive or dead.

Haniya Yutaka 埴谷雄高

(1910–). Novelist and literary critic. Real name Hannya Yutaka. Born in Taiwan; studied at Nihon University. He joined the Japan Communist Party in 1931 but abandoned his Marxist activities after being imprisoned (1932–33) for his views. After World War II, he helped found the magazine KINDAI BUNGAKU (1946–64), which serialized the beginning of his monumental and still unfinished novel *Shirei* (Dead Souls) from 1946 to 1949. His vehemently anti-Stalinist stance and unusual existentialist theory of eternal revolution significantly influenced the new-left intellectuals of the late 1950s and 1960s. In 1976 he finally published five chapters of *Shirei* in book form. A sixth chapter was published as a separate volume in 1981. The novel won the 1976 Japan Literary Prize. Other works include *Yami no naka no kuroi uma* (1970, Black Horse in Darkness), a collection of short stories, and *Genshi no naka*

no seiji (1960, The Politics of Illusion), a collection of essays about politics.

Hankampu 藩翰譜

A 13-volume historical work of the Edo period (1600–1868), compiled by the scholar-statesman ARAI HAKUSEKI at the order of TOKUGAWA IENOBU, *daimyō* of the Kōfu domain (now part of Yamanashi Prefecture), who later became the sixth Tokugawa shōgun. Completed in 1702, the *Hankampu* ("genealogy of those who protect the shogunate") records the enfeoffment and later development of 337 daimyō families from 1600 to 1680. The work, which also includes biographies and genealogical tables, is generally considered an objective account of the daimyō families' relationship with the house of Tokugawa. A supplement was written in 1806.

hanko → seals

hankō 藩校

(domain schools). Official schools established during the Edo period (1600–1868) by each *daimyō* domain (HAN) to educate the children of its retainers. These schools existed until 1871, when the domains were abolished after the Meiji Restoration (1868). The *hankō* were at first narrowly defined as schools of Confucian studies for the cultivation of the *samurai* elite, and attendance was both expected of and limited to the children

499

hankō

hansharo The reverberatory furnace in the town of Nirayama, Shizuoka Prefecture, is a relic of Japan's first steps into the industrial era.

of this class. Late in the period, however, children of other social classes were permitted to attend, and the curriculum was expanded from its core in the Confucian classics to include training in classical Japanese studies (KOKUGAKU), medicine, and the various branches of WESTERN LEARNING, including mathematics, astronomy, military science, and ballistics. Students entered at age 7 or 8 and usually completed their courses of study between the ages of 15 and 20. By the 1860s there were about 255 *hankō* nationwide.

Hankyū Corporation 阪急電鉄[株]

(Hankyū Dentetsu). Private passenger railway company in the Kinki (Kyōto-Ōsaka-Kōbe) area. Founded in 1906 as Minoo Arima Railway by KOBAYASHI ICHIZŌ and others. Some of the ideas he implemented to increase demand for the railway system were the construction of housing developments along the rail lines and of a department store at the line's terminus station. As of March 1989 total trackage was 141 kilometers (87.6 mi). In the fiscal year ending March 1991 revenue was ¥161.8 billion (US $1.2 billion), of which railway lines earned 57 percent and real estate 43 percent. The company was capitalized at ¥69.5 billion (US $506.6 mil-

happi Edo-period-style *happi* coats are worn by participants in a New Year's fire-brigade demonstration featuring acrobatic stunts performed atop a ladder.

lion) in the same year. Headquarters are in Ōsaka. See also HANKYŪ DEPARTMENT STORES, INC.

Hankyū Department Stores, Inc
[株]阪急百貨店

(Hankyū Hyakkaten). Leading department store chain with its main store in Ōsaka. Established by the HANKYŪ CORPORATION in 1929, it became independent in 1947 but remains a core member of the Hankyū group of transportation, distribution, real estate, and leisure industry companies. It has a total of eight stores in Tōkyō, Ōsaka, Kyōto, and Kōbe, as well as overseas offices in Los Angeles, London, Paris, and Milan. Sales for the fiscal year ending March 1991 totaled ¥349.7 billion (US $2.5 billion). Clothing accounted for 40 percent of its total sales volume; foods, 24 percent; sundries, 12 percent; household goods and furniture, 10 percent; and other merchandise, 14 percent. The company was capitalized at ¥16.8 billion (US $122.4 million) in the same year. Headquarters are in Ōsaka.

Hannan 阪南[市]

Textile-manufacturing city facing Ōsaka Bay on the northwestern slopes of the Izumi Mountains in southwestern Ōsaka Prefecture, central Honshū. Rice and onions are grown here. In recent years housing construction has been increasing. Pop: 54,073.

Hannō 飯能[市]

City in southern Saitama Prefecture, central Honshū, on the river Irumagawa. According to local tradition the area was settled by Korean immigrants (KIKAJIN) in the 8th century. Situated at the junction of several railways, Hannō is the distribution center for lumber and agricultural products. The city has long been a textile center, and there are also electrical-appliance industries. More recently it has become a residential area for commuters to Tōkyō. Pop: 73,214.

Hannya shingyō → Heart Sutra

hanrei → judicial precedents

hansatsu 藩札

(domainal paper money). Paper currency (*satsu*) issued during the Edo period (1600–1868) by various *daimyō* domains (*han*) and fiefs held by senior vassals (*hatamoto*) of the Tokugawa shogunate. Valid only in the domain in which it was issued, *hansatsu* was in theory convertible into the coinage issued by the Tokugawa shogunate. It was first issued by the Fukui domain (now part of Fukui Prefecture) in 1661, and other domains quickly followed suit, issuing *hansatu* in large amounts, despite injunctions by the shogunate. This caused devaluation, rampant inflation, and general confusion in domainal finances. *Hansatsu* continued to circulate after the Meiji Restoration of 1868. Between 1871 and 1879 the new government assumed responsibility for converting all *hansatsu* to the new national currency.

hansharo 反射炉

(reverberatory furnace). A type of furnace in which heat is radiated from the roof onto the material treated. Introduced into Japan on an experimental basis in the 1840s, the reverberatory furnace enabled the Japanese to build large iron artillery pieces, something that could not be accomplished with the existing crucible furnaces. In 1850, the Saga domain (in what is now Saga Prefecture) built the first working reverberatory furnace in

Japan, using a description in a translation of a Dutch work. The Tokugawa shogunate's (1603–1867) huge furnace, built under the direction of EGAWA TARŌZAEMON at Nirayama, Izu Province (now part of Shizuoka Prefecture), began partial operation in 1855 and was completed in 1857. By the mid-1860s several other domains also had reverberatories.

Hanshin Electric Railway Co, Ltd
阪神電気鉄道[株]

(Hanshin Denki Tetsudō). Railway company operating in the Kansai region. Incorporated in 1899. The KŌSHIEN STADIUM and the Hanshin Tigers, a professional baseball team, are operated through subsidiaries of the firm. Sales for the fiscal year ending March 1991 totaled ¥53.7 billion (US $391.4 million), of which railways accounted for 49 percent; buses, 9 percent; and other revenues, 42 percent. The company was capitalized at ¥28.4 billion (US $207.0 million) in the same year. Headquarters are in Ōsaka.

Hanshin Industrial Zone 阪神工業地帯

(Hanshin Kōgyō Chitai). Extends along the northeastern shore of Ōsaka Bay with Ōsaka and Kōbe as the principal cities. Only the KEIHIN INDUSTRIAL ZONE is larger. As a result of recent expansion west to Himeji, northeast to Kyōto and Ōtsu, and south to Wakayama and Arida, the zone is also called the Keihanshin Industrial Zone or Kinki Industrial Zone. The major industrial products are metals, iron and steel, electric machinery and equipment, general machinery and equipment, textiles, chemicals, and foodstuffs.

Hanwa Co, Ltd 阪和興業[株]

(Hanwa Kōgyō). Firm chiefly engaged in the export, import, and domestic sale of steel, but also handling oil, synthetic goods, specialty steel, machinery, food products, and lumber. Incorporated in 1947, it was the first in the industry to erect a modern, large-scale center on the seacoast for the storage of mass-produced steel. The company controls four foreign subsidiaries and more than 20 overseas offices. Sales for the fiscal year ending March 1991 totaled ¥773.3 billion (US $5.6 billion), and capitalization stood at ¥142.5 billion (US $1.0 billion). Headquarters are in Ōsaka and Tōkyō.

Hanyū 羽生[市]

City in northeastern Saitama Prefecture, central Honshū, on the southern bank of the river Tonegawa. Hanyū is a clothing manufacturing city, and there is an emerging automobile parts industry. When still a small town, Hanyū provided the setting for *Inaka kyōshi* (1909, Country Teacher), a story by TAYAMA KATAI. Pop: 53,764.

hanzei 半済

(literally, "half payment"). A tax system in which the Muromachi shogunate (1338–1573) assigned to its vassals, for one-year terms, one-half of the land tax (NENGU) collected from private landed estates (SHŌEN); proprietors retained the other half. These grants, ostensibly for the support of troops in the field, were calculated to win support for the shogunate. Conferral documents, usually authorized by provincial military governors (SHUGO), survive from the 1330s. In 1352 the shogunate issued a law standardizing the area, length of tenure, and proportion of yield for *hanzei* grants in certain provinces. The enforcement of these guidelines was left to the *shugo*, who increasingly abused their power, especially during the ŌNIN WAR of 1467–77 (see SHUGO DAIMYŌ). *Hanzei*, together with earlier practices of WAYO and SHITAJI CHŪBUN, contributed to the final disappearance of *shōen*.

haori 羽織

A traditional jacket worn over a *kimono*. The *haori* may fall to a length anywhere between the hip and the knee; its front is slightly longer than its back. The garment is closed by fastening two short cords at chest level. Traditional formal dress for men consists of a *haori* imprinted with the family crest and pleated loose-fitting trousers called HAKAMA; the degree of formality depends upon the number of crests. For women, however, a crest-decorated *haori* denotes simple rather than formal dress.

happi 法被

1. A traditional straight-sleeved coat made of indigo or brown cotton or linen and imprinted with a family crest. *Happi* extend to the hips or knees and are worn mainly by men. During the Edo period (1600–1868) *happi* were worn by servants in the employ of *samurai* or wealthy families. Today, *happi* bearing a house name (YAGŌ) or shop name are worn by some carpenters, gardeners, and other workers; those bearing the name of a neighborhood association, or CHŌNAIKAI, are often worn by participants in summer festivals.

2. An outer garment with wide sleeves that is worn as part of the costume of certain male characters—such as a military commander or a vengeful ghost (GORYŌ)—in Nō theater.

Happō One 八方尾根

(Happō Ridge). Ridge extending to the east from Karamatsudake (2,696 m; 8,843 ft), a peak in the northern HIDA MOUNTAINS. Located in northwestern Nagano Prefecture, central Honshū. Happō One is famous for its skiing grounds.

hara 腹

(abdomen, stomach, belly, viscera, womb). In addition to referring to actual body parts, the word *hara* is used in a number of Japanese idioms having to do with emotions, thoughts, intentions, or character. For example, when a person is angry, it is said that his "*hara* stands up" (*hara ga tatsu*). When one tries to probe another's plans, intentions, or thoughts without verbal communication, one "gropes around," "reads," or "gauges" the other's *hara* (*hara o saguru*). A person having a frank talk with another "cuts his *hara* open" (*hara o waru*). A wicked man's *hara* is "black" (*haraguroi*). *Haragei*, or "belly play," is supposed to be a way to reach mutual understanding without direct verbal communication.

In the practice of Zen meditation and the martial arts, the student concentrates on the center of the abdominal region (*seika tanden*) to become at the same time relaxed and alert. The ritual suicide by disembowelment developed by Japanese warriors (HARAKIRI) testified to their belief that *hara* is the locus of life and character. See also KI; MUSHI; NONVERBAL COMMUNICATION.

Harada Magoshichirō 原田孫七郎

(fl late 16th century). Trader of the Azuchi-Momoyama period (1568–1600). Born in Higo Province (now Kumamoto Prefecture). Magoshichirō made voyages to the Philippines for the Nagasaki trader Harada Kie-

mon. The two men encouraged TOYOTOMI HIDEYOSHI to annex the islands of the southern seas, and in 1592 Magoshichirō went to Manila to urge the Spanish to pay tribute to Japan. In 1593 he went to Taiwan for the same purpose. Both missions failed.

Harada Naojirō 原田直次郎

(1863–99). Western-style painter of the Meiji period (1868–1912). Born in Edo (now Tōkyō). He graduated from the Tōkyō School of Foreign Languages (Tōkyō Gaikokugo Gakkō) in 1881 and began studying oil painting with TAKAHASHI YUICHI. From 1884 to 1887 he studied painting in Munich, where he specialized in genre and history painting in the style of the German realists. When he returned to Japan he helped to found the Meiji Bijutsukai (Meiji Fine Arts Society) in 1889. He established a private art school, the Shōbikan, in Hongō, Tōkyō; among his students was WADA EISAKU.

Harada Yasuko 原田康子

(1928–). Novelist. Real name Sasaki Yasuko. Born in Tōkyō; raised in Hokkaidō. *Banka* (1955–56, Elegy), set in Hokkaidō, was a best seller. Harada's other works include *Bōkyō* (1964, Nostalgia).

Harada Yoshito 原田淑人

(1885–1974). Archaeologist. Born in Tōkyō. Harada graduated from Tōkyō University and later joined its faculty. After participating in the excavation of the SAITOBARU TOMB CLUSTER, he studied in Europe and the United States in 1921–23. In 1925 he founded the Far Eastern Archaeological Society with HAMADA KŌSAKU. Harada is also known for his studies of clothing and accessories in Central Asia and Han (206 BC–AD 220) and Tang (T'ang; 618–907) China, as well as for his excavations of fortress sites in China and on the Korean peninsula. Among his works are *Kan rikuchō no fukushoku* (1937, Clothes and Accessories of the Han and the Six Dynasties) and *Tōa kobunka kenkyū* (1940, Studies on Ancient East Asian Culture).

harae 祓

(also pronounced *harai*). General term for a wide range of Shintō rites of purification, atonement, and penitence; the term comes from the verb *harau* (to cleanse). *Harae* rites permeate Shintō and reflect its preoccupation with the process of purification. Standing in opposition to purification and atonement are a variety of states of pollution and transgression (see KEGARE; TSUMI). One of the basic functions of *harae* has been ceremonial purification to prepare participants in Shintō observances for visitations from and union with gods. Some of the basic methods of purification have been (1) ritual ablution or MISOGI, which is said to have originated with Izanagi no Mikoto's act of purification with water after returning from his visit to the underworld (see IZANAGI AND IZANAMI), (2) the waving of *harae-gushi* (sacred mulberry paper called *nusa* attached to a stick) by priests over those to be purified, (3) the recitation of *harae kotoba* (prayers of purification, a type of NORITO), believed to purify by their sacred power, and (4) the presentation of offerings to the gods.

As illustrated in Japanese mythology by accounts of the penance (*harae*) extracted from SUSANOO NO MIKOTO following his offenses (*tsumi*) against AMATERASU ŌMIKAMI, *harae* has also included acts of atonement and punishment for transgression of the sacred, political, and social orders. In addition,

harae New Year's Day *harae* at the Kashima Shrine, Fukushima Prefecture. The Shintō priest (right center) waves a *harae-gushi* in this purification rite.

harae might also be viewed as forming the end goal of Shintō practice. *Ōharae*, for instance, is a grand rite of purification and renewal of the entire country traditionally performed on the last day of the 6th and 12th months and before the imperial rite of thanksgiving (DAIJŌSAI) celebrated after a new emperor's formal enthronement. See also SHINTŌ RITES.

Harajuku 原宿

District in the eastern part of Shibuya Ward, Tōkyō. It encompasses an area centered on Omote Sandō, the main approach to MEIJI SHRINE. Its restaurants, drinking establishments, and the specialty clothing and accessory shops along the street known as Takeshita-Dōri have made it a mecca for young people. On Sundays and holidays motorists are barred from certain streets, and street performers provide entertainment. Yoyogi Park, the headquarters of the Japan Broadcasting Corporation (NHK), and the Yoyogi National Stadium are located in the western part of the district.

Hara Kei → Hara Takashi

harakiri 腹切り

Japanese ritual suicide by self-disembowelment. The word *harakiri*, written with the Chinese characters for "abdomen" and "cutting," is better known in the Western world than the more formal term *seppuku*, which is written with the same Chinese characters in reverse order. *Seppuku* is the preferred term in Japan. The abdomen (*hara*) was chosen as the target of the suicidal knife inasmuch as ancient Japanese regarded it as the place where the soul resides and the source of action-derived tension. Additionally, the abdomen, at the physical center of the body, came to be regarded as the cradle of the individual's will, boldness, spirit, anger, and generosity.

One of the first legendary instances of *harakiri* was that of the bandit Hakamadare

Harajuku Lined with clothing shops and restaurants, Takeshita-Dōri attracts crowds of teenagers.

harakiri An act of ritual suicide is carried out by a samurai in this scene from the kabuki play Kanadehon chūshingura.

Hara Setsuko The actress in Ozu Yasujirō's film Bakushū (1951, Early Summer). Hara, representing a widespread ideal of Japanese femininity, has been admired for her graceful and unpretentious beauty.

Hara Takashi Known as the "commoner" prime minister, Hara was one of the principal architects of party government in modern Japan.

Yasusuke, who, when faced with capture by the police in 988, disemboweled himself, leaning against a pillar in his own home. He did not die until the following day. According to an apocryphal account in the military romance Heike monogatari (tr The Tale of the Heike, 1988), Minamoto no Yorimasa (1104–80), defeated in battle and wounded, sought refuge in the Byōdōin, a temple south of Kyōto. Leaving behind a farewell poem, he sat on his fan and pressed the point of a long sword to his abdomen, then, leaning forward, forced the blade into his body.

During Japan's early feudal period, suicide by self-disembowelment gradually became more ritualized, and by the time of the Edo period (1600–1868) it had become one of the five grades of punishment for wrongdoers among the samurai class. All aspects of the seppuku ritual were prescribed with precision: apparel, site, time, witnesses, inspector, and assistant. When the site had been readied and the witnesses, guards, and inspectors assembled, the doomed man would open his kimono, stretch out his right hand to grasp his knife, and cut into his abdomen from left to right. Often this wound was neither deep nor intended to bring on death. He would then make a prearranged signal to his kaishakunin (assistant), whereupon the kaishakunin's sword slashed down, severing his head. A famous instance of mass seppuku is that of the 47 rōnin (masterless samurai), who were ordered to commit seppuku after they had murdered KIRA YOSHINAKA (1641–1703), whom they regarded as responsible for the death of their master Asano Naganori (see FORTY-SEVEN RŌNIN INCIDENT).

Harakiri (i.e., seppuku) was not mentioned in the revised criminal code promulgated in 1873, but the nationalism of the Meiji period (1868–1912) and the partial reversion to traditional values combined to keep the practice alive. Instances of harakiri have continued to dot the pages of the modern history of Japan, the most famous being that of General NOGI MARESUKE, who, in 1912, chose to follow the emperor Meiji in death. A considerable number of persons committed harakiri in front of the Imperial Palace in Tōkyō shortly after the announcement of Japan's surrender to the Allied Forces in 1945. In November 1970 the novelist MISHIMA YUKIO committed harakiri in a sensational and theatrical manner.

Haramachi 原町[市]

City in northeastern Fukushima Prefecture, northern Honshū, on the Pacific coast. Haramachi developed as a post-station town on the highway Hamakaidō. Principal industries are electrical equipment, paper, and machine manufacturing. The city is known for the Sōma Nomaoi (literally, "wild horse

chase") Festival, held in July, which it shares with the nearby city of Sōma. Pop: 49,055.

Hara Martinho 原マルチノ

(ca 1570–1629). One of the young envoys sent by the CHRISTIAN DAIMYŌ of Kyūshū on the MISSION TO EUROPE OF 1582. Born in Hasami in the Ōmura domain (now part of Nagasaki Prefecture), he studied at the Jesuit seminary in Arima. The mission returned to Japan in 1590 after visiting Spain, Portugal, and Italy. Hara's eulogy in praise of the Jesuit missionary Alessandro VALIGNANO was published in Goa under the title Oratio Habita A Fara D. Martino (1588). He entered the Society of Jesus in 1591 and was ordained in 1608; when the Tokugawa shogunate intensified its persecution of Christianity, he went to Macao in 1614. There he assisted Fr. Rodrigues Tçuzzu with his Historia da Igreja do Japão (1620–34) and taught Japanese at the Jesuit college. He died in Macao on 23 October 1629.

Hara Setsuko 原節子

(1920–). Film actress. Real name Aida Masae. Born in Yokohama. Known in the Japanese film world as the "eternal virgin." She joined what is now the NIKKATSU CORPORATION in 1935 and made her motion-picture debut the same year in Taguchi Satoshi's (1903–84) Tamerau nakare wakōdo yo (Youth! Don't Hesitate!). She was the Japanese heroine in Arnold Fanck and ITAMI MANSAKU's joint German-Japanese film Atarashiki tsuchi (1937, The New Earth). Her quiet beauty and talent were featured in such favorite OZU YASUJIRŌ films as BANSHUN (1949, Late Spring), Bakushū (1951, Early Summer), TŌKYŌ MONOGATARI (1953, Tōkyō Story), and Akibiyori (1960, Late Autumn). She retired from films in 1963.

Hara Takashi 原敬

(1856–1921). Influential politician of the early 20th century, recognized as one of the principal architects of party government in modern Japan. Also known as Hara Kei or Hara Satoshi. He served as home minister (1906–08, 1911–12, 1913–14) and prime minister (1918–21). As the first Japanese prime minister who was neither a member of the peerage nor of the domainal cliques (HAMBATSU) that had dominated the governments of the Meiji period (1868–1912), Hara is frequently known as the "commoner" prime minister (heimin saishō).

Born on 15 March 1856 into a samurai family in the Morioka domain (now part of Iwate Prefecture) in north-central Japan, Hara was educated in the domain school. In 1871 he went to Tōkyō, where he was baptized into the Catholic faith as David. Having joined the law school of the Ministry of Justice in 1876, he left it without graduating, assuming responsibility for a student protest against the room and board system. He joined the newspaper Yūbin hōchi shimbun in 1879 as a reporter but left it three years later after a disagreement with other reporters, including YANO RYŪKEI and INUKAI TSUYOSHI, who sought to make the paper an organ of the RIKKEN KAISHINTŌ, the political party of ŌKUMA SHIGENOBU. Such actions foreshadowed the ambivalence toward authority Hara continued to show throughout his career.

In 1882, having become editor of the newspaper Daitō nippō in Ōsaka, Hara left to take a position in the Ministry of Foreign Affairs, for which he had been recommended by Foreign Minister INOUE KAORU.

Impressed with the views about the future of Japanese politics that Hara expressed to him during a trip that both took to Korea in 1884, Inoue quickly elevated Hara to consul general in Tianjin (Tientsin), and then to first secretary in the embassy in Paris. From 1890 to 1891 Hara served as personal secretary to MUTSU MUNEMITSU and later as his vice-minister of foreign affairs; then, through the auspices of Mutsu, he was appointed ambassador to Korea. Within a year, however, he had resigned from government service to return to journalism, becoming editor in chief of the newspaper Ōsaka mainichi shimbun.

In 1900 Hara joined the RIKKEN SEIYŪKAI, the party of ITŌ HIROBUMI, as its secretary-general. He ran the party with Matsuda Masahisa (1845–1914) and SAIONJI KIMMOCHI (the party president beginning in 1903) from 1901 until 1914, and then took sole charge until his death in 1921. Also in 1900, during Itō's fourth cabinet, Hara succeeded HOSHI TŌRU as minister of communications. He ran successfully for the lower house of the Diet in 1902 as a representative of Iwate Prefecture and was reelected seven times thereafter. Hara served as home minister in cabinets formed in 1906, 1911, and 1913. Following the resignation of the TERAUCHI MASATAKE cabinet after the RICE RIOTS OF 1918, Hara formed his own cabinet—the first in Japanese parliamentary history to be headed by an elected member of the majority party in the lower house of the Diet.

Hara identified the fundamental political tension within Japan's constitutional order as being between the elected lower house and the bureaucracy. He realized that the only way to overcome the strength of the bureaucracy would be through one-party domination in the lower house. He also perceived that maintenance of that majority must involve a long-term economic policy, the coordination and satisfaction of regional interests, and the pursuit of an investment policy emphasizing economic needs. Hara's political career after he joined the Seiyūkai can be seen as a series of efforts aimed toward promoting the growth of the party as an undeniable force within the constitutional order. His policies as a party politician, aimed at weakening the position of the bureaucracy, made for considerable tension in his relationship with Itō, Inoue, and Mutsu; he himself had had an illustrious bureaucratic career due to their patronage.

Hara's popularity declined during his time as prime minister (1918–21). One of the reasons for this was that he did not use the absolute majority he had in the lower house to endorse the UNIVERSAL MANHOOD SUFFRAGE MOVEMENT. According to his personal records, he did hope to achieve manhood suffrage gradually, but the public expected quicker moves toward democracy from a "commoner" prime minister. Liberals and socialists, as well as traditional moralists and nationalists, began to accuse him of being concerned only with power. As party politician, he did not find favor among ultrarightist radicals either: he was in fact stabbed to death by one of their number in Tōkyō Station on 4 November 1921, while on his way to a regional party rally in western Japan.

Hara Tamiki 原民喜

(1905–51). Poet and author. Born in Hiroshima Prefecture; graduate of Keiō University. His works exhibit a delicate sensibility and a pessimistic view of life and reflect the influence of dadaism and art modes of the

1930s. In 1945 he was living in Hiroshima when the atomic bomb was dropped. From this experience he wrote a series of short stories published as *Natsu no hana* (1947, Summer Flowers). The title story, an ominous account of a family dispute just prior to the bombing, is considered not only his best work but one of the best on the subject. In 1951 he committed suicide.

Hara Yasusaburō   原安三郎

(1884–1982). Businessman. Born in Tokushima Prefecture and graduated from Waseda University, Hara assisted in the revitalization of some 70 faltering corporations. He became president of Chūgai Mining in 1932 and, in 1935, president of NIPPON KAYAKU CO, LTD, of which he became the chairman. Hara served as chairman of the National Railways Council and the Customs Tariff Council.

Harbin   ハルビン

(Harubin; Ch: Haerbin or Ha-erh-pin). Once cosmopolitan city on the south bank of the Sungari River in Heilongjiang (Heilungkiang) Province, northeastern China. Founded by Russians in 1897 as a railway construction settlement at the junction of the CHINESE EASTERN RAILWAY trunk lines to Vladivostok and Dalny (J: Dairen; Ch: Dalian or Ta-lien), Harbin developed into the economic hub of northern Manchuria. The Japanese presence in Harbin, largely commercial during the 1920s, became predominant following Japan's seizure of Manchuria in 1931–33 (see MANCHURIAN INCIDENT). From 1932 until 1945 the GUANDONG (KWANTUNG) ARMY, a semiautonomous Japanese military unit in Manchuria, used Harbin as field headquarters for intelligence operations against the USSR. The Soviet army occupied Harbin on 19 August 1945 and handed the city over to the Chinese communists in April 1946. Harbin is currently a food-processing and industrial center with a population of 2,930,000.

hari → acupuncture

haribako   針箱

(sewing box; literally, "needle box"). Traditional box or basket used for sewing equipment. Considered essential belongings for Japanese women, *haribako* were traditionally included in dowries. Some were simply made of lacquered paper or bamboo; more elaborate ones of lacquered wood had several drawers and sometimes gold or silver decoration. Since World War II, the traditional sewing boxes have been largely replaced by more easily portable ones with top-mounted handles.

hari kuyō   針供養

(literally, "needle memorial service"). An annual event originating in the Edo period (1600–1868). On 8 February or 8 December, or both days in some districts, women take a day off from their sewing chores and collect all their old needles. Sticking them into cakes of *tōfu* (bean curd) or of *konnyaku* (a paste made from the root of a plant called devil's tongue), they pray for the repose of the needles, improvement in their sewing skills, and safety from injury while sewing.

Harima   播磨［町］

Town in southern Hyōgo Prefecture, western Honshū. Fertilizer and textile manufacturers were located here during the Meiji period (1868–1912), and after World War II

Harima became a modern industrial town with large-scale steel and chemical factories. Harima constitutes one part of the Harima Coastal Industrial Region. Pop: 30,813.

Harima Coastal Industrial Region
播磨臨海工業地域

(Harima Rinkai Kōgyō Chiiki). Industrial zone located on the coast of the Harima Sea in Hyōgo Prefecture, western Honshū, extending from the city of Akashi to the city of Akō. In addition to the textile and food-processing industries traditionally found here, there are now steel mills, electrical machinery factories, and petrochemical complexes.

Harima Plain → Himeji Plain

Harima Sea   播磨灘

(Harima Nada). Part of the INLAND SEA. Bounded by western Honshū (Hyōgo Prefecture) on the north, northeastern Shikoku (Tokushima and Kagawa prefectures) on the south, and the islands of Awajishima on the east and Shōdoshima on the west. Formerly a fine fishing ground, the sea is now polluted due to land reclamation and industrial development. Area: approximately 2,500 sq km (965 sq mi); deepest point 40 m (130 ft).

Harinoki Pass   針ノ木峠

(Harinoki Tōge). Located on the border of Nagano and Toyama prefectures, central Honshū. It is on a trans–Northern Alps route, from Ōmachi in Nagano Prefecture to the Kurobe and Toyama regions in Toyama Prefecture. Altitude: 2,541 m (8,337 ft).

haritsu-zaiku   破笠細工

Decorative technique used in making LACQUER WARE. In *haritsu-zaiku*, materials such as shells, ceramic fragments, and ivory are used to create designs along with the MAKI-E technique of sprinkling powders or filings—usually of gold or silver—on damp lacquer. *Haritsu-zaiku* is named for Ogawa Haritsu (1663–1747), a mid-Edo period (1600–1868) practitioner of the technique. Haritsu, who studied with the TOSA SCHOOL, also worked in ceramics, painted, and composed *haiku*. *Haritsu-zaiku*, which exhibits considerable Chinese influence, is characterized by its bold use of materials.

Harp of Burma → Biruma no tategoto

Harris, Merriman Colbert
ハリス, M. C.

(1846–1921). American Methodist missionary to Japan and Korea. Born in Beallsville, Ohio; graduate of Allegheny College. In 1873 he became American consul to Hakodate while serving as the first Protestant missionary to Hokkaidō. There he baptized a number of students, including NITOBE INAZŌ and UCHIMURA KANZŌ, and began what matured into a lifelong acquaintance with Chinda Sutemi (1856–1929), a diplomat. Harris returned to America in 1898 to work with Japanese immigrants in San Francisco until he became a bishop, first in Japan and then in Korea, 1904–16. His acceptance of Japan's colonial policies helped him become, for his time, the foreigner most decorated by the Japanese government.

Harris, Thomas Lake   ハリス, T. L.

(1823–1906). American poet, socialist, and spiritualist. Founder of the Brotherhood of the New Life. Born in Fenny Stratford, England, he emigrated with his parents to Utica, New York, in 1828. Harris's unortho-

dox Christian ministry was a blend of transcendentalism, universalism, and Swedenborgian theology.

Harris established the brotherhood in New York State in 1861. Laurence OLIPHANT, a former diplomat in Japan, promoted Harris as a "living Confucius," and some 20 Japanese (including MORI ARINORI) entered the brotherhood, although most eventually returned to Japan. ARAI ŌSUI brought Harris's ideas to Japan, and Kanaye NAGASAWA became Harris's lieutenant and heir. Harris moved in 1875 to California with selected followers, including Nagasawa, who led the brotherhood from 1892 until 1934.

Harris, Townsend   ハリス, T.

(1804–78). New York merchant; first US consul general in Japan, a post established as a result of the KANAGAWA TREATY. He arrived in Japan in August 1856 with instructions to secure a full commercial treaty with Japan.

In December 1857 the Tokugawa shogunate (1603–1867) reluctantly granted Harris an audience at Edo Castle. Harris secured a draft treaty the following February. When the senior councillor HOTTA MASAYOSHI was unable to win prior approval from the imperial court in Kyōto, the wealthy and powerful *daimyō* II NAOSUKE arranged for the formal signing of the United States–Japan Treaty of Amity and Commerce (HARRIS TREATY) at Edo (now Tōkyō) on 29 July 1858. Taking effect in July 1859, the treaty set the pattern for commercial agreements (see ANSEI COMMERCIAL TREATIES) with other Western nations and helped intensify agitation against the shogunate.

Promoted to minister resident in June 1859, Harris remained in Japan until 1862; he encouraged the shogunate's plans to send an embassy to Washington (see UNITED STATES, MISSION OF 1860 TO) and assisted local authorities in framing the regulations necessary for the establishment of foreign residence and facilitation of international trade. Harris resigned his post and left Japan in May 1862 for New York, where he retired from public life.

Harris Treaty   日米修好通商条約

(United States–Japan Treaty of Amity and Commerce; Nichibei Shūkō Tsūshō Jōyaku). The first commercial treaty between Japan and the United States, signed on 29 July 1858. The American consul general, Townsend HARRIS, arrived in Shimoda in August 1856 to secure provisions for free trade, which the KANAGAWA TREATY, signed in 1854, lacked. In December 1857, Harris had an audience with the shōgun in Edo (now Tōkyō). Thereafter, he negotiated with shogunal representatives and by 25 February 1858 had secured a draft treaty. A formal treaty was finally signed without imperial sanction.

hari kuyō In this ceremony discarded needles are stuck into a piece of *tōfu* while the participants give thanks for the service the needles have rendered and pray for their repose. Pictured is a ceremony at the temple Sensōji in Tōkyō.

Townsend Harris In 1858 this diplomat concluded the first commercial treaty between the United States and Japan.

Harunobu *Secrets on the Veranda.* In this full-color woodcut an older girl (kneeling) tells a boy about his secret admirer, the shy young girl peering from behind the sliding screen. Late 1760s. 28 × 20 cm. Tōkyō National Museum.

Harunasan The summit floor of this volcano group, with Haruna Fuji rising above the far shore of Lake Haruna.

The treaty stipulated the exchange of diplomatic agents and consuls; the opening of various Japanese ports; the right of American citizens to reside in those ports, trade without interference, and enjoy extraterritorial privileges; the opening of Edo and Ōsaka for trade; and a moderate, fixed scale of import and export duties. Similar treaties were concluded within a few weeks with the Netherlands, Russia, Great Britain, and France (see ANSEI COMMERCIAL TREATIES). The unequal terms of these treaties and the Harris Treaty plagued the shogunate for 10 years and then the new Meiji government until 1899, when a new treaty with the United States went into effect (see UNEQUAL TREATIES, REVISION OF).

Hartmann, Carl Sadakichi

ハートマン, C. S.

(1867–1944). Poet, writer, and art critic. He was born on Dejima, in Nagasaki, the second son of Oskar Hartmann, a German trader and member of the German consulate. His mother was Japanese. After early education in Hamburg, Germany, he went to the United States where he began writing. After traveling in Europe and associating with literary celebrities there, he became an avant-garde artist in New York City's Greenwich Village and later in California. His major works include *Christ* (play, 1893), *Conversations with Walt Whitman* (1895), *Buddha* (play, 1897), *Japanese Art* (1904), *The Whistler Book* (1910), *My Rubaiyat* (poetry, 1913), *Tanka and Haikai* (1915), and *The Last Thirty Days of Christ* (novel, 1920).

Haruma wage

波留麻和解

(Halma Translated). The first Dutch-Japanese dictionary published in Japan. Based on François Halma's (1653–1722) Dutch-French dictionary *Woordenboek der Nederduitsche en Fransche Taalen* (1708), it was compiled by INAMURA SAMPAKU and several other scholars of Rangaku (Dutch Learning), as WESTERN LEARNING was then known. The 27-volume work, with its more than 80,000 entries, took over 13 years to complete. It was printed at Edo (now Tōkyō) in 1796. Another Dutch-Japanese dictionary, similarly based on the Halma work, was completed in 1812–33 under the editorship of Hendrik DOEFF, head of the Dutch trading post at Nagasaki. In distinction to the earlier "Edo Haruma," Doeff's work is known as the "Nagasaki Haruma." Both contributed greatly to the advance of Western studies in Japan.

Haruna, Lake

榛名湖

(Harunako). Crater lake in central Gumma Prefecture, central Honshū. Located on the summit of Mt. Haruna (HARUNASAN). Ice-skating is possible in winter. Area: 1.2 sq km (0.5 sq mi); circumference: 5 km (3 mi); depth: 13.3 m (43.6 ft); altitude: 1,084 m (3,556 ft).

Harunasan

榛名山

Composite stratovolcano in central Gumma Prefecture, central Honshū. On the summit are Haruna Fuji (1,391 m; 4,564 ft), the central cone, and Lake Haruna, a crater lake to the west. On the crater rim is Kamongadake (1,448 m; 4,751 ft), the highest point. Harunasan forms Haruna Prefectural Park.

Harunobu

春信

(1725?–70). UKIYO-E artist. Full name Suzuki Harunobu. Harunobu's life, like that of many Japanese artists, is shrouded in uncertainty, but his place in the history of Japanese art is assured by his delicate and exquisitely designed color prints of women and other subjects. He was also the first major Japanese print artist to produce full-color woodcuts (nishiki-e). His work in this technique, using 4 to 10 pigments in addition to the black key-block outline, rendered obsolete the old two- and three-color prints.

His early works, datable to the early 1760s (one perhaps to 1757), are in the style of Edo (now Tōkyō), where he was active, and most depict KABUKI actors in character for particular performances. Most of the early prints, in the old two- or three-color technique, are in the small, narrow hosoban format. Harunobu made a group of prints in mizu-e technique (using a color outline), probably in 1764. In 1765 and 1766 he was the principal artist selected to design pictorial calendars (e-goyomi) that were privately printed for groups of Edo connoisseurs, whose names frequently appear on the print together with or instead of that of the artist. The best of these calendars, and other prints commissioned by the same men, were in the new full-color technique and in the large chūban format, and they led directly to the commercial production of nishiki-e.

Between 1765 and his early death in 1770, Harunobu produced hundreds of single-sheet color prints, about 20 illustrated books, and a number of paintings. The single-sheet prints are mainly in the chūban or hashira-e (long "pillar-print") formats, are on a superior hōsho paper, and may use embossing, size, mica dusting, and other special techniques. They cover a wide variety of subjects: many are whimsical illustrations of classical or sometimes contemporary poems; others depict courtesans or beauties of the day; others are parodies of mythical and literary subjects; others show scenes of domestic life; and as with all ukiyo-e artists, there is also a group of erotic prints (SHUNGA). Many of the prints belong to sets, some of which may have been issued originally as portfolios or albums. Harunobu's illustrated books, with two exceptions, are in black and white, and nearly all were published in Edo by Yamazaki Kimbei.

After Harunobu's death, imitations with his signature were made for a few years by SHIBA KŌKAN; reprints also appeared, using original blocks that had survived the Edo fire of 1772. Further reprints were produced during the 19th century, and reproductions were also made, especially from the Meiji period (1868–1912) onward.

Hasaki

波崎[町]

Town at the mouth of the river Tonegawa in southeastern Ibaraki Prefecture, central Honshū. It is a commercial fishing port and has several processing plants for marine products. The northern section of the township is part of the Kashima Coastal Industrial Region. Watermelons and other melons are grown in the coastal sand dunes. Pop: 37,245.

Hase

初瀬

Also known as Hatsuse. District in the eastern part of the city of Sakurai, northern Nara Prefecture, central Honshū. It developed as a post-station town on the Ise Road (Ise Kaidō) and as a temple town around HASEDERA. It was a favorite resort of court nobles in the Heian period (794–1185).

Hasebe Kotondo

長谷部言人

(1882–1969). Anthropologist. Born in Tōkyō; graduate of Tōkyō University School of Medicine in 1906. After graduation he continued his study of anthropology and anatomy under the noted anthropologist ADACHI BUNTARŌ and lectured on anatomy at Kyōto and Tōhoku universities. He studied in Europe from 1921 to 1922, principally at Munich University in Germany. In 1939 he established the first full-scale department of anthropology in Japan within the Faculty of Science at Tōkyō University and concentrated on the study and teaching of comprehensive anthropology centered on morphological studies. He excavated SHELL MOUNDS and carried out extensive anthropological studies on the human skeletal remains from burial mounds. Hasebe held that Jōmon-period (ca 10,000 BC–ca 300 BC) man was a direct ancestor of modern Japanese man and opposed the theory that the AINU were the direct ancestors of the Japanese.

Hasedera

長谷寺

Also called Chōkokuji. Head temple of the Buzan branch of the SHINGON SECT of Buddhism; located in the city of Sakurai, Nara Prefecture. According to tradition, the Hasedera was founded by the monk Dōmyō on the order of Emperor Temmu (r 672–686).

In 747 the cleric GYŌGI is said to have consecrated the image of the Eleven-Headed KANNON (Jūichimen Kannon), the bodhisattva who became the main object of worship at the temple. The Hasedera originally belonged to the HOSSŌ SECT, but in 1588 it was converted to a center of the Shingi (New) Shingon sect by the monk Sen'yo (1530–1604). In 1900 it established itself as the head temple of the Buzan branch.

Hasegawa Kazuo 長谷川一夫

(1908–84). Actor. Born in Kyōto. Hasegawa joined what is now SHŌCHIKU CO, LTD, in 1927. He won recognition for his performance in the highly successful *Yukinojō henge* (1935–36, Yukinojō's Disguise; refilmed in 1963). After World War II, he appeared in *Jigokumon* (1953, Gate of Hell), which won the Grand Prix at the Cannes Film Festival. Altogether he appeared in more than 300 films. Later he turned to directing; *Berusaiyu no bara* (1974, The Rose of Versailles), which he directed for the all-female TAKARAZUKA KAGEKIDAN, was a great success. He was posthumously awarded the People's Honor Award (Kokumin Eiyo Shō).

Hasegawa Kiyoshi 長谷川潔

(1891–1980). Print designer. Born in Yokohama. He studied line drawing with KURODA SEIKI and oil painting with OKADA SABURŌSUKE and FUJISHIMA TAKEJI. About 1912 he also began experimenting with woodcuts and copperplates. In 1918 he visited the United States and went on to Paris the following year, where he revived the art of *manière noire*, a kind of mezzotint. He was accepted as a member of the Salon d'Automne, was awarded the Légion d'Honneur in 1935, and received the French Order of Merit in 1966. Hasegawa is identified with the School of Paris style.

Hasegawa Machiko 長谷川町子

(1920–92). Cartoonist. Born in Fukuoka Prefecture. Attended Yamawaki Girls' High School. Hasegawa studied under the cartoonist TAGAWA SUIHŌ. Her comic strip *Sazae san* ran for 3 years in the newspaper *Yūkan fukunichi* and, from 1949, for 25 years in the newspaper *Asahi shimbun*. Centering on the young housewife Sazae san and the daily life of her extended family, the comic strip has humorous plots reflecting current affairs and concerns. Popular with children and adults alike, *Sazae san* is available in book form and has been made into an animated television show. Hasegawa also created *Ijiwaru bāsan* (Granny the Tease) and other comic strips. She received the People's Honor Award posthumously.

Hasegawa Norishige 長谷川周重

(1907–). Businessman; president of SUMITOMO CHEMICAL CO, LTD (1965–77). Born in Kumamoto Prefecture. After graduating from Tōkyō University, Hasegawa joined Sumitomo Gōshi Kaisha in 1931. In 1934 he began working for Sumitomo Chemical Co, becoming its president in 1965. Hasegawa played a key role in making the company an integrated chemical enterprise. He served as executive secretary of the JAPAN ASSOCIATION OF CORPORATE EXECUTIVES (1959–78), vice-president of KEIDANREN (Federation of Economic Organizations; 1974–86), and chairman of the Japan-US Business Council (1981–89).

Hasegawa Nyozekan 長谷川如是閑

(1875–1969). Social critic and journalist. Real name Hasegawa Manjirō. Born in Tōkyō.

Hasegawa studied criminal law at Tōkyō Hōgakuin (now Chūō University) and graduated in 1898. He joined the staff of KUGA KATSUNAN's newspaper *Nihon* in 1903. In 1907 he moved to the periodical *Nihon oyobi nihonjin*, headed by MIYAKE SETSUREI. He then joined the newspaper *Ōsaka asahi shimbun* and established a reputation as a political liberal. In 1918, together with ŌYAMA IKUO, TORII SOSEN, and other staff members, he resigned in the wake of the ŌSAKA ASAHI HIKKA INCIDENT, in which the newspaper was censured by the government. The following year he and Ōyama founded the influential periodical *Warera* (We). Through his writings, Hasegawa sought to provide a theoretical underpinning for political and social democracy and to combat the growing fanaticism of militarist cliques. He remained true to his principles throughout World War II, and in 1948 he was awarded the Order of Culture. His writings are collected in *Hasegawa Nyozekan senshū* (8 vols, 1969–70).

Hasegawa Roka 長谷川路可

(1897–1967). Painter. Real name Hasegawa Ryūzō. Born in Kanagawa Prefecture. In 1921, after graduating from the Tōkyō Bijutsu Gakkō (now Tōkyō University of Fine Arts and Music), he went to France and studied the technique of fresco. Hasegawa returned to Japan in 1927 and showed works in the exhibitions of the Imperial Academy and the Japan Art Institute. After World War II, he produced fresco and mosaic wall-paintings in Japan and Italy in addition to Japanese-style paintings. He died while visiting Italy.

Hasegawa school 長谷川派

(Hasegawaha). School of painters founded by HASEGAWA TŌHAKU (1539–1610). It is clear that Tōhaku and his followers were in competition with KANŌ SCHOOL artists and with UNKOKU TŌGAN and KAIHŌ YŪSHŌ as well, for they all specialized in the Chinese academic style of painting (*kanga*). The Hasegawa school was probably located in Kyōto in or near Hompōji, a Nichiren sect temple affiliated with Tōhaku's family temple in Sakai, near Ōsaka. Records indicate that Tōhaku had at least four artist sons: Kyūzō (1568–93), Sōtaku and Sakon (both active before 1650), and Sōya (d 1667). The school seems to have disappeared by the end of the 17th century. The large-scale sliding-wall paintings (*fusuma-e*) at CHISHAKUIN in Kyōto were

executed in 1592 by Tōhaku, his son Ryūzō, and possibly other disciples.

Hasegawa Shin 長谷川伸

(1884–1963). Writer of POPULAR FICTION and drama; known for his historical novels and plays dealing with *samurai* and gamblers. Born Hasegawa Shinjirō in Yokohama, Kanagawa Prefecture; he later took his pen name Shin as his legal name. Hasegawa began by writing theater reviews and later joined the newspapers *Japan Gazette* and *Miyako Shimbun*. His first published fiction was the story "Yomosugara kengyō" (1924), after which he became a full-time writer.

In 1928 Hasegawa's play *Kutsukake Tokijirō* generated a vogue in *matatabi-mono*, a literary, and later cinema, genre portraying the world of gamblers and gangsters. His most famous work of this type is the play *Mabuta no haha* (1930, Mother in My Dreams); another *matatabi-mono* drama by Hasegawa is *Ippon-gatana dohyōiri* (1931, A One-Sworded Outlaw Enters the Ring).

Hasegawa also dealt with revenge, an important theme in popular literature. Major works include the historical novel *Araki Mataemon* (1936–37) and *Nihon katakiuchi isō* (1961–63, Different Faces of Revenge in Japan), a series of portrayals that closely follow historical fact. Hasegawa's *Nihon horyo shi* (1949–50, A Study of Japan's Prisoners of War) is a monumental work in which he attempts to explain the Japanese attitude toward war captives in its historical context.

Hasegawa also served as a mentor for writers of popular literature. Following his death, the Hasegawa Shin Prize and the

Hasegawa Kazuo This prolific actor and stage director is probably best remembered for his stunning performance in the 1963 film *Yukinojō henge* (Yukinojō's Disguise), in which he played three roles.

Hasegawa Machiko Book covers of this newspaper cartoonist's best-known creations: *Sazae san* (left and center) and *Ijiwaru bāsan* (below)

Shin'yōkai, an organization to promote literature, were established in his memory.

Hasegawa Shirō   長谷川四郎

(1909–87). Novelist and poet. Born in Hakodate, Hokkaidō; brother of the novelist HAYASHI FUBŌ. A graduate of Hōsei University, he taught German literature there after World War II. At the end of World War II, he was taken prisoner by the Soviet Army in Manchuria and sentenced to five years at hard labor in Siberia, an experience that inspired the novel *Shiberiya monogatari* (1951–52). He is also known for his poetry and translations of such Western authors as Samuel Beckett, Bertolt Brecht, and Franz Kafka.

Hasegawa Tai   長谷川泰

(1842–1912). Medical educator and administrator. Born in Echigo Province (now part of Niigata Prefecture). Hasegawa studied Western medical science under Tsuboi Hōshū and Satō Shōchū (1827–82). From 1869 he taught at Daigaku Tōkō, a predecessor of the present Faculty of Medicine of Tōkyō University, and in 1876 he established the Saisei Gakusha, a private medical school, in Hongō, Tōkyō. In 1878 Hasegawa entered the Home Ministry and worked under NAGAYO SENSAI, the first director of its Bureau of Public Health; Hasegawa was appointed its director in 1898. He became a member of the House of Representatives in the first general election of 1890.

Hasegawa Tenkei   長谷川天渓

(1876–1940). Literary critic. Real name Hasegawa Seiya. Born in Niigata Prefecture; graduate of Tōkyō Semmon Gakkō (now Waseda University). A writer for the journal

TAIYŌ, he translated many Western works into Japanese. He was one of the earliest theoreticians of Japanese literary NATURALISM. In an article entitled "Genjitsu bakuro no hiai" (1908, The Pain of Exposing Reality), he wrote that the true purpose of literature is to lay bare reality in all its darkness and ugliness. The title of this essay became the motto for the naturalist movement.

Hasegawa Tōhaku   長谷川等伯

(1539–1610). Painter. Founder of the HASEGAWA SCHOOL of painting. Records suggest that his original family name was Okumura but that he was adopted by the Hasegawa, a family of dyers in Noto Province (now part of Ishikawa Prefecture). He is said to have studied KANŌ SCHOOL painting in Kyōto under Kanō Shōei (1519–92) or KANŌ EITOKU.

Tōhaku considered himself the successor of SESSHŪ TŌYŌ. Until the present century, Tōhaku was known mainly for his INK PAINTING, often depicting monkeys or gibbons, of the sort done by Zen priests since the 13th century. He is credited with the pair of sixfold *Pine Trees*, screens now in the Tōkyō National Museum. In the early 1930s art historians added a sizable body of large-scale polychrome works to Tōhaku's known oeuvre. All of these works are decorative sliding-wall paintings in Kyōto temples. Scholars have also attributed a large number of monochromatic ink paintings to Tōhaku.

Haseko Corporation   ［株］長谷工コーポレーション

(Haseko Kōporēshon). General housing contractor and developer and a leading builder of condominiums. Incorporated in 1946. Haseko also builds office buildings and industrial facilities and has been expanding into the deluxe condominium market. The company launched its overseas development activities in 1973 in Hawaii. It has offices in Hawaii, Los Angeles, San Francisco, New York, and Guam. Sales for the fiscal year ending March 1990 totaled ¥489.0 billion (US $3.1 billion), and capitalization stood at ¥80.3 billion (US $524.6 million). Headquarters are in Tōkyō.

Hasekura Tsunenaga   支倉常長

(1571–1622). Retainer of DATE MASAMUNE; also known as Hasekura Rokuemon. He led an embassy to Mexico and Europe (1613–20) and was the first official Japanese envoy to

visit the American continent. In July 1611 an embassy under Sebastian VISCAINO brought back from New Spain (Mexico) the Japanese merchants who had traveled there with Rodrigo VIVERO Y VELASCO the previous year. This inspired Date Masamune, the *daimyō* of Sendai (now Miyagi Prefecture), to send an embassy to seek trade with Mexico and southern Europe. Date named Hasekura, a veteran of the INVASIONS OF KOREA IN 1592 AND 1597, as his representative.

In October 1613 Hasekura, at the head of 180 Japanese, set out for Acapulco in a galleon built by Japanese shipwrights under Spanish supervision. He had audiences with the Mexican viceroy in 1614 and with the Spanish monarch Philip III and Pope Paul V in 1615. While in Spain he was baptized a Christian. In February 1614, however, TOKUGAWA IEYASU had issued an edict expelling Christian priests from Japan, and this resulted in a hardening of the Spanish attitude toward trade with Japan; thus, Hasekura's mission failed. After two years in the Philippines Hasekura returned to Japan in September 1620.

hashi → chopsticks

Hashida Sugako   橋田寿賀子

(1925–). Television scriptwriter. Real name Iwasaki Sugako. Born in Seoul. Graduate of Japan Women's University and Waseda University. Hashida is known for her ability to capture the spirit of a particular period from a woman's point of view. Her works include *Tonari no shibafu* (1984, The Grass Is Always Greener; televised in 1976), *Oshin* (1983, Oshin; televised in 1983–84), and *Inochi* (1986, Life; televised in 1986). *Oshin* was awarded the Kikuchi Kan Prize in 1984.

Hashiguchi Goyō   橋口五葉

(1880–1921). Painter and printmaker. Born in Kagoshima Prefecture, he studied NIHONGA (Japanese-style painting) with HASHIMOTO GAHŌ. In 1905 Goyō graduated from the Western-style painting division of the Tōkyō Bijutsu Gakkō (now Tōkyō University of Fine Arts and Music). He entered the first BUNTEN exhibition in 1907. Goyō achieved overnight success in 1911 by winning a poster contest; he subsequently abandoned oil painting and threw himself wholeheartedly into a study of woodblock prints (see UKIYO-E; MODERN PRINTS). Goyō gained

distinction as a designer of magazine covers and dust jackets for books.

Hashikuiiwa 橋杭岩
Group of rocks in southern Wakayama Prefecture, central Honshū. Formed by the erosion of dolerite by the sea, these huge pillar-like rocks extend in a line from a point off the coast of the town of Kushimoto to the island of Ōshima. They are a natural monument and are located in Yoshino-Kumano National Park.

Hashima 羽島[市]
City in southern Gifu Prefecture, central Honshū, between the rivers KISOGAWA and NAGARAGAWA. Hashima is known for its woolen cloth cottage industry. It is in a grain-producing area. Pop: 61,460.

Hashima 端島
Small mining island west of Nagasaki Peninsula, Nagasaki Prefecture, northwestern Kyūshū; part of Nagasaki Prefecture. In 1890 the Mitsubishi Mining Co (now Mitsubishi Mining and Cement Co, Ltd) started mining coal approximately 1,000 m (3,300 ft) under the sea here. The mine once had a significant annual output, but it closed in 1974 and the island is presently uninhabited. Area: 0.1 sq km (0.04 sq mi).

Hashimoto 橋本[市]
City in northeastern Wakayama Prefecture, central Honshū, on the river Kinokawa. At the intersection of the highways Yamato and Kōya Kaidō, Hashimoto developed as a regional transportation center. It is known for its fishing rods and other bamboo ware. It is a residential suburb for commuters to Ōsaka. Pop: 46,594.

Hashimoto Gahō 橋本雅邦
(1835–1908). One of the last KANŌ SCHOOL painters. Born in Edo (now Tōkyō), he was the son of the painter Hashimoto Seien Yōhō, who served the Matsudaira family (see TOKUGAWA FAMILY). Gahō studied under Kanō Shōsen'in. After mastering Kanō-school techniques, he set up his own studio in 1860. Along with KANŌ HŌGAI he introduced Western-style painting into the Kanō school to create a new kind of Japanese painting. In the early 1880s in the first and second Domestic Painting Competitive Exhibitions (Naikoku Kaiga Kyōshinkai), he won silver medals. On OKAKURA KAKUZŌ's recommendation, Gahō became the chief professor of painting at the Tōkyō Bijutsu Gakkō (now Tōkyō University of Fine Arts and Music) at its inception in 1889. In 1890 he was among the first to be named an artist for the imperial household (teishitsu gigeiin). In 1898, when Okakura founded the JAPAN FINE ARTS ACADEMY (Nihon Bijutsuin), Gahō accompanied him to become the principal teacher at the academy. He taught there until his death.

Hashimoto Heihachi 橋本平八
(1897–1935). Sculptor. Born in Mie Prefecture. Hashimoto studied with the sculptor Satō Chōzan (1888–1963) and at the JAPAN FINE ARTS ACADEMY. In 1927 he became a regular exhibitor at the Inten (Exhibition of the Japan Fine Arts Academy). An admirer of the wooden Buddhas of the sculptor ENKŪ (1632–95), Hashimoto developed an original style that was a synthesis of the Japanese sculptural tradition with Western figurative techniques. His work breathed new life into the world of contemporary wood sculpture.

Hashimoto Kansetsu 橋本関雪
(1883–1945). Japanese-style painter. Born in Kōbe, the son of the Confucian scholar and literati painter Hashimoto Kaikan. He first studied the MARUYAMA-SHIJŌ SCHOOL of painting and in 1903 became a disciple of the Kyōto literati painter TAKEUCHI SEIHŌ. Kansetsu developed an eclectic style, a blend of traditional literati painting (BUNJINGA), Maruyama-Shijō school realism, and elements of European impressionism, that was heralded as the "new literati style." Among his most often depicted subjects are monkeys and Chinese historical themes. He was appointed a member of the Teikoku Bijutsuin (Imperial Fine Arts Academy) in 1935. His former residence in Kyōto, the Hakusa Sonsō, is now a museum.

Hashimoto Kingorō 橋本欣五郎
(1890–1957). Army officer. Born in Okayama Prefecture. He graduated from the Army Academy in 1911 and the Army War College in 1920. An advocate of military expansion, he organized a secret society of army officers called the SAKURAKAI in 1930 and is generally believed to have masterminded two abortive coups in 1931 (see MARCH INCIDENT and OCTOBER INCIDENT). In 1936, after the FEBRUARY 26TH INCIDENT, he was put on reserve status. That same year he founded the profascist Dai Nippon Seinentō (Great Japan Youth Party). In 1937, he was recalled to active duty but was again retired for his part in the LADYBIRD INCIDENT. Tried as a class A war criminal after World War II (see WAR CRIMES TRIALS), he was sentenced to life imprisonment but released in 1955.

Hashimoto Meiji 橋本明治
(1904–91). Japanese-style (NIHONGA) painter. Born in Shimane Prefecture. Graduate of Tōkyō Bijutsu Gakkō (now Tōkyō University of Fine Arts and Music). Hashimoto studied under the painter MATSUOKA EIKYŪ. His paintings, with their emphasis on line drawing, have a quality of freshness. He received the Order of Culture in 1974.

Hashimoto Osamu 橋本治
(1948–   ). Novelist. Born in Tōkyō. Graduate of Tōkyō University. Hashimoto received the Shōsetsu Gendai Prize for New Talent for Momojiri musume (1977, Peach-Bottom Girl). In addition to his ongoing Momojiri musume series, Hashimoto's works include Momojirigo yaku "Makura no sōshi" (1987), a translation of the Heian-period (794–1185) classic MAKURA NO SŌSHI (Pillow Book) into the language of today's Japanese youth.

Hashimoto Sanai 橋本左内
(1834–59). Physician and political reformer of the late Edo period (1600–1868). Born in the castle town of the Fukui or Echizen domain (now part of Fukui Prefecture); son of the domainal physician. Erroneously esteemed by some as a martyr of the campaign to topple the Tokugawa shogunate (1603–1867), he actually supported the shogunal system, advocating only limited reform.

Following medical training and other study, he became head of the domainal school, Meidōkan. In 1857 he was summoned to Edo (now Tōkyō) by MATSUDAIRA YOSHINAGA, the daimyō of Echizen, to help promote reform of the shogunate. In 1858 Hashimoto was sent to Kyōto to seek backing among the court aristocracy for the selection as shōgun of Hitotsubashi Yo-

Hashimoto Gahō White Clouds and Autumn Trees. 1890. Ink and colors on paper. 266 × 160 cm. Tōkyō University of Fine Arts and Music.

shinobu (TOKUGAWA YOSHINOBU), who was a sympathizer with the reform faction. Hashimoto was executed in 1859, during the ANSEI PURGE, which was initiated by II NAOSUKE to eradicate a perceived threat on the part of the reformers to the powers of the shogunate and to suppress opposition to the signing of the HARRIS TREATY. In his thought Hashimoto combined Western Learning and the nationalism of the MITO SCHOOL, which were to supply theoretical support for the imperial restoration in 1868 and the sweeping reforms of the Meiji period (1868–1912).

Hashimoto Shinkichi 橋本進吉
(1882–1945). Linguist and Japanese grammarian. Born in Fukui Prefecture, he graduated from Tōkyō University in 1906, majoring in linguistics. He served as assistant to UEDA KAZUTOSHI from 1909 until 1927, when he succeeded Ueda as professor of Japanese at Tōkyō University.

Hashimoto's most noted research was perhaps his account of Old Japanese vowels, based on the earliest systems of KANA. His investigation of the Christian literature of the

Hashimoto Meiji Actress. 1967. Colors on paper. 170 × 115 cm. National Museum of Modern Art, Tōkyō.

507

16th and 17th centuries similarly shaped the study of the Japanese language of that period. Hashimoto's grammatical system is based on the *bunsetsu* (phonological phrase). He was responsible for the *Shin bunten bekki* (1931, 1936, 1938, 1939, Supplement to the New Grammar), the official school reference grammar established by the Ministry of Education. Thus his grammatical ideas enjoyed the widest possible distribution and remain influential to the present time. See JAPANESE LANGUAGE STUDIES, HISTORY OF.

Hashimoto Shinobu 橋本忍

(1918–). Screenwriter. Born in Hyōgo Prefecture. He studied scenario writing with ITAMI MANSAKU. His first screenplay to be made into a movie was the celebrated RASHŌMON (1950), written with and directed by KUROSAWA AKIRA. Following this, Hashimoto collaborated on a number of other Kurosawa films, including IKIRU (1952, To Live), *Shichinin no samurai* (1954, SEVEN SAMURAI), *Kumonosujō* (1957, Throne of Blood), and *Kakushi toride no san akunin* (1958, The Hidden Fortress). He wrote the scripts for the acclaimed television drama *Watashi wa kai ni naritai* (1958, A Clam Is What I Want to Be) and the films SEPPUKU (1962), directed by KOBAYASHI MASAKI; *Shiroi kyotō* (1966, The White Tower), directed by YAMAMOTO SATSUO; *Nihon no ichiban nagai hi* (1967, Japan's Longest Day), directed by OKAMOTO KIHACHI; and *Nihon chimbotsu* (1973, Japan Sinks), directed by Moritani Shirō (1931–84).

hasu→lotus

Hasuda 蓮田[市]

City in eastern Saitama Prefecture, central Honshū. Rice and fruit are grown in the area. About 40 km (25 mi) from Tōkyō, Hasuda is rapidly being urbanized. Pop: 59,706.

Hasumi Shigehiko 蓮実重彦

(1936–). Literary critic and scholar of French literature. Born in Tōkyō. Graduate of Tōkyō University. His *Han nihongo ron* (Against a Theory of the Japanese Language) won the Yomiuri Literary Prize in 1977. In his *Natsume Sōseki ron* (1978, On Natsume Sōseki), Hasumi maintained that the critic should read the surface of an individual work—the actual language of the text—rather than search for "deeper meanings" in the writer's complete oeuvre, psychology, or personal history. This theory was systematized in his *Hyōsō hihyō sengen* (1979, Manifesto of Surface Criticism).

Hata family 秦氏

(Hatashi). Influential family or clan (UJI) of ancient Japan; descended from continental immigrants (KIKAJIN). According to family legend, its more important members were descendants of YUZUKI NO KIMI, who arrived from the Korean state of PAEKCHE around 400. He brought with him a large number of people, whose descendants became known as *hatahito*. The Hata are associated in early historical accounts with sericulture, weaving, and metallurgy (techniques they may have helped introduce to Japan), as well as land development, supervision of government storehouses, and diplomatic service. Although branches of the Hata spread to many parts of Japan, their principal settlement was in the Kyōto basin. Hata no Kawakatsu, a friend of the regent Prince SHŌTOKU, founded the temple KŌRYŪJI in the

early 7th century; other family members are said to have founded the FUSHIMI INARI SHRINE and other Shintō shrines in the Kyōto area. At the end of the 8th century the Hata provided financial assistance for the building of the new capital city HEIANKYŌ.

Hatakeyama family 畠山氏

(Hatakeyamashi). Warrior family of Musashi Province (now Saitama, Tōkyō, and part of Kanagawa prefectures) in the Kamakura (1185–1333) and Muromachi (1333–1568) periods. Although a TAIRA FAMILY descendant, HATAKEYAMA SHIGETADA helped MINAMOTO NO YORITOMO destroy the Taira and became a retainer (GOKENIN) of the KAMAKURA SHOGUNATE. In 1205 Shigetada's son was killed by the shogunal regent HŌJŌ TOKIMASA; Shigetada rebelled, was killed, and his line was extinguished. His widow, a daughter of Tokimasa, married Ashikaga Yoshizumi, a descendant of the MINAMOTO FAMILY; he succeeded to the Hatakeyama domains and adopted their name. The Hatakeyama helped ASHIKAGA TAKAUJI found the MUROMACHI SHOGUNATE (1338–1573) and were made military governors (SHUGO) of several provinces. In 1398 Hatakeyama Motokuni (1352–1406) became first of his line to serve as shogunal deputy (KANREI). Conflicts over family headship were one cause of the ŌNIN WAR (1467–77), after which the Hatakeyama never regained power.

Hatakeyama Museum 畠山記念館

(Hatakeyama Kinenkan). Located in Tōkyō. The collection of Hatakeyama Issei (1881–1971), a descendant of the HATAKEYAMA FAMILY; housed in a contemporary Japanese-style building opened in 1964. The collection includes Chinese and Japanese paintings, calligraphy, sculpture, metalwork, and ceramics; Japanese lacquer, tea-ceremony objects, and costumes; and Korean ceramics. The Japanese paintings range from those of the Muromachi period (1333–1568) to those in the RIMPA style.

Hatakeyama Shigetada 畠山重忠

(1164–1205). Warrior of the early Kamakura period (1185–1333); son of an estate (SHŌEN) manager of Hatakeyama in northern Musashi Province (now part of Saitama, Tōkyō, and Kanagawa prefectures). The HATAKEYAMA FAMILY were descended from a branch of the TAIRA FAMILY, and Shigetada initially fought against MINAMOTO NO YORITOMO; however he took a prominent part in Yoritomo's struggle against the Taira. He distinguished himself in the Battle of DANNOURA (1185) and served in the 1189 campaign against the ŌSHŪ FUJIWARA FAMILY. In 1205 his son was killed by the shogunal regent HŌJŌ TOKIMASA. Shigetada took up arms against the Hōjō and was killed in battle later that year. His exploits have been celebrated in popular literature.

Hata Kōhei 秦恒平

(1935–). Novelist. Born in Kyōto. Graduate of Dōshisha University. Hata's surreal prose style serves as a vehicle for his unusual perspectives on life and death. His works include *Kiyotsune jusui* (1969, Kiyotsune's Watery Grave), *Atsuko* (1972), and *Migomori no umi* (1974, Sea of Conception).

Hata Masanori 畑正憲

(1935–). Essayist. Born in Fukuoka Prefecture. Graduate of Tōkyō University. Trained in zoology, he worked as a maker of documentary nature films before moving to Hok-

kaidō and establishing the "Mutsugorō Animal Kingdom," a farm and nature preserve where he and his family live together with a variety of wild and domesticated animals. His "Mutsugorō" series, several collections of humorous and affectionate essays based on this experience, won Hata the Kikuchi Kan Prize in 1977. The series includes *Warera dōbutsu mina kyōdai* (1967, All of Us Animals Are Brothers and Sisters) and *Mutsugorō no hakubutsushi* (1975, Mutsugorō's Natural History).

hatamoto 旗本

(bannermen). Direct *samurai* retainers of the TOKUGAWA SHOGUNATE (1603–1867). About 5,000 in number, they occupied positions analogous to the officer corps in a standing army or the bureaucracy of a central government. Nearly all of the *hatamoto* were descendants of warriors who had helped TOKUGAWA IEYASU establish the shogunate. The *hatamoto* received from the shogunate annual stipends of at least 100 *koku* of rice (1 *koku* = about 180 liters; see KOKUDAKA); the amount and type of payment depended on rank. Direct shogunal retainers ranking below the *hatamoto* and usually receiving less than 100 *koku* were called GOKENIN.

Though the status of *hatamoto* could be revoked, it was in principle hereditary, as were the specific positions the *hatamoto* held. The military positions ranged from captain of the Great Guard (Ōban) to unranked members of less prestigious guard units. The civil positions ranged from grand chamberlain (SOBAYŌNIN), directly under the senior councillors (RŌJŪ), to financial or record clerks. Many *hatamoto* held positions in Edo (now Tōkyō), but others were assigned elsewhere as intendants (DAIKAN) or as guards.

The *hatamoto* were loyal to the Tokugawa to the end and served them well, in part because a *hatamoto* would designate a younger or adopted son as heir to his stipend if the eldest son was less competent. Major problems for *hatamoto* during the late Edo period (1600–1868) included a decline in income relative to that of many merchants and even some peasants, growing indebtedness, and faltering morale, as they spent their days performing ceremonial or routine bureaucratic functions. Other than ENOMOTO TAKEAKI and KATSU KAISHŪ, few *hatamoto* rose to any position of significance after the MEIJI RESTORATION (1868).

hatamoto yakko 旗本奴

A type of *samurai* ruffian of the early Edo period (1600–1868). YAKKO was a term for footmen and other attendants (*hōkōnin*) of samurai families, some of whom dressed extravagantly to compensate for their low rank. Some HATAMOTO (direct retainers of the Tokugawa shōgun) imitated this swaggering fashion and became known as *hatamoto yakko*. One reason for the phenomenon may have been the lack of opportunity, in the Tokugawa realm of peace, to demonstrate manliness by military valor; flaunting irregular behavior to show "style" became an alternative way of proving that one was a "real man" (*otoko o tateru* or *otokodate*). Not content with this virile pose, *hatamoto yakko* organized gangs (*kumi*) and engaged in violence in the streets of Edo (now Tōkyō), on occasion coming into conflict with their townsman equivalents, the MACHI YAKKO. The Tokugawa shogunate imposed severe countermeasures and by 1687 had suppressed both the *hatamoto yakko* and the *machi yakko.* Various kinds of *otokodate* have been immortalized in *kabuki* and other popular theater.

Hatano Kanji 波多野完治

(1905–). Psychologist. Born in Tōkyō, Hatano graduated from Tōkyō University. He became a professor at the Tōkyō Women's Higher Normal School (now Ochanomizu Women's University) in 1947 and was its president from 1969 to 1971. He conducted research in child development, communication, and audiovisual education. His use of the theories of psychologists such as Jean Piaget furthered the study of child development in Japan.

Hatano Seiichi 波多野精一

(1877–1950). Scholar and specialist in the history of philosophy and the philosophy of religion. Born in Nagano Prefecture. Hatano studied the history of Western philosophy with Raphael Koeber (1848–1923) at Tōkyō University, where he concentrated on Spinoza and the Greek philosophers. While studying in Germany he attended the lectures of C. G. A. von Harnack (1851–1930) and E. Troeltsch (1865–1923) and was deeply influenced by their ideas on Christianity and Christian theology. He embarked upon a historical study of the Bible, establishing his own philosophy of religion. Hatano sought to explain the religious experience—the highest experience attained by man—as it related organically and psychologically to other life experiences. The idea of eternity was first introduced academically to Japan in his book *Toki to eien* (1943, Time and Eternity). He was a professor at Kyōto University and president of Tamagawa University.

Hata Sahachirō 秦佐八郎

(1873–1938). Bacteriologist. Born in Shimane Prefecture. Hata completed a full medical course at the Third Higher School in Kyōto. He studied epidemic diseases under KITASATO SHIBASABURŌ at the Institute for Infectious Diseases in Tōkyō; immunology at the Koch Institute, Berlin; and chemotherapy under Paul Ehrlich at the National Institute for Experimental Therapeutics in Frankfurt am Main, Germany. He assisted Ehrlich in research that led to the discovery in 1910 of arsphenamine (Salvarsan), a compound of arsenic that proved effective against syphilis. After returning to Japan he helped establish the Kitasato Institute. He was appointed a director and vice-president of the institute and professor at Keiō University.

Hata Toyokichi 秦豊吉

(1892–1956). Producer; translator; writer. Born in Tōkyō; attended Tōkyō University. He translated Goethe and Remarque. In 1933 he joined the theater group Tōkyō Takarazuka Gekijō, establishing himself as a producer and later becoming its president. Taking the pen name Maruki Sado, a wordplay on "Marquis de Sade," he wrote on humorous and erotic subjects. He founded the Nichigeki Dancing Troupe.

Hatogaya 鳩ケ谷[市]

City in southeastern Saitama Prefecture, central Honshū. It is noted for its tree nurseries. In recent years many housing complexes and small and medium-size industrial plants have been built. Pop: 56,440.

Hatoyama Haruko 鳩山春子

(1861–1938). Educator. Born in Matsumoto (now in Nagano Prefecture); maiden name Taga. She graduated in 1881 from the Women's Normal School (now Ochanomizu Women's University), where she later taught. She was married in 1881 to HATOYAMA KAZUO, a politician and lawyer. Their children included future prime minister HATOYAMA ICHIRŌ and legal scholar HATOYAMA HIDEO. In 1886 she helped Miyagawa Hozen (1852–1922) found the women's vocational school Kyōritsu Joshi Shokugyō Gakkō (now Kyōritsu Joshi Gakuen) and served as its president from 1925 until her death.

Hatoyama Hideo 鳩山秀夫

(1884–1946). Scholar of law and politician. Born in Tōkyō. After graduating from Tōkyō University in 1908, he was appointed assistant professor there in 1910 and the following year went to study in France and Germany. On his return in 1916 he was appointed professor and taught civil law at Tōkyō University until 1926. After his retirement he became a lawyer and was elected to the House of Representatives in 1932. His interpretation of civil law in the Germanic tradition was highly influential during the Taishō period (1912–26). Among his principal works were *Nihon saiken hō sōron* (1918, An Outline of the Law of Obligations in Japan) and *Saikenhō ni okeru shingi seijitsu no gensoku* (1924, The Principles of Trust and Sincerity in the Law of Obligations). His elder brother was the politician HATOYAMA ICHIRŌ.

Hatoyama Ichirō 鳩山一郎

(1883–1959). Prime minister from December 1954 to December 1956. Born in Tōkyō; the eldest son of the politician HATOYAMA KAZUO and his wife, the educator HATOYAMA HARUKO. Graduate of Tōkyō University. Hatoyama was first elected to the Diet in 1915 and eventually became secretary-general of his party, the RIKKEN SEIYŪKAI. He was director of the Cabinet Secretariat (1927–29) and served as minister of education (1931–34). After the MANCHURIAN INCIDENT (1931) Hatoyama dismissed liberal teachers from the universities (see KYŌTO UNIVERSITY INCIDENT).

After World War II, Hatoyama organized the Japan Liberal Party (Nihon Jiyūtō) and became its president. In 1946, on the eve of becoming prime minister, he was purged by the Occupation authorities (see OCCUPATION PURGE) and did not participate in politics until his rehabilitation in 1951. In 1954 Hatoyama aligned himself with the Kaishintō (Reform Party) to form a new party, the NIHON MINSHUTŌ (Japan Democratic Party). He became prime minister in December 1954 and soon hinted that the 1947 constitution, including article 9 (RENUNCIATION OF WAR), might be amended. In October 1956 Hatoyama concluded a treaty with the Soviet Union, ending the state of war that had existed between the two nations since August 1945. It was during Hatoyama's term as prime minister that the LIBERAL DEMOCRATIC PARTY was formed, effecting a merger of all the conservative parties.

Hatoyama Kazuo 鳩山和夫

(1856–1911). Politician and lawyer. Born in Edo (now Tōkyō). He attended Kaisei Gakkō (now Tōkyō University) and studied law at Columbia and Yale universities. Upon returning to Japan, he taught at Tōkyō University but left teaching to practice law. In 1885 he entered the Ministry of Foreign Affairs to help in the revision of the so-called Unequal Treaties with Western nations (see UNEQUAL TREATIES, REVISION OF). In 1892 he was elected to the House of Representatives as a member of the RIKKEN KAISHINTŌ party and became speaker of the House in 1896. He also served as president of Waseda University. His wife, HATOYAMA HARUKO, was a well-known educator; the politician and prime minister HATOYAMA ICHIRŌ was his eldest son.

Hatsukaichi 廿日市[市]

City in southwestern Hiroshima Prefecture, western Honshū, on Hiroshima Bay. Hatsukaichi developed early as a market and post-station town. Its main occupations are farming and the manufacture of wood products. The city is a satellite community of Hiroshima. Pop: 63,441.

hatsumōde 初詣

("first shrine or temple visit"). Word used to refer to a person's first visit to a Shintō shrine or Buddhist temple during the New Year. Because it was customary to visit the shrine or temple located in the direction from one's home considered to be the most auspicious that year (*ehō*), this practice was also called *ehōmairi* ("visiting the shrine or temple in the *ehō*"). Today, however, it has become more common to visit well-known shrines and temples, regardless of their location. These visits, which begin at midnight on New Year's Eve, are made annually by large numbers of Japanese. Tōkyō's MEIJI SHRINE, Kamakura's TSURUGAOKA HACHIMAN SHRINE, and Kyōto's YASAKA SHRINE each receive several million visitors over the first three days of January.

Hatsushima 初島

Small island in Sagami Bay, 10 km (6 mi) southeast of the city of Atami, Shizuoka Prefecture, central Honshū. A fishing community from the early Edo period (1600–1868) until just after World War II, it has developed in recent years as a vacation spot. Area: 0.4 sq km (0.2 sq mi).

Hatsuuma 初午

The first "day of the horse" in February as determined by Chinese and Japanese zodiacal traditions (see JIKKAN JŪNISHI); also, the event held on that day. It is connected with the belief in INARI (the deity of cereals). Since the 8th century many Inari shrines have held festivities on Hatsuuma. At the FUSHIMI INARI SHRINE in Kyōto, it was the custom for worshipers to break off branches of cedars growing nearby to take home. Today, shrines give worshipers cedar leaves with consecrated paper streamers and sell seeds, fox statues (the fox is one of the forms of Inari), and insect-shaped bells. Many regions celebrate a horse or ox festival on Hatsuuma, and in eastern Japan the silkworm deity is honored.

Hatta, Mohammad ハッタ, M.

(1902–80). The first vice-president (1945–56) and later prime minister (1948–50) of the Republic of Indonesia. Born in West Sumatra, Hatta studied for 10 years in the Netherlands and was active in an anticolonial organization of Indonesian students. After returning to the Dutch East Indies, he was arrested and imprisoned from 1934 until 1942, when he was released by the Japanese. During the Japanese occupation, he served as an adviser to the military administration. After Japan indicated in September 1944 that independence would be granted the East Indies, Hatta served as a member of a number of preparatory and investigatory committees. Two days after the Japanese surrender on 15

Hatoyama Ichirō
As prime minister, Hatoyama negotiated the formal suspension of hostilities between Japan and the Soviet Union in 1956.

hawks and eagles
1 A falconer hunting with a *kumataka* (Hodgson's hawk eagle). Popular with the military elite from the 16th to 19th centuries, today falconry has all but died out.
2 Native to mountain forests north of Kyūshū, the *kumataka* feeds on birds and small mammals.
3 The *ōwashi* (Steller's sea eagle), which can grow to 95 cm in length, is the largest eagle in Japan. It breeds in eastern Siberia and winters in Hokkaidō.

August 1945, SUKARNO and Hatta declared an independent republic. Dissenting from Sukarno's views, Hatta resigned the vice-presidency in 1956. See also INDONESIA AND JAPAN.

Hattori Kintarō 服部金太郎

(1860–1934). Entrepreneur. Founder of K. Hattori & Co, Ltd (now SEIKŌ CORPORATION), and Seikōsha Co, Ltd, the maker of Seikō-brand products. Born in Edo (now Tōkyō), Hattori became apprentice to a watch dealer in 1874. In 1881 he started K. Hattori & Co, which repaired and sold timepieces. He established Seikōsha in 1892 and became a leading producer of wall clocks and watches. He won first prizes for his timepieces at the Second Tōkyō Industrial Exposition of 1912. Hattori established a measuring instrument plant in 1929 and started production of measuring instruments and fuses for military use.

Hattori Nankaku 服部南郭

(1683–1759). Confucian scholar, poet, and painter of the Edo period (1600–1868). Born in Kyōto, as a youth he went to EDO (now Tōkyō) to serve under YANAGISAWA YOSHIYASU, a senior councillor (RŌJŪ) of the Tokugawa shogunate (1603–1867). He also studied under OGYŪ SORAI, founder of the KOBUNJIGAKU school of Confucianism, which emphasized philological studies of the original Confucian classics. Nankaku opened his own school in 1716.

Hattori Ransetsu 服部嵐雪

(1654–1707). HAIKU poet of the Edo period (1600–1868) and founder of the Setsumon school of haiku. Real name Hattori Hikobei. Born in Edo (now Tōkyō). A leading disciple of BASHŌ, he carried on the master's tradition in his own verses and trained many young poets. Ransetsu's earlier haiku are characterized by a graceful lyricism, and later examples convey a sense of inner peace and enlightenment. His main collections are *Sono fukuro* (1690) and *Ransetsu bunshū* (1774).

Hattori Shirō 服部四郎

(1908–). Linguist. Born in Mie Prefecture, Hattori was educated at Tōkyō University, where he became professor and later professor emeritus of linguistics. He was awarded the title Contributor to Culture and became a member of the Japan Academy. He was awarded the Order of Culture in 1983. His research, which concentrated on Altaic languages, also included studies on several non-Altaic Asian languages. Although he often employed modern Western (especially American) linguistic research methods, he also endeavored to establish a Japanese tradition of systematic linguistic study. His published works include *Onseigaku* (1951, Phonology), *Nihongo no keitō* (1959, The Genealogy of the Japanese Language), and *Gengogaku no hōhō* (1960, Methods in Linguistics). See also JAPANESE LANGUAGE STUDIES, HISTORY OF.

Hattori Shisō 服部之総

(1901–56). Historian. Born in Shimane Prefecture; graduate of Tōkyō University. While a student, Hattori joined the progressive study group SHINJINKAI and became interested in Marxism. In 1928 he published *Meiji ishin shi*, a groundbreaking study of the MEIJI RESTORATION (1868). With HANI GORŌ he was a contributor to the series NIHON SHIHON SHUGI HATTATSU SHI KŌZA (7 vols, 1932–33; Studies on the History of the Development of Japanese Capitalism). After World War II, he published works on the FREEDOM AND PEOPLE'S RIGHTS MOVEMENT and the 13th-century religious figure SHINRAN. See also NIHON SHIHON SHUGI RONSŌ.

Hattori Tohō 服部土芳

(1657–1730). Also known as Hattori Dohō; real name Hattori Yasuhide. HAIKU poet of the early Edo period (1600–1868). Born in Ueno, Iga Province (now part of Mie Prefecture), also BASHŌ's hometown. He is best known for the *Sanzōshi* (1702), his recording of Bashō's later teachings about haiku, which, with the *Kyoraishō* by MUKAI KYORAI, is considered the most authoritative source on Bashō's poetics. It deals with the concepts of *fūga no makoto*, the "truth of haiku," and *fueki ryūkō*, the dialectic of permanence and change in haiku. *Minomushian shū*, compiled by Tohō between 1688 and 1729, is a valuable record of his own verses and those of the other members of the Iga haiku circles.

Hausknecht, Emil ハウスクネヒト, E.

(1853–1927). German educator who brought the educational theories of Johann Friedrich Herbart (1776–1841) to Japan. Hausknecht studied languages and history at Berlin's Friedrich-Wilhelm University and became a teacher after graduation. He went to Japan in 1887 at the invitation of the Ministry of Education. In 1889 the curriculum for secondary-school teacher training was established in accordance with his proposals. Among his students were many leading educators of the Meiji (1868–1912) and Taishō (1912–26) periods, such as TANIMOTO TOMERI. Hausknecht left Japan in 1890.

hawks and eagles 鷹と鷲

(*taka to washi*). Some 28 species of birds of prey belonging to the order Falconiformes are found in Japan, including 22 of the family Accipitridae and 6 of the family Falconidae; of these, 7 of the larger species are called *washi* (eagles) by the Japanese, and the other 21 are called *taka* (hawks). Since the distinction between hawks and eagles is based mainly on size, with different standards employed in Japan and the West, some species known as eagles in English are classified as *taka* by the Japanese.

The following 5 *taka* species are peculiar to Asia: the *tsumi* (Japanese lesser sparrow hawk; *Accipiter gularis*), the *sashiba* (gray-faced buzzard eagle; *Butastur indicus*), the *kumataka* (Hodgson's hawk eagle; *Spizaetus nipalensis*), the *akaharadaka* (Chinese sparrow hawk; *A. soloensis*), and the *madarachūhi* (pied harrier; *Circus melanoleucos*). Other species generally called *taka* in Japan include the *nosuri* (Japanese buzzard; *Buteo buteo*), the *hayabusa* (Siberian peregrine falcon; *Falco peregrinus*), the *chōgembō* (Japanese kestrel; *F. tinnunculus*), and the *chūhi* (marsh harrier; *C. aeruginosus*). Species generally called *washi* in Japan include the *inuwashi* (Japanese golden eagle; *Aquila chrysaetos*), the *ōwashi* (Steller's sea eagle; *Haliaeëtus pelagicus*), and the *ojirowashi* (white-tailed sea eagle; *H. albicilla*).

The earliest record of hawks used for hunting in Japan is found in the KOJIKI (712). The practice continues on a small scale today. See also FALCONRY; KITE, BLACK.

Hayabusa 隼

("Falcon"). Japanese army fighter plane in World War II. Officially designated Nakajima Isshiki Sentōki (Nakajima Mark I Fighter), it was the army's principal fighter aircraft. Construction of the first test model began in 1937. The model was officially adopted in April 1941, and a total of 5,751 were manufactured before the conclusion of the war.

Hayachinesan 早池峰山

Mountain in central Iwate Prefecture, northern Honshū. It is the highest peak in the Kitakami Mountains, a monadnock composed of basic rocks such as serpentine. Its alpine flora belt is designated a natural monument. Hayachine Shrine is on the summit. Height: 1,917 m (6,289 ft).

Hayaishi Osamu 早石修

(1920–). Biochemist. Born in Kyōto. A graduate of Ōsaka University, he later taught at Kyōto University and Tōkyō University. He discovered the enzyme oxygenase while conducting research in the United States and has continued to explore new areas of biochemical research. He was awarded the Order of Culture in 1972.

Hayakawa Sesshū 早川雪洲

(1889–1973). Film actor. Known abroad as Sessue Hayakawa. Born in Chiba Prefecture, his real name was Hayakawa Kintarō. In 1909 he went to the United States to attend the University of Chicago. He later joined an amateur theater group there and made his movie debut in *Typhoon* (1914). Hayakawa was the most successful Japanese actor in Hollywood, making a total of 40 films there. However, his roles were invariably portrayals of Japanese as seen through Western eyes. He gained critical acclaim for his performance in Max Ophuls's *Yoshiwara* (1937) and was much praised for his portrayal of the shrewd, iron-willed Japanese army officer in *Bridge over the River Kwai* (1957), directed by David Lean. He returned to Japan in 1949.

Hayama 葉山[町]

Town in southern Kanagawa Prefecture, central Honshū, on the Miura Peninsula. Because of its mild climate, Hayama developed as a resort. There is a marina located here. Pop: 29,536.

Hayama Yoshiki 葉山嘉樹

(1894–1945). Novelist and short-story writer; one of the leading writers of the PROLETARIAN LITERATURE MOVEMENT of the 1920s and early 1930s. Hayama was born in the village of Toyotsu in Fukuoka Prefecture in northern Kyūshū. He briefly attended Waseda University. He then worked as a seaman and later drifted from one job to another.

In June 1920 Hayama became a reporter with the *Nagoya shimbun.* When a strike broke out at the Aichi Tokei Denki Co, Ltd, in October of that year, he joined the strikers. He was arrested and sentenced to two months in jail. For the next several years Hayama was in and out of prison, where he wrote the half-dozen stories and one long novel that are regarded as his most important works.

In 1925 Hayama published the short story "Imbaifu" (The Prostitute) in the journal *Bungei sensen* (Literary Battlefront). Written in a highly lyrical style, it was unusual among proletarian literary works, which were often little more than schematic representations of ideological convictions. The long novel *Umi ni ikuru hitobito,* published by Kaizōsha in 1926 and hailed as a masterpiece of the Japanese proletarian novel describes a group of seamen on a coal-carrier and the inhuman conditions under which they are forced to work.

From the mid-1930s to the early 1940s Hayama and his family moved from village to village in the mountains of Gifu and Nagano prefectures. In June 1945 he moved to a farming settlement in Manchuria with his eldest daughter. He died from a stroke while returning to Japan in October of that year.

Hayami Gyoshū 速水御舟

(1894–1935). Japanese-style painter. Born in Tōkyō, Gyoshū began the study of traditional Japanese painting at the age of 15 under Matsumoto Fūko (1840–1923). Two years later his talent was recognized by IMAMURA SHIKŌ, and he became a member of

the Kōjikai, a group that Shikō had organized composed of leading young artists. He also joined the revived Nihon Bijutsuin (Japan Fine Arts Academy). He practiced many styles of painting, including YAMATO-E, RIMPA, and BUNJINGA. Gyoshū's style gradually moved toward detailed realism, especially after his study of Chinese painting of the Song (Sung; 960–1126) and Yuan (Yüan; 1279–1368) dynasties. Later his style changed to a fantasy-rich symbolism.

Hayami Masaru 速水優

(1925–). Business leader. Born in Kōbe. Graduated from the Tōkyō Higher Commercial School (now Hitotsubashi University). In 1947 he joined the Bank of Japan, where he spent the greater part of his career stationed in various locations abroad. In 1981 he moved to NISSHŌ IWAI CORPORATION, where he became president in 1984 and chairman in 1987. In April 1991 he became chairman of the JAPAN ASSOCIATION OF CORPORATE EXECUTIVES (Keizai Dōyūkai).

Hayasaka Akira 早坂暁

(1929–). Radio and television writer. Real name Tomita Shōji. Born in Ehime Prefecture, Hayasaka graduated from Nihon University. His writings have a keen sense of sympathy for the social underdog. Among his most important scripts are *Shura no tabishite* (broadcast 1979), *Yumechiyo nikki* (broadcast 1981; published 1983), and *Hana henro, kaze no Shōwa nikki* (broadcast 1985, 1986, and 1988).

Hayasaka Fumio 早坂文雄

(1914–55). Composer. Born in Miyagi Prefecture. Self-taught, he founded the Shin Ongaku Remmei (New Music League) in 1934 with fellow composer Ifukube Akira (b 1914). Rather than simply following the Western musical tradition, Hayasaka contributed to contemporary musical development by creating a new Eastern style. Out of this approach came his 1938 piece for orchestra, *Kodai no bukyoku* (Ancient Dance Music), which was awarded the Weingartner Prize. His most famous work is *Saho no mai to uhō no mai* (1942, Classical Dance of the Left and Right). In 1939 he became music director for the film production company TŌHŌ CO, LTD, creating the music for such famous films as SEVEN SAMURAI, RASHŌMON, UGETSU MONOGATARI, and IKIRU.

hayashi 囃子

Broad term covering different types of musical accompaniment or vocal "encouragement" for dancers, singers, instrumentalists, actors, and other kinds of performers; it may also indicate the performers themselves. The term derives from the Japanese verb *hayasu,* meaning "to encourage" or "spur on." In traditional FOLK PERFORMING ARTS (*minzoku geinō*) it refers to the instrumental accompaniment, generally drums and flutes. In the music of the KANDA FESTIVAL, GION FESTIVAL, and similar festivals, the *hayashi* itself constitutes the performance (often called *matsuri-bayashi,* or "festival *hayashi*"). In the NŌ drama the *hayashi* instrumental group consists of one flute plus two or three TAIKO and TSUZUMI drums. In KABUKI MUSIC the *hayashi* is provided by an instrumental group similar to that of Nō. This group, along with the singers and SHAMISEN players, forms the kabuki onstage orchestra (*debayashi*). Offstage music (*geza ongaku*) is provided by a varied group of musicians and noisemakers referred to as the *kage-bayashi.*

Hayashi Chūshirō 林忠四郎

(1920–). Astrophysicist. Born in Kyōto. Upon graduating from Tōkyō University, Hayashi studied under YUKAWA HIDEKI at Kyōto University, and in 1957 he became a professor there. He is internationally known for his theoretical research on the evolution of stars, and his explication of the transition phase between protostar and main-sequence star (known as the Hayashi phase) is a basic theory of stellar evolution. Hayashi received the Order of Culture in 1986.

Hayashi Fubō 林不忘

(1900–1935). Novelist. Real name Hasegawa Umitarō. Born on the island of Sado in Niigata Prefecture; brother of novelist HASEGAWA SHIRŌ. After he left middle school he lived in the United States for six years. After his return to Japan in 1924, he began writing, under the pen name Tani Jōji, about the Japanese community in America in a popular series known by the general title *Meriken Jappu,* the first of which was *Jappu shōbai ōrai* (1927, A Jap Businessman's How-to Book). He also wrote mystery stories and stories of family life under the pen name Maki Itsuma. Under his third pen name, Hayashi Fubō, he is known for a number of pseudohistorical romances, including *Shimpan Ōoka seidan* (1927–28), whose hero is Tange Sazen, a one-eyed, one-armed super swordsman. His other works include the novel *Chijō no seiza* (1932–34, The Terrestrial Constellation) and *Tekisasu mushuku* (1929, Homeless in Texas), a collection of his *Meriken Jappu* stories.

Hayashi Fukusai 林復斎

(1800–59). Confucian scholar of the Edo period (1600–1868); sixth son of HAYASHI JUSSAI.

511

Hayashi Fumiko One of the premier Japanese woman writers of the 20th century, Hayashi is known for her compassionate portrayals of the urban working class.

Fukusai was appointed head of the shogunate academy for Confucian studies (SHŌHEIKŌ) in 1853. The following year he represented the shogunate in the signing of the KANAGAWA TREATY, which opened Japan after 200 years of NATIONAL SECLUSION.

Hayashi Fumiko   林芙美子

(1903–51). Novelist. Born in Yamaguchi Prefecture; the fourth illegitimate child, all by different fathers, of Hayashi Kiku. When Fumiko was about 7 years old, Kiku ran off with her common-law husband's store manager, over 20 years her junior, taking Fumiko along as they peddled goods throughout Kyūshū. While at Onomichi Higher Girls' School in Hiroshima Prefecture, Fumiko published her poetry in local newspapers. Her relationship with a Meiji University student, whom she followed to Tōkyō, ended when he broke their engagement in 1923. She then began a rootless life while continuing to write poetry. The diary she began around the time her lover left her became the basis of her first novel, HŌRŌKI (1928–48; partial tr *Journal of a Vagabond*, 1951).

In 1924 she met Tanabe Wakao (1889–1966), leader of the theater group Shiminza, and through him she became acquainted with a circle of anarchist poets and other avant-garde writers. She lived briefly with Tanabe and later, again briefly, with the poet Nomura Yoshiya (b 1903), who often beat her. During this period she became friends with the poet TSUBOI SHIGEJI and his wife the novelist TSUBOI SAKAE, as well as with the novelist HIRABAYASHI TAIKO. She married the painter Tezuka Ryokubin (b 1902) in late 1926.

A wanderer since her childhood, she continually traveled even after her marriage, with visits to Europe (1931–32) and to China, Manchuria, and Southeast Asia as a reporter. Although sometimes criticized for melodramatic tendencies, she maintained the popularity she earned with *Hōrōki* throughout her life by repeatedly and compassionately capturing the dark misery of war, of rootless women, or of couples tortured by stale marriages.

While such earlier stories as "Fūkin to sakana no machi" (1931, Town of the Accordion and Fish) and "Seihin no sho" (1931, Record of Clean Poverty) are autobiographical, later short stories are works of pure fiction. "Dauntaun" (1949; tr "Downtown," 1961) and "Hone" (1949; tr "Bones," 1966) are among her most highly regarded short stories.

Hayashi Fusao   林房雄

(1903–75). Novelist and literary critic. Real name Gotō Toshio. Also known as Shirai Akira. Born in Ōita Prefecture. Attracted to Marxism while a student at Tōkyō University, he joined the PROLETARIAN LITERATURE MOVEMENT with the publication of his short story "Ringo" in 1926. After he was jailed four times in the 1930s for political activities, his views shifted profoundly to ultranationalism (see TENKŌ). After World War II, he established himself as a writer of apolitical family novels. In the 1960s he reemerged as a polemicist against left-wing pacifism with *Daitōa sensō kōtei ron* (1963), an apologia for Japan's actions in World War II. His principal works include the novels *Seinen* (1932, Youth) and *Musuko no endan* (1954).

Hayashi Gahō   林鵞峯

(1618–80). Confucianist of the early Edo period (1600–1868). Son of HAYASHI RAZAN, a Confucian scholar and adviser to the Tokugawa shogunate (1603–1867). A native of Kyōto, he went to live in Edo (now Tōkyō), where he instructed the shōgun TOKUGAWA IEMITSU in Confucian classics. He wrote, with his father, *Kan'ei shoka keizu den*, a genealogy of warrior families, and *Honchō tsugan*, a history of Japan; his own works are collected in *Gahō bunshū*.

Hayashi Hōkō   林鳳岡

(1644–1732). Confucian scholar of the Edo period (1600–1868). Born in Edo (now Tōkyō); grandson of HAYASHI RAZAN and son of HAYASHI GAHŌ, Confucian scholars to the Tokugawa shogunate (1603–1867). He lectured at EDO CASTLE to the shōgun TOKUGAWA TSUNAYOSHI. When the private academy of the Hayashi family was designated as the official shogunate school (see SHŌHEIKŌ) in 1691, Hōkō became its first head. The post (*daigaku no kami*) became a hereditary prerogative of the Hayashi family. At Hōkō's suggestion Confucian scholars were permitted to discard their priestlike robes and to be entered on *samurai* registers. After Tsunayoshi's death Hōkō continued to serve as lecturer and adviser to succeeding shōguns.

Hayashi Jussai   林述斎

(1768–1841). Confucian scholar of the late Edo period (1600–1868). Son of Matsudaira Norimori, *daimyō* of Iwamura (now part of Gifu Prefecture), he was chosen by MATSUDAIRA SADANOBU to head the Hayashi family, hereditary Confucian advisers to the Tokugawa shogunate (1603–1867), when Hayashi Nobutaka died without an heir in 1793. Jussai became head of the official shogunal academy (see SHŌHEIKŌ) in 1794, part of Sadanobu's program to establish the Zhu Xi (Chu Hsi) school of Neo-Confucianism (see SHUSHIGAKU) as the shogunate's official doctrine (see also KANSEI REFORMS). With the help of Koga Seiri (1750–1817), BITŌ NISHŪ, and SHIBANO RITSUZAN, Jussai reorganized the curriculum of the school, which under him became Japan's most important center of learning. Jussai also supervised the compilation of the TOKUGAWA JIKKI, a history of the Tokugawa family.

Hayashi Kyōko   林京子

(1930–). Real name Miyazaki Kyōko. Born in Nagasaki Prefecture; lived in Shanghai until she was 14. In 1945 Hayashi was injured in the atomic bombing of Nagasaki. She won the Akutagawa Prize in 1975 for "Matsuri no ba" (Festival Site), which described that experience. She has published many works dealing with the atomic bombing, her experiences in Shanghai, and her family life, including *Shanhai* (1983, Shanghai) and *Sangai no ie* (1984, A Home in the Threefold World).

Hayashi Razan   林羅山

(1583–1657). An important Neo-Confucian scholar of the early Edo period (1600–1868). In his long and conspicuous career as adviser to the Tokugawa shogunate, propagandist, historiographer, and educator, he promoted Zhu Xi (Chu Hsi) Neo-Confucianism (see SHUSHIGAKU) as the shogunate's favored school of Confucian learning and contributed to its diffusion in the society of his day.

Born in Kyōto, the son of Hayashi Nobutoki, Razan was adopted by his father's elder brother Yoshikatsu, a rice dealer. The family claimed *samurai* ancestry but had declined during the late 16th century. Following some Zen study, he read Zhu Xi's edition of the Confucian classics, and in 1604 he was introduced to FUJIWARA SEIKA, whom he regarded as his mentor though there remained openly declared differences between them. Razan's Neo-Confucianism, more exclusively loyal to Zhu Xi's interpretation than Seika's, may have been influenced by the similarly orthodox style of Korean Confucianism. In 1605 Razan first appeared before the retired shōgun TOKUGAWA IEYASU, beginning a sequence of events that led to the establishment of Neo-Confucianism as an independent school of learning in the Edo period. In 1607 Razan was summoned to Ieyasu's castle at Sumpu where he was ordered against his own inclination to take the tonsure in the manner of the Zen-Confucian advisers of the Muromachi period (1333–1568) and to assume the name Dōshun. Thus began Razan's long service with the shogunate.

Razan moved closer to the center of shogunal counsels in 1633. In 1635 he and his younger brother Nobuzumi drafted the second BUKE SHOHATTO (Laws for the Military Houses) and the Hatamoto Shohatto (Laws for the Shōgun's Vassals). For the remainder of his life Razan continued in shogunal service, drafting official documents, participating in diplomacy with Korea, advising on shogunal ceremonial matters, helping formulate the anti-Christian program, and participating in historiographical projects. After Razan's death the office of shogunal Confucian adviser became hereditary in the Hayashi family. In 1790, Zhu Xi Confucianism became the officially adopted government orthodoxy, and in 1797 the Hayashi family academy was reorganized into the official shogunal college known as the SHŌHEIKŌ.

Hayashi Senjūrō   林銑十郎

(1876–1943). Army general; served briefly as prime minister in 1937. Born in Ishikawa Prefecture; graduate of the Army War College. After serving as head of the Army War College and the Konoe (Imperial Guard) Division, he was sent to command the Japanese army in Korea. During the MANCHURIAN INCIDENT (1931) Hayashi dispatched his troops to support the Japanese GUANDONG (KWANTUNG) ARMY without authorization from the Tōkyō government. He was appointed army minister in the SAITŌ MAKOTO cabinet in 1934. As army minister in the OKADA KEISUKE cabinet in 1935, he dismissed the extremist general MAZAKI JINZABURŌ. His action aggravated the rivalry between the KŌDŌHA and TŌSEIHA factions in the army and contributed to the FEBRUARY 26TH INCIDENT, an attempted coup d'état by Kōdōha officers sympathetic to Mazaki. After the attempt was quashed, Hayashi retired from military service. In 1937 he became prime minister, formed a cabinet without party representation, and dissolved the Diet. The two major parties, the RIKKEN SEIYŪKAI and the RIKKEN MINSEITŌ, won in the April 1937 election, and Hayashi was forced to resign.

Hayashi Shihei   林子平

(1738–93). Military and administrative expert of the Edo period (1600–1868). Born in Edo (now Tōkyō). In 1757 Hayashi moved to the Sendai domain (now Miyagi Prefecture), where his elder brother was in service to the DATE FAMILY. From 1767 on, he went several times to study in Edo, where his contacts with ŌTSUKI GENTAKU and KATSURAGAWA

Hayashi Fusao Originally active in Japan's proletarian literature movement, this novelist recanted his ideological views while in prison and subsequently became an avowed ultranationalist.

HOSHŪ, eminent scholars of WESTERN LEARNING, deepened his knowledge of world conditions. Alarmed by the growing Russian presence in East Asia, he became convinced of the need to strengthen national defenses. In 1785 Hayashi wrote *Sangoku tsūran zusetsu* (Illustrated Survey of Three Countries), a geographical treatise on Korea, the Ryūkyū Islands, and Ezo (now Hokkaidō), advocating the development of Japan's northern frontiers to forestall Russian encroachment.

Hayashi is best known for *Kaikoku heidan* (1791, Discussion of the Military Problems of a Maritime Nation), which stressed the need to prepare for naval warfare, praised European legal systems and military techniques, and called for the reeducation of the warrior *samurai* class. Eight months after the book's publication, Hayashi was arrested for criticizing official policies. However, a few months later the Russians arrived in Ezo, and subsequent events confirmed the work's significance. Several later editions appeared.

Hayashi Tadahiko   林忠彦

(1918–90). Photographer. Born in Yamaguchi Prefecture, where his family operated a photography studio. He graduated from the Orientaru Shashin Gakkō and in 1937 took a position as a news photographer at Tōkyō Kōgei Sha. In 1947–48 he published photographic portraits of writers such as DAZAI OSAMU in the magazine *Shōsetsu shinchō*. These vivid depictions of authors' lives had considerable influence on the photographic portrait genre. Hayashi was also a major figure in landscape photography. *Nihon no sakka* (1971, Japanese Authors) is one collection of his works.

Hayashi Tadasu   林董

(1850–1913). Diplomat. Born in Shimōsa Province (now part of Chiba Prefecture). Studied in England from 1866 to 1868. After the Meiji Restoration (1868) he joined the group of Tokugawa loyalists led by ENOMOTO TAKEAKI and fled to Hokkaidō but was captured at the Battle of GORYŌKAKU. Released in 1870, he accompanied the IWAKURA MISSION to Europe and the United States. He later served in the Ministry of Public Works (Kōbushō) and held governorships and diplomatic posts. As minister to Britain from 1900 he worked to bring about the ANGLO-JAPANESE ALLIANCE of 1902. On becoming foreign minister in the first SAIONJI KIMMOCHI cabinet (1906), he concluded agreements with France (see FRANCO-JAPANESE AGREEMENT OF 1907) and with Russia (see RUSSO-JAPANESE AGREEMENTS OF 1907–1916). He served as minister of communications in the second Saionji cabinet (1911–12).

Hayashi Takeshi   林武

(1896–1975). Western-style painter. Real name Hayashi Takeomi. Born in Tōkyō. Hayashi studied at the Nihon Bijutsu Gakkō (Japan School of Art). One of his paintings won the Chogyū Prize at the 1921 Nikaten (Exhibition of the Nika Society). In 1930 he helped found the Dokuritsu Bijutsu Kyōkai (Independent Art Association). He possessed an original style of composition involving simplified shapes, which gave his paintings a feeling of massiveness and weight. He taught at Tōkyō University of Fine Arts and Music from 1952 to 1963. He received the Order of Culture in 1967.

Hayashi Tsuruichi   林鶴一

(1873–1935). Mathematician. Born in Tokushima Prefecture. A graduate of Tōkyō Uni-

versity. In 1911 he became the first professor to be appointed to the mathematics department of Tōhoku University. In the same year he established Japan's first mathematics periodical, *Tōhoku sūgaku zasshi* (Tōhoku Mathematical Journal; still published as of 1991), to which he contributed numerous papers on the traditional Japanese system of mathematics, WASAN. He also wrote several widely used mathematics textbooks.

Hayashi Yūzō   林有造

(1842–1921). Politician. Born in the Tosa domain (now Kōchi Prefecture), he was active in the movement to overthrow the TOKUGAWA SHOGUNATE (1603–1867). After the MEIJI RESTORATION (1868) he joined the Ministry of Foreign Affairs but resigned in 1873 following the defeat of the proposal to invade Korea (see SEIKANRON). He joined the RISSHISHA and helped to form the AIKOKU KŌTŌ (Public Party of Patriots). He was jailed briefly for procuring weapons during the SATSUMA REBELLION (1877). In 1890 Hayashi was elected to the Diet in the first general election. He served as minister of communications in the first ŌKUMA SHIGENOBU cabinet and, after helping to form the RIKKEN SEIYŪKAI (Friends of Constitutional Government Party), was appointed minister of commerce and agriculture in the fourth ITŌ HIROBUMI cabinet.

Hayasui Strait   速吸瀬戸

(Hayasui Seto). Strait between eastern Ōita Prefecture, Kyūshū, and western Ehime Prefecture, Shikoku; also called the Hōyo Strait. The strait is the southwestern entrance to the Inland Sea. A ferryboat linking Kyūshū and Shikoku runs here. Width: 13 km (8 mi); depth: approximately 100 m (328 ft).

Hayato   隼人

Tribal people who lived in southern Kyūshū in ancient times, mainly on the Ōsumi and Satsuma peninsulas (now Kagoshima Prefecture). The term Hayato was used pejoratively for those peoples in the south who resisted subjugation by the YAMATO COURT. The accounts of the submission of Hoderi no Mikoto to Hoori no Mikoto in the mythological sections of the KOJIKI (712) and the NIHON SHOKI (720) (see MYTHOLOGY: the myths of the *Kojiki* and *Nihon shoki*) are believed to reflect the submission of the Hayato to the rulers of Yamato, although there are some doubts about the date. It is thought, however, that by the beginning of the 9th century the government was able to implement its land allotment system (see HANDEN SHŪJU SYSTEM) in the area. A central office, the Hayato no Tsukasa, was established under the RITSURYŌ SYSTEM of administration to su-

pervise the Hayato in the service of the court.

Hazama Corporation   [株]間組

(Hazama-Gumi). Leading engineering and construction firm specializing in heavy civil-engineering projects, both in Japan and abroad. Hazama has also built many high-rise, "intelligent" commercial buildings. Active in international markets, it has overseas offices in 20 countries, including the United States, Australia, and the United Kingdom. Sales for the fiscal year ending March 1991 totaled ¥687.1 billion (US $5.0 billion); capitalization stood at ¥24.3 billion (US $177.1 million) in the same year. Headquarters are in Tōkyō.

haze →gobies

Hazuki →calendar, dates, and time

HDTV →high-definition television

headgear   被り物

(*kaburimono*). Traditional Japanese headgear can be classified into three categories: *kammuri* (literally, "crown"), *kasa*, and headcloths (TENUGUI and *zukin*). In 604 noblemen were ordered to wear *kammuri* as part of their ceremonial or court dress following the customs of Sui (589–618) China (see KAN'I JŪNIKAI). For less formal occasions and for those without rank, a plain *kammuri* such as a *keikan* or a *tokin* made of soft, thin, black silk was worn. *Kammuri* were gradually replaced by the *eboshi*, a soft or hard roundish hat of silk or gauze, later made of lacquered paper. During the Muromachi period (1333–1568), when the *chommage* hairstyle (see HAIRSTYLES) came into use, the popularity of the *eboshi* declined.

The *kasa* was a functional hat, woven of rush, sedge, straw, or bamboo, in a variety of shapes. *Sugegasa* (sedge *kasa*) were worn when working outdoors; women wore sedge *ichimegasa* for traveling. Of the variety of mesh-woven *kasa* called *amigasa*, the *ayaigasa* and the cone-shaped *kumagaigasa* were worn by warriors and the crescent-shaped *oriamigasa* by ordinary people. Wandering SHAKUHACHI-playing priests called *komusō* wore a large cylindrical *tengai* that concealed the entire head. During the Edo period (1600–1868), express messengers called HIKYAKU wore a dome-shaped *sandogasa*, a popular accoutrement for *samurai* in modern television series. Some *kasa* were lacquered, such as the metal *jingasa* worn in battle.

Traditional Japanese Headgear

kammuri   tate eboshi   kazaore eboshi   ichimegasa   tsunokakushi

jingasa   ayaigasa   okoso zukin   maruzukin   anesan kamuri

Lafcadio Hearn The writings and translations of Hearn, who became a Japanese citizen under the name Koizumi Yakumo, gave many Westerners their first glimpse of Japan.

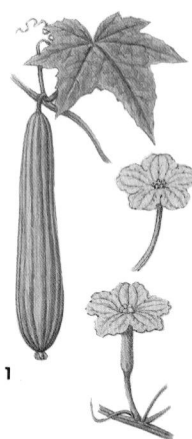

hechima
1 The fruit of the loofah (above left), edible when young, grows to a length of 30 to 60 cm. To its right, the male flower (above) and female flower.
2 Sponges are made from the loofah's mature fruit. It is first soaked in water, and the pericarp is allowed to rot. It is then washed and dried out.

Tenugui, long rectangular pieces of cotton gauze, are still made as towels and sometimes used for head coverings. In the Edo period there were many fashionable styles such as the *anesan kamuri* ("elder sister covering") or *hōkamuri* ("cheek covering"). *Tenugui* or any other long cloths may be rolled and tied as headbands called *hachimaki*.

The cloth *zukin* was most popular during the Edo period, when the many different types included the circular *maruzukin*, square *sumizukin*, or sleeve-shaped *sodezukin*. The most popular *zukin* worn by women during the Meiji (1868–1912) and Taishō (1912–26) periods was the *okoso zukin*, which covered the head except for the eyes and nose.

With the opening of Japan to Western commerce in the Meiji period, Western-style hats and caps became the accepted fashion. Traditional Japanese weddings, however, still require a *tsunokakushi* (literally, "horn covering") for the bride. An oblong white silk cloth lined with red silk, it covers the forehead and fastens at the back.

health food 健康食品

(*kenkō shokuhin*). A growing public consciousness of health issues in Japan during the 1980s was accompanied by a boom in sales of health foods. In 1986 the Japan Health Food Association, an organization created in 1985, established its own independent standards for health food. Compliance with these standards is designated by a seal affixed to the product at the time of purchase. The National Institute of Nutrition classified health foods under three categories: (1) nutritional supplements such as vitamins, protein, calcium, and wheat-, rice-, or corn-germ oil; (2) health-maintenance supplements such as ginseng and dietary fibers; (3) foods for adjusting nutritional balance such as low-sodium and diet foods. In addition, foods free of additives as well as unrefined foods such as whole wheat are also generally referred to as health foods. In 1984 the Ministry of Health and Welfare established a Health Food Policy Office to take responsibility for ensuring the safety of health foods.

Hearn, Lafcadio ハーン, L.

(1850–1904; Japanese name Koizumi Yakumo). Author, translator, and educator. With their exotic, romantic view of Japanese people, customs, and folklore, his books were widely read and influential in shaping Western views on Japan from the late 19th century.

Hearn was born on the Greek island of Lefkas, son of an Anglo-Irish surgeon major in the British army and a Greek mother. He was brought up by a great-aunt in Dublin, later moving to Cincinnati, Ohio, where he became a newspaper reporter.

In 1889 he decided to go to Japan and upon his arrival in Tōkyō in 1890 was befriended by Basil Hall CHAMBERLAIN. While working at a government college, Hearn completed his book *Glimpses of an Unfamiliar Japan* (1894). Hearn, who married the daughter of a *samurai*, also became a Japanese citizen, taking the name Koizumi Yakumo. In 1894 he accepted a position with the English-language *Kobe Chronicle*, but soon Chamberlain arranged for him to teach English literature at Tōkyō University, a post Hearn held until 1903.

Hearn's most famous work is a collection

of lectures entitled *Japan: An Attempt at Interpretation* (1904). His other books on Japan include *Exotics and Retrospective* (1898), *In Ghostly Japan* (1899), *Shadowings* (1900), *A Japanese Miscellany* (1901), and *Kwaidan* (1904).

Heart Institute of Japan
日本心臓血圧研究所

(Nihon Shinzō Ketsuatsu Kenkyūjo). Institute devoted to research into the cardiovascular system. Founded in 1955 in Shinjuku Ward, Tōkyō, as an adjunct of the Tōkyō Women's Medical College. The institute conducts basic research in the fields of electrobiology, blood circulation properties, molecular biology, immunology, and micromorphology. The institute's clinical research is based on cases in its affiliated hospital, focusing particularly on cardiovascular problems such as ischemic heart disease (IHD), arrhythmia, and congenital heart disease.

Heart Mountain Relocation Center ハートマウンテン収容所

(Hāto Maunten Shūyōjo). Wartime relocation facility for Japanese Americans from California and Washington State; located near Cody, Park County, Wyoming. In operation from 12 August 1942 until 10 November 1945, it held a maximum of 10,767 persons at any one time; a total of 14,025 persons were confined there. It was the focal point of draft resistance in the camps. See also JAPANESE AMERICANS, WARTIME RELOCATION OF; WAR RELOCATION AUTHORITY.

Heart Sutra 般若心経

(*Hannya shingyō*; Skt: *Prajñāpāramitā-hṛdaya-sūtra*). Extremely brief distillation of the essence of the *Prajñāpāramitā* (Perfection of Wisdom) sutras, a body of scriptures written during the early developmental stages of Mahāyāna (Greater Vehicle) Buddhism that expounds the doctrine of EMPTINESS (J: *kū*; Skt: *śūnyatā*). The oldest extant text, written in Sanskrit on *tāla* leaves, was brought into Japan in AD 609 and is kept in the temple HŌRYŪJI. The translation of this sutra into classical Chinese by the Chinese Buddhist priest Xuanzang (Hsüan-tsang [602–664]; J: Genjō) is the version most commonly used by Buddhist temples. Daily recitation of the Heart Sutra is common to many Buddhist sects, and numerous Buddhist priests including KŪKAI have written commentaries on it. It is also the sutra most frequently used for SHAKYŌ, the practice of copying sutras. As such, the Heart Sutra remains one of the most popular Buddhist scriptures in Japan.

heaven 天

(*ten*). In Japanese mythology, as recorded in the KOJIKI (712), heaven, or the High Celestial Plain (TAKAMAGAHARA), is depicted as the abode of the deities. The sun goddess, AMATERASU ŌMIKAMI, was given the highest place in the Shintō pantheon and is described as the progenitor of the imperial line in the mythology. In Mahāyāna BUDDHISM, heaven is conceived of as the future dwelling place of the virtuous. In the popular mind it was understood to mean the Pure Land (Jōdo) or Paradise (Gokuraku) to which one went through the saving power of the Buddha. The Chinese concept of heaven (*tian* or *t'ien*) as the ultimate principle of the moral and physical universe was accepted by Confucianists but never gained wide acceptance in Japan. The Christian heaven is translated as *ten* or *tengoku*.

Hebei-Qahar (Hopeh-Chahar) Political Council → Ji-Cha (Chi-Ch'a)
Autonomous Political Council

hechima 糸瓜

(loofah). *Luffa aegyptiaca*. An annual vine of the family Cucurbitaceae native to tropical Asia and commonly cultivated in Japan as a summer shade plant. The plant grows climbing and coiling its tendrils around other objects, and its vine reaches a height of 5–6 meters (16.4–19.7 ft). The alternate, palmately lobed leaves are 30 centimeters (11.8 in) long. From summer to autumn the plant bears a five-lobed yellow corolla of unisexual flowers. The ellipsoid fruits are 30–60 centimeters (11.8–23.6 in) long and are fleshy and edible when young. The mature fruit can be used as a sponge after the fleshy pericarp has been removed. The liquid that flows out when the *hechima* vine is cut is used as a cosmetic lotion and as a folk remedy for coughs.

Heco, Joseph → Hamada Hikozō

Hegurajima 舳倉島

Also known as Hekurajima. Volcanic island in the Sea of Japan, 47 km (29 mi) north of the Noto Peninsula, Ishikawa Prefecture, central Honshū; part of Ishikawa Prefecture. It is composed of andesite and lava. Women divers from the mainland city of Wajima travel to the island in the summer and dive for abalone and *sazae* (turban shell; *Turbo cornutus*) in the nearby reefs. Area: 1.2 sq km (0.5 sq mi).

Heiankyō 平安京

(literally, "Capital of Peace and Tranquillity"). Original name of KYŌTO; capital of Japan from 794 to 1868, when Tōkyō was made the capital. Heiankyō was situated between the rivers Kamogawa and Katsuragawa in the Kadono District of Yamashiro Province (now Kyōto Prefecture). The word *kyōto* (capital, or site of the imperial palace) had been used earlier as an informal name for the capital at Nara (HEIJŌKYŌ), and it was also applied to Heiankyō. By the late 11th century, Kyōto had for practical purposes become the name of the city.

In 784 Emperor KAMMU moved the seat of government from Nara to NAGAOKAKYŌ to eliminate the excessive political power of the Nara Buddhist sects (see DŌKYŌ) and to bring new vigor to the RITSURYŌ SYSTEM of government. However, the assassination in 785 of Fujiwara no Tanetsugu, the leading advocate of the transfer, and the subsequent banishment and death of Kammu's brother Crown Prince Sawara (d 785) were followed by a series of natural disasters that were attributed to Sawara's angry spirit, and construction of the capital halted. In 793, on the advice of WAKE NO KIYOMARO, the emperor ordered Fujiwara no Oguromaro (733–794) to build a new capital in the village of Uda (now Ukyō Ward, Kyōto).

City Plan——Heiankyō was patterned after Chang'an (Ch'ang-an), the capital of Tang (T'ang) China. The course of the Kamogawa was shifted to flow around the city and canals were dug parallel to the major north-south avenues. The new capital measured approximately 4.5 kilometers (2.8 mi) east to west and 5.2 kilometers (3.2 mi) north to south. With the exception of the state-sponsored TŌJI and Saiji, constructed near the gate Rajōmon, no temples were to be allowed within Heiankyō. The residence of the emperor and imperial government offices were located in an area called the *daidairi* (outer palace grounds) in the northernmost part of the city. Also located there was the hall called the DAIGOKUDEN, from which, initially, the emperor governed the country. The palace of the emperor stood at the right center of the *daidairi* within the *dairi* (inner palace grounds). Directly south of the *daidairi* was a large park, Shinsen'en.

Heiankyō was divided by the broad avenue Suzaku Ōji (84 m or 276 ft wide) into two districts, Sakyō to the east and Ukyō to the west. In each of these districts was an office called Kyōshiki; these together administered the affairs of the capital. The two main districts were subdivided into large square sectors called *bō* by streets running east to west and avenues running north to south. The east-to-west rows of *bō* sectors were called *jō* and were numbered north to south. The east-to-west cross streets were named after them, e.g., Ichijō Ōji (First Jō Street) and so on. The district south of the fourth cross street, Shijō Ōji, was the center of industry and commerce. The Ukyō quarter was a damp lowland, and the city developed toward the east, straddling the Kamogawa, with its population center near the west bank of the river. During the INSEI period of rule by retired emperors (late 11th to mid-12th centuries), Shirakawa, a suburb of the capital east of the Kamogawa, flourished as the locus of political authority.

Destroyed, Then Rebuilt—In the Kamakura period (1185–1333) Heiankyō changed from a political to an economic center. Under the Muromachi shogunate (1338–1573) the city again became the seat of power, but during the ŌNIN WAR (1467–77) more than half of it was destroyed. However, the city and the imperial palace were gradually rebuilt by ODA NOBUNAGA and TOYOTOMI HIDEYOSHI in the 16th century. The palace was moved to its present site in the north central section of modern Kyōto in the 18th century, but the present buildings, now known as the Kyōto Imperial Palace, date from the 19th century.

Heian literature   平安時代の文学

(Heian *jidai no bungaku*). The literature of the Heian period (794–1185) may be divided into three parts: the first characterized by an intense interest in the composition of works in Chinese and a renascence of WAKA (classical Japanese poetry) after a few decades of neglect, the second notable for the emergence of prose literature in Japanese, and the third marked by the appearance of new prose genres and the continued evolution of Japanese poetic styles.

Works in Chinese and the Revival of Waka (794–905)—Whereas the pre-Heian anthology MAN'YŌSHŪ (mid-8th century) commemorated the first flowering of poetry in Japanese, the three anthologies that appeared in the first decades of the 9th century show how little prestige the native *waka* then enjoyed at the imperial courts, for these are devoted to Chinese verse. Early Heian *kanshi* (Chinese poetry; see POETRY AND PROSE IN CHINESE) was diligently imitative, not of contemporary Tang (T'ang) dynasty (618–907) works but of poems from the earlier Six Dynasties (222–589), which were known in Japan through anthologies that documented the era's later decadent phase. Chinese taste delighted in artifice, a delight that was later scorned as excessive but that the Japanese of the early Heian period deemed the height of literary style. This style avoided direct statement in favor of oblique formulations laden with ornate metaphor, "elegant confusion" (pre-

tended inability to discern differences between similar phenomena), and antithetical parallelism.

Prose works like NIHON RYŌIKI were also written in Chinese. A collection of over 100 anecdotes put together by the Buddhist monk Kyōkai around 822, this was the earliest example of a genre known as SETSUWA BUNGAKU. The *Nihon ryōiki* drew on Chinese tales used to illustrate the sermons of Buddhist preachers and show, through supposedly true examples, how good deeds are infallibly rewarded and evil punished in this and lives to come.

The rage for writing in Chinese waned when the emperors lost their struggle with the powerful FUJIWARA FAMILY. Ironically, this was when the greatest Heian *kanshi* poet, SUGAWARA NO MICHIZANE (845–903), lived. A brilliant student and teacher, Michizane rose to become minister of the right under Emperor DAIGO (r 897–930), an almost unprecedented accomplishment for a scholar. His writings reveal him as a compassionate, humanistic scholar-poet in the best Chinese tradition, one whose *kanshi* effectively echo the plain, direct, and quiet voice of the great Tang poet Bo Juyi (Po Chu'i; 772–846). Writing on such topics as his grief for a lost son, or his reaction to disgrace, Michizane revealed more of his own personality and feelings in his Chinese poetry than most poets writing in their native tongue.

Even when *kanshi* was most prized as a public art, native poetry did not vanish. Amorous repartee was highly developed long before the Heian period began, and since few women, even in court society, learned to write in Chinese, wooing continued to be done through *waka*, especially the 31-syllable *tanka* (short poem). But as the earliest Heian *waka* poets were also producing *kanshi*, their native poetry reflected stylistic influences from the Six Dynasties. Obliquity, ornate metaphor and hyperbole, elegant confusion, questioning of logic and sense experience, pretended paradoxes, archness, and plays on double meanings—all these characterized poetry collected in the first imperial *waka* anthology, the KOKINSHŪ (ca 905). The "*Kokinshū* style" marks a significant departure from the more direct declarations and archaic simplicity of viewpoint of ancient *Man'yōshū* poems. Retained were certain themes, such as a love tradition of passionate avowal, sometimes declarative and sometimes metaphorical, and a nature tradition that emphasized the beauties of the different seasons. To these, the "*Kokinshū* style" added elements of intellectual play, indirectness, and a courtly distancing from common life.

Two of the greatest of the early poets whose work later figured prominently in the *Kokinshū* are ONO NO KOMACHI (fl mid-9th century) and ARIWARA NO NARIHIRA (825–880). Legends grew up about the mysterious Komachi, emphasizing her reputed beauty, cruelty in love, and her miserable old age. Komachi's small body of about 100 poems are passionately forthright as well as rich in wordplay and highly inflected verbs, expressing fine gradations of feeling and perception. Often employing the theme of meeting in dreams a lover impossible to find in life, her poetry possesses a dark intensity and melancholy beauty. Narihira, son of an imperial prince demoted to nonroyal status, became the beau ideal of the gallant lover. His poetry shows wit, a characteristic of much Heian verse, and an intense questioning of what is real and what is not, a style of "passionate confusion" that is a deeper

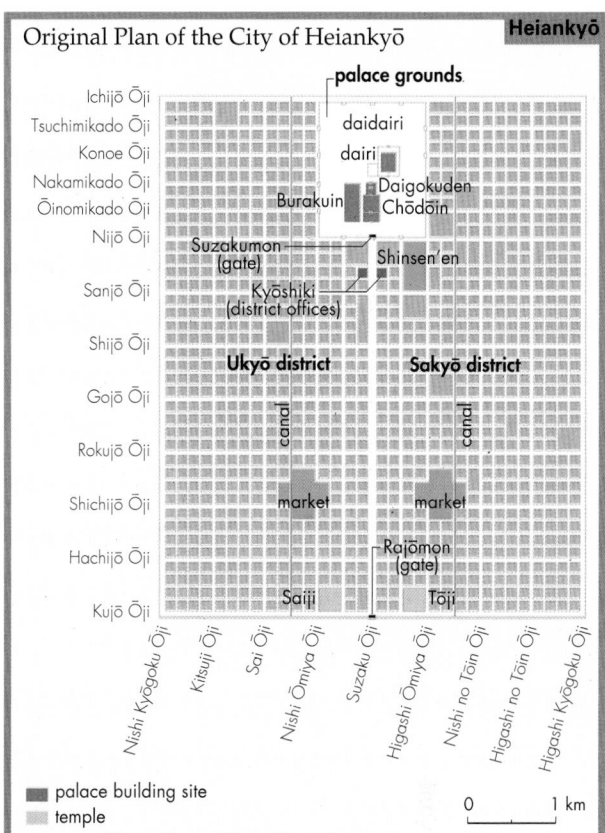

Original Plan of the City of Heiankyō **Heiankyō**

palace grounds

Ichijō Ōji
Tsuchimikado Ōji
Konoe Ōji
Nakamikado Ōji
Ōinomikado Ōji
Nijō Ōji
Sanjō Ōji
Shijō Ōji
Gojō Ōji
Rokujō Ōji
Shichijō Ōji
Hachijō Ōji
Kujō Ōji

daidairi
dairi
Burakuin
Daigokuden
Chōdōin
Suzakumon (gate)
Shinsen'en
Kyōshiki (district offices)
Ukyō district   **Sakyō district**
canal   canal
market   market
Rajōmon (gate)
Saiji   Tōji

Nishi Kyōgoku Ōji
Kitsuji Ōji
Sai Ōji
Nishi Ōmiya Ōji
Suzaku Ōji
Higashi Ōmiya Ōji
Nishi no Tōin Ōji
Higashi no Tōin Ōji
Higashi Kyōgoku Ōji

■ palace building site   0   1 km
■ temple

version of the "elegant confusion" that mistakes plum blossoms for snow.

The revived interest in *waka*, which culminated in the compilation of the *Kokinshū*, is also evident in the advent of the UTA-AWASE, or poetry match, in which poets, divided into two rival teams, gathered with their supporters and a judge to match poems and decide which was superior. Many of the early *uta-awase* combined matching poems with matching flowers, roots, shells, perfumes, fans, and other things. Such matching games were among the chief amusements of the Heian court.

The *Kokinshū*, the first of what became a string of 21 IMPERIAL ANTHOLOGIES of poetry stretching into the 15th century, was put together by four compilers in 20 volumes containing 1,111 poems and prose prefaces in both Chinese and Japanese. The 20-volume format, standard in later anthologies, grouped seasonal poems at the beginning of the series, love poems in the second half, and allocated to separate volumes poems on parting or grief or miscellaneous topics. Within their categories, poems were arranged in patterns of association and progression to give the order of a season, or of a love affair. The Japanese "Kana Preface" is the first extended piece of pure Japanese prose, a sign that the native tongue had come of literary age. By advocating a classical balance of form (*kotoba*; literally, "words") and content (*kokoro*; literally, "heart"), the "Kana Preface"—and the anthology as a whole—set a standard of limited, courtly diction that had a profoundly conservative effect on Japan's poetic tradition.

The Birth of Prose Literature (905–1020)—KI NO TSURAYUKI (872?–945), who as chief compiler of the *Kokinshū* and author of its "Kana Preface" was influential in shaping the literary taste of generations, also instituted what became a staple of expression, the literary diary. His TOSA NIKKI (tr *The Tosa Diary*, 1981), written in 935, marks the beginning of Japanese prose literature. Like his Japanese preface to the *Kokinshū*, the *Tosa nikki* is written in the phonetic script, *kana*, used mostly by women. Eschewing the *kambun* (Chinese prose) of an educated man was such a new idea that Tsurayuki created a fictive female narrator to write about a journey he made from Shikoku to the capital. Extant diaries in *kambun* are hardly literary works, unlike the *Tosa nikki*, which is a "poetic diary" interspersed with *waka* composed as expressions of emotions aroused by events of the journey.

Tsurayuki's work was experimental, however, and had no immediate followers. The next literary diary, KAGERŌ NIKKI (tr *The Gossamer Years*, 1964), appeared in the second half of the 10th century. Covering 21 years in the life and rueful marriage of a Fujiwara noblewoman (FUJIWARA NO MICHITSUNA NO HAHA), *Kagerō nikki* is important for its psychological and social realism. It also initiated a succession of glorious prose works by highborn, educated women.

The earliest extant fictional narrative in Japanese appeared toward the mid-10th century. TAKETORI MONOGATARI (tr *The Tale of the Bamboo Cutter*, 1956) is the story of Kaguyahime, a magical infant found by an old bamboo cutter, and of how she grew up to set tasks for her five ultimately unsuccessful suitors. The story draws on generic fairy tale motifs, such as magic birth, tasks for suitors, and origin myths.

Another new genre was the *uta monogatari* (poem tale; see MONOGATARI BUNGAKU) in which prose and *waka* were combined in a fictional narrative. The most admired of these works, ISE MONOGATARI (tr *The Tales of Ise*, 1972), included 125 brief stories, each centered on one or more poems and usually describing a love that ends badly. It was always believed that the hero was Ariwara no Narihira and indeed the work contains all 30 of the poems attributed to Narihira in the *Kokinshū*. Its unknown author apparently drew on various sources—one of which may have been an early collection of Narihira's poems—for verses, which he made the subject of explanatory anecdotes. In so doing, he preserved the legend of the poet-lover Narihira and helped foster the ideal of Heian courtly love, with its belief in the primacy of romantic sensibilities. Another poet-lover, Taira no Sadabumi (d 923), as notorious for his failures as Narihira was for conquests, is featured in HEICHŪ MONOGATARI. Though its stories are more highly developed, with extended prose passages not tied to poems, and its use of irony sophisticated, *Heichū monogatari* does not achieve the poetic quality of *Ise.*

The second half of the 10th century is also notable as the probable time of composition of the first attempts at a Heian novel. Of the larger number of long *monogatari* that circulated at the time, two survive. They are entitled UTSUBO MONOGATARI (The Tale of the Hollow Tree) and OCHIKUBO MONOGATARI (tr *Ochikubo Monogatari, or The Tale of Lady Ochikubo*, 1970). The story of *Utsubo monogatari* falls into four parts, beginning with an opening chapter of fantastic happenings that introduces the theme of magic music. The second section describes the wooing of Atemiya, a beautiful young girl who finally rejects all her suitors and marries the crown prince, the third is a realistic description of a power struggle between factions at court, and in the final section the

losing side recoups its glory. An attempt at a thematic novel, the work suffers from extreme unevenness and a jerky story line. *Ochikubo monogatari*, a Cinderella story of an abused stepdaughter and her devoted Prince Charming, is more down-to-earth and much better organized.

Heian literature entered its heyday in the 990s, when FUJIWARA NO MICHINAGA (966–1028) began his long dominance of the court, and consorts to the boy emperor ICHIJŌ (r 986–1011) set up rival coteries of talented ladies-in-waiting. One of these ladies, SEI SHŌNAGON, wrote MAKURA NO SŌSHI (tr *The Pillow Book of Sei Shōnagon*, 1967), a ZUIHITSU, or collection of random jottings, fictional and nonfictional. Very much an individual, Sei Shōnagon was all sharp angles and sharper opinions; she was also a writer who could render a scene with deftness and economy.

Another court lady of the period, IZUMI SHIKIBU, was as famous for her ardor as Sei Shōnagon was for her wit. Her more than 1,500 *waka* continue the tradition of the passionate poetess, showing her to have brash and witty moods offset by moments of intense passion, languor, and a desire for the peace of Buddhist renunciation. She is also the subject of the work *Izumi Shikibu nikki* (tr *The Diary of Izumi Shikibu*, 1969). This is a third-person account, which she may or may not have written, of the beginning of her love affair with Prince Atsumichi (981–1007). The work presents a considerably more melancholy picture of Izumi Shikibu than is to be derived from her collected poems.

Early in the 11th century MURASAKI SHIKIBU, a woman in service to the second of Emperor Ichijō's principal consorts, produced *Genji monogatari* (the TALE OF GENJI), immortalizing Heian society in the greatest of the courtly novels. Murasaki's diary reveals that parts of the novel's manuscript circulated at court; it also shows its author to have been a defensive and unpopular introvert. For her hero, she created the dashing, amorous Genji, a very attractive figure who brings pain and disaster to some of the many women he loves. Lover, man of taste and accomplishments, intensely alive and generous, Genji is also lecherous, hypocritical, and a master of self-deceit. Nothing in the Japanese literary tradition (including the few *monogatari* that survive from the previous century) prepares us for the sudden emergence of a psychological novel with such thematic resonance. At the end, Genji is long dead, the world is in decline, the main characters are shallow or neurotic, and love—the search for which is the novel's grand theme—is seen as an illusory dream.

Later Growth of Prose and Poetry (1020–1185)—That the *Genji* was popular—and influential—is evident in later writings, such as SARASHINA NIKKI (tr *As I Crossed a Bridge of Dreams*, 1971), an autobiographical work by SUGAWARA NO TAKASUE NO MUSUME (b 1008). She is credited with having written four novels, of which two have partly survived. The first of these, YORU NO NEZAME (Nights of Fitful Waking) is a highly introspective account of frustrated love derivative of *Genji monogatari;* but whereas in the latter work fate emerges from character, in *Nezame* it comes from heavenly preordination. The second work, HAMAMATSU CHŪNAGON MONOGATARI (Tale of the Hamamatsu Middle Counselor), set in China with a plot that embraces an unbelievably tangled web of liaisons, births, and rebirths

across generations (the hero ends up becoming stepfather to his own reincarnate father), veers into fantasy. Another work, SAGOROMO MONOGATARI (Tale of Sagoromo), from the court of Princess Baishi (1039–96), includes motifs and events modeled on the *Genji*, such as the passing off of a child born illegitimately to an imperial consort as the emperor's son.

Techniques and conventions of the novel were well developed by the 11th century, when they were turned to the narration of history. EIGA MONOGATARI (tr *A Tale of Flowering Fortunes*, 1980), covering events from 887 to 1092 in two sections by different unknown authors, displays an eye for colorful detail and an interest in anecdote not found in earlier national histories. Its theme is the glory of the Fujiwara family as epitomized in Fujiwara no Michinaga, the protagonist of a work that treats history as if it were an episodic novel. It was soon imitated by other historical narratives using a lively storytelling style, including the ŌKAGAMI (late 11th century?), a critical history that examined Fujiwara fortunes with a view to why things happened as they did and that inspired a new series of works, *kagami-mono* (mirror pieces), which continued past the Heian period.

In the early 12th century, there appeared the dominant work in the above-mentioned genre of *setsuwa bungaku*, a major collection of more than 1,000 tales known as KONJAKU MONOGATARI (partial tr *Tales of Times Now Past*, 1979). In *Konjaku monogatari* appears a style of prose that was heavily influenced by the Chinese in which the first *setsuwa* were written and which marked a new direction in the evolution of Japanese prose. The purity of the old native tongue was ultimately preserved only in *waka;* the harsher, more masculine quality of *Konjaku monogatari*, with its heavy seasoning of Chinese loanwords and grammatical borrowings, led the way to modern Japanese. The style of *Konjaku monogatari* also differs from courtly writings in being determinedly explanatory, paradoxically at once terse and prolix, but never vague and misty. Writing in Chinese continued as well, but, as official contacts between the two countries had ended two centuries earlier, the *kambun* (Chinese prose) diaries of court officials show some lapses in language.

It was in poetry, however, that the last years of the Heian era saw the greatest changes. Formal poetry contests, which peaked in the mid-11th century, had been a conservative force, poems being subject to criticism for violating technical rules of diction and decorum. Experimental poems were composed outside such contests, rarely being admitted into imperial anthologies but occasionally earning the admiration of later generations, as with the earthy imagery of SONE NO YOSHITADA (fl ca 985). But in the 12th century there were new trends, new talents, and a strongly revived interest in *waka*, beginning with *Horikawa hyakushu* (ca 1105). At the order of Emperor Horikawa (r 1087–1107), some 15 or 16 poets took part in composing 100-poem sequences on individual, precisely defined topics often arranged in the manner of an imperial anthology. The Horikawa sequences led to fairly bold experimentation with colloquial and archaic diction.

The last half of the 12th century saw cataclysmic political changes that ultimately affected Japanese literature profoundly. Although autobiographical works by court

ladies continued to be written into the 13th century, as the feudal Kamakura period (1185–1333) replaced the Heian, they eventually died out with the decline of the court. One poet whose life points toward the new age was the Buddhist monk SAIGYŌ (1118–90), who spent most of his life either in retreat or on pilgrimage. To later ages, he became the image of the wandering poet, free of all earthly ties and seeking only the truth.

A more conventional figure was FUJIWARA NO TOSHINARI (1114–1204), better known as Fujiwara no Shunzei. Dedicating his life to the renascence of *waka*, he sought a middle ground between the conservatives and innovators with the formula "old words, new heart," that is, a fidelity to classical diction combined with freshness of conception. In a departure from custom, Shunzei introduced positive criteria into judging at poetry contests, instead of confining himself to finding disqualifying faults. He also compiled the seventh imperial anthology, SENZAI WAKASHŪ (ca 1187), which included a large number of poems from the innovative MINAMOTO NO TOSHIYORI (1055?–1129), who had contributed to *Horikawa hyakushu*, as well as poems, listed as "anonymous," from members of the rebel Taira clan. In his own poetry, Shunzei valued YŪGEN, a deep and suggestive allusiveness, often somber, that came to be a major aesthetic ideal of succeeding generations.

Ironically, the Heian era ended before the finest testament to its poetic sensibility was produced. The SHIN KOKINSHŪ, one of the canons in the *waka* tradition, was compiled in the early 13th century, making it technically a work of MEDIEVAL LITERATURE.

Heian period 平安時代

(794–1185; Heian *jidai*). As defined in this encyclopedia, the Heian period is a span of nearly 400 years extending from 794, when Emperor KAMMU established HEIANKYŌ (now Kyōto) as the imperial capital of Japan, to 1185, when MINAMOTO NO YORITOMO's forces defeated those of the TAIRA FAMILY, thus setting the stage for the establishment of the KAMAKURA SHOGUNATE. The name of the period is taken from that of the capital and

means "peace and tranquility." Some classifications begin the period in 781, the year of Kammu's accession to the throne, or in 784, when the capital was removed from HEIJŌKYŌ (now Nara) to NAGAOKAKYŌ; some end it in 1180, when Yoritomo took up arms and established his headquarters at Kamakura, or in 1183, when the Taira family fled Heiankyō before the advancing army of MINAMOTO NO YOSHINAKA.

Heian has long been an established division of history, regarded as the apogee of the nation's aristocratic age, which produced one of the world's most exquisitely refined cultures. During Heian times, Japan fully assimilated the elements of Chinese society that the architects of the Japanese state had long emulated. While the Chinese ideals never died out completely, in economics, government, and cultural style, the Japanese created indigenous institutions that bore only a slight resemblance to Chinese prototypes.

From Nara to Nagaoka to Kyōto—In 784 Emperor Kammu moved the capital from Heijōkyō (now Nara) northwest to Nagaokakyō, and only a decade later he moved it to Heiankyō. Political rivalries at court lay behind these removals. One major consideration was to escape the baneful influence of a Buddhist clergy that had come to exercise considerable influence in secular affairs, especially under the leadership of the priest Dōkyō during the reign of Empress Shōtoku (r 764–770; see KŌKEN, EMPRESS).

There were other political problems. The FUJIWARA FAMILY, then headed by Momokawa (732–779), was responsible for the exile of Dōkyō after Shōtoku's death and for the enthronement of Emperor Kōnin (r 770–781) and then arranged for Kammu to succeed by eliminating Crown Prince Osabe. For the imperial house this represented a shift from the line of Emperor TEMMU, which remained powerful around Nara, to that of TENJI, which was dominant in Yamashiro, location of both Nagaokakyō and Heiankyō. Thus several factors—desire to escape Buddhist influence, desire to move into the area of Tenji-line strength, and fear of the spirits of the deceased Prince Osabe and his mother—motivated Kammu to move from Nara.

Momokawa's nephew Fujiwara no Tanetsugu (737–785) was placed in charge of construction at Nagaokakyō, to which Kammu moved long before the city itself was completed. Tanetsugu supported Kammu's eldest son, Prince Ate, to succeed his father but was opposed by Crown Prince Sawara. One night Tanetsugu was set upon and assassinated, and Sawara, among others, was implicated; exiled to Awaji, he died within a few weeks but always has been considered innocent. Sawara's figure seemed to haunt the court, and Kammu, fearful that several untoward events (including the deaths of his mother and empress) were the result of Sawara's vengeful spirit, ordered the construction of, and removal to, Heiankyō.

Heian Institutions—Heian political, social, and economic institutions were shaped by the RITSURYŌ SYSTEM, based on the penal (*ritsu*) and administrative (*ryō*) codes of Tang (T'ang) China (618–907). Ever since the time of Prince SHŌTOKU in the early 7th century, imperial house members and their close associates had sought to invoke august Chinese symbols of authority and power to assert their hegemony over society. By the early Nara period (710–794) they had succeeded in creating a reasonable approximation of the Chinese model, complete with a detailed administrative and penal code and an impressive capital that demonstrated the transcendent magnificence of the emperor.

Although it functioned imperfectly from the outset, the *ritsuryō* system remained the fountainhead of Japanese political and economic ideas, even during the Heian period, when considerable movement away from the system occurred. Especially entrenched was the concept of a "public" system of peasantry and land in the sense that they belonged to the emperor, as opposed to a system in which land and people were controlled by "private" interests. The latter had been the case under the earlier UJI (powerful kin groups) society, and private interests reasserted control over the course of the Heian period to replace the *ritsuryō* system.

A Glimpse into Heian Court Life

Between the 10th and mid-11th centuries, a highly cultivated circle of ladies-in-waiting created the diaries, narratives of courtly romance, and observations of daily life that constitute the most enduring legacy of Heian culture. Most prominent among these ladies were the empress and the other consorts whose residences were clustered behind that of the emperor. Dwelling within these confines they created an enclosed, self-referential universe of nuance and allusion as they passed their days exchanging poems on the seasons, playing music, and engaging in games or witty conversation.

The Heian imagination found shadows and silhouettes more alluring and suggestive than well-lit, clearly-seen figures. The architecture of the time conspired to sustain this mystique. Broad, low-slung eaves isolated vast horizontal interiors broken up by the folding screens, rattan blinds, and trailing curtains used by court ladies to accentuate their charming elusiveness. In the sunless hush, scents and whispers, barely glimpsed expressions, and the rustle of silk garments took on deep meanings. The Japanese preference for what is only faintly revealed, sometimes called the aesthetic of indirection, is displayed in Heian masterpieces like Sei Shōnagon's *Makura no sōshi* (The Pillow Book) and Murasaki Shikibu's *Tale of Genji*, as well as the latter's diary.

Heian court ladies and their attendants in a scene from the *Genji monogatari emaki* (*Tale of Genji* Scrolls). A story is read aloud as one lady has her hair brushed. 12th century.

Heian reverence for protocol meant that every detail of rituals like this imperial visit was documented in the *Nenchū gyōji emaki* (Scrolls of Annual Rites and Ceremonies) for subsequent imitation. 17th-century copy of a 12th-century work.

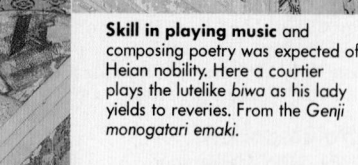

Skill in playing music and composing poetry was expected of Heian nobility. Here a courtier plays the lutelike *biwa* as his lady yields to reveries. From the *Genji monogatari emaki*.

Servants ready boats aboard which musicians and dancers are to perform for the entertainment of the emperor. From the *Murasaki Shikibu nikki emaki* (Diary of Lady Murasaki Scroll). 13th century.

Lurking in the shadows behind curtains, blinds, and screens, elusive Heian ladies kept their faces out of view. At right, a would-be lover steals a glimpse. From the *Genji monogatari emaki*.

Politics and Government——The political history of Heian Japan can be divided in several ways, most simply by postulating early and late Heian periods, divided near the mid-10th century. The early period represents various attempts to reinvigorate the *ritsuryō* system, with its emperor-dominated polity and nationally controlled rice fields. In the late Heian period, systemic contradictions allowed Fujiwara regents (and then retired sovereigns) to dominate the political system and *shōen* (private landed estates) to become the principal form of landholding.

A more precise division of the period requires a four-phase scheme. In the first phase, which ended in the early 9th century, Kammu attempted to reinvigorate the *ritsuryō* system through various governmental reforms and military campaigns. His work was carried on by Emperor SAGA, who created certain extrastatutory offices outside the *ritsuryō* system to enhance government efficiency. These offices, however, created new avenues to power for nonimperial royal families, most important among them the Fujiwara, who had been a leading family in Nara times. Through skillful political maneuvering in several plots at court, the Fujiwara eliminated a number of rival families and drew close to the imperial house as regents (SESSHŌ or KAMPAKU).

In the second phase, from the late 9th century until 967, the imperial house managed to preserve power and authority in the face of the rise of the Fujiwara under Emperors UDA, DAIGO, and MURAKAMI, all of whom ruled without Fujiwara "assistance." But the court faced both political and fiscal problems at this juncture. Daigo tried to solve the matter by regulating *shōen* and reforming provincial government and tax collection. But his efforts were in vain as court control of land and people continued to weaken due to the collaboration of local landholders with central nobles and religious institutions to create *shōen.*

The third phase is dated from 967, when Fujiwara no Saneyori (900–970) became regent after a hiatus of 20 years. With the exile of his rival Minamoto no Takaakira in 969, Saneyori was supreme. The next century was the period of Fujiwara regency politics (*sekkan seiji*), when the northern branch of the Fujiwara family established a permanent regency. Emperors were born of Fujiwara mothers and dominated by uncles, fathers-in-law, or grandfathers, in whose households they usually were raised. The two greatest Fujiwara regents were FUJIWARA NO MICHINAGA, father of four daughters married to emperors and grandfather of three emperors, and his son FUJIWARA NO YORIMICHI, who held the post of regent for 52 years.

The fourth phase of the Heian period is recognized as commencing when Go-Sanjō, the first emperor in a century who had not been born of a Fujiwara mother, came to the throne in 1068. It is called the phase of INSEI, or rule by "cloistered emperor," so named because three successive retired emperors—SHIRAKAWA, TOBA, and GO-SHIRAKAWA—replaced emperors and also regents as the supreme political figures at Heiankyō, fully utilizing and expanding upon a private base of power for the imperial house created by Go-Sanjō.

This was a period of imperial revival, as the imperial house, no longer simply the repository of sovereignty as it had been under Fujiwara domination, regained control over the imperial position, reorganized itself into a strong private house with aristocratic and military clients, and competed with the Fujiwara and others for *shōen* acquisition.

The *ritsuryō* system virtually disappeared during this phase, however, as cliques of local powerful individuals threatened state control over lands, Buddhist institutions quarreled with each other and with the court, and public law and order broke down. The rising military class became increasingly necessary to maintain civil government even in Heiankyō, as demonstrated by the HŌGEN DISTURBANCE (1156) and the HEIJI DISTURBANCE (1160). One warrior-courtier, TAIRA NO KIYOMORI, rose so high in court rank that some scholars postulate the existence of yet a fifth phase of the Heian period, one of Taira warrior domination, from 1160 to 1185.

Landholding System——Facing a shaky hegemony over other *uji* at the Yamato court in the mid-7th century, the Yamato *uji*, or imperial family, centralized the government, establishing the *ritsuryō* system. At the core of the system was the idea of imperial control over both land and people, replacing earlier control by individual *uji*. The imperial house lacked the power to force others to accept the new arrangements and achieved acquiescence only by appointing other *uji* members to bureaucratic posts that allowed them to maintain their economic interests under the new system.

Under the *ritsuryō* system the government asserted the right to control and tax the land, which was allotted to free and slave cultivators, both male and female. Lands, which could be held throughout the recipient's lifetime, were pooled by household units for cultivation purposes. A complex system of land allotment required a census every six years to reallocate lands according to population increase or decrease in households. The state levied three kinds of taxes on cultivators: a rice tax (*so*), a tax in kind (*chō*), and corvée (YŌEKI), the heaviest burden of all, which was levied on males aged 17 to 65. Military duty also was required.

From the outset the system worked only imperfectly, largely due to compromises needed to maintain the support of great *uji*. The nobility and large temples had the capital to open new lands, and they were able to entice cultivators of allotment fields unable to sustain themselves on their own lands. The government, faced with the problem of increasing population demands without a concomitant increase in productive lands, could do little to stop this process. Although it announced a project in 722 to open new lands, little cooperation was forthcoming until a law the next year offered proprietary control for periods of one or three generations to those opening new fields (see SANZE ISSHIN NO HŌ). By 743 the government had to grant permanent ownership to anyone reclaiming new rice fields (see KONDEN EISEI SHIZAI HŌ).

These actions paved the way for extensive private land ownership by temples and nobles, a movement counter to the spirit of the *ritsuryō* system but supported by government officials who found it profitable. Several attempts to halt this development in the late Nara and early Heian periods failed, and reallotment was accomplished only twice in the 9th century, during which time noble lands, acquired through reclamation, purchase, occupation of abandoned fields, or placing them into vassalage, expanded. Many of these were in the form of *shōen*, and in 902 an edict was promulgated to stop their growth, but it succeeded only in curtailing lands of the imperial house.

Onerous *ritsuryō* levies forced peasants to abscond, to falsify census records, or to collude with temples or nobles to form *shōen*, seriously eroding the resources of the government. To alleviate the crisis, two major changes in the provincial government and taxation systems were introduced in the early 10th century. First, *ritsuryō* levies were now made on lands rather than individuals since the former were easier to calculate. A new administrative unit, called the *myō*, was established, a taxation unit on which both rent and corvée could be levied. The second change was that local administration was entrusted to those governors or their deputies in return for a stipulated amount of tax revenue, calculated for each province.

Allotment no longer being practiced, all government lands—that is, taxable lands—were now listed as *kōden* ("public lands"). The amount for each province was set and divided for exploitative purposes into *myō*. Nonpublic lands were mostly *shōen*, and their growth over the 11th and 12th centuries was so great that by the end of the Heian period more than half the paddy fields were within *shōen*, forcing the nobility to look for ever more private land to replace declining public revenues. Although *kōden* survived well into the Kamakura period (1185–1333), the *ritsuryō* ideal of national control over people and land was long dead by the end of the 12th century.

Heian Cultural Life——If the dominant view of Heian political and economic developments is negative, resulting from an ill-advised move away from the institutions borrowed from China in the *ritsuryō* system, the evaluation of Heian cultural developments moving away from Chinese prototypes is positive: the experience is seen as one in which the Japanese created a truly native culture for the first time. The absorption of continental Buddhist ideas, the perfection of a native written language that made possible a truly Japanese form of literary expression, and the emergence of a secular artistic tradition that freed Japanese artists from the rigid traditions learned from China—it is for these cultural achievements that the Heian period is best known by most Japanese.

Religion——Although escaping the undue influence of Buddhism was one of the reasons for removing the capital to Heiankyō, Emperor Kammu and his successors were not hostile to Buddhism. Buddhism flourished in Heian times, and in combination with native SHINTŌ beliefs it dominated the religious and philosophical lives of the nobility. But Heian-period Buddhism differed from earlier Buddhism.

New forms of Buddhism were brought to the Heian court by two monks who had gone to China in search of Buddhist truth. SAICHŌ, who had founded the temple ENRYAKUJI on Mt. Hiei (Hieizan), established the TENDAI SECT, dedicating himself to creating a monastic order that would truly serve the nation. Indeed, a large number of Japan's subsequent religious leaders came from the Tendai headquarters at Enryakuji. Situated in the critically dangerous northeast, from which it was believed evil spirits invaded, Enryakuji came to be regarded as the protector of the capital.

KŪKAI, better known by his posthumous name Kōbō Daishi, returned to found his temple on Mt. Kōya (Kōyasan), far from the

Heian Shrine The shrine oratory, built in 1895, is a two-thirds scale replica of the Great Hall of State of the Heian-period Kyōto palace. Two shrine attendants, called *miko*, stand in the foreground.

court in Kii Province (now Wakayama Prefecture). Kūkai introduced tantric Buddhism into Japan in the form of the SHINGON SECT. Because it emphasized rituals, incantations, and powerful visual representations of the Buddhist cosmology—in cosmic diagrams called MANDALA—Shingon Buddhism proved immensely popular with the Japanese court, as a means of personal comfort and as a spur to artistic developments. Furthermore, Kūkai's own talents and strength of character helped to make esoteric Shingon more influential than Tendai among the nobility.

The headquarters of the new sects of Buddhism were located outside the capital, reflecting Kammu's desire to avoid the negative influence of priests. Only two temples, both located far south of the palace near Heiankyō's main gate, were included in the original city plan, and other temples were constructed in the suburbs. But from mid-Heian times the aristocracy had built numerous private temples within the city, and monks from suburban temples were as common a sight in Heiankyō as they had been in Nara. In fact, they proved more threatening, for they often were armed.

Major temples recruited WARRIOR-MONKS (*sōhei*) for protection in bitter doctrinal disputes within and among temples and in conflicts over *shōen* holdings. These monks were also effective in pressing demands at court, when they would march into the capital bearing the sacred palanquin of the protective Shintō deity associated with their temple. Ironically, it was the warrior-monks of Mt. Hiei at the capital's protective temple of Enryakuji who most terrified the court and the citizens of Heiankyō. Yet despite occasional intimidation, the separation of religion and politics was largely maintained. The court nobles remained devout, however, and frequent pilgrimages to major Buddhist and Shintō institutions were common, even for emperors.

In Heian times Buddhism did not spread widely among commoners, but the faith began to be popularized through the belief in the saving grace of AMIDA, the Buddha of Boundless Light, into whose Western Paradise souls could be reborn. Amida supposedly made an original vow that all who called on his name—a practice known as NEMBUTSU—would be welcome in the Western Paradise, or Pure Land (see PURE LAND BUDDHISM). This Pure Land doctrine was introduced from China in the 9th century by ENNIN and was popularized to some degree by KŪYA (903–972), who preached it in the streets. The most important Heian figure in Pure Land development was GENSHIN, who wrote graphically of the horrors of hell and the delights of the Pure Land. See ŌJŌYŌSHŪ.

Pure Land Buddhism achieved great popularity from mid-Heian times. The key to its popularity was the Mahāyāna Buddhist idea of *mappō* (see ESCHATOLOGY), the concept that Buddhist law would develop through three stages after the death of the Buddha: prosperity of 500 years, decline of 1,000 years,

and finally disappearance in the latter days (*mappō*). Once *mappō* began, widely believed in Japan to have been in 1052, it would not be sufficient to achieve enlightenment through one's own efforts, as most Buddhist sects preached; the only hope was faith in the saving grace of Amida. Thus, court nobles and ladies chanted the *nembutsu* with great fervor or built Amida halls within their residences to show their faith. The most famous example of such private Amida temples is the Phoenix Hall of the BYŌDŌIN in Uji, which was built by Fujiwara no Yorimichi.

Although Buddhism flourished in the Heian period, there was no strict sectarian division among devotees. Apart from members of the religious community itself, religious belief for most Japanese was highly eclectic. Courtiers seemingly made little distinction among different sects of Buddhism, Shintō beliefs, and imported Confucian lore centering on the pseudoscientific concepts of *yin* and *yang* and the "five elements." See OMMYŌDŌ.

Literature——The field of literature represented the height of the Heian creative spirit. As in other spheres, a convenient psychological dividing point in Heian literary history is the year 838, when the last official mission was sent to China. After that the Japanese, while continuing to value Chinese books, pictures, and other artifacts and while retaining Chinese philosophical tendencies, turned increasingly to a more native means of expression.

The outburst of literary creativity was made possible by the development of the *kana* syllabary with its some 50 phonetic symbols, which made writing much simpler. While it was now theoretically possible to write in Japanese without reliance on any Chinese characters, the Japanese had by this time borrowed such an enormous corpus of Chinese terms that in practice both *kana* and Chinese characters were used. Moreover, Heian courtiers remained intellectually committed to the written Chinese language, which they employed in private diaries, court records, and official documents, using *kana* only when composing Japanese poetry. Thus, the use of *kana* was left largely to court ladies, and by and large it was these women who produced the greatest works of Heian literature.

As direct interest in China waned, courtiers turned increasingly to the cultivation of the 31-syllable WAKA poem. In fact, poetry composition became a crucial aspect of the world of the Heian courtier. Poetry competitions were held (some at imperial command), lovers commonly exchanged poems, and the inability to compose a credible poem or recognize a poetic allusion could condemn one to social disgrace. Although none matched the earlier MAN'YŌSHŪ, anthologies of Japanese poetry were compiled, the KOKINSHŪ being perhaps the greatest.

The *kana* syllabary was a stimulus to the creation of a native prose literature, of which there were essentially two types in Heian times, the *monogatari* (tale) and the *nikki* (diary). The former was a narrative tale, which reached unparalleled heights in MURASAKI SHIKIBU's *Genji monogatari* (TALE OF GENJI), while the latter was more a record of intimate, private impressions of daily events at court. The two genres did share the common feature of interspersing poems throughout the narrative. In fact, one type of tale, the *uta monogatari*, or poem tale, was little more than a large number of poems

linked by brief introductory remarks. ISE MONOGATARI (Tales of Ise), thought to be the best of this genre, is regarded as a classic of Japanese literature.

The *nikki* is regarded as having its beginning with TOSA NIKKI (Tosa Diary), an account by KI NO TSURAYUKI of his trip to Tosa Province (now Kōchi Prefecture) in the early 10th century. The genre was later taken over by women, the two most representative works being the KAGERŌ NIKKI (The Gossamer Years) by the "mother of Michitsuna" and *Murasaki Shikibu nikki* by the author of *Genji*.

In a slightly different vein from the diary is SEI SHŌNAGON's MAKURA NO SŌSHI (Pillow Book), a collection of reminiscences, anecdotes, and very candid opinions about the world of the court. The tone is light and witty, expressing the ideal of amusement or delight that Heian courtiers referred to as *okashi*, and it pioneered the popular genre of essays known as ZUIHITSU.

The *Tale of Genji* remains the classic work of Japanese literature, a massive work in 54 chapters dealing with the life of the court and focusing on the hero, Hikaru Genji, the "shining prince." In contrast to the *Pillow Book*—which stressed the aesthetic of *okashi*—*Genji* is the epitome of another Heian ideal, a sense of MONO NO AWARE, or the sadness inherent in the things of this world. See also HEIAN LITERATURE.

Art——Heian art is usually divided into two periods hinging on the break in official relations with China in 838. The first 100-year period is known by one of two era names, Kōnin (810–824) or Jōgan (859–877), and the last three centuries are called the Fujiwara age. In the Jōgan era Chinese influence remained strong, and the development of arts related to esoteric Buddhism was especially striking. The two major art forms were Buddhist sculpture and mandalas.

In the Jōgan era the Japanese began to rely on wood for their sculpture, moving away from early bronze, lacquer, and clay figures. It was common to carve an entire statue from one large block of wood, left unpainted except for the lips to preserve the natural aroma (sandalwood was especially favored). Decline of court patronage of the Buddhist establishment from the level evident in the Nara period reduced the necessity for massive Buddhist sculptures, which were as much nationalistic as religious, and consequently also reduced the need for large numbers of government artisans, so that from the Jōgan era the tendency toward individual craftsmen became strong. The two greatest examples of Jōgan sculpture are the Yakushi Nyorai (healing Buddha) at Kyōto's JINGOJI and the Shaka Nyorai (historical Buddha) at Murōji, south of Nara. See also BUDDHIST SCULPTURE.

Among the few surviving examples of early Heian painting are mandalas, used as aids in meditation, and fierce representations of Fudō Myōō, a manifestation of the cosmic Buddha, always depicted as grotesque, muscular guardians who subdued enemies of the faith with the ropes and swords they usually carried.

Just as in literature, the art of the long period of Fujiwara domination shows great changes. One of the most important determinants of the new art was the growing popularity of Amida. Images of Amida became popular, the most remarkable being that sculpted by JŌCHŌ in the Phoenix Hall of the Byōdōin. Amida's gentle and serene countenance contrasts with the more severe Bud-

dhist figures of the Jōgan era. There were also sculptural representations of Amida coming to lead the believer to the Pure Land.

The most marked departure from earlier art forms was the development of secular painting, known as YAMATO-E or "Japanese (style) pictures" to distinguish them from "Chinese pictures" (KARA-E). Compared to the few earlier examples of religious portraits or copies of Chinese-style landscapes, the Fujiwara era witnessed an outburst of secular painting, both landscapes and scenes of daily court life, painted on folding screens (*byōbu*) and on paper doors (*fusuma*). We know them only by description since none survives.

Perhaps the finest examples of Fujiwara painting are the narrative scrolls (EMAKIMONO) that came into vogue in the 11th and 12th centuries. Some dealt with famous historical incidents—the Hōgen Rebellion, for example, or the fate of the wronged courtier SUGAWARA NO MICHIZANE—while some were more religious in nature, depicting the horrors of Buddhist hell or the origins of a temple. Perhaps the most celebrated is the 12th-century GENJI MONOGATARI EMAKI, which depicts in elegant color the world of Murasaki's great novel.

Freed from the constraints of religion, painting developed in many directions, and the *yamato-e* influenced the development of a singularly Japanese form of decorative art. Even though new Chinese forms of painting, such as ink painting, continued to be introduced, Japanese painters continued to produce new forms of quite distinct character by going back to the *yamato-e* style.

☎ *518*

Heian Shrine 平安神宮

(Heian Jingū). Shintō shrine in Sakyō Ward, Kyōto; dedicated to the spirits of Emperor Kammu (r 781–806), in whose reign Heian-kyō (now Kyōto) was established as the capital of Japan, and of Emperor Kōmei (r 1846–67), the last emperor to sit on the throne in Kyōto before the capital was moved to Tōkyō in 1868. The shrine was built in 1895 to commemorate the 1,100th anniversary of the founding of the capital. Festivals are held annually on 13 April in honor of Emperor Kammu and on 30 January in honor of Emperor Kōmei. In addition, the shrine sponsors

a spectacular procession, the JIDAI FESTIVAL (Festival of the Ages), on 22 October.

Heibonsha, Ltd, Publishers
[株]平凡社

(Heibonsha). Publisher, mainly of encyclopedias, dictionaries, and books in the fields of science and philosophy. Heibonsha was established in 1914 by SHIMONAKA YASABURŌ. Heibonsha published a large general encyclopedia entitled *Dai hyakka jiten* in 28 volumes between 1931 and 1935. Since World War II, Heibonsha has published not only encyclopedias but also books on art and literature, including the series Tōyō Bunko (The Eastern World Library). In 1963 Heibonsha launched the general-interest magazine *Taiyō* (Sun).

Heichū monogatari 平中物語

Work of the *uta monogatari* (poem tale) genre, made up of 39 episodes and containing 152 WAKA and 1 *chōka*. The central hero, Heichū, is identified as Taira no Sadabumi (d 923; also known as Taira no Sadafun). The author of the work, which was probably compiled between 959 and 965, is unknown. In both *Heichū monogatari* and another poem tale, YAMATO MONOGATARI, Heichū emerges as a dismal failure as a lover, a striking contrast to ARIWARA NO NARIHIRA, featured in the poem tale ISE MONOGATARI. These stories of bumbling or gracious lovers were transmitted to MURASAKI SHIKIBU, who introduced both themes, often alluding to their literary antecedents, into the narrative of the TALE OF GENJI.

Heiji Disturbance 平治の乱

(Heiji no Ran). A clash between MINAMOTO NO YOSHITOMO and TAIRA NO KIYOMORI in January 1160 (Heiji 1.12). They had shared the victory in the HŌGEN DISTURBANCE of 1156, but Kiyomori had received greater rewards and, with FUJIWARA NO MICHINORI, exerted great influence over the retired emperor GO-SHIRAKAWA. While Kiyomori was on a pilgrimage Yoshitomo seized power with the aid of Fujiwara no Nobuyori (1133–60). He imprisoned Go-Shirakawa and Emperor Nijō (1143–65) and killed Michinori before Kiyomori returned to crush the uprising. Yoshitomo and Nobuyori were killed and Minamoto influence was swept from the court, leaving the Taira family in control.

These events are depicted in the war tale HEIJI MONOGATARI and in the scrolls known as the HEIJI MONOGATARI EMAKI.

Heiji monogatari 平治物語

One of a pair of war tales (GUNKI MONOGATARI) that tell the story of the succession struggles of the mid-12th century that resulted in the eclipse of Fujiwara power and the rise to supremacy of the TAIRA FAMILY, more commonly known as the Heike. The first phase of the struggles, in 1156, is treated in HŌGEN MONOGATARI; the second and decisive phase in 1160, in *Heiji monogatari* (see HEIJI DISTURBANCE). A significant difference between the two tales is that in *Hōgen* the warriors supporting the court factions are not shown (despite the depiction of MINAMOTO NO TAMETOMO as an almost superhuman hero) as dominating or directing events to the same extent as in *Heiji*.

The Taira leader was TAIRA NO KIYOMORI. The Minamoto leader was MINAMOTO NO YOSHITOMO, aided by his eldest son, Akugenta Yoshihira, and his third son, MINAMOTO NO YORITOMO. In many of the 33 different extant texts, the work ends after the rout of the Minamoto. Some texts, however, go on to events of later years, with Yoshitomo's son MINAMOTO NO YOSHITSUNE's flight to northeast Japan, Yoritomo's revolt, the defeat of the Taira, and even Yoritomo's death in 1199. *Heiji monogatari* is referred to at the end of the 13th century as a chanted text; thus it is meaningless to assign a date of composition. There are in existence three superb scrolls (see HEIJI MONOGATARI EMAKI) illustrating in YAMATO-E style sections of book 1 of the Heiji story.

Heiji monogatari emaki
平治物語絵巻

(Tale of Heiji Scrolls). Handscrolls illustrating scenes from the HEIJI MONOGATARI (Tale of Heiji), a chronicle of the brief war between the Taira and Minamoto clans in 1160 (see HEIJI DISTURBANCE). There are four complete scrolls and fragments of a fifth, all polychrome; however, these belong to different sets of scrolls, suggesting that originally there were many more.

The five scrolls date from the late 13th

Original Plan of the City of Heijōkyō

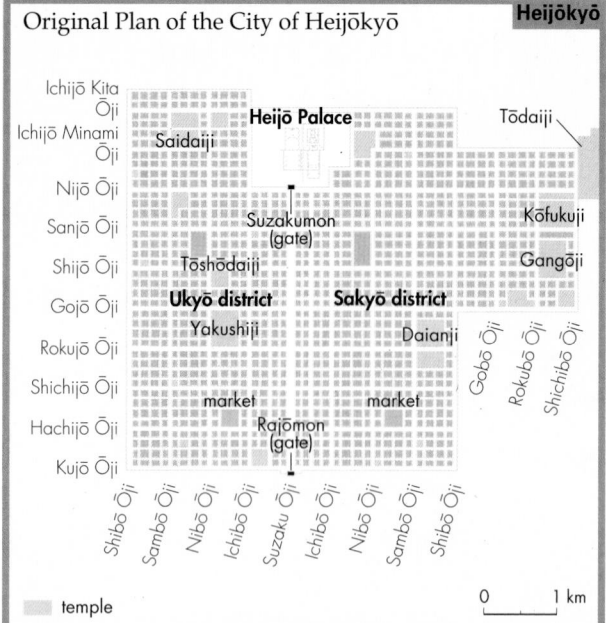

Ichijō Kita Ōji
Ichijō Minami Ōji
Saidaiji
Heijō Palace
Tōdaiji
Nijō Ōji
Suzakumon (gate)
Kōfukuji
Sanjō Ōji
Tōshōdaiji
Gangōji
Shijō Ōji
Gojō Ōji
Ukyō district
Sakyō district
Yakushiji
Daianji
Rokujō Ōji
Gobō Ōji
Rokubō Ōji
Shichibō Ōji
Shichijō Ōji
market
market
Hachijō Ōji
Rajōmon (gate)
Kujō Ōji

Shibō Ōji Sambō Ōji Nibō Ōji Ichibō Ōji Suzaku Ōji Ichibō Ōji Nibō Ōji Sambō Ōji Shibō Ōji

☐ temple

0   1 km

NOTE: In the system of street identification used at Heijōkyō, rows of blocks running north-to-south were called *bō*, and those running east-to-west were called *jō*. The *jō* were numbered from north to south, and the *bō* were numbered counting outward from Suzaku Ōji. The main east-to-west cross streets were named after the numbered *jō*; for example, Ichijō Ōji (First Jō Street), of which there were two (north and south), Nijō Ōji (Second Jō Street), and so on. The main north-to-south streets were named after the numbered *bō*; for example, Ichibō Ōji (First Bō Street), Nibō Ōji (Second Bō Street), and so on.

century. The earliest seem to be *The Burning of the Sanjō Palace* (Boston Museum of Fine Arts) and *Shinzei*. *The Flight to Rokuhara* (Tōkyō National Museum) and *The Battle of Rokuhara* (preserved in 14 fragments) are usually attributed to another school. *Lady Tokiwa* is stylistically different from the other scrolls. It is also smaller in format than the other three complete scrolls. It is apparently the work of a different school and may have appeared later than the other scrolls. Despite slight differences in style and date, all of these scrolls are remarkable examples of war pictures, executed with a strong sense of drama and distinguished by an acute observation of detail. See also EMAKIMONO.

Heijōkyō   平城京

City in the Nara Basin in use from 710 to 784 as the capital of Japan (usually referred to as NARA). Located 20 kilometers (12 mi) almost due north from the preceding capital of FUJIWARAKYŌ, in the western sector of the present city of Nara, the city was built on a plain crossed by the rivers Sahogawa and Akishinogawa where there had previously been villages and mounded tombs (KOFUN). After two years of construction Empress Gemmei (661–721; r 707–715) moved her court there in 710, and Heijōkyō remained the seat of government for eight successive rulers, until NAGAOKAKYŌ was constructed by Emperor KAMMU in 784.

The city was laid out on a grid pattern of square blocks modeled on that of the Chinese Tang (T'ang) dynasty (618–907) capital at Chang'an (Ch'ang-an). Major streets intersected so as to form 72 large blocks—eight rows of blocks running north to south and nine rows running east to west. Each large block was subdivided into 16 smaller blocks. Later 12 additional large blocks were added on the northeast side of the city and 3 partial blocks in the northwest.

After Heijōkyō was abandoned the temples, which included SAIDAIJI, TŌSHŌDAIJI,

YAKUSHIJI, KŌFUKUJI, Gangōji, DAIANJI, TŌDAIJI, and SHIN YAKUSHIJI, remained the object of pilgrimages. Archaeological excavations have provided a wealth of information about the area. Ceramics found have included SUE WARE and HAJI WARE; metal objects found include tools and examples of the so-called twelve coinages of the imperial court (KŌCHŌ JŪNISEN); and almost 100,000 of the wooden tablets called MOKKAN have been found. The inscribed *mokkan* provide a detailed record of business transactions and taxation, as well as the kinds and quantities of goods known in Heijōkyō during its prime.

Heike monogatari   平家物語

(tr *The Tale of the Heike*, 1975). The most important of the Kamakura (1185–1333) and Muromachi (1333–1568) period prose tales known as GUNKI MONOGATARI, or "war tales." It deals with the short heyday of the TAIRA FAMILY (the 20 years following the HŌGEN DISTURBANCE [1156] and the HEIJI DISTURBANCE [1160], when they not only defeated their rivals, the MINAMOTO FAMILY, but also ousted the FUJIWARA FAMILY from its dominant position at court) and the five years of the TAIRA-MINAMOTO WAR. The war began with the Minamoto rising again in 1180 and ended with the crushing defeat of the Taira in 1185. The tale divides into roughly three parts. The central figure in the first is TAIRA NO KIYOMORI. Arrogant, evil, and ruthless, he is above all so consumed by the fires of hatred for the Minamoto that he dies in agony, his feverish body beyond all cooling, even when he is immersed in water. The main figures of the second and third parts are generals on the Minamoto side, first MINAMOTO NO YOSHINAKA and then, after his death, the heroic MINAMOTO NO YOSHITSUNE, a youthful military genius wrongly suspected of treachery by his elder brother MINAMOTO NO YORITOMO.

Heike monogatari abounds in stirring scenes of battle, recounting brave deeds by warriors proud of their lineage and military prowess and prizing loyalty above life. Dealing with the cataclysmic upheavals of this time of Taira and Minamoto rivalry, it undoubtedly has a grand sweep about it that can be described as "epic." Whether it may truly be termed an epic is debatable, principally because of its lyrical and emotional content. Several episodes about tragic lovers or love affairs have an atmosphere redolent of the MONO NO AWARE of Heian court literature. Also, the emphasis throughout is very much on the pathos of the situation of the Taira, a warrior family that rose to importance at court, only to be forced out by uncouth rivals from eastern Japan. The atmosphere of the whole work is permeated by the Buddhist doctrine that all human activity is ephemeral and illusory, that the mighty are soon cast down, and that nothing avails but faith in the grace of the Buddha Amida.

Such Buddhist sentiments are not uncommon in the literature of the time, but the reason for their prominence in *Heike monogatari* is that those responsible for the development of this work were chanters (BIWA HŌSHI), lute-playing priests who traveled the country reciting this and other chronicles. They were blind men who used no fixed text but rather recreated the work at each performance on the basis of oral formulae. The original *Heike* text, dating from the early 13th century, comprises material from various sources, including oral tales about the wars, some of which may have been first told as religious rituals for the benefit of the

dead warriors. From the mid-13th century, two traditions developed. One was a line of texts for silent reading, culminating in GEMPEI SEISUIKI, and the other was a line of texts for oral chanters, which contained many passages in the 7-5 syllable rhythm of classical poetry. The chanted tradition continued well into the Muromachi period, but of all the approximately 100 texts of the *Heike*, the accepted standard is the version dictated by a master *Heike* performer, Akashi Kakuichi, just before his death in 1371. *Heike* texts vary not only in wording but also in content, revealing the development of social attitudes and ideals of conduct.

Heike monogatari contains so much of varied human interest that it has been almost as popular a source for later Japanese writers as has *Genji monogatari* (TALE OF GENJI). It has provided material for a number of NŌ plays. Some of these, such as *Atsumori*, are "warrior pieces," but several are based on more lyrical episodes about tragic lovers, particularly women, such as *Giō*, *Senju*, and *Kogō*.

heikyoku   平曲

Episodes from the HEIKE MONOGATARI (The Tale of the Heike), chanted to the accompaniment of the BIWA (lute). Yoshida Kenkō (ca 1283–ca 1352), in his TSUREZUREGUSA, section 226, ascribes the *Heike monogatari* to one Yukinaga, a former official and courtier of the cloistered emperor Go-Toba (r 1183–98), and later a Tendai monk at the monastery Enryakuji on Mt. Hiei. Yukinaga collaborated with a blind monk, Shōbutsu, who was the first to chant the text. This probably all occurred before 1220. The *heikyoku* style of biwa music (also called Heike biwa) incorporated elements of court music, Buddhist chant, and *mōsō biwa* (blind monks' lute). Other military tales were also being set to music, but by the 13th century they had been eclipsed by *heikyoku*. The *heikyoku* repertoire contains 200 pieces, of which 176 are *hira-mono* (ordinary items), 19 are *hikyoku* (secret pieces), and 5—the most weighty—are *hiji* (secret material). Another classification is *fushi-mono* (melodic, lyrical pieces), *hiroi-mono* (narrative pieces, often about battles), and *yomi-mono* (recitative pieces).

heimin   平民

(commoners). One of the three classes of society in a system adopted by the Meiji government in 1869. The other two classes were the *kazoku* (court nobles and former *daimyō*; see PEERAGE) and the SHIZOKU (former *samurai*). The word *heimin* had long been used to refer to the common people, but in the Meiji period (1868–1912) it became part of an official class that included the three lower categories of the Edo-period (1600–1868) division of society (SHI-NŌ-KŌ-SHŌ). In 1870 *heimin* were permitted for the first time to have surnames, and in 1871 certain outcast groups were included as *heimin*. The class status of each family was noted in the HOUSEHOLD REGISTERS. Marriage and adoption between classes also became legal, and theoretically all three classes were now equal, but the custom of social ranking persisted. After World War II, Japan's new constitution outlawed the class system that was reflected by such terms as *kazoku*, *shizoku*, and *heimin*.

Heiminsha   平民社

(Society of Commoners). A socialist organization founded in October 1903 by KŌTOKU

SHŪSUI and SAKAI TOSHIHIKO soon after their departure from the newspaper YOROZU CHŌHŌ in protest over its prowar stance on the eve of the RUSSO-JAPANESE WAR (1904–05); the center of early-20th-century socialist activities. The group included a number of Christian socialists, most notably ISHIKAWA SANSHIRŌ and KINOSHITA NAOE, and published a newspaper, *Heimin shimbun,* enlisting the contributions of such writers as UCHIMURA KANZŌ and TAOKA REIUN. The newspaper was discontinued in 1905 because of government repression and lack of resources. Another weekly, *Chokugen* (Straight Talk), took its place, but after eight months this, too, was prohibited. A short time later the Heiminsha itself was forced by internal dissension and financial difficulties to disband. In January 1907 both the society and the *Heimin shimbun* were revived, but they were forced to disband in April, again because of internal disunity and government prohibition.

Heimin shimbun 平民新聞

("Commoner's News"). Socialist weekly newspaper launched in Tōkyō in November 1903 by KŌTOKU SHŪSUI and SAKAI TOSHIHIKO. As the official voice of its parent organization, the HEIMINSHA, the paper quickly became the country's foremost leftist news publication. Regular contributors included well-known socialist thinkers such as ISHIKAWA SANSHIRŌ. When it carried the first Japanese translation of the *Communist Manifesto* in November 1904, the government suspended publication. The paper struggled briefly to survive but on 29 January 1905 printed its final edition. In 1907 a brief attempt to revive the paper ended in failure.

heimon 閉門

(house arrest; literally, "closed gate"). A form of punishment established by the Tokugawa shogunate (1603–1867) as part of an elaborately codified body of civil and criminal law (see KUJIKATA OSADAMEGAKI). Like *enryo* and *hissoku* (two other forms of domiciliary confinement), it was imposed on *samurai* and priests. The analogous punishment for commoners was known as *tojime* ("door-shutting"). When one was sentenced to *tojime, enryo,* or *hissoku,* one's front gate was nailed shut but discreet exit was permitted at night. In the case of *heimon* one was forbidden to go out even at night, and entry of others was restricted. *Chikkyo,* a similar type of confinement, was applied to *samurai* and aristocrats. Persons subjected to this punishment, which does not appear in the Kujikata Osadamegaki, were confined in a single room of their domicile. These forms of punishment were abolished after the Meiji Restoration of 1868.

Heisei Boom 平成景気

(Heisei Keiki). Economic boom that began at the end of 1986. With the death of Emperor Shōwa in January 1989 the NENGŌ (era name) changed from Shōwa to Heisei to mark the commencement of the reign of the new emperor. The economic boom then in progress, which had been called the Shōwa Boom, was promptly renamed the Heisei Boom. Ending in early 1991, the Heisei Boom rivaled the longest previous period of uninterrupted business expansion in the postwar era, the 57-month IZANAGI BOOM of 1965–70.

The Heisei Boom was primarily fueled by domestic demand. In response to the sudden rise in the value of the yen following the PLAZA ACCORD of September 1985, the government moved to prevent an economic down-

turn by cutting the official discount rate five times beginning in 1986; by February 1987 it had dropped to 2.5 percent, its lowest level since World War II. Significantly lowered interest rates induced prodigious levels of capital investment and construction, and personal consumption levels also rose to an all-time high. Moreover, in fiscal 1987 government efforts to stimulate domestic demand took the form of public investments totaling ¥6 trillion (US $41.5 billion). In addition to these factors, the Heisei Boom was also supported by the fact that the high value of the yen during this period aided imports of raw materials, while at the same time doing little to inhibit the performance of Japanese exports in the world market. See also BUSINESS CYCLES.

Heisei period 平成時代

(1989– ; Heisei *jidai*). The reign of the present emperor, AKIHITO, who ascended the throne at the death of his father, Emperor SHŌWA, on 7 January 1989. The era name Heisei is based on two quotations from the Chinese classics *Shi ji* (Shih chi; Book of History) and *Shu jing* (Shu ching; Book of Documents) that signify the attainment of peace in heaven and on earth, at home and abroad. It is the first era name to be selected and given official recognition under the Gengō Law of 1979. See NENGŌ.

Heishi → Taira family

Hekinan 碧南[市]

City in south-central Aichi Prefecture, central Honshū, at the mouth of the river YAHAGIGAWA. A port town during the Edo period (1600–1868), Hekinan has traditionally been known for tile making, brewing, and spinning, and more recently for emerging metal, machinery, and food-processing industries. Its chief agricultural product is carrots. Many residents commute to NAGOYA and TOYOTA. Pop: 65,899.

Hekizan nichiroku 碧山日録

Diary of Taikyoku (pen name Hekizan; 1421–86?), a priest of the Rinzai sect of Zen

Heike monogatari
A detail from the Edo-period (1600–1868) folding screen *Episodes from the Taira-Minamoto War* depicts the Battle of Yashima in 1185, as described in the *Tale of the Heike.*

Buddhism who lived in the temple TŌFUKUJI in Kyōto. Surviving sections of the diary cover 1459–63 and 1465–68. The diary provides important information on the social unrest preceding the ŌNIN WAR (1467–77).

hell 地獄

(*jigoku*). Although ancient Japanese myths mention Yomi no Kuni, an underworld of the dead much like the Greek Hades, the concept of hell (*jigoku*) as a place of punishment for the damned was introduced with BUDDHISM. The Buddhist hell itself was of Hindu origin (Skt: *naraka*). Hindu sacred texts usually refer to many distinct hells, which include Avīci (J: Abi Jigoku or Muken Jigoku; "Interminable Hell") and Raurava (J: Kyōkan Jigoku; "Hell of Sorrowful Crying"). The ruler of hell is known as EMMA (Skt: Yama), a fearful judge, who, after reviewing a person's past deeds, consigns him to the appropriate hell. The concept of hell became increasingly widespread from the late Heian period (794–1185), as PURE LAND BUDDHISM preached salvation in the Pure Land in contrast to punishment in hell. Many JIGOKU-ZŌSHI (Scrolls of Hells) produced in this period depict the torments of hell. See also NIHON RYŌIKI; ŌJŌYŌSHŪ.

Henderson, Harold Gould ヘンダーソン, H. G.

(1889–1974). American scholar of Japanese language and literature. Born in New York City; graduate of Columbia University in chemical engineering. In 1929 he was appointed curator of Far Eastern art at the Metropolitan Museum of Art. He went to Japan in 1930 to study the language and compile material for his first book, *Bamboo Broom,* a collection of *haiku* translations. From 1935 to 1945 he taught at Columbia. After World War II, he returned to Japan as head of the Education, Religion, Arts, and Monument Division of SCAP (Supreme Commander for the Allied Powers). He later resumed teaching at Columbia and wrote *Handbook of Japanese Grammar* (1948) and *An Introduction to Haiku* (1958).

herbs and spices

1 *Wasabi.* This pungent root, pictured here on a sharkskin grater, is used to flavor *sushi* and *sashimi.*

2 *Yuzu.* Thin slices of citron peel are used to flavor clear soups; the juice is sometimes added to soy sauce to make a *sashimi* dipping sauce.

3 *Myōga.* The sharp-tasting *myōga* root is used as a garnish and also marinated or pickled.

4 *Hamabōfū.* The leaves and wine-red stems of the *hamabōfū* are used as a garnish for *sashimi,* but only the stems are eaten.

5 *Shiso.* The aromatic leaves and buds of this herb are used as a *sashimi* garnish. The leaves are also deep-fried, *tempura* style.

6 *Mitsuba.* The leaves and stems of the *mitsuba* are often added to the steamed egg-custard dish called *chawan-mushi.*

7 *Shōga.* Ginger root is sliced and pickled for use as a *sushi* condiment. Freshly grated ginger is also used as a flavoring.

Henjō 遍昭

(816–890). Classical (WAKA) poet and Buddhist prelate. His lay name was Yoshimine no Munesada. After taking Buddhist orders in 850, he rose rapidly in ecclesiastical ranks, becoming a bishop (*sōjō*) in 885. Henjō is one of the so-called Six Poetic Geniuses (ROKKASEN). Some 36 of his poems are included in imperial anthologies beginning with the KOKINSHŪ.

hensachi 偏差値

(deviation). Statistical term frequently used in Japanese education to express a student's performance on a standardized examination relative to a mean average score. Since the early 1960s *hensachi* figures have been used in Japan to calculate an individual's percentile ranking for practice ENTRANCE EXAMINATIONS. Guidance counselors often base their assessment of how likely a student is to gain admission to certain educational insitutions by comparing the student's *hensachi* with the average *hensachi* of other students applying to the same schools. The industry of private tutoring schools (JUKU) and CRAM SCHOOLS also calculates *hensachi* figures for students, based on the results of large-scale practice examinations, to advise them on test-taking strategies.

hentai kambun 変体漢文

(literally, "variant Chinese"). A now defunct hybrid form of literary Japanese combining both Chinese and native Japanese elements. It is often called *kirokutai,* meaning "Japanese used in documents," because it was used for the writing of court and shogunate records. This language was also used in the private diaries of male courtiers, clerics, and military men.

The Japanese learned to write Chinese (KAMBUN) from immigrant Korean teachers in the 5th century, some two centuries before a system for writing their own language was developed. Chinese studies in Japan and the ability of the bureaucrats to write Chinese reached their height in the early 9th century, only to decline with the termination of official missions to China in 894. Thereafter, Chinese written in Japan became increasingly corrupted by Japanese words and constructions and a hybrid language emerged as a separate entity. Before the end of the Heian period (794–1185) "variant Chinese" had become the dominant mode of written expression in the conduct of day-to-day business.

The term *hentai kambun* refers to a spectrum of Chinese styles ranging from the slightly ungrammatical to a style that has a heavy admixture of Japanese words and grammatical forms. The latter end of the spectrum contains distinctive vocabulary not found in either orthodox Chinese or other kinds of Japanese prose and is regarded as a special form of literary Japanese. The bulk of historical materials surviving from the premodern period are recorded in the more corrupt style of *hentai kambun.*

In the Heian period *hentai kambun* achieved a degree of uniformity of vocabulary and phraseology and reached maturity as a style of writing. It was more practical and easier to use than pure Chinese, yet retained much of the latter's value as an indication of status compared to Japanese, which was written in the KANA syllabary. The language of the AZUMA KAGAMI, a record of the political achievements of the Kamakura shogunate (1192–1333), is considered to be archetypal of the mature form. Thus, the term *Azuma kagami tai* (the *Azuma kagami* style) is often used synonymously with the term *hentai kambun.*

Hentai kambun continued to be used with some variation throughout the Edo period (1600–1868) and was still being used in the SŌRŌBUN epistolary form in the early decades of the 20th century. Despite the lengthy duration and broad extent of its use in Japan, *hentai kambun* has been the object of little linguistic research.

Hepburn, James Curtis ヘボン, J. C.

(1815–1911). Physician. Popularizer of the Hepburn system of romanizing Japanese. Born in Milton, Pennsylvania; graduate of the College of New Jersey (now Princeton University) in 1832 and the University of Pennsylvania medical school in 1836. Hepburn served as a Presbyterian medical missionary in Singapore and Xiamen (Amoy) from 1841 to 1845. He then returned to New York City, where he practiced medicine before going to Japan in 1859. There he operated a dispensary in Kanagawa (now part of Yokohama) and taught Western medicine. Hepburn was one of the founders of MEIJI GAKUIN UNIVERSITY and served as its first president. He compiled *A Japanese and English Dictionary* (1867, *Waei gorin shūsei*), the first work of its kind. The system of ROMANIZATION OF JAPANESE that he adopted for the third edition of his dictionary is still widely used, and it is named after him though he did not originate it. He also played a major role in translating the Bible into Japanese (see BIBLE, TRANSLATIONS OF). He returned to the United States in 1892.

herbs and spices 香味料

(*kōmiryō*; also called *yakumi*). Japanese cuisine has traditionally used very few herbs and spices, probably as a result of the reliance from early times on rice, fish, and vegetables rather than on fats, meat, and dairy products. The techniques of preserving fish and vegetables by salting and drying and of making SOY SAUCE (*shōyu*) and MISO (bean paste) also date from early times. The strongly flavored *miso* was used to season *iwashi* (sardines), *saba* (mackerel), and other fish considered low grade, and GINGER has been in use since at least the 8th century. Until the Meiji Restoration (1868) the herbs and spices used in Europe were known in Japan by their Chinese names and considered part of the pharmacopoeia of traditional Chinese medicine. With the opening of Japan to foreign influences in the Meiji period (1868–1912), curry powder and Worcestershire sauce were introduced. Since World War II, the eating habits of the Japanese have changed considerably, and a wide variety of herbs and spices is now used. The following are some of the more commonly used herbs and spices in Japanese cooking: *bōfū* or *hamabōfū* (*Glehnia littoralis*; family Umbelliferae); GOMA (sesame; *Sesamum orientale*); *mitsuba* (honewort, wild chervil; *Crytotaenia japonica*); *myōga* (*Zingiber mioga*); *negi* (WELSH ONION); *nira* (*Allium odorum*); *sanshō* (Japanese pepper; *Zanthoxylum piperitum*); *shichimi tōgarashi* (a mixture of *tōgarashi* [cayenne pepper], *sanshō,* *aonori* [a kind of seaweed], poppy seed, sesame seed, dried orange peel, and *shiso* seed); SHISO (beefsteak plant; *Perilla frutescens*); *shōga* (ginger); *tōgarashi* (cayenne pepper); *wasabi* (horseradish; *Eutrema wasabi*); *yuzu* (citron).

herons 鷺

(*sagi*). In Japanese, *sagi* is the common name for wading birds of the family Ardeidae. They have long legs, necks, and bills and range from 37 to 95 centimeters (15–37 in) in length. Some 18 species are found in Japan, including the *sankanogoi* (Eurasian bittern; *Botaurus stellaris*), three species of *yoshigoi* (little bitterns; *Ixobrychus* spp.), three species of *shirasagi* (white egrets; *Egretta* spp.), the *goisagi* (night heron; *Nycticorax nycticorax*), and the *mizogoi* (Japanese night heron; *Gorsakius goisagi*).

Herons standing gracefully on one leg have long been a favorite subject for Japanese artists and also figure as a theme in some folk dances. Before they were designated a protected species, the plumes (aigrettes) of herons were used to decorate hats, and their flesh was eaten.

hero worship 英雄崇拝

(*eiyū sūhai*). In Japan myths and cults centering on heroes are common. Since the line of demarcation separating deities (KAMI) from humans is not easily drawn, the spirits of those who led extraordinary lives or died under remarkable circumstances are often said to function as guardian spirits. Often of noble birth and charismatic personality, heroes contribute to the general good while alive, but often incur official disfavor; they meet death calmly for the sake of glory and often leave farewell poems.

The mythical prince YAMATOTAKERU, who appears in the KOJIKI (712), offers one example of such a hero. His father, Emperor KEIKŌ, grew afraid of his military prowess and sent him on difficult missions to conquer aboriginal tribes; returning from a mission, he incurred divine disfavor, fell under a curse, and died (see ATSUTA SHRINE).

SUGAWARA NO MICHIZANE (845–903) is perhaps the most famous of Japan's noble heroes. A scholar, poet, and calligrapher, Michizane was slandered by a political rival, fell into ignominy, and died in exile. After a series of incidents at the capital in which it was thought his angry spirit was involved, the KITANO SHRINE was set up to appease him. In time he came to be regarded as the patron deity of learning (see TEMMANGŪ).

In modern times cults surrounding war heroes such as TŌGŌ HEIHACHIRŌ (1848–1934) and NOGI MARESUKE (1849–1912) were officially encouraged. Shrines have also been dedicated to folk heroes such as NINOMIYA SONTOKU (1787–1856).

herring 鰊

(nishin). In Japanese, nishin is the common name of the Pacific herring (Clupea pallasi), a migratory fish of the family Clupeidae, order Clupeiformes, class Osteichthyes. It grows to 30 centimeters (12 in). It is distributed in the temperate and subarctic zones of the northern Pacific Ocean and adjoining seas, feeding mainly on plankton. The annual catch in Japan fluctuates from about 1 million metric tons (1.1 million short tons) to between 20,000 and 30,000 metric tons (22,000–33,000 short tons).

Herring roe was commonly used for New Year's dishes and wedding feasts until the outbreak of World War II. Sharp declines in the size of the catch have made it expensive in recent years, and such foods as dried, smoked herring and herring pickled in *sake* lees are now expensive delicacies.

He-Umezu (Ho-Umezu) Agreement 梅津・何応欽協定

(Umezu–Ka Ōkin Kyōtei). An agreement concluded on 10 June 1935 between General HE YINGQIN (Ho Ying-ch'in), acting as CHIANG KAI-SHEK's military deputy, and Lieutenant General UMEZU YOSHIJIRŌ, commander of the Japanese army's Tianjin (Tientsin) garrison. China agreed to transfer all armies of the central government and all organs of the Guomindang (Kuomintang; Nationalist Party) out of the province of Hebei (Hopeh), which included the cities of Beijing (Peking) and Tianjin. China also agreed to suppress the activities of the Lanyi She (Lan-i She; "Blue Shirts"; a paramilitary group formed by Chiang in 1932) in that province and to prohibit anti-Japanese movements throughout China. These provisions eliminated the possibility of more aggressive measures by Japan for the moment and allowed Chiang Kai-shek to proceed with his highest priority, a campaign to exterminate the communists. Although the He-Umezu Agreement was made in secret, its revelation led to an outburst of Chinese patriotic indignation. See also SINO-JAPANESE WAR OF 1937–1945.

Heusken, Henry Conrad Joannes ヒュースケン, H. C. J.

(1832–61). Secretary and translator to Townsend HARRIS, the first American resident consul in Japan. Given name Hendrik. Born in the Netherlands, he was fluent in Dutch, English, and French. Arriving in Japan in 1856 with Harris, he acted as a Dutch-English interpreter—Dutch being the diplomatic language favored by the Japanese—during negotiations surrounding the ANSEI COMMERCIAL TREATIES. In January 1861 Heusken was murdered by an antiforeign extremist from

hibachi Inside this ceramic *maruhibachi* are an iron kettle resting on a tripod and, at left, *hibashi* (tongs) for arranging the burning charcoal.

the Satsuma domain (now Kagoshima Prefecture). Harris negotiated an indemnity of 10,000 Mexican dollars to be paid to Heusken's mother.

He Yingqin (Ho Ying-ch'in) 何応欽

(1889–1987; J: Ka Ōkin). Nationalist China's minister of war from 1930 to 1944 and army chief of staff from 1938 to 1944. Like many leaders of republican China, he received his professional education in Japan; he was a graduate of the Rikugun Shikan Gakkō (Army Academy) in Tōkyō. In 1935, when Japanese expansionists were endeavoring to exclude the Nationalists from North China, CHIANG KAI-SHEK ordered He to negotiate with the local Japanese commander, Lieutenant General UMEZU YOSHIJIRŌ. The resulting HE-UMEZU (HO-UMEZU) AGREEMENT represented a capitulation by the Nationalist government to Japanese demands for a withdrawal of Nationalist troops from the province of Hebei (Hopeh). He visited Japan on numerous occasions following the Sino-Japanese War of 1937–45, either privately or in his capacity as president of the Sino-Japanese Cultural and Economic Association.

hibachi 火鉢

Charcoal brazier used as a source of heat. In ancient days the *hibachi* was also called *hioke* and *hibitsu*. Several copper and nickel *hibachi* made during the Nara period (710–794) are at the SHŌSŌIN repository in Nara. Until the mid-Edo period (1600–1868) *hibachi* were mainly for the use of the ruling class. There are several types of *hibachi*: the *maruhibachi*, made from a hollowed-out log or of ceramic; the boxlike *hakohibachi* and *nagahibachi*, made by fitting together boards of hardwood; and those made of metal. The *hibachi* is filled with ash, and pieces of charcoal are arranged in the center. A trivet is sometimes placed over the burning charcoal to hold a kettle. The *hibachi* was used essentially for warmth and only incidentally for heating water or food. Today the *hibachi* has been largely replaced by more efficient and safer heating appliances.

Hibara, Lake 桧原湖

(Hibarako). On the Bandai Azuma highland, Fukushima Prefecture, northern Honshū. Located within Bandai-Asahi National Park. In 1888 Mt. Bandai (Bandaisan) erupted, damming a river and creating this lake. Area: 10.4 sq km (4 sq mi); circumference: 47 km (29 mi); depth: 31 m (102 ft); altitude: 822 m (2,697 ft).

Hibi Ōsuke 日比翁助

(1860–1931). Businessman. Born in what is now Fukuoka Prefecture, he graduated from Keiō Gijuku (now Keiō University) in 1884. Hibi worked for Mosurin (Muslin) Shōkai, then joined Mitsui Bank, Ltd, in 1896, becoming manager of Mitsui Gofukuten (Mitsui Dry Goods Store) in 1898. He participated in the modernization of Mitsui Gofukuten (now MITSUKOSHI, LTD) and became its executive director. His policy of

"small profits and quick returns" turned Mitsukoshi into the first modern department store in Japan.

Hibiya Incendiary Incident 日比谷焼打事件

(Hibiya Yakiuchi Jiken). A citywide riot in Tōkyō arising from a mass rally held at Hibiya Park on 5 September 1905 to protest the Treaty of PORTSMOUTH, which concluded the RUSSO-JAPANESE WAR (1904–05). The Japanese public, ignorant of the actual war situation, attacked the government for concluding what it considered a humiliating peace with Russia. The Kōwa Mondai Dōshi Rengōkai (literally, "Joint Council of Fellow Activists on the Peace Question") defied a government ban and held a mass rally at Hibiya Park on the day of the treaty signing. After the rally some participants marched to the Imperial Palace grounds and clashed with the police. Martial law was declared the next day, and the riot soon subsided. During the riot more than 350 buildings, including the official residence of the home minister, were either smashed or burned down. The recorded casualties, including 17 dead, numbered 450 policemen, 48 firemen and soldiers, and more than 500 civilians. Similar disturbances subsequently took place throughout Japan.

Hibiya Park 日比谷公園

(Hibiya Kōen). In Chiyoda Ward, Tōkyō, next to the Imperial Palace. Formerly the site of several *daimyō* mansions and later an army drill ground, it was opened as a public park in 1903. It is laid out partly in Western style. Tōkyō Metropolitan Hibiya Library and Hibiya Public Hall are located here. Area: 16 hectares (40 acres).

Hiburishima 日振島

Island in the Uwa Sea, west of Ehime Prefecture, western Shikoku. FUJIWARA NO SUMITOMO gathered warships and led a revolt from this island in 939. Fishing is the chief activity. Area: 3.3 sq km (1.3 sq mi).

hichiriki 篳篥

Short cylindrical-bore oboe, used as a melody instrument in GAGAKU music. Its body, 18 centimeters (7 in) long, is of bamboo bound with thinly split cherry bark, lacquered

Hibiya Incendiary Incident Opinion is divided over the historical significance of this 1905 Tōkyō riot, seen here in an artist's recreation. Some have seen it as a precursor of mass political consciousness, while others have interpreted it as a manifestation of chauvinism.

hichiriki A musician playing one of these oboelike bamboo instruments during a court-music performance at the temple Shitennōji in Ōsaka.

Hida Mountains The peaks of the Hida Mountains, often called the Northern Alps, seen from the city of Ōmachi in northwestern Nagano Prefecture.

brown on the outside and red inside; it has seven elliptical finger holes on top, two thumbholes underneath, and an integral double reed fitted with a bridle (and cover, when not in use). The sound is heavy but not strident. The *hichiriki* is related directly to the old Chinese *bili* (*pili*), which was used in Tang (T'ang; 618–907) court music. It found its way to Japan in the 7th century and is played for both the *tōgaku* and the *komagaku* repertoires of *gagaku*.

Hidagawa　　　　　　飛驒川

River in northeastern Gifu Prefecture, central Honshū; it originates on the southern slopes of Norikuradake, flows through the Hida Mountains, and joins the river Kisogawa at the city of Mino Kamo. The lower reaches of the river are part of Hida-Kisogawa Quasi-National Park. Length: 147 km (91 mi). Area of drainage basin: 2,170 sq km (838 sq mi).

Hidaka　　　　　　　日高[市]

City in southern Saitama Prefecture, central Honshū. The area was originally settled during the Nara period (710–794) by immigrants from the Korean peninsula. In recent years it has become a commuter suburb of Tōkyō. Pop: 53,169.

Hieizan
1 View of the aerial ropeway ascending the mountain. Lake Biwa is visible in the distance.
2 The Kompon Chūdō, central structure of the Tōtō complex at the temple Enryakuji, was reconstructed beginning in 1630 by the Tokugawa shogunate. National Treasure.

Hidaka Mountains　　　日高山脈

(Hidaka Sammyaku). Mountain range running 150 km (93 mi) north to south, south-central Hokkaidō. Its highest peak is Poroshiridake (2,052 m; 6,732 ft). This watershed between the Ishikari and Tokachi plains consists of many peaks in the 1,500–2,000 m (4,920–6,560 ft) range. The foothills are covered with subarctic coniferous forests.

Hida Mountains　　　飛驒山脈

(Hida Sammyaku). Mountain range running north to south through Niigata, Toyama, Nagano, and Gifu prefectures, central Honshū. It is the northernmost of the three ranges forming the JAPANESE ALPS and is often called the Northern Alps. There are several peaks over 3,000 m (10,000 ft) high, including YARIGATAKE, HOTAKADAKE, TATEYAMA, TSURUGIDAKE, and NORIKURADAKE. The snow grouse (*raichō*) and the Japanese serow (KAMOSHIKA) living here have been designated as protected species. The range is known as the birthplace of modern mountain climbing in Japan. Most of the peaks in the Hida Mountains are included in the Chūbu Sangaku National Park.

Hidari Jingorō　　　左甚五郎

(fl late 16th–early 17th century). Temple carpenter and sculptor. Real name Itami Toshikatsu. Born in Akashi (now part of Hyōgo Prefecture). A disciple of a master carpenter of the imperial court, he assisted in the reconstruction of the temple Negoroji in Kii Province (now Wakayama Prefecture) and in

the construction of the bell tower of the temple Hōkōji in Kyōto. He later went to Edo (now Tōkyō), where he married the daughter of the Tokugawa family's master carpenter. He has been credited with many famous works from the early Edo period (1600–1868). These include the *nemurineko* or "sleeping cat" of the shrine TŌSHŌGŪ in Nikkō and the so-called nightingale floors of the temple CHION'IN in Kyōto, which "sing" loudly when walked on.

Hidari Sachiko　　　左幸子

(1930–). Actress and film director. Born in Toyama Prefecture. She became a film actress in 1952 and had her first major roles in two of director GOSHO HEINOSUKE's films, *Ōsaka no yado* (1954, An Inn at Ōsaka) and *Niwatori wa futatabi naku* (1954, The Cock Crows Again). In 1957 she received the award for best actress at the Cork Film Festival in Ireland for her role in *Kamisaka Shirō no hanzai* (1956, The Crime of Shiro Kamisaka), directed by Hisamatsu Seiji (b 1912).

In 1956 she left NIKKATSU CORPORATION, one of the major studios, to become an independent film performer. She starred in director IMAMURA SHŌHEI's *Nippon konchū ki* (1963, The Insect Woman); HANI SUSUMU's *Kanojo to kare* (1963, She and He), for which she won the award for best actress at the Berlin Film Festival; and Hani's *Andesu no hanayome* (1966, Bride of the Andes). In 1977, after directing several short films in Paris, Hidari made her debut as both a producer and director of a major feature film, *Tōi ippon no michi* (Far Road).

hiden'in　　　　　　悲田院

Also known as *hiden-dokoro*. Refuges for the poor and orphaned; sponsored by both the government and Buddhist temples from the 8th century. Both the *hiden'in* and the SEYAKUIN for the sick are said to have been started by Prince SHŌTOKU (574–622), but the first clear records date from 723, when such institutions were established at the temple KŌFUKUJI in the capital city of Nara. In 730 both types of refuge came under the sponsorship of the empress KŌMYŌ. The *hiden'in* in the temple Sennyūji in Kyōto endured into the 15th century and was revived under the Tokugawa shogunate (1603–1867).

Hieda no Are　　　稗田阿礼

(650?–?). Attendant (TONERI) of Emperor TEMMU; commissioned by the court to quote from memory the imperial genealogy and ancient legends so that Ō NO YASUMARO could record them in what became Japan's first written chronicle, the KOJIKI. It is not known whether Hieda no Are was a man or a woman. See also KATARIBE.

Hieizan 比叡山

(Mt. Hiei). Mountain on the border between Kyōto and Shiga prefectures, central Honshū. On the eastern slope is the temple EN-RYAKUJI, an important center of the Tendai sect of Buddhism founded by the priest SAI-CHŌ in 788. HIE SHRINE, on the same slope, houses the guardian deity of Enryakuji. Height: 848 m (2,782 ft).

Hie Shrine 日吉大社

(Hie Taisha; also known as Hiyoshi Taisha). Shintō shrine in the city of Ōtsu, Shiga Prefecture. The shrine is divided into two parts: the East Shrine, dedicated to Ōyamakui no Kami (the deity of Mt. Hiei; see HIEIZAN), and the West Shrine, dedicated to Ōnamuchi no Mikoto (the deity of the mountain Miwayama in Nara Prefecture). The Hie Shrine was regarded as the guardian (known by the Buddhist name Sannō Gongen) of the Buddhist temple ENRYAKUJI built on Mt. Hiei in 788 and hence came to be closely associated with it (see SANNŌ ICHIJITSU SHINTŌ). It developed subsidiary shrines, and the 21 larger shrines, including the two main shrines mentioned above, were collectively called the Sannō Nijūissha (Twenty-One Shrines of the Sannō). The Hie Taisha is regarded as the central shrine for Japan's more than 3,800 Hie Sannō shrines. The two main shrines are designated National Treasures. Its annual festival is on 12–15 April.

Hie Shrine 日枝神社

(Hie Jinja). A Shintō shrine in Chiyoda Ward, Tōkyō; dedicated to Ōyamakui no Kami, the deity who presides over Mt. Hiei (HIEIZAN), and three other deities. The Tokugawa shōguns (1603–1867) regarded its central deity as the protector of Edo (now Tōkyō). The Hie Shrine grew into one of the most popular shrines in Edo. The SANNŌ FES-TIVAL, held at the shrine on 7–16 June, is one of the major shrine celebrations in Tōkyō, along with the festival of the KANDA SHRINE. (The two festivals are held in alternate years.) Until the official separation of Buddhism and Shintō in 1868, the Hie Shrine was known as the Sannō Gongen.

higaki kaisen →kaisen

higambana 彼岸花

Lycoris radiata. Also known as *manjushage.* Perennial herb of the family Amaryllidaceae; widely found from Honshū to Kyūshū in fields, along roadsides, and on ridges between rice paddies. In early September the bulb produces a flower shoot (30 cm; 12 in). Toward the end of the month, corresponding with the autumnal equinox (*higan*), clusters of red flowers appear on the tip of the stem. The six petals face directly outward from the stalk and are wrinkled at the edges. After flowering the plant sends out shiny, dark leaves, which wither the following spring.

higan 彼岸

(literally, "the other shore"). A seven-day Buddhist memorial service held twice a year, centering on the vernal and autumnal equinoxes. More formally called *higan'e*, it is common to all Japanese Buddhist sects but is not found in India, China, or other Buddhist countries. The word *higan* is derived from the Chinese equivalent of the Sanskrit word *pāramitā*, which refers to the eternal paradise awaiting those who achieve enlightenment (SATORI), as opposed to "this shore" (*shigan*), in which one wanders through the pain of living. The *higan'e* rites are intended to help souls pass from the world of confusion to the world of enlightenment. In a rite formerly conducted at the temple SHITENNŌJI in Ōsaka, believers worshipped the sunset while praying for rebirth into paradise. *Higan* is an important event even today. It is a time for family gatherings, visiting family graves, and offering "*higan* dumplings." A proverb associates it with the change of seasons: "Winter cold and summer heat end at *higan.*"

Higashi Hiroshima 東広島[市]

City in central Hiroshima Prefecture, western Honshū, contiguous with the city of Hiroshima. It is fast being urbanized. Its Saijō district has long been known for its *sake.* Principal industries are electric equipment and machinery. Pop: 94,209.

Higashi Honganji 東本願寺

The head temple of the Shinshū Ōtani branch of the Buddhist True Pure Land sect (Jōdo Shinshū; see JŌDO SHIN SECT); located in Shimogyō Ward, Kyōto. The temple was founded in 1603 (the traditional foundation date of 1602 is based on suspect sources) as the result of a succession dispute between two sons of the HONGANJI's 11th abbot (*hossu*), Kennyo Kōsa (1543–92), which split the great religious organization of the Honganji into two rival branches. After the death of Kennyo Kōsa in 1592, his eldest son, Kyōnyo Kōju (1558–1614), assumed the abbacy. He was forced into retirement in 1593, when his younger brother Junnyo Kōshō's (1577–1631) claim to their father's inheritance was established and TOYOTOMI HIDEYOSHI recognized the latter as the temple's abbot. Kyōnyo soon established ties with the future shōgun TOKUGAWA IEYASU, however, and he may have had Ieyasu's support when he left retirement for his own new temple in 1603. That temple came to be called Higashi (eastern) Honganji to distinguish it from its rival, Nishi (western) Honganji, located a few city blocks to the west, which remained in the possession of Junnyo and his successors. It was not until 1619 that the Tokugawa shogunate (1603–1867) officially recognized the establishment founded by Kyōnyo as an independent branch of the Jōdo Shinshū. Thereafter the two Honganji enjoyed equal status, dividing between them the major portion of the True Pure Land sect's adherents. In 1989 the Higashi Honganji had 5,533,194 members

and 8,682 branch temples. See also NISHI HONGANJI.

Higashikuni Naruhiko 東久邇稔彦

(1887–1990). Imperial prince, prime minister (1945), and army general. Born in Kyōto, the ninth son of Prince Kuni no Miya Asahiko (1824–91), he married one of the daughters of Emperor MEIJI. He was given the name Higashikuni in 1906. He graduated from the Army Academy and the Army War College and studied in France. After holding various posts, he became general commander of defense during World War II. Following the decision to surrender in August 1945, he was appointed prime minister. It was the only time that a member of the imperial family headed a cabinet. He presided over the formal signing of the surrender on 2 September 1945 and the dissolution of the armed forces but resigned in October 1945 in opposition to an order from the Occupation authorities to abolish the PEACE PRESERVATION LAW OF 1925 and the SPECIAL HIGHER POLICE. In 1947 he formally renounced membership in the imperial family.

Higashi Kurume 東久留米[市]

City in north-central Tōkyō Prefecture. Situated on the Musashino Plateau, the city is a residential area for commuters to Tōkyō. Pop: 113,818.

Higashi Matsuura Peninsula 東松浦半島

(Higashi Matsuura Hantō). Located in northwestern Saga Prefecture, northwestern

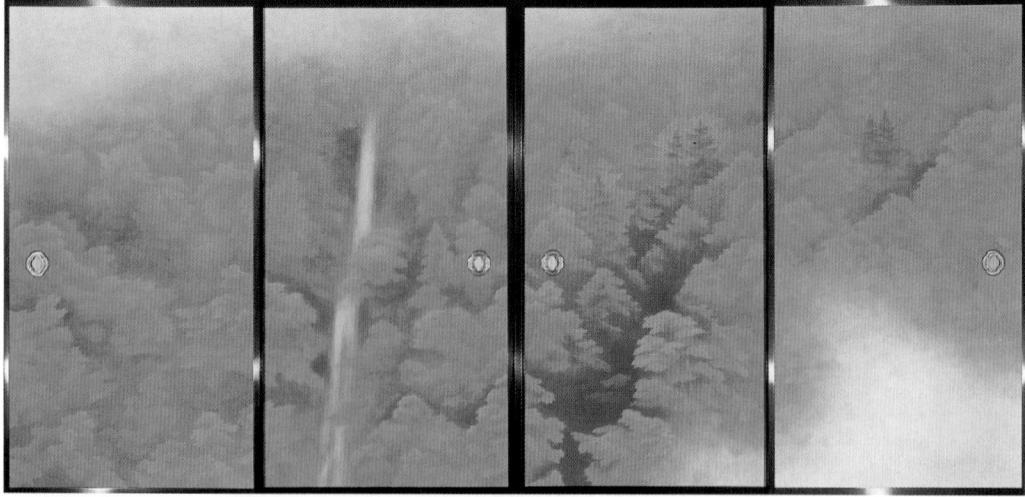

Higashiyama Kaii Four panels from this *nihonga* artist's landscape on sliding screens, titled *San'un* (Mountain Clouds). 1975. 178 × 376 cm. Part of a set of screen and wall paintings done by Higashiyama in the *mieidō*, or founder's hall, Tōshōdaiji, Nara.

Kyūshū; part of Genkai Quasi-National Park. Extending into the Genkai Sea, its heavily indented coastline has numerous promontories as well as hundreds of inlets. Several good harbors are found here.

Higashi Matsuyama 東松山[市]

City in central Saitama Prefecture, central Honshū. Originally an agricultural town, it has become rapidly industrialized and urbanized. Tourist attractions are the Iwadono Kannon, a statue of the bodhisattva at the temple Shōhōji, and the Yakyū Shrine. Pop: 84,394.

Higashi Murayama 東村山[市]

City in north-central Tōkyō Prefecture. Once an agricultural district, it has become a residential suburb of Tōkyō. Several hospitals and convalescence homes are located here. Pop: 134,002.

Higashine 東根[市]

City in central Yamagata Prefecture, northern Honshū. Formerly a castle town. Principal agricultural products are rice, safflower, and fruit, particularly apples and cherries. Recently an electronics industry has devel-

oped in the area. It is the site of Yamagata Airport. Higashine Hot Spring is in the northwestern part of the city. Pop: 42,751.

Higashi Ōsaka 東大阪[市]

City in Ōsaka Prefecture. Established in 1967 with the merger of the three cities of Fuse, Kawachi, and Hiraoka; it is now a satellite city of Ōsaka and adjacent to it. Industry and commerce flourish in the Fuse district. The electric appliance and textile industries are active in the Kawachi district, and machinery manufacturing prospers in the Hiraoka district. Numerous sites of historical interest are located on the mountain Ikomayama to the east. Pop: 518,319.

Higashiyama culture 東山文化

(Higashiyama *bunka*). The culture that flourished during the rule and retirement of the eighth Muromachi shōgun ASHIKAGA YO-SHIMASA (1436–90; r 1449–74), who spent his last years at his villa (popularly known as GINKAKUJI) in the Higashiyama section of Kyōto. It was distinguished by its blend of the aristocratic traditions of the Heian court nobility, the religious influences of ZEN Buddhism, and the tastes and ethos of the dominant warrior society. Yoshimasa's reign as shōgun was marked by grave political unrest, largely stemming from his own negligence and mismanagement. At the start of his rule he had had every intention of wielding governmental power, but on realizing that he was too weak-willed to combat more astute political rivals, he quickly gave himself over to sensual and artistic pleasures and eventually decided to retire. The succession dispute that followed was one of the major causes of the ŌNIN WAR (1467–77), which decimated Kyōto and destroyed Ashikaga political power.

While Kyōto burned, Yoshimasa pursued his interests, settling in 1483 at Ginkakuji, which soon became the center for the arts, attracting *daimyō* and townspeople alike. Yoshimasa's patronage of the TEA CEREMONY awakened a new interest in implements, MAKI-E lacquer work, architecture, garden design, and flower arrangement. Inspired by Chinese Ming-dynasty (1368–1644) paintings, the genre of the *suibokuga* (INK PAINTING) was perfected by SHŪBUN and SESSHŪ TŌYŌ. There were also technical refinements in NŌ drama by KOMPARU ZENCHIKU and in linked-verse poetry (RENGA) by SŌGI. Studies on the classics by such scholars as ICHIJŌ KANEYOSHI and SANJŌNISHI SANETAKA were encouraged as well.

The aesthetic canons of Higashiyama culture—YŪGEN and WABI—have come to typify Japanese art. An aura of mystery and ineffability rather than descriptive realism, a stress on sparseness, understatement, and

rusticity rather than artifice represent to this day the highest ideal of aesthetics in Japan.

Higashiyama Hot Spring 東山温泉

(Higashiyama Onsen). Located in a deep valley in the city of Aizu Wakamatsu, Fukushima Prefecture, central Honshū. A common salt spring; maximum water temperature 61°C (142°F).

Higashiyama Kaii 東山魁夷

(1908–). Japanese-style (NIHONGA) painter. Real name Higashiyama Shinkichi. Born in Kanagawa Prefecture. After graduating from Tōkyō Bijutsu Gakkō (now Tōkyō University of Fine Arts and Music), he studied art history at the University of Berlin. In 1947 one of his paintings won the highest award at the Nitten (Japan Art Exhibition). A highly regarded landscape painter, Higashiyama has done murals at the Tōgū Palace, the Imperial Palace, and the temple Tōshōdaiji. In 1969 he was awarded the Order of Culture.

Higashi Yamato 東大和[市]

City in north-central Tōkyō Prefecture. Formerly a farming village, it developed as a residential area from 1955 with the construction of large housing complexes. The city has numerous electrical machinery, appliance, and food-processing factories. Lake Tama is located in the northern part of the city. Pop: 75,132.

Higeki kigeki 悲劇喜劇

(Tragedy, Comedy). Influential theater journal. Founded by a drama study group headed by KISHIDA KUNIO, the journal has had three series. Series one (October 1928–July 1929) published works by KUBOTA MANTARŌ, YAMAMOTO YŪZŌ, KOBAYASHI HIDEO, KINOSHITA MOKUTARŌ, and FUNAHASHI SEIICHI. Contributors to series two (November 1947–June 1964) included TANAKA CHIKAO, HINO ASHIHEI, TERAYAMA SHŪJI, and YAMAZAKI MASAKAZU. In late 1950 it changed from a quarterly to a monthly. This postwar series included special issues on contemporary and historical drama and encouraged the development of amateur and school dramatic programs. Series three began in January 1966 and published works by TOITA YASUJI, IIZAWA TADASU, and INOUE HISASHI.

high-definition television 高品位テレビ

(HDTV; J: *kōhin'i terebi*). Next-generation television system capable of producing pictures with an image quality comparable to that of 35-millimeter motion picture film. The HDTV system developed by NHK (Japan Broadcasting Corporation) Science and Technology Research Laboratories, commonly referred to as Hi-Vision (Haibijon), utilizes a screen with a 9:16 height/width ratio, instead of the 3:4 ratio in current television, and has a resolution of 1,125 scanning lines, more than double the present 525 lines. HDTV is capable of high-quality sound reproduction and visual effects. Consequently, its applications extend beyond television to such areas as motion picture production, satellite distribution of movies, large-scale displays at public events, and the production, manipulation, and storage of still images for art and archival purposes.

Development of HDTV technology in Japan began in the mid-1960s. Extensive research into the physiology of human vision led to the development of new specifications for screen size and image quality capable of producing a greatly enhanced visual impact on the television viewer. HDTV was broad-

high-definition television
1 A 1,125-line high-definition television picture (left) and Japan's current 525-line television image.
2 Sales of high-definition televisions, such as this Sony model, have been slow because of high prices and limited HDTV broadcasting.

cast experimentally during EXPO '85, and in June of 1989 one-hour daily broadcasts by satellite were begun. The Gifu Prefectural Museum and the Saison Museum of Art in Tōkyō began using HDTV systems to display still images of art, referred to as videographs, in 1989.

High Energy Physics, National Laboratory for 高エネルギー物理学研究所

(Kōenerugī Butsurigaku Kenkyūjo). Government research center under the administration of the Ministry of Education. Located in the city of Tsukuba, Ibaraki Prefecture. Opened in 1976, it is the largest research center for high-energy physics in Japan and carries out studies of elementary particles with such equipment as TRISTAN, a 30-giga electron-volt proton accelerator.

higher education 高等教育

(kōtō kyōiku). Japan's higher education system enrolled roughly 2.5 million students in universities and colleges in 1989, with about 60 percent of high school graduates attending some type of higher education institution.

The Development of the System— Higher education institutions were established in Japan as early as the 8th century AD, but it was only following the Meiji Restoration (1868) that they began to assume their present forms and to place primary emphasis on so-called WESTERN LEARNING. In 1877 the new government established TŌKYŌ UNIVERSITY, with departments of jurisprudence, liberal arts, natural science, and medicine taught by European or American faculty in their own languages (see FOREIGN EMPLOYEES OF THE MEIJI PERIOD). In addition, the government established a normal school, an engineering school, and several other higher education and research institutions. Smaller schools started by scholars or religious groups during the Edo period (1600–1868) also expanded to become full-fledged institutions of higher education after 1868. Keiō Gijuku (later KEIŌ UNIVERSITY) was started by FUKUZAWA YUKICHI and the Tetsugakukan (later TŌYŌ UNIVERSITY) by INOUE ENRYŌ. Leading statesmen ŌKUMA SHIGENOBU and MORI ARINORI founded WASEDA UNIVERSITY and the Shōhō Kōshūjo (later HITOTSUBASHI UNIVERSITY), respectively. Western Christian groups helped establish such universities as Dōshisha, Meiji Gakuin, Aoyama Gakuin, and Kansei Gakuin.

Tōkyō University was reorganized as the first of the IMPERIAL UNIVERSITIES in 1886, and five higher middle schools (later HIGHER SCHOOLS) were established throughout Japan to prepare students for study there. The Imperial University in Tōkyō became the center for academic research and the training of civil servants and scholars "in accordance with the needs of the state." It comprised six schools: law, medicine, technology, liberal arts, natural science, and agriculture; a graduate school and courses were set up in each school. By the late 1890s some classes were taught in Japanese by qualified native instructors. In 1897 the second imperial university was established in Kyōto (see KYŌTO UNIVERSITY), followed by five more over the next three decades. Renamed national universities and expanded after World War II, they still occupy a central position in Japanese higher education.

From 1918, under the University Order (Daigaku Rei), private institutions that maintained prescribed standards were permitted official university charters. By 1935

Japan had 45 universities (25 of them private) and a total of 356 institutions of higher education. Following World War II, the Allied Occupation authorities proposed that the various existing universities, higher schools, professional and vocational schools (SEMMON GAKKŌ), and normal schools be consolidated into a smaller number of four-year universities offering both general and specialized education on an equal opportunity basis. The SCHOOL EDUCATION LAW of 1947 embodied these proposals. Some semmon gakkō lacked proper facilities and teaching staff to qualify as universities and, as a relief measure, they were temporarily recognized as two-year JUNIOR COLLEGES, for which permanent recognition came only in 1964. In addition, provisions were made for qualified institutions to establish GRADUATE SCHOOLS with two-year master's and three-year doctor's programs. By 1952 some 220 universities (with 399,513 students) and 205 junior colleges (with 53,230 students) had been recognized. Today Japan's diverse system of higher education, still centered on the universities, also includes junior colleges, technical colleges, MISCELLANEOUS SCHOOLS (kakushu gakkō), and special training schools (senshū gakkō).

Finance—National universities are totally dependent on the national government; other public institutions rely heavily on prefectural or local governments. Until recently, private universities drew their revenues primarily from student tuition, supplemented by loans, income from attached businesses, and gifts. These sources proved insufficient, forcing private universities to press parents of incoming students for enormous "contributions" and to raise the student-teacher ratio. By the mid-1960s, there were 100 students per full-time staff member at several private schools, and it was not uncommon for 500 or more students to be enrolled in a class. Such conditions helped lead to the STUDENT MOVEMENT that troubled higher education between 1965 and 1970. In 1970 the government finally acted to relieve the financial plight of private universities by establishing the JAPAN PRIVATE SCHOOL PROMOTION FOUNDATION, which in 1989 provided about 15 percent of the operating funds of all private institutions. Tuitions at national universities have meanwhile been raised to a level more in line with those at private universities, a ratio of about 2:3 in 1990. See also UNIVERSITIES AND COLLEGES.

higher schools 旧制高等学校

(kyūsei kōtō gakkō, or "old-system high schools"). Three-year institutions of learning that existed before the EDUCATIONAL REFORMS of 1947; they prepared students for IMPERIAL UNIVERSITIES. Five higher schools were set up at the same time as the establishment of the imperial university system in 1886. (At the time of their inception, they were called "higher middle schools" [kōtō chūgakkō] but came to be called higher schools from 1894.) Students had to pass an arduous examination to enter the higher schools, but once there they were virtually assured of entrance into imperial or other government universities. Foreign languages dominated the curriculum. Unlike at universities, students lived in dormitories, which were noted for their free atmosphere. All higher schools were abolished in 1947.

high school baseball 高校野球

(kōkō yakyū). High school baseball is dominated by the National Invitational Senior

High School Baseball Tournament, which is held each year in March and April, and the All-Japan High School Baseball Championship Tournament, which is held in August. These events, which trace their origins back to 1924 and 1915, respectively, are held at KŌSHIEN STADIUM in Nishinomiya, Hyōgo Prefecture, and are commonly known as the spring and summer Kōshien tournaments. They receive extensive coverage in the press, are broadcast live nationwide via radio and television, and consistently rival professional baseball in popularity. More than 4,000 high school teams participated in the qualifying rounds for the 1990 summer tournament.

high schools 高等学校

(kōtō gakkō). Japanese high schools are a noncompulsory stage of SECONDARY EDUCATION, open to graduates of the compulsory MIDDLE SCHOOLS. In 1989, 94.5 percent of middle school students chose to attend high school programs, which require three years of full-time study to complete. Most students (74 percent in 1989) enroll in general education course programs, but high schools specializing in business, industrial arts, agriculture, homemaking, or fishery also exist (see VOCATIONAL EDUCATION). The school year runs from April to March. In 1989 28.4 percent of Japan's high school students were enrolled in private schools. The total number of high school graduates who entered universities or junior colleges in 1989 constituted a figure equal to 30.7 percent of the number of students who completed high school that year. ▶▶530-531

high school baseball
Japan's national pastime is taken very seriously, especially at the high school level. A television audience of millions views the annual national championship tournaments broadcast from Kōshien Stadium.
1 At the conclusion of a game played in Kōshien Stadium, the winning team's school song is played and the school flag raised.
2 A losing team collects dirt from the Kōshien playing field to bring back for scattering on the team's home field as an inspiration to work harder.

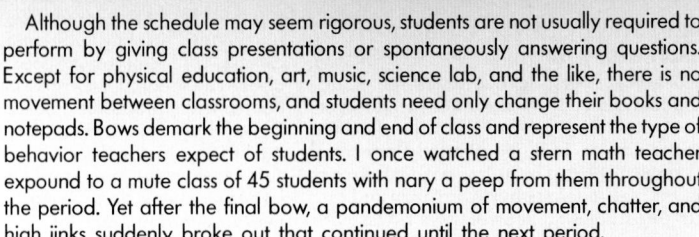

Life in a Japanese High School

A former teacher sheds light on the behind-the-scenes workings of Japan's educational system.

Japan's continuing accomplishments in education have drawn the attention of the international media to its school system. But while the press has praised Japanese education, particularly in math and science, a number of writers have criticized Japanese middle schools and high schools for their stark atmosphere.

Many of the images presented in the media have focused on the shocking and sensational aspects of Japanese secondary education. Adolescent suicide, "examination hell," and cheating scandals have been featured topics for two decades, giving the impression that the Japanese high school is a test factory run with militaristic precision. Such a narrow focus by the press has prevented any real understanding of the successes and failures of Japan's educational establishment.

The Japanese high school is a total institution that pervades every aspect of student life and is the center of social interaction for students. But average, healthy adolescents are not the stuff of news articles, so the world knows little of the day-to-day life in Japan's high schools.

The School Day

Before they reach the school gates, Japanese high school students have already entered their daily cycle of social time and study time. The school, like the Japanese company, pervades one's life, but not as a single-minded endeavor. The school is a totality—a mosaic of playfulness and seriousness.

The day begins with students converging on the streets and lanes near school. As the density of bodies increases, so too does the decibel level. Upon entering the building, students change out of their street shoes into their school shoes. They do not have lockers other than shoe boxes. When they arrive in the classroom, boys and girls break into smaller groups. In the summer, groups usually spread out; in winter everyone congregates around the heater. Students chat: girls with girls, boys with boys. Some hurry to finish assignments—the average first-year student logs in more than an hour and a half of homework every day. But even last-minute studiers tend to form pairs and threesomes.

As the warning bell chimes, tardy students make a break for the classroom. Teachers keeping watch at the entrance gate urge stragglers to hurry. When the class bell rings, the teachers nicknamed "fire engines" (because they appear as soon as the alarm sounds) will be mounting the podium, while more relaxed educators will be finishing up their tea in the teachers' room. Within five minutes of the bell, the halls are deserted and quiet. Students rise when the monitor barks "stand up," and at the command "bow," 40 heads bend in unison. Class has now begun, and the social atmosphere has come to an end. For the next 50 minutes, academics will dominate.

The school day is highly structured. There are usually seven subjects covered each day, although the last period is not formally part of the Ministry of Education curriculum. On Saturdays, classes end at around 1 PM. During the college exam preparation period—from September to January—some teachers convene early morning classes for drilling special subjects. At many high schools, third-year students are divided into separate tracks (usually science or humanities), but for the first year or two, students spend virtually the whole day studying the same subjects with the same group of people. Throughout Japan, some form of the following schedule takes place Monday through Friday:

8:40–8:50	Homeroom Period	12:40–1:15	Lunch
8:50–9:40	English	1:15–1:25	Cleaning
9:50–10:40	Math	1:30–2:20	Social Studies
10:50–11:40	Physics	2:30–3:20	Japanese Literature
11:50–12:40	Art/Music	[3:30–4:20]	Chemistry/Biology

Although the schedule may seem rigorous, students are not usually required to perform by giving class presentations or spontaneously answering questions. Except for physical education, art, music, science lab, and the like, there is no movement between classrooms, and students need only change their books and notepads. Bows demark the beginning and end of class and represent the type of behavior teachers expect of students. I once watched a stern math teacher expound to a mute class of 45 students with nary a peep from them throughout the period. Yet after the final bow, a pandemonium of movement, chatter, and high jinks suddenly broke out that continued until the next period.

The school day, then, is punctuated with lively moments of free time and conversation. The social interaction that goes on at school is, for most students, the heart of their social lives. While engaged in silent study, students prefer to sit in groups of three and four. Even when going to the restroom, both boys and girls tend to go in groups. And in the library, few students are seen reading alone, for being alone is synonymous with being lonely.

Teachers and Coaches

The nature of the teacher-student relationship is emotionally charged in Japan. While the school holds overall responsibility for the moral development of the child, the homeroom teacher is directly responsible for the welfare of his or her class. For a good part of the day—during class, homeroom period, cleaning time, and sometimes lunch—the homeroom teacher is with the students. He or she also performs with the class at all school events. Disciplinary matters are usually left in his or her hands as well, and the principal is generally called only when expulsion may be necessary. The homeroom teacher acts as counselor for the students, guiding them in their choice of college or consoling them when they have troubles. Through this constant interaction over a yearlong period, the homeroom teacher becomes well acquainted with each student.

Good homeroom teachers demonstrate their caring and responsibility by working hard and by always being accessible to students. It is the homeroom teacher who calls a week of early morning math review if the class average slips. It is the homeroom teacher who dons a warm-up suit and scrubs the floor with the students, and it is the homeroom teacher who comes to the house to drop off homework when a student has been out sick for a few days.

A teacher's responsibilities do not end once the students leave the campus. The conduct of the homeroom teacher in the community must reflect his or her status and position. To the extent that homeroom teachers fulfill all of these roles with compassion and dignity, they are respected and admired by their pupils.

For many students, however, particularly those who are not on track to prestigious colleges, their athletic coach may be the most important adult at school. During trips to various matches or on long, cold rainy days of practice, it is the coach who displays the characteristics that invoke respect—patience, hard work, and devotion to the students. One English teacher I knew was also the baseball coach of his school. During the baseball season he literally spent seven days a week at school, often arriving at 7:30 in the morning and departing at 7 at night. In a society sensitive to effort and self-sacrifice, this kind of dedication has a profound psychological effect on the recipients.

Discipline

In some areas of student life, Japanese high schools are far more restrictive than their Western counterparts. Much has been made of the strict disciplinary codes, which many in the West see as unnecessarily severe.

A number of schools have stern policies, one example being the stringent dress code imposed on students. The majority of schools, public and private, require students to wear uniforms. The schools in which I taught were particularly strict about dress: skirt length, trouser width, and color of hair ribbon were regulated and inspected monthly. Caps, scarves, and nonstandard rain gear were prohibited.

Infractions of the rules brought punishment, which ranged from scolding to having students' parents come in for a meeting. But, of course, students found ways around these rules—a judicious use of tape allowed girls to adjust their hemlines for inspection and put them back to where they wanted afterward.

The aim of uniform regulations is to instill in young people a sense of precision and seriousness. A student is a student in school and out, and his or her responsibilities do not end off campus. In Japan, an individual is seen as an extension of the group to which he or she belongs, so care must be taken to project a proper image to the world. This emphasis on form and appearance is not limited to schools, but is a basic fact of Japanese life. Students must assume the responsibility of representing the school, just as they will someday represent a company or a family in later life.

The mandatory cleaning ritual has been viewed favorably by Western educators. Each day a period is set aside for a cleaning session in which students, and sometimes teachers, take part. At the beginning of every month and before important events, cleaning period is extended. Teachers assign special team tasks: window washing, floor waxing, etc.

Many in the West link the daily cleaning sessions with the absence of graffiti in Japanese high schools. The reasoning is that if students are required to clean their environment, they are less likely to mess it up. But this is an oversimplification. The aim of the cleaning session is not merely to tidy up the school, which could be done more efficiently once a week. What daily cleaning aims to do is to instill in students a sense of responsibility. The cleaning ritual itself is regarded as a form of moral training, a concept that has its origins in monastic Buddhism. Having students and teachers engage in this daily ritual not only fosters a communal sense of duty, but also emphasizes the continual care and nurturing that learning in general requires.

As for high-school romances, couples are virtually invisible on Japanese campuses. But this does not necessarily mean that the students are all deprived of experiencing young love. Couples often find clever ways around rules that restrict dating—meeting after school or on weekends, sitting in snack shops, or strolling along covered sidewalks. At school, the innocuous shoe box is often put to use as a secret postal route for love letters. For the lucky, a small envelope, highly embossed and neatly sealed, may await them when they change into their school shoes at the start of the day.

I recall a boy and girl who, every morning, would stand back to back on opposite sides of a fire door at the corner of a stairwell. They weren't facing anyone nor could they see each other, but every day there they were. Once, in coming down the stairs rather quickly, I caught them unawares. They were actually chatting with each other through the fire door, which was thin enough for their voices to carry through. While not everyone may have resorted to these particular means, for many Japanese, high school will be sure to bring back some fond memory of their *hatsukoi*, or first love.

Extracurricular Activities

Though school officially ends at around 4:30 each day, the number of students going home is small. At some schools, where a large percentage of students hope to apply to national or private universities, there may be a mass exodus to exam preparatory schools (*juku*). At the average school, there is a mix of students heading for *juku*, staying to talk with teachers, and joining after-school clubs. Students who head straight home get the reputation for being members of the *kitaku kurabu*, or the "go home club," a distinction which implies a lack of seriousness and a dash of laziness.

Extracurricular activities are varied and may include everything from English and broadcasting clubs to athletic clubs. For many students, these activities are their raison d'être. Students in athletic clubs train from 4:30, when classes end, until 6 or 8 in the evening. Practice for freshmen is tough, as the older students tend to run the clubs with a high hand. The junior members (*kōhai*) must use polite language, run errands, put in extra hours to show proper deference to their seniors (*sempai*), and prove that they are dedicated to the team. The resulting bonds that form among club members are strong and will often last a lifetime.

The School Year

Social activity peaks during the special events that highlight the school year: the cultural festival (*bunkasai*), sports festival (*taiikusai*), and the field trip (*ensoku*). Preparation for the cultural festival takes months, and everyone eagerly anticipates the day when their accomplishments will be displayed for all to see. The school, usually devoid of decoration, is for a few days filled with art. Good-natured fun is essential, and hand-drawn cartoons mocking teachers' physiognomies often grace the walls. The cultural festival is also a time when teachers can show students a different side of themselves—for example, everyone may be amazed to see that their homeroom teacher is a fine watercolor artist.

The sports festival is to athletes what the cultural festival is to musicians, artists, and writers. At the sports festival, however, talent is acknowledged within the framework of group performance. The school is divided into teams, each one having its own color: blue, red, or yellow. Each team competes for the championship of the school, and in striving for the team, individual runners and jumpers can make their mark. Participation of all is essential, and a portion of the judging rests on the performance of the cheering teams, or *ōendan*. Boys turn into a legion of kicking kung fu dancers, while crepe paper and ribbon transform the girls into a festive pom-pom squad. Each cheering team performs in a show that is half boisterousness and half coordinated drills, and the team with the most creativity and spirit wins the most points.

But students probably look forward most to the yearly field trip, which is usually planned months in advance. Some classes are more creative than others, but no matter what the outing—a simple picnic at the beach or a trip to the nearest cultural center—everyone is enthusiastic.

For high school seniors, the annual class trip can last up to 10 days. These extended excursions give students a chance to travel to more distant parts of the country. While Tōkyō residents may relish Hokkaidō snow or a glimpse of Sakurajima's awesome volcanic force, students from other areas like to visit Tōkyō—and in particular Disneyland. Recently, overseas trips to places such as Taiwan and Australia have also become popular.

Field trips foster lasting bonds among fellow classmates. Hundreds of photographs are taken and then painstakingly arranged into neat albums that will be pulled out and dusted off at later reunions with old friends. The pictures, and some *sake* or beer, can do wonders to revive memories of those jolly times.

English slogans of dubious meaning abound in Japan, but one phrase that graced a student's jacket summed up the high school experience for me: "vibrant life." Compared to the devil-may-care atmosphere of college, high school in Japan is indeed a time of serious and intensive study, especially for those who must prepare for the competitive university entrance exams. But high school is not all drudgery and memorization. It is a dynamic period of social interaction and intellectual growth—a time when students prepare for their future roles in society.

After 20 or 30 years of work, child rearing, and fulfilling the duties expected of a *shakaijin* ("solid citizen"), school may seem like a pleasant dream. At reunions, whether formal or informal, many people will undoubtedly reminisce about the enjoyable and—in retrospect—carefree years of their youth. For the all-consuming nature of school is both constrictive and supportive. School is a fabric of interwoven academic and social time that defines and gives meaning to life.

Gerald K. LeTendre

Hikawa Shrine At this shrine's annual festival in April, young girls costumed as *miko* (shrine maidens), wearing cherry blossoms in their hair, perform a dance to placate evil spirits.

high-temperature supercon-ductivity research 高温超電導研究

(*kōon chōdendō kenkyū*). Superconductivity, the loss of all resistance to electric current, occurs in various materials when they are cooled below about 20 K (-253°C; -423.4°F). In 1986 a research group at Tōkyō University confirmed the presence of superconductive properties in an oxide material at 40 K (-233°C; -387.4°F), sparking worldwide interest in "high-temperature" superconductivity research. Various Japanese industries and government agencies began separate research projects, but in 1988 the MINISTRY OF INTERNATIONAL TRADE AND INDUSTRY (MITI) established a joint public/private consortium, the International Superconductivity Technology Center (ISTEC), to strengthen and unify Japanese research. In 1990 the ISTEC-affiliated Superconductivity Research Laboratory confirmed superconductivity at 127 K (-146°C; -230.8°F). Superconductive materials are used in the construction of strong electromagnets and in various electronics applications.

High Treason Incident of 1910 大逆事件

(Taigyaku Jiken). Also known as the Kōtoku Incident. An anarchist plot to assassinate Emperor Meiji that led to mass arrests of leftwing activists in 1910 and culminated in the execution of KŌTOKU SHŪSUI and 11 other alleged conspirators in 1911.

On 20 May 1910 Nagano prefectural police searched the room of Miyashita Takichi (1875–1911), a young lumber-mill employee, and uncovered materials that could be used for the construction of bombs. Within five days the police had amassed sufficient evidence to arrest Miyashita, Nitta Tōru (a local accomplice; b 1880), and, in quick succession, Niimura Tadao (1887–1911), Niimura Zembei (dates unknown), and Furukawa Rikisaku (1884–1911). Kōtoku Shūsui and KANNO SUGA, his common-law wife, were apprehended soon afterward. Questioning of these people and further investigation by the police soon uncovered what the prosecutor general's office regarded as a nationwide conspiracy against the throne.

After a preliminary investigation conducted by government prosecutors, in which hundreds of left-wing activists and sympathizers were interrogated, 25 men and 1 woman were brought to trial on charges of violating article 73 of the Criminal Code, which prohibited harming or intending harm to the emperor or the imperial family. The case was tried in closed extraordinary sessions before the GREAT COURT OF CASSATION. The prosecution was headed by HIRANUMA KIICHIRŌ.

Higuchi Ichiyō The first major female writer of the modern period, Ichiyō wrote stories about young women growing up in Tōkyō's poorer quarters.

Although evidence against the 5 principal conspirators seemed conclusive, that dealing with the other 21 defendants was often less than adequate. Despite such circumstances, the court found all of the defendants guilty as charged on 18 January 1911. Twenty-four were sentenced to death by hanging for violations of article 73; the remaining two were sentenced to 8 and 11 years respectively for violations of the laws governing the manufacture and possession of explosives. On 19 January 1911 an imperial rescript commuted the sentences of 12 of those condemned to life imprisonment. Twelve conspirators, including Kōtoku and Kanno, were executed on 24 and 25 January.

Intellectuals were rightly concerned that the case showed a shift from the open intellectual environment of the early Meiji years to increased government control in the area of thought. With the conclusion of the High Treason Incident, the Japanese socialist movement entered what has often been described as the "winter years" (*fuyu no jidai*) from which it was not to emerge until the stimulus of the Russian Revolution and the more liberal environment of TAISHŌ DEMOCRACY.

Higuchi Ichiyō 樋口一葉

(1872–96). The most prominent female writer of the Meiji period (1868–1912), Higuchi Ichiyō was the author of some 20 short and medium-length stories treating primarily the unhappy and circumscribed lives of young women of her day. She also composed some 3,800 TANKA (31-syllable poems in the classical WAKA genre), several essays, and a highly regarded diary.

Ichiyō was the pen name of Higuchi Natsu, born the daughter of a minor official in the Tōkyō city government. In late 1883 she completed her formal education at the end of the fourth year of elementary school, at the head of her class. Her mother opposed further education on the grounds that too much learning was not good for a woman.

Ichiyō showed an early interest in literature. Hiding from her mother, she immersed herself in romances and adventure stories. She had already begun to write *tanka* while in primary school, but it was only after 1886, when she entered a poetry academy, the Haginoya, directed by the woman poet Nakajima Utako (1844–1903), that she developed her poetic talents. Since almost all the other students were young women of the upper class, Ichiyō felt out of place as the daughter of a minor official. Yet her economic inferiority undoubtedly spurred her to excel in the area of poetry. This determination to overcome all obstacles characterized Ichiyō for the remainder of her life.

With the death of Ichiyō's eldest brother in 1887, followed by the business failure, illness, and death of her father in 1889, the Higuchi family fell into dire poverty. The Shibuya family broke off the engagement between their son Saburō and Ichiyō, a bitter blow because she and Saburō had been childhood sweethearts. Ichiyō began writing fiction in 1890, and in the following year she became the pupil of Nakarai Tōsui (1861–1926), a writer for the *Tōkyō asahi shimbun*, a daily newspaper. Under his tutelage she published her first story, "Yamizakura" (1892, Cherry Blossoms in the Dark), in the first issue of *Musashino*, a magazine Tōsui was editing. This story, treating the unhappy love of a boy and a girl, dealt with a theme common to many of her later works. Ichiyō fell deeply in love with Tōsui, but

the relationship was broken off. This rupture with Tōsui and her consequent suffering, following upon her broken engagement with Shibuya Saburō, reinforced Ichiyō's belief that she would not find fulfillment in love, and she poured forth her unhappiness in the pages of her diary.

Although she continued publishing stories in various magazines, including the influential *Bungakukai*, and in newspapers, she received so little financial compensation that she decided to give up writing. She moved in July 1893, with her mother and sister, to Ryūsenji near the Yoshiwara prostitution quarter of Tōkyō. Her 10-month stay at Ryūsenji provided her with the material for her best-known and most highly praised story, TAKEKURABE (1895–96, Comparing Heights; tr "Growing Up," 1956), which treated the lives of young people growing up in a licensed prostitution quarter and focused on the heroine Midori, destined to follow her older sister into prostitution.

In May 1894 Ichiyō moved to the Hongō district of Tōkyō, where she resumed her writing and also began to teach at the Haginoya. In rapid succession she produced her best stories, on which her fame is based. The superbly crafted "Ōtsugomori" (1894, The Last Day of the Year) deals with the plight of a maid who steals money from her employer to aid her uncle. While "Takekurabe" was still being serialized, Ichiyō wrote "Nigorie" (1895; tr "Muddy Bay," 1958), a compelling portrait of the fatal love affair of Oriki, a bar girl and occasional prostitute. "Jūsan'ya" (1895; tr "The Thirteenth Night," 1960–61) treats the unhappy marriage of Oseki, who wishes to leave her cruel husband but is persuaded by her parents to return to him. Overwork and economic hardship both contributed to Ichiyō's terminal illness, tuberculosis.

Hiikawa 斐伊川

River in eastern Shimane Prefecture, western Honshū, originating in the Chūgoku Mountains and emptying into Lake Shinji. It figures in the legend of "Yamata no Orochi" (Eight-Headed Dragon). Length: 153 km (95 mi); area of drainage basin: 2,070 sq km (799 sq mi).

Hijikata Tatsumi 土方巽

(1928–86). BUTŌ dancer. Real name Motofuji Kunio. Born in Akita Prefecture. After studying modern dance with Eguchi Takaya (b 1900), he went on to contribute to the creation of the avant-garde dance form *butō* with such powerfully erotic and violent dances as *Kinjiki* (1959, Forbidden Colors), *Amma* (1963, Massage), and *Tomato* (1966). Based on stillness rather than movement, his style of *butō* exerted a great influence on avant-garde theater during the 1960s. Beginning with his *Nikutai no hanran* (1968, Rebellion of the Flesh), he incorporated the gestures of Japanese folk culture into dance. He is known as the founder of *ankoku butō*, or the "dark" school of *butō*.

Hijikawa 肱川

River in western Ehime Prefecture, Shikoku, originating in the Uwa Mountains and flowing northwest into the Iyo Sea. Length: 103 km (64 mi); area of drainage basin: 1,210 sq km (467 sq mi).

hijiki 鹿尾菜

Hizikia fusiformis. Perennial brown alga of the family Sargassaceae that grows attached

hikeshi This detail from a contemporary hand-scroll shows fire fighters battling a blaze that raged through Edo in 1772. Large white standards with tassels attached (some spade-shaped, others cylindrical) identify the units to which they belong.

to rocks in coastal waters of the sea. Young plants are edible and are rich in vitamins A, B, and C, calcium, and iron. *Hijiki* may be cooked with *aburaage* (fried bean curd) or used in *sunomono* (vinegared dishes). See also SEAWEED.

hijiri 聖

(holy man). Although the term *hijiri* dates from pre-Buddhist times and was even an appellation of the emperor, by the middle of the Heian period (794–1185) it came to mean Buddhist holy men who led lives of itinerancy or ascetic retreat. Some were ordained, others were not. Initially they were independent of, and occasionally in opposition to, the official Buddhist institutions. Notable among these early *hijiri* was KŪYA, the "hijiri of the market," who urged the common people to chant the name of the Buddha Amida. Many other *hijiri* were devoted to the Lotus Sutra.

In the 11th and 12th centuries, *hijiri* were organized into formal groups chartered by the great Buddhist temples for purposes of fund-raising. Chief among these groups were several based at Mt. Kōya (Kōyasan). Perhaps the most prestigious *hijiri* organization was that founded by Chōgen (1121–1206), who was appointed in 1181 to rebuild the temple TŌDAIJI after it had burned in the warfare of the period. His *hijiri* were so successful in raising funds that other temples organized similar groups.

Hijiri thus became a permanent feature of medieval Japanese Buddhism and a major factor in the spread of Buddhism to the Japanese masses. From institutions usually called *bessho* (literally, "separate places"), which enjoyed a franchise granted by a parent temple, they traveled throughout the country preaching and raising funds.

Hikaku Sangensoku 非核三原則

(Three Nonnuclear Principles). Japan's nuclear policy that specifies that "Japan will not produce, possess, or let others bring in" nuclear weapons. Declared as a national policy by Prime Minister SATŌ EISAKU in January 1968 and adopted by the ruling Liberal Democratic Party as part of its party platform, the three principles were unanimously adopted as a resolution by the Diet in 1972. The Nobel Peace Prize was awarded in 1974 to

Satō largely because of his nonnuclear policy. It has been suggested that the phrase "let others bring in" be deleted to accommodate the national defense requirements under the United States–Japan Security Treaty. See also ATOMIC BOMB.

hikan → oyakata and hikan

Hikari 光[市]

City in southeastern Yamaguchi Prefecture, western Honshū. Originally a farming village, Hikari was the site of a naval arsenal before World War II. Pharmaceutical and steel industries are now concentrated there. Tourists enjoy the beach at Nijigahama and Mishima Hot Spring. Pop: 47,611.

Hikari Agata 干刈あがた

(1943–92). Novelist. Real name Asai Kazue. Born in Tōkyō; attended Waseda University. Hikari is known for her humorous accounts, interspersed with witty dialogue, about a mother and child's life after divorce. Her works include *Juka no kazoku* (1982, The Family under the Tree) and *Kiiroi kami* (1987, Yellow Hair).

Hikawa Shrine 氷川神社

(Hikawa Jinja). A Shintō shrine in the city of Ōmiya, Saitama Prefecture; dedicated to SUSANOO NO MIKOTO and two other deities. The origins of the shrine are shrouded in obscurity. The shrine has enjoyed great popularity because of the close association Susanoo no Mikoto has had with both agriculture and military prowess. In Saitama Prefecture 162 offshoot shrines bear this name; in Tōkyō there are 59 such shrines. The annual festival is held on 1 August.

hikeshi 火消

Fire fighters during the Edo period (1600–1868). Japanese cities, consisting largely of closely built wooden structures, were repeatedly ravaged by fire. Fire-fighting brigades, like most groups in Tokugawa society, were organized according to major status categories. In the great cities of Edo (now Tōkyō), Kyōto, and Ōsaka fire-fighting units were organized by the shogunate. *Daimyō* and HATAMOTO formed *hikeshi* units both in Edo and in their own castle towns (*jōka machi*) and fief headquarters (*jin'ya*), while

urban commoners set up fire-fighting units in their neighborhoods. The best-known brigades were those of Edo: the shogunate's fire brigades (*jōbikeshi* or *jōhikeshi*) and those of daimyō (*daimyō hikeshi*) and townsmen (*machi hikeshi*).

The *jōbikeshi* (also called *yoriai hikeshi* or *jūnin hikeshi*) were first established as 4 units (*kumi*) in 1650, expanded after the disastrous MEIREKI FIRE of 1657, and stabilized at 10 units in 1704. These were treated as regular shogunate offices under the authority of the junior councillors (WAKADOSHIYORI). From 1819 they were restricted to the area bounded by the outer moat of Edo Castle. *Daimyō hikeshi* appeared from 1629 at the behest of the shogunate and evolved into a well-organized system of fire fighters and lookouts (*hinoban*).

The *machi hikeshi* of Edo were established in 1718 to protect commercial establishments; two years later, they were reorganized and expanded to 47 units and eventually numbered 48. Placed under the authority of the city commissioners (EDO MACHI BUGYŌ), each unit included a commander and his assistants, standard bearers, ladder carriers, plain firemen, and coolies (*ninsoku*). *Machi hikeshi* were often assisted by volunteers called *tobi ninsoku* who were sometimes more interested in betting on the outcome of fires than in fighting them and often became rowdy public nuisances. Perhaps because of the dubious reputation of the volunteers and perhaps for reasons of class prejudice or economic rivalry, *machi hikeshi* were not authorized to function in *samurai* districts of the city, these being left to the *jōbikeshi* and *daimyō hikeshi*.

hikidemono 引出物

Commemorative souvenir given to guests at banquets for special occasions. The most frequent occasions for giving *hikidemono* are wedding banquets, but those observing someone's 60th or 77th birthday or those celebrating a person's receipt of a special award such as commendation for a long teaching career also require *hikidemono*. Elegant utensils or flower vases, as well as sweets, are common souvenirs. The initials or the name of the person or persons hon-

Himeji Castle
A National Treasure, Himeji Castle—also known as the White Egret Castle—combined beauty of design with security against attack.

ored and the occasion commemorated are inscribed on the gift. See also GIFT GIVING; SHŪGI.

hikimawashi 引廻し

(literally, "dragging around"). An extra penalty imposed in the Edo period (1600–1868) when a criminal offense was considered to deserve something beyond the death penalty. The criminal was led on horseback through the city to the execution grounds, accompanied by a parade of HININ (the lowest social class). Flags and plaques inscribed with the nature of the offense were displayed at the head of the procession.

Hikitsuke 引付

(High Court). An organ of both the Kamakura (1192–1333) and Muromachi (1338–1573) shogunates for the adjudication of lawsuits. It was first established in 1249 by the fifth shogunal regent (*shikken*), HŌJŌ TOKIYORI, to aid the HYŌJŌSHŪ (Council of State). It was composed of a president (*tōnin*) and several coadjutors (*hikitsukeshū*) from the Hyōjōshū, assisted by several secretaries (*bugyōnin*). There were three, later five, such tribunals, which served in rotation. Hikitsuke were established both at Kamakura and in the office of the Rokuhara deputies in Kyōto. Originally they heard only suits involving shogunate vassals, but later their jurisdiction included general matters of landholding and taxation.

Hiki Yoshikazu 比企能員

(?–1203). General of the early Kamakura period (1185–1333). The adopted son of the nurse of MINAMOTO NO YORITOMO, founder of the Kamakura shogunate (1192–1333). Rendering distinguished service in various battles, he won Yoritomo's confidence; his daughter was married to Yoritomo's son MINAMOTO NO YORIIE, the second shōgun. Yoshikazu exercised strong influence as Yoriie's father-in-law and held important posts in the shogunate. When Yoriie became seriously ill in 1203, shogunal regent HŌJŌ TOKIMASA, whose authority had been challenged by Yoshikazu, planned to reduce Yoriie's son's birthright by transferring half to Yoriie's brother MINAMOTO NO SANETOMO. Infuriated, Yoshikazu plotted to overthrow the Hōjō family. The plan was discovered and Yoshikazu was assassinated, Yoriie's son was killed, and Yoriie was replaced by Sanetomo.

Hikone 彦根[市]

City in eastern Shiga Prefecture, central Honshū, on the eastern shore of Lake Biwa. A castle town under the powerful Ii family during the Edo period (1600–1868). Besides traditional goods, such as Buddhist altars and textiles, the city produces valves, machinery, and tires. The site of the castle has been made into a park, with several lovely gardens. Pop: 99,519.

Hikone domain 彦根藩

(Hikone *han*). Edo-period (1600–1868) domain that extended along the eastern shore of Lake Biwa in Ōmi Province; part of present-day Shiga Prefecture. It was granted in 1601 to II NAOMASA, who, having served TOKUGAWA IEYASU since 1575, received the status of FUDAI (hereditary vassal). A number of lords of Hikone held high positions in the shogunal government, including II NAOSUKE, who was appointed TAIRŌ (great elder) in 1858. A chain of events that began with his signing the ANSEI COMMERCIAL TREATIES without imperial approval led to a reduction of domain lands in 1862. OMOTEDAKA (estimated annual production of rice): 350,000 KOKU (1 *koku* = 180 liters or 5 US bushels).

Hikosan 英彦山

Mountain on the border of Fukuoka and Ōita prefectures, Kyūshū. Known from ancient times as a center for religious exercises of the SHUGENDŌ sect. Hikosan Shrine is located on Nakadake, one of Hikosan's three peaks. There are strange rock formations, beech forests, and numerous cultural properties. Hikosan is known for its rare insects. Height: 1,200 m (3,937 ft).

Hikoshima 彦島

Island in the western mouth of the Kammon Strait, city of Shimonoseki, Yamaguchi Prefecture, western Honshū. The site of numerous metalworking, shipbuilding, chemical, and fish-processing plants, Hikoshima is an important heavy-industry location. Area: 9.8 sq km (3.8 sq mi).

hikyaku 飛脚

(literally, "flying feet"). Couriers or runners who carried messages and small packages on foot along established routes. Known by a variety of names, such runners date from the Kamakura period (1185–1333). During the Edo period (1600–1868) a *hikyaku*-based postal system linked the cities of Edo (now Tōkyō), Kyōto, and Ōsaka. TOKUGAWA IEYASU requisitioned runners and packhorses from POST-STATION TOWNS along the TŌKAIDŌ (Eastern Sea Road) for official use.

Major *daimyō* also set up courier services (*daimyō hikyaku*) early in the Edo period to link Edo with their castle towns, stationing men at rest stops on the route. In 1663 merchants in Ōsaka, Kyōto, and Edo jointly established a daily tri-city courier service. At Nihombashi in Edo, and at comparable places in Ōsaka and Kyōto, a person could deposit a letter together with postage coins at collection points during the day, and in the evening the courier would pick up the mail pouch and depart. Known as *machi hikyaku* ("common couriers"), these runners made the trip between Ōsaka and Edo in six days. The regularity, reliability, and economy of the service enabled *machi hikyaku* to displace the other services, except for emergency deliveries by shogunate couriers. The *machi hikyaku* system flourished until the 1860s, after which it was replaced by mari-

time, vehicular, and telegraphic communications.

Hill, James Jerome ヒル, J. J.

(1838–1916). American railroad magnate. Born in Ontario, Canada. He held a strong interest in China, Japan, and India. Together with a Japanese shipping line, the NIPPON YŪSEN KAISHA, in 1896 he formed a short-lived steamship company to promote trade between the United States and the Far East.

himachi and tsukimachi 日待ちと月待ち

(*himachi to tsukimachi*; literally, "waiting for the sun" and "waiting for the moon"). Traditional social gatherings, held on predetermined nights, at which neighbors talked and feasted while awaiting dawn or moonrise. Such parties originally had some religious significance, and they were often held by the various types of religious groups called KŌ. The parties frequently coincided with major annual events, such as the end of harvest or the "Little New Year" (Koshōgatsu; see NEW YEAR). Some gatherings were for women only and were held on nights when it was considered unlucky to become pregnant. The dates varied widely from place to place, and they were sometimes determined by the traditional sexagenary calendar cycle (JIKKAN JŪNISHI). Groups that held such parties often set up commemorative stone tablets by the roadside or in temple or shrine precincts, where some can still be found today.

Himeji 姫路[市]

City in southern Hyōgo Prefecture, western Honshū, on the river Ichikawa. A castle town since the 14th century, Himeji is most noted for HIMEJI CASTLE, completed by IKEDA TERUMASA in 1610. It is the main city of the Harima region and a part of the Harima Industrial Zone; major industries are electrical machinery, food processing, steel, and oil refining. The temple Enkyōji is on the outskirts. Pop: 454,360.

Himeji Castle 姫路城

(Himejijō). Castle located in the city of Himeji, Hyōgo Prefecture; also known as Shirasagi (White Egret) Castle because of an alleged resemblance to an egret in its tall, white elegance. First constructed during the mid-14th century by the AKAMATSU FAMILY, the castle soon came into the hands of the Kodera family and in 1580 was ceded to TOYOTOMI HIDEYOSHI, who added 30 turrets. A later lord of the castle, IKEDA TERUMASA, added 20 more turrets. The main compound is located on a hill 45 meters (148 ft) high; the main and the adjoining west compounds are surrounded by three rings of outer compounds. The main donjon, five stories high on the outside and seven on the inside, is connected to three minor donjons. The Himeji Castle ranked second to ŌSAKA CASTLE in size. Most of the original structures survive; the grounds have been designated a Historic Site and the castle a National Treasure. See also CASTLES.

Himeji Plain 姫路平野

(Himeji Heiya). Also known as Harima Plain or Banshū Plain. Located in southern Hyōgo Prefecture, western Honshū, bordering the Inland Sea. It consists of the deltas of the rivers Kakogawa and Ibogawa, flowing parallel north to south. Despite the low precipitation, numerous ponds and reservoirs allow the cultivation of rice. Industries have developed along the coastal region. The major city is Himeji. Length: 10 km (6 mi); width: 40 km (25 mi).

Himeyuri Butai　　　ひめゆり部隊
(Star Lily Corps). A corps of 221 field hospital nurses in Okinawa; organized on 23 March 1945 in response to the American invasion of Okinawa. It was composed of local female high-school and normal-school students and their teachers. Many of its members committed suicide in June as Japan's defeat neared. The Himeyuri Butai is particularly remembered by the Japanese because of the novel *Himeyuri no tō* (1950) by Ishino Keiichirō (1909–90) and its movie version (1953).

Himi　　　氷見[市]
City in northwestern Toyama Prefecture, central Honshū, on Toyama Bay at the base of the Noto Peninsula. Himi is a flourishing fishing port (yellowtail, sardines, and cuttlefish) with a marine-food–processing industry. Pop: 60,766.

Himiko　　　卑弥呼
(fl ca 3rd century). Also known as Pimiko. Female ruler of the early Japanese political federation known as YAMATAI, as described in the WEI ZHI (*Wei chih*), a Chinese chronicle of the 3rd century.

Yamatai, perhaps in either northern Kyūshū or the Yamato (now Nara Prefecture) region, was at one time controlled by male rulers. According to what the Japanese call the "Wajinden," the section in the *Wei zhi* dealing with Japan (the "Land of Wa"), warfare erupted among the various countries inhabited by the Wa people around 170–180. Himiko, possibly still in her teens, eventually was "jointly established" as sovereign by the chieftains of the various political entities.

Himiko enjoyed a great following among her subjects, largely because of her mastery of *kidō* ("the way of the demons"), probably a form of SHAMANISM. After she became queen, very few persons were allowed to see her. She is said to have had 1,000 female slaves in her service, and only one male was allowed to enter her living quarters, in order to bring food, drink, and messages. Her private quarters and their outer enclosure were guarded at all times by soldiers.

Because Himiko was sequestered by a set of taboos, someone else presumably had to take charge of actual affairs of state. According to the account in the *Wei zhi*, "she had a younger brother who assisted her in ruling the country," and we may suppose that this brother was in fact a second sovereign, a nonspiritual ruler who could show himself to the populace and who looked after the concrete details of politics.

Himiko sent envoys to Wei China in 239. The Wei emperor Ming granted Himiko the title *qin wei wowang* (*ch'in wei wo-wang;* J: *shingi waō;* "Wa ruler friendly to Wei"); sent a mission to Japan, and received later ones from Yamatai. It is likely that Himiko's later missions to Wei China were to request aid in a war between Yamatai and a Japanese country called Kuna.

Hina Matsuri → Doll Festival

Hinatsu Kōnosuke　　　日夏耿之介
(1890–1971). Poet and scholar of English and Japanese literature. Real name Higuchi Kunito. Born in Nagano Prefecture; graduate of and later professor of English literature at Waseda University. He translated romantic and gothic poetry and became known for the self-described "gothic romanticism" of his own poetry. The arcane symbolism of his first collection, *Tenshin no shō* (1917), stood in stark opposition to the simple "people's poetry" (*minshūshi*) then in fashion. His 1929 study, *Meiji Taishō shi shi*, was the first systematic history of modern Japanese poetry and received the 1950 Yomiuri Literary Prize. His works are collected in the eight-volume *Hinatsu Kōnosuke zenshū* (1973–78).

hinawajū　　　火縄銃
Name given to the European harquebus or matchlock musket, first introduced to Japan in 1543 by the Portuguese at the island of Tanegashima (now part of Kagoshima Prefecture); hence, it is sometimes also called *tanegashima*. The harquebus had a bore size of about 15 millimeters (0.6 in) and a length of about 1 meter (3 ft). The use of firearm units in the armies of military leaders such as ODA NOBUNAGA (1534–82) and TAKEDA SHINGEN (1521–73) brought about a revolution in military strategy. The harquebus continued to be used until the mid-19th century. See also FIREARMS, INTRODUCTION OF.

hinin　　　非人
(literally, "nonhumans"). People who belonged to the lowest social class—along with the outcast group now known as *eta* (see BURAKUMIN)—in the Edo period (1600–1868). Under the Tokugawa shogunate (1603–1867), *hinin* were prohibited from making a living by any means other than begging. They were compelled to undertake disagreeable jobs such as caring for victims of contagious diseases and taking criminals to execution grounds. They were not allowed to tie their hair or cover their heads; their clothes had to end above the knee; women had to leave their eyebrows unshaved and their teeth undyed. Legally, there were two divisions in the *hinin* class: those who were born into the class and those who were demoted to that status because of crime or poverty. The latter could move back up to their original class under certain conditions. The class was legally abolished in 1871.

Hino　　　日野[市]
City in southwestern Tōkyō Prefecture, at the confluence of the rivers Tamagawa and Asakawa. An industrial city since the 1920s, Hino is noted for its automobile, electrical-appliance, film, and watch industries. It is fast becoming a residential area for commuters to Tōkyō. Tourist attractions include Tama Zoological Park, the temple Takahata Fudōson, and the Mogusaen Botanical Garden. Pop: 165,928.

Hino Ashihei　　　火野葦平
(1907–60). Novelist. Real name Tamai Katsunori. Born in Fukuoka Prefecture, he studied at Waseda University until drafted into the army in 1928. In 1932 he was arrested as a leftist sympathizer but was released after recanting his beliefs (see TENKŌ). His short story about a city sanitation worker, "Funnyō tan" (1937), won the sixth Akutagawa Prize, awarded after he had left for military service in China in the SINO-JAPANESE WAR OF 1937–1945. He became known as a war novelist with his popular trilogy about military life, which included *Mugi to heitai* (1938; tr *Barley and Soldiers*, 1939). Among his postwar works *Hana to ryū* (1952–53, The Flowers and the Dragon), a novel about his parents, is noted for its combination of warmth

and keen observation. After completing the autobiographical novel *Kakumei zengo* (1959, Before and After the Revolution), which dealt with his early involvement in leftist causes, Hino committed suicide.

hinoe uma　　　丙午
The 43rd year in the traditional sexagenary cycle (JIKKAN JŪNISHI). It was traditionally believed that many fires and other natural disasters occur during this year of the cycle. There was also a superstition that women born during this year had a wild disposition and ate their husbands, and such women were shunned as brides. These beliefs became widespread during the Edo period (1600–1868). Today there is still a tendency for pregnancy and childbirth to be avoided during *hinoe uma;* the most recent occurrence of that year, 1966, saw a marked drop in the birth rate.

Hino family　　　日野氏
(Hinoshi). Courtier family descended from the northern branch of the FUJIWARA FAMILY. Their name derived from a place in the Uji district of Yamashiro Province (now part of Kyōto Prefecture) where Fujiwara no Iemune founded the temple Hōkaiji in 822. In 1051 Iemune's fifth-generation descendant Sukenari (990–1070) took holy orders, retired to the Hōkaiji, and adopted the name Hino. The family produced poets and Confucian scholars who served as court officials; one of them, Hino Suketomo (1290–1332), was involved in Emperor GO-DAIGO's plot to overthrow the Kamakura Shogunate (see SHŌCHŪ CONSPIRACY). Nariko (1352–1405), daughter of Hino Tokimitsu (1328–67), married the third Muromachi shōgun, ASHIKAGA YOSHIMITSU. Perhaps the family's most famous member was Hino Katsumitsu (1429–76), who persuaded the eighth shōgun, ASHIKAGA YOSHIMASA, to marry his sister HINO TOMIKO.

Hino Keizō　　　日野啓三
(1929–). Literary critic; novelist. Born in Tōkyō; graduate of Tōkyō University. Hino's critical works include *Sonzai no geijutsu* (1967, The Art of Existence) and *Genshi no bungaku: Genjitsu o koeru mono* (1968, The Literature of Hallucination: Transcending the Real). In 1975 he received the Akutagawa Prize for *Ano yūhi* (1974, That Sunset). Hino has also written fantasy novels such as *Hōyō* (1982, The Embrace) and *Yume no shima* (1985, Isle of Dreams) which

Hirafuku Hyakusui
Reefy Coast, a pair of folding screens. 1926. Colors on silk. Each screen 152 × 143 cm. National Museum of Modern Art, Tōkyō.

Hirabayashi Taiko
This prolific writer and committed left-wing activist was a major figure in Japan's proletarian literature movement.

depict contemporary life within surreal settings of urban alienation and decay.

hinoki→cypresses

Hinomaru→national flag

Hinomisaki　　　　日御碕
Cape on western Shimane Peninsula, northern Shimane Prefecture, western Honshū; part of Daisen-Oki National Park. Located on the Sea of Japan, it is the site of the ancient Hinomisaki Shrine, with the Izumo Shrine nearby.

Hino Motors, Ltd　　日野自動車工業[株]
(Hino Jidōsha Kōgyō). Manufacturer of diesel-engine vehicles sold under the Hino brand name. The company was established in 1910 and in 1966 became affiliated with the TOYOTA MOTOR CORPORATION. It is known for its diesel engines featuring the Hino micromixing system (HMMS), a highly efficient fuel-air mixing and combustion method. Hino has 7 subsidiaries, 27 associated companies, and 78 distributors overseas. Sales for the fiscal year ending March 1991 totaled ¥657.1 billion (US $4.8 billion), with diesel trucks and buses accounting for 46 percent; passenger cars and pickup trucks, 43 percent; and engine components and other goods, 11 percent. The company was capitalized at ¥24.7 billion (US $180.0 million) in the same year. Headquarters are in the city of Hino, Tōkyō Prefecture.

Hino Sōjō　　　　　日野草城
(1901–56). HAIKU poet. Real name Hino Yoshinobu. Born in Tōkyō. Graduate of Kyōto University. He attracted the attention of the haiku world with his collection *Sōjō kushū* (1927). In 1935 he started the haiku magazine *Kikan* (1935–41) and became a central figure in the modern haiku movement. After World War II he founded the magazine *Seigen* (1949–　). In his later years the fresh brilliant style of his early work mellowed to an elegant simplicity, as in his haiku collection *Jinsei no gogo* (1953, The Afternoon of Life).

Hino Tomiko　　　　　日野富子
(1440–96). Wife of ASHIKAGA YOSHIMASA (married 1455), eighth shōgun of the MUROMACHI SHOGUNATE (1338–1573). Born into the HINO FAMILY, who traditionally provided wives for Ashikaga shōguns. In her first 10 years of marriage Tomiko bore two daughters so Yoshimasa named his younger brother Yoshimi

(1439–91) as his successor. Tomiko then unexpectedly bore him a son, Yoshihisa (1465–89), and gained for her child the right of succession by forming an alliance with the powerful military leader YAMANA SŌZEN. The succession dispute was a major cause of the ŌNIN WAR (1467–77).

Hinuma　　　　　涸沼
Lagoon in eastern Ibaraki Prefecture, central Honshū, on the Pacific coast. It is a good fishing ground for both freshwater and ocean fish. Hinuma was once a valley of the river Hinumagawa and became an inlet that later formed the lagoon. Area: 8.8 sq km (3.4 sq mi); circumference: 20 km (12.4 mi); depth: 3 m (10 ft).

Hirabayashi Hatsunosuke
　　　　　　　　　平林初之輔
(1892–1931). Literary critic. Born in Kyōto Prefecture; graduate of Waseda University. While working as a translator for a news agency, he became a contributor to the proletarian magazine TANE MAKU HITO (The Sower). He became a spokesman for the PROLETARIAN LITERATURE MOVEMENT with his criticism collection *Musan kaikyū no bunka* (1923), the first expression in Japan of a literary theory based on dialectical materialism. Later, in the article "Seijiteki kachi to geijutsuteki kachi" (1929), he advocated the equal importance of artistic and political values. This article met strong criticism from those in the movement who considered art to be subordinate to political activity.

Hirabayashi Taiko　　　平林たい子
(1905–72). Writer known for stories on the lives of the poor and on her own hardships as a left-wing activist. Born in Nagano Prefecture. She graduated from Suwa Girls' High School.

Hirabayashi went to Tōkyō in 1922 to meet those responsible for the leftist magazine TANE MAKU HITO (The Sower), especially SAKAI TOSHIHIKO. After the Tōkyō Earthquake of 1923, she and her lover, the anarchist Yamamoto Toshio, were arrested and banished from Tōkyō. They traveled to Manchuria, where Hirabayashi gave birth to a baby girl, who soon starved to death. This tragedy later became the basis for one of her best-known stories, "Seryōshitsu nite" (1927, At the Charity Clinic).

Returning alone to Tōkyō in 1924, she began living with an anarchist named Iida Tokutarō. She described the poverty and disillusion of their life together in another early story, "Azakeru" (1926, To Mock). In 1927 Hirabayashi married Kobori Jinji (1901–59),

a member of the group producing the radical magazine *Bungei sensen* (Literary Battlefront). She became a major figure in the PROLETARIAN LITERATURE MOVEMENT.

Her later works cover a broad range of subjects. They include "Hitori yuku" (1946, To Go Alone), "Kōiu onna" (1946, This Kind of Woman), *Sabaku no hana* (1955–57, Desert Flowers), "Himitsu" (1967, Secrets), and *Miyamoto Yuriko* (1971–72).

Hirado　　　　　平戸[市]
City in northwestern Nagasaki Prefecture, Kyūshū, composed of the islands of Hiradoshima and Takushima. Hirado flourished as a trading port from 1550, when Portuguese ships cast anchor, until 1641, when the Dutch trading post was transferred to DEJIMA in Nagasaki. Its principal industry is tourism. Historical sites include the remains of Hirado Castle, the former Dutch trading post, and Orandabashi ("Holland Bridge"). Pop: 26,864.

Hiradoshima　　　　平戸島
Island off the Kita Matsuura Peninsula, northwestern Nagasaki Prefecture, northwestern Kyūshū. The city of Hirado covers the entire island, which is connected to the mainland by a bridge. Principal activities are cattle raising and the growing of rice, vegetables, and mandarin oranges. Many historical traces remain from the 16th and 17th centuries when Dutch merchants and secret Christians (KAKURE KIRISHITAN) lived here. Area: 165 sq km (64 sq mi).

Hirafuku Hyakusui　　　平福百穂
(1877–1933). Japanese-style painter. Born in Akita Prefecture, he was the son of the painter Hirafuku Suian (1844–90). In 1894 he went to Tōkyō and studied with KAWABATA GYOKUSHŌ. Three years later he entered the Japanese-style painting (NIHONGA) division of the Tōkyō Bijutsu Gakkō (now Tōkyō University of Fine Arts and Music) and graduated in 1899. The following year, along with Yūki Somei (1875–1957) and other artists, he formed the Museikai group, which advocated naturalism in opposition to the romantic idealism of the Nihon Bijutsuin (JAPAN FINE ARTS ACADEMY) headed by OKAKURA KAKUZŌ.

Hyakusui worked as an illustrator for several newspapers in Tōkyō and in 1907 joined the staff of the KOKUMIN SHIMBUN, becoming well known for his lively sketches. He was represented at the Ministry of Education–sponsored annual BUNTEN exhibition from 1909. In 1917 Hyakusui, KABURAGI KIYOKATA, and others formed the Kinreisha society of artists. Hyakusui was appointed to the Teikoku Bijutsuin (Imperial Fine Arts Academy) in 1930 and two years later to a professorship at the Tōkyō Bijutsu Gakkō.

Hiraga Gennai　　　　平賀源内
(1728–80). Naturalist and writer of the Edo period (1600–1868). Born in the Takamatsu domain in Sanuki Province (now Kagawa Prefecture), the son of Shiroishi Mozaemon, a low-ranking *samurai;* he changed his family name to Hiraga upon becoming family head. After a year of study in Nagasaki (1752) he studied herbal medicine (*honzōgaku*). Around 1757 he went to Edo (now Tōkyō) to continue his studies under Tamura Gen'yū (or Ransui; 1718–76). NAKAGAWA JUN'AN was in the same school, and through him Gennai became acquainted with SUGITA GEMPAKU, a scholar of WESTERN LEARNING. Gennai prevailed upon Tamura to

join them in sponsoring a *yakuhin'e*, a kind of symposium of naturalists, to evaluate new and unusual products (see BUSSANGAKU). From these symposia came Gennai's magnum opus, the *Butsurui hinshitsu* (1763, Classification of Various Materials). In the same year he also produced two satirical novels, *Nenashigusa* (Rootless Weeds) and *Fūryū Shidōken den* (Gallant History of Shidōken), works that marked the start of his career as a successful writer of comic literature known as KOKKEIBON.

Gennai experimented in making asbestos cloth (*kakanfu*), thermometers, and Dutch-style pottery. His activities also included conducting surveys for ore deposits, wool manufacturing, and Western oil painting. Gennai also produced several JŌRURI (puppet-play texts). In 1777 he finished his *Hōhiron* (Treatise on Breaking Wind), a self-satirical memoir. Frustrated by lack of recognition and success, he had already begun to show signs of psychological deterioration, and during a fit of madness in 1779, he killed a disciple with a sword. He died in prison in 1780.

Hiraga Motoyoshi　　平賀元義

(1800–1865). WAKA poet. Originally a *samurai* of the Okayama domain (now part of Okayama Prefecture), he gave up his domain affiliation and traveled through western Honshū studying martial arts, history, Shintō, and *waka* on his own resources. A devotee of the 8th-century anthology MAN'YŌSHŪ, he wrote virile, passionate *waka*, often on martial and patriotic themes. His poetry was admired and rescued from obscurity by the Meiji-period (1868–1912) poet MASAOKA SHIKI. His main collection is *Hiraga Motoyoshi kashū* (1906).

hiragana → kana

Hiraga Renkichi　　平賀練吉

(1902–85). Leading figure in the Japanese immigrant community in Brazil. Hiraga was born in Tōkyō and graduated from Tōkyō University's Forestry Department. He settled in Brazil's Pará state in 1931 as a member of the Nambei Takushoku Kabushiki Kaisha (South America Colonization Co, Ltd). A trusted leader and hard-working researcher in tropical agriculture, he provided a model for farmers in the Amazon Basin and won great respect not only among Japanese settlers but also from the government and people of Brazil.

Hiraga Yuzuru　　平賀譲

(1878–1943). Vice admiral in charge of shipbuilding for the Imperial Japanese Navy and president of Tōkyō University. Born in Hiroshima Prefecture. Upon graduating in 1901 from Tōkyō University, he entered the navy. He served in the RUSSO-JAPANESE WAR of 1904–05 and then studied at the Greenwich School of Naval Shipbuilding and Engineering in England. Hiraga was responsible for planning the buildup of the so-called Eight Eight Fleet (HACHIHACHI KANTAI) and for the construction of the battleship YAMATO and other ships. He became a professor at Tōkyō University in 1931 and served as its president from 1938 to 1943.

Hiragushi Denchū　　平櫛田中

(1872–1979). Sculptor. Born in Okayama Prefecture. In 1898 he moved to Tōkyō, where he learned traditional wood sculpture techniques from TAKAMURA KŌUN. With the support of OKAKURA KAKUZŌ, in 1907 he and a group of sculptors, including Yonehara

Unkai (1869–1925) and Yamazaki Chōun (1867–1954), founded the Nihon Chōkoku Kai (Japan Sculpture Association), which held exhibitions from 1908. In 1937 he was elected to the Teikoku Geijutsuin (Imperial Art Academy). He taught for eight years at what is now Tōkyō University of Fine Arts and Music and was awarded the Order of Culture in 1962. Denchū's sculpture of Okakura is representative of the realistic, colorful portraits in wood for which he is most well known.

Hiraide site　　平出遺跡

(Hiraide *iseki*). An ancient settlement site in the city of Shiojiri, Nagano Prefecture, occupied from the Middle Jōmon period (ca 3500 BC–ca 2000 BC) to the Heian period (794–1185). First discovered in 1947, the site was excavated by an interdisciplinary team in 1950–51 and yielded 17 round or oval PIT HOUSES belonging to the Middle Jōmon period, 49 square or rectangular pit houses from the Kofun (ca 300–710) through Heian periods, 1 oval-shaped stone formation centering on a stone-lined fireplace, and 3 groups of postholes thought to have held the supports for raised storehouses. Artifacts recovered from the site include JŌMON POTTERY, STONE TOOLS such as axes, adzes, and projectile points, and JŌMON FIGURINES; and, from the Kofun occupation, HAJI WARE and SUE WARE, a green-glazed pitcher, and iron arrowheads.

Hiraiwa Gaishi　　平岩外四

(1914–). Businessman; chairman of TŌKYŌ ELECTRIC POWER CO, INC (1984–). Born in Aichi Prefecture. After graduating from Tōkyō University in 1939, he joined Tōkyō Electric Power Co. Hiraiwa promoted diversification of power resources in order to lower the industry's dependence on oil following the 1973 oil crisis. He was president of the Federation of Electric Companies (1977–84) and has served as chairman of the Economic Council (the long-range planning bureau of the ECONOMIC PLANNING AGENCY) since 1987 and as chairman of KEIDANREN (Federation of Economic Organizations) since 1990.

Hiraiwa Yumie　　平岩弓枝

(1932–). Novelist. Born in Tōkyō; graduated from Japan Women's University. Studied under HASEGAWA SHIN and participated in the literary group Shin'yōkai. Hiraiwa won the Naoki Prize for *Taganeshi* (1959, The Engraver). With works such as *On'yado kawasemi* (1974–77, Kingfisher Inn), Hiraiwa established a reputation as a writer of popular fiction. In addition to writing plays and scripts for television dramas, she is involved in a wide range of activities, including directing.

Hiraizumi　　平泉

Town in southwestern Iwate Prefecture, northern Honshū. Seat of the ŌSHŪ FUJIWARA FAMILY and cultural center of northern Japan during the 11th and 12th centuries. Since the 8th century Hiraizumi, situated on the Kitakami River (Kitakamigawa), had been an important military stronghold, and it was there that in 1094 Fujiwara no Kiyohira (1056–1128) settled with his followers. The area was rich in gold, and with the wealth it brought him Kiyohira built the temple CHŪSONJI and established Hiraizumi as a semi-independent provincial metropolis. Kiyohira's son Motohira (d 1157) rebuilt the temple MŌTSUJI, and his grandson Hidehira (d 1187),

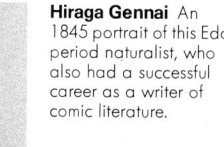
Hiraga Gennai An 1845 portrait of this Edo-period naturalist, who also had a successful career as a writer of comic literature.

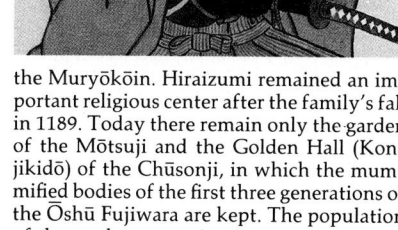

the Muryōkōin. Hiraizumi remained an important religious center after the family's fall in 1189. Today there remain only the garden of the Mōtsuji and the Golden Hall (Konjikidō) of the Chūsonji, in which the mummified bodies of the first three generations of the Ōshū Fujiwara are kept. The population of the modern town is 9,493.

Hirakata　　枚方〔市〕

City in northeastern Ōsaka Prefecture, central Honshū, on the eastern bank of the river Yodogawa. The city developed as a post-station town during the Edo period (1600–1868). It is now a satellite city of Ōsaka. Its principal products are machinery, metals, and clothes. Of historic interest are several tumuli (KOFUN). Pop: 390,788.

Hira Mountains　　比良山地

(Hira Sanchi). Mountain range running north to south along the west bank of Lake Biwa between Shiga and Kyōto prefectures, central Honshū. It has three main peaks: Hōraisan (1,174 m; 3,852 ft), Bunagadake (1,214 m; 3,983 ft), and Uchimiyama (1,103 m; 3,619 ft). "Evening Snow on Mount Hira" is one of the famous "Eight Views of Ōmi" (see ŌMI HAKKEI). The slopes and surrounding area are popular with hikers, mountain climbers, and skiers.

Hirano Ken　　平野謙

(1907–78). Literary critic. Real name Hirano Akira. Born in Kyōto Prefecture; graduate of Tōkyō University. While a student, he participated in the PROLETARIAN LITERATURE MOVEMENT, and after World War II, he contributed articles on political and literary issues to the progressive KINDAI BUNGAKU. His principal critical works are *Shimazaki Tōson* (1947), a biography of SHIMAZAKI TŌSON; *Seiji to bungaku no aida* (1956), on the relationship between literature and politics; and *Geijutsu to jisseikatsu* (1958), on fiction and writers' private lives. In 1975 he won the Noma Literary Prize for his *Samazama na seishun.*

Hirano Kuniomi　　平野国臣

(1828–64). Proimperial activist of the late Edo period (1600–1868). In 1858 he abandoned his domain (Fukuoka; now part of Fukuoka Prefecture) to participate in the antiforeign, antishogunate movement in Kyōto led by *samurai* from the Chōshū domain (now Yamaguchi Prefecture). With other activists he planned to raise an anti-Tokugawa army on the occasion of an 1862 visit to Kyōto by SHIMAZU HISAMITSU. He was arrested after the TERADAYA INCIDENT in which several of the activists were killed for refusing Hisamitsu's order to abandon their plan. After his release from prison in 1863, Hirano returned to Kyōto, only to be driven out again in the COUP D'ETAT OF 30 SEPTEMBER 1863. He then went to the Ikuno district of Tajima

Hiraiwa Gaishi In 1990 this businessman was appointed chairman of Keidanren, Japan's most powerful organization of business leaders.

Hiratsuka Raichō The feminist and founder of the Bluestocking Society in a 1911 photograph.

(now in Hyōgo Prefecture) to mobilize some 2,000 peasants, but they were easily suppressed by troops from neighboring domains (see IKUNO DISTURBANCE). Hirano was captured and executed.

Hirano Yoshitarō   平野義太郎

(1897–1980). Marxist scholar. Born in Tōkyō, he graduated from Tōkyō University, where he became an assistant professor in 1923. During studies in Germany from 1927 to 1930, he deepened his knowledge of Marxism. After returning to Japan, Hirano was arrested in 1930 as an alleged communist sympathizer. He collaborated with NORO EITARŌ, YAMADA MORITARŌ, and Ōtsuka Kinnosuke (1892–1977) in writing and editing the seven-volume NIHON SHIHON SHUGI HATTATSU SHI KŌZA (1932–33, Lectures on the History of the Development of Japanese Capitalism), thus establishing himself as a prominent spokesman for the KŌZAHA group of Marxist theorists (see also NIHON SHIHON SHUGI RONSŌ). After World War II, he was active in movements to improve Japan's relations with China, Southeast Asia, and Africa. Hirano collected and published his articles from the *Kōza* under the title *Nihon shihon shugi shakai no kikō* (1934, Structure of Capitalist Society in Japan). His writings compared the absolutist nature of Japan's imperial institution with the modern political history of European countries.

Hiranuma Kiichirō   平沼騏一郎

(1867–1952). Ministry of Justice official, prime minister, and prominent prewar RIGHT WING leader; a powerful political figure in the 1920s and 1930s. The son of a low-ranking *samurai* retainer of the Tsuyama domain (now part of Okayama Prefecture), Hiranuma graduated in 1888 from Tōkyō University with a degree in English law.

Hiranuma entered the Ministry of Justice after graduation. In 1909 he secured the convictions of 25 current and former members of the Diet for receiving bribes from the Japan Sugar Company. In 1915 he forced ŌURA KANETAKE, home minister in the ŌKUMA SHIGENOBU cabinet, to retire because of suspected bribery. Hiranuma's attacks on political party "venality" and "immorality" persisted. He objected to the "internationalist" tendencies of Japan's party governments, opposing liberalism, democracy, and socialism as "foreign ideologies." Hiranuma served as justice minister from September 1923 to January 1924 and was then appointed to the PRIVY COUNCIL. In 1924 he created the KOKUHONSHA nationalist society. He also promoted the development of Japan's "thought police" to combat the spread of liberal and left-wing ideas.

In April 1926 he became vice-president of the Privy Council, a position he held for the next 10 years. He led opposition to the WAKATSUKI REIJIRŌ cabinet's plan for rescuing the Bank of Taiwan in 1927, spearheaded opposition to ratification of the London Naval Conference Treaty in 1930 (see LONDON NAVAL CONFERENCES), mobilized support for the seizure of Manchuria (1931) and the creation of Manchukuo, and directed from behind the scenes the prosecution of the Banchōkai in the TEIJIN INCIDENT of 1934. In 1936 Hiranuma became president of the Privy Council. In 1939 he became prime minister for eight months. Under his leadership the cabinet debated at length whether to form a military alliance with Nazi Germany in order to neutralize the Soviet Union. It was feared that Japan would be committed to supporting Germany against the Anglo-American powers as well. Upon the conclusion of the German-Soviet Non-Aggression Pact in August 1939, the futility of the cabinet's European policy was exposed, and Hiranuma resigned. He was appointed to the KONOE FUMIMARO cabinet in December 1940, but withdrew from the government with Konoe's resignation in October 1941. He served during World War II as one of the JŪSHIN, unofficial senior advisers to the emperor. In April 1945 he was reappointed president of the Privy Council. After the war he was arrested as a class A war criminal by the Occupation authorities and sentenced to life imprisonment. He died a prisoner.

Hiranuma Ryōzō   平沼亮三

(1879–1959). Head of numerous sports organizations, including the Japan Amateur Sports Association, the Japan Amateur Athletic Federation, and the Japan Olympic Committee. Born in Yokohama; graduated from Keiō University. Hiranuma served as mayor of Yokohama (1951). He led the Japanese delegation to the 1932 Los Angeles and the 1936 Berlin Olympic Games. In 1946 he founded the NATIONAL SPORTS FESTIVAL and in 1955 was awarded the Order of Culture.

Hiraodai   平尾台

Limestone plateau in southeastern Kokura Minami Ward, city of Kita Kyūshū, Fukuoka Prefecture, Kyūshū. The southern half is covered with terra rossa while the northern half has a well-developed lapis field (Karrenfeld) as well as limestone caves. Vegetables are cultivated, and limestone is quarried. Part of Kita Kyūshū Quasi-National Park. Elevation: 360–680 m (1,180–2,230 ft); length: approximately 7 km (4.3 mi); width: approximately 2 km (1.2 mi).

Hirara   平良[市]

City on Miyakojima, an island belonging to the Miyako Islands, Okinawa Prefecture. The principal city of the islands, it is the site of government agencies and company branch offices. Sugarcane cultivation, bonito fishing, and shell crafts are Hirara's main activities. Pop: 32,599.

Hirase Sakugorō   平瀬作五郎

(1856–1925). Botanist. Born in what is now Fukui Prefecture. After working as a drawing teacher in Gifu Prefecture, he became botanical illustrator at Tōkyō University and engaged in the production of scientific drawings and microscope specimens. During that time he became interested in botany and, under the guidance of IKENO SEIICHIRŌ, studied the growth of gymnospermous plants. He discovered ginkgo spermatozoa in 1896 and greatly influenced the study of plant systematics.

Hirashimizu ware   平清水焼

(*hirashimizu-yaki*). Glazed ceramics, sometimes with underglaze or overglaze decoration, made in Hirashimizu, Uzen Province (now the city of Yamagata, Yamagata Prefecture) from the early 1800s to the present. Sometimes called Chitose ware after the nearby mountain that provides the source of clay. Both stoneware and porcelain wares have been produced. Typical decoration includes porcelain slip; matte-white glaze streaked with muted green and brown (called *zansetsu* or "lingering snow"); and a crisp, pale-green glaze with dark spots (called *nashi seiji* or "pear celadon"). In addition, copper red, *temmoku*, "oil spot," and the bright blue-green Oribe glaze are widely used. Unglazed surfaces are also utilized. Five kilns operate today. The Yamagata Museum contains a collection of Hirashimizu.

Hirata   平田[市]

City in eastern Shimane Prefecture, western Honshū, on Lake Shinji. Hirata prospered during the Edo period (1600–1868) as a market town dealing in cotton cloth. The main activity today is rice cultivation, although the town has several emerging industries. Pop: 30,632.

Hirata Atsutane   平田篤胤

(1776–1843). KOKUGAKU (National Learning) scholar and Shintō theologian. Literary name Ibukinoya. Leader of the RESTORATION SHINTŌ movement known as Fukko Shintō, which strove to revive Shintō by freeing it of debilitating Buddhist and Confucian influences. His nationalist thought strongly influenced the *shishi*, loyalist *samurai* who sought the restoration of direct imperial rule in the late 19th century.

Hirata was the fourth son of a low-ranking samurai of the Akita domain (now part of Akita Prefecture). He began training in the branch of Confucianism founded by YAMAZAKI ANSAI (1619–82). His interest turned to the Chinese philosopher Zhuangzi (Chuang-tzu), Taoism, and the works of MOTOORI NORINAGA (1730–1801), a founder of the National Learning movement. Hirata rejected Confucianism and Buddhism, advocating, instead, a revival of the "ancient way" and reverence for the emperor.

One of Hirata's first publications was *Kamōsho* (1803), in which he criticized the Confucian thinker DAZAI SHUNDAI's (1680–1747) treatise on Buddhism titled *Bendōsho*. He was invited by the Yoshida family, the head family of YOSHIDA SHINTŌ, to become a teacher. Hirata's pupils included ŌKUNI TAKAMASA and SUZUKI SHIGETANE. Representative works are *Kodō taii* (1811), *Koshichō* (1811), *Tama no mihashira* (1812), *Tamadasuki* (1824), and *Koshiden* (1825).

Hirata Gōyō   平田郷陽

(1903–81). Doll maker. Real name Hirata Tsuneo. Born in Tōkyō. He was trained from an early age by his father, Gōyō I, a doll maker best known for realistic dolls. In 1936 Gōyō became the first doll maker chosen to participate in the Imperial Academy's annual art exhibition. He was designated as one of the LIVING NATIONAL TREASURES in 1955. Gōyō founded an organization of doll makers known as the Yōmonkai and instructed a talented group of followers in this art. He was considered Japan's foremost realistic doll maker.

Hirata Tokuboku   平田禿木

(1873–1943). Scholar of English literature. Real name Hirata Kiichirō. Born in Tōkyō. Graduate of Tōkyō Higher Normal School (now Tsukuba University). Hirata joined the literary magazine *Bungakukai* and introduced the works of Pater, Keats, and Dante. He translated NŌ drama texts into English for Ernest F. FENOLLOSA. Hirata's work was later used in Fenollosa and Ezra Pound's books on the Nō theater.

Hirata Tōsuke   平田東助

(1849–1925). Bureaucrat and politician. Born in the Yonezawa domain (now part of

Yamagata Prefecture), he studied at Daigaku Nankō (now Tōkyō University). In 1871 he accompanied the IWAKURA MISSION to the United States and Europe and remained in Germany to study. In 1876 he joined the government and in 1890 was named to the House of Peers. As a member of the Saiwai Kurabu, a political club of members of the House of Peers, he supported YAMAGATA ARITOMO. He served as minister of commerce and agriculture and later as home minister in two KATSURA TARŌ cabinets (1901–06; 1908–11) and in 1922 was appointed lord keeper of the privy seal.

Hiratsuka 平塚[市]

City in south-central Kanagawa Prefecture, central Honshū, at the mouth of the river SAGAMIGAWA. A post-station town in the Edo period (1600–1868), the city now produces vehicles, tires, and foodstuffs. Every July people flock to see Hiratsuka's TANABATA FESTIVAL. Pop: 245,950.

Hiratsuka Raichō 平塚らいてう

(1886–1971). Feminist. Born in Tōkyō; original name Hiratsuka Haru. Daughter of a government official. Graduated from Japan Women's University. She first aroused public criticism in 1908 when she allegedly planned to commit suicide with the writer MORITA SŌHEI. Raichō and others founded the SEITŌSHA (Bluestocking Society) in 1911 and, aiming at the "development of women's talent," published the literary magazine Seitō (Bluestocking). She introduced the first number with a famous manifesto entitled Genshi josei wa taiyō de atta (In the Beginning Woman Was the Sun).

In 1914 Raichō left her parents' home to live with the painter Okumura Hiroshi (1891–1964); she gave birth to a daughter and son. With ICHIKAWA FUSAE and OKU MUMEO in 1920 she founded the SHIN FUJIN KYŌKAI (New Woman's Association) and engaged in a battle to reform the social and legal position of Japanese women. In 1922 the group achieved the first political success of the women's movement with the amendment of the Public Order and Police Law (Chian Keisatsu Hō), thus making it legal for women to participate to some degree in political activities. After World War II, she continued her campaign for peace and women's rights, becoming the first president of the Nihon Fujin Dantai Rengōkai (Federation of Japanese Women's Societies) in 1953.

Hiratsuka Tsunejirō 平塚常次郎

(1881–1974). Businessman and politician. Born in Hokkaidō; studied at a Russian language school in Sapporo. Hiratsuka established a fishing company, NICHIRO CORPORATION, in 1907, soon after Japan negotiated fishing rights on the Russian coast. After World War II, he was elected to the House of Representatives and joined the first YOSHIDA SHIGERU cabinet as minister of transportation. He was subsequently purged by Allied Occupation authorities but returned to the business world in 1955 when he became president of Nichiro Corporation. In his later years, as chairman of the Dai Nippon Suisankai (Japan Fisheries Association) and a member of the House of Representatives, he played an important role in Russo-Japanese fishery negotiations.

Hiratsuka Un'ichi 平塚運一

(1895–). Print artist. Born and raised in Matsue, Shimane Prefecture. When the Western-style painter and printmaker Ishii

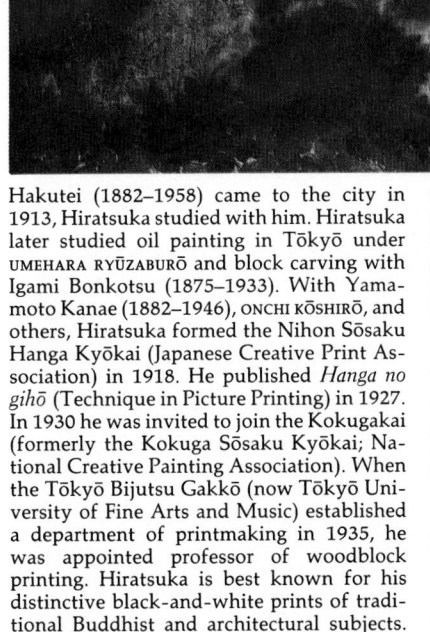

Hakutei (1882–1958) came to the city in 1913, Hiratsuka studied with him. Hiratsuka later studied oil painting in Tōkyō under UMEHARA RYŪZABURŌ and block carving with Igami Bonkotsu (1875–1933). With Yamamoto Kanae (1882–1946), ONCHI KŌSHIRŌ, and others, Hiratsuka formed the Nihon Sōsaku Hanga Kyōkai (Japanese Creative Print Association) in 1918. He published Hanga no gihō (Technique in Picture Printing) in 1927. In 1930 he was invited to join the Kokugakai (formerly the Kokuga Sōsaku Kyōkai; National Creative Painting Association). When the Tōkyō Bijutsu Gakkō (now Tōkyō University of Fine Arts and Music) established a department of printmaking in 1935, he was appointed professor of woodblock printing. Hiratsuka is best known for his distinctive black-and-white prints of traditional Buddhist and architectural subjects. Although his work draws on the Japanese tradition in subject matter, his viewpoint and technique put him squarely in the tradition of modern art. His work is represented in numerous American collections.

Hirayama Ikuo 平山郁夫

(1930–). Japanese-style painter. Born in Hiroshima Prefecture. After graduating from Tōkyō Bijutsu Gakkō (now Tōkyō University of Fine Arts and Music), he studied under MAEDA SEISON. Hirayama is known for works on Buddhist themes and works depicting the landscape of the Silk Road with a touch of fantasy. He was commissioned to copy the wall paintings in the ancient TAKAMATSUZUKA TOMB.

Hirayama Kiyotsugu 平山清次

(1874–1943). Astronomer. Born in Miyagi Prefecture. Graduate of Tōkyō University. In 1915 he went to the United States for study and in 1919 published the hypothesis, based on statistics and theories of celestial mechanics, that asteroids with uniform characteristics, such as eccentricity and mean motion, form a "family" that derives from the destruction of a single planet. He served as professor at Tōkyō University from 1919 to 1935, and from 1921 was a researcher at the Tōkyō Astronomical Observatory (now NATIONAL ASTRONOMICAL OBSERVATORY).

Hirayu Hot Spring 平湯温泉

(Hirayu Onsen). Located on the northern slope of Norikuradake at an altitude of 1,230 m (4,035 ft), northeastern Gifu Prefecture,

central Honshū. A bicarbonate spring; water temperature 46°–96°C (115°–205°F). Located in Chūbu Sangaku National Park, it has been designated as a National Health Resort Hot Spring. It is presently the base for climbing Norikuradake.

Hirohata 広畑

District of the city of HIMEJI, Hyōgo Prefecture, western Honshū, facing the INLAND SEA. After the establishment of a giant steel mill here in 1939, it became a center of the Harima Coastal Industrial Region.

Hirohito, Emperor → Shōwa, Emperor

Hiroi Isamu 広井勇

(1862–1928). Civil engineer who led the early development of bridge and harbor design in Japan. Born in the Tosa domain (now Kōchi Prefecture), he graduated from Sapporo Agricultural School (now Hokkaidō University). In 1883 Hiroi went to the United States, where he worked on several bridge construction projects. After study in Germany he returned to Japan in 1889 and became a professor at his alma mater. From 1899 he taught at Tōkyō University. Hiroi designed Hakodate, Otaru, and several other harbors.

Hironaka Heisuke 広中平祐

(1931–). Mathematician. Born in Yamaguchi Prefecture. A graduate of Kyōto University, he continued his studies at Harvard University, where he later taught. Hironaka was awarded the Fields Prize in 1970 for his research on algebraic manifolds and the resolution of singularities in analytic spaces. He received the Order of Culture in 1975.

Hirosaki 弘前[市]

City in western Aomori Prefecture, northern Honshū. A castle town during the Edo period (1600–1868), it is now the political, economic, and cultural center of the Tsugaru region. Hirosaki is noted for its rice, apples, sake, and tsugaru-nuri, a local lacquer ware. The remains of the castle are in Hirosaki Park, famous for its cherry blossoms. The city is known for the NEBUTA FESTIVAL and for its colorful kites and other folk crafts. Pop: 174,704.

Hironaka Heisuke This mathematician, a recipient of the Fields Prize, taught at Harvard University.

Hiroshige
1 The *Kambara* print from the artist's best-known woodblock print series, *Fifty-Three Stations of the Tōkaidō Road*. Hiroshige designed a total of 20 sets of prints depicting scenes along the highway from Edo to Kyōto. Series printed 1833–34. 24 × 37 cm. Tōkyō National Museum.
2 The *Shōno* print from *Fifty-Three Stations of the Tōkaidō Road*. 24 × 37 cm. Tōkyō National Museum.

Hirose Gen　　　　　弘世現

(1904–). Businessman and chairman of NIPPON LIFE INSURANCE CO. Born in Tōkyō, Hirose graduated from Tōkyō University in 1928 and entered Mitsui & Co, Ltd, in the same year. In 1944 he joined, as a director, Nippon Life Insurance Co, the enterprise his grandfather had created. Hirose became president in 1948 and chairman in 1982. He has made many contributions to the Japanese life insurance industry. A connoisseur of art and music, Hirose created the Nissei Theater in 1963 and has been active in promoting international cultural exchanges.

Hirose Saihei　　　　広瀬宰平

(1828–1914). Businessman; leader of the SUMITOMO *zaibatsu* (financial and industrial combine) in the late 19th century. Born in what is now Shiga Prefecture, Hirose started working at age 11 at the Sumitomo family's Besshi Copper Mine in what is now Ehime Prefecture, later becoming general manager. After the Meiji Restoration of 1868 he contributed to the formation and development of the Sumitomo *zaibatsu*, while serving as "prime minister" for the Sumitomo family. With GODAI TOMOATSU, Hirose established the Ōsaka Shōhō Kaigisho (forerunner of the Ōsaka Chamber of Commerce) and the Ōsaka Stock Exchange.

Hirose Shrine　　　　広瀬神社

(Hirose Jinja). Shintō shrine in the Kita Katsuragi District, Nara Prefecture; dedicated to the goddess of cereals, Wakaukanome no Mikoto, and two other deities. Besides its reputation for protecting crops, the shrine is believed to offer protection from water-related disasters, and for this reason it is often associated with the TATSUTA SHRINE, which supposedly protects against winds. Its annual festival is celebrated on 4 April.

Hirose Takeo　　　　広瀬武夫

(1868–1904). Naval officer. Born in what is now Ōita Prefecture. A graduate of the Naval Academy in 1889, from 1897 to 1902 Hirose studied in Russia. He participated in the RUSSO-JAPANESE WAR of 1904–05 as torpedo officer on the battleship *Asahi.* He commanded two smaller craft in the attempt to seal the entrance to the harbor of PORT ARTHUR and was killed while searching for one of his men. He was posthumously appointed to the rank of commander and until Japan's defeat in 1945 was revered as a *gunshin* ("war god"), together with Lieutenant Colonel TACHIBANA SHŪTA.

Hirose Tansō　　　　広瀬淡窓

(1782–1856). Confucian scholar and educator of the late Edo period (1600–1868). Born in Bungo Province (now Ōita Prefecture). In 1817 he founded the Kangien, a Confucian-oriented school, in his hometown of Hita. The Dutch-studies scholar TAKANO CHŌEI and the military strategist ŌMURA MASUJIRŌ studied there. Tansō's friends and associates included RAI SAN'YŌ, YANAGAWA SEIGAN, the Confucian scholar HOASHI BANRI, and the painter TANOMURA CHIKUDEN. His works are collected in *Tansō zenshū* (3 vols, 1925–27).

Hiroshige　　　　　広重

(1797–1858). Full name Andō Hiroshige. UKIYO-E print designer, illustrator, and painter; best known for his many tranquil landscapes, which succeeded in infusing the woodblock print with certain techniques and poetry of brush painting. Born in the Yayosugashi district (now Yaesu) of Edo (now Tōkyō). Original name Andō Tokutarō.

Tokutarō entered the studio of UTAGAWA TOYOHIRO around 1811 and sometime afterward was given the name Hiroshige and the right to use the Utagawa name (see UTAGAWA SCHOOL). Hiroshige's first signed works seem to have been book illustrations published in the spring of 1818. His first single-sheet woodblock prints, undistinguished full-length portraits of actors and beauties, began to appear late the same year. His first *kachōga* prints (see BIRD-AND-FLOWER PAINTING) were painterly subjects in the narrow, upright format of paintings with calligraphic inscriptions and seals, printed with a full range of color. These proved a popular success and during his career Hiroshige designed nearly 1,000 bird-and-flower subjects.

Around 1830 the publisher Kawaguchi Shōzō invited Hiroshige to design a set of 10 views of the city of Edo. The prints were the first full expression of Hiroshige's brilliant ability to combine startling designs with a sense of atmosphere and poetry that made the pictures familiar and accessible in spite of their striking novelty. For the next 20 years he designed thousands of horizontal landscape prints, over 1,000 of them views of his beloved city of Edo. In 1832 Hiroshige traveled from Edo to Kyōto and back. This prompted the set of woodblock prints for which he is best known both in Japan and in the West, *Tōkaidō gojūsantsugi* (Fifty-Three Stations of the Tōkaidō Road), which was issued in parts by the publisher Takeuchi Hoeidō. Before his death, Hiroshige designed 20 sets of views of the TŌKAIDŌ. The Hoeidō set is often called the Great Tōkaidō, to distinguish it from the Reisho Marusei Tōkaidō, also in large horizontal format; the Upright or Vertical Tōkaidō of 1853; the Gyōsho Tōkaidō, published in a slightly smaller horizontal format in the early 1840s; and the many small sets.

It was perhaps as a result of this journey to Kyōto that Hiroshige designed the Eight Views of Ōmi and sets of 10 views each of famous places in Kyōto and Ōsaka. Around 1835 Hiroshige took over from KEISAI EISEN the responsibility of completing a set of 70 horizontal views of another more mountainous route from Edo to Kyōto, the Kiso Kaidō (see NAKASENDŌ). In the mid-1840s Hiroshige illustrated many albums and booklets of comic KYŌKA poetry. In the early 1850s he chose a new, vertical format for his landscape sets, including *Rokujūyoshū meisho zue* (Views of Over Sixty Famous Places), a set of 69 views of the provinces; *Meisho Edo hyakkei* (One Hundred Views of Edo), a set that included 118 prints; and *Fuji sanjūrokkei* (Thirty-Six Views of Mt. Fuji), which was published posthumously.

Hiroshige II (1826–69)——Suzuki Chimpei was accepted as one of Hiroshige's pupils and was given the name Shigenobu. After the death of Hiroshige, he married his master's daughter Tatsu and took the name of Ichiryūsai Hiroshige II. He designed vertical landscapes of the provinces and Edo, several prints of foreigners, and views of Yokohama.

Hiroshige III (1841–94)——A pupil of Hiroshige whose early work was signed Shigemasa adopted the name Hiroshige III, probably after Shigenobu's death in 1869. He designed many garish triptychs of Western buildings, trains, and ships in Yokohama and Tōkyō.

Hiroshima 広島[市]
Capital of Hiroshima Prefecture, western Honshū; located on the Inland Sea coast at the delta of the river Ōtagawa. Hiroshima developed as a castle town during the Edo period (1600–1868). By the early 1940s it had expanded into the seventh largest city in Japan and served as an important military center. On 6 August 1945 the world's first atomic bomb was dropped on Hiroshima, destroying 90 percent of the city and ultimately killing about 200,000 people (see ATOMIC BOMB). Now completely rebuilt, it is one of the most important cities in western Honshū. Major industries are machinery, automobiles, and food processing.

At what was the epicenter of the bomb there are located the Peace Memorial Park (with the Peace Memorial Hall, Peace Memorial Museum, and a memorial cenotaph for victims of the bomb), the Atomic Bomb Dome (the only building left unreconstructed), and the World Peace Memorial Cathedral. A commemorative ceremony on 6 August has become Hiroshima's most important annual event. Area: 737 sq km (285 sq mi); pop: 1,085,705.

Hiroshima 広島[町]
Town in western Hokkaidō, on the outskirts of the city of SAPPORO. Founded in 1884 by settlers from Hiroshima Prefecture. The local economy once centered on agriculture and dairy farming, but due to the town's proximity to Sapporo the number of factories and housing developments has been increasing rapidly. Pop: 47,758.

Hiroshima Bay 広島湾
(Hiroshima Wan). Inlet of the western Inland Sea, on the coast of southwestern Hiroshima and southeastern Yamaguchi prefectures, western Honshū. Bounded by the islands of Kurahashijima on the east and Ōshima on the south and by Honshū on the west and north. It provides harbors for the cities of Hiroshima, Ōtake, Kure, and

Iwakuni. There are numerous islands in the bay. Oyster farming has been endangered by increasing industrialization. The bay was the site of a major naval base until the end of World War II.

Hiroshima Museum of Art
ひろしま美術館
(Hiroshima Bijutsukan). Located in the city of Hiroshima, Hiroshima Prefecture. Opened in 1978. Established by the Bank of Hiroshima, the museum focuses on European paintings, primarily by the French impressionists (some 150 works), and early modern and contemporary Japanese paintings (approximately 160 works). The former include works by Manet, Renoir, van Gogh, Picasso, and Utrillo; the latter include works by UEMURA SHŌEN, HAYAMI GYOSHŪ, ASAI CHŪ, SAEKI YŪZŌ, and UMEHARA RYŪZABURŌ.

Hiroshima Peace Memorial Museum 広島平和記念資料館
(Hiroshima Heiwa Kinen Shiryōkan). Museum in Hiroshima Peace Memorial Park in the city of Hiroshima. Opened in 1955. On exhibit are objects and models related to the 1945 atomic bombing of the city, including photographs, damaged clothing, melted roof tiles and glass, and stone and cement onto which human shadows were imprinted.

Hiroshima Plain 広島平野
(Hiroshima Heiya). Located in western Hiroshima Prefecture, western Honshū. This low-lying plain bordering the Inland Sea consists of the delta of the river ŌTAGAWA with its six branches. The industrialized southern part comprises land that has been reclaimed. The major city is HIROSHIMA, which covers much of the plain. Area: approximately 30 sq km (10 sq mi).

Hiroshima Prefecture 広島県
(Hiroshima Ken). Located in western Honshū and bounded by Shimane and Tottori prefectures to the north, Okayama Prefecture to the east, the Inland Sea to the south, and Yamaguchi Prefecture to the west. The northern portion of the prefecture is occupied by the CHŪGOKU MOUNTAINS and is relatively thinly populated. Its climate tends to be cool and humid. The southern area, composed of highlands and coastal plains, has a milder, drier climate. Most of the population is concentrated in urban areas along the Inland Sea coast.

Under the ancient provincial system (KOKUGUN SYSTEM) the area was divided into the provinces of Aki and Bingo. It developed as a center for Inland Sea shipping. Toward the end of the Heian period (794–1185),

when the TAIRA FAMILY was in power, TAIRA NO KIYOMORI lavished support on the ITSUKUSHIMA SHRINE and established HIROSHIMA BAY as a base for commercial activities. During the Edo period (1600–1868) the cities of HIROSHIMA and FUKUYAMA developed as castle towns. The present prefectural boundaries were established in 1876. In 1945 Hiroshima became the first city in the world to suffer an atomic bomb attack.

While agriculture, forestry, and fishing have declined steadily in recent years, industrial growth has been rapid in the coastal cities. Major industries include shipbuilding, automobiles, steel, machinery, textiles, petrochemicals, and food processing. Traditional industries such as weaving, *sake* brewing, and the manufacture of *tatami* mats also continue to exist.

Parts of the coast are included in the INLAND SEA NATIONAL PARK. The atomic bomb memorial and Peace Memorial Park in Hiroshima bring visitors from around the world. Area: 8,467 sq km (3,269 sq mi); pop: 2,849,847; capital: Hiroshima. Other major cities include KURE, ONOMICHI, and Fukuyama.

Hiroshima University 広島大学
(Hiroshima Daigaku). National university; main campus located in the city of Higashi Hiroshima. The university is made up of eight formerly independent institutions of higher learning that were merged in 1949. Hiroshima University maintains faculties of arts and sciences, letters, education, teacher education, economics, science, medicine, dentistry, engineering, fisheries, and animal husbandry. Enrollment was 12,521 in 1989.

Hirota Kōki 広田弘毅
(1878–1948). Diplomat and prime minister (1936–37). Born in Fukuoka Prefecture. After graduating from Tōkyō University he held several overseas posts in the Ministry of Foreign Affairs. While foreign minister (1933–36), he negotiated the purchase of the CHINESE EASTERN RAILWAY in Manchuria, and on 28 October 1935 he announced his "three principles" (Hirota *sangensoku*): the establishment of a Japan-China-Manchukuo bloc (Manchukuo being the name of the puppet state that the Japanese had established in Manchuria), the suppression of anti-Japanese activities in China, and the organization of a Sino-Japanese front against communism. He became prime minister in March 1936 as a result of the FEBRUARY 26TH INCIDENT and reinstituted the system of appointing only generals and admirals on ac-

hirugao This twining perennial is often seen along mountain roads. Because the flowers are open only during the day, the plant is called hirugao, "daytime face."

Hirota Kōki This diplomat and prime minister actively supported the militarization of Japan during the pre–World War II period.

tive duty as army and navy ministers (GUMBU DAIJIN GEN'EKI BUKAN SEI). Hirota also signed the Japanese-German-Italian ANTI-COMINTERN PACT. He was named foreign minister in the first KONOE FUMIMARO cabinet (1937–39). During World War II he was a JŪSHIN ("senior statesman"). After the war he was tried as a class-A war criminal and was executed on 23 December 1948, the only civilian to be so sentenced.

Hirota Shrine　　　広田神社

(Hirota Jinja). A Shintō shrine in the city of Nishinomiya, Hyōgo Prefecture; dedicated to the "rough spirit" (aramitama; see TAMA) of the sun goddess and so-called imperial ancestress, AMATERASU ŌMIKAMI. According to shrine tradition, after the legendary empress JINGŪ successfully completed her campaign in Korea and returned to Japan, she received an oracle instructing her to establish a shrine in an area distant from the imperial residence to house the "rough spirit" of Amaterasu Ōmikami. The shrine is also believed to afford encouragement and protection to those who write traditional Japanese verse (WAKA). The annual festival is observed on 16 March.

Hirotsu Kazuo　　　広津和郎

(1891–1968). Novelist and literary critic. Born in Tōkyō; graduate of Waseda University. Second son of novelist HIROTSU RYŪRŌ. He started writing critical articles for various literary magazines around 1910. In his short story "Shinkeibyō jidai" (1917, The Neurotic Age) he depicted the nihilism and decadence of modern intellectuals. In the early 1930s he was sympathetic to the PROLETARIAN LITERATURE MOVEMENT but later grew displeased with its inefficacy and fragmentation. He defended the accused saboteurs in the MATSUKAWA INCIDENT in Izumi e no michi (1953–54, The Road to the Spring) and Matsukawa saiban (1954–58, The Matsukawa Trial). His autobiography, Nengetsu no ashioto (The Footsteps of Time), serialized from 1961 to 1963 in the magazine Gunzō, won the 1963 Noma Literary Prize. He became a member of the Japan Art Academy in 1950.

Hirotsu Ryūrō　　　広津柳浪

(1861–1928). Novelist. Creator of the "tragic novel" (hisan shōsetsu); father of the novelist and critic HIROTSU KAZUO. Born Hirotsu Naoto in what is now Nagasaki Prefecture, he moved to Tōkyō in 1874 and graduated from school in 1877. He was an official in the Agriculture and Commerce Ministry from 1881 to 1885. In 1889 Ryūrō met OZAKI KŌYŌ and joined the KEN'YŪSHA, a literary group. He published two novels during 1895 that brought him wide literary fame: Hemeden and Kurotokage. These were the first of his numerous hisan shōsetsu, the most famous of which is Imado shinjū (1896, Suicide at Imado). After 1908 he retired from writing.

Ryūrō's tragic novels are never entirely free of influence from the Edo-period (1600–

1868) GESAKU tradition. They are filled with exaggeration and extremes, improbable or incredible events, rampant romanticism, melodramatic emotion, and wooden posturing. Plot focus is on a relentless progression through a series of pathetic circumstances and wretched experiences toward a destructive finale governed by hostile fate.

hirugao　　　昼顔

(bindweed). Calystegia japonica. Twining perennial of the family Convolvulaceae that grows wild in grassy fields and mountains throughout Japan. It is also found in Korea and China. Long twining stems grow from white creeping underground stems, and leaves are alternate and arrow-shaped. In summer, pink funnel-shaped flowers about 5 centimeters (2 in) across bloom during the day. These flowers have been appreciated by poets since the time of the 8th-century poetry anthology Man'yōshū. See also MORNING GLORIES.

Hiruzen Kōgen　　　蒜山高原

Highland in northern Okayama Prefecture, western Honshū. It has good skiing and camping grounds and is noted for its alpine flora. Part of Daisen-Oki National Park. Elevation: 500–600 m (1,600–2,000 ft).

hisago　　　瓠

Also called hyōtan. Dried and hollowed-out bottle gourd traditionally used as a container. Large hisago containing sake or tea were hung at the waist for picnics and when traveling. Small ones were, and are, used for spices or pills. Hisago halved lengthwise were used as ladles.

Hisai　　　久居[市]

City in central Mie Prefecture, central Honshū. Hisai is fast becoming a residential area. Pears and rice are grown along the river Kumozugawa. Sakakibara Hot Spring draws many visitors. Pop: 39,682.

Hisaita Eijirō　　　久板栄二郎

(1898–1976). Playwright. Born in Miyagi Prefecture; graduate of Tōkyō University. He was one of the central figures of the proletarian movement in drama in the 1920s. Later, in the realistic drama Hokutō no kaze (1937, The Northeast Wind), he described the life of a textile factory manager. After World War II, Hisaita wrote screenplays, including Ōsoneke no asa (1946, Morning for the Ōsone Family), which he wrote with its director KINOSHITA KEISUKE, and Waga seishun ni kui nashi (1946, No Regrets for Our Youth), directed by KUROSAWA AKIRA.

Hisamatsu Shin'ichi　　　久松真一

(1889–1980). Philosopher of religion. Born in Gifu Prefecture. Hisamatsu was a student of the philosopher NISHIDA KITARŌ at Kyōto University and later a professor at the same university (1946–49). He undertook a comparison of Eastern and Western culture from a religio-philosophical point of view. He led a Zen-oriented group called the FAS Association, its name taken from its motto, "To awake to Formless self, to stand for the

standpoint of All mankind, to create Super-historical history." A collection of his works, Hisamatsu Shin'ichi chosakushū (1969–80), includes Tōyōteki mu (1939, Eastern Nothingness).

Hisao Jūran　　　久生十蘭

(1902–57). Author. Real name Abe Masao. Born in Hokkaidō. After participating in the modern theater movement of the 1920s led by KISHIDA KUNIO, he went to France to study theater. After his return to Japan, Hisao wrote many mystery stories, historical novels, and works of popular fiction. His short story "Suzuki Mondo" (1951) won the Naoki Literary Prize. Other works include "Boshizō" (1954, The Mother), Usuyuki shō (1952), and Hadairo no tsuki (1957, Flesh-Colored Moon).

Hishida Shunsō　　　菱田春草

(1874–1911). Japanese-style painter. Born in Iida, Nagano Prefecture. In 1889 he went to Tōkyō to study the KANŌ SCHOOL–style of painting with Yūki Masaaki (1834–1904). He attended the Tōkyō Bijutsu Gakkō (now Tōkyō University of Fine Arts and Music) from 1890 to 1895. There he studied with the painter HASHIMOTO GAHŌ and was much influenced by Ernest F. FENOLLOSA and OKAKURA KAKUZŌ. After graduation he worked at copying old religious paintings in Kyōto and Nara for the Imperial Household Museum (now Tōkyō National Museum) and taught at the Tōkyō Bijutsu Gakkō. In 1898, when Okakura established the JAPAN FINE ARTS ACADEMY (Nihon Bijutsuin), Shunsō followed him. From 1903 to 1905 Shunsō traveled and exhibited his works in India, the United States, and Europe. In his final years he experimented with the RIMPA style. Shunsō successfully competed in many exhibitions, including the government-sponsored BUNTEN.

Hishikawa Moronobu→

Moronobu

Historical Museum of Hokkaidō
北海道開拓記念館

(Hokkaidō Kaitaku Kinenkan). A museum located in the city of Sapporo, Hokkaidō, devoted to the history of the settlement and development of the region. Opened in 1971, the museum's exhibits are organized under such themes as daily life, industry, education, and culture. There are also exhibits on the AINU people and their culture.

historic preservation districts
重要伝統的建造物群保存地区

(jūyō dentōteki kenzōbutsugun hozon chiku). General term for areas, towns, and villages designated by the government for preservation because of their historic importance. The Ancient Cities Law was enacted in 1966, but it affected only the ancient capitals of Nara and Kyōto and certain other historic areas. In 1975 a revision of the CULTURAL PROPERTIES LAW opened the way for that law's application to the preservation of other urban districts and historic buildings. In 1976 the Agency for Cultural Affairs cooperated with local governments in selecting areas for designation as Preservation Districts for Groups of Historic Buildings. In February 1991 there were 29 districts so designated throughout Japan. These included samurai residences from the Edo period (1600–1868), such as those in KAKUNODATE, Akita Prefecture; the remains of POST-STATION TOWNS from the same period; houses

built by foreign residents in Ikuta Ward, Kōbe; and historic farmhouses such as those in the village of SHIRAKAWA, Gifu Prefecture.

Historiographical Institute, Tōkyō University 東京大学史料編纂所

(Tōkyō Daigaku Shiryō Hensanjo; often abbreviated as Shiryō Hensanjo). Research institute devoted to the study and publication of historical materials on Japan. Established in 1869, it became a part of Tōkyō University in 1888 and received its present name in 1929. Originally charged with compiling a "great history of Japan," since 1895 it has taken on the broader task of collecting material for historical research. Today it is known as the central institution and principal library for the study of Japanese history. Among its continuing projects are the DAI NIHON SHIRYŌ and DAI NIHON KOMONJO collections. Another undertaking was the publication of *Historical Documents Relating to Japan in Foreign Countries* (15 vols, 1963–88), a catalog of the institute's extensive Western-language microfilm collection.

historiography 歴史学

(*rekishigaku*). The writing of histories in Japan is thought to have begun in the mid-6th century, by which time a small number of Japanese had gained an incipient mastery of the Chinese system of writing. The early histories TEIKI and KYŪJI, neither of which survives, were probably written by members of the YAMATO COURT (ca 4th century–ca mid-7th century). Although in chronicles and documents of the Nara period (710–794) only the titles of these works are recorded, the former appears to have been a genealogical record of the imperial line, and the latter to have contained myths of the Shintō gods and legends of emperors and culture heroes.

The Imperial Age——In order to establish the legitimacy of the Yamato emperors' authority over other lineage groups (UJI), Prince SHŌTOKU collaborated with SOGA NO UMAKO in 620 to compile the TENNŌKI AND KOKKI (Record of the Emperors; Record of the Nation), which, however, were destroyed by fire in 645. In 681 Emperor TEMMU (r 672–686) commanded HIEDA NO ARE to read and commit to memory selected passages of various historical and other narratives, which, some 30 years later, Hieda recited to Ō NO YASUMARO, who compiled the KOJIKI (712, Record of Ancient Matters). The oldest extant Japanese history, it recounts the descent of the Yamato emperors from the gods who, myth held, created the islands of Japan. Although both the *Kojiki* and the much longer NIHON SHOKI (720, Chronicles of Japan) were written almost wholly in classical Chinese (KAMBUN), the latter work was more profoundly influenced by the format of Chinese dynastic histories.

The *Nihon shoki* was the first of the RIKKOKUSHI (Six National Histories), which were compiled by a bureau of the imperial government and cover the country's history up until the year 887. The study of Chinese history was encouraged by the government, which established the Confucian-oriented court university DAIGAKURYŌ, and editors of the *Rikkokushi*, among them ŌMI NO MIFUNE and SUGAWARA NO MICHIZANE, possessed a comprehensive knowledge of Chinese, the language in which the early histories of Japan were written. The RITSURYŌ SYSTEM of government, which was based on the Chinese model, was already in decline by the 9th century, and the sixth of the national histories, *Nihon sandai jitsuroku* (901), was

the last that was sponsored by the government. Unofficial histories, however, such as the NIHON KIRYAKU and the HONCHŌ SEIKI, continued to be written by members of the court aristocracy.

In the 11th century there developed a genre of historical writing in Japanese that introduced the narrative techniques and prose style of contemporary vernacular fiction (see MONOGATARI BUNGAKU). The first such history was the EIGA MONOGATARI, which chronicled the rise of the FUJIWARA FAMILY to political power between 887 and the mid-11th century. It was followed by the ŌKAGAMI, which employed the rhetorical device of dialogue to relate contrasting views of the history of the Fujiwara family from 850 to 1025. Although the Fujiwara are glorified in both works, the wistful tone in which their appropriation of political power from the emperors is described conveys a deep sympathy with the imperial cause and reflects the then-dominant Buddhist belief that the world had entered a cycle of decay (see ESCHATOLOGY).

Another type of historical writing was the military chronicle (GUNKI MONOGATARI), the first example of which is the SHŌMONKI, a mid-10th-century account of the unsuccessful rebellion of TAIRA NO MASAKADO. Although the *Shōmonki* was written in HENTAI KAMBUN, a hybrid type of Chinese that employed numerous Japanese usages, later works in the genre were written in Japanese; HŌGEN MONOGATARI, HEIJI MONOGATARI, and HEIKE MONOGATARI, which appeared from the late 12th century to the early 13th century, dramatically depict the final stages of decline of the imperial order and the usurpation of power in 1185 by MINAMOTO NO YORITOMO.

The Age of the Medieval Shogunates (1192–1573)——The GUKANSHŌ (ca 1220), written by the aristocratic Buddhist monk JIEN, presents arguments that display the inevitability of the collapse of the imperial order and posit the possibility of its restoration. It is the first Japanese history to introduce a system of periodization based on theoretical principles of historical change. Another analytical history was KITABATAKE CHIKAFUSA'S JINNŌ SHŌTŌ KI, which was written for the instruction of the young emperor Go-Murakami (1328–68; r 1339–68). Based upon the Shintō religious tradition, the work contends that the distinctive feature of the polity of Japan is that the nation has been ruled by an unbroken succession of descendants of the god AMATERASU ŌMIKAMI and that the imperial line offers the sole means of ethical government. The AZUMA KAGAMI, which was written in *hentai kambun*, was apparently compiled by officials of the Kamakura shogunate (1192–1333) and chronicles the

origin and development of military rule in the period 1180–1266. The GODAI TEIŌ MONOGATARI, which was written in Japanese, records the affairs of the imperial court during the reigns of five emperors, beginning with Go-Horikawa (r 1221–32) and ending with Kameyama (r 1260–74).

In the ensuing era of the Muromachi shogunate (1338–1573) there appeared two important works that followed in the tradition of the military chronicle *Heike monogatari.* The TAIHEIKI recounts the rivalry for imperial supremacy of the NORTHERN AND SOUTHERN COURTS during the period 1318–67, while the much shorter and more accurate BAISHŌRON begins with an account of the Kamakura shogunate and ends with a discussion of the origins of the conflict over succession that led to the establishment of the Southern Court by Emperor GO-DAIGO (r 1318–39) in 1337. The first Japanese histories devoted to a subject other than political history were GENKŌ SHAKUSHO (1322), an account by the Zen monk KOKAN SHIREN of the introduction and development of Buddhism in Japan, and ZENRINKOKU HŌKI (1470), a history of Japan's relations with its continental neighbors.

The Edo Period (1600–1868)——The Tokugawa shogunate (1603–1867) had no sooner reunified the country than it set historians to producing works designed to legitimize its rule. HAYASHI RAZAN began compilation in 1644 of the comprehensive national history *Honchō tsugan*, a work completed by his son, HAYASHI GAHŌ, in 1670. Although Razan and Gahō were rigorous scholars, they were also proselytizers of Neo-Confucianism (SHUSHIGAKU), which was adopted by the shogunate as a semiofficial orthodoxy,

Hishida Shunsō *Fallen Leaves.* One of a pair of six-panel folding screens. 1909. Colors on paper. 157 × 362 cm. Eisei Bunko Museum, Tōkyō.

historic preservation districts The old inns of Tsumago in Nagano Prefecture were designated as official historic sites in 1971. The town was once a stop along the Nakasendō, a major thoroughfare during the Edo period.

and their history is deeply influenced by a Neo-Confucian world view. Another work that was compiled on the basis of Neo-Confucian principles was the 397-volume DAI NIHON SHI, a national history begun in 1657 at the order of TOKUGAWA MITSUKUNI, a domainal lord and grandson of TOKUGAWA IEYASU, but not completed until 1906. Both the *Honchō tsugan* and the *Dai Nihon shi* give a negative view of Buddhism and condemn the old aristocratic regime as decadent, while extolling the moral uprightness of the military governments that followed. Nevertheless, the *Dai Nihon shi* is considered the chief monument of Tokugawa historiography, and its influence upon later historical scholarship has been profound.

In contrast to the Neo-Confucian interpretation of history that predominated early in the Edo period, YAMAGA SOKŌ and OGYŪ SORAI, whose chief concern was with the Chinese classics, insisted that the fundamental responsibility of the scholar was not to moralize but merely to record facts on the basis of primary sources (see KOGAKU). A similar philological approach to texts was introduced into the study of the Japanese classics by KEICHŪ, who asserted that rigorous critical study of the language of the classics was the sole means of gaining an understanding of ancient culture. The tradition of National Learning (KOKUGAKU) initiated by Keichū was further developed by KADA NO AZUMAMARO, KAMO NO MABUCHI, and MOTOORI NORINAGA.

The increasing concern among historians and classicists with textual study led in the late 18th and early 19th centuries to the compilation of collated texts of literary and historical works by Kokugaku scholars such as HANAWA HOKIICHI and YASHIRO HIROKATA. The first series of the GUNSHO RUIJŪ, a collection of some 1,270 texts, the oldest of which are of 9th-century provenance, was begun by Hanawa in 1779. Completed in 1819, it remains an important resource for historians.

The Modern Age—The introduction of Western historiographical methodology in the wake of the Meiji Restoration of 1868 led to the appearance of works that adopted new approaches to the study of history. FUKUZAWA YUKICHI, whose BUMMEIRON NO GAIRYAKU (Outline of a Theory of Civilization) appeared in 1875, held that history should be understood not through the achievements of those in power but in terms of the development of civilization, and TAGUCHI UKICHI, in his study of the MEIJI ENLIGHTENMENT titled *Nihon kaika shōshi* (1877–82), discussed the historical significance of certain aspects of the Japanese economy.

A committee of scholars appointed by the Meiji government began work in 1881 on a new history of Japan. In 1888 three of the scholars, SHIGENO YASUTSUGU, KUME KUNITAKE, and Hoshino Hisashi (1839–1917), became professors at Tōkyō University, under whose auspices the project was thereafter carried on. The editors of the new history held deep reservations concerning the prevalence of Neo-Confucian ideology in the *Dai Nihon shi* and were convinced that a purely objective textual-critical approach to records of the past was absolutely necessary. In 1892 an article by Kume calling for the study of Shintō on the basis of rigorous historiographical methods appeared in the magazine *Shikai*. Kume held that Shintō was a form of heaven worship similar to that of a number of East Asian cultures and that its later application as the ideological underpinning of imperial authority had no basis in fact. Nationalists were outraged and, with the concurrence of the Imperial Household Ministry, Kume was forced to resign.

In 1893 the compilation of the new history was abandoned, but in 1895 the committee of scholars turned to the gathering and publication of primary historical materials (DAI NIHON SHIRYŌ) and public documents (DAI NIHON KOMONJO; see also DIPLOMATICS), arranged chronologically from 887 to 1867. Far from complete even today, these two collections have nevertheless laid the foundation for all Japanese research on the premodern era (see HISTORIOGRAPHICAL INSTITUTE, TŌKYŌ UNIVERSITY).

From the second decade of the 20th century, a number of histories appeared that drew on economic and cultural as well as political history. TSUDA SŌKICHI's *Bungaku ni arawaretaru waga kokumin shisō no kenkyū* (1916–21, Studies on the Thought of Our People as Expressed in Literature), MIURA HIROYUKI's *Kokushijō no shakai mondai* (1920, Social Problems in Japanese History), and WATSUJI TETSURŌ's *Nihon seishin shi kenkyū* (1926, Studies on the History of Japanese Thought) made important contributions to Japanese historiography.

From the late 1920s a number of Japanese historians were influenced by Marxist theory. *Meiji ishin shi* (1928, History of the Meiji Restoration) by HATTORI SHISŌ and *Nihon shihon shugi hattatsu shi* (1930, History of the Development of Japanese Capitalism) by NORO EITARŌ applied the principles of historical materialism to the study of Japanese history (see NIHON SHIHON SHUGI RONSŌ). By the mid-1930s, however, all writings by Marxist historians had been suppressed by the increasingly militarist Japanese government, and in 1940 Tsuda Sōkichi, who had presented conclusive evidence that the first 14 Japanese emperors were mere fabrications arising from the political ideology of the Yamato court, was convicted of lese majesty.

In the post–World War II period all restrictions on scholars were removed. In 1946 MARUYAMA MASAO published *Chōkokka shugi no ronri to shinri* (The Logic and Psychology of Ultranationalism), a study of the formerly sacrosanct EMPEROR system, and scholars such as Ishimoda Shō (1912–86) and Tōma Seita (b 1913) reintroduced the methodology of dialectical materialism, which predominated in the early postwar era. By the 1960s, however, the weaknesses of the rigidly theoretical Marxist approach became evident to most historians, while scholars of the traditionalist school, who previously had been concerned largely with the recounting of fact, came to recognize the value of theoretical structure in the study of history. Among the various fields of research pursued over the latter part of the 20th century, those that have made the most significant strides are probably social and economic history, local history, and the history of the Japanese masses, commonly referred to as *minshūshi*.

history of Japan　日本史

(*nihonshi*). For a people who are pressing toward the 21st century at the forefront of economic and technological development, the Japanese are intensely aware of their past. History is an important subject at every level of the school and university curricula. Historical sites all over the country draw crowds of visitors, and major archaeological finds fill the front pages of morning newspapers. The television networks regularly broadcast historical documentaries and lavish historical spectacles. Bookstores have large historical sections, and special occasions, such as the accession of Emperor AKIHITO in 1989, invite a flood of historical reflection on the part of the publishing industry and the mass media. In short, the Japanese possess a strong awareness of their history and explain many of their attitudes to themselves and the outside world in historical terms.

Observers in Europe and the United States are naturally tempted to view Japanese history in terms of its encounters with the West. From this perspective, the "Christian Century" from ca 1540 to ca 1640, and the century and a half from the arrival of Commodore Matthew PERRY's fleet and the "Opening of Japan" in the mid-19th century to the present, tend to be viewed as the major phases of Japanese history. The Japanese themselves, of course, see these periods of contact with the West, especially in modern times, as vital phases of their historical development, but they also look to their relations with the Asian continent. They prize the formative contacts with China and Korea in the premodern era and recall with regret Japan's imperialist aggression in Korea, China, and Manchuria in the period leading to World War II, a tragic episode that has shaped their modern history in numerous ways and with which they are still coming to terms.

Despite the importance of these contacts with other societies, however, it is the unfolding history of the Japanese people within the islands of the Japanese archipelago itself that must take center stage in any discussion of the Japanese past. That past can be divided into seven major phases: prehistoric (*senshi*), protohistoric (*genshi*), ancient (*kodai*), medieval (*chūsei*), early modern (*kinsei*), modern (*kindai*), and contemporary (*gendai*). Each of these major phases is usually further subdivided into several briefer units of PERIODIZATION.

The Prehistoric Period—The Japanese islands have been inhabited for at least 30,000 years and probably much longer. Because reliable written records were not produced in Japan before the early 8th century AD, most of Japan's earliest history has to be gleaned from archaeological finds or from the few references to Japan in Chinese and Korean records dating from the 1st century AD and after.

The scientific study of Japanese archaeology has made great strides in the past century, and we now have a very complete record of Japan's prehistoric and protohistoric development. Archaeologists who specialize in the earliest phase of Japanese social development usually divide the prehistoric phase (see PREHISTORY) into four major periods: a long paleolithic preceramic period prior to ca 10,000 BC; the JŌMON PERIOD (ca 10,000 BC–ca 300 BC), which saw the introduction of ceramics; the YAYOI PERIOD (ca 300 BC–ca AD 300), when metals and sedentary agriculture became widespread; and the KOFUN PERIOD (ca 300–710), age of the great burial mounds and the beginnings of political centralization. However, this latter period, which was one of transition to the era of written records, is also known—and is classified by this encyclopedia—as the protohistoric period.

The first inhabitants of the Japanese islands were paleolithic hunter-gatherers from the continent who used sophisticated stone blades but had no ceramics or settled agriculture. This paleolithic culture persisted until the close of the Pleistocene epoch, about 13,000 years ago, when the Japanese climate ameliorated and sea levels began to rise. In these changing climatic circumstances a new culture began to overlay the older paleolithic culture. This new culture is known as Jōmon (literally, "cord marked") from the magnificent pottery that characterized it. Although it has been commonly thought that the Jōmon people were hunter-gatherers who did not practice cultivation, recent research suggests that by about 1000 BC in Kyūshū they were cultivating a green-leaf condiment known as SHISO and had begun to cultivate rice, which was not native to Japan.

From about 300 BC Jōmon culture was overlaid by a distinctly different culture, the Yayoi, characterized by less flamboyant ceramics, a knowledge of bronze and iron technologies, including fine weaponry, and the systematic development of wet-field rice agriculture. These developments laid the basis for the strong martial current found in Japan's early history and for the agricultural way of life that profoundly shaped Japanese society into the modern era. They also contributed to greater social stratification and the emergence of a hierarchy of local clans (*uji*), ruling service groups (*be*), and slaves. Yayoi culture had spread through Kyūshū, Shikoku, and Honshū by the mid-3rd century AD.

The Protohistoric Period—Before the close of the Yayoi period, from about the mid-3rd century, clans in the Yamato region at the eastern end of the Inland Sea and in other areas of central and western Japan were building impressive mounded stone tombs for the burial of their chieftains. The largest of these KOFUN, huge keyhole-shaped tumuli covering several acres, were built in the Yamato region and are said to be the mausoleums of the first powerful political dynasty in Japan, the Yamato, which eventually asserted political control over the entire country.

Tumuli continued to be built in Japan until the end of the 7th century. By then, however, the old clan society was being restructured and Japan was already well on the way to the articulation of a Chinese-inspired centralized imperial administration. The ASUKA PERIOD (593–710) marks the final phase of this transition between protohistory and history proper. The Asuka period dates from the establishment of the court of Empress SUIKO (r 593–628) at the Toyoura Palace in the Asuka region of Yamato, south of the present-day city of Nara. That same year (593) Prince SHŌTOKU (574–622) began to serve as her regent. For more than a century the area was the site for the palaces of the rulers of the Yamato lineage and the powerful *uji* supporting it. Buddhism had been introduced to this region in the mid-6th century and it was here that Prince Shōtoku labored to elevate the power and prestige of the imperial line and set the country on the course of centralized reform heralded in his SEVENTEEN-ARTICLE CONSTITUTION. The Japanese court sponsored Buddhism; built temples, palaces, and capitals after Korean and later Chinese models; began to write histories using Chinese characters; and laid out a blueprint for a Chinese-style imperial state structure later known as the RITSURYŌ SYSTEM. These innovations were further extended in the TAIKA REFORM of 645 and the *ritsuryō* codes of the late 7th and early 8th centuries.

The Ancient Period—In 710 a magnificent new capital, called HEIJŌKYŌ and modeled on the Chinese Tang (T'ang) dynasty (618–907) capital at Chang'an (Ch'ang-an), was established at Nara. During the course of the NARA PERIOD (710–794) Japan received even more direct cultural and technological influences from China. Japan's first chronicles, the KOJIKI (712) and NIHON SHOKI (720), were compiled at this time. Buddhism and Confucianism were harnessed to support political authority, and temples were constructed in the capital and in each of the provinces. Centralized systems for the administration of taxation, census, and landholding were instituted. By the closing years of the 8th century, however, the centralized imperial administration and public land system were showing signs of strain. Politics in Nara were upset by rivalries among nobles and clerics. In 784 Emperor KAMMU (r 781–806) decided to make a new start and tried to revive the *ritsuryō* system by moving the capital to a new site. In 794 a new capital, called HEIANKYŌ (literally, "Capital of Peace and Tranquillity"), was established where the modern city of Kyōto now stands. This was to serve as the home of the imperial court and the capital of Japan until the 19th century, when the capital was moved to Edo, which was renamed Tōkyō.

The period from 794 to 1185, which was the heyday of the imperial government's rule of Japan from Heiankyō, is known as the HEIAN PERIOD. It saw the full assimilation of Chinese culture and the flowering of an elegant courtly culture. Politically, however, the imperial court and the imperial office itself came to be dominated by nobles of the FUJIWARA FAMILY, and the court had difficulty controlling the proliferation of private estates (SHŌEN) and in maintaining its control over the administration of the provinces. In the absence of an effective centralized military system, warrior bands began to assume more power, first in the provinces and then over the court itself when the TAIRA FAMILY seized power in the capital in the mid-12th century.

The Medieval Period—The Taira were overthrown in 1185 by warriors led by MINAMOTO NO YORITOMO, who was granted the title of SHŌGUN and established a military government, called the KAMAKURA SHOGUNATE, in the small town of Kamakura in eastern Japan. The first four centuries of warrior domination, covering the KAMAKURA PERIOD (1185–1333) and the MUROMACHI PERIOD (1333–1568), are usually described as Japan's feudal era. The court was not displaced by the creation of a military government in Kamakura but its influence steadily weakened. The shogunate assumed control of the administration of justice, the imperial succession, and the defense of the country against the attempted MONGOL INVASIONS OF JAPAN in the late 13th century. Headed first by Yoritomo and his sons and then by child shōguns who were controlled by regents from the Hōjō warrior family, the Kamakura shogunate was the first in a series of warrior regimes that dominated Japan until the mid-19th century. It was overthrown in 1333 by a coalition led by Emperor GO-DAIGO, who was seeking to restore direct imperial rule (see KEMMU RESTORATION).

Go-Daigo himself was ousted in 1336 by ASHIKAGA TAKAUJI, who had helped bring him to power. Takauji, using a rival emperor as a puppet sovereign, established a new shogunate in the Muromachi district of Kyōto (see MUROMACHI SHOGUNATE). After several decades of civil war between the rival NORTHERN AND SOUTHERN COURTS the shogunate was put on a firm footing by ASHIKAGA YOSHIMITSU, the third shōgun. Yoshimitsu was able to assert shogunal control over the powerful provincial warriors (SHUGO) who provided support for the shogunate. Later Ashikaga shōguns were less successful in controlling

the feudal coalition. Beginning with the ŌNIN WAR (1467–77), the country slipped into the century of sporadic civil war known as the Warring States period (SENGOKU PERIOD; 1467–1568), in which local feudal lords (DAIMYŌ) ignored the shogunate and the imperial court and struggled with each other for local hegemony.

The Early Modern Period—From the mid-16th century, a movement toward national reunification gradually emerged out of the violence of the warring feudal domains and was carried through by three powerful hegemons, ODA NOBUNAGA, TOYOTOMI HIDEYOSHI, and TOKUGAWA IEYASU. The short but spectacular epoch during which Nobunaga and Hideyoshi established their military control over the country and began to reshape its feudal institutions is known as the AZUCHI-MOMOYAMA PERIOD (1568–1600) after their magnificent castle-residences. This was an age of gold, grandeur, and openness to the outside world. Hideyoshi sought to pacify the countryside by confiscating swords and by separating *samurai* from peasants. He had visions of conquering Korea and establishing an enduring dynasty, though he lived to see his Korean invasions end in brutal failure. His death in 1598 left his heir vulnerable to rival daimyō. One of these, Tokugawa Ieyasu, after a striking victory over pro-Toyotomi warriors at the Battle of SEKIGAHARA in 1600, assumed the title of shōgun and established a powerful and enduring shogunate in the city of Edo, ushering in the EDO PERIOD (1600–1868) in Japanese history.

Ieyasu's victory gave him preponderant power and allowed him to rearrange the political map of Japan. He established a carefully balanced political structure known as the BAKUHAN SYSTEM in which the TOKUGAWA SHOGUNATE directly controlled Edo and the heartland of the country while the daimyō (classified on the basis of their loyalty to the Tokugawa) governed the 250 or so domains (*han*). Ieyasu and his shogunal successors were able to maintain a strong centralized feudal structure by balancing the daimyō domains; enforcing status distinctions between samurai, merchants, artisans, and peasants; instituting a hostage system of alternate-year attendance by daimyō in Edo (SANKIN KŌTAI); eradicating Christianity; controlling contacts with the outside world, especially the West; and enforcing regulations for samurai, nobles, and temples. This structure was dominated by samurai and relied heavily on the tax yield of the peasants, but it also gave scope to the merchants of Edo, Ōsaka, Kyōto, and the castle towns to develop commerce and a lively urban culture.

The Modern Period—The Tokugawa system, oppressive as it was in many respects, gave the country more than two centuries of peace and relative seclusion from the outside world. This was threatened in the 19th century as Russian, British, and American vessels began to probe Asian waters and press for trade with China and Japan. The shogunate's failure to "expel the barbarians," the concession of unequal treaties, and the opening of ports after Perry's visit in 1853 set in motion a chain of events that led the powerful domains of Satsuma, Chōshū, and Tosa to use the imperial court to challenge the shogunate, which was overthrown in the MEIJI RESTORATION of 1868. The young samurai who carried through the restoration wanted to preserve, revitalize, and strengthen the country. This process moved ahead rapidly during the course of the MEIJI PERIOD (1868–1912). The slogan of the new leadership of Japan was FUKOKU KYŌHEI (Enrich the Country, Strengthen the Military). This meant reforming most social, political, and economic institutions along Western lines. Japan adopted a constitution in 1889, opening the way to parliamentary government. It achieved industrial progress and built up sufficient military power to defeat China in 1895 and Russia in 1905, and to annex Korea in 1910, emerging as the major imperialist power in East Asia.

The TAISHŌ PERIOD (1912–26) was marked by Japan's acceptance as a major power, a period of party government sometimes known as TAISHŌ DEMOCRACY, domestic economic growth, and international diplomacy. The SHŌWA PERIOD (1926–89) began on a note of optimism but quickly descended into military aggression in Manchuria and China and Japan's departure from the League of Nations. Ultranationalism and political oppression at home eventually led to war with the United States and the Allied powers in Asia and the Pacific (see WORLD WAR II).

The Contemporary Era—The defeat of Japan in 1945 under atomic clouds brought the Allied OCCUPATION, demilitarization, dismantling of the old industrial combines (ZAIBATSU), renunciation of divinity by the emperor, a new constitution, democratization, and a new educational system. After a painful period of postwar rehabilitation, the Japanese economy began to surge ahead in the 1960s and 1970s. The Tōkyō Olympics in 1964 brought Japan renewed international recognition. The nation's continued prosperity has been based on a security treaty with the United States, a consistent stress on economic growth and business-oriented policy making, an emphasis on education, and the frugality, energy, and sustained efforts of the Japanese people. In recent years the Japanese, under international pressure to liberalize trade, have been moving from an export-oriented economy to one that is more accessible to foreign imports. This is part of a larger effort by the Japanese to overcome a strong historical tendency to view themselves as somehow unique and aloof from other nations. They are now attempting to truly internationalize their society and bring it into fuller cooperation with an increasingly interdependent world.

Hita   日田[市]

City in northwestern Ōita Prefecture, Kyūshū, on the river Chikugogawa. Hita was a prosperous castle town during the Edo period (1600–1868). Today its chief industry is lumbering and the manufacture of *geta* (wooden clogs) and other wood products. Sightseeing spots are Tsukikuma Park and the remains of Kangien, a school built in 1817 by the scholar HIROSE TANSŌ. Special products of the city are ONTA WARE pottery and Hita lacquer ware. Pop: 64,695.

Hita Basin   日田盆地

(Hita Bonchi). In western Ōita Prefecture, Kyūshū. Consisting of the floodplain of the river Mikumagawa, this small basin is surrounded by andesite mountains with flattish summits. Orchards are located on the uplands, and rice is grown in the lowlands, while Japanese cedar grows on the surrounding mountains. The remains of ancient ornamented tombs have been discovered in the area. Hita is the major city. Length: 6 km (4 mi); width: 8 km (5 mi).

Hitachi   日立[市]

City in northeastern Ibaraki Prefecture, central Honshū, on the Pacific Ocean coast. Once a post-station town, it was surrounded by farming villages during the Edo period (1600–1868). With the exploitation of the Hitachi Mines (the forerunner of the NIKKŌ KYŌDŌ CO, LTD) in 1905 and the establishment of HITACHI, LTD, in 1910, it developed rapidly into a mining and manufacturing city. A number of its factories are engaged in the smelting of copper and the production of electrical machinery and appliances. The port of Hitachi, opened in 1959, is used for importing industrial raw material and exporting finished products. Pop: 202,141.

Hitachi Cable, Ltd   日立電線[株]

(Hitachi Densen). Manufacturer of a wide variety of wires and cables as well as rolled copper products, industrial rubber products, and electronic components. Third largest in the electric wire industry, the company was incorporated in 1956 when the electric wire division of HITACHI, LTD, was made an independent firm. It has six production plants in Southeast Asia and three in the United States. The firm is also pursuing the development of new products such as superconductors, optical fiber communication cables, and gallium arsenide substrate for semiconductors. Sales for the fiscal year ending March 1991 totaled ¥348.6 billion (US $2.5 billion), of which wires and cables accounted for 52 percent; rolled copper products, 17 percent; industrial rubber goods, 5 percent; engineering work, 7 percent; and electronic components and other products, 19 percent. In the same year capitalization was ¥25.8 billion (US $188.0 million). Headquarters are in Tōkyō.

Hitachi Chemical Co, Ltd
日立化成工業[株]

(Hitachi Kasei Kōgyō). Manufacturer of a wide variety of products, including electronic materials and components, organic chemical products, synthetic resin molded parts, inorganic chemical products, housing equipment, environmental facilities, and pharmaceuticals. Incorporated in 1962, when the chemical products division of HITACHI, LTD, became an independent firm. The company has a broad technological capacity in both organic and inorganic chemistry. Overseas operations are in the United States, Germany, Taiwan, Singapore, Hong Kong, and China. Sales for the fiscal year ending March 1991 totaled ¥314.7 billion (US $2.3 billion), and capitalization was ¥15.0 billion (US $109.3 million). Headquarters are in Tōkyō.

Hitachi Kōki Co, Ltd   日立工機[株]

(Hitachi Kōki). Manufacturer of power tools, computer printers, and scientific instruments. Incorporated in 1948. An affiliate of HITACHI, LTD. The company is diversifying into precision machining and electronic control technology. It is also expanding its home-power-tool markets in Europe, the United States, and Asia. Sales for the fiscal year ending March 1990 totaled ¥116.7 billion (US $762.3 million), and capitalization stood at ¥17.7 billion (US $115.8 million). Headquarters are in Tōkyō.

Hitachi, Ltd   [株]日立製作所

(Hitachi Seisakusho). Electric machinery manufacturer producing heavy electrical equipment, consumer products, communications and electronic equipment, and transportation equipment. It is the largest electric machinery maker in Japan. It was established under its present name in 1910 in the town of Hitachi (Ibaraki Prefecture) as an electric machinery repair plant for Kuhara Kōgyōsho, a company founded by ODAIRA NAMIHEI. It became independent in 1920 and in the 1930s solidified its position as a comprehensive producer of electric machinery. In 1959 Hitachi entered the field of electronic computers and, later, integrated circuits and other advanced electronic products. It has established over 30 subsidiary and affiliated firms in Southeast Asia, the United States, and Europe. The company places considerable emphasis on research and development. Sales for the fiscal year ending March 1991 totaled ¥3.8 trillion (US $27.7 billion), of which heavy electrical machinery accounted for 19 percent; consumer products, 14 percent; communications and electronics equipment, 48 percent; industrial machinery, 10 percent; and transportation equipment, 9 percent. In the same year the export ratio was 24 percent, and the company was capitalized at ¥270.0 billion (US $2.0 billion). Headquarters are in Tōkyō.

Hitachi Maxell, Ltd   日立マクセル[株]

(Hitachi Makuseru). Manufacturer of dry batteries, magnetic tapes, and floppy disks. Established in 1961 as a member of the Hitachi group. The company has developed technology in the fields of opto-electronics and electronic devices. It has three overseas production subsidiaries in the United States and the United Kingdom, along with overseas sales subsidiaries in the United States, the United Kingdom, Germany, the Netherlands, Sweden, and Hong Kong. Sales for the fiscal year ending March 1991 totaled ¥139.8 billion (US $1.0 billion), and capitalization stood at ¥9.1 billion (US $66.3 million). Headquarters are in the city of Ibaraki, Ōsaka Prefecture.

Hitachi Metals, Ltd   日立金属[株]

(Hitachi Kinzoku). Manufacturer of high-grade special steels (under the brand name YSS), pipe fittings, malleable castings, and magnets. Incorporated in 1956 as a member of the Hitachi group, the company was a pioneer in the fields of casting and special steels. Its export ratio has diminished to 13 percent, reflecting an increase in overseas production. The company is developing new materials, such as a super-alloy for airplanes and electronics-related components. Sales for the fiscal year ending March 1991 totaled ¥350.4 billion (US $2.6 billion), and capitalization stood at ¥19.8 billion (US $144.3 million). Headquarters are in Tōkyō.

Hitachi Ōta   常陸太田[市]

City in northern Ibaraki Prefecture, central Honshū. During the Sengoku period (1467–1568) it flourished as a castle town of the SATAKE FAMILY. In the Edo period (1600–1868) it became a part of the Mito domain ruled by a branch of the TOKUGAWA FAMILY. Traditional products are Japanese paper (*washi*) and tobacco. Agricultural produce includes rice, fruits, and vegetables. Many residents commute to the cities of Mito and Hitachi. Of historic interest are Seizansō, where TOKUGAWA MITSUKUNI retired, and Zuiryūzan, the family grave of the Mito *daimyō*. Pop: 37,624.

Hitachi Plant Engineering & Construction Co, Ltd

日立プラント建設[株]

(Hitachi Puranto Kensetsu). Comprehensive engineering and construction firm specializing in the construction of power plants, industrial plants, pollution-control facilities, and air-conditioning and water-treatment equipment. Incorporated in 1929, the company joined the Hitachi group in 1935 and assumed its present name in 1968. It is engaged in research and development in cooperation with research institutes of HITACHI, LTD, and is diversifying its business into electronics and biotechnology. Sales for the fiscal year ending March 1991 totaled ¥236.4 billion (US $1.7 billion). The company was capitalized at ¥7.2 billion (US $52.5 million) in the same year. Headquarters are in Tōkyō.

Hitachi, Prince

常陸宮正仁親王

(1935– ; Hitachi no Miya Masahito Shinnō). The second son of Emperor SHŌWA and Empress Nagako (now the empress dowager). As a youth he was known as Yoshi no Miya. He graduated from Gakushūin University in 1958 and continued his studies at Tōkyō University. In 1964 he married Tsugaru Hanako, fourth daughter of former count Tsugaru Yoshitaka, and established the princely house of Hitachi. He is third in line for succession to the throne after Crown Prince NARUHITO and Prince AKISHINO.

Hitachi Sales Corporation

[株]日立家電

(Hitachi Kaden). General wholesale agent for electrical household appliances produced by HITACHI, LTD. The firm was incorporated in 1955 when it became independent of Hitachi, Ltd. Since it initiated export operations in 1967, sales companies have been established in the United States, Canada, England, and elsewhere. Sales for the fiscal year ending March 1991 totaled ¥637.4 billion (US $4.6 billion). In the same year capitalization stood at ¥7.8 billion (US $56.9 million). Headquarters are in Tōkyō.

Hitachi Scholarship Foundation

日立国際奨学財団

(Hitachi Kokusai Shōgaku Zaidan). A foundation established in 1984 by HITACHI, LTD, to promote mutual understanding between Japan and the countries of Southeast Asia and to support industrial modernization in that region. The foundation provides research fellowships to faculty and graduate students from various Southeast Asian universities and awards scholarships for study in Japan. In 1989 total assets were ¥3.0 billion (US $21.7 million). Headquarters are in Tōkyō.

Hitachi Zōsen Corporation

日立造船[株]

(Hitachi Zōsen). Company engaged in shipbuilding and the manufacture and sale of various types of machinery, steel structures, and environmental protection equipment and plants. Hitachi Zōsen's forerunner was Ōsaka Iron Works, established by a British trader in Ōsaka in 1881. It is one of the three largest shipbuilders in Japan. The company has technical tie-up contracts with Westinghouse Electric Co in the United States and with companies in Denmark, Switzerland, and the Federal Republic of Germany. Sales for the fiscal year ending March 1991 totaled ¥266.3 billion (US $1.9 billion). The company was capitalized at ¥50.3 billion (US

$366.6 million) in the same year. Headquarters are in Ōsaka.

hitobashira

人柱

(literally, "human pillar"). A legendary type of human sacrifice. Many Japanese legends claim that during the construction of bridges, dikes, and castles in ancient times a human being was buried alive to ensure the durability of the structure and as a prayer for safe completion of construction. The earliest mention of such a sacrifice appears in the chronicle *Nihon shoki* (720) in the section on the reign of Emperor NINTOKU. The legend concerning the building of the Nagara Bridge at Tarumi (in present-day Hyōgo Prefecture) is particularly well known. Many of the victims in the legends are women, who are sometimes accompanied by their children. The legends are believed to have been spread by female shamans (MIKO) who participated in rituals to placate water deities (SUIJIN).

hitodama

人魂

Spirit that is supposed to depart from the human body at the time of death and afterwards; commonly believed to take the form of a bluish white ball of fire with a tail. Seeing *hitodama* was traditionally regarded as a premonition of one's own death, although various ways of exorcising them are mentioned in medieval literature. Shooting stars, phosphorescence, and other natural phenomena are sometimes taken for *hitodama*.

hitogaeshi

人返し

(literally, "returning the people"). Policies designed in 1790 and 1843 to encourage peasants in urban areas to return to the countryside. Attracted by the wealth of the cities and burdened by heavy taxation, many peasants left the villages during the Edo period (1600–1868), especially after 1700. In 1790 the *rōjū shuseki* (chief senior councillor) MATSUDAIRA SADANOBU, as part of his KANSEI REFORMS, encouraged peasants in Edo (now Tōkyō) to return to their villages by supplying transportation money, but this was basically unsuccessful. In 1843 the *rōjū shuseki* MIZUNO TADAKUNI, in carrying out the TEMPŌ REFORMS, issued an order (the Hitogaeshi no Hō) requiring peasants in Edo to return to the countryside, which had been ravaged by the famines of 1833 and 1836. Since wages in the city far exceeded those in the countryside, this order had little long-term effect.

hitojichi

人質

(hostage). The offering of hostages in political agreements, such as alliance and surrender, was particularly common during the Sengoku (Warring States) period (1467–1568). A famous child *hitojichi* was TOKUGAWA IEYASU, held hostage for about 12 years. The Tokugawa shogunate's (1603–1867) policy requiring *daimyō* to leave their families in Edo (now Tōkyō) may be seen as an institutionalized form of the practice (see SANKIN KŌTAI).

Hitomi Kinue

人見絹枝

(1907–31). The first Japanese woman athlete of international stature. Born in Okayama Prefecture; graduated from Nihon Joshi Taiiku Semmon Gakkō (now Tōkyō Women's College of Physical Education). In 1926 at the Second Women's World Athletic Championship in Sweden, Hitomi set a new world record in the long jump (5.5 m; 18 ft) and became the first Japanese woman athlete to win an international championship. She

was singled out as the most valuable participant in the competition. In the 1928 Amsterdam Olympic Games she placed second in the 800-meter run, becoming the first Japanese woman to win an Olympic medal. She set world records 10 times in seven different events from 1926 to 1929.

hitorishizuka

一人静

Chloranthus japonicus. Perennial herb of the family Chloranthaceae that grows wild on thinly forested mountains and in shady thickets in the hill areas throughout Japan. The single stem (10–20 cm; 4–8 in) has three or four nodes; from the lower nodes grow small scaly leaves, while two pairs of opposite, dark green, elliptical leaves grow from the top node. In spring a flower stalk from the top of the stem bears a spike of numerous white blossoms. Another variety with two or more spikes, known as the *futarishizuka* (*C. serratus*), blooms in May. The family includes a small evergreen tree SENRYŌ (*Sarcandra glabra*), which, with its clusters of red round fruits, is a favorite cut flower for the New Year holidays.

Hitotsubashi University

一橋大学

(Hitotsubashi Daigaku). National university located in the city of Kunitachi, Tōkyō Prefecture. Its predecessor was the Shōhō Kōshūjo (School for Commercial Law), which was established by MORI ARINORI in 1875. It became a government institution in 1884, changing its name to Tōkyō Shōgyō Gakkō (Tōkyō School of Commerce). There were a number of subsequent name changes, including Tōkyō Shōka Daigaku (Tōkyō University of Commerce) in 1920 and finally Hitotsubashi Daigaku in 1949. It maintains faculties of economics, law, social science, and commerce, and the Institute of Economic Research. Enrollment was 4,383 in 1989.

hitotsume kozō

一つ目小僧

Goblin with a single eye in the middle of its forehead; one of the fantastic and grotesque creatures (see BAKEMONO) that appear in Japanese folktales. It generally takes the form of a young boy (*kozō*) but is sometimes associated with the Shintō gods of mountain or field (YAMA NO KAMI; TA NO KAMI). In the Kantō and Tōhoku regions it was believed to appear on the night of *kotoyōka*, a taboo day falling on the eighth day of the 2nd and 12th lunar months, and was warded off by attaching an open mesh basket upside down to a pole set up before a house.

hitoyogiri

一節切

(literally, "one node cut"). Vertical bamboo flute with a notched mouthpiece and five finger holes, closely related to the SHAKUHACHI but shorter and thinner with only one node along its length. Although the name *hitoyogiri* is often used to designate those

hiwatari In a test of spiritual strength, members of the Shugendō sect of Buddhism walk barefoot on burning embers at the temple Yakuōin, city of Hachiōji, Tōkyō Prefecture.

vertical flutes that appeared in Japan during the 14th and 15th centuries, and especially those played by mendicant *komusō* (straw-hat priests) in the 16th century, not until the beginning of the 17th century did the distinction between the standard *hitoyogiri* (with one node along its length) and the standard *shakuhachi* (with three, and later seven, nodes along its length) become clear. The *hitoyogiri* reached its zenith in the late 17th century when, in addition to maintaining its own repertoire of short solo pieces, it was used in a variety of popular musical genres. It declined rapidly in the 18th century and had virtually disappeared by the end of the 19th century.

Hitoyoshi 人吉[市]

City in southern Kumamoto Prefecture, Kyūshū, on the river Kumagawa. During the Kamakura period (1185–1333) Hitoyoshi was a prosperous castle town of the Sagara family. Lumbering is its principal industry. Hitoyoshi Hot Spring and boat excursions down the Kumagawa are popular with tourists. Pop: 40,173.

Hitoyoshi Basin 人吉盆地

(Hitoyoshi Bonchi). In southern Kumamoto Prefecture, Kyūshū. Surrounded by the Kyūshū Mountains, this basin consists of the floodplain of the river Kumagawa's upper reaches and alluvial fans below the fault scarp. Rice and tobacco are grown, melons and Japanese pears are cultivated, and dairy farming is practiced. The major city is Hitoyoshi. Area: approximately 72 sq km (28 sq mi).

Hiuchigadake 燧ヶ岳

Also known as Hiuchidake. Conical volcano in southwest Fukushima Prefecture, northern Honshū. Its lava flow has dammed the river Tadamigawa to form the swampy regions of OZE. It is part of Nikkō National Park. Height: 2,356 m (7,730 ft).

hiwatari 火渡り

Ritual of the SHUGENDŌ sect of Buddhism in which wooden sticks called *goma-gi* are burned and believers walk barefoot on the embers uttering incantations. A test of the strength the practitioner has derived from the ascetic practices of the sect, this ritual is believed to burn away the sins and filth of the world and unite the practitioner with Buddhist deity Fudō Myōō (Skt: Acalanātha; see MYŌŌ).

Hiyoshi Shrine → Hie Shrine (Hie Taisha)

Hizen domain 肥前藩

(Hizen *han*). Also known as Saga domain. Edo-period (1600–1868) domain that extended over much of Hizen Province (parts of present-day Saga and Nagasaki prefec-

tures). It was granted in 1607 to Nabeshima Katsushige (1580–1657; see NABESHIMA FAMILY), who received the status of TOZAMA (outside vassal). In the late Edo period the domain gained a monopoly trade in such products as coal and porcelain and was instrumental in introducing Western military technology. It produced a number of leading political figures of the Meiji period (1868–1912), including ŌKUMA SHIGENOBU. OMOTEDAKA (estimated annual production of rice): 357,036 KOKU (1 *koku* = 180 liters or 5 US bushels).

Hoan Jōrei → Peace Preservation Law of 1887

Hoashi Banri 帆足万里

(1778–1852). Scholar and educator of the late Edo period (1600–1868). Born in Bungo Province (now Ōita Prefecture). His many works combined WESTERN LEARNING with Confucian and Buddhist philosophy and his own speculation. His *Kyūritsū* (1836, Mastery of Truth) discussed planets, constellations, the earth, and gravity; his other books included a work on political economy called *Tōsempu ron* (Treatise by an Eastern Recluse) and *Igaku keimō* (Instruction in Medicine).

Hōchi shimbun 報知新聞

A large sports and recreation tabloid published daily in Tōkyō and Ōsaka. Originally known as the YŪBIN HŌCHI SHIMBUN, it was founded in Tōkyō in 1872. In 1894 it was reorganized as the *Hōchi shimbun* and became a leader among large commercial newspapers. In the 1920s the *Hōchi* faced strong competition from other large dailies such as the ASAHI SHIMBUN and the YOMIURI SHIMBUN, with which it briefly merged in 1942. In 1946 it came back as an evening paper, and then in 1950 it became a sports and recreation morning newspaper. Its circulation in 1991 was 710,000 in Tōkyō and 400,000 in Ōsaka.

Hodosan 宝登山

Mountain in western Saitama Prefecture, central Honshū. It is famous for its views of the gorge NAGATORO, the Chichibu Mountains, and the Kantō Plain. Hodosan Shrine is at its foot. Height: 497 m (1,631 ft).

Hoechst Japan, Ltd ヘキストジャパン[株]

(Hekisuto Japan). Manufacturer of chemical products and pharmaceuticals. Incorporated in 1966 as a wholly owned subsidiary of the German firm Hoechst AG. It produces industrial and agricultural chemicals, electronic and engineering materials, and pharmaceuticals. Sales for the fiscal year ending December 1990 totaled ¥108.2 billion (US $788.6 million), and capitalization stood at ¥4.7 billion (US $34.3 million) in the same year. Headquarters are in Tōkyō.

Hoffmann, Johann Joseph ホフマン, J. J.

(1805–78). German scholar of the Japanese and Chinese languages. He worked in Amsterdam as an assistant to Philipp Franz von SIEBOLD, a scholar of Japanese culture. Hoffmann later served as the first professor of Japanese at Leiden University and laid the foundation for Japanese studies in Europe. He died in Leiden, never having set foot in Japan. He published several research works on Japan, including *Japansche Spraakleer* (1867–68), a grammar of the Japanese language.

Hōfu 防府[市]

City in central Yamaguchi Prefecture, western Honshū. Hōfu was a provincial capital in ancient times and a post-station town on the San'yōdō highway during the Edo period (1600–1868). Salt was shipped to various parts of the country from the port of Mitajiri to the south. Today textile and automobile plants are located in the coastal industrial zone. Historical sites include Hōfu Temmangū Shrine and the remains of an 8th-century provincial temple (KOKUBUNJI). Pop: 117,634.

hōgaku → music, traditional

Hōgen Disturbance 保元の乱

(Hōgen no Ran). Military conflict arising from rivalries within the imperial family, the FUJIWARA FAMILY, the MINAMOTO FAMILY, and the TAIRA FAMILY following the death of the retired emperor TOBA in 1156 (Hōgen 1). The reigning emperor, GO-SHIRAKAWA, had the support of the regent Fujiwara no Tadamichi (1097–1164), but Tadamichi's brother Yorinaga (1120–56) sided with the retired emperor SUTOKU. Sutoku had the backing of the Seiwa Genji leader Minamoto no Tameyoshi (1096–1156), while Tameyoshi's son MINAMOTO NO YOSHITOMO joined TAIRA NO KIYOMORI in support of Go-Shirakawa. When Sutoku's faction attempted to seize power, Yorinaga was killed in the fighting, Tameyoshi was executed, and Sutoku was exiled. Despite Go-Shirakawa's victory, real political power passed to the Taira and Minamoto families, who immediately contested for supremacy (see HEIJI DISTURBANCE).

Hōgen monogatari 保元物語

War tale (GUNKI MONOGATARI) of the early Kamakura period (1185–1333); an account of the power struggle for the imperial succession in the HŌGEN DISTURBANCE of 1156. It is often paired with HEIJI MONOGATARI, a tale of rebellion to gain control of the imperial court in 1160. In the early middle ages *Hōgen* was chanted by itinerant "lute priests" (BIWA HŌSHI) but was overshadowed in popularity by HEIKE MONOGATARI, a narrative account of the TAIRA-MINAMOTO WAR, which was also chanted. Later versions of *Hōgen monogatari* seem intended to be read.

Volume 1 describes the disposition of the throne by the retired emperor TOBA to successors unsatisfactory to his son, the retired emperor SUTOKU. Volume 2 describes the successful attack by TAIRA NO KIYOMORI on Sutoku. Volume 3 concerns the aftermath. The major theme of the tale is the tragic consequences of violations of the natural order of human relationships, which is preserved by propriety and harmony. In the disturbances, factions of both the Fujiwara family and the imperial family are pitted against their own blood relatives; Taira family members fight each other, as do the Minamoto. Throughout the tale, the focus is on the figure of MINAMOTO NO TAMETOMO as a valiant *samurai* and tragic hero.

hōhei kōshō 砲兵工廠

(arsenals). At Tōkyō in 1868 and at Ōsaka in 1870 the new Meiji government established army arsenals with munitions facilities confiscated from the Tokugawa shogunate (1603–1867) and *daimyō* domains. They received the name *hōhei kōshō* with the issuance of the Arsenal Ordinance (Hōhei Kōshō Jōrei) in October 1879. The facilities were expanded during the Sino-Japanese

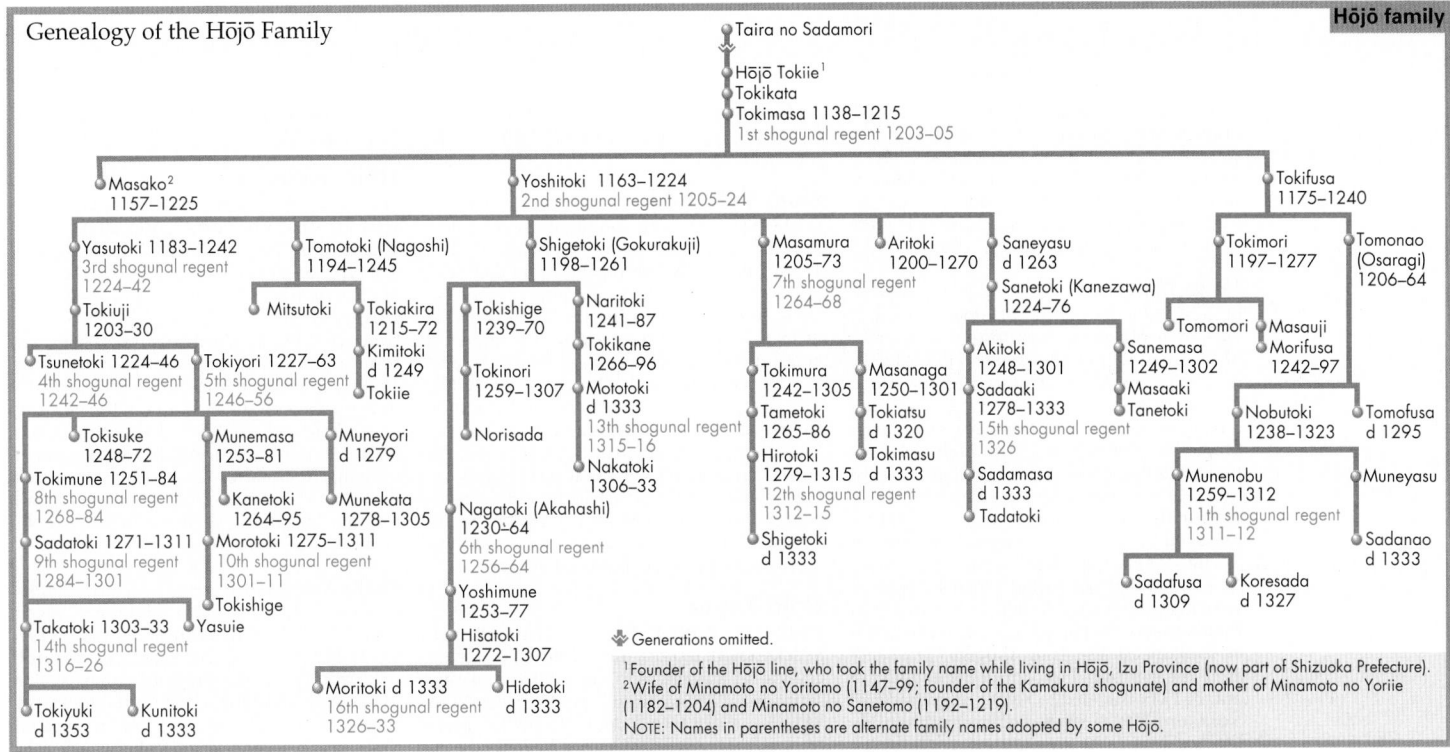

Genealogy of the Hōjō Family

Generations omitted.

[1] Founder of the Hōjō line, who took the family name while living in Hōjō, Izu Province (now part of Shizuoka Prefecture).
[2] Wife of Minamoto no Yoritomo (1147–99; founder of the Kamakura shogunate) and mother of Minamoto no Yoriie (1182–1204) and Minamoto no Sanetomo (1192–1219).
NOTE: Names in parentheses are alternate family names adopted by some Hōjō.

(1894–95) and Russo-Japanese (1904–05) wars. See also GOVERNMENT-OPERATED FACTORIES, MEIJI PERIOD.

Hōitsu → Sakai Hōitsu

Hōji Conflict   宝治合戦

(Hōji Kassen). A battle in 1247 in which the HŌJŌ FAMILY destroyed the MIURA FAMILY and consolidated its authority as regents (shikken) of the Kamakura shogunate (1192–1333). HŌJŌ TOKIYORI, with the aid of his maternal grandfather, ADACHI KAGEMORI, forced over 500 members and retainers of the rival Miura family to commit suicide.

hōjin   法人

(juristic person). An entity other than a natural person possessing a personality under law. Hōjin may be a public corporation, private corporation, foundation, stock company, or nonprofit corporation. Chapter II of the CIVIL CODE, consisting of 52 articles, deals with juristic persons. The code provides that no juristic person can come into existence except under provisions set forth in the code or other laws. The code recognizes two general categories of juristic person: those relating to the public interest (in such fields as religion, charity, science, the arts, etc, which do not have gain or profit as their motive) and those relating to private interest.

Juristic persons have rights and duties, subject to the provisions of laws and ordinances and within the limits of their objectives as set forth in their articles of incorporation. In addition, they are responsible for any damage done to others by their directors or other representatives in the execution of their duties. See also GAIKOKU HŌJIN (foreign juristic person).

Hōjō   北条[市]

City in northern Ehime Prefecture, Shikoku, on the INLAND SEA. Main industries are textiles, roof tiles, fishing, and agriculture (mandarin oranges, poultry, and onions). The main tourist attraction is the island of Kashima, part of the INLAND SEA NATIONAL PARK. Pop: 29,418.

Hōjō Dansui   北条団水

(1663–1711). HAIKU poet and writer of UKIYO-ZŌSHI, a genre of popular fiction of the Edo period (1600–1868). A disciple of SAIKAKU, he edited and published his master's manuscripts after Saikaku's death. His best-known work is Chūya yōjin ki (1707, An Account of Unrelenting Vigilance).

Hōjō family   北条氏

(Hōjōshi). 1. Warrior family of the Kamakura period (1185–1333); hereditary regents (SHIKKEN) of the KAMAKURA SHOGUNATE, the Hōjō ruled Japan for more than a century until destroyed in the KEMMU RESTORATION. The family was founded by Taira no Tokiie, who took the name Hōjō. His grandson HŌJŌ TOKIMASA (1138–1215) befriended MINAMOTO NO YORITOMO. Yoritomo married Tokimasa's daughter HŌJŌ MASAKO (1157–1225), and when Yoritomo set up his military government at Kamakura in 1185 he was assisted by his father-in-law. Yoritomo died in 1199, and Tokimasa, with Masako, took control of the shogunate, becoming regent in 1203. He was succeeded by his son HŌJŌ YOSHITOKI (r 1205–24), who crushed a conspiracy (the JŌKYŪ DISTURBANCE). Under HŌJŌ TOKIMUNE (r 1268–84), the shogunate defended the nation against the MONGOL INVASIONS OF JAPAN in 1274 and 1281. The last Hōjō regent of importance was HŌJŌ TAKATOKI (r 1316–26), who retained control of the shogunate even after his retirement. In 1333, his principal commanders, ASHIKAGA TAKAUJI and NITTA YOSHISADA, turned against him and joined Emperor GO-DAIGO's imperial restoration movement. Takatoki and his family committed suicide.

2. Another Hōjō family, of the late Muromachi (1333–1568) and the Azuchi-Momoyama (1568–1600) periods, were regional lords (SENGOKU DAIMYŌ). They were unrelated to the earlier Hōjō and are sometimes called the Go-Hōjō (Later Hōjō). Founded by HŌJŌ SŌUN (1432–1519), the family was destroyed by TOYOTOMI HIDEYOSHI in the ODAWARA CAMPAIGN of 1590. See also HŌJŌ GODAI KI.

Hōjō godai ki   北条五代記

(Chronicle of the Hōjō Family through Five Generations). A chronologically arranged collection of military episodes and anecdotes belonging to the genre GUNKI MONOGATARI (war tales); date of compilation uncertain. It recounts the history of the Later Hōjō family (Go-Hōjō; see HŌJŌ FAMILY), from HŌJŌ SŌUN (1432–1519) until Hōjō Ujinao (1562–91). It is composed of selections from the KEICHŌ KEMMON SHŪ (Collections of Things Seen and Heard during the Keichō Era [1596–1615]) by Miura Jōshin (1565–1644).

Hōjō Hideji   北条秀司

(1902–). Playwright. Real name Iino Hideji. Born in Ōsaka. A graduate of Kansai University, he studied with the dramatists OKAMOTO KIDŌ and HASEGAWA SHIN. In the mid-1930s he joined the SHIMPA (New School) modern drama movement. He became a troupe playwright for the SHINKOKUGEKI (New National Theater) acting company and became important in Japan's commercial theater. Among his many plays is the masterpiece Ōshō (1947, Chess Master).

Hōjōki   方丈記

(1212; tr The Ten Foot Square Hut, 1928; tr An Account of My Hut, 1955). A brief work in the ZUIHITSU (essay) mode by the elderly recluse KAMO NO CHŌMEI (1156?–1216). In its opening passage the impermanence of life (MUJŌ) is conveyed by likening man and his dwellings to the flow of a river and the bubbles that form and vanish along its surface. To convey the perils that await those who wed their fates to the worldly splendors of the capital, Chōmei then relates five disasters he has witnessed: a devastating fire, a terrible whirlwind, the ill-fated attempt to move the capital, an awful famine, and an earthquake. By contrast, the second half of the Hōjōki describes the simple joys and tranquillity of Chōmei's existence after he has taken the tonsure and become a Buddhist recluse in the shadows of Mt. Hino. In the terse closing passage, however, the author questions whether his own love of the contemplative life is not itself a form of earthly desire inconsistent with the rigorous demands of Buddhist renunciation. The Hōjōki and the TSUREZUREGUSA (ca 1330; tr Essays in Idleness, 1967) of YOSHIDA KENKŌ exemplify the numerous meditations on impermanence written by Japanese Buddhist monks living in seclusion. Similarities in style and content between the Hōjōki and a short essay in Chinese, the *Chiteiki* (982, Pond Bower Notes) by YOSHISHIGE NO YASU-TANE, have led critics to suggest that Chōmei may have been influenced by this work; in turn, the *Hōjōki* is cited as an influence on Matsuo BASHŌ's *Genjūan no ki* (1690; tr *Prose Poem on the Unreal Dwelling*, 1955).

Hōjō Masako 北条政子

(1157–1225). Daughter of HŌJŌ TOKIMASA; wife of MINAMOTO NO YORITOMO, the founder of the Kamakura shogunate (1192–1333); mother of MINAMOTO NO YORIIE and MINAMOTO NO SANETOMO. Masako married Yoritomo during his exile in Izu Province (now part of Shizuoka Prefecture). Although Masako took Buddhist vows after Yoritomo's death in 1199, she gradually became involved in shogunate politics. She and her father removed the politically incompetent shōgun Yoriie, replacing him with Sanetomo. Masako exiled her father when he plotted with his second wife, Maki no Kata, to install their son-in-law Hiraga Tomomasa (d 1205) as shōgun. As the "nun shōgun" (*ama shō-gun*) she continued to control the shogunate and in 1219 traveled to Kyōto to invite Kujō Yoritsune (1218–56) to be heir to the childless Sanetomo. At the outbreak of the JŌKYŪ DISTURBANCE (1221) she induced shogunate vassals to reaffirm their loyalty. Masako remained powerful in shogunate councils until her death.

Hōjō no umi 豊饒の海

(The Sea of Fertility). A tetralogy by MISHIMA YUKIO (1925–70), published 1965–71, consisting of the following novels: *Haru no yuki* (1965–67; tr *Spring Snow*, 1971), *Homba* (1967–68; tr *Runaway Horses*, 1973); *Akatsuki no tera* (1968–70; tr *The Temple of Dawn*, 1973), and *Tennin gosui* (1970–71; tr *The Decay of the Angel*, 1974). The protagonist, who dies tragically in the love story *Spring Snow*, is reborn in *Runaway Horses* as a political activist who commits suicide, and in *The Temple of Dawn* as a Thai princess. In the final novel, *The Decay of the Angel*, it comes to light that the fourth reincarnation is a sham. The idea of transmigration is thus ultimately denied, and a secondary character, Honda, who has acted as an observer throughout the four novels, is forced into a direct confrontation with nothingness. Mishima completed the final installment of the tetralogy immediately before his own suicide.

Hōjō Sanetoki → Kanazawa Bunko

Hōjō Sōun 北条早雲

(1432–1519). Military and political leader. Real name Ise Shinkurō Nagauji. He later adopted the surname Hōjō and used the religious name Sōun. To distinguish his surname from that of the HŌJŌ FAMILY regents of the KAMAKURA SHOGUNATE (1192–1333), he and his descendants are often called the Go-Hōjō or Later Hōjō. Around 1475, he became a retainer of Imagawa Yoshitada (1442–76), the military governor (*shugo*) of Suruga (now part of Shizuoka Prefecture). In 1476 he helped suppress a revolt in which Yoshitada was killed; Yoshitada's son Imagawa Ujichika rewarded Sōun with Kōkokuji Castle. In 1491 Sōun seized control of Izu Province (now part of Shizuoka Prefecture) and in 1495 took over Odawara Castle. By 1516 he also held Musashi and Sagami provinces (now Saitama, Tōkyō, and Kanagawa

prefectures). His descendants controlled the Kantō region until their defeat by TOYOTOMI HIDEYOSHI in 1590.

Hōjō Takatoki 北条高時

(1303–33). The 14th shogunal regent (SHIK-KEN) of the Kamakura shogunate (1192–1333); son of the 9th regent, Hōjō Sadatoki (1271–1311). Takatoki became regent in 1316, but, because of his youth, the powers of his office were exercised by his maternal grandfather, Adachi Tokiaki (d 1333), and the minister Nagasaki Takasuke (d 1333). The shogunate was in decline, and the SHŌ-CHŪ CONSPIRACY of 1324, Emperor GO-DAIGO's first attempt to overthrow the regime, weakened it further. In 1326 Takatoki resigned the regency. Go-Daigo struck again in the GENKŌ INCIDENT of 1331. When NITTA YOSHISADA attacked Kamakura in 1333, Takatoki and most of his family committed suicide.

Hōjō Tamio 北条民雄

(1914–37). Author. Born in Seoul, Korea. Stricken with leprosy and admitted to a leper asylum at the age of 20, he sent the manuscript of "Maki rōjin" (1935, Old Man Maki), a story based upon his own experience, to KAWABATA YASUNARI, who helped him publish it in the magazine BUNGAKUKAI. This and his other stories about life in a leper asylum affirm the value of life in the face of suffering. His works include the short stories "Inochi no shoya" (1936, The First Day of Life) and "Raiin jutai" (1936, A Pregnancy in the Leper Asylum).

Hōjō Tokimasa 北条時政

(1138–1215). First regent (SHIKKEN) of the Kamakura shogunate (1192–1333). He gave shelter to MINAMOTO NO YORITOMO, who was exiled by TAIRA NO KIYOMORI in 1160. His daughter HŌJŌ MASAKO married Yoritomo. When Yoritomo rebelled against Taira rule, Tokimasa came to his son-in-law's aid (see TAIRA-MINAMOTO WAR). He went to Kyōto in 1185 on the pretext of apprehending MINA-MOTO NO YOSHITSUNE, Yoritomo's estranged brother; there he persuaded the court to grant Yoritomo the power to appoint JITŌ (estate stewards) and SHUGO (military governors) throughout the country. Tokimasa helped Yoritomo consolidate his rule after the Kamakura shogunate was formed in 1192. After Yoritomo's death Masako and Tokimasa stripped the ineffectual shōgun MINAMOTO NO YORIIE of political power and created the office of regent for Tokimasa in 1203. He had Yoriie murdered (1204) and installed MINAMOTO NO SANETOMO as shōgun. In 1205 he plotted to replace Sanetomo with Hiraga Tomomasa (d 1205) but was foiled by Masako and his son HŌJŌ YOSHITOKI, who forced him out of office.

Hōjō Tokimune 北条時宗

(1251–84). The eighth shogunal regent (SHIK-KEN) of the Kamakura shogunate (1192–1333). Son of HŌJŌ TOKIYORI and of a daughter of Hōjō Shigetoki (1198–1261). Tokimune became cosigner (RENSHO) in 1264 and regent in 1268. Throughout his regency Tokimune faced the threat of the MONGOL INVASIONS OF JAPAN. He strengthened the defenses of southwestern Japan and mobilized Kyūshū warriors to repel the first invasion in 1274. He had a long stone wall constructed along Hakata Bay against another attack, which came in 1281; again he organized the shogunate's successful defense of Japan. A follower of Zen Buddhism, he invited the priest Wuxue (Wu-hsüeh; J: Mugaku) from

Song (Sung) China and built the temple EN-GAKUJI in 1282.

Hōjō Tokiyori 北条時頼

(1227–63). The fifth shogunal regent (SHIK-KEN) of the KAMAKURA SHOGUNATE (1192–1333); son of Hōjō Tokiuji (1203–30). Tokiyori became regent in 1246 on the death of his brother Tsunetoki (1224–46) and crushed a plot, led by the former shōgun Kujō (Fujiwara) Yoritsune (1218–56) and some of his own kinsmen, to overthrow him. The next year he was able to destroy the powerful vassal MIURA FAMILY in the HŌJI CONFLICT. Tokiyori established the High Court (HIKITSUKE) in 1249 to adjudicate lawsuits involving shogunal vassals. Although he took Buddhist vows and relinquished the regency to Hōjō Nagatoki (1230–64) in 1256, Tokiyori retained the actual power.

Hōjō Yasutoki 北条泰時

(1183–1242). The third shogunal regent (SHIKKEN) of the Kamakura shogunate (1192–1333). Eldest son of HŌJŌ YOSHITOKI. Yasutoki successfully led the shogunal forces against those of the imperial court in the JŌKYŪ DISTURBANCE of 1221. He remained in Kyōto as the first ROKUHARA TANDAI (Rokuhara deputy) to oversee the court, and on his father's death in 1224 he became regent. Appointing his uncle Hōjō Tokifusa (1175–1240) as RENSHO (cosigner), Yasutoki began to systematize shogunal rule. He established the Council of State (HYŌJŌSHŪ) in 1226, and in 1232 he promulgated the GOSEIBAI SHIKIMOKU, the first codification of warrior house law (BUKEHŌ). Yasutoki was instrumental in laying the foundations for WARRIOR GOVERNMENT in medieval Japan.

Hōjō Yoshitoki 北条義時

(1163–1224). The second shogunal regent (SHIKKEN) of the Kamakura shogunate (1192–1333). Yoshitoki followed his father, HŌJŌ TOKIMASA, in the TAIRA-MINAMOTO WAR as a supporter of MINAMOTO NO YORITOMO, husband of his sister HŌJŌ MASAKO. With Masako's help he ousted and replaced his father as regent in 1205. Having destroyed the Wada family in 1213, he also took the headship of the Board of Retainers (SAMURAI-DOKORO), which WADA YOSHIMORI had held. After the assassination of the shōgun MINAMOTO NO SANETOMO in 1219, Yoshitoki and Masako gained complete control of the shogunate. In the JŌKYŪ DISTURBANCE of 1221, retired emperor GO-TOBA attempted to overthrow the Hōjō; Yoshitoki crushed the uprising and extended the shogunate's rule over the entire country.

hōka 放下

1. Type of street performance popular from the Muromachi (1333–1568) to the Edo (1600–1868) period, featuring juggling, acrobatics, and distinctive singing accompanied by striking two short bamboo sticks together. The performers were called *hōka*, *hōkashi*, or *hōkasō*; many were dressed as priests.

2. Present-day folk performance of central Japan (especially Aichi Prefecture), featuring a vigorous dance accompanied by flutes and drums. The dancers carry giant fans on their backs.

Hōkaiji 法界寺

SHINGON SECT Buddhist temple; located in Fushimi Ward, Kyōto. Originally a TENDAI SECT monastery, Hōkaiji became affiliated with Shingon in the Edo period (1600–1868). According to legend, Hōkaiji was founded in the 9th century when a courtier, Hino Iemune (d 877), received a small image of the Buddha Yakushi Nyorai made by the monk SAICHŌ and built a family temple on his land to enshrine the image. Later Hino Sukenari (d 1070) built a Yakushi hall, an Amida hall, and a Kannon hall. Of these, only the Amida hall (1051), partially rebuilt during the late Heian period (794–1185), survives.

hōkan   幇間

Also called *taikomochi.* Jesterlike male GEISHA whose role is to entertain people at banquets by creating an atmosphere of merriment. *Hōkan* first became established during the Hōreki era (1751–64). Their performances consisted of improvised humor and could encompass a variety of techniques, including parody, singing, dancing, mimicry, and impersonation. *Hōkan* routines are depicted in such Ihara SAIKAKU works as *Kōshoku ichidai otoko* (1682; tr *The Life of an Amorous Man,* 1964). There are very few *hōkan* still performing in present-day Japan.

hōkei shūkōbo   方形周溝墓

(literally, "square, ditched graves"). A prehistoric form of burial consisting of square or roundish mounds of earth ranging from 6 to 25 meters (19.7 to 82.0 ft) in length, 1 meter (3.3 ft) in height, and surrounded by a moat 1 to 2 meters (3.3 to 6.6 ft) wide. Developed in the Ōsaka region at the end of the Early Yayoi period (ca 300 BC–ca 100 BC), they spread throughout Japan in Middle Yayoi (ca 100 BC–ca AD 100) and lasted through the early part of the Kofun period (ca 300–710). *Hōkei shūkōbo* sites contained several burials in simple pits, wood coffins, or jars. See also DOLMEN BURIALS; FLEXED BURIALS; JAR BURIALS.

Hokekyō→Lotus Sutra

Hokkaidō   北海道

The northernmost and second largest of Japan's four main islands. It is separated from Honshū to the south by the Tsugaru Strait and bounded by the Sea of Japan on the west, the Sea of Okhotsk on the northeast, and the Pacific Ocean on the south and east. Several mountain ranges cross Hokkaidō, and those belonging to the Ezo Mountains run from north to south across the center of the island, separated into two strands by a series of basin areas. To the west of these mountains lies the broad ISHIKARI PLAIN. To the southwest of the plain is a long peninsula, which is the area closest to Honshū and the first part of the island to be inhabited by the Japanese. The climate is unlike that of the rest of Japan, being notably colder and drier.

The prehistoric culture of Hokkaidō seems to have shared many of the characteristics of the early culture of Honshū, except that it lacked a YAYOI CULTURE. Hokkaidō, or EZO, as it was known, was inhabited by the AINU and not included in Japan proper. In the Edo period (1600–1868) the Matsumae domain was established in the extreme southwestern corner of the island. After the Meiji Restoration of 1868, the new government placed great emphasis on Hokkaidō's economic development, setting up a colonial office (KAITAKUSHI) and encouraging settlers to come from other parts of Japan. The name of the island was changed to Hokkaidō (literally, "Northern Sea Circuit") in 1869 on MATSUURA TAKESHIRŌ's suggestion. Hokkaidō was divided into three prefectures from 1882 to 1886. These were abolished, and the present prefectural form of administration was

established in 1886. (Within Japan's prefectural system, Hokkaidō alone is called a *dō* [circuit] rather than a *ken* [prefecture]; however, it is the equivalent of a prefecture.)

The main agricultural crop is rice; grain and vegetable farming as well as dairy farming are active. Fishing, forestry, and mining have long been an important part of Hokkaidō's economy, forming a sizable percentage of Japan's total production. They also form the basis for much of Hokkaidō's industrial activity, including food-processing, woodworking, pulp, and paper industries.

Hokkaidō is noted for its dramatic and unspoiled scenery, which includes active volcanoes, large lakes, and vast virgin forests. Major tourist attractions are Shikotsu-Tōya, Akan, Daisetsuzan, Shiretoko, and Rishiri-Rebun-Sarobetsu national parks. Area: 83,520 sq km (32,247 sq mi); pop: 5,643,647; capital: SAPPORO. Other major cities include HAKODATE, ASAHIKAWA, OTARU, MURORAN, TOMAKOMAI, OBIHIRO, and KUSHIRO.

Hokkaidō Colonization Office Scandal of 1881   開拓使官有物払下げ事件

(Kaitakushi Kan'yūbutsu Haraisage Jiken). Political scandal in 1881 centering on the government's proposed sale of the assets of its Hokkaidō Colonization Office (KAITAKU-SHI), established in 1869. The office proved unprofitable, and in 1881, one year after the government had decided to sell off many of its enterprises to private entrepreneurs (see KAN'EI JIGYŌ HARAISAGE), KURODA KIYOTAKA, the director of the Colonization Office, proposed the sale of its Hokkaidō assets to the Kansai Bōeki Shōkai, a trading consortium led by his old colleague from the former Satsuma domain, GODAI TOMOATSU. The cost was nominal, about ¥380,000 to be paid over 30 years at no interest. The sale received the tacit approval of ITŌ HIROBUMI and other government leaders. When the terms of the sale leaked out, members of the FREEDOM AND PEOPLE'S RIGHTS MOVEMENT, as well as opposition leaders in the government—especially ŌKUMA SHIGENOBU—expressed outrage. Government leaders were forced to cancel the sale and issue an imperial rescript promising a national assembly by 1890. In retaliation, however, they dismissed Ōkuma from office. See also POLITICAL CRISIS OF 1881.

Hokkaidō Development Agency   北海道開発庁

(Hokkaidō Kaihatsu Chō). Agency of the national government, attached to the Prime Minister's Office and headed by a cabinet minister. It was established under the 1950 Hokkaidō Development Law (Hokkaidō Kaihatsu Hō) and charged with formulating and implementing the central government's plans for Hokkaidō's development, including construction of roads, ports and harbors, transportation and communications facilities, and irrigation projects. It is also involved in planning the development of housing, cities, and industry, and it supervises the Hokkaidō and Tōhoku Development Corporation.

Hokkaidō Electric Power Co, Inc   北海道電力[株]

(Hokkaidō Denryoku). Supplier of electricity to the island of Hokkaidō. Incorporated in 1951. As of 1989, 49 percent of the company's power was generated from coal, 20 percent from hydroelectric sources, 20 percent from nuclear sources, and 11 percent from thermoelectric sources. In the fiscal

year ending March 1991 income totaled ¥478.5 billion (US $3.5 billion), and capitalization stood at ¥114.0 billion (US $831.0 million). Headquarters are in Sapporo, Hokkaidō.

Hokkaidō shimbun   北海道新聞

A leading Hokkaidō daily newspaper. The *Hokkaidō shimbun* was formed through the wartime merger of 11 different Hokkaidō dailies in 1942. Its progressive editorials and news stories have contributed to the paper's popularity with local residents. The main publishing office is located in Sapporo, with branch offices in Hakodate, Asahikawa, and Kushiro. The *Hokkaidō shimbun* maintains 8 overseas news bureaus. Circulation: 1.1 million (1987).

Hokkaidō Takushoku Bank, Ltd   [株]北海道拓殖銀行

(Hokkaidō Takushoku Ginkō). City bank controlling a national network of branches. It was incorporated in 1900 as a specialized financial institution to supply long-term capital loans for the development of Hokkaidō. In 1955 it was reclassified as a regular commercial bank. The bank has 205 domestic branches with overseas branches in New York, Los Angeles, Seattle, London, Hong Kong, Singapore, and Shenzhen (Shenchen), China. As of March 1991 the bank's total assets were ¥11.4 trillion (US $83.1 billion), deposits were ¥8.3 trillion (US $60.5 billion), and capitalization stood at ¥109.5 billion (US $798.1 million). Headquarters are in Sapporo, Hokkaidō.

Hokkaidō University   北海道大学

(Hokkaidō Daigaku). National university located in Sapporo, Hokkaidō. Its predecessor was the Sapporo Agricultural College, which was established in 1876 as Japan's first agricultural institute of higher learning. In 1907 it became the College of Agriculture of Tōhoku Imperial University, and in 1918 an independent institution. In 1919 a faculty of medicine was created, and it was made a comprehensive university under the name Hokkaidō Imperial University. It was renamed Hokkaidō University in 1949. It maintains faculties of letters, education, law, economics, science, medicine, pharmaceutical sciences, engineering, dentistry, agriculture, veterinary medicine, and fisheries. Enrollment was 10,826 in 1989.

Hokkaidō University Botanic Garden   北海道大学農学部附属植物園

(Hokkaidō Daigaku Nōgakubu Fuzoku Shokubutsuen). Full name Botanic Garden, Faculty of Agriculture, Hokkaidō University. Botanic garden founded in 1886 containing plants native to Hokkaidō. It also provides ethnobotanical descriptions of plants important to the Ainu, Uilta, and Gilyak peoples, and displays products derived from them. A part of the garden is given over to alpine plants.

Hokkeji   法華寺

Convent-temple of the Shingon Ritsu sect of Buddhism, located in the suburbs of Nara. Also known as Himuro Gosho. In 747 the empress KŌMYŌ, consort of the emperor SHŌMU (r 724–749) and daughter of FUJIWARA NO FUHITO, converted her father's residence into a nunnery in keeping with Shōmu's edict of 741 calling for the establishment of temples (monasteries and convents) in each

Hokkaidō
Location and
Prefectural Crest

Hokkeji The Eleven-Headed Kannon, central icon of this Buddhist convent-temple, dates from the 9th century and is a National Treasure.

province (see KOKUBUNJI). The Hokkeji was traditionally regarded as the headquarters for all provincial nunneries (all called Hokkeji). It became a temple of the Shingon Ritsu sect (see EIZON) in the mid-13th century and was refurbished by TOYOTOMI HIDEYORI and his mother in 1601. Its chief icon is a wooden statue of the Eleven-Headed Kannon (Jūichimen Kannon), a National Treasure that dates from the 9th century.

Hōkō Fishing Co, Ltd   宝幸水産[株]

(Hōkō Suisan). Fishery company. Incorporated in 1946. The company grew rapidly after expanding its operations to the Sea of Okhotsk area in 1955 and is now one of Japan's leading fishery companies, dealing in fresh and processed fish and seafood. Sales for the fiscal year ending January 1990 totaled ¥115.8 billion (US $756.5 million), and capitalization stood at ¥3.0 billion (US $19.6 million). Headquarters are in Tōkyō.

Hokuetsu Paper Mills, Ltd
北越製紙[株]

(Hokuetsu Seishi). Manufacturer of pulp, paper, and paperboard. Incorporated in 1907. Its main products are wood-free printing and writing paper, coated paper, coated art board, coated white boxboard, fiberboard, and a range of papers. Sales for the fiscal year ending March 1991 totaled ¥106.2 billion (US $774.1 million), of which paper-related products accounted for 96 percent; fiber, 2 percent; and other products, 2 percent. The company was capitalized at ¥13.7 billion (US $99.9 million) in the same year. Headquarters are in Nagaoka, Niigata Prefecture.

Hokuetsu seppu   北越雪譜

("Annals of Snow in the Hokuetsu Region"). Collection of essays by the Edo-period (1600–1868) writer Suzuki Bokushi (1770–1842), a native of Shiozawa in Echigo Prov-

ince (now Niigata Prefecture). His work was stimulated by close association with such contemporary literary figures as ŌTA NAMPO and BAKIN. *Hokuetsu seppu* was published with the help of Bakin. Part 1 (1836) consists of three volumes; part 2 (1842) consists of four volumes. The work was edited extensively by Santō Kyōzan (1769–1858) and illustrations were done by the author and Santō Kyōsui (dates unknown). Suzuki describes in detail winter life in the snow country. His illustrated descriptions of snow crystals—which he observed under a microscope—are notable for their accuracy. He also recorded local products, customs and manners, and annual observances, making his work a valuable source for studying the folk customs of the Echigo area. The essays were edited anew by Okada Takematsu (1874–1956) and republished in 1936.

hokumen no bushi   北面の武士

(literally, "warriors of the northern quarter"). Type of warrior-official in the service of the retired emperors of the 12th century (see INSEI); also called *in no hokumen.* The name *hokumen no bushi* derives from the area of a retired emperor's palace (*in no gosho*) in which they met. First appointed by the retired emperor SHIRAKAWA, they provided the military power for former sovereigns, serving as palace guards and as troops in the event of a serious disturbance. There was never any formal hierarchy, although they were later divided into upper and lower divisions. The retired emperor GO-TOBA further strengthened his forces by adding another type of official called *saimen no bushi* (warriors of the western quarter). However, after the JŌKYŪ DISTURBANCE (1221), the *saimen no bushi* were disbanded and *hokumen no bushi* were stripped of their military role.

Hokuriku Bank, Ltd   [株]北陸銀行

(Hokuriku Ginkō). Regional bank based in Toyama Prefecture. Its predecessor was established in 1877. Hokuriku Bank has a network of some 190 branches in 13 prefectures in Japan, and, through its New York branch, its Hong Kong branch, and its London representative office, the bank maintains a high volume of foreign exchange transactions. Its total assets for the fiscal year ending March 1991 reached ¥8.2 trillion (US $39.8 billion), and total deposits were ¥6.3 trillion (US $45.9 billion). The bank was capitalized at ¥83.2 billion (US $606.4 million) in the same year. Headquarters are in the city of Toyama, Toyama Prefecture.

Hokuriku Electric Power Co, Inc
北陸電力[株]

(Hokuriku Denryoku). Supplier of electric power, chiefly to the three prefectures of the Hokuriku region: Toyama, Ishikawa, and Fukui. It was incorporated in 1951 after the reorganization of the electric power industry following World War II. In 1988 the company operated 117 hydroelectric and 4 thermoelectric plants. In the fiscal year ending March 1991 its income totaled ¥394.3 billion (US $2.9 billion), and capitalization stood at ¥117.0 billion (US $852.8 million). Headquarters are in Toyama, Toyama Prefecture.

Hokuriku region   北陸地方

(Hokuriku *chihō*). The part of central Honshū that encompasses Niigata, Toyama, Ishikawa, and Fukui prefectures. The Hokuriku region corresponds to the Hokurikudō of the old GOKI SHICHIDŌ system of administrative units in Japan. There is

heavy snowfall in winter and high temperatures in summer. The region is Japan's principal single-crop rice production area. Both hydroelectric and nuclear power plants are located here, and heavy and chemical industries have been introduced. Other industries include fibers and textiles. Among traditional products of the region are lacquer ware and ceramics.

Hokusai   北斎

(1760–1849). Also known as Katsushika Hokusai. UKIYO-E painter, draftsman, illustrator, print designer, and author; one of the great masters of Japanese pictorial art. Born, it is said, in the Warigesui section of the Honjo district of Edo (now Tōkyō). His given name was Tokitarō; throughout his career he adopted numerous pseudonyms. At the age of 18 he entered the studio of the actor portraitist and *ukiyo-e* painter KATSUKAWA SHUNSHŌ, and in 1779 he created a series of capably designed actor portraits.

In 1791 he was invited to design a few woodblock prints for the publisher Tsutaya Jūzaburō. After the death of his teacher Shunshō in 1792, Hokusai, who was passed over for headship of the KATSUKAWA SCHOOL in favor of KATSUKAWA SHUN'EI, seems to have stopped painting actor portraits. The relatively inactive years of 1793 and 1794 were crucial in Hokusai's career because they marked not only the end of his attempts to accommodate his vision to the trite prevailing styles of *ukiyo-e*, but also his integration of RIMPA and TOSA SCHOOL influences and Western perspective into a unique style.

In 1795 he designed an illustration for *Kyōka Edo murasaki*, a verse anthology. Between 1796 and 1799 he designed many single-sheet prints and album illustrations. His SURIMONO, as these special-order prints were called, were immediately successful and were imitated by many other artists.

It was in 1796 that he began using the name Hokusai, by which he is best known. From 1798 he used the name Hokusai for prints and paintings, Tatsumasa for certain privately published illustrations, Tokitarō for illustrations accompanying commercial fiction, and Kakō (or Sorobeku) for other commercial prints and books. In 1800, at the age of 41, he began to call himself Gakyōjin Hokusai, "mad-about-painting Hokusai." From about this time, though he lived as a recluse, Hokusai enjoyed a certain amount of notoriety and gave public demonstrations of his skills. In 1804 he painted, within the precincts of an Edo temple, a half-length picture of the Zen patriarch Bodhidharma that measured about 240 square meters (2,600 sq ft). Between 1804 and 1813 Hokusai produced illustrations for the comic-book-format YOMIHON of Kyokutei BAKIN and RYŪTEI TANEHIKO.

In 1812 Hokusai began a lifelong friendship with the artist Bokusen (1775–1824) that resulted in the *Hokusai manga* (Sketches by Hokusai), a series of picture books published in Nagoya between 1814 and 1834. Hokusai's celebrated series of landscape prints *Fugaku sanjūrokkei* (Thirty-Six Views of Mt. Fuji) had begun to appear by 1831, and in the early 1830s Hokusai designed the woodblock prints of waterfalls, bridges, birds, and ghosts for which he is now best known. Late in 1834, just before the publication of *Fugaku hyakkei* (One Hundred Views of Mt. Fuji), his masterpiece of book illustration, he left Edo and lived for over a year in a rural district near Uraga on the Miura Peninsula south of Edo. During his

Hokusai

▶ This sketch of a roadside prostitute is among Hokusai's earliest works. Light colors on paper. Private collection.

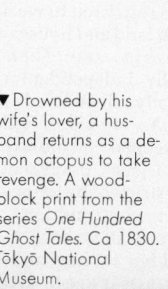

▼ Drowned by his wife's lover, a husband returns as a demon octopus to take revenge. A woodblock print from the series *One Hundred Ghost Tales.* Ca 1830. Tōkyō National Museum.

▲ *Beneath the Wave off Kanagawa*, a woodblock print from Hokusai's most famous series, *Thirty-Six Views of Mt. Fuji.* Ca 1831. Tōkyō National Museum.

▼ Horses from *Hokusai manga* (Sketches by Hokusai), a series of picture books. 1817. Woodblock print.

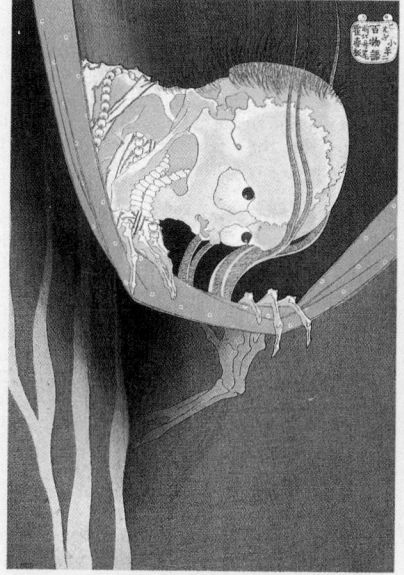

▲ Facing pages from an illustrated book titled *Scenes from Both Banks of the Sumidagawa.* 1801–06. Kanagawa Prefectural Museum.

absence, his last important series of woodblock prints, *Hyakunin isshu uba ga etoki* (Illustrations of the One Hundred Poems), began to appear. This series of illustrations for the poetry anthology *Hyakunin isshu* was interrupted after 27 pictures were published and was never resumed. In 1836 Hokusai returned to Edo to find the city ravaged by famine but managed to support himself by selling pictures for measures of rice. In 1839, Hokusai's lodgings burned and all his study sketches and painting materials were destroyed. Thereafter he seems to have produced relatively few paintings and practically no prints and book illustrations. Perhaps the most famous of his pupils was the illustrator and *surimono* designer TOTOYA HOKKEI.

holding companies 持株会社

(*mochikabu kaisha*). Business organizations that control many diverse corporations through stock ownership. They are thus able to coordinate the activities of all the corporations. Holding companies may be divided into two types: "pure" holding companies, which exist only to hold the stock of other companies (typified in Japan by some of the holding companies of the pre–World War II ZAIBATSU), and others that engage in a variety of business activities in addition to holding stocks. As the result of the 1947 ANTIMONOPOLY LAW, holding companies per se do not exist in postwar Japan. See also KEIRETSU.

holidays and vacations 休日

(*kyūjitsu*). In fiscal year 1989, Japanese working people had an average of 114 days off. This included weekends, 13 national holidays, paid vacation, 3–7 days (average 4.2) at New Year's, and 3–7 days (average 3.5) of summer vacation. Overall, Japanese have relatively few days off compared with citizens of other countries; for example, the French have 138 days off; the British, 136; and Americans, 132. The two main reasons for this gap are that the five-day workweek is still not widespread in Japan, and only a small percentage of paid vacation days are actually taken. Some 40.3 percent of all companies (16.4% of all employees) have a six-day workweek, while 58.3 percent (82.7% of employees) use some form of a five-day workweek. However, many companies in this second group have a two-day weekend only every other week or once a month, and a true five-day workweek exists for only 9.6 percent of all companies (36.9% of all employees).

The average number of paid vacation days allotted to an employee is 15.4, but only an average of 7.9 days are actually taken, with the rest going unused. The government is encouraging workers to take more paid vacation in an effort to reduce international criticism that the Japanese work too hard. At the same time because of the labor shortage, in an effort to attract and keep employees, many companies are allowing more flexibility in the timing of vacations and the number of days that can be taken at once. See also HOLIDAYS, NATIONAL. — *See graph, next page.*

holidays, national 国民の祝日

(*kokumin no shukujitsu*). As of 1992, there were 13 national holidays authorized under Japanese law. Nine of these were established under the Law concerning National Holi-

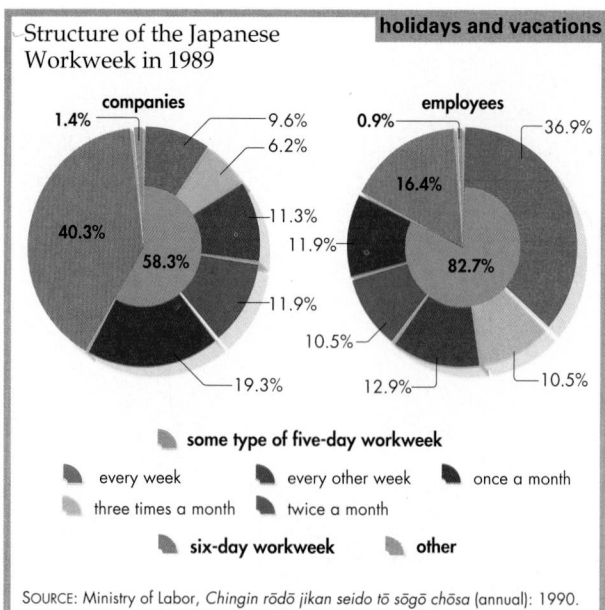

holidays and vacations

Structure of the Japanese Workweek in 1989

companies

1.4% — 9.6%
6.2%
40.3% — 11.3%
58.3% — 11.9%
— 11.9%
19.3% — 10.5%

employees

0.9% — 36.9%
16.4%
82.7% — 12.9%
10.5% — 10.5%

■ some type of five-day workweek

■ every week   ■ every other week   ■ once a month
■ three times a month   ■ twice a month
■ six-day workweek   ■ other

SOURCE: Ministry of Labor, *Chingin rōdō jikan seido tō sōgō chōsa* (annual): 1990.

days (Kokumin no Shukujitsu ni kansuru Hōritsu), which was enacted in 1948. Four additional holidays were created by revision of this law. The 13 national holidays are as follows:

Ganjitsu (New Year's Day). 1 January. See NEW YEAR.

Seijin no Hi (Coming-of-Age Day). 15 January. This holiday honors people who attain the age of 20 years anytime between 2 April of the previous year and 1 April of the current year. This is specified in the Japanese Civil Code as the age at which adulthood is reached.

Kenkoku Kinen no Hi (National Foundation Day). 11 February. Nationalistic commemoration of the legendary enthronement of Japan's first emperor, JIMMU (see KIGENSETSU CONTROVERSY).

Shumbun no Hi (Vernal Equinox Day). 21 March. Visits to family graves and family reunions occur on this day, the central day of a seven-day Buddhist memorial service (HIGAN). A similar holiday is celebrated at the time of the autumnal equinox (see Shūbun no Hi below).

Midori no Hi (Greenery Day). 29 April. In 1989 this was designated as a day for nature appreciation. Prior to that the birthday of Emperor SHŌWA was celebrated on this day.

Kempō Kinembi (Constitution Memorial Day). 3 May. Commemoration of the day the CONSTITUTION OF JAPAN became effective in 1947.

Kodomo no Hi (Children's Day). 5 May. Day set aside for praying for the health and happiness of Japan's children. See CHILDREN'S DAY.

Keirō no Hi (Respect-for-the-Aged Day). 15 September. Day honoring Japan's elderly and celebrating their longevity. Established to commemorate the enactment of the Law concerning Welfare for the Aged (Rōjin Fukushi Hō) in 1966.

Shūbun no Hi (Autumnal Equinox Day). 23 September. Visits to family graves and family reunions occur on this day, the central day of a seven-day Buddhist memorial service (HIGAN). A similar holiday is celebrated at the time of the vernal equinox (see Shumbun no Hi above).

Taiiku no Hi (Sports Day). 10 October. Day on which good physical and mental health are fostered through physical activity. Established to commemorate the Tōkyō Olympic Games, which were held 10–24 October 1964.

Bunka no Hi (Culture Day). 3 November. Day on which the ideals articulated in Japan's postwar constitution—the love of peace and freedom—are fostered through cultural activities.

Kinrō Kansha no Hi (Labor Thanksgiving Day). 23 November. Day on which people express gratitude to each other for their labors throughout the year and for the fruits of those labors.

Tennō Tanjōbi (Emperor's Birthday). 23 December. Celebration of the birthday of Japan's present emperor, AKIHITO.

History—The majority of the national holidays adopted by Japan during the Meiji period (1868–1912) were based on religious rites of the imperial household. Prior to that the shogunate's recurring annual events (NENCHŪ GYŌJI) and seasonal festivals (*gosekku;* see SEKKU) were celebrated as holidays by the general public.

Special ceremonies were held in government offices and schools on the following days until 1945: Shinnensetsu (1 January), Kigensetsu (11 February; the date in the Western calendar corresponding to the accession of Japan's legendary first emperor, Jimmu), Tenchōsetsu (29 April; the birthday of Emperor Shōwa), and Meijisetsu (3 November; the birthday of Emperor Meiji). In addition to these 4 days, 8 days were designated as days of important state ceremonies, including Shunki (around 21 March, the time of the vernal equinox), Shūki (around 23 September, the time of the autumnal equinox), and NIINAMESAI (23 November), for a total of 12 pre–World War II holidays. The Shunki and Shūki equinoctial festivals honored the souls of past emperors and members of the imperial family, and Niinamesai was an imperial thanksgiving rite.

After World War II, these holidays were abolished and the present holidays were adopted under Japan's new constitution. Although they were given new names, many of the new holidays correspond to the former Meiji holidays.

Holy Orthodox Church   正教会

(Seikyōkai). The history of the Orthodox Church in Japan began in 1861 with the arrival of the Russian priest NIKOLAI at Hakodate, Hokkaidō. Nikolai aspired to build an indigenous church and took most of his clergy from among the Japanese. He built a mission society that maintained close relations with the mother church in Moscow and introduced many aspects of Russian culture into Japan. Church membership did not increase during the late Meiji (1868–1912) and early Taishō (1912–26) periods, partly because of ideological currents that developed during the Russo-Japanese War (1904–05) and the Russian Revolution (1917). In 1919 the church became independent of the Russian Orthodox Church and was renamed the Nippon Harisutosu Seikyōkai (Orthodox Church in Japan). In 1965 it normalized relations with the Russian Orthodox Church, becoming in 1970 an autocephalous church. There were approximately 9,400 members in 1989. The Byzantine-style Cathedral of the Holy Resurrection, popularly known as the Nikorai-dō, is a famous Tōkyō landmark.

Holy Spirit Association for the Unification of World Christianity
世界基督教統一神霊協会

(Sekai Kirisutokyō Tōitsu Shinrei Kyōkai). Commonly known as the Unification Church. The church was founded in 1954 by Sun Myung Moon (b 1920) in Seoul, Korea,

and its first Japanese branch was established in Tōkyō in 1964. The sect teaches Christianity as interpreted by Moon, especially in his book *The Divine Principle* (1977). Emphasis is on perfecting the self, family, and society through belief in the coming of the Messiah in the present day. The church claimed some 348,000 members in Japan in 1989.

hombyakushō   本百姓

(literally, "basic peasants" or "basic farmers"). Members of the peasant class during the Edo period (1600–1868) who, in contrast to the landless MIZUNOMI-BYAKUSHŌ, had rights to land and paid taxes (NENGU). Early in the period the term was restricted to wealthier peasants who owned land and houses and were liable for labor taxes (BUYAKU). The *hombyakushō* were basically independent cultivators who eventually diversified into commercial ventures. As organs of village self-government developed, *hombyakushō* served as headmen (see OSABYAKUSHŌ; SHŌYA). They were restricted by shogunal authorities in conduct, consumption, and various other ways (see KEIAN NO OFUREGAKI), and were even forbidden to buy and sell land (see TAHATA EITAI BAIBAI KINSHI REI). In protest against heavy taxes, the *hombyakushō* often rose in rebellion (see HYAKUSHŌ IKKI). With the development of the money economy, stratification of the *hombyakushō* became more pronounced. The wealthier *hombyakushō* acquired more land, while the poorer lost their land and were reduced to tenancy and wage labor.

Home Ministry   内務省

(Naimushō). Government ministry responsible for local administration, police, public works, and elections. It was originally created in November 1873, with ŌKUBO TOSHIMICHI as minister, to control the social unrest, especially among dispossessed *samurai,* that troubled the early Meiji period (1868–1912). Initially the ministry had responsibility for the promotion of domestic industry in addition to its public security duties, but this was taken over by the Ministry of Agriculture and Commerce (NŌSHŌMUSHŌ) when it was established in 1881.

After YAMAGATA ARITOMO became head of the Home Ministry in 1883 it was reorganized into bureaus for general administration, local government, police, public works, public health, topographical survey, census, religious institutions, and budget. During Yamagata's tenure the ministry strengthened its controls over free speech and assembly and tightened police surveillance of political activity. It became a strong arm of the central government in local administration, achieving a virtual monopoly over local government appointments. The Home Ministry was able to suppress labor movements and antigovernment activity through its use of the SPECIAL HIGHER POLICE and the PEACE PRESERVATION LAW OF 1925, and was also notorious for meddling in elections (see SENKYO KANSHŌ).

The activities of the Home Ministry were drastically curtailed by OCCUPATION authorities in October 1945, and in December 1947 it was abolished altogether, its functions divided among the MINISTRY OF HOME AFFAIRS, MINISTRY OF CONSTRUCTION, and MINISTRY OF LABOR.

Hommonji   本門寺

One of the four ranking temples of the NICHIREN SECT of Buddhism, located in Ikegami,

Ōta Ward, Tōkyō. The Hommonji is built on the site where NICHIREN died in 1282. The main hall of the temple was completed in 1317 under the supervision of Nichirō (1245–1320), one of Nichiren's six leading disciples. Destroyed in a fire in 1710, the Hommonji was rebuilt by the eighth Tokugawa shōgun, TOKUGAWA YOSHIMUNE (1684–1751). Much of the temple was burned down in an air raid in 1945, but it has now been restored. A ceremony known as Oeshiki, commemorating Nichiren's death, is held here on 11–13 October.

homosexuality   同性愛

(*dōseiai*). Male homosexuality has a long and well-documented history in Japan. There is almost no extant documentation of female homosexuality, however, since sexuality was traditionally expressed from the male perspective in the Japanese language.

Prior to the introduction of Western moral concepts to Japan after the Meiji Restoration of 1868, attitudes toward homosexuality were quite relaxed. During the Edo period (1600–1868), a homosexual subculture flourished along with the erotic world of the pleasure_quarters in urban areas such as Kyōto, Ōsaka, and Edo (now Tōkyō). The era could be called the "golden age" of homosexuality in Japan, and it spawned a substantial corpus of writings called *shudo bungaku* (homosexual literature) that dealt fictionally with homoerotic themes; chief among them was Ihara SAIKAKU's *Nanshoku ōkagami* (1687, The Great Mirror of Male Love).

Origins — The practice of homosexuality in Japan is traditionally said to date from the early Heian period (794–1185), when Buddhist monks introduced it upon their return from Tang (T'ang) China. Homosexuality surely existed in Japan before then, but the traditional account of its origins helps explain why homosexuality became a preferred form of sexual expression among the Buddhist priesthood, for whom sexual relations with women were forbidden. The priest GENSHIN's famous treatise on Buddhist doctrine, ŌJŌYŌSHŪ (985, Essentials of Pure Land Rebirth), includes an account of the fiery punishments awaiting homosexuals in purgatory. Genshin's terrifyingly vivid descriptions may or may not have deterred homosexual activity, but the fact that such warnings were necessary perhaps indicates how widespread the practice of homosexuality had become.

By the end of the Heian period, homosexuality had become popular among the Kyōto aristocracy, perhaps because of the increased contact with the Buddhist clergy. During the reigns of the tonsured emperors SHIRAKAWA (r 1073–87) and TOBA (r 1107–23), attractive young boys were routinely engaged in court service as entertainers and sexual partners. This practice was adopted by the military elite and continued throughout the Kamakura (1185–1333) and Muromachi (1333–1568) periods. By the advent of Tokugawa rule in the 17th century, homosexuality was an integral part of the social fiber of the military and religious elites. When the Jesuit priest Francis XAVIER arrived to proselytize among the Japanese in the 16th century, he was astonished at how openly homosexuality was practiced and dubbed it the "Japanese vice."

Homosexuality and the Arts — A link between homosexuality and entertainment, especially theater, developed early. The shōgun ASHIKAGA YOSHIMITSU's patronage of the young actor ZEAMI during the late 14th century stemmed from homosexual attraction and resulted in the establishment of NŌ as the official theater of the military elite. Youthful male physical beauty and the attraction it excited were integral to early Nō and later became important to the popularity of KABUKI during the Edo period. Actors of female roles, ONNAGATA, brought to the kabuki theater an electrifying homoerotic element.

Recent Times — The present legal status of homosexuals is similar to that in many Western countries, where unofficial toleration is not backed by legal protection. However, since World War II there have been no specific provisions dealing with homosexuality in the legal code. Female homosexuality has never received attention in the legal codes. However, social pressures exist that make many homosexuals in Japan feel a definite lack of freedom to disclose their homosexuality openly and without fear, especially at their workplaces. As a result, much homosexual expression remains hidden.

Hōmushō → Ministry of Justice

Honami   穂波［町］

Town in central Fukuoka Prefecture, Kyūshū. From the middle of the Meiji period (1868–1912), Honami rapidly developed as a coal-mining town, but, with the decline of the coal industry and the closing of the last of its mines in 1966, the population shrank drastically. Today it is chiefly an agricultural area, although there are also chemical, pharmaceutical, and food-processing industries. Pop: 26,704.

Hon'ami Kōetsu   本阿弥光悦

(1558–1637). Artist widely admired for his calligraphy, pottery, and lacquer designs and for inspiring the revival of classical court traditions that led to what was later called the RIMPA style. Little is known of Kōetsu prior to 1603. In 1615 he retired to Takagamine (northwest of Kyōto), where he organized a small community of craftsmen.

Beginning in 1604 Kōetsu collaborated with the wealthy Kyōto merchant and scholar Suminokura Soan (1571–1632) in designing and publishing a set of beautifully printed books called *sagabon*, which included NŌ play texts and selections from classical literature. Kōetsu showed great interest in the TEA CEREMONY from his early days and was regarded as one of the outstanding pupils of FURUTA ORIBE. In addition to becoming proficient in the design of lacquer ware and ceramics, Kōetsu excelled in CALLIGRAPHY. His style can be seen in his surviving *shikishi* (cardboard-backed paper used in painting and calligraphy), WAKA scrolls, sutra copies, and letters. Characteristic are the smooth, flowing brushlines, fluctuating in thickness from full and fleshy to delicate and threadlike. Kōetsu became known as one of the Kan'ei no Sampitsu (Three Brushes of the Kan'ei Era), sharing the honor with his friend KONOE NOBUTADA and the monk SHŌKADŌ SHŌJŌ. The painter Tawaraya SŌTATSU is believed to have decorated the papers for much of Kōetsu's calligraphy, resulting in sumptuous works reminiscent of the Heian period (794–1185).

Honda Sōichirō In 1989 the founder of Honda Motor Co became the first Japanese to be inducted into the US Automotive Hall of Fame.

Honchō monzui 本朝文粋

Heian-period (794–1185) anthology of poetry and prose in classical Chinese; compiled around 1060 by FUJIWARA NO AKIHIRA. In its division into categories, 39 in this case, it is patterned after the 6th-century Chinese anthology *Wen xuan* (*Wen hsüan*; J: *Monzen*). The collection consists of 427 selections by some 70 contributors and includes the best work in Chinese by Japanese authors from the previous two centuries, the years from the reign of Emperor Saga (r 809–823) to that of Emperor Go-Ichijō (r 1016–36). It is often quoted or alluded to in diaries, NŌ plays, and war tales (GUNKI MONOGATARI) of the late Heian and Kamakura (1185–1333) periods.

Honchō seiki 本朝世紀

(Chronicle of the Reigns of the Imperial Court; also called *Shikanki* and *Geki nikki*.) An official history (*seishi*) of Japan compiled in the mid-12th century by FUJIWARA NO MICHINORI at the command of the retired emperor TOBA. It was intended as a continuation of the Six National Histories (RIKKOKUSHI) but was never completed. Twenty chapters survive, many in fragmentary form. It is an important historical source for the second half of the Heian period (794–1185).

Honchō shojaku mokuroku 本朝書籍目録

(Catalog of Japanese Books). One-volume catalog of books, presumably compiled between 1278 and 1292; believed to be the oldest work of its kind. Also known as *Ninnaji shojaku mokuroku* and *Omuro shojaku mokuroku*. The catalog is divided into some 20 categories, such as Shintō gods and ceremonies and imperial affairs. There are 493 entries, including books that were no longer extant when the catalog was compiled.

Honda Kōtarō 本多光太郎

(1870–1954). Physicist known for his developmental research in materials science, particularly in metallurgy. Born in what is now Aichi Prefecture, he graduated from Tōkyō University in 1897. After studying in Germany from 1907 to 1911, he returned to Japan to become a professor at Tōhoku University. Honda developed a number of high-performance magnetic alloys, including KS Magnetic Steel in 1917 and New KS Magnetic Steel (with MASUMOTO HAKARU) in 1933. He served as president of Tōhoku University from 1931 to 1940 and received the Order of Culture in 1937.

Honda Motor Co, Ltd 本田技研工業[株]

(Honda Giken Kōgyō). Manufacturer of motorcycles, four-wheel vehicles, and industrial engines. It is the leading maker of motorcycles in the world and the third leading domestic producer of passenger vehicles. Founded in 1946 by HONDA SŌICHIRŌ as Honda Gijutsu Kenkyūjo, it was reorganized two years later as a corporation, taking on its present name. Honda met initial success when it developed a motorbike by attaching a small engine to a bicycle.

After the company established American Honda Motor Co, Inc, in 1959, 11 overseas sales companies, fully capitalized by the parent firm, were set up. Overseas production plants, including those under joint ventures and technology exchange agreements, numbered 75 in 1989 and were based in 40 countries. Among Japanese auto manufacturers Honda was the first to declare its intention to produce passenger cars in the United States. Sales for the fiscal year ending March 1991 totaled ¥2.8 trillion (US $20.4 billion), of which export sales accounted for 61 percent. In the same fiscal year, 10 percent of total sales was earned by motorcycles, 78 percent by four-wheel vehicles, and 12 percent by general-purpose engines and other products. In March 1991 capitalization stood at ¥85.3 billion (US $622.0 million). Headquarters are in Tōkyō.

Honda Seiroku 本多静六

(1866–1952). Dendrologist. Born in what is now Saitama Prefecture; graduate of Tōkyō Agriculture and Forestry School (now part of Tōkyō University). He studied forestry and economics at Munich University in Germany and served as assistant professor and professor at Tōkyō University from 1893. A pioneer of modern dendrology, he became chairman of the Imperial Society of Dendrology late in life. He also made a lasting contribution to the beautification and preservation of the natural environment, including the design of the Meiji Shrine gardens and the establishment of a number of national parks. He is the author of *Zōringaku kakuron* (1927, Studies on Afforestation).

Honda Shūgo 本多秋五

(1908–). Literary critic. Born in Aichi Prefecture; graduate of Tōkyō University. He participated in the PROLETARIAN LITERATURE MOVEMENT of the early 1930s, gaining recognition as a critic. After World War II, he joined the progressive literary magazine KINDAI BUNGAKU (1946–64) and published *Tenkō bungaku ron* (1957, The Literature of Ideological Conversion; see TENKŌ). A humanist who was significantly influenced by Tolstoy's thought, Honda sought human liberation from political ideology. His principal works include *Shirakaba ha no bungaku* (1954), a survey of the humanist writers of the SHIRAKABA SCHOOL, and *Monogatari sengo bungaku shi* (1958–63), a historical study of post–World War II Japanese literature, which won the 1965 Mainichi Book Award.

Honda Sōichirō 本田宗一郎

(1906–91). Founder of HONDA MOTOR CO, LTD. Born in Shizuoka Prefecture. He studied at Hamamatsu Technical Higher School (now Shizuoka University). A highly innovative engineer, Honda organized Honda Motor in 1948 and revolutionized the motorcycle industry by successfully developing a series of powerful new models, which were exported throughout the world. In 1960 he built the world's largest motorcycle plant in Mie Prefecture. In the following year, his vehicles placed first in the international motorcycle race on the Isle of Man. After that, Honda placed extra emphasis on motorcycle exports, laying the groundwork for the company to become the world's largest motorcycle manufacturer. In 1963 Honda Motor entered the four-wheeled vehicle market; a series of innovative designs, such as the low-pollution engine called CVCC (combined vortex controlled combustion), helped the company become a major automobile manufacturer. Aggressive in overseas development, Honda Sōichirō built motorcycle and automobile plants in various parts of the world, including the United States and Europe. He became the company's "supreme adviser" in 1973.

Honda Toshiaki 本多利明

(1744–1821). Mathematician, astronomer, ship captain, and political economist of the late Edo period (1600–1868). Born in Echigo Province (now Niigata Prefecture), he went to Edo (now Tōkyō) at age 18 to study mathematics and astronomy. Within six years he opened his own school and was learning Dutch. An accomplished navigator, he maintained close relations with northern explorers such as MOGAMI TOKUNAI and MAMIYA RINZŌ, and in 1801 he captained a vessel that surveyed Ezo (now Hokkaidō). Honda became convinced that Japan's economic problems could be overcome by emulating European models, particularly England. In *Keisei hisaku* (1798, A Secret Plan for Governing the Country) Honda identified Japan's four top priorities as gunpowder, metals, shipping, and the colonization of Ezo. In SAIIKI MONOGATARI (1798, Tales of the West) he proposed that the capital be moved from Edo to Kamchatka to share the same latitude with London. He also advised that Japan abandon its isolation (see NATIONAL SECLUSION) in favor of state-managed foreign trade and overseas colonization.

Hondo 本渡[市]

The principal city of the Amakusa Islands off western Kyūshū; located on adjoining portions of the islands Shimoshima and Kamishima, Kumamoto Prefecture. Prawn cultivation is an important local industry. Of historical interest are several sites connected with the SHIMABARA UPRISING and 17th-century Christians. Pop: 41,216.

Hōnen 法然

(1133–1212). Real name Genkū. Buddhist priest and founder of the JŌDO SECT who spearheaded the Kamakura Buddhist "reformation." Born in Mimasaka Province (now part of Okayama Prefecture). The son of a *samurai*, Hōnen entered the Buddhist order at age eight after the death of his father. He studied at the temple ENRYAKUJI on Mt. Hiei (Hieizan) and became a monk of the TENDAI SECT at age 15. Disenchanted with the secular politics at Hiei, he decided to become a mountain ascetic (HIJIRI) and retired to Kurotani, a monastery in another part of Mt. Hiei, in 1150. He mastered the Tendai doctrines and the scholarship of the Nara sects, but he still felt spiritually unfulfilled. Hōnen finally came to the realization that NEMBUTSU, the recitation of the Buddha AMIDA's name, was the only way to achieve *ōjō*, rebirth in Amida's Pure Land (Jōdo; see PURE LAND BUDDHISM). In 1175 Hōnen began to preach the path of *nembutsu* in the city of Kyōto and founded the Jōdo sect. Urged by his patron-disciple KUJŌ KANEZANE, he wrote the *Senchaku hongan nembutsushū* (The Selection of the Nembutsu of the Original Vow; see SENCHAKUSHŪ). In 1204 the Buddhist establishment launched a campaign against Hōnen's movement, leading to the execution of four of his disciples in 1206. Hōnen himself was laicized and exiled in 1207. He was finally allowed to return to Kyōto in 1211, just a few months before his death.

Hōnen Corporation [株]ホーネンコーポレーション

(Hōnen Kōporēshon). Manufacturer of vegetable oils and oilseed meals, animal feeds, cornstarch, and synthetic resins; incorporated in 1922. The company leads the industry in the production of soybean oil. It is dependent on overseas sources for all of its raw

materials, including soybeans, rapeseed, and corn. For the year ending March 1990, total sales were ¥91.0 billion (US $663.2 million) and capitalization was ¥8.7 billion (US $63.4 million). Headquarters are in Tōkyō.

Honest John Incident
オネスト・ジョン事件

(Onesuto Jon Jiken). Incident surrounding the announcement on 28 July 1955 that the US Department of Defense planned to send "Honest John" rocket launchers, capable of using atomic warheads, to Japan. Strong public interest, reflecting the sensitivity of the Japanese to the nuclear issue, gradually waned when it became known that no atomic warheads were involved. In 1960 the UNITED STATES–JAPAN SECURITY TREATIES provided for consultation in cases of this kind.

honeysuckle, Japanese
忍冬

(suikazura). Lonicera japonica. Also known in Japanese as nindō. Evergreen shrub of the family Caprifoliaceae native to mountain areas throughout Japan. Its oblong leaves remain all year; hence the name nindō, which means "endures winter." In early summer fragrant, five-lobed flowers bloom in pairs. The flower is white or pink, later changing to yellow. The Japanese honeysuckle also grows wild along the eastern coast of the United States.

hongaku
本覚

A priori, original, or primordial enlightenment, in contradistinction to shigaku ("incipient enlightenment"), which refers to the gradual process of attaining enlightenment. Hongaku (Ch: benjue or pen-chüeh) first appeared as a concept in the Daijō kishinron (Treatise on the Awakening of Faith in the Mahāyāna; Ch: Dasheng qixin lun or Ta-sheng ch'i-hsin lun). The Daijō kishinron postulates a symmetry between the mind of sentient beings and the Buddhist absolute, or Suchness (tathatā), thanks to which the essence of enlightenment of hongaku is already present within one's deepest consciousness. The concept of hongaku, basic to Mahāyāna Buddhism, permeated Buddhist philosophy in the Heian period (794–1185), encouraging an optimistic perception of enlightenment, or Buddhahood, as immanent in all things-as-they-are. In the late Heian period HŌNEN, founder of the JŌDO SECT of PURE LAND BUDDHISM, initiated a critique of hongaku philosophy. Hongaku tendencies reemerged in later Buddhist thinkers.

Honganji
本願寺

Major temple of the Buddhist True Pure Land sect (Jōdo Shinshū; see JŌDO SHIN SECT). During the Sengoku period (1467–1568), the Honganji surpassed its rivals within the sect, developing an extensive ecclesiastical organization that bound its adherents (monto) with religious and secular ties, mobilized armed leagues (IKKŌ IKKI), and ruled entire provinces. The secular power of this religious monarchy was destroyed by ODA NOBUNAGA (1534–82) in a 10-year war (1570–80). At the beginning of the 17th century, the Honganji split into two rival branches, headquartered at NISHI HONGANJI and HIGASHI HONGANJI in Kyōto, which today are still vast religious establishments.

The Honganji originated in a small memorial chapel (goeidō, or portrait hall) enshrining an image of SHINRAN (1173–1263), the True Pure Land sect's patriarch, which was built in 1272 by Shinran's daughter Kakushin Ni (1224–83?). This hall was located at Yoshimizu in the Ōtani district at the foot of the Higashiyama hills in Kyōto (on grounds now part of the Jōdo sect's temple Chion'in and occupied by its subtemple Sūtaiin), and Shinran's remains were reinterred on the site. In 1282 Kakushin Ni deeded this property to the Shinshū community of faith. Her grandson Kakunyo Sōshō (1270–1351) obtained the status of a temple for the mausoleum, and it was redesignated Honganji (Temple of the Original Vow) by 1321.

Kakunyo asserted the Honganji's preeminence by claiming direct descent from Shinran, by blood through Kakushin Ni and by spiritual transmission through the patriarch's grandson Nyoshin (1235–1300); Shinran, Nyoshin, and Kakunyo therefore are the first three names in the Honganji's pontifical lineage. The Honganji's fourth to seventh abbots (hossu)—Zennyo Shungen (1333–89), Shakunyo Jigei (1350–93), Gyōnyo Genkō (1376–1440), and Zonnyo Enken (1396–1457)—continued to press their temple's claims. Under the leadership of RENNYO Kenju (1415–99), who became its eighth abbot in 1457, the Honganji did establish its preeminence in the True Pure Land sect. Rennyo strove for doctrinal and organizational unity among the Shinshū believers, using pastoral letters (gobunshō; also called ofumi) written in simple language to preach a return to Shinran's original doctrine of salvation through faith in the grace of the Buddha Amida. Rennyo won the Honganji many adherents, including defectors from the Bukkōji and SENJUJI factions of the Shinshū sect. In 1465 the Tendai sect monastery ENRYAKUJI on Mt. Hiei (Hieizan) northeast of Kyōto reacted to Rennyo's incursion into territories in which they had a proprietary interest by causing the Ōtani Honganji to be ransacked and torn down. Rennyo moved first to Ōmi (now Shiga Prefecture) and then in 1471 to Yoshizaki in Echizen (now Kanazu Chō, Fukui Prefecture). Yoshizaki Gobō, the temple he founded there, became the center of the Honganji's network of affiliated temples in the Hokuriku (northern Honshū) region.

The ŌNIN WAR (1467–77) provided the context for the emergence of Honganji's armed leagues (the Ikkō ikki) as a powerful force in Japanese politics when the monto (adherents) of the temple intervened militarily in Hokuriku's regional conflicts, ignoring Rennyo's appeals that they return to farming. Hence, Rennyo in 1475 left Yoshizaki and returned to the Kansai (western Honshū) region. At Yamashina, immediately east of Kyōto, the first truly impressive Honganji, a great new temple headquarters, was built by Rennyo between 1479 and 1483.

The Honganji fully evolved into a religious monarchy under Shōnyo Kōkyō (1516–54), who became its 10th abbot in 1525 and whose relatives and advisers involved the Honganji in ambitious military enterprises. After the Ikkō ikki occupied the city of Sakai and ravaged Nara in 1532, the Yamashina Honganji was burned by forces of the daimyō Rokkaku Sadayori (1495–1552) of Ōmi and the Lotus Confederation (Hokke ikki) of Kyōto's Nichirenist townsmen. Shōnyo moved to Ōsaka, where in 1533 he established the ISHIYAMA HONGANJI as his new headquarters. In 1549 the imperial court appointed Shōnyo provisional high priest of Buddhism (gon no sōjō); his son Kennyo Kōsa (1543–92), the 11th hossu, obtained the status of an imperial abbacy (monzeki) for the Honganji in January 1560. In short, the hossu of the Honganji was priest, daimyō, and imperial noble all at once.

The Honganji became the major obstacle in the career of Oda Nobunaga as a national unifier; its major areas of strength coincided precisely with his primary sphere of interest in central Japan. Ikkō ikki mobilized by Kennyo Kōsa fought Nobunaga from 1570 to 1580. In the spring of 1580 Kennyo finally made peace with Nobunaga, agreeing to surrender the Ishiyama Honganji and leaving the temple fortress for Saginomori in Kii (now Wakayama Prefecture). Kennyo's son and designated successor Kyōnyo Kōju (1558–1614), however, refused to honor the agreement. Kennyo therefore disowned Kyōnyo (with whom he was later reconciled) in favor of a younger son, Junnyo Kōshō (1577–1631), thus laying the ground for a schism in the Honganji.

The Ishiyama Honganji burned on the day of its surrender, 10 September 1580. Kennyo moved the Honganji's headquarters to Kaizuka in Izumi Province (now part of Ōsaka Prefecture) in 1583. In 1584 TOYOTOMI HIDEYOSHI (1537–98) moved into Ōsaka Castle, the great fortress he built on the site of the Ishiyama Honganji. In 1585 Hideyoshi endowed Kennyo with land at Temma in his new castle town, reestablishing the Honganji in Ōsaka. In 1591, however, Hideyoshi again ordered Kennyo to move his head temple, and it was relocated on the present site of the

Hōnen The founder of the Jōdo sect of Buddhism preaches in Settsu Province in this detail from a series of early-14th-century scrolls entitled A Pictorial Record of the Priest Hōnen.

Japanese honeysuckle The fragrant flowers of this evergreen shrub bloom in early summer. The leaves are dried and made into a diuretic tea.

Nishi Honganji in Kyōto. In 1603 Kyōnyo established the Higashi Honganji a few city blocks to the east of Nishi Honganji. Both Honganji put the turmoil of their background behind them and became pillars of establishment religion during the Edo period (1600–1868).

Hong Kong and Japan 香港と日本

(Honkon *to* Nihon). Toward the end of the 19th century a number of Japanese companies established branch offices in the British crown colony of Hong Kong, which then became a jumping-off point for Japanese immigrants to Southeast Asia. Following the outbreak of World War II in the Pacific, Japan swiftly seized Hong Kong in late December 1941 and made it a vital link in its supply line to Southeast Asia, continuing its occupation until 1945.

When the SAN FRANCISCO PEACE TREATY came into effect in 1952, Japan reopened its consulate general in Hong Kong, and Japanese banks, trading firms, and shipping companies established branch offices there. During Hong Kong's period of high economic growth and industrialization during the 1960s, ties with Japan became increasingly close, and between 1960 and 1970 Japan's share of Hong Kong's import-export trade rose from 12 percent to 16 percent. Japan exports to Hong Kong a great deal of production machinery as well as appliance parts, which are assembled locally and the finished products re-exported. Throughout the 1980s the balance of trade between the two nations was in Japan's favor. As of 1989 there were 180 Japanese and Japanese-affiliated manufacturing companies in Hong Kong, producing mainly electric and electronic goods, as well as 11 Japanese department stores and supermarkets, and branch offices of 60 Japanese banks. Hong Kong is important as a commercial link to the People's Republic of China, and, despite the prospect of its reversion to China in 1997, Japanese investment remains active. In 1990 Japan's exports to Hong Kong totaled US $13.1 billion and its imports, chiefly textiles and other manufactured goods, $2.2 billion.

Hon'imbō 本因坊

Title of the grand master of the game GO. The name Hon'imbō originally referred to a residence for monks in Jakkōji, a temple of the Nichiren sect of Buddhism in Kyōto. One of the monks of this temple, Nikkai (1558–1623), won renown for his mastery of *go* under the name Hon'imbō Sansa and was chosen to instruct the warlords ODA NOBUNAGA, TOYOTOMI HIDEYOSHI, and TOKUGAWA IEYASU in the game. *Go* masters continued to receive the title Hon'imbō after Sansa. The Tokugawa shogunate (1603–1867) patronized *go* by establishing stipends for masters and by formally recognizing several hereditary lines of masters (IEMOTO), including the Hon'imbō line. The JAPAN GO ASSOCIATION was established in 1924 through a merger of the Hon'imbō line and another *go* group. Since 1939 the successor to the title has been decided by an annual professional competition.

honjibutsu 本地仏

The original Buddhist prototype of a native Japanese deity. According to the religious syncretism that prevailed in Japan after the 9th century, Shintō deities (KAMI) were believed to be indigenous Japanese incarna-

tions of universalistic Buddhist divinities. Thus AMATERASU ŌMIKAMI (the divine imperial ancestress identified with the sun) was regarded as the Japanese manifestation of Dainichi Nyorai (Skt: Mahāvairocana; literally, "Great Sun Buddha"), the Shintō deity ŌKUNINUSHI NO MIKOTO was viewed as the manifestation of Yakushi Nyorai (Skt: Bhaiṣajyaguru), and so on; however, the identifications between specific Buddhist and Shintō deities were not always the same. In this syncretic system, the Buddhist divinity was termed *honjibutsu* ("a Buddha who is the original source"), whereas his incarnation in Japan as an indigenous Shintō deity (*kami*) was designated *gongen* ("expedient manifestation"). See also HONJI SUIJAKU.

honjin 本陣

Special inns established for *daimyō*, nobles, shogunal officials, and other important personages at post stations along the main highways during the Edo period (1600–1868). Used during the journeys to and from Edo (now Tōkyō) under the SANKIN KŌTAI system, *honjin* were operated by local officials. The name dates from 1363, when the shōgun Ashikaga Yoshiakira (1330–67) named his lodgings en route to Kyōto the *honjin*, or "principal headquarters." *Honjin* were abolished two years after the Meiji Restoration of 1868.

honji suijaku 本地垂迹

The theory that the native Shintō deities (KAMI) are Japanese incarnations or manifestations (*suijaku*) of Indian Buddhist divinities who are their original and eternal prototypes (*honji*). As the Buddhist religion gained a foothold in Japan in the 7th century, local Shintō deities came to be viewed as protectors of Buddhism and Buddhist temples. From around the 10th century the *honji suijaku* theory became popular and Shintō deities were seen as incarnations of Buddhas and bodhisattvas who had manifested themselves in Japan in the form of Shintō deities (*gongen*) in order to deliver the Japanese from their suffering and ignorance. By the 13th century the deities of most major shrines were identified with specific Buddhist divinities.

Shintō theorists such as YOSHIDA KANETOMO (1435–1511) tried to refute the concept of *honji suijaku* by asserting that it was rather the Shintō deities who were the true and eternal prototypes, whereas the Buddhas and bodhisattvas were merely Indian manifestations of them. Despite strong opposition from Shintō scholars throughout the Edo period (1600–1868), the *honji suijaku* concept continued to be almost universally accepted among the Japanese people until the government issued a ban in 1868 forbidding Buddhist-Shintō syncretic practices at shrines. See also SHINTŌ AND BUDDHISM, SEPARATION OF.

Honjō 本庄[市]

City in northwestern Saitama Prefecture, central Honshū. Honjō developed as a post-station town. Its silk industry, begun in the Meiji period (1868–1912), has been replaced by chemical, electrical-appliance, and foodstuff industries. Pop: 59,098.

Honjō 本荘[市]

City in southwestern Akita Prefecture, northern Honshū, on the Sea of Japan. A castle town during the Edo period (1600–1868). *Honjōmai* rice is produced here; lumber processing is also important. Pop: 44,442.

Honjō Mutsuo 本庄陸男

(1905–39). Novelist. Born in Hokkaidō. Graduate of Aoyama Normal School. He participated in the PROLETARIAN LITERATURE MOVEMENT in the 1920s and wrote fiction protesting against social injustice. His historical novel *Ishikarigawa* (1938–39) describes the hardships endured by a band of former *samurai* who settled in the primeval forestland beside the river Ishikarigawa in Hokkaidō during the early Meiji period (1868–1912).

Honjō Shigeru 本庄繁

(1876–1945). Commander in chief of the GUANDONG (KWANTUNG) ARMY, the Japanese field army that overran Manchuria during 1931–32 (see MANCHURIAN INCIDENT). Born in Hyōgo Prefecture into a farming family, Honjō graduated from the Army Academy in 1897 and the Army War College in 1907 and served in numerous army posts in Japan and on the continent. During 1920–24 he acted as military adviser to ZHANG ZUOLIN (Chang Tso-lin), the Manchurian warlord. In August 1931 he was made head of the Guandong Army. On 6 April 1933 Honjō was appointed chief aide-de-camp to the emperor. He resigned from his post following the attempted coup d'état by KŌDŌHA (Imperial Way faction) officers in the FEBRUARY 26TH INCIDENT (1936) because his son-in-law was implicated in the affair. He later served as head of the Disabled Veterans Administration (Shōhei Hogo In) and briefly as a member of the Privy Council (Sūmitsuin). Honjō was charged as a war criminal by the Allied Powers after World War II. He committed suicide before he could be arrested.

honkadori 本歌取

(literally, "taking from an original poem"). Technique in WAKA of echoing a phrase or image from a well-known poem or using it verbatim in a different context in the creation of a new one, thus, by association, giving an added depth to the new poem. Although the device appears in the 8th-century anthology MAN'YŌSHŪ, it was with FUJIWARA NO TOSHINARI (Fujiwara no Shunzei) and other leading poets of the anthology SHIN KOKINSHŪ (1205) that it came to be used consciously as a poetic technique. Toshinari's son FUJIWARA NO SADAIE (Fujiwara no Teika), in *Eiga no taigai* (ca 1222), and the ex-emperor JUNTOKU (1197–1242), in *yakumo mishō*, set guidelines governing the usage of *honkadori*. The device was also employed in the linked verse (RENGA) that emerged in the mid-Kamakura period (1185–1333).

honke and bunke 本家と分家

(*honke to bunke*). Terms used to describe the relationship between the main household (*honke*) and branch households (*bunke*) of extended families. Also used to describe certain fictive kinship relationships in Japanese society. The head of a household and his successor reside in the *honke*, and married younger sons usually build new homes apart, creating *bunke*. Even when the establishment of the *bunke* occurred long ago and actual kinship is unclear, as long as both parties recognize a relationship, the *honke-bunke* relation continues. A *honke* and the *bunke* associated with it are referred to in sociological literature as *dōzoku*, a corporate group of kin composed of a number of families, usually residing in the same town. The *honke-bunke* relationship may be based on ties other than blood, such as when an employee of the *honke* creates a new household

or a new shop (in this case called *norenwake*). In general, *honke* maintain greater social and economic responsibilities for community festivities and ANCESTOR WORSHIP, and even today they exert great authority in rural areas. The pattern of *honke-bunke* is one of the paradigms of Japanese society, seen also in the relationship between companies and their subsidiaries. See also KINSHIP; IE.

honke and ryōke　本家と領家

(*honke to ryōke*). Persons or institutions who had proprietary rights on a landed estate (SHŌEN). The rights of proprietorship were separated in a threefold division by the end of the 10th century. The RYŌSHU was the original or local proprietor who managed the cultivators, but in many cases, in order to prevent government interference, the *ryōshu* commended his land to a more powerful proprietor, called a *ryōke* (central proprietor), who had more influence in the capital. In return for his patronage, the *ryōke* was entitled to a share (*ryōke shiki*) of the revenues. In order to guarantee title to the *shōen* as well as certain immunities (see FUYU AND FUNYŪ), however, the *ryōke* often commended the estate to an even more exalted personage or religious institution, called *honke* (titular proprietor), who in turn received a share (*honke shiki*) of the revenues.

Honnōji Incident　本能寺の変

(*Honnōji no Hen*). The assassination of the hegemon ODA NOBUNAGA by his vassal AKECHI MITSUHIDE on 21 June 1582 (Tenshō 10.6.2). Nobunaga had arrived in Kyōto two days previously, taking up quarters at the temple Honnōji. Only a few attendants were with him, the armed retinue of his son Nobutada (1557–82; also killed on 21 June) was quartered elsewhere in the city, and none of his principal captains was in the vicinity. Mitsuhide, the *daimyō* of Kameyama in Tamba Province (just west of Kyōto), had orders to march his army of 13,000 to the Chūgoku region to engage Mōri Terumoto (1553–1625) for control of the area, but instead perpetrated a surprise attack on Nobunaga, who died in the burning temple. TOYOTOMI HIDEYOSHI returned from the Chūgoku front and defeated Mitsuhide in the Battle of YAMAZAKI 11 days after the Honnōji Incident.

hōnoki　朴の木

Magnolia obovata. Deciduous tree of the magnolia family (Magnoliaceae) that grows wild in mountain areas of Japan and is cultivated. It grows to 3 meters (10 ft) in height, and its diameter reaches 1 meter (3 ft). Large, alternate, oval leaves (20–45 cm [8–18 in] long) grow on branch tips. Fragrant white flowers (about 15 cm [6 in] wide) bloom in May and June; conical fruits (15 cm [6 in] long) ripen in the fall.

In ancient times the large leaves were used as plates, and an extract of *hōnoki* bark was used as a remedy for stomachache and worms. *Hōnoki* wood is highly valued for making furniture, drafting boards, lacquer ware, sword sheaths, and wooden sandals. Charcoal made of *hōnoki* wood was used in polishing gold and silver. The *hōnoki* was first exported to Europe in 1790 and was introduced to the United States in 1865.

honor　名誉

(*meiyo*; literally, "glory of the name"). A fundamental concept that has regulated Japanese society in various ways since ancient times. The Japanese traditionally attached

overwhelming importance to one's "name." In the 8th-century poetic anthology MAN'YŌSHŪ, ŌTOMO NO YAKAMOCHI frequently alluded to "pure names" (*kiyoki sono na*) and "brilliant names" (*akirakeki na*). The names he referred to were those of *uji* (clans or families) and reflected the authority accorded to heads of powerful *uji* in the pyramidal hierarchy with the imperial family at its apex.

With the rise of the warrior class in the 12th century, the idea of "valuing one's name" (*na o oshimu*) came to occupy a central place in the psychological makeup of the Japanese. It is highly significant that the constant references to "name" (*na*) and "shame" (*haji*) in the warrior tales written during the Kamakura (1185–1333) and Muromachi (1333–1568) periods are not limited to the honor of an individual but also encompass that of one's family and ancestors.

In the Meiji period (1868–1912), when the state was presented as a patriarchal family, the historic lord-vassal relationship was held up as the model, and a renewed emphasis was given to the importance of honor. It was only with defeat in World War II that the Japanese began to reconsider the nature of honor in more personal and individual terms.

honorific language　敬語

(*keigo*). Often referred to in English as "polite speech" or "honorifics." The Japanese language has an extensive system of honorific language to show respect by the speaker to the addressee. *Keigo* in the broad sense refers to the entire system of speech levels. In its narrow sense *keigo* means "terms of respect" and refers to honorific words and expressions. In speaking, a choice is made as to the degree of politeness to be expressed. Depending on the status of the speaker relative to the addressee and on the context of the conversation, a simple question can be phrased in as many as two dozen different ways.

Choice of Speech Style—The speech style adopted in any two-person interaction is basically determined by the status of the speaker and the addressee and the degree of intimacy between them. The general rule is that when the addressee is of higher status than the speaker, or when the two are not very intimate, the polite style (with *desu-masu* verb forms) is to be used. Relative status is determined by a combination of factors, such as age, sex, rank, or social status and favors done or owed. Observance of the status hierarchy is particularly strict within an in-group situation. Being members of the same club or working in the same section of the company results in greater intimacy than otherwise. In general, however, status superiority supersedes intimacy in the above cases, and the junior-ranking person normally is expected to use the polite style of speech in addressing friends or colleagues of a slightly higher status. In the reverse case, where the speaker is of higher status in an in-group situation, the speaker has a choice of plain (with *da* verb forms) or polite style. The choice depends partly on how great the status difference is and partly on the personal preference of the person of higher status. When two individuals who do not belong to the same group meet for the first time, both individuals will use the polite style unless there are some obvious differences in age or social status as reflected in dress, manner, or occupation.

The speech style chosen by women is often a step politer than that selected by

men. Women are not as likely to speak in the plain style to a junior-ranking adult as men are. They tend to use the polite style much more widely and indiscriminately, restricting the use of the plain style to immediate family members, close friends, and children.

Types of Honorifics—The final verb phrase of the sentence that differentiates the speech styles is only one aspect of *keigo*. There are innumerable other honorifics to be found in various parts of speech, including nouns, pronouns, verbs, adjectives, adverbs, and conjunctions. These honorifics, also referred to as *keigo*, are normally classified into three groups: *sonkeigo* (exalted terms), *kenjōgo* (humble terms), and *teineigo* (polite terms). Exalted terms are used to refer to the addressee and anything directly associated with the addressee, such as kin, house, or possessions, while humble terms are used to refer to the speaker and anything associated with the speaker. By elevating the addressee through exalted terms and lowering the speaker through humble terms, a greater distance is created between the two, thereby expressing deeper respect for the addressee. Exalted terms are also used to refer to a third person of higher status if he is not a member of the speaker's in-group. *Teineigo* or polite terms are used without reference to the addressee or speaker and are found in increasing numbers as the speech level goes up.

The give-receive verbs play an important role in the *keigo* system. These verbs are used as main verbs in describing the giving and receiving of gifts and as auxiliary verbs in compound verb phrases to express the giving and receiving of actions done as a favor. The rules in using the give-receive verbs are complex, and group membership becomes an important factor.

In comparison with verbs, honorific nouns are relatively simple. There are underived exalted and humble nouns, but the majority of these are used in writing. Most exalted nouns are created through grammatical rules. In general, the prefix *o-* is attached to neutral nouns of Japanese origin, such as *oniwa* (garden), *otegami* (letter); and the prefix *go-* to Chinese compounds, such as *gobyōki* (illness), *goiken* (opinion). In the case of nouns referring to people, *-san* is suffixed in addition to the prefix *o-*, such as *otetsudaisan* (maid), *oishasan* (doctor).

Rules exist for the use of *keigo* in referring to a third person, as well as for first- and second-person pronouns. The result is an all-pervasive system that allows for fine gradations in the level of politeness within each speech style.

"honors"　→eiten

honryō ando→ando

Honsaroku　本佐録

A 17th-century treatise on statecraft. The title implies the authorship of Honda Sado no Kami Masanobu (1538–1616), combining *hon* and *sa*, the first syllables of his family name (Honda) and his title (Sado no Kami), with *roku* (account). Honda was one of the

Bridge Routes between Honshū and Shikoku

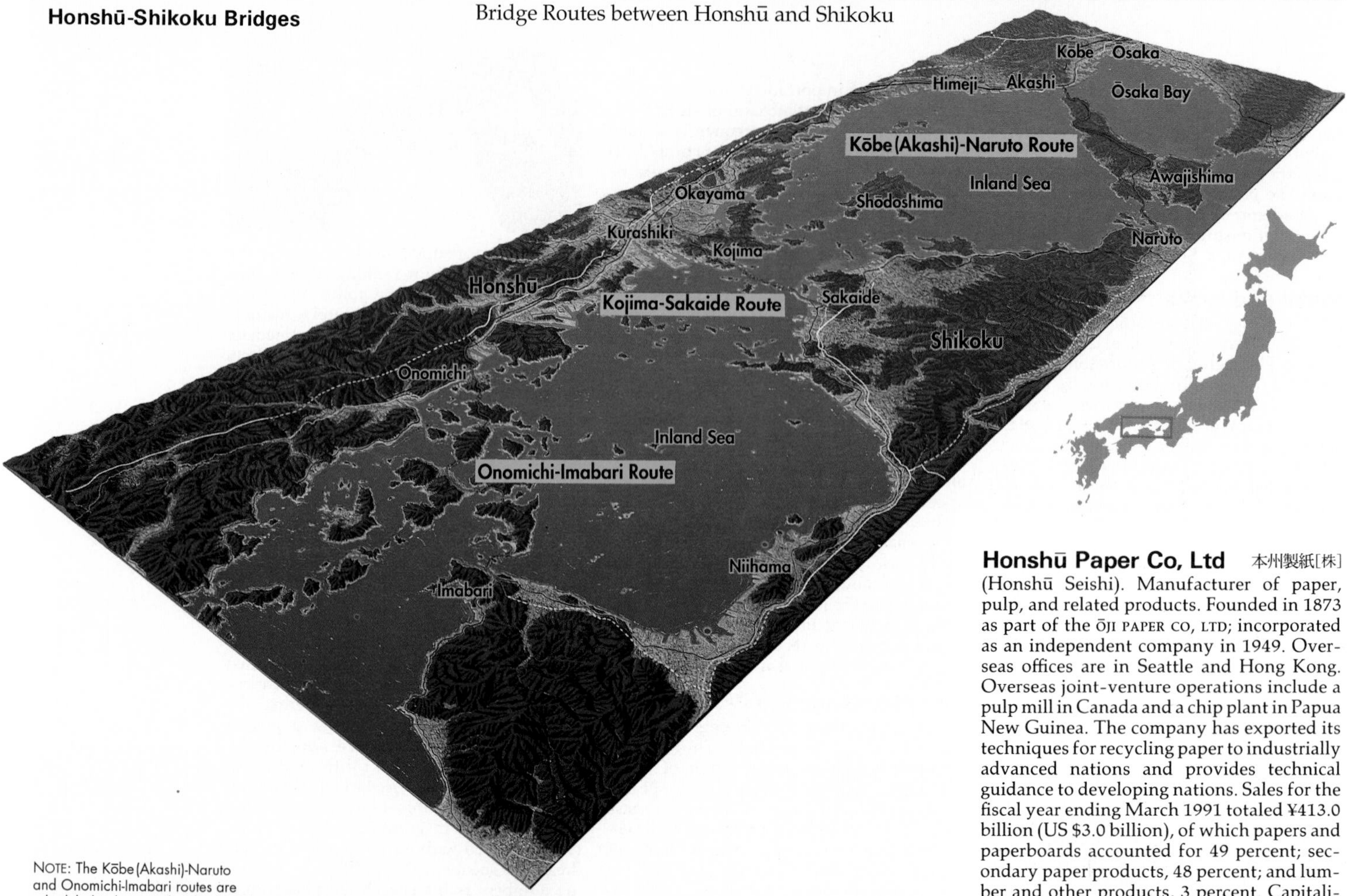

Kōbe　Ōsaka

Himeji　Akashi

Ōsaka Bay

Kōbe (Akashi)-Naruto Route

Inland Sea

Awajishima

Okayama

Shodoshima

Kurashiki

Naruto

Kojima

Sakaide

Honshū

Kojima-Sakaide Route

Shikoku

Onomichi

Inland Sea

Onomichi-Imabari Route

Niihama

Imabari

NOTE: The Kōbe (Akashi)-Naruto
and Onomichi-Imabari routes are
scheduled to be completed in 1998.

One of three series of bridges linking Honshū and the
island of Shikoku, this route runs from Kojima in Okayama Prefecture to Sakaide in Kagawa Prefecture.

most influential men of the early Tokugawa shogunate (1603–1867) and is said to have written the work for the guidance of the second shōgun, TOKUGAWA HIDETADA (r 1605–23). The treatise circulated under several other titles, including *Tenka kokka no yōroku* (How to Rule the Realm) and *Chiyō shichijō* (The Seven Essentials of Government), and was attributed also to FUJIWARA SEIKA (1561–1619), the first purveyor of Neo-Confucian ideology to the Tokugawa; in fact, neither the author nor the date of composition is known. The work draws examples from Chinese and Japanese history, guaranteeing success to a lord who "maintains the principle of *tentō* (the Way of Heaven) and unselfishly exerts himself for the realm."

Honshū　本州

The largest of Japan's four major islands. The majority of the country's population and industries are concentrated on this island. Its terrain is predominantly mountainous, with plains along the coast. The climate is temperate, and the annual precipitation generally exceeds 1,000 mm (40 in). Districts on the coast of the Sea of Japan have long winters and heavy snowfall. The coastal districts of the Pacific Ocean and the Inland Sea extending from southern Kantō to Yamaguchi Prefecture are the most industrialized and urbanized regions in Japan (including the cities of Tōkyō, Kyōto, and Ōsaka. Together with northern Kyūshū, these districts are called the Pacific Coastal Belt (Taiheiyō Beruto Chitai). Along the Sea of Japan the economy centers on agriculture and fishery. Area (including offshore islands): 230,940 sq km (89,166 sq mi); pop (including that of surrounding islands): 99,254,194.

Honshū Paper Co, Ltd　本州製紙［株］
(Honshū Seishi). Manufacturer of paper, pulp, and related products. Founded in 1873 as part of the ŌJI PAPER CO, LTD; incorporated as an independent company in 1949. Overseas offices are in Seattle and Hong Kong. Overseas joint-venture operations include a pulp mill in Canada and a chip plant in Papua New Guinea. The company has exported its techniques for recycling paper to industrially advanced nations and provides technical guidance to developing nations. Sales for the fiscal year ending March 1991 totaled ¥413.0 billion (US $3.0 billion), of which papers and paperboards accounted for 49 percent; secondary paper products, 48 percent; and lumber and other products, 3 percent. Capitalization in the same year was ¥48.5 billion (US $353.5 million). Headquarters are in Tōkyō.

Honshū-Shikoku Bridges
本州-四国連絡橋

(Honshū-Shikoku Renrakukyō). Three separate series of island-hopping bridges across the Inland Sea, connecting Honshū and Shikoku. The middle route, using five islands and six bridges to link Kojima in Okayama Prefecture with Sakaide in Kagawa Prefecture, was opened in April 1988. The bridges are built with two levels, the upper for automobiles and the lower for trains. The eastern route, via the island Awajishima and using two double-deck bridges, will link Akashi (near Kōbe) in Hyōgo Prefecture with Naruto in Tokushima Prefecture, and the western route, using eight islands and nine single-level bridges, will link Onomichi in Hiroshima Prefecture with Imabari in Ehime Prefecture. The projected completion date for the latter two routes is 1998. The Honshū-Shikoku Bridge Authority was established in 1970 and construction was initiated in 1975. Of the total of 17 bridges, 11 had been completed by 1990.

honto mononari　本途物成

(annual land tax). The major tax levied on peasants during the Edo period (1600–1868). Also called *honto, mononari, shomu, narika, torika,* or *hommen.* Calculation of the tax was based on several factors: the assessed value of all agricultural and residential land in a village (expressed as KOKUDAKA, the putative annual rice yield); estimates of the actual yield of the village's arable land; and, in some cases, the overall economic condition of the village. Prior to TOYOTOMI HIDEYOSHI's land surveys (KENCHI) in 1582, similar taxes had been levied in cash on rice paddies

(see KANDAKA). Thereafter, the tax base was expanded to include dry fields and residential lands. In principle, the tax was to be paid in rice, but in fact a portion of the land tax was frequently commuted to other in kind or cash payment.

Honto mononari formed the bulk of taxes during the Edo period. After the Meiji Restoration (1868) it was replaced by a tax system based on the market value of the land (see LAND TAX REFORM OF 1873–1881).

honzen ryōri 本膳料理

One of the three basic styles of traditional Japanese cooking (see also KAISEKI RYŌRI; TEA CEREMONY). *Honzen ryōri* is a highly ritualized form of serving food in which prescribed types of food are carefully arranged and served on legged trays (*honzen*). *Honzen ryōri* has its main roots in the so-called *gishiki ryōri* (ceremonial cooking) of the nobility during the Heian period (794–1185). Although today it is seen only occasionally, chiefly at wedding and funeral banquets, its influence on modern-day Japanese cooking has been considerable. The basic menu of *honzen ryōri* consists of one soup and three types of side dishes—for example, SASHIMI (raw seafood), a broiled dish of fowl or fish (*yakimono*), and a simmered dish (*nimono*). This is the minimum fare. Other combinations are 2 soups and 5 or 7 side dishes, or 3 soups and 11 side dishes. The dishes are served simultaneously on a number of trays. The menu is designed carefully to ensure that foods of similar taste are not served. Strict rules of etiquette are followed concerning the eating of the food and drinking of the *sake*. For example, it is proper to eat a bit of rice before passing from one side dish to the next.

hōō 法皇

Abbreviation of *daijō hōō* (priestly retired sovereign), a formal title given to retired emperors who became Buddhist priests. In 899, Emperor UDA (r 887–897) was the first to receive the title when he took holy orders and moved to the temple NINNAJI after his abdication. Retired sovereigns remained politically active, especially in the last century of the Heian period (794–1185), when the former emperors SHIRAKAWA, TOBA, and GO-SHIRAKAWA ruled from retirement (see INSEI). Emperor Reigen (r 1663–87) was the last to receive the title.

Hōōzan 鳳凰山

Mountain in the northern part of the Akaishi Mountains (Southern Alps), western Yamanashi Prefecture, central Honshū. It is a prominent part of SOUTHERN ALPS NATIONAL PARK. Height: 2,841 m (9,321 ft).

Hopeh-Chahar Political Council → Ji-Cha (Chi-Ch'a) Autonomous Political Council

Hoppō Ryōdo mondai → Northern Territories issue

horagai 法螺貝

A horn formed by attaching a simple mouthpiece to the end of a conch shell. Of Indian origin, the instrument entered Japan via Korea in the Nara period (710–794). It was employed in Buddhist ceremonies and as one of the religious accoutrements of the ascetic SHUGENDŌ practitioners. The *horagai* was also used to sound commands in premodern warfare.

Hōraijisan 鳳来寺山

Mountain in eastern Aichi Prefecture, central Honshū. It is noted for Hōraiji, an ancient Buddhist temple of the Shingon sect, and for its screech owls. Birds, animals, and rare rocks abound. It has a natural-science museum. Height: 695 m (2,280 ft).

Hōrei 法例

(Law on the Applicability of Laws). Law that came into effect in 1898 establishing the basic principles for the application of laws. It comprises rules concerning the date of execution of laws (art. 1), rules concerning the validation of customary law (art. 2), and rules of PRIVATE INTERNATIONAL LAW (arts. 3–34). With the aim of resolving conflicts between the private laws of Japan and foreign countries, the rules of private international law regulate CAPACITY TO ACT, property law, CONSANGUINITY and INHERITANCE LAW, standards of determination of personal law, *renvoi*, public order, and exception to application. In 1989 there was a major revision of the rules of private international law, dealing primarily with those pertaining to marriage and to parent-child relationships. Whereas previously the nationality of the husband or father was taken as the point of contact between Japanese and foreign legal systems, now, based on the EQUALITY OF THE SEXES UNDER THE LAW, the nationality of either the husband or the wife or of either the father or the mother has become the standard. One consequence of this provision is that children of a Japanese mother and foreign father have become eligible for Japanese citizenship. At the same time new rules relaxed the previous emphasis on the nationality principle in conflict of laws and introduced the concept of "habitual residence" (*jōkyosho*) in determination of the applicability of laws.

Hōreki Incident 宝暦事件

(Hōreki Jiken). The censure by the Tokugawa shogunate (1603–1867) of TAKENOUCHI SHIKIBU and several antishogunate nobles in 1758 (Hōreki 8). Shikibu, a Shintō scholar for the house of Tokudaiji, had been lecturing on Shintō, Confucianism, and military arts from a proimperial viewpoint to Tokudaiji Kimmura and other nobles at the court of Emperor Momozono (1741–62; r 1747–62). The imperial regent reported this to the shogunal deputies (*shoshidai*) in Kyōto, worrying that the nobles' practicing of military arts would exacerbate problems in court-shogunate relations. In 1758 Tokudaiji and several other nobles were dismissed by the *shoshidai* from their court positions and put under house arrest; the following year Shikibu was banished from Kyōto. The incident, along with the MEIWA INCIDENT of 1767, is an early instance of shogunate repression of the nascent movement to restore the emperor to full power.

Horie Ken'ichi 堀江謙一

(1938–). Yachtsman; international racer. Born in Ōsaka. In 1962 he became the first Japanese to make a solo crossing of the Pacific Ocean, from Nishinomiya (Hyōgo Prefecture) to San Francisco, in 94 days. He sailed around the world in 275 days (August 1973–May 1974) and set a world record for sailing alone nonstop. In 1989 he made a solo nonstop crossing of the Pacific Ocean in 136 days in a small yacht 2.8 meters (9.2 ft) long and 1.8 meters (6 ft) wide.

Horie Shigeo 堀江薫雄

(1903–). Banker. Born in Tokushima Prefecture. Graduate of Tōkyō University. A longtime employee of the Yokohama Shōkin Ginkō (YOKOHAMA SPECIE BANK), Horie played a leading role in reorganizing it as the BANK OF TŌKYŌ, LTD, after World War II. He became the bank's president in 1957 and chairman in 1965. Horie played an international role as an expert in businesses involved in foreign exchange in the post–World War II period.

Horiguchi Daigaku 堀口大学

(1892–1981). Poet and translator. Born in Tōkyō; studied at Keiō University. His collection of translated poems, *Gekka no ichigun* (1925), introduced modern French poets (including Jean Cocteau, Raymond Radiguet, and Guillaume Apollinaire) and greatly influenced Japanese poetry in the mid-1920s and early 1930s. His translation of Paul Morand's *Ouvert la nuit* (*Yoru hiraku*, 1924) particularly influenced the SHINKANKAKU SCHOOL. He also wrote more than 20 books of poems, including *Gekkō to piero* (1919) and *Ningen no uta* (1947).

Horiguchi Sutemi 堀口捨己

(1895–). Architect and architectural historian. Born in Gifu Prefecture. Graduate of Tōkyō University. He visited Europe in 1923–24 and on his return to Japan published an introduction to modern Dutch architecture. Interested in Japanese tradition, he studied the tea ceremony and the tearoom or *sukiya* (see SUKIYA-ZUKURI). His buildings include the European-influenced villa Shiensō (1926), Wakasa House (1939), and the *sukiya*-style Miyuki no Ma, a room at the inn Hasshōkan (1950). He wrote *Rikyū no cha* (1951), a study of the tea master SEN NO

561

Japanese horse chestnut The large flower clusters of the *tochinoki* (top left) appear in early spring. The smooth, edible fruits (top right) ripen and split open around October.

RIKYŪ, and *Katsura rikyū* (1952), on the KATSURA DETACHED PALACE.

Hori Hidemasa　　　　堀秀政

(1553–90). Warrior of the Azuchi-Momoyama period (1568–1600). Born in Mino (now part of Gifu Prefecture). He helped ODA NOBUNAGA in suppression of the JŌDO SHIN SECT rebellions (IKKŌ IKKI) and other campaigns. After Nobunaga's death he served under TOYOTOMI HIDEYOSHI in the Battle of YAMAZAKI and the KOMAKI NAGAKUTE CAMPAIGN before dying in the ODAWARA CAMPAIGN.

Hori Ichirō　　　　堀一郎

(1910–74). Scholar of religious folklore. Born in Mie Prefecture, Hori graduated from Tōkyō University and taught there and at Tōhoku University. By introducing folklore research methods into the study of religion, he pioneered a new discipline, religious folklore studies. Hori's principal works include *Minkan shinkō* (1951, Folk Religious Beliefs) and *Wagakuni minkan shinkōshi no kenkyū* (2 vols, 1953 and 1955, Research on the History of Japanese Folk Religious Beliefs).

Horikoshi Jirō　　　　堀越二郎

(1903–82). Aeronautical engineer. Designer of the famous Japanese ZERO FIGHTER of World War II. Born in Gumma Prefecture, he graduated from Tōkyō University in 1927. He joined what later became MITSUBISHI HEAVY INDUSTRIES, LTD, and was sent to study in Germany and the United States from 1929 to 1930. After his return to Japan, he directed the design of such fighter aircraft as the Zero, the Raiden, and the Reppū. He remained with Mitsubishi until his retirement in 1967.

Horikoshi Kubō　　　　堀越公方

(Lord of Horikoshi; 1435–91). Popular name of Ashikaga Masatomo, younger brother of ASHIKAGA YOSHIMASA, eighth shōgun of the MUROMACHI SHOGUNATE. In 1457 Masatomo was sent to regain control of the Kantō region from Ashikaga Shigeuji (1434–97), son of the last Kamakura *kubō* (governor-general of the Kantō). Shigeuji defied the shogunate from Koga in Shimōsa Province (now Ibaraki Prefecture), calling himself KOGA KUBŌ. Masatomo established a base at Horikoshi in Izu Province (now part of Shizuoka Prefecture), taking the name Horikoshi Kubō. Masatomo had little power, however, and Shigeuji made peace with the shogunate on his own in 1482. Masatomo was given the province of Izu, which was taken over by HŌJŌ SŌUN after his death.

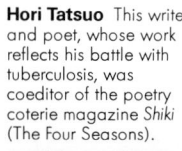

Hori Tatsuo This writer and poet, whose work reflects his battle with tuberculosis, was coeditor of the poetry coterie magazine *Shiki* (The Four Seasons).

Hori Kyūsaku　　　　堀久作

(1900–1974). Businessman and director of the NIKKATSU CORPORATION, a major Japanese movie company. Born in Tōkyō, he graduated from Ōkura Commercial Higher School (now Tōkyō University of Eco

nomics). After serving as secretary to well-known businessman Matsukata Otohiko, Hori became director of Nikkatsu in 1935. He played an early role in the production of "talkies" and expanded his own network of movie houses. He was the head of Nikkatsu during the company's first successful years.

Hori Ryūjo　　　　堀柳女

(1897–1984). Dollmaker. Born in Tōkyō; real name Yamada Matsue. In her youth she joined a handicraft group led by TAKEHISA YUMEJI and began making dolls. She later developed her own style of *kimekomi ningyō* (wooden dolls dressed in *kimono*). In 1936 her work appeared for the first time in the annual Imperial Academy Exhibition, a prestigious government-sponsored art exhibition. In 1955 she became the first woman honored as a Bearer of an Important Intangible Cultural Asset (Jūyō Mukei Bunkazai Hojisha; see LIVING NATIONAL TREASURES).

Hori Tatsuo　　　　堀辰雄

(1904–53). Novelist and poet. Born in Tōkyō; graduate of Tōkyō University. While still a student he participated in a literary coterie sponsored by the poet MUROO SAISEI and contributed translations of modern French poets to its magazine *Roba*. His own poems and novelettes, characterized by the atmosphere of mountain resort sanatoriums and a thematic preoccupation with death, reflect his long battle with tuberculosis, which eventually took his life. Impressionistic and often plotless, Hori's writings describe a fragile world of love and beauty. Among his works are the short story "Seikazoku" (1930; tr "The Holy Family," 1976) and the novelettes *Kaze tachinu* (1936–38; tr *The Wind Has Risen*, 1947) and *Naoko* (1941; tr *Naoko*, 1967).

hōritsu　　　　法律

(law; statute). Term commonly used to denote laws in general, but technically referring to that form of law that has been enacted by the Diet according to its procedure for enacting laws. *Hōritsu* (as statutes enacted by the Diet) rank below the constitution and above other forms of laws such as cabinet orders (*seirei*) and ordinances (*jōrei*) in binding force.

As a general rule, *hōritsu* must be passed by both the House of Representatives and the House of Councillors, but the constitution recognizes some exceptions. First, when the House of Representatives passes a bill and the House of Councillors passes a modified version of the same bill, the resolution of the House of Representatives alone will become law if passed again in the House of Representatives by two-thirds of those members present. The second exception covers interim actions passed by the House of Councillors in emergency session. Third, a *hōritsu* that is to affect only certain local public bodies requires not only passage by the Diet but also majority approval by the local residents in a referendum. The minister responsible for the bill signs it, the prime minister countersigns it, and the emperor promulgates it. As a general rule, *hōritsu* become effective 20 days after promulgation.

Horiuchi Masakazu　　　　堀内正和

(1911–). Modern sculptor. Born in Kyōto. He studied sculpture at the Tōkyō Kōtō Kōgei Gakkō (Tōkyō Higher School of Arts and Crafts) before joining the artists' group Nikakai. In the 1930s Horiuchi produced his

first abstract works, but during World War II he temporarily abandoned sculpture. After the war, when the Nikakai was reorganized, Horiuchi resumed his artistic activity, experimenting with a variety of new media. After 1954 he worked primarily in metal, using iron wire and sheet metal to create monumental geometric forms. From 1950 to 1974 he taught sculpture at what is now Kyōto City University of Arts. He received the TAKAMURA KŌTARŌ Prize in 1963 and the grand prize at the first International Exhibition of Contemporary Sculpture in 1969.

Hōrōki　　　　放浪記

(partial tr *Journal of a Vagabond*, 1951). Autobiographical novel by HAYASHI FUMIKO (1903–51), based on the diary she kept for several years after arriving in Tōkyō in 1922. *Hōrōki* was serialized sporadically between 1928 and 1948. Parts of the novel were published in book form in two separate volumes in 1930, and a third and final volume was published in 1949. The three volumes were eventually combined into one. The protagonist is a young woman who, despite extreme poverty, mistreatment by men, and a succession of menial jobs as a maid, factory hand, and café waitress, never loses her will to survive; she possesses a vitality and sense of humor that allow her to rise above her difficulties. The work resembles an I-NOVEL in content, yet the writing—including poetry, surprising shifts in scene, and lively narration—gives the novel a mark of distinction. *Hōrōki*, a novel that captures the atmosphere of the early Shōwa period (1926–89), established Hayashi's place in Japan's literary world and was a best seller in its time.

hōroku　　　　焙烙

A flat, lidded cooking vessel; used especially for roasting sesame seeds, beans, rice, salt, tea leaves, medicinal herbs, and the like over a flame or live coals. Once a standard utensil, it has in modern times been supplanted by metal cookware. The *hōroku* lent its name to a cooking method broadly known as *hōroku-yaki*, or "*hōroku*-grilling." According to an old Japanese belief, throwing a *hōroku* from a high place and breaking it protects a person from evil.

Horoshiridake→Poroshiridake

horsecars　　　　鉄道馬車

(*tetsudō basha*). Horse-drawn streetcars on rails, generally using two horses and carrying 20 to 30 passengers. The first horsecar line in Japan was opened between Shimbashi and Nihombashi in Tōkyō in 1882. Horsecars quickly supplanted rickshaws in the major cities, and rickshawmen organized to protest the loss of their livelihood (see SHAKAITŌ). After 1895 the horsecars were gradually replaced by electric streetcars.

horse chestnut, Japanese　　　　栃

(*tochinoki*). *Aesculus turbinata*. Deciduous tree of the family Hippocastanaceae that grows wild in mountain areas throughout Japan and is sometimes cultivated. Many trees reach a height of 30 meters (98 ft) and a circumference of 2 meters (7 ft). The leaves are palmate and compound, made up of five to seven leaflets (20–30 cm [8–12 in] long) with sharp pointed tips and serrated edges. The tree flowers about May with numerous four-petaled, white flowers in large (20 cm; 8 in), erect clusters. The funnel-shaped fruit splits into three when ripe, releasing reddish

brown seeds. In northern Honshū mountain villages, starch from these seeds is used to make *tochimochi*, a food resembling rice cake (*mochi*). The wood is used for floorboards, ceilings, alcove pillars, and Western-style furniture.

The common horse chestnut (French: *marronier*; *A. hippocastanum*), called *seiyō tochinoki* (Western *tochinoki*), is often planted along streets in Tōkyō. It is similar to the Japanese species but is distinguished by the thornlike projections of the fruit.

horsemanship 馬術

(*bajutsu*). Horse riding had become widespread among the elite in Japan by the mid-Kofun period (ca 300–710). Toward the end of the 12th century, with the ascendancy of the warrior class, activities such as horseback riding and archery became very popular. Gradually, different schools of *bajutsu* were formed. Although the Meiji period (1868–1912) marked the end of traditional horsemanship, several traditional events are still performed at certain festivals, including *dakyū* (a kind of polo) and YABUSAME (shooting arrows from galloping horses).

Japanese equestrians trained in Western horsemanship were first sent to the Olympics in 1928, and at the 10th Olympic Games in 1932 NISHI TAKEICHI won Japan's first equestrian gold medal. After World War II, horsemanship went into a decline when the military was virtually abolished. But since the 18th Olympics in Tōkyō in 1964, horsemanship has once again become popular in Japan. An equestrian event called the Concours de Saut International Tōkyō (Tōkyō Kokusai Bajutsu Taikai) has been held annually since 1984.

horse racing 競馬

(*keiba*). Ritual horse racing in Japan dates from the early 8th century. The competitions of that time were part of Shintō religious functions and no wagering was involved. Western-style horse racing with betting was introduced to Japan in the early 1860s by British and American residents of Yokohama. A number of private racing clubs were established, and in 1936 these clubs joined to form the Japan Racing Society, which oversaw virtually every aspect of horse racing in Japan.

In 1948 the Japan Racing Society was dissolved and horse racing was nationalized: all assets were transferred to the government and what is now known as National Racing began. In 1954 the government-supervised Japan Racing Association (JRA; Nihon Chūō Keiba Kai) was established to act as the sport's main governing body in Japan. In addition to JRA-supervised National Racing, various local municipalities conduct "Regional Public Racing" under the auspices of a second governing body, the Japan Regional Public Racing Association (Chihō Keiba Kai). The betting and types of races conducted under the two systems are virtually identical, but there are certain restrictions on the exchange of horses and jockeys. As of 1989 there were 12 National Racing tracks in Japan and 30 Regional Public Racing tracks.

Races are of three types: Thoroughbred flat races, Thoroughbred steeplechase races, and Anglo-Arab races. Wagering is under the pari-mutuel system; a horse may win, place, or show, and winning bettors share the total amount bet minus a percentage for the racetrack. There is also a specialty bet, the quinella. In recent years Japanese Thoroughbred breeders have been attempting to im-

prove their horses through breeding with superior stock from the United States and Europe. Among the better known large-stakes horse races held in Japan are the Ōka Shō (Cherry Blossom Cup), the Tennō Shō (Emperor's Cup), the Arima Kinen (Arima Memorial Stakes), and the Japan Cup, an international invitational race. See also GAMBLING.

horse-rider theory 騎馬民族説

(*kiba minzoku setsu*). Controversial theory proposed by Egami Namio (b 1906), a professor of Asian history at Tōkyō University, that seeks to explain the process by which the first unified Japanese state was established and, in a larger sense, frames a hypothesis on the formation and constitution of the Japanese people themselves. Egami proposed the theory during a symposium held in 1948 and refined the idea in several later articles and a book, *Kiba minzoku kokka* (1967, The Horse-Rider State). It generally holds that the unified state was founded by a group of horse-riding warriors, who entered or invaded the Japanese islands, conquered the native rulers, and established themselves as Japan's ruling class. The original Asiatic home of the supposed intruders, their ethnic identity, their relationship to Koreans and to Korean history, the circumstances and time of their arrival in Japan, and the process by which they might have come to dominate Japanese society are all matters on which various proponents of this theory differ. Although there is thus no single horse-rider theory, most Japanese historians recognize Egami's as standard.

The controversy arises in part from the fact that most Japanese have been accustomed to seeing their history as more or less self-generated and self-contained. Scholars long ago abandoned literal belief in the legends of Japan's origin found in the classical works KOJIKI (712) and NIHON SHOKI (720), according to which the first emperor, JIMMU, was descended directly from the gods, who themselves had created the Japanese islands. But, aside from the conclusion—evident from linguistics, comparative mythology, and anthropology—that the earliest Japanese may have had some vague connections with early Asiatic and Oceanic peoples, before Egami no link had been proposed with any specific people or group of peoples and no specific historical process had been hypothesized to explain how these alien peoples and cultures might have entered Japan.

For about a decade prior to the end of World War II in 1945, discussion of Japanese origins beyond the legendary accounts had been discouraged. In 1948, however, the "Symposium on the Origins of the Japanese People and Culture and the Formation of the Japanese State" was organized by the cultural anthropologist ISHIDA EIICHIRŌ and included, in addition to Egami Namio, the ethnologist Oka Masao (1898–1982) and the archaeologist YAWATA ICHIRŌ.

Oka sought to examine the cultural strata in the Japanese ethnological record for evidence of earlier constituent cultures. He identified four, of which the last, the "imperial race" (*tennō zoku*), dominating the Tomb or KOFUN PERIOD (ca 300–710), came to be associated with the horse riders of Egami. Oka believed that this group had originated in eastern Manchuria as a mixed herding and farming people and that in the 2nd or 3rd century it had moved through the Korean peninsula and into the Japanese ar-

chipelago, conquering the peoples of the earlier cultural strata. Oka did not specifically identify this conquering people, but suggested that it was in close relationship, culturally and ethnically, with the ancient Puyŏ (J: Fuyo) and KOGURYŎ (J: Kōkuri) states on the peninsula.

Egami's Theory—Egami's starting point was the nature of the Tomb age associated by Oka with the "imperial race." Egami argued that the Tomb age should be divided into two contrasting periods that he called early and late. The Early Tomb burials (generally 4th century) differed from those of the Late Tomb (5th and 6th centuries) both in tomb structure and in the character of the burial objects interred with the deceased. Early assemblages included BRONZE MIRRORS, ritual knives, comma-shaped beads known as *magatama*, and other items that Egami characterized as "magical, religious, agricultural, and Southeast Asian." Late assemblages included weapons, armor, horse trappings, and ceramic figurines (HANIWA) of houses and of warriors and other persons, all of which Egami characterized as "realistic, warlike, baronial, horse-riding, and North Asian."

Egami enunciated his theory in seven statements: (1) the Early and Late Tomb periods were fundamentally different; (2) the transition from one to the other was not evolutionary, but sudden and dramatic; (3) agricultural societies, such as that of Yayoi-period (ca 300 BC–ca AD 300) Japan, did not aggressively borrow foreign culture or reform their own, and thus horse-rider culture was not peacefully imported into Japan, but rather both southern Korea and Japan were conquered by horse-riding people; (4) Japan's adoption of horse-rider culture was not partial but total and was "completely in common" with horse-rider culture on the mainland; (5) the horses did not come to Japan by themselves, but with their riders; (6) the Late Tomb culture was baronial in character and was spread over Japan by force; and (7) horse-riding peoples did not stop when they reached the sea, but, like the Vandals, Mongols, and others, got into boats and continued their conquests.

Egami believed that a southern-Korean hegemon king, called the "Chin king" in a 3rd-century Chinese source, was of horse-rider origin and had some connection with Puyŏ or Koguryŏ, and that he ruled much of southern Korea through a dynasty of conquest. Toward the end of the 3rd century, he or one of his descendants, pressed by a changing strategic situation on the peninsula, would have migrated with his followers to Japan. Egami thought that SUJIN, the 10th Japanese emperor listed in the classical books and the earliest to be considered a historical figure by most historians, was linked to or identical with the Chin king line. Many historians, both Japanese and Western, remain skeptical of Egami's theory. Egami has countered various criticisms, but the lack of direct historical sources and the as yet incomplete archaeological work leave room for doubt. Whether accepted or rejected, Egami's theory has done much to stimulate new research.

horses 馬

(*uma*). Judging from skeletons and teeth unearthed from archaeological sites such as SHELL MOUNDS, small- and medium-sized horses may have been introduced to Japan

During the isolationist Edo period (1600–1868) Japan's horticultural efforts were confined to the amateur cultivation of certain traditional plants such as IRISES, PRIMROSES, MORNING GLORIES, CHRYSANTHEMUMS, CAMELLIAS, OMOTO (*Rhodea japonica*), YABUKŌJI (*Ardisia japonica*), and BONSAI (dwarf trees). Early in the Meiji period (1868–1912) plants now common in Japanese horticulture, such as the cyclamen, rose, carnation, kaffir lily (*Clivia miniata*), western orchid, cactus, saintpaulia, and various foliage plants, were introduced. The Taishō period (1912–26) saw the first commercial cultivation of the rose, carnation, sweet pea, and dahlia, as well as the creation of markets to sell them. As of 1990 approximately 5.3 billion cut flowers were grown on about 16,609 hectares (41,041 acres). In addition, 205 million potted plants, about 473 million flower bulbs such as tulips, and 183 million flowering trees such as AZALEAS are produced annually. Horticulture is enjoyed as an avocation by roughly 10 million Japanese. The extremely limited space available in homes has led to the cultivation of potted plants. See also FARMING TECHNIQUES.

Hōryūji 法隆寺

A monastery temple, also known as Ikarugadera, located in the town of Ikaruga, some distance north of the Asuka region, Nara Prefecture. Originally it was a modest temple said to have been built in the early 7th century by order of Prince SHŌTOKU, the prince regent, whose palace, Ikaruga no Miya, was being erected nearby. In time Hōryūji was enlarged into a monastery famous for Buddhist studies, especially the doctrines of the HOSSŌ SECT. Always associated with the life of Shōtoku, who was popularly regarded as the patron saint of Japanese Buddhism, Hōryūji became the focus of a widespread Shōtoku cult. After World War II, Hōryūji was designated head temple of the newly created Shōtoku sect. Hōryūji, which owns one of the finest collections of Buddhist art in Japan, is unsurpassed in masterpieces from the Asuka period (593–710; see ASUKA CULTURE; HAKUHŌ CULTURE). The buildings extant today are arranged for the most part around a major compound known as the Western Precinct (Saiin), to which a subtemple compound, the Eastern Precinct (Tōin), was added during the 8th century. The nucleus of the Western Precinct, erected primarily during the late 7th century, constitutes the oldest temple compound extant in Japan.

Temple Buildings—Excavations in 1939, southeast of the Western Precinct, disclosed the main buildings of the original Hōryūji built in the SHITENNŌJI style. The compound was destroyed by a conflagration in 670. Shortly thereafter, Hōryūji was rebuilt on a larger scale, northwest of the original site, within the compound later designated as the Western Precinct. The extant pagoda, main hall (*kondō*), inner gate (*chūmon*), and part of the surrounding corridors are the oldest wooden buildings in the world. In the *kondō* is the triad of the Buddha Śākyamuni with two attending bodhisattvas made by the celebrated sculptor KURATSUKURI NO TORI in 623 to commemorate the death of Prince Shōtoku. The Four Heavenly Kings were made around 650 by the sculptor YAMAGUCHI NO ATAI ŌGUCHI.

The Western Precinct of Hōryūji was completed in 711. The lecture hall, sutra repository, and belfry, originally located north of the Western Precinct, were joined to the corridors during the 10th century. Outside

---

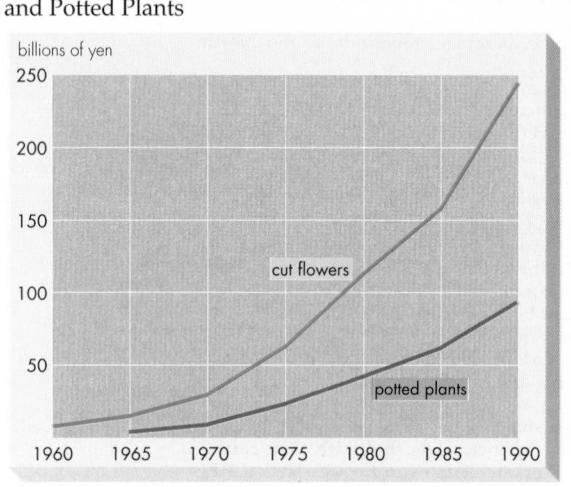

Japanese Production of Cut Flowers and Potted Plants

horticulture

billions of yen

250

200

150

cut flowers

100

50

potted plants

1960 1965 1970 1975 1980 1985 1990

SOURCE: Ministry of Agriculture, Forestry, and Fisheries, *Kakirui no seisan jōkyō tō chōsa* (annual): 1990.

---

from the Asian continent as early as the mid-Jōmon period (ca 10,000 BC–ca 300 BC). The small horse had a shoulder height of about 110–120 centimeters (3.5–4.0 ft) and is thought to be the same as the Tokara *uma*, which inhabited the Ryūkyū Islands until recently. The medium-sized horse was about 130–150 centimeters (4–5 ft) high and is thought to be the same as the *misaki uma* and Kiso *uma*, raised extensively until the Meiji period (1868–1912). Both are thought to be derived from the Mongolian horse.

Horses were primarily used as draft animals and for war. After the Meiji period the government bred larger horses for military purposes. Since World War II, horses have been bred mainly for racing.

horseshoe crab This female horseshoe crab, approximately 60 cm in length, was found on the beach near the city of Kasaoka, Okayama Prefecture. Pollution and waterfront development threaten the *kabutogani* in this area with extinction, and they have been accorded government protection.

The religious custom of dedicating horses to Shintō gods dates back to ancient times. Even today, horses are kept by Shintō shrines as divine horses (*shimme*) and paraded on festival days. In medieval times a fine horse was indispensable to a warrior; the horse figures frequently in military chronicles.

horseshoe crab 兜蟹

(*kabutogani*). *Tachypleus tridentatus*. In Japanese, *kabutogani* is a general name for a marine arthropod with a black helmetlike shell and a long swordlike tail. Its distribution ranges from western Japan to Southeast Asia, with two species of this genus and one species of another genus found in the tropics and one species of the genus *Limulus* found in North America. Considered a "living fossil," it lives on relatively deep sea bottoms, but in summer it appears on shallow sandy bottoms near the shore. The female lays small, spherical eggs on sandy beaches at high tide at night between 10 July and 10 August, always accompanied by a male. The horseshoe crab sheds its shell several times in the first year, once a year thereafter; it may live for over five years.

horse trappings, ancient 馬具

(*bagu*). Horse trappings used as funerary objects have been recovered from 5th-century mounded tombs (KOFUN) and are also clearly depicted on funerary HANIWA horse sculptures from the mid-Kofun period (ca 300–710). They include iron bits, ring stirrups, nose guards, gilt bronze fittings, small bronze horse bells, bell ornaments, and gold openwork decorations. In the Nara period (710–794) a Chinese style of saddlery was adopted. Known as *karakura*, the accoutrements became increasingly elaborate during the Heian period (794–1185) and were used on state occasions. Subsequent modification to suit native tastes resulted in the *yamatogura*, or Japanese saddle. See also ARMS AND ARMOR.

horticulture 園芸

(*engei*). The Japanese have only comparatively recently begun the full-scale development of home gardening as it is known in Western countries. Although Japan has a large number of native tree species, it has few species of annual flowering plants; the traditional Japanese garden is composed of such elements as stones, trees, and water, all arranged to give the impression of natural scenery.

The Flowering of Ancient Buddhism

First completed in 607, the temple Hōryūji serves as a monument to the role its founder, Prince Shōtoku, played in promoting the adoption of Buddhism from China and Korea. Although the original Hōryūji burned down in 670, the main hall, inner gate, and pagoda were rebuilt by Shōtoku's admirers over the next three decades and form the nucleus of Japan's oldest temple compound. Hōryūji's growth in scale and stature in the centuries since testifies to the awe that Shōtoku continues to inspire. The striking similarities between the masterpieces from the Asuka period (593–710) collected at Hōryūji and the works then being produced in Korea and China prove that for the Japanese of Shōtoku's day, Buddhism was still a new and barely assimilated influence. Only gradually did the basis for an artistic and architectural style that could be called uniquely Japanese begin to emerge.

The world's oldest wooden buildings can be glimpsed through the south gate of Hōryūji. The pagoda and inner gate were rebuilt in the late 7th century, while the gate in the foreground dates from 1438. All the structures and sculptures on this page have been designated National Treasures.

A nine-ringed finial adorns the 7th-century pagoda, the oldest pagoda in Japan.

A continuous roofed gallery encloses the pagoda and main hall. Latticed windows are set into the gallery's outer walls. The gallery was built in the 7th century; new sections were added in the 10th.

The 7th-century Kudara Kannon, two meters tall, is a bodhisattva carved from a block of camphor wood. Its name links it to Kudara (Paekche), a Korean kingdom.

The Shaka Triad showing the Buddha Śākyamuni flanked by bodhisattvas was cast in 623 by Kuratsukuri no Tori to commemorate the death of Shōtoku.

Yumechigai Kannon. According to legend, this 7th-century bronze statue of the bodhisattva Kannon possesses the power to change inauspicious dreams into felicitous ones.

The 8th-century Yumedono (Dream Hall) was built on the site of Shōtoku's chapel. According to legend, the prince was instructed by a golden being who appeared to him in a dream.

Hoshi Tōru This politician participated in the formation of the Rikken Seiyūkai, one of the leading political parties in Japan from 1900 to 1940.

the enclosure, to the east and west, monks' quarters (the Higashimuro and Nishimuro) were built; these contained the Shōryōin and Sangyōin chapels. The present Shōryōin chapel was erected in 1284. On the slope northwest of the main compound is the octagonal chapel, the Saiendō, reconstructed in 1250. Through the Hossō scholar-priest Gyōshin's (d 750) efforts, the devastated site of Ikaruga Palace was converted by 739 into the Eastern Precinct, which centers around the well-preserved octagonal chapel, the Yumedono or "Hall of Dreams."

The Daihōzōden (Great Treasure House)—In 1941, a museum called the Daihōzōden was built to the east of the Western Precinct. In it are exhibited numerous works of Buddhist art assembled from other Hōryūji buildings. Outstanding is the Kudara Kannon, a slender, tall image with gently curving scarves, carved during the Asuka period. Two magnificent miniature shrines were also placed in the Daihōzōden: the Tamamushi Shrine and the Shrine of Lady Tachibana.

The Hōryūji complex with its many works of art represents living proof of the great variety of artistic traditions that were transmitted to Japan from Korea and China during the 7th century. They were copied, absorbed, and gradually transformed in accordance with Japanese aesthetic preferences. See also BUDDHIST ARCHITECTURE.

☛ 565

Hōryūji Great Treasure House 法隆寺大宝蔵殿

(Hōryūji Daihōzōden). Located at the temple HŌRYŪJI in Ikaruga, Nara Prefecture. One of the older (it was established in 1939 and opened in 1941) and more important Buddhist temple treasure houses, it is particularly famous for its Buddhist sculptures, which date from the Asuka period (593–710) through the Kamakura period (1185–1333). Among its holdings are the Kudara Kannon, the Tamamushi Shrine (Tamamushi no Zushi), and the Shrine of Lady Tachibana (Tachibana Fujin no Zushi) with its AMIDA triad in bronze. The Hōryūji Treasure House (Hōryūji Hōmotsukan), a separate building at the TŌKYŌ NATIONAL MUSEUM in Tōkyō, houses many other items from the temple. See HŌRYŪJI, TREASURES OF.

Hōryūji, treasures of 法隆寺献納宝物

(Hōryūji Kennō Hōmotsu; literally, "Treasures Donated by Hōryūji"). A collection of precious objects preserved in the Hōryūji Treasure House (Hōryūji Hōmotsukan) located on the grounds of the TŌKYŌ NATIONAL MUSEUM in Ueno Park, Tōkyō. The collection includes sculpture, painting, metal and lacquer articles, Buddhist and secular documents, GIGAKU masks, and musical instruments. The 319 objects, of which 11 are National Treasures, were made over a period of nearly 1,300 years, beginning with the founding of the temple HŌRYŪJI in Nara in 607. The Hōryūji collection focuses on the life and subsequent veneration of Prince SHŌTOKU, the founder of Hōryūji. The buildings of Hōryūji originally housed the treasures, many of which had been objects of worship over the centuries. In 1878 the temple authorities donated these treasures to the imperial household. The collection was then exhibited in the Imperial Museum (Teishitsu Hakubutsukan), later called the Tōkyō National Museum.

Among the most remarkable objects in the collection are the largest group of small-scale gilt-bronze devotional images extant in Japan. The Japanese call them the SHIJŪHATTAI BUTSU ("The 48 Buddhas") even though there are more than 50 pieces in the collection. Averaging 30 centimeters (11.8 in) high, these statuettes include the earliest known Japanese Buddhist images. There are 38 nimbuses in the collection, widely varied in magnificence of design. There are also 11 reliefs hammered out of copper in repoussé and a gilt-bronze Buddhist banner, 5 meters (16.5 ft) high, suspended from a canopy, that is known as *Kanchōban.* Prince Shōtoku is the subject of several important Hōryūji paintings, 5 two-fold screens, and 4 hanging scrolls.

The extensive collection of written documents comprise manuscripts of every period in Japanese history beginning with the Asuka period (593–710) and ending with the Edo period (1600–1868). A Sanskrit text, known in Japanese as the *Hannya shingyō,* was written in India during the Gupta dynasty on *tāla* leaves. The *Hokke gisho,* one of the earliest Japanese documents, is a manuscript commentary on the LOTUS SUTRA attributed to Prince Shōtoku. Another important manuscript is the *Kokon mokuroku shō,* a major biography of Shōtoku and a sourcebook for information on the architecture, images, and other works of art at Hōryūji.

Textiles include silk banners, embroideries, brocades, and dyed fabrics. The collection also contains robes, shoes, writing equipment, an incense burner, bows and arrows, and other objects that, according to tradition, belonged to Prince Shōtoku. See also HŌRYŪJI GREAT TREASURE HOUSE; BUDDHIST ART.

Hōsa Bunko 蓬左文庫

(Hōsa Library). Collection of books originally owned by the Owari branch of the TOKUGAWA FAMILY. Among the 100,000 volumes in the library are valuable works from the collection of TOKUGAWA IEYASU. The library, which is housed in Nagoya, contains such works as 15th- and 16th-century Korean printed books, several books from the KANAZAWA BUNKO, and manuscripts of the Kamakura period (1185–1333).

Hōseidō Kisanji 朋誠堂喜三二

(1735–1813). Mid-Edo-period (1600–1868) writer of the light fictional genres KIBYŌSHI and SHAREBON, and KYŌKA ("mad verse") poet. Born in Edo (now Tōkyō). Adopted by the *samurai* Hirasawa family of the Akita domain (now part of Akita Prefecture), he served that domain as a liaison officer in Edo. His real name was Hirasawa Tsunetomi, but he is better known by several literary aliases, including Hōseidō Kisanji, Hirasawa Heikaku, Tegara no Okamochi, and Kisanjin. He was a friend and literary collaborator of KOIKAWA HARUMACHI. The Tokugawa shogunate (1603–1867) banned his most famous *kibyōshi, Bumbu nidō mangoku-dōshi* (1788, Sifting for Practitioners of the Dual Paths of Literary and Martial Learning), which satirized the general degeneracy of the samurai class and the KANSEI REFORMS. His domain ordered him to stop writing fiction, and he turned exclusively to the writing of *kyōka,* which he continued well into his later years. See also GESAKU.

Hōsei University 法政大学

(Hōsei Daigaku). A private university; main campus located in Chiyoda Ward, Tōkyō. Its

predecessor was the Tōkyō Hōgaku Sha, which was established in 1880 as the first private law school in Japan. It was named Hōsei University in 1903 and became an officially accredited university in 1920. It maintains faculties of law, letters, economics, social sciences, engineering, and business administration. Hōsei University is known for the Institute of Okinawan Culture, the Nogami Memorial Noh-Play Research Center, the Boissonade Institute of Modern Law, and the Ōhara Institute for Social Research. It has affiliated junior high and high schools. Enrollment was 27,277 in 1989.

Hoshina Masayuki 保科正之

(1611–73). *Daimyō* of the early Edo period (1600–1868). A son of the second Tokugawa shōgun, TOKUGAWA HIDETADA, and half-brother of the third shōgun, TOKUGAWA IEMITSU. He was adopted by the Hoshina family and succeeded to the lordship of the Takatō domain (in what is now Nagano Prefecture) in 1631. In 1643 he was made daimyō of the Aizu domain (now part of Fukushima Prefecture). In 1651 Hoshina became official guardian (*hosa*) of the infant shōgun TOKUGAWA IETSUNA. He was responsible for the construction of the TAMAGAWA AQUEDUCT and the Ryōgoku Bridge in Edo (now Tōkyō), and he proposed banning the practices of JUNSHI (suicide as an act of loyalty following the death of one's lord) and HITOJICHI (the holding of hostages). As a serious student of the Zhu Xi (Chu Hsi) school of Confucianism (SHUSHIGAKU), Hoshina could be narrowly moralistic, but he is generally remembered for his benevolent leadership.

Hoshino site 星野遺跡

(Hoshino *iseki*). Archaeological site in Hoshino, in the city of Tochigi, Tochigi Prefecture. Excavations begun in 1965 by Serizawa Chōsuke (b 1919) of Tōhoku University have yielded thousands of STONE TOOLS from the paleolithic period (pre-10,000 BC). A group of chert implements from the lower eight layers underlying a volcanic pumice, dated by radiocarbon and fission track to about 40,000 years ago, supports interpretations for an early occupation of Japan. See also PALEOLITHIC CULTURE.

Hoshi Shin'ichi 星新一

(1926–). Author; chiefly known for his science fiction. Born in Tōkyō; graduate of Tōkyō University. He published his first science-fiction work, "Sekisutora," in 1957. With such works as "Jinzō bijin" (1958, Man-Made Beauty) and "Bokko chan" (1958; tr "Bokko Chan," 1963), he established the science-fiction "short short story" form in Japan. Other works include *Sofu Koganei Yoshikiyo no ki* (1974), a biography of his grandfather KOGANEI YOSHIKIYO, a pioneering anthropologist.

Hoshi Tōru 星亨

(1850–1901). Politician. Born in Edo (now Tōkyō), he studied law in England (1874–77). Under the patronage of MUTSU MUNEMITSU he entered the government, working as lawyer for the Ministry of Justice. He joined the JIYŪTŌ (Liberal Party) at its founding in 1881. Critical of the domination of politics by HAN cliques (HAMBATSU), Hoshi was twice jailed for antigovernment activities. He was elected to the House of Representatives (1892) and named chairman, but he was soon ousted for receiving bribes. In 1896 he was appointed minister to the United States, but in 1898, hearing of the formation of a coalition cabinet under ŌKUMA SHIGENOBU and ITAGAKI TAISUKE, he rushed back to Japan without permission. Hoshi later helped ITŌ HIROBUMI form the RIKKEN SEIYŪKAI (Friends of Constitutional Government Party) and was rewarded with the post of communications minister in the fourth Itō cabinet (1900). Forced to resign after two months in office when he was implicated in a financial scandal, he was then named head of the Tōkyō municipal assembly. Hoshi was assassinated in 1901 by Iba Sōtarō (1851–1903), who blamed him for corruption in Tōkyō's city government.

hoshō→suretyship

Hōshō school   宝生流

(Hōshōryū). One of the five major *shite kata* (principal player) schools (or troupes) of professional NŌ theater actors. Also known as the Kamigakari Hōshō school. The school claims direct descent from the Tobiza (Tobi troupe), one of the original four Yamato SARUGAKU Nō troupes. After the MEIJI RESTORATION of 1868 the 16th troupe head (*tayū*), Hōshō Kurō (1837–1917), attempted to revive Nō, which was suffering a decline. His successor also made great efforts to preserve the characteristically severe acting style of the school. Other famous actors who were members of the school include Noguchi Kanesuke (1879–1953) and Kondō Kenzō (1890–1988).

Hōshō is also the name of a leading *waki* (secondary player) school of Nō actors whose outstanding members included Matsumoto Kenzō (1899–1980) and Hōshō Yaichi (1908–85).

hōshosen   奉書船

Vessels (*sen*) licensed to trade overseas by administrative directives (*hōsho*) issued for the Tokugawa shogunate by its senior councillors (RŌJŪ). After 1631 such endorsement was required, in addition to the traditional "vermilion seal" credentials (SHUINJŌ), for all foreign voyages, giving the shogunate tighter control than it had had under the VERMILION SEAL SHIP TRADE licensing system. In 1635 the *hōshosen* were terminated (see KAIGAI TOKŌ KINSHI REI) in accord with the policy of NATIONAL SECLUSION.

Hosoda Eishi   細田栄之

(1756–1829). UKIYO-E artist. Also known as Chōbunsai Eishi. Real name Hosoda Tokitomi. Ranked with UTAMARO and TORII KIYONAGA as one of the three great masters of *bijinga*, or pictures of beautiful women. Born to a *samurai* family in Edo (now Tōkyō), Eishi first studied painting with Kanō Eisen'in (1753–1811). He is said to have been a pupil of the *ukiyo-e* artist Torii Bunryūsai, and his use of the professional name "Chōbunsai" on his earlier works emphasizes his connection to the TORII SCHOOL. Later, he increasingly used his KANŌ SCHOOL name, Eishi. In his pictures of beautiful women Eishi developed the elegant, elongated figure style that became his hallmark.

Hōsō Hō→Broadcasting Law

Hosoi Heishū   細井平洲

(1728–1801). Confucian scholar of the Edo period (1600–1868). Born in the Owari domain (now part of Aichi Prefecture), he studied in Nagoya with Nakanishi Tan'en (1709–52), a scholar associated with the SETCHŪGAKUHA, or eclectic school of Confucianism.

After further study in Kyōto and Nagasaki he went to Edo (now Tōkyō) and opened a school. In 1772 Heishū was invited by UESUGI HARUNORI, *daimyō* of the Yonezawa domain (now part of Yamagata Prefecture), to assist in educational reform and teach in the domainal school. In 1780 he was invited back to Owari as lecturer to the daimyō and three years later was named head of the Meirindō, the domainal school.

Hosoi Kōtaku   細井広沢

(1658–1735).   Chinese-style   calligrapher. Also known as Hosoi Kōkin. Born in Tōtōmi (now part of Shizuoka Prefecture). As a young man Kōtaku went to Edo (now Tōkyō) to study Confucian philosophy with Sakai Zenken and calligraphy with Kitajima Setsuzan (1636–97). He later served as a retainer of and adviser on firearms to shogunate councillor YANAGISAWA YOSHIYASU. Widely talented, Kōtaku excelled in seal carving, astronomy, mathematics, painting, and poetry, but he eventually devoted himself to calligraphy. Kōtaku published several woodblock books on calligraphy, the most influential being the *Shibi jiyō* (1724). Kōtaku's bold and strong calligraphy survives in both scroll and screen formats.

Hosokawa family   細川氏

(Hosokawashi). Warlords and shogunal deputies of the Muromachi period (1333–1568); subsequently *daimyō* in the Edo period (1600–1868). A branch of the Ashikaga family, the Hosokawa took their name from their estate in Hosokawa, Mikawa Province (now part of Aichi Prefecture). Hosokawa Akiuji (d 1352) helped ASHIKAGA TAKAUJI found the Muromachi shogunate. The Hosokawa were made military governors (SHUGO) of seven provinces in Shikoku and central Honshū and traditionally held the post of shogunal deputy (KANREI). They reached the peak of their power under HOSOKAWA KATSUMOTO (1430–73). After the ŌNIN WAR (1467–77) they remained in control of the declining shogunate. HOSOKAWA YŪSAI (1534–1610), a *waka* poet and scholar, restored family prominence through service with ODA NOBUNAGA and TOYOTOMI HIDEYOSHI. His son HOSOKAWA TADAOKI (1563–1646) fought under Tokugawa Ieyasu at the Battle of SEKIGAHARA in 1600; as lords of the Higo domain (now Kumamoto Prefecture), assessed at 540,000 *koku* (see KOKUDAKA), the Hosokawa were among the most important TOZAMA (outer) daimyō.

Hosokawa Gracia   細川ガラシア

(1563–1600; Japanese name: Hosokawa Tama). Christian convert often held up as a model of the virtuous *samurai* wife. Hosokawa Tama was the third daughter of AKECHI MITSUHIDE. In 1578 she was married to HOSOKAWA TADAOKI, eldest son of the *daimyō* HOSOKAWA YŪSAI. When Akechi rose against ODA NOBUNAGA in the HONNŌJI INCIDENT of 1582, Tadaoki refused to assist his father-in-law, and Tama was obliged to retire to Mitono in the Okutango Peninsula. Two years later the new ruler, TOYOTOMI HIDEYOSHI, allowed her to take up residence in Ōsaka. Tama became a Christian in 1587, receiving the baptismal name Gracia. In 1598 Tadaoki sided with TOKUGAWA IEYASU, leaving instructions to put his wife to death rather than allow her to fall into the hands of his enemies. When Ieyasu's chief rival, ISHIDA MITSUNARI, attempted to seize Gracia as a hostage, Ogasawara Shōsai, the senior retainer of the family, executed her in ac-

cordance with Tadaoki's orders and then committed suicide.

Hosokawa Karoku   細川嘉六

(1888–1962). Journalist and politician. Born in Toyama Prefecture; graduate of Tōkyō University. From 1921 he was a member of the ŌHARA INSTITUTE FOR SOCIAL RESEARCH. He also wrote for various journals, consistently taking a critical view of Japan's expansionist policies. In 1942 he was arrested for writing an article with alleged communist tendencies (see YOKOHAMA INCIDENT) and spent the rest of World War II in prison. He was elected to the House of Councillors in 1947 as a Communist, but was forced to resign in 1951 during the RED PURGE.

Hosokawa Katsumoto   細川勝元

(1430–73). Military leader of the Muromachi period (1333–1568). Son of Hosokawa Mochiyuki (1400–1442); succeeded his father as military governor (SHUGO) of Settsu (now part of Ōsaka and Hyōgo Prefectures), Tamba (now part of Hyōgo and Kyōto Prefectures), Sanuki (now Kagawa Prefecture), and Tosa (now Kōchi Prefecture). The HOSOKAWA FAMILY, with the SHIBA FAMILY and the HATAKEYAMA FAMILY, had alternated in the post of shogunal deputy (KANREI) in the Muromachi shogunate; Katsumoto occupied the office for three terms (1445–49; 1452–64; 1468–73). He and YAMANA SŌZEN came into conflict when succession disputes broke out in the shogunal ASHIKAGA FAMILY and in the Hatakeyama and Shiba families. This confrontation was one of the chief causes of the ŌNIN WAR (1467–77), in which the armies of Katsumoto and Sōzen devastated the city of Kyōto. Katsumoto died of illness during the struggle. An adherent of Zen Buddhism, Katsumoto built the temple RYŌANJI in Kyōto.

Hosokawa Tadaoki   細川忠興

(1563–1646). Also known as Hosokawa Sansai. *Daimyō*. Son of HOSOKAWA YŪSAI and husband of HOSOKAWA GRACIA. He participated in several of ODA NOBUNAGA's campaigns, including the conquest of the TAKEDA FAMILY in 1582. When Nobunaga was killed by AKECHI MITSUHIDE later that year, Tadaoki refused his father-in-law Mitsuhide's request for assistance, instead joining TOYOTOMI HIDEYOSHI to destroy Mitsuhide. Tadaoki succeeded his father as daimyō of Tango Province (now part of Kyōto Prefecture) in 1582; he rose in Hideyoshi's service and fought in many campaigns. At the Battle of SEKIGAHARA in 1600 Tadaoki fought on the side of TOKUGAWA IEYASU and was rewarded with a large domain including Buzen province and two districts in Bungo Province (now parts of Fukuoka and Ōita prefectures). He retired in 1619. A poet, painter, and expert on etiquette and ceremonial matters (YŪSOKU KOJITSU), Tadaoki ranked as one of the tea master SEN NO RIKYŪ's "Seven Great Disciples" (Rikyū Shittetsu) and was the author of works on the art of tea.

Hosokawa Yūsai   細川幽斎

(1534–1610). Also known as Hosokawa Fujitaka. *Daimyō* and poet of the Azuchi-Momoyama period (1568–1600). The son of Mitsubuchi Harukazu (d 1570), an intimate of several Ashikaga shōguns, he was adopted by Hosokawa Mototsune (d 1553), another important shogunal vassal. Yūsai was a key intermediary between ASHIKAGA

Hotakadake This mountain in central Honshū has four peaks; here, 3,090-meter Mae Hotakadake (center) is viewed from 3,106-meter Kita Hotakadake.

hototogisu The flowers of this mountain lily resemble the breast markings of the *hototogisu* (cuckoo), after which it is named.

YOSHIAKI and the hegemon ODA NOBUNAGA, who in 1580 made him daimyō of Tango Province (now part of Kyōto Prefecture). Upon Nobunaga's assassination in 1582, Yūsai retired, passing on his domain to his son HOSOKAWA TADAOKI and assuming the priestly style Yūsai. Thereafter he devoted himself to cultural pursuits, becoming known as the outstanding authority on WAKA (classical Japanese poetry). He instructed the national unifier TOYOTOMI HIDEYOSHI (1537–98) in that art and initiated Prince Hachijō Toshihito (1579–1629) into the secret traditions of the 10th-century KOKINSHŪ anthology (see KOKIN DENJU). Among his literary works are the poetry collection *Shūmyōshū* (Collection of Many Marvels) and the commentary *Hyakunin isshu shō* (Notes on One Poem Each by One Hundred Authors).

Hossō sect 法相宗

(Hossōshū; Ch: Faxiang Zong or Fa-hsiang Tsung). One of the six sects of NARA BUDDHISM. The sect draws on the doctrine of the Indian Buddhist school Vijñānavāda ("mind only" school; J: Yuishikishū). This school, also known as the Yogācāra ("practice of yoga") school, is represented by Vasubandhu (4th century; J: Seshin) and Asaṅga (4th century; J: Mujaku), who emphasized the workings of consciousness (Skt: *vijñāna*) in its interrelation with environment. The basic scriptures for this school include the work known in Japanese as *Jōyuishiki ron* (Treatise on the Establishment of the Doctrine of Consciousness Only), which was originally a collection of commentaries on one of Vasubandhu's works but was modified when translated into Chinese so as to center on the interpretation of the 6th-century Indian commentator Dharmapāla. The school, transplanted from China to Japan by monks such as DŌSHŌ and GEMBŌ during the period from 653 to 735, was located at KŌFUKUJI, HŌRYŪJI, and YAKUSHIJI, the three institutions that served as representative centers of Buddhist studies during the medieval period (mid-12th–16th centuries). In 1950 Hōryūji seceded from the sect, which now has two main temples, Kōfukuji and Yakushiji, and some 55 other temples.

Hotakadake 穂高岳

Mountain on the border of Nagano and Gifu prefectures, central Honshū. It comprises the four peaks of Kita Hotakadake (3,106 m; 10,190 ft), Oku Hotakadake (3,190 m; 10,466 ft), Mae Hotakadake (3,090 m; 10,138 ft), and Nishi Hotakadake (2,909 m; 9,544 ft). It is Japan's third highest mountain and the highest of the HIDA MOUNTAINS. Ice-scoured areas, including the Karasawa Cirque, are found on the eastern side of the mountain. Mae Hotakadake was first climbed by Wil-

liam Gouland, an Englishman, in 1880. One of the two most popular rock-climbing areas in the JAPANESE ALPS, Hotakadake forms a principal part of Chūbu Sangaku National Park.

Hotakayama 武尊山

Stratovolcano in northern Gumma Prefecture, central Honshū. On the northwest side are a wide plateau, Hotaka Shrine, and several spas with hot springs. Height: 2,158 m (7,080 ft).

hotarugari → firefly viewing

Hotel Ōkura Co, Ltd
[株]ホテルオークラ

(Hoteru Ōkura). Hotel company. Incorporated in 1958. It has hotels in Tōkyō, Kōbe, Guam, Shanghai, and Amsterdam and operates a chain of affiliate hotels—seven in Japan, two in Hawaii, one in South Korea, and one in China. For the fiscal year ending March 1990, sales totaled ¥40.9 billion (US $267.2 million) and capitalization stood at ¥3.0 billion (US $19.5 million). Headquarters are in Tōkyō.

Hototogisu ホトトギス

Leading HAIKU magazine launched in 1897 in conjunction with the haiku reform movement of MASAOKA SHIKI; by 1920 it had become one of the most influential organs in haiku circles. *Hototogisu* was first published in the city of Matsuyama (Ehime Prefecture) in January 1897. Yanagihara Kyokudō (1867–1957) was the publisher and Masaoka Shiki the editor. In 1898 Shiki's disciple TAKAHAMA KYOSHI took over as editor and publisher and the magazine moved to Tōkyō. By 1906 Kyoshi had become more interested in prose and *shaseibun* (sketch pieces), and *Hototogisu* was temporarily changed from a poetry to a general literary arts magazine. In 1912 Kyoshi took up the cause of preserving the traditional haiku style, which emphasized objective reflection of the natural world. The leading poets MIZUHARA SHŪŌSHI, AWANO SEIHO, YAMAGUCHI SEISHI, and TAKANO SUJŪ were regular contributors after 1915. As of 1990 the magazine was still being published.

Hototogisu 不如帰

(tr *Nami-ko*, 1904). Novel by TOKUTOMI ROKA (1868–1927); published 1898–99. The work portrays the marriage between Baron Kawashima Takeo, a navy ensign, and Namiko, the daughter of an army general. Takeo and Namiko are extremely happy, but Namiko falls ill with tuberculosis and as a result cannot bear children. Her mother-in-law, intent on continuing the family line, mercilessly dissolves the marriage while Takeo is away on fleet maneuvers. Despite their deep love for one another, husband and wife are never reunited; Namiko dies, vowing that she will never be reborn as a woman. *Hototogisu*, set during the Sino-Japanese War of 1894–95, is noteworthy for dealing with the problem of the status of women in Meiji-period (1868–1912) Japan. The novel was one of the best sellers of the period.

hototogisu 杜鵑草

(toad lily). *Tricyrtis hirta.* Perennial herb of the lily family (Liliaceae) that grows wild in mountain areas throughout Japan; it is also planted in gardens. The straight or slanted stem reaches 60 centimeters (2 ft). Leaves are alternate, elliptical, and pointed. Lily-like, six-lobed flowers, white on the outside

and with deep purplish spots inside, bloom in the fall. Similar species native to Japan include the *yamajino hototogisu* (*T. affinis*) and species with yellow flowers with purple spots, such as the Tamagawa *hototogisu* (*T. latifolia*), the *kibana no hototogisu* (*T. flava*), and the *chabo hototogisu* (*T. nana*).

hototogisu → cuckoos

hot springs 温泉

(*onsen*). Hot springs are numerous in Japan, and for centuries the Japanese people have enjoyed hot spring bathing. Visits to hot spring resorts were hailed not only as a means of relaxation but also for the beneficial medicinal properties attributed to thermal spring water. Hot springs are still major attractions for vacationing Japanese, and many have been modernized and developed into large-scale resort complexes. Under the 1948 Hot Spring Law (Onsen Hō), the Japanese government recognizes as *onsen* only those hot springs that reach certain standards regarding temperature and mineral composition; the number of these as of 1990 was about 2,300. Since 1954 the Ministry of Health and Welfare has accorded special recognition to 64 hot spring resorts capable of providing medical treatment.

Definition—A hot spring is defined by the Hot Spring Law as "hot water, mineral water, water vapor and other gases (except natural gas containing hydrocarbons as the main element) that issue from the ground with a temperature in excess of 25°C (77°F) or that contain more than a prescribed amount of designated substances." Thus a cool mineral spring under 25°C but containing more than a prescribed amount of the designated substances may be called a hot spring; even volcanic gas or volcanic vapor may be called a hot spring, creating cases that do not agree with the general concept of hot spring water.

History of Utilization—The Japanese take special pleasure in mineral and hot spring bathing. The popularity of hot springs for such purposes in ancient Japan is described in the regional chronicles called FUDOKI. The *Izumo fudoki* reports that TAMATSUKURI HOT SPRING was continually thronged with visitors and that by "bathing once, the visitor was made fair of face and figure; bathing twice, all diseases were healed; its effectiveness has been obvious since of old."

DŌGO HOT SPRING in Iyo Province (now Ehime Prefecture) is reputedly the oldest hot spring in Japan. It was the site, according to tradition, of therapeutic bathing by several legendary or early historical emperors. Buddhist monks developed hot springs for medicinal purposes and used hot springs for the bathing that is part of the Buddhist purification ritual. Farmers and fishermen engaged in ritualistic baths at various times of the year.

GOTŌ KONZAN, a doctor in Edo (now Tōkyō), noticed the effectiveness of hot spring bathing as a cure for certain disorders and in 1709 initiated the first medical study of hot springs, advocating the use of baths as therapy for various ailments. In 1874 the Japanese government undertook the chemical analysis of mineral springs. After the founding of the Balneotherapy Institute (now called the Medical Institute of Bioregulation) at Beppu Hot Spring in Ōita Prefecture by Kyūshū University in 1931, the medical study of hot springs began to be systematized, with many universities establishing research facilities at various hot springs. After World War II, national hot spring hospitals were created, making hot springs for

medical treatment available around the country. Hot springs are utilized in the treatment of chronic rheumatism; neuralgia; chronic diseases of the stomach, intestines, liver, and gallbladder; hypertension; hemiplegia; glucosuria; and gout. They are also used for treating external injuries and for postoperative treatment and rehabilitation.

Although hot springs are used mainly for bathing, in some places the heat they release is utilized for heating rooms and hothouses, for cooking food, for brewing *sake*, or for making *miso* (bean paste). In addition, certain hot springs that reach very high temperatures are now being utilized as energy sources for geothermal electricity generation. The first geothermal generation of electricity in Japan was carried out in 1925 in BEPPU, producing 1 kilowatt. During the 1950s and 1960s more power was produced, and, spurred by the oil crisis of 1973, 50-megawatt power stations were constructed during the 1970s. As of 1990, 12 geothermal power stations were operating in Japan, altogether producing a total of 269,950 kilowatts. Despite a national program to promote it, however, geothermal electricity generation remains relatively small in scale, limited by concern for the environment and tourism.

Hotta Masatoshi   堀田正俊

(1634–84). Great elder (TAIRŌ) of the TOKUGAWA SHOGUNATE (1603–1867). On orders from the shōgun TOKUGAWA IEMITSU he was adopted by KASUGA NO TSUBONE, Iemitsu's nurse. After serving as personal attendant to the fourth shōgun, TOKUGAWA IETSUNA, he was promoted to junior councillor (*wakadoshiyori*) in 1670 and to senior councillor (*rōjū*) in 1679. When Ietsuna died without an heir in 1680, Masatoshi successfully supported Ietsuna's brother TOKUGAWA TSUNAYOSHI, in opposition to Great Elder SAKAI TADAKIYO's candidate for the succession. Tsunayoshi appointed him great elder in 1681, but he was increasingly shunned by other officials and eventually assassinated by the junior councillor Inaba Masayasu (1640–84).

Hotta Masayoshi   堀田正睦

(1810–64). *Daimyō* of the Sakura domain (now part of Chiba Prefecture) and senior councillor (*rōjū*) of the Tokugawa shogunate. As a daimyō Hotta was known for his progressive views and encouragement of the study of Western medicine and military science. In 1855 he became chief senior councillor and immediately faced pressure from Western powers to conclude agreements similar to the KANAGAWA TREATY signed with the United States the previous year. In 1857 he signed an agreement with the Dutch and negotiated the HARRIS TREATY with American representative Townsend HARRIS. Hotta then went to Kyōto to gain Emperor KŌMEI's approval, but failed. The controversy over the treaty was complicated by a shogunal succession dispute in which Hotta supported TOKUGAWA YOSHINOBU against the great elder (*tairō*) II NAOSUKE's candidate. Ii's choice prevailed, and Hotta was forced to resign. Ii eventually signed the Harris Treaty without imperial sanction.

Hotta Shōzo   堀田庄三

(1899–1990). Banker. Born in Aichi Prefecture. After graduating from Kyōto University, Hotta joined SUMITOMO BANK, LTD, becoming president in 1952 and chairman in 1970. Under the banner of stabilized and rationalized management, he successfully turned Sumitomo Bank into the third largest bank in Japan (in deposits). Using his bank's financial resources, he played a key role in the post–World War II regrouping of the Sumitomo corporations.

Hotta Yoshie   堀田善衛

(1918–). Novelist. Born in Toyama Prefecture; graduate of Keiō University. After serving as a Japanese army propagandist in China in World War II, he wrote of his experiences in *Sokoku sōshitsu* (1950, Loss of the Motherland) and other novels. Hotta received the Akutagawa Prize for *Hiroba no kodoku* (1951, Alone in the Marketplace), which described the psychological impact of the Korean War on a Japanese intellectual. His works deal with the dilemmas faced by the modern intellectual in critical situations. Other works by Hotta include the novels *Jikan* (1953, Time) and *Uminari no soko kara* (1960–61, From Beneath the Sea Roar), a historical novel that deals with the conflict of native and foreign ways of thinking during the Christian SHIMABARA UPRISING, and

Ransei no bungakusha (1958), a collection of essays.

Ho-Umezu Agreement→He-Umezu (Ho-Umezu) Agreement

House, Edward Howard

ハウス, E. H.

(1836–1901). American journalist who played an important role in shaping 19th-century American opinion about Japan and the Japanese. Born in Boston, House arrived in Japan in 1871 to teach at the Kaisei Gakkō, one of the predecessors of Tōkyō University. His pro-Japanese views made him very popular with the Japanese government, especially ŌKUMA SHIGENOBU. In 1873 he resigned his teaching post to serve as a war correspondent accompanying the Japanese army on the TAIWAN EXPEDITION OF 1874. With a government subsidy, in 1877 House founded an English-language newspaper, the *Tōkyō Times*, which he edited until 1880, championing the Japanese position on such issues as treaty revision and foreign policy. He was decorated and pensioned by the Japanese government in recognition of his services.

House Food Industrial Co, Ltd

ハウス食品工業[株]

(Hausu Shokuhin Kōgyō). Manufacturer, processor, and vendor of spicy foods such as curry, as well as dry foods, wheat products, and instant foods. Incorporated in 1947. The company has developed techniques for producing a wide variety of processed foods ranging from curry and spices to snack foods and packaged noodles. Sales for the fiscal year ending March 1991 totaled ¥164.1 billion (US $1.2 billion), and capitalization was ¥9.5 billion (US $69.2 million). Headquarters are in Ōsaka.

household electrical products industry   家電産業

(*kaden sangyō*). The industry producing goods classified as either consumer electronics (63.1 percent of the industry in 1988), such as videocassette recorders (VCRs) and color televisions, or as electrical appliances (36.9 percent of the industry), such as air conditioners, refrigerators, and washing ma-

hot springs
1 *Rotemburo* (open-air baths), such as this one at Hanamaki Hot Spring in Iwate Prefecture, are popular year round.
2 A bather enjoys the warm water in a natural pool at Seseki Hot Spring in Shiretoko National Park, Hokkaidō.
3 Steam fills the air at the springhead of Yumura Hot Spring, Hyōgo Prefecture. The 98°C water flows from the source at a rate of 415 liters per minute.

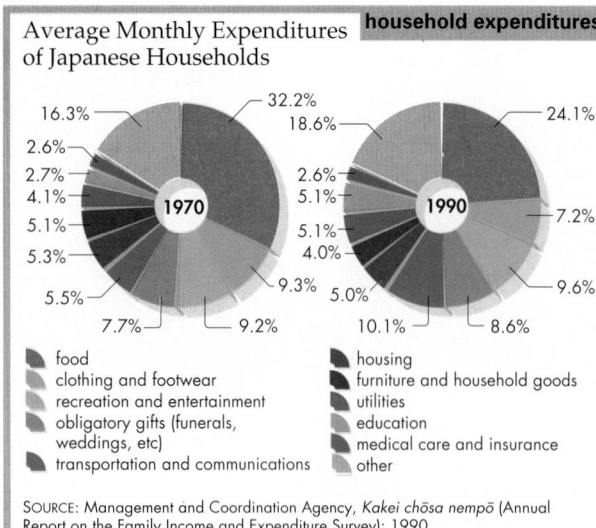

Average Monthly Expenditures of Japanese Households

household expenditures

1970
- 32.2%
- 16.3%
- 2.6%
- 2.7%
- 4.1%
- 5.1%
- 5.3%
- 5.5%
- 7.7%
- 9.2%
- 18.6%

1990
- 24.1%
- 2.6%
- 5.1%
- 5.1%
- 4.0%
- 5.0%
- 10.1%
- 8.6%
- 9.6%
- 9.3%
- 7.2%

- food
- clothing and footwear
- recreation and entertainment
- obligatory gifts (funerals, weddings, etc)
- transportation and communications
- housing
- furniture and household goods
- utilities
- education
- medical care and insurance
- other

SOURCE: Management and Coordination Agency, *Kakei chōsa nempō* (Annual Report on the Family Income and Expenditure Survey): 1990.

chines. One special characteristic of Japan's household electrical products industry is its sudden growth in a short period of time, based on the two principles of new product development through technological innovation and cost reduction through high-volume production. For example, in 1955 only 140,000 televisions were produced, and by 1957 only 3 percent of all households owned televisions. By 1959, however, yearly production had risen to 3 million sets and television ownership exceeded 20 percent of all households. Similarly, washing machines and refrigerators spread very quickly throughout the population, whereas before World War II, very few families had owned them.

A huge market emerged after World War II, as a result of the increase in per-capita income, changes in lifestyle, and the concentration of population in cities. Growth of the industry continued with expanding sales of key products such as color televisions and tape recorders in the 1970s and VCRs in the early 1980s. Expectations are that the next major product following VCRs will be high-definition television, the demand for which is predicted to go from 10,000 units in fiscal 1991 to 200,000 in 1993 and to 650,000 in 1995.

Types of Companies and Sales Percentages—The companies in the industry can be divided into three groups: (1) general electrical machinery and appliance manufacturers such as HITACHI, LTD; TŌSHIBA CORPORATION; and MITSUBISHI ELECTRIC CORPORATION; (2) general household electrical product manufacturers such as MATSUSHITA ELECTRIC INDUSTRIAL CO, LTD; SAN'YŌ ELECTRIC CO, LTD; and SHARP CORPORATION; and (3) companies specializing in the manufacture of consumer electronics such as SONY CORPORATION and PIONEER ELECTRONIC CORPORATION.

The industry's sales of ¥6.8 trillion (US $53.1 billion) in 1988 (63 percent consumer electronics, 37 percent electrical appliances) were second only to 1985's ¥7.2 trillion (US $30.2 billion). VCRs generated 28 percent of consumer electronics sales in 1988, followed by color televisions, 19 percent; tape recorders, 17 percent; and video cameras, 15 percent. Electrical appliance sales included air conditioners, 48 percent; refrigerators, 17 percent; microwave ovens, 8 percent; and washing machines, 6 percent.

Product Exports and Imports—Domestic demand increased, and some domestic production was shifted overseas as a result of trade friction and the increase in the value of the yen following the 1985 Plaza

Accord. After a peak of ¥4.4 trillion (US $18.4 billion; 60.8 percent of all exports) in 1985, household electrical product exports fell to ¥2.6 trillion (US $20.3 billion; 37.9 percent of all exports) in 1988. In contrast, household electrical product imports rose each year during the same period from ¥43.7 billion (US $183.2 million; 1.5 percent of all imports) in 1985 to ¥145.7 billion (US $1.1 billion; 3.4 percent of all imports) in 1988.

A key task for companies in this industry is to develop new high-value-added products in order to differentiate their own products from those of competitors in a market strongly affected by the entry of products from the Asian NIEs (newly industrializing economies). Another important task is to establish an integrated management structure linking Japan, the United States, Europe, and Asia.

household expenditures 家計

(*kakei*). Household expenditures, which accounted for 56 percent of the gross national expenditure of Japan in 1990, exert considerable influence on the entire Japanese economy. The Statistics Bureau of the Management and Coordination Agency (Sōmuchō Tōkei Kyoku) conducts comprehensive annual surveys of total household expenditures. The average annual increase in disposable income in real terms was 0.9 percent between 1974 and 1978, declining to 0.7 percent between 1979 and 1983. Between 1984 and 1990 disposable income grew by 3.5 percent per year. According to the *Annual Report on the Family Income and Expenditure Survey*, the average monthly household income in Japan in 1990 was ¥521,757 (US $3,604), and the average disposable income (excluding taxes and social security payments) was ¥440,539 (US $3,043), 75 percent of which was spent on consumables. Rising disposable income naturally led to higher household consumption expenditures in the late 1980s, particularly for luxury goods.

In recent years rising income levels and decreasing household sizes have resulted in decreases in the percentage of income spent on food. Changing consumption patterns, based on more affluent lifestyles, coupled with rising public utility charges have caused the percentage expended for fuel, light, and water to increase. Transportation, communication, and education expenditures have also risen. At the same time, social expenditures and miscellaneous expenditures are on the rise, an indication that discretionary spending is becoming a larger part of the average household budget in Japan. See also STANDARD OF LIVING.

household precepts→kakun

household registers 戸籍

(*koseki*). Official documents that record important information about a household, which in Japan is defined as consisting of a married couple, a married couple and their unmarried children (natural or adopted) of the same surname, an individual with unmarried children (natural or adopted) of the same surname, or an individual. Every Japanese national is listed in a *koseki*, which constitutes legal proof of his or her status. The *koseki* contains such information as the members' names, dates of birth and death, reasons for entry into the *koseki* (e.g., marriage or birth), and the names of the natural (or foster) mother and father of each household member.

The first member listed in the *koseki* is

called the *hittōsha*. The *hittōsha* is the spouse whose surname the couple has taken; after the *hittōsha* are listed the other spouse and the children in order of birth. The location of the permanent domicile listed in the *koseki* is called the *honseki*. The *koseki* is compiled in the city, town, or village that is the person's *honsekichi* (place of permanent domicile).

Koseki are arranged in the order of house-lot numbers and bound together in *kosekibo* (household register books). The original *kosekibo* is kept at the local municipal office, and a duplicate is deposited with the regional bureau of the Ministry of Justice. When a person enters another *koseki* (e.g., in the case of marriage), his or her name is stricken from the former *koseki* (a line is drawn through his or her name). In the event all persons listed in a *koseki* are stricken from it, the *koseki* is removed from the *kosekibo* and placed in another register, the *jōsekibo* (removal register).

History—*Koseki* were apparently compiled as early as the 6th century. Under the RITSURYŌ SYSTEM of government that developed in the late 7th century, *koseki* came to be institutionalized as a means of facilitating government control and land distribution (see KŌGONEN-JAKU; HANDEN SHŪJU SYSTEM) and were to be compiled every six years.

With the decline of the *ritsuryō* system and the development of private landed estates (SHŌEN) in the Heian period (794–1185), compilation of *koseki* virtually ceased until early in the Edo period (1600–1868), when the shogunate ordered the domains to compile household registers (see SHŪMON ARATAME). These registers were compiled throughout the Edo period and became the basis for the *koseki* compiled under the Meiji government, which in 1871 enacted the Koseki Hō (Household Register Law), resulting in the JINSHIN KOSEKI of 1872, the first nationwide compilation of family records. The CIVIL CODE of 1898 established the IE (household) system, under which a register was compiled for each family unit and the family head (*koshu*) was held responsible for their welfare. After World War II, the *ie* system as a legal entity was abolished and the Koseki Hō was amended to place more emphasis on the individual.

House of Councillors 参議院

(Sangiin). One of the two elective bodies (the HOUSE OF REPRESENTATIVES is the other) that make up the DIET, the legislative branch of the Japanese government. Under Japan's post–World War II constitution, the House of Councillors replaced the hereditary, appointive House of Peers, which had been established under the Meiji Constitution of 1889. Although the House of Councillors and the House of Representatives share power, the latter predominates in decisions on legislation, designation of the prime minister, budgetary matters, and international treaties. Every three years, half of the 252 representatives in the House of Councillors are elected by popular vote to a six-year term of office that is not terminated in the event of dissolution of the House of Representatives. One hundred of the seats are filled on a proportional representation system; the remaining 152 seats are filled on a system of prefectural districts. See also REAPPORTIONMENT ISSUE.

House of Peers 貴族院

(Kizokuin). One of two legislative chambers of the IMPERIAL DIET as mandated by the 1889

Meiji Constitution. Membership was by appointment. It was composed of adult males of the imperial family, heads of the hereditary PEERAGE, and other imperial nominees that included certain of the nation's biggest taxpayers and a few illustrious scholars. Males of the imperial family became members at 20 (the Crown Prince at 18) years of age, while all other members were required to be 30 or older. Moreover, while princes, marquis, and some imperial nominees were granted lifetime membership, the rest were appointed to seven-year terms. The house thus represented the ruling class and functioned as a conservative check on the popularly elected House of Representatives. The House of Peers was superseded by the House of Councillors under the 1947 constitution.

House of Representatives 衆議院

(Shūgiin). The lower house of Japan's supreme legislative body, the national DIET. According to the provisions of the CONSTITUTION OF JAPAN, the House of Representatives and its collective decisions take precedence over the upper house (the HOUSE OF COUNCILLORS) in the areas of legislation, the budget, treaty ratification, and the selection of the prime minister. The representatives, who have numbered 512 since May 1986, are elected by popular vote. Their term of office is four years, unless the House has been dissolved before their term has elapsed. In recent years the average term of office has actually been about three years.

housewives 主婦

(shufu). Being a housewife is still the most widely expected and most socially approved role for a Japanese woman; it is generally seen as a respected job requiring the skill, training, and devotion of a full-time professional. Modernization since the Meiji Restoration of 1868 and democratization following World War II have brought many changes to the lives of Japanese women, but the importance of the housewife as mother, as nurturing caretaker of the family, has not changed.

Traditional Confucian-inspired rules requiring a woman to be subservient to her father, her husband, or her son have been displaced by the post–World War II constitution, which proclaims legal equality of the sexes. The small nuclear family has become common, so daughters-in-law have generally been freed from bondage to their mothers-in-law. Modern technology allows housewives to spend less time on household chores; time is available to pursue part-time jobs, traditional hobbies like tea ceremony and flower arranging, or newer activities like sports or participation in volunteer and community-service activities such as the CONSUMER MOVEMENT. Because of widespread FAMILY PLANNING, the norm is now one or two children per couple. Despite these changes, the essential nature of the housewife's role remains the same. A large majority of women keep to the traditional ideal of "the good wife and wise mother" (ryōsai kembo). The Japanese still call a wife okusan (referring to someone else's wife) or kanai (referring to one's own wife), both terms meaning the one inside the house.

Yet it must be noted that over half of all married women are also employed in some other way as well (see WOMEN IN THE LABOR FORCE). Moreover, although the husband is the nominal head of the household the sexual division of labor gives the housewife autonomy in her own sphere. She is effectively in charge of family finances as well as housekeeping, child rearing, and educational planning. The husband typically turns his paycheck over to his wife, who then does the shopping and budgeting and even gives her husband his spending allowance.

Today some Japanese housewives are pushing for shared household chores, more companionship with their husbands, and more equality in employment opportunities, but most housewives still prefer to protect their autonomy and control over their homes. They value the lifetime security of a stable family system with little threat of divorce and take pride in their central role in the family. See also FAMILY; WOMEN, RURAL.

Housing and Urban Development Corporation 住宅・都市整備公団

(Jūtaku Toshi Seibi Kōdan). Special corporation whose purpose is to accelerate the supply of housing and residential land for middle-income people as well as to undertake urban development and redevelopment. The Housing and Urban Development Corporation (HUDC) was established in 1981 as a government agency under the Housing and Urban Development Corporation Law with the amalgamation of Japan Housing Corporation and the New Town Development Public Corporation. The Japan Housing Corporation had been created in 1955 to provide inexpensive apartment complexes for workers in districts lacking adequate housing. Following the oil crisis of 1973, land prices soared and the proposed complexes were forced farther from places of work. Rents rose, housing became constricted, and in 1975 the New Town Development Public Corporation was established and began building comprehensive, multifunctional communities. As of March 1989 HUDC and its two predecessor corporations had supplied a total of 1.3 million housing units and developed more than 43,000 hectares of land since 1955. The corporation's staff numbers 5,000. It was capitalized at ¥103.4 billion ($753.6 million) as of March 1991.

housing, history of 住宅史

(jūtakushi). The history of housing in Japan reflects two primary factors: the requisites of indigenous climatic conditions, land formation, and natural occurrences (such as earthquakes and typhoons), and successive encounters with the architecture and construction methods of foreign cultures. In premodern times, influence from China, Korea, and India was transmitted largely through religious institutions and then assimilated into traditional housing styles. In modern times, the influence of Europe and the United States has been dominant.

Prehistoric Dwellings—The first known Japanese dwellings were the PIT HOUSES (tateana) that were inhabited by people of the Jōmon period (ca 10,000 BC–ca 300 BC). According to archaeological evidence, Jōmon dwellings were constructed over a shallow rectangular pit, from which slanting rafters rose directly to support lintel beams. The rafters themselves formed both the frame of the house and the roof. The roof was covered with bark and grass, and open ridges allowed smoke to escape. See also JŌMON CULTURE.

Around 300 BC the Yayoi people appeared. Unlike the Jōmon—who, though now believed to have been of the same ethnic origin, were essentially hunting tribes— the people of the Yayoi period (ca 300 BC–ca AD 300) engaged in agriculture and had an organized architectural system. Archaeological evidence shows that the Yayoi people created an elevated-floor (takayuka) structure that was originally used as a granary, probably because it served to protect crops from humidity and from animals. In this stable society, there evolved a noble class who may have gradually taken to using the granaries as dwellings (see STOREHOUSES, TRADITIONAL). Around the 5th century AD, the takayuka dwelling with a balcony appeared. The elevated floor became a fundamental element of the Japanese house and has remained unchanged apart from some refinement. See also YAYOI CULTURE.

Clay house models excavated from the mounded tombs (KOFUN) of noble chieftains of the Kofun period (ca 300–710) attest to the existence of katsuogi, or wooden logs attached to the roof ridge of noble dwellings. An architectural symbol of distinction, this was later restricted to imperial architecture and Shintō shrines. Large windows found in some of the excavated clay models might have been developed originally for taking in light for inside work and for emitting smoke from an inside hearth.

Ancient Religious Influence—Shintō beliefs were already widespread when written history began late in the Kofun period. Deities, human beings, and objects in nature were thought to be closely interrelated; Shintō shrines were considered the residences of deities and were always located in natural surroundings, often around rocks and trees, believed to have a divine spirit (kami). Shintō buildings are constructed of hinoki (Japanese cypress), which is planed smooth and left unpainted, relying upon the absolute purity of the material for its effect. Strips of hinoki bark are used for roofing. The preference for natural surfaces remains one of the main characteristics of residential buildings in modern Japan. See also SHINTŌ ARCHITECTURE.

With the introduction of Buddhism around the 6th century, Buddhist temples were imported from China, bringing new elements of grandeur to Shintō architecture, such as decorative brass ornaments on a balustrade or steps. Surviving monuments of the Nara period (710–794) include the Hokkedō of TŌDAIJI (733), the Yumedono of HŌRYŪJI (739), and the SHŌSŌIN (756), all in Nara. See BUDDHIST ARCHITECTURE.

Emergence of Residential Styles—During the Heian period (794–1185) the cultural connection with China was temporarily severed, leading to the emergence of the first Japanese style of residential court dwelling—SHINDEN-ZUKURI. The essential features of this style are the placement of individual halls around a central main hall (moya) with interconnecting corridors, and the asymmetric positioning of the building complex in an elaborate garden. See GARDENS.

In the Kamakura period (1185–1333) the samurai regime reestablished cultural ties with China, which brought the introduction of Zen Buddhism. Zen doctrines held that discipline and simplicity were required in order to exist harmoniously with nature, a belief that yielded a domestic architecture that is aesthetically straightforward and organic. The elements of Zen Buddhist buildings were gradually adapted in the secular residences of the nobility and warrior class.

The gradual transformation of shinden-zukuri continued into the Muromachi period (1333–1568), when Kyōto again became the

Trends in Japanese Housing

Type of dwelling	1968	1973	1978	1983	1988
	(percentage of all households)				
Detached houses	66.5	64.8	65.1	64.3	62.3
Town houses[1]	14.7	12.3	9.6	8.3	6.7
Apartments in buildings less than three stories high	13.7	14.1	13.0	11.6	11.6
Apartments in buildings three stories and higher	4.7	8.4	11.7	15.3	18.9
Other[2]	0.3	0.4	0.5	0.5	0.5

[1]Rows of dwellings that share at least one wall with their neighbors.
[2]Includes dwellings that are part of factories or office buildings.
SOURCE: Economic Planning Agency, *Kokumin seikatsu hakusho* (annual): 1990.

political center of Japan under a samurai regime. A new residential style, called SHOIN-ZUKURI, included the TOKONOMA (a decorative alcove, with *chigai-dana* or staggered shelves) and the *shoin* (study-alcove). Chinese architectural features such as the raked roof, roof tiles, and portable screens were also adopted and modified and refined over time. The portable screen of Chinese origin, for instance, was transformed into Japanese opaque sliding panels (*fusuma*).

Fundamental Elements of Japanese Architecture——The main structure, materials, and principles of Japanese architecture, even as it persists today, were fully established by the 16th century. A skeleton frame of wooden post-and-beam construction with an elaborate joinery system is the main feature of a Japanese house. The floor is raised above the ground, and its posts rest on foundation stone, not only to prevent moisture from rotting them but also to allow the entire structure to bounce during earthquakes.

Protruding eaves protect the structure from frequent rain, allowing winter sunlight to penetrate into the interior but blocking strong summer glare. SHŌJI or *shōji-do* (sliding doors; made of thin wood covered with translucent paper) allow diffuse daylight to illuminate the interior and maintain a sense of closeness with the outdoors. Interior space is partitioned by *shōji-do* or *fusuma* and sometimes by folding screens. TATAMI (straw mats) cover the floors; FUTON (sleeping quilts; see also BEDDING) are stored in an *oshiire* (closet) during the day. Without any large or specialized furniture, room functions are totally interchangeable. The *tokonoma* with a raised floorboard is the focal point of the *zashiki* (sitting room) and is reserved for the display of a hanging scroll (KAKEMONO), a flower arrangement, or a ceramic object.

In the Edo period (1600–1868) *kawarabuki yane* (tiled roofs) were extensively utilized in domestic architecture (see MINKA), especially after the development of a new tiling technique in the late 17th century that made less expensive tiling possible (see ROOF TILES). The main features of the Japanese house, however, remained largely in the form that had been developed by the Azuchi-Momoyama period (1568–1600).

Modern Housing——Japan was completely cut off from the West under the Tokugawa shogunate (1603–1867). With the reestablishment of Western contact during the Meiji period (1868–1912), new institutional buildings in the Western style (*yōkan*) began to be built in Japan. Houses in the Western style were built by some upper-class Japanese, some of whom had traveled to Europe or America. However, the majority of the Japanese continued to live in traditional houses.

Thorough modernization of Japanese housing occurred mainly after the end of World War II. In 1945 the shortage of houses in Japan was extreme because of wartime air raid destruction. Individual, single-family houses were mass-produced, and the concentration of population in the urban centers spurred the construction of apartments. Multistory apartments of concrete have been constructed at an unprecedented pace (see DANCHI). However, most new houses, including apartment buildings, have retained vestiges of traditional Japanese architecture. At the same time, new designs and housing plans have been developed by aspiring young architects. See also ARCHITECTURE, TRADITIONAL DOMESTIC; HOUSING, MODERN.

Housing Loan Service Co, Ltd

［株］住宅ローンサービス

(Jūtaku Rōn Sābisu). Finance company specializing in housing loans. It was incorporated in 1971 with capital participation from seven major city banks including DAI-ICHI KANGYŌ BANK, LTD; FUJI BANK, LTD; MITSUBISHI BANK, LTD; and SUMITOMO BANK, LTD. In March 1990, its loan balance totaled ¥1.3 trillion (US $8.5 billion) and capitalization stood at ¥5.4 billion (US $35.3 million). Headquarters are in Tōkyō.

housing, modern

現代の住まい

(*gendai no sumai*). Housing in Japan has changed dramatically in the past century as a result of rapid urbanization, population pressures, changes in family and social relationships, and the influence of Western architecture. Especially in large cities, multiunit dwellings have become the norm, although the majority of people still aspire to own their homes.

In 1988 there were 42,007,300 housing units in Japan, of which 37,413,400 were permanently occupied units, with an average of 3.2 persons per unit, and the remainder were second houses, resort condominiums, and so forth. Of the total, 62.3 percent were single-family units and 37.7 percent multiple-unit dwellings. Of the single-family units, 80.8 percent were owned and 10.2 percent rented; of the multiple-unit dwellings, 15.1 percent were owned and 79.4 percent rented.

The Modern Japanese House——There has been a progressive shrinking of the living space available to the middle-class household, from an average total floor space of 165 square meters (1,776 sq ft) at the turn of the century to 100 square meters (1,076 sq ft) by the beginning of the Shōwa period (1926–89), and by 1988 average total floor space had shrunk to 89 square meters (958 sq ft). In the 1980s this trend was exacerbated by the rapid rise in the cost of land, which forced would-be homeowners into the suburbs and into the market for small *tateuri jūtaku* (developer-built houses). Large tracts of *tateuri jūtaku* housing have become a common sight within a two-hour commuting distance of major urban centers such as Tōkyō, Ōsaka, and Nagoya.

Whether built by the owner on his or her own property or by a developer, the two-story detached house with a tiled roof, a small (sometimes tiny) ornamental garden enclosed by a high stone wall or hedge, and garage space for the family automobile remains the ideal for the majority of Japanese. Such houses are basically wooden structures with overlaid plaster walls. The average total floor area in a house built by a salaried worker about 40 years of age is about 115.48 square meters (1,242 sq ft). There is a dining room–kitchen, two or three Japanese-style rooms with TATAMI mats, and one or two Western-style rooms with carpeted, tiled, or wooden floors.

Passage through traditional houses was from room to room rather than along a corridor. Rooms were separated by sliding screens and sliding doors (SHŌJI and *fusuma*), which allowed for a more flexible multipurpose use of the rooms than is possible in Western houses, in which rooms tend to have fixed functions. The introduction of Western features such as corridors, hinged rather than sliding doors, Western-style furniture, and beds has tended to make many modern Japanese houses more compartmentalized and somewhat more private than traditional houses. Eighty percent of all newly constructed single-family dwellings have Western-style toilets and living or dining rooms; the entry (*genkan*) of 60 percent has Western-style doors rather than sliding doors. However, since almost 90 percent of these new houses also have a traditional Japanese TOKONOMA (alcove), it is clear that many Japanese prefer a blend of Japanese and Western styles. Modern elements are common in urban areas, while rural homes often retain the multifunctional rooms of the old style. Rural homes tend to be larger, reflecting the lower price of land in rural areas, and ceremonial functions still take place at home there rather than in restaurants or community buildings.

Multiunit Dwellings——Overall, multiunit dwellings increased to 52.8 percent of total housing constructed from 1986 to 1988. Wood-construction rental apartments (*mokuzō chintai apāto*) continue to be a widespread form of multiunit housing. The earlier small units had shared kitchens and toilets, but in recent years the majority of apartments of this type have private kitchen and toilet facilities.

The first American-style apartment house (*apāto*) in Japan may have been the Bunka Apartment (1925) in the Ochanomizu area of Tōkyō. The apartments built by the Dōjunkai (Mutual Benefit Association), formed after the Tōkyō Earthquake of 1923 to provide housing for victims of the quake (see DŌJUNKAI APARTMENTS), made Western-style accommodations widely available to the middle class. A typical unit had two rooms with a small kitchen and an average floor space of 33 square meters (355 sq ft). Apartment houses became increasingly popular in the 1930s, because they symbolized progress and offered convenience, better sanitation and maintenance, and greater protection from fire, earthquakes, and burglaries. Many early apartments were of wood construction; reinforced-concrete apartment buildings came into their own only after World War II.

In 1955 the Japan Housing Corporation (JHC; see HOUSING AND URBAN DEVELOPMENT CORPORATION) was established, and apartment buildings and housing projects (DANCHI) became a familiar sight in Japan. The JHC standardized apartment layouts, introducing the concept of the dining room–kitchen ("dining-kitchen"; DK), a space of about 8 square meters (86 sq ft) used for both cooking and dining. This soon became a popular feature.

The most common unit in early JHC housing was the 2DK, or two rooms and the dining-kitchen area; in such apartments one of the rooms would serve as a living room during the day. An enlarged DK is called an LDK, or living room–dining-kitchen area. The emphasis in recent JHC housing has been on 3DK and 3LDK units.

In addition to the publicly subsidized *danchi* apartments, there are a great number of mid- to high-rise buildings constructed by private developers since the 1960s; these have individual units for sale or rent and are known as *manshon* (the English word "mansion" was borrowed to distinguish them from the more spartan 1960s public *danchi* apartment buildings). Townhouses—basically, connected rows of single-unit, rather more expensive dwellings—are an increasingly popular alternative to apartment dwelling.

From the standpoint of affordability, the housing situation continues to worsen, especially in Tōkyō and other large cities. Land prices are rising drastically throughout most of the country, although prices in the Tōkyō area, which skyrocketed in the mid-1980s, have stabilized somewhat since 1989 (see HOUSING PROBLEMS). High land prices are blamed for increases in housing construction costs and rents and for the increase in construction of one-room apartments (50 percent of new rental apartments built in Tōkyō in 1987 consisted of one room or one room plus a dining-kitchen). The average floor space of all types of urban dwellings continues to shrink, and people are going far out into the suburbs in search of affordable housing. New "bed-towns" continue to spring up on the fringes of Tōkyō; in 1990 they accounted for 25.7 percent of the metropolitan area population. Not just a Tōkyō problem, the drastic increase in land costs is also causing major difficulties for Ōsaka, Nagoya, and other Japanese cities. See also ARCHITECTURE, MODERN; ARCHITECTURE, TRADITIONAL DOMESTIC; HOUSING, HISTORY OF.

☎ 574–575

housing problems 住宅問題

(*jūtaku mondai*). Urban housing problems in Japan arose as the country entered the stage of industrialization and urbanization around 1900. Before the end of World War II, no public measures were taken except for emergency housing after the Tōkyō Earthquake of 1923 and wartime housing for military procurement.

In the 1950s three major pieces of legislation on housing established a general framework for Japanese housing policy. The GOVERNMENT HOUSING LOAN CORPORATION (Jūtaku Kin'yū Kōko) founded in 1950 was a means of channeling public funds for low-interest, long-term loans for owner-occupied housing. Under the Public Housing Law (Kōei Jūtaku Hō) of 1951 local authorities were empowered to build public housing for rental to low-income households with subsidies from the central government. Finally, the Japan Housing Corporation (Nihon Jūtaku Kōdan; see HOUSING AND URBAN DEVELOPMENT CORPORATION) was founded in 1955 as a public nonprofit developer to supply housing units for urban dwellers.

In 1966 the Housing Construction Planning Law (Jūtaku Kensetsu Keikaku Hō) was enacted to coordinate public policy measures for housing. The act mandated that the central government formulate five-year comprehensive housing construction plans at five-year intervals starting in 1966. The first Five-Year Housing Construction Plan aimed at achieving "one housing unit for one household" in five years by constructing a total of 6.7 million housing units.

The second Housing Construction Plan, initiated in 1971, aimed at achieving "one room for each member of the household." Although the plan was to construct 9.6 million housing units in five years, only 8.26 million units were actually built.

The third Housing Construction Plan, approved in 1976, stated explicitly that the main priority of housing policy should be shifted from an emphasis on quantity to the improvement of quality. The purpose of the fourth Housing Construction Plan, begun in 1981, was to continue to improve housing quality, especially in urban areas.

High prices for land have forced many people to buy housing at a considerable distance from their workplaces. The rise in residential land prices in the Tōkyō metropolitan region has been particularly explosive: in 1988 the average price increase was 68.6 percent over the previous year. In all of Japan's intensely crowded urban areas it is becoming increasingly difficult for the average "salaryman" or wage-earner to purchase a single-family dwelling. Multistory buildings with individual units for sale, similar to condominiums in the United States, have become the standard form of urban housing.

The fifth Housing Construction Plan (1986–91) set forth a number of guidelines, including new standards for residential housing floor space and facilities. Other issues also remain, including the problems of the nearly 24.5 percent of all Japanese families who live in substandard private rental housing, as well as the difficulties faced by the aged, the handicapped, and other socially disadvantaged members of Japanese society in securing adequate housing. See also STANDARD OF LIVING; HOUSING, MODERN.

Hōya 保谷[市]

City in northern Tōkyō Prefecture, contiguous with Nerima Ward. With the construction of many housing projects, Hōya has become a dormitory suburb for nearby Tōkyō. Pop: 95,146.

Hōya Corporation ホーヤ[株]

(Hōya). Major manufacturer of optical glass. Incorporated in 1944. The company also produces crystal glassware and glass products for the manufacture of integrated circuits. Hōya maintains worldwide production and sales networks for eyeglasses. Manufacturing facilities are located in the United States, Australia, Thailand, and Europe. Sales for the fiscal year ending March 1991 totaled ¥109.9 billion (US $801.0 million), and capitalization stood at ¥5.7 billion (US $41.5 million). Headquarters are in Tōkyō.

Ho Ying-ch'in → He Yingqin (Ho Ying-ch'in)

Hōyo Strait → Hayasui Strait

Hozugawa 保津川

River in Kyōto Prefecture, central Honshū. A section of a longer river that originates in the Tamba Mountains and flows into the river YODOGAWA in the Kyōto Basin. The Hozugawa is that part of the river between Kameoka and Arashiyama. The upper reaches, above Kameoka, are called the Ōigawa, and the lower reaches, from Arashiyama, are called the KATSURAGAWA. Length: 12 km (7 mi).

hōzuki 酸漿

1. The ground cherry or Chinese-lantern plant (*Physalis alkekengi*) of the potato family (Solanaceae).

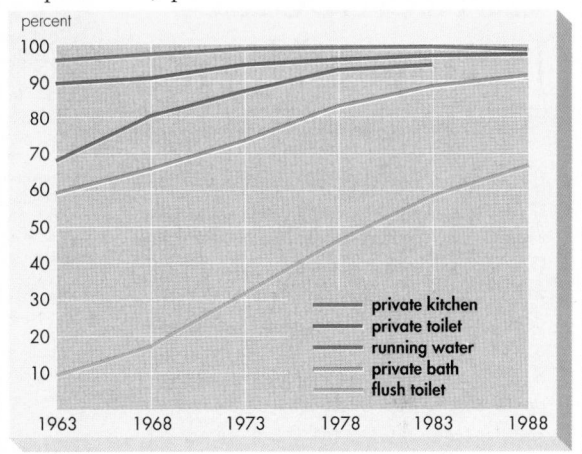

Year	Total number of housing units (millions)	Average size of housing unit	
		Number of rooms*	Total area (square meters)
1963	21.09	3.82	72.52
1968	25.59	3.84	73.86
1973	31.06	4.15	77.14
1978	35.45	4.52	80.28
1983	38.61	4.73	85.92
1988	42.01	4.86	89.29

Housing Units in Japan — housing problems

*Does not include bathrooms. Kitchens are included only when their total floor space, excluding sink, is 5 square meters or more.
SOURCE: Ministry of Construction, *Nippon no jūtaku to kenchiku* (annual): 1991.

Proportion of Japanese Homes with Modern Facilities

percent

— private kitchen
— private toilet
— running water
— private bath
— flush toilet

NOTE: Data for running water was not collected in the 1988 survey.
SOURCE: Ministry of Construction, *Nippon no jūtaku to kenchiku* (annual): 1991.

2. A noisemaking toy improvised from the fruit of the Chinese-lantern plant. The noisemaker (traditionally a toy for girls) is made by taking the cherrylike fruit from its lantern-shaped pod and kneading it carefully until soft. The pulp and seeds are removed through a small hole, and the empty skin is then pressed between the tongue and the roof of the mouth to make a squeaking noise. Imitations of this toy were made from the egg pouches of shellfish (the so-called *umi hōzuki*), and manufactured versions have been made of rubber or other substances. See also HŌZUKI ICHI.

hōzuki ichi 酸漿市

Fair at which HŌZUKI (Chinese lantern plants) are sold; held at the temple Asakusa Kannon in Tōkyō on 10 July. This fair is also known as Shimanrokusennichi ("46,000 days") because one visit to the temple on this particular day is said to be as meritorious as 46,000 ordinary visits. During the Edo period (1600–1868) the fair drew throngs who came to pray and to purchase not only *hōzuki*, but

Continued on page 576 ►

hōzuki ichi Customers select *hōzuki* (Chinese lantern plants) at this fair held every July in Tōkyō. Among their various decorative functions, the plants are used for adorning altars during the Buddhist Bon Festival.

A Look into a Contemporary Japanese Home

Private homes and massive apartment blocks stand side by side in Japan. A house of one's own has long been the ideal, but overpopulation and astronomical land prices have made apartment living the only choice for many Japanese.

Modern Japanese houses have been shaped by the climate, the aristocratic tastes of an earlier age, and the American Dream. With their steep, tiled roofs and protruding eaves, houses are designed to provide comfort and shelter from Japan's abundant rainfall and scorching summers. Other traditional features, including sliding doors, *tokonoma*, *tatami* floor mats, and a reliance on wood as the primary building material, are remnants of the influence of Japan's old ruling class and its residential style. In today's homes, the traditional elements coexist with Western features—living rooms, combination kitchen-dining rooms, and separate bedrooms for parents and children—that attest to postwar Japan's enthusiasm for the housing style prevalent in the United States.

Compared to contemporary American houses, however, which have an average 188 square meters (2,018 sq ft) of floor space, the modern Japanese house is quite small—a mere 127 square meters (1,363 sq ft) on average. Single-family housing had been a part of rural life even before World War II, but it was the image of American suburbia, widely glorified in the postwar era, that led to the profusion of freestanding, privately owned homes in Japan, even in urban areas. Today the incorporation of sophisticated electronic appliances, an offshoot of remarkable industrial growth, is again changing Japanese homes.

Miyawaki Mayumi

Bath and toilet. It has long been the custom in Japan for the toilet and bathtub to be located in separate rooms, and even today this arrangement is far more prevalent than the one-room Western-style bathroom.

Tatami room. Most Japanese houses have at least one room done in the traditional style, with *tatami* flooring and sliding doors. Originally thought of as a place to practice traditional arts like the tea ceremony or as a formal guest room, nowadays it may be converted into a bedroom for the grandparents.

Oshiire. A standard feature of *tatami* rooms, this spacious built-in closet is primarily designed to hold bedding but can also be used to store a variety of other items.

Tokonoma. This alcove, virtually the only decorative element in the otherwise austerely furnished *tatami* room, reflects the influence of Zen on domestic architecture. The items displayed here—calligraphy, flower arrangements, and traditional works of art—vary according to the season.

Butsudan. Nearly every Japanese household reserves space, preferably in a *tatami* room, for a Buddhist altar where prayers can be offered to the family ancestors. Many homes also have a small Shintō altar.

Engawa. This characteristic feature of Japanese domestic architecture—once an open veranda—has gradually been incorporated into the interior of the house.

Shoe cabinet. Since street shoes are not worn inside the house, every Japanese home has a cupboard for shoes, usually located just inside the front door.

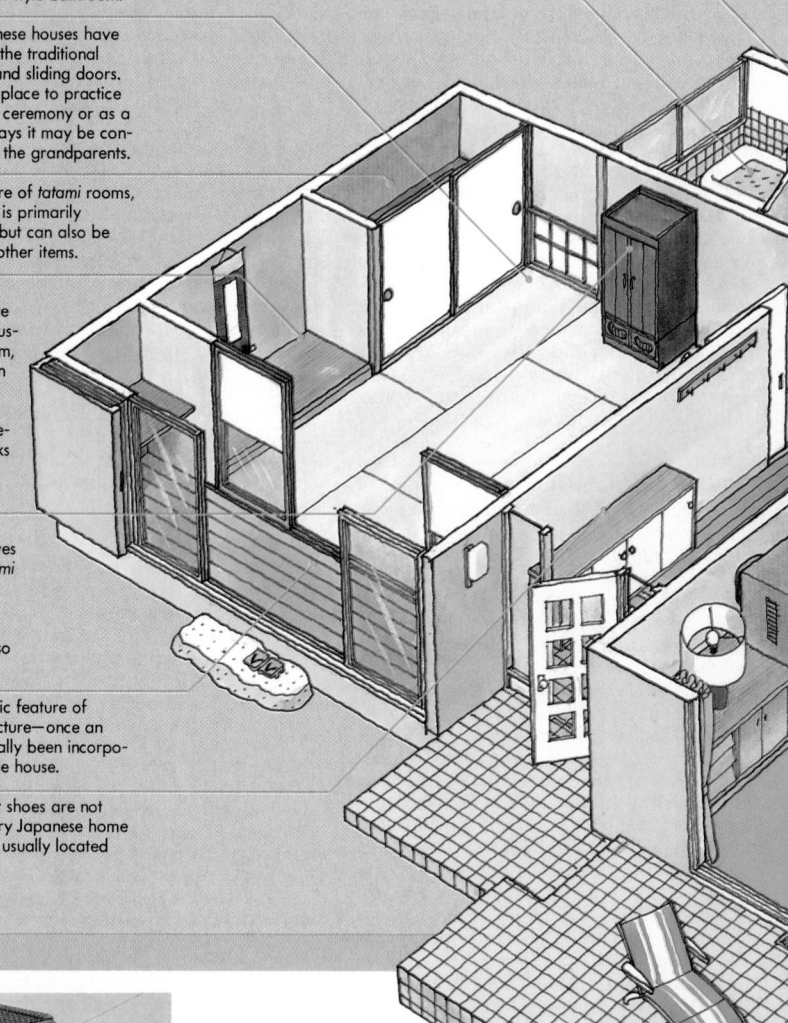

The exterior of this single-family house reveals a mixture of styles—traditional terra cotta roof tiles and modern brickwork.

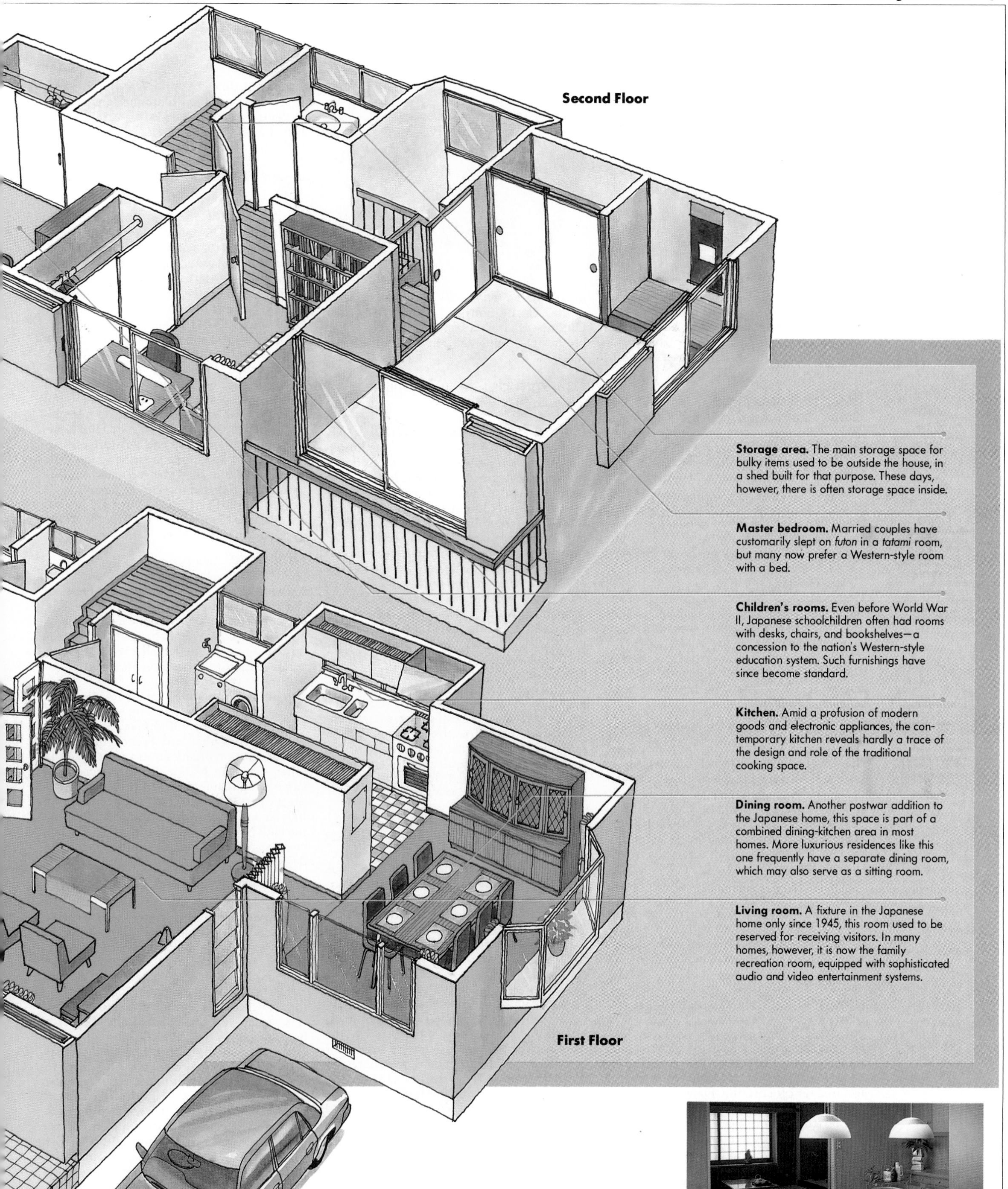

Second Floor

Storage area. The main storage space for bulky items used to be outside the house, in a shed built for that purpose. These days, however, there is often storage space inside.

Master bedroom. Married couples have customarily slept on *futon* in a *tatami* room, but many now prefer a Western-style room with a bed.

Children's rooms. Even before World War II, Japanese schoolchildren often had rooms with desks, chairs, and bookshelves—a concession to the nation's Western-style education system. Such furnishings have since become standard.

Kitchen. Amid a profusion of modern goods and electronic appliances, the contemporary kitchen reveals hardly a trace of the design and role of the traditional cooking space.

Dining room. Another postwar addition to the Japanese home, this space is part of a combined dining-kitchen area in most homes. More luxurious residences like this one frequently have a separate dining room, which may also serve as a sitting room.

Living room. A fixture in the Japanese home only since 1945, this room used to be reserved for receiving visitors. In many homes, however, it is now the family recreation room, equipped with sophisticated audio and video entertainment systems.

First Floor

A hybrid design is the hallmark of many Japanese homes. In this house one passes directly from a Western-style dining room into a traditionally furnished *tatami* room.

Illustration by Hozumi Kazuo

575

Hyakunin isshu This 13th-century poetry anthology is the basis for a card game called *uta karuta*, which has been popular since the Edo period.
1 A famous *uta karuta* competition is held each year on 3 January at the Yasaka Shrine in Kyōto, with the participants clad in traditional Japanese court dress.
2 Two sets of cards are used in *uta karuta*. The complete texts of 31-syllable *waka* poems are inscribed on one set. As these are read aloud, players try to match the concluding lines, which are inscribed on cards of the other set.

also ears of corn, used to ward off thunder and lightning; the cosmetic used by women to blacken their teeth; and bamboo tea whisks. The potted plants are placed inside bamboo baskets to which WIND-BELLS (*fūrin*) are attached.

Hozumi Nobushige   穂積陳重

(1856–1926). Scholar of legal history and drafter of the CIVIL CODE. Born in what is now Ehime Prefecture. Hozumi studied at Kaisei Gakkō (now Tōkyō University) and from 1876 to 1881 in England and Germany. As a professor at Tōkyō University from 1881 onward, he actively promoted the study of German law. In 1888 he became Japan's first doctor of laws (*hōgaku hakushi*). With UME KENJIRŌ and TOMII MASAAKI he drafted the Civil Code of 1898. He was appointed to the House of Peers in 1890 and to the Privy Council in 1916, becoming president of the latter body in 1925. His writings include *Goningumi seido ron* (1921, On the Goningumi System) and *Hōritsu shinka ron* (1924–27, Theory of the Evolution of Law). He was a brother of the constitutional scholar HOZUMI YATSUKA and the father of legal scholar HOZUMI SHIGETŌ.

Hozumi Shigetō   穂積重遠

(1883–1951). Legal scholar. Born in Tōkyō, the son of HOZUMI NOBUSHIGE and nephew of HOZUMI YATSUKA, both distinguished scholars of law. He graduated from Tōkyō University in 1908 and taught there until his retirement as dean of the law faculty in 1943. He specialized primarily in the family-law provisions of the CIVIL CODE. His academic works include *Rikon seido no kenkyū* (1924, Studies on Divorce Law), *Shinzokuhō* (1933, Family Law), and *Sōzokuhō* (1946, Inheritance Law). Hozumi also wrote popular books on the law, such as *Hyakumannin no hōritsugaku* (1950, Law for the Millions). He was appointed to the Supreme Court in 1949.

Hozumi Yatsuka   穂積八束

(1860–1912). Scholar of constitutional law. Born in what is now Ehime Prefecture, he graduated from Tōkyō University in 1883 and studied at the University of Strasbourg under Paul Laband (1838–1918) from 1884 to 1888. As a professor at Tōkyō University he lectured on constitutional law from 1889 to 1912 and served as chairman of the Faculty of Law from 1897 to 1911. Hozumi's theories on the constitution supported and strengthened imperial sovereignty. An enemy of parliamentary government, he opposed giving political parties power over both legislation and administration. A defender of Japan's traditional virtues, he criticized the original draft (1890) of the Civil Code, based on the French model, saying that its enactment would mean "the death of loyalty and filial piety" (see CIVIL CODE CONTROVERSY). His writ-

ings include *Kempō taii* (1896, The Essence of the Constitution) and *Kempō teiyō* (1910, Outline of the Constitution). His older brother was the legal scholar HOZUMI NOBUSHIGE.

Hsin-min Hui → Xinmin Hui
(Hsin-min Hui)

Huang Xing (Huang Hsing)   黄興

(1874–1916; J: Kō Kō). Chinese revolutionary. Along with SUN YAT-SEN, cofounder of the United League (Tongmeng Hui or T'ung-meng Hui) and leader of the overthrow of the Manchu Qing (Ch'ing) dynasty in 1911. As a student in Tōkyō from 1902 to 1903 Huang met a number of anti-Manchu students. Returning to Hunan, he founded the Huaxing Hui (Hua-hsing Hui; Society for the Revival of China). After a failed uprising he returned to Tōkyō, where he met Sun Yat-sen through MIYAZAKI TŌTEN, a Japanese sympathizer with the Chinese revolutionary cause. In 1905 they formed the Tongmeng Hui. In 1913 Huang and Sun led an unsuccessful revolt against YUAN SHIKAI (Yüan Shih-k'ai), who had become president of the new Chinese republic after the 1911 Revolution and whose rule was becoming increasingly authoritarian. Forced to flee to Japan, Huang broke with Sun over the latter's insistence on an oath of personal loyalty from all members of his newly organized (July 1914) Chinese Revolutionary Party.

Huang Zunxian (Huang Tsun-hsien)   黄遵憲

(1848–1905; J: Kō Junken). Chinese diplomat, reformer, poet, and author of a book about Japan that was the chief source of information on the Meiji-period (1868–1912) reforms for the Chinese reformers of the 1890s. In 1877 Huang was appointed counselor to the Chinese legation in Tōkyō. He remained in Japan until 1882 and wrote the *Riben guozhi* (*Jih-pen kuo-chih*, 1887), a political history of Japan from the Meiji Restoration (1868) to 1882 that praised both Japan's selective adoption of Western institutions and the FREEDOM AND PEOPLE'S RIGHTS MOVEMENT of the 1880s. Huang's history of Japan had a great impact on those Chinese of the late Qing (Ching) period (1644–1912) who sought reform of the imperial system, such as KANG YOUWEI (K'ang Yu-wei) and LIANG QICHAO (Liang Ch'i-ch'ao).

Hukbalahap   フクバラハップ

(J: Fukubarahappu). Abbreviation for the Hukbo ng Bayan Laban sa Hapon (Tagalog for People's Anti-Japanese Army) of World War II or its postwar successor, Hukbong Mapagpalaya ng Bayan (HMB; People's Liberation Army). Commonly called "the Huks." It was first organized on 29 March 1942 as the Army of the Communist Party of the Philippines. Under the leadership of Luis Taruc (b 1913), the Huks fought 1,200 en-

gagements during World War II with Japanese forces and the Philippine constabulary in central Luzon. The HMB's activities declined after a peak in 1949–51, when membership was estimated at between 12,000 and 20,000. Taruc surrendered in 1954, and the organization became inactive by the mid-1960s.

Hull, Cordell   ハル, C.

(1871–1955). US political leader and secretary of state (1933–44). Born in Tennessee, he received a law degree from Cumberland University in 1891. Hull belonged to the Democratic Party, representing his district in the US House of Representatives for 22 years (1907–21; 1923–31) and in the Senate (1931–33) until he was appointed secretary of state by President Franklin D. Roosevelt in 1933. He improved US relations with Latin America by implementing the "Good Neighbor Policy." Before the outbreak of World War II in 1941, Hull handled the delicate negotiations with Japan. In the so-called Hull Note, he strongly supported the territorial integrity of China and urged Japan to abandon its military conquests. The uncompromising tone of his note led directly to Japan's decision to attack Pearl Harbor. In 1945 he was awarded the Nobel Peace Prize for his efforts in organizing the United Nations.

Hull Note   ハル・ノート

(Haru Nōto). Diplomatic documents produced in the course of negotiations between the United States and Japan on the eve of World War II; delivered to the Japanese government on 26 November 1941 by US Secretary of State Cordell Hull (1871–1955), it summed up the US position on the issues dividing the two countries.

The Hull Note called for the conclusion of a nonaggression treaty among the nations of the Pacific region, withdrawal of Japanese forces from China and French Indochina, nonrecognition of any government in China other than the Nationalist government in Chongqing (Chungking), and abrogation of the Tripartite Pact of Japan, Germany, and Italy. The Japanese government interpreted the Hull Note as an ultimatum and, in an imperial conference on 1 December, made the decision to go to war with the United States.

Hundred Regiment Offensive
百団大戦

(J: Hyakudan Taisen). Large-scale offensive by the Chinese communist Eighth Route Army and Shanxi (Shansi) New Army against Japanese forces in five northern provinces of China. Launched on 20 August 1940, the Hundred Regiment Offensive was the sole instance during the SINO-JAPANESE WAR OF 1937–1945 of a conventional offensive by the Chinese communists, who otherwise relied on guerrilla tactics against the Japanese. One of its major aims was to prove to the CHONGQING (CHUNGKING) GOVERNMENT the Chinese communists' ability to resist Japan in North China and thereby to dissuade Chongqing from negotiating a compromise peace with Japan. It was not until October that the Japanese regained the initiative. The Japanese responded to the offensive with harsh policies of punishment and destruction in North China that lasted through early 1943.

hunting   狩猟

(*shuryō*). Archaeological findings show that the early inhabitants of Japan lived by hunting and gathering. Nuts, fruits, wild boar, and deer were their staple foods. Later, when an agricultural economy was firmly established, hunting remained a livelihood only for those special small groups scattered in the mountains (see MATAGI). Hunting was also considered a method of martial training.

In modern times the number of birds and animals has diminished despite regulatory laws and administrative guidance. To solve this problem the Meiji government promulgated the Wildlife Hunting Law in 1873 and further established the Hunting Law in 1895. These regulations, however, proved powerless against the rising tide of modernization. In an effort to save some of Japan's wilderness from development, the law regarding Wildlife Protection and Hunting was enacted in 1963. This law requires a hunting license and limits hunting weapons, seasons, and areas. There are also limits on the variety and numbers of birds and animals that may be hunted.

The maximum possible hunting season fixed by law is from 15 October to 15 April (1 October to 31 January in Hokkaidō), but these dates may change from year to year. Permissible hunting equipment includes small firearms, snares, falcons, and bows and arrows.

hyakudo mairi   百度参り

The practice of going to a specially designated shrine or temple every day for 100 days to ensure that a prayer will be answered; also, the act of making 100 continuous circuits of the precincts of a shrine or temple. This custom originated in the Heian period (794–1185). Because of the belief that the prayer will not be answered if the worshiper is seen by others, hyakudo mairi usually take place in the early morning or late at night.

Hyakunin isshu   百人一首

(Single Poems by 100 Poets). Also known as the Ogura hyakunin isshu. Collection of 100 WAKA (31-syllable poems), each by a different poet, organized in roughly chronological order beginning with Emperor Tenji (626–671) and ending with retired emperor Juntoku (1197–1242). FUJIWARA NO SADAIE (Fujiwara no Teika) probably compiled the collection, although it may have been revised by his son FUJIWARA NO TAMEIE. The entry for 14 June 1235 in Teika's journal MEIGETSUKI (1180–1235, Bright Moon Diary) tells how Utsunomiya no Yoritsuna prevailed on Teika to write out single poems by 100 poets to decorate a set of sliding doors. If these poems became the Hyakunin isshu, the collection must date from between 1235 and 1241, the year of Teika's death. As the basis for the popular card game uta karuta (see PLAYING CARDS), the poems of the Hyakunin isshu have been memorized since the Edo period (1600–1868). The game is still widely played today.

Hyakurenshō   百練抄

Historical work compiled late in the 13th century; author unknown. Written in classical Chinese (KAMBUN), it covers the years 968 through 1259. The first 3 of the original 17 volumes are now missing. It is a valuable source for information about Kyōto during the early Kamakura period (1185–1333).

hyakushō   百姓

Term for peasants or farmers, particularly in reference to their social status. In ancient times this term was pronounced hyakusei or ōmitakara; it originally meant "people with family names" (it is written with Chinese characters that mean literally "the hundred names") and referred to those who worked in imperial rice fields (miyake). With the institution of the RITSURYŌ SYSTEM of government and the TAIKA REFORM of 645, hyakushō came to mean subjects of the sovereign (kōmin).

With the rise of private estates (SHŌEN) in the mid-Heian period (794–1185), the term hyakushō was generally reserved for free cultivators who worked on shōen or on public lands (kōryō or kokugaryō) and paid land taxes (NENGU) and other levies (KUJI). The term hyakushō connoted a social status distinguishable from the governing classes, such as court nobles and warriors, above and from others, such as bondsmen (GENIN), below.

Under the shōgun-daimyō system (BAKUHAN SYSTEM) established by the Tokugawa shogunate (1603–1867), the people were classified as warriors, farmers, artisans, or merchants (SHI-NŌ-KŌ-SHŌ), and hyakushō became synonymous with farmer or peasant. The burden of taxes fell heavily on the hyakushō during the Edo period (1600–1868), and more than 2,500 uprisings (HYAKUSHŌ IKKI) are recorded.

Since the Meiji Restoration (1868) and the abolition of the class system, the term hyakushō has been used for peasants or farmers in general. Today, however, nōka is the preferred term. See also LAND TAX REFORM OF 1873–1881.

hyakushō ikki   百姓一揆

(peasant uprisings). Popular uprisings and other forms of peasant defiance against government authorities during the Edo period (1600–1868). There were more than 2,600 recorded instances of hyakushō ikki that took place in every part of the country during over 260 years of Tokugawa rule. Statistics indicate that uprisings occurred more frequently during the latter half of the Edo period, with peak periods roughly corresponding to periods of famine and political uncertainty.

The hyakushō ikki of the early phase of Tokugawa rule usually took the form of mild resistance. Peasants would desert the land to avoid tax responsibilities or make direct (JIKISO) or indirect appeals to protest against economic burdens. More important, the peasant protests of the early period were initiated by influential members of the village, such as the village head, whose prestigious positions enabled them to incite the peasant masses to rise against the authorities. For example, an ikki involving more than 200 villages in the Sakura domain (now part of Chiba Prefecture) in the 1640s was led by village head SAKURA SŌGORŌ. The peasants protested the high land taxes and forced labor imposed by the daimyō of Sakura.

The hyakushō ikki that occurred after 1750 took on more complex features. First, the ikki often became violent and were larger, involving thousands of peasants from village communities under the jurisdiction of several domainal governments and the shogunate. Second, the ikki of this period were well organized and hence more effective in putting up resistance against the authorities. Third, and most important, peasants planned and executed these ikki themselves, thus taking the initiative away from the village officials. Finally, the rebellious peasants of this period not only attacked the government authorities but also set upon merchants and other privileged

Period	Number of uprisings		
1590–1600	34	1731–40	86
1601–10	35	1741–50	130
1611–20	60	1751–60	116
1621–30	45	1761–70	108
1631–40	38	1771–80	78
1641–50	30	1781–90	229
1651–60	36	1791–1800	122
1661–70	42	1801–10	98
1671–80	44	1811–20	166
1681–90	46	1821–30	133
1691–1700	40	1831–40	279
1701–10	55	1841–50	129
1711–20	73	1851–60	170
1721–30	70	1861–67	194
		Total	**2,686**

Peasant Uprisings, 1590-1867   **hyakushō ikki**

SOURCE: Aoki Kōji, Hyakushō ikki no nenjiteki kenkyū (1966).

segments of rural communities for rent-gouging, loan-sharking, and other exploitive practices.

Development of Political Ikki—Peasant uprisings that occurred during the post-1830 period were often started by peasants to bring about political reforms within the village organization, such as the dismissal of corrupt local officials, although economic motivations were still important. For example, the ikki in the Chōshū domain (now Yamaguchi Prefecture) in the 1830s occurred because villagers wanted to dismiss the incumbent village head and introduce a more democratic procedure permitting the election of village officials. In other ikki rebels challenged village authorities by burning the land registers and other tax-related documents.

Both the shogunate and domainal governments quickly perceived the changed nature of these uprisings and tried to deal with them by adopting stronger measures. For example, in 1769 the shogunate issued a directive to local officials specifying ways to suppress ikki within its own domain (TENRYŌ). In another directive issued in 1770, the shogunate stressed the need to coordinate the military forces of various domains in the event of large-scale uprisings transcending their respective boundaries.

The peasants' resistance had become a formidable threat that obliged shogunal and domainal governments to reassess traditional tactics and to adopt a series of unprecedented measures, such as the use of combined military forces, to quell the rebellions. Marxist and non-Marxist scholars of the 20th century disagree on whether or not the peasant uprisings were revolutionary in design, but there is no disagreement over the complexity of their role in social change during the Edo period. See also YONAOSHI REBELLIONS; UCHIKOWASHI.

hyakushōuke   百姓請

(peasant tax contracts). Also called jigeuke. A form of tax farming developed in the 14th century in which the whole populace of a village or its representatives, such as MYŌSHU (local landholders) and JIZAMURAI (farmer-samurai), took joint responsibility for delivering annual taxes to the proprietor. The spread of such contracts through the 16th century is often regarded as an indication of increased village autonomy (see SŌ). While this may have been true when contracts were made with an entire village, it was less clearly the case when proprietors successfully evaded villagers' demands by contract-

Japanese hydrangea
1 The path to the inner gate of the temple Meigetsuin, known as Ajisaidera ("Hydrangea Temple"), in Kamakura. More than 2,000 bushes grow within the grounds, attracting many visitors from early June to early July.
2 Flowers grow in a rounded cluster at the tip of the branch. The common Western hydrangea is a hybrid based on the Japanese ajisai.

Hyōgo Prefecture
Location and Prefectural Crest

ing only with the wealthy and more influential villagers. This latter form of contract seems to have been common. Similar tax arrangements were sometimes made with townsmen (see EGŌSHŪ).

hydrangea, Japanese 紫陽花

(ajisai). *Hydrangea macrophylla.* Deciduous shrub of the family Saxifragaceae, developed in Japan as a horticultural variety from the wild *gakuajisai* (*H. macrophylla* f. *normalis*) and cultivated widely as a decorative plant. Its stems grow in clusters to 1.5 meters (5 ft); the leaves are opposite, ovate to broadly ovate, thick, and dark green, with serrated margins. In summer numerous small flowers appear in ball-shaped clusters (corymbs) composed mostly of sterile flowers, each with four or five large, light blue to deep purple petallike sepals. The acidity of the soil changes the color of the plant's flowers: acid soils produce more bluish blossoms and alkaline soils more pink ones.

References to *ajisai* in Japanese literature appear as far back as the *Man'yōshū*, an 8th-century poetry anthology. Mention of *ajisai* usually alludes to the spring rainy season.

Hyōgo Prefecture 兵庫県

(Hyōgo Ken). Located in western Honshū, bordered by the Sea of Japan to the north, Kyōto and Ōsaka prefectures to the east, Ōsaka Bay and the INLAND SEA to the south, and Okayama and Tottori prefectures to the west. The middle portion is occupied by a ridge of mountains and highlands; the area to the south of these mountains contains some broad coastal plains traversed by rivers. Most of Hyōgo's population is concentrated in this area, where the climate is temperate and comparatively dry. The area to the north is hillier and more humid, with snowy winters typical of the Sea of Japan coast. The island of AWAJISHIMA in the Inland Sea is one of the largest of Japan's offshore islands.

The Hyōgo area was inhabited early on, and remains of primitive people were found there near the city of AKASHI (see JAPANESE PEOPLE, ORIGIN OF). Under the ancient system of provinces (KOKUGUN SYSTEM), the area was designated as the three provinces of Harima, Tajima, and Awaji and as part of Settsu and Tamba provinces. From the 8th to 12th cen-

turies the port of Hyōgo (now KŌBE) was a base for trade with the Asian continent. Hyōgo's position between the Nara-Kyōto capital regions and western Japan added to its importance. It was the site of numerous battles between contending warlords and of the TAIRA-MINAMOTO WAR. During the Edo period (1600–1868) it was divided into many small domains; these were combined into the present single prefecture in 1876.

Formerly a flourishing agricultural and fishing area, the prefecture is now dominated by industry, especially along the Inland Sea coast. Products include ships, steel, transportation equipment, ceramics, and textiles. Kōbe developed into one of Japan's major port cities in the late 19th century.

Most of its tourist attractions are located within the Inland Sea and SAN'IN COAST NATIONAL PARK. ROKKŌSAN, a mountain located behind the city of Kōbe, is a favorite summer resort. HIMEJI CASTLE is known as one of Japan's most distinctive historical structures. Awajishima is the home of a folk puppet theater with a long tradition, and its beaches attract vacationers from the Ōsaka-Kōbe area. Area: 8,382 sq km (3,236 sq mi); pop: 5,405,040; capital: Kōbe. Other major cities include NISHINOMIYA, AMAGASAKI, and HIMEJI.

Hyōgo Shipyards 兵庫造船所

(Hyōgo Zōsensho). Predecessor of Kawasaki Shipyards, now part of KAWASAKI HEAVY INDUSTRIES, LTD; located in Kōbe's Hyōgo district. Built by the Kanazawa domain (now part of Ishikawa Prefecture) in 1870, it was taken over by the central government in 1872. In 1887, as part of the government's program of selling state enterprises to private interests (see KAN'EI JIGYŌ HARAISAGE), it was sold to Kawasaki Shōzō (1837–1912) who combined it with other shipyards to form Kawasaki Shipyards.

Hyōjōshū 評定衆

(Council of State). The highest office of the Kamakura (1192–1333) and Muromachi (1338–1573) shogunates, where administrative matters and legal disputes were discussed in council. Established in 1226 by HŌJŌ YASUTOKI, a shogunal regent (SHIKKEN), it originally had 11 members (later around 15), including heads of offices, Hōjō kinsmen, legal specialists and scholars from the Ōe and Kiyohara families, and warriors from the

Sasaki, Chiba, MIURA, and other eastern vassal houses. Meetings were presided over by the shogunal regent and cosigner (RENSHO) and decisions were reached by majority vote. Originally set up to allow broader participation in government, by the mid-14th century it was dominated by the Hōjō family. Retained by the Muromachi shogunate, it gradually lost powers and was abolished during the Sengoku period (1467–1568).

hyōjungo → kyōtsūgo

Hyō, Lake 瓢湖

(Hyōko). Irrigation pond in the town of Suibara, central Niigata Prefecture, central Honshū. Known for the white swans that migrate from Siberia from January to March and also for the mute swans that were presented to the town by the Soviet Union. Area: 0.1 sq km (0.04 sq mi); circumference: 1.2 km (0.75 mi).

hyōrōmai 兵糧米

(commissariat rice). A rice tax levied by the Kamakura (1192–1333) and Muromachi (1338–1573) shogunates to pay for military provisions. First imposed in 1180 by TAIRA NO KIYOMORI during the TAIRA-MINAMOTO WAR, it was formalized in 1185 by MINAMOTO NO YORITOMO. Discontinued the following year, the tax was reinstated as need arose. The government tried to prevent stewards (JITŌ) of private estates (SHŌEN) from demanding it regularly for their own profit. Early in the Muromachi period ASHIKAGA TAKAUJI assigned certain *shōen* lands (*hyōrō ryōsho*) to his military supporters; the *hyōrōmai* that they levied often amounted to one-half of the income of the *shōen* (see HANZEI). Military governors (SHUGO) also collected *hyōrōmai* to maintain their armies. During the period of the NORTHERN AND SOUTHERN COURTS (1337–92), the Southern Court relied on this tax for support.

hypothec 抵当権

(*teitōken*). In Japanese law, a right created to secure an obligation to a creditor even though there is no actual prior transfer of possession of immovable property owned by the debtor (or a third party). The creditor has the right to receive payment prior to other creditors from the immovable property if the obligor does not fulfill his obligatory duty (Civil Code, art. 369). A hypothec may also be created in superficies and perpetual land leases. Special laws, such as the Automobile Hypothec Law, allow a hypothec in certain movable property. A hypothec is most commonly used to secure financial loan obligatory duties and is usually recorded. If, after the repayment period, the debtor has not fulfilled his obligation, the creditor may request a court to auction the hypothecated property for the benefit of the hypothec right holder.

Hyūga 日向[市]

City in northeastern Miyazaki Prefecture, Kyūshū, on the Hyūga Sea. Sugar refining, chemical, and textile factories, as well as oil-storage and lumbering facilities, were constructed here during the 1960s. Hyūga is noted for its white GO stones, made from clamshells. Pop: 58,442.

Hyūga Sea 日向灘

(Hyūga Nada). Part of the Pacific Ocean off eastern Miyazaki Prefecture, Kyūshū, noted for its strong currents. Offshore fisheries are rich in sardines, bonito, and tuna.

I

iai 居合

Technique of swordsmanship that includes the skill of cutting one's adversary on the draw, usually at the temple or at eye level; believed to have been founded by Hayashizaki Jinsuke Shigenobu (b 1542). When attacked, *iai* involves drawing, parrying, and riposte with a lethal blow through the shoulder and spine. When the blade is freed it is swung to shake off the blood and then wiped clean before being returned to the scabbard. In practice the wiping of the blade is omitted. *Iai* was an essential part of *kenjutsu* (fencing) during the Edo period (1600–1868). The *samurai* trained himself to attack or parry a blow and riposte against a single opponent or several opponents while seated, standing, or walking. In recent years the term *iaidō* (the Way of *iai*) has come into common usage. The All Japan Kendō Federation has created an eclectic *iai* form, derived from several historical schools.

Ibara 井原[市]

City in southwestern Okayama Prefecture, western Honshū. Known for its textiles, especially work clothes and blue jeans, Ibara also has automotive, electronics, machinery, and metal industries. Farm products are tobacco and grapes. Pop: 36,076.

Ibaragi Noriko 茨木のり子

(1926–). Poet. Real name Miura Noriko. Born in Ōsaka Prefecture. Graduate of Teikoku Women's Pharmaceutical College. Using plain language, Ibaragi expresses the sentiments of everyday life in a direct, cheerful style. Her poetry collections include *Taiwa* (1955, Dialogue), *Mienai haitatsufu* (1958, Invisible Deliveryman), and *Jibun no kanjusei kurai* (1977, As Much As I Feel).

Ibaraki 茨木[市]

City in northern Ōsaka Prefecture. A castle town during the late 16th–early 17th centuries, it underwent large-scale land development and population growth during the 1950s. Ibaraki's main products are electrical equipment, metals, and processed food. A cluster of mounded tombs (the Shikinzan KOFUN) and an inn (the Kōriyama Honjin) once used by traveling *daimyō* are of interest. Pop: 254,078.

Ibaraki Prefecture 茨城県

(Ibaraki Ken). Located in central Honshū and bounded by Fukushima Prefecture to the north, the Pacific Ocean to the east, Chiba Prefecture to the south, and Tochigi and Saitama prefectures to the west. The northern part is occupied by mountains of the Abukuma and Yamizo ranges, and the larger southern section is an extension of the Kantō Plain. The prefecture contains several large lakes and lagoons. The climate is relatively mild.

It was known as Hitachi Province under the ancient provincial system (KOKUGUN SYSTEM). The city of MITO was the seat of an important branch (see GOSANKE) of the TOKUGAWA FAMILY in the Edo period (1600–1868) and became a center of scholarship. The present prefectural name and boundaries were established in 1875 after the Meiji Restoration.

Relative abundance of level land and proximity to the great market of Tōkyō help to make Ibaraki a leading agricultural prefecture. Rice, other grains, and a wide variety of fruits and vegetables are produced in great quantity. Fishing has long been important.

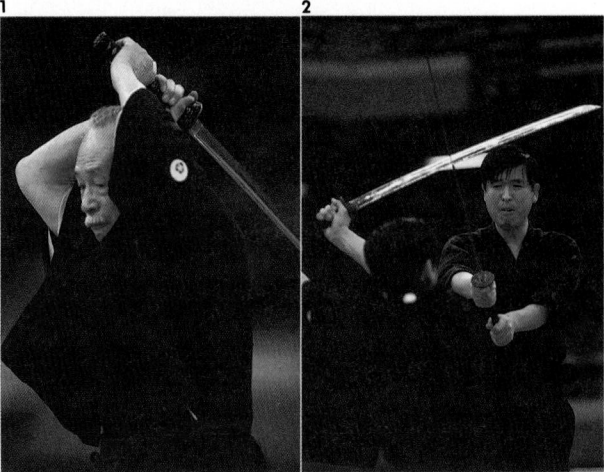

iai
1 Having drawn and raised his sword, this *iai* practitioner is about to execute an overhead cut.
2 Cut and parry techniques demonstrated as part of a two-man formal exercise.

More recently, Ibaraki's proximity to the Keihin Industrial Zone has led to the development of electrical-equipment, food-processing, steel, and petrochemical industries. Recent large-scale projects include the Kashima Coastal Industrial Region and Tsukuba Academic New Town (see TSUKUBA).

Tourist attractions include the KAIRAKUEN in Mito, one of Japan's most famous gardens, and lakes, lagoons, and sandy beaches. One of Japan's larger waterfalls is located near the hot-spring resort of Fukuroda (see FUKURODA FALLS). Area: 6,095 sq km (2,352 sq mi); pop: 2,845,382; capital: Mito. Other major cities include HITACHI, TSUCHIURA, and KOGA.

Iba site 伊場遺跡

(Iba *iseki*). Archaeological site in the city of Hamamatsu, Shizuoka Prefecture. The principal features are wooden artifacts, a large ditch 12–16 meters (39.3–52.5 ft) wide, PIT HOUSES from the Yayoi (ca 300 BC–ca AD 300) and Kofun (ca 300–710) periods, and building remains that are believed to have been a provincial seat during the Nara period (710–794). More than 75 inscribed wooden tablets (MOKKAN) have been recovered from the site. Despite scholarly objections, a large part of the site was covered by a railroad building in 1973; the remainder is preserved as a park.

Ibigawa 揖斐川

River in Gifu Prefecture, central Honshū, originating in the Ryōhaku Mountains at the border between Fukui and Gifu prefectures and emptying into Ise Bay. It is one of the three great rivers of the Nōbi Plain together with the Kisogawa and the Nagaragawa. Farming settlements called WAJŪ are found on the delta of its lower reaches. The three dams on the upper reaches are used by electric power plants. Length: 120 km (75 mi); area of drainage basin: 1,839 sq km (710 sq mi).

IBM Japan, Ltd 日本アイ・ビー・エム[株]

(Nihon Ai Bī Emu). Japanese subsidiary of the International Business Machines Corporation (IBM). It was incorporated in 1937 as Watson Business Machines of Japan, Ltd, to sell IBM's punch card system. In 1949 the company took its present name. With the Japanese government's adoption of this system for compiling the 1950 national census, the company increased its sales tremendously. In 1958 the ATOMIC ENERGY RESEARCH INSTITUTE, JAPAN, purchased the country's first IBM computers. In 1960 the company commenced production of computers in Japan and since then has controlled a large share of the nation's computer market. Since 1961 IBM Japan has exported its computers, and Japan remains one of the most important production bases for the corporation. The

Ibaraki Prefecture
Location and Prefectural Crest

Ibuka Masaru This cofounder of Sony Corporation was in charge of the research and development side of the business.

Ibuse Masuji Ibuse's trademark as a writer is his detached and often dryly humorous tone, employed to considerable effect in his masterwork, *Kuroi ame* (1965–66, Black Rain).

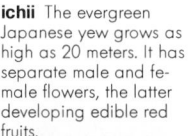

ichii The evergreen Japanese yew grows as high as 20 meters. It has separate male and female flowers, the latter developing edible red fruits.

company deals in personal computers and small to mid-size office computers as well as large systems, the area in which it has traditionally been strongest. Annual sales in 1990 totaled ¥1.3 trillion (US $9.7 billion); capitalization, wholly controlled by the IBM World Trade Co, stood at ¥135.3 billion (US $1.0 billion). Headquarters are in Tōkyō.

Ibuka Masaru   井深大

(1908–). Entrepreneur and cofounder of the SONY CORPORATION. Born in Tochigi Prefecture. After graduating from Waseda University, he established Tōkyō Tsūshin Kōgyō (Sony's predecessor) in 1946 with MORITA AKIO and others. In 1950 they developed and marketed the first tape recorders produced in Japan, thereby laying the groundwork for the company's spectacular success. In 1953 Ibuka acquired the patent rights on transistors from Western Electric Co of the United States and began developing transistor radios, which he started marketing to the world in 1955. The success led to the creation of a powerful semiconductor industry in Japan. Later, Ibuka was instrumental in introducing small-sized televisions, videocassette recorders, and many other highly successful new products. He handled the research and development end of Sony's business, while Morita devoted himself to market development. Ibuka became the company's president in 1950 and served as chairman from 1971 to 1976. Honorary chairman of Sony since 1976, Ibuka is one of the leading engineer-entrepreneurs of post–World War II Japan. He is also president of the Early Development Association, an educational facility for preschool children.

Ibukiyama   伊吹山

Limestone mountain located on the border of Gifu and Shiga prefectures, central Honshū. Approximately 1,700 plant varieties are found on the mountain. Height: 1,377 m (4,518 ft).

Ibuse Masuji   井伏鱒二

(1898–1993). Novelist, short-story writer, essayist, and poet. Born in Kamo, Hiroshima Prefecture. Ibuse carefully experimented with a number of styles. In his books the conventions of the I-NOVEL (*watakushi shōsetsu*) are enlivened; the ancient stock of romantic nature-lyricism acquires a robust, epic quality; and into the often serious or sentimental art of modern Japanese prose writing he introduces his own brand of dry humor.

Ibuse was born into a family of independent farmers. He moved to Tōkyō in 1917 to study literature at Waseda University and painting at the Nihon Bijutsu Gakkō (Japan School of Art). French literature was his major, but Russian literature, especially Tolstoy and Chekhov, also engaged his attention. In 1923 his first successful story, "Yūhei," appeared in a student magazine. This gentle satire on intellectual pretense is better known by its later title, "Sanshōuo" (1929; tr "Salamander," 1971). Another story, "Yofuke to ume no hana" (1928; tr "Plum Blossom at Night," 1971), casts his self-mockery in a dreamlike, symbolic mode. In "Koi" (1926; tr "Carp," 1971) Ibuse uses a typical Japanese I-novel mode.

During the following years his interest shifted from Tōkyō to the rural areas of southern Japan, where he was born. A painstaking craftsman, he always spent more time revising and polishing his stories than taking sides in ideological polemics. When his literary friends joined the popular PROLETARIAN LITERATURE MOVEMENT in the late 1920s, Ibuse found himself an outsider.

His native countryside was the setting of some of his best stories, as in "Tange shi tei" (1931; tr "Life at Mr. Tange's," 1971) and "Kawa" (1931–32, The River). During the 1930s Ibuse worked steadily on the most remarkable of his works on historical themes, a long novella called *Sazanami gunki* (1930–38), set against the decline and annihilation of the Taira family in the late 12th century. It shows the initiation of a sensitive young Taira *samurai* into a brutal world. In 1937 Ibuse published another historical novella, *Jon Manjirō hyōryūki* (1937; tr *John Manjirō, the Cast-away: His Life and Adventure*, 1940), which dealt with the actual experiences of a shipwrecked Japanese fisherman who was taken all the way to America and back at a time when contacts outside Japan were strictly forbidden (see NAKAHAMA MANJIRŌ). Ibuse's last major prewar work was "Tajinko Mura" (1939; tr "Tajinko Village," 1971). He wrote little during the war, and his unwilling induction into the army as a war correspondent probably inspired the biting satire on army drill in "Yōhai taichō" (1950; tr "Lieutenant Lookeast," 1971).

His longest and most important novel is KUROI AME (1965–66; tr *Black Rain*, 1969), which deals with the atomic bombing of Hiroshima. Rather than trying to deal with the disaster in its totality, Ibuse chose to bring out the beauty of the southern landscape and the manners and colorful foibles of its people against the absurd brutality of the holocaust. Ibuse has received numerous awards, including the Naoki Prize, the Noma Literary Prize, and the Order of Culture; in 1960 he was nominated to the Japan Art Academy.

Ibusuki   指宿[市]

City in Kagoshima Prefecture, Kyūshū, on Satsuma Peninsula. Ibusuki is noted for its hot springs. The Experimental Station for Tropical Plants of Kagoshima University is here. Pop: 32,008.

ichien chigyō   一円知行

(sole or exclusive proprietorship). Also known as *ichien ryōchi*. Type of landownership in the Kamakura (1185–1333) and Muromachi (1333–1568) periods whereby an area of land was owned and administered completely and exclusively by a single authority. *Ichien* means whole or entirety; CHIGYŌ means direct control of property.

The government land-allotment system (see HANDEN SHŪJU SYSTEM) that had been instituted under the late-7th-century RITSURYŌ SYSTEM of administration gradually collapsed early in the Heian period (794–1185), and the private ownership of landed estates (SHŌEN) developed. At first it was unusual for a *shōen* to be held under a single, exclusive authority (see HONKE AND RYŌKE). For example, one proprietor might hold the right to collect land rent (see NENGU), while another had the right to corvée labor (see BUYAKU). This kind of multiple management was known as *kakubetsu chigyō* (separate or divided proprietorship). However, when one person or authority assumed complete administrative and fiscal rights, he was said to hold *ichien chigyō*. The elimination of competing rights and claims became particularly pronounced from the Kamakura period onward through

the agency of military land stewards (JITŌ). Proprietary rights to land were redefined under the nationwide cadastral survey (KENCHI) carried out after 1582.

Ichigō Sakusen→ Operation Number One

Ichihara   市原[市]

City on Tōkyō Bay in central Chiba Prefecture, central Honshū. Once a post-station town on the highway Kisarazu Kaidō, it is now part of the KEIYŌ INDUSTRIAL REGION. Its main industries are oil and shipbuilding. The eastern section remains residential and agricultural. Pop: 257,716.

ichii   一位

(Japanese yew). *Taxus cuspidata*. Evergreen of the family Taxaceae that grows wild in the mountainous regions of Hokkaidō, northern and central Honshū, and Shikoku; it is also planted in home gardens and as hedges. Some trees grow to 20 meters (66 ft). The trunk is straight and the bark reddish brown. The tree has separate male and female flowers; the female flowers develop into succulent red fruits, the fleshy seed coverings (arils) of which are sweet and edible. The hard, fine-grained, flexible, glossy wood is used for carvings, tools, and furniture. The *ichii* was introduced to England and the United States in the 19th century.

Ichijitsu shintō ki   一実神道記

(Record of Ichijitsu Shintō). A theoretical work probably written in the late 1820s by the Tendai monk Jihon (1795–1869). It sets forth the history and doctrines of SANNŌ ICHIJITSU SHINTŌ, a syncretic school that held that Ōyamakui no Kami, the Shintō deity who presides over Mt. Hiei (HIEIZAN), site of the main TENDAI SECT temple, was essentially an embodiment of the highest truth of the Tendai school of Buddhism. The *Ichijitsu shintō ki* deals with such subjects as the Shintō creation myths, the founding of ENRYAKUJI (the Tendai temple complex on Mt. Hiei) and its relation to the HIE SHRINE, and biographies of prominent monks connected with Mt. Hiei. It includes many medieval documents that are important in tracing the doctrinal development of Sannō Ichijitsu thought.

Ichijō, Emperor   一条天皇

(980–1011; Ichijō Tennō). The 66th sovereign (*tennō*) in the traditional count (which includes several legendary emperors); reigned 986–1011. Son of Emperor En'yū (r 969–984) and Senshi (961–1001), a daughter of the imperial regent FUJIWARA NO KANEIE. During Ichijō's reign Kaneie's son FUJIWARA NO MICHINAGA brought the Fujiwara family to the height of its political influence, obliging Ichijō to balance the family's two principal factions by maintaining two nearly equal-ranking empresses (see CHŪGŪ). Some of the greatest literature of the Heian period (794–1185) was written in the courts of these two consorts, where SEI SHŌNAGON, MURASAKI SHIKIBU, and AKAZOME EMON were ladies-in-waiting.

Ichijō family→ Gosekke

Ichijō Kaneyoshi   一条兼良

(1402–81). Also known as Ichijō Kanera. Courtier, scholar, classical (WAKA) poet, and critic. Grandson of the regent NIJŌ YOSHIMOTO and son of the regent Tsunetsugu. He became grand minister of state (*dajō daijin*) in

1446 and regent (KAMPAKU) and head of the Fujiwara family in 1447. Reduced to virtual penury during the ŌNIN WAR (1467–77), he resigned the regency in 1470. His works include the following: on traditional customs and practices, *Kuji kongen* (ca 1422, Origins of Court Ritual), *Gōshidai shō* (Notes on Ōe Masafusa's Writings on Court Ceremonial), and *Nenchū gyōji taigai* (Outline of Annual Rites and Observances); on the classic court romance, *Kachō yojō* (1472, Atmosphere of Blossoms and Birds) and *Gengo hiketsu* (1477, Secret Wisdom on *The Tale of Genji*); on government, *Sayo no nezame* (ca 1477–78, Wakeful Thoughts in the Small Hours) and BUMMEI ITTŌKI (ca 1479, On the Unity of Learning and Culture). He also wrote on religion, classical poetry, and song. His works on RENGA (linked verse) include *Renju gappeki shū* (ca 1476, Gems of Linked Verse) and, with the *renga* master TAKAYAMA SŌZEI, an expanded and updated edition of the official rules of linked verse composition, *Renga shinshiki* (1452, New Rules of Linked Verse).

Ichijō Norifusa 一条教房

(1423–80). Court noble of the Muromachi period (1333–1568). Eldest son of ICHIJŌ KANEYOSHI, he became imperial regent (KAMPAKU) in 1458. He resigned the post in 1463. In 1467, when the ŌNIN WAR broke out, he moved to Nara to escape the fighting. The following year he moved to Tosa Province (now Kōchi Prefecture), where his family owned land. With the support of the CHŌSOKABE FAMILY, he made the town of NAKAMURA a cultural center.

Ichijō Sanetsune 一条実経

(1223–84). Court noble of the Kamakura period (1185–1333); third son of Kujō Michiie (1193–1252), founder of the Ichijō family (see GOSEKKE). Briefly KAMPAKU (regent) for Emperor GO-SAGA, then SESSHŌ (regent for a minor) for Emperor GO-FUKAKUSA (1246), he served a second term (1263) as minister of the left (*sadaijin*), and in 1265 he became *kampaku* for Emperor KAMEYAMA.

Ichijō Tsunetsugu 一条経嗣

(1358–1418). Court noble of the early Muromachi period (1333–1568). Son of NIJŌ YOSHIMOTO, he was adopted by Ichijō Fusatsune. In 1388 he was named inner minister (*naidaijin*) and in 1391 achieved junior first rank in the imperial court. In 1394 he became minister of the left (*sadaijin*) as well as regent (KAMPAKU) for the first of three terms under Emperor GO-KOMATSU.

Ichikawa 市川[市]

City in northwestern Chiba Prefecture, central Honshū, on the river EDOGAWA. Mainly a residential district for commuters to Tōkyō, it is also part of the KEIYŌ INDUSTRIAL REGION, with many heavy-industry and chemical plants. Pears and vegetables are still grown in the northern district. Also here are Jōmon-period (ca 10,000 BC–ca 300 BC) shell mounds and the remains of an 8th-century provincial temple (KOKUBUNJI). Pop: 436,596.

Ichikawa Beian 市河米庵

(1779–1858). Calligrapher of the Edo period (1600–1868). Also known as Ichikawa Sangai, Kōyō, or Rakusai. Born in Edo (now Tōkyō). As a young man Beian devoted himself to calligraphy, particularly following the style of Mi Fu of Song (Sung) dynasty (960–1279) China. His brushwork is relaxed, strong but not rigid, and often rather thick

in line. It is estimated that by his death he had taught over 5,000 pupils. His published works include *Beika shoketsu* (Mi-Style Calligraphy), *Beian bokudan* (Beian's Discussions of Ink), his own poetry, and a number of books on calligraphy and writing materials.

Ichikawa Danjūrō 市川団十郎

The most illustrious of the major acting family lines in the KABUKI tradition identified with the Edo (now Tōkyō) region. Danjūrō I (1660–1704) created the *aragoto* (rough business) style of acting. He also wrote plays under the pen name Mimasuya Hyōgo. His son Danjūrō II (1688–1758) firmly established the prestige of the Ichikawa name. He premiered a majority of the celebrated works known as the KABUKI JŪHACHIBAN and also adapted JŌRURI puppet plays for the kabuki stage.

Danjūrō IV (1711–78) carried on the *aragoto* tradition and excelled as a *jitsuaku* (villainous *samurai*). His son Danjūrō V (1741–1806) also acted skillfully in both male and female roles. Danjūrō VII (1791–1859) is best remembered as the compiler of the *kabuki jūhachiban*, which he formally established as the special repertory of the Ichikawa family. Danjūrō IX (1838–1903) promoted the *katsureki-mono* ("living history" plays), which stressed greater factual accuracy and pictorial realism. Both he and Morita Kan'ya XII (1846–97; see MORITA KAN'YA), a prominent theater manager, helped to elevate the status of kabuki to a theater of respectability and contributed to the stability of the kabuki theater as it underwent sweeping social and cultural changes. Danjūrō XI (1909–65) performed heroic and romantic roles in the traditional repertory as well as kabuki plays based on works by contemporary novelists. Danjūrō XII (real name Horikoshi Natsuo; b 1946), eldest son of Ichikawa Danjūrō XI, assumed the name in April 1985.

Ichikawa Ennosuke 市川猿之助

Professional name of a family of KABUKI actors. Ennosuke I (1855–1922) was the pupil of Ichikawa Danjūrō IX (1838–1903; see ICHIKAWA DANJŪRŌ). Ennosuke II (1888–1963), the eldest son of Ennosuke I, founded the troupe Shunjūza, performing both foreign plays in translation and original works. He also traveled to Europe to observe theater there. Ennosuke III (b 1939), the grandson of Ennosuke II, graduated from Keiō University. He assumed the professional name Ennosuke III in 1963. Known for his innovations in tailoring kabuki to the tastes of today's audiences, he has guided it in the di-

rection of fast-moving visual spectacle, with quick costume changes, airborne stage effects, and so on. He has also revived older, lesser-known plays with vigorous new productions. In 1989, he produced and starred in *Ryūō*, the first joint production of kabuki and the Peking Opera.

Ichikawa Fusae 市川房枝

(1893–1981). Feminist and politician; leader of the prewar WOMEN'S SUFFRAGE movement. Born in Aichi Prefecture. Completing her teacher training education in Nagoya, Ichikawa taught elementary school, then became the first woman reporter for the newspaper *Nagoya shimbun*. Concerned with both labor and feminist issues, in late 1919 and early 1920 Ichikawa joined HIRATSUKA RAICHŌ and OKU MUMEO in establishing the SHIN FUJIN KYŌKAI (New Woman's Association). In December 1924 she helped found the FUSEN KAKUTOKU DŌMEI (Women's Suffrage League). For the next 16 years she tried to persuade liberal politicians to support legislation that would grant women political rights. After World War II, she devoted much of her time to the League of Women Voters (Nihon Fujin Yūkensha Dōmei), which she founded in 1945, and to the Women's Suffrage Hall (Fusen Kaikan), a research institute designed to increase women's political consciousness. She was elected five times to the House of Councillors on the basis of her campaigns for social equality and against government corruption.

Ichikawa Kon 市川崑

(1915–). Film director. Born in Mie Prefecture. From 1933 he worked on cartoon designs in the animation department of the J. O. Studio. The first film he directed, *Hana hiraku* (1948, The Flower Opens), was a melodrama, as were most of his other early assignments. His 1955 adaptation of KOKORO, a novel by NATSUME SŌSEKI, was the first Ichikawa film based on a literary work. Among the many others are *Enjō* (1958,

Ichikawa Kon
1 The actor Yasui Shōji in a scene from Ichikawa's 1956 version of *Biruma no tategoto* (Harp of Burma), which the director remade in 1985.
2 Ichikawa, who has brought many Japanese novels to the screen.

581

Ichikawa Kon

Ichikawa Raizō
A *kabuki* actor in his younger days, Ichikawa became widely known as a film actor who played the role of a heroic swordsman in a popular series of period dramas.

ichirinsō This perennial wild herb blooms in the spring. Its flower is formed by five white sepals resembling petals.

ichirizuka This is the only milestone mound in Tōkyō to remain at its original location, the Nishigahara area of Kita Ward. It is two *ri* (approximately 7.8 km) from Nihombashi, a bridge historically regarded as the center of the city.

Conflagration), based on the MISHIMA YUKIO novel KINKAKUJI (The Temple of the Golden Pavilion); *Kagi* (1959, The Key; shown abroad as *Odd Obsession*) and *Sasameyuki* (1983, The Makioka Sisters) are both based on TANIZAKI JUN'ICHIRŌ novels. In his first foray into documentary film, *Tōkyō Orimpikku* (1965, Tōkyō Olympiad), Ichikawa sparked a controversy by placing more emphasis on the athletes as people than on the sports events. Ichikawa has also directed historical films and many comedies. His wife, Wada Natsuto (1920–83), worked on the scripts for many of his films, including both the 1956 and 1985 versions of BIRUMA NO TATEGOTO (Harp of Burma).

Ichikawa Raizō　市川雷蔵

(1931–69). Actor. Born in Kyōto. Ichikawa made his stage debut in 1946 at the Kabukiza in Ōsaka. In 1951 Ichikawa Jukai (1886–1971), the reigning elder of KABUKI in the Kansai (Kyōto–Ōsaka) region, adopted the young actor and gave him a new stage name, Ichikawa Raizō VIII. Beginning in 1954 the movie studio DAIEI CO, LTD, cast him in the lead role in many period dramas (JIDAIGEKI) and contemporary dramas, including MIZOGUCHI KENJI's *Shin Heike monogatari* (1955, New Tales of the Taira Clan), ICHIKAWA KON's *Enjō* (1958, Conflagration), and Tanaka Tokuzō's (b 1925) *Kyōshirō sappō chō* (1963, Enter Kyōshirō Nemuri the Swordsman).

Ichikawa Shōichi　市川正一

(1892–1945). One of the leading figures of the JAPAN COMMUNIST PARTY (JCP) before World War II. Born in Yamaguchi Prefecture. A graduate of Waseda University, he worked as a newspaperman and later started a Marxist magazine, *Musan kaikyū* (Proletariat), with AONO SUEKICHI and others. In January 1923 he joined the JCP and became an editor of the party organ *Sekki* (later renamed *Akahata*; both names mean "Red Flag"). He escaped arrest in the MARCH 15TH INCIDENT of 1928 and attended the sixth Comintern meeting in Russia. Ichikawa was arrested in 1929 (see APRIL 16TH INCIDENT). His testimony during the subsequent trial was published posthumously as *Nihon kyōsantō tōsō shōshi* (A Short History of the Struggle of the Japan Communist Party). Given a life sentence, Ichikawa refused to recant his political beliefs and died in prison of malnutrition.

Ichikawa Utaemon　市川右太衛門

(1907–). Period-film actor whose career began in silent movies. Real name Asai Zennosuke. Born in Kagawa Prefecture. Formerly a KABUKI actor, Ichikawa made his film debut in *Kurokami jigoku* (1925, Hell of Black Hair). He appeared in more than 350 pictures and became a box-office star. Ichikawa specialized in period dramas, only rarely appearing in films with contemporary settings such as *Jiruba no Tetsu* (1950, Jitterbugging Tetsu), written by KUROSAWA AKIRA. Ichikawa is especially remembered for the movie series *Hatamoto taikutsu otoko* (1930–63, The Samurai with Time on His Hands). He has made only occasional film appearances since the mid-1960s.

Ichiko Teiji　市古貞次

(1911–). Scholar of classical Japanese literature. Born in Yamanashi Prefecture. After graduating from Tōkyō University, he became a professor there and later director of

the Kokubungaku Kenkyū Shiryōkan (National Institute of Japanese Literature). He has made important contributions in compiling and organizing documents on Japanese literature. Among his major works is *Chūsei shōsetsu no kenkyū* (1955, A Study of Medieval Novels), in which he classified more than 300 OTOGI-ZŌSHI. He played a leading role in the compilation of the nine-volume *Kokusho sōmokuroku* (1963–76), a comprehensive catalog of books, anthologies, and translated works in Japanese up to 1867. It indicates where original handwritten copies or imprints are preserved, as well as giving such basic information as number of volumes, library classification, author, and date of publication. Ichiko received the Order of Culture in 1990.

Ichimura Kiyoshi　市村清

(1900–68). Businessman. Born in Saga Prefecture. Studied at Chūō University. With a recommendation from ŌKŌCHI MASATOSHI, director of the Institute of Physical and Chemical Research (Rikagaku Kenkyūjo), Ichimura was invited in 1933 to join Rikagaku Kōgyō Co, a company related to Rikagaku Kenkyūjo. In 1936 he established a company to make photosensitive paper, Riken Kankōshi (now RICOH CO, LTD), and later founded other new companies, including Nihon Kōkū Heiki, San-Ai, San-Ai Oil, and Ricoh Watch. He also formed the Ricoh-San-Ai business group.

Ichimura Sanjirō　市村瓚次郎

(1864–1947). Scholar of Asian history. Born in what is now Ibaraki Prefecture. A graduate of Tōkyō University, he became a professor there in 1905. His most famous work is the four-volume *Tōyōshi tō* (1939–50, Comprehensive History of East Asia).

Ichinomiya　一宮〔市〕

City in northern Aichi Prefecture, central Honshū. Ichinomiya developed in the Edo period (1600–1868) as a shrine town around the Masumida Shrine, and as a market town. Its principal industry is textiles, particularly wool. Pop: 262,434.

Ichinoseki　一関〔市〕

City in southern Iwate Prefecture, northern Honshū. Ichinoseki developed as a castle town in the Edo period (1600–1868). Rice, dairy goods, and apples are its principal products. Many electronics and precision-instrument companies have built factories here. GEMBIKEI, a gorge on the river Iwaigawa, and Sukawa Hot Spring, a part of the Kurikoma Quasi-National Park, draw visitors. Pop: 61,967.

ichirinsō　一輪草

(literally, "one-flower plant"). *Anemone nikoensis*. Perennial herb of the family Ranunculaceae that grows in mountain woods and on grassy foothills in Honshū, Kyūshū, and Shikoku. The straight stem grows to 18–25 centimeters (7–10 in). Three pinnate leaflets compose each compound leaf. A single white flower, often tinged with pink and 4 centimeters (1.6 in) across, opens in April. *Ichirinsō* is related to *nirinsō* (*A. flaccida*), which usually has two flowers.

ichirizuka　一里塚

(milestone mounds). Markers to indicate distances in *ri* (approximately 2.44 mi or 3.9 km) from Nihombashi, a bridge regarded as the central point in Edo (now Tōkyō). They were placed in pairs along major highways

in the Edo period (1600–1868), one on each side of the road. Each *ichirizuka* consisted of a 30-foot-square mound, 10 feet high, planted with nettle or pine trees.

ichō→ginkgo

Idemitsu Art Gallery　出光美術館

(Idemitsu Bijutsukan). Located in Tōkyō. Large private collection founded by IDEMITSU SAZŌ. Opened in 1966, it includes Japanese paintings, Chinese and Japanese calligraphy and ceramics, Chinese bronzes, and Southeast Asian objects. The representation of UKIYO-E and BUNJINGA painters is extensive; particularly notable is the group of paintings and calligraphy by SENGAI GIBON. The Chinese ceramic section is one of the largest in Japan, as is an equally large collection of shards from kiln sites in Japan, China, Korea, and the Middle East.

Idemitsu Kōsan Co, Ltd　出光興産〔株〕

(Idemitsu Kōsan). Company engaged in petroleum refining, petrochemical production, development and extraction of petroleum and other mineral resources, marine transportation, ship chartering, and other related business operations. Founded originally as Idemitsu Shōkai by IDEMITSU SAZŌ in 1911. Incorporated under its present name in 1940.

The company operates refineries with a total daily capacity of 640,000 barrels (102,000 kl) in Hokkaidō, Yamaguchi, Chiba, Hyōgo, and Aichi prefectures. To ensure a stable supply of oil, Idemitsu operates a tanker fleet of 1.9 million tons, owned by Idemitsu Tanker Co, Ltd, including the *Idemitsu maru* (250,000 tons), the world's first supertanker. The company is also engaged in oil exploration on the continental shelf of the Sea of Japan and in other areas of the world. Idemitsu Oil Development Co, Ltd, was incorporated in 1976 to promote further development. Idemitsu has also entered the field of alternative energy sources (coal, uranium, and geothermal).

The company has some 9,000 filling stations and a sales network of 43 branch offices across the nation. It also maintains branch offices in New York, Los Angeles, Denver, London, Kuwait, Teheran, Abu Dhabi, Singapore, Sydney, and Rio de Janeiro. Total sales amounted to ¥1.7 trillion (US $11.1 billion) at the end of March 1990; its stock is not publicly offered. Headquarters are in Tōkyō.

Idemitsu Sazō　出光佐三

(1885–1981). Entrepreneur. Born in Fukuoka Prefecture, he was a graduate of Kōbe Commercial Higher School (now Kōbe University). In 1911 Idemitsu established Idemitsu Shōkai (forerunner of IDEMITSU KŌSAN CO, LTD), an oil products dealership. He rapidly expanded his business into a broad retail enterprise and turned the company into a major oil corporation financed by Japanese capital. Idemitsu had a 130,000-ton tanker constructed in 1951 and started importing high-octane gasoline from the United States as well as crude oil from Iran. His large collection of Asian art is housed in the IDEMITSU ART GALLERY.

Ide Takashi　出隆

(1892–1980). Philosopher. Born in Okayama Prefecture, he graduated from Tōkyō University, where he later became a professor (1935–51). Based on a classical bibliographical methodology, he opened the way for serious research in Japan in classical Greek philosophy. He found the focus of his thought in his study of Socrates, who viewed philosophical life as consisting in the unity of theory and practice. In his study of Aristotle, Ide approved of the realistic approach to investigating the nature of particulars, while criticizing the idea of a life devoted solely to contemplation. His works include *Tetsugaku izen* (1921) and *Girishia no tetsugaku to seiji* (1943).

Idojiri Archaeological Hall
井戸尻考古館

(Idojiri Kōkokan). Located in the town of Fujimi, Nagano Prefecture. The hall houses artifacts, including JŌMON POTTERY and STONE TOOLS, that were excavated from several sites in the Idojiri area at the southeastern foot of the mountain Yatsugatake. The artifacts are mainly from the Middle Jōmon period (ca 3500 BC–ca 2500 BC; also dated as ca 3500 BC–ca 2000 BC). See also TOGARIISHI SITE.

ie
家

(household). Traditional primary unit of social organization in Japan. *Ie* is often translated as "family," but the term "household" comes closer to conveying the Japanese concept of *ie.* Usually formed around an elementary family as its nucleus, it will often include other relatives and even nonrelatives. Once established, a household is expected to exist through generations.

In Japan, communities are built on the basis of households. It is the custom in many areas for a well-established household to have an exclusive house-name (see YAGŌ) in contrast to a family surname often shared by others. The *ie* is seen not simply as a contemporary household but as a continuum, embracing not only current living members but also their deceased predecessors and successors yet unborn. Members come and go, through birth, marriage, and death, but the *ie* persists.

Rules of Succession——Two important rules of succession to the headship of an *ie* are common throughout Japan. The first is that the head must be succeeded by a "son." Any male, related or not, can be the son provided he has been legally adopted into the family as its adopted son (*yōshi*) or adopted son-in-law (*muko yōshi*). Even if the head already has a son of his own, if he considers him unfit to be his successor, he may adopt another, as is occasionally done among *ie* that maintain family businesses.

ADOPTION to ensure succession to a headship has been very common in Japan. An adopted son or adopted son-in-law has the same rights in succession and inheritance as a real son and assumes the reciprocal obligation of caring for his adoptive parents in their old age and for other household members.

The second rule of succession is that it is never joint. In a household occupied by two brothers there is a sharp distinction in status between the successor and the nonsuccessor, with the wife and children of the latter being considered less than "full members" of the household. In fact, it is rare for two married brothers to reside in the same household, since nonsuccessors are supposed to leave upon marriage. Once they have established their own independent households, these become separate property-holding units in which the same principles operate. See also HONKE AND BUNKE.

The customs of succession ensure that the new head receives the father's house and the lion's share of the father's property. Although the 1947 Civil Code gives equal inheritance rights in the father's property to all sons and daughters, among agricultural families nonsuccessors almost invariably sign over their rights and leave the house and land intact for the brother who succeeds and assumes responsibility for their parents.

Human relationships within the traditional household group are seen as more important than relationships based merely upon consanguinity; the genealogical relationship between individual members of different households has no specific importance unless the households are involved in a common economic or political relationship. A brother who has established his own household is thought of as belonging to another social group, whereas a son-in-law, once a complete outsider, assumes more importance upon marriage than a brother living apart.

The concept of *ie* was manifested in both rural and urban areas, as family continuity was greatly valued by those with property or businesses to manage. It was the basic unit of the *samurai* community in the Edo period (1600–1868); the status of samurai was assigned to the household so that the household head alone could enjoy its privileges and transmit them to his successor alone, one man to one household being the rule of the *ie* system.

The decline of the *ie* institution came about because of changing economic conditions following World War II. The population of urban areas burgeoned, increasing the numbers of those who lived on salaries rather than from the management of household property. Ensuring the continuity of the household became meaningless when the household had no significant property to manage and conserve. The growth of salaried workers, the exodus of the younger population from rural areas, and the growing reluctance of women to submit to living with in-laws all contributed to the decline of the *ie.*

The Modern Ie——Today the institution is found mostly among farmers and men of traditional occupations (such as traditional arts and crafts), where techniques are handed down to the next generation, or in professions with fairly fixed clientele, such as doctors or temple priests. The majority of contemporary Japanese households are nuclear families. Older parents may live by themselves or with their married daughters, not necessarily with their eldest son's families.

Despite the decline of the *ie* system as a family institution, the basic concept has in fact survived as a structural basis for contemporary Japanese groups. A company is conceived of as an *ie,* all its employees qualifying as members of the household, with the employer as its head. The company envelops the employee's personal family, taking social and economic responsibility for it, and the employee's family in turn considers the company its primary concern. In this sense the role of the *ie* institution is now played by the company, or any unit of work organization, and the concept of the *ie* persists in group identity as the basis of Japanese social structure.

Iejima
伊江島

Island west of the Motobu Peninsula of the main island of Okinawa; part of Okinawa Prefecture. Except for a rock mountain in the east, Iejima is generally flat. The island was the site of fierce fighting between Japanese and American forces during World War II. Area: 23 sq km (9 sq mi).

iemoto
家元

A term used in traditional Japanese arts, such as music, dance, flower arrangement, tea ceremony, and Nō, to refer to either the founder of a school or the current head of the school, who is usually a direct descendant of the founder. The *iemoto* is one of many manifestations in Japanese society of the hierarchical pattern of relationships modeled on the *ie* (household) and *dōzoku* (extended kin group).

The *iemoto* of each school inherits the secret traditions and prized art objects of the school from the previous *iemoto.* He (or less typically she) is the final arbiter regarding orthodox practices of the school. He also has the sole right to award certificates of achievement, publish the school's secret techniques, and expel members of the school. Each *iemoto* is followed by disciples, whom he recognizes as accredited teachers (*natori*). They are in turn masters of their own disciples.

Ienaga textbook review case
教科書裁判

(*kyōkasho saiban*). Also known as Ienaga *soshō.* A series of lawsuits initiated by Ienaga Saburō (b 1913), a historian and textbook writer, challenging the constitutionality and legality of the Japanese government's textbook review system. In 1965 Ienaga, then a professor at the Tōkyō University of Education, filed a suit seeking recovery of royalties lost due to the Ministry of Education's 1963 disapproval and 1964 conditional approval of the fifth edition of his high school textbook *Shin nihonshi* (New History of Japan). In 1967 Ienaga filed a second suit seeking to reverse the ministry's 1966 rejection of a new application for approval of his partially revised version of the book.

The Tōkyō District Court, deciding the second case in 1970, found that the review in question was in effect an examination by an administrative agency of the substance of the thoughts and ideas of the writer, and therefore not only exceeded the limits set by the Basic Law on Education, but also constituted censorship in violation of article 21 of the CONSTITUTION OF JAPAN. The Tōkyō High Court agreed and dismissed the Ministry of Education's appeal in 1976. In 1982, however, the Supreme Court overturned the decisions of the lower courts and remanded the case for further review. In June 1989 the Tōkyō High Court, relying on the highly technical ground of mootness, repealed its original judgment.

In the meantime, the Tōkyō High Court also ruled on Ienaga's first suit in 1986, holding that the review in question fell short of unconstitutional censorship, even if it went so far as to constitute an examination of the substance of the ideas of the writer.

Two years before this judgment, Ienaga filed another lawsuit, this time challenging the validity of the "recommendations" issued by the Ministry of Education in 1980–83 for revision of his textbook in order to modify his descriptions of brutal behavior by the Imperial Japanese Army during World War II. In October 1989 the Tōkyō District Court, while upholding the constitutionality of the textbook review system, awarded the plaintiff partial damages on the grounds that there had been an excessive exercise of discretionary authority by the ministry.

Iga ware This water jar is named *Yabure-bukuro* (Torn Pouch) after the large cracks and rifts that crisscross it, which are features of Iga ceramics. Late 16th century. Height 22 cm. Gotō Art Museum, Tōkyō.

igusa The stems and flowers of this perennial. The sturdy stems, about 2 mm in diameter, are used for woven mats and footwear.

Iha Fuyū The founder of modern linguistic study of the Okinawan language was also known as a devoted Christian and prohibitionist.

Ie no hikari 家の光

(The Light of the Home). Monthly magazine designed especially for the members of AGRICULTURAL COOPERATIVE ASSOCIATIONS. Founded in 1925 by the Sangyō Kumiai Chūōkai, forerunner of the central coordinating body of the cooperatives, for the purpose of popularizing the agricultural cooperative movement. After World War II, a more popular format was introduced, aimed toward the rural housewife and offering reading entertainment for the rural population in general. It had 1.2 million subscribers in 1990.

ienoko and rōtō 家子と郎党

(*ienoko to rōtō;* warriors' vassals). Subordinate members of a warrior band (BUSHIDAN) in the mid-Heian period and the Kamakura period (i.e., 10th–14th centuries). *Ienoko* (literally, "children of the house") were blood kinsmen of the chief of the warrior band, holding their own estates (*honryō*) and managing their family affairs independently of the lineage chief (*sōryō*), although their actions were under his supervision. Family members without landed inheritance were called *kenin.* In the Kamakura period (1185–1333) direct retainers of the shōgun were called GOKENIN, and their branch-family members were called *ienoko.*

Rōtō originally signified warriors who had no blood ties to the band they joined and who came from low-ranking *samurai* families. They held no land of their own. Later the term was applied to nonlineage members, even those who held land. Under the Kamakura shogunate the *rōtō* of the *gokenin* were considered the shōgun's secondary vassals (BAISHIN), but not members of the samurai class. The two terms were eventually combined into one, *ienoko rōtō,* to designate all of a warrior's retainers. See also SŌRYŌ SYSTEM.

Ieshima Islands 家島諸島

(Ieshima Shotō). Archipelago in the western HARIMA SEA. Also called the Ejima Islands. Part of Hyōgo Prefecture. They are located along an important transportation route in Japan's coastal waters. The main islands include Ieshima; Nishijima, where young yellowtail are cultivated; Bōzejima; and Tangajima, where stone quarries are located. The remaining 40 islands are uninhabited.

Iga Basin → Ueno Basin

Igakusho 医学所

School of Western medicine founded in 1858 in the Kanda district of Edo (now Tōkyō) as a smallpox vaccination clinic by ITŌ GEMBOKU and other scholars of WESTERN LEARNING. The clinic was placed under the supervision of the Tokugawa shogunate (1603–1867) in 1860, and after a reorganization of its activities under OGATA KŌAN, it was named the Igakusho (Medical School) in 1863. Taken

over by the Meiji government in 1868, the Igakusho later became the medical school of Tōkyō University.

Igarashi Chikara 五十嵐力

(1874–1947). Scholar of Japanese literature. Born in Yamagata Prefecture. Graduate of Tōkyō Semmon Gakkō (now Waseda University), where he later lectured on HEIAN LITERATURE and war chronicles (GUNKI MONOGATARI). He pioneered the study of rhetoric in Japan with *Bunshō kōwa* (1905, Lectures on Writing) and subsequent works.

Iga ware 伊賀焼

(*iga-yaki*). Ceramics made in Iga Province (now Mie Prefecture; near the city of Iga Ueno). Iga ware was most highly prized for TEA CEREMONY use, the height of production being in the late Azuchi-Momoyama period (1568–1600) and early Edo period (1600–1868). Up to the late 16th century Iga ware had been crude, rustic, and primarily for local domestic use; it was then discovered by the tea masters FURUTA ORIBE and KOBORI ENSHŪ and introduced as tea-ceremony ware. In the late 17th century production slowed down, and by the late 18th century it stopped altogether. In 1937 Kikuyama Taneo resumed production, which continues today. Cracks or splits on the surface of Iga ware are desired, and the primitive appearance, with twisted and rugged shapes, more closely resembles a product of nature than of man.

Igaya Chiharu 猪谷千春

(1931–). Skier; the first Japanese to win a Winter Olympics medal. Born on one of the Kuril Islands, he began receiving ski instruction from his father at the age of three. Later, Igaya transferred from Rikkyō University to Dartmouth College in the United States to take advantage of its skiing instruction. He won the silver medal in the slalom in the 1956 Olympic Games held in Italy. He became a member of the International Olympic Committee in 1982.

igo → go

igusa 藺草

(mat rush). *Juncus effusus* var. *decipiens.* Also known as *i* and *tōshinsō.* A perennial plant of the family Juncaceae that grows in marshy ground throughout Japan. In the wild the rush reaches a height of 25–100 centimeters (10–40 in), but when cultivated as a winter crop in rice paddies it reaches 120–150 centimeters (47–59 in). Dried *igusa* is woven to make *goza* mats and the covering of TATAMI mats and ZŌRI. The pith was formerly used to make lamp wicks (*tōshin*). *Igusa* is cultivated chiefly in Kumamoto, Okayama, and Kōchi prefectures.

Iha Fuyū 伊波普猷

(1876–1947). Linguist, ethnologist, and folklorist; founder of modern linguistic study of the Okinawan language. Also known as Iba Fuyū. Iha was born and raised in Naha, Okinawa. His interest in the linguistic study of Okinawan culture developed while he was attending the Third Higher School in Kyōto (1900–1903) and the linguistics department of Tōkyō University (1903–06).

Iha returned to Okinawa and in 1909 was appointed the first director of the Okinawa Prefectural Library. In 1924 he resigned from the library directorship and moved to Tōkyō to devote the rest of his life to various re-

search projects, including the textual study of *Omoro sōshi,* an anthology of poems (1531–1623?) of the Okinawan kingdom, and the compilation of a dictionary of the Okinawan language. His significant works are collected in the 11-volume *Iha Fuyū zenshū* (1974–76).

Ihara Saikaku → Saikaku

Iha shell mound 伊波貝塚

(Iha *kaizuka*). Prehistoric site in Iha, in the city of Ishikawa, Okinawa Prefecture; contemporaneous with the Late Jōmon period (ca 2500 BC–ca 1000 BC; also dated as ca 2000 BC–ca 1000 BC) culture in Japan proper. A shell stratum about 60 centimeters (24 in) thick extends over an area of 150 square meters (1,614 sq ft) on a limestone fault slope. Excavated in 1920, it is one of the few Okinawan SHELL MOUNDS to have been investigated. The site yielded STONE TOOLS; shell and BONE ARTICLES; and deep, flat-bottomed pots with rim punctuate design. See also OGIDŌ SHELL MOUND.

Iida 飯田[市]

City in southern Nagano Prefecture, central Honshū. Iida developed as a castle town in the Edo period (1600–1868). Mulberry trees are grown for silkworm cultivation. Other products are pears, apples, *kōri-dōfu* (dried bean curd), and MIZUHIKI (paper strings used for decorations). In recent years an electronics and precision-instruments industry has been set up. The flowering apple trees on the main street and boating on the Tenryūgawa attract tourists. Pop: 91,859.

Iida Dakotsu 飯田蛇笏

(1885–1962). HAIKU poet. Real name Iida Takeharu; also known as Sanro. Born in Yamanashi Prefecture; attended Waseda University. Influenced by the naturalist literary movement (see NATURALISM) and one of the foremost disciples of TAKAHAMA KYOSHI, the leader of the Hototogisu school of traditional haiku, he contributed to HOTOTOGISU magazine. His haiku are characterized by forceful descriptions of nature. Collections of his works include *Sanroshū* (1932) and *Kodamashū* (1940, Echoes).

Iida Incident 飯田事件

(Iida Jiken). An unsuccessful plot by activists of the FREEDOM AND PEOPLE'S RIGHTS MOVEMENT to overthrow the government in 1884. In April 1884 members of the Kōdō Kyōkai (Justice Society), a political society based in Nagoya, collaborated with members of the Aikoku Seirisha (Patriotic Truth Society), a political society in Iida, Nagano Prefecture. Their avowed purpose was to awaken people to the necessity of parliamentary constitutional government, first through underground publications, and later, if necessary, by force. Muramatsu Aizō (1857–1939) of the Kōdō Kyōkai engineered the conspiracy, which aimed at organizing the peasant unrest caused by the deflationary policies of Finance Minister MATSUKATA MASAYOSHI into a general uprising against the central government, but the plot was discovered before it could get underway. In early December its leaders were tracked down and imprisoned.

Iida Makoto 飯田亮

(1933–). Businessman; chairman of SECOM CO, LTD (1976–). Born in Tōkyō. After graduating from Gakushūin University, he established the first security company in Japan, Security Patrols Co (now Secom Co, Ltd), with Toda Juichi in 1962. Iida served as president and director until becoming chairman. He transformed Secom into an integrated information-service enterprise equipped with sophisticated technology.

Iida Ryūta 飯田龍太

(1920–). HAIKU poet. Born in Yamanashi Prefecture; graduated from Kokugakuin University. His father was the haiku poet IIDA DAKOTSU. He published his first collection of haiku, *Hyakko no tani* (One Hundred Valleys), in 1954. After the death of his father in 1962 he became editor of the haiku magazine *Unmo*. (*Unmo* ceased publication in 1992.) Iida received the Yomiuri Literary Prize for his fourth haiku collection, *Bōon* (1968, Forgotten Sound).

Iide Mountains 飯豊山地

(Iide Sanchi). Mountain range extending across Yamagata, Niigata, and Fukushima prefectures, central Honshū. The highest peak is Iidesan (2,105 m; 6,904 ft). Part of BANDAI-ASAHI NATIONAL PARK, the range's principal attractions are its virgin forests and magnificent mountain formations.

Iimoriyama 飯盛山

Hill in the northeastern part of the city of Aizu Wakamatsu, Fukushima Prefecture, northern Honshū. Famous as the burial place of the BYAKKOTAI (White Tiger Brigade), a group of youths who committed suicide after failing to defend Wakamatsu Castle against imperial troops in 1868 in the BOSHIN CIVIL WAR. Their 20 tombstones stand beside a monument erected in their memory. Height: 380 m (1,247 ft).

Ii Naomasa 井伊直政

(1561–1602). Warrior of the Azuchi-Momoyama period (1568–1600) and a chief vassal of TOKUGAWA IEYASU. When Ieyasu was given extensive territory in the Kantō region by TOYOTOMI HIDEYOSHI in 1590, Naomasa was appointed lord of Minowa Castle in Kōzuke (now Gumma Prefecture). After the Battle of SEKIGAHARA in 1600, he was also given a fief in Ōmi (now Shiga Prefecture), which became the family seat.

Ii Naosuke 井伊直弼

(1815–60). Thirteenth *daimyō* of the Hikone domain (now part of Shiga Prefecture) who, as TAIRŌ (great elder) of the Tokugawa shogunate (1603–1867), was effectively the dictator of Japan for 23 months in 1858–60. During his rule Ii temporarily stemmed the erosion of shogunal primacy in Japan. However, he failed to initiate any vigorous policies that could protect the shogunate against Western encroachment from without and dissension within.

Born in Hikone, Ii succeeded his older brother Naooki (1796–1850) as daimyō. The arrival of Commodore PERRY's ships in 1853 turned Ii's attention from Hikone to national affairs. Ii supported the KANAGAWA TREATY (1854), clashing with TOKUGAWA NARIAKI of the Mito domain (now part of Ibaraki Prefecture) over the question. Two new issues—the negotiation of a commercial treaty with the West and the choosing of a successor for the ailing shōgun Iesada (1824–58)—led to turmoil. The former issue was of immense importance to the nation as a whole, so the daimyō were anxious to ensure a satisfactory outcome. The succession issue assumed great importance because the choice of a successor was the key to shaping all future shogunate policy.

After his appointment as *tairō* Ii moved

promptly to secure his control of the shogunate, shunting aside uncooperative officials and warning others to obey his instructions. He hoped to secure daimyō support and imperial sanction for the HARRIS TREATY, a commercial treaty with the United States, which he would then have the shōgun formally approve. Unfortunately for Ii's strategy, American consul Townsend HARRIS grew impatient with the delays and threatened that a British armada would soon arrive and extort a more punitive treaty if his own draft were not accepted as a model for later negotiations. Reports of naval movements lent weight to Harris's warning, and Ii concluded that he must sign the treaty even without imperial approval. On 29 July 1858 his delegates signed the Harris Treaty. A new burst of concerted opposition from the great daimyō and concurrent agitation involving politicized *samurai* only reinforced Ii's determination to settle the succession issue as well, and six days later he had TOKUGAWA IEMOCHI designated heir. Immediate issues were thus settled, but Ii correctly saw the unprecedented political activism by the court, great daimyō, and samurai during the treaty negotiations as a threat to political order, and he resolved to stop it. Known as the ANSEI PURGE, this policy of repression was to be brought to an end by Ii's assassination in March 1860.

By the autumn of 1859, however, most signs of political disruption had subsided, and Ii felt encouraged to move to a policy of gradual reconciliation. He now planned to arrange a marriage between the new shōgun, Iemochi, and Princess KAZU, a sister of Emperor KŌMEI. Negotiations progressed during the winter, and as spring approached it appeared that a more harmonious political period was dawning (see also MOVEMENT FOR UNION OF COURT AND SHOGUNATE).

The one area of domestic political difficulty that clouded Ii's policy of reconciliation was the shogunate's relationship to the Mito domain. His conviction that Tokugawa Nariaki was the source of his difficulties led him to pursue a policy of exceptional harshness, punishing not only Nariaki but also many of his supporters in Mito. As a result the factional tension that had plagued Mito reached unprecedented levels. Within days of Nariaki's incarceration in July 1858, large numbers of Mito retainers began to maneuver against Ii, the shogunate, and one another. As bitterness, fear, and overt military activity grew in Mito during 1859, Ii responded by increasing the pressure. On 24 March 1860 a band of men intercepted Ii on his way to Edo Castle and murdered him (see SAKURADAMONGAI INCIDENT).

Iinuma Yokusai 飯沼慾斎

(1782–1865). Botanist and doctor of medicine who introduced modern European botany into *honzōgaku* (traditional pharmacognosy) studies in Japan. Born in Ise (now Mie Prefecture), he studied medicine and practiced in Mino (now Gifu Prefecture). He engaged in Dutch Learning (Rangaku) under UDAGAWA YŌAN in Edo (now Tōkyō) and studied *honzōgaku* under ONO RANZAN and Mizutani Toyobumi (1779–1833). His *Sōmoku zusetsu* (1856, Plant Atlas) is in 20 volumes and contains 1,215 species of herbs arranged in the Linnaean system of plant classification rather than in the traditional system.

Iiyama 飯山[市]

City in northeastern Nagano Prefecture, central Honshū, on the river Chikumagawa. A

castle town since 1579, Iiyama has long been the commercial center of northern Nagano. Local products are rice, skis, Buddhist altars, and Japanese paper (*washi*). There is a fast-growing electronics industry. Heavy snows make it a popular skiing area. SHIMAZAKI TŌSON's novel *Hakai* (1906; tr *The Broken Commandment*, 1974) was set in Iiyama. Pop: 28,114.

Ii Yōhō 伊井蓉峰

(1871–1932). Actor. Born in Tōkyō. Real name Ii Shinzaburō. In 1891 he joined the KAWAKAMI OTOJIRŌ troupe, popular for its social satire plays. In 1895 he founded the Isami Engeki drama troupe, whose wide repertoire ranged from CHIKAMATSU MONZAEMON to Shakespeare. Around 1915, Ii, KITAMURA ROKURŌ, and Kawai Takeo (1877–1942), who had joined forces some 10 years earlier, came to be called "the SHIMPA (new school) three."

Iizaka Hot Spring 飯坂温泉

(Iizaka Onsen). Located in the city of Fukushima, northern Fukushima Prefecture, northern Honshū. A simple thermal spring; water temperature 40°–70°C (104°–158°F). Situated along the river Surikamigawa, it is one of the most famous spas in the Tōhoku region.

Iizawa Tadasu 飯沢匡

(1909–). Playwright. Real name Izawa Tadasu. Born in Wakayama Prefecture; son of Izawa Takio (1869–1949), a bureaucrat-politician, and nephew of the educator IZAWA SHŪJI. Following graduation from Bunka Gakuin in 1933, Iizawa worked as an editor for the newspaper *Asahi shimbun*. He served as editor in chief of such magazines as *Fujin asahi* and *Asahi gurafu*. He began writing plays in the 1930s and was recognized for his humorous works that drew on the comic KYŌGEN tradition. During World War II, his plays criticized government repression and expressed his pacifist sentiments. He received the first Kishida Prize for Drama in 1950 for *Nigō* (Mistress). Throughout the 1960s he wrote radio and television dramas for children. His best-known stage play is *Mō hitori no hito* (1970, Another Person), a satire on Japanese leadership during the war.

Iizuka 飯塚[市]

City in central Fukuoka Prefecture, Kyūshū, on the river Ongagawa. It developed as one of the post-station towns along the highway Nagasaki Kaidō during the Edo period (1600–1868). From 1882 it was the main coal-mining town of the Chikuhō Coalfield. All the mines are now closed. Machinery, food-processing, and electrical-appliance plants as well as a Self Defense Forces base are located here. Pop: 83,131.

Iizuka Kōji 飯塚浩二

(1906–70). Geographer and critic. Born in Tōkyō, Iizuka graduated in 1930 from Tōkyō University, where he majored in economics. He later studied geography at the Sorbonne and translated Paul Vidal de La Blache's *Principes de la géographie humaine* (Principles of Human Geography) into Japanese. His own works include *Chirigaku hihan* (1947, Criticism of Geography) and *Sekai to Nihon* (1955, The World and Japan). Iizuka taught at Rikkyō University in Tōkyō and served as head of the INSTITUTE OF ORIENTAL CULTURE, TŌKYŌ UNIVERSITY. He was known for his theories on the comparative study of cul-

Ikebukuro This Tōkyō district's most famous landmark, the 60-story Sunshine 60 Building, towers over narrow local streets.

tures, his criticism of histories that centered on the West, and his advocacy of the historical significance of the Third World.

ijime→bullying

Ijūin family　　　　伊集院氏
(Ijūinshi). Provincial leaders in southern Kyūshū from the 13th century. Descended from a branch of the SHIMAZU FAMILY, in the 1340s the Ijūin opposed the main Shimazu line by siding with Prince KANENAGA in skirmishes following the KEMMU RESTORATION. From the 16th century through the Edo period (1600–1868), the Ijūin served as retainers of the Shimazu. Ruins of the family castle remain near the present-day city of Ijūin.

ika→squid and cuttlefish

Ikaho　　　　伊香保[町]
Town in central Gumma Prefecture, central Honshū. Situated on the eastern slope of Mt. Haruna (Harunasan), Ikaho is chiefly known as a health resort, with hot springs. Nearby Lake Haruna and the fields of wildflowers on Harunasan also attract tourists. Pop: 4,593.

ikai→court ranks

Ikaruga　　　　斑鳩[町]
Town in northern Nara Prefecture, central Honshū. It is the site of IKARUGA NO MIYA, the palace of the 7th-century leader Prince SHŌTOKU, as well as the temples HŌRYŪJI and CHŪGŪJI associated with him. Pop: 27,595.

Ikaruga no Miya　　　　斑鳩宮
Palace at IKARUGA built by Prince SHŌTOKU in 601, according to the chronicle NIHON SHOKI. The destruction of the palace in 643 by SOGA NO IRUKA and the suicide of Shōtoku's son YAMASHIRO NO ŌE at that time signaled the end of the princely family. What is now the East-

Ikeda Masuo Sentimental Journey. 1970. Copperplate print. 40 × 36 cm. Private collection.

ern Precinct of the temple HŌRYŪJI was built on the palace's site in 739. Remains of the palace were found in 1939.

ikebana→flower arrangement

Ikebe Sanzan　　　　池辺三山
(1864–1912). Meiji-period (1868–1912) journalist. Real name Ikebe Kichitarō. Born in the city of Kumamoto in Kyūshū, he studied at Keiō Gijuku (now Keiō University) in Tōkyō. In 1890 he began working for the newspaper *Nihon*. In 1892 he went to Paris, where, under the pen name Tekkonron, he wrote for the *Nihon* a series of articles entitled *Pari tsūshin* (News from Paris). Returning to Japan, he served in 1896 as editor of the newspaper *Ōsaka asahi shimbun;* in 1897 he became the chief editor of the *Tōkyō asahi shimbun* (see ASAHI SHIMBUN). Ikebe introduced the serialized newspaper novel (SHIMBUN SHŌSETSU) to the *Asahi*, providing such well-known writers as FUTABATEI SHIMEI and NATSUME SŌSEKI with a publishing outlet.

Ikebukuro　　　　池袋
A commercial district that centers on Ikebukuro Station in the central part of Toshima Ward, Tōkyō. In the course of the Meiji (1868–1912) and Taishō (1912–26) periods, Ikebukuro grew from a farm village into a suburban rail terminus. With the development of residential communities along the suburban rail lines in the period after World War II, Ikebukuro rapidly expanded into one of the three biggest subcenters in the metropolis of Tōkyō (the other two being Shinjuku and Shibuya). In addition to being an important nexus in Tōkyō's subway and rail network, the district has a large concentration of department stores, banks, restaurants, bars, and movie theaters.

Ikeda　　　　池田[市]
City in northern Ōsaka Prefecture, central Honshū, northwest of Ōsaka. It is said that the art of weaving was first introduced to Japan by Chinese immigrants (KIKAJIN) who settled here in the 4th century. Ikeda is known for its plants, flower nurseries, and *sake* brewing, but because of its proximity to Ōsaka, much of its farmland is being converted into residential land. Ōsaka International Airport occupies the southern fringe of the city. Pop: 104,218.

Ikeda　　　　池田[町]
Town in northwestern Tokushima Prefecture, Shikoku, on the river Yoshinogawa. Ikeda is the focal point of routes leading to all four prefectures on the island. Its climate is suited to tobacco, and Japan Tobacco, Inc, has a plant here. Many people come to see the nearby gorges IYADANI and ŌBOKE. Pop: 19,616.

Ikeda Daisaku　　　　池田大作
(1928–). Religious leader. Born in Tōkyō. Third president of the SŌKA GAKKAI, one of the NEW RELIGIONS. He helped bring the Sōka Gakkai into the national political arena in 1964 by creating a Sōka Gakkai–related political party, the KŌMEITŌ. In 1970 he adopted a policy of separation of politics and religion. Ikeda was elected president of Sōka Gakkai International in 1975 and retired as president of Sōka Gakkai in 1979.

Ikeda Hayato　　　　池田勇人
(1899–1965). Prime minister from July 1960 to November 1964. Born in Hiroshima Pre-

fecture. Upon graduation from Kyōto University in 1925, he joined the Finance Ministry and served in prefectural tax offices. In 1947 he was named vice-minister of finance. In 1949 he was elected to the House of Representatives as a member of the Democratic Liberal Party (Minshu Jiyūtō) and appointed minister of finance. In October 1952 he was named minister of international trade and industry; a month later he was forced to resign after giving an inflammatory speech. Ikeda visited Washington in October 1953 as Prime Minister YOSHIDA SHIGERU's representative. In his talks with Walter S. Robertson, assistant secretary of state, Ikeda recognized the necessity of increasing Japan's Self Defense Forces in order to reduce the US defense burden (see IKEDA-ROBERTSON TALKS). In 1960 Ikeda became prime minister. His policies to maximize Japan's growth potential— expansion of public expenditures, reduction of taxes, and implementation of low interest rates—resulted in a rapidly expanding economy. See INCOME-DOUBLING PLAN.

Ikeda-Kennedy Agreements
池田・ケネディ協定
(Ikeda-Kenedī Kyōtei). Three agreements for cooperation between the United States and Japan reached by Prime Minister IKEDA HAYATO and President John F. Kennedy during their Washington meetings and announced on 22 June 1961. Separate agreements established three bilateral committees: a United States–Japan Joint Committee of Trade and Economic Affairs, consisting of five cabinet officers from each government; a committee to expand educational and cultural cooperation; and a United States–Japan Joint Scientific Committee to increase scientific cooperation. The Committee of Trade and Economic Affairs held nine meetings in which senior officials consulted on key economic issues; other forms of economic consultation proved more effective, however, and the committee has not met since 1973. The committee on educational and cultural cooperation, known as CULCON, and the committee on scientific matters have both proven extremely active and effective.

Ikeda Kikunae　　　　池田菊苗
(1864–1936). Chemist prominent in the development of physical chemistry in Japan in the early 1900s. He also extracted monosodium glutamate (MSG) from *kombu* (kelp); MSG was later developed into a commercial seasoning product known as Ajinomoto (see AJINOMOTO CO, INC). Born in Kyōto, he graduated from Tōkyō University, where he became a full professor in 1901. He helped establish the INSTITUTE OF PHYSICAL AND CHEMICAL RESEARCH, becoming the first director of its chemistry department.

Ikeda, Lake　　　　池田湖
(Ikedako). Caldera lake in the southwestern Satsuma Peninsula, southwestern Kagoshima Prefecture, Kyūshū. The largest freshwater lake in Kyūshū. Its water is used for irrigation and drinking. Area: 11 sq km (4 sq mi); circumference: 15 km (9 mi); depth: 233 m (764 ft); altitude: 66 m (217 ft).

Ikeda Masuo　　　　池田満寿夫
(1934–). Copperplate printmaker and novelist. Born in China. He won the International Grand Prix for printmaking at the 1966 Venice Biennale. His work is characterized by a lyrical eroticism and irony. In 1977 his novel *Ēge Kai ni sasagu* (Homage to

the Aegean) won the Akutagawa Prize. Ikeda is also active as an essayist.

Ikeda Mitsumasa 池田光政

(1609–82). *Daimyō* of the early Edo period (1600–1868), renowned for his authoritarian but enlightened rule. Mitsumasa inherited a large domain at Himeji in Harima Province (now part of Hyōgo Prefecture), but in 1617 he was transferred by the TOKUGAWA SHOGUNATE (1603–1867). In 1632 he was transferred again to Okayama, a domain comprising Bizen and a portion of Bitchū (now part of Okayama Prefecture). Mitsumasa's reputation as a model administrator rests on his use of Confucian principles as a rationale for government and on his employ of Confucian scholars, such as KUMAZAWA BANZAN, as political advisers. In 1641 he founded the Hanabatake Kyōjō, often called the first domain school (*hankō*) in Japan, which was in 1666 replaced by a new college for SAMURAI, Karigakkan. In 1668 he embarked on a scheme to establish 123 elementary schools (*tenaraijo*) "for peasant youths," a progressive but costly program that was abandoned by his successor. Only one of the educational institutions planned by Mitsumasa—the famous Shizutani Gakkō—survived throughout the Edo period.

Ikeda Nagaoki 池田長発

(1837–79). Retainer of the Tokugawa shogunate (1603–1867). Born in Edo (now Tōkyō), Ikeda rose swiftly in the bureaucratic ranks. He was selected in 1863 to head a shogunate mission to France (see SHOGUNATE MISSIONS TO THE WEST). He advocated an early opening of Japan to the West, a view that led to his dismissal as commissioner of foreign affairs (*gaikoku bugyō*). Reinstated as a naval commissioner (*gunkan bugyō*) in 1867, he soon retired, pleading illness.

Ikeda-Robertson Talks
池田・ロバートソン会談

(Ikeda-Robātoson Kaidan). Discussions between the United States and Japan in October 1953 regarding US military assistance and increasing Japan's defense forces. A joint statement was issued on 30 October 1953 by IKEDA HAYATO, personal representative of Prime Minister YOSHIDA SHIGERU of Japan, and Walter S. Robertson, assistant secretary of state for Far Eastern affairs, who had been meeting in Washington for several weeks. Their statement reported agreement that Japan should increase its self-defense forces. It was agreed that the United States should supply Japan with agricultural commodities and that Japan should use the proceeds from the sale of these commodities to promote the development of its defense production and industrial potential through offshore procurement and investment. These discussions led to the conclusion of the UNITED STATES–JAPAN MUTUAL DEFENSE ASSISTANCE AGREEMENT on 8 March 1954.

Ikeda Shigeaki 池田成彬

(1867–1950). Businessman and politician; also called Ikeda Seihin. Born into a *samurai* family of the Yonezawa domain (now part of Yamagata Prefecture). A graduate of Keiō Gijuku (now Keiō University), Ikeda also studied in the United States, receiving a BA degree from Harvard College in 1895. He then entered the Mitsui Bank, Ltd, where his talents were recognized by the bank's director, NAKAMIGAWA HIKOJIRŌ, whose daughter he later married. By 1909 Ikeda had become managing director, a position he held until

1933. In that year he succeeded DAN TAKUMA as managing director of the Mitsui holding company, the Mitsui Gōmei Kaisha. He retired from Mitsui in 1936. The following year Ikeda was appointed governor of the Bank of Japan. He was finance minister and minister of commerce and industry in the first KONOE FUMIMARO cabinet (1937–39). He was appointed to the Privy Council in 1941. After World War II Ikeda was barred from public office under the OCCUPATION PURGE.

Ikeda Terumasa 池田輝政

(1564–1613). *Daimyō* of the Azuchi-Momoyama period (1568–1600). With his father he served ODA NOBUNAGA and TOYOTOMI HIDEYOSHI. When his father and brother died in the KOMAKI NAGAKUTE CAMPAIGN (1584), Terumasa became the lord of Ōgaki Castle in Mino (now part of Gifu Prefecture). In 1590 he was moved to Yoshida Castle in Mikawa (now part of Aichi Prefecture) with a domain assessed at 152,000 *koku* (see KOKUDAKA). He supported TOKUGAWA IEYASU at the Battle of SEKIGAHARA in 1600 and was given the domain of Harima (now part of Hyōgo Prefecture), assessed at 520,000 *koku*, where he extensively renovated HIMEJI CASTLE.

Ikedaya Incident 池田屋事件

(Ikedaya Jiken). Armed encounter in July 1864 between antishogunate, proimperial *samurai* and the shogunate's special police force, the SHINSENGUMI, at the Ikedaya, an inn located in the center of Kyōto. After the COUP D'ETAT OF 30 SEPTEMBER 1863, in which extremists from the Chōshū domain (now Yamaguchi Prefecture) were expelled from Kyōto, pro-Chōshū loyalists sought to regain control of Kyōto and plotted the assassination of Tokugawa leaders and pro-shogunate court nobles. On the night of 8 July the Shinsengumi, led by KONDŌ ISAMI, attacked a gathering of these activists at the Ikedaya. Eight activists were killed, 4 wounded, and more than 20 arrested. News of this encounter was an important factor in Chōshū's decision to attempt to retake Kyōto by military force (see HAMAGURI GOMON INCIDENT). See also MEIJI RESTORATION.

Ikeda Yōson 池田遥邨

(1895–1988). Japanese-style (NIHONGA) painter. Real name Ikeda Shōichi. Born in Okayama Prefecture. Ikeda graduated from Kyōto Shiritsu Kaiga Semmon Gakkō (now Kyōto City University of Arts) and studied under the *nihonga* painter TAKEUCHI SEIHŌ. He received the highest award at the 1930 Teiten (Exhibition of the Imperial Fine Arts Academy). He painted in a style at once elegant and joyous. Ikeda was awarded the Order of Culture in 1987.

Ikegai Shōtarō 池貝庄太郎

(1869–1934). Inventor and industrial pioneer. Born in Tōkyō. After working as an apprentice in a machine tool shop, in 1889 he established Ikegai Tekkōsho, the first facility in Japan to manufacture industrial lathes. His designs for the Ikegai-type semidiesel engine and numerous other inventions contributed to the modernization of numerous Japanese industries.

Ikehara Dam 池原ダム

(Ikehara Damu). Power-generating dam located on the river Kitayamagawa, a tributary of the Kumanogawa, in southeastern Nara Prefecture, central Honshū. Completed in 1964. The gorge DOROKYŌ, located near the

dam, is part of YOSHINO-KUMANO NATIONAL PARK. Height: 111 m (364 ft); storage capacity: 220 million cu m (7.8 billion cu ft).

Ikejima Shimpei 池島信平

(1909–73). Editor and president of BUNGEI SHUNJŪ, LTD, one of Japan's major publishing houses. Born in Tōkyō. He entered the company after graduating from Tōkyō University in 1933 and quickly proved himself a skilled interviewer in informal discussions. Appointed chief editor in 1956 of *Bungei shunjū*, the firm's leading magazine, he increased its circulation to 1 million. He was president of the firm from 1966 until his death. A mild conservative, to the end he remained a constructive critic of political extremes.

Ikenami Shōtarō 池波正太郎

(1923–90). Novelist and playwright. Born in Tōkyō. Ikenami began his career as a SHINKOKUGEKI dramatist. In 1960 he received the Naoki Prize for *Sakuran* (1960, Confusion), later establishing himself as an author of period novels with three major series: "Onihei hankachō" (1967–90, The Court Records of Onihei), "Kenkaku shōbai" (1972–89, This Sword for Hire), and "Shikakenin Fujieda Baian" (1972–90, Fujieda Baian, the Mastermind). Other works include *Sanada taiheiki* (1974–82, War Chronicles of the Sanada Clan) and his personal collection *Ikenami Shōtarō sakuhin shū* (10 vols, 1976). Ikenami is also remembered for his essays.

Ikenishi Gonsui 池西言水

(1650–1722). *Haikai* (prototype of HAIKU) poet. Born in Nara, he lived in Edo (now Tōkyō), traveled extensively, then settled in Kyōto in the early 1680s. Like BASHŌ, he sought to raise *haikai* to a serious mode of artistic expression. His main collections are *Edo shimmichi* (1678, New Streets in Edo) and *Miyakoburi* (1690, Tunes from the Capital).

Ikenobō 池坊

The oldest school of FLOWER ARRANGEMENT (*ikebana*) in Japan. Its first head was the Tendai sect Buddhist priest Ikenobō Senkei (fl mid-15th century). Senkei is said to have originated the *rikka* ("standing flowers") style of arrangement. The headquarters of Ikenobō are at Rokkakudō, a Buddhist temple in Naka-Gyō Ward, Kyōto. Ikenobō Sen'ei (b 1933) became the 45th-generation head of the school in 1945. In 1992 there were some 60,000 teachers of Ikenobō style flower arrangement worldwide, and there were said to be 1.5 million students. In the same year there were 356 chapters in Japan and 64 foreign chapters in countries including the United States, Taiwan, Canada, Brazil, South Korea, the Philippines, and Germany.

Ikenobō A traditional Ikenobō flower arrangement in the *rikka* ("standing flowers") style. The materials include pine, bamboo, narcissus, chrysanthemum, and *umemodoki*.

Ikenami Shōtarō This novelist and playwright is best known for his historical fiction.

Ike no Taiga The Convenience of Firewood, a leaf from the landscape series album *Jūben jūgi* (Ten Conveniences and Ten Pleasures). 1771. Colors and ink on paper. 18 × 18 cm. Kawabata Yasunari Kinen Kai, Kanagawa Prefecture. National Treasure.

Ike no Gyokuran　　池玉瀾

(1728?–84). BUNJINGA (literati painting) artist and WAKA poet. Also known as Tokuyama Gyokuran; real name Ike no Machi. Her grandmother, Kaji, and her mother, Yuri, were well-known *waka* poets who operated a teahouse, which Gyokuran inherited, in the Gion district of Kyōto. Gyokuran studied under the literati painter YANAGISAWA KIEN and married the literati master IKE NO TAIGA. Her painting style closely resembles that of her husband. She specialized in fan paintings.

Ikeno Seiichirō　　池野成一郎

(1866–1943). Botanist. Born in Edo (now Tōkyō). A graduate of Tōkyō University, he later taught there. He proved the presence of motile spermatozoa in some gymnosperms while working with HIRASE SAKUGORŌ in 1896. Ikeno used the Japanese sago palm (*sotetsu*; *Cycas revoluta*) in making the discovery, and Hirase used the gingko (*ichō*). This discovery greatly influenced botanical studies. Ikeno later became interested in genetics, analyzing the genes of rice and other plants. He wrote *Zikken idengaku* (*Jikken idengaku*; 1906) in Japanese, but using the Roman alphabet.

Ike no Taiga　　池大雅

(1723–76). Artist and calligrapher in the BUNJINGA (literati painting) tradition. He was born in the Kyōto area, where his father worked in the silver mint. From an early age Taiga showed extraordinary talent; at six he was taken to the Ōbaku Zen temple MAMPUKUJI in Uji, an important repository of Chinese art and culture, where he gave a calligraphy demonstration that won him praise and prizes. YANAGISAWA KIEN, one of the pioneers of Japanese *bunjin* painting, became his teacher and benefactor. In 1751 Taiga met GION NANKAI, also prominent in the early *bunjinga* movement, from whom he received a Chinese woodblock-print style manual. He was also influenced by the techniques of SŌTATSU and KŌRIN and by Zen painting (ZENGA) and Western painting.

In all, some 2,000 existing paintings have been attributed to Taiga. The majority are landscapes, although he also painted figures of the "Four Gentlemen" (SHIKUNSHI: orchid, bamboo, plum, and chrysanthemum).

Taiga's reputation as a calligrapher is predicated on the same mastery of the brush and originality that characterize his painting. He was one of the earlier Edo-period calligraphers to make extensive use of archaic Chinese script styles, which are employed in the two earliest of his surviving paintings. He was married to the *bunjinga* artist IKE NO GYOKURAN.

Ike no Zenni　　池禅尼

(fl mid–12th century). Wife of TAIRA NO TADAMORI; stepmother of the powerful leader TAIRA NO KIYOMORI. After the HEIJI DISTURBANCE of 1160, she persuaded Kiyomori to commute the death sentence of MINAMOTO NO YORITOMO, who later instigated the TAIRA-MINAMOTO WAR (1180–85), which ended with the downfall of the Taira. The 13th-to-14th-century chronicle AZUMA KAGAMI states that Yoritomo restored 34 confiscated estates to Ike no Zenni's son Taira no Yorimori (1131–86) out of gratitude for her intercession.

Iki　　壱岐

Island in the Genkai Sea, 27 km (17 mi) northwest of the town of Yobuko, Saga Prefecture, northwestern Kyūshū. The highest point is the volcano Takenotsuji (213 m; 699 ft). Iki was a vital point in transportation between Japan and the Asian continent in ancient times. Farming is the chief activity; crops are sweet potatoes, mandarin oranges, and tobacco. Other activities include cattle raising, fishing, and pearl culture. The island is part of the Iki-Tsushima Quasi-National Park. Area: 134 sq km (52 sq mi).

iki and sui　　粋と粋

(*iki to sui*). Aesthetic and moral ideals of urban commoners in the Edo period (1600–1868). The concept of *sui* was cultivated initially in the Ōsaka area during the late 17th century, while *iki* prevailed mostly in Edo (now Tōkyō) during the early 19th century. Aesthetically both pointed toward an urbane, chic, bourgeois type of beauty with undertones of sensuality. Morally they envisioned the tasteful life of a person who was wealthy but not attached to money, who enjoyed sensual pleasure but was never carried away by carnal desires, and who knew all the intricacies of earthly life but was capable of disengaging himself from them. In their insistence on sympathetic understanding of human feelings, *sui* and *iki* resembled the Heian courtiers' ideal of *aware* (see MONO NO AWARE), yet they differed from it in their inclusion of the more plebeian aspects of life.

The origin of the word *sui* is not clear. In modern Japanese it is usually written with a Chinese character meaning "pure essence" (Ch: *cui* or *ts'ui*) but other characters like "sour" (*suan*), "to infer" (*tui* or *t'ui*), "water" (*shui*), and "leader" (*shuai*) were also used for transcribing the word. *Sui* comprised all these meanings: it described the language and deportment of a person who fully knew the sour taste of this life and was able to infer other people's suffering, adapt himself to various human situations with the shapelessness of water, and become a leader in taste and fashion for his contemporaries. *Sui* is frequently manifest in the characters of the genre of fiction called UKIYO-ZŌSHI, particularly in those of Ihara SAIKAKU (1642–93).

Iki originally denoted "spirit" or "heart." Later it came to mean "high spirit" or "high heart" and referred also to the way in which a high-spirited person talked, behaved, or dressed. As it became expressive of the Edo commoners' ideal, its connotations were affected by the Ōsaka concept of *sui* and moved closer to the latter. Indeed, *iki* was sometimes used as an equivalent of *sui*. Yet usually it carried a slightly different shade of meaning. As an aesthetic concept *iki* leaned toward a beauty somewhat less colorful than *sui*. Also, *iki* seems to have had a slightly more sensual connotation than *sui*. It was often applied to the description of a woman, especially a professional entertainer who knew exactly how much display of eroticism was desirable by the highest standard of taste. *Iki* had its best literary expression in works of the NINJŌBON genre. *Shunshoku umegoyomi* (1832–33, Spring Love: A Plum-Blossom Almanac) by TAMENAGA SHUNSUI presents especially fine examples of people who conducted themselves in accordance with the ideal of *iki*.

Iki Channel　　壱岐水道

(Iki Suidō). Channel between the Higashi Matsuura Peninsula, Saga Prefecture, Kyūshū, and the island of Iki. Situated on the shortest route between Kyūshū and the Korean peninsula, it has been an important transportation route since ancient times. Width: 20 km (12.4 mi); depth: approximately 50 m (164 ft).

ikigai　　生き甲斐

(that for which life is worth living; from *iki*, "living," and *kai*, "value, effectiveness, meaning"). A popular phrase often used in discussions of individual life goals and a frequent subject of public opinion surveys in Japan. A Japanese mother will often say that her children are her only *ikigai*, or a man will find his *ikigai* in his job. Individuals may commit suicide when they no longer have an *ikigai*. Since the early 1960s this word has become a focal point for public concern. With Japan's defeat in World War II, many old values and beliefs were lost. The Japanese began to look for *ikigai* in material comforts and a happy family life, no doubt in reaction to the traditional stress upon frugality, hard work, and selfless dedication to collective causes. A number of opinion surveys on *ikigai* seem to confirm this new attitude. Women consistently rank a happy home and children highest and service to society very low. For men, work ranks highest until their forties, when they split into work-oriented and family-oriented groups.

ikigami　　生き神

(living human deity). Living individual revered as a deity (KAMI). Emperors were called *akitsukami* or *arahitogami* (living deity) until 1946, when the status, which had been supported by the STATE SHINTŌ (Kokka Shintō) system, was renounced by the emperor himself. Generally individuals with extraordinary charisma were deified after their death until the Edo period (1600–1868), when the concept was also applied to the living. Some recent charismatic religious leaders, such as NAKAYAMA MIKI and KITAMURA SAYO, were declared *ikigami*.

Iki no Muraji Hakatoko no fumi
伊吉連博徳書

Journal kept by Iki no Hakatoko, a diplomat in a mission to Tang (T'ang) China in 659. Although the journal is no longer extant, passages are quoted in the 8th-century chronicle *Nihon shoki*. Its descriptions of the missions to China are valuable for studying relations between the two countries (see SUI AND TANG [T'ANG] CHINA, EMBASSIES TO).

Ikiru 生きる

(To Live). KUROSAWA AKIRA's 1952 film about a civil servant dying of cancer who comes to question his life and attempts at the end to redeem it. The film breaks naturally into two parts. In the first the civil servant, Watanabe Kanji (played by SHIMURA TAKASHI), attempts in various ways to escape or ignore the reality of his illness. In the second half of the picture Watanabe has died, and we, attending his wake, learn from workers in his office that he had ended by devoting himself to his work, but for the first time in a truly meaningful way. He had pushed through the completion of a playground in the face of the type of bureaucratic indifference that he himself had once personified. In discovering a way to be responsible for others he had found out what it means to live.

Ikkei Dōsan → Manase Dōsan

ikki 一揆

A term that originally meant to do something in agreement, but which came to denote both a league formed for military purposes and an uprising by local warriors and peasants in the Muromachi period (1333–1568). By the Edo period (1600–1868) it was used to refer to any kind of peasant revolt. The most common forms of uprisings were the TSUCHI IKKI and KUNI IKKI of the Muromachi period and the HYAKUSHŌ IKKI of the Edo period.

The earliest *ikki* were an outgrowth of the struggle to establish Ashikaga rule in the first half of the 14th century. Leagues of local warriors united to thwart attempts by SHUGO (military governors) to control the provinces. Originally many of these leagues were united by blood ties, but land soon became the unifying factor. This latter form of *ikki*, operating on pledges of mutual loyalty, evolved into the *kuni ikki*. At about the same time the peasants of central Japan were also forming leagues called *tsuchi ikki* (or *doikki*) that were directed against SHŌEN (estate) proprietors. The early *tsuchi ikki* of the second half of the 14th century were generally concerned with the reduction of taxes and corvée or the removal of unpopular estate officials.

By the 15th century the motivation for revolt changed to inducing the shogunate to proclaim a cancellation of debts (TOKUSEI). Starting with the Shōchō Uprising of 1428, more than 100 *tsuchi ikki* followed before the end of the century. The Kakitsu Uprising of 1441 expanded to include tens of thousands of peasants before winning its demand for debt cancellation. The *bashaku* (teamster) and *tokusei* (debt cancellation) *ikki* also fell under this classification.

Although local warrior groups had formed leagues in the 14th century, it was not until the 15th century that provincial uprisings, known as *kuni ikki*, became important. The first important *kuni ikki* was in Harima Province (now Hyōgo Prefecture) in 1429, while the largest was the YAMASHIRO NO KUNI IKKI of 1486. It was not until some of these local landowners and warriors (*kokujin*) had emerged as autonomous territorial lords (Sengoku *daimyō*) that anyone had sufficient military strength to destroy this form of *ikki*. The large-scale uprisings by followers of the Jōdo Shin sect of Buddhism in the late 15th and 16th centuries—referred to as IKKŌ IKKI—were a special type of *kuni ikki*. These uprisings, which began in the 1470s, continued until 1580, when ODA NOBUNAGA destroyed their military power.

During the Edo period *ikki* came to refer to any kind of peasant revolt (*hyakushō ikki*), and it is estimated that more than 2,500 took place during that period. Besides the *hyakushō ikki*, YONAOSHI REBELLIONS ("world renewal" rebellions), protesting a precipitous rise in prices, also occurred in the late Edo period and the early Meiji period (1868–1912).

From the beginning of the Muromachi period to the end of the Edo period, the *ikki* served as the major vehicle for organizing local warriors and peasants to challenge the rule of government authorities. How these authorities reacted to the *ikki* helped determine both the form and strength of government rule in Japan for more than 500 years.

Ikkō ikki 一向一揆

Large-scale uprisings in the late 15th and 16th centuries by adherents of the JŌDO SHIN SECT of Buddhism. Ikkō (single-minded) is another name for the sect; IKKI (league or uprising) is a term for organized lawless activity. Militant acts by Ikkō sectarians began in the 1470s, when the abbot RENNYO, fleeing religious persecution, established his base in the Hokuriku region (now Toyama, Ishikawa, and Fukui prefectures). By 1488 the Ikkō *ikki* had killed the military governor (*shugo*) of Kaga Province (now part of Ishikawa Prefecture) and taken control there, retaining power for nearly a century. Uprisings spread to neighboring provinces and then beyond. Rennyo disapproved of insurrection, and after his death the temple HONGANJI in Kyōto, the center of the sect, was reluctant to assume leadership. In 1563 TOKUGAWA IEYASU suppressed an Ikkō uprising in his native Mikawa Province (now part of Aichi Prefecture). Their defeat in 1580 by ODA NOBUNAGA finally crushed the military power of the Ikkō *ikki*. The tenets of the Jōdo Shin sect encouraged peasant solidarity and millenarian goals, but the local lords (KOKUJIN) who led early Ikkō *ikki* were motivated by more worldly ambitions. Nonetheless, the growth of Ikkō *ikki* into a coordinated national force can be explained only in terms of Jōdo Shin doctrine and organization.

Ikkoku Ichijō Rei 一国一城令

(literally, "Law of One Castle per Province"). Order by TOKUGAWA IEYASU designed to trim *daimyō* power by reducing the number of castles under their control. After Ōsaka Castle fell to Tokugawa forces in 1615 (see ŌSAKA CASTLE, SIEGES OF), Ieyasu issued a regulation ordering daimyō to demolish all castles in their domains except those in which they were living. In following years some 400 castles were torn down, most of them in western Japan. See also BUKE SHOHATTO.

Ikkyū 一休

(1394–1481). Also known as Ikkyū Sōjun. ZEN monk of the RINZAI SECT and eccentric who played a major role in the rebuilding and revitalization of Kyōto's temple DAITOKUJI after the ŌNIN WAR (1467–77). He was a noted poet and calligrapher and an important contributor to the infusion of Japanese art and literature with Zen attitudes and ideals. He is known to most Japanese primarily as a comic Zen character, famed for his unconventional behavior.

It is generally held that Ikkyū was the son of Emperor GO-KOMATSU (r 1382–1412) and a court noblewoman. Ikkyū was placed in the temple Ankokuji in Kyōto as an acolyte at the age of five. In 1410 Ikkyū left Ankokuji

Ikkyū Late-15th-century portrait of the eccentric Zen monk Ikkyū by his disciple Bokusai. The inscription is a poem by Ikkyū rendered in Bokusai's calligraphy.

to become the disciple of Ken'ō Sōi, under whose tutelage he undertook a strict program of meditation and study. After Ken'ō's death in 1415, Ikkyū left Kyōto to join the demanding master Kasō Sōdon (also known as Kesō Shūdon; 1352–1428) at a small hermitage in Katata, a commercial town on the shores of Lake Biwa.

By the late 1420s Ikkyū settled in the port town of SAKAI, where he began to express himself in the unconventional style of "mad Zen." He spent more time in brothels and wineshops than in temples and hermitages, going out of his way to amaze and offend the citizenry of Sakai. During a subsequent wandering period, he began to attract the interest of a number of literary and artistic figures, including the Nō playwright KOMPARU ZENCHIKU, the linked-verse (*renga*) masters SŌGI and SŌCHŌ, and several painters of the emerging SOGA SCHOOL.

In 1455 Ikkyū circulated a collection of poems called the *Jikaishū* (The Self-Admonition Anthology) in which he shifted his attack on the "inauthentic" Zen of the GOZAN temples to excesses that he felt were destroying Zen at the Daitokuji. In 1474 Ikkyū accepted an appointment as the temple's 47th abbot. Though his tenure as abbot was brief, he managed to marshal financial support for the temple and to heal some of the factional divisions that had plagued it. Ikkyū's final years were spent mostly at his Shūon'an hermitage in Takigi, a village halfway between Kyōto and Sakai.

His chief poetic work is the *Kyōunshū* (The Crazy-Cloud Anthology), a collection of over 1,000 Chinese poems. Eight prose pieces are attributed to Ikkyū. Most are simple sermons intended for a popular audience. They include "Gaikotsu" (1457, Skeletons; tr "Ikkyū's Skeletons," 1973), "Bukkigun" (tr "The Buddha's Great War against Hell," 1980), and the *Maka-hannyaharamita shingyō ge* (Explication of the *Mahāprajñāpāramitā-hṛdaya-sūtra*), a highly poetic commentary on the Heart Sutra.

Ikoku nikki 異国日記

(Register of Foreign Affairs). A register of Japan's relations with foreign countries, compiled in the 17th century by SŪDEN, a Zen priest active in affairs of state under the first three Tokugawa shōguns, and Saigaku Genryō (d 1657). The first of its two parts contains accounts of the conduct of foreign affairs and external trade, as well as copies of diplomatic correspondence (much of it drafted by Sūden), from the years 1608–29. The second includes information on the Korean embassies (CHŌSEN TSŪSHINSHI) of 1636, 1643, and 1655 and examples of diplomatic notes drafted by Zen monks dating back to the 13th century.

Ikokusen Uchiharai Rei→
Gaikokusen Uchiharai Rei

Ikoma   生駒[市]
City in northwestern Nara Prefecture, central Honshū, 17 km (11 mi) east of Ōsaka. Formerly a farming village, with the opening of a railway line in the Taishō period (1912–26) and the construction of a cable car line to the temple Hōzanji, the city has flourished. A special local product is *chasen*, bamboo whisks used in the tea ceremony. The grave of the Buddhist monk GYŌGI (668–749) is at the temple Chikurinji. Pop: 99,604.

Ikomayama   生駒山
Mountain on the border between Nara and Ōsaka prefectures, central Honshū; highest peak in the Ikoma Mountains. A Buddhist temple, Hōzanji, is located on the eastern slope. It is a developed recreational center with cable cars and roads. On the summit are a playground and an observatory of Kyōto University. Height: 642 m (2,106 ft).

Ikukunitama Shrine   生国魂神社
(Ikukunitama Jinja; popularly known as Ikutama Jinja). Shintō shrine in Tennōji Ward, Ōsaka; dedicated to the deities Ikushima no Kami and Tarushima no Kami, who are believed to be protectors of the Japanese islands. It has been located at its present site since around 1583. Its annual festival is observed on 9 September.

Ikuno Disturbance   生野の変
(Ikuno no Hen). Armed uprising in November 1863 by proimperial *samurai* and peasants in Ikuno, a silver-mining town under shogunate rule in Tajima Province (now part of Hyōgo Prefecture). Having learned of the uprising of the antishogunate Tenchūgumi (see TENCHŪGUMI REBELLION) in the Nara area two months earlier, HIRANO KUNIOMI and other proimperial samurai under the figurehead leadership of SAWA NOBUYOSHI organized about 2,000 peasants in the Ikuno area. Joined by samurai from the KIHEITAI, the mixed militia that had recently been organized in Chōshū (now Yamaguchi Prefecture), they attacked the shogunal deputy's office. The shogunate immediately ordered neighboring domains to subdue the rebels; the samurai became divided among themselves, the peasants deserted, and within three days the uprising was crushed. The uprising was ostensibly a protest against the expulsion of antishogunate Chōshū samurai from Kyōto (see COUP D'ETAT OF 30 SEPTEMBER 1863).

Ikuno Silver Mine   生野銀山
(Ikuno Ginzan). Located in Ikuno, Hyōgo Prefecture; discovered as early as 807 and developed intensively in the 16th century by the local *daimyō*, Yamana Suketoyo (d 1580). Toward the end of that century the mine came under direct control of the hegemons ODA NOBUNAGA and TOYOTOMI HIDEYOSHI, and ownership later passed to the Tokugawa shogunate. It was the most productive silver mine in Japan during much of the Edo period (1600–1868). The Meiji government then controlled it until the Mitsubishi company bought it in 1896. The largest tin refinery in Japan was located at Ikuno. Its silver exhausted, the mine mainly produced copper and zinc until it was closed in 1973.

Ikuta Chōkō   生田長江
(1882–1936). Literary critic. Real name Ikuta Kōji. Born in Tottori Prefecture; graduate of Tōkyō University. A free thinker influenced by Nietzsche, Ikuta was a literary and social critic and a supporter of the women's movement. Among his works are translations of Nietzsche's *Thus Spake Zarathustra*, D'Annunzio's *The Triumph of Death*, and Dante's *The Divine Comedy* and a commentary on contemporary authors, *Saikin no shōsetsuka* (1912).

Ikutama Shrine→ Ikukunitama Shrine

Ikuta Shungetsu   生田春月
(1892–1930). Poet. Real name Ikuta Seihei. Born in Tottori Prefecture. Although his early poetry expresses a Christian humanism, after 1917 his writing increasingly tends toward nihilism and anarchism. Among his works are collections of poetry, *Reikon no aki* (1917, Autumn of the Soul) and *Shōchō no ika* (1930, The Cuttlefish Symbol); translations of Heinrich Heine's poetry; and an autobiographical novel in three volumes, *Aiyoru tamashii* (1921–24, Spirits That Gather).

Ikuta Yorozu, Rebellion of
    生田万の乱
(Ikuta Yorozu no Ran). An uprising in Echigo (now Niigata Prefecture) staged by Ikuta Yorozu (1801–37) and a small band of his students and local farmers in July 1837. Ikuta had studied in Edo (now Tōkyō) under the KOKUGAKU (National Learning) scholar HIRATA ATSUTANE. He returned to his home domain of Tatebayashi (now part of Gumma Prefecture) but was expelled for criticizing the domain administration. After several years in Edo, in 1836 he moved to Kashiwazaki in Echigo, where he opened a school. Like most of the country Echigo was then suffering from famine (see TEMPŌ FAMINE); domain officials and rice brokers had cornered the rice market, causing prices to rise. Yorozu unsuccessfully made repeated appeals to domain officials for relief. In desperation, he and his followers attacked the local deputy's stronghold at Kashiwazaki. The rebellion was quickly quelled, and Yorozu committed suicide. There was also an unsuccessful rebellion in Ōsaka led by ŌSHIO HEIHACHIRŌ earlier in the year.

Imabari   今治[市]
City in northern Ehime Prefecture, Shikoku, on the Hiuchi Sea. Imabari developed as a castle town after TŌDŌ TAKATORA built Imabari Castle in 1600. A cotton-textile industry grew thereafter, and today is Japan's largest producer of cotton towels. A bridge system is under construction that will link Shikoku to Honshū at Imabari (see HONSHŪ-SHIKOKU BRIDGES). Pop: 123,114.

Imagawa family   今川氏
(Imagawashi). Warrior family of the Muromachi period (1333–1568). The family was descended from Ashikaga Kuniuji, who inherited an estate at Imagawa in Mikawa Province (now part of Aichi Prefecture). His grandson Norikuni (1304?–84) served under ASHIKAGA TAKAUJI, founder of the MUROMACHI SHOGUNATE; the Imagawa were later made military governors (SHUGO) of Suruga and Tōtōmi provinces (now parts of Shizuoka Prefecture). The most famous family member was the poet and general IMAGAWA SADAYO (Imagawa Ryōshun; b 1326). Imagawa Ujichika (1473–1526) and his son IMAGAWA YOSHIMOTO (1519–60) were overlords of Suruga, Tōtōmi, and Mikawa provinces. Ambitious for power, Yoshimoto in 1560 marched on Kyōto but was killed by ODA NOBUNAGA in the Battle of OKEHAZAMA. TAKEDA SHINGEN and TOKUGAWA IEYASU seized the Imagawa domain. Descendants of the Imagawa served the TOKUGAWA SHOGUNATE (1603–1867) as masters of court ceremony (KŌKE). The family's domainal code was the IMAGAWA KANA MOKUROKU.

Imagawa Kana Mokuroku
    今川仮名目録
(The Kana List of Articles of the Imagawa). A domainal law code (BUNKOKUHŌ) of the Sengoku period (1467–1568) enacted by Imagawa Ujichika (1473–1526), lord of Suruga and Tōtōmi provinces (now parts of Shizuoka Prefecture), on 25 May 1526 in 33 articles (31 in an alternate version). Ujichika had been appointed SHUGO (military governor) of the two provinces by the MUROMACHI SHOGUNATE, but this code testifies to his transformation into a SENGOKU DAIMYŌ, the independent ruler of a regional domain. The code reiterates the supremacy of the daimyō and his officers. The privilege of immunity from entry (see FUYU AND FUNYŪ) by *shugo* officials into private landholdings is abridged if not totally abrogated (arts. 22–23). A 21-article supplement (*tsuika*), issued by Ujichika's son IMAGAWA YOSHIMOTO in 1553, further stresses a daimyō's right to pass laws for his domain without reference to the shogunate. A 13-article set of regulations (*sadame*) governing lawsuit procedures, undated but assumed to be Yoshimoto's provision, is commonly attached to the other two documents.

Imagawa Sadayo   今川貞世
(1326–?). Warrior and general, classical (WAKA) poet, and poet of linked verse (RENGA). Commonly known as Imagawa Ryōshun after entering the priesthood in 1367. Born in Kyōto, he succeeded his father, Norikuni (1304?–84), as military governor (SHUGO) of Tōtōmi Province (now part of Shizuoka Prefecture) and was later assigned a position in the shogunal courts of law. In 1371 Sadayo, now Ryōshun, was dispatched as shogunal deputy (*tandai*) to Kyūshū, where for nearly 25 years he fought to establish the shōgun's authority. In 1395 the retired shōgun ASHIKAGA YOSHIMITSU, made suspicious by slanders against Ryōshun, shunted him off as *shugo* of Suruga Province (now part of Shizuoka Prefecture). In 1398 he retired and devoted himself to religious pursuits, to poetry, and to the study of old ceremonial lore and precedents. He died sometime between 1414 and 1418. Only 98 of his poems survive; his literary importance rests on his narrative and polemical writings, ranging from a travel diary to rebuttals and manifestos against the conservative Nijō school of poetry. Ryōshun's works include *Gonjinshū* (1406, Collection of Verbal Trash), a brief account of changes in poetic style through

the ages and the state of contemporary poetry; *Ryōshun isshi den* (1409, Ryōshun's Testament to His Heir; also called *Ben'yōshō* [Notes on the Fundamentals of Poetry]); *Rakusho roken* (about 1412, The Anonymous Document Revealed), a refutation of Nijō attacks on the poet Tamemasa; and *Nan taiheiki* (1402, Errors in the *Taiheiki*), an attack on the historical work TAIHEIKI.

Imagawa Yoshimoto 今川義元

(1519–60). Prominent *daimyō* of the Sengoku period (1467–1568); third son of Ujichika (1473–1526), the *shugo* (military governor) of Suruga and Tōtōmi provinces (now parts of Shizuoka Prefecture). Having established ties by marriage with the TAKEDA FAMILY of Kai Province (now Yamanashi Prefecture), he fought intermittently against the Later Hōjō family (see HŌJŌ FAMILY) of Odawara until an alliance of the three houses was formed in 1554. By 1548 he had gained control of most of Mikawa Province (now part of Aichi Prefecture). His westward advance had brought him in conflict with the ODA FAMILY of Owari Province (now part of Aichi Prefecture); in 1560 he was surprised in his encampment by the inferior force of ODA NOBUNAGA and died in the Battle of OKEHAZAMA. Yoshimoto is known for his attempts to consolidate daimyō power in his domains through land surveys (KENCHI) and for the 1553 set of 21 supplements to the IMAGAWA KANA MOKUROKU, a domainal law code (BUNKOKUHŌ) originally formulated by his father in 1526.

Imaichi 今市[市]

City in central Tochigi Prefecture, central Honshū. During the Edo period (1600–1868) Imaichi flourished as a market and post-station town on the highway leading to the mausoleum of TOKUGAWA IEYASU. Once a major producer of lumber, furniture, and *senkō* (incense sticks), it now has several electrical-appliance and ceramic factories. It is the gateway to the Nikkō National Park. Pop: 56,008.

Imai Isao 今井功

(1914–). Physicist. Born in Dalian (Talian; J: Dairen), China. Graduate of Tōkyō University, where he became a professor in 1950. In 1975 he was appointed professor at Ōsaka University. Imai solved a number of important problems in fluid mechanics through an advanced analytic method based on the theory of complex analysis. He received the Order of Culture in 1988.

Imai Sōkyū 今井宗久

(1520–93). Merchant and tea connoisseur of the Sengoku (1467–1568) and Azuchi-Momoyama (1568–1600) periods. Sōkyū was an influential citizen of the port city of SAKAI, where he was engaged in warehousing and the medicine and arms trades; accordingly, he came into contact with some of the era's most eminent personages, whose acquaintance he cultivated through the medium of the cult of tea. In 1568 he presented two priceless tea ceremony utensils to ODA NOBUNAGA. Nobunaga installed him as intendant (*daikan*) in the northern part of Sakai the next year. Sōkyū served Nobunaga as master of the tea ceremony and as purveyor of munitions. After Nobunaga's death in 1582, Sōkyū for a time enjoyed high favor under TOYOTOMI HIDEYOSHI, as one of his premier tea masters (*sadō*) alongside TSUDA SŌGYŪ and SEN NO RIKYŪ, but he lost favor after 1584.

Imai Tadashi 今井正

(1912–91). Film director. Born in Tōkyō. He studied literature at Tōkyō University, where he participated in radical activities as a member of a communist youth league, for which he was arrested. In 1935 he joined J. O. Studios as an assistant director, later moving to TŌHŌ CO, LTD, when J. O. merged with Tōhō in 1937. He joined the Japan Communist Party after World War II and was later blacklisted by the film industry.

Imai's filmmaking style might be referred to as "*nakanai* realism," or "realism without tears." He was influenced by Italian neorealists such as Vittorio De Sica, as evidenced in *Dokkoi ikiteiru* (1951, And Yet We Live). Imai's finest work includes *Nigorie* (1953, Muddy Waters), MAHIRU NO ANKOKU (1956, Darkness at Noon), and *Yoru no tsuzumi* (1958, Night Drum). Imai differs from other masters of the Japanese film in the informality with which he works. At his best, Imai displays a richness of social perception and an ongoing critique of injustice that render his films evocative studies of the workings of Japanese society.

Imakagami 今鏡

("Mirror of the Present"). Historical tale of the late Heian period (794–1185). Author unknown; possibly Fujiwara no Tametsune. Compiled in 1170, it recounts the events at court during the 150 years from the reign of Emperor Go-Ichijō (r 1016–36) to that of Emperor Takakura (r 1168–80). It presents recollections by a fictional narrator, who claims to have served the author MURASAKI SHIKIBU and who presents herself as the granddaughter of the ŌKAGAMI's narrator Ōyake no Yotsugi. Modeled on the *Ōkagami*, it continues the narrative from 1025, where the older work left off. It resembles the *Genji monogatari* (TALE OF GENJI) and the EIGA MONOGATARI in its treatment of Heian aristocratic life.

Imamura Arao 今村荒男

(1887–1967). Internist. Born in Nara Prefecture. Graduate of Tōkyō University. The author of a series of studies on BCG, a tuberculosis vaccine, he was an indefatigable pioneer in the use of BCG inoculation in Japan. He also stressed the importance of examinations to detect tuberculosis. He was professor at and president of Ōsaka University and a member of the Japan Academy from 1951.

Imamura Hitoshi 今村均

(1886–1968). Army general. Born in Miyagi Prefecture, he graduated from the Army Academy in 1907 and from the Army War College in 1915. In 1931 he directed strategic planning in the early phases of the MANCHURIAN INCIDENT as head of the operations section of Army General Staff. With the outbreak of World War II, Imamura commanded the Japanese invasion of Java and was named commander of the 8th Army in 1942. Even though he managed to set up a self-sufficient supply network for the isolated 70,000-man force he commanded at Rabaul, they were defeated. After Japan's surrender, Imamura was convicted of war crimes and sentenced to imprisonment.

Imamura Shikō 今村紫紅

(1880–1916). Painter instrumental in the modernization of Japanese-style painting (NIHONGA). Born in Yokohama, Shikō went to Tōkyō in 1897 to study under Matsumoto Fūko (1840–1923). In 1901, along with

YASUDA YUKIHIKO and others, he organized and became the leader of the Kōjikai artists' group. Shikō became increasingly influenced by the RIMPA-school style and the work of HISHIDA SHUNSŌ. Shiko's masterpiece, *Nekkoku no maki* (1914, The Tropics), a two-volume set of handscrolls in an idiosyncratic style, caused great excitement in the Tōkyō art world. His style was innovative, and his works were among the first to combine BUNJINGA style with elements of northern European realism.

Imamura Shikō *Asa no maki* (Morning). One of a pair of handscroll paintings. 1914. Colors on paper. 46 × 966 cm. Tōkyō National Museum.

Imai Tadashi A director whose films have been characterized by a realistic approach and a concern with social issues reminiscent of the Italian neorealists.

Imamura Shōhei 今村昌平

(1926–). Film director. Born in Tōkyō. Graduate of Waseda University. He joined the film company SHŌCHIKU CO, LTD, in 1951 and debuted as a director with *Nusumareta yokujō* (1958, Stolen Desire). Imamura has consistently portrayed in his works the resilience and energy of common people, a preoccupation that is prominent in *Buta to gunkan* (1961, Pigs and Battleships), which established his reputation as a director. *Nippon konchūki* (1963, The Insect Woman) and *Akai satsui* (1964, Unholy Desire) are representative of Imamura's brand of realism with its heavy reliance on location shooting. In both films he presents the tenacious hold on life of lower-class, uneducated women forced to rely on their sexual instincts for survival.

Imamura begins all his projects with thorough research. His first documentary, *Ningen jōhatsu* (1967, A Man Vanishes), about a woman's search for her missing fiancé, made the process of research itself the focus of the film. After this work, he directed a series of television documentaries on the plight of expatriate prostitutes and soldiers abandoned overseas after World War II. Imamura's films include *Fukushū suru wa ware ni ari* (1979, Vengeance Is Mine), *Narayamabushi kō* (1983, The Ballad of Narayama), and *Kuroi ame* (1989, Black Rain).

Imanishi Kinji 今西錦司

(1902–92). Biologist and anthropologist. Born in Kyōto. A graduate of Kyōto University, he began his research career by studying the ecology of the mayfly. Based on these studies, he developed the biological theory

Imamura Shōhei
1 Actor Ogata Ken carries actress Sakamoto Sumiko in a scene from the film *Narayamabushi kō* (1983, The Ballad of Narayama), Imamura's film about a man who is forced by ancient custom to abandon his aged mother on a mountain. The film took the 1983 Cannes Film Festival Grand Prize. **2** The director, whose brand of film realism centers on portrayals of the energy and resiliency of ordinary Japanese people.

Imanishi Kinji This anthropologist was also an expert mountain climber who scaled 1,500 peaks in Japan.

of "habitat segregation," according to which different species inhabiting a single area maintain spatially and temporally different living habits. After he joined the Kyōto University faculty, Imanishi's interest in mountain climbing and exploration led him to carry out various research expeditions in Inner Mongolia (1938–39, 1944–46), Ponape Island (1941), the Himalayan Mountains in Nepal (1952), and many other places. After World War II, he became a member of the KYŌTO UNIVERSITY RESEARCH INSTITUTE FOR HUMANISTIC STUDIES, where he initiated behavioral studies on primates; his studies of the Japanese monkey (*Macaca fuscata*) have attracted considerable attention outside of Japan. Imanishi received the Order of Culture in 1979.

Imari 伊万里[市]

City in western Saga Prefecture, Kyūshū, on Imari Bay. The city developed in the Edo period (1600–1868) as a shipping port for Imari ware ceramics (see ARITA WARE). From the early Meiji period (1868–1912) to the 1950s, it flourished as a coal-mining town; today its principal industries are ceramics, plywood, and shipbuilding. Special local products are Imari ware, *kamaboko* (boiled fish paste), and pears. Pop: 60,882.

Imari ware→Arita ware

Imbanuma 印旛沼

Lake in northern Chiba Prefecture, central Honshū, located west of the city of Narita. It was created by deposits of the river Tonegawa damming a valley in the plateau of Shimōsa. It is currently divided into two lakes, north and west, because of the completion of a land reclamation project in 1969. The water is utilized for irrigation, industry, and drinking. Area of the lake before land reclamation: 21.3 sq km (8.2 sq mi); present area: 13.1 sq km (5 sq mi).

Imbe family 忌部氏, 斎部氏

(Imbeshi). Family that, with the Nakatomi family, oversaw religious affairs at the YAMATO COURT (ca 4th century–ca mid-7th century). Originally of low status at court, the family grew influential as the imperial institution became invested with secular and sacerdotal powers. After the 7th century the Imbe were eclipsed by the FUJIWARA FAMILY. In 807, in a vain attempt to give credit to the family's achievements and revive its fortunes, Imbe no Hironari wrote the KOGO SHŪI.

IMF 国際通貨基金

(International Monetary Fund; J: Kokusai Tsūka Kikin). The IMF was established in 1944 along with the WORLD BANK. Its purpose is to promote international monetary cooperation and to expand world trade. Japan became a member of the IMF in 1952. Originally Japan was exempted from the requirement that it eliminate all restrictions on foreign exchange, as stipulated in article 8 of the IMF charter. After abolishing such restrictions Japan in 1964 assumed the status of an "article 8 member." The exchange rate of the yen was established under the IMF rules in 1949 at ¥360 per US dollar, and it remained at this level until the Smithsonian talks in December 1971, when the yen was officially revalued to ¥308 per US dollar. Japan adopted a floating exchange rate system in February 1973.

At the end of 1988, Japan's IMF quota, which among other things determines its approximate voting power within the IMF, stood at 4.2 billion SDRs (special drawing rights; one SDR equaled ¥169.4 in 1988). This represented 4.7 percent of the total of IMF quotas, making Japan the IMF's fifth largest voting member. At the end of 1988, Japan's SDR reserves totaled 2.2 billion SDRs.

Japan is striving to expand the flow of funds to developing countries through its 1987–92 Capital Recycling Plan, as well as increased support for the IMF. In particular, Japan's IMF contributions have been used to bolster its standby credit loan programs and have gone to the Enhanced Structural Adjustment Facility, which provides concessional loans to low-income countries.

imikotoba→taboo expressions

Imo Mutiny 壬午事変

(J: Jingo Jihen). Revolt of traditionalist Korean troops in 1882 (*imo* in the sexagenary system of year designations as pronounced in Korean; *jingo* in Japanese). In 1881 Japanese military advisers had arrived in Korea to initiate the modernization of the Korean army. A newly organized select unit was given benefits that aroused the anger of traditional units, unpaid for over a year. These troops mutinied, killed prominent Korean government officials and Japanese officers, and attempted unsuccessfully to assassinate Queen MIN. Both China and Japan dispatched troops to Korea, and the Chinese seized the TAEWŎN'GUN, the king's father, who was believed to have incited and directed the mutiny, and held him in exile. The mutiny set the stage for the Chinese-Japanese rivalry in Korea that culminated in the SINO-JAPANESE WAR OF 1894–1895.

imori 井守

Triturus pyrrhogaster. Small newt of the family Salamandridae commonly found throughout Japan except Hokkaidō. The body (8–12 cm; 3–5 in) is black or blackish brown above and bright red below. Large numbers gather in the fresh water of swamps, ponds, paddy fields, and streams to spawn from spring through summer. The larva metamorphoses after three to five months. In autumn it leaves the water and hibernates on land. Its attractive colors make it a prized pet in Japan, Europe, and the United States.

The unusual appearance of its red belly created superstitious fears that the *imori* was poisonous or would never release anything it bites. According to another superstition, a man who sprinkled the powder of charred *imori* on the object of his love, or let her drink *sake* with the powder, would gain her heart.

impeachment 弾劾

(*dangai*). Proceedings for the removal from office of JUDGES and commissioners of the NATIONAL PERSONNEL AUTHORITY. Japanese law does not provide for impeachment of the prime minister or other high government officials. The 1947 CONSTITUTION OF JAPAN provides that judges shall not be removed except by impeachment (art. 78) and that the Diet shall establish an impeachment court for the trial of judges (art. 64). The Law for the Impeachment of Judges (Saibankan Dangai Hō) enacted in 1947 establishes a Committee for the Prosecution of Judges (Saibankan Sotsui Iinkai). Any person may request a charge of impeachment from the committee. Grounds for impeachment are conspicuous failure to discharge responsibilities, extreme neglect of duties, or misconduct in or out of court that causes a conspicuous loss of dignity as a judge.

A member of the three-person National Personnel Authority may also be impeached. In such cases the Diet brings charges, and the Supreme Court hears the case and renders the verdict.

imperial anthologies 勅撰集

(*chokusenshū*). Anthologies of Japanese court poetry (WAKA) compiled at the direct command of an emperor or retired emperor. Altogether, 21 were compiled, the first in 905 and the last in 1439. Inclusion of a poem in one of these prestigious anthologies was the highest accolade and an honor eagerly sought by every poet, while the even greater honor of being appointed a compiler was yet more avidly coveted by the leading poets and was a source of bitter rivalry. The command by Emperor DAIGO for the compilation of the first imperial anthology, the KOKINSHŪ (Collection from Ancient and Modern Times; 905), marks the rise of *waka* to full literary and social acceptance after more than a century of obscurity, and was a conscious attempt to establish its status and produce an equivalent in Japanese of the three imperial anthologies of Chinese poetry (*chokusen shishū*), which had been ordered in the mid-9th century. The *Kokinshū*, divided into 20 books and with its poems arranged not by poet but in carefully regulated order of topic, became the model for all subsequent imperial anthologies. The development of *waka* can be traced through the first 8 anthologies, which are collectively known as the *hachidaishū* (collections of eight generations): the *Kokinshū, Gosenshū* (GOSEN WAKASHŪ; Later Collection; ca 955–966), *Shūishū* (SHŪI WAKASHŪ; Collection of Gleanings; ca 996–1007), *Go shūishū* (Later Collection of Gleanings; 1086), *Kin'yōshū* (KIN'YŌ WAKASHŪ; Collection of Golden Leaves; 1124–27), *Shikashū* (SHIKA WAKASHŪ; Collection of Verbal Flowers; 1152–53), *Senzaishū* (SENZAI WAKASHŪ; Collection of a Thousand Years; ca 1187–1188), and SHIN KOKINSHŪ (New Collection from Ancient and Modern Times; ca 1205). However, most critical and scholarly attention is focused on the *Kokinshū* and the *Shin kokinshū*. Of the 13 anthologies following the *Shin kokinshū*, only three, the *Shin chokusenshū* (New Imperial Collection; 1232), *Gyokuyōshū* (GYOKUYŌ WAKASHŪ; Collection of Jeweled Leaves; 1312–49), and *Fūgashū* (*Fūga wakashū;* Collection of Elegance; 1344–49) are worthy of note, with the others, and particularly the last four, showing a sad state of stagnation and then decline.

imperial conferences→gozen kaigi

Imperial Diet 帝国議会

(Teikoku Gikai). Bicameral national assembly established by the CONSTITUTION OF THE EMPIRE OF JAPAN in 1889. It was first convoked on 25 November 1890 and dissolved in 1947 after World War II.

The government leaders of the early Meiji period (1868–1912) sought to contain the political demands of the FREEDOM AND PEOPLE'S RIGHTS MOVEMENT. Although they saw the wisdom of making some concessions to popular demands for a parliamentary assembly, they firmly believed that sovereignty should reside in the emperor and that popular participation in the political process should be kept at a minimum. It was on these principles that the 1889 constitution was framed. Under the provisions of the constitution, the emperor combined in his person the rights of sovereignty, exercising all legislative, administrative, and judicial powers. The Imperial Diet was an organ designed to "assist and approve" (kyōsan) the emperor's exercise of these rights. The emperor convoked, opened, closed, and prorogued the Imperial Diet; he could also dissolve the lower house, the House of Representatives. Since in actuality the emperor exercised his rights with the advice and consent of his governmental ministers, government dominance of the Diet was ensured by the constitution. Apart from these sovereign rights, the emperor was empowered to issue imperial ordinances (chokurei) and special imperial ordinances (kinkyū chokurei) for emergencies, determine the organization of different branches of the administration, and appoint and dismiss all civil and military officials. The emperor had supreme command over the army and navy, determined the organization and size of the military, declared martial law and war, made peace, and concluded treaties. Thus, the Imperial Diet from its inception was severely limited in its powers.

The Diet's primary power was to initiate legislation. Both it and the government were authorized to introduce bills, and the emperor as a matter of course sanctioned all laws passed by the Diet. The emperor's sovereign rights were exempted from parliamentary debate and laws concerning the Diet's election and tenure of office had to be first reviewed by the PRIVY COUNCIL (Sūmitsuin). The Diet also held the power to determine the annual budget, but appropriations fixed by the emperor's exercise of his sovereign rights (e.g., imperial household and military expenses) could neither be reduced nor rejected by the Diet without the concurrence of the government. The Diet was authorized to present memorials to the emperor, make representations to the government concerning laws or any other subject, and receive petitions from the people.

Organization—The Diet consisted of two houses, the HOUSE OF PEERS (Kizokuin) and the House of Representatives (Shūgiin). The House of Peers was composed mainly of members of the imperial family, the nobles (kazoku; see PEERAGE), and other eminent members of society. Members received appointments for either seven-year terms or, in many cases, for life.

In contrast, members of the House of Representatives were elected to four-year terms by popular vote. The electorate was initially limited to about 1.25 percent of the population, however, since the first election law stipulated that only males over 25 years of age who paid ¥15 or more in national tax could vote. A movement to extend the franchise arose from about 1897, and in 1925 universal manhood suffrage (see UNIVERSAL MANHOOD SUFFRAGE MOVEMENT) was enacted.

As a rule, deliberations in the Diet were held in public. Upon demand of the government or by a resolution of the House, deliberations could be held in camera. Thus, whenever it chose, the government could conceal its debates from the public. Because a session could not be prolonged, Diet failure to pass a bill within the brief term of a session amounted to its rejection.

History—The first session was convoked by Emperor MEIJI on 25 November 1890. The first six sessions, up to 1894, were dominated by the heirs to the people's rights movement, the opposition JIYŪTŌ (Liberal Party) and RIKKEN KAISHINTŌ (Constitutional Reform Party). With the outbreak of the SINO-JAPANESE WAR OF 1894–1895 and the emergence of a spirit of "national unity," the so-called popular parties (MINTŌ) decided to compromise with the government to participate, however feebly, in political decision making.

In September 1900 the GENRŌ (elder statesman) ITŌ HIROBUMI formed the RIKKEN SEIYŪKAI (Friends of Constitutional Government Party) as a progovernment party. For the first time, the government could count on a firm base of support in the lower house. In the following decades, the Seiyūkai expanded its influence in opposition to the KENSEI HONTŌ (True Constitutional Party). During the Meiji period, the House of Peers on the whole vigorously opposed party politics.

With the development of capitalism, political parties also gained in power. During the TAISHŌ POLITICAL CRISIS of 1912–13 the Seiyūkai, RIKKEN KOKUMINTŌ (successor to the Kensei Hontō), and nonparty intellectuals organized the MOVEMENT TO PROTECT CONSTITUTIONAL GOVERNMENT (Kensei Yōgo Undō) and succeeded in toppling the KATSURA TARŌ cabinet. Later, in the wake of the RICE RIOTS OF 1918 and the resignation of the TERAUCHI MASATAKE cabinet, the politician HARA TAKASHI formed Japan's first genuine party cabinet. After Hara was assassinated, conservative, promilitary elements in the House of Peers gained power. As a result, three nonparty cabinets were formed between 1922 and 1924.

In the face of these undemocratic tendencies, the popular call for a return to party government—the so-called TAISHŌ DEMOCRACY—and for reform in the House of Peers grew stronger. In 1924 the KENSEIKAI (Constitutional Association), Seiyūkai, and KAKUSHIN KURABU (Reform Club) organized a second movement to protect constitutional government. They gained an overwhelming majority in the May elections, and in June KATŌ TAKAAKI formed a coalition cabinet. Party government was once again firmly established, and the prestige of political parties and the Diet within the framework of an imperial monarchy reached new heights.

Party politics during the early Shōwa period (1926–89) revolved around the struggle between the Seiyūkai and the RIKKEN MINSEITŌ (Constitutional Democratic Party). The passage of the NATIONAL MOBILIZATION LAW in the year following the outbreak of the SINO-JAPANESE WAR OF 1937–1945 struck a fatal blow to the political parties: the government arro-

gated political powers on a wide scale, and the Diet was reduced to being an "imperial assistance Diet" (yokusan gikai) that rubber-stamped all government policies.

After World War II, political parties reestablished themselves. With the approval of the new constitution in the 90th session of 1946, and the closing of the 92nd session on 31 March 1947, the Imperial Diet was formally dissolved. See also DIET.

imperial edict 詔書

(shōsho). Document used to relay imperial orders. Under the RITSURYŌ SYSTEM of government, instituted in the late 7th century, the imperial order called mikotonori (also pronounced shō) was used for extraordinary matters and that called choku for routine matters. Shōsho refers to the document that embodies a mikotonori or shō. From the Heian period (794–1185), shōsho were written exclusively in kambun, or classical Chinese, and differentiated from SEMMYŌ, which were written in pure Japanese (using Chinese characters). Under the Meiji Constitution (1889), imperial edicts were divided into kammu shōsho, relating to the imperial family, and seimu shōsho, relating to the declaration of war and the convocation of the IMPERIAL DIET. Under the present constitution (1947), imperial edicts are issued only for matters involving the emperor as head of state. Cabinet approval is required, and the prime minister signs in addition to the emperor. See also DIPLOMATICS.

Imperial Hotel, Ltd [株]帝国ホテル

(Teikoku Hoteru). Operator of the Imperial Hotel, one of Tōkyō's oldest luxury hotels. The company was established in 1887 as the operator of a residence for visiting guests of the state. The Imperial Hotel is especially famous for its former building, which was designed by Frank Lloyd WRIGHT. It was completed in 1922, after six years of construction. The building survived the Tōkyō Earthquake of 1923 and remained in use until 1967, when it was demolished and replaced by the present structure. The lobby of the old building was preserved and is on display at the MEIJI MURA open-air museum. The Imperial Hotel, Ltd, also operates the Kamikōchi Imperial Hotel in Kamikōchi, a valley in Nagano Prefecture, and is involved in building leasing and management. Revenues for the fiscal year ending March 1990 totaled ¥4.6 billion (US $310.9 million), and capitalization stood at ¥1.5 billion (US $9.8 million). Headquarters are in Tōkyō.

Imperial Diet Japan's bicameral national assembly (1890–1947) was severely limited in its powers; however, it was part of the first successful implementation of Western-style parliamentary democracy in Asia. This woodblock-print triptych depicts the 1890 convocation ceremony. The text set into the print is a list of the members of the House of Representatives.

The Imperial Family

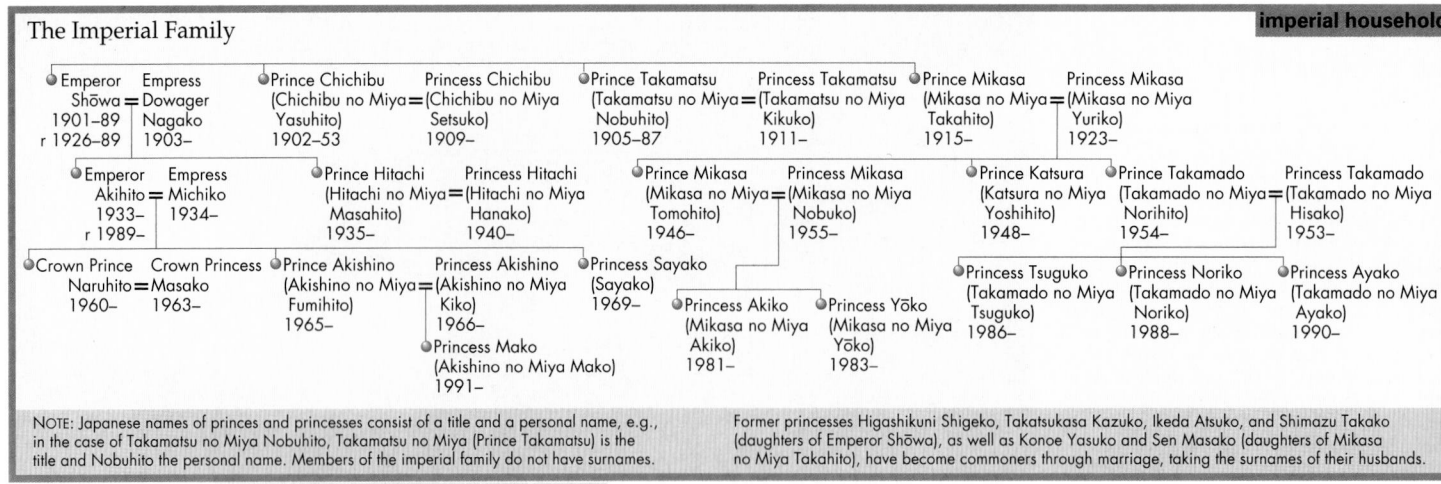

- Emperor Shōwa 1901–89 r 1926–89 = Empress Dowager Nagako 1903–
  - Emperor Akihito 1933– r 1989– = Empress Michiko 1934–
    - Crown Prince Naruhito 1960– = Crown Princess Masako 1963–
    - Prince Akishino (Akishino no Miya Fumihito) 1965– = Princess Akishino (Akishino no Miya Kiko) 1966–
      - Princess Mako (Akishino no Miya Mako) 1991–
    - Princess Sayako (Sayako) 1969–
- Prince Chichibu (Chichibu no Miya Yasuhito) 1902–53 = Princess Chichibu (Chichibu no Miya Setsuko) 1909–
  - Prince Hitachi (Hitachi no Miya Masahito) 1935– = Princess Hitachi (Hitachi no Miya Hanako) 1940–
- Prince Takamatsu (Takamatsu no Miya Nobuhito) 1905–87 = Princess Takamatsu (Takamatsu no Miya Kikuko) 1911–
  - Prince Mikasa (Mikasa no Miya Tomohito) 1946– = Princess Mikasa (Mikasa no Miya Nobuko) 1955–
    - Princess Akiko (Mikasa no Miya Akiko) 1981–
    - Princess Yōko (Mikasa no Miya Yōko) 1983–
- Prince Mikasa (Mikasa no Miya Takahito) 1915– = Princess Mikasa (Mikasa no Miya Yuriko) 1923–
  - Prince Katsura (Katsura no Miya Yoshihito) 1948–
  - Prince Takamado (Takamado no Miya Norihito) 1954– = Princess Takamado (Takamado no Miya Hisako) 1953–
    - Princess Tsuguko (Takamado no Miya Tsuguko) 1986–
    - Princess Noriko (Takamado no Miya Noriko) 1988–
    - Princess Ayako (Takamado no Miya Ayako) 1990–

NOTE: Japanese names of princes and princesses consist of a title and a personal name, e.g., in the case of Takamatsu no Miya Nobuhito, Takamatsu no Miya (Prince Takamatsu) is the title and Nobuhito the personal name. Members of the imperial family do not have surnames.

Former princesses Higashikuni Shigeko, Takatsukasa Kazuko, Ikeda Atsuko, and Shimazu Takako (daughters of Emperor Shōwa), as well as Konoe Yasuko and Sen Masako (daughters of Mikasa no Miya Takahito), have become commoners through marriage, taking the surnames of their husbands.

imperial household
The imperial family in June 1993. Standing behind Emperor Akihito and Empress Michiko are, from left to right, Princess Sayako, Crown Prince Naruhito, Crown Princess Masako, Prince Akishino, and Princess Akishino.

imperial household　皇室

(*kōshitsu*). General term applied to the emperor (*tennō*) and the imperial family. The imperial family consists of the empress (*kōgō*), the grand empress dowager (*tai kōtaigō*), the empress dowager (*kōtaigō*), imperial princes (*shinnō*) and their wives (*shinnōhi*), imperial princesses (*naishinnō*), princes (*ō*) and their wives (*ōhi*), and princesses (*jōō*).

Only males can succeed to the imperial throne. The order of succession as established by law is as follows: the eldest son, the eldest son's eldest son, other sons and grandsons of the eldest son, the second eldest son and his sons and grandsons, other imperial sons and grandsons, imperial brothers and their sons and grandsons, and imperial uncles and their sons and grandsons. The crown prince (*kōtaishi*) is the eldest son of the emperor. The affairs of the imperial household are governed by the IMPERIAL HOUSEHOLD LAW, enacted by the National Diet in 1947. See also IMPERIAL HOUSEHOLD AGENCY.

Imperial Household Agency　宮内庁

(Kunaichō). Government agency responsible for the personal, ceremonial, and official affairs of the emperor and his family. Formed in 1947 and named Kunaichō in 1949 to replace the former Imperial Household Ministry (Kunaishō), it takes charge of the administrative duties concerning the emperor's acts in matters of state and takes custody of the imperial seal (*gyoji*) and the seal of state (*kokuji*). It is responsible for maintaining imperial records and documents and caring for imperial tombs and any state property used by the imperial family. Administratively attached to the Prime Minister's Office, with responsibility for its official actions borne by the cabinet, the agency is headed by a grand steward (Kunaichō *chōkan*) who is appointed by the prime minister but is not a cabinet member. The agency's divisions include the ARCHIVES AND MAUSOLEA DEPARTMENT.

Imperial Household Law　皇室典範

(Kōshitsu Tempan). The law concerning matters related to the IMPERIAL HOUSEHOLD, such as succession to the throne, membership in the imperial family, titles of family members, regency, and the establishment of the advisory Imperial Household Council. There have been two such laws, one under the Meiji Constitution (1889) and the other under the present constitution (1947).

Imperial Japanese Army　大日本帝国陸軍

(Dai Nippon Teikoku Rikugun). Official name of the Japanese army established under the direct command of the emperor Meiji in 1868 and disbanded in 1945. It fought the SINO-JAPANESE WAR OF 1894–1895, the RUSSO-JAPANESE WAR of 1904–05, the SINO-JAPANESE WAR OF 1937–1945, the Pacific phase of WORLD WAR II (1941–45), and several other major military actions. During World War II, the army expanded to a peak strength of 6.4 million, organized into at least 172 infantry divisions, 4 armored divisions, and 13 air units. The central organization consisted of the ARMY MINISTRY, charged with administration, and the ARMY GENERAL STAFF OFFICE, charged with command. See also ARMED FORCES, IMPERIAL JAPANESE.

Imperial Japanese Navy　大日本帝国海軍

(Dai Nippon Teikoku Kaigun). Founded in 1868 following the Meiji Restoration, Japan's prewar naval force rose to world rank after its victories in the SINO-JAPANESE WAR OF 1894–1895, the RUSSO-JAPANESE WAR (1904–05), and WORLD WAR I. It was virtually annihilated in the Pacific War and formally dissolved on 30 November 1945 (see WORLD WAR II). The central structure consisted of the NAVY MINISTRY, charged with administration, and the NAVAL GENERAL STAFF OFFICE, charged with command. See also ARMED FORCES, IMPERIAL JAPANESE.

Imperial Military Reservists' Association　帝国在郷軍人会

(Teikoku Zaigō Gunjinkai). Also translated as Imperial Veterans' Association. Pre-World War II organization of veterans or men who were eligible for military service. Founded in 1910 by Army Minister TERAUCHI MASATAKE and TANAKA GIICHI (then at the Military Affairs Bureau) to promote patriotism and military ideals. Branches were established on the city, town, and village levels. The association became increasingly politicized in the 1930s, taking an active part in the rightist movement to discredit the emperor-as-organ theory (TENNŌ KIKAN SETSU) of Minobe Tatsukichi (1873–1948; see KOKUTAI DEBATE). It was put under the

war ministries in 1936 and was dissolved in August 1945.

Imperial New Year's Poetry Reading　歌会始

(Utakai Hajime). Poetry (TANKA) reading held at the Imperial Palace to celebrate the New Year. It was held irregularly in the Heian period (794–1185) and was rarely observed during the Muromachi (1333–1568) and Edo (1600–1868) periods. Since 1869, however, the year following the Meiji Restoration, it has been held annually on or about 10 January. Initially only the imperial family and guests offered poems, but since 1879 contributions have been solicited from the public. Poems are written on a subject chosen by the emperor, usually a natural theme such as cherry blossoms.

imperial ordinance　勅令

(*chokurei*). A type of law issued by the emperor under the CONSTITUTION OF THE EMPIRE OF JAPAN (1889). Because the administration could enact such imperial orders without approval of the Imperial Diet, these orders played an important role in maintaining the superior position of the executive branch under the 1889 Constitution. In addition to orders enacted with specific statutory authority, imperial orders included so-called independent orders (*dokuritsu meirei*), intended to preserve public peace and order or to advance the welfare of the citizens (art. 9), and so-called emergency imperial orders (*kinkyū chokurei*), which were to be issued in crisis situations (art. 8). Imperial orders generally ranked below statutes (HŌRITSU) and could not alter their provisions, but emergency orders were accorded the same effect as statutes. Under the 1947 CONSTITUTION OF JAPAN, there is no provision for the imperial orders as a form of law.

Imperial Palace　皇居

(Kōkyo). Official residence of the emperor. Situated in Chiyoda Ward, Tōkyō, on grounds occupying 1.15 square kilometers (0.44 sq mi). Japanese emperors and their families have resided here since after the Meiji Restoration of 1868, when EDO CASTLE was designated the official imperial residence (before the Meiji Restoration, emperors resided in Kyōto). The part of Edo Castle that served as the imperial residence was destroyed by fire in 1873. A new palace was completed in 1888, but this was destroyed in air raids in 1945. The present palace complex, the Kyūden, was completed in 1968. Its individual buildings are in the traditional style with the gently sloping roofs known as *irimoya* (semigabled roofs). These include the Omote Gozasho, the emperor's office for affairs of state; the Seiden, for official ceremonies; the Hōmeiden, for banquets enter-

The Emperor's Official Residence

The grounds of the Imperial Palace occupy a portion of central Tōkyō that was once part of Edo Castle, seat of the Tokugawa shogunate. Emperors took up official residence there after the Meiji Restoration of 1868. In the years since, fires and the air raids of World War II have destroyed most of the castle, and new buildings have replaced it. Vestiges of the castle, such as its moats, watchtowers, and gates, still stand, serving as reminders of its scale and the central role it has played in the city's history.

The complex known as the Kyūden, where the emperor presides over many official functions, is the heart of the palace today. A new imperial residence, located on the palace grounds, was completed in 1993.

Moats and greenery set off the palace grounds. The turquoise roofs are those of the Kyūden.

Two watchtowers from Edo Castle. The two-storied Tatsumi Yagura (foreground) and the three-storied Fujimi Yagura (in the distance) overlook the moat.

The Seiden State Hall is divided into three main staterooms—the Takenoma, Matsunoma, and Umenoma.

The Matsunoma Stateroom. The emperor and empress sit before a folding screen during official functions.

The South Lobby of the Chōwaden Reception Hall. The wood, marble, and other materials were collected from various parts of Japan.

Emperor Akihito welcomes state visitors in the Hōmeiden State Banquet Hall.

Irises bloom in a garden within Higashi Gyoen, a portion of the palace grounds open to the public.

taining guests of state; and the Chōwaden, for evening receptions. These buildings are connected by corridors surrounding a large central courtyard. To the northwest is the Fukiage Gosho, formerly the private residence of Emperor SHŌWA, now occupied by his widow. A new palace residence for Emperor AKIHITO was completed in May 1993. Other buildings on the palace grounds are occupied by the Imperial Household Agency. Part of the palace grounds is open to the public. ☎ 595

imperial regalia 三種の神器

(sanshu no jingi). Collective name for the three sacred objects that are the symbols of the legitimacy and authority of the emperor. The regalia consist of the curved jewels (yasakani no magatama) that, according to mythology, were presented by the deities of heaven to AMATERASU ŌMIKAMI, the sun goddess, when she reappeared after secluding herself in a cave; the sacred mirror (yata no kagami) that was used to entice Amaterasu from the cave and then presented to her; and the sacred sword (Ame no Murakumo no Tsurugi; later renamed Kusanagi no Tsurugi), that was removed from the tail of the serpent YAMATA NO OROCHI by Amaterasu's brother, SUSANOO NO MIKOTO, and presented to the goddess as a sign of his submission.

The three regalia were entrusted by Amaterasu to her grandson, NINIGI NO MIKOTO, when he descended to the Japanese islands. They are said to have been passed from emperor to emperor until the 9th century, when replicas of the sword and mirror were made for the emperor to keep in his possession. The original mirror and sword are purportedly kept at the Ise and Atsuta shrines, respectively, where they are the most famous of the sacred objects known as SHINTAI.

The original curved jewels are purportedly kept in the Imperial Palace, along with the replicas of the mirror and sword. (The original replica sword was lost in the Battle of DANNOURA in 1185 and was replaced shortly thereafter.) The replica mirror, three times damaged by fire, is enshrined in the Kashikodokoro (Place of Awe), one of the three palace shrines. The supposed original curved jewels and the replica sword are stored in a special room of the palace, known as the Kenji no Ma (Room of the Sword and Seal). The accession of a new emperor is accomplished when he receives the transfer of the replica sword and "original" jewels, a solemn ritual known as the Kenji Togyo no Gi. See also DAIJŌSAI.

Imperial Rescript on Education 教育勅語

(Kyōiku Chokugo). Rescript issued in the name of Emperor MEIJI on 30 October 1890 articulating the guiding principles of education in Japan. The rescript served as a powerful instrument of political indoctrination and remained in effect until the end of World War II.

During the 1870s and 1880s there was a struggle at the highest levels of the Meiji government to reconcile the conflicting goals of rapid modernization and the legitimation of a political order centered on the imperial institution. In reaction to the relatively liberal EDUCATION ORDER OF 1872, MOTODA NAGAZANE and other conservatives called for a revival of Confucian thought and morality. By 1890, when Prime Minister YAMAGATA

ARITOMO ordered the drafting of the rescript, it had been decided that greater efforts would be made to incorporate Confucian ideology into public education, particularly at the primary level.

The 315-word text, prepared by INOUE KOWASHI, Motoda, and several other educators and government leaders, states that Japan's unique national polity (KOKUTAI) is based on the historical bonds uniting its benevolent rulers and their loyal subjects and that the fundamental principles of education in Japan are based upon this. The rescript then exhorts all Japanese subjects to cultivate a list of virtues, central among them loyalty (chū) and filial piety (kō), for the greater glory of the imperial house.

The Ministry of Education distributed certified copies of the rescript to every school in Japan. It was given ceremonial readings at all important school events and functions, and students were required to study and to memorize the text for their moral education classes. After World War II, the formal reading of the Imperial Rescript was forbidden by OCCUPATION authorities. The rescript was officially rescinded by the Diet in June 1948. See EDUCATION, FUNDAMENTAL LAW OF.

Imperial Rescript to Soldiers and Sailors 軍人勅諭

(Gunjin Chokuyu). Rescript issued by Emperor MEIJI on 4 January 1882. The most important document in the development of the modern Japanese armed forces, aside from the CONSCRIPTION ORDINANCE OF 1873. Intended as the official code of ethics of all soldiers and sailors, it is often cited, along with the IMPERIAL RESCRIPT ON EDUCATION (1890), as having provided the moral underpinning for the prewar national ideology that defined service to the state in terms of absolute loyalty to the emperor.

The Rescript to Soldiers and Sailors had the distinction of being presented directly to the army minister by the emperor at a special ceremony at the palace. This unprecedented act was meant to symbolize the personal bond between the emperor and the military service, as if he were giving private instructions to his personal army, and it elevated the observance of these precepts to a sacred obligation to the throne. Servicemen returning to their home villages transmitted to civilians the rescript's values, which in time became part of the national ideology.

Many of the rules and regulations issued by the military during the first 15 years of the Meiji period were the work of the Army Ministry bureaucrat and Western scholar NISHI AMANE. Nishi prepared a draft of the 1882 rescript, but numerous revisions were made to it, most notably by INOUE KOWASHI. The revised rescript stressed absolute loyalty to the emperor (chūsetsu). Inoue retained Nishi's warnings to the military not to be led astray by current opinions and to avoid politics, but excluded Nishi's ideas about respecting civil authority.

Imperial Rule Assistance Association 大政翼賛会

(IRAA; J: Taisei Yokusankai). Association established on 12 October 1940 to promote the goals of the NEW ORDER MOVEMENT. Originally conceived as the nucleus of a mass-based "reformist" political party, the IRAA instead became an instrument for governmental control of popular morale and resources during World War II and included every Japanese subject as a member.

During the summer of 1940 Prime Minis-

ter KONOE FUMIMARO launched plans for a totalitarian political system that would absorb all existing political parties. He appointed 37 members to a Preparatory Commission for Establishing a New Political Order (Shin Taisei Jumbi Kai) representing a broad political spectrum that had great difficulty agreeing on reforms. Konoe proposed originally to assign new-party members to branches according to their occupation or cultural group; the new party would then provide the masses with channels for spontaneous political participation (i.e., "assisting the imperial rule," or taisei yokusan).

However, the permanent directors and advisers Konoe selected to guide the IRAA represented all political viewpoints, thereby preventing the IRAA from becoming unified even at the outset. Also, the HOME MINISTRY set up local IRAA branches according to existing territorial administrative units, not according to vocation or cultural group. Existing local governmental leaders at each level automatically headed their local IRAA branches. After late November 1940 Konoe himself decided to weaken the reformist character of the IRAA, guaranteeing that the IRAA remained under the control of the existing alignment of political elites.

In 1941 and 1942 the army attempted to establish local support groups through the Yokusan Sōnendan (Imperial Rule Assistance Men's Associations). General TŌJŌ HIDEKI's government tried to eradicate the influence of Diet leaders through an officially sponsored election-nomination commission in March 1942. Following the 1942 general elections, virtually all Diet members were obliged to join a single party, the Yokusan Seijikai (Imperial Rule Assistance Political Association). But none of these ventures led to the creation of a mass totalitarian party, and the old Diet leadership retained control of the Yokusan Seijikai.

The Home Ministry used the IRAA to extend its local administration to every city, town, village, and hamlet. Citizens were organized into small neighborhood associations called tonarigumi or rimpohan. Until its dissolution on 13 June 1945 the IRAA focused largely on enlisting popular support and work for the wars in China and the Pacific. Its campaigns encouraged higher productivity, increased savings and less consumption, and civil defense. OCCUPATION authorities believed that the IRAA had played a political role analogous to that of the Nazi Party in Germany and purged thousands of officials and community leaders from public life for their IRAA activities.

imperial universities 帝国大学

(teikoku daigaku). National universities established by the Imperial University Order of 1886 to train Japanese scholars and bureaucrats. Initially there was only one imperial university, established in 1886 through a reorganization of TŌKYŌ UNIVERSITY; this was followed by Kyōto (1897), Tōhoku (1907), Kyūshū (1910), Hokkaidō (1918), Ōsaka (1931), and Nagoya (1939) imperial universities.

The period of study at the imperial universities was three to four years, but this presupposed three years of preparatory education at a higher school (kōtō gakkō). Students at the imperial universities enjoyed many special privileges, including deferment of military service and exemption from the state licensing examinations for medicine, law, and middle-school teaching. Imperial university graduates occupied the most important positions in the state bureaucracy and private corporations. Although the imperial university system was abolished after World War II, the national universities that succeeded them continue to dominate the higher education system in Japan. See also UNIVERSITIES AND COLLEGES.

"Imperial Way" faction→Kōdōha

Imphal Campaign インパール作戦

(Impāru Sakusen). Aborted military operation undertaken by the Japanese army to seize Imphal in northeastern India during the final stages of WORLD WAR II. The campaign is an example of the failure to take into account the problems of logistics and topography. The original purpose of the campaign was to eliminate the Anglo-Indian forces controlling the Imphal Basin, a strategic point in the northern Arakan mountains on the Indian-Burmese border. Three Japanese divisions under Lieutenant General Mutaguchi Ren'ya (1888–1966) started to advance from the Burma front in March 1944. Because of unanticipated difficulties in maintaining supply routes, the Japanese exhausted their food and munitions. A powerful Allied counteroffensive extended the planned campaign period into the monsoon season, destroying the already fragile system of communications and transportation. The Japanese army gave up the campaign on 9 July 1944. It is estimated that the total number of Japanese casualties in the campaign approached 73,000.

import promotion policy 輸入促進策

(yunyū sokushin saku). Series of government measures implemented since 1985 with the objective of reducing Japan's balance-of-trade surplus (US $40 billion in 1985) by increasing imports, especially imports of manufactured goods. In addition to market-opening measures such as tariff reductions (see TARIFFS) and the lifting of import restrictions, there have also been campaigns to increase Japanese demand for imported goods and to provide indirect support for export expansion by foreign companies. Government actions have included (1) requests by the MINISTRY OF INTERNATIONAL TRADE AND INDUSTRY (MITI) for industry cooperation in increasing imports; (2) a request to major department stores and supermarkets to implement a plan for making use of the high yen to increase purchases of foreign goods; (3) sponsorship of an "import promotion month" campaign; (4) support for various kinds of import bazaars and fairs; and (5) the activities of the MANUFACTURED IMPORTS PROMOTION ORGANIZATION (MIPRO).

in→seals

Ina 伊那[市]

City in southern Nagano Prefecture, central Honshū, on the river Tenryūgawa. In the Edo period (1600–1868) it developed as a post-station town and as a river port. The main agricultural products are rice, pears, and tomatoes; dairy farming also flourishes. There is an emerging electronics and precision-instruments industry. Ina Park is noted for its cherry blossoms. Ina serves as a base camp for excursions into the Kiso Mountains. Pop: 60,062.

Ina Basin 伊那盆地

(Ina Bonchi). In southern Nagano Prefecture, central Honshū. Flanked by the Kiso and Akaishi mountains, this long fault basin consists of piedmont alluvial fans below the fault scarp in the west, river terraces along the river Tenryūgawa's upper reaches, and a floodplain on its lower reaches. Orchards and rice fields are found here. The major cities are Ina, Komagane, and Iida. Length: 70 km (43 mi); maximum width: 15 km (9 mi).

Inada Ryōkichi 稲田竜吉

(1874–1950). Internist. Also known as Inada Ryūkichi. Born in Aichi Prefecture. A graduate of Tōkyō University, where he studied under AOYAMA TANEMICHI, Inada pursued further studies in Germany. He became a professor at the Fukuoka Ika Daigaku (now the medical department of Kyūshū University). In 1915, with Ido Yutaka (1881–1919), he discovered the pathogen *Leptospira icterohaemorrhagiae*, which causes Weil's disease. After moving to Tōkyō University in 1918, he studied influenza and internal medicine. He was director of Kōraku Hospital, attached to the Japanese Foundation for Cancer Research. He received the Imperial Prize of the Japan Academy in 1916 and the Order of Culture in 1944.

Inadome Naoie 稲富直家

(1552–1611). Also known as Inatomi (or Inadome) Ichimu. Authority on gunnery and founder of the Inatomi school of gunnery. Born in Tango Province (now part of Kyōto Prefecture). He entered the service of Hosokawa Tadaoki (1563–1645), the *daimyō* of Tango, and subsequently served TOKUGAWA IEYASU and his successor TOKUGAWA HIDETADA.

Inagaki Hiroshi 稲垣浩

(1905–80). Film director. Born in Tōkyō. Inagaki began his career as an actor before becoming a director in 1928. He is known outside Japan chiefly for his three-part *Miyamoto Musashi* (1954–56, Samurai) and for *Muhō Matsu no isshō* (1958, The Life of Matsu the Untamed; shown abroad as *Rickshaw Man*), each of which he had made previously in the 1940s. Inagaki was one of several directors who flourished in the 1930s making serious period films that bore some allegorical message for modern man. Many of his films were versions of popular historical legends grounded in fact and centered on actual figures from Japanese history. Inagaki himself said that the true period film died with the 1930s, being subsumed into such categories as historical romances and literary adaptations.

Inagaki Taruho 稲垣足穂

(1900–1977). Author and poet. Born in Ōsaka; graduate of Kansei Gakuin Middle School. In 1923 he published his first work, *Issen ichibyō monogatari* (The Tale of 1,001 Seconds). After World War II, he wrote the novels *Miroku* (1946, Maitreya) and *Karera* (1948, Them); the latter dealt with pederasty, a topic of continuing interest to him. After his marriage and move to Kyōto in 1950, Inagaki began contributing regularly to the literary coterie magazine *Sakka*, in which he published the short essay "Tosotsu jōshō" (1950, Rebirth in the Tuṣita Heaven). In 1969 his *Shōnen'ai no bigaku* (1968, The Aesthetics of Pederasty) won the Japan Literary Prize.

Inagi 稲城[市]

City in southern Tōkyō Prefecture, on the river Tamagawa, contiguous with the city of Kawasaki, Kanagawa Prefecture. Formerly a farming area, since the 1960s Inagi has undergone urbanization. Several electrical appliance manufacturers are located here. Pop: 58,635.

Inaka kyōshi 田舎教師

(tr *Country Teacher*, 1984). Novel by TAYAMA KATAI (1872–1930); published 1909. At the outset of the novel, the young Hayashi Seizō, burdened by his family's poverty, accepts a lowly teaching post at a country elementary school. The job, demeaning and unrewarding, falls far short of Seizō's youthful ambition to move to Tōkyō and become a success in the literary world. Enviously watching his wealthier friends move away, Seizō falls deeper into frustration and despair as he is forced to abandon his dreams one by one. Dispirited in the heady days of the RUSSO-JAPANESE WAR, he is stricken with tuberculosis and dies a miserable and ironically timed death: in his last moments, news of the Japanese victory at Liaoyang reaches his ears. The novel is written using an impressionistic technique known as *heimen byōsha* (single-plane description), and its sensitivity and restraint make *Inaka kyōshi* one of Katai's best and most representative works.

Inamori Kazuo 稲盛和夫

(1932–). Businessman and chairman of KYŌCERA CORPORATION (1985–). Born in Kagoshima Prefecture; graduate of Kagoshima University. In 1959 he was one of the founders of the Kyōto Ceramic Co, forerunner of Kyōcera, and was named president in 1966. The company grew rapidly as a result of his commitment to developing technologies for the production of fine industrial ceramics. In 1983 Inamori merged Yashica, the camera manufacturer, into Kyōcera, and in 1984 he established DDI Corporation, Japan's first private telecommunications company, becoming its chairman. He also created the Inamori Foundation and the Kyōto Prize in 1984 to promote the development of human resources in the field of high technology.

Inamura Sampaku 稲村三伯

(1758–1811). Scholar of Dutch Learning (Rangaku). Born in the Tottori domain (now part of Tottori Prefecture), he studied under ŌTSUKI GENTAKU. Because of the NATIONAL SECLUSION policy limiting Japan's contact with the Western world to Dutch traders in Nagasaki, Dutch was then the principal medium of Western knowledge. With the help of Udagawa Genzui (1755–97) and others, in 1796 Sampaku completed the HARUMA WAGE; containing over 80,000 entries, it was the first reliable Dutch-Japanese dictionary. Though only 30 copies of it were made, it contributed significantly to WESTERN LEARNING. Sampaku's dictionary was also known as *Edo Haruma*, to distinguish it from the later *Nagasaki Haruma* by the Dutch trade commissioner in Nagasaki, Hendrick DOEFF.

Inari 稲荷

Originally one of the names of the deity of cereals. Inari has been the deity most widely worshiped by the Japanese because of its close association with the nation's rice-centered agriculture. Inari has also been regarded as a guardian of commerce and success. During the Edo period (1600–1868) merchants who desired prosperity and many warriors who wished for success erected Inari shrines in their homes. In modern times Inari has been installed as a guardian deity in

Inagaki Taruho
Initially recognized for his stories of the fantastic, this 20th-century author later wrote numerous works on the theme of pederasty.

Inari A stone fox stands before a row of gates (*torii*) at the entrance to a shrine venerating Inari, the deity of cereal crops. The fox's red bib has been given in gratitude for prayers answered.

some households (*yashikigami*) and companies.

In medieval times (mid-12th–16th centuries), belief in the sacredness of the fox, especially the white fox, was common. Eventually the fox came to be regarded as Inari's messenger. Thus the fox as a symbol has often been referred to as *inari*, and a piece of fried soybean curd, offered to an Inari shrine in the belief that it was the fox's favorite food, has also been called *inari*.

Based on the myths in such works as the KOJIKI and NIHON SHOKI, Shintō ideology identifies the deity Inari as Uka no Mitama (or Uganomitama) no Kami, the deity of cereals. Shrine histories, however, trace the origins of the deity back to the FUSHIMI INARI SHRINE in Kyōto, where the tutelary deity of the ancient HATA FAMILY was enshrined by Hata no Kimi Irogu. (The related legend seems to indicate that Inari was originally the god of the fields, or TA NO KAMI.) This shrine remains among the more eminent of the 30,000 Inari shrines that are legally designated as incorporated religious institutions. There are several hypotheses concerning the etymology of the name Inari, but none is certain. According to one theory, the name is an abbreviation of *ine-nari* (ripening of rice). See also HATSUUMA.

Inaridai inscribed iron sword
稲荷台一号墳出土鉄剣

(Inaridai Ichigōfun *shutsudo tekken*). Iron sword with inscriptions in silver inlay discovered in Inaridai Tomb Number One (Ichigōfun) in the city of Ichihara, Chiba Prefecture. Inaridai Tomb Number One is a round tomb mound with a diameter of approximately 30 meters (98 ft) that was excavated in December 1976. The sword was found in four pieces in a wooden coffin buried in the mound. Its total length is about 73 centimeters (29 in). In 1987 it became apparent that there were inscriptions on the sword, five characters on one side and two on the reverse. Two of the characters are read *ōshi*, meaning "presented by the king." It is conjectured that the sword was presented by a king to one of his warriors sometime during the mid- to late 5th century.

Inariyama tomb
稲荷山古墳

(Inariyama *kofun*). An early-6th-century mounded tomb (KOFUN), one of a cluster of 10 tombs (generally known as Sakitama Tomb Cluster) located in the city of Gyōda, Saitama Prefecture. It was originally keyhole-shaped, measuring about 120 meters (394 ft) in length. Excavations in 1968 revealed fragments of HANIWA funerary sculptures and two coffin enclosures, one of which yielded horse trappings (see HORSE TRAPPINGS, ANCIENT), small bells, BRONZE MIRRORS, curved *magatama* (see BEADS, ANCIENT), belt fittings, and iron weapons and armor. In 1978 a 115-character inscription was discovered on one of the swords; several of the characters referred to a ruler of the YAMATO COURT known posthumously as Emperor Yūryaku (late 5th century). Together with a sword from the ETA FUNAYAMA TOMB in Kyūshū with a similar inscription, it is considered evidence of the far-ranging authority of the Yamato court in the 5th century.

Ina Tadatsugu
伊奈忠次

(1550–1610). Civil administrator of the Azuchi-Momoyama (1568–1600) and Edo (1600–1868) periods. Born in Mikawa Province (now part of Aichi Prefecture). Ina was an attendant to TOKUGAWA IEYASU before the latter's rise to power and distinguished himself in the ODAWARA CAMPAIGN (1590) by his brilliant handling of provisions, supplies, and other logistical operations. He was subsequently appointed intendant of the eight Kantō provinces (Kantō GUNDAI). The survey and tax-assessment methods he devised were adopted as models by the Tokugawa shogunate.

Inatori Hot Spring
稲取温泉

(Inatori Onsen). Located on the eastern shore of the IZU PENINSULA in the town of Higashi Izu, Shizuoka Prefecture, central Honshū. A common salt spring; maximum temperature 60°C (140°F). There is a sports center and golf course nearby.

Inawashiro Kensai
猪苗代兼載

(1452–1510). RENGA, or linked verse, poet and a disciple of SHINKEI. Born in Aizu (now part of Fukushima Prefecture). With SŌGI, he compiled the second honorary imperial *renga* anthology, SHINSEN TSUKUBASHŪ. In 1489 he was appointed to succeed Sōgi as master of the Kitano Shrine *renga* office, the highest honor for a *renga* poet at that time. His verses written 1469–1508 are collected in *Sono no chiri*.

Inawashiro, Lake
猪苗代湖

(Inawashiroko). In central Fukushima Prefecture, northern Honshū. Located on the southern slopes of the mountain Bandaisan within Bandai-Asahi National Park. It is the water source of the ASAKA CANAL. The house in which the bacteriologist NOGUCHI HIDEYO was born (now the Noguchi Memorial Museum) is located on the northern bank. Area: 104 sq km (40 sq mi); circumference: 63 km (39 mi); depth: 94 m (308 ft); altitude: 514 m (1,686 ft).

Inax Corporation
[株]イナックス

(Inakkusu). World's largest manufacturer of ceramic tiles and second largest sanitary ceramics producer in Japan. Incorporated in 1924. The company also manufactures bathroom fixtures, faucets, and other household facilities and units. Inax has joint ventures in Malaysia and Germany and technical tie-ups with companies in Taiwan, Korea, Indonesia, Germany, and Sweden. Sales for the fiscal year ending October 1990 totaled ¥245.7 billion (US $1.9 billion), and the company was capitalized at ¥48.5 billion (US $373.9 million). Headquarters are in Tokoname, Aichi Prefecture.

Inayama Yoshihiro
稲山嘉寛

(1904–87). Business leader. Born in Tōkyō, he graduated from Tōkyō University in 1927 and entered the Ministry of Commerce (forerunner of the Ministry of International Trade and Industry), where he was assigned to the government-operated YAWATA IRON AND STEEL WORKS. In 1970, as president of the private-sector Yawata Steel, he joined with NAGANO SHIGEO of Fuji Steel in the formation by merger of the NIPPON STEEL CORPORATION. Inayama became its president and was chairman of the board (1973–81). He campaigned for a more flexible application of the antitrust laws. In 1968 he became vice-chairman of KEIDANREN (Federation of Economic Organizations); he later became its fifth chairman (1980–86).

Inazawa
稲沢[市]

City in western Aichi Prefecture, central Honshū. Inazawa is noted for its tree nurseries. It is fast becoming a satellite city of NAGOYA. The Kōnomiya Festival at the Owari Ōkunitama Shrine is a major tourist attraction. Pop: 96,274.

incense ceremony
香道

(*kōdō*). An aesthetic pursuit in which participants appreciate the fragrance emitted by the burning of scented wood or combinations of wood and other substances. The art of *kōdō* was brought to Japan in the 6th century, with the introduction of Buddhism. It reached the height of its popularity in the late 17th century, as a highly refined secular accomplishment.

Incense was originally burnt as an offering to Buddhist images in temples, but by the 8th century the burning of incense to scent rooms and clothing had become fashionable among the upper classes. During this period incense competitions at court were also popular.

Eventually this aristocratic entertainment was adopted by commoners. Recognizing the need for rules, literary figures, such as SANJŌNISHI SANETAKA, Shino Munenobu (d 1480), SŌGI, and SHŌHAKU, helped create a format for the burning of incense. The Sanjōnishi and Shino schools, which have since become the core of the incense tradition, continue to the present day, although, unlike the tea ceremony and flower arrangement, *kōdō* attracts few adherents.

Various Ceremonies——*Single scent.* The burning of a single variety of aromatic wood may be enjoyed in a solitary or social setting.

Incense competition. Participants try to guess the name of an incense; this is difficult because there are as many as 2,500 varieties.

Matching incense. A participant burns one kind of incense, and someone else burns another that will combine pleasantly with the first.

Combined fragrances. Using two or more kinds of incense, the participant tries to create the atmosphere of a particular literary work, for example, a combination that will call to mind the poems of the KOKINSHŪ. There are about 700 such combinations, each having its own literary association.

income distribution
所得分布

(*shotoku bumpu*). Household income differentials in Japan narrowed sharply after

World War II, especially in the high-growth period of the 1960s and 1970s. Compared with the United States and the United Kingdom, Japan has quite small income differentials and a relatively "equal" population as far as income distribution is concerned.

However, income differentials have started to widen in recent years. There are a number of factors accounting for this trend. First, wage levels of workers in large corporations often differ markedly from those of their counterparts in smaller firms. In the 1950s this situation was referred to as the DUAL STRUCTURE of the economy. This dual structure was more or less eliminated in the high-growth period as nearly full employment in the economy narrowed wage gaps. In the 1980s, however, wage differentials based on corporate size began to expand again, especially among young employees. Although difficult to measure statistically, the considerably higher levels of nonmonetary compensation provided by large corporations, including expense accounts and housing and other benefits, further exacerbate the effects of the dual structure.

A second feature of wage differentials in Japan is that they are far greater among different age groups than in other developed countries. This is primarily due to the SENIORITY SYSTEM followed by most Japanese corporations.

The third factor concerns women in the workplace. In previous decades an increasing number of Japanese women in households with lower incomes sought employment in order to supplement their husbands' limited incomes. This development originally served to equalize Japanese family incomes. Recently, however, supplementary incomes earned by working women have tended to widen income differences between families, as many women in high-income-bracket households are now also gainfully employed.

The wage gap between the sexes remains conspicuous in Japan. In 1988 the average monthly salary (excluding overtime pay) of a female worker amounted to only 61 percent of the salary of her male counterpart. This is primarily because the average working woman's career is only half as long as the average man's, a definite disadvantage in a wage system based on seniority; women are more often employed in comparatively low-paying industries and smaller firms and are seldom promoted to management positions; and many women are part-time workers, usually putting in fewer hours than their male counterparts.

Although income distribution in Japan is still relatively equal when measured in terms of employment income, the gap between rich and poor is seen as much wider when considered in terms of asset ownership (financial assets, real estate, stock, etc). Although the gaps in asset ownership had been narrowing in the postwar perod, they have begun to widen conspicuously in recent years because of skyrocketing land prices, especially in the Tōkyō Metropolitan Area. This widening in wealth differentials measured in asset terms is likely to further widen income differentials in the coming years as huge capital gains are generated by these assets.

Income-Doubling Plan 所得倍増計画

(Shotoku Baizō Keikaku). An economic plan developed by the ECONOMIC PLANNING AGENCY under Prime Minister IKEDA HAYATO in 1960. The plan was designed to bring about the doubling of the real national income during the decade from 1961 to 1970. The key elements of the plan called for an increase in social capital, revision of the industrial structure to make it suited for rapid growth, development of trade and international economic cooperation, investment in science and technology, and maintenance of social stability. The plan aimed to achieve an annual growth rate of at least 7.8 percent. In actuality, the economy grew at a much faster pace, averaging about 10.0 percent during the decade. However, rapid growth was accompanied by a rise in the cost of living, and criticism of the plan's focus on growth at the expense of social welfare became widespread. As a result, the plan was dropped in 1965 by the cabinet of SATŌ EISAKU. The goal of a doubled national income was reached sometime in 1967 or 1968.

Independence Club 独立協会

(Kor: Tongnip Hyŏphoe; J: Dokuritsu Kyōkai). Political coalition advocating Korean independence from all foreign control. It was founded in 1896 by Sŏ Chae-p'il (1866–1951), a former member of the KAEHWAP'A (Enlightenment Faction) who had fled to the United States in 1884 after the group's unsuccessful KAPSIN POLITICAL COUP. He became a US citizen and took the name Philip Jaisohn. During the KABO REFORM (1894–95) he returned to Korea and began its first mass newspaper, the *Tongnip sinmun* (The Independent), which gave birth to the Independence Club. The club rallied support from Christian, anti-Japanese, anti-Westernization, and anti-Russian leaders including Syngman RHEE (Yi Sŭng-man). The group encouraged King KOJONG to declare Korea the TAEHAN EMPIRE in 1897. Eventually, however, it came to be seen as a threat to the established political order. In the spring of 1898 Sŏ was persuaded to return to the United States, and a few months later the king ordered the club disbanded and its leaders arrested.

independent movie productions 独立プロ

(*dokuritsu puro*). Motion-picture production firms established by directors, actors, or actresses who are not under contract with the giant movie production companies. The first independent movie production companies in Japan were those formed by such stars of the 1920s and 1930s as KATAOKA CHIEZŌ and ARASHI KANJŪRŌ. After World War II, people in the Japanese motion-picture industry who were driven from their companies by the RED PURGE formed independent production companies. At present there are a number of independent film production companies, mostly established by movie stars, as well as production ventures that function as subcontractors for the large movie companies.

India and Japan インドと日本

(Indo *to* Nihon). Despite Japan's early interest in some elements of Indian culture, especially BUDDHISM, there was little direct contact between the countries until relatively recently. After the opening of Japan in the mid-19th century, contacts with India were governed by Japan's relations with Great Britain, as India was a British colony. Japan accepted Britain's claim to India and even agreed to protect British interests there under the revised ANGLO-JAPANESE ALLIANCE of 1905.

However, Japan's victory in the RUSSO-JAPANESE WAR in 1905 was a source of inspiration to Indians engaged in the struggle for freedom from British imperialism and kindled hope that Japan would assist in the Asian resistance against the West. Indian students in Japan formed a base for Indian revolutionaries who looked to Japan as a place of refuge.

Following the outbreak of World War II in the Pacific, the Japanese government perceived the strategic advantages of befriending the large ethnic Indian populations in Southeast Asian nations. Japan helped in the creation of an Indian military force, the INDIAN NATIONAL ARMY (INA), which was dedicated to the overthrow of British rule and was led by Subhas Chandra BOSE. However, the majority of Indian nationalists condemned Japanese aggression in China and doubted the wisdom of accepting Japanese assistance, suspecting that Japan wished to substitute its own domination for that of Britain. Furthermore, the INA set up its own independent command and refused to be employed by the Japanese in the suppression of rebellions against Japan in occupied Southeast Asian nations. Meanwhile, Japan's military occupation of India was restricted to the sparsely populated Andaman and Nicobar Islands. Eventually Japan was defeated in the IMPHAL CAMPAIGN and proved unable to help the INA in liberating India. Yet, the wartime experience promoted a close relationship between Indians and Japanese without leaving a legacy of hatred, as it did in other Asian nations.

As a member of the FAR EASTERN COMMISSION, India participated in the formulation of policies for the postwar Allied OCCUPATION of Japan. An Indian army unit participated in the Occupation but was withdrawn once India became independent. India terminated its state of war with Japan on 28 April 1952, although it was not a signatory to the SAN FRANCISCO PEACE TREATY, which was implemented on the same date. The Indian government objected to the exclusion of the People's Republic of China from the conference at which the peace treaty was signed, and argued that the security treaty between Japan and the United States (signed immediately after the peace treaty) should be negotiated after Japan regained independence. The bilateral peace treaty between India and Japan, concluded on 9 June 1952, was the first treaty Japan signed on terms of equality after regaining its sovereignty. In the 1950s the people of Japan had high expectations that India would carve out a new path for the Asian nations under the leadership of Prime Minister Jawaharlal Nehru, but in the 1960s this assessment was adversely affected by India's inability to solve basic social and economic problems, as well as by India's armed conflicts with China and Pakistan and the shifting political relations between India and both China and the Soviet Union.

Since the 1970s economic ties have assumed a central position in Indo-Japanese relations. Iron ore gradually replaced cotton as the main commodity imported from India. Japan has become India's principal creditor, supplying a total of US $1.8 billion from 1986 to 1990. Indo-Japanese trade totaled US $3.8 billion in 1990, with Japan importing raw materials such as iron ore, manganese ore, chromium ore, diamonds, and prawns, and exporting machinery, steel, and capital goods. As a result of economic liberalization within India, lower wage levels, and its stable currency, India is attracting capital investment and joint ventures and is being targeted as a market with huge potential by Japanese business.

Indian National Army インド国民軍

(INA; J: Indo Kokumin Gun). The Indian National Army, organized in 1942 with the support of Japan, consisted of Indian soldiers taken prisoner during the fall of Singapore. This force was to return home to fight for the liberation of India from the British. Major Fujiwara Iwaichi (1908–86), who headed the intelligence group FUJIWARA KIKAN, or Efu (F) Kikan, suggested that Captain Mohan SINGH form an Indian volunteer force to support the Japanese army. Singh raised an army of 40,000 but disbanded the INA after falling out with another Indian leader, Rash Behari BOSE, as well as the Japanese liaison officer, Colonel Iwakuro Hideo (1897–1970). The Indian nationalist leader Subhas Chandra BOSE took over a revived INA in 1943. Subhas Bose wanted to attack in his home province of Bengal but was overruled by the Japanese military headquarters, which instead ordered an attack on Imphal in 1944 (see IMPHAL CAMPAIGN). The INA, now numbering some 8,000 troops, joined a force of 83,000 Japanese in the march on Imphal, only to share in defeat.

indigo 藍

(*ai*). A blue liquid obtained from the indigo plant that has been used as a dye since ancient times. The variety most commonly used in Japan is *tadeai* (*Polygonum tinctorium Lour*), native to the Indochina peninsula. The earliest example of Japanese indigo-dyed fabric is kept in the Nara temple HŌRYŪJI and dates from about 620. Indigo-dyed material was used only by the aristocracy through the Nara period (710–794), but became accessible to the common people with the advent of vat dyeing. Indigo is an extremely fast dye, particularly to light and water. With repeated dipping and oxygenating, deep shades of blue are possible.

The earliest known dye method in Japan (*namahazome*; raw-leaf dyeing) involved using fresh *tadeai* leaves. The vat-dye method (*tatezome*), thought to date from the Nara period, allowed for more shades of blue. There are various recipes, but the most common involves the preparation through fermentation of the indigo dye known as *sukumo*.

Tokushima Prefecture in Shikoku has traditionally produced the most indigo, but the introduction of synthetic indigo in the 20th century all but crushed the industry. See also DYES AND DYE COLORS.

Indochina, Japanese occupation of 仏印進駐

(*Futsuin shinchū*). The Japanese takeover of France's colonies in Indochina in the early stages of World War II. Following the fall of France in 1940, Japan negotiated with the Vichy government to allow the stationing of Japanese forces in northern French Indochina (now Vietnam). In July 1941, Japan deployed troops in southern French Indochina as well, and negotiated a new "joint defense" agreement that left the Vichy government with only nominal authority. The United States then placed a total embargo on exports to Japan and froze Japanese assets in the United States. The quickly deteriorating relations between the two countries led to war in December 1941.

Indonesia and Japan インドネシアと日本

(Indoneshia *to* Nihon). The earliest known contacts between Indonesia and Japan date from the late 16th century, when Japanese settled in a number of Indonesian towns. The Portuguese began visiting Japan in 1543 and took some Japanese to Southeast Asian countries, including Indonesia. Japanese traders also began to visit Indonesian ports, and some settled there; European colonial authorities as well as local Asian rulers welcomed the Japanese as mercenaries, merchants, and craftsmen.

The policy of NATIONAL SECLUSION enacted by the Tokugawa shogunate (1603–1867) prohibited Japanese abroad from returning home, and the Japanese in Indonesia gradually were assimilated. Following the rescinding of the National Seclusion policy and the overthrow of the shogunate in 1868, Japanese again began to arrive in Southeast Asia. Initially, the majority were women known as KARAYUKI SAN, who settled in port towns as prostitutes, but they soon were followed by men of various professions.

World War II Occupation—During World War II, initial Japanese military successes in Southeast Asia gave some Indonesian nationalists the hope of terminating Dutch rule with Japan's assistance; after Japanese forces occupied all of the archipelago early in 1942, SUKARNO, Mohammad HATTA, and a few other political prisoners were released and used by the Japanese occupation authorities as collaborators. The Indonesians' hopes for self-rule soon faded into frustration as the Japanese imposed strict controls on speech and assembly, forced deliveries of foodstuffs, and drafted manpower for public works and military training.

In September 1944 Prime Minister KOISO KUNIAKI stated that Japan would grant independence to the East Indies in the near future. As the war situation worsened, the Japanese gave military training to Indonesian youths (see PETA ARMY). Although Japan surrendered to the Allies before carrying out its plans to sponsor Indonesian independence, the Republic of Indonesia declared its own independence under Sukarno on 17 August 1945. Their wartime experience provided the Indonesians with valuable lessons for their subsequent struggle with the Dutch, which ended with transfer of sovereignty in 1949.

Postwar Relations—The Indonesian government signed but did not ratify the SAN FRANCISCO PEACE TREATY of 8 September 1951 because its conditions for war reparations remained ambiguous. Prolonged bilateral talks between Indonesia and Japan resulted in the 20 January 1958 Agreement on Reparations, stipulating that Japan would pay US $223 million in services and goods over a 12-year period. After Sukarno's fall in 1967, his successor, President Suharto, adopted a more pro-Western policy, asking noncommunist countries for economic aid. The Indonesian economy, however, remained stagnant, and in the early 1970s the highly visible Japanese economic presence in Indonesia led to the buildup of anti-Japanese sentiments that erupted into violent protests during Prime Minister TANAKA KAKUEI's visit to Jakarta in 1974.

In more recent years, relations have been marked by a deepening of bilateral economic ties. It is increasingly recognized in Japan that the health of the Japanese economy depends greatly on trade with Indonesia, which is the largest non–Middle East supplier of petroleum to Japan. Largely because of imports of petroleum and other raw materials, Japan has run a consistent trade deficit vis-à-vis Indonesia. In 1990, for example, Japan exported products valued at US $5.0 billion while importing goods worth US $12.7 billion. Petroleum and natural gas accounted for 71.4 percent of Indonesia's exports; other major export items included prawns, lead, rubber, and timber. Japan's exports were mainly chemicals, steel, and machinery.

Japanese investments in Indonesia underscore the level of economic interaction: between 1951 and 1988 Japan invested a total of US $9.2 billion, mainly to develop petroleum and other raw material sources. In 1988 alone, 18 Japanese firms were set up in Indonesia with total investments valued at US $586.0 million.

Since 1987 Indonesia has been the largest recipient of Japanese official development assistance (ODA). Japan's disbursements of grants, loans, and technical assistance to Indonesia in 1987 totaled US $707.0 million, representing more than a quadrupling of aid given the previous year. In 1986–90 bilateral ODA totaled US $3.9 billion.

Industrial Bank of Japan, Ltd （株）日本興業銀行

(Nippon Kōgyō Ginkō). Private bank specializing in long-term credit to industrial enterprises. Incorporated in 1902, the bank is the largest of the three such credit banks in Japan. With the increase in Japan's foreign currency reserves in the 1970s, the bank began issuing yen-based bonds through the Asian Development Bank and the World Bank. It also underwrote bonds issued by various governments and enterprises around the world, playing an increasingly important role in the international financial market. Beginning with subsidiary banks in Germany (Industriebank von Japan) and Hong Kong (IBJ Asia), the bank has increased its international network of operations. Now there are subsidiaries in Luxembourg, New York, London, and Zurich, among others. At the end of March 1991, the total assets were ¥43.6 trillion (US $317.8 billion), and total debentures and deposits were ¥32.9 trillion (US $239.8 billion), 64 percent of which was obtained through the issuance of debentures. The bank was capitalized at ¥352.0 billion (US $2.6 billion) in the same year. Headquarters are in Tōkyō.

industrial design インダストリアル・デザイン

(*indasutoriaru dezain*). The beginning of modern industrial design in Japan dates from the early post–World War II period, although original product design was not a major consideration in Japan at this early stage. Rather, early postwar Japanese manufacturers, operating under economic and technological constraints, concentrated on producing large numbers of technically reliable, inexpensive products, such as watches, for the export market. The design aesthetic that did exist was largely influenced by American product design, a natural choice since the United States constituted most of Japan's export market. This trend of American-influenced design continued through the mid-1950s as Japan's overseas markets grew. Japanese-made transistor radios of this period, for example, displayed many of the same automobile-inspired chrome embellishments that characterized much of American industrial design of the same period.

Despite this tendency to imitate American and other Western models, the industrial design scene in Japan was far from static. Japanese newspapers began sponsoring product design contests, and the Japan External Trade Organization (JETRO) sent students of design to Europe and the United States in an effort to foster young talent. A number of designers' organizations were also established, including the Japanese Industrial Designers' Association (JIDA), established in 1951.

From the mid-1950s on, Japanese manufacturers became more concerned with original styling and design of products. While most industrial design was produced by teams of designers rather than individual "stars," a few names stand out as representative of this period. One of the early figures in Japanese automobile design was Kosugi Jirō (1915–81), who produced a number of successful designs for Mazda. Ekuan Kenji (b 1929), a JETRO design student, established his own studio in 1957. In addition to motorcycle designs for Yamaha and camera designs for Olympus, Ekuan's studio produced a number of well-known home products, such as soy sauce containers. Akioka Yoshio (b 1920), who worked as a free-lance industrial designer after the war, participated in designs for a wide variety of products, including railroad cars, motorcycles, and stationery products. These men and a number of other designers remained active through the 1960s and 1970s.

The World Design Conference was held in Tōkyō in 1960, and by the time of the Tōkyō Olympics in 1964 Japan had produced internationally respected designs for such products as cameras, electronics, automobiles, and motorcycles. The sleek, modern styling of the locomotives and cars of the SHINKANSEN, Japan's high-speed passenger railway, was especially admired and exemplified one of the key characteristics of Japanese consumer product design in the 1960s: the "high-tech" look, a modern, functional styling that mirrored growing awareness of Japan as a leader in the creation and mass production of high-technology products. The high-tech design sense was especially evident in such products as calculators and audio equipment.

In the 1970s and 1980s Japanese industrial design became identified with miniaturization. As markets became saturated and consumers became more selective, product design that stressed convenient size and portability became even more important as a marketing tool. The drive to create smaller and smaller versions of various products was directly tied to advances in technology, especially the development of the microchip and microcircuitry, which enabled engineers to reduce the size of many products drastically. Perhaps the best example of this trend is Sony's Walkman portable cassette player, which became a phenomenal success worldwide and which was followed by miniature televisions and other electronic products.

One of the chief concerns of Japanese industrial design in the late 1980s and early 1990s was adapting products to consumer lifestyles. There was a move to address the individuality of consumers, both at home and abroad, through various design combinations of technical features, compact size, color, and styling. Designers and engineers were also attempting to "humanize" high technology, as evidenced by the FUZZY ENGINEERING boom, designing such items as office machines and home electrical products for

greater ease of operation. These and other design trends further strengthened Japan's reputation as a world leader in industrial design.

industrial history 産業史

(*sangyōshi*). Japan's present INDUSTRIAL STRUCTURE has its roots in the industrial and economic development that took place during the Edo period (1600–1868). This period was characterized by the encouragement of the work ethic by the Confucian values of the *samurai* class, the spread of primary education, the development of a nationwide distribution system, and the accumulation of large amounts of capital in the hands of merchants and landowners.

The country's modern industrial history can be roughly divided into two periods: first, the early modern era from the MEIJI RESTORATION (1868) to the end of World War II, during which capitalism was established in Japan, and second, the contemporary period, from the end of the war to the present, which has seen reconstruction and rapid economic growth.

Early Modern Industry (1868–1945)
Japan's industrial revolution began in the late 1880s. Light industry, notably the TEXTILE INDUSTRY, grew especially rapidly between 1887 and 1896, while a second wave of industrialization between 1897 and 1906 led to the establishment of many heavy industries. The Meiji government took the lead in developing such basic industries as railroads and mining, as well as a number of manufacturing industries such as the SHIPBUILDING INDUSTRY, the IRON AND STEEL INDUSTRY, the MACHINE TOOL INDUSTRY, and the cement and glass industries. Most of these enterprises were later turned over to the private sector (see KAN'EI JIGYŌ HARAISAGE).

During World War I Japanese industry experienced significant growth, as it benefited greatly from the inability of European suppliers, preoccupied with events at home, to trade in Asian markets. Japan received many orders for military supplies and munitions from the Allies, and there was great demand for Japanese shipping; by the end of the war Japan had become the world's third largest shipbuilding nation. An industrial boom took place during the period of the war as the values of Japanese exports rose threefold, their volume increased by about 50 percent, and there was a rapid accumulation of capital. Industrial production overtook agricultural production during the war, and by the war's end almost half of nonagricultural labor was employed in industry; capitalism in Japan had become fully entrenched.

Despite economic hardships caused by a depression in 1920, the TŌKYŌ EARTHQUAKE OF 1923, and the SHŌWA DEPRESSION, the productivity of Japanese industry continued to increase as a result of technological progress, greater efficiency in production techniques, the government's relatively successful suppression of the nascent trade union movement, and the development of managerial techniques designed to secure employee loyalty and commitment (see LABOR). Japan's heavy industries, such as iron and steel and shipbuilding, grew especially rapidly in the 1930s. The output of the CHEMICAL INDUSTRY and the machine tool, electric machinery, and ceramics industries all increased greatly during this period. Exports rose sharply, led by shipments of textile products and sundry goods. In the PRECISION MACHINERY INDUSTRY, which became the foundation for Japan's munitions industry, domestic products were

almost meeting domestic demand, except for certain specialized items.

Throughout this period there was no antimonopoly policy in Japan. Since the Meiji Restoration the overriding concern of the nation's political oligarchs (see GENRŌ) had been Japan's national survival in the face of the perceived political and economic threat of Western domination. Neither political individualism nor economic individualism was seen as an ideal to be guided by, and in the period before Japan's defeat in World War II it is not clear that the government placed a premium on economic competition in itself. On the contrary, administrations considered that the national interest would best be served by supporting the interests of large, powerful, and well-established companies such as MITSUI, MITSUBISHI, and SUMITOMO—the ZAIBATSU (literally, "financial cliques")—that had the resources to lead the nation's industrial progress. Governments did all they could to promote the interests of such companies—for example, by encouraging trade associations (*kumiai*) in the 1920s and industrial cartels in the 1930s. The *zaibatsu* dominated industry in this period, exercising an oligopolistic control over a wide range of industries such as manufacturing, mining, and transportation, as well as finance and overseas trade.

Despite the growing industrial power of the *zaibatsu*, manufacturing still accounted for no more than 16 percent of the national labor force in the early 1930s. A DUAL STRUCTURE had developed within the manufacturing industry itself, between, on the one hand, the relatively small number of firms in the more modern sector with its capital-intensive production methods, and, on the other hand, vast numbers of low-capital, labor-intensive small firms and family concerns, many of which were more or less wholly dependent on the business of a single larger firm. In 1930, 60 percent of the nation's manufacturing labor force was employed by firms with fewer than 10 workers. Although this figure had fallen to just 9 percent by 1986, the "dual structure"—the high proportion of smaller-scale businesses in dependency relationships with larger firms—has continued to be a key characteristic of the Japanese economy in the post–World War II period.

A great many new industries emerged in the years between the world wars. For instance, the development of the electric power industry gave a great boost to the domestic aluminum-smelting industry. While originally used as a material in the new AIRCRAFT INDUSTRY, aluminum gradually came to be utilized for household consumer products. The development of the radio led to the beginning of domestic vacuum tube production. Large phonographs became coveted items and many new businesses entered this area, including the companies now known as TŌSHIBA CORPORATION; VICTOR CO OF JAPAN, LTD; and NIPPON COLUMBIA CO, LTD. Many other major Japanese manufacturing companies of the present day were founded at this time, such as TOYOTA MOTOR CORPORATION and NISSAN MOTOR CO, LTD, in automobiles and MITSUBISHI HEAVY INDUSTRIES, LTD, in military aircraft.

Various governmental policies encouraged industrial growth. Subsidies supported the production of military vehicles and the substitution of domestic production for the import of cargo ships. The birth of Nippon

Seitetsu (Nippon Steel Co), an iron and steel trust centered on YAWATA IRON AND STEEL WORKS, was the result of government guidance. Industrial growth was also fostered by laws enacted for individual industries, with emphasis placed on automobiles, the PETROCHEMICAL INDUSTRY, iron and steel, machine tools, and aircraft manufacturing. For example, the infant AUTOMOTIVE INDUSTRY was promoted by the Automobile Manufacturing Industry Law of 1935. Such laws served as prototypes for the industry-specific laws, such as those for the machinery and electronics industries, that were enacted in the post–World War II period.

Contemporary Industrial History (from 1945)—During the reconstruction period following World War II, the recovery of key industries was aided by an INDUSTRIAL POLICY known as the PRIORITY PRODUCTION PROGRAM. Underdeveloped capacity in certain areas was seen as a bottleneck limiting overall growth, so the electric power, iron and steel, marine transportation, and coal industries were targeted for rapid reconstruction.

The Allied OCCUPATION period (1945–52) was fraught with economic difficulties, however, as Japanese industry strove to rebuild its shattered plants and regain its international markets. The Korean War (1950–53) enabled Japanese industry to climb out of the stagnant situation in which it was mired at the end of the 1940s. By supplying the United Nations forces serving in Korea with the vast quantities of matériel (known as special procurements or TOKUJU) that they required to prosecute the war, Japan was able to earn the foreign exchange necessary to pay for vital imports; the war thus provided the stimulus for the economic recovery of the 1950s.

During the rapid-growth period from the late 1950s to the early 1970s, industries such as iron and steel, the CONSTRUCTION INDUSTRY, the CONSTRUCTION MACHINERY INDUSTRY, and the PHARMACEUTICAL INDUSTRY grew quickly, and the HOUSEHOLD ELECTRICAL PRODUCTS INDUSTRY and the petrochemical industry developed. The international economic environment at this time was favorable for Japanese exports; in the 1960s, Japan's average dollar-base export increase of 18.4 percent per year was 2.5 times the overall increase in world trade. This period saw the establishment of an industrial structure based on imported raw materials that were domestically processed for export.

In the wake of the export successes of the iron and steel and shipbuilding industries, other industries such as the precision machinery industry and electronic and optical equipment also turned to export-led growth. Huge investments were made in production facilities for heavy industry, primarily located in the Tōkaidō megalopolis that stretches along Honshū's Pacific coast from Tōkyō to Ōsaka and Kōbe. Total plant and equipment investments by business exceeded profits, and the ratio of borrowed capital increased.

Aggressive management created an increasing demand for funds, which banks satisfied using their large volumes of household savings deposits. Relationships between corporations and their main banks became closer, and industrial groups of affiliated companies formed around major banks (see KEIRETSU). This aggressive corporate capitalism and strong reliance on indirect financing were characteristic of the Japanese industrial

structure and were the basic mechanisms responsible for the strong economic growth Japan enjoyed. Japan's NATIONAL INCOME more than doubled in the 1960s, and in 1968 its gross national product became the second largest among the world's market economies. The spring labor offensive (SHUNTŌ), first organized in 1955, became in the 1960s the established mechanism by which labor bargained for more equitable INCOME DISTRIBUTION.

Efforts to reduce costs and increase efficiency in response to the OIL CRISIS OF 1973 strengthened the competitiveness of major export industries such as electric machinery, electrical consumer goods, and automobiles. The jump in petroleum prices had less effect on the machinery industry, given its relatively low consumption of energy and raw materials, than on industries with greater energy consumption such as iron and steel, petrochemicals, aluminum refining, and cement. Successful conservation efforts were made by both management and labor; as a result, energy demand fell by 37 percent in the chemical industry and, eased by the introduction of continuous casting technology, by more than 20 percent in the iron and steel industry. In the automobile industry energy-saving efforts led to lighter automobiles and increased fuel economy, which further increased export competitiveness.

The oil crisis of 1979 also caused distinctive changes in the country's industrial structure. The heavy industries, which had previously supported rapid economic growth, stagnated, and the industrial emphasis shifted to industries that utilize high technology and sophisticated machinery (see ECONOMIC PLANNING). Technological advances contributed to growth in the electronics and automobile industries. Productivity increased through innovations such as the mounting of small computers on machine tools to develop numerically controlled equipment. It was also during the late 1970s that the COMPUTER INDUSTRY and the SEMICONDUCTOR INDUSTRY began to grow rapidly.

Although the yen has appreciated greatly since the PLAZA ACCORD of 1985, thus reducing the price competitiveness of Japanese exports, export volume remains high. Japan, which had relied on exports for its economic recovery since the oil crises, has been strongly criticized for not taking action to stimulate domestic demand, and TRADE FRICTION has become a pressing issue.

In their view of Japanese industry, many outside observers tend to emphasize the role of the intimate relationship between business and government in increasing industrial competitiveness (see MINISTRY OF INTERNATIONAL TRADE AND INDUSTRY). Since the Meiji Restoration, Japanese administrations have indeed worked closely with industry to develop Japan's economy, a process that some trace back to the policies of the Meiji oligarchs. Throughout the 20th century, it is argued, and particularly since World War II, the government has identified key industrial sectors for development and then actively encouraged major corporations to undertake the necessary research, investment, and development. Recent examples were the official encouragements in the early 1980s to Japanese manufacturers to overtake the US computer giant IBM, and also to establish an ADVANCED CERAMICS industry. However, other observers have insisted that much of the credit for Japan's rapid economic growth must be given to the private sector rather than the government. They claim that the in-

troduction of new technologies and the development of new products owe more to the mechanisms of market competition than they do to the promotion efforts and the leadership of government, and that in many key areas, such as robotics, the government was slow to respond to the challenge of the new technology, the pace being set by the intensity of interfirm competition. See also ECONOMIC HISTORY; ECONOMY, CONTEMPORARY.

industrial policy　　　産業政策

(sangyō seisaku). Policies with the objective of changing the industrial structure by strengthening, developing, and protecting priority industries and realigning depressed industries. Also included in the category are policies concerning pollution, industry location, small and medium-sized companies, and foreign trade.

Changes in Japanese industrial policy since World War II can be divided into three stages: (1) In the initial recovery period, the priority production program emphasized restarting production. This was followed by an industrial rationalization policy to regain export competitiveness and by measures to promote development of new industries and growth industries. (2) During the period of rapid economic growth there was a move toward policies of industrial reorganization and development of priority industries in response to the transition to an open economic system with trade and capital liberalization. (3) Following the oil crisis of 1973, emphasis came to be placed on structural realignment policies and cross-industry policies in response to international developments, including the consumer movement, increasing environmental problems, and the intensification of trade friction. With the growing international role of the Japanese economy in recent years, more emphasis is being placed on industrial policies for stimulation of domestic demand.

A special characteristic of postwar Japanese industrial policy was the method whereby the INDUSTRIAL STRUCTURE COUNCIL, consisting of representatives from the public and private sectors and universities, would first build a consensus on policy objectives and the measures needed to achieve them. This would be followed by the government ministries (primarily the Ministry of International Trade and Industry [MITI]) providing guidance for achieving the objectives.

industrial property　　　工業所有権

(kōgyō shoyūken). Legal concept first formally used in Japan in the 1894 trade and navigation treaty between Japan and England, when Japan agreed to the Paris Convention for the protection of industrial property. Article 1 states, "The protection of industrial property has as its object patents, utility models, designs, trademarks, trade names, indications of source on goods or appellations of origin and the prevention of unfair competition." The convention also provides that "industrial property taken in its broadest sense extends not only to industry and commerce but also to fields such as agriculture and the harvesting industry."

In Japan, the term "industrial property" is not used in its broad sense but commonly refers to only four rights: patent, utility-model, design, and trademark. These are regulated by very similar legal provisions, and their administration is handled by the Patent Office, a special bureau of the Ministry of International Trade and Industry. Thus it is necessary to distinguish between industrial property in the narrow sense (see PATENT LAW; UTILITY-MODEL LAW; DESIGN LAW; TRADEMARK LAW) and industrial property in the broad sense, which, along with copyrights, is considered to lie within the domain of incorporeal property.

Industrial property is divided into two classes. The first, industrial production activities, includes inventions, devices, and designs. The second, markings for the maintenance of industrial order, includes trademarks, trade names, service marks, indications of source on goods, appellations of origin, product containers, wrappings, shape, etc.

The establishment, change, and extinction of patents, registered designs, trademarks, and trade names are clarified by means of a registration or recording system. Product markings other than trademarks and trade names initially carry no monopoly use rights. Once these markings have become commonly known through wide usage, they receive exclusive monopoly protection under the Unfair Competition Prevention Law (Fusei Kyōsō Bōshi Hō).

Because the objects of industrial property have no international boundaries, there is a strong need for their international protection. Beginning with the Paris Convention, various international treaties have been concluded on the matter. In 1978 the Patent Cooperation Treaty became effective, and the Japanese Patent Office is an important international searching and preliminary examining authority.

industrial reorganization 産業再編成

(sangyō saihensei). Efforts of leading corporations within an industry to realign affiliations and investments in order to increase production efficiency and stabilize business operations. Examples include the new enterprise groups (see KEIRETSU) that were formed in the high-growth period of the 1960s as major industries expanded production and modernized equipment.

A somewhat different type of industrial reorganization was prevalent in the 1980s as large corporations tried to use excess financial and personnel resources to take advantage of new opportunities outside their traditional line of business. This was done in two different ways. The first was to utilize the technical and business expertise of existing personnel to set up new subsidiaries, as was done by large steel firms such as NIPPON STEEL CORPORATION and NKK CORPORATION on their entry into the new fields of electronics and biotechnology. The second method was to expand the company group through mergers and acquisitions, an example being the KYŌCERA CORPORATION's acquisition of Yashica Co, Ltd.

industrial revolution in Japan
日本の産業革命

(Nihon no sangyō kakumei). The term "industrial revolution" generally refers to the classic case of internally generated English industrial development from the mid-18th to the mid-19th century. In Japan, by contrast, the industrial revolution was a piecemeal process. It began in the late 1880s, after the deflationary MATSUKATA FISCAL POLICY had achieved a "primitive accumulation" of capital, and lasted until about 1910. Because Japan suffered political and economic encroachment by Western powers (see UNEQUAL TREATIES, REVISION OF), its industrialization had to be rushed, directed largely by government fiat. The state's active role in

fostering industrialism while encouraging the private sector distinguished the Japanese industrial revolution from its English counterpart.

In accord with its policy of promoting trade and industry (SHOKUSAN KŌGYŌ), the Meiji government in the early 1870s had purchased foreign machinery for the domestic textile industry. The privately owned ŌSAKA SPINNING MILL independently imported the latest steam-powered machinery from England and raw cotton from China, India, and the United States. The highly successful Ōsaka mill set an example for the cotton textile industry. To pay for foreign raw materials and textile machinery, the government encouraged the domestic production of raw silk for export. As with the cotton industry, the government-owned filatures did not fare as well as their privately operated counterparts, which combined traditional and Western techniques, used cooperative marketing, and relied on the labor of peasant girls who received subsistence wages.

The development of heavy industry began in the late 1880s with the government's decision to sell many of its industrial enterprises, most of them unprofitable, to private entrepreneurs (see KAN'EI JIGYŌ HARAISAGE). In 1887 the NAGASAKI SHIPYARDS were sold to MITSUBISHI, and two years later the MIIKE COAL MINES were sold to MITSUI, signaling the beginning of the shipping and coal industries, which played a central role in the development of Japanese capitalism. (See also ZAIBATSU.) The government established its own steel mill at Yawata, in Kyūshū, after the Sino-Japanese War of 1894–95 (see YAWATA IRON AND STEEL WORKS). The army and navy arsenals were tied in with the Yawata mill. After the Russo-Japanese War of 1904–05, the government established the Anshan Steel Works in Manchuria. In this manner the state took the lead over private concerns in a critical sector of modern industry.

industrial structure 産業構造

(sangyō kōzō). The structure of an economy by industry, typically measured by the percentage distribution of economic activities (in terms of output, capital, and labor) by major sectors and industries. National economies are conventionally divided into three sectors—primary industries (agriculture, forestry, and fisheries), secondary industries (mining, manufacturing, construction, transportation, and communications), and tertiary industries (retail and wholesale trade, banking, finance and real estate, business services, personal services, and public administration). In general, national economies in the early stages of development are dominated by primary production related to land (often including mining). As the economy develops and income rises, the primary sector shares of output, capital, and labor tend to fall, and those of the secondary sector tend to rise. In late stages of development, the primary sector accounts for only a small fraction of total economic activities, the secondary sector begins to decline in relative terms, and the tertiary sector comes to the fore.

Historical Experience of Japan— Japan's economic development since the MEIJI RESTORATION (1868) is an excellent illustration of these patterns. In the distribution of the labor force between agriculture (including forestry) and nonagriculture, changes were relatively slow until the first decade of the 20th century, considerably ac-

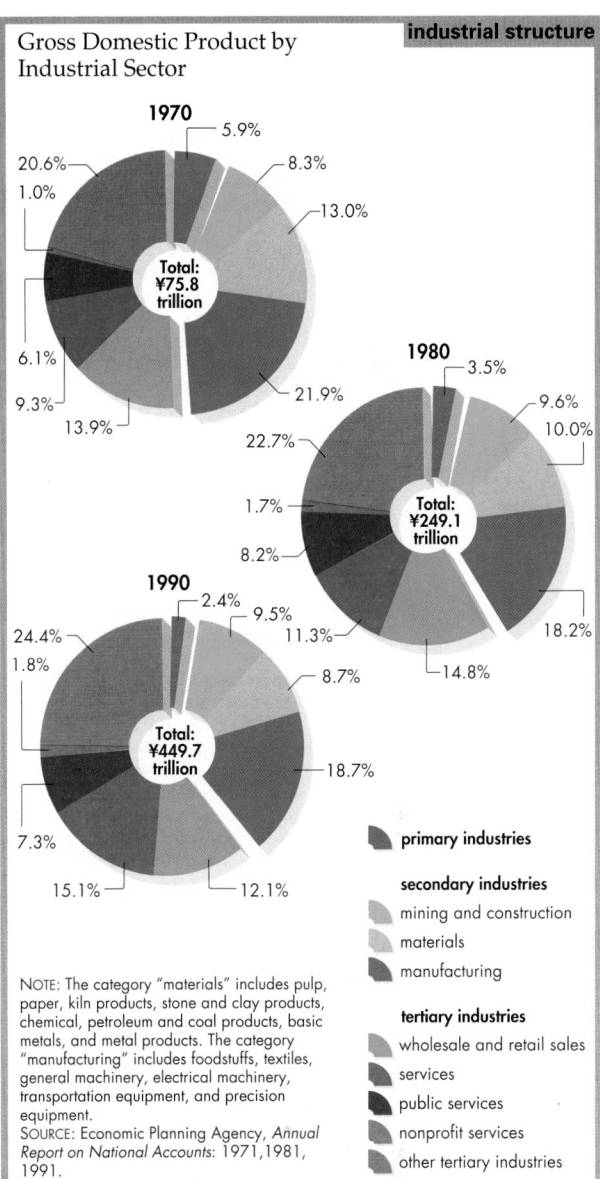

Gross Domestic Product by Industrial Sector

1970

5.9%
8.3%
13.0%
20.6%
1.0%
Total: ¥75.8 trillion
21.9%
6.1%
9.3%
13.9%

1980

3.5%
9.6%
10.0%
22.7%
1.7%
8.2%
Total: ¥249.1 trillion
18.2%
14.8%

1990

2.4%
9.5%
11.3%
24.4%
1.8%
8.7%
Total: ¥449.7 trillion
18.7%
7.3%
15.1%
12.1%

- ■ primary industries
- **secondary industries**
  - mining and construction
  - materials
  - manufacturing
- **tertiary industries**
  - wholesale and retail sales
  - services
  - public services
  - nonprofit services
  - other tertiary industries

NOTE: The category "materials" includes pulp, paper, kiln products, stone and clay products, chemical, petroleum and coal products, basic metals, and metal products. The category "manufacturing" includes foodstuffs, textiles, general machinery, electrical machinery, transportation equipment, and precision equipment.
SOURCE: Economic Planning Agency, Annual Report on National Accounts: 1971,1981, 1991.

celerated from then up to World War II, temporarily reversed in direction after the war owing to the disruption caused by the destruction of urban industry and infrastructure, and very rapid during the following decades. After 1960 the agricultural labor force began to contract in absolute terms, and even those who remained on farms worked only part-time as farmers.

In the secondary sector, statistics show a continued relative expansion in employment and production until the mid-1970s, except for a temporary reversal in World War II. The tertiary sector maintained a relatively stable share in net domestic product before World War II, although its share of the national labor force expanded. After World War II, its share of employment continued to increase, while its share of gross domestic product (GDP) remained stable until the early 1960s when it, too, started to rise. See also LABOR MARKET.

Changes in Manufacturing—A broad comparison of light and heavy manufacturing reveals that light manufacturing accounted for as much as 85 percent of total production until 1900. From then on, the share steadily declined, and after 100 years the relative positions of light and heavy manufacturing were reversed. Among light manufacturing industries, the FOOD PROCESSING INDUSTRY was the most important in the early Meiji period (1868–1912), accounting for 60 percent of total production, but its share shrank steadily over the next 100 years. The decline of the TEXTILE INDUSTRY was much slower. The industry was, in fact, the dynamic catalyst in Japan's industrialization. It was in this industry that the factory system was first introduced. Textile output was less than 10 percent of the total in the 1870s but jumped above 25 percent in the 1890s and stayed close to 30 percent until World War II. The continued expansion of textile mills through the prewar period provided significant employment opportunities, especially for surplus female labor in agriculture. This feature of *dekasegi*, or temporary migration, was a salient feature of prewar labor mobility. After World War II, the textile industry began to decline because of the development of synthetic fibers and competition from emerging producers in less developed countries; by 1990 the industry accounted for only 3.1 percent of the national labor force.

In heavy manufacturing, basic metals (see IRON AND STEEL INDUSTRY) initially accounted for a very small fraction of total output. The industry began to expand in the decade beginning in 1910, but government protection was necessary to shield it from international competition; the largest steel mill, YAWATA IRON AND STEEL WORKS, was run by the government until 1934. After World War II, basic metals maintained a stable share of manufacturing output. On the other hand, the MACHINE TOOL INDUSTRY, after making relatively slow progress in the pre–World War II period, experienced a spectacular expansion in the three decades after 1945; it accounted for less than 20 percent of manufacturing output in 1950 but exceeded 40 percent by 1972. Japan is now one of the world's leading exporters of machinery. The CHEMICAL INDUSTRY maintained a comparatively stable 10 percent share before World War II and rose to 20 percent after the war.

The most recent stage in the development of national economies has been called post-industrialism, which is marked by a decrease in the employment share of the secondary sector, a shift from production of goods to services, and the growing importance of knowledge as a factor in production. This "service revolution" brings the continuing growth of tertiary industries; it seems to have begun in Japan in the mid-1970s, when manufacturing employment started to decline. In 1990 the tertiary sector accounted for 60.8 percent of total output and employed 59.0 percent of the national labor force.

Relationship to the Foreign Trade Structure——The composition of a nation's exports and imports closely reflects its stage of industrialization. Japan's main exports were tea and raw silk when the country opened its doors to foreign powers in the 1860s, and raw silk remained the most important export item until 1929, thanks to the rapidly growing demand for silk goods in the United States. Cotton textiles followed raw silk. Cotton exports were initially in cotton yarns and then shifted to cotton fabrics. In the 1930s, cotton replaced raw silk as the most important category of Japan's exports. In the early postwar period, more than half of Japan's exports were in light manufacturing, but with the expansion of heavy industries Japanese exports continued to shift to heavy manufactured goods, which came to account for more than 87 percent

of the total value of exports by 1990.

Japan's imports consisted almost entirely of manufactured products in the early Meiji period. Industrialization in the subsequent decades enabled Japan to carry on import substitution of consumer goods and to increase imports of crude materials. Thus, in the 1930s, Japan's imports consisted of light manufactures (12 percent), heavy manufactures (30 percent), foodstuffs (18 percent), raw materials (33 percent), and fuels (7 percent). Comparable figures in 1988–90 were 16, 31, 14, 14, and 22 percent (others 3 percent), respectively. See also FOREIGN TRADE.

Industrial Structure Council
産業構造審議会

(Sangyō Kōzō Shingikai). Also known as Sankōshin. An advisory council sponsored and controlled by the MINISTRY OF INTERNATIONAL TRADE AND INDUSTRY (MITI), whose purpose is to study and make recommendations on questions posed by the minister concerning the industrial structure of the national economy. The council was created in 1964 by combining the Industrial Structure Study Commission (Sangyō Kōzō Chōsakai) and the Industrial Rationalization Council (Sangyō Gōrika Shingikai). It analyzes the long-term prospects of the development pattern of the national economy, thereby providing a broad policy vision to MITI.

industrial waste
産業廃棄物

(*sangyō haikibutsu*). Waste products resulting from manufacturing and business operations. In 1971 the Waste Disposal and Public Cleaning Law specified treatment procedures for 19 designated types of waste, including sludge, oil, acids, and construction materials. Domestically produced industrial waste is surveyed every five years by the Ministry of Health and Welfare. In 1985 there was 312 million metric tons (343 million short tons) of waste. The largest component, sludge, which made up 34 percent of the total, amounted to 113 million metric tons (124 million short tons).

Excluding recycled materials, the amount of waste for final disposal was 90 million metric tons (99 million short tons) in 1985, but that amount has been increasing yearly. Due to inadequate treatment facilities, incidents of waste from Tōkyō and other large cities being illegally dumped in outlying areas have increased, becoming a serious social issue. According to a National Police Agency survey, illegally dumped industrial waste reached 1.7 million metric tons (1.8 million short tons) in 1990. Recently, in addition to the 10 types of waste designated by the Waste Disposal and Public Cleaning Law, such high-technology waste materials as beryllium, selenium, and antimony have become a problem.

According to the "polluter pays principle" (PPP), businesses are responsible for the treatment of the industrial waste they produce. Despite limitations on the construction of new treatment facilities, national and local governments are establishing strong policies regarding industrial waste, as well as fostering programs for recycling and using refuse materials as a resource.

industrial zones
工業地帯

(*kōgyō chitai*). Industrial zones were first created in Japan during the mid-Meiji period (1868–1912) when modern industries were introduced into Japan. Most of Japan's principal industrial regions have developed around ports and river mouths, chiefly be-

cause Japanese industry depends heavily on imported raw materials. Also, a large proportion of manufactured goods is shipped to foreign markets. The major industrial zones are the KEIHIN INDUSTRIAL ZONE, HANSHIN INDUSTRIAL ZONE, CHŪKYŌ INDUSTRIAL ZONE, and KITA KYŪSHŪ INDUSTRIAL ZONE.

Industry and Labor Roundtable Conferences
産業労働懇話会

(Sangyō Rōdō Konwakai). Series of conferences, the first in January 1970, held by a private advisory group reporting to the minister of labor. These meetings bring together representatives from the academic world, business circles, and trade unions and also include bureaucrats from related government ministries and the prime minister's office; the prime minister himself sometimes participates. Conferences are held eight or nine times a year to discuss the dominant labor issues of the day and are considered the most influential "think tank" on Japanese labor policy.

inflation and price stability
インフレーションと物価の安定

(*infurēshon to bukka no antei*). In the 1950s, the wholesale price index and the consumer price index in Japan were fairly stable, the annual rate of increase being 0.3 percent for the former and 2.8 percent for the latter. During the 1960s, a new trend set in: wholesale prices remained fairly stable, but consumer prices began rising at a faster pace. The annual rate of increase was 1.3 percent for the wholesale price index and 5.8 percent for the consumer price index. One important factor contributing to the stability of wholesale prices was rising labor productivity in heavy industry. The major factor accelerating consumer price inflation was the rising cost of services. During the early 1970s, wholesale prices as well as consumer prices rose sharply. The annual rate of increase for 1970–75 was 9.4 percent for wholesale prices and 11.3 percent for consumer prices. This phase coincided with the worldwide inflation associated with the oil price hikes of the 1970s and the commodity price explosion, which contributed to rising inflation in Japan through the late 1970s. In the early 1980s the consumer price index again stabilized at an annual rate of increase of approximately 2.0 percent. The sharp increase in the value of the yen in 1985 (see PLAZA ACCORD) contributed to a considerable drop in wholesale prices. As of the early 1990s, however, the effects of the high yen had not been fully reflected in consumer prices, and price levels in Japan were still quite high considered internationally.

Information Network System
アイエヌエス

(INS; J: Ai Enu Esu). The name of the integrated services digital network (ISDN) developed by the Nippon Telegraph and Telephone Corporation (NTT). The system combines previously separate phone, facsimile, and data communication lines into a single telecommunications network, thereby providing information and visual communication simultaneously. Through a home terminal unit, users can shop by television, bank, utilize data services, and enjoy home study and other activities. The system was introduced to Japan in 1984 as a 30-month experiment in the cities of Mitaka and Musashino, Tōkyō Prefecture. In 1988 INS became the world's first large-scale commercial service using ISDN technology, and as of 1991

the service was operative in 1,351 areas throughout Japan. Subscribers to INS number more than 40,000. Technical characteristics of the system are digitization of electrical signals and the use of large-capacity optical fiber cables.

inga 因果

(cause and effect; Skt: *hetu* and *phala*). An important concept of Buddhism. The term *in* refers to an inner and direct cause, while another term, *en* (Skt: *pratyaya*), refers to an external and indirect cause. The two combine to produce effect (J: *ka* or *ga*). In the Buddhist conception of karmic retribution (*inga ōhō*), a good karmic cause will invariably produce a good karmic result, and a bad karmic cause will produce a bad karmic result. Depending on one's good or bad actions, one will obtain pleasurable or painful karmic retribution. The karmic realm of cause and effect, with its perpetual cycle of death and rebirth, is called *rinne* (Skt: *saṃsāra*). The devout Buddhist hopes to achieve deliverance from karmic retribution, the cause of suffering, and enter *nirvāna*.

Ingen 隠元

(1592–1673). Also known as Ingen Ryūki (Ch: Yinyuan Longji or Yin-yüan Lung-chi). Chinese Zen monk and founder of the ŌBAKU SECT of Zen Buddhism in Japan. The son of a poor family in Fujian (Fukien) Province, China, Ingen became a Zen monk of the Rinzai sect at the age of 29 and eventually abbot of the temple Wanfusi (Wan-fu-ssu) in Fujian. At the third request of ITSUNEN and other Chinese Zen monks and laymen in Nagasaki, Ingen at the age of 63 left China a decade after the fall of the Ming dynasty (1368–1644), arriving in Nagasaki in 1654.

Through contact with the government rulers and the imperial family, Ingen was given an audience with the fourth shōgun, TOKUGAWA IETSUNA. In 1659 he was granted a large tract of land in Uji, near Kyōto, where he built a major temple of his sect. This temple was named MAMPUKUJI (Japanese pronunciation of Wanfusi), and his sect was called Ōbaku (Ch: Huangbo or Huang-po), after the mountain on which the temple in Fujian was located. Ingen's highly regarded calligraphic skills were important in making the Ōbaku style of calligraphy popular.

ingo 隠語

(secret language; argot). A general term for the specialized vocabulary and idioms employed by a particular group in order to exclude outsiders or to reinforce in-group feelings. *Ingo* particularly appears among certain professional groups, in the restaurant and entertainment business, and among thieves, gamblers, vagrants, and others on the fringe of society. Many *ingo* words result from abbreviation, as in *yaji* from *oyaji* (father); inversion, as in *doya* from *yado* (lodgings); association, as in *uji* (from Uji, a city famous for its tea) for *cha* (tea); or extension of meaning, as in *morau* (receive, take) for *nusumu* (steal). Some are references to the way a word is written, as in *sanzui* for *sake* (rice wine, liquor), *sanzui* being the name of one of the two elements that make up the Chinese character for *sake*.

Ingo words from the criminal subculture include *satsu* for police (from *keisatsu*, police) and *shoba* for place or territory (from *basho*, place). Conversely, the police have their own vocabulary: *hoshi* (star) for suspect, *tataki* (beating) for armed robbery, and so on.

inheritance law 相続法

(*sōzoku hō*). The inheritance system was vital to the functioning of premodern Japanese society, for it dictated succession to the family leadership. The traditional system ended with World War II, and freedom in the disposition of one's assets became the central legal principle.

The basic principle in the Japanese CIVIL CODE is freedom to dispose of one's assets as one wishes (although legally secured portions may not be infringed upon). In fact, intestacy or intestate succession is overwhelmingly the most frequent case. Of 793,014 deaths in 1988, the number of cases in which a holographic will was probated in family court was 4,499 (a notarial will is not required for the probate proceedings). In the same year 36,468 estates, inherited by 107,253 heirs, paid inheritance taxes.

In regard to heirs (*sōzokunin*), the order of inheritance is as follows: (1) the children (including unborn children) and spouse; (2) if there are no children, then the lineal ascendants and spouse; (3) if there are no lineal ascendants, then the siblings and the spouse; (4) if there are no siblings, then the spouse; (5) if none of the above exist, procedures to prove the nonexistence of an heir are initiated. If it is confirmed that there is no heir, assets still remaining after the debts and obligations related to the succession are settled escheat to the state, except where a family court recognizes the partial or total acquisition of the property by parties such as the wife in a *naien* (de facto marriage), a de facto adopted child who lived with the decedent, or those who had had some kind of special relationship with the decedent, such as caring for the deceased during medical treatment.

Disqualification from inheritance. Heirs punished for murder or attempted murder of the decedent or of an heir with superior or equal inheritance rights, and heirs who forge, destroy, or conceal a will, fall within provisions of the Civil Code that disqualify such parties from inheriting.

Disinheritance. During his life or by his will, an individual, via a petition to the family court, may with good cause disinherit heirs.

Acceptance and renunciation. The heir is free to decide whether or not to inherit. An heir's manifestation of intent to consent to inheritance is called acceptance of inheritance (*sōzoku no shōnin*), and his manifestation of intent to refuse inheritance is called renunciation of inheritance (*sōzoku hōki*). Among the former type of manifestations are acceptance without reservation, called absolute acceptance (*tanjun shōnin*), and qualified acceptance (*gentei shōnin*), in which the heir limits his or her acceptance of the obligations of the decedent (the decedent's debts and bequests) to the extent of the positive assets he receives in the inheritance. Renunciation of inheritance was in-

tended for use in situations where the obligations of the estate exceeded the assets. However, there are many cases where it is used to leave the assets to one child.

Statutory shares. The statutory shares of heirs are determined by the order of the heirs. (1) Where there are children and the surviving spouse as heirs, the surviving spouse receives half and the other half is divided among the children. (2) Where there are a surviving spouse and lineal ascendants, the surviving spouse receives two-thirds and lineal ascendants one-third. (3) Where there are a surviving spouse and siblings, a surviving spouse receives three-fourths and the siblings one-fourth. (4) Where there is only a surviving spouse, the surviving spouse takes the entire estate. (5) Where there is no surviving spouse, the other heirs take the entire estate. (6) Where there is more than one child or party on the same level in the inheritance order, each receives an equal share. But illegitimate children receive one-half that of legitimate children, while siblings born of different parents (half-blood siblings) receive one-half that of full-blood siblings. (7) Where there are heirs who received gifts from the decedent at the time of a wedding, adoption, and the like (for example, a gift of capital), the amount given will be added to the total value of the estate. Each heir's share is then decided by multiplying the total amount by the percentage of his statutory share, less the amount he has already received.

Secured portions. The law requires that a fixed portion of the estate be reserved for spouses and lineal descendants. This portion is known as the secured portion (*iryūbun*). See also WILLS; PARENT AND CHILD, LEGAL DEFINITION OF.

injiuchi 印地打

Also called *inji* or *ishigassen*. A game once traditionally played on Boy's Day (5 May) and at New Year's; a mock battle in which boys divided themselves into two groups and threw pebbles at each other. It originated as a game for men in the Heian period (794–1185). However, it became increasingly violent, often resulting in injury or even death. The practice was forbidden for a time in the Edo period (1600–1868).

ink painting 水墨画

(*suibokuga*; literally, "water-ink painting"; Ch: *shuimohua*). Also called *sumi-e* or "ink pictures." A Chinese style of painting adopted by Japanese painters in the 14th century. Gradually adapted to Japanese tastes, *suibokuga* emerged by the end of the 15th century as the mainstream of Japanese painting. Having absorbed elements from YAMATO-E, the indigenous mode of painting, *suibokuga* in turn became the medium out of which the Sino-Japanese synthesis of the KANŌ SCHOOL emerged. In later centuries its

Detail of a landscape by Sesshū Tōyō in his *haboku* or "splashed ink" style. 1495. Ink on paper. 148 × 33 cm. Tōkyō National Museum. National Treasure.

Detail of a hanging scroll painting by the Japanese Zen monk Kaō Ninga of the legendary Chinese Zen eccentric Hanshan (J: Kanzan). Early 14th century. Ink on paper. Entire scroll 99 × 33 cm. Private collection. National Treasure.

Chinese paintings of the Song period like this winter scene by the Chinese artist Li Di were an important influence on ink painting in Japan. 12th century. Ink and light colors on silk. 24 × 24 cm. Yamato Bunkakan, Nara Prefecture. National Treasure.

influence was evident even in such mutually exclusive styles as those of the RIMPA school and literati painting (BUNJINGA).

Suibokuga is monochrome painting, characterized by the use of black ink (*sumi*), a solid form of charcoal or soot-based Chinese ink, which is ground on an inkstone and diluted with water, then applied with a brush to paper or silk. Monochrome offers an infinite range of tonal values, which the Chinese long ago recognized as the "colors" of ink. The medium does allow for occasional use of color but limits it to subtle, transparent washes that always remain subordinate to the ink line. Ink painting shares with CALLIGRAPHY the essential disciplines of controlled expression and technical mastery of form; quality in ink painting, as in calligraphy, resides in the integrity and tensile strength of the ink-drawn line, which sustains the work of art as bone supports tissue.

Ink-painting techniques used by Chinese painters, particularly of the Tang (T'ang) dynasty (618–907), were first introduced to Japan in the 8th century. But it was only after the introduction of the monochrome painting of the Song (Sung; 960–1279) and Yuan (Yüan; 1279–1368) dynasties, which came to Japan from China and Korea along with ZEN Buddhism and other elements of Chinese culture in the Muromachi period (1333–1568), that Chinese ink painting was transformed by Japanese Zen monks and adopted into the mainstream of Japanese painting. Among the first Zen monks to paint *suibokuga* in the 14th century were KAŌ NINGA and MOKUAN REIEN. In the 15th century the ink-painting master SHŪBUN was associated with the painting academy of the temple SHŌKOKUJI in Kyōto; his more famous successor SESSHŪ TŌYŌ left an important artistic legacy. Sesshū's *Haboku sansuizu* (1495, Haboku Landscape) is an example of the "splashed-ink" style, an untrammeled, expressive ink-painting style first associated

with the 8th-century eccentric Chinese painter Wang Mo.

Zen monks who spent long hours in the study of the Chinese literary classics identified with Confucian scholars who rejected the vulgar world to commune with nature and to pursue the fine arts of music, poetry, painting, and calligraphy (see KINKI SHOGA). Among the earliest Muromachi-period ink paintings are several idealized depictions of the scholar's rustic studio retreat (*shosaizu*). Often painted as farewell gifts given in recognition of mutual spiritual goals and inscribed with poems, these paintings belong to the *shigajiku* ("poem-painting scroll") classification and are exemplified by MIN-CHŌ's *Keiin shōchiku zu* (1413, Cottage by a Stream).

Landscape became an important ink-painting theme. Early Japanese ink landscapes often depict fantastically towering peaks and deep gorges that are ultimately derived from Chinese landscape painting and alien to the native topography. As ink painting was gradually naturalized, however, so was the ink landscape. Sesshū began the process with his depiction of real Japanese landscapes, as in his masterpiece *Amanohashidate* (ca 1501). The style of the ink landscape was further naturalized by the AMI SCHOOL and SOGA SCHOOL, whose soft, watery-ink landscapes incorporated elements from *yamato-e* as practiced by the TOSA SCHOOL.

Portraits of Zen patriarchs and the enigmatic personalities of KANZAN AND JITTOKU were also common themes of ink painting, along with depictions of the bodhisattva KANNON and Bodhidharma (J: DARUMA), the legendary founder of Zen. The broader category of Zen monochrome figure painting also includes animals, birds and flowers (see BIRD-AND-FLOWER PAINTING), plants, fruits, and vegetables.

Ink painting was gradually secularized and separated from Zen Buddhism in the late Muromachi period, beginning with the

works of Ami school artists NŌAMI, GEIAMI, and SŌAMI, who were attached to the court of the shogunate. The trend culminated in the early Edo period (1600–1868) in the works of the Kanō school, whose Sino-Japanese synthesis of monochrome ink and gold-ground polychrome responded to patrons from the newly risen military class who were bored with the austerity of monochrome and required grand compositions for large-scale architectural settings.

Ink painting continued to develop as a vibrant medium throughout the Edo period in the hands of painters working in such disparate stylistic domains as Rimpa and *bunjinga*. SŌTATSU, a master of the Rimpa school, invented a visually rich puddling effect (*tarashikomi*) achieved by dropping ink onto still-wet ink strokes and washes. Japanese scholar-gentlemen painters such as Yosa BUSON and URAGAMI GYOKUDŌ, like the earlier Zen monks, painted ink landscapes and other Chinese themes. Although the first generation of *bunjin* (literati) artists based their work on Chinese models, which they knew mainly from woodblock-printed manuals of painting, later scholar-painters developed their own idiosyncratic styles. After 1868, the tradition of *suibokuga* was kept alive by such NIHONGA (Japanese-style) painters as YOKOYAMA TAIKAN, HISHIDA SHUNSŌ, and SHIMOMURA KANZAN. See also PAINTING.

inkyo   隠居

Traditional Japanese practice of retirement of the household head. In colloquial speech *inkyo* (literally, "seclusion") indicates retirement in general, a retired person, or an old person. A household head need not become old or incapacitated before relinquishing his role, nor need he cut back on other activities when doing so. The position of head of household has had no legal standing since 1947, but it remains important in everyday thought and conduct.

Japanese ideals hold that the incumbent

head of a household should be a person of vigor and competence in order to maintain the household descent line intact generation after generation. This ideal has tended to favor early retirement, with the head yielding the position once an able successor (most often the eldest son) is ready for it. Another ideal is that the retired head and spouse and the succeeding head and spouse remain members of a single family unit (IE), but in order to avoid intergenerational discord they should set up housekeeping separately, in different houses or different parts of the main house. It is also considered ideal that when retired members grow old, juniors in the household should provide for their care.

Inland Sea 瀬戸内海

(Seto Naikai). Bounded by Honshū on the north and east, Shikoku on the south, and Kyūshū on the west. Encompasses the Harima, Bingo, Hiuchi, Iyo, and Suō seas. It is dotted with over 1,000 islands and islets, the largest of which is Awajishima, and is connected to outer seas by the Kii Strait and NARUTO STRAIT to the east, the Hayasui Strait and Bungo Channel to the southwest, and KAMMON STRAIT to the west.

Since ancient times the Inland Sea and its coasts have played an important role in transportation. Rapid industrialization and population growth in recent decades have made the Inland Sea Industrial Region one of Japan's major industrial regions. The area is now suffering the effects of industrial pollution.

A spectacular coastline, mountains in the background, and the pine-covered islands and islets make the Inland Sea a major tourist spot. It forms the Inland Sea National Park. As of 1993 the construction of a series of bridges connecting Honshū and Shikoku (HONSHŪ-SHIKOKU BRIDGES) via the larger islands of the Inland Sea was near completion. Average depth: 44 m (144 ft).

Inland Sea Industrial Region 瀬戸内工業地域

(Setouchi Kōgyō Chiiki). Consists of a long row of industrial cities along the Inland Sea coasts on Honshū and Shikoku. Excellent marine and land transportation is available. Prominent cities are Tokuyama (oil refining); Iwakuni and Kurashiki (steel and petrochemicals); Matsuyama (oil refining and petrochemicals); Kudamatsu and Fukuyama (steel); Niihama (chemicals and metals); Hiroshima (automobiles); and Sakaide, Kure, Innoshima, and Tamano (shipbuilding). Industrial complexes have been constructed at Iwakuni, Tokuyama, Kurashiki, Harima, and Niihama.

Inland Sea National Park 瀬戸内海国立公園

(Seto Naikai Kokuritsu Kōen). National park covering the entire expanse of the INLAND SEA. The park spans ten prefectures and extends some 400 km (250 mi) east to west and has a maximum width of 60–70 km (37-43 mi). It is characterized by the irregular shoreline of the Inland Sea and the over 1,000 islands in it. AWAJISHIMA, the largest of the islands, is located between the Kii Peninsula of central Honshū and northeastern Shikoku and is separated from the latter by the NARUTO STRAIT, known for its violent whirlpools. To the island's west lies SHŌDOSHIMA, the second largest island.

The Inland Sea has a number of ancient shrines, such as KOTOHIRA SHRINE (also called Kompira Shrine) in northeastern Shikoku,

Ōyamatsumi Shrine on the island of ŌMI-SHIMA, and the ITSUKUSHIMA SHRINE southeast of the city of Hiroshima. The famous historical sea battles of Yashima and Dannoura, between the Taira and Minamoto families, were fought in this area. Land area: 628 sq km (242 sq mi).

Innoshima 因島[市]

City in southeastern Hiroshima Prefecture, western Honshū. The city incorporates the entire island of Innoshima and a part of the island of Ikuchishima in the Inland Sea.

Products include mandarin oranges, olives, peaches, and chrysanthemums. It is now linked to the main island of Honshū by the Innoshima Bridge. Pop: 32,640.

Innoshima 因島

Island in the central Inland Sea, Hiroshima Prefecture. One of the GEIYO ISLANDS. The Murakami pirates operated from Innoshima during the Muromachi period (1333–1568). Today the island is a link in a series of bridges

Inland Sea National Park This park, founded in 1934, encompasses the more than 1,000 islands and rugged coastline of the Inland Sea.
1 The Inland Sea as seen from the peak Ōjigatake in Okayama Prefecture. At center is the island Ōtsuchijima; in the distance is Shikoku.
2 The island of Shishijima. Farmers on Inland Sea islands use even the steepest slopes in cultivating citrus fruit and flowers. Kagawa Prefecture.
3 Completed in 1985, the Great Naruto Bridge spans the turbulent waters of the Naruto Strait.

Inō Tadataka A post-
humous portrait of Inō
painted by his surveying
partner, Aoki Katsujirō.
Ca 1821.

Inoue Hisashi Much
of this playwright-
novelist's finest work is
in the tradition of the
satirical *gesaku* writers
of the Edo period.

connecting Honshū and Shikoku. It is
known for its shipbuilding industry. Area:
34 sq km (13 sq mi).

inns 旅館

(*ryokan*). Lodging facilities, generally with
Japanese-style architecture, accommodations, and service, in contrast to Western-
style hotels. At an inn, guest rooms have
TATAMI mat floors and Japanese bedding
(FUTON). The food served at inns is almost
always Japanese. Two meals are included in
the rate for a night's lodging. Reservations
may be made in person or by a Japanese
travel agent.

Of the some 80,000 Japanese inns, many
have one or more Western-style rooms for
the convenience of foreigners. About 2,200
inns specialize in accommodating foreign
guests. Known as International Travel Inns
(Kokusai Kankō Ryokan), each carries a special mark to aid the visitor in identifying it.
See also MINSHUKU. ■▶610–611

Inō Jakusui 稲生若水

(1655–1715). Specialist in *honzōgaku* (traditional pharmacognosy) and an early scholar
of Japanese natural history during the Edo
period (1600–1868). Born in Edo (now
Tōkyō), he studied medicine, pharmacognosy, and Confucianism and started a private school in Kyōto. MATSUOKA JOAN and
NORO GENJŌ were among his students. The
work for which he is known is *Shobutsu rui-
san*, a 1,000-volume herbal originally compiled from Chinese texts on medicinal herbs
and later used as a reference for the study of
natural history. He began the work in 1697
and completed 362 volumes before his
death. The series was continued after his
death by his students, with the cooperation
of the shōgun TOKUGAWA YOSHIMUNE.

Inokuchi Ariya 井口在屋

(1856–1923). Mechanical engineer. A leading figure in the early development of his
field in Japan, Inokuchi is known for his
work on the centrifugal pump. Born in
Kanazawa domain (now part of Ishikawa
Prefecture), he graduated from what is now
the Department of Mechanical Engineering
at Tōkyō University. He taught there and at
the Naval War College.

Inoue Kaoru Inoue's
service in a series of
high offices and his
close ties to Meiji-
period financial circles
gained him great
political power.

Inomata Tsunao 猪俣津南雄

(1889–1942). Marxist economist and politi-
cal commentator. Born in Niigata Prefecture,
Inomata graduated from Waseda University.
From 1915 to 1921 he studied in the United
States, becoming a Marxist under the influ-
ence of Japanese labor leader KATAYAMA SEN.
Upon his return to Japan, Inomata joined the
Waseda faculty and in 1922 participated in
the formation of the JAPAN COMMUNIST PARTY
(JCP). He was arrested in 1923 and dismissed
from the university. With YAMAKAWA HITOSHI
and ARAHATA KANSON, he founded the period-

ical *Rōnō* in 1927 and served as a spokesman
for the group of Marxist theorists known as
the RŌNŌHA in their debates with the rival
KŌZAHA over the nature of capitalism and
revolution in Japan (see NIHON SHIHON SHUGI
RONSŌ). He was arrested again in the 1937
POPULAR FRONT INCIDENT. His works include
Kin'yū shihon ron (1925, Theory of Financial
Capital).

Inō Tadataka 伊能忠敬

(1745–1818). Geographical surveyor of the
late Edo period (1600–1868). Inō was the first
to use Western scientific methods in his surveys of Japan. His magnum opus was a collection of maps covering the entire country,
based on an actual coastal survey.

Inō was born on the coast of Kujūkuri,
Kazusa Province (now part of Chiba Prefecture). At age 17 he was adopted into the Inō
family in Sawara, Shimōsa Province (now
part of Chiba Prefecture). While attending to
his family's business, he studied calendar
making and astronomy on his own, and at
age 49 he went to Edo (now Tōkyō) to study
under the Tokugawa shogunate astronomer
TAKAHASHI YOSHITOKI. Beginning in 1800 Inō
surveyed all of Japan, using precision instruments for his astronomical observations. The
number of days he had spent surveying
throughout Japan by the age of 70 totaled
3,737, and he had covered over 43,700 kilometers (27,160 mi), a distance exceeding the
circumference of the earth.

After his death his friends and pupils
completed his maps. In 1821 they compiled
the DAI NIHON ENKAI YOCHI ZENZU (225 sheets of
maps) and the 14-volume *Dai Nihon enkai jis-
sokuroku* (Records of an Actual Survey of
the Japanese Coast). His maps, popularly referred to as "the Inō maps," served as the
basis for Japanese mapmaking during the
Meiji period (1868–1912) and later. Maps
based on Inō's were used as late as 1924. A
large number of Inō's books, his own works,
diaries, maps, and instruments are preserved
at the Inō Tadataka Memorial Hall in
Sawara. See also MAPS.

Inoue Enryō 井上円了

(1858–1919). Buddhist thinker and educator
whose lifelong endeavor was the popularization of philosophy. Born in Niigata of a family belonging to the JŌDO SHIN SECT of Buddhism, he graduated from Tōkyō University
in 1885. In 1887 he founded the institute of
philosophy known as the Tetsugakukan, the
forerunner of Tōyō University. He attempted a synthesis of the thought of the
Buddha Gautama, Confucius, Socrates, and
Kant; his interpretation of Buddhism in the
light of Western philosophy is unique. He
wrote over 120 books and is known for his
study of spirit phenomena, *Yōkaigaku kōgi*
(1895, Lectures on Ghosts).

Inoue Hisashi 井上ひさし

(1934–). Playwright and novelist. Real
name Uchiyama Hisashi. Born in Yamagata
Prefecture; graduate of Sophia University.
Inoue's writings are in the tradition of the satirical GESAKU writers of the Edo period
(1600–1868). He first gained recognition for
such comic plays as *Omoteura Gennai kaeru
gassen* (1970) and *Chin'yaku seisho* (1973).
He won the Naoki Prize for his novel
Tegusari shinjū (1972, Handcuffed Double
Suicide). *Kirikirijin* (1981, The People of
Kirikiri) won the Yomiuri Literary Prize and
the Japan Science Fiction Award for its humorous treatment of the residents of a small
village who secede from Japan to form their

own independent city-state. In 1984 Inoue
formed the theater troupe Komatsuza. The
troupe has performed some of his brilliantly
energetic works, such as the 1984 stage biographies *Zutsū katakori Higuchi Ichiyō* and
Nakimushi namaiki Ishikawa Takuboku, about
the Meiji-period (1868–1912) writers HIGU-
CHI ICHIYŌ and ISHIKAWA TAKUBOKU, and his
1988 comic trilogy—*Kirameku seiza, Yami ni
saku hana,* and *Yuki ya kon kon*—depicting
the lives of ordinary Japanese during the
turbulent Shōwa period (1926–89). Inoue
also has turned his talents to the problems of
the modern Japanese language in *Jikasei bunshō tokuhon* (1984, A Homemade Writing
Primer).

Inoue Junnosuke 井上準之助

(1869–1932). Politician and banker. Born in
what is now Ōita Prefecture, he graduated
from Tōkyō University in 1896. Entering the
BANK OF JAPAN, he became head of the
YOKOHAMA SPECIE BANK (now Bank of Tōkyō,
Ltd) in 1913 and governor of the Bank of
Japan in 1919. In 1923 he was named finance
minister in the YAMAMOTO GONNOHYŌE cabinet
and was appointed to the House of Peers
when the cabinet resigned the same year. In
1927 he again became governor of the Bank
of Japan, helping to overcome the FINANCIAL
CRISIS OF 1927. In 1929 he was named finance
minister in the HAMAGUCHI OSACHI cabinet and
joined the RIKKEN MINSEITŌ political party. To
stabilize exchange rates and prices, he returned Japan to the gold standard. Inoue remained in office in the succeeding WAKATSUKI
REIJIRŌ cabinet, as Japan sank into the SHŌWA
DEPRESSION. The cabinet resigned in 1931 in
the crisis resulting from the military's takeover of Manchuria (see MANCHURIAN INCI-
DENT). Inoue was assassinated by a member
of the ultranationalist terrorist group Ketsumeidan (see LEAGUE OF BLOOD INCIDENT).
Inoue's orthodox financial policy of 1929–31
was reversed by his successor as finance minister, TAKAHASHI KOREKIYO, who took Japan off
the gold standard and increased government
spending through deficit financing.

Inoue Kaoru 井上馨

(1836–1915). Politician of the Meiji period
(1868–1912) who held several ministerial
posts in the Meiji government. He eventually became an influential elder statesman
(GENRŌ).

Born into a *samurai* family of the Chōshū
domain (now Yamaguchi Prefecture), he
participated in the SONNŌ JŌI (Revere the Emperor, Expel the Barbarians) movement that
began in the late 1850s. In January 1863 he
joined TAKASUGI SHINSAKU and other nationalists in an attack on the British legation in
Edo (now Tōkyō). Recognizing Japan's need
to learn further from the West, he set forth
in June 1863 to study in England. During the
voyage Inoue became friends with ITŌ
HIROBUMI and Yamao Yōzō (1837–1917).
After six months in England Inoue and Itō
returned to Chōshū and led negotiations between Chōshū and the Western powers (see
SHIMONOSEKI BOMBARDMENT). Later Inoue
played a key role in the formation of the
SATSUMA-CHŌSHŪ ALLIANCE against the Tokugawa shogunate (1603–1867).

After the establishment of the Meiji government, Inoue served in several positions
before being appointed vice-minister of finance in September 1871. He advocated the
LAND TAX REFORM OF 1873–1881, the termination
of samurai and aristocratic stipends (see
CHITSUROKU SHOBUN), and the promotion of industry. Conservative elements forced Inoue

and his assistant SHIBUSAWA EIICHI to resign in May 1873. Inoue then began to develop close ties with Japanese businesses, especially the MITSUI group. He helped establish the Senshū Kaisha trading company, one of the two companies that later merged to form a predecessor of what is now MITSUI & CO, LTD.

After acting as mediator at the ŌSAKA CONFERENCE OF 1875, Inoue returned to the government, eventually becoming minister of public works in 1878 and minister of foreign affairs in 1879. As foreign minister, Inoue unsuccessfully set about to recover rights Japan had earlier ceded to the Western powers (see UNEQUAL TREATIES, REVISION OF). On 16 September 1887 Inoue resigned. He subsequently served as adviser to the imperial household, minister of agriculture and commerce, and minister of home affairs. From 1901 Inoue served as an elder statesman (genrō), considering himself the government's foremost adviser on financial matters.

Inoue Kiyonao   井上清直

(1809–67). Official of the Tokugawa shogunate; younger brother of KAWAJI TOSHIAKIRA. Born in Edo (now Tōkyō). Inoue was appointed commissioner (bugyō) of the port of Shimoda in 1855. He negotiated with Townsend HARRIS and in 1857 signed supplementary agreements to the KANAGAWA TREATY. In July 1858 Inoue and IWASE TADANARI were given full powers to conclude the HARRIS TREATY, first of the ANSEI COMMERCIAL TREATIES.

Inoue Kowashi   井上毅

(1844–95). Bureaucrat. Born in Higo Province (now Kumamoto Prefecture). He fought on the imperial side in the BOSHIN CIVIL WAR. After the MEIJI RESTORATION (1868) Inoue joined the Ministry of Justice and was sent to study in France and Germany (1872–73). He became a protégé of ŌKUBO TOSHIMICHI and accompanied him to Beijing (Peking) for negotiations following the TAIWAN EXPEDITION OF 1874. After Ōkubo's death Inoue became closely associated with ITŌ HIROBUMI and IWAKURA TOMOMI. Soon after the POLITICAL CRISIS OF 1881 he was appointed to the House of Councillors. Under the supervision of Itō and working closely with K. F. Hermann ROESLER, the government's German adviser, he prepared drafts that became the base for the CONSTITUTION OF THE EMPIRE OF JAPAN and the Imperial Household Laws. He was also responsible, with MOTODA NAGAZANE, for the IMPERIAL RESCRIPT ON EDUCATION. He was appointed to the Privy Council in 1890 and in 1893 became minister of education in the second Itō cabinet.

Inoue Mitsuharu   井上光晴

(1926–92). Novelist. Born in Manchuria, where his father worked as an itinerant potter. After World War II, he joined the Japan Communist Party and began to write for the Marxist literary magazine SHIN NIHON BUNGAKU. In 1950 he was expelled from the Communist Party for his short story "Kakarezaru isshō," which dealt with the frustrations of a party member forced to follow the party's impractical, bureaucratic orders. He continued to criticize the deteriorating party leadership in "Yameru bubun" (1951), establishing his name as an independent Marxist writer. In 1956 he founded the magazine Gendai hihyō, which serialized his Kyōkō no kurēn (published in 1960), a novel about the mental anguish of a youth beset with self-doubts about his participation in

World War II. He is known for his exploration of controversial topics, including Japan's actions in World War II, the role of the emperor, the position of the Communist Party, and discrimination against minorities. His novel Tsukareta hito (1981, The Possessed) depicts the psychological state of a radical leader imprisoned for seven years for a murder he did not commit.

Inoue Nisshō   井上日召

(1886–1967). Rightist ideologue of the 1930s. Born Inoue Akira, in Gumma Prefecture. He left school to go to China and Manchuria, gathering information for the Japanese military. Upon returning to Japan in 1921 he joined the NICHIREN SECT, a militant, nationalistic Buddhist sect, and took the name Nisshō. In 1928 he founded a school, the Risshō Gokoku Dō, in Ibaraki Prefecture to propagate agrarian nationalism (NŌHON SHUGI) and social reform. Gradually convinced that force could bring national reform, he established contacts with young military officers. After the aborted coup d'état by rightist officers and civilians in the OCTOBER INCIDENT (1931), he formed his own terrorist group, the Ketsumeidan (League of Blood), and directed the assassinations of DAN TAKUMA, chairman of the MITSUI company, and INOUE JUNNOSUKE, the former finance minister (see LEAGUE OF BLOOD INCIDENT). Sentenced to life imprisonment in 1934, he was released in the general amnesty of 1940.

Inoue Shigeyoshi   井上成美

(1889–1975). Admiral. Born in Miyagi Prefecture, he graduated from the Naval Academy in 1909. Inoue, YONAI MITSUMASA, and YAMAMOTO ISOROKU were known as the "liberal trio" of the Imperial Navy. Inoue opposed the TRIPARTITE PACT allying Japan with Germany and Italy. Advocating a closer relationship with the United States, Inoue argued that Japan could never win a war with that country and opposed starting one. Placed in charge of the Naval Academy in 1942, he maintained his commitment to liberal policies and later engaged in clandestine efforts to bring an early end to the war. He attained the rank of admiral in 1945.

Inoue Tetsujirō   井上哲次郎

(1855–1944). Philosopher and educator. Born in what is now Fukuoka Prefecture, he graduated from Tōkyō University in 1880 and spent his academic career teaching philosophy there. Inoue is credited with introducing German idealism to the Japanese academic world. Interested also in Buddhism and Confucianism, he sought to synthesize Eastern and Western thought. He was an ardent nationalist, criticizing Christianity as being inimical to Japan's unique national polity (KOKUTAI). His works are collected in Inoue Hakase kōronshū (2 vols, 1894–95) and Sonken rombunshū (2 vols, 1899–1901).

Inoue Yachiyo IV   井上八千代 4 世

(1905–). Dancer, choreographer, and dance school head. Real name Katayama Aiko. Born in Kyōto Prefecture, she became a pupil of Inoue Yachiyo III (1838–1939) at the age of four. In 1947 she succeeded her as head of the Inoue school of kyō-mai dance, maintaining its unique style, which incorporates aspects of NŌ and the movements of BUNRAKU puppets into the zashiki-mai technique of dance developed in the Kyōto-Ōsaka area. She annually choreographs the Miyako Odori dance festival in Kyōto. She was designated one of Japan's LIVING NA-

Inoue Yachiyo IV The dancer performing a kyō-mai dance in a 1984 appearance at the National Theater in Tōkyō. Inoue, whose work draws on Nō and bunraku puppet theater, has been designated a Living National Treasure.

TIONAL TREASURES in 1955 and was awarded the Order of Culture in 1990.

Inoue Yasushi   井上靖

(1907–91). Novelist. Born in Asahikawa, Hokkaidō, where his father, an army medical officer, was temporarily stationed. He spent most of his childhood living with his grandmother on the Izu Peninsula, not far from Mt. Fuji (Fujisan). He graduated at the age of 29 from Kyōto University with a degree in art history. Although Inoue had already received professional recognition as a writer of fiction, he chose to become a newspaperman and wrote for the MAINICHI SHIMBUN for the next dozen years, except for seven months spent as a soldier in northern China in 1937.

Early Works—Inoue found the subject for his novel Tōgyū (1949, The Bullfight) in the chaotic postwar society of Japan. It depicts the frenzied activities of an enterprising newspaper executive who is promoting a bullfight, the success or failure of which will determine the fate of his firm. This work earned him the Akutagawa Prize in 1949. A simultaneous success was Ryōjū (1949; tr The Hunting Gun, 1961), on the theme of loneliness and world-weariness in modern society.

Inoue became one of Japan's most prolific and respected authors, writing in various genres and for all levels of readers. His Kuroi ushio (1950, The Black Tide), a dramatization of the mysterious murder of a prominent public figure, encouraged the vogue for novelistic treatment of contemporary social and political events. Hyōheki (1956–57, Wall of Ice), about a love triangle culminating in sudden death as the antagonists scale an alpine slope, was published serially in a daily newspaper. It won the Japan Art Academy Award (Geijutsuin Shō) in 1959.

Historical and Autobiographical Fiction—Inoue's most important works are historical and autobiographical narratives, often thinly disguised as fiction. TEMPYŌ NO IRAKA (1957; tr The Roof Tile of Tempyō, 1975), for which he received the Ministry of Education Prize, is an artistic reconstruction of the drama of 8th-century Japanese and Chinese monks who dedicated their lives to transmitting Buddhist ideals from Tang (T'ang; 618–907) China to Japan. Other historical novels that exhibit the same preference for authenticity and a straightforward, spare style are Fūtō (1963, Wind and Waves), a poignant portrayal of the struggles of Korean monarchs to keep their nation independent despite the predatory Mongol invaders, and Go-Shirakawa In (1972), a portrait of a medieval Japanese monarch based upon diaries kept by close attendants. In Saiiki monogatari (1968–69; tr

Continued on page 612 ➤

Inoue Yasushi A prolific author in several genres, Inoue is best known for his historical and autobiographical fiction.

A Traveler's Guide to Overnight Accommodations

*From the quintessentially Japanese ryokan to deluxe Western-style hotels
to no-frills economy lodgings, Japan's vast array of accommodations
offers something to suit every taste and pocketbook.*

Traveling in a distant and culturally diverse land is like opening the door to adventure. Even if the door slides instead of swings, Japan is unparalleled in its ability to make visitors feel at home. With the Japanese emphasis on service, travelers may rest assured that whatever type of accommodation they choose will be clean and efficient. Large, modern Western hotels are much the same in Japan as in other parts of the world, but Japanese-style accommodations have certain characteristics worth noting.

One is the way room rates are calculated. While Western-style hotels charge by the room, with the rate increasing only marginally if more than one person occupies it, Japanese-style lodgings (*ryokan*, *minshuku*, and so on) charge on a per-person basis. Since the bedding is laid out each night, as many as four people can sleep comfortably in one room. The per-person price quoted almost always includes two Japanese-style meals—breakfast and dinner. Although Western food is not usually prepared in such establishments, some Western items such as coffee are becoming more readily available. Expect to be charged extra for these.

When planning a trip, keep in mind that the Japanese are inveterate travelers themselves. Be sure to make advance reservations by telephone (preferably in Japanese for Japanese-style accommodations). Tourist or information offices, which are located in or near railway stations of popular tourist spots, can help you find a place to stay if you need some assistance.

The 1992 prices that are quoted in this essay are intended only as a general guide because prices vary tremendously even among listings in the same category. In the more expensive hotels, both Western and Japanese style, you will find a 10–15 percent service charge and a 3–6 percent consumption tax added to your bill. Individual tipping is not expected.

Western-Style Hotels

These range from internationally renowned luxury hotels to basic but perfectly adequate "business hotels." Although some of the larger hotels may have rooms with *tatami* mats, the unique Japanese experience of sleeping on *tatami* is lost in the Western-style ambience and facilities.

Even the smallest Western hotels are equipped with central heating and air-conditioning, private baths and toilets, TVs, restaurants, and bars. The larger ones often have a swimming pool and sauna, tennis courts, money-changing facilities, interpreters, babysitting services, and doctors on call who speak various languages. In metropolitan centers, the large hotels generally have multilingual staff, facilities for making travel arrangements, organized sightseeing tours, and airport and station shuttle buses.

The "business hotels"—so called because they are frequented by business travelers—are both practical and economical. As a matter of convenience, they are usually located near large train stations. For ¥5,000–¥10,000 (US $41–$81) per night, you get a small room with bath and toilet. Sometimes a light breakfast is included in the price.

A decidedly modern Japanese phenomenon is the "capsule hotel," which caters primarily to male office workers, many of whom have been out drinking and have missed the last train home. For about ¥4,000 ($33) per night, you get a small sleeping area rather like a berth, compactly equipped with lighting, heating, air-conditioning, stereo, and television set. Once inside your tiny compartment, you can imagine yourself going off on a long space voyage! Communal facilities in such hotels usually include a bath (toiletries provided), sauna, snack bar, and lounge. Lockers are also available. Located in or around train stations of big cities, capsule hotels are surprisingly comfortable.

Ryokan

When you are in Japan, nothing can rival the experience of staying at a traditional Japanese inn, or *ryokan* (literally, "travel lodge"). There are 80,000 such inns scattered throughout the country. They vary enormously in class and price, but for a night at an average inn expect to spend about ¥10,000 ($81) per person (excluding tax and service), a figure that can easily triple at the more famous or luxurious inns. Two lavish meals, breakfast and dinner, both often of gourmet quality, are served on the low table in your room. Check-in time is usually 3 PM and check-out 10 AM.

The high-class *ryokan* is the ultimate in Japan's luxurious accommodations. Upon your arrival a maid will welcome you with a low bow and escort you to your room, where you will be served Japanese green tea (*ocha*), accompanied by a Japanese cookie. In the room you will find a *yukata*, the patterned cotton robe worn after bathing and also in bed, as well as a thicker outer robe (*haori*) worn over the *yukata* if it is cold or if you wish to go outdoors for a stroll (perfectly acceptable, particularly at hot-spring resorts).

By day, the room is designed for lounging and eating, but after the evening meal the *futon* bedding will be laid out, transforming it into a bedroom (the bedding will be put away the next morning). Some *ryokan* have private Japanese-style baths in the rooms, but there will always be a large communal bath, which for the Japanese is an essential part of the pleasure of staying at such places.

Minshuku

By far the best accommodation for those seeking a cross-cultural experience while keeping costs down is the *minshuku* (guesthouse). This is usually a large family home or a farmhouse with a few rooms for paying guests, who are made to feel like part of the family. Just as in a *ryokan*, a *minshuku* offers a *tatami*-matted room and two ample meals. Although you cannot expect a meticulously manicured garden, room service, *yukata*, or private bath, you may find sometimes that you get these anyway! But, in general, service and amenities are limited. You will be expected to lay out your own bedding in the evening and put it away in the morning. The meals served may not be as refined as those at a *ryokan*, but they can be delicious. Often, in fact, the services of a good *minshuku* outshine those of a mediocre *ryokan*, and the cost is considerably less. The average *minshuku* charge, including two meals, runs about ¥6,500–¥8,000 ($53–$65) per person. Of the roughly 25,000 such

Entrance to the Tawaraya Inn, a famous *ryokan* in Kyōto. The stacked rice cakes and tangerine at left are a traditional New Year's decoration.

establishments in Japan, about 200 are accustomed to accommodating foreign guests.

Kokumin Kyūka Mura and Kokumin Shukusha

Kokumin kyūka mura (national vacation villages) are government-sponsored resort facilities, numbering 32 in 1991 and found in popular vacation spots, especially inside national and quasi-national parks. The *kyūka mura* are furnished with various sports and recreational facilities, and staff will often provide instruction in activities such as hiking, tennis, or skiing. They are open to anyone, but because of their reasonable prices they tend to be fully booked well in advance, so be sure to reserve early. Although the rooms are private, toilets and baths are often communal. Prices include two meals and usually start at ¥7,000 ($57) per person.

Kokumin shukusha (people's lodges) also offer pleasant accommodations in scenic areas and are slightly cheaper than national vacation villages since they do not offer as wide a range of facilities. Usually managed by local governments, there are approximately 300 of them throughout the country. They charge about ¥5,500 ($45) per person, which includes two meals. Non-Japanese, though rarely encountered, are welcomed.

Since both types of accommodations are especially popular during the summer, reservations can take up to one week to confirm.

Penshon

A relatively recent phenomenon in Japan, *penshon* take their name from the French word *pension*. Offering Western-style rooms and a wide range of foods and services, they are found in rural locations popular for sight-seeing or for outdoor sports and are particularly suited to families. The owners will often go to great lengths to make your stay comfortable, sometimes acting as tour guides for the area. Fishing, hiking, or skiing equipment may also be provided as part of the stay package. Many *penshon* offer activities for children, along with babysitting services during the evening. Prices at most establishments start at around ¥8,000 ($65) per person and include two meals (usually Western style or a mixture of Western and Japanese styles).

Youth Hostels

There are approximately 450 youth hostels, of which 40 are operated by Japan Youth Hostels, Inc (JYH). Most are operated privately or by local governments. They come in all shapes and sizes, ranging from dull concrete blocks to converted temples or former *minshuku* or *ryokan*. To stay at a youth hostel you must have a membership card from your own country or an International Guest Card, which can be obtained from JYH for ¥2,800 ($23) or at the front desk of any youth hostel.

Youth hostels in Japan follow the worldwide youth-hostel codes, with separate dormitories for men and women, although family rooms are sometimes available. Mealtimes are generally from 6 to 8 AM and 5 to 7 PM. Baths are taken at specified times in the evenings. You should try to arrive before 8 PM as lights go out at 10 PM. In general, expect to spend ¥2,300 ($19) for the overnight charge or ¥3,800 ($31) including two meals. There are extra charges for sheets (sleeping bags are not acceptable), kitchen privileges, and heating and air-conditioning (in private units only).

Temples

More than 40 Buddhist temples function as youth hostels and are listed in Japan Youth Hostels booklets. There are also *shukubō*, or temples that accept overnight guests, lodging them in communal *tatami* rooms and providing *shōjin ryōri* (vegetarian food). Many of these temples can be found in the Kyōto-Nara area, as well as on the island of Shikoku, which has a famous pilgrimage route that visitors can take to see 88 temples. Lists of *shukubō* in the Tōkyō and Kyōto areas can be obtained from the local Tourist Information Center (TIC) and the Japan National Tourist Organization (JNTO). Some temples will allow guests to participate in or observe meditation sessions, while others only offer lodging. The average price per night, including two meals, is ¥4,500 ($37).

Clad in light cotton robes known as *yukata*, travelers at a hot-spring resort in Tochigi Prefecture gather around an open hearth (*irori*) for their evening meal.

Cycling Inns and Campgrounds

Designed for the growing number of people touring Japan by bicycle, cycling inns cost about the same as youth hostels and offer similar facilities. The eventual aim is to have at least one such inn every 100 kilometers (60 mi) or so, but so far there are only 52 of them.

Although the Japanese love nature, camping is not yet as popular as in the West, partly because many of the national parks do not allow it. There are quite a few campsites, however, and these range from the primitive, with only pit toilets, to those with hot showers, tennis courts, swimming pools, and even cabins. In the countryside you can put up a tent wherever you find a likely spot, but if it is near a farmhouse, you should ask for permission first. There is usually no problem about camping on beaches.

Services and Information

The Japan National Tourist Organization (JNTO; head office: 10-1, Yūrakuchō 2-chōme, Chiyoda Ku, Tōkyō 100) operates three suboffices called Tourist Information Centers (TICs):

Airport office:
New Tōkyō International Airport
Airport Terminal Bldg. No. 1
Narita, Chiba 282
Tel. (0476) 32-8711

Tōkyō office:
6-6, Yūrakuchō 1-chōme
Chiyoda Ku, Tōkyō 100
Tel. (03) 3502-1461

Kyōto office:
Kyōto Tower Bldg.
Higashi Shiokōjichō
Shimogyō Ku, Kyōto 600
Tel. (075) 371-5649

The offices' multilingual staff provide information and brochures but do not make reservations, except at the Kyōto office. If you are lost or in need of advice or a place to stay, call Japan Travel Phone, a service provided by JNTO, open daily from 9 AM to 5 PM. In eastern Japan, call (0120) 222-800; in western Japan, call (0120) 444-800. The number for the Tōkyō area is (03) 3503-4400; in Kyōto call the local TIC listed above.

Ryokan—JNTO and the TICs offer a booklet entitled *Ryokan Guide* that lists *ryokan* by area, with prices included. Reservations and prepayments can be made at any travel agency. Two organizations listing inexpensive *ryokan* that welcome foreigners are the Japanese Inn Group, c/o Hiraiwa Ryokan, 314 Hayao chō, Kaminoguchi agaru, Ninomiyachō-Dōri, Shimogyō Ku, Kyōto 600, tel. (075) 351-6748, and the Welcome Inn Reservation Center, c/o International Tourism Center of Japan, Second Floor, Kotani Bldg., 6-6, Yūrakuchō 1-chōme, Chiyoda Ku, Tōkyō 100, tel. (03) 3580-8353.

Minshuku—Japan Minshuku Association, 29-5-505, Takadanobaba 1-chōme, Shinjuku Ku, Tōkyō 160, tel. (03) 3232-6561. This organization has an excellent booklet describing the etiquette required at *minshuku*, together with a list of *minshuku* and directions. JNTO and the TICs also provide brochures.

Kokumin Kyūka Mura—Kokumin Kyūka Mura Kyōkai, 10-1, Yūrakuchō 2-chōme, Chiyoda Ku, Tōkyō 100, tel. (03) 3216-2085.

Youth Hostels—Japan Youth Hostels, Inc, Third Floor, Hoken Kaikan Bldg., 2, Sadoharachō 1-chōme, Ichigaya, Shinjuku Ku, Tōkyō 162, tel. (03) 3269-5831. The TICs and JNTO have a booklet in English and in other languages entitled *Youth Hostels in Japan*. This lists all youth hostels in Japan and gives rudimentary directions. It is best to use this booklet in conjunction with the Japanese *Youth Hostel Handbook* available from JYH, or at many front desks of youth hostels. Although in Japanese, the latter book is easy to follow, and can be shown to any Japanese passerby for help with directions.

Cycling Inns—Japan Bicycle Promotion Inst., Nihon Jitensha Kaikan Bldg., 9-3, Akasaka 1-chōme, Minato Ku, Tōkyō 107, tel. (03) 3583-5444.

J. D. Bisignani

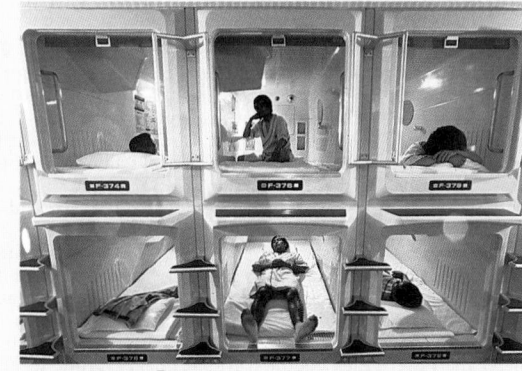

A capsule hotel in Ōsaka.

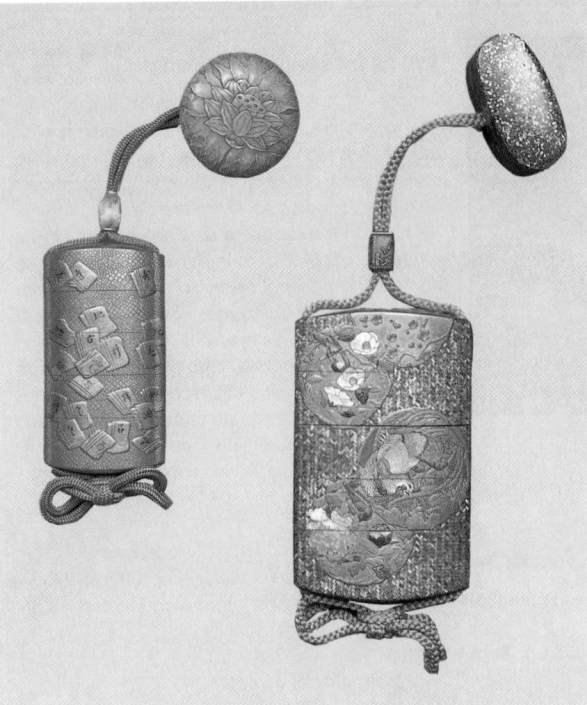

inscriptions

1 The hilt of a sword excavated from the 6th-century Inariyama tomb; visible are some of the characters inscribed in gold inlay on the sword's blade. Sakitama Archaeological and Folkloristic Data Museum. National Treasure.

2 There are 115 characters inscribed on the sword: 57 on the front of the blade (pictured) and 58 on the back.

Journey beyond Samarkand, 1971), Inoue writes primarily as a historian and traveler depicting the past and present of ancient central Asian cities and the caravan route that had once connected them. *Waga haha no ki* (1975, A Record of My Mother) is heavily invested with the characteristics of the traditional Japanese poetic diary as well as the classical ZUIHITSU.

Inoue received every major literary prize in Japan. In 1964 he was elected to the Japan Art Academy and in 1976 received the Order of Culture (Bunka Kunshō). Among his later novels is *Kōshi* (1987–89), which deals with the life and teachings of Confucius.

I-novel   私小説

(*shishōsetsu*). Also called *watakushi shōsetsu.* A type of modern Japanese fiction that relies on "self-directed" narration, usually with the author as the central character. Analogous to European forms such as the *Ich Roman* or *roman personnel*, the I-novel is best described as autobiographical or personal fiction. The narration may be in first or third person and is typically devoid of such structural elements as plot, characterization, and dramatic tension. Although loosely described as "novels," *shishōsetsu* may range in length from brief stories to massive works of 500 pages or more.

The evolution of the I-novel dates from the Meiji period (1868–1912). It was a product of the movement toward NATURALISM that dominated the Japanese literary establishment during the first two decades of the 20th century. The first I-novel is often considered to be TAYAMA KATAI's novel *Futon* (1907), an embarrassingly honest account of the feelings of its central character, a writer, toward a young female pupil. This novel opened up new territory for the Japanese novelist: the realistic depiction of the course of events (often mere trivialities) in his or her daily life. Novels with a similar approach were written by authors such as SHIMAZAKI TŌSON, TOKUDA SHŪSEI, and KASAI ZENZŌ; a characteristic of many of these works is their confessional tone, frequently associated with the *shishōsetsu* genre as a whole.

The other major type of I-novel is also known as the *shinkyō shōsetsu*, or the novel of mental states. Generally briefer than the

confessional form, these works are usually essaylike sketches focusing on the mental, emotional, or spiritual state of the author and have much about them that is suggestive of the traditional genre of ZUIHITSU (essays or random jottings). The best examples of this subgenre of Japanese fiction are the masterful short pieces of SHIGA NAOYA such as "Kinosaki nite" (1917; tr "At Kinosaki," 1956).

The I-novel emerged as the main current of modern Japanese fiction during the Taishō period (1912–26), attracting such practitioners as MUSHANOKŌJI SANEATSU, UNO KŌJI, and MUROO SAISEI. Post–World War II writers such as DAZAI OSAMU, DAN KAZUO, and KAWASAKI CHŌTARŌ continued the tradition, and MISHIMA YUKIO also explored the confessional form in his novel KAMEN NO KOKUHAKU (1949; tr *Confessions of a Mask*, 1958).

In postwar criticism, the I-novel has received both praise and blame. Many critics felt its lack of plot and narrow perspective had stunted the growth of the modern novel in Japan. None, however, could deny its enduring popularity and dominant place in 20th-century Japanese fiction, a phenomenon attested to by the appearance since the 1960s of a new breed of I-novelists, such as SHIMAO TOSHIO, SHŌNO JUNZŌ, YASUOKA SHŌTARŌ, YOSHIYUKI JUNNOSUKE, ABE AKIRA, and TOMIOKA TAEKO.

inrō   印籠

(literally, "seal basket"). Small containers usually made of LACQUER WARE and decorated by MAKI-E artists. They consisted of snugly fitted compartments covered by a lid and worn suspended by a cord and toggle from OBI, sashes used to secure the KIMONO. *Inrō* were used to carry medicines, although the name suggests an earlier association with the seals and seal-paste stamped on documents as marks of personal identity. *Inrō* apparently came into use during the 17th century and became an important personal accessory for Japanese men of the middle and late Edo period (1600–1868). Their decoration encompasses in miniature virtually the entire range of Edo lacquering styles and techniques. The rich variety of themes and styles among *inrō* reflects their importance as an emblem of the taste, status, and wealth of the owner. *Inrō* usually have a rectangular face and a flattened, elliptical cross section. A silk cord is threaded through channels on either side, and the ends are passed through a bead and then secured to a toggle (usually a miniature carving known as NETSUKE). Their use declined during the Meiji period (1868–1912) as Western clothing became more popular.

INS → Information Network System

In school   院派

(Impa). Kyōto school of Buddhist sculptors who worked in the style of JŌCHŌ (d 1057); active from the late Heian period (794–1185) through the early Kamakura period (1185–1333). There were two In-school workshops (BUSSHO) in Kyōto: the Shichijō-Ōmiya *bussho*, established by Injo (d 1108), a grandson of Jōchō; and the Rokujō Madenokōji *bussho*, set up by Inchō (fl mid-12th century). The sculptors from these two workshops came to be known as the In school because most of them included in their names the Chinese character for "in" to demonstrate their common artistic lineage. From the middle to the end of the 12th century the In school flourished and temporarily domi-

nated the field. Their chief rivals were in the EN SCHOOL.

inscriptions   金石文

(*kinsekibun;* literally, "metal and stone writings"). *Kinsekibun* is a generic term referring to all types of inscriptions recorded on metal, stone, clay, wood, and other durable materials by such methods as carving, casting, impression, brush writing, and inlay. The appearance of inscriptions in Japan probably coincided with the introduction of the Chinese language and script, and their number and variety grew with the spread of writing.

Some of the objects on which inscriptions have been discovered were made to be seen (for example, Buddhist images, bells, mirrors, swords, and stone monuments); others, such as tiles, stones, and other objects inscribed with passages from Buddhist scripture, were buried in the ground immediately after manufacture. These were often buried in SUTRA MOUNDS, which were built to ensure the survival of Buddhist doctrine through the period of decay (*mappō*) prophesied in numerous sutras.

The earliest *kinsekibun* recovered to date are of continental origin and include inscriptions on metal mirrors and swords and a gold seal (KAN NO WA NO NA NO KOKUŌ NO IN) thought to have been presented to the ruler of Nakoku ("the state of Na") by the founding emperor of the Later Han dynasty (25–220) of China. The inscriptions on the SHICHISHITŌ in the Isonokami Shrine are important for understanding Japan's relationship with Korea in the 4th century. The oldest extant native Japanese inscriptions, thought to date from the 5th and 6th centuries, occur on swords excavated from the Inaridai Tomb (see INARIDAI INSCRIBED IRON SWORD), the ETA FUNAYAMA TOMB, the INARIYAMA TOMB, and the Okadayama Tomb (see NUKATABE NO OMI SWORD INSCRIPTIONS), and on a bronze mirror (see BRONZE MIRRORS) in the possession of the Suda Hachiman Shrine in Wakayama Prefecture, probably from the early 6th century. With the exception of many recently excavated wooden tallies (MOKKAN), only about 85 *kinsekibun* can be accurately dated from before 794. Most numerous are stone memorials (see KŌZUKE MONUMENTS), metal statues, and burial tablets.

Kinsekibun are extremely valuable as a source of information on history, religion, language, archaeology, art history, and culture. Those that can be dated to the Nara period (710–794) and earlier are especially useful to researchers, for there are few other existing early written sources. *Kinsekibun* have revealed inaccuracies in historical records and have enabled historians to interpret more correctly events described in diaries and other writings.

Kinsekibun were not systematically collected and studied until the 17th century. Scholars included TOKUGAWA MITSUKUNI (1628–1700), MATSUDAIRA SADANOBU (1759–1829), Kariya Ekisai (1775–1835), and Kizaki Aikichi (1865–1944). These inscriptions are now studied according to the type of object or geographical area.

insects   昆虫

(*konchū*). Many endemic species of insects inhabit Japan. Among them are the *gifuchō*, related to the swallowtails; the *usubashiro-chō*, a species of Apollo butterfly; the *tsumajiro urajanome* (speckled-wood; *Lasiommata interrupta*) and the *hikagechō* (*Lethe*

Reigning emperor	Reign dates	Senior retired emperor	Junior retired emperor
Go-Sanjō	1068–1073	—	—
Shirakawa	1073–1087	—	—
Horikawa	1087–1107	Shirakawa	—
Toba	1107–1123	Shirakawa	—
Sutoku	1123–1129	Shirakawa	Toba
Sutoku	1129–1142	Toba	—
Konoe	1142–1155	Toba	Sutoku
Go-Shirakawa	1155–1156	Toba	Sutoku
Go-Shirakawa	1156–1158	—	—
Nijō	1158–1165	Go-Shirakawa	—
Rokujō	1165–1168	Go-Shirakawa	—
Takakura	1168–1180	Go-Shirakawa	Rokujō (to 1176)
Antoku	1180–1185	Go-Shirakawa	Takakura (to 1181)
Go-Toba	1183–1192	Go-Shirakawa	—
Go-Toba	1192–1198	—	—

SOURCE: Adapted from George Sansom, *A History of Japan to 1334* (1958).

sicelis), relatives of the wood nymphs; the Fuji *midori shijimi* (hairstreak), a relative of the blue butterflies; the *yamamayuga* (Japanese oak silk-moth; *Antheraea yamamai*), a relative of the moths; and the snail-eating genus *Damaster*, related to the ground beetles. In the Ryūkyū Islands there are many milkweed butterflies of the South Seas group, including the *ōgomadara* with a 12-centimeter (4.7-in) wingspread; its relative the *asagimadara* is found as far north as Hokkaidō. In the mainland there are many swallowtails of the South Seas group, with eight species of genus *Papilio* alone. The high mountains are inhabited by alpine butterflies of the Siberian group. The large-sized, violet *ōmurasaki*, considered a representative Japanese butterfly, is found also in Korea and China and is not endemic to Japan.

Apart from BUTTERFLIES, there are many other insect groups, including 180 species of DRAGONFLIES (there are about 20 species of the genus *Sympetrum*), such as the *oniyamma* with a body length of 7.5 centimeters (3 in) and the scarlet *shōjōtombo* (*Crocothemis servilia*). There are 20–30 species of CICADAS, as well as numerous long-horned grasshoppers and CRICKETS. FIREFLIES also are plentiful, with about 25–30 species in Japan.

The *garoamushi* (grylloblattids; *Galloisiana nipponensis*), which lives under stones in mountainous regions, and the *mukashitombo*, a dragonfly that spends seven to eight years in the larva stage in mountain streams, are noted living fossils. The *mukashitombo* is a remnant of an animal that flourished more than 190 million years ago in the Triassic period; only two species are now known, one each in Japan and the Himalayas. See also ANTS; BEES AND WASPS; GOLD BEETLE; KIRIGIRISU.

insei   院政

(literally, "cloister government"). The system of government that prevailed between the abdication of Emperor SHIRAKAWA in 1087 and the establishment of WARRIOR GOVERNMENT in 1192. Political control was restored to the imperial house from the Fujiwara regents but was exercised primarily by retired emperors rather than by the titular rulers and the official bureaucracy. *In* refers to the buildings (often a cloister or monastery) where a former emperor resided; *sei* is an abbreviation of *seiji* (politics or government).

For much of the Heian period (794–1185) the imperial house had been controlled and its powers exercised by the FUJIWARA FAMILY, which had established a REGENCY GOVERNMENT based on close marital ties with the imperial line. In 1068, however, Emperor GO-SANJŌ (r 1068–73), who had weak Fujiwara connections, was allowed to ascend the throne. His accession marked the decline of the Fujiwara regency. Go-Sanjō's abdication in 1073 brought to the throne his son Emperor Shirakawa (r 1073–87) whose Fujiwara connection was also weak. Though Shirakawa diverted the succession from Go-Sanjō's other sons to his own Fujiwara-descended sons, he prevented the Fujiwara regents from regaining control. Shirakawa abdicated in 1087 in favor of his son Emperor Horikawa (1079–1107; r 1087–1107) but continued to govern the country from retirement for more than 40 years. During Shirakawa's retirement, *insei* became fully institutionalized.

There was often more than one retired emperor at a given time. However, only one of them exercised real power as senior clois-

tered emperor (*hon'in*), a position held by only three men in this period: Shirakawa (cloistered 1087–1129), his grandson TOBA (cloistered 1129–56), and Toba's son GO-SHIRAKAWA (cloistered 1158–92). Effectively excluded from power, junior retired emperors were frequently a cause of political unrest. See HŌGEN DISTURBANCE.

Japanese historians traditionally held that Go-Sanjō and Shirakawa deliberately established the cloister system as a new form of government to free the imperial house from domination by the Fujiwara regents. Recent scholars, however, argue that the Cloister Office was not a separate "court," but rather a family administrative office (see MANDOKORO) designed to compete more effectively for economic and political resources and for power within the existing political system.

insider trading regulations   インサイダー取引の規制

(*insaidā torihiki no kisei*). Insider trading is the utilization for securities trading of information not available to the general public. In Japan it is regulated by the SECURITIES EXCHANGE LAW as an unfair trading practice. This law (art. 190 [2, 3]) prohibits the buying and selling of the securities of a company by those in a special relationship to it who have made use of that relationship to obtain information on "important facts" before they have been made public. This particularly applies to parties closely connected to the company such as company directors, major stockholders, and customers. Important facts include knowledge of a merger, a new allotment of shares, or any other factor that will influence the company's stock price.

In the autumn of 1987, Tateho Chemical Industries Co, Ltd, suffered huge losses as a result of unsuccessful bond speculation. Before this information had been made public, a large volume of the company's stock was sold. Although the bank that sold the stock had clearly engaged in insider trading, the MINISTRY OF FINANCE judged that the Securities Exchange Law provision in effect at that time was vague, and did not prosecute. As a result of this incident the revision to the Securities Exchange Law implemented in June 1989 strengthened the regulation of insider trading.

Inson   院尊

(1120–98). Buddhist sculptor of the late Heian period (794–1185) and early Kamakura period (1185–1333); lived and worked in Heiankyō (now Kyōto). The leading representative of the IN SCHOOL and a member of the Shichijō-Ōmiya workshop, Inson received many important commissions including the main restoration work at the Nara temples Tōdaiji and Kōfukuji, destroyed by fire in the Taira-Minamoto War (1180–85). After Inson's death the quality and fortunes of the In school gradually declined. No sculpture that can be definitely attributed to Inson has survived.

Installment Sales Law   割賦販売法

(*Kappu Hambai Hō*). A law enacted in 1961 to ensure fairness in installment sales transactions and to protect the interests of purchasers. Frequently amended to strengthen its consumer protection aspects, the current law comprises 6 chapters and 55 articles. Merchants who sell products by the installment sale method must disclose to purchasers the cash price, the installment sale price,

the number and periods for payments, the annual rate for charges, and, for layaway installment sales in which the purchase price is paid before delivery of the goods, the time of delivery. The merchant must provide the purchaser with a written contract. See also DOOR-TO-DOOR SALES LAW.

instant foods   インスタント食品

(*insutanto shokuhin*). The earliest "instant food" in Japan was *hoshi-ii*, or dried boiled rice, which was an essential provision for travelers and warriors in ancient times. In the 1920s instant *shiruko* (a thick sweet soup made of azuki beans) and instant curry sauce were introduced to the marketplace. During World War II, powdered *misoshiru* (bean-paste soup) and dried vegetables were used by the army. Since the mid-1950s, with the appearance of instant *rāmen* (Chinese noodles), instant foods have become familiar to the Japanese public. Instant foods currently in use include vacuum-packed rice, frozen foods, and microwavable foods.

Institute for the Science of Labor   労働科学研究所

(*Rōdō Kagaku Kenkyūjo*). Institute in the city of Kawasaki, Kanagawa Prefecture, devoted to research on all aspects of labor science. Founded in 1921 as part of the ŌHARA INSTITUTE FOR SOCIAL RESEARCH, the institute came under the control of the Ministry of Education in 1951. It carries out medical, psychological, and economic studies pertaining to such labor issues as contractual working conditions, the physical workplace, and workers' health care management.

Institute for Virus Research, Kyōto University   京都大学ウイルス研究所

(*Kyōto Daigaku Uirusu Kenkyūjo*). Research institute founded in 1956. Located in Kyōto, the institute performs a broad range of research in nine areas ranging from the physicochemical characteristics of viruses to viral pathology and infectious mechanisms.

instant foods Two types of instant *rāmen*. On the left, cup *rāmen*—the most "instant" of instant noodles—is ready to eat after hot water is added. On the right, *rāmen* with separate packets of soup base, ready after a few minutes of boiling.

Institute of Cetacean Research 日本鯨類研究所

(Nihon Geirui Kenkyūjo). Institute in Chūō Ward, Tōkyō, that conducts research on whales and other marine mammals. The institute, which is under the jurisdiction of the Ministry of Agriculture, Forestry, and Fisheries, was founded in 1987 to survey the world's whale populations and to study the classification of whales and other marine mammals.

Institute of Developing Economies アジア経済研究所

(Ajia Keizai Kenkyūjo). A nonprofit organization founded in 1958 to conduct research on the economies of developing countries and to promote the expansion of trade and economic cooperation with those areas. Reorganized in 1960 as a quasi-governmental body under the jurisdiction of the MINISTRY OF INTERNATIONAL TRADE AND INDUSTRY, the institute is located in Shinjuku Ward, Tōkyō. The institute collects books, documents, and statistical data concerning the developing countries, publishes research reports and periodicals including the monthly *Ajia keizai* (Asian Economies), and holds international symposia. The institute maintains a staff of 260 and is funded primarily by government subsidies.

Institute of Low Temperature Science, Hokkaidō University 北海道大学低温科学研究所

(Hokkaidō Daigaku Teion Kagaku Kenkyūjo). Research institute in the city of Sapporo, Hokkaidō, for the study of low-temperature phenomena. The institute was founded in 1941 to study the nature of snow and ice, weather in cold regions, low-temperature physiology, and other phenomena that occur in low-temperature environments.

Institute of Medical Science, Tōkyō University 東京大学医科学研究所

(Tōkyō Daigaku Ikagaku Kenkyūjo). Institute for basic and clinical research in all fields of medical science. Located in Minato Ward, Tōkyō, the institute was founded in 1892 for research on epidemic diseases. Such diseases now having been largely eradicated, the institute's research focus has shifted to such areas as cancer, viral infections, allergic disease, and organ transplants.

Institute of Oriental Culture, Tōkyō University 東京大学東洋文化研究所

(Tōkyō Daigaku Tōyō Bunka Kenkyūjo). Established in 1941, the institute now consists of the Asian Studies Documents Center and four major research divisions specializing in Asian humanities, social sciences, law, and economics. The institute publishes the journals *Tōyō bunka kenkyūjo kiyō* and *Tōyō bunka;* library resources number more than 300,000 volumes.

Institute of Pacific Relations 太平洋問題調査会

(IPR; Taiheiyō Mondai Chōsakai). Research institute founded in Honolulu in 1925. Organized and financed by private citizens from a number of Pacific countries, including the United States and Japan, the institute consisted of councils in each participating country, plus a Pacific Council made up of one representative from each national council. Thirteen Pacific Council meetings were held, including one at Kyōto in 1929. The subjects discussed at the council meetings, in the IPR magazine, *Pacific Affairs*, and in the several hundred books and pamphlets it published covered a broad range of political, economic, and social issues such as US immigration legislation, Japan's China policy, and the Chinese civil war. Japan's IPR council played an important role in Japanese-American relations until the mid-1930s, and it resumed active participation after World War II. However, the American council of the IPR came under political attack in the 1950s because of the alleged pro-communist sympathies of some of its leading members, and the IPR eventually dissolved itself in 1961.

Institute of Physical and Chemical Research 理化学研究所

(Rikagaku Kenkyūjo). Laboratory established in 1917 to advance and improve Japanese science and technology. Located in the city of Wakō, Saitama Prefecture. The demand for the establishment of a national scientific laboratory by the chemist TAKAMINE JŌKICHI in 1913 led to the creation of the institute. One of the institute's founders was ŌKOCHI MASATOSHI. It was initially headed by KIKUCHI DAIROKU. Researchers have included such chemists as IKEDA KIKUNAE, SUZUKI UMETARŌ, and MAJIMA TOSHIYUKI. Outstanding physicists have included NAGAOKA HANTARŌ, TERADA TORAHIKO, HONDA KŌTARŌ, and NISHINA YOSHIO. The institute was made a public corporation in 1958. Publications include the *Scientific Papers of the Institute of Physical and Chemical Research.*

Institute of Space and Astronautical Science 宇宙科学研究所

(Uchū Kagaku Kenkyūjo). A national institute for space science research. Located in the city of Sagamihara, Kanagawa Prefecture, the institute was founded under the supervision of the Ministry of Education in 1981. The institute conducts experiments using satellites, rockets, and weather balloons.

intellectual property 知的所有権

(*chiteki shoyū ken*). The official definition of this term is found in article 2(viii) of the Convention Establishing the World Intellectual Property Organization, signed in Stockholm on 14 July 1967. Japan adopted *chiteki shoyū ken* (literally, "intellectual ownership right") as the official term for intellectual property when Japan ratified the convention in 1975. This Japanese term is possibly a direct translation from the French original *la propriété intellectuelle*, as in the case of *kōgyō shoyū ken* for industrial property or *la propriété industrielle*, which was adopted in 1899 when Japan acceded to the Paris Convention of 20 March 1883 for the Protection of Industrial Property. Intellectual property consists mainly of copyright and industrial property, the latter including patents, utility models, industrial designs, and trademarks, and protection against unfair competition. The term *chiteki zaisan*, which is a literal equivalent of the English "intellectual property," is also in frequent use.

"intelligent" buildings インテリジェントビルディング

(*interijento birudingu*). The concept of the "intelligent" or "smart" building—an ultramodern office building equipped with computer-based office operations and telecommunications systems—was developed in the United States and imported to Japan in the early 1980s. The key element in an intelligent building is provision for advanced electronic communications technology and for the systems of interconnected computers and other devices known as local area networks (LAN). The Tōshiba Building, completed in 1984 as the main office building for the Tōshiba Corporation, and the Honda Aoyama Building, completed in 1985 and serving as the main office building for the Honda Motor Co, Ltd, were equipped with office automation systems that clearly reflected the concept of the intelligent building. Following the deregulation of the telecommunications industry in April 1985, construction of large new buildings and reconstruction of existing structures incorporated the latest technology. Representative are the main office building of the NEC Corporation, completed in 1990, and the Tōkyō Metropolitan Government Offices, completed in 1991.

Interest Limitation Law 利息制限法

(Risoku Seigen Hō). Law that imposes limits on interest. The current law was promulgated in 1954, completely revising the 1877 Interest Limitation Law. The maximum rate of interest is 20 percent per year if the loan principal is under ¥100,000 (US $667 at $1 = ¥150), 18 percent if principal is ¥100,000 or more but below ¥1 million, and 15 percent if principal is ¥1 million or more.

The Interest Limitation Law is not strictly observed in Japan. Although a Supreme Court decision theoretically allows a borrower to demand the return of excess interest payments, in actual practice it is usually not possible. There is a regulatory law that imposes a fine on lenders for charging interest in excess of 109.5 percent per year (0.3% per day), but, by the same token, the charging of interest up to that rate, even if in violation of the Interest Limitation Law, is in practice acknowledged. See also SARAKIN KISEI HŌ.

interest rate structure 金利体系

(*kinri taikei*). With the increasing deregulation of interest rates since the mid-1980s, Japan's interest rate structure is shifting from a relatively rigid system to one with greater flexibility. As of late 1989, principal interest rates included the Bank of Japan's official discount rate, which is the rate at which the central bank discounts prime commercial notes; the short-term prime lending rate, which is now set above a moving average of rates on various bank sources of funds, including large time deposits with negotiable rates, money market certificates, and certificates of deposit; and the long-term prime lending rate, which is a negotiated rate set in discussions with various groups, including the BANK OF JAPAN, the MINISTRY OF FINANCE, long-term credit banks, trust banks, and securities companies. As deregulation of interest rates proceeds, various rates are expected to become increasingly sensitive to changes in market conditions. The central bank is expected to rely increasingly on open market operations involving buying and selling of short-term securities to influence interest rates. At the same time, regulated rates will apply to an increasingly smaller percentage of deposits. See also MONETARY POLICY.

International Christian University 国際基督教大学

(ICU; J: Kokusai Kirisutokyō Daigaku). Private, coeducational university located in the city of Mitaka, Tōkyō Prefecture. It was established in 1953 by a foundation composed of 15 different Protestant denominations in the United States and a group of Japanese Christians, for the purpose of providing higher education based on Christian values through bilingual instruction (Japanese and English). YUASA HACHIRŌ was the first president of the university. The administrative and educational system resembles an American college of liberal arts, with courses in humanities, social science, natural science, languages, and education. An affiliated high school provides EDUCATION FOR CHILDREN OF RETURNEES from abroad. Enrollment stood at 2,086 in 1989.

international communications
国際通信

(*kokusai tsūshin*). The principal means and sources of Japanese communications with the rest of the world community are news agencies (both foreign and domestic), news correspondents, communications satellites, business networks, and international telegraph and telephone.

Japanese News Agencies—The major Japanese news agencies are the KYŌDŌ NEWS SERVICE and JIJI PRESS. Kyōdō and Jiji, as well as NHK (Japan Broadcasting Corporation) and leading newspapers, each have from 29 to 37 branch offices in foreign countries where they station correspondents. Of the 150 or 200 news articles that Kyōdō distributes daily to newspapers and broadcasting stations, telegrams from their own correspondents account for approximately three-fourths, the other one-fourth being supplied by foreign news agencies.

Foreign News Agencies—Japanese newspapers and broadcasting stations mainly use for their sources of international news and events the news agencies of the Western countries, such as Associated Press, United Press International, Reuters, and Agence France-Presse. In addition to contracting directly with foreign news agencies, leading Japanese newspapers and broadcasting stations contract with the Kyōdō News Service and Jiji Press, which themselves contract with 50 and 14 foreign news agencies, respectively. In 1990 the Japanese news media paid over ¥2.5 billion (over US $17.0 million) to foreign news agencies in total yearly fees under contract, which made Japan a major market for foreign news agencies.

Business Communications—General trading companies and large businesses actively handle a much greater volume of information than the agencies. For example, MITSUI & CO, LTD, has a network connecting 552 overseas points with 1,598 overseas representatives (as of January 1989) and over 150,000 local employees. The main branch in Japan receives an average of 65,000 pieces of information daily. Foreign news agencies and information organizations have also been successful in marketing business-related information to Japanese companies.

Television Relay—Television picture and sound was relayed to and from Japan by satellite for the first time on 23 November 1963, when NHK received and relayed news of the assassination of US president John F. Kennedy. In 1964 the Tōkyō Olympic Games were transmitted worldwide by satellite. Japanese television networks make hundreds of international relays each year.

International Telephone and Telegraph—In 1989 there were 700,000 international telegraphic messages dispatched to and from Japan and 21 million messages sent via subscribed international telex. Over 323 million international telephone calls were made the same year.

international crimes
国際犯罪

(*kokusai hanzai*). Crimes involving offenses or persons in more than one country. The criminality of an offense is determined in each nation according to its own criminal law, and infringements upon the laws of each country become subject to punishment in its domestic courts. Under Japanese criminal law, certain serious crimes committed by Japanese abroad, such as sedition, murder, and arson, are still punishable in Japan as "overseas crimes" (*kokugaihan*). Acts such as piracy, buying or selling of slaves, and illicit drug dealing are considered international crimes.

In international law, war and other exercises of military force have come to be prohibited as offenses against international society as a whole. The Nuremburg Trials and the WAR CRIMES TRIALS in Tōkyō after World War II led to the first instances of punishment for this type of international crime. Subsequently, the provisions of Japanese criminal law pertaining to overseas crimes were revised in accordance with the conclusion of the Convention of 1973 on the Prevention and Punishment of Crimes against Internationally Protected Persons, including Diplomatic Agents, and the International Convention of 1979 against the Taking of Hostages. See also EXTRADITION.

international cultural exchange
国際文化交流

(*kokusai bunka kōryū*). Between the OPENING OF JAPAN to foreign contact in the late 19th century and World War I, Japan's international cultural relations stressed the importation of Western culture rather than the introduction abroad of its own culture. Behind this effort was the intention of creating a modern state based on the Western model. Following World War I, the importance of promoting international understanding of Japan through cultural exchange was recognized, and in 1934 the Kokusai Bunka Shinkōkai (KBS; the Society for International Cultural Relations) was established.

In the period of recovery following World War II, there was little Japanese involvement in international cultural exchange. Rapid economic growth in the 1960s and increased visibility of Japan in the international community, however, prompted greater interest in Japanese culture and society among countries overseas. With the aim of conducting Japan's international cultural relations on a more systematic basis, the Japanese government created a new cultural exchange organization, the Kokusai Kōryū Kikin (JAPAN FOUNDATION), in 1972.

Japan's international cultural exchange activities are handled mainly by the Cultural Affairs Department of the Ministry of Foreign Affairs, the Science and International Affairs Bureau of the Ministry of Education, and two public corporations attached to these ministries: the Japan Foundation and the JAPAN SOCIETY FOR THE PROMOTION OF SCIENCE. Among the programs administered by these governmental and semigovernmental agencies are (1) educational exchange, including the exchange of students, teachers, and trainees; (2) academic exchange, including the exchange of scholars and researchers, support of Japanese studies, and promotion of Japanese language teaching abroad; (3) ar-

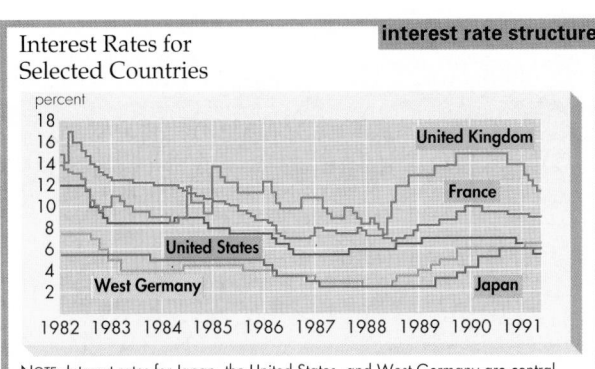

Interest Rates for Selected Countries

interest rate structure

NOTE: Interest rates for Japan, the United States, and West Germany are central bank discount rates. Interest rates for the United Kingdom and France are central bank market intervention rates.
SOURCE: Bank of Japan.

tistic exchange, including the exchange of artists and artworks and the sponsorship of visual- and performing-arts programs; (4) cultural materials exchange, including the exchange of books, films, and radio and television programs; and (5) multilateral cultural exchange, including cooperation with UNESCO, the Southeast Asian Ministers of Education Organization, and other international cultural exchange organizations.

International organizations such as the LIONS CLUB, ROTARY CLUB, and KIWANIS CLUB have branches in Japan. Friendship societies link Japan with individual nations, and, in the cases of China and the Soviet Union, have played important roles at a time when those nations did not have normal diplomatic relations with Japan. Private organizations, local governments, and citizens' groups have promoted cultural exchange to increase mutual understanding and to address social issues of mutual concern, such as Third World development aid, the environment, and international peace.

There are also some 500 private organizations and foundations in Japan today that are engaged in the promotion of international cultural exchange. They include such organizations as the INTERNATIONAL HOUSE OF JAPAN, the Japan Association of International Education, the Japan Center for International Exchange, the Commemorative Association for the Japan World Exposition, the Hōsō Bunka Foundation, the TOYOTA FOUNDATION, and the Yoshida International Education Foundation.

International House of Japan
国際文化会館

(Kokusai Bunka Kaikan). A private, non-profit organization established in 1952 through the efforts of MATSUMOTO SHIGEHARU for the purpose of deepening international understanding. Situated in the Roppongi district of Tōkyō. Its principal functions include administering exchange programs for intellectuals and scholars, organizing lectures and discussions, and providing accommodations and assistance to visiting scholars and artists.

international legal cooperation
国際司法共助

(*kokusai shihō kyōjo*). Japan's cooperation with foreign countries in regard to civil and criminal law proceedings is systematized in a variety of ways. When Japan requests the assistance of a foreign country with regard to civil proceedings, such as in obtaining documents related to litigation or in examining evidence, it does so either on the basis of a bilateral agreement (as of 1989 Japan was a party to 23 such agreements) or on the basis of a multilateral convention, such as

615

Country[1]	Type of diplomatic mission in Japan (20 March 1992)	Type of Japanese diplomatic mission (20 March 1992)	Exports to Japan, 1991 (in thousands of US dollars)	Imports from Japan, 1991 (in thousands of US dollars)	Foreign nationals residing in Japan[2] (31 December 1990)	Japanese nationals residing there[3] (1 October 1990)
Asia						
Republic of Afghanistan	E	E	2,971	116,037	142	0
People's Republic of Bangladesh	E	E	66,668	242,047	2,109	426
Kingdom of Bhutan	NR	NR	134	9,187	22	26
Negara Brunei Darussalam	E	E	1,500,358	128,637	9	94
Cambodia	—[4]	NR	5,466	6,690	1,171	0
People's Republic of China	EC	EC	14,215,837	8,593,143	150,339	8,269
India	EC	EC	2,190,366	1,522,802	3,107	1,190
Republic of Indonesia	EC	EC	12,769,673	5,612,456	3,623	7,031
Republic of Korea	EC	EC	12,339,218	20,067,881	687,940	5,826
Democratic People's Republic of Korea	—	—	283,574	223,993	—[5]	—
Lao People's Democratic Republic	E	E	4,465	21,353	959	60
Malaysia	E	EC	6,471,323	7,634,605	4,683	6,116
Republic of Maldives	—	NR	5,199	12,309	4	60
Mongolia	E	E	21,516	46,997	27	29
Union of Myanmar	E	E	49,348	82,405	1,221	183
Kingdom of Nepal	E	E	1,695	97,510	447	363
Islamic Republic of Pakistan	E	EC	648,349	1,360,551	2,067	681
Republic of the Philippines	EC	EC	2,351,476	2,659,301	49,092	4,025
Republic of Singapore	EC	E	3,414,516	12,213,087	1,194	12,701
Democratic Socialist Republic of Sri Lanka	E	E	131,734	291,465	1,206	625
Kingdom of Thailand	EC	E	5,251,950	9,431,136	6,724	14,289
Socialist Republic of Viet Nam	E	E	661,686	217,266	6,233	99
(Taiwan)	—	—	9,492,501	18,254,581	—[6]	7,729
(Hong Kong)	—	CG	2,063,736	16,314,613	—[7]	13,980
Middle East						
State of Bahrain	—	E	449,395	165,402	2	35
Islamic Republic of Iran	E	EC	2,791,965	2,472,552	1,237	394
Republic of Iraq	E	E	213	314	55	—
State of Israel	E	E	736,738	737,982	398	269
Hashemite Kingdom of Jordan	E	E	25,191	85,856	65	90
State of Kuwait	E	E	57,250	435,454	12	—
Republic of Lebanon	E	E	1,569	107,519	42	9
Sultanate of Oman	E	E	2,163,661	612,673	0	99
State of Qatar	E	E	2,156,896	209,295	0	42
Kingdom of Saudi Arabia	E	EC	10,080,950	3,893,162	89	423
Syrian Arab Republic	E	E	3,976	118,111	70	123
United Arab Emirates	E	E	10,524,336	2,153,812	2	770
Republic of Yemen	E	E	165,798	142,596	8	65
Oceania						
Australia	EC	EC	13,011,325	6,493,072	3,975	15,154
Republic of Fiji	E	E	40,093	53,177	41	195
Republic of Kiribati	NR	NR	5	4,797	33	27
Republic of the Marshall Islands	E	NR	910	3,859	5	37
Federated States of Micronesia	E	NR	3,115	18,200	22	119
Republic of Nauru	—	NR	601	123	0	0
New Zealand	E	EC	1,819,359	1,081,055	1,275	2,006
Papua New Guinea	E	EC	372,840	163,203	23	252
Solomon Islands	NR	NR	40,338	23,023	0	229
Kingdom of Tonga	—	NR	16,989	4,083	27	58
Tuvalu	—	NR	2	24	1	6
Republic of Vanuatu	—	NR	5,279	26,885	1	60
Western Samoa	—	NR	4,571	8,262	37	63
Africa						
Democratic and People's Republic of Algeria	E	E	120,736	365,737	56	344
People's Republic of Angola	—	NR	3,245	138,598	1	13
Republic of Benin	NR	NR	499	13,785	3	4
Republic of Botswana	—	NR	6,480	23,457	4	9
Burkina Faso	NR	NR	2,317	19,444	2	13
Republic of Burundi	E	NR	1,867	18,099	3	9
Republic of Cameroon	E	NR	8,583	42,501	6	18
Republic of Cape Verde	—	NR	162	3,941	1	15
Central African Republic	E	E	288	10,049	2	19
Republic of Chad	NR	NR	10,391	4,529	1	5
Federal Islamic Republic of the Comoros	—	NR	118	3,243	1	0
Republic of Congo	—	NR	1,790	20,957	5	10
Republic of Côte d'Ivoire	E	E	20,381	67,343	17	175
Republic of Djibouti	E	NR	81	24,772	2	0
Arab Republic of Egypt	E	E	88,965	545,692	368	925
Republic of Equatorial Guinea	NR	NR	7	115	0	0
Ethiopia	E	E	49,189	55,457	45	91

the Hague Convention relating to Civil Procedure or the Hague Convention on the Service Abroad of Judicial and Extrajudicial Documents in Civil or Commercial Matters, both of which took effect in Japan in 1970. Japan's response to similar requests from foreign countries is also rendered on the basis of these agreements and conventions as well as the Law concerning Assistance with Requests from Foreign Courts (1905, Gaikoku Saibansho no Shokutaku ni yoru Kyōjo Hō).

Japan is not a party to any multinational convention regarding criminal proceedings. When Japan asks a foreign country for this type of assistance, it is rendered exclusively on the basis of bilateral agreements. When a foreign country requests this type of assistance from Japan, it is given on the basis of bilateral agreements and the Law concerning Assistance with Requests from Foreign Courts. A relatively recent example of bilateral cooperation in a criminal case took place between Japan and the United States during the Lockheed scandal in 1976.

The Law for Assistance with International Investigations (Kokusai Sōsa Kyōjo Hō), enacted in 1980, provides for international cooperation among investigative organizations. This law regulates the gathering and presentation of evidence required in foreign criminal investigations as well as cooperation with the International Criminal Police Organization (Interpol). See also EXTRADITION.

International Monetary Fund→IMF

international relations, history of 国際関係史

(*kokusai kankei shi*). Japan's relations with foreign nations, following abandonment of the shogunal policy of NATIONAL SECLUSION in 1854, can be divided into the period before and the period after the close of World War II. The earlier period includes the entrance of Japan into the community of nations, its participation as an equal in international affairs, and the creation and collapse of the GREATER EAST ASIA COPROSPERITY SPHERE. The later period embraces the Allied OCCUPATION (1945–52), the SAN FRANCISCO PEACE TREATY (1951), admission to the United Nations (1956), and the gradual reestablishment of an independent diplomatic policy.

The Opening of Japan and the "Unequal Treaties"——The arrival in Japan of Commodore Matthew PERRY and his "black ships" (KUROFUNE) in 1853 led to the signing by representatives of the United States and the Tokugawa shogunate of the KANAGAWA TREATY of 1854, which effected the OPENING OF JAPAN. Formal diplomatic relations were soon established with the United Kingdom, Russia, the Netherlands, and other Western countries. The various friendship and commercial treaties (see ANSEI COMMERCIAL TREATIES) that Japan concluded with these countries provided for broad grants of extraterritoriality and restrictions on Japan's right to levy customs duties and were the means by which Japan was forcibly incorporated into a system of international relations developed by the Western powers. Following the formation of the Meiji government in 1868, Japan embarked on a program of forthright Westernization, with the goal of establishing Japan as a great power. Revision of the Unequal Treaties became a crucial concern, and, though it was not achieved until the end of the Meiji period (1868–1912), the issue was raised, to little effect, in the United States by members of the IWAKURA MISSION of 1871–73 and by a succession of foreign ministers, but the nations of the West were disinclined to relinquish their vested privileges. It was not until the signing of the ANGLO-JAPANESE COMMERCIAL TREATY OF 1894 that the extraterritorial rights of a foreign power were first abolished. Japan did not fully recover autonomous customs rights or attain equal status with Western nations until 1911. See UNEQUAL TREATIES, REVISION OF.

Expansion on the Asian Mainland—In 1876, through a display of military power, Japan compelled Korea to sign the Treaty of KANGHWA, gaining for itself access to three Korean ports, extraterritorial rights, and full exemption from customs duties. Japan thus succeeded in concluding an unequal treaty with Korea ahead of the Western powers. China, however, held considerable influence over Korean diplomatic and domestic affairs, and rivalry with Japan was inevitable. An attempt by the Korean reform faction led by Queen MIN to modernize the military with the aid of Japanese advisers led to the disaffection of elements of the army, who rose in revolt (see IMO MUTINY). Military units were dispatched from Japan but arrived after the insurrection had been put down by Chinese forces. Nevertheless, in addition to indemnities and other concessions, Japan extracted from Korea the right to station troops in Seoul. In the wake of the KAPSIN POLITICAL COUP of 1884, Japan and China agreed to withdraw their troops from Korea (see TIANJIN [TIENTSIN] CONVENTION); however, in the spring of 1894 the TONGHAK REBELLION broke out, and the Korean government called on the Chinese for military assistance. Japan too sent an expeditionary force, which clashed with the Chinese in July 1894, leading to the SINO-JAPANESE WAR OF 1894–1895. The Treaty of SHIMONOSEKI, which ended hostilities, provided for the cession by China of TAIWAN and the Pescadores, giving Japan its first colonies. Reparation money received from China played a significant role in the industrialization of Japan, while the opening of numerous Chinese ports and cities to Japanese commerce and industry enabled entrance into the Chinese domestic market. The TRIPARTITE INTERVENTION by Russia, Germany, and France, however, forced Japan to relinquish the Liaodong (Liaotung) Peninsula, which it had also obtained from China.

Following the severance of China's interest in Korea, a new rivalry developed between Japan and Russia, which now increasingly involved itself in Korean domestic affairs. Furthermore, after the BOXER REBELLION (1900) Russia stationed troops in Manchuria, which Japan considered a grave threat to its position on the Korean peninsula. It was under these circumstances that Japan signed with Britain the ANGLO-JAPANESE ALLIANCE (1902), the first military treaty concluded by Japan with a foreign country. Renewed in 1905 and 1911, for 20 years it remained the pillar of Japanese foreign policy.

On 6 February 1904 Japan broke off diplomatic relations with Russia over the issues of China and Korea and on 10 February declared war (see RUSSO-JAPANESE WAR). The terms of the Treaty of PORTSMOUTH, which ended hostilities, gave to Japan the southern half of Sakhalin and the Russian lease concessions in China, including the Liaodong Peninsula; the latter provided a foothold for eventual Japanese political domination of southern Manchuria. Russia also agreed not to intervene in Korean affairs, and

Country[1]	Type of diplomatic mission in Japan (20 March 1992)	Type of Japanese diplomatic mission (20 March 1992)	Exports to Japan, 1991 (in thousands of US dollars)	Imports from Japan, 1991 (in thousands of US dollars)	Foreign nationals residing in Japan[2] (31 December 1990)	Japanese nationals residing there[3] (1 October 1990)
Gabonese Republic	E	E	151,748	60,052	8	16
Republic of the Gambia	—	NR	41,562	10,589	2	7
Republic of Ghana	E	E	70,587	76,610	598	200
Republic of Guinea	E	E	1,815	23,474	13	20
Republic of Guinea-Bissau	—	NR	71	6,255	0	0
Republic of Kenya	E	E	17,158	206,328	118	828
Kingdom of Lesotho	NR	NR	76	3,540	16	2
Republic of Liberia	E	E	5,586	798,334	13	—
Socialist People's Libyan Arab Jamahiriya	E	E	1,136	138,531	23	147
Democratic Republic of Madagascar	E	E	37,517	24,110	23	101
Republic of Malawi	E	NR	77,067	40,212	11	124
Republic of Mali	NR	NR	5,866	9,087	10	25
Islamic Republic of Mauritania	E	NR	125,926	6,177	0	0
Republic of Mauritius	NR	NR	3,148	78,102	15	61
Kingdom of Morocco	E	E	301,643	127,481	71	192
Republic of Mozambique	NR	NR	22,230	38,790	3	83
Republic of Namibia	—	—	9,415	3,477	0	4
Republic of Niger	NR	NR	266	13,423	1	56
Federal Republic of Nigeria	E	E	8,171	410,483	193	235
Republic of Rwanda	E	NR	698	9,336	1	37
Democratic Republic of Sao Tome and Principe	—	NR	9	1,360	0	1
Republic of Senegal	E	E	13,230	26,461	19	207
Republic of Seychelles	NR	NR	413	7,176	7	9
Republic of Sierra Leone	NR	NR	2,202	8,099	2	—
Somali Democratic Republic	—	NR	37	2,285	2	3
Republic of South Africa	E	EC	1,819,338	1,634,746	108	530
Republic of the Sudan	E	E	30,671	52,496	35	71
Kingdom of Swaziland	—	NR	4,443	4,715	1	14
United Republic of Tanzania	E	E	22,521	97,901	84	279
Republic of Togo	NR	NR	622	30,251	4	8
Republic of Tunisia	E	E	29,008	63,470	57	91
Republic of Uganda	NR	NR	2,773	39,116	18	25
Republic of Zaire	E	E	96,732	38,399	98	83
Republic of Zambia	E	E	333,846	69,603	52	289
Republic of Zimbabwe	E	E	164,521	79,345	17	89
Western Europe						
Republic of Austria	E	E	772,829	1,918,683	309	1,568
Kingdom of Belgium	EC	E	1,353,264	4,189,639	402	4,551
Republic of Cyprus	NR	NR	2,648	358,527	10	6
Kingdom of Denmark	E	E	1,289,598	915,935	450	870
Republic of Finland	E	E	403,131	779,494	432	458
French Republic	EC	EC	5,813,239	6,116,760	3,166	15,026
Federal Republic of Germany	EC	EC	10,738,726	20,605,352	3,606	21,086
Hellenic Republic (Greece)	E	E	85,446	1,005,085	169	907
Republic of Iceland	NR	NR	137,296	76,285	26	6
Ireland	E	E	823,688	874,636	671	472
Republic of Italy	EC	EC	4,534,011	3,787,869	940	4,849
Principality of Liechtenstein[8]	—	—	—	—	4	7
Grand Duchy of Luxembourg	E	NR	55,064	175,035	14	310
Republic of Malta	NR	NR	5,269	58,539	6	13
Principality of Monaco	—	—	1,989	6,016	1	24
Kingdom of the Netherlands	EC	E	1,227,229	7,218,633	749	4,334
Kingdom of Norway	E	E	817,077	1,073,029	360	466
Portuguese Republic	E	E	181,827	666,989	319	424
Republic of San Marino[9]	—	—	—	—	1	2
Spain	E	EC	673,513	2,562,453	856	4,195
Kingdom of Sweden	E	E	1,272,097	1,795,621	586	1,510
Swiss Confederation	EC	EC	3,628,917	3,007,769	980	4,456
Republic of Turkey	E	EC	305,146	827,498	251	645
United Kingdom of Great Britain and Northern Ireland	EC	EC	5,016,838	11,039,528	10,206	44,351
Vatican City State[9]	E	E	—	—	0	0
Eastern Europe						
Republic of Albania	NR	NR	8,336	113	9	0
Republic of Bulgaria	E	E	44,776	35,617	90	104
Republic of Croatia[10]	—	—	—	—	—	—
Czech and Slovak Federal Republic	E	E	125,743	68,586	88	179
Republic of Estonia	—	—	—	175	—[11]	—[11]
Republic of Hungary	E	E	152,815	224,566	165	284
Republic of Latvia	—	—	—	1,334	—[11]	—[11]
Republic of Lithuania	—	—	88	53	—[11]	—[11]
Republic of Poland	E	E	189,570	360,945	359	252

Country[1]	Type of diplomatic mission in Japan (20 March 1992)	Type of Japanese diplomatic mission (20 March 1992)	Exports to Japan,1991 (in thousands of US dollars)	Imports from Japan, 1991 (in thousands of US dollars)	Foreign nationals residing in Japan[2] (31 December 1990)	Japanese nationals residing there[3] (1 October 1990)
Romania	E	E	94,497	56,462	42	99
Republic of Slovenia[10]	—	—	—	—	—	—
Socialist Federal Republic of Yugoslavia	E	E	72,531	175,095	117	172
CIS and Georgia						
Republic of Armenia[12]	—	—	—	—	—	—
Azerbaidjan Republic[12]	—	—	—	—	—	—
Republic of Belarus[12]	—	—	—	—	—	—
Republic of Kazakhstan[12]	—	—	—	—	—	—
Republic of Kyrgyzstan[12]	—	—	—	—	—	—
Republic of Moldova[12]	—	—	—	—	—	—
Russian Federation	EC	EC	3,316,831	2,113,711	440	957
Republic of Tadzhikistan[12]	—	—	—	—	—	—
Turkmenistan[12]	—	—	—	—	—	—
Ukraine[12]	—	—	—	—	—	—
Republic of Uzbekistan[12]	—	—	—	—	—	—
Republic of Georgia[12]	—	—	—	—	—	—
North America						
Antigua and Barbuda	—	NR	267	12,773	0	0
Commonwealth of The Bahamas	—	NR	17,565	385,526	58	2
Barbados	—	NR	741	25,608	48	14
Belize	—	NR	902	8,593	7	8
Canada	EC	EC	7,698,426	7,251,165	4,909	21,846
Republic of Costa Rica	E	E	27,799	78,448	63	280
Republic of Cuba	E	E	141,817	35,671	41	236
Commonwealth of Dominica	—	NR	3,410	4,664	14	0
Dominican Republic	EC	E	21,618	103,932	53	622
Republic of El Salvador	E	NR	17,508	61,918	69	34
Grenada	—	NR	1,411	6,357	0	7
Republic of Guatemala	E	E	47,334	87,327	48	161
Republic of Haiti	EC	NR	1,356	20,636	5	24
Republic of Honduras	E	E	103,251	66,431	58	209
Jamaica	—	NR	16,646	69,176	37	71
United Mexican States	E	E	1,741,532	2,817,601	786	3,286
Republic of Nicaragua	EC	E	41,802	30,641	30	33
Republic of Panama	EC	E	98,182	3,945,636	37	420
Saint Christopher and Nevis	—	NR	78	2,500	0	1
Saint Lucia	—	NR	110	11,907	1	19
Saint Vincent and the Grenadines	—	NR	7,105	6,280	1	0
Republic of Trinidad and Tobago	NR	E	35,232	82,002	14	32
United States of America	EC	EC	53,317,255	91,537,637	38,364	236,401
South America						
Argentine Republic	EC	E	603,418	448,307	2,656	12,663
Republic of Bolivia	E	E	10,981	49,959	496	2,593
Federative Republic of Brazil	E	EC	3,179,938	1,225,809	56,429	105,060
Republic of Chile	EC	E	1,887,871	630,855	263	868
Republic of Colombia	E	E	274,035	494,841	425	963
Republic of Ecuador	E	E	107,172	193,122	68	337
Co-operative Republic of Guyana	NR	NR	18,474	15,016	7	12
Republic of Paraguay	EC	EC	9,710	147,939	672	4,388
Republic of Peru	E	EC	395,644	181,232	10,279	2,458
Republic of Suriname	—	NR	19,663	19,404	0	61
Oriental Republic of Uruguay	E	E	25,481	71,875	56	327
Republic of Venezuela	E	E	468,149	529,441	144	819

E Embassy.
EC Embassy plus consulate(s) general and/or consulates.
NR Nonresident legations.
CG Consulate general.

[1]Includes the 182 nations formally recognized by Japan as of 20 March 1992, as well as Taiwan, the Democratic People's Republic of Korea, the British colony of Hong Kong, and the Republic of Georgia, which Japan recognized on 3 April 1992.
[2]Includes aliens, resident in Japan for over 90 days, who have registered with the Japanese government, and some 600,000 Korean and 25,000 Chinese permanent residents. US figures do not include military personnel.
[3]Includes Japanese citizens there who have dual nationality, those who have been resident in that country for over 90 days, and some 101,000 permanent residents in Brazil and 77,000 in the United States. A dash indicates that the number is unknown.
[4]A diplomatic mission was first sent to Japan in March 1954. Since April 1975, however, there has not been a mission.
[5]Included under the Republic of Korea.
[6]Included under the People's Republic of China.
[7]Included under either the United Kingdom or the People's Republic of China.
[8]Trade statistics for Liechtenstein are included among those of Switzerland, which handles its foreign affairs.
[9]Trade statistics are included among those of Italy.
[10]All statistics are included among those of Yugoslavia.
[11]Included under the Russian Federation, whose figures include those of the former Union of Soviet Socialist Republics.
[12]All statistics are included among those of the Russian Federation.

SOURCES: Ministry of Foreign Affairs, Sekai no kuni ichiranhyō (annual): 1992; Kaigai zairyū hōjin sūchōsa tōkei (annual):1991; Japan Tariff Association, Gaikoku bōeki gaikyō (monthly): March 1992; Ministry of Justice, Zairyū gaikokujin tōkei (biennial): 1991.

618

international relations, history of

in 1910 Korea became a Japanese colony (see KOREA, ANNEXATION OF).

In a series of agreements with Russia in 1907, 1910, and 1912, Japan established a sphere of influence in southern Manchuria and the eastern part of Inner Mongolia (see RUSSO-JAPANESE AGREEMENTS OF 1907–1916). By means of the SOUTH MANCHURIA RAILWAY, Japan strengthened its position in the two areas with the ultimate aim of monopolizing their natural resources and markets. This activity, however, was in conflict with the OPEN DOOR POLICY of the United States, which was based on the principle of equal access to Chinese markets, and led to a dispute between Japan and the United States over the issues of railway rights and interests in Manchuria. Friction was exacerbated by restrictions placed by the United States on immigration from Japan (see GENTLEMEN'S AGREEMENT) and by reports of discriminatory treatment of Japanese immigrants (see SEGREGATION OF JAPANESE SCHOOLCHILDREN IN THE UNITED STATES), as well as by rivalry between the US and Japanese navies in the Pacific Ocean.

World War I and Its Aftermath—With the attention of the Western powers turned to Europe, Japan moved to strengthen its position in southern Manchuria and eastern Inner Mongolia. Moreover, in the TWENTY-ONE DEMANDS, presented to the Republic of China in January 1915, Japan sought formal recognition of its occupation of German holdings on the Shandong (Shantung) Peninsula, extension of tenure for its leaseholds in China, and appointment by the Chinese government of Japanese as political, financial, and military advisers.

Following World War I, Japan was one of the five victorious nations at the Paris Peace Conference in 1919 (see VERSAILLES, TREATY OF); it received confirmation of its occupation of the Shandong Peninsula and the mandate for the Pacific Islands formerly held by Germany. However, Japan's strong pressure on China sparked antagonism, and tension and confrontation between Japan and China increased (see MAY FOURTH MOVEMENT). Following the Bolshevik revolution in Russia in November 1917, Japan joined the Allied SIBERIAN INTERVENTION. An initial contingent of troops arrived in Vladivostok in August 1918, and by November more than 70,000 Japanese were entrenched in northern Manchuria and the Maritime Province. The forces of the United States, the United Kingdom, and France completed their withdrawal by April of 1920, but Japan, which had hoped to establish a sphere of influence in eastern Siberia, did not withdraw the last of its forces until October 1922.

At the WASHINGTON CONFERENCE of 1921–22 a plan for international cooperation in East Asia, the so-called Washington System, was formulated. Japan agreed to remove its military forces from the Shandong Peninsula, and during the 1920s, while also working to develop its established interests, Japan made an effort not to disturb the political equilibrium in Asia. However, when the Chinese Nationalist Party (Guomindang or Kuomintang) extended its sphere of activity to Manchuria and Inner Mongolia, Japan replied with extreme measures, such as the SHANDONG (SHANTUNG) EXPEDITIONS (1927 and 1928) and the assassination of ZHANG ZUOLIN (Chang Tso-lin), which were condemned by the United States.

Growing Japanese Military Activity in China—The MANCHURIAN INCIDENT of September 1931 and the establishment of the Japanese-controlled puppet state MANCHUKUO in 1932 brought the Japan–United States confrontation in Asia close to the flash point. Japan ignored the NINE-POWER TREATY, which it had signed at the Washington Conference in 1922, and used military force to protect its interests in Manchuria. The United States, which opposed all of Japan's activities in Manchuria, responded with the Stimson Doctrine (see NONRECOGNITION POLICY).

The Japanese challenge to the Washington System was denounced by a large majority of the member countries of the League of Nations, which supported the LYTTON COMMISSION recommendations of 1932 for an accommodation between Japan and China. Japan responded by leaving the League of Nations in March 1933 (see LEAGUE OF NATIONS AND JAPAN). Japan's economy suffered due to its estrangement from Britain and the United States, and to compensate for its losses Japan extended its influence from Manchuria into northern China. The military dominance of Japan over the entire area of Manchuria created tension with the Soviet Union and led to the signing of the ANTI-COMINTERN PACT in November 1936 by Germany and Japan. Triggered by the MARCO POLO BRIDGE INCIDENT of July 1937, Japan's expansion into northern China escalated into general armed conflict (see SINO-JAPANESE WAR OF 1937–1945). As the scope of military activity in China increased, the United States reacted by declaring an embargo against Japan.

World War II—The 1938 declaration of the TŌA SHINCHITSUJO (New Order in East Asia), which encompassed China, Manchukuo, and Japan, and the announcement in August 1940 of the Greater East Asia Coprosperity Sphere, which included Southeast Asia as well, gave notice of Japan's intention to create a new non-Western political order throughout Asia. It was in the context of the "New Order" that, with assurances from Prime Minister KONOE FUMIMARO of an equal partnership between China and Japan, the puppet REORGANIZED NATIONAL GOVERNMENT OF THE REPUBLIC OF CHINA was established.

The sweeping victories of Germany, following the outbreak of WORLD WAR II in September 1939, convinced Japan of the value of an alliance, and in September 1940 it negotiated the TRIPARTITE PACT with Germany and Italy. In the same month, Japan invaded the northern part of French Indochina in order to gain access to strategic raw materials and to further its Asia policy (see INDOCHINA, JAPANESE OCCUPATION OF).

The collapse of Japan–United States relations appeared imminent; negotiations in Washington proved fruitless. The SOVIET-JAPANESE NEUTRALITY PACT, concluded in April 1941, provided assurance against an attack from the north, and Japan advanced into the southern part of French Indochina. In retaliation the United States froze Japanese assets and banned oil exports to Japan. A Japanese proposal for the resumption of amicable relations was presented to the United States; on 26 November the US secretary of state, Cordell Hull, replied with the HULL NOTE, which called for radical changes in Japan's Asia policy. This was construed by Japan as an unacceptable ultimatum that left it with no alternative but war.

Overwhelming victories in the Pacific theater in the initial stages of World War II opened the way for Japanese occupation and military administration of French Indochina, the Philippines, the Dutch East Indies, Malaya, and Burma. However, defeat in the naval battle at MIDWAY in June 1942 put Japan

on the defensive, and, at the height of its power, imperial Japan was on the verge of collapse.

Allied Occupation and Dependence on US Military Strength—Japan conceded defeat on 15 August 1945 and formally surrendered to the Allied powers on 2 September. The right of Japanese to rule their nation was made subject to the authority of the supreme commander for the Allied powers (SCAP). As supreme commander, Douglas MACARTHUR, who had played a leading role in Japan's defeat, presided over General Headquarters (GHQ) and set about implementing plans for the demilitarization and democratization of Japan.

Following the victory of the communists in China in 1949 and the establishment of the People's Republic of China (PRC), and the outbreak of the KOREAN WAR in 1950, the United States moved to restore Japan's independence. In September 1951 Japan and the Allied powers (excluding the Soviet Union, China, India, and Burma) signed the San Francisco Peace Treaty, which became effective in April 1952, enabling Japan to reenter the community of independent nations. Prohibited by the new CONSTITUTION OF JAPAN from possessing land, sea, or air military forces, Japan was faced with the problem of national security. The issue was partially resolved when, at the signing of the peace treaty, it concluded the first of the UNITED STATES–JAPAN SECURITY TREATIES, bringing Japan under the protective umbrella of the US military. Bases used by the army of occupation remained in the hands of US forces, and during the Korean War the Japanese economy was stimulated by massive US military procurements (see TOKUJU). With US backing, Japan was accepted in 1955 as a member of the General Agreement on Tariff and Trade (GATT) and in 1956 as a member of the United Nations (see UNITED NATIONS AND JAPAN). At the end of the 1950s, Japan announced its intention to adhere to "three principles" in the determination of its foreign policy: membership in the Asian community, diplomacy centered on the United Nations, and maintenance of Japan's position in the free world. Throughout the 1960s, however, Japan's foreign policy was strongly influenced by that of the United States. Opponents of this relationship were particularly vocal in 1960, when the United States–Japan Security Treaty was revised, and again following the outbreak of the Vietnam War (see PEACE MOVEMENT).

Emergence of Japan as an Economic Power—Whereas in the pre–World War II era Japan's diplomatic policies were in large measure directed toward the development of its colonial empire, in the postwar era Japan's expanding foreign trade has played an increasingly influential role in the formation of its diplomacy. In the latter part of the 1960s Japan's economy reached a level competitive with those of the United States and the European Community (EC). Friction over trade issues and, from the standpoint of Japan, the apparent abandonment by the United States of the practice of close policy coordination caused Japan–United States relations to enter a new phase. In the midst of a textile dispute between the two countries in 1969–71, President Richard Nixon announced in July 1971, without prior consultation with Japan, that he would visit Beijing to negotiate the establishment of diplomatic relations with China. Out of deference to US anticommunist policy and despite domestic agitation for the normalization of relations with the People's

Republic of China, Japan had maintained close ties with the Republic of China on Taiwan, and this radical shift in policy without notification was construed as a humiliation. On the heels of this "shock" came the announcement by President Nixon, again without consultation, of his New Economic Policy, which resulted in a major increase in the value of the yen and the unsettling of Japan's foreign trade (see NIXON SHOCKS).

In the late 1970s friction with the United States, which continued to be Japan's chief trade partner, again grew heated due to several factors: the trade balance was overwhelmingly in favor of Japan; increasing imports of Japanese steel and electronic products had grave consequences for corresponding US industries; and the United States sharply criticized Japan for not opening domestic markets to US goods, such as high-technology products, oranges, and beef. Economic friction with the United States persisted through the 1980s, and the criticism was voiced in the US Congress that Japanese trade practices were "unfair." The formation of this perception was influenced by a serious US foreign trade imbalance, of which, in 1989, trade with Japan accounted for some 40 percent. See also UNITED STATES AND JAPAN; UNITED STATES, ECONOMIC RELATIONS WITH.

A similar trade dispute developed between Japan and the nations of Western Europe. Trade imbalances arising from the enormous export volumes of Japanese steel, electronic products, ships, and automobiles caused friction, which intensified in the 1980s and was stimulating the formation of a new protectionism and of new economic blocs in the early 1990s. See EUROPEAN COMMUNITY, ECONOMIC RELATIONS WITH.

Relations with the Soviet Union and China—The conclusion of the first United States–Japan Security Treaty in 1952 inevitably brought Japan into confrontation with the Soviet Union and China. In 1955, during the post-Stalin-era thaw in the cold war, the Soviet Union initiated negotiations on the restoration of normal relations with Japan. However, the talks were suspended in mid-1956 due to a dispute over a number of islands off the coast of Hokkaidō that had come under Soviet dominion at the close of World War II and that Japan demanded be returned (see NORTHERN TERRITORIES ISSUE). Two months later, during a visit to Moscow by Prime Minister HATOYAMA ICHIRŌ, it was decided that an interim agreement terminating the state of war between the two nations would be put into effect, while negotiations continued on a peace treaty. The SOVIET-JAPANESE JOINT DECLARATION to this effect was signed in October 1956, and diplomatic relations were resumed. Trade and cultural exchanges were initiated and joint economic projects inaugurated for the development of timber and natural gas resources in Siberia (see SOVIET-JAPANESE DEVELOPMENT OF SIBERIA).

In the 1980s, following the political ascendance in the Soviet Union of Mikhail Gorbachev, international tensions were reduced, bringing an end to the cold war that had dominated world politics for more than 40 years. The state visit to Japan by President Gorbachev in April 1991—the first ever by a Soviet leader—contributed to the amelioration of Soviet-Japanese relations. However, when the Soviet Union dissolved at the end of 1991, the issue of the Northern Territories had still not been resolved and a peace treaty

inu hariko In the Edo period these colorfully painted dogs served as charms for both safe childbirth and the protection of children.

Inukai Tsuyoshi This veteran politician became prime minister in 1931 but was assassinated the next year during a failed military coup.

had still not been concluded. It seemed clear that these issues would now have to be negotiated between Japan and the Russian Federation. See also SOVIET UNION AND JAPAN.

When the San Francisco Peace Treaty was implemented in April 1952, Japan, at the urging of the United States, established diplomatic relations with the Nationalist government on Taiwan, which it recognized as the official government of China. Until 1972 contact with the People's Republic of China was maintained on a largely nongovernmental basis, and only limited and intermittent trade was conducted. In the early 1960s Japanese overtures that were intended to improve relations with the PRC resulted in the disaffection of the Nationalist government on Taiwan, and in 1969 a joint statement with the United States expressing concern for the security of Taiwan in turn offended the PRC.

In the 1970s growing dissension within the communist bloc led to changes in the structure of international cold-war relationships, and the eruption of armed conflict between China and the Soviet Union in 1969 was a factor in the decision of the United States to negotiate with China for the establishment of diplomatic relations. The China–United States rapprochement paved the way for the issuance of a joint communiqué in September 1972 establishing formal diplomatic relations between Japan and the People's Republic of China (of which Japan recognized Taiwan to be a territory) and the signing in 1978 of the CHINA-JAPAN PEACE AND FRIENDSHIP TREATY. See also CHINA AND JAPAN.

Relations with Korea—In 1948 the Korean peninsula was divided at the 38th parallel between the Democratic People's Republic of Korea (North Korea) and the Republic of Korea (South Korea), with which Japan was urged by the United States to establish diplomatic relations. This effort, however, was fraught with difficulties due to the deep resentment felt by Koreans toward the nation that had colonized it. The anti-Japanese policies of President Syngman RHEE, the declaration in 1952 of the RHEE LINE restricting Japanese fishing in the Sea of Japan, and indemnity claims were major obstacles to progress. Following the assumption of power by the government of PAK CHŎNG-HŬI, negotiations were resumed and resulted in the signing of the KOREA-JAPAN TREATY OF 1965, in which Japan recognized South Korea as the only lawful government on the Korean peninsula. The economies of the two countries have since grown increasingly close. Contacts with North Korea have been largely unofficial, but in 1990 negotiations were initiated to normalize relations. See KOREA AND JAPAN.

Relations with Southeast Asia and the Pacific Basin—Japan's postwar relations with Southeast Asia began with negotiations concerning war reparations. The first country with which Japan reached an agreement was Burma, followed by the Philippines, Indonesia, and the Republic of Vietnam, all between 1954 and 1959 (see REPARATIONS FOR SOUTHEAST ASIA). In the 1960s Japan established close economic relations with many countries in the region, and since then, in accord with its assertion of a special relationship with nations of the Asian community, Japan has placed particular emphasis on foreign aid. In 1967 Thailand, Malaysia, Singapore, Indonesia, and the Philippines organized the Association of Southeast Asian

Nations (ASEAN). Its member countries worked to increase economic cooperation, particularly in trade and industry, and their industrial development was accelerated by Japanese capital funding and technology. See SOUTHEAST ASIA AND JAPAN.

Remarkable advances were made in the early 1980s by South Korea, Taiwan, Hong Kong, and Singapore, the Asian nations known collectively as the NIEs (newly industrializing economies). With the ASEAN countries, Japan, and a number of other nations in the East Asia–western Pacific area, they have become the most dynamic regional influence upon the world's economy. As providers of raw materials, Australia, Canada, New Zealand, and Mexico have become increasingly important to Japan and the other industrialized nations of the region, and growing economic interdependence has lent itself to the idea of a "Pacific Basin Economic Sphere" (see PACIFIC BASIN ECONOMIC COUNCIL). In November 1989 government representatives of Canada, the United States, New Zealand, Australia, South Korea, Japan, and the six ASEAN nations (Brunei joined in 1984) met for their first roundtable conference, at which they established principles for economic cooperation. Japan, which has the strongest economy in the East Asia–western Pacific area and is a major beneficiary of global free trade, considers the advancement of regional economic stability and expansion of the international system of free trade to be essential to its well-being.

Japan and the Middle East—Japan possesses only marginal petroleum resources and is dependent on the import of oil to meet its needs. In the years since the OIL CRISIS OF 1973, Japan has established strong economic relations with the countries of the Middle East, not only in regard to the import of oil but also the export of manufacturing and refining plants and other industrial as well as consumer goods. During this period Japan chose to support the Arab nations vis-à-vis Israel, but in the wake of the Persian Gulf War of 1990–91 it is likely that Japan's foreign policy will assume a broader view. See MIDDLE EAST AND JAPAN.

Economic Assistance to Developing Nations—During the 1970s the Third World nations, utilizing their natural resources as a diplomatic weapon, emerged as a force in international politics. However, in the 1980s the problem of accumulated debt afflicted many of these nations, and economic inequality between countries of the northern and southern hemispheres has grown increasingly grave. At the same time, total direct government economic assistance provided by Japan had steadily increased to US $9.2 billion by 1990, exceeding that of all other economically advanced nations. Nevertheless, because in that year less than 50 percent of Japanese aid—as opposed to 98.1 percent of British foreign aid and 92.6 percent of US aid—was in the form of outright grants, critics have argued that its effectiveness was severely circumscribed. In step with government aid, private investment by Japanese in developing countries is also increasing, and the scope of Japanese technological cooperation with the developing nations is also expanding. See FOREIGN AID.

Future Prospects—Japan has grown into a major economic power, and the opinions of its leaders concerning world affairs have become increasingly influential; nevertheless, due to its renunciation of war (art. 9 of the Constitution of Japan), the nation has been wary of involvement as a mediator in

international conflicts. In recent years, however, it has sought to expand its role in international affairs, and it is anticipated that in the 1990s Japan will play a role in the maintenance of world peace, contribute to projects for the preservation of the environment, and offer substantial economic and technological assistance to developing nations.

International Research Center for Japanese Studies
国際日本文化研究センター
(Kokusai Nihon Bunka Kenkyū Sentā). Interuniversity facility under the jurisdiction of the Ministry of Education and located in the city of Kyōto. The center was founded in 1987 to conduct interdisciplinary research on Japanese culture in cooperation with scholars of Japanese studies throughout the world. It provides information and research materials to research institutions and scholars in Japan and overseas, as well as guidance and assistance to Japanese and foreign graduate students. Under its director-general, Umehara Takeshi (b 1925), there is a staff of 67, including resident professors and associate professors.

international schools → gaikokujin gakkō

International University of Japan
国際大学
(Kokusai Daigaku). A coeducational private graduate school located in the Minami Uonuma District of Niigata Prefecture. Founded in 1982, it has graduate schools of international relations and international management. All lectures are given in English and 30 percent of the instructors are non-Japanese. The student body is composed of foreign students, Japanese company personnel sent to the university to study, and a small number of ordinary Japanese graduate students. The school's dormitory system also helps foster an international environment. Enrollment in 1989 was 224.

In the Realm of the Senses
愛のコリーダ
(Ai no korīda). A 1976 film directed by ŌSHIMA NAGISA and starring Fuji Tatsuya (b 1941) and Matsuda Eiko (b 1952) that has been called the first hard-core pornographic film that is also art. Although it was produced by Argos Films of France, the cast and crew were all Japanese and Ai no korīda was shot in Japan. (Because full frontal nudity in films is illegal in Japan, the film was developed and edited in France.) It depicts the infamous 1936 incident in which a young woman named Abe Sada (b 1905) strangled her lover to death with a scarf during an extended round of lovemaking and then cut off his penis and kept it as a memento of their love. Because it presents Abe more as a victor in love than as a murderer, some see the film as an attack on Japan's suppression of the dark, melancholy aspects of sexuality.

Inubōzaki
犬吠埼
Cape on Chōshi Peninsula, northeastern Chiba Prefecture, central Honshū; part of Suigō-Tsukuba Quasi-National Park. Noted for its lighthouse, built in 1874, and its beautiful beaches.

inu hariko
犬張子
A papier-mâché dog popular during the Edo period (1600–1868) as a talisman for safe

childbirth and the protection of children. During the Heian period (794–1185) a forerunner of *inu hariko* was used by the nobility as a talisman against difficult birth. During the Edo period the *inu hariko* was included in a bride's trousseau and was also displayed at festivals with *hina* dolls (see DOLL FESTIVAL). A newborn infant was given an *inu hariko* by relatives on the child's first visit to the family's tutelary shrine. Today *inu hariko* are used mainly as toys for children. *Inu hariko* are called Azuma *inu* in the Kyōto-Ōsaka area.

Inukai Tsuyoshi 犬養毅

(1855–1932). Statesman and prime minister (1931–32). Born at Niwase in what is now Okayama Prefecture. He studied at Keiō Gijuku (now Keiō University) in Tōkyō and had an early career as a journalist. Beginning with his involvement in the formation of a political party called the RIKKEN KAISHINTŌ in 1882, Inukai supported liberal political causes and was invariably critical of the domination of the government by political leaders from the former Chōshū (now Yamaguchi Prefecture) and Satsuma (now Kagoshima Prefecture) domains (see HAMBATSU). Elected to the House of Representatives in the first general election in 1890 and reelected 17 times, he was a leading figure first in the SHIMPOTŌ and then in the KENSEITŌ. In 1910 he organized the RIKKEN KOKUMINTŌ. With OZAKI YUKIO, Inukai was instrumental in the campaign that led to the resignation in 1913 of General KATSURA TARŌ's cabinet (see TAISHŌ POLITICAL CRISIS).

The Kokumintō was reorganized in 1922 as the KAKUSHIN KURABU. This party joined forces with the KENSEIKAI and RIKKEN SEIYŪKAI to form the KATŌ TAKAAKI cabinet in 1924, with Inukai as minister of communications. The Kakushin Kurabu later merged with the Seiyūkai, and Inukai continued to be elected to the House of Representatives as a senior member of the Seiyūkai. With the death of TANAKA GIICHI, Inukai became president of the Seiyūkai in 1929 and was asked to organize his own cabinet in 1931. Japan was in serious economic straits as a result of the world depression and Japan's untimely return to the gold standard. Inukai's cabinet immediately announced the reembargo on gold and set about trying to reflate the Japanese economy. Inukai tried to curb the military's designs on China after the MANCHURIAN INCIDENT in 1931. His tight control of the army prompted a 1932 uprising of military officers, the MAY 15TH INCIDENT, during which Inukai was assassinated.

Inukai unfailingly fought for parliamentary democracy and friendly relations with China. Since his death his followers have assembled every May 15th in his memory.

inuoumono 犬追物

(literally, "dog chasing"). A sport of the warrior class that involved warriors on horseback shooting arrows at dogs. It originated during the Kamakura period (1185–1333) and was especially popular during the Muromachi period (1333–1568). After a period of decline it was revived during the Edo period (1600–1868) but never achieved its former popularity and disappeared soon after the Meiji Restoration of 1868. A large circle was roped off within a riding ground, and a smaller circle was made inside the larger one. Warriors on galloping horses outside the outer rope shot their arrows at dogs released inside the inner circle. See also YABUSAME; KASAGAKE.

Inu tsukubashū 犬筑波集

(ca 1540; Collection of Doggerel Linked Verse). Also known as *Shinsen inu tsukubashū*. One of the oldest and most influential anthologies of humorous *hokku* (HAIKU) and two-strophe linked verse (*tsuke-ai*); compiled by YAMAZAKI SŌKAN. Its name is a facetious allusion to the anthology of serious RENGA (linked verse) of TSUKUBASHŪ (1356–57) and marks a reaction to the restrictive rules and belletristic diction of that genre. Although the names of poets are not given, some of the verses also appear in other texts and can be attributed to the *renga* masters SŌGI, INAWASHIRO KENSAI, TAKAYAMA SŌZEI, and ARAKIDA MORITAKE, as well as to Sōkan himself; however, the majority remain anonymous. Alternately witty, broadly comic, salacious, and parodistic, the collection had a strong influence on the development of the DANRIN SCHOOL of haiku.

Inuyama 犬山[市]

City in northern Aichi Prefecture, central Honshū, on the river KISOGAWA. It is the site of Inuyama Castle, which has one of the oldest donjons in Japan. Because of its proximity to NAGOYA, it is fast becoming a satellite city, with emergent machinery and food-processing industries. Tourists are drawn to Inuyama Castle, MEIJI MURA, a complex of Meiji-period (1868–1912) buildings, the Japan Monkey Center, and boating and CORMORANT FISHING (*ukai*) on the Kisogawa. Pop: 69,801.

invasions of Korea in 1592 and 1597 文禄·慶長の役

(Bunroku Keichō no Eki). TOYOTOMI HIDEYOSHI's two invasions of Korea were launched in 1592 (Bunroku 1) and 1597 (Keichō 2). One major cause was Korea's refusal to allow passage of Japanese troops for Hideyoshi's planned conquest of China.

The Bunroku Campaign (1592–1593)—Hideyoshi's plans to invade Korea became concrete soon after his unification of Japan in 1590. When the attack actually began with the invasion of Pusan on 23 May 1592, Korean regular army forces were ill prepared. Japan's armies moved quickly through the peninsula. The two vanguard divisions under KONISHI YUKINAGA and KATŌ KIYOMASA took separate attack routes, but both arrived in Seoul on 11 June. Konishi pushed forward and occupied P'yŏngyang on 23 July; Katō moved to the northeast and by 30 August reached the Tumen River.

The Japanese attack then began to lose momentum as serious problems developed. Korean naval forces under Admiral YI SUN-SIN had begun to decimate the Japanese supply fleet, preventing maritime supplies from reaching Konishi's armies via the Yellow Sea. Also, Korean irregulars constantly harassed the overland supply lines and kept Japanese forces from consolidating their positions.

Meanwhile, Korea had appealed to the Chinese Ming dynasty (1368–1644) for help. A small Chinese detachment attacked P'yŏngyang in August but was easily defeated by Konishi. China proposed a 50-day truce that Konishi, deeply troubled by supply problems, accepted. A Chinese attack by 40,000 men (February 1593) overwhelmed Konishi and forced him to retreat to Seoul, opening the way for long peace negotiations.

Peace Negotiations (1593–1596)—Hideyoshi's demands included a restoration of the TALLY TRADE previously conducted

between the Ming and the Muromachi shogunate (1338–1573). In Chinese eyes, formal trade involved a tributary relationship in which the Ming emperor invested the Japanese ruler as "king." Although it conflicted with Japanese attitudes of parity with China, the Japanese accepted the investiture to ease the negotiations. The day after the investment ceremony in October 1596, Hideyoshi had the investiture documents read aloud. He was infuriated by the condescending tone of the Chinese document and the failure to mention his demand for a marriage alliance between the Chinese and Japanese imperial families and the cession of part of Korea. He broke off talks and embarked on a new campaign.

The Keichō Campaign (1597–1598)—Throughout the negotiations Japan had maintained some of its coastal fortresses in Korea, but with the exception of a brutal massacre at Chinju there had been little military activity. Konishi and Katō now raced back to Korea to reopen the war. As in 1592, surprise and solid organization secured initial victories. A Japanese intrigue led to the dismissal of Yi Sun-sin as commander of the Korean fleet, which was then defeated in a major battle on 27 August 1597. With the sea secure, Japanese units advanced successfully into Chŏlla Province (southwestern Korea) and prepared to march on Seoul. Redeployment of Ming forces at Chiksan stopped the Japanese advance, however, and Yi Sun-sin, vindicated and reappointed as naval commander, achieved a dramatic victory over the Japanese fleet.

As a strategic stalemate was developing between huge Chinese naval and land forces and impregnable Japanese coastal fortresses, Japanese commanders learned that Hideyoshi had died (18 September 1598) and had left a deathbed order for the withdrawal of troops from Korea. Katō's forces were evacuated, but Konishi was forced to fight his way out, suffering many casualties. The Korean hero Yi Sun-sin also lost his life in this final action, the Battle of Noryang (16 December 1598). See also KOREA AND JAPAN.

invasions of Korea in 1592 and 1597 The warlord Toyotomi Hideyoshi was the moving force behind these failed Japanese attempts to conquer Korea and China.
1 Detail of a 1709 Korean painting depicting Japanese military leader Konishi Yukinaga's attack on Pusan Castle in 1592.
2 Korean naval hero Yi Sun-sin, pictured here, was killed in 1598 during fighting that impelled the retreat of Japanese forces from Korea.

The most common of the symbolic hand positions used for seated images of the Buddha Amida is the one shown at right on the great Buddha at Kamakura.

Buddhist Mudrā

Semui in (Skt: *abhaya-mudrā*), raised right hand, shows the Buddha bestowing fearlessness.

Yogan in (Skt: *varada-mudrā*), lowered open hand, expresses the Buddha's charity and vow to strive for the salvation of all sentient beings.

Sokuchi in (Skt: *bhūmisparśa-mudrā*) shows the Buddha touching the ground to disperse demons obstructing his enlightenment.

Tembōrin in (Skt: *dharmacakra-mudrā*) shows the Buddha teaching, symbolically turning the wheel of the Buddhist Law.

Chiken in (Skt: *jñānamuṣṭi-mudrā*) expresses the enlightened wisdom of the Buddha Dainichi (Skt: Mahāvairocana).

Zenjō in (Skt: *dyāna-mudrā*) or *hokkaijō in* (Skt: *dharmadhātu-mudrā*) expresses the Buddha's absorption in deep meditation.

investment trusts　　投資信託

(*tōshi shintaku*). Japanese investment trusts or investment trust funds are essentially the same as mutual funds in the United States. Investment trust companies are firms that develop various types of investment trust funds to meet investor requirements, such as those of individuals or pension funds, and manage moneys invested in these funds. Such investment trust funds are generally

marketed by one securities company or more. Funds are typically invested in domestic and foreign bonds, stocks, and other financial instruments, including the short-term money market. However, each fund will generally have a specialty, such as high-growth equities or medium-term government bonds. Although most investment trust funds are run by fund managers on an "active" basis, there is a trend toward more "passive" funds for equity investments, where decisions are based upon a computer-based investment model that seeks to match the performance of the market as a whole. See also CORPORATE FINANCE.

inzō　　印相

(Skt: *mudrā*). Also known as *ingei* or *in*. In Buddhist art, the symbolic positioning of the hands, including objects held in the hands, which represent the contents of a Buddha's or bodhisattva's enlightenment, powers, or vows. An important part of the practice of esoteric Buddhism is to identify oneself with a particular enlightenment and receive its powers through the imitation of the *inzō*.

Ioffe (Joffe), Adolf Abramovich
ヨッフェ, A. A.

(1883–1927). Soviet diplomat active in negotiations with Japan. Known also as Victor Krymsky. Although born to wealth and educated as a physician, Ioffe became a Menshevik (a member of a moderate faction of the Russian Social Democratic Party) in 1903, and in 1917 he joined the more radical Bolsheviks. Following the Bolshevik Revolution, Ioffe was in charge of the peace negotiations with Germany at Brest-Litovsk in 1918 and became the first Soviet ambassador to Germany the same year. In early 1923 Ioffe took part in the negotiations between Japan and the Soviet FAR EASTERN REPUBLIC regarding the withdrawal of Japanese troops sent in the SIBERIAN INTERVENTION. He then traveled to Japan and opened informal preliminary negotiations with Foreign Minister Kawakami Toshitsune (1861–1935) seeking Japanese recognition of the USSR. Although no agreement was reached, he succeeded in improving Soviet-Japanese relations. Ioffe, who had supported Leon Trotsky, committed suicide when Joseph Stalin gained the upper hand in their intra-party struggle.

Iō Islands　　硫黄列島

(Iō Rettō). Also known as the Iwo Islands; known internationally as the Volcano Islands. They are part of the OGASAWARA ISLANDS. Located in the Pacific Ocean at latitude 24°–25° north, the three Iō Islands are Kita Iōjima, Naka Iōjima, and Minami Iōjima. Naka Iōjima, the largest, is usually called Iōjima (also known as Iwojima). It was the scene of fierce fighting between American and Japanese forces in World War II. Following a period of American rule, in 1968 these islands came under the jurisdiction of the Tōkyō prefectural government. Area: Kita Iōjima, 5.5 sq km (2.1 sq mi); Naka Iōjima, 22.4 sq km (8.65 sq mi); Minami Iōjima, 3.7 sq km (1.4 sq mi).

Iōjima　　硫黄島

Volcanic island, approximately 50 km (30 mi) south of the Satsuma Peninsula, Kagoshima Prefecture, southern Kyūshū. Part of Kagoshima Prefecture. Sulfur was mined from ancient times until 1964, hence the name "sulfur island." Today the chief activi-

ties are small-scale farming and fishing. Iōjima is believed to be the Kikaigashima to which the priest SHUNKAN was exiled in 1177. There is an island of the same name in the IŌ ISLANDS. Area: 11.7 sq km (4.5 sq mi).

Iōjima (Iwojima), Battle of
硫黄島作戦

(Iōjima Sakusen). Fiercely fought battle on the island of Iōjima (also known as Iwojima) during WORLD WAR II. The US forces were anxious to acquire Iōjima, part of the Iō Islands (also known as the Volcano Islands), as a base for flying escort missions for the B-29 bombing campaign against mainland Japan. They also hoped to use the island to effect a blockade of Japanese sea-lanes and to ensure the defense of primary US bomber bases in the Mariana Islands. Landing of the US forces began on 19 February 1945. The Japanese forces were commanded by General Kuribayashi Tadamichi. Casualties were high on both sides, and it was one of the fiercest battles in the Pacific War, lasting almost a month before the island was taken by the US forces.

Ionushi　　いほぬし

(The Hermit). Late-10th-century work attributed to the priest Zōki (fl ca 950–1000). It consists of three sections: (1) a lyrical account, containing 30 poems, of a pilgrimage to the KUMANO SANZAN SHRINES in the Kii Peninsula; (2) 43 poems on famous pilgrimage centers and scenic spots; (3) 50 poems with brief headnotes dealing chiefly with a journey through the province of Tōtōmi (now part of Shizuoka Prefecture). The reputation of the work rests largely on its first section, often referred to as *Kumano kikō* (Journey to Kumano). Among works in the genre of *kikō*, or poetic travel diaries in the vernacular, this part of the text is regarded as second in importance only to the *Tosa nikki* (Tosa Diary) of KI NO TSURAYUKI.

Ippen　　一遍

(1239–89). Founder of the JI SECT of PURE LAND BUDDHISM; known as a "wayfaring saint" (*yugyō shōnin*) and "a saint of abandonment" (*sute hijiri*), who emphasized the importance of reciting the name of the Buddha Amitābha (J: Amida Butsu; see NEMBUTSU) for salvation. Born to a prominent family in Iyo Province (now Ehime Prefecture) on Shikoku. His mother's death when he was 10 years old led him to become a Buddhist monk, taking the name Zuien. He first studied Tendai Buddhism at the monastery EN-RYAKUJI on Mt. Hiei, but, feeling unfulfilled, in 1251 went to Dazaifu in Kyūshū to study under Shōtatsu, a disciple of Shōkū (1177–1247), the founder of the Seizan branch of JŌDO SECT Buddhism. Changing his name to Chishin, he became a devout Pure Land Buddhist.

In 1263, upon the death of his father, he returned to his homeland. It is believed that he resumed a secular life, taking a wife. He renounced the world once again in 1271, however, and returned to Shōtatsu in Dazaifu before embarking on a series of extensive pilgrimages. He discovered that in the utterance of Amitābha's name all dualities dissolved: life and death, this world of desires and the afterworld—Amida's Pure Land of unsurpassed bliss. This conviction gave Ippen a profound sense of mission, and he spent the remainder of his life traveling throughout the country preaching the importance of reciting Amitābha's name. Thus was born the Ji sect, Ippen's unique religion,

Ippen This detail from a series of scrolls entitled *A Pictorial Biography of Monk Ippen* (1299) depicts shogunal regent Hōjō Tokimune refusing Ippen entrance into Kamakura.

combining Pure Land Buddhism with elements of Shingon Buddhism and folk Shintō that he had encountered in his travels.

In 1279 Ippen started preaching the "dancing *nembutsu*" in the manner of the Heian-period (794–1185) Pure Land monk KŪYA. His ecstatic dancing and preaching won a great popular following. In contrast to the teachings of SHINRAN, the founder of the Jōdo Shin sect, which centered around rebirth in the Pure Land and emphasized the believer's faith, Ippen's teaching of the ecstatic incantation of Amitābha's name focused on abandonment, entrusting oneself totally to the Buddha.

Ippitsusai Bunchō 一筆斎文調

(fl ca 1768–90). UKIYO-E artist active in Edo (now Tōkyō). A contemporary of HARUNOBU, Bunchō was one of the foremost innovators of full-color woodblock printing; he specialized in pictures of beautiful women and courtesans (*bijinga*) and actors (*yakusha-e*), in all of which he displayed great individual portrait realism. In 1770 he collaborated with KATSUKAWA SHUNSHŌ on a popular three-volume edition of fan-shaped actor portraits called *Ehon butai ōgi.*

Iragomisaki 伊良湖岬

Cape on western Atsumi Peninsula, southern Aichi Prefecture, central Honshū; part of Mikawa Bay Quasi-National Park. Noted for its coastal scenery consisting of towering rocks, especially a rock formation known as the Stone Gate of Hii.

Irako Seihaku 伊良子清白

(1877–1946). Poet and physician. Real name Irako Teruzō. Born in Tottori Prefecture; graduate of Kyōto Prefectural Medical School. He gained recognition as a TANKA poet around 1900, publishing in Tōkyō literary magazines thematically modern poems written in the classical language. His one collection, *Kujakubune* (1906, The Peacock Boat; repr 1929), displays a richly imaginative romanticism and was highly praised by the poets HINATSU KŌNOSUKE, KITAHARA HAKUSHŪ, and SAIJŌ YASO.

Iran and Japan イランと日本

(Iran *to* Nihon). Contact between Japan and Iran (then Persia) began in 1878 when the Japanese ambassador to Russia, ENOMOTO TAKEAKI, was received at St. Petersburg by King Nasr-ed-Din of the Kajar dynasty. However, formal diplomatic relations were not established until 1926. A treaty of amity was signed in 1939 and the two nations maintained cordial relations until 1942.

Iran declared war on Japan in March 1945, but diplomatic relations were restored in 1953. A cultural agreement was signed in 1957 and an economic and technological cooperation agreement in the following year. Japan's dependence on Iranian oil has contributed to the forging of strong economic ties between the two countries. In 1973 the Iran-Japan Petrochemical Co, a joint venture funded equally by the Mitsui group of Japan and the Iran Chemical Development Co, Ltd, was established. After investing ¥300 billion (US $1.4 billion in 1981 dollars), Mitsui withdrew from the project by mutual agreement in 1990 due to the consequences of the Iran-Iraq war. Since the conclusion of the war in August 1988, Japanese exporters to Iran have found an increasingly important market in the nation's reconstruction program. In 1990 Japan's exports to Iran totaled

US $1.6 billion and its imports, chiefly petroleum, US $3.5 billion.

irezumi → tattoos

iriai 入会

(literally, "to enter collectively"). A term referring to the time-honored system of collective ownership of nonarable or "mountain" (*yama*) areas and of offshore fisheries in Japan before the Meiji period (1868–1912). Collective ownership entailed the sharing of these natural resources. Mountain areas included such lands as forests, marshes, bamboo groves, and dry riverbeds. They were open to all rural inhabitants who possessed entry rights and who observed the rigid regulations for collecting their portion of its resources: grass, foliage, and other vegetation used for fodder, fertilizer, and thatch, as well as edible plants, roots, and firewood. The right to enter, called *iriaiken*, was jealously guarded by the collective.

Types of Iriai—Various types of *iriai* were distinguished according to ownership. In *murajū iriai*, an area was owned and controlled collectively by the population of a single village. *Mura mura iriai*, the collective ownership by the inhabitants of several neighboring villages, was the most common form of *iriai* in the late Edo period (1600–1868). In this type of *iriai*, the collectively owned land was designated as *iriaichi*. Other forms of *iriai* holdings in the Edo period included mountain districts owned either by the domainal or shogunal government or by private persons. The former was called *han'yūchi iriai* and the latter *shiyūchi (jitsukiyama) iriai*. The use of government or privately owned mountain sites required the payment of fees, known variously as *yama yakugin* or *yama yakuei*.

The Origins of Iriai—Before the TAIKA REFORM of 645, collective ownership and utilization of both agricultural and other types of land resources was predominant. Thus both arable and nonarable land resources were managed collectively by local farming communities organized hierarchically. No individual claims had yet been laid to the exclusive ownership or use of the land.

After the Taika Reform, following the Chinese example, the central government proclaimed public ownership of all rice-producing land in the nation. It subsequently distributed this land to able-bodied peasants in return for taxes. Under this new system, the cultivators never enjoyed exclusive ownership of the land they occupied but instead possessed the exclusive right to use it (see HANDEN SHŪJU SYSTEM). Land not cultivated for rice remained outside the control of public

authority, and local communities continued to use its resources.

After about the 10th century the weakened central government in the capital city (Kyōto) could not prevent noble families and powerful religious organizations from illicitly appropriating its landholdings. This absorption of public land by private interests gave rise to the SHŌEN system. Rice land was taken over by groups of individuals or organizations, such as temples and shrines, which in turn claimed a certain portion of the harvest from these estates as income. The local inhabitants, now incorporated into *shōen* units, could still utilize the mountain resources.

Edo and Meiji Periods—During the Edo period the amount of land used for agriculture increased, as did the demand for the resources from mountain areas. Disputes over the use of these lands also increased and were often resolved by governmental intervention to decide whether the land belonged to a claimant or was to be held in common.

After the MEIJI RESTORATION of 1868 the government established a modern landholding system. In the 1870s it formally recognized private ownership of land resources and conferred land titles to protect the properties of legitimate title holders. As for resources under collective management, the government usually classified those designated as *iriaichi* during the Edo period as "public" domain and seized them to enrich its coffers.

It is important to note here that when conflicts arose, the Meiji government often neglected the welfare of the actual cultivators by giving preferential treatment to powerful rural landholders. For example, it often accepted claims filed by litigants who could provide some form of legal documentation, while it usually rejected claims filed by poor cultivators who could not submit any written documents. It may be argued, then, that the Meiji government's land policy promoted the concentration of landholdings, a tendency that was to create serious socioeconomic problems in the late 19th century and the first half of the 20th century.

Irie Takako 入江たか子

(1911–). Film actress. Real name Higashibōjō Hideko. Born in Tōkyō. In the 1930s Irie became a popular star of NIKKATSU CORPORATION films. She starred in several of director MIZOGUCHI KENJI's films, including *Taki no Shiraito* (1933, Taki no Shiraito, the Water Magician). In later years she starred in mysteries such as *Kaidan Saga yashiki* (1953,

Iriomote National Park This maritime park is home to diverse subtropical vegetation and wildlife.
1 The decorated roofs and black coral walls on the island of Take-tomijima create a tropical atmosphere.
2 Mangrove swamps at the mouth of the river Nakamagawa on Iriomotejima contain *suōnoki*, or *sappan* trees. Their strangely shaped roots were once used to make boat rudders.

Ghostly Tales from Saga Mansion) and *Kai-byō Arima goten* (1953, The Ghostly Cat at Arima Castle).

Iriomotejima   西表島

Island approximately 440 km (270 mi) southwest of Okinawa. The largest island of the YAEYAMA ISLANDS, it is hilly, with mountains averaging 400 m (1,310 ft) high. Some 96 percent of the island is covered with subtropical forests, and mangroves flourish at the mouths of the rivers. The island is the habitat of the Iriomote *yamaneko* (see WILDCATS), a wildcat unique to the island. The island has been developed as a tourist area in recent years. Part of IRIOMOTE NATIONAL PARK. Area: 284 sq km (110 sq mi).

Iriomote National Park   西表国立公園

(Iriomote Kokuritsu Kōen). Situated in the YAEYAMA ISLANDS, in the RYŪKYŪ ISLANDS chain, 1,000 km (620 mi) southwest of Kyūshū. The major part of the park is on the hilly island of IRIOMOTEJIMA, and it includes the small islands of Kobamajima, Kuroshima, and TAKETOMIJIMA and their surrounding waters to the east of Iriomotejima. The two islands of Kobamajima and Taketomijima are situated in the largest coral reef in Japan, which measures 20 km (12.4 mi) east to west and 15 km (9.3 mi) north to south. The park has dense subtropical forests and vegetation, poisonous snakes, rare butterflies, and mangrove swamps. In 1965 a species of wildcat (Iriomote *yamaneko;* see WILDCATS) was discovered on Iriomotejima. Land area: 125 sq km (48 sq mi).

Iriomote yamaneko → wildcats

irises   菖蒲・杜若

(*ayame; kakitsubata*). Perennial herbs of the family Iridaceae, genus *Iris*, many of which are indigenous to Japan and frequently cultivated as ornamentals. Among the best-known iris species in Japan is the *ayame* (*Iris sanguinea* or *I. sibirica* var. *orientalis*), which is common in fields and on mountains from Hokkaidō to Honshū and Kyūshū as well as in eastern Siberia and northeastern China. It grows 30–50 centimeters (12–20 in) high. The purple flower, 7–8 centimeters (3 in) across, usually opens early in summer at the top of the stem. Cultivated varieties include the white-flowered *shiroayame*, the *kuru-maayame* with large inner petals (standards),

and the *chaboayame*, a small plant with a purple or white flower. Until the Heian period (794–1185) the name *ayame* was used to refer to the plant now known as SHŌBU, or sweet flag (*Acorus calamus* var. *asiaticus*). *Shōbu* is often translated as "iris," but the plant is not an iris and should not be confused with the *hanashōbu*, which is.

The *hanashōbu* (*Iris ensata* var. *ensata*) averages 60–80 centimeters (24–32 in) in height. It grows in clusters. The leaves are sword-shaped and prominently veined. In early summer violet, white, and violet-white variegated flowers bloom, with a diameter of 8–24 centimeters (3–9 in). The *nohanashōbu* (*I. ensata* f. *spontanea*) is the mother species. At present there are approximately 500 varieties of *hanashōbu*.

The *kakitsubata* (*I. laevigata*) has long been cultivated, but it also grows wild in moist places in various parts of Japan as well as in Korea, northern China, and eastern Siberia. It reaches a height of 50–70 centimeters (20–28 in). The leaves are sword-shaped or broad and linear, with pointed tips but without conspicuous midribs. Early in summer two to three dark bluish purple flowers, 12 centimeters (5 in) across, open at the top of the stem. The flowers consist of wide drooping outer petals (falls), yellow at the center bottom, and erect inner petals (standards).

The *shaga* (*I. japonica*) grows wild in large colonies on moist wooded slopes all over Japan and is also widely cultivated. The bright green leaves, which develop in two rows from a shallow rhizome, are swordlike and glossy. Around May a flower stalk (scape) produces light bluish white flowers 5–6 centimeters (2–2.5 in) across with distinctive yellow spots and a crest-shaped projection in the center of the toothed outer petals. The flowers wither after blooming for one day.

A miniature species called *himeshaga* (*I. gracilipes*) grows in fields and mountains and is also cultivated. It has light purple or, more rarely, white flowers.

Iroha jirui shō   色葉字類抄

A Japanese-language dictionary compiled in the late Heian period (794–1185) by the courtier Tachibana no Tadakane (fl late 12th century). A 2-volume version and a 3-volume version exist. This dictionary classifies the standard vocabulary of the period into 47 divisions according to the traditional *iroha* syllabic alphabet (see IROHA POEM), further

subdividing the contents according to meaning and supplying the Chinese characters (KANJI) used to write the word and examples of usage. It considerably influenced later dictionaries. Another work with the same name dating from the Kamakura period (1185–1333) is a 10-volume expansion of the former work. See also DICTIONARIES.

iroha karuta   伊呂波カルタ

A simple recognition game based on 47 of the 48 written symbols of the Japanese phonetic syllabary (see KANA), using cards printed with pictures and proverbs. (The omitted symbol is that for syllable-final *n;* most sets have a 48th card using the Chinese character for *kyō*, or capital.) The name derives from the first three syllables of an older traditional arrangement of the *kana* syllabary (*i-ro-ha* and so on; see IROHA POEM) and the Japanese transliteration of the Portuguese word for card (*carta*). There are 96 cards divided into two equal sets, one for "reading" and one for "taking." On each card of the reading set is a proverb that begins with a particular syllable, while on each of the taking set is a single syllable written in cursive script (*hiragana*) and a picture illustrating the proverb that begins with that syllable. The picture cards are spread in front of the players on the floor. One person reads the proverb cards in random order. The object of the game is to spot and seize the corresponding picture card as the proverb is being read. The player holding the most cards at the end of the game wins. Invented in Kyōto around 1850, *iroha karuta* is a children's game with educational overtones, teaching the alphabet and traditional wisdom as well. See also PLAYING CARDS.

iroha poem   伊呂波歌

(*iroha uta*). Poem dating from the Heian period (794–1185) made up of 47 characters of the phonetic KANA syllabary, excluding only the 48th (for syllable-final *n*). It has traditionally been ascribed to the Buddhist monk KŪKAI.

In the *iroha* poem the signs are arranged in the following order:

i	ro	ha	ni	ho	he	to	chi	ri	nu
ru	(w)o	wa	ka	yo	ta	re	so	tsu	ne
na	ra	mu	u	(w)i	no	o	ku	ya	ma
ke	fu	ko	e	te	a	sa	ki	yu	me
mi	shi	(w)e	hi	mo	se	su			

The poem is read (with voicing of some consonants) in modern pronunciation as:

Iro wa nioedo chirinuru o
Waga yo tare zo tsune naran
Ui no okuyama kyō koete
Asaki yume miji ei mo sezu

This can be roughly translated as:

The colors blossom, scatter, and fall.
In this world of ours, who lasts forever?
Today let us cross over the remote
mountains of life's illusions,
And dream no more shallow dreams nor
succumb to drunkenness.

The *iroha* poem was used to organize
words in dictionaries, though the chart
known as the GOJŪON ZU is now more frequently used.

Irohazaka いろは坂

Popular name for two toll roads in NIKKŌ NA-
TIONAL PARK, western Tochigi Prefecture, central Honshū. The roads ascend a towering
ridge from Umagaeshi near the city of Nikkō
to the vicinity of Lake Chūzenji. The name
Irohazaka is derived from the fact that the
two roads have a total of 48 hairpin curves,
the same number as the *iroha* arrangement of
the Japanese *kana* syllabary (see IROHA
POEM). The descending road (6.5 km; 4 mi)
has 28 hairpin curves, while the ascending
road (9.5 km; 6 mi) has 20 hairpin curves.

Irokawa Takehiro 色川武大

(1929–89). Novelist. Born in Tōkyō. Irokawa
received the Naoki Prize for *Rikon* (1978,
Divorce). Other serious works include
Hyaku (1982, One Hundred) and the Yomiuri Literary Prize–winning *Kyōjin nikki*
(1988, Diary of a Madman). He also published popular fiction, such as *Mājan hōrōki*
(1969–74), Memories of a Mah-Jongg
Tramp), under the pen name Asada Tetsuya.

iron and steel 鉄鋼

(*tekkō*). Iron has been known in Japan since
ancient times. In about AD 300 various kinds
of ironware and an iron-making process
were introduced from China, by way of
Korea, and iron production began on a very
small scale. Primitive forms of the *tatara*
iron- and steel-making process (see TATARA-
BUKI) were in use by the Nara period (710–
794), and variations of the process were
widely used until the beginning of the Meiji
period (1868–1912), when modern European
processes using the blast furnace were introduced into Japan.

The *tatara* process used iron sand instead
of iron ore, and iron made by this process
was in great demand for the manufacture of
arms and agricultural implements. The high
quality of iron sand found in Japan helps
account for the excellent metallurgical properties of the traditional Japanese sword.
Using different grades of steel made by the
tatara process, Japanese swordsmiths developed a complex system of layering, folding,
differential cooling, and forging that created
composite blades of extreme hardness and
sharpness (see SWORDS).

In 1896 a government enterprise, the
YAWATA IRON AND STEEL WORKS, was established to form the foundation of the modern
steel industry. By 1912 the private enterprises that are now known as SUMITOMO METAL
INDUSTRIES, LTD; KŌBE STEEL, LTD; the KAWASAKI
STEEL CORPORATION; and the NKK CORPORATION
had been organized. In 1934 Nippon Steel
was established as a national company. After
World War II, this company was broken up
into Yawata Steel and Fuji Steel. In March
1970 these two companies were again amal-

gamated as the NIPPON STEEL CORPORATION. In
the 1970s and 1980s Japan aggressively developed its steel-making industry and became a major steel-exporting country. See
also IRON AND STEEL INDUSTRY.

iron and steel industry 鉄鋼業

(*tekkōgyō*). Modern iron-making techniques
and steel production began in Japan in 1901
with the opening of the state-owned
YAWATA IRON AND STEEL WORKS, an integrated
steel plant. Later, private steel makers such
as KŌBE STEEL, LTD, and a branch factory of
Kawasaki Shipyard Co began production,
but they used separate pig-iron and steel
production operations rather than integrated techniques. The worldwide economic
crisis in 1929 spurred debate in Japan over
amalgamation of public and private steel
companies as a means of increasing the international competitiveness of the industry.
In 1933 the Nippon Steel Co Law was
passed, and in 1934 state-owned Yawata
was combined with six private companies to
form Nippon Steel. The goal was to expand
the use of integrated production techniques,
but most of the private steel makers did not
participate. Japan's maximum yearly production of crude steel prior to the end of
World War II was 7.7 million tons in 1943;
this was 9.5 percent of US production for the
same year.

Postwar Growth—Following the war,
Nippon Steel was broken up into Yawata
Steel and Fuji Steel, and intense competition
developed within the industry. Supported
by rapid economic growth, production facilities were expanded, and Japan became the
world's largest steel-exporting nation.

A new Nippon Steel was created in 1970
through the merger of Yawata Steel and Fuji
Steel, and today the five major Japanese steel
producers are NIPPON STEEL CORPORATION,
KAWASAKI STEEL CORPORATION, NKK CORPORA-
TION, SUMITOMO METAL INDUSTRIES, LTD, and
Kōbe Steel. Although Nippon Steel is a descendant of the government-owned Yawata
Iron and Steel Works, the other four companies have been private steel makers since
their inceptions. The product breakdown for
fiscal 1990 production was pig iron, 80.9 million tons; crude steel, 111.7 million tons; carbon steel products, 91.5 million tons; alloy
steel products, 20.2 million tons; and ferro-
alloy, 1.2 million tons.

The Japanese steel industry is totally dependent on imports of iron ore and coal, but
it has maintained its international competitiveness through a high-quality labor force
and the implementation of new production

facilities and technology. In 1991 Nippon
Steel was the largest producer of crude steel
in the world outside the Soviet Union, and 4
of the world's top 10 companies were Japanese.

Problems and Prospects—Although
Japan remains a key steel-exporting country,
VOLUNTARY EXPORT RESTRICTIONS to the United
States (begun in 1969), the rise in value of the
yen, the increase in domestic demand, and
the increase in steel production by China and
the newly industrializing economies of
Southeast Asia have led to decreases in the
quantity and monetary value of Japan's steel
exports. In response to this trend many of the
steel companies are restructuring through
diversification into such new businesses as
electronics, biotechnology, and new-materi-
als development.

irori 囲炉裏

Open wood-burning hearth found in traditional Japanese-style houses (MINKA). *Irori*
were usually square in shape, about 1 meter
(3.28 ft) on a side, and sunk into the floor.
In addition to its functions as a heating and
lighting device, the *irori* was also used for
cooking: an iron kettle was suspended over
it with a device called a JIZAIKAGI. A shelf was
often built above the *irori*, allowing its heat
to be used for drying foods as well. At meal-

irises Several species
of iris grow wild in
Japan, and many more
are cultivated as
ornamentals.
1 *Hanashōbu* at the
Heian Shrine, Kyōto.
The shrine's garden
contains more than 200
of the some 500
varieties of this species.
2 The *hanashōbu*.
3 *Ayame*. This species is
also cultivated in white-
flowered varieties.
4 The *kakitsubata* was
the earliest known of the
irises among the
Japanese; its juice was
used as a dye in
ancient times.

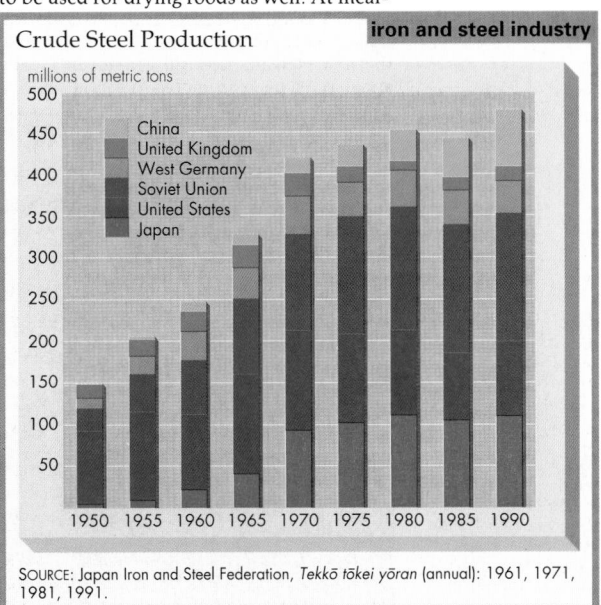

Crude Steel Production — iron and steel industry

millions of metric tons

China
United Kingdom
West Germany
Soviet Union
United States
Japan

1950 1955 1960 1965 1970 1975 1980 1985 1990

SOURCE: Japan Iron and Steel Federation, *Tekkō tōkei yōran* (annual): 1961, 1971,
1981, 1991.

Ise-Shima National Park The "Wedded Rocks" off Futamigaura beach. The sacred nature of the two rocks is indicated by the ropes linking them and by the Shintō gate (*torii*) at the pinnacle of the larger one.

time and when guests came the *irori* was the center of household activity. The seating arrangement around it was strictly prescribed: specific seats were reserved for the head of the household, his wife, other family members, and guests. With the introduction of electricity and modern methods of heating to Japan, the *irori* fell almost entirely out of use.

Irōzaki 石廊崎

Cape on southern Izu Peninsula, Shizuoka Prefecture, central Honshū; part of Fuji-Hakone-Izu National Park. It ends with a large sea cliff and fantastically shaped rocks that rise above the sea. Tourist attractions include a lighthouse and Ishimuro Shrine.

Iruma 入間[市]

City in southern Saitama Prefecture, central Honshū. A prosperous market center and post-station town in the Edo period (1600–1868), Iruma has long been famous for its tea. It is rapidly being urbanized, with textile and brewing industries. A former US military base is now used by the Self Defense Force. Pop: 137,585.

Irwin, Robert Walker
アーウィン, R. W.

(1844–1925). American businessman and diplomatic representative of the Kingdom of Hawaii in Japan. Born in Pennsylvania. Irwin went to Japan in 1866 to work for the trading firm of Walsh, Hall and Co; in 1876 he joined the MITSUI company. He was later appointed the first Hawaiian consul general in Japan, and, having been promoted to special envoy,

irori A traditional *irori* hearth, set for guests. At one time widely used in country households for cooking as well as heating, the *irori* has virtually disappeared from daily life in Japan.

in 1884 he negotiated the first formal immigration treaty between Hawaii and Japan. He ensured that Japanese immigrants were transported safely and given jobs on the sugar plantations of Hawaii. In 1900 he established the Taiwan Seitō Co, a sugar refinery in Taiwan. Irwin became a naturalized Japanese citizen and was awarded the Order of the Rising Sun and the Order of the Sacred Treasure by the Japanese government.

Isahaya 諫早[市]

City in southern Nagasaki Prefecture, Kyūshū. A former castle town, the city is the terminus of several railways and national highways. Rice is grown on reclaimed land. Commerce and industry, particularly the metal industries, flourish. Tourist attractions include Isahaya Park. Pop: 90,683.

Isawa 石和[町]

Town in central Yamanashi Prefecture, central Honshū, on the river Fuefukigawa. In the Edo period (1600–1868) Isawa was a post-station town on the highway Kōshū Kaidō. Products include grapes, peaches, and persimmons. The Isawa Hot Spring is located here. Pop: 21,809.

Ise 伊勢

(ca 877–938). Court lady and classical (WAKA) poet. Her real name is unknown. Ise was the name of a province of which her father, Fujiwara no Tsugikage, was governor, and it became her sobriquet when she was a lady-in-waiting at court. She is thought to have entered the service of Empress Onshi, consort of Emperor Uda (867–931; r 887–897), around 892. She caught the eye of the emperor and later became a favorite of his fourth son, Prince Atsuyoshi, to whom she bore a daughter, known as Lady Nakatsukasa, who became a famous poet in her own right. One of the Thirty-Six Poetic Geniuses (SANJŪROKKASEN), Ise and ONO NO KOMACHI rank as the two most accomplished women poets of the late 9th and early 10th centuries. The compilers of the first imperial anthology of Japanese classical poetry, the KOKINSHŪ, included 22 of Ise's poems. Seventy are contained in the second imperial anthology, GOSEN WAKASHŪ. Her personal anthology is entitled *Iseshū*.

Ise 伊勢[市]

Formerly Uji-Yamada. City in southeastern Mie Prefecture, central Honshū. The site of ISE SHRINE, it welcomes thousands of pilgrims and tourists every year. Ise is also a commercial city, with electrical-appliance and textile industries and shipyards in the Ōminato district. Numerous educational and cultural facilities as well as shrines affiliated with the

Ise Shrine are located here. Ise is part of the Ise-Shima National Park. Pop: 104,164.

Ise Bay 伊勢湾

(Ise Wan). Inlet of the Pacific Ocean, on the coast of Mie and Aichi prefectures, central Honshū. Extends from the Atsumi Peninsula on the east to the Shima Peninsula on the west. In addition to Nagoya to the north, various industrial and fishing ports are located on this bay. In recent years the fishing industry has declined due to expanding industrialization. The bay includes the Ise-Shima National Park and the Mikawa Bay Quasi-National Park.

Ise ebi 伊勢海老

(Japanese spiny lobster). *Palinurus japonicus*. A large crustacean of the family Palinuridae, it reaches a length of some 35 centimeters (14 in). The Ise *ebi*, which lives among rocks in water 10 to 30 meters (33 to 99 ft) deep, is found along the Pacific coast from the Kantō region in central Honshū to Kyūshū and Taiwan. It has through the centuries been considered a symbol of long life and thus an appropriate food to serve on occasions of celebration. It may be prepared raw and served as *sashimi*, steamed, or grilled whole in the shell.

Isehara 伊勢原[市]

City in central Kanagawa Prefecture, central Honshū. Isehara developed around the Afuri Shrine on the mountain Ōyama. Today plants produce auto parts and electrical appliances. Pop: 89,567.

Iseki & Co, Ltd 井関農機[株]

(Iseki Nōki). Manufacturer of agricultural machinery and garden equipment. Founded in 1926. It designs, manufactures, and markets in four principal categories: tractors and tilling machinery, rice transplanters, harvesting machinery such as combine harvesters, and other agricultural implements. Iseki products are exported to over 50 countries. The company operates six overseas subsidiaries and affiliates located in Australia, Belgium, the United Kingdom, and other countries. Sales for the fiscal year ending November 1990 totaled ¥121.0 billion (US $937.4 million), of which approximately 10 percent came from export sales, and capitalization was ¥22.5 billion (US $174.3 million). Headquarters are in Tōkyō.

Ise monogatari 伊勢物語

(Tales of Ise). Mid-10th-century collection of some 125 brief lyrical episodes (variant texts range from 110 to 140 or more episodes), combining elements of prose and poetry of anonymous authorship. It is the oldest of the *uta monogatari* (collections of short tales built around one or more poems). Familiarity with the *Ise monogatari* and the KOKINSHŪ (ca 905, Collection from Ancient and Modern Times) was indispensable for well-bred courtiers in the late Heian period (794–1185).

The *Ise monogatari* collection is probably based upon the *Narihira kashū* (Narihira Collection) by the 9th-century poet ARIWARA NO NARIHIRA, to whom authorship of the collection was traditionally ascribed. It also contains materials from other sources and popular traditions, all woven into an organic whole. The theory that Narihira was the author is no longer accepted, but to some extent the collection gives the impression of being a quasi-biography of this famous poet, emphasizing his love adventures. The most reliable manuscript is the *Den Teika*

◀Aerial view showing the current Inner Shrine buildings and the adjacent empty lot in which they will be rebuilt as part of a rite carried out every 20 years.

▼ One of the two treasure repositories of the Outer Shrine. Its simple design is believed to derive from that of the granaries and storehouses of prehistoric Japan.

hitsu hon, one of three versions going back to a handwritten copy made by FUJIWARA NO SADAIE.

The *Ise monogatari* exerted a tremendous influence upon later Japanese literature and art. The first part of the YAMATO MONOGATARI consists of short stories centered around poems similar to the *Ise monogatari,* from which it uses material. Other important *monogatari* influenced by the *Ise monogatari* are the UTSUBO MONOGATARI, *Genji monogatari* (see TALE OF GENJI), and KONJAKU MONOGATARI. Four Nō plays have plots inspired by the *Ise monogatari: Unrin'in, Kakitsubata, Izutsu,* and *Oshio.* In the Edo period (1600–1868) several authors wrote imitations of it, such as the *Nise monogatari* (Imitation Tales) ascribed by some to KARASUMARU MITSUHIRO.

Picture scrolls (*emakimono*) were made to illustrate various episodes of the *Ise monogatari.* In the Edo period an enormous number of printed editions with illustrations appeared as early as 1608. An especially beautiful album of paintings based on the *Ise monogatari* was done by the early-Edo-period artist Tawaraya SŌTATSU. See also MONOGATARI BUNGAKU.

Ise Plain 伊勢平野

(Ise Heiya). Located in Mie Prefecture, central Honshū, with Ise Bay on the east. These alluvial and diluvial plains, where rice, tea, and tobacco are cultivated, have long been a rich agricultural region. The major cities are Yokkaichi, part of the Chūkyō Industrial Zone; Tsu; Matsusaka; and Ise. Length: 80 km (50 mi); width: 15 km (9 mi).

Ise Province 伊勢国

(Ise no Kuni; also called Seishū). One of the 15 provinces of the Tōkaidō (Eastern Sea Circuit) in central Honshū; established under the KOKUGUN SYSTEM in 646, at which time it comprised most of what is now Mie Prefecture. In ancient times much of its land was owned by Shintō shrines, the largest and most important of which was the ISE SHRINE in Uji-Yamada (now the city of Ise). In the late Heian period (794–1185) it was the home base of a branch of the TAIRA FAMILY, and at the end of the Muromachi period (1333–1568) ODA NOBUNAGA controlled it. In the Edo period (1600–1868) it was divided into seven *daimyō* domains (HAN). In 1871 Ise was combined with Iga and Shima provinces to form Watarai and Anotsu prefectures, and in 1876 these two prefectures became MIE PREFECTURE.

Ise Rebellion 伊勢暴動

(Ise Bōdō). Peasant uprising on 18 December 1876 in the Ise district of Mie Prefecture; the largest of several uprisings against the new Meiji government, protesting the LAND TAX REFORM OF 1873–1881. The land tax had previously been assessed as a fixed percentage of crops, but in 1873 the government established a system requiring cash payment of the assessed value of land. Taxes increased in some cases, and the rate remained constant regardless of good or bad harvests. In the Ise district over 50,000 dissatisfied peasants attacked prefectural offices. Violence spread to the neighboring prefectures of Aichi and Gifu. Though the rioting was suppressed by late December, the government was persuaded to reduce the land tax.

Isesaki 伊勢崎[市]

City in southeastern Gumma Prefecture, central Honshū. Known for its silk, called Isesaki *meisen.* Textiles, machinery, and electrical and communications equipment are made here. Pop: 115,938.

Ise-Shima National Park 伊勢志摩国立公園

(Ise-Shima Kokuritsu Kōen). Situated in central Honshū on the SHIMA PENINSULA, Mie Prefecture, this maritime park, encompassing the hilly hinterland of the peninsula and its surrounding coastal waters, is characterized by a heavily indented coastline that features numerous small bays and islets. The two main cities are ISE (famed for the ancient ISE SHRINE), lying at the northern edge of the park, and TOBA, a port to its east, which is the center of the Mikimoto pearl industry. Between the two cities is FUTAMIGAURA beach, with its "Wedded Rocks" (Meotoiwa), which are two sacred rocks linked by ropes. In the south of the peninsula is AGO BAY, a fishing and pearl cultivation center. The women divers (*ama*) employed by the pearl industry are a major tourist attraction of the park. Land area: 555 sq km (214 sq mi).

Ise Shintō → Watarai Shintō

Ise Shrine 伊勢神宮

(Ise Jingū). One of the most important Shintō shrines. Located in the city of Ise in Mie Pre-

▲ The imperial representative leaving the Inner Shrine after ceremonies performed as part of the annual Kannamesai rite, when the new rice crop is dedicated.

fecture and comprising the Inner Shrine (Kō Taijingū or Naikū) and the Outer Shrine (Toyouke [also called Toyuke] Daijingū or Gekū), with other affiliated shrines. Beginning in the 10th century, Ise became a popular pilgrimage site. Since then, strong ties have been formed between the Ise Shrine and the Japanese people.

Inner Shrine——The Inner Shrine is said to date from the 3rd century and to enshrine AMATERASU ŌMIKAMI, the mythical ancestor of the imperial family, who is represented by the sacred mirror (*yata no kagami*), one of the three IMPERIAL REGALIA. According to legend, Princess YAMATOHIME, daughter of the emperor Suinin, traveled throughout the country in search of an eternal resting place for the sacred mirror. At Ise, she heard the voice of Amaterasu Ōmikami, saying, "This is a good place, and I would like to stay here." The princess thereupon built a shrine for the goddess.

The main building of the Inner Shrine is designed in a special form of *shimmei-zukuri* architectural style (see SHINTŌ ARCHITECTURE) that is prohibited for other shrines. The shrine is razed and rebuilt every 20 years in a rite called *shikinen sengū.* The most important rite at the shrine is the Kannamesai in October, when the new rice crop is dedicated; other rites include the Toshigoi no Matsuri, to pray for a rich harvest, and Tsukinamisai, conducted every month.

The preparation of food offered to the deities follows ancient practices. Fire for cooking is made by rubbing sticks of wood, food is grown in special places, and earthenware vessels are made in a special shrine kiln and thrown away after one use.

Outer Shrine——The Outer Shrine is said to date from the late 5th century and to enshrine Toyouke (Toyuke) no Ōkami, the god of food, clothing, and housing. It also is razed and reconstructed at regular intervals.

The Cult of Ise Shrine——Ise Shrine has long had a special significance for the Japanese. It is mentioned in the 8th-century poetry anthology, the MAN'YŌSHŪ. During the 15th century *oshi* (lower-ranking clerics of the shrine) went around the provinces proselytizing, collecting funds, and preaching the benefits of visiting Ise, adding that seven pilgrimages ensured salvation. Ise *kō* (see KŌ), or associations for pilgrimages to the shrine, were formed in various provinces. In the more secularized modern period, Ise Shrine is significant more for its literary and historic associations and for its architecture than as a place of worship.

Isetan Co, Ltd   [株]伊勢丹

(Isetan). Department store in the Tōkyō Metropolitan Area with five retail stores, as well as nine overseas outlets. Its predecessor, Iseya Tanji Dry Goods, was founded in 1886. Established in its present form in 1930, Isetan achieved success by anticipating the emergence of Tōkyō's Shinjuku district as an important urban center and by developing market research geared toward the age and sex of its customers. Sales for the fiscal year ending March 1991 totaled ¥430.9 billion (US \$3.1 billion), of which the sale of clothing constituted 47 percent; food products, 16 percent; accessories, 9 percent; sundry goods, 12 percent; household goods, 9 percent; and other products, 7 percent. In the same year capitalization stood at ¥34.6 billion (US \$252.2 million). Headquarters are in Tōkyō.

isharyō→solatium

Ishibashi Masashi   石橋政嗣

(1924–   ). Politician. Born in the city of Taibei (Taipei; J: Taihoku) in Taiwan, then a Japanese colony. Ishibashi graduated from the Taibei Economics Professional School in 1944. In 1955 he was elected to the House of Representatives from Nagasaki Prefecture as a candidate of the left faction of the JAPAN SOCIALIST PARTY. He served as the party's secretary-general under the chairmanship of NARITA TOMOMI for seven years from 1970. In 1983 he became the ninth chairman of the party. After the July 1986 election Ishibashi resigned as chairman. He retired from politics in 1990.

Ishibashi Museum of Art
石橋美術館

(Ishibashi Bijutsukan). Museum founded in 1956 in the city of Kurume, Fukuoka Prefecture. The museum's collection of modern Japanese Western-style paintings (YŌGA) originally belonged to ISHIBASHI SHŌJIRŌ, founder of Bridgestone Corporation, and contains approximately 500 items. The collection focuses on artists from Kyūshū—such as AOKI SHIGERU, SAKAMOTO HANJIRŌ, KOGA HARUE, KURODA SEIKI, and FUJISHIMA TAKEJI—who have made major contributions to the development of modern painting in Japan.

Ishibashi Ningetsu   石橋忍月

(1865–1926). Literary critic and novelist. Real name Ishibashi Tomokichi. Born in Fukuoka Prefecture; graduate of Tōkyō University. He contributed literary criticism to *Kokumin no tomo,* an influential magazine of the 1890s. His methodical approach to criticism based on Aristotelian aesthetics stimulated Meiji literature and criticism. Originally trained in German law, he worked as an attorney in his later years. His son, YAMAMOTO KENKICHI, is a contemporary critic. Ishibashi's criticism is collected in *Ishibashi Ningetsu hyōron shū* (1939).

Ishibashi Shōjirō   石橋正二郎

(1889–1976). Businessman and founder of the tire manufacturer BRIDGESTONE CORPORATION. Born in Fukuoka Prefecture. Ishibashi expanded his family's footwear (see TABI) business through mass production of inexpensive goods. He established the Bridgestone Corporation in 1931. The company prospered during World War II because of mounting demand from the military. In 1950 he signed a contract for technical cooperation with the Goodyear Tire and Rubber Co of the United States, greatly improving the quality of domestically manufactured tires. A famous art collector, Ishibashi established the BRIDGESTONE MUSEUM OF ART in 1952 and the ISHIBASHI MUSEUM OF ART in 1956.

Ishibashi Tanzan   石橋湛山

(1884–1973). Journalist, Keynesian economist, and politician who held postwar cabinet posts and was briefly prime minister. Born in Tōkyō, he graduated from Waseda University. He wrote for magazines and newspapers, including *Waseda bungaku, Tōkyō mainichi shimbun,* and TŌYŌ KEIZAI SHIMPŌ. He was an outspoken critic of the militarists during the 1930s. After World War II, he joined the Liberal Party (Nihon Jiyūtō) and served as finance minister (1946). He was barred from office (1947–51) by the OCCUPATION PURGE but later served as minister of international trade and industry

in the HATOYAMA ICHIRŌ cabinet (1954). He became prime minister in 1956 but resigned after two months because of illness. After regaining his health he devoted himself to normalizing relations between Japan and the People's Republic of China.

Ishibutai tomb   石舞台古墳

(Ishibutai *kofun*). A 7th-century mounded tomb (KOFUN) located in Asuka, Nara Prefecture; believed to be that of SOGA NO UMAKO, a powerful figure at the YAMATO COURT. The tomb originally consisted of a square earthen platform, about 50 meters (164 ft) to a side, possibly topped by a round earthen mound and surrounded by a wide moat. Gradual erosion exposed the ceiling rocks of the corridor-type stone burial chamber embedded within, thus giving the tomb its name, meaning "rock platform." Excavated in 1933 by HAMADA KŌSAKU, the chamber interior measures 7.7 meters (25.3 ft) long, 3.4 meters (11.2 ft) wide, and 4.8 meters (15.7 ft) high; the larger of the two ceiling rocks weighs 77 metric tons (84.7 short tons).

Ishida Baigan   石田梅岩

(1685–1744). Religious and moral teacher; founder of the SHINGAKU movement. Born in a farming village in Tamba Province (now part of Kyōto Prefecture), he spent his youth working on the family farm and became deeply interested in Shintō. He went to Kyōto to preach, and, despite an early lack of success, he continued studying Neo-Confucianism, Shintō, and Buddhism while working at a merchant house. At age 45 he opened his own lecture hall and eventually built a substantial following. Baigan's doctrines were called Shingaku ("Heart Learning"). He preached in terms of "heart" and "knowing the nature." The purpose of devotion was to overcome one's "selfish heart," thereby discovering one's "true heart." This meant realizing that conventional morality (as epitomized by Confucius' Five Relationships) was completely natural and in accord with the laws of the universe.

Baigan's disciples included Saitō Zemmon (1700–1761), Kimura Shigemitsu (1703–56), and TESHIMA TOAN (1718–86). Toan proved to be the most successful in propagating his teacher's beliefs. Baigan's principal writings are *Tohi mondō,* a four-volume catechism based on his lectures, completed in 1739, and *Seikaron* (1744).

Ishida Eiichirō   石田英一郎

(1903–68). Pioneer of cultural anthropological studies in Japan. Born in Ōsaka, Ishida attended Kyōto University (he was forced to leave because of his leftist political activities) and studied ethnology under Wilhelm Schmidt and William Koppers at the University of Vienna. In 1951 he was appointed to the newly founded chair of cultural anthropology at Tōkyō University. Ishida examined what are regarded as certain peculiar features of Japanese culture in light of a wider East Asian cultural context by using the comparative ethnological method known as *Kulturkreislehre.* His comparative study of the KAPPA (mythical creatures that appear in Japanese folklore) legend, *Kappa komahiki kō* (1948), is one of the major products of this research. Later he developed a theory of culture correlating the materialist-Marxist view of history and society and the anthropological concept of culture as defined by the neo-evolutionist school. His collected works are found in *Ishida Eiichirō zenshū* (8 vols; 1970–72).

Ishida Hakyō   石田波郷

(1913–69). HAIKU poet. Real name Ishida Tetsuo. Born in Ehime Prefecture; studied at Meiji University. He began writing haiku after the style of the magazine HOTOTOGISU, but he was later inspired by the works of MIZUHARA SHŪŌSHI, who rejected objective nature descriptions in favor of a more subjective style. He wrote for Mizuhara's new coterie magazine *Ashibi*. In 1935 he published his first collection and became a leading figure in the new-style haiku movement of the 1930s. His collection *Shakumyō* (1950, Desire for Life) is noted for its sharp, clear images and the passionate conviction of their expression.

Ishida Kōshirō   石田幸四郎

(1930–). Politician. Born in Hokkaidō, Ishida graduated from Meiji University. He was first elected to the House of Representatives in 1968 as a KŌMEITŌ candidate from Aichi Prefecture. Known as a practical man well versed in party affairs, Ishida has served as deputy secretary-general and vice chairman of the Kōmeitō. In May 1989 he became party chairman in place of YANO JUN'YA.

Ishida Mitoku   石田未得

(1587?–1669). KYŌKA and *haiku* poet. Born in Edo (now Tōkyō). He was a disciple of MATSUNAGA TEITOKU and (with NAKARAI BOKUYŌ) the leading figure in early-Edo-period (1600–1868) *kyōka*. His *kyōka* anthology, *Gogin wagashū* (1649, the title parodying the early-10th-century anthology *Kokin wakashū*; see KOKINSHŪ), influenced later generations of *kyōka* poets.

Ishida Mitsunari   石田三成

(1560–1600). Warlord of the Azuchi-Momoyama period (1568–1600). Born in Ōmi Province (now Shiga Prefecture). As a youth he became an attendant to TOYOTOMI HIDEYOSHI. When Hideyoshi assumed the highest court title of *kampaku* in 1585, Mitsunari was appointed one of the 12 ministers (*shodayū*). Upon Hideyoshi's unification of Japan, Mitsunari became the most important figure on his administrative staff. He was endowed by Hideyoshi with a large domain at Sawayama in Ōmi. Mitsunari served as a general in the first of Hideyoshi's invasions of Korea in 1592–93 (see INVASIONS OF KOREA IN 1592 AND 1597) and was a major figure in the nationwide land survey known as the Taikō KENCHI. After Hideyoshi's death in 1598 Mitsunari championed the cause of Hideyoshi's son TOYOTOMI HIDEYORI and organized forces against TOKUGAWA IEYASU. He and several major *daimyō* confronted Ieyasu and his allies at the Battle of SEKIGAHARA in 1600. Losing the battle, Mitsunari was captured and executed.

Ishida Reisuke   石田礼助

(1886–1978). Businessman and president (1963–69) of the Japanese National Railways (JNR). Born in Shizuoka Prefecture. After graduating from Tōkyō University of Commerce (now Hitotsubashi University) in 1907, he joined MITSUI & CO, LTD, becoming representative director in 1939. Because of his opposition to World War II, Ishida had to retire from the corporation in 1941. During World War II, he worked as president of Kōeki Eidan, an organization that regulated foreign trade. Ishida joined JNR in 1956. As its president he contributed considerably to the revitalization of the national railways by inaugurating the SHINKANSEN "bullet-train" line.

Ishida Taizō   石田退三

(1888–1979). Businessman. Born in Aichi Prefecture. After graduating from middle school, he took various jobs before joining the Toyoda Spinning & Weaving Co in 1927. He rose through the ranks to become president of TOYODA AUTOMATIC LOOM WORKS, LTD, in 1948. While still in this position he took over the presidency of TOYOTA MOTOR CORPORATION in 1950. Ishida established an efficient production system, and under his leadership Toyota began its rise to its current position as one of the world's leading motor vehicle manufacturers. Ishida served on the board of many Toyota group companies and contributed substantially to the group's prosperity.

Ishigaki   石垣[市]

City on Ishigakijima, the principal island of the YAEYAMA ISLANDS, Okinawa Prefecture. The city is the political, economic, and cultural center of the islands. Pineapple cultivation is the principal industry. Serving the many tourists, air flights and ship and ferry routes connect the city with Naha, the prefectural capital. Pop: 41,245.

Ishigakijima   石垣島

Island, surrounded by coral reefs, approximately 400 km (250 mi) southwest of Okinawa. One of the YAEYAMA ISLANDS. The city of Ishigaki covers the entire island. Pineapples are produced. The highest peak in Okinawa Prefecture, Omotodake (526 m; 1,726 ft), is located here. Area: 221 sq km (85 sq mi).

Ishigaki Rin   石垣りん

(1920–). Poet. Born in Tōkyō. Using clear, direct language, Ishigaki bases her socially conscious poetry on her own daily experience as a working woman. Her first poetry collection was *Watashi no mae ni aru nabe to okama to moeru hi to* (1959, The Pots, Pans, and Fire in Front of Me). Other works include *Hyōsatsu nado* (1968, Nameplates,

Etc), winner of the 1969 H-Shi Prize, and the personal poetry collection *Ishigaki Rin shishū* (1971). Ishigaki is a regular contributor to the poetry magazine REKITEI.

Ishiguro Munemaro   石黒宗麿

(1893–1968). Ceramist, best known for the iron glazes called *temmoku*, inspired by Chinese wares of the Song (Sung) dynasty (960–1279). Born in Shimminato, Toyama Prefecture, Ishiguro left school in 1912. He experimented with RAKU WARE, IGA WARE, MISHIMA WARE, *hakeme* (brushed design) pieces, southern Song Jun (Chün) ware porcelain, Tang (T'ang) dynasty (618–907) three-color ware, Korean-style decorated Kōrai (Kor: Koryŏ) pieces, and KARATSU WARE. He perfected the first even persimmon *temmoku* glaze in Japan (1939), the first tree-leaf *temmoku* outside China (1940), and versions of partridge-spotted ware and Henan (Honan) *temmoku*. He won top prizes at the Paris International Exposition (1937) and the Ministry of Commerce and Industry Crafts Exhibition (1941). Because of his work in *temmoku* glazes, he was designated one of the LIVING NATIONAL TREASURES in 1955.

Ishiguro Tadaatsu   石黒忠篤

(1884–1960). Agricultural administrator. Born in Tōkyō. After graduating from Tōkyō University, he entered the Ministry of Agriculture and Commerce (later the Ministry of Agriculture and Forestry), where he served as bureau director, vice-minister, and twice as minister before the end of World War II. His administrative philosophy, based upon concepts of agrarian nationalism (NŌHON SHUGI), exercised a great influence on government agricultural policy in the 1920s and 1930s.

Ishihara Kanji →Ishiwara Kanji

Ishihara Shinobu   石原忍

(1879–1963). Ophthalmologist. Born in Tōkyō. After graduating from Tōkyō University in 1905, he entered the army as a medical doctor. He went to Germany for further study in 1912. Ishihara taught at Tōkyō University from 1922 to 1940. A color-blindness test table he devised is widely used throughout the world. He received the Japan Academy Prize (1941) for his work on the causes of idiopathic nyctalopia (1930).

Ishihara Shintarō   石原慎太郎

(1932–). Novelist and politician. Born in Kōbe; graduate of Hitotsubashi University. Ishihara started writing in 1954, publishing "Hai iro no kyōshitsu" (The Gray Classroom) in *Hitotsubashi bungaku*, a literary

Ishihara Yūjirō The savvy "tough guy" who was Japan's top male film star of the late 1950s and early 1960s.

magazine. His *Taiyō no kisetsu* (1955, Season of the Sun; tr *Season of Violence*, 1966) won the Bungakukai's newcomer's award and the Akutagawa Prize. Depicting the life of postwar Japanese youth opposed to all established morals and customs, the novel gave the name *taiyōzoku* ("sun tribe") to a generation of alienated youth. Ishihara's other novels include *Kiretsu* (1956–58, The Crevice), *Shokei no heya* (1956; tr *The Punishment Room*, 1966), and *Kanzen naru yūgi* (1957, Utter Decadence). He was elected to the House of Councillors in 1968 as a Liberal Democratic Party candidate and since 1972 has been a member of the House of Representatives. He collaborated with MORITA AKIO in writing *"No" to ieru Nihon* (1989, The Japan That Can Say No), a revised version of which was published in English in 1991 under Ishihara's name.

Ishihara Takashi 石原俊

(1912–). Businessman; chairman of NISSAN MOTOR CO, LTD (1985–). Born in Tōkyō. After graduating from Tōhoku University in 1937, he joined Nissan Motor Co, becoming its president in 1977 and chairman in 1985. Under his leadership Nissan increased its domestic auto production to 2.45 million units in 1980, a historic high. In 1980 he established Nissan Motor Manufacturing Corporation, USA, and in 1984 he established Nissan Motor Manufacturing, UK, Ltd. As chairman of the JAPAN ASSOCIATION OF CORPORATE EXECUTIVES (1985–), he transformed that organization into an active policy-making group. While president of the Japan Automobile Manufacturers' Association (1980–86), he was involved in implementation of Japan's voluntary restrictions on auto exports to the United States.

Ishihara Yoshirō 石原吉郎

(1915–77). Poet. Born in Shizuoka Prefecture. Graduate of Tōkyō University of Foreign Studies. Ishihara began writing poetry in reaction to his experience of internment in Siberia after World War II. Freed in 1953, he returned to Japan and became a regular contributor to the poetry magazine ARECHI during its final phase. Ishihara won the H-Shi Prize for the poetry collection *Sancho Pansa no kikyō* (The Return of Sancho Panza) in 1964.

Ishihara Yūjirō 石原裕次郎

(1934–87). Actor and singer. Born in Kōbe. Ishihara appeared in the 1956 film version of his elder brother ISHIHARA SHINTARŌ's novel *Taiyō no kisetsu* (1955; tr *Season of Violence*, 1966) while still a student at Keiō University. Over the next decade he acted in numerous action dramas produced by the NIKKATSU CORPORATION. Managing to appear well bred, tough, and streetwise all at once, he became the top male film star of the time. He was also a professional singer. His most important roles were in *Kurutta kajitsu* (1956, Crazed Fruit) and *Hi no ataru sakamichi* (1958, Street in the Sun).

Ishii Kikujirō 石井菊次郎

(1866–1945). Diplomat of the Meiji (1868–1912) and Taishō (1912–26) periods; Japan's foreign minister (1915–16). Born in Kazusa Province (now part of Chiba Prefecture). After graduating from Tōkyō University, Ishii began a diplomatic career that included posts in China and Korea, service as ambassador to France (1912–15, 1920–27) and to the United States (1918–19), and two terms as president of the Council and Assembly of the League of Nations (1923, 1926).

Americans remember Ishii for his efforts during World War I to smooth relations between Japan and other states at war with the Central Powers. As foreign minister, and then as head of a special mission to the United States in 1917, he faced an increasingly tense American-Japanese rivalry rooted in conflicts over China and over American treatment of Japanese living in the United States. His approach reflected the conviction of an influential group of Japanese businessmen and politicians that an accommodation with the United States was vital to Japan's continuing growth as a power. Ishii's talks in 1917 with US secretary of state Robert LANSING produced the LANSING-ISHII AGREEMENT, but the "agreement" was limited by their governments' unwillingness to make substantial concessions. Ishii returned to Washington in 1918, where as ambassador he continued to wrestle with American-Japanese tensions as they were exacerbated by conflicts in Siberia (see SIBERIAN INTERVENTION) and at the Paris Peace Conference.

Ishii Mitsujirō 石井光次郎

(1889–1981). Politician. A graduate of Tōkyō Higher School of Commerce (now Hitotsubashi University), he was a career journalist before being elected to the House of Representatives in 1946. He was appointed minister of transportation in 1953 and subsequently held numerous cabinet posts. He played a major role in the formation of the LIBERAL DEMOCRATIC PARTY (LDP). He was elected Speaker of the House of Representatives in 1967 and later became one of the "elder statesmen" of the LDP.

Ishii Ryōsuke 石井良助

(1907–93). Legal historian. Born in Tōkyō, he graduated from Tōkyō University in 1930 and received a Doctor of Laws degree in 1937. In 1942 he succeeded NAKADA KAORU as professor of Japanese legal history at Tōkyō University and became professor emeritus in 1968. After 1950 he was a director of the Japan Legal History Society (Nihon Hōseishi Gakkai). His prodigious publications began with a study of medieval immovable-property law and later expanded to broad studies of public and private law in all periods. He was awarded the Order of Culture in 1990. His works include *Nihon hōseishi gaisetsu* (1948, An Outline of Japanese Legal History); *Japanese Legislation in the Meiji Era*, tr and adapted by W. T. Chambliss (1958); and *A History of Political Institutions in Japan* (1980).

Ishikari Bay 石狩湾

(Ishikari Wan). Bay on the Sea of Japan on the west coast of Hokkaidō. Herring fishing formerly flourished here. The river Ishikarigawa feeds into the bay; ferries connecting Hokkaidō and Honshū use it as a landing.

Ishikari Coalfield 石狩炭田

(Ishikari Tanden). Located in the western Yūbari Mountains, central Hokkaidō. Japan's largest and most productive coalfield; famous for its high-quality coking coal. Its development began in the early Meiji period (1868–1912), and at its peak in 1966 it produced 17.5 million metric tons (19.3 million short tons) of coal. Since then, the decreased demand for coal has led to a succession of mine closures. In 1988 its output was 4.5 mil-

lion metric tons (4.9 million short tons). Length: 90 km (56 mi); width: 30 km (19 mi); estimated volume of deposits: 6.4 billion metric tons (7 billion short tons).

Ishikaridake 石狩岳

Mountain in central Hokkaidō. It is the source of the rivers Ishikarigawa and Otofukegawa. Primeval forests of Yeddo spruce (*ezomatsu*) and Sakhalin fir (*todomatsu*) cover the mountain. It forms the central part of Daisetsuzan National Park. Height: 1,967 m (6,453 ft).

Ishikarigawa 石狩川

River in central Hokkaidō, originating in the mountain ISHIKARIDAKE in the Daisetsuzan National Park, flowing through the Kamikawa Basin and Ishikari Plain, and emptying into the Sea of Japan. The name is derived from the Ainu word *ishikaribetsu*, meaning a zigzagging river. It is the largest river in Hokkaidō. Large peat bogs along the lower reaches have been formed by deposits of the Ishikarigawa and its tributary, the Yūbarigawa. Floods were frequent in the past, but dams and embankments have been built. Scenic spots include the gorge SŌUNKYŌ on its upper reaches. Length: 268 km (167 mi); area of drainage basin: 14,330 sq km (5,533 sq mi).

Ishikari Mountains 石狩山地

(Ishikari Sanchi). Mountain range in central Hokkaidō. Part of the Ezo Mountains, it forms the watershed between the Pacific Ocean to the east, the Sea of Japan to the west, and the Sea of Okhotsk to the northeast. The major peaks are Asahidake (2,290 m; 7,513 ft), the highest, and ISHIKARIDAKE (1,967 m; 6,453 ft). The range forms part of Daisetsuzan National Park.

Ishikari Plain 石狩平野

(Ishikari Heiya). Alluvial plain in western Hokkaidō. Bordering on the Sea of Japan and formed by the meandering river Ishikarigawa, it has numerous oxbow lakes and marshes. The establishment of Sapporo in 1869 and the subsequent arrival of colonist militia (TONDENHEI) have made the region one of the most productive farmlands in Hokkaidō. The major cities are SAPPORO and IWAMIZAWA. Area: approximately 4,000 sq km (1,500 sq mi).

Ishikawa 石川[市]

City on the island of Okinawa, Okinawa Prefecture. After World War II, Ishikawa was the site of a refugee camp operated by the American Occupation forces. It is still economically dependent on American military bases, although efforts are being made to introduce various enterprises. Its principal farming activity is the cultivation of sugarcane and rice. The IHA SHELL MOUND is located here. Pop: 20,733.

Ishikawa Chiyomatsu 石川千代松

(1861–1935). Zoologist who helped spread the theory of evolution in Japan. Born in Edo (now Tōkyō). A graduate of Tōkyō University, he later taught there. He studied in Germany under August Weismann (1834–1914). Ishikawa published notes on the theory of evolution from lectures given in Japan by the American Edward S. MORSE and wrote *Shinka shinron* (1891) and other books about evolution. He was also active in applied zoology, experimenting with the artificial breeding of AYU (sweetfish).

Ishikawa Ichirō 石川一郎

(1885–1970). Businessman. Born in Tōkyō. After graduating from Tōkyō University in 1909, Ishikawa became an assistant professor of engineering there. He had planned to become a scholar, but in 1915 he left the university and joined Kantō Oxygen (now NISSAN CHEMICAL INDUSTRIES, LTD), then run by his father, becoming president of the company in 1941. Although most business leaders and executives were purged after World War II, Ishikawa remained active and reorganized various economic organizations. He became president of KEIDANREN (Japan Federation of Economic Organizations) in 1948. He played an important role in the reconstruction of the war-torn Japanese economy until 1956, when ISHIZAKA TAIZŌ took over as chairman of Keidanren.

Ishikawajima-Harima Heavy Industries Co, Ltd 石川島播磨重工業[株]

(Ishikawajima-Harima Jūkōgyō). Manufacturer of land-based machinery, plants, ships, and jet aircraft engines; commonly known as IHI. Established in 1960 through a merger of Ishikawajima Heavy Industries and Harima Zōsenjo. The history of Ishikawajima Heavy Industries dates back to 1853, when the Mito domainal authorities constructed a shipyard on Ishikawajima, an island at the mouth of the Sumidagawa in Edo (now Tōkyō). This facility also manufactured machinery. Harima Zōsenjo, which developed its own technology for the construction of large ships, was established in 1907 in Hyōgo Prefecture and developed as an affiliate of the SUZUKI SHŌTEN. It merged with KŌBE STEEL, LTD, in 1921 but became independent in 1929.

IHI has established wholly owned subsidiaries and joint ventures overseas and is actively involved in technical assistance abroad. IHI remains devoted to the development and manufacture of high-technology machinery, such as aircraft engines and space equipment. Sales for the fiscal year ending March 1991 totaled ¥731.3 billion (US $5.3 billion). The company was capitalized at ¥64.9 billion (US $473.0 million) in the same year. Headquarters are in Tōkyō.

Ishikawa Jōzan 石川丈山

(1583–1672). Confucian scholar and writer of *kanshi* (poems in Chinese; see POETRY AND PROSE IN CHINESE). He studied with FUJIWARA SEIKA, founder of Neo-Confucian studies in Japan. At 58 he retired to a hermitage called Shisendō (Hall of the Immortal Poets) at the foot of Mt. Hiei. His principal work of poetry is the *Fushōshū* (1671).

Ishikawa Jun 石川淳

(1899–1987). Novelist, translator, and critic. Born in Asakusa, Tōkyō; educated in French literature at Tōkyō School of Foreign Languages. Early in his career he translated works by Anatole France and André Gide.

In 1935 he began publishing a series of *récits*, commencing with "Kajin" (The Lady) and "Hinkyū mondō" (Dialogue on Poverty), that depict a solitary urban writer who is engaged in a desperate struggle to create a Parnassian fiction. Ishikawa's novel *Fugen* (1936, The Bodhisattva) was awarded the Akutagawa Prize in 1936. During World War II, he produced several important nonfiction works (including critical and biographical studies of MORI ŌGAI and WATANABE KAZAN), and adopted the pen name Isai ("the

kyōka poet at his desk") out of his deep interest in the KYŌKA or comic verse of the Temmei era (1781–89).

Ishikawa is numbered among the "first wave" of writers of the immediate postwar era. The short stories that Ishikawa wrote from 1946 to 1948, such as "Ōgon densetsu" (1946, Legenda Aurea) and "Yakeato no Iesu" (1946, Christ amidst the Ruins), are his most representative pieces.

His critical essays, beginning with *Isai hitsudan* (1950–51, Isai's Discourses), form an ongoing "Isai" series. They are conceived in an irreverent and acerbic style and cover a wide range of topics on art and literature. Ishikawa also pioneered in the revival of the lost art of the *kijinden*, a cycle of sketches concerning unusual personalities from Japanese history, with his *Shokoku kijinden* (1955–57, Eccentrics and Gallants from around the Country).

Ishikawa is recognized as not only a superb craftsman but also a thoroughgoing methodologist of the novel, the latter making him an anomaly among Japanese writers. At the same time that he belongs to the modernist tradition within 20th-century fiction, he can be seen as part of the "literati" (*bunjin*) tradition that originates in the poets and BUNJINGA painters of the Temmei years and that descends through Mori Ōgai and NAGAI KAFŪ. Indeed, Ishikawa is often called Japan's "last belletrist" (*saigo no bunjin*).

Ishikawa Masamochi 石川雅望

(1753–1830). KYŌKA poet and KOKUGAKU scholar of the late Edo period (1600–1868). Son of the *ukiyo-e* artist ISHIKAWA TOYONOBU. Ishikawa was an innkeeper in Edo (now Tōkyō). His *kyōka* pen name was Yadoya no Meshimori ("Maid at the Inn"). He was a disciple of ŌTA NAMPO and eventually founded his own school of *kyōka*, stressing satire and wit as opposed to the pseudoclassical elegance advocated by his rival SHIKATSUBE MAGAO. He also wrote philological studies of the classics and compiled the still-valuable dictionary of the classical language, *Gagen shūran* (1826–49). His *kyōka* are found in the anthology *Manzai kyōka shū* (1783).

Ishikawa Prefectural Museum of Art 石川県立美術館

(Ishikawa Kenritsu Bijutsukan). Museum in the city of Kanazawa, Ishikawa Prefecture. Opened in 1983. The museum houses such items as an incense burner by the 17th-century ceramic artist NONOMURA NINSEI that has been designated a National Treasure, traditional Ishikawa KUTANI WARE and lacquer ware, and sculptures and paintings by artists associated with Ishikawa Prefecture.

Ishikawa Prefecture 石川県

(Ishikawa Ken). Located in central Honshū and bounded by the Sea of Japan on the west and north, Toyama Bay and Toyama and Gifu prefectures on the east, and Fukui Prefecture on the south. It is divided into two main areas, the Kaga region to the south and the NOTO PENINSULA to the north. There are also several islets north of Noto in the Sea of Japan, the largest of which is HEGURAJIMA. The southern portion of the Kaga region is largely mountainous, and the area around the city of KANAZAWA forms the prefecture's largest plain, with several small rivers and lakes. The Noto Peninsula is hilly, with an uneven coastline forming many natural harbors. Both areas are warmed by the Tsushima Current; precipitation is heavy, and the weather is frequently cloudy.

The area that is now Ishikawa Prefecture was once part of Echizen Province as established under the KOKUGUN SYSTEM in 646. In 718 part of this area was made Noto Province, and in 823 another part was made Kaga Province. In the 15th century a religious sect overthrew the local ruler of Kaga (see IKKŌ IKKI) and controlled the province for nearly a century. Later both Kaga and Noto came under the rule of the powerful MAEDA FAMILY, who encouraged scholarship and the arts. Noto and Kaga were combined in 1872 to form Ishikawa Prefecture. (The remainder of the original Echizen Province is now part of Fukui Prefecture.)

Agriculture is dominated by the produc-

Ishikawa Takuboku
Considered by many to be Japan's finest modern poet, Takuboku, shown here in a 1904 photograph, wrote in a highly innovative style.

tion of rice, which is grown mainly on the KANAZAWA PLAIN. Fishing is a major industry on the Noto Peninsula. Although industry is not highly developed, there are textile and heavy-machinery plants. The area is also known for several traditional handicrafts such as *wajima-nuri* lacquer ware and KUTANI WARE.

Tourist attractions include the rugged scenery of both the Kaga and Noto seacoasts and Kanazawa, which was the castle town of the Maeda family. There are many hot-spring resorts, the most representative being Yamanaka, Yamashiro, and Awazu. Area: 4,197 sq km (1,620 sq mi); pop: 1,164,628; capital: Kanazawa. Other major cities include KOMATSU, KAGA, and NANAO.

Ishikawa Sanshirō 石川三四郎

(1876–1956). Socialist and later anarchist. Born in Saitama Prefecture, he graduated from Tōkyō Hōgakuin (now Chūō University). In 1902 he began work for the newspaper YOROZU CHŌHŌ but left in 1903, together with KŌTOKU SHŪSUI and SAKAI TOSHIHIKO, when the paper supported the RUSSO-JAPANESE WAR. He joined the socialist group HEIMINSHA (until it disbanded in 1905) and wrote for its newspaper, the *Heimin shimbun*. Drawn to Christianity, Ishikawa was baptized by EBINA DANJŌ. In 1905 he joined ABE ISOO and KINOSHITA NAOE in founding *Shinkigen* (New Era), a Christian-socialist journal. He also helped revive the Heiminsha in 1907.

After the HIGH TREASON INCIDENT OF 1910, which resulted in executions of socialists, Ishikawa went to Europe (1913–20), where he became attracted to anarchism. Returning to Japan he promoted anarchism through his group the Kyōgakusha (Mutual Study Society) and its journal *Dynamic*. In 1946 he helped found the Anarchist League of Japan (Nihon Anākisuto Dōmei). His autobiography was published in two volumes as *Jijoden* (1956).

Ishikawa Tairō 石川大浪

(1765–1817). Shogunate official and Western-style illustrator of the Edo period (1600–1868) who cultivated friendships with scholars of WESTERN LEARNING. Born in Edo (now Tōkyō), he served in the Great Guard (Ōban) of the Tokugawa shogunate (1603–1867). He studied painting and illustrated several medical texts.

Ishikawa Takeyoshi 石川武美

(1887–1961). Editor and publisher who created the prototype of the Japanese magazine for housewives. Born in Ōita Prefecture, he left middle school, moved to Tōkyō in 1906, and became a live-in apprentice to a magazine publisher. In 1917 he founded *Shufu no tomo* (The Homemaker's Friend), which in three years became the most popular of WOMEN'S MAGAZINES in Japan.

Ishikawa Takuboku 石川啄木

(1886–1912). Poet and novelist; especially known for his *tanka*, the traditional Japanese short poem of 31 syllables (see WAKA). Takuboku was born in the village of Hinoto, Iwate Prefecture. Encouraged by the publication of some of his poems in MYŌJŌ, one of the leading literary magazines of the day, Takuboku dropped out of school in 1902 and went to pursue connections in Tōkyō with YOSANO TEKKAN, editor of *Myōjō*, and his wife, YOSANO AKIKO, both prominent poets in

the romantic movement. However, illness and lack of funds forced him to return home in 1903.

Takuboku's New-Style Poetry——Takuboku continued to write during his recuperation, and his first volume of poetry, *Akogare* (Longing), was published in 1905. Written in the free verse manner of the SHINTAISHI ("new-style poetry," after the example of European poetry), *Akogare* attracted immediate public and critical attention for its startling imagery and outspokenness. That same year, Takuboku married and assumed responsibility for support of his entire family. He took a position as a substitute teacher in Shibutami, then moved to Hokkaidō in 1907. These years were marked by periodic separations from his wife and child, illness in the family, and unremitting financial difficulties.

Becoming interested in NATURALISM, Takuboku began to write fiction during this period but met with limited success and later abandoned these efforts. While in Hokkaidō he wrote several new collections of poems in the modern style, but after his return to Tōkyō in 1908, Takuboku began to turn more and more to the traditional *tanka* form. At the height of his career Takuboku devoted himself almost exclusively to the writing of *tanka*, and it is on the quality of these short poems and on his innovations within the form that his considerable fame as a poet rests.

His first collection of *tanka*, *Ichiaku no suna* (tr *A Handful of Sand*, 1934), was published in 1910 and contains 551 poems written in simple, direct language. Dealing with emotions and experiences taken from his daily life, these poems have a frankness and vitality all but unprecedented in Japanese poetry. During this period Takuboku also published a statement of his poetics in an essay entitled "Kurōbeki shi" (1909, Poems to Eat), in which he challenged the prevalent notion that poets or poetic experiences are in any way exalted and advocated a poetry that is down-to-earth and based on real life. Takuboku also kept a diary from 1902 to 1912. The portion for the year 1909, which he wrote in romanized Japanese, is regarded as a classic in the diary genre. Parts of the latter were published in 1909 as *Rōmaji nikki*. It was not published in full until 1977.

Influence——Deeply shocked by the arrests of socialists in the HIGH TREASON INCIDENT OF 1910, Takuboku began to take a serious interest in the socialist movement but soon fell ill, dying at the age of 26. A second *tanka* collection, *Kanashiki gangu* (tr *Sad Toys*, 1977), was published a few months later. Considered by many to be Japan's finest modern poet, Takuboku exercised a major influence upon the subsequent development of *tanka* written in the modern language. Takuboku societies have sprung up in many parts of Japan, devoted to the study of his works and the perpetuation of his literary ideals. Since the 1920s, Takuboku has attained international stature; his poetry has been translated into most Western European languages and into Russian and Chinese as well.

Ishikawa Tatsuzō 石川達三

(1905–85). Novelist. Born in Akita Prefecture; studied at Waseda University. Intending to emigrate to Brazil, he went to São Paulo but returned in two months. He wrote about this experience in a long novel, *Sōbō* (1935–39), the first part of which was awarded the first Akutagawa Prize in 1935. Writing in the journalistic style typical of

much of his work, Ishikawa described the life of poor Japanese emigrants to Brazil in the 1930s. After a trip to the war front in China following the Japanese invasion in 1937, Ishikawa wrote a novella, *Ikite iru heitai* (1938, Living Soldiers), whose treatment of the behavior of Japanese troops was too frank for government officials. The book was banned and Ishikawa and his publisher were convicted for violation of the PRESS LAW OF 1909, serving as one of the first test cases for wartime media censorship. After World War II, he became known as a major novelist with such works as *Kaze ni soyogu ashi* (1949–51, A Reed Bowed by the Wind) and *Ningen no kabe* (1957–59, The Human Wall).

Ishikawa Toyonobu 石川豊信

(1711–85). UKIYO-E artist who specialized in portraits of beautiful women (*bijinga*) and actor prints (*yakusha-e*). Born in Edo (now Tōkyō). As a student of the *ukiyo-e* artist Nishimura Shigenaga (d 1756), he worked under the name Nishimura Shigenobu and produced actor prints in the style of the TORII SCHOOL. Later he began signing his work with the name Ishikawa Toyonobu and developed a style of his own, especially in his portraits of warm and elegantly beautiful women. Along with OKUMURA MASANOBU, he experimented in the utilization of wood-grain patterns (*kimezuri*) in the backgrounds of his prints. The literary figure ISHIKAWA MASAMOCHI was his son.

Ishimure Michiko 石牟礼道子

(1927–). Writer. Born in Kumamoto Prefecture, she grew up in the city of Minamata, where she continues to reside. In 1969 Ishimure published *Kugai jōdo: Waga minamatabyō* (tr *Paradise in the Sea of Our Sorrow*, 1989), a realistic account of the tragedy of Minamata disease (see POLLUTION-RELATED DISEASES) based on her own interviews with its victims. The work has been acclaimed for its evocative and virtually poetic use of the interview form and local dialect to convey its difficult subject. In addition to her work as a writer, Ishimure has been a leader of the movement to aid the victims of Minamata disease and redress their grievances. Two other works by Ishimure, *Ten no uo* (1974, Heavenly Fish) and *Tsubaki no umi no ki* (1976, Story of the Sea of Camellias), form a trilogy with *Kugai jōdo*.

Ishinomaki 石巻[市]

City in eastern Miyagi Prefecture, northern Honshū, at the mouth of the river Kitakamigawa. Principal activities are fishing and the cultivation of seaweed (*nori*) and oysters; the pulp and marine food-processing industries are also active. An industrial port has been completed. Pop: 121,976.

Ishioka 石岡[市]

City in central Ibaraki Prefecture, central Honshū, on Lake Kasumigaura. Once the site of a provincial capital (*kokufu*), Ishioka developed as a lake port. Today it is a residential and industrial city. It is known for its *sake* and *miso* (bean paste). Pop: 50,618.

Ishiwara Jun 石原純

(1881–1947). Theoretical physicist. Responsible for the introduction and promotion of relativity and quantum theory in Japan; the enthusiasm that he generated for this new approach to PHYSICS contributed to the emergence of such eminent Japanese physicists as YUKAWA HIDEKI and TOMONAGA SHIN'ICHIRŌ. Born in Tōkyō, Ishiwara graduated from

Ishikawa Tatsuzō This writer's novella *Living Soldiers* (1938), banned by wartime authorities, features a frank treatment of the taking of Nanjing, which he visited as a war correspondent in the wake of the Nanjing Massacre.

Tōkyō University in 1906. He studied in Germany with Arnold Sommerfeld (1868–1951) and later with Albert Einstein (1879–1955) in Switzerland. In 1914 he returned to Japan and became a professor at Tōhoku University. His publications include *Sōtaisei genri* (1921, Principles of Relativity).

Ishiwara Kanji 石原莞爾

(1889–1949). Also called Ishihara Kanji. Army officer and nationalist writer. Born 18 January 1889 in the city of Tsuruoka, Yamagata Prefecture. He graduated from the Army Academy in 1909. Commissioned a lieutenant, Ishiwara was assigned to regimental garrisons in Korea and Honshū. He graduated in 1918 from the Army War College and was a lecturer in military history there from 1925 to 1928. His research into the history of war and the apocalyptic doctrines of the medieval Buddhist monk NICHIREN led him to formulate a theory of the evolution and future of war. Based on this theory Ishiwara taught that Japan must prepare for "The Final War" between Japan and the United States by harnessing the resources of Asia (particularly Manchuria) and reordering domestic affairs. In 1929 Ishiwara became operations officer of the GUANDONG (KWANTUNG) ARMY in Manchuria, where he was instrumental in planning the 1931 Japanese military takeover (see MANCHURIAN INCIDENT).

Ishiwara returned to Japan in 1932 and spent two years as regimental commander in Sendai. In 1935 he was assigned as section chief in the Operations Division of the General Staff and drafted plans for a "national defense state," designed to prepare Japan for major hostilities. In 1936 Ishiwara was instrumental in suppressing the FEBRUARY 26TH INCIDENT, an uprising by young officers. However, Ishiwara dissipated the influence and prestige he had gained by a series of futile political maneuvers in 1936–37. Although he was promoted to major general and appointed chief of the Operations Division of the General Staff in March 1937, his advocacy of a policy of greater accommodation toward China brought him into conflict with other officers who advocated a hard-line attitude toward China. His policy of military moderation on the Asian continent was fatally compromised when the SINO-JAPANESE WAR OF 1937–1945 broke out in July 1937. Ishiwara found his remaining influence drained by September and held a series of backwater assignments until 1941. He became a lieutenant general that year, but was soon forced out of the army by old enemies, including Army Minister TŌJŌ HIDEKI. In 1942 he returned to Tsuruoka, where for the duration of World War II he and his small agricultural community turned to the problems of rural self-sufficiency. Japan's defeat shattered much of his theory of war. Purged from public life by Occupation authorities, he spent the remainder of his life in discouragement and infirmity.

Ishiwara Ken 石原謙

(1882–1976). Historian of Christianity. Born in Tōkyō; graduate of Tōkyō University. He was named associate professor of Tōkyō University in 1921, and in 1924 became professor at Tōhoku University. He was president (1940–48) of Tōkyō Women's Christian University and in 1953 became a member of the Japan Academy. He worked with the entire history of Christian thought with particular interest in Augustine and Luther. Ishiwara's works include *Kirisutokyō shi*

(1934, A History of Christianity), *Kirisuto-kyō shisō shi* (1949, A History of Christian Thought), and *Chūsei kirisutokyō kenkyū* (1952, Studies on Medieval Christianity). In 1973 he was awarded the Order of Culture.

Ishiyamadera 石山寺

A ranking temple of the TŌJI branch of the SHINGON SECT of Buddhism, located in the city of Ōtsu, Shiga Prefecture. Ishiyamadera is said to have been founded in 749 by the eminent monk RŌBEN, who converted his hermitage into the temple. He installed a newly carved large image of KANNON (Nyoirin Kannon) as the object of worship.

The sectarian affiliation of Ishiyamadera was changed from the TŌDAIJI temple to the Shingon sect after the learned Shingon cleric Kanken (853–925) took up residence there. Ishiyamadera was completely gutted by fire in 1078, although there is some controversy over whether the original sacred image was lost at that time. The temple was rebuilt some 20 years later. It is known for its valuable collection of early Buddhist manuscripts. Ishiyamadera is the 13th of the 33 holy places of Kannon visited by pilgrims in western Japan (see PILGRIMAGES).

Ishiyama Honganji 石山本願寺

A temple and town, located on Naniwa Bay in the estuary of the rivers Yodogawa and Yamatogawa, which was from 1533 to 1580 the headquarters of the religious and secular organization of the HONGANJI, the major branch of the Buddhist True Pure Land sect (Jōdo Shinshū; see JŌDO SHIN SECT); the origin of the modern city of Ōsaka.

The temple was founded in 1496 as the Ishiyama *dōjō* (chapel) by RENNYO Kenju (1415–99). It grew into an elaborate complex containing great halls of prayer, a residence, and gardens; the whole was an almost impregnable temple fortress, surrounded by moats and walls. A large town (*jinai machi*) grew up within the temple precincts (*jinai*). The Ishiyama Honganji served as a center of religion, commerce, and culture. Above all, it was the governing center of the Honganji's vast power structure, fittingly called a religious monarchy, which by the 1570s encompassed entire provinces.

After that religious monarchy lost a 10-year war with ODA NOBUNAGA, its leader, Kyōnyo Kōju (1558–1614), reluctantly surrendered the Ishiyama Honganji on 10 September 1580. The temple burned that day, presumably set afire on Kyōnyo's orders. Because of its strategic location, the national unifier TOYOTOMI HIDEYOSHI built Ōsaka Castle on the same site; he moved into the new fortress in 1584, restoring Ōsaka's central place in Japanese affairs and assuring its development into a major city.

Ishizaka Kimishige 石坂公成

(1925–). Immunologist. Born in Tōkyō; graduate of Tōkyō University. In 1948 he became a researcher at the National Institute of Health in Tōkyō. After studying at the California Institute of Technology, in 1962 he was appointed director of research at the Children's Asthma Research Institute in Denver, Colorado. Between 1960 and 1966 he succeeded in isolating immunoglobulin E (IgE), an antibody that contributes to certain allergic syndromes, such as bronchial asthma and pollen reactions. From 1970 to 1989 Ishizaka was a member of the Faculty of Medicine at Johns Hopkins University, and from 1974 to 1980 he served concurrently as a professor at Kyōto University. In 1989 he

became the director of the La Jolla Institute for Allergy and Immunology in California. In 1972 he received the Passano Award for distinguished accomplishment in the field of immunology. He received the Order of Culture in 1974.

Ishizaka Taizō 石坂泰三

(1886–1975). Businessman. Born in Tōkyō. After graduating from Tōkyō University, Ishizaka joined the Communications Ministry (now the Ministry of Posts and Telecommunications), but shifted to the Daiichi Seimei insurance firm in 1915 at the invitation of YANO TSUNETA. He served as its president from 1938 to 1946. Although purged by the Allied Occupation authorities after World War II, he later returned to public life, and in 1949, as president of the faltering Tōkyō Shibaura Electric (TŌSHIBA CORPORATION), supervised the company's reconstruction. He served as the second president of KEIDANREN (Japan Federation of Economic Organizations) from 1956 to 1968. Ishizaka opposed government intervention in economic affairs, particularly in trade and capital liberalization, and led the business-industrial community toward policies conducive to good relations with the United States.

Ishizaka Yōjirō 石坂洋次郎

(1900–1986). Novelist. Born in Aomori Prefecture; graduate of Keiō University. While teaching at a girls' high school, he contributed short stories to literary magazines. His novel *Wakai hito* (1933–37), serialized in the magazine MITA BUNGAKU, is about the dilemma of a young male teacher who falls in love with two uninhibited women. It became the prototype for his *seishun-mono*, novels dealing with teenage life. Characterized by sympathetic and humorous descriptions of youth freed from feudalistic social conventions, many of his works have been made into films. He was one of the most popular writers of the 1950s.

Ishizuchisan 石鎚山

Mountain in central Ehime Prefecture, Shikoku; chief peak in the Shikoku Mountains, composed of andesite. Rare plants grow here. The Ishizuchi Shrine is located on the summit. Thousands of worshipers yearly go to the mountain for the 1–10 July summer mountain festival. It is designated the Ishizuchi Quasi-National Park. Height: 1,982 m (6,503 ft).

Ishizuka Tatsumaro 石塚竜麿

(1784–1823). National Learning (KOKUGAKU) scholar; known for his discovery of a special form of ancient KANA orthography. Born in Tōtōmi Province (now Shizuoka Prefecture), he was a student of the much respected classicist and philologist MOTOORI NORINAGA. He conducted an exhaustive study of the literature of the Nara period (710–794), including the KOJIKI (712, Records of Ancient Matters) and NIHON SHOKI (720, Chronicle of Japan), the two oldest extant histories of Japan. As a result of his research, he demonstrated the existence of two special categories of characters within the writing system known as *man'yōgana*, an early Japanese orthography derived from Chinese characters (KANJI). Among Ishizuka's writings, *Kanazukai oku no yamamichi*, a three-volume orthographic study probably completed before 1798, and *Kogen seidaku kō* (1801) are especially well known.

Ishimure Michiko A writer whose major work chronicles the human suffering caused by industrial pollution in her hometown of Minamata, site of one of the worst pollution incidents in Japan.

Ishiwara Kanji A military theorist and army officer who helped plan Japan's takeover of Manchuria in 1931.

Ishizaka Yōjirō Much of the work by this 20th-century author is focused on teenage life. His novel *Aoi sammyaku* (1947, Blue Mountains) was made into a 1949 hit movie with the same name.

Isozaki Arata Isozaki's recent designs, such as that of the Kita Kyūshū International Conference Center (1990), pictured here, are characterized by an eye-catching, inventive play of geometric forms.

Ishō nihonden 異称日本伝

(Foreign Accounts of Japan). Collection of excerpts from Chinese and Korean documents concerning Japan's contacts with the Asian continent; the first known attempt to compile a history of Japanese diplomacy. It was compiled over 30 years by the Confucian and National Learning (KOKUGAKU) scholar Matsushita Kenrin (1637–1703), who completed it in 1688 and published it in 1693 in 15 volumes.

Isoda Kōichi 磯田光一

(1931–87). Literary critic. Born in Yokohama; graduate of Tōkyō University. A scholar of the English romantic poets, in the early 1960s he began to write literary criticism, which is collected in *Junkyō no bigaku* (1964). His extremely laudatory critique of MISHIMA YUKIO is philosophically consistent with Isoda's other work; he believed in an indigenous Japanese traditional "mentality," which he claimed transcends political ideology. Other works include *Shisō toshite no Tōkyō* (1978, Tōkyō as an Idea); *Nagai Kafū* (1979), a critical study of the writer; and *Hagiwara Sakutarō* (1987), an analysis of the poet and his work left incomplete at the time of Isoda's death.

Isoda Koryūsai 磯田湖竜斎

(18th century). UKIYO-E artist. Real name Isoda Masakatsu. The son of a *rōnin* (masterless *samurai*), he is thought to have studied under Nishimura Shigenaga (d 1756), a master of *bijinga*, and to have been strongly influenced by Suzuki HARUNOBU. His style resembles Harunobu's, and his earlier works are often signed Haruhiro or Koryūsai Haruhiro, the name Haruhiro being patterned on Harunobu. Koryūsai's *ukiyo-e* are marked by a sensual directness. He produced numerous *abuna-e* (mildly erotic *ukiyo-e*), *nishiki-e* (full-color prints), and SHUNGA (erotic pictures). In his later years he produced paintings rather than prints.

Isoho monogatari 伊曽保物語

A 17th-century Japanese translation of *Aesop's Fables* by an unknown translator. It was the first, and remained the only, Western literary work widely read in Japan until the 19th century. Appearing in various editions from early in the century, it appealed to educated adults and influenced subsequent Japanese fiction considerably. Many of its stories were used later by professional storytellers (see RAKUGO). An earlier translation, *Esopo no fabulas*, published in 1593 by Portuguese missionaries in romanized, colloquial Japanese, is a valuable source for linguistic studies. See JESUIT MISSION PRESS.

Isonokami no Yakatsugu 石上宅嗣

(729–781). Courtier and poet of the Nara period (710–794). A descendant of the MONONOBE FAMILY, he held a variety of court posts during his distinguished public career and was appointed great counselor (*dainagon*) in 780. Several of his verses were anthologized in the KEIKOKUSHŪ (827). A noted Buddhist scholar and bibliophile, he established the UNTEI library, perhaps the earliest important private collection in Japan.

Isonokami Shrine 石上神宮

(Isonokami Jingū). Shintō shrine in the city of Tenri, Nara Prefecture; dedicated to Futsunomitama no Ōkami, a sacred sword presented to the legendary first emperor, Jimmu, by the deity Takemikazuchi no Kami. The shrine holds many treasures, including the famous seven-pronged sword SHICHISHITŌ. The oratory (*haiden*) of the shrine is one of the oldest examples of *haiden* architecture and is designated as a National Treasure. The annual festival is held on 15 October.

Isozaki Arata 磯崎新

(1931–). Architect. Born in Ōita Prefecture. Graduated from Tōkyō University in 1954 and completed doctoral studies there in 1961. Isozaki's early designs were marked by a futuristic quality current in Japanese architecture in the 1960s; his most recent designs display a highly inventive play of geometrical forms. His works include the Ōita Prefectural Medical Association Hall (1960), the Ōita Prefectural Library (1966), the Fukuoka Mutual Bank main office (1971), the Gumma Prefectural Modern Art Museum (1974), and the Kita Kyūshū Municipal Art Museum and Library (1974). More recently, his projects have included the Tsukuba Center Building (1983), designed for EXPO '85; the Los Angeles Museum of Contemporary Art (1986); the Sports Hall in Barcelona (1990); the Brooklyn Museum in New York; and the Tōkyō Panasonic Globe (1983).

Israel and Japan イスラエルと日本

(Isuraeru to Nihon). Japan extended diplomatic recognition to the State of Israel in 1948 and formal relations were established in 1952. Israel opened a legation in Tōkyō that year, and Japan reciprocated in 1955 with the establishment of a legation in Tel Aviv. Both legations were elevated to the status of embassies in 1963.

Japan's relations with Israel have been complicated by the former's dependence on oil supplies from the Arab nations of the Middle East, but ties between the two nations have grown closer since the middle of the 1980s. Israeli foreign minister Itzhak Shamir visited Japan in 1985 and President Haim Hertzog attended the funeral of Emperor SHŌWA (Hirohito) in 1989 and the enthronement ceremonies for Emperor AKIHITO in 1990. Japanese foreign ministers Uno Sōsuke (b 1922) and Nakayama Tarō (b 1924) responded with formal visits to Israel in 1988 and 1991.

As of 1990 Israel had maintained a favorable trade balance with Japan for several years: imports from Japan in that year, chiefly automobiles and machinery, totaled US $509.0 million; exports to Japan, mainly diamonds, stood at $879.4 million. Japan was the second largest importer of Israeli goods after the United States.

Issa 一茶

(1763–1827). Also known as Kobayashi Issa. HAIKU poet of the late Edo period (1600–1868). Real name Kobayashi Nobuyuki. In addition to Issa, which means "a cup of tea," he used a number of other pen names. Born as the first son of a middle-class farmer in Kashiwabara, Shinano Province (now Nagano Prefecture), he was educated by a village teacher who wrote haiku under the pen name of Shimpo. Issa's mother died when he was three, and five years later his father married again. The stepmother was cold to Issa, and a lifelong family struggle began.

In 1777 he went to Edo (now Tōkyō). In 1787 he was studying haiku under Chikua, a poet of the Katsushika group, which was interested in reviving the style of BASHŌ. Following Chikua's death in 1790, Issa decided to live the life of a poet-priest. He spent the following 10 years or so on a series of wandering journeys. During this period, Issa visited many poets, especially in the Kansai (Kyōto-Ōsaka) area, and gathered his poems in such collections as *Kansei kikō* (1791) and *Kansei kuchō* (1794).

In 1801 his father died, and Issa wrote about this experience in *Chichi no shūen nikki* (1801, Diary of My Father's Death). Carrying out his father's wish, he decided to settle in his native village, but negotiations with his half-brother prevented his settling until 1813. During this period, he went back and forth between Edo and Kashiwabara and gathered his poems in collections that included *Kyōwa kuchō* (1803) and *Bunka kuchō* (1804–08).

In 1814 Issa married a 27-year-old woman named Kiku. Four children were born in quick succession, but none of them lived long. The birth and death of his second child, Sato, inspired Issa to write ORAGA HARU (1820; tr *The Year of My Life,* 1972), the best known of all his works; it was written in HAIBUN (haiku mixed with prose passages). Poems written after settling in his native village were gathered in such collections as *Shichiban nikki* (1810–18), *Hachiban nikki* (1819–21), *Kuban nikki* (1822–24), and *Bunsei kuchō* (1822–25). His style is characterized by a bold acceptance of down-to-earth language, by the introduction of animal images, by the use of personification and the free exercise of a comic spirit, and by the frequent expression of a stepson mentality and an obsession with poverty. These unconventional elements were, however, combined with the high seriousness Issa inherited from Bashō.

Issan Ichinei　一山一寧

(1247–1317; Ch: Yishan Yining or I-shan I-ning). Chinese Zen monk considered the founder of GOZAN LITERATURE (Chinese learning in medieval Japanese Zen monasteries). Born in Zhejiang (Chekiang) Province. After the unsuccessful MONGOL INVASIONS OF JAPAN of 1274 and 1281, Khubilai's successor sent him to Japan as a goodwill gesture. He became abbot of the temple Nanzenji in Kyōto. His disciples included KOKAN SHIREN and SESSON YŪBAI.

Issey Miyake →Miyake Issei

Issumbōshi　一寸法師

(One-Inch Boy). Folktale. A couple pray for a child and are finally granted an extraordinarily small boy, whom they fondly call Issumbōshi (literally, "One-Inch Monk"). The boy seeks his fortune in Kyōto and vanquishes demons on an island; thanks to a miraculous mallet that they have left behind, he becomes a tall man and makes a fortunate marriage. The story gained wide circulation when it was printed as an OTOGI-ZŌSHI (companion story) during the Edo period (1600–1868). Similar "small-boy" legends are found throughout Japan.

Isuzu Motors, Ltd　いすゞ自動車[株]

(Isuzu Jidōsha). Comprehensive automotive manufacturer producing commercial vehicles and passenger cars; widely known for its diesel engines. It started operations in 1916. Isuzu is Japan's largest manufacturer of trucks. It became affiliated with General Motors Corporation of the United States in 1971. The company's export ratio reached 44 percent in 1988. Sales for the fiscal year ending October 1990 totaled ¥1.2 trillion (US $9.2 billion), of which commercial vehicles generated 57 percent; passenger cars, 15 percent; and engines and other products, 28 percent. Capitalization stood at ¥63.3 billion (US $488.0 million) in 1990. Headquarters are in Tōkyō.

Itabashi Ward　板橋区

(Itabashi Ku). One of the 23 wards of Tōkyō. A residential area on the Musashino Plateau and bordered by the river Arakawa. In the Edo period (1600–1868) Itabashi was a post-station town. After World War II, large housing complexes were constructed, and the population grew rapidly. There are many small and medium-sized machinery, pharmaceutical, and chemical plants in the ward. Pop: 518,943.

itadori　虎杖

(Japanese knotweed). *Reynoutria japonica*. Large perennial herb of the buckwheat family (Polygonaceae), found in fields and mountains throughout Japan as well as in Korea and China. The unusually thick, strong stems grow from rhizomes. They are hollow and grow to 30–150 centimeters (1–5 ft). The leaves are alternate and ovate or ovately elliptic. Separate male and female plants develop panicles with numerous small white flowers in summer. The *beniitadori*, also called *meigetsusō*, is a variety with red flowers.

Raw young stems are edible but taste sour. The dried rhizome is used as a laxative and diuretic and for relieving pain. Reference to the plant as *tajii* appears in the KOJIKI (712), the oldest Japanese chronicle.

Itagaki Seishirō　板垣征四郎

(1885–1948). Army general. Born in Iwate Prefecture. He was a graduate of the Army Academy (1904) and the Army War College (1916). At the time of the MANCHURIAN INCIDENT (1931) he and ISHIWARA KANJI worked out details for the military occupation of Manchuria, and engineered the bombing that started the incident. He was named commander of the Fifth Division at the time of the outbreak of the SINO-JAPANESE WAR OF 1937–1945 but was recalled to Japan to serve as army minister in the first KONOE FUMIMARO cabinet. In 1939 he became chief of the general staff of the China Expeditionary Army. Itagaki was tried at the Tōkyō WAR CRIMES TRIALS. He was executed in 1948.

Itagaki Taisuke　板垣退助

(1837–1919). Politician of the Meiji period (1868–1912). He was a leader of the FREEDOM AND PEOPLE'S RIGHTS MOVEMENT and a founder of Japan's first major political party, the JIYŪTŌ. Itagaki was born into a *samurai* family of Kōchi, Tosa domain (now Kōchi Prefecture). After studies in Kōchi and Edo (now Tōkyō) supported by his *daimyō*'s patronage, he was appointed as a domainal official. In 1861 he was transferred to the Edo residence of the Tosa daimyō to take charge of accounts and military matters. Shortly before the MEIJI RESTORATION of 1868 Itagaki met with SAIGŌ TAKAMORI of the Satsuma domain (now Kagoshima Prefecture) and agreed to help overthrow the TOKUGAWA SHOGUNATE (1603–1867). Itagaki fought against shogunate troops in February 1868 in the BOSHIN CIVIL WAR, becoming a powerful Tosa leader.

In 1869 he entered the new government in Tōkyō and became involved in several key reforms, including the abolition of the domains and the creation of prefectures (see PREFECTURAL SYSTEM, ESTABLISHMENT OF). Itagaki, Saigō, and others resigned in protest in 1873 when the government refused to send a punitive expedition to Korea (see SEIKANRON). The following year Itagaki, along with GOTŌ SHŌJIRŌ of Tosa and ETŌ SHIMPEI and SOEJIMA TANEOMI of the Hizen domain (now Saga Prefecture), organized the AIKOKU KŌTŌ (Public Party of Patriots) in Tōkyō. In January 1874 they submitted to the government the so-called Tosa Memorial (Minsen Giin Setsuritsu Kempakusho), criticizing it for its arbitrary exercise of power and calling for the establishment of a national assembly. This document marked the beginning of the Freedom and People's Rights Movement, a nationwide movement for popular rights that would occupy a central place in Japanese politics for at least a decade. Inspired by a fusion of the samurai ethos with concepts of freedom, equality, and representative government borrowed from Western liberalism, Itagaki and his associates founded a series of organizations to agitate for their beliefs, including the RISSHISHA (Self-Help Society, 1874) and the AIKOKUSHA (Society of Patriots, 1875).

Government leaders met at the ŌSAKA CONFERENCE OF 1875, offering concessions that enticed Itagaki to return as a *sangi* (councillor). But in October of that year he resigned again, opposing the concentration of power in the DAJŌKAN (Grand Council of State).

In 1880 the Aikokusha was renamed the Kokkai Kisei Dōmei (LEAGUE FOR ESTABLISHING A NATIONAL ASSEMBLY). In October 1881 Itagaki and others formed Japan's first genuine political party, the Jiyūtō (Liberal Party).

In 1884 the Jiyūtō disbanded as a result of government repression and growing factionalism within the party itself, but by 1890 the party (now called the Rikken Jiyūtō) was revived in time for the first session of the Diet. In April 1896 Itagaki was persuaded to enter the second ITŌ HIROBUMI cabinet as home minister.

In 1898 the followers of Itagaki and ŌKUMA SHIGENOBU successfully unified the two major political parties, Itagaki's Jiyūtō and Ōkuma's SHIMPOTŌ (formerly the Rikken Kaishintō); Itagaki and Ōkuma agreed to form a joint party, the KENSEITŌ (Constitutional Party). The new party formed Japan's first party cabinet (see ŌKUMA CABINET). Itagaki served as home minister, but after four months the short-lived cooperation between the two factions broke down. Itagaki soon retired from politics and spent the rest of his life writing.

itai itai disease →pollution-related diseases

Itako　潮来[町]

Town in southeastern Ibaraki Prefecture, central Honshū, southeast of Lake Kasumigaura. An important center of water and land transportation in the Edo period (1600–1868), Itako declined after the opening of the Jōban railway line. Occupations include rice cultivation and garden farming. The town's Iris Festival is held in June. Pop: 24,445.

Itakura Katsukiyo　板倉勝静

(1823–89). *Daimyō* of the Matsuyama domain (now part of Okayama Prefecture) and a close adviser of TOKUGAWA YOSHINOBU, the last shōgun of the Tokugawa shogunate (1603–1867). After the restoration of imperial rule and the defeat of Tokugawa forces in the Battle of TOBA-FUSHIMI in early 1868, Itakura returned to Edo (now Tōkyō) to resist an imperial takeover (see BOSHIN CIVIL WAR). Unsuccessful, he fled to Hakodate, where in 1869 Itakura and other Tokugawa diehards, including ENOMOTO TAKEAKI, capitulated; he was pardoned in 1871.

Itakura Katsushige　板倉勝重

(1545–1624). Administrator of the early Tokugawa regime. Born in Mikawa Province (now part of Aichi Prefecture), Katsushige assumed the headship of his *samurai* family in 1581. Katsushige served TOKUGAWA IEYASU as a city commissioner (*machi bugyō*) of Sumpu (now the city of Shizuoka), Ieyasu's headquarters from 1587. Upon Ieyasu's transfer to Edo (now Tōkyō) in 1590, he became an EDO MACHI BUGYŌ. In 1601 Katsushige was made a city commissioner of Kyōto; he served the TOKUGAWA SHOGUNATE

Itakura Katsushige

Itami Jūzō

1 Itami, who is one of the most popular of Japan's current film directors. He is known for his offbeat views of contemporary life.
2 The film *Osōshiki* (1984, The Funeral), Itami's directorial debut, won many of Japan's motion picture awards. *Clockwise from top:* Edoya Nekohachi, Miyamoto Nobuko (Itami's wife), Yamazaki Tsutomu, Ōtaki Shūji, Sugai Kin.
3 A scene from *Marusa no onna* (1987, A Taxing Woman), with Miyamoto Nobuko in the lead role. The film took tax evasion as its theme and became a big hit in Japan.

(1603–1867) as KYŌTO SHOSHIDAI (the shogunal deputy in Kyōto) from 1603. His responsibilities included not only the administration of civil affairs and criminal justice in the city and surrounding countryside but also the supervision of the shogunate's direct holdings (TENRYŌ) in the Kyōto-Ōsaka region and the surveillance of the *daimyō* of western Japan. The cordial relations he enjoyed with the Kyōto aristocracy may have been the reason for his replacement in 1619. Katsushige's son Shigemune (1586–1656) succeeded him as Kyōto *shoshidai*.

Italy and Japan イタリアと日本

(Itaria *to* Nihon). The first contact between Italy and Japan took place in the late 16th century with the arrival of Italian Catholic missionaries in Japan. On the initiative of the missionary Alessandro VALIGNANO, four Japanese youths representing the CHRISTIAN DAIMYŌ were dispatched to the Vatican on the MISSION TO EUROPE OF 1582, and in 1613 the daimyō DATE MASAMUNE sent HASEKURA TSUNENAGA to Rome to negotiate a trade agreement. Italian-Japanese contact was soon halted, however, by the anti-Christian policies of the Tokugawa shogunate (1603–1867).

Cultural Exchange After 1868——Regular intercourse between Italy and Japan began after the Meiji Restoration of 1868. Among the many Western technological and cultural imports brought to Japan during the Meiji (1868–1912) and Taishō (1912–26) periods were modern Italian military technology and, especially, Italian art and music.

Italians contributed significantly to the development of Western art in Japan. In 1876 Japan established its first art academy, the Kōbu Bijutsu Gakkō, and invited a number of Italian artists and art critics to teach at the school. Among these Italian instructors were Antonio FONTANESI and Vincenzo RAGUSA. The Italian engraver Edoardo CHIOSSONE, who was employed by the Japanese government, designed Japan's first modern paper currency.

Italy's contribution to Western music in Japan took place largely during the Taishō period. Adolfo Sarcoli (1867–1936) transmitted knowledge of Western music in general and also contributed much to the development of vocal music. Giovanni Vittorio Rossi was active in the introduction of dance, operetta, and vocal music. He also played a key role in the first visit of an Italian opera company to Japan, in 1929.

The War Years——By the 1930s Italy had a fascist government and Japanese politics had taken on strong fascist tendencies. Close Italian-Japanese political and military relations were established through the conclusion of the ANTI-COMINTERN PACT (1937) and the TRIPARTITE PACT (1940). Attempts were also made to enhance relations between the people of Italy and Japan through the establishment of the Italo-Japanese Society (forerunner of the present-day Japan-Italy Institute) in Japan in 1937 and the Società Amici del Giappone in Italy in 1938. In 1941 an agreement for the monthly ex-

change of music and news broadcasts was concluded.

Relations after World War II——After World War II and the restoration of democratic forms of government in Japan and Italy, political and economic exchange increased significantly. Diplomatic relations were friendly throughout the postwar period, and regular consultations between the foreign ministers of the two countries began in 1965. The first Italian prime minister to visit Japan officially was Giulio Andreotti, in 1973, and a number of Japanese prime ministers have paid official visits to Italy in the postwar years.

The postwar period also initiated an increase in trade between the two countries. The principal imports from Italy have included food products (olive oil, canned tomatoes, and cheese), leather goods, and textiles. Principal Japanese exports to Italy through the postwar years included ships and other steel products, electrical appliances, and motorcycles, but these have gradually been supplanted by such electronic products as televisions, videocassette recorders, and computers. As of 1989, however, the volume of trade between Japan and Italy remained small compared to their trade with numerous other countries. This was partly due to Italy's attempt to protect its domestic industries, especially its automotive industry, by imposing import restrictions on Japanese products. In August 1989, however, the Italian government announced a four-stage plan for liberalizing trade with Japan. In 1990, exports from Japan to Italy reached US $3.4 billion, while imports to Japan from Italy totaled US $5.0 billion, making Italy one of the few countries to register a trade surplus with Japan.

Itami 伊丹[市]

City in southeastern Hyōgo Prefecture, western Honshū. Originating as a castle town in the mid-16th century, it later developed as a *sake*-brewing center and is now a satellite city of Ōsaka. Itami's major industries are food-processing, machinery, and electrical machinery. Ōsaka International Airport is here. Pop: 186,134.

Itami Jūzō 伊丹十三

(1933–). Actor, scenarist, film director, and essayist. Real name Ikeuchi Yoshihiro. The son of ITAMI MANSAKU, he was born in Kyōto. First hired as a film actor by DAIEI CO, LTD, in 1960, he turned in superb performances in supporting roles, his forte being the cynical intellectual. Itami appeared in *Nihon shunka kō* (1967, A Treatise on the Japanese Bawdy Song), directed by ŌSHIMA NAGISA, and *Kazoku gēmu* (1983, The Family Game), directed by Morita Yoshimitsu (b 1950), before writing and directing *Osōshiki* (1984, The Funeral) to great acclaim. He also wrote, produced, and directed *TAMPOPO* (1986), *Marusa no onna* (1987, A Taxing Woman), *Marusa no onna 2* (1988, A Taxing Woman Returns), and *Ageman* (1990, Lady Luck).

Itami Mansaku 伊丹万作

(1900–1946). Film director and scenarist. Real name Ikeuchi Yoshitoyo. Born in Ehime Prefecture. He became a director in 1928 with *Adauchi ruten* (Perpetual Vendetta). Itami became known for his skillful direction of period films with intellectual and modernistic themes, and is noted for such movies as *Kokushi musō* (1932, Peerless Patriot) and *Akanishi Kakita* (1936). *Akanishi Kakita* was one of the first films to treat the *samurai* tradition (embodied in its eponymous hero)

with a satirical touch. Itami is also known for his work as a scenarist, beginning with *Tenka taiheiki* (1928, The Wandering Gambler), directed by INAGAKI HIROSHI. Other works include *Muhōmatsu no isshō* (1943, The Life of Matsu the Untamed) and *Te o tsunagu kora* (1948, Children Hand in Hand), also directed by Inagaki.

Itaya Hazan 板谷波山

(1872–1963). Porcelain artist, best known for his low relief and lightly lustrous matte-glaze polychrome designs. Real name Itaya Kashichi. Born in Shimodate, Ibaraki Prefecture; graduate of the Tōkyō Bijutsu Gakkō (now Tōkyō University of Fine Arts and Music) and a teacher of sculpture and ceramics at the Ishikawa Prefectural Industrial School. In 1903 he left for Tōkyō to teach at Tōkyō Industrial College and established his own kiln. He won a number of gold medals at exhibitions, including the 1928 Teiten. In 1953 he received the Order of Culture. Hazan's porcelains (about 1,000 survive) range from celadon, white-and-cinnabar pieces, and iron-glaze *temmoku* tea wares emulating ancient Chinese models to the matte-glaze, powdery, pastel polychrome works for which he was famous.

Itō 伊東[市]

City in eastern Shizuoka Prefecture, central Honshū, on the Izu Peninsula. Its mild climate and hot springs have made it a popular resort. Itō is also a base for deep-sea fishing. A part of the FUJI-HAKONE-IZU NATIONAL PARK, the city also has a marine park; a cactus park; and historical sites associated with MINAMOTO NO YORITOMO, NICHIREN, and William ADAMS. Pop: 71,223.

Itōchū Corporation 伊藤忠商事[株]

(Itōchū Shōji). Named C. Itoh & Co, Ltd, until 1992. One of Japan's major GENERAL TRADING COMPANIES (*sōgō shōsha*). Founded in 1858 as a textile wholesaler, it has been traditionally strong in the fields of textiles and fuel. After World War II, it was divided into C. Itoh & Co and the MARUBENI CORPORATION. Itōchū has 41 offices and branches in Japan and subsidiaries, branches, and representatives in 84 countries. Sales for the fiscal year ending March 1991 totaled ¥20.6 trillion (US $150.1 billion), of which textiles constituted 11 percent; machinery and construction, 26 percent; metal and ore, 28 percent; food and agriculture products, 11 percent; forest products and general merchandise, 5 percent; and energy and chemicals, 19 percent. Capitalization stood at ¥174.7 billion (US $1.3 billion) in March 1991. Headquarters are in Ōsaka.

Itō Chūta 伊東忠太

(1867–1954). Architect and pioneering architectural historian. Born in Yamagata Prefecture. In 1892 he graduated from Tōkyō University, where he later served as a professor from 1905 to 1928, and began postgraduate studies in the history of Japanese architecture. His research took him to China, where he encountered the 5th-century cave temples at Yungang (Yün-kang) and helped establish their significance in the history of Buddhist architecture. He also traveled to Burma and India in search of the roots of the Buddhist architectural tradition. As a practicing architect his designs include the HEIAN SHRINE (1895), the MEIJI SHRINE (1920), the Shūkokan Museum (1927), and the Tsukiji Honganji temple (1934). In 1943 he became the first architect to be awarded the Order of Culture.

Itō Daisuke 伊藤大輔

(1898–1981). Film director. Born in Ehime Prefecture. In 1920 he entered the acting school affiliated with what is now SHŌCHIKU CO, LTD. He joined the company's scriptwriting department and then its contemporary drama section. His debut as a director came in 1924 with *Shuchū nikki*, after which he founded the independent Itō Eiga Kenkyūjo (Itō Movie Research Center) in 1926. Despite great financial strain, he managed to produce *Kyōko to Shizuko* (1926, Kyōko and Shizuko) and *Nichirin* (1926, The Sun) but incurred tremendous debts. His films *Chōkon* (1926, Lingering Resentment) and *Chūji tabi nikki* (1927, Chūji's Travels) were, however, great successes. In the early "talkies" era he directed *Tange Sazen* (1933) and *Satsuma hikyaku* (1938, The Courier of Satsuma). With his historical period works he broke away from the tradition of heroic films by portraying tragic, rebellious protagonists and gained the sympathy of the antiestablishment proletarian class. In the post–World War II era, he directed *Ōshō* (1948, The Chess King) and *Hangyakuji* (1961, The Rebel).

Itō Gemboku 伊東玄朴

(1800–1871). Physician; the foremost authority on Western medicine in the late Edo period (1600–1868). Born in what is now Saga Prefecture, he studied the Dutch language under Inomata Denjiemon and medicine under Philipp Franz von SIEBOLD. In 1826 he established the Shōsendō, a school of Western sciences in Edo (now Tōkyō) from which many prominent physicians and scholars graduated. In 1831 he was appointed physician of the Saga domain and in 1858 physician to the TOKUGAWA SHOGUNATE (1603–1867). He pioneered the use of the smallpox vaccine in Japan, and the vaccination center he established in 1857 in Edo evolved into Tōkyō University's School of Medicine. His written works include *Iryō seishi*, a 24-volume translation, from the Dutch, of Austrian medical texts.

Itōham Foods, Inc 伊藤ハム[株]

(Itō Hamu). Processed-food manufacturer, specializing in ham, sausage, and processed meats. The largest producer of ham and sausage in Japan, the company was established in 1928 in Ōsaka by Itō Denzō. It has joint ventures in the United States and Brazil. Sales for the fiscal year ending March 1991 totaled ¥421.0 billion (US $3.1 billion); capitalization stood at ¥22.3 billion (US $162.5 million) in the same year. Headquarters are in Nishinomiya, Hyōgo Prefecture.

Itō Hirobumi 伊藤博文

(1841–1909). Preeminent statesman of modern Japan. In a career that spanned nearly the entire Meiji period (1868–1912), Itō played a leading role in guiding Japan in its formative years as a modern nation-state. He was the chief architect of Japan's first constitution and served four terms as prime minister.

Itō was born in the Chōshū domain (now Yamaguchi Prefecture). His father was the adopted son of a low-ranking *samurai* family. As a young man Itō was active in the SONNŌ JŌI movement, which held that Japan should be united under imperial rule and that incursions by foreign nations should be repelled. In 1863 Chōshū officials awarded Itō samurai status and, despite Japan's policy of NATIONAL SECLUSION, sent him to England for study. While abroad Itō abandoned his anti-Western stance and came to favor the diplomatic and commercial opening of Japan. Upon his return he and INOUE KAORU led the negotiations following the bombing of Chōshū by Western forces (see SHIMONOSEKI BOMBARDMENT).

With the MEIJI RESTORATION (1868) Itō was appointed *san'yō* (junior councillor; see SANSHOKU), with responsibility for foreign affairs. In 1870 he went to the United States to study Western currency systems. Returning to Japan in 1871, he was made director of the Tax Division and then vice-minister of public works. Later that year he accompanied the IWAKURA MISSION to Europe and the United States. In 1873 Itō was appointed SANGI (councillor) and minister of public works, and in 1875 he presided as chairman of the first Assembly of Prefectural Governors.

The death of KIDO TAKAYOSHI in 1877 and the assassination of ŌKUBO TOSHIMICHI in 1878 signaled a change in Japanese political leadership. Itō, now home minister, and Finance Minister ŌKUMA SHIGENOBU emerged as the most powerful figures in government. Ōkuma's ouster in the POLITICAL CRISIS OF 1881 left Itō in a position of unchallenged power.

In 1883, having returned from nearly one and a half years of study in Europe (notably in Germany) under leading constitutional scholars, Itō and others set to work in drafting the CONSTITUTION OF THE EMPIRE OF JAPAN. He also wrote the draft of the IMPERIAL HOUSEHOLD LAW, and to further bolster the prestige of the imperial family he issued the Peerage Act of 1884 (see PEERAGE). Upon the establishment of a modern cabinet system in 1885, Itō became the first prime minister, serving concurrently as imperial household minister and chairman of the Constitutional Commission. In 1888 Itō resigned as prime minister to head the PRIVY COUNCIL, a supracabinet body he had established to give formal approval to the constitution. In 1889 he was granted the title *genkun*, or elder statesmen (see GENRŌ). The constitution was promulgated on 11 February of that year.

Itō was prime minister again from 1892 to 1896, during which time Japan defeated the superior forces of China in the SINO-JAPANESE WAR OF 1894–1895. He represented Japan in negotiating the Treaty of SHIMONOSEKI, which formally concluded the war. The landmark victory signaled Japan's emergence as the dominant East Asian power, but it also marked the point at which Japanese foreign policy began to emphasize Western-style territorial expansion. Earlier, Itō had helped Japan achieve its first important success in removing extraterritorial rights held by Western countries in Japan (see ANGLO-JAPANESE COMMERCIAL TREATY OF 1894). In Japanese eyes these events represented the culmination of Japan's long quest for great-power status on the level of Western nations.

In 1898 Itō began a third term as prime minister. Both the JIYŪTŌ (Liberal Party) and the SHIMPOTŌ (Progressive Party) opposed his proposal for extra land taxes. In response Itō dissolved the Diet, an action that prompted the two parties to merge into the KENSEITŌ (Constitutional Party), which won a Diet majority in the next election. Itō resigned as prime minister soon after. His experiences with obstructionist party politicians convinced him of the need for a progovernment party, and in 1900 he organized the RIKKEN SEIYŪKAI (Friends of Constitutional Government Party) and began a fourth and final term as prime minister. Obstructive tactics continued, however, this time in the House of Peers. In 1901, weary of politics and of dealing with party members, each with his own constituency to answer to, Itō resigned.

Itō returned to politics in 1903 as head of the Privy Council. In 1904 Japan went to war with Russia for control of both Korea and Manchuria (see RUSSO-JAPANESE WAR). With Japan's victory in 1905, Itō went to Korea to sign the KOREAN-JAPANESE CONVENTION OF 1905, which gave Japan full control of Korea's foreign relations. Itō returned to Korea the next year as the first Japanese resident general. In 1907 he forced the Korean emperor to abdicate and established a full Japanese protectorate over Korea, thus paving the way for annexation (see KOREA, ANNEXATION OF). Itō resigned as resident general in 1909. During a tour of Manchuria later that year he was assassinated in Harbin by AN CHUNG-GŬN, a Korean nationalist.

Itō Hirobumi The preeminent statesman of the Meiji period, Itō was chief architect of Japan's first constitution and served four terms as prime minister.

Itoigawa 糸魚川[市]

City in southwestern Niigata Prefecture, central Honshū, on the Sea of Japan. A castle town during the Edo period (1600–1868), Itoigawa has been traditionally known for its hot springs and jade. Its abundant supply of limestone provides material for local cement and related industries. Itoigawa lies on the starting point of the Itoigawa-Shizuoka Tectonic Line (see FOSSA MAGNA). Pop: 34,047.

Itō Jakuchū 伊藤若冲

(1716–1800). Painter known for his meticulously detailed, almost surrealistic, depictions of exotic birds and fowl. Born in Kyōto. He began by studying the techniques of the KANŌ SCHOOL but, unsatisfied, went on to study Chinese BIRD-AND-FLOWER PAINTING.

Beginning around 1758 Jakuchū worked on a spectacular set of 30 large hanging scrolls as a votive offering to the temple SHŌKOKUJI. In the mid-1770s, he retreated to the mountains of Tamba Province (now part of Kyōto Prefecture) and embarked on a project at the temple Sekihōji: to erect an outdoor sculptural series of the eight phases of the Buddha Śākyamuni's life (Shaka hassō), which included 500 stone images of arhats, or RAKAN. In order to support himself, Jakuchū exchanged paintings for rice, often signing his paintings Tobeiō (Old Man Bushel of Rice).

Itō Jinsai 伊藤仁斎

(1627–1705). Confucian philosopher and educator. Founder of the Kogigaku (Study of Ancient Meaning) school. Born in Kyōto. Jinsai dedicated himself to the study of Confucian teachings, concentrating on Neo-Confucian doctrines, chiefly those derived from the philosophy of Zhu Xi (Chu Hsi, 1130–1200; see SHUSHIGAKU). Confident that he had comprehended the essence of these concepts, he developed his own ideas, which he expounded in his works *Taikyokuron* (A Treatise on the Ultimate), *Seizenron* (On the Goodness of Human Nature), and *Shingaku genron* (Principles in the Study of Mind).

Later, however, he became skeptical of the Zhu Xi school philosophy and explored the teachings of Wang Yangming (1472–1529; see YŌMEIGAKU) and Zen. He came to believe that the path of the sages should be understood by direct readings in such Confucian classics as the *Analects* or *Mencius*, and he discouraged reliance upon later interpretations. Jinsai's studies are generally referred to by the name Kogigaku because the aim was the clarification of the original meanings of the classics. Kogigaku is considered part of the KOGAKU (Ancient Learning) school. Jinsai established a private

Itō Midori The popular figure skater glides to a first place finish at the 1991 First Asia Cup Figure Skating Competition in Yokohama.

school in Kyōto named Kogidō (the Hall of Ancient Meaning). He remains the most noteworthy Confucian philosopher of the Edo period (1600–1868), whose stress upon loyalty and faithfulness led to the general emphasis on *makoto* (sincerity) that was characteristic of ethical thought in the Edo period.

Itojō   怡土城

(Ito Castle). Fortress built in the Nara period (710–794) in the western part of Chikuzen Province (now the town of Maebaru, Fukuoka Prefecture). According to the chronicle *Shoku nihongi* (797), construction began in 756 and took 13 years to complete. Located on the western slope of Mt. Takasu, the castle covered about 250 hectares (618 acres). Built under KIBI NO MAKIBI's supervision as a base for a proposed invasion of Korea, the castle was abandoned soon after its completion, when the invasion did not materialize. Excavation of the ruins in 1936 revealed remains of the gate and a watchtower.

Itokawa Hideo   糸川英夫

(1912–). Aeronautical engineer and leading figure in the development of the Japanese space program in the 1950s and 1960s. Born in Tōkyō, he graduated from Tōkyō University in 1935. During World War II, he helped to design the HAYABUSA and other fighters at Nakajima Airplane Co (now FUJI HEAVY INDUSTRIES, LTD). In 1951 he began his study of high-speed projectiles and rockets at Tōkyō University's Institute of Industrial Science. He also served as professor at Tōkyō University from 1948 to 1967. In 1967 he established and became director of the Systems Research Institute.

Itō Keiichi   伊藤桂一

(1917–). Novelist. Born in Mie Prefecture. Completed secondary school in Tōkyō. He served in Manchuria and China in World War II. Although most of his novels are based on his wartime experiences, they have a lyrical quality that stresses man's intimate connection with the natural world. His best-known novels include *Hotaru no kawa* (1961, River of Fireflies), which won the Naoki Prize, and *Kanashiki senki* (1962–63, Sad Tales of the War).

Itō Keisuke   伊藤圭介

(1803–1901). Specialist in *honzōgaku* (traditional pharmacognosy) and botany who helped modernize the study of pharmacognosy in the Edo period (1600–1868). Born in the city of Nagoya. He first studied traditional medicine and went into private practice. He wrote *Taisei honzō meiso* (1829) based on Carl Peter THUNBERG's *Flora Japonica*. In his book he used the Linnaean plant classification system and the Latin names of plants for the first time in Japan. In 1881 he became a professor at Tōkyō University, and in 1888 he became the first doctor of science in Japan.

Itokin Co, Ltd   イトキン[株]

(Itokin). Apparel manufacturer specializing in women's wear. Incorporated in 1955. It has more than 70 brand names on its production roster. The company has production and sales subsidiaries in Hong Kong, Seoul, New York, Paris, and Milan. For the fiscal year ending January 1991, sales totaled ¥150.1 billion (US $1.1 billion) and capitalization

Itsuki Hiroyuki This prolific writer of essays and contemporary romances was one of Japan's best-selling authors during the 1960s and 1970s.

stood at ¥1.0 billion (US $7.5 million). Headquarters are in Ōsaka.

Itokoku   伊都国

A dependent state of the ancient Japanese state YAMATAI, mentioned in the WEI ZHI (*Wei chih*), a 3rd century Chinese history. It is believed to have been situated in the area of the town of Maebaru in the Itoshima district of Fukuoka Prefecture. The Maebaru area is now the site of archaeological excavations. Artifacts discovered there, including mirrors and other bronze objects, indicate that Itokoku was the cultural center of western Japan in the Yayoi period (ca 300 BC–ca AD 300).

Itoman   糸満[市]

City on the southern tip of the island of Okinawa, Okinawa Prefecture. Itoman has long been known for its daring fishermen, who ventured in small boats as far as the Indian Ocean. Fishing remains the principal industry. Southern Itoman was a battlefield during the last months of World War II; the area, designated as the Okinawa Old Battlefield Quasi-National Park, has several memorials to the dead. Pop: 49,636.

Itō Mancio   伊東マンショ

(ca 1570–1612). Nominal leader of the MISSION TO EUROPE OF 1582 sent by the CHRISTIAN DAIMYŌ of Kyūshū. Real name Itō Sukemasu. Born in Hyūga Province (now Miyazaki Prefecture), he is believed to have been a grandson of the warlord Itō Yoshisuke (1513–85) and a relative of ŌTOMO SŌRIN, *daimyō* of Bungo (now Ōita Prefecture). He was baptized Mancio in 1580 and studied at the seminary in Arima. In 1582 he and three other boys left for a tour of southern Europe that culminated in a papal audience in 1585. Returning to Japan in 1590, Itō entered the Society of Jesus the following year and was ordained in 1608.

Itoman Corporation   イトマン[株]

(Itoman). Trading firm primarily handling textile goods. Founded in 1883. Initially the company sold cotton and other textile goods in Japan, Korea, Manchuria, and Taiwan, but in the 1960s it diversified into the fields of steel, machinery, and foodstuffs and in the 1970s into the real estate and leisure industries. Hurt financially by real estate investment losses, Itoman announced in 1992 that it would cease to exist on 1 April 1993, when it was expected to merge with Sumikin Bussan Co, Ltd, an unlisted steel-products trading company in the Sumitomo group.

Itō Masami   伊藤正己

(1919–). Scholar of Anglo-American and constitutional law. Born in Kōbe. A graduate of Tōkyō University, Itō served as a professor there from 1957 to 1980. He was a Supreme Court justice from 1980 to 1989. Itō has done important work on the parliamentary system and rules of law of Great Britain and on the right of privacy. His *Genron, shuppan no jiyū* (1959, Freedom of Speech and of the Press), a study of standards for judicial review based on US precedential materials, was a pioneering achievement of Japanese legal scholarship. During his tenure on a relatively conservative Supreme Court, Itō wrote supplementary and dissenting opinions on many important cases.

Itō Masatoshi   伊藤雅俊

(1924–). Businessman; president of ITŌ-YŌKADŌ CO, LTD (1958–). Born in Tōkyō, he

graduated from Yokohama City University in 1944. In 1958 he established Itō-Yōkadō and became its president. He established DENNY'S JAPAN CO, LTD, and SEVEN-ELEVEN JAPAN CO, LTD, in 1973 and is president of both. He is managing director of the Japan Chain Store Association (1987–) and a member of the board of directors of KEIDANREN (Federation of Economic Organizations; 1982–).

Itō Midori   伊藤みどり

(1969–). Figure skater. Born in Aichi Prefecture; graduated from Tōkai Junior College for Women. The first woman to perform a triple axel in competition, Itō reproduced this feat to win the silver medal at the 1992 Winter Olympics in Albertville, France, Japan's first Olympic figure skating medal.

Itō Miyoji   伊東巳代治

(1857–1934). Bureaucrat and politician. Born in what is now Nagasaki Prefecture. He accompanied statesman ITŌ HIROBUMI to Europe in 1882 and later, with INOUE KOWASHI and KANEKO KENTARŌ, assisted him in drafting the CONSTITUTION OF THE EMPIRE OF JAPAN. He served as Itō's chief cabinet secretary (1892) and as his minister of commerce and agriculture (1898). As president (1891–1904) of the progovernment newspaper *Tōkyō nichinichi shimbun* (now *Mainichi shimbun*) he consistently defended stable government bureaucracy. In 1899 he was appointed privy councillor. During the FINANCIAL CRISIS OF 1927 he brought about the collapse of the first WAKATSUKI REIJIRŌ cabinet. He criticized the administration of HAMAGUCHI OSACHI for infringing on the "prerogative of [the emperor's] supreme command" (see TŌSUIKEN) by accepting the proposals of the LONDON NAVAL CONFERENCES for limiting the size of the Japanese navy.

Itō Noe   伊藤野枝

(1895–1923). Feminist and anarchist. Born in Fukuoka Prefecture. After graduating from Ueno Girls' High School in Tōkyō, she was forced into an arranged marriage in her native village, but soon fled back to the city. There she joined the feminist group SEITŌSHA (Bluestocking Society) and edited its magazine, *Seitō* (Bluestocking), from 1915 to 1916. In 1916 she left her second husband, the writer TSUJI JUN, and began living with anarchist ŌSUGI SAKAE. Itō worked with him in promoting the anarchist movement. She helped to found the socialist women's group SEKIRANKAI in 1921. She and Ōsugi were killed by military police during the chaos following the massive TŌKYŌ EARTHQUAKE OF 1923, when many left-wing activists were arrested or killed.

Itō Sachio   伊藤左千夫

(1864–1913). TANKA poet and novelist. Real name Itō Kōjirō. Born in Chiba Prefecture. In 1900 his interest in poetry spurred him to visit MASAOKA SHIKI, and he became one of Shiki's most faithful disciples. Itō was instrumental in establishing the poetry magazine *Ashibi* in 1903, serving as its editor until its demise in 1908. With other members of the Negishi Tanka Kai (a poetry group founded by Shiki) he founded the magazine *Araragi* in 1908; there he published poems, critical works on *tanka*, and studies of the MAN'YŌSHŪ. SAITŌ MOKICHI and SHIMAKI AKAHIKO are two poets whom Itō encouraged. *Sachio kashū*, a collection of his poems, was published in 1920. His sentimental love story *Nogiku no haka* (1906, Grave amid Asters) has become a popular classic.

Itō Sei 伊藤整

(1905–69). Literary critic, author, and translator. Real name Itō Hitoshi. Born and educated in Hokkaidō. His first literary effort was a collection of poems titled *Yukiakari no michi* (1926, Snow-Lit Path).

Itō embarked on a literary career at a time when the Japanese literary establishment was shaken by the impact of the Marxist-oriented PROLETARIAN LITERATURE MOVEMENT. He emerged firmly in the antiproletarian camp as the leader of a modernistic movement: the so-called new psychological literature (*shin shinri shugi bungaku*), which introduced 20th-century European writers to Japan.

In 1950 Itō was named as a defendant in the LADY CHATTERLEY'S LOVER CASE on account of his allegedly obscene translation of D. H. Lawrence's *Lady Chatterley's Lover*. The litigation continued until the Supreme Court issued a guilty verdict seven years later.

His works include the essay collections *Shin shinri shugi bungaku* (1932) and *Shōsetsu no hōhō* (1948, The Method of the Novel), the novels *Yūki no machi* (1937, A Ghost Town) and *Yūki no mura* (1938, A Ghost Village), and the short-story collection *Seibutsusai* (1932, Festival of the Living). He was posthumously awarded the Shinchō Prize in 1970 for his last novel, *Hen'yō*. He was a cofounder of the MUSEUM OF MODERN JAPANESE LITERATURE (Nihon Kindai Bungakukan). His 18-volume *Nihon bundan shi* (1952–73) is considered a classic study of the history of modern Japanese literature.

Itō Shinsui 伊東深水

(1898–1972). Japanese-style painter and print designer, best known for his *bijinga* (pictures of beautiful women). Born in Tōkyō, he studied under KABURAGI KIYOKATA. Itō made his first color print in 1916; it immediately established his reputation. His most famous series, the ŌMI HAKKEI (Eight Views of Ōmi), produced in 1917, established the close relationship of his work to traditional Japanese prints in both style and subject matter. However, unlike traditional UKIYO-E, his prints were made by craftsmen from finished paintings. His paintings of beautiful women are painted in the soft, misty palette of modern Japanese-style painting (*nihonga*) and are generally considered his finest works.

Itō Shizuo 伊東静雄

(1906–53). Poet. Born in Nagasaki Prefecture; graduate of Kyōto University. He contributed poetry to the magazines *Kogito* and *Nihon rōmanha*. In 1935 he published his first collection of poems, *Waga hito ni atauru aika* (Sad Poems for My Lady), which was highly praised by symbolist poet HAGIWARA SAKUTARŌ. During World War II, Itō published two more collections: *Natsuhana* (1940, Summer Flowers) and *Haru no isogi* (1943, Spring's Haste). Itō's poems are characterized by recurrent death imagery and a lyrical quality reminiscent of the European poet Rainer Maria Rilke.

Itō Sukechika 伊東祐親

(?–1182). Warrior of the late Heian period (794–1185). Sukechika's appropriation of his nephew Kudō Suketsune's estate in Izu Province (now part of Shizuoka Prefecture) led Suketsune to instigate the murder of Sukechika's son. (Later, in 1193, Sukechika's grandsons, the Soga brothers, murdered Suketsune; see SOGA MONOGATARI.) Sukechika had had charge of MINAMOTO NO YORITOMO when the latter was exiled by TAIRA NO KIYOMORI. In 1180, however, Sukechika fought against Yoritomo and was captured; although released in 1182, he committed suicide.

Itō Tōgai 伊藤東涯

(1670–1738). Confucian scholar and teacher. Born in Kyōto. Tōgai was the eldest son of ITŌ JINSAI. Refusing public office, he devoted himself to writing and teaching. He carried on the work of his father, who rejected the Zhu Xi (Chu Hsi; see SHUSHIGAKU) and Wang Yangming (YŌMEIGAKU) interpretations and emphasized the study of the *Analects* and other Confucian classics (KOGAKU). Although he lacked his father's originality of thought, Tōgai was proficient in Confucian classics and literature, Japanese and Chinese institutional history, linguistics, and Korean literature. The noted scholar AOKI KON'YŌ was one of his outstanding disciples. Tōgai wrote a total of 53 works.

itowappu 糸割符

System under which certain merchants were granted a monopoly of the Chinese raw-silk trade during the Edo period (1600–1868); also called *shiraitowappu*. During the late 16th century all raw silk was imported by Portuguese merchants, who alone had access to trade with China. Under a system known as *pancada*, the Japanese merchants would buy a year's supply of silk from the Portuguese at a fixed price determined by negotiation. In a narrow sense, this term also referred to the fixed price itself. In order to strengthen its control of foreign trade, in 1604 the Tokugawa shogunate established the *itowappu* system, granting a group of merchants from Sakai, Nagasaki, and Kyōto exclusive power to buy, allocate, and negotiate the import price of raw silk. The *itowappu* system was applied to trade with the Chinese in 1631 and, after the shogunate's enactment of the NATIONAL SECLUSION policy and its expulsion of the Portuguese in 1639, to trade with the Dutch in 1641. The system was abolished in 1655 because of strong opposition from Chinese traders, was reimposed in 1685, and endured until the opening of Japan in the 1850s. See also GOKASHO SHŌNIN.

Itō-Yōkadō Co, Ltd ［株］イトーヨーカ堂

(Itō-Yōkadō). Chain store chiefly engaged in retail sale of clothing, household goods, and food products through its large facilities known as "superstores." Incorporated in 1913. The firm has 138 stores, mainly in the Tōkyō area. Among its affiliates are the convenience store chain SEVEN-ELEVEN JAPAN CO, LTD, and the restaurant chain DENNY'S JAPAN CO, LTD. Sales for the fiscal year ending February 1991 totaled ¥1.4 trillion (US $10.7 billion) and capitalization stood at ¥37.0 billion (US $283.6 million). Headquarters are in Tōkyō.

Itsuki Hiroyuki 五木寛之

(1932–). Novelist. Born in Fukuoka Prefecture; lived in Korea until the end of World War II; attended Waseda University. After working as an editor and free-lance journalist, he published *Saraba Mosukuwa gurentai* (1966, Farewell to the Moscow Misfits), a novel about a Japanese jazz pianist's unsettling encounter in Moscow with a misfit Russian youth who wants to play the jazz trumpet. The following year, Itsuki won the Naoki Prize for *Aozameta uma o miyo* (1966,

See the Pale Horse). He was one of Japan's best-selling writers of popular fiction in the 1960s and 1970s. The first segments of his ongoing autobiographical novel, *Seishun no mon* (The Gate of Youth), begun in 1969, were made into a movie and serialized on television. Other works include the novel *Kaze no ōkoku* (1985, Kingdom of the Wind).

Itsukushima 厳島

Also known as Miyajima. Island in Hiroshima Bay, west central Inland Sea, 20 km (12 mi) southwest of the city of Hiroshima, Hiroshima Prefecture. The island is covered with forests, with little level ground. It is famous for the ITSUKUSHIMA SHRINE on the northern shore, with its vermilion *torii* (gateway) in the bay between the island and Honshū. This forms one of the NIHON SANKEI, the three most beautiful views in Japan. Area: 30.2 sq km (11.7 sq mi).

Itsukushima Also known as Miyajima, this island in the Inland Sea is the site of the Itsukushima Shrine, which is dedicated to three tutelary deities of fishing.
1 The great Itsukushima *torii*, symbol of the shrine and its sacred entrance.
2 Taira no Kiyomori, a powerful provincial governor who eventually came to control the imperial institution, provided the funds to build the main shrine and to amass the treasures that fill it.

Iwaki Hiroyuki This orchestral conductor, one of the few to regularly incorporate modern works into the traditional classical orchestral program, is shown here leading the NHK Symphony Orchestra.

Itsukushima Shrine 厳島神社

(Itsukushima Jinja). Sometimes called Aki no Miyajima. A Shintō shrine on the island of ITSUKUSHIMA in the Saeki district of Hiroshima Prefecture; dedicated to Ichikishimahime no Mikoto and two other deities, originally of the MUNAKATA SHRINES, who protect seamen and oversee fishing. According to tradition the shrine was established in 593 after the three deities appeared at its present site and instructed a local inhabitant to erect a shrine there. TAIRA NO KIYOMORI provided lavish support for the shrine, building a predecessor of the present large TORII gate 160 meters (525 ft) out into Hiroshima Bay. Much of the shrine, including its many corridors connecting various buildings, is constructed over water so that when the tide rises it appears to be floating. Itsukushima Shrine is rich in national treasures, such as the richly ornamented scrolls of the LOTUS SUTRA, which were dedicated to the shrine by the Taira family. In addition to the annual festival on 17 June, many observances take place throughout the year. The shrine is well known as one of the most scenic sights in Japan.

Itsunen 逸然

(1601–68; Ch: Yiran or I-jan). Chinese painter. One of the first ŌBAKU SECT Zen monks to come to Japan; he left China in 1644 and went to Nagasaki. He was appointed the third abbot of the temple Kōfukuji and subsequently persuaded the Chinese abbot INGEN to come to Nagasaki. Ingen became the first patriarch of the Ōbaku sect in Japan and was granted land in Uji to build a major Ōbaku temple, MAMPUKUJI. Like many Ōbaku monks Itsunen was a talented artist. His paintings generally depicted Buddhist subjects. He especially inspired artists of the KANŌ SCHOOL and NAGASAKI SCHOOL. See also ZENGA.

Itsuō Art Museum 逸翁美術館

(Itsuō Bijutsukan). Located in Ikeda, Ōsaka Prefecture. The museum houses a choice collection of Japanese painting, calligraphy, and lacquer; Chinese sculpture; and Japanese, Chinese, Korean and Western ceramics. All were assembled by KOBAYASHI ICHIZŌ and are shown in a Western-style house opened in 1957 and in an adjoining gallery added in 1973. Among the paintings are scrolls of the Kamakura (1185–1333) and Muromachi (1333–1568) periods and a large group of works by BUSON and MATSUMURA GOSHUN, as well as many other Edo-period (1600–1868) artists. Nearly all the well-known ceramic kilns are represented, and there are also pieces by CHŌJIRŌ, NIN'AMI DŌHACHI, and HON'AMI KŌETSU.

Iwafune no ki 磐舟柵

Also known as Iwafune *no saku*. A fortified frontier post (SAKU) established in 648 near what is now the city of Murakami in Niigata Prefecture as part of a military campaign by the YAMATO COURT against the EZO tribes of northeastern Honshū. In 1957 remains believed to be those of Iwafune *no ki* were discovered in the vicinity of Iwafune Shrine, north of Murakami. See also NUTARI NO KI.

Iwai 岩井[市]

City in southwestern Ibaraki Prefecture, central Honshū, on the river Tonegawa. After the opening of a bridge creating a more direct route to Tōkyō in 1958, Iwai witnessed rapid urbanization and industrialization. Principal products are electrical appliances and pulp. Pop: 43,102.

Iwai Akira 岩井章

(1922–). A leader of Japan's labor movement. Born in Nagano Prefecture, he served as secretary-general of SŌHYŌ (General Council of Trade Unions of Japan) from 1955 through 1970. Becoming active in the post–World War II labor union movement as a member of the Japan National Railways Union, he joined the JAPAN SOCIALIST PARTY, in which he remained influential after his retirement in 1970. With his colleague ŌTA KAORU, he helped establish the annual wage offensive known as SHUNTŌ.

Iwai, Rebellion of 磐井の乱

(Iwai no Ran). Rebellion of the early 6th century, traditionally dated 527–528. Said to have been led by Iwai, a chieftain (KUNI NO MIYATSUKO) of the territory of Tsukushi in Kyūshū, it is the first recorded instance of rebellion against the YAMATO COURT. According to the early-8th-century chronicle NIHON SHOKI, Iwai, supported by the Korean kingdom of SILLA, obstructed the attempts of the Yamato court to send a relief force to the Korean region of KAYA (thought by some to have been a Japanese enclave on the Korean peninsula). Iwai was defeated and killed by court forces under the chieftains of the MONONOBE FAMILY and the ŌTOMO FAMILY, and his son surrendered to them. Although the authenticity of some of the details is questionable, the traditional account is useful for the insights it affords into Korean-Japanese relations in the early historical period. Iwai is said to be buried in the so-called IWATOYAMA TOMB in the city of Yame, Fukuoka Prefecture.

Iwajuku site 岩宿遺跡

(Iwajuku *iseki*). Paleolithic site discovered in 1946 by AIZAWA TADAHIRO; located in the Iwajuku section of Nitta District, near the city of Kiryū, Gumma Prefecture. Aizawa's recovery of STONE TOOLS from Iwajuku's KANTŌ LOAM strata provided the first convincing evidence that the Japanese islands were occupied by human groups before 10,000 BC. Excavations by Sugihara Sōsuke (1913–83) in 1949 confirmed the existence of two cultural strata. The older Iwajuku I stratum is believed to be about 20,000 years old; it contained large, oval quartz tools originally described as hand axes but with evidence of polishing along the edges. The younger Iwajuku II stratum contained small tools such as points and blades made of obsidian and agate. In 1970 another part of the site was excavated by Aizawa and Serizawa Chōsuke (b 1919); thousands of pieces of chert were recovered from a formation called the Iwajuku Zero stratum, more than 40,000 years old. See also PALEOLITHIC CULTURE; HOSHINO SITE; NOGAWA SITE.

Iwaki いわき[市]

City in southeastern Fukushima Prefecture, northern Honshū. Iwaki was created in 1966 with the merger of the five cities of Taira, Iwaki, Uchigō, Jōban, and Nakoso with four other towns and five villages. The complex of cities prospered with the opening of the Jōban Coalfield in 1883. Mining ceased in 1976. The Taira district is the center of government, commerce, transportation, and education. The Onahama Port district is Iwaki's industrial center. Tourist attractions include the remains of NAKOSO NO SEKI, a medieval barrier station (SEKISHO) celebrated in literature. Pop: 355,812.

Iwakigawa 岩木川

River in western Aomori Prefecture, northern Honshū, originating in the in Shiragami Mountains, changing to a northerly course at the city of Hirosaki, passing through the Tsugaru Plain, and emptying into Lake Jūsan on the western coast of the Tsugaru Peninsula. It is the largest river in the prefecture. The Meya Dam is located on the upper reaches. Length: 102 km (63 mi); area of drainage basin: 2,544 sq km (982 sq mi).

Iwaki Hiroyuki 岩城宏之

(1932–). Orchestra conductor. Born in Tōkyō. Attended Tōkyō University of Fine Arts and Music and studied conducting as an intern with the NHK SYMPHONY ORCHESTRA, which he conducted in 1960 on a tour of Europe and the United States. He was appointed its regular conductor in 1969 and in 1974 was engaged as principal conductor of the Melbourne Symphony Orchestra, filling both positions concurrently. He also became musical director of the Tōkyō Philharmonic Chorus. Iwaki is known for having conducted the premier performances of over 1,000 works of new music, a feat that earned him the sobriquet of "First-Performance Demon."

Iwakisan 岩木山

Conical composite volcano in the Chōkai Volcanic Zone, western Aomori Prefecture, northern Honshū; composed of andesite. Also called Tsugaru Fuji. Iwakisan Shrine is in the foothills. The summit abounds in alpine flora. Skiing is popular. Iwakisan is part of Tsugaru Quasi-National Park. Height: 1,625 m (5,331 ft).

Iwakuni 岩国[市]

City in eastern Yamaguchi Prefecture, western Honshū, on the river Nishikigawa. During the Edo period (1600–1868) Iwakuni was a castle town of a branch of the MŌRI FAMILY. In the early 20th century it became an industrial center with the establishment of pulp and spinning industries. After World War II, a giant petrochemical complex and oil storage base were constructed on former military land. Pop: 109,530.

Iwakura 岩倉[市]

City in western Aichi Prefecture, central Honshū. A farming area, it is fast becoming a suburb of Nagoya. Special products are carp streamers (*koinobori*) for CHILDREN'S DAY and tent cloth. Of historic interest are a Yayoi-period (ca 300 BC–ca AD 300) archaeological site and the ruins of Iwakura Castle. Pop: 43,807.

Iwakura mission 岩倉遣外使節

(Iwakura Kengai Shisetsu). Eighteen-month embassy to the United States and Europe in 1871–73 by leading members of the early Meiji government. Commissioned by Emperor MEIJI and reputedly costing a million dollars, the mission was led by senior minister IWAKURA TOMOMI and included his close political allies ŌKUBO TOSHIMICHI, KIDO TAKAYOSHI, and ITŌ HIROBUMI. Associated with them were several high-ranking officials, including SASAKI TAKAYUKI and TANAKA FUJIMARO, representing each of the departments of the central bureaucracy. In all there were about 50 members, ranging from ambassadors and commissioners to secretaries, interpreters, clerks, attendants, and baggage handlers, most of whom had never been outside Japan. Many students accompanied the mission, including five girls ranging from 6 to 15 years in age (see TSUDA UMEKO), the first Japanese females to go abroad for study.

The members of the mission were to pay goodwill visits on behalf of the emperor to the monarchs and heads of state of the 15 Western countries with which Japan had concluded treaties (see ANSEI COMMERCIAL TREATIES). The ambassadors were also to discuss the actual operation of the treaties with the heads of foreign offices, with a view to future revisions. Another purpose of the mission was to examine Western society closely. The mission was the most dramatic of the many ways in which Japan during the era of *bummei kaika* (civilization and enlightenment; see MEIJI ENLIGHTENMENT) was systematically acquiring Western Learning. Before departure the ambassadors and leading members of the caretaker government, such as SAIGŌ TAKAMORI, ITAGAKI TAISUKE, and ŌKUMA SHIGENOBU, signed a pledge to remain in frequent communication, to concentrate for the time being only on those reforms that were crucial to the centralization of power, and to refrain from making new high-level political appointments.

Escorted by the US minister to Japan, the mission set sail from Yokohama on 23 December 1871 and arrived in San Francisco in January 1872 for a seven-month stay in the United States. The mission's attempt to negotiate a revision of the HARRIS TREATY was rebuffed, and thereafter, in Europe, it confined its diplomacy to polite discussion. The mission traveled in Britain for four months (August–December 1872) and on the continent for over seven months (December 1872–July 1873). During the long tour, the mission was received with much pomp and ceremony by presidents and prime ministers, kings and queens, and titled aristocrats. The leaders, Iwakura, Ōkubo, and Kido, came to understand more clearly the requirements of modern economic life, especially factory production, the application of technology to industry and agriculture, and mass transportation and communications. American and German advocacy of economic protectionism convinced them that the Meiji government should offer encouragement to businessmen in initiating modern enterprises and that the government itself should act vigorously as an entrepreneur. Their survey of military and naval establishments assured them that the West, especially Russia, was not an immediate threat to Japan's security. Ōkubo and Kido, at the urgent request of the caretakers, returned early, Ōkubo in May and Kido in July 1873. Iwakura arrived in Tōkyō with the main party in September.

Instead of the expected policy debate, the mission returned to domestic unrest, a power struggle, and a crisis in foreign relations. The main issue, ostensibly whether to send a punitive expedition to Korea (see SEIKANRON), was actually much broader, encompassing who should take charge of the government and the extent and pace of reforms. When the chief councillor of state, SANJŌ SANETOMI, collapsed in late October, Iwakura took his place, counseled the young emperor, and helped force the resignation of many of the caretakers. Iwakura and his allies, now with a firmer hand on the reins of government, drew on their experiences in the West and promoted policies of internal reconstruction at home and national rights diplomacy abroad.

To help create a public mood receptive to

change, Iwakura supported the publication in 1878 of a five-volume account of the journey, *Tokumei zenken taishi: Beiō kairan jikki* (A True Account of the Tour in America and Europe of the Special Embassy), compiled by his private secretary, KUME KUNITAKE.

Iwakura Tomomi   岩倉具視

(1825–83). Statesman who played an important role in the MEIJI RESTORATION. Born in Kyōto, the second son of a low-ranking courtier, he was adopted into the Iwakura family. He became a chamberlain to Emperor KŌMEI in 1854. In 1858, when HOTTA MASAYOSHI sought imperial sanction for the HARRIS TREATY, Iwakura, with other court nobles, persuaded the emperor to withhold approval. He later became a supporter of the MOVEMENT FOR UNION OF COURT AND SHOGUNATE and helped to arrange the marriage of Princess KAZU to the shōgun TOKUGAWA IEMOCHI. For this he was forced to leave the court. With ŌKUBO TOSHIMICHI and SAIGŌ TAKAMORI, leaders of the antishogunate movement, he engineered the seizure of the Imperial Palace on 3 January 1868, which initiated the Restoration (see ŌSEI FUKKO).

Iwakura, who strongly influenced the emperor, was largely responsible for the CHARTER OATH and the establishment of the prefectural system. Soon after his appointment in 1871 as minister of the right (*udaijin*), he led a mission abroad (see IWAKURA MISSION). In 1873 he vigorously opposed plans to send a military expedition to Korea (see SEIKANRON). Iwakura believed in a strong imperial institution and opposed the FREEDOM AND PEOPLE'S RIGHTS MOVEMENT. At the same time, he realized the wisdom of adopting a constitutional system, and in 1881 he ordered INOUE KOWASHI to draw up guiding principles for the CONSTITUTION OF THE EMPIRE OF JAPAN. In 1882 he sent ITŌ HIROBUMI to Europe to study various forms of constitutional government.

Iwami Silver Mine   石見銀山

(Iwami Ginzan). Mine in Nima District, Iwami Province (now the city of Ōda, Shimane Prefecture), discovered early in the 14th century; the most important source of silver during the Edo period (1600–1868). From 1533 the application of a new method of silver recovery imported from China by way of Korea made possible the extraction of great quantities of silver from the Iwami mine. This led to armed struggles for its possession and its eventual control by the MŌRI FAMILY. The Tokugawa shogunate (1603–1867) assumed direct control of the mine in the early 17th century, and under the direction of commissioner ŌKUBO NAGAYASU it annually produced as much as 14.88 tons of silver. By the late 17th century production of silver was severely reduced, but beginning in the 18th century copper was also extracted. In 1887 the mine became the property of a private firm, Fujita-Gumi, which in 1923 abandoned it.

Iwamizawa   岩見沢[市]

City in central Hokkaidō, some 40 km (25 mi) northeast of Sapporo. Food processing, brewing, and ceramics are the principal industries. Agricultural products include onions and potatoes. Iwamizawa is becoming a satellite city of Sapporo. Pop: 80,417.

Iwamoto Yoshiharu   巌本善治

(1863–1942). Educator; chief editor and co-founder with Kondō Kenzō (d 1886) of JOGAKU ZASSHI (Magazine of Women's Learning). Born in Hyōgo Prefecture. Becoming

interested in women's rights and education, Iwamoto advocated women's economic independence and the abolition of prostitution. In 1884 he helped found the women's magazine *Jogaku shinshi*, renamed *Jogaku zasshi* the following year. In 1885 he helped Kimura Kumaji (1845–1927) and his wife Tōko (1848–86) start the Meiji Jogakkō, a Christian-oriented secondary school for women. Iwamoto headed the school after Tōko's death in 1886 until it closed in 1908.

Iwanaga Yūkichi   岩永裕吉

(1883–1939). News agency director. Born in Tōkyō; graduate of Kyōto University. In

Route of the Iwakura Mission   **Iwakura mission**

Yokohama
departed 23 December 1871
returned 13 September 1873

Pacific Ocean

Japan   Kōbe
Nagasaki   Shanghai   Hong Kong
Saigon
Singapore

San Francisco
arrived 15 January 1872

North America   Arctic Ocean   Asia

Boston
departed 6 August 1872

Ceylon

Washington
President Grant
4 March 1872   Europe   Indian Ocean

Atlantic Ocean   Port Said

Africa   Aden

Audiences with Heads of State on the European Tour

King William III
25 February 1873
The Hague

Tsar Alexander II
3 April 1873
St. Petersburg

King Oscar II
25 April 1873
Stockholm

arrived
17 August 1872
Liverpool ❶

London ❷
Queen Victoria
5 December 1872

Copenhagen
King Christian IX
19 April 1873

❻ **Brussels** King Leopold II
18 February 1873

Berlin
Emperor William I
11 March 1873

Paris ❸
President Thiers
26 December 1872

Vienna ⓫
Emperor Francis Joseph I
8 June 1873

Bern ⓬
President Cérésole
21 June 1873

Marseilles ⓭
departed
20 July 1873

Rome ❿
King Victor Emmanuel II
13 May 1873

Iwakura mission The leaders of this mission in 1872. *Left to right*: Kido Takayoshi, Yamaguchi Naoyoshi, Iwakura Tomomi, Itō Hirobumi, and Ōkubo Toshimichi.

Iwasaki Yatarō The son of a farmer, Iwasaki founded the Mitsubishi business combine during the early 1870s.

1920 he started the Iwanaga News Agency and later became managing director of the Nippon Shimbun Rengōsha (Japan Associated Press). For many years Iwanaga advocated an amalgamation of the national news agencies to form a state-represented news firm. In 1936 he became president of the DŌMEI TSŪSHINSHA (Dōmei News Agency), which closely followed government policy lines.

Iwanai   岩内[町]

Port town on the Shakotan Peninsula in western Hokkaidō. Herring fishing flourished here until the end of the Meiji period (1868–1912). Principal industries now include asparagus canning and walleyed pollack fishing. Pop: 19,372.

Iwanami Shigeo   岩波茂雄

(1881–1946). Founder of IWANAMI SHOTEN, PUBLISHERS. Born in Nagano Prefecture. Attended Tōkyō University as an auditor. Iwanami opened a secondhand bookstore in the Kanda district of Tōkyō in 1913. In 1914 he published NATSUME SŌSEKI's novel KOKORO, which proved so successful that Iwanami was encouraged to convert his store into a publishing company. His early publications consisted of literary and philosophical essays by former classmates at the university. These sold well, and Iwanami continued to publish scholarly works in the fields of philosophy, the natural sciences, and the social sciences. In 1927, when the inexpensive editions of literary works known as EMPON ("one-yen books") had become popular, Iwanami launched his well-known paperback series of classics, the Iwanami Bunko (Iwanami Library). His company eventually became one of Japan's most distinguished publishing houses and an opinion leader among liberal intellectuals. He received the Order of Culture in 1946.

Iwanami Shoten, Publishers
[株]岩波書店

(Iwanami Shoten). Publishing house founded by IWANAMI SHIGEO. Starting in 1913 as a secondhand book dealer in the Jimbōchō section of Tōkyō, Iwanami became a successful publisher of novels, scholarly journals, and paperback book series. These ventures attracted many leading scholars as contributors. With the Iwanami Bunko (Iwanami Library) series, begun in 1927, the firm became definitely associated with a serious, elitist, intellectual culture known as "Iwanami culture." The NIHON SHIHON SHUGI HATTATSU SHI KŌZA, an Iwanami series of articles on Japanese capitalism begun in 1932, became a forum for Marxist scholars before World War II. The Iwanami Shinsho series (begun in 1938) dealt with what were considered urgent, even controversial, topics. SEKAI, begun in 1946, became one of the leading journals of opinion in postwar Japan.

Iwano Hōmei   岩野泡鳴

(1873–1920). Poet, playwright, critic, and novelist. Born in Sumoto on the island of Awaji in the Inland Sea. His real name was Yoshie; his pseudonym, Hōmei (literally, "foam and roar"), was an allusion to Awa, the domain to which his family belonged. While at Meiji Gakuin, a Christian college, his interest in literature was stimulated by SHIMAZAKI TŌSON.

Hōmei began his career as a poet by publishing his *shintaishi* (new style poetry) in

the magazine *Bundan* (Literary World), which he helped found in 1890. Between 1901 and 1915 he published five poetry anthologies. His critical works include a detailed study of Japanese metrics, *Shintaishi no sahō* (1907, The Composition of New Style Poetry), and *Shintaishi shi* (1907–08, The History of New Style Poetry). His first tragedy was *Tama wa mayou getchū no yaiba* (1894, The Wandering Soul and the Moonlit Sword), later retitled *Katsura Gorō*. In 1906 Hōmei published a philosophical work, *Shimpiteki hanjū shugi* (The Principle of the Mystic Demi-Animal).

Hōmei is considered one of the chief representatives of Japanese NATURALISM. He expounded his concept of naturalism in *Shin shizen shugi* (1908, New Naturalism) and therein developed the idea of "naturalistic symbolism," an interpretation of Japanese MYTHOLOGY that became the basis of the magazine *Shin Nihon shugi* (New Japanism), which he founded in 1916. He is best known for his autobiographical works: *Tandeki* (1909; usually translated as "Indulgence," although Hōmei himself preferred "Decadence") and *Hōmei gobusaku* (1910–19, The Pentalogy of Iwano Hōmei), a series of novels sharing the same hero. Together these works exemplify Hōmei's view that literature is action; they employ a powerful, occasionally rough, and often symbolic language.

Iwanuma   岩沼[市]

City in southern Miyagi Prefecture, northern Honshū. An important terminus for railway, road, and air transportation, it is rapidly becoming a satellite city of SENDAI. Pulp and rubber factories have been constructed here in recent years. The Takekoma Inari Shrine attracts visitors to Iwanuma. Pop: 38,091.

Iwasaki Kan'en   岩崎灌園

(1786–1842). Specialist in *honzōgaku* (traditional pharmacognosy). Born in Edo (now Tōkyō). He learned pharmacognosy from ONO RANZAN and lectured on the subject. He may have painted Philipp Franz von SIEBOLD's portrait when Siebold came to Edo. His *Honzō zufu* in 92 volumes is highly valued for its color illustrations.

Iwasaki Koyata   岩崎小弥太

(1879–1945). Businessman and leader of the MITSUBISHI *zaibatsu*, a powerful industrial and financial combine before World War II. Born in Tōkyō. He studied at Tōkyō University and Cambridge University. Upon his return to Japan in 1906, Iwasaki became vice-president of Mitsubishi, Ltd, and, in 1916, president. He separated various divisions of Mitsubishi, Ltd, into independent companies, creating Mitsubishi Shipbuilding (now MITSUBISHI HEAVY INDUSTRIES, LTD) in 1917, Mitsubishi Mining (now MITSUBISHI MATERIALS CORPORATION) and MITSUBISHI CORPORATION in 1918, MITSUBISHI BANK, LTD, in 1919, and MITSUBISHI ELECTRIC CORPORATION in 1921. He was enthusiastic about overseas expansion and eagerly sought development rights in Asian countries. In 1931 Iwasaki also introduced imported technology and established MITSUBISHI OIL CO, LTD, in a joint venture with an American oil company.

Iwasaki Yatarō   岩崎弥太郎

(1835–85). Founder of the MITSUBISHI financial empire. Born in the Tosa domain (now Kōchi Prefecture); eldest son of a farmer. As *samurai* status was essential to obtain a position in the domainal government, at age 20

Iwasaki managed to buy the status of GŌSHI (the lowest-ranked rural samurai). He became an assistant at the Kaiseikan (Industry Promotion Office) of Tosa, and in 1867 was hired to manage its Nagasaki office, where the domain had accumulated a huge debt as a result of large-scale arms purchases. Iwasaki succeeded in refinancing the debt by borrowing 300,000 RYŌ from an American merchant in exchange for exclusive rights to deal in the domain's camphor production. He consummated the negotiations by employing what would become standard Iwasaki tactics: coaxing, cajoling, hinting at nonexistent rivals, and extensive "wining and dining." Tosa officials recognized his ability to serve as the domain's financial agent.

When the domains were abolished in 1871, the Tosa government withdrew from all commercial activities, and Iwasaki was chosen to take over the former domainal enterprises. The domain is said to have given Iwasaki its fleet of 11 ships, 230,000 *ryō* in cash, and all the assets and privileges connected with its business in camphor, tea, silk, lumber, and coal mining. Iwasaki then began to acquire ships that were being sold by former domains and foreign merchants. The profits, however, were small compared to what he earned through clever dealing in the conversion of domain notes into the new national government notes (DAJŌKAN SATSU).

In 1873 Iwasaki founded the Mitsubishi Shōkai trading company, with shipping as its principal business. He eliminated most competitors by undercutting prices and by offering longer and better-integrated shipping routes. The TAIWAN EXPEDITION OF 1874 proved to be a godsend to Iwasaki; for transporting troops and provisions for the government, his company was rewarded handsomely. By the mid-1870s his ships were serving the Shanghai-Japan route, and in 1875 he bought the competing American Pacific Mail Steamship Company and in 1876 forced the British Peninsular and Oriental Navigation Company (P&O) from the Shanghai-Yokohama route. The SATSUMA REBELLION of 1877 enriched Iwasaki even more than the earlier Taiwan Expedition. By 1877 Iwasaki owned over 80 percent of all the ships in Japan, and despite a major MITSUI-backed challenge to his shipping empire in 1882, he succeeded in diversifying into mining, banking, insurance, iron foundry, and other fields. The ZAIBATSU established by Iwasaki was to become a cornerstone of the rapid industrialization of Japan.

Iwasa Matabei   岩佐又兵衛

(1578–1650). Painter of classical themes in the YAMATO-E style. Also known as Iwasa Katsumochi. The son of Araki Murashige, the lord of Settsu Province (now part of Ōsaka and Hyōgo prefectures), Matabei was raised in the temple Honganji in Kyōto after his father's unsuccessful revolt against ODA NOBUNAGA. Iwasa was Matabei's mother's maiden name.

Matabei is said to have studied painting in Sakai with Tosa Mitsunori (1583–1638). In 1617 he became official painter to MATSUDAIRA TADANAO, the lord of Echizen Province (now Fukui Prefecture). He moved to Edo (now Tōkyō) in 1637 to serve the shōgun TOKUGAWA IEMITSU. In 1640 he painted a set of the Thirty-Six Poetic Geniuses (SANJŪROKKASEN) and in them signed himself "The last of the line of Tosa Mitsunobu" (see TOSA SCHOOL). Matabei's service under the shogunate and a certain element of sensuality in his style also connect him with UKIYO-E, the artistic tradition of the Edo commoners.

Iwasa Yoshizane 岩佐凱実

(1906–). Businessman; chairman of FUJI BANK, LTD (1971–75). Born in Ehime Prefecture. After graduating from Tōkyō University in 1928, he joined Yasuda Bank (now Fuji Bank, Ltd), becoming its president in 1963. He aggressively promoted the bank's overseas activities and turned it into one of the most influential banks in Japan. Iwasa was chairman of the JAPAN ASSOCIATION OF CORPORATE EXECUTIVES (1959–60) and vice-chairman of KEIDANREN (Federation of Economic Organizations; 1968–80).

Iwase Tadanari 岩瀬忠震

(1818–61). Official of the Tokugawa shogunate (1603–1867). In 1854 he was appointed inspector (metsuke) by the senior councillor (rōjū) ABE MASAHIRO and entrusted with strengthening coastal defenses. In 1857 he was sent to Nagasaki to negotiate supplements to trade agreements signed with the Dutch and the Russians, and in 1858 he and INOUE KIYONAO assisted senior councillor HOTTA MASAYOSHI in negotiating a commercial treaty with Townsend HARRIS, American consul in Shimoda. He accompanied Hotta to Kyōto to obtain imperial approval of the HARRIS TREATY and to try to convince court nobles of the necessity of opening the country to foreign intercourse. Iwase was eventually dismissed and ordered into permanent retirement when he supported the losing candidate in the 1858 shogunal succession dispute.

Iwase "thousand-mound" tomb cluster 岩橋千塚古墳群

(Iwase senzuka kofungun). A cluster of 500 to 600 mounded tombs (KOFUN), most of them built in the 6th and 7th centuries; located in the hills south of the river Kinokawa in Iwase, Wakayama Prefecture. This tomb cluster is representative of burial patterns of the late Kofun period (ca 300–710). It consists mostly of round tumuli ranging from 4 to 30 meters (13 to 98 ft) in diameter, although some are keyhole-shaped or square. The majority of the tombs have corridor-type stone chambers constructed of local green schist, the larger ones being constructed with stone partitions, beams, and drainage facilities.

iwashi → sardines

Iwashimizu Hachiman Shrine 石清水八幡宮

(Iwashimizu Hachimangū). Also known as Otokoyama Hachimangū. Shintō shrine in the city of Yawata, Kyōto Prefecture, dedicated to the spirits of Emperor ŌJIN (late 4th to early 5th century), popularly worshiped as HACHIMAN, and the legendary Empress JINGŪ and to the deity Hime Ōkami (also known as Himegami). The shrine was established in 859 by the Buddhist monk Gyōkyō and has been greatly venerated by the court and the imperial family throughout Japanese history. In the 11th and 12th centuries the Minamoto family regarded Hachiman as their clan deity (UJIGAMI) and the first Kamakura shōgun, MINAMOTO NO YORITOMO, established a branch of this shrine, TSURUGAOKA HACHIMAN SHRINE, in Kamakura. This led to the establishment of Hachiman shrines throughout the country. The annual festival, known as the Iwashimizu Festival, is held on 15 September.

Iwashita Shima 岩下志麻

(1941–). Actress. Born in Tōkyō, she made her acting debut on television in 1958 and was hired by SHŌCHIKU CO, LTD, in 1960, going on to appear in more than 100 films. She has won many awards for her performances, which have shown considerable range and depth. Among her most important films are Shinjū Ten no Amijima (1969, Love Suicide at Amijima) directed by her husband, SHINODA MASAHIRO, and Samma no aji (1962, An Autumn Afternoon), the last picture directed by OZU YASUJIRŌ.

Iwashita Sōichi 岩下壮一

(1889–1940). Catholic priest, theologian, and philosopher. Born in Tōkyō, he studied philosophy under Raphael Koeber (1848–1923) at Tōkyō University and went on to teach at the Seventh Higher School in Kagoshima Prefecture. He studied in Europe from 1919 to 1925, was ordained to the priesthood in Rome in 1925, and was a pioneer in Japanese research on medieval European philosophy. He worked actively for the propagation of the Christian faith among university students. His collected works in nine volumes have been published as Iwashita Sōichi zenshū (1961–64).

Iwata 磐田[市]

City in western Shizuoka Prefecture, central Honshū. Formerly a provincial capital (kokufu), Iwata developed as a post-station town on the TŌKAIDŌ, the major highway during the Edo period (1600–1868). Principal products are tea, sweet potatoes, and melons; there are several textile, automobile, and ball-bearing plants. Of interest are the ruins of an 8th-century provincial temple. Pop: 83,521.

Iwatahara 磐田原

Diluvial upland along the eastern bank of the river Tenryūgawa, Shizuoka Prefecture, central Honshū. Vegetables, tea, and tobacco are grown. In the southern part, industrial plants and residences are increasing. Elevation: 10–130 m (30–430 ft).

Iwate Prefecture 岩手県

(Iwate Ken). Located in northern Honshū and bounded by the Pacific Ocean on the east, Aomori Prefecture on the north, Akita Prefecture on the west, and Miyagi Prefecture on the south. The terrain consists of mountain and plateau areas, with the ŌU MOUNTAINS running through the western section of the prefecture and the KITAKAMI MOUNTAINS rising in the east. Between them lies the basin of the river KITAKAMIGAWA, the prefecture's main level area and population center. The climate is generally cool and dry.

Formerly known as Mutsu Province and inhabited by the ancient indigenous people known as EZO, the area came under the control of the central government only in the Heian period (794–1185). During the 11th and 12th centuries it was ruled independently by the ŌSHŪ FUJIWARA FAMILY, whose capital at HIRAIZUMI became northern Japan's major cultural center. It then came under the control of the Kamakura shogunate. The Nambu family and the DATE FAMILY ruled the area in the 16th century, and in the Edo period (1600–1868) the province was divided into several domains. The present prefectural name and boundaries were established in 1876.

Agriculture is centered on rice production

and livestock farming. Both forestry and fishing are important. Although the prefecture is not extensively industrialized, food-processing, lumber, and electrical-appliance industries are growing. It is also one of Japan's leading sources of both iron and copper ore.

Iwate offers some of Japan's most dramatic coastal scenery, and much of its shoreline is included in RIKUCHŪ COAST NATIONAL PARK. TOWADA-HACHIMANTAI NATIONAL PARK is also a major tourist attraction, and the prefecture has many hot-spring resorts such as Hanamaki, Getō, and Tsunagi. Hiraizumi has several historic sites. Iwate is also known for its traditional folk crafts and customs, such as Nambu cast-iron ware, KOKESHI dolls, kembai (a sword dance), and the SHISHI ODORI (deer dance). Area: 15,278 sq km (5,899 sq mi); pop: 1,416,928; capital: MORIOKA. Other major cities include MIYAKO, HANAMAKI, and ICHINOSEKI.

Iwatesan 岩手山

Conical composite volcano in the Nasu Volcanic Zone, western Iwate Prefecture, northern Honshū. Also called Nambu Fuji and Iwate Fuji. It is composed of two peaks, Higashi Iwatesan and Nishi Iwatesan, and numerous hot springs are found in the vicinity. Japan's first geothermal electric plant was constructed in the Matsukawa Hot Spring area on the northwestern slopes of the mountain in 1966. On the mountain's southern skirts is Japan's largest dairy farm, the Koiwai Farm. Iwatesan is part of the TOWADA-HACHIMANTAI NATIONAL PARK. Height: 2,038 m (6,686 ft).

Iwate University 岩手大学

(Iwate Daigaku). A coeducational national university located in the city of Morioka, Iwate Prefecture. Founded in 1949, the university maintains faculties of agriculture, engineering, and education as well as a college of liberal arts and social sciences. The faculty of agriculture stems from Japan's first agricultural and forestry college (founded 1902). Enrollment in 1989 was 5,321.

Iwato Boom 岩戸景気

(Iwato Keiki). Term used to describe the 42 months of economic expansion between July 1958 and December 1961. The period saw the most rapid economic advancement in the history of Japan. The INCOME-DOUBLING PLAN and other strong economic growth measures taken by the government increased plant investment, but deterioration in the balance of payments in 1961 led to stagnation in the years that followed. See also ECONOMIC PLANNING.

Iwatoyama tomb 岩戸山古墳

(Iwatoyama kofun). Tomb mound in the city of Yame, Fukuoka Prefecture. The Iwatoyama tomb is a keyhole-shaped mound about 135 meters (443 ft) in length; its base faces west, and there are traces of the tomb's ditch and outer bank. Shields, jars, and stone figures of people, horses, and chickens have been discovered in and around the tomb. These items match descriptions concerning Iwai, a chieftain of the territory of Tsukushi in Kyūshū that appears in the Nara-period (710–794) compilation Chikugo no Kuni fudoki. As a result, the Iwatoyama tomb is thought to be the tomb of Iwai, who died in the early 6th century.

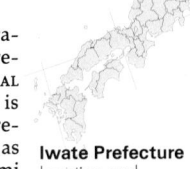

Iwate Prefecture
Location and Prefectural Crest

Iwatsuki 岩槻[市]

City in eastern Saitama Prefecture, central Honshū, about 30 km (19 mi) from Tōkyō. A castle town during the 15th century, in the Edo period (1600–1868) it prospered as a post-station town on the highway leading to the mausoleum of TOKUGAWA IEYASU. In recent years there has been an increase in factory construction and residential land development. The city has long been known for its *hina ningyō* (dolls) and HAGOITA (battledores). Pop: 106,462.

Iwaya Sazanami 巌谷小波

(1870–1933). Novelist and scholar of juvenile literature. Real name Iwaya Sueo. Born in Tōkyō, he was a member of the literary circle KEN'YŪSHA. His 1891 children's story, *Koganemaru*, was a popular success. He edited the 24-volume *Nihon mukashibanashi* (1894–96), a collection of Japanese folktales and legends, which formed the basis of modern juvenile literature.

Iwaya Sazanami This writer of children's stories was also a noted anthologizer of juvenile literature.

Iwojima → Iō Islands

Iyadani 祖谷渓

Gorge on the middle reaches of the river Iyagawa (a tributary of the Yoshinogawa) in western Tokushima Prefecture, Shikoku. Located in the foothills of the mountain Tsurugisan, it is said to have been the place where the warriors of the Taira family (Heike) hid after their defeat, giving rise to many legends. Famous for its rugged beauty and Kazura Bridge (Kazurabashi; a bridge made of vines). Length: approximately 20 km (12 mi).

Iyo 伊予[市]

City in central Ehime Prefecture, Shikoku. Situated on the Iyo Sea, Iyo developed as a fishing port in the Edo period (1600–1868). Mandarin oranges and loquats are cultivated here; the area is also known for *kezuribushi* (a mixture of shavings of dried mackerel, bonito, Japanese sardine, etc), used for flavoring stock. Pop: 29,803.

Iyo Mishima 伊予三島[市]

City in eastern Ehime Prefecture, Shikoku, on the Hiuchi Sea. Its paper industry, together with that of the neighboring city of KAWANOE, is second only to the city of Fuji in Shizuoka Prefecture. The city is also known for its MIZUHIKI, paper strings used for ornamentation. Pop: 38,351.

Iyo Sea 伊予灘

(Iyo Nada). Area in the western reaches of the Inland Sea between Yamaguchi Prefecture, western Honshū; Ehime Prefecture, Shikoku; and Ōita Prefecture, Kyūshū. It is a sardine fishery and whales migrate here. Depth: 40–60 m (131–197 ft).

Izanagi and Izanami 伊弉諾と伊弉冉

(Izanagi *to* Izanami). Full names: Izanagi no Mikoto and Izanami no Mikoto; an alternate pronunciation of Izanagi is Izanaki. Male and female deities appearing in the KOJIKI (712, Records of Ancient Matters) and NIHON SHOKI (720, Chronicle of Japan). According to legend, entrusted by the Heavenly Deities with the task of creating the land, the two stood on the Floating Bridge of Heaven and thrust down the Heavenly Jeweled Spear into the ocean below. The brine that dripped from the spear became the island of

Onogorojima, where the two performed a marriage rite. Izanami gave birth to the islands of Japan and their deities. But in giving birth to the fire deity, Kagutsuchi no Kami, Izanami was burned and died. Izanagi pursued Izanami to the netherworld (Yomi no Kuni) where he found her horribly transformed by death. Ashamed and enraged that he had disregarded her entreaty not to look at her, Izanami and the Eighty Ugly Females of Yomi pursued Izanagi, who escaped by blocking the exit of Yomi with a large boulder; thus the worlds of the living and the dead are separated. Izanagi then performed a ceremony of ablution (MISOGI) that produced the sun goddess AMATERASU ŌMIKAMI, the moon god Tsukuyomi no Mikoto, and the important deity SUSANOO NO MIKOTO. See also MYTHOLOGY.

Izanagi Boom いざなぎ景気

(Izanagi Keiki). Period of business expansion lasting 57 months from October 1965 to July 1970. Following the prosperous period of the Olympic Boom, which peaked in 1964, business conditions worsened in 1965. The Bank of Japan lowered the prime interest rate, and the government used economic policy to bolster the economy by increasing its 1966 budget and issuing ¥730 billion (US $2 billion) in government bonds. At the same time, the world economy began to improve, and as a result exports increased. From the spring of 1966 investment in plant and equipment increased with expansion in such areas as labor-saving devices and pollution control facilities.

Izawajō 胆沢城

Heian-period (794–1185) fortress built in 802 in the province of Mutsu (now Iwate Prefecture) near the confluence of the rivers Kitakamigawa and Izawagawa. The military leader SAKANOUE NO TAMURAMARO transferred his headquarters (CHINJUFU) there for the purpose of subjugating the EZO. The ruins of the fortress are located in the city of Mizusawa, Iwate Prefecture.

Izawa Shūji 伊沢修二

(1851–1917). Educational leader in the Meiji period (1868–1912). Born in the Takatō domain (now part of Nagano Prefecture), he studied at the Daigaku Nankō (now Tōkyō University). In 1875 he went to the United States to study the US educational system. After returning to Japan in 1878, he served as head of the Tōkyō Normal School and chief of the editorial bureau of the Ministry of Education. In 1888 he became the first head of the Tōkyō School of Music (now Tōkyō University of Fine Arts and Music), which he organized with the help of his former teacher, Luther W. MASON. Izawa also served as chief of the educational bureau in the government-general of Taiwan. He actively supported education for the blind and deaf, creating the Japanese braille system and adapting sign language for use in Japan. One of his major works on education is *Kyōikugaku* (1882, Pedagogy).

Izayoi nikki 十六夜日記

(ca 1280; tr *The Izayoi Nikki*, 1951). A minor classic of the poetic TRAVEL DIARIES genre, written by ABUTSU NI (d 1283), WAKA poet and secondary wife of FUJIWARA NO TAMEIE (1198–1275), head of the foremost poetic family at court. When Tameie died, Abutsu worked to obtain for her own children, especially REIZEI TAMESUKE (1263–1328), a share of her husband's land, property, and poetic prestige. To plead their cause, she traveled to Kamakura about 1279. *Izayoi nikki* recounts her reasons for going, describes the trip, records letters and poetic exchanges, and ends with a 151-line CHŌKA (long poem) and envoy, setting forth her grievances in verse. The work contains 116 short poems, of which 86 are by Abutsu.

Izu Gold Mine 伊豆金山

(Izu Kinzan). Collective name for several gold mines in Izu Province (now part of Shizuoka Prefecture) that were operated by the Tokugawa shogunate during the Edo period (1600–1868). Toi, Yugashima, and Nawaji, the principal mines, were first developed at the end of the 16th century. Production increased under ŌKUBO NAGAYASU, who was commissioner from 1606 to 1613.

Izu Islands 伊豆諸島

(Izu Shotō). Group of volcanic islands in the Pacific Ocean, southeast of the Izu Peninsula, including the islands of ŌSHIMA, TOSHIMA, Niijima, Kōzushima, MIYAKEJIMA, Mikurajima, HACHIJŌJIMA, Shikinejima, and Udonejima. The islands are administratively under the Tōkyō prefectural government. Extending for approximately 540 km (335 mi) north to south, they form part of the Fuji-Hakone-Izu National Park.

Izumi 和泉[市]

City in southern Ōsaka Prefecture, central Honshū. Contiguous with Sakai to the north, Izumi is a satellite city of Ōsaka. Its principal industry is textiles. Farm products include flowers and mandarin oranges. Because it was the site of an ancient provincial capital (*kokufu*), Izumi has several noteworthy temples. Pop: 146,127.

Izumi 出水[市]

City in northwestern Kagoshima Prefecture, Kyūshū. Local products include rice, mandarin oranges, sweet potatoes, saplings, poultry, seaweed, and prawns. Izumi also has alcohol, paper, and electric industries. Migrating cranes winter here. Pop: 39,729.

Izumi Kyōka 泉鏡花

(1873–1939). Novelist. Real name Izumi Kyōtarō. Born in Kanazawa (Ishikawa Prefecture) to an artisan family. His mother introduced him at an early age to the KUSAZŌSHI, a genre of Edo-period (1600–1868) fiction. Because of his family's straitened circumstances, he attended the tuition-free Hokuriku English-Japanese School run by Christian missionaries. In 1890 he left for Tōkyō, where in the following year he came under the tutelage of the celebrated novelist OZAKI KŌYŌ. Under Kōyō's auspices, Kyōka's first work, *Kammuri Yazaemon* (the title is the name of the protagonist), was serialized in a newspaper in 1892.

Two years later Kyōka made his mark as a writer with the publication of *Giketsu kyōketsu* (The Righteous and the Chivalrous). Although he was no longer under the patronage of Kōyō, Kyōka found that Kōyō still exercised a considerable influence on his personal life. Because of Kōyō's objections, Kyōka's marriage was delayed until after Kōyō's death.

Eccentric and superstitious, Kyōka distinguished himself as a writer of the grotesque and fantastic. "Kōya hijiri" (1900, The Itinerant Monk) exemplifies his style—a mixture of grace, the grotesque, and the supernatural. It is a tale recounting the adventures of a monk as he journeys through mountain recesses, encountering strange and frightening experiences. Kyōka was particularly fascinated by the supernatural, borrowing and embellishing themes from Edo fiction, NŌ, and folklore. More than two-thirds of his some 300 works incorporate a supernatural element of some kind.

As a novelist, Kyōka is often linked with NAGAI KAFŪ and TANIZAKI JUN'ICHIRŌ because they shared their love for Edo culture and their depiction of life in the pleasure quarters. Kyōka's style was very much influenced by Edo culture, especially the *kusazōshi*. His use of a complex and suspenseful plot development was a common technique found in the GŌKAN, a type of *kusazōshi* that flourished at the end of the Edo period. He also incorporated the narrative techniques of RAKUGO (storytelling), a traditional genre, and adapted certain types of dramatic dialogues from KABUKI.

The theme of a beautiful, gentle older woman loving and caring for a young boy or youth can often be seen in Kyōka's works. *Teriha kyōgen*, published in 1896, is an example of this theme, which is supposedly linked to the death of his mother when he was nine.

Kyōka spent the latter part of his life in the idyllic environs of Zushi, a summer resort area not far from Tōkyō. There he wrote some of his better-known works, including *Onna keizu* (1907, The Genealogy of Women), *Shirasagi* (1909, The White Heron), and *Uta andon* (1910).

Izumi Mountains   和泉山脈

(Izumi Sammyaku). Mountain range running east to west, forming a natural boundary between Wakayama and Ōsaka prefectures, central Honshū. The range consists of numerous peaks under 1,000 m (3,280 ft) and is known for citrus fruit production.

Izumi Ōtsu   泉大津[市]

City in southern Ōsaka Prefecture, central Honshū. Located on Ōsaka Bay, it was a prosperous port town during the Edo period (1600–1868). It is now a textile center, producing 95 percent of the blankets made in Japan. Pop: 67,035.

Izumi Sano   泉佐野[市]

City in southern Ōsaka Prefecture, central Honshū, on Ōsaka Bay. During the Edo period (1600–1868) Izumi Sano was the site of many fish and cotton wholesale houses. It is now a textile center, producing about 30 percent of the towels that are made in Japan. Pop: 88,866.

Izumi school   和泉流

(Izumiryū). One of the three major schools of KYŌGEN. Its founder was Yamawaki Izumi no Kami Motoyoshi (d 1659). The Izumi school was particularly influential in Nagoya and Kyōto (the home of the school), often performing for the imperial court, whereas the other two major kyōgen schools, the Ōkura and the Sagi, were patronized by the shogunate in Edo (now Tōkyō). In 1881, after the Meiji Restoration (1868), Motokiyo, the head of the school, unsuccessfully tried to establish the school in Tōkyō, the new capital of Japan. When his son died at an early age in 1916, the main family line of the school came to an end. Miyake Yasuyuki (b 1937), the son of Miyake Tōkurō (b 1901), a leading member of the school, succeeded to the headship. Other leading families of the school include those of Nomura Matasaburō and Nomura Manzō.

Izumi Seiichi   泉靖一

(1915–70). Cultural anthropologist who was instrumental in establishing cultural anthropology as an academic discipline in Japan. Born in Tōkyō, Izumi studied social anthropology at Keijō University in Korea (then a Japanese colony). While teaching at Keijō University he conducted anthropological fieldwork in Korea and other areas of northeast Asia. His special interest was the culture of Cheju Island (off the Korean peninsula in the East China Sea). In 1951 Izumi was appointed to the faculty of Tōkyō University. With ISHIDA EIICHIRŌ he was responsible for founding its department of cultural anthropology. In his later years his interest turned to ancient Andean culture. He organized large expeditions to Peru, and his excavation work at the pre-Columbian site of Kotosh near the city of Huánuco in Peru received worldwide recognition. His works are collected in *Izumi Seiichi chosakushū* (1971–72).

Izumi Shikibu   和泉式部

(fl ca 1000). Poet of the mid-Heian period (794–1185); author of a collection of over 1,500 WAKA (31-syllable poems). Izumi's birth and death dates are unknown; she was probably born in the 960s or 970s, and there are traces of her activity into the late 1020s. Brought up at court, she was twice married. Between her two marriages she was the mistress, successively, of two imperial princes who were brothers. The younger brother, Prince Atsumichi (981–1007), was the great love of her life; she mourned his death in more than a hundred poems.

She is famous for her intense love poetry and exploitation of Buddhist themes. Izumi's poetry shows her possessed of two strongly contrasting sides of character: an amorous tendency, now playful, now serious, and an earnest, even prayerful urge which seeks release from the toils of passion through Buddhist enlightenment and renunciation. Both aspects speak with a conviction that allows us to see her as we can few other poets in the classical tradition. Her poetry itself is exceptionally skilled. She mastered every style and manner current in her day, from simple descriptive nature poetry to the most artful of introspective conceits. She was fond of verbal games, indulging in outrageous repetitions of a single word. Her tone is often arch and deliberately wicked, and multiple meanings are put to superlative use in some of her finest verse. And yet, she could write with the most classic simplicity, creating poems of seemingly effortless transparency. A single such verse, a plea for enlightenment on the "dark path" of mortal love and death, has been preserved in the *Shūishū*, the third imperial *waka* anthology, compiled during her lifetime. Her fame after death was so great that the fourth imperial *waka* anthology, the *Goshūishū* of 1086, contains 67 of her poems, the largest number by any single poet. She was certainly the most gifted poet of her day. Her poems are preserved principally in two collections, the *Seishū* (Main Collection) and the *Zokushū* (Continued Collection). A fictionalized version of the love story of Izumi Shikibu and Prince Atsumichi is told in the IZUMI SHIKIBU NIKKI.

Izumi Shikibu nikki   和泉式部日記

(ca 1010; tr *The Diary of Izumi Shikibu*, 1969). Although its title contains the word *nikki*, this Heian-period (794–1185) work is not a diary, but a third-person narrative account of the love affair between IZUMI SHIKIBU, one

of the most gifted poets of her era, and Prince Atsumichi (981–1007). It is a strong possibility that Izumi Shikibu herself wrote the work the year after Atsumichi's death; despite recent controversy concerning its authorship, scholars still favor this traditional attribution. Their affair began in the spring of 1003 with an impassioned exchange of poems; these are incorporated into the narrative, which cleaves to the facts but discusses events and dialogues Izumi Shikibu could not have witnessed firsthand. When, after ten months, the poetess goes to live with the prince, the work lapses into prose and ends abruptly. It is memorable both as a paradigm of the courtly romances celebrated in the imperial WAKA (classical Japanese poetry) anthologies and as an evocation of the poetess and her fated love.

Izumiya Co, Ltd   イズミヤ[株]

(Izumiya). Supermarket operator. Incorporated in 1949. Izumiya is mainly engaged in the retail sale of clothing, foods, and household goods such as electrical appliances, furniture, furnishings, and sundries. The company originally developed its supermarket chain in the Kansai region and has since expanded into other parts of Japan. AIC, Inc, a company established jointly by several supermarket operators including Izumiya, is engaged exclusively in the import business and has representative offices in Hong Kong, Taipei, Shanghai, Singapore, and Bangkok. Izumiya's sales for the fiscal year ending February 1991 totaled ¥371.5 billion (US $2.8 billion), and capitalization stood at ¥25.7 billion (US $197.0 million). Headquarters are in Ōsaka.

Izumo   出雲[市]

City in eastern Shimane Prefecture, western Honshū. A market town from the 14th century, with the opening of the San'in Line of the Japanese National Railways (now Japan Railways or JR) in 1911, it became a textile center. Roof tiles and *sake* are also made. It is the gateway to IZUMO SHRINE, one of the most venerable Shintō shrines in Japan. Pop: 82,679.

Izumo no Okuni→Okuni

Izumo Plain   出雲平野

(Izumo Heiya). Located in eastern Shimane Prefecture, western Honshū. Formed by the deltas of the rivers Hiikawa and Kandogawa filling up the graben valleys of the Chūgoku Mountains in the south and the Shimane Peninsula in the north. Peculiar to the area are the stands of native pine trees (*tsuiji matsu*) that surround farmhouses to protect them from the strong westerly winds in winter. The major city is IZUMO. Area: approximately 130 sq km (50 sq mi).

Izumo Province   出雲国

(Izumo no Kuni; also known as Unshū). One of the eight provinces (*kuni*) of the San'indō region along the Sea of Japan in southern Honshū. It is now the eastern half of SHIMANE PREFECTURE. Izumo, which is associated with many myths and legends recorded in the oldest Japanese histories, is thought to have once been a religious and political center that rivaled the YAMATO COURT of the Nara region. It was controlled successively by the Sasaki, YAMANA, KYŌGOKU, and AMAKO families until the mid-16th century. Early in the Edo period (1600–1868) the Horio fam-

Izumi Kyōka The writer, shown here in 1933, enlivened his fictional world with supernatural beings and events, resisting the naturalist style fashionable among his contemporaries.

ily built a castle in MATSUE, but in 1634 it passed to the Kyōgoku, who in turn were supplanted by the Matsudaira family (see TOKUGAWA FAMILY) in 1638. From that time until the MEIJI RESTORATION (1868) the Matsudaira served there as *daimyō*, ruling over the three domains of Matsue, Hirose, and Mori, into which the province was divided in 1684.

Izumo Shrine   出雲大社

(Izumo Taisha; also called Izumo no Ōyashiro). One of the most important Shintō shrines; located in the town of Taisha (Taishamachi), Shimane Prefecture. The chief god of the shrine is ŌKUNINUSHI NO MIKOTO. The mythic origin of the shrine as described in the 8th-century chronicles KOJIKI and NIHON SHOKI is as follows: Ōkuninushi no Mikoto had first started developing the world of mortal man, but when NINIGI NO MIKOTO, the grandson of the sun goddess AMATERASU ŌMIKAMI, descended to earth from the heavens, Ōkuninushi no Mikoto turned over this land to him. This so pleased Amaterasu Ōmikami that she had a large shrine erected in honor of Ōkuninushi no Mikoto at the present location of the Izumo Shrine and put it under the care of Amenohohi no Mikoto. In ancient times people said to be the descendants of Amenohohi no Mikoto served

as the KUNI NO MIYATSUKO or local chieftains of Izumo.

The shrine is built in the *taisha-zukuri* style, considered the oldest of shrine architectural styles in Japan. The present main building (*honden*) was built in 1744, the 25th building since the original structure. Now approximately 24 meters (79 ft) high, it was reportedly once 96 meters (315 ft) high.

The main festival at Izumo Shrine occurs on 14 May. Another festival, the Kamiari Matsuri (the "gods being present" festival), is held on 11–17 October, by the old lunar calendar. It is said that at this time the gods gather from throughout Japan and confer with each other about their respective realms. For this reason the ancient name for October (in other parts of Japan) was Kannazuki, or the "Month without Gods." During this period small box-shaped houses are lined up in the shrine precincts to house the gods. The god of Izumo has traditionally been regarded as the god of marriage, good fortune, and agriculture.

Izu Nagaoka   伊豆長岡[町]

Town in eastern Shizuoka Prefecture, central Honshū, on the Izu Peninsula. Noted for its hot springs, it commands a fine view of Mt. Fuji (FUJISAN). Its climate is suited to mandarin orange and strawberry cultivation. An iris festival is held here in early July. Pop: 14,899.

Izu no odoriko   伊豆の踊子

(1926; tr "The Izu Dancer," 1955). Story by KAWABATA YASUNARI (1899–1972) that first brought him fame. A lonely 20-year-old higher-school student on a walking tour of the Izu Peninsula falls in love with a 14-year-old dancer who is a member of a group of itinerant performers that he encounters along the way. The resulting story of the purity of young love is told lyrically and sensually.

Izu Ōshima → Ōshima

Izu Peninsula   伊豆半島

(Izu Hantō). Located in Shizuoka Prefecture, central Honshū, extending south into the Pacific Ocean between Suruga Bay and the Sagami Sea. It has a long, indented coastline, much of which is part of Fuji-Hakone-Izu National Park. A major portion of the volcanic group AMAGISAN dominates the peninsula. It has a subtropical climate and many beautiful beaches and contains numerous hot spring spas. Earthquakes have occurred here in recent years.

Izura   五浦

Coastal area in the city of Kita Ibaraki, northeastern Ibaraki Prefecture, central Honshū. Located on the Pacific Ocean, the coast is noted for its picturesque scenery including craggy cliffs. OKAKURA KAKUZŌ transferred the JAPAN FINE ARTS ACADEMY here in 1906, and the building is currently used as the Izura Art Research Institute.

Izutsu   井筒

(The Well Curb). Nō play by ZEAMI. Classified as a *sambamme-mono* ("part-three play"), it is based on the ISE MONOGATARI. An itinerant Buddhist priest (the *waki* or subordinate character) visits the temple Ariwaradera in Yamato Province and encounters a young woman (the *maejite* or main character at the beginning of a play). She tells him that the poet ARIWARA NO NARIHIRA and his wife lived in the temple long ago. After recounting the story of their love, which blossomed from the intimacy of shared childhood experiences such as peering together over a well curb (*izutsu*) into a well, the young woman disappears. In the second half of the play, the ghost of Narihira's wife (the *nochijite* or main character at the end of a play) dances clad in her husband's clothes. Standing at a well curb, she gazes down at the mirrorlike surface of the water and sees a reflection of Narihira's face there. As dawn breaks, she vanishes.

J

Jagatara-bumi ジャガタラ文

(letters from Jakarta). Letters sent to Japan in the 17th century by persons of Japanese descent who found themselves exiled in the Dutch colony on Java by the Tokugawa shogunate's (1603–1867) policy of NATIONAL SECLUSION. Many of these people were the wives and offspring of Dutch traders, who in 1639 had been forbidden by the shogunate "to have children in Japan." The most famous of these letters, that of Oharu (Jeronima Simonsen; d 1697), was a fabrication of the Nagasaki savant NISHIKAWA JOKEN; others are authentic.

Jahana Noboru 謝花昇

(1865–1908). Pioneer leader in the movement for popular rights in Okinawa. Born to a middle-class farming family, he went to Tōkyō as one of the first government scholarship students from Okinawa and graduated from the agriculture division of Tōkyō University in 1891. He returned home to become an agriculture specialist for the Okinawa prefectural government and two years later became the first Okinawan to enter Japan's higher civil service. He came into conflict with the prefectural governor, Narahara Shigeru (1834–1918), over the latter's decision to sell forest land that had been used as commonage by local farmers. Resigning from office in 1898, Jahana formed the Okinawa Kurabu (Okinawa Club), which criticized prefectural policies. He was also active in the unsuccessful movement to secure Okinawan representation in the national government. See also OKINAWA.

Jakkōin 寂光院

Convent in Ōhara, Sakyō Ward, Kyōto, belonging to the TENDAI SECT of Buddhism. Although the temple records variously attribute the origins of the Jakkōin to Prince SHŌTOKU (574–622), the monk KŪKAI (744–835), or the monk RYŌNIN (1073–1132), there is little reliable information about Jakkōin until the famous KENREI MON'IN (1155–1213), daughter of TAIRA NO KIYOMORI (1118–81), took up residence there.

The convent, which figures in the HEIKE MONOGATARI (13th century; tr *Tale of the Heike*, 1975) and the Nō drama *Ohara gokō* (The Imperial Visit to Ōhara), contains many relics of the Taira family. After a period of decline, the temple was refurbished by YODOGIMI (1567?–1615), concubine of TOYOTOMI HIDEYOSHI (1537–98). The central image of worship is the bodhisattva JIZŌ (Skt: Kṣitigarbha).

Jakuchū → Itō Jakuchū

Jakugon 寂厳

(1702–71). Monk, Sanskrit expert, and outstanding calligrapher of the Edo period (1600–1868). Born in Asaguchi, Bitchū Province (now part of Okayama Prefecture). Jakugon studied Buddhism, but later concentrated on Sanskrit textual studies. With JIUN ONKŌ, RYŌKAN, and Meigetsu (1726–97), Jakugon is known as one of the Four Monk-Writers.

Jakuren 寂蓮

(ca 1139–1202). Classical (WAKA) poet, Buddhist priest, and one of six compilers of the eighth imperial anthology, SHIN KOKINSHŪ (1205). Jakuren's lay name was Fujiwara no Sadanaga. His father was a brother of the great poet FUJIWARA NO TOSHINARI (Shunzei), who apparently intended Sadanaga as his heir. However, Shunzei later sired two male children—the untalented Nariie and the gifted FUJIWARA NO SADAIE. Sadanaga resigned as Shunzei's adoptive son and took holy orders and his priestly name, Jakuren. As his older contemporary SAIGYŌ had done, he composed poems on his travels. His best poems create the atmosphere of SABI (loneliness). His disputes with KENSHŌ over poetic theory on the occasion of the "Poetry Contest in 600 Rounds" (*Roppyakuban uta-awase*) of 1193 are particularly famous. Some 117 of Jakuren's poems are included in various imperial anthologies, beginning with the SENZAI WAKASHŪ (ca 1188, Collection of a Thousand Years).

Jakushitsu Genkō 寂室元光

(1290–1367). Also known as Ennō Zenji and Shōtō Kokushi. Zen monk of the RINZAI SECT and founder of its Eigenji subsect. Born in Mimasaka Province (now part of Okayama Prefecture), he became a monk at the age of 15 under Mui Shōgen of the temple Sanshōji in Kyōto. Later he entered Zenkōji in Kamakura to study with Yakuō Tokuken, an eminent disciple of RANKEI DŌRYŪ. Accompanying his master, he moved successively to KENNINJI, KENCHŌJI, and NANZENJI. He visited China (1320–26), where he received the name Jakushitsu, and then resided in various areas of Japan. In 1360 he founded the Eigenji subsect in Ōmi Province (now Shiga Prefecture).

JAL Foundation 日航財団

(Nikkō Zaidan). A foundation established in 1990 by the JAPAN AIRLINES CO, LTD (JAL). It promotes international exchange of aviation experts, awards scholarships for study in Japan to students from the countries of the Pacific Rim, and sponsors international student exchanges and sister city programs. It also sponsors a worldwide children's *haiku* contest. Total assets in 1990 were ¥2.0 billion (US $13.8 million). Headquarters are in Tōkyō.

Janes, Leroy Lansing ジェーンズ, L. L.

(1838–1909). US educator who taught in Japan early in the Meiji period (1868–1912). A graduate of the US Military Academy, in 1871 Janes accepted an invitation to teach at the KUMAMOTO YŌGAKKŌ, the Kumamoto domainal school for Western studies. His classes in mathematics, history, and natural sciences were given entirely in English. Janes also acted as a moral guide, waiting three years to discuss Christianity until he thought his students had learned enough English to understand the relation between Christianity and Western learning. Under his influence 35 students were converted, the so-called Kumamoto Band. Many of its members, among them EBINA DANJŌ and UKITA KAZUTAMI, eventually became Christian leaders in education and politics. Conservative elements in Kumamoto forced the school to close in August 1876, and members of the Kumamoto Band moved to the Dōshisha school (now Dōshisha University) in Kyōto. Janes returned to the United States in 1878 but again taught in Japan from 1893 to 1899.

janken じゃん拳

Children's game of "scissors-paper-rock," one of many KEN (literally, "fist") games. In *janken* the players call out "*jan, ken, pon*" and make one of three forms with one hand: stone (closed fist), scissors (two fingers extended), or paper (hand opened flat). Stone

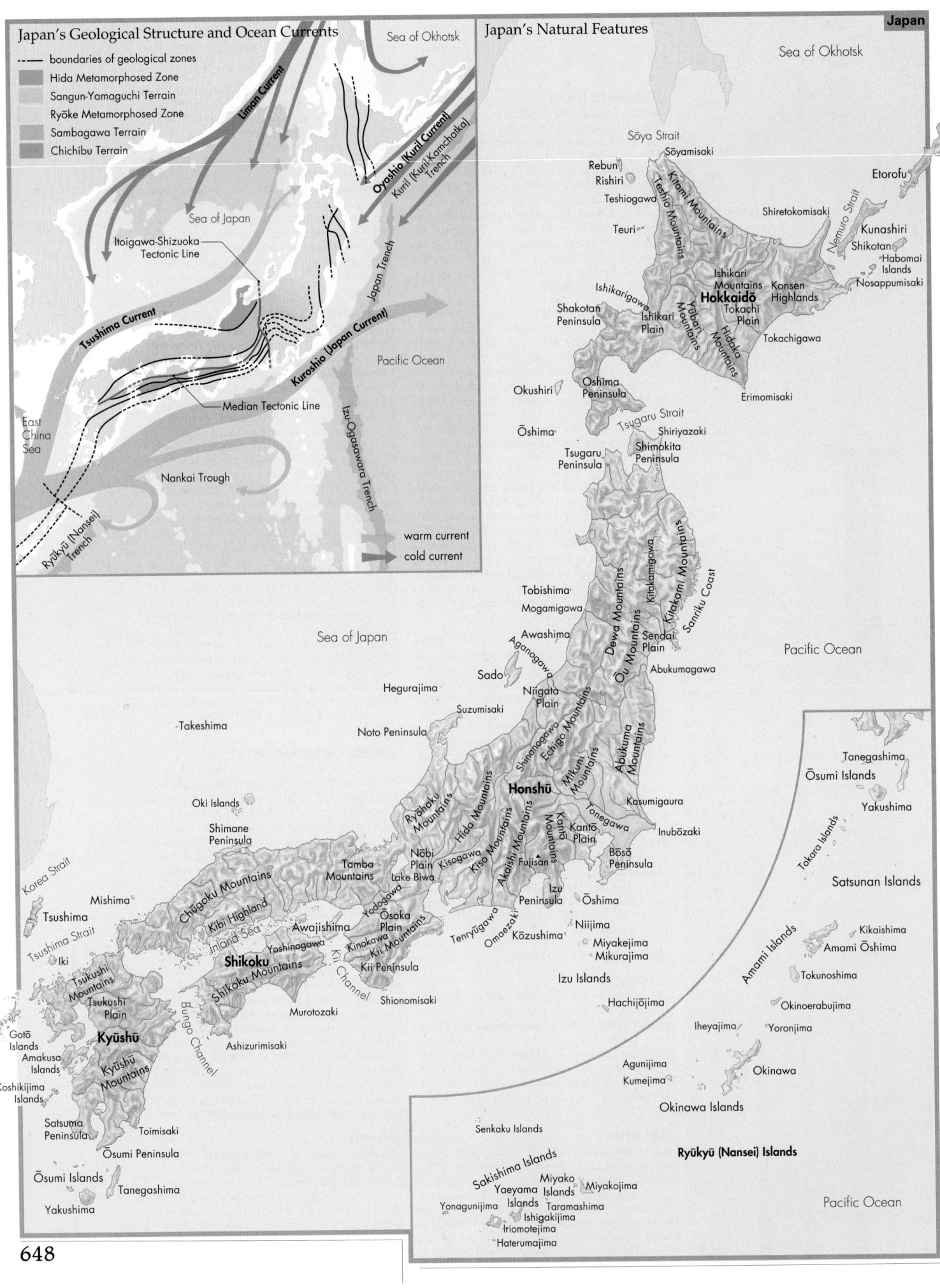

Japan's Geological Structure and Ocean Currents

- - - boundaries of geological zones
- Hida Metamorphosed Zone
- Sangun-Yamaguchi Terrain
- Ryōke Metamorphosed Zone
- Sambagawa Terrain
- Chichibu Terrain

Sea of Okhotsk

Liman Current

Oyashio (Kuril Current)

Kuril (Kuril-Kamchatka) Trench

Sea of Japan

Itoigawa-Shizuoka Tectonic Line

Tsushima Current

Japan Trench

Kuroshio (Japan Current)

Pacific Ocean

Median Tectonic Line

Izu-Ogasawara Trench

East China Sea

Nankai Trough

Ryūkyū (Nansei) Trench

→ warm current
→ cold current

Japan's Natural Features

Japan

Sea of Okhotsk

Sōya Strait

Sōyamisaki

Rebun
Rishiri
Teshiogawa
Teuri

Etorofu

Shiretokomisaki

Kunashiri
Shikotan
Nemuro Strait
Habomai Islands
Nosappumisaki

Kitami Mountains
Teshio Mountains

Ishikarigawa

Ishikari Mountains
Konsen Highlands

Hokkaidō

Yūbari Mountains
Tokachi Plain

Shakotan Peninsula
Ishikari Plain

Hidaka Mountains

Tokachigawa

Okushiri

Oshima Peninsula

Erimomisaki

Ōshima

Tsugaru Strait

Shiriyazaki
Shimokita Peninsula

Tsugaru Peninsula

Tobishima

Mogamigawa

Awashima

Aganogawa

Sado

Hegurajima

Suzumisaki

Noto Peninsula

Sea of Japan

Dewa Mountains

Kitakamigawa

Sendai Plain

Ōu Mountains

Abukumagawa

Kitakami Mountains

Sanriku Coast

Pacific Ocean

Niigata Plain

Shinanogawa

Echigo Mountains

Abukuma Mountains

Kasumigaura

Mikuni Mountains

Honshū

Takeshima

Oki Islands

Shimane Peninsula

Ryōhaku Mountains

Hida Mountains

Kantō Mountains

Tonegawa

Kanto Plain

Inubōzaki

Tamba Mountains

Nōbi Plain

Kisogawa

Kiso Mountains

Akaishi Mountains

Fujisan

Bōsō Peninsula

Chugoku Mountains

Kibi Highland

Lake Biwa

Izu Peninsula

Ōshima

Mishima

Inland Sea

Yodogawa

Ōsaka Plain

Niijima

Korea Strait

Tsushima

Yoshinogawa

Kinokawa

Kii Mountains

Kōzushima

Miyakejima

Mikurajima

Shikoku

Awajishima

Tsushima Strait

Iki

Shikoku Mountains

Kii Peninsula

Tenryūgawa

Omaezaki

Izu Islands

Tsukushi Mountains

Kii Channel

Shionomisaki

Hachijōjima

Bungo Channel

Tsukushi Plain

Murotozaki

Ashizurimisaki

Gotō Islands

Kyūshū

Amakusa Islands

Kyūshū Mountains

Koshikijima Islands

Satsuma Peninsula

Toimisaki

Ōsumi Peninsula

Ōsumi Islands

Tanegashima

Yakushima

Tanegashima

Ōsumi Islands

Yakushima

Satsunan Islands

Tokara Islands

Amami Islands

Kikaishima

Amami Ōshima

Tokunoshima

Okinoerabujima

Iheyajima

Yoronjima

Agunijima

Kumejima

Okinawa

Okinawa Islands

Senkaku Islands

Ryūkyū (Nansei) Islands

Sakishima Islands

Yaeyama Islands

Miyako Islands

Miyakojima

Yonagunijima

Taramashima

Ishigakijima

Iriomotejima

Haterumajima

Pacific Ocean

"breaks" scissors, scissors "cuts" paper, and paper "covers" stone. *Janken* is often played to determine who shall be "it" in games of tag or who shall go first in selecting teams.

Janome Sewing Machine Co, Ltd
蛇の目ミシン工業[株]

(Janome Mishin Kōgyō). Sewing machine manufacturing company; second to BROTHER INDUSTRIES, LTD, in the production of home sewing machines. Founded in 1921. After World War II, it grew steadily by adopting a direct-sales system. Janome had nine overseas subsidiaries in 1989 and is expanding its production capacity abroad. Sales for the fiscal year ending March 1991 totaled ¥78.9 billion (US $575.1 million), the export ratio was 20 percent, and capitalization stood at ¥7.6 billion (US $55.4 million). Headquarters are in Tōkyō.

Japan
日本

(Nippon or Nihon). This article describes the territory and administrative divisions, the natural features, and the geological structure of Japan.

TERRITORY AND ADMINISTRATIVE DIVISIONS

Japan consists of an archipelago extending approximately from northeast to southwest. It lies off the east coast of the Asian continent. The total land area as of October 1989 was 377,688 square kilometers (145,825 sq mi), only slightly larger than that of Finland or Italy and about the same size as the US state of Montana. The four major islands of Japan are HOKKAIDŌ, HONSHŪ, Shikoku (see SHIKOKU REGION), and Kyūshū (see KYŪSHŪ REGION). Claimed by the Japanese, the northernmost islands of Kunashiri (Kunashir), Etorofu (Iturup), the Habomai Islands, and Shikotan were occupied by the Soviet Union at the end of World War II and were still occupied by the Russian Federation in late 1992 (see TERRITORY OF JAPAN; NORTHERN TERRITORIES ISSUE). The OGASAWARA ISLANDS and OKINAWA ISLANDS, under American rule after World War II, were returned to Japan in 1968 and 1972, respectively. The areas of the main geographical divisions of Japan (including offshore islands under their administrative control) are as follows:

Hokkaidō	83,520 sq km (32,247 sq mi)
Honshū	230,940 sq km (89,166 sq mi)
Shikoku	18,808 sq km (7,262 sq mi)
Kyūshū	42,164 sq km (16,279 sq mi)
Okinawa Prefecture	2,256 sq km (871 sq mi)
Total	377,688 sq km (145,825 sq mi)

Following the recent tendency among countries to enlarge TERRITORIAL WATERS, Japan set its territorial limit at 12 nautical miles from the coast in 1977.

Population——At the time of the Meiji Restoration (1868) Japan's POPULATION was about 33 million. In 1990 it was 123,612,000, seventh largest in the world. The density per square kilometer (0.386 sq mi) was 332 persons in 1990. Although this figure is comparable to 359 persons in the Netherlands and 325 in Belgium, the density of the Japanese population per unit area under cultivation is the highest in the world, because over two-thirds of Japan is occupied by mountainous terrain, and alluvial plains occupy only 13 percent. Among the main islands the density is highest in Honshū, followed by Kyūshū and Shikoku.

The population was distributed comparatively equally all over the country about a century ago, when Japan was still predominantly agricultural. With industrialization, however, there was a strong tendency toward regional concentration. This became even more pronounced in the postwar years; as a result, 43.1 percent of Japanese live in the three major urban areas of Tōkyō, Ōsaka, and Nagoya. The Tōkyō Metropolitan Area in particular, although less than 2.0 percent in terms of area, has a concentration of 23.4 percent of the national population.

Formation of the Country——Among the various theories on the formation of Japan as a nation-state, one school holds that, because of its proximity to the Asian continent, northern Kyūshū was the site of the first political center. By the 4th century a sovereign court had emerged, which by conquest and alliance eventually unified the country. The YAMATO COURT repeatedly dispatched expeditionary forces to northeastern Honshū and succeeded in subduing it in the 7th century, thus establishing the prototype of a unified Japan consisting of Honshū, Shikoku, and Kyūshū. Under the TAIKA REFORM of 645, the KOKUGUN SYSTEM of administration was instituted, and the country was divided into 58 (later 66) provinces (*kuni*) with subunits called *gun*. This division remained in effect nominally until the Meiji Restoration (1868). However, under the BAKUHAN SYSTEM of the Tokugawa shogunate (1603–1867), a system of feudal *daimyō* domains (*han*) whose boundaries did not for the most part coincide with those of the ancient provinces was superimposed on the *kokugun* system.

Changes in Territory——The territory of Japan has remained essentially the same from the 7th century, but its history is nonetheless one of numerous modifications. In 1609 the daimyō of the Satsuma domain (now Kagoshima Prefecture) established control over the Ryūkyū Kingdom (see OKINAWA). The Ogasawara Islands (also known as the Bonin Islands) were discovered by the Japanese in 1593 and were officially incorporated into Japan in 1876. Hokkaidō, once called EZO, was settled by the Japanese in the Edo period (1600–1868). As trade developed with the AINU people in the interior, the Japanese gradually made their way into the southern part of SAKHALIN (J: Karafuto) and the Kuril Islands, where they came into conflict with the Russians. In 1875 Japan concluded the Treaty of ST. PETERSBURG with Russia and gave up the southern part of Sakhalin in exchange for the Kuril Islands. After the SINO-JAPANESE WAR OF 1894–1895 Japan acquired TAIWAN, and after the RUSSO-JAPANESE WAR (1904–05) it acquired the southern half of Sakhalin and leased the southern part of the Liaodong (Liaotung) Peninsula. It annexed Korea in 1910 (see KOREA, ANNEXATION OF) and secured a mandate over former German territories in the South Sea Islands after World War I (see VERSAILLES, TREATY OF). Thus at the time of the outbreak of World War II, the total land area was 680,729 square kilometers (262,830 sq mi). However, after its defeat Japan was stripped of all territories acquired during its period of colonialism and, until the restoration of Okinawa in 1972, was left with essentially the four main islands.

Modern Administrative System——After the Meiji Restoration the country was administratively reorganized into the prefectural system (see PREFECTURAL SYSTEM, ESTABLISHMENT OF). Tōkyō, Ōsaka, and Kyōto were made *fu* (urban prefectures) in 1871, and the rest of the country was divided into 302 *ken* (prefectures). By 1888 this system had been integrated into a system of 3 *fu* and 43 *ken*. Hokkaidō was initially administered directly by the central government but later came to be treated equally with other prefectures, although it was called a *dō* (circuit) rather than a *ken*. In 1943 Tōkyō Fu was designated as a special administrative area and named Tōkyō To (officially translated as Tōkyō Metropolis). At present Japan is administratively divided into 1 *to* (Tōkyō To), 1 *dō* (Hokkaidō), 2 *fu* (Ōsaka Fu and Kyōto Fu), and 43 *ken*. See also LOCAL GOVERNMENT.

NATURAL FEATURES OF JAPAN

Topography——The chief feature of the Japanese archipelago is its geological instability, including frequent volcanic activity and many EARTHQUAKES. This implies more than the facts that earthquakes are numerous and that volcanic activity is severe; it also demonstrates that the rise and fall of the land and the amount of horizontal migration are extensive. Another distinctive characteristic of the topography is the fact that the Japanese archipelago is made up almost entirely of steep mountain districts with very few plains.

High, precipitous mountains of about 1,500–3,000 meters (5,000–10,000 ft) run along the Pacific Ocean side of southwestern Japan. Deep, V-shaped valleys are cut into these mountain districts. The mountain ranges and mountainous districts of Akaishi, Kii, Shikoku, and Kyūshū are representative of this zone. In contrast, on the Sea of Japan side of southwestern Japan are groupings of plateaus and low mountain districts with a height of about 500–1,500 meters (1,600–5,000 ft), such as the Hida, Tamba, and Chūgoku mountain districts; the Kibi Highland; and the Tsukushi Mountains.

The large number and variety of VOLCANOES found throughout the Japanese archipelago constitute another remarkable feature. There have been 188 volcanoes active at some time or another since the Quaternary geological period, and more than 40 of these remain active today. Among these are volcanoes that have had numerous violent eruptions, such as Asamayama and Bandaisan. Further, a special characteristic of Japan's volcano zone is the development of large craters or calderas such as those at Akan, Daisetsu, Hakone, Aso, and Aira. The caldera at Aso is on a scale unrivaled anywhere in the world.

A small number of large rivers, such as the Ishikarigawa, Shinanogawa, Tonegawa, Kisogawa, Yodogawa, and Chikugogawa, have fair-sized delta plains at their mouths. Diluvial uplands and river and marine terraces have developed in many coastal areas of Japan, and these are utilized along with the plains for both agriculture and habitation.

Climate——Located in the monsoon zone of the eastern coast of the Asian continent, the most notable features of the CLIMATE of the Japanese archipelago are the wide range of yearly temperatures and the large amount of rainfall. However, because of the complexity of the land configuration, there are numerous regional differences throughout the seasons.

Continued on page 658➤

A Bird's-Eye View of Japan

The Japanese archipelago unfolds like a continent in miniature. Seen from the air, the land reveals surprising diversity—pack ice and palm trees, mountains and farmland, ultramodern cities and old-fashioned villages. This section presents aerial views of northern, central, and southern Japan and metropolitan Tōkyō.

Northern Japan

Hokkaidō

Tōhoku

The northern third of Japan comprises the island of Hokkaidō and the Tōhoku region, which covers the northernmost part of the island of Honshū. The landscape of Hokkaidō, which remained essentially undeveloped until the late 19th century, has retained much of its pristine beauty. Hokkaidō's mountains, lakes, and forests are popular among tourists, while its farms produce a sizable percentage of the vegetables, grain, and dairy products consumed in Japan. Agriculture is also important in the Tōhoku region, which is well known for its vegetables, rice, and fruit. With their long winters and abundant snow, Tōhoku and Hokkaidō are especially alluring to skiers, and some of Japan's most popular ski resorts are located there.

1 Cape Notoro, Hokkaidō. Every year between February and April, pack ice forms in the Sea of Okhotsk north of Hokkaidō, making the waters off this promontory impassable.
2 Teshikaga, Hokkaidō. Open-range cattle raising and other types of large-scale agriculture, rare in other parts of Japan, are common in Hokkaidō.
3 Kushiro Shitsugen, Hokkaidō. This primeval peat marsh, located in Kushiro Shitsugen National Park, is a breeding ground for the *tanchō*, or Japanese crane.
4 Lake Saroma, Hokkaidō. A lake in name only, this body of water is actually a lagoon separated by a large sandbar from the Sea of Okhotsk, at right.
5 Lake Mashū, Hokkaidō. The waters of this caldera lake are among the clearest in the world; visibility is an amazing 36 meters.
6 Shirakawa, Fukushima Prefecture, Tōhoku region. Stacks of rice straw lie arrayed across a drained paddy after the harvest. Rice farming remains vital to Tōhoku's agricultural economy.
7 Daisetsuzan National Park, Hokkaidō. Japan's largest national park is named for the group of towering volcanoes at its center. Among the park's attractions are hiking, mountain climbing, and hot-spring bathing.
8 Shizukuishi, Iwate Prefecture, Tōhoku region. Ski resort areas like the one pictured here now abound in Tōhoku, following the development of expressway networks and high-speed railway lines linking the region to Tōkyō and other major cities.

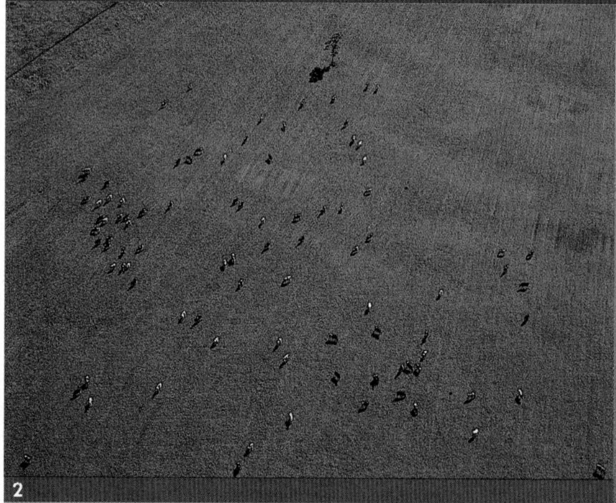

All the photographs in this section are by Toyotaka Ryozō

Central Japan

Kantō

Chūbu

The middle third of Japan consists of the Chūbu region in central Honshū and the Kantō region to the east. The mountainous Chūbu region is divided by the Japanese Alps, a series of three mountain ranges running through the region from north to south. Northwest of these, along the Sea of Japan, is the area known as Hokuriku, where much of Japan's rice is grown. On the other side of the Japanese Alps, the Pacific Ocean side, lies the largest and best known of Chūbu's many volcanoes—the majestic Mt. Fuji.

The Kantō region in east-central Honshū is Japan's most heavily populated region and the nation's political and economic hub. The Kantō Plain, the country's largest, covers over half of this region, including most of the Tōkyō metropolitan area, where nearly a quarter of the Japanese population resides. Tōkyō Bay is host to some of the country's busiest ports, among them Yokohama, which handles more trade than any other port in Japan. Kantō, like Chūbu, is warmer than northern Japan, and its beaches and coastal waters attract millions of visitors every year.

1 Kan'eiji, Tōkyō. Located in what is now Ueno Park, this temple was built in 1625 as the family temple of the ruling Tokugawa clan. Nowadays it is a popular place for cherry-blossom viewing.
2 Shinjuku, Tōkyō. Once a post-station town on the old Kōshū Highway, Shinjuku has developed into one of Tōkyō's main commercial and entertainment districts. With the completion in 1991 of the new Tōkyō Metropolitan Government Offices (the two towerlike buildings at left in the photo), this area has also become the city's administrative center.
3 Tōkyō Bay. The Yokohama Bay Bridge, which opened in 1989, rises over the main channel into the Port of Yokohama, at right, from Tōkyō Bay, at left.
4 Enoshima, Kanagawa Prefecture, Kantō region. Located in Sagami Bay near the city of Kamakura, this island attracts hordes of swimmers and beachcombers every summer.
5 Mt. Fuji, Yamanashi and Shizuoka prefectures, Chūbu region. Mt. Fuji is most often admired from ground level. The view from above provides a glimpse into its crater and a reminder that this celebrated symbol of Japan is also an active volcano.
6 Tōjimbō, Fukui Prefecture, Chūbu region. Centuries of erosion by waves have created this spectacular geological formation on the Sea of Japan coast. Tōjimbō is in the Echizen-Kaga Coast Quasi-National Park.
7 Wajima, Ishikawa Prefecture, Chūbu region. The use of terraced paddies facilitates the cultivation of rice in mountainous regions. Areas like this one are known as *semmaida*, or "thousand paddies."
8 Hida Mountains, Chūbu region. Part of the Japanese Alps, the Hida range extends through four prefectures and includes five mountains over 3,000 meters high.

Tōkyō

Tōkyō

The spectacle that Tōkyō presents when seen from the air reveals some basic features of the city's character: its staggering dimensions and teeming populace, its profusion of concrete and paucity of wooded land, its labyrinthine streets and sprawling railway network. But Tōkyō has other facets it does not disclose so readily—resilience, for example. Gazing out over its prosperous, bustling precincts, one may be surprised to learn that this enormous city has been virtually destroyed twice within the past 60 years: once by the Tōkyō Earthquake of 1923 and again by firebombing during World War II. Both times it has emerged from the rebuilding process as a larger, more dynamic city. Even now it seems that the metropolis is constantly being redefined, redesigned, and rebuilt. In recent years, hardly a structure has been left unchanged in trendier neighborhoods such as Shibuya and Shinjuku, while rivers like the Sumidagawa have been the focus of ambitious efforts to improve Tōkyō's physical environment. Even the outlines of historic sections like Asakusa and Ueno are being altered, and the relentless drive to expand into and exploit every available space is being carried straight out into Tōkyō Bay.

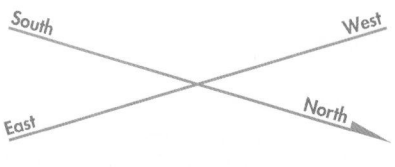

Tōkyō Tower

National Diet Bu

Hama Detached Palace Garden

Hibiya Park

Ginza

Tōkyō Station

Kokugikan

Mt. Fuji

Shibuya

Shinjuku

Meiji Shrine

State Guesthouse

Shinjuku Gyoen National Garden

Imperial Palace

Kitanomaru Park

Tōkyō Dome

Ueno Park

Sumidagawa

Asakusa

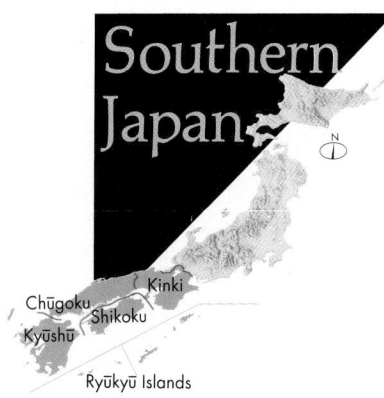

Southern Japan

Chūgoku　Kinki
Kyūshū　Shikoku
Ryūkyū Islands

Japan's southern third is composed of the Kinki, Chūgoku, Shikoku, and Kyūshū regions and the Ryūkyū Islands. Kinki, in west-central Honshū, and Chūgoku, on the island's western tip, are covered by mountains, small basins, and coastal plains. The Kinki region includes the Ōsaka-Kōbe area, the nation's second most important commercial and industrial district, as well as the Kyōto-Nara area, the ancient heart of Japan. The Chūgoku and Shikoku regions, often regarded as two parts of a single district, face one another across the Inland Sea. The Shikoku region consists of Shikoku, the smallest and least populated of Japan's four main islands, and the many islands that surround it.

Kyūshū is the southernmost of Japan's four main islands. Its warm climate is ideal for agriculture, but the Kyūshū region, which includes the surrounding islands, has relatively little arable land. Active volcanoes abound here, as do sulfurous hot springs. Trailing away to the southwest of Kyūshū are the Ryūkyū Islands, the largest of which is Okinawa. Nearly all these islands are in the subtropical zone—closer to Taipei than to Tō-kyō. Tourism, especially in Okinawa, is an important industry.

1 Ōsaka Castle, Ōsaka Prefecture, Kinki region. This extensively restored fortress is located in the heart of the city of Ōsaka. The original structure was completed in 1586 at the behest of Toyotomi Hideyoshi.
2 Ago Bay, Mie Prefecture, Kinki region. The many rafts that can be seen floating on the waters of this inlet, part of the Ise-Shima National Park, are used for the cultivation of pearls.
3 Tōdaiji, Nara Prefecture, Kinki region. This temple's 52-meter-high main hall, the roof of which appears in the foreground, is the largest wooden structure in Japan.
4 The Inland Sea. Bounded by Honshū on the north and east, by Shikoku on the south, and by Kyūshū on the west, this body of water has been an important transportation route for centuries. Shown here is a segment of one of the Honshū-Shikoku Bridges.
5 Amanohashidate, Kyōto Prefecture, Kinki region. Some 7,000 pine trees grow on this sandbar in the interior of Wakasa Bay. Amanohashidate is famous for its unique setting and natural beauty, often cited in classical poetry.
6 Tottori Sand Dunes, Tottori Prefecture, Chūgoku region. These dunes, part of the San'in Coast National Park, rise to a height of over 90 meters, making this area an ideal spot for paragliding.
7 Ryūkyū Islands. These small islands surrounded by coral reefs are typical of the more than 160 islands that make up the Ryūkyū chain.
8 Asosan, Kumamoto Prefecture, Kyūshū. This volcano's caldera is one of the largest in the world; all but the most distant formations shown here fall within its 80-km circumference. Asosan is located in the Aso-Kujū National Park.

— Continued from page 649

Spring. When low-pressure areas pass over the Pacific coast of Japan in March, the temperature rises with each rainfall. When low-pressure areas start to develop over the Sea of Japan, the strong wind from the south called *haru ichiban* (the first tidings of spring) blows over Japan. This wind causes flooding due to suddenly melting mountain snow and the foehn phenomenon, which sometimes results in great fires on the Sea of Japan side. The approaching rainy season (*baiu* or *tsuyu*) can be felt in mid-May.

Summer. The onset of the rainy season takes place around 7 June. It starts in the southern part of Japan and moves northward. The position of the *baiu* front varies each year; when it leans to the south, northeastern Japan suffers damage from cold summers, and when it leans to the north, southwestern Japan suffers drought. With the end of the rain around 20 July, the Ogasawara air masses blanket Japan, and the weather takes on a summer pattern. The peak of summer is late July, and the summer heat lingers on into mid-August.

Fall. September is the typhoon season. Weather resembling that of the rainy season also occurs because of the autumnal rain fronts. The weather clears in mid-October, and the winter winds start to blow. The atmospheric pressure configuration gradually changes to the winter pattern, and snow begins to fall in northern Japan.

Winter. In December, when the atmospheric pressure configuration has completely changed to the winter pattern, northwest winds bring snow to the mountains and to the plains on the Sea of Japan side, and a dry wind blows on the Pacific Ocean side. The peak of winter comes around 25 January.

Life and Nature—Japan's land area is small but its configuration is complex, so that the climate and the flora and fauna vary regionally, extending from the subarctic zone in the north to the subtropical zone in the south (see PLANTS); there is also much seasonal change. An abundance of HOT SPRINGS, which are popular as health resorts, accompany the many volcanoes.

Japan's seasonal changes and geological structure bring many natural disasters. Heavy rains due to the *baiu* front and the autumn typhoons bring about landslides, floods, and wind damage. Heavy winter precipitation causes snow damage as well as flooding and cold damage because of the unusually low temperature of the rivers when the snows melt. In addition, earthquakes on the scale of the TŌKYŌ EARTHQUAKE OF 1923 strike somewhere in Japan every several decades. Typhoons and the tidal waves accompanying earthquakes also inflict damage on heavily populated, low-lying coastal areas. Flooding and land subsidence have also occurred as the result of LAND RECLAMATION and excessive pumping of groundwater.

GEOLOGICAL STRUCTURE

The Japanese archipelago is a part of the island arc that borders the eastern edge of the Asian continent and corresponds to the edge of the continental crust that forms the Asian continent. The eastern side of the Japanese islands directly touches the oceanic crust of the Pacific Ocean. The fact that the islands are located near the border of the two crusts has much to do with their geological characteristics.

Topography—Topographically, the Kuril Arc; the Sakhalin-Hokkaidō Arc; the Honshū Arc, connecting Kyūshū, Shikoku, Honshū, and the western part of Hokkaidō; and the Ryūkyū and Izu-Ogasawara arcs make up the Japanese islands, with each arc assuming a form projecting toward the Pacific Ocean. The Kuril, Japan, and Izu-Ogasawara trenches constitute one continuous trench that assumes the form of an arc projecting toward the west. This trench is a narrow, submarine channel with a depth of about 9,000 meters (30,000 ft) in some areas. The Japan Trench, however, is not connected to the shallower Nankai Trough in the offing of Shikoku and Kyūshū, nor is the Nankai Trough connected to the Ryūkyū Trench. The Philippine Basin is separated from the Pacific Ocean by the Izu-Ogasawara Arc, and the Nankai Trough and the Ryūkyū Trench together correspond to the northern edge of the Philippine Basin.

The Sea of Okhotsk, the Sea of Japan, and the East China Sea separate Japan topographically from the Asian continent. They are called marginal seas, which are generally shallow, although some basins in the Sea of Okhotsk and the Sea of Japan are 3,000–4,000 meters (9,800–13,000 ft) deep.

The geological structure of Japan is reflected in the facts that the Japan Trench is not connected to the Nankai Trough and that the Kuril Arc, the northeastern part of the Honshū Arc, and the Izu-Ogasawara Arc are one continuous island arc. The southwestern part of the Honshū Arc and the Ryūkyū Islands are a separate arc formed in a comparatively older period. Geologically the former is called northeastern Japan and the latter southwestern Japan.

The border of northeastern Japan and southwestern Japan is a great fault called the Itoigawa-Shizuoka Tectonic Line. The belt-like area east of this fault and running from the western part of Niigata Prefecture to the central part of Nagano Prefecture and from Yamanashi Prefecture to the eastern part of Shizuoka Prefecture forms a single valley crossing Honshū that is called the FOSSA MAGNA. The mountain ranges and volcanic zones that form northeastern Japan turn south-southeast at the Fossa Magna and are connected to the Izu Islands; southwestern Japan is cut off diagonally at the Itoigawa-Shizuoka Tectonic Line. Southwestern Japan is divided into an inner belt (the side facing the Sea of Japan) and an outer belt (the side facing the Pacific Ocean) by the great fault called the Median Tectonic Line, which runs lengthwise along the axis of southwestern Japan from the Ina Mountains to Ōita Prefecture. These belts can be traced as far as the Ryūkyū Islands, and the entirety of southwestern Japan is characterized by a considerably regular beltlike structure. In southwestern Japan there are fewer volcanoes than in northeastern Japan, and they are concentrated in the area facing the Sea of Japan and Kyūshū. Volcanic activity is vigorous in northeastern Japan, and two volcanic zones are present, one running along the coast of the Sea of Japan and the other along the Ōu Mountains.

Crustal Movement—The Japanese islands have severe crustal movements, which are still progressing. Crustal movements include movements of short duration, such as seismic activity, and also slow movements of long duration. Volcanic activity, gravity anomaly, and crustal heat flow are also directly caused by the crustal deformation. Volcanoes have been particularly active in

northeastern Japan since the Quaternary period. There is a narrow nonvolcanic zone along the Pacific coast, the rest of the region being volcanic.

History of the Japanese Islands—The Japanese islands were formed as the result of several orogenic movements and are not the product of a single crustal movement. Their history goes back at least to the Silurian period in the Paleozoic era (about 400 million years ago). As shown by fossil evidence, the oldest stratum is that of the mid-Silurian period. The principal part of the Japanese islands had been under the surface of the sea from this period through the end of the Paleozoic era or through the beginning of the Mesozoic era.

The greater part of the Japanese islands became land in the Paleocene period. It was only after the Neocene period that the sea again began to invade the land. The present northeastern part of the Honshū Arc originated after the Cretaceous period. As the newly produced orogenic zone intersected obliquely with the island arc that had already existed, the northeastern extension of southwestern Japan was curved like a reverse S, forming a block. The sea moved into the hollow created behind it, and volcanic activity began. This is the Green Tuff zone.

Sedimentation took place during the Quaternary period, progressing gradually from east to west in the Green Tuff zone, and foldings occurred. This crustal movement still continues, and volcanic and seismic activities are regarded as representing this movement. Thus the shape of the present Japanese islands had nearly been formed by the Quaternary period, when sedimentation took place in the lowlands scattered all over the Japanese islands, creating plains.

☎ 650–657

Japan Academy　日本学士院

(Nihon Gakushiin). The preeminent learned society of Japan, established in 1879 to honor scholars who have made outstanding contributions to their fields of study. Election to the academy is considered the highest distinction a Japanese scholar can receive. Academicians enjoy life tenure and a yearly stipend. The academy awards two annual prizes—the Academy Prize (Gakushiin Shō) and the Imperial Prize (Gakushiin Onshi Shō)—for important scholarly work and publishes *Gakushiin kiyō* (*Proceedings of the Japan Academy*).

Japan Advertisers Association
日本広告主協会

(Nihon Kōkokunushi Kyōkai). An organization of some 272 major advertisers in such media as newspapers, magazines, radio, and television. It was organized in 1956 to take countermeasures against the rising cost of advertising. The association offers training in advertising techniques to member firms and publishes the results of its research on advertising technology. It also provides information concerning overseas marketing procedures and advertising methodologies.

Japan Advertising Review Organization　日本広告審査機構

(Nihon Kōkoku Shinsa Kikō). A consumer-advocate organization established in 1974 for the self-regulation of the advertising industry. Modeled on the US Better Business Bureaus, its members include all major advertisers, the media, advertising agencies, and producers of television commercials. It accepts complaints about advertisements

from consumers and requests the suspension of advertisements if, in the judgment of the organization, the complaints are justified. See also ADVERTISING; ADVERTISING AGENCIES.

Japan Airlines Co, Ltd 日本航空[株]

(Nihon Kōkū). Often called JAL. Air transport company. With international flights to 47 cities in 23 countries, it is one of the world's largest airlines. It also operates domestic routes. The company was founded in 1951 as a joint-stock company and reorganized in 1953 as a semigovernmental enterprise under the provisions of the Japan Air Lines Law. JAL was completely privatized in 1987.

In 1991 the JAL fleet comprised 101 aircraft. The company also operates hotels and other businesses through affiliated firms. The Japan Airlines Development Co operates hotels in Paris and at the NEW TŌKYŌ INTERNATIONAL AIRPORT at Narita and also has chain contracts with 210 hotels around the world, forming the JAL Hotel System International. The Japan Creative Tours Co sells package tours under the brand names JAL-PAK and AVA. Annual revenue totaled ¥1.1 trillion (US $8.0 billion) in the fiscal year ending March 1991. In the same year the company's capitalization stood at ¥188.3 billion (US $1.4 billion). Headquarters are in Tōkyō.

Japan Air System Co, Ltd [株]日本エアシステム

(Nihon Ea Shisutemu). Air transport company; also engaged in leasing helicopters. It is the third largest airline in Japan. Incorporated in 1964 as the Japan Domestic Airlines Co (Nihon Kokunai Kōkū), and later called Tōa Domestic Airlines (1971), it took a new corporate identity in 1988 to reflect the inauguration of international services. In 1991 it served a network of 44 cities and operated some 372 flights a day, covering 68 routes. Sales for the fiscal year ending March 1991 totaled ¥243.5 billion (US $1.8 billion), and the company was capitalized at ¥23.5 billion (US $171.3 million). Headquarters are in Tōkyō.

Japan Amateur Sports Association 日本体育協会

(Nihon Taiiku Kyōkai). National organization for the regulation, promotion, and funding of amateur sports and recreation. Founded in 1911 to prepare Japan for participation in its first Olympics, the association quickly broadened its role in amateur sports and became the governing body for such sports as track and field, swimming, *karate*, and *jūdō*. It sponsors national competitions and supervises participation in international events. Present membership includes 43 amateur athletic organizations and 47 prefectural sports associations. The first chairman was KANŌ JIGORŌ. See also SPORTS.

Japan-America Student Conference 日米学生会議

(Nichibei Gakusei Kaigi). A series of conferences planned and administered by students from Japan and the United States to promote Japanese-American understanding and cooperation. The conferences, roughly one month long, are held each year alternately in Japan and the United States. The conferences were first proposed by Japanese students after the MANCHURIAN INCIDENT of 1931, when relations between the two countries began to deteriorate. The first meeting was held at Aoyama Gakuin University in 1934; the sec-

ond was at Reed College in Portland, Oregon. Suspended during World War II, the conferences resumed in 1947. The 41st conference was held in Japan in 1989 with 80 participants.

Japan Art Academy 日本芸術院

(Nihon Geijutsuin). Organization, established in 1947 and placed under the control of the Ministry of Education in 1949, that deliberates art-related issues, promotes art, and advises the minister of education on matters concerning art. It is composed of up to 200 lifetime members, who receive an annual stipend (there were 107 members in 1990). The history of the academy can be traced back to the Bijutsu Shinsa Iinkai (Fine Art Screening Committee) of 1907, which in 1919 became the Teikoku Bijutsuin (Imperial Fine Arts Academy), headed by MORI ŌGAI. The organization was reestablished as the Teikoku Geijutsuin (Imperial Art Academy) in 1937. The academy annually presents the Japan Art Academy Awards for contributions in the fields of fine arts; literature; and music, drama, and dance. See also BUNTEN.

Japan Associated Finance Co, Ltd 日本合同ファイナンス[株]

(JAFCO; J: Nihon Gōdō Fainansu). Venture capital company, a member of the Nomura Securities group. Incorporated in 1973. Sales for the fiscal year ending September 1991 totaled ¥43.3 billion (US $315.6 million), of which investment business accounted for 26 percent; fund management, 27 percent; consulting, 3 percent; and financing, 44 percent. The company was capitalized at ¥20.3 billion (US $148.0 million) in the same year. Headquarters are in Tōkyō.

Japan Association of Corporate Executives 経済同友会

(JACE; J: Keizai Dōyūkai). Economic organization for policy studies, made up of leading Japanese businessmen. Founded in 1946. The Japan Association of Corporate Executives is a private, nonprofit, and nonpartisan body, entirely financed by members' subscriptions. In 1989 its membership included 1,500 business executives from throughout Japan, and it was governed by a 270-member board of trustees elected by the membership at the annual general meeting. The organization has a strong influence on national and corporate policy formation. Because the membership comprises autonomous individuals, its members can express their views clearly and frankly without heeding the interests of any particular company or industry.

Japan Association of National Universities 国立大学協会

(Kokuritsu Daigaku Kyōkai). Association established in 1950 to promote cooperation among four-year national universities. General meetings and committee meetings of the association are presided over by the presidents of the member universities; executives of the association are presidents and professors of universities that have doctoral degree programs. The association influences the formation of government policies on higher education. In 1991 it had 97 member universities.

Japan Association of Private Colleges and Universities 日本私立大学連盟

(JAPCU; J: Nihon Shiritsu Daigaku Remmei). An association formed in 1951 when 24 member institutions of the ASSOCIATION OF

PRIVATE UNIVERSITIES IN JAPAN (APUJ) split off to form an independent body. Some of Japan's most prestigious private universities, among them Waseda and Keiō, joined the JAPCU. In 1990 the JAPCU had 112 member schools. The JAPCU sponsors faculty training programs, engages in public relations and opinion sampling, and attempts to influence new legislation affecting private universities. Unlike its American counterparts, the JAPCU plays no role in accreditation.

Japan Atomic Power Company 日本原子力発電[株]

(Nihon Genshiryoku Hatsuden). Manufacturer and operator of nuclear power plants and supplier of electrical power. Capitalized by nine major electric power companies, it was incorporated in 1957. In 1966 it began operation of Japan's first commercial nuclear power plant, in Tōkai Mura, Ibaraki Prefecture. Subsequently two more nuclear power plants were constructed by Japan Atomic Power: one in Tsuruga, Fukui Prefecture, and one in Tōkai Mura. In 1990 electric power generation capacity was 2,783,000 kilowatts. In the same year total sales were ¥193.8 billion (US $1.3 billion), and capitalization stood at ¥120.0 billion (US $783.9 million). Headquarters are in Tōkyō.

Japan-Australia Business Co-operation Committee 日豪経済委員会

(Nichigō Keizai Iinkai). Private enterprise organization in Japan concerned with economic relations with Australia. The committee was organized in 1963 in response to the rapid growth in trade between the two countries that followed the 1957 Agreement on Commerce. The committee's Australian counterpart is the Australia-Japan Business Co-operation Committee. Both committees operate entirely under private auspices. An important initiative taken at the committees' 1966 joint meeting in Canberra led to the formation of the PACIFIC BASIN ECONOMIC COUNCIL by businessmen from Australia, Japan, the United States, Canada, and New Zealand.

Japan Automobile Research Institute, Inc 日本自動車研究所

(Nihon Jidōsha Kenkyūjo). Institute in the city of Tsukuba, Ibaraki Prefecture, that does basic research in such areas as automobile safety and pollution control technology. Founded in 1961 by the Ministry of International Trade and Industry and various Japanese automobile manufacturers, the institute also conducts automobile performance tests.

Japan Aviation Electronics Industry, Ltd 日本航空電子工業[株]

(Nihon Kōkū Denshi Kōgyō). Manufacturer of connectors for industrial use. Incorporated in 1950. The firm also makes aeronautical inertial navigation equipment and automatic control equipment. It has two subsidiaries in the United States and one in Taiwan. For the fiscal year ending March 1991, sales totaled ¥77.4 billion (US $564.1

659

million) and capitalization stood at ¥10.6 billion (US $77.3 million). Headquarters are in Tōkyō.

Japan Book Publishers Association 日本書籍出版協会

(Nihon Shoseki Shuppan Kyōkai). Organization of leading publishing companies formed in 1957. As of January 1991 it had 482 member companies. It was founded to ensure the continuing growth of the publishing industry and to contribute to the cultural education of the reading public. The association and the JAPAN MAGAZINE PUBLISHERS ASSOCIATION (Nihon Zasshi Kyōkai) cooperate to formulate ethical guidelines for publishers. The Japan Book Publishers Association was also instrumental in the founding in April 1991 of the Japan Authors and Publishers Reprographic Rights Clearance Center in order to protect the rights of copyright holders. In 1968 it published the *Nihon shuppan hyakunen shi nempyō*, a detailed chronology of Japanese publishing over the last 100 years, and since 1977 it has annually published the *Nihon shoseki sōmokuroku*, a general catalog of books in print in Japan.

Japan Braille Library 日本点字図書館

(Nihon Tenji Toshokan). Social welfare institution for the visually handicapped, located in Shinjuku Ward, Tōkyō. It opened in 1940 with a small collection of braille books owned by Homma Kazuo (b 1915), who is himself blind, and it was established as a social welfare corporation in 1952. The library publishes braille and tape-recorded books; its holdings of some 141,302 braille books and 394,882 reels of tape were available to borrowers in 1989. The library provides braille instruction and distributes items such as games and small household appliances for the use of the blind.

Japan Buddhist Federation→
Zen Nihon Bukkyō Kai

Japan Chamber of Commerce and Industry 日本商工会議所

(Nihon Shōkō Kaigisho; commonly abbreviated Nisshō). Central organ of regional chambers of commerce situated in 501 Japanese cities. In 1878 the first chambers of commerce and industry were established in Tōkyō, Ōsaka, and Kōbe. Nisshō was created in 1922 to represent the views of member organizations. It is especially concerned with international commerce, and business offices of such economic organizations as the Pacific Basin Economic Council, the Japan-Australia-New Zealand Economic Committee, and the Federation of Asian Chambers of Commerce and Industry, among others, have been set up within Nisshō. See KEIDANREN.

Japan College of Social Work 日本社会事業大学

(Nihon Shakai Jigyō Daigaku). A coeducational, private four-year university in the city of Kiyose, Tōkyō Prefecture. Founded in 1958, it is devoted exclusively to social welfare research and education. It is subsidized by the Ministry of Health and Welfare. Enrollment in 1989 was 564.

Japan Communist Party 日本共産党

(JCP; J: Nihon Kyōsantō). A leading opposition party of the post–World War II era. Founded on 15 July 1922 as a branch of the Comintern by a group of socialist activists including YAMAKAWA HITOSHI, ARAHATA KANSON, SAKAI TOSHIHIKO, and TOKUDA KYŪICHI. The party initially attracted socialists such as NOSAKA SANZŌ; younger intellectuals such as SANO MANABU, ICHIKAWA SHŌICHI, and SHIGA YOSHIO; and workers such as WATANABE MASANOSUKE.

History through 1945—In the beginning the party was dominated intellectually by Yamakawa Hitoshi, who emphasized the need to "go to the masses." His logic led him to call for the dissolution of the JCP to lead the way for the formation of a legal united-front mass party, and the JCP was formally dissolved in 1924. In the same year, a young communist named FUKUMOTO KAZUO returned from two years of intensive study of Marxism in Germany and France and strongly criticized Yamakawa's ideas. Fukumoto argued in favor of the theoretical need for a vanguard party on the basis of "division before unity." He took part in the reestablishment of the party at the end of 1926.

In July 1927 the Comintern issued a thesis to direct the activities and ideology of the burgeoning Japanese communist movement (see COMINTERN 1927 THESIS). It attacked the ideas of Yamakawa as "opportunist" and those of Fukumoto as "sectarian" and called for a revolution in two stages: bourgeois-democratic and socialist (see NIHON SHIHON SHUGI RONSŌ). The JCP drafted a new thesis in 1931 that urged moving directly into a socialist revolution. This radical approach led to factionalism and blistering attacks against social democrats, but it did not receive Comintern approval. However, the COMINTERN 1932 THESIS also called for a two-stage revolution and claimed that the emperor system fostered "military feudal imperialism."

Until it was legalized after World War II, the party remained a small secretive organization subject to frequent suppression by government authorities opposed to its aim of creating a workers' state free of monarchy. Two communist-backed candidates of the RŌDŌ NŌMINTŌ (Labor-Farmer Party) were elected to the Diet in 1928. However, by 1935 JCP activity virtually ceased after the government arrested its leaders and dissolved supporting organizations. See MARCH 15TH INCIDENT; APRIL 16TH INCIDENT; TENKŌ.

Postwar History—The JCP was legally constituted on 4 October 1945 by veteran communists released from prison the preceding month. They were later joined by members who returned from their wartime haven in China, notably Nosaka Sanzō. Portraying themselves as peace-loving moderates free of any outside influence, they captured 5 seats in the House of Representatives and 2.1 million votes in the 1946 election. In a whirl of feverish activity, party membership and influence on organized labor grew rapidly until General Douglas MACARTHUR banned the GENERAL STRIKE OF 1947. This event signaled the displeasure of the OCCUPATION authorities (SCAP) with the JCP and caused a split within the ranks of labor. Nonetheless, the communists at first increased their influence, winning 35 seats and almost 3 million votes in the 1949 election as voters critical of the Occupation's "reverse course" (*gyaku kōsu*) shifted their support from the socialists to the communists after the fall of the socialist-led cabinet (1947–48) of KATAYAMA TETSU.

However, this success evaporated quickly in the heightened cold war atmosphere of the early 1950s. SCAP on 6–7 June 1950 ordered the purge from politics of the top JCP leadership, which, it said, was endangering the Occupation. After the outbreak of the Korean War on 25 June 1950, the RED PURGE was extended to suspected communist sympathizers in government and private industry. The JCP leaders reacted by adopting a policy of violent revolution to achieve their aims. The terrorist acts committed by JCP members resulted in the loss of public support, and the government listed it as a subversive group under the SUBVERSIVE ACTIVITIES PREVENTION LAW. In the 1952 election the party lost all of its 35 seats in the House of Representatives.

In the mid-1950s the party gradually moderated its policies and activities, and party leaders began to reappear. Throughout most of the postwar period the party's leader was MIYAMOTO KENJI, whose influence shaped the party's new basic program, which was approved in 1961 and remained in force until 1982; the program stressed the possibility of a peaceful transition to socialism after the achievement of a bourgeois-democratic revolution. The JCP broke with the Russian Communist Party in 1963–64 and with the Chinese Communist Party in 1966–67. In 1976 the JCP added a "Manifesto of Freedom and Democracy" to its party program. It advocates parliamentary democracy and denies the need for "dictatorship" as practiced in the Soviet Union. Although the JCP has opposed the US–Japan Security Treaty (see UNITED STATES–JAPAN SECURITY TREATIES) and took part in the two biggest campaigns against its renewal (1960, 1970), it was criticized by leftist student groups for not being militant enough.

The JCP has broadened its appeal by adopting an independent and nationalist stance, demanding the return to Japan of Soviet-held islands north of Hokkaidō. It has also become less critical of the United States and has modified its opposition to the existence of Japan's SELF DEFENSE FORCES.

Party Strength—After its debacle in the 1952 election, the JCP gradually recovered and consistently held a handful of seats in the lower house of the Diet, winning for example 26 seats in the elections of both 1983 and 1986. The turnover in party membership has apparently been high, although, until the LIBERAL DEMOCRATIC PARTY's whirlwind membership registration campaign in 1977–78, the JCP had the largest membership (370,000) of any postwar Japanese party. The leadership, unlike that of the JAPAN SOCIALIST PARTY, has been stable and has not suffered any major splits. The party's newspaper, AKAHATA, had a circulation of about 3 million in 1990. This and other publications, rather than funds from labor federations, provide the bulk of the party's income.

However, the end of the communist order in Eastern Europe in 1989–90 and the Tiananmen (T'ienanmen) Square Incident in China in June 1989 had an inevitable effect on the party. As a result of the general election of February 1990, the number of JCP representatives in the lower house of the Diet dropped sharply from 26 to 16, although it seems unlikely that popular support for the JCP has reached a permanent plateau. Despite this rapid succession of tumultuous developments in the history of the international communist movement, including the breakup of the Soviet Union itself in late 1991 (accompanied by the suspension of activities of the Communist Party there), the JCP continues to insist on the correctness of its own socialist ideology. There seems little prospect of any substantial change in policy in the foreseeable future.

Japan Current→Kuroshio

Japan Development Bank
日本開発銀行

(Nihon Kaihatsu Ginkō). Government financial institution. Established in 1951 pursuant to the Japan Development Bank Law "to supplement and encourage lending by private financial institutions by supplying long-term funds in order to promote industrial development and economic and social progress." Lending activities are carried out in accordance with an annual policy determined by the cabinet. Lending categories are urban development, regional development, improvement of national living standards, resources and energy, ocean shipping and aircraft, and development of technology. Domestic funds for lending operations come from the government, loan repayments, and reserves. Outstanding borrowings from the government amounted to ¥8.1 trillion (US $59.0 billion) at the end of March 1991. Funds from nondomestic sources come from issuance of foreign bonds and notes guaranteed by the government. New loans and equity participation extended in fiscal 1990 amounted to ¥1.5 trillion (US $10.9 billion), and outstanding loans and equity participation totaled ¥9.6 trillion (US $67.0 billion) at the end of the same year. Headquarters are in Tōkyō.

Japanese Alps
日本アルプス

(Nihon Arupusu). Three mountain ranges extending north to south in central Honshū, consisting of the HIDA MOUNTAINS (also called the Northern Alps), the KISO MOUNTAINS (Central Alps), and the AKAISHI MOUNTAINS (Southern Alps). The highest peak is KITA-DAKE (3,192 m; 10,472 ft). There are more than 10 mountains over 3,000 m (10,000 ft) in height. The Chūbu Sangaku and Southern Alps national parks are situated in the Japanese Alps.

Japanese American Citizens League
全米日系市民協会

(JACL; J: Zembei Nikkei Shimin Kyōkai). Political and civil rights organization of the Japanese American community. At its founding in 1930 it was an organization exclusively for *nisei* (second-generation JAPANESE AMERICANS).

After the bombing of Pearl Harbor, the JACL supported the US war effort against Japan. It also chose an accommodationist stance when in early 1942 the US government decided to relocate and incarcerate the Japanese American population of the West Coast, citizens as well as aliens (see JAPANESE AMERICANS, WARTIME RELOCATION OF). Although this stance was unpopular with many, it ensured that the organization's views were listened to by at least some key federal officials.

In the postwar era the JACL campaigned for an equitable immigration system that no longer discriminated against Asians (see UNITED STATES IMMIGRATION ACTS OF 1924, 1952, AND 1965). In the early 1980s it engaged in a campaign for some kind of redress for Japanese Americans who were incarcerated during World War II; the drive culminated with the passage of the Civil Liberties Act of 1988, which stipulated payment to some 60,000 people who had been confined in relocation camps. Although many now question the need for such an organization, since overt statutory discrimination against Japanese Americans is a thing of the past, the JACL

continues to enjoy influence and prestige. As of April 1990 it had some 26,000 members.

Japanese Americans
日系アメリカ人

(*nikkei amerikajin*). Ethnic minority group in the United States consisting of immigrants from Japan and their descendants. According to the 1990 US census, there were 847,562 Japanese Americans, with the largest concentrations in California (312,989), Hawaii (247,486), New York (35,281), Washington (34,366), and Illinois (21,831). Japanese Americans have at times been victims of racial discrimination, the most tragic episode being incarceration during World War II. They have nonetheless made numerous important contributions to US society.

The Japanese American experience in the United States can be analyzed as follows: (1) 1868–1924 was the major period of Japanese immigration to Hawaii and the United States, as well as the first major phase of organized anti-Japanese agitation, culminating with the Immigration Act of 1924, which in effect barred further immigration from Japan (see UNITED STATES IMMIGRATION ACTS OF 1924, 1952, AND 1965). During this period approximately 270,000 Japanese immigrants (*issei*) settled in the United States. More than 125,000 came during the peak years 1901–08. (2) 1924–41 was the major period of Japanese settlement and community development in the United States and of the emergence of American-born Japanese Americans (*nisei*). (3) 1941–45 were the years of wartime incarceration, when 112,000 Japanese Americans from the Pacific Coast were placed in American concentration camps called relocation centers. (4) 1945 to the present was the postwar recovery period, when Japanese Americans rebuilt their lives and communities. It also was during this period that the third (*sansei*) and fourth (*yonsei*) generations emerged.

Immigration Background—In 1868 a shipload of 148 contract laborers arrived in Honolulu to work on Hawaii's flourishing sugar plantations. These laborers, known as *gannen-mono* or "first-year men" because they came in the first year of Emperor Meiji's reign, were recruited from Tōkyō and Yokohama.

Japanese immigration to the mainland had its symbolic beginning in 1869 with the arrival in California of the so-called Wakamatsu colony, whose 20-odd members came from the Aizu Wakamatsu area of Japan. Large-scale immigration to Hawaii and the US mainland, however, did not begin until 1885–86, when the Japanese government relaxed restrictions against emigration. In early years Japanese immigrants tended to be young, single men who came from farming backgrounds in the southern and western prefectures of Hiroshima, Yamaguchi, Wakayama, Kumamoto, and Fukuoka. Before 1908, when the GENTLEMEN'S AGREEMENT between the United States and Japan went into effect and placed restrictions on the types of individuals who could emigrate, the ratio of men to women was 7 to 1. However, for the remaining years of large-scale immigration to the United States, more women than men migrated, most coming as so-called PICTURE BRIDES of immigrant men. Permanent residence in the United States gradually replaced the dream of returning to Japan for many immigrant laborers who saved enough money to start small businesses and farms. Marriage and the creation of families further reinforced permanent settlement in America.

Japanese Americans
A festival in the Little Tōkyō section of Los Angeles. Like many other immigrant groups, Japanese Americans have preserved a number of traditions and customs from their country of origin.

The Meiji government's ambitious drive for industrialization and international parity generated internal political conflicts and severe economic dislocations, which had an unusually adverse impact on the agricultural sector. Emigration was viewed by the Japanese government as one means of coping with difficult economic conditions. A major distinguishing feature of Japanese emigration was the active role of the Japanese government in monitoring and controlling the process. Government measures included the creation of a special government bureau and government-sponsored emigration companies to ensure that emigrants would be treated fairly and that they would not undermine Japan's rising international status or its relations with the United States. The close attention Japanese government officials paid to the immigration situation in the United States, coupled with the American government's view of Japan as an emerging major power, elevated many regionally based controversies and issues, such as the San Francisco school board's decision in 1906 to segregate Japanese schoolchildren (see SEGREGATION OF JAPANESE SCHOOLCHILDREN IN THE UNITED STATES), to major areas of negotiation and contention between the two countries.

The Evacuation during World War II—The World War II incarceration of 112,000 Japanese Americans from the Pacific Coast in American concentration camps (see JAPANESE AMERICANS, WARTIME RELOCATION OF) is the most tragic event in Japanese American history. The roots of what has been called "America's worst wartime mistake" reach back to decades of anti-Japanese hatred and agitation in the western states. Research indicates that the evacuations had an all-encompassing economic impact on Japanese Americans involving not only personal loss of property, income, and savings but also the destruction of a viable, ethnically based economy. The evacuation served to disperse a sizable proportion of the Japanese American population to cities in the Midwest and East Coast, where few Japanese Americans had resided before the war; to destroy a number of previously existing Japanese American communities; and to cause various forms of social disorganization for the Japanese American family unit in adapting to the abnormal situation of life in concentration camps.

Japanese American Organizations—Beginning with the founding in 1877 of the Japanese Gospel Society of San Francisco, an *issei* Christian and English-language study group, Japanese Americans have formed an extensive network of organizations to advance their economic, social, religious, cultural, and political goals. During the pre–World War II era, the JAPANESE ASSOCIATIONS

OF AMERICA comprised the most important and multifunctional groups in the Japanese American community. The JAPANESE AMERICAN CITIZENS LEAGUE (JACL), founded in 1930 by *nisei* along the Pacific Coast, came to prominence during and after World War II. During the postwar period it played a major role in overturning prewar anti-Japanese laws and statutes. In 1990 the organization had more than 30,000 members and local chapters in all parts of the mainland.

Military Service——The involvement of Japanese Americans, especially *nisei*, in America's military ventures during the 20th century has received wide recognition. This is due, in large part, to the exploits of the 442ND REGIMENTAL COMBAT TEAM and the 100th Battalion, all-*nisei* fighting units formed during World War II. Guided by their motto, Go for Broke, they became America's most decorated military units during the war.

Political Involvement——The political history of Japanese Americans differs from that of other American immigrant groups because of *issei* disenfranchisement. Since *issei* were ineligible for citizenship, they could not vote and therefore could not use electoral politics for advancing their goals as did other immigrant groups. Instead, they had to resort to alternative strategies such as legal advocacy, public relations, and appeals to the Japanese government to seek remedies for their situation. During the prewar period, the JACL and other Japanese American groups launched voter registration drives aimed at increasing the political awareness and participation of American-born Japanese Americans in American electoral politics, but it was not until the late 1960s that Japanese Americans in the mainland states won elected offices (the situation was slightly different in Hawaii, where Japanese Americans were elected to Congress as early as 1959).

Cultural Change and Adaptation——Like other American immigrant groups, Japanese immigrants carried with them a unique set of cultural traditions, which contained values, beliefs, behavioral practices, culinary arts, and folkways of the homeland they left. Although a good deal of commentary has attempted to demonstrate the maintenance of these cultural characteristics, Japanese Americans, like other American immigrant groups, have developed a unique ethnic culture and social system, which shares ingredients from both their American and Japanese heritages and experiences.

Current Issues——Although they have now gained formal redress and reparations for their World War II incarceration, members of the Japanese American community continue to debate how they will remember the tragedy and apply the lessons learned from it. Japanese Americans continue to face racial discrimination and prejudice. Other issues include providing adequate housing and social services for an increasingly large elderly population consisting of *issei* and *nisei*, planning redevelopment projects in traditional Japanese American communities and determining the role of Japanese multinational corporations in those projects, providing for the special needs of a growing postwar immigrant sector among the Japanese American population, and increasing the political representation of Japanese Americans in local and national governments.

Japanese Americans in Hawaii
ハワイの日系アメリカ人

(Hawai *no nikkei amerikajin*). Japanese immigrants to Hawaii and their American descendants. In 1990 the 247,486 residents of Japanese ancestry made up 22.3 percent of Hawaii's total population and 29.2 percent of the Japanese American population of the entire United States. First-generation Japanese immigrants (*issei*) came to Hawaii in the Meiji (1868–1912) and Taishō (1912–26) periods, primarily to work on Hawaii's sugar plantations. Their American-born descendants—the second generation (*nisei*), third generation (*sansei*), and fourth generation (*yonsei*)—now vastly outnumber the *issei* and are widely and prominently distributed in the state's occupational and political structures. Like JAPANESE AMERICANS on the West Coast, although less traumatically, Hawaii's Japanese Americans experienced discriminatory treatment during World War II, but they are now an integral part of Hawaii's multiracial society.

Between 1868 and 1924, the year that Japanese immigration to the United States was stopped, nearly 220,000 arrived in Hawaii and about 150,000 left, either to return to Japan or to move on to the continental United States. Arrivals until 1907 were overwhelmingly male indentured laborers, but the coming of PICTURE BRIDES (women affianced through the mail) greatly increased the number of resident Japanese families. By 1940, a year before war broke out between Japan and the United States, there were already more than three times as many Japanese American citizens born in Hawaii as there were immigrant Japanese, although the average age of the former group was only 16. The 1940 Japanese-ancestry population of 185,000 made up 37 percent of Hawaii's people. Although nearly all the Japanese prefectures were represented, the great majority of immigrants came from the four prefectures of Hiroshima, Yamaguchi, Kumamoto, and Okinawa.

Only a limited degree of socioeconomic mobility was possible for the immigrants owing to handicaps of language and lack of American citizenship. Deteriorating relations between the United States and Japan in the 1920s and 1930s brought attention to the existence of a large Japanese population in a vital outpost of the American military. However, despite Hawaii's strategic importance, after the attack on Pearl Harbor only about 1,000 Japanese, nearly all *issei*, were shipped to mainland internment centers in contrast to the wholesale relocation of Japanese and Japanese Americans from the West Coast. The status of *nisei* as Americans of Japanese parentage prevented them from being conscripted into the armed forces, nor were they permitted to volunteer until 1943, when they were allowed to join a special segregated combat team. This unit fought with great distinction in Europe (see 442ND REGIMENTAL COMBAT TEAM). Others served primarily in the Pacific as military interpreters.

With the coming of age of the *nisei* and *sansei* citizens the Japanese moved out of the plantation communities, took advantage of educational opportunities, and began moving into white-collar positions in technical and professional fields, most notably in the legal profession. Although *issei* were prohibited from direct participation in political affairs, their Hawaiian-born children and grandchildren were citizens by birth and possessed the rights to vote, run for public office, and seek government employment. In the period just before World War II, there was only a handful of Japanese in the local legislature or in positions of responsibility in local governments. But in 1989, 27 of the 76 state legislators, 3 of the 5 state supreme court justices, and 3 of the 4 members of Congress from Hawaii were of Japanese ancestry. The first Japanese American to be elected governor, George Ariyoshi (b 1926), served from 1974 to 1986.

Due to the larger number of families in the immigrant generation after 1900, the Japanese community not only grew rapidly but also exercised effective social control over its members. Most *nisei* studied Japanese, absorbed the parental emphasis on family cohesion and honor, and married within their own group. However, more recent figures indicate that nearly half of the *sansei* marry non-Japanese. Few among the younger generations today speak Japanese or have visited Japan, and most are wholly American in their political, economic, and cultural orientations.

Japanese Americans, wartime relocation of
日系アメリカ人の戦時転地収容

(*nikkei amerikajin no senji tenchi shūyō*). The incarceration and relocation of the entire Japanese American population of the Pacific coastal area of the United States in 1942. More than two-thirds of the approximately 112,000 persons imprisoned were native-born citizens of the United States. This massive evacuation program should not be confused with the selective internment of several thousand *issei* (first-generation JAPANESE AMERICANS) presumed to be dangerous.

Immediately after the attack on Pearl Harbor on 7 December 1941, a public hue and cry began for some kind of confinement for all persons of Japanese ancestry. On 19 February 1942 President Franklin Delano Roosevelt signed Executive Order 9066, which delegated authority to the secretary of war "to prescribe military areas . . . from which any or all persons may be excluded." The military authorities designated most of the Pacific Coast as such an area. The only persons actually excluded were those of Japanese birth or descent. Congress, without a dissenting vote, passed legislation supporting the evacuation.

Evacuation and Relocation——The army set up the Wartime Civil Control Administration, which divided the entire Pacific slope into 108 areas of unequal size but containing about 1,000 Japanese each. Beginning with Civilian Exclusion Order No. 1, dated 24 March 1942, Japanese were collected and taken to assembly centers. In many cases the evacuees were domiciled in quarters intended for livestock. Almost the entire Japanese American population complied with these orders without overt resistance. Apart from untold psychic damage, the property losses of the West Coast Japanese were staggering. Between 1948 and 1965 some $38 million in compensation was paid under terms of the Japanese American Claims Act of 1948. This was less than 10 cents on the dollar without allowing for interest or inflation.

The assembly centers were only a temporary stop for the evacuees; their ultimate destinations were relocation centers run by a newly established civilian agency, the WAR RELOCATION AUTHORITY. Located in desolate parts of the United States, they were surrounded by barbed wire and guarded by troops. Treatment was generally humane, and the diet was more than sufficient; births outnumbered deaths. And, almost from the start, there were ways to gain release from camp. Young citizens could leave to attend college. Individuals and families could at first receive furloughs to harvest crops and later obtain leave to resettle in the midwestern or eastern United States. In addition, Japanese American citizens of military age could enter the armed forces. At first this was done by enlistment, but eventually the draft was extended to those in relocation centers. It was in relation to the draft that the major "resistance" of the relocation occurred. About 10 percent of those ordered to report for induction into the armed forces refused and were tried, convicted, and sent to federal penitentiaries.

A few Japanese Americans challenged the evacuation process by instituting legal proceedings contesting its constitutionality. Three of these suits eventually figured in major decisions of the US Supreme Court. In *Hirabayashi* v *US* (320 US 81), decided in 1943, the Court unanimously upheld various preevacuation orders affecting the rights of Japanese American citizens. In *Korematsu* v *US* (323 US 214), decided in December 1944, the Court upheld the legality of the evacuation of US citizens of Japanese ancestry. On the same day, the Court also ruled in *Ex parte Endo* (323 US 283) that once loyal Japanese American citizens had been evacuated, it was illegal for the War Relocation Authority to keep them imprisoned. Despite this ruling, some Japanese remained in relocation centers until March 1946.

On 19 February 1976, on the 34th anniversary of Roosevelt's order that made the evacuation possible, President Gerald R. Ford formally declared: "We know now what we should have known then—not only was the evacuation wrong, but Japanese Americans were and are loyal Americans."

In 1980 a presidential fact-finding commission began investigation of the causes and consequences of the wartime relocation and incarceration and submitted a report recommending appropriate remedies and compensation in 1983. Finally, after a decade of grass-roots lobbying by the JAPANESE AMERICAN CITIZENS LEAGUE (JACL) and other Japanese American groups, Congress passed the Civil Liberties Act of 1988, which provided for monetary reparations—$20,000 to each of the 60,000 survivors, for a total of $1.2 billion—and a formal apology by the US government. See also articles on individual relocation centers: AMACHE; GILA RIVER; HEART MOUNTAIN; JEROME; MANZANAR; MINIDOKA; POSTON; ROHWER; TOPAZ; TULE LAKE.

Japanese and the Altaic languages
日本語とアルタイ語

(*nihongo to arutaigo*). Altaic is the designation for a large and important family of genetically related languages. Its principal subbranches consist of Turkic, Mongolian, and Tungusic, each embracing many different but related languages. The Altaic elements that may be traced in Japanese show important isoglosses (clusters of similar linguistic features) that are respectively shared with both Turkic and Tungusic. Features relating Japanese to Mongolian are less evident, though present. In particular, elements of Japanese that may be shown to be of Altaic origin are the number system, the pronouns and interrogatives, and a major portion of the verb and adjective morphology, especially the Japanese verb stem suffixes.

The original homeland of the Altaic speakers was most likely located somewhere in the Trans-Caspian steppes. Sometime in the first half of the second millennium BC they began to migrate eastward, still maintaining a unified linguistic group, and eventually reached a site on the Central Asiatic steppes. From this second Altaic homeland, the Altaic linguistic community later split up, with various subgroups of the original community moving away from the main body. Ancestors of the Tungusic speakers appear to have been the first of the subgroups to break away, migrating into Northeast Asia, where they brought the Altaic languages into geographical proximity with the Korean peninsula and the Japanese islands. Turkic migrations away from the homeland took place later, probably not before the Chinese drove the Huns out of Mongolia during the Han dynasty (206 BC–AD 220).

The presence in Japanese of important isoglosses with both Turkic and Tungusic, therefore, suggests the existence of proto-Japanese elements in the Altaic linguistic unity in the second Altaic homeland before the earliest movements away from this community by the proto-Tungusic speakers. The many points of formal and semantic detail by means of which the Japanese verb corresponds to the formation of the verb in Tungusic languages provide especially striking evidence for proto-Japanese membership in that part of the second Altaic homeland where these proto-Tungusic elements were located prior to their early severance from the bulk of the original Altaic community.

As is the case in all language families, intrafamily relationships are complicated by extensive lexical borrowing back and forth as a result of early contacts. These borrowed forms must be distinguished from genetically related works, which are later, changed forms of earlier common terms inherited from the original linguistic unity, in this case ancient proto-Altaic. Discrimination between borrowed and genetically inherited forms, particularly in the absence of early written records, is not always easy. Although there is little question that Japanese has numerous forms borrowed from other Altaic languages, some of them entering the language as late as the Kofun period (ca 300–710), these forms are over and above the Japanese inherited stock of words (lexicon), word formations (morphology), and syntactic patterns that are genetically inherited from proto-Altaic. Once regular phonological correspondences between Japanese words and words of other Altaic languages with identical or closely related meanings have been established, thus permitting reconstruction of now-lost proto-Altaic phonemes, it is relatively easy to demonstrate the Altaic origin of much of Japanese vocabulary, morphology, and syntax.

Japanese and the Malayo-Polynesian languages
日本語とマライ・ポリネシア語

(*nihongo to marai-porineshia go*). Malayo-Polynesian is a name used by linguists to identify a protolanguage (or "parent language"), for which we have no written records and that has been reconstructed from contemporary languages that are historically ("genetically") related to it. This same language family has also often been called Austronesian. A surprisingly large number of languages, covering an enormous geographical expanse, has survived from this original Malayo-Polynesian linguistic unity. Today they extend from Taiwan to Easter Island

wartime relocation of Japanese Americans
A large group of Japanese Americans waiting to board a train that will take them part way on their forced journey to a relocation center.

and are found in such diverse places as Madagascar, the Philippines, and New Zealand. They include such languages as Indonesian, Tagalog, Hawaiian, and Tahitian.

In view of the pan-Pacific distribution of the surviving Malayo-Polynesian languages, it is hardly surprising that attempts should have been made to establish some kind of historical connection between this language family and Japanese. Certainly there are elements in the Japanese vocabulary stock that cannot be explained historically by comparison with the other Altaic languages, and a few of these words may very well have originated through extremely remote historical contact with Malayo-Polynesian speakers. This lends support to the "mixed language" hypothesis proposed between 1918 and 1938 in papers by Soviet scholar E. D. POLIVANOV, which suggested that Japanese is formed of both Malayo-Polynesian and Altaic elements. Polivanov's studies were largely ignored for many years, until they were revived by Murayama Shichirō (b 1908), who in 1968 began publishing important studies along these lines. Murayama subsequently refined and elaborated the Polivanov hypothesis in an attempt to support it with more lexical evidence than Polivanov had at his command. In Murayama's opinion, the Japanese lexical stock is particularly in debt to Malayo-Polynesian, while the major grammatical elements (the verb morphology in particular) he holds to be almost entirely Altaic.

In certain specialized areas of the vocabulary, particularly for words that have to do with marine life and types of flora for which the Altaic peoples were, by reason of their original geographical setting, most unlikely to have had specific terms, the discovery of likely Malayo-Polynesian etymologies for Japanese words occasions little surprise. It has also been suggested that a number of isolated Old Japanese terms found in the early FUDOKI texts and fragments, where they are identified as "popular" or "vulgar" words, may have resulted from ancient Malayo-Polynesian lexical contacts.

Probably the most satisfactory evaluation of the Murayama hypothesis at present is to recognize the presence of important Malayo-Polynesian elements in the pre-Japanese lexical stock and to interpret their role in the historical formation of the Japanese language as having been somehow analogous to the process generally known to linguists as creolization, if indeed those elements are more than simply an early stratum of loanwords resulting from ancient landings of Malayo-Polynesian–speaking wanderers in the Japanese archipelago. See also JAPANESE AND THE ALTAIC LANGUAGES.

Japanese as a foreign language
外国語としての日本語

(*gaikokugo to shite no nihongo*). The study of Japanese as a foreign language is a subject of

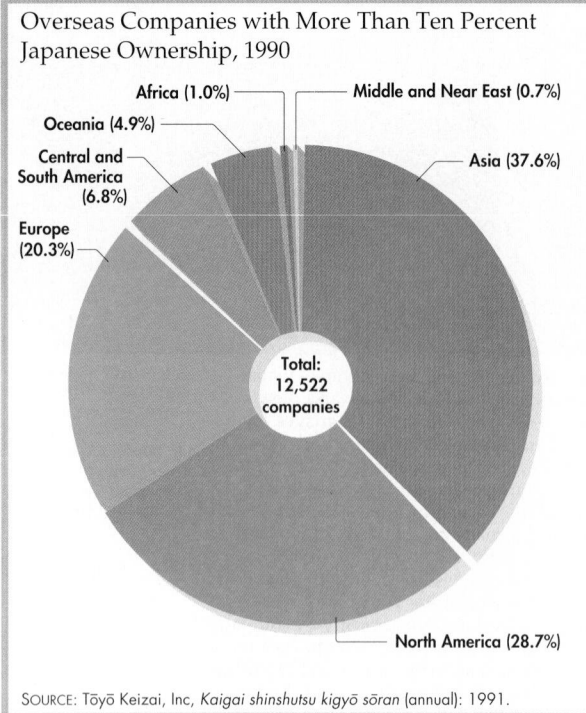

Overseas Companies with More Than Ten Percent Japanese Ownership, 1990

Africa (1.0%)
Middle and Near East (0.7%)
Oceania (4.9%)
Central and South America (6.8%)
Europe (20.3%)
Asia (37.6%)

Total: 12,522 companies

North America (28.7%)

SOURCE: Tōyō Keizai, Inc, *Kaigai shinshutsu kigyō sōran* (annual): 1991.

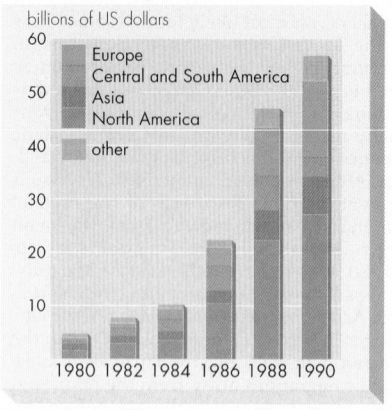

Direct Overseas Investment by Japanese Companies

billions of US dollars

Europe
Central and South America
Asia
North America
other

1980 1982 1984 1986 1988 1990

SOURCE: Ministry of Finance, *Kokusai kin'yūkyoku nempō* (annual): 1991

increasing interest around the world. The expansion of programs has been especially marked since the 1970s, as Japan has emerged as one of the world's major economic powers.

The Pre–World War II Period—Prior to World War II, a few major universities around the world offered limited opportunities that focused on the reading of Japanese—for the most part the translation of literary works and historical documents—but such study was regarded as esoteric in the extreme. Diplomats and missionaries with a work-related interest in learning Japanese usually satisfied this need by studying in Japan.

The World War II Period—With the outbreak of World War II, huge language programs were organized by the military in the United States, enrolling thousands of military personnel. A whole new approach to language study was launched, utilizing new analyses of hitherto uncommonly taught languages, based on the principles of modern linguistics and new pedagogical approaches.

The Post–World War II Period—As Japan rejoined the international community following World War II, interest in the Japanese language in other nations began to grow at a rapid pace. According to a survey conducted in 1967 by the Japanese Ministry of Foreign Affairs, Japanese was being taught at 428 institutions in 37 foreign countries. The number of teachers was 1,027 and the number of students 36,694. The corresponding figures in a survey conducted in 1986 by the Ministry of Foreign Affairs and the JAPAN FOUNDATION were 2,600 institutions, 75 countries, 7,200 teachers, and 1 million students. Growing interest in Japan and closer international relationships dramatically increased these numbers, especially during the second half of the 1980s. The largest numbers of foreign students of Japanese lived in nations situated around the rim of the Pacific Ocean, such as the nations of East Asia, Southeast Asia, Oceania (including Australia and New Zealand), North America, and Central and South America. In some of the nations of East Asia, Southeast Asia, and Oceania, Japanese was now being taught at the secondary-school level (chiefly in high schools). In

some countries, such as South Korea, China, and Australia, Japanese had become one of the foreign languages included in college entrance examinations. According to the US Modern Language Association, post-secondary school enrollment in Japanese in the period 1986–90 increased by 95 percent, the highest rate of increase for any foreign language. The 1990 enrollment figure of 45,717 made Japanese the fifth most popular foreign language studied in the United States. At the precollegiate level more than 860 US schools were teaching Japanese in 1990. Japanese was also being taught by radio and television in South Korea, China, Australia, and the United States. Some foreigners were even beginning to learn Japanese as a medium for the study of advanced technology.

Similar trends were seen in Japanese-language study for foreigners in Japan itself. According to a 1990 survey by the Ministry of Education, Japanese was being taught to 60,600 foreign residents of Japan in 821 institutions, including universities and Japanese-language schools. The administration of a Japanese-language proficiency test to foreigners residing in Japan and in various other countries began in 1984. The 1988 test was taken by 27,000 people in 43 cities in 22 countries, including Japan.

The Japan Foundation provides various forms of support and assistance to Japanese-language programs in foreign countries. Assistance to Japanese-language programs for foreigners in Japan is the responsibility of the Ministry of Education and the Agency for Cultural Affairs. The Society for Teaching Japanese as a Foreign Language (Nihongo Kyōiku Gakkai), which was founded in 1962 and has headquarters in Tōkyō, had 3,300 members in 1991, of whom 360 were overseas members. The society publishes *Nihongo kyōiku* (Journal of Japanese Language Teaching) and sponsors conferences for specialists in the field. See also JAPANESE LANGUAGE.

Japanese Associations of America　在米日本人会

(*zaibei nihonjin kai*). General term for the major organizations of *issei*, first-generation JAPANESE AMERICANS, in the United States. Between 1891 and 1908, Japanese consular officials in San Francisco had created a series of ephemeral organizations, but, in assuming special responsibilities for Japanese residents in the United States under the GENTLEMEN'S AGREEMENT of 1907–08, the Japanese government felt that it needed a more effective vehicle for social control. In February 1908 the Japanese consulate general in San Francisco created the Japanese Association

of America, which organized regional or local groups. In theory all Japanese residents in the United States belonged to one of these lesser bodies, but in practice many Japanese residents never joined.

The Japanese government made the associations the intermediaries through which *issei* had to pass if they were to maintain official connections with the Japanese government. The associations charged fees to provide *issei* with the documents they needed to have family members join them in the United States or to register marriages, divorces, and births. The organizations played important community roles until shortly after Pearl Harbor, when their leaders were interned (see JAPANESE AMERICANS, WARTIME RELOCATION OF) and the organizations ceased to exist. See also JAPANESE AMERICAN CITIZENS LEAGUE.

Japanese beetle　豆黄金

(*mamekogane*). *Popillia japonica*. A beetle of the order Coleoptera, f. Scarabaeidae. It measures 9–12 millimeters (0.4–0.5 in) in length. The body is oval and black tinged with a glossy copper green; the wings are brown with green edges. The adult beetle appears in late spring and feeds on the leaves of various plants such as soybean, *kunugi* (a kind of oak), wild roses, and grapes; the larva damages lawns and sapling roots. It takes from one to two years for an egg to develop into an adult. The beetle is indigenous to Japan, but its larvae apparently entered the United States in 1911 in the soil around bulbs of *hanashōbu* (a kind of iris) and spread rapidly, feeding on soybeans and white potatoes and becoming a major pest in some areas.

Japanese businesses overseas　海外進出日本企業

(*kaigai shinshutsu Nihon kigyō*). Overseas business operations by Japanese companies began in 1876 when Mitsui & Co, Ltd, established a branch in Shanghai. Mitsui also opened branches in Hong Kong and Paris in 1877 and in New York in 1878. The primary purpose of these branches was the direct export of silk thread and silkworm eggs. Following trade-related enterprises such as trading companies, banks, and insurance companies, in the 1890s spinning companies set up operations in Chinese cities, including Shanghai and Tianjin (Tientsin). Japanese heavy-industry companies were active in Manchuria in the 1930s, although these overseas assets were all lost following defeat in World War II. Overseas investment and business operations, including manufacturing, were restarted in the second half of the 1960s. These overseas activities increased considerably in the mid-1980s with the ending of restrictions on foreign investment, and they have been expanding dramatically since fiscal 1988.

Distribution of Investment—During the first half of the 1980s there were about 2,500 cases a year of direct overseas investment by Japanese companies. This exceeded 3,000 cases in 1986 and rose to more than 4,000 cases in 1987. Investments of US $10.2 billion in 1984 jumped to US $22.3 billion in 1986, and 1988 investments of US $47.0 billion expanded to US $56.9 billion in 1990. The regional breakdown of fiscal 1990 investments was North America, 47.8 percent; Central and South America, 6.4 percent; Asia, 12.4 percent; Europe, 25.1 percent; and other areas, 8.3 percent. In fiscal 1980 the corresponding figure for North America had been 34.0 percent; for Asia, 25.3 percent; and for Europe, 12.3 percent. The apparent shift of investments in recent years from Asia to North America and Europe is the result of a drastic increase in investments in European and US securities and real estate by non-manufacturing companies such as financial institutions, insurance companies, and real estate companies. However, if the number of local companies established to date in each country is considered, it is clear that the ratio of Asian operations continues to be high. Of the 12,522 local companies with more than 10 percent capital participation by Japanese companies as of 1990, the United States had the most with 26.2 percent (3,282), followed by Hong Kong with 6.1 percent, Thailand with 5.9 percent, Singapore with 5.8 percent, and Taiwan with 5.6 percent.

Approximately half (51.4%) of the companies listed on the Japanese stock exchanges have set up operations overseas. If the industry sectors are considered separately, more than 70 percent of the electrical equipment and transportation equipment companies have ongoing overseas operations.

The reasons for setting up businesses abroad include (1) to find inexpensive labor and parts supplies as a cost-control measure, (2) to avoid trade friction, (3) to maintain a business relationship with the overseas operations of a parent company, and (4) to create an international company capable of carrying on business worldwide. Although a key trend in overseas business development has been the setting up of operations in developing countries in Southeast Asia in order to reduce costs, emphasis recently has shifted to establishing operations in the United States and Europe in order to protect the companies' markets and to avoid trade friction. One special characteristic of recent activity has been the move overseas by small and medium-sized companies in the automobile industry, such as manufacturing subcontractors, as a means of maintaining their business relationships with major automobile manufacturers.

In addition, some new Japanese companies are emphasizing overseas business development over domestic operations from the start. For example, Yaohan Japan Corporation of Shizuoka Prefecture opened a Singapore store in 1974 and by 1992 had established 3 more stores in Singapore and a total of 22 stores in Thailand, Hong Kong, Taiwan, Malaysia, Brunei, China, the United States, and Costa Rica. In May 1990 Yaohan moved the headquarters of its international operations to Hong Kong. In the manufacturing industries, medium-sized companies such as Mabuchi Motor Co, Ltd, and Yoshida Kōgyō KK are making extensive use of production facilities abroad.

▷▷ 666–667

Japanese Cities, A Geographical Approach　日本の都市—地理学的接近

(Nihon no Toshi: Chirigakuteki Sekkin). A collection of English monographs published by the ASSOCIATION OF JAPANESE GEOGRAPHERS in 1970. The chief editor was KIUCHI SHINZŌ. These monographs cover the results of projects and research undertaken since 1958 by the association's Study Group on Urbanization and its successor, the Study Group on Urban Geography.

Japanese Exclusion Act　排日移民法

(Hainichi Imin Hō). Although such phrases as "Japanese Exclusion Act" or "Exclusion Act of 1924" are often encountered, there never was a Japanese Exclusion Act in US law. Exclusion of Japanese was effected by the Immigration Act of 1924, which did not refer specifically to the Japanese. See UNITED STATES IMMIGRATION ACTS OF 1924, 1952, AND 1965.

Japanese Foundation for Cancer Research　癌研究会

(Gan Kenkyūkai). Foundation supporting basic research in the diagnosis, clinical study, and treatment of cancer and other neoplasms. It began operations in 1908 as a cancer research association and became a legally chartered foundation in 1933. The foundation established the Cancer Institute in 1934 and the Cancer Chemotherapy Center in 1973. The foundation is also involved in the training of nurses and the dissemination of information on the prevention of cancer. Foundation offices are in Tōkyō.

Japanese language　日本語

(nihongo). The native language of the overwhelming majority of the more than 100 million inhabitants of the Japanese archipelago, including the Ryūkyū Islands, and significant numbers of Japanese immigrants in other countries, especially in North and South America. Japanese is spoken as a second language by many Chinese and Korean residents of Japan and by older residents of areas once dominated by the Japanese such as Korea and Taiwan. Comparative figures are difficult to assess because of inconsistency in the types of speakers included, but by any account Japanese is one of the major languages of the world.

The only other indigenous language of the Japanese islands is the apparently unrelated AINU LANGUAGE, which was, during historic times, gradually confined to the northern island of Hokkaidō and then overwhelmed by Japanese and is now close to extinction. The RYŪKYŪ DIALECTS are closely related to Japanese, though mutually unintelligible.

Although the Japanese and Chinese languages are entirely unrelated genetically, the Japanese writing system derives from that of Chinese. Chinese characters were introduced sometime in the 6th century, if not before, and the modern writing system is a complex one in which Chinese characters are used in conjunction with two separate phonetic scripts developed from them in Japan. Japanese has also absorbed LOANWORDS freely from other languages, especially Chinese and English, the former chiefly from the 8th to the 19th century and the latter in the 20th century.

Genetic Relationships——Some scholars have maintained that no genetic relationship of Japanese to any known language can be demonstrated. However, the syntactic similarity of Japanese to Korean is widely acknowledged, as is its resemblance in certain respects to the Altaic languages in general. The situation is complicated by similarities in vocabulary between Japanese and the Malayo-Polynesian languages. There seems to be a growing consensus among Japanese scholars that syntactically Japanese shows an Altaic affinity, but that at some time in its prehistory it received an influence in vocabulary and morphology from the Malayo-Polynesian languages to the south. See JAPANESE AND THE ALTAIC LANGUAGES; JAPANESE AND THE MALAYO-POLYNESIAN LANGUAGES.

The Japanese Dialects and the Speech of Tōkyō——Modern Japanese language has a large number of local dialects, existing alongside, but gradually being overwhelmed by, the officially recognized standard language (hyōjungo), which is based on the speech of the capital, Tōkyō. The Japanese dialects, however, show less variety in syntax and morphology than do the strong regional languages of Italy, for example, or Austria. Although it is true that a speaker of the Kagoshima dialect in the southwest of Kyūshū and a speaker of the Aomori dialect in the northeast of Honshū will be unable to understand each other, the distance separating these two dialects is 1,300 kilometers (about 800 mi), whereas in some of the smaller countries of Europe in which dialects persist, a distance of 50 kilometers (about 30 mi) is sufficient for them to be mutually unintelligible. Japan has differences of this magnitude only among the dialects of the Ryūkyū Islands, and there, too, the pressure of the standard language is considerable.

Two important urban dialects that flourish alongside the standard language of Tōkyō are those of the cities of Kyōto and Ōsaka. Kyōto was the imperial capital for more than 1,000 years, and, though it was not always the seat of real political or economic power, both it and its language continued to have the highest prestige. The language of its court nobility during the Heian period (794–1185) as preserved in the literary works of that period became the basis of CLASSICAL JAPANESE, which remained the standard for the written language until the beginning of the 20th century. During the Edo period (1600–1868), Edo (now Tōkyō), which was the seat of the TOKUGAWA SHOGUNATE, grew into an important commercial and administrative city. Both it and the older commercial city of Ōsaka became thriving centers of the culture and language of the merchant classes (CHŌNIN), and the language of Edo in particular—the locus of political power and the home of the samurai bureaucracy—gradually developed a prestige of its own. When Edo was renamed Tōkyō and made the new imperial capital shortly after the Meiji Restoration of 1868, the language of its educated elite was gradually systematized and transformed. Incorporated into this language were a number of expressions from the language of the nobility who accompanied Emperor MEIJI on his move from Kyōto. The resulting mixture became what is now the standard language, sometimes loosely referred to as "the Tōkyō dialect." During the 20th century the standard language spread throughout Japan, first by means of centralized compulsory education and later even more effectively by radio and television. It is probably safe to say that 99 percent of the population now understands the standard language, even though some speakers employ a strong touch of some local dialect.

The Phonology of the Standard Language——The short or unit vowels of standard Japanese, a, i, u, e, and o, are pronounced more or less as in Spanish or Italian. (In this description the phonemes of Japanese will be written in the standard Hepburn romanization used throughout this encyclopedia, phonetic symbols being added only when necessary for clarity.) The long vowels, $\bar{a}$, ii, $\bar{u}$, ei, and $\bar{o}$, are pronounced double the length of the short vowels ([a:], [i:], [u:], [e:], and [o:]), except that ei is often pronounced as a sequence of

Continued on page 668 ➡

Overseas Investment: The Experience of Japanese Multinationals

The profound effect of Japan's direct investments abroad can be felt from factory floors to corporate boardrooms in companies all over the world.

From the 1960s on, the rapid growth of Japan's economy gave rise to the beginnings of significant direct investment abroad by Japanese manufacturing firms. At first, companies chose to invest mostly in East and Southeast Asian economies because of the lower costs of labor and materials and because they wanted to penetrate the local markets.

These early efforts were too small to have any great financial impact on the parent companies. They did, however, provide a good learning experience for the Japanese. Local workers held protests, notably in Bangkok and Jakarta, against those who came to be called "the economic animals"—the Japanese managers of these overseas subsidiaries. Clearly, the epithet hit home, since it resulted in much self-examination on the part of Japanese business, as well as efforts to increase the local acceptance of Japanese operations.

Complaints by host countries are common to all discussions of Japanese foreign investment. One such complaint, which has taken on serious political overtones, stems from Japan's fear of the "boomerang effect." When South Korea's Pohang Iron and Steel Co was starting up its operations, for example, Nippon Steel Corporation did the engineering design. As a result of the superior design provided by the Japanese, Pohang became a low-cost producer and began successfully exporting to Japan. Thus, the Japanese technology was used by the Koreans to reap profit in Japan, in what has come to be known as the boomerang effect. So, when Pohang asked Nippon Steel for assistance in a major expansion, Nippon Steel declined to help, relenting only after vigorous South Korean government pressure. (Ironically, Japanese firms have exploited American technology and used it to great advantage in US markets, thereby creating a boomerang effect of their own.)

Another major complaint of developing host countries has to do with corporate staffing and what is perceived to be an abundance of overpaid Japanese managers, who monopolize the decision-making process and prevent the career advancement of local hires.

During the past decade, the great wave of Japanese investment has shifted from developing to developed economies. This investment drive was fueled largely by an increase in US protectionist measures, initially applied to steel imports and subsequently applied to consumer electronics, autos, semiconductors, and machine tools. In each case, the response to US protectionism, or the threat of it, was direct investment by Japanese firms in US industry. The investment drive was greatly accelerated by the abrupt doubling of the exchange value of the yen against the dollar in the mid-1980s, making exports from Japan more expensive and sharply reducing the cost of acquiring US assets in yen.

By 1990, 1,433 US manufacturing firms, with more than 300,000 employees, were owned by the Japanese. In addition, considerable Japanese funds moved into the US real estate market and into service sectors such as banking and securities brokerage. Unlike earlier Japanese investments in East and Southeast Asia, investments in the United States were primarily motivated by opportunities in the marketplace and became quite substantial. They were followed by increased investment in the United Kingdom and Europe, in a similar context of increased protectionism against Japanese imports.

These market-driven investments in the developed economies raise real questions regarding the applicability of Japanese management methods abroad and the impact on Japanese companies of large-scale direct investment in other countries.

The "Green Field" Approach

When considering the experience of Japanese firms investing in the developed economies, a distinction needs to be drawn between two of the common forms of investment: acquisition of an existing company and the establishment of an entirely new entity, called a "green field" investment.

While important acquisitions have been made, Japanese firms have generally chosen—by a ratio of about 2 to 1—to invest in the United States by the green field route. The difference is important, since a newly established company builds its own facilities and provides its own staff without encumbrance from existing structures.

Many newly established Japanese firms in the United States have been successful. A significant impact has been made, for instance, within the American automotive industry. Honda led the way into the US market with motorcycles in 1979 and automobiles in 1982, building new plants on farmland in Ohio. Honda was followed by Nissan, Mazda, Toyota, Mitsubishi, Subaru, Isuzu, and Suzuki. The US auto market was penetrated on two fronts: by Japanese firms on North American soil and by imports from Japan. By the beginning of the 1990s, the Japanese controlled more than 30 percent of the market, and their share continued to increase. Along the way, Honda also became the largest exporter of US-made autos to Japan.

Lest I paint too positive a picture, some cases of failure should be mentioned. One example is Fujitec Co, which ranked fourth in the elevator and escalator market in Japan, but enjoyed greater success abroad, especially in Singapore and Latin America. Fujitec assumed that, like Honda, it could use foreign

operations, especially in the United States, as a way to end-run entrenched competition at home. Fujitec set up a plant in Ohio and, like Honda, had considerable local assistance. It then embarked on an aggressive sales campaign, winning major orders across America. The company felt so successful that it announced it would move

its corporate headquarters to the United States. Shortly after, however, in the mid-1980s, Fujitec was forced to announce substantial losses in its US operations. Production problems had made it impossible for the firm to fill its orders in time to meet construction schedules.

Japanese companies in the United States illustrate both the strengths and weaknesses of Japan's direct investments abroad. At the shop-floor level, the Japanese system has worked well. By massive majority vote of their employees, companies like Honda,

Nissan, and Toyota have remained non-unionized. Honda has built an engine plant in Ohio to go with its assembly operations, thus making its US products largely with locally manufactured parts. In 1990 Honda's Accord became the single best-selling model in the American market. Periodic surveys of product quality consistently

place the US-made Accord among the two or three highest-quality autos sold in the United States. Moreover, all of the Japanese auto producers have announced increases in their US capacity.

As far as management style is concerned, the egalitarian emphasis of the Japanese company seems to appeal to US workers. Characteristics typical of Japanese factories—production systems that emphasize group output and job rotation; compensation levels commensurate with position (instead of being merit related); employee cafeterias, parking facilities, and uniforms—have worked well abroad both in terms of business and human relations.

A success story, it appears. Yet with these successes have come failures. Honda, for example, was charged with discriminating against women, blacks, and older workers and paid penalties for the offenses. Indeed, a number of Japanese companies, including Sumitomo, San'yō Electric, Matsushita Electric, Nikkō Securities, and C. Itoh (now Itōchū Corporation) have faced lawsuits alleging discrimination on the basis of race, gender, or age.

Another personnel problem stems from the propensity of Japanese firms to assign large numbers of Japanese to management positions. Complaints by local employees about exclusion from the decision-making process, slow career advancement, and tight control from the home office are not new in the history of foreign investment. Similar charges have been leveled against European and US companies abroad; however, the problem appears severe in the Japanese case. For instance, two US nationals in senior management positions at NEC Electronics sued the parent company, NEC Corporation, charging that control by Tōkyō was excessive and that Japanese managers in America were preventing them from carrying out their jobs.

One conclusion that could be drawn is that the Japanese management system, when moved abroad, deals reasonably well with the blue-collar work force but does not deal well with white-collar and middle-management work forces. There is evidence to suggest, however, that Japanese firms are taking steps to address their managerial problems. Increasingly, US nationals are being included in the top management of US subsidiaries. An outstanding example was Marvin Runyon, president of Nissan before he moved to head the Tennessee Valley Authority. Americans in top positions represent, if not solutions, at least preliminary efforts to deal with personnel problems.

Community relations pose another unfamiliar challenge faced by Japanese firms abroad. Since there is no real tradition of corporate philanthropy in Japan—nor any tax or other incentives for it—Japanese companies are not accustomed to playing a role in the community. It has been suggested that Japanese firms are supportive of those inside (*uchi*) the organization but feel no special responsibility for those outside (*soto*). In the United States, as in the West in general, the boundary is not as clearly drawn. Companies are expected to play a part in the community and to encourage their staffs to do so as well. In this area, too, Japanese firms are making an effort, as evidenced by philanthropic foundations established by Hitachi, Toyota, and others.

The Acquisitions Approach
The Japanese acquisition of US companies and assets is a tempting target for American politicians. "The buying of America" is an oft-invoked theme, especially in times of economic malaise.

Acquisitions pose different problems than green field investments, both in managerial and political terms. A green field investment aids the host community by providing jobs and boosting the local economy. A constituency of supporters develops for the investor. An acquisition, on the other hand, is an exchange of money for assets and does not usually generate community support. The acquired firm is often a troubled one, compounding the problems of foreign investment with the internal problems of the firm. The acquired companies have labor forces, histories of labor relations, established production systems, and the like that are deeply embedded and hard for a new owner to change.

The inherent risks, both implicit and explicit, associated with large-scale acquisition are considerable. When Mitsubishi Estate Co bought into Rockefeller Center in 1990, for example, there was a public outcry. The same thing had happened in 1989 when Sony Corporation bought Columbia Pictures Entertainment. To Americans, these purchases were symbols of Japan's economic prowess. Yet the manner in which Japanese firms handled these and other acquisitions suggests insensitivity in the area of public relations. The Japanese will have to improve their public relations abilities or risk serious political consequences that may result in tight restrictions on Japanese direct investment in the US economy.

Future Prospects
A further political risk for Japanese firms arises from their very success, especially in the automotive industry. Japanese direct investment in auto production in the United States is adding considerable new capacity to an industry that already had more capacity than needed. The Japanese factories have the latest equipment and are staffed by young workers who are largely non-unionized. Factories are centrally located in the national market and are supported by grants and various other kinds of aid from local governments. When plants are inevitably closed in response to excess production, it is unlikely to be the Japanese plants that shut down. Instead, it will probably be the outmoded and inefficient plants owned by the "Big Three" US automakers. The political backlash in areas where employment falls is sure to add to the tension already created by Japan's conspicuous industrial and real estate acquisitions.

The assumption is often made that it will be necessary for Japanese firms to integrate non-Japanese employees into their culture and organizations. Experience to date indicates that a different approach may prevail—one in which foreign subsidiaries combine Japanese production methods and factory management techniques with local practices for white-collar recruitment and employment, as well as community relations. Thus, instead of integrating foreign subsidiaries and their staffs, Japanese parent companies are treating their overseas operations as separate and distinct entities.

Setting up shop in a country and culture other than one's own is a learning experience of the highest order. Just as Western companies find it extremely challenging to establish integrated businesses in Japan, Japanese companies confront similar problems when going abroad. But there is little doubt that the Japanese will continue to invest overseas and, in doing so, will learn effective ways of dealing with the complex issues facing multinational organizations.

James C. Abegglen

two separate vowels. (When transcribing the Japanese pronunciation of loanwords from Western languages, in this encyclopedia *ii* and *ei* are written *ī* and *ē*, respectively.) The distinction between long and short vowels is essential for meaning. Aside from *ei*, sequences of vowels such as *ai*, *au*, *ae*, *oi*, *ue*, and so forth are so pronounced that the individual vowels retain their identity, although a glide often occurs; they are treated as separate syllables.

The consonants are *k*, *s*, *sh*, *t*, *ch*, *ts*, *n*, *h*, *f*, *m*, *y*, *r*, *w*, *g*, *j*, *z*, *d*, *b*, and *p*. The fricative *sh* ([ʃ] as in English "shoe") and the affricates *ch*, *ts*, and *j* ([tʃ] as in English "church," [ts] as in German *zu* or English "patsy," and [dʒ] as in English "judge," respectively) are treated as single consonants. *G* is always pronounced as in English "good" (never as in "genetics"); however, it is often nasalized as [ŋ]. The rest are pronounced more or less as in English except that *f* is a bilabial rather than labiodental fricative, *r* is flapped, and *t*, *d*, and *n* are dental. When *n* is used at the end of a syllable as opposed to the beginning, it expresses a uvular syllabic nasal [N]; this changes to one of three different types of nasals when followed by certain consonants: *n* (dental) before *t*, *d*, or *n*; [ŋ] (velar, as in English "thank") before *k* or *g*; and *m* (bilabial) before *p*, *b*, or *m*. The older Hepburn spelling used in this encyclopedia reflects the last named of these pronunciations by changing *n* to *m* before *p*, *b*, or *m* as in *san* (three) versus *sammai* (three sheets); however, the modified Hepburn romanization used in many recent publications retains the *n* in all cases (*sanmai*). When followed by a vowel or *y*, this syllable-final *n* must be distinguished from syllable-initial *n*. In this encyclopedia an apostrophe is used after the former for this purpose (e.g., *jin'in* "personnel" as opposed to *jinin* "resignation"). In the double consonants, -*kk*-, -*pp*-, -*tt*-, and -*ss*-, and in the combinations -*ssh*- [ʃʃ] and -*tch*- (all of which are always medial) the consonants are pronounced—without release but with, in effect, a short interval of silence—much as in the English "bookcase," "shirttail," and "hatcheck."

Japanese has no stress accent like that of English. Each syllable is given equal stress, successions of syllables being pronounced with metronomic regularity. Standard Japanese and a number of the dialects do have, however, a high-low pitch accent system, accent in a word or sequence of words being marked by the syllable after which the pitch drops. The way in which the same word (or the same set of contrasting homophones) is accented can differ significantly among those dialects that have pitch accents. See ACCENT IN THE JAPANESE LANGUAGE.

Another characteristic of standard Japanese is the strong tendency to devoice the vowels *i* and *u* when they fall between two voiceless consonants, so that *shitakusa* (undergrowth) becomes *sh'tak'sa* [ʃtaksa]. The vowels are not always dropped entirely, however: often they are sounded faintly, or at least their metronomic beat preserved. The vowel *u* at the end of a word after a voiceless consonant is also often devoiced or dropped, most notably in *desu*, the polite form of the copula, and in the polite verb ending -*masu*, which are often pronounced *des'* and *mas'*, respectively.

The Grammar of Modern Japanese

Nouns. Japanese nouns are uninflected words that have neither number nor gender and do not influence the inflection of the adjectives modifying them. There do exist a number of pluralizing suffixes that can be attached to nouns referring to human beings, and a few nouns can be pluralized by reduplication, as in *hitobito* (people) from *hito* (person); however, in most cases there is no explicit indication of plurality.

In Japanese the grammatical function of nouns within a sentence is not indicated by word order as in English; neither are nouns inflected for grammatical case as in some languages. Instead grammatical function is indicated by grammatical particles (sometimes called postpositions), which follow the noun. Among the more important of these are *ga*, *o*, *ni*, and *no*, which function as case markers, *ga* indicating subject of verb, *o* direct object of verb, *ni* dative or indirect object, and *no* genitive. For example, in *kaze ga fuku* (the wind blows/will blow), *ga* marks *kaze* as the subject of the verb *fuku*; in *kodomo ga tomodachi no inu ni mizu o yaru* (the child gives/will give water to his/her friend's dog), *ga* marks *kodomo* (child) as the subject of the verb *yaru*, *no* marks *tomodachi* (friend) as possessor of *inu* (dog), *ni* marks *inu* as indirect object, and *o* marks *mizu* (water) as direct object of the verb. A particularly important particle is *wa*. This is not a case marker but rather marks the topic or theme of the sentence. In *zō wa hana ga nagai* (elephants have long noses; literally, "as for elephants, the nose is long"), *wa* marks *zō* (elephant/elephants) as the topic of the sentence and *ga* marks *hana* (nose/noses) as the subject of the adjective *nagai* (is long). All of these particles also have various other functions and meanings depending on grammatical structure and context. There are a number of other postpositions that function much as prepositions do in English.

Verbs. Japanese verbal inflections do not indicate person or number. The dictionary forms of all verbs in the modern language end in the vowel -*u*. When citing the dictionary form of Japanese verbs in English, it is conventional to refer to them by the English infinitive; thus *kaku* is often cited as "to write," although this form is actually the present (more precisely the nonpast) tense, which means "write/writes" or "will write." Other inflectional forms include *kakanai* (negative: "does not/will not write"), *kakō* (tentative or hortatory: "[someone] may write"; "let's write"), *kakitai* (often called "desiderative": "wants to write"), *kaita* (past: "wrote"), *kakeba* (provisional or conditional: "if [someone] writes"), and *kake* (nonpolite imperative: "write!"). Verbs can be used not only to form the predicate of a sentence or clause but also attributively to modify nouns (e.g., *kaku hito*, "the person who writes").

Verb conjugations are classified in two main types. One of these consists of the consonant-stem verbs (verbs whose stems end in consonants), including verbs such as *kaku* (write), *hanasu* (talk), and *utsu* (hit), whose stems are *kak*-, *hanas*-, and *uts*-, respectively (as mentioned above, *ts* is treated as a single consonant). The other type comprises the vowel-stem verbs, which are themselves of two types, with stems ending in either the vowel *i* or the vowel *e*; e.g., *miru* (see) and *taberu* (eat), whose stems are *mi*- and *tabe*-, respectively. (The dictionary forms of vowel-stem verbs all end in -*iru* or -*eru*; however, not all verbs so ending are vowel-stem verbs. Some are consonant-stem verbs with stems ending in *r*; e.g., *kiru* "cut"). In modern Japanese there are two fully conjugated irregular verbs, *kuru* (come) and *suru* (do), bringing the total number of standard verb conjugations to five.

The copula. The Japanese copula or linking verb (plain form *da*; polite form *desu*) is used to link two nouns (or nominal phrases) in the pattern *A wa B da* or *A wa B desu* (A is B). The literal meaning of this pattern is "as for A, it is B" or "as for A, it is in the category of B," e.g., *neko wa dōbutsu da* (cats are animals; literally, "as for cats, they are animals"). For this reason the Japanese copula cannot always be translated by the English "to be." For example, *watakushi wa bīru desu* does not mean "I am beer" but "I am having beer" (literally, "as for me, [it] is beer").

Adjectives. Japanese adjectives are inflected in some ways like verbs, and like verbs they can function either attributively, coming before the nouns they modify, or as the predicates of sentences or clauses, in the latter case appearing at the end of the sentence or clause. The dictionary forms of all adjectives end in one of four vowels (*a*, *i*, *u*, or *o*) followed by a final *i*. The stem of the adjective is obtained by dropping the final *i*; e.g., *takai* (high; stem *taka*), *utsukushii* (beautiful; stem *utsukushi*), *samui* (cold; stem *samu*), and *shiroi* (white; stem *shiro*).

Levels of speech. Japanese expresses a consciousness of social relationships by various grammatical means. Plain versus polite verb forms distinguish between easy informality and abruptness on the one hand and a correct, neutral politeness on the other. In the system of levels known as HONORIFIC LANGUAGE (*keigo*), the speaker chooses among a number of alternative ways of saying the same thing, the choice being determined by such factors as relative age, sex, and social status. One uses respectful or exalting forms with reference to an addressee or third person of higher status and humble terms with reference to oneself or a third person who falls into the same category as oneself.

Some actions often referred to in social situations, such as "go," "come," "be," "say," "look," "eat," "give," and "receive," are represented by sets of three completely different verbs, one neutral, one humble, and one exalting. There are also sets of humble and exalting nouns for common kinship terms, and so forth. The passive forms of verbs are also often used as honorific verbs (with active meaning) when referring to actions of the exalted.

The sentence. The typical Japanese sentence is built on the pattern of subject-object-verb (SOV), as in *neko ga nezumi o tsukamaeta* (the cat caught the mouse). However, since the particle *ga* marks *neko* (cat) as the subject, and the particle *o* marks *nezumi* (mouse) as the object of the verb *tsukamaeta*, a certain amount of inversion, as for stylistic purposes, is possible; *nezumi o neko ga tsukamaeta* (OSV) would have virtually the same meaning as the SOV sentence, whereas in English such inversion of subject and object would change the meaning entirely. To return to the basic SOV sentence, if an adverbial modifier, for instance *subayaku* (swiftly), is inserted, it may come before the subject, the object, or the verb, with slight differences of emphasis. As noted before, adjectival modifiers always precede the nouns they modify. There is a strong tendency in Japanese to omit the subject or the object or even both if the speaker or writer feels that it is clear from the context what they would be, so that, depending on the situation, this sentence might be stated *nezumi o tsukamaeta* (it caught the mouse), *neko ga tsukamaeta* (the cat caught it), or simply *tsukamaeta* (it caught it).

There are no relative pronouns in Japanese as in the English "the cat that caught the mouse died." In Japanese the entire subordinate clause is placed directly in front of the noun as a modifier: *nezumi o tsukamaeta neko ga shinda* (literally, "the caught-the-mouse cat died"). A sentence can also be made into a subordinate clause in another sentence by inserting either the nominalizing particle *no* (not to be confused with the genitive particle *no* mentioned earlier) or the function word *koto* (thing; matter) after the final verb of the sentence, which then modifies the particle, forming a noun clause. For example, the sentence *kodomo ga tabako o suu* (the child smokes cigarettes) is in this way used as the object of the main verb in the sentence *hahaoya wa kodomo ga tabako o suu no* [or *koto*] *o shiranai* (the mother does not know that her child smokes cigarettes). The elements in this sentence are *hahaoya* (mother), *wa* (the topic marker), *kodomo* (child), *ga* (the subject particle), *tabako* (cigarettes), *o* (the object particle), *suu* (smoke; literally, "suck": the verb in the subordinate clause), *no* or *koto* (the nominalizer), *o* (the object particle), *shiranai* ("does-not-know": the main verb of the sentence). A fairly literal rendering of the whole would be "as for the mother, (she) does not know the child-smokes-cigarettes matter."

Vocabulary. Japanese has an extremely rich and varied vocabulary, not only its large stock of native words, which are felt to be particularly expressive and sonorous, but also a great quantity of words of Chinese origin. To these are added the many loanwords from English and other European languages that have come into Japanese, especially during the 20th century. Many of the loanwords from Chinese have been so thoroughly absorbed into the daily vocabulary that their foreign origin is no longer felt. Much of the intellectual and philosophical vocabulary is of Chinese origin, but not all of this is due entirely to Chinese cultural influence; an important part of the modern intellectual vocabulary consists of words coined in Japan in the late 19th and early 20th centuries by devising new combinations of Chinese characters as translations of concepts then being introduced from the West. This process of coinage still continues, but there is a growing tendency, particularly in the sciences, to use Western words intact. Aside from the sciences, words are often used with meanings quite different from those of their original languages, and new Japanese words are sometimes coined by combining parts of Western language words in startling ways. One particularly interesting feature of the native Japanese vocabulary is the large number of established onomatopoeic words it contains. These include not only words imitating sounds but also words expressing abstract qualities or subjective feelings (see ONOMATOPOEIA).

Writing System—The Japanese writing system uses Chinese characters (KANJI) in combination with two separate forms of the phonetic syllabic script known as KANA: *hiragana* and *katakana*. Some words are written entirely in *kana*, others entirely in Chinese characters, and others in a combination of the two. In the latter case the stem of the word is written with a Chinese character, or characters, and inflectional endings or other suffixes with *kana*. Grammatical particles and function words (such as demonstratives and auxiliary verbs) are written in *kana*. The resulting text is sometimes sprinkled with Roman letters (e.g., acronyms such as PTA, model numbers, and occasionally entire foreign words), so that the number of scripts needed to write modern Japanese actually comes to four.

Of the two *kana* scripts or syllabaries, *hiragana* is a cursive script and *katakana* an angular one. Both were derived from Chinese characters used phonetically, the present forms being either stylized or abbreviated versions of the original characters. Although in a few cases their symbols for a particular sound resemble each other, they are in essence entirely separate scripts for producing the same set of sounds. Each script contains 48 symbols, each symbol representing the sound of one Japanese syllable (to be precise, short syllable or mora). For example, the syllables *a, ka, sa, ta,* and *na* are written あ, か, さ, た, and な in *hiragana* and ア, カ, サ, タ, and ナ in *katakana*. The syllable-final *n* ([N]) is written ん in *hiragana* and ン in *katakana*. By using diacritical marks to indicate the voiced consonants in such syllables as *ga, za,* and *da,* and by using combinations of *kana* symbols to represent the postconsonantal *y* glides of some syllables (e.g., *kya, myo*), all of the possible syllables of Japanese can be written with either script. It is possible to write Japanese entirely in *kana,* and, although that is not normally done, there is a fair amount of individual discretion in writing particular words with *kana* instead of Chinese characters in the mixed writing system described above. The *hiragana* script is the one that is normally used together with the Chinese characters for writing Japanese. *Katakana* is used to write the numerous loanwords from Western languages as well as onomatopoeic words, and Japanese words are occasionally written in *katakana* for emphasis or some other technical reason.

There are 1,945 Chinese characters in the JŌYŌ KANJI, the list approved by the government for use in publications for the general public and for writing personal names. There are an additional 284 characters approved for writing names alone. The *jōyō kanji* are learned (or at least taught) by the end of the ninth grade. *Kanji* in scholarly publications may exceed the government guidelines. Tens of thousands of *kanji* are contained in large dictionaries; however, the number of characters in actual use probably did not exceed 5,000 or 6,000 even before the post–World War II language reforms that led to adoption of the government-approved list.

Most Chinese characters have more than one pronunciation or "reading." There are two types: ON READINGS and KUN READINGS. The former are the pronunciations that result when characters are used to write Chinese loanwords. They reflect an original Chinese pronunciation of the character, but as pronounced in Japan. Some characters have two or three possible *on* readings, reflecting loanwords brought in from different parts of China or in different historical periods. *Kun* readings are native Japanese words that have the same meaning as the character (or more precisely, the Chinese morpheme the character represents); they are, in effect, the Japanese words that the character stands for. Often several Japanese words of similar meaning have become associated with a particular character, with the result that it may have several *kun* readings. It is not unusual for commonly used characters to have 2 or more readings of each type, and in extreme cases a single character may have a total of 10 or more possible pronunciations.

Japanese is normally written or printed in vertical lines reading from top to bottom, with the lines starting at the right-hand side of the page and proceeding across from right to left. For this reason most ordinary books open from what would be the back of an English book, and most ordinary newspapers and magazines are arranged in the same way. However, books and periodicals on certain special subjects—including scientific and technical matter—are usually printed in horizontal lines reading from left to right as in English, and these also open in the Western manner.

Japanese language reforms
国語国字問題

(*kokugo kokuji mondai*). The term language reform refers, in the context of Japanese, to extensive and radical changes in prescriptive linguistic usage as a conscious response to the evolution of customary usage and to such language problems as external cultural influence and the use of a vast number of Chinese characters. Although much of the development of modern Japanese proceeded spontaneously, the role of planned development was considerable. After the Meiji Restoration (1868), the language styles and dialects ranged from the language of classical Chinese texts to a dialect spoken in a single village of northeastern Japan. It was necessary to select a single variety of Japanese as a national language, to increase literacy, to create an extensive modern vocabulary, and to codify grammatical and stylistic usage. The written language had to be liberated from its dependence on classical Chinese. The only way to modernize the language—and the minds of the people who spoke it—was in affiliation with the languages by means of which the knowledge of the developed West was introduced. The post-Meiji history of language reform in Japan can be divided into three major periods.

First Period, 1868–1900—The first period was characterized by considerable activity by language reform organizations but no major language reforms. The changes that did occur were largely spontaneous.

Two separate varieties of Japanese emerged: the Classical Standard, based on the written styles of pre-Meiji Japanese (*bungo*) and used only in writing, and the Colloquial Standard, based on the spoken language (*kōgo*) and basically identical with present-day Standard Japanese. The undesirability of this "diglottic" situation and the need to remove the difficult Classical Standard were extensively discussed during the GEMBUN ITCHI movement, but no radical decision to change usage resulted.

The issue of the most suitable system of writing for the language appeared early in the first period. MAEJIMA HISOKA became famous for his early plea (1866) to abandon Chinese characters in favor of the KANA syllabary. In 1869 Nambu Yoshikazu (1840–1917) suggested the use of romanization. However, these radical ideas lacked sufficient support for implementation, and Chinese characters and *kana* were retained as the basic orthographic components. An amazingly fast development of the Japanese vocabulary occurred in this period. The modern vocabulary used Chinese characters as constituent elements, but its conceptual structure was either purely Japanese or identical with that of the Western languages that served as models. Radical extension of literacy was achieved through the introduction of general and compulsory education.

Second Period, 1900–1960——The second period saw adjustments that aimed at increasing the efficiency of the standard language as well as completing the process of modernization and spreading the modern changes throughout the community. An early successful reform was the unification of the shapes of *kana* (1900). Especially important was the proposal of 1923, which listed 1,962 Chinese characters for standard use. It was partly implemented in 1925 by the major newspapers. The Ministry of Education created its own specialized language-study agencies, resulting in the creation of the COUNCIL ON THE NATIONAL LANGUAGE (Kokugo Shingikai) in 1934.

The defeat of Japan in World War II created excellent conditions for the reformists, who had the support of the Allied OCCUPATION authorities. The Classical Standard was removed from its last stronghold, the area of administration and law, and the style of the language of Japanese officialdom was thoroughly modernized. A series of writing reforms was begun in 1946 by "phoneticizing" certain phonically anomalous *kana* usages and restricting the number of characters used in public life to 1,850. These characters were called *tōyō kanji* (Chinese characters for daily use). A strongly restrictive list of approved readings of the *tōyō kanji* appeared in 1948, and the shapes of the characters were standardized in 1949. It was decided that 881 characters out of the *tōyō kanji* list should be taught during the nine years of compulsory school education (later reduced to the six years of elementary school). The last reform in this first postwar series, promulgated in 1959, concerned the spelling of words that consist of a character and affixed *kana* (*okurigana*).

Third Period, 1960–Present——In 1960 there was a change in the balance of power within the Council on the National Language, and toward the end of the decade it issued a series of recommendations, later implemented, that softened the restrictions on public usage imposed by the postwar reforms. The number of characters to be taught during compulsory school education was raised from 881 to 996 (1968) and then to 1,006 (1989), the number of approved readings for the *tōyō kanji* was increased (1973), and the list of *tōyō kanji* was expanded. The new JŌYŌ KANJI list of 1981 includes 1,945 characters, an increase of 95. Despite various problems, there is no reason to expect that a radical reform of the writing system or of any other aspect of the language will take place in the coming decades. However difficult the present-day writing system may be, it has become obvious that it is not incompatible with the functioning of a modern society.

Japanese language studies, history of 国語学史

(*kokugogaku shi*). Japanese language studies may be defined in a narrow sense as attempts to describe the various properties of the Japanese language. The history of these endeavors may be divided into three major periods: the seminal period, up to 1600; the

formative period, which coincides with the Edo period (1600–1868); and the modern period, after the Meiji Restoration of 1868.

The Seminal Period——The first system of writing mastered by the Japanese was that of Chinese, and Chinese remained the language of scholarship into the Edo period. It was read or written by means of interlinear notations (*kunten*) that allowed conversion into or from Japanese (see KAMBUN), and it was in this context that a method for transcribing the sounds of Japanese developed. Certain Chinese characters (KANJI) whose pronunciations in Chinese were roughly similar to Japanese phonemes were used to denote the latter; the abbreviation and standardization of these characters led to the formation of the Japanese phonetic syllabary (KANA). Other unabbreviated Chinese characters were read using the Japanese word to which they corresponded semantically. Although more appropriately classified as studies of Chinese, such dictionaries as SHINSEN JIKYŌ (ca 900), WAMYŌ RUIJU SHŌ (ca 934), RUIJŪ MYŌGI SHŌ (ca 1100), and SETSUYŌSHŪ (ca 1450) record the development of these usages. SIDDHAM, a phonetic script used to record Sanskrit, was introduced to Japan in the 8th century and influenced the formation of the inventory of *kana*, the GOJŪON ZU (table of the 50 sounds). Other early examples of the study of the Japanese language are the *kana* spelling manuals associated with Fujiwara no Teika (FUJIWARA NO SADAIE; 1162–1241).

The Formative Period——In the Edo period the KOKUGAKU (National Learning) movement, which considered Buddhism and Confucianism to be extraneous to the essential culture of Japan, raised the philological study of the Japanese language to the status long held by Chinese. A case in point is the work of KEICHŪ (1640–1701). In his studies of the 8th-century poetry anthology MAN'YŌSHŪ, Keichū noted many discrepancies between the *kana* spelling in that work and 17th-century usage; in WAJI SHŌRAN SHŌ (1695) he showed that the system of spelling adopted by Fujiwara no Teika was historically arbitrary and he offered a new system based on the usage of the *Man'yōshū.*

MOTOORI NORINAGA (1730–1801) and FUJITANI NARIAKIRA (1738–79) initiated work on the development of a Japanese grammar. The concern with grammatical particles in Noringa's *Kotoba no tama no o* (1785) and Nariakira's *Ayuishō* (1778) grew out of a desire to appreciate and revive the classical WAKA poetic form. Nariakira set up a consistent part-of-speech system for Japanese that was further developed by students of Norinaga, in particular his son MOTOORI HARUNIWA (1763–1828) and SUZUKI AKIRA (1764–1837). Haruniwa's study of Japanese inflection, *Kotoba no yachimata* (1806–08), and Akira's treatise on grammatical categories, *Gengyo shishu ron* (1824), represent the culmination of this work, which was systematized as the received traditional grammar of Japanese by TŌJŌ GIMON (1768–1843). This period also witnessed the emergence of comprehensive dictionaries, such as the WAKUN NO SHIORI, the GAGEN SHŪRAN, and the RIGEN SHŪRAN.

The Modern Period——Under the influence of Western linguistics, Japanese language studies in the Meiji period (1868–1912) turned to the historical study of Japanese and the question of its relationship to other East Asian languages. UEDA KAZUTOSHI (1867–1937), the first Japanese trained in

Western linguistics, and SHIMMURA IZURU (1876–1967) pursued historical and comparative research, while YANAGITA KUNIO (1875–1962) and TŌJŌ MISAO (1884–1966) were instrumental in the development of Japanese dialectology.

Phonetic studies that gave close attention to accent were carried out by Jimbō Kaku (1883–1965) and SAKUMA KANAE (1888–1970). Using comparative methods, ARISAKA HIDEYO (1908–52) and HASHIMOTO SHINKICHI (1882–1945) did studies in historical phonology that built upon the Edo-period research of ISHIZUKA TATSUMARO (1764–1823). Ōno Susumu (b 1919) and Mabuchi Kazuo (b 1918) adopted related philological approaches in the post–World War II era, and Hirayama Teruo (b 1909) and Kindaichi Haruhiko (b 1913) have combined a dialectological perspective with the phonological tradition. The study of grammar has been affected by the gradual shift in the early 20th century from the classical to the colloquial style of writing. The grammarians YAMADA YOSHIO (1878–1958) and MATSUSHITA DAISABURŌ (1878–1935) dealt primarily with CLASSICAL JAPANESE, and Hashimoto Shinkichi and TOKIEDA MOTOKI (1900–1967) with colloquial Japanese.

Among comprehensive theories of language developed in the West, the structuralist approach is best represented in the work of HATTORI SHIRŌ (b 1908), who has contributed to the study of both phonology and grammar as well as doing research in the fields of historical and comparative linguistics. The transformational-generative approach is employed by Inoue Kazuko (b 1919), Kuno Susumu (b 1933), and Kuroda Shigeyuki (b 1934).

The government has played a decisive role in language reform and standardization since the Meiji period, when the need to define and promulgate a standard Japanese language was considered to be an issue of the utmost importance. The first modern dictionary of Japanese, the *Genkai* (1889–91), was compiled at the command of the Ministry of Education by ŌTSUKI FUMIHIKO (1847–1928), and from 1902 to 1913 the government-administered Kokugo Chōsa Iinkai (Commission to Investigate the National Language) met to formulate an agenda of language reforms. Government involvement in language reform has continued in the post–World War II period through the Kokugo Shingikai (COUNCIL ON THE NATIONAL LANGUAGE) and the Kokuritsu Kokugo Kenkyūjo (NATIONAL LANGUAGE RESEARCH INSTITUTE).

Japanese Mothers' Congress 日本母親大会

(Nihon Hahaoya Taikai). An annual convention of members from local mothers' congresses in all parts of Japan. The national and local gatherings provide mothers with an opportunity to discuss their concerns about their children's welfare and education, world peace, and other issues. Rather than having a set structure and by-laws, the Japanese Mothers' Congress maintains contact with the local groups by means of a liaison committee.

The origins of the Japanese Mothers' Congress date back to March 1954, when a group of Japanese women submitted a petition for the banning of nuclear weapons to the Women's International Democratic Federation. Their cause was taken up, and plans were laid for a Worldwide Mothers' Congress aimed at protecting children from nuclear war. In preparation for that event, the first Japanese Mothers' Congress was held in Tōkyō in June 1955, with approximately 2,000 people attending. The Worldwide Mothers' Congress was held in Switzerland in July of the same year.

Japanese nationality 国籍

(*kokuseki*). Legal status denoting membership in, allegiance to, and protection by the Japanese state. Article 18 of the Meiji Constitution of 1889 provided that the conditions of Japanese nationality be stipulated by law. Accordingly, in 1899 the Nationality Law (Kokuseki Hō) of Japan (Law No. 66) was promulgated. The statutory provisions contained therein set the criteria for determining who shall be Japanese nationals.

Under the provisions set forth in article 10 of the new 1947 CONSTITUTION OF JAPAN, a new Nationality Law (Law No. 147) was enacted on 4 May 1950. It introduced some important changes to the old law concerning the acquisition and loss of nationality, recognizing the individual's right of choice and equality of the sexes in such matters. The proviso of the old law based upon the Japanese traditional family system (IE) was abolished, and people were given the freedom to renounce their Japanese nationality. The new law, like the old, adopted the rule of *jus sanguinis* ("right of blood," whereby one acquires nationality by virtue of one's descent or parentage) through the father only.

Acquisition of Nationality—On 25 May 1984 the Diet unanimously approved an amendment to the Nationality Law that made important changes to that law. Under this amendment Japanese nationality can be acquired by birth, legitimization, or naturalization. In the first instance, a child is a Japanese national if, at the time of its birth, the father *or* the mother is a Japanese national (art. 2, para. 1). The recognition of *jus sanguinis* through the mother followed lawsuits charging unconstitutional discrimination by sex. A child under 20 years of age who is recognized as a legitimate child by parents of Japanese nationality is entitled to obtain Japanese nationality (art. 3).

Nationality acquired through naturalization falls into three categories:

Ordinary naturalization. The following are the conditions for ordinary naturalization (art. 5): the applicant (1) has had his or her domicile in Japan consecutively for five years or more; (2) is 20 years of age or older and is a person of mental competency under the law of the country of his or her origin; (3) is a person of upright conduct; (4) has property or ability permitting him or her to maintain an independent livelihood; (5) has no nationality or has one that acquisition of Japanese nationality will cause him or her to lose; (6) since the promulgation of the Japanese constitution, has never plotted or advocated, organized, or belonged to a political party or other organization that has plotted or advocated the forceful overthrow of the Japanese constitution or the government.

Special naturalization. Any alien who comes under one of the following classifications may be permitted naturalization even though he or she does not meet conditions for ordinary naturalization: (1) the husband or wife of a Japanese national who has been married to the Japanese national for 3 years or more and has had a domicile in Japan for 1 full year or more (art. 7); (2) the child of a former Japanese national (excluding an adopted child) who has had a domicile or

residence in Japan consecutively for 3 years or more; (3) a person born in Japan who has had a domicile or residence in Japan consecutively for 3 years or more, or whose father or mother (excluding a father or mother by adoption) was born in Japan; (4) a person who has resided in Japan consecutively for 10 years or more. The minister of justice may also permit the naturalization if the alien is, despite his or her intentions, unable to deprive himself or herself of his or her current nationality and the minister finds exceptional circumstances (art. 5, para. 2).

Grand naturalization. An alien who has rendered especially meritorious service to Japan may be permitted naturalization with the approval of the Diet, waiving the conditions for ordinary naturalization. No such case of naturalization has been registered.

Choice of Nationality—A Japanese national having a foreign nationality must choose either of the nationalities (1) before reaching 22 years of age if he or she acquired both nationalities before reaching 20 years of age, or (2) within two years after acquiring the second nationality if he or she acquired such nationality after reaching 20 years of age. Choice of Japanese nationality must be made either by depriving oneself of the foreign nationality or by a sworn declaration that one chooses to be a Japanese national, renouncing the foreign nationality.

Loss of Nationality—A Japanese national who voluntarily acquires a foreign nationality or who acquires a foreign nationality by reason of birth in a foreign country shall lose his or her Japanese nationality retroactively unless within three months after birth the national (or his or her parents) manifests the intention to preserve Japanese nationality according to the provisions of the Family Registration Law of 1947 (revised 1984). Furthermore, a Japanese national having a foreign nationality may renounce and lose his or her Japanese nationality by notifying the minister of justice.

Japanese National Railways 国鉄

(JNR; J: Nihon Kokuyū Tetsudō; commonly abbreviated Kokutetsu). Former public corporation, founded in 1949, which operated national railway, ferry, and bus services as well as various subsidiary concerns. Prior to its breakup in 1987 (see JR), it was Japan's largest enterprise. With assets totaling ¥22.6 trillion (US $134.1 billion) in 1986, the JNR formed the mainstay of the nation's railway network.

Background—In 1869 the Japanese government decided to embark upon railway construction as a public undertaking, completing in 1872 the nation's first railway line, which linked Tōkyō's Shinagawa with Yokohama. Owing to its strained finances, however, the government also permitted private construction, which began in 1881. Private railways soon outstripped the state lines in extent and by 1905 accounted for just over two-thirds of the entire network. Under the Railway Nationalization Law of 1906, the major private lines were purchased by the government in 1906 and 1907. This action left only small local lines in private hands. Between 1917 and 1945 the government extended its ownership and control by buying up 69 more private local lines. In 1949, with the aim of rationalizing the enterprise and increasing its efficiency, the state railways were reorganized under the Japanese National Railways Law as a public corporation, independent of the Ministry of Transporta-

tion. The government, however, provided all the capital and retained powers of supervision.

Organization and Development—The officers of the JNR consisted of a president appointed by the cabinet, a vice president, a chief engineer, and several directors and auditors. With some 276,000 employees, the corporation operated just over 22,000 kilometers (13,662 mi) of railway line in 1986. In the same year the volume of traffic on the JNR amounted to about 200 billion passenger-kilometers (124 billion passenger-mi) and 20.6 billion ton-kilometers (12.8 billion ton-mi) of freight.

The national railways were hard hit by competititon from private automotive transport, which began in the late 1950s and increased rapidly in the 1960s as a network of expressways was extended throughout the country. Between 1960 and 1970 the corporation's share of domestic passenger traffic declined from 51 percent to 32 percent despite the JNR's successful development and inauguration during the same period of the internationally renowned high-speed "bullet train" service (see SHINKANSEN). By 1986 the JNR's share of domestic passenger traffic had dropped to 22 percent, and its share of domestic freight traffic had declined from 51 percent in 1950 to just over 4 percent. Added to the problem of competition from automotive transport was the financial burden of maintaining nonpaying local lines, which made up some 40 percent of the total state network. In 1984 the railway's net loss was over ¥1.7 trillion (US $7.2 billion), its cumulative deficit exceeded ¥12.3 trillion (US $51.8 billion), and its long-term debt was more than ¥21.8 trillion (US $91.8 billion).

The Ministry of Transport and the JNR took steps to remedy the situation in June 1983 by organizing the Japanese National Railways Reform Commission. Against the background of a 1980s trend in the capitalist world toward the deregulation and privatization of industry, in July 1985 the commission proposed a drastic reform plan whereby the company's passenger division would be divided into six regional companies, all of which were to be placed under private management. Measures were taken to relocate to other firms the 93,000 employees made idle by the plan. Part of the JNR's long-term and other debts, amounting to over ¥37.3 trillion (US $157.0 billion), was liquidated by creating new corporations and by selling JNR-owned land; the balance fell on the shoulders of the taxpayers. The legislation necessary to execute the plan was duly approved by the Diet and in 1987 the Japanese National Railways ceased to exist. See also RAILWAYS.

Japanese nationals residing abroad 海外在留日本人

(*kaigai zairyū nihonjin*). According to Ministry of Foreign Affairs statistics, in 1989 there were 586,972 Japanese nationals residing overseas, either as permanent resident aliens or as nonpermanent long-term residents (defined as those residing abroad for at least three months). This figure represents an increase of 7.0 percent over the 1988 statistics and 22.8 percent over the statistics for 1984. The largest population of Japanese residing abroad was in the United States (213,300), the second largest in Brazil (109,311), and the third largest in Great Britain (37,335). Statistics showed that 51.5 percent of the

Japanese population resident abroad was male and 48.5 was female.

Of the total number of Japanese nationals residing abroad in 1989, there were 246,043 permanent residents; 53.2 percent of those lived in South America and 35.2 percent in North America. The number of Japanese residing abroad on a long-term basis in 1989 was 340,929. Of these long-term residents, 43.2 percent lived in North America, 26.6 percent in Western Europe, and 20.1 percent in Asia. Sixty-four percent of the long-term residents were employed by private companies. The next largest group—20.4 percent—was engaged in educational or cultural occupations.

Japanese people, origin of
日本人の起源

(*nihonjin no kigen*). The development of the Japanese people has been markedly influenced by geography and climate. In glacial periods the central mountain range was capped with ice, but the coastal zone and mountain slopes were habitable, and lowered sea levels exposed three major migration routes: from Sakhalin and Siberia in the north, from China and Korea to the west, and from Okinawa and the Ryūkyūs in the south. During interglacial periods the islands were isolated, but navigation had replaced the land corridors by the time the sea level had risen at the end of the last glacial period, about 10,000 BC.

Thousands of artifacts and caches of broken animal bones have been recovered from rock shelters, limestone fissures, and glacial loam sites, some dating from as early as the end of the second glacial period a half a million years or more ago. A few associated hominid bone fragments have been found but are identifiable only as belonging to the genus *Homo*. The oldest identified human (*Homo sapiens*) remains, although incomplete, date from about 30,000 BC. The oldest remains satisfactory for comparative analysis are from the early part of the Jōmon period (ca 10,000 BC–ca 300 BC), but Jōmon skeletal assemblages satisfactory for statistical analysis date from about 5000 BC. Altogether there are approximately 500 Jōmon-period skeletal assemblages useful for comparative purposes and probably no more than that from the Yayoi period (ca 300 BC–ca AD 300).

The Jōmon population was generally short-statured with heavy skeletal structure; skulls were longheaded, and faces were short and broad with markedly concave nasal profiles. Multivariate discriminant analyses place Jōmon skulls between those of the native AINU and modern Japanese but closer to the Ainu and more variable.

Crania of the early-historic-period Japanese are shorter and slightly narrower than those of Jōmon times, and there are marked increases in cranial height and both cranial and facial indexes. The historical Japanese known as the Yamato (Yamatobito) are probably mainly descendants of the Yayoi cultivators with regionally varying admixtures of the earlier Jōmon population and a continually increasing immigrant population from the insular south and, more especially, Korea and China. See also ARCHAEOLOGY.

Japanese Red Cross Society
日本赤十字社

(Nihon Sekijūjisha). Affiliate of the International Red Cross. Its predecessor was the Hakuaisha, a relief organization established by SANO TSUNETAMI in 1877 for casualties in the SATSUMA REBELLION. The Hakuaisha joined the International Red Cross in 1887 and changed its name to the Japanese Red Cross Society. In 1952 it was given legal status as a special nonprofit corporation. Its activities include training nurses, managing medical institutions, and setting up blood banks.

Japanese spaniel
狆

(*chin*). Also called Japanese chin in English. A small breed of pet dog. It is generally thought that the etymology of *chin* is *chi-inu* or *chinu*, "small dog." Its body resembles the Pekingese breed but has a somewhat more delicate build and longer and more slender legs. Its weight is about 2.5–4.0 kilograms (5.5–8.8 lb) and its height is about 22–30 centimeters (8–12 in). The head is high domed, with a snub nose and large, round eyes. The hair is long, silky, and straight. The ears are V-shaped and pendulous, and the tail curls over the back and is covered with tufty hair. The coat is usually black and white in color, but red and white is also seen.

The Japanese chin seems to have developed around the beginning of the Edo period (1600–1868), based on a Pekingese-like toy breed imported from China. The breed first became known in the West after Commodore Matthew Perry's expedition to Japan in 1853, when he brought some of these dogs back to the United States.

Japanese studies abroad
海外での日本研究

(*kaigai de no Nihon kenkyū*). "Japanese studies" (Nihon *kenkyū*) refers to education and research on Japan in the humanities, social sciences, and fine arts conducted overseas by universities and other institutions of higher education as well as research institutes. Scholarly study of Japan is undertaken by institutions in many different regions of the world.

Europe—Japanese studies in Europe goes back to the reports sent back by Francis XAVIER and other Jesuit missionaries who came to Japan in the 16th century. After Japan adopted its policy of NATIONAL SECLUSION in the early 17th century, the Dutch, Germans, and French visited and resided at the foreign enclave in Nagasaki on Kyūshū, and they continued to write about Japan throughout its two and a half centuries of isolation. Scholarly study began with the arrival of the British diplomat and scholar Ernest SATOW in the 19th century and continued into the early 20th century through the efforts of pioneer researchers such as Sir George B. SANSOM and Arthur WALEY. Their work, relying chiefly on traditional philological methodology, remained the mainstream of Japanese studies in the West until World War II.

In Britain, Japanese studies focused on literature and the arts before the war but shifted after the war to interdisciplinary research using the area studies approach that had become established in the United States. The postwar centers of Japanese studies were Cambridge and Oxford universities, as well as the School of Oriental and African Studies (University of London). In 1963 a regular course in Japanese studies was included in the curriculum at Sheffield University, which has developed a strong program of research and education focused on contemporary Japan.

On the European continent post–World War II Japanese studies has tended to focus on the humanities, carrying on the prewar tradition of Japanology. Among the many major centers of Japanese studies in Europe are the Institut National des Langues et Civilization Orientales and Université de Paris VII, in France; Ruhr-Universität Bochum, Universität zu Köln, and Humboldt-Universität (Berlin), in Germany; and Universita Degli Studi di Venezia and Istituto Universitario Orientale di Napoli, in Italy. There are also Japanese studies specialists in Austria at the Universität Wien, in Switzerland at the Université de Genève, and in the Netherlands at the Rijksuniversiteit te Leiden.

In Eastern Europe, Japanese studies is pursued in Hungary at Eötvös Lóvánd University (Budapest), and in Czechoslovakia at Karlova Univerzita (Charles University) and at the Orientálí Ústav Csav (Oriental Institute of the Czechoslovak Academy of Sciences). In Poland a Japanese language course is offered at the Uniwersytetu Warszawskiego (Warsaw University). Japanese language courses were also established at the University of Sofia, in Bulgaria; the University of Bucharest, in Romania; and the University of Belgrade, in Yugoslavia.

In Russia the leading role in Japanese studies is played by the Academy of Sciences. Japan-related courses are also available at the universities of Moscow and St. Petersburg.

North America—Early Japanese studies in the United States passed through three phases. The first phase, beginning around the time of the MEIJI RESTORATION (1868), was characterized by writings on Japan mainly by foreign advisers involved in the modernization effort, such as the physician James C. HEPBURN and the student of Asian art Ernest FENOLLOSA. Then came a phase during which Japan-related courses were taught as part of a Far Eastern studies program set up at the Berkeley campus of the University of California in 1896. The third phase was marked by the invitation of Serge ELISSÉEFF, a French scholar born in Russia, to the Harvard-Yenching Institute in 1932. Among the scholars who led the field in those days were ASAKAWA KAN'ICHI at Yale University and TSUNODA RYŪSAKU at Columbia. Still, Japanese studies in the United States was relatively undeveloped, causing such pre–World War II Japanologists as Edwin O. REISCHAUER to pursue their studies abroad.

The outbreak of World War II prompted intensive language training programs launched by the US armed forces with an eye to postwar occupation. The cold war and polarization during the postwar period served to facilitate the inclusion of Japanese studies as one aspect of area studies. This generation of scholars includes Donald KEENE, Edward SEIDENSTICKER, and John W. Hall (b 1916).

Steady progress was made in the field of Japanese studies through assistance provided by Fulbright Program fellowships begun in 1952 (see JAPAN–UNITED STATES EDUCATION COMMISSION), Ford Foundation grants, and other philanthropic support. Later, funds for Japanese studies began to grow scarce. The JAPAN FOUNDATION, established in 1972, and the Japan–United States Friendship Commission, set up in 1975, have been key sources of funds for Japanese studies in the United States.

In Canada, Japanese studies and language education tended until the early 1970s to be confined to the University of British Columbia and the University of Toronto. It was not until around 1972 that Japanese studies were begun at other Canadian universities such as McGill University and the University of Montreal.

According to a 1988 survey there were 295 academic institutes in the United States and 31 in Canada that offered Japanese language courses and/or other Japan-related courses. There were a total of 1,224 scholars in the field in the United States and 196 in Canada.

Latin America——In Latin America the leading Japanese studies institutes are at El Colegio de Mexico, in Mexico, and Centro de Estudos Japoneses, Universidade de São Paulo, in Brazil. Japanese studies courses have also been established in Peru at the Pontificia Universidad Católica de Peru, in Argentina at the Universidade de Buenos Aires, and in Colombia at the Pontificia Universidad Javeriana.

Asia——In South and Southeast Asia the Europe-oriented tradition of higher education as well as the legacy of World War II long remained obstacles to the development of Japanese studies. Courses began to be offered in the 1960s in Malaysia, Hong Kong, Thailand, the Philippines, Indonesia, and India with assistance from the Japanese government.

On the undergraduate level, it is possible to obtain a degree in Japanese studies/language in Indonesia at the University of Indonesia and at Padjadjaran University, in Thailand at Thammasat University and at Chulalongkorn University, and in Singapore at the National University of Singapore. On the graduate level the University of the Philippines' Asian Center, University of Delhi, Jawaharlal Nehru University, and others have Japanese language/studies programs.

In China, since normalization of diplomatic relations with Japan in 1972, leading institutions have been Beijing (Peking) University, the Chinese Academy of Social Sciences, and Fudan (Fu-tan) University.

In South Korea the Korean Society of Japanology was launched in 1973. Japan-related courses are offered in more than 50 institutions of higher education, including Seoul University, Yonsei University, and Korea University. Nineteen of the 50 have Japanese studies and/or language courses on the graduate level.

Oceania——Among the major centers of Japanese studies in Australia are Australian National University, the University of Adelaide, and the University of Sydney. In Australia there is also the Australia-Japan Research Centre (within Australian National University) and the Japanese Studies Centre (Monash University). New Zealand's centers are at the University of Auckland, Massey University, and Victoria University of Wellington.

Middle East and Africa——The major Japanese research institutes in the Middle East are at the Hebrew University of Jerusalem, in Israel; Ankara University, in Turkey; and the University of Cairo, in Egypt.

In Africa, Japanese studies is in the early stages of development. Japanese studies scholars may be found at Kenya's University

of Nairobi and other large African universities.

By the early 1990s many Japanese studies specialists had succeeded in breaking out of the area studies framework and obtaining posts in such traditional disciplines as history and sociology. The spectrum of people now involved in Japanese studies is much broader than before, with programs being incorporated into the curricula not only of law, business, and other professional schools but of high schools as well. In the United States and many other countries throughout the world, the growth of Japanese studies has been given increased impetus because of economic ties with Japan.

Japanese-style painting → nihonga

Japanese Sword Museum
刀剣博物館

(Tōken Hakubutsukan). Museum established in 1968 in Shibuya Ward, Tōkyō, that houses Japanese swords, *tsuba* (sword guards) and other sword fittings, as well as some 1,200 historical documents dealing with Japanese swords. Of the approximately 520 swords housed in the museum, some 400 are on loan from collectors; 11 of these are National Treasures. The museum itself owns the remaining swords, including 1 National Treasure.

Japanese terrier
日本テリア

(Nippon *teria*). A breed of dog developed from small foreign toy terriers during the Taishō (1912–26) and Shōwa (1926–89) periods. Small, slender pet dogs with smooth short hair similar to European toy terriers are described in books of the Edo period (1600–1868). They were supposedly of foreign origin and were called *shika-bane* or *shika-bone* (deer skeleton). Today's breed was probably bred from the black-and-tan terrier and the toy smooth fox terrier brought to Japan in the mid-Meiji period (1868–1912).

The Japanese terrier has exceptionally fine, velvety short hair. The coat is white with small black markings, and there is often a trace of tan on the face. The breed was very popular between World War I and World War II but is rarely seen today.

Japanese Trade Union Confederation → Rengō

Japan External Trade Organization → JETRO

Japan Federation of Bar Associations
日本弁護士連合会

(JFBA; J: Nihon Bengoshi Rengōkai; abbreviated Nichibenren). The national association of private attorneys (exclusive of judges and prosecutors). It was created by statute. The Lawyers' Law (Bengoshi Hō) of 1949 requires every lawyer to register as a member of one of the 52 local bar associations and of the Japan Federation of Bar Associations. The JFBA has almost complete autonomy in the governance of the private legal profession, including the legal responsibility to screen entrants and to discipline members.

In 1990, the JFBA had more than 48 committees (including the Qualification Screening Committee and the Disciplinary Committee), as mandated by the Lawyers' Law. It is engaged in areas such as the defense of human rights, research and recommendations for law reform, the representation of the interests of private attorneys in relation to the other branches of the legal profession, and the supervision of the bar associations' role in the training of new attorneys.

Japan Federation of Employers' Associations → Nikkeiren

Japan Fine Arts Academy
日本美術院

(Nihon Bijutsuin). Association of artists in the NIHONGA (Japanese-style painting) tradition. Founded in Tōkyō in 1898 by OKAKURA KAKUZŌ and a group of artists including HASHIMOTO GAHŌ, YOKOYAMA TAIKAN, SHIMOMURA KANZAN, and HISHIDA SHUNSŌ. In 1906 the academy moved to Izura, Ibaraki Prefecture. In 1913 Okakura died, and the academy almost dissolved. In 1914, however, Yokoyama Taikan reorganized the academy, after which it was often referred to as the Saikō Nihon Bijutsuin or Reorganized Japan Fine Arts Academy. The academy holds its exhibition of Japanese-style paintings, the Inten, twice a year.

Japan Folk-Craft Museum
日本民芸館

(Nihon Mingeikan). The first and most important folk-craft museum in Japan; located in Komaba, Meguro Ward, Tōkyō. Founded in 1936 by YANAGI MUNEYOSHI, the leader of the folk-craft movement, and others, with financial assistance provided by ŌHARA MAGOSABURŌ. Yanagi served as the first curator of the museum. The collection includes paintings, pottery, porcelain, prints, textiles, lacquer, masks, toys, furniture, metalwork, and costumes from various regions of Japan. Aside from its exhibitions the museum conducts research on folk craft and encourages interest in contemporary folk arts and crafts. It publishes the monthly magazine *Mingei*.

Japan Forum 国際文化フォーラム

(Kokusai Bunka Fōramu). A nonprofit organization established in 1987 by KŌDANSHA, LTD; ŌJI PAPER CO, LTD; JŪJŌ PAPER CO, LTD; DAI NIPPON PRINTING CO, LTD; TOPPAN PRINTING CO, LTD; and MITSUBISHI BANK, LTD. It provides support for international seminars and symposia that promote cultural exchange and attempts to further the teaching of Japanese as a foreign language. It also publishes *World Plaza*, a bimonthly magazine devoted to international cultural exchange. In 1990 total assets were ¥373 million (US $2.6 million). Headquarters are in Tōkyō.

Japan Foundation 国際交流基金

(Kokusai Kōryū Kikin). Public corporation under the jurisdiction of the Ministry of Foreign Affairs, commissioned to administer programs for INTERNATIONAL CULTURAL EXCHANGE. It was established in 1972 through the reorganization of the Kokusai Bunka Shinkōkai (KBS; founded in 1934). The foundation undertakes exchange programs for scholars, artists, and specialists; provides financial support for research on Japan and the promotion of Japanese-language teaching abroad; participates in the presentation of various cultural events; produces and distributes materials on Japanese culture; and performs surveys and research related to the administration of international cultural exchange programs. Headquarters are in Tōkyō, with a branch office in Kyōto. The foundation maintains a cultural center in Jakarta, cultural institutes in Cologne and Rome, and liaison offices in Bangkok, Kuala Lumpur, London, Los Angeles, New York, Mexico City, Paris, São Paulo, Sydney, and Toronto. It established the Japan Foundation Japanese-Language Institute in 1989 and the Japan Foundation ASEAN Culture Center in 1990. The foundation's 1990 budget was ¥8.7 billion (US $57 million), which came from the proceeds on a government endowment amounting to about ¥55 billion (US $362 million).

Japan Foundation Library
国際交流基金図書館

(Kokusai Kōryū Kikin Toshokan). Collection of books and journals about Japan. It was started in the early 1930s by the Kokusai Bunka Shinkōkai (KBS; Japan Cultural Society) and transferred to the JAPAN FOUNDATION in 1972. The library holds some 40,000 volumes focusing on the humanistic and social sciences. About 22,000 of these are written in English or other European languages. There are an additional 3,000 PhD dissertations on Japanese studies written by US students. Landmark studies of Japan by Lafcadio HEARN, Philipp Franz von SIEBOLD, and Engelbert KAEMPFER are among the library's most notable holdings. The library also published *Law and Justice in Tokugawa Japan* (9 vols, 1988).

Japan Freight Railway Co
日本貨物鉄道［株］

(Nippon Kamotsu Tetsudō). The only Japanese freight railway company with a nation-

wide network; operates railway freight transport services and provides a wide range of services in such fields as warehousing insurance, travel, and advertising. The company was established in 1987 as part of the JR group when the JAPANESE NATIONAL RAILWAYS (JNR) was privatized. It uses containers specifically designed for the transport of products requiring special care, such as live fish, meat, fruit, and chemical products. The company also operates special freight cars to transport oil, cement, and paper. For fiscal year 1990, sales totaled ¥192.2 billion (US $1.3 billion) and capitalization stood at ¥19.0 billion (US $124.1 million). Headquarters are in Tōkyō.

Japan Go Association 日本棋院

(Nihon Kiin). Leading organization of Japan's professional GO players. Established in 1924 through a merger of several major *go* groups, it acts to advance and popularize the game and exerts a strong influence on amateurs. Today the association's main activities include organizing professional matches and tournaments sponsored by newspapers and television, issuing rankings, publishing *go* literature, and introducing the game to foreign audiences. There are 1,170 branch organizations and a membership of approximately 300 professionals that accounts for 80 percent of the nation's top players. The head office is in Chiyoda Ward, Tōkyō.

Japan Herald ジャパン・ヘラルド

(Japan Herarudo). Influential English-language newspaper whose existence spanned the Meiji period (1868–1912); launched as a weekly in Yokohama in November 1861 by Albert W. Hansard. Its motto was "The Most Thorough Independence." It expanded to become a daily, the *Daily Japan Herald*, in October 1863 under the capable editorship of John Reddie BLACK. An evening edition was added later. The paper was sold to a German syndicate in 1905 and ceased publication in 1914.

Japan Highway Public Corporation 日本道路公団

(Nihon Dōro Kōdan). Public corporation that constructs and administers the nation's major toll roads and related facilities. Capitalized wholly by the government, it was established in 1956. At the time of its establishment, the corporation took over all the toll roads belonging to the national and prefectural governments. In July 1963, the corporation's Meishin Expressway between Nagoya and Kōbe, the first road of its kind in Japan, was partially opened to traffic. By March 1989, the corporation was operating a total of 36 expressways throughout the country, including the Tōmei, Meishin, Chūō, Tōhoku, Hokuriku, Chūgoku, and Kyūshū expressways, with a total length of approximately 4,869 kilometers (3,025 mi). The corporation also manages other general toll roads with a total length of 660 kilometers (410 mi). An average of 1 billion automobiles utilize the corporation's toll roads each day. See also METROPOLITAN EXPRESSWAY PUBLIC CORPORATION.

Japan Housewives Association
→Shufuren

Japan Housing Loan, Inc
日本ハウジングローン［株］

(Nippon Haujingu Rōn). Housing finance company. Incorporated in 1976. Its parent

companies are two long-term credit banks (INDUSTRIAL BANK OF JAPAN, LTD, and NIPPON CREDIT BANK, LTD) and three securities companies (DAIWA SECURITIES CO, LTD; NIKKŌ SECURITIES CO, LTD; and YAMAICHI SECURITIES CO, LTD). At the end of March 1991, outstanding loans totaled ¥1.6 trillion (US $10.5 billion) and capitalization stood at ¥5.2 billion (US $34.0 million). Headquarters are in Tōkyō.

Japan Incorporated 日本株式会社

(Nihon *kabushiki kaisha*). Term coined in the late 1960s suggesting that the reason for Japan's economic success lay in its unique government-business relationship. Among journalists, businesspeople, and government officials outside Japan, and particularly those in the United States, it was popular during the early 1970s to use such terms as Japan Incorporated and "Japan Inc" to account for the so-called Japanese economic miracle. Of the many formulations of the concept, one common feature is the assertion of a close correspondence between the structure of the Japanese economic-political system and that of a giant, multidivisional, conglomerate corporation. According to this analogy, the role of government in the Japanese economy is like that of a corporate headquarters responsible for the formulation of long-term policies and investments as well as general planning and coordination. Large corporations are viewed as akin to corporate divisions, possessing considerable operating autonomy but nevertheless subject to the ultimate control of central authority. Since the mid-1970s, the popularity of the concept has declined. A major criticism has been its failure to account for variations by sector in Japanese government-business relations, as well as analogous patterns of public-private sector collaboration in the United States and Europe.

Japan Institute of International Affairs 日本国際問題研究所

(Nihon Kokusai Mondai Kenkyūjo). An organization founded in 1960 to further research and study in international politics, law, and economics. Affiliated with the Ministry of Foreign Affairs. The institute is located in Minato Ward, Tōkyō. Its chief activities are disseminating information on international issues and exchanging research findings with organizations and individuals specializing in international affairs. It also serves as the secretariat for the PACIFIC ECONOMIC COOPERATION CONFERENCE (PECC). The institute's publications include the *Japan Review of International Affairs*, issued five times a year in English.

Japan International Cooperation Agency 国際協力事業団

(JICA; J: Kokusai Kyōryoku Jigyōdan). Special public corporation established to promote international cooperation through the provision of overseas development assistance. It was founded in 1974 in accordance with the International Cooperation Agency Law.

JICA's main activities include (1) the strengthening of technical assistance programs to developing countries provided by the Japanese government by bringing technical trainees to Japan and by dispatching specialists and providing needed equipment and materials for projects overseas, (2) the facilitation and promotion of grant assistance programs, (3) the extension of loans and equity investment related to development projects, (4) the training and dispatching of JAPAN OVERSEAS COOPERATION VOLUN-TEERS (JOVC), and (5) the facilitation of Japanese emigration abroad.

JICA's activities are administered by the Ministry of Foreign Affairs; the Ministry of Agriculture, Forestry, and Fisheries; and the Ministry of International Trade and Industry (MITI). Its head office is in Tōkyō, with other domestic offices and subsidiary agencies, such as the International Training Center, spread throughout the country. JICA maintains 49 offices overseas. In 1990, its staff numbered 1,030, of whom about 200 worked abroad.

Japan Junior Chamber, Inc
日本青年会議所

(Nihon Seinen Kaigisho). The Japan Jaycees. Nonprofit organization founded in 1949 and engaged in community development, leadership cultivation, personal improvement, and international cooperation. The Japan Jaycees, with a total membership as of January 1991 of 60,900 in 752 cities, is the second largest component of Junior Chamber International, the umbrella organization for 86 national Junior Chambers around the globe, with an aggregate membership of 420,000. Headquarters are in Tōkyō.

Japan Labor-Farmer Party→
Nihon Rōnōtō

Japan Leasing Corporation
[株]日本リース

(Nihon Rīsu). Independent leasing company. Incorporated in 1963. It has 14 overseas offices in 9 countries. Sales for the fiscal year ending March 1990 totaled ¥471.6 billion (US $3.1 billion), of which leasing accounted for 62 percent; installment credit, 21 percent; and other revenues, 17 percent. The company was capitalized at ¥20.3 billion (US $132.6 million) in the same year. Headquarters are in Tōkyō.

Japan Magazine Publishers Association
日本雑誌協会

(JMPA; J: Nihon Zasshi Kyōkai). Organization established in 1956 with a membership of 30 major magazine publishers, which had increased to 74 by 1991. Its objective is to maintain ethical standards in the magazine-publishing industry, and toward this end it established in October 1963 a set of general principles of ethical magazine editing. In 1966 it joined the International Federation of the Periodical Press. See also JAPAN BOOK PUB-LISHERS ASSOCIATION.

Japan Medical Association
日本医師会

(Nihon Ishikai). Organization of physicians. In 1906 voluntary medical associations were formed in various parts of Japan, but it was not until 1919, with the inauguration of the health insurance system, that the Japan Medical Association was legally established. During World War II, it was made a part of the government and charged with national medical policy, but in 1948 it was reorganized completely and membership was made voluntary. In the same year it was legally recognized as a nonprofit corporation with the aim of enhancing professional ethics, developing and spreading medical science and art, improving public health, and promoting social welfare. In 1950 the association absorbed the Japanese Association of Medical Sciences (Nihon Igakukai) and organized sectional meetings of medical specialists. With 121,514 members in 1990, most of whom are

practicing doctors, the association exerts great influence on government medical policies. Haneda Haruto (b 1915) has served as president since 1984.

Japan Metals & Chemicals Co, Ltd
日本重化学工業[株]

(Nihon Jūkagaku Kōgyō). Steel company. Japan's largest producer of ferroalloys, the company also manufactures fertilizers and constructs geothermal electrical power plants. It is affiliated with the NIPPON STEEL CORPORATION. It was established in 1917 as a carbide manufacturer and later converted to the production of ferroalloys. During the 1970s, the company absorbed numerous steel firms. It is also working on the development of new energy sources; it began a geothermal project in 1957 and in 1966 constructed Japan's first geothermal electric plant. Annual sales totaled ¥78.3 billion (US $586.3 million) in December 1990; capitalization stood at ¥6.8 billion (US $50.9 million) in the same year. Headquarters are in Tōkyō.

"Japan money"
ジャパンマネー

(Japan manē). A voguish Japanese-English term commonly used by the Japanese media to indicate the massive overseas investments, chiefly in foreign securities, made by Japanese institutional investors. Such investment has grown substantially since the early 1980s, reaching a high of US $102 billion in 1986 and subsequently exceeding the level of US $80 billion per annum. The increase in individual financial assets and the reduction in corporate demand for funds contributed to a structural surplus of funds. Growing interest rate advantages prompted the movement of this money from domestic to overseas investments. The largest investment target was the United States, accounting for 40–50 percent of total Japanese overseas investment. Large-scale Japanese purchases of government bonds came to play a large role in providing capital to fund the US fiscal and current account deficits. These funds are invested by financial institutions including banks, securities companies, and insurance companies. Recently the foreign securities investments of insurance companies received considerable attention because they have increased significantly since 1988. Reducing risk through diversified investment and the use of financial futures has become important because of the currency exchange risks not found in domestic investments. See also CAPITAL MAR-KETS; DEREGULATION; FOREIGN EXCHANGE CONTROL.

Japan Monkey Center
日本モンキーセンター

(Nihon Monkī Sentā). Center for the scientific study of primates. Located in the city of Inuyama, Aichi Prefecture. Established in 1956. In addition to its role as a primate study center, the Monkey Center maintains a primate zoo, which is open to the public, as well as a rare monofamilial outdoor enclosure where wild Japanese macaques are maintained in their natural habitat. The zoo houses about 1,000 specimens of some 90 species of monkeys and apes. The center, including the zoo, covers an area of about 30 hectares (72 acres).

Japan Newspaper Publishers and Editors Association
日本新聞協会

(Nihon Shimbun Kyōkai; NSK). A cooperative organization founded in July 1946, whose membership comprises major daily

Japan Monkey Center Visitors to this primate study center are able to observe monkeys closely in a natural setting.

newspaper publishers, news agencies, and broadcasting companies. In 1991 it had 172 member companies. The association is not affiliated with any political party or special interest group. Its activities include research on newspapers, communication, and broadcasting; the encouragement of high journalistic standards; the establishment of standard guidelines under which its member publishers edit news articles; and the collection, cataloging, and microfilming of the newspapers of member publishers. The association publishes a regular bulletin, a yearbook, and other collected data. It also publishes in English an edition of the NSK newsletter and a yearbook, *The Japanese Press.*

Japan Olympic Committee
日本オリンピック委員会

(JOC; J: Nihon Orimpikku Iinkai). Organization approved under the terms of the charter of the International Olympic Committee (IOC) to engage in the promotion of Olympic athletic activities within Japan, which is its principal objective. The JOC was founded in 1911, when Japan became a member of the IOC. It was part of the JAPAN AMATEUR SPORTS ASSOCIATION from its establishment until August 1989, when it became an autonomous organization. The JOC includes the Japan University Sports Board and a headquarters for strengthening players, as well as special committees on sports science, sports information, Olympic strategies, and internationalization.

Japan Overseas Cooperation Volunteers
青年海外協力隊

(JOCV; J: Seinen Kaigai Kyōryoku Tai). Often called the Japanese Peace Corps. Program founded by the Japanese government in 1965 to provide technical services and instruction to developing countries. Originally under the Overseas Technical Cooperation Agency (absorbed by the new JAPAN INTERNATIONAL COOPERATION AGENCY in 1974) and financed exclusively by the Japanese government, the JOCV sent out 10,255 volunteers between 1965 and 1990.

The volunteers, all young people, serve a term of two years and receive a monthly living allowance of not less than US $250; their housing is provided by the host country, and they work as members of that country's government. The JOCV places strong emphasis on technical qualifications and experience, and nearly half of its volunteers have been in agriculture, fishing, and other areas of primary industry.

Japan P.E.N. Club
日本ペンクラブ

(Nihon Pen Kurabu). Japanese branch of the International Association of Poets, Playwrights, Editors, Essayists, and Novelists. Founded in 1935, its first president was SHIMAZAKI TŌSON. Following an interruption of its activities during the war, the club was reestablished nationally in 1947, with a new president, KAWABATA YASUNARI. In 1957 the club hosted the 29th International P.E.N. Conference, and in 1984 the 47th conference was held in Tōkyō. The club publishes *Japanese Literature Today.* In 1989 there were 1,367 members.

Japan Philharmonic Symphony Orchestra 日本フィルハーモニー交響楽団

(Nihon Firuhāmonī Kōkyō Gakudan). Orchestra established in Tōkyō in 1956 by Nippon Cultural Broadcasting, Inc. Watanabe Akeo (1919–90) served as its first principal conductor. In 1972 its backers withdrew their sponsorship, but the orchestra's enthusiastic fans and other members of the general public rallied to its support and the organization has since been able to operate under its own management; it incorporated in 1985.

Japan Private School Promotion Foundation 日本私学振興財団

(Nihon Shigaku Shinkō Zaidan). A special corporation set up in 1970 to distribute subsidies provided by Japan's central and municipal governments to private schools. All direct support for private schools is channeled through the foundation. The Law concerning the Promotion and Support of Private Schools (1975) declared that 50 percent of the operating expenses of private schools should be subsidized, but in 1989, due to insufficient government funding, the foundation distributed subsidies of only 15 percent.

Japan Productivity Center 日本生産性本部

(Nihon Seisansei Hombu). Headquarters of the Japanese movement to increase industrial productivity—part of a worldwide movement that began in the late 1940s. The center was established as a foundation in 1955. Since its early days the center has closely adhered to the guiding principles of the productivity movement: (1) improved productivity should ultimately lead to business restructuring and increased employment; (2) management and labor should cooperate to improve productivity; and (3) the benefits of improved productivity should be distributed fairly among management, labor, and consumers. The center is engaged in management development, management guidance, productivity research, promotion of joint labor-management consultations in industry, international productivity information exchange, and technical cooperation. Headquarters are in Tōkyō.

Japan Pulp & Paper Co, Ltd 日本紙パルプ商事[株]

(Nihon Kami Parupu Shōji). Firm engaged in the export, import, and domestic sale of paper, paperboard, pulp, and machinery. Incorporated in 1916. It is the industry leader in the domestic sale and export of paper products. The firm has numerous overseas offices, including several in Southeast Asia, one in New York, and one in Düsseldorf. Sales for the fiscal year ending March 1991 totaled ¥470.3 billion (US $3.4 billion), and capitalization stood at ¥15.2 billion (US $110.8 million). Headquarters are in Tōkyō.

Japan Railway Construction Public Corporation 日本鉄道建設公団

(JRCC; J: Nihon Tetsudō Kensetsu Kōdan). Public corporation engaged in railway construction and related projects with the aim of strengthening the nation's infrastructure. Established in 1964. The SEIKAN TUNNEL and SHINKANSEN lines are some of the major projects JRCC has undertaken. JRCC is also active in overseas feasibility studies on railway projects. The corporation fund stood at ¥134.7 billion (US $981.8 million) as of March 1991. Headquarters are in Tōkyō.

Japan Religious League 日本宗教連盟

(Nihon Shūkyō Remmei). A loosely affiliated council of religious groups, organized in 1946 to promote fellowship among religious organizations. It is composed of five federations of groups: the Association of Shintō Shrines (Jinja Honchō; see SHINTŌ SHRINES, ASSOCIATION OF), the Association of Sect Shintō (Kyōha Shintō Rengōkai; see SECT SHINTŌ, ASSOCIATION OF), the Japan Buddhist Federation (ZEN NIHON BUKKYŌ KAI), the Japan Association of Christian Churches (Nihon Kirisutokyō Rengōkai; see CHRISTIAN CHURCHES, JAPAN ASSOCIATION OF), and the UNION OF NEW RELIGIOUS ORGANIZATIONS OF JAPAN (Shin Nihon Shūkyō Dantai Rengōkai).

Japan Securities Finance Co, Ltd 日本証券金融[株]

(Nihon Shōken Kin'yū). Japan's largest securities financing company. Incorporated in 1927. In 1956 the company obtained a license under the Securities and Exchange Law. Its main lines of business include loans for margin transactions, bond financing, and general loans. Additionally, it initiated general stock loans in 1977 and bond loans in 1989. Its clients are largely securities companies but also include corporations and individuals. Operating income during the fiscal year ending March 1991 totaled ¥172.2 billion (US $1.3 billion). In the same year, capitalization stood at ¥10.0 billion (US $72.9 million). Headquarters are in Tōkyō.

Japan Shōgi Federation 日本将棋連盟

(Nihon Shōgi Remmei). The official association of SHŌGI (Japanese chess) players. Established in 1949. Its governing structure consists of over 160 active players of the fourth rank and above and retired professional players. The federation decides on promotions in rank (*shōgi* players are ranked at nine levels, or *dan;* below these are a number of classes, or *kyū*) and jointly sponsors with various newspaper publishing companies such title matches as the *meijin-sen, ryūō-sen, ōshō-sen, kisei-sen,* and *ōi-sen.* It also issues licenses to amateur players, trains new professionals, and publishes the monthly magazines *Shōgi sekai* (Shōgi World) and *Shōgi magajin* (Shōgi Magazine). The federation has 568 chapters (including overseas branches) and a total membership of about 20,000. Its head office is located in Tōkyō.

Japan Socialist Party 日本社会党

(JSP; J: Nihon Shakaitō). Political party; in 1991 it adopted the appellation Social Democratic Party of Japan (SDPJ) as the official English translation of its name. The first Japan Socialist Party was founded on 28 January 1906 by a coalition of radical and moderate socialists, including the radical SAKAI TOSHIHIKO and the moderates NISHIKAWA MITSUJIRŌ, KATAYAMA SEN, and TAZOE TETSUJI. However, the government disbanded the party on 22 February 1907 after radical members, such as KŌTOKU SHŪSUI, began to call for "direct action." The radical-moderate coalition dissolved along with the party, both factions going on to found a succession of other short-lived socialist parties and to engage in underground activities.

The post–World War II Japan Socialist Party was founded in November 1945 by socialists of various ideological positions who had been active in left-wing parties before World War II. Since then the party has been the major political opponent of conservative rule, principally that of the LIBERAL DEMOCRATIC PARTY (LDP). The JSP's sole experience as ruling party lasted only 15 months (1947–48), when it participated in a three-party coalition government headed first by the JSP chairman KATAYAMA TETSU and later by ASHIDA HITOSHI of the political party MINSHUTŌ. In the 1949 elections, however, the JSP suffered a drastic loss of seats (from 143 to 48) in the House of Representatives, in part due to its involvement in the SHŌWA DENKŌ SCANDAL.

During the early 1950s the JSP was riven by feuding between its left- and right-wing factions over foreign policy. The left opposed both the SAN FRANCISCO PEACE TREATY and the United States–Japan Security Treaty, advocated neutralism, and opposed rearmament, whereas the right was much more positive toward the peace settlement. Although from 1951 to 1955 the two factions had separate party organizations, the socialist movement gained ground electorally—particularly the left-wing socialists, who consolidated their ties with the SŌHYŌ group of labor unions.

In October 1955 the two socialist parties reunited, and the JSP rose to the height of its influence and popularity. In the 1958 elections for seats in the House of Representatives, the socialists won 166 seats, more than the one-third portion of total seats (467) that were required to block revision of the constitution, which had become a distinct possibility when the LDP established the COMMISSION ON THE CONSTITUTION in 1956. During the late 1950s the party gradually moved toward the left on a number of issues, and in 1959 a right-wing faction broke away, forming the DEMOCRATIC SOCIALIST PARTY in 1960.

The JSP led the attack on the policies of Prime Minister KISHI NOBUSUKE during the security treaty revision crisis of May and June 1960 (see PEACE MOVEMENT); in October 1960 the JSP chairman ASANUMA INEJIRŌ was assassinated by a rightist fanatic. From the mid-1960s the party entered a period of disarray as its leadership engaged in extreme left-wing rhetoric in a political atmosphere charged with disagreement over the Vietnam War. At its 27th party congress in 1966 the JSP adopted at the urging of left-wing members a rigorously Marxist-Leninist party platform, which it called "The Road to Socialism in Japan."

The JSP suffered a serious reverse in the 1969 lower-house general election, when its total of seats fell from 140 to 90. Some improvement of the party's electoral fortunes occurred under the seven-year joint leadership of its chairman NARITA TOMOMI and secretary-general ISHIBASHI MASASHI, but feuding continued between the left-wing faction and more moderate elements of the party. Early in 1977 EDA SABURŌ, secretary-general of the JSP in the early 1960s, defected from the party after losing his seat in the previous year's lower-house general elections and founded the Shakai Shimin Rengō (Social Citizens' League; now UNITED SOCIAL DEMOCRATIC PARTY). In late 1977 a number of prominent figures on the right of the party were expelled, and in December 1977, after a long period of strife and indecision, ASUKATA ICHIO became the chairman of the party. Although intraparty differences abated somewhat under Asukata's leadership, there were no significant innovations in policy or organization. The JSP remained closely dependent on the Sōhyō group for electoral backing (see also PRESSURE GROUPS).

From 1960 until the early 1970s the JSP joined forces with the JAPAN COMMUNIST PARTY (JCP) and won the election of a number of progressive mayors in major cities, including Tōkyō and Kyōto. However, from the mid-1970s the Democratic Socialist Party and the KŌMEITŌ gained increasing public support, and the JSP began to move away from the JCP and to develop a cooperative relationship with the Kōmeitō. In January 1980 the JSP and the Kōmeitō agreed to work toward the establishment of a coalition government that would exclude participation by the JCP.

Under Ishibashi Masashi, who assumed chairmanship of the party in September 1983, the JSP mounted a fierce attack on the policy of PRIVATIZATION of public corporations set forth by the LDP government of Prime Minister NAKASONE YASUHIRO, but the JSP failed to develop a viable alternative. In order to win a broader base of public support the JSP abandoned its Marxist-Leninist platform and at the 50th party congress held in January 1986 adopted a "New Declaration" of social democracy. Nevertheless, in the general election held in July 1986 the number of party seats in the House of Representatives fell from 112 to 85, and in September the party chairmanship passed from Ishibashi to DOI TAKAKO, Japan's first woman party leader.

Under Doi, public support of the party increased significantly, especially among women. In elections for the House of Councillors in July 1989, party seats increased from 20 to 46, and in lower-house elections in February 1990 the number of its seats rose from 85 to 136. However, in local elections held nationwide in March and April 1991 the party suffered unexpected reverses, and in July of that year Doi was replaced as chairman by TANABE MAKOTO.

Japan Society for the Promotion of Science   日本学術振興会

(Nihon Gakujutsu Shinkōkai). Semiofficial organization that helps implement Japanese government policies pertaining to the development of the sciences. Established in 1967; a predecessor with the same name had been established in 1932. The society provides postdoctoral fellowships and visiting professorships to researchers; carries on international scientific cooperation in accordance with the Japanese-American, the Japanese-French, and other formal agreements for scientific cooperation; arranges for exchanges of scholars; and publishes scholarly books in Japanese and English on the sciences and on Japanese culture.

Japan Society, Inc
ジャパン・ソサエティー（ニューヨーク）
(Japan Sosaetī [Nyū Yōku]). Private, nonprofit organization dedicated to the promotion of understanding and cooperation between the United States and Japan. Located in New York City, it was founded in 1907 by a group of US business leaders and revitalized after World War II under the leadership of John D. Rockefeller 3rd. Today, the society is an important source of knowledge on Japan. It sponsors cultural, educational, and public affairs programs and maintains the Japan House Gallery and the Japan Film Center.

Japan Steel Works, Ltd
［株］日本製鋼所
(Nihon Seikōsho). Integrated steel and machinery manufacturer. Established in 1907. The company caters to a variety of industries, including the automobile, electric machinery, information equipment, electric power, and shipbuilding industries, and is branching out into fields such as new materials, optical instruments, electronics, biotechnology, and communications equipment. In the fiscal year ending March 1991, sales totaled ¥133.3 billion (US $971.6 million) and capitalization stood at ¥20.0 billion (US $145.8 million). The company shipped 27 percent of its products overseas. Headquarters are in Tōkyō.

Japan Synthetic Rubber Co, Ltd
日本合成ゴム［株］
(Nihon Gōsei Gomu). Leading manufacturer of synthetic rubber. Its products, including rubber and plastics, are marketed under the brand name "JSR." The company was incorporated in 1957. Overseas offices are maintained in London and New York. Sales for the fiscal year ending March 1991 totaled ¥203.4 billion (US $148.3 billion), of which synthetic rubber accounted for 47 percent; emulsion, 14 percent; and synthetic resins and other products, 39 percent. Capitalization stood at ¥23.1 billion (US $168.4 million) in the same year. Headquarters are in Tōkyō.

Japan Teachers' Union→
Nikkyōso

Japan Times   ジャパンタイムズ
(Japan Taimuzu). The first English-language newspaper in Japan to be put out by Japanese publishers; started in 1897 by Zumoto Motosada (1862–1943) and Yamada Sueji (1848–1916) with the backing of government leader ITŌ HIROBUMI and with the support of educator FUKUZAWA YUKICHI. It was for many years the sole foreign-language news publication in Japan. The paper's news format was patterned on that of *The Times* of London and aimed at explaining Japan's position on international affairs. Dating back to the years before World War II, the *Japan Times* had close ties with the Ministry of Foreign Affairs, from which it received financial support during the war; however, it is no longer tied to any government agency. Between the years 1943 and 1956 the name was changed to *Nippon Times.* It continues to publish actively and, in addition to a daily edition, puts out the *Japan Times Weekly,* the *Student Times,* and various books and dictionaries, all in English. The paper's motto is All the News without Fear or Favor. Circulation was 75,000 in 1989.

Japan Tobacco, Inc
日本たばこ産業［株］
(Nihon Tabako Sangyō). Company that has a monopoly on the manufacture of tobacco products in Japan. Created in 1985 through the privatization of the Japan Tobacco and Salt Public Corporation, it is Japan's exclusive producer of cigarettes, although import and distribution have been liberalized to allow private enterprise participation. It had 24,200 employees in 1990. The company also holds a monopoly on the sale of salt. It is diversifying its business into seedlings and gardening supplies, real estate, pharmaceuticals, and engineering. Sales for the fiscal year ending March 1990 totaled ¥2.6 trillion (US

Japantown The Peace Pagoda (center) is a landmark in this San Francisco district.

$17.0 billion), and capitalization stood at ¥100.0 billion (US $653.3 million). Headquarters are in Tōkyō.

Japantown   ジャパンタウン
(Japantaun). Economic and symbolic center of the Japanese-American community in San Francisco. Although Japanese immigrants arrived as early as 1860, Japantown was not established until after the San Francisco Earthquake of 1906. Residents there built Japanese-style shrines and shops and began to refer to the area as Nihommachi, or Japantown. Today, numerous Japan-related businesses and cultural organizations are located in the area. Japantown hosts a variety of cultural events catering to the 12,000 Japanese Americans living in the area and is a popular attraction for visitors to San Francisco. Japantown underwent a major program of commercial redevelopment in the 1960s and 1970s.

Japan Travel Bureau, Inc
［株］日本交通公社
(Nihon Kōtsū Kōsha; commonly known as JTB). Japan's largest travel agency. Founded in 1912 as the Japan Tourist Bureau for the purpose of attracting foreign tourists, it was incorporated in 1945 as a nonprofit foundation (*zaidan hōjin*), changing its name to the Japan Travel Bureau. In 1963 the foundation's business department was reorganized as an independent private corporation, Japan Travel Bureau, Inc. The agency sponsors the sale of tickets for JR (Japan Railways) and other transport organizations, sale of accommodation coupons for hotels and inns, development of tourist resorts, and publication of travel literature and maps. The firm has about 309 branch offices in Japan and 54 offices overseas. Sales for the fiscal year ending March 1991 totaled ¥1.4 trillion (US $10.6 billion). In the same year capitalization stood at ¥1.9 billion (US $14.0 million). Headquarters are in Tōkyō.

Japan Ukiyo-e Museum
日本浮世絵博物館
(Nihon Ukiyo-e Hakubutsukan). Located in the city of Matsumoto, Nagano Prefecture. Opened in 1982. The museum holds a collection of approximately 100,000 prints ranging from early UKIYO-E works to modern prints. The collection was assembled over a 200-year span, beginning in the late Edo period (1600–1868), by five generations of the Sakai family (rich merchants based in the city of Matsumoto).

Japan–United States Educational Commission   日米教育委員会
(Nichibei Kyōiku Iinkai). Often referred to as the (Japan) Fulbright Commission. Based on the exchange program introduced by US Senator J. William FULBRIGHT in 1946, the

jar burials
1 From early through middle Yayoi times, jar burials, such as these at the Kanenokuma site in Fukuoka Prefecture, were apparently quite common.
2 A headless but remarkably well preserved skeleton was discovered in a burial jar at the Yoshinogari site in Saga Prefecture. Middle Yayoi period.

commission was established to administer educational and cultural activities between Japan and the United States. Its governing board is composed of 10 members, 5 each from Japan and the United States. The commission was established in 1952; until 1981 it was called the United States Educational (Fulbright) Commission in Japan. Since December 1979, however, the governments of the two countries have financed the commission on an equal basis, and, as a result, the name of the commission was changed to its present one. From the commission's inception until 1988, Fulbright grants were awarded to approximately 6,000 Japanese and 1,450 Americans. Grants are also provided by the commission under the Visiting American Lecturer Program to Americans who wish to teach or lecture in Japan. See also STUDY ABROAD.

Japan–United States textile talks
日米繊維交渉

(Nichibei Sen'i Kōshō). Contentious negotiations on bilateral textile trade carried out over a two-year period beginning in 1969. The talks began when US President Richard Nixon requested in February 1969 that Japan voluntarily restrain its exports of chemical and synthetic fibers to the United States. The Japanese government refused this request, and in June 1970 talks in Washington eventually broke down.

Complicating the negotiations was the linkage between progress in the talks and the reversion of Okinawa to Japan, scheduled for 1972, which gave the United States an additional bargaining advantage. After significant concessions from Japan, the textile talks concluded in October 1971 with an agreement consistent with the original proposal, under which Japan extended existing VOLUNTARY EXPORT RESTRICTIONS from cotton textiles to include all textile products. The textile talks proved to be one of the most acrimonious episodes in postwar US-Japan economic relations.

Japan Women's University
日本女子大学

(Nihon Joshi Daigaku). Private women's university located in Bunkyō Ward, Tōkyō. NARUSE JINZŌ founded the school in 1901 as the first liberal arts college for women in Japan. Under such educational principles as "true conviction," "creativity," and "service," the aim of the university is to educate its students as human beings, as women, and as Japanese citizens. In 1948 the school was given university status. Faculties are home

economics and letters. The university has its own kindergarten, elementary school, and junior and senior high schools. Enrollment was about 5,000 in 1989. See also WOMEN'S EDUCATION.

Japan Wool Textile Co, Ltd
日本毛織[株]

(Nippon Keori; also known as Nikke). Japan's oldest manufacturer of woolen textiles. Incorporated in 1896. The company is a major supplier of cloth for uniforms of civil servants. Sales for the fiscal year ending November 1990 totaled ¥73.9 billion (US $572.5 million), of which fabrics accounted for 53 percent; woolen yarns, 19 percent; carpets and blankets, 6 percent; nontextiles, 7 percent; and other products, 15 percent. The company was capitalized at ¥6.4 billion (US $49.6 million) in the same year. Headquarters are in Kōbe.

JAPIO
日本特許情報機構

(Japan Patent Information Organization; J: Nihon Tokkyo Jōhō Kikō). Nonprofit organization that collects, processes, and provides information on domestic and foreign patents and operates the PATOLIS (Patent On-Line Information System) data base. Established in 1985, JAPIO combines the services previously rendered by the Japan Patent Information Center and the Japan Institute of Invention and Innovation. PATOLIS stores information on more than 24 million domestic and foreign patents and provides on-line access to details concerning patents, utility models, designs, and trademarks belonging to corporations.

japonaiserie→japonisme

japonisme
ジャポニズム

(japonizumu). Also called japonaiserie. Type of artistic exoticism that appeared, along with phenomena such as chinoiserie and turquerie, in the latter half of the 19th century, predominantly in France. After the OPENING OF JAPAN to the West in the 1850s and 1860s, much Japanese art—primarily UKIYO-E and decorative arts—was imported into Europe and the United States, influencing France's impressionists and postimpressionists and England's Pre-Raphaelites in a variety of ways. Claude Monet, Edgar Degas, and Vincent van Gogh, for example, were well-known collectors of ukiyo-e. The influence of Japanese art was manifested both superficially, as in the use of fans, screens, and other Japanese objects as artistic subjects, and in more fundamental ways, with the use of bold colors and designs, the adoption of two-dimensional perspective and well-defined brush strokes, and the incorporation of nature in a specifically Japanese manner. Japonisme originated in the field of painting and later spread to music, architecture, and literature. 🔗 680–681

jar burials
甕棺葬

(kamekansō). A common form of burial in the prehistoric Jōmon (ca 10,000 BC–ca 300 BC) and Yayoi (ca 300 BC–ca AD 300) periods was in large, wide-mouthed jars (kamekan). Such jars usually were used for the bodies of children but only for the secondary burial of bones of adults; however, in northern Kyūshū during the Middle Yayoi period (ca 100 BC–ca AD 100) very large jars were made especially for the burial of adult bodies. These were deposited in unmarked pits or beneath dolmens. Usually burial jars were capped

with stones or other smaller vessels. See also FLEXED BURIALS; DOLMEN BURIALS; HŌKEI SHŪKŌBO.

JAS
日本農林規格

(Japanese Agricultural Standard; J: Nihon Nōrin Kikaku). The body of uniform standards based on a 1950 law regulating the content and description of agricultural and forestry products. The JAS was established with the objectives of increasing agricultural and forestry product quality, standardizing product descriptions, and protecting fair trade and the consumer. Items are designated by government ordinance according to the JAS law and stamped with a distinctive mark to indicate that they meet its standards. As of December 1990, 390 standards existed.

JCB Co, Ltd
[株]ジェーシービー

(Jēshībī). Largest credit card company in Japan. Incorporated in 1961. It issues the JCB Card, the sole international-caliber credit card of Japanese origin. JCB provides a variety of services to its 21 million members. In 1989 JCB signed cooperative agreements with the Bank of America and Société Générale of France. For the fiscal year ending March 1991, sales totaled ¥3.0 trillion (US $21.9 billion) and capitalization stood at ¥6.6 billion (US $48.1 million). Headquarters are in Tōkyō.

JDC Corporation
日本国土開発[株]

(Nihon Kokudo Kaihatsu). General contractor, principally engaged in the planning, designing, and construction of civil engineering works and buildings. Incorporated in 1951. For the fiscal year ending March 1991, sales totaled ¥343.6 billion (US $2.5 billion) and capitalization stood at ¥12.7 billion (US $92.6 million). Headquarters are in Tōkyō.

jellyfish
水母

(kurage). Floating animals belonging to classes Hydrozoa and Scyphomedusae of phylum Coelenterata and to phylum Ctenophora (comb jellies). The most common species in Japan is the mizukurage (Aurelia aurita), which has a translucent, whitish color and is found in bays. The akakurage (Dactylometra pacifica) has nematocysts (stinging cells) in its tentacles and may harm swimmers. The katsuo no eboshi (Physalia physalis utriculus), also known as denki kurage or electric jellyfish, is especially poisonous. The bizenkurage (Rhopilema esculenta) lacks tentacles with nematocysts and grows to 40 centimeters (about 16 in); it is salted for use in Chinese cooking. The mamizukurage (Craspedacusta sowerbyi) is a freshwater species said to have originated in China.

The jellyfish appears as a symbol of chaos in the opening section of cosmogony in the KOJIKI (completed in 712) and in 10th-century works that show Chinese influence. The Chinese have favored cooked dried jellyfish since ancient times, and its popularity at the imperial court in early Japan is thought to have been an imitation of the Chinese practice.

Jerome Relocation Center
ジェローム収容所

(Jerōmu Shūyōjo). Wartime relocation facility for Japanese Americans from California; located near the town of Jerome, in Chicot and Drew counties, Arkansas. In operation from 6 October 1942 until 30 June 1944, it held a maximum of 8,497 persons at any one time; a total of 10,241 persons were confined there. See JAPANESE AMERICANS, WARTIME RELOCATION OF; WAR RELOCATION AUTHORITY.

Jesuit mission press 切支丹版

(*kirishitan-ban*). The printing and publishing activities of the Jesuit missionaries in the late 16th and early 17th centuries, using a European printing press they imported into Japan.

The introduction of a European printing press to Japan in 1590 was due to the initiative of the Italian Jesuit Alessandro VALIGNANO. Owing to the unsettled situation of the Christian mission during the next decade (see CHRISTIANITY), the press was first operated in Japan in the remote areas of Kazusa in Hizen Province (now Nagasaki Prefecture) and Amakusa in Higo Province (now Kumamoto Prefecture). It was later transferred to the city of Nagasaki, where printing was begun in 1598. With the expulsion of the missionaries from Japan in 1614, the press was sent back to Macao, where it was used to print at least one more book.

The press was the first in Japan to use movable metal type. During its 25 years of activity in Japan it produced books and pamphlets (known collectively as *kirishitan-ban*). Religious works made up the largest category; these included liturgical manuals, prayer books, catechisms, and spiritual classics translated into Japanese and printed in either *rōmaji* (romanized Japanese) or Japanese script. A second category, language books, included dictionaries and grammars of the Japanese language and also Latin textbooks. A miscellaneous literary category included anthologies of Japanese and Chinese poetry, a translation of *Aesop's Fables*, and abridged versions of *Heike monogatari* and *Taiheiki*.

Relatively few copies of the original editions have survived. Copies of about 30 titles are preserved in institutions in Japan and Europe.

Jesuits イエズス会士

(*Iezusukaishi*). The Society of Jesus is a Catholic religious order for men founded by Ignatius of Loyola in Paris in 1534. One of its founders, Francis XAVIER, reached Kagoshima in 1549 and began the Christian mission in Japan. Numerous members of the order were martyred during the Tokugawa persecution. The Jesuits returned to Japan at the beginning of the 20th century and established Sophia University (Jōchi Daigaku) in Tōkyō in 1913. The order also runs Elizabeth University of Music in Hiroshima (Erizabēto Ongaku Daigaku), four high schools, and various parishes. As of 1991 there were 344 Jesuits in Japan. See also CHRISTIANITY; CATHOLIC MISSIONARIES.

JETRO 日本貿易振興会

(Jetoro). Acronym of the Japan External Trade Organization (Nihon Bōeki Shinkōkai); former English name Japan Export Trade Research Association. Japan's official trade promotion association, supervised by the Ministry of International Trade and Industry. Established in 1958. Although originally set up to promote exports from Japan, JETRO's activities have stressed both import and export promotion in recent years. JETRO offices overseas provide information on overseas markets to Japanese exporters and information to foreign concerns interested in the Japanese market. Other activities include sponsorship of market research, trade exhibitions, lectures, and missions to promote trade.

JGC Corporation 日揮[株]

(Nikki). Engineering firm. Established in 1928. Originally a specialist designer-builder of energy and chemical plants, the company recently has moved into factory automation, communications, biochemistry, regional development, and environment-related fields. The company has built more than 10,000 plants in 40 countries since 1965. For the fiscal year ending March 1991, sales totaled ¥279.0 billion (US $2.0 billion). Capitalization stood at ¥7.1 billion (US $51.7 million) in the same year. Headquarters are in Tōkyō.

Jiaozhou (Kiaochow) concession 膠州湾租借地

(*Kōshūwan soshakuchi*). Also spelled Chiaochou. Former Japanese territory in present-day Jiao County, along the southern shore of the Shandong (Shantung) Peninsula in China. Wrested from China by Germany in 1898, it was seized by Japan in November 1914 after Japan had declared war on Germany. The concession included the city of QINGDAO (Tsingtao), a surrounding leasehold between the Yellow Sea and Jiaozhou Bay, several offshore islands, railway rights to the provincial capital Jinan (Tsinan), and Jiaozhou Bay, an ideal site for a modern naval base. In 1915 Japan forced the Chinese government to accept in secret its acquisition of Germany's former rights to the Jiaozhou concession (see TWENTY-ONE DEMANDS). Japan's refusal to return these holdings after World War I led eventually to the MAY FOURTH MOVEMENT. At the WASHINGTON CONFERENCE in 1922, Japan agreed to return the concession to China.

JICA → Japan International Cooperation Agency

Ji-Cha (Chi-Ch'a) Autonomous Political Council 冀察政務委員会

(J: Kisatsu Seimu Iinkai). Council established in December 1935 to administer two North China provinces: Hebei (Hopeh) and Qahar (Chahar). Following the HE-UMEZU (HO-UMEZU) AGREEMENT and DOIHARA-QIN (DOIHARA-CH'IN) AGREEMENT, both of June 1935, the Guomindang (Kuomintang; Nationalist Party) agreed to withdraw from Hebei and Qahar. Chinese warlords there formed an independent council to act as a pro-Japanese buffer for the puppet state of MANCHUKUO. The two provinces, however, remained formally a part of Nationalist China, and the head of the council, General SONG ZHEYUAN (Sung Cheyüan), refused to act as a puppet of the Japanese. The council lasted until Japan's occupation of Beiping (Peiping; now Beijing or Peking) in the aftermath of the MARCO POLO BRIDGE INCIDENT of 7 July 1937.

Jichi Medical School 自治医科大学

(Jichi Ika Daigaku). A coeducational private medical school in Kawachi District, Tochigi Prefecture. Founded in 1972 by the prefectural governments of Japan in a joint effort to improve medical services in remote areas, the school is administered by a private foundation created for that purpose. Students receive loans for the six-year course of study and may be exempted from repayment if they agree to work at a medical facility in a remote area of their home prefecture after graduation. The facility and length of the assignment (usually nine years) are assigned by the prefectural government. Enrollment in 1988 was 634.

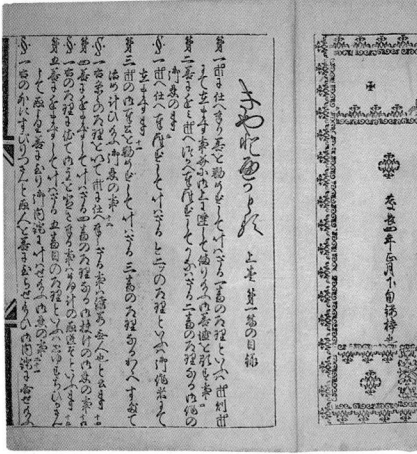

Jesuit mission press Set in movable metal type, the volume pictured here is *Giya do pekadoru* (1599, Leading the Evil to Good), a Japanese translation of a Christian religious tract.

Jichirō 自治労

(abbreviation of Zen Nihon Jichi Dantai Rōdō Kumiai; All-Japan Prefectural and Municipal Workers' Union). The largest labor organization in Japan, with a membership of over 1,250,000 in 1989. The union's membership comprises employees of local governments and public entities. Organized in 1954, Jichirō was affiliated with the General Council of Trade Unions of Japan (SŌHYŌ). When Sōhyō disbanded in 1989, Jichirō joined the Japanese Trade Union Confederation (RENGŌ). At that time some members opposed to joining Rengō left Jichirō and formed a separate organization. Under the Local Civil Service Law (Chihō Kōmuin Hō), union members do not have the right to bargain collectively or to strike. Attainment of these rights has been a primary goal of Jichirō, and the union has gone so far as to organize illegal strikes (see PUBLIC EMPLOYEES).

Jichishō → Ministry of Home Affairs

Jidai Festival 時代祭

(Jidai Matsuri; "Festival of the Ages"). Festival of the HEIAN SHRINE in Kyōto. Held annually on 22 October, it is one of the major festivals and tourist attractions of the city. It was begun in 1895 when the shrine was built to commemorate the 1,100th anniversary of the founding of the ancient capital HEIANKYŌ (now Kyōto). The main event of the festival is a procession of people dressed in costumes representing various periods of Japanese history and famous historical personages.

jidaigeki 時代劇

(period films). A general term for films set in various periods of Japanese history. Edo-period (1600–1868) *jidaigeki* featuring *samurai*, YAKUZA, and common folk are among the most popular. *Jidaigeki* range from low comedy to high drama and revisionist social criticism. They continue to attract a large audience.

Jidai Festival The procession of the "Festival of the Ages" departs from the Kenreimon, the southern gate of the Kyōto Imperial Palace, en route to the Heian Shrine.

Echoes of Japan in Western Art

In the late 19th century, Japanese art—represented most prominently by the *ukiyo-e* print—had a profound influence on artists in the West. The impact of *japonisme*, as this phenomenon is known, is probably most evident in the paintings of the French impressionists. But manifestations can also be seen in the works of other European and American painters, as well as in the forms, subjects, and techniques employed by various sculptors, designers, and architects of the late 1800s. For Western artists struggling to transcend artistic traditions that had remained essentially unchanged since the Renaissance, Japanese art represented a good deal more than mere exotica. *Japonisme* provided a rich source of inspiration and new approaches to composition and the use of line and color that, once assimilated, significantly transformed Western art.

Yano Yōko

Portrait of Père Tanguy by Vincent van Gogh. 1887. Oil on canvas. 92 x 75 cm. Musée Rodin, Paris.

La Japonaise by Claude Monet. 1876. Oil on canvas. 231 x 142 cm. Museum of Fine Arts, Boston.

Subjects

At its simplest level, *japonisme* is represented by the use of objects from Japan—lanterns, porcelain, folding screens, and the like—as artistic subjects. In the work at left by Vincent van Gogh, the European artist most closely identified with *japonisme*, six *ukiyo-e* prints provide the background motif. For the Monet portrait above, the artist dressed his wife in a flamboyant red *kimono* and surrounded her with an array of Japanese fans.

Approach to Nature

Western art had traditionally been dominated by human concerns; rarely did European artists select their principal subjects from the animal world. The arrival from Japan of affectionate portraits of birds, fish, insects, and other living creatures, depicted not as symbols or scientific specimens but simply as inhabitants of the animal kingdom in their natural state, was a revelation for Western artists. Illustrations from a picture book series by the Japanese artist Hokusai inspired a wide variety of decorative objects later produced in the West, including plates, vases, and bowls.

Gyoran Kanzeon by Hokusai, from *Sketches by Hokusai*. 1814. Woodblock print. Uragami Sōkyū-dō Co, Ltd.

The Carp by Emile Gallé. 1878. Colored glass. Height 45 cm. Musée des Arts Décoratifs, Paris.

Use of Color

The vivid coloring used in *ukiyo-e* prints helped transform the use of color in Western painting. European artists found new avenues for expression in the Japanese techniques of minimizing shading and defining structure with blocks of color. The work of Paul Gauguin, an avid collector of *ukiyo-e* prints, clearly reflects their influence. In the painting shown here, Gauguin's structural use of color has created a one-dimensional effect.

Plum Garden at Kameido by Hiroshige, from *One Hundred Views of Edo*. 1857. Color woodblock. Kanagawa Prefectural Museum.

Jacob Wrestling with the Angel by Paul Gauguin. 1888. Oil on canvas. 73 x 92 cm. National Galleries of Scotland, Edinburgh.

At left, *In Front of the Mirror* by Edgar Degas. Ca 1889. Pastels on canvas. 49 x 64 cm. Hamburger Kunsthalle, Hamburg. Below, *Woman Trimming Her Sidelock* by Utamaro. Ca 1789–1811. Color woodblock. Tōkyō National Museum.

Ornamentation

In Japan, not only artisans but also painters and printmakers produced works that were designed to have decorative or ornamental value. In *ukiyo-e* prints, this decorative quality was often created by the clever interplay between straight and curved lines in geometric patterns featured in the background and on the sumptuous kimono worn by the people pictured. The juxtaposition of a checkered dress with a striped background in the Bonnard painting below echoes the *ukiyo-e* technique of placing strikingly different patterns in the same plane.

The Close-Up

The practice of presenting a truncated view of a subject and magnifying one aspect, a common feature of *ukiyo-e* prints, was a radical departure from the traditional European approach to composition and was immediately adopted by the impressionists. Here, Degas's close-up study of a woman arranging her hair reveals the influence of artists like Utamaro.

Designs from Nature

Japanese artists had long found inspiration for their designs in nature—the flowing of a stream or the rise and fall of the waves on the sea—and were adept at capturing such images in abstract patterns. These patterns provided the stimulus for many of the swirling designs typical of the art nouveau style. Austrian painter Gustav Klimt's fabric patterns and background designs were heavily influenced by the Nō costumes and kimono in his own collection.

A depiction of two *kabuki* actors by Toyokuni III. 1861. Color woodblock. Private collection.

Detail from the *Beethoven Frieze* by Gustav Klimt. 1902. Paint on stucco. Österreichische Galerie, Vienna.

The Bird's-Eye View

The elevated perspective often used in *ukiyo-e* prints offered an alternative to Western art's one-point perspective, opening up fresh compositional possibilities. The American artist James Whistler, an admirer of the landscapes of Hiroshige, adopted the bird's-eye perspective for many of his own works.

Above, *Variations in Violet and Green* by James Abbott McNeill Whistler. 1871. Oil on canvas. 61 x 36 cm. Marlborough International Fine Art Est. At right, *Shinagawa Suzaki* by Hiroshige, from *One Hundred Views of Edo*. 1856. Color woodblock. Kanagawa Prefectural Museum.

A portrait of a woman holding wind chimes by Toyokuni III. Ca 1843–1847. Color woodblock. Private collection.

Woman in Checkered Dress by Pierre Bonnard. 1891. Oil on canvas. 160 x 48 cm. Musée d'Orsay, Paris.

Jigoku-zōshi An illustration from the *Scrolls of Hells* depicting the Iron Mill Hell, one of the various Buddhist hells awaiting the wicked. Late 12th century. Colors on paper. 27 × 435 cm. Nara National Museum. National Treasure.

jidan 示談

(settlement). A contract to resolve a civil dispute through discussion and mutual concession between parties rather than through litigation. In Japan most legal disputes are resolved by such settlements. In recent years there have been many negotiations involving groups of people adversely affected by pollution, by the unwanted side effects of drugs, or by a new building that blocks sunlight. In such cases, issues of criminal law sometimes complicate the matter, and settlement is often used as a supralegal means to resolve the conflict. Settlements often entail less time and expense than a court procedure. See also WAKAI.

Jidōsha Sōren 自動車総連

(abbreviation of Zen Nihon Jidōsha Sangyō Rōdō Kumiai Sōrengōkai; Japan Confederation of Automobile Workers' Unions). National organization of automobile workers' unions. Jidōsha Sōren was established in 1972 as the result of the reorganization of Jidōsha Rōkyō (Japan Council of Automobile Workers' Unions). It includes the workers' unions of the TOYOTA MOTOR CORPORATION; ISUZU MOTORS, LTD; HONDA MOTOR CO, LTD; NISSAN MOTOR CO, LTD; and other companies. Politically moderate, the organization became a member of IMF-JC (International Metal Workers' Federation–Japanese Committee; see KINZOKU RŌKYŌ) immediately after formation. It also joined RENGŌ (Japanese Trade Union Confederation) in 1987. Jidōsha Sōren had 697,000 members in 1989.

jieiken → self-defense, national right of

Jieitai → Self Defense Forces

Jien 慈円

(1155–1225). Buddhist prelate, poet, and historian. A member of the leading branch of the FUJIWARA FAMILY, Jien was the sixth son of the imperial regent Fujiwara no Tadamichi (1097–1164) and thus the uncle of FUJIWARA NO YOSHITSUNE. On the 13th anniversary of his death the court honored him with the posthumous name Jichin, by which he is also commonly known.

Jien became a Buddhist novice at the age of 10 and took orders at 14 at ENRYAKUJI, headquarters of the Tendai sect, where he received the priestly name Dōkai. He rose rapidly through the ecclesiastical ranks, as his birth entitled him, becoming abbot of the Hosshōji in 1178 and receiving the highest Buddhist rank bestowed by the court (Hōin; literally, "Seal of the Law") in 1181. At this time he changed his name to Jien. He was appointed palace chaplain to Emperor GO-TOBA (1180–1239; r 1183–98), who placed great confidence in him.

Over the years Jien exerted considerable political influence as a kind of gray eminence, assisting the proshogunate policy of his brother Kanezane and the SAIONJI FAMILY and attempting to dissuade Go-Toba from his design to overthrow the shogunate. To this end he wrote his famous GUKANSHŌ, the first historical work in Japan that attempted to deal critically and morally with the record of human events. He was also an eminent poet, believing that poetry was a way of life (*michi*) and an art that could lead to enlightenment. Ninety-two of his poems—second only in number to SAIGYŌ's 94—were included in the *Shin kokinshū*, and some 225 in other imperial anthologies. From the time of the JŌKYŪ DISTURBANCE, Go-Toba's abortive uprising of 1221, Jien was beset by frequent illness, and he finally died at a hermitage at the foot of Mt. Hiei.

jige 地下

(literally, "below, on the ground"). Also called *jigenin* ("people on the ground"). Low-ranking court officials of the Heian period (794–1185) who were not allowed to enter the Seiryōden, the emperor's personal quarters in the palace. An alternate term was *shimobito* (people below), in contrast to the *uebito* (people above) or TENJŌBITO, officials who had access to the emperor. *Jige* was also used more broadly to refer to commoners in general. See also COURT RANKS.

jigoku → hell

Jigoku-zōshi 地獄草紙

(Scrolls of Hells). A group of late-12th-century handscrolls (EMAKIMONO) alternating textual descriptions and paintings of the torments encountered by sinners in the Bud-

dhist hells. In all, 23 sections of text and 24 illustrations survive from the *Jigoku-zōshi*. There are also two later copies of hell scrolls in the Tōkyō National Museum. The surviving scrolls and detached segments from the original *Jigoku-zōshi* belong to several collections: in the Nara National Museum, whose scroll is considered to be of the highest quality, in the Tōkyō National Museum, and in the Seattle Art Museum. The Museum of Fine Arts in Boston possesses a segment of text and painting stylistically consistent with the Nara National Museum scroll. The *Jigoku-zōshi* segments are among the most important of the surviving early Japanese narrative paintings. The artists were probably highly trained professional Buddhist painters (EBUSSHI).

The short sections of text describing the hells come from Buddhist sutras such as the *Kisekyō*, the *Shōbōnenjokyō*, and the *Butsumyōkyō*. In Buddhist belief 8 great hells and 16 lesser hells are included among the so-called Six Realms of Existence (Rokudō) into which a person could be reborn repeatedly until attaining release from the cycle.

Jiji Press 時事通信社

(Jiji Tsūshinsha). Major Japanese news agency. Established in 1945 upon the demise of the Dōmei News Agency (DŌMEI TSŪSHINSHA). In its early years the firm concentrated on providing specialized news and information for use by companies, organizations, and government offices. After 1959 it expanded into a general news service for newspapers and broadcasting stations.

Jiji shimpō 時事新報

Newspaper started by the educator FUKUZAWA YUKICHI in Tōkyō in 1882. Fukuzawa's editorial policy was politically nonpartisan; he stressed news stories and feature articles on economics. After the Tōkyō Earthquake of 1923, financial management deteriorated, and the paper was absorbed in 1936 by the *Tōkyō nichinichi shimbun* (now the MAINICHI SHIMBUN). It was revived in 1946 and published for nine years before being absorbed in 1955 by the *Sangyō keizai shimbun* (now the SANKEI SHIMBUN).

jikan → vice-ministers

jikata 地方

Term referring to local administration during the Muromachi (1333–1568) and Edo (1600–1868) periods. During the former it referred to urban administration; during the latter, when it was in much wider use, it referred to rural administration.

Muromachi period. During the Muromachi period those shogunate officials who handled questions involving residences, estates, and legal disputes within Kyōto were designated *jikata*. The *jikata* office included a chief *jikata* (*tōnin*) and his subordinates. By 1379 the authority of the chief included the supervision of residences, estates, shops, and roads within the larger Kyōto metropolitan district.

Edo period. Whereas the Muromachi shogunate had been based on Kyōto and the considerable income it generated, the Tokugawa shogunate attempted to base itself on rural tax sources. Accordingly, Tokugawa leaders used the term *jikata* to mean rural administration rather than urban and to embrace a broader conception of civil governance. *Jikata* involved supervision of agriculture; encouragement of sound agronomics; management of resources; resolution of peasant disputes; and most important, operation of the complex land-tax system. Proper local administration was intended to bolster rural productivity and tranquillity in order to assure tax income and social stability.

The term *jikata* was also used to distinguish those SAMURAI (*jikatatori*) who held assigned fiefs from those (*kuramaitori* or *kirimaitori*, see KURAMAI and KIRIMAI) who received stipends. Such landholding vassals were also known as *jitō* or *chigyōtori.* The term *jikatatori* reflected the fact that such landholders were responsible for administering the lands assigned them and were supported by taxes they collected directly from the producers. In the cases of both shogunate and domains, it was the greater vassals who were *jikatatori,* while the stipendiaries tended to be minor vassals; and so the political role of *jikatatori* in the Tokugawa polity was appreciably greater than their numbers suggest.

Jikata hanrei roku　地方凡例録

(Principles of Rural Management). Eleven-volume work on local administration (JIKATA) during the Edo period (1600–1868) by Ōishi Hisataka (1725–94), who was an official of the Takasaki domain (now part of Gumma Prefecture). Citing precedents from history and local custom, the work discusses land surveys (KENCHI), land and miscellaneous taxes (NENGU; KOMONONARI), tax assessment (JŌMEN; KEMI), corvée labor services (SUKEGŌ), coinage, weights and measures, and rules of behavior for village officials (MURA YAKUNIN).

Jikei University School of Medicine　東京慈恵会医科大学

(Tōkyō Jikeikai Ika Daigaku). A coeducational private medical school located in Minato Ward, Tōkyō. Founded in 1881 as the Seiikai Medical Training Institute, it became Japan's first private medical college in 1921. Along with a faculty of medicine and four affiliated hospitals, the school maintains two research facilities. Enrollment in 1989 was 721.

jikifu　食封

(sustenance allotments). A part of the stipendiary system from the 7th century onward under which imperial kinsmen, high-ranking nobles, and temples and shrines were assigned a certain number of "vested households" (FUKO). These allotments, which entitled the assignee to half of the rice tax and all of the other taxes paid by those households, were originally instituted as compensation for local chieftains dispossessed by the TAIKA REFORM of 645, but they soon became an important source of income for the central ruling class under the RITSURYŌ SYSTEM of government. From the mid-Heian period (794–1185), the importance of such allotments diminished as many vested households were absorbed into privately held estates (SHŌEN).

jikiso　直訴

Direct appeal to high authorities, bypassing official channels; a form of osso. The term was used in the Edo period (1600–1868) to refer especially to petitions for the redress of grievances addressed to the shōgun or *daimyō. Jikiso* took various forms, including peasant uprisings (HYAKUSHŌ IKKI), written appeals presented directly to the ruler as he passed through the streets in his palanquin (*kagoso*), and pleas written and placed in an "appeals" box (MEYASUBAKO) to be read by the shōgun. Only the last form of *jikiso,* instituted in 1721, was sanctioned; others were punishable by death. After the Meiji Restoration of 1868, *jikiso* meant a direct appeal to the emperor. The Meiji government prohibited this form of protest but could not prevent it entirely. After World War II, when the doctrine of imperial sovereignty was abandoned, *jikiso* lost all of its meaning.

jikkan jūnishi　十干十二支

(literally, "10 stems and 12 branches"). Usually referred to in English as the sexagenary cycle or "Chinese zodiacal symbols"; also called *eto* in Japanese. An ancient system, originally Chinese, for counting days, months, and years; also used to indicate directions and the divisions of the day. The system consists of two ordered sets of symbols (Chinese characters): one of 10 units called the 10 stems or trunks (J: *jikkan;* Ch: *shi gan* or *shih kan*), and the other of 12 units called the 12 branches (J: *jūnishi;* Ch: *shier zhi* or *shih-erh chih*). The two sets were used together in 2-symbol combinations, 1 from each set (with the *jikkan* repeating six times and the *jūnishi* five times) to create a cycle of 60. In counting years the cycle was repeated ad infinitum.

It is thought that the 10 stems were first used to count days of the month (in three

The Ten Stems and Twelve Branches

The 10 stems or trunks *(jikkan)*

Chinese character	甲	乙	丙	丁	戊	己	庚	辛	壬	癸
On reading	*kō*	*otsu*	*hei*	*tei*	*bo*	*ki*	*kō*	*shin*	*jin*	*ki*

NOTE: The *on* reading is the Japanese approximation of the Chinese pronunciation of the character.

The 5 elements combined with yin and yang to give alternate names to the 10 stems

Five elements	木 *ki* (wood)		火 *hi* (fire)		土 *tsuchi* (earth)		金 *kane* (metal)		水 *mizu* (water)	
E and *to* (yang and yin)	*e* (elder)	*to* (younger)	*e*	*to*	*e*	*to*	*e*	*to*	*e*	*to*
Name	*kinoe*	*kinoto*	*hinoe*	*hinoto*	*tsuchinoe*	*tsuchinoto*	*kanoe*	*kanoto*	*mizunoe*	*mizunoto*

NOTE: The *no* in these combinations is the genitive particle. *Kane* becomes *ka* in its two combinations.

The 12 branches *(jūnishi)*

Chinese character	子	丑	寅	卯	辰	巳	午	未	申	酉	戌	亥
On reading	*shi*	*chū*	*in*	*bō*	*shin*	*shi*	*go*	*bi*	*shin*	*yū*	*jutsu*	*gai*
Animal name	*ne* (rat)	*ushi* (ox)	*tora* (tiger)	*u* (hare or rabbit)	*tatsu* (dragon)	*mi* (snake)	*uma* (horse)	*hitsuji* (sheep or ram)	*saru* (monkey)	*tori* (rooster)	*inu* (dog)	*i* (boar)

The stems and branches combined to form the cycle of 60

1 甲子 *kōshi (kasshi)* *kinoe ne*	11 甲戌 *kōjutsu* *kinoe inu*	21 甲申 *kōshin* *kinoe saru*	31 甲午 *kōgo* *kinoe uma*	41 甲辰 *kōshin* *kinoe tatsu*	51 甲寅 *kōin* *kinoe tora*
2 乙丑 *itchū* *kinoto ushi*	12 乙亥 *itsugai* *kinoto i*	22 乙酉 *itsuyū* *kinoto tori*	32 乙未 *itsubi* *kinoto hitsuji*	42 乙巳 *isshi* *kinoto mi*	52 乙卯 *itsubō* *kinoto u*
3 丙寅 *heiin* *hinoe tora*	13 丙子 *heishi* *hinoe ne*	23 丙戌 *heijutsu* *hinoe inu*	33 丙申 *heishin* *hinoe saru*	43 丙午 *heigo* *hinoe uma*	53 丙辰 *heishin* *hinoe tatsu*
4 丁卯 *teibō* *hinoto u*	14 丁丑 *teichū* *hinoto ushi*	24 丁亥 *teigai* *hinoto i*	34 丁酉 *teiyū* *hinoto tori*	44 丁未 *teibi* *hinoto hitsuji*	54 丁巳 *teishi* *hinoto mi*
5 戊辰 *boshin* *tsuchinoe tatsu*	15 戊寅 *boin* *tsuchinoe tora*	25 戊子 *boshi* *tsuchinoe ne*	35 戊戌 *bojutsu* *tsuchinoe inu*	45 戊申 *boshin* *tsuchinoe saru*	55 戊午 *bogo* *tsuchinoe uma*
6 己巳 *kishi* *tsuchinoto mi*	16 己卯 *kibō* *tsuchinoto u*	26 己丑 *kichū* *tsuchinoto ushi*	36 己亥 *kigai* *tsuchinoto i*	46 己酉 *kiyū* *tsuchinoto tori*	56 己未 *kibi* *tsuchinoto hitsuji*
7 庚午 *kōgo* *kanoe uma*	17 庚辰 *kōshin* *kanoe tatsu*	27 庚寅 *kōin* *kanoe tora*	37 庚子 *kōshi* *kanoe ne*	47 庚戌 *kōjutsu* *kanoe inu*	57 庚申 *kōshin* *kanoe saru*
8 辛未 *shimbi* *kanoto hitsuji*	18 辛巳 *shinshi* *kanoto mi*	28 辛卯 *shimbō* *kanoto u*	38 辛丑 *shinchū* *kanoto ushi*	48 辛亥 *shingai* *kanoto i*	58 辛酉 *shin'yū* *kanoto tori*
9 壬申 *jinshin* *mizunoe saru*	19 壬午 *jingo* *mizunoe uma*	29 壬辰 *jinshin* *mizunoe tatsu*	39 壬寅 *jin'in* *mizunoe tora*	49 壬子 *jinshi* *mizunoe ne*	59 壬戌 *jinjutsu* *mizunoe inu*
10 癸酉 *kiyū* *mizunoto tori*	20 癸未 *kibi* *mizunoto hitsuji*	30 癸巳 *kishi* *mizunoto mi*	40 癸卯 *kibō* *mizunoto u*	50 癸丑 *kichū* *mizunoto ushi*	60 癸亥 *kigai* *mizunoto i*

NOTE: The first of the two names for each of the combinations consists of the *on* readings of the two symbols. The combination of *kō* and *shi* (number 1) can be pronounced *kasshi. Otsu* becomes *itsu* in combination and undergoes other sound changes. The second of the two names combines an alternate name of the stem with the animal name for the branch.

groups of 10) and the 12 branches to count months of the year. The two series were subsequently combined into the cycle of 60. The 12 branches were also used to mark the time of day in combination with the concepts of yin-yang (see OMMYŌDŌ) and the five elements (wood, fire, earth, metal, and water). The two series were used to determine auspicious and inauspicious days and directions. It became the custom to refer to the 12 branches as animals; this contributed to the system's increasing use as a means of divination analogous to astrology.

This calendric and geomantic complex is said to have been first implemented in Japan by the empress SUIKO in 604. Two methods developed of naming the combinations of the cycle of 60. The simpler method was to use the *on* readings of the symbols (the Japanese pronunciation of their original Chinese sounds). These names are the first of the 2 names below each combination of symbols in the table. In the other, more complex method, each of the 12 branches was given the name of an animal: *ne* (rat), *ushi* (ox), *tora* (tiger), *u* (hare or rabbit), *tatsu* (dragon), *mi* (snake), *uma* (horse), *hitsuji* (ram or sheep), *saru* (monkey), *tori* (rooster), *inu* (dog), and *i* (boar). Each of the 10 stems was identified as either *yang* (*e* or elder brother) or *yin* (*to* or younger brother) and then a *yin-yang* pair of the stems connected with each of the five elements, as in *kinoe* (wood-*yang*) and *kinoto* (wood-*yin*). These names were combined with the animal names of the 12 branches to form names for the 2-symbol combinations of the cycle. These names are the second of the 2 names below each combination of symbols in the table. Thus the first unit in the cycle, the *on* reading of which is *kasshi*, becomes *kinoe ne* (wood-*yang* rat).

Among divinatory methods introduced with the 10 stems and 12 branches was *shier zhi* (shih-erh chih; J: *jūnichoku*, the 12 watches). These were a series of values, such as fulfillment or failure, applied to consecutive days beginning with the first day of the rat in the 11th month, the first day of the ox in the 12th month, and so forth through the first day of the boar in the 10th month of the succeeding calendar year. The casting of fortunes by this or similar means was often used when planning some endeavor, and there developed numerous indigenous superstitions surrounding the practice. Like the Chinese the Japanese believed that one took on the character of the animal of one's birth year: those born in the year of the rat (i.e., any year for which *ne*, or the symbol for rat, appeared in the combination) were restless, while those born in the year of the ox were patient. In Japan women born in the year *hinoe uma* (fire-*yang* horse), the 43rd year of the 60-year cycle, were thought to be particularly headstrong and inclined to oppress their husbands. See also CALENDAR, DATES, AND TIME; PERIODIZATION; KANREKI; KŌSHIN.

Jikkoku Pass   十国峠

(Jikkoku Tōge). Also called Hikanesan. Located in the western part of the city of Atami, eastern Shizuoka Prefecture, central Honshū. Situated within the Fuji-Hakone-Izu National Park, the Jikkoku Pass offers a panoramic view of 10 former provinces from Hitachi Province (now Ibaraki Prefecture) in the east to Tōtōmi Province (now part of Shizuoka Prefecture) in the west. Altitude: 774 m (2,539 ft).

Jikkunshō   十訓抄

Also known as *Jikkinshō*. Kamakura-period (1185–1333) collection of tales with moral lessons for the young. Published in 1252; authorship uncertain. The 280 stories, divided into 10 categories, are mostly gathered from various Heian-period (794–1185) works as well as from China and India. The stories, full of commonsense teachings and anecdotes, are humorous and often bizarre.

Jimmin Sensen Jiken→Popular Front Incident

Jimmu, Emperor   神武天皇

(Jimmu Tennō). The legendary first sovereign (*tennō*) of Japan, according to the ancient chronicles KOJIKI (712) and NIHON SHOKI (720). The *Nihon shoki* gives Jimmu's reign dates as 660 BC–585 BC—however, these impossibly early dates were arrived at arbitrarily, and there is doubt as to whether Jimmu ever existed.

The chronicles relate that Jimmu was the great-great-grandson of the sun goddess AMATERASU ŌMIKAMI. After growing up in the Takachiho Palace in Hyūga (probably what is now Miyazaki Prefecture in Kyūshū), he resolved at age 45 to conquer the YAMATO region. In an expedition that lasted several years he made his way along the Inland Sea and landed his forces northwest of Yamato. At first defeated by local chieftains, he ultimately subdued the area with the aid of a golden bird and was enthroned as Japan's first emperor.

Some scholars maintain that the myth surrounding Jimmu reflects the spread of YAYOI CULTURE from Kyūshū to the Kinai region (the general area around Yamato); some hold that it explains the origins of Japan's imperial line in terms of the conquest of the Kinai region by a horse-riding people from the Asian continent (see HORSE-RIDER THEORY); others consider Jimmu a composite of several figures including the legendary emperor SUIJIN and Emperor KEITAI (early 6th century). Whatever the case, it is likely that the ancestors of the present imperial house came to Yamato from Kyūshū.

jimoku   除目

Court ceremonies for the appointment of all but the most senior officials in the Heian period (794–1185). The two principal *jimoku* ceremonies were for appointment to offices in the capital (the so-called Tsukasameshi no Jimoku), and for appointing provincial officials (the Agatameshi no Jimoku). These ceremonies began to lose their importance in medieval times.

Jimokuji   甚目寺[町]

Town on the western border of the city of Nagoya in western Aichi Prefecture, central Honshū. The temple Jimokuji is located here. Pop: 31,282.

Jimpūren Rebellion   神風連の乱

(Jimpūren no Ran). Rebellion in 1876 by former *samurai* (see SHIZOKU) in Kumamoto Prefecture. In 1872 dissident former samurai of the former Kumamoto domain organized themselves as the Jimpūren (League of the Divine Wind). Angered by loss of privilege, they perceived the ordinance of March 1876 forbidding the wearing of swords (HAITŌREI) as the final indignity. About 170 Jimpūren members, led by Ōtaguro Tomoo (1835–76), attacked the Kumamoto garrison on 24 October but were subdued the following day.

Their action inspired the HAGI REBELLION, the AKIZUKI REBELLION OF 1876, and other uprisings.

jinaimachi   寺内町

(literally, "town within the precincts of a temple"). Also called *jinaichō*. A form of walled, fortified town that grew up around temples in the Muromachi period (1333–1568). *Jinaimachi* were particularly associated with the JŌDO SHIN SECT, whose adherents were deeply involved in the military struggles of the late 15th and 16th centuries (see IKKŌ IKKI). The various *jinaimachi* became major commercial centers. The *jinaimachi* may thus be considered halfway between temple towns (MONZEN MACHI) and CASTLE TOWNS. The modern city of Ōsaka originated as the *jinaimachi* for ISHIYAMA HONGANJI, one of the main religious centers. Other notable examples include Inami in Etchū Province (now Toyama Prefecture) and Kaizuka in Izumi Province (now part of Ōsaka Prefecture).

Jindai Botanical Park   神代植物公園

(Jindai Shokubutsu Kōen). Botanical park in the city of Chōfu, Tōkyō Prefecture. Opened in 1961. The 38-hectare (94-acre) park contains camellia, azalea, and peony gardens, among others, and flowering plum and cherry trees. Its main attractions are a huge greenhouse and a rose garden boasting 300 varieties of roses.

Jindaiji   深大寺

Temple in the city of Chōfu, Tōkyō Prefecture, belonging to the TENDAI SECT of Buddhism. According to tradition, Jindaiji was built in 733 as a temple of the HOSSŌ SECT but changed its affiliation to Tendai during the Jōgan era (859–877). Under the patronage of the MINAMOTO FAMILY, Jindaiji became a major center in eastern Honshū for the practice of ESOTERIC BUDDHISM. The temple was also patronized by the TOKUGAWA FAMILY. Of the many festivals associated with Jindaiji, the most popular is the Darumaichi (Daruma Fair; see DARUMA), celebrated on 3–4 March, which is believed to bring prosperity and good fortune to participants.

jingi   仁義

(Ch: renyi or jen-i). Moral concept formulated by the Chinese Confucian philosopher Mencius (ca 371 BC–ca 289 BC), who integrated what had been two separate virtues in the philosophy of Confucius: ren (jen; J: jin; benevolence or brotherly love) and yi (i; J: gi; righteousness or proper conduct). *Renyi* was the objective of the Kingly Way or ideal government; at the same time it is found potentially in everyone in the form of feelings of compassion and shame. In the Edo period (1600–1868) in Japan, the Japanese Confucian scholar ITŌ JINSAI maintained that *jingi* (renyi) was the most basic tenet of orthodox Confucianism. In a corrupted usage the word *jingi* in modern Japan refers to the code of conduct or formal greetings among gangsters (*yakuza*).

Jingikan→Dajōkan

Jingoji   神護寺

A temple-monastery of the esoteric SHINGON SECT of Buddhism. It was founded in the 9th century on the mountain Takaosan, just west of the river Kiyotakigawa, in the northwest sector of Kyōto. A temple complex called Takaosanji had been built on the same site by at least the end of the 8th century. WAKE

NO KIYOMARO, the most important early patron of Takaosanji, founded another temple, Jinganji, in Kawachi Province (now part of Ōsaka Prefecture) between 782 and 805. In 809 KŪKAI, the founder of Shingon esoteric Buddhism in Japan, arrived at the monastery on Takaosan and began giving instruction in Shingon Buddhism. In 824 Kiyomaro's son Wake no Matsuna moved Jinganji and its treasures (some of which survive today) to the present Jingoji site. The already existing Takaosanji and Jinganji merged to form an imperial temple, Jingo Kokuso Shingonji, commonly called Jingoji from then on.

Eleven of the monastery's art holdings have been declared National Treasures, including the image of Yakushi (Skt: Bhaiṣajyaguru), the Buddha of Healing, probably the best surviving example of Jōgan sculpture (late 9th century); the Takao mandala, dated 824–834, the oldest surviving painted mandala in Japan; and portraits of TAIRA NO SHIGEMORI and MINAMOTO NO YORITOMO, said to have been painted in the early Kamakura period (1185–1333) by FUJIWARA NO TAKANOBU.

Jingū Bunko 神宮文庫

(Shrine Library). Library known for its unequaled holdings on Japan's native SHINTŌ religion. It contains the collections formerly held by the Inner and Outer Shrines (Naikū and Gekū) of ISE SHRINE. The Outer Shrine Library, the Toyomiyazaki Bunko, was built in 1648. The Inner Shrine Library, the Hayashizaki Bunko, was built in 1687, housing ancient records pertaining to Shintō deities and to the emperors. The Inner Shrine collections were consolidated in 1873, and the library was placed under the Grand Shrine Office (Jingūshichō). In 1907 a new building was erected and officially named the Jingū Bunko; the Outer Shrine collection was added to it in 1911. The library's collection currently numbers some 250,000 volumes.

Jingū, Empress 神功皇后

(Jingū Kōgō). Also known as Empress Jingō. Legendary nonreigning empress (KŌGŌ). According to the chronicle NIHON SHOKI (720) she ruled as regent for 69 years in the late 4th–early 5th centuries, between the reigns of the legendary emperor Chūai and the emperor ŌJIN (her son), when there was no official sovereign. Modern scholars believe that the figure of Jingū, who was credited with great military exploits, is a composite of several ancient shaman-rulers. See also HIMIKO.

jinin → jinin

Jinkaishū 塵芥集

(Collection of Dust and Ashes). A domainal law code (BUNKOKUHŌ) of the Sengoku (Warring States) period (1467–1568); enacted by Date Tanemune (1488–1565; see DATE FAMILY), the lord of an extensive region in the provinces of Mutsu and Dewa, the northeastern region of Honshū, on 4 May 1536. The most complete extant version comprises 171 articles, making the Jinkaishū the most detailed code of its type. A major part of the text (arts. 16–75) is devoted to criminal law; other articles deal with the relations between military gentry and farmers (76–83), the regulation of trade in the domain (93–120), and marital problems (162–167). The absolute supremacy of the *daimyō* and his law is stressed. A related document in 13 articles, Kurakata no Okite (Regulations for Pawnbrokers), dated 7 April 1533, is attached. See also SENGOKU DAIMYŌ.

Jinkōki → Yoshida Mitsuyoshi

jinnin 神人

Also known as *jinin.* Dependents of Shintō shrines (*jinja*); one of several groups originating in the Heian period (794–1185) among people who sought to escape agricultural labor and public duties by subordinating themselves to powerful institutions or individuals and providing various services in exchange for protection. Religious functions were only a part of the relationship between the *jinnin* and their shrines. Some *jinnin* were tradesmen, artisans, and theatrical performers; others performed menial tasks. At the end of the 16th century the specialized functions of the *jinnin* disappeared, but the term was applied to certain low-ranking shrine personnel in the Edo period (1600–1868).

Jinnō shōtō ki 神皇正統記

(Chronicle of the Direct Descent of Divine Sovereigns). A history of Japan from the mythical founding of the country by the gods (*kami*) until the mid-14th century. It was written between 1339 and 1343 by KITABATAKE CHIKAFUSA (1293–1354)—a leader of the Southern Court at Yoshino after the failure of the KEMMU RESTORATION in 1336 (see NORTHERN AND SOUTHERN COURTS).

Jinnō shōtō ki states that "Great Japan is a divine land (*shinkoku*)." To many Japanese this meant that Japan was divinely protected by the gods. But to Chikafusa the most important reason why Japan was a *shinkoku*, and superior to other countries, was that it had "always been ruled by the line of the sun goddess, AMATERASU ŌMIKAMI." Behind his theory of a direct line (*shōtō*) of generational descent—that is, one sovereign per generation—there lay a desire to equate hereditary emperorship in Japan with ethical rule. A corollary to Chikafusa's theory was the belief that the repository of imperial virtue was the IMPERIAL REGALIA (mirror, sword, and jewels). Chikafusa also argued that when Amaterasu mandated the imperial family to reign over Japan eternally, she also granted certain other families, led by the Nakatomi (later called the FUJIWARA FAMILY), an equally sacred right to assist the throne.

Jinnō shōtō ki is probably best known as a historical tract designed to support the Southern Court's claim to legitimacy over the Northern Court, although, in fact, most of Chikafusa's contemporaries already accepted the Southern Court's legitimacy. Chikafusa also attempted to persuade leading warrior chieftains to join the Yoshino side, but his reactionary political views most likely alienated more chieftains than he persuaded. Nevertheless, his work was received by succeeding generations as a classical study of imperial loyalism and was even elevated to the status of a canonical text by nationalist scholars from the Edo period (1600–1868) on (see NAMBOKUCHŌ SEIJUN RON).

Jinsei gekijō 人生劇場

(The Theater of Life). Novel by OZAKI SHIRŌ (1898–1964). *Jinsei gekijō*, a bildungsroman with strong autobiographical elements, appeared in a variety of publications between 1933 and 1959; the first portion published in book form appeared in 1935 and was widely read and praised. The protagonist, Aonari Hyōkichi, an only son, leaves his village for the urban life of Tōkyō. The idealistic Aonari (whose name suggests the maturation of youth) undergoes a variety of experi-

ences in the city: he becomes involved with a student group, encounters romance, participates in a left-wing political movement, and begins to write novels. The story, spanning the years from the early Taishō period (1912–26) to the onset of the SINO-JAPANESE WAR OF 1937–1945, takes place against the background of a political situation that grows increasingly tense. At the close of the novel, Aonari feels a sense of nostalgia for his lost youth. *Jinsei gekijō*, praised for the warmth and color of its description, is Ozaki's best-known novel.

Jinshin Disturbance 壬申の乱

(Jinshin no Ran; Civil War of 672). War of succession following the death of Emperor TENJI, in which Prince Ōama, Tenji's younger brother, deposed Prince Ōtomo, Tenji's son and designated heir. The insurrection is named for the sexagenary cyclical designation, *jinshin*, of the year corresponding to AD 672.

At that time there was no fixed rule of succession. Tenji had expressed his preference for Ōtomo by appointing him grand minister of state (*dajō daijin*). Prince Ōama withdrew from the court and secured the support of local rulers, who resented the provisions of the TAIKA REFORM of 645, a policy of centralization which Emperor Tenji had devoted his reign to implementing and which Ōtomo seemed likely to continue. Within two months of the outbreak of hostilities in mid-672 the forces of the Ōmi court were defeated and Prince Ōtomo committed suicide. (Centuries later, in 1870, he was designated Emperor KŌBUN.) Late in 672 Prince Ōama took power as Emperor TEMMU (r 672–686). Ironically, as Emperor Temmu, Ōama vigorously carried out the reforms of the Taika edicts.

Jinshin Koseki 壬申戸籍

A census registration carried out in 1872–73 by the Meiji government; the first attempt at a nationwide census in Japan. It was named *jinshin* after the designation of the year 1872 in the traditional calendar and conducted pursuant to the Family Registration Law (Koseki Hō) of 4 April 1871. The last census carried out under this law was in 1886.

The basic unit for the Jinshin Koseki was the domicile or household (*ie*), and registration was based on the Confucian principle

of patrilineal descent. The male head (*koshu*) of each household was given full authority over its members and required to provide detailed census information on them and to record marriages, adoptions, the establishment of branch families, and any other changes in household composition. Such transactions were not legal until the *koshu* had formally registered them at a prefectural office.

The Home Ministry delegated collection and maintenance of the census registers to prefectural and local authorities, who sent statistical abstracts of them to the central government. This allowed the government to collect vital information for the formulation of public policy in areas such as taxation, conscription, and education. Though the Meiji government had an avowed policy of equalizing the four traditional social classes, in practice the Jinshin census continued to record class distinctions between nobility, former *samurai*, commoners, and former outcastes. For that reason, free access to these family registers is no longer permitted.

jinushisei → landlordism

Jinzūgawa 神通川

River in Gifu and Toyama prefectures, central Honshū, flowing north from northern Gifu Prefecture into Toyama Prefecture and emptying into Toyama Bay. The upper reaches, sometimes called the Miyagawa, converge with the Takaharagawa to form the Jinzūgawa. Numerous electric power plants are located along the river, and the port of Toyama forms a part of its mouth. In the 1960s the waters, contaminated with cadmium from a smelting plant, caused an outbreak of *itai itai* disease (see POLLUTION-RELATED DISEASES). Length: 120 km (75 mi); area of drainage basin: 2,720 sq km (1,050 sq mi).

Jippensha Ikku 十返舎一九

(1765–1831). GESAKU fiction writer and playwright; artist. Real name Shigeta Sadakazu. Born in the province of Suruga (now part of Shizuoka Prefecture). One of the most popular and prolific writers of the early 19th century, he is best known for his comic novel series TŌKAIDŌCHŪ HIZAKURIGE (1802–22; also known as *Dōchū hizakurige; tr Shank's Mare*, 2nd ed 1960). Renouncing *samurai* status, he began a career around 1790 as a JŌRURI playwright in Ōsaka. In 1794 he returned to Edo (now Tōkyō) and became a protégé of the publisher Tsutaya Jūzaburō. His first work of fiction, a KIBYŌSHI ("yellow cover") entitled *Shingaku tokeigusa*, was published in 1795. Thereafter Ikku published as many as 20 *kibyōshi* in a single year. In spite of his reputation as a humorist, the most reliable accounts describe him as having been somewhat cheerless in person and, at his worst, surly and at times even violent.

In a career spanning four decades he produced not only his *Hizakurige* series but also a staggering total of about 360 *kibyōshi* and GŌKAN ("bound volumes"). He wrote a large number of SHAREBON and NINJŌBON dealing with the pleasure quarters, many YOMIHON ("reading books"), and occasional nonfiction works, among them a commentary on the famous puppet play *Kanadehon chūshingura* (1748, The Treasury of Loyal Retainers) entitled *Chūshingura okame hyōban* (1803). He was active in the field of comic verse (KYŌKA and SENRYŪ) and was an accom-

plished artist, illustrating many of his own works (including *Hizakurige*). According to his contemporary Takizawa BAKIN, Ikku was the first fiction writer in Japan able to earn a living solely from the proceeds of his books.

Tōkaidōchū hizakurige depicts the comic adventures of a pair of commoners from Edo as they travel along the highway Tōkaidō from Edo to Kyōto and Ōsaka. Its first volume appeared in 1802, expanding finally to eight volumes in 1809. Capitalizing on its success, in 1810 Ikku began to publish a sequel, *Zoku hizakurige*, which grew to 12 volumes by 1822.

jiriki → tariki

JIS 日本工業規格

(Japanese Industrial Standard; J: Nihon Kōgyō Kikaku). Official standard for mining and industrial products approved by the Japanese Industrial Standards Committee in compliance with the Industrial Standardization Law (Kōgyō Hyōjunka Hō) of 1949. The 1949 law was designed to improve the quality of mining and industrial products and to elevate productivity through standardization. Areas covered include technical terminology, symbols, and signs; quality and performance of products; and testing and measuring methods. Products complying with the JIS standard are allowed to carry the JIS label. As of February 1991, 8,340 specifications had been set by the Ministry of International Trade and Industry (MITI), which supervises the standards program. The JIS system has been made applicable to foreign manufacturers since 1980.

Ji sect 時宗

(Jishū). Originally a mendicant order of Pure Land (Jōdo) Buddhists (see PURE LAND BUDDHISM), prominent from the 13th through the 15th centuries, which was transformed into a sect in the Edo period (1600–1868) and continues to the present. The Jishū was founded by IPPEN (1239–89), a wayfaring holy man (HIJIRI) trained in the Seizan school of the Jōdo sect. Ippen emphasized that the name of the Buddha AMIDA contained within it both Amida's attainment of Buddhahood and the salvation of all beings, united as a single, timeless event. Accordingly, he distributed paper talismans (*fuda*) inscribed with this name. He also practiced the *nembutsu* dance (*odori nembutsu;* a form of NEMBUTSU ODORI), originally an ecstatic dance celebrating the immediacy of salvation available in the name of Amida Buddha.

In his travels Ippen acquired many disciples, whom he organized into the Jishū. The name Jishū translates literally as "hourly group," but means "24-hours-a-day group," referring to its incessant devotion to the name Amida. The ideal Jishū life was one of impoverished, mendicant wayfaring, distributing paper talismans with Amida's name and thus saving all who received them.

The Jishū found its support largely among the warrior class, for whom it provided both ordinary funerals and services for battlefield deaths. Among Pure Land Buddhist groups, the Jishū alone strongly advocated the worship of native deities, since it regarded them as ultimately manifestations of Amida. Thus the Pure Land Buddhism of the Jishū was compatible with the local and clan religious requirements of the warriors.

Chief among the permanent institutions (*dōjō*) established by the Jishū was Shōjōkoji, also called YUGYŌJI, in Fujisawa

(Kanagawa Prefecture). The Jishū may have been the leading Pure Land Buddhist group in the 14th and 15th centuries, but it has so diminished in importance that today many Japanese have not heard of it.

jisha bugyō 寺社奉行

(commissioners of temples and shrines). An office of the Tokugawa shogunate (1603–1867). Its antecedents dated from the Kamakura (1185–1333) and Muromachi (1333–1568) periods, when commissioners (BUGYŌ) were appointed by the shogunate to supervise the affairs of major Shintō shrines and Buddhist temples. In 1635 the shōgun TOKUGAWA IEMITSU formalized the office of *jisha bugyō*, appointing four FUDAI *daimyō* who served in rotation at monthly intervals (*tsukibansei*). In addition to supervising the affairs of temples and shrines throughout the country, they oversaw judicial matters in HATAMOTO lands outside the Kantō region and supervised professional musicians, linked-verse (*renga*) poets, and *go* players, as well as service personnel in the shogun's household.

jishi 地子

Also called *chishi;* land rent, a term variously used from the establishment of the RITSURYŌ SYSTEM in the 7th century. It originally referred to the annual rent from state-owned rice lands (*kōden*) under the field-allotment system (see HANDEN SHŪJU SYSTEM). These lands were rented yearly, and the *jishi*, set at one-fifth of the crop, was collected by the central government. From the mid-Heian period (794–1185) the rent charged on private landed estates (SHŌEN) for rice land was known as *jishi*, the rent for other productive fields as *hatajishi*, and that for land occupied by dwellings as *yajishi*. From the late Muromachi period (1333–1568) land rent paid in rice was called *jishimai*, while that paid in cash was called *jishisen*. During the Edo period (1600–1868) *jishi* became the general term for taxes on urban residential land, paid in silver or copper coins. In some areas it referred to rent that was paid by tenant farmers.

jishimban and tsujiban 自身番と辻番

(*jishimban to tsujiban*). Two major forms of neighborhood civil patrol during the Edo period (1600–1868), making supplemental forces available to the city commissioners (MACHI BUGYŌ). *Jishimban* were officially approved patrol groups manned and supported by neighborhoods of commoners. Those in Edo (now Tōkyō) were formed during the late 1600s, and by the mid-19th century there were some 990 *jishimban* posts strategically located throughout commoners' sections of the city. *Jishimban* members patrolled at night, served as fire lookouts (*hinoban*), and apprehended and escorted suspicious persons to the city commissioners' offices. Initially these units were staffed on a rotating basis by neighborhood residents, but later the posts were filled by hire, often with diminished effectiveness.

Tsujiban were similar to *jishimban* except that they were manned and supported through regular levies imposed on *daimyō*, HATAMOTO, and GOKENIN. First established in Edo in 1629 to prevent murders and other street violence (see TSUJIGIRI), some 890 *tsujiban* were situated at strategic points in *samurai* residential areas.

Jishōji → Ginkakuji

Jissen Women's University
実践女子大学

(Jissen Joshi Daigaku). A private women's university in the city of Hino, Tōkyō Prefecture. The university traces its origins back to the Jissen Girls' School, which was founded by SHIMODA UTAKO in 1899. It became a university in 1949. It maintains faculties of literature and domestic science. Enrollment was 3,307 in 1989.

jitō
地頭

(estate stewards). Also called *jitō shiki.* Officials appointed by the KAMAKURA SHOGUNATE from among its warrior vassals. Along with the office of SHUGO (constable or military governor), the *jitō* was distinctive of the Kamakura period (1185–1333).

During the fighting in the TAIRA-MINAMOTO WAR (1180–85), local warriors began to style themselves as *jitō* (and also as *gesu,* a comparable but more common title) to justify seizure of administrative control over estates (see SHŌEN). The Minamoto chieftain, MINAMOTO NO YORITOMO, had been casting about for a reward system that would be acceptable to his followers but not grant them complete autonomy. He ultimately hit upon a disbursement scheme using the newly current title *jitō.* Recipients of that title would be guaranteed tenure in the office and the right to fees for estate services provided to proprietors. In 1185 the emerging Kamakura shogunate secured an authorization from the court to appoint *jitō. Jitō* were given rights confiscated from warriors associated with the Taira. This meant two things: that true fiefs were not granted since actual title to the land did not change hands and that the range of *jitō* appointments remained strictly limited. Large sections of the country had no *jitō.*

Jitō were the country's first land stewards who stood outside the estate system's regular chain of command. Early on, estate proprietors began directing their complaints of *jitō* lawlessness to the shogunate, and it was from this practice that the warrior regime's system of justice evolved. Throughout the period, reconciling antagonisms between *jitō* and proprietors was to be the shogunate's principal governmental concern.

After the Taira-Minamoto War, the next occasion on which large numbers of *jitō* were appointed was the JŌKYŪ DISTURBANCE of 1221, an attempt by the imperial court to regain ascendancy. Nevertheless, estates with a *jitō* were never more than a minority. The new *jitō* were assigned to the estates of the defeated aristocrats in central and western Japan, making the *jitō* a national institution. *Jitō* were especially prominent as local policemen and tax collectors, with the precise extent of authority determined by precedent. Whether these rights coincided with a domain's boundaries or were defined in some other way would thus vary widely. The *jitō*'s authority also gave him access to peasant labor, domain storage facilities, and specialty products. It was Kamakura's clear intention that most *jitō shiki* be hereditary, the shogunate merely reserving the right to renew investitures with each generation. The shogunate also served as arbitrator of family disputes over an inheritance. Vassal houses might hold multiple *jitō* rights scattered across the country, which meant that deputies (*jitōdai*) had to be appointed to administer far-flung territories.

The historical importance of *jitō* lies principally in their role in the warrior class's struggle against absentee proprietors based in Kyōto: *jitō* gained control over estates largely through infringement of older privileges. Estate owners bearing grievances against them had to lodge formal complaints with the shogunate, which could not afford to move too harshly against its own men. The most common abuses concerned taxes, either short delivery or unauthorized levies. The *jitō* could also exploit his police powers: extortion became a way of life, and the residents of an estate were often gradually reduced to subject status. A direct outgrowth of this was a decline in the proprietors' own powers of enforcement, which in turn led them to seek new solutions to their problem. One device, called *jitōuke,* involved the surrendering of full control over an estate in return for the *jitō*'s promise, confirmed by the shogunate, to deliver a fixed annual tax. A second device, *shitaji chūbun,* involved the physical partitioning of a domain between *jitō* and proprietor. Both of these bore witness to the worsening plight of estate owners.

By the period of the NORTHERN AND SOUTHERN COURTS (1337–92) *jitō* came to be subsumed under a more generalized category of local magnates—the "provincial men" (KOKUJIN). The assault against the traditional proprietors of estates was completed in the 15th and 16th centuries at the hands of a new class of warrior lords, SENGOKU DAIMYŌ.

Jitō, Empress
持統天皇

(645–703; Jitō Tennō). The 41st sovereign (*tennō*) in the traditional count (which includes several nonhistorical emperors); reigned 686–697. Second daughter of Emperor TENJI; wife of Prince Ōama (Tenji's younger brother), who later became Emperor TEMMU. After Temmu's death in 686, she gained control of state affairs and, following the death of the crown prince, formally ascended the throne as reigning empress in 690. During her reign she was responsible for completing and enacting the ASUKA KIYOMIHARA CODE, Japan's first set of administrative and penal laws. She relinquished the throne to her grandson (Emperor MOMMU) and became the first to assume the official title of *dajō tennō* (retired sovereign). She is also known as a talented *waka* poet. See also FUJIWARAKYŌ.

Jitsugyō Dōshikai
実業同志会

(Businessmen's Association). Small political party founded in 1923 by MUTŌ SANJI, president of Kanegafuchi Bōseki (Kanegafuchi Spinning Co). Its call for business tax cuts and further industrialization initially won support among financial circles in the Kansai region, though its laissez-faire economic policy did not sit well with small and middle-sized companies that preferred to rely on government protection and financial aid. Its electoral support never gave it more than 10 Diet seats. Often aligned with the RIKKEN SEIYŪKAI, it participated in the TANAKA GIICHI cabinet of 1927. Reorganized under the name Kokumin Dōshikai in April 1929, it disbanded in January 1932.

jitsugyō gakkō
実業学校

(vocational schools). A system of three-year vocational schools established in 1899 as an alternative to the general educational programs offered in the middle schools of the pre–World War II system. The *jitsugyō gakkō* provided training in fields such as engineering, agriculture, or commerce. There were two separate programs: one for graduates of the four-year compulsory elementary schools and the other for graduates of the KŌTŌ SHŌGAKKŌ (higher elementary schools). Most of the students were male. After World War II many of these vocational schools became regular high schools.

jitsurokumono
実録物

Documentary stories of the late Edo period (1600–1868). They were popular chronicles of historical events and the lives of folk heroes, often dealing with such themes as vendettas, succession disputes in the houses of feudal lords, shogunal tribunals, valiant warriors, brigands, or the tragic fate of star-crossed lovers. The *jitsurokumono,* which borrowed the practice of embellishing historical fact from KABUKI plays and YOMIHON, developed into a distinct genre of historical fiction by the beginning of the Kansei era (1789–1801). SAN'YŪTEI ENCHŌ, a Meiji-period (1868–1912) professional storyteller, entertained his audiences with narratives drawn from *jitsurokumono.* Taken down in shorthand and published, they attracted the notice of the writer-critic TSUBOUCHI SHŌYŌ, who advised the novelist FUTABATEI SHIMEI to adopt Enchō's conversational style.

jitte
十手

Iron weapon with a shaft about 46 centimeters (1.5 ft) long and an L-shaped hook parallel to the shaft just below the hilt; used to catch an opponent's sword blade and twist it from his grasp. Introduced from China, the use of this weapon developed as one of the martial arts during the Sengoku period (1467–1568). In the Edo period (1600–1868) *jitte* were used as a mark of office by shogunal constables (YORIKI AND DŌSHIN).

Jiun Onkō
慈雲飲光

(1718–1804; also known as Jiun Sonja). Monk of the SHINGON SECT, outstanding calligrapher, and Japan's greatest Sanskrit scholar. Born in Ōsaka. He received a Confucian education in his youth. When his father died, the young Jiun entered a Shingon temple in Ōsaka. He was then sent by the abbot to Kyōto to pursue an understanding of the Chinese classics under ITŌ TŌGAI.

Jiun was an outstanding scholar. His works were reprinted in 1926 by Hase Tamahide under the title *Jiun Sonja zenshū.* This collection, however, contains only the table of contents of Jiun's greatest work, the 1,000-volume Sanskrit study *Bongaku shinryō.* This opus exists only in manuscript form; it consists of literary references to and commentaries on Sanskrit in China and Japan, as well as the first thorough study of Sanskrit grammar in East Asia.

jiuta
地唄

(literally, "local songs"). A genre of traditional Japanese music. In its most common usage the term *jiuta* refers to the songs of the Kyōto-Ōsaka region, as distinguished from those of Edo (now Tōkyō). Written for voice with SHAMISEN accompaniment, these songs originated in the 17th century.

The varieties of *jiuta* pieces include the *shamisen kumiuta,* NAGAUTA, *hauta, tegotomono, jōruri-mono,* and *sakumono.* The distinctions between the various types of *jiuta* are based on the relative importance of the instrumental and vocal passages, the content, the strictness of form, and the sources of the songs. The most characteristic form is the song in two or three parts.

Although the *shamisen* is the characteris-

jitte An Edo-period example of this weapon, which was used to defend against sword attacks. Criminological Museum of Meiji University, Tōkyō.

Jizō A statue of the deity stands in a rice field. Jizō images are often placed along roadsides and dressed in bibs by worshipers.

tic instrument, it is the two major schools of KOTO (a thirteen-stringed plucked zither) music, the Ikuta and the Yamada schools, that are the present guardians of the *jiuta* tradition. With the appearance of instrumental virtuosi in the late 17th century, the *jiuta* also played an important role in theatrical music. Composers and musicians were sometimes known as *kengyō,* or master. One such man, Sayama Kengyō (d 1694), moved to Edo where he founded Edo *nagauta.* This school eventually broke with the *jiuta* tradition to become the primary music of KABUKI theater.

The current repertoire of *jiuta* includes both traditional and modern pieces. Many of the latter show Western influences, although more frequently in an increased formal freedom than in details of content. In recent times *koto* players far outnumber performers on the more demanding *shamisen,* and *jiuta* pieces are now usually heard in public as supplements to *koto* recitals.

Jiyū Minken Undō →Freedom and People's Rights Movement

Jiyū Minshutō →Liberal Democratic Party

Jiyūtō 自由党

(Liberal Party). 1. In 1880 the LEAGUE FOR ESTABLISHING A NATIONAL ASSEMBLY petitioned to create a national assembly. Even earlier ITAGAKI TAISUKE and other leaders of the FREEDOM AND PEOPLE'S RIGHTS MOVEMENT had advocated the formation of a political party in preparation for parliamentary government. On 29 October 1881 the Jiyūtō, Japan's first national political party, was founded. Other political parties, such as the Kaishintō (see RIKKEN KAISHINTŌ) and the progovernment RIKKEN TEISEITŌ, were founded soon after, but only the Jiyūtō could claim to be a direct outgrowth of the people's rights movement. Itagaki assumed the position of party president and NAKAJIMA NOBUYUKI was appointed vice-president; the standing committee included GOTŌ SHŌJIRŌ, BABA TATSUI, SUEHIRO TETCHŌ, and other prominent political leaders. UEKI EMORI and NAKAE CHŌMIN, both influenced by French political liberalism,

served as intellectual spokesmen for the new party.

The Meiji government amended the PRESS ORDINANCE OF 1875, issued restrictions on assembly (SHŪKAI JŌREI) and in other ways attempted to obstruct the growth of the new parties. The Jiyūtō was susceptible to these attacks, having become divided in its response to the FUKUSHIMA INCIDENT and other violent uprisings instigated by local Jiyūtō politicians, including ŌI KENTARŌ. On 29 October 1884, just before the CHICHIBU INCIDENT, a party convention voted to dissolve the Jiyūtō.

2. In October 1887 Gotō Shōjirō began to regroup the former members of the Jiyūtō to prepare for the 1890 elections for the new Diet (see DAIDŌ DANKETSU MOVEMENT). By 1890 three competing parties had emerged, but Itagaki united the three factions in September 1890, establishing the Rikken Jiyūtō (renamed Jiyūtō in March 1891).

In 1898 Itagaki and ŌKUMA SHIGENOBU, head of the SHIMPOTŌ (formerly the Kaishintō), combined their two parties into the KENSEITŌ. Japan's first party cabinet (see ŌKUMA CABINET) quickly disintegrated, but it was clear the government could no longer ignore the political parties. After the Kenseitō split in 1898, former Jiyūtō members rallied around ITŌ HIROBUMI when he formed the RIKKEN SEIYŪKAI in 1900.

3. Post–World War II party formed in 1945 by HATOYAMA ICHIRŌ; more properly called the Nihon Jiyūtō. It won the election of 1946 and YOSHIDA SHIGERU assumed the premiership. In 1948 the Jiyūtō merged with dissidents from the MINSHUTŌ to form the Minshu Jiyūtō (Democratic Liberal Party), but two years later it reorganized as the Jiyūtō (LIBERAL PARTY). In 1955 it merged with the NIHON MINSHUTŌ to form the Jiyū Minshutō (LIBERAL DEMOCRATIC PARTY). See also POLITICAL PARTIES.

Jiyūtō shi 自由党史

(History of the Liberal Party). Two-volume official history of the JIYŪTŌ (Liberal Party) compiled in 1901 by a committee of its successor, the KENSEITŌ (Constitutional Party), and published in 1910 after editing by ITAGAKI TAISUKE, the first president of the Jiyūtō. It emphasizes the role of Itagaki and other men from Kōchi Prefecture and ends

with the promulgation of the Meiji Constitution in 1889.

jizaikagi 自在鈎

Apparatus for suspending cooking pots over a traditional Japanese hearth, allowing for rotation of the pot and adjustment of the distance between pot and fire. It usually consisted of a vertically hung bamboo tube through which an iron rod, bent into a hook at the bottom end, was passed. The hooked end of the rod was fed through a hole in a horizontal crosspiece whose pressure against the rod held it at the adjusted height. The horizontal piece was often carved in the shape of a fish, fan, or good luck mallet (*uchide no kozuchi*). Traditionally the *jizaikagi* was considered the hearth god's lodging place.

jizamurai 地侍

Medieval yeoman warriors (*bushi*) who retained power as local magnates not in service to the shogunate. The decline of shogunate power late in the Kamakura period (1185–1333) allowed landholders (MYŌSHU) to seize actual ruling power in the villages; those who became militarized were known as *jizamurai. Jizamurai* gradually became regional military rulers (SENGOKU DAIMYŌ), their retainers, or simply rural warriors (GŌSHI). See also SAMURAI.

Jizō 地蔵

(Skt: Kṣitigarbha; "womb of the earth"). One of the most popular bodhisattvas in Japanese Buddhism. Jizō is usually represented as a monk with a jewel in one hand and a staff in the other. Jizō's vow to aid and benefit all suffering beings has made him an object of popular veneration from the Heian period (794–1185) onward. Jizō is often syncretized with native deities. He is particularly regarded as the savior of children and those beings suffering in hell. See also BODHISATTVA; DŌSOJIN.

Jōban Coalfield 常磐炭田

(Jōban Tanden). Located in southeastern Fukushima and northeastern Ibaraki prefectures, northern Honshū. It produced about 10 percent of the national coal yield at its peak, but all of the mines here were closed down by 1976.

Jōchō 定朝

(?–1057). Preeminent Buddhist sculptor in the Kyōto area during the mid-Heian period (794–1185). He is credited with creating an elegant Japanese style of sculpture (*wayō*), perfecting the assembled woodblock sculptural technique called *yosegi-zukuri,* and instituting the workshop system (BUSSHO) for the production of Buddhist sculpture. Jōchō received unprecedented recognition: in 1022, in honor of his work at the temple Hōjōji, he was given the rank of *hokkyō* by FUJIWARA NO MICHINAGA; in 1048, for his sculpture and restoration work at the temple Kōfukuji, he was elevated by the court to the rank of *hōgen.* Jōchō was the first Buddhist sculptor to be honored with these titles, formerly reserved for the highest-ranking members of the Buddhist clergy. Jōchō's single surviving work is the image of Amida carved in 1053 as the main icon of the Hōōdō (Phoenix Hall) of the temple BYŌDŌIN at Uji.

jochūgiku 除虫菊

(Dalmatian pyrethrum). Chrysanthemum spp. A perennial herb of the family Compositae. The species known as *shiro mushiyokegiku* (C. *cinerariifolium*) is native to

Dalmatia in the Balkan Peninsula and is cultivated in Hokkaidō and on the coast of the Inland Sea. The stem is 30–60 centimeters (11.8–23.6 in) long and the leaves are pinnately lobed. Both stem and leaves are covered with white hairs. The stem forms a single white head with yellow disk flowers inside. The dried, powdered head is used to make *katori senkō*, an incense that repels mosquitoes. The literal meaning of *jochūgiku* is "insect-repellent chrysanthemum."

jōdai   城代

(castellan or keeper of the castle). From the 16th century onward, it was customary for warrior lords to place trusted vassals called *jōdai* in charge of their castles during their absence. During the Edo period (1600–1868) the title was used to designate those officials commanding certain castles on behalf of the Tokugawa shōgun. Initially these officials included the *jōdai* of NIJŌ CASTLE in Kyōto, Sumpu Castle (see SUMPU), ŌSAKA CASTLE, and FUSHIMI CASTLE; after 1699 only two remained: the Sumpu *jōdai* as a post for a high-ranking bannerman (HATAMOTO) and the Ōsaka *jōdai* as a major post for middle-ranking hereditary (FUDAI) *daimyō*. Holders of the Ōsaka *jōdai* post frequently were promoted to the posts of Kyōto deputy (KYŌTO SHOSHIDAI) and senior councillor (RŌJŪ).

Jōdogahama   浄土ヶ浜

Coastal area, east of the city of Miyako, Iwate Prefecture, northern Honshū; faces the Pacific Ocean. Part of Rikuchū Coast National Park, it is noted as a swimming resort.

Jōdokyō → Pure Land Buddhism

Jōdo sect   浄土宗

(Jōdoshū). School of PURE LAND BUDDHISM founded by HŌNEN (1133–1212), known for its advocacy of NEMBUTSU, the practice of chanting the phrase *Namu Amida Butsu* (I take my refuge in the Buddha Amida), for the purpose of *ōjō*, rebirth in the Buddha AMIDA's Pure Land in the West. The first of the new Buddhist sects to emerge in the late Heian period (794–1185), it remains the second largest after its independent subsect, the JŌDO SHIN SECT, which was founded by SHINRAN.

Doctrinal Basis——The Pure Land faith is based on the early Mahāyāna corpus of Pure Land (Skt: *Sukhāvatī*) sutras: the Larger *Sukhāvatī-vyūha-sūtra* (J: *Muryōjukyō*), the Smaller *Sukhāvatī-vyūha-sūtra* (J: *Amidakyō*), and the *Amitāyurdhyāna-sūtra* (J: *Kan muryōju kyō*). Hōnen called these the Threefold Pure Land Sutras (Jōdo Sambu Kyō). Pure Lands (*jōdo*) are realms of purity, the residences of Buddhas and bodhisattvas, in contradistinction to the impure and polluted human realm. The Pure Land of Amida promises both the illuminating wisdom and eternal presence of its resident Buddha, known according to these attributes as Amitābha (Eternal Light) or Amitāyus (Eternal Life). Amida is also characterized as a Buddha of compassion: formerly the bodhisattva Dharmākara (J: Hōzō), he created his Pure Land through an aeons-long accumulation of merit and power and a series of 48 vows. The 18th vow, the most important, promises rebirth in this realm to all who call on Amida's name 10 times at death; this exemplifies Amida's compassionate response to sinful worldlings.

Foundation of the Jōdo Sect——The founding of the Jōdo sect is traditionally dated to 1175, the year Hōnen left his moun-

tain hermitage and descended to the capital of HEIANKYŌ (now Kyōto) to preach the selective or exclusive practice of *nembutsu*. It is now thought by some that Hōnen no more anticipated founding a new sect than Luther intended to split his church. It is likely that as he offered his interpretation of the Threefold Pure Land sutras in an exegesis of 1190, his departure from tradition was such that his pioneering and definitive personal statement of 1198, the *Senchaku hongan nembutsu shū* (also known as the SENCHAKUSHŪ), became inevitable. In a trance (*samādhi*) Hōnen had a vision of a manifestation of Amida. This mystical experience, reported in 1198 in the privately circulated editions of Hōnen's *Senchakushū*, legitimized a divinely instituted beginning for the Jōdo sect.

No school could be established without the permission of the state. Hōnen's willingness to forgo this world for the Pure Land and his renunciation of the monastic precepts as a criterion for salvation challenged both state and church officialdom, and consequently he was banned and exiled.

Hōnen did not advocate an abstract faith (*shinjin*) but favored the "10 recitations" of the *nembutsu* for achieving *ōjō*. Although in the Edo period (1600–1868) the influence of Shinran's understanding of the Pure Land as an ever-present state of grace came to be felt, the Jōdo sect largely retained its original abhorrence of the world and desire for the pure beyond.

Jōdo Shin sect   浄土真宗

(Jōdo Shinshū; often called the True Pure Land sect in English). One of the traditional 13 schools of Japanese Buddhism and a major form of PURE LAND BUDDHISM. Its founder, SHINRAN (1173–1263), used the term Jōdo Shinshū to denote the "true essence" (*shinshū*) of Pure Land teaching as expounded by his teacher HŌNEN, but the term later came to designate the sect (*shū*) that evolved around Shinran's teachings. The year 1224, one of the dates suggested for the compilation of his major work, the KYŌGYŌSHINSHŌ, is considered to be the year of the sect's founding. Until 1872, however, the sect was called Ikkōshū, Montoshū, or HONGANJI. Today it is frequently referred to simply as Shinshū, and sometimes in the West as Shin Buddhism. Jōdo Shinshū, consisting of 10 branches, claims the largest following among the Buddhist sects in Japan.

According to Shinran, the Pure Land tradition originated in the Primal Vow of the Buddha AMIDA to save all mankind, especially in a time when human degradation becomes manifest in ineffectual religious practices, spiritual bankruptcy, brutish egoism, and social chaos. Historically, such an age was called *mappō* (literally, "the end-time of the Buddhist Law"; see ESCHATOLOGY). It was in the midst of *mappō* that Hōnen founded an independent JŌDO SECT in 1175. Rejecting all existing forms of Buddhism, he proclaimed the recitation of the name of the Buddha Amida (NEMBUTSU) to be the sole practice suited for the age and relevant to human needs. Among his many disciples was Shinran.

When the emerging *nembutsu* movement, centered in Kyōto, was persecuted in 1207 for both real and imagined social abuses, Hōnen was exiled, several of his disciples were executed, and Shinran was banished. Though subsequently pardoned, Hōnen died in the spring of 1212 shortly after his return to Kyōto. Shinran was pardoned in 1211. When he returned to Kyōto around

1235, he found several of Hōnen's disciples preaching the *nembutsu* path, each according to his own interpretation. Thus Shinran attempted to transmit his master's true teaching. The *nembutsu* path taught by Hōnen's disciples eventually developed into the five branches of the Jōdo sect, and Shinran's teaching led to the formation of the Jōdo Shin sect. The basic goal of Shin Buddhism coincides with that of Mahāyāna Buddhism: realizing the wisdom to see things, including the self, as they truly are. In this tradition, however, such wisdom is brought forth from within each person by the transforming powers of Amida's Primal Vow and not through calculative thinking or self-generated effort.

The sect declined after Shinran's death in 1263. His mausoleum was named Honganji, Temple of the Primal Vow. With the appearance of the energetic RENNYO (1415–99), the eighth head abbot of Honganji, the sect showed a sudden, dramatic growth. The Jōdo Shin sect became one of the most influential Buddhist movements, especially among the masses. Later, because of a succession struggle, the Honganji split into two factions, the Honganji branch (Nishi or West Honganji) and the Ōtani branch (Higashi or East Honganji). In addition, there developed eight other rather small branches. During the Edo period (1600–1868) the Jōdo Shin sect secured a permanent place in society.

Jōei Shikimoku → Goseibai Shikimoku

Jōetsu   上越[市]

City in southwestern Niigata Prefecture, central Honshū, on the Sea of Japan. Formed by the merger of the cities of Naoetsu and Takada in 1971, it is the political, cultural, and industrial center of the region. Naoetsu was designated a provincial capital in the 8th century and prospered as a post-station town and port from the 14th century. Takada developed as a castle town under the UESUGI FAMILY and later under the Matsudaira. At present heavy and chemical industries predominate in the Naoetsu district, and light industries are being developed in the Takada district. Of interest are the remains of the fortress built by UESUGI KENSHIN. Jōetsu, known as the birthplace of skiing in Japan (see Theodor von LERCH), has an annual ski festival. Pop: 130,114.

Joffe, Adolf Abramovich→Ioffe
(Ioffe), Adolf Abramovich

Jogaku zasshi　女学雑誌
(Magazine of Women's Learning). First major women's magazine in Japan, with 526 issues published between 1885 and 1904. Originally called *Jogaku shinshi*, it was founded in 1884 by Kondō Kenzō, IWAMOTO YOSHIHARU, and Ōba Sōkichi. Iwamoto became its chief editor after Kondō's death in 1886. Starting as a Christian ethics magazine devoted to enlightening Japanese women about education, foreign affairs, and culture, it later focused more on literature and published works by such women writers as KISHIDA TOSHIKO (under the pen name Shōen), WAKAMATSU SHIZUKO, SHIMIZU SHIKIN, and MIYAKE KAHO.

Jōganjigawa　常願寺川
River in eastern Toyama Prefecture, central Honshū, originating in the Hida Mountains and flowing into Toyama Bay. It forms an alluvial fan at the entry into the Toyama Plain. The Shōmyō Falls of the Shōmyōgawa, a tributary, are the highest falls in Japan, with a head of 350 m (1,148 ft). Water is used for irrigation and for generating electric power. Length: 56 km (35 mi).

Jōgashima　城ヶ島
Island off the tip of the Miura Peninsula, Kanagawa Prefecture, central Honshū. It is connected with the Miura Peninsula by a bridge. The island, a tourist area, is famous because of KITAHARA HAKUSHŪ's poem "Jōgashima no ame" (The Rain of Jōgashima). Area: 0.9 sq km (0.3 sq mi).

Jōgū Shōtoku Hōōtei setsu
上宮聖徳法王帝説
(Traditions concerning His Holiness, Prince Shōtoku). Title of a small corpus of documents concerning Prince SHŌTOKU, one of the most influential political leaders of the early 7th century. One volume; compiler unknown. The original book is said to have been stored at the temple HŌRYŪJI in Nara. The only extant copy is a manuscript preserved at the temple CHION'IN in Kyōto that is believed to have been copied from the original some time during the Heian period (794–1185). The documents are valuable because they supplement the information given in the KOJIKI (712) and the NIHON SHOKI (720), Japan's earliest chronicles.

Jōhei and Tengyō rebellions→
Fujiwara no Sumitomo; Taira no Masakado

jōheisō　常平倉
(literally, "ever-normal granary"). Government granaries established to stabilize the price of rice. In years of abundant harvest the government bought rice cheaply and stored it; in years of famine or drought the government sold the stored rice to lower the price. The idea was originally developed under the Former Han dynasty (206 BC–AD 8) of China and was first introduced to the provinces of Japan in 759. The *jōheisō* were only occasionally effective during the Heian period (794–1185) and were abolished during the

Kamakura period (1185–1333). The idea was revived by several *daimyō* domains after the TEMPŌ FAMINE in the 1830s.

Johnston Report　ジョンストン報告
(Jonsuton Hōkoku). Also known as the Draper-Johnston Report. Report of a 15-member committee (headed by Percy H. Johnston, a New York banker, and William H. Draper, assistant secretary of the army) sent to Japan in March 1948 by the secretary of the US Army to evaluate political and economic conditions in Japan and Korea. Aside from discussion of currency exchange rates and foreign investment, the report recommended a lenient reparations settlement and other measures to accelerate Japan's economic recovery. It reflected a shift in US OCCUPATION policy from political and social reform to economic stability and rehabilitation. See also DODGE LINE; SHOUP MISSION.

joint and several obligation→
rentai saimu

Joint Staff College　統合幕僚学校
(Tōgō Bakuryō Gakkō). Educational institution for field grade officers in the SELF DEFENSE FORCES. It specializes in teaching and research in the field of joint military operations and administration. The college is supervised by the JOINT STAFF COUNCIL and is located in Tōkyō.

Joint Staff Council　統合幕僚会議
(Tōgō Bakuryō Kaigi). Advisory organization for the director-general of the DEFENSE AGENCY. It consists of the chairman, who is the highest ranking officer of the SELF DEFENSE FORCES, and the chiefs of staff of the Ground, Maritime, and Air Self Defense Forces. The council's principal function is to assist the director-general of the Defense Agency in drawing up an overall defense plan and in coordinating joint military operations. The council also supervises the JOINT STAFF COLLEGE.

joint-stock company　株式会社
(kabushiki kaisha, also pronounced *kabushiki-gaisha*; abbreviated as KK). The *kabushiki kaisha* is the Japanese equivalent of the joint-stock company or limited liability public company and the most common form of business entity in Japan. Most *kabushiki kaisha* are small by American standards; the overwhelming majority are capitalized at less than $460,000. Any business enterprise, large or small, is free to incorporate as a *kabushiki kaisha*. Virtually all such business entities are domestically run; the number of foreign-controlled *kabushiki kaisha* is small. The *kabushiki kaisha* is a juristic entity created by the COMMERCIAL CODE.

Formation—The *kabushiki kaisha* must be formed by at least seven promoters, who must prepare, subscribe to, and register articles of incorporation in the prescribed form. A heavy onus is placed on the promoters, or incorporators, who among other things are personally liable for all acts performed in establishing the company. They owe a fiduciary duty to the company in relation to those acts and must personally take up shares in the company. The promoters must also appoint directors and auditors at the time of formation, and these appointees are immediately required to petition the courts for the appointment of an inspector who must examine the promoters' activities. The promoters meanwhile call for subscriptions to the share capital of the company, and

when the shares have been fully paid for and allotted they must call a STOCKHOLDERS' GENERAL MEETING, which receives reports from the inspector and the promoters and appoints directors and auditors.

Shares in the *kabushiki kaisha* are transferable, although prior approval of the directors may be required. The Japanese corporation may acquire its own shares when it wishes to reduce its capital, when it takes over a company that is in fact one of its own shareholders, or when it is required by the Commercial Code to purchase shares from disgruntled shareholders.

Management—The management of the company is divided among the stockholders' general meeting, the board of directors, and the statutory auditors. The first two organs play roles similar to those of their Anglo-American counterparts, but the auditors potentially may play a more significant part in the management of the affairs of the company. Legal reforms during the Occupation period (1945–52) significantly altered the balance of power among these three organs of management. Prior to 1949 the general meeting was the supreme authority in all matters. Now, under article 230-10 of the Commercial Code, the general meeting has power only to pass resolutions on matters prescribed in the Commercial Code or in the articles of incorporation. There must be an annual general meeting, and other meetings may be held at the request of the board of directors or 3 percent of the shareholders. In general each share carries one vote, although the company may not vote its own shares, and preference shareholders may be denied a vote.

The concept of a board of directors was also introduced in 1949. Prior to that date each director possessed a general agency authority and could bind the company subject to any limitations prescribed in the articles. The board is now elected solely by the general meeting, and the articles of incorporation may not require that the directors be shareholders. There must be at least three directors, each of whom may be appointed for a term of up to two years subject to reappointment. The general meeting may also remove a director at any time by special resolution. The affairs of the corporation are now entrusted to the board, whose decisions are arrived at by a simple majority vote at a board meeting.

joint ventures　合弁会社
(gōben kaisha). Companies jointly owned by Japanese and foreign interests. In Japan the joint venture is a more common form of entry for foreign capital than it is in the United States or Europe for many reasons. Because of restrictions on direct foreign investment in Japan in the 1950s, 1960s, and early 1970s, non-Japanese companies were obliged to seek a Japanese partner. For foreign companies the joint venture offers the advantage of having access to Japanese staff and expertise, which it would otherwise have to acquire on its own. The most successful joint ventures appear to have been those in which the two partners have complementary strengths and objectives, with the Japanese side providing some of its best talent and resources and the foreign company supplying technology, capital, and other resources. Joint ventures between companies that have conflicting or competitive objectives have usually been less successful and have often been dissolved or bought out by one of the partners. Since the

1970s there have been increasing numbers of joint ventures involving Japanese firms in foreign countries.

Jōjitsu school 成実宗

(Jōjitsushū). Buddhist school centered on the study of the *Jōjitsuron* ("Treatise on Establishing Reality"), written by the Indian Buddhist scholar Harivarman (ca 250–350). The Sanskrit original has been lost, and the text survives only in a 4th or 5th century translation into Chinese. The treatise emphasizes *śūnyatā* (J: *kū;* see EMPTINESS) as the middle way, negating the dichotomy between the all-things-non-existent and all-things-existent theories. It draws upon central teachings of Mahāyāna Buddhism to interpret critically the Hīnayāna Sarvastivādin school and appears as a bridge between the two Buddhist traditions. It arrived in Japan via Korea with the SANRON SCHOOL and was counted among the six Buddhist schools of Nara (see NARA BUDDHISM).

jōka machi → castle towns

jōkō 上皇

Abbreviation of *dajō tennō* (retired sovereign), the character for *nō* being also read as *kō.* A formal title given to sovereigns upon abdication, although from the mid-Heian period (794–1185) onward they were more commonly known as *in* ("cloistered" sovereigns; see HŌŌ). The title *jōkō* was first assumed by Empress JITŌ at her abdication in 697 and became standard thereafter. In the period 1087–1192, when retired emperors dominated the government (see INSEI), there were often several retired emperors at any given time.

Jokō aishi 女工哀史

(Tragic History of Women Workers). Book about female textile workers by Hosoi Wakizō (1897–1925); published in 1925. With the writings of YOKOYAMA GENNOSUKE and the 1903 government report SHOKKŌ JIJŌ, it is one of the best-known books on workers during Japan's early stages of industrialization. *Jokō aishi,* which gives a comprehensive description of the extremely poor working conditions in textile mills, was based on the personal experiences of Hosoi and his wife Toshio (1902–83) as textile workers and labor activists. Japanese companies justified their exploitation of young farm girls by claiming the role of surrogate parents who taught traditional virtues while providing close supervision. However, many women tried to escape, and others frequently fell ill and died. Appearing only one month before his death, Hosoi's book was widely read but failed to produce any substantial changes in policy or practice. See also WOMEN IN THE LABOR FORCE.

jokōba 女紅場

Schools for girls of the early Meiji period (1868–1912). The first of its kind was established in Kyōto in 1872, with sewing, crafts, and English as the main subjects for the students, who ranged from age 12 to older married women. Similar schools founded in Kyōto and elsewhere also came to be known as *jokōba.* The Kyōto school, renamed the Kyōto Jogakkō in 1876 (now Ōki High School), created a training institute for *jokōba* teachers.

jokotoba 序詞

(preface). Also called *joshi.* Phrase of variable length preceding the main statement of a WAKA poem and joined to it by a metaphorical relationship or by a pun (KAKEKOTOBA) or other wordplay. In the following poem by Taira no Sadabumi (also called Taira no Sadafun; d 923) from the KOKINSHŪ, the first three lines are a preface linked to the statement of the poem by a pun on the word *uramite* ("to feel bitter" or "to see the underside"):

*Akikaze no
Fukiuragaesu
Kuzu no ha no
Uramite mo nao
Urameshiki kana*

But a glance is all,
White underleaves of arrowroot
Tossed by autumn winds—
Bitter though my thoughts have been,
Yet, still bitter do I feel.

The preface resembles the MAKURA KOTOBA ("pillow word" or conventional epithet) in that it modifies the main theme of the poem. The *makura kotoba,* however, is a set phrase of five syllables that modifies a set word, while the *jokotoba* is a freely composed image that may extend over two or more lines and modifies the remaining lines of a poem.

Jōkyū Disturbance 承久の乱

(Jōkyū no Ran). Attempt by retired emperor GO-TOBA in 1221 (Jōkyū 3) to overthrow the KAMAKURA SHOGUNATE. The death in 1199 of the shogunate's founder, MINAMOTO NO YORITOMO, sowed seeds of unrest among the vassals (*gokenin*) of the shogunate, and the murder in 1219 of the third shōgun, MINAMOTO NO SANETOMO, brought further internal strife. Court nobles seized this opportunity to issue a decree in 1221 calling for chastisement of the shogunal regent (*shikken*) HŌJŌ YOSHITOKI. In response Yoshitoki and HŌJŌ MASAKO, Yoritomo's widow, rallied shogunate forces under HŌJŌ YASUTOKI, who marched on Kyōto and defeated the supporters of the court. The shogunate deposed Emperor Chūkyō (1218–34), placed Emperor Go-Horikawa (1212–34; r 1221–32) on the throne, and exiled retired emperors Go-Toba and JUNTOKU. The shogunate assigned lands of the losers to vassals designated *shimpo* or "newly appointed" JITŌ (estate stewards); in Kyōto it established special shogunal deputies (ROKUHARA TANDAI) to keep the court under surveillance, making it clear that the shogunate ruled Japan.

jōmen 定免

Method used during the Edo period (1600–1868) to assess the annual land tax (NENGU). In contrast to the earlier KEMI, which assessed taxes according to the actual yield and differed from year to year, the *jōmen* method was determined by averaging the harvest over a span of time (commonly 5, 10, or 20 years) and remained fixed thereafter, except for times of exceptionally poor harvests. The method was introduced by the Tokugawa shogunate in 1722 as part of the KYŌHŌ REFORMS in order to ensure a steady income, and it was subsequently adopted by many domainal governments. Although it caused hardship initially, productivity increased while the tax did not, and it worked to the advantage of the farmers.

Jōmon culture 縄文文化

(Jōmon *bunka*). The Jōmon period (ca 10,000 BC–ca 300 BC) received its name from the cord-marked (*jōmon*) pottery that is present in most sites. Lasting more than 8,000 years, it witnessed early contributions to Japanese culture, including shamanistic practices, views of nature and higher life, fishing and shellfish gathering techniques, and certain features of the language. The Jōmon embodies some neolithic characteristics in the sense that it was not metal-using and was probably not exclusively a hunting and gathering economy. Opinions differ, however, as to whether any simple forms of agriculture existed during the later millennia of the period.

While some archaeologists include Incipient or Subearliest Jōmon (ca 10,000 BC–ca 7500 BC)—marked by the first appearance of pottery—as the threshold of Jōmon culture, others begin Jōmon with the earliest shellfish gatherers of the east coast, who left their remains at the Natsushima shell mound in the city of Yokosuka. These were the Earliest or Initial Jōmon people (ca 7500 BC–ca 5000 BC), who built simple surface shelters supported by thin poles and used bullet-shaped pots covered with a primitive cord-marking. Other cultural remains are sparse.

Early Jōmon people (ca 5000 BC–ca 3500 BC) developed small villages consisting of several square-shaped PIT HOUSES. They cooked and stored food in cord-marked, flat-bottomed pots and wicker baskets and used arrowheads, stone awls, all-purpose tanged scrapers, and chipped and occasionally some ground axes. (See also STONE TOOLS.) Earrings and other ornaments were worn.

The culture of the Middle Jōmon period (ca 3500 BC–ca 2500 BC; also dated as ca 3500 BC–ca 2000 BC) rose first in the central mountains and diffused toward the coasts. Many large sites in the Kantō and Chūbu regions consist of numerous house pits yielding vast quantities of pottery and other remains, suggesting considerable economic stability. These communities were usually located 2 or more kilometers (1.2 mi) apart, always close to springs. The diet consisted chiefly of nuts, fruits, wild animals, fish, and tubers and other sources of starch. The ideal pit house evolved with a superstructure supported by five or six posts around an open center with a central fireplace. Storage pits were common and were supplemented by large vessels, often heavily encrusted with decoration.

Pottery vessels in mountain sites were shaped for specific uses, and the use of various symbolic motifs reflected the feeling of closer contact with the supernatural. Female figurines increased in number and stone phalli appeared. Lamps or "incense burners" were made, and clay drum bodies were the trappings for ceremonies.

Artifact characteristics transcended regional boundaries, as deteriorating climatic conditions at the end of Middle Jōmon drove most of the population out of the mountains, sending people north and south in search of subsistence.

Late Jōmon (ca 2500 BC–ca 1000 BC or ca 2000 BC–ca 1000 BC) people settled in rather large groups along the east coast and used the same sites for long periods, their debris forming immense shell middens. Technical improvements included the toggle harpoon, which was employed extensively in the Tōhoku maritime zone by the end of this stage. The northern population hoped to ensure its survival by elaborating its ceremonies. In Late Jōmon, independent ceremonial sites consisting of stone circles came into existence (see ŌYU STONE CIRCLES). Repeated patterns on the pottery, coordinated with rim

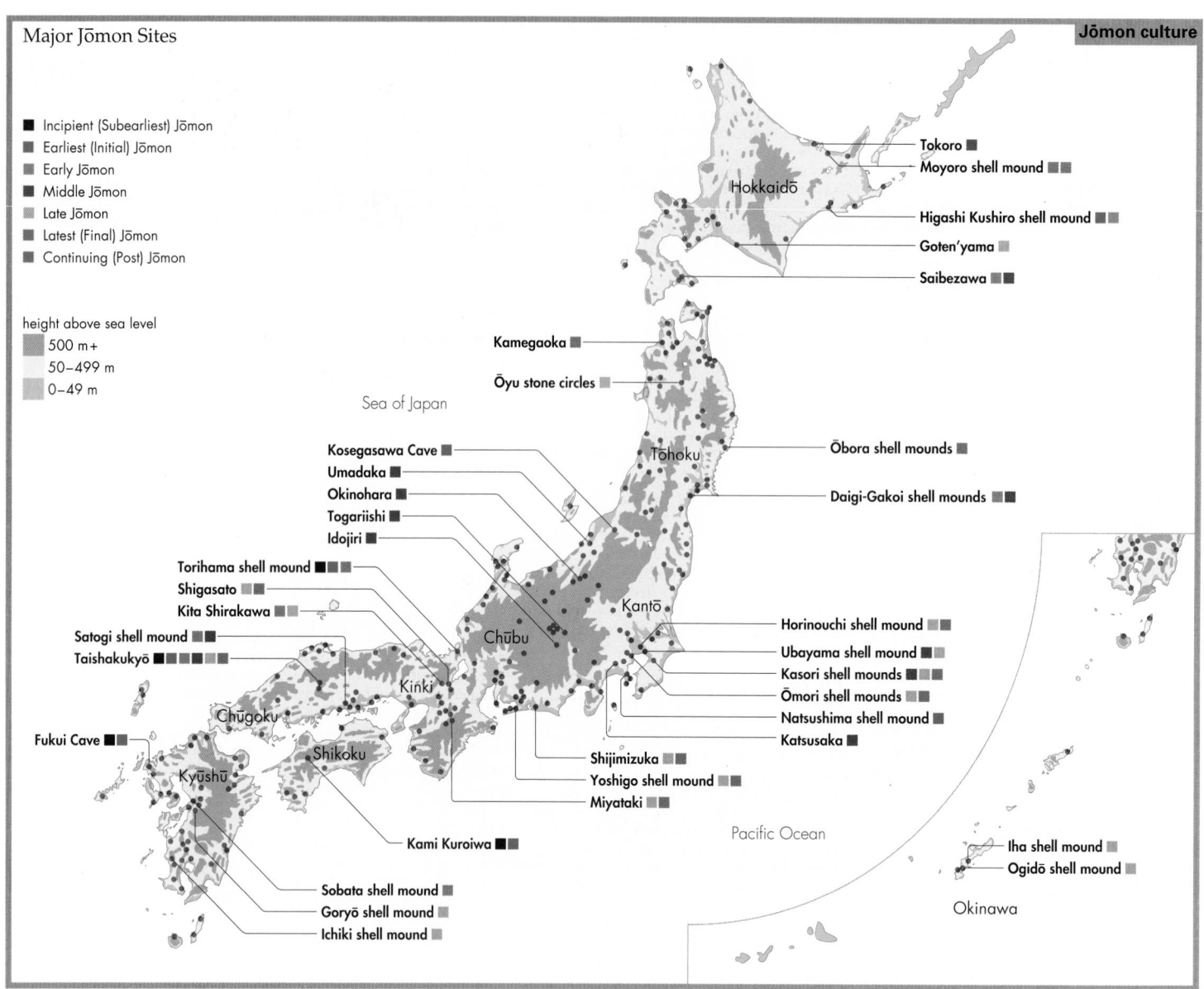

Major Jōmon Sites

■ Incipient (Subearliest) Jōmon
■ Earliest (Initial) Jōmon
■ Early Jōmon
■ Middle Jōmon
■ Late Jōmon
■ Latest (Final) Jōmon
■ Continuing (Post) Jōmon

height above sea level
■ 500 m+
■ 50–499 m
■ 0–49 m

Tokoro ■
Moyoro shell mound ■ ■
Higashi Kushiro shell mound ■ ■
Goten'yama ■
Saibezawa ■ ■

Hokkaidō

Kamegaoka ■
Ōyu stone circles ■

Sea of Japan

Tōhoku

Ōbora shell mounds ■
Daigi-Gakoi shell mounds ■ ■

Kosegasawa Cave ■
Umadaka ■
Okinohara ■
Togariishi ■
Idojiri ■
Torihama shell mound ■ ■ ■
Shigasato ■ ■
Kita Shirakawa ■ ■
Satogi shell mound ■ ■
Taishakukyō ■ ■ ■ ■

Chūbu

Kantō

Horinouchi shell mound ■ ■
Ubayama shell mound ■ ■
Kasori shell mounds ■ ■ ■
Ōmori shell mounds ■ ■
Natsushima shell mound ■ ■
Katsusaka ■

Fukui Cave ■ ■

Kinki

Chūgoku

Shikoku

Kyūshū

Shijimizuka ■ ■
Yoshigo shell mound ■ ■
Miyataki ■ ■

Pacific Ocean

Kami Kuroiwa ■ ■

Sobata shell mound ■
Goryō shell mound ■
Ichiki shell mound ■

Iha shell mound ■
Ogidō shell mound ■

Okinawa

projections and ornaments, for the first time produced a predictable decorative system. Smaller vessels had simple, trim shapes. Clay figurines simulating pregnant women with heart-shaped or triangular faces exist in large enough numbers in many sites for every household to have had at least one of its own. See JŌMON FIGURINES.

Latest or Final Jōmon (ca 1000 BC–ca 300 BC) marked a return to strong regionalism. The cultural differences are most striking between northern and southern Japan, the former becoming a more ritualized and tightly organized society, the latter fragmenting into more mobile and informal groups. In Hokkaidō, where rice cultivation was not introduced until much later, the surviving Jōmon-like stage is usually termed Zoku Jōmon, that is, Continuing Jōmon or Post-Jōmon.

In the south, in Kyūshū, the Latest (Final) Jōmon period saw the beginning of rice cultivation in Japan. However, it seems to have taken several centuries before paddy farming, agricultural villages, water management systems, and community ceremonies characteristic of the Yayoi culture developed. See also JŌMON POTTERY.

Jōmon figurines   土偶

(dogū). Clay images of humans and animals from 10 to 30 centimeters (4 to 12 in) high made by the hunters and gatherers of the Jōmon period (ca 10,000 BC–ca 300 BC). Figurines were already being made in eastern Japan as early as the Initial Jōmon period (ca 7500 BC–ca 5000 BC) and had become quite numerous by Middle Jōmon times (ca 3500 BC–ca 2500 BC; also dated as ca 3500 BC–ca 2000 BC). First crafted as flat, two-dimensional images, they were made three-dimensional in the Late Jōmon period (ca 2500 BC–ca 1000 BC; also dated as ca 2000 BC–ca 1000 BC). In the Final Jōmon period (ca 1000 BC–ca 300 BC), large figurines with distinctive faces were common. Some clay images continued to be made into the Yayoi period (ca 300 BC–ca AD 300), but these should not be confused with the HANIWA funerary sculptures of the ensuing Kofun period (ca 300–710). Most of the figurines represent human females and may symbolize pregnancy or fertility. See also JŌMON CULTURE.

Jōmon period   縄文時代

(ca 10,000 BC–ca 300 BC; Jōmon jidai). Prehistoric period during which the peoples of Japan followed a hunting and gathering way of life. It was preceded by the PALEOLITHIC PERIOD (pre–10,000 BC), from which it is distinguished by the presence of pottery, and was followed by the YAYOI PERIOD (ca 300 BC–ca AD 300), the distinguishing characteristics of which are the use of metals and wet-rice cultivation.

The Jōmon period is studied in terms of six subperiods, although archaeologists are not in complete agreement over the dates of the various Jōmon phases. The Incipient Jōmon period (ca 10,000 BC–ca 7500 BC) is a transitional period, marked by the combining of pottery making with late paleolithic stone-working techniques. It is not clear how pottery making originated in Japan, but it is clear that the world's oldest known pottery dates from between 10,750 and 10,000 BC and was excavated from FUKUI CAVE and other sites in southern Japan. Whether introduced from the Asian mainland or locally developed, the appearance of pottery does not appear to have been caused by or to have resulted in immediate changes in paleolithic subsistence or settlement patterns.

Initial and Early Jōmon Periods—The major innovation of the Initial Jōmon period (ca 7500 BC–ca 5000 BC) was the utilization of marine and coastal resources leading to the accumulation of the first SHELL MOUNDS. At this time the Jōmon cultural assemblage—including basic stone tool types, PIT HOUSES, clay figurines (see JŌMON FIGURINES), and cord-marked (jōmon) pottery vessels—was also established. The evidence of shell middens indicates that the economy was well rounded: not only were fish and shellfish collected, but deer and wild pigs were hunted and wild seeds and plant foods were gathered. From this time Jōmon culture was divided into two spheres, roughly corresponding to the deciduous forests of eastern Japan and the broadleaf evergreen forests of

the southwestern end of the archipelago, which preserved their differences until the end of the Jōmon period.

High sea levels caused by warm climates during the Early Jōmon period (ca 5000 BC–ca 3500 BC) turned coastal lowlands into tidal marshes, and huge accumulations of seashells and fish bones attest to the utilization of this resource through coastal gathering. In western Japan deep-sea fishing may also have been undertaken; similarities between the Sōbata pottery of Kyūshū and comb-pattern pottery of Korea indicate that there was waterborne contact.

Middle, Late, and Final Jōmon—The cultural center shifted from the coasts to the interior of the Kantō district, where large semisedentary villages developed during the Middle Jōmon period (ca 3500 BC–ca 2500 BC; also dated as ca 3500 BC–ca 2000 BC). This may have been a result of improved methods of exploiting available plant resources. Most archaeologists feel, however, that although the economy of this period drew on a wide range of wild resources, it cannot be considered a true agricultural one. A strikingly elaborate pottery appeared during the period. In the Late Jōmon period (ca 2500 BC–ca 1000 BC; also dated as ca 2000 BC–ca 1000 BC) a more vigorous marine economy developed along the Pacific coast of eastern Japan. The fishermen of this period invented a vast array of tools and techniques that allowed them to undertake true deep-sea fishing. The Final Jōmon period (ca 1000 BC–ca 300 BC) saw the spread of a series of elaborate pottery styles—called Kamegaoka-type pottery—along the Pacific coast from northern Tōhoku to the Inland Sea region. Throughout the Late and Final Jōmon periods, southwestern Japan was a largely separate cultural sphere. Ceramic similarities strongly suggest that there was regular contact between Kyūshū and western Japan and the Korean peninsula during the Final Jōmon period.

The introduction of rice farming to Kyūshū and the rapid spread of YAYOI CULTURE brought an end to the Jōmon lifestyle. Remnants of the Jōmon tradition—called the Zoku Jōmon—persisted in Hokkaidō until it developed into the SATSUMON CULTURE in the 8th century. See also JŌMON CULTURE; JŌMON POTTERY.

Jōmon pottery 縄文土器

(Jōmon *doki*). Earthenware made during the Jōmon period (ca 10,000 BC–ca 300 BC). Jōmon pottery is distributed throughout

Japan, from the Kuril Islands in the north to the Ryūkyū Islands in the south. It is brown to reddish in color and characterized by a cord-marked surface. Coil- or ring-built, it was not thrown on a potter's wheel. First called "shell mound pottery" and "Ainu pottery," it was eventually called Jōmon ("cord-marked"), a translation of the English term used in the ŌMORI SHELL MOUNDS excavation report by Edward S. MORSE in 1879. However, not all pottery of the Jōmon period is decorated with cord-marking.

The oldest pottery, belonging to the Incipient (also called Subearliest) Jōmon period (ca 10,000 BC–ca 7,500 BC) or earlier, was discovered in FUKUI CAVE in Nagasaki Prefecture. It has a coarse, linear-relief decoration (*ryū-semmon*). Widely used techniques of decoration in the Earliest (also called Initial; ca

7500 BC–ca 5000 BC) and Early (ca 5000 BC–ca 3500 BC) Jōmon periods include marking by a rolled carved stick (*oshigatamon;* rouletting) incising, shell-marking, and nail-marking with a split bamboo stick. The earliest forms of cord-marking did not appear until about 7500 BC and were done with simple strands of plant fibers. In Early Jōmon there was much twisting and knotting of multiple strands. Application of cord-marking within incised zones of decoration during Late Jōmon (ca 2500 BC–ca 1000 BC; also dated as ca 2000 BC–ca 1000 BC) was the only decorative technique to encompass the entire country; this tradition survived into the Latest (also called Final) Jōmon (ca 1000 BC–ca 300 BC) in the Kantō and Tōhoku regions.

Jōmon pottery

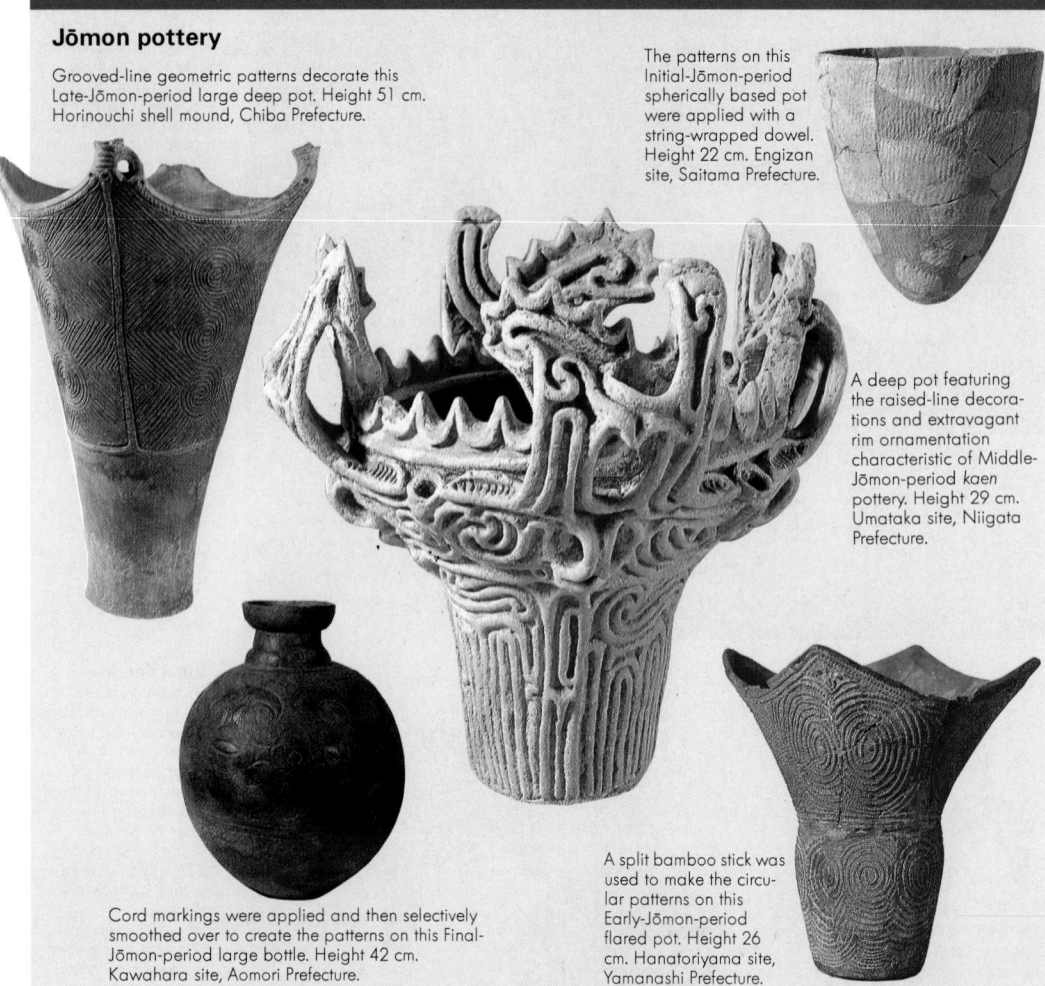

Grooved-line geometric patterns decorate this Late-Jōmon-period large deep pot. Height 51 cm. Horinouchi shell mound, Chiba Prefecture.

The patterns on this Initial-Jōmon-period spherically based pot were applied with a string-wrapped dowel. Height 22 cm. Engizan site, Saitama Prefecture.

A deep pot featuring the raised-line decorations and extravagant rim ornamentation characteristic of Middle-Jōmon-period *kaen* pottery. Height 29 cm. Umataka site, Niigata Prefecture.

Cord markings were applied and then selectively smoothed over to create the patterns on this Final-Jōmon-period large bottle. Height 42 cm. Kawahara site, Aomori Prefecture.

A split bamboo stick was used to make the circular patterns on this Early-Jōmon-period flared pot. Height 26 cm. Hanatoriyama site, Yamanashi Prefecture.

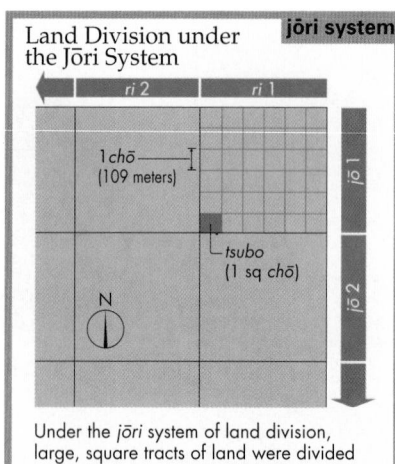

jōri system

Land Division under the Jōri System

1 *chō* (109 meters)

tsubo (1 sq *chō*)

ri 2   *ri* 1

jō 1   *jō* 2

N

Under the *jōri* system of land division, large, square tracts of land were divided into 36 smaller squares called *tsubo*.

Kamegaoka-type pottery (see KAMEGAOKA SITE) marked a cultural florescence in the Latest Jōmon period of northern Japan.

Initially pots were designed for boiling foods, but later in the Jōmon period some served as steamers, bowls without bottoms lined fireplaces, lamps or incense burners were hung from the rafters of PIT HOUSES, and foods were stored in large pots. Large jars were occasionally used for burials (see JAR BURIALS). More variety in shapes in the Latest Jōmon period took the form of cups, bowls, plates, pots, vases, ewers, and incense burners. See also JŌMON CULTURE; CERAMICS.

Joosten van Lodenstijn, Jan

ヤン・ヨーステン

(1556?–1623). One of the first Dutchmen in Japan. Born in Delft, the Netherlands. In 1600 Joosten was second mate on the Dutch trading vessel LIEFDE, which landed disabled in Kyūshū. Joosten, the English pilot William ADAMS, and other survivors were received by TOKUGAWA IEYASU. Joosten and Adams later became Ieyasu's advisers. Given a residence in Edo (now Tōkyō)—the place name Yaesu near Tōkyō Station is thought to be a corruption of his name—Joosten married a Japanese and received permission to engage in overseas trade. After the establishment of the DUTCH FACTORY at Hirado, he became a middleman between Dutch traders and the shogunate. Later, hoping to return to the Netherlands, he sailed as far as Batavia (now Jakarta) in Java but was denied permission by the Dutch authorities to proceed. On his way back to Japan, Joosten drowned when his ship sank in the South China Sea.

jōrei→local ordinances

jōri

条理

(natural reason). A Japanese legal term that essentially means "the nature of things" or "the right way of being." It is a translation of the German phrase "Natur der Sache." *Jōri* is important because of a proclamation by the Grand Council of State (DAJŌKAN) in 1875, which states that "civil courts of law shall base their judgments with reference to custom when statutory law is lacking and upon natural reason (*jōri*) when applicable custom is not to be found." As this statement is not negated by the present constitution, it should be understood as still being valid today. *Jōri* is also important because it functions as a standard of interpretation. As the substance of laws or legal acts must not be contrary to natural reason (*jōri*), the ultimate standard for the interpretation of laws and legal acts is *jōri*. This is also made clear in court decisions.

jōri system

条里制

(*jōrisei*). System of land division in the 7th and 8th centuries. Under the TAIKA REFORM of 645, tracts of land were divided into squares measuring 6 *chō* to a side (1 *chō* = 109 m or 358 ft). Counting from north to south, these units were designated *jō* 1, *jō* 2, etc; from east to west, the same units were called *ri* 1, *ri* 2, etc. Each of these units was further divided into 36 equal and numbered squares, called *tsubo*, each having an area of 1 square *chō*. Thus it was possible to indicate any parcel of land by specifying in which *tsubo*, *ri*, *jō*, *gun* (district), and *kuni* (province) it lay.

The system made it possible for the government to allocate land smoothly to individual cultivators (see HANDEN SHŪJU SYSTEM), and the rationalization of field boundaries

also encouraged cultivation of new lands. The designations went out of existence only with TOYOTOMI HIDEYOSHI's nationwide cadastral survey (KENCHI) of 1582, although land development under the *jōri* system had been discontinued at the beginning of the Heian period (794–1185). To this day, fields in the Kyōto-Nara-Ōsaka region retain the dimensions and contours of the ancient *jōri* system.

jōruri

浄瑠璃

Form of dramatic narrative chanting to SHAMISEN accompaniment that is commonly associated with the BUNRAKU puppet theater and that flourished during the Edo period (1600–1868). As applied to the puppet theater, *jōruri* refers to the part of the performance that does not involve the puppets, their manipulation, or the staging—i.e., the texts and their recitation.

According to legend, Jōruri was the name given to a rich man's daughter who had a one-night love affair with the warrior hero MINAMOTO NO YOSHITSUNE and later rescued him when he fell ill and was abandoned. References to the story occur from the late 15th century. By some time in the 16th century the *Jōruri hime monogatari* (Tale of the Lady Jōruri) had become part of the repertoire of minstrels who chanted popular pieces like it to the accompaniment of the *shamisen* (which had recently been introduced to Japan), and this style of chanting came to be called *jōruri*.

Development—*Jōruri* reached early maturity in the late 16th and early 17th centuries, by which time it was being used together with puppets to present dramatic performances in Kyōto. The period 1600–1686 is known as that of old *jōruri*, with separate developments in Edo (now Tōkyō) and the Kamigata, or Kyōto-Ōsaka, region. Works of this period are always recorded with the name of the chanter. The puppets enact the story of the text and are under the ultimate control of the chanter's words. The earliest *jōruri* playbook extant is *Takadachi* (1625), probably belonging to Satsuma Tayū (later called Jōun), a reciter who typified the violent Edo style of theater that appealed to audiences of low-ranking, underemployed *samurai*. Most popular were the Kimpira *jōruri*, tales of the fictional hero Kimpira. After the great fire of 1657 in Edo, some Edo chanters moved to Kyōto, taking with them the Kimpira *jōruri*.

It seems that Edo *jōruri* remained static until the end of the 17th century, but in Ōsaka, Inoue Harima no Jō (1632–85) com-

bined the violence of the Kimpira tales with elements of the traditional "soft" style of Kyōto and developed a new style, known as the Harima school, in the 1670s. Another contribution was made in Kyōto by Uji Kadayū (later known as Uji Kaga no Jō; 1635–1711), who had been trained in NŌ and helped change *jōruri* from a simple narrative to a more structured dramatic form, often in five acts. The greatest chanter of all, Takemoto Gidayū I (1651–1714), emerged from the Harima school in Ōsaka and was the founder of the GIDAYŪ-BUSHI style that still bears his name and prevails in the modern puppet theater. Gidayū I engaged in a rivalry with Kaga no Jō until the latter's death in 1711.

The great CHIKAMATSU MONZAEMON was Gidayū I's playwright. Although *Shusse Kagekiyo* (1686, Kagekiyo Victorious) is usually designated as the first of Chikamatsu's new *jōruri*, perhaps the greatest step forward was in 1703 with his *Sonezaki shinjū* (tr *The Love Suicides at Sonezaki*, 1961), the first puppet drama of contemporary life (*sewa-mono*).

Although *gidayū-bushi* is the most significant style of *jōruri*, there are others in addition to the Kimpira *jōruri* mentioned above. The different styles of *jōruri* chanting are known as *fushi* (*-bushi*). Most of the early chanters had *fushi* named after them (*satsuma-bushi*, *harima-bushi*, etc), but since the introduction of *gidayū-bushi* no other school of chanting has been successful. The live KABUKI theater, apart from the *gidayū-bushi* that serves mainly as a chorus in plays borrowed from the puppets, uses other styles of *jōruri* chanting such as TOKIWAZU-BUSHI (founded in Edo ca 1750) and KIYOMOTO-BUSHI (Edo, 1814).

Jōruriji 浄瑠璃寺

Also known as Kutaiji. A temple of the Shingon Ritsu sect of Buddhism (see EIZON). Located in Kamo Chō, Kyōto Prefecture. It is noted for the 12th-century architecture of its main hall and pagoda, its statuary, and the charm of its remote setting. There are legends suggesting that the temple was founded either in 739 or 982, but a 14th-century manuscript describes the construction by the monk Gimyō in 1047 of the main hall housing the image of Yakushi (the healing Buddha; Skt: Bhaiṣajyaguru). The main hall, reconstructed in 1108 to house nine images of AMIDA (Skt: Amitābha), was moved to its present site in 1157. The name Jōruriji (literally, "clear lapis lazuli temple") is thought to derive from the association of this jewel with the land of the Buddha Yakushi, formerly the main image enshrined there. Its statue of Kichijōten (Skt: Śrīmahādevī), dating from 1212, is now one of the best-known statues in Japan.

joseigo→feminine language

Josetsu 如拙

(early 15th century). Buddhist monk-painter of the temple SHŌKOKUJI in Kyōto and an early master of INK PAINTING (*suibokuga*). The earliest reference to Josetsu is found in the diary of Zuikei Shūhō (1391–1473), a scholar-monk of the Shōkokuji, which mentions Josetsu as the stonecutter commissioned by the shōgun Ashikaga Yoshimochi (1386–1428) in 1405 to carve a stone inscription honoring the memory of the great Zen master MUSŌ SOSEKI.

Several paintings are attributed to Josetsu, and at least two are firmly accepted as his: *Hyōnenzu* (ca 1413, Catching a Catfish with a Gourd; Taizōin, Kyōto) and *Ō Gishi shosen zu* (Wang Xizhi [Wang Hsi-chih] Writing on Fans; Kyōto National Museum). The *Hyōnenzu* has special importance as one of the earliest examples of Japanese ink landscape painting. The evocative range of hills in the distance, rendered in filmy ink washes, reveals Josetsu's interest in spatial tonality.

Jōshin'etsu Kōgen National Park
上信越高原国立公園

(Jōshin'etsu Kōgen Kokuritsu Kōen). Situated in central Honshū, in Niigata, Gumma, and Nagano prefectures. Comprises two separate mountainous regions (the Jōshin'etsu and the Myōkō-Togakushi regions) and has active volcanoes, a plateau, lakes, and hot-spring resorts. It is a popular mountain-climbing and skiing area.

In the Jōshin'etsu region lie the volcanoes TANIGAWADAKE and NAEBASAN, the latter of which slopes southwest to SHIGA KŌGEN, an extensive highland with marshland, small lakes, and forests of silver birch. South of the highland are two active volcanoes: SHIRANE-SAN, on whose slopes are MANZA HOT SPRING and Kusatsu Hot Spring (see KUSATSU), and ASAMAYAMA, at whose foot lies the summer resort town of KARUIZAWA. Myōkō-Togakushi, the smaller region, to the northwest, contains the peaks of MYŌKŌSAN, KUROHIMEYAMA, and TOGAKUSHIYAMA and has extensive forests of Japanese beech (*buna*) and many alpine plants. Area: 1,890 sq km (730 sq mi).

Jōsō Plateau 常総台地

(Jōsō Daichi). Group of diluvial uplands of the eastern KANTŌ PLAIN, stretching from southern Ibaraki Prefecture to northern Chiba Prefecture, central Honshū, on either side of the river TONEGAWA. The area is noted for the cultivation of Chinese cabbage and peanuts. In recent years many housing developments and industrial complexes have been constructed here. Elevation: 10–150 m (33–492 ft).

Jōtō Mon'in 上東門院

(988–1074). The "palace name" (*ingō*) of Fujiwara no Shōshi, daughter of FUJIWARA NO MICHINAGA. Shōshi entered the women's quarters of Emperor ICHIJŌ in 999 and became CHŪGŪ (empress) in 1000 when the former *chūgū*, FUJIWARA NO TEISHI, was appointed KŌGŌ. The writers MURASAKI SHIKIBU and IZUMI SHIKIBU were among Shōshi's ladies-in-waiting. Shōshi's sons became the emperors GO-ICHIJŌ and Go-Suzaku (1009–45; r 1036–45). In 1026 she became a Buddhist nun and retired to the palace for which she is named.

Jōwa Conspiracy 承和の変

(Jōwa no Hen). A political plot of 842 (Jōwa 9) believed to have been fabricated by FUJIWARA NO YOSHIFUSA, the powerful head of the Fujiwara family, to effect the downfall of the Tomo family. After the deaths of the retired emperor Junna (r 823–833) in 840 and the retired emperor SAGA (r 809–823) in 842, the officials Tomo no Kowamine and TACHIBANA NO HAYANARI were accused by Yoshifusa, apparently unjustly, of plotting a rebellion to enthrone Prince Tsunesada (825–884), a son of Junna and grandson of Saga who was the designated heir apparent to the reigning emperor, Nimmyō (r 833–

Jōshin'etsu Kōgen National Park
1 The steep walls on the eastern face of Tanigawadake are a popular challenge for rock climbers.
2 One of three crater lakes of the active volcano Shiranesan, Yugama bubbles continuously with mineral-rich water.

Josetsu Detail from *Wang Xizhi Writing on Fans*, showing the famous Tang-dynasty Chinese calligrapher at work. Early 15th century. Fan painting remounted as a hanging scroll. Ink and faint colors on paper. 84 × 33 cm. Kyōto National Museum.

Japan Railways Companies

	Hokkaidō Railway Co	East Japan Railway Co	Central Japan Railway Co	West Japan Railway Co	Shikoku Railway Co	Kyūshū Railway Co	Japan Freight Railway Co	Total
Route length								
Kilometers	2,629	7,498	1,983	5,108	856	2,101	10,136	20,175*
Miles	1,633	4,659	1,232	3,174	532	1,305	6,297	12,535
Employees	12,060	79,883	21,669	47,987	4,201	13,883	11,526	191,209
Operating revenue (in billions of yen)	106.3	1,949.9	1,130.7	917.2	51.0	160.4	215.2	4,530.7
Equity capital (in billions of yen)	9.0	200.0	112.0	100.0	3.5	16.0	19.0	459.5

*Totals for route length do not include figures for the Japan Freight Railway Co, which shares track with other companies. Route length figures are as of 31 December 1990; all other figures are as of the end of the 1990 fiscal year (31 March 1991).
SOURCE: Ministry of Transport.

850). Kowamine and Hayanari were exiled, and Prince Tsunesada was deposed. His replacement by Prince Michiyasu, Yoshifusa's nephew, eventually paved the way for a permanent Fujiwara REGENCY GOVERNMENT.

joya no kane   除夜の鐘

(New Year's Eve bells). Beginning on New Year's Eve and continuing into New Year's Day, the bells in Buddhist temples in Japan are rung each year to announce the passing of the old year and the coming of the new. Because of the Buddhist belief that human beings are plagued by 108 earthly desires or passions (*bonnō*), the bells are rung a total of 108 times; with each toll of the bell, one desire is dispelled.

Jōyō   城陽[市]

City in southern Kyōto Prefecture, central Honshū, some 19 km (12 mi) south of Kyōto. Farm products include rice, pears, sweet potatoes, and tea. With convenient transportation Jōyō has become a suburb of Kyōto. The gold and silver thread used in Nishijin fabrics (see NISHIJIN-ORI) is manufactured in Jōyō. Pop: 84,770.

Jōyō Bank, Ltd   [株]常陽銀行

(Jōyō Ginkō). Regional bank based in Ibaraki Prefecture. Incorporated in 1935. It has 163 domestic branches, a branch in New York, and a representative office in London. Its total assets for the fiscal year ending March 1991 reached ¥7.4 trillion (US $53.9 billion), and total deposits were ¥6.2 trillion (US $45.2 billion). The bank was capitalized at ¥68.8 billion (US $501.4 million) in the same year. Headquarters are in the city of Mito, Ibaraki Prefecture.

jōyō kanji   常用漢字

(Chinese characters for common use). A list of 1,945 Chinese characters (KANJI) officially designated by the Japanese government on 1 October 1981 for common use in writing Japanese. The 1981 list superseded the 1,850-character *tōyō kanji* (Chinese characters for daily use), a similar list that had been officially adopted in November 1946.

joya no kane The ritual ringing of Buddhist temple bells on New Year's Eve is usually done by temple priests. Some temples, however, allow the public to participate in taking a turn at "ringing out" one of the 108 earthly passions. Zōjōji, Tōkyō.

Tōyō Kanji—Along with a reform of the spelling rules for the native phonetic syllabary (KANA) that was also announced in 1946, the *tōyō kanji* simplified what had been an extremely complex writing system, in which several thousand Chinese characters were used, and made the written Japanese language easier both to learn and to use. They thus had a great impact on both Japanese education and daily life; however, the *tōyō kanji* were criticized as placing undue restrictions on the number of characters that could be used and on the ways that those characters could be used to write words. For example, no provision was made for many important proper and place names. There were many inconsistencies in the choice of characters generally. Many persons found that the restrictions made reading awkward and felt that the characters had been selected too arbitrarily.

Jōyō Kanji—Consequently, in June 1966 the minister of education requested the Council on National Language to draft recommendations for further language reforms. Changes in the pronunciation of characters on the *tōyō kanji* list and changes in the ways that the *kana* syllabary could be used to express the inflectional endings of verbs and adjectives were adopted in June 1973. Changes in the characters themselves were adopted in October 1981 under the title *Jōyō kanji hyō* (Table of Chinese Characters for Common Use), a comprehensive table that includes not only the designated characters in their designated physical form but also their designated pronunciations and examples of their use in writing words. It increases the number of Chinese characters officially designated for general use by 95. The characters in the table are arranged according to the radical (the characteristic or identifying structural element) under which they belong, following the basic principles of the *tōyō kanji* table and its later modifications. The issuance of the new table, however, makes one important change in language policy. Whereas the *tōyō kanji* were understood as restricting the use of characters not on the table in publications intended for the general public, the *jōyō kanji* are understood as a guideline. They present a standard for the use of Chinese characters in daily life, but the necessity of additional characters in specialized areas is recognized.

Specialized Characters—Along with the announcement of the *jōyō kanji* table, the list of 881 characters designated to be learned within the first six years at school (the so-called KYŌIKU KANJI) was also formally updated to 996 and in 1989 to 1,006 characters. A list modified by the Japanese Newspaper Association has been adopted for use by newspapers and broadcast media in Japan. The number of characters in the supplementary list (to the *tōyō kanji*) approved for use only in personal names was increased to 166 (it was increased to 284 in 1990). Since the 1,945 characters of the *jōyō kanji* can also be used for personal names,

the number of characters available for naming newborn infants has thus been brought up to a total of 2,229. See also JAPANESE LANGUAGE REFORMS.

Jōzankei Hot Spring   定山渓温泉

(Jōzankei Onsen). Located in the southwestern part of the city of Sapporo, southwestern Hokkaidō. Also called Shikanoyu Hot Spring. A weak saline hot spring; maximum water temperature 94°C (201°F). Situated on the upper reaches of the river Toyohiragawa, it is in Shikotsu-Tōya National Park. The name "Jōzan" is taken from the Zen priest Jōzan, who is said to have opened the spa in 1866. This area, within the Hōhei Gorge, is noted for its scenery.

JR   ジェーアール

(Japan Railways; J: Jē Āru). Acronym for the Japan Railways group, a nationwide network of private railways and related service companies. In 1987 the JAPANESE NATIONAL RAILWAYS (JNR), long plagued by financial difficulties, was privatized, creating the JR group, which consists of the JAPAN FREIGHT RAILWAY CO as well as six independent passenger railways: CENTRAL JAPAN RAILWAY CO, EAST JAPAN RAILWAY CO, Hokkaidō Railway Co, KYŪSHŪ RAILWAY CO, Shikoku Railway Co, and WEST JAPAN RAILWAY CO. Management changes following privatization have resulted in improved profit margins among JR group members. See also SHINKANSEN; TRANSPORTATION.

JTB→ Japan Travel Bureau, Inc

jūbako   重箱

(literally, "stacked-up boxes"). Small lacquered wooden boxes, stacked in groups of two, three, or five, and used for storing, carrying, or serving food. They are most commonly lacquered black on the outside and red on the inside, but some are elaborately decorated with gold lacquer (MAKI-E). *Jūbako* became very popular in the Edo period (1600–1868) when they were used for picnic boxes, for giving rice cakes or SEKIHAN (a dish of *azuki* beans and rice cooked on auspicious occasions), or for storing and presenting precooked food for guests at wedding or New Year's festivities. It is still customary at New Year's to serve *jūbako* filled with special seasonal foods (see OSECHI RYŌRI).

judges   裁判官

(*saibankan*). As of 1990, in Japan there were 15 Supreme Court justices and some 280 high court judges, 910 judges and 460 assistant judges of the district courts, 200 judges and 150 assistant judges of the family courts, and 810 summary court judges. Post-university legal training is given at the LEGAL TRAINING AND RESEARCH INSTITUTE to those who pass the national LAW EXAMINATION. A trainee chooses one of three legal careers—that of judge, public prosecutor, or lawyer in private practice—during the two years spent at the institute. See also JUDICIAL SYSTEM; LEGAL SYSTEM.

judicial precedents   判例

(*hanrei*). Precedents established by previous court decisions. In Japan, judicial precedents are recognized as having binding force, but whether or not they should be considered a source of law is currently a matter of debate among scholars of jurisprudence. Judicial precedents are considered binding for the following reasons: since the SUPREME COURT has the final power of decision in litigation,

Japan's Court System

```
                    Supreme Court

              8 high courts (6 branches)

          50 district courts (201 branches)        50 family courts
                                                 (201 branches, 79 subbranches)
      452 summary courts

  minor offenses punishable    civil cases involving    serious offenses and civil    domestic and
  by fine or light sentence    less than ¥900,000       cases involving ¥900,000 or   juvenile cases
                               in claims                more in claims
```

lower courts tend to follow its lead in handing down decisions; modification of a previous position held by the Supreme Court can be made only by the Grand Bench of the Supreme Court (Court Law, art. 10, item 3); and decisions rendered by lower courts contrary to judicial precedents set by the Supreme Court become grounds for appeal (Rules of Civil Procedure, art. 48; Code of Criminal Procedure, art. 405). Judicial precedents have considerable significance; they play a major role in determining legal questions in such matters as common-law marriage and the transfer of securities, which have not yet become subject to legislation.

judicial review　違憲立法審査権

(*iken rippō shinsa ken;* also referred to as *hōrei shinsa ken*). Power of the courts to determine the constitutionality of legislative and administrative acts. The 1947 CONSTITUTION OF JAPAN is characterized by a strong emphasis on fundamental human rights. Under the previous system, the courts had no power to protect these rights from infringement by the legislature or the executive. In applying the principles of separation of powers and checks and balances, the new charter freed the judiciary from ministerial tutelage, established it as a truly independent third branch of government, and entrusted it with the power of judicial review under the following provision: "The Supreme Court is the court of last resort with power to determine the constitutionality of any law, order, regulation or official act" (art. 81). It further provides that "this Constitution shall be the supreme law of the nation and no law, ordinance, imperial rescript or other act of government, or part thereof, contrary to the provisions hereof, shall have legal force or validity" (art. 98, para. 1).

Japanese legal scholars were initially divided as to the meaning of these provisions of the constitution. According to the predominant school of thought, these articles provided a US-style system of judicial review, in which ordinary courts exercise the power of judicial review in connection with specific cases or controversies. Another interpretation of the articles maintained that such power should be vested exclusively in the Supreme Court, which, like the German Constitutional Court, would perform that sole function for general and abstract as well as specific questions. The former view has been adopted by the Supreme Court of Japan (see NATIONAL POLICE RESERVE CASE), and, in their actual operation of judicial review, Japanese courts tend to give weight to the example of US courts.

Japanese courts have actively dealt with constitutional issues but have been reluctant to hold legislation unconstitutional. In only five cases has the Supreme Court invalidated a statute. Critics maintain that the Supreme Court weighs excessively the public welfare against the rights of the individual. Whether courts have the power to review treaties is a question that divides Japanese jurists. See also TŌKYŌ ORDINANCE DECISION.

judicial scrivener　司法書士

(*shihō shoshi*). A legal functionary who can be engaged by the public to act as an agent in matters relating to the registration of transfers of title to land or the making of deposits at a public deposit office and to draft documents to be filed in a court of law (Hōmukyoku), public prosecutor's office, or one of the eight regional Legal Affairs Bureaus. This status is granted to persons who

have passed the judicial scriveners' examination or who have been recognized by the minister of justice as having the necessary qualifications to perform such duties (in actual practice the Ministry of Justice usually only recognizes experienced persons such as those who have previously served as administrative officers of courts, procurators' offices, or one of the Legal Affairs Bureaus). In rural areas judicial scriveners often play a large role in the legal affairs of their clients. There are currently over 16,000 persons who have qualified as judicial scriveners.

judicial system　司法制度

(*shihō seido*). The unified national structure of courts for the administration of justice. The 1947 constitution (art. 76) provides that "the whole judicial power is vested in a Supreme Court and in such inferior courts as are established by law." All courts on all levels are parts of a single system under the sole and complete administration of the Supreme Court. There are no separate municipal, county, state, or federal systems as in the United States and a jury system does not exist.

The structure of the judicial system is as follows: the SUPREME COURT (Saikō Saibansho); 8 high courts (*kōtō saibansho*), with 6 branches, located in the eight principal geographical subdivisions of the country; 50 district courts (*chihō saibansho*), in the principal administrative units, with 201 branches; 50 family courts (*katei saibansho;* see FAMILY COURT), with 201 branches and 79 subbranches; and 452 summary courts (*kan'i saibansho*), located throughout the country. The DIET as the sole law-making organ of the state can change the organization of the courts by passing the necessary legislation, but the administration of the court system remains constitutionally vested in the Supreme Court.

The Supreme Court is headed by the chief justice, who is appointed by the emperor after designation by the cabinet. The other 14 justices (the number being determined by law) are appointed by the cabinet. The court is organized into a grand bench consisting of all 15 justices and three petty benches of 5 justices each. When the full court considers administrative matters of the judiciary, it sits as the judicial assembly. All cases before the Supreme Court are appeals; it possesses original jurisdiction over no cases. The constitution (art. 81) also provides that the Supreme Court is the court of last resort "with power to determine the constitutionality of any law, order, regulation or official act."

The high courts are essentially appellate courts. They are courts of first instance for the crimes of insurrection, preparation for or plotting of insurrection, and of assistance in the acts enumerated.

District courts have original jurisdiction over most cases with the exception of offenses carrying minor punishment and a few others reserved for other courts. In addition, they are courts of appeal for actions taken by

the summary courts. Family courts came into existence under the Allied Occupation (1945–52). They have jurisdiction over such matters as juvenile crime (the age of majority being 20), problems of minors, divorce, and disputes over family property. Summary courts have jurisdiction over minor cases involving less than ¥900,000 (about $7,000) in claims or fines or offenses carrying lighter punishments. See also DISPUTE RESOLUTION SYSTEMS OTHER THAN LITIGATION.

jūdō　柔道

(literally, "the Way of softness"). One of the MARTIAL ARTS; a form of unarmed combat that stresses agile motions, astute mental judgment, and rigorous form rather than sheer physical strength. The Chinese character for *jū* derives from a passage in the ancient Chinese military treatise *Sanlüe* (*San-lüeh*), which states, "softness (*jū;* Ch: *rou* or *jou*) controls hardness well." *Jūdō* techniques (*waza*) include throwing (*nagewaza*), grappling (*katamewaza*), and attacking vital points (*atemiwaza*). The first two techniques are used in competition, but the *atemiwaza* is used only in practice. Developed as a sport by KANŌ JIGORŌ (1860–1938) from *jūjutsu,* *jūdō* has been valued as a method of exercise, moral training, and self-defense.

Jūjutsu began with *sechie-zumō* (court banquet wrestling), a court event popular in the Nara (710–794) and Heian (794–1185) periods. During the sustained peace of the Edo period (1600–1868) *jūjutsu* developed as a self-defense martial art and was used in making arrests. *Jūjutsu* schools proliferated during this period but declined with the collapse of the *samurai* class after the Meiji Restoration of 1868. In 1882 Kanō Jigorō organized the KŌDŌKAN *jūdō* school at Eishōji, a temple in Tōkyō.

The Peers' School (see GAKUSHŪIN UNIVERSITY) was the first to include *jūdō* in a school curriculum in 1883. Immediately after World War II, school *jūdō* was prohibited by the Allied Occupation. In 1949, however, the Zen Nihon Jūdō Federation (Zen Nihon Jūdō Remmei) was organized. In 1951 school *jūdō* was revived and leagues were established at the various levels. *Jūdō* clubs were also set up in various large companies. Tōkyō hosted the first world *jūdō* championships in 1956. In 1964 *jūdō* was made a formal entry in the Olympics for the first time at the Tōkyō games.

Kanō Jigorō set up a system of ranks (*dan*) and classes (*kyū*) as an encouragement for his disciples. These designations have been recognized internationally. There are ranks from 1 to 10, with 10 the highest. Those in ranks 1 to 5 wear a black belt, ranks 6 to 8 have a scarlet and white striped belt, and those in ranks 9 to 10 have a scarlet belt. The classes are below the ranks and range from the fifth class to the first and highest class. Adults in the first to third class wear a brown belt; children in the first to third class

Jūdō Techniques

Nagewaza (throwing techniques)

jūdō

seoinage
(shoulder throw)

hanegoshi
(spring-hip throw)

taiotoshi
(body drop)

ōsotogari
(major outer cut)

ōgoshi
(full hip throw)

ukiwaza
(floating throw)

hizaguruma
(knee wheel)

ōuchigari
(major inner cut)

tomoenage
(circular throw)

Katamewaza (grappling techniques)

kesagatame
(diagonal hold)

kami shihōgatame
(upper four-corner hold)

katagatame
(shoulder hold)

hadakajime
(naked choke)

kata jūjijime
(half cross-choke)

tate shihōgatame
(lengthwise four-corner hold)

yoko shihōgatame
(side four-corner hold)

udehishigi jūjigatame
(arm-crushing cross-hold)

NOTE: The wrestler in red is executing the techniques.

jūdō The red-belted wrestler falls victim to an *uchimata* leg-trip during the All-Japan Jūdō Championship, 1991.

wear a purple belt. Those in the fourth and fifth class wear a white belt.

Jūhachi Daitsū 十八大通

("The 18 Connoisseurs"). A group of wealthy men who dominated the *beau monde* of Edo (now Tōkyō) during the An'ei (1772–81) and Temmei (1781–89) eras. The group was not necessarily limited to 18, the number being chosen as auspicious. Most of the Jūhachi Daitsū were wealthy merchants but some were also high-ranking *samurai.* See also IKI AND SUI.

Jūjō Paper Co, Ltd 十条製紙[株]

(Jūjō Seishi). Manufacturer of paper and pulp; incorporated in 1949 when the Ōji Paper Co, Ltd, was divided into three companies. It controls a large share of Japan's newsprint and printing-paper markets. The North Pacific Paper Corporation, a joint-venture company established by Jūjō with the Weyerhaeuser Co of the United States, began production of newsprint in 1979. The company is also participating in joint enterprises for pulp production in Brazil. Sales for the fiscal year ending March 1991 totaled ¥402.9 billion (US $2.9 billion), with paper and pulp making up 90 percent of the sales. The company was capitalized at ¥47.6 billion (US $347.0 million) in the same year. Headquarters are in Tōkyō.

Jūjūshin ron 十住心論

(Treatise on the Ten Stages of the Development of Mind). Full title, *Himitsu mandara jūjūshin ron.* Work in 10 volumes by KŪKAI, founder of the SHINGON SECT of Japanese Buddhism. A treatise explaining the Shingon philosophy, it was most probably written in 830. Using a scheme of 10 stages to rank the profundity of various Buddhist and non-Buddhist doctrines, Kūkai places Shingon at the highest stage and each of the other doctrines at one of the lower 9 stages. The 10 stages also describe the spiritual ascent of a Shingon monk. The more popular *Hizōhōyaku* (The Precious Key to the Secret Treasure) is a condensed edition of this work.

jūjutsu → jūdō

juka bijin 樹下美人

(literally, "beauty under a tree"). Pictorial motif that can be traced from its appearance in India (ca 100 BC) across Central Asia, through China, to Japan. It is the subject of a famous folding screen (the *Torige ryūjo no zu byōbu*) in the SHŌSŌIN repository in Nara. Each of the six extant panels depicts a single lady standing or seated on a rock beneath a tree. Originally their hair and garments glistened with colorful pheasant feathers, but now only the ink underdrawing and the flesh tones on faces and hands remain. Besides being an important dated example of 8th-century pictorial style, this work documents the eastern terminus of a widely diffused motif.

juku 塾

(private tutoring schools). In the Edo period (1600–1868) the term *juku* referred to small schools founded by individual scholars or educators specifically for the teaching of martial arts, some other special skill, or the doctrines of a particular school of philosophy. In the early Meiji period (1868–1912) *juku* came to mean privately run tutoring establishments, often specializing in a particular subject. Modern *juku* may offer lessons in nonacademic subjects such as arts

and sports or in the academic subjects that are important in school ENTRANCE EXAMINATIONS. *Juku* for high school students must compete for enrollments with *yobikō* (CRAM SCHOOLS), which are solely geared to helping students pass university entrance examinations. According to a 1989 survey, 38.2 percent of elementary school students, 74.9 percent of middle school students, and 37.6 percent of high school students in Tōkyō were attending *juku.* Recently there has been a trend toward enlarging the major *juku* and expanding them into chain or franchise operations. At the same time, a number of smaller, innovative *juku* have sprung up to serve a particular clientele, helping students who are unable to keep up with regular classwork or who have had problems with irregular attendance or dropping out of school.

jūmin soshō 住民訴訟

(resident's lawsuit). A legal action by a resident of a locality to seek rectification of an illegality in the financial administration of local government. Such suits are authorized by article 242 of the Local Autonomy Law (Chihō Jichi Hō, 1947).

This system was patterned after the American system of taxpayers' suits and was instituted after World War II. These suits are brought by residents for the sake of the public good, not for the purpose of seeking relief from the direct infringement of individual rights by local government. In the event of an illegal act or forbearance in financial accounting by an executive organ or official of a local government, a resident may first file a demand for an audit with a member of the auditing commission of the local government. If this action does not suffice to achieve the purpose, the resident may then file a *jūmin soshō* in court.

jūmin tōroku → resident registration

jūnihitoe 十二単

(literally, "12-layered garment"). Popular name for the layered formal court ensemble worn by Heian period (794–1185) ladies-inwaiting. The innermost layer of a *jūnihitoe* ensemble was an unlined robe (*hitoe*); over that were a number of lined robes (*uchiki*), a lustrous silk robe (*uchiginu*), a jacket (*uwagi*), and a pleated rectangular train (a vestige of a type of skirt known as a *mo*). The *karaginu* ("Chinese coat"), a short coat with half sleeves, constituted the outermost layer. Loose crimson trousers (*hakama*) completed the ensemble. A common number of layers was 12, but layers could number as many as 20. The sleeves and hems of the outer robes were progressively shorter so that their edges remained visible, displaying bands of silk in contrasting colors. During the Heian period the choice of colors displayed was considered an important expression of the wearer's aesthetic response to the changing seasons. During the Kamakura period (1185–1333), the number of layers decreased to 5, and the resulting garment was called an *itsutsuginu*.

junior colleges   短期大学

(*tanki daigaku*). Two- or three-year colleges associated mainly with WOMEN'S EDUCATION, since they accommodate around two-thirds of the women who continue their schooling after high school. As of 1989 there were 584 junior colleges in Japan with about 460,000 students. The majority were private colleges (490 schools with 420,000 students). Approximately 12 percent of the Japanese who continue their education after high school attend junior colleges; of these, 94 percent are women. Recently, in order to compete with special training schools (SENSHŪ GAKKŌ) for students, junior colleges have added vocational training to their curricula.

junrei → pilgrimages

junshi   殉死

Self-immolation of a nobleman's retainer following the death of his lord. Historically derived from *junsō* (Ch: *xunzang* or *hsün-tsang*), the ancient Chinese custom of burying attendants alive with the lord's body. The annotation to the *Book of Rites* (Ch: *Li ji* or *Li chi*), one of the Chinese classics, defines *xun* (J: *jun*) as "the killing of a person or persons to guard a dead man." Thus the practice did not originally mean suicide.

It is not certain whether this custom was practiced in ancient Japan. Historically speaking, in Japan the term *junshi* is applied to the suicide of a *samurai* for the purpose of following his lord into death. In most cases this took the form of disembowelment (HARAKIRI), which in the case of *junshi* was variously called *oibara* ("disembowelment to follow") or *tomobara* ("disembowelment to accompany"). With the emergence of the warrior class in the 10th century, it was not uncommon for retainers to perish with their lord in battle or to commit suicide immediately afterward if their lord was killed. The motivating force for the custom of *junshi* was derived from the Way of the warrior (BUSHIDŌ), a long-revered code that demanded unconditional loyalty, even unto death.

It was not until the 17th century, when peace was established by the Tokugawa shogunate (1603–1867), that it became customary for a retainer to commit *junshi* on the death of his lord through illness or natural causes. Such acts were considered ultimate expressions of loyalty and gratitude for favors received, and retainers who committed suicide were honored by being buried beside their lord and having their families well provided for. Moreover, some *daimyō* came to regard the number of self-immolating retainers as a mark of prestige.

The growing number of deaths by *junshi* laid bare its negative aspects—the loss of men of ability and the formalization of a custom that was observed not out of loyalty but to save face. A contemporary document, the *Meiryō kōhan*, lists three types of *junshi*: *gibara*, performed from the depths of the heart according to the moral ties between lord and retainer; *rombara*, performed upon the reasoning that, since others committed suicide, one had no choice but to die; and *shōbara*, committed for mercenary purposes to benefit one's descendants.

Prohibition of Junshi—Criticism of the custom arose from several quarters, and in 1663 the shōgun TOKUGAWA IETSUNA orally forbade *junshi*. The prohibition against *junshi* was formally added to the BUKE SHOHATTO (Laws for Military Houses) during the rule of the shōgun TOKUGAWA TSUNAYOSHI.

During the Tokugawa rule the prohibition of *junshi* was violated in the celebrated FORTY-SEVEN RŌNIN INCIDENT. In Japan's modern period there has been one isolated case of *junshi*—the suicide of General NOGI MARE-SUKE on the day of Emperor Meiji's (1852–1912) funeral. His act drew criticism from several young intellectuals at the time, but the majority of people were deeply moved. The novelist MORI ŌGAI was impelled by the incident to write "Okitsu Yagoemon no isho" (1913, The Last Will of Okitsu Yagoemon) and "Abe ichizoku" (1913; tr "The Abe Family," 1977), the latter a historical short story centering on the *junshi* of retainers of Hosokawa Tadatoshi (1586–1641). Nogi's death plays an important part in NATSUME SŌSEKI's novel *Kokoro* (1914; tr *Kokoro*, 1957). It should be noted that Nogi was subsequently enshrined by the government and held up as a shining example of loyalty to the emperor.

Juntendō University   順天堂大学

(*Juntendō Daigaku*). A private university located in Bunkyō Ward, Tōkyō. It originated as a private school of Dutch medicine founded in Edo (now Tōkyō) in 1838, became the Juntendō Medical School in 1943, and was renamed Juntendō University in 1951. Juntendō University maintains a school of medicine and a school of health and physical education, the former being coeducational and the latter all male. Enrollment in 1989 was 1,368.

Juntoku, Emperor   順徳天皇

(1197–1242; Juntoku Tennō). The 84th sovereign (*tennō*) in the traditional count (which includes several legendary emperors); reigned 1210–21. Third son of Emperor GO-TOBA, who ruled from retirement throughout Juntoku's reign (see INSEI). In 1221 Juntoku abdicated in favor of his son Emperor Chūkyō (1218–34; r 1221), mobilized his forces against the KAMAKURA SHOGUNATE, and was quickly defeated by the shogunate. For his part in the JŌKYŪ DISTURBANCE, Juntoku was exiled to the island of Sado (now part of Niigata Prefecture), where he died 21 years later. Juntoku was the author of poetry criticism and of KIMPI-SHŌ, a work on court ceremonial.

jurisprudence   法哲学

(*hōtetsugaku*). Study of the nature and the origin and development of law. The term jurisprudence has been used in England (since the 1830s) and the United States to denote theoretical studies of law, as distinguished from legal learning from a purely practical point of view. This field may be divided into three problem areas: definition and analysis, legal reasoning, and the criticism of law.

Modern jurisprudence in Japan began in the 1880s with HOZUMI NOBUSHIGE, a gifted and original thinker who played a leading role in drafting the Civil Code. After Hozumi, however, the Anglo-Saxon tradition of empirically oriented jurisprudence receded to the background, giving way to metaphysical philosophy in the grand tradition of German idealism, which was often mingled with strains of nationalism.

After 1945 there came a burst of research and literature in the field of philosophy of law. As a result of extensive personnel exchanges under various projects, there has been a remarkable fusion of the Continental (and above all German) tradition of legal learning (including the field of jurisprudence) with the Anglo-Saxon tradition. At present, a broad consensus seems to prevail among the leading specialists in the field of jurisprudence in Japan regarding the major areas for research. These are the methodology of legal studies in the broader sense of the word, the history of social and political thought, and "theories of justice" (or of "the just law").

juristic act   法律行為

(*hōritsu kōi*). Action regarding which the actor's intended effect is accorded recognition by law. Juristic acts are classified according to the nature of the intent expressed. A juristic act that can be established by a unilateral expression of intent is called an independent act (*tandoku kōi*). The bilateral concurrence of mutual and interdependent expressions of intent is called a contract (*keiyaku*). Juristic acts established by the concurrence of a multiplicity of mutual expressions of intent, such as the establishment of a company, are called joint acts (*gōdō kōi*).

The Japanese concept of the juristic act is derived from the German civil code. Both the Japanese and German systems attempt to explain all private legal relationships on the basis of the intent of the parties involved. By

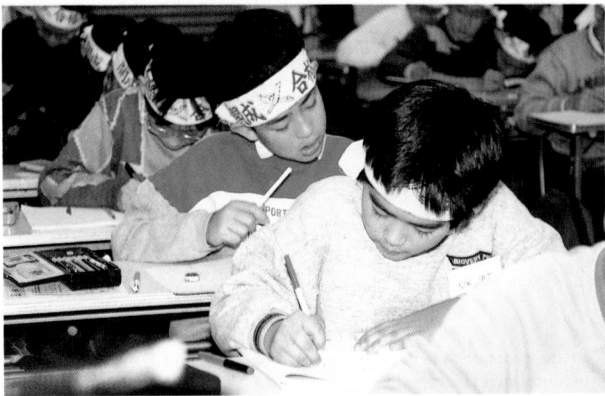

juku These private tutoring schools provide supplementary coursework designed to help students pass entrance examinations. The headbands worn by these students announce their goal of admission to a prestigious junior high school.

jūnihitoe During the 1990 wedding ceremony of Prince Aya, the emperor's second son, and Kawashima Kiko, the bride (pictured) wore this layered style of formal court dress.

Juvenile and Adult Crime, 1990

Crime type		Juvenile	Adult
		(percentage*)	
Murder, robbery, arson, rape		0.7	2.6
Other violent crimes:	Assault	1.7	3.9
	Infliction of bodily harm	5.7	11.1
	Extortion	3.2	2.6
	Other	0.2	0.6
	Total	10.8	18.2
Theft:	Shoplifting	24.8	20.2
	Motorcycle theft	20.8	0.3
	Bicycle theft	10.2	9.2
	Other	14.6	18.5
	Total	70.4	48.2
Misappropriation of a lost or stolen article		15.1	12.7
Fraud, embezzlement, forgery		0.5	6.9
Vice (obscenity, gambling, etc)		0.4	6.5
All other crimes		2.1	4.9

*Percentages represent the proportion of all people arrested in each age group who were arrested for that type of crime. Traffic-related offenses are not included.
SOURCE: National Police Agency.

contrast, in Anglo-American law, which views rights and duties stemming from legal relationships as incidental to those relationships, the juristic act does not exist.

juristic person→hōjin

jūroku musashi 十六武蔵

Children's game, dating from the mid-17th century, that uses a board with 1 master piece and 16 secondary pieces. The master piece, named after legendary warrior-monk Musashibō BENKEI, can take subordinate pieces when they fall on both sides of it in a straight line. The person who drives Benkei into a corner wins.

Jūsan, Lake 十三湖

(Jūsanko). Lagoon on the western coast of the Tsugaru Peninsula, northwestern Aomori Prefecture, northern Honshū. Connected by a canal to the Sea of Japan. *Shijimi* or corbicula (a small shellfish) is the principal catch. Swans gather at Lake Jūsanko in winter. Area: 21 sq km (8.1 sq mi); circumference: 30 km (18.6 mi); depth: 1.5 m (4.9 ft).

Jusco Co, Ltd ジャスコ[株]

(Jasuko). Company that operates chain stores selling foodstuffs, clothing, and household goods. Jusco is an acronym for Japan United Stores Company. The company was established in 1969 with the merger of three store chains. During the 1970s Jusco expanded its network by absorbing small- and medium-sized supermarkets and small department stores. Jusco has six stores in Thailand, Malaysia, and Hong Kong. In 1989 it acquired Talbots, Inc, an American chain of women's wear stores. In the fiscal year ending February 1991 its 170 stores generated annual sales of ¥995.4 billion (US $7.6 billion). The company was capitalized at ¥27.9 billion (US $213.8 million) in February 1991. Headquarters are in Tōkyō.

Jūshichijō no Kempō→Seventeen-Article Constitution

jūshin 重臣

A group of senior statesmen who acted as unofficial advisers to the emperor in the selection of prime ministers from the early 1930s until the end of World War II. From the mid-Meiji period (1868–1912) the elder statesmen (GENRŌ) performed that function, but with the deaths of YAMAGATA ARITOMO in 1922 and MATSUKATA MASAYOSHI in 1924, the responsibility fell to SAIONJI KIMMOCHI, the last surviving *genrō*. In the 1930s, a new ad-

visory group, the *jūshin*, was formed to replace the *genrō*. They included the lord keeper of the privy seal (*naidaijin*), the president of the Privy Council (Sūmitsuin), and former prime ministers. *Jūshin* were also summoned by the emperor on extraordinary occasions; for example, when Japan declared war against the Allies in December 1941 and accepted defeat in August 1945.

juvenile crime 少年犯罪

(*shōnen hanzai*). Illegal acts committed by a person under 20 years of age fall under the jurisdiction of the JUVENILE LAW in Japan. Persons under 14 years of age are not subject to the Penal Code, and acts committed by them in violation of criminal laws and ordinances are not called crimes. The CHILD WELFARE LAW is sometimes applied to a person under the age of 18 when he or she commits a crime.

Juveniles arrested for criminal acts are turned over to the juvenile department of the FAMILY COURT, unless it is a serious offense, in which instance the case is turned over to the public prosecutor for an opinion on criminal prosecution. Juveniles under 14 years of age are turned over to a child consultation center, a social welfare office, or in some cases to the juvenile department of the family court. Nearly 95 percent of the juveniles who are arrested for a criminal offense are turned over to their guardians after interrogation by the police without being placed in confinement. More than 70 percent of juveniles under 14 are returned to their guardians and are not committed to the consultation center.

More than 45 percent of the arrested juveniles are released without punishment on the grounds of probable rehabilitation, and another 30 percent are released on the grounds of low criminality. About 8 percent are punished with posttrial probation under the supervision of the Ministry of Justice. See also CRIME; PENAL SYSTEM; PUBLIC PROSECUTORS.

juvenile labor 年少労働

(*nenshō rōdō*). The Ministry of Labor's Women's and Minors' Bureau, which handles young workers' legal problems, defines juveniles (*seishōnen*) as persons between 15 and 24 years old. In 1988 the juvenile work force, of which 95.1 percent was employed, totaled 7,820,000. This constituted 42.6 percent of the total population of juveniles and 12.6 percent of the entire labor force. Because of demographic changes and the increasing percentage of people entering postsecondary educational institutions in recent years, the youth labor force has been decreasing in relative terms.

The Labor Standards Law of 1947 (see LABOR LAWS) prohibits employment of children under 15 years old except in certain types of light labor. The law also has special protective provisions for workers under 18 years of age. Labor law administrators investigate violations of the law and offer guidance and leisure-hour activities through Youth Labor Homes (Kinrō Seishōnen Hōmu).

Juvenile Law 少年法

(Shōnen Hō). The present Juvenile Law went into effect in 1949; it emphasizes rehabilitation. The law defines a juvenile as a person under 20 years of age. The law assigns jurisdiction over the misdeeds of juveniles to the FAMILY COURT. Juveniles under 14 years of age who commit acts that would constitute a criminal offense are sent to a consultation office for children (*jidō sōdansho*). At the

family court a trained examiner conducts an investigation of the character and environment of the juveniles sent there. A decision on punishment is made by the judge after examining the report of the investigation.

The law requires that preference be given to probation, of which there are three kinds: rehabilitative supervision, dispatch to a reformatory, and dispatch to a correctional school or a children's home. The cases of juveniles 16 years or older can be referred to a prosecutor for disposition in criminal court. The vast majority of misbehaving minors are returned to their homes without punishment. A minority are subjected to criminal penalties, such as being sent to reformatories or given supervised probation.

juvenile reformatories and classification centers 少年院・少年鑑別所

(*shōnen'in; shōnen kambetsusho*). Government institutions under the jurisdiction of the Ministry of Justice for internment of juvenile delinquents who are dispatched to them by a FAMILY COURT order. There are four types of juvenile reformatory: (1) reformatories for the internment of 14- and 15-year-olds without serious physical or emotional disabilities; (2) reformatories for the internment of 16- to 19-year-olds without serious disabilities; (3) special juvenile reformatories for 16- to 22-year-olds who, though free from serious disabilities, have displayed advanced criminal tendencies; and (4) reformatories for the internment of 14- to 25-year-olds with serious disabilities. At juvenile reformatories, in addition to academic and social guidance, vocational training is stressed. A juvenile who has already been interned may be placed by the family court into a juvenile classification center for examination and judgment. There various medical and psychological tests are conducted, and the juvenile's problems are diagnosed.

juvenile workers, protective legislation for 年少者の労働法上の保護

(*nenshōsha no rōdō hō jō no hogo*). Special protection extended to juvenile workers. The Labor Standards Law (Rōdō Kijun Hō) divides juveniles into those under 15, those between 15 and 18, and those under 20. Prohibitions on the employment of children are based on article 27, paragraph 3 of the constitution (prohibition of exploitation of children). Children over 12 can be employed in nonmanufacturing industries where their health or welfare is not in danger, and children under 12 years of age may be employed in theatrical or motion picture productions. The employer must have at the place of employment an age certificate, a certificate from the school principal, and written permission from a parent or guardian. As a rule, late night work, work on holidays, and extension of the 8-hour workday and 48-hour workweek are prohibited. Employment in dangerous industries and coal mines is also prohibited. See also LABOR LAWS.

juzu→Buddhist rosary

Jyūsō, Inc [株]住総

(Jūsō). Finance company, specializing in housing loans. Incorporated in 1971. Its loan balance surpassed ¥1.9 trillion (US $13.8 billion) in 1991. For the fiscal year ending March 1991, total assets were ¥2.1 trillion (US $15.3 billion) and capitalization stood at ¥3.0 billion (US $21.9 million). Headquarters are in Tōkyō.

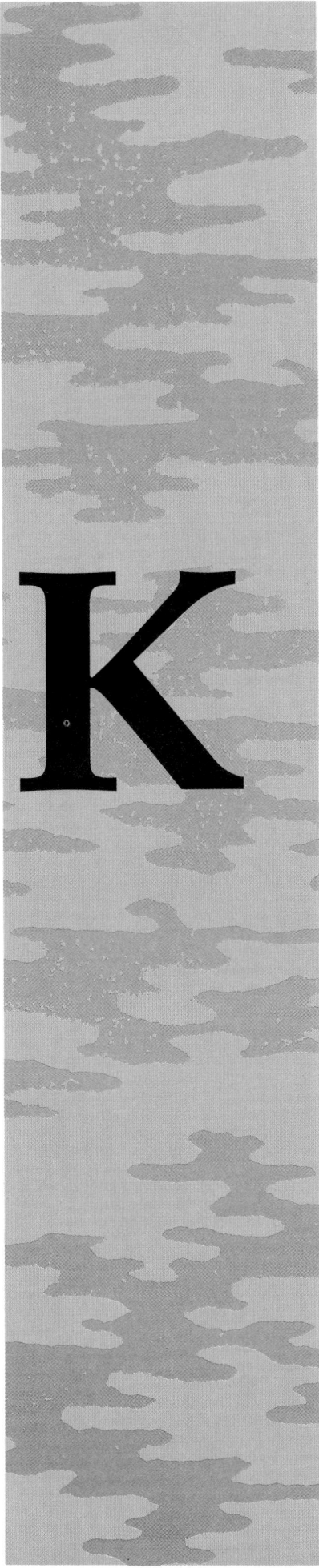

K

kabane 姓

A hereditary title indicating the social rank and specific duty of the *uji no kami*, the chieftain of a lineage group (UJI) who served the YAMATO COURT from the late 5th through the late 7th century. *Kabane* were also borne by the *uji no kami*'s close kin and came to form a sociopolitical hierarchy. These titles may have originated in the terms of deference with which the *uji-bito* (the constituent members of *uji*) addressed their chieftain. The titles *omi*, *muraji*, or *miyatsuko* were traditionally conferred on chieftains in service at the court and the titles of *kimi*, *atae*, or *obito* on regional chieftains. The title of *imiki* or *fuhito* was often conferred on lineage groups of continental origin (KIKAJIN). In 684 the *kabane* system was reorganized into a new YAKUSA NO KABANE system but did not die out completely until the 10th century. See also UJI-KABANE SYSTEM.

Kabasan Incident 加波山事件

(Kabasan Jiken). Unsuccessful revolutionary plot by radical members of the JIYŪTŌ (Liberal Party) to assassinate leaders of the Meiji government and then establish a democratic system of government. The plot reached its climax on 23 September 1884, when 16 of the rebels issued a revolutionary manifesto to the residents of the Mt. Kaba (Kabasan) region, Makabe District, Ibaraki Prefecture. Local policemen and troops sent from Tōkyō engaged the rebels in combat on 24 September, resulting in the death of 1 policeman and 1 rebel. By February 1885 the remaining 15 rebels had been apprehended, and in July 1886, 7 were sentenced to hang and the others to prison terms.

The Kabasan Incident was one of a dozen similar incidents occurring in the early 1880s. Most of these incidents took place in the Kantō region of eastern Japan. In general the incidents shared two characteristics: ties with the FREEDOM AND PEOPLE'S RIGHTS MOVEMENT (Jiyū Minken Undō) and largely economic demands aimed at alleviating the plight of indebted farmers, whose fortunes had declined because of the deflation policy (1881) of MATSUKATA MASAYOSHI.

This incident was a reaction to the government's violent suppression of participants involved in the FUKUSHIMA INCIDENT of 1882. Assassination targets of the Kabasan rebels included MISHIMA MICHITSUNE, YAMAGATA ARITOMO, and other high-ranking officials of the central government who had been responsible.

Prominent among the rebels was Kōno Hiromi (1864–1941), the nephew of Jiyūtō leader KŌNO HIRONAKA, and Koinuma Kuhachirō, a Jiyūtō activist. Ironically, such incidents served to discredit the Jiyūtō and probably strengthened the oligarchic government rather than furthering the rebels' democratic cause.

Kabayama Sukenori 樺山資紀

(1837–1922). Admiral and politician from the Satsuma domain (now Kagoshima Prefecture). He took an active role on the imperial side in the BOSHIN CIVIL WAR and on the government side in the SATSUMA REBELLION, distinguishing himself in the latter by his defense of Kumamoto Castle. Kabayama served as navy minister in the first YAMAGATA ARITOMO cabinet (1889) and the first MATSUKATA MASAYOSHI cabinet (1891). Following active duty in the SINO-JAPANESE WAR of 1894–1895, he was appointed admiral and first governor-general of Taiwan. He later served in Japan as home minister and education minister. Kabayama was named a field marshal in 1903.

kabegaki 壁書

(also called *hekisho;* literally, "wall writings"). Placards posted on walls or written on notice boards. The term occurs in *Ruijū fusen shō*, a collection of official documents from the years 737–1093, as a notation to a decree dated 807; it is defined in SATA MIRENSHO, an early-14th-century manual of legal terms, as an announcement of interruption of litigation when one of the parties is forced by a taboo, such as mourning, into abstinence from action; but it assumed a wider meaning in the Muromachi period (1333–1568), when it was applied to public notices issued by various offices of the MUROMACHI SHOGUNATE and incorporated into the body of shogunal law (see BUKEHŌ). *Kemmu irai tsuika*, the supplementary articles to the shogunate's fundamental constitution (the KEMMU SHIKIMOKU), contain items identified as *kanrei kabegaki* and Mandokoro *kabegaki*, that is, proclamations issued by the shogunate's chief executive officer (KANREI) and its central Administrative Board (MANDOKORO). The term *kabegaki* also came to be used for the laws and regulations themselves, as in the ŌUCHIKE KABEGAKI, a domainal code.

Kabo Reform 甲午改革

(J: Kōgo Kaikaku). Program to modernize the Korean government and society, instituted at Japanese insistence in 1894. (*Kabo* [J: *kōgo*] is the designation for 1894 in the sexagenary cycle.) Japan's goals were to force Korea to abandon its traditional ways and to lay the groundwork for increased Japanese influence on the peninsula. The most significant reforms were the establishment of a cabinet system of administration and the replacement of Korea's five-century-old civil and military examination system with government schools that trained candidates for officialdom in Western categories of knowledge. Korean cooperation was undermined by the assassination of Queen MIN by Japanese troops in 1895 and the flight of King KOJONG to the Russian legation in 1896. Russian influence became dominant in Korea until the RUSSO-JAPANESE WAR of 1904–05.

Kabuki 歌舞伎

Monthly drama journal; 175 issues were published between January 1900 and January 1915 by the Kabuki Hakkōjo. Miki Takeji (1867–1908), younger brother of MORI ŌGAI, was its first managing editor; he was succeeded by Ihara Seiseien (1870–1941). *Kabuki* published criticism, commentary, research, production notes, and original plays from all dramatic genres, as well as Japanese translations of modern Western drama. The journal played a significant role in the development of the Japanese theatrical genre known as SHINGEKI. Principal contributors included Ōgai, TSUBOUCHI SHŌYŌ, OSANAI KAORU, AEBA KŌSON, and OKAMOTO KIDŌ.

kabuki 歌舞伎

One of the three major classical theaters of Japan, together with the NŌ and the BUNRAKU puppet theater. Kabuki began in the early 17th century as a kind of variety show performed by troupes of itinerant entertainers. By the Genroku era (1688–1704), it had achieved its first flowering as a mature thea-

▶ In the set-piece gesture called *mie*, the actor pauses and assumes a pose, often with eyes crossed, to emphasize an especially dramatic moment. Matsumoto Kōshirō VIII is pictured here striking a *mie* in *Ichinotani futaba gunki*.

▼ The theater Kabukiza in Tōkyō, originally built in 1925, was destroyed in a 1945 air raid; it was rebuilt in the same grand style in 1951.

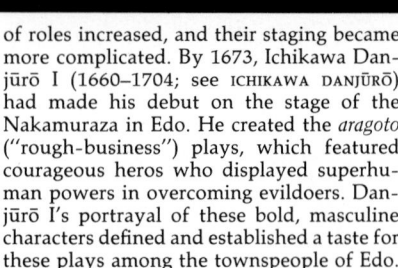

▶ Playing the character Benkei in the final scene of *Kanjinchō*, Ichikawa Danshirō executes a *roppō*, a dramatic exit accompanied by exaggerated gestures.

ter, and it continued, through much of the Edo period (1600–1868), to be the most popular form of stage entertainment. Kabuki reached its artistic pinnacle with the brilliant plays of Tsuruya Namboku IV (1755–1829; see TSURUYA NAMBOKU) and Kawatake MOKUAMI (1816–93). Through a magnificent blend of playacting, dance, and music, kabuki today offers an extraordinary spectacle combining form, color, and sound and is recognized as one of the world's great theatrical traditions.

Origin of Kabuki—The creation of kabuki is ascribed to OKUNI, a female attendant at the IZUMO SHRINE, who, documents record, led her company of mostly women in a light theatrical performance featuring dancing and comic sketches on the dry bed of the river Kamogawa in Kyōto in 1603. Her troupe gained nationwide recognition and her dramas—and later the genre itself—became identified as "kabuki," a term connoting its "out-of-the-ordinary" and "shocking" character.

The strong attraction of *onna* (women's) kabuki, which Okuni had popularized, was largely due to its sensual dances and erotic scenes. Because fights frequently broke out among the spectators over these entertainers, who also practiced prostitution, in 1629 the Tokugawa shogunate (1603–1867) banned women from appearing in kabuki performances. Thereafter, *wakashu* (young men's) kabuki achieved a striking success, but, as in the case of *onna* kabuki, the authorities strongly disapproved of the shows, which continued to be the cause of public disturbances because the adolescent actors also sold their favors.

Kabuki after 1652—In 1652 *wakashu* kabuki was forbidden, and the shogunate required that kabuki performances undergo a basic reform to be allowed to continue. In short, kabuki was required to be based on KYŌGEN, farces staged between Nō plays that used the spoken language of the time but whose style of acting was highly formalized. The performers of *yarō* (men's) kabuki, who now began to replace the younger males, were compelled to shave off their forelocks, as was the custom at the time for men, to signify that they had come of age. They also had to make representations to the authorities that their performances did not rely on the provocative display of their bodies and that they were serious artists who would not engage in prostitution.

In the 1660s a broad platform, the forerunner of the HANAMICHI in use today, extending from the main stage to the center of the auditorium, was introduced to provide an auxiliary stage on which performers could make entrances and exits. In 1664 two theaters located in Ōsaka and Edo (now Tōkyō) introduced the draw curtain, which brought unlimited theatrical possibilities to the previously curtainless stage by permitting the lengthening of plays through the presentation of a series of scenes and providing the freedom to effect complicated scene changes unobtrusively. In the meantime the roles played by the ONNAGATA (female impersonator) gradually increased in importance; mastery of them came to require many years of training. By the mid-17th century, the major cities, Kyōto, Ōsaka, and Edo, were permitted to build permanent kabuki playhouses.

During its formative years important elements from other theatrical forms—particularly *kyōgen*, Nō, and the puppet theater—were introduced. The strongest single influence came from *kyōgen*, which, by government fiat, had served as a model for reorganizing the basic structure of the kabuki theater. By introducing the dialogue, acting techniques, and realism of *kyōgen*, kabuki developed from a variety show featuring dance and music into a new form of drama. The kabuki stage was originally derived from the Nō stage, although later modified by the addition of the draw curtain and the *hanamichi* in the 17th century and the abandonment of the distinctive roof in the 18th century. Many Nō plays were also adapted for performance as kabuki. The simple texts borrowed from Nō, *kyōgen*, and early JŌRURI (narratives recited during bunraku puppet plays) were gradually supplanted by works written for the kabuki stage. The plots became longer and more involved, the number

of roles increased, and their staging became more complicated. By 1673, Ichikawa Danjūrō I (1660–1704; see ICHIKAWA DANJŪRŌ) had made his debut on the stage of the Nakamuraza in Edo. He created the *aragoto* ("rough-business") plays, which featured courageous heros who displayed superhuman powers in overcoming evildoers. Danjūrō I's portrayal of these bold, masculine characters defined and established a taste for these plays among the townspeople of Edo.

Genroku Era Kabuki—By the beginning of the Genroku era in 1688 there had developed three distinct types of kabuki performance: *jidai-mono* (historical plays), often with elaborate sets and a large cast; *sewa-mono* (domestic plays), which generally portrayed the lives of the townspeople and which, in comparison to *jidai-mono*, were presented in a realistic manner; and *shosagoto* (dance pieces), consisting of dance performances and pantomime. In the Kyōto-Ōsaka (Kamigata) area, SAKATA TŌJŪRŌ I (1647–1709), whose realistic style of acting was called *wagoto*, was enormously popular for his portrayal of romantic young men, and his contemporary YOSHIZAWA AYAME I (1673–1729) consolidated the role of the *onnagata* and established its importance in the kabuki tradition. For a period of some 10 years until about 1703, when he returned to the puppet theater, CHIKAMATSU MONZAEMON (1653–1724) wrote a number of kabuki plays, many of them for Tōjūrō I, which gained public recognition for the craft of the playwright. The commanding stage presence and powerful acting of Danjūrō I made him the premier kabuki performer in Edo, and as a playwright, under the name Mimasuya Hyōgo, he was once considered the rival of the great Chikamatsu.

Kabuki and the Puppet Theater—The spectacular success of kabuki in the Kyōto-Ōsaka area during the late 17th century was followed by a period of diminished popularity due to the flourishing of the bunraku puppet theater. In the years following the departure of Chikamatsu, *maruhon-mono* (kabuki adaptations of puppet plays) were staged in an attempt to draw back the spectators who were now flocking to the puppet theater. The musical and narrative accompaniment of the puppet plays was transported to kabuki performances, and even stage techniques of bunraku, such as the distinctive movement of the manipulated dolls, were imitated by kabuki actors. Chikamatsu's KOKUSEN'YA KASSEN (1715), an early example of the *maruhon-mono*, enjoyed tremendous success in both the Kamigata area and in Edo when it was per-

◀A stagehand runs from stage left to stage right, drawing the curtain (jōshikimaku) on a scene.

▼A ship sinks at sea in this scene from the modern play Chinsetsu yumiharizuki (1969) by Mishima Yukio.

▶Stylized acrobatic fighting (tate) demands precise choreography. The play Yamato-gana Ariwara keizu is known for its vigorous sword fights; in this scene, a fight takes place on a ladder that is carried onto the hanamichi.

The Kabuki Stage

- choboyuka (box for chorus)
- geza (box for musicians)
- ōzeri (large trapdoor)
- mawaributai (revolving stage)
- seri (trapdoor)
- jōshikimaku (draw curtain)
- kamite (stage left)
- agemaku (curtain)
- shimote (stage right)
- suppon (trapdoor on hanamichi)
- hanamichi (elevated runway)
- karihanamichi (auxiliary elevated runway)
- sajiki (box seats)

▲The trapdoor located on the hanamichi is known as the suppon. Because action on the hanamichi is considered to be in "another dimension" from that on stage, only ghostly or superhuman characters enter and exit through the suppon. Here a magical warrior appears in a cloud of smoke.

formed soon after its presentation as a puppet play. The works of later writers which are considered masterpieces in both theaters include: SUGAWARA DENJU TENARAI KAGAMI (1746), YOSHITSUNE SEMBON-ZAKURA (1747), and KANADEHON CHŪSHINGURA (1748). In Edo, despite the growing popularity of the bunraku theater, kabuki remained in the ascendancy due to the undiminished power of the Ichikawa Danjūrō family of actors and the regional preference for the *aragoto* style of performance, which was not suited for the puppet stage. Nevertheless the tight logical structure of the puppet plays and their realistic character portrayal eventually influenced the Edo kabuki theater. After enjoying immense success during the first half of the 18th century, the puppet theater rapidly declined in the Kamigata area, and kabuki recaptured the support of the townspeople. Today, half of the plays presented on the kabuki stage are adaptations of bunraku plays.

After the mid-17th century, the cultural center of Japan gradually shifted from the Kamigata region to Edo. During this transitional period, one of the more notable Kamigata playwrights was Namiki Shōzō I (1730–73; see NAMIKI SHŌZŌ), best known as the inventor of the revolving stage (*mawaributai*). It was a pupil of Shōzō I, the dramatist Namiki Gohei I (1747–1808; see NAMIKI GOHEI), along with Sakurada Jisuke I (1734–1806; see SAKURADA JISUKE), who was instrumental in transmitting the social realism traditionally associated with the *sewamono* (domestic plays) of the Kyōto-Ōsaka area to Edo. Their plays laid the foundation for the development of the realistic *kizewa-mono* ("bare" domestic plays) written by Tsuruya Namboku IV, Segawa Jokō III (1806–81; see SEGAWA JOKŌ), and Kawatake Mokuami.

Kabuki Music and Dance——During the 18th century, the rise of the Tokiwazu (see TOKIWAZU-BUSHI) and Tomimoto schools of narrative and music and the Edo school of NAGAUTA (songs accompanying dances, sung to the music of the SHAMISEN) enriched kabuki performances. In the early 19th century, the Kiyomoto (see KIYOMOTO-BUSHI) school flourished at the expense of the Tomimoto school, which rapidly declined. The first half of the 19th century was the golden age of KABUKI MUSIC and was accompanied by the spectacular growth of the dance-oriented dramas, *shosagoto*.

Late-Edo- and Meiji-Period Kabuki—— After the death of Namboku IV in 1829, kabuki did not produce any prominent playwrights until the mid-1850s, when Jokō III

and Mokuami began to write for the theater. Their early successes, embellishments on the genre *kizewa-mono*—the masterpiece of which had been TŌKAIDŌ YOTSUYA KAIDAN (1825) by Namboku IV—intermingled brutality, eroticism, and macabre humor and introduced characters from the underworld. Mokuami created the *shiranami-mono* (thief plays), which had robbers, murderers, confidence men, and cunningly vicious women in the leading roles.

The Meiji Restoration of 1868 marked the collapse of the social order ruled by the *samurai*, whose loss of status was symbolized by a ban on the wearing of swords and by government discouragement of the continued wearing of topknots. During the early years of the Meiji period Mokuami developed the *zangiri-mono* ("cropped-hair" plays), which introduced soldiers dressed in Western-style uniforms and *onnagata* characters wearing Western dresses. These dramas were little more than caricatures of modern life and failed to draw audiences. Actors such as Ichikawa Danjūrō IX (1838–1903) and Onoe Kikugorō V (1844–1903; see ONOE KIKUGORŌ) urged the preservation of classical kabuki, and in the later years of their careers agitated for the continued staging of the great plays of the kabuki tradition and trained a younger generation of actors in the art that they would inherit.

The immediate successors of Kikugorō V and Danjūrō IX, including Kikugorō VI (1885–1949), Matsumoto Kōshirō VII (1870–1949; see MATSUMOTO KŌSHIRŌ), and Nakamura Kichiemon I (1886–1954; see NAKA-

MURA KICHIEMON), also worked to maintain the spirit and integrity of traditional kabuki. However, they also experimented with plays by writers who were not professionally affiliated with the kabuki theater and who wrote plays in the modern vernacular, freely incorporating elements that they had learned from the Western dramatic tradition, such as graphic realism and the detailed character study. Among writers associated with this *shin kabuki* (new kabuki) movement were OKAMOTO KIDŌ (1872–1939), MAYAMA SEIKA (1878–1948), HASEGAWA SHIN (1884–1963), and KUBOTA MANTARŌ (1889–1963).

Post–World War II Kabuki—In the postwar era the popularity of kabuki has been maintained and the great plays of the Edo period, as well as a number of the modern classics, continue to be performed in Tōkyō at the Kabukiza and the National Theater. However, offerings have become considerably shortened and, particularly at the Kabukiza, limited for the most part to favorite acts and scenes presented together with a dance piece. The National Theater continues to present full-length plays. The average length of a kabuki performance is about five hours, including intermissions. The roles once played by the great postwar actors Morita Kan'ya XIV (1907–75; see MORITA KAN'YA), Ichikawa Danjūrō XI (1909–65), Nakamura Kanzaburō XVII (1910–88; see NAKAMURA KANZABURŌ), Onoe Shōroku II

Continued on page 706 ➤

A Spectacle Larger Than Life

Falsely labeled as a daughter of the Taira, Yoshitsune's wife prepares to commit suicide to vindicate his honor. Her actual father assists her in the act.

Yoshitsune and his mistress are in danger and must part. Two figures urge them to flee. Prevailing on the mistress is the fox, disguised as a servant.

The five-act drama known as *Yoshitsune sembon-zakura* (The Thousand Cherry Trees of Yoshitsune) is one of the three *kabuki* plays most often performed. Its plot has everything: betrayal, self-sacrifice, vengeance, romance, suicide, bravery, sorcery, and a larger-than-life historic hero. To tell the story, a startling profusion of stagecraft elements—dance, live music, acrobatics, rapid-fire costume changes, revolving backdrops, and magic effects—are brought into play. Based on the 12th-century Taira-Minamoto War, the narrative follows three Taira generals as they seek revenge on Yoshitsune of the Minamoto, who had defeated them in battle. Yoshitsune is in double jeopardy because his jealous older brother suspects him of treason. Audiences with a taste for fleeting glory and "beauty in doom" are thrilled to watch Yoshitsune fight his losing battle with the world.

The play consists of vignettes featuring characters torn between ideals of loyalty and realities of deception and betrayal. Dogged by fatal misunderstandings, false accusations, or defeat in battle, they surrender to the inevitable. Like the cherry blossoms that fall around the hero's mistress as she seeks him in the Yoshino hills, these characters radiate a poignant beauty; they are not long for this life.

One of the major figures is a fox able to assume human form. Ironies arise as this creature, the personification of deceit and cunning in Japanese myths, takes its place among the human players, for its motives are far purer than theirs: it is devoted to the memory of its dead parents. (Humans killed them and fashioned a drum from their skins, and the fox has disguised itself as a human to obtain it.) The filial piety of the animal is seen in contrast to the treachery of the hero's human sibling, for as the audience knows, the historic Yoshitsune was in the end hunted down and killed at his brother's command. The play's ironic use of the Yoshitsune legend and its spectacular stagecraft have made this 1747 work a perennial favorite.

Fujita Hiroshi

A vengeful Taira general who plans to eliminate Yoshitsune restrains two of his own retainers, who would kill Yoshitsune themselves. The general, Tomomori, will mount a sneak attack at sea.

Tomomori prepares to die after his attempt to destroy Yoshitsune fails. With the anchor tied to his waist, he will somersault into the waves.

The makeup worn by kabuki actors often possesses a symbolic meaning. The red *kumadori* makeup worn by the loyal servant at left symbolizes righteousness.

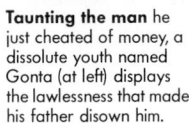

Yoshitsune's mistress (photo at right) makes her way toward his hideout through the cherry forest of Yoshino. In the photo at lower right, the loyal fox appears in the forest disguised as the lady's bodyguard (center), warding off a would-be attacker (left).

Taunting the man he just cheated of money, a dissolute youth named Gonta (at left) displays the lawlessness that made his father disown him.

Stabbed by his father, who thought he betrayed an ally, Gonta reveals that his act was a ruse to allow the ally to escape. His father (at left) bewails Gonta's imminent death.

The fox's deception is exposed by the arrival of the real bodyguard. Brandishing a sword, Yoshitsune's mistress forces the fox to reveal its true identity.

The major figures in the drama go their separate ways in the play's finale.

(1913–89; see ONOE SHŌROKU), Onoe Baikō VII (b 1915; see ONOE BAIKŌ), and Nakamura Utaemon VI (b 1917; see NAKAMURA UTAEMON) are now performed by younger actors, such as Ichikawa Ennosuke II (b 1939; see ICHIKAWA ENNOSUKE), Matsumoto Kōshirō IX (b 1942), Nakamura Kichiemon II (b 1944), BANDŌ TAMASABURŌ V (b 1950), Kataoka Takao (b 1944), and Nakamura Kankurō (b 1955). Dramas in which Tamasaburō V appears in the role of the onnagata and Takao that of the leading man, or tachiyaku, are always well attended. Performances by kabuki actors in other theatrical genres and the broadcasting of kabuki on television have served to increase popular interest in the tradition. The adaptation for new-style theater (SHINGEKI) and the avant-garde theater of kabuki plays by Tsuruya Namboku offers further evidence that the kabuki tradition continues to play a vital role in modern Japanese theater.

Kabuki and Tokugawa Thought—The kabuki theater often incorporates the prevailing moral notions of Tokugawa society as the mechanism upon which plots turn. For example, inga ōhō (law of retributive justice), a Buddhist notion, may result in the destruction of an evildoer or the bestowal of prosperity and happiness upon a long-suffering woman. The notion of mujō (the impermanence of all things), also derived from Buddhism, may be illustrated by the fall of a powerful military leader or the demise of a proud family. Certain ethical notions based on Confucian traditions, such as duty, obligation, and filial piety, may come into direct conflict with personal desires and passions, leading to a series of dramatic situations (see GIRI AND NINJŌ).

The Kabuki Stage—The kabuki theater uses a draw curtain. It has broad black, green, and orange vertical stripes and is normally drawn open from stage right to stage left accompanied by the striking of wooden clappers. The curtain may also serve as a backdrop for brief scenes given before or after the performance on the main part of the stage. Kamite (stage left) is regarded as the place of honor and is occupied by characters of high rank, guests, and important messengers or official representatives. Shimote (stage right) is occupied by characters of low rank and members of a household; most entrances and exits take place on this side, usually by way of the hanamichi. A unique feature of the kabuki stage is the mawaributai, a circular platform that can be rotated to permit a second scene to be performed simultaneously with the scene already in progress or to dramatize a flashback.

Roles in Kabuki Plays—Yakugara, or types of dramatic role, are determined on the basis of the personality, age, or social position of characters. Onnagata are assigned to such roles as housewife, samurai lady, heroic woman, and wicked woman. Within the rich repertory of kabuki plays, the roles of Agemaki in SUKEROKU YUKARI NO EDO-ZAKURA and Masaoka, the loyal nanny in MEIBOKU SENDAI HAGI, are regarded as among the most challenging. Standard male roles are virtuous hero, handsome lover, evil courtier, wicked samurai, and unscrupulous rake. Versatile performers sometimes play both male and female roles.

Kabuki Dialogue—The dialogue in kabuki plays ranges from the extremely stylized to the intensely realistic. Generally jidai-mono contain more formalized speech and

the sewa-mono more colloquial speech. In general, lines tend to be marked by a seven-five syllabic pattern (similar to that of classical Japanese poetry) and are delivered with a distinctive rhythm and tempo that is closely identified with kabuki. The tsurane, a long declamatory speech occurring in jidai-mono, effectively employs this rhythmic pattern. Maruhon-mono, kabuki adaptations from bunraku puppet plays, are in particular noted for their mellifluous lines in the seven-five pattern.

Acting Forms—The powerful influence of a long theatrical tradition is graphically illustrated by kata (forms), the stylized gestures and movements of kabuki performers. Since kata are not subject to rejection at the whim of the actor, they have helped to maintain the artistic integrity of kabuki. Tate (stylized fighting), roppō (dramatic exit accompanied by exaggerated gestures), mie (striking an attitude), and dammari (silent scene) all belong to this category. The performing of kata occurs more often in jidai-mono, which deal with members of the warrior class and in which larger-than-life action is always expected, but sewa-mono also contain instances of kata in the apparently casual movements of actors as they walk, speak, or sit.

Costumes—Costume, wig, and makeup are carefully matched with the nature of a role. In general, the costumes in jidai-mono are more stlylized and elegant, befitting members of the nobility and the samurai class. By contrast, the prevailing fashions of society at large during the Edo period are portrayed quite realistically in sewa-mono plays. The costumes used in shosagoto dance pieces are especially noted for their color, design, and workmanship. Wigs are classified according to age of characters, historical period, social status, occupation, and other considerations. Makeup varies widely depending on the role. The most striking example is KUMADORI, an established set of masklike makeup styles numbering about 100 and used in jidai-mono.

Stage Assistants—In addition to the regular performers, the kōken (stage assistant) serves a valuable function on the stage. He is especially important in dance pieces. During the demanding hayagawari (quick costume change), the kōken must carefully follow the movements of the dancer, all the while remaining close behind him, and at the crucial moment assist in the hikinuki ("pulling out"), by which a layer of clothing is quickly removed revealing a costume of different pattern and color. The kōken is also known as kurogo ("black costume") since he is often dressed all in black.

Acting Families—Each performer belongs to an acting family by whose name he is known. Professionally, he is part of a closely knit hierarchical organization, headed by one of the leading actors, and must spend many years as an apprentice. An actor may eventually receive a new name as a mark of his elevation to a higher position within the professional organization. It is awarded at a shūmei (name-assuming) ceremony, and in the company of his colleagues he then delivers from the stage an address (kōjō) in which he requests the continued patronage of the audience. The name Ichikawa Danjūrō, which can be traced back to the formative years of kabuki, is regarded even today as the most illustrious of honors a kabuki actor can receive. In 1985 Ichikawa Ebizō X (b 1951) became Danjūrō XII at a shūmei ceremony held at the Kabukiza,

which was reported with considerable fanfare in the popular press. For synopses of individual kabuki plays see AOTO-ZŌSHI HANA NO NISHIKI-E; KAGAMIJISHI; KANADEHON CHŪSHINGURA; KANJINCHŌ; KENUKI; KOKUSEN'YA KASSEN; KURUWA BUNSHŌ; KYŌ-GANOKO MUSUME DŌJŌJI; MEIBOKU SENDAI HAGI; NARUKAMI; SANJA MATSURI; SHIBARAKU; SOGA NO TAIMEN; SONEZAKI SHINJŪ; SUGAWARA DENJU TENARAI KAGAMI; SUKEROKU YUKARI NO EDO-ZAKURA; TSUMORU KOI YUKI NO SEKI NO TO; YA NO NE; YOSHITSUNE SEMBON-ZAKURA; YO WA NASAKE UKINA NO YOKOGUSHI. ☎ 704–705

kabuki jūhachiban　　　歌舞伎十八番

(literally, "eighteen KABUKI numbers"). Inventory compiled by the actor Ichikawa Danjūrō VII (1791–1859; see ICHIKAWA DANJŪRŌ) of the most notable plays, acts, and scenes from plays in the repertory of the Ichikawa acting-family dynasty, the most illustrious in kabuki history. The plays are Fuwa (1680), Shibaraku (1697), Fudō (1697), Uwanari (1699), Zōbiki (1701), Sukeroku (1713), Uirōuri (1718), Ya no ne (1720), Oshimodoshi (1727), Kan U (1737), Kagekiyo (1739), Nanatsumen (1740), Kenuki (1742), Narukami (1742), Gedatsu (1760), Jayanagi (1763), Kamahige (1774), and Kanjinchō (1840). Of these only 6 are often performed in the modern repertory: NARUKAMI, SHIBARAKU, Sukeroku (see SUKEROKU YUKARI NO EDO-ZAKURA), YA NO NE, KENUKI, and KANJINCHŌ. Only the last, a one-act play, is complete in itself; the other 5 are single acts from long plays. All of the other 12 titles have been reconstructed and revived in modern times but have not found a place in the repertory. With the exception of 3 plays (Uirōuri, Nanatsumen, and Jayanagi) the central character is a larger-than-life hero who acts and declaims in an exaggerated, unrealistic style called aragoto ("rough business"). A specialty of the Ichikawa line, this bombastic style came to be seen as typical of the Edo (now Tōkyō) kabuki, in contrast to the realistic mode favored in the Kyōto-Ōsaka area.

kabuki music　　　歌舞伎音楽

(kabuki ongaku). A variety of vocal and/or instrumental music that has accompanied dances or enhanced dramatic situations in the popular KABUKI theater from the 17th century to the present. The first kabuki theaters used singing plus the drums and flute of the classical NŌ drama. The lyrics of surviving pieces and the plebeian nature of the theater show that this kabuki music was derived from popular and folk forms. By the 17th century, the major melodic instrument used in kabuki was the three-stringed plucked lute called the samisen or SHAMISEN. Throughout the 18th and 19th centuries, a great variety of shamisen musical styles appeared both on the kabuki stage and in the neighboring amusement quarters. These styles differed in repertoire, in the size and sound of the shamisen, and in the vocal style of the singers. The constant elaboration of kabuki productions also included the use of new percussion instruments derived from folk and religious sources. Overall, kabuki showed the kind of creative eclecticism indicative of good theater music.

Music Types—The kinds of shamisen music used in kabuki can be divided first into those that are primarily narrative (called jōruri or katarimono) and those that are lyrical (called utamono). Though historically almost every genre of shamisen music has appeared on stage, only four are common today. The dominant lyrical genre is NAGAUTA ("long song"), while KIYOMOTO-BUSHI, TOKIWAZU-BUSHI, and GIDAYŪ-BUSHI are classified as narrative music. Each genre in kabuki is performed by different musicians since their lineages and styles are different.

Another set of *shamisen* musicians are those who perform various old popular lyrical genres (such as *hauta* and KOUTA) offstage or work with other offstage musicians in special effects needed for a given scene. Their music, along with that of their percussion and flute-playing colleagues, is called offstage (*geza*) music. The drummers and flutists who perform on stage with the other *shamisen* genres are known collectively as the HAYASHI, while the term for all music performed on stage is *debayashi*.

Functions—Music on stage is generally used to accompany dance. Offstage music has many functions. It may accompany specific stage actions, set moods, establish locations or even weather conditions, identify characters, create sound effects, or reflect the unspoken thoughts of the actors. The most effective support of a specific stage gesture or pose is created by the clack of two wooden sticks (*ki* or *hyōshigi*), struck on a wooden board at stage left at the precise moment of the movement. These same sticks struck together signal the opening or ending of a scene and always have a dramatic impact on kabuki audiences.

Perhaps the most striking fact for Western musicians is that the music for a kabuki performance is communally composed. The singer and *shamisen* player are responsible for their own parts, while the percussion and offstage music are added in consultation with the head of the guild of percussionists (the *hayashi-gashira*) and the actors and directors of the performance. If performers from a different guild play the same piece, the result may be audibly different. Thus, there is no "correct" rendition of a piece; instead, there may be several correct ways in which music can operate in a kabuki performance.

kabunakama 株仲間

Monopolistic trade associations sanctioned by the Tokugawa shogunate and various *daimyō* domains during the Edo period (1600–1868). *Nakama* meant an association of merchants who banded together with official approval to restrict access to trade and to set prices. *Kabu* meant a "share" or membership in such an association. In theory, each member held only one *kabu*, symbolized by a wooden placard called a *kabufuda*. In return for the right to monopolize a trade or some aspect of it, the *kabunakama* made "contributions" (known as MYŌGAKIN) to the authorities.

Monopolistic trade associations called ZA had flourished during the Muromachi period (1333–1568), but most of them had been abolished during the 16th century (see RAKUICHI AND RAKUZA). In the late 17th century the Tokugawa shogunate came to recognize the usefulness of such associations for regulating trade and began to approve them. Their "contributions" were regularized as annual taxes. However, *kabunakama* came under increasing opposition, and during the KANSEI REFORMS (1787–93) many of them were dissolved. During the TEMPŌ REFORMS (1841–43) the shogunate dissolved all *kabunakama*. But this action resulted in high inflation, and in 1851 the *kabunakama* system was revived with broader membership and prohibitions on the payment of *myōga-*

kin. The associations were abolished soon after the Meiji Restoration of 1868.

Kaburagi Kiyokata 鏑木清方

(1878–1972). Japanese-style painter and leading modern master of genre painting. He specialized in *bijinga* (pictures of beautiful women). He was born Kaburagi Ken'ichi in the Kanda district of Tōkyō. His father was president of the newspaper *Nichinichi shimbun* and a writer of popular novels. In 1891 Kaburagi entered the studio of Mizuno Toshikata (1866–1908) and began the study of UKIYO-E. He was soon producing illustrations for newspapers and magazines. In 1901 he helped found the Ugōkai (1901–12), an organization that sought to revive genre painting. When the Bunten exhibitions were established in 1907, Kaburagi began to paint full time and exhibit at the Bunten. In 1916 with HIRAFUKU HYAKUSUI, MATSUOKA EIKYŪ, Yūki Somei (1875–1957), and Kikkawa Reika (1875–1929), he helped found the Kinreisha, the nucleus of the Japanese-style painting (NIHONGA) associations in Tōkyō. He was appointed a member of the Imperial Fine Arts Academy (Teikoku Bijutsuin) in 1929 and artist for the imperial household (*teishitsu gigeiin*) in 1944. Kaburagi was awarded the Order of Culture in 1954.

kabushiki kaisha → joint-stock company

kabutogani → horseshoe crab

Kachikachi yama かちかち山

(Kachikachi Mountain). Folktale about the mischievous deeds of a TANUKI (raccoon dog, a badger-like creature), a common trickster figure in Japanese folklore. A *tanuki* teases an old man and woman who become so angry that they threaten to make soup out of him. The *tanuki* deceives the old woman and kills her. He then assumes her shape, gives the old man soup made from the old woman, and escapes. A rabbit comes along and decides to avenge the old woman; he persuades the *tanuki* to carry some firewood and sets fire to the twigs with a flintstone. (The *kachikachi* of the title refers to the sound of striking flints.) He then irritates the *tanuki's* burns by applying a spicy bean-paste mixture and finally tricks the *tanuki* into boarding a boat made of mud, which immediately sinks. In some versions, the trickster is a wolf or a monkey.

kachōga → bird-and-flower painting

Kada no Arimaro 荷田在満

(1706–51). KOKUGAKU (National Learning) scholar and WAKA poet. Nephew and adopted son of KADA NO AZUMAMARO. Born in Kyōto. Opposing the views of KAMO NO MABUCHI and TAYASU MUNETAKE, he advocated the *waka* poetry style of the SHIN KOKINSHŪ over that of the MAN'YŌSHŪ. He wrote *Kokka hachiron* (1742), the foremost work on poetics of its time.

Kada no Azumamaro 荷田春満

(1669–1736). KOKUGAKU (National Learning) scholar and poet. Born into a priestly family of the Fushimi Inari Shrine in Kyōto, he was educated in the traditions of WAKA poetry and Shintō scholarship. He was summoned to Edo (now Tōkyō) to collate documents held in the shogunal library. He also gave private lectures on the KOJIKI, NIHON SHOKI, and MAN'YŌSHŪ and published works on Shintō and on Man'yō poetics. Considered one of the founders of the Kokugaku tradi-

tion, he urged that it be officially adopted in place of Confucianism as the ethical underpinning of the state. His student KAMO NO MABUCHI built upon his master's attainments by employing the philological methods of KEICHŪ. Azumamaro's *waka* are collected in *Shun'yōshū* (1798); a modern edition of his complete works, *Kada zenshū*, appeared in 1928.

Kadena 嘉手納[町]

Town on the island of Okinawa, Okinawa Prefecture. Approximately 80 percent of Kadena is occupied by the Kadena US Air Force Base, upon which the economy depends. Small amounts of sugarcane and pineapple are produced. Pop: 13,865.

Kades, Charles Louis ケーディス, C. L.

(1906–). US lawyer and government official. As deputy chief of the Government Section of SCAP (the headquarters of the Allied Occupation of Japan) from 1945 to 1949, he played a leading role in making and carrying out OCCUPATION policies for Japan's constitutional and legal reforms and the purge of wartime officials. Born in Newburgh, New York, he graduated from Cornell University in 1927 and from Harvard Law School in 1930. He practiced law in New York and was assistant general counsel of the Treasury Department from 1941 to 1942.

Kadokawa Publishing Co, Ltd [株]角川書店

(Kadokawa Shoten). One of Japan's leading publishing houses. Founded in 1945 by Kadokawa Gen'yoshi (1917–75), a scholar of Japanese literature and student of ORIKUCHI SHINOBU. The company originally focused on the publishing of belles lettres. When Kadokawa's son Haruki (b 1942) became the second president of the company in 1975, he began publishing paperback editions and undertook for the first time in Japan the simultaneous production of a single work in book and film form, supported by coordinated advertising on television and radio.

707

kadomatsu In this *kadomatsu* display, a pair of arrangements featuring pine, bamboo, Japanese plum, and bamboo grass adorn the gate of a Kyōto restaurant at New Year's.

His activities have changed the publishing house into a multimedia organization.

Kadoma 門真[市]

City in central Ōsaka Prefecture, central Honshū, contiguous with Ōsaka. Kadoma has traditionally been known for its lotus roots (*renkon*), used in Japanese cooking. Matsushita Electric Works, Ltd, has its headquarters here. Pop: 142,297.

kadomatsu 門松

An arrangement of tree sprigs used to decorate the inside and outside of Japanese homes at New Year's. Although there are regional variations in the type of tree used and the places where these arrangements are displayed, most commonly an arrangement featuring pine is placed on the gate to the house, giving rise to the name *kadomatsu*, literally, "gate pine." Bamboo, SAKAKI (a low evergreen of the tea family), and Japanese chestnut are among the other types of trees used in *kadomatsu*; in some parts of Japan two or three different ones are combined. When displayed outside the house, *kadomatsu* are usually arranged in pairs, one to the left and one to the right of the entrance. Inside, they are displayed singly. The origin of this custom lies in the fact that *kadomatsu* are believed to serve as a dwelling place (*yorishiro*) for the god who brings good luck at the beginning of the year (TOSHIGAMI). *Kadomatsu* are usually displayed until 7 January, but this varies regionally as well.

Kadoya Shichirobei 角屋七郎兵衛

(1610–72). Overseas trader of the early Edo period (1600–1868). Born in Matsuzaka in Ise Province (now part of Mie Prefecture). In 1631 he sailed to Annam (now Vietnam) and settled permanently in a Japanese community near Tourane (now Da Nang). The NATIONAL SECLUSION policy limited his trade and communication with Japan for nearly 30 years until the Kambun era (1661–73), when he reestablished contact with his homeland.

kadozuke 門付

Entertainers who go door-to-door performing for food (usually uncooked rice) or money. The performance itself is also called *kadozuke*. From earliest recorded times, people dressed as gods would visit each house at certain seasons of the year to offer the blessings of the gods to its occupants. The religious significance gradually faded, but the custom persisted as an entertainment for a reward. *Kadozuke*'s ranks include seasonal visitors, such as the SHISHI-MAI groups and *daikoku* dancers, whose performances are to guarantee good fortune for the year, and year-round *kadozuke*, whose performances usually are more for entertainment than for

religious purposes. Since World War II, the number of *kadozuke* has greatly diminished.

kaede → maples

Kaehwap'a 開化派

(J: Kaikaha; Enlightenment Faction). Also called the Independence Party. A Korean political clique promoting Westernization and independence from China; formed after the IMO MUTINY of 1882. Two of the leaders, KIM OK-KYUN and PAK YŎNG-HYO, had traveled to Japan and had come under the influence of the pro-Western scholar FUKUZAWA YUKICHI. The group clashed with the SUGUP'A, a conservative, pro-Chinese faction of the government, in an unsuccessful Japanese-supported attempt to seize power in 1884 (see KAPSIN POLITICAL COUP). See also KOREA AND JAPAN.

Kaei sandai ki 花営三代記

(Record of Three Generations of Flowery Rule). Also called *Muromachi ki* or *Buke nikki*. A record of the Muromachi shogunate; author unknown. It covers political and economic matters from 1367 to 1425, encompassing the rule of the shōguns ASHIKAGA YOSHIMITSU (r 1369–95), Yoshimochi (r 1395–1423), and Yoshikazu (r 1423–25).

Kaempfer, Engelbert ケンペル, E.

(1651–1716). German physician and historian. Born at Lemgo in the Duchy of Lippe (now part of Germany), Kaempfer received an excellent medical and humanistic education and in March 1683 became secretary of a Swedish embassy to Persia. He entered the service of the Dutch East India Company, spending 1686–88 at Bandar Abbas (Gombrun, Persia).

Reaching Batavia (now Jakarta, Indonesia) in 1689, he left for Japan via Siam (now Thailand) in May 1690. In September 1690 he arrived at Nagasaki to become physician at the Dutch factory on the island of DEJIMA in Nagasaki Harbor. In 1691 and 1692 Kaempfer accompanied the annual Dutch tribute mission (EDO SAMPU) to the shōgun's court at Edo (now Tōkyō). His meticulous accounts of these journeys are published in his two-volume *History of Japan* (1727–28), which appeared in Dutch, French, and German editions. It remained the standard European work on Japan until the publication in the 19th century of the works of Izaak TITSINGH and Philipp Franz von SIEBOLD. Despite the ban against foreigners' acquiring any materials on Japan, Kaempfer contrived to smuggle out a collection of books, manuscripts, and maps that were fairly representative of literature in Japan during the GENROKU ERA (1688–1704). Kaempfer returned to Europe in 1693. In April 1694 he took his medical degree at Leiden and then settled at Lemgo as physician to the prince of Lippe.

kaeshi 返し

(paying back; literally, "return"). Gift or favor given in return for same. In some cases Japan has relatively formal and explicit rules as to what should be paid back and when and how. For funeral gifts (KŌDEN) that it has received, for example, the bereaved family must give a return gift equivalent to about one-third to one-half the value of the *kōden*. Gifts given in situations of social equality always require a return gift. When return of an equivalent gift is not required, as in the case of the midyear gift (CHŪGEN) or the

year-end gift (SEIBO), a hierarchical relationship is usually involved, in which an inferior gives to his social superior to express gratitude for a past favor. These customs express and create mutual trust, as well as the obligation of readiness to help each other, sometimes felt more strongly when reciprocity is entailed. As such they are an important part of the Japanese social network. See also GIFT GIVING; YUINŌ; KAIKI IWAI.

kaezeni 替銭

(money exchange). Also called *kaesen* or *kawashi*. Payment by a bill of exchange called SAIFU employed during the Kamakura (1185–1333) and Muromachi (1333–1568) periods. It originated in the 13th century mainly as a substitute for the payment of rice and other taxes (NENGU) from landed estates (SHŌEN) in remote areas to their proprietors in Kyōto. It was especially convenient since currency was not standard at the time. The business of money exchange was handled by specialized merchants called *kaezeniya* or *saifuya*. With the expansion of commercial activities the *kaezeni* system came to be widely used in general business transactions.

Kaga 加賀[市]

City in southwestern Ishikawa Prefecture, central Honshū, on the Sea of Japan. Kaga developed as a castle town during the Edo period (1600–1868). It produces silk fabrics known as Kaga *habutae* and is also noted for its KUTANI WARE. Hot springs (Katayamazu and Yamashiro) and famous tombs (at Hōōzan and Kitsuneyama) attract visitors. Pop: 69,196.

Kaga domain 加賀藩

(Kaga *han*). Also known as Kanazawa domain. Edo-period (1600–1868) domain that extended over much of Kaga, Noto, and Etchū provinces; most of present-day Ishikawa and Toyama prefectures. The MAEDA FAMILY, lords of the domain, were granted the major parts of their lands by TOYOTOMI HIDEYOSHI and received the status of TOZAMA (outside vassal) from TOKUGAWA IEYASU. The commercial and administrative center of the domain was the castle town of Kanazawa. OMOTEDAKA (estimated annual production of rice): 1,025,020 KOKU (1 *koku* is 180 liters or 5 US bushels).

Kagaku Gijutsu Chō → Science and Technology Agency

Kagamijishi 鏡獅子

(The Lion at the New Year's Banquet). Original title *Shunkyō kagamijishi*. KABUKI dance piece (*shosagoto*) by Fukuchi Ōchi and others, in two contrasting parts; first performed in 1893. At a New Year's banquet in the ladies' quarters of Edo Castle, the young attendant Yayoi performs a graceful dance until, picking up a hand puppet of a lion, she is possessed by the lion's spirit and driven from the scene. In the second part she reappears in lion makeup and puts on a spectacular show of the great beast twirling its mane.

Kagami Kenkichi 各務鎌吉

(1868–1939). Businessman who developed the general insurance industry in Japan. Born in Gifu Prefecture. Graduate of Tōkyō Higher Commercial School (now Hitotsubashi University). Kagami joined TOKIO MARINE & FIRE INSURANCE CO, LTD, in 1891 and became chairman in 1925. He is credited with transforming Tokio Marine into a large, internationally known firm. He also became chairman of Meiji Fire & Marine in 1922, of Tōmei Fire & Marine in 1925, and of Mitsubishi Marine & Fire in 1933. He was concurrently chairman of NIPPON YŪSEN KAISHA and MITSUBISHI TRUST & BANKING CORPORATION.

Kagami Shikō　　　各務支考

(1665–1731). HAIKU poet. Born in Mino Province (now part of Gifu Prefecture). One of the 10 major disciples of BASHŌ. Shikō is credited for his part in consolidating Bashō's teachings into a coherent poetic theory and for popularizing haiku and Bashō's work. He wrote *Kuzu no matsubara* (1692), the first critical essay on Bashō's style, and coedited *Zoku sarumino* (1698), the last item in the collection HAIKAI SHICHIBUSHŪ. The Mino school, which he founded, was later ridiculed for its facile, vulgarized version of the orthodox style. Shikō remains, however, the foremost theorist of haiku, as evidenced in such critical works as *Haikai jūron* (1719) and *Jūron ibenshō* (1725).

Kaga no Chiyo　　　加賀千代

(1703–75). HAIKU poet. Born in Kaga Province (now part of Ishikawa Prefecture). She gained fame by the age of 18, when she attracted the attention of KAGAMI SHIKŌ, a prominent disciple of BASHŌ. She became a nun in her later years and was referred to as Chiyo Ni (the Nun Chiyo). *Chiyo Ni kushū* (1763) and its sequel, *Matsu no koe* (1771, The Voice of the Pines), are collections of her poems.

Kaga Otohiko　　　加賀乙彦

(1929–). Novelist and psychiatrist. Real name Kogi Sadataka. Born in Tōkyō; graduate of Tōkyō University Medical School. After working in several Tōkyō hospitals, he studied in Paris from 1957 to 1960. He gained recognition with *Furandoru no fuyu* (1966), a novel based upon his experiences in France. Other works include the critical essay "Bungaku to kyōki" (1971) and the novels *Kaerazaru natsu* (1973) and *Senkoku* (1979).

Kaga Province　　　加賀国

(Kaga no Kuni). Present-day Ishikawa Prefecture, excluding the Noto Peninsula. The lands were separated from Echizen Province in 823. From the Nara period (710–794), TŌDAIJI and other major temples established estates (SHŌEN) here, and the area supplied a variety of goods to the capital. In the 14th and 15th centuries the province was under the sway of military governors (SHUGO) of the TOGASHI FAMILY; they gave way at the end of the 15th century to adherents of the Jōdo Shin sect of Buddhism (see IKKŌ IKKI), who controlled Kaga for almost a century. ODA NOBUNAGA suppressed the sect and the province passed into the hands of MAEDA TOSHIIE and his descendants, who ruled over Kaga (see KAGA DOMAIN) until the Meiji period (1868–1912).

Kagawa Canal　　　香川用水

(Kagawa Yōsui). Canal in southern Kagawa Prefecture, Shikoku. It provides water to the entire prefecture for agricultural, industrial, and household use. The canal supplies approximately 250 million metric tons (275 million short tons) of water yearly, drawn from the Ikeda Dam on the upper reaches of the river Yoshinogawa in Tokushima Prefecture. Total length including branch channels: 106 km (66 mi).

Kagawa Gen'etsu　　　賀川玄悦

(1700–1777). Physician and founder of the Kagawa school of obstetrics. Also known as Kagawa Shigen; original family name Miura. A native of Hikone, Ōmi Province (now Shiga Prefecture), Kagawa studied medicine of the classicist school (*koihō*) in Kyōto. In one instance of extreme prolongation of labor, he used an iron hook from a paper lantern; this is said to be Japan's first forceps delivery. He also developed other methods for facilitating delivery and published his findings in a four-volume work, *Sanron* (1765, On Childbirth).

Kagawa Kageki　　　香川景樹

(1768–1843). WAKA poet and theorist. Founder of the Keien school of *waka*. Born in the Tottori domain (now Tottori Prefecture), in 1793 he went to Kyōto, where he studied under and was adopted into the family of Kagawa Kagemoto, court poet of the conservative Nijō school of *waka*. Kageki's true mentor, however, was OZAWA ROAN, who advocated simplicity, intelligibility, and the use of everyday language in poetry. Kageki's group, which came to be known as the Keien school, dominated *waka* poetic circles through the end of the Edo period (1600–1868). Central to Kageki's poetics is the idea of *shirabe*, the spontaneous flow of verse in harmonious response to feelings evoked by a particular scene or object. He stressed direct, sincere emotion as the source of all poetry and spurned intellectually contrived embellishment based on theory and lacking the immediacy of experience. His principal *waka* collection is *Keien isshi* (1830); his principal critical works include *Niimanabi iken* (1815) and *Kokin wakashū seigi* (1835–95).

Kagawa Prefecture　　　香川県

(Kagawa Ken). Located in northeastern Shikoku and bounded by the Inland Sea to the north, east, and west, and Ehime and Tokushima prefectures to the south. The SANUKI MOUNTAINS cover the southern part of the prefecture, and the northern area is composed largely of coastal lowlands. Numerous small Inland Sea islands also fall within Kagawa's territory. As the main transport link between Shikoku and Honshū, the city of TAKAMATSU has become the economic and administrative center of the Shikoku region. A Honshū-Shikoku bridge system between the cities of SAKAIDE, Kagawa Prefecture, and KURASHIKI, Okayama Prefecture, was opened in 1988. The climate is generally mild and dry, except in the rainy season in June and early July.

Known after the TAIKA REFORM of 645 as Sanuki Province, it developed as a rice-producing area and later added salt, sugar, and cotton to its economy. In the Edo period (1600–1868) it was divided into small domains, with some areas under the direct rule of the Tokugawa shogunate. The present prefectural name and boundaries were established in 1888.

Agriculture is dominated by the production of rice, livestock, and fruit. Kagawa once led Japan in salt production, but the salt fields were closed in 1972. Fishing is also important. Manufacturing industries are not highly developed and consist of light industries such as food processing, textiles, and paper, as well as some heavy industries such as shipbuilding.

Tourist attractions include seashore areas that are part of the INLAND SEA NATIONAL PARK, KOTOHIRA SHRINE in Kotohira, and RITSURIN PARK in Takamatsu. Area: 1,883 sq km (727 sq mi); pop: 1,023,412; capital: Takamatsu. Other major cities include Sakaide and MARUGAME.

Kagawa Shūtoku　　　香川修徳

(1683–1755). Physician of the classicist school (*koihō*). Also known as Kagawa Shūan or Ippondō. Born in Harima (now Hyōgo Prefecture), he studied medicine with GOTŌ KONZAN and Confucianism with ITŌ JINSAI. Kagawa advocated *jui ippon*, the doctrine holding that Confucianism and medical art originated from the same principles.

Kagawa Toyohiko　　　賀川豊彦

(1888–1960). Christian social reformer and labor leader. Born in Kōbe; studied at Meiji Gakuin, Kōbe Shingakkō, and Princeton Theological Seminary. A versatile, resourceful Christian who worked among the poor in Kōbe, Kagawa advocated a kind of "social gospel" modeled in part on guild socialism. Among his numerous publications were *Shisen o koete* (1920, Crossing the Deathline; tr *Before the Dawn*, 1924), an autobiographical novel, and *Himmin shinri no kenkyū* (1915, The Psychology of the Poor), a study

Kagamijishi In this exciting *kabuki* dance, performed here by Nakamura Ganjirō III, a young woman possessed by the spirit of a lion twirls her "mane" ferociously.

Kagawa Prefecture Location and Prefectural Crest

Kagawa Toyohiko This Christian evangelist was also active in the labor movement.

709

Kagawa Toyohiko

kago
1 A *yamakago*, a simple type of palanquin used by commoners, is depicted in this woodblock print from Hiroshige's 19th-century series *Fifty-Three Stations of the Tōkaidō Road*.
2 A *norimono*, used by people of higher rank.
3 A *machikago*, used by commoners.

based on knowledge and data collected while he lived in the slums.

Kagawa was active in the labor movement until the failure of the large-scale dockyard strikes in Kōbe in 1921 led to its radicalization. For his labor activities he was briefly imprisoned that year. He then turned his attention to the farmers' movement and worked to establish agricultural cooperatives. Kagawa was also one of the most prominent mass evangelists Japan produced. A pacifist, he was harassed by the military during World War II. After the war he was active in the world federation movement.

Kagerō nikki 蜻蛉日記

The diary, or memoirs, of a lady who lived in the 10th century and who is known as the mother of Michitsuna (FUJIWARA NO MICHITSUNA NO HAHA). The author was married to a distant kinsman, FUJIWARA NO KANEIE, who was at the end of his life head of the Fujiwara family and the most powerful statesman in the land. Kaneie was the father of FUJIWARA NO MICHINAGA, under whom the Fujiwara hegemony had its greatest day. Her only son had a moderately successful career at court but was never a serious rival of his brilliant half brother. *Kagerō nikki* (tr *The Gossamer Years*, 1964), divided into three books, covers 21 years (954–974) and is chiefly concerned with the author's unhappy marriage. As a secondary wife in a system of uncodified polygamy, her position was uncertain, and the *nikki* soon turns to her reasons for feeling betrayed and rejected. At the end of the third book she is completely estranged from Kaneie. The psychological description that distinguishes the work is considered to have influenced the development of MONOGATARI BUNGAKU, beginning with *Genji monogatari* (the TALE OF GENJI).

Kagetsu sōshi 花月草紙

(Book of Blossoms and Moon). Six-volume collection of essays (ZUIHITSU) by political reformer MATSUDAIRA SADANOBU; published 1818. A compilation of 156 pieces written by Sadanobu after he stepped down from his post as RŌJŪ (senior shogunal councillor) in 1812, it covers a variety of topics drawn from daily life and contemporary events. Sadanobu's literary and scholarly pronouncements, descriptions of nature, and discussions of natural phenomena are recorded in an elegant and floating style. Although his views are strongly marked by Confucian didacticism, he displays a quick wit and good-tempered humanity.

kageyushi 勘解由使

(audit officers). Extrastatutory officials (RYŌGE NO KAN) appointed to supervise the rotation of official personnel; the post was established during the Enryaku era (782–806). The

kago The weaving of a large *kago*. Long strips of bamboo are gradually curved while being woven through vertical bamboo standards.

kageyushi were originally established to investigate the misappropriation of funds by provincial governors (KOKUSHI), but in time their auditing duties extended to other areas as well. *Kageyushi* remained in office throughout the Heian period (794–1185) except between 806 and 824, when they were replaced by the Rokudō *kansatsushi* (investigators for the Six Circuits); but in the latter part of the period, with the rise of the provincial military aristocracy and the central government's loss of provincial control, their functions gradually became nominal.

kago 駕籠

Traditional means of conveyance, especially for one person, consisting of a covered palanquin suspended from a long pole carried on two men's shoulders. Originally constructed of bamboo, *kago* were later also made of wood. Only the back and front of the palanquin were covered, with the sides open or equipped with fold-up screens. *Kago* came into use during the mid-Muromachi period (1333–1568) and developed into an important mode of transportation during the Edo period (1600–1868). Types of *kago* and occasions for their use were controlled by the Tokugawa shogunate and depended on the social status of the rider. Elaborate *kago* called *norimono* were decorated in lacquer finish and were strictly for use by court nobles, *daimyō*, physicians, and high-ranking priests.

kago 籠

General term for various kinds of woven baskets made of plant material, such as AKEBI (*Akebia quinata;* a woody vine), BAMBOO, cane, or wisteria vine; it also refers to baskets made from woven leather strips or metal wire. *Kago* are roughly woven, though some show a certain intricacy of design and are comparatively large in mesh and size. This differentiates them from more finely meshed, woven containers such as sieves (*zaru*). *Kago* remains have been excavated in Japan from the Jōmon period (ca 10,000 BC–ca 300 BC). The varieties and uses of *kago* are numerous: as containers and winnowers in sericulture and agriculture, fishing creels, back baskets for transporting goods, WARIGO (a traditional lunch box), TSUZURA (clothes boxes), or storage containers. See also BAMBOO WARE.

Kagome Co, Ltd カゴメ[株]

(Kagome). Food processor, concentrating on tomato products, juices, and sauces. Founded in 1899 and incorporated in its present form in 1949. A pioneer in its field, it has become the industry leader in the processing of tomatoes, with a near monopoly in tomato products. The company has moved into the fields of fruit drinks and instant foods. Sales for the fiscal year ending March 1991 totaled ¥110.3 billion (US $803.9 million), and capi-

talization was ¥4.8 billion (US $35.0 million). Headquarters are in Nagoya and Tōkyō.

kagome kagome 籠目籠目

Children's game. The child who is "it" crouches in the middle with eyes closed while the others hold hands and circle around singing "*kagome, kagome.*" At the end of the song all crouch down and the one in the middle tries to guess who is directly behind him or her. If the guess is correct, the child whose name was called becomes "it."

Kagoshima 鹿児島[市]

Capital of Kagoshima Prefecture, southern Kyūshū. The city prospered after a castle was constructed by the SHIMAZU FAMILY in 1602. Devastated during World War II, the city has fully recovered. Food processing, wood crafts, and Ōshima *tsumugi* (a silk fabric) are the major industries. Kagoshima is the point of departure for ships leaving for Okinawa and the other Nansei Islands. As part of the KIRISHIMA-YAKU NATIONAL PARK, with SAKURAJIMA, a volcanic island soaring up in Kagoshima Bay, the city has been compared to Naples, its sister city. The people of the area have long been known for their Spartan virtues and spirit of independence; many leaders of the Meiji Restoration, such as SAIGŌ TAKAMORI and ŌKUBO TOSHIMICHI, were born here. Shiroyama, a hilly section of the city, was the site of the last battle of the SATSUMA REBELLION (1877), an uprising against the Meiji government by former *samurai*. Other spots of interest are the remains of Tsurumaru Castle, the garden Iso Teien, and a museum next to the garden displaying objects associated with SHIMAZU NARIAKIRA's attempts at modernization in the 1850s. Pop: 536,752.

Kagoshima Bay 鹿児島湾

(Kagoshima Wan). Also known as Kinkō Bay. Deep bay on the southern coast of Kyūshū between the Satsuma and Ōsumi peninsulas, Kagoshima Prefecture. The active volcano SAKURAJIMA, linked to the Ōsumi Peninsula by lava flows, juts into the northern section of the bay. An important area for shipping, the bay is also the site of a large storage base for crude oil. Kagoshima Bay forms the center of the Kirishima-Yaku National Park.

Kagoshima Bombardment 薩英戦争

(Satsuei Sensō). Exchange of cannon fire between a British naval squadron and the Satsuma domain (now Kagoshima Prefecture) in Kagoshima, on 15 August 1863. In September 1862 a British subject was killed by Satsuma *samurai* (see RICHARDSON AFFAIR); Britain responded with demands for indemnities from the Tokugawa shogunate and from Satsuma in addition to the execution of the murderers. Satsuma refused to pay, and in August 1863 a squadron of seven British warships entered Kagoshima Bay to negotiate directly. After fruitless talks, the British seized three Satsuma steamers anchored offshore. In the exchange of fire that followed, large parts of the city of Kagoshima were destroyed, but the British also suffered substantial losses and were forced to retreat when a typhoon struck. As a result, Satsuma became convinced of the superiority of Western military technology, while Britain decided on a peaceful settlement. An agreement was reached in December; Satsuma promised to punish the murderers and pay the indemnity.

Kagoshima domain →Satsuma domain

Kagoshima Juzō 鹿児島寿蔵

(1898–1982). Dollmaker and poet. Born in Fukuoka Prefecture. Kagoshima created the *shiso* doll, made by applying layers of paper (WASHI) to unglazed pottery. He first exhibited his work at the Imperial Academy Exhibition in 1936. He also made finely crafted ceramic dolls. In 1961 he was designated one of the LIVING NATIONAL TREASURES. Kagoshima was also active in the ARARAGI group of TANKA poets. In 1973 he published a book about his dollmaking, *Juzō tōgei ningyō.*

Kagoshima Prefecture 鹿児島県

(Kagoshima Ken). Located on the southern end of Kyūshū and bordered by Kumamoto and Miyazaki prefectures to the north, the Pacific Ocean to the east and south, and the East China Sea to the west. Includes several island groups to the south. The southern portion of the prefecture is divided by Kagoshima Bay into the Satsuma and Ōsumi peninsulas. The terrain consists mostly of low hilly areas, with a few large volcanoes, including KIRISHIMAYAMA, SAKURAJIMA, and KAIMONDAKE. The climate is warm, with frequent precipitation. The southern islands are generally flat, with the exception of YAKUSHIMA and AMAMI ŌSHIMA; MIYANOURADAKE on Yakushima is the highest mountain in the Kyūshū region. The vegetation on these islands is subtropical. Typhoons are frequent.

Remains of both Jōmon (ca 10,000 BC–ca 300 BC) and Yayoi (ca 300 BC–ca AD 300) cultures attest to the prefecture's early settlement. In early historical times the area was part of Hyūga Province and was inhabited by the KUMASO and HAYATO tribes. In the Nara period (710–794) the area was administratively divided into the provinces of Satsuma and Ōsumi. From the late Heian period (794–1185) until the Meiji Restoration (1868) it was under the control of the SHIMAZU FAMILY. Because of its location, it was among the first areas in Japan to come into contact with Europeans in the 16th century. Its geographical isolation also encouraged a spirit of independence from the Tokugawa shogunate, and several Satsuma men, including SAIGŌ TAKAMORI and ŌKUBO TOSHIMICHI, were leaders in the Meiji Restoration and the establishment of the modern Japanese state. The present prefectural boundaries were established in 1896.

Kagoshima's economy remains predominantly agricultural: the main crops are rice, sweet potatoes, and vegetables. Local specialty crops are sugarcane, citrus fruits, tea, and tobacco. Livestock farming and forestry are also important. General economic stagnation and low income levels, however, have led to a steady decline in Kagoshima's population since 1955.

Tourist attractions include KIRISHIMA-YAKU NATIONAL PARK and the subtropical vegetation and giant cryptomeria trees on the island of Yakushima. Area: 9,167 sq km (3,539 sq mi); pop: 1,797,824; capital: KAGOSHIMA. Other major cities include SENDAI, KANOYA, and NAZE.

Kagoshima University 鹿児島大学

(Kagoshima Daigaku). A coeducational national university located in the city of Kagoshima, Kagoshima Prefecture. Founded in 1949, the university contains faculties of law and letters, education, science, medicine, dentistry, engineering, agriculture, and fisheries. The university's Research Center for the South Pacific is Japan's leading institution in its field. Enrollment in 1989 was 8,900.

kagura 神楽

Type of performance or ritual of Shintō origin that dates from early times and is still found widely in contemporary Japan. In popular usage *kagura* means any performance—often one of masked dancing—that is part of the annual festival of a local Shintō shrine. To scholars of the performing arts, however, *kagura* is one of three primary categories in a widely accepted classification system of Japanese FOLK PERFORMING ARTS (*minzoku geinō*). In this context *kagura* is essentially the invocation of gods followed by the performance of song or dance or both, the whole event serving as prayer for the prolongation or revitalization of man's life.

The forms of *kagura* are extremely diverse. They are usually grouped into two large categories: the *kagura* performed at the imperial court or in major shrines closely related to it (*mikagura*), and that performed outside the court (*sato kagura*). The latter is further subdivided into *miko kagura*, which involves the dances of Shintō priestesses; *Ise kagura*, in which boiling water is offered to the gods; *Izumo kagura*, in which objects are held while dancing; and *shishi kagura*, which involves a lion dance. This diversity is made even richer by differences due to geographical, historical, and other factors.

Kagura is documented from at least the early 9th century, and it is assumed that even before these earliest records the evocation of KAMI (Shintō gods) in a community setting was practiced in Japan—with or without the concomitant performance aspect. In ancient times there was a belief that the soul—which departed the body at death—could be kept from leaving or even resummoned after leaving the body by means of various rituals, including the performance of song or dance. These rituals are referred to by the general term *chinkon*, which means literally to quiet or pacify a spirit. The account in the KOJIKI of how the sun goddess AMATERASU ŌMIKAMI was lured from her hiding place in a cave by the performance of a dance is thought by some to be a representation in myth of this belief. *Kagura* shares basic elements of the *chinkon* ritual. The order of events is as follows: establish a place for and invoke the god, celebrate formally by eating and drinking, hold performance events, send off the god, and then perhaps repeat the drinking, eating, and performance section in a more relaxed setting. Summoning and dispatching *kami* and gaining the revitalization of energy bestowed through participation in such an occasion are central characteristics of *kagura.*

Mikagura— At an early period the term *kagura* referred to several types of performance in the imperial court or in closely related shrines. The honorific form *mikagura* is now used to distinguish this type of *kagura.* At one time performers of *mikagura* included courtiers as well as court musicians. Today it is the responsibility of the musicians of the imperial household. *Kagura* was performed on a wide range of occasions throughout the year. Today the most important are that of the Daijōe (or DAIJŌSAI), a ceremony held in the year when a new emperor is enthroned, and the annual Naishidokoro *mikagura*, named after the place in the court where it was formerly performed. The Daijōe was formerly held in the 11th lunar month and the Naishidokoro *mikagura* in the 12th. (They are now held in November and December, respectively.) The Naishidokoro *mikagura* was first performed very early in the 11th century, and by that century's end it had apparently become an annual event.

kagura uta 神楽歌

Originally, the songs (*uta*) of Shintō ritual dance (see KAGURA). More specifically, a fixed body of ancient court songs in the musical style of GAGAKU. In the 9th century they were incorporated in the DAIJŌSAI accession ceremony. During the 11th century the *kagura* concert became an independent annual event with a fixed repertory, which was subsequently used for all *kagura* ceremonies.

Modern performances generally consist of short selections from the standard repertory of about 88 pieces. The program schedule is arranged as follows: (1) *niwabi*—the introductory fire song; (2) *torimono*—songs on the various religious implements carried by the dancers; (3) *karakami*—interlude with songs on the god known as Karakami; (4) *saibara*—pieces in the style of folk songs; and (5) the finale consisting of miscellaneous selections.

All *kagura* songs consist of two parts: *moto* (the rise) and *sue* (the close), to be sung by two groups sitting opposite each other.

kagura Dancers and musicians perform the Izumo-style *kagura* piece "Orochi" (Giant Serpent).

Kagoshima Prefecture Location and Prefectural Crest

There are distinct differences among the various categories of song in meter, style of singing, and instrumental arrangement. Accompanying instruments are the *wagon*, or six-string zither; the *kagurabue*, a six-hole horizontal flute; the HICHIRIKI, a kind of oboe; and the *shakubyōshi*, or wooden clappers. See also EARLY JAPANESE SONG; MUSIC, TRADITIONAL.

Kahokugata　河北潟

Also called Hasuko. Lagoon in the northwestern part of the city of Kanazawa, Ishikawa Prefecture, central Honshū. Two-thirds of the lagoon has been reclaimed and is used for rice cultivation. It is known for its white swans. Area of original lake: 23 sq km (9 sq mi); present area: 5.1 sq km (2 sq mi); circumference: 25 km (16 mi); depth: 2 m (6.6 ft); altitude 1 m (3.3 ft).

kai-awase　貝合せ

A shell-matching game popular among aristocrats of the Heian period (794–1185). One of many matching games of the period, *kai-awase* was at first played by simply comparing the shape, color, size, and rarity of natural shells. Toward the end of the Heian period another game, using different kinds of clamshell, emerged called *kai-ōi*. In *kai-ōi* one half shell of each clam was placed outside-up, and players competed in selecting the matching halves from a separate pile. Later, each half shell was painted or inscribed with lines of WAKA poetry, and players had to choose matching shells to complete a picture or poem. Eventually, *kai-ōi* came to be called *kai-awase*, although its rules differed from the original *kai-awase* game. *Kai-awase* was the ancestor of *utagai* and *uta-garuta*, which became popular in the Edo period (1600–1868). See PLAYING CARDS.

Kaibara Ekiken　貝原益軒

(1630–1714). Confucian scholar of the Edo period (1600–1868). Born into the family of a retainer of the Fukuoka domain (now part of Fukuoka Prefecture). He entered the service of the domainal lord Kuroda Tadayuki but in 1649 came into disfavor with Tadayuki and was deprived of his stipend and forced to become a RŌNIN. During this period he studied medicine and botany in Nagasaki. In 1656 his stipend was restored by the new *daimyō* Kuroda Mitsuyuki. Ekiken spent the rest of his life in the service of the Fukuoka domain.

From his interest in Confucianism and natural science Ekiken expounded a philosophy that emphasized experience and practical knowledge. In 1708 he wrote *Yamato honzō*, in which he classified 1,300 kinds of medicinal herb from China and Japan. In 1713, drawing on Japanese and Chinese sources, he wrote YŌJŌKUN, a work on health improvement. ONNA DAIGAKU, a widely read manual for the moral training of women, has been mistakenly attributed to Ekiken.

kaidō　街道

(main highways). Term for trunk highways developed before the modern period. Their number, location, rank, and importance varied from period to period. In the Nara (710–794) and Heian (794–1185) periods there were seven government-administered highways linking the Nara and Kyōto area with the outlying provinces. A network of POST-STATION TOWNS was established to provide for the needs of travelers (see also EKISEI). In the Edo period (1600–1868) the TOKUGAWA SHOGUNATE maintained five main highways (GOKAIDŌ) under its direct control to link the provinces with the shogunal capital at Edo (now Tōkyō). These highways were utilized by the *daimyō* in their periodic journeys to Edo (see SANKIN KŌTAI). In recent years modern highways have been built on or near the courses of the old *kaidō*. The original names are still popularly used to identify the routes.

Kaidōki　海道記

Kamakura-period (1185–1333) diary of a journey from Kyōto to Kamakura, probably in April 1223 along the highway TŌKAIDŌ. Author unknown. The work captures the pathos of the JŌKYŪ DISTURBANCE of 1221 and ruminates on tenets of Amida Buddhism. With the TŌKAN KIKŌ, it is admired for the beauty of its *wakan konkō* prose style—classical Japanese with a heavy admixture of words and phrases from classical Chinese literature—but it is also an important source of historical information on Kamakura Buddhism and government.

kaieki　改易

Term for *samurai* declassment during the Edo period (1600–1868). Originally *kaieki* referred to the transfer or dismissal from office of a *shōen* (estate) administrator (SHŌKAN). Later, during the Kamakura (1185–1333) and Muromachi (1333–1568) periods, it referred to dismissal of JITŌ (military land stewards) and other samurai officials and gradually to the deprivation of samurai status itself. The Tokugawa shogunate used the term *kaieki* specifically to mean deprivation of rank and samurai or *kuge* (court noble) status. *Kaieki* was a major instrument of political control and was imposed for violation of regulations such as the BUKE SHO-HATTO or for failure to assure stable succession in one's house (see OIE SŌDŌ), among other reasons. It was enforced most widely between 1600 and 1652, when 197 *daimyō* houses were declassed and lands assessed at 16 million *koku* (see KOKUDAKA) were redistributed by the first three Tokugawa shōguns.

Kaien　海燕

(Stormy Petrel). Monthly literary journal. Founded in 1982; published by Fukutake Publishing Co. Its emphasis is on works of high literary quality and the discovery of new talent. It has published works by established writers such as IBUSE MASUJI, KURAHASHI YUMIKO, and YOSHIMOTO TAKAAKI, and new authors such as HIKARI AGATA and SHIMADA MASAHIKO debuted in *Kaien* and have developed their talents in its pages.

Kaientai　海援隊

(Naval Auxiliary Force). Name of trading and shipping company organized by SAKAMOTO RYŌMA, an antishogunate *samurai* from the Tosa domain (now Kōchi Prefecture). In 1864, with help from the Satsuma domain (now Kagoshima Prefecture), Sakamoto and 20 other samurai who had abandoned their domains gathered in Nagasaki and formed a small organization known as the Shachū (Company). With a small fleet of ships at its command, it bought goods, especially arms, from Western traders in Nagasaki for Satsuma and Chōshū (now Yamaguchi Prefecture), another domain active in the antishogunate movement. In 1866 Sakamoto brought together the two rival domains in the so-called SATSUMA-CHŌSHŪ ALLIANCE. The following year Sakamoto reestablished ties with his domain, and his organization, renamed the Kaientai, received Tosa's support. It was disbanded in 1868, after Sakamoto's assassination in Kyōto by shogunate henchmen.

Kaifūsō　懐風藻

(Verses in Memory of Poets Past). Oldest extant Japanese anthology of *kanshi* (poems written in Chinese by Japanese poets; see POETRY AND PROSE IN CHINESE). It was compiled in 751, before completion of the MAN'YŌSHŪ (759), the oldest extant anthology of Japanese WAKA poetry. Its compiler is unknown, although it has been ascribed variously to ŌMI NO MIFUNE, Fujii no Hironari (fl ca mid-8th century), and ISONOKAMI NO YAKATSUGU. The *Kaifūsō* contains 120 poems by 64 poets, covering almost 100 years (ca 661–758), and is arranged in chronological order. There are poems by imperial princes, including Prince Ōtomo (see Emperor KŌBUN); nobles, including FUJIWARA NO FUHITO; and Buddhist monks. Nine poets are introduced by short biographies; the others are represented only by their poems. Twenty-one authors of the *Kaifūsō* are known also as poets of the *Man'yōshū*.

The poems of the *Kaifūsō* are traditionally Chinese in wording, phrasing, and metrical pattern. The *Wen xuan* (*Wen hsüan;* J: *Monzen*), the great Chinese anthology of the Six Dynasties period (220–589), seems to have served as a model. The *Kaifūsō* was succeeded by other court compilations of Chinese verse: *Ryōunshū* (814; see SAGA, EMPEROR), BUNKA SHŪREISHŪ (818), and KEIKOKU-SHŪ (827).

Kaifu Toshiki　海部俊樹

(1931–). Politician; prime minister from August 1989 to November 1991. Born in Aichi Prefecture, Kaifu graduated from Waseda University. He was first elected to the House of Representatives in 1960 as a LIBERAL DEMOCRATIC PARTY (LDP) candidate from his home prefecture. In November 1974 Kaifu was appointed deputy chief cabinet secretary in the MIKI TAKEO cabinet, and in December 1976 he became minister of education in the FUKUDA TAKEO cabinet. In August 1989, Kaifu became prime minister, replacing UNO SŌSUKE. In February 1990 Kaifu formed his second cabinet. His inability to get a number of political reform bills passed contributed to his decision in September 1991 to step down. MIYAZAWA KIICHI SUCceeded Kaifu as prime minister in November of that year.

Kaigai Tokō Kinshi Rei 海外渡航禁止令

(Prohibitions of Foreign Voyages). Major steps in the formation of the Tokugawa shogunate's NATIONAL SECLUSION (Sakoku) policy in the 1630s. These were not discrete regulations but were included in administrative directives dealing comprehensively with the control of foreign trade and of Christianity. One of these directives, dated 1633, prohibited Japanese travel to foreign lands except on trading vessels endorsed by the senior councillors (*rōjū;* see HŌSHOSEN). Japanese residing overseas, except for those cast abroad by mischance, were forbidden to reenter the country. Even these exceptions were eliminated in 1635; however, the Tokugawa regime in actuality sanctioned the repatriation of castaways. Moreover, two overseas destinations remained legally open to certain rigidly circumscribed groups of Japanese. They were Ryūkyū, which after 1609 was not a sovereign foreign country but a dependency of the *daimyō* of Kagoshima; and Pusan in Korea, where the daimyō of Tsushima maintained a trading factory ("Japan House"; Kor: Waegwan; J: Wakan) from 1611 throughout the Edo period (1600–1868).

Kaigetsudō school 懐月堂派

(Kaigetsudō Ha). School of UKIYO-E painters and print artists in Edo (now Tōkyō) during the early 18th century, specializing in large-scale paintings and prints of courtesans. The founder and first master of the school was Kaigetsudō Ando (also known as Kaigetsudō Yasunori). Ando was followed by his pupils Anchi (Yasutomo), Dohan (Norishige), Doshin (Noritatsu), Doshu (Noritane), and Doshū (Norihide), all using the Kaigetsudō name and flourishing during the 1710s. Ando, who was active from shortly after 1700 until 1714, was an *ukiyo-e* painter who had an atelier in Asakusa, Edo, at which his students assembled. The influence of Hishikawa MORONOBU and SUGIMURA JIHEI can be seen in his work.

Despite the excellence of their genre paintings—of which several dozen by Ando are extant—the Kaigetsudō masters are known today primarily for their work as print artists. Only 23 designs, all from the 1710s, are extant. No prints by Ando survive; what remains is entirely the work of his pupils Anchi, Doshin, and Dohan.

Kaigo Tokiomi 海後宗臣

(1901–87). Educator. Born in Ibaraki Prefecture; graduate of Tōkyō University, where he later became professor of education. A leading theoretician, he played a major role in postwar educational reforms. He was chairman (1959–73) of the Japanese Society for the Study of Education. Kaigo's scholarly works center upon Japanese education during the Meiji period (1868–1912). His best-known work includes a study of the drafting of the IMPERIAL RESCRIPT ON EDUCATION, *Kyōiku chokugo seiritsushi no kenkyū* (1965).

Kaigun Denshūjo 海軍伝習所

Training center for the study of navigation and other maritime technology, established in Nagasaki in 1855; the first naval-officer training school in Japan. In 1853 the Tokugawa shogunate (1603–1867) had lifted its longtime prohibition against building large oceangoing vessels and instituted plans for a modern, Western-style navy. The Netherlands sent 22 Dutch officers and crewmen to teach at the new school. There were many prominent graduates, among whom were KATSU KAISHŪ, ENOMOTO TAKEAKI, GODAI TOMOATSU, and SANO TSUNETAMI. In 1859 the school was absorbed into the naval training facility at Tsukiji in Edo (now Tōkyō).

Kaihaku Goshi Shinrei → Shōtoku Nagasaki Shinrei

Kaihō school 海北派

(Kaihōha). Family of painters, started by KAIHŌ YŪSHŌ, that continued for seven generations until the end of the Edo period (1600–1868). Yūshō developed a highly individualistic style, but from Yūsetsu (1598–1677), the second generation, on, the family style is hardly distinguishable from that of the dominant KANŌ SCHOOL. Following Yūsetsu, successive generations were represented by Yūchiku (1654–1728); Yūsen, who died in his fifties in the Gembun era (1736–41); Yūsan, who received the court title of *hokkyō* in 1766; Yūtoku (fl 1818–30); and Yūshō (1817–68). Few paintings by the generations after Yūsetsu are extant.

Kaiho Seiryō 海保青陵

(1755–1817). Political economist of the Edo period (1600–1868). Born in Edo (now Tōkyō). Of SAMURAI background, he spent most of his life studying the growing commercial economy. He studied with the Confucian scholar Usami Shinsui (1710–76), a disciple of OGYŪ SORAI. In contrast to most of his class Kaiho held that samurai should take advantage of the money economy to enrich their domains. A thoroughgoing mercantilist, he even saw the lord-vassal relationship as ultimately a commercial contract. As practical measures, he advocated the establishment of domainal monopolies (HAN'EI SEMBAI) and of cottage industries in samurai households. After briefly serving the domains of Owari (now Aichi Prefecture) and Miyazu (now part of Kyōto Prefecture), Kaiho traveled around the Kantō region and the western provinces and in his later years settled in Kyōto, where he founded his own academy.

Kaihō Yūshō 海北友松

(1533–1615). A master of Azuchi-Momoyama period (1568–1600) painting and founder of the KAIHŌ SCHOOL. The son of Kaihō Zen'emon Tsunachika, a military commander of Ōmi Province (now Shiga Prefecture). Sent as a child novice to Tōfukuji, a major Zen temple in Kyōto, Yūshō is said to have left the temple at 41 to become a layman and later a professional painter.

Yūshō studied under KANŌ MOTONOBU or KANŌ EITOKU. He worked in both ink on paper and ink and color on a gold ground. His output includes examples from the two main currents in Momoyama-period painting: the one deriving from Chinese INK PAINTING and the other from highly colored native Japanese YAMATO-E decorative painting.

Most of Yūshō's works were large-scale paintings on sliding doors or folding screens. Many of the small paintings were originally single panels for folding screens. A major part of Yūshō's extant work consists of a large series of sliding-door paintings executed for the Zen monastery KENNINJI in Kyōto.

Kaihō Yūshō *Clouds and Dragons.* Sliding-door panel remounted as a hanging scroll. Ca 1600. Ink on paper. Height 198 cm. Kenninji, Kyōto.

Kaike Hot Spring 皆生温泉

(Kaike Onsen). Located on the Sea of Japan coast in the city of Yonago, Tottori Prefecture, western Honshū. First discovered in 1900 when the spring welled up from the seashore on this spot, it has been a popular resort since the 1920s. A common salt spring; maximum water temperature 86°C (187°F).

Kaikei 快慶

(fl late 12th–early 13th century). Sculptor of Buddhist images in the Kamakura period (1185–1333). A member of the KEI SCHOOL, he was the disciple of KŌKEI and, along with Kōkei's son UNKEI, was considered one of the outstanding sculptors of his time. Kaikei was commissioned by his religious mentor, the monk Chōgen (1121–1206), to create works for the reconstruction of the temple TŌDAIJI in Nara. Among his extant works are the statue of Sōgyō Hachiman and the statue of AMIDA, both housed in Tōdaiji, and the image of MIROKU in the Boston Museum of Fine Arts. His style, known as the An'ami style, while realistic, is more graceful and elegant than that of other members of his school. See also BUDDHIST SCULPTURE.

Kaikō Ken The most powerful work by this writer is the fiction and reportage that grew out of his experiences as a war correspondent in Vietnam.

kaiki iwai 快気祝い

The celebration of recovery after hospitalization or a long illness. In the past, *kaiki iwai* was celebrated by inviting relatives and close friends to partake in a meal of foods traditionally considered auspicious, such as SEKIHAN (rice cooked with adzuki beans). In recent years, however, *kaiki iwai* has come to consist merely of the presentation of simple gifts such as *sekihan*, sugar, and soap as tokens of thanks (KAESHI) to those who had expressed their sympathies to the invalid (see MIMAI). See also GIFT GIVING.

Kaikō Ken 開高健

(1930–89). Novelist, essayist, and journalist. Real name Kaikō Takeshi. He is regarded as one of the leaders of the generation of young Japanese writers known as the "pure postwar group" (*junsui sengo ha*). One of his main themes is the self versus the crowd or organization.

The son of an elementary-school teacher, Kaikō was born in Ōsaka. In 1948 he was admitted to Ōsaka City University, where he enrolled in the law department. He was habitually absent from class because he had to

Kairakuen At the center of this landscape garden stands the Kōbuntei pavilion, surrounded by the red and white plum blossoms for which the Kairakuen is famous.

take on odd jobs to earn a living. While in school, Kaikō avidly read the works of KAJII MOTOJIRŌ, KANEKO MITSUHARU, and NAKAJIMA ATSUSHI; he also began translating Louis Aragon and Sherwood Anderson and writing fiction. During this time he met and married the poet Maki Yōko (real name Kotani Shōko; b 1923). Kaikō graduated from college in 1953 and moved to Tōkyō.

His literary career began the same year with the publication of "Na no nai machi" (Nameless City) and a handful of other short stories in KINDAI BUNGAKU. He first attracted critical attention with the publication in SHIN NIHON BUNGAKU of the short story "Panikku" (1957; tr "Panic," 1977), about a dedicated public servant, employed in the forestry section of a prefectural administration, who encounters high-level bureaucratic bungling, corruption, and intractability. Literary recognition came with the publication of "Hadaka no ōsama" (1957; tr "The Naked King," 1977), an Akutagawa Prize–winning story about the pressures brought to bear on young schoolchildren by the Japanese educational system.

Kaikō's best novel, Kagayakeru yami (1968; tr Into a Black Sun, 1980), is an intensely moving evocation of Vietnam in the mid-1960s as told by a Japanese journalist experiencing firsthand the atrocities of war. It won the Mainichi Book Award. The novel Natsu no yami (1971; tr Darkness in Summer, 1973) recounts the love affair between a reporter and an expatriate Japanese woman living in Europe. Other significant works include the autobiographical novel Mimi no monogatari (1986, The Story of an Ear).

Kaikoku →Opening of Japan

Kai Komagatake →Komagatake

Kaimondake 開聞岳
Also called Satsuma Fuji. Conical volcano in southern Satsuma Peninsula, Kagoshima Prefecture, Kyūshū. A subtropical botanical garden is located in its foothills. It is part of Kirishima-Yaku National Park. Height: 922 m (3,025 ft).

Kainan 海南[市]
City in northwestern Wakayama Prefecture, central Honshū, on the Kii Channel. Once a center of traditional crafts, including Kuroe lacquer ware, Kainan is today an industrial city with oil-refining and chemical plants on reclaimed land along the coast. Pop: 48,596.

Kainō Michitaka 戒能通孝
(1908–75). Legal scholar and lawyer. Prominent leader of the movement to modernize the Japanese court system after World War II. Born in Nagano Prefecture, he studied at Tōkyō University, graduating in 1930. His early research culminated in two ambitious books: Iriai no kenkyū (1943, A Study of the

Right of Commonage), an elaborate historical treatment of the issues involved in claims to the right of use of undivided open land (iriaiken), and Hōritsu shakaigaku no shomondai (1943, Various Problems in Sociological Jurisprudence).

Kainō taught at Chūō University for a brief period and was a professor at Waseda (1940–54) and Tōkyō Metropolitan (1954–64) universities. After World War II, he served as legal counselor for the International Military Tribunal for the Far East during the Tōkyō WAR CRIMES TRIALS. Kainō advocated the modernization and democratization of the Japanese court system. His constant emphasis on people's rights had considerable effect on the study and teaching of legal science.

Kaionji Chōgorō 海音寺潮五郎
(1901–77). Novelist. Real name Suetomi Tōsaku. Born in Kagoshima Prefecture. Graduate of Kokugakuin University. He wrote grand-scale, lyric historical novels, often about warriors, as in Taira no Masakado (1954–57) and Ten to chi to (1960–62, Heaven and Earth), both of which became popular television series. His earlier novel Tenshō onna gassen (1936), about the tea master Sen no Rikyū and his daughter Ogin, won the Naoki Prize.

Kai Province 甲斐国
(Kai no Kuni). Present-day Yamanashi Prefecture. Established after the TAIKA REFORM (645). In the late Heian period (794–1185), Minamoto no Yoshimitsu (1045–1127) was appointed governor (kami) of Kai. His descendants became known as the Kai Genji (i.e., the Kai branch of the Minamoto family), the dominant line of which was the TAKEDA FAMILY. Military governors (shugo) during the Kamakura period (1185–1333), the Takeda remained the leading power in the region until they were defeated by ODA NOBUNAGA at the Battle of NAGASHINO (1575). After Nobunaga's death, control of the region was assumed by TOYOTOMI HIDEYOSHI, and then by TOKUGAWA IEYASU. Throughout the Edo period (1600–1868) most of Kai Province was directly controlled by the Tokugawa shogunate (see TENRYŌ).

Kairakuen 偕楽園
Municipal park in Mito, Ibaraki Prefecture, central Honshū. With KENROKUEN and KŌRAKUEN one of the three most celebrated landscape gardens in Japan. It was built by TOKUGAWA NARIAKI in 1842. The park is known for its ume (Japanese plum) blossoms, which attract visitors from late February to March. Area: 7.5 hectares (18.5 acres).

Kaisakuhō 改作法
(Laws of Cultivation). Administrative reforms enacted largely between 1651 and 1656 in the Kaga domain (now Ishikawa and Toyama prefectures). The Kaisakuhō were promulgated by Maeda Toshitsune (1593–1658), regent for his young grandson, MAEDA TSUNANORI. They implemented an innovative fixed land-tax motivated by concern over the Kaga domain's fiscal condition. Toshitsune wished to increase the domain's revenues and control over landholding retainers.

Although the fixed tax rate generally constituted a tax increase, some relief was provided for the peasants, who were excused from debts incurred during earlier crop failures. The domain arranged to lend peasants money or rice at the relatively low interest

rate of 20 percent a year. The domain also invested large sums in irrigation to increase agricultural productivity and conducted periodic land redistributions to standardize the quality of landholdings.

To increase the efficiency of tax assessment and collection, tax functions were taken from the county commissioner (kōri bugyō) and vested in a new official, the kaisaku bugyō (cultivation commissioner). Tomuragumi (districts) were enlarged to include 50 or more villages, and officials were selected from among the district administrators (tomura) to form a new level of peasant official, the gofuchinin tomura, who supervised the district administrators.

kaiseki ryōri 会席料理
One of the three basic styles of traditional Japanese cooking. Kaiseki ryōri is a type of cuisine served at sake parties and developed in its present form as restaurants became popular in Japan in the early 19th century. Although the basic features of kaiseki ryōri can be traced to the more formal styles of Japanese cooking—HONZEN RYŌRI and cha-kaiseki ryōri—in kaiseki ryōri diners are able to enjoy their meal in a relaxed mood, unrestricted by elaborate rules of etiquette. Today this type of cooking can be found in its most complex form at first-class Japanese-style restaurants (ryōtei). Sake is drunk during the meal, and, because the Japanese customarily do not eat rice while drinking sake, rice is served at the end. Appetizers (sakizuke or otōshi), SASHIMI (sliced raw fish; also called tsukuri), suimono (clear soup), yakimono (grilled foods), mushimono (steamed foods), nimono (simmered foods), and aemono (dressed saladlike foods) are served first, followed by MISO SOUP, tsukemono (PICKLES), rice, Japanese sweets, and fruit. Tea concludes the meal. The types and order of foods served in kaiseki ryōri are the basis for the contemporary full-course Japanese meal.

kaisen 廻船
(literally, "circuit ships"). Cargo ships used in premodern times for transport and trade within the Japanese archipelago. Kaisen were most active during the Edo period (1600–1868). Typical of vessels of this type were the higaki kaisen and taru kaisen, which transported goods between the Kyōto-Ōsaka area and Edo (now Tōkyō). Cargo ships came into regular use around the 8th century to transport tribute to the capital in Kyōto. With the rise of the SHŌEN (estate) system in the 10th century, kaisen were used to forward the rice tax (nengu) to absentee proprietors in Kyōto.

During the 14th century kaisen began to be used to transport commercial goods. In the 15th and 16th centuries harbors were built to accommodate the sea trade, and kaisen shikimoku (maritime regulations) were issued. In the 17th century the TOKUGAWA SHOGUNATE and various daimyō made a concerted effort to develop new sea routes between Ōsaka and Edo. By order of the shogunate, KAWAMURA ZUIKEN opened two new routes—the higashi mawari (eastern circuit), which connected ports on the Sea of Japan and Edo by way of the Tsugaru Strait and the Pacific, in 1671; and the nishi mawari (western circuit), which connected the Sea of Japan ports with Ōsaka by way of the Shimonoseki Strait and the Inland Sea, in 1672. It was about this time that the higaki kaisen and taru kaisen became active. Higaki kaisen were used by the SAKAI MERCHANTS to transport cotton, oil, *sake*, vinegar, and soy sauce to Edo. From the end of the 17th century they were managed by the NIJŪSHIKUMI-DOIYA in Ōsaka and the TOKUMI-DOIYA in Edo. *Taru kaisen* were used mainly to transport *sake* from Ōsaka to Edo. The two types of ship competed vigorously for cargo. *Kaisen* were gradually supplanted by steamboats, which appeared in the late 19th century.

kaishi 懐紙

(literally, "bosom paper"). Also known as *tatōgami* (folded paper). A fine-grained crepe paper carried in the breast-fold opening of the KIMONO and used for tissue paper (*hanagami*) and letter writing. The word also refers to the paper originally used in court circles when composing WAKA and RENGA poetry. This paper came in different colors and sizes, according to one's sex and social rank. Court dress codes required that men carry white *kaishi* and women carry red *kaishi*. The *kogikushi* paper used in the TEA CEREMONY is also called *kaishi*.

Kaishintō → Rikken Kaishintō

Kaita 海田[町]

Town in southwestern Hiroshima Prefecture, western Honshū. Kaita developed as a post-station town on the highway San'yōdō. Today there are automobile and chemical factories here, and small-scale agriculture and oyster cultivation take place. In recent years Kaita has become a residential suburb of the city of Hiroshima. Pop: 30,744.

Kaitai shinsho 解体新書

(1774, New Book of Anatomy). Anatomical text. As the first complete Japanese translation of a Western medical work, *Kaitai shinsho* was a landmark in the history of science in Japan. The Japanese text, compiled by a team of translators headed by SUGITA GEMPAKU and MAENO RYŌTAKU, was based on a 1734 Dutch translation by Gerardus Dicten of the third edition of *Anatomische Tabellen* (1732) by the German scholar Johann Adam Kulmus. *Kaitai shinsho* served to deepen Japanese understanding of Western medical science and its roots in the study of anatomy; it also inspired a wave of new Japanese translations from Dutch texts. The arduous four-year struggle to translate *Kaitai shinsho* is described in detail in Sugita Gempaku's *Rangaku kotohajime* (1815, The Beginning of Dutch Learning).

Kaitakushi 開拓使

(Hokkaidō Colonization Office). Government office of the early Meiji period (1868–1912) charged with the administration and development of Hokkaidō. Recognizing the strategic importance of Ezochi (or EZO), as Hokkaidō and islands further north were called, the Meiji government established the Kaitakushi in August 1869 and renamed the area Hokkaidō and Karafuto (the Japanese name for SAKHALIN). Under the provisions of the Treaty of St. Petersburg (1875; see ST. PETERSBURG, TREATY OF), Sakhalin became a Russian possession and the Kuril Islands were placed under the jurisdiction of the Kaitakushi. After KURODA KIYOTAKA was appointed as director, the office became a stronghold of former Satsuma (now Kagoshima Prefecture) *samurai*.

The Kaitakushi employed many foreign advisers, founded the Sapporo Agricultural College (now Hokkaidō University), and actively promoted settlement in Hokkaidō. However, it summarily deprived the indigenous AINU people of their fishing, hunting, and land rights. In 1881 a major scandal erupted over the proposed sale of the Kaitakushi's assets (see HOKKAIDŌ COLONIZATION OFFICE SCANDAL OF 1881; POLITICAL CRISIS OF 1881). The Kaitakushi was abolished the following year. Three prefectures—Hakodate, Sapporo, and Nemuro—were created in 1882, but in 1886 these were done away with and the entire island of Hokkaidō became one political unit with a prefectural form of government.

Kaitei Ritsurei 改定律例

(Revised Statutes). Criminal code drawn up in 1873 as an amendment and supplement to the SHINRITSU KŌRYŌ (1870). The earlier code was a codification of 17th-century Chinese legal concepts; the Kaitei Ritsurei was influenced by Western, in particular French, criminal codes. The new Criminal Code of 1880 (effective 1882) replaced them.

Kaiten 回天

Special naval attack weapon used by the Japanese navy during World War II. Also known as the "human torpedo," the weapon was a vessel 15 meters (49 ft) in length and 1 meter (3 ft) in diameter that was designed to carry 1.5 metric tons (1.7 short tons) of explosive charge and one man. Kaiten were first produced in the summer of 1944 (some 420 were made by the end of the war).

Kaitokudō 懐徳堂

Also known as Kaitoku Shoin. School for commoners founded in Ōsaka in 1724. Because the shōgun TOKUGAWA YOSHIMUNE encouraged the education of commoners, the school received shogunal support. MIYAKE SEKIAN, appointed first head of the school, was succeeded by Nakai Shūan (1693–1758), who had played an important role in founding the school. The curriculum was based on the philosophy of Zhu Xi (Chu Hsi; see SHUSHIGAKU). It also included introductory expositions of Wang Yangming's doctrines (see YŌMEIGAKU). The school reached its peak under Shūan's son, Nakai Chikuzan (1730–1804), but it began to decline after his death and was finally closed in 1869.

Kaizei Yakusho 改税約書

(Tariff Convention). Trade agreement signed 25 June 1866 by the Tokugawa shogunate and Great Britain, France, the Netherlands, and the United States. Under the agreement, drafted by British minister Sir Harry PARKES, import tariffs, which had been set by the ANSEI COMMERCIAL TREATIES at 5 to 35 percent of average selling price, were reduced to a uniform 5 percent of declared value, payable in silver, and other terms favoring foreign traders were established. In 1894 this agreement was supplanted by more equitable trade treaties. See also UNEQUAL TREATIES, REVISION OF.

Kaizō 改造

(Reconstruction). General-interest magazine published between 1919 and 1955 by Kaizōsha, a publishing firm founded by innovative newspaperman YAMAMOTO SANEHIKO. *Kaizō* became a major forum for Marxist and socialist debate in the 1920s, with regular contributions by SAKAI TOSHIHIKO, YAMAKAWA HITOSHI, ŌSUGI SAKAE, KAWAKAMI HAJIME, KAGAWA TOYOHIKO, and other leading socialists. Yamamoto, who long served as editor in chief, also solicited articles from such foreign luminaries as Bertrand Russell and Albert Einstein, making *Kaizō* a voice of new trends in thought and science. It was also a major publishing outlet for literature.

Kaizuka 貝塚[市]

City in southern Ōsaka Prefecture, central Honshū. Kaizuka developed as a temple town of the temple Gansenji in the late 1500s and later as a center for Izumi cotton cloth. Its modern textile industry centers on Unitika, Ltd. Pop: 79,234.

kaizuka → shell mounds

Kaizuka Shigeki 貝塚茂樹

(1904–87). Scholar of Chinese history. Born in Tōkyō. Kaizuka studied Chinese history under NAITŌ KONAN and others at Kyōto University, where he became a professor in 1949. He is highly regarded for his studies emphasizing the importance, as historical materials, of the "oracle bones," bronze and stone inscriptions, and other Chinese archaeological finds. He organized the approximately 3,000 oracle bone fragments housed at the Research Institute for Humanistic Studies, Kyōto University. His collected works are in 10 volumes, *Kaizuka Shigeki chosaku shū* (1976–78). He was awarded the Order of Culture in 1984.

Kajii Motojirō 梶井基次郎

(1901–32). Short-story writer of the Taishō period (1912–26). Although overshadowed by AKUTAGAWA RYŪNOSUKE, TANIZAKI JUN'ICHIRŌ, and SHIGA NAOYA, he shared their influences—Tolstoy, Baudelaire, and Poe—and their great intellectual dilemma, i.e., how to reconcile the activist demands of Marxism (newly introduced to Japan) with a basic orientation toward aestheticism.

Born in Ōsaka, Kajii attended the Third Higher School in Kyōto (1919–24) and Tōkyō University (1924–27). He founded the coterie magazine *Aozora* (1925–27, Blue Skies) along with other Third Higher School graduates, including Tonomura Shigeru (1902–61), KITAGAWA FUYUHIKO, MIYOSHI TATSUJI, Yodono Ryūzō (1904–67), and Nakatani Takao (b 1901). A collection of his first 18 short stories was published under the title *Remon* (1931, The Lemon). His novella *Nonki na kanja* (1932, The Carefree Patient) appeared in the magazine CHŪŌ KŌRON shortly before his death.

Recognition of his talent came only after his death, especially in the 1950s when his works enjoyed a revival among young readers. A collection of Kajii's correspondence titled *Wakaki shijin no tegami* (Letters of a Young Poet) was published in 1955.

Kajima Corporation 鹿島建設[株]

(Kajima Kensetsu). Japan's largest engineering and construction company. Founded in 1840 and established in its present form in 1930, the firm engages in operations ranging from design, engineering, financing, and construction to land development. It built the first Japanese skyscraper and controls a large share of the market for the construction of such facilities as nuclear power plants, steel mills, and petrochemical plants. Kajima has participated in numerous projects of various types in some 50 nations throughout the world. The company controls more than 50 subsidiary firms in Japan as well as overseas in the fields of engineering, finance, commerce, publishing, and audiovisual products. In the fiscal year ending March 1991 total sales were ¥1.7 trillion (US $12.4 billion), of

Kaizuka Shigeki This scholar's extensive research into ancient inscriptions—especially those found on "oracle bones"—made a lasting contribution to the study of Chinese antiquity.

Kajii Motojirō The talents of this Taishō-period short-story writer went largely unnoticed until the 1950s, when his work enjoyed a revival.

kakashi The divine power of the god of the fields is said to reveal itself through scarecrows fashioned in human form, such as this one standing in the middle of a rice field.

which 73 percent was derived from construction, 22 percent from public works projects, and 5 percent from development projects. Two percent of sales was gained in the overseas market. In the same year capitalization stood at ¥62.2 billion (US $453.4 million). Headquarters are in Tōkyō.

Kajimaya   加島屋

Wealthy merchant house of Ōsaka in the Edo period (1600–1868); founded by Masanori (also called Kyūemon). The family later expanded their prosperous rice-polishing business to include money-changing, and in 1731 the Kajimaya became brokers in the DŌJIMA RICE MARKET. The family also made extensive loans to *daimyō* (see DAIMYŌ LOANS). Like many other merchant houses, the Kajimaya had difficulties after the MEIJI RESTORATION (1868) but survived to establish the Kajima Bank in 1887.

Kajiwara Kagetoki   梶原景時

(?–1200). Warrior. Kagetoki initially fought on the Taira side in the TAIRA-MINAMOTO WAR, but rescued MINAMOTO NO YORITOMO at the Battle of Ishibashiyama and became a trusted vassal, governor of several provinces, and a member of the Board of Retainers (SAMURAI-DOKORO). He fought under Yoritomo's brother MINAMOTO NO YOSHITSUNE in the destruction of the Taira but later turned against him, contributing to the growing rift between the two brothers. After Yoritomo's death in 1199, Kagetoki served briefly as an elder adviser to MINAMOTO NO YORIIE, the second shōgun. When he slandered a prominent vassal, Kagetoki earned the wrath of the leading warrior houses of the Kamakura shogunate. Ousted from office, he planned to go to Kyōto to support Takeda Ariyoshi as shōgun but was discovered and killed in fighting in Suruga (now part of Shizuoka Prefecture).

Kajiwara Shōzen   梶原性全

(1266–1337). Buddhist priest and scholar of Chinese medicine. Born in Sagami Province (now Kanagawa Prefecture). He practiced medicine in Gokurakuji, a temple in Kamakura. He wrote *Ton'ishō* (1303, Jottings on Medicine), a book in simple syllabic Japanese; and *Man'anhō* (1327, Prescriptions for Felicity), a revised version in classical Chinese.

Kajiyama Toshiyuki   梶山季之

(1930–75). Novelist. Born in Seoul, Korea. Graduate of Hiroshima Higher Normal School (now Hiroshima University). He

kakemono *Haiga* (haiku sketch) by Buson (1716–84), mounted as a hanging scroll. Ink and light color on paper. 98 × 27 cm. Yuki Museum of Art, Ōsaka.

wrote popular mysteries and erotic novels. An investigative reporter, he gained recognition with his documentary-style novel *Kuro no shisōsha* (1962, The Black Test Model Car), leading to a boom in industrial spy novels. He also wrote *Akai daiya* (1962–63, Red Diamonds).

Kakamigahara   各務原[市]

City in southern Gifu Prefecture, central Honshū, on the river Kisogawa. The site of an airport and aircraft plant since World War II, Kakamigahara also produces automobiles and textiles. Pop: 129,680.

kakari-musubi   係結び

Rule of grammatical agreement in the CLASSICAL JAPANESE language. When a certain grammatical particle or *joshi* (the *kakari*) occurs in the middle of a sentence, a particular verb-adjective conjugational form (the *musubi*, literally, "tying up") is used at the end of the sentence. The particles *zo*, *namu*, *ya*, and *ka* require the *rentaikei* (attributive) form of the verb at the end of the sentence, while the particle *koso* requires the *izenkei* (perfective) form of the verb. The term *kakari-musubi* is usually applied only to these special cases in which a conjugation other than the usual *shūshikei* (sentence final) form of the verb is required; but some grammarians feel that the same grammatical principle applies to the general correspondence between the particles *wa* and *mo* and the *shūshikei* form of the verb. Established during the Heian period (794–1185), *kakari-musubi* now appears only in a few dialects of modern Japanese.

kakashi   案山子

(scarecrows). Objects set up in fields to frighten away birds and animals that damage crops. Various kinds of *kakashi* have been used in Japan since ancient times. One kind is the human-shaped figure through which the divine power of the god of the fields (TA NO KAMI) is believed to manifest itself. In its presence farmers offer prayers for abundant crops in the spring and of thanksgiving after the harvest. It is typically made of straw, dressed in old clothing, and holds a bow and arrow. Chunks of rotting meat, clumps of hair or fur, or other objects having a repulsive smell are also used as scarecrows. Other *kakashi* employ frightening noises, as in bird rattles (NARUKO), or shiny materials, such as aluminum foil, placed about the fields.

kakebotoke → mishōtai

Kakegawa   掛川[市]

City in southwestern Shizuoka Prefecture, central Honshū, on the river Sakagawa. A castle town and post-station town during the Edo period (1600–1868), Kakegawa is known for its tea, *shiitake* (a variety of mushroom), and roses. Transport-related machinery and musical instruments are also produced. *Kuzufu*, a grass cloth, has been made here since the Edo period. Attractions include Sayo no Nakayama Park and the ruins of Kakegawa Castle. Pop: 72,795.

Kakei Katsuhiko   筧克彦

(1872–1961). Scholar of constitutional law; Shintō thinker. Born in Nagano Prefecture, Kakei graduated from Tōkyō University in 1897 and went on to postgraduate research in Germany. In 1903 he became a full professor at Tōkyō University, where he lectured on such subjects as administrative law, constitutional law, and legal theory. He was an ad-

herent of the ancient Shintō belief as set forth by the mid-19th-century KOKUGAKU (National Learning) theorists. A conservative scholar who advocated the theory that the emperor equals the state (*tennō soku kokka*), Kakei was appointed to the Bunkyō Shingikai, a prewar advisory council of the Ministry of Education. His writings include *Dai Nippon teikoku kempō no kompongi* (1936, The Basic Meaning of the Constitution of the Empire of Japan).

kakekomidera   駆込寺

(refuge temples). Also known as *enkiridera* (divorce temples). From the 13th through 19th centuries, certain convent-temples offered refuge to women fleeing their husbands; after serving in such a temple for two full years, a woman could be granted the right of divorce by the commissioners of temples and shrines (*jisha bugyō*) despite her husband's objection. The best-known temple of this kind, TŌKEIJI in Kamakura, was founded in 1285. Mantokuji, founded in the 13th century in what is now Gumma Prefecture, also came to be known as a refuge temple. In the late Edo period (1600–1868) only Mantokuji and Tōkeiji were officially recognized as refuge temples. Tōkeiji alone is said to have harbored about 2,000 absconding wives in the 150 years before new divorce laws were instituted by the Meiji government in 1873. See also DIVORCE.

kakekotoba   懸詞

("pivot word"). In WAKA poetry, a type of wordplay or pun through which a word or series of syllables takes on two meanings. One meaning is evoked by the association of the pivot word with the phrase that precedes it, and a completely different meaning is evoked by its association with the words that follow. For example, in the following poem from the HEICHŪ MONOGATARI (mid-10th century, The Tale of Heichū), the syllables *tatsu*, when read with the preceding phrase *uki na nomi*, complete the meaning "one's love life gives rise to rumor"; when read with the following phrase, as *Tatsuta no kawa*, they give the meaning "river Tatsuta."

Uki na nomi
Tatsuta no kawa no
Momijiba wa
Mono omou aki no
Sode ni zo arikeru

This autumn as
I brood upon the shame
That stains my name
The river Tatsuta's colored leaves
Rage red upon my tear-soaked sleeves.

Kakekotoba reached their fullest development in the 9th century with the decline of the CHŌKA, or long poem, and predominance of the brief 31-syllable TANKA, or short poem. The *kakekotoba* later came to be exploited as a technique for heightening language in prose fiction and drama as well as in other poetic forms such as linked verse (RENGA).

kakemono   掛け物

(hanging scroll). Painting or calligraphy mounted with strips of luxurious fabric on flexible backing paper so that it can be rolled up for storage. In contrast to *makimono* (handscrolls), which are unrolled laterally on a flat surface and can be viewed by only one or two persons at a time, *kakemono* are designed to be used as part of the interior decoration of a room. Since the Muromachi period (1333–1568) *kakemono* have been the major artwork on the wall of the TOKONOMA, the alcove especially designed for the display of prized objects. In contrast to wall paintings (*shōhekiga*) and folding screens (*byōbu*), *kakemono* can be easily changed to suit the season or the occasion.

The scroll was introduced to Japan in the early Heian period (794–1185) in the form of Buddhist paintings and scriptures from the Asian continent. The preferences of tea masters during the late Muromachi period greatly influenced the form, since the major object of contemplation in the tearoom is the scroll displayed in the alcove. Preferred subjects for scroll paintings are landscapes, flowers and birds, and figures; in calligraphy the more valued scrolls display writing by virtuous men or respected priests and lines of poetry by famous poets.

kakeya 掛屋

Accounting agents of the Edo period (1600–1868) who handled accounts at the warehousing offices (KURAYASHIKI) of the shogunate and *daimyō* where tax rice and other commodities were sold. Generally based in Ōsaka, these agents were given the authority to hold the money obtained and to make monthly remittances to the domains or the daimyō residences in Edo (now Tōkyō). In times of a bad harvest or extraordinary expenditures, *kakeya* lent money at interest to the daimyō, holding warehouse goods as security (see DAIMYŌ LOANS). Among the most powerful *kakeya* were the KŌNOIKE FAMILY.

Kakeya Sōichi 掛谷宗一

(1886–1947). Mathematician. Known for his work on the properties of algebraic and simultaneous integral equations. Born in Hiroshima Prefecture, he graduated from Tōkyō University. After teaching at Tōhoku University and studying in the United States, he became a professor at Tōkyō University in 1935. He became the first director of its Institute of Statistical Mathematics in 1944.

Kakeyu Hot Spring 鹿教湯温泉

(Kakeyu Onsen). Located in the town of Maruko, central Nagano Prefecture, central Honshū. A simple thermal spring; maximum water temperature 53°C (127°F). Many guests come for lengthy stays at the therapeutic facilities here.

Kakiemon ware 柿右衛門

(*kakiemon*). Porcelain ware. A type of underglaze blue and white or polychrome overglaze enameled porcelain made from 1643 in Arita, Hizen Province (now Saga and Nagasaki prefectures). According to traditional accounts, Sakaida Kizaemon (later renamed Kakiemon; 1596–1666) made Japan's first polychrome porcelains in 1643 with overglaze pigments imported from China. After 1672 Kakiemon ware was imitated by other Japanese potters. It was copied after 1700 in China, and in the 18th century throughout Europe, starting with Meissen, Germany, in 1728. Typical forms include dishes, bowls, bottles, jars, teabowls, incense burners, and flower vases, as well as candlesticks, handled ewers, teapots, and, mostly for the Western market, ornamental figures. At their best, Kakiemon pieces have a milk-white body, an almost transparent matte glaze full of bubbles with a glossy sheen, and spur marks on the base. In polychrome pieces soft orange-red and azure

blue predominate, sometimes with light yellow, light green, aubergine, and brown. Bird-and-flower motifs are most common. In modern times Kakiemon XIII (1906–82) and his son (b 1934) have carried on the family tradition.

kakiire 書入

System of nonpossessory collateral for loans in the Edo period (1600–1868). Also called *hikiate*. In contrast to *shichiire* (pawnage), *kakiire* did not involve transfer of the possession of the collateral to the creditor and instead required only a written pledge. Real estate, movable property, and human beings could all be offered as *kakiire* collateral. In legal proceedings, *kakiire*, unlike *shichiire*, was accepted only as a *kanekuji* (money suit), which received less legal protection than a *honkuji* (main suit). Under the new Civil Code of 1898, *kakiire* was abolished.

Kakinomoto no Hitomaro 柿本人麻呂

(fl ca 685–705). Most important poet of the MAN'YŌSHŪ, the earliest anthology of Japanese verse. He was a low-ranking member of the courts of Emperor TEMMU (r 672–686), Empress JITŌ (r 686–697), and Emperor MOMMU (r 697–707). His authentic poems appear in the *Man'yōshū*, which also includes poems attributed to a *Hitomaro kashū* (Hitomaro collection), a SHIKASHŪ (personal poetry collection) no longer extant and not necessarily composed exclusively of verses by Hitomaro. Poems attributed to Hitomaro in later anthologies (e.g., SHIN KOKINSHŪ, 3:190) are suspect on various grounds. A conservative view of his canon allows for 18 CHŌKA (long poems) from the first three books of the *Man'yōshū* and over 60 *tanka* (short poems; see WAKA), almost entirely from the first four books and often appearing as *hanka* (envoys) to the long poems.

Excluding many poems attributed to him and ignoring some poems of lesser interest, we are left with others of such quality as to demonstrate why many people consider Hitomaro the greatest Japanese poet. His art is at once the most natural and complex in the *Man'yōshū*. He masters numerous techniques—complex parallelism, pillow words (MAKURA KOTOBA), overturelike paeans to the divinity of the land or royal line, and irony. He infuses public events with personal emotion and universalizes the intimate.

Public and Personal Poems——Two of Hitomaro's public poems relate to the JINSHIN DISTURBANCE of 672. *Man'yōshū* poem 2:199–201 mourns Prince Takechi, who, as son of the sovereign Temmu, commanded the victorious forces in the Jinshin War and served as prime minister and heir apparent under the subsequent reign of his mother, Jitō, dying before he could succeed her. This *chōka* is the longest in the collection (149 lines, with 2 envoys) and is vivid in its description of battle scenes. Sometime after that war, Hitomaro visited Ōmi (now Shiga Prefecture) and the ruins of the rival court there that Prince Takechi had overwhelmed in 672. In *Man'yōshū* poem 1:29–31 Hitomaro questions why a capital was perversely established so far away, mourning the waste and the irreparable loss of people and their aspirations.

More personal poems include two *chōka* on the death of one wife (2:207–209, 210–212) and two on parting from another (2:131–133, 135–137). The first elegy depicts the poet distractedly visiting a market his wife frequented. He stands vainly calling

Kakiemon ware Edo-period (1600–1868) bowl. This example has the white body and bird-and-flower motif typical of Kakiemon ware. Height 13 cm. Tōkyō National Museum.

kakizome This New Year's calligraphy ritual is sometimes conducted in large groups at shrines or other locations. Here, a young girl writes the characters for "Japan" at the Kitano Shrine in Kyōto.

out her name, waving his sleeves—yet not a single person even looks like her. Hitomaro's parting poems likely imply his being recalled to the capital for other service. The first *chōka* concludes with the poet's wretched thought on crossing the mountains that hide his wife from view: "I wish these mountains would bow down." The second poem is especially lovely in its imagery and in Hitomaro's characteristically skillful integration of the envoys with the *chōka*. Foremost among *Man'yōshū* poets, Hitomaro remains, along with SAIGYŌ and BASHŌ, one of the three most esteemed poets in Japanese history.

kakitsubata → irises

kakizome 書初め

The act of writing in calligraphy or painting a picture at the beginning of the year as a way to refresh the spirit and pray for progress in writing and painting that year. *Kakizome* is usually done on 2 January. Traditionally water drawn on the morning of New Year's Day (WAKAMIZU) was used to prepare the ink, and the calligraphy was done while facing in the direction considered to be most auspicious that year (*ehō*). The products of *kakizome* are usually displayed until 15 January, which is called Koshōgatsu, or Small New Year.

Kakogawa 加古川〔市〕

City in southern Hyōgo Prefecture, western Honshū, on the river Kakogawa. Kakogawa developed as a post-station town on the highway San'yōdō and as a river port during the Edo period (1600–1868). Now part of the Harima Coastal Industrial Zone, it produces woolens, fertilizer, steel, and silk thread. Many burial mounds (KOFUN) have been discovered here, indicating that the area was settled in ancient times. Pop: 239,803.

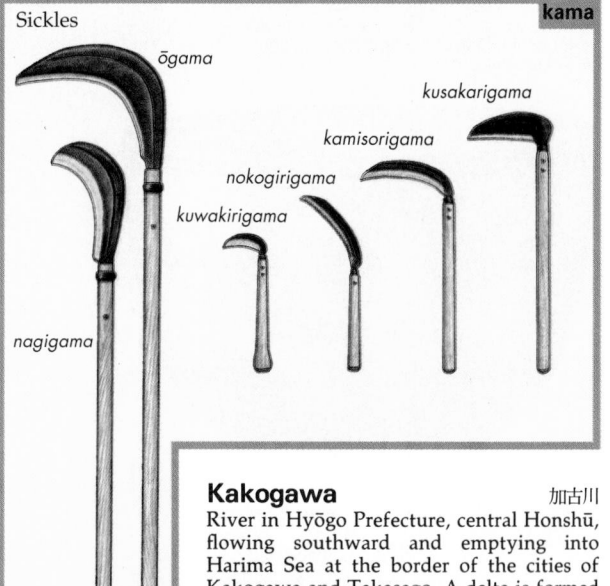

Sickles

kama

ōgama

kusakarigama

kamisorigama

nokogirigama

kuwakirigama

nagigama

Kakogawa

加古川

River in Hyōgo Prefecture, central Honshū, flowing southward and emptying into Harima Sea at the border of the cities of Kakogawa and Takasago. A delta is formed at the lower reaches. The water is used for drinking, irrigation, and industry. Length: 96 km (60 mi); area of drainage basin: 1,730 sq km (668 sq mi).

kakoimai

囲米

(stored rice). Rice stored by order of the Tokugawa shogunate and many *daimyō* during the Edo period (1600–1868) for use during famines, to stabilize rice prices, or for military purposes. The rice was stored in sheaves (*momi*) to prevent spoilage and so was sometimes called *kakoimomi*; it was also known as *okimai* or *tsumemai*. The practice of reserving rice for military use had long been in existence, but it was in 1683 that the shogunate first ordered daimyō domains to set aside a stipulated percentage of their annual rice crop for use during famines. Daimyō began issuing similar orders on their own initiative, especially after the KYŌHŌ FAMINE of the 1730s.

Kakuban

覚鑁

(1095–1143). Also known as Kōgyō Daishi. Buddhist priest of the SHINGON SECT. Regarded as the founder of the Shingi ("new

kamado One of these traditional stoves in use in the Ōhara district of Kyōto.

interpretation") branch of Shingon. Born in Fujitsu in Hizen Province (now part of Saga Prefecture). Kakuban entered monastic life as a child and in 1110 became a monk at the temple NINNAJI in Kyōto. In 1121 he was ordained a Shingon master (*ajari;* Skt: *ācārya*) there, receiving Dembō Kanjō or Kanjō (Skt: Abhiṣeka; an initiation ceremony of aspersion from the eminent master Kanjo (1057–1125) of the Hirosawaryū school.

In 1134 Kakuban was put in charge of KONGŌBUJI, the main temple of the monastery complex on Mt. Kōya. His reform movement, however, met stiff resistance from the clerical establishment at Kongōbuji and TŌJI in Kyōto, the latter then being the central temple of the Shingon sect. Kakuban integrated Pure Land worship, which was then gaining popularity even among Shingon Buddhists, into Shingon teachings. He believed that each person, upon realizing oneness with the Buddha Mahāvairocana (DAINICHI), can embody the Pure Land. He was above all concerned, however, for a spiritual reinvigoration of the Shingon tradition. For the two main divisions within the Shingi branch, see HASEDERA and CHISHAKUIN.

kakubei-jishi

角兵衛獅子

Dance common in the Edo period (1600–1868); performed by young boys who wore lion (*shishi*) headdresses and high GETA (clogs). Beating on small drums, they performed acrobatic stunts to the accompaniment of flute and drum. The dance is also known as *echigo-jishi* from its place of origin in Kambara, Echigo Province (now Niigata Prefecture); *kakubei* has been explained as the name of the originator or as a corruption of Kambara. Some of its features were incorporated into KABUKI dance. See also SHISHIMAI; KADOZUKE.

Kakuda

角田[市]

City in southern Miyagi Prefecture, northern Honshū, on the river Abukumagawa. Kakuda developed as a castle town and collection point for rice and silk cocoons transported on the Abukumagawa. Kakuda's mainstay is agriculture. Factory construction has increased in recent years. Pop: 35,431.

Kakuijima

鹿久居島

Island in the eastern Inland Sea, off southeastern Okayama Prefecture; largest of the Hinasa Islands. Part of Okayama Prefecture. This mountainous island was used as a hunting ground for the lords of the Okayama domain; wild deer still roam the island. Chief activities are fishing and the cultivation of mandarin oranges. Area: 10 sq km (4 sq mi).

kakun

家訓

(household precepts). Instructions composed by the head of a household for members of his family or group; an exposition of the values and modes of action that the household head considers requisite to the success of the person or persons addressed and to the prosperity of his house. Documents classifiable in this broad category have a long history in premodern Japan, one that extends from the "Assorted Private Teachings" (Shikyō Ruijū) of the 8th-century *udai-*

kamaboko This steamed or grilled fish paste is an easily digestible source of highly concentrated protein.

jin (minister of the right) KIBI NO MAKIBI and the "Admonitions" (Kujō Ujōshō Ikai) of the 10th-century *udaijin* Fujiwara no Morosuke (908–960) to a multitude of prescriptions of conduct for *samurai,* townsman, and farmer households of the Edo period (1600–1868). Regulations issued for religious institutions are also sometimes called *kakun,* as in the case of Rinsen Kakun, compiled in 1339 for the monastic community of the Rinsenji, a Zen temple in Kyōto, by its founding abbot, MUSŌ SOSEKI. *Kakun* are closely related to the hortatory type of another broad category, OKIBUMI, testamentary documents that are similarly concerned with the perpetuation of a family's or religious institution's interests. *Okibumi* tend to be less elaborate statements than *kakun,* but a precise distinction between the two documentary forms cannot be drawn in all cases.

Kakun of the Kamakura period (1185–1333) and Muromachi period (1333–1568) are excellent illustrations of the ethical and political attitudes of the dominant samurai class. *Kakun* are also related to *kahō* or BUNKOKUHŌ (domainal law codes). *Kakun* were expressions of the "house" as a private entity, whereas *bunkokuhō* were representations of the "house" as a legal public person. Whereas household precepts essentially offer advice and establish rules for the behavior of a person or group, *bunkokuhō* were intended as binding legal regulations in the governing of a domain. See also ASAKURA TOSHIKAGE, 17-ARTICLE CODE OF; SŌUNJI DONO NIJŪIKKAJŌ.

Kakunodate

角館[町]

Town in eastern Akita Prefecture, northern Honshū. A castle town during the Edo period (1600–1868), Kakunodate retains several *samurai* residences. It is known especially for boxes, tea canisters, and similar articles made from wild-cherry bark. Pop: 15,846.

Kakure Kirishitan

隠れキリシタン

(Hidden or Clandestine Christians). Christian believers of the Edo period (1600–1868) who survived the ANTI-CHRISTIAN EDICTS of the Tokugawa shogunate (1603–1867) and the period of NATIONAL SECLUSION, and whose descendants escaped detection during succeeding waves of persecution (see PERSECUTIONS AT URAKAMI). In 1614 there were at most 300,000 baptized members of the Catholic church. The expulsion of the Catholic clergy that was decreed in 1614 and the general persecution of Christianity that followed were designed to eliminate the foreign faith from Japan. The response of some of the faithful to persecution was to declare their faith and embrace martyrdom, but most Christians concealed their belief and went underground. Some groups of Christians chose emigration of their entire communities to remote areas where it was relatively easier to remain hidden.

The shogunal Inquisition Office (Kirishitan Shūmon Aratame Yaku; see SHŪMON ARATAME), established in 1640, aimed at total extermination of Christians. The practice of *efumi* (trampling on holy pictures; see FUMIE), instituted in 1629 as a means of identifying believers, was well established by 1640. Small groups of priests secretly entered the country after 1636, but they were quickly detected and eliminated. Thus from 1637, in matters of faith and practice, Christian communities were wholly dependent on lay leadership. Because they were often forced to outwardly conform with Buddhist and Shintō practice by the Tokugawa shogunate, hidden Christians developed a double religious life in which they secretly preserved their Christian belief and practice. When Japan was opened to international communication in the mid-19th century, more than 30,000 believers in the old faith (*mukashi* Kirishitan) came forward from various remote areas. In the absence of any priest or printed texts, the entire body of doctrine and liturgy was passed on by word of mouth.

A related term, Hanare Kirishitan (Separated Christians), refers to the descendants of old Christians whose faith survived the National Seclusion period but who refused reconciliation with the Roman Catholic Church after the abolition of Christian prohibition laws in the mid-19th century. Pockets of Hanare Kirishitan still exist in Japan.

Kakushin Kurabu   革新俱楽部
(Reform Club). A small political party formed in November 1922 by former members of the RIKKEN KOKUMINTŌ, independents, and disaffected members of the KENSEIKAI. Headed by INUKAI TSUYOSHI, its 45 members included OZAKI YUKIO and SHIMADA SABURŌ. The Kakushin Kurabu represented the most liberal wing of the Diet and drew its main support from the urban middle class and prosperous farmers. Its goals were to achieve universal suffrage, to reduce the size of the military, and to abolish the system that allowed only generals and admirals on active duty to head the war ministries (GUMBU DAIJIN GEN'EKI BUKAN SEI). In 1924 it joined with the RIKKEN SEIYŪKAI and the Kenseikai in forming the second MOVEMENT TO PROTECT CONSTITUTIONAL GOVERNMENT and ousted the cabinet of KIYOURA KEIGO. Inukai subsequently served in the coalition cabinet of KATŌ TAKAAKI. Members became divided over passage of the PEACE PRESERVATION LAW OF 1925, and the club dissolved in 1925; most members joined the Seiyūkai.

Kakuyū→Toba Sōjō

Kakuzenshō   覚禅鈔
Collection of studies and documents on esoteric Buddhist rituals and iconography compiled by the SHINGON SECT monk Kakuzen from approximately 1176 to 1213. In addition to ritual and historical documents of the Shingon sect, the more than 100 volumes in this collection include line drawings and writings on Buddhist iconography that Kakuzen collected from his direct study of temple images and conversations with senior monks.

kama   鎌
(sickle). The sickle's use in Japan began in the Yayoi period (ca 300 BC–ca AD 300) and became widespread by the late Kofun period (ca 300–710). Over the centuries it became an indispensable harvesting tool and is still used by Japanese farmers today. The basic Japanese sickle has a crescent-shaped blade attached to a short wooden handle, but there is considerable variation depending on the locale. A straight, wide blade is common in the Kantō (eastern Honshū) region around Tōkyō, while in the Kansai (Kyōto-Ōsaka) region the blade is considerably thinner and crescent-shaped. Regardless of region, the Japanese sickle is distinguished by the positioning of the blade, which is attached at nearly a right angle to the handle. In addition to its agricultural uses, it also often serves as an offering to the deities in local harvest festivals.

kamaboko   蒲鉾
A food made from fish paste—the chief source for which is the walleye pollack—that is seasoned, mounded on a rectangular board, and steamed or grilled. Often served sliced and eaten with soy sauce, it is also an ingredient in clear soup (*sumashijiru*).

Kamada Ryūō   鎌田柳泓
(1754–1821). SHINGAKU scholar of the late Edo period (1600–1868). Born in Kii Province (now Wakayama Prefecture). He was adopted by his uncle Kamada Issō (1721–1804), who had studied with TESHIMA TOAN, a disciple of ISHIDA BAIGAN, the founder of Shingaku. Kamada also studied with Teshima and traveled throughout the Kyōto-Ōsaka region spreading the teachings of the school. He tried to incorporate his knowledge of Buddhism and Western science into his system of Shingaku.

kamado   竈
Traditional Japanese stove; an earthen, stone, brick, or cement oven-like structure designed with a hollow center in which fuel is burned to provide heat and with openings on the top surface for holding pots and kettles (*kama*). Also known as *hettsui* or *kudo* in some locales. *Kamado* are known to have been in use in Japan from the Kofun period (ca 300–710). There are two types: movable and fixed (the latter usually being built into the earthen floor of the kitchen area). An altar dedicated to the *kamadogami* (literally, "oven deity") is often installed nearby (see also SHINTŌ FAMILY ALTARS). This deity is called Kōjinsama (see KŌJIN) in western Japan. Like the hearth in the West, the *kamado* has been looked upon as the symbolic center of the home in Japan. In the past when a branch house of a family was established (for example by marriage), fire from the *kamado* of the main house was used to light the fire in the new house.

Kamagaya   鎌ケ谷[市]
City in northwestern Chiba Prefecture, central Honshū. Formerly a farming area, it is now a suburb of Tōkyō, with a machinery industry. Pop: 95,052.

Kamaishi   釜石[市]
City in southeastern Iwate Prefecture, northern Honshū. An important steel-producing center since 1858 when ŌSHIMA TAKATŌ constructed Japan's first Western-style blast furnace. The city's steel industry is now in decline. Magnetite, pyrite, and copper are mined. Its port is used by deep-sea fishing boats. Pop: 52,484.

Kamakura   鎌倉[市]
City in southeastern Kanagawa Prefecture, central Honshū, 45 km (28 mi) southwest of Tōkyō. Overlooking Sagami Bay and favored with a mild climate, Kamakura is an exclusive residential area for commuters to Tōkyō. Its historical importance dates to the 12th century, when MINAMOTO NO YORITOMO chose it as the seat of the Kamakura shogunate, Japan's first military government. It remained the political center of the country until the shogunate was destroyed in 1333. Among its many historical sites are the TSURUGAOKA HACHIMAN SHRINE; the Zen Buddhist temples KENCHŌJI, ENGAKUJI, Jōchiji, Jufukuji, and Jōmyōji (collectively known as the Kamakura GOZAN); Myōhonji of the Nichiren sect; Kōmyōji of the Jōdo sect; and TŌKEIJI. Famous Buddhist images include the

bodhisattva Kannon at the temple Hasedera and the DAIBUTSU (great Buddha) at Kōtokuin. Pop: 174,307. — *See map, next page.*
☞721

☞721

kamakura-bori This 16th-century carved and lacquered wooden box in the *kamakura-bori* style was used to hold perfume or incense. Diameter 24 cm. Yamato Bunkakan, Nara.

kamakura-bori   鎌倉彫
(Kamakura carving). A lacquer technique in which lacquer is applied to a carved wooden base. The term is derived from the town of Kamakura in Sagami Province (now Kanagawa Prefecture), the most important place of its manufacture. The distinctive feature of *kamakura-bori* is the carved wooden base. *Kamakura-bori* should be distinguished from the technique of carving the lacquer, which it was initially intended to resemble. *Kamakura-bori* became an important lacquer technique in its own right, particularly during the 19th and 20th centuries. Examples of *kamakura-bori* are usually executed in red or, more rarely, in black lacquer, with traditional floral and geometric designs. There are few surviving pieces that predate the 16th century.

Kamakura Gozan→Gozan

Kamakura Museum   鎌倉国宝館
(Kamakura Kokuhōkan). Museum in the city of Kamakura, Kanagawa Prefecture. Established in 1928. The museum houses and displays cultural properties from temples and shrines in Kamakura. Among its 3,500 items, many of which date from the Kamakura (1185–1333) and Muromachi (1333–1568) periods, are Buddhist figures, paintings, and handicrafts such as KAMAKURA-BORI. The museum holds five National Treasures.

Kamakura Museum of Modern Art   神奈川県立近代美術館
(Kanagawa Kenritsu Kindai Bijutsukan). Located in Kamakura, Kanagawa Prefecture. The museum collects and exhibits Japanese and foreign art from the 19th century to the present. Opened in 1951, the museum has played an active part in the contemporary art field, organizing important exhibitions of Japanese and Western art and publishing excellent catalogs.

Kamakura ōzōshi   鎌倉大草紙
Military chronicle in three volumes; author unknown. Probably written in the late Muromachi period (1333–1568), it describes events in the Kantō region between 1379 and 1479, focusing on the Kamakura KUBŌ, the governor-general of the Kantō, and the KANTŌ KANREI, his assistant. It continues the TAIHEIKI and is sometimes called *Taihei kōki* (Postscript to the *Taiheiki*).

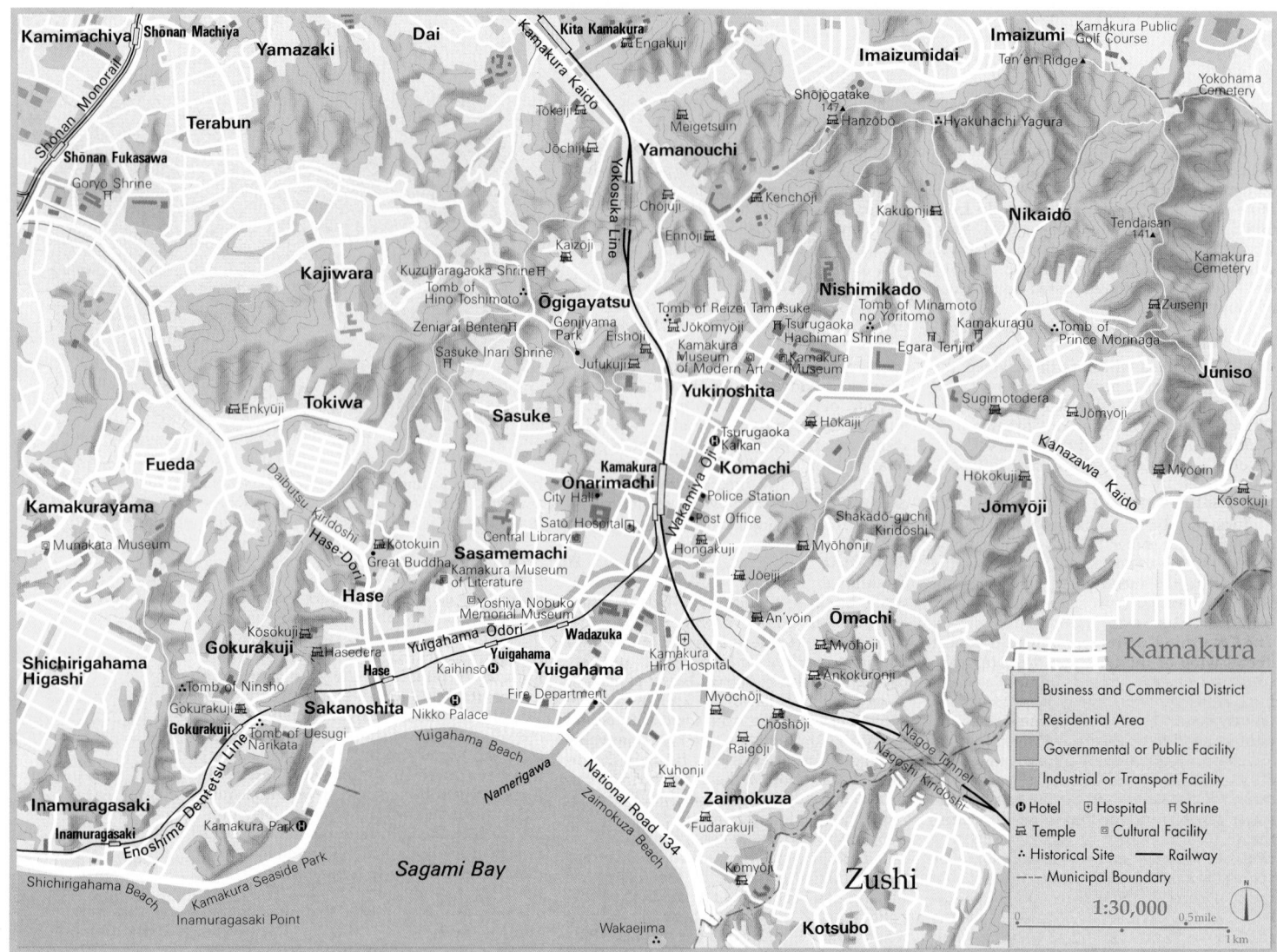

Kamakura

- Business and Commercial District
- Residential Area
- Governmental or Public Facility
- Industrial or Transport Facility
- ⊕ Hotel   ⊞ Hospital   ∏ Shrine
- ⌂ Temple   ▣ Cultural Facility
- ∴ Historical Site   —— Railway
- ----- Municipal Boundary

1:30,000

Kamakura period　　　　鎌倉時代

(1185–1333; Kamakura *jidai*). The Kamakura period corresponds roughly to the span of the KAMAKURA SHOGUNATE (1192–1333) and is named after the city of Kamakura (located in what is now Kanagawa Prefecture), the seat of the government. Distinguishing characteristics of the period are the rise to political power of the provincial warrior class (*bushi*) and the establishment of a military government; the emergence of new and strongly proselytizing sects of Buddhism and the spread of Buddhism from the aristocracy to the common people; and a new vitality in literature and the fine arts. These developments also reflect the continued diminution of Chinese cultural influence, a process that had begun in the late 9th century.

Historians agree that the terminal year of the Kamakura shogunate is 1333, when it was destroyed; however, opinions diverge concerning the year of its inception. Some historians hold that the period begins in 1192, the year in which Emperor GO-TOBA (r 1183–98) recognized the de facto military rule of MINAMOTO NO YORITOMO by conferring on him the title of SHŌGUN. Others have proposed 1180, when Yoritomo established his base in Kamakura. In this encyclopedia, however, the period's beginning is understood as 1185, the year in which Yoritomo destroyed the TAIRA FAMILY and established his military government through the appointment of SHUGO (constables; later, mili-

tary governors) to provinces and JITŌ (stewards) to SHŌEN (private estates) and *kokugaryō* (lands administered by provincial governments).

Background—In 1185 Minamoto forces defeated their old rivals, the Taira family, in the Battle of DANNOURA at the western end of the Inland Sea, finally bringing to a close the TAIRA-MINAMOTO WAR, which had lasted for five years and which had been fought over a wide area from eastern to western Japan, including Kyōto. Earlier, as a result of the HŌGEN DISTURBANCE (1156) and the HEIJI DISTURBANCE (1159) the Taira had gained control of the imperial court and had driven the Minamoto out of Kyōto. The small headquarters that Yoritomo, the leader of the Minamoto, set up in 1180 to prosecute the Taira-Minamoto War had grown by 1184 into a formidable organization of three boards: the SAMURAI-DOKORO, or Board of Retainers, which disciplined and controlled vassals; the KUMONJO, or Public Documents Office, which was later absorbed into the MANDOKORO, or Administrative Board; and the MONCHŪJO, or Board of Inquiry, which heard and reviewed claims and lawsuits. Moreover, within a few months after Dannoura, Yoritomo was given the authority by the imperial court to appoint and post two types of officials throughout the country; a *shugo* to each province to maintain law and order, and *jitō* to private estates and provincial government lands to oversee the fulfillment of obligations, such as the submission of taxes. In addition the Kamakura government was empowered to levy a tax to help defray the expense of keeping the

peace. The delegation of such broad powers to Yoritomo, coupled with the conferral on him in 1192 of the title *seii tai shōgun* ("barbarian-subduing generalissimo") by the imperial court following his conquest of northern Honshū, the only remaining enclave of resistance to his rule, amounted to a formal recognition of the Kamakura government by the imperial government at Kyōto. After 1192 Yoritomo's government may properly be termed a shogunate, and it was the first of a succession of military governments, or shogunates, that ruled Japan for much of the ensuing seven centuries. It was also the beginning of a system of dual rule characterized by the coexistence of a *de jure* sovereign, the emperor, and a de facto ruler, the shōgun.

Structure of Warrior Society—Although the majority of Yoritomo's followers were of humble origin and from the remote and backward region of eastern Honshū, the warrior society that he headed was in outlook and structure a distinct military aristocracy. Its leadershp consisted for the most part of descendants of former governors, holders of military commissions, and managers of private estates who had been sent out to the provinces from Kyōto. A few, like Yoritomo, were descendants of emperors.

Kamakura society was strictly ranked into three classes. At the top were the shōgun's vassals (GOKENIN). Comparatively few in number, they were men of proven loyalty who commanded followings of subvassals. To assure their continued support, Yoritomo accorded them privileged status, assigning special places to them in processions and at

Kamakura, Stronghold of the First Shōguns

Kamakura was only a small seaside village until late 1180, when Minamoto no Yoritomo made it his headquarters and began a successful campaign to become the military leader of a united Japan. By the time Yoritomo officially received the title of shōgun in 1192, the feudal bureaucracy he had created there to oversee his vassals made Kamakura the center of political power in the nation.

Kamakura offered two major advantages: it was far removed from the intrigues and refined influences of the imperial court in Kyōto, and it was a natural stronghold. Bordered by Sagami Bay to the south, Kamakura was protected at the other three compass points by an unbroken crescent of hills.

Easily defendable passes were cut through these hills at strategic points to enable overland travel to and from the town without jeopardizing its security.

The priest Kugyō is said to have hidden behind this ginkgo at the Tsuru-gaoka Hachiman Shrine before killing the third Kamakura shōgun in 1219.

Their hold on power firmly established, the leaders of the Kamakura shogunate began to patronize Buddhist temples, particularly those of the Rinzai Zen sect. The directness and emphasis on self-discipline of Zen strongly appealed to the military class, and the sect's monks served not only as religious guides but also as literati, creators and connoisseurs of art, and valued advisers to the shogunate.

The unadorned and vigorous culture of Kamakura—which stood in clear contrast to the cultivated delicacy of the aristocratic culture evolved by the courtiers of Kyōto—sprang in large measure from the affinity that developed between the warrior leaders and the Zen monks.

The dance of Shizuka Gozen is performed every April at the Tsurugaoka Hachiman Shrine, where in the spring of 1186 Minamoto no Yoritomo forced Shizuka, a celebrated dancer and the mistress of his estranged brother Yoshitsune, to perform for him.

The bell tower gate at Jōchiji, one of the Kamakura Gozan (five main Zen temples of Kamakura), was built in 1283.

The 13th-century Kamakura Daibutsu, an 11.5-meter bronze image of the Buddha Amida, has become a symbol of the city. National Treasure.

The Asahina Kiridōshi pass, which was cut through the hills to the east of the city, looks much as it did in the days of the Kamakura shōguns.

Kamakura period The provincial warriors pictured in this detail from a 13th- or 14th-century scroll typify the class that rose to political power during the Kamakura period.

state functions, and bestowed on them letters of confirmation (*andojō;* see ANDO) that recognized their proprietorship and governance of their lands.

Below them were the *samurai.* In later periods the term came to denote any and all warriors, but in the Kamakura period it referred to a definite rank. The rigid hierarchical relationship that obtained between samurai and *gokenin* is apparent in a passage from a contemporary chronicle: "If a man is made a samurai, he will forget his status and want to be a *gokenin."* Like the *gokenin,* the samurai was mounted and well equipped, and he had a following of subvassals. That both had been elevated to the top of the military aristocracy from lesser origins is apparent in their titles of rank—*gokenin* means "houseman" or "retainer"; samurai, "one who waits on (another)."

At the bottom of warrior society were the foot soldiers (*zusa*). Lightly armed and, early in the period, not especially numerous, they grew considerably in number toward the period's close when the shogunate weakened and warfare increased. The hierarchy was strictly observed at Kamakura, for the leadership felt that once laxity was admitted, greater laxity would ensue.

Life in Kamakura contrasted sharply with that of the court at Kyōto. The *bushi* was dedicated to the martial arts, such as swordsmanship, archery, and horsemanship, while the courtier, who eschewed violence, devoted his time to poetry and other genteel pursuits. Kamakura society exalted loyalty, honor, and frugality—ideals that were later to inspire the cult of the warrior, or BUSHIDŌ.

The Hōjō Regency—The power that Yoritomo wielded did not remain in his family for long. When he died in 1199, there were no Minamoto of any importance to succeed him except two young sons, for in the process of defeating the Taira and establishing Minamoto rule he had eliminated all potential rivals, including his younger brother MINAMOTO NO YOSHITSUNE, who had emerged as the hero of the Taira-Minamoto War. Real power passed to the HŌJŌ FAMILY, the family of Yoritomo's widow, HŌJŌ MASAKO, and for the remainder of the Kamakura period they ruled the country as regents (SHIKKEN) to Minamoto shōguns, none of whom was more than a figurehead.

On the whole, Hōjō rule was firm and ef-

ficient. For example, when the retired emperor Go-Toba attempted to take back the reins of government in the JŌKYŪ DISTURBANCE of 1221, HŌJŌ YOSHITOKI, the second *shikken,* quelled the uprising within a month and sent Go-Toba and two other former emperors into exile, summarily deposed the reigning emperor and designated his successor, and seized lands of court nobles who had supported Go-Toba and awarded them to Hōjō vassals. Finally, he stationed in Kyōto two shogunal deputies (ROKUHARA TANDAI), to watch over the court.

The most resourceful and politically astute of the Hōjō leaders was HŌJŌ YASUTOKI, the third *shikken.* In 1224, at the outset of his regency, he created a new office called REN-SHO, or cosigner, and appointed his uncle to the post. The *rensho* cosigned with the regent all decrees and important documents and was, in effect, an associate regent. By sharing the authority of his office with another prominent Hōjō, Yasutoki was able to minimize factionalism and succession disputes within the family.

In 1225 Yasutoki also established the HYŌJŌSHŪ (Council of State), which was the chief advisory, administrative, and judicial body of the Kamakura government. Its comparatively large membership of 11 (later 15) allowed broader participation—especially of non-Hōjō families—in the decision-making process than was the case under Minamoto no Yoritomo, who had ruled autocratically. Under HŌJŌ TOKIYORI, the fifth regent, yet another body, the HIKITSUKE (High Court), was created in 1249 to assist the Council of State by passing swift judgment on the increasing number of suits and claims pertaining to land.

An outstanding accomplishment of Yasutoki's regency was the promulgation in 1232 of a legal code for the warrior class, the GOSEIBAI SHIKIMOKU. Drawn up by the Hyōjō-shū and consisting of 51 articles, the code embodied customary law of the warrior class and judicial precedents established by the Kamakura government. It enunciated the rights not only of the warriors but also of women, who were allowed to adopt heirs if they were widows and to inherit and perpetuate fiefs. It clarified the duties and responsibilities of Kamakura-appointed officials, such as the *shugo* and the *jitō,* and acted as a restraint on warriors by exhorting them, for example, to respect the rights of shrines and temples and of *shōen* proprietors. The code also reflected the practical na-

ture of justice of the period and the reliance of Kamakura officials on *dōri,* or "common sense," rather than on the laws of earlier times that had been modeled on Chinese laws and institutions. In fact, with the promulgation of the Goseibai Shikimoku, the entire RITSURYŌ SYSTEM, which had been established in the late 7th century, was swept away and replaced by laws that arose from the structure and requirements of warrior society.

The Mongol Invasions—Among the most dramatic of events of the Kamakura period were the MONGOL INVASIONS OF JAPAN during the regency of HŌJŌ TOKIMUNE, the eighth *shikken.* The first was launched in 1274 after the Japanese brusquely rejected a Mongol demand that they acknowledge the suzerainty of Khubilai Khan (1215–94). Fortunately for the defenders, only a day after the invading force of about 40,000 men landed near Hakata in northern Kyūshū, a storm suddenly arose, destroying a good part of the fleet and causing many of the invaders to drown.

Seven years later, after the Japanese had rejected his demands once again and, moreover, beheaded his envoys, Khubilai dispatched a huge invasion force of between 140,000 and 150,000 men to Hakata Bay. Again, after nearly two months of fighting, a fierce typhoon arose, forcing the invaders to retreat. Until the end of the century the Japanese remained apprehensive. Fortifications that had been built on the shore of the bay following the first invasion were extended and a series of Hōjō family members were appointed special deputies (Chinzei TANDAI) to resolve disputes between shogunal vassals in Kyūshū and to lead them in battle in the event of another attack.

The repulse of the invasions nourished a certain amount of national pride and temporarily raised the prestige of the Hōjō regency; however, the regency could not make good on promises of reward to warriors and the consequence was increased domestic strife. Because the invaders had come from overseas, the Hōjō took no war booty in the form of land to grant to its victorious vassals. Furthermore, Shintō and Buddhist priests also pressed for rewards, insisting that their prayers had generated the KAMIKAZE ("divine wind") that decimated the invaders. The expediencies that the shogunate resorted to, such as referring the claims of vassal and priest to the Hikitsuke, which delayed judgment, served only to erode confidence in the judicial system and ultimately in the Hōjō regency itself. In an attempt to prevent the increasing impoverishment of its retainers the shogunate issued decrees forbidding the sale or foreclosure of lands held by its retainers. Called TOKUSEI, or "acts of virtuous government," they pleased some but alienated the creditors, whose support the shogunate could ill afford to lose.

The Kamakura-Period Economy—Two economic institutions that arose early in and continued through the Kamakura period were the TOIMARU and the ZA. The former were shipping agents who took rice and other products of the *shōen* on consignment and distributed them over a wide market. The latter were trade guilds that often engaged in monopolistic practices. Both institutions developed more fully in the succeeding MUROMACHI PERIOD (1333–1568).

Popularization of Buddhism—In the Kamakura period Buddhism, which had been chiefly an ornament of the ruling class, turned its attention to the common people. A

The Emergence of the Warrior Class

By the late 12th century the political authority of the Heian court in Kyōto had been successfully challenged by warrior bands formed in outlying areas, with Yoritomo of the Minamoto clan emerging as de facto ruler of Japan. Based in Kamakura, Yoritomo and his vassals made the cult of the warrior the dominant force in Japanese culture. The commitment to stoic self-discipline and the emphasis on action rather than words that these warriors shared with Zen Buddhist monks set the spiritual tone for an age that saw the battlefield, rather than the court, as the arena in which men established their worth.

Samurai anxious to perfect and demonstrate their military prowess chafed under the restraints that were imposed in times of peace. They were therefore quick to seize opportunities like the attempted Mongol invasions of 1274 and 1281 to actively prove their devotion to the martial ideal.

Pride in his military exploits led Takezaki Suenaga, a Kyūshū vassal whose valor the shogunate awarded with an estate, to commission the *Scrolls of the Mongol Invasion*. At top, the mounted Takezaki reviews shore defenses. Above, he ignores enemy arrows to slash throats after boarding a Mongol ship. At right, he displays heads he has taken.

Provincial warriors hone their fighting skills in the late-13th-century *Tale of Obusuma Saburō Scroll*. Perfecting bowmanship and swordsmanship was a constant preoccupation. Mansions became strongholds, and guards moved quickly against potential intruders.

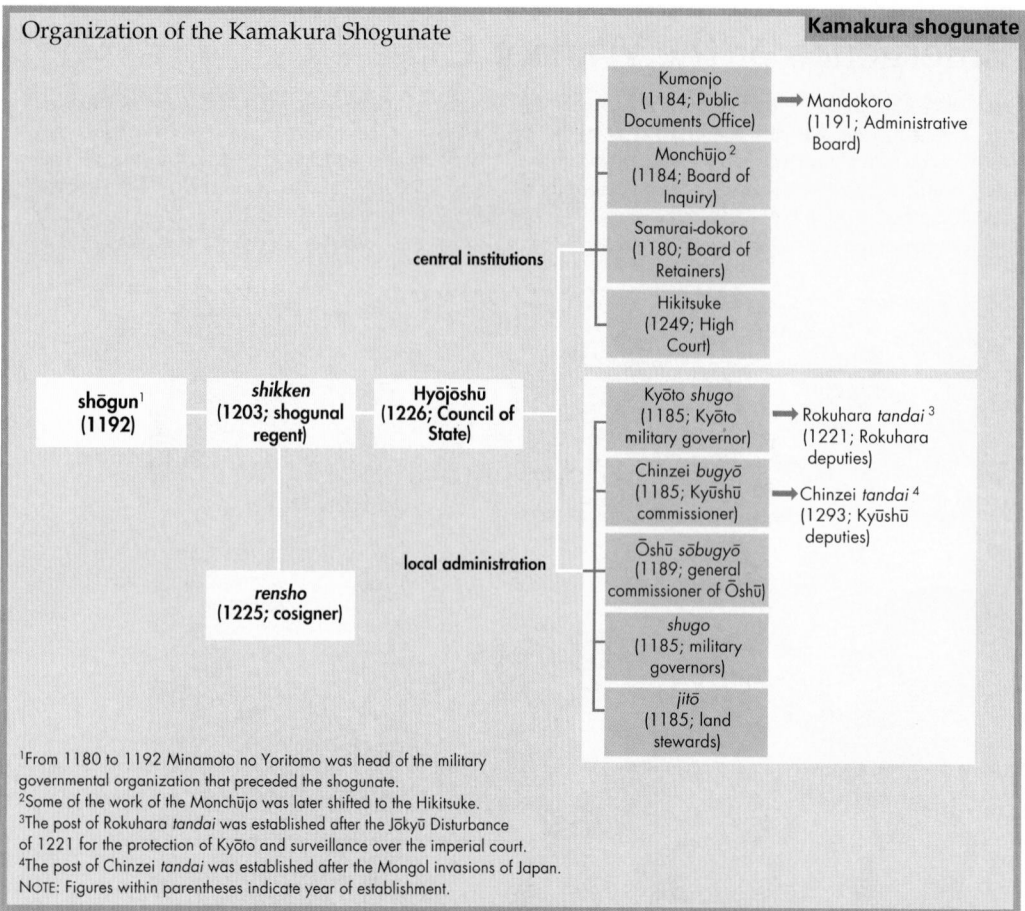

central institutions

shōgun[1]
(1192)

shikken
(1203; shogunal regent)

Hyōjōshū
(1226; Council of State)

rensho
(1225; cosigner)

Kumonjo
(1184; Public Documents Office) → Mandokoro (1191; Administrative Board)

Monchūjo[2]
(1184; Board of Inquiry)

Samurai-dokoro
(1180; Board of Retainers)

Hikitsuke
(1249; High Court)

Kyōto shugo
(1185; Kyōto military governor) → Rokuhara tandai[3] (1221; Rokuhara deputies)

Chinzei bugyō
(1185; Kyūshū commissioner) → Chinzei tandai[4] (1293; Kyūshū deputies)

Ōshū sōbugyō
(1189; general commissioner of Ōshū)

shugo
(1185; military governors)

jitō
(1185; land stewards)

local administration

[1]From 1180 to 1192 Minamoto no Yoritomo was head of the military governmental organization that preceded the shogunate.
[2]Some of the work of the Monchūjo was later shifted to the Hikitsuke.
[3]The post of Rokuhara tandai was established after the Jōkyū Disturbance of 1221 for the protection of Kyōto and surveillance over the imperial court.
[4]The post of Chinzei tandai was established after the Mongol invasions of Japan.
NOTE: Figures within parentheses indicate year of establishment.

major role was played in this movement by the tradition of Amida, the Buddha who, doctrine holds, enables believers to be reborn in the Western Pure Land (Saihō Jōdo) in answer to the sincere invocation of his name (see NEMBUTSU). HŌNEN, founder of the JŌDO SECT, taught that reliance on the grace of Amida was more efficacious than personal effort toward enlightenment. His disciple SHINRAN, founder of the JŌDO SHIN SECT, held that faith, not acts, was the one essential qualification for salvation, which could be achieved by a single invocation of Amida's name. Shinran was also the first Japanese Buddhist to take a wife. Although marriage eventually became normal practice in all sects of Japanese Buddhism, the immediate consequence for both Shinran and Hōnen was their exile.

An equally controversial religious figure was NICHIREN, founder of the NICHIREN SECT, who stressed the importance of personal effort toward enlightenment and insisted that the essential teachings of Buddhism were contained in the LOTUS SUTRA. He was intolerant of all other forms of Buddhism and of the Kamakura government for patronizing them.

Another form of Buddhism that flourished in this period was ZEN. Its simplicity and emphasis on self-discipline and meditation as the means to enlightenment particularly appealed to the warrior class. Unlike the founders of the other major new Buddhist sects of the period, both EISAI, who introduced the RINZAI SECT, and DŌGEN, who introduced the SŌTŌ SECT, considered themselves disciples of Chinese Zen masters from whom they received teachings, ritual, and even the names of their sects.

Literature and the Fine Arts—Although deprived of its political role, the court remained the center of Japanese culture. The SHIN KOKINSHŪ, a poetry anthology

that many scholars consider to be the crowning achievement of courtly WAKA (chiefly 31-syllable verse), appeared in 1205. KAMO NO CHŌMEI, who in 1204 became a Buddhist monk, had witnessed the terrible events that accompanied the transfer of power from the court to the provinces, and in the HŌJŌKI (1212; tr *The Ten Foot Square Hut*, 1928), he dwells upon the impermanence of all human endeavor (MUJŌ).

The characteristic form of Kamakura prose literature, however, was the GUNKI MONOGATARI, or war tale. The most famous of these was the chronicle of the Taira-Minamoto wars, HEIKE MONOGATARI (13th century; tr *The Tale of the Heike*, 1988). Recited to the accompaniment of the *biwa*, a plucked string instrument, the story recounts the rise and fall of the Taira in the context of the Buddhist philosophy of impermanence. The priest JIEN, whose writing was also deeply influenced by Buddhist philosophy, produced the first interpretive history of Japan, GUKANSHŌ (1220; tr *The Future and the Past*, 1978). In 1275 Hōjō Sanetoki, nephew of the regent Hōjō Yasutoki, established a library and learning center, whose collection of Chinese and Japanese manuscripts became the nucleus of the still-extant KANAZAWA BUNKO.

Among accomplishments in the fine arts during the Kamakura period the wood sculptures of UNKEI and KAIKEI, who collaborated on the two huge guardian deities of the great south gate (*nandaimon*) at TŌDAIJI, are of particular note. Painters of the era showed a great interest and skill in portraiture, a particularly renowned example of which is the portrait of Minamoto no Yoritomo done in the YAMATO-E style and attributed to FUJIWARA NO TAKANOBU. Another important genre was EMAKIMONO (picture scrolls). Although the genre arose in the Heian period, it continued to flourish in the Kamakura period. Though much reduced in scale in comparison to earlier eras, the influence of Chinese

artistic traditions can yet be seen in INK PAINTING and in the style of temple architecture known as *karayō* (Chinese style), both of which were introduced by Zen monks.

Decline and Fall of the Shogunate—The Kamakura shogunate came to a sudden end in 1333 when two important vassals turned against their leader. ASHIKAGA TAKAUJI had been sent on a punitive expedition against the retired emperor GO-DAIGO, who had recently escaped from the island of Oki to which he had been banished for having defied the shogunate, but Takauji chose instead to support Go-Daigo (see KEMMU RESTORATION). Another vassal of the shogunate, NITTA YOSHISADA, was ordered to proceed against Takauji, but he too turned against his superiors and forced HŌJŌ TAKATOKI, the 14th regent, to take his own life. Thus ended the 150-year rule of the country's first military regime.

There had been signs of a deterioration of the power of the shogunate in the 1280s, when it had been unable to fulfill its obligation to reward its worthy vassals following the Mongol invasions. Equally significant was the fact that Takatoki, the last Hōjō regent, had neither the inclination nor the skills necessary to administer the government, and spent much of his time dancing and watching dogfights. A further contributing factor was the mounting resentment of senior vassals against the virtual monopolization of shogunal offices by the Hōjō. Thus the fall of the Kamakura shogunate in 1333 was not as unexpected as it appeared to be.
☛723

Kamakura shogunate   鎌倉幕府

(1192–1333; Kamakura *bakufu*). Japan's first military or warrior government; established by MINAMOTO NO YORITOMO in Kamakura. Although many scholars date the beginning of the shogunate from 1192, when Yoritomo was given the title of SHŌGUN, the bakufu itself, the warrior governmental organization, had been set up in 1180, and the system of appointed military governors (SHUGO) and land stewards (JITŌ) by which it controlled the country began in 1185.

In 1180 Yoritomo rebelled against the TAIRA FAMILY (see TAIRA-MINAMOTO WAR). Vast numbers of warriors pledged fidelity to him as GOKENIN (housemen). After defeating a Taira force at the Battle of FUJIGAWA that year, Yoritomo established a bakufu (literally, "tent government") and consolidated his control over the eastern provinces. By the end of 1183 Yoritomo's generals had expelled the Taira from Kyōto, and his de facto control of these eastern provinces was recognized by the imperial court. In 1185 he sought and received from the court the right to appoint *shugo* in each province and *jitō* in the SHŌEN (landed estates) throughout the country. In 1192 Yoritomo was given the title of *seii tai shōgun* ("barbarian-subduing generalissimo"; usually abbreviated as shōgun).

Character of the Shogunate—Particularly in this early period, the power of the shogunate was far from being nationwide. The right to appoint *jitō* in the Kinai (capital area) and western provinces did not come until the triumph of the shogunate over the imperial court in the JŌKYŪ DISTURBANCE of 1221. The Kamakura shogunate's system of granting land rights (*shiki*) through appointment to the post of *jitō* differed distinctly from the *daimyō* system of later times, under which land was directly bestowed. Yoritomo used these *jitō* appointments as a means of rewarding his vassals with land. This system, based on the combination of the lord-vassal relationship and the bestowal of land (more accurately, land rights), has been described by many historians as feudal.

Development of the Shogunate— Yoritomo set up the SAMURAI-DOKORO, the MANDOKORO, and the MONCHŪJO to handle, respectively, the *gokenin*, general and financial affairs, and legal matters. After Yoritomo's death in 1199, his successors were MINAMOTO NO YORIIE and MINAMOTO NO SANETOMO. Their mother, HŌJŌ MASAKO, took on the role of guardian. Through her, the HŌJŌ FAMILY took control of the shogunate as SHIKKEN (shogunal regent), and the Hōjō regency was established.

The shogunate formulated the legal precedents of the military government in the GOSEIBAI SHIKIMOKU and strengthened its institutional structure by setting up the Council of State (HYŌJŌSHŪ), a supreme governing body made up of 11 *gokenin* (there were later about 15 members). Under the Hyōjōshū was the *hikitsukeshū* (see HIKITSUKE), a group of coadjutors who dealt with land claims.

In the late 13th century, at around the time of the MONGOL INVASIONS OF JAPAN, the council system gradually declined and the vast majority of the *gokenin* were deprived of political influence. Concurrently the direct descendants of the main branch of the Hōjō family, known as the *tokusō*, and the private family council, the YORIAI, came to monopolize power. Dissatisfaction with the Hōjō grew, and in 1333 the Kamakura shogunate was overthrown by Emperor GODAIGO (see KEMMU RESTORATION). The shogunate can be said to have ruled for almost 150 years from the early 1180s to its overthrow in 1333. Its appearance marked a major turning point in Japanese history, representing the first in a series of military governments that ruled Japan until the collapse of the TOKUGAWA SHOGUNATE (1603–1867) and the imperial restoration in 1868.

Kamanashigawa 釜無川

River in western Yamanashi Prefecture, central Honshū, originating in the northern Akaishi Mountains and flowing in a southerly direction. It joins the FUEFUKIGAWA in the Kōfu Basin to form the FUJIKAWA. The water is used for irrigation. Length: 64 km (40 mi).

kamasu 叺

A bag made by folding a length of hemp cloth or straw matting in half and sewing up the sides. Large ones were used for transporting and storing coal, fertilizer, grain, salt, and so forth. Small ones were used as tobacco pouches and purses. The bags were made during the agricultural off-season. With the increased availability of paper bags, the use of *kamasu* has decreased dramatically.

Kamba Falls 神庭滝

(Kamba no Taki). Located in the town of Katsuyama, northern Okayama Prefecture, western Honshū. It is on a minor tributary of the river Asahigawa. The surrounding area is inhabited by wild monkeys. Height: 140 m (459 ft); width: 27 m (89 ft).

kamban system かんばん方式

(*kamban hōshiki*). Also known as the Toyota production system because it was developed by TOYOTA MOTOR CORPORATION, or as the "just-in-time" (JIT) system because parts and materials are delivered and produced only at the time and in the quantity needed.

The *kamban* system utilizes a "pull" method of production, in which the production plan is made only for the final assembly. Demand for materials then flows backward as each process in the sequence withdraws the parts it needs from the previous process, which then produces only the amount that was withdrawn. The *kamban*, for which the system is named, is the document used to request parts from previous processes.

The *kamban* or JIT system depends on a factory layout that follows the production flow, short changeover times, and level scheduling. Advantages of the system include increased productivity, reduction in work-in-process inventory, and increased flexibility for producing a variety of different products or models with the same facilities.

Kambara 蒲原[町]

Town at the mouth of the river Fujikawa in central Shizuoka Prefecture, central Honshū. Kambara has a growing industrial district; mandarin oranges are also produced. Pop: 14,688.

Kambara Ariake 蒲原有明

(1876–1952). Poet. Real name Kambara Hayao. Born in Tōkyō. He was a devotee of Dante Gabriel Rosetti. *Kusawakaba* (1902), his first collection of poetry, contains lyrical pieces, ballads, and sonnets. *Dokugen aika* (1903), another collection of his poems, also shows lyrical and sonnet influences. With SUSUKIDA KYŪKIN, he became a leading figure in Japanese symbolist poetry at the beginning of the 20th century. A collection of his symbolist poems, *Shunchōshū*, was published in 1905. He later published translations of European poets as well as works of literary criticism.

Kambayashi Akatsuki 上林暁

(1902–80). Author. Real name Tokuhiro Iwaki. Born in Kōchi Prefecture; graduate of Tōkyō University. He began writing fiction while working as an editor of the magazine KAIZŌ. After publishing *Bara tōnin* (1933), a collection of short stories, he began to write full time. His autobiographical fiction derives from his personal and family life. A series of his short stories deals with his affection for and care of his wife, who died after a long mental illness. His works include the short stories "Anjū no ie" (1938) and "Sei Yohane Byōin nite" (1946).

kambun 漢文

(Chinese writing). The term *kambun* broadly denotes all compositions in classical Chinese, whether written by Chinese or Japanese authors. In the broadest sense, it also embraces a hybrid form of literary Japanese known as HENTAI KAMBUN ("variant *kambun*"), which is often found in such premodern nonliterary documents as contracts and diaries. Until late in the 19th century, classical Chinese occupied a position in Japan analogous to that which Latin held to the end of the 17th century in Europe as the written language of scholarship, high literature, and religion. The study of *kambun* made up the core of higher education during the Edo period (1600–1868), and today it is still taught in high schools as part of the curriculum.

Method of Reading Kambun—In Japan, classical Chinese is normally read by a standard method of translation known as *kundoku*. In *kundoku*, the order of words in the Chinese original (typically subject, ob-

ject, verb) is inverted in reading to conform to Japanese word order (subject, object, verb), and Japanese verb endings (Chinese is uninflected) and grammatical particles are added. Verb endings and particles, as well as Japanese readings of certain Chinese characters, are indicated by small phonograms (KANA) to the right of or directly below the characters to which they adhere. Changes in word order are indicated by small symbols, called *kaeriten* (transposition marks), on the left side of the vertical line of characters. Of the five varieties of *kaeriten*, the one most frequently used is a simple checklike mark that can be placed between any two graphs to indicate that in Japanese they are read in the reverse order. The other four varieties are sequences of ordinal signs that are used to show in what order Chinese words are to be read in the Japanese translation of a sentence in cases where it is necessary to move them to a place two or more characters distant from their original position. More than one sequence is necessary because in complex sentences there are sometimes grammatical sequences contained within other grammatical sequences. The standardized system of marks now in use is the outcome of centuries of experimentation, reaching completion only shortly after 1600.

The style of Japanese generated in the manner described above is called *kundoku kambun* (literally, "translated Chinese"). It has two general peculiarities. One of these is that the language itself is CLASSICAL JAPANESE (i.e., the vocabulary, spelling, and morphology reflect the language of the 9th-century aristocracy). The other general characteristic is that, being a partial as well as a literal translation, it preserves a strong flavor of Chinese; it is replete with such Chinese rhetorical devices as the double negative and with many words and phrases characteristic of *kambun*. Many of these found their way into the written classical Japanese language as part of the general influence of *kambun* on Japanese.

Cultural Influence of Kambun—*Kambun* secular literature enriched the intellectual and aesthetic life of a progressively widening circle of the population from the late 6th century until well into the 20th, and in the fields of ethics, history, essay writing, and poetry, Japanese authors of *kambun* have made no small contribution to the heritage. In effect, *kambun* kept Japan in contact with one of the world's great civilizations and continued to be influential until new intellectual currents in the world at large reduced its status in the present century. See also POETRY AND PROSE IN CHINESE.

Kambun Master 寛文巨匠

(fl ca 1660–73; Kambun Kyoshō). Name given to the anonymous mentor of the UKIYO-E pioneer Hishikawa MORONOBU. It was at one time assumed that all of the *ukiyo-e–*style book illustrations and prints done in Edo (now Tōkyō) during the second half of the 17th century were the work of Moronobu. Modern research, however, has established the identity of at least two other important *ukiyo-e* artists of that time, the Kambun Master and SUGIMURA JIHEI.

The Kambun Master, who left no signed works, receives his name from the Kambun era (1661–73) in which he flourished. He was the first known artist of Edo *ukiyo-e*. His work consists of at least 50 illustrated books and several dozen prints; many of these are

Kambara Ariake
One of Japan's leading early-20th-century symbolist poets.

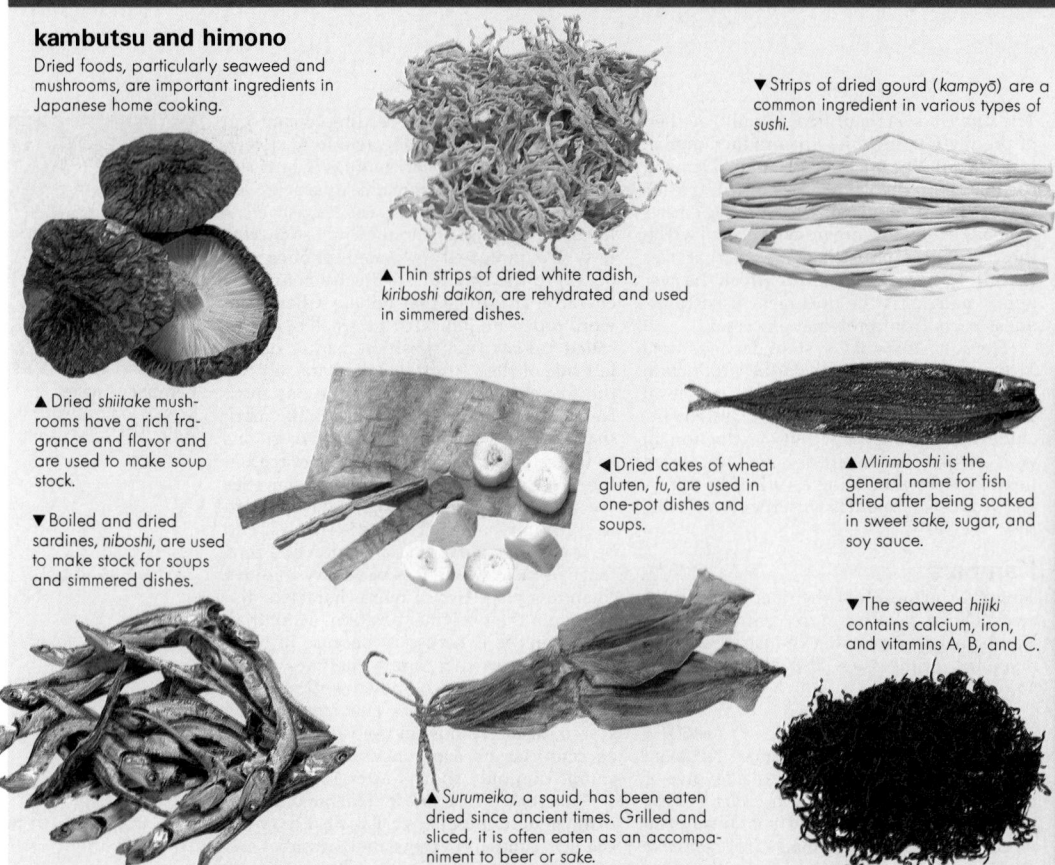

kambutsu and himono

Dried foods, particularly seaweed and mushrooms, are important ingredients in Japanese home cooking.

▲ Thin strips of dried white radish, *kiriboshi daikon*, are rehydrated and used in simmered dishes.

▼ Strips of dried gourd (*kampyō*) are a common ingredient in various types of *sushi*.

▼ Approximately 50-percent protein, freeze-dried *tōfu* is extremely nutritious and easy to digest.

▼ Horse mackerel (*aji*) salted and spread out to sun dry, Chiba Prefecture.

▲ Dried *shiitake* mushrooms have a rich fragrance and flavor and are used to make soup stock.

▼ Boiled and dried sardines, *niboshi*, are used to make stock for soups and simmered dishes.

◄ Dried cakes of wheat gluten, *fu*, are used in one-pot dishes and soups.

▲ *Mirimboshi* is the general name for fish dried after being soaked in sweet *sake*, sugar, and soy sauce.

▼ The seaweed *hijiki* contains calcium, iron, and vitamins A, B, and C.

▲ *Surumeika*, a squid, has been eaten dried since ancient times. Grilled and sliced, it is often eaten as an accompaniment to beer or *sake*.

SHUNGA (erotica). He created the unique Edo style that formed the basis for Moronobu's later consolidation of the nascent *ukiyo-e* school.

kambutsu and himono 乾物と干物

(*kambutsu to himono*). Two general terms for traditional Japanese dried foods. *Kambutsu* refers to dried foods in general, and *himono* to dried fish and shellfish. Before the wide availability of frozen food, drying was a common means of preserving foods, and such foods continue to be important in Japanese cooking. Many, in particular plant foods, are softened in cold or lukewarm water before they are cooked. Some of the more common dried foods are *hoshi shiitake* (dried SHIITAKE mushrooms), *kiriboshi daikon* (white radish sliced in narrow strips and dried), *kampyō* (dried gourd strips), *kōyadōfu* (frozen and dried *tōfu*), and *fu* (dried cakes made with wheat gluten). Among dried seaweeds are *hijiki*, *kombu*, and *wakame*. *Surume* is dried squid, *niboshi* are boiled and dried sardines, and *mirimboshi* is fish soaked in a mixture of *mirin* (sweetened *sake*), soy sauce, and sugar and then dried.

Kameda 亀田[町]

Town in central Niigata Prefecture, central Honshū. The town is located in an agricultural area between the rivers Shinanogawa and Aganogawa. Cultivation of Japanese

pears and food processing are the chief industries. Kameda has become a commuter suburb of the city of Niigata. Pop: 29,977.

Kameda Bōsai 亀田鵬斎

(1752–1826). Confucian philosopher, poet, calligrapher, and painter in the *nanga* or literati style (see BUNJINGA). Also known as Kameda Hōsai. Born in Edo (now Tōkyō), where he studied Confucianism under Inoue Kinga (1732–84), a leader in the new eclectic Kogaku school of Confucianism. Bōsai eventually opened a school of his own, but was forced to close it when MATSUDAIRA SADANOBU, the leader of the KANSEI REFORMS, decreed that only the Zhu Xi (Chu Hsi) school of Confucianism (see SHUSHIGAKU) should be considered orthodox.

Bōsai was especially famous for his calligraphy, which somewhat resembled that of his friend the monk RYŌKAN. He contributed inscriptions to many paintings, including those of his friends SAKAI HŌITSU of the Rimpa school and TANI BUNCHŌ of the *nanga* school. Bōsai's paintings, generally of landscapes, were published in woodblock form in *Kyōchūzan* (Mountains of the Spirit).

Kamegaoka site 亀ケ岡遺跡

(Kamegaoka *iseki*). Archaeological site of the Final Jōmon period (ca 1000 BC–ca 300 BC); located in Kamegaoka, Kizukuri Chō, Aomori Prefecture. First discovered in 1623 and excavated many times since the 19th century, the site has yielded STONE TOOLS, JŌMON FIGURINES, beads, and Final Jōmon Kamegaoka-type pottery distinguished by its artistic cloud motifs, for which it serves as the type site. Unusual recoveries of BONE ARTICLES, wooden objects, and lacquer ware have also been made from the lowland peat stratum.

Kameido Incident 亀戸事件

(Kameido Jiken). The murder by military police of militant laborers in the working-class Tōkyō district of Kameido on the night of 4

September 1923. Martial law had been declared in the wake of the catastrophic TŌKYŌ EARTHQUAKE on 1 September. Amid rumors that Koreans and leftists were rioting, police arrested many innocent Koreans, socialists, and labor union members. Over 700 were detained at the police station in Kameido, an area with a particularly active labor movement. On the night of 4 September, 10 labor union members and 4 other men who were part of a temporary patrol group were imprisoned and killed by military police. Their deaths were not reported in the news until 10 October. Members of the Nihon Rōdō Sōdōmei (Japan Federation of Labor) led a protest movement, and the following February a memorial service was held in honor of the victims.

Kamei Fumio 亀井文夫

(1908–87). Documentary filmmaker. Born in Fukushima Prefecture, Kamei was one of the foremost socialist filmmakers in the history of Japanese film, standing by his principles from the prewar through the postwar years. His *Tatakau heitai* (1939, Fighting Soldiers), although it was banned from public screening, is important as the only Japanese antiwar film to be made during the war years of 1937–45. Kamei was arrested and imprisoned for his filmmaking activities. After the war, he took a stand against nuclear weapons with such films as *Ikite ite yokatta* (1956, Glad to Be Alive) and *Sekai wa kyōfu suru* (1957, The World Is Terrified).

Kamei Katsuichirō 亀井勝一郎

(1907–66). Literary critic. Born in Hakodate, Hokkaidō. In 1926 Kamei entered Tōkyō University, where he studied aesthetics. Soon after entering the university, he joined the SHINJINKAI (New Man Society), a Marxist study group. He was imprisoned but renounced his Marxist beliefs through the process that came to be known as TENKŌ and was released in 1930.

In 1932 Kamei became actively involved

1

2

726

in the PROLETARIAN LITERATURE MOVEMENT. In 1934 he helped found the progressive literary journal *Genjitsu* (Reality) and published a collection of literary essays entitled *Tenkeiki no bungaku* (Literature in a Period of Change). Disillusioned with proletarian literature, in 1935 Kamei and YASUDA YOJŪRŌ founded the coterie NIHON RŌMANHA (Japanese Romantic school).

Kamei became deeply interested in traditional Japanese culture, as is reflected in his "Return to Japan" series: *Yamato koji fūbutsushi* (1943, A Pilgrimage to Old Temples in Yamato), *Shinran* (1944, Shinran), and *Shōtoku Taishi* (1946, Prince Shōtoku). His autobiography, *Waga seishin no henreki* (The Pilgrimage of My Spirit), was published in 1948. He received the Yomiuri Literary Prize in 1951 for his *Gendaijin no kenkyū* (1950, A Study of Modern Man) and the Kikuchi Kan Prize in 1965 for his lifework, *Nihonjin no seishin shi kenkyū* (A Study of the Spiritual History of the Japanese People), four volumes of which had been completed at his death.

kamekan→jar burials

Kamekura Yūsaku   亀倉雄策

(1915–   ). Graphic designer. Born in Niigata Prefecture, Kamekura studied at the New Institute of Applied Architecture (Shin Kenchiku Kōgei Gakuin). In 1938 he took a position at Japan Studio (Nihon Kōbō), where he eventually became the art director for the English-language magazine *NIPPON*. A leader in the field of Japanese design, Kamekura participated in the establishment of the Japan Advertising Artists Club in 1951 and Nippon Design Center, Inc, in 1960. The poster and symbol he created for the 1964 Tōkyō Olympic Games received international acclaim. *Kamekura Yūsaku no dezain* (1983) is a collection of his works.

Kamen no kokuhaku   仮面の告白

(tr *Confessions of a Mask*, 1958). Novel by MISHIMA YUKIO (1925–70); published in 1949. The work, which established Mishima's reputation as a writer, depicts the sexual awakening of the narrator, a boy from an upper-class family. Unable to sustain a relationship with a member of the opposite sex because of his latent homosexuality, he is finally rejected by the woman he loves. The protagonist's loneliness can be said to epitomize the alienation experienced after World War II by Japanese young people who could not adapt successfully to the unsettled conditions of their society. The title itself mocks the pretension to unadorned confession characteristic of the I-NOVEL genre and hints at an important aspect of Mishima's aesthetic: his emphasis on the beauty of artifice.

Kameoka   亀岡[市]

City in central Kyōto Prefecture, central Honshū. A provincial capital (*kokufu*) during the Nara period (710–794), it came under the rule of AKECHI MITSUHIDE in the late 16th century. During the Edo period (1600–1868) Kameoka was a post-station town. Today it is a commercial center of the Kameoka Basin, though its principal occupation was once farming. Textile and precision-instrument industries are developing rapidly. Tourist attractions include a boat ride down the rapids of the HOZUGAWA. Pop: 85,283.

Kameyama   亀山[市]

City in northern Mie Prefecture, central Honshū. Kameyama developed as a castle town and post-station town during the Edo period (1600–1868). The area is known for its rice, tea, and decorative candles. Pop: 37,632.

Kameyama, Emperor   亀山天皇

(1249–1305; Kameyama Tennō). The 90th sovereign (*tennō*) in the traditional count (which includes several legendary emperors); reigned 1260–74. A son of Emperor GO-SAGA. Kameyama, his father's favorite, replaced his elder brother, the emperor GO-FUKAKUSA, who was forced to abdicate. After his own abdication, Kameyama continued to rule from retirement during the reign of his son Emperor GO-UDA. Go-Fukakusa's son succeeded Go-Uda as Emperor FUSHIMI, beginning the tradition of alternating succession between the senior Jimyōin line (descended from Go-Fukakusa) and the junior Daikakuji line (descended from Kameyama). This practice was made official by the KAMAKURA SHOGUNATE. Kameyama took holy orders in 1289 and in 1291 converted his palace into the Zen temple that later became NANZENJI.

kami   神

Term used to refer to the divine in Shintō religion, traditionally interpreted as a superior and mysterious force of either creative or destructive character, which resides in natural elements, animals, and certain human beings; causes ambivalent feelings of fear and gratitude; and is the focus of ritual behavior. *Kami* are usually worshiped in shrines. Worship includes mental and physical preparations, purification, offerings of food, expression of the community's gratitude and desires, and offerings of dances and music. See FESTIVALS.

Whereas heavenly divinities tend to reside in the High Celestial Plain (TAKAMAGAHARA) and to be worshiped at shrines, earthly divinities tend to reside in natural phenomena and to manifest themselves either spontaneously or through summoning by priests. On the whole, *kami* appear to be benevolent if properly worshiped. However, natural calamities were attributed to the spirits of humans wrongly accused who had therefore committed suicide or died in exile, leaving a "vengeful spirit" (GORYŌ) needing to be pacified and transformed into a benevolent force. Each *kami* is endowed with a particular force, or will, called TAMA, which may have a "coarse" aspect (*aramitama*) and "gentle" aspect (*nigimitama*) and is worshiped accordingly in ritual. As Shintō interacted with Buddhism, Confucianism, and Taoism, the notion of *kami* developed philosophically and ethically. Within the Shintō-Buddhist syncretic systems (see HONJI SUIJAKU) beginning around the 10th century, particular Shintō *kami* were associated with particular Buddhist divinities and thus transformed in important ways. Attempts to establish an all-encompassing *kami* at the very top of the pantheon failed, and many *kami* retain their local and historical character. See also UJIGAMI; ONI; TA NO KAMI; MOUNTAINS, WORSHIP OF; YAMA NO KAMI.

Kamichika Ichiko   神近市子

(1888–1981). Writer and politician. Born in Nagasaki Prefecture. In 1912 she joined the feminist group SEITŌSHA (Bluestocking Society) while still a student at Tsuda College. She then became a reporter for the newspaper *Tōkyō nichi-nichi shimbun* (now *Mainichi shimbun*). In 1916 she precipitated a notorious scandal (the so-called Hikage Teahouse Incident) when she stabbed and wounded her lover, the anarchist ŌSUGI SAKAE, because he had begun living with ITŌ NOE. After two years in prison she continued her writing career. In 1935 she edited the magazine *Fujin bungei* (Women's Literary Arts) with Suzuki Atsushi (her husband from 1920 to 1937). From 1953 to 1969 she served in the House of Representatives as a Japan Socialist Party member, campaigning against prostitution and for human rights.

kamidana→Shintō family altars

Kami Fukuoka   上福岡[市]

City in southern Saitama Prefecture, 30 km (19 mi) from Tōkyō. Formerly a farming area, it is now a residential suburb for commuters to Tōkyō. Pop: 58,761.

Kamigumi Co, Ltd   [株]上組

(Kamigumi). Firm chiefly engaged in harbor transport that is diversifying into related businesses such as warehousing and land transport; one of the top-ranked companies in the integrated transport business in Japan. Incorporated in 1947. The company has overseas subsidiaries and representative offices in the United States, Hong Kong, Taiwan, Singapore, Malaysia, and other countries. Sales for the fiscal year ending September 1991 totaled ¥118.5 billion (US $863.7 million). The company was capitalized at ¥18.1 billion (US $131.9 million) as of March 1991. Headquarters are in Kōbe.

Kamiiso   上磯[町]

Town in southwestern Hokkaidō on Hakodate Bay. Oil refineries and cement plants are located in the Nanaehama district of the town. Japan's only Trappist monastery is situated here. Pop: 30,950.

kamikakushi   神隠し

(literally, "hiding by the spirits"). The sudden and unexplained disappearance of a person from home that was traditionally believed to be the work of the supernatural beings called TENGU, of foxes, and of other malevolent spirits. When someone fell victim to *kamikakushi*, it was customary for the entire community to conduct a search of the village and neighboring mountains with ringing of bells and beating of drums. It was believed that the victim—usually a sickly child—had been carried off to the world of spirits (*reikai*) and that he would return after a day or two, or even after several years.

Kamikawa Basin   上川盆地

(Kamikawa Bonchi). In central Hokkaidō. Bounded by the Kitami and Ishikari mountains on the east and the Teshio and Yūbari mountains on the west, this fault basin consists of a floodplain on the upper river Ishikarigawa. The area is one of the northernmost regions of rice cultivation in Japan and also produces vegetables. The major city is Asahikawa. Area: approximately 450 sq km (174 sq mi).

kamikaze   神風

Meaning "wind of the gods" or "divine wind," *kamikaze* was used as a literary "pillow word" (MAKURA KOTOBA) for the province of Ise (now Mie Prefecture) and was also applied to strong prevailing winds off its coast. However, in common usage, *kamikaze* refers to the storms that destroyed the invading Mongol armadas off northwestern

Kamei Katsuichirō This literary critic, jailed in 1928–30 for his leftist politics, renounced Marxism while in prison and later became a nationalist and leading writer on traditional Japanese culture.

Kamichika Ichiko This newspaper reporter, essayist, translator, and Diet member worked for women's rights throughout her long life.

Kamikōchi
1 The volcano Yakedake provides a backdrop for autumn foliage and the waters of the river Azusagawa. **2** The Taishō Pond was formed in 1915 when lava flows from Yakedake dammed the river Azusagawa.

Kyūshū in 1274 and 1281 (see MONGOL INVASIONS OF JAPAN) and were thought to represent divine intervention by the gods of ISE SHRINE in Japan's defense. The myth of the *kamikaze* reinforced the Japanese belief that their land was protected by Shintō gods. During World War II, the term *kamikaze* was applied to pilots who flew suicide attacks on Allied ships. See KAMIKAZE SPECIAL ATTACK FORCE.

Kamikaze Special Attack Force
神風特別攻撃隊

(Kamikaze Tokubetsu Kōgekitai or Tokkōtai). General name given to units of specially trained pilots who attacked Allied ships in suicide dives toward the end of World War II. Named for the *kamikaze*, or "divine wind," that had repelled the MONGOL INVASIONS OF JAPAN in the 13th century, they were used when it became apparent that conventional means could not prevent the Allied fleet from retaking the Philippines.

The first Kamikaze attack took place on 25 October 1944, when five navy Zero Fighters, each carrying a 250 kilogram (550 lb) bomb, plunged into US warships and transports off the coast of Leyte. Encouraged by the results, Vice Admiral Ōnishi Takijirō (1891–1945) of the First Air Fleet hastily recruited new suicide forces. Army air force units soon followed suit. Until Japan's surrender in August 1945, and especially in the Battle of Okinawa, the Japanese employed more than 2,000 planes for suicide attacks. According to US figures, 34 ships were sunk and 288 damaged by these "suicide squads." See also KAITEN.

Kamikōchi
上高地

Scenic valley in western Nagano Prefecture, central Honshū. On the river Azusagawa and surrounded by HOTAKADAKE, YAKEDAKE, and other mountains, it is noted for its beautiful alpine scenery, hot springs, and ponds. It is considered the best starting point for mountain climbing in the Northern Alps (Hida Mountains). Average elevation: 1,500 m (5,000 ft).

Kaminoyama
上山[市]

City in southeastern Yamagata Prefecture, northern Honshū. It prospered as a castle town and post-station town during the Edo period (1600–1868). Primarily a farming area today, Kaminoyama also has silk-reeling plants and factories manufacturing pharmaceuticals and cast-iron products. It is a hot-springs resort and a base camp for climbing the Zaōzan mountain range. There is a museum honoring the *tanka* poet SAITŌ MOKICHI, who was born here. Pop: 38,237.

Kamioka Mine
神岡鉱山

(Kamioka Kōzan). Japan's largest zinc and lead mine, located on the river Takaharagawa at the northern tip of Gifu Prefecture, central Honshū. Excavation of the mine began in the 1590s, and in the middle of the Meiji period (1868–1912) the Mitsui ZAIBATSU bought it and developed it. Liquid waste from the mine, which is owned by Mitsui Mining & Smelting Co, Ltd, was determined to be the cause of an outbreak of *itai itai* disease (see POLLUTION-RELATED DISEASES).

Kamisu
神栖[町]

Town in southeastern Ibaraki Prefecture, central Honshū. Kamisu rose in the Edo period (1600–1868) as a port on the waterway connecting the lake Kasumigaura and the river Tonegawa. The development of the Kashima Coastal Industrial Region has led to the establishment of petrochemical complexes. Pop: 40,351.

Kami Suwa Hot Spring
上諏訪温泉

(Kami Suwa Onsen). Located near Lake Suwa, in the city of Suwa, central Nagano Prefecture, central Honshū. A simple thermal spring; water temperature 65°–80°C (149°–176°F). The nearby highlands KIRIGAMINE and TATESHINA KŌGEN attract many visitors.

Kamitsukasa Shōken
上司小剣

(1874–1947). Author. Real name Kamitsukasa Nobutaka. Born in Nara Prefecture. While a journalist for *Yomiuri shimbun*, he began writing essays and short stories. Early stories were about the local Ōsaka culture of his youth, but his later works reflect the influence of his socialist friends, such as SAKAI TOSHIHIKO and KŌTOKU SHŪSUI. His works include *Hamo no kawa* (1914, Sea Eel's Skin), a novel.

Kamiyama Sōjin
上山草人

(1884–1954). Movie actor. Real name Mita Tadashi. Born in Miyagi Prefecture, he studied at the Tōkyō Drama School and joined the SHINGEKI (new theater) movement. In 1919 he went to the United States, where he won acclaim for his role as a Mongolian prince in *The Thief of Baghdad* (1924). Returning to Japan in 1929, he played leading roles in SHIMAZU YASUJIRŌ's *Ai yo jinrui to tomo ni are* (1931, Love, Be with Mankind) and Shimizu Hiroshi's *Tōyō no haha* (1934, Mothers of Asia). Kamiyama was never widely popular in Japan.

Kamiya Sōtan
神屋宗湛

(1553–1635). Famous merchant and tea connoisseur of the Azuchi-Momoyama (1568–1600) and early Edo (1600–1868) periods; along with SHIMAI SŌSHITSU, the representative Hakata (now part of Fukuoka) townsman of his age. The Kamiya family's wealth came from the IWAMI SILVER MINE and smelting techniques newly introduced from China. They were also active in wax and textile manufacture. Sōtan formed close ties with TOYOTOMI HIDEYOSHI. Sōtan's tea diary, *Kamiya Sōtan nikki*, offers interesting glimpses into the relationship between the two men and the interplay of politics, commerce, and the tea ceremony characteristic of the period. With the establishment of the Tokugawa regime Sōtan lost his prominence. See also HAKATA MERCHANTS.

kamiyui
髪結

Traditional-style hairdresser. *Kamiyui* first appeared early in the Edo period (1600–1868) when diverse and complex men's HAIRSTYLES required professional care. In the late 18th century a separate profession of women's hairdressers developed. Hairdressers practiced either in their own shops or visited private residences, and famous salons developed in large cities, such as Edo (now Tōkyō) and Ōsaka. In 1871 the DAMPATSUREI law discouraged the traditional *chommage* (topknot) for men, and Western-style barbers began to appear. A limited number of *kamiyui* carry on their trade for women, such as *geisha*.

Kammon gyoki
看聞御記

(Record of Things Seen and Heard). Also known as *Kammon nikki*. Diary of imperial prince Fushimi no Miya Sadafusa (1372–1456). His original manuscript survives almost complete. The diary chronicles the period 1416–48 and ranges over personal matters, court affairs, gossip, and political events at the height of the Muromachi shogunate (1338–1573).

Kammon Strait
関門海峡

(Kammon Kaikyō). Also known as Shimonoseki Strait. Narrow strait between the city of Shimonoseki, Yamaguchi Prefecture, western Honshū, and the city of Kita Kyūshū, Fukuoka Prefecture, northern Kyūshū. It connects the western Inland Sea and the Sea of Japan. It is a vital point in maritime transportation in western Japan. An underwater tunnel for the Japanese National Railways' (now Japan Railways) San'yō Main Line was completed in 1942, a state road tunnel in 1958, and a Shinkansen (super-speed train) tunnel in 1975. A highway bridge spans the strait. Narrowest point: 0.6 km (0.4

mi); widest point: 2.5 km (1.6 mi); depth: 10–21 m (33–69 ft).

Kammu, Emperor 桓武天皇

(737–806; Kammu Tennō). The 50th sovereign (*tennō*) in the traditional count (which includes several nonhistorical emperors); reigned 781–806. Eldest son of Emperor Kōnin (709–782; r 770–781). Because his mother was a commoner of Korean origin, Kammu was not originally in the line of succession, but he was named crown prince in 772 through the efforts of his father-in-law, the court official Fujiwara no Momokawa (732–779). Kammu moved the capital from Nara to NAGAOKAKYŌ and then to HEIANKYŌ (Kyōto) and reformed the provincial administrative system. Although he opposed the economic and political power of the Buddhist establishment, he was a generous patron of the monks SAICHŌ and KŪKAI. The power and prestige of the throne reached a peak during his reign.

Kammuriyama 冠山

Also called Kamuriyama. Mountain at the junction of Hiroshima, Shimane, and Yamaguchi prefectures, western Honshū; principal peak of the Kammuriyama Mountains. Surrounded by an extension of the KIBI KŌGEN highland, it is a monadnock with level land on its summit. Height: 1,339 m (4,393 ft).

Kamo 加茂[市]

City in central Niigata Prefecture, central Honshū. Its name comes from the KAMO SHRINES in Kyōto, which came into possession of this area in 794. It developed as a market town in the Middle Ages. It manufactures electrical appliances, textiles, and furniture and is also Japan's largest producer of paulownia chests. Pop: 34,863.

Kamo 賀茂

NŌ play by KOMPARU ZENCHIKU. It is classified as a *shobamme-mono* ("part-one play"). A Shintō priest (the *waki* or subordinate character) visits the KAMO SHRINES in Kyōto. Seeing a white-feathered arrow displayed on a ceremonial dais on the bank of the nearby river Kamogawa, he approaches two women (one is the *maejite* or main character at the beginning of a play; the other is the *tsure* or "companion" character) who are drawing ritual water to ask about the deity worshiped at the shrine. They tell him that long ago a woman saw a white-feathered arrow floating downstream and plucked it from the current. She became pregnant as a result, giving birth to the thunder god Wakeikazuchi no Kami. The god, the woman, and the arrow became the three deities of the Kamo Shrines. In the second half of the play, Wakeikazuchi no Kami (the *nochijite* or main character at the end of a play) performs a thunderous dance.

Kamochi Masazumi 鹿持雅澄

(1791–1858). KOKUGAKU (National Learning) scholar. Born in the Tosa domain (now Kōchi Prefecture), he was a self-educated librarian and professor at the official domainal school. In 1856, after 30 years' labor, he completed his chief work, the *Man'yōshū kogi*, a massive compilation of previous annotations on the 8th-century anthology MAN'YŌSHŪ.

Kamogawa 鴨川[市]

City in southern Chiba Prefecture, central Honshū, on the Pacific Ocean. A commercial center and base for inshore fishing, Kamogawa also produces citrus fruit and vegetables. Pop: 31,226.

Kamogawa 鴨川・賀茂川

River in the city of Kyōto, Kyōto Prefecture, central Honshū, originating in the Tamba Mountains and flowing south to join the KATSURAGAWA. It was a line of defense for Kyōto in ancient times. Parks have been constructed on the dry areas of the riverbed. Length: 35 km (22 mi).

Kamogawa Sea World 鴨川シーワールド

(Kamogawa Shī Wārudo). Aquarium in the city of Kamogawa, Chiba Prefecture, in central Honshū. Opened in 1970. The aquarium is designed around displays that show how a mountain stream grows to become a river and empties into the sea. Over 7,000 freshwater and saltwater fish and shellfish of 400 varieties are on exhibit. The aquarium has an ocean sunfish breeding program and also presents shows featuring dolphins, killer whales, and sea lions.

Kamo no Chōmei 鴨長明

(1156?–1216). Poet, critic, and essayist. Scion of the Kamo family, hereditary Shintō priests of the KAMO SHRINES, he lived in the troubled transitional years between the Heian (794–1185) and Kamakura (1185–1333) periods. He has come to typify the literary recluse who abandons the world for a life of refined tranquillity in a small mountain hut. He was active in the literary world of FUJIWARA NO TOSHINARI, FUJIWARA NO SADAIE, and SAIGYŌ. A poetic disciple of the priest SHUN'E (1113–ca 1190?), Chōmei cultivated a complex style, examples of which appear in the SHIN KOKINSHŪ (1205) and other imperial anthologies, as well as in his personal collection of verse (SHIKASHŪ), the *Kamo no Chōmei shū* (1181).

In 1200 Chōmei presented to the former emperor GO-TOBA a 100-poem sequence entitled *Shōji ninen nido hyakushu* (Second Hundred-Poem Sequence of the Shōji Era). In 1201 Go-Toba appointed Chōmei to the newly established Bureau of Poetry (Wakadokoro). Chōmei excelled as a literary critic and aesthetician. His *Mumyōshō* (post-1211, Nameless Notes) consists of 78 chapters of varying length covering a wide range of topics, including the nature and history of WAKA (classical Japanese poetry). Like most poetic treatises (*karon*), it is written in the question-and-answer format. In it, Chōmei advocated the aesthetic ideal of YŪGEN (literally, "mystery and depth").

In his early thirties he left his ancestral home to live in a small cottage near the river Kamogawa in Ōhara, northeast of Kyōto. A fragmentary poetic diary, *Iseki* (ca 1186, Accounts of Ise), remains from his travels. His name has also been spuriously linked to two later travel accounts, the *Kaidōki* (ca 1223, Sea Route Journal) and *Tōkan kikō* (ca 1242, Trip to the Eastern Barrier). Chōmei's taste for worldly success seems to have paled altogether when in his late forties he was denied a hereditary post at the Kamo Shrines, and in 1204 he became a Buddhist monk and secluded himself in the mountains of Ōhara. In 1208 he moved to Toyama on Mt. Hino (Hinoyama), south of Kyōto near Uji, where he constructed a small hut. Chōmei defined the ideal of the literary recluse in the HŌJŌKI (1212; tr *The Ten-Foot-Square Hut*, 1928; *An Account of My Hut*, 1955), a short commentary on life that has become a landmark in the Japanese literary and philosophical consciousness. His last work was probably the collection of 102 Buddhist exemplary tales

(*setsuwa;* see SETSUWA BUNGAKU) known as the *Hosshinshū* (ca 1214, Collection of Religious Awakenings).

Kamo no kurabeuma 賀茂の競馬

Horse race held yearly on 5 May at the Kami-Gamo Shrine in Kyōto (see KAMO SHRINES) to ask for a rich harvest and peace. Modeled on a race that used to be held at the Imperial Palace, it was first held on the fifth day of the fifth month of 1093. It was subsequently held every year using horses sent from around the country as offerings to the shrine. The race was discontinued for a time following the ŌNIN WAR (1467–77), but was eventually revived and has continued to the present day. Twenty colorfully dressed riders, after first paying homage at the main shrine building, take turns racing their horses two by two.

Kamo no Mabuchi 賀茂真淵

(1697–1769). KOKUGAKU (National Learning) scholar and WAKA poet. Mabuchi is known for his contributions to the development of the National Learning school through his studies of the ancient Japanese classics (particularly the MAN'YŌSHŪ, the oldest anthology of Japanese verse, compiled late in the 8th century). He combined the comparative philological research methods of KEICHŪ with the ethical system of KADA NO AZUMAMARO. Mabuchi emphasized a Shintō creed of simplicity and spontaneity. As a poet, he favored the so-called Man'yō style and unsuccessfully attempted to revive the CHŌKA ("long poem").

Mabuchi was born in the province of Tōtōmi (now part of Shizuoka Prefecture). In 1733 he moved to Kyōto, to study with Kada no Azumamaro, and in 1737 to Edo (now Tōkyō), where he set himself up as a teacher of the classics. In 1746 Mabuchi succeeded Azumamaro's nephew, Kada no Arimaro (1706–51), as tutor in Japanese literature to TAYASU MUNETAKE, son of the shōgun TOKUGAWA YOSHIMUNE (r 1716–45). Mabuchi wrote commentaries on the Japanese classics *Man'yōshū*, ISE MONOGATARI (mid-10th century), and TALE OF GENJI (ca 1000). He retired in 1760 at age 63, thereafter writing and teaching. Most of Mabuchi's books and tracts date from this period.

Interpretations of the *Man'yōshū* make up his magnum opus, the *Man'yōkō* (1760–68), which discusses the linguistic aspects and literary value of the *Man'yōshū*. Other works by Mabuchi are the *Kanjikō* (1757), *Genji monogatari shinshaku* (1758), *Niimanabi* (1765), and a five-volume set of commentaries in the Kokugaku tradition, which includes the *Bun'ikō* (1762), *Kaikō* (1764), *Kokuikō* (1765), *Shoikō* (ca 1765),

kamoshika A herbivorous animal found only in Japan, the kamoshika was hunted for its fur and horns before being designated a protected species.

and *Goikō* (1769). Among the disciples of Mabuchi were MOTOORI NORINAGA (his chief disciple and successor as leader of the Kokugaku movement), KATŌ CHIKAGE, KATORI NAHIKO, and MURATA HARUMI.

kamoshika 羚羊

(Japanese serow). *Capricornis crispus.* Primitive, even-toed, hoofed mammal of the family Bovidae found only in Japan. The *kamoshika* inhabits the high mountain areas of Honshū, Shikoku, and Kyūshū, usually singly or in pairs. It resembles a mountain goat in shape, but is smaller, with a combined head and body length of about 1 meter (3 ft) and a shoulder height of about 70 centimeters (28 in). It is usually brown in color, but some are white or black. Both sexes have horns about 14 centimeters (6 in) long. The *kamoshika*'s chief natural enemy is the Asiatic black bear (*Selenarctos thibetanus*). It was once hunted extensively for its fur and its horns but is now a protected species.

Kamo Shrines 賀茂神社

(Kamo Jinja). Two independent but closely associated Shintō shrines in Kyōto: the Kamo Wakeikazuchi Jinja (popularly Kami-Gamo Sha) in Kita Ward, dedicated to the deity Kamo Wakeikazuchi no Kami, and the Kamo Mioya Jinja (Shimo-Gamo Sha) in Sakyō Ward, dedicated to the deities Tamayorihime no Mikoto (the mother goddess of Wakeikazuchi) and Kamo Taketsunumi no Mikoto (the father god of Tamayorihime). According to the tradition of the Kamo Shrines, they were built at their present locations in 678, although their origins are said to go back to the reign of the legendary first emperor, Jimmu. After the capital was moved from Nagaoka to Kyōto in 794, the shrines enjoyed great popularity because of the protection they provided to the city. The AOI FESTIVAL and other annual ceremonies are held at both shrines.

kampaku 関白

Imperial regent for an adult emperor, as opposed to SESSHŌ, a regent for a minor emperor. The extrastatutory office of *kampaku* was modeled after an office mentioned in Chinese documents. The *kampaku* assisted the emperor in governing. The first to take the title was Fujiwara no Mototsune (836–891), who was appointed *kampaku* in 887 to assist Emperor Kōkō (r 884–887) after having ruled as de facto regent since 884. He and his

adoptive father, FUJIWARA NO YOSHIFUSA, had already served as *sesshō*, and their descendants held a monopoly on these titles until the Meiji Restoration of 1868 (with the exception of a brief period in the late 16th century when the title was held by TOYOTOMI HIDEYOSHI and his son TOYOTOMI HIDETSUGU), establishing what historians call REGENCY GOVERNMENT. The political power of the *kampaku* declined with the institution of the INSEI system of government by retired emperors in the 11th century. See also TAIKŌ.

Kampan Batabiya shimbun 官板バタビヤ新聞

First Japanese-language newspaper published in Japan. It was put out by the Tokugawa shogunate in the late Edo period (1600–1868) and was devoted to the translation of foreign news items. Publication started in 1862; 23 issues appeared during January and February of that year before it ceased publication. Translations for the paper were done at the Institute for the Investigation of Western Books (Yōsho Shirabesho; see BANSHO SHIRABESHO) from selected news stories taken from a Dutch colony publication in Batavia (now Jakarta), the *Javasche Courant.*

Kampō → Official Gazette

kampō → medicine, traditional

kampu 官符

Official orders (*fu*) issued by either the Grand Council of State (DAJŌKAN) or the Office of Shintō Worship (Jingikan) to their subordinate offices under the RITSURYŌ SYSTEM of government established in the late 7th century. The term most often referred to *dajō kampu*, orders issued by the Dajōkan, the chief administrative organ of the central government. *Kampu* were issued by the Dajōkan in conjunction with or independently of imperial edicts, with specified forms for each case. They were always signed by two officials of the Benkankyoku (Controllers' Office). Although *kampu* had become a mere formality by the late Heian period (794–1185), they continued in use until the early years of the Meiji period (1868–1912), when political power was restored to the imperial court.

Kampūzan 寒風山

Composite volcano in the central Oga Peninsula, western Akita Prefecture, northern Honshū; composed of pyroxene andesite. Skiing is available. Height: 355 m (1,165 ft).

Kamuikotan 神居古潭

Canyon in the city of Asahikawa, central Hokkaidō. Formed by the river Ishikarigawa, the canyon is famous for its rugged scenery and fantastically shaped rocks. In ancient times it was believed by the AINU to be the abode of the gods and thus unapproachable. Length: approximately 10 km (6.2 mi).

Kamura Isota 嘉村礒多

(1897–1933). Author. Born in Yamaguchi Prefecture. He went to Tōkyō, where he became an editor of the coterie magazine *Fudōchō*. He was encouraged in his writing by KASAI ZENZŌ, an author of the naturalist school. Most active in the 1920s, Kamura wrote autobiographical fiction (see I-NOVEL) that exposed his personal life to an extreme degree, even for this genre. His works include "Gōku" (1928) and "Tojō" (1932).

kan 勘

An important Japanese concept referring to a form of intuitional cognition. *Kan* encompasses a number of attributes including intuition, the so-called sixth sense, premonition, a knack for doing things, inspiration, and sudden realization. *Kan* is considered essential in many spheres of Japanese life that involve certain traditional skills or techniques, such as the martial arts and artistic endeavors. This traditional concept was examined by the psychologist Kuroda Ryō (1890–1947), who attempted to identify and establish *kan* as an essential concept in Japanese psychology, which he examined in his book *Kan no kenkyū* (1933, A Study of *Kan*).

Kuroda discerned two distinct aspects of *kan*. The first is an intuitive power revealed in cognition and judgment. This aspect of *kan* resembles the Western notion of intuition. A second aspect is *kotsu* (a knack or physical skill), which manifests itself in the handling of objects or in other voluntary acts. It is *kotsu* that Japanese artists and artisans have traditionally sought to attain in their works and performances. In common parlance, however, these two nuances of *kan* are not distinguished. See also SATORI.

kana 仮名

General term for a number of syllabic writing systems developed in Japan, all based on Chinese characters (KANJI), used to express the sounds of Japanese rather than the meanings of individual words. The etymology of *kana* is *kari* ("temporary," "nonofficial," "nonregular") plus *na* ("name" or "writing"), an expression of the feeling that the use of Chinese characters not for their meaning but for their pronunciation was "not regular."

Since *kana* can express all the sounds of Japanese, the language can be written entirely in *kana*. However, the normal practice is to use a mixture of Chinese characters and *kana*; the Chinese characters are used to express the meanings of most words (from which the pronunciation can be inferred) and the *kana* to write inflectional endings, grammatical particles, and certain words officially designated not to be written in characters (see JAPANESE LANGUAGE). Two sets of *kana* are used in the present-day Japanese writing system: *hiragana*, a cursive form (and the one commonly used for native words and any words of Chinese origin not to be written in characters), and *katakana*, a noncursive form. The latter can be used in place of *hiragana*, but it is most typically used to write LOANWORDS from other languages, for emphasis, or for representation of onomatopoeic words, thus performing functions similar to the use of italics in Western orthography. Both *katakana* and *hiragana* derive from an earlier set of *kana* known as *man'yōgana*, and *hiragana* in particular derives from the cursive form of *man'yōgana* known as *sōgana*.

Man'yōgana—*Man'yōgana* are a set of unmodified Chinese characters that were once used as phonetic symbols to represent Japanese syllables. As the name suggests, *man'yōgana* (*man'yō* + *kana*) was the writing system used in the MAN'YŌSHŪ, an 8th-century poetry anthology. Most attempts to write Japanese prior to the Heian period (794–1185) fall into the category of *man'yōgana*.

The *man'yōgana* differs from the two currently used *kana* systems in at least three

Hiragana and Katakana

Development of modern *hiragana* and *katakana* from Chinese characters

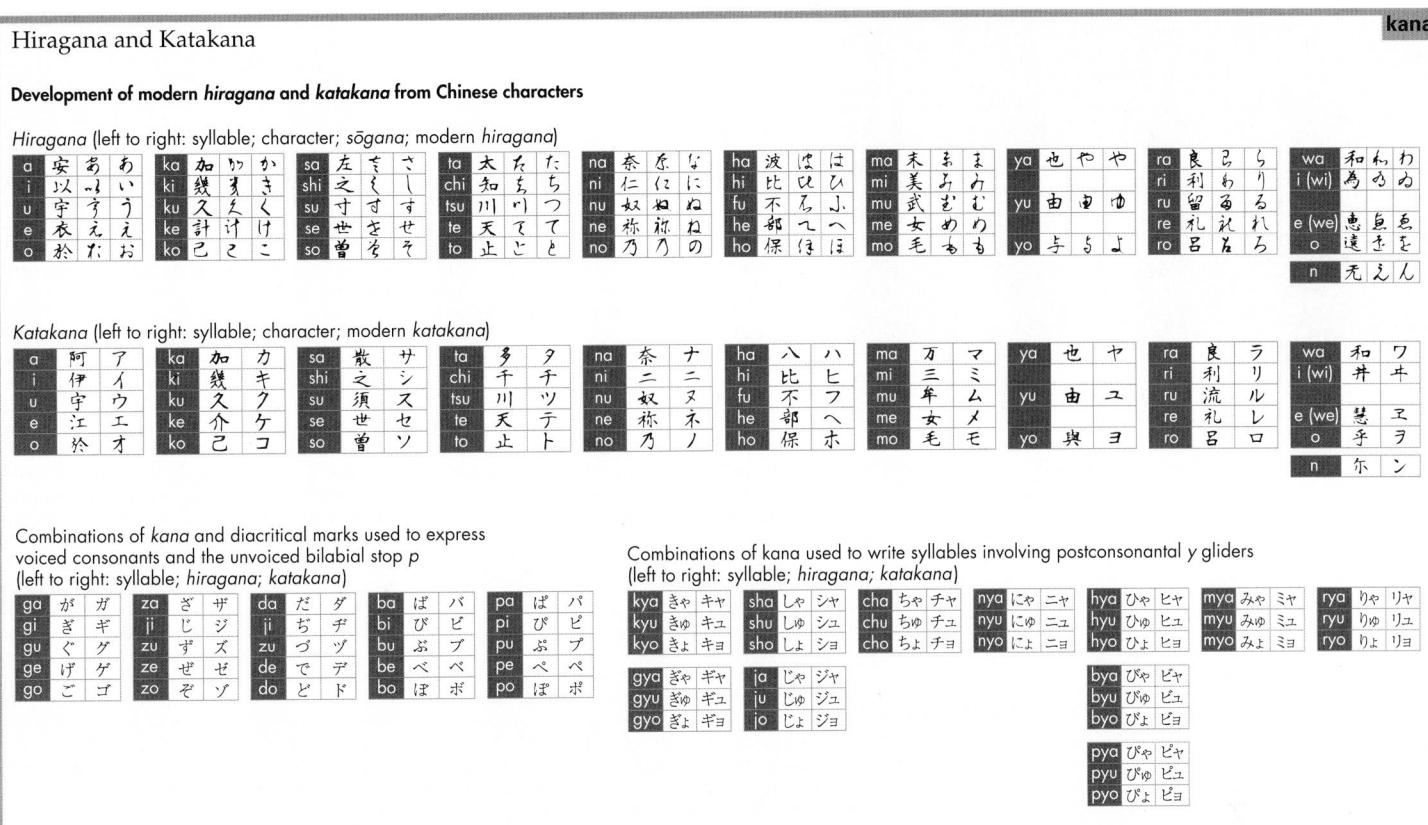

Hiragana (left to right: syllable; character; *sōgana*; modern *hiragana*)

Katakana (left to right: syllable; character; modern *katakana*)

Combinations of *kana* and diacritical marks used to express voiced consonants and the unvoiced bilabial stop *p* (left to right: syllable; *hiragana*; *katakana*)

Combinations of kana used to write syllables involving postconsonantal *y* gliders (left to right: syllable; *hiragana*; *katakana*)

NOTE: The *hiragana* and *katakana* tables contain the 48-character syllabary, including the symbols for *wi* and *we*, which were removed from the official *kana* list in 1946.

---

important aspects. First, there is no one-to-one relationship between syllables and characters. There were 87 syllable types in 8th-century Japanese (88 in the language of the KOJIKI), but more than 970 Chinese characters were used to write them. Second, the Chinese characters were used as written in Chinese, without modification or simplification. For this reason a text written in *man'yōgana* superficially resembles a text in Chinese; however, because many of the characters are used only for their pronunciation and not for their meaning and because the language represented is Japanese, the text is likely to be unintelligible to a Chinese reader. Third, the types of character pronunciation represented in *man'yōgana* are more varied than in *hiragana* and *katakana*, including the *on* reading and *kun* reading of the character as well as the type of reading called *gisho* (literally, "playful writing").

The *on* reading is a Japanized version of the Chinese pronunciation for the character. For example, the Chinese character 阿, which means "mountain ridge," was pronounced ʔa in the rising tone in Middle Chinese—the language of Chang'an (Ch'ang-an) around 600. The Japanese used this character to represent the syllable [a] in Japanese.

The *kun* reading is the pronunciation of a Japanese word with the same meaning as the Chinese character. For example, the Chinese character 吾, which means "I," was pronounced ŋo in the even tone in Middle Chinese. The 8th-century Japanese word for "I" was *a*. The character was assigned the latter pronunciation as a *man'yōgana*, and thus it too was used to represent the syllable [a].

The *gisho* or playful writing involves, among other things, onomatopoeia. An example is the two-character combination of 蜂音. The first character, 蜂, means "bee" or "wasp" and was pronounced pʼïoŋ in the even tone in Middle Chinese; the second, 音, pronounced ʔïəm (even tone), meant "sound." The sound or buzzing of bees was

apparently represented as *bu* in 8th-century Japanese, and the two characters together were used to represent the Japanese syllable [bu].

Sōgana—*Sōgana* consists of the Chinese characters of the *man'yōgana* system written in the *sōsho* or cursive style (see SHOTAI). Three differences between the modern *kana* (i.e., *katakana* and *hiragana*) and *sōgana* are that (1) in *sōgana*, as in *man'yōgana*, there is no one-to-one correspondence between syllables and characters, the number of the latter exceeding the former; (2) Chinese characters are used in their full cursive forms and not in stylized, reduced cursive forms such as those associated with *hiragana*; and (3) the *kun* as well as *on* readings are reflected in the pronunciation. What characterizes *sōgana* is its cursive or *sōsho* form, and it is an intermediate stage of simplification between the fully regular or *kaisho* (noncursive) form of the Chinese characters that is used in *man'yōgana* and the totally stylized modern *hiragana*.

Katakana—In its modern, standard form, *katakana* is a system of 48 syllabic writing units for writing non-Chinese loanwords, onomatopoeia, emphasized words, and the names of flora and fauna. The *kata* in *katakana* means "partial," "not whole," "fragmentary." It is so named because many of the *katakana* are a part and not the whole of a Chinese character. In its earlier stages, *katakana* was used as a mnemonic device for pronouncing Buddhist tests written in Chinese. Next appeared Japanese texts written in a mixture of Chinese characters and *katakana*. This writing system is called *kanamajiri bun* (sentences mixing *kana* and characters). By the middle of the 10th century, anthologies of Japanese verse (WAKA) came to be written in *katakana* and by the 12th century collections of folktales came to be written in a mixture of Chinese characters and *katakana*.

Hiragana—In its modern, standard form, *hiragana* is a system of 48 syllabic writing units for writing indigenous Japa-

nese words and often for Chinese loanwords that cannot be written with the 1,945 characters officially approved for general use (see JŌYŌ KANJI). *Hira* means "commonly used," "easy," "rounded." *Hiragana* is so named because the letters are considered rounded and easy to write compared with the full forms of the original Chinese characters. In its early forms *hiragana* was used by women, while the unsimplified Chinese characters were used by men; for this reason, the earliest *hiragana* was also called *onnade* (women's hand). By the end of the 9th century *onnade* ceased to be a system limited to women and became an accepted device for recording poems. *Hiragana* gained full acceptance when the imperial poetic anthology *Kokin wakashū* (KOKINSHŪ, 905) was written in *onnade*.

Kanadehon chūshingura

仮名手本忠臣蔵

(tr *Chūshingura: The Treasury of Loyal Retainers*, 1971). Popular title *Chūshingura*. KABUKI play by Takeda Izumo II (see TAKEDA IZUMO), Miyoshi Shōraku (1696?–1772?), and Namiki Senryū (NAMIKI SŌSUKE). Originally written as a puppet play that was first performed in 1748, *Chūshingura* is categorized as a *jidaimono* (historical play) although it also contains important *sewa-mono* (domestic play) elements. Based on the celebrated FORTY-SEVEN RŌNIN INCIDENT of 1701–03 but transposed into the world of the TAIHEIKI in the early Muromachi period (1333–1568), it recounts in 11 acts how the villainous KŌ NO MORONAO (in the actual incident, Kira Yoshinaka) humiliated En'ya Hangan (the *daimyō* Asano Naganori of Akō), provoking him into drawing his sword in the shogunal palace of Kamakura (Edo)—an act for which Hangan was sentenced to commit suicide—and how Ōboshi Yuranosuke (Asano's chief counselor ŌISHI YOSHIO) and 46 other loyal retainers of Hangan avenged their lord's death.

Kanazawa This city's many tile-roofed houses, here crowding the banks of the river Asanogawa, recall its history as a castle town.

Kanagawa Prefecture Location and Prefectural Crest

kanamugura The short spines of this weed vine act as hooks, enabling the *kanamugura* to wrap itself around other plants.

Kanagaki Robun 仮名垣魯文

(1829–94). Author and journalist. Real name Nozaki Bunzō. Born in Edo (now Tōkyō). In the tradition of the late Edo period (see GESAKU), he wrote humorous descriptions of the introduction of Western culture in the early Meiji period (1868–1912). His principal works are *Seiyō dōchū hizakurige* (1870–76, Through the West by Shank's Mare) and *Agura nabe* (1871–72, Stew Pot Tales).

Kanagawa Prefectural Museum
神奈川県立博物館

(Kanagawa Kenritsu Hakubutsukan). Located in the city of Yokohama, Kanagawa Prefecture. Established in 1967. The museum has exhibits on the history, folklore, and natural life of Kanagawa Prefecture. It also houses the well-known Tamba Collection of some 6,000 *ukiyo-e* (woodblock prints). The museum building, which has been designated an Important Cultural Property, is the former head office of the Yokohama Specie Bank.

Kanagawa Prefecture 神奈川県

(Kanagawa Ken). Located on the southern edge of the Kantō Plain in central Honshū and bounded by Tōkyō on the north, Tōkyō Bay on the east, Sagami Bay on the south, and Shizuoka and Yamanashi prefectures on the west. The terrain of the western part of the prefecture is mountainous, and the southern and eastern sections are coastal plains. Principal rivers are the SAGAMIGAWA, flowing south through the center of the prefecture into Sagami Bay, and the TAMAGAWA, which flows eastward into Tōkyō Bay. The climate is generally mild, especially along the southern coast.

The area was known as Sagami Province under the ancient provincial system (see KOKUGUN SYSTEM). The city of KAMAKURA served as the seat of the Kamakura shogunate from 1192 to 1333, and during the Edo period (1600–1868) the area became a vital transportation link between Edo (now Tōkyō), the seat of the Tokugawa shogunate, and the western half of Japan. The arrival of Commodore Matthew C. PERRY off the coast of URAGA in 1853 and the signing of the KANAGAWA TREATY ushered in a new era in the nation's history. The prefecture's present name was established in 1876, but its boundaries were not settled until 1893. Although it suffered severe damage in the TŌKYŌ EARTHQUAKE OF 1923 and during World War II, it has developed into one of Japan's major industrial centers. Industries include machinery, electrical equipment, food processing, chemicals, and steel. Many of the factories are concentrated along Tōkyō Bay in KAWASAKI and YOKOHAMA. Yokohama also ranks as one of Japan's leading ports for international trade.

The Hakone area in southwestern Kanagawa is part of the FUJI-HAKONE-IZU NATIONAL PARK. Kamakura is known for its enormous statue of the Buddha (DAIBUTSU) and numerous historical sites. The mountains of Tanzawa and the beaches of Sagami Bay attract many vacationers. Area: 2,403 sq km (928 sq mi); pop: 7,980,391; capital: Yokohama. Other major cities include Kawasaki, YOKOSUKA, FUJISAWA, SAGAMIHARA, and HIRATSUKA.

Kanagawa Treaty 日米和親条約

(Nichibei Washin Jōyaku). Officially, Treaty of Peace and Amity between the United States and the Empire of Japan. Signed 31 March 1854 at Kanagawa (now Yokohama, Kanagawa Prefecture) during Commodore Matthew C. PERRY's visit to Japan. The treaty included the following terms: (1) the ports of Shimoda and Hakodate would be open to American ships; (2) provisions would be supplied to these vessels; (3) shipwrecked sailors would receive good treatment; and (4) an American consulate would be established in Shimoda. Conclusion of the treaty between Tokugawa shogunate officials and Perry signaled the end of Japan's 200-year policy of NATIONAL SECLUSION; the shogunate concluded similar treaties with the British that same year, with the Russians in 1855, and with the Dutch in 1856. See OPENING OF JAPAN.

Kanai Mieko 金井美恵子

(1947–). Poet and novelist. Born in Gumma Prefecture; graduate of Takasaki Girls' High School. She depicts the loneliness of love in the modern world in a language rich in images and poetic resonance. Her novels include *Ai no seikatsu* (1967, Love Life), *Puraton-teki ren'ai* (1979, Platonic Love), and *Tama ya* (1987). Her collections of poetry include *Madamu Juju no ie* (1971, The House of Madame Juju) and *Haru no e no yakata* (1973, The Mansion of Spring Pictures).

Kanai Noburu 金井延

(1865–1933). Economist. Born in what is now Shizuoka Prefecture. After graduating from Tōkyō University in 1885, he studied governmental approaches to social problems in Germany and England. Becoming a professor at Tōkyō University in 1890, he followed the German model in advocating governmental legislation of social policy. He was one of the seven professors involved in the so-called SHICHIHAKASE JIKEN at the outbreak of the Russo-Japanese War of 1904–05. In 1919 he became the first dean of the School of Economics at Tōkyō University. Among his books are *Shakai keizaigaku* (1902, Social Economics) and *Shakai mondai* (1892, Social Problems).

Kan'ami 観阿弥

(1333–84). Full name Kan'ami Kiyotsugu. Born in Yamato Province (now Nara Prefecture). Early NŌ (SARUGAKU) actor and playwright and father of the celebrated ZEAMI. One source says he was a nephew of the *samurai* warrior KUSUNOKI MASASHIGE. Kan'ami founded the Yūzaki troupe, from which the modern KANZE SCHOOL claims descent. His great triumph occurred in Kyōto in 1374, when he danced *Okina* for the shōgun ASHIKAGA YOSHIMITSU. This was the first time a ruler had deigned to watch the then plebeian *sarugaku*. The secret of Kan'ami's success is said to have been that he introduced into *sarugaku* the highly popular *kuse-mai*, a lively song-and-dance form. He was a great artist, and Zeami, who in his early critical writings claims only to pass on his father's teachings, gave him the highest possible praise. Kan'ami's plays have not survived intact, but masterpieces based on his originals include *Eguchi*, *Motomezuka*, and MATSUKAZE.

Kanamori Tokujirō 金森徳次郎

(1886–1959). Government official and politician. Born in Aichi Prefecture. After graduation from Tōkyō University in 1912, Kanamori entered the Ministry of Finance and in 1934 was appointed director-general of the Cabinet Legislative Bureau (Hōseikyoku). He resigned two years later under attack from rightists for supporting the constitutional theories of MINOBE TATSUKICHI (see also TENNŌ KIKAN SETSU). In 1946 he became minister of state in the first YOSHIDA SHIGERU cabinet. In this capacity he was responsible for answering inquiries from the Diet on the draft of the new constitution. In response to questions about the emperor's new symbolic role, Kanamori responded that the emperor would remain "the center of national aspirations." With the promulgation of the new constitution in 1946, he resigned and in 1948 became the first head of the NATIONAL DIET LIBRARY.

kanamugura 金葎

(Japanese hop). *Humulus japonicus*. Annual climbing vine of the mulberry family (Moraceae), which grows wild in fields and empty lots and along roadsides throughout Japan. Its hard stem and stalks have short spines, and its opposite palmlike leaves are coarsely toothed. The *kanamugura* is dioecious; male flowers are pale yellow and bloom in long clusters; female flowers are small and conelike. The fruits (achenes) are egg shaped and 5 millimeters (0.2 in) long. The *kanamugura* has appeared in literature since ancient times in descriptions of desolate dwelling places.

Kanaya 金谷[町]

Town in central Shizuoka Prefecture, central Honshū. Kanaya developed as a post-station town during the Edo period (1600–1868). The town produces tea-processing machinery and is the site of the National Research Institute of Tea. Pop: 22,048.

Kanazawa 金沢[市]

Capital of Ishikawa Prefecture, central Honshū. The political, economic, and cultural center of the HOKURIKU REGION. Kanazawa developed during the 15th century as a virtually autonomous temple town of the Ikkō sect (see JŌDO SHIN SECT). After 1580 the city came under the rule of the powerful MAEDA FAMILY. Kanazawa is still known for its KUTANI WARE, Kaga *yūzen* (printed silk), MAKI-E (a type of decorated lacquer ware), and embroidery. Spared by the bombings of World War II, it retains much of its character as a castle town. Tourist attractions are KENROKUEN, a garden begun in the early 19th century by the Maeda family and now a park, and the remains of Kanazawa Castle. Pop: 442,868.

Kanazawa Bunko 金沢文庫

(Kanazawa Library). Also known as the Kanesawa (or Kanezawa) Bunko. Library in Kanazawa Chō, Kanazawa Ku, in the city of Yokohama, Kanagawa Prefecture; with the ASHIKAGA GAKKŌ library, it was one of the two most important centers of learning in medieval Japan (mid-12th–16th centuries). The library was opened in 1275 by Hōjō Sanetoki (also known as Kanezawa [or Kanesawa] Sanetoki; 1224–76), a grandson of HŌJŌ YOSHITOKI, second regent (*shikken*) of the Kamakura shogunate (1192–1333). The library was enlarged by his son Hōjō (Kanezawa) Akitoki (1248–1301) and grandson Kanezawa Sadaaki (1278–1333). Among its holdings are the *Issaikyō* (Complete Collection of the Buddhist Scriptures), copied in the Liu-Song (Sung) period (420–479) in China, and the manuscript of TSUREZUREGUSA by the essayist YOSHIDA KENKŌ. Originally the collection was open to the members of the Kanezawa family, scholars, and priests, but books did not circulate. Since 1955 the Kanazawa Bunko has functioned as a museum and is open to the public.

Kanazawa domain→Kaga domain

Kanazawa Plain   金沢平野

(Kanazawa Heiya). Located in south-central Ishikawa Prefecture, central Honshū. Situated along the Sea of Japan, it consists of alluvial fans of the river Tedorigawa and the floodplain of the river Saigawa. Two lagoons, Kahokugata and Shibayamagata, are in the interior of this rice-producing region. Around the city of Kanazawa, commercial, industrial, and residential areas are expanding. The major cities are Kanazawa and Komatsu. Area: 600 sq km (230 sq mi).

Kanazawa University   金沢大学

(Kanazawa Daigaku). A coeducational national university located in the city of Kanazawa, Ishikawa Prefecture. Founded in 1949, the university maintains faculties of letters, education, law, economics, science, pharmaceutical science, and technology as well as a school of medicine. Enrollment in 1989 was 7,348.

kana-zōshi   仮名草子

A general term in literary history for popular works published between 1600 and 1682, the date of SAIKAKU's KŌSHOKU ICHIDAI OTOKO (The Life of an Amorous Man). The term literally refers to a book in *kana* (Japanese phonetic characters), hence a book in pure Japanese rather than in the Chinese or sinicized Japanese in which learned books were written. *Kana-zōshi* number roughly 200 and account for most of the nonscholarly or nonclassic books printed during their time. They were succeeded by the genre of popular literature known as UKIYO-ZŌSHI, the first example of which is the above work by Saikaku.

Movable type had reached Japan from Korea at the close of the 16th century; however, the Japanese found it easier to print their cursive script, with copious illustrations, from whole-page blocks. With the peace and prosperity of early Tokugawa rule, bookstores began to appear. *Kana-zōshi* authors were often *samurai* of modest rank whose livelihood in peacetime was uncertain; others were monks, physicians, or even needy court nobles. Confucian scholars wrote *kana-zōshi* with missionary intent.

Few *kana-zōshi* are well-constructed stories; some provide only the thinnest fictional setting for static exposition of a message, while others resemble rambling gossip. There are tales of desperate romance, stories of merchants who made good, Buddhist homilies, Confucian portraits of ideally noble women, guides to the pleasure quarters, parodies of the classics, and even a very successful translation of *Aesop's Fables*

(ISOHO MONOGATARI). Many offer, besides entertainment, religious and ethical instruction or practical information. For example, a *kana-zōshi* author might work into his hero's trip down the highway TŌKAIDŌ all sorts of sermons, curious incidents, and tips on what to see and how best to travel. Of particular interest are such works as *Ukiyo monogatari* (after 1661, Tales of the Floating World) by ASAI RYŌI, at once the best and the most prolific of the *kana-zōshi* authors. This Pure Land Buddhist monk was perhaps Japan's first professional writer.

kanazukai   仮名遣い

KANA orthography, or conventions for the usage of the Japanese phonetic scripts *hiragana* and *katakana*. By the late Heian period (794–1185) there had arisen a need for agreement on which of the various *kana* symbols used to represent individual sounds of Japanese should be adopted; the confusion was due to changes in the spoken language whereby formerly distinct syllables had come to be pronounced alike, resulting in the retention of a number of symbols for what had become a single sound. The "historical" approach was simply to retain multiple and interchangeable symbols. "Contemporary" or "phonetic" orthographies, however, followed current pronunciation more closely and abandoned the *kana* that represented disused sounds. The following are three of the most important *kana* orthographies.

Teika kanazukai is the orthographic convention used by Fujiwara no Teika (FUJIWARA NO SADAIE; 1162–1241) and by his followers. Teika had no intention of making prescriptive rules, but established for his own purposes a system of usage for the following *kana*: お *o*, を *o*, え *e*, ゑ *e*, へ *he*, い *i*, ゐ *i*, and ひ *hi*. Teika followed a contemporary approach for お *o* and を *o* and a historical approach for the remaining six *kana*.

Rekishiteki kanazukai (historical *kana* usage) is the orthographic convention proposed by KEICHŪ (1640–1701) and his followers. Through his study of the 8th-century poetry anthology MAN'YŌSHŪ, Keichū discovered that, on the basis of contemporary Edo-period (1600–1868) pronunciation, *Teika kanazukai* did not always agree with Keichū's own reconstruction of the sounds of Japanese current in the 8th century. Unaware that Teika and others had used both historical and contemporary approaches, Keichū wrote WAJI SHŌRAN SHŌ (1693) to correct the "mistakes" of Teika. Keichū's historical approach gained support among scholars of the Japanese classics, and in the Meiji period (1868–1912) his system was introduced into the curriculum of elementary schools, where it remained until 1946.

Gendai kanazukai (contemporary *kana* usage) is the system of *kana* in use today. Adopted in 1946, it reflects the pronunciation of the spoken language more accurately than does the classically based *rekishiteki kanazukai*. One of its few inconsistencies involves the grammatical particles [wa], [o], and [e], which are written with the *kana* symbols は *ha*, を *o*, and へ *he*, respectively, preserving historical practice. Another inconsistency is the writing of the long vowel ō, which developed from paired conjunctions of *kana* terminating, in historical usage, with う *u*, ふ *fu*, ほ *ho*, or を *o*, and now customarily terminating with う *u*, as in そう *sou* ("to accompany" or "to be parallel to"; formerly そふ) and すもう *sumō* ("sumō wrestling"; formerly すまう or すまふ). In cer-

tain cases, however, the terminal *kana* is now written お *o*, as in おおかみ *ōkami* ("wolf"; formerly おほかみ) and とお *tō* ("ten"; formerly とを).

Kanchūki   勘仲記

Also known as *Kanenaka Kyō ki* and *Kanenaka ki*. Diary of the Kamakura period (1185–1333) courtier and archivist Kadenokōji Fujiwara no Kanenaka (1244–1308). Only later copies are extant. It records the period 1268–1300, covering SHŌEN (landed estate) disputes, the MONGOL INVASIONS OF JAPAN, relations between the imperial court and the KAMAKURA SHOGUNATE, and the alternating succession between two branches of the imperial house.

Kanda   苅田[町]

Town in eastern Fukuoka Prefecture, Kyūshū, on the Inland Sea. Cement and automobiles are manufactured here and exported from Kanda Port, the gateway to the Kita Kyūshū Industrial Zone. Pop: 33,732.

Kanda   神田

District in the northeastern part of Chiyoda Ward, Tōkyō. A commercial and residential area since the early Edo period (1600–1868), in modern times it has been known primarily as a student quarter because of the many colleges and universities clustered in the Surugadai section of the district and as a center for secondhand bookstores, publishing houses, and printers, most of which are clustered in the Jimbōchō area.

Kanda Aqueduct   神田上水

(Kanda Jōsui). In Tōkyō, central Honshū. Extends from Inokashira Pond to Sekiguchi through the Takaido, Nakano, and Yodobashi districts of Tōkyō. It was one of the three main aqueducts of Edo (now Tōkyō) during the Edo period (1600–1868). Construction began in the late 16th century. It supplied water to the Kanda, Nihombashi, and Kyōbashi districts until 1900. Length: approximately 17 km (11 mi).

Kanda Festival   神田祭

(Kanda Matsuri). Major festival of the KANDA SHRINE in Tōkyō. The gods presently enshrined are Ōnamuchi no Mikoto and Sukunahikona no Mikoto. However, according to popular legends, the shrine was originally built to placate the angry spirit of the rebel TAIRA NO MASAKADO (d 940). Originally held on 15 September, the Kanda Festival now takes place on 15 May every other year. Pa-

Kanda Festival This major festival of the Kanda Shrine is held in May. Shown is one of the portable shrines that are carried through the streets.

rishioners parade floats (DASHI) and portable shrines (MIKOSHI) through a large area of downtown Tōkyō.

kandaka 貫高

(valuation in terms of *kan*). A means of designating the tax value of agricultural land from the late Kamakura period (1185–1333) through the 16th century. The value was expressed in a monetary unit called *kammon* (*kan-mon*), hence the term *kandaka*. (When expressed in EIRAKUSEN, another currency, it was referred to as EIDAKA.) Although the value was stated in money, the tax was not necessarily paid in cash; payment in products was also practiced. By the 17th century the *kandaka* system was largely replaced by the KOKUDAKA system, in which value was expressed in terms of potential rice yield.

Kanda Shrine 神田神社

(Kanda Jinja; also called Kanda Myōjin). A Shintō shrine in Chiyoda Ward, Tōkyō; dedicated to Ōnamuchi no Mikoto (see ŌKUNINUSHI NO MIKOTO) and Sukunahikona no Mikoto, two deities figuring in myths about the pacification of the Japanese islands. In the medieval period (13th–16th centuries), however, the shrine was closely associated with the propitiation of the spirit of TAIRA NO MASAKADO, a rebel against the central government who was killed in 940. Its celebrated festival, known as the Kanda Matsuri (KANDA FESTIVAL), is held on 15 May in alternate years.

Kanda Takahira 神田孝平

(1830–98). Also known as Kanda Kōhei. Scholar and bureaucrat. Born in what is now Gifu Prefecture. Kanda applied himself to WESTERN LEARNING and became a teacher at the BANSHO SHIRABESHO, the shogunate school for Western studies. After the Meiji Restoration (1868) he worked for the new government, doing research on economics and government. Kanda was also a member of the MEIROKUSHA, the society of scholars who introduced Western thought to Japan. His proposal and implementation of the LAND TAX REFORM OF 1873–1881 and his work in setting up organs of local government established his reputation. He was appointed to the House of Peers in 1890. His *Keizai shōgaku* (1867, Introduction to Economics), essentially a translation of William Ellis's *Outlines of Social Economy,* is the earliest Japanese work on Western economics.

Kandenkō Co, Ltd [株]関電工

(Kandenkō). Japan's largest electrical engineering company. Incorporated in 1944. It has close ties with TŌKYŌ ELECTRIC POWER CO, INC. It specializes in electrical engineering and related construction and datacommunications engineering. Overseas offices are located in Singapore, Hong Kong, and Malaysia. Sales for the fiscal year ending March 1991 totaled ¥480.6 billion (US $3.5 billion), and capitalization stood at ¥8.3 billion (US $60.5 million). Headquarters are in Tōkyō.

Kanebō, Ltd 鐘紡[株]

(Kanebō). Company engaged in the manufacture and sale of textiles, cosmetics, food, pharmaceuticals, industrial and housing materials, and electronics and information systems. The company began as a small spinning mill in Tōkyō in 1887. It has more than 100 subsidiaries and affiliates in Japan and more than 20 overseas in the United States, Brazil, Indonesia, and other countries. Sales for the fiscal year ending March 1991 totaled ¥527.8 billion (US $3.8 billion), distributed as follows: natural fibers, 16 percent; synthetic fibers, 18 percent; fashion, 17 percent; cosmetics, 28 percent; food, 9 percent; pharmaceuticals, 4 percent; industrial materials and other products, 8 percent. The company was capitalized at ¥29.8 billion (US $217.2 million) in 1991. Headquarters are in Ōsaka.

Kaneda Masaichi 金田正一

(1933–). Professional baseball pitcher and manager. Born in Aichi Prefecture. His professional career began with the Kokutetsu Swallows in 1950. He played with the Yomiuri Giants from 1964 until his retirement in 1969. Kaneda won more than 400 games and set a then world record of 4,490 strikeouts. He also set a Japanese record of more than 20 victories a year for 13 consecutive seasons (1951–64). He served as manager of the Lotte Orions from 1972 to 1978, and returned to this post at the end of the 1989 season.

Kanegafuchi Chemical Industry Co, Ltd 鐘淵化学工業[株]

(Kanegafuchi Kagaku Kōgyō). Leading manufacturer of PVC (polyvinyl chloride) resins and soda; incorporated in 1949. Product lines include synthetic resin, plastic products, chemicals, foodstuffs, pharmaceuticals, medical devices, electronic materials, and synthetic fibers. The company manufactures PVC reinforcing agents (MBS resin) and polyolefin foam in plants located in Belgium, the United States, and Japan. HPG, a material used in production of antibiotics, is produced in its Singapore plant. Super heat-resistant polyimide film, esssential for production of flexible printed circuits and other electronic materials, is being produced in the United States by a joint venture with Allied-Signal, Inc. Kaneka MS polymer, the principal material used to make elastic sealants, is now under research and development in co-operation with Union Carbide Corporation, with plans for a joint venture for local manufacturing and sales in the United States. Sales for the fiscal year ending March 1991 totaled ¥232.6 billion (US $1.7 billion) and capitalization stood at ¥29.8 billion (US $217.2 million). Headquarters are in Ōsaka.

Kan'eiji 寛永寺

Temple in Ueno Park, Daitō Ward, Tōkyō, belonging to the TENDAI SECT of Buddhism. The Kan'eiji was built in 1625 (Kan'ei 2) at the urging of the influential monk Tenkai (1536–1643), who convinced the shōgun TOKUGAWA IEMITSU that a temple should stand to the northeast of Edo Castle, since it was commonly believed that evil spirits emanated from that direction. Thus Kan'eiji was to perform the same function for Edo Castle that ENRYAKUJI performed for the Imperial Palace in Kyōto. Kan'eiji was richly supported by the Tokugawa family, and six Tokugawa shōguns are interred there. Its main hall (*hondō*) was destroyed in the BOSHIN CIVIL WAR of 1868 and replaced in 1879.

kan'ei jigyō haraisage 官営事業払下げ

(sale of government enterprises). The sale of factories, mines, and other government enterprises by the Meiji government to private interests, mainly in the 1880s. Part of the government's financial retrenchment program, these sales marked a major shift in government economic policy from direct state involvement in the economy to promotion of private industry. The immediate objective was to restore government finances, so that enterprises scheduled for sale initially were restricted largely to those government-operated factories running deficits (see GOVERNMENT-OPERATED FACTORIES, MEIJI PERIOD). After 1884, as the MATSUKATA FISCAL POLICY began to show results, the government added such profitable operations as mines to the list of enterprises for sale. The state sold off many of its enterprises, except military and communication works, to such concerns as MITSUI, MITSUBISHI, and FURUKAWA. The sales helped these so-called SEISHŌ, or businesses with political connections, to develop into the giant combines known as ZAIBATSU.

Kan'ei shoka keizu den 寛永諸家系図伝

(Kan'ei House Genealogies). The first comprehensive collection of genealogies of *daimyō* and *hatamoto* (direct shogunal vassal) houses; named for its year of completion, Kan'ei 20 (1643). Compiled by order of the Tokugawa shogunate under the direction of the Confucian scholar HAYASHI RAZAN, the genealogies were classified into five groups according to the lineages from which the houses claimed descent: Matsudaira (see TOKUGAWA FAMILY), Seiwa Genji (see MINAMOTO FAMILY), Taira (see TAIRA FAMILY), Fujiwara (see FUJIWARA FAMILY), and miscellaneous.

Kaneko, Josephine Conger カネコ, J. C.

(1872–1939). American feminist, socialist, and journalist who married a Japanese man and helped inform Americans about Japanese women. Born in Centralia, Missouri, she studied at Christian College (Columbia, Missouri) and at Ruskin College (Trenton, Missouri). From 1903 (when she became a member of the Socialist Party) until 1905, she was an editor of *Appeal to Reason,* a popular socialist paper published in Girard, Kansas. In 1905 she married Japanese socialist Kaneko Kiichi (1875–1909). In June 1907 she and her husband founded in Chicago a monthly magazine, *The Socialist Woman* (renamed *The Progressive Woman* in 1909), that was unique for its frequent coverage of Japanese women. She later worked as editor of *Home Life Magazine* and *The Mother's Magazine.* Her writings include *Stray Thoughts* (1901), *Little Love and Nature Poems* (1903), *Women's Slavery* (1913), and *Woman's Voice: An Anthology* (1918).

Kaneko Kentarō 金子堅太郎

(1853–1942). Government official. Born to a *samurai* family in the Fukuoka domain (now part of Fukuoka Prefecture); graduate of Harvard College (1878). He became a lecturer in the preparatory course at Tōkyō University, and in 1880 he was appointed a secretary in the GENRŌIN (Senate). In 1884 he was assigned to the Seido Torishirabe Kyoku (Office for the Investigation of Institutions), the government office responsible for drafting the Meiji Constitution, together with ITŌ HIROBUMI, INOUE KOWASHI, and ITŌ MIYOJI. In 1885 Kaneko became secretary to Itō Hirobumi, Japan's first modern prime minister. In 1886 he was appointed a lecturer at Tōkyō University.

After Kaneko was named to the House of Peers in 1890, he was appointed vice-minister (1894) and then minister (1898) of agriculture and commerce and became minister of justice in 1900. During the RUSSO-JAPANESE WAR (1904–05) he was sent to Washington, DC, as a spokesman for Japan. From 1906 until his death he served as a member of the Privy Council. Kaneko was made a baron in 1900, a viscount in 1907, and a count in 1934.

Kaneko Kun'en   金子薫園

(1876–1951). TANKA poet. Real name Kaneko Yūtarō. Born in Tōkyō. In 1893 he joined the Asakasha (a coterie of *tanka* poets founded that year by OCHIAI NAOBUMI). In 1902 he published the poetry collection *Jokeishi* with ONOE SAISHŪ. Opposing the sensual romanticism championed by the publishers of MYŌJŌ magazine, *Jokeishi* exemplified a classical aesthetic based on descriptions of natural scenery, which itself gave rise to a new movement. The following year Kaneko formed the *tanka*-poet coterie Shiragikukai. His poetry collections include *Sametaru uta* (1910, Awakened Songs) and *Shirasagishū* (1937, The White Heron Collection). Kaneko's poetic style is characterized by elegant simplicity.

Kaneko Mitsuharu   金子光晴

(1895–1975). Poet and essayist. Real name Ōshika Yasukazu. Attended the Tōkyō School of Fine Arts (now Tōkyō University of Fine Arts and Music) and Waseda and Keiō universities. In an early poem entitled "Hantai" (1917, Opposition) Kaneko wrote, "To oppose is to be alive." After a yearlong (1919–20) stay in Europe, he returned to Japan to publish a collection of poetry entitled *Koganemushi* (1923, A Golden Beetle). In 1924 he married Mori Michiyo (1901–77), a poet and novelist. Subsequent travels to China, Southeast Asia, and Europe deepened Kaneko's existing sense of alienation from society, as can be seen in his *Marē Ran'in kikō* (1940, Malay–Dutch East Indies Travelogue). The revulsion with which he viewed power, tradition, war, and colonialism is forcefully expressed in *Same* (1937, Sharks), a small but monumental book of poems. During World War II, Kaneko was the only major Japanese poet who wrote antiwar poems, most of which were published in *Rakkasan* (1948, Parachute), *Ga* (1948, Moths), and *Oni no ko no uta* (1949, Songs of a Devil's Child). With his reputation as an outsider established, Kaneko developed a distinct, often experimental style, which combined earthy description, veiled erudition, and the tone of a perpetual complainer. Notable among his postwar books of poetry are *Ningen no higeki* (1952, The Tragedy of Man), which won the Yomiuri Literary Prize; *Suisei* (1956, The Force of Water); and *Wakaba no uta* (1967, Songs on Wakaba). Prose works include the autobiographical trilogy *Dokuro hai* (1971, Skull Bowl), *Nemure Pari* (1973, Sleep, Paris), and *Nishi higashi* (1974, West East).

Kaneko Naokichi   金子直吉

(1866–1944). Pre–World War II entrepreneur and chief manager of SUZUKI SHŌTEN. Born in what is now Kōchi Prefecture, Kaneko joined Suzuki Shōten in Kōbe in 1886, transforming it from a small camphor and sugar importer into a leading general trading firm that rivaled Mitsui and Mitsubishi during the economic boom of World War I. Suzuki Shōten collapsed during the FINANCIAL CRISIS OF 1927; however, TEIJIN, LTD, KŌBE STEEL, LTD, and ISHIKAWAJIMA-HARIMA HEAVY INDUSTRIES CO, LTD (all companies fostered by Kaneko under the aegis of the giant trader), went on

to become leading corporations in their own right.

Kaneko Ōtei   金子鷗亭

(1906–). Calligrapher. Real name Kaneko Kenzō. Born in Hokkaidō. Kaneko graduated from Hakodate Normal School (now Hokkaidō University of Education) in 1929 and became an advocate of the use of modern Japanese prose and poetry in calligraphy, thus making it more accessible to contemporary audiences, as opposed to strict adherence to the use of classical (often Chinese) writing. His style is known for its firm character and refinement. Kaneko received the Japan Art Academy Prize in 1967 and the Order of Culture in 1990.

Kaneko Tōta   金子兜太

(1919–). HAIKU poet. Born in Saitama Prefecture; graduate of Tōkyō University. Kaneko studied under KATŌ SHŪSON and was a contributor to Shūson's haiku magazine *Kanrai*. In 1955 he published the haiku collection *Shōnen* (Boy). From about this time Kaneko began to write more abstruse, avant-garde haiku without the traditional seasonal references and established himself as a leading avant-garde theoretician. In 1962 he founded and began editing his own magazine, *Kaitei*. His works are collected in *Kaneko Tōta zenkushū* (1975).

Kanematsu Corporation   兼松[株]

(Kanematsu). One of the leading Japanese GENERAL TRADING COMPANIES. Incorporated in 1889, it assumed its present name in 1960 with the merger of F. Kanematsu & Co, Ltd, and the Gōshō Co, Ltd. The company has 78 overseas and 23 domestic offices; 39 affiliates operate overseas and 100 in Japan. Sales for the fiscal year ending March 1991 totaled ¥5.9 trillion (US $43.0 billion), distributed as follows: textiles, 12 percent; metals, 27 percent; machinery and construction, 10 percent; fuels and chemicals, 43 percent; foodstuffs, 6 percent; and general merchandise, 3 percent. The firm was capitalized at ¥32.1 billion (US $234.0 million) in 1991. Headquarters are in Tōkyō, Ōsaka, and Nagoya.

Kanemi Kyō ki   兼見卿記

Diary of Yoshida Kanemi (1535–1610), head of the Yoshida Shintō branch of Shintō. Entries date from 1570 to 1610, with occasional gaps. The military takeover of Kyōto by ODA NOBUNAGA and his death at Honnōji, and the construction of Ōsaka Castle and Jurakudai by TOYOTOMI HIDEYOSHI are some of the events described. There are also references to Hideyoshi's land surveys and valuable information on the arts of the period.

Kanemi Oil Poisoning Incident
カネミ油症事件

(Kanemi Yushō Jiken). The world's largest and first major episode of food poisoning by polychlorinated biphenyls (PCBs). It took place in 1968, affecting 14,000 persons who had consumed contaminated cooking oil produced by the Kanemi Sōko Co. Victims experienced chloracne, a severe skin disease, as well as cardiovascular and central nervous system disorders. By 1982 the government had officially designated 1,858 sufferers of the disease. Although the medical data are uncertain, over 100 people are believed to have died as a result of the incident.

In October 1977, more than 9 years after their tragedy had begun and eight and a half years after entering court, 44 victims of

Kanemi oil disease won a total legal victory against the companies involved: Kanemi Sōko, producer of the oil, and Kanegafuchi Chemical, manufacturer of the PCBs. The Fukuoka District Court found both companies guilty of negligence under civil law and instructed them to pay the plaintiffs ¥682.0 million (US $2.5 million). A similar decision was rendered by the Kokura branch of the same district court, which in March 1978 awarded 729 plaintiffs ¥6.1 billion (US $28.8 million) in damages to be paid by the two companies. In all, seven appeals cases were heard, and the Kanemi Oil Poisoning Incident finally came to an end in 1989, when the last of the claimants accepted out-of-court settlements. The court cases significantly advanced the concept of product liability in Japan.

Kanenaga, Prince   懐良親王

(?–1383; Kanenaga Shinnō). Also known as Prince Kaneyoshi. A son of Emperor GO-DAIGO who fought on for his father after the failure of the KEMMU RESTORATION. Go-Daigo's restoration of direct imperial rule had been cut short by the revolt of one of his generals, ASHIKAGA TAKAUJI. In 1336 Takauji set up a rival emperor and Go-Daigo established the Southern Court at Yoshino (see NORTHERN AND SOUTHERN COURTS). In 1338 Kanenaga was sent to Kyūshū to command Southern Court forces, and by 1361 he was in control of most of Kyūshū. Ashikaga Takauji dispatched General IMAGAWA SADAYO to destroy him. In 1375 the defeated prince withdrew to Yabe in Chikugo Province (now Fukuoka Prefecture), where he died in obscurity.

Kaneshige Tōyō   金重陶陽

(1896–1967). Potter. Born Kaneshige Isamu in the Imbe district of the city of Bizen, Okayama Prefecture, to a family said to have been making BIZEN WARE since the Azuchi-Momoyama period (1568–1600). Tōyō inherited the family kiln in 1915. He conducted exhaustive research and experiments on firing in an effort to recreate the quality of the Azuchi-Momoyama period wares, and eventually succeeded in doing so. Intricate bird and animal sculptures comprise his earlier work, while wheel-thrown TEA CEREMONY vessels with simple contours and rugged surfaces characterize his later pieces. Tōyō was declared one of Japan's LIVING NATIONAL TREASURES by the government in 1956.

kangaku   官学

(government school). General term for government institutions of higher learning, as opposed to private ones. In the Nara (710–794) and Heian (794–1185) periods, the term referred to the government-established DAIGAKURYŌ in the capital and the *kokugaku* in the provinces, in contrast to the educational facilities of Buddhist temples and private schools for the aristocracy (see KANGAKUIN). In the Edo period (1600–1868) it referred to the Zhu Xi (Chu Hsi) school of Confucianism (see SHUSHIGAKU) and to the academy of this school, the SHŌHEIKŌ. During and after the Meiji period (1868–1912) the term was used to refer to universities and colleges set up by the national government.

Kangakuin   勧学院

Private educational facility established for students in the DAIGAKURYŌ by the Fujiwara

Kaneko Mitsuharu This poet and essayist, who traveled extensively in Europe and Asia in the 1920s and 1930s, is known for his fiercely independent verse and evocative autobiographical prose.

Character Styles

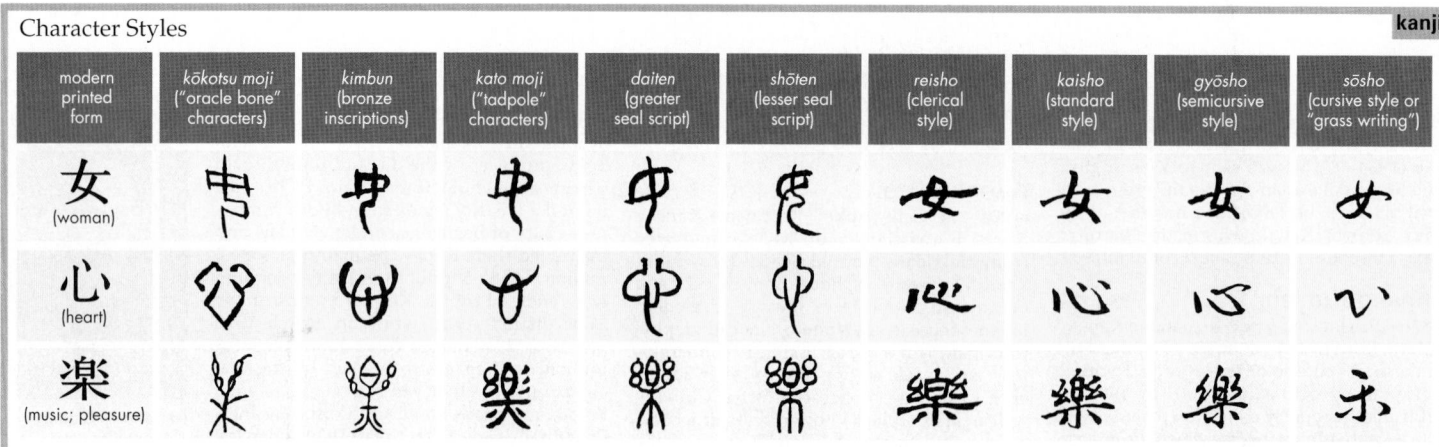

modern printed form	*kōkotsu moji* ("oracle bone" characters)	*kimbun* (bronze inscriptions)	*kato moji* ("tadpole" characters)	*daiten* (greater seal script)	*shōten* (lesser seal script)	*reisho* (clerical style)	*kaisho* (standard style)	*gyōsho* (semicursive style)	*sōsho* (cursive style or "grass writing")
女 (woman)									
心 (heart)									
楽 (music; pleasure)									

family during the Heian period (794–1185). Founded in 821, this boarding school (also known as Daigaku Bessō) educated Fujiwara family heirs for a career in the bureaucracy. For instructors, they enlisted the doctors (HAKASE) from the Daigakuryō. With the rise of the Fujiwara family, it became the best-organized private school of the day. The school's fortunes declined with those of the Fujiwara family.

kangeiko
寒稽古

The term for rigorous training exercises performed early in the morning or at night during midwinter, usually in January. Followers of Buddhism and Shintō carried on this practice in ancient times, and it became part of the traditional training program in the martial and performing arts. It is still practiced at KENDŌ and JŪDŌ halls. At the KŌDŌKAN martial arts hall midwinter training still takes place.

Kanghwa, Treaty of
日朝修好条規

(known in Japan as the Nitchō Shūkō Jōki or Japan-Korea Treaty of Amity). Korea's first modern treaty with Japan, signed on the island of Kanghwa (J: Kōkatō) on 27 February 1876. Japan was determined to secure trade rights and political influence in Korea, which had for centuries been a tributary state under Chinese suzerainty. The bilateral treaty led to the SINO-JAPANESE WAR OF 1894–1895 and was a step toward Japan's ultimate annexation of Korea in 1910. Negotiated after Japan sent two gunboats to Pusan, the treaty recognized Korea as an independent and sovereign nation; an exchange of diplomatic representatives was arranged; the opening of Pusan and two additional ports for trade with Japan was agreed upon; and Japan's right to establish consulates in three Korean ports with extraterritorial jurisdiction over Japanese nationals was recognized.

Kanginshū
閑吟集

(Songs Sung in Tranquility). The first extant collection of 311 songs of the type known as KOUTA, compiled in 1518; the editor is unknown. Three-quarters of the songs were chosen from what was sung on private occasions, while the remainder came from the repertoires of diverse performance groups popular in the late Kamakura period (1185–1333) and in the Muromachi period (1333–1568). Fifteen percent of the latter are from the NŌ theater. *Kouta* has no fixed prosodic pattern, though a stanza of 7-5-7-5–syllable lines predominates. Love is a main theme. Songs in the anthology are grouped first into those on the seasons, then into those on love. The basic guidelines to this system were inherited from traditional collections of WAKA. There is a sense of various relationships possible between adjacent songs, fos-

tered by the practice of linked verse (see RENGA).

kangō bōeki → tally trade

Kang Youwei (K'ang Yu-wei)
康有為

(1858–1927; J: Kō Yūi). Chinese Confucian scholar and leader of the Hundred Days' Reform (June–September 1898). Looking to reforms in Meiji-period (1868–1912) Japan as a model, he led a movement for constitutional monarchy that rivaled the revolutionary movement of SUN YAT-SEN and HUANG XING (Huang Hsing) before the 1911 Revolution. In 1895 Kang sent a petition to the emperor Guangxu (Kuang-hsü; r 1875–1908) urging him to begin a series of reforms and to reject the Treaty of SHIMONOSEKI concluding the SINO-JAPANESE WAR OF 1894–1895. Kang's action inaugurated a reform movement among the educated elite that was to culminate in the Hundred Days' Reform attempted by the emperor. Kang wrote a history of modern Japan for the edification of the emperor, using accounts by WANG TAO (Wang T'ao) and HUANG ZUNXIAN (Huang Tsun-hsien). The reforms were cut short in a coup d'état by the empress dowager Cixi (Tz'u-hsi; 1835–1908), and Kang fled to Japan. He was received by ŌKUMA SHIGENOBU, foreign minister and founder of the SHIMPOTŌ (Progressive Party), and by Prince KONOE ATSUMARO, founder of the Tōa Dōbunkai (East Asia Common Culture Society). After China's 1911 Revolution his monarchist views became increasingly irrelevant.

Kan Hasshū
関八州

(Eight Provinces of Kantō). An old designation for the eight provinces that constituted what is now known as the KANTŌ REGION. They are Musashi, Sagami, Kazusa, Shimōsa, Awa, Kōzuke, Hitachi, and Shimotsuke provinces, corresponding to the present-day prefectures of Tōkyō, Saitama, Kanagawa, Chiba, Gumma, Ibaraki, and Tochigi.

Kani
可児 [市]

City located at the confluence of the rivers Kisogawa and Hidagawa in southern Gifu Prefecture, central Honshū. Sight-seeing boats leave here for excursions down the Kisogawa. The Aichi Canal provides water for irrigation agriculture. In recent years a number of factories have been established and housing developments have been built for commuters to Nagoya. Pop: 80,012.

Kanie
蟹江 [町]

Town on the western border of the city of Nagoya in western Aichi Prefecture, central Honshū. Formerly the distribution center for a rice-producing area, Kanie now has numerous metal, textile, and food-processing

plants, and it is rapidly developing as a commuter suburb of Nagoya. Pop: 34,428.

kan'i jūnikai
冠位十二階

("twelve grades of cap rank"). The first system of courtly ranks (*i*) in Japan. Colored caps (*kan* or *kammuri*) were used to designate each of the 12 ranks. Devised by Prince SHŌTOKU, it was promulgated in 604. In contrast to the earlier hereditary titles (KABANE) based on clan membership, the *kan'i jūnikai* system was designed to reward individual merit and promote loyalty to the emperor. Ranks were named after the six Confucian virtues: *toku* (moral excellence), *jin* (benevolence), *rei* (decorum), *shin* (fidelity), *gi* (righteousness), and *chi* (wisdom); and each was subdivided, making 12 ranks. The *kan'i jūnikai* system was replaced by a 13-rank system in 647, and the use of caps to indicate rank was abolished in 701 with the adoption of the elaborate court hierarchy created under the RITSURYŌ SYSTEM. See also COURT RANKS.

Kan'in, House of
閑院宮

(Kan'in no Miya). One of the four princely houses, with Fushimi, Arisugawa, and Katsura, during the Edo period (1600–1868). The house was established in 1710 at the recommendation of the scholar-statesman ARAI HAKUSEKI, with a son of Emperor Higashiyama (r 1687–1709) as its first head. The family died out after five generations but was revived in 1872 when a Fushimi scion, Prince Kotohito (1865–1945), was adopted. In 1947, along with other princely houses, the Kan'in family was relegated to commoner status.

kanji
漢字

(Chinese characters). Ideographs of ancient Chinese origin that are still used in China, Korea, and Japan and were formerly used in other areas influenced by Chinese culture such as Vietnam. Chinese characters are ideographs in that essentially each character or graph symbolizes a single idea and, by extension, the sound (i.e., spoken word or morpheme) associated with that idea. For example, the Chinese character 犬 is "dog" in English, *quan* (*ch'üan*) in modern standard Chinese, and *ken* or *inu* in Japanese. In ancient Chinese each word consisted of a single syllable represented by one character; thus the characters were originally, properly speaking, logographs in that one character represented both the meaning and sound of an entire word. However, in the course of the centuries compound words became more and more common, with the result that the one-to-one correspondence between word and character weakened.

In Japan, Chinese characters are used in combination with the Japanese phonetic script known as KANA. Although any word can be written in the phonetic script, words of Chinese origin are normally written in Chinese characters alone as in Chinese, one character per Chinese syllable; however, the Japanese pronunciations of these Chinese syllables are often bisyllabic. In writing native Japanese words, Chinese characters are used either singly or in combination to indicate the meaning—and, by association, the sound—of the word. In the case of inflected words, the Chinese character or characters represent the stem of the word, inflectional suffixes being added in the phonetic script. Thus in Japanese a number of pronunciations are possible for most characters, the choice being dictated by context. See also the section on the writing system in JAPANESE LANGUAGE.

Types of Chinese Characters—Chinese characters were classified by Xu Shen (Hsü Shen) of the Later Han dynasty (25–220) into six types, which he called the Six Scripts (Liu Shu; J: Rokusho). Only the first four of these are really different types of characters, the other two being extended or "borrowed" uses of characters of these four types. The first two of the four main types are simple characters. Characters of type one are pictographs (Ch: xiangxing or hsiang-hsing; J: shōkei), being originally pictorial representations of the things indicated—e.g., 日 (originally written ☉) "sun." Characters of type two are diagrammatic (Ch: zhishi or chih-shih; J: shiji), i.e., symbolic representations of concepts or ideas—e.g., 一 "one," 二 "two." Types three and four are complex characters, combinations of two or more simple characters of either type. In type three, "combined meanings" (Ch: huiyi or hui-i; J: kaii), two simple characters are combined to indicate the meaning of a word—e.g., 明 "bright" (composed of 日 "sun" and 月 "moon"). In type four, phonetic characters (Ch: xingsheng or hsing-sheng; J: keisei), one element of the character suggests the general area of meaning and the other indicates the sound—e.g., 梅 (Ch: mei; J: bai, ume) "plum" (composed of 木 "tree" and 每, a character of unrelated meaning, used here only for the sound, that is pronounced mei in Chinese; hence "the tree that is pronounced mei").

Xu Shen's remaining two categories consist of extended usage of existing characters of the first four types to represent words other than (or in addition to) the ones with which they were originally associated. In type five, "extension" (Ch: zhuanzhu or chuan-chu; J: tenchū), one character is used to represent a word of the same or similar meaning but different pronunciation and thus acquires an additional pronunciation—e.g., 楽 (Ch: yue or yüeh; J: gaku) "music," which when pronounced le (J: raku) means "pleasure, enjoyment." In type six, "borrowing" (Ch: jiajie or chia-chieh; J: kasha), a character is used to represent phonetically a word with the same sound but different meaning—e.g., 萬 (Ch: wan) "scorpion," used to write the word wan (J: man) "ten thousand."

There is also a seventh type, consisting of a limited number of characters coined in Japan by combining elements from existing Chinese characters. These are known as kokuji or domestic characters. An example is 働 (J: dō, hataraku) "work" (composed of 人 "person" and 動 "move").

Character Styles—The oldest known Chinese characters are the so-called oracle bone characters engraved on tortoise shells and animal bones that have been unearthed from archaeological sites assigned to the

Shang (or Yin) dynasty (1766 BC–1027 BC) in China. These shells and bones, which are estimated to date from about the 13th century BC, were used by rulers in divinations to determine matters of policy or ritual, the oracle being read from the cracks formed when the items were subjected to intense heat. The characters scratched on them are a record of the divination. Comprising both simple and complex characters, the oracle bone characters represent a fairly advanced stage in the development of the Chinese writing system.

A variety of standardized styles for writing the characters flourished and declined during the course of Chinese history, with the chief styles now still in use developing by the 5th and 6th centuries. In the bronze and stone inscriptions of the Zhou (Chou) dynasty (1027 BC–256 BC) the characters of the oracle bones, already somewhat standardized and systematized, are known in Japanese as kimbun and sekibun, respectively. Another style developed during the Zhou dynasty is that of the so-called tadpole characters (J: kato moji), which were written on bamboo or wooden slips in lacquer by means of a stylus. The decorative style known as greater seal script (J: daiten) became the standard style late in this period. During the Qin (Ch'in) dynasty (221 BC–206 BC) an official standardization of the writing system resulted in a refinement of the greater seal script; this is known as the lesser seal script (J: shōten).

Scribes of the Former Han dynasty (206 BC–AD 8) wrote in an angular, straight-lined style known as the clerical script (J: reisho), which developed during the Later Han dynasty into the style known in Japanese as kaisho. The angular kaisho style remains to this day the standard, noncursive form for Chinese characters. During the 5th and 6th centuries the diffusion of writing on paper by means of brush and ink resulted in the semicursive style known in Japanese as gyōsho and the fluid cursive style known as sōsho or "grass writing." The gyōsho style—and to a more limited extent, the sōsho—continue to be used widely along with the kaisho. Some of the older styles, particularly the seal scripts and the clerical script, are still occasionally used for decorative purposes.

On and Kun Readings—Since in the Japanese writing system Chinese characters can be used to write either words of Chinese origin or native Japanese words, the pronunciations that can be assigned to them in reading fall naturally into two categories: (1) the Japanese imitations or approximations of the sound of the original Chinese syllable and (2) the native Japanese word that translates the meaning of the character. The former are called ON READINGS (on yomi), on being written with a character that means "sound" (i.e., the original Chinese sound); these are often referred to as "Sino-Japanese" readings in English. The latter are called KUN READINGS (kun yomi), kun being written with a character that originally meant "to interpret the meaning" (i.e., the meaning of the character as expressed by the Japanese word).

Number of Characters in Use—The number of Chinese characters currently used in Japan is limited to a small percentage of the 40,000 to 50,000 contained in the larger dictionaries. A list of characters called tōyō kanji (Chinese characters for daily use) was selected by the Ministry of Education in 1946, limiting the number of characters for official and general public use to 1,850. In

1981 this list was superseded by a similar but larger one (the JŌYŌ KANJI) containing 1,945 characters.

kanjiki 樏

Special footgear or crampons used for walking on snow, ice, or mud. Those used for walking on snow or ice are traditionally made of wooden hoops with rope straps and metal cleats.

Kanjinchō 勧進帳

(The Subscription List). KABUKI play; one of the 18 celebrated kabuki plays known as the KABUKI JŪHACHIBAN. A jidai-mono (historical play) by Namiki Gohei III (1790–1855), it was first performed in 1840. Arguably the most popular play in the kabuki repertory, it deals with the exploits of BENKEI, the legendary retainer of MINAMOTO NO YOSHITSUNE (1159–89), who was a tragic (and therefore romantic) figure in Japanese history—a brilliant general hounded to death by an insanely jealous elder brother. An earlier play on the same theme, written and enacted by Ichikawa Danjūrō I (1600–1704) in 1702, did not survive. The play as now presented was adapted by Namiki from the NŌ play ATAKA at the request of Ichikawa Danjūrō VII (1791–1859). It deals with Yoshitsune's flight north disguised as a porter serving Benkei and four retainers who were disguised as monks.

kanjō bugyō 勘定奉行

(commissioners of finance). The principal financial officials of the Tokugawa shogunate. The office was usually staffed by four men of relatively high HATAMOTO rank. In 1721–22 the shōgun TOKUGAWA YOSHIMUNE divided the tasks of the four commissioners, assigning two of them responsibility for fiscal matters as kattekata and the other two charge of judicial affairs as kujikata. Directly responsible to the individual senior councillor (RŌJŪ) who held the special title of kattegakari rōjū, the four officers supervised an army of subordinates. Most of this staff

Kanjinchō In a scene from this celebrated kabuki play, Benkei, at left with staff, and his traveling companions encounter Togashi, a barrier-station guard. Benkei is played here by Matsumoto Kōshirō IX, Togashi by Kataoka Takao.

kanjiki Traditional footgear designed to aid traction on snow or ice, kanjiki are still used in some regions of Japan.

Kannamesai

In this annual rite at the Ise Shrine, newly harvested rice and other food is offered to the goddess Amaterasu Ōmikami at both the Inner and Outer shrines.

▶ A purification ceremony is held at the Inner Shrine to confirm the ritual purity of the participants and the sacred food.

▲ Here, new rice is offered at the Outer Shrine by an imperial representative (in black) and shrine priests. The rice is stacked in front of the gate of the Outer Shrine's inner compound.

▼The imperial representative bows before the sacks of rice, which have been sent from all over Japan.

served in the tax-collection offices of intendants (DAIKAN and GUNDAI) that were scattered about the shogunate's own domains (TENRYŌ). In times of natural disaster or political crises, commissioners of finance were commonly assigned emergency authority. Because of the importance of the office of *kanjō bugyō* to the shogunate, its occupants were usually among the most able and powerful figures in the regime. See also KANJŌ GIMMIYAKU.

kanjō gimmiyaku   勘定吟味役

(comptrollers). Investigative officials of the Tokugawa shogunate (1603–1867) who ranked below but were independent from the KANJŌ BUGYŌ (commissioners of finance). They were first appointed in 1682 and reestablished in 1712 after a 13-year hiatus.

Kankakei A ropeway offers visitors a superb view of the autumn foliage in this gorge on the island of Shōdoshima.

Kannon Long popular in Chinese and Japanese Buddhism, the bodhisattva Kannon is represented here by a sandalwood image imported to Japan from Tang-dynasty China in 719. Height 38 cm. Hōryūji, Nara Prefecture. National Treasure.

The post was usually filled by four middle-ranking HATAMOTO who had served as shogunal intendants (DAIKAN) and were knowledgeable about financial matters. They served one-year terms, usually working in Edo (now Tōkyō), and were responsible to the senior councillors (RŌJŪ). Assisted by small staffs of subordinates, two of the comptrollers (known as *kattekata*) maintained surveillance over fiscal matters and two (known as *kujikata*) over judicial matters.

Kankakei   寒霞渓

Gorge in the eastern part of the island of Shōdoshima, Kagawa Prefecture, Shikoku. It is known for its strangely shaped rocks and spectacular autumn foliage.

Kankaku Securities Co, Ltd   勧角証券[株]

(Kankaku Shōken). Securities company providing a full range of financial services. Incorporated in 1922 as Nippon Kangyō Shōken, the company later merged with Kakumaru Shōken and adopted its present name in 1967. Affiliated with the DAI-ICHI KANGYŌ BANK, LTD, the company has expanded into financing for mergers and acquisitions and venture businesses abroad through its overseas offices. Revenue for the fiscal year ending March 1990 totaled ¥180.3 billion (US $1.2 billion), and capitalization stood at ¥66.0 billion (US $431.1 million). Headquarters are in Tōkyō.

Kankyōchō → Environment Agency

Kannamesai   神嘗祭

An annual rite at the ISE SHRINE in which the emperor makes offerings of newly harvested rice to AMATERASU ŌMIKAMI, the divine imperial ancestress. Kannamesai, which literally means "the festival in which the deities taste [the new rice]," is one of the most important rites in the imperial calendar. According to tradition, it has been observed since the founding of the Ise Shrine (probably in the 3rd century). Originally celebrated in September, since 1889 the Kannamesai has been performed over a three-day period beginning on 15 October.

The ceremony begins with a rite (called *miura*) to confirm the ritual purity of the participants. Then the sacred food, known as *yuki ōmike* ("pure and sacred rice"), consisting of new rice, sacred rice wine (*miki*), and other food, is offered at both the Outer and Inner shrines at Ise. The ceremony concludes with recitations by the imperial representative and the high priest, followed by the presentation of additional offerings and a sacred dance (*mikagura;* see KAGURA). On the 17th at the Imperial Palace, the emperor, other imperial family members, and specially chosen individuals worship in the direction of Ise (*yōhai*), and the emperor makes his own offering at the Kashikodokoro

("Place of Awe") in the palace. See also NIINAMESAI; DAIJŌSAI.

Kannami   函南[町]

Town on the river Kanogawa in the northern part of the Izu Peninsula, eastern Shizuoka Prefecture, central Honshū. The Tanna (7.8 km; 4.8 mi) and Shin Tanna (8.0 km; 5.0 mi) railway tunnels pass underneath the center of the township. Major economic activities are dairy farming and the cultivation of strawberries. Pop: 35,191.

Kannazuki → calendar, dates, and time

Kannō Disturbance   観応の擾乱

(Kannō no Jōran). Conflict between the shōgun ASHIKAGA TAKAUJI and his younger brother ASHIKAGA TADAYOSHI, who opposed the influence of General KŌ NO MORONAO on the shōgun's affairs. In 1350 Tadayoshi launched a campaign against Takauji and Moronao. When Moronao was killed in 1351 the brothers appeared to have reconciled their differences, but the conflict was renewed later that year. In 1352, after an apparent second reconciliation, Tadayoshi's sudden, unexplained death brought the conflict to a close.

Kannon   観音

(Skt: Avalokiteśvara; Ch: Guanyin or Kuanyin). Also known in Japanese as Kanzeon or Kanjizai. With JIZŌ, one of the most popular of all bodhisattvas in Japan. As the personification of infinite compassion, Kannon is believed to deliver all beings from danger when the name Kannon, meaning "the one who hears their cries," is invoked.

PURE LAND BUDDHISM regards Kannon as the major attendant of the Buddha AMIDA (Skt: Amitābha). Kannon is said to provide protection in the present life and help transport the faithful after death to Amida's Pure Land. PILGRIMAGES to temples to view famous Kannon images have been popular for many centuries.

As Avalokiteśvara in India, Kannon was originally male. However, Kannon in female form became especially popular as a bodhisattva for women who desired to become mothers or who wanted reassurance during childbirth. The most popular female image of Kannon is the White-Robed Kannon (Byakue Kannon) found in Tang (T'ang; 618–907) China from the 8th century and in Japan from the 10th century. The most famous images in Japan, designated as National Treasures, are the 7th-century wooden image of Kannon in the Hall of Dreams (Yumedono) at the temple HŌRYŪJI in Nara, and the array of 1,001 small statues of the Thousand-Armed Kannon in the 12th-century temple SANJŪSANGENDŌ in Kyōto.

Kannonzaki   観音崎

Cape at the mouth of Tōkyō Bay on the eastern tip of the MIURA PENINSULA in Kanagawa Prefecture, central Honshū. Kannonzaki

Lighthouse, built in 1869, is one of Japan's oldest Western-style lighthouses. A prefectural park is located here.

Kanno Suga 管野スガ

(1881–1911). Anarchist. Born in Ōsaka. After a three-year forced marriage she became a journalist in 1902 and the next year joined the KYŌFŪKAI (Japan Woman's Christian Temperance Union). While working for a socialist newspaper in 1906 in Wakayama Prefecture, she began living with leftist ARAHATA KANSON. Arrested with him and imprisoned for nearly two months in the RED FLAG INCIDENT OF 1908, she came to believe in the need for violent revolution. While Arahata remained in prison, she began living with anarchist KŌTOKU SHŪSUI, and she was again imprisoned briefly in 1909 for helping him publish two issues of a magazine called *Jiyū shisō* (Free Thought). Kanno and Kōtoku were implicated in the HIGH TREASON INCIDENT OF 1910, an alleged plot to assassinate the emperor Meiji. Along with 10 others she and Kōtoku were sentenced to death and hanged in 1911.

Kannoura 甲浦

District in the town of Tōyō, eastern Kōchi Prefecture, Shikoku. It was a fishing port in the Edo period (1600–1868) and is now a base for offshore fishing and a shipping port for lumber and marine products. Many scenic islands and inlets are found along the coast.

Kan no Wa no Na no kokuō no in 漢委奴国王印

(seal of the king of the state of Na of Wa, [vassal] of Han). A gold seal (see SEALS) discovered in 1784 on Shikanoshima in Chikuzen Province (now Fukuoka Prefecture). The base of the seal measures 2.4 centimeters (0.95 in) square and 0.9 centimeters (0.4 in) in height; the handle, carved in the shape of an animal with a snake's head, stands 1.5 centimeters (0.6 in) high. The inscription consists of five Chinese characters in three columns, written in *shōten* or "lesser seal script"; rendered into Japanese, it reads: *Kan no Wa no Na no kokuō* (King of the state of Na of Wa [Japan], [vassal] of the Han [dynasty]). Seals of this design were commonly given to "barbarian" rulers by the Han dynasty (206 BC–AD 220) of China. Moreover, the "Basic Annals" of the Chinese work *Hou Han shu* (History of the Later Han Dynasty) record a presentation of tribute by the king of the Wa state of Na in AD 57, and the chapter "Records of the Eastern Barbarians" in the same work reports that he was given a seal. It is widely accepted that this is the very seal mentioned in the Chinese records, although some scholars regard it as spurious.

kannushi 神主

A general designation for Shintō priests. The terms *kannushi* and *shinkan* often refer to Shintō priests in general, although, because of the lack of centralization in Shintō, priestly functions, ranks, titles, and names vary greatly depending upon individual shrines as well as on the period of history. Originally the term *kannushi* was used to designate those who performed a priestly function in religious ritual, mediating between the people and the divine. *Kannushi* became an institution at some of the larger shrines, such as the Kamo, Iwashimizu, Kasuga, and Matsunoo shrines, during the Heian period (794–1185), when *kannushi* were made the head priests.

Once established, the position of *kannushi* tended to be transmitted hereditarily. This is how some major priestly families (*shake*) emerged, each connected with a particular shrine. At small village shrines there was no institution of professional priesthood prior to the Edo period (1600–1868). Rather, there was the MIYAZA and *tōya* system in which lay people, often the heads of powerful households, presided by turns over the annual village festival. There is the suggestion in this of the original form of the *kannushi* role. At present the Jinja Honchō (see SHINTŌ SHRINES, ASSOCIATION OF) uses the terms *gūji* and *negi* to refer to priests concerned mainly with administrative and liturgical functions respectively (see PRIESTHOOD). *Kannushi*, however, remains a general term for Shintō priest in popular usage.

Kanō Eitoku 狩野永徳

(1543–90). KANŌ SCHOOL painter. Real name Kanō Kuninobu. Eldest son of Kanō Shōei (1519–92); grandson of KANŌ MOTONOBU, from whom he received his initial artistic training. Contemporary diaries indicate that Eitoku was the most sought-after artist of his day. His dramatic, monumental style of color-and-gold screen and wall painting for the decoration of castles and palaces during the Azuchi-Momoyama period (1568–1600) became a legacy for generations of Japanese artists, though many of his major works for military patrons such as ODA NOBUNAGA and TOYOTOMI HIDEYOSHI were destroyed in the warfare characteristic of the era.

An example of Eitoku's early style can be seen in the panel paintings (*fusuma-e*) in the Jukōin, the memorial chapel in the DAITOKUJI complex built in 1566, when Eitoku was in his early twenties. Another important surviving work done in the detailed style associated with YAMATO-E painting is his *Scenes in and around Kyōto* (*Rakuchū rakugai zu*), screens in the Uesugi Collection, Yamagata Prefecture. A group of works of varying degrees of authenticity illuminate Eitoku's activity during the final decade of his life. These include a pair of hanging scrolls, *Xu You* and *Chao Fu* (*Hsü Yu* and *Ch'ao Fu*; J: *Kyoyū* and *Sōfu*; Tōkyō National Museum) and two screens, *Chinese Lions* (*Karajishi zu*; Imperial Household Collection) and *Cypress Trees* (*Hinokizu*; Tōkyō National Museum). Eitoku died while working on an Imperial Palace commission in Kyōto.

Kanogawa 狩野川

River in IZU PENINSULA, Shizuoka Prefecture, central Honshū, originating in the AMAGI PASS and flowing north through the Tagata Plain to empty into Suruga Bay at the city of Numazu. A flood-control canal was constructed after the great flood of 1958, caused by the Kanogawa typhoon. Numerous hot springs, including Shuzenji and Yugashima, are located along the gorges of its upper reaches. Length: 46 km (29 mi).

Kanō Motonobu One of a pair of six-panel folding screens titled *Four Elders on Mt. Shang and Seven Sages in the Bamboo Grove*. 16th century. Ink on paper. Each screen 153 × 360 cm. Tōkyō National Museum.

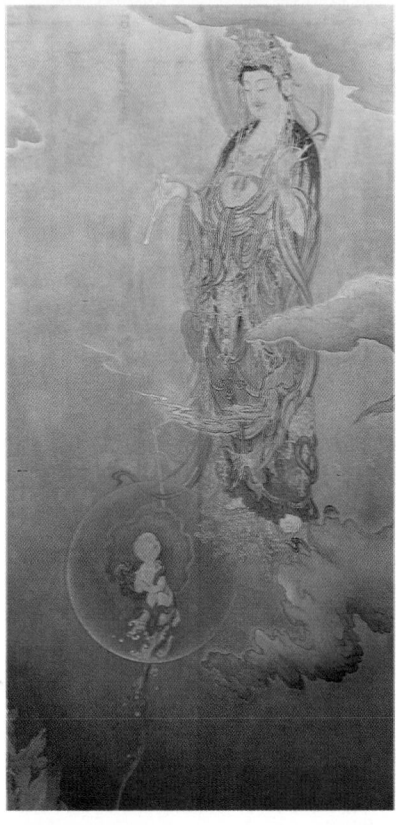

Kanō Hōgai *Merciful Mother Kannon*, one of this painter's best-known works. 1888. Hanging scroll. Colors on silk. 196 × 87 cm. Tōkyō University of Fine Arts and Music.

Kanō Jigorō At his Kōdōkan school in Tōkyō, Kanō developed *jūdō* as a modern sport based on the techniques of the martial art *jūjutsu*.

Kanō Hōgai 狩野芳崖

(1828–88). KANŌ SCHOOL painter. Born in Chōfu, Nagato Province (now part of Yamaguchi Prefecture), the son of Kanō Seikō, a painter for the local *daimyō*. In 1846 Hōgai was sent to Edo (now Tōkyō) to study painting with Kanō Shōsen'in (1823–80). In 1859 he received a commission to do ceiling paintings for the inner citadel of Edo Castle. Later, one of his paintings was selected for the 1876 Paris international exposition. Despite these honors he suffered financial difficulties and had to earn his living from other pursuits. The US art critic Ernest F. FENOLLOSA, impressed by Hōgai's work at the Second Domestic Painting Competitive Exhibition (Naikoku Kaiga Kyōshinkai) in 1884, bought several of his paintings. They became close friends. Fenollosa, Hōgai, HASHIMOTO GAHŌ, and OKAKURA KAKUZŌ participated in the Kangakai (Painting Appreciation Society). Hōgai adapted techniques of Western painting, such as the use of bright colors and chiaroscuro, to the tradition of Buddhist painting. His best-known paintings are *Niō sokki* (1886, Deva Seizing a Demon), *Fudō Myōō* (1887), and *Hibo Kannon* (1888, Merciful Mother Kannon).

Kanō Jigorō 嘉納治五郎

(1860–1938). Founder of the Kōdōkan school of JŪDŌ. Born in Settsu Province (now Hyōgo Prefecture); graduate of Kaisei Gakkō (now Tōkyō University). A disciple of the Tenjin Shin'yō and the Kitō schools of *jūjutsu*, Kanō transformed what had been primarily a martial art into a sport with spiritual and educational value. He established the Kōdōkan jūdō hall in Shitaya, Tōkyō, in 1882. In 1909 he became the first Japanese member of the International Olympic Committee; in 1912 he led the Japanese delegation to Stockholm for Japan's first appearance at the Olympics. He also helped found the JAPAN AMATEUR SPORTS ASSOCIATION and served as its first head. He was president of Tōkyō Higher Normal School.

Kanō Kōkichi 狩野亨吉

(1865–1942). Scholar. Born in what is now Akita Prefecture. Kanō graduated from Tōkyō University and served as principal of the First Higher School (Daiichi Kōtō Gakkō) in Tōkyō and as the first chairman of the humanities department at Kyōto University. A rationalist, he taught that God, free will, and the imperishable soul were the three great delusions of mankind. His interest in scientific thought of the Edo period (1600–1868) led to the discovery of two original thinkers, ANDŌ SHŌEKI and SHIZUKI TADAO.

Kanō Masanobu 狩野正信

(1434–1530). Painter. Traditionally called the founder of the KANŌ SCHOOL of painting. Masanobu was the son of a warrior from the village of Kanō in Izu Province (now Shizuoka Prefecture). Most scholars now believe that he studied with SHŪBUN at the temple SHŌKOKUJI in Kyōto. The *Inryōken nichiroku*, a log kept by one of the subtemples of Shōkokuji during the mid-15th century, lists many works by Masanobu, including paintings done in polychrome and ink.

The Kanō school's formal alliance with the ruling military regime began in 1481 when Masanobu succeeded OGURI SŌTAN as the official painter (*goyō eshi*) of the Muromachi shogunate. In the next generation, when leadership fell to Masanobu's son KANŌ MOTONOBU, Kanō painting was codified into a distinct style.

Kanō Mitsunobu 狩野光信

(1561 or 1565–1608). KANŌ SCHOOL painter. Author of a gentle, elegant version of the Azuchi-Momoyama–period (1568–1600) color-and-gold painting style. The earliest recorded mention of Mitsunobu is in conjunction with the AZUCHI CASTLE commission of 1581 given to his father, KANŌ EITOKU. He also worked with Eitoku at the Jurakudai, ŌSAKA CASTLE, and the Imperial Palace in Kyōto. Mitsunobu headed the painting project for Nagoya Castle, erected around 1592 in Hizen Province (now part of Saga and Nagasaki prefectures) in Kyūshū. In 1600 he executed a series of paintings for the Kangakuin subtemple of the Miidera (in what is now Shiga Prefecture).

Kanō Motonobu 狩野元信

(1476–1559). KANŌ SCHOOL painter; eldest son and heir of KANŌ MASANOBU. He is credited with establishing the orthodox style of the Kanō school and securing its position as the leading school of Chinese-inspired painting in Japan. He inherited from his father the position of painter-in-attendance (*goyō eshi*) to the Ashikaga shōgun and later became the chief painter (*edokoro azukari*) at the Imperial Court Academy. Extant paintings and literary records testify to Motonobu's artistic lineage in Zen-inspired Chinese INK PAINTING (*suibokuga*), his training in the indigenous Japanese painting tradition, or YAMATO-E, and his familiarity with Chinese polychrome BIRD-AND-FLOWER PAINTING (*kachōga*). He is best known for his *fusuma-e* (sliding-door paintings) that integrated all the above in his own style.

Two sets of bird-and-flower sliding-door paintings (now hanging scrolls) executed for the Daisen'in at the temple DAITOKUJI (ca 1513) and for the Reiun'in at the temple MYŌSHINJI (1543) best illustrate Motonobu's accomplishment. With so unorthodox a meeting of native and foreign heritages, the orthodox *wakan* ("Japanese-Chinese") style of the Kanō school was born. Motonobu's grandson KANŌ EITOKU further developed and perfected the style Motonobu originated.

kan on 漢音

(the Han pronunciation). One of the several varieties of ON READINGS of Chinese characters (KANJI) as used in Japan. *On* readings are Japanese approximations of the way the characters were pronounced in Chinese. For any one character there may be two or three possible *on* readings (reflecting the Chinese pronunciations of different periods and different regions). *Kan on*, introduced during the 7th and 8th centuries, differ markedly from GO ON (the Wu pronunciation), which were introduced in the 6th century and before along with Buddhism and the Chinese writing system. *Kan on* were declared the official pronunciations in Japan in 793. However, go on had already become deeply entrenched in Buddhist usage and in many commonly used words. As a result, *kan on* did not replace go on completely. Instead, it came to exist alongside go on, becoming established especially in newly introduced words and in certain academic contexts.

Kano Naoki 狩野直喜

(1868–1947). Scholar of Chinese literature and philosophy. Born in Kumamoto Prefecture. Graduate of Tōkyō University. A professor at Kyōto University, Kano served as director of the Institute of Oriental Culture (now Kyōto University Research Institute for Humanistic Studies). He made a substantial contribution to Chinese studies in Japan, particularly with his bibliographical study of the Qing (Ch'ing) dynasty (1644–1912) classics. His writings include *Chūgoku tetsugakushi* (1953, A History of Chinese Philosophy). He received the Order of Culture in 1944.

Kan'onji 観音寺〔市〕

City in western Kagawa Prefecture, Shikoku, on the Hiuchi Sea. Principal activities are sardine and shrimp fishing, marine-food processing, and the cultivation of rice, tobacco, and mandarin oranges. Textile mills and agricultural-machine plants are also located here. Pop: 45,500.

Kanō Sakujirō 加能作次郎

(1885–1941). Naturalist writer (see NATURALISM). Born in Ishikawa Prefecture. Graduate of Waseda University. While editor of *Bunshō sekai*, a literary magazine, he wrote *Yo no naka e* (1918), an autobiographical description of life in a poor fishing village. Other works include *Yakudoshi* (1911, A Critical Year) and *Chichi no nioi* (1941, Mother's Milk), collections of short stories.

Kanō Sanraku 狩野山楽

(1559–1635). Painter and leader of the Kyōto KANŌ SCHOOL of painting in the early Edo period (1600–1868). Born Kimura Mitsuyori. His father is said to have been a Kanō-style painter and retainer of the warlord TOYOTOMI HIDEYOSHI. Sanraku was trained in Kyōto and became a protégé of KANŌ EITOKU, the leading master of the Kanō school. He became an adopted member of the Kanō family through marriage to Eitoku's daughter. When Kanō Shōei, Eitoku's immediate successor, died in 1592, the leadership of the Kanō school became the shared responsibility of Sanraku and KANŌ MITSUNOBU. With the latter's death in 1608 Sanraku became the head of the school. Among the paintings scholars attribute to Sanraku, those considered his masterpieces include two pairs of six-fold screens in private collections: *Birds of Prey* and the *Imperial Mirror*. More paintings of birds can be seen in the temple Daikakuji in Kyōto, as well as Sanraku's paintings of tree peonies and other plant-and-animal themes. A four-fold screen in the Tōkyō National Museum, the *Battle of the Carriages*, is done in the native YAMATO-E manner, in colors and gold leaf.

Kanō Sansetsu 狩野山雪

(1589–1651). Painter. Leader of the Kyōto KANŌ SCHOOL of painting from 1635 until his death. He is thought to have been born in Kyūshū (according to some sources he was born in 1590) and brought up by Kanō-school artists in Kyōto. He became KANŌ SANRAKU's principal disciple and ultimately his son-in-law, adopted son, and successor.

Sansetsu began a compilation on the history of Japanese painting from his notes on 183 artists, which his son Kanō Einō (1631–97) edited and published in its final form in five volumes in 1693 as the *Honchō gashi*. The only important work actually signed by Sansetsu is a pair of screens, entitled *Winter Seascape with Birds*, now in a private collection. However, many major works have been attributed to him. From his works it is apparent that Sansetsu stayed close to Chinese models, which he refined and often adapted to a large-scale format with a delicacy that became the hallmark of Kyōto Kanō-school painting from his time on.

Kanō school 狩野派

(Kanōha). School of professional artists, patronized from the late Muromachi (1333–1568) through the Edo (1600–1868) periods by successive military governments. The Kanō were the most enduring and influential of the so-called Japanese schools of Chinese

painting (*kanga*). The chief strength and glory of the school were its monumental landscape, figure, and bird-and-flower compositions. Kanō artists produced works of every variety, ranging from fans and handscrolls (EMAKIMONO) to hanging scrolls (KAKEMONO) and votive plaques (EMA). The Kanō school was also well known for its INK PAINTING.

History——The first important Kanō master and founder of the school, KANŌ MASANOBU (1434–1530), emigrated to Kyōto sometime prior to the 1460s from his native village of Kanō in the Izu-Suruga region (now Shizuoka Prefecture). Masanobu is said to have trained under the painter-priest SHŪBUN (d ca 1460) at the atelier of the temple SHŌKOKUJI, at that time a bastion of the conservative Chinese Southern Song (Southern Sung; 1127–1279) and Yuan (Yüan; 1279–1368) academic style. During the 1480s Masanobu inherited the position of painter-in-attendance, or *goyō eshi*, to the Muromachi shogunate. Thus the position of the Kanō school was established as the first strictly secular and professional artists' group to practice and benefit from the stylistic tradition and patronage previously controlled by Zen painter-priests. The Kanō school grew into a vast network of artists, linked by family ties or by training, who held hegemony for nearly 250 years over public and private commissions from the shogunate, affluent monasteries, provincial lords, and wealthy merchants.

Masanobu's eldest son, KANŌ MOTONOBU (1476–1559), created the orthodox Kanō style, a monumental *wakan* (literally, "Japanese-Chinese") style that synthesized elements drawn from *kanga* and YAMATO-E (indigenous Japanese painting). He also instituted the studio system that ensured in perpetuity the professionalism of Kanō-trained artists.

Motonobu's grandson KANŌ EITOKU (1543–90) forged a style of SCREEN AND WALL PAINTING (*shōbyōga*) that proved the classic expression of the heroic and parvenu spirit of the Azuchi-Momoyama period (1568–1600). His son-in-law KANŌ SANRAKU (1559–1635) in Kyōto and grandson KANŌ TAN'YŪ (1602–74) in Edo (now Tōkyō) continued what had become, by the second half of the 16th century, a pattern in which major figures would emerge in successive ages, each serving as the pivot for a complex community of Kanō and Kanō-trained artists. For example, the next generation included Eitoku's sons, KANŌ MITSUNOBU (1561 or 1565–1608) and Kanō Takanobu (1571–1618), and Sanraku's son-in-law KANŌ SANSETSU (1589–1651), as well as a number of less talented artists who helped preserve and transmit the Kanō style.

The successful lineage continued into the early Edo period, when Takanobu's sons Tan'yū and Naonobu (1607–50) established the Kajibashi and Kobikichō branches, respectively, of the Kanō line in Edo. Meanwhile a third son, Yasunobu (1613–85), later adopted by Mitsunobu's son Sadanobu (1597–1623), founded the Nakabashi branch in Edo.

During the Meiji period (1868–1912) Kanō-school artists KANŌ HŌGAI (1828–88) and HASHIMOTO GAHŌ (1835–1908) helped found the Tōkyō Bijutsu Gakkō (now Tōkyō University of Fine Arts and Music), where Hashimoto, the last of the Kanō artists, taught a blend of Kanō and Western techniques.

Kanō Ink Painting——The Kanō ink painting (*suibokuga*) lineage can easily be

Kanō Sanraku Detail from the four-fold screen *Battle of the Carriages*, based on a chapter from the 11th-century novel *Tale of Genji*. First half of the 17th century. Colors and gold leaf on paper. 176 × 371 cm. Tōkyō National Museum.

traced from Motonobu's 1543 cycle of wall paintings at the Myōshinji subtemple Reiun'in, where he demonstrated mastery of Chinese landscape, bird-and-flower, and figural themes in the formal, informal, and cursive modes of ink painting, through the vast number of extant Kanō *suiboku* paintings dated from the late Muromachi through the Edo periods. Each generation of Kanō masters preserved the *kanga* foundation of their tradition by mastering and reinterpreting the standard models, both Chinese and Japanese, of Muromachi *suibokuga*, while at the same time adapting their ink styles and subject matter to the requirements of their patrons. The Kanō tradition of progressive experimentation is particularly noteworthy in Tan'yū's descriptive nature studies, which anticipated the naturalistic style of the MARUYAMA-SHIJŌ SCHOOL.

Kanō Screen Painting——All the trends of Kanō painting, from *suibokuga* to *yamato-e*, from *kanga* to genre painting, from conservatism to progressivism, are best represented by the monumental paintings for which the school is most noted. The Three Great Brushes of Kanō painting—Motonobu, Eitoku, and Tan'yū—together with the fourth central figure, Sanraku, emerge as successive authors of the mainstream styles of screen and wall painting associated with military patronage of the mid-16th through the 18th centuries.

Eitoku spawned a style that was to influence strongly the rival HASEGAWA SCHOOL and KAIHŌ SCHOOL but that, except for a brief revival at the hands of Tan'yū and Naonobu, would be abandoned by Eitoku's immediate circle and followers. Eitoku's vision showed the fullest possible exploitation of the monumental dimensions of the wall plane, as can be seen in reconstructions of the grand painting cycles he designed for warlords ODA NOBUNAGA and TOYOTOMI HIDEYOSHI. His compositions of heroically proportioned and broadly stroked single-theme motifs sweeping across multiple panels established the classic formula for the decoration of shogunal and imperial audience halls and residences.

In the compositions of Mitsunobu, Sanraku, and Sansetsu, smaller-scale, naturalistically described motifs are articulated with

Kanō Tan'yū Detail from one of the five scrolls making up the *Tōshōgū engi*, illustrating the life of the shōgun Tokugawa Ieyasu. Here he is depicted on horseback (at center) directing the siege of Ōsaka Castle in the summer of 1615. 1640. Colors on paper. This scroll 34 × 2,217 cm. Tōshōgū, Nikkō.

elegant brushwork and deeply saturated color against a ubiquitous gold ground, producing quiet, yet splendidly patterned and decorative effects that recall the origins of Kanō painting in classical *yamato-e* and *kanga* of the Song (Sung; 960–1278) and Yuan periods.

Kanō Tan'yū　狩野探幽

(1602–74). The foremost KANŌ SCHOOL painter of the Edo period (1600–1868). Real name Kanō Morinobu. The eldest son of Kanō Takanobu (1571–1618) and grandson of KANŌ EITOKU. In 1617 he was requested by the Tokugawa shogunate to come to Edo (now Tōkyō) as an official artist, and in 1621 he established an atelier. In his position as *goyō eshi* (official painter) he was engaged to work on the most prestigious painting commissions. Among his most important early large-scale commissions were EDO CASTLE (1622), ŌSAKA CASTLE (1623–24), NIJŌ CASTLE (1626), NAGOYA CASTLE (ca 1634), and the shrine TŌSHŌGŪ in Nikkō (1634–36). At the temple NANZENJI alone he painted portions of the interior decorations of four subtemples, in addition to the main temple buildings. His most famous work in the *yamato-e* style is the *Tōshōgū engi*, a set of five scrolls executed in 1639 and 1640 depicting the life of the shōgun TOKUGAWA IEYASU.

Kanoya　鹿屋[市]

City in southern Kagoshima Prefecture, Kyūshū. Sweet potatoes, rice, tea, and peanuts are grown; stock breeding and dairy farming are also important. Kanoya is the site of an air base for the Maritime Self Defense Force. Pop: 77,655.

kanrei　管領

(shogunal deputy). Also called *kanryō*. High official post in the MUROMACHI SHOGUNATE (1338–1573). The *kanrei* assisted the shōgun in all important government affairs, especially in mediating between the shogunate and the increasingly powerful SHUGO (provincial military governors). The *kanrei* office was not hereditary like the post of SHIKKEN or shogunal regent in the preceding Kamakura shogunate, but was rotated among members of the SHIBA FAMILY, HOSOKAWA FAMILY, and HATAKEYAMA FAMILY, who were thus known as the Sankanrei or "Three Deputies." See also KANTŌ KANREI.

kanreki　還暦

Celebration of a person's 60th birthday (61st as reckoned by *kazoedoshi*, the traditional

way of counting age, in which one is considered to be a year old at birth). The significance of age 60 is that the traditional calendar was organized on 60-year cycles (see JIKKAN JŪNISHI), and on the 60th birthday one begins a new cycle, returning to the calendar sign under which one was born (*honke-gaeri*). The celebration of *kanreki* began in the medieval period (mid-12th–16th centuries) and became popular during the Edo period (1600–1868). On the day of a person's 60th birthday, relatives and friends are invited to a celebratory feast. In some areas it is customary for the person to wear something red, this traditionally being the color for infants' clothes and hence symbolizing the beginning of a new cycle. Until recently, a man of 60 was expected to become, with his spouse, an INKYO (retired person). See also GA NO IWAI.

Kanrin maru　咸臨丸

The first modern warship to cross the Pacific under Japanese command. Purchased from Holland in 1857 by the Tokugawa shogunate, the *Kanrin maru*, a 300-ton, three-masted, screw-propelled steamer, was used to train a new Western-style navy in Japan. In 1860, under the command of Admiral KIMURA YOSHITAKE and Captain KATSU KAISHŪ, the *Kanrin maru* accompanied the ship taking the Tokugawa embassy to the United States to ratify the 1858 HARRIS TREATY (see UNITED STATES, MISSION OF 1860 TO). It took 35 days to complete the trip between Uraga and San Francisco. The voyage was a great achievement for the Tokugawa navy, formed less than five years earlier.

Kanroku　観勒

(fl early 7th century). Buddhist priest from the Korean kingdom of PAEKCHE who came to Japan in 602, during the reign of Empress SUIKO. Kanroku was a scholar and teacher of calendrical science, astronomy, geography, and astrology. When the government in 624 established an official Buddhist hierarchy to oversee monks and nuns, Kanroku was appointed its first primate (*sōjō*).

Kansai Electric Power Co, Inc

関西電力[株]

(Kansai Denryoku). Company supplying electricity to most of Ōsaka, Kyōto, Nara, Shiga, Wakayama, and Hyōgo prefectures and parts of Fukui, Gifu, and Mie prefectures. It is the second largest electric power company in Japan. The company was incorporated in 1951. Kansai Electric put a nuclear power plant in operation at Mihama in 1970, and it has since built 8 atomic reactors

at Takahama and Ōi. The company is constructing large-scale steam-generating plants in Ōsaka and Kyōto prefectures and increasing its capacity at the Ōi nuclear power plants. It operates a total of 138 hydroelectric plants, 20 thermoelectric plants, and 3 nuclear power plants. Annual revenue totaled ¥2.2 trillion (US $16.0 billion) in March 1991; capitalization stood at ¥484.8 billion (US $3.5 billion) in that year. Headquarters are in Ōsaka.

Kansai International Airport

関西国際空港

(Kansai Kokusai Kūkō). International airport for the Kansai (Ōsaka-Kyōto-Kōbe) region under construction since 1987 and scheduled to open in the summer of 1994. Construction of the new airport, on an artificial island in Ōsaka Bay, is being financed jointly by private enterprise and the national and local governments. The airport will be the first in Japan to operate 24 hours a day. The Kansai International Airport Co, Ltd, the primary agency involved in its construction, was established in October 1984, when it became evident that the existing Ōsaka International Airport was unable to meet demands for increased capacity. The first stage of construction calls for an airport of 511 hectares (1,263 acres) with one 3.5-kilometer (2.2-mi) runway.

Kansai Paint Co, Ltd　関西ペイント[株]

(Kansai Peinto). Manufacturer of paints and coatings. Incorporated in 1918. In 1926 it became the first domestic producer of lacquer paints. It has joint-venture factories in several Asian countries, including India, Thailand, Singapore, and Taiwan. It also has offices in New York, London, Hamburg, Hong Kong, and other cities. In the fiscal year ending March 1991 total sales were ¥166.5 billion (US $1.2 billion), of which 82 percent came from the sale of synthetic resin paints; capitalization was ¥25.7 billion (US $187.3 million). Headquarters are in Ōsaka.

Kansai region　関西地方

(Kansai *chihō*). A term loosely applied to the area centering on the cities of Ōsaka, Kyōto, and Kōbe. It is sometimes defined as equivalent to the KINKI REGION, but the latter is an official geographical designation with clearly defined boundaries. The term Kansai is rather a cultural and historical one, the definition of which has changed over the years. Kansai (literally, "west of the barrier") was first used sometime before the 10th century in contradistinction to the word Kantō. Kantō ("east of the barrier") referred to the area east of the barrier station (SEKISHO) at Ōsaka (in what is now Shiga Prefecture, not to be confused with the major city of the same name), and Kansai referred to the area west of the station. From the Kamakura period (1185–1333) the dividing line between Kantō and Kansai was marked by the three barrier stations at Suzuka (in what is now Mie Prefecture), Fuwa (in what is now Gifu Prefecture), and Arachi (in what is now Fukui Prefecture). It was later fixed farther east at the barrier station at Hakone (in what is now Kanagawa Prefecture). The term is also used to describe local speech patterns (as in Kansai *ben* or Kansai *namari*) and manners and customs, and thus closely resembles *kamigata*, another word used loosely to cover the Kyōto-Ōsaka area. In broader usage, Kansai includes Shikoku and the CHŪGOKU REGION. See also KINAI.

Kansai University 関西大学

(Kansai Daigaku). A coeducational private university located in the city of Suita, Ōsaka Prefecture. Founded in 1886 as the Kansai Law School, it changed its name to Kansai University in 1905 and achieved university status in 1922. The university has faculties of law, letters, economics, commerce, sociology, and engineering. Enrollment in 1989 was 24,066.

Kan Sazan 菅茶山

(1748–1827). Confucian scholar and writer of Chinese verse. Real name Kan Shinsui. Born in Bingo Province (now Hiroshima Prefecture). Influenced by Song (Sung) poetry, his realistic evocations of everyday life influenced poets in western Japan who wrote in Chinese. He opened a school, the Kōyō Sekiyō Sonsha, in his home province. The school was attended by the poet and historian RAI SAN'YŌ. His principal works include the prose piece *Fude no susabi* (1857) and a renowned anthology of his poetry, *Kōyō sekiyō sonsha shi* (1812, 1823).

Kansei chōshū shoka fu 寛政重修諸家譜

(Revised Kansei Genealogies). An official compilation (1812) by the Tokugawa shogunate of the genealogies of *daimyō*, *hatamoto*, and other Tokugawa vassal houses. The project stemmed from plans made during the Kansei era (1789–1800) to add a supplement to the earlier compilation KAN'EI SHOKA KEIZU DEN (1643). The project took 14 years to complete and involved about 60 scholars, including YASHIRO HIROKATA and HAYASHI JUSSAI. The *Kansei chōshū shoka fu*, though unreliable for the period before 1600, is valued particularly for its record of family histories for the Edo period (1600–1868).

Kansei Gakuin University 関西学院大学

(Kansei Gakuin Daigaku). Private, coeducational university located in Uegahara, in the city of Nishinomiya, Hyōgo Prefecture. The school was founded in 1889 by Walter R. Lambuth, an American missionary. In 1910 the Japanese, US, and Canadian Methodist churches became joint sponsors of the school, and in 1929 the campus moved to its present location. University status was granted in 1932. It has faculties of theology, humanities, sociology, law, economics, commerce, and science. It also has an affiliated kindergarten; elementary, junior high, and senior high schools; and a two-year women's junior college. Enrollment in 1989 was 13,839.

Kansei Reforms 寛政の改革

(Kansei no Kaikaku). The Kansei Reforms (1787–93; Temmei 7–Kansei 5) were the second of three reform programs undertaken by the Tokugawa shogunate (1603–1867), falling between the KYŌHŌ REFORMS (1716–45) and the TEMPŌ REFORMS (1841–43). MATSUDAIRA SADANOBU, chief senior councillor (*rōjū shuseki*) from 1787 to 1793, was their architect and implementer. Because many *daimyō* followed his example, the term also refers to all domainal reforms of the period.

The reforms achieved central administrative efficiency through a major purge of officials at all levels and restored power to the senior councillors (RŌJŪ) from the chamberlain (SOBAYŌNIN), who had held it during the preceding regime under TANUMA OKITSUGU. In the countryside the reforms restored tax farming, built up rice reserves for bad years, and abolished the abusive collector guilds of licensed merchants (*osameyado*). Peasants, who had flocked to urban areas in search of work, were ordered to return to the land (see HITOGAESHI).

The shogunal capital of Edo (now Tōkyō), which had proven vulnerable during a rice riot in June 1787, was the focus of the Kansei Reforms. By manipulating the official rate of exchange, Sadanobu strengthened Edo's financial position vis-à-vis Ōsaka and reduced the upward pressure on commodity prices. He further bolstered Edo's economic independence from Ōsaka by developing the *sake*, oil, cotton, and paper industries in Edo's hinterland, the Kantō region.

The Kansei Reforms restored financial solvency, revitalized the bureaucracy, and reduced feudal-bourgeois tensions. They provided temporary remedies but did not check social and economic trends that would further undermine Tokugawa society.

kanshi → poetry and prose in Chinese

Kantan 邯鄲

NŌ play. Author unknown. It is classified as a *yobamme-mono* ("part-four play"). Uncertain about the meaning of life and determined to find an answer, the Chinese youth Rosei (Ch: Lu Sheng; the *shite* or main character) embarks on a journey to discover truth. He stops overnight at a village inn in the Kantan (Ch: Handan or Hantan) region. The proprietress of the inn urges on him a pillow that is said to bring enlightenment to anyone who lays his head upon it. Rosei borrows the pillow and dreams a marvelous dream: an imperial messenger (the *waki* or subordinate character) arrives and makes him emperor. He lives in a great palace, drinks from the fountain of youth, and dances to lovely music; 50 years elapse in a moment. However, when Rosei wakens, he finds that his dream has lasted only as long as it has taken the proprietress to prepare a bowl of millet.

Kantei style 勘亭流

(Kanteiryū). Style of calligraphy conceived in 1779 by Okazakiya Kanroku, an employee of the theatrical company Nakamuraza. Its thick, curved strokes form compact characters with few open areas between them, suggesting a "full house," and it quickly won favor in the theatrical world. Easily recognized from a distance, the style was used in posters advertising the productions of *kabuki* troupes as well as in writing their playbooks. To this day the style is used in kabuki posters and in bills (*banzuke*) announcing the ranking of *sumō* wrestlers.

Kantō 竿灯

The major event of the TANABATA FESTIVAL as celebrated in the city of Akita, Akita Prefecture, from 4 August to 7 August; also, the bamboo poles hung with lanterns used in this event. Twenty-four or 46 paper lanterns are suspended from nine horizontal crosspoles attached to a long, vertically held bamboo pole. At night, brightly costumed young men balance these long poles on their palms, shoulders, hips, and foreheads as they parade through the city to the accompaniment of drums and chanting.

Kantō Auto Works, Ltd 関東自動車工業[株]

(Kantō Jidōsha Kōgyō). Manufacturer of passenger car bodies. Incorporated in 1946, it

Kantei style These signboards with actors' names written in the Kantei style of calligraphy are displayed outside the Minamiza *kabuki* theater in Kyōto.

is affiliated with TOYOTA MOTOR CORPORATION. Other product lines include prefabricated buildings and school furniture. Sales for the fiscal year ending March 1991 totaled ¥411.1 billion (US $3.0 billion), and capitalization stood at ¥6.9 billion (US $50.3 million). Headquarters are in Yokosuka, Kanagawa Prefecture.

Kantō Daishinsai → Tōkyō
Earthquake of 1923

Kantō Earthquake → Tōkyō
Earthquake of 1923

Kantōgun → Guandong (Kwantung)
Army

Kantō kanrei 関東管領

(shogunal deputy for the Kantō region). Official post created in Kamakura by the MUROMACHI SHOGUNATE (1338–1573) to assist governors-general of the Kantō region (Kantō *kubō* or Kamakura *kubō*; see KUBŌ). After the appointment of Uesugi Noriaki (1306–68) in 1363, the post was held in rotation by members of the four branches of the powerful UESUGI FAMILY, who retained the title until the end of the 16th century.

Kantō loam 関東ローム

(Kantō *rōmu*). Four thick layers of ash laid down by several volcanoes to form the KANTŌ PLAIN around present-day Tōkyō. The layers of deposition are the Tama loam (300,000–200,000 years ago), the Shimo Sueyoshi loam (200,000–100,000 years ago), the Musashino loam (100,000–30,000 years ago), and the Tachikawa loam (30,000–10,000 years ago). The surface of the plain is black humus averaging 1 meter (3.3 ft) thick, near the bottom of which occur artifacts of the JŌMON CULTURE (ca 10,000 BC–ca 300 BC). Those of the PALEOLITHIC CULTURE (pre-10,000 BC) occur throughout the underlying Tachikawa loam.

Kantō At the Tanabata Festival held in the city of Akita, neighborhood groups compete to display the best technique of holding the *kantō* aloft. The shape of the *kantō*, modeled after an ear of rice, represents the hope for a bountiful harvest.

From the 10th through the 19th century, *kaō* (personal marks or monograms) were used in place of signatures on a wide range of documents. Pictured here are the *kaō* of several historical figures.

Fujiwara no Yukinari (972–1027). Court noble and famous calligrapher.

Shinran (1173–1263). Founder of the Jōdo Shin sect of Buddhism.

Emperor Go-Toba (1180–1239). Reigned from 1183 to 1198.

Rankei Dōryū (1213–78). Chinese monk and early Zen master in Japan.

Issan Ichinei (1247–1317). Considered to be the founder of Gozan literature.

Ashikaga Yoshimitsu (1358–1408). Third shōgun of the Muromachi shogunate.

Toyotomi Hideyoshi (1537–98). Warlord instrumental in the reunification of Japan.

Date Masamune (1567–1636). Warrior who ruled the Sendai domain.

In this letter written by Tokugawa Ieyasu, announcing the end of the Komaki Nagakute military campaign, his *kaō* appears at the bottom of the second line from the left.

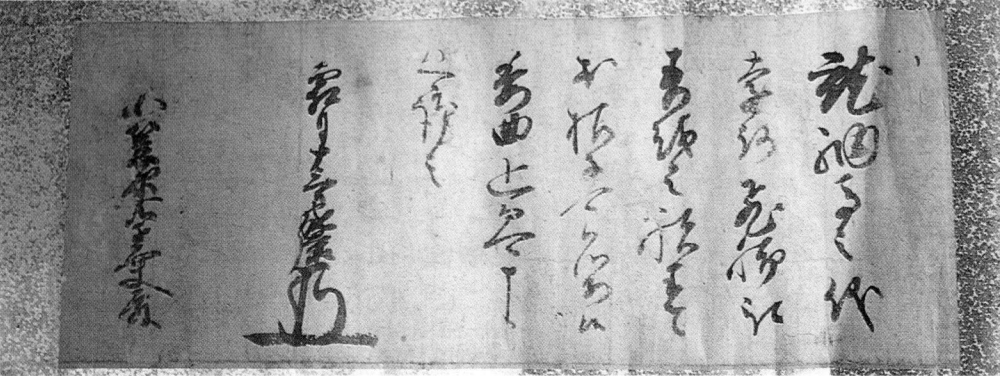

Kantō Mountains   関東山地

(Kantō Sanchi). Mountain range in the western Kantō region, central Honshū. It runs north to south through Nagano, Gumma, Saitama, Yamanashi, Kanagawa, and Tōkyō prefectures for a distance of about 130 km (80 mi) and is divided into the Chichibu Mountains (see OKU CHICHIBU) in the north and the Tanzawa Mountains in the south. Peaks include KOBUSHIGADAKE (2,483 m; 8,146 ft) and KIMPUSAN (2,599 m; 8,526 ft), the highest in the range.

Kantō Plain   関東平野

(Kantō Heiya). Located in central Honshū. The largest plain in Japan, it occupies more than half the KANTŌ REGION. Volcanic ash known as the KANTŌ LOAM layer covers more than half of this plain; the remainder consists of alluvial areas and the deltas of the rivers Tonegawa, Arakawa, and Tamagawa. Lakes and marshland lie on the lower Tonegawa, and on the Pacific seaboard are the sandy beaches of Kujūkurihama, Kashima, and Shōnan. The region is undergoing rapid change as land is reclaimed in Tōkyō Bay and as the hills are turned into residential areas for the swelling Tōkyō metropolitan area that includes Tōkyō, Yokohama, Kawasaki, and their suburbs. Area: 17,000 sq km (6,564 sq mi).

Kantō region   関東地方

(Kantō *chihō*). Located in east central Honshū, consisting of Tōkyō, Chiba, Saitama, Kanagawa, Gumma, Ibaraki, and Tochigi prefectures. This is Japan's most heavily populated region and is the political, economic, and cultural center of the nation. The regional center is the metropolitan area that includes Tōkyō, Yokohama, Kawasaki, and

Chiba. The region is dominated by the Kantō Plain.

The term Kantō (literally, "east of the barrier") originally referred to the area east of the barrier station (SEKISHO) at Ōsaka in what is now the city of Ōtsu, Shiga Prefecture (not to be confused with the city of Ōsaka); the term was used in contradistinction to the KANSAI REGION west of the station. The border was later moved twice, finally being set much farther east at the barrier station at Hakone (in what is now Kanagawa Prefecture).

The Tōkyō-Yokohama district in the center of the region is Japan's leading commercial and industrial area. Agriculture plays a declining but still important role in the region's economy. Coastal fishing in the Pacific Ocean and Tōkyō Bay has declined because of vastly increased catches by deep-sea fishing trawlers and because of increased pollution and land reclamation in Tōkyō Bay. Area: 32,385 sq km (12,504 sq mi); pop: 38,543,517.

Kan U   関羽

(?–219; Ch: Guan Yu or Kuan Yü). Powerful Chinese general of Shu (Szechuan) who became a popular subject for Japanese ink painters. During the Three Kingdoms (220–265) he was deified as a protector of warriors in China. With the diffusion of secular Confucian culture in Edo-period Japan (1600–1868), Guan Yu's military exploits became a popular pictorial theme.

Kanuma   鹿沼［市］

City in central Tochigi Prefecture, central Honshū. Kanuma developed in the Edo period (1600–1868) as a post-station town leading to the mausoleum of TOKUGAWA IEYASU in Nikkō. Known for its wooden household furnishings (*tategu*) and for a planting soil called *kanumatsuchi*, the city

now has lumbering, metal, and machine industries. Pop: 90,043.

Kanzaki Paper Mfg Co, Ltd
神崎製紙［株］

(Kanzaki Seishi). Company specializing in the production of processed paper products such as art paper and coated paper. Incorporated in 1948, the company concentrates its efforts on the development of special paper products such as high-quality printing paper, carbonless paper, and thermal paper. Sales for the fiscal year ending March 1991 totaled ¥157.5 billion (US $1.1 billion), while capitalization stood at ¥18.1 billion (US $131.9 million). The company's 18-percent export rate was the highest among Japanese paper manufacturers. Headquarters are in Tōkyō.

Kanzan and Jittoku   寒山と拾得

(Kanzan *to* Jittoku; Ch: Hanshan and Shide or Han-shan and Shih-te). Legendary Tang (T'ang) dynasty (618–907) eccentrics who became popular subjects in Chinese and Japanese INK PAINTING. Hanshan (literally, "cold mountain") was a poet-recluse in the Tiantai (T'ien-t'ai) mountain region of Zhejiang (Chekiang) near the temple of Guoqingsi (Kuo-ch'ing-ssu), where his friend Shide worked in the kitchen. Shide (literally, "foundling") had been an abandoned child retrieved and reared by the Chan (Ch'an; J: Zen) master Fenggan (Feng-kan; J: Bukan), another unconventional personality, who is said to have ridden about on a tiger.

Kanzanji   館山寺

Resort area on the shore of Lake HAMANA in the city of HAMAMATSU, western Shizuoka Prefecture, central Honshū. The temple Kanzanji, reputedly built by the priest KŪKAI, is famous for moon viewing. A scenic outlook, ropeway, and hot spring are also in this area.

kanzashi   簪

Ornaments used in traditional Japanese HAIRSTYLES. The immediate ancestor of the *kanzashi* is said to be the *kazashi*, a hair ornament of the medieval period (mid-12th–16th centuries). During the 18th and 19th centuries, as new hairstyles became popular, *kanzashi* came into wide use, and many were products of fine artistic workmanship. Materials such as wood, bamboo, tortoiseshell, ivory, glass, and metal were used. See also KŌGAI.

Kanze Motokiyo→Zeami

Kanze Motomasa   観世元雅

(1394?–1432). Also known as Kanze Jūrō. NŌ actor and playwright. Motomasa succeeded his father ZEAMI as head of the KANZE SCHOOL, or troupe, in 1422. Zeami lamented his son's early death in *Museki isshi* (1433, A Page on the Ruin of a Dream). Motomasa's best-known plays are *Yoroboshi* and SUMIDAGAWA.

Kanze Nobumitsu   観世信光

(1435–1516). Also known as Kanze Kojirō. NŌ actor and playwright. Member of the KANZE SCHOOL. Nobumitsu's plays, which include *Funa Benkei*, *Dōjōji*, MOMIJIGARI, and *Rashōmon*, are among the most enduringly popular in the repertoire. Many of his plays give *waki* (subordinate actor) roles unusual prominence. They are generally far more showy than the plays of ZEAMI and foreshadowed KABUKI.

kanzashi Decorative hair ornaments such as the one shown here were popular among women of the 18th and 19th centuries. Especially finely crafted *kanzashi* were often handed down from mother to daughter as heirlooms.

Kanze school 観世流

(Kanzeryū). One of the five major *shite kata* (principal player) schools (or troupes) of professional NŌ theater actors. The school is directly descended from the Yūzakiza (Yūzaki troupe), one of the four original SARUGAKU Nō troupes of the Kamakura period (1185–1333). Established during the period of the Northern and Southern Courts (1337–92), its name derives from the childhood name of its founder, the early Nō master KAN'AMI. Kan'ami and his talented actor-playwright son ZEAMI were patronized by the third Muromachi shōgun, ASHIKAGA YOSHIMITSU. During the Edo period (1600–1868) the Kanze school ranked foremost among Nō schools. After the Meiji Restoration (1868), Kanze Kiyotaka, the 22nd hereditary head of the troupe, moved with the deposed shōgun TOKUGAWA YOSHINOBU to Shizuoka. The school is currently led by Kanze Kiyokazu (b 1959), the 26th hereditary head. The Kanze school is known for its elegant and colorful style of acting.

kao 顔

(literally, "face"). An important concept in Japanese interpersonal relationships. The word *kao* is used in a number of idioms with implications similar to those of the Chinese word *mianzi* (*mien-tsu;* J: *mentsu*) and the English word "face." If a person has a wide circle of acquaintances, his *kao* is "broad" (*kao ga hiroi*); if he is influential, his *kao* "works" (*kao ga kiku*). When a person "smears his *kao* with dirt" (*kao o yogosu*) or his *kao* is "crushed" (*kao o tsubusareru*), he is disgraced. When one's face is saved, one's *kao* is "made to stand" (*kao o tateru*). *Kao* is almost synonymous with *memboku* (Ch: *mianmu* or *mien-mu;* "face"). *Memboku* may also be "sullied," "ruined," or "smeared with ash." What is signified by these words is the individual's social self or the self as properly presented to the public. To maintain one's good reputation and to avoid shame to one's name have long been cardinal principles of personal conduct in Japan.

kaō 花押

(monograms). Personal marks or signs that developed from signatures. In the 10th century they began to be used in place of signatures on a vast range of public and private documents. The word *kaō* is a compound of two Chinese characters: *ka* ("flower") and *ō* ("to impress one's signature"); together they convey the sense of "a beautiful, flowerlike signature." *Kaō* were later called *kakihan*, from *kaki* ("to write") and *han* ("to distinguish"; in this case, "to distinguish self from others").

During the 8th and 9th centuries all official documents were signed by the person responsible for them. Signatures were usually in formal, regular script, but even when they were not, they were always quite legible. On private correspondence, however, one was free to write in running or cursive styles, and the stroke order and basic shape of characters might be altered until they were no longer immediately recognizable. Such highly individualized, often illegible, signatures came to be called *kaō*. Far more than simply an expedient, they resulted from the desire for unique personal marks that could not be imitated.

Kaō first appeared during the same period when the *hiragana* syllabary was being developed by a similar process of abbreviation

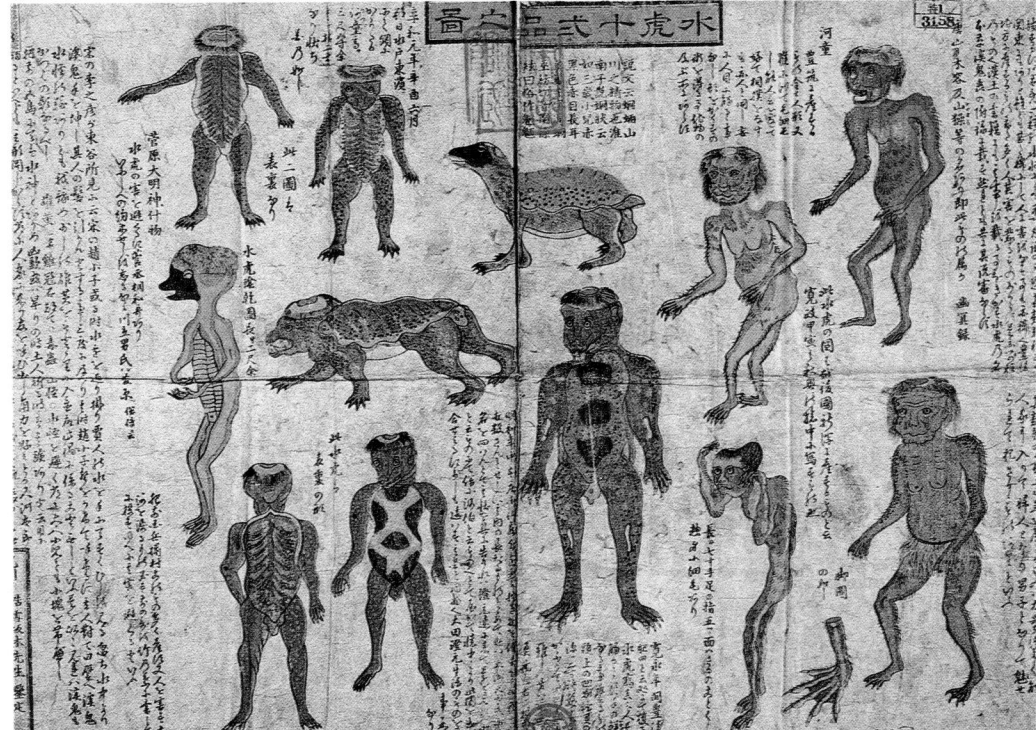

of Chinese characters (see KANA). Throughout the Heian period (794–1185) *kaō* were based upon the actual characters of a person's name and thus might be described as artistic signatures. Yet, because they were not legible to others, they resembled monograms. Over the centuries *kaō* changed according to styles developed in each historical period.

From the time of the shōgun TOKUGAWA YOSHIMUNE (1684–1751), it was customary to have the *kaō* design carved into a wooden seal, from which rubbings could be taken. *Kaō* lost their original meaning and significance and became little different from seals. After the Meiji Restoration (1868) the government ruled that *jitsuin* (registered seals) be used on all important documents. *Kaō* were seldom used after this ruling (see SEALS).

Kaō are often the only clue to the identity of the author and the authenticity of certain documents. Carried out within the larger field of DIPLOMATICS ("the study of old documents"), the study of *kaō* is of immeasurable importance.

Kaō Corporation 花王[株]

(Kaō). Chemical firm producing primarily soaps, cosmetics, and household goods such as detergents, but also industrial products such as plasticizers and edible oils. Founded in 1887 as Nagase Shōten, the firm had established a solid base for commercial growth within five years. The company manages its nationwide network of sales firms and automated factory warehouses by a computer in its main office. In addition to 9 wholly owned domestic factories, Kaō Corporation has established 13 overseas joint-venture companies. Sales for the fiscal year ending March 1991 totaled ¥570.2 billion (US $4.2 billion), of which sales of household products constituted 87 percent and products for industrial use 13 percent. In the same year capitalization was ¥61.6 billion (US $449.0 million). Headquarters are in Tōkyō.

Kaō Ninga 可翁仁賀

(fl early 14th century). Painter whose name is known from two signature seals found on some ink paintings dating from the early 14th century. A painting listed in the *Koga bikō*, an early-19th-century dictionary of painters, as bearing the signatures "Kaō" and "Ryōzen," provided support for the tradition that the two signatures represent the same artist, but this theory is now largely rejected, and paintings bearing the Ryōzen signatures are usually regarded as the work of a different master. Another possibility is that Kaō Ninga was actually the famous Zen priest Kaō Sōnen, the abbot of the temple Kenninji in Kyōto who died in 1345. However, Kaō Ninga's seal suggests that Kaō may have been a professional Buddhist painter or EBUSSHI associated with the TAKUMA SCHOOL. Confusion over Kaō's identity does not detract from his importance as an artist. Such paintings as the hanging scroll depicting the Chinese Zen eccentric Hanshan (J: Kanzan) in the Hattori Collection, Tōkyō, demonstrate a seemingly casual freedom of line, which, with rapid ink-wash passages, conveys a quality of spontaneity and humor that is profoundly expressive both of the subject and of the spirit of Zen Buddhism.

kappa 河童

An amphibious supernatural creature said to inhabit Japan's waters. Thought to be a transformation of a water deity. The description and name of the *kappa* vary from region to region. Generally, the *kappa* is believed to be about the size and shape of a 12- or 13-year-old child, with a face like a tiger with a snout; its hair is bobbed, and a saucer-like depression on top of the head contains water. When the supply of water diminishes, the *kappa*'s supernatural power on land is impaired. The *kappa*'s slippery body is covered with blue-green scales and emits a fishy odor. It has webbed feet and hands. Human beings can recognize the *kappa* by its ability to rotate arm and leg joints freely. In other variations, *kappa* have beaks and wings or resemble turtles or otters. Although in some areas *kappa* help with rice-planting or irrigation, usually they prey on humans and animals. In particular the *kappa* delights in grabbing its victim and tearing out the liver through the anus. The *kappa* is also said to be fond of cucumbers and partial to SUMŌ wrestling. AKUTAGAWA RYŪNOSUKE wrote a popular novel entitled *Kappa*.

kappa The malicious water imp of Japanese folklore is depicted in a number of its regional variations in this 1820 drawing. Children swimming in lakes or rivers, the home of the *kappa*, are said to be the creature's favorite prey. National Diet Library.

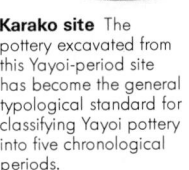

Karako site The pottery excavated from this Yayoi-period site has become the general typological standard for classifying Yayoi pottery into five chronological periods.
1 A pedestaled bowl probably used to hold individual food servings. Middle Yayoi period. Height 16 cm, diameter 21 cm. Kyōto University. **2** A ring- or coil-built unglazed jar. Early Yayoi period. Height 29 cm. Kyōto University.

Kapsin Political Coup 甲申事変

(J: Kōshin Jihen). Unsuccessful attempt by the Korean KAEHWAP'A (Enlightenment Faction), with Japanese support, to seize control of the Korean government in December 1884. (Kapsin [J: kōshin] is the designation for 1884 in the sexagenary cycle.) Led by KIM OK-KYUN and PAK YŎNG-HYO, the Kaehwap'a urged rapid Westernization on the model of Japanese modernization. Thwarted by the pro-Chinese SUGUP'A (Conservative Faction) then in control of the government, the young reformers seized the royal palace on 4 December and held it for three days before their revolt was put down by Chinese garrison forces. The Japanese legation was burned and 40 Japanese killed. Japan received reparations and an apology from Korea in the Treaty of SEOUL in January 1885, while China and Japan agreed to withdraw troops from Korea in the TIANJIN (TIENTSIN) CONVENTION in April 1885. See also KOREA AND JAPAN.

kara-e 唐絵

(Chinese-style painting). A term often contrasted with YAMATO-E (Japanese-style painting). In its earliest 8th-century use kara-e referred to works done by Chinese artists of the Tang (T'ang) dynasty (618–907) that were imported to Japan. Its meaning was subsequently extended to copies of Chinese paintings done by Japanese artists and then to Japanese depictions of Chinese scenery or Chinese subjects. Throughout the Heian period (794–1185) kara-e carried overtones of the dignity and opulence of Tang China in contrast to the familiarity of themes from Japanese literature.

During the 13th and 14th centuries ink paintings by Chinese artists of the Song (Sung; 960–1279) and Yuan (Yüan; 1279–1368) dynasties began to enter Japan. Japanese called these newly imported Chinese paintings kara-e. In the Edo period (1600–1868) kara-e designated the colorful style of Tang China, yamato-e referred to the classical Heian style, and kanga ("Chinese painting") indicated the Japanese translation of Song and Yuan painting styles.

karaoke Partygoers look on while a man and woman sing to the accompaniment of prerecorded music and a video interpretation of the song that includes a display of the lyrics.

Karafuto →Sakhalin

Karafuto-Chishima Kōkan Jōyaku
→St. Petersburg, Treaty of

Karagoromo Kisshū 唐衣橘洲

(1743–1802). KYŌKA poet. Real name Kojima Gennosuke. Born in Edo (now Tōkyō) to a samurai family, he was an advocate of delicately humorous verse evincing the technical intricacy and classical grace of traditional WAKA. With ŌTA NAMPO and Akera Kankō (1740–1800) he headed a group of kyōka poets formed of both samurai and townsmen (chōnin). Kyōka first became popular in Edo following the publication of Nampo's Manzai kyōkashū, but after the KANSEI REFORMS the more reserved kyōka of Kisshū and Kankō came into vogue. Kisshū's works include the anthologies Kyōka wakabashū (1783) and Suichikushū (1802).

Karai Senryū 柄井川柳

(1718–90). Anthologist and founder of the poetic genre SENRYŪ. Born Karai Hachiemon in Edo (now Tōkyō). In his forties he became a master of the maeku-zuke ("verse-capping") style of haikai and was soon so prominent that verses anthologized by him came to be known as senryū. From 1757 until his death he selected and published poems in annual collections known as Senryūhyō mankuawase. These collections include some 80,000 of the more than 2.3 million verses judged by Senryū. His disciple Goryōken Arubeshi (d 1788) chose 756 of these poems that could be understood separately without their maeku couplets and published them under the title of Haifū yanagidaru in 1765. This established the 17-syllable form as an independent genre, the modern senryū. Editions of Senryūhyō mankuawase and Haifū yanagidaru continued to be published under different editors until 1797 and 1838(?), respectively. Senryū is the only genre of Japanese literature that is named after a person.

Kara Jūrō 唐十郎

(1940–). Leading "post-postwar" playwright, director, and actor. Kara, whose real name is Ōtsuru Yoshihide, graduated from the theater department of Meiji University. He organized the Jōkyō Gekijō (Situation Theater) troupe in 1963 and began to write plays. The group subsequently acquired a distinctive red tent that could be readily set up anywhere and that became both the symbol and the prime vehicle for realizing Kara's goal of integrating contemporary theater with everyday life.

The dialogue in Kara's plays is a highly literary, humorous amalgam of nonsense words and onomatopoeia, incessant puns, current slang, and unexpected images and allusions. He often reworks his archetypal characters through a series of plays and uses stories and characters from many times and cultures. Representative works include Jon Shirubā (1965, Long John Silver), Giri ninjō i ro ha ni ho he to hen (1967, The ABCs of Obligation vs Feeling), Aribaba (1967, Ali Baba), Kyūketsu ki (1971, The Vampire Princess), Nito monogatari (1972, A Tale of Two Cities), and Bengaru no tora (1973, Bengal Tiger). In recent years Kara has turned his hand to fiction, winning the Akutagawa Prize in 1982 for the novella Sagawa kun kara no tegami (1982, A Letter from Master Sagawa).

karakami 唐紙

Type of decorative paper, originally imported from China, hence the name ("Chinese paper"). Often used for calligraphy and as stationery during the Heian period (794–1185). Also known as kira ("glittering") because of the sparkling surface created by gofun (chalk wash) and mica. From the Muromachi period (1333–1568) on, karakami was manufactured in Japan, where it came to be used mainly as fusuma (sliding door) paper. This use persists today, and the term karakami has hence become a synonym for fusuma.

Karakhan, Lev Mikhailovich カラハン, L. M.

(1889–1937). Soviet diplomat. Born in Tiflis. He graduated from the University of St. Petersburg. In 1917 he joined the Bolsheviks and assumed a series of posts in the People's Commissariat for Foreign Affairs, rising to the position of deputy commissar. He issued the "Karakhan Manifestos" of 25 July 1919 and 27 September 1920, which renounced privileges and concessions in China acquired by the tsarist regime. As envoy to China (1923–26), Karakhan negotiated treaties that established Soviet diplomatic relations with China (31 May 1924) and with Japan (20 January 1925; see SOVIET-JAPANESE BASIC CONVENTION). In 1928 he negotiated a fisheries convention with Japan. He was executed during the Stalin purges.

Karaki Junzō 唐木順三

(1904–80). Critic. Born in Nagano Prefecture; graduated from Kyōto University. He first attracted attention in 1932 with the publication of Gendai Nihon bungaku josetsu (An Introduction to Contemporary Japanese Literature). In 1943 he published Ōgai no seishin (The Spirit of Mori Ōgai), which analyzed MORI ŌGAI's position in the history of modern Japanese thought. After World War II he continued his critical studies of modern culture while at the same time developing an interest in the medieval period (mid-12th–16th centuries). Other important works include Gendaishi e no kokoromi (1949, An Essay in Contemporary History), Chūsei no bungaku (1955, Medieval Literature), and Muyōmono no keifu (1960, A Genealogy of the Superfluous).

Karako site 唐古遺跡

(Karako iseki). Archaeological site of the Yayoi period (ca 300 BC–ca AD 300); located in alluvial lowlands of Nara Prefecture. The many types of YAYOI POTTERY that were excavated in 1936–37 were subsequently assigned to five categories or phases that have since served as the standard typology for Yayoi pottery of the Kinki region (the seven prefectures centering on the Kyōto-Ōsaka-Nara area). Karako was also the first site to yield wooden artifacts and agricultural implements that shed light on the daily life of Yayoi peoples. Also excavated were PIT HOUSES, storage-pit and ditch remains, BONE ARTICLES and STONE TOOLS, and clay and stone molds for casting bronze bells (DŌTAKU). See also YAYOI CULTURE.

karamatsu →larch, Japanese

karaoke カラオケ

(literally, "empty orchestra"). Prerecorded musical accompaniment, usually on compact or laser disc. An essential part of one of the most popular leisure-time activities in Japan:

the singing of songs backed by *karaoke* musical accompaniment at bars and pubs, at parties, or at home. Recording studios and radio stations started using music-only *karaoke* tapes in the mid-1960s, and in the 1970s bar owners hit upon the idea of outfitting their establishments with *karaoke* sound systems so that patrons could sing along (today's systems display the song lyrics on a separate video monitor, and smaller systems are available for home use). Most *karaoke* establishments have a large and eclectic catalog of songs; the sentimental songs known as *enka* and contemporary music are among the most popular selections.

kara-ori 唐織

A heavy, profusely decorated brocade cloth (NISHIKI); also, the small-sleeved *kimono* made of this cloth. Long strands of thick, glossy silk, appearing much like loose embroidery, stand out against the ground in multicolored designs. The name *kara-ori* ("Chinese weave") referred first to cloths imported from Ming China woven with pictorial brocade patterns, and later to similar textiles produced in Japan. During the 15th and 16th centuries men and women of the upper classes wore *kara-ori*, often under a broad-sleeved cloak. Around 1600 a special style of *kara-ori* became the basis of the subsequent NŌ theater costume with which the term is primarily associated today. The designs are generally floral. The standard method of wearing *kara-ori* is to wrap it tightly over the hips, secure it with a band, and loosely fold the upper portion over the chest.

Karasawa 涸沢

Valley lying amid the multiple peaks of HOTAKADAKE in Nagano Prefecture, central Honshū. Surrounded by Kita Hotakadake (3,106 m; 10,188 ft), Karasawadake (3,110 m; 10,203 ft), Oku Hotakadake (3,190 m; 10,463 ft), and Mae Hotakadake (3,090 m; 10,135 ft), it drains into the river Azusagawa. Elevation at the base of the cirque at its upper end is 2,550 meters (8,364 ft). Length: 3.0 km (1.9 mi).

Karasumaru Mitsuhiro 烏丸光広

(1579–1638). WAKA poet and court noble of the early Edo period (1600–1868). A member of the conservative Nijō school, he studied poetry under his father-in-law, HOSOKAWA YŪSAI, from whom he received the secret, orally transmitted poetic tradition known as the KOKIN DENJU. He is regarded as the moving spirit behind the poetic revival following the wars of the 16th century. He bridges the *waka* style of traditional court poetry and that of the Edo period. He is also known for his calligraphy. His principal works include *Kōyō wakashū* (published posthumously in 1669) and *Jiteiki* (ca 1602).

Karatani Kōjin 柄谷行人

(1941–). Literary critic. Real name Karatani Yoshio. Born in Hyōgo Prefecture. Graduated from Tōkyō University. Karatani launched his career with *"Ishiki" to "shizen": Sōseki shiron* (1969, "Consciousness" and "Nature": Essays on Natsume Sōseki), an analysis of Sōseki's works centering on the consciousness of being that won the Gunzō Prize for New Talent. Karatani's other works include *Nihon kindai bungaku no kigen* (1980, The Origins of Modern Japanese Literature), *In'yu to shite no kenchiku* (1983, Architecture as Metaphor), and *Tankyū* (1985, Investigations), a series of essays.

karate 空手

(literally, "empty hand"). Art of self-defense that uses no weapons and relies instead on three main techniques: arm strikes (*uchi*), thrusts (*tsuki*), and kicks (*keri*). A distinction is made between offensive and defensive techniques, which are modified according to the position of one's opponent. For defense, there are various parrying methods (*uke*) corresponding to each of the methods of offense. There are two sections in karate competitions: form (*kata*) competition and sparring (*kumite*) matches.

Karate was historically most widely practiced in China and Okinawa and thus is not considered one of the traditional Japanese MARTIAL ARTS; it is, however, loosely referred to as such outside of Japan. Current forms of *karate* developed from a style of Chinese boxing called *quanfa* (*ch'üan-fa*, literally, "rules of the fist"; known as kung fu in the West; J: *kempō*), which is thought to have been transmitted by the Indian Buddhist monk Bodhidharma (d ca 532) along with ZEN (Ch: Chan or Ch'an) Buddhist teachings to Chinese disciples at Shaolin temple (J: Shōrinji) in the southern province of Henan (Honan). The method of self-defense traced to these beginnings is called Shōrinji *kempō* in Japan; it had spread widely through China by the time of the medieval Ming dynasty (1368–1644), but it was suppressed in the Qing (Ch'ing) period (1644–1912) because it was used by a secret society aspiring to reestablish Ming rule. The subsequent development of *karate* took place primarily in OKINAWA. Chinese fighting techniques (referred to in Japanese as *tōde*; literally, "Tang [T'ang] hand") merged with indigenous techniques (called *te*; literally, "hand") to produce the *karate* style. A karate club was established at a middle school in Okinawa in 1905 after the islands had become a prefecture of modern Japan, and the sport thereafter began to emerge from obscurity. It became known throughout mainland Japan in 1922, when FUNAKOSHI GICHIN, an Okinawan master, performed a demonstration in Tōkyō. In the late 1920s a *karate* club was founded at Keiō Gijuku (now Keiō University), and thereafter the development of the sport centered on the universities. Two schools developed, one of which emphasized strengthening the body, and the other, quick movements. Numerous styles (*ryū*) have emerged over the years.

After World War II, *karate* and the other martial arts experienced a decline that lasted until around 1955. After that the sport increased in popularity, and it is more widespread now than ever. A federation of student *karate* organizations was established in 1962. A general federation of the various karate organizations in Japan was established in 1964, after *karatedō* (the Way of *karate*) had achieved a large following abroad.

Karatsu 唐津[市]

City in northwestern Saga Prefecture, Kyūshū, on Karatsu Bay. Important as the point of embarkation for Korea in ancient times, Karatsu became a castle town in the Edo period (1600–1868). After the Meiji period (1868–1912) it developed as a port for shipping coal from Karatsu Coalfield and as a base for fishing. Principal industries are the manufacture of machine tools and construction materials and the processing of foodstuffs. It is noted for its KARATSU WARE. Tourist attractions include the ruins of Karatsu

Castle and the NIJI NO MATSUBARA, a stand of pines on the bay. Pop: 79,207.

Karatsu Bay 唐津湾

(Karatsu Wan). Bay on the Genkai Sea, extending from western Fukuoka Prefecture to northern Saga Prefecture, northern Kyūshū. There are many campsites and beaches along the bay.

Karatsu ware 唐津焼

(*karatsu-yaki*). Collective name for diverse ceramics produced south of the city of Karatsu, an ancient port in Hizen Province (now Saga and Nagasaki prefectures), Kyūshū. Over 100 kilns produced high-fired stonewares from the mid-16th century for shipment in great quantities to the rest of Japan. Often with a finely crackled, hard feldspathic glaze, many pieces had underglaze-painted designs of simple reeds and flowers or patterns. The smaller pieces were all wheel-thrown and had trimmed, unglazed foot rims. Despite its great diversity, the Karatsu style can be classified into three major types: plain Karatsu (*muji karatsu*), having a single glaze; Korean Karatsu (Chōsen *karatsu*), combining an opaque white glaze (*madara* or *namako*) with a dark brown or black iron glaze; and underglazed decorated Karatsu (*ekaratsu*), using a milky or semitransparent glaze over iron-oxide painted underglaze designs. Some pieces were fashioned specifically for the TEA CEREMONY.

One of the earliest kilns, Handōgame, operated from at least the mid-16th century. Production reached its peak in the early 17th century. Nakazato Tarōemon XII (1895–1985), a descendant of the early potters, was designated one of Japan's LIVING NATIONAL TREASURES. Nakazato Tarōemon XIII (b 1923), his oldest son, continues the production of Karatsu ware in the ancient, traditional style.

karayuki san からゆきさん

(literally, "one who goes to China," i.e., abroad). Japanese women who went to work as prostitutes in Asia, the South Pacific, India, and even America and Africa after the

karate
1 The contestant on the right slips a punch past his opponent's block.
2 A right roundhouse kick lands during a sparring match.

Karuizawa A villa in Karuizawa. The area has been a popular site for summer homes since the late 19th century.

Meiji Restoration of 1868. The majority were natives of western Kyūshū. Girls in early adolescence were either sold by their parents or unwittingly signed themselves over to procurers, who then sold them to overseas brothels. As many as 100,000 women may have been involved, though their numbers decreased greatly in the 1920s when the government moved to suppress the traffic. After Japan's surrender in 1945, *karayuki san* as such completely disappeared. See also MURAOKA IHEIJI; YAMADA WAKA.

karē raisu カレーライス

(curry and rice). Vegetables and meat or seafood in a curry-flavored sauce that is thickened with flour and served over rice. The curry roux is commonly sold in prepackaged blocks for easy preparation. The Japanese version of curry and rice is usually quite mild and is especially popular among children and young adults. Curry powder first came into use in Japan at the end of the Edo period (1600–1868), when it was brought there by the English. During the late Meiji period (1868–1912) the Japanese version of curry roux was developed, and curry and rice began to be served in Japanese restaurants. Early in the Shōwa period (1926–89) a number of restaurants specializing in this dish appeared. Pickled shallots (*rakkyōzuke*) and sliced vegetables pickled in soy sauce (*fukujinzuke*) are often served as condiments with curry and rice.

Karikachi Pass 狩勝峠

(Karikachi Tōge). Located in the northern Hidaka Mountains, central Hokkaidō. The pass offers a panoramic view of the Tokachi Plain. A new railway tunnel (length: 5,810 m; 19,061 ft) runs under the pass. Altitude: 644 m (2,113 ft).

Kariya 刈谷[市]

City in central Aichi Prefecture, 24 km (15 mi) southeast of NAGOYA. Kariya developed as a castle town in the Edo period (1600–1868). It was rapidly industrialized after the opening of the Tōkaidō main rail line and the establishment of the Toyota Spinning Co in 1926. Many Toyota-affiliated plants manufacturing steel, automobiles, machine tools, and other products are here. Pop: 120,126.

Karlgren, Bernhard カールグレン, B.

(1889–1978). One of the great philologists of the 20th century. Born in Jönköping, Sweden. After pursuing his early interest in linguistics at Uppsala University, in 1910 he left for field work in China, spending 18 months in Northern China (Taiyuan or T'ai-yüan) to compare dialects and begin the work of reconstructing ancient Chinese. The revolution in 1911 forced him to cut short his stay,

karē raisu This curry dish has been popular in Japan since the 1920s. It is usually served with condiments such as the red pickles (*fukujinzuke*) shown in the separate dish.

and he returned via Siberia to Sweden. There he continued his work on Chinese phonology and published his monumental work *Etudes sur la phonologie chinoise* (1915–26).

Karlgren received in 1918 a personal chair of Far Eastern Linguistics and Culture at the University of Göteborg, where he stayed until 1939. He was president of the university between 1931 and 1936. China and the Chinese language were of course his main interests here, but it should be noted that while at Göteborg Karlgren established the first Japanese program in the Scandinavian countries; the first student in Japanese graduated in 1923.

karō 家老

(literally, "house elders"). Sometimes called TOSHIYORI (and in the Tokugawa shogunate known as RŌJŪ), *karō* were the highest-ranking officials in the governments of *daimyō* during the Edo period (1600–1868). Usually drawn from vassal families of high rank, two to four *karō* commonly held office at one time and had general responsibility for the administration of domainal affairs.

Karuizawa 軽井沢[町]

Town in eastern Nagano Prefecture, central Honshū, on a plateau 900–1,100 m (2,952–3,608 ft) high on the southern slope of Mt. Asama (Asamayama), the highest active volcano in Japan. A post-station town during the Edo period (1600–1868), since the late 1800s Karuizawa has grown rapidly as a summer retreat. Tourist attractions include Shiraito Falls and ONIOSHIDASHI, a massive flow of lava formed by the eruption of Mt. Asama in 1783. Pop: 15,464.

karuta →playing cards

kasagake 笠懸

("hat-hanging"). A form of mounted archery originating in the Heian period (794–1185). The term derives from the fact that archers initially shot arrows at a straw hat (*kasa*). As a martial sport *kasagake* flourished in the Kamakura period (1185–1333) along with YABUSAME and INUOUMONO. Bowmen galloped their horses down a course. At its midpoint they shot arrows at a leather-covered wooden target about eight bow lengths to the side. The arrows were called *kaburaya* and had hollow, bullet-shaped, wooden heads that whistled as they flew towards the target. Interest in the sport declined in the Muromachi period (1333–1568).

Kasagi Mountains 笠置山地

(Kasagi Sanchi). A chain of plateaulike horst mountains extending across the borders of Nara, Mie, Shiga, and Kyōto prefectures, central Honshū. Emperor GO-DAIGO fled here after his unsuccessful attempt to overthrow the KAMAKURA SHOGUNATE in 1331.

Kasai 加西[市]

City in south-central Hyōgo Prefecture, western Honshū, on the river KAKOGAWA. Traditionally known for its *banshū-ori* (a cotton fabric), *tatami* matting, and *goza* (straw mats), Kasai's more modern industries include electrical appliances and textiles. The 7th-century temple Ichijōji and the Gohyaku Rakan, a group of some 404 stone Buddhist images, draw visitors. Pop: 51,784.

Kasai Zenzō 葛西善蔵

(1887–1928). Novelist. Born in Aomori Prefecture; received primary education only. Kasai settled in Tōkyō in 1905 and became a follower of TOKUDA SHŪSEI. His novels, written in an autobiographical naturalist style (see I-NOVEL), describe his struggles with loneliness, illness, and poverty. Major works include *Kanashiki chichi* (1912), *Akuma* (1912), and "Kohan shuki" (1924).

Kasa jizō 笠地蔵

(The Bamboo-Hat Jizō). Folktale. A poor but kind-hearted old couple have no money to buy rice cakes for the New Year. The old man makes bamboo hats and sets off to sell them. On his way to town, he sees six statues of JIZŌ (the guardian deity of children) standing in the snow. Feeling sorry for them, he covers their heads with the bamboo hats and returns home. That night the statues reward him by leaving a huge mound of rice cakes and gold at his gate. The folktale is based on the popular belief that gods come to visit on New Year's Eve (see ŌTOSHI NO KYAKU).

Kasama 笠間[市]

City in central Ibaraki Prefecture, central Honshū. Kasama was a castle town and post-station town during the Edo period (1600–1868) and a shrine town of the Kasama Inari Shrine in the Meiji period (1868–1912). Stone quarrying is its main activity. Utensils for the tea ceremony, flower vases, and *sake* containers called Kasama ware are produced here. Pop: 30,811.

Kasamatsu 笠松[町]

Town in southern Gifu Prefecture, central Honshū; center of the Mino textile industry. Kasamatsu originally developed as an important river port; today, the textile industry, whose products include cotton, rayon, and chemical fibers, is active. Pop: 22,299.

Kasa no Kanamura 笠金村

(fl ca 715–733). Poet and courtier of the early Nara period (710–794). An important poet of the so-called third period of Man'yō poetry (see MAN'YŌSHŪ), he was one of a group of "poets laureate" during an age when poetry was being transformed from an art close to the ancient bardic tradition to a literary accomplishment of the entire court class. Of the 43 poems—11 CHŌKA (long poems) and 32 *tanka* (short poems; see WAKA)—associated with him in the *Man'yōshū*, 30 (8 *chōka* and 22 *tanka*) are specifically labeled as his; the others are indicated as from the Kanamura Collection (*Kanamura kashū*) and are believed to have been by him.

Kasaoka 笠岡[市]

City in southwestern Okayama Prefecture, western Honshū. Aside from its chemical and textile industries, the manufacture of *tansu* (wooden chests) and hats is important. Steel mills have also been constructed here. Farm products are flowers, fruit, and poultry. Kanaura Bay is a breeding area for the HORSESHOE CRAB. Pop: 59,619.

Kasaya Yukio 笠谷幸生

(1943–). Ski jumper; the first Japanese to win a gold medal in the Winter Olympics. Born in Hokkaidō; graduated from Meiji University. In the 1972 Sapporo Winter Olympic Games he won first place in the 70-meter jump.

Kaseda 加世田[市]

City in southwestern Kagoshima Prefecture, Kyūshū. It is known for its *shōchū* (distilled Japanese spirits) and its man-made gems. Rice, tobacco, mandarin oranges, grapes, tea, and vegetables are grown. Cattle raising also flourishes. The sand dunes on the coast, a part of FUKIAGEHAMA, attract tourists. Pop: 25,088.

kasen-e 歌仙絵

("pictures of immortal poets"). Idealized portraits of famous Japanese poets drawn from the artists' imaginations but following set conventions; usually painted in a series. A popular theme in the indigenous YAMATO-E painting tradition, especially during the Kamakura (1185–1333) and Muromachi (1333–1568) periods. The tradition originated in the early 12th century when pictures of the illustrious late-7th-century poet KAKINOMOTO NO HITOMARO became popular with courtiers. Sets of his portraits also illustrated two famous anthologies of WAKA poems: the *Sanjūrokunin sen* (ca 1008, Selection of Thirty-Six Poets) assembled by FUJIWARA NO KINTŌ, and the *Jidai fudō uta-awase* (Competition of Poems of Different Periods) compiled by the retired emperor GO-TOBA in the early 13th century. The 36 poets selected by Kintō became a popular subject, but other selections of 36 poets were also painted (see SANJŪROKKASEN).

Artists of the Edo period (1600–1868) reinterpreted the theme of *kasen-e* in strikingly new ways. A card game was devised based on the HYAKUNIN ISSHU, a poetry anthology by FUJIWARA NO SADAIE (Fujiwara no Teika; 1162–1241). The 100 cards used in this game, each depicting a poet with a representative poem, are a type of modern *kasen-e*. The game is still widely enjoyed, especially at New Year's.

kashi→oaks

kashiage 借上

Also called *kariage*. Usury or usurers of the Kamakura (1185–1333) and early Muromachi (1333–1568) periods. As a money economy developed, usurers became conspicuous in the Kamakura period, when many shogunal vassals (GOKENIN) fell deeply in debt to them. In 1239 the shogunate forbade estate stewards (JITŌ) to appoint creditors as deputies, and in 1240 it prohibited purchase of vassals' lands by usurers and proclaimed that such properties would be confiscated. Such measures did little to check this business, and it continued throughout the Muromachi period under the name DOSŌ.

Kashiba 香芝[市]

City in the west section of the Nara Basin, northern Nara Prefecture, central Honshū. Kashiba has been an important link between the cities of Nara and Ōsaka since ancient times. Vegetables, strawberries, and chrysanthemums are grown here. Kashiba is also a producer of socks and stockings, sandpaper, and cast-metal products. In recent years it has become a commuter suburb of Ōsaka. Pop: 52,817.

Kashihara 橿原[市]

City in northwestern Nara Prefecture, central Honshū. According to tradition, Kashihara was the site where JIMMU, Japan's legendary first emperor, is said to have been enthroned. Historical sites include the remains of the ancient capital FUJIWARAKYŌ, the mausolea of several emperors, and Kashihara Shrine. Pop: 115,554.

Kashihara Shrine 橿原神宮

(Kashihara Jingū). A Shintō shrine in the city of Kashihara, Nara Prefecture; dedicated to the spirits of the legendary first emperor,

JIMMU, and his consort, Himetataraisuzuhime no Mikoto. Built in 1889 to commemorate the founding of the Japanese nation, the shrine was refurbished and further expanded in 1940 to celebrate the 2,600th anniversary of Jimmu's supposed accession to the throne. The shrine is situated on the southeast slope of the mountain Unebiyama, the legendary site of the enthronement of Jimmu. The annual festival is held on 11 February, the traditional date for Jimmu's enthronement, which is a national holiday (formerly called Kigensetsu, now Kenkoku Kinembi).

Kashii Shrine 香椎宮

(Kashiigū). Shintō shrine in the Kashii district of the city of Fukuoka, Fukuoka Prefecture, Kyūshū; dedicated to the spirits of the legendary emperor Chūai and the legendary empress JINGŪ. Originally an imperial mausoleum, it was converted into a shrine in the second half of the 10th century. The main hall is built in a unique architectural style known as the *kashii-zukuri*. An annual festival is held on 29 October.

Kashikojima 賢島

Island in Ago Bay, town of Ago, southeastern Mie Prefecture, central Honshū. Separated from Honshū by a strip of water only 20 m (66 ft) wide. The chief activity is pearl culture. Area: 0.7 sq km (0.3 sq mi).

Kashima 鹿島[市]

City in southwestern Saga Prefecture, Kyūshū, on the Ariake Sea. The city developed in the Edo period (1600–1868) as a castle town. Local products are rice, mandarin oranges, *sake*, dairy products, seaweed (*nori*), and processed seafood. Its industries include machinery, pharmaceuticals, and readymade suits. Asahigaoka Park and Yūtoku Inari Shrine draw visitors. The city is the base for climbing the mountain TARADAKE. Pop: 34,336.

Kashima 鹿島[町]

Town in southeastern Ibaraki Prefecture, central Honshū, on the Pacific Ocean. The town developed as a shrine town around the KASHIMA SHRINE. Farm products include rice, sweet potatoes, and watermelons. In recent years, it has become a center of the Kashima Coastal Industrial Zone, producing steel, petrochemicals, metals, and machinery. Pop: 45,227.

Kashima Coastal Industrial Region 鹿島臨海工業地域

(Kashima Rinkai Kōgyō Chiiki). Industrial zone along the Pacific coast of Ibaraki Prefecture, central Honshū. Abundant water resources and the proximity of the Keihin (Tōkyō-Yokohama) region have contributed to the development of industries including steel, petroleum refining, petrochemicals, machinery, and electric power generation.

Kashima Oil Co, Ltd 鹿島石油[株]

(Kashima Sekiyu). Oil-refining company. Incorporated in 1967. Its products include liquefied petroleum gas (LPG), gasoline, naphtha, kerosene, gas oil, fuel oil, asphalt, and sulfur. The company supplies raw materials for the petrochemical industry and fuel for consumer and industry use. For the fiscal year ending March 1990, the company had annual sales of ¥252.8 billion (US $1.7 billion), and capitalization was ¥20.0 billion (US $130.7 million). Headquarters are in Tōkyō.

Kashima Sea 鹿島灘

(Kashima Nada). Arm of the Pacific Ocean off Ibaraki Prefecture, central Honshū. Extends approximately 70 km (43 mi) from the mouth of the river Nakagawa to the cape Inubōzaki. The meeting of cold and warm currents makes this area a rich fishing ground, and the coastal regions abound in shellfish. The Kashima Coastal Industrial Region is located along the southern section of the coast.

Kashima Shrine 鹿島神宮

(Kashima Jingū). Shintō shrine in the Kashima District of Ibaraki Prefecture; dedi-

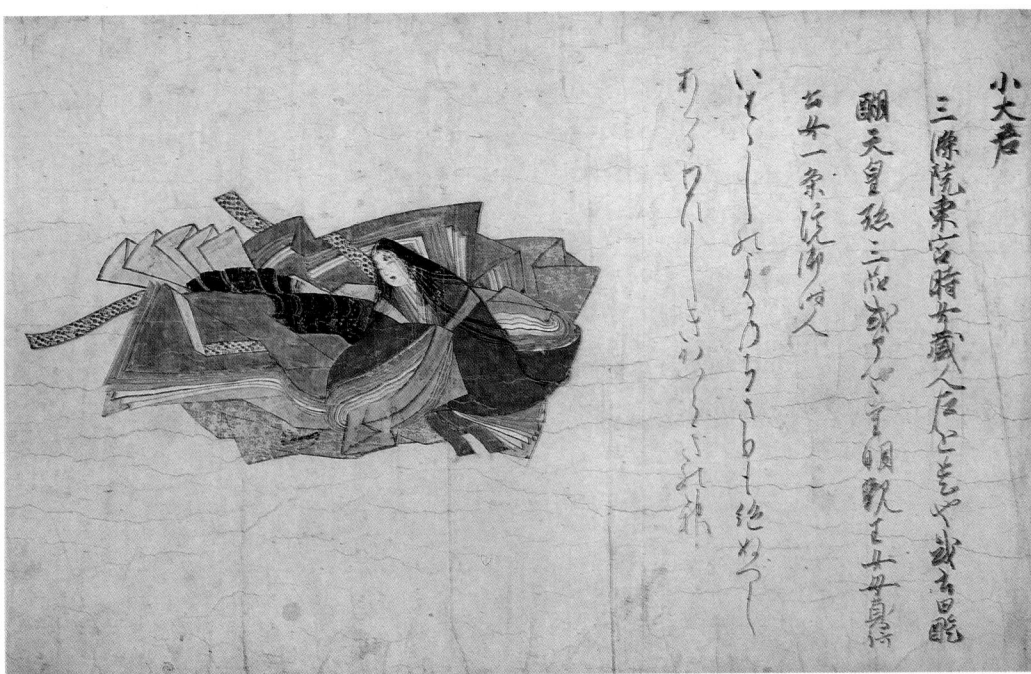

kasen-e The "immortal poet" depicted in this *kasen-e* is Kodai no Kimi. From the 13th-century *Satake-bon* handscroll, one of the earliest extant illustrated versions of Fujiwara no Kintō's *Selection of Thirty-Six Poets*. Colors on paper. 36 × 60 cm. Yamato Bunka-kan, Nara.

Kashii Shrine This shrine was converted from its original function as an imperial mausoleum in the late 10th century. Pictured is the shrine's central gate.

Kasuga Shrine Each of the four structures pictured enshrines a separate deity. Together they constitute the main hall of this shrine, noted for its unique style of architecture. The current buildings date from 1863. National Treasure.

Kasori shell mounds
1 This Final-Jōmon-period bowl uses an incised design rather than applied cord marks. Height 8 cm.
2 The patterns on this Final-Jōmon-period wide-mouth jar were created by the application of cord marks that were subsequently erased in selected areas. Height 24 cm.

cated to Takemikazuchi no Mikoto. This deity is believed to have descended to the Japanese islands together with Futsunushi no Kami (see KATORI SHRINE), ahead of NINIGI NO MIKOTO, to arrange for the transfer of the land to AMATERASU ŌMIKAMI's descendants. The deity has been associated with military prowess as well as with the imperial cause. An annual festival is held on 1 September. On 2 September of every 12th year the shrine observes the colorful ritual of sending a portable shrine (MIKOSHI) down the river Tonegawa to the Katori Shrine and back again. See also KASUGA SHRINE.

Kashimaura   鹿島浦

Coastal region composed of sand dunes along the Kashima Sea in southeastern Ibaraki Prefecture, central Honshū. The construction of Kashima Port, which was carved out of the southern part of the coast, led to the establishment of the Kashima Coastal Industrial Region. There are many beaches and campgrounds in the area. Length: 70 km (43 mi).

Kashima Yarigatake   鹿島槍ケ岳

Mountain on the border between Toyama and Nagano prefectures, central Honshū; one of the Hida Mountains. Composed of granite, the summit is divided into two peaks. The narrow northern ridge is marked by a series of deep sawtooth notches. The mountain is part of Chūbu Sangaku National Park. Height: 2,889 m (9,478 ft).

Kashiwa   柏[市]

City in northwest Chiba Prefecture, central Honshū. A post-station town on the high-

way Mito Kaidō during the Edo period (1600–1868), it developed into a commercial center with the opening of railway lines in the Meiji period (1868–1912). It is now primarily a residential district for commuters to Tōkyō, although vegetables are still grown. There is also a textile industry. Pop: 305,058.

Kashiwabara Hyōzō   柏原兵三

(1933–72). Novelist. Born in Chiba Prefecture; graduate of Tōkyō University. He was a professor of German literature at Meiji Gakuin University and later at Tōkyō University of Fine Arts and Music. His story "Tokuyama Dōsuke no kikyō" (1967, The Homecoming of Tokuyama Dōsuke), a humorous account of an old ex–army general similar to Kashiwabara's own grandfather, was awarded the Akutagawa Prize. Other works include his long autobiographical novel, *Nagai michi* (1969, The Long Road), and *Berurin hyōhaku* (1972, Wanderings in Berlin).

Kashiwagi Gien   柏木義円

(1860–1938). Also known as Kashiwagi Yoshimaru. Christian thinker and pastor. Born in what is now Niigata Prefecture; attended the Tōkyō Normal School (later Tōkyō University of Education); graduate of Dōshisha (now Dōshisha University), where he came under the influence of NIIJIMA JŌ. Kashiwagi became a pastor in the Annaka Church in Gumma Prefecture in 1897 and served there until his death. From 1898 until 1936 he published the *Jōmō kyōkai geppō* (Jōmō Church Monthly; 459 issues), advocating Christian pacifism and commenting on public affairs.

Kashiwara   柏原[市]

City in southeastern Ōsaka Prefecture, central Honshū. Traditional handicrafts include dyeing, bleached cotton, and shell products. There are also chemical and machinery plants. Principal farm products are grapes, strawberries, and vegetables. A cluster of ancient tombs (KOFUN) at Matsuoka and cave dwellings at Takaida are noteworthy. Pop: 76,819.

Kashiwazaki   柏崎[市]

City in central Niigata Prefecture, central Honshū, on the Sea of Japan. A post-station town on the highway Hokuriku Kaidō during the Edo period (1600–1868), it developed

as an oil town with the discovery of oil in nearby Nishiyama in the Meiji period (1868–1912). Machinery, metal, glass, and lumber-processing industries flourish. It is the site of a nuclear power plant. Pop: 88,309.

kasho   過所

Certificates of passage used from the Nara (710–794) to the Azuchi-Momoyama (1568–1600) periods. *Kasho* granted the bearer permission to pass through a barrier station (SEKISHO) or gave him exemption from tolls (SEKISEN) and served as a means of regulating internal traffic. From the Kamakura period (1185–1333) onward, when tolls were levied at barriers, *kasho* came to mean a certificate of waiver issued by the shogunate, a *daimyō*, or a large religious institution. In the Edo period (1600–1868) passage certificates came to be called *tegata*.

kasō   家相

Physical aspect (i.e., location, direction, construction) of buildings according to the art of geomancy. The basic concepts of geomancy (Ch: *fengshui*) originated in China during the Shang (Yin) dynasty (16th to 11th centuries BC) and were practiced, along with astrology and other forms of divination, in predicting the flooding of the Yellow River, in laying out palaces and cities, and in carrying on daily activities, e.g., determining directional taboos (KATATAGAE) and taboo days. In Japan *kasō* was used in the planning of two early capitals, FUJIWARAKYŌ (694–710) and HEIJŌKYŌ (710–784), and so was probably introduced to Japan from the continent about that time. A concept central to this form of geomancy is *kimon*, or inauspicious direction, generally regarded as the northeast. Even today houses are located and constructed to avoid this direction in the positioning of entrances and certain rooms such as the bath and toilet.

Kasori shell mounds   加曽利貝塚

(Kasori *kaizuka*). Archaeological site of the Middle (ca 3500 BC–ca 2000 BC) to Final (ca 1000 BC–ca 300 BC) Jōmon period; located in the city of Chiba, Chiba Prefecture, on a Pleistocene terrace cut by the river Miyakogawa. The site covers an area extending about 350 meters (1,150 ft) north to south and about 200 meters (650 ft) east to west and consists of two tangential ring-shaped SHELL MOUNDS and many small middens with deposits up to 2 meters (6.6 ft) thick. Excavations since 1887 have yielded PIT HOUSES, FLEXED BURIALS, STONE TOOLS, BONE ARTICLES, and JŌMON POTTERY.

Kasuga   春日[市]

City in northwestern Fukuoka Prefecture, Kyūshū. Once a farming village, during World War II it was the site of munitions plants. After the war a military base for the American OCCUPATION forces was located here. Returned to Japan in 1972, it became a base for the Self Defense Forces. Kasuga is known for the SUKU SITE, where Yayoi-period (ca 300 BC–ca AD 300) burial jars were excavated. Pop: 88,699.

Kasugai   春日井[市]

City in northwestern Aichi Prefecture, central Honshū, contiguous with NAGOYA to the northeast. Numerous paper and electrical-appliance factories were established after World War II, although peaches and cactus are still cultivated in its hilly areas. Mitsuzōin, a TENDAI SECT temple built over 600 years ago, is here. Pop: 266,599.

kasutera The recipe for this sponge cake, popular in Japan since the early Edo period, originally came from Portuguese traders in Nagasaki.

Kasuga Ikkō　春日一幸

(1910–89). Politician. Born in Gifu Prefecture, Kasuga studied at a communications school. After serving in the Aichi Prefectural Assembly, he was elected in 1952 to the House of Representatives as a candidate of the JAPAN SOCIALIST PARTY (JSP). Identified with the right wing of the JSP, he left in 1960 to help form the DEMOCRATIC SOCIALIST PARTY, becoming secretary in 1967 and serving as chairman from 1971 to 1977.

Kasuga no Tsubone　春日局

(1579–1643). Nurse of TOKUGAWA IEMITSU, the third Tokugawa shōgun. Given name Fuku. A daughter of Saitō Toshimitsu (d 1582), a retainer of AKECHI MITSUHIDE, she married and bore four children. She was asked by the shogunate to become Iemitsu's nurse and accepted the position after her husband Inaba Masanari divorced her. Through her skillful maneuvers Iemitsu became shōgun in 1623, and she later brought the entire women's quarters (ŌOKU) under her control.

Kasuga Shrine　春日大社

(Kasuga Taisha). Shintō shrine in the city of Nara; dedicated to the four deities of three shrines associated with the Fujiwara family: the KASHIMA SHRINE (the deity Takemikazuchi no Mikoto), the KATORI SHRINE (the deity Futsunushi no Kami), and Hiraoka Shrine (in the city of Higashi-Ōsaka; the married deities Amenokoyane no Mikoto and Hime no Kami). Kasuga Shrine was founded in 709 by FUJIWARA NO FUHITO to protect the new capital at Nara, on which construction was to begin the following year. Around 768 the shrine, which had been on the nearby mountain Mikasayama, was moved to its present location nearer the capital. The sacred symbol (*shimboku*, literally, "sacred wood") of the Kasuga Shrine was often carried into Kyōto in the 11th and the 12th centuries by protesting shrine servants (JINNIN) and WARRIOR-MONKS (*sōhei*) of the nearby KŌFUKUJI, a major Buddhist temple associated with the shrine, in an effort to intimidate the government. The shrine is noted for its unique style of architecture (*kasuga-zukuri*) and the many deer that inhabit the park around it. The deer are considered sacred messengers from the gods and often constitute a symbolic element in the so-called *Kasuga mandara* (see MANDALA). The annual festival (Kasuga Matsuri) is now celebrated on 13 March.

Kasugayama　春日山

Hill in the eastern part of the city of Nara, Nara Prefecture, central Honshū. It has been regarded since ancient times as a holy abode of various deities; its sacred trees have never been cut. At the foot of the hill is KASUGA SHRINE. Height: 497 m (1,631 ft).

Kasukabe　春日部〔市〕

City in eastern Saitama Prefecture, central Honshū, on the river Furu Tonegawa, about 30 km (20 mi) north of Tōkyō. During the Edo period (1600–1868) it prospered as a post-station town and market town. It is now a residential town for commuters to Tōkyō, although its traditional products, such as chests (*tansu*), battledores (HAGOITA), and clogs (GETA), are still manufactured. Pop: 188,823.

Kasumigaseki　霞ケ関

District in the southern part of Chiyoda Ward, Tōkyō, where Japan's central governmental institutions are located. During the Edo period (1600–1868) many *daimyō* mansions were situated in Kasumigaseki; from the Meiji period (1868–1912) it became a center for both civil and military bureaucracies. Today, the offices of most of the national government ministries are located in Kasumigaseki, along with the Tōkyō High Court, the Supreme Public Prosecutor's Office, the Metropolitan Police Department, and other administrative and judicial agencies. Japan's first modern high-rise, the 36-story Kasumigaseki Building, was built here in 1968.

Kasumigaura　霞ケ浦

Lake in southeastern Ibaraki Prefecture, central Honshū. Japan's second largest freshwater lake after Lake Biwa. Located within Suigō-Tsukuba Quasi-National Park. During the Edo period (1600–1868) it flourished as a transportation route. Smelt, eels, carp, crucian carp, prawns, goby, and corbicula are found in the lake. Area: 168 sq km (65 sq mi); circumference: 137 km (85 mi); depth: 7 m (23 ft).

kasuri　絣

(ikat). A kind of cloth, typically of hemp, ramie, or cotton, with hazed patterns of reserved white against a deep indigo-blue ground. The patterns are made by selectively reserving sections of thread to be used for warp or weft from the dye (as by binding some sections tightly with thread) in order to weave a predetermined pattern into the finished cloth. In the 14th century ikat was introduced to the Ryūkyū Islands from the south. The techniques and motifs developed there formed the basis of later Japanese *kasuri* weaving.

The earliest recorded *kasuri* weaving in Japan was in the mid-17th century in the remote Sea of Japan province of Echigo (now Niigata Prefecture). In the late 18th century there was a rapid proliferation and popularization of *kasuri* weaving throughout the country, and particular local characteristics and patterns emerged. The 19th and early 20th centuries saw the development of increasingly complex patterns, a proliferation of technical innovations, and the emergence of small cottage industries that were later replaced by modern factories.Today textile artists and fashion designers explore the rich potential of Japan's *kasuri* heritage. At the same time, old processes and designs are preserved in Niigata Prefecture (Ojiya *chijimi*), in Okinawa Prefecture, and in Kyūshū (*kurume-gasuri*).

kasutera　カステラ

Type of sponge cake made with wheat flour, eggs, and sugar, the preparation of which was learned from Portuguese who came to Nagasaki during the Sengoku period (1467–1568). It attained widespread popularity in Japan at the beginning of the Edo period (1600–1868) and thereafter developed independently of its Western origins. In recent years *kasutera* prepared with powdered green tea or with red *azuki* beans have appeared. The word *kasutera* is the Japanese approximation of the Portuguese pronunciation of the Spanish place name Castilla.

Kasumigaura Traditional fishing boats like these were once common on this lake but are now primarily tourist attractions. Nets for freshwater smelt are hung from lines stretching from the upper spar, bow, and stern.

Kasuya　粕屋〔町〕

Town in northern Fukuoka Prefecture, Kyūshū. Located east of the city of Fukuoka, with convenient transportation to the city, Kasuya has developed as a commuter suburb, and its population is growing rapidly. Flowers and vegetables are grown here. Pop: 29,697.

Katagami Noboru　片上伸

(1884–1928). Literary critic and scholar of Russian literature. Pen name Katagami Tengen. Born in Ehime Prefecture; graduate and later a faculty member of Tōkyō Semmon Gakkō (now Waseda University). In 1913 a collection of his literary criticism, *Sei no yōkyū to bungaku*, was published. His second visit to Russia, in 1924, reinforced his interest in the proletarian movement. He later became a pioneer of left-wing literary criticism. His principal works are the critical studies *Shizen shugi no shukanteki yōso* (1910), *Mugen no michi* (1915), and *Naizai hihyō ijō no mono* (1926).

katagi　気質

(character, turn of mind, spirit). An important concept of character in Japanese traditional popular psychology. The word originally meant a wooden board with carved designs used to print designs on paper and cloth. It later came to mean customs and habits and, eventually, the spirit, traits, or type of mind common to members of an occupational, age, or status group. Stories describing the *katagi* of members of various social categories (such as mistress, merchant, student, and farmer) constituted a genre (*katagi-mono*) of popular literature in the Edo period (1600–1868). *Katagi* among artisans (*shokunin katagi*), for example, was characterized by a fastidious devotion to one's work and pride in one's product, to the point of ignoring profit. It also implied the artisan's lack of social tact, his indifference to complicated interpersonal relations, and his honesty and naïveté.

Katagiri Katsumoto　片桐且元

(1556–1615). Warrior of the Azuchi-Momoyama (1568–1600) and early Edo (1600–1868) periods. Katsumoto gained fame as one of the "Seven Spears" (Shichihon'yari) of TOYOTOMI HIDEYOSHI in the 1583 Battle of SHIZUGATAKE; in 1595 he attained *daimyō* status. After Hideyoshi's death Katsumoto drew close to TOKUGAWA IEYASU and through his backing obtained a position in the household of TOYOTOMI HIDEYORI, becoming in effect the Tokugawa agent within the Toyotomi stronghold at Ōsaka Castle. Caught in the conflict between the Toyotomi and the Tokugawa that came to a head with the SHŌMEI INCIDENT

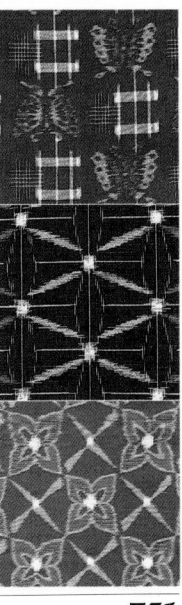

kasuri Three examples of *kurume-gasuri*, a style of ikat weaving with cotton.

katakuri This perennial mountain lily is now much depleted as a result of early spring flower hunters.
1 *Katakuri* blooming in clusters.
2 The flower, which typically faces sideways or downward, and the bulb.

Kataoka Chiezō This popular actor starred in many period films.

Kataoka Tamako
Portrait of Katsushika Hokusai. 1971. Folding screen. Colors on paper. 198 × 182 cm. Kamakura Museum of Modern Art, Kanagawa Prefecture.

(1614), Katsumoto unsuccessfully pleaded Hideyori's case before Ieyasu. Suspecting him of treason, Toyotomi hard-liners, such as ŌNO HARUNAGA and KIMURA SHIGENARI, planned to assassinate Katsumoto, but he was later allowed to leave Ōsaka unharmed. At the command of Ieyasu, he fought against Hideyori in the Ōsaka campaigns of 1614–15 (see ŌSAKA CASTLE, SIEGES OF), which ended in Toyotomi destruction. Katsumoto was rewarded by a large increase in his domains, but died three weeks after the castle's fall.

katakana→kana

katakiuchi　敵討

Blood revenge for the killing of an elder relation or, less often, a feudal superior. This type of vendetta was regularly justified in Japan by reference to the Chinese Confucian classics. The *Nihongi* (or NIHON SHOKI, 720), for instance, echoes such classic Confucian moral pronouncements as that found in the *Li ji* (*Li chi*; *The Book of Rites*): "No one should live under the same Heaven as his father's enemy." The archetype of the practice was for centuries the revenge exacted by the two Soga brothers in 1193, whose legend has been celebrated in literature from the SOGA MONOGATARI down to modern times. The cult of the vendetta rapidly gained momentum in the medieval period (mid-12th–16th centuries) and increasingly during the Edo period (1600–1868). Perhaps the most noteworthy feature of the Japanese practice of blood revenge is that the vendetta was not allowed to continue after the first revenge was taken. Furthermore, acts of revenge could only be aimed at the original murderer, not another member of his household.

Though *katakiuchi* flourished right up to the opening of Japan to the West, the Meiji government could not countenance the con-

tinuance of a practice that allowed avengers to usurp one of the functions of central authority, public justice. In 1873 a government decree formally declared blood revenge to be illegal, but it remains a popular subject of drama (see FORTY-SEVEN RŌNIN INCIDENT).

katakuri　片栗

(trout lily or dogtooth violet). *Erythronium japonicum.* Also known archaically as *katakago.* Perennial herb of the lily family (Liliaceae) growing wild mainly in wooded mountain areas throughout Japan. The rhizomes are white, succulent, scaly, and clustered deep under the ground. Early in spring a soft stalk (scape) sprouts 20–30 centimeters (8–12 in) high, a reddish purple flower (4–5 cm; 1.5–2.0 in) grows at the summit, and a pair of narrow, purple-spotted leaves grows at the lower middle.

The boiled young leaves and cooked bulbs are edible, but the bulbs, harvested from May to June, when the flower and leaves are gone, have generally been used to make a starch called *katakuriko,* which is used for food as well as for medicinal purposes. Dissolved in boiling water, it is used as an aid for intestinal problems.

katanagari→sword hunt

Katano　交野[市]

City in northeastern Ōsaka Prefecture, central Honshū. Formerly a rice-producing area, it is now a residential town for commuters to Ōsaka. Pop: 65,308.

Kataoka Chiezō　片岡千恵蔵

(1903–83). Actor. Real name Ueki Masayoshi. Born in Gumma Prefecture. He joined the Kataoka Youth Theater at age nine but left the stage to become a movie actor. He starred in Nakajima Hōzō's (life dates unknown) *Mange jigoku* (1927, Hill of Flowers) and gained popularity as a handsome swordsman. In 1928 Kataoka set up an independent production company that produced such excellent works as INAGAKI HIROSHI's *Tenka taihei ki* (1928, The Wandering Gambler), *Mabuta no haha* (1931, Visions of Mother), and *Ippon gatana dohyōiri* (1931, A Sword and the Sumo Ring), and ITAMI MANSAKU's *Kokushi musō* (1932, Peerless Patriot). The company dissolved in 1937, but Kataoka went on to star in such box-office successes as Inagaki's *Dokuganryū Masamune* (1942, One-Eyed Dragon: Masamune), UCHIDA TOMU's *Chiyari Fuji* (1955, Bloody Spear at Mt. Fuji), and Matsuda Sadatsugu's (also known as Matsuda Teiji; b 1906) *Ninkyō Tōkaidō* (1958).

Kataoka Kenkichi　片岡健吉

(1844–1903). Politician of the Meiji period (1868–1912). He was born into a *samurai* family in the Tosa domain (now Kōchi Prefecture). In 1868 he joined a squad of Tosa soldiers under the command of ITAGAKI TAISUKE and fought in the BOSHIN CIVIL WAR. After traveling to the United States and Europe to study foreign military systems (1871–73), he became a commander in the Imperial Navy, but in 1874 he joined Itagaki Taisuke in resigning from government service when a scheme to invade Korea was rejected (see SEIKANRON). The same year, he and Itagaki established the RISSHISHA, a political association, and Kataoka became an active proponent of the FREEDOM AND PEOPLE'S RIGHTS MOVEMENT. In 1875 he helped Itagaki found the AIKOKUSHA. In 1877 and again in 1880 he presented petitions to the govern-

ment demanding a national assembly, the second time as the representative of the LEAGUE FOR ESTABLISHING A NATIONAL ASSEMBLY. Kataoka was a key figure in the organization of Japan's first true political party, the JIYŪTŌ, in 1881. Arrested and imprisoned for antigovernment agitation in 1887, he was pardoned in 1889. After the Diet was established in 1890, Kataoka served in the House of Representatives until his death. He was instrumental in the formation of the KENSEITŌ and RIKKEN SEIYŪKAI political parties.

Kataoka Tamako　片岡球子

(1905–). Japanese-style (NIHONGA) painter. Born in Hokkaidō. Graduate of Joshi Bijutsu Semmon Gakkō (now Women's College of Fine Arts). Her work was first shown in 1930 at the semiannual Inten (Exhibition of the Japan Fine Arts Academy), which subsequently became the main outlet for her work. Kataoka opened up new territory for *nihonga* with an individualistic style involving intentional distortion of the subject. She received the Order of Culture in 1989.

Kataoka Teppei　片岡鉄兵

(1894–1944). Author. Born in Okayama Prefecture. A college dropout, he worked for several newspapers. In 1924 he participated in BUNGEI JIDAI, a magazine that gave birth to a coterie of talented new writers known as the SHINKANKAKU SCHOOL (School of New Sensibilities). He became a leading figure in the group, but his interest soon turned to the PROLETARIAN LITERATURE MOVEMENT. Imprisoned because of his Communist Party involvement, he left the movement in 1934. In his later years, he wrote popular fiction. His works include the short stories "Tsuna no ue no shōjo" (1926) and "Aijō no mondai" (1931).

kataribe　語部

A hereditary occupational group (BE) that specialized in reciting orally transmitted texts at court ceremonies in ancient times. According to the legal formulary ENGI SHIKI (927), during the Nara (710–794) and Heian (794–1185) periods *kataribe* were summoned from several provinces to recite at the court on the occasion of enthronement and thanksgiving ceremonies (DAIJŌSAI). Their recitations probably recounted legendary feats of military valor, such as passages from the chronicles KOJIKI (712) and NIHON SHOKI (720) describing the exploits of Emperor JIMMU. The *kataribe* members were long thought to have held official positions, but this has been conclusively disproved by the historian TSUDA SŌKICHI.

katashiro　形代

Object employed as a scapegoat in the exorcism of ritual impurities or evil influences (see KEGARE) in Shintō rites. The malignant influences are drawn into the *katashiro,* which is then floated away or burned. *Katashiro* are also termed *hitogata* (literally, "dolls"), from their common occurrence in the form of dolls or human effigies, or *nademono* ("things for rubbing"), from the practice of rubbing the scapegoat against the worshiper's body to absorb evil influences. Formerly, the observance of the DOLL FESTIVAL on the third day of the third month included a "Snake Day Exorcism" in which a doll was rubbed against the body and then set adrift on a river. Rites employing *katashiro* occur throughout Japan during the NAGOSHI observance. Local tutelary shrines distribute paper *katashiro* among their parishioners; the names and ages of family members are written upon the *katashiro*, which are then returned to the shrine for purification.

katatagae 方違え

Taboos about directions, based on OMMYŌDŌ (the ancient Chinese body of knowledge that sought to explain natural phenomena in terms of the *yin-yang* theory). During the Heian period (794–1185), it was customary to stay overnight at another place if one had to travel in the direction from one's home that was presided over by the god Nakagami (also known as Nagagami). Nakagami was believed to govern people's fortunes, both good and bad. He descended from heaven on a certain day, traveled from one direction to another in a prescribed order for a total of 44 days, and returned to his celestial abode for 16 days. The cycle was repeated endlessly, and it was in order to avoid Nakagami that *katatagae* was observed. It was considered safe to travel in any direction while the god was in heaven.

katauta 片歌

An early-8th-century poetic form of three lines in the pattern 5-7-7 (or sometimes 4-7-7) syllables. The *katauta* ("half poem") rarely appears alone and is usually set in the form of a dialogue, the second *katauta* answering a question posed by the first. *Katauta* are included in the chronicles KOJIKI (712) and NIHON SHOKI (720), but as the poetry anthology MAN'YŌSHŪ (ca 759) includes none, *katauta* seem to have disappeared early in the history of Japanese poetry.

Katayama Nampū 堅山南風

(1887–1980). Japanese-style (NIHONGA) painter. Real name Katayama Kumaji. Born in Kumamoto Prefecture. He studied under Takahashi Hirogo (1875–1912) and modeled his work after that of YOKOYAMA TAIKAN. His work was first shown at the 1913 BUNTEN exhibition. Katayama's mature style melded realistic and decorative elements. He received the Order of Culture in 1968.

Katayama Sen 片山潜

(1859–1933). A pioneering social worker, trade union organizer, and leader of radical political parties and movements. Born Yabuki Sugatarō in what is now Okayama Prefecture; he was adopted by the Katayama family and took the personal name Sen. Katayama studied in Tōkyō and then moved to the United States in 1884, attending various schools and finally studying at Andover Theological Seminary and Yale Divinity School. More important than his formal American schooling, however, was his conversion to the "socialistic" ideas then being spread by several Protestant denominations. Following a trip to England and Scotland to observe local social work, he returned to Japan in 1895.

In 1897 he became director of Kingsley Hall in Tōkyō, Japan's first modern settlement house. A few months later he was chosen as a leader in Japan's budding trade union movement. Katayama also became editor of *Rōdō sekai* (Labor World), Japan's first trade-union newspaper. Just before the RUSSO-JAPANESE WAR (1904–05) Katayama joined with KŌTOKU SHŪSUI and others in forming several socialist groups and parties, some of them pacifistic.

In December 1903 Katayama went to the United States and Europe for two years. His antiwar stance won him international fame, but intramovement quarrels among social-

ists in Japan muted his influence there. Returning to the United States in September 1914, Katayama became a permanent expatriate. Late in 1921 he went to Moscow and lived there until his death on 5 November 1933. Greatly respected by the Soviets as a spokesman for the struggling masses of Asia, Katayama was repeatedly appointed to the Presidium of the Third International (Comintern) and upon his death was honored by burial within the Kremlin Wall.

Katayama Tetsu 片山哲

(1887–1978). Politician and socialist leader; prime minister (1947–48). Born in Wakayama Prefecture; graduate of Tōkyō University. Katayama established a law office in Tōkyō. In 1926 he was a founder of the SHAKAI MINSHŪTŌ (Socialist People's Party). He was elected to the Diet in 1930. In 1932 Katayama joined the SHAKAI TAISHŪTŌ (Socialist Masses Party), but later left it to protest some of its actions. Immediately after World War II, Katayama helped form the JAPAN SOCIALIST PARTY. He headed a coalition cabinet in 1947, becoming Japan's first socialist prime minister, but resigned after eight months. As prime minister he created a new Ministry of Labor, revised the criminal code and Labor Standards Law, enacted the Antimonopoly Law, and oversaw the dissolution of the ZAIBATSU. He helped form the DEMOCRATIC SOCIALIST PARTY in 1960 and retired from politics in 1963.

katazome 型染め

(stencil dyeing). Textile-dyeing method. Stencils were used in dyeing from at least the late Muromachi period (1333–1568). A cutpaper stencil is placed over the cloth and glutinous-rice paste-resist (*nori*) is applied over it. When dry, the uncovered areas of the cloth are hand-dyed to allow for the production of either a repeated or a continuous pattern. Other methods include resist stenciling both sides of the fabric and then vat dyeing (*chūgata*); and direct dyeing by adding dye to the paste-resist before stenciling (*utsushizome*). Stencils (*katagami*) are most often made of mulberry paper treated with a prepared persimmon juice (*shibu*). Knife-cut stencils have a characteristic flowing line. After the paste-resist dries, the cloth is generally brush-dyed so that colors flow into one another, causing a misty blurring effect known as *bokashi*.

katei saibansho →family court

Katō Chikage 加藤千蔭

(1735–1808). Also known as Tachibana Chikage. KOKUGAKU (National Learning) scholar and WAKA poet. Born in Edo (now Tōkyō), he studied Kokugaku with KAMO NO MABUCHI. After his teacher's death in 1769, Katō became recognized as a leading figure in Kokugaku scholarship. Serving in a number of official posts for the shogunate until he was forced to retire from office in 1788, Katō also earned a reputation as a poet of the Edo school of *waka* with his elegant, urbane compositions. Principal works include a major commentary on the MAN'YŌSHŪ, the *Man'yōshū ryakuge* (1796–1812), which remains in high esteem today, and a collection of his *waka*, *Ukeragahana* (1802).

Katō Gen'ichi 加藤元一

(1890–1979). Physiologist known for his theory concerning nerve excitation and conduction. Born in Okayama Prefecture. Graduate of Kyōto University and professor at Keiō University. Katō succeeded in isolating

(or extirpating) single nerve fibers, and at the International Congress of Physiology in Rome in 1932 he demonstrated by means of motion pictures that the intensity and the conduction rate of excitation of nerve fibers was without decrement. Katō wrote *Seirigaku* (1925, Physiology), the first systematic textbook on physiology in Japanese.

Katō Hajime 加藤土師萌

(1900–1968). Ceramist. Best known for his reworking of late-Ming-dynasty (1368–1644) Chinese polychrome porcelain styles. He was born in the city of Seto, a ceramics center in Aichi Prefecture. He started his career as a ceramics designer but soon became a potter. Hajime opened his own kiln in Yokohama in 1940 and divided his time between potting and teaching. His many prizes include grand prizes at the 1938 Paris international exposition and the 1939 Brussels World's Fair. He also won the Chūnichi Cultural Prize in 1952.

Hajime was an authority on Oribe ware (see FURUTA ORIBE). He made outstanding MINO WARE and SETO WARE pottery and excelled in delicate Oribe-style pieces. His accomplished porcelains include re-creations of Chinese Song (Sung) dynasty (960–1279) white porcelain; colorful green-and-yellow-ground works with gold or silver decoration; strongly designed red, green, and yellow pieces (*aka-e*); subtle but strong underglazed-red works; and the first successful revival of the Ming-dynasty yellow-ground decorated pieces overglazed in red. In 1961 he was honored as one of the LIVING NATIONAL TREASURES for his polychrome porcelains.

Katō Hiroharu 加藤寛治

(1870–1939). Admiral. Also known as Katō Kanji. Born in what is now Fukui Prefecture; graduate of the Naval Academy. After serving as head of the Naval War College, he attended the WASHINGTON CONFERENCE of 1921–22 as a member of the delegation headed by KATŌ TOMOSABURŌ. In 1926 he was appointed commander in chief of the Combined Fleet. As head of the naval command, he opposed signing the disarmament treaty that resulted from the LONDON NAVAL CONFERENCES. When the cabinet of HAMAGUCHI OSACHI ratified the treaty, Katō accused the prime minister of interfering with the navy's prerogative of supreme command (see TŌSUIKEN).

Katō Hiroyuki 加藤弘之

(1836–1916). Political thinker and educational official of the Meiji period (1868–1912) who introduced German studies and Social Darwinism into Japan. Katō served the gov-

753
Katō Hiroyuki

ernment as president of Tōkyō University (1877–86; 1890–93), head of the Imperial Academy (1905–09), lecturer to the emperor, adviser to the Imperial Household Ministry, and member of the Senate (GENRŌIN) and House of Peers.

Born into a *samurai* family in the Izushi domain in Tajima Province (now northern Hyōgo Prefecture), Katō studied Western military science under SAKUMA SHŌZAN and WESTERN LEARNING with Ōki Nakamasu in Edo (now Tōkyō) from 1852 to 1859. As a teacher at the shogunate's BANSHO SHIRABE-SHO and Kaiseijo schools for Western studies between 1860 and 1868, he became the first Japanese to study German language and thought. He commended Western constitutionalism and democratic politics in *Rikken seitai ryaku* (1868, Survey of Constitutional Systems), *Shinsei taii* (1870, Outline of True Government), and *Kokutai shinron* (1875, New Thesis on the National Polity). In 1874 he joined the MEIROKUSHA society of Westernizing intellectuals. However, Katō was later drawn intellectually to a statist point of view, finding in Darwin, Spencer, and others the ingredients for his own evolutionary, positivist interpretation of the Japanese polity. From 1882 onward he defended state supremacy against the FREEDOM AND PEOPLE'S RIGHTS MOVEMENT. He propounded his doctrines of the organic state and of rights acquired through survival of the fittest in *Jinken shinsetsu* (1882, A New Theory of Human Rights).

Katō Shizue The feminist and politician at a press conference following her receipt of the United Nations Population Award in 1988.

Katō Takaaki In 1925, during this politician's term as prime minister, the vote was granted to almost all male citizens over the age of 25.

Katō Ichirō   加藤一郎

(1922–). Scholar of civil law. Born in Tōkyō, Katō graduated from Tōkyō University in 1943 and became a professor there in 1957. He served as president of Tōkyō University from 1969 to 1973 and as vice rector of the United Nations University from 1975 to 1976. In 1983 he became chancellor of Seijō Gakuen, a university and affiliated elementary and secondary schools in Tōkyō. Katō has done extensive research in the field of torts in order to aid victims of traffic accidents, environmental pollution, and medical malpractice. He has also published research on medical law and bioethics. Katō is a member of the Health and Welfare Minister's Committee on Life and Ethics and chairman of the Bioethics Committee of the Japan Medical Association. His publications include *Fuhō kōi* (1961, Torts).

Katō Kanji → Katō Hiroharu

Katokichi Co, Ltd   ［株］加ト吉

(Katokichi). Producer of frozen foods. Incorporated in 1956. The company has plants in Hong Kong, Korea, and Thailand. Sales for the fiscal year ending November 1990 totaled ¥93.6 billion (US $725.1 million), of which frozen foods accounted for 69 percent; frozen marine products, 28 percent; and other goods, 3 percent. The company was capitalized at ¥26.0 billion (US $201.4 million) in the same year. Headquarters are in Kannonji, Kagawa Prefecture.

Katō Kiyomasa   加藤清正

(1562–1611). *Daimyō* of the Azuchi-Momoyama period (1568–1600). Supposedly born in Nakamura (now part of the city of Nagoya) in Owari Province (now part of Aichi Prefecture). He served TOYOTOMI HIDEYOSHI (whose origins were in the same village), gained fame as one of his "Seven

Spears" (Shichihon'yari) at the Battle of SHIZUGATAKE in 1583, and was awarded a small fief. In 1588 Hideyoshi assigned him and KONISHI YUKINAGA the task of restoring order in Higo (now Kumamoto Prefecture), a province that had experienced a massive SAMURAI uprising. Higo was divided between the two, and Kiyomasa was allotted a large domain, centering on Kumamoto Castle, that established his status as a *daimyō*. In 1592 Yukinaga and Kiyomasa led Hideyoshi's invasion of Korea (see INVASIONS OF KOREA IN 1592 AND 1597). In 1597 Kiyomasa again led a force into Korea, but the Japanese withdrew after Hideyoshi's death in 1598. Kiyomasa then took the side of TOKUGAWA IEYASU; he helped secure northern Kyūshū for Ieyasu's party and was rewarded with most of Yukinaga's former holdings when Yukinaga and his allies were defeated by Ieyasu in the Battle of SEKIGAHARA; he thus became the master of a great domain. Kiyomasa died before relations between the Toyotomi and Tokugawa families had deteriorated into armed conflict (see ŌSAKA CASTLE, SIEGES OF).

Katō Kōmei → Katō Takaaki

Katō Kyōtai   加藤暁台

(1732–92). HAIKU poet from Nagoya. Along with Yosa BUSON, he tried to reform haiku along the lines that had been established by BASHŌ. Kyōtai was responsible for the first printing of the *Kyoraishō* (1775), an authoritative record of Bashō's teachings as set down by his disciple MUKAI KYORAI. Similarly, in *Aki no hi* (1772), a collection of verse sequences by Kyōtai and his disciples, he included an unpublished manuscript of verses composed by Bashō and others during a visit to Nagoya in 1688. Some 1,153 of his verses are collected in the *Kyōtai kushū* (1809).

Katō Michio   加藤道夫

(1918–53). Playwright. Born in Fukuoka Prefecture. Graduate of Keiō University. Inspired by the Japanese classics, he wrote *Nayotake* (1946), a poetic play based on the ancient tale TAKETORI MONOGATARI. After World War II, he joined BUNGAKUZA, a modern theater group, and started writing antirealistic plays that reflected the influence of the French playwright Jean Giraudoux. Other plays are *Episōdo* (1948, Episode) and *Omoide o uru otoko* (1951, The Man Who Sells Memories).

Katori Hotsuma   香取秀真

(1874–1954). Sculptor and poet. Real name Katori Shūjirō. Born in Chiba Prefecture. Graduate of Tōkyō Bijutsu Gakkō (now Tōkyō University of Fine Arts and Music). Katori was prominent among the artists who worked in metal casting during the first half of the 20th century. A TANKA poet and contributor to the magazine ARARAGI, he also wrote extensively on the history of metalworking. He was awarded the Order of Culture in 1953.

Katori Nahiko   楫取魚彦

(1723–82). KOKUGAKU (National Learning) scholar and WAKA poet. Born in Shimōsa (now Chiba Prefecture). Studied *kokugaku* under KAMO NO MABUCHI and in 1765 published *Kogentei*, a dictionary of classical words. In his *waka* verse, collected in *Katori Nahiko kashū* (1777), he employed the archaic diction of the 8th-century poetry anthology MAN'YŌSHŪ.

Katori Shrine   香取神宮

(Katori Jingū). Shintō shrine in the city of Sawara, Chiba Prefecture; dedicated to Futsunushi no Kami, a clan deity (UJIGAMI) of the FUJIWARA FAMILY. The date of the shrine's origin is not known. The shrine was believed to offer protection to military men. An annual festival is held on 14 April; it is celebrated in a particularly colorful fashion on 15 April every 12th year, when shrine parishioners, dressed in traditional warrior garb, transport a portable shrine (MIKOSHI) up the river Tonegawa to KASHIMA SHRINE and back.

Katō Sawao   加藤沢男

(1946–). Gymnast. Born in Niigata Prefecture; graduate of Tōkyō University of Education. He took first place in the men's individual combined exercises (all-around) at the 1968 Mexico City and the 1972 Munich Olympic Games. In the 1976 Montreal Olympics he won the gold medal in the parallel bars and led the Japanese men's gymnastics team to its fifth consecutive team championship. The eight gold medals he won during these three Olympic Games were a record number for a Japanese athlete.

Katō Shizue   加藤シヅエ

(1897–). Feminist and politician. Born in Tōkyō. In 1914 she graduated from the Joshi Gakushūin (Peeresses' School) and married Baron Ishimoto Keikichi. Accompanying her husband to the United States in 1919, she met the birth control advocate Margaret SANGER. Shizue returned to Japan the next year and began to campaign for safe FAMILY PLANNING and other women's rights. After her husband left her, Shizue supported herself and her two sons through writing and other work promoting social reform. This brought her in contact with labor leader Katō Kanjū (1892–1978); they married in 1944. In the first postwar election in 1946, Shizue and Katō were elected to the House of Representatives as candidates of the JAPAN SOCIALIST PARTY. She was then elected to the House of Councillors in 1950, remaining a member until 1974. She wrote two autobiographies: *Facing Two Ways* (1935; translated into Japanese, 1985) and *Hitosuji no michi* (1956, A Straight Road). In 1988 she received the United Nations Population Award.

Katō Shūichi   加藤周一

(1919–). Literary critic, author, and medical doctor. Born in Tōkyō; graduate of Tōkyō University. He taught at foreign universities and later at Sophia University, Tōkyō. His literary career began with *1946 bungakuteki kōsatsu* (1947), a collection of essays by Katō as well as NAKAMURA SHIN'ICHIRŌ and others. Among his writings are an antiwar novel, *Aru hareta hi ni* (1949); a collection of essays on Japanese culture, *Zasshu bunka* (1956); his autobiography, *Hitsuji no uta* (1968); a collection of essays on Japanese art, *Shōshin dokugo* (1972); and a history of Japanese literature, *Nihon bungaku shi josetsu* (1975).

Katō Shūson   加藤楸邨

(1905–93). HAIKU poet. Real name Katō Takeo. Born in Tōkyō; graduate of Tōkyō Bunrika Daigaku (now Tsukuba University). In the late 1920s he contributed haiku to *Ashibi*, a haiku magazine, and became a disciple of its chief editor, MIZUHARA SHŪŌSHI. He shifted, however, from the lyrical style of the Ashibi group to a more abstract and introspective style. As a poet of the so-called "human quest" school of abstract haiku in the mid-1930s and as the founder in 1940 of the magazine *Kanrai*, he exerted a significant influence on young haiku poets after World War II. He also contributed to the study of BASHŌ, the famous 17th-century haiku poet.

Katō Takaaki　加藤高明

(1860–1926). Statesman and politician. Also known as Katō Kōmei. Born Hattori Sōkichi, second son of a retainer of the Owari domain (now part of Aichi Prefecture). He was adopted at age 13 by Katō Buhei and educated at the Tōkyō Foreign Language School and at the Tōkyō Kaisei Gakkō (which was soon incorporated into Tōkyō University), where he studied English law. He maintained a lifelong admiration for the English parliamentary system, which he regarded as a model for Japan.

Katō joined the Mitsubishi company and enjoyed the patronage of IWASAKI YATARŌ, the company's founder. After two years of study in Britain, he became an assistant manager in the Mitsubishi home office in 1885 and married Iwasaki's eldest daughter the following year.

Katō turned to government service in 1887, becoming private secretary to Foreign Minister ŌKUMA SHIGENOBU in 1888 and participating in plans for the revision of the Unequal Treaties (see UNEQUAL TREATIES, REVISION OF). In 1894 he was appointed minister to Britain and worked to lay the foundation for the Anglo-Japanese Alliance concluded in 1902.

Between 1900 and 1913 Katō was appointed three times as foreign minister and served once again as minister to Britain, a post he had resigned in 1900 in a policy dispute. He also began a career in parliamentary politics, winning election to the Diet from Kōchi Prefecture in 1902 and becoming leader of the RIKKEN DŌSHIKAI party upon the death of its founder, KATSURA TARŌ, in 1913.

In April 1914 Katō returned as foreign minister and was largely responsible for Japan's decision to enter World War I, which angered the GENRŌ (elder statesmen), with whom he had not fully consulted. Katō aroused further controversy in January 1915 when he sent the so-called TWENTY-ONE DEMANDS to China, sparking fierce domestic and foreign opposition. Katō soon resigned as foreign minister, and in 1916 he was elected president of the newly formed KENSEIKAI party, which built its program around extension of suffrage, opposition to the *genrō*, and concession to growing popular demands for reform in areas such as labor, education, civil rights, and constitutional government.

In June 1924 Katō became prime minister at the head of a three-party coalition cabinet. Compared with the other cabinets of the Taishō period (1912–26) its legislative accomplishments were significant. The Universal Manhood Suffrage Law of April 1925 finally granted the vote to almost all male citizens over the age of 25. On the other hand, the PEACE PRESERVATION LAW of 1925, aimed at the repression of radical political organizations, had been passed only two months earlier.

Katō Takeo　加藤武男

(1877–1963). Banker. Born in Tochigi Prefecture. After graduating from Keiō Gijuku (now Keiō University), Katō joined Mitsubishi Gōshi Kaisha's banking division (now MITSUBISHI BANK, LTD) in 1901. He became the bank's president in 1943 and con-

currently served as a director in the central office of the MITSUBISHI *zaibatsu*, where his power was exceeded only by that of IWASAKI KOYATA. After World War II, Katō played a crucial role in regrouping Mitsubishi's firms.

Katō Tōkurō　加藤唐九郎

(1898–1985). Ceramist. Famous for his reproductions of Azuchi-Momoyama-period (1568–1600) TEA CEREMONY wares. Born in Seto, Aichi Prefecture, to an old potting family, he learned traditional techniques as a child and became an independent potter at age 15. In 1935 he established a kiln in Nagoya. Tōkurō played an important role in founding the Japan Ceramics Society (1947) and the Japan Crafts Society (1955).

In 1959 a pot thought to date from the Einin era (1293–99) was designated an Important Cultural Object by a committee of which Tōkurō was a member. A scandal erupted when ceramics researchers raised doubts about the pot's origin, and Tōkurō declared that he himself had made the pot in 1937. The designation was removed, and Tōkurō resigned his official positions.

Tōkurō was also a prolific author of articles and books on ceramics. His finely glazed and modeled Shino, Oribe, yellow-and-black Seto, Karatsu, IGA WARE, and SHIGARAKI WARE pieces are very similar to the ancient wares.

Katō Tomosaburō　加藤友三郎

(1861–1923). Admiral; prime minister (1922–23). Born in the Aki domain (now part of Hiroshima Prefecture); graduate of the Imperial Naval Academy. During the RUSSO-JAPANESE WAR (1904–05) he participated in the Battle of TSUSHIMA as chief of staff under Admiral TŌGŌ HEIHACHIRŌ. After serving as navy vice-minister and commander of the Kure Naval Station in 1915, he was named navy minister in the second ŌKUMA SHIGENOBU cabinet. He remained in that post for three succeeding cabinets. In 1921 Katō headed Japan's delegation to the WASHINGTON CONFERENCE and there signed the Naval Limitation Treaty of 1922. Named prime minister in 1922, he formed a cabinet mainly of bureaucrats and members of the House of Peers. He implemented the naval treaty and also saw to the withdrawal of Japanese troops stationed on the Shandong (Shantung) Peninsula since World War I. Katō died in office in August 1923.

Katō Works Co, Ltd　［株］加藤製作所

(Katō Seisakusho). Manufacturer of construction machinery. Incorporated in 1935. Noted for its oil hydraulic technology, the company has cultivated markets in Europe, Asia, and the United States. For the fiscal year ending March 1991, sales totaled ¥103.9 billion (US $757.3 million), of which exports accounted for 22 percent, and capitalization stood at ¥2.9 billion (US $21.1 million). Headquarters are in Tōkyō.

Katō Yukiko　加藤幸子

(1936–). Novelist. Real name Shiraki Yukiko. Born in Hokkaidō; graduated from Hokkaidō University. She received the Akutagawa Prize for *Yume no kabe* (1982, Wall of Dreams), which depicts the relationship between a Japanese girl and a Chinese father and child in Beijing (Peking) after World War II. Other works include *Hisui iro no messeiji* (1983, Jade Green Message) and *Toki no ikada* (1988, The Raft of

Time). Katō is also active in the conservationist movement.

katsudon　カツ丼

One-dish meal consisting of a bowl of rice topped with a mixture of ingredients, chief among which are egg and TONKATSU (a breaded deep-fried pork cutlet). To make it, the *tonkatsu* and sliced onions are simmered in a small pan in broth seasoned with soy sauce and *mirin* (sweet sake). Beaten eggs are added and the mixture is cooked until the egg is almost set, then removed from the pan and placed over the cooked rice in the bowl.

Katsu Kaishū　勝海舟

(1823–99). Statesman active during transition from the Tokugawa shogunate (1603–1867) to the new Meiji government. Also known as Katsu Rintarō and Katsu Awa. Born in Edo (now Tōkyō), Katsu was the eldest son of an impoverished, low-ranking retainer of the shogunate. He gained a reputation as an expert in Western military technology and was instrumental in the formation of the modern Japanese navy. At the time of the MEIJI RESTORATION in 1868 he acted as the chief negotiator for the Tokugawa shogunate, supervising its demise and ensuring that the transfer of power took place in an orderly, peaceful fashion.

By the 1850s Katsu had established a reputation as an expert in Western military technology and had been given an official appointment as a translator dealing with foreign affairs. In 1855 he was sent with other shogunal retainers to the KAIGUN DENSHŪJO in Nagasaki for naval training under Dutch instructors. In 1860 the mission to ratify the HARRIS TREATY sailed to the United States; Katsu was appointed captain of the KANRIN MARU, a Japanese warship built by the Dutch and the first modern Japanese ship to sail across the Pacific (see UNITED STATES, MISSION OF 1860 TO). Upon returning to Japan, Katsu was appointed commissioner of warships (*gunkan bugyō*) in 1862, and he established the Kōbe Naval Training Center.

In 1866 Katsu was called upon to negotiate a peace settlement between the shogunate and Chōshū (now Yamaguchi Prefecture), which was the most extremist of the antishogunate domains. When the shogunate collapsed in late 1867, some Tokugawa retainers argued for a last-ditch resistance, but Katsu argued that surrender was the only realistic course of action. Eventually Katsu's argument was accepted. On 5 and 6 April 1868 Katsu presented to SAIGŌ TAKAMORI, chief spokesman of the imperial forces, a series of proposals that would allow the Tokugawa family to retain considerable autonomy. Initially accepted, Katsu's compromise settlement was destroyed after the SHŌGITAI, a squad of prowar Tokugawa retainers, refused to accept defeat. After a brief battle, on 3 May Edo Castle was surrendered to the imperial forces and the Tokugawa family was stripped of its vast landholdings. Katsu followed the last shōgun, TOKUGAWA YOSHINOBU, into retirement in what is now Shizuoka Prefecture. From 1872 to 1875 Katsu returned to government service as the Meiji government's minister of the navy, becoming one of the more prominent of the many Tokugawa retainers who served the new regime. He spent the remainder of his life in scholarly pursuits, and in 1887 he was awarded the title of count.

katsudon This pork-cutlet-and-rice dish, one of the most popular of the various *domburi-mono* (one-bowl rice dishes), is often served with *miso* soup and pickles.

Katsu Kaishū This 19th-century statesman and expert in Western military technology was captain of the first modern Japanese ship to cross the Pacific.

Katsukawa school 勝川派

(Katsukawaha). School of UKIYO-E founded by KATSUKAWA SHUNSHŌ that flourished in the late 18th century. Because its branch schools produced numerous *yakusha-e* (portraits of actors), the Katsukawa school was referred to as the school of *yakusha-e* masters. In contrast to the traditional style of the TORII SCHOOL, the style of the Katsukawa school was realistic, and the school helped establish the *nigao-e* style ("likeness portrait" style) of *yakusha-e*. However, the school was overshadowed by the UTAGAWA SCHOOL and gradually fell into decline.

Katsukawa Shun'ei 勝川春英

(1762–1819). UKIYO-E illustrator, print designer, and comic artist specializing in portraits of SUMŌ wrestlers and KABUKI actors. His given name was Isoda Kyūjirō. His first prints, portraits of actors modeled on the work of his teacher KATSUKAWA SHUNSHŌ, were published in 1782.

In the 1780s the Katsukawa artists had a virtual monopoly on full-color woodblock portraits of kabuki actors. Monopoly led to demand, and in 1790 after Shunshō had retired and Shunkō, his eldest pupil, had fallen ill, the task of meeting these demands fell upon Shun'ei, who drastically simplified his style of composition and drawing. In 1792 Shun'ei simplified his drawing style even further and began designing prints with broad expanses of color, which influenced SHARAKU, UTAGAWA TOYOKUNI, and other actor portraitists of the 1790s. His 20 portraits of actors in scenes from *Chūshingura* (Treasury of Loyal Retainers) published in 1795 are of superior quality. From 1800 he concentrated on portraits of wrestlers and comic prints.

Katsukawa Shunshō 勝川春章

(1726–93). Painter and UKIYO-E print designer. Born in the Kamigata (Kyōto–Ōsaka) region; his family name was Fujiwara and his given name was Yōsuke (later Yūsuke). Active in Edo (now Tōkyō) during the 1760s through the 1780s, Shunshō is noted for his realistic portraits of *kabuki* actors, *sumō* wrestlers, and legendary warriors. He was the primary force behind the KATSUKAWA SCHOOL of ukiyo-e artists. His actor prints utilized fully the multicolor technique refined by HARUNOBU. By assigning each actor readily recognizable, individual features he revolutionized kabuki actor portraiture.

A student of Miyagawa Shunsui, as a painter he first called himself Miyagawa (and Katsumiyagawa) but eventually settled on the name Katsukawa Shunshō. Throughout his long career he signed his paintings and prints using various names. Because of the jar-shaped seal that he sometimes used, he is also known as Tsuboya or Tsubo Shunshō (from the Japanese word for jar, *tsubo*). His many pupils—all with names that begin with "Shun"—include Shunrō (later Katsushika HOKUSAI).

Katsuki Yasuji 勝木保次

(1905–). Physiologist. Born in Ishikawa Prefecture. Graduate of Tōkyō University. Professor at Tōkyō Medical and Dental University from 1949 to 1970. Katsuki carried out research on the auditory mechanism and made notable contributions in the field of sensory physiology and the development of the auditory function. His research into the lateral line organ of various species of fish confirmed that the evolutionary origins of the organs of hearing and taste are the same. He received the Order of Culture in 1973.

Katsumoto Seiichirō 勝本清一郎

(1899–1967). Literary critic. Born in Tōkyō; graduate of Keiō University. A Marxist, he became involved in the PROLETARIAN LITERATURE MOVEMENT in the late 1920s and lived in Germany from 1929 to 1933. After returning to Japan in 1933, he began critical study of modern Japanese literature. In 1935 he helped found the JAPAN P.E.N. CLUB but was expelled from it in 1938 for his political views. After World War II, he served as chairman of the Japan Commission for UNESCO and lectured at Keiō and other universities. His principal works of criticism are *Zen'ei no bungaku* (1930) and *Kindai bungaku nōto* (1948).

Katsunuma 勝沼[町]

Town in central Yamanashi Prefecture, central Honshū. It developed as a post-station town on the highway Kōshū Kaidō in the Edo period (1600–1868). The area is Japan's oldest center for the production of grape wine. Pop: 8,649.

Katsunuma Seizō 勝沼精蔵

(1886–1963). Physician. Born in Shizuoka Prefecture. Graduate of Tōkyō University. He elaborated on the histochemical study of oxidase. In 1919 he histocytologically described oxidoreductases (redox enzymes) in cells and clarified their relationship to tissue iron. For this work he received the Imperial Prize of the Japan Academy in 1926. He also carried out comprehensive studies on geriatrics and aeromedicine. He was a member of the Japan Academy from 1947 and became president of Nagoya University in 1949. He received the Order of Culture in 1954.

katsuo → bonito

katsuobushi 鰹節

Bonito fillet that has been steamed and dried. *Katsuobushi* is shaved into paper-thin flakes and used as an ingredient in many types of Japanese cooking. Stock (*dashi*) made from *katsuobushi* and *kombu* (a type of seaweed) is used to impart flavor to many Japanese dishes. *Katsuobushi* flakes are also sprinkled on TŌFU when it is served cold and on dishes such as *ohitashi*, parboiled leafy greens.

Katsura Bunraku VIII 桂文楽8代

(1892–1971). RAKUGO (comic monologue) storyteller. Real name Namikawa Masuyoshi. Born in Tōkyō, he studied with Katsura Konan I (1880–1947). In 1920 he assumed the name Katsura Bunraku VIII, though he was only sixth in the Katsura Bunraku line, because the Chinese character for 8 is thought to bring good luck. Although he specialized in *rakugo* classics, he made them seem modern with his lively storytelling style. Among the stories for which he was best known were "Nedoko" (Sleeping Place) and "Akegarasu" (Crows Cawing at Dawn).

Katsurada Fujirō 桂田富士郎

(1867–1946). Pathologist. Born in what is now Ishikawa Prefecture. Graduate of Ishikawa Prefectural Medical School. A pioneer in the field of parasitology in Japan, Katsurada is known for his research on distomiasis, an endemic disease in Okayama Prefecture, and for his discovery of *Schistosoma japonicum* (1904). He taught at Okayama Igaku Semmon Gakkō (now the medical faculty of Okayama University). He was awarded the Japan Academy Prize in 1918.

Katsura Detached Palace 桂離宮

(Katsura Rikyū). The 17th-century country villa of the imperial princely family Hachijō no Miya. The estate is situated on the west bank of the Katsura River (Katsuragawa) in Nishikyō Ward, Kyōto, and maintained by the Imperial Household Agency. It includes a main house, or hall, with special quarters for imperial visits; four smaller pavilions for entertaining in the estate's various gardens; several belvederes for landscape viewing; and a small Buddhist chapel. The estate compound is about 7 hectares (17 acres) in area and contains a large pond for boating with several islands connected by bridges and paths.

The principal structures are among the finest examples of the SUKIYA-ZUKURI style of residential architecture. Prince Toshihito (1579–1629) of the Hachijō no Miya family built the section of the main house known as the Old Shoin (Ko Shoin) and some of the other buildings between around 1620 and around 1625. His son Prince Toshitada (1619–62) built the Middle Shoin (Chū Shoin), the Music Room (Gakki no Ma), and most of the other buildings between around 1641 and around 1662, using deliberately rustic details in the teahouses and garden pavilions.

Katsura Detached Palace has acquired a considerable reputation among 20th-century architects in Europe and the United States, among them Bruno TAUT, who have been impressed by its simplicity of form, natural materials, interpenetration of interior and exterior spaces, and richness of detail. Permission to visit the estate must be obtained from the Imperial Household Agency.

☎ 758–759

Katsuragawa 桂川

River in western Kyōto, Kyōto Prefecture. A section of a longer river that originates in the Tamba mountains and flows into the Yodogawa. The Katsuragawa is the part of the lower reaches of the river between ARASHIYAMA and the point where it joins the Yodogawa. The section above Arashiyama as far as Kameoka is called the Hozugawa, and the part above Kameoka is called Ōigawa. Numerous ancient tombs and remains of Nagaokakyō Palace are located along the river. Length: 31 km (19 mi).

Katsuragawa Hoshū 桂川甫周

(1751–1809). Physician and scholar of WESTERN LEARNING. Together with MAENO RYŌTAKU and SUGITA GEMPAKU, he undertook the first translation into Japanese of a Western anatomy book, *Ontleedkundige Tafelen* (1734, Anatomical Tables), a Dutch version of a German work. Their translation was published as KAITAI SHINSHO (1744, New Book of Anatomy). Carl Peter THUNBERG, a physician at the Dutch trading post in DEJIMA, wrote admiringly of Hoshū, as did the trade commissioner Izaak TITSINGH. In 1777 Hoshū became shogunal physician, the fourth family member to hold the position. He also taught at the Igakukan, the shogunate's school of medicine. Among his works are *Hokusa bunryaku*, (1794) which chronicled the adventures in Russia of the shipwrecked sailor DAIKOKUYA KŌDAYŪ, and a work on coastal defense strategy.

Katsura Bunraku VIII This *rakugo* storyteller was regarded as one of the 20th-century masters of the art.

Katsura Tarō This Meiji-period prime minister promoted Japan's development as a major imperialist power in East Asia.

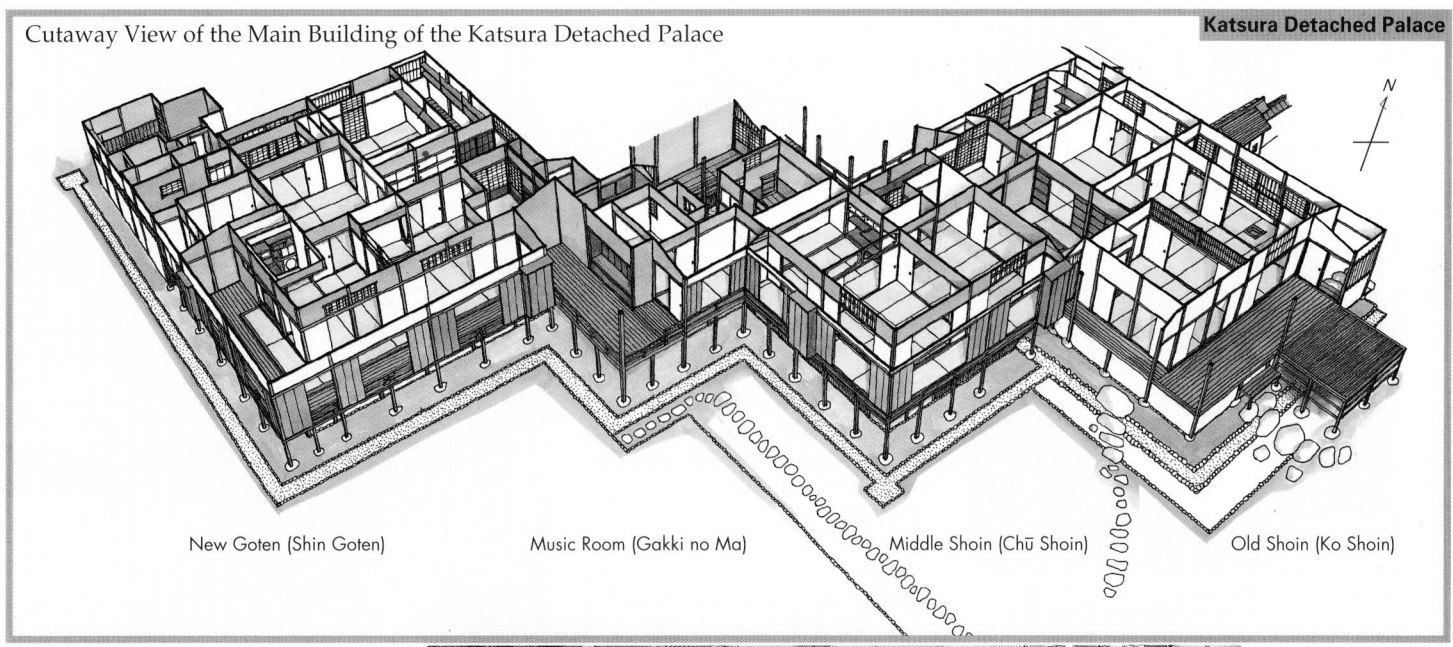

Cutaway View of the Main Building of the Katsura Detached Palace

New Goten (Shin Goten)   Music Room (Gakki no Ma)   Middle Shoin (Chū Shoin)   Old Shoin (Ko Shoin)

Katsurahama   桂浜

Coastal area located on Urado Bay in the southern part of the city of Kōchi, central Kōchi Prefecture, Shikoku. White-sand beaches lined by pines and rocks and reefs are notable and have made the area a tourist and resort spot. An aquarium and a bronze statue of SAKAMOTO RYŌMA are located here. Length: approximately 700 m (2,300 ft).

Katsura Kogorō → Kido Takayoshi

Katsura-Taft Agreement
桂・タフト協定

(Katsura-Tafuto Kyōtei). Memorandum signed by American Secretary of War William Howard Taft and Japanese Prime Minister KATSURA TARŌ on 29 July 1905, immediately before the termination of the RUSSO-JAPANESE WAR (1904–05). The agreement included Japanese recognition of US sovereignty in the Philippines, endorsement of close working relations between the two countries, and American recognition of Korea as a Japanese protectorate. The agreement, kept secret until 1924, was not legally binding and was meant to clarify Japanese-US relations.

Katsura Tarō   桂太郎

(1847–1913). Army general and politician of the Meiji period (1868–1912) who held key positions in the army command and served as prime minister in three cabinets (1901–06, 1908–11, 1912–13). Born in Hagi, the castle town of the Chōshū domain (now Yamaguchi Prefecture). At age 17 he joined the movement in Chōshū against the Tokugawa shogunate and fought in some of the major campaigns leading up to the MEIJI RESTORATION of 1868. In the early 1870s he studied military science in Germany, and served as military attaché to the Japanese embassy in Germany from 1875 to 1878. In 1884 and 1885 he again visited Europe to study military systems. Promoted to major general in 1885, he served in several key military posts, including vice-minister of the army. After serving as general of the Third Division under the command of his mentor, YAMAGATA ARITOMO, during the SINO-JAPANESE WAR OF 1894–1895, Katsura was appointed governor-general of Taiwan in 1896 and then army minister in successive cabinets from 1898 to 1900.

In 1901 Katsura became prime minister, and in the succeeding years he presided over

a series of foreign policy moves that established Japan as a major imperialist power in East Asia: the ANGLO-JAPANESE ALLIANCE of 1902, the RUSSO-JAPANESE WAR of 1904–05, and Japan's annexation of Korea in 1910 (see KOREA, ANNEXATION OF). In domestic politics, Katsura engaged in a complex struggle for power with the RIKKEN SEIYŪKAI, the majority party in the lower house of the Diet. He sustained his prime ministerships through a compromise with the party by which he agreed to alternate the premiership with SAIONJI KIMMOCHI, the party's president. Although this period is often referred to as the Katsura-Saionji decade, it was primarily through HARA TAKASHI, the party secretary, that this compromise arrangement was worked out. Katsura became increasingly unpopular through the course of the decade, however, as a symbol of domainal and military clique politics (see HAMBATSU; GUMBATSU) and as the sentiment spread that he was using his office to further his personal ambitions and the interests of the military at the expense of the people. This mistrust exploded into popular riots in late 1912 and

1913, shortly after the death of the Emperor Meiji, in what is known as the TAISHŌ POLITICAL CRISIS. Instead of compromising, Katsura responded to this unrest by organizing his own political party, the RIKKEN DŌSHIKAI, in an attempt to establish an independent base of support for himself. Popular opinion and Seiyūkai opposition, mobilized in the so-called MOVEMENT TO PROTECT CONSTITUTIONAL GOVERNMENT, forced Katsura's resignation as prime minister in February 1913. He died eight months later.

katsura tree   桂

(katsura). Cercidiphyllum japonicum. Deciduous tree of the family Cercidiphyllaceae that grows wild in mountainous regions throughout Japan. It is known for the beauty of its spring and autumn foliage. The erect trunk reaches a towering height of 27 meters (89 ft) with a diameter of 1.3 meters (4.3 ft). The leaves are opposite, broadly ovate, heart-shaped at the base, and slightly

Continued on page 760 →

Katsura Detached Palace A bird's-eye view of the estate compound. Overlooking the large artificial pond at the center of the photograph are the main house (left) and a teahouse (right).

757

katsura tree

Katsura Detached Palace: Modern Design before Its Time

A view of the main house with the section known as the Old Shoin (Ko Shoin) prominent in the foreground.

A shōji screen and a sliding door inside the Shōkintei teahouse.

Architects throughout the world have long admired the Katsura Detached Palace for its clean lines, its prominent display of natural materials, and its seamless integration of interior and exterior space. Although this country retreat was built by 17th-century Japanese aristocrats who prized stark simplicity and a rustic look for religious and aesthetic reasons, it anticipates many of the innovations created by modernist architects. The rhythmic repetition of plain rectangular elements—*tatami* mats, *shōji* screens, or paving stones, for example—creates a dynamic set of interlocking grids reminiscent of a Mondrian painting. Larger expanses, like the whitewashed or earthen walls and the verandas with overlapping eaves, are broken up by borders of plain trim or slim pillars into smaller segments which maintain the proportional rhythms of the composition at large. Offsetting the rectilinear modules that dominate the architecture are the irregular shapes of natural forms. The latter are not only present in the gardens but have been incorporated into structural elements of the buildings as well.

The imperial princes who built the Katsura Detached Palace had certainly never heard of modernist principles. They stressed natural materials, stripped away decoration, and laid structure bare because they equated purity of design with clarity of perception. By pursuing these values with unrelenting rigor, they created a villa that seems refreshingly "modern" even in the wake of modernist architecture.

The Shōkintei teahouse, situated to the east of the main house.

Paving stones at the entrance to the Old Shoin.

A garden view from inside the Middle Shoin (Chū Shoin) section of the main house. The ink painting on the sliding door is attributed to Kanō Naonobu, a member of the famous Kanō family of painters.

Kawabata Ryūshi
Kokaji (The Blacksmith). This work, in which a manifestation of the deity Inari assists a master smith in forging a famous sword, was inspired by a scene from the Nō play of the same name. 1955. Six-panel screen. Colors on paper. 243 × 728 cm. Ryūshi Memorial Hall, Tōkyō.

pointed at the tip, with serrated edges. The tree is dioecious, and flowers lacking sepals and petals grow before the leaves in late spring.

At the AOI FESTIVAL held each May in Kyōto, branches of *katsura* are used to decorate the oxen and horses, apparently because *katsura* leaves resemble those of the *futaba aoi* plant (*Asarum caulescens*) from which the festival takes its name. The lightweight, warp-resistant wood has wide uses in construction and carpentry. The leaves are used to make incense; the bark, which contains tannin and resists decay, is used as roofing material.

Katsushika Hokusai → Hokusai

Katsushika Ward   葛飾区

(Katsushika Ku). One of the 23 wards of Tōkyō. Between the rivers Arakawa and Edogawa. A residential area, it is undergoing rapid industrialization. Tourist attractions are Mizumoto Park and the temple Shibamata Taishakuten. Pop: 424,801.

Katsu Shintarō   勝新太郎

(1931–). Actor and director. Real name Okumura Toshio. Born in Tōkyō. He made his acting debut in Tasaka Katsuhiko's (1914–79) *Hana no byakkotai* (1954, White Tiger Brigade). He won popular acclaim as the reckless outlaw Asakichi in Tanaka Tokuzō's (b 1925) *Akumyō* (1961, The Rogue) and as the blind swordsman ZATŌICHI in the film series (begun in 1962) of the same name. Katsu also starred in MASUMURA YASUZŌ's *Heitai yakuza* (1965, Hoodlum Soldier). In 1967 he founded Katsu Productions.

Katsuta   勝田〔市〕

City in eastern Ibaraki Prefecture, central Honshū, on the river Nakagawa. Originally a farming village, Katsuta became industrialized after the establishment of a plant by Hitachi, Ltd, in 1940. Pop: 109,825.

Katsuura   勝浦〔市〕

City in southeastern Chiba Prefecture, central Honshū, on the Pacific Ocean. Katsuura is principally a fishing port, with the largest catch in the prefecture after CHŌSHI. The morning fish and vegetable market is said to have a history of 300 years. The view from OSENKOROGASHI, a precipice, draws many visitors. Pop: 25,334.

Katsuyama   勝山〔市〕

City in northeastern Fukui Prefecture, central Honshū, on the river KUZURYŪGAWA. It developed as a castle town in the Edo period (1600–1868) and as a terminus for river transportation. Originally a tobacco-growing region, Katsuyama was the home of a textile industry during the Meiji period (1868–1912). Today a synthetic fiber industry flourishes. Pop: 29,805.

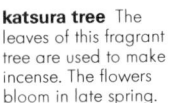

katsura tree The leaves of this fragrant tree are used to make incense. The flowers bloom in late spring.

Kauffman, James Lee

カウフマン, J. L.

(1886–1968). American lawyer and teacher. Born in Pennsylvania, he studied at Princeton and at Harvard, where he earned an LLB in 1911. From 1913 to 1919 he taught Anglo-American law at Tōkyō University. He later founded an architectural firm and was responsible for the Marunouchi Building and other modern structures in Tōkyō. After World War II, he worked for Japan's economic recovery, giving advice to the supreme commander for the Allied powers (SCAP) and facilitating the introduction of foreign capital. He was decorated by Japan with the Order of the Sacred Treasure and the Order of the Rising Sun.

Kawabata Bōsha   川端茅舎

(1900–1941). HAIKU poet. Real name Kawabata Nobukazu. Born in Tōkyō. Around 1920 he became a disciple of TAKAHAMA KYOSHI, the leader of the school of traditional haiku associated with the magazine HOTOTOGISU, and contributed frequently to the magazine. Although he adopted Kyoshi's basic style of objective description of flowers and birds, Bōsha's haiku contain bold metaphors and have a spirit of religiosity. His principal haiku collection is *Kegon* (1939).

Kawabata Gyokushō   川端玉章

(1842–1913). MARUYAMA-SHIJŌ SCHOOL painter and book illustrator. Real name Kawabata Takinosuke. Born in Kyōto to a family of lacquerers. He studied with the Maruyama-school painter Nakajima Raishō (1796–1871) and also trained in BUNJINGA (literati painting) with Oda Kaisen (1785–1862). In 1866 he settled in Edo (now Tōkyō). He briefly studied Western-style painting with Charles WIRGMAN in Yokohama. He won bronze medals at national painting competitions in 1882 and 1884, which earned him recognition.

Gyokushō screened the Japanese-style paintings submitted to the world fairs in Paris (1900) and St. Louis (1904). He taught Japanese-style painting at the Tōkyō Bijutsu Gakkō (now Tōkyō University of Fine Arts and Music) from 1890 to 1912. In 1909 he established his own painting school. In 1896 he was appointed an artist for the imperial household (*teishitsu gigeiin*). His style tended to employ strong outlines contrasting with areas of color and wash, a compromise between the softer, traditional approach and Western realism.

Kawabata Ryūshi   川端龍子

(1885–1966). Japanese-style painter and principal advocate of *kaijō geijutsu* ("art for the exhibition place"), a philosophy that emphasized the public nature of art. Real name Kawabata Shōtarō. Born in Wakayama Prefecture, he moved to Tōkyō in 1895. He studied Western-style painting (YŌGA) at the studios of the White Horse Society (HAKUBAKAI) and the Pacific Painting

Society (Taiheiyō Gakai). In 1914 he took up Japanese-style painting (NIHONGA). In 1928 he formed his own group, the Seiryūsha. In 1959 he was awarded the Order of Culture.

Kawabata Yasunari   川端康成

(1899–1972). Japanese novelist; the only Japanese to be awarded the Nobel Prize in literature (1968). Born in Ōsaka. He was orphaned at an early age and soon lost his only sister and the grandmother with whom he lived. The death of his grandfather, his last near relative, is described in his earliest surviving work, "Jūrokusai no nikki" (1925, Diary of a Sixteen-Year-Old).

For some years thereafter he lived in school dormitories in suburban Ōsaka. In 1917 he entered the First Higher School in Tōkyō and in 1920 the English literature department of Tōkyō University. A year later he transferred to the Japanese literature department and graduated in 1924. His literary activities as a student attracted the attention of such eminent literary figures as KIKUCHI KAN, and he was one of the earliest contributors to Kikuchi's magazine, BUNGEI SHUNJŪ. He was also a member of a literary group, the SHINKANKAKU SCHOOL.

The novelist MISHIMA YUKIO described Kawabata as "the eternal traveler." Kawabata once said of himself that he was chiefly attracted by "islands in a distant sea." The first of several traveler's lodgings that are important to his writing was on the Izu Peninsula south of Tōkyō. "Izu no odoriko" (tr "The Izu Dancer," 1955), based on a visit to Izu, was published in two installments in 1926 and made him famous. It tells of a despondent high-school student who, on a walking trip down the Izu Peninsula, makes friends with the young dancer of the title and returns to Tōkyō in much improved spirits. The story is successful because of the dashes of melancholy and even bitterness that cut through what might otherwise be cloying sweetness.

Kawabata left many of his writings unfinished. His notions of form were such that the incidents along the way were more important than the conclusions. He was fond of likening himself to a practitioner of RENGA, or linked verse. Another striking aspect of the Kawabata novel is the delicate balance between the actors and the background against which the action takes place. Human life seems very fragile and precarious and constantly on the point of fading away into nature.

In his early professional years Kawabata was the chief exponent of a form called *tanagokoro no shōsetsu* or "palm-of-the-hand story," which might more freely be rendered "vignette" or "short, short story." He thought of the form as peculiarly Japanese, in the tradition of HAIKU. Some of his best stories are in collections called *Tanagokoro no shōsetsu*. For some two decades, beginning while still a student at Tōkyō University, Kawabata regularly wrote critical reviews of new writing, and his part in discovering new writers was considerable. From a later period, his most important find was probably Mishima. Kawabata also busied himself in cinema. His script for *Kurutta ippeiji* (1926, A Page of Madness), directed by KINUGASA TEINOSUKE, has become a classic of the experimental cinema.

Asakusa, Snow Country, War Years

From the late 1920s the Asakusa district in Tōkyō, then the most lively of the plebeian entertainment districts, became for Kawabata an island in a distant sea. His most significant "Asakusa piece" is *Asakusa kurenaidan* (Scarlet Gang of Asakusa), serialized in 1929 and 1930, with an unfinished sequel in 1934 and 1935. The influence of Edo-period (1600–1868) literature is so strong as to make it seem almost imitative; *Kurenaidan* is not typical Kawabata. The investigation of lonely lives on the edges of the Asakusa demimonde, however, brings it close to the central preoccupations of Kawabata's writing. His most famous essay, "Matsugo no me" (1933, Eyes in Their Last Extremity), is from the same period. It is a meditation on death, another of his central preoccupations. *Suishō gensō* (1931, Crystalline Fantasy) is his main exercise in stream-of-consciousness writing.

The next traveler's lodging or distant island to become important in his writing was the "snow country" along the Sea of Japan. It is the setting for *Yukiguni* (tr *Snow Country*, 1956), which is generally numbered among his masterpieces and parts of which were published in several magazines from early 1935. After some rewriting it appeared in book form in 1937. There were subsequent additions and an attempt at a conclusion that did not satisfy Kawabata. Not until 1948 was the final version published in book form. Although the chronological sequence of the story is complex, the plot is simple, telling of an affair between a Tōkyō dilettante and a mountain-town *geisha* and of the man's resolve not to visit the snow country again. The meeting of the traditional in the form and in the natural description and of the modern in the theme and characterization is most effective.

Never a prolific writer, Kawabata published little during the war years. The first installment of *Meijin* (tr *The Master of Go*, 1972) appeared in 1942. The work was not published in book form until 1954. It is a delicately fictionalized account of a *go* match that took place in 1938 and that Kawabata reported on for a major newspaper. The "master" of the title entered the match, which was to be his last, as an undefeated champion and lost.

Postwar Years—Kawabata was by now among the recognized leaders of the literary world. As president of the JAPAN P.E.N. CLUB and one of the more frequently translated of modern authors, he had gained considerable international fame even before he was awarded the Nobel Prize in 1968.

His two most important postwar works, *Sembazuru* (tr *Thousand Cranes*, 1959) and *Yama no oto* (tr *The Sound of the Mountain*, 1970), were written around the same time. The first installment of *Sembazuru* appeared in 1949, and the work was, to all appearances, finished in 1951. In 1953, however, with a short story treating the same characters, Kawabata began what seems to have been intended as a sequel of considerable length. It was never finished. The first installment of *Yama no oto* also appeared in 1949, and the last in 1954. The gradual accretion of the two works is typical of Kawabata's methods. *Sembazuru* was brought to what may seem an adequate conclusion, then continued, and finally left dangling.

Sembazuru centers upon the tea ceremony and upon hopeless love. The hero is drawn to the mistress of his deceased father, and, after her suicide, to her daughter, who flees from him. At the end of the 1951 version, the hero is left alone with a remarkably

unpleasant teacher of the tea ceremony, also a former mistress of his father's. The tea ceremony seems not so much to provide a beautiful foil for ugly human affairs as to emphasize Kawabata's fascination with death. People die, but the vessels of the tea ceremony remain, still bearing the marks of the dead.

Yama no oto, also a tale of impossible love, is set in Kamakura, Kawabata's home from 1936 until his death. The hero is an old man who has little affection for his children and for whom his wife is an object of a certain wry amusement but not of passion. He is strongly drawn to someone whom he cannot have, his daughter-in-law, and over much of the action hovers the ghost of someone whom he could not have, his sister-in-law. At the end of the story he thinks of going back to the old family home, but the story does not see him on his way.

Last Years, Death—In his last years Kawabata became a master of what might be called the literature of the aged, of which *Yama no oto* is an example. An even better example is *Nemureru bijo* (tr *House of the Sleeping Beauties*, 1969), a novelette or long story published in several installments in 1960 and 1961. An old man frequents a most unusual house of pleasure, which purveys drugged maidens to old men no longer sexually capable. Old men spend nights fondling girls and going no further, and the girls are too deeply drugged to respond.

Nemureru bijo and other works of Kawabata's late years also feature a withdrawal from society. Kawabata experimented with increasingly extreme aspects of isolation. The most extreme example, perhaps, is "Kataude" (tr "One Arm," 1969), published serially in 1963 and 1964. In it a man spends a night with the severed but still living arm of a young girl. For the man as well as for Kawabata, society has withered quite away, and attempts to bring it back in his last writings are somehow wanting in conviction.

On the evening of 16 April 1972, Kawabata was found dead in a gas-filled room in an apartment he owned not far from his Kamakura home. Everything suggested suicide, and the consensus is that he died by his own hand. There was no suicide note, however, and among his close associates there are those who still argue accident.

kawabiraki 川開き

("river opening"). Annual festival celebrating the beginning of summer. Though the festival is held in a number of cities, the one in the Ryōgoku section of Tōkyō is particularly famous and has a long, intermittent history. In the Edo period (1600–1868) the festival marked the start of a three-month period during which city dwellers went out to enjoy the cool of evening. Since the Meiji period (1868–1912) it has been celebrated on the last Saturday in July with an elaborate display of fireworks. The term *kawabiraki* also refers to the opening day of the river fishing season.

Kawachi Nagano 河内長野[市]

City in southern Ōsaka Prefecture, central Honshū. Metal and *sake*-brewing industries are active. The city is also known for its toothpicks. Farm products include rice and mandarin oranges. Tourist attractions include the temple Kanshinji, associated with the warrior KUSUNOKI MASASHIGE, and the temple Emmeiji, said to have been founded by KŪKAI. Pop: 108,767.

Kawagoe 川越[市]

City in central Saitama Prefecture, central Honshū. Kawagoe developed as a castle town. The city still has traditional warehouse-style merchant houses, built of wattle and daub (*dozōzukuri*). Although chemical and foodstuff industries thrive, Kawagoe is chiefly a commuter suburb of Tōkyō. Tourist attractions are the Kitain temple and the Kawagoe Festival in October. Pop: 304,854.

Kawaguchi 川口[市]

City in southeastern Saitama Prefecture, central Honshū. The river Arakawa separates the city from Tōkyō. The principal occupation is iron casting. Machinery, textiles, and electrical-appliance industries are also well developed. In recent years it has virtually become a suburb of Tōkyō. The Angyō section in the northeastern part of the city is known for its BONSAI and tree nurseries. Pop: 438,680.

Kawaguchi Ekai This Buddhist monk and scholar made two lengthy expeditions to Tibet, India, and Nepal in search of Buddhist texts in their original languages.

Kawaguchi Ekai 河口慧海

(1866–1945). Buddhist monk, scholar, and explorer. Born in Sakai. He studied at INOUE ENRYŌ's institute of philosophy known as the Tetsugakukan and in 1890 became a monk of the ŌBAKU SECT of Zen Buddhism in Tōkyō. He twice embarked on trips to Tibet, India, and Nepal in search of original Sanskrit and Tibetan Buddhist texts. On his second sojourn in India and Tibet (1905–13), he exchanged with the Panchen Lama complete sets of Japanese and Tibetan Buddhist texts (DAIZŌKYŌ). Known for his progressive views, Kawaguchi renounced his priestly status in 1935. He taught at Taishō University. Among his publications are *Chibetto ryokōki* (1904), published in London in 1909 in an English version titled *Records of a Tibetan Journey*, and a Tibetan grammar book.

Kawaguchi, Lake 河口湖

(Kawaguchiko). In southeastern Yamanashi Prefecture, central Honshū. One of the FUJI FIVE LAKES, it is located directly north of Mt. Fuji (FUJISAN) and was created by a dam formed by lava flows. The upside-down image of Mt. Fuji reflected in the lake is a tourist attraction. Area: 5.6 sq km (2.2 sq mi); circumference: 21 km (13 mi); depth: 14.6 m (47.9 ft); altitude: 831 m (2,726 ft).

Kawaguchi Matsutarō 川口松太郎

(1899–1985). Novelist, playwright, and stage and film producer. Born in Tōkyō. Raised in a poor family, he left home at age 14. He started to write while working at various jobs. In 1935 he won the first Naoki Prize for his short story "Tsuruhachi Tsurujirō" (1934). His serialized novel *Aizen katsura* (1936–38), a melodramatic love story about a nurse and a doctor, gained him tremen-

Kawaguchi Matsutarō A popular writer and successful stage and film producer.

Kawai Gyokudō
Cormorant Fishing. 1931.
Colors on silk. 87 × 117
cm. Tōkyō University of
Fine Arts and Music.

dous popularity. He was long associated with DAIEI CO, LTD, a motion picture company. In 1965 he was elected to the Japan Academy of the Arts.

Kawahara Keiga   川原慶賀

(ca 1786–ca 1860). Painter of Edo-period (1600–1868) Western-style pictures (see WESTERN-STYLE PICTURES, EARLY). He sometimes signed his works "Tojosky," a Westernization of his given name Toyosuke. Born in Nagasaki, Keiga was an apprentice in his family's print shop and later became the disciple of Ishizaki Yūshi (1768–1846), who chronicled the artifacts and activities of the Hollanders residing on the island of DEJIMA in Nagasaki Bay.

Over a period of six years Keiga worked with Dr. Philipp von SIEBOLD (1796–1866), a German physician who arrived in Japan in 1823, illustrating von Siebold's botanical and ethnological studies. Scandal involving von Siebold's attempt to smuggle from the country maps of the Japanese coastline brought an end to Keiga's official relationship with Dejima in 1829. After a brief exile, Keiga returned and, changing his name to Taguchi, continued to produce secular and religious portraits, landscapes, *ukiyo-e* paintings, and woodblock prints. His pictures reflect in varying degrees the amalgamation of European and indigenous YAMATO-E styles.

Kawahigashi Hekigotō   河東碧梧桐

(1873–1937). HAIKU poet. Real name Kawahigashi Heigorō. Born in Ehime Prefecture. He began writing haiku under the guidance of MASAOKA SHIKI, a leader in the modern haiku movement. He contributed many haiku to HOTOTOGISU, the magazine founded by Shiki in 1897. He and TAKAHAMA KYOSHI became Shiki's two most important disciples. After Shiki's death in 1902, he left the magazine. He advocated a more progressive form called *shinkeikō haiku* (new trend haiku), which discarded both the traditional

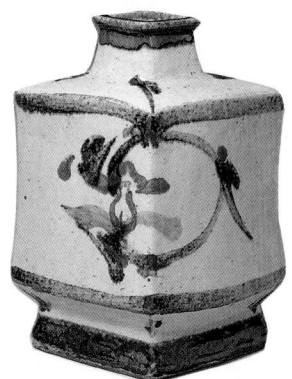

Kawai Kanjirō Flask
with floral design. 1939.
Height 33 cm. National
Museum of Modern Art,
Kyōto.

metric pattern of 5–7–5 syllables and the use of "season words" (*kigo*). His principal works include the collection of travel essays *Sanzenri* (1906–08) and the haiku collection *Hekigotō kushū* (1916).

Kawai Eijirō   河合栄治郎

(1891–1944). Scholar and publicist. He was born in Tōkyō, studied political science at Tōkyō University, and taught social and industrial relations policy there (1920–39). Kawai was particularly influenced by the thought of English idealist Thomas Hill Green (1836–82), who stressed the importance of the individual's self-realization. While still a student Kawai learned about the desperate living conditions of Japanese industrial workers. To help promote their well-being he became a factory inspector in the Ministry of Agriculture and Commerce. When his superiors rejected the position paper he wrote for the first conference of the International Labor Organization (1919), he resigned and became a university professor.

Kawai advocated extensive public ownership of the means of production, along the lines of the British Labour Party, and opposed Marxism, communism, and fascism. He continued to voice his dissent from Japan's increasingly totalitarian politics in the 1930s. Indicted in 1938 for dissemination of dangerous ideas from the West in violation of the PUBLICATION LAW OF 1893, he was forced to surrender his faculty position. The Kawai Eijirō case, the biggest "thought trial" of the time, lasted six years and ended in his conviction. He died soon afterward.

Kawai Gyokudō   川合玉堂

(1873–1957). Japanese-style painter. Real name Kawai Yoshisaburō. Born in Aichi Prefecture. He went to Kyōto in 1887 to study with KŌNO BAIREI, a teacher of the MARUYAMA-SHIJŌ SCHOOL of painting. He also studied with HASHIMOTO GAHŌ, a master of the KANŌ SCHOOL. In 1907 he was a judge for the first annual Ministry of Education exhibit, the BUNTEN. He was invited to teach at the Tōkyō Bijutsu Gakkō (now Tōkyō University of Fine Arts and Music) in 1915 and was elected to the Imperial Fine Arts Academy (Teikoku Bijutsuin) in 1919. In 1940 he received the Order of Culture. Most of his paintings are preserved and exhibited at the Gyokudō Art Museum in Ōme, outside Tōkyō.

Kawai Kanjirō   河井寛次郎

(1890–1966). Artist-potter. Born in Shimane Prefecture; graduate of the Ceramics Department at Tōkyō Industrial College. Kawai, HAMADA SHŌJI, and YANAGI MUNEYOSHI organized the Nihon Mingei Kyōkai (Japan Folk Art Association), which began publishing the crafts magazine *Kōgei* in 1931 and opened the JAPAN FOLK-CRAFT MUSEUM in Tōkyō in 1936. Kawai's ceramics before World War II remained close to Japanese and Korean folk-art traditions, with considerable influence from English slip-decorated folk pottery (see Bernard H. LEACH). After the war Kawai developed his own distinctive, personal style of ceramic art. His slab-mold bottle-vases and boxes are prized for their original, sculpturesque shapes. These pieces often have lively, high-relief, slip-trailed decoration touched with various brightly colored glazes, such as *gosu* (poorly refined cobalt-oxide blue with interesting iron-oxide brown inclusions) and *shinsha* (underglaze copper red). Kawai spent most of his adult life in Kyōto. His kiln and tradi-

tional Japanese house there are now a museum. See also FOLK CRAFTS.

Kawai Michi   河井道

(1877–1953). Educator and Christian activist. Born in Mie Prefecture. She attended a mission school in Sapporo and graduated in 1904 from Bryn Mawr College in Pennsylvania. She helped TSUDA UMEKO and others establish Japanese branches of the Young Women's Christian Association (YWCA). She became the first general secretary of the Japanese YWCA. In 1929 she founded Keisen Jogakuen (Keisen Girls' School). After World War II, she helped establish Japan's system of two-year junior colleges.

Kawai Musical Instruments Mfg Co, Ltd   [株]河合楽器製作所

(Kawai Gakki Seisakusho). Manufacturer and vendor of musical instruments such as pianos, digital pianos, electronic organs, and electronic keyboards. Founded in 1927, it was incorporated in its present form in 1951. The firm's growth is based on a national direct-sale system, the operation of music and physical fitness classrooms, and subscription sales. It has subsidiary companies in the United States, Germany, Canada, and other countries and exports to over 80 countries. Sales for the fiscal year ending March 1991 totaled ¥101.4 billion (US $739.1 million). In the same year the export ratio was 15 percent and capitalization stood at ¥3.6 billion (US $26.2 million). Headquarters are in the city of Hamamatsu, Shizuoka Prefecture.

Kawai Sora   河合曽良

(1649–1710). HAIKU poet. Disciple of BASHŌ. Born in Shinano Province (now Nagano Prefecture). He went to Edo (now Tōkyō), where he studied SHINTŌ and WAKA. He accompanied Bashō on several journeys, including the one that resulted in Bashō's OKU NO HOSOMICHI (1694; tr *The Narrow Road to the Deep North*, 1966). Sora's diary of that journey is indispensable for the study of this famous work.

Kawai Suimei   河井酔茗

(1874–1965). Poet. Real name Kawai Matahei. Born in Ōsaka Prefecture. He gained recognition for his romantic and lyrical poems, which appeared in the literary magazine *Bunko* during his 13-year editorship through 1907. He encouraged the poets YOKOSE YAU, KITAHARA HAKUSHŪ, and KAWAJI RYŪKŌ. Around 1910 he began to write poems in the vernacular and advocated free-verse poetry written in modern Japanese. He was elected to the Japan Art Academy (Nihon Geijutsuin) in 1937. His principal collections include *Mugenkyū* (1901) and *Tōei* (1905).

Kawai Tsugunosuke   河井継之助

(1827–68). Official of the Nagaoka domain (now part of Niigata Prefecture). He assisted the *daimyō* in carrying out financial reforms. At the time of the BOSHIN CIVIL WAR (1868–69) he recommended that Nagaoka remain neutral, but when the domain's stance was interpreted as hostility Kawai decided to fight the imperial forces and died in battle.

Kawaji Hot Spring   川治温泉

(Kawaji Onsen). Located near the upper reaches of the river Kinugawa, northwestern Tochigi Prefecture, central Honshū. A simple thermal spring; water temperature 42°–47°C (108°–117°F). Located within Nikkō National Park, the site has been in continual use since the Edo period (1600–1868). Scenic spots in the area include Lake Ikari and the gorge called Ryūōkyō.

Kawaji Ryūkō 川路柳虹

(1888–1959). Poet and critic. Real name Kawaji Makoto. Born in Tōkyō; graduate of the Tōkyō School of the Arts (now Tōkyō University of Fine Arts and Music), where he studied Japanese painting. His poems published in 1907, especially the free-verse poem "Hakidame," had a great impact as the first to be composed in the modern spoken language. He received the 1957 Japan Art Academy Award for his poetry collection *Nami* (1957, Waves). Other works include the poetry collections *Robō no hana* (1910, Flowers by the Wayside) and *Ayumu hito* (1922, Walking Man) and numerous essays on art.

Kawaji Toshiakira 川路聖謨

(1801–68). Official of the Tokugawa shogunate (1603–1867); major participant, with his brother INOUE KIYONAO, in the events that terminated Japan's two centuries of NATIONAL SECLUSION. Kawaji distinguished himself as an administrator and rose rapidly in the shogunate hierarchy. In 1852 he was appointed commissioner of finance (*kanjō bugyō*) and placed in charge of coastal defense. The following year he was sent to Nagasaki to negotiate with the Russian envoy Evfimii Vasil'evich PUTIATIN, who sought to open commercial relations with Japan. In 1855 he concluded a treaty of friendship with Russia modeled after the KANAGAWA TREATY with the United States. In 1858 Kawaji accompanied HOTTA MASAYOSHI to Kyōto in an unsuccessful attempt to win imperial sanction for the HARRIS TREATY. Kawaji was placed under house arrest in 1859 by the great elder (*tairō*) II NAOSUKE for supporting the losing faction in the 1858 shogunal succession dispute, but he returned to prominence after Ii's assassination in 1860. As commissioner of foreign affairs (*gaikoku bugyō*), he was later active in shaping the foreign policy of the shogunate. He committed suicide the day after Edo Castle, the seat of the Tokugawa regime, was surrendered to imperial forces.

Kawakami Bizan 川上眉山

(1869–1908). Novelist; poet. Originator of the so-called *kannen shōsetsu* (idea or concept fiction). Real name Kawakami Akira. Born in Ōsaka, he studied at Tōkyō University. Bizan associated with such writers as OZAKI KŌYŌ and YAMADA BIMYŌ and in late 1886 joined the group known as the KEN'YŪSHA. He later associated with writers from the magazine *Bungakukai* (ca 1893) and with the literary group known as the Ryūdokai (ca 1904).

Bizan's earliest works fall into two categories: melodramatic love stories and short, floridly descriptive pieces. The latter category was crowned by *Futokoro nikki* (1897), a HAIBUN-style travel account considered Bizan's masterpiece. Bizan's fiction became deeply pessimistic as he moved toward the social criticism that marks his brief *kannen shōsetsu* period. Generally limited to 1895, this period produced such works as *Ōsakazuki*, *Shokikan*, and *Uraomote*. Bizan earned his greatest critical acclaim for these works, which were vaguely anchored in philosophical concepts and contained a blend of bitter misanthropy and slashing social censure. Bizan's works of 1902–03, all of which were set in agricultural villages, can be viewed as an extension of the *kannen shō-*

setsu or as forerunners of the *shakai shōsetsu* (social novel). In his last period Bizan showed some influence from NATURALISM; *Kannon iwa* (1903–07), *Harin* (1907), and other novels exhibit the standard naturalistic concentration on sex. As a novelist Bizan made a determined effort to break with old patterns of fiction, but too often his characterizations are stereotyped, plots are romantic and subjective, and structure is sketchy and disjunctive.

Kawakami Gen'ichi 川上源一

(1912–). Businessman. Born in Shizuoka Prefecture. Graduated from Takachiho Commercial School (now Takachiho Commercial University). Kawakami joined Nippon Gakki Co, Ltd (now YAMAHA CORPORATION), in 1938. He replaced his father, Kawakami Kaichi (1885–1964), as president in 1950. In 1955 he separated the motorcycle division from his company and turned it into an independent firm, YAMAHA MOTOR CO, LTD. He retired from Yamaha in 1992. Kawakami established the Yamaha Music Foundation, which now operates a nationwide chain of music schools.

Kawakami Hajime 河上肇

(1879–1946). Economist instrumental in introducing Marxism into Japan in the period following World War I. Born in Iwakuni, Yamaguchi Prefecture, the eldest son of a former *samurai*. Graduate of the Law Faculty of Tōkyō University in 1902. In 1905 he published the first Japanese translation of E. R. A. Seligman's *The Economic Interpretation of History* (1902) and a series of articles entitled "Shakai shugi hyōron" (A Critique of Socialism), which established his reputation as a social critic. He was professor of economics at Kyōto University from 1908 to 1928. His most famous work, *Bimbō monogatari* (Tale of Poverty), was written after he had visited England and seen social conditions there. Serialized in the newspaper *Ōsaka asahi shimbun* in 1916 and published in book form in 1917, *Bimbō monogatari* was Kawakami's last major publication before his conversion to Marxism.

Kawakami initiated his study of Marxism in 1919, but his persistent call for moral as well as institutional reform and his failure to view history in terms of dialectical materialism led critics to question his grasp of it. A series of academic exchanges in the 1920s with two of his major critics—KUSHIDA TAMIZŌ, his former student, and FUKUMOTO KAZUO, leader of the newly reorganized Japan Communist Party—forced Kawakami to revise his interpretations. Under pressure from Fukumoto he also felt compelled to engage in revolutionary practices. In 1932 he joined the Communist Party, and in January 1933 he was arrested. He was released in 1937 but spent the remaining years of his life in seclusion writing his autobiography, which became a best seller immediately after World War II.

Kawakami Jōtarō 河上丈太郎

(1889–1965). Politician. Born in Tōkyō; graduate of Tōkyō University. Influenced by KINOSHITA NAOE, he became interested in socialism. He was elected to the House of Representatives (1928) as a member of the Nihon Rōnōtō (Japan Labor-Farmer Party). He participated in forming the postwar Japan Socialist Party (Nihon Shakaitō) but was barred from office under the OCCUPATION PURGE for having served in the IMPERIAL RULE ASSISTANCE ASSOCIATION (Taisei Yokusankai). He was de-

purged in 1951, and in 1952 he became chairman of the right wing (*uha*) of the Japan Socialist Party. He resigned after both wings were reunited in 1955. After the assassination of ASANUMA INEJIRŌ in 1960, he became chairman of the party, resigning in 1965 because of ill health.

Kawakami Otojirō 川上音二郎

(1864–1911). Actor and theatrical entrepreneur. He was the principal originator of the SHIMPA theatrical tradition. Born in Hakata (now in Fukuoka Prefecture), Kawakami moved with his family to Tōkyō, where he joined the FREEDOM AND PEOPLE'S RIGHTS MOVEMENT (Jiyū Minken Undō) as a traveling agitator. Kawakami later became a humorous balladeer in YOSE (Japanese vaudeville theater), which brought him national fame.

In 1891 Kawakami organized his fellow agitators into a theatrical troupe that barnstormed the country with contemporary political plays performed in a style that imitated KABUKI. In 1893 he traveled to Paris to study theater and switched to producing apolitical melodramas upon his return. During the Sino-Japanese War (1894–95), he staged patriotic plays set in the battle zones. Between 1899 and 1902, the Kawakami company made two tours of Europe and America with a repertoire composed principally of kabuki adaptations.

Between 1903 and 1906 Kawakami staged and starred in Japan's first professional productions of Shakespearean and other European plays in translation. He gradually abandoned acting to concentrate on reforming the way in which plays were produced and theaters were managed in Japan. His wife and costar, Kawakami Sadayakko (1872–1946), is considered to be the first Japanese actress of the modern era.

Kawakami Otojirō
This pioneer of *shimpa* theatrical productions also established one of the first schools for actresses in 1908.

Kawakami Sadayakko→

Kawakami Otojirō

Kawakami Sōroku 川上操六

(1848–99). Army general. Born in the Satsuma domain (now Kagoshima Prefecture), the son of a *samurai*. He fought for the imperial side in the BOSHIN CIVIL WAR of 1868 and helped to quell the SATSUMA REBELLION of 1877 as commander of the 13th Regiment. Kawakami studied military science in Europe. During the SINO-JAPANESE WAR OF 1894–1895, he served as the senior army staff officer at Imperial General Headquarters (DAIHON'EI) and distinguished himself as a brilliant strategist.

Kawakami Tetsutarō 河上徹太郎

(1902–80). Critic. Born in the city of Nagasaki. Graduate of Tōkyō University. A friend of the critic KOBAYASHI HIDEO, Kawakami wrote criticism on literature, music, and religion from a symbolist viewpoint and translated French literature and literary criticism. His *Nihon no autosaidā* (1958–59, Japan's Outsiders) won the Shinchōsha Prize. In 1961 he received the Japan Art Academy Award and in 1962 was made an academy member.

Kawakami Tōgai 川上冬崖

(1827–81). Literati painter; early scholar of Western painting (YŌGA). Born in Shinano Province (now Nagano Prefecture), he went to Edo (now Tōkyō) at age 15 and studied literati painting (BUNJINGA) with Ōnishi Chinnen (1792–1851). Between 1856 and

kawaraban
1 An 18th-century book illustration shows sellers of these newssheets reading out selected passages in order to attract customers. This practice gave rise to the term *yomiuri* ("sell by reading"), an alternate name for *kawaraban*.
2 Natural disasters, such as the eruption of Asamayama in 1783 pictured in this *kawaraban*, were a staple of *kawaraban* reporting.

Kawakubo Rei This dramatic and innovative designer's formal training was in philosophy, not fashion—which may account for the austere intricacy of her best work.

1868 Tōgai worked at the Bansho Shirabesho, the shogunate school for the study of European science and technology. He established a private studio and school for the study of Western-style painting, the Chōkō Dokuga Kan, in the Okachimachi district of Tōkyō.

Kawakita Nagamasa 川喜多長政

(1903–81). Importer and distributor of foreign films. Born in Tōkyō. Kawakita studied in China and Germany. He founded the company Tōwa Shōji (now Tōhō-Tōwa Co, Ltd) to import and distribute European films, mostly French and German classics, in Japan. He also produced such films as *Atarashiki tsuchi* (1937, The New Earth), which was the first Japanese-German coproduction, and the Japanese-Italian *Chōchō fujin* (1955, Madame Butterfly).

Kawakubo Rei 川久保玲

(1942–). Fashion designer. Born in Tōkyō. Graduated from Keiō University. Kawakubo founded her own company, Comme des Garçons, in 1973. Her designs are distinguished by their unconventional shaping, achieved by clever manipulation of the fabric, such as hidden tucks and flaps and asymmetrical closures. Though originally noted for her dark palette, her recent collections have employed more color. She won the Mainichi Fashion Grand Prize in 1983.

Kawamata Katsuji 川又克二

(1905–86). Businessman and chairman of NISSAN MOTOR CO, LTD (1973–85). Born in Ibaraki Prefecture. He graduated from Tōkyō University of Commerce (now Hitotsubashi University) in 1929 and, after working in the Industrial Bank of Japan, Ltd, entered Nissan Motor Co as executive director in 1947. He personally dealt with the labor upheavals there in 1953, successfully established new labor-management relations, and became president in 1957. He developed the small passenger car "Bluebird" in 1959, thereby virtually opening the door to widespread ownership of automobiles in Japan. He thereafter successively developed the medium-sized "Cedric" in 1960, the luxury model "President" in 1965, and the mass-market model "Sunny" in 1966. Kawamata merged Prince Motor Co into Nissan in 1966, making Nissan one of the largest automobile companies in the world.

Kawamori Yoshizō 河盛好蔵

(1902–). Scholar, critic, and translator of French literature. Born in Ōsaka; graduated from Kyōto University. He won the Yomiuri Literary Prize with *Furansu bundan shi* (1954–57, History of the French Literary World). His *Pari no yūshū: Bōdorēru to sono*

jidai (1978, Paris Melancholy: Baudelaire and His Age), is a compilation of his life's work, research on Baudelaire. Among his other works is *Ibuse Masuji zuimon* (1986, Conversations with Ibuse Masuji). In 1970 he became a member of the Japan Art Academy, and in 1988 he received the Order of Culture.

Kawamoto Kihachirō 川本喜八郎

(1925–). Animator. Born in Tōkyō. Kawamoto first worked for TŌHŌ CO, LTD, from 1946 to 1950. In 1958 he joined Shiba Production, an animation production company, and in 1963 he went to Czechoslovakia to study. After returning to Japan he began to produce shows for NHK (Japan Broadcasting Corporation). His animated puppet series *Sangokushi* (1982–84, Romance of the Three Kingdoms) helped make him Japan's leading puppet animator. Among his major productions are *Oni* (1972, Demon) and *Dōjōji* (1976, Dōjōji Temple).

Kawamoto Kōmin 川本幸民

(1810–71). Scholar of WESTERN LEARNING. Born in Settsu (now part of Hyōgo Prefecture), he studied medicine. With establishment in 1856 of the BANSHO SHIRABESHO, the shogunal school for Western studies, he was appointed instructor in physics and chemistry. He advised SHIMAZU NARIAKIRA, *daimyō* of the Satsuma domain (now Kagoshima Prefecture) on the manufacture of armaments, chemicals, and machinery. Apart from treatises on chemistry, Kawamoto wrote the 15-volume treatise on physics, *Kikai kanran kōgi* (1851–58, Observing the Waves in the Sea of Ether, Expanded).

Kawamura Jirō 川村二郎

(1928–). Literary critic and scholar of German literature. Born in Aichi Prefecture. Graduate of Tōkyō University. Kawamura started his career with essays on and translations of modern German literature. In *Ginga to jigoku* (1973, The Milky Way and Hell) he examines works of fantasy by such authors as IZUMI KYŌKA and KŌDA ROHAN to explore the illusionary nature and imaginative power of fiction. His other works include *Genkai no bungaku* (1969, The Literature of Limitation) and *Uchida Hyakken ron* (1983, On Uchida Hyakken).

Kawamura Zuiken 河村瑞賢

(1617–99). Wealthy merchant of the early Edo period (1600–1868). Born to an impoverished family in the province of Ise (now Mie Prefecture), at the age of 12 Zuiken went to Edo (now Tōkyō), where he established himself in the lumber business. In the rebuilding of Edo that followed the great MEIREKI FIRE of 1657, he made enormous profits. Zuiken developed new sea routes for transporting rice

from northeastern Honshū to Edo using the cargo ships called KAISEN and devised means of controlling the river Yodogawa in the Ōsaka region. He was made a direct shogunal vassal (*hatamoto*) in recognition of his contributions.

Kawanabe Gyōsai 河鍋暁斎

(1831–89). UKIYO-E artist and painter, sometimes called the second HOKUSAI. Also known as Kawanabe Kyōsai, he was born Kawanabe Noriyuki to a *samurai* family in Koga, Shimōsa Province (now part of Ibaraki Prefecture), and brought up in Edo (now Tōkyō). At age 7 he entered the atelier of the *ukiyo-e* master UTAGAWA KUNIYOSHI, and from the age of 11 he studied with KANŌ SCHOOL artists. From around 1858–59 he established himself as an independent artist in the Hongō section of Edo. He was arrested and imprisoned in 1869 for caricatures politically offensive to the newly established Meiji government. His independence and powerful artistic style, together with his tremendous productivity, made him very popular. He participated in the Vienna Exposition of 1873 and the Paris Exposition of 1878. Among his many pupils was the English architect Josiah CONDER. Among his illustrated books are the *Gyōsai gadan* (1887) and *Gyōsai manga* (date unknown).

Kawanakajima, Battles of 川中島の戦い

(Kawanakajima no Tatakai). A series of inconclusive engagements fought between two prominent *daimyō* of the Sengoku period (1467–1568), UESUGI KENSHIN of Echigo Province (now part of Niigata prefecture) and TAKEDA SHINGEN of Kai Province (now Yamanashi Prefecture), in the same general locale. All the battles were fought between the rivers Chikumagawa and Saikawa in northern Shinano Province (now Nagano Prefecture). There were no less than five clashes: in 1553, 1555, 1557, 1561, and 1564. Only the second and the fourth, however, were substantial battles. The fame of these combats is attributable to Edo-period (1600–1868) chronicles and treatises on military strategy, beginning with the KŌYŌ GUNKAN (ca 1625), which romanticized the two rival *daimyō*.

Kawanishi 川西[市]

City in southeastern Hyōgo Prefecture, western Honshū. Situated on the river Inagawa, Kawanishi developed as a land and river transportation center. Local products are leather goods and *yūzen-zome* (a dyed cloth). Modern industries include precision machinery. Kawanishi is now a growing suburb of Ōsaka. Pop: 141,253.

Kawanoe 川之江[市]

City in eastern Ehime Prefecture, Shikoku, on the Hiuchi Sea. It has been a focal point of land and sea transportation since ancient times. An intendant's office (*daikansho*) of the Tokugawa shogunate was established here in the Edo period (1600–1868). Kawanoe's paper industry, together with that of neighboring IYO MISHIMA, is second only to that of Fuji in Shizuoka Prefecture. Pop: 38,991.

kawaraban 瓦版

Edo-period (1600–1868) commercial newssheets. It is thought that the name *kawaraban* ("roof-tile print") derives from the engraved roofing tiles once used as printing plates; the tiles were replaced by woodblocks. The oldest extant *kawaraban* was printed in Kyōto in 1615 to inform the populace of TOKUGAWA IEYASU's victory over TOYOTOMI HIDEYORI at Ōsaka. The earliest presses were clandestine operations producing crude newssheets 24.1 by 12.7 centimeters (9.5 by 5.0 in) in size. Later, large bookstores, which customarily doubled as printshops, published single or occasionally multiple newssheets of a similar size reporting ribald gossip from the bordello districts; coverage later broadened to include current events and politics. The newssheets were sold in the streets by hawkers who read out selected passages to attract buyers, giving rise to the alternate appellation *yomiuri* or "sell by reading" (now the name of a leading newspaper). *Kawaraban* flourished until the introduction of Western-style daily newspapers early in the Meiji period (1868–1912).

Kawaradera remains 川原寺跡

(Kawaradera *ato*). Site of Kawaradera (also known as Gufukuji), an important temple in the ancient capital FUJIWARAKYŌ; located in the village of Asuka, Nara Prefecture. The *Fusō ryakki*, a 12th-century history, states that the temple was built in 655. Kawaradera was prominent throughout the Nara period (710–794) but began to decline after it was designated a subtemple of TŌJI in the 9th century. Excavations of the site in 1957 and 1958 revealed the plan of the original temple compound: the great south gate and middle gate, the west main hall, the pagoda, an enclosing corridor, the middle main hall, the lecture hall, and the priests' quarters. See also BUDDHIST ARCHITECTURE.

kawaramono 河原者

("dry riverbed people"). Term used during the premodern age for members of the lowest stratum of Japanese society. They traditionally lived along *kawara* (dry riverbeds) and often performed the most menial tasks or were engaged in occupations that involved contact with corpses and carcasses. Hence, *kawaramono* as a whole were stigmatized as unclean and unfit to mingle with the rest of society.

Among the *kawaramono*, a variety of entertainers—singers, dancers, musicians, acrobats, puppeteers—performed on the dry riverbed, a place where the government did not demand a share of their receipts or require official permission to set up facilities for public viewing. These free, unrestricted areas gradually developed into large entertainment centers. KABUKI actors were closely identified with the *kawaramono* throughout the Edo period (1600–1868).

kawara nadeshiko→fringed pink

Kawasaki 川崎[市]

City in northeastern Kanagawa Prefecture, central Honshū, a commuting suburb between Tōkyō and Yokohama. The center of the KEIHIN INDUSTRIAL ZONE. During the Edo period (1600–1868), it developed as a post-station town and as a temple town of the KAWASAKI DAISHI. From 1913, an industrial district was created on land reclaimed from Tōkyō Bay. After World War II, petrochemical and other industrial complexes were established. Today, oil and coal products, electrical machinery and appliances, steel, cars, cement, chemicals, and flour are produced. The port is one of the largest in Japan, importing oil, iron ore, coal, and foodstuffs. The city is also a center for land transportation.

Tourist attractions include the temple Heigenji (popularly known as Kawasaki Daishi), Mukōgaoka Amusement Park, and Inadazutsumi, an area on the banks of the TAMAGAWA famous for its cherry blossoms. Pop: 1,173,603.

Kawasaki Chōtarō 川崎長太郎

(1901–85). Author. Born in Kanagawa Prefecture. He helped found the anarchist poetry magazine *Aka to kuro* in 1923, although he soon turned away from the anarchist movement. He began writing semiautobiographical novels and short stories, attracting the attention of KIKUCHI KAN and other writers. After World War II, he wrote sentimental short stories depicting the love affair of an old man and a prostitute. His works include the novel *Michikusa* (1934) and the short stories "Makkō Chō" (1950) and "Hōsenka" (1952).

Kawasaki Daishi 川崎大師

Formally Heigenji. Popular temple in the city of Kawasaki, Kanagawa Prefecture, belonging to the Chizan branch (see CHISHAKUIN) of the SHINGON SECT of Buddhism. According to tradition Heigenji was built in 1127 by an exiled warrior, Hirama Kanenori, who recovered from the sea a wooden image of KŪKAI (popularly known as Kōbō Daishi; 774–835), the founder of the Shingon sect. The image, which is housed in the temple, is thought to help worshipers in warding off evils (*yakuyoke*). Festivals are held on the 21st day of January, March, May, and September.

Kawasaki disease 川崎病

(*kawasakibyō*). Also known as acute febrile mucocutaneus-lymph-node syndrome (MCLS). Acute disease that mainly attacks children under four years old; named after Kawasaki Tomisaku (b 1925), who reported the syndrome in 1967. It should not be confused with Kawasaki asthma (see POLLUTION-RELATED DISEASES). Each year there are some 5,000 cases of the disease with an estimated fatality rate of 0.5–1 percent. The illness is characterized by six main symptoms: (1) high fever that lasts for more than five days; (2) hyperemia of both conjunctiva bulbi; (3) redness, dryness, and bleeding of the lips; (4) swelling of neck lymph nodes; (5) exanthema of the body; and (6) redness of palms and soles and desquamation membranosa from the tops of the fingers and toes after swelling of the hands and feet. Although its cause has not yet been discovered, aspirin therapy is recognized as being effective. However, patients who respond well to treatment still need careful monitoring, as a tendency to contract coronary arterial disease has been found to be an aftereffect of Kawasaki disease.

Kawasaki Heavy Industries, Ltd 川崎重工業[株]

(Kawasaki Jūkōgyō). Manufacturer of ships, industrial machinery, engines, aircraft, motorcycles, rolling stock, and industrial plants. A member of the Kawasaki group, its forerunner was the Kawasaki Tsukiji Shipyard, established in 1878 in Tōkyō by Kawasaki Shōzō. Kawasaki also opened the Kawasaki Hyōgo Shipyard in Kōbe in 1886, and in 1896 the two were merged to form the Kawasaki Shipyard Co. The company took its present name in 1939.

The company developed original technologies through the construction of large-size tankers and liquefied natural gas (LNG) carriers. In the 1970s it placed heavy empha-

Kawasaki One of Japan's busiest ports, Kawasaki is also a major industrial center.

Kawasaki Daishi The street leading to the gate of this temple is thronged with visitors, especially at New Year's and on festival days; the temple's main image is believed by the faithful to prevent ill fortune.

sis on the development of overseas markets for plant exports. Kawasaki-brand motorcycles are exported in great volume. Kawasaki has 16 overseas subsidiaries and 10 offices in the Philippines, Brazil, the United States, and elsewhere. Sales for the fiscal year ending March 1991 totaled ¥891.6 billion (US $6.5 billion), and the company was capitalized at ¥66.5 billion (US $484.7 million). Headquarters are in Kōbe.

Kawasaki Kisen Kaisha, Ltd 川崎汽船[株]

(Kawasaki Kisen). Japanese ocean freight carrier. It is affiliated with both Kawasaki Heavy Industries, Ltd, and Kawasaki Steel Corporation. Incorporated in 1919, when it was separated from Kawasaki Shipbuilding Co (a forerunner of Kawasaki Heavy Industries). Under the name "K" Line, the firm offers comprehensive ocean freight service, including container ships, specialty ships, and tankers. The firm operates approximately 200 ships, owned and chartered, for an aggregate of 10 million deadweight tons. Total revenues for the fiscal year ending March 1991 were ¥363.9 billion (US $2.7 billion), and capitalization was ¥29.2 billion (US $212.8 million). Headquarters are in Tōkyō.

Kawasaki Natsu 河崎なつ

(1889–1966). Feminist and educator. Born in Nara Prefecture. A graduate of Tōkyō Women's Higher Normal School (now Ochanomizu Women's University), she taught writing there and at Tōkyō Women's Christian University and Tsuda College. In 1921 she joined the poet YOSANO AKIKO and others to found the coeducational Bunka Gakuin (Culture Academy) for training in creative arts. She participated in prewar women's movement groups, such as the SHIN

kawauso A good swimmer that feeds on fish, crayfish, and crabs, the Japanese otter is now almost extinct, despite a hunting ban that dates to 1928.

FUJIN KYŌKAI and the FUSEN KAKUTOKU DŌMEI. During World War II, she was appointed to several committees concerned with welfare and women's problems. In 1947 she was elected to the House of Councillors. She helped organize peace movement and social reform activities, especially the Nihon Fujin Dantai Rengōkai (Japan Federation of Women's Groups) in 1953 and the annual JAPANESE MOTHERS' CONGRESS (Nihon Hahaoya Taikai), which began in 1955.

Kawasaki Steel Corporation
川崎製鉄［株］

(Kawasaki Seitetsu). Steel producer; ranked among the top five in Japanese crude steel production. A member of the Kawasaki group. Its forerunner was established in 1906 in Kōbe by Kawasaki Shipbuilding Co (now Kawasaki Heavy Industries, Ltd, a separate company). The corporation became independent in 1950. The company is organized into four basic sectors: steel, the production of which is gradually being reduced in favor of nonsteel diversification; engineering and construction services; chemicals; and new businesses such as electronics and information and communication services. It has 13 overseas subsidiaries, including Companhia Siderurgica de Tubarao; Philippine Sinter Corporation; California Steel Industries, Inc; NBK Corporation; and Armco Steel Co, LP. Sales for the fiscal year ending March 1991 totaled ¥1.2 trillion (US $8.7 billion). The company was capitalized at ¥239.6 billion (US $1.7 billion) in the same year. Headquarters are in Tōkyō and Kōbe.

kawase kaisha
為替会社

(exchange companies). Financial institutions established in 1869 as part of the Meiji government's program to promote foreign trade. Together with the TSŪSHŌ KAISHA (commercial companies), whose operations they were meant to finance, the kawase kaisha were set up under the direction of government commercial offices (tsūshōshi) in eight cities: Tōkyō, Ōsaka, Kyōto, Yokohama, Kōbe, Niigata, Ōtsu, and Tsuruga.

Kawashima Takeyoshi
川島武宜

(1909–92). Legal scholar; specialist in the CIVIL CODE and the sociology of law. Born in Gifu Prefecture. A 1932 graduate of Tōkyō University, where he studied the Civil Code under WAGATSUMA SAKAE, Kawashima joined its faculty in 1934 and became a full professor in 1945. He served as chairman of the Japan Private Law Association (Nihon Shihō Gakkai) and as a member of the Legislative Council of the Ministry of Justice (Hōsei Shingikai). After his retirement from Tōkyō University, he practiced as an attorney.

Kawashima's 1949 work Shoyūken hō no riron (Theory of the Law of Ownership) greatly influenced post–World War II legal theory. He was also a leader in the postwar development of the relatively new field of legal sociology, being noted especially for his study Nihon shakai no kazokuteki kōsei (1948, The Familial Structure of Japanese Society).

Kawashō Corporation
川鉄商事［株］

(Kawatetsu Shōji). Trading firm specializing in iron and steel manufactured goods. Directly affiliated with KAWASAKI STEEL CORPORATION, it was incorporated in 1954 when the trading department of the parent firm was made independent. The firm has subsidiary companies in Thailand, Singapore, and Malaysia. In Hong Kong, Canada, and the United States, affiliated corporations handle export and import operations. Kawashō has diversified into such fields as lumber, chemicals, coal, and resort development. Sales for the fiscal year ending March 1991 totaled ¥1.7 trillion (US $12.4 billion), and capitalization stood at ¥12.5 billion (US $91.1 million). Headquarters are in Tōkyō and Ōsaka.

kawauso
獺

(otter). Lutra lutra whiteleyi. The kawauso is a subspecies of the common Eurasian otter, of the family Mustelidae. It is small in size, with a head and body length of about 70 centimeters (28 in) and a tail of about 45 centimeters (18 in). Until about 50 years ago kawauso were common in rivers and lakes throughout Hokkaidō, Honshū, Shikoku, and Kyūshū, but overhunting and water pollution exterminated them in freshwater areas by about 1950. At present a limited number of individuals inhabit the coast of southwestern Shikoku, where they make nests among seaside rocks. Measures to protect the kawauso have shown little success.

Kawayu Hot Spring
川湯温泉

(Kawayu Onsen). Located in the town of Teshikaga, eastern Hokkaidō. Situated within the AKAN NATIONAL PARK, Kawayu is a starting point for tours of Lake MASHŪ and Lake KUSSHARO. A hydrogen sulfide spring; water temperature 30°–75°C (86°–167°F).

Kawazu, Seven Falls of
河津七滝

(Kawazu Nanadaru). Located south of Amagi Pass on the upper river Kawazugawa, Izu Peninsula, Shizuoka Prefecture, central Honshū. The biggest waterfall is Ōdaru Falls, with a height of 27 m (89 ft) and a width of 7 m (23 ft).

Kaya
伽耶

Region of southern Korea where some tribes formed a league named Kaya in the 4th or 5th century. Many Japanese scholars refer to the area as Mimana and claim that it was controlled by Japan in the Kofun period (ca 300–710). Located between the ancient Korean kingdoms of SILLA and PAEKCHE, it was conquered by Silla in two stages in 532 and 562. See also KOREA AND JAPAN.

Kayaba Industry Co, Ltd
カヤバ工業［株］

(Kayaba Kōgyō). Manufacturer of shock absorbers and hydraulic equipment. The company also produces aircraft components and special-purpose vehicles. Founded as a hydraulics laboratory in 1919, Kayaba is known for hydraulics, electronics, and pneumatics. It has 5 manufacturing affiliates overseas and exports to 90 countries. For the fiscal year ending March 1991, sales totaled ¥190.8 billion (US $1.4 billion) and capitalization stood at ¥15.0 billion (US $109.3 million). Headquarters are in Tōkyō.

Kayama Matazō
加山又造

(1927–). Japanese-style painter. Born in Kyōto. Kayama's style as a painter owes much to his background as the son of a pattern designer of nishijin-ori silk fabrics. After graduating from the Tōkyō Bijutsu Gakkō (now Tōkyō University of Fine Arts and Music), he studied under YAMAMOTO KYŪJIN. Kayama's works are known for their modern ornamental style and his treatment of nature and animals; he has also done nudes and screen paintings in the RIMPA style.

kayari
蚊遣り

Smoke to drive away insects such as mosquitoes and gnats. The word kayari appears in the Wamyō ruiju shō (931–937), Japan's first encyclopedia. At first, branches of the kaya (Japanese nutmeg tree) or sawdust mixed with sulphur were burned to create smoke. Mugwort (yomogi) was used by farming families. In the late 19th century, pyrethrum (jochūgiku), a kind of chrysanthemum, was cultivated, ground into a powder, and burned to ward off insects. This powder was eventually pressed into a spiral form called katori senkō and in this form remains in wide use today.

Kaya Seiji
茅誠司

(1898–1988). Physicist who explored the properties of ferromagnetic crystals. Born in Kanagawa Prefecture, he graduated from Tōhoku University in 1923. After teaching at Hokkaidō University for 13 years, Kaya became a professor at Tōkyō University in 1943. After World War II, he played a key role in the founding of the SCIENCE COUNCIL OF JAPAN (Nihon Gakujutsu Kaigi) for the purpose of restructuring Japan's educational and research systems. He was president of Tōkyō University from 1957 to 1963 and received the Order of Culture in 1964.

Kaya Shirao
加舎白雄

(1738–91). HAIKU poet. Born in Shinano Province (now Nagano Prefecture), he was active in the effort to bring BASHŌ's haiku back into favor. In his essay Kazarinashi (1771, Without Artifice), he rejected subjectivism and technical artifice in haiku in favor of direct, natural expression. He inspired disciples who became leading poets of the next generation.

kayōkyoku →ryūkōka

Kazan, Emperor
花山天皇

(968–1008; Kazan Tennō). The 65th sovereign (tennō) in the traditional count (which includes several nonhistorical emperors); reigned 984–986. Eldest son of Emperor Reizei (950–1011; r 967–969) and grandson of Fujiwara no Koretada (924–972). During his reign, his maternal relatives incurred the wrath of the main line of the Fujiwara family. FUJIWARA NO KANEIE contrived Kazan's abdication and installed Emperor ICHIJŌ, Kaneie's grandson, gaining total control of the succession for the Fujiwara regents (see REGENCY GOVERNMENT).

Kazo
加須［市］

City in northeastern Saitama Prefecture, central Honshū, on the river Furu Tonegawa. Kazo has long been known for its cotton textiles. Its special products include carp streamers (KOINOBORI) for CHILDREN'S DAY and JŪDŌ wear. Pop: 56,401.

kazoku → peerage

kazoku kokka   家族国家
("family-state"). A term likening the national structure of Japan to that of an extended family with the EMPEROR as its head and his subjects as his children. It was used from the Meiji period (1868–1912) through World War II to justify the absolute authority of the emperor.

Kazuno   鹿角[市]
City in northeastern Akita Prefecture, northern Honshū, on the river YONESHIROGAWA. Copper mining was formerly an important occupation in the area. A part of TOWADA-HACHIMANTAI NATIONAL PARK, the city has hot springs and a Jōmon-period (ca 10,000 BC–ca 300 BC) site (see ŌYU STONE CIRCLES). Pop: 42,407.

Kazu, Princess   和宮
(1846–77; Kazu no Miya). Sister of Emperor Kōmei (r 1846–67) and wife of the 14th Tokugawa shōgun, Iemochi. She was the object of a political marriage arranged by the senior councillors (rōjū) ANDŌ NOBUMASA and KUZE HIROCHIKA as part of the attempt to bolster the shogunate's tottering prestige by more closely associating it with the imperial court (see MOVEMENT FOR UNION OF COURT AND SHOGUNATE). The marriage was pushed through in March 1862, even though Princess Kazu was betrothed to an imperial prince, Prince ARISUGAWA. The union, however, did not have the desired effect. Rather, antishogunate radicals were so enraged by the event that a group attempted to assassinate Nobumasa (see SAKASHITAMONGAI INCIDENT). When Iemochi died in 1866 Princess Kazu became a Buddhist nun.

KDD → Kokusai Denshin Denwa Co, Ltd

kebiishi   検非違使
(imperial police). Extrastatutory office (RYŌGE NO KAN) established by Emperor SAGA (r 809–823) to maintain order in the capital. The kebiishi gradually assumed wide-ranging powers to arrest, try, and punish offenders, while also taking over many of the functions of the Board of Censors (Danjōdai), the Ministry of Punishments (Gyōbushō), and the Office of Municipal Affairs (Kyōshiki). After the establishment of the Muromachi shogunate (1338–1573), the functions of the kebiishi were absorbed by the head of the SAMURAI-DOKORO or Board of Retainers.

Keenan, Joseph Berry   キーナン, J. B.
(1888–1954). US chief counsel for the Allied prosecution in the WAR CRIMES TRIALS of Japanese World War II leaders in Tōkyō. Born in Pawtucket, Rhode Island, he graduated from Brown University in 1910 and from Harvard Law School in 1913. He served with the US armed forces in France during World War I, entered the US Justice Department in 1933, and was appointed chief prosecutor for the Tōkyō Trial in 1945. He was the author, with Brendan F. Brown, of Crimes against International Law (1950).

Keene, Donald   キーン, D.
(1922–   ). US scholar and translator of Japanese literature. Born in New York City.

Keene graduated from Columbia University, where he received a PhD in 1949. He studied Japanese literature at Cambridge University in England and Kyōto University. Keene's scholarly studies include The Japanese Discovery of Europe (1952; revised edition, 1969) and a series of volumes on the history of Japanese literature that began with World Within Walls (1976) and continued with Dawn to the West (2 vols, 1984). His translations of Japanese literary works include The Tale of the Bamboo Cutter (TAKETORI MONOGATARI; tr 1956), Essays in Idleness (TSUREZUREGUSA; tr 1967), The Treasury of Loyal Retainers (KANADEHON CHŪSHINGURA; tr 1971), and fiction by MISHIMA YUKIO and DAZAI OSAMU. Keene became a member of the American Academy of Arts and Letters in 1986. The Donald Keene Center for Japanese Culture was established at Columbia University in the same year.

kegare   穢れ
(ritual impurity or defilement). The concepts of clean and unclean, pure and impure, have been of cultural and social significance in Japan from ancient times to the present. One special characteristic of the concept of kegare in ancient times was its close ties to the concept of TSUMI (sin or crime). Thus, good was understood as pure and clean, while evil implied something dirty that defiled or contaminated the good. Consequently, the two concepts were fused in the term tsumi-kegare, inclusive of all that was abhorred by the Shintō deities (KAMI). Another characteristic of sinful and unclean things is that they can be passed from one person to another through direct contact. Hence, persons thought to have been contaminated were required to undergo purification (MISOGI) or to separate themselves from everyday life for a period of time. The prototype for this process is the story of a deity who goes to visit his deceased wife in the land of the dead (see IZANAGI AND IZANAMI) and then must be purified.

Such early Shintō writings as the collection of NORITO contained in the ENGI SHIKI (927) enumerate several categories of kegare. The first includes things unclean from a sanitary viewpoint; the second involves human blood; the third involves everything related to death, including not only human death but also the death of animals. Killing or wounding birds and beasts and cooking them for food also constitutes kegare. Fourth, subjection to all sorts of natural disasters was considered a form of kegare. Fifth are all actions that serve to disturb life in human society. In the area of sexual acts,

incest and bestiality were treated as kegare. The kegare involving blood was largely associated with women. Such events as childbirth and menstruation ranked along with death as forms of kegare that were particularly abhorred by the Shintō deities.

Kegon Falls   華厳滝
(Kegon no Taki). Located in northwestern Tochigi Prefecture, central Honshū, on the river Daiyagawa, which has its source in Lake Chūzenji; part of Nikkō National Park. This is Japan's most famous waterfall. An elevator takes visitors to the bottom of the gorge for a spectacular view of the falls. Height: 97 m (318 ft).

Kegon sect   華厳宗
(Kegonshū). One of the schools that flourished in the early centuries of Japanese Buddhism and one of the six sects of NARA BUDDHISM. The Kegon (Ch: Huayan or Hua-yen) school was introduced from China first by the Chinese monk Daoxuan (Tao-hsüan; J: DŌSEN, 702–760) and then by the Korean monk known in Japan as Shinjō (d 742). ROBEN, a priest of the temple TŌDAIJI in Nara, was an early expert on the school's basic scripture, the Kegonkyō (Skt: Avataṃsaka-sūtra). The monk-scholars GYŌNEN of Tōdaiji and KŌBEN (MYŌE) of KŌZANJI in Kyōto were considered the highest authorities during the Kamakura period (1185–1333). Today, Tōdaiji in Nara is the central temple of this small sect, with 58 other temples.

Kehi Shrine   気比神宮
(Kehi Jingū). Shintō shrine in the city of Tsuruga, Fukui Prefecture; dedicated to Izasawake no Mikoto and six other deities. According to tradition, Izasawake was worshiped by Homutawake no Mikoto (the personal name of Emperor ŌJIN; late 4th to early 5th century) on the instruction of his mother, the empress JINGŪ, during a visit to this area after her successful campaign in Korea. The Kehi Jingū soon became the largest shrine in the region. It enjoyed particular patronage from warrior families. The shrine, which is noted for its huge four-legged gateway (torii) built in 1645, has its annual festival on 4 September.

Keian Genju   桂庵玄樹
(1427–1508). ZEN priest of the RINZAI SECT and promoter of Zhu Xi (Chu Hsi) Neo-Confucian learning (see SHUSHIGAKU) in Japan. Born in Nagato Province (now part of Yamaguchi Prefecture). Genju came in contact with

Kayama Matazō Detail from Cranes, a pair of six-panel folding screens. 1970. Colors on silk. Each screen 168 × 374 cm. Private collection.

Donald Keene This US scholar and translator was awarded the Order of the Rising Sun in 1974 for his contribution to the study of Japanese literature.

Neo-Confucianism while training in Kyōto in the Rinzai monasteries known as the GOZAN. He went to China as a member of the 1465 embassy headed by Ten'yo Seikei, abbot of KENNINJI. When that mission returned in 1469, Genju remained behind to study Confucian classics. He came back to Japan in 1473 to find the country embroiled in the ŌNIN WAR; he sought refuge with several lords in Kyūshū, to whom he preached Buddhism and taught Neo-Confucianism. His most prominent patron was Shimazu Tadamasa (d 1508) of Satsuma (now part of Kagoshima Prefecture), who endowed a temple for him. The lineage of Zhu Xi Neo-Confucian studies that he established is known as the Satsunan school.

Keian Incident   慶安事件

(Keian Jiken). An unsuccessful coup d'état undertaken against the Tokugawa shogunate by a group of masterless *samurai* (RŌNIN) in 1651 (Keian 4); also known as the Yui Shōsetsu Disturbance after the name of its leader, YUI SHŌSETSU, a teacher of "military science." The accession of the 10-year-old TOKUGAWA IETSUNA as shōgun in 1651 was deemed opportune by the plotters, who planned to burn SUMPU (now the city of Shizuoka) and to create a crisis by blowing up the shogunate's arsenal and setting fire to Edo (now Tōkyō). The putsch was discovered before any action could be undertaken, possibly because of an indiscretion on the part of Shōsetsu's lieutenant, MARUBASHI CHŪYA. Informers reported the cabal to the shogunal senior councillor (*rōjū*) MATSUDAIRA NOBUTSUNA, Chūya and his group were captured and executed in Edo, and Shōsetsu committed suicide in Sumpu. Shōsetsu left behind a note insisting that he had only intended a remonstrance against bad government. Shōsetsu and Chūya became heroes of popular literature and theater.

Keian no Ofuregaki   慶安の御触書

(Instructions of the Keian Era). Ordinance directed toward farmers, issued in 1649 (Keian 2) by the shōgun TOKUGAWA IEMITSU. Comprising 32 articles and written from a Confucian point of view, the ordinance instructed peasants on morality in their everyday life and especially on the virtue of obedience. The ordinance also extolled self-sufficiency and frugality. It is clear that the instructions were designed to ensure proper and prompt payment of taxes (NENGU); in fact, the ordinance states that "once he paid his taxes, there was no calling as easy as a peasant's."

keibatsu   閨閥

A clique (BATSU) in which access to political or economic power is controlled through marriage alliances between influential families. Often a man of a less influential family marries a daughter of a more influential one. This kind of marriage alliance has a long history in Japan as it has elsewhere in the world, the most notable instances in Japan being the marriage politics of the FUJIWARA FAMILY during the Heian period (794–1185) and those of warring *daimyō* families, particularly during the 16th century. The word *keibatsu*, however, came into prominence in the late 19th and early 20th centuries, when the family system played an important role in political and industrial circles and when many bureaucrats advanced themselves by means of strategic marriages. A related term, *mom-*

batsu, is often used interchangeably with *keibatsu;* however, *mombatsu* is broader, referring to cliques based on various kinds of family connections.

keichō   計帳

Tax registers compiled in ancient Japan beginning in the late 7th or early 8th century. Also called *daikeichō* or *daichō.* Each year heads of households were required to report to the provincial governors (KOKUSHI) on the number of people in the household; their age, sex, and physical characteristics; and, most important, which members were taxable and which were exempt. The governors then used this information to compile registers (*keichō*) and forwarded them to the Grand Council of State (Dajōkan) at the capital. These registers formed the basis for government land allotment and taxation. The system fell out of use in the 9th century.

Keichō kemmon shū   慶長見聞集

(Things Seen and Heard in the Keichō Era [1596–1615]; also called *Kembunshū*). A 10-volume collection of anecdotes by Miura Jōshin (1565–1644). The main value of the work is in its depiction of the ordinary life of Edo (now Tōkyō) as it was being transformed from a backwater to a metropolis at the dawn of the 17th century. It contains sketches of such events as the introduction of a water supply, the foundation of the Yoshiwara pleasure quarters, and early *kabuki* performances. The collection's preface is dated 1614, but later incidents are included in the contents.

Keichū   契沖

(1640–1701). Shingon priest, scholar, and poet. Born at Amagasaki in Settsu Province (now part of Hyōgo Prefecture). He entered the Buddhist priesthood at the age of 11. His studies included classical Chinese and Japanese literature and Shittan (Skt: SIDDHAM, a script used to write Sanskrit). From his midtwenties, Keichū was friendly with the WAKA poet and classical scholar SHIMOKŌBE CHŌRYŪ (1624–86). Almost all of Keichū's works were written in the last 20 years of his life.

Keichū is known primarily for classical commentaries and language studies. There is a close link between the two categories; for example, Keichū's research into KANA (the Japanese phonetic syllabary) usage directly resulted in important progress in the interpretation of old texts. The most important of his classical commentaries is undoubtedly *Man'yō daishō ki* (ca 1683–90), a commentary on the MAN'YŌSHŪ. Keichū also wrote commentaries on the *Genji monogatari* (TALE OF GENJI), KOKINSHŪ, and ISE MONOGATARI. His main works on language relate to *kana* usage; the most important of these is WAJI SHŌRAN SHŌ (completed 1693). As a result of his *Man'yōshū* studies, Keichū had perceived the consistent usage of *man'yōgana* (Chinese characters used phonetically) in the *Man'yōshū* and other early works such as WAMYŌ RUIJU SHŌ (10th century); he urged that contemporary *kana* conform to their conventions.

Keichū's academic writings are characterized by an objective spirit of independent inquiry. This new objectivism, based on empirical and inductive procedures, formed the methodological basis for research among the KOKUGAKU (National Learning) scholars. Traditionally the Kokugaku movement was regarded as centering around four main scholars: KADA NO AZUMAMARO, KAMO NO MABUCHI, MOTOORI NORINAGA, and HIRATA ATSUTANE. Kei-

chū was not normally included, partly it seems because his writings are characterized by a Buddhist viewpoint that was considered incompatible with the stand of the Kokugaku scholars. Recently there has been a reappraisal of Keichū's work by Japanese scholars, and the importance of his role in the early development of Kokugaku is now generally recognized.

Keidanren   経団連

(abbreviation of Keizai Dantai Rengōkai; Federation of Economic Organizations). One of Japan's four main business organizations (the other three being NIKKEIREN, the JAPAN ASSOCIATION OF CORPORATE EXECUTIVES, and the JAPAN CHAMBER OF COMMERCE AND INDUSTRY). Keidanren's members include 119 industrywide groups representing such major industries as mining, manufacturing, trade, finance, and transportation, in addition to 916 of Japan's largest corporations.

Keidanren was established in 1946 as part of a general reorganization of business groups. The organization's principal functions are to adjust and mediate differences of opinion among its various member industries and businesses and to submit proposals to the government regarding policies to stimulate the economy. Keidanren has a total of 36 permanent committees and consulting organs, including committees concerned with general economic policy, energy, economic cooperation, foreign trade, and ocean resources. It also has provisional committees on defense production and the promotion of space activities.

As Keidanren is the representative of big business in Japan, its proposals and demands have exerted a strong influence in Japanese political life. This power was clearly demonstrated in 1955 when Keidanren and the business community demanded that the two conservative political parties, the Japan Democratic Party (NIHON MINSHUTŌ) and the Liberal Party (JIYŪTŌ), merge to form a large conservative party. The result was the birth of the LIBERAL DEMOCRATIC PARTY, which has been the ruling party in Japan ever since its formation.

keigo → honorific language

Keihan Electric Railway Co, Ltd
京阪電気鉄道[株]

(Keihan Denki Tetsudō). Private railway company engaged in the transportation of passengers between Ōsaka, Kyōto, and Ōtsu (in Shiga Prefecture). Established in 1906. Since World War II, the company's earnings have grown, not only from the railway line, but also from its businesses along the line, which include housing developments, department stores, and leisure facilities. In 1988, to meet the increase in passengers, the firm completed a decentralized traffic control system using optical fibers. At the end of March 1991 annual income totaled ¥98.4 billion (US $717.2 million). Capitalization in the same year was ¥46.6 billion (US $339.7 million). Headquarters are in Ōsaka.

Keihin Electric Express Railway Co, Ltd
京浜急行電鉄[株]

(Keihin Kyūkō Dentetsu). Chiefly a railroad company, it also sells real estate and operates a bus line, hotels, and recreation facilities. Founded in 1898. Its main rail line runs through the industrial area between Tōkyō and the two cities of Kawasaki and Yokohama. The firm controls 63 affiliated companies. Sales for the fiscal year ending March 1991 totaled ¥123.1 billion (US $897.2

million). In the same year capitalization stood at ¥31.6 billion (US $230.3 million). Headquarters are in Tōkyō.

Keihin Industrial Zone 京浜工業地帯
(Keihin Kōgyō Chitai). Extends along the shores of Tōkyō Bay and nearby inland areas. Tōkyō, Kawasaki, and Yokohama are the zone's principal cities. It ranks first in Japan in the value of industrial goods produced. Factors that contributed to its growth are its proximity to Japan's greatest consumer markets and labor force and to the ports of Tōkyō and Yokohama. The heart of the zone is the coastal industrial belt between Kawasaki and Yokohama, where giant steel mills, oil refineries, petrochemical plants, shipyards, primary food-processing plants, thermoelectric plants, and other plants are located. Automobile, electric machinery, secondary food-processing, and precision machine plants are located further inland. The country's largest publishing houses and printing plants are located in the Tōkyō area. Since the 1970s, overpopulation, pollution, and a shortage of industrial water have caused many plants in the central part of the zone to relocate.

keihō→criminal law

Keikō, Emperor 景行天皇
(Keikō Tennō). The legendary 12th sovereign (tennō) in the traditional count (which includes several other nonhistorical emperors). According to the chronicle NIHON SHOKI (720) he is supposed to have reigned 71–130, an implausibly early period. After establishing his court in the Yamato region, he reputedly led an expedition to Kyūshū to suppress an uprising of the KUMASO tribes. When they rose up again, he sent his son, Prince YAMATOTAKERU, to chastise them and later to subdue the EZO tribes of northern Honshū.

Keikokushū 経国集
Early-Heian-period (794–1185) anthology of verse and prose written in Chinese. Compiled under the supervision of Yoshimine no Yasuyo at the command of Emperor Junna in 827, it is one of the three imperial anthologies in Chinese, along with *Ryōunshū* (814) and *Bunka shūreishū* (818). Only 6 of 20 chapters are extant. The contributions in several forms and styles by 178 authors cover 120 years.

Keiō Gijuku→Keiō University

Keiō Teito Electric Railway Co, Ltd 京王帝都電鉄[株]
(Keiō Teito Dentetsu). Railway operator. Incorporated in 1948. The company operates two main railway lines through the western suburbs of the Tōkyō Metropolitan Area. The firm also operates hotels in Shinjuku and Sapporo. The Keiō group consists of over 40 companies. Sales for the fiscal year ending March 1991 totaled ¥99.2 billion (US $723.0 million), of which railway operations accounted for 60 percent; bus operations, 20 percent; and other activities, 20 percent. The company was capitalized at ¥49.6 billion (US $361.5 million) in the same year. Headquarters are in Tōkyō.

Keiō University 慶応義塾大学
(Keiō Gijuku Daigaku). Private, coeducational university; main campus located in Minato Ward, Tōkyō. It was founded as a private academy in Edo (now Tōkyō) in 1858 by FUKUZAWA YUKICHI (1835–1901), a noted propagator of WESTERN LEARNING. Begun as a

school for Dutch studies (*rangaku*), in 1863 it turned to English as a means of introducing Western knowledge; by 1868, when it took the name Keiō Gijuku, it had grown into one of the leading schools of Western Learning in Japan. It continued to expand throughout the Meiji period (1868–1912), adding schools of finance, law, and literature in 1890, and offering the first private college-level curriculum in Japan. By 1898 it became the first private institution in the country with a comprehensive educational program from elementary school through college. Renamed Keiō Gijuku Daigaku in 1910, it was given full university accreditation by the Ministry of Education in 1920. It now has faculties of literature, economics, law, commerce, medicine, science and engineering, policy management, and environmental information. There are also several specialized institutes and laboratories. The university offers correspondence curricula in humanities, economics, and law and has affiliated elementary, junior high, and high schools. In 1989, 537 foreign students attended the school. Of those, 143 were undergraduates, 252 were graduate students, and 142 were students in the Japanese language program. Total enrollment was 23,354 in 1989.

keiretsu 系列
Group of affiliated private business enterprises; often, one of the loose groupings of former subsidiaries of the giant ZAIBATSU (financial and industrial combines) that have appeared since the ZAIBATSU DISSOLUTION program following World War II. The former *zaibatsu keiretsu* include the MITSUI *keiretsu*, the MITSUBISHI *keiretsu*, and the SUMITOMO *keiretsu*. Other forms of *keiretsu* include *kin'yū* (finance), *shihon* (capital), and *kigyō* (enterprise) *keiretsu*. A more general term for such affiliations is enterprise groups.

A *kin'yū keiretsu* is a group of companies that do their largest borrowing from the bank that gives the grouping its name. The BANKING SYSTEM has provided the bulk of corporate funds in postwar Japan and plays a more important role than shareholders' equity in CORPORATE FINANCE. A *shihon keiretsu* is a group of companies with a common parent company. The parent company in a *shihon keiretsu* must, by definition, hold more than 50 percent of the stock of the SUBSIDIARY COMPANIES. A *kigyō keiretsu* is a group of companies that do the bulk of their work for the same firm as subcontractors.

As *keiretsu*, Sumitomo, Mitsui, and Mitsubishi are substantially different in form from their *zaibatsu* predecessors. First and foremost, there are no top HOLDING COMPANIES to serve as command centers for the groups. Holding companies were outlawed by the ANTIMONOPOLY LAW. Ownership ties are weaker than those in the prewar *zaibatsu*, with intercompany shareholding usually not exceeding 3 to 5 percent. Additionally, bank lending and borrowing occur across *keiretsu* lines, and trading companies may no longer bind companies to purchases and sales through them alone. Coordination of *keiretsu* activities is achieved through "presidents' clubs," made up of the presidents of the most important companies in each group. GENERAL TRADING COMPANIES and *keiretsu* banks also serve a coordinating function in these groups.

keirin 競輪
(professional bicycle racing). Bicycle races mounted by local government bodies to gen-

erate income through controlled betting. The city of Kokura (now Kita Kyūshū in Fukuoka Prefecture) held the first *keirin* in 1948. Created to stimulate local economies, *keirin* also serve to promote bicycle manufacturing and raise funds for public projects. Seventy-five percent of the proceeds raised through the sale of betting tickets is paid out to those holding winning tickets, with the remaining 25 percent going to prize money or to finance the construction of local roads and schools. By 1989 there were 50 active velodromes throughout Japan, and 4,491 professional *keirin* cyclists. Since 1981, top European and American cyclists have been invited to join the International Keirin Competition, held annually in Japan in spring.

Keirō no Hi→holidays, national

Keisai Eisen 渓斎英泉
(1790–1848). Popular and prolific painter, book illustrator, designer of UKIYO-E woodblock prints, playwright, novelist, biographer, and amateur historian. He was born Ikeda Yoshinobu in the Hoshigaoka district of Edo (now Tōkyō). His earliest works are thought to be two illustrated novelettes published in 1808 and 1809 and signed Keisai Shōsen. He adopted the name Eisen in 1816. He wrote plays as Chiyoda Saiichi, fiction as Ippitsuan Kakō, biography as Mumeiō, and historical essays as Kaedegawa Shiin. He designed erotica (SHUNGA) as Insai and Insai Hakusui and is said to have used the names Keisai, Kokushunrō, and Hokutei or Hokkatei on conventional pictures. Today he is remembered for hundreds of prints of young women—brazen, distant, somewhat harsh, yet intimate, elegant, graceful, and subtly aroused—for many SURIMONO and landscape prints, and for numerous erotic books and albums. As a writer he is best remembered for *Mumeiō zuihitsu* (1833, Essays of a Nameless Old Man), a manuscript revision of *Ukiyo-e ruikō*, a compilation of biographies of *ukiyo-e* artists. He also is remembered for a set of landscape prints, *Kiso kaidō rokujūkutsugi* (1835, 69 Stations of the Kiso Kaidō Road), which he started but which HIROSHIGE was asked to finish.

Kei school 慶派
(Keiha). Group of sculptors of Buddhist images active mainly in the Kamakura period (1185–1333). These sculptors belonged to the Shichijō workshop (BUSSHO) in Nara and traced their ancestry to the 11th-century sculptor JŌCHŌ. Since they often took *kei* as part of their names, they became known to later generations as the Kei school. Their realistic style and depictions of virile, muscular male torsos gained the approval of warriors in the Kamakura period. As repre-

kemari A popular amusement of Japan's ancient nobility, this kickball-like game later gained popularity among samurai and common folk. A game is in progress in this 17th-century copy of the *Nenchū gyōji emaki,* a Heian-period scroll depicting annual court events.

sented in the works of important sculptors such as KŌKEI, UNKEI, KAIKEI, and TANKEI, the Kei school flourished over the older EN SCHOOL and IN SCHOOL.

Keisei Electric Railway Co, Ltd
京成電鉄[株]

(Keisei Dentetsu). Railroad and real estate company that also operates a bus line. Incorporated in 1909. The firm's main rail line connects the Tōkyō International Airport in Narita, Chiba Prefecture, with the metropolitan area. Its special express trains carry passengers nonstop from the airport to Tōkyō. Sales for the fiscal year ending March 1991 totaled ¥82.0 billion (US $597.7 million). In the same year capitalization was ¥13.6 billion (US $99.1 million). Headquarters are in Tōkyō.

keishi
家司

(house stewards). Clerks who administered the household affairs of imperial princes, regents, court nobles, high-ranking officials, and other great men of the Heian period (794–1185). Also known as *ietsukasa*. The term came to be used in warrior houses as well, and with the rise of WARRIOR GOVERNMENT under the Kamakura shogunate (1192–1333), functionaries in such governmental organs as the Administrative Board (MANDOKORO), the Council of State (HYŌJŌSHŪ), the High Court (Hikitsukeshū), and the Board of Inquiry (MONCHŪJO) were all designated *keishi.* The succeeding Muromachi shogunate (1338–1573) adopted substantially the same system.

Keishichō→Tōkyō Metropolitan
Police Department

Keitai, Emperor
継体天皇

(first half of the 6th century; Keitai Tennō). The 26th sovereign (*tennō*) in the traditional count (which includes several nonhistorical emperors). According to the chronicle NIHON SHOKI (720) he supposedly reigned 507–531, but modern scholars reject these dates. According to the *Nihon shoki,* when Emperor Buretsu (late 5th century) died without an heir, the court military leaders ŌTOMO NO KANAMURA and Mononobe no Arakabi (see MONONOBE FAMILY) discovered Keitai and installed him as emperor. Although he was alleged to be a fifth-generation descendant of Emperor ŌJIN, some scholars have speculated that he was unrelated to the original imperial house. Among the events at-

tributed to his troubled reign are the loss (in 512?) of four districts of KAYA, the supposed Japanese enclave in Korea; the Rebellion of IWAI in Kyūshū; and civil wars in Japan.

Keiyō Industrial Region
京葉工業地域

(Keiyō Kōgyō Chiiki). Industrial zone extending along the shore of Tōkyō Bay from the city of Urayasu to the city of Futtsu in Chiba Prefecture, central Honshū. Part of the PACIFIC COASTAL BELT industrial zone, the area supports such industries as steel, petroleum, petrochemicals, shipbuilding, and electric power generation.

keizai kanchō→economic agencies

Keizai Kikaku Chō→Economic
Planning Agency

Keizan Jōkin
瑩山紹瑾

(1268–1325). Monk of the SŌTŌ SECT of Zen Buddhism. Born in Echizen Province (now Fukui Prefecture). As a child he entered the Buddhist order at the temple EIHEIJI where he studied under Gikai (1219–1309), a disciple of DŌGEN. Later he also studied esoteric Buddhist tradition in Kyōto. In 1321 he founded the temple SŌJIJI, to which Emperor Go-Daigo contributed an imperial plaque. Along with Eiheiji, Sōjiji became a center of the sect, and Keizan helped to firmly establish Japanese Sōtō Zen. His writings include the well-known collection of monastic rules, *Keizan oshō shingi,* and a collection of his speeches titled *Denkōroku.*

Kellner, Oskar
ケルナー, O.

(1851–1911). German agricultural chemist. Invited to teach by the Japanese government, he traveled to Japan in 1881 and was an instructor in agricultural chemistry at Komaba Agricultural School and its successor, the Tōkyō Agriculture and Forestry School (now part of Tōkyō University), while also doing research in soil types and fertilizers. During his 11 years' stay, he laid the foundations of Japanese agricultural chemistry. His method of nutritional analysis of livestock feed, which he worked out after returning to Germany, is called Kellner's feeding standard and was used for a long time in the Japanese cattle industry.

Kellogg-Briand Pact
不戦条約

(Fusen Jōyaku, literally, "Antiwar Treaty"). Agreement signed in Paris on 27 August 1928 by Japan and 14 other countries, denouncing "recourse to war for the solution of international controversies"; also known as the Pact of Paris. Its terms derived from the June 1927 proposal of French Foreign Minister Aristide Briand to the US government to bar all war between their respective governments and from US Secretary of State Frank B. Kellogg's reply suggesting that other countries join them in such an agreement. The pact was initially signed by 15 nations, including France, Germany, Great Britain, Italy, and the United States. Later, 48 other nations joined them. Japan was requested to sign the pact in April 1928. The Japanese government was reluctant to do so, because it was unwilling to deny itself the right to intervene militarily in Chinese affairs in order to protect its nationals in China and its interests in Manchuria. Though the Japanese Privy Council finally ratified the pact in June 1929, Japan proceeded to invade Manchuria in 1931. See MANCHURIAN INCIDENT.

kemari
蹴鞠

Also known as *shūkiku.* Traditional game in which the players (usually eight) form a circle and kick a ball back and forth without letting it fall to the ground. It is thought to have come to Japan from China. There are records of its being played at the imperial court as early as the mid-7th century. *Kemari* achieved wide popularity among the *kuge* (court nobles) during the Nara (710–794), Heian (794–1185), and Kamakura (1185–1333) periods and later spread among both warriors and commoners. The playing field was known as the *kakari* and consisted of an area about 6 meters (20 ft) square with one tree planted at each of the four corners (a willow, a cherry, a pine, and a maple). Players wearing leather shoes shouted as they kicked the *mari,* a deerskin ball 24 centimeters (9.4 in) in diameter.

kemi
検見

(or *kemmi;* crop inspection). An Edo-period (1600–1868) procedure for inspecting crop yields in order to calculate the amount of land tax (see HONTO MONONARI). In principle the inspections occurred annually. Crop inspections were carried out from the Kamakura period (1185–1333) onward, but they did not become widespread until the late 16th century, when they are thought to have been systematized through nationwide implementation of TOYOTOMI HIDEYOSHI's land survey (see KENCHI).

Inspections were made by officials of different levels. In the Tokugawa house lands (TENRYŌ), inspections by village officials of the yield of each plot in the village were called *naimi.* A *kokemi* was an investigation of yields by the shogunal intendant's (DAIKAN) assistant, who reviewed and checked the reports that village officials prepared by taking sample cuttings (*tsubogari*) in the village. If the *daikan* himself checked the work of his representative in a similar manner, it was called *ōkemi.* Taxes based on these forms of inspection were discontinued after the Meiji LAND TAX REFORM OF 1873–1881. See also JŌMEN.

Kemmu nenchū gyōji
建武年中行事

Three-volume work completed about 1334 (Kemmu 1) describing annual events and ceremonies at the imperial court and compiled by order of Emperor GO-DAIGO. It was an attempt to revive discarded court ceremonies on the occasion of the KEMMU RESTORATION. In contrast to similar works up to that date, the book was written in Japanese instead of classical Chinese. It was known by a variety of names before the present title was chosen in the Edo period (1600–1868).

Kemmu nenkan ki
建武年間記

(Chronicle of the Kemmu era). A record of the Kemmu era (1334–36) compiled anonymously about 1336 during the reign of Emperor GO-DAIGO, who had succeeded in retrieving political power from the Kamakura shogunate in the KEMMU RESTORATION. It includes administrative regulations, dispositions concerning SHŌEN proprietary rights, lists of officials, legal decisions, and transcriptions of NIJŌGAWARA NO RAKUSHO, satirical verses about government and fashions of the time.

Kemmu Restoration
建武の中興

(Kemmu no Chūkō). The attempt by Emperor GO-DAIGO in 1333–36 to restore direct imperial rule following the overthrow of the

KAMAKURA SHOGUNATE. Kemmu refers to the era name (NENGŌ) Go-Daigo inaugurated in 1334. Within three years his restoration government was overthrown by ASHIKAGA TAKAUJI, who established the MUROMACHI SHOGUNATE (1338–1573).

Despite the founding of the Kamakura shogunate in 1185 and the subsequent expansion of its power, the court and courtiers in Kyōto retained considerable landed estates (SHŌEN) and the potential, at least, to reassert themselves politically. The court was subordinated to Kamakura following the unsuccessful attempt in 1221 by the retired emperor GO-TOBA to overthrow the shogunate (see JŌKYŪ DISTURBANCE). Thereafter even the succession to the throne was dictated by Kamakura. Upon the death of retired emperor GO-SAGA in 1272, no firm decision was made as to which line the succession should go to—that of his older son, the former emperor GO-FUKAKUSA, or his younger son, the emperor KAMEYAMA. By the end of the 13th century, the shogunate had accepted the practice of alternate succession to the throne by members of the senior (Go-Fukakusa or Jimyōin) and the junior (Kameyama or Daikakuji) lines.

By the time Go-Daigo ascended the throne in 1318, the quality of Kamakura rule had declined greatly, and Go-Daigo determined not only to end alternate succession but also to overthrow the "eastern barbarians" in Kamakura and restore imperial power. An antishogunate plot was uncovered in Kyōto in 1324 (see SHŌCHŪ CONSPIRACY) and in 1331 Go-Daigo was arrested and sent into exile (see GENKŌ INCIDENT).

Go-Daigo returned to Kyōto in 1333 to "restore" imperial power. This was made possible when shogunate generals Ashikaga Takauji and NITTA YOSHISADA switched allegiance to Go-Daigo and defeated shogunate forces. In selecting the name Go-Daigo ("The Latter Daigo"), he clearly expressed his desire to model his regime on that of Emperor DAIGO, who had ruled from 897–930.

Takauji coveted the title of shōgun (more formally, seii tai shōgun). Go-Daigo, however, steadfastly refused to comply with Takauji's wishes, even when the Ashikaga leader directly requested that he be made shōgun in 1335. Shortly thereafter the court dispatched an army under Nitta Yoshisada, Takauji's arch rival, to defeat Takauji. Thus began the conflict that eventually led to the overthrow of the restoration government, the flight of Go-Daigo to Yoshino, and the establishment by Takauji of the Muromachi shogunate in Kyōto. At this time began the war (1337–92) that pitted the Southern (Yoshino) Court of Go-Daigo and his descendants of the junior branch of the imperial house against the Northern Court of the senior branch in Kyōto supported by the Ashikaga shōguns. See NORTHERN AND SOUTHERN COURTS.

Go-Daigo's Kemmu Restoration was little more than an anachronistic pause between the overthrow of the first shogunate and the founding of the second. Yet it gave rise to the only major dynastic schism in Japanese history, and later generations of historians felt impelled to deal with the fundamental issue of imperial legitimacy that had been raised by Takauji's treatment of Go-Daigo and by the subsequent division of the court into northern and southern branches.

Kemmu Shikimoku 建武式目

(Kemmu Code). Code of governmental principles and policies promulgated in 1336 by ASHIKAGA TAKAUJI, founder of the MUROMACHI SHOGUNATE (1338–1573). Drawn up by a commission of scholars and officials in consultation with Takauji, the code is a list of general precepts for the guidance of the ruling class. It comprises 17 articles that enjoin frugality, maintenance of law and order, respect for property rights, selection and reward of officials on the basis of merit and honesty, scrupulous fairness in judicial decisions, resistance to the influence and demands of courtiers and monks, and attention to the grievances of the poor. The Kemmu Shikimoku is modeled on the SEVENTEEN-ARTICLE CONSTITUTION issued by Prince SHŌTOKU in 604 and in content is comparable to the GOSEIBAI SHIKIMOKU (1232), the rigid military code of the Kamakura shogunate (1192–1333).

Kempō gige 憲法義解

(Commentary on the Constitution). Official commentary on the CONSTITUTION OF THE EMPIRE OF JAPAN and the IMPERIAL HOUSEHOLD LAW; published under the general supervision of ITŌ HIROBUMI in 1889. The actual author, however, was INOUE KOWASHI, who worked with the advice of the PRIVY COUNCIL.

Kempō Kinembi → holidays, national

Kempō satsuyō 憲法撮要

(Outline of the Constitution). A treatise on the CONSTITUTION OF THE EMPIRE OF JAPAN (the Meiji Constitution), published in 1923 by MINOBE TATSUKICHI, professor of administrative law at Tōkyō University. In opposition to conservative scholars such as HOZUMI YATSUKA and UESUGI SHINKICHI, who saw the emperor as absolute and mystically identified with the body of the state, Minobe described the state as a legal person possessing both sovereignty and the authority to rule, the emperor being merely the highest organ of the state (see TENNŌ KIKAN SETSU). Minobe's theory prevailed until the 1930s, when it was denounced by militarists and rightists associated with the movement to "clarify the national polity" (see KOKUTAI DEBATE). Minobe was attacked in the Diet, and his works were proscribed in 1935.

ken 拳

(literally, "fist"). Any of a number of games played by two or more people matching extended hand gestures. The most common form of ken is the familiar "scissors-paper-rock" (see JANKEN). Other well-known forms of the game include kazuken and kitsuneken (also called tōhachiken). In kazuken ("numbered fist") one player tries to guess and match the number of fingers extended by the other player. In kitsuneken ("fox fist") the hand shape representing the hunter beats the one for fox, the village headman fist beats the hunter, and the fox beats (outwits) the village headman.

kenchi 検地

A general term applied to cadastral surveys in Japan, particularly from the 16th century through the Edo period (1600–1868). From early historic times surveys of cultivated land were carried out by government officials or by landed proprietors for purposes of administration and taxation. During the medieval period (mid-12th–16th centuries) these surveys were called kenchū. Under the Kamakura shogunal rule (1192–1333), the shōgun's superior provincial agents (SHUGO) were ordered to collect cadastral records (kenchū) from local officials in both the

kenchi This Tempō-era (1830–44) illustration portrays government officials conducting a cadastral survey. The people at the right are measuring the area of a field.

kokugaryō (public lands) and the SHŌEN (private estates).

During the last half of the Muromachi period (1333–1568), and particularly with the appearance of the so-called SENGOKU DAIMYŌ after 1500, new land registrations (now called kenchi) were initiated by the large military lords. Such surveys were not yet systematically carried out, nor did most DAIMYŌ have the power to intrude their own survey teams onto lands held in fief by their vassals or by powerful religious proprietors. Thus, the usual practice was for the daimyō to require the submission of cadastral documents from the fief and estate holders themselves, a procedure known as sashidashi. Among the Sengoku daimyō, the most powerful, such as the IMAGAWA FAMILY of Suruga and Tōtōmi provinces (now parts of Shizuoka Prefecture), the TAKEDA FAMILY of Kai and Shinano provinces (now Yamanashi and Nagano prefectures), and the Later Hōjō family (see HŌJŌ FAMILY) of Odawara (in what is now Kanagawa Prefecture), were noteworthy for their reliance on the kenchi as a tool in local governance.

Soon after his entrance into Kyōto in 1568, ODA NOBUNAGA ordered a full survey of lands in Ōmi Province (now Shiga Prefecture), a province adjoining the home province of Yamashiro (now part of Kyōto Prefecture) and the future location of his castle headquarters at Azuchi. In the next few years, as Nobunaga extended his conquests, local civil and military proprietors were obliged to submit cadastral records on their landholdings. In most cases Nobunaga did not send his own surveyors to conduct the actual survey, but in certain instances he did dispatch his own cadastral commissioners (kenchi bugyō) to check for accuracy.

It was under TOYOTOMI HIDEYOSHI that the system of land registration was designed that was to remain in use throughout the early modern period. Although Hideyoshi alone cannot be credited with the series of surveys begun in 1582 that extended into the 1590s, it is common practice to call this national effort the Taikō kenchi. (TAIKŌ is the title by which Hideyoshi was known in his later years.) The Taikō kenchi worked a revolution in land administration and tenure practices in Japan. By virtue of its comprehensiveness, it swept away all previous landholding systems. The national military hegemon now stood as the sole possessor of the rights of proprietorship throughout Japan.

Kenchi were carried out in a variety of ways. In many parts of the country, where the local daimyō power was strongly entrenched, Hideyoshi allowed the daimyō to conduct their own surveys according to his specifications. This was the case for the TOKUGAWA FAMILY, Ukita family, CHŌSOKABE FAMILY, and MŌRI FAMILY. In other instances Hideyoshi sent his own survey commissioners to oversee or to do the job directly.

The enforcement of the Taikō kenchi program in all parts of the country did more

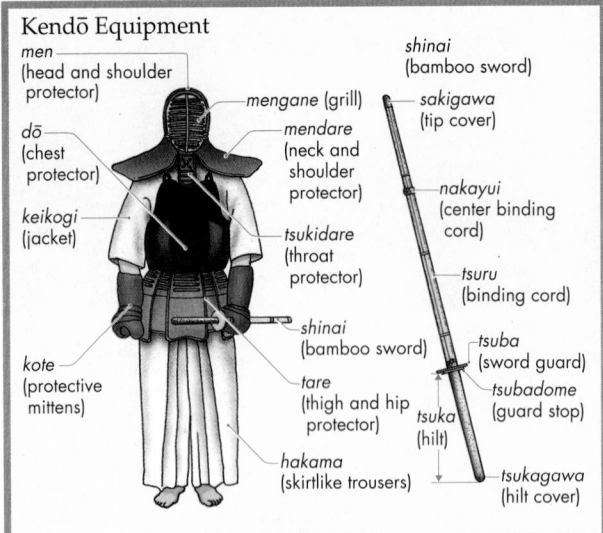

Kendō Equipment

men (head and shoulder protector)

mengane (grill)

mendare (neck and shoulder protector)

dō (chest protector)

keikogi (jacket)

tsukidare (throat protector)

kote (protective mittens)

shinai (bamboo sword)

tare (thigh and hip protector)

hakama (skirtlike trousers)

shinai (bamboo sword)

sakigawa (tip cover)

nakayui (center binding cord)

tsuru (binding cord)

tsuba (sword guard)

tsubadome (guard stop)

tsuka (hilt)

tsukagawa (hilt cover)

Strike Zones **kendō**

kote (forearm)

men (head)

tsuki (throat)

dō (trunk)

kendō A practice session of Japanese fencing in a training hall.

than provide systematic land registration; it had numerous political and social ramifications. With respect to the relationship between the daimyō and the national overlord, since the daimyō were now granted their domains in terms of agreed-upon KOKUDAKA (the total tax assessment base for a village measured in *koku* of rice; 1 *koku* = about 180 liters or 5 US bushels) totals, the identification of a daimyō with any specific location lost much of its significance. This facilitated the practice initiated by Nobunaga, perfected by Hideyoshi, and continued by the Tokugawa shogunate (1603–1867) whereby the national hegemon could move daimyō from location to location for strategic or political purposes.

The *kenchi* also contributed to the flow of rural *samurai* into the daimyō's CASTLE TOWNS, for it presented to the rural samurai two clearcut choices: to remain on the land and be classed as farmers (HYAKUSHŌ) or to preserve samurai status by moving to the daimyō's castle. The result was an irreversible legal separation of the samurai from the farming class—a phenomenon called *heinō bunri* by Japanese historians. The withdrawal of the entire samurai class of lower landed military gentry from the land and its conversion into an urban-dwelling, military-administrative officer corps attached to national and regional centers of administration had a profound effect upon the Japa-

nese nation for the next two and a half centuries.

Whether or not, as some scholars contend, the Taikō *kenchi* was intended to work a feudal revolution (*hōken kakumei*), the work was a mammoth undertaking, occupying the energies of Japan's rulers for many years. By their very nature cadastral surveys are never finished, since the land base is continually changing. There is no firm evidence that before Hideyoshi's death in 1598 all provinces had been subjected directly to the Taikō *kenchi*, although if there were neglected areas, the succeeding Tokugawa regime discovered them. The use of land registers (*kenchichō*) as the basic cadastral document for land tax purposes came to an end with the LAND TAX REFORM OF 1873–1881. Nationwide surveys conducted between 1875 and 1878 became the basis for the modern transformation of land ownership and the land tax practices under the Meiji government.

kenchiku girei 建築儀礼

Collective term for various religious and magic ceremonies and rites observed in Japan in the process of building a house. Such ceremonies are conducted in order to invoke divine protection in keeping misfortune from falling on the house while under construction. *Kenchiku girei* are said to have originated in the Heian period (794–1185) under the influence of the Chinese cosmological concept of *yin-yang*.

The only *kenchiku girei* observances commonly performed today are the *jichinsai*, or groundbreaking ceremony, and the *muneage*, the setting up of the framework of the house. The former involves a ritualized blessing by a Shintō priest, carried out around a square arrangement of bamboo branches tied with a *shimenawa* (straw rope). In the latter, sacred strips of paper (*GOHEI*) are tied to the ridgepole when the framework is erected to invoke the blessing of the gods, and rice cakes (*mochi*) are thrown from the ridge of the house to people who have gathered below.

Kenchōji 建長寺

Head temple of the Kenchōji branch of the RINZAI SECT of Buddhism, located in the city of Kamakura, Kanagawa Prefecture. Kenchōji was founded in 1249 by the fifth Kamakura shogunal regent (SHIKKEN), Hōjō Tokiyori (1227–63), to serve as a major Zen center in Kamakura for RANKEI DŌRYŪ (Ch: Lanqi Daolong or Lan-Ch'i Tao-lung, 1213–78), a distinguished Chinese Zen master who had arrived in Japan three years earlier. It was ranked first among the five great Zen monas-

teries (GOZAN) in Kamakura. The site was selected by Tokiyori's teacher, the famous Zen monk ENNI (1202–80), who sought to establish in Japan a Zen temple modeled after the great Chinese monastery on Jingshan (Ching-shan) in Hangzhou (Hangchow), where Enni had studied. Over the centuries Kenchōji suffered extensive damage from fires and earthquakes but has been rebuilt after each disaster. The last catastrophe to strike was the great Tōkyō Earthquake of 1923, which destroyed virtually the entire temple aside from the main gate (*sammon*), built in 1755, and the lecture hall (*hattō*), built in 1814.

Kenchōji-bune 建長寺船

Ship sent in 1325 on a trade mission to China's Yuan dynasty (1279–1368) by the Kamakura shogunate (1192–1333). The shogunate authorized and provided protection for the mission for a share of the profits, to be used to rebuild Kenchōji, a ZEN temple at Kamakura. The mission was a predecessor of the TENRYŪJI-BUNE trade missions.

kendan 検断

Policing and adjudication authority—including the power to pursue, arrest, incarcerate, try, and sentence criminals—legally vested in various officials from late in the Heian period (794–1185) through the Muromachi period (1333–1568) and arrogated by local magnates in times of disruption.

kendō 剣道

(the Way of the sword). Japanese fencing based on the techniques of the two-handed sword of the *samurai*. Before the Shōwa period (1926–89) it was customarily referred to as *kenjutsu* or *gekken*. *Kendō* is a relatively recent term that implies spiritual discipline as well as fencing technique.

Fencing with the single-edged, straight-blade sword was probably introduced from Sui (589–618) or early Tang (T'ang; 618–907) China. The cultivation of sword skills flourished during the Kamakura shogunate (1192–1333). With the establishment of nationwide peace by the Tokugawa shogunate in the early 17th century, *kenjutsu* went into a decline. The moral and spiritual element became prominent, drawing on Confucianism, Shintō, and Buddhism, especially Zen. *Kenjutsu* became an element for training the mind and body. In the late 18th century protective equipment and bamboo training swords (*shinai*) were introduced.

Following the Meiji Restoration (1868), the practice of *kenjutsu* again went into a temporary decline, but in 1879 the Tōkyō

kenchiku girei The traditional ceremonies that attend the construction of a house include the *muneage*, which is observed upon the completion of the framework. In the photo, branches of bamboo with colored streamers, used here in place of the usual *gohei*, sway above the ridgepole, while carpenters toss rice cakes to the crowd below.

police force instituted a *kenjutsu* course. In 1895 the Dai Nihon Butokukai (All Japan Martial Virtue Society) was established to encourage *kenjutsu* and other martial arts. At the end of World War II, the Occupation authorities banned *kendō* on the basis of its use before the war to cultivate militarism. But following the end of the Occupation period in 1952, the All Japan Kendō Federation (Zen Nihon Kendō Remmei) was established, and in 1957 the practice of *kendō* was returned to Japanese middle schools.

The weapon is a hollow cylinder made of four shafts of split bamboo. It is bound with a leather grip and cap connected by a silk or nylon cord and a leather thong wound three times around the bamboo cylinder and knotted. The length varies for different age groups. Fencers are protected by the *men* (face mask); the trunk of the body is protected by the *dō* (chest protector). The thighs are protected with five overlapping quilted panels, the *tare*, and the hands with padded mittens (*kote*). Training is based on a variety of movements of attack and defense known as *waza*. Most fundamental are stance, footwork, cuts, thrusts, feints, and parries. Today *kendō* has ten grades and three teaching degrees, with the higher ranks regulated by the All Japan Kendō Federation. The International Kendō Federation, founded in 1970, oversees international *kendō* tournaments.

kenin 家人

(servant; houseman). A term for someone who had entered into a client relationship with a court noble or warrior chieftain. In the 7th and 8th centuries *kenin* were one of the five classes of servants of aristocratic families (see SEMMIN). In the Heian period (794–1185) *kenin* were attached as servants to the houses of major nobles and warrior leaders. In the Kamakura period (1185–1333) and Edo period (1600–1868) vassals of the shogunate were called GOKENIN (housemen).

kenka ryōseibai 喧嘩両成敗

Principle according to which both parties in a private fight are punished. It was first institutionalized in the Nambokuchō (Northern and Southern Courts) period (1337–92), when the Muromachi shogunate (1338–1573) issued the interdict Kassen no Toga no Koto (1350) in order to prevent the increasing fights among *samurai*. According to this interdict, when two samurai engaged in a fight over territorial rights rather than seeking the shogunate's judgment, the shogunate confiscated all the land of the samurai who had started the fight and half the land of the one who had been forced into the fight. This law was reissued by the Muromachi shogunate in 1516. After the Ōnin War (1467–77), SENGOKU DAIMYŌ (warlord) families established similar codes in their domains. During the Sengoku (Warring States) period (1467–1568) *kenka ryōseibai* was also applied to priests and commoners. In the Edo period (1600–1868), the practice continued, although the principle was not officially part of the KUJIKATA OSADAMEGAKI, the fundamental code of the Tokugawa shogunate.

Kenkoku Kinen no Hi → holidays, national

Kennaiki 建内記

Full title *Kenshō In Naifu ki*. Diary of Madenokōji Tokifusa (1394–1457), who be-

came inner minister (NAIDAIJIN or *naifu*) in 1445; Kenshō In is his posthumous title. The diary, an important source for the study of courtier society in the Muromachi period (1333–1568), covered the years 1414–55, but only the 50 volumes for 1428–47 survive.

Kenninji 建仁寺

ZEN monastery of the RINZAI SECT located in Higashiyama Ward, Kyōto; established by EISAI (or Yōsai), who served as its first abbot. In 1202 the shōgun MINAMOTO NO YORIIE commissioned Eisai to found a monastery in the southern part of Kyōto. Eisai modeled it on the Baizhang (Pai-chang) monastery in China, built during the Tang (T'ang) dynasty (618–907). The monastery was named Kenninji after the era (Kennin) in which it was built. Eisai transmitted the teachings of the Rinzai sect of Zen Buddhism, being careful to combine Zen with SHINGON SECT and TENDAI SECT teachings in order to avoid antagonizing the two dominant Japanese Buddhist establishments of the day. The 10th abbot, ENNI, renovated the temple and further promoted Zen teachings. In 1334 it was designated as one of the GOZAN temples, the five most important Zen monasteries patronized by the Kamakura and Muromachi shogunates, and from 1380 it ranked third in importance.

Over the years temple buildings were destroyed by fire and reconstructed so that most of the present buildings date from the Edo period (1600–1868). It houses a number of finely executed screen paintings (*fusuma-e*; see SCREEN AND WALL PAINTING) by the 16th-century artist KAIHŌ YŪSHŌ, as well as paintings by Tawaraya SŌTATSU and HASEGAWA TŌHAKU.

kenrei 県令

(prefectural governor). Title used for the governor of a prefecture from 1871 to 1886. With the return of domain registers to the new imperial government (*hanseki hōkan*) a year after the MEIJI RESTORATION of 1868, the former *daimyō* had been designated governors (*chiji*) of their domains. In 1871 the government instituted a prefectural system (see PREFECTURAL SYSTEM, ESTABLISHMENT OF), and the title for prefectural governors was changed to *kenrei* or *gonrei*, although the governors of Tōkyō, Kyōto, and Ōsaka continued to be called *chiji*. The *kenrei* was appointed by the central government and was in full charge of the administrative business of his prefecture. In 1886 the title of a prefectural governor was changed back to *chiji*.

Kenrei Mon'in 建礼門院

(1155–1213). "Palace name" (*ingō*) of Taira no Tokuko, a daughter of TAIRA NO KIYOMORI. In 1172 she was married to Emperor Takakura (r 1168–80) and six years later gave birth to the boy emperor ANTOKU (r 1180–85). When the Taira (Heike) forces were defeated in the naval battle of DANNOURA (1185), she threw herself into the sea after the boy emperor. Although the child was lost, Kenrei Mon'in was rescued. Grief-stricken, she entered a remote Buddhist convent called JAKKŌIN, where she spent the remainder of her life.

Kenrei Mon'in Ukyō no Daibu shū 建礼門院右京大夫集

(tr *The Poetic Memoirs of Lady Daibu*, 1980). Lyrical autobiography of Lady Daibu, a court lady of the late-12th–early-13th century, made up of 361 poems arranged in basically chronological order and furnished

with prose headnotes (*kotobagaki*). The memoirs consist of two volumes, the first of which describes Lady Daibu's early days at court in the service of Empress Tokuko, later known as KENREI MON'IN (1155–1213). She writes of her love affairs with the noted poet and portrait painter FUJIWARA NO TAKANOBU and with Taira no Sukemori, a grandson of TAIRA NO KIYOMORI. It is the affair with Sukemori that forms the main theme of her work. The second volume tells of the death of Sukemori in the TAIRA-MINAMOTO WAR and her attempts to overcome her grief. She continues with an account of her reentry into service at the court of Emperor GO-TOBA in about 1196. An epilogue consisting of an exchange with FUJIWARA NO SADAIE helps to date the work no later than 1233.

kenrikin → key money

Kenrokuen 兼六園

Garden in Kanazawa, Ishikawa Prefecture, central Honshū. With KAIRAKUEN and KŌRAKUEN, one of the three most famous gardens in Japan. It was laid out in 1822 as the garden of the *daimyō* Maeda Narinaga (1782–1824). The remains of Kanazawa Castle are located near the garden. Area: 10 hectares (25 acres).

kensatsu → public prosecutors

Kensei Hontō 憲政本党

(True Constitutional Party). Political party formed in November 1898 by the former SHIMPOTŌ faction of the KENSEITŌ. In December 1900 ŌKUMA SHIGENOBU became the Kensei Hontō president. The following year 34 members left the party out of opposition to its support for the fourth ITŌ HIROBUMI cabinet's proposal to increase taxes to pay for BOXER REBELLION expenses. In 1903 it allied with Itō's party, the RIKKEN SEIYŪKAI, to oppose the first KATSURA TARŌ cabinet. In January 1907 Ōkuma resigned from the presidency. In the 1909 election the party won 65 seats compared to the Seiyūkai's 204. It decided to merge with other Diet groups to form the RIKKEN KOKUMINTŌ in March 1910. See also POLITICAL PARTIES.

Kenseikai 憲政会

(Constitutional Association). Political party founded in October 1916 through a merger of the RIKKEN DŌSHIKAI, CHŪSEIKAI, and Kōyū Kurabu. Its 197 seats in the House of Representatives immediately made it the majority

Kenzan
1 Teabowl with flowering plum design and calligraphic inscription. Transparent glaze over iron-oxide decoration. Early 18th century. Height 8 cm. Umezawa Memorial Gallery, Tōkyō.
2 *Flower Baskets.* Early 18th century. Colors on paper. 110 × 49 cm. Fukuoka Art Museum.

party and nourished the expectation that its president, KATŌ TAKAAKI, would be named prime minister by the elder statesmen (GENRŌ). The unexpected appointment of General TERAUCHI MASATAKE and his subsequent dissolution of the Diet in the face of a Kenseikai no-confidence motion initiated a decade of political isolation for the Kenseikai. In 1924 it allied with the RIKKEN SEIYŪKAI and KAKUSHIN KURABU to bring down KIYOURA KEIGO's nonparty cabinet and won more than 150 seats to become the majority party. With Katō heading a three-party coalition cabinet (GOKEN SAMPA NAIKAKU), the Kenseikai favored international cooperation and further domestic political reform. Its liberal reputation, however, was sullied by its passage of the repressive PEACE PRESERVATION LAW OF 1925. In June 1927 the party merged with the Seiyū Hontō to form the RIKKEN MINSEITŌ. See also POLITICAL PARTIES.

Kenseitō　　　　　　　　　　憲政党

(Constitutional Party). Political party of the late Meiji period (1868–1912). Formed in June 1898 by an alliance of the JIYŪTŌ (Liberal Party) and the SHIMPOTŌ (Progressive Party), with ŌKUMA SHIGENOBU as president. Following the dissolution of the Diet by ITŌ HIROBUMI, whose cabinet had been unsuccessful in its efforts to increase taxes, the Jiyūtō, headed by ITAGAKI TAISUKE, and the Shimpotō formed the Kenseitō. Ōkuma and Itagaki formed a new cabinet, and, in the election that followed, the Kenseitō won a majority. Members of the old Jiyūtō faction felt they had not been given their share of cabinet appointments and joined YAMAGATA ARITOMO and other conservative elements in criticizing Minister of Education OZAKI YUKIO for his "Republic Speech." Ozaki resigned, but factionalism continued, leading to the resignation of Itagaki, and the cabinet's dissolution. The former Jiyūtō faction reorganized as the new Kenseitō, with Itagaki as its head, and the Ōkuma faction reformed as the KENSEI HONTŌ (True Constitutional Party). The new Kenseitō was absorbed in 1900 by Itō's RIKKEN SEIYŪKAI (Friends of Constitutional Government Party).

Kensetsushō → Ministry of Construction

Kenshō　　　　　　　　　　顕昭

(ca 1130–1210). WAKA poet and Buddhist prelate; adopted son of FUJIWARA NO AKISUKE and a leader of the conservative Rokujō school of poets. Kenshō wrote commentaries on the MAN'YŌSHŪ, KOKINSHŪ, and other classical anthologies. He participated as both poet and judge in several major poetry contests, in

which he served as a principal proponent of Rokujō poetic ideals; his disputes with JAKUREN over poetic theory on the occasion of the "Poetry Contest in 600 Rounds" (*Roppyakuban uta-awase*) of 1193 are particularly famous. Thirteen of his poems are included in the imperial anthology SENZAI WAKASHŪ (ca 1188, Collection of a Thousand Years).

kentōshi → Sui and Tang (T'ang) China, embassies to

Kenuki　　　　　　　　　　毛抜

(The Tweezers). KABUKI play; one of the celebrated kabuki numbers known as the KABUKI JŪHACHIBAN. A *jidai-mono* (historical play) by Tsuuchi Hanjūrō, Yasuda Abun, and Nakada Mansuke, it was first performed in 1742. Originally act 3 of a longer play called *Narukami Fudō Kitayama-zakura*, *Kenuki* is a classic example of a kabuki plot—the usurpation by an evil faction in a feudal domain of the privileges of the ruling house. To end a severe drought, the emperor has commanded the Ono family to present a poem by an Ono clan ancestress that possesses the magic power of causing rain. To its consternation, the Ono family discovers that the poem is missing. Moreover, their daughter's marriage has had to be postponed because of a strange affliction: her long hair stands on end. An emissary from her fiancé's family, the central figure in the play, solves both mysteries by discovering that villains trying to prevent the marriage had put a magnet in the attic to pull the girl's hair ornaments upward and had stolen the poem as well.

Kenwood Corporation　[株]ケンウッド

(Ken'uddo). Company manufacturing and selling home and car audio equipment, communications equipment, and testing instruments. Incorporated in 1946. It was the first to market transistorized amplifiers in 1962. In 1958 it established a sales company in the United States, and it now has 10 sales companies in Europe, Australia, Hong Kong, and Canada as well as manufacturing companies in France and Singapore. Kenwood has expanded its activities to include satellite-related communications development and other new business areas. Sales for the fiscal year ending March 1991 totaled ¥182.1 billion (US $1.3 billion), and capitalization stood at ¥22.0 billion (US $160.3 million). Headquarters are in Tōkyō.

ken'yakurei　　　　　　　　倹約令

(sumptuary edicts). Edicts issued during the Edo period (1600–1868) by the Tokugawa shogunate and domainal governments to enforce frugality in finances, dress, food, housing, and almost every other aspect of life. See also KEIAN NO OFUREGAKI; KYŌHŌ REFORMS; KANSEI REFORMS; TEMPŌ REFORMS.

Ken'yūsha　　　　　　　　　硯友社

Literary coterie. Formed in February 1885 as a casual fraternity of college students to dabble in literature, the Ken'yūsha became Japan's first major modern literary clique. Their coterie journal, *Garakuta bunko* (Library of Odds and Ends), launched the careers of several major novelists before the group dissolved in 1903.

The four charter members, ranging in age from 17 to 19, were OZAKI KŌYŌ, YAMADA BIMYŌ, Ishibashi Shian (1867–1927), and Maruoka Kyūka (1865–1927). Under the group name Ken'yūsha ("Friends of the Inkstone"), they inaugurated their journal,

Garakuta bunko, which first circulated among friends in handwritten copies and later was printed for private distribution. By the time the magazine went on sale (16 issues, May 1888–February 1889), membership had swollen to 85, including KAWAKAMI BIZAN and IWAYA SAZANAMI, soon joined by Emi Suiin (1869–1934). Shortening its name to *Bunko* (nos. 17–27, March–October 1889), the journal attracted new members, one of whom was HIROTSU RYŪRŌ, and guest contributors such as KŌDA ROHAN. Between 1889 and 1892, the Ken'yūsha published three more periodicals, *Shōbungaku, Edo murasaki*, and *Senshi bankō*.

Members who had established a reputation, particularly through the ambitious fiction series *Shincho hyakushu* (A Hundred New Volumes) inaugurated by the bookshop Yoshioka Shosekiten in 1889, found themselves besieged by aspiring young writers begging to be disciples. Out of this second generation of Ken'yūsha members and associates emerged authors whose historical significance ultimately matched or surpassed that of the first generation: IZUMI KYŌKA, TOKUDA SHŪSEI, NAGAI KAFŪ, and TAYAMA KATAI.

Ken'yūsha literary contributions included replacing abstract concepts with a realistic portrayal of the human dilemma; bringing a degree of psychological depth, analytical insight, and social perspective to literature; making stylistic innovations (see GEMBUN ITCHI); and contributing to the development of POPULAR FICTION and the novel of manners (FŪZOKU SHŌSETSU). Although many now seem elaborate and maudlin melodramas, the best of the Ken'yūsha works stand as important expressions of indigenous aesthetic and literary traditions in the transitional period before the mainstream of Japanese literature entered fully into the Western-oriented phase of its evolution.

Kenzan　　　　　　　　　　乾山

(1663–1743). Potter and painter. Also known as Ogata Kenzan. Real name Ogata Shinsei. The third son of Ogata Sōken (1621–87), a wealthy Kyōto textile merchant, he was the younger brother of the Edo-period (1600–1868) artist Ogata KŌRIN.

Kenzan built a scholarly retreat near the kiln of the prominent Kyōto potter NONOMURA NINSEI, and contacts with Ninsei and his sons were instrumental in moving Kenzan toward an active career as an artist. In 1699 Kenzan established a kiln at Narutaki, northwest of Kyōto. Since the northwesterly direction is called *inui*, Kenzan called the kiln Inuiyama (Northwest Mountain). The same characters used to write Inuiyama can be read *kenzan*, which became his best-known art name. His brother Kōrin joined him, and some of the finest surviving examples of Ogata ceramic art are the result of their collaboration.

By 1712 Kenzan was forced for financial reasons to give up his adventurous and creative work at Narutaki. He opened a retail pottery store in Kyōto and rented facilities for the production of more routine pieces that emphasized the strong overglaze enamel colors popularized by Ninsei. In 1731 he accepted the patronage of a priestly aristocrat in the city of Edo (now Tōkyō). This financial reprieve gave him a new creative impetus, and he remained active in scholarly and artistic endeavors until his death. Kenzan is noted for his imaginative combination of the poetic sensibilities of the Chinese literati-painter tradition (using bold blackish iron-oxide brush strokes on a ground of white slip) with the decorative verve and invention of the great Japanese artist-artisans who flourished in the 17th and early 18th centuries. See also KYŌTO CERAMICS.

kenzuishi→Sui and Tang (T'ang) China, embassies to

keppan 血判
("blood seal"). A fingerprint stamped with blood drawn from one's fingertip; affixed on or beside a signature to show one's responsibility for and adherence to the terms of various contractual and ceremonial documents. This custom, which can be traced back to the 14th century, became popular among the warrior class during the Sengoku period (1467–1568), a time of war and treachery. During the Edo period (1600–1868), it spread to other social classes and was used, for example, to seal pledges of love.

Kerama Islands 慶良間諸島
(Kerama Rettō). Group of some 20 small islands approximately 30 km (19 mi) west of the main island of Okinawa, clustered around the larger islands of Tokashikijima and Zamamijima. Part of Okinawa Prefecture. There is coastal fishing but relatively little farming because of the hilly terrain.

Kesennuma 気仙沼[市]
City in northeastern Miyagi Prefecture, northern Honshū, on the Pacific coast. A fishing port since ancient times, Kesennuma also has several seafood-processing plants. Pop: 65,578.

keshin→avatar

Ketsumeidan Jiken→League of Blood Incident

ketsuzei ikki 血税一揆
("blood tax" riots). Also called chōhei hantai ikki. Riots by peasants in opposition to the CONSCRIPTION ORDINANCE OF 1873 (ketsuzei or "blood tax" was a metaphor for compulsory military service that had been used in official notices). More than 15 riots took place, mostly in western Japan, in which peasants attacked and burned government offices, schools, and police stations. The riots were eventually quelled, the leaders executed, and more than 60,000 others punished.

keyaki→zelkova

key money 権利金
(kenrikin). A payment by the lessee (tenant) of a specified sum to the lessor (landlord) at the commencement of a lease agreement for land or structures. This payment is a premium that is not returned to the lessee upon the expiration of the lease. It is sometimes referred to as fee money (reikin) or an honorarium (shakin). The practice of requiring a lessee to pay key money originated in the large urban areas of Japan and has no legal basis. Whether a lessee is required to pay key money theoretically depends upon the mutual agreement of the parties in the lease agreement, but in reality, if a lessor requests such a fee as a condition of the lease contract, it is very difficult for a lessee to refuse. The amount of key money is usually set unilaterally by the landlord.

The reasons for paying key money vary, as do the legal consequences. In a lease of land or a building for business purposes, key money is often paid as compensation for the

benefit the lessee obtains in acquiring the lease of a preferred business location. In a lease for residential purposes, key money may be a prepayment of part of the rent or compensation to the lessor for granting consent (which is legally required) to the assignment of a lease right by a lessee to a third party. See also RENTAL DEPOSIT.

ki 気
An important concept in Japanese traditional popular psychology and in interpersonal relationships. The word ki, which means loosely "mind," "spirit," or "heart," is used in over 40 idiomatic expressions to describe various states of mind. They may be classified roughly into the following categories. (1) Consciousness, awareness, or sanity: when a person becomes insane, it is said that his "ki is out of kilter" (ki ga kuruu); when he faints, his "ki becomes distant" (ki ga tōku naru); when he is distracted, his "ki becomes scattered" (ki ga chiru). (2) Interest, intention, or volition: when an individual is willing, his "ki proceeds" (ki ga susumu); when he loses his initial interest, his "ki changes" (ki ga kawaru). (3) Mood, feelings, or emotions: when a person feels depressed, his "ki sinks or becomes closed" (ki ga shizumu/fusagu); when he is nervous, his "ki becomes ruffled" (ki ga kusha kusha suru). (4) Temperament, heart, or mind: of a quick-tempered person it is said that his "ki is short" (ki ga mijikai); of a good-natured person that his "ki is good" (ki ga ii); of a patient person that his "ki is long" (ki ga nagai). However, in most expressions it is ki, not the individual, that is the subject of the statement. When a person is patient, it is not he but the ki (in him) that is long. When an individual feels depressed, it is not he but ki that sinks.

Kiaochow concession→Jiaozhou (Kiaochow) concession

Ki Baitei 紀梅亭
(1734–1810). Painter of the literati (BUNJINGA) manner. A native of Ōtsu in Ōmi Province (now Shiga Prefecture). A disciple of BUSON (1716–84) both in painting and haiku poetry, Baitei was often referred to as Ōmi Buson and Ōtsu Buson. Baitei's paintings show much of the lyricism found in the work of Buson, though in general they are less meticulously executed, their rough brushwork giving the impression of tremendous power and dramatic energy. His specialty was landscape painting, but he numbered among his accomplishments haiga (haiku paintings), giga (humorous paintings), ŌTSU-E (folk-style pictures from Ōtsu), bijinga (paintings of beautiful women), and kyōga (satirical paintings).

Kibi Kōgen 吉備高原
(Kibi Highland). Series of low-lying mountains. Southern corner of the Chūgoku Mountains. Extends from Okayama Prefecture to Hiroshima Prefecture, western Honshū. In the valleys are paddy fields, while in the uplands are limestone quarries and cement plants. Stock farming and vegetable farming flourish on the highland. Elevation: 200–600 m (660–2,000 ft).

Kibi no Makibi 吉備真備
(695–775). Scholar-official of the Nara period (710–794). Born into a powerful family of the Kibi region (now part of Okayama Prefecture). In 717 he was sent, with the scholar ABE NO NAKAMARO, the priest GEMBŌ, and others, to study in China (see SUI AND

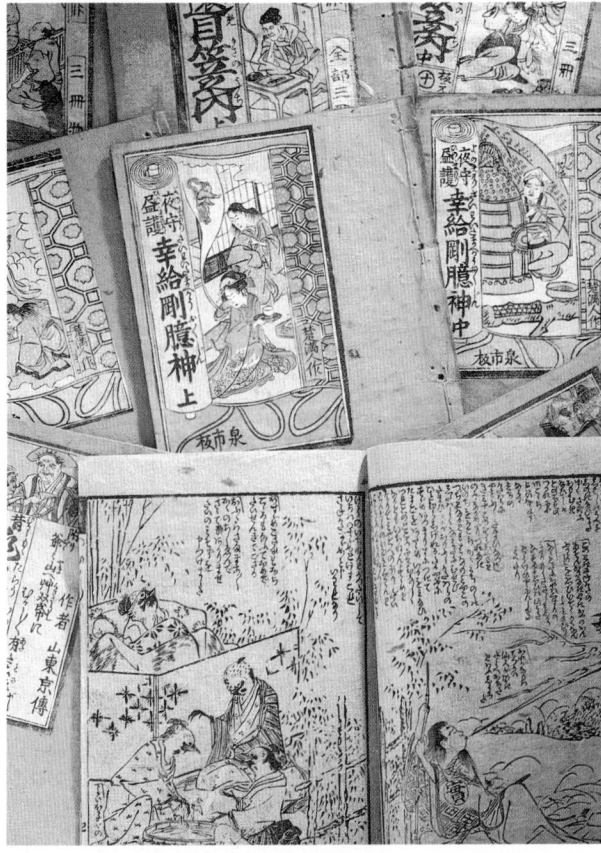

kibyōshi This genre of popular illustrated fiction, widely read during the late Edo period, derived its name from the yellow-jacketed booklets in which it was published.

TANG [T'ANG] CHINA, EMBASSIES TO). Following their return in 735, Makibi and Gembō became influential in government under the regime of TACHIBANA NO MOROE, but they were demoted after the rise to power of FUJIWARA NO NAKAMARO. In 764 Makibi played a central role in the suppression of a revolt led by Nakamaro. In 766 he was promoted to minister of the right (udaijin). However, with the death of Empress Shōtoku (Empress KŌKEN) and the ensuing succession dispute, he retired from office in 771. Makibi was well versed in the Confucian classics as well as in astronomy, military science, and law; he also directed the construction of the temple TŌDAIJI. His first trip to China is depicted in the scroll Kibi Daijin nittō ekotoba.

Kibuneyama 貴船山
Mountain in northern part of the city of Kyōto. It is the site of Kibune Shrine, dedicated to the god of rain. Noted for forests of cedar, it has numerous hiking trails. Height: 700 m (2,297 ft).

kibyōshi 黄表紙
(literally, "yellow covers"). Major form of GESAKU literature, the generic designation for all prose fiction from the mid-18th century to the end of the Edo period (1600–1868). Kibyōshi is one of the main subgenres of the KUSAZŌSHI (grass books), a distinctive genre of popular illustrated fiction produced mainly by writers and artists in the city of Edo (now Tōkyō), ranging from juvenile tales to elaborate stories. The name kibyōshi derives from the bright yellow color of these jacketed booklets, similar to earlier species of the kusazōshi genre—the kurobon (black books) and aohon (green books).

The format of the kibyōshi is a 13-by-18-centimeter (5-by-7-in) bound pamphlet of woodblock-print illustrations, with narrative and dialogue inscribed in the blank spaces in the drawings. Five double pages are bound in a yellow cover; most stories are made up of three such pamphlets. Among

Kido Takayoshi One of the *samurai* leaders of the Meiji Restoration, Kido became a central figure in the new government, advocating political centralization and modernization.

the illustrators were such prominent UKIYO-E artists as TORII KIYONAGA and UTAGAWA TOYOKUNI.

The *kibyōshi* emerged as a distinct category of fiction with the success of *Kinkin sensei eiga no yume* (1775; tr *Mr Glitter 'n' Gold's Dream of Splendor*, 1970). *Kinkin sensei* was written and illustrated by a *samurai* who wrote many *kibyōshi* using the pen name KOIKAWA HARUMACHI. The best *kibyōshi* were written in the decade before 1791, the year in which the fury of the moral austerity program initiated by MATSUDAIRA SADANOBU was directed at writers of fiction. Provocative writers of that period were Tōrai Sanna (1744–1810), SANTŌ KYŌDEN, and HŌSEIDŌ KISANJI. More than 2,000 titles were published between 1775 and 1806, after which reader preference shifted to the GŌKAN (bound volumes).

kidai → kigo

Kida Minoru
きだみのる

(1895–1975). Writer. Real name Yamada Yoshihiko. Born in Kagoshima Prefecture; studied at Keiō University. From 1933 to 1939 he studied sociology at the University of Paris and worked as a reporter. His *Kichigai buraku shūyū kikō* (1946), a novel in essay form satirizing postwar Japanese society, received the 1948 Mainichi Book Award. In collaboration with Hayashi Tatsuo (1896–1984), Kida published a 20-volume translation, entitled *Fāburu konchū ki* (1958), of Jean Henri Fabre's work on insects, *Souvenirs entomologiques.* He also translated French works on sociology.

Kido Kōichi
木戸幸一

(1889–1977). Politician. Born in Tōkyō; grandson of KIDO TAKAYOSHI, one of the leaders of the MEIJI RESTORATION (1868); graduate of Kyōto University. Kido held minor bureaucratic posts before becoming minister of education in the first KONOE FUMIMARO cabinet (1937) and home minister in the HIRANUMA KIICHIRŌ cabinet (1939). As lord keeper of the privy seal (NAIDAIJIN) from 1940, he called a meeting of JŪSHIN (senior statesmen) and recommended that Konoe succeed YONAI MITSUMASA as prime minister. He did so again in 1941, this time recommending that TŌJŌ HIDEKI succeed Konoe. Kido is generally credited with persuading the government toward the end of the war to accept the conditions of the POTSDAM DECLARATION. Sentenced by the International Military Tribunal (see WAR CRIMES TRIALS) to life imprisonment as a class-A war criminal, he was released in 1955. His diary, *Kido nikki* (1966), covering January 1930–December 1945, is an important historical source for the last days of World War II.

Kido Kōin → Kido Takayoshi

Kido Shirō
城戸四郎

(1894–1977). Film producer. Born in Tōkyō. Graduating from Tōkyō University in 1919, he joined what is now SHŌCHIKU CO, LTD. Becoming the head of the Shōchiku Kamata studio in 1924, he actively encouraged OZU YASUJIRŌ, KINOSHITA KEISUKE, and other directors to make films with an optimistic humanitarian content. Such films appealed especially to female audiences and were labeled as "Ōfuna-style" movies after the site of Shōchiku's Ōfuna studios in Kanagawa Prefecture. In 1940 he became the

president of the Nan'yō Eiga Kyōkai, and in 1943 he became the chairman of the Dai Nihon Eiga Kyōkai, two film organizations that promoted the war effort. After World War II, Shōchiku revived the Ōfuna-style movie with such films as Ōba Hideo's KIMI NO NA WA (1953, What Is Your Name?) and Kinoshita Keisuke's NIJŪSHI NO HITOMI (1954, Twenty-Four Eyes). Kido served as president of Shōchiku from 1954 to 1971.

Kidōtai → Riot Police

Kido Takayoshi
木戸孝允

(1833–77). Statesman of the Meiji period (1868–1912). Also known as Kido Kōin. With SAIGŌ TAKAMORI and ŌKUBO TOSHIMICHI, one of the "three heroes" of the MEIJI RESTORATION of 1868. As representative of the Chōshū domain (now Yamaguchi Prefecture) he negotiated the secret alliance (1866) with the Satsuma domain (now Kagoshima Prefecture) that eventually overthrew the TOKUGAWA SHOGUNATE (1603–1867); his initiatives between 1868 and 1871 as a Meiji government official brought about the abolition of the feudal system and the creation of a centralized bureaucratic state.

Kido was born in the Chōshū castle town of Hagi into the *samurai* household of the domain physician. Adopted by the Katsura family at age seven, until 1865 he was known as Katsura Kogorō. He received an orthodox education at the Meirinkan, the domain school, and he then attended the private academy of YOSHIDA SHŌIN, where he was introduced to imperial loyalism.

In 1852 Kido went to Edo (now Tōkyō) to study swordsmanship. There he established ties with loyalists from Mito (now part of Ibaraki Prefecture) and other domains. He studied artillery with EGAWA TARŌZAEMON and, after observing foreign shipbuilders at Shimoda and Nagasaki, designed the first Western-style schooner to be constructed (1856) in Chōshū.

After 1858 Kido acted as a liaison between the radical lower-samurai loyalists and the regular domain bureaucracy. In 1862 he fell under shogunate suspicion for his ties with Mito loyalists who had attempted to assassinate the senior councillor (*rōjū*) ANDŌ NOBUMASA. Kido was transferred from Edo to Kyōto, where he joined the inner circle of Chōshū officials who guided their domain to a loyalist-exclusionist SONNŌ JŌI policy.

As chief domain officer in Kyōto, he failed to obtain advance warning of the COUP D'ETAT OF 30 SEPTEMBER 1863, in which Satsuma and Aizu drove Chōshū forces out of the city. He was involved in the HAMAGURI GOMON INCIDENT of 20 August 1864, an unsuccessful attack by Chōshū forces on Kyōto. Kido went into hiding with the *geisha* Ikumatsu, who later became his wife. Summoned back to Chōshū when the radical clique under TAKASUGI SHINSAKU regained control of the domain in 1865 (see CHŌSHŪ EXPEDITIONS), Kido negotiated a secret anti-Tokugawa alliance with Satsuma in 1866 (see SATSUMA-CHŌSHŪ ALLIANCE).

Following the restoration of imperial rule, Kido became the chief Chōshū spokesman in the new government, itself largely a Satsuma-Chōshū creation (see HAMBATSU). He shared in drafting the CHARTER OATH. He promoted policies of centralization and modernization, most notably as SANGI (councillor) in 1870–74 and 1875–76. He directed the surrender of domain registers (*hanseki hōkan*) in 1869 and worked for the abolition of domains and the establishment of prefectures

in 1871 (see PREFECTURAL SYSTEM, ESTABLISHMENT OF).

As associate ambassador to the United States and Europe with the IWAKURA MISSION (1871–73), he was able to study Western political and educational systems. On his return he presented a memorial on constitutional government. In the cabinet debate of October 1873 he and the peace faction barely defeated the war faction of Saigō Takamori, who espoused an expedition against Korea (see SEIKANRON). After 1873 Kido lost the dominant position in the government to Ōkubo and resigned from it in protest against the TAIWAN EXPEDITION of 1874.

Following the ŌSAKA CONFERENCE OF 1875, Kido returned to the government as councillor. In June he presided over the ASSEMBLY OF PREFECTURAL GOVERNORS. In his last years Kido oversaw the young emperor MEIJI's education.

kienrei
棄捐令

Debt moratoriums declared by the Tokugawa shogunate (1603–1867) to save its retainers from destitution. The retainers habitually sought cash advances against their rice stipends from FUDASASHI (rice brokers); these debts, with interest, rose beyond the retainers' ability to pay. The shogunate attempted to control interest rates and *samurai* expenditures, but the debts continued to mount. In 1789 the senior councillor (*rōjū*) MATSUDAIRA SADANOBU canceled all debts to *fudasashi* incurred before 1784, a total of some 1.2 million *ryō*. The shogunate decreed another *kienrei* in 1843 as part of the TEMPŌ REFORMS, and various *daimyō* instituted similar orders at different times, bankrupting many *fudasashi*.

Ki family
紀氏

(Kishi). Influential family (UJI) of ancient Japan. They claimed descent from Ki no Tsuno no Sukune, son of TAKENOUCHI NO SUKUNE, a legendary warrior of the YAMATO COURT (ca 4th century–ca mid-7th century). According to the early chronicle KOJIKI (712), Takenouchi was the common ancestor of the HATA FAMILY, Kose family, SOGA FAMILY, Heguri family, Ki family, and other prominent families. However, the SHINSEN SHŌJIROKU, a 9th-century genealogy, lists the Ki and Soga families as descended from the imperial line. Prominent Ki family members included the poets KI NO TSURAYUKI and KI NO TOMONORI.

kigen
紀元

(era). A chronological system such as the Christian era or the Islamic era in which events are dated from a specified base year; also, the base year itself or the period of time reckoned from it. In 1872, four years after the Meiji Restoration, the Japanese government officially inaugurated the use of the "imperial era" (*kōki*), reckoned from 660 BC, the year in which the legendary first emperor, JIMMU, was said to have ascended the throne. According to the imperial era, 1990 would have been *kigen* (or *kōki*) 2650.

The reckoning of historical dates from the year of Jimmu's accession was used only infrequently—although the year *kigen* 2600 was greeted with considerable fanfare in 1940—and has been rarely used since the end of World War II. The method traditionally preferred was based on an emperor's reign or, later, on the use of era names (NENGŌ; see also PERIODIZATION; CALENDAR, DATES, AND TIME).

A national holiday named Kigensetsu was

established by the Meiji government to commemorate the date of Jimmu's accession. The holiday was abolished in 1948 but was restored in 1966 as Kenkoku Kinen no Hi (National Foundation Day) and is celebrated on 11 February. See KIGENSETSU CONTROVERSY.

Kigensetsu controversy　紀元節論争

(Kigensetsu *ronsō*). Post–World War II debate over the revival of Kigensetsu (see KIGEN; now known as Kenkoku Kinen no Hi, or National Foundation Day) as a national holiday. There had always been an argument as to the validity of dating the founding of Japan from the legendary enthronement of Emperor JIMMU in 660 BC. In 1872 the leaders of the new Meiji government had officially adopted this dating. By declaring in 1873 that the 11th of February would thenceforth be a national holiday to commemorate the founding of the Japanese empire, they hoped to give further legitimacy to the imperial institution. In 1948 the *kigen* system of dating and most traditional holidays were abolished; Kigensetsu in particular had come to be associated with the "emperor system" and with the excesses of nationalism during the pre–World War II period. Therefore, when Prime Minister YOSHIDA SHIGERU advocated the revival of Kigensetsu in 1951, there was strong opposition, especially from leftists and intellectuals. Nevertheless, in 1966 a bill was passed declaring 11 February a national holiday, Kenkoku Kinen no Hi.

kigo　季語

(seasonal words). Also called *kidai.* Words with fixed seasonal connotations used in the traditional Japanese verse forms of RENGA and HAIKU. *Kigo* are essential to the aesthetics and form of these genres, in which people, things, and events can be fully appreciated and take on their proper meanings only in the context of temporal flow and the rhythms of nature. Obvious examples of *kigo* are the use of cherry blossoms to indicate spring; cicadas, summer; chrysanthemums, autumn; and snow, winter.

Kigo became a required element in *renga* during the Muromachi period (1333–1568); during the Edo period (1600–1868), when haiku became established as an independent verse form, glossaries of seasonal words known as SAIJIKI were published as aids to haiku composition. Wide distribution of such glossaries helped fix most of the standard repertoire of *kigo* at about this time, though new *kigo* continue to enter the lexicon, reflecting changes in lifestyle and customs—the use in contemporary haiku of words such as "skiing" and "Christmas" to indicate winter are an example of this.

Perhaps the most significant function of *kigo* is the way in which they extend the temporal and spatial range of characteristically brief traditional verse forms, permitting them to attain the compression, intensity, and allusiveness that is their hallmark.

Kiguchi Kohei　木口小平

(1873–94). Soldier and war hero of the SINO-JAPANESE WAR OF 1894–1895. Born in Okayama Prefecture. Serving as bugler at a battle in Korea, he was wounded but continued to sound the charge until he died. His heroic death was cited in moral and ethics primers for schoolchildren until the end of World War II.

kihachijō　黄八丈

("yellow silk cloth"). Type of silk textile made on the island of HACHIJŌJIMA in the Izu Islands, Tōkyō Prefecture. *Kihachijō* features stripes or cross stripes in colors such as yellow, brown, black, and white. Silkworms, their mulberry fodder, and materials for dyes used to make these textiles are all native to Hachijōjima. A mordant is used to fix the natural dyes, resulting in a colorfast textile with an elegant luster. During the latter part of the Muromachi period (1333–1568), *kihachijō* was used to pay taxes. During the Edo period (1600–1868), it was prized by *daimyō* and ladies who served the shōguns. Gradually it came to be used by the general public as well. *Kihachijō* is still made today and has been designated an Intangible Cultural Property.

Kihara Hitoshi　木原均

(1893–1986). Geneticist. Born in Tōkyō. Graduate of Hokkaidō University. He became a professor at Kyōto University in 1927. His most important research concerned the cytogenetics of wheat. He succeeded in tracing the original ancestry of wheat. His other research includes work on the seedless watermelon and the sex chromosomes of *suiba* (a variety of sorrel). He founded the Kihara Institute for Biological Research in 1942 and served as director of the National Institute of Genetics. He was awarded the Order of Culture in 1948.

Kiheitai　奇兵隊

(Irregular Militia). A crack volunteer militia unit organized by the Chōshū domain (now Yamaguchi Prefecture) in 1863. Formed by TAKASUGI SHINSAKU, the unit comprised 300–400 men of all social classes, including the peasantry, from Chōshū and other domains. Leaders were chosen for ability rather than hereditary status, and the unit was known for its strict discipline, Western-style training and armament, and overall effectiveness. Funds were contributed both by the domainal government and by wealthy farmers and merchants. The unit played a crucial role in the events surrounding the MEIJI RESTORATION, serving as the military arm of the proimperial reformist faction in Chōshū. It saw action in the SHIMONOSEKI BOMBARDMENT of 1864, the overthrow of the proshogunate conservative faction within Chōshū, the repulsion of the second Chōshū Expedition in 1866, and the BOSHIN CIVIL WAR of 1868. The Kiheitai was disbanded in 1869 after the establishment of the Meiji government, but the success of this mixed unit against traditional *samurai* forces was a factor in the establishment of a modern system of universal conscription in Japan.

Kihira Tadayoshi　紀平正美

(1874–1949). Philosopher. Born in Mie Prefecture, he graduated from the Department of Philosophy of Tōkyō University in 1900. In 1919 he became a professor at the Peers' School (now Gakushūin University) and from 1932 to 1943 was an active member of Kokumin Seishin Bunka Kenkyūjo (Institute for Research on National Spirit and Culture), a government-operated organ for the propagation of nationalist ideology. Although he pioneered the Japanese study of Hegel's philosophy, after the publication of *Gyō no tetsugaku* (1923, Philosophy of Spiritual Discipline), he concentrated on the Japanese spiritual tradition and championed nationalist philosophy in such publications as *Nihon seishin* (1930, The Spirit of Japan).

Kii Channel　紀伊水道

(Kii Suidō). Between eastern Shikoku and the western coast of the Kii Peninsula, Wakayama Prefecture, central Honshū, connecting the Inland Sea and Ōsaka Bay with the Pacific Ocean. It is a major shipping artery. Length: 50 km (30 mi); width: 30–50 km (19–30 mi).

Kii domain　紀伊藩

(Kii *han*). Edo-period (1600–1868) domain that extended over Kii Province and part of ISE PROVINCE; present-day Wakayama Prefecture and part of Mie Prefecture. It was granted in 1619 to Tokugawa Yorinobu (1602–71), who, as a son of TOKUGAWA IEYASU, received the status of SHIMPAN (collateral vassal) and became founder of one of the three cadet houses of the Tokugawa family (GOSANKE). The fifth lord of Kii, TOKUGAWA YOSHIMUNE, revived the domain economy through a series of reforms and subsequently became the eighth shōgun. OMOTEDAKA (estimated annual production of rice): 555,000 KOKU (one *koku* = 180 liters or 5 US bushels).

Kii Mountains　紀伊山地

(Kii Sanchi). Mountain range covering the Kii Peninsula in Nara, Wakayama, and Mie prefectures, central Honshū. The highest peak is Hakkenzan (1,915 m; 6,283 ft). The area has abundant water resources. The mountains are covered with forests of cryptomeria and cypress, and lumbering is important. Yoshino-Kumano National Park and Kōya-Ryūjin Quasi-National Park are the area's main attractions.

Kii Peninsula　紀伊半島

(Kii Hantō). Located in the southern Kinki region, central Honshū. Jutting out into the Pacific Ocean, it encompasses Mie, Nara, and Wakayama prefectures. The greater part of the peninsula is covered by the rugged Kii Mountains. Heavily indented coasts surround the peninsula. There is heavy precipitation, with the annual rainfall of the city of Owase exceeding 400 cm (160 in). The principal industries are forestry, fishing, and tourism.

Kiire, Port of　喜入港

(Kiire Kō). Port located in the town of Kiire on KAGOSHIMA BAY in the eastern part of SATSUMA PENINSULA in southern Kagoshima Prefecture, Kyūshū. Japan's first crude oil storage facility, and the world's largest, was established here in 1975.

kiji → pheasants

kijiya　木地屋

Traditional woodworkers who mainly produced round wooden objects such as bowls, trays, and KOKESHI dolls, using a lathe (ROKURO). Also called *kijishi, kijibiki,* and *rokuroshi.* They built temporary huts in the mountains as base camps for collecting wood, changing locations when the proper kind of wood became scarce. Their traditional base was in the Ogura valley of Ōmi Province (now Eigenji Machi, Kanzaki District, Shiga Prefecture). The two shrines located there are dedicated to the supposed *kijiya* ancestor, Prince Koretaka (844–897), first son of Emperor Montoku (r 850–858). *Kijiya* credit the prince with the invention of the lathe. After the Meiji Restoration (1868), *kijiya* were unable to traverse the mountains freely and so turned to valley agriculture or woodworking in the city. The contribution

Kikaishima The reefs surrounding this island in the Amami group are formed of fossilized coral.

Kikuchi Kan This author and playwright also established the monthly magazine *Bungei shunjū* and two major literary prizes.

Kikuta Kazuo This stage and radio playwright's accomplishments include the production of Japanese versions of such Broadway musicals as *My Fair Lady*.

of *kijiya* to Japanese crafts is noteworthy, as several of the areas now famous for LACQUER WARE or WOODENWARE developed around *kijiya* communities.

Kikaishima 喜界島

Island approximately 25 km (16 mi) east of the island of AMAMI ŌSHIMA, Kagoshima Prefecture, Kyūshū. One of the AMAMI ISLANDS, it is rather flat and surrounded by coral reefs. Some 90 percent of this subtropical island is arable. The chief crops are sugarcane and melons. Stock raising, sugar production, and the manufacture of such products as Ōshima *tsumugi* (pongee) are important. Area: 56 sq km (22 sq mi).

kikajin 帰化人

Immigrants from the Asian continent (particularly the Korean peninsula) who settled in early Japan, especially the group led by YUZUKI NO KIMI, ancestor of the HATA FAMILY, from the Korean state of PAEKCHE in about AD 400. The term *kika*, meaning to change country of allegiance (*jin* means people), was applied to this group by the chronicle NIHON SHOKI (720). The term *kikajin*, as first defined in the mid-9th-century legal commentaries, RYŌ NO SHUGE, follows earlier Chinese usage and has ethnocentric connotations of "grateful change of allegiance" (J: *kinka naiki*) to new rulers. Many scholars today prefer a more neutral term like *toraijin* ("people from overseas") or *ijūmin* (immigrants). Historians have commonly used the term *kikajin* to refer, also, to several generations of the newcomers' descendants.

Records suggest that the *kikajin* came for a variety of political and economic reasons. Aside from pre-4th-century immigrants of whom no written record exists, the newcomers arrived in three roughly definable periods. The first was at the end of the 4th century and the beginning of the 5th century. This group introduced silkworm culture, horse breeding, and SUE WARE. The second phase, from the late 5th century until the beginning of the 7th century, brought immigrants associated with the development of learning, government administration and technology, the BE system of organized economic production, and the introduction of BUDDHISM. The third wave of immigrants came in the late 7th century and included many people fleeing from the warfare and political changes that accompanied the unification of Korea by the kingdom of SILLA in the 660s. Over the years these groups, through intermarriage and cultural assimilation, lost any distinguishing traits.

Kikakuin Jiken → Planning Board Incident

Kikawada Kazutaka 木川田一隆

(1899–1977). Businessman. Born in Fukushima Prefecture. Graduate of Tōkyō University. In 1926 Kikawada joined Tōkyō Dentō Kabushiki Kaisha (reorganized in 1951 as TŌKYŌ ELECTRIC POWER CO, INC). After World War II, Kikawada promoted the private ownership of the electric power industry in cooperation with nine regional companies under the leadership of MATSUNAGA YASUZAEMON. He became director of Tōkyō Electric Power Co in 1951 and president in 1961. From 1963 to 1975 Kikawada served as chairman of the JAPAN ASSOCIATION OF CORPORATE EXECUTIVES (Keizai Dōyūkai). From 1966 to 1977 he also served as chairman for the Economic Council, an advisory organ for the ECONOMIC PLANNING AGENCY. A leading business theorist, he worked for the development of a harmonious relationship between industry and society.

Kike wadatsumi no koe きけわだつみのこえ

Collection of letters and other writings of Japanese students who died in World War II; published posthumously in 1949 by a committee organized by survivors, which was later formally organized as the Nihon Sembotsu Gakusei Kinen Kai (Association for a Memorial to Japanese Students Fallen in Battle), more popularly known as the Wadatsumikai. The book has been translated into many languages; an English translation, *Hearken to the Ocean's Voice!*, appeared in 1968.

Kikkōman Corporation キッコーマン[株]

(Kikkōman). Japan's largest soy sauce producer. Kikkōman also produces wines, other sauces, and processed foods; it is expanding its restaurant chains in Japan and overseas. Its predecessor was the Noda Shōyu Co, established in 1917 by the Mogi and Takanashi families. In 1957 it established Kikkōman International, Inc, a sales subsidiary, in San Francisco. In 1979 Kikkōman Trading Europe GmbH was established as a European sales subsidiary for soy sauce and other foods. In addition, through agreements with overseas food manufacturers, Kikkōman is the distributor in Japan for Del Monte tomato products, Ragu spaghetti sauces, Lea & Perrins Worcestershire sauces, and Coca-Cola. In 1990 sales totaled ¥140.0 billion (US $1.0 billion), of which soy sauce constituted 53 percent. Capitalization stood at ¥11.4 billion (US $85.4 million) in the same year. Headquarters are in Noda, Chiba Prefecture.

kikō bungaku → travel diaries

kikoku shijo kyōiku → education for children of returnees

kiku → chrysanthemums

Kikuchi 菊池[市]

City in northern Kumamoto Prefecture, Kyūshū, on the river Kikuchigawa. The base of the Kikuchi warrior family from the 10th to the 14th century, Kikuchi also prospered as a village on the route connecting Kumamoto with Hita. Principal products are rice, chestnuts, and *shiitake* (Japanese mush-

rooms). Tourist attractions include a hot spring, Kikuchi Gorge, and Kikuchi Shrine. Pop: 28,166.

Kikuchi Dairoku 菊池大麓

(1855–1917). Mathematician and educational administrator noted for furthering the study of mathematics in Japan. Born in Edo (now Tōkyō). After attending the BANSHO SHIRABESHO, the shogunal institute for Western studies, he studied in England from 1866 to 1868. In 1870 he again went to England to study physics and mathematics at Cambridge University. After returning to Japan in 1877, he became a professor at Tōkyō University, where he later founded the mathematics department. His *Shotō kikagaku kyōkasho* (1888, Elementary Geometry Textbook) was the most widely used textbook in Japan until the end of World War II. Kikuchi served as president of Tōkyō University (1898–1901), minister of education (1901–03), and the first head of the INSTITUTE OF PHYSICAL AND CHEMICAL RESEARCH. He is also known for his research into WASAN, the native mathematics of Japan.

Kikuchi family 菊池氏

(Kikuchishi). Warrior family based in the Kikuchi district of Higo Province (now Kumamoto Prefecture) in Kyūshū. The heroism of Kikuchi Takefusa in the defense of Kyūshū against the second of the MONGOL INVASIONS OF JAPAN in 1281 is depicted in the famous scroll *Mōko shūrai ekotoba*. Takefusa's grandson Taketoki fought for Emperor GO-DAIGO during the GENKŌ INCIDENT, dying in battle in 1333. Thereafter the Kikuchi served the Southern Court (see NORTHERN AND SOUTHERN COURTS). After the two courts were reunited in 1392, however, the Kikuchi declined, and they were ultimately destroyed by the ŌTOMO FAMILY in the Sengoku period (1467–1568). Later a branch family, the Mera, revived the name.

Kikuchi Kan 菊池寛

(1888–1948). Author, playwright, and editor and founder of the influential monthly BUNGEI SHUNJŪ. Real name Kikuchi Hiroshi. Born in Takamatsu, Kagawa Prefecture, into a poor family of *samurai*-scholar ancestry. In 1908 he was admitted to the tuition-free Tōkyō Higher Normal School (later Tōkyō University of Education). He was forced to leave school, however, after he was wrongly accused of involvement in a minor theft in the school dormitory. The following year he entered the National First Higher School (now part of Tōkyō University), where he became friends with many future authors, most notably AKUTAGAWA RYŪNOSUKE, YAMAMOTO YŪZŌ, and KUME MASAO. He went on to study at Kyōto University, where he majored in English literature, graduating in 1916.

In 1920 his *Shinju fujin* (Madam Pearl), a monumental popular novel and the first of numerous melodramatic works, was serialized in two newspapers in Ōsaka and Tōkyō. In the same year his play *Chichi kaeru* (1917; tr *The Father Returns*, 1925) was staged at a major commercial theater in Tōkyō. The play created a sensation because of its originality, and he achieved belated recognition as a playwright. Kikuchi's works include the short stories "Mumei sakka no nikki" (1918, The Diary of an Unknown Writer) and "Tadanao Kyō gyōjō ki" (1918; tr "On the Conduct of Lord Tadanao," 1961).

In 1923 he launched his own magazine,

Bungei shunjū, partly motivated by his concern over the increasing aggressiveness of Marxist writers (see PROLETARIAN LITERATURE MOVEMENT). Although the magazine suffered a temporary setback due to losses incurred in the TŌKYŌ EARTHQUAKE OF 1923, it quickly recovered and grew into a popular magazine with unprecedented circulation.

One of Kikuchi's greatest contributions to Japan's literary world was the establishment of two important literary prizes, the Akutagawa Ryūnosuke Literary Prize (abbreviated as the AKUTAGAWA PRIZE) and the Naoki Sanjūgo Literary Prize (abbreviated as the NAOKI PRIZE). He was instrumental in forming what later developed into the Professional Writers' Guild of Japan, and he used his magazine to help further the careers of younger writers. He also established the KIKUCHI KAN PRIZE for creative contributions to the fields of literature, drama, journalism, and the mass media.

Kikuchi Kan Prize 菊池寛賞

(Kikuchi Kan Shō). Prize awarded for meritorious cultural activity. Established in 1938 by the Society for the Promotion of Japanese Literature at the suggestion of the writer KIKUCHI KAN, it is awarded annually. The recipients of the first six prizes were selected by a committee of writers and critics under 45 years of age to honor senior writers. The prize was not awarded between 1945 and 1952. Since 1953 the Kikuchi Kan Prize has been given to individuals and groups that have made original contributions in any of a number of cultural areas, including literature, drama, film, broadcasting, journalism, and publishing. See also LITERARY PRIZES.

Kikuchi Seishi 菊池正士

(1902–74). Nuclear physicist and a leader in the development of nuclear physics in Japan. Born in Tōkyō, the son of mathematician and educator KIKUCHI DAIROKU, he graduated from Tōkyō University in 1926. Working at the INSTITUTE OF PHYSICAL AND CHEMICAL RESEARCH (Rikagaku Kenkyūjo), in 1928 he produced cathode ray diffraction in a mica crystal. Kikuchi was the first director of the Tōkyō University Institute for Nuclear Study and also directed the construction of two cyclotron facilities at Ōsaka University. He received the Order of Culture in 1951.

Kikumura Itaru 菊村到

(1925–). Author. Real name Togawa Yūjirō. Born in Kanagawa Prefecture. A graduate of Waseda University, he worked as a newspaper correspondent during World War II. In 1957 his short story "Iōjima" (Iwojima) was awarded the Akutagawa Prize. Kikumura's works (fiction, documentaries, mysteries, and biographies) often deal with the uncertainties and distorted perceptions that his generation experienced because of the war.

Kikuta Kazuo 菊田一夫

(1908–73). Popular stage and radio playwright and show-business innovator. Born in Kanagawa Prefecture, Kikuta began his career as a writer of short comedies for small theaters in the Asakusa amusement area of Tōkyō. His first success, at age 22, was a parody of the KABUKI classic *Kanadehon chūshingura* (1748, The Treasury of Loyal Retainers; tr *Chūshingura*, 1971), titled *Akō gishi meimei den* (The Wanderings of the Forty-Seven Samurai), which he created for the leading Asakusa comedian Enoken (ENOMOTO KEN'ICHI). His successes increased during the 1930s and World War II. During the Occu-

pation period, Kikuta turned from stage comedy to write three immensely popular dramatic serials for radio, including *Kimi no na wa* (broadcast 1952–54, What's Your Name?).

Kikuta became head of the stage division of the TŌHŌ CO, LTD, in 1955. There he set up HASEGAWA KAZUO's "Tōhō Kabuki" to integrate the classic form with contemporary popular theater. His cosmopolitan touch was evident in the Tōhō stage musicals he wrote during the early 1950s, such as *Morugan Oyuki* (Oyuki Morgan), which were the forerunners of Japan's contemporary musical theater.

Kikutake Kiyonori 菊竹清訓

(1928–). Architect. Born in Fukuoka Prefecture. After graduating from Waseda University in 1950, he worked first for the Takenaka Corporation and then for the firm of Murano and Mori. In 1953 he opened his own office. In 1960, with the architect KUROKAWA KISHŌ, Kikutake helped found the Metabolist group, which attempted to express the dynamic, cyclical quality of urban growth. He designed futuristic marine cities, which were partly realized in the Aquapolis for the Okinawa Expo '75. His buildings include Sky House (1958), his private residence; Hotel Tōkōen (1964); and the Kurume Civic Center (1969).

Kikutake Sunao 菊竹淳

(1880–1937). Journalist known for his antimilitary views. Pen name Rokko. Born in Fukuoka Prefecture. In 1903 he joined the newspaper *Fukuoka nichinichi shimbun* after graduating from Waseda University. As editor (1911) and later as managing editor (1926), he was known for the moral integrity rather than the analytical incisiveness of his editorials. In 1932, at the time of the MAY 15TH INCIDENT, when public sentiment favored the "patriotism" of the conspirators, Kikutake steadfastly criticized the military for acting outside legitimate political channels.

kikyō 桔梗

(balloonflower or Chinese bellflower). *Platycodon grandiflorum.* Perennial herb of the family Campanulaceae that grows wild in grassy mountain highlands throughout Japan and much of the temperate zone of Asia. It is also cultivated as an ornamental plant. The roots are thick, succulent, and yellowish white. Its straight stems grow over 1 meter (40 in), and the leaves are alternate and lanceolate-oblong with serrated margins. In August and September it opens bluish purple, bell-shaped flowers measuring 4–5 centimeters (1.6–2.0 in) across.

There are also garden varieties with white and pink flowers and a miniature variety. It is one of the seven flowers of autumn (*aki no nanakusa*). In mountain villages roots are eaten either pickled or boiled then fried.

Kim Dae-jung Incident 金大中事件

(Kin Daichū Jiken). An incident in August 1973 in which the influential South Korean opposition leader Kim Dae-jung (b 1925) was kidnapped from a Tōkyō hotel and released in Seoul one week later. The kidnappers were identified by Tōkyō police as agents of the Korean Central Intelligence Agency, and the Japanese public was outraged at what it considered an infringement of Japan's sovereignty. The crisis in South Korea–Japan relations continued despite a formal South Korean apology, and was complicated in 1974 by an attempt on the life of President PAK CHŎNG-HŬI by a Korean resident of Japan, before finally being resolved in July 1975.

In 1980, however, Kim was tried before a military court on charges that included his activities in Japan—a direct contravention of an agreement reached in November 1973—and sentenced in September to death. In November Japanese prime minister SUZUKI ZENKŌ informed the South Korean ambassador to Japan that Japan would "find it difficult to maintain cooperative relations with South Korea if Kim were executed." Kim's sentence was reduced to life imprisonment, and in December 1982, shortly before a visit to South Korea by Prime Minister NAKASONE YASUHIRO, Kim was allowed to go to the United States. He returned to South Korea in February 1985. In 1987 Kim was granted amnesty and formed the P'yŏnghwa Minju Dang (Party for Peace and Democracy).

Kim Gu 金九

(1876–1949; J: Kin Kyū). A leader of the Korean independence movement and the post–World War II struggle for unification. Also known as Kim Ch'ang-am and Kim Ch'angsu. Kim was arrested in 1896 and convicted of murdering a Japanese soldier in retaliation for the assassination of Queen MIN; he escaped from prison in 1898 and lived in hiding. He later helped to organize the anti-Japanese demonstrations of 1 March 1919 (see SAMIL INDEPENDENCE MOVEMENT), after which he fled to Shanghai. There he served the PROVISIONAL GOVERNMENT OF KOREA in various capacities. Kim established a military academy for Koreans in Nanjing (Nanking) and organized a Korean division, which fought with the Chinese Nationalist army against the Japanese during World War II.

Kikutake Kiyonori
The architect's Aquapolis (1975), in Okinawa Prefecture, is an experimental "marine city" connected to the mainland by a bridge, crossed on foot or by electric bus.

kikyō The corolla of the *kikyō*, or balloonflower, swells out just before opening. It grows in sunny, dry locations.

A Woman's Lined Kimono

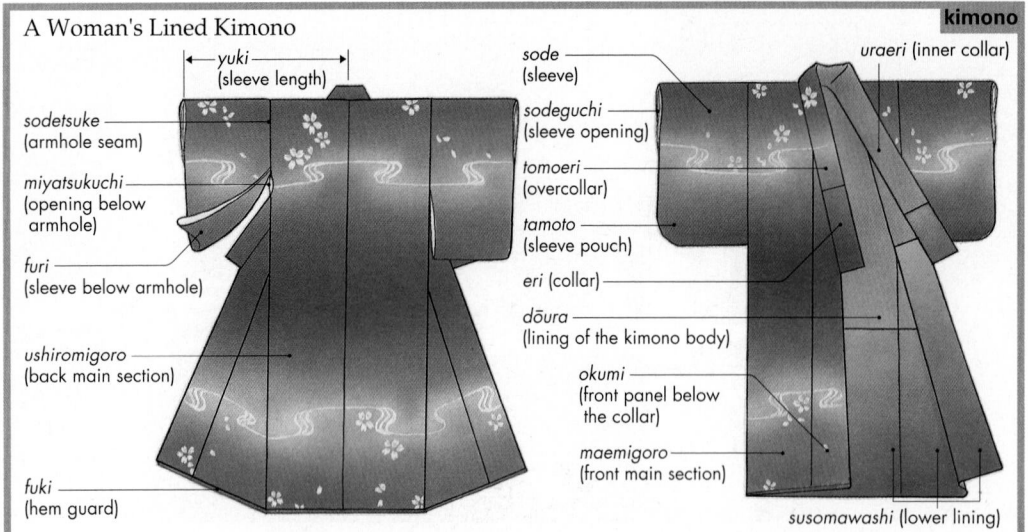

yuki (sleeve length)

sodetsuke (armhole seam)

miyatsukuchi (opening below armhole)

furi (sleeve below armhole)

ushiromigoro (back main section)

fuki (hem guard)

sode (sleeve)

sodeguchi (sleeve opening)

tomoeri (overcollar)

tamoto (sleeve pouch)

eri (collar)

dōura (lining of the kimono body)

okumi (front panel below the collar)

maemigoro (front main section)

uraeri (inner collar)

susomawashi (lower lining)

Kim returned to Korea as president of the provisional government in November 1945. He advocated disengagement of foreign powers from Korea and self-determined reunification. Kim was assassinated by a South Korean military officer in June 1949.

Kimigayo→national anthem

Kimiidera
紀三井寺

Popular name of the temple Kimiisan Kongōhōji Gokokuin, located in the city of Wakayama, Wakayama Prefecture. The temple belongs to the Guze Kannon branch of the SHINGON SECT of Buddhism. It is said to have been founded in 770 when the Chinese priest Ikō (Ch: Weiguang or Wei-Kuang) donated an image of the Senju Kannon (Avalokiteśvara with a Thousand Arms). The temple is known as Kimiidera or the Miidera of Kii (Kii Province, now Wakayama Prefecture) to differentiate it from the MIIDERA in Ōtsu, Ōmi Province (now Shiga Prefecture). It was designated an imperial temple in the 12th century under the aegis of retired emperor GO-SHIRAKAWA. Many of the original buildings are intact.

Kim Il-sŏng
金日成

(1912–   ; J: Kin Nissei). Premier of the Democratic People's Republic of Korea (DPRK; North Korea) from 1948 to 1972; DPRK president since 1972. Also written Kim Il-sung. Born Kim Sŏng-ju (sometimes spelled Kim Sung-chu) near P'yŏngyang. His father had a long record of anti-Japanese activities, and Kim became active against the Japanese soon after joining the Communist Youth League in 1927. He was elected the league's secretary in 1929 and entered the Chinese Communist Party in 1931.

Kim rose to prominence as the leader of an anti-Japanese guerrilla group called the Kapsan Faction, which operated in Manchuria and northern Korea between 1932 and 1940.

Kimi no na wa The lovers, played by Sada Keiji (left) and Kishi Keiko, meet in a scene from the third part of this popular film.

By 1941 he commanded the Korean People's Liberation Army attached to the Soviet army. In early October 1945 Kim was elected first secretary of the Korean Communist Party's Central Bureau. He became premier of the DPRK when it was established in September 1948 and has been the nation's dominant political leader ever since.

Kimi no na wa
君の名は

(What's Your Name?). A film released in three parts between 1953 and 1954, directed by Ōba Hideo (b 1910), starring Kishi Keiko (b 1932) and SADA KEIJI. Based on the radio drama series written by KIKUTA KAZUO, the film takes place during World War II, when a man and woman meet for the first time during an air raid. Upon parting, they vow to meet again. When they encounter each other after the war, she is already married to another. Although they are in love, they must overcome numerous obstacles to be together, parting and reuniting again and again. Altogether, some 30 million tickets were sold for the three parts of this extremely sentimental, romantic melodrama.

Kimi Pass
紀見峠

(Kimi Tōge). Located on the border of Ōsaka and Wakayama prefectures, central Honshū, bisecting the Izumi Mountains. The ancient route Kōya Kaidō (now National Route No. 170), extending from Ōsaka to the mountain KŌYASAN, was built along the pass. A railroad runs through a tunnel under the pass. Altitude: 380 m (1,247 ft).

Kimitsu
君津〔市〕

City in southwestern Chiba Prefecture, central Honshū, on Tōkyō Bay. Long known for its seaweed (*nori*), it is now part of the KEIYŌ INDUSTRIAL REGION. The mountains to the southeast, including Kanōzan, belong to a prefectural natural park. Pop: 89,242.

Kimmei, Emperor
欽明天皇

(509–571; Kimmei Tennō). The 29th sovereign (*tennō*) in the traditional count (which includes several legendary emperors). According to the chronicle NIHON SHOKI (720) he reigned from either 531 or 539 to 571 and was the third son of Emperor KEITAI. On Keitai's death, Kimmei is said to have contested the succession for several years with his elder half-brothers, emperors Ankan and Senka. However, Ankan and Senka soon died, leaving Kimmei sole possession of the throne. According to tradition it was during his reign (in either 538 or 552) that Buddhism was introduced from Korea, causing a conflict between the pro-Buddhist SOGA FAMILY and the anti-Buddhist MONONOBE FAMILY that was not resolved for decades.

Kimmon Incident→Hamaguri
Gomon Incident

kimoiri→shōya

Kim Ok-kyun
金玉均

(1851–94; J: Kin Gyokukin). Early advocate of Korea's Westernization; organizer of the KAEHWAP'A (Enlightenment Faction or Independence Party). He was born to a Ch'ungch'ŏng Province branch of the Andong Kim clan. A civil servant, he was sent to Japan in 1881 to study the Meiji government. Influenced by FUKUZAWA YUKICHI's interpretation of Westernization and pan-Asianism, he and other Koreans formed a political group, the Kaehwap'a, and set out to lead Korea's Westernization. With Japanese encouragement the group attempted unsuccessfully to seize control of the Korean government in 1884 (see KAPSIN POLITICAL COUP), after which Kim fled to Japan. In 1894 he left for Shanghai, where he was assassinated by a Korean government agent.

kimono
着物

The word *kimono* (literally, "clothing") is usually used in the narrow sense for the traditional Japanese wrap-around garment, worn by both men and women, with rectangular sleeves, and bound with a sash (OBI). The word is occasionally used in the broad sense as a term for clothing or for the native dress in general as opposed to Western-style clothing (*yōfuku*). The predecessor of the kimono is the *kosode* ("small sleeves"), which was worn as an undergarment from about the Nara period (710–794) and as the everyday outer garment from about the mid-16th century. The term kimono gained favor over *kosode* only in the 18th century (see also CLOTHING).

In the Meiji period (1868–1912) many men began wearing Western-style clothes, reserving kimono for formal occasions or when relaxing at home, but only from the beginning of the Shōwa period (1926–89) did the new style of dress become popular among women. Today most women wear kimono mainly for social and ceremonial events or when performing certain traditional arts. Children and young men and women may wear kimono for such occasions as NEW YEAR, the SHICHIGOSAN festival, Adulthood Day (see GEMPUKU), graduations, and WEDDINGS.

Kimono may be unlined (*hitoe*), lined (*awase*), or cotton-quilted (*wataire*). Unlined kimono are worn from June through September; for everyday wear, stencil-dyed cotton YUKATA are most common. For street or formal wear, materials such as silk gauze (RO AND SHA) or fine linen (*jōfu*) are used. Lined kimono are worn from October through May and are mainly made of silk or wool. Today synthetic materials are often used, and one-layer wool kimono are often worn in winter. Cotton quilted kimono, or cotton-quilted robes called *tanzen* worn over kimono, are for midwinter at home.

The ceremonial kimono for men is made of black *habutae* silk and decorated in several places with the family crest (*mon;* see CRESTS) in white. Women wear different types of formal kimono. The dazzling wedding costume consists of a white or red silk kimono with embroidery or brocade. Married women wear dark-colored silk, with a lighter design, for festive occasions and black silk, without a design, for funerals.

Generally when dressing one first dons TABI (socks); top undergarment and wrap-around underskirt; and then the under-kimono (*nagajuban*), which is tied tightly with a wide belt (*datemaki*). The *nagajuban* has a collar (*han'eri*), usually white, which should show about 2 centimeters (1 in) above the collar of the kimono that is worn over it. The left side of the kimono is lapped over the right in front; the opposite is done only when dressing a body for burial. The technique of donning kimono and *obi* was traditionally passed on from mother to daughter, but today women often go to a special school to learn how to achieve the correct effects.

A silk kimono is usually not cleaned as a whole unit but is first taken apart along the straight, hand-sewn seams, then washed and laid or stretched out to dry. After every wearing the kimono should be aired. For storage, the kimono is folded in a set order along the seams, wrapped in special paper (*tatōgami*), and laid flat in a drawer.
☎ 782–783

Kimpishō 禁秘抄

(Summary of Court Practices). Also known as *Kinchūshō, Juntoku In mishō,* or *Kenryaku gyoki.* A three-volume compilation by Emperor JUNTOKU pertaining to court appointments and ceremonial, completed in 1213 or 1221. The contents cover administrative practice, annual observances, festivals, ceremonies, edicts, and the like. Because of its detail *Kimpishō* became a model for later generations.

Kimpokusan 金北山

Mountain on the island of Sado, Niigata Prefecture, off central Honshū. The island's highest peak, this young mountain is composed of pyroxene andesite and liparite. Kimpokusan Shrine is on the summit. It is part of Sado-Yahiko-Yoneyama Quasi-National Park. Height: 1,172 m (3,845 ft).

Kimpusan 金峰山

Mountain on the border between Yamanashi and Nagano prefectures, central Honshū; composed of granite. It was formerly a source of quartz, but the supply is now exhausted. Height: 2,599 m (8,526 ft).

Kimpusenji 金峰山寺

Head temple of the Kimpusen Shugen Honshū, a sect of the Buddhist-Shintō ascetic tradition called SHUGENDŌ; located in Yoshino District (see YOSHINOYAMA), Nara Prefecture. According to tradition the temple was founded by EN NO GYŌJA (late 7th century), a semi-legendary mountain ascetic. Kimpusenji offered a haven to Prince MORINAGA (1308–35) and then to his father Emperor GO-DAIGO (r 1318–39) during their campaign to restore imperial rule (see KEMMU RESTORATION). It was thus at one time the seat of the Southern Court. The chief divinity enshrined in the main hall is Zaō Gongen, the bodhisattva who is believed by devotees to be capable of suppressing all evil.

Kim Sŏk-pŏm 金石範

(1925– ; J: Kin Sekihan). Novelist. Born in Ōsaka. Graduate of Kyōto University. As a second-generation Korean resident of Japan, Kim explores political and racial problems in his works, portraying the anguish of the oppressed. His *Karasu no shi* (1967, Death of a Crow) depicts the armed insurrection against the Syngman RHEE administration that took place on the American-occupied island of Cheju in 1948. Kim used

the Cheju rebellion again as his theme in *Kazantō* (1983, Volcanic Island).

Kim Tal-su 金達寿

(1919– ; J: Kin Tatsuju). Author. Born in Korea. He moved to Japan with his mother at the age of 10. He worked his way through Nihon University and then became a newspaper reporter for *Kanagawa shimbun* until the outbreak of World War II. After the war, he edited a Japanese-language news magazine about Korea called *Minshu Chōsen.* He turned to fiction with the novel *Genkai Nada* (1954), based upon his experiences as a Korean reporter during the war years. His works capture, often with humor and grace, the dilemma of the Koreans who suffered during the Japanese occupation of their country and those who presently must live with the discrimination against them that is prevalent in Japan. Recently his interests have turned to investigations of Japanese archaeological sites of Korean origin, the results of which he published as *Nihon no naka no Chōsen bunka* (1970–84). Other works include *Pakutari no saiban* (1959).

Kimura Hisashi 木村栄

(1870–1943). Astronomer. The first director of the Latitude Observatory of Mizusawa from 1899 to 1941, he was known for discovering the Z-term (or Kimura-term) of latitude variation. Born in Ishikawa Prefecture, he graduated from Tōkyō University. In 1937 he became one of the first recipients of the Order of Culture.

Kimura Ihei 木村伊兵衛

(1901–74). Photographer. Born in Tōkyō. Graduate of the Keika Commercial School. In 1932 he helped launch the magazine *Kōga* (Photo Image) and the following year began to work with NATORI YŌNOSUKE and Natori's atelier, Nihon Kōbō. Kimura was also active as a news photographer. His photographs, frequently portraits and character studies, have an unaffected spontaneity that led him to be called a master of the snapshot. *Kimura Ihei kessaku shashinshū* (1954) is a collection of some of his best work.

Kimura Kaishū → Kimura Yoshitake

Kimura Kenjirō 木村健二郎

(1896–1988). Inorganic chemist. Born in Aomori Prefecture. Graduate of Tōkyō University. After graduation he continued his studies under SHIBATA YŪJI, conducting geochemical and analytic chemical research on rare earths. Kimura also studied analytic chemistry at the Bohr Institute in Denmark and at institutes in France and the United States. In 1933 he was appointed a professor at Tōkyō University. In 1940 he succeeded in synthesizing a new isotope of uranium (uranium 237). After World War II Kimura was in charge of the analysis of radioactive fallout in Hiroshima and Nagasaki.

Kimura Ki 木村毅

(1894–1979). Literary historian and critic. Born in Okayama Prefecture; graduated from Waseda University. He was a founding member of the Japan Fabian Society and the Japan Labor-Farmer Party (NIHON RŌNŌTŌ). His works include *Shimabara bishōnen roku* (1927), a historical novel, and *Nichibei bungaku kōryūshi no kenkyū* (1960), a study of literary exchanges between Japan and the United States.

Kimura Motoo 木村資生

(1924–). Geneticist. Born in Aichi Prefecture. A graduate of Kyōto University. He has been a staff member of the National Institute of Genetics since 1949, engaging in research in population genetics. Based on findings concerning the mutation level of DNA molecules, he opposed the theory of natural selection current since the time of Darwin and in 1968 advocated a "neutral" theory of evolution. He received the Weldon Prize for his studies in population genetics. In 1976 he was awarded the Order of Culture.

Kimura Shigenari 木村重成

(1592?–1615). A warrior who served TOYO-TOMI HIDEYORI and was a stalwart of the

Kimura Ihei
1 Kimura's 1932 portrait of a cleaner and repairer of hats at his street stall.
2 Kimura, a photographer who was noted for the spontaneity of his work.

Continued on page 784►

Kimono Images

While Japan's indigenous clothing traditions have evolved considerably since ancient times, the styles, colors, and forms of the *kimono* worn today became standardized over a century ago. By late in the Edo period (1600–1868) an independent sense of style—one marked by flamboyance and ostentation—had developed among Japan's emerging merchant class. In order to curb extravagance and promote more temperate modes of dress, the Tokugawa shogunate issued a series of regulations prohibiting commoners from wearing gilded or gaudily embroidered kimono and restricting the colors and materials they could use. The townspeople responded by searching out richer colors and more uninhibited designs for their dyed kimono, until these features too became the focus of sumptuary regulations. For most people, the only way to cope with this imposed austerity was by revising their notions of finery and by finding new ways to dress with taste and style using plain patterns and simple fabrics.

One result of this process was the emergence of a remarkable variety of kimono styles, each with its own symbolic and aesthetic pedigree—a diversity still seen today. For those who wear kimono, the appropriate style reflects the occasion, the setting, the season, and the time of day. As in the past, however, the decisive factor is the identity of the wearer, the personality that lends the garment its essential character. Indeed, the kimono's most enduring virtue is said to be its capacity to reveal the wearer's inner nature.

The three women depicted in *Falling Cherry Blossoms*, a 1908 hanging scroll by Kaburagi Kiyokata, are clad in sumptuous kimono of the sort favored by townspeople of the Edo period. The mother, center, wears her *obi* tied in the front, as was customary for married women. At left, the younger daughter catches petals in an outstretched sleeve. The cherry-blossom pattern on the lining of her kimono was considered an elegant touch.

Chic
For parties and other semiformal occasions—a visit to the theater, dinner at a posh restaurant, or, as here, an open-air tea ceremony—a Japanese woman might choose to appear attired in *hōmongi*. Like an artist's canvas, this type of kimono is covered with imaginative designs; along with the colors, designs are selected to suit the occasion and the season. While the event may be semiformal, *hōmongi* is nevertheless considered formal dress, and the woman who wears one must be careful not to outshine the guest of honor.

Purity

In traditional Japanese wedding ceremonies, the bride's role is that of a virtuous maiden serving the gods. For this reason, she is clad in pure white from head to toe, wearing the kimono known as *shiromuku*. A variety of auspicious ornamental symbols are woven into the immaculate fabric of this garment, inviting fortune to smile upon the marriage. The groom is traditionally attired in full formal dress—black kimono, *hakama* (long pleated skirt), and a black *haori* (half-coat) adorned in five places with his family crest.

Maidenhood

The most dazzling of all kimono are worn only by girls and young single women—the style known as *furisode*. The *furisode* ("flowing sleeves") is customarily the most formal garment in a young woman's wardrobe, and as the name suggests, is distinguished by its long billowy sleeves. Made of brilliantly colored fabric often emblazoned with bold floral patterns, the *furisode* is tied with a gorgeous sash, accentuating the wearer's youth.

Innocence

It is the custom in Japan for parents to take their five-year-old sons and three- and seven-year-old daughters to a Shintō shrine on 15 November to commemorate an observance known as Shichigosan ("Seven-Five-Three"). The children are turned out in traditional finery for this event, the boys wearing dark-hued silk kimono, *haori*, and *hakama* and the girls wearing brightly colored kimono, carefully arranged hairstyles, and makeup.

Conviviality

The sight of a group of men dressed in *yukata*, or summer kimono, enjoying a drink outdoors on a balmy evening has special resonance for many Japanese people. Made of lightweight cotton, *yukata* were originally worn to and from the bath by members of the upper class. By the Edo period they had become standard warm-weather attire for the common people, and today they are still worn at summer festivals and at inns and hot-spring resorts. While women wear this type of kimono as well, a man in a crisply starched *yukata* with *geta* (wooden sandals) on his bare feet can cut a very masculine figure, calling to mind a bygone era.

Simplicity

For some kimono, the pattern is the definitive characteristic. The pattern called Edo *komon* is made up of delicate geometric designs that repeat over the entire surface of the garment, imparting a simple elegance. Unlike the graceful patterns that adorn more formal kimono, Edo *komon* is appropriate for casual outings—a shopping excursion, an informal gathering, or lunch with a friend.

Subtlety

Tsumugi has a rustic, almost primitive quality that reflects this fabric's humble origins—it was created on farms out of leftover raw silk and used to make work clothes for the farmers and their families. Woven by hand from hand-spun yarn, the quietly tasteful *tsumugi* found favor among the Edo-period merchant class as an alternative to the gaudier kimono fabrics that had been banned by the government. Stripes, checks, and other subtle patterns commonly adorn *tsumugi* kimono, which are admired partly for the casual way they are worn—as if they were cotton rather than silk.

Kindaichi Kyōsuke
This philologist was known for his studies on the Ainu language.

Kingu The cover of the first issue of *King*, a general-interest magazine that was published from 1925 to 1957. It was Japan's first magazine to attain a circulation of one million.

Toyotomi party in its showdown with the Tokugawa regime in 1614 and 1615 (see ŌSAKA CASTLE, SIEGES OF). During the Tokugawa assault on Hideyori's Ōsaka Castle, Shigenari fought UESUGI KAGEKATSU and Satake Yoshinobu (1570–1633) to a draw in 1614. During the armistice, the young Shigenari was sent as ambassador to the shōgun TOKUGAWA HIDETADA. When the conflict was resumed in the Summer Campaign of 1615, Shigenari and his troop sallied from Ōsaka Castle in an attempt to surprise the shogunate's main force but were intercepted by TŌDŌ TAKATORA and Ii Naotaka (1590–1659), and in the ensuing encounter, which took place on 2 June 1615, Shigenari was killed. Ōsaka Castle fell the next day.

Kimura Takeyasu   木村健康

(1907–73). Economist. Born in Fukuoka Prefecture. He graduated from Tōkyō University in 1934. When Professor KAWAI EIJIRŌ was forced to resign from the university in 1939 because of his opposition to Japan's growing militarism, Kimura, a disciple of Kawai's, also left his position on the faculty. He returned to Tōkyō University after the war and served as a professor of modern theoretical economics (1953–73). Kimura was instrumental in popularizing W. W. Rostow's theory that economic development proceeds in distinct stages.

Kimura Yoshitake   木村喜毅

(1830–1901). Also known as Kimura Kaishū. Advocated creation of a modern navy during the 1860s. Born in Edo (now Tōkyō); appointed supervisor of the Nagasaki Naval Training Academy (KAIGUN DENSHŪJO) in 1856. In 1859 he was promoted to the office of commissioner of warships (*gunkan bugyō*) and was commanding officer aboard the KANRIN MARU in 1860 when it became the first Japanese vessel to sail across the Pacific.

Kinai   畿内

(Capital Provinces). General term for the provinces surrounding the ancient capitals of Nara and Kyōto. It is a Japanese rendering of an old Chinese term that referred to the 1-million-square-*ri* (450,000-sq-km) area centered on the imperial residence. Until the mid-7th century the term was loosely applied to the general region around the imperial capitals in YAMATO (now Nara Prefecture). The area was officially defined at the time of the TAIKA REFORM of 645 to include specifically the four provinces of Yamato, Yamashiro (now part of Kyōto Prefecture), Kawachi (now part of Ōsaka Prefecture), and Settsu (now part of Hyōgo Prefecture). Later, with the creation of Izumi Province from part of Kawachi, the Capital Provinces came to number five. See also GOKI SHICHIDŌ.

Kin Bay   金武湾

(Kin Wan). Inlet of the Pacific Ocean, on the eastern coast of the main island of Okinawa, Okinawa Prefecture. Bounded by Kimmisaki, a cape on the north, and the Yokatsu Peninsula on the south.

Kinchū Narabi ni Kuge Shohatto
禁中並公家諸法度

(Laws Governing the Imperial Court and Nobility). Laws issued by the Tokugawa shogunate (1603–1867) in 1615 to regulate the imperial court and Kyōto nobility; drafted by the Buddhist priest SŪDEN. Issued at the same time as the laws governing the

daimyō (BUKE SHOHATTO) and religious institutions (Jiin Hatto), these regulations defined the proper role and limits of the emperor and his court. The emperor was to occupy himself with scholarship and the arts, and the political role of the court was limited to tasks assigned by the shogunate. Thus, although the shōgun in theory derived his authority from his appointment by the emperor, these regulations clearly were a major step in the Tokugawa effort to put all potential rivals under strict shogunal control.

Kindai bungaku   近代文学

(Modern Literature). Literary journal published from January 1946 to August 1964. Founded after World War II by a newly formed coterie of critics and writers, it became a central pillar of modern literary criticism and helped restore some sense of intellectual order during the chaotic postwar period by critically examining events of the recent past. Its original members included HONDA SHŪGO, HIRANO KEN, ARA MASAHITO, HANIYA YUTAKA, and ODAGIRI HIDEO. Later participants included NOMA HIROSHI, UMEZAKI HARUO, SHIINA RINZŌ, ABE KŌBŌ, KATŌ SHŪICHI, and SHIMAO TOSHIO. Having experienced the collapse of the PROLETARIAN LITERATURE MOVEMENT and its aftermath, *Kindai bungaku* coterie members opposed the attempt by the Shin Nihon Bungaku Kai (New Japanese Literature Society; see SHIN NIHON BUNGAKU) to establish a new leftist literary movement. *Kindai bungaku* broke new ground in the study of modern Japanese literature, provided an outlet for experimental works by new writers, and nurtured a new generation of critics.

Kindaichi Kyōsuke   金田一京助

(1882–1971). Philologist. Born in Morioka, Iwate Prefecture. He graduated from Tōkyō University, where he became professor of linguistics; he later served as a professor at Kokugakuin University. Kindaichi devoted much of his career as a scholar to the study of the AINU LANGUAGE. He left numerous publications on Ainu language studies, including *Ainu jojishi yūkara no kenkyū* (2 vols, 1931), a valuable written record of Ainu oral literature as recounted in the epic tradition *yukar.* His studies of the Japanese language are also highly regarded. Among his other principal works is *Kokugoshi keitō hen* (1938, On the Systems of the History of the Japanese Language). *Kindaichi Kyōsuke senshū* (1960–62) is a three-volume collection of his selected works. In 1954 he received the Order of Culture.

Kinden Corporation   [株]きんでん

(Kinden). Firm chiefly engaged in electrical engineering, but also in plant construction and installation of air-conditioning systems and instrumentation. It was incorporated in 1944 with the merger of over 50 electrical engineering companies, initially to erect power lines for KANSAI ELECTRIC POWER CO, INC. But in 1991, 70 percent of its income was derived from other private and public construction projects. Sales for the fiscal year ending March 1991 totaled ¥430.3 billion (US $3.1 billion). Capitalization was ¥24.3 billion (US $177.1 million) in the same year. Headquarters are in Ōsaka and Tōkyō.

kindergartens → preschool education

Kineya Jōkan II   稀音家浄観２世

(1874–1956). Singer and composer of NAGAUTA (a major form of lyric song in the

KABUKI theater; also performed in concerts) who accompanied himself on the SHAMISEN. Born in Tōkyō; the son of Kineya Jōkan I (1839–1917). In 1902 he formed the Kenseikai Society with YOSHIZUMI KOSABURŌ IV and worked to foster appreciation of *nagauta* on its own terms, apart from its function as accompaniment to *kabuki* and dance performances. In 1929 he set up a *nagauta* course at Tōkyō Music School (now Tōkyō University of Fine Arts and Music). By composing highly acclaimed original *nagauta* works, *Yuya* and *Genkō* among them, Kineya redefined the genre. He took the professional name Jōkan II in 1939 and was awarded the Order of Culture in 1955.

Kingu   キング

(King). Popular, general-interest monthly magazine founded in 1925 by NOMA SEIJI, the president of KŌDANSHA, LTD, who launched it with the promotional slogan "Japan's most entertaining and enlightening magazine." Geared for the general reading public, it featured special sections on literature, humor, fashion, human interest stories, sports, and new trends, as well as extensive coverage of current events. The press run for the first issue was 740,000 copies; in 1928 the circulation exceeded 1.5 million copies. Its name was changed to *Fuji* in 1943. Renamed *Kingu* in 1946, it ceased publication in 1957.

Kinkai wakashū   金槐和歌集

(The Collection of the Kamakura Minister of the Right). Commonly called the *Kinkaishū.* Containing 663 WAKA poems, it was the personal poetry collection of MINAMOTO NO SANETOMO (1192–1219), second son of MINAMOTO NO YORITOMO and shōgun from 1203 to 1219. The earliest version of his collection is thought to have been compiled by Sanetomo himself before 1213 and was probably sent to his teacher, FUJIWARA NO SADAIE (Fujiwara no Teika), for comment. It appears to have been a collection of practice poems, for there are many sequences of poems having the same topic and with only the smallest variations in wording. A second and larger version containing 716 of his poems was compiled on the basis of the earlier version probably soon after his death. Compelled by his position to live in the military capital, Kamakura, and thus cut off from the center of poetic activity at court, Sanetomo trained himself largely by study of poetic treatises and anthologies, so that the bulk of his poetry is purely imitative of the dominant SHIN KOKINSHŪ style of his day. However, some 20 poems written in his later years show a refreshing boldness and a keen attention to the details of life.

Kinkakuji   金閣寺

(Temple of the Golden Pavilion). Formally known as Rokuonji. Temple in Kita Ward, Kyōto, belonging to the SHŌKOKUJI branch of the RINZAI SECT of Zen Buddhism. Kinkakuji is built on the site of an estate of the aristocrat Saionji Kintsune (1171–1244) in the hills of the Kitayama district. The third Muromachi shōgun, Ashikaga Yoshimitsu (r 1369–95), took possession of the estate in 1397 with the intention of turning it into an elegant retreat. Over the next 10 years various buildings were erected there at enormous cost. The resulting complex, which was called Kitayama-dono (Kitayama Palace), was the center of Ashikaga power at the time. After Yoshimitsu's death in 1408, the Kitayama-dono was converted into a temple

in accordance with his last wishes and given the name of Rokuonji, Rokuon being Yoshimitsu's posthumous religious title. The great Zen master Musō Soseki (1275–1351) was designated the honorary first abbot.

The Kinkakuji suffered severe damage during the ŌNIN WAR (1467–77) but was largely restored. Only the Kinkaku (Golden Pavilion) survived the conflagration that swept the temple around 1565. Some reconstruction occurred, but the temple gradually declined during the Edo period (1600–1868). With the advent of the Meiji period (1868–1912) the temple underwent extensive renovations.

The Kinkaku was completely destroyed by arson in 1950. The writer MISHIMA YUKIO fictionalized the events surrounding the fire in his novel KINKAKUJI (1956; tr *The Temple of the Golden Pavilion*, 1959). An exact reproduction of the building was completed in October 1955.

The Kinkaku is a gilded three-story structure. The ground floor (known as the Hōsui-in) is built in the SHINDEN-ZUKURI architectural style. The middle floor (the Chōonkaku) is representative of *buke-zukuri* ("*samurai*-style") architecture, and the top floor (the Kukyōchō) follows the Zen architectural style. More than half of the Kinkakuji precincts is taken up by a fine landscape garden. The temple is also noted for its collection of art treasures. See also KITAYAMA CULTURE.

Kinkakuji 金閣寺

(tr *The Temple of the Golden Pavilion*, 1959). Novel by MISHIMA YUKIO (1925–70); published 1956. Based on an incident that took place in 1950 when a youth set fire to the Golden Pavilion of the Kyōto temple KINKAKUJI. In the novel, the youth, Mizoguchi, an acolyte from a remote village on the Japan Sea coast, serves at the temple in training for the Zen priesthood. A physically unattractive young man with a stutter, Mizoguchi has carried the image of the Golden Pavilion with him since his youth, when his father spoke of the structure's unparalleled beauty. The beauty of the temple becomes an obsession, directing Mizoguchi's every thought and action. In an effort both to possess its beauty fully and to liberate himself from its power, he decides to burn the Golden Pavilion. *Kinkakuji* is con-

sidered by many critics to be Mishima's finest work.

Kinkazan 金華山

Island 1 km (0.6 mi) southeast of the Oshika Peninsula, Miyagi Prefecture, northern Honshū. The Koganeyama Shrine, located here, commemorates the guardian god of gold and silver. Wild monkeys and deer inhabit the island. Area: 9 sq km (3.5 sq mi).

Kinki Nippon Railway Co, Ltd
近畿日本鉄道[株]

(Kinki Nippon Tetsudō; commonly called Kintetsu). Japan's second largest private railroad operator; also engaged in the operation of bus lines and department stores and in the sale of real estate. Founded in 1910 as the Nara Railway Co, Ltd. The company's rail lines connect Ōsaka with such major tourist and commercial centers as Kyōto, Nara, Ise, and Nagoya. The company was incorporated under its present name in 1944, and through a merger in 1963 it initiated service to Kyōto. The Kintetsu group consists of 156 related companies. Overseas, Kintetsu affiliates are engaged in hotel management in San Francisco and Los Angeles. Kinki Nippon Tourist Co, Ltd, and Kintetsu World Express, Inc, both affiliates of Kinki Nippon Railway, also have overseas subsidiaries. Sales for the fiscal year ending March 1991 totaled ¥237.5 billion (US $1.7 billion). In the same year capitalization stood at ¥90.6 billion (US $660.3 million). Headquarters are in Ōsaka.

Kinki Nippon Tourist Co, Ltd
近畿日本ツーリスト[株]

(Kinki Nippon Tsūrisuto). Japan's second largest travel agency. Incorporated in 1947, it is a member of the KINKI NIPPON RAILWAY CO, LTD, group. It has 264 branches in Japan. Sales for the fiscal year ending December 1990 totaled ¥82.7 billion (US $602.8 million), of which domestic travel accounted for 63 percent; overseas travel, 34 percent; and other revenues, 3 percent. The company was capitalized at ¥4.7 billion (US $34.3 million) as of December 1990. Headquarters are in Tōkyō.

Kinki region 近畿地方

(Kinki *chihō*). Located in west central Honshū and consisting of Ōsaka, Hyōgo, Kyōto, Shiga, Mie, Wakayama, and Nara prefec-

tures. It is the nation's second most important industrial region. The terrain is mountainous with many small basins in between and numerous coastal plains on the Inland Sea, Ōsaka Bay, and the Kii Channel. The Kii Peninsula has some of the heaviest precipitation in Japan and is warm even in winter. The northern part of the region faces the Sea of Japan and is noted for its heavy snowfall.

The Kyōto-Nara area was the cultural and political center of Japan in ancient days, but it lost its political significance after the capital was moved to Tōkyō in 1868. The Ōsaka-Kōbe district is the center of commerce and industry for western Japan. This area, called the HANSHIN INDUSTRIAL ZONE, is dominated by chemical and heavy industries. Rice and citrus fruit production, lumbering, and fishing are important activities. Principal cities include ŌSAKA, KYŌTO, and KŌBE, one of the country's most important ports. See also KANSAI REGION. Area: 33,075 sq km (12,767 sq mi); pop: 22,206,747.

kinki shoga 琴棋書画

(Ch: *qinqi shuhua* or *ch'in-ch'i shu-hua*). Chinese painting subject illustrating the four accomplishments of the cultivated Chinese gentleman: music (specifically, playing the Chinese string instrument called the *qin*), the game of GO (Ch: *qi;* also called *weiqi*), CALLIGRAPHY (Ch: *shu*), and painting (Ch: *hua*). Depicted in China since ancient times, the theme was established in Japan by the end of the 15th century and became a popular subject related to the diffusion of Confucian ideas during the Edo period (1600–1868).

Kinki University 近畿大学

(Kinki Daigaku). A coeducational private university located in the city of Ōsaka. Founded in 1949, it was the first university in Japan to have both a nuclear reactor and a nuclear research laboratory. It maintains faculties of law, economics and business administration, science and technology, pharmacy, agriculture, medicine, and engineering. Enrollment in 1989 was 23,291.

kinkyōrei→anti-Christian edicts

Kinoshita Junji This leading Japanese playwright has also published many important works on the theory of the stage.

Ki no Kaion 紀海音

(1663–1742). Dramatist for the puppet theater (BUNRAKU) who wrote about 50 JŌRURI plays, mostly *jidai-mono* (historical plays). Real name Enami Kiemon. Born in Ōsaka. Kaion and CHIKAMATSU MONZAEMON are often mentioned as professional rivals. In 1708 Kaion introduced the now-familiar romance of Kyūemon, the wooden-bowl dealer, and Matsuyama, the courtesan, in *Wankyū sue no Matsuyama*, and soon thereafter he was the first to describe the tragic love affair of Sankatsu, the umbrella dealer, and Hanshichi, the courtesan, in *Sankatsu Hanshichi nijūgonen ki* (1719). Both were later developed into major KABUKI dramas by other playwrights.

Kinokawa 紀ノ川

River in northern Wakayama Prefecture, central Honshū, originating in Nara Prefecture, where it is known as the Yoshinogawa. It flows west through the Wakayama Plain to enter the Kii Channel at the city of Wakayama. Many dams have been constructed along the river. The water is used for irrigation and for industry. Length: 136 km (84 mi); area of drainage basin: 1,660 sq km (640 sq mi).

Kinokuniya Bunzaemon 紀伊国屋文左衛門

(late 1660s?–1734?). Wealthy merchant of the middle Edo period (1600–1868). Probably born in Kii Province (now Wakayama Prefecture), he became a lumber merchant in the Hatchōbori district of Edo (now Tōkyō). He secured exclusive rights to supply building material for the main halls of the temple Kan'eiji in Ueno, the largest and most influential in Edo. As an official purveyor to the Tokugawa shogunate, Bunzaemon was able to obtain choice lumber and maintain a flourishing business.

Bunzaemon was famed for his extravagant living. His guests included high shogunate officials, such as YANAGISAWA YO-SHIYASU, who reciprocated his hospitality with special privileges. A generous patron of the theater and entertainment world, he ransomed Miuraya no Kichō, the most famous courtesan of the time. With Yoshiyasu's fall from power, Bunzaemon's fortunes dwindled, and his final years were spent in comparative austerity.

Kinosaki 城崎[町]

Town in northern Hyōgo Prefecture, western Honshū, on the river Maruyamagawa. Known for its hot spring since the 8th century, it is closely associated with SHIGA NAOYA's *An'ya kōro* (1921–37; tr *A Dark Night's Passing*, 1976) and "Kinosaki nite" (1917; tr "At Kinosaki," 1956). Located nearby are Hiyoriyama coastal park and the GEMBUDŌ cave. Pop: 4,748.

Kinoshita Chōshōshi 木下長嘯子

(1569–1649). WAKA poet. Real name Kinoshita Katsutoshi. Born in Owari (now part of Aichi Prefecture). Nephew of Kita no Mandokoro, the wife of TOYOTOMI HIDEYOSHI. Connected to the shōgun TOKUGAWA IEYASU by marriage, Chōshōshi led a life of elegant ease. He was a student of the *waka* master HOSOKAWA YŪSAI and the Neo-Confucian scholar FUJIWARA SEIKA. Among his friends were ANRAKUAN SAKUDEN, KOBORI ENSHŪ, and

HAYASHI RAZAN. Chōshōshi wrote in a fresh and uniquely personal style. His verse, collected in *Kyohakushū* (1649) and *Wakasa no Shōshō Katsutoshi Ason shū*, influenced the poetry of BASHŌ.

Kinoshita Jun'an 木下順庵

(1621–98). Neo-Confucian scholar of the early Edo period (1600–1868). Born in Kyōto, he studied with MATSUNAGA SEKIGO, a disciple of FUJIWARA SEIKA. After a brief stay in Edo (now Tōkyō) he returned to Kyōto, where he remained for the next 20 years, until he was invited to the Kanazawa domain (now Ishikawa Prefecture) by its *daimyō*, MAEDA TSUNANORI. In 1682 he was appointed Confucian scholar to the shogunate and lecturer to shōgun TOKUGAWA TSUNAYOSHI. His many disciples included the scholar-statesmen ARAI HAKUSEKI, MURO KYŪSŌ, AMENOMORI HŌSHŪ, and MIYAKE KANRAN.

Kinoshita Junji 木下順二

(1914–). One of Japan's foremost modern playwrights. Born in Tōkyō. He studied English literature at Tōkyō University. Kinoshita's first work was *Fūrō* (1947, Wind and Waves), staged in 1954. Between the 1940s and the late 1970s Kinoshita wrote more than 40 plays, mostly based on Japanese folklore or contemporary history. He also published many important works on dramatic theory.

YANAGITA KUNIO's *Zenkoku mukashibanashi kiroku* (Compendium of Japanese Legends) led Kinoshita to material for a new type of modern play, later to be known as *minwageki* (folktale play). In the immediate postwar years Kinoshita published several *minwageki*, a translation of *Othello*, and several radio plays. He also helped found a SHINGEKI (new drama) group, Budō no Kai (Grape Society), which staged the first performance of his most famous folktale play, *Yūzuru* (1949; tr *Twilight Crane*, 1956). It generated widespread interest in Japanese folktales. During the early 1950s Kinoshita became known as a leading spokesman on the modern Japanese theater and its problems.

Kinoshita is also famous for his *gendaigeki* (plays of the present). His plays from 1960 on reflect his concern with individuals who are forced to stand against the momentum of history. These include *Okinawa* (1961), *Ottō to yobareru nihonjin* (1962, A Japanese Called Ottō), *Fuyu no jidai* (1964, The Winter Season), and *Kami to hito to no aida* (1972; tr *Between God and Man: A Judgment on War Crimes*, 1979). During the 1970s Kinoshita wrote a number of important theoretical works and published a complete translation of Shakespeare's plays.

His interest in the medieval romance HEIKE MONOGATARI (The Tale of the Heike) led to a series of record albums entitled *Heike monogatari ni yoru gundoku: Tomomori* (Group Readings from *Heike monogatari*: Tomomori; released in 1969) and a full-length play with Tomomori as its hero, *Shigosen no matsuri* (1978, The Dirge of the Meridian). Kinoshita's stature as a playwright derives mainly from his conception of the dramatic hero, who is often placed in environments or against forces that are bound to overwhelm him. It is the resistance to such forces that is central to Kinoshita's thought. Theoretically and intellectually, Kinoshita has made important contributions to postwar *shingeki*. In 1982 he published the critical work *Gikyoku no nihongo* (Japanese Language in the Drama).

Kinoshita Keisuke 木下恵介

(1912–). Film director. Born in Shizuoka Prefecture. Kinoshita joined what is now SHŌCHIKU CO, LTD, in 1933; he directed his first film in 1943. Especially fond of themes related to contemporary social problems, he has treated such problems as comedy, in *Karumen kokyō ni kaeru* (1951, Carmen Comes Home), and as tragedy, in *Nihon no higeki* (1953, A Japanese Tragedy). Kinoshita's most successful and famous film is NIJŪSHI NO HITOMI (1954, Twenty-Four Eyes), which won the Kinema Jumpō Award as the best film of 1954. Kinoshita has won that award for two other films as well: *Ōsoneke no asa* (1946, Morning for the Ōsone Family) and *Narayama-bushi kō* (1958, The Ballad of Narayama). A hallmark of Kinoshita's work is his fondness for long, panoramic, postcardlike shots that give the viewer a feel for the setting of his films. For a time he involved himself almost exclusively in work for television, but in recent years he has returned to directing films.

Kinoshita Mokutarō 木下杢太郎

(1885–1945). Physician, poet, playwright, and novelist. Real name Ōta Masao. Born in Shizuoka Prefecture. Kinoshita began writing poetry as a student in the Medical School of Tōkyō University. In 1908 he became a member of PAN NO KAI, a group of poets and artists that included KITAHARA HAKUSHŪ and YOSHII ISAMU. He contributed novels, dramas, and poems to journals such as SUBARU and *Okujō teien;* by the time of his graduation in 1911 he had established his reputation as a writer. The theme of his works was usually the conflict between intellect and emotions. In 1916 he became a hospital director in Manchuria and traveled extensively in China. He later served as professor of dermatology at several universities, including Tōkyō University. His complete works are collected in the *Kinoshita Mokutarō zenshū* (12 vols, 1948–51).

Kinoshita Naoe 木下尚江

(1869–1937). Author, socialist, and Christian pacifist. Born in Matsumoto (in what is now Nagano Prefecture), he graduated from Tōkyō Semmon Gakkō (now Waseda University). He cultivated an interest in Western socialism, and in a number of forcefully written articles he attacked a wide range of social abuses. An eloquent orator, he spoke out against the Sino-Japanese War of 1894–95. The most striking affirmation of both his socialism and his pacifism is his first novel, *Hi no hashira* (1904; tr *Pillar of Fire*, 1972), which was banned in 1910 and not republished in full until 1950.

In 1900 Kinoshita compiled a series of newspaper reports on the pollution caused by poisonous effluent from the giant Ashio Copper Mine (see ASHIO COPPER MINE INCIDENT). Inspired in part by a meeting with TANAKA SHŌZŌ, the courageous politician who had campaigned for the peasant victims of the effluent, Kinoshita's reports from the contaminated areas were later published as a book.

From about 1910, however, he began to feel a need for an inwardness that his writing and political activity could not satisfy. Acknowledging a debt to both Christianity and Buddhism, he spent the rest of his life as a near-recluse, advocating the form of meditation known as *seiza* (sitting in silence).

Kinoshita Keisuke A number of this director's films are searching, often satiric examinations of post–World War II Japanese society.

Kinoshita Rigen 木下利玄

(1886–1925). TANKA poet. Real name Kinoshita Toshiharu. Born in Okayama Prefecture; graduate of Tōkyō University. Together with his classmates SHIGA NAOYA and MUSHANOKŌJI SANEATSU, he founded the literary magazine *Shirakaba* (see SHIRAKABA SCHOOL) in 1910. His poetry, colloquial in language but elegant in style, has an undertone of humanism. His poetry collections include *Kōgyoku* (1919) and *Ichiro* (1924).

Kinoshita Takafumi 木下幸文

(1779–1821). Late-Edo-period (1600–1868) WAKA poet from Bitchū Province (now Okayama Prefecture). He studied *waka* with KAGAWA KAGEKI, but while Kageki modeled his poetry on the KOKINSHŪ, the greatest influence on Takafumi's poetry collection, *Sayasaya ikō*, is that of the MAN'YŌSHŪ. "Hinkyū hyakushu," a series of 100 poems on poverty included in the collection, is particularly original and noteworthy.

Ki no Tomonori 紀友則

(fl ca 900). Classical (WAKA) poet, one of four courtiers commanded by Emperor DAIGO to compile the first imperial anthology of native poetry, the KOKINSHŪ (completed 905). There are 46 poems in the *Kokinshū* by Tomonori, who died before the anthology was completed. He was a master of the elegant style, given to witty conceits, that was esteemed in his day.

Ki no Tsurayuki 紀貫之

(872?–945). A leading WAKA poet of the Heian period (794–1185). Born into a family of the middle aristocracy and of poets, Tsurayuki served in official capacity both at the imperial court and in the provinces. After service as a vice-governor, Tsurayuki was appointed governor of Tosa (now Kōchi Prefecture) in 930.

Tsurayuki's first appearance as a poet in an official capacity dates back to the two poetry contests (UTA-AWASE) of the Kampyō era (889–898). In 905 the ruling emperor, DAIGO, entrusted Tsurayuki and other leading poets with the compilation of Japan's first imperial anthology of poetry—the *Kokin wakashū* (or KOKINSHŪ). That he wrote one of the two prefaces of this work suggests his leading role in its compilation. Tsurayuki's preface, which was in Japanese (the other was in Chinese) and called *Kokin wakashū jo*, was written in KANA (the Japanese syllabary) and constitutes the first known critical work on poetry in the Japanese language. In it Tsurayuki discusses poetry and then gives his critical views on six leading poets of his time. He says, for example, that ARIWARA NO NARIHIRA had "too much heart and too few words," reflecting his own basic differentiation between *kotoba* (diction) and *kokoro* (heart) in poetry. In spite of the shortcomings, Tsurayuki accused his fellow poets of, they were later revered as the Six Poetic Geniuses (ROKKASEN), probably because they were mentioned in this preface.

The renewed emphasis on native elements in Japanese culture, after the overwhelming influence of Chinese culture of the 9th century, is further expressed in Tsurayuki's TOSA NIKKI (Tosa Diary), which describes his return voyage in 934–935 to the Kyōto capital from Tosa in Shikoku, as if written by a female companion. Fifty-seven *waka* mark the emotional high points of the diary. The inclusion of *Tosa nikki* poems in imperial

anthologies of poetry under Tsurayuki's name led to the theory that Tsurayuki must have written the *Tosa nikki* through the persona of a female companion, since it was uncommon for a man to write a diary of an official voyage in *kana*.

Other works by Tsurayuki are the prefaces of the collection *Ōigawa gyōkō waka* and of the anthology *Shinsen wakashū*. About 500 poems have been preserved in imperial anthologies (the *Kokinshū* includes over 100) and in private collections such as the *Tsurayuki shū*.

kinran and ginran 金襴と銀襴

(*kinran to ginran*; gold brocade and silver brocade). Sumptuous fabrics made by weaving a pattern into twill, satin, or gauze cloth with either gold or silver leaf, or gold or silver thread. The technique was introduced from China into Japan through the port city of Sakai during the late 16th century and later brought to the Nishijin weaving district of Kyōto. These fabrics are used for Buddhist priests' robes, costumes for NŌ plays, and traditional accessories such as bags and sashes (OBI) worn with KIMONO.

Kinrō Kansha no Hi → holidays, national

kinroku kōsai 金禄公債

Public bonds issued in 1877 by the Meiji government in commutation of the hereditary stipends (*chitsuroku*) of nobles and members of the former *samurai* class. The bonds were issued on a sliding scale, the interest rates and the dates of maturity varying according to the amount of the original rice stipend. Many of the poorer former samurai, who had no business experience, were forced to sell their bonds at a loss. See CHITSUROKU SHOBUN.

Kinsei kijin den 近世畸人伝

(Tales of Unusual Men of Our Day). A collection of biographical sketches of more than 100 outstanding men, mostly *samurai* and men of letters, but also farmers and townsmen, of the Edo period (1600–1868); written by poet and scholar Ban Kōkei (1733–1806), illustrated by Mikuma Katen, and published in 1790. *Kinsei kijin den* strongly influenced later Japanese literature, particularly the KIBYŌSHI genre.

Kinshi Kunshō 金鵄勲章

(Order of the Golden Kite). Award given by the emperor to members of the military before World War II for bravery in action. First given on 11 February 1890 to commemorate the traditional anniversary of the accession of the legendary first emperor JIMMU, it had seven ranks.

kinship 親族

(*shinzoku*). The basic pattern of the Japanese kinship system is bilateral. Both the paternal and maternal sides are symmetrically referred to and addressed by the same terms. Differences from the Anglo-American categories are found only in the terms for siblings. Both brothers and sisters are differentiated according to relative age: *ani* for elder brothers and *otōto* for younger brothers; likewise, *ane* for elder sisters and *imōto* for younger sisters. The range of kinship terms extends to first cousins.

Another characteristic of the Japanese use of kinship terms is found in the tendency to equate cognates (relatives by blood) and affines (relatives by marriage): spouses of un-

cles, aunts, and siblings are referred to and addressed by the same terms as those related by blood, and the same range and terms apply to the cognates and affines of one's spouse. As reflected in this usage of kinship terms, the Japanese tend to conceptualize their kinship universe without differentiating between cognates and affines. This is closely related to the concept of the IE (household), the members of which are grouped as a distinctive social unit. A set of relatives called *shinrui* (or *shinseki*) is conceptualized in terms of households rather than individuals. The *shinrui* includes a certain number of households whose family members are related to one through the bilateral extension of kinship, normally including first cousins. Although it is not a constant group of kin, it has important functions: it is the *shinrui* who assemble and are indispensable at weddings and funerals.

Tendency toward Dominance by the Male Side—The Japanese kinship system is often labeled "patrilineal" in sociological literature. This description derives from the tendency toward virilocal marriage (in which wives come to live with husbands' families after marriage), which became the dominant pattern in the feudal age and after. During the Edo period (1600–1868), when the *ie* institution became prevalent, it was advantageous for management of a household that the head be succeeded by his son, who had been his active collaborator. As a result, patrilocal marriage became the predominant pattern in the society. However, in the absence of a son, normally the daughter's husband became an adopted son-in-law, assuming the position of *de jure* as well as de facto successor of his wife's father. Therefore, the Japanese kinship system should not strictly be called patrilineal in the usage of current social anthropology.

Another phenomenon that sometimes gave the impression that the Japanese had a patrilineal system was the existence of the *dōzoku*, a set of households that split off from an original one: the original household is called the *honke* and the branch household is called the *bunke* (see HONKE AND BUNKE). The *dōzoku* group was normally created around the households of brothers, so that it might appear to be a patrilineal group. However, here too, some branch households were created by adopted sons-in-law. Thus, strictly speaking, the *dōzoku* cannot be called a patrilineal descent group.

Importance of Women in the Kinship Network—The tradition of virilocal marriages, including the *dōzoku* organization, suggests the dominance of the male line in Japanese kinship in spite of its bilateral character. The father and eldest brother occupy higher seats than the mother and sister

Kintarō The ruddy-cheeked mountain boy of Japanese folklore cheers on his animal playmates in a wrestling match on Mt. Ashigara. This scene is from a 1949 children's book illustrated by Yonai Suihō.

Kinugasa Sachio Known as "Iron Man" to his fans and the Japanese sports press, the Hiroshima Tōyō Carp infielder set a record by appearing in 2,215 consecutive games over 17 years.

in a gathering of *shinrui;* relatives of the father's (husband's) side are given priority on formal occasions. However, it is the mother, wife, and sisters who play key roles in communication among relatives. This often leads to a household's having more effective links with relatives on the wife's side. Today, with the decline of traditional formality, it has become increasingly common for young people to visit the wife's natal house first, more frequently, and for longer periods than the husband's. Thus the recent tendencies disclose the latent importance of women in the Japanese kinship system and strengthen the interpretation of its essential nature as bilateral.

Kinshō-Mataichi Corporation
金商又一[株]

(Kinshō Mataichi). Trading company handling various types of metals; incorporated in 1947 as Kinzoku Shōji. The company assumed its current name in 1960 when it merged with Mataichi Co. It joined the Mitsubishi group in the mid-1960s. The company's overseas network now links 16 major cities. For the fiscal year 1991, sales totaled ¥278.6 billion (US $2.0 billion) and capitalization stood at ¥1.6 billion (US $11.7 million). Headquarters are in Tōkyō.

Kintarō
金太郎

Popular figure in Japanese folklore. Kintarō (Golden Boy) was the childhood name of Sakata no Kintoki, one of the four trusted followers of the warrior MINAMOTO NO YORIMITSU. Although he seems to have been a historical figure, appearing in the 11th-century anthology KONJAKU MONOGATARI, Sakata is depicted in later stories as the son of a YAMAMBA (mountain witch), born on Mt. Ashigara, and as a prodigy of Herculean strength who wrestled with bears and other beasts. Kintarō appears in the 17th- and 18th-century ballads (JŌRURI) and KABUKI plays, often by the name of Kaidōmaru. The tales of his supernatural birth, his red complexion, and his possession of a hatchet said to be the thunder-god's weapon point to the fusion of his historical life with a belief in the thunder god—the ensurer of a bountiful crop.

Kintetsu Department Store Co, Ltd
[株]近鉄百貨店

(Kintetsu Hyakkaten). One of the companies of the Kintetsu department store group based in the Kinki and Ōsaka areas. It began as a member of Kintetsu Corporation (KINKI NIPPON RAILWAY CO, LTD) and was incorporated as an independent company in 1972. It has seven department stores. Overseas offices are located in Paris, New York, and Hong Kong. Annual sales for the fiscal year ending February 1990 totaled ¥264.8 billion (US $1.7 billion). Capitalization in the same year was ¥3.4 billion (US $22.2 million). Headquarters are in Ōsaka.

Kinugasa Sachio
衣笠祥雄

(1947–). Professional baseball player. Born in Kyōto. A catcher during his Heian High

Kinugasa Teinosuke Initially an *onnagata* (female impersonator) on both stage and screen, Kinugasa became an innovative film director.

School days, he switched to the infield when he joined the Hiroshima Carp (now Hiroshima Tōyō Carp). From 19 October 1970, when he took the field against the Yomiuri Giants, until his retirement in 1987, he played in 2,215 consecutive games over 17 years, surpassing the record set by Lou Gehrig of the New York Yankees, and became known as "Iron Man." In 1987 he received the People's Honor Award.

Kinugasa Teinosuke
衣笠貞之助

(1896–1982). Film director. Initially famous as one of the first great innovators of Japanese cinema, later noted for his lavish and spectacular productions. He began his acting career as an ONNAGATA (female impersonator) with several SHIMPA theater troupes. He continued as an *onnagata* at the Nikkatsu (see NIKKATSU CORPORATION) film studios beginning in 1917, but found within a few years that actresses had begun to replace *onnagata.* He then turned to other aspects of the film industry, writing his first screenplay in 1920 and directing his first feature in 1922. Kinugasa's most important films of the period were KURUTTA IPPEIJI (1926, A Page of Madness) and *Jūjiro* (1928, Crossroads), both of which employed unconventional narrative techniques and used visual imagery to present the story. Following World War II, he specialized in conventional but lavish costume dramas and remakes of some of his earlier films. Of this body of work only one film is well known: *Jigokumon* (1953, Gate of Hell), the first successful Japanese color film. It won the Grand Prix at the Cannes Film Festival in 1954 and the Academy Award as Best Foreign Film in 1955.

Kinugawa
鬼怒川

River in Tochigi and Ibaraki prefectures, central Honshū. Originating in the Taishaku Mountains in northwest Tochigi Prefecture and flowing south, it joins the Tonegawa at the city of Mitsukaidō. Numerous dams and hot springs are located along the upper reaches. The water is utilized for drinking, irrigation, and electric power. Length: 177 km (110 mi); area of drainage basin: 1,760 sq km (680 sq mi).

Kinugawa Hot Spring
鬼怒川温泉

(Kinugawa Onsen). Located near the Kinugawa Gorge, northwestern Tochigi Prefecture, central Honshū. A simple thermal spring; water temperature 34°–53°C (93°–127°F). Located within Nikkō National Park, it is one of the most famous spas in the Kantō region, abounding in natural scenic spots such as the gorge called Ryūōkyō.

Kin'yō wakashū
金葉和歌集

(Collection of Golden Leaves). Usually abbreviated to *Kin'yōshū.* Fifth imperial anthology (*chokusenshū*) of classical Japanese poetry (WAKA). It was ordered in 1124 by the retired emperor SHIRAKAWA, and drafts were completed between 1124 and 1127. The standard version is the second draft. Compiled by MINAMOTO NO TOSHIYORI, it consists of 10 books. The number of poems varies, depending on draft and manuscript copy; the second draft commonly has 712 poems; the third draft, 648.

Toshiyori showed a disregard for tradition by making the anthology the shortest to date and by limiting it to 10 books instead of the 20 considered standard since the first imperial anthology, the KOKINSHŪ (ca 905). Another departure was the inclusion in the last book of a major subcategory headed *renga,* "linked poems"—standard five-line, 31-

syllable poems of which one person had composed the first three lines and another the last two. These were witty single-poem precursors of the later extended forms of linked verse known as RENGA, and, though they had occasionally been included in imperial anthologies, they had not before been considered worthy of a distinct heading. Poetry of Toshiyori's own generation and the previous one accounts for the bulk of the anthology, with only about one-tenth by older poets. Violently attacked by poetic conservatives (who objected to its title, format, and choice of poems), the *Kin'yōshū* came to be admired in later centuries as an important milestone in the development of descriptive symbolism (see SHIN KOKINSHŪ).

Kin'yū Kyōkō→Financial Crisis of 1927

kinza, ginza, and zeniza
金座, 銀座と銭座

(*kinza, ginza to zeniza*). The gold (*kin*), silver (*gin*), and lesser coin (*zeni*) mints (*za*) of the Tokugawa shogunate (1603–1867). Today the major commercial district of Tōkyō is named Ginza after the silver mint that was situated in that area from 1612 to 1800. Control of money and commerce was important to political leaders from the late Muromachi period (1333–1568) onward. As TOKUGAWA IEYASU extended his power during the 1590s and early 1600s, he set up mints as part of his larger strategy to regularize commercial and political life and establish direct control over the output of gold and silver mines. After incidents of corruption, in 1800 both *kinza* and *ginza* (which had been located in several cities) were consolidated in Edo (now Tōkyō). Minting activities were run as hereditary monopolies under the supervision of the commissioners of finance (KANJŌ BUGYŌ).

The *kinza* dates from 1594, when Ieyasu ordered GOTŌ MITSUTSUGU to mint gold coins (KOBAN and *ichibu kin;* ŌBAN were minted there from 1601), a task for which he and his descendants were paid a stipend. Ieyasu established a *ginza* in Fushimi in 1601. In 1608 it was moved to Kyōto, where until 1800 the actual minting process was overseen by the descendants of Daikoku (Yuasa) Sakuhei (d 1636; later known as Daikoku Jōze, or Daikoku the "sealer" or "certifier"). In 1606 Ieyasu established another *ginza* in Sumpu (now the city of Shizuoka), later moving it to Edo. From their origins until the Empō era (1673–81) all *ginza* operations were directly responsible through Gotō to the senior councillors (*rōjū*). During the Genroku era (1688–1704), however, they were placed directly under the *kanjō bugyō.*

The *zeniza* was first established in 1636, when the shogunate ordered a copper mint established in Edo and another at Sakamoto in Ōmi Province (now Shiga Prefecture). During the following century coin use increased dramatically, and a great variety of copper and iron coins was minted, reducing their value. In 1745 the shogunate shut down all *zeniza.* A new *zeniza* was erected in Edo, and from the 1770s onward all copper, iron, and brass coins were produced under *kinza* and *ginza* supervision, mostly at the Edo mint.

Kinzoku Rōkyō
全日本金属産業労働組合協議会

(abbreviation of Zen Nihon Kinzoku Sangyō Rōdō Kumiai Kyōgikai; the Japan Council of Metalworkers' Unions). Also known as the

International Metalworkers' Federation–Japan Council (IMF-JC). Founded in 1964 to help individual unions join the International Metalworkers' Federation (IMF), Kinzoku Rōkyō was at first a loose organization, but after 1967 it became actively involved in collective bargaining and it has taken a leading role in the annual SHUNTŌ (spring wage offensive). As an influential labor federation, it acts in unison with the umbrella national labor confederation, RENGO (Japanese Trade Union Confederation), in pursuing an anticommunist policy and in seeking harmony between workers and employers. One of its current major priorities is the reduction of working hours. Kinzoku Rōkyō's membership includes eight major federations in the metal-manufacturing industry, among which are the Confederation of Japan Automobile Workers' Unions (JIDŌSHA SŌREN), the Japanese Federation of Iron and Steel Workers' Unions (TEKKO-RŌREN), and the Japanese Federation of Electrical Machine Workers' Unions (Denki Rōren), as well as a few independent enterprise-based unions. As of September 1990 Kinzoku Rōkyō had a total membership of 2,418,000.

Kira Yoshinaka   吉良義央

(1641–1703). Also known as Kira Kōzukenosuke. Official of the TOKUGAWA SHOGUNATE (1603–1867) who was killed by 46 men led by ŌISHI YOSHIO in the famous FORTY-SEVEN RŌNIN INCIDENT. Born in Edo (now Tōkyō), he belonged to a select group of families (KŌKE) responsible for shogunate protocol and enjoying close ties with YANAGISAWA YOSHIYASU. In April 1701 he was wounded by Asano Naganori (1665–1701), *daimyō* of Akō (now part of Hyōgo Prefecture), for supposedly keeping Asano ignorant of fine points of protocol. To draw a sword in the shogunal castle was a serious offense, and Asano was deprived of his domain and ordered to commit suicide. Kira was not even reprimanded, although he was later relieved of his office. Asano's retainers vowed vengeance and in 1703 killed Kira.

kiri → paulownia

kiribi   切火

Sacred fire, principally for ceremonial or ritual use, ignited by friction, such as rubbing together pieces of cypress (*hinoki*) wood or by striking flint. In ancient times special wooden mortar and pestle sets were also commonly used for starting fires, especially at Shintō shrines. Fire struck in this manner was believed to be sacred, and the sparks were believed to have a purifying effect on persons and objects. Today, the fire used in ceremonies at the ISE SHRINE is still ignited by mortar and pestle. The related custom of scattering sparks on a person about to leave the house is still observed by some members of the tradition-bound world of the *geisha* and other entertainers.

Kirigamine   霧ケ峰

Highland northeast of Lake Suwa, central Nagano Prefecture, central Honshū. Shield-shaped and covered with grass, it is used for flying gliders. It has several beautiful marshlands and is part of Yatsugatake Chūshin Kōgen Quasi-National Park. The main peak is Kurumayama (1,925 m; 6,316 ft). Average elevation: 1,700 m (5,577 ft).

kirigirisu   螽蟖

(katydid). *Gampsocleis buergeri*. Insect of the order Orthoptera, family Tettigoniidae. This species is green or light brown with black spots on the forewings. The body is long (about 40 mm; 1.5 in) with very long antennae and hind legs. It is seen from summer through late autumn in grassy plains and dry riverbeds; it chirps day and night. The male makes sounds by rubbing the forewings together. There are about 80 related species, among them the *yabukiri* (*Tettigonia orientalis*), *tsuyumushi* (*Phaneroptera falcata*), and *kutsuwamushi* (*Mecopoda nipponensis*).

It is thought that in ancient times the word *kirigirisu* was used to refer to CRICKETS, which are now called *kōrogi*. It has also been suggested that *kirigirisu* was the common name for insects that chirp in autumn and that only in the Heian period (794–1185) did the word take on its present meaning of katydid.

kirikane   切り金

Thin gold- or silver-leaf decorative technique used on paintings and LACQUER WARE; also, the gold and silver used. Introduced to Japan in the Nara period (710–794) from Tang-dynasty (T'ang; 618–907) China. From the Heian period (794–1185) through the Kamakura period (1185–1333) this technique was widely used on Buddhist paintings and statuary. The earliest known example of *kirikane* is found on the 7th-century Shitennō images in the *kondō* (main hall) of the temple HŌRYŪJI in Nara. For use in paintings, two or three sheets of thin gold leaf are baked into one leaf, which is then shredded and applied with glue and brush. The use of *kirikane* for lacquer ware can also be traced to the Nara period. The gold or silver adheres permanently to the lacquer as it hardens, forming rich decoration that highlights or adds variety to a design.

kirimai   切米

Rice stipend given to *daimyō* or shogunal retainers who did not hold fiefs (CHIGYŌ) that yielded tax income; also known as KURAMAI. As most daimyō strengthened direct control over their domains throughout the Edo period (1600–1868), their retainers (including many of the highest rank) lost their fiefs and received a rice stipend instead, paid in seasonal installments. Although the entire stipend was usually specified in terms of rice alone, part of it was frequently paid in cash according to the official exchange rates. *Samurai* employed brokers (FUDASASHI) for these transactions and for loans.

Kirin Brewery Co, Ltd   麒麟麦酒[株]

(Kirin Bīru). Beer-brewing company; also produces soft drinks and food products. A member of the MITSUBISHI group of companies, it was incorporated in 1907. At the end of World War II, Kirin was third in the beer industry. Through the expansion of production and aggressive promotional efforts, it became the industry leader in 1954. Seeking product diversity, the firm established in 1972 Kirin-Seagram, Ltd, in cooperation with Joseph E. Seagram & Sons, Inc, for the production of distilled liquors. Sales for the fiscal year ending December 1990 totaled ¥1.4 trillion (US $10.5 billion), of which the sale of beer contributed 89 percent and soft drinks and other products 11 percent. In the same year capitalization stood at ¥102.0 billion (US $763.8 million). Headquarters are in Tōkyō.

Kirishima Volcanic Zone   霧島火山帯

(Kirishima Kazantai). Volcanic zone extending south from ASOSAN, a volcano in Kumamoto Prefecture, Kyūshū, whose caldera is one of the largest in the world, to northern Taiwan via the RYŪKYŪ ISLANDS. The major volcanoes in the zone are Asosan, SAKURAJIMA, and KIRISHIMAYAMA. Ash and lava from the zone's volcanoes spread over a large area of central and southern Kyūshū. The volcanic ash called *shirasu* is found as far south as Kagoshima Prefecture.

Kirishima-Yaku National Park   霧島屋久国立公園

(Kirishima-Yaku Kokuritsu Kōen). Situated in southern Kyūshū in Kagoshima and Miyazaki prefectures. The park includes volcanoes, mountains, lakes, caldera lakes, forests, and an island off the southern Kyūshū coast. The Kirishima Volcanic Group, consisting of 23 volcanoes, is dominated by the peaks of Karakunidake and TAKACHIHONOMINE. The latter is sacred to the Japanese because it is the spot where the god Ninigi no Mikoto is said to have descended from heaven. To the northwest is the highland EBINO KŌGEN, and in the southwest is the Kirishima Hot Spring.

South of Kirishima are SATSUMA PENINSULA and ŌSUMI PENINSULA, with KAGOSHIMA BAY in between. KAGOSHIMA, the principal city in southern Kyūshū, lies on the bay directly op-

Kirigamine Named "misty ridge" for the haze that often floats over it, this highland is also well known for its abundant day lilies.

kirigirisu The chirping of the adult katydid can be heard throughout Japan between June and September.

Kirishima-Yaku National Park This park contains a wide variety of natural habitats and lush vegetation that reflect its southern location.
1 One of Japan's most active volcanoes, Sakurajima emits smoke and ash almost continuously, often dusting the city of Kagoshima across the bay.
2 The subtropical island of Yakushima is home to a forest of giant cryptomeria (*sugi*) that includes the tree pictured—popularly known as the Jōmon Sugi, it is more than 7,000 years old.
3 Takachihonomine, a craterless stratovolcano, is known for its fields of *miyamakirishima*, an alpine azalea that blooms in early June.

posite SAKURAJIMA, an island with an active volcano. At the tip of the Satsuma Peninsula is Ibusuki Hot Spring, Lake IKEDA, and the mountain KAIMONDAKE. Lying 60 km (37 mi) south of Ōsumi Peninsula is YAKUSHIMA, an island noted for its giant cedars (*yakusugi*), some over 1,000 years old. Area: 548 sq km (212 sq mi).

Kirishimayama　霧島山

Volcanic group on the border between Kagoshima and Miyazaki prefectures, Kyūshū. Of 1 composite and 22 simple volcanoes, there are 15 with perfect craters in this unusual volcanic group. One of the group erupted in 1959. The mountains are covered with mixed forests. On the summits grow rare plants such as *miyamakirishima* (a kind of rhododendron) and the Japanese green alder. Hot springs abound in the foothills. Kirishimayama is the center of KIRISHIMA-YAKU NATIONAL PARK; its highest peak is Karakunidake (1,700 m; 5,577 ft).

Kirishitan Bunko, Sophia University　上智大学キリシタン文庫

(Jōchi Daigaku Kirishitan Bunko). Library in Chiyoda Ward, Tōkyō, that houses materials related to the history of Christianity in Japan and other Asian countries. The Kirishitan Bunko was established by the Jesuit priest

and Sophia University professor Johannes Laures (1891–1959) in 1932. The collection contains some 10,000 works, including histories of Japanese Christianity published in various European countries; books, pamphlets, and scholarly works published by the JESUIT MISSION PRESS in Japan in the late 16th and early 17th centuries; anti-Christian polemics from the Azuchi-Momoyama (1568–1600) and Edo (1600–1868) periods; and works relating to Roman Catholicism in China and Korea published by Jesuits in China during the late Ming (1368–1644) and early Qing (Ch'ing; 1644–1912) dynasties.

Kirishitan monogatari　吉利支丹物語

(Tales of Christians). An anonymous chapbook dated 1639, the progenitor of a profuse genre of anti-Christian fictional narratives that were widely read during the Edo period (1600–1868). The work begins with a grotesque portrayal of the first missionary to arrive in Japan, denigrates basic Christian practices, depicts a one-sided debate between the Christian apologist FABIAN and an expert in Buddhist doctrine, and ends with a semihistorical account of the SHIMABARA UPRISING.

Kirishitan Yashiki　切支丹屋敷

(Christian Mansion). The seat of the Tokugawa shogunate's (1603–1867) anti-Christian inquisition (see SHŪMON ARATAME), located in Kobinata in Edo (now Tōkyō). It was originally the villa of the shogunate's inspector-general (*ōmetsuke*) Inoue Masashige (1585–1661), a former Christian who was the first to hold the inquisitor's post (1640–58). The Kirishitan Yashiki was officially designated a prison for Christian missionaries around 1646, housing under protective custody the Jesuits of the so-called Second Rubino Group, who had apostatized under torture. The "fallen padre" (*korobi bateren*) Giuseppe Chiara, also known as Okamoto San'emon (d 1685), is the best known of the group. After its last member died in 1700, the Kirishitan Yashiki was destined to be the prison of only one other missionary, Giovanni Battista SIDOTTI, who was incarcerated there from 1709 until his death in 1714. The establishment was abolished in 1792 together with the office of the inquisition, which was no longer considered necessary.

kirisute gomen　切捨御免

(permission to kill). A privilege enjoyed by the *samurai* class during the Edo period

(1600–1868) whereby they were permitted to kill members of the lower classes (farmers and townsmen) on serious provocation, especially on points of honor. The samurai was expected to report his action to the authorities if a death resulted, facing punishment if he were found to have exceeded his rights.

Kiritake Monjūrō II　桐竹紋十郎2世

(1900–70). Master puppeteer in the BUNRAKU puppet theater of Japan. Real name Isakawa Sakichi. Born in Ōsaka Prefecture, Monjūrō became a disciple of the noted puppeteer Yoshida Bungorō III in 1909 and became one of Japan's great puppet operators. Monjūrō was acclaimed especially for his masterful handling of puppets cast in various feminine roles. His activities also included popularization of puppetry as an art and experimentation with puppetry theatricals set to Western music. In 1965 he was designated one of the LIVING NATIONAL TREASURES.

Kiroku Shōen Kenkeijo　記録荘園券契所

(Office for the Investigation of Shōen Documents). Better known in English as the Records Office, from the Japanese abbreviation Kirokusho. An extrastatutory office established by Emperor GO-SANJŌ in 1069 in an attempt to regulate the illegal acquisition of land by noble houses and religious institutions. It disappeared after Go-Sanjō's death but was revived in 1156 by Emperor GO-SHIRAKAWA, to adjudicate land disputes between local officials and SHŌEN proprietors, and again in 1187 by MINAMOTO NO YORITOMO. During Emperor Go-Daigo's KEMMU RESTORATION (1333–36) the Records Office became the central organ of the imperial government.

Kiryū　桐生[市]

City in eastern Gumma Prefecture, central Honshū. Long known for its fine silks, Kiryū rivals KYŌTO's Nishijin district both in quality and quantity. In addition to textiles, there are electrical-appliance, automobile-parts, machine, and metal industries here. Pop: 126,446.

Kiryū Yūyū　桐生悠々

(1873–1941). Liberal journalist. Born Kiryū Masatsugu in Ishikawa Prefecture. Graduated from the law faculty of Tōkyō University. He became editor in chief of the *Shinano mainichi shimbun* in 1910 and drew attention with his editorial policies of antimilitarism and liberalism. In 1933 strong opposition to one of his editorials from organizations such as the Veterans' Association forced him to resign. The next year he began *Tazan no ishi*, a privately circulated magazine in Nagoya, continuing his outspoken opposition to fascism until his death.

Kisakata　象潟[町]

Town on the Sea of Japan in southwestern Akita Prefecture, northern Honshū. Situated at the foot of the mountain Chōkaisan. Dairy farming is an important local industry. The many lagoons that made Kisakata a picturesque area were completely destroyed by an earthquake in 1804. Pop: 14,203.

Kisaragi →calendar, dates, and time

Kisarazu　木更津[市]

City in western Chiba Prefecture, central Honshū, on Tōkyō Bay. Kisarazu prospered in the Edo period (1600–1868) as a port for ships bound to and from Edo (now Tōkyō).

A naval base during World War II, after the war it became a base for the Self Defense Forces. Land has been reclaimed to create an industrial zone. Shōjōji, a temple made famous in a nursery song, is located here. Pop: 123,433.

Kisegawa 黄瀬川

River in eastern Shizuoka Prefecture, central Honshū. It originates in the city of Gotemba at the eastern slope of Mt. Fuji (Fujisan) and flows south, converging with the Hakone Canal, to join the Kanogawa at the city of Numazu. Length: 32 km (20 mi).

kisei 帰省

(homecoming). Word used to refer to the return to their hometowns of people working and attending school away from home, usually at New Year's and around the time of the BON FESTIVAL, a Buddhist observance held in July or August to commemorate the souls of ancestors. In most cases people are traveling from Tōkyō to rural areas, and the major highways and railroad lines out of Tōkyō become terribly congested, a condition referred to as *kisei* rush. Additional trains and buses are added to the schedules to ease crowding.

Kishibojin 鬼子母神

Also known as Kishimojin, or Karitei, from the Sanskrit Hārītī; guardian deity of children. She is said originally to have been a malevolent goddess who ate the children of others, although she had 1,000 of her own. In order to chastise her, Buddha hid her youngest and favorite child. When she went to him to ask its whereabouts, she was converted to Buddhism. In Japan childless women pray to Kishibojin to become pregnant, and she is regarded as the tutelary deity of safe childbirth and conjugal harmony. Although Kishibojin is sometimes represented as a demon, she is more often depicted as a beautiful celestial being robed in silken garments, with a pomegranate in her right hand and her favorite child in her left. As the guardian deity of the LOTUS SUTRA, she is especially venerated by followers of the NICHIREN SECT.

Kishida Ginkō 岸田吟香

(1833–1905). Pioneer journalist of the Meiji period (1868–1912). Born Kishida Ginji in what is now Okayama Prefecture. Kishida assisted James Curtis HEPBURN in the compilation of his Japanese-English dictionary. Together with HAMADA HIKOZŌ, he published one of Japan's first modern newspapers, the *Kaigai shimbun*. In 1873 he became a reporter for the *Tōkyō nichinichi shimbun* (now the MAINICHI SHIMBUN), writing articles in the spoken language rather than the classical Japanese that was normal in newspapers of the time. He was one of Japan's first modern war correspondents, covering the Taiwan Expedition of 1874.

Kishida Kunio 岸田国士

(1890–1954). Playwright who helped raise the standards of modern theater in Japan during the period before World War II. Born in Tōkyō. Kishida graduated from the Army Academy in 1912 and studied in Paris with the celebrated French director Jacques Copeau in 1921 and 1922. Returning to Japan, he spent the rest of his career composing plays and writing critical essays in an attempt to create a theater responsive to the literary and humanistic values he felt to be important. He was one of the founders of the

Kishibojin A Buddhist goddess best known as the guardian of children. This wooden image of Kishibojin dates from the late Heian period (794–1185). Height 42 cm. Tōdaiji, Nara.

BUNGAKUZA (Literary Theater), an important theatrical troupe that began its activities in 1937. Among his plays are short poetic sketches of considerable charm, such as *Chiroru no aki* (1924; tr *Autumn in the Tyrol*, 1968) and *Kamifūsen* (1925; tr *A Paper Balloon*, 1965), as well as longer comedies of manners, such as *Ochiba nikki* (1927; tr *Fallen Leaves, a Diary*, 1961) and *Sawa shi no futari musume* (1935, Mr. Sawa's Two Daughters), which portray with wit and considerable irony the emotional attitudes of the Europeanized upper-middle class in prewar Japan. Kishida can well be credited with the creation of stage dialogue in modern Japanese theater; his plays are eloquent and wholly colloquial.

Kishida Kunio zenshū (1954–55) contains texts of his plays and critical writings. See also SHINGEKI.

Kishida Ryūsei 岸田劉生

(1891–1929). Painter. Born in Tōkyō, the son of the progressive journalist KISHIDA GINKŌ (1833–1905). He left school in 1908 to study Western-style painting with KURODA SEIKI at the White Horse Society (HAKUBAKAI) studio. His earliest works, exhibited beginning in 1910 at the BUNTEN, the annual Ministry of Education art exhibition, show the influence of Kuroda's plein-air style. Through his friendship with MUSHANOKŌJI SANEATSU he became involved with the White Birch school (SHIRAKABA SCHOOL), a literary group whose journal was instrumental in disseminating French cubism and fauvism in Japan. Kishida formed the Fyūzankai (Fusain Society; 1912–13) with other artists. In 1915 he founded the Sōdosha (1915–22). Around 1917 Kishida began to be influenced by the realism of Northern Renaissance painting, especially Dürer and Van Eyck. His well-known series of portraits of his daughter combines the seemingly disparate elements of photographic realism and decorative surface effects. In the early 1920s Kishida abruptly shifted his focus to Japanese-style painting (*nihonga*).

Kishida Toshiko 岸田俊子

(1863–1901). Writer and political activist, called Japan's first woman orator. Also known as Nakajima Toshiko; pen name Nakajima Shōen. Born in Kyōto, she became in 1880 a companion to Empress Shōken (1850–1914). In 1882 she began speaking tours for the new JIYŪTŌ (Liberal Party). (See also FREEDOM AND PEOPLE'S RIGHTS MOVEMENT.) She was married in 1884 to Jiyūtō leader NAKAJIMA NOBUYUKI. She taught school in Yokohama and contributed to the magazine JOGAKU ZASSHI. Her works include *Shōen nikki* (1903, Shōen's Diary).

Kishida Ryūsei *Reiko Smiling*, one of a series of portraits of the painter's daughter. 1921. Oil on canvas. 44 × 36 cm. Tōkyō National Museum.

Kishi Nobusuke 岸信介

(1896–1987). Bureaucrat, politician, and prime minister (February 1957 to July 1960). Born in Yamaguchi Prefecture. He took the name Kishi when adopted into his uncle's family. Upon graduation from Tōkyō University in 1920, he entered the Ministry of Agriculture and Commerce and soon became a leader of the so-called new bureaucrats (*shinkanryō*). From 1936 to 1939 he served in the government of MANCHUKUO.

A member of the cabinet of TŌJŌ HIDEKI from 1941 through 1944, he was in charge of Japan's economic mobilization for World War II and was imprisoned by the OCCUPATION authorities as a war criminal. In 1953 Kishi was elected to the House of Representatives as a member of the LIBERAL PARTY (Jiyūtō), but he later aligned with the Japan Democratic Party (NIHON MINSHUTŌ). Kishi was the main architect of the conservative coalition known as the LIBERAL DEMOCRATIC PARTY (LDP), formed in November 1955, and became its secretary-general. As prime minister, Kishi promoted revision of the United States–Japan Security Treaty in hopes of restoring independent diplomacy for Japan and cementing close US relations. His high-handed tactics in obtaining ratification of the revised treaty caused wide public protest and forced his resignation. See also UNITED STATES–JAPAN SECURITY TREATIES.

Kishi Seiichi 岸清一

(1867–1933). Leading figure in Japanese amateur sports; lawyer. Born in Shimane Prefecture; graduate of Tōkyō University. In 1921 he became the second president of the JAPAN AMATEUR SPORTS ASSOCIATION. He also served as a member of the International Olympic Committee and headed the Japanese athletic delegations to the 1924 (Paris) and the 1928 (Amsterdam) Olympic Games.

Kishiwada 岸和田［市］

City in southern Ōsaka Prefecture, central Honshū, on Ōsaka Bay. Kishiwada was a castle town of the Okabe family during the Edo period (1600–1868). Since the late 1800s Kishiwada has been known for its Izumi cot-

Kishi Nobusuke The moving force behind the creation of the Liberal Democratic Party in 1955, this conservative politician served as prime minister from 1957 to 1960.

Kiso Mountains
Hōkendake (2,931 m), one of the peaks that make up Komagatake, the highest mountain in the Kiso range.

ton. More recently, industrial complexes for lumber, steel, and metal production have been constructed on reclaimed land. Farm products include rice, onions, and mandarin oranges. The remains of Kishiwada Castle and the annual Kishiwada Danjiri Festival draw tourists. Pop: 188,563.

Kiska   キスカ島

(Kisukatō). One of the American Aleutian Islands occupied by Japanese forces in June 1942. After ATTU fell to American forces in May 1943, the Imperial Japanese Navy went to great lengths to evacuate its considerable garrison on Kiska, succeeding on the fifth attempt. It was the only major effort by the Japanese to relieve a garrison during the war.

Kisodani   木曽谷

Valley on the upper reaches of the river Kisogawa, southwestern Nagano Prefecture, central Honshū. The highway Nakasendō passed through this long and narrow valley, which bustled with travelers and processions of *daimyō* journeying between Edo (now Tōkyō) and their fiefs in the Edo period (1600–1868). Its forest, composed mainly of Japanese cypress, is counted as one of the three most beautiful in Japan.

Kiso Fukushima   木曽福島[町]

Town in southwestern Nagano Prefecture, central Honshū. Located in the KISODANI (Kiso Valley) on the highway Nakasendō, the town was the site of a shogunate commissioner's office (*bugyōsho*) and a toll barrier (*sekisho*) during the Edo period (1600–1868). More recently, it has relied on its lumber, woodwork, and musical-instrument (notably violins) industries. Tourist attractions are a folk museum and several hot springs. Kiso Fukushima is the base for pilgrims climbing the sacred mountain ONTAKE-SAN. Pop: 9,101.

Kisogawa   木曽川

River in Nagano, Gifu, Aichi, and Mie prefectures, central Honshū. It originates in the northern Kiso region, flows southwest be-

tween the Hida and Kiso mountains, and empties into Ise Bay. It flows through a granite plateau, creating gorges, and enters the Nōbi Plain near the city of Inuyama. Regions along the river are covered with Kiso cypress (Kiso *hinoki*) and are counted as one of the three most beautiful forest areas of Japan. Numerous WAJŪ (farming settlements protected by circular embankments) are found along the lower reaches. The water is used for drinking, irrigation, electric power, and industry. Popular tourist attractions include the gorges called NEZAMENOTOKO and ENAKYŌ and the area referred to as the Japan Rhine. Length: 227 km (141 mi); area of drainage basin: 9,100 sq km (3,513 sq mi).

Kiso Komagatake →Komagatake

Kiso Mountains   木曽山脈

(Kiso Sammyaku). Mountain range; referred to as the "Central Alps," the range is part of the JAPANESE ALPS. It runs northeast to southwest for about 100 km (60 mi) in Nagano Prefecture, central Honshū. It is noted for its towering, rugged peaks and its cirques. The highest mountain in the range, KOMAGATAKE (2,956 m; 9,698 ft), is rich in alpine flora.

Kiso Ontake →Ontakesan

Kiso Yoshinaka →Minamoto no Yoshinaka

kissaten →coffeehouses

Kitabatake Akiie   北畠顕家

(1318–38). Supporter of the attempt by Emperor GO-DAIGO to reassert imperial rule over Japan (see KEMMU RESTORATION). The eldest son of KITABATAKE CHIKAFUSA, Akiie was appointed in 1333 by Go-Daigo as civil governor of Michi no Oku, responsible for the vast provinces of Mutsu (now Fukushima, Miyagi, Iwate and Aomori prefectures) and Dewa (now Akita and Yamagata prefectures) in northern Honshū. He was given the ancient title Chinjufu shōgun (general of the Headquarters for the Pacification of Ezo) in 1335, the year in which ASHIKAGA TAKAUJI turned against Go-Daigo. The following year Akiie expelled Takauji from Kyōto. Upon Akiie's return north, Takauji defeated Go-Daigo's other armies and installed the rival emperor Kōmyō (1322–80; r 1336–48) of the Northern Court in Kyōto (see NORTHERN AND SOUTHERN COURTS). By early 1337 Takauji had founded the Muromachi shogunate, and Go-Daigo had fled to the Southern Court at Yoshino. Akiie fell in battle against Takauji's general KŌ NO MORONAO in 1338.

Kitabatake Chikafusa   北畠親房

(1293–1354). Courtier, scholar, and political figure of the period of the NORTHERN AND SOUTHERN COURTS (1337–92). Scion of the Murakami branch of the MINAMOTO FAMILY, Chikafusa was in 1324 appointed *dainagon* (great counselor) and invested with offices emblematic of that family's headship (Genji no Chōja). In 1330 he took the tonsure. In 1337, after the failure of the KEMMU RESTORATION, the attempt by Emperor GO-DAIGO to reassert direct imperial rule, Chikafusa counseled Go-Daigo to leave Kyōto and establish a separate imperial court at Yoshino, an act that initiated a severe dynastic schism. Defeated in his effort to rally provincial support by the forces of the MUROMACHI SHOGUNATE, which supported the rival Northern Court, Chikafusa fled to Yoshino in late 1343. Under Chikafusa's leadership

the Southern Court briefly recaptured Kyōto in 1352, but was unable to hold it. Chikafusa is the author of the imperial loyalist history JINNŌ SHŌTŌ KI (Chronicle of the Direct Descent of Divine Sovereigns), *Gengenshū* (a Shintoist account of Japan's origins), and SHOKUGENSHŌ (a study of official posts in Japanese history).

Kitabatake family   北畠氏

(Kitabatakeshi). Court nobles of the Kamakura (1185–1333) and Muromachi (1333–1568) periods. Founded by Nakanoin Masaie, the family was descended from the Murakami branch of the MINAMOTO FAMILY. Masaie's great-grandson KITABATAKE CHIKAFUSA and his son KITABATAKE AKIIE supported Emperor GO-DAIGO in the KEMMU RESTORATION (1333–36). In 1338 Kitabatake Akiyoshi (d 1383), another son of Chikafusa, became governor (*kokushi*) of Ise (now Mie Prefecture), where the family maintained power until Kitabatake Tomonori (1528–76) was defeated by ODA NOBUNAGA in 1576.

Kita Daitōjima   北大東島

Island approximately 350 km (220 mi) east of Okinawa. One of the Daitō Islands; part of Okinawa Prefecture. A coral island with steep cliffs. The central part is level land; some 46 percent of the island is arable and is utilized for sugarcane production. Area: 13 sq km (5 sq mi).

Kitadake   北岳

Mountain in western Yamanashi Prefecture, central Honshū, in the northern part of the AKAISHI MOUNTAINS. It is Japan's second highest mountain; one of a group of three mountains called SHIRANE SANZAN. It is composed primarily of argillite and phyllite. It has a great variety of alpine flora and fauna. The Kitadake buttress on the mountain's eastern slopes is popular with rock climbers. Height: 3,192 m (10,472 ft).

Kitagawa Fuyuhiko   北川冬彦

(1900–1990). Poet; film critic. Real name Taguro Tadahiko. Born in Shiga Prefecture; graduate of Tōkyō University. He started to write poems under the influence of French surrealists and dadaists and in 1928 founded the magazine *Shi to shiron* (Poetry and Poetics). A participant in the PROLETARIAN LITERATURE MOVEMENT of the late 1920s, he combined its ideology with his avant-garde poetry. The result was a unique kind of anti-war poetry, collected in *Sensō* (1929). His other poetry collections include *Iyarashii kami* (1936) and *Jikkenshitsu* (1941).

Kitagawa Morisada →Morisada mankō

Kitagawa school   喜多川派

(Kitagawaha). A school of UKIYO-E artists active in the late Edo period (1600–1868). Its origin, as an offshoot of the Toriyama Sekien school, can be traced to the master printmaker UTAMARO (1753–1806), who was acclaimed for his highly sophisticated prints of beautiful women (*bijinga*). Although Utamaro's prominence ensured the school's success in the Kansei era (1789–1801), none of his many followers, including Utamaro II, Tsukimaro, and Fujimaro, could match his brilliant style. The Kitagawa school disappeared soon after Utamaro's death, unable to compete with newer rival schools.

Kitagawa Tamiji   北川民次

(1894–1989). Western-style painter. Born in Shizuoka Prefecture. Kitagawa went to the

United States in 1913 and studied under John Sloan (1871–1951) at the Art Students League in New York. Later he traveled in South America and became an art teacher in Mexico. After Kitagawa returned to Japan in 1936, his works dealt mainly with Mexico and social issues.

Kitagawa Utamaro →Utamaro

Kitahara Hakushū　北原白秋

(1885–1942). A versatile poet recognized for both his TANKA and his modern poetry and an influential figure in poetry circles during the early 20th century. Real name Kitahara Ryūkichi. Born in Fukuoka Prefecture; attended Waseda University. The first book of poetry he read with passion was SHIMAZAKI TŌSON's *Wakanashū* (1897, Collection of Young Herbs), an early collection of poems in the SHINTAISHI (new-style poetry) form. In 1904 he moved to Tōkyō, where his poems immediately won praise. In 1908, with several other poets and Western-style painters, he formed the PAN NO KAI (the Pan Society), which, after adding a number of musicians and actors, soon became the most important gathering of "aesthetes."

In 1909 he published his first book of poems, *Jashūmon* (Heretics). Because of its rich imagery and dazzling diction, *Jashūmon*, along with YOSANO AKIKO's *tanka* collection *Midaregami* (1901; tr *Tangled Hair*, 1971), is credited with liberating the senses and imagination in modern Japanese poetry. In 1911 Hakushū published his second book of poems, *Omoide* (Memories), a brilliant evocation of a child's world that compares with NAKA KANSUKE's famous novel *Gin no saji* (1913–15; tr *The Silver Spoon*, 1976).

In 1912 he was convicted of adultery and jailed for two weeks. The incident is touched on in his first collection of *tanka*, *Kiri no hana* (1913, Paulownia Blossoms), which was welcomed as a fresh stimulus to the *tanka* form. More important, the experience gave a religious turn to Hakushū's outlook. This is evident in *Shinju shō* (1914, Selection of Pearls), which consists mainly of one-line poems, and in *Hakkin no koma* (1914, Platinum Top), which includes poems in WASAN (Buddhist prayer) form. Hakushū's religious feelings led him to a state of "oriental simplicity" (*tōyōteki kotan*), to which he gave expression in *Suibokushū* (1923, Collection of Ink Drawings) and in *Suzume no tamago* (1921, Sparrow Eggs). His interest in early classical poetic forms culminated in *Kaihyō to kumo* (1929, Seals and Clouds), in which he experimented with forms from the KOJIKI and other ancient books.

Hakushū remained active even after nearly going blind in 1937, and he published almost 200 books in his lifetime. He also brought out a number of poetry magazines, notably *Chijō junrei* (Earthly Pilgrimage), to which HAGIWARA SAKUTARŌ, MUROO SAISEI, and ŌTE TAKUJI, among others, contributed. In addition, he was poetry editor of the children's magazine *Akai tori* (Red Bird). Many of his poems for children were set to music by YAMADA KŌSAKU, and some remain popular today.

Kitahara Takeo　北原武夫

(1907–73). Novelist and critic. Born in Kanagawa Prefecture. While still a student at Keiō University, he published his first novel. His early novels, such as *Tsuma* (1938, Wife), center on his first wife, who died in a mental hospital. His second wife was nov-

elist UNO CHIYO; from 1936 they published the women's fashion magazine *Sutairu*. Kitahara established himself as a commentator on issues concerning women as well as a critic of contemporary fiction. Many of his later novels depict promiscuous women vainly searching for love in the decadent city.

Kitahara Tasaku　北原多作

(1870–1922). Marine scientist and oceanographer. Born in Gifu Prefecture. Graduate of Tōkyō University. Kitahara implemented numerous projects dealing with marine resources and technology in the belief that the development of the fishing industry should be based on scientific oceanographic investigation. He designed various marine instruments that bear his name and discovered Kitahara's law, which states that the area where two ocean currents come together is where schools of fish gather. His published works include *Gyoson yawa* (1921), a popular book on oceanography.

Kita Ibaraki　北茨城[市]

City in northeastern Ibaraki Prefecture, central Honshū, on the Pacific Ocean. The city was formerly a coal-producing area, occupying the southern part of the JŌBAN COALFIELD. Efforts are being made to introduce new industries. Artists, such as OKAKURA KAKUZŌ and YOKOYAMA TAIKAN, built a hall for contemplation, Rokkakudō, on the IZURA coast, noted for its sea-eroded cliffs. Pop: 51,093.

Kita Ikki　北一輝

(1883–1937). Leader of the movement for national socialism during the Taishō (1912–26) and Shōwa (1926–89) periods. Born in Sado in Niigata Prefecture, his real name was Kita Terujirō. He attended Waseda University in Tōkyō. While in Tōkyō he became friends with KŌTOKU SHŪSUI, SAKAI TOSHIHIKO, and other thinkers of the socialist organization HEIMINSHA.

Before the Chinese Revolution of 1911 Kita joined the United League (Tongmeng Hui or T'ung-meng Hui), a Chinese revolutionary group, and met SONG JIAOREN (Sung Chiao-jen). At the outbreak of the revolution Kita journeyed to China to take part, but returned to Japan, disillusioned, in 1919. That year, he joined ŌKAWA SHŪMEI and others in establishing the YŪZONSHA, an ultranationalist organization. Thereafter he devoted his time to writing and political activities, becoming a leading theorist of the RIGHT WING movement.

Kita's political philosophy is discussed in *Kokutai ron oyobi junsei shakai shugi* (1906, National Polity and Pure Socialism) and *Nihon kaizō hōan taikō* (1923, An Outline Plan for the Reorganization of Japan). Two themes running through his writings were Japan's evolution toward a socialism identical with the national polity (KOKUTAI) and an "Asian nationalism," through which Japan would lead a united and free Asia. Kita's plan depended on a radical revision of Japan and Japanese society. He proposed a military coup that would result in an authoritarian regime based on the promise of a direct relationship between the emperor and the people. The emperor would suspend the constitution, declare martial law, and authorize a National Reorganization Diet that would be free of corruption. The Diet would nationalize Japan's principal industries, confiscate excess wealth, limit private property, and enact a land reform program to benefit im-

poverished farmers. Japan, according to Kita, could then fulfill its destiny as the bearer of liberation to other societies suffering under Western imperialism. Kita's ideas inspired those army officers who advocated a "SHŌWA RESTORATION" and led the unsuccessful 1936 revolt known as the FEBRUARY 26TH INCIDENT. Kita was arrested for complicity in planning the revolt, tried by a military court, and executed in 1937.

Kitakami　北上[市]

City in southern Iwate Prefecture, northern Honshū, on the river KITAKAMIGAWA. Kitakami formerly flourished as a river port and as a post-station town on the highway Ōshū Kaidō. Rice and fruit growing and stock raising are the traditional principal occupations, and industrialization is under way. Pop: 58,782.

Kitakami Basin　北上盆地

(Kitakami Bonchi). In Iwate Prefecture, northern Honshū. Flanked by the Kitakami and Ōu mountains, it consists of piedmont alluvial plains below the fault scarps of the Ōu Mountains, diluvial uplands, and the narrow floodplain of the river Kitakamigawa. The principal crop is rice. The major cities are Morioka and Ichinoseki. Length: approximately 180 km (110 mi).

Kitakami Canal　北上運河

(Kitakami Unga). Canal passing through the city of ISHINOMAKI and the district of Monou in eastern Miyagi Prefecture, northern Honshū; used as an irrigation and drainage channel. Completed in 1882, the canal had its origins during the Edo period (1600–1868) in the plans of the lord of the Sendai domain Date Masamune (1567–1636). Length: 12 km (7.5 mi).

Kitakamigawa　北上川

River in Iwate and Miyagi prefectures, northern Honshū. It originates in the volcano Nanashigureyama in northern Iwate Prefecture and flows south between the Kitakami and Ōu mountains. After winding through the Sendai Plain, it enters the bays of Ishinomaki and Oppa in Miyagi Prefecture. It is the largest river in the Tōhoku region. It was important for the transportation of goods before the Japanese National Railways (now JR) Tōhoku Main Line was opened. Numerous dams have been constructed on the river for flood prevention, electric power, and irrigation. Length: 249 km (155 mi); area of drainage basin: 10,150 sq km (3,919 sq mi).

Kitakami Mountains　北上山地

(Kitakami Sanchi). Plateaulike mountain range extending 250 km (155 mi) from Aomori Prefecture to Miyagi Prefecture, northern Honshū. The highest peak is Hayachinesan (1,917 m; 6,289 ft). The mountains end abruptly at the Pacific Ocean, forming a beautiful backdrop for Rikuchū Coast National Park.

Kitakata　喜多方[市]

City in northwestern Fukushima Prefecture, northern Honshū. Kitakata developed during the Edo period (1600–1868) as the site of a local governmental office of the Aizu domain and as a market town. Industries include traditional *sake* brewing and lacquer ware, as well as aluminum smelting. Farm products include rice and hops. Pop: 37,288.

Kitahara Hakushū Highly regarded for both his *tanka* and modern poetry, Hakushū also composed more than 1,000 poems for children, many of which were set to music by the composer Yamada Kōsaku.

Kita Ikki Advocating a hybrid of national socialism and "Asian nationalism," this early-20th-century right-wing theorist believed Japan had a mission to liberate Asia from Western imperialism.

Kita Morio Trained as a neurologist, Kita became a professional writer in 1960 with the success of *Dokutoru Mambō kōkai ki*, a comic novel based on his experiences as a ship's doctor.

Kitamura Tōkoku Before suicide ended his brief career, this poet and essayist tried to fuse Eastern and Western thought into a harmonious whole that would transcend both.

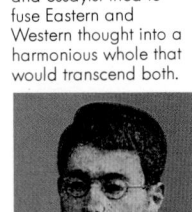

Kita Kyūshū   北九州［市］

City in northern Fukuoka Prefecture, Kyūshū. Located on the Sea of Japan. In 1963 the five cities of Moji, Kokura, Wakamatsu, Yawata, and Tobata merged to become Kita Kyūshū, the center of the KITA KYŪSHŪ INDUSTRIAL ZONE. Until the first half of the Meiji period (1868–1912), the area was composed of fishing and farm villages, except for the castle town of Kokura and the port and post-station town of Kurosaki in Yawata. With the development of the CHIKUHŌ COALFIELD, Moji and Wakamatsu became ports for shipping coal. In 1901 the government-operated YAWATA IRON AND STEEL WORKS (now Nippon Steel Corporation, a private corporation) was founded. Today the steel and iron, chemical, machinery, ceramics, food-processing, and electrical-appliance industries dominate the 30-km (19-mi) coastline. Moji is connected directly with SHIMONOSEKI on Honshū by an undersea tunnel and a bridge. Local attractions include the limestone plateau HIRAODAI and the annual Kokura Gion Daiko festival. Area: 481.3 sq km (185.8 sq mi); pop: 1,026,455.

Kita Kyūshū Industrial Zone
北九州工業地帯

(Kita Kyūshū Kōgyō Chitai). Centered on the city of KITA KYŪSHŪ in northern Kyūshū as well as on the extreme western tip of Yamaguchi Prefecture, Honshū. It is noted for the production of iron and steel, cement, chemicals, fertilizer, glass, ceramics, and metals. It was the site of Japan's first modern iron and steel mills. The zone grew rapidly after 1900 because of both its proximity to the CHIKUHŌ COALFIELD and the availability of resources imported from China. Its importance declined after World War II when these imports temporarily ceased; other factors were the switch from coal to oil as an energy source and a shift in the industrial structure away from heavy industries such as iron, steel, and cement.

Kitami   北見［市］

City in northeastern Hokkaidō. Kitami was settled in 1897 by government-sponsored colonist militia (TONDENHEI). Today it is the political, commercial, and educational center of the Kitami Basin. Principal industries are flour processing, sugar refining, dairy farming, lumber, furniture, and pulp. It is the nation's largest producer of peppermint and menthol. Pop: 107,247.

Kitami Mountains   北見山地

(Kitami Sanchi). Mountain range in north-central Hokkaidō. The highest peak is Teshiodake (1,558 m; 5,111 ft). The mountains, though mined extensively, are covered by dense primeval forests as well as forests utilized by major lumber companies.

Kitamori Kazō   北森嘉蔵

(1916–). Protestant theologian. Born in Kumamoto; studied at the Lutheran Theological School in Tōkyō and Kyōto University. He has been a professor at Tōkyō Union Theological Seminary since 1949. Kitamori was deeply influenced by Martin Luther and the philosopher Tanabe Hajime (1885–1962). The central concept of his theology, the pain of God, combines in a paradoxical way the wrath of God against the sins of humanity and the love of God toward humans who are sinners. Among his many writings are *Kami no itami no shingaku* (1946; tr *Theology of the Pain of God*, 1961) and *Shūkyō kaikaku no shingaku* (1960, Theology of the Reformation).

Kita Morio   北杜夫

(1927–). Novelist and neurologist. Real name Saitō Sōkichi. Born in Tōkyō, he is the second son of SAITŌ MOKICHI, the TANKA poet and psychiatrist. He graduated from Tōhoku University Medical School. In 1960 his *Yoru to kiri no sumide* won the Akutagawa Prize. Also published in 1960 was *Dokutoru Mambō kōkai ki* (tr *Doctor Manbo at Sea*, 1987), based upon his travels and experiences as a ship's physician. The first of his popular "Doctor Mambō" series, it was followed in 1961 by *Dokutoru Mambō konchū ki* and in 1968 by *Dokutoru Mambō seishun ki*. Other major works include NIREKE NO HITOBITO (1964; tr in 2 vols, *The House of Nire*, 1984–85, and *The Fall of the House of Nire*, 1985), a fictionalized account of three generations of his family, which received the Mainichi Book Award. *Kagayakeru aoki sora no shita de* (1979–86) is a novel that deals with Japanese immigrants in South America.

Kitamoto   北本［市］

City in east-central Saitama Prefecture, central Honshū. Since the late 1950s it has rapidly become an industrial and residential center. The area is noted for its chrysanthemums and orchids. Pop: 63,929.

Kitamura Kigin   北村季吟

(1624–1705). Classical scholar and WAKA and HAIKU poet of the early Edo period (1600–

1868). Born in Ōmi Province (now Shiga Prefecture). A student of the haiku masters YASUHARA TEISHITSU and MATSUNAGA TEITOKU, he sought to preserve the authority of the declining Teimon school of *haikai*, for a time instructing the young BASHŌ in the art. He later became the official *waka* instructor of the Tokugawa shogunate (1603–1867). His principal works include *Yama no i* (1648), *Shin zoku inu tsukubashū* (1660), *Genji monogatari kogetsu shō* (1673), and *Makura no sōshi shunsho shō* (1674).

Kitamura Kusuo   北村久寿雄

(1917–). Olympic swimmer. Born in Kōchi Prefecture; graduated from Tōkyō University. At the age of 14 he won the 1,500-meter freestyle at the 1932 Los Angeles Olympic Games with a long-unchallenged record time of 19:12.4. The record-setting achievements of Kitamura and 16-year-old MIYAZAKI YASUJI were widely publicized.

Kitamura Rokurō   喜多村緑郎

(1871–1961). Actor. Born in Tōkyō. He later moved to Ōsaka and founded the drama group Seibidan. He returned to Tōkyō in 1906 and with II YŌHŌ became one of the great actors of the SHIMPA theater. His teaching methods were strict and demanding, but he was also exacting about his own acting. Known for his sensitive portrayal of women, Kitamura had his greatest dramatic success in IZUMI KYŌKA's *Onna keizu* (Genealogy of Women). His only film appearance was in *Noroi no fue* (1958, The Cursed Flute). In 1947 he became a member of the JAPAN ART ACADEMY and in 1955 was designated one of Japan's LIVING NATIONAL TREASURES (*ningen kokuhō*).

Kitamura Sayo   北村サヨ

(1900–1967). Religious leader; founder of the Tenshō Kōtai Jingū Kyō religious movement. Claiming to have heard a divine voice, she later declared herself the only daughter and living shrine of the goddess Tenshō Kōtaijin (i.e., the sun goddess, AMATERASU ŌMIKAMI) and began preaching and faith healing. Her followers regarded her as the goddess incarnate, and their religious organization, the Tenshō Kōtai Jingū Kyō, was established in 1945. Her movement, popularly known as the "dancing religion" (*odoru shūkyō*) for its use of dance to express bliss, has gained a following among overseas Japanese. As of 1989 the movement had over 450,000 followers.

Kitamura Seibō   北村西望

(1884–1987). Sculptor. Born in Nagasaki Prefecture. Graduate of Tōkyō Bijutsu Gakkō (now Tōkyō University of Fine Arts and Music). After winning several prizes in BUNTEN exhibitions, he was made a Teiten (Exhibition of the Imperial Fine Arts Academy) judge in 1919. In 1921 he became a professor at Tōkyō Bijutsu Gakkō. Among his major works is the Statue of Peace in Nagasaki Peace Park. Kitamura's work is characterized by monumental human figures in dramatic poses. He received the Order of Culture in 1958.

Kitamura Tōkoku   北村透谷

(1868–94). Poet, essayist, and leader of the BUNGAKUKAI literary coterie. Real name Kitamura Montarō. In five brief years of activity that ended with his suicide in 1894, Kitamura sowed the seeds of many later developments in Japanese literature and thought.

Kitano Shrine The middle gate of this shrine, which is dedicated to the scholar and court official Sugawara no Michizane. The shrine oratory is visible in the background.

Kitao Shigemasa *Herb Gathering.* 1780s. Colors on silk. 79 × 133 cm. Tōkyō National Museum.

Born in Odawara in Kanagawa Prefecture, he was attracted to the FREEDOM AND PEOPLE'S RIGHTS MOVEMENT at an early age but soon shifted his interest to writing. He attended Tōkyō Semmon Gakkō (later Waseda University) for a time and was married at age 19. The next year he wrote "Soshū no shi," the first Japanese poem of any great length to be written in free verse. Influenced by his wife's Christianity, which he also adopted, and by Byron, Carlyle, and Emerson, he wrote essays exalting what he saw as "the life-espousing view" of the West over the nihilistic "life-denying view" of Japan's Buddhist and Shintō tradition. Later essays reveal that the latter had a strong hold over him, although his search for a view of life that would rescue the individual self from ultimate annihilation continued. His attempt to explore the nature and potentialities of the individual self, set forth in "Naibu seimei ron" (The Inner Life), has been called the starting point of modern Japanese literature, and the influence of his romantic notions on later writers, particularly SHIMAZAKI TŌSON, is incontestable.

Kitano Shrine   北野天満宮

(Kitano Temmangū). A Shintō shrine, also known as Kitano Jinja and Kitano Tenjin, in Kamigyō Ward, Kyōto; dedicated to the spirits of the scholar and court official SUGAWARA NO MICHIZANE (845–903), his wife, and his son. Shortly after Michizane's death in Dazaifu, Kyūshū, a series of disasters struck the capital, Kyōto. It was soon believed that these misfortunes were the work of Michizane's vengeful spirit (*onryō;* see GORYŌ) chafing at the injustices that he had suffered at the end of his career. To placate his spirit, the court conferred upon him the name Karai Tenjin (God of Thunder). The Kitano Shrine was built on the 44th anniversary of his death. The present main shrine building was rebuilt in 1607 and is the oldest remaining example of the *gongen* style (see SHINTŌ ARCHITECTURE). In addition to the annual festival on 4 August, special ceremonies are held during the year. One treasure owned by the shrine is the famous *Kitano Tenjin engi,* a scroll (EMAKIMONO) depicting the life of Michizane and the building of the shrine. See also TEMMANGŪ.

Kitanoumi   北の湖

(1953–). SUMŌ wrestler; the 55th grand *sumō* champion (*yokozuna*). Real name Obata Toshimitsu. Born in Hokkaidō. He

entered the Mihogaseki stable in 1966, achieving top-division (*makuuchi*) status in 1972 and champion (*ōzeki*) status in 1974. The same year, at age 21, he became the youngest wrestler to date to achieve *yokozuna* status. He wrestled in 50 consecutive *sumō* tournaments, in which he had more wins than losses (*kachikoshi*). Kitanoumi retired in 1985, having won a total of 24 tournaments, and established his own *sumō* stable.

Kitan Strait → Tomogashima Channel

Kitaōji Rosanjin   北大路魯山人

(1883–1959). Artist-potter. Real name Kitaōji Fusajirō. Born in Kyōto. Rosanjin began his art career as a calligrapher. From 1915 to 1917 he studied porcelain production at a Kutani kiln in Kanazawa (see KUTANI WARE). He subsequently moved to Kita Kamakura and built his own kiln there. Rosanjin began to design and produce ceramics partly through his passion for fine Japanese food and his conviction that the ceramics of his day were inadequate for serving it. He imitated an astonishing assortment of earlier Japanese wares, creating his own individual, contemporary versions. Most of his output before World War II consisted of porcelain inspired by Imari blue-and-white (see ARITA WARE) as well as Kutani overglaze enamel wares. After the war he concentrated on stoneware in the manner of various old Japanese wares, such as BIZEN WARE and MINO WARE.

Kitao Shigemasa   北尾重政

(1739–1820). UKIYO-E illustrator and print designer, calligrapher, and poet. Born in Edo (now Tōkyō), the eldest son of a bookseller, Suharaya Saburobei, he left the family business to a younger brother in order to be an artist. Apparently self-taught, he took the family name Kitao and the working name Shigemasa. His first signed work, an illustrated book, was published in 1760, and was followed by several actor portraits, most of which were printed in three colors. In 1765 he designed a full-color calendar print that he signed Karan, a name he had received from his teacher of *haikai* verse, Tani Sogai. In the early 1770s he collaborated with UTAGAWA TOYOHARU and KATSUKAWA SHUNSHŌ. *Seirō bijin awase sugata kagami* (1776, Mirror Images of the Green House Beauty Contest), which he published in three volumes, is a masterpiece of the Japanese illustrated book.

His pupils included Kitao Masanobu (better known as SANTO KYŌDEN) and KUBO SHUMMAN.

Kitarō   喜多郎

(1953–). Composer and performer of electronic music. Real name Takahashi Masanori. Born in Aichi Prefecture. After graduating from high school he formed a rock group, the Far East Family Band. After it broke up in 1976, he began his solo career, releasing the album *Tenkai* (Astral Voyage) in 1978. Kitarō makes his home in the mountain village of Yasaka in Nagano Prefecture; his innovative synthesizer contributions are inspired by nature and the cosmos. He wrote the score for the popular NHK (Japan Broadcasting Corporation) television documentary series *Silk Road* (1980) and has produced a succession of recordings that have gained him an international reputation in the field of so-called New Age music, including *Tenkū* (1986, The Firmament) and *Kojiki* (1990, Record of Ancient Matters).

Kita Roppeita   喜多六平太

(1874–1971). Head of the KITA SCHOOL of NŌ theater and *shite* (player of leading Nō roles). Born in Tōkyō. His mother was the daughter of Nō actor Kita Roppeita Nōsei XII, and he was made heir to the leadership of the Kita family as a young child. His stately, original, and soulful style earned Roppeita a reputation as a master of his art and enabled him to revive the fortunes of the Kita school of Nō. He became a leading figure in the Nō world and an influential mentor to the younger generation of Nō actors. He received the Order of Culture in 1953. In 1955 he was designated a Living National Treasure.

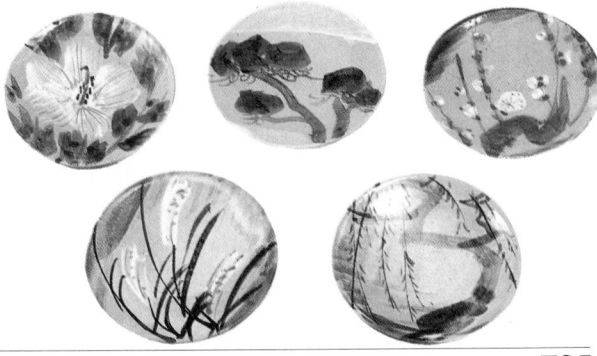

Kitaōji Rosanjin These plates, produced by Rosanjin in the late 1930s, are styled after the work of the famed potter Kenzan (1663–1743). Private collection.

Kita Sadakichi 喜田貞吉

(1871–1939). Historian. Born in Tokushima Prefecture; graduate of Tōkyō University. In 1899 he founded the Nihon Rekishi Chiri Kenkyūkai (Japan Historical Geography Society) and began to publish the journal *Rekishi chiri*. As an official of the Ministry of Education, he edited standardized history textbooks for the national elementary school system, but resigned in 1911 under attack by rightists. He founded the journal *Minzoku to rekishi* (Race and History) and was one of the first to study Japan's BURAKU-MIN minority group.

Kitasato Shibasaburō 北里柴三郎

Kitasato Shibasaburō
In the late 19th century this German-trained bacteriologist isolated the toxin used in tetanus inoculations and identified the bubonic plague bacillus.

(1853–1931). Bacteriologist. Born in what is now Kumamoto Prefecture. Graduate of the medical school Kumamoto Igakkō and Tōkyō University. From 1885 to 1891 Kitasato studied bacteriology under Robert Koch in Germany. In 1889 he obtained a pure culture of *Clostridium tetani*, the bacterium that causes tetanus, and in the following year he cooperated with Emil Behring in developing a serum therapy for tetanus, employing tetanus toxin that Kitasato had isolated. Returning to Japan in 1892, he established the Institute for Infectious Diseases with the assistance of FUKUZAWA YUKICHI. Kitasato went to Hong Kong during an outbreak of the bubonic plague in 1894 and identified *Pasteurella pestis* independently of Alexandre Yersin, to whom credit is generally given in the West for discovery of the bacterium in the same year and place. In 1915 Kitasato and his colleagues established the Kitasato Institute. He was the first dean of the Faculty of Medicine of Keiō University, served in the House of Peers, and was the first president of the Japan Medical Association.

Kita school 喜多流

(Kitaryū). One of the five major *shite kata* (principal player) schools (or troupes) of professional NŌ theater actors. Founded by Kita Nagayoshi (professionally known as Kita Shichidayū; 1586–1623). Although not born into a family of Nō actors, Shichidayū studied the Nō of the KONGŌ SCHOOL from his childhood and became a skilled actor. Early in his career he was patronized by the hegemon TOYOTOMI HIDEYOSHI and served for a time as troupe head (*tayū*) of the Kongō school. His techniques derived mainly from the Kongō school, but he adapted the strong points of the various schools in perfecting an independent acting style. The Kita school declined in the Meiji period (1868–1912), but it was revived by KITA ROPPEITA, the 14th hereditary troupe head, and performances continue to be given.

Kitaura 北浦

Lake in southeastern Ibaraki Prefecture, central Honshū. Situated east of Lake Kasumigaura. The water is used for industrial purposes by the Kashima Coastal Industrial Region. Freshwater smelt, crucian carp, and carp are found in the lake. Area: 36 sq km (13.9 sq mi); circumference: 68 km (42 mi); depth: 7 m (23 ft).

Kitaura Kiichirō 北裏喜一郎

(1911–85). Businessman and chairman of NOMURA SECURITIES CO, LTD (1978–81). Born in Wakayama Prefecture. Kitaura graduated from Kōbe University of Commerce (now Kōbe University) in 1933 and joined Nomura Securities Co. In 1968 he became the company's fifth president. During his tenure as president, Kitaura completed an extensive on-line system to automate the company's business transactions, established NOMURA RESEARCH INSTITUTE, LTD, and promoted the company's internationalization by creating overseas offices. Kitaura also served as trustee of the JAPAN ASSOCIATION OF CORPORATE EXECUTIVES (Keizai Dōyūkai; 1953–85).

Kita Ward 北区

(Kita Ku). One of the 23 wards of Tōkyō. South of the river Arakawa. Many metal, textile, printing, machinery, and chemical plants, as well as housing complexes, are located here. Pop: 354,647.

Kitayama culture 北山文化

(Kitayama *bunka*). The culture of the early Muromachi period (1333–1568), particularly from 1369 to 1408, when the third Muromachi shōgun, ASHIKAGA YOSHIMITSU, ruled, first as shōgun and, after 1395, as retired shōgun. It is named for the location of Yoshimitsu's villa at Kitayama in northern Kyōto. Encompassing recent cultural influence from China and the native cultures of both the court nobility and the newly risen warrior class, Kitayama culture found expression in a remarkably wide range of artistic accomplishments. Chief among them were the cultivated Zen literature of the Five Mountains (GOZAN LITERATURE); monochrome INK PAINTING, strongly influenced by Chinese painting of the Song (Sung; 960–1279) and Yuan (Yüan; 1279–1368) periods and exemplified by JOSETSU and MINCHŌ; the perfection of NŌ drama by KAN'AMI and his son ZEAMI; linked verse (RENGA); and an eclectic architecture incorporating both the Japanese court style and the Chinese Tang (T'ang) dynasty (618–907) style, the former epitomized by Yoshimitsu's official residence, the Hana no Gosho (Palace of Flowers), and the latter by the Golden Pavilion (KINKAKUJI). All of the arts flourished in this period, fostered by the social stability of the times and by Yoshimitsu's generous patronage. Kitayama culture is often compared with the HIGASHIYAMA CULTURE of the reign (1449–74) of the eighth Muromachi shōgun, ASHIKAGA YOSHIMASA.

Kitazono Katsue 北園克衛

(1902–78). Poet. Real name Hashimoto Kenkichi. Born in Mie Prefecture. Graduate of Chūō University. In the late 1920s he associated with several avant-garde poetry coteries and wrote experimental surrealistic verses. He founded the poetry magazine *VOU* in 1935. His poetry collections include *Shiro no arubamu* (1929, White Album) and *Kuroi hi* (1951, Black Fire). He is also known for his translations of Paul Eluard and Stéphane Mallarmé.

kite, black 鳶

(*tobi*). *Milvus migrans*. A large hawk of the family Accipitridae. Its total length is around 64 centimeters (25 in). It has a notched tail and blackish brown feathers except for white spots at the base of the primary wing feathers that are visible when in flight. The black kite is distributed throughout Eurasia, Africa, and Australia. It is a resident bird in all parts of Japan northward from Kyūshū and is especially common along the seashore. Since the kite eats kitchen waste and the remains of small animals and fish, it has long been valued as a scavenger in Japan. It makes its nest by piling dead branches at the top of a large tree.

The NIHON SHOKI (720) says that when Japan's legendary first emperor, Jimmu Tennō, was fighting to conquer the Yamato region, a glittering golden kite alighted on his bow and flashed like lightning so that his enemies were defeated. The Order of the Golden Kite (KINSHI KUNSHŌ), awarded for exceptional military service between 1890 and 1945, took its name from this legend. Kites often appear in proverbs and folk sayings.

kites 凧

(*tako*). Japan's kites are among the most spectacular in the world, treasured as much for their aesthetic worth as for the pleasure they give as toys. The traditional kite consists of a light bamboo or wood frame over which is affixed paper painted with various bold motifs. Japanese kites are made in many shapes and sizes, from miniature kites of only a few square inches to immense ones of over a thousand square feet. Many of them require considerable skill in handling if they are to be airborne successfully.

Kites in Premodern Japan——Kites may be indigenous to Japan or may have been imported, most likely from China. The earliest mention of kites in Japan is in the WAMYŌ RUIJU SHŌ, a 10th-century dictionary of Chinese characters. It provides Japanized pronunciations of the Chinese words written by two sets of characters, both denoting a contrivance "made of paper in the shape of a hawk, which rides the wind and flies well": *shiroshi* ("paper venerable hawk") and *shien* ("paper kite," i.e., paper hawk).

The words *ikanobori* and its shortened version *ika*—neither of which is used today—are considered the oldest Japanese terms for "kite." In the illustrated encyclopedia WAKAN SANSAI ZUE of 1712, *ikanobori* and *ika* are cited as the standard Japanese readings for the characters "paper hawk." The current Japanese word *tako* derives from Kantō-region speech of the Edo period (1600–1868). Both words make punning reference to a common premodern kite shape: *ika* is a homophone for the word meaning "squid," and *tako* for the word meaning "octopus." The Chinese character now used to write "kite" (*tako*) in Japan is composed of two Japanese elements meaning "wind" and "scrap of cloth."

The relationship binding kites to the myriad KAMI (gods, deities, spirits) of Japan's indigenous SHINTŌ religion is apparently an old one. Kites have been interpreted as prayers in concrete form linking heaven and earth and as offerings to the gods. Kites and kite-flying events still sometimes maintain a religious association. Kites also have a military history. Stories abound in which kites serve as signals, message carriers, and even primitive airborne transport for daredevil warriors.

In the Edo period kites became a popular form of amusement largely detached from traditional associations. If the illustrations in contemporary woodblock prints are any indication, there were times when the skies of Edo (now Tōkyō) were literally filled with kites. Kite battles (*tako-gassen*) in particular attracted enthusiastic crowds and, periodically, the wrath of public officials.

The brilliantly painted kite known today developed by the end of the 17th century. Families of the warrior class began to have their children's kites illustrated with dragons or Chinese lions in imitation of the TOSA SCHOOL and KANŌ SCHOOL paintings on the

kites

Japanese kites are not merely children's toys. Kites from many regions served various historical purposes that continue today through festivals and contests. The kites themselves preserve traditional decorative motifs.

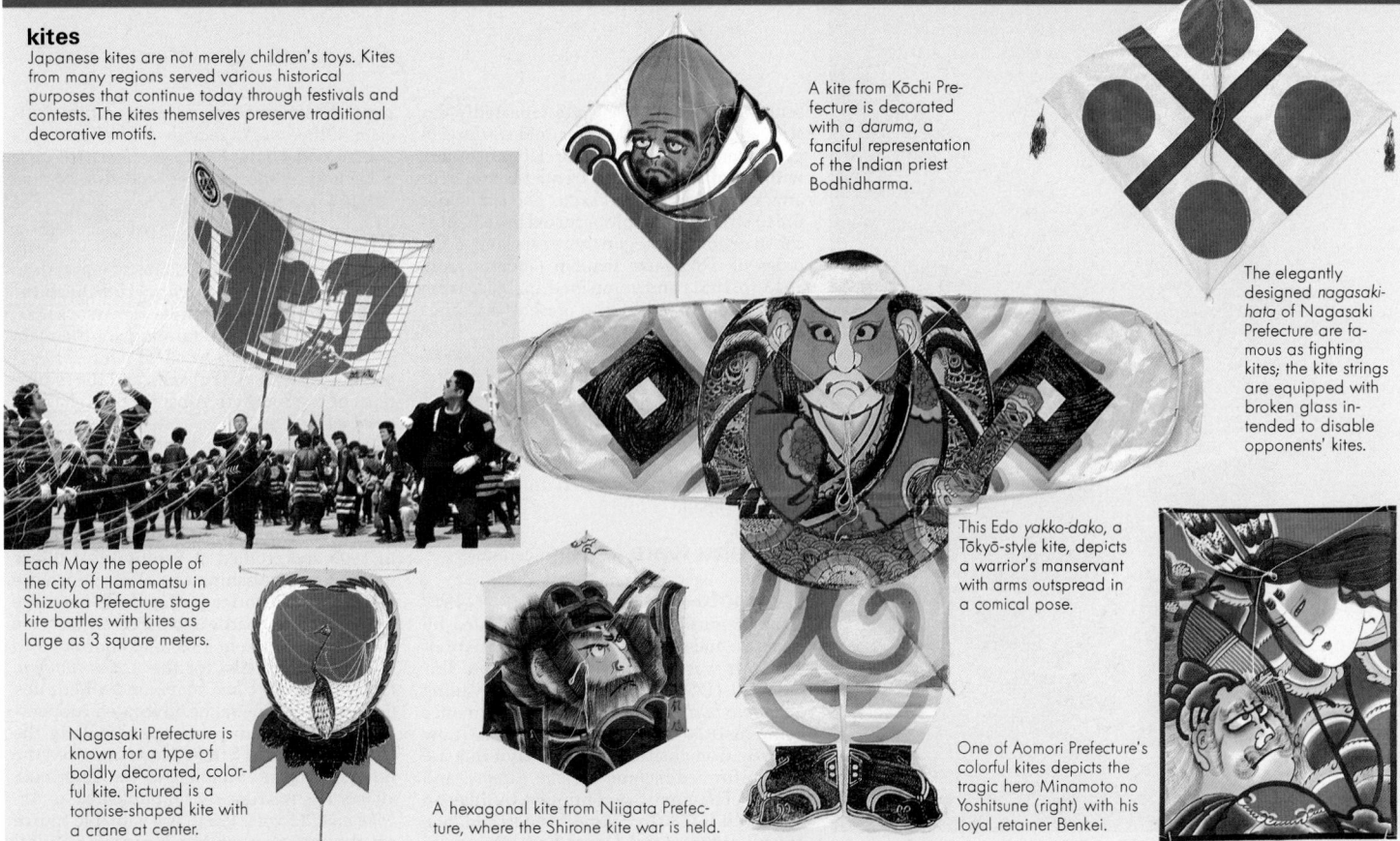

A kite from Kōchi Prefecture is decorated with a *daruma*, a fanciful representation of the Indian priest Bodhidharma.

The elegantly designed *nagasaki-hata* of Nagasaki Prefecture are famous as fighting kites; the kite strings are equipped with broken glass intended to disable opponents' kites.

Each May the people of the city of Hamamatsu in Shizuoka Prefecture stage kite battles with kites as large as 3 square meters.

This Edo *yakko-dako*, a Tōkyō-style kite, depicts a warrior's manservant with arms outspread in a comical pose.

Nagasaki Prefecture is known for a type of boldly decorated, colorful kite. Pictured is a tortoise-shaped kite with a crane at center.

A hexagonal kite from Niigata Prefecture, where the Shirone kite war is held.

One of Aomori Prefecture's colorful kites depicts the tragic hero Minamoto no Yoshitsune (right) with his loyal retainer Benkei.

---

fusuma (sliding doors) and hanging scrolls of their homes. The warrior figures prevalent on late Edo kites are believed to have developed as a CHŌNIN (merchant class) phenomenon. Wealthy merchants enjoyed the military romances in vogue at the time and apparently transferred this enthusiasm to kites.

By the close of the Edo period, kites from Edo had made their way into the provinces as souvenirs. Most popular were the *nishikie-dako*, which featured UKIYO-E woodblock-print subjects and were fancied by warrior households, and the ironic *yakko-dako* favored by merchant families, which depicted a warrior's manservant (*yakko*) with his arms outspread in a silly pose.

Kites in Modern Japan—The modern Japanese kite has its roots firmly planted in the Edo period, when its standard shapes and motifs were established. Aside from abstract geometric motifs, four subjects are common as kite decoration. Most prominent is the warrior hero of legend or drama, such as the tragic hero MINAMOTO NO YOSHITSUNE. Folk images also find their way onto kites; the DARUMA doll is a popular figure, as are the comic masks OKAME AND HYOTTOKO. Various Chinese written characters and Japanese *kana* syllables form another category of designs. For many kite fanciers, birds and insects (especially the cicada) present the most entertaining subjects, as they dictate the form of the kite itself. Many kites utilize a shape or motif unique to the town or district in which they were made.

Today kites are fashioned in a variety of two- and three-dimensional shapes; many are equipped with brightly colored tails. Intricate box kites, linked kites, and tube kites are among the most popular. Kites painted with figural motifs generally remain square, oblong, or hexagonal in shape but are constructed so as to flap and flutter, giving them a three-dimensional quality. Kites are built to ride and buck with the wind, sometimes spinning in circles or shooting from side to

side. Undulating *mukade-dako* ("centipede" kites), formed of jointed sections, are the most complex of the kites based on bird or insect form. Kites are also built to create noise by flapping and snapping; they are frequently fitted with hummers or whistles. Kite battles still attract an enthusiastic following.

The launching of enormous kites (*ōdako*) rivals kite wars as a popular spectacle. The district of Hōshubana in Saitama Prefecture is renowned for the immense kites it sends aloft annually on 3 and 5 May. The coordinated teamwork of 50 men is required before the kite, approximately 15 by 11 meters (49 by 36 ft) and weighing about 800 kilograms (1,760 lb), lifts skyward in ponderous majesty. In March 1980 the city of Shirone, Niigata Prefecture, broke the Guinness world record by launching a kite measuring 19.07 by 14.10 meters (62.6 by 46.3 ft).

Because kites are appreciated as works of art, they are collected by some as a form of folk craft, though many such kites are also flown.

Kitsuki   杵築[市]

City in northeastern Ōita Prefecture, Kyūshū, on north BEPPU BAY. Kitsuki is known for its *shichitōi*, a reed used for *tatami* mats. Mandarin oranges are also grown. Since the 1980s it has been luring high-technology industries and moving towards industrialization. Pop: 21,936.

kitsunebi   狐火

("fox fires"). Japanese legendary belief that the strange rosy pink fires sighted at such places as hills, fields, and graveyards are lit by foxes. These fires, which are often seen in chains rather than singularly, moving forward as they appear to be lit and then extinguished, are also referred to as *kitsune no chōchin gyōretsu* (processions of fox lanterns) and *kitsune no yomeiri* (foxes' wedding processions).

Kiuchi Sekitei   木内石亭

(1724?–1808). Mineralogist and collector of fossils, stone-age tools, and other archaeological artifacts. A native of Ōmi Province (now Shiga Prefecture), from an early age he was fond of collecting unusual rocks. From about 1750 Kiuchi traveled throughout Japan, collecting and classifying stones and artifacts. He published his findings in *Unkon-shi* (15 vols, 1773–1801; Treatise on Rocks) and left several other works in manuscript.

Kiuchi Shinzō   木内信蔵

(1910–   ). Scholar of human geography and urban studies specialist. Born in Tōkyō, Kiuchi graduated in 1935 from Tōkyō University, where he later became professor of geography. He served as president of the ASSOCIATION OF JAPANESE GEOGRAPHERS and as vice-president of the TŌKYŌ GEOGRAPHICAL SOCIETY and the International Geographical Union. Among his published works are *Toshi no chirigakuteki kenkyū* (1949, Geographical Studies of Cities) *Toshi chirigaku kenkyū* (1951, Study of Urban Geography), *Chiiki gairon* (1968, Introduction to Regional Studies), and *Toshi chirigaku genri* (1979, Principles of Urban Geography). He was the recipient of the Carl Ritter silver medal from the Geographische Gesellschaft zu Berlin in 1959 and the George Davidson Prize from the American Geographical Society.

Kiwanis Club   キワニス・クラブ

(Kiwanisu Kurabu). The first Japanese chapter of the Kiwanis Club was established in 1964 in Tōkyō. In 1968 the Japan Kiwanis Committee was organized, and charter clubs were also formed in Nagoya, Ōsaka, Kyōto, Hiroshima, Kōbe, Sendai, Sapporo, Yokohama, Chiba, Takamatsu, and Fukuoka. Kiwanis clubs organize lectures and promote local craftsmanship and various charities. Membership in 1991 was 1,433.

Kiyomizudera This temple's main hall, constructed in 1633, is famous for its wide veranda built out over a cliff overlooking Kyōto. The hall has been designated as a National Treasure.

Kiyosato This primarily agricultural district has also become a popular summertime resort. Pictured is Seisenryō, a hotel with a fine view of the peak Yatsugatake.

Kiyokawa Masaji 清川正二

(1913–). Olympic swimmer, businessman. Born in Aichi Prefecture; graduated from Tōkyō Shōka Daigaku (now Hitotsubashi University). In the 1932 Los Angeles Olympic Games he took the gold medal in the 100-meter backstroke. The silver and bronze medalists were also Japanese, marking the first time Japan took all the medals in one Olympic event. At the 1936 Berlin Olympics Kiyokawa took third place in the backstroke. In 1969 he became a member of the International Olympic Committee, serving as vice chairman from 1979 to 1983.

Kiyomizudera 清水寺

Temple of the HOSSŌ SECT of Buddhism; located on a high hill in Higashiyama Ward, Kyōto. Kiyomizudera, also known as Seisuiji, was founded about 798 by the monk Enchin with support from General SAKANOUE NO TAMURAMARO. According to one account, in 798 the two men erected a temple, which they named Kiyomizudera (Temple of Clear Water), to house an image of the Eleven-Faced Kannon (Jūichimen Kannon; see KANNON).

In 810 Kiyomizudera was designated a temple at which prayers were to be offered for the protection of the empire. Over the centuries the buildings were repeatedly destroyed by fires, earthquakes, and warfare. In particular, the affiliation of Kiyomizudera with KŌFUKUJI made it a frequent target for attack by the rival ENRYAKUJI. The last major fire to strike the temple occurred in 1629. Reconstruction was begun two years later at the order of Tokugawa Iemitsu (shōgun from 1623 to 1651) and completed in 1633, from which time many of the present buildings date.

Kiyomizudera now consists of seven halls, a three-story pagoda, and several minor structures. The main hall, one end of which is built out over a cliff, has a spacious veranda that affords a panoramic view of Kyōto. Kiyomizudera is the 16th of the 33 places of pilgrimage sacred to Kannon in western Japan.

Kiyomizu ware → Kyōto ceramics

kiyomoto-bushi 清元節

Type of music for KABUKI, accompanied by SHAMISEN and other instruments; a variety of JŌRURI. It was developed by Kiyomoto Enjudayū I (1777–1825) out of the prevailing tomimoto-bushi style, the first performance being in 1814, at the Ichimuraza, Edo (now Tōkyō). Compositions by Enjudayū that are still performed include Yasuna, Kasane, and Toba-e. The line was continued by his son Enjudayū II (1801–55) and his descendants, as well as by several branch lines. Enjudayū I and II also performed in compositions written for them by Kawaguchi Onao (d 1845), formerly a geisha in the Yoshiwara pleasure quarters. Her works include Ume no haru (1827) and the well-known Hokushū (1818), the text of which was written by ŌTA NAMPO (1749–1823). Other early kiyomoto were written for plays by Tsuruya Namboku IV (1755–1829; see TSURUYA NAMBOKU). Of some 300 kiyomoto pieces, 40 have been maintained in the kabuki repertoire, including Kanda matsuri, Bun'ya, Seigaiha, Unohana, Sumidagawa, and Yoshiwara suzume. Kiyomoto has a more narrative character than NAGAUTA or TOKIWAZU-BUSHI, also music of the kabuki theater. The general effect of the music is light and cheerful. The vocal tessitura is high, and the singer uses a declamatory, nasal style of delivery.

Kiyonaga → Torii Kiyonaga

Kiyono Kenji 清野謙次

(1885–1955). Pathologist and anthropologist. Born in Okayama Prefecture. The son of a medical doctor, Kiyono graduated from Kyōto University in 1909. He studied in Germany from 1912 to 1914 under the German pathologist Ludwig Aschoff at the University of Freiburg. His specialty was the study of vital staining, and he is said to have established this discipline in Japan. He was a professor at Kyōto University from 1921 to 1938. Kiyono excavated a large number of ancient SHELL MOUNDS throughout Japan, concluding that the Stone Age people of Japan were partly of Korean origin and the direct ancestors of the present Japanese people.

Kiyooka Takayuki 清岡卓行

(1922–). Poet and novelist. Born in China; graduate of Tōkyō University. He taught French at Hōsei University and became one of the few surrealist poets in Japan. Kōtta honoo (1959) is a collection of his poems. His novel Akashiya no Dairen won the Akutagawa Prize for 1969. He has also produced news documentaries and written film criticism. Other works include Nichijō (1962), a poetry collection; Furūto to ōboe (1970), a collection of short stories; and Rito no kuni de (1986), a novel.

Kiyosato 清里

District in the town of Takane, northwestern Yamanashi Prefecture, central Honshū. Situated in the eastern foothills of YATSUGATAKE. Agriculture and dairy farming are the main activities. With an excellent view of Yatsugatake, Mt. Fuji (Fujisan), and the mountains of the Southern Alps, Kiyosato has developed as a resort.

Kiyosawa Kiyoshi 清沢洌

(1890–1945). Journalist and specialist on foreign affairs. Born in Nagano Prefecture. Kiyosawa traveled to the United States in 1906 and studied at Whitworth College in Spokane, Washington, after which he worked as a reporter for Japanese-language newspapers in Seattle and San Francisco. He returned to Japan in 1920 and continued to work as a journalist for the Asahi shimbun, Hōchi shimbun, Chūō kōron, and other publications. As a liberal he advocated cooperation with Western powers, particularly the United States and Britain, and supported the internationalist diplomacy of SHIDEHARA KIJŪRŌ. His wartime diary, published as Ankoku nikki (3 vols, 1954), is a valuable source on the activities of the Japanese political elite; Nihon gaikō shi (1942), a history of Japanese diplomacy, is also highly regarded.

Kiyose 清瀬[市]

City in northern Tōkyō Prefecture. Formerly a farming village, Kiyose's population has increased rapidly since the 1950s. It is the site of many housing projects and hospitals. Pop: 67,539.

Kiyosumiyama 清澄山

Hill in the town of Amatsu Kominato, southern Bōsō Peninsula, Chiba Prefecture, central Honshū. It is the site of a Nichiren sect temple, Seichōji (also known as Kiyosumidera). The temple is surrounded by a dense forest that has been used as an experimental station by the agriculture department of Tōkyō University. Height: 377 m (1,237 ft).

Kiyotsune 清経

NŌ play by ZEAMI. It is classified as a nibammemono ("part-two play"). In the final stage of the TAIRA-MINAMOTO WAR, the warrior-courtier Taira no Kiyotsune (the shite or main character) has abandoned all hope of victory. On a moonlit night he takes a boat out to sea, plays a lonely melody on his favorite flute, chants a Buddhist prayer, and throws himself into the water. Later Kiyotsune's armor-clad ghost appears at the bedside of his wife (the tsure or "companion" character), describes scenes of war and carnage, and explains the motive for his suicide.

Kiyoura Keigo 清浦奎吾

(1850–1942). Politician; prime minister (1924). Born in what is now Kumamoto Prefecture; attended the Kangien, a school founded by HIROSE TANSŌ. Kiyoura joined the justice ministry in 1876 and helped draft the PEACE PRESERVATION LAW OF 1887. Allied with YAMAGATA ARITOMO, he held numerous cabinet posts. By 1922 he was president of the Privy Council. In January 1924 Kiyoura formed a cabinet, but he was attacked by

kitchen knives

Knives are very important in Japanese cookery, in which appearance is much emphasized. The Japanese word for chef is *itamae*—literally, "in front of the cutting board."

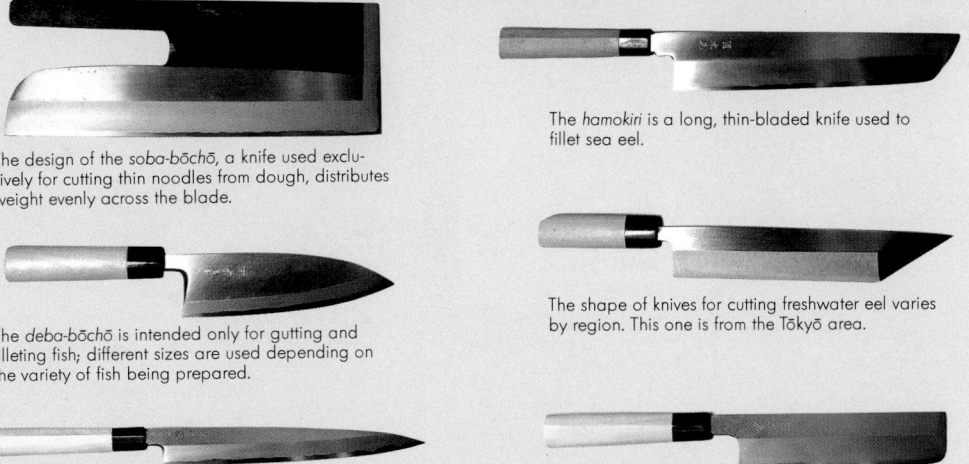

The design of the *soba-bōchō*, a knife used exclusively for cutting thin noodles from dough, distributes weight evenly across the blade.

Using a variety of knives, a chef creates garnishes for a meal.

The *deba-bōchō* is intended only for gutting and filleting fish; different sizes are used depending on the variety of fish being prepared.

This *sashimi* knife is known as a "willow blade" for its resemblance to a willow leaf.

The *nakiri-bōchō* is a strong and easily sharpened knife designed for chopping vegetables.

The *hamokiri* is a long, thin-bladed knife used to fillet sea eel.

The shape of knives for cutting freshwater eel varies by region. This one is from the Tōkyō area.

The thin blade of the *usuba-bōchō* is ideal for paring vegetables.

Knives for slicing *sashimi* (raw fish) come in various shapes but are usually long and narrow.

---

several political parties (see MOVEMENT TO PROTECT CONSTITUTIONAL GOVERNMENT) and soon forced to resign.

Kiyozawa Manshi   清沢満之

(1863–1903). Buddhist priest and philosopher. Born in Nagoya; eldest son of Tokunaga Naganori, a low-ranking *samurai.* In 1878 Kiyozawa entered the priesthood. He later attended Tōkyō University, where he studied Western philosophy with Ernest F. FENOLLOSA and Ludwig Busse (1862–1907). Kiyozawa taught at various schools before moving to Kyōto in 1888 to serve as head of a middle school his sect supported. At about the same time he married, taking his wife's family name, Kiyozawa. In 1890 he resigned his position.

Kiyozawa initiated reforms aimed at spiritually reinvigorating and democratizing the JŌDO SHIN SECT OF PURE LAND BUDDHISM but met with stiff opposition from conservative elements. This led him to retreat to a temple in Aichi Prefecture to study the early teachings of the Buddha Gautama collected in the Āgamas, SHINRAN'S KYŌGYŌSHINSHŌ and TANNISHŌ, and Epictetus's *Discourses.* From Epictetus Kiyozawa learned Stoicism, which helped to sustain him during his nine-year bout with tuberculosis, which caused his death at age 40. Kiyozawa was convinced of the need for moral fiber, a quality he found lacking in Jōdo Shin teachings, which emphasized reliance on the saving grace of the "other power" (TARIKI), that is, the Buddha AMIDA (Skt: Amitābha).

In 1901 Kiyozawa became dean of Shinshū University in Tōkyō (now Ōtani University, relocated in Kyōto). He founded the *seishin shugi* (spiritualism) movement in Tōkyō. His major works include *Shūkyō tetsugaku gaikotsu* (1892, A Skeletal Outline of the Philosophy of Religion).

Kiyū shōran   嬉遊笑覧

(Diversions for One's Amusement). A compendium of miscellaneous information written by scholar and bibliographer Kitamura Nobuyo (also called Kitamura Tokinobu; 1784–1856); published in 1830 in 12 volumes with an appendix. The work consists mainly of excerpts from works read by the author with his own commentaries and covers numerous topics, including clothing, deportment, music, festivals, language, and trade. It

is a rich source of information on the manners and customs of urban commoners during the Edo period (1600–1868).

Kizokuin → House of Peers

Kizugawa   木津川

River in southern Kyōto Prefecture, central Honshū, joining the Yodogawa at the southern part of the Kyōto Basin. Known as Izumigawa in antiquity, it has long been remembered in poems and songs. Length: 51 km (32 mi).

knives, kitchen   包丁

(*hōchō*). Great emphasis is placed in Japanese cuisine on the appearance of a meal when served, and this is reflected in the manner in which foods are cut or sliced. There are dozens of types of kitchen knives, each of which is designed to fulfill a specific function, and their choice, use, and sharpening are given careful consideration by professionals.

The *deba-bōchō*, which has a broad, heavy, pointed blade, is used to gut and fillet fish. The *sashimi-bōchō* has a long, narrow blade, also pointed, measuring 20 to 25 centimeters (8 to 10 in), and is used to slice *sashimi* (raw fish). Similar in shape to the willow (*yanagi*) leaf, it is alternately referred to as *yanagiba* or "willow blade." There is a special knife for filleting sea eel (*hamo*) and another for Japanese common eel (*unagi*). These knives are of the type called *katahabōchō*; that is, they are made by laminating a thin layer of very hard steel to a thicker layer of softer steel from which side alone they are sharpened, thus remaining flat on the reverse.

The *usuba-bōchō*, which also is a *katahabōchō*, is used for paring vegetables, such as the Japanese radish (*daikon*), and has a rectangular blade. The *nakiri-bōchō* is sharpened from both sides and has a rectangular blade with a slightly convex edge; it is used for slicing and chopping vegetables. The function of the *soba-bōchō* is to cut noodles from sheets of dough, and that of the *saikubōchō* to cut foods into various shapes pleasing to the eye.

In most Japanese households multipurpose stainless-steel knives are customarily used. There are also knives designed specifically for cutting meat, paring vegetables, or

slicing bread. Recently knives with ceramic blades have come into use.

Knott, Cargill Gilston   ノット, C. G.

(1856–1922). British physicist. One of the FOREIGN EMPLOYEES OF THE MEIJI PERIOD (1868–1912). Born in Scotland. Graduate of the University of Edinburgh. Knott arrived in Japan in 1883 and taught mechanics, acoustics, and electromagnetism at Tōkyō University. He also performed geomagnetic measurements throughout Japan with the geophysicist TANAKADATE AIKITSU. Knott's research included the study of earthquakes and volcanoes.

know-how   ノウ・ハウ

(*nō-hau*). The English colloquial expression "know-how," in the sense of technical knowledge or information kept as trade secrets, has come into daily use in the Japanese business world, especially in technology transfer and licensing arrangements between Japanese and foreign companies. This term is officially used by the Japanese government. For example, the term is used throughout the Fair Trade Commission's Guidelines on Unfair Trade Practices with Respect to Patent and Know-How Licensing Agreements published in February 1989, which superseded the commission's Antimonopoly Act Guidelines for International Licensing Agreements of 1968. Know-how is protected as trade secrets against misappropriation or unauthorized disclosure under a set of provisions newly established in the Unfair Competition Prevention Law (Fusei Kyōsō Bōshi Hō, 1934) by 1990 amendment (art. 1[3] and [4], art. 1-2[3] and [4]). Under these provisions, the proprietors of trade secrets are entitled to civil remedies of injunction and damages against persons who misappropriated the trade secrets.

ko   戸

(household). Smallest administrative unit of the KOKUGUN SYSTEM of land division that was inaugurated by the RITSURYŌ SYSTEM of government in the mid-7th century. The *ko* (also known as *gōko*) was a subunit of the RI (hamlet or village, later renamed GŌ), 50 *ko* making up 1 *ri* or *gō*. The *ko* served as the basic unit for the allocation of land (see HAN-

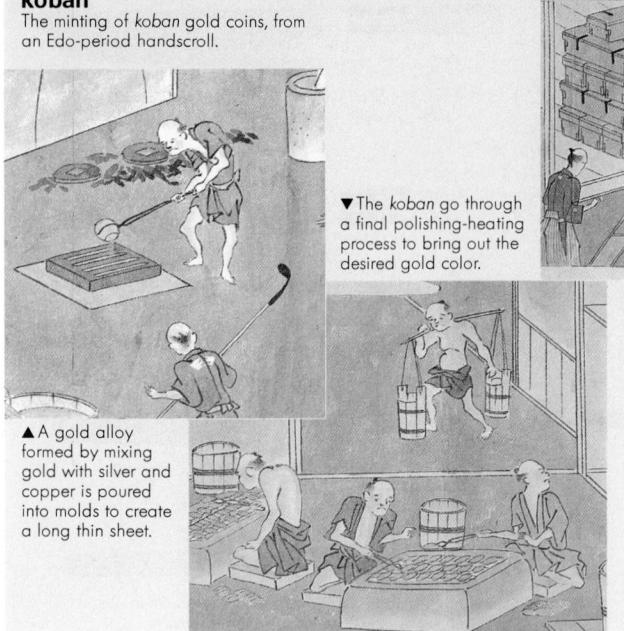

koban
The minting of *koban* gold coins, from an Edo-period handscroll.

▼ The *koban* go through a final polishing-heating process to bring out the desired gold color.

▲ A gold alloy formed by mixing gold with silver and copper is poured into molds to create a long thin sheet.

▲ The finished *koban* are packed 2,000 to a box and stored in a warehouse.

▶ The Keichō *koban* was the first gold coin in general nationwide use; initially issued in 1601 on the orders of Tokugawa Ieyasu, it was 84.29-percent gold and had a face value of one *ryō*.

DEN SHŪJU SYSTEM) and various taxes (see SO, YŌ, AND CHŌ). *Ko* differed in size, ranging from around 10 to 100 people and, in addition to husbands, wives, parents, and children, also included such people as cousins, nephews, nieces, other relatives and close friends called *kiko*, slaves, and vassals.

Each *ko* was entered into a family register (*koseki*). The practice fell into disuse in the mid-Heian period (794–1185) with the collapse of the *ritsuryō* system. See also HOUSE-HOLD REGISTERS.

kō 講

Religious or fraternal associations that developed from lecture meetings on Buddhist sutras and later spread among the Shintō faithful. *Kō* such as the Saishōkō, Ninnōkō, and the Hokkekō, all lecture meetings on Buddhist sutras, were popular among the aristocracy during the Nara (710–794) and Heian (794–1185) periods. The institution spread rapidly during the Kamakura period (1185–1333). Several Buddhist *kō* formed at this time, such as the Daishikō and the Amidakō, survive to this day. Within Shintō, the Isekō and the Kumanokō are among the oldest and largest. Many Shintō sects that became independent in the Meiji period (1868–1912), such as the Izumo Ōyashirokyō and the Ontakekyō, could not have done so without the structural base provided by their *kō*. Many *kō* are regional organizations, with those related to SHU-GENDŌ (mountain worship) being particularly prominent. The *kō* also came to function as mutual assistance associations, leading to the development of the *tanomoshi* and the MUJIN, both *kō* for financial assistance.

Kōa Fire & Marine Insurance Co, Ltd 興亜火災海上保険[株]

(Kōa Kasai Kaijō Hoken). Nonlife insurance company. Incorporated in 1944. Its main business is automobile, fire, and casualty insurance. Total assets for the fiscal year ending March 1991 reached ¥1.1 trillion (US $8.0 billion). Net premium income was ¥240.6 billion (US $1.8 billion) in the same year, and capitalization stood at ¥29.0 billion (US $211.3 million). Headquarters are in Tōkyō.

koan 公案

(Ch: *gongan* or *kung-an;* literally, "public cases"). Conundrums or propositions used by the RINZAI SECT (Ch: Linji, or Lin-chi) of Buddhism as an aid to meditation and enlightenment. "Does a dog have Buddha-nature?"; "What is the sound of one hand clapping?"; and "Buddha preached 49 years, and yet his broad tongue never once moved" are typical *kōan*. The rational impasse created by these *kōan* paradoxes helps to free the mind from its normal conceptual frame and open the novice to a pure encounter with reality-as-is. In Japan the *kōan* tradition was systematized by HAKUIN. The Rinzai tradition claims *kōan* as effecting the true "sudden enlightenment," but the SŌTŌ SECT tradition gives it less validity. See also ZEN.

Kōan Chōsa Chō →Public Security Investigation Agency

kōan jōrei 公安条例

(prefectural public safety ordinance). Generic term for ordinances made by local governments for the regulation of assemblies, parades, and other types of demonstration. Most *kōan jōrei* require that permits for public meetings or demonstrations be obtained from the police or respective public safety commission before the day of the proposed gathering.

Kōa Oil Co, Ltd 興亜石油[株]

(Kōa Sekiyu). Oil-refining firm affiliated with Caltex Co. The company was incorporated in 1933 for the domestic production of high-grade lubricating oil but later turned to the production of airplane fuel and other materials. Following World War II, Caltex bought a 50 percent interest in the company and supplied it with crude oil, which it refined and sold to NIPPON OIL CO, LTD. In 1955 Kōa Oil joined with companies of the Mitsui

group to establish MITSUI PETROCHEMICAL IN-DUSTRIES, LTD, to which it now supplies raw materials. Sales for the fiscal year ending March 1991 were ¥292.7 billion (US $2.1 billion), and capitalization stood at ¥7.3 billion (US $53.2 million). Headquarters are in Tōkyō.

koban 小判

Gold coins with a face value of one *ryō* (a standard monetary unit), in general circulation during the Edo period (1600–1868). The earliest *koban* issued in large quantities and circulated nationwide were the Keichō *koban*, which were 84.29 percent gold. *Koban* were recalled and reissued nine times during the Edo period in order to increase their number while reducing their gold content. As with the larger ŌBAN coins, this practice substantially debased their value. See also KINZA, GINZA, AND ZENIZA; MONEY, PRE-MODERN.

kōban 交番

(usually translated as "police box"). *Kōban*—or more correctly *hashutsujo* in urban areas and *chūzaisho* in the countryside—are the primary mechanism of police deployment in Japan. *Kōban* range in size from 1 or 2 men per shift to the over-10-man shifts at *kōban* in several Tōkyō entertainment districts. *Kōban* usually have an office in the front part and sleeping quarters and storage areas in the rear or upstairs. Police officers (*omawari san*) assist callers and patrol the surrounding neighborhood on foot or bicycle. A typical *chūzaisho* is a small house in which a police officer (called a *chūzai san*) lives with his family; an office is attached to the front for handling police business. See also POLICE SYSTEM.

kobanashi 小咄

(literally, "little story"). Term that refers generally to a variety of brief humorous stories popular from the 17th to the 19th century and specifically to the Edo *kobanashi*, a type of short humorous story produced in Edo (now Tōkyō) during the late 18th century. Initially called *karukuchihon* (books of "light-mouthed" stories) in the Kyōto-Ōsaka area and *otoshibanashibon* (books of punch-line stories) in Edo, compilations of humorous tales ultimately came to be known collectively and generically as *hanashibon* (talk books) and later, in popular usage, as *shōwahon* (books of funny stories) or *kobanashibon* (books of short humorous stories).

Approximately 1,000 *hanashibon* were published during the 200 years or so in which the genre was in vogue. One of the earliest was the *Seisuishō* (Laughs to Wake You Up), completed in 1623, according to the accompanying preface, and traditionally attributed to ANRAKUAN SAKUDEN. It was probably preceded by the *Gigen yōkishū* (Collection of Jokes to Buoy Up the Spirits) and the *Kinō wa kyō no monogatari* (Events of Yesterday, the Tales of Today), anonymous works presumably compiled by OTOGISHŪ (companion entertainers) of military hegemon Toyotomi Hideyoshi (1537–98). Works following the *Seisuishō* included *Hyaku monogatari* (1659, One Hundred Tales), attributed to ASAI RYŌI, and *Shikatabanashi* (1659, Tales Told with Gestures), compiled by Nakagawa Kiun (1636–1705).

The *kobanashi* genre is intimately connected to the development of the art of comic storytelling that later in the 19th century came to be called RAKUGO. It persists

today as a device used at the beginning of *rakugo* performances to warm up the audience for the long humorous story (*nagabanashi*).

Kobayakawa Hideaki 小早川秀秋

(1582–1602). *Daimyō* of the Azuchi-Momoyama period (1568–1600). A nephew of Kita no Mandokoro (1548–1624), wife of TOYOTOMI HIDEYOSHI. Adopted as Hideyoshi's son, Hideaki was by 1594 readopted by Kobayakawa Takakage (1533–97), the daimyō of a domain assessed at 307,000 *koku* (see KOKUDAKA) at Najima in Chikuzen (now the city of Fukuoka), and the next year succeeded to this domain. In 1597 Hideaki was appointed commander (*sōdaishō*) of Hideyoshi's invasion forces in Korea (see INVASIONS OF KOREA IN 1592 AND 1597) but the next year incurred Hideyoshi's disfavor and was saved only by the intercession of the future shōgun TOKUGAWA IEYASU, being demoted to a smaller fief at Kitanoshō in Echizen (now the city of Fukui). In 1599, the year after Hideyoshi's death, he was restored to his previous domain in northern Kyūshū. In the Battle of SEKIGAHARA in 1600, Hideaki nominally adhered to ISHIDA MITSUNARI; he had, however, sent secret pledges to Tokugawa Ieyasu and at a crucial point attacked and routed his supposed ally Ōtani Yoshitsugu (1559–1600), thus ensuring Ieyasu's victory. Hideaki was rewarded with a 510,000-*koku* domain at Okayama, but died without issue in 1602.

Kobayashi 小林[市]

City in southwestern Miyazaki Prefecture, Kyūshū. The area is known for its rice and its cattle. Grapes and sweet potatoes are also grown. Pop: 41,048.

Kobayashi Ataru 小林中

(1899–1981). Businessman. Born in Yamanashi Prefecture. After studying at Waseda University, he joined the Isawa Bank in his native prefecture. In 1929 he moved to Fukoku Chōhei Hoken (now Fukoku Mutual Life Insurance Co) and later became general manager. He became the first president of the JAPAN DEVELOPMENT BANK in 1951 and also served as chairman of the board for ARABIAN OIL CO, LTD, and JAPAN AIRLINES CO, LTD. He was a strong supporter of mainstream conservative politicians, including YOSHIDA SHIGERU and IKEDA HAYATO, and was considered one of the four most powerful leaders in the postwar business-industrial community (see SAKURADA TAKESHI; MIZUNO SHIGEO; NAGANO SHIGEO).

Kobayashi Hideo 小林秀雄

(1902–83). Critic. Born in Tōkyō. Graduated from Tōkyō University. Inspired by the SHIRAKABA SCHOOL novelist SHIGA NAOYA, Kobayashi became a critic. He made his debut in 1929 by publishing a prize-winning essay, "Samazama naru ishō" (All Manner of Designs), in a contest sponsored by the magazine KAIZŌ.

Kobayashi joined with KAWABATA YASUNARI, TAKEDA RINTARŌ, HAYASHI FUSAO, and others in 1933 to launch the literary journal *Bungakukai*. He published *Watakushi shōsetsu ron* (1935), a vigorous attack on the Japanese I-NOVEL (*watakushi shōsetsu*), which had shaped the mainstream of modern Japanese literature since the early 1900s. He also completed *Dosutoefusukī no seikatsu* (1935–37), a critical biography of Dostoevsky.

Following the outbreak of World War II, Kobayashi turned to the traditional arts and literature of Japan, particularly the literature of the medieval period (mid-12th–16th centuries) as represented by such figures as SAIGYŌ and MINAMOTO NO SANETOMO. His new interests are reflected in a collection of essays entitled *Mujō to iu koto* (1946, On *Mujō*). Between 1965 and 1976 Kobayashi wrote his study of MOTOORI NORINAGA, the 18th-century scholar of National Learning (KOKUGAKU). Kobayashi was a member of the Japan Art Academy and a recipient of the Order of Culture (1967). Other works include *Mōtsuaruto* (1946), on the life of Mozart; *Gohho no tegami* (1951–52), a study of the letters of van Gogh; and *Kindai kaiga* (1954–58), on modern painters. Kobayashi has exerted great influence on Japanese literature since the 1930s and helped to establish criticism as an independent literary form.

Kobayashi Ichizō 小林一三

(1873–1957). Businessman and politician. Born in Yamanashi Prefecture. Graduate of Keiō Gijuku (now Keiō University). Kobayashi joined Mitsui Bank, Ltd, in 1893. In 1907 he helped establish Minoo Arima Railway (now HANKYŪ CORPORATION), becoming president in 1927 and chairman in 1934. He developed a unique way of managing the railroad company by combining it with housing and land developments, an amusement park, and a department store. Kobayashi became involved in the entertainment business by establishing the TAKARAZUKA KAGEKIDAN (Takarazuka Girls' Opera Company) in 1913 and TŌHŌ CO, LTD, in 1932. Kobayashi served as commerce and industry minister in the second Konoe cabinet (1940) and as state minister in the Shidehara cabinet (1945).

Kobayashi Issa → Issa

Kobayashi Kiyochika 小林清親

(1847–1915). Painter, illustrator, and UKIYO-E print designer. One of the first traditional artists to formally study Western painting, he is particularly noted for his atmospheric landscapes and reportorial prints published during the Sino-Japanese War of 1894–95 and the Russo-Japanese War of 1904–05.

Kiyochika was born in the Asakusa district of Edo (now Tōkyō), the ninth son of a government warehouse supervisor, Kobayashi Mohei. His career as an artist took form when he met Shimooka Renjō (1822–1914), the pioneer of photography in Japan, and Charles WIRGMAN, the expatriate English painter, who taught him the rudiments of Western oil painting. He acquired more skill in Japanese-style painting from KAWANABE GYŌSAI and SHIBATA ZESHIN.

The 100 or more horizontal landscape prints for which he is most remembered today and which have earned him the title of the HIROSHIGE of the Meiji period (1868–1912)

were published between 1876 and 1881, mostly by Matsuki Heikichi and Fukuda Kumajirō. During the wars with China and Russia Kiyochika designed heroic triptychs to glorify the Japanese, which, with their snowfalls, explosions, and bursts of light, have pictorial and technical qualities that link traditional woodblock prints of the *ukiyo-e* school with modern "creative prints," or *sōsaku hanga*.

Kobayashi Kōji 小林宏治

(1907–). Businessman; chairman of NEC CORPORATION (1976–88). Born in Yamanashi Prefecture. After graduating from Tōkyō University in 1929, he joined NEC Corporation, becoming its president in 1964. Kobayashi developed a nonloaded cable-carrier telephone system connecting Japan and Manchuria in 1937. He also opened ways for the practical application of multiplex cable-carrier communications equipment and of television relay networks. In 1977 Kobayashi launched the C & C (computers and communications) strategy, which transformed NEC into one of the world's largest and most advanced communications enterprises.

Kobayashi Kokei 小林古径

(1883–1957). Japanese-style painter. Real name Kobayashi Shigeru. Born in Niigata Prefecture. Orphaned at an early age, he went to Tōkyō in 1899 to study with Kajita Hanko (1870–1917). His paintings in this period show a gradual change from representational art to the more decorative styles of YAMATO-E and RIMPA. He produced one masterpiece after another in the so-called neoclassic style, based on a study of traditional *yamato-e* scrolls (see EMAKIMONO). He taught at the Tōkyō Bijutsu Gakkō (now Tōkyō University of Fine Arts and Music) from 1944 to 1950 and was awarded the Order of Culture in 1950.

Kobayashi Masaki 小林正樹

(1916–). Film director noted for works that criticize Japanese social mores. Born in Hokkaidō, Kobayashi graduated from Waseda University. He joined SHŌCHIKU CO, LTD, in 1941 but was drafted into the military in January 1942. He was taken prisoner in Okinawa, an experience that served as the subject for his first feature film, *Kabe atsuki heya* (1953, The Thick-Walled Room). NINGEN NO JŌKEN (1959–61, The Human Condition) is a six-part work (often shown in three parts) on the struggle of a soldier to survive World War II with his values intact. SEPPUKU (1962, shown abroad as *Harakiri*), a critical examination of the 17th-century warrior code of ethics, is universally recog-

Kobayashi Kokei
Crane and Turkey, a pair of two-panel folding screens. 1928. Colors on paper. Each screen 169 × 192 cm. Eisei Bunko Museum, Tōkyō.

Kobayashi Hideo This literary critic wrote on a broad range of subjects, both Japanese and Western, and contributed to the establishment of literary criticism as an independent discipline in Japan.

Kobayashi Masaki This film director's work has been widely praised for its critical perspective on Japanese society and culture.

Kōbe This major city in western Honshū is well known for its international connections and cosmopolitan atmosphere.
1 Kōbe Harbor with (left to right) the *Kaiō maru*, Kōbe City Hall, the *Nippon maru*, and the Kōbe Commerce, Industry, and Trade Center Building.
2 A foreign-style residence built in 1922.

nized as Kobayashi's finest film. *Kaidan* (1964, shown abroad as KWAIDAN), adapted from several tales of Lafcadio HEARN, also garnered international attention. Kobayashi's 1983 documentary *Tōkyō saiban* (The Tōkyō Trial) was based on extensive US government footage of the Tōkyō War Crimes Trial.

Kobayashi Takiji 小林多喜二

(1903–33). Author. The most famous writer in the PROLETARIAN LITERATURE MOVEMENT in Japan. Born in Akita Prefecture. Takiji entered Otaru Commercial School in 1916 and Otaru Higher Commercial School in 1921. After graduating from school in 1924, Takiji found employment as a bank clerk. On the side he founded and edited, with friends, the magazine *Clarté*.

In 1927 he secretly took part in organizing two strikes. On 15 March 1928, leftists were rounded up throughout Japan (see MARCH 15TH INCIDENT). Takiji then wrote his first major work, "Senkyūhyakunijūhachinen sangatsu jūgonichi" (The Fifteenth of March, 1928), in which he described the activities of the underground and the arrest and torture of its leaders. The work was published the same year in *Senki* (Battle Flag), the organ of the All-Japan Federation of Proletarian Arts. The magazine was banned.

In 1929 Takiji wrote "Kani kōsen" (tr "The Factory Ship," 1973), the most celebrated work in Japanese proletarian literature. In it the fierce response of the Imperial Navy toward workers striking against brutal conditions aboard a factory ship in the Sea of Okhotsk exposes the link between capitalism and militarism and the resultant exploitation of workers.

His bank's role as an agent in the exploitation of farmers and land in Hokkaidō was exposed by Takiji in 1929 in "Fuzai jinushi" (tr "The Absentee Landlord," 1973). As a result, he was summarily dismissed from his post. He then went underground. On 20 February 1933, he was lured to a rendezvous by an undercover police agent and arrested. He was tortured during interrogation and died the same day.

Kobayashi Takiji One of the most talented figures in the proletarian literature movement of the 1920s and 1930s, Kobayashi was arrested for his Communist Party activities and died as a result of police torture in 1933.

Kobayashi Yōtarō 小林陽太郎

(1933–). Businessman; president of FUJI XEROX CO, LTD (1978–). Born in Tōkyō. After graduating from Keiō University in 1956 and studying at Pennsylvania State University, Kobayashi joined FUJI PHOTO FILM CO, LTD, in 1958. He began working at Fuji Xerox Co shortly after it was established in 1963. Through his implementation of programs such as total quality control (TQC), the company became the largest photocopier manufacturer in Japan, and an important

part of the multinational Xerox group. In 1987 he became a Xerox Corporation board member.

Kōbe 神戸[市]

Capital of Hyōgo Prefecture, western Honshū. Overlooking OSAKA BAY and sheltered on the north by the Rokkō Mountains (Rokkō-san). Its importance as a port goes back to the Nara period (710–794). It prospered in the trade with China and particularly in the 15th- and 16th-century TALLY TRADE with the Ming dynasty. Under the ANSEI COMMERCIAL TREATIES (1858) Kōbe (then known as Hyōgo) was designated an open port. In total value of international trade the port of Kōbe now ranks second in Japan, after YOKOHAMA.

Kōbe produces ships, railway cars, steel and iron, textiles, matches, and rubber, as well as *sake*. The central shopping areas of Motomachi-Dōri and "Sanchikatown," an underground mall, are especially popular. The Hakutsuru Art Museum houses Chinese and Japanese art. The hot springs on Rokkōsan and numerous historical sites are also of interest. Area: 546.7 sq km (211 sq mi); Pop: 1,477,410.

Kōbe College 神戸女学院大学

(Kōbe Jogakuin Daigaku). A private women's college located in the city of Nishinomiya, Hyōgo Prefecture. Founded as a girl's school in 1875 by two female missionaries sent by the American Board of Commissioners for Foreign Missions, it became a four-year women's college in 1948. The college maintains faculties of literature, music, and home economics. Enrollment in 1989 was 2,246.

Kōbe Steel, Ltd [株]神戸製鋼所

(Kōbe Seikōsho). Producer of iron and steel, nonferrous metals (aluminum, copper, and titanium), and machinery (industrial, chemical, and construction) and provider of comprehensive engineering services. Incorporated in 1911. Kōbe Steel is also branching out into electronics, biotechnology, the service sector, and real estate development. The company has established manufacturing subsidiaries and research laboratories overseas, with most of the activity focused on North America, Europe, and Southeast Asia. In 1988 Kōbe Steel established a US subsidiary, Kōbe Steel USA, Inc, to coordinate the activities of its US-based companies. Sales for the fiscal year ending March 1991 totaled ¥1.3 trillion (US $9.5 billion), of which sales of iron, steel, and welding consumables constituted 49 percent; machinery and engineering, 30 percent; and aluminum and copper, 21 percent. In the same period the export ratio was 18 percent, and capitalization stood at ¥213.6 billion (US $1.6 billion). Headquarters are in Tōkyō and Kōbe.

Kōbe University 神戸大学

(Kōbe Daigaku). National, coeducational university located in the city of Kōbe, Hyōgo Prefecture. Originally the Kōbe Higher Commerce School, founded in 1902, it became Kōbe University of Commerce in 1929 and then Kōbe University of Economics in 1944. This school was combined with Himeji Higher School, Kōbe Technical College, Hyōgo Normal School, and Hyōgo Youth Normal School in 1949 to establish Kōbe University, which later merged with Kōbe Medical College and Hyōgo Agricultural College as well. It maintains faculties of letters, education, law, economics, business management, science, medicine, engineering, and agriculture. Enrollment was 11,051 in 1989.

Kōbō Daishi→Kūkai

Kobori Enshū 小堀遠州

(1579–1647). Prominent tea master, pottery connoisseur, garden designer, architect, calligrapher, and poet. Born in Ōmi Province (now Shiga Prefecture), the son of the commissioner of public works (*fushin bugyō*) under TOYOTOMI HIDEYOSHI, Enshū served as *fushin bugyō* under the first three Tokugawa shōguns, overseeing construction work on FUSHIMI CASTLE, NIJŌ CASTLE, and EDO CASTLE. In his youth he studied the tea ceremony under FURUTA ORIBE and founded his own school of tea. He also excelled at garden design, a field in which he created a number of masterpieces. Only a few examples of his work remain, among them the gardens of the Sentō Palace, the Konchiin subtemple of the NANZENJI, and the Kohōan subtemple of the DAITOKUJI, all of which are in Kyōto. As a tea master, Enshū was also an important patron of ceramics production.

Kobotoke Pass 小仏峠

(Kobotoke Tōge). Located on the border of Tōkyō and Kanagawa prefectures, central Honshū. Situated northwest of the mountain TAKAOSAN, it was formerly a pass on the road Kōshū Kaidō, and remains of a former barrier station (*seki*) can still be seen. Presently the Chūō Main Line of the JR (Japan Railways) runs through tunnels under the pass. Altitude: 590 m (1,936 ft).

Kōbu Gattai Undō→Movement for Union of Court and Shogunate

Kōbun, Emperor 弘文天皇

(648–672; Kōbun Tennō). The 39th sovereign (*tennō*) in the traditional count (which includes several legendary emperors); said to have reigned January–August 672. Known to history as Prince Ōtomo, he was the eldest son and designated heir of Emperor TENJI. Soon after Tenji's death in early 672, however, Ōtomo was challenged for the throne by his uncle Prince Ōama (see JINSHIN DISTURBANCE). Within six months Ōtomo was defeated and obliged to commit suicide. Prince Ōama ascended the throne as Emperor TEMMU in the following year. Although the NIHON SHOKI (720) makes no mention of Prince Ōtomo's enthronement, the compilers of the DAI NIHON SHI (1657–1906) asserted that he had formally acceded as Emperor Ōtomo shortly before the rebellion. In 1870 Emperor MEIJI concluded that Ōtomo had indeed reigned for several months during 672 and gave him the posthumous name Kōbun.

Kobunjigaku 古文辞学

(School of Ancient Rhetoric). Also known as the Ken'engaku school. One of the schools of Confucianism in the Edo period (1600–1868). Its most outstanding exponent was OGYŪ SORAI, who opposed the teachings of Wang Yangming (see YŌMEIGAKU) and Neo-Confucianism (see SHUSHIGAKU) as well as the Kogigaku school (School of Ancient Meaning) of ITŌ JINSAI. Sorai claimed that the purpose of Confucian scholarship was the understanding of the original Confucian classics through the close study of the meaning of ancient words. Other representative scholars of the school were HATTORI NANKAKU and DAZAI SHUNDAI.

kōbusen 洪武銭

(more correctly, Kōbu *tsūhō;* Kōbu currency). Chinese copper coins cast during the Hongwu (Hung-wu; J: Kōbu) era (1368–98) of the Ming dynasty. The coins were of five different sizes, with denominations ranging from 1 *mon* to 10 *mon,* imported to Japan during the Muromachi period (1333–1568). Along with EIRAKUSEN, coins of the Yongle (Yung-le) era (1403–24), they remained in use until the Edo period (1600–1868). Although the number in circulation was never very great, they were accepted as sound currency in business transactions (see ERIZENI). In the late Muromachi period facsimiles of *kōbusen,* called *kajikisen,* were cast in Japan.

kobushi 辛夷

Magnolia kobus. Deciduous tree of the family Magnoliaceae that grows wild in mountainous regions throughout Japan as well as in southern Korea. It is also widely planted as an ornamental. It reaches a height of about 8 meters (26 ft). The twigs are green and give off a pleasant scent when broken. The leaves are alternate and oval. The fragrant white flowers open before leafing in spring and have six perianths, each about 6 centimeters (2.4 in) long. Fruits split open in autumn to reveal red seeds hanging from white strings.

A variety called *kitakobushi,* which grows wild in mountainous areas of the Sea of Japan coast in Hokkaidō and northern and central Honshū, has larger flowers and leaves than those of the *kobushi.* The *kobushi* was exported to the United States and England in the early 19th century as an ornamental tree.

Kobushigadake 甲武信ケ岳

Also called Kobushidake. Mountain at the junction of Saitama, Yamanashi, and Nagano prefectures, central Honshū. In the Chichibu Mountains, Kobushigadake is part of CHICHIBU-TAMA NATIONAL PARK. Height: 2,475 m (8,120 ft).

kobushin 小普請

Vassals of the Tokugawa shogunate (1603–1867), largely HATAMOTO or GOKENIN with limited fiefs or stipends of rice, who were assigned to no official posts because of age, illness, or incompetence. The term literally means "minor construction" and was originally applied to vassals assigned to such work as the repair of castles rather than military duties. Divided into 5 to 12 groups, they were at first supervised by the Edo Castle administrators (RUSUI) and, after 1719, by the shogunal senior councillors (RŌJŪ).

Kobutori jijii 瘤取爺

(The Old Man Who Lost His Wen). Folktale. An old man with a wen on his cheek comes

kobushi This hardy species of magnolia has been discovered to be remarkably resistant to pollution.

upon a company of carousing demons (ONI; TENGU in some versions) and entertains them with song and dance. As a reward the demons remove his wen. Hearing of this, his neighbor, also afflicted with a wen, performs for them too, but he is so clumsy that the angry demons put a wen on his other cheek. This comic tale is found in the 13th-century UJI SHŪI MONOGATARI.

Kōchi 高知[市]

Capital of Kōchi Prefecture, Shikoku, on Urado Bay. The city developed after a castle was constructed in 1603 by YAMANOUCHI KAZUTOYO. Kōchi is the main economic, cultural, and transportation center of the prefecture. Cement, steel, chemicals, lumber, shipbuilding, paper, and foodstuff industries flourish. Attractions include the ruins of Kōchi Castle, Godaisan Park, the scenic coastline of KATSURAHAMA, and Tosa Shrine, built by CHŌSOKABE MOTOCHIKA. Pop: 317,069.

Kōchi domain → Tosa domain

Kōchi Plain 高知平野

(Kōchi Heiya). Located in central Kōchi Prefecture, Shikoku. Bordering the Pacific Ocean and separated by step faults from the Shikoku Mountains in the north, it consists of alluvial sediment of the rivers Monobegawa and Niyodogawa. A warm climate allows two rice crops a year in some areas; vegetables are grown in greenhouses. The major city is Kōchi. Area: approximately 140 sq km (55 sq mi).

Kōchi Prefecture 高知県

(Kōchi Ken). Located in southern Shikoku and bounded by Ehime Prefecture to the northwest, Tokushima Prefecture to the northeast, and the Pacific Ocean to the south. The terrain consists of the Ishizuchi Mountains, with small level areas concentrated along rivers. The climate is among the warmest in Japan, with heavy precipitation. Subtropical vegetation flourishes in the southern coastal regions.

It was known as Tosa Province under the ancient provincial system (KOKUGUN SYSTEM). During the Sengoku period (1467–1568) it came under the control of several warrior families, including the Chōsokabe and the Yamanouchi. In the late Edo period (1600–1868) *samurai* from Tosa, including SAKAMOTO RYŌMA and NAKAOKA SHINTARŌ, were prominent in the movement to overthrow the Tokugawa shogunate. The prefecture's present name dates from 1871, and its current boundaries were established in 1880.

Agriculture is the main occupation, and Kōchi is one of the few places in Japan with a climate that permits the harvesting of two rice crops annually (in some areas). Forestry and fishing are also important. Apart from woodworking and papermaking, which draw on the prefecture's abundant lumber

Kōchi Vermilion railings mark the spot at the heart of this city's business district where Harimayabashi, a famous bridge, once stood.

resources, there is very little industry.

Tourist attractions include the coastal scenery of the cape ASHIZURIMISAKI (the main attraction of ASHIZURI-UWAKAI NATIONAL PARK), the cape MUROTOZAKI of the KATSURAHAMA seacoast, and the unspoiled mountain areas to the north. Kōchi is also known as a center for the breeding of fighting dogs. Area: 7,107 sq km (2,744 sq mi); pop: 825,034; capital: KŌCHI. Other major cities include NANKOKU, TOSA, and NAKAMURA.

kōchō jūnisen 皇朝十二銭

(twelve coinages of the imperial court). Twelve types of copper coin minted in ancient Japan; they were issued by the court during the Nara (710–794) and Heian (794–1185) periods to demonstrate its authority to the people. The first Japanese coins, called WADŌ KAIHŌ, were modeled on those of the Chinese Tang (T'ang) dynasty (618–907) and were minted in 708; they were circular, with a square hole in the center and four Chinese characters inscribed on one side. In the following 250 years, 11 other types of coin appeared, all similar to the Wadō *kaihō.* The coins circulated only around the capital and were used exclusively by the aristocracy. After the minting of 958, Japanese coins gradually disappeared, and imported Chinese coins (SŌSEN; KŌBUSEN; EIRAKUSEN) were used increasingly until the end of the 16th century, when the Japanese began minting again.

Kōda Aya 幸田文

(1904–90). Novelist and essayist. Born in Tōkyō; daughter of the novelist KŌDA ROHAN. After World War II, she wrote a series of essays about her late father, including "Shūen" (1947, Last Moments). She went on to write autobiographical fiction and won the Yomiuri Literary Prize for "Kuroi suso" (1954; tr "The Black Kimono," 1960). Other works include *Nagareru* (1955, To Flow), *Otōto* (1956–57, Younger Brother), and the essay collection *Chigiregumo* (1956, Tattered Clouds). In 1957 she received the Japan Art Academy Award for *Nagareru.*

Kōdaiji maki-e 高台寺蒔絵

A type of MAKI-E lacquer ware popular in the Azuchi-Momoyama period (1568–1600). Named after the temple Kōdaiji in Kyōto, which owns some of the most important examples of this ware. Kōdaiji *maki-e* designs are often clear representations of flowers or grasses and are highly ornamental. The lacquer surface is frequently divided into contrasting fields, each with its own design. Characteristic Kōdaiji *maki-e* designs employ *hira maki-e* ("level sprinkled-picture") in which gold or silver flakes are sprinkled

Kōchi Prefecture
Location and
Prefectural Crest

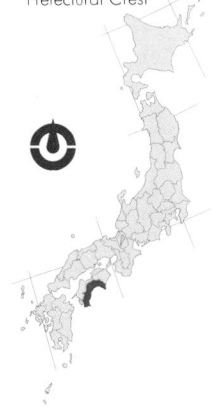

kōdan jūtaku The Hikarigaoka apartment complex (pictured), in Nerima Ward, Tōkyō, is typical of these large public-housing projects.

onto black lacquer; although this is normally covered with a coat of raw lacquer and ground down to a flat surface, here it is left without being polished or ground down. This technique results in a distinctive gold tone and is known as *makihanashi* ("left as sprinkled"). Additional design elements may be added by "needle drawing" (*harigaki*). These techniques are frequently used in combination with sprinkled gold or silver dust, *nashiji* ("pear-skin ground"), used in the decoration as well as the background. See also LACQUER WARE.

Kodai kenkyū 古代研究

(The Study of Ancient Times). Collection of essays by folklorist ORIKUCHI SHINOBU, published in three volumes, 1929–30. One volume deals with Japanese literature, the other two with FOLKLORE STUDIES. The essays present Orikuchi's views concerning Japanese traits as reflected in folklore and early literature. The literature volume includes original studies on such subjects as the 8th-century poetry anthology MAN'YŌSHŪ, the TALE OF GENJI, and SETSUWA BUNGAKU ("tale litera-

kōdan Kanda Kurenai, a practitioner of this storytelling art, holds a sheet of paper as a prop while reciting a story about Edo-period (1600–1868) playwright Chikamatsu Monzaemon.

ture"). Also included are extensive studies of ancient religious beliefs as revealed in folk customs. In addition, there are Orikuchi's reports on his research trips to Okinawa and to the island of Iki.

Kodaira 小平[市]

City in central Tōkyō Prefecture. A flourishing village in the Edo period (1600–1868), from the 1920s it was the site of military installations, schools, and factories. It is now the site of large factories and housing complexes. Tsuda College and Musashino Art University are located here. Pop: 164,013.

Kodaira Kunihiko 小平邦彦

(1915–). Mathematician. Known internationally for his extensive work in various fields of mathematics, including harmonic analysis, differential operators, complex analytic manifolds, and algebraic geometry. Born in Tōkyō, he received from Tōkyō University a mathematics degree in 1938 and a physics degree in 1941. In 1949 Kodaira was invited to the Institute for Advanced Study at Princeton University, and, until his return to Japan in 1967 to teach at Tōkyō University, he taught at Princeton, Johns Hopkins, and other US universities. He received the Fields Prize in 1954 and the Order of Culture in 1957.

Kodama Gentarō 児玉源太郎

(1852–1906). Army general. Born in Suō Province (now part of Yamaguchi Prefecture). Kodama fought in the BOSHIN CIVIL WAR, the SAGA REBELLION, and the SATSUMA REBELLION. As head of the Army Staff College, he worked for the adoption of the German military system. He served in the SINO-JAPANESE WAR OF 1894–1895 and, afterward, as governor-general of Taiwan. Kodama was army minister in the fourth ITŌ HIROBUMI cabinet (1900) and in the succeeding KATSURA TARŌ cabinet, in which he was also minister of both home affairs and education. Promoted to full general in 1904, during the RUSSO-JAPANESE WAR of 1904–05 he served as chief of general staff of the Manchurian Army and assisted in the capture of PORT ARTHUR. In 1906 he was named chief of the Army General Staff Office.

Kodama Yoshio 児玉誉士夫

(1911–84). Right-wing political leader. Born in Fukushima Prefecture and raised in Tōkyō. He was involved in right-wing politics from his youth and was imprisoned on two separate occasions (1931, 1932). In 1937 he went to MANCHUKUO and North China on a fact-finding mission for the Foreign Ministry. In 1941 he was commissioned by the Naval Air Force to set up a network (known as the "Kodama Kikan") in Japanese-occupied Shanghai to procure war matériel. After World War II, Kodama was imprisoned by the OCCUPATION authorities as a class-A war criminal. Released in 1948, he resumed his right-wing activities, becoming a powerful behind-the-scenes manipulator who used capital he had amassed during the war to finance conservative parties and politicians. In 1976 he was prosecuted for his involvement in the LOCKHEED SCANDAL.

kōdan 講談

Genre of oral storytelling. Initially termed *kōshaku*, it has been known as *kōdan* since the Meiji period (1868–1912). The word is used to refer to either the art or the story itself. Originally, lectures on historical and literary texts given before high-ranking per-

sonages were known as *kōshaku*, and these developed into the entertainment now known as *kōdan*. Because of this heritage, even today the narrator often sits behind a desk, marking the rhythm of his words with a fan or wooden clappers. Though artists seldom read from texts, recitals are still called "readings." The recitations were derived mainly from historical tales and martial chronicles but later came to include incidents in the lives of townsmen, succession disputes in *daimyō* households, and tales of vendettas, thieves, and heroic protectors of the downtrodden. After the Meiji Restoration (1868) newly created material helped make *kōdan* more popular than ever. Transcriptions of *kōdan* were made during the Meiji period. From these "written" *kōdan* the contemporary genre of popular fiction (*taishū bungaku*) evolved.

Kōdan languished during the early 20th century in the face of new amusements such as movies, while dated material and a dearth of new performers contributed to its further decline after World War II. Since about 1985, however, the emergence of female *kōdan* narrators has contributed to a renewed interest in the storytelling art. The new narrators employ topical themes, such as women's issues, in the creation of new *kōdan* material. See also TACHIKAWA BUNKO, RAKUGO, NANIWA-BUSHI.

kōdan jūtaku 公団住宅

(public housing). Middle- to high-rise apartment buildings constructed by the Japan Housing Corporation (now the HOUSING AND URBAN DEVELOPMENT CORPORATION) for families in urban areas. As part of the effort to resolve the housing shortage after World War II, the corporation (funded by the national and local governments) built good-quality, fire-resistant housing in large numbers in metropolitan areas where population clustered in response to the concentration of industry. Compared to the public housing built by local governments, the *kōdan jūtaku* complexes tend to be on a larger scale and charge higher rents. Among the newer residential communities consisting of large-scale *kōdan jūtaku* complexes are TAMA NEW TOWN in Tōkyō (30.1 sq km [11.6 sq mi]; pop: 300,000), KŌHOKU NEW TOWN in Yokohama (25.3 sq km [9.8 sq mi]; pop: 300,000), and SENRI NEW TOWN in Ōsaka (11.6 sq km [4.5 sq mi]; pop: 150,000). See also HOUSING, MODERN.

Kōdansha, Ltd [株]講談社

(Kōdansha). Major Japanese publishing house. The Dai Nippon Yūben Kai (Greater Japan Oratorical Society), the forerunner of Kōdansha, was established in November 1909 by NOMA SEIJI, and its first periodical publication, *Yūben* (Oratory), appeared in February 1910. A second firm, Kōdansha, was set up in 1911 to publish *Kōdan kurabu*, a magazine that Noma intended to be as entertaining as *Yūben* was serious. In 1925 the two publishing houses merged and by 1926 the company was publishing nine magazines, the most popular of which were SHŌNEN KURABU, a magazine for boys, and KINGU.

Following World War II the firm was widely criticized for its forthright support of the war effort, and its president, NOMA SHŌICHI, was purged by OCCUPATION authorities. However, in 1949 Noma was permitted to resume his duties and through drastic restructuring was able to save the company. Although the firm's major emphasis continued to be on the publication of magazines, it also began to publish an increasing number of books; in 1963 Kōdansha International, Ltd, was established for the publication of books in English. In 1990 Kōdansha published 52 magazines and 1,500 books. Sales for the fiscal year ending November 1990 totaled ¥170 billion (US $1.3 billion).

Kōda Rohan   幸田露伴

(1867–1947). Novelist, essayist, and poet. Rohan captured much of the vitality and constructive idealism of late-19th-century Japanese society, then in the early stages of modernization. Writing in a pithy, pseudo-classical prose style modeled on that of the great 17th-century master Ihara SAIKAKU, Rohan was the last of a breed of well-educated men of letters schooled in the classical East Asian tradition and a precursor of Japanese romanticism and symbolism. Born Kōda Shigeyuki in Edo (now Tōkyō), Rohan's education was irregular for financial reasons. Prompted by the need to support himself, he graduated from the government-financed telegraphers school in 1884.

Rohan devoted a major part of his life to study, which earned him a doctoral degree in literature in 1911. He was awarded the Order of Culture in 1937. From his literary debut with "Tsuyu dandan" (1889, Dewdrops), a Christian love story set in New York, until his last work, published in 1947, a prodigious commentary on the *Shichibushū* (Seven Collections) of the BASHŌ school of HAIKU, Rohan produced a massive amount of writing in diverse fields. His pen name, Rohan, means companion of the dew.

Isanatori (1891–92, The Whaler) is Rohan's only completed novel; it focuses on the ethical issue of karma versus human conscience. Rohan is best known for his early idealistic short stories, including "Fūryūbutsu" (1889, Love Bodhisattva), "Tai dokuro" (1890, Encounter with a Skull), and the novella GOJŪ NO TŌ (1891–92, The Five-Storied Pagoda), Rohan's best work. Beginning with "Yoritomo" in 1908, Rohan fashioned a new genre of historical fiction. Besides composing a quantity of haiku and WAKA (31-syllable poems), Rohan wrote several long poems, a play, juvenile literature, travelogues, essays, scholarly discourses, and commentaries.

Rohan synthesized Buddhist metaphysics, Taoist mysticism, Christian humanism, Confucian activism, and Japanese aestheticism into a bright microcosm of ideals and aspirations. His heroes and heroines memorialize those nameless individuals who made Japan's modernization possible.

kōden   香典

(condolence gifts; literally, "incense money"). A monetary or material gift given to the family of a deceased person. Until very recently in rural Japan, staples such as rice, *sake* (rice wine), and vegetables were common condolence gifts; these were cooked and served at the banquet after the funeral. Today, *kōden* is almost always in the form of money, which is used to defray part of the cost of the funeral, including the banquet, and to purchase return gifts (*kōdengaeshi*). The money is placed in a special envelope, which is tied with a decorative string (MIZUHIKI) dyed half of its length in white and half in black, gray, or yellow—color combinations that symbolize mourning. The name of the donor is written on the envelope to facilitate return gifts. It is customary to write the amount enclosed on the back.

kōden   公田

(public fields). Also pronounced *kuden*. The type of cultivated land most stringently controlled by the state under the RITSURYŌ SYSTEM of government established in the late 7th century. At first *kōden* were defined as fields to which the cultivator was not given exclusive right of usufruct. There were three main types of *kōden*: excess land (*jōden*) remaining after the distribution of field allotments (KUBUNDEN) to individual cultivators; government land (*kanden*) supervised by the Ministry of the Imperial Household; and land set aside to award to holders of high government office, possessors of high court rank, or temples and shrines. *Kōden* were distinguished from SHIDEN (private fields) or lands with fixed rights of usufruct.

After 743, with the promulgation of a law permitting permanent possession of newly opened fields (see KONDEN EISEI SHIZAI HŌ), the distinction between *kōden* and *shiden* underwent a change and all lands other than those newly developed for private use and those granted to religious institutions were known as *kōden*. With the development of the SHŌEN (landed estate) system in the 10th century, lands subject to government taxation (*denso*) or high-interest loans of rice seed (SUIKO) were designated *kōden*. In the 12th century the term came to refer to all cultivated lands registered with the government.

Kōdōha   皇道派

("Imperial Way" faction). Army faction during the 1930s led by generals ARAKI SADAO and MAZAKI JINZABURŌ. The Kōdōha stressed spiritual training, an almost mystic devotion to the emperor, and "direct action" to achieve total national reform and military success over the Soviet Union. Its struggle with a rival faction, the TŌSEIHA, intensified in 1935 when Mazaki was dismissed from his appointment as inspector general of military education for his complicity in a 1934 plot to murder prominent politicians (see NOVEMBER INCIDENT). In retaliation Aizawa Saburō (1889–1936), a Kōdōha officer, murdered General NAGATA TETSUZAN, a Tōseiha figure. In February 1936 pro-Kōdōha junior officers led an insurrection to establish a military government (FEBRUARY 26TH INCIDENT). General Araki resigned and Kōdōha members holding top army posts were purged. Control of the army then passed into the hands of the Tōseiha.

Kōdōkan   講道館

An educational foundation for the teaching and promotion of JŪDŌ; also, the gymnasium

belonging to the foundation. Kōdōkan was established in the Shitaya district of Tōkyō by KANŌ JIGORŌ in 1882; it is now located in Bunkyō Ward, Tōkyō. In the late 1980s membership was about 1.5 million. Holders of ranks (*dan*) numbered about 1.3 million.

Kōdōkan ki jutsugi   弘道館記述義

A two-volume commentary on FUJITA TŌKO's *Kōdōkan ki* (1838, Record of the Kōdōkan); written 1845–47 by Tōko, a scholar of the MITO SCHOOL. Tōko had written the *Kōdōkan ki* at the behest of the Mito *daimyō* TOKUGAWA NARIAKI to set forth the educational principles of the Kōdōkan, the Mito domainal school that Nariaki planned to establish; he wrote the commentary after the school opened. Tōko's argument that everyone, each according to his station, should loyally serve his lord—and, by extension, the emperor—was to exert great influence on the proimperial, antiforeign SONNŌ JŌI thought of the mid-19th century.

Kodomo no Hi→holidays, national

Kōetsu→Hon'ami Kōetsu

Kōfu   甲府[市]

Capital of Yamanashi Prefecture, central Honshū. Business, cultural, and transportation center of Yamanashi Prefecture. The base of the TAKEDA FAMILY during the 16th century, Kōfu flourished as a castle town and as a post-station town during the Edo period (1600–1868). Its industries are foodstuffs and textiles. It is also known for its wine and crystal ware. Attractions are the park at the site of Kōfu Castle, Takeda Shrine, and Yumura Hot Spring. Pop: 200,626.

Kōfu Basin   甲府盆地

(Kōfu Bonchi). In central Yamanashi Prefecture, central Honshū. Bounded by the fault scarps of the Akaishi and Misaka mountains, it consists of piedmont alluvial plains of the rivers Fuefukigawa and Kamanashigawa (the upper reaches of the Fujikawa). Grapes and peaches flourish there, and rice is grown on the flood plain. Industrial areas are rapidly growing. The major city is Kōfu. Area: approximately 190 sq km (73 sq mi).

Kōfukuji   興福寺

One of the two head temples of the HOSSŌ SECT of Buddhism, located in the city of Nara, Nara Prefecture. Kōfukuji originated in 669, when Kagami no Ōkimi (d 683), consort of FUJIWARA NO KAMATARI (614–669), established a temple at the family estate in Yamashina

Kōda Rohan Best known for his early fiction, this writer was also a literary scholar who produced a magisterial commentary on the seven *haiku* collections of the Bashō school.

Kōfukuji Treasure House

1 This painted dry-lacquer statue of an *ashura* (a type of Buddhist guardian deity) is a major example of 8th-century style and technique. 734. Height 152 cm. National Treasure.
2 Head of a cast-bronze statue of the healing Buddha Yakushi. 685; only the exquisitely sculpted head survived a fire in 1411. Height 98 cm. National Treasure.

(in what is now Kyōto Prefecture) on behalf of her ailing husband. With the establishment of the capital at Nara in 710, the temple was renamed Kōfukuji and moved to its present location.

Kōfukuji grew rapidly as the family temple (*ujidera*) of the FUJIWARA FAMILY. In 723 a SEYAKUIN to provide medical care for the orphaned and impoverished and a HIDEN'IN to offer them refuge were established at the temple. From the mid-8th century until the Meiji period (1868–1912), Kōfukuji was Japan's leading center for Hossō studies. The Hossō doctrines were brought to Kōfukuji in 735 by the monk GEMBŌ (d 746), who was followed by a line of distinguished Hossō scholars.

Owing to its strong Fujiwara backing, Kōfukuji became the dominant force in the province of Yamato (now part of Nara Prefecture) and owned extensive estates, from which it derived great revenue. To protect its interests it maintained an army of WARRIOR-MONKS (*sōhei*), which it did not hesitate to use in its struggles with TŌDAIJI and EN-RYAKUJI after the 10th century. In 1180 the Heike warrior leader TAIRA NO KIYOMORI had Kōfukuji razed, but it was rebuilt under the sponsorship of the founder of the Kamakura shogunate (1192–1333), MINAMOTO NO YORITOMO.

In 1600 TOKUGAWA IEYASU sought to revive the then-impoverished Kōfukuji through an annual endowment that made possible the renovation and reconstruction of many of the temple buildings. In 1717, however, a disastrous fire gutted much of the temple complex. With the independence of the Kasuga Shrine, which was associated with the temple and had also been founded by the Fujiwara family, in 1868 and the confiscation of most of the temple precincts three years later, Kōfukuji became virtually defunct. In 1872 it formally affiliated itself with the powerful SHINGON SECT, but 10 years later declared its independence as a head temple of the Hossō sect. Kōfukuji houses a rich collection of art treasures. See KŌFUKUJI TREASURE HOUSE.

Kōfukuji Treasure House
興福寺国宝館

(Kōfukuji Kokuhōkan). Located at the temple KŌFUKUJI in Nara. A collection, opened in 1959, of some of the finest sculpture in Japan dating from the 7th century through the Kamakura period (1185–1333). There are pieces attributed to such Kamakura sculptors as Jōkei, UNKEI, and KōKEI. The few paintings include a 14th-century Kasuga mandala (see MANDALA). This collection is essential to the study of Japanese sculpture, but many of the pieces are occasionally on extended loan to the national museums at Tōkyō, Kyōto, or Nara.

kofun
古墳

(tomb mounds). Large tombs of mounded earth built mainly for the ruling elite during the 4th to 7th centuries. Ranging in size from 15 meters (50 ft) in diameter to 32.3 hectares (80 acres) in area, these tombs are an important source of information on the social and political organization and material culture of the Kofun period (ca 300–710).

Early-Kofun-Period Tombs—The earliest tomb mounds of the Kofun period were built in the Kinai (Kyōto-Ōsaka-Nara) region. Tomb building spread to northern Kyūshū through the Inland Sea region in the early 4th century. Early tombs had either round or keyhole-shaped mounds. The first tombs were constructed on hilltops overlooking fertile agricultural land. Burial facilities consisted of a wooden coffin buried directly in the summit or placed in a pit-style stone chamber called *tateana sekishitsu* (literally, "vertical hole, stone chamber"). Clay cylinders and various funerary sculptures (see HANIWA) were often embedded over the grave. The funerary goods of the early tombs were mainly ceremonial in nature, with some iron weapons, armor, Chinese-made BRONZE MIRRORS, and necklaces and bracelets (see BEADS, ANCIENT).

In the late 4th century tomb building spread further. The tombs assumed a greater variety of shapes—square or gourd-shaped, formed by two round mounds joined together. Alternate burial facilities were also developed: large stone coffins were placed in pit-style chambers or directly into the ground, and wooden coffins were embedded in prepared clay enclosures rather than stone chambers.

Tombs of the Middle and Late Kofun Period—In the 5th century the character of the tombs underwent drastic changes. In-

stead of being built on natural hillocks, they were mounded up from flatter terrace surfaces. Wide moats became a common feature, dramatically increasing the area of the tombs (see NINTOKU MAUSOLEUM; ŌJIN MAUSO-LEUM). Accessory mounds (*baichō*) often accompanied the highest-status tombs of this period, acting as depositories for tremendous volumes of funerary goods, including iron swords and tools, imported gold ornaments (see EAR ORNAMENTS, ANCIENT), SUE WARE, and horse trappings (see HORSE TRAP-PINGS, ANCIENT).

The idea for a new type of tomb chamber called *yokoana sekishitsu* (literally, "horizontal hole, stone chamber") was transmitted from the Korean peninsula in the 5th century. The tomb had a corridor entrance so that one could walk into the chamber rather than access through the top as in the pit-style chamber. The corridor allowed the tomb to be used several times, and during the Late Kofun period family tombs became common.

Tombs of the 6th and 7th centuries shrank in size and increased in number as they came to be used by a greater segment of the population. Entire hillsides were devoted to cemeteries of small, round mounds averaging 15 meters (50 ft) in diameter, each containing a corridor-style chamber (see IWASE "THOU-SAND-MOUND" TOMB CLUSTER; SAITOBARU TOMB CLUSTER; IWATOYAMA TOMB). Funerary goods of this period were increasingly utilitarian in nature, and included *sue* ware, HAJI WARE, personal weapons, jewelry, and tools. In northern Kyūshū, bold geometric designs and animate figures were painted on the interior walls of the chambers (see ORNA-MENTED TOMBS). With the introduction of Buddhism in the mid-6th century, an increasing number of the elite built temples instead of tombs for posterity, and tomb building gradually ceased during the 7th century. See also ARCHAEOLOGY.

Kofun period
古墳時代

(ca 300–710; Kofun *jidai*). Protohistoric period during which large tumuli (KOFUN) were built for deceased members of the ruling elite. The period is variously dated as ca 250–552, ca 300–552, ca 300–645, ca 300–710, and so forth, and it may be divided into either two or three phases: Early (4th and 5th centuries) and Late (6th and 7th centuries), or Early (4th century), Middle (5th century), and Late (6th and 7th centuries). This encyclopedia has adopted the three-phase division and the dates ca 300–710 for the period; thus, it encompasses the ASUKA PERIOD (593–710). The first state in Japan, Yamato, emerged during the Kofun period, and diplomatic relations were established with the Korean states and the Chinese courts. Based on rice agriculture continuing from the YAYOI PERIOD (ca 300 BC–ca AD 300), the economy was reorganized in the late 5th century in the form of the BE system to provide the supplies necessary to support palace life. Buddhism was introduced from the kingdom of PAEKCHE on the Korean peninsula in the mid-6th century, and the state administrative structure was reorganized on the Tang (T'ang) dynasty (618–907) model through the TAIKA REFORM in the mid-7th century.

Mounded Tombs and Social Stratification—The large tombs of the Kofun period resulted from the formation, in the late 3rd century, of a class society consisting of aristocrats and commoners. Social stratification is reflected in the size, labor required for

Main Types of Tomb Mounds

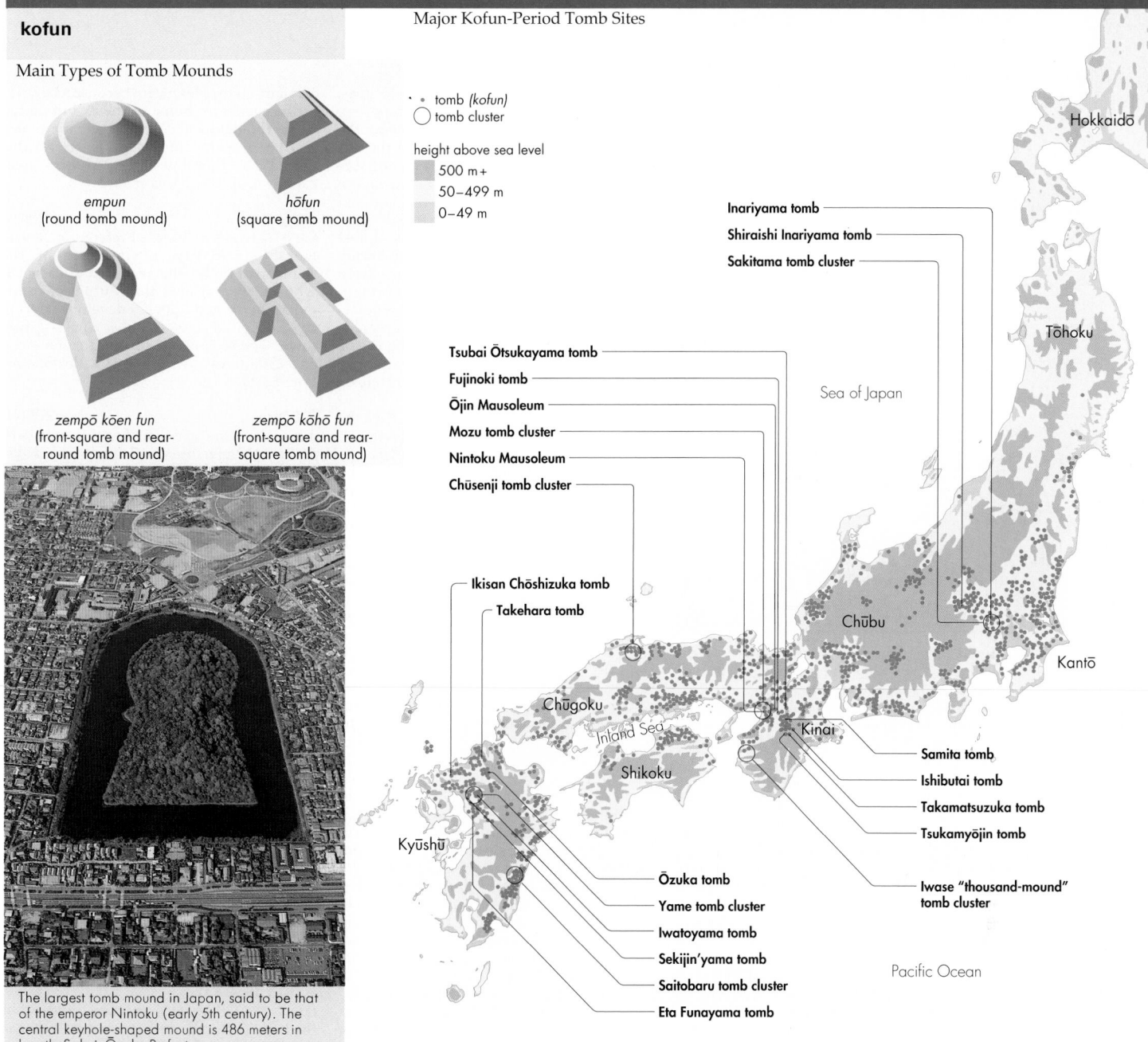

empun
(round tomb mound)

hōfun
(square tomb mound)

zempō kōen fun
(front-square and rear-round tomb mound)

zempō kōhō fun
(front-square and rear-square tomb mound)

Major Kofun-Period Tomb Sites

`·` `•` tomb *(kofun)*
◯ tomb cluster

height above sea level
500 m+
50–499 m
0–49 m

Inariyama tomb
Shiraishi Inariyama tomb
Sakitama tomb cluster

Tsubai Ōtsukayama tomb
Fujinoki tomb
Ōjin Mausoleum
Mozu tomb cluster
Nintoku Mausoleum
Chūsenji tomb cluster

Ikisan Chōshizuka tomb
Takehara tomb

Hokkaidō

Tōhoku

Sea of Japan

Chūbu

Kantō

Chūgoku

Inland Sea

Shikoku

Kinai

Kyūshū

Samita tomb
Ishibutai tomb
Takamatsuzuka tomb
Tsukamyōjin tomb

Iwase "thousand-mound"
tomb cluster

Ōzuka tomb
Yame tomb cluster
Iwatoyama tomb
Sekijin'yama tomb
Saitobaru tomb cluster
Eta Funayama tomb

Pacific Ocean

The largest tomb mound in Japan, said to be that of the emperor Nintoku (early 5th century). The central keyhole-shaped mound is 486 meters in length. Sakai, Ōsaka Prefecture.

construction, and isolation of the aristocratic burials in contrast to the humble graves of the masses—most of which are unknown. The tombs range in size from 15 meters (50 ft) in diameter to 32.3 hectares (79.8 acres) in area. A unique tomb shaped like an old-fashioned keyhole when viewed from above was used for the burials of the highest-ranking members of the ruling elite. Many of these keyhole-shaped tombs are assigned as imperial mausolea of specific emperors listed in the early historical chronicles, the KOJIKI and NIHON SHOKI, both compiled in the 8th century. Round tombs, present from the beginning of the period, served as burials for the lower-ranking aristocrats; from the early 6th century, they became family repositories clustered together in clan cemeteries on hillsides. Square tombs, also present from early on, became the preferred shape for the highest-ranking aristocratic burials at the end of the Kofun period.

The earliest tombs were built in the KINAI (Kyōto-Ōsaka-Nara) region, spreading from there through the Inland Sea to northern Kyūshū in the 4th century and into other regions of western and eastern Japan thereaf-

ter. The predecessor of the mounded tomb was probably the Yayoi-period mound burial; but Yayoi mound burials did not often contain lavish grave goods, whereas sumptuous funerary deposits always occur in Kofun-period tombs. Burial facilities changed through time, at first consisting of a wooden coffin buried directly in the tomb summit or in a pit lined with stone slabs and covered ceiling rocks. Earthenware cylinders were often embedded in the tomb surface surrounding the burial, and some supported earthenware sculptures of shields, sunshades, and houses—symbolic representations to protect and/or house the spirit of the deceased. These cylinders and sculptures are called HANIWA. Later, stone coffins were used, and, finally, in the Late Kofun period, stone chambers with horizontal entrance passages were constructed. These allowed reentry into the chamber, leading to their development as family repositories and also contributing to the development of ideas about *yomi*, the Japanese underworld.

The grave goods deposited in Kofun-period tombs chronicle the changing nature of leadership and status during the period of

state emergence. In the Early Kofun period, funerary goods were mainly ceremonial, with some iron weapons and armor, an indication that the deceased had considerable magico-religious powers as well as military might. The ceremonial goods consisted of bronze mirrors, necklaces of curved and cylindrical beads made from precious jade and jasper (see BEADS, ANCIENT), and other jasper and green-tuff ornaments including unusually shaped bracelets. Tomb contents from the Middle Kofun period—vast numbers of iron weapons and agricultural implements and imported gold ear ornaments, stoneware, and horse trappings in the continental style—attest to the rulers' limitless access to the resources of society and to new contacts with the Korean peninsula. The character of ritual objects changed dramatically from the carefully made jasper, jade, and green-tuff beads and bracelets to hoards of quickly roughed-out talc imitations of sheathed knives and daily objects. The significance of the knife imitations is still unknown. From the Late Kofun period on, in addition to per-

Koga Harue *Outdoor Cosmetics.* 1930. Oil on canvas. 161 × 129 cm. Kamakura Museum of Modern Art, Kanagawa Prefecture.

sonal ornaments and weapons worn by the deceased, SUE WARE and food were deposited to provide for the afterlife.

By the 6th century, tomb burial was not confined to the rulers per se but was afforded to all aristocrats; thus the sizes of the tombs were much smaller and the contents more religious than political in that they provided for the individual's existence in the next life. As Buddhism took hold, many elites invested their resources in temple building rather than tomb building for aggrandizement of their status. In combination with cremation, these trends led to the demise of tomb building by the end of the 7th century.

Formation of the State—It is known from Chinese chronicles that Japan housed many small polities called *kuni* at the end of the Yayoi period. Although one of these was named YAMATAI, it is still not known whether Yamatai and the early state of Yamato can be equated. Equally unclear is exactly when the Yamato polity became a state. Japanese historians speak of the YAMATO COURT existing in the 4th century and tend toward recognizing a unified state in the mid- to late 5th century. Archaeologists tend to equate the mounded tomb culture (stratified society) with state organization. The appearance of horse trappings in the 5th-century tombs led one school of Japanese scholars to postulate an invasion of "mounted warriors" from the Asian mainland, who subsequently formed the imperial Yamato line. This HORSE-RIDER THEORY of state formation has been adopted by many historians and woven into their accounts of Yamato development because it dovetails nicely with a break in the imperial genealogies as reconstructed from the chronicles. Archaeologists vehemently reject this hypothesis, saying that the material evidence on which the original thesis was based had been skewed to fit the theory.

In any case, it is clear both archaeologically and historically that the Japanese were in close contact with the continent from the late 4th century. Virtually all the grave goods in the early tombs, except for the stone orna-

kōgai Decorative hairpins such as the one pictured here came into wide use among women during the Edo period.

ments, have Korean or Chinese prototypes, and many appear to have been imported. Contemporary Chinese records of the southern Chinese courts make mention of the FIVE KINGS OF WA (Japan), who may be identifiable with some of the emperors known from the *Nihon shoki.* From 369, Yamato was in touch with Paekche on the Korean peninsula, and the court provided refuge for many skilled craftspeople and court functionaries during Paekche's retreat in the 5th century from invasions by Koguryŏ—another northern peninsular state. It is the influx of knowledge and skills, which demanded the reorganization of court administration into the *be* system, that contributed most significantly to the emergence of a strong centralized Yamato state in the 6th century.

Be is a word adopted from the Paekche language; however, in Paekche *be* were territorial administrative units, whereas in Yamato they were groups of people. The appointment of nobles to administer the *be* signaled the emergence of a service nobility, which gathered strength from its positions and formed the nuclei of emergent aristocratic clans, the UJI. It was once thought that *uji* were the primeval units of social organization, but now scholars see them as a late development and outgrowth of the *be* system. This system of administration was short-lived, being replaced in the mid-6th century by the Chinese administrative model.

Urbanization—The center of the Yamato state was the Kinai area, especially the Nara Basin in the old province of Yamato. Imperial tombs and palaces, as identified in the chronicles, cluster mainly in the Nara Basin and the Ōsaka Plain. The location of the imperial residence changed with each new emperor, giving rise to what is known as the "shifting palace system." Actual palace buildings are unknown archaeologically before the 6th century, but the locations mentioned for earlier palaces coincide with areas of concentrated craft production and ritual remains. These provide the earliest evidence of urban conglomerates in the Nara Basin.

In the 6th century, elite domestic architecture was heavily influenced by Buddhist temple construction—especially in the use of roof tiles and stone foundations. In the Asuka region of southern Nara, where most of the earliest temples were built, early imperial palaces such as the Itabuki Palace of Empress Kōgyoku (see SAIMEI, EMPRESS) have been excavated. These have stone-lined drainage ditches and foundation stones upon which a wooden building was erected. This new style of architecture differed from the traditional thatched pit house in having load-bearing pillars integrated into a wooden-board wall structure.

In the mid-7th century, with the Taika Reform initiating the sinicization of the administrative system, the Chinese gridded city plan was adopted. The first capital built on this model was FUJIWARAKYŌ, north of Asuka in the southern Nara Basin. In 710 the capital was moved to HEIJŌKYŌ in the northern Nara Basin, marking the end of the Kofun period as here defined and leading into the fully historic NARA PERIOD (710–794). Soon after the removal the court chronicles still extant today were compiled: the *Kojiki* in 712 and the *Nihon shoki* in 720. These documents were politically aimed at legitimizing the imperial and aristocratic families by recounting their genealogies and their forebears' roles in the development of the

Yamato state. However, because they describe events for much of the Kofun period in mythological and semilegendary terms, and because the chronology is not reliable before 500, they must be used with great care in analysis of this period.

Koga   古河[市]

City in western Ibaraki Prefecture, central Honshū. The base of members of the Ashikaga family (the so-called KOGA KUBŌ) who rebelled against the Muromachi shogunate in the mid-1400s, it developed during the Edo period (1600–1868) as a post-station town. Today Koga is mainly a commercial city. Of interest are the Koga Castle remains. Pop: 58,231.

Koga   古賀[町]

Town on the Genkai Sea in northern Fukuoka Prefecture, Kyūshū. Many *kofun* (tomb mounds) and other historical sites are located here. Today it is a commuter suburb of the city of Fukuoka. Pop: 45,725.

Koga Harue   古賀春江

(1895–1933). Avant-garde Western-style painter. Real name Koga Yoshio. Born in Fukuoka Prefecture; studied Western painting with the Taiheiyō Gakai artists' group. He won the Nikakai Prize in 1922. His work was influenced by many styles of art, such as cubism, expressionism, Paul Klee's manner of dreamlike fantasy, and surrealism.

kōgai   笄

Long hairpins used for traditional Japanese HAIRSTYLES. Originally *kōgai* were used by both men and women for parting and styling the hair, as well as for scratching the scalp. During the Edo period (1600–1868), they also functioned as women's hair ornaments. *Kōgai* were made of wood, bamboo, metal, glass, tortoiseshell, or the shinbones of cranes and were sometimes decorated with gold and silver lacquerwork. See also KANZASHI.

kogaisha → subsidiary companies

Koga Issaku   古賀逸策

(1899–1982). Electrical engineer. Inventor of the high-performance quartz crystal resonator (1932). Born in Saga Prefecture, he graduated from Tōkyō University in 1923. He devised a new cutting method making it possible to produce crystals with excellent frequency-stability under variations in temperature, improving the performance of communications equipment. He became a professor at Tōkyō University in 1944 and dean of engineering in 1958. He received the Order of Culture in 1963.

Kogaku   古学

(Ancient Learning). Revival movement in Japanese Confucianism advocating a return to the works of ancient Chinese Confucian sages in order to understand their content correctly without resorting to the interpretations of later scholars. YAMAGA SOKŌ (1622–85), ITŌ JINSAI (1627–1705), and OGYŪ SORAI (1666–1728) spearheaded the movement, which emerged in the mid-Edo period (1600–1868). It represented no unified philosophical school but rather a mature phase in Japanese understanding of the Confucian tradition.

Earlier Japanese scholars had attempted to interpret the teachings of such Neo-Confucianists as Zhu Xi (Chu Hsi) and Wang Yangming within a Japanese context (see

SHUSHIGAKU; YŌMEIGAKU). It became apparent to some, however, that the teachings that had evolved in Chinese society were not readily adaptable to Japan. Rejecting the interpretations of Zhu Xi and Wang Yang-ming, the Kogaku movement instead promoted direct knowledge of the original teachings of the Confucian sages (see FOUR BOOKS AND FIVE CLASSICS).

Sokō and Jinsai—The first work in which Ancient Learning was clearly presented was Yamaga Sokō's SEIKYŌ YŌROKU (1665, Essentials of the Sacred Teachings). To Sokō, the Zhu Xi school, which made "principle" (Ch: *li;* J: *ri*) the metaphysical basis of all things, idealized an unacceptably static, otherworldly enlightenment. For him, the universe was an entity pulsing with vitality but governed by certain inevitable principles (*jōri*). The sages, comprehending these principles, had presented them in the form of right conduct (*reigi*), and it was mastery of these rules that should be the aim of learning. A "sincere" or "truthful" life (see MAKOTO) was one that adhered to the principles of right conduct, which permitted those who followed them to make contact with what was vital and dynamic in their spirits. A scholar of military affairs, Sokō detailed the proper behavior of a warrior (see BUSHIDŌ), yet his criticism of Zhu Xi aroused the suspicion of the Tokugawa shogunate, which supported the Zhu Xi school.

Quite independently of Sokō, Itō Jinsai, whose position was based on a philological study of the Four Books, considered the *Analects* and *Mencius* to be of central importance and rejected Zhu Xi's teaching of the Four Books. Jinsai emphasized the dynamism of human relations built upon mutual love and friendship. This led him to propose that the true way of life for man, as taught by the sages, must be lived within these bounds of friendship and love. He used the term MICHI (Way) to describe such a life. For Jinsai, *michi* was based upon *jin* (benevolence, charity). In this he referred not only to the emotional aspect of love but to the desire to do good for others. The proper basis for an ethical code was *chūshin* (fidelity), a supreme form of sincerity, free of guile or deceit; when realized in one's life, *jin* followed naturally. Both Confucius and Mencius had emphasized *chūshin*, Jinsai contended, while their later interpreters omitted the concept.

Ogyū Sorai—A generation after Sokō and Jinsai, the scholar Ogyū Sorai rejected all philosophical works after Confucius and Mencius as consisting of subjective, factional arguments. The only reliable works were the traditional Six Classics, that is, the Five Classics and the *Zhou li* (*Chou li;* Rituals of Chou); to understand them one had to study classical rhetoric. Sorai's emphasis on knowledge of rhetoric led his theories to be known as the School of Ancient Rhetoric (KOBUNJIGAKU).

According to Sorai, the true essence of the universe was known only to the ancient sages, who had superhuman powers, and to protect and govern mankind they had codified their understanding and established the Way by which man should live. This Way was divided into rites (*rei*) and music (*gaku*): observation of rites preserved the social order, while music or poetry inspired the heart. Zhu Xi's rigid conception of *ri* as the basis for human conduct ignored the emotions. Likewise, Sorai rejected the focus of both Zhu Xi and Wang Yangming upon training the inner self to find the virtuous

essence within. While affirming the usefulness of developing one's innate abilities and traits by referring to the sages' teachings, Sorai also recognized the emotional release needed by man and provided by music. Official institutions, he held, would have to guide the citizenry toward morality rather than depend upon each individual's attempts at self-improvement. Moreover, the Zhu Xi school taught that society had arisen in accordance with an immutable, heaven-bestowed *ri*, but Sorai countered that social institutions erected by humans were not a direct realization of heaven's principle and certainly were not eternal. Rejecting Zhu Xi's conception of *ri* strengthened the position Sorai inherited from Sokō and Jinsai and effected a significant retreat from the idea of *ri* as the universal unchangeable.

The teachings of Sorai were very popular for a while, although his decreased emphasis on individual morality drew criticism. The scholarship of Sorai and his predecessors, however, made it impossible to continue viewing the Neo-Confucianists as absolute authorities and gave rise to an eclectic approach that drew from different interpretations of the classics to find what best suited Japanese society. The argument that only direct knowledge of the original classics could bring about awareness of truth largely died out with the demise of Sorai's philosophical school. Sorai's approach, however, did influence a later scholar, MOTOORI NORINAGA (1730–1801), who was a leader in the KOKUGAKU (National Learning) movement, which sought to define the essence of Japanese thought by studying native classics.

Koga kubō   古河公方

("ruler at Koga"). Term applied to Ashikaga Shigeuji (1434–97) and four of his descendants while they held an independent power base at Koga in Shimōsa Province (now part of Ibaraki Prefecture) in the years 1455–1583. Shigeuji's father, Mochiuji (1398–1439), had defied the Ashikaga shogunate and had been defeated by the shogunal deputy UESUGI NORIZANE in the incident known as the Eikyō Rebellion. In 1455 Shigeuji killed Uesugi's son Noritada (1433–55) in revenge. Fleeing the armies sent against him by the Uesugi and the shogunate, Shigeuji made his stand at Koga and called himself Koga *kubō*. Ashikaga Masatomo (1435–91), younger brother of the shōgun, meanwhile established a base at Horikoshi on the Izu Peninsula and styled himself HORIKOSHI KUBŌ. Shigeuji eventually made peace with the Uesugi in 1478 and with the shogunate in 1482; his heirs held the Koga area until 1583.

Koga Masao   古賀政男

(1904–78). Composer of popular Japanese music, particularly of the genre called *kayōkyoku*. Born in Fukuoka Prefecture, he attended Meiji University. His sentimental melodies, such as *Kage o shitaite* (1931, Yearning for the Shadow) and *Sake wa namida ka tameiki ka* (1931, Is Wine a Tear or a Sigh?), and *Kanashii sake* (1966, Melancholy Wine) are extremely popular. During his life he published some 5,000 songs. From 1964 until his death he was chairman of the Japanese Society of Rights of Authors, Composers, and Publishers. In 1978 he received the People's Honor Award (Kokumin Eiyo Shō) posthumously.

Koganei   小金井[市]

City in central Tōkyō Prefecture. A residential suburb of Tōkyō. Tōkyō Gakugei Uni-

versity, Tōkyō University of Agriculture and Technology, and Hōsei University are located here. Pop: 105,899.

Koganei Yoshikiyo   小金井良精

(1859–1944). Anatomist; anthropologist; one of the initiators in Japan of the study of physical anthropology. Born in what is now Niigata Prefecture, Koganei graduated from Tōkyō University School of Medicine in 1880. After five years in Germany studying anatomy and histology, he became a lecturer on anatomy at Tōkyō University in 1885 and was appointed to a professorship the following year. Koganei studied the anatomy and bone structure of the AINU and published his findings in *Ainu zoku no kenkyū* (1904–05), where he claimed that the paleolithic people of Japan were Ainu.

koganemushi → gold beetle

kōgi   公儀

("authorities"; "government"; "public" as opposed to "private"). Term widely used from the 7th century through the Edo period (1600–1868). It referred primarily to public authorities, such as the imperial court, the shogunate, or the *daimyō*, and secondarily to the public or society at large. The character for *kō* is also read *ōyake*, meaning a large residence. The character for *gi* means "rule," "affair," or "case."

From the 7th century until the Kamakura period (1185–1333) *kōgi* referred to the emperor or the imperial court. With the decline of imperial authority, it came to mean the shōgun (or shogunate) or the daimyō (i.e., whoever held political power). *Kōgi* in the sense of public place or public opinion dates from the Muromachi period (1333–1568), when it referred to the collective power of regional lords (*ryōshu*) or to a consensus among urban groups.

Kogidō   古義堂

Also known as the Horikawa Gakkō. A private school for commoners founded in 1662 in the Higashi Horikawa district of Kyōto by the Confucian scholar ITŌ JINSAI. Its teaching was centered on the exposition of such works as the Confucian *Analects, Mencius,* and the *Doctrine of the Mean (Zhong yong* or *Chung yung*). Jinsai's ideas on moral education greatly influenced the academic world of the day. His heirs continued the Kogidō after his death until the early Meiji period (1868–1912).

kōgi seitai ron   公議政体論

(argument for government by public discussion). Political argument of the 1860s calling for the adoption of elements of the Western parliamentary system into the Tokugawa shogunate (1603–1867); propounded by pro-Tokugawa factions who hoped to restore the failing regime. MATSUDAIRA YOSHINAGA, an important *daimyō*, felt that a Western-style parliamentary system, with an upper house of daimyō and a lower house of *samurai* and commoners, would create a new sense of national unity. In 1867 another daimyō, YAMANOUCHI TOYOSHIGE, urged the shōgun TOKUGAWA YOSHINOBU to return his political mandate to the emperor and to support a bicameral parliamentary system. Although those ideas never materialized, they influenced political reform movements after the Meiji Restoration of 1868.

kogitte → commercial paper

Koga Masao This prolific composer of popular sentimental tunes published some 5,000 songs during his lifetime.

Koganei Yoshikiyo This German-trained anatomist played a key role in establishing physical anthropology as an academic discipline in Japan.

Koide Narashige *The "N" Family*. 1919. Oil on canvas. 79 × 91 cm. Ōhara Museum of Art, Okayama Prefecture.

kōgō　皇后

Nonreigning empress (a reigning empress being called *tennō*). The title *kōgō* was reserved for the principal consort of an emperor, that is, the one who gave birth to the heir apparent. According to the RITSURYŌ SYSTEM, only women of imperial blood were eligible for that honor, but in 729 FUJIWARA NO FUHITO's daughter became *kōgō* to Emperor SHŌMU (see KŌMYŌ, EMPRESS) and the first of many Fujiwara empresses. In 1000 Emperor ICHIJŌ initiated the practice of having two empresses at once—one called *kōgō*, the other CHŪGŪ. In forms of address, honorific terms, and general deference, the *kōgō* was equal to the sovereign. The title *kōgō* was sometimes honorary—for example, as conferred on the wife of a deceased crown prince or on a woman (usually an imperial princess) who had given birth to an heir apparent. The title is still in use today; under the IMPERIAL HOUSEHOLD LAW, the wife of the crown prince automatically assumes it on the death of the emperor.

kōgoishi　神籠石

Stone fortifications of the 6th century ringing the mountain summits in northern Kyūshū and the Inland Sea's western coast; probably built in anticipation of invasions from Korea. The best examples are in Fukuoka Prefecture. Called *kōgoishi* ("divine protection stones") by archaeologist TSUBOI SHŌGORŌ, who thought they were religious sanctuaries, they are distinguished from mountain fortifications such as ITOJŌ, Ōnojō, and Kiijō (all outposts of DAZAIFU) by walls of cut stone as much as 3 kilometers (1.9 mi) in length.

Kōgon, Emperor　光厳天皇

(1313–64; Kōgon Tennō). The first sovereign (*tennō*) of the Northern Court; reigned 1331–33. Eldest son of retired emperor Go-Fushimi (1288–1336; r 1298–1301). As a member of the Jimyōin line of the imperial family, Kōgon became crown prince under Emperor GO-DAIGO of the Daikakuji line in accordance with the KAMAKURA SHOGUNATE's policy of alternating the two lines on the throne. He became emperor in 1331, after Go-Daigo fled from the palace (see GENKŌ INCIDENT). Kōgon was forced to abdicate, however, when Go-Daigo later succeeded in restoring direct imperial rule (see KEMMU RESTORATION). Go-Daigo's rule came to a quick end in 1336, when ASHIKAGA TAKAUJI established the Muromachi shogunate, placing Emperor Kōmyō (1322–80; r 1336–48),

Kōgon's brother, on the throne. Go-Daigo, in turn, set up a separate Southern Court in Yoshino (see NORTHERN AND SOUTHERN COURTS). Kōgon, as retired emperor, headed the cloister government of the Northern Court for 15 years. He is known as a co-compiler of the poetry anthology *Fūga wakashū* (1346).

Kōgonen-jaku　庚午年籍

(Register of the Kōgo Year). A set of household registers compiled in the year corresponding to 670, designated *kōgo* in the sexagenary cycle. Although it is no longer extant, several references to it appear in such historical sources as the *Shoku nihongi* (797) and the SHINSEN SHŌJIROKU (815). Registers had been compiled every six years since the time of the TAIKA REFORM (645), but the Kōgonen-jaku is believed to have been the first of nationwide scope. While registers were normally destroyed after 30 years, the Kōgonen-jaku remained in use until the mid-Heian period (794–1185) to verify a family's social pedigree.

Kogosho Kaigi　小御所会議

(Kogosho Conference). The first meeting of the leaders of the new Meiji government, held in the Kogosho, part of the Imperial Palace in Kyōto, on 3 January 1868, the day of the coup d'état that restored imperial rule (ŌSEI FUKKO). A number of court nobles, major *daimyō*, and other political activists met in the presence of Emperor Meiji to decide the future status of the Tokugawa shōgun. A compromise faction (led by YAMANOUCHI TOYOSHIGE, GOTŌ SHŌJIRŌ, and MATSUDAIRA YOSHINAGA) urged that the shōgun, TOKUGAWA YOSHINOBU, should be included in the new government and tried to arrange for him to participate in the meeting. However, others (including IWAKURA TOMOMI and ŌKUBO TOSHIMICHI) who had long plotted the overthrow of the shogunate refused. They succeeded in persuading the compromise faction that the shōgun must be ordered to resign all offices, surrender his domains to the emperor, and apologize for his lack of leadership. This intransigence by the shogunate's opponents led to the BOSHIN CIVIL WAR.

Kogo shūi　古語拾遺

Historical work compiled in 807 by Imbe no Hironari. It is a collection of myths and legends originating before the reign of the legendary emperor JIMMU. Transmitted orally through the descendants of the IMBE FAMILY, it contains material not found in the KOJIKI and NIHON SHOKI, the oldest extant histories of Japan, and records the Imbe family's achievements.

Koguryŏ　高句麗

(J: Kōkuri). One of Korea's three ancient kingdoms (see KOREAN THREE KINGDOMS PERIOD). Formed by tribes in southern Manchuria between 37 BC and 19 BC, Koguryŏ dominated northern Korea from AD 313 until overwhelmed by the southeastern Korean kingdom of SILLA and Tang (T'ang) Chinese forces in 668. As a result, Japan, which had earlier sent a naval force to help PAEKCHE against Silla and China (see HAKUSUKINOE, BATTLE OF), lost its influence on the Korean peninsula.

Kōgyō iken　興業意見

(Opinions on Promoting Industry). Record of industrial production of the first 17 years of the Meiji period (1868–1912); completed in 1884. Maeda Masana (1850–1921) led the

compilation of this 30-volume work. The *Kōgyō iken* is invaluable for its information on economic conditions of the early Meiji period.

Kōgyoku, Empress → Saimei, Empress

Kōhoku New Town　港北ニュータウン

(Kōhoku Nyū Taun). Planned residential community in the city of Yokohama, Kanagawa Prefecture, central Honshū. The town has been under development since 1965 by the Yokohama city government and the national government's Housing and Urban Development Corporation. Area: 23.5 sq km (9.1 sq mi). Projected pop: 300,000.

Koichijō In　小一条院

(994–1051). Alternative name of Prince Atsuakira, eldest son of Emperor SANJŌ (r 1011–16) and Fujiwara no Jōshi; briefly heir apparent to the throne. In 1016 Emperor Sanjō was succeeded by Emperor GO-ICHIJŌ (r 1016–36), son of the previous emperor ICHIJŌ (r 986–1011) and Fujiwara no Shōshi (JŌTŌ MON'IN), daughter of the regent (*sesshō*) FUJIWARA NO MICHINAGA; it was at this time that Atsuakira was named heir apparent. However, Fujiwara no Shōshi had borne Emperor Ichijō another son, later Emperor Go-Suzaku (1009–45; r 1036–45), whom Michinaga wished to make heir apparent. Atsuakira was pressured into giving up his position as heir to the throne in 1017, and retired to the palace Koichijō In, from which he took his name.

Koide Narashige　小出楢重

(1887–1931). Western-style painter; born in Ōsaka. He studied both Japanese-style (NIHONGA) and Western-style (YŌGA) painting at the Tōkyō Bijutsu Gakkō (now Tōkyō University of Fine Arts and Music). At the 1919 exhibit of the Nikakai (an artists' association) he received the Chogyū Prize, and in 1920 he was awarded the Nikakai Prize. In 1924 with other painters in the Kyōto-Ōsaka area, he founded the Shinanobashi Yōga Kenkyūjo (Shinanobashi Western-style Painting Study Institute) in Ōsaka. Koide is best known for his nudes.

Koikawa Harumachi　恋川春町

(1744–89). Author and illustrator of KIBYŌSHI. *Samurai* of a small domain in Suruga Province (now part of Shizuoka Prefecture). Real name Kurahashi Kaku. He was stationed in Edo (now Tōkyō) and studied *ukiyo-e* painting. He is credited with being the originator of *kibyōshi* (small illustrated books of prose fiction bound in yellow covers). He wrote 30 *kibyōshi*, but his *Ōmugaeshi bumbu no futamichi* (1789), a great popular success, was censured by the government as a satire on the KANSEI REFORMS. He also wrote KYŌKA poetry under the pen name of Saka no Ue no Furachi and popular fiction in the SHAREBON genre, of which his *Mudaiki* (1779) is the most notable.

kōiki shichōson ken　広域市町村圏

(wide area municipal districts). Local administrative districts established since 1969 by the MINISTRY OF HOME AFFAIRS for the integrated administration of large regions. With the consent of the localities concerned and with some central government subsidy, they provide such services as road construction, waterworks, garbage disposal, and fire fighting. The standard *kōiki shichōson ken* was meant to have jurisdiction over a central city and neighboring towns and villages with a total population of 100,000. In 1990 the 336 designated districts comprised 2,944 cities, towns, and villages.

koinobori 鯉幟

(carp streamers). Banners in the form of carp that are flown outside houses on 5 May, CHILDREN'S DAY, to celebrate male children and as an expression of hope for their health and prosperity. This custom originated during the middle of the Edo period (1600–1868). Because of an ancient Chinese legend about a carp that swam upstream and became a dragon, carp had long been a symbol of success in Japan. At first the banners were small and made of paper. Today the sizes and the materials used to make carp streamers vary, with smaller ones being more common in cities. The practice is still alive in Japan today; parents look forward to the flying of streamers on a son's first Children's Day especially eagerly.

Koishikawa Botanic Garden
小石川植物園

(Koishikawa Shokubutsuen). Botanic garden located in Bunkyō Ward, Tōkyō, with an adjunct in the city of Nikkō, Tochigi Prefecture. The full name is Botanical Gardens, Faculty of Science, Tōkyō University. The garden is maintained for research purposes and is open to the public. It was originally established as an herb garden under the Tokugawa shogunate in 1684. After the Meiji restoration in 1868, it was placed under the control of the Tōkyō city government. In 1877 control was transferred to Tōkyō University. Since then it has contributed greatly to research undertaken by the biology department of Tōkyō University.

Koishikawa Yōjōsho 小石川養生所

Charitable hospital in Edo (now Tōkyō) established by the Tokugawa shogunate in 1722 at the recommendation of a local physician, Ogawa Shōsen (1672–1760). Placed under the jurisdiction of the Edo city commissioners (Edo *machi bugyō*), it had accommodations for 40 (later 170) patients. Only those who had been certified as having no means of support were admitted. In 1868 the Koishikawa Yōjōsho was made part of the government-sponsored medical school (IGAKUSHO) and later became the medical school of Tōkyō University.

Koishiwara ware 小石原焼

(*koishiwara-yaki*). Sometimes referred to as Koishibara ware (*koishibara-yaki*). Pottery made in and around Sarayama, in the village of Koishiwara, Fukuoka Prefecture. It is believed to have first been made in 1682. Pottery was produced on a small scale during the 18th and 19th centuries and consisted almost entirely of everyday wares. Glazes most commonly used were translucent honey (*ame*) and transparent (*tōmei*) over a white slip, with drips or splashes of green, white, or yellow overglazing (*uchigake* and *nagashigake*). Production virtually ceased with the depression of the 1930s and was only resuscitated after the war by the efforts of YANAGI MUNEYOSHI, leader of the folk craft (*mingei*) movement. In 1952–53 potters mechanized clay preparation techniques, a decision that led to considerable expansion and social change, including the breakup of the cooperative kilns. There are now almost 40 households independently firing kilns in Koishiwara.

Koiso Kuniaki 小磯国昭

(1880–1950). Army general; prime minister (1944–45). Born in Tochigi Prefecture; graduate of the Army War College. He entered the General Staff Office in 1913 and was involved in plans to use the MANCHURIAN-MONGOLIAN INDEPENDENCE MOVEMENT to Japan's advantage. He later played a leading role in the MARCH INCIDENT of 1931, in which young army officers attempted to establish a military cabinet. Koiso served as minister of colonial affairs (1939–40) and, after World War II began, as governor-general of Korea. He became prime minister after the fall of TŌJŌ HIDEKI in July 1944. Following the fall of Okinawa he resigned. Sentenced to life imprisonment as a class-A war criminal (see WAR CRIMES TRIALS), he died in prison.

Koiso Ryōhei 小磯良平

(1903–88). Western-style painter known for his paintings of women and groups done in a style that combines precise realism with Western classicism. Born in Hyōgo Prefecture, Koiso graduated from the Tōkyō Bijutsu Gakkō (now Tōkyō University of Fine Arts and Music). His painting *Kyōdai* (Brother and Sister) was selected for exhibition at the Teiten (Exhibition of the Imperial Fine Arts Academy) in 1925. He studied in France from 1928 to 1930 and participated in the forming of the Shin Seisakuha Kyōkai (New Creative Association) in 1936. He taught at the Tōkyō University of Fine Arts and Music from 1950, becoming professor emeritus there in 1971. He became a member of the Japan Art Academy in 1982 and received the Order of Culture in 1983.

Koito Gentarō 小絲源太郎

(1887–1978). Western-style painter. Born in Tōkyō, Koito studied at Tōkyō Bijutsu Gakkō (now Tōkyō University of Fine Arts and Music). He first showed at the BUNTEN (Ministry of Education Fine Arts Exhibition) in 1910. In 1953 his painting *Shunsetsu* (Spring Snow) won the Japan Art Academy Prize. He was a professor at both Tōkyō University of Fine Arts and Music and Kanazawa College of Art. In his early work he pursued a minutely detailed realism; in later years he turned to landscapes rendered in brilliant colors. He received the Order of Culture in 1965.

Koito Mfg Co, Ltd [㈱]小糸製作所

(Koito Seisakusho). Company specializing in the manufacture, development, and sale of lighting equipment for cars and airplanes. Incorporated in 1936. The company has a consolidated subsidiary producing traffic signals and sanitary equipment and is also expanding into the production of aircraft parts. In 1990 Koito management was involved in a public controversy with the American investor T. Boone Pickens, who purchased 26 percent of the company's stock and demanded more say for stockholders in the running of the company. Sales for the fiscal year ending March 1991 totaled ¥143.6 billion (US $1.0 billion). Capitalization in the same year stood at ¥14.1 billion (US $102.8 million). Headquarters are in Tōkyō.

Koizumi Chikashi 古泉千樫

(1886–1927). TANKA poet. Real name Koizumi Ikutarō. Born in Chiba Prefecture. While teaching primary school, he began to write *tanka*. First recognized by ITŌ SACHIO, he was active as a member of the ARARAGI group (founded in 1908), which played a signifi-

cant role in revitalizing traditional *tanka* poetry. His poetry collections include *Kawa no hotori* (1925) and *Okujō no tsuchi* (1928).

Koizumi Shinzō 小泉信三

(1888–1966). Economist. Born in Tōkyō, he graduated from Keiō Gijuku (now Keiō University) in 1910. His father served as president of Keiō Gijuku and manager of Yokohama Specie Bank (now Bank of Tōkyō, Ltd). Koizumi studied economics while teaching at Keiō Gijuku. After studying in Europe from 1912 to 1916, he became professor at Keiō and served as the university's president from 1933 to 1947. Koizumi was educational adviser to Crown Prince (now Emperor) Akihito after World War II. A specialist in economic history and social thought, he was a longtime critic of Marxism. He also was a specialist in the studies of FUKUZAWA YUKICHI. Koizumi's works include *Marukusu shigo gojūnen* (1933, Fifty Years after the Death of Marx) and *Rikādo kenkyū* (1934, A Study of Ricardo).

Koizumi Yakumo→Hearn, Lafcadio

Kojidan 古事談

(Stories about the Past). Six-volume collection of historical anecdotes, mostly didactic in tone, believed to have been compiled about 1212–15 by Minamoto no Akikane (1160–1215). *Kojidan* directly influenced such later works as UJI SHŪI MONOGATARI and JIKKUNSHŌ.

Kojiki 古事記

(Record of Ancient Matters; tr *Kojiki*, 1969). Japan's oldest extant chronicle, recording events from the mythical age of the gods up to the time of Empress SUIKO (r 593–628). The compiler, Ō NO YASUMARO, states in the preface that it was presented to the reigning empress, Gemmei (661–722; r 707–715), on 9 March 712.

The Three Sections——The first section, known as "Jindai no maki" (Book on the Age of the Gods), records the creation of heaven and earth as well as myths concerning the founding of Japan. It describes the descent from heaven of NINIGI NO MIKOTO, grandson of AMATERASU ŌMIKAMI, progenitor of the imperial line, to the mountain TAKACHIHONOMINE in Kyūshū (see MYTHOLOGY). The second section covers the period from Emperor JIMMU's reign through the reign of Emperor ŌJIN at the beginning of the 5th century. The third section records events from the reign of Emperor NINTOKU until the rule of Suiko in the early 7th century. Beginning with the passage in the third section dealing with Emperor Kensō (late 5th century), almost all story elements disappear and the narrative consists mainly of records on imperial succession and the imperial family. This contrasts sharply

with the NIHON SHOKI (720), in which the information beginning with the reign of Emperor Yūryaku in the late 5th century becomes increasingly detailed. The *Kojiki*, which places emphasis on myths, legends, and historical and pseudohistorical narratives, may thus be called *furukotobumi*, i.e., a literary work dealing with matters in ancient times.

The *Kojiki* is transcribed in Chinese characters (*kanji*) because the Japanese had yet to develop their own phonetic script. The main text, in prose, is written in HENTAI KAMBUN, a form of literary Japanese that borrows heavily from classical Chinese, while the verse sequences make phonetic use of Chinese characters. The main text includes glosses indicating accent patterns, the pronunciations of characters in Japanese and Chinese, and definitions of terms. Unlike the *Nihon shoki*, the *Kojiki* does not present variant or supplementary versions of a story.

History—According to Ō no Yasumaro's preface, sometime during the late 7th century Emperor TEMMU issued a decree stating that the TEIKI (the genealogical record of the imperial family) and the KYŪJI (a collection of myths, legends, and songs connected with the forebears of the imperial and other leading families) had ceased to be accurate and would have to be corrected. The compilation of accurate historical records would "clarify the basis of the state and the foundations for the moral teachings of the emperors." Temmu ordered HIEDA NO ARE to memorize the contents of the *Teiki* and *Kyūji*. On 3 November 711 Empress Gemmei ordered Ō no Yasumaro to transcribe the information memorized by Are, and the completed records were presented to the court the following year.

The oldest surviving manuscript of the *Kojiki* is a scroll copied in the years 1371–72. It is known as the Shimpukuji-bon after the temple Shimpukuji in Nagoya where it is stored. The postscript to this edition notes that copies from the Kamakura period (1185–1333) existed at the time, but that no copies from the Nara (710–794) or Heian (794–1185) periods had been found. Moreover, in other historical records from the Nara period there is no mention of the *Kojiki*. In the Edo period (1600–1868) speculation arose that the *Kojiki* was a forgery from a later age. The 8th-century anthology MAN'YŌSHŪ, however, includes quotations from the work, and the *Shōhei no shiki* (936, Private Record of the Shōhei Era) describes the *Kojiki* as Japan's oldest historical work.

Scholarly research on the *Kojiki*, however, began only in the Edo period, with MOTOORI NORINAGA's *Kojiki den* being the most famous and influential study. Scholars of the KOKUGAKU school of historical studies, such as Motoori, regarded the *Kojiki* as a "classic among classics." Most scholars accept TSUDA SŌKICHI's conclusion that these oral traditions were first written down in the mid-6th century. In addition to being a history, the *Kojiki* is also one of the classics of Japanese literature, valuable for an understanding of the mythology, traditions, religious beliefs, and arts of Japan.

Kōjima 幸島

Island approximately 300 m (980 ft) off the southern coast of Miyazaki Prefecture, southeastern Kyūshū. The island is covered with subtropical vegetation and inhabited by wild monkeys (*Maccaca fuscata*). The behavior of these monkeys, who wash their food and are able to swim, has been studied by Kyōto University anthropologists since 1947. Area: 0.4 sq km (0.2 sq mi).

Kojima Bay 児島湾

(Kojima Wan). Inlet of the Inland Sea south of the city of Okayama, southern Okayama Prefecture, western Honshū. Much of the bay's original area was converted to farmland by reclamation projects beginning in the Edo period (1600–1868), and a manmade lake was constructed for irrigation purposes. The only part of the original bay remaining is the part that is adjacent to the Inland Sea.

Kojima Iken 児島惟謙

(1837–1908). Jurist. Also known as Kojima Korekata. Born in what is now Ehime Prefecture. He joined the Ministry of Justice in 1871 and became chief justice of the Great Court of Cassation (Daishin'in) in 1891. He served as a member of the House of Peers (1894) and House of Representatives (1898). As chief justice of the Great Court of Cassation, he heard evidence relating to the ŌTSU INCIDENT (1891), in which the crown prince of Russia (later Tsar Nicholas II), then visiting Japan, was wounded by an escort policeman named Tsuda Sanzō (1854–91) at Ōtsu. Though the government put pressure on the court to sentence Tsuda to death, Kojima resisted and imposed only a life sentence. His decision was significant in demonstrating both at home and abroad the independence of the Japanese judiciary.

Kojima Nobuo 小島信夫

(1915–). Author. Born in Gifu Prefecture; graduate of Tōkyō University; professor of English at Meiji University. In 1954 his "Amerikan Sukūru" (tr "The American School," 1977), which humorously described the helpless lot of postwar Japanese intellectuals, won the Akutagawa Prize. He later turned to serious criticism of the disintegration of society and the family in postwar Japan, as in *Hōyō kazoku* (1965), which received the Tanizaki Jun'ichirō Prize in 1965. Other works include *Watakushi no sakka hyōden* (1972–75), a three-volume collection of critical biographies of modern writers.

Kojima Takanori 児島高徳

(fl 1330s). Legendary warrior of the Nambokuchō period (NORTHERN AND SOUTHERN COURTS period; 1337–92). During the GENKŌ INCIDENT of 1331 he raised an army in support of Emperor GO-DAIGO, who hoped to overthrow the Kamakura shogunate and restore direct imperial rule. He remained loyal to Go-Daigo even after the failure of the emperor's short-lived KEMMU RESTORATION (1333–36). From the Meiji period (1868–1912) through the end of World War II, references to Takanori often appeared in elementary-school textbooks and songs, and his story was used by the government to promote patriotism.

kōjin 荒神

Category of folk deities. *Kōjin* are said to cast evil spells on people unless properly revered; they fall into the category of malevolent deities (*aramitama*) that are juxtaposed in the Shintō tradition against beneficent deities (*nigimitama*). *Kōjin* include: (1) A god of the kitchen fire who dislikes uncleanliness. In northeastern Japan it is thought to bring vigor to newborn babies on whose foreheads soot from the kitchen fire has been rubbed. Also believed to prevent fires, it has been adopted into Buddhism as the three-headed, six-armed god *sampō kōjin*, who protects the faithful. (2) Gods worshiped in southwestern Japan, known as *jikōjin* (earth *kōjin*), that are treated as protectors of houses, family gods, or community gods. (3) A god widely worshiped as a guardian deity of horses and cattle.

Kōjindani site 荒神谷遺跡

(Kōjindani *iseki*). Archaeological site of the YAYOI PERIOD (ca 300 BC–ca AD 300); located in the town of Hikawa, Shimane Prefecture. In 1984, 358 bronze swords dating from the 1st to 2nd centuries were discovered there as a group. The bronze swords are medium-narrow ones, about 50 centimeters (20 in) in length. This was the first discovery of such a large number of buried swords. In 1985 a group of 6 DŌTAKU (bronze bells), all approximately 20 centimeters (8 in) high, and 16 medium-breadth bronze spearheads, ranging from 64 to 84 centimeters (25.2 to 33.1 in) in length, were discovered buried together at the same site. This was the first time that objects representing both of the two great cultural spheres of Japan's bronze age—bronze spearheads representing northern Kyūshū and *dōtaku* representing the capital provinces (the present-day Kyōto-Ōsaka-Nara area)—had been discovered in the same place, leading to the theory that these two great cultural spheres stood in opposition to each other to be reexamined.

Kojinteki na taiken 個人的な体験

(tr *A Personal Matter*, 1968). Novel by ŌE KENZABURŌ (b 1935) published in 1964. It depicts the struggle of a young father forced to accept responsibility for the welfare of a son born with brain damage. Based on the author's experience with his eldest son, who was born with a congenital abnormality of the skull, the novel transcends conventional human interest to address forcefully the existential anguish of a person faced with overwhelming responsibilities. *Kojinteki na taiken* is representative of Ōe's works of the 1960s in that it depicts suffering yet ultimately manages to affirm life.

Koji ruien 古事類苑

Government-sponsored encyclopedia of premodern Japan. Initially undertaken by the Ministry of Education at the instigation of NISHIMURA SHIGEKI, the project was ultimately entrusted to the Bureau of Shintō Shrines (Jingū Shichō) and published in 350 volumes from 1896 to 1913. Information concerning Japan is arranged under 30 categories based on traditional Chinese encyclopedic conventions. Following an introductory essay on each topic, relevant primary and early secondary documents (all written by Japanese authors prior to 1867) are extensively cited. A third revised edition in 60 volumes was issued by the Koji Ruien Kankō Kai (Committee for the Publication of the *Koji ruien*) in 1931–36. The Bureau of Shintō Shrines published a fourth edition in 51 volumes between 1967 and 1971.

Kojong, King 高宗

(1852–1919; J: Kōsō). The next-to-last monarch (r 1864–1907) of the Korean YI DYNASTY. Personal name Yi Chae-hwang. Kojong ascended the throne when only 12 years old, and his father (the TAEWŎN'GUN) played a dominant role at court between 1864 and 1873. Kojong's wife, Queen MIN, was assassinated by the Japanese in 1895, and the Jap-

Ten types of regional *kokeshi* dolls (pictured here) have been produced in Japan since the Edo period.

Left to right: **Hijiori**, Hijiori Hot Spring, Yamagata Prefecture. **Kijiyama**, city of Yuzawa, Akita Prefecture. **Tsugaru**, Nuruyu and Ōwani hot springs, Aomori Prefecture. **Nambu**, cities of Hanamaki and Morioka, Iwate Prefecture. **Tsuchiyu**, Tsuchiyu Hot Spring, Fukushima Prefecture. **Tōgatta**, Tōgatta Hot Spring, Miyagi Prefecture. **Narugo**, Narugo Hot Spring, Miyagi Prefecture. **Yajirō**, city of Shiroishi, Miyagi Prefecture. **Sakunami**, cities of Yamagata in Yamagata Prefecture and Sendai in Miyagi Prefecture. **Zaō Takayu**, Zaō Hot Spring, Yamagata Prefecture.

anese minister ITŌ HIROBUMI used military force to pressure him into abdicating the throne in July 1907. In 1910, Kojong's kingdom was transformed from a Confucian monarchy into a Japanese colony (see KOREA, ANNEXATION OF). Koreans erupted in violent nationalistic demonstrations against Japan on 1 March 1919, on the eve of Kojong's funeral (see SAMIL INDEPENDENCE MOVEMENT). He is remembered as a symbol of Korean nationalism.

kōjo ryōzoku 公序良俗

(public order and good morals). Basic standard of Japan's CIVIL CODE. Acts that are contrary to this standard are not valid (Civil Code, art. 90). Accordingly, primary actors and third parties may assert the invalidity of such acts and thus prevent ratification. A demand for return of a thing delivered pursuant to a JURISTIC ACT contrary to the *kōjo ryōzoku* standard is denied legal protection as a delivery in respect of illicit consideration. Such invalid acts include acts contrary to orderly property interests, acts contrary to public morals, acts that impinge on human rights, and acts contrary to notions of right.

Kōjunsha 交詢社

A social and political club made up of graduates of FUKUZAWA YUKICHI's Keiō Gijuku (now Keiō University) and business figures connected with the school. The club was formed in 1880 by Fukuzawa, BABA TATSUI, and others to exchange information and advise the government. Membership at the time of its founding was 1,800. The club published a periodical, *Kōjun zasshi*. In 1881 members of the Kōjunsha submitted a draft constitution based on the British system. The club was active in the MOVEMENT TO PROTECT CONSTITUTIONAL GOVERNMENT during the TAISHŌ POLITICAL CRISIS of 1912–13. The Kōjunsha still exists in Tōkyō as a social club.

Kokan Shiren 虎関師錬

(1278–1346). Zen monk of the RINZAI SECT. With SESSON YŪBAI, one of the two great figures in early GOZAN LITERATURE. Born in Kyōto. His writings include *Saihokushū*, an anthology; *Shubun inryaku* (1306), a dictionary of Chinese rhymes; GENKŌ SHAKUSHO, the first history of Japanese Buddhism; and *Butsugo shinron* (1325), a treatise on the *Lankāvatāra-sūtra*.

kōke 高家

(literally, "elevated families"). Hereditary officials of the Edo period (1600–1868); masters of rites and ceremonies for the Tokugawa shogunate. The 26 families eligible for the post included the Kira family (see KIRA YOSHINAKA), ŌTOMO FAMILY, HATAKEYAMA FAMILY, and KYŌGOKU FAMILY, all of whom traced their lineage to the Muromachi period

(1333–1568). Apart from their ceremonial functions, the *kōke* received emissaries from the imperial court and served as the shōgun's representatives at the court and at major shrines and temples, including the Ise Shrine and the Tōshōgū at Nikkō. They enjoyed honorary *daimyō* status.

Kokedera → Saihōji

Kōkei 康慶

(fl late 12th century). Sculptor of Buddhist images. His work strongly influenced the development of Kamakura-period (1185–1333) sculpture and enabled the KEI SCHOOL to flourish. He was the father of UNKEI and the teacher of KAIKEI, both prominent Kei-school sculptors. Kōkei often collaborated with his followers in restoration projects for major temples in the Kyōto and Nara areas, such as the temple TŌDAIJI. Among the few authenticated examples of his work is the *Fukū Kensaku Kannon* in the temple KŌFUKUJI in Nara. The strong emotions and physical movement expressed in his sculpture won favor over the elegant grace of the IN SCHOOL and EN SCHOOL.

Kokei sanshō 虎渓三笑

("The Three Laughers of Tiger Ravine"; Ch: Husi san xiao or Hu-ssu san hsiao). A Chinese allegorical story illustrating that spiritual purity is not limited by artificial boundaries. The Buddhist monk Huiyuan (Hui-yüan; 334–416) practiced religious austerities in his monastery on the mountain Lushan, vowing never to cross the bridge over the bordering Tiger Ravine. However, the poet Tao Yuanming (T'ao Yüan-ming; ca 365–427) and the Taoist Lu Xiujing (Lu Hsiu-ching; ca 406–477) came to visit him and, after an evening of penetrating discussion, Huiyuan escorted his guests out. Still deep in conversation, no one noticed when they crossed the bridge. Realizing that Huiyuan had broken his vow, the three men burst out laughing, understanding that Huiyuan's moral integrity was unimpaired. The story subsequently became a subject for Japanese INK PAINTING.

koken 沽券

Bill of sale, or deed, used from the Heian (794–1185) to the Meiji (1868–1912) periods in sales of property (*kokyaku*), particularly real estate such as farmlands or residential lots. Also called *baiken*, *baikenjō*, and *kokyakujō*. A *koken* was given by the seller to the buyer as legal confirmation of the sales contract. Under the administrative provisions of the RITSURYŌ SYSTEM (7th–11th centuries), *koken* were official documents certified with the seals of provincial governors (KOKUSHI) or district officials (GUNJI). From the mid-Heian period onward, *koken* were simply exchanged by the parties concerned.

During the Edo period (1600–1868) it was required that *koken* bear the seals of town or village officials or those of the semiofficial neighborhood leaders' groups known as GONINGUMI. After the MEIJI RESTORATION (1868) the *koken* deed system was retained by the authorities in large cities such as Tōkyō and Kyōto.

Kōken, Empress 孝謙天皇

(718–770; Kōken Tennō). The 46th and 48th sovereign (*tennō*) in the traditional count (which includes several legendary emperors); reigned 749–758 as Kōken and 764–770 as Shōtoku. She was the second daughter of Emperor SHŌMU and Empress KŌMYŌ. She was strongly influenced by her cousin, the powerful FUJIWARA NO NAKAMARO, and following his advice abdicated in 758 in favor of Prince TONERI's seventh son, who became the 47th emperor, Junnin (r 758–764). When the retired empress came to favor the monk DŌKYŌ, the outraged Nakamaro rose up in arms but was soon captured and killed. Charging Junnin with responsibility for the uprising, Kōken had him deposed and exiled; she then reascended the throne in 764 as the reigning empress Shōtoku. After this headstrong woman sovereign, no woman was allowed to reign until the two figurehead empresses (Meishō and Go-Sakuramachi) of the Edo period (1600–1868).

kōkennin 後見人

(guardian). A person lawfully invested with the power and charged with the duty of taking care of and supervising a person incapable of administering his or her own affairs (CIVIL CODE, arts. 838–876). The ward of a guardianship (*kōken*) may be either a minor or an incompetent. A guardianship for a minor is established when there is no one to exercise parental authority over the minor. If the person who last exercised parental authority over the minor child did not designate a guardian by will, the family court appoints a guardian. With respect to incompetent wards, if a married person is adjudged incompetent, the spouse becomes his or her guardian. If there is no spouse, a guardian is appointed by the family court. A ward cannot have more than one guardian.

kokeshi 小芥子

Wooden doll with a round head attached to a cylindrical body with no limbs. *Kokeshi* are thought to have originated in the Edo period (1600–1868) as a folk toy made by woodworkers of the Tōhoku district (northeastern Japan). Many *kokeshi* are painted with floral designs on the body and a girl's face. They are classified into 10 types according to manufacturing techniques, shape, decoration, and so forth. There were once as many

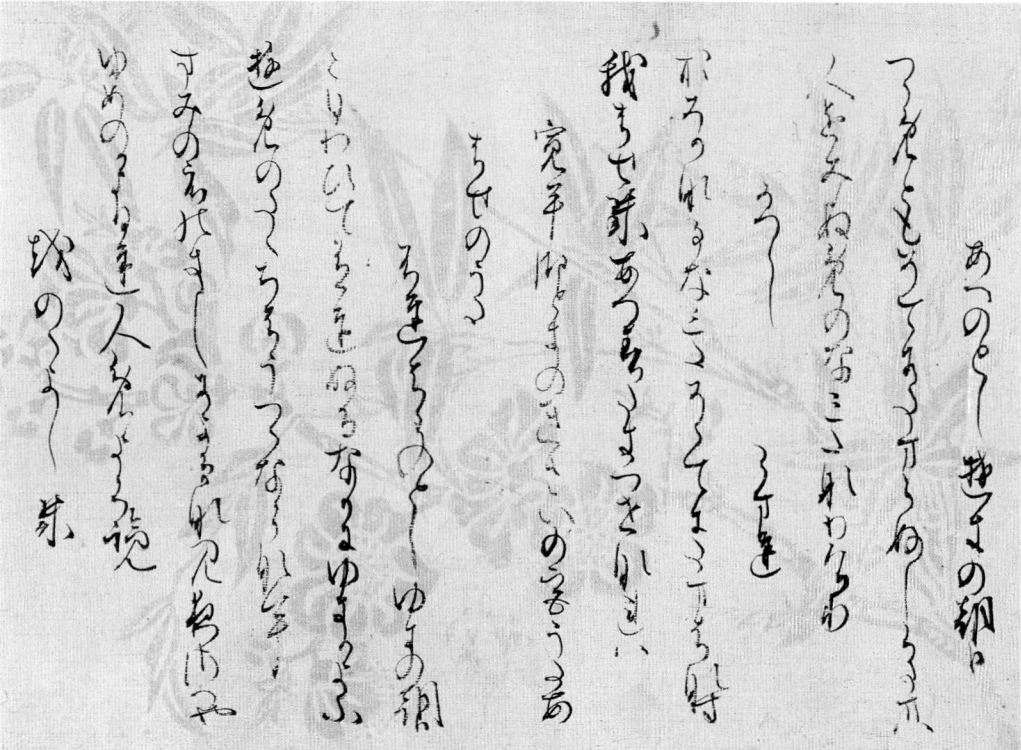

Kokinshū A calligraphic scroll of selected poetry from this 10th-century anthology. Early 12th century. Ink on paper. 17 × 317 cm. Kyōto National Museum. National Treasure.

as 60 different local names for the doll. Since World War II, *kokeshi* have become popular among collectors.

koki 古希

The name given to the rite of passage (see GA NO IWAI) celebrated at age 70, by the traditional Japanese way of reckoning age (*kazoedoshi*), according to which a person is considered to be one year of age in the year of birth and one year older at the beginning of each subsequent year. The origin of *koki* is traced to a poem by China's Tang (T'ang) dynasty (618–907) poet Du Fu (Tu Fu; 712–770). Originally *ga no iwai* began in Japan when one turned 40 in *kazoedoshi* and continued to be celebrated once every ten years, but in the latter part of the Muromachi period (1333–1568) they came to begin at age 61 (KANREKI). Today, as life expectancy continues to increase, many people feel that this rite should begin with *koki*.

Kokin Denju 古今伝授

("Transmission of the *Kokinshū*"). Tradition of handing down, from teacher to chosen disciple, a body of secret teachings concerning the poems of the 10th-century classic poetry anthology KOKINSHŪ. The term *denju* refers to the transmission of secret teachings, a convention common to Buddhism and many Japanese arts.

The tradition of Kokin Denju began when the Nijō and Kyōgoku-Reizei literary families, descended from the great poet FUJIWARA NO SADAIE (Fujiwara no Teika; 1162–1241), contested inheritance of his poetic tradition. The conservative Nijō version remained in the family until NIJŌ TAMEYO (1250?–1338) handed it down to his disciple TON'A (1289–1372). It was bestowed, through TŌ NO TSUNEYORI (1401–84), on the RENGA (linked verse) poet SŌGI (1421–1502), from whom it was passed to SANJŌNISHI SANETAKA (1455–1537) and his family, and then to HOSOKAWA YŪSAI (1534–1610) and Prince Toshihito

(1579–1629), from whence came the so-called Gosho (Imperial Palace) Denju. A second line of transmission began with Sōgi's disciple SHŌHAKU (1443–1527). This became known as the Sakai Denju, from Shōhaku's residence in the city of Sakai, near Ōsaka.

Kokinshū 古今集

(Collection from Ancient and Modern Times). More properly known as the *Kokin wakashū* (Collection of Japanese Poems from Ancient and Modern Times). Although its compilation was already under way during the reign of Emperor Uda (r 887–897), the *Kokinshū* was officially commissioned under Emperor Daigo (r 897–930). It was completed about 905. Although the compilers of the 8th-century collection of Japanese verse, the MAN'YŌSHŪ, had also been royally commissioned, the *Kokinshū* was in fact the first in a series of anthologies of native verse compiled by royal command, the *chokusenshū* or *nijūichidai shū*, "collections from 21 eras." Next to being chosen as a compiler of such a collection, having one's poems included was the highest poetic honor.

Contents—The four compilers of the *Kokinshū* were KI NO TSURAYUKI, his cousin KI NO TOMONORI, ŌSHIKŌCHI NO MITSUNE, and MIBU NO TADAMINE. Tsurayuki wrote the Japanese preface to the *Kokinshū* and Ki no Yoshimochi (d 919), the Chinese preface. The collection's 1,111 poems were chosen from three groups: anonymous poems from older and more recent times; poems from the period of the "six poetic sages" (ROKKASEN; mid-9th century); and poems by the compilers and their contemporaries. The six poetic sages, who attained their status by having been discussed in Tsurayuki's preface, include Bishop HENJŌ (17 poems), ARIWARA NO NARIHIRA (30 poems), Fun'ya no Yasuhide (or Bun'ya no Yasuhide; 5 poems), Priest Kisen (1 poem), ONO NO KOMACHI (18 poems), and Ōtomo no Kuronushi (3 poems). The compilers themselves are represented by 244 poems: Tsurayuki, with over 100, has more

poems than any other poet; Tadamine, with 36, is the least represented of the compilers. Another 6 poets, including Lady ISE and Priest SOSEI, are represented by 10 or more poems each, accounting for 121 poems in all. Over 120 named poets are represented, including almost 100 men and almost 30 women; however, more than 450 anonymous poems, some of great attractiveness, make up the largest single group in the collection.

Arrangement of Poems—The *Kokinshū* set the practice of arranging poems not by single author canons but by topics, and the ensuing 20 royal collections use its basic organization, whether in its 20 books or in the occasional variant of 10. Topics include seasonal poems (books 1–6); love poems (books 11–15); congratulatory, parting, travel, and acrostic poems; laments; miscellaneous topics; miscellaneous poetic forms; and poems from the Bureau of Poetry (Wakadokoro). The proportions make it clear that seasonal and love poetry were considered the essential topical concerns of Japanese lyric poetry.

The *Kokinshū* also pioneered in arranging poems in meaningful sequences within a given topic. The seasonal poems follow the course of natural phenomena in themselves and as ordered by annual court rites (NENCHŪ GYŌJI). The love poems detail the course of lovers' affairs from their inception, through countless vicissitudes of arrest and renewal, to their ends.

Systematic Japanese poetics also begin with Tsurayuki's and Yoshimochi's prefaces to the *Kokinshū*. The latter especially exhibits the influence of the great preface to the Chinese *Shijing* (*Shih-ching; Book of Songs*). Yoshimochi posits three poetic concepts: feeling (Ch: *qing* or *ch'ing;* J: *jō* or *nasake*); words (Ch: *ci* or *tz'u;* J: *shi* or *kotoba*); and style (Ch: *ti* or *t'i;* J: *tai*). Tsurayuki's equivalents are heart or mind (*kokoro*), words (*kotoba*), and style (*sama*), although the last yields to total effect (*sugata*).

Japanese usually compare the *Kokinshū* with the SHIN KOKINSHŪ (ca 1205, New Collection from Ancient and Modern Times), and the latter collection is conventionally preferred for its profundity. The *Kokinshū* is more original, however, and more responsive to immediate life. The *Kokinshū* represents the most creative period of the Japanese court. See also WAKA; HEIAN LITERATURE.

kokiroku 古記録

(ancient private records). The term *kokiroku*, as used by Japanese historians, is almost synonymous with "ancient diary." From the late 9th century it was customary for members of the aristocracy to keep diaries. In later periods this custom spread throughout society. Large numbers of these diaries, central to the study of Japanese history, survive.

The earliest *kokiroku* were not diaries in the ordinary sense but private records of certain incidents. By the Heian period (794–1185), diaries were often kept by members of the imperial family or by court nobles. Only fragments remain of the diaries kept by the emperors UDA (r 887–897) and DAIGO (897–930), but many diaries by court nobles have been preserved almost in their entirety. The more notable ones are SHŌYŪKI, MIDŌ KAMPAKU KI, CHŪYŪKI, and TAIKI. Most of them are copies, but in some of them, such as *Midō Kampaku ki*, a large part of the original manuscript has been preserved.

In the Kamakura period (1185–1333), the diaries of the emperors FUSHIMI and

Hanazono, as well as diaries by nobles, such as the GYOKUYŌ and MEIGETSUKI, are noteworthy. During the Northern and Southern Courts period (1337–92), the ENTAIRYAKU and MOROMORIKI are notable. During the Muromachi period (1333–1568), the Azuchi-Momoyama period (1568–1600), and the Edo period (1600–1868), a large number of diaries appeared. Among the most important are the diary of Emperor Go-Nara (r 1526–57), the KAMMON GYOKI by Prince Fushimi no Miya Sadafusa, the KENNAIKI, and SANETAKA KŌ KI. Temple officials and priests kept diaries such as MANSAI's *Mansai Jugō nikki*, DAIJŌIN JISHA ZŌJI KI, and TAMON'IN NIKKI. UWAI KAKUKEN NIKKI is famous as the private diary of a *samurai*. For literary diaries see NIKKI BUNGAKU.

Kokka   国華

(National Essence). Influential monthly magazine specializing in East Asian, particularly Japanese, art. It was founded in 1889 by the art patron Kuki Ryūichi (1852–1931), the art critic OKAKURA KAKUZŌ, and the *Asahi shimbun* editorial writer Takahashi Kenzō (1855–98) to counterbalance what they regarded as excessive Japanese enthusiasm for Western art and to awaken Japanese and Western interest in East Asian art. It remains one of Japan's most distinguished art journals.

Kokkai→Diet

Kokkai Kisei Dōmei→League for
Establishing a National Assembly

Kokka Kōan Iinkai→National
Public Safety Commission

Kokka Sōdōin Hō→National
Mobilization Law

kokkeibon   滑稽本

(literally, "funny books"). Highly heterogeneous body of comic writing, largely but not exclusively fiction, produced for the most part in Edo (now Tōkyō) from the mid-18th century until the end of the Edo period (1600–1868). All *kokkeibon* are humorous in intent, but not all humorous works of the period are called *kokkeibon;* those whose subject matter or format places them in other categories, such as SHAREBON and KIBYŌSHI, are not designated *kokkeibon*. Most *kokkeibon* are distinguished by the fact that they were printed originally as *chūbon*, "middle-size books" whose page size set them apart physically from other formats for fiction. A great many *kokkeibon* consist in large part of vivid, highly colloquial dialogue. This importance of realistic dialogue is perhaps the greatest contribution of *kokkeibon* to Japanese literature.

Literary historians trace the origin of the *kokkeibon* to the *dangibon*, books of sermons or ethical discourses (*dangi*), often satiric in tone, modeled on the sermons of proselytizing priests of the Jōdo sect. Later writers revered the Dutch scholar and naturalist HIRAGA GENNAI (1728–80) as the spiritual father of the form. Two other writers closely identified with the *kokkeibon* are JIPPENSHA IKKU (1765–1831) and SHIKITEI SAMBA (1776–1822). See also GESAKU.

kokkuri   狐狗狸

(literally, "nodding"). Type of popular divination, the Japanese counterpart of planchette or Ouija. A medium holds the top of a tripod of loosely tied sticks over a board on which are written numbers from 1 to 10 and the 50 letters of the Japanese *kana* syllabary. As the medium, usually blindfolded, goes into a trance, the sticks begin to slide over the letters on the board and, letter by letter, a message appears. The name *kokkuri* refers to the movement of the medium, who nods involuntarily like a person dozing off. It has been popular since the mid-Meiji period (1868–1912).

kōkoku shikan   皇国史観

(emperor-centered historiography). A nationalistic school of historiography that stressed the centrality and permanence of the imperial line as the embodiment of Japan's national polity (KOKUTAI) as well as its role in the shaping of Japanese history. In the late 1930s and early 1940s this historical school provided the basis for the wartime ideology of the Japanese state.

According to the *kōkoku shikan*, Japan was "the country of the gods" (*shinkoku*), "reigned over and governed by a line of emperors unbroken for ages eternal," who were themselves possessed of divinity. The Japanese nation was conceived of as a "family state" (KAZOKU KOKKA) in which the people were bound to their sovereign as subjects by familistic ties of loyalty (*chū*) and filial piety (*kō*). In addition, the school stressed that the glory of the Japanese national polity as defined in this manner should be extended to other nations in order to bring "the whole world under one roof" (HAKKŌ ICHIU), a belief that served as an ideological glorification of imperialist aggression and Japan's domination of other nations and peoples. Needless to say, the school's unquestioning advocacy of the legitimacy of Japanese state power resulted in a brand of historiography fatally marred by a lack of objectivity and scholarly validity.

The *kōkoku shikan* was an instrument of the emerging modern Japanese state in its struggle to establish power and authority in the face of countervailing currents of modern rationalist thought recently introduced from the West. In 1869 the newly established Meiji government issued an imperial rescript creating a historiographical institute (now the HISTORIOGRAPHICAL INSTITUTE, TŌKYŌ UNIVERSITY) charged with the compilation of a history of Japan based upon the Confucian theory of loyalty (*meibunron*). In 1881 the *Taisei kiyō*, political history of the country, was completed under government sponsorship. It was a highly partisan document and contained an implicit critique of the radical parliamentarianism of certain elements of the FREEDOM AND PEOPLE'S RIGHTS MOVEMENT. Stressing the immutability of the Japanese imperial line and the bonds of loyalty uniting subjects and sovereign, it was the prototype for the theory of *kokutai* that formed the core of the *kōkoku shikan*.

The style of Confucianism advocated in the *Taisei kiyō* also became the foundation of the state's educational policies. With the promulgation of the Imperial University Order in 1886, a clear separation was created between scientific scholarship and the highest levels of the educational system and the education offered to the mass of the Japanese people at the elementary and secondary level. The latter became a vehicle for the indoctrination of the people with the values of loyalty to the emperor and love of country (*chūkun aikoku*), resulting in the formation of an ideological system that sustained and perpetuated the concept of *kokutai*.

This system was strengthened and given further articulation by the promulgation in

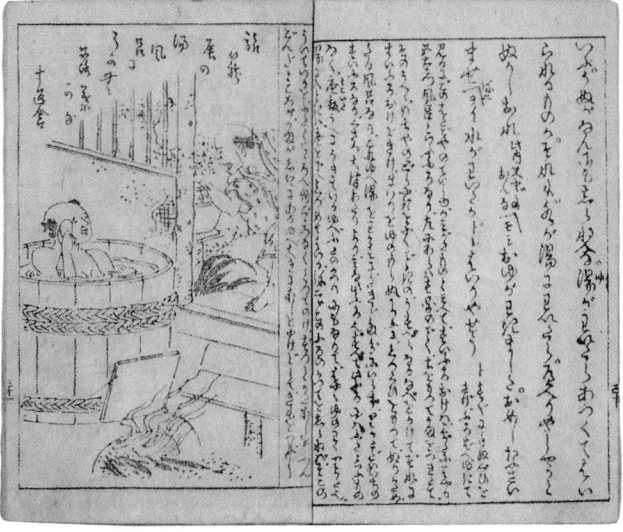

1898 of the chapters of the CIVIL CODE treating domestic relations and inheritance, which provided a legal basis for a patriarchal and patrilineal family system (see IE), and by Japan's imperialistic expansion onto the Asian continent, which began in earnest with the SINO-JAPANESE WAR OF 1894–1895 and the RUSSO-JAPANESE WAR of 1904–05. Though challenged in the 1920s and 1930s by the "organ theory" (TENNŌ KIKAN SETSU) of the Japanese state propounded by MINOBE TATSUKICHI and other liberal scholars, and attacked from a Marxist perspective by the participants in the debate on Japanese capitalism (NIHON SHIHON SHUGI RONSŌ), the ideology of *kokutai* hardened into an absolute system of values with its own fixed interpretation of the meaning and nature of Japanese history. This historiographical vision—the *kōkoku shikan*—was given its final and most complete articulation in two wartime works published by the state: KOKUTAI NO HONGI (1937, The Cardinal Principles of the National Entity of Japan) and *Kokushi gaisetsu* (1943, An Outline of the Nation's History).

With Japan's defeat in World War II, the *kōkoku shikan* also collapsed, but in recent years some Japanese have feared its revival in modified form, giving rise to controversy over such issues as the treatment of history in Japanese high school textbooks (see IENAGA TEXTBOOK REVIEW CASE; TEXTBOOK ISSUE) and official visits by the prime minister and other governmental officials to Yasukuni Shrine (see YASUKUNI SHRINE OFFICIAL VISIT CONTROVERSY).

Kokon chomonjū   古今著聞集

(Record of Things Heard, Past and Present). Collection of tales with moral lessons for the young. Compiled by Tachibana no Narisue in 1254, it was later amended. Sixty-one of its 697 stories also appear in the JIKKUNSHO and are divided into 30 categories ranging from "Buddhism," "Government," and "Loyal Retainers" to "Animals," "Thieves," and "Gambling." AKUTAGAWA RYŪNOSUKE used it as a source for some of his short stories. See SETSUWA BUNGAKU.

Kokontei Shinshō V   古今亭志ん生5代

(1890–1973). RAKUGO (comic monologue) storyteller. Born Minobe Kōzō in Tōkyō, he began to study *rakugo* under Tachibanaya Enkyō (1865–1912) in 1907. He also studied with other *rakugo* masters, each time undergoing a change of name. He was known by a total of 16 names before becoming Kokontei Shinshō V in 1939. Audiences were attracted to his free, large-spirited style, and he is consideered the premier *rakugo* storyteller of the Shōwa period (1926–89).

Kokontei Shinshō V
This comic storyteller is considered to be the premier *rakugo* artist of the Shōwa period.

Kokoro　こゝろ

(tr *Kokoro,* 1957). Novel by NATSUME SŌSEKI (1867–1916); serialized in the newspaper *Asahi shimbun* in 1914. *Kokoro,* narrated by its two principal characters, tells of the peculiar friendship that develops between a university student and the enigmatic "Sensei," one of the many tormented intellectuals who appear in Sōseki's novels. In a letter to the student, Sensei reveals the event that has made him the dour person he is today: as a young man he was part of a lovers' triangle—a familiar pattern in Sōseki's novels—in which he stole the woman his best friend loved and so prompted the friend's suicide. As the Meiji period (1868–1912) ends, Sensei, pained by guilt and fearful of a future in which egoism flourishes—a theme that Sōseki pursued in his famous lecture of 1914, "Watakushi no kojin shugi" (My Individualism), and elsewhere—feels it is time that his own life came to a close. Following the example of General NOGI MARESUKE, who committed ritual suicide after the death of Emperor MEIJI, Sensei decides to take his own life. *Kokoro,* in which Sōseki's skills in characterization reached a high level of maturity, is one of the most widely read works of modern Japanese literature.

Kokoro no hana　心の花

(Flower of the Heart). Japan's oldest TANKA poetry monthly. Founded in February 1898 by SASAKI NOBUTSUNA. In addition to publishing poetry in traditional forms, which was its raison d'être, the magazine reflected Sasaki's commitment to research in the Japanese classics, publishing numerous scholarly articles on Japan's literary tradition. KINOSHITA RIGEN and YANAGIHARA BYAKUREN were among the poets who found a voice in the magazine's pages. As of 1991 its editor was Sasaki Yukitsuna (b 1938), Nobutsuna's grandson.

kokorozuke　心付け

(token of appreciation; tip). Money or articles given, as an expression of appreciation for services, to a person of lower status, such as a maid in a Japanese-style inn, a *geisha,* or a chauffeur. Also referred to as SHŪGI. If extra service is desired, one gives a little more than the prevailing rate in advance. For a person whose services one uses often or in a place that one frequents, *kokorozuke* need not be given. To such a person or establishment, one would give seasonal gifts, such as CHŪGEN (at midyear) or SEIBO (at the end of the year). Money is the most common form of *kokorozuke.* It is placed in a special gift-money envelope with ornaments (MIZUHIKI and NOSHI) usually printed on the envelope. At the top of the envelope the Chinese characters for *shūgi* (literally, "in celebration") or *sunshi* ("a trifle") may be written. See also GIFT GIVING.

koku　石

A measure of volume or capacity, used generally for rice but sometimes for other dry substances and liquids as well. In the Edo period (1600–1868) a *koku* of grain equaled about 0.18 cubic meter, 180.39 liters, or 5.12 US bushels, theoretically enough rice to feed one person for a year. Land productivity, tax assessments, the stipends of *samurai,* and the wealth of *daimyō* were all measured in *koku* (see KOKUDAKA; KENCHI). As early as the 7th century, under the RITSURYŌ SYSTEM, the following hierarchy of measurement units was adopted from China: one *koku* equaled 10 *to;* one *to* equaled 10 *shō;* and one *shō* equaled 10 *gō.* When the varying sizes of these units were standardized by the national unifier TOYOTOMI HIDEYOSHI late in the 16th century, the *koku* was set at more than twice the size it had been in the 7th century. See also WEIGHTS AND MEASURES.

Kokubu　国分［市］

City on Kagoshima Bay in central Kagoshima Prefecture, Kyūshū. It takes its name from the provincial temple (KOKUBUNJI) established here in the 8th century. The city's fame derives mainly from its tobacco, grown since about 1600. A Self Defense Force base is located here. Pop: 46,557.

Kokubungaku Kenkyū Shiryōkan　国文学研究資料館

(National Institute of Japanese Literature). Government center for the preservation of classical Japanese literature. Established in 1972; located in Shinagawa Ward, Tōkyō. The institute collects and preserves on microfilm research materials for the study of classical Japanese literature. In addition to collecting manuscript and block-printed documents and making them available for use by scholars, the institute also conducts a variety of research activities. As of January 1989 the collection contained 15,000 manuscripts and block-printed books, 60,000 modern volumes, 336 periodical titles, and 20,000 reels of microfilmed documents.

Kokubunji　国分寺［市］

City in central Tōkyō Prefecture. It takes its name from the provincial temple (KOKUBUNJI) established here in the 8th century. An agricultural district before World War II, it is now a residential area and is the site of precision-instruments plants and colleges, including the Railway Technical Research Institute and Tōkyō College of Economics. The Man'yō Botanical Gardens and the remains of the provincial temple are noteworthy. Pop: 100,982.

kokubunji　国分寺

(provincial temple). Temples built by the government during the Nara period (710–794) in imitation of a system in Tang (T'ang) dynasty (618–907) China. In 741 Emperor SHŌMU decreed that a *kokubunji* and a *kokubunniji* (provincial nunnery) be built in each province. State funds as well as donations from major families (*uji*) financed their building, and peasants serving the annual 60-day corvée labor (*zōyō;* see YŌEKI) were enlisted for the project. By 780 most of these temples were completed. The official name of the *kokubunji* was Konkōmyō Shitennō gokoku no tera, and that of the *kokubunniji* was Hokke *metsuzai no tera,* indicating that the former was built to pray for the protection of the state and the latter for the atonement of sin. In 752 the TŌDAIJI, enshrining the 16-meter (52.5-ft)-high statue of the Buddha Vairocana, was built in Heijōkyō (now Nara) as the head *kokubunji.*

kokudainō　石代納

The practice during the Edo period (1600–1868) of paying the annual tax (NENGU) in cash instead of rice, the customary medium of payment. As the money economy grew after the mid-18th century, the shogunate placed limitations on *kokudainō* because of concern over the shortage of stored rice (see KURAMAI).

kokudaka　石高

(assessed tax base in terms of *koku*). An estimate of the annual yield of farmland, measured in KOKU (1 *koku* = about 180 liters or 5 US bushels) of unpolished rice; the uniform basis of land taxes throughout the Edo period (1600–1868). Established nationwide by TOYOTOMI HIDEYOSHI at the time of his cadastral survey of 1582 to 1596 (see KENCHI), this kind of assessment remained in use until the LAND TAX REFORM OF 1873–1881. Paddy fields were classified in four grades with average annual yields (*kokumori*) of 1.5, 1.3, 1.2, and 1.1 *koku* for each *tan* (about 0.1 hectare or 0.25 acre) of area. Multiplying the *kokumori* of a paddy field by its number of *tan* produced its *kokudaka,* or assessed tax base. The productivity of dry fields was similarly computed. *Kokudaka* replaced KANDAKA (the agreed-upon annual tax calculated in terms of money), which had been used in the Kamakura (1185–1333) and Muromachi (1333–1568) periods. *Kokudaka* protected the farmers from the vagaries of rice prices in an increasingly money-based economy.

Kokudo Chiriin →Geographical Survey Institute

Kokudochō →National Land Agency

kokufu　国府

(provincial capitals). Seats of provincial governments under the RITSURYŌ SYSTEM of government begun in the late 7th century; also known as *fuchū* or *funai.* Located at strategic points throughout Japan, they apparently had the same "checkerboard" layout as the capital cities HEIJŌKYŌ (Nara) and HEIANKYŌ (Kyōto) and were surrounded by earthen walls and moats. The main government offices (*kokuga*), located in the north central section of each city, served as the headquarters of the provincial administrators (KOKUSHI), who were responsible for collecting the central government's taxes and maintaining law and order. A government-sponsored Buddhist temple (KOKUBUNJI) and a major local Shintō shrine (*sōja* or *sōsha*) were usually situated nearby. Traces of some of these administrative centers still exist, the best-known example being in Hōfu City, the capital of Suō Province (now part of Yamaguchi Prefecture).

Kokugaku　国学

(National Learning). General name for the textual and interpretive study of Japanese classical literature and ancient writings that began in the 17th century. Four scholars have traditionally been cited as forming the lineage of orthodox Kokugaku in the Edo period (1600–1868): KADA NO AZUMAMARO (1669–1736), KAMO NO MABUCHI (1697–1769), MOTOORI NORINAGA (1730–1801), and HIRATA ATSUTANE (1776–1843). This lineage, although beginning with Kada no Azumamaro, was conceived and propagated by Hirata Atsutane and his followers to serve their nationalist ideology. In contrast, modern philologically oriented scholars see KEICHŪ (1640–1701) as the forerunner of Kokugaku.

A monk of the Shingon sect, Keichū completed the *Man'yō daishō ki* (ca 1683–90), an annotated text of the 8th-century poetry anthology MAN'YŌSHŪ, at the request of TOKUGAWA MITSUKUNI. In his study of this earliest extant Japanese poetic anthology, Keichū demonstrated a strong affinity for the ancient poets, insisting that their simple humanity had been obscured by the interposition of contemporary concepts. This humanistic spirit influenced many later classicists. Another early influence in Kokugaku studies was Kada no Azumamaro, who came from a family of Shintō priests. He founded a school in Kyōto to promote National Learning that was later highly praised by Hirata Atsutane and other nationalists. Kada no Azumamaro was the teacher of Kamo no Mabuchi, who was also from a Shintō family. Mabuchi praised the "lofty and honest spirit" of the *Man'yōshū* poets, emphasizing that, previous to the absorption into Japanese culture of Buddhist and Confucian influence, WAKA poetry had been composed to express straightforwardly the feelings of the ancient poets. The poetry of later times he found artificial and false. This view constituted an important aspect of the ideological basis of Kokugaku.

Motoori Norinaga was a student of Kamo no Mabuchi, but he did not share Mabuchi's enthusiasm for the *Man'yōshū*. Before his contact with Mabuchi, however, he had already been profoundly influenced by Keichū's literary outlook. On the basis of his study of the TALE OF GENJI and *waka* literature, Norinaga felt that literary creation was dependent upon sensitivity to what he called MONO NO AWARE, a sensibility genuinely and sympathetically responsive to the nuances of objects and events in the human and natural worlds. He believed that this sensibility was the principle behind all Japanese literature and insisted that literature was an artistic, not an ideological, mode of expression. It took approximately 34 years for Norinaga to complete his *Kojiki den* (1764–98), the greatest annotation of a classical work in the Edo period. Norinaga stated that the historical chronicle KOJIKI (712) contained the purest record of ancient oral Japanese and so was more valuable than the NIHON SHOKI (720), a chronicle written in classical Chinese (*kambun*). He did not extol ancient times with the vehement restorationist passion of Kamo no Mabuchi. Yet Norinaga did maintain that early Japanese writings did not contain the word MICHI (way), used in the sense of the "right moral path," precisely because they tacitly assumed a right way of living, which he called Kodō, the Way of the Ancients. Furthermore, Norinaga stated that because the ancient Japanese acted correctly without moralizing, ancient Japan had been superior to Confucian China.

In the late Edo period the focus of classical studies began to shift as the ideological character of Kokugaku gradually strengthened, a tendency that crystallized in the work of Hirata Atsutane. Although he never met Norinaga, Atsutane believed that he himself most closely adhered to Norinaga's thought and ideals and was his obvious successor. Kokugaku, in his view, was the study of the Japanese classics and ancient Japan undertaken with a nationalistic orientation that accorded with Shintō thought as he conceived it. For Atsutane, ancient documents were a means of determining the Way of the gods (Shintō). He constructed a Shintoist cosmology and world view that encompassed salvation of the soul after death, as well as a cosmogony. Unique in Atsutane's cosmogony was the importance he placed on the deity Musubinokami (the God of Procreation), who ruled the production of all things, preceded all things, and was the source of all existence, divine and human. Atsutane regarded this Japanese cosmology

not only as the truth about existence, but as a truth superior to any other nation's.

Later Interpretations——ŌKUNI TAKAMASA (1792–1871) and many other thinkers active in the imperial restoration movement were Atsutane's disciples. These scholars believed that the activities of people in this world, directed toward realizing the divine will of the God of Procreation, arise from a subject's obligatory duty to the emperor. A new concept of the nation, with strong emphasis on the obligation of its subjects to give reverent service to the exalted figure of the divine emperor, was thus created.

In the years before World War II, nationalist zealots used Kokugaku as the ideological framework for the imperial Japanese state. The scholar YAMADA YOSHIO (1873–1958) rejected Kokugaku as a purely philological study and insisted in *Kokugaku no hongi* (1942, Principle of National Learning) that its principal goal was the "clarification of the national polity (KOKUTAI)." The ideological effort to determine and propound the essence of the Japanese spirit through Kokugaku studies ended with Japan's defeat in World War II.

Kokugakuin University 国学院大学

(Kokugakuin Daigaku). A private, coeducational university whose main campus is located in Shibuya Ward, Tōkyō. Its predecessor was the Kōten Kōkyūjo, a research institute of National Learning (KOKUGAKU) and Japanese history, founded in 1882. In 1890 the school was renamed Kokugakuin, and in 1906 it adopted its present name. It was officially granted university status in 1920. After World War II, the university expanded its faculties to include letters, law, and economics. Enrollment was 10,930 in 1989.

Kokugikan 国技館

SUMŌ wrestling stadium operated by the Japan Sumō Association (Nihon Sumō Kyōkai). The first Kokugikan was built in the Ryōgoku section of Tōkyō in 1909 and its successor in the Kuramae section in 1954. The latter has been torn down, and in 1985 a new Kokugikan was opened, again in the Ryōgoku district. Three of the six annual main *sumō* tournaments are held here, in January, May, and September. The stadium accommodates nearly 11,000 people when it is used for *sumō*; the *sumō* ring can be lowered beneath the floor so that the stadium can be used for other purposes. The complex also contains a *sumō* museum, training school, and clinic.

Kokugogaku daijiten 国語学大辞典

(Dictionary of Japanese Language Studies). A one-volume dictionary compiled by the Society for the Study of the Japanese Language and published in 1980. The *Kokugogaku daijiten* is a revision of the 1955 *Kokugogaku jiten*, incorporating 25 years of further research in the field of Japanese language studies. The short-entry system of the earlier work was changed to 1,600 medium-length entries in the revised version. In addition to Japanese language studies, the dictionary covers subjects from a variety of related disciplines, including Japanese language education, JAPANESE LANGUAGE REFORMS, and sociolinguistics.

Kokugo nenkan 国語年鑑

(Japanese Language Yearbook). Yearbook published by the NATIONAL LANGUAGE RESEARCH INSTITUTE since 1954. It reviews devel-

Kokugikan Banners announcing the names of the wrestlers are displayed outside this stadium during a *sumō* tournament.

opments during the preceding year in areas such as spoken and written Japanese, governmental linguistic and language-education policies, Japanese language studies, and linguistic usage in the mass media. Other major features of the yearbook include an annual bibliography of books and periodical articles dealing with the Japanese language, a directory of specialists in the field, a list of prize-winning monographs and their topics, general news relating to the discipline of Japanese language studies, and a variety of other reference materials.

Kokugo Shingikai →Council on the National Language

kokugun system 国郡制

(*kokugunsei*). The administrative division of Japan into PROVINCES (*kuni* or *koku*) and districts (*kōri* or *gun*) under the RITSURYŌ SYSTEM of government. The chronicle *Nihon shoki* (720) claims that the *kokugun* system was established in 646 as part of the TAIKA REFORM, but Japanese scholars have shown that the Chinese character read *gun* (or *kōri*) was not used for administrative divisions until the early 8th century. Under the TAIHŌ CODE (701) Japan was divided into 58 *kuni* and three island provinces (changed by the mid-9th century to 66 *kuni* and two island provinces). Categorized by size, the *kuni* were administered by central-government officials and the *gun* within the *kuni* by powerful local families.

The *kokugun* system was established to strengthen the local authority of the central YAMATO COURT; by the mid-Heian period (794–1185), however, it had been undermined by the growth of private estates (SHŌEN). Nonetheless, the basic territorial divisions were retained in the shogunal administrative systems of the Kamakura (1185–1333) and Muromachi (1333–1568) periods, and even to some extent in the domainal system of the Edo period (1600–1868).

Kokuhonsha 国本社

(National Foundation Society). Nationalist society of the 1920s and 1930s, formed by the conservative bureaucratic politician HIRANUMA KIICHIRŌ in 1924. The word *kokuhon* or "nation-based" was considered antithetical to the term *mimpon* or "people-based" (*mimpon shugi* was the term then used as a translation of "democracy"), hence the organization's name suggested a nationalist society that was opposed to democracy. Kokuhonsha theorists called upon patriots to reject foreign "isms" and to adhere to the traditional national spirit.

Members included Hiranuma's Justice Ministry colleagues and protégés SUZUKI KISABURŌ, Shiono Suehiko (1880–1949), and

Hara Yoshimichi (1867–1944); Takeuchi Kakuji (1875–1946); and Ōta Kōzō (1889–1981). Though the Kokuhonsha's roster boasted many high-ranking officials and military officers such as ARAKI SADAO, MAZAKI JINZABURŌ, Obata Toshishirō (1885–1947), KATŌ HIROHARU, and Admiral TŌGŌ HEIHACHIRŌ, they did not necessarily support Hiranuma on political issues. By 1936 Hiranuma claimed 80,000 adherents. After the FEBRUARY 26TH INCIDENT of 1936, Hiranuma dissolved the society because of its fascist reputation.

kokujin 国人

Also called *kunishū*, both terms meaning "provincials." Provincial barons, in general originating from the more powerful local landholding warriors (SAMURAI), especially those assigned as land stewards (JITŌ) during the Kamakura period (1185–1333). From early in the Muromachi period (1333–1568) *kokujin* were the dominant political and military figures on the local level. Their allegiance was essential to the military governor (SHUGO), who generally lacked a base in his province of assignment. *Kokujin* frequently took advantage of the *shugo*'s weakness to expand their own control in the province. *Kokujin* sometimes formed confederations or leagues (IKKI) among themselves and provided leadership for uprisings by provincial groups (KUNI IKKI) of the 15th and early 16th centuries. By the late Muromachi period the more powerful of these barons had succeeded in displacing the military governors and becoming autonomous territorial rulers (SENGOKU DAIMYŌ).

Kokumin Chōyō Rei → National Service Draft Ordinance

Kokumin Dōmei 国民同盟

(National Alliance). Ultranationalist political party formed in December 1932 by ADACHI KENZŌ and NAKANO SEIGŌ. When Adachi was prevented by the RIKKEN MINSEITŌ from returning to its ranks after his withdrawal in 1931, he set up the Kokumin Dōmei, consisting mostly of defectors from the Minseitō. The party advocated government control of strategic industries and financial institutions and creation of a Japan-Manchuria economic bloc. In 1934 it demanded an inquiry into the TEIJIN INCIDENT to bring down the SAITŌ MAKOTO cabinet. From 1935, when the Yamaji Jōichi (1882–1942) faction returned to the ruling Minseitō, the Kokumin Dōmei's Diet representation fell in stages from its original strength of 32 to 11 after the 1937 election. Nakano left the party in 1936 and formed his own party, the TŌHŌKAI, the following year. In July 1940 the remaining Kokumin Dōmei members joined the IMPERIAL RULE ASSISTANCE ASSOCIATION. See also POLITICAL PARTIES.

Kokumin Eiyo Shō → People's Honor Award

kokumin gakkō 国民学校

(national people's schools). Name given to the Japanese compulsory school system between 1941 and 1947. Influenced by the concept of the German *Volksschule*, the idea was a product of the jingoistic atmosphere of World War II. The curriculum under the *kokumin gakkō* system was dedicated to training "loyal subjects of the emperor." Under the National People's School Order (Kokumin Gakkō Rei) of 1941, the nation's compulsory education system, which had consisted of six years of primary school, was to be reorganized to consist of eight years (six primary and two secondary). Wartime conditions prevented practical application of the new system. After World War II, the system was reorganized as the present elementary and secondary system under the SCHOOL EDUCATION LAW OF 1947. See also ELEMENTARY EDUCATION.

Kokumin Jissen Yōryō 国民実践要領

(Guidelines for Popular Practical Morality). A set of proposed guidelines for moral education in Japan's public schools drawn up in 1951 by the minister of education, AMANO TEIYŪ. The nationalistic moral training course, SHŪSHIN, was withdrawn following World War II. Amano's guidelines advocated a morality based on individualism while stressing the need for love and loyalty to society and the state. Popular opposition forced him to withdraw the proposal.

Kokumin Kenkō Hoken → National Health Insurance

Kokumin Kyōdōtō 国民協同党

(People's Cooperative Party). Centrist political party founded in March 1947 with the merger of the People's Party (Kokumintō) and the Cooperative Democratic Party (Kyōdō Minshutō). The party's platform emphasized class harmony, cooperation, and modernization of rural areas. In April 1950 the party merged with the conservative Democratic Party (MINSHUTŌ) to form the People's Democratic Party (Kokumin Minshutō), which was reorganized as the Kaishintō (Reform Party) in 1952 and ultimately merged with the LIBERAL DEMOCRATIC PARTY (Jiyū Minshutō).

Kokumin Kyōkai 国民協会

(Nationalist Association). 1. A progovernment political group organized in 1892 by SHINAGAWA YAJIRŌ, SAIGŌ TSUGUMICHI, and others, with the aim of countering opposition parties, such as the JIYŪTŌ and RIKKEN KAISHINTŌ, that obstructed the government's legislative program. Despite the group's antiparty bias it sided in 1893 with the opposition parties in attacking the government's plan for treaty revision (see UNEQUAL TREATIES, REVISION OF). In 1898 the position of the Kokumin Kyōkai as the sole progovernment faction in the Diet was weakened with the formation of an alliance between the KENSEITŌ (Constitutional Party) and the second Yamagata cabinet. The group was therefore dissolved in 1899 and reorganized as the TEIKOKUTŌ (Imperial Party). 2. Ultranationalist political group founded by AKAMATSU KATSUMARO and others in July 1933. It attacked theories skeptical of the "divine nature" of the emperor (see TENNŌ KIKAN SETSU). In July 1937 it joined other nationalistic associations to form the Nihon Kakushintō (Japan Reform Party). See also POLITICAL PARTIES.

kokumin kyūka mura → national vacation villages

Kokumin Nenkin → National Pension

Kokumin no tomo 国民之友

(The Nation's Friend). Opinion journal founded by TOKUTOMI SOHŌ in February 1887 and published by the Min'yūsha. It occupied a central position in the intellectual world of the 1890s and drew upon some of the best writers of the day—FUTABATEI SHIMEI, YAMADA BIMYŌ, TOKUTOMI ROKA, KUNIKIDA DOPPO, and UCHIDA ROAN—as contributors. Chiefly devoted to political, social, economic, and literary commentary, *Kokumin no tomo* carried provocative essays on current issues and reflected Sohō's interest in Christian-inspired humanism and the FREEDOM AND PEOPLE'S RIGHTS MOVEMENT. After the Sino-Japanese War of 1894–95, as Sohō shifted to a more conservative and nationalistic position, the magazine lost its following, ceasing publication with its 372nd issue in August 1898.

Kokumin Seishin Sōdōin Undō → National Spiritual Mobilization Movement

Kokumin shimbun 国民新聞

Meiji-period (1868–1912) political tabloid launched in Tōkyō in 1890 by writer-critic TOKUTOMI SOHŌ. In its early days the paper was popular because of its moderate approach to people's rights. After the Russo-Japanese War (1904–05), however, Sohō shifted his position and began to advocate an expansionist policy. Because of its support of the conservative Katsura Tarō cabinet, the *Kokumin shimbun* came to be regarded as a government mouthpiece. During the era of TAISHŌ DEMOCRACY, the company offices were attacked by members of the Freedom and People's Rights Movement. The paper eventually ran into financial difficulty, for which Sohō took responsibility. He resigned from the company in 1929. Continuing to publish until 1942, the *Kokumin* merged with the MIYAKO SHIMBUN to form the present TŌKYŌ SHIMBUN.

kokumin shukusha 国民宿舎

Publicly sponsored lodging houses. Erected at scenic locations, these lodges provide inexpensive accommodations for Japanese vacationers and foreign tourists. Started in 1956, the lodges are built and maintained with long-term, low-interest loans obtained through the Ministry of Health and Welfare and are managed by local government organizations. Facilities and meals (included in the cost) are generally Japanese-style, though a few lodges have beds and Western-style meals. Most can accommodate an average of 110 guests; they are primarily located within national and prefectural parks. As of 1990 there were 292 such lodging houses.

Kokura 小倉

District in the city of Kita Kyūshū in northern Fukuoka Prefecture, Kyūshū. During the 17th century Kokura was a busy castle town. Today it is divided into Kokura Kita and Kokura Minami wards. The former is a commercial and industrial center and the latter a residential area.

Kōkuri → Koguryŏ

Kokuryūkai → Amur River Society

Kokusai Denshin Denwa Co, Ltd 国際電信電話[株]

(Kokusai Denshin Denwa; KDD). Firm that has the largest share of international telecommunications services between Japan and foreign countries; linked with 215 nations and territories. Incorporated in 1953. Providing over 20 types of services including an international integrated services digital network (ISDN), telephone, telex, leased circuit communications, data transfer, video conferencing, and television transmissions,

KDD plays a leading role in satellite and optical communication technology development. The company has international telephone offices in Tōkyō, Oyama (Tochigi Prefecture), Ōsaka, and Okinawa and also has five satellite communication centers and six cable landing stations. Overseas offices are located in more than 20 major foreign cities. Sales for the fiscal year ending March 1991 totaled ¥240.7 billion (US $1.8 billion), and capitalization stood at ¥34.5 billion (US $251.5 million). Headquarters are in Tōkyō.

Kokusai Electric Co, Ltd
国際電気[株]

(Kokusai Denki). Manufacturer of electrical communications equipment, industrial electronics equipment, data-processing equipment, electrical measuring instruments, and medical equipment. Incorporated in 1949. The company belongs to the Hitachi group. Products are exported to 61 countries worldwide. Sales for the fiscal year ending March 1991 totaled ¥128.4 billion (US $1.1 billion); capitalization stood at ¥8.3 billion (US $60.5 million). Headquarters are in Tōkyō.

Kokusai Kōgyō Co, Ltd 国際航業[株]

(Kokusai Kōgyō). Largest aerial surveying contractor in Japan. Incorporated in 1947. Its diverse operations include civil engineering, environmental research, and groundwater and waste disposal development. The company has a joint venture in Malaysia and branches in Thailand and Korea. Sales for the fiscal year ending March 1991 totaled ¥39.3 billion (US $286.4 million), and capitalization stood at ¥16.9 billion (US $123.1 million). Headquarters are in Tōkyō.

Kokusai Securities Co, Ltd
国際証券[株]

(Kokusai Shōken). Securities company. Incorporated in 1948 as Yachiyo Securities, it merged with Kōa Securities and Nomura Securities Investment Trust and changed to its present name in 1981. Noted for management of stocks, bonds, and investment trusts, the company has subsidiaries in Hong Kong, Singapore, New York, London, and Zurich and representative offices in Beijing, Geneva, and Bangkok. Revenue for the fiscal year ending March 1991 totaled ¥168.3 billion (US $1.2 billion), and capitalization was ¥55.5 billion (US $404.5 million). Headquarters are in Tōkyō.

kokusan kaisho 国産会所

(local production associations). Also called *bussan kaisho.* Offices established by domainal governments in the Edo period (1600–1868) to encourage and gain more complete control over production operations (see HAN'EI SEMBAI). They furnished loans, materials, and technical guidance. Many of them were established in the wake of the Tokugawa shogunate's KYŌHŌ REFORMS. During the early 1880s *kaisho* officials attempted to increase domainal revenues by encouraging production of specialized local goods (see BUSSANGAKU). Most of the *kokusan kaisho* were partly staffed by chartered merchants (GOYŌ SHŌNIN) whose wealth and financial expertise were valuable, although their presence was not always to the advantage of the producers. In an effort to strengthen its own finances, the shogunate prohibited domainal monopolization of products in 1842. Plans to regulate the *kokusan kaisho* in the late 1850s, however, never materialized. The *kokusan kaisho* and the domains were abolished in 1871.

kokusei chōsaken 国政調査権

The power of the national DIET to investigate matters relating to government. The 1947 CONSTITUTION OF JAPAN states: "Each House may conduct investigations in relation to government, and may demand the presence and testimony of witnesses, and the production of records" (art. 62). The Law concerning the Oath and Testimony by Witnesses before the National Diet (Giin ni okeru Shōnin no Sensei oyobi Shōgen Tō ni kansuru Hōritsu; generally referred to as Giin Shōgen Hō) was enacted in 1947. This law compels a person to appear, testify, and produce records under oath before a House of the Diet whenever asked to do so by that House. There are some exceptions; for example, a public official may refuse to testify about confidential matters of his office or matters that gravely affect national interests. The law establishes penalties for failure to appear, failure to submit subpoenaed documents, refusal to take an oath or to testify, and perjury.

kokuseki → Japanese nationality

Kokusen'ya kassen 国姓爺合戦

(tr *The Battles of Coxinga,* 1951). A *jidaimono* (historical drama) written by CHIKAMATSU MONZAEMON (1653–1724) in 1715 that is still performed by both BUNRAKU and KABUKI troupes. Among Chikamatsu's most successful works, it had an unprecedented 17-month run when first staged. Watōnai, the hero, a fantastic treatment of the historical figure, ZHENG CHENGGONG (Cheng Ch'eng-kung), is a half-Chinese, half-Japanese fisherman who goes off to China to restore the Ming dynasty (1368–1644) after its overthrow. *Kokusen'ya kassen* is a play of violent contrasts, ranging from rough humor and comic comparisons between Chinese and Japanese to scenes of bloodshed and eye gouging, a famous fight with a tiger, and other gory moments that brilliantly exploit the limitations of the bunraku puppets for which originally written.

kokushi 国司

(provincial governors). Administrators (*shi*) of provinces (*kuni* or *koku*) under the RITSURYŌ SYSTEM of government established in the mid-7th century. There were four major ranks: governor (*kami*), vice-governor (*suke*), commissioner (*jō*), and inspector (*sakan*). The title *kokushi* was originally applied to all these officials but in later years mainly referred to the governors. Usually chosen from the central-government bureaucracy, they were assigned to provincial headquarters (KOKUFU) for terms of four to six years and were given the income from state lands for their support. Their principal duties involved supervision of the militia, police, land registry, and tax bureau. In the 10th century, with the rise of private landed estates (SHŌEN), central authority declined, and *kokushi* soon became an empty title, although it was used for its prestige throughout the Muromachi period (1333–1568).

Kokushi taikei 国史大系

(Compilation of Japanese History). A major collection of standard sources for Japanese history from the earliest times to the Meiji Restoration (1868), including official histories, private records, genealogies, laws, and literary works; published in two editions. The first series (32 vols, 1897–1904) was edited by economist and cultural historian

TAGUCHI UKICHI; the second series, a careful revision of the first, entitled *Shintei zōho kokushi taikei* (66 vols, 1929–64; Revised and Enlarged Compilation of Japanese History), was begun under the general editorship of KUROITA KATSUMI, professor of Japanese history at Tōkyō University.

The methods used in compiling the *Kokushi taikei* reflect both the native tradition of textual collation and criticism and the positivist techniques of Western historical scholarship that influenced Japanese historiography after the Meiji Restoration.

kokuso 国訴

(provincial appeals; also read *kuniso*). Demands by peasants late in the Edo period (1600–1868) for the redress of grievances, particularly against the monopoly trade guilds (KABUNAKAMA). The petitioners presented their complaints to the *daimyō* or to the *kabunakama* authorities. In contrast to the frequently violent peasant uprisings (HYAKUSHŌ IKKI) of the time, the *kokuso* followed legal procedures. The first major *kokuso* took place in 1823, when more than 1,000 villages engaged in cotton and rapeseed production in the Ōsaka region joined to present an appeal.

kokutai 国体

Usually translated as "national polity," "national essence," or "national entity." The term has been commonly used to refer to what was seen as the uniquely Japanese polity, the most important elements of which were rule by an unbroken imperial line and the concept of the state as a family, in which the relationship between the emperor and his subjects is like that between a father and his children.

The idea that Japan is different from all other countries in its origins and in the organization of the state is a very old one. From earliest times, there are frequent references to Japan as "the land of the gods." It was not until the Edo period (1600–1868), however, that the uniqueness of Japan's polity became a subject for scholarly discussion. Stimulated by greater knowledge of early Japanese history, scholars of the time began to feel resentment at the dominance of Confucian thought and the "worship" of all things Chinese. YAMAGA SOKŌ asserted that Japan, not China, was the true "middle kingdom." Japan's ethics and system of government had not been learned from China; on the contrary, SHINTŌ led where Confucianism followed. In the later Edo period, with the rise of KOKUGAKU (National Learning) and in particular of the MITO SCHOOL of historical studies, *kokutai* became the subject of heated debate.

The "family concept of the state," in which the emperor was seen as being directly descended from AMATERASU ŌMIKAMI, the sun goddess, and his subjects were regarded as an extension of the imperial family, became the pivot of popular education from the 1890s on, following the IMPERIAL RESCRIPT ON EDUCATION (1890). Read in the schools on important occasions, the rescript was the basis of Japanese ethics for half a century.

Persecution of persons or groups for expressing views held to be contrary to the orthodox interpretation of *kokutai* occurred frequently until the end of World War II. The most famous was the 1935 Affair of the "Emperor-as-an-Organ-of-the-State" Theory (TENNŌ KIKAN SETSU), involving MINOBE

kokyū
1 The melancholy tones of this instrument waft through the town of Yatsuo in Toyama Prefecture each year during the festival Kaze no Bon. Performed at the peak of the typhoon season, the music and dance are intended to pacify the god of wind. **2** The kokyū is a hybrid of European and Okinawan ancestry. It is held vertically and played with a horsehair bow.

TATSUKICHI. This incident was representative of the new, more intense campaign against "unorthodox" ideas that had begun with the enactment of the PEACE PRESERVATION LAW OF 1925 (Chian Iji Hō), the first law in which the term *kokutai* was used. It forbade membership in any association advocating changes in the *kokutai* or the overthrow of the system of private property.

This intensified attack on heresy gave rise to the "clarification of the *kokutai*" movement (*kokutai meichō undō;* see KOKUTAI DEBATE), one result of which was the book KOKUTAI NO HONGI (1937; tr *Kokutai no hongi: Cardinal Principles of the National Entity of Japan,* 1949), published by the Ministry of Education and used as a textbook for ethics classes in schools. It presented the Japanese origin myths as historical facts and was extremely xenophobic in tone, though it offered no more precise definition of the *kokutai* than that it was "the everlasting rule over the Great Japanese Empire of an unbroken line of emperors in obedience to the commands of their ancestors."

As a result of Japan's defeat in World War II and the ensuing Occupation reforms the concept of *kokutai* fell into disuse and has little meaning to most Japanese today.

kokutai debate 国体明徴問題

(*kokutai meichō mondai;* literally, "debate concerning the clarification of the national polity"). Major political controversy in 1935 instigated by extremist elements in the army, right-wing politicians, and civilian groups in an attempt to discredit the theory of MINOBE TATSUKICHI that the emperor was merely an organ of the state (TENNŌ KIKAN SETSU). Traditionalists subscribing to an absolutist view of imperial sovereignty in February 1935 denounced Minobe in the Diet for violating the "national polity" (KOKUTAI) and accused him of lese majesty. The RIKKEN SEIYŪKAI tried to use the affair to overthrow the OKADA KEISUKE cabinet. In conjunction with right-wing organizations, the Seiyūkai initiated a campaign for "the clarification of the national polity." The government was

komainu Symbolic shrine and temple guardians. These pairs of lionlike figures are usually slightly asymmetrical: only one has its mouth open in a roar. Kanda Shrine, Tōkyō.

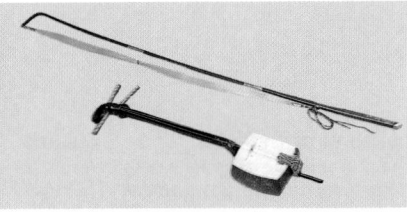

finally pressured into banning three of Minobe's works; it issued statements declaring the organ theory to be "contrary to the true meaning of the national polity." Minobe was forced to resign from the House of Peers. The *kokutai* debate added fuel to right-wing demands for a radical reconstruction of the political order and accelerated the trend toward ultranationalist thinking.

kokutai meichō mondai→kokutai debate

Kokutai no hongi 国体の本義

(Cardinal Principles of the National Entity of Japan). A political tract published on 30 March 1937 by the Ministry of Education. It was regarded by the Japanese government as a statement of the fundamental principles of the KOKUTAI (national entity or national polity), the state structure unique to Japan. Considered by OCCUPATION authorities to be militarist propaganda, it was banned in December 1945.

As stated in its introduction and conclusion, the avowed purpose of *Kokutai no hongi* was to combat social unrest, which was seen largely as stemming from Western influence. Divided into two books, the text was intended for the masses, including schoolchildren, but contains recognizable quotations from political and religious sources cited for intellectual credibility. Its fundamental thesis is Japan's divine character and mission, and it explores Japanese customs, culture, rites, BUSHIDŌ, and direct rule by the emperor to justify its conclusions.

Kokuyo Co, Ltd コクヨ[株]

(Kokuyo). Manufacturer of school and office supplies and furniture. The company was established in 1905 by Kuroda Zentarō (1881–1966). It manufactures approximately 90,000 products and has a near monopoly on the domestic market through a nationwide network of retailers. A computer network links management and production plants to customers. Sales for the fiscal year ending March 1991 totaled ¥308.0 billion (US $2.2 billion), of which furniture produced 60 percent and stationery 40 percent. Capitalization was ¥15.7 billion (US $114.4 million) in the same year. Headquarters are in Ōsaka.

Kōkyo→Imperial Palace

kokyū 胡弓

Long-necked bowed lute. Japan's only bowed musical instrument, the *kokyū* was derived partly from the Portuguese rebec and partly from the SHAMISEN, and entered Japan from the Ryūkyū Islands, probably at the end of the 16th century. In the 17th century it was still rare, but by the early 18th century it was being widely used as a folk instrument, and spread to Edo (now Tōkyō), where by mid-century it was played in *sankyoku* (trios with *shamisen* and KOTO). During the 1780s a fourth string was added to the Edo *kokyū*.

koma→tops

komadori 駒鳥

(Japanese robin). *Erithacus akahige.* A bird of the family Muscicapidae. One section of its

rhythmical song resembles the whinny of a horse, hence the name *komadori* ("horse bird"). It measures about 14 centimeters (5.5 in) in length and has an orange-red breast. Its eggs are blue. A subspecies, the *tanekomadori* (*E. akahige tanensis*), is found on the Izu Islands.

Noted for its beautiful appearance and song, the *komadori* has been kept in homes since early times. Although celebrated with the *uguisu* (BUSH WARBLER) and *ōruri* (blue-and-white flycatcher) as one of the "three songbirds of Japan," it has rarely been used as a poetic or pictorial subject.

Komae 狛江[市]

City in south-central Tōkyō Prefecture, central Honshū. Formerly a farming district, it is now a residential suburb of greater Tōkyō. Pop: 74,189.

Komagane 駒ケ根[市]

City in southern Nagano Prefecture, central Honshū, on the river Tenryūgawa. Rice and pears are grown. There is also an electronics and precision-instrument industry. It is a base camp for the mountain Kiso Komagatake and the highland Komagane Kōgen, popular with climbers and campers. The temple Kōzenji, with its magnificent stand of cypresses, is of interest. Pop: 32,771.

Komagatake 駒ケ岳

Mountain on the border of Yamanashi and Nagano prefectures, central Honshū, in the northern Akaishi Mountains; composed of granite. Also called Kai Komagatake and Kaikoma. Alpine flora abound. Komagatake is located in the SOUTHERN ALPS NATIONAL PARK. Height: 2,967 m (9,734 ft).

Komagatake 駒ケ岳

Mountain in southwestern Nagano Prefecture, central Honshū; the highest peak in the Kiso Mountains. Also called Kiso Komagatake and Kisokoma. Composed of granite. The summit's eastern side has a glacial erosion area, and the Senjōjiki cirque is famous. Alpine flora abound. There is a ropeway to Komagatake Shrine, which is on the summit. Height: 2,956 m (9,698 ft).

Komagatake 駒ケ岳

Mountain in the village of Hinoemata, southwestern Fukushima Prefecture, northern Honshū. Also called Aizu Komagatake and Aizukoma. There are deep valleys on the slopes. Swamps and ponds are located near the summit. Summer skiing is available because of late-lasting snow. Height: 2,133 m (6,998 ft).

Komagatake 駒ケ岳

Mountain in southeastern Niigata Prefecture, central Honshū. Part of the ECHIGO MOUNTAINS. Alpine flora grow around the summit. The region is noted for its many hot springs and heavy snowfall. Height: 2,003 m (6,571 ft).

Komagatake 駒ケ岳

Mountain in the northernmost part of the HIDA MOUNTAINS in central Toyama Prefecture, central Honshū. KUROBE KYŌKOKU, one of Japan's steepest gorges, is located on the eastern slopes. Height: 2,003 m (6,571 ft).

Komagatake 駒ケ岳

Composite volcano, in the Nasu Volcanic Zone, on the border between Akita and Iwate prefectures, northern Honshū. Also called Akita Komagatake and Akitakoma.

The peak Medake is in the volcano's central crater, and Odake is on the crater rim. Medake erupted in 1970 and 1971. Alpine flora, designated as natural monuments, abound. Komagatake is in Towada-Hachimantai National Park. Height: 1,637 m (5,371 ft).

Komagatake　駒ケ岳

Active conical volcano in the Nasu Volcanic Zone, Oshima Peninsula, southwestern Hokkaidō. Also called Oshima Fuji. It last erupted in 1942. Its slopes are covered with mixed broad-leaved and coniferous forests. It is the dominant peak in Ōnuma Quasi-National Park. Height: 1,133 m (3,717 ft).

Komai Kazuchika　駒井和愛

(1905–71). Archaeologist. Born in Tōkyō, Komai graduated from Waseda University. He was a professor at Tōkyō University from 1951 to 1965. Komai was a member of the team that excavated Shizuoka Prefecture's TORO SITE, a site opened in 1946 that dated to the Late Yayoi period (ca AD 100–ca AD 300). He also made significant contributions to archaeological excavations and research in Hokkaidō. Komai's publications include *Ohōtsukukai engan: Shiretoko Hantō no iseki* (2 vols, 1963–64, The Coast of the Sea of Okhotsk: Archaeological Sites on the Shiretoko Peninsula).

komainu　狛犬

Mythical lionlike beasts, statues of which are customarily placed in pairs in front of the gates or main halls of many shrines and temples to repel evil. The images may be made of stone, wood, or bronze. This custom came to Japan from continental Asia during the Heian period (794–1185).

Komaki　小牧[市]

City in northern Aichi Prefecture, central Honshū. Komaki developed as a post-station town during the Edo period (1600–1868). Served by several expressways, it is a satellite city of Nagoya. Industries include rubber, machinery, and textiles. Of historic interest is the site of the KOMAKI NAGAKUTE CAMPAIGN (1584). Pop: 124,441.

Komaki Nagakute Campaign　小牧・長久手の戦い

(Komaki Nagakute no Tatakai). Campaign fought in 1584 by the national unifier TOYOTOMI HIDEYOSHI against the combined forces of the future shōgun TOKUGAWA IEYASU and Oda Nobukatsu (or Nobuo; 1558–1630), ODA NOBUNAGA's son; the second and final stage of the succession struggle that had broken out among Nobunaga's generals after his assassination in 1582. In the first stage, which ended with Hideyoshi's victory at the Battle of SHIZUGATAKE in 1583, Nobukatsu took Hideyoshi's side and Ieyasu was passive. Disaffected by Hideyoshi's spectacular rise, Ieyasu and Nobukatsu formed an alliance, and in the spring of 1584 Nobukatsu provoked hostilities. After Ieyasu defeated Hideyoshi's forces in May at Nagakute (now the town of Nagakute, Aichi Prefecture), the war soon settled into fruitless skirmishing at nearby Komaki. In the winter of 1584 Hideyoshi marched on Oda Nobukatsu's domain at Ise (now part of Mie Prefecture), but the object of this offensive was to make peace with Nobukatsu rather than conquer him. This goal was achieved on 16 December 1584, in effect ending the campaign. Ieyasu welcomed the accommodation with Hideyo-

shi, who was left free to pursue his plans for the reunification of Japan.

Komatsu　小松[市]

City in southwestern Ishikawa Prefecture, central Honshū, on the Sea of Japan. Komatsu developed as a castle town after a *daimyō* of the Kanazawa domain retired here in 1639. Traditionally known for its KUTANI WARE and silk, its attractions are the Awazu Hot Spring; the temple Natadera; and the site of Ataka no Seki, a barrier station associated with the tragic hero MINAMOTO NO YOSHITSUNE. Pop: 106,075.

Komatsubara Eitarō　小松原英太郎

(1852–1919). Journalist and statesman of the Meiji period (1868–1912). Born in Okayama Prefecture, he studied at Keiō Gijuku (now Keiō University). He entered the Ministry of Foreign Affairs in 1880. He was appointed chief of the police department under the Home Ministry (Naimushō) in 1891, director of general affairs of the same ministry in 1899, and member of the House of Peers in 1900. He later became known as the main spokesman of the house's bureaucratic clique. In 1900 he also became managing editor of the *Osaka mainichi shimbun* (predecessor of the MAINICHI SHIMBUN) and president in 1901.

Komatsu, Ltd　[株]小松製作所

(Komatsu Seisakusho). Integrated manufacturer of construction machinery. Incorporated in 1921. Offering a full-line of construction equipment, presses, and industrial machinery such as robots and laser machines, Komatsu has production plants in Brazil, Indonesia, the United States, and the United Kingdom and serves customers in more than 150 countries. Consolidated net sales for the fiscal year ending March 1991 totaled ¥674.5 billion (US $4.9 billion), with ¥69.7 billion (US $508.0 million) in capital. Headquarters are in Tōkyō.

Komatsu Sakyō　小松左京

(1931–). Novelist. Real name Komatsu Minoru. Born in Ōsaka Prefecture; graduate of Kyōto University. He turned to writing science fiction in the early 1960s. With his novel *Nihon Apatchi zoku* (1964), Komatsu's reputation as a writer skilled in humor and satire became established. In his best-selling novel *Nihon chimbotsu* (1973; tr *Japan Sinks*, 1976), which was made into a film, he depicts the catastrophic end of the Japanese islands by earthquake while preserving hope and sympathy for the human race.

Komatsushima　小松島[市]

City in eastern Tokushima Prefecture, Shikoku. A port town since the Edo period (1600–1868), it is now the center of pulp, textile, and seafood-processing industries. Pop: 43,188.

Komatsu Tatewaki　小松帯刀

(1835–70). High-ranking *samurai* of the Satsuma domain (now Kagoshima Prefecture) active in the overthrow of the Tokugawa shogunate in 1867–68; later a high official in the Meiji government. He became a senior elder (KARŌ) in 1862 and after 1864 was Satsuma's representative in Kyōto, acting as coordinator of the various factions in the anti-Tokugawa movement. With SAKAMOTO RYŌMA and others, he was instrumental in bringing about the SATSUMA-CHŌSHŪ ALLIANCE. After the MEIJI RESTORATION Komatsu

served in the Meiji government as a junior councillor (*san'yo*) and briefly as vice-minister of foreign affairs.

Komazawa University　駒沢大学

(Komazawa Daigaku). A coeducational private university located in Setagaya Ward, Tōkyō. Founded in 1926, the university traces its origins back to the Sendanrin, an educational institution established in 1592 by the Sōtō sect of Zen Buddhism. Komazawa University seeks to provide an education infused with the spirit of Zen. Faculties include Buddhist studies, arts and sciences, economic science, law, and business management. Enrollment in 1989 was 14,682.

kombu　昆布

(kelp; also translated as sea tangle). Kelp of the family Laminariaceae. In Japan, *kombu* grows in the waters north of Miyagi Prefecture, northern Honshū, particularly on reefs deep in the ocean off Hokkaidō. The Japanese have eaten certain species of *kombu* since the Nara period (710–794) and it traditionally appears among foods prepared on occasions of celebration. Dried *kombu* is softened by soaking in water and used as an ingredient in stocks (*dashi*) and in the simmered dishes known as *nimono*. It is also simmered in soy sauce to make TSUKUDANI, wrapped around herring and simmered to make *kobumaki*, and processed into sweets. *Tororokombu* is a soft, thin kelp that is dried and shredded and used as an ingredient in clear soups (*sumashijiru*).

Kōmei, Emperor　孝明天皇

(1831–67; Kōmei Tennō). The 121st sovereign (*tennō*) in the traditional count (which includes several legendary emperors). He reigned from 1846 to 1867, a time when Japan faced two crises. Within, the movement to overthrow the Tokugawa shogunate (1603–1867) threatened to divide the country; without, the Western powers stood poised to open Japan by force. Kōmei favored continuing the 200-year policy of NATIONAL SECLUSION. After the visit by Commodore Matthew PERRY in 1853, Kōmei accepted the KANAGAWA TREATY of 1854 but in 1859 gave only conditional approval of the HARRIS TREATY. He opposed the military overthrow of the shogunate, preferring the MOVEMENT FOR UNION OF COURT AND SHOGUNATE (Kōbu Gattai Undō). He accordingly consented to the marriage of his sister Princess KAZU to the shōgun TOKUGAWA IEMOCHI in March 1862. This gesture further inflamed the antishogunate movement. Under pressure from SONNŌ JŌI (Revere the Emperor, Expel the Barbarians) extremists, Kōmei issued an edict in 1863 ordering all foreigners from the country. The extremists were driven out of Kyōto in the COUP D'ETAT OF 30 SEPTEMBER 1863. Political power reverted to the moderate *kōbu gattai* faction, and in 1865 the emperor belatedly approved the Harris Treaty and other agreements. Kōmei died of smallpox in January 1867. It was rumored that he had been poisoned. See also MEIJI RESTORATION.

Kōmeitō　公明党

(Clean Government Party). The second largest opposition political party in Japan, after the JAPAN SOCIALIST PARTY. What is now the Kōmeitō began in the 1950s as the political

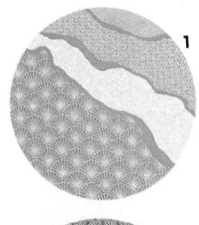

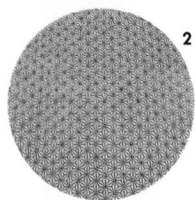

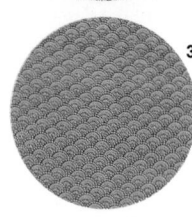

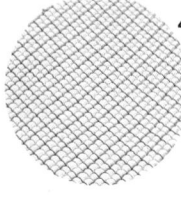

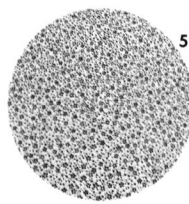

komon *Komon* (literally, "fine patterns") is a general term for detailed textile designs. **1** *Kimono* fabric on which a succession of tiny patterns produce a large-scale design. *Top to bottom:* sharkskin, waves, hail, chrysanthemums. **2** Hemp leaves. **3** Waves. **4** Geometric pattern. **5** Flowers.

wing of the SŌKA GAKKAI, a large lay organization affiliated with the Nichiren Shōshū sect of Buddhism. In 1961 this evolved into the Kōmei Political Federation, and on 17 November 1964 the organization adopted its present name and ran its first list of candidates for the House of Representatives. In 1969 the Kōmeitō was involved in a dispute contesting the publication of a book critical of the Sōka Gakkai, resulting in public disapproval and a decline in the party's strength in the Diet. In the wake of this incident, the Kōmeitō labored to break free of its image as a religiously oriented political party and adhere to the principle of the separation of politics and religion. In 1970 the party's national convention resolved to cut its organizational ties to the Sōka Gakkai and overhaul its platform to remove the strongly religious coloration it had previously possessed. By the late 1970s the Kōmeitō had regained its strength, and throughout the 1980s it served as the mainstay of the centrist forces in the Diet. In terms of policy, the party espouses peaceful coexistence with all nations, preservation of the 1947 constitution, strong support for social welfare programs, and the elimination of POLITICAL CORRUPTION. In recent years certain policy statements have brought the party closer to the more conservative positions held by the LIBERAL DEMOCRATIC PARTY and the DEMOCRATIC SOCIALIST PARTY—among them the Kōmeitō's official acceptance of the UNITED STATES–JAPAN SECURITY TREATIES and the constitutionality of the SELF DEFENSE FORCES, as well as its recognition of the Republic of Korea. In addition to its prominent position within the national Diet, the Kōmeitō is also a significant political force at the prefectural and local levels. See also POLITICAL PARTIES.

kome kitte 米切手

(rice certificates). Security certificates issued during the Edo period (1600–1868) to merchants upon purchase from a *daimyō* of rice stored in the latter's warehousing offices (KURAYASHIKI) in Ōsaka and other major commercial centers. The purchaser or recipient of the certificate held title to the amount of stored rice stipulated in the document. Though valid for only a limited time, *kome kitte* were widely circulated and became the principal instrument of rice transactions. The practice arose of redeeming part of the value of the certificate in silver rather than rice; *kome kitte* came to be used as security and were used increasingly in transactions involving amounts greater than their face value.

kome sōdō → rice riots of 1918

kōminkan → community centers

Komiya Toyotaka 小宮豊隆

(1884–1966). Literary critic. Born in Fukuoka Prefecture. Graduate of Tōkyō University. Professor of Tōhoku University and, after World War II, of Gakushūin University. A pupil of the Meiji-period (1868–1912) novelist NATSUME SŌSEKI, he wrote mainly on the *kabuki* and Nō theater; on the *haiku* poet BASHŌ; and on Sōseki, most notably in *Natsume Sōseki* (1938) and in *Sōseki no geijutsu* (1942, Sōseki's Art).

Kommintō 困民党

("Indigents' Party"). Also known as Shakkintō ("Debtors' Party"). Formed by peasants who rebelled in the western part of the

Kantō region and the southeastern part of the Chūbu region from 1883 to 1885 to demand lower interest rates and cancellation of debts (see also MATSUKATA FISCAL POLICY; FREEDOM AND PEOPLE'S RIGHTS MOVEMENT; CHICHIBU INCIDENT).

komon 小紋

Textile pattern of fine dots made from stencils and paste-resist; also fabrics with such patterns. The dots are usually from 1 to 2 centimeters in diameter (0.4 to 0.8 in), but the finest patterns have as many as 600 to 700 dots per 3 square centimeters (0.5 sq in). Early in the Edo period (1600–1868) *komon* was used mainly on a monochrome background for *kamishimo*, the warriors' formal upper garment, and later for unlined *haori*, *kosode*, and *nagajuban* (see CLOTHING). Since it was particularly popular in Edo (now Tōkyō), it is also known as Edo *komon*. In the Meiji period (1868–1912) its popularity declined, but it has recently come into use again. See also TEXTILES.

komonjo → diplomatics

komononari 小物成

Miscellaneous taxes, as opposed to the annual land taxes (HONTO MONONARI), levied by the shogunate and the domains during the Edo period (1600–1868). These taxes, abolished during the LAND TAX REFORM OF 1873–1881, were imposed on certain businesses and crafts, on products such as tea and fish, and on peasants' use of forests, mountains, and fields, which were not covered by *honto mononari*. They were paid in rice or cash. Some *komononari*, assessed annually at a fixed rate, were called *jō komononari* and were recorded in the village tax registers. Others fluctuated in amount; these were called *uki komononari* or UKIYAKU and were not recorded. *Komononari* assessed on various businesses were further classified as UNJŌ, MYŌGAKIN, etc. See also NENGU.

Komoro 小諸[市]

City in eastern Nagano Prefecture, central Honshū, on the slopes of the mountain Asamayama. A castle town and a post-station town during the Edo period (1600–1868), Komoro is associated with the poems of SHIMAZAKI TŌSON (1872–1943). Vegetables, apples, and peaches are grown. There is also an emerging electronics industry. Kaikoen, a park on the river Chikumagawa, contains the remains of Komoro Castle. Pop: 44,888.

Komparu school 金春流

(Komparuryū). One of the five major *shite kata* (principal player) schools (or troupes) of professional Nō theater actors. It claims descent from the Emaiza (Emai troupe; also known as the Takedaza), the oldest of the four Yamato SARUGAKU Nō troupes of the Kamakura period (1185–1333). The present name of the school is said to derive from the name of Komparu Gonnokami of the Nambokuchō period (Northern and Southern Courts period; 1337–92). Actor-playwright KOMPARU ZENCHIKU is credited with reviving the school in the mid-15th century. Komparu Zempō (b 1454), Zenchiku's grandson, is another well-known Komparu school playwright. In the Meiji period (1868–1912) the school produced a number of famous actors, including Sakurama Sajin (1835–1917). In 1951 Komparu Nobutaka (b 1920) became the 79th hereditary head of the school, whose members included Sakurama Michio (1897–1983), who was designated a Living National Treasure in 1970.

Komparu Zenchiku 金春禅竹

(1405–70?). Nō actor and playwright; head of the Emman'i troupe (ancestor of the modern KOMPARU SCHOOL of Nō). Real name Komparu Ujinobu. He studied with ZEAMI, married Zeami's daughter, and was Zeami's successor but was overshadowed by On'ami, favorite of the shōgun ASHIKAGA YOSHINORI. In 1466 Zenchiku retired to a hermitage near that of his friend, the Zen master IKKYŪ. A record from 1471 refers to Zenchiku as already deceased. Zenchiku wrote such respected critical treatises as *Kabu zuinō ki* (1456, The Essence of Song and Dance) and *Rokurin ichiro* (1455, The Six Wheels and the Drop of Dew). He also left several fine plays, including *Teika*, KAMO, and *Bashō*.

Kompira Shrine → Kotohira Shrine

kōmuin → public employees

Kŏmundo Incident 巨文島事件

(J: Kyobuntō Jiken). Also known as the Port Hamilton Incident. An 1885 dispute between Great Britain and Russia over Kŏmundo (J: Kyobuntō), a small island off Korea's southwest coast at the entrance to the Yellow Sea and midway between China and Japan. Russia's increased influence in Korea following the IMO MUTINY in 1882 aroused British interest in using the island as a commercial and naval base to counter Russia. British naval forces seized the island in 1885. China, Russia, and Japan immediately joined Korea in demanding their withdrawal, accomplished in 1887 after China and Russia promised neither to approve nor attempt occupation of Korean territory.

Komura Jutarō 小村寿太郎

(1855–1911). Foreign minister who vigorously promoted Japan's continental expansion. Born in the southern Kyūshū domain of Obi (now part of Miyazaki Prefecture), Komura studied law at the Daigaku Nankō (later Tōkyō University). He graduated from Harvard Law School in 1878. In 1880 he entered the Ministry of Justice and in 1884, the Ministry of Foreign Affairs.

In 1893 Komura became first secretary of the legation in Beijing (Peking). During the SINO-JAPANESE WAR OF 1894–1895 he served as civil administrator of Japanese-occupied areas in Manchuria and later drafted the Japanese peace demands (see SHIMONOSEKI, TREATY OF).

In May 1896 he signed an agreement with Russia, the Komura-Vaeber Memorandum, allowing joint interference in Korean internal affairs. He was vice–foreign minister until September 1898, when he was named minister to Washington.

In September 1901 Komura became foreign minister in the first KATSURA TARŌ cabinet and soon helped to conclude the ANGLO-JAPANESE ALLIANCE (January 1902). During the RUSSO-JAPANESE WAR (1904–05) he drafted peace terms that aimed at making Korea Japan's de facto sphere of sovereignty and southern Manchuria Japan's sphere of interest. Under instructions from Tōkyō he signed the highly unpopular Treaty of PORTSMOUTH, which brought the war to its conclusion. Komura further succeeded in forcing China to sign the Treaty of Beijing in December 1905, which transferred Russian rights in southern Manchuria to Japan.

In January 1906 Komura was appointed to the Privy Council (Sūmitsuin). In June he was named ambassador to England. In August 1908 he again became foreign minister and later that year arranged the signing of the TAKAHIRA-ROOT AGREEMENT with the United States. He played a key role in 1910 in Japan's takeover of Korea (see KOREA, ANNEXATION OF) and in 1911 in concluding international agreements that restored Japan's tariff autonomy.

Kōmyō, Empress   光明皇后

(701–760; Kōmyō Kōgō). Nonreigning empress (KŌGŌ); consort of the 45th emperor, SHŌMU (r 724–749). Daughter of the court official FUJIWARA NO FUHITO and the court lady AGATA NO INUKAI NO TACHIBANA NO MICHIYO, her personal names were Kōmyōshi and Asukabehime. In 729, through the influence of her family, she became the first woman not of royal blood to attain the rank of empress. She assumed sponsorship of the HIDEN'IN and SEYAKUIN, charitable foundations for the poor and sick, and generously patronized temples, especially the Shingon Ritsu sect temple Hokkeji. After her husband's death she dedicated some 600 valuable objects used by him and his court to the Great Buddha (DAIBUTSU) in Nara, of which more than 100 are preserved today in the SHŌSŌIN, treasure house of the temple TŌDAIJI. Empress Kōmyō is said to have wielded the real power of government during the rule of her daughter, the empress KŌKEN.

kōnai bōryoku→school violence

Konami Industry Co, Ltd   コナミ[株]

(Konami). Computer software maker. Incorporated in 1973. The company develops a variety of software, from action games, role-playing games, and communication games to business application and educational software. Konami has subsidiaries in Chicago, London, and Frankfurt. Sales for the fiscal year ending February 1991 totaled ¥50.8 billion (US $399.3 million), and capitalization stood at ¥8.1 billion (US $62.1 million). Headquarters are in Kōbe.

Kōnan   江南[市]

City in northern Aichi Prefecture, on the river KISOGAWA; 17 km (11 mi) north of NAGOYA. Kōnan was long known for its vegetables and sericulture, but the latter has been replaced by the synthetic-fiber, foodstuff, machinery, and metal industries. Pop: 93,837.

Kōnan University   甲南大学

(Kōnan Daigaku). A coeducational private university in the city of Kōbe, Hyōgo Prefecture. Originally founded in 1918 as the Kōnan Middle School, it achieved university status in 1951. The university maintains faculties of liberal arts, science, economics, law, and business administration. Enrollment in 1989 was 7,710.

kondei   健児

(literally, "able-bodied young men"). Militia established during the Nara period (710–794). Men between the ages of 20 and 40 with skills in archery and horsemanship were selected to serve in the provinces for periods of 60 days in exchange for temporary exemption from corvée labor (*zōyō*) and the rice tax (see YŌEKI; SO, YŌ, AND CHŌ). Although the *kondei* system was first created in 733, it was not until 792 that it replaced the earlier conscription system (*gundan*) established under the TAIHŌ CODE of 701. It attained a maximum strength of some 3,000

men but had been disbanded by the latter half of the Heian period (794–1185).

Konden Eisei Shizai Hō

墾田永世私財法

(also called Konden Einen Shizai Hō). Nara-period (710–794) law that granted private ownership of newly opened agricultural land to the individuals who developed it. Under the RITSURYŌ SYSTEM all land was owned by the government, which then distributed it for use (see HANDEN SHŪJU SYSTEM). In order to encourage reclamation the government enacted the SANZE ISSHIN NO HŌ, a law granting individuals ownership of reclaimed land through three generations. This 723 law proved to be ineffective, and in 743 the Konden Eisei Shizai Hō replaced it to encourage further land reclamation. Although the new law set some restrictions, it represented the abandoning of the basic principle of public ownership of land, and it allowed wealthy nobles and temples to amass huge private estates (SHŌEN).

kondō butsu   金銅仏

("gilt-bronze Buddhist image"). Japanese bronze Buddhist images produced in large numbers mainly from the 6th century through the 8th century. Two main techniques of casting were employed. In the lost-wax method a beeswax model was constructed around a small clay core. Clay was then applied to the exterior of the model to make a mold. When the mold was heated the wax burned away, allowing the molten bronze to be poured in. The second method was often used in the casting of large images and employed a model of either clay or wood. A clay mold was made of the model, which was then pared down to form the inner core. This pared core was secured within the hollow of the outer mold, and molten bronze was poured into the space between the core and the outer mold. After the casting of a statue, an amalgam of gold and mercury was applied to the bronze surface. By the Heian period (794–1185), wood had virtually replaced bronze as the main sculptural material.

Kondō Heisaburō   近藤平三郎

(1877–1963). Organic chemist and pharmaceutical scientist. Born in Shizuoka Prefecture. Graduate of the Faculty of Pharmaceutical Science, Tōkyō University. Kondō contributed to studies on the components of medicinal plants in Japan, especially the chemistry of alkaloids. He discovered new types of alkaloids through his structural determination of menispermaceous alkaloids, opening a new avenue in the field of organic chemistry. Kondō served as army pharmacist superintendent general, as a professor at Tōkyō University, and as director of the Otou Laboratory. He received the Order of Culture in 1958.

Kondō Isami   近藤勇

(1834–68). Shogunal loyalist and police official of the Tokugawa shogunate (1603–1867). Born into a farming family in Musashi Province (now part of metropolitan Tōkyō). In 1863 Kondō joined the SHINSENGUMI, a police force created to check increasing antishogunate activities in Kyōto. He became its commander and in 1864 led a bloody attack against antishogunate *samurai* in Kyōto (see IKEDAYA INCIDENT). After the defeat of Tokugawa forces in the 1868 Battle of TOBA-FUSHIMI, Kondō returned to Edo (now Tōkyō) and formed the Kōyō Chimbutai, a

shogunal loyalist unit. He led this force in attacks against imperial strongholds in the Kantō region until his capture and execution in 1868.

Kondō Jūzō   近藤重蔵

(1771–1829). Retainer of the Tokugawa shogunate (1603–1867) who explored EZO, as Japan's northern frontier was then called. Real name Kondō Morishige; pen name Seisai. Born in Edo (now Tōkyō). In 1798 Kondō was sent to explore and survey Ezo. Altogether he made four trips to the area, which he urged the shogunate to colonize. In his explorations Kondō was helped in no small measure by a resident merchant, TAKATAYA KAHEI. In 1808 Kondō was appointed shogunal commissioner of documents (*shomotsu bugyō*). Besides writing on geography and defense he edited *Gaiban tsūsho*, a collection of shogunate documents concerning foreign relations, and *Kenkyō ruiten*, a collection of shogunate laws.

Kondō Keitarō   近藤啓太郎

(1920–). Novelist. Born in Mie Prefecture. Studied painting at Tōkyō Bijutsu Gakkō (now Tōkyō University of Fine Arts and Music). His early stories reflect his experiences in a fishing village after World War II. His best-known short story about the sea is "Amabune" (1956, Women Divers), which was awarded the Akutagawa Prize. Other works include the novel *Umi* (1967, The Sea).

Kondō Yoshimi   近藤芳美

(1913–). TANKA poet. Born in Korea; graduated from Tōkyō Institute of Technology. In 1932 Kondō joined the group of poets publishing the magazine ARARAGI. With the publication of the two poetry collections *Sōshunka* (Poems of Early Spring) and *Hokori fuku machi* (Dust-Blown Streets) in 1948, Kondō established himself as a postwar poet. His works include *Kurohyō* (1968, Black Panther) and other poetry collections, as well as numerous critical essays.

Kongōbuji   金剛峰寺

Buddhist temple complex that is the central headquarters of the more than 3,600 temples in Japan belonging to the Kōyasan Shingonshū (Mt. Kōya Shingon sect) of Buddhism (see SHINGON SECT). Located on Mt. Kōya (KŌYASAN) in Wakayama Prefecture, it is one of Japan's foremost holy places. Kongōbuji was originally the general name for all the temples and buildings on Mt. Kōya, but in 1869 two of the temples, Seiganji and Kōzanji, merged to become the temple Kongōbuji. The temple's origins date to 816, when Emperor SAGA granted Mt. Kōya to the priest KŪKAI (commonly known as Kōbō Daishi). Kūkai opened there the first training center for Shingon *mikkyō*, a new school of ESOTERIC BUDDHISM with Indian origins that he had introduced to Japan from China and further systematized. The temple suffered destruction several times because of factional disputes and fire, but it was restored after each episode.

Kongōkai   金剛界

(Skt: Vajradhātu; Diamond or Thunderbolt Realm). Realm symbolizing one of two aspects of the Dharmakāya Buddha Mahāvairocana (J: DAINICHI), the central Buddha in ESOTERIC BUDDHISM, more particularly the SHINGON SECT. The Kongōkai reveals the wis-

Komura Jutarō
A career diplomat who actively promoted Japanese expansion on the Asian continent during two terms as foreign minister.

kondō butsu This 7th-century gilt-bronze statue from the temple Hōryūji in Nara is one of a group popularly known as the Shijūhattai Butsu ("48 Buddhas"). Height 42 cm. Tōkyō National Museum.

konnyaku
1 The *konnyaku* plant. **2** *Konnyaku* foods: a block of jelly (above), thin noodles called *shirataki* (below left), thick noodles called *ito konnyaku* (center and right).

dom aspect of this Buddha, who is also ultimate reality, without beginning or end. The essence of this wisdom is unchanging, indestructible, and powerful enough to destroy all delusions; it is therefore called "diamond." The Kongōkai is further divided into five spheres of wisdom, each symbolizing a particular realm. The *Kongōkai mandara* (MANDALA of the Vajradhātu) is a pictorial representation of this world, a square mandala divided vertically and horizontally into nine sections. The Kongōkai and the TAIZŌ-KAI (Matrix or Womb Realm), which is the other aspect of Mahāvairocana, can be seen as either dual entities or one and the same, depending on the interpretation. See also RYŌBU MANDARA.

Kongō Mountains　　　　金剛山地

(Kongō Sanchi). Mountain range running from north to south along the borders of Ōsaka and Nara prefectures, central Honshū. The highest peak is KONGŌSAN (1,125 m; 3,690 ft). The religion SHUGENDŌ is practiced here.

Kongōsan　　　　　　　金剛山

Also known as Kongōsen. Mountain on the border between Ōsaka and Nara prefectures, central Honshū; the highest peak in the Kongō Mountains. On its western slopes are the remains of Chihaya Castle, built by KUSUNOKI MASASHIGE in 1332. On the summit are the Katsuragi Shrine and the temple Tempōrinji. Height: 1,125 m (3,690 ft).

Kongō school　　　　　　金剛流

(Kongōryū). One of the five major *shite kata* (principal player) schools (or troupes) of professional NŌ theater actors. The school claims direct descent from the Sakadoza (Sakado troupe) of the Nambokuchō period (Northern and Southern Courts period; 1337–92), originally one of the four Yamato SARUGAKU Nō troupes. The present name of the school is said to derive from the childhood name, Kongōmaru, of Saburō Masaaki (1449–1526), who succeeded as troupe head (*tayū*). Ukon Ujinari (1815–84), head of the school from the late Edo period (1600–1868) through the early Meiji period (1868–1912), was a well-known Nō actor. The Sakado Kongō family line, however, ended with his grandson Ukyō Ujiyasu (1872–1936). Kongō Iwao (1886–1951) of Kyōto later succeeded as school head; his son Iwao II (b 1924) became the 25th hereditary head of the school.

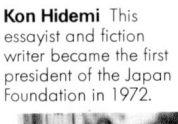

Kon Hidemi This essayist and fiction writer became the first president of the Japan Foundation in 1972.

Kon Hidemi　　　　　　今日出海

(1903–84). Literary critic and author. Born in Hokkaidō; younger brother of writer KON TŌKŌ. Graduate of Tōkyō University. *Sanchū hōrō* (1949) was based upon his war experiences in the Philippines. He received the Naoki Prize in 1950 for his short story "Tennō no bōshi." As director of the Ministry of Education's art department and founder of the annual Japan Art Festival, he was active in promoting Japanese literature and the arts. He directed the government's Agency for Cultural Affairs from 1968 until

he became the president of the Japan Foundation in 1972. His works include *Miki Kiyoshi ni okeru ningen no kenkyū* (1950), a fictional portrait of philosopher MIKI KIYOSHI (1897–1945).

Konica Corporation　　コニカ[株]

(Konika). Manufacturer of photographic film, sensitized paper, cameras, optical instruments, and copy machines, as well as medical, printing, and industrial machinery. Established in its present form in 1936, the firm was founded in 1873 as a manufacturer of photographic and lithographic materials. In 1987 the company developed the world's fastest color film, ISO 3200. Total sales for the fiscal year ending April 1991 were ¥369.4 billion (US $2.7 billion), of which 71 percent came from photographic materials and photo-related industrial equipment, 21 percent from business machines, and 8 percent from cameras and other sources. In the same year capitalization was ¥37.4 billion (US $272.6 million). Headquarters are in Tōkyō.

Konishi Raizan　　　　小西来山

(1654–1716). *Haikai* (see HAIKU) poet of the Edo period. Born in Ōsaka. He studied with NISHIYAMA SŌIN, the founder of the DANRIN SCHOOL of *haikai*, and was a friend of *haikai* poet UEJIMA ONITSURA, whose aesthetic of MAKOTO (sincerity) influenced his verse. Raizan's style is considered closer to the elegant restraint of BASHŌ than to the poetry of the Danrin group, although he profited from their freedom from the restrictions of traditional WAKA and linked verse. Chief among his works is a posthumous collection of poetry and prose, *Imamiyagusa* (1734).

Konishi Yukinaga　　　　小西行長

(?–1600). A principal lieutenant of TOYOTOMI HIDEYOSHI; known to contemporary Europeans as the CHRISTIAN DAIMYŌ Dom Agostinho. Yukinaga's father, Konishi Ryūsa Joachim (d 1594), was a merchant who became Hideyoshi's fiscal intendant (*kurairibun daikan*) in Kawachi Province (now part of Ōsaka Prefecture). Yukinaga entered Hideyoshi's service by 1581 and distinguished himself as a fleet commander in Hideyoshi's campaigns in 1585 and 1587. In 1588 Hideyoshi sent Yukinaga and KATŌ KIYOMASA to restore order in Higo Province (now Kumamoto Prefecture), which they divided between them. Yukinaga's domain, centered at Uto, included the Amakusa Islands, where in 1589–90 he had to subdue a rebellion of local barons who were fellow Christians. In May 1592 Yukinaga and Kiyomasa led the first two waves of Hideyoshi's invasion of Korea (see INVASIONS OF KOREA IN 1592 AND 1597). Following Hideyoshi's death in 1598, Yukinaga joined the league of *daimyō*, led by ISHIDA MITSUNARI, that opposed TOKUGAWA IEYASU but met defeat at Sekigahara (see SEKIGAHARA, BATTLE OF) in 1600. As a Christian, Yukinaga refused to commit suicide and was put to death in Kyōto.

Konjaku monogatari　　　今昔物語

(partial tr *Tales of Times Now Past*, 1979). Collection of more than 1,000 short tales said to have been compiled at a retreat in Uji, southwest of Kyōto, by a nobleman, Minamoto no Takakuni (1004–77), from tales told him by passersby. This tradition has been discredited, partly because the work contains references to events after 1077 but mostly because, although many of the tales are evidently based upon oral tradi-

tion, others derive from literary sources including Buddhist scriptures, Chinese histories, and secular Japanese works. (One of these sources seems not to have been brought to Japan until 1120.)

The work is divided into 31 books: 5 are about India, mostly concerning the Buddha and the growth of Buddhism; 5 about China (1 not extant), including some non-Buddhist as well as many Chinese Buddhist tales; and 21 about Japan (2 not extant), approximately evenly divided between Buddhist and secular themes. Notably, the tales include no myths, and Shintō themes play a very small part. The title is derived from the opening words of each story, the same "Once-upon-a-time" formula used in fairy tales. The modern writer AKUTAGAWA RYŪNOSUKE, greatly attracted to this collection, dealt with its material in several of his stories.

Konjiki yasha　　　　　　金色夜叉

(tr *The Golden Demon*, 1905). Novel by OZAKI KŌYŌ (1867–1903), written 1897–1903 and left unfinished at his death. The work poses romantic love against lust for material riches, reflecting concern for the widespread advance of capitalist values at the time. The protagonist, Hazama Kan'ichi, a promising student who will soon enter a university, plans to marry Shigisawa Miya, the beautiful daughter of Kan'ichi's benefactor. Miya, however, is infatuated with Tomiyama Tadatsugu, the son of a banker, and breaks with Kan'ichi to marry this wealthy young man. Incensed by her betrayal, Kan'ichi abandons his academic career and vows to amass a enormous fortune of his own. He becomes a clerk to a particularly devious usurer and soon turns as heartless as his mentor. Passages of *Konjiki yasha*, such as the seaside scene at Atami, in which Kan'ichi violently refuses to accept Miya's apology, may seem melodramatic by modern standards. However, the novel's very theatricality (it was also made into a SHIMPA drama) and its rather ornate style, which combined both classical and vernacular Japanese (*gazoku setchū*), made *Konjiki yasha* one of the top best sellers of the Meiji period (1868–1912).

Konkōkyō　　　　　　　金光教

Syncretist SHINTŌ sect; founded in 1859 by Kawate Bunjirō (1814–83) of Bitchū Province (now part of Okayama Prefecture). His recovery from illness, following supplication to the vengeful deity Konkō Daijin (also called Konjin), confirmed his faith in this god, and in 1859 Kawate took the god's name as his own and converted his home into a shrine. Konkōkyō believes Konjin to be the parent god of heaven and earth and the god of love. It holds that the life of Kawate, the living manifestation (IKIGAMI) of Konjin, is its doctrine. It teaches that all beings are equal and that if a person worships Konjin, works diligently, avoids selfishness, and is kind to others, that person will receive the god's blessing.

Konkōkyō spread through the area along the Inland Sea by the end of the Edo period (1600–1868), and Kawate was licensed to conduct worship in 1864 and confirmed as the priest (KANNUSHI) of Konjin Shrine in 1867. In the early years of the Meiji period (1868–1912), however, these offices were revoked by the government. During his lifetime Kawate opposed any subordination to STATE SHINTŌ, but, to avoid suppression, the officers of Konkōkyō later made efforts to conform to its doctrines, and in 1900 Konkōkyō was officially recognized as an independent sect (see SECT SHINTŌ). Its headquarters are in Konkō Chō, Okayama Prefecture. In 1990 it claimed some 450,000 followers.

konnyaku　蒟蒻

Amorphophallus konjak. Bulbous perennial herb that has been cultivated in Japan from ancient times; also a jellylike noncaloric food derived from the plant's bulb. To make the latter, the bulb is sliced, dried, and then boiled; a coagulant is added and the material is molded into blocks. It is also formed into thick noodles (*ito konnyaku*) or fine ones (*shirataki*). Slices of *konnyaku* are an ingredient in simmered dishes (*nimono*) such as ODEN. *Shirataki* is used in *sukiyaki* and other *nabemono* (vegetable and fish or meat dishes prepared in a pot).

Kōno Bairei　幸野楳嶺

(1844–95). MARUYAMA-SHIJŌ SCHOOL painter, book illustrator, and teacher. Born in Kyōto, he studied with the Maruyama school artist Nakajima Raishō (1796–1871) and then with the Shijō school painter Shiokawa Bunrin (1808–77). He also studied calligraphy and Chinese literature with Confucian scholars Kamiyama Hōyō and Miyahara Setsuan. Bairei was instrumental in founding the Kyōto Prefectural Painting School (Kyōto Fu Gagakkō) in 1880 and opened his own school in 1881. After he retired from teaching in 1890, he helped establish the Kyōto Art Association (Kyōto Bijutsu Kyōkai). In 1893 he was appointed artist for the imperial household (*teishitsu gigeiin*).

Konoe Atsumaro　近衛篤麿

(1863–1904). Political leader and pan-Asianist; scion of the KONOE FAMILY and father of Prime Minister KONOE FUMIMARO. Born in Kyōto; studied at the University of Leipzig. He received the title of prince under the PEERAGE system instituted in 1884 and was named to the House of Peers in 1890. Konoe openly criticized the monopoly of government power held by the Satsuma and Chōshū cliques (see HAMBATSU) in the early 1890s. In 1895 Konoe became head of the Peers' School (see GAKUSHŪIN UNIVERSITY). The following year he became chairman of the House of Peers and after his resignation in 1903 was appointed to the Privy Council.

In 1898 he founded the TŌA DŌBUNKAI, a society to promote a pan-Asian movement to end European influence in East Asia. Konoe pressed for resolution of tsarist Russia's occupation of Manchuria and in 1903 formed the Tairo Dōshikai to incite public opinion against Russia.

Konoe family　近衛家

(Konoeke). The senior of five houses (GOSEKKE) of the Northern Branch (Hokke) of the FUJIWARA FAMILY whose members were eligible for the post of regent (SESSHŌ or KAMPAKU). The Konoe house was established in the late Heian period (794–1185) by Fujiwara (Konoe) Motozane (1143–66); the family took its name from the Konoedono residence of Motozane's son Motomichi (1160–1233) in Kyōto. Family members served for generations as regents and grand ministers of state (*dajō daijin*); many were scholars, poets, and calligraphers (see KONOE NOBUTADA). After the Meiji Restoration (1868) and the establishment of a new peerage (*kazoku*), the head of the family was given the rank of prince (*kōshaku*). Perhaps the best-known member of the family, KONOE FUMIMARO, son

of KONOE ATSUMARO, served three times as prime minister just before World War II.

Konoe Fumimaro　近衛文麿

(1891–1945). Politician and prime minister (1937–39; 1940–41). The son of KONOE ATSUMARO, he inherited the title of prince. A native of Tōkyō, he graduated from Kyōto University in 1917. Seated in the House of Peers in 1916, he served as a member of the Japanese delegation to the Paris Peace Conference in 1919. He was an active leader of the House of Peers, becoming its vice-president in 1931 and its president from 1933 to 1937. He was a staunch defender of the nobility, which he believed should preserve a high-minded "impartial" position as defenders of the imperial polity (KOKUTAI). Konoe advocated the reduction of Western influence in Asia and the enhancement of Japan's power and prestige in its place. After Chinese nationalists refused to support Japanese expansion on the Asian mainland, Konoe supported the conversion of Manchuria into a Japanese puppet state (MANCHUKUO).

He was first nominated to the post of prime minister after the FEBRUARY 26TH INCIDENT of 1936 but declined and did not form his first cabinet until June 1937. Konoe's first cabinet (4 June 1937–5 January 1939) presided over the outbreak of the SINO-JAPANESE WAR OF 1937–1945 in July 1937 and the Japanese government's initial steps toward mobilizing the populace into a "national defense state" (see NATIONAL MOBILIZATION LAW). Because of his inability to end the war in China on his terms, Konoe resigned in early 1939.

Throughout the rest of 1939 Konoe was president of the PRIVY COUNCIL. In early 1940 he sought to launch the NEW ORDER MOVEMENT and in July was reappointed prime minister. His second two terms, which were consecutive (22 July 1940–18 July 1941; 18 July 1941–18 October 1941), saw a worsening of Japan's position at home and abroad and the creation of the IMPERIAL RULE ASSISTANCE ASSOCIATION. Konoe proclaimed the establishment of a Japan-dominated GREATER EAST ASIA COPROSPERITY SPHERE as part of his program to have Japan recognized as the master of East Asia. He promoted Japan's entry into a military alliance with the Axis powers in Europe in September 1940 (see TRIPARTITE PACT) and then sought the Soviet Union's support of this accord in order to secure Japan's northern flank and deter British and US intervention in China and Southeast Asia. Hitler's attack on the Soviet Union in June 1941 ruined Konoe's plans for a quadripartite alliance. In the summer of 1941, perceiving that Japan's overseas expansion could not succeed in the face of US economic and military pressure, he proposed, in vain, a summit meeting with President Franklin D. Roosevelt. Unwilling to accept any further responsibility for Japan's dilemma, he resigned from office on 16 October. Throughout the remainder of World War II, Konoe held no public office but retained influence. In the first postwar cabinet, he served as vice–prime minister and worked on revising Japan's constitution to conform with the wishes of the OCCUPATION authorities, who withdrew their support of his constitutional reforms and indicted him as a war criminal. On 16 December 1945 he committed suicide.

Konoe Iehiro　近衛家熙

(1667–1736). Courtier, master calligrapher, and cultural leader in Kyōto. Born into the highest-ranking family of courtiers, Iehiro

was a grandson of Emperor GO-MIZUNOO and married the daughter of Emperor Reigen (1654–1732; r 1663–87). He became regent in 1709, the youngest man ever to hold this position. Iehiro's position was largely ceremonial; he retired in 1725 and became a monk with the name of Yorakuin.

Iehiro was a great cultural figure in Kyōto, with his own schools of tea ceremony and flower arrangement. His collection formed the core of the Konoe Collection, now housed in the YŌMEI BUNKO in Kyōto. He was also a poet, painter, and garden designer, but his greatest achievements were in calligraphy. His brushwork follows the models of the previous masters of the Konoe school, but he expanded the stylistic range of his predecessors. He wrote in all of the five Chinese script styles as well as in Japanese KANA.

Konoe Nobutada　近衛信尹

(1565–1614). Courtier and calligrapher. As the son of the regent Konoe Sakihisa (1536–1612), Nobutada was a scion of the leading family among Kyōto courtiers. He held various exalted posts, but these were ceremonial, since the Tokugawa shogunate (1603–1867) in Edo (now Tōkyō) controlled the country. Nobutada developed his calligraphy following family traditions, but he also incorporated the style of Heian-period (794–1185) masters. With HON'AMI KŌETSU and SHŌKADŌ SHŌJŌ, Nobutada has been classed as one of the Kan'ei no Sampitsu ("Three Brushes of the Kan'ei Era"), although he died before the Kan'ei era (1624–44) began. His brushwork is characterized by a sense of blunt power and movement.

Kōno Hironaka　河野広中

(1849–1923). Political activist and politician. Born into a rural *samurai* (GŌSHI) family of the Miharu domain (now part of Fukushima Prefecture). He met ITAGAKI TAISUKE and later joined Itagaki's FREEDOM AND PEOPLE'S RIGHTS MOVEMENT and JIYŪTŌ (Liberal Party). Elected chairman of the Fukushima Prefectural Assembly in 1881, Kōno in 1882 organized popular resistance to Prefectural Governor MISHIMA MICHITSUNE's plan to levy compulsory labor service for road-building projects (see FUKUSHIMA INCIDENT). He was arrested and imprisoned but was released in 1889. In the first Diet election, in 1890, Kōno was elected to the first of 14 consecutive terms in the House of Representatives. He left the Jiyūtō in 1897 and joined the rival KENSEI HONTŌ (True Constitutional Party). In 1905 Kōno helped to organize a mass meeting in Tōkyō to protest the Treaty of PORTSMOUTH with Russia, which led to the HIBIYA INCENDIARY INCIDENT. Kōno was imprisoned but was released the next year. In 1914 Kōno became minister of agriculture and commerce. He spent his last years working for the UNIVERSAL MANHOOD SUFFRAGE MOVEMENT.

Kōno Ichirō　河野一郎

(1898–1965). Politician. Born in Kanagawa Prefecture; graduate of Waseda University. He worked as a reporter for the newspaper *Tōkyō asahi shimbun* before his election to the House of Representatives as a member of the RIKKEN SEIYŪKAI party in 1932. In 1945 Kōno helped HATOYAMA ICHIRŌ form the Japan Liberal Party (Nihon Jiyūtō). Barred from office (1946–51) during the OCCUPATION PURGE, he became minister of agriculture and forestry under Hatoyama in 1954 and worked toward restoring relations with the

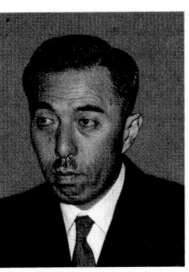

Konoe Fumimaro
One of the most important political figures of the 1930s and 1940s, Konoe served three terms as prime minister.

Soviet Union. He was again minister of agriculture and forestry under IKEDA HAYATO in 1961.

Kōnoike family   鴻池家

(Kōnoikeke). A major Ōsaka merchant house during the Edo period (1600–1868), founded by Yamanaka Shinroku (1570–1650). Around 1600 Shinroku, a man of *samurai* origin who became a brewer in the village of Kōnoike in Settsu Province (now part of Hyōgo Prefecture), discovered how to make clear *sake*, and demand grew rapidly. In 1619 he moved to Ōsaka and opened a brewery. By 1630 the family were major shippers as well as brewers. Shinroku became an agent for sales of *daimyō* tax rice stored in their warehouses in Ōsaka, which gave him access to rice for his *sake* production (see KURAMAI). By 1637 the Kōnoike were engaged in making loans to various daimyō (see DAIMYŌ LOANS) whose finances were often strained by the SANKIN KŌTAI system, which required them to reside in Edo on alternate years. Shinroku was succeeded by his son Zen'emon (1608–93), the first of 13 generations of family heads to use the name Kōnoike Zen'emon. He opened a successful money-changer shop (see RYŌGAE-SHŌ), which for two generations was the primary business of the house. Daimyō loans increased under Zen'emon III (1667–1736), and by 1704 they accounted for 73.5 percent of total house capital.

In the early 19th century daimyō interest payments declined, and the Kōnoike were increasingly subjected to forced levies by the Tokugawa shogunate (1603–1867). The financial base of the house was strong enough to withstand both these levies and the shocks of the MEIJI RESTORATION of 1868, but the fortunes of the family declined in the late 19th and early 20th centuries. Active in banking, insurance, real estate, and other enterprises, they have survived, however, as prestigious members of the Ōsaka commercial community.

Kōno Kenzō   河野謙三

(1901–83). Politician. Born in Kanagawa Prefecture; graduate of Waseda University. He served in the House of Representatives from 1949 to 1953, when he was elected to the House of Councillors. There he was a member of the RYOKUFŪKAI until leaving it in 1958 to join the Liberal Democratic Party (LDP). He quickly became an influential Diet member and served as vice-speaker of the House of Councillors (1965–68) and as its president (1971–77). He was the brother of KŌNO ICHIRŌ and the uncle of KŌNO YŌHEI.

Kōno Michiari   河野通有

(?–1311). Warrior of Iyo Province (now Ehime Prefecture). In the defense of northern Kyūshū against the second of the MONGOL INVASIONS OF JAPAN (1281), he led a successful attack on the Mongol fleet. Kōno is depicted in the *Mōko shūrai ekotoba* (Mongol Invasions Picture Scroll), a scroll commissioned by his fellow warrior TAKEZAKI SUENAGA.

Kō no Moronao   高師直

(?–1351). General of the period of the NORTHERN AND SOUTHERN COURTS (1337–92). Member of a family of hereditary retainers (*hikan*) of the Ashikaga, Moronao served ASHIKAGA TAKAUJI, founder of the MUROMACHI SHOGUNATE, as his chief executive officer (*shitsuji*) from 1336. Moronao fought Southern ar-

mies, destroying KITABATAKE AKIIE in 1338 and Kusunoki Masatsura in 1348. In shogunate politics, Moronao is identified as the leader of a "radical" faction opposed to the "legalists" headed by ASHIKAGA TADAYO-SHI, Takauji's brother and his right hand in civil administration. In 1349 Tadayoshi unsuccessfully sought to displace Moronao. The next year Tadayoshi formally adhered to the Southern Court and raised an army that in 1351 inflicted defeats on Takauji and Moronao. Although Tadayoshi agreed to be reconciled with Takauji on condition that Moronao take the tonsure and withdraw from political affairs, Moronao was subsequently killed by troops loyal to Tadayoshi. Moronao's image as an arrogant parvenu was established by the 14th-century war tale TAIHEIKI. He is also famous as the villain of the popular 18th-century *bunraku* and *kabuki* play *Chūshingura* (The Treasury of Loyal Retainers). See also KANNŌ DISTURBANCE.

Kōnosu   鴻巣[市]

City in central Saitama Prefecture, central Honshū. Kōnosu developed as a post-station town during the Edo period (1600–1868). Now a satellite city of Tōkyō with numerous industries, it is also known for its dolls. Pop: 72,435.

Kōno Taeko   河野多恵子

(1926–). Novelist. Real name Ichikawa Taeko. Born in Ōsaka. Graduate of Ōsaka Women's University. Kōno first attracted public attention with *Yōji-gari* (1961, Baby Hunt) and received the Akutagawa Prize for *Kani* (1963, Crabs). In both works Kōno presents everyday human reality, while at the same time brilliantly illuminating the dark passions of the subconscious. Other works include the novels *Fui no koe* (1968, Sudden Voice) and *Ichinen no bokka* (1980, A Year of Pastorals) and the critical study *Tanizaki bungaku to kōtei no yokubō* (1976, The Literature of Tanizaki and the Desire for Affirmation).

Kōno Togama   河野敏鎌

(1844–95). Politician active during the Meiji period (1868–1912). Born in the Tosa domain (now Kōchi Prefecture). In 1861 he joined a local proimperial league and in 1863 he and others in the league were imprisoned by domain authorities for antishogunate activities. In 1869, after the MEIJI RESTORATION, Kōno was introduced to ETŌ SHIMPEI, who was working for the Ministry of Punishments (Gyōbushō). Etō secured an official appointment for Kōno, who gradually rose to become chief justice. Kōno later presided over the trial of Etō, who had broken with the Meiji government to lead the SAGA REBELLION in 1874. Kōno also tried the leaders of the SATSUMA REBELLION in 1878. In 1881 he was appointed minister of agriculture and commerce but was forced to retire as a result of the POLITICAL CRISIS OF 1881. With ŌKUMA SHIGENOBU he founded the RIKKEN KAISHINTŌ political party. In 1888 Kōno served on the PRIVY COUNCIL, newly created to review ITŌ HIROBUMI's draft of the proposed constitution (see CONSTITUTION OF THE EMPIRE OF JAPAN). In 1892 he served as minister of agriculture and commerce and thereafter held several ministerial posts.

Kōno Yōhei   河野洋平

(1937–). Politician; founder (1976) and first chairman of the New Liberal Club (Shin Jiyū Kurabu), a political party. A graduate of Waseda University, he attended Stanford

University in California in 1961. Previously a member of the ruling LIBERAL DEMOCRATIC PARTY (LDP), he was elected to the House of Representatives in 1967 at age 29, succeeding his late father, KŌNO ICHIRŌ, who had been a faction leader in the LDP. Kōno Yōhei became parliamentary vice-minister of education in 1973. In 1985 he became director-general of the Science and Technology Agency. The New Liberal Club disbanded in 1986, and that year Kōno returned to the LDP.

Konrad, Nikolai Iosifovich   コンラッド, N. I.

(1891–1970). Soviet orientalist. In 1912 he graduated from the Japanese-Chinese Section of the Department of Oriental Languages of St. Petersburg University and the Japanese Section of the Practical Oriental Academy. In 1912 and from 1914 to 1917 he studied in Japan. Konrad headed the Japanese language and literature sections of the Oriental Department of the St. Petersburg University, the A. S. Enukidze Leningrad Oriental Institute (1922–38), and the Moscow Oriental Institute (1941–49). He wrote a grammar of conversational and literary Japanese as well as a number of works on Japanese and Chinese literary history. Konrad was also the founder of the Soviet school of scientific translation and commentary on major texts of classical Japanese literature. He edited the two-volume *Large Japanese-Russian Dictionary* (1970). In 1969 he was awarded the Order of the Rising Sun, the highest Japanese decoration given to foreigners.

konsei   金精

Type of deity. Often referred to as *konsei sama*. The *konsei* is worshiped primarily as a god ensuring safe delivery of babies and as a god of marriage. This god is considered a variation of the *sae no kami* (DŌSOJIN). Found frequently in eastern Japan, most notably in the Tōhoku and Kantō regions, it takes the form of a phallus of stone, wood, or, rarely, bronze.

Konsei Pass   金精峠

(Konsei Tōge). Located on the border of Tochigi and Gumma prefectures, central Honshū. Situated within Nikkō National Park, it is famed for its spectacular views of the wooded slopes of the mountain Nantaisan. A 755 m (2,477 ft) tunnel through the pass and a toll road were completed in 1965. Altitude: 2,024 m (6,640 ft).

Konsen Highlands   根釧台地

(Konsen Daichi). Diluvial upland, northeast of the city of Kushiro, eastern Hokkaidō. An abrasion platform averaging about 200 m (660 ft) in elevation, covered by volcanic ash. This land, long unused because of sea fog in the summer, was finally cleared, and dairy farming began in 1955. Potatoes and sugar beets are also cultivated here. Area approximately 5,000 sq km (2,000 sq mi).

Kon Tōkō   今東光

(1898–1977). Novelist, Buddhist priest, and politician. Born in Kanagawa Prefecture. Elder brother of novelist KON HIDEMI. He participated in the avant-garde literary movement of the 1920s, led by such notable writers as KAWABATA YASUNARI and YOKOMITSU RIICHI. He was a maverick of the group and participated briefly in the PROLETARIAN LITERATURE MOVEMENT before becoming a Buddhist priest in 1930. He resumed writing with the best-selling novel *Ogin sama* (1956, The

Bard), winner of the Naoki Prize. In 1966 he assumed the position of abbot at the temple CHŪSONJI, and in 1968 he was elected to the House of Councillors. Most of his works are amorous anecdotes narrated with uninhibited eloquence. Important works include *Shundei Ni shō* (1957, The Story of the Nun Shundei) and *Akumyō* (1960–61, Notorious).

Kōrai → Koryŏ

Korai fūtei shō   古来風体抄

(Notes on Poetic Style through the Ages). Two-volume treatise on poetics written by FUJIWARA NO TOSHINARI in 1197 at the request of Princess SHIKISHI; revised 1201. Volume 1 contains discussions of the nature and history of Japanese verse (WAKA) and explications of 191 verses selected from the 8th-century collection MAN'YŌSHŪ. In volume 2, Toshinari gives examples that display the variety of expressive effects that can be achieved with *waka* and analyzes verses drawn from seven IMPERIAL ANTHOLOGIES, beginning with the KOKINSHŪ (ca 905) and ending with the SENZAI WAKASHŪ (ca 1187). He also records verses that he considers to be the finest of the tradition and asserts that the essence of *waka* is best displayed in the verse of the *Kokinshū*. Toshinari's definition of the aesthetic power of *waka* as arising from the conjunction of graceful cadence and deeply resonant image (YŪGEN) strongly influenced poetry of the medieval period (mid-12th–16th centuries). An autograph manuscript of the first version of *Korai fūtei shō* held by the REIZEI FAMILY SHIGURETEI MUSEUM has been designated a National Treasure.

Kōrakuen   後楽園

Landscape garden in Okayama, Okayama Prefecture, western Honshū. It is considered an outstanding representative of the KOBORI ENSHŪ school of landscape gardening. Completed in 1702 by Ikeda Tsunamasa, the local *daimyō*, it was donated to Okayama Prefecture in 1871 and opened to the public in 1884. Along with KENROKUEN and KAIRAKUEN it is one of the three most celebrated landscape gardens in Japan. It has tea-ceremony houses, ponds, waterfalls, a miniature tea plantation and rice paddy, and a stage for the Nō drama. Area: 13.3 hectares (33 acres).

Kōrakuen Garden   後楽園

(Kōrakuen). Municipal park in Bunkyō Ward, Tōkyō; also called Koishikawa Kōrakuen. Built around a large pond with a small island, Hōraijima, in the center, it reflects a strong Chinese influence in its design. Several miniature hills represent famous Chinese and Japanese scenes from nature. The garden was originally laid out in the early 17th century by Tokudaiji Sahei on the orders of Tokugawa Yorifusa (1603–61) and TOKUGAWA MITSUKUNI, *daimyō* of the Mito domain (now part of Ibaraki Prefecture). Adjoining the garden is an amusement center with sports facilities, including the TŌKYŌ DOME. Area: 6.9 hectares (17 acres).

Korea and Japan   朝鮮・韓国と日本

(Chōsen, Kankoku *to* Nihon). Contact between the peoples of the Korean peninsula and the Japanese archipelago existed before the dawn of history and continued, largely in a friendly fashion, until the 19th century. Following the Meiji Restoration (1868), however, Japan extended its influence over the Korean peninsula, and from 1910 to 1945 Korea was a colony of Japan. Since the 1960s Japan has conducted friendly relations

with the Republic of Korea, and economic ties between the two countries have grown steadily closer. As of 1991 Japan had not established diplomatic relations with the Democratic People's Republic of Korea.

Prehistory to the 16th Century — JŌMON POTTERY, the ware characteristic of the prehistoric Japanese Jōmon period (ca 10,000 BC–ca 300 BC), bears resemblances to "comb-pattern" pottery unearthed in Korea, and the basic elements of the culture of the Yayoi period (ca 300 BC–ca AD 300)—rice cultivation, bronze, and iron—were most likely brought to Japan by immigrants from Korea. Archaeological findings and historical documents indicate that from the latter half of the 4th century Japan was in close contact with the Asian continent, and over the next few centuries groups of people arrived from Korea, bringing with them more products of continental culture. Some of them established powerful clans that wielded considerable political influence and whose daughters were, on occasion, received as consorts by scions of the Japanese imperial family (see KIKAJIN).

The YAMATO COURT maintained close relations with the Korean kingdom of PAEKCHE, from which Buddhism, Confucianism, and Chinese characters were transmitted to Japan, and was also in contact with the kingdoms KOGURYŎ and SILLA, which lay to the north and east of Paekche, respectively. Formal relations with Silla, which had established undisputed control over the peninsula by 676, ceased in 779, but trade between Korea and Japan thrived, continuing into the period that followed the overthrow of Silla and the establishment of KORYŎ in 918. However, the MONGOL INVASIONS OF KOREA (1231–59) and the subsequent MONGOL INVASIONS OF JAPAN (1274 and 1281) rendered trade impossible, and in the wake of this turmoil bands of pirates (WAKŌ), largely Japanese, made an increasing number of attacks on coastal areas of China and Korea. In 1404 Japan was permitted by Ming dynasty (1368–1644) China to become a tributary nation—and thus to enjoy the fruits of trade—on the condition that the MUROMACHI SHOGUNATE (1338–1573) suppress the pirates. An eventual consequence of this development was the establishment of relations between Japan and the YI DYNASTY (1392–1910) of Korea, which was also a tributary of China. The early rulers of the Yi dynasty permitted trade and conducted diplomatic relations through the SŌ FAMILY, lords of the island of Tsushima in the Korea Strait. See also ŌEI INVASION.

Invasions of Korea and Korean Embassies to Edo — The INVASIONS OF KOREA IN 1592 AND 1597 were executed by TOYOTOMI HIDEYOSHI, who in 1590 had established control over all of Japan, in order to extend his power to Korea and China. The campaigns, which ended in defeat at the hands of a combined force of Koreans and Ming Chinese, contributed to the collapse of the Toyotomi suzerainty. For Korea, however, the consequences were widespread desolation and the removal to Japan of some 50,000 to 60,000 of its citizens as well as many books and copper movable type. Among Koreans brought to Japan were numerous potters, who initiated the manufacture of KARATSU WARE, ARITA WARE, and HAGI WARE.

Hideyoshi's successor as suzerain and founder of the Tokugawa shogunate (1603–1867), TOKUGAWA IEYASU, who wished to resume trade, initiated negotiations with Korea on a basis of equality. In 1607 formal relations were restored and a mission of sev-

eral hundred Koreans was received and feted at Edo (now Tōkyō). A total of 11 such embassies (*tsūshinshi;* Kor: *t'ongsinsa;* see CHŌSEN TSŪSHINSHI) arrived in Edo during the Edo period (1600–1868), providing an important diplomatic contact during this era of Japanese NATIONAL SECLUSION. In 1618 the Sō family of Tsushima reopened the trade station, or WAEGWAN (Japanese residence), at Pusanp'o (now Pusan), and Japanese exports included silver, copper, and pepper, while the Koreans exported cotton, ginseng, and Chinese silks. Although formal relations between the two countries ended with the mission of 1811, which came only as far as Tsushima, trade through the Sō family continued.

Meiji Restoration to the Annexation of Korea — Following the opening of Japan by the Western powers and the resumption in 1868 of direct imperial rule, the nation swiftly embarked upon a new era of development as a modern capitalist state. Korea, however, maintained a policy of seclusion and sank an armed US commercial ship that in 1866 sailed up the Taedong River to the vicinity of P'yŏngyang, and fired on French (1866) and US (1871) naval fleets that entered the mouth of the Han River near the capital city of Seoul. In 1869 the Korean government refused to accept a communication, transmitted through the Sō family, informing it of the Meiji Restoration (1868), because terms used in reference to Emperor MEIJI (r 1867–1912) implied a parity with the emperor of China, of which Korea remained a tributary state. The Meiji government then divided into camps for and against the military conquest of Korea (see SEIKANRON). In 1875 a Japanese warship, dispatched for the ostensible purpose of surveying the Korean coast, was fired upon by a Korean shore battery when it entered the mouth of the Han River; on the pretext of gaining satisfaction for this insult, a fleet of six naval vessels was sent early in the following year to force the signing of the Treaty of KANGHWA, which provided for the opening of three Korean ports, the appointment to each of a Japanese consul with extraterritorial jurisdiction over Japanese nationals, and exemption from customs duties.

Although Japan had thus succeeded in gaining a march on the Western powers by concluding an unequal treaty with Korea, rivalry with China was inevitable. An attempt by the reform faction led by Queen MIN, with the assistance of Japanese advisers, to modernize the Korean army led to disaffection of elements of the army, which rose in revolt (see IMO MUTINY). Military units were dispatched from Japan but arrived after the insurrection had been put down by Chinese forces. Nevertheless, in addition to indemnities, Japan extracted the right to station troops in Seoul. In the wake of the KAPSIN PO-

Kōrakuen Behind the ponds and trees of this noted landscape garden rises a modern reconstruction of Okayama Castle, former headquarters of the *daimyō* who commissioned the Kōrakuen in the early 18th century.

LITICAL COUP of 1884, Japan and China agreed to withdraw their troops from Korea (see TIANJIN [TIENTSIN] CONVENTION); however, in the spring of 1894 the TONGHAK REBELLION broke out, and the Korean government called on the Chinese for military assistance. Japan too sent an expeditionary force, which clashed with the Chinese in July 1894, leading to the SINO-JAPANESE WAR OF 1894–1895.

Victory in that war and in the RUSSO-JAPANESE WAR of 1904–05 enabled Japan to stem the influence in Korea of China and Russia, and, under threat of military force, to gain affirmation by Korea of Japanese ascendancy through the three Korean-Japanese conventions of 1904, 1905, and 1907. The first of these gave Japan the right to install advisers to the Korean government on financial and diplomatic affairs and required Korea to seek Japanese approval of all important diplomatic dealings. Japan secured the consent of the United States, Great Britain, and Russia to its special interest in Korea through the KATSURA-TAFT AGREEMENT of July 1905, the second ANGLO-JAPANESE ALLIANCE of August 1905, and the Treaty of PORTSMOUTH of September 1905. The signing in November of the KOREAN-JAPANESE CONVENTION OF 1905 gave Japan full administrative control over Korea's foreign affairs, thus making it a protectorate, and provided for establishment of the Office of Resident General in Korea (see RESIDENT GENERAL IN KOREA, OFFICE OF). The third convention was signed in July 1907, just five days after the forced abdication of King KOJONG of Korea, and gave comprehensive administrative power over Korean domestic affairs to the resident general. This was followed on 1 August by the disbanding of the Korean army. Elements of the army rose against the Japanese but were suppressed; anti-Japanese guerrilla activity broke out throughout the country and persisted into 1914.

Colonial Period—In September 1909 ITŌ HIROBUMI, resident general in Korea, was assassinated by AN CHUNG-GUN, and in December an attack was made on Itō's protege, Korean prime minister YI WAN-YONG. On 22 August 1910 a treaty annexing Korea to Japan was signed by Yi and became effective on 29 August (see KOREA, ANNEXATION OF), bringing to an end the dynasty founded by YI SŎNG-GYE in 1392 and the Taehan Cheguk (TAEHAN EMPIRE; since 1897 the official name of Korea). Authority over the military, the judiciary, the legislature, and the civil administration was vested in the GOVERNMENT-GENERAL OF KOREA, presided over by a governor-general appointed by the Japanese emperor. Regulations issued by the government-general, which was essentially a military government presided over by an army general or navy admiral, were enforced by a Japanese military police force (kempei keisatsu), which assumed the duties of the regular police and was charged not only with the enforcement of criminal law but also that of public health regulations and the use of the Japanese language. Under the Chōsen Kyōiku Rei (Education Law of Korea) of August 1911, Japanese was made the primary language of Korean schools.

Immediately after annexation, the government-general banned all meetings, rallies, and political parties. All existing newspapers were suppressed and replaced by government newspapers, one each in Korean, Japanese, and English. The Companies Law (Kaisha Rei) of 1910 placed the estab-lishment of private enterprises under a licensing system that militated against the accumulation of capital by Koreans. Land surveys were carried out from 1910 to 1918 to establish property rights; land that was not reported or whose ownership was undocumented was nationalized and the tillers made tenant farmers. Japanese, under their constitution, were guaranteed trial before a judge. Koreans, under Law (Seirei) 10 promulgated in December 1910, were subject to administrative trial by captains of police stations or equivalent officials in instances in which punishment for an offense was ¥100 or less, or three months of confinement or less. In December 1912, under Directive (Kunrei) 40, the punishment of whipping (chikei), administered only to Koreans, was instituted. Harsh and prejudicial treatment by the Japanese provoked increasing resentment.

The call by President Woodrow Wilson of the United States for the self-determination of nations, and the death of King Kojong in January 1919, contributed to the formation of a movement for independence. On 1 March 1919, while the Paris Peace Conference was in session, a declaration of independence was read in Seoul to a cheering audience of 5,000, who were joined by tens of thousands of others as they marched through the city (see SAMIL INDEPENDENCE MOVEMENT). The movement spread throughout the country, involving as many as 2 million participants and issuing in numerous violent confrontations with the Japanese police and military. In April 1919 the PROVISIONAL GOVERNMENT OF KOREA was founded by Korean patriots in Shanghai as a government-in-exile. As a result of the independence movement the governor-general was recalled, the kempei keisatsu was replaced by a much larger civil police force, the Companies Law was revised, and the publication of magazines and newspapers and the formation of community organizations was permitted. Censorship, however, remained strict.

In the 1920s Korean rice production was stepped up to meet shortages in Japan: in 1919, 22 percent of the rice produced in Korea was shipped to Japan, but by 1931 exported rice amounted to 57 percent of the total crop. Many owners of small plots were unable to meet the costs imposed on them by land-improvement and irrigation projects, and their paddies were bought up by large landholders with low-interest loans guaranteed by the Japanese government. Between 1919 and 1933 the number of tenant farmers increased by some 550,000. Moreover, many Koreans were forced to seek land in Manchuria or employment in Japan: at the time of the MANCHURIAN INCIDENT in September 1931 there were 700,000 Koreans in Manchuria, and between 1910 and 1929 the number of Koreans in Japan rose from 790 to 270,000. The antipathy felt toward Korean immigrants by the Japanese is reflected in the fact that in the wake of the TŌKYŌ EARTHQUAKE OF 1923 rumors spread that Koreans were rioting and pillaging, and more than 6,000 innocent Koreans were killed by vigilante organizations, mobs, and the police.

Following the outbreak of the SINO-JAPANESE WAR OF 1937–1945, efforts were stepped up to assimilate Koreans. Worship at Shintō shrines was enforced and the principles of Japanese emperor worship were introduced into the curriculum of Korean schools. In 1940 all Koreans were forced to assume Japanese names. Between 1939 and 1945 some 1.2 million Koreans were transported to Japan to perform forced labor, and toward the end of WORLD WAR II Koreans were made subject to military conscription.

1945–1952—On 15 August 1945 Emperor SHŌWA (Hirohito) announced Japan's surrender and its acceptance of the POTSDAM DECLARATION, putting into effect the CAIRO DECLARATION, under which the independence of Korea was established. However, under an agreement between the United States and the Soviet Union the peninsula was occupied by Soviet forces north of the 38th parallel and by US troops south of that line. This resulted in the founding in August 1948 of the Republic of Korea (Taehan Minguk; J: Daikan Minkoku; hereafter South Korea) under President Syngman RHEE in the south, and the founding during the following month of the Democratic People's Republic of Korea (Chosŏn Minjujuui Inmin Gonghwa-guk; J: Chōsen Minshushugi Jimmin Kyōwakoku; hereafter North Korea) under KIM IL-SŎNG in the north.

At the close of World War II there were some 2.3 million Koreans residing in Japan. The majority chose to be repatriated and by March 1946 the population had been reduced to 640,000. Nearly all of the Japanese military personnel and civilians in Korea—710,000 in 1944—had been repatriated by the end of 1946. In October 1945 the Association of Korean Residents in Japan (Zai Nihon Chōsenjin Remmei) was formed to assist repatriation and to protect the livelihoods of Koreans in Japan. The organization came under the influence of the Japan Communist Party (JCP) and was disbanded by government order in 1949; however, a new body, the General Federation of Korean Residents in Japan (Zai Nihon Chōsenjin Sō Rengō Kai), which distanced itself from the JCP, was formed in 1955 to represent the overseas interests of North Korea. The Korean Residents' Association in Japan (Zai Nihon Chōsen Kyoryūmin Dan; later Zai Nihon Daikan Minkoku Kyoryūmin Dan) was set up in October 1946 and supports South Korea. See KOREANS IN JAPAN.

With the invasion of South Korea by North Korea on 25 June 1950, war broke out between the two Korean states, and forces of the United Nations, chiefly US troops, sided with South Korea while China sided with North Korea. After three years and several phases of intense fighting an armistice was signed on 27 July 1953, restoring a line near the 38th parallel as the border between the two Koreas (see KOREAN WAR). Throughout the war Japan served as the chief military supply base for UN forces, and its economy benefited immensely by the expenditure of some US $2.4 billion to US $3.6 billion for goods and services (see TOKUJU).

Relations with South Korea, 1952–1990—With the restoration of Japan's independence on 28 April 1952, it regained the right to conduct diplomatic relations with the nations of the world. At the urging of the United States, formal talks were initiated in February 1952 toward the establishment of relations with South Korea. Differences over such issues as the demarcation of territorial waters in the Sea of Japan (see RHEE LINE) and rights of Japanese to property in South Korea, and anger on the part of South Koreans over the remark by Japanese delegate Kubota Kan'ichirō at the third session in October 1953 that Korea had benefited from the 35-year Japanese occupation, contributed to the breakdown of negotiations. A fourth series of talks began in April 1958 but was broken off due to the repatriation of Koreans to North Korea by Japan in 1959. The sixth session in 1961–64 ended due to an impasse over the issue of territorial waters and claims and counterclaims of property rights. In 1962 President PAK CHŎNG-HŬI announced the commencement of a five-year economic plan, and, in order to fund the plan, resolution of the issue of Japanese war reparations became an urgent priority.

Although the United States continued to urge the normalization of relations, opposition by groups in South Korea claiming that the treaty would open the way for a new era of Korean political and economic dependency on Japan, by the Japan Socialist Party, by the Korean residents' associations in Japan, and by North Korea contributed to the delay of negotiations. On 20 February 1965, however, Japan and South Korea agreed that the treaty to be signed would declare void all treaties and agreements signed on or before 22 August 1910. Japan also confirmed UN Resolution 195, which specified that South Korea was the only lawful government of Korea. The KOREA-JAPAN TREATY OF 1965 and supplementary agreements were signed on 22 June. Mutual property claims were abandoned, but Japan agreed to provide to South Korea US $800 million in economic assistance. The Rhee line was abolished and South Korean territorial waters were set at 12 miles (19.3 km) from its shores. It was also agreed that Koreans in Japan who had been living there prior to World War II would be given permanent resident status. The one remaining unresolved issue was that of territorial rights to the island TAKESHIMA (Kor: Tokto) in the Sea of Japan. As a result of the treaty political and economic relations rapidly improved. Regular ministerial conferences between the two countries were initiated in 1967, and in 1969 leading Japanese and Korean businessmen and financiers formed the Japan-Korea Cooperative Committee (Nikkan Kyōryoku Iinkai; Kor: Il-Han Hyŏpryŏk Wiwŏnhoe).

The rapid development of South Korea's economy in the 1970s contributed greatly to the establishment of stable and close economic relations with Japan. Nevertheless a series of unfortunate incidents that marred diplomatic relations between the two countries indicated that there remained considerable mistrust and hostility due to Japan's pre–World War II colonial ambitions. Prominent among these issues were the kidnapping and removal to Seoul in 1971 of opposition leader Kim Dae-jung by agents of the Korean Central Intelligence Agency (see KIM DAE-JUNG INCIDENT), the attempted assassination in 1974 of President Pak Chŏng-hŭi by a Korean resident of Japan, and the so-called TEXTBOOK ISSUE, in which China and South Korea formally objected in August 1982 to what they alleged were distortions of fact introduced at the insistence of the Japanese government into passages in history textbooks dealing with Japan's pre–World War II activities in Asia.

The government of NAKASONE YASUHIRO, formed in November 1982, placed a high priority on the improvement of relations with South Korea, and in January 1983 Prime Minister Nakasone visited South Korea, where he announced the start of a new era in relations between the two countries and promised US $4 billion in economic aid. During a visit to Japan in September 1984 President Chŏn Du-hwan of Korea was received by Emperor Shōwa, who, in reference to prewar Japanese aggression against Korea, expressed "sincere regret" for the "unfortunate past." However, the effectiveness of Prime Minister Nakasone's diplomacy vis-à-vis South Korea, which was based on his personal relationship with President Chŏn, was seriously prejudiced by mounting criticism in South Korea of the Chŏn regime. Relations worsened when in September 1986 Japanese minister of education Fujio Masayuki (b 1917), whose ministry had approved revisions in Japanese history textbooks, caused a furor by declaring that Korea was in part responsible for its annexation in 1910 by Japan. The education minister resigned and Prime Minister Nakasone immediately went to South Korea to tender an apology. In 1990 changes in procedure relating to fingerprinting for identification cards that resident aliens are required to possess, and amelioration of restrictions on the civil rights of Koreans residing in Japan, led to the improvement of South Korea–Japan relations. In an audience in May 1990, Emperor AKIHITO expressed to South Korean president Roh T'ae-u his "deep regret" for the "suffering" the Korean people had been forced to endure during the period of Japanese colonial rule.

The steady improvement in diplomatic relations between South Korea and Japan has been accompanied by the expansion of trade relations, and in 1990 South Korea was Japan's third largest trading partner, while Japan was South Korea's second largest. In that year Japan's exports to South Korea totaled US $17.5 billion and its imports US $11.7 billion. Japan accounted for 26.6 percent of South Korea's total imports and 19.5 percent of its exports, while South Korea accounted for 5.0 percent of total Japanese imports and 6.1 percent of exports. In the same year some 653,000 South Korean tourists and businessmen visited Japan and 1.37 million Japanese visited South Korea.

Relations with North Korea, 1952–1990——Following the restoration of its independence Japan had no contact with North Korea until the late 1950s. However, many Koreans residing in Japan expressed a desire to be repatriated to North Korea and negotiations were initiated through the mediation of the International Red Cross. Despite strong opposition by South Korea an agreement was signed in August 1959, and 88,611 Koreans had been repatriated to North Korea by December 1967.

Japan's foreign policy concerning the Korean peninsula has been to honor the spirit of its agreements with the United States and South Korea and to take no action vis-à-vis North Korea that would contradict that policy. However, it is hoped that a consequence of the rapprochement between the East and the West in the late 1980s and early 1990s will be an improvement in relations with North Korea. In September 1990 Kanemaru Shin (b 1914), a former secretary-general of the Japanese Liberal Democratic Party (LDP), visited North Korea bearing a letter of apology for Japan's pre–World War II activities in Korea from Prime Minister KAIFU TOSHIKI in his capacity as president of the LDP, and in November preliminary negotiations were initiated toward the reestablishment of diplomatic relations. The normalization of relations with North Korea is one of Japan's greatest unresolved diplomatic problems of the post–World War II period.

Korea, annexation of　日韓併合

(Nikkan Heigō). Korea was annexed by Japan on 22 August 1910. On the eve of the SINO-JAPANESE WAR OF 1894–1895 Japan's policymakers were divided between those who favored helping Korea modernize so that it could resist Western imperialism and those who wanted to absorb the country into the Japanese empire. After Japan's victory over China, Russia assumed the role of Japan's rival on the Korean peninsula. Under the YAMAGATA-LOBANOV AGREEMENT Russia and Japan pledged to preserve Korea's independence, but after the outbreak of the RUSSO-JAPANESE WAR in 1904 Japan moved military units into Korea and declared it a Japanese protectorate. Nonintervention by Western powers was assured by the KATSURA-TAFT AGREEMENT, the ANGLO-JAPANESE ALLIANCE, and the Treaty of PORTSMOUTH. Japan forced Korea to sign a protectorate treaty on 18 November 1905 (see KOREAN-JAPANESE CONVENTION OF 1905). ITŌ HIROBUMI became resident general of a Japanese-staffed administration that paralleled the Korean bureaucracy and instituted economic development programs that benefited Japanese immigrants and investors. The Korean monarch KOJONG secretly authorized an unsuccessful appeal of the protectorate treaty before the second Hague Conference on World Peace, but this led to his forced abdication on 19 July 1907, and on 24 July Itō assumed complete control of the Korean government. In 1909 the Japanese prime minister KATSURA TARŌ informed Itō that annexation was inevitable. Itō, who resisted immediate annexation, resigned as resident general of Korea in June, but his assassination in October by AN CHUNG-GŬN hastened the process. In 1910 Korea's prime minister, YI WAN-YONG, and Japan's minister of war, TERAUCHI MASATAKE, signed a treaty that transformed Korea into Chōsen, which remained a colony of Japan until 15 August 1945. See also KOREA AND JAPAN.

Korea-Japan Treaty of 1965

日韓基本条約

(J: Nikkan Kihon Jōyaku). Formally known as the Treaty on Basic Relations between Japan and the Republic of Korea (ROK; South Korea). Concluded on 22 June 1965 after 14 years of negotiations, the treaty provides for diplomatic and consular relations (art. 1). It also confirms that all treaties or agreements concluded between Japan and Korea on or before 22 August 1910, the date of the annexation of Korea to Japan, are already null and void (art. 2). It affirms that the government of the ROK is the only lawful government in Korea as specified in Resolution 195 (III) of the United Nations General Assembly (art. 3). It provides that the two countries will be guided by the principles of the Charter of the United Nations in their mutual relations (art. 4).

Agreements in addition to the Treaty on Basic Relations covered such areas as fisheries, settlement of problems concerning property and claims, economic cooperation, the legal status and treatment of ROK nationals residing in Japan, cultural cooperation, and the settlement of disputes. See also KOREA-JAPAN TREATY OF 1965, SUPPLEMENTARY AGREEMENTS.

Korea-Japan Treaty of 1965, supplementary agreements

日韓基本条約付属協定

(J: Nikkan Kihon Jōyaku *fuzoku kyōtei*). The 26 documents concerning disputes between Japan and the Republic of Korea (ROK) signed on 22 June 1965 along with the

Korean War
A Japanese tank factory in the early 1950s, when Japan served as a staging area and supply depot for the US military effort in Korea. Japanese industry received millions of dollars' worth of contracts for supplies.

Treaty on Basic Relations. The agreements involved property claims, fishing rights, the legal rights of KOREANS IN JAPAN, and the return of certain Korean cultural properties in Japanese possession. Most of these disputes arose out of the period of Japanese colonial occupation of Korea (1910–45), which had intensified long-standing animosities between the Japanese and Koreans and made the post–World War II normalization of relations a long and difficult process.

Over a 10-year period negotiations began to bear fruit because of strong US pressure and the economic policies of the PAK CHŎNG-HŬI government after 1961. In late 1962 a secret agreement was reached under which Japan was to provide US $800 million in grants and government and commercial credits to the ROK. Although the secrecy of the negotiations was denounced by Koreans and Japanese, the so-called Kim-Ōhira Memorandum provided the framework for the 1965 agreement on property claims and economic cooperation.

A second major area of dispute resulting directly from the forced withdrawal of the Japanese from Korea was the fate of Koreans who had elected to remain in Japan. At the end of World War II, about three-fourths of the Koreans in Japan were repatriated, and the status of the approximately 600,000 Koreans remaining in Japan became an issue. The ROK demanded that residents be given special status, with the full benefits of Japanese citizenship and the right to remain ROK citizens. Negotiations on the issue of the legal rights of Korean residents began in October 1951 but stalled in the late 1950s after a serious dispute arose between the ROK and Japan over the repatriation of approximately 51,000 Koreans to the Democratic People's Republic of Korea (DPRK; North Korea). Agreement was finally reached after Japan made a number of concessions, including the classification of all Koreans as nationals of the ROK and the recognition of demands concerning privileges of permanent residence, favorable treatment, and the removal of property and funds.

The agreement allowed each country to establish an exclusive fishing zone with a 12-nautical-mile limit, allowed for the establishment of joint regulations, and set maximum limits with respect to the number of fishing vessels in the area, the size of the vessels, and the type of fishing. In addition, Japan extended US $120 million in commercial credits to the ROK for the development of its fishing industry.

No final agreement was reached with respect to sovereignty over the island of TAKE-SHIMA (Kor: Tokto); the two countries simply pledged to settle disputes through negotia-

tions. However, the serious negotiations and subsequent agreements of 1965 represented a turning point in improving relations between the ROK and Japan. See also KOREA AND JAPAN; KOREA-JAPAN TREATY OF 1965.

Korean campaigns of 1592 and 1597 → invasions of Korea in 1592 and 1597

Korean-Japanese Convention of 1905   第二次日韓協約
(J: Dainiji Nikkan Kyōyaku). Known in Korea as the Ŭlsa Treaty (Ŭlsa is the designation in the sexagenary cycle for the year corresponding to 1905) or Protectorate Treaty. The convention established Korea as a Japanese protectorate and was a major step toward Japan's 1910 annexation of Korea. ITŌ HIROBUMI presented it to the Korean cabinet, which signed it on 18 November 1905 after Japanese soldiers occupied the Korean royal palace. Japan assumed complete responsibility for Korea's foreign affairs. Trade in Korean ports was placed under Japanese supervision. The Residency General of Korea was established to advise the Korean government. King KOJONG sent a secret mission to the Second Hague Conference on World Peace in 1907 to contest the convention, but the effort failed. See also KOREA, ANNEXATION OF.

Koreans in Japan   在日韓国人と朝鮮人
(zainichi kankokujin to chōsenjin). The presence of a large ethnic minority of Koreans in Japan, most of whom are legally aliens, is mainly a legacy of Japanese colonialism. When Japan annexed Korea in 1910, there were only about 2,500 Koreans in Japan. However, during World War II, Koreans were brought to Japan as forced laborers, many to the coal or gold mines, to solve the wartime manpower shortage. At the end of World War II, there were more than 2 million, many of whom were repatriated after Japan's surrender. In 1990 approximately 688,000 Koreans resided in Japan, constituting the largest ethnic minority. About 90 percent of this population consists of Japanese-born, second- and third-generation Koreans, many of whom have never been to Korea nor learned to speak Korean. (Birth in Japan does not legally assure Japanese citizenship, unless one parent is a Japanese national. See FOREIGNERS IN JAPAN.)

During the colonial period Koreans had been granted Japanese nationality, but the Japanese government disenfranchised them in 1952 and declared them aliens, excluded from the benefits reserved for Japanese citizens. Koreans remaining in Japan endured economic hardship as a result, eking out an uncertain livelihood as day laborers or workers in the service and entertainment industries. Recently the number of Koreans entering professional and clerical positions is increasing, but as before they must confront the reality of discrimination in the workplace.

Two groups which have been at the center of the struggle to abolish discrimination and improve daily life for Koreans in Japan are Mindan (Zai Nihon Daikan Minkoku Kyoryūmin Dan; Korean Residents Association in Japan), founded in 1946, which is affiliated with the Republic of Korea (South Korea), and Chōsen Sōren (Zai Nihon Chōsenjin Sō Rengō Kai; General Federation of Korean Residents in Japan), founded in 1955 and affiliated with the Democratic People's Republic of Korea (North Korea). Since the

1970s, citizen groups have also become active, stimulated in part by the success of the Korean plaintiff in the renowned *Pak Chong-sŏk* v *Hitachi, Ltd*, case of 1974. Pak Chong-sŏk sued Hitachi when the company withdrew an offer of employment after learning of his Korean ancestry, which he had concealed on his application by using the Japanese form of his name. In June 1974 the court ruled that Hitachi's cancellation of Pak's employment offer was "an arbitrary breach of the labor contract" and recognized that Japanese society had compelled Pak to hide his Korean name to escape discrimination.

Since the Hitachi case, the clauses making Japanese citizenship a requirement have been dropped for entrants into the LEGAL TRAINING AND RESEARCH INSTITUTE, for employees in local government, and for schoolteachers, widening the range of employment opportunities for Korean nationals. In recent years Koreans in Japan have also distinguished themselves in such areas as theater, music, sports, and literature. Notable Korean authors include LEE HWE-SONG, KIM TAL-SU, and KIM SŎK-PŎM.

In 1982 the Japanese government granted permanent resident status to Koreans who had lived in Japan prior to the end of World War II, and to their children. In 1991, this right was extended to third-generation Koreans in Japan as well. Since the late 1970s the Japanese government has made considerable progress toward guaranteeing Korean residents access to the same social security benefits enjoyed by Japanese citizens. As of January 1993, Korean and other permanent residents were no longer required to be fingerprinted as a part of ALIEN REGISTRATION procedures, a concession to prolonged protests against this requirement (see REFUSAL TO BE FINGERPRINTED). Such improvements in their legal status, however, have not eliminated the discrimination many Koreans in Japan still face in their daily lives.

Korean Three Kingdoms period   三国時代
(J: Sangoku *jidai;* Kor: Samguk *sidae*). The period in Korea from approximately 300 to 668 when three states (KOGURYŎ in the north, PAEKCHE in the southwest, and SILLA in the southeast) were founded and fought for control of the Korean peninsula. The era began with Koguryŏ's conquest of the Han Chinese colony LELANG (Lolang; Kor: Nangnang) and ended with Silla's unification of the peninsula in 668. Chinese culture, institutions, technology, and Buddhist traditions filtered through Paekche to Japan during this period. See also SAMGUK SAGI; SAMGUK YUSA.

Korean War   朝鮮戦争
(J: Chōsen Sensō). Major military confrontation between the Republic of Korea (ROK), the United States, and the United Nations on one side and the Democratic People's Republic of Korea (DPRK), the People's Republic of China (PRC), and the Soviet Union on the other. The war began on 25 June 1950, when the DPRK sought by force to reunite the Korean nation, divided at the 38th parallel into a Soviet-occupied north and a US-occupied south at the conclusion of World War II. Hostilities continued until an armistice was concluded on 27 July 1953.

When fighting broke out, US President Harry S. Truman ordered General Douglas MACARTHUR to rush troops from Japan to Korea in support of the ROK. The UN Secu-

rity Council approved UN military intervention against the DPRK, which was designated the aggressor. During the summer of 1950, DPRK forces pushed UN and ROK forces into a small area around the southeastern port of Pusan. However, on 15 September US forces made an amphibious attack at Inch'ŏn, a port on Korea's western coast, reversing the tide of battle. DPRK forces crumbled into retreat. In October UN–ROK armies struck across the 38th parallel into North Korea, driving toward the Yalu River, Korea's border with China.

China responded with a massive counteroffensive, and by June 1951 both sides were stalemated in positions along the 38th parallel. Armistice negotiations continued for two years in P'anmunjŏm, until an agreement was signed leaving Korea divided by a demilitarized zone along the 38th parallel. Casualties amounted to approximately 4 million, including 1 million civilians on each side and 900,000 Chinese. Some 50,000 US soldiers died in the conflict. During the war Japan became a staging area and supply depot for the military effort in Korea and also received millions of dollars of contracts for supplies. The policy of the US OCCUPATION of Japan also shifted from an emphasis on reform to the reconstruction of Japan as a new ally.

Korea Strait　朝鮮海峡

(Chōsen Kaikyō). Between the Korean peninsula and the island of TSUSHIMA, connecting the Sea of Japan and the East China Sea. This strait has long been important in transportation between Japan and the continent. In recent years Japan and South Korea have had disputes over the rich fishing ground here. Narrowest point: 50 km (30 mi); deepest point: 210 m (690 ft).

Kōrin　光琳

(1658–1716). Painter and designer of the Edo period (1600–1868). Also known as Ogata Kōrin; real name Ogata Koretomi. Working in the RIMPA style, he imbued the classical themes of HON'AMI KŌETSU (1558–1637) and Tawaraya SŌTATSU (d 1643?) with a cool elegance and decorative sense of design. Even his most formalized and simplified bird-and-flower paintings are enhanced by a lifelike naturalism based on sketches from life.

Kōrin was the second son of an upper-class merchant, Ogata Sōken (1621–87), the proprietor of a successful Kyōto textile shop.

Through self-indulgence and poor investments, Kōrin quickly squandered his inheritance. His financial difficulties led him to take up painting as a serious profession from the 1690s. He was already well trained in the techniques of KANŌ SCHOOL ink painting, which he had studied with Yamamoto Soken (d 1706), and there is also evidence that he was an accomplished designer of textile patterns. Around 1700 and again between 1709 and 1712 Kōrin collaborated with his younger brother KENZAN, who had chosen pottery as a profession. Kōrin painted quick sketches in iron oxide on the flat surfaces of the square plates designed by his brother. In 1701 at age 43, Kōrin achieved official recognition with the award of the honorary title *hokkyō*.

He is most admired for his gorgeous screens in rich colors against a gold ground. The earliest of these are thought to be the *Iris Screens* (*Kakitsubatazu*) in the Nezu Art Museum in Tōkyō. Several clusters of iris are identical, executed with a stencil technique obviously adopted from the artist's early training in textile design. His first dated work is a 1704 portrait of his lifelong friend and patron, Nakamura Kuranosuke. That year Kōrin moved to Edo (now Tōkyō), and for seven years he served a succession of wealthy *daimyō* lords and merchant clients. His only other dated work, a long handscroll of plants and flowers, was executed in 1705 for the daimyō of Tsugaru. The style reflects his deep understanding and study of the paintings of Sōtatsu. Kōrin's twofold screen of *Rough Waves* (*Hatōzu*) in the New York Metropolitan Museum of Art is also based closely on a painting by Sōtatsu. In 1711 the need for artistic freedom drove him back to Kyōto where, although eventually reduced to poverty, he produced some of his most complex and best work. His masterpiece, the screens of *Red and White Plum Trees* (*Kōhakubai zu*) in the MOA Museum of Art in Atami, is thought to date from this final period.

Kōriyama　郡山[市]

City in central Fukushima Prefecture, northern Honshū. A post-station town in the Edo period (1600–1868), it was rapidly industrialized after the opening of the ASAKA CANAL in the Meiji period (1868–1912). Chemicals, electrical appliances, food processing, and precision instruments are its main industries. Pop: 314,642.

Kōriyama Basin　郡山盆地

(Kōriyama Bonchi). In central Fukushima Prefecture, northern Honshū. Bounded by the Ōu and Abukuma mountains, the basin consists mostly of diluvial uplands and the floodplain of the upper river Abukumagawa. The major city is Kōriyama. Area: approximately 150 sq km (58 sq mi).

kōrogi → crickets

Kōrokan　鴻臚館

Government offices set up in 608 in the port of Naniwa (now Ōsaka), in 688 at DAZAIFU, and sometime after 794 in Heiankyō (now Kyōto) for the reception and accommodation of foreign embassies and merchants. When regular diplomatic relations with China and the Korean state of SILLA ended in the 9th

Kōrin This versatile artist of the mid-Edo period was known as both a painter and designer.
1 A pair of two-panel folding screens titled *Red and White Plum Trees*. Ca 1711. Colors and gold leaf on paper. Each screen 157 × 173 cm. MOA Museum of Art, Shizuoka Prefecture. National Treasure.
2 A subtly colored autumn flower motif decorates this white silk *kimono*. Early 18th century. Tōkyō National Museum.

koshi This detail from a 1309 picture scroll shows several types of these palanquins, which were originally used only by the emperor and imperial kinsmen.

century, these offices fell into disuse, and the buildings were used to accommodate Chinese and Korean merchants. By the 12th century they had fallen into private hands.

Koryŏ   高麗

(J: Kōrai). A medieval Korean state established by Wang Kŏn (r 918–943) in 918. It became the ruling state on the Korean peninsula in 935. Koryŏ dynastic rule was weakened after the state withstood three invasions by the Khitan Liao dynasty of northeastern China between 993 and 1018. Rival military families usurped the monarch's authority during the 12th century only to be subdued by the Mongols in the 13th century (see MONGOL INVASIONS OF KOREA). Finally YI SŎNG-GYE rebelled against Koryŏ authority and established the YI DYNASTY in 1392. See also KOREA AND JAPAN.

Kōryūji   広隆寺

Temple in the Uzumasa section of Ukyō Ward, Kyōto, belonging to the Omuro branch (see NINNAJI) of the Shingon sect of Buddhism. Also known as Hachiokadera, Uzumasadera, and Hatanokimidera, it is said to have been founded in 603 by a high official, Hata no Kawakatsu, to house an image of the future Buddha MIROKU (Maitreya) that he had received from Prince SHŌTOKU.

Kōryūji was originally built to serve the needs of the HATA FAMILY, a powerful family of Chinese or Korean origin living in the Yamashiro region outside Kyōto, where the temple was situated until it was moved to its present site around 794. The original Kōryūji was destroyed in a fire in 818 but was rebuilt in the Jōwa era (834–848).

Kōryūji was devastated by fire a second time in 1150 and rebuilt by imperial command 15 years later. The present lecture hall (kōdō), popularly called the Akadō (Red Hall), dates from this time. Enshrined in the lecture hall is a huge wooden seated image of the Buddha Amida dating from 836, a standing image of an Eleven-Faced, Thousand-Armed Kannon dating from the Kōnin era (810–824), and an image of Fukū Kensaku (Amoghapāśa) Kannon dating from the Tempyō era (729–749).

Kosai   湖西［市］

City in western Shizuoka Prefecture, central Honshū, on Lake HAMANA (Hamanako). The birthplace of TOYODA SAKICHI, the inventor of the Toyoda-type loom, Kosai was long the center of the silk-reeling and textile industries. Now its principal industries are automobile parts and precision instruments. Pop: 43,055.

Kōsei Nenkin Hoken →Employees' Pension Insurance

Kōsei shimpen   厚生新編

A partial translation into Japanese, with annotations, of the Dutch translation of M.

Noël Chomel's Agronome français: Dictionaire économique (1709). Undertaken in 1811 by ŌTSUKI GENTAKU and other scholars under the official sponsorship of the Tokugawa shogunate, the translation was never completed, although work continued until 1839. The Kōsei shimpen (literally, "a new book to promote public welfare") stimulated the development of Rangaku (Dutch Learning), as WESTERN LEARNING was then known.

Kōseishō →Ministry of Health and Welfare

koseki →household registers

Koseki San'ei   小関三英

(1787–1839). Physician and scholar of Rangaku (Dutch Learning; see WESTERN LEARNING) during the late Edo period (1600–1868). Also known as Ozeki San'ei. Born in Dewa Province (now Yamagata Prefecture), Koseki studied Dutch in Edo (now Tōkyō). He became a student of Philipp Franz von SIEBOLD and later practiced medicine. From 1833 he served as a translator in the shogunate's astronomical observatory. Shortly before this, Koseki, with WATANABE KAZAN, TAKANO CHŌEI, and other Rangaku scholars, formed the informal study group SHŌSHIKAI. When the shogunate initiated a purge of Western scholars in 1839 (see BANSHA NO GOKU) Koseki committed suicide.

Kose no Kanaoka   巨勢金岡

(fl 9th century). Court painter of the early Heian period (794–1185); founder of the KOSE SCHOOL. No authenticated work by him survives, though he is known to have painted portraits of the Confucian sages for the wall of the Imperial University (Daigakuryō) in 880 and a screen for a member of the powerful FUJIWARA FAMILY in 885. He introduced native subjects and a new Japanese style to the prevalent Chinese mode; as a consequence, he has sometimes been referred to as the founder of YAMATO-E painting.

Kose school   巨勢派

(Koseha). The earliest school of painters in Japan and one of the longest lived. The school began with KOSE NO KANAOKA near the end of the 9th century in the capital (now Kyōto), and survived into the 15th century. Paintings by early Kose masters have not survived, but fragmentary primary documents suggest that these artists played a central role in transforming the style imported from China during the 7th and 8th centuries into an inherently Japanese mode of secular art. They are credited with initiating the classical Heian-period (794–1185) style that later became known as YAMATO-E. During the late Heian period Kose-school artists were eshi (professional artists) at the Kyūtei Edokoro (Imperial Court Painting Bureau); in the Kamakura period (1185–1333) a branch of the Kose school established itself as EBUSSHI (professional priest-painters) in the EDOKORO (painting bureau) of the temple KŌFUKUJI in Nara; and in the period of the NORTHERN AND SOUTHERN COURTS (1337–92) another branch served the edokoro of the Kyōto temple TŌJI as well as the Kyūtei Edokoro of the Northern Court.

koshi   輿

A covered palanquin resting on long horizontal poles borne on men's shoulders or hips. During the Nara (710–794) and Heian (794–1185) periods, only the emperor and imperial kinsmen rode in these conveyances,

formally called ren. From the late Heian period such palanquins were also used by nobles and priests; their use was later extended to samurai and commoners. In the Edo period (1600–1868) koshi were supplanted by the KAGO. MIKOSHI (portable shrines carried in festival processions) are the only kind of koshi in use today.

Kōshien Stadium   阪神甲子園球場

(Hanshin Kōshien Kyūjō; commonly called Kōshien Kyūjō). Baseball stadium in the city of Nishinomiya, Hyōgo Prefecture, built by Hanshin Electric Railway Co, Ltd. Constructed in 1924, the Kōshien Stadium was Japan's first real stadium and has a capacity of 70,000. It is widely known as the site of the extremely popular HIGH SCHOOL BASEBALL championship tournaments held every spring and summer. The stadium has also been the home of the Hanshin Tigers, a professional baseball team in the Central League, since 1935.

Koshigaya   越谷［市］

City in southeastern Saitama Prefecture, central Honshū, on the river Moto Arakawa. A market, and post-station town in the Edo period (1600–1868), it is now an industrial and commercial center, as well as a commuter suburb of Tōkyō. Major agricultural products include rice, vegetables, and flowers. Pop: 285,259.

Koshikijima Islands   甑島列島

(Koshikijima Rettō). Group of islands 40 km (25 mi) west of the city of Kushikino, Kagoshima Prefecture, Kyūshū; part of Kagoshima Prefecture. Composed of Kami Koshikijima, Naka Koshikijima, Shimo Koshikijima, and smaller islands. These hilly islands are frequently struck by typhoons, and fishing has declined. While farming is poor, sweet potatoes and wheat are grown on terraced land; a well-known local product is lily bulbs. Area: 119 sq km (46 sq mi).

kōshin   庚申

Year or day designation in the sexagenary cycle, a system of Chinese origin for reckoning years and other calendar units (see JIKKAN JŪNISHI; CALENDAR, DATES, AND TIME). Kōshin designates any year or day that falls on the combination of kō (Ch: geng or keng), the 7th of the "10 stems," and shin (Ch: shen), the 9th of the "12 branches" or zodiacal symbols, a combination representing the 57th year or day of a complete cycle of 60.

According to Taoist tradition, on the night of a kōshin day the "three worms" (J: sanshi) believed to dwell in the human body escape during sleep and report a person's sins to the Celestial God, resulting in a shortening of that person's life. During the Heian period (794–1185) the Taoist custom of staying awake all night to prevent the worms' escape was practiced among Japanese court nobility, who fought off sleep with games of SUGOROKU and GO and the playing of music. This custom, known as kōshin machi, became widespread among the general populace during the Edo period (1600–1868). All-night kōshin machi are a thing of the past, but the custom survives in some areas in an abbreviated form.

Kōshin'etsu region   甲信越地方

(Kōshin'etsu chihō). An area of central Honshū encompassing Yamanashi, Nagano, and Niigata prefectures. (The name was formed by combining the first characters of the old names of these prefectures.) The region is largely mountainous, with elevations ranging from 2,000 to 3,000 meters (6,600–9,800 ft). The three prefectures are also considered parts of other regions; the use of the name Kōshin'etsu to refer to them as a unit began after World War II, when close economic ties with the KANTŌ REGION, especially Tōkyō, began to develop. Today the Kōshin'etsu region is almost as much a part of the Tōkyō economic sphere as the prefectures immediately surrounding Tōkyō, and its mountains and highlands provide summer resorts and recreation areas for residents of the capital.

Koshino Hiroko コシノヒロコ

(1937–). Fashion designer. Born in Ōsaka Prefecture. After graduating from Bunka Fashion College, Koshino opened her own haute couture studio in Ōsaka. Her designs are noted for their extremely fluid lines.

Koshino Junko コシノジュンコ

(1939–). Fashion designer. Real name Suzuki Junko. Born in Ōsaka Prefecture. A graduate of Bunka Fashion College, Koshino was active in the psychedelic fashion movement in the late 1960s, designing see-through and Chinese-look clothing. In 1978 she had her first showing at the Paris Collection and since then she has become known internationally.

koshirae 拵え

(sword mountings). Also known as *tōsō* or *gaisō*. The parts of a Japanese sword excluding the blade; these generally consist of the *tsuka* (handle), *saya* (scabbard), and TSUBA (guard). The original purpose of the mountings was to protect the blade, but in time they became increasingly ornate and functioned as status symbols or as displays of authority. *Koshirae* may be made of metal, lacquer, leather, or textiles.

From the Heian period (794–1185) swords often featured black lacquer on the hilt, scabbard, and sword guard and other metal fittings. This type of *koshirae* was used by warriors and monk-soldiers through the Kamakura period (1185–1333). From the Muromachi period (1333–1568) on, sword guards in particular became more elaborate and refined, followed by the development of other accessories, most notably the *kozuka* (small knife), *kōgai* (an awl-like instrument), and *menuki* (hilt ornament). See SWORDS.

koshiro and nashiro 子代と名代

(*koshiro to nashiro*). Hereditary groups of workers (BE) who, along with the lands they worked on, were considered the property of the imperial family, from perhaps as early as the 5th century up to the TAIKA REFORM of 645. The two terms seem to have been used interchangeably, but when a distinction is made, *koshiro* may indicate *be* designated for the support of an imperial consort, prince, or princess; *nashiro* would indicate *be* set up in the name of an emperor without issue. In both cases, they were usually taken over from local chieftains (KUNI NO MIYATSUKO) and assigned to members of the imperial family, constituting their main source of support. After the Taika Reform, the members of all these *be* were considered the property of the central government and were relabeled *kōmin* ("public people").

koshō 小姓

(page or attendant). A title used during the period of warrior rule to identify personal attendants of major leaders. During the Muromachi period (1333–1568) it referred generally to those who attended to the daily needs of warrior lords. In the Edo period (1600–1868) it denoted specific personal attendants of the shōgun. About 50 Nakaoku *koshō* (also called Omote *koshō*) attended the shōgun and performed duties in those parts of Edo Castle (the Omote or "Exterior," and Nakaoku or "Middle Interior") where the shōgun handled affairs of state. Another 50 or so Oku *koshō* were assigned to facilitate movement between the "Middle Interior," the shōgun's personal chambers, and the "Great Interior" (ŌOKU), the chambers of the shōgun's wife and ladies. The *koshō* were under the authority of the junior councillors (WAKADOSHIYORI), were directly supervised by four overseers (*tōdori*), and generally were recruited from bannermen (HATAMOTO) families.

Kōshoku 更埴[市]

City in northern Nagano Prefecture, central Honshū. It is known for its knitted-goods, foodstuff, and machine industries and for its carnations and Easter lilies. The more than 50,000 apricot trees in the southeastern section attract visitors in April. Pop: 36,923.

kōshokubon 好色本

("amorous books"). Genre of popular fiction of the Edo period (1600–1868) that dealt with the amorous affairs of the merchant class and with the licensed pleasure quarters. Subgenre of UKIYO-ZŌSHI. Outstanding examples are SAIKAKU's KŌSHOKU ICHIDAI OTOKO (1682; tr *The Life of an Amorous Man*, 1964) and *Kōshoku ichidai onna* (1686; tr *The Life of an Amorous Woman*, 1963). Besides Saikaku, writers of these mildly erotic books included NISHIZAWA IPPŪ, EJIMA KISEKI, and Hachimonjiya Jishō (d 1745). After 1716, with increasing shogunate control of published materials, works of this type were suppressed.

Kōshoku ichidai otoko 好色一代男

(1682; tr *The Life of an Amorous Man*, 1964). Ihara SAIKAKU's first prose work and the first example of the UKIYO-ZŌSHI (tales of the floating world) genre. It is a picaresque account of a ridiculously amorous hero named Yonosuke, who as a boy of 6 makes advances to a maid; at 9 he has his calligraphy teacher write a love letter for him; eventually he seduces 3,742 women and 725 boys. The work is divided into 54 chapters, as is the 11th-century classic *Genji monogatari* (TALE OF GENJI); Yonosuke, unencumbered by sentiment or aristocratic pedigree but free-spending and high-spirited, is a version of Prince Genji in the spirit of Saikaku's own era. His erotic quest carries Yonosuke throughout the provinces and into the arms of bath girls, shrine maidens, and boy actors; Saikaku, also a poet, describes each new conquest in very brief chapters that have the formal balance and wayward irreverence of a linked-verse sequence. Contemporary guidebooks to the pleasure quarters serve as frames of reference when Yonosuke, having received an inheritance from his late father, dissipates it in the company of the ranking courtesans of the time. At the age of 60, Yonosuke turns philosophical and sails off to seek the fabulous Island of Women (Nyogo no Shima).

Kōshoku Tsuihō → Occupation Purge

Kōshū Kaidō → Gokaidō

Kosugi 小杉[町]

Town in northern Toyama Prefecture, central Honshū. Formerly an agricultural area, Kosugi has rapidly become urbanized since the construction of the Hokuriku Expressway and a port at Toyama Shinkō. Pop: 30,701.

Kosugi Tengai 小杉天外

(1865–1952). Novelist. Forerunner of French naturalism in modern Japanese literature. Real name Kosugi Tamezō. Born in what is now Akita Prefecture. He moved to Tōkyō in 1886 and entered college, but soon withdrew. In 1891, he became a student of SAITŌ RYOKUU. He joined the magazine *Shincho gekkan* in 1897 but later transferred to the staff of the newspaper *Hōchi shimbun*. Tengai was elected to the JAPAN ART ACADEMY (Nihon Geijutsuin) in 1948 in recognition of such works as *Hatsusugata* (1900) and *Hayariuta* (1902).

Because of his pioneering role in furthering the concept and practice of realism, in experimenting with Zola's ideas, and in pointing the way toward fuller realization of naturalism in Japan, Tengai remains an important figure in literary history. He attempted to create fiction that was objective and realistic, without the thoughts or values of the author intruding into the work. However, his objectivism resulted in two-dimensional characters who met predictable fates based on hereditary and environmental determinism.

Kotani Kimi 小谷喜美

(1901–71). Cofounder and leader of REIYŪKAI, a lay religious organization. Born in Miura, Kanagawa Prefecture. In 1924 she married Kotani Yasukichi (1885–1929) and received religious instruction from his brother, Kubo Kakutarō (1892–1944; his name had been changed to Kubo by adoption). She and the two brothers founded Reiyūkai in 1925. Kotani served as the group's president and assumed complete control upon Kubo's death in 1944. A proselytizer and faith healer, she taught that suffering arises from moral deficiencies and neglect of ancestral spirits and that genuine repentance can lead to worldly benefits, including healing. She also championed the values of the traditional Japanese family system.

Kotani Masao 小谷正雄

(1906–93). Theoretical physicist. Born in Kyōto Prefecture. Graduate of Tōkyō University. Although Kotani's research was mainly concerned with atomic and molecular quantum mechanics and electromagnetic conductor theory, his achievements have crossed disciplinary boundaries to include chemistry and biology, including research in biopolymers. He was a professor at Kyōto University from 1943 to 1966 and at Ōsaka University from 1965 to 1969 and served as president of the Science University of Tōkyō from 1972 to 1982. He received the Order of Culture in 1980.

kotatsu 炬燵

Traditional type of heater-table said to have originated during the Muromachi period (1333–1568). There are two kinds of *kotatsu* in use today. One consists of a table with an electric heater attached to the underside of the frame. The legs, which are about 36 centimeters (14 in) high, rest directly on the floor. The other type of *kotatsu* is a pit about

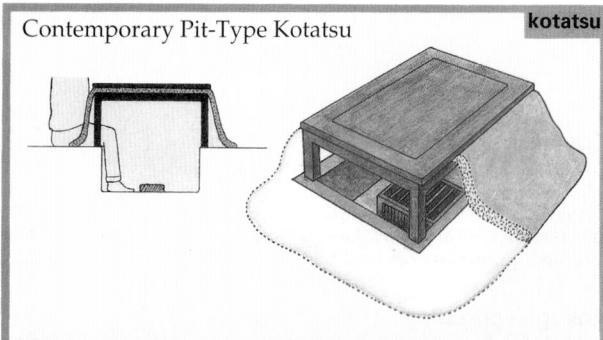

Contemporary Pit-Type Kotatsu · kotatsu

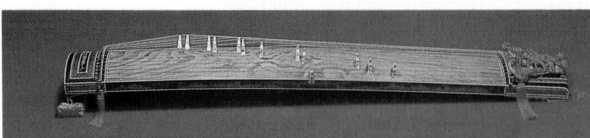

koto

1 A *tsukushigoto*. This type of *koto* was developed during the 16th century in Chikugo Province in northern Kyūshū by Kenjun, a Buddhist monk.
2 A *koto* performance given during the annual autumn festival at the Meiji Shrine in Tōkyō.

40 centimeters (16 in) deep that is cut into the floor. An electric heater is placed inside and a tabletop and frame arranged over it. In either case, a FUTON is draped over the frame under the tabletop. To sit, one places one's legs under the table close to the heater and wraps the *futon* snugly around one's lower body. Before World War II, charcoal was used as the heat source for *kotatsu*.

koto 琴

Thirteen-stringed, half-tube (semicylindrical) plucked zither. The earliest *koto* (*yamatogoto* or *wagon*) had only 5 strings and was about 1 meter (3 ft) long. A 6th string was added in the Nara period (710–794). The 13-stringed *koto*, modeled on the Chinese *zheng* (*cheng*) and about 2 meters (6 ft) long, also dates from Nara times and under the name *gakusō* was and is used in the court music ensemble. Starting in the late 15th century there was a series of new schools of solo *koto* (see SŌKYOKU). The *koto* is made of paulownia wood, has movable bridges for each string (and many tunings), and is played with small picks on the thumb and first two fingers of the right hand (the left meanwhile may raise the pitch of strings or modify the tone). See also MUSICAL INSTRUMENTS; GAGAKU; SHICHIGENKIN.

Kōtō 江東

Area of Tōkyō east of the river SUMIDAGAWA that comprises 5 of Tōkyō's 23 wards:

Kotohira Shrine More than 700 steps lead to the main hall of this Shintō shrine. Sedan-chair bearers do a brisk business transporting those not up to making the long climb on their own.

Sumida, Kōtō, Katsushika, Edogawa, and Adachi. The term can also be used to refer only to the Sumida and Kōtō wards. Part of the Keihin Industrial Zone, Kōtō encompasses a large portion of Tōkyō's SHITAMACHI with its concentration of assorted small and medium-sized factories, residences, and, more recently, high-rise apartment buildings. Most of the area is below sea level.

kotobagaki 詞書

(headnotes). Prefatory notes to WAKA poems found in collections of verse. Explaining the poem's theme or circumstances of its composition, *kotobagaki* were sometimes elaborate, fictional narratives, apparently written by someone other than the poet. Certain *uta monogatari* (poem tales) may have developed from *kotobagaki* and their poems.

kotodama 言霊

A belief, reflected in the earliest Japanese sources, that a sacred power or spirit dwells in the words of the traditional Japanese language. Particularly when expressed in certain forms, such as NORITO (ritual prayers) or WAKA poetry, it was believed that the words of the Japanese language could exert a special influence on people, the gods, and even the course of the world. Extreme care thus needed to be taken with words to utilize their power properly, for good or for ill. Although the notion is similar to beliefs in the magical power of words found in most traditional societies, it has been employed by some modern Japanese thinkers to explain what they believe are the special characteristics of Japanese language and culture. See also TABOO EXPRESSIONS.

Kotohira 琴平[町]

Town in western Kagawa Prefecture, Shikoku. Kotohira developed in the Edo period (1600–1868) as a shrine town around the KOTOHIRA SHRINE and is still a popular pilgrimage center. Pop: 12,632.

Kotohira Shrine 金刀比羅宮

(Kotohiragū). Shintō shrine, popularly known as "the Kompirasan [Kompira Shrine] of Sanuki Province," in the Nakatado district of Kagawa Prefecture, Shikoku; dedicated to the deity Ōmononushi no Kami (see ŌKUNINUSHI NO MIKOTO) and to Emperor Sutoku (r 1123–42). The latter died in exile in Sanuki, where he had become a devotee of this shrine. Founded at the beginning of the 11th century, the shrine was first dedicated to Kompira Daigongen, a Buddhist-Shintō syncretic deity believed to be a benevolent protector of fishermen and sailors. There are numerous offshoot shrines throughout the country. After the forcible separation of Buddhism and Shintō in 1868, the syncretic Kompira Daigongen was reidentified as the purely Shintō deity Ōmononushi no Kami. The annual festival is held on 9–11 October. See also HONJI SUIJAKU.

kōtō jogakkō 高等女学校

Girls' secondary schools of the period from the late 19th century to just after World War II. The term means, literally, "girls' high school," but the schools were actually counterparts of the middle schools (*chūgakkō*) for boys (see SECONDARY EDUCATION). The earliest were the Tōkyō Girls' High School (Tōkyō Jogakkō), founded in 1872, and the Girls' High School attached to the Tōkyō Women's Normal School (Tōkyō Joshi Shihan Gakkō; now OCHANOMIZU WOMEN'S UNIVERSITY), founded in 1882. Most girls'

schools were privately operated (see MISSION SCHOOLS), but in 1899 the Directive on Girls' High Schools (Kōtō Jogakkō Rei) provided for the establishment of a secondary education system for girls. All primary school graduates were eligible for entrance, and the course of study was four to five years. Yet education there was designed primarily to make each student a "good wife and wise mother" (*ryōsai kembo*). Since 1947 coeducation has become the norm in public schools (see EDUCATION, FUNDAMENTAL LAW OF). See also WOMEN'S EDUCATION.

Kōtoku, Emperor 孝徳天皇

(597–654; Kōtoku Tennō). The 36th sovereign (*tennō*) in the traditional count (which includes several legendary emperors); reigned 645–654. He succeeded his sister Empress Kōgyoku (see SAIMEI, EMPRESS) with the support of his cousin Prince Naka no Ōe (later Emperor TENJI) and Nakatomi no Kamatari (later FUJIWARA NO KAMATARI). Kōtoku transferred his residence from Asuka (now Nara Prefecture) to Naniwa (now Ōsaka) and ordered work begun on the TAIKA REFORM. Throughout his reign, policies were determined by Naka no Ōe and Kamatari. In addition to far-reaching reforms in government, land tenure, and taxation, relations with Korea and China were strengthened during his reign.

Kōtoku Shūsui 幸徳秋水

(1871–1911). Socialist and anarchist leader. Real name Kōtoku Denjirō. Born in Nakamura, in the Hata district of Kōchi Prefecture. He developed an early interest in the FREEDOM AND PEOPLE'S RIGHTS MOVEMENT. After graduating from the Kokumin Eigakkai, a Tōkyō school of English, Kōtoku wrote for newspapers, including the *Jiyū shimbun* and the YOROZU CHŌHŌ. In 1898 he joined KATAYAMA SEN and Murai Tomoyoshi (1861–1944) in the newly founded SHAKAI SHUGI KENKYŪKAI (Society for the Study of Socialism). In 1901 Kōtoku, Katayama, and ABE ISOO formed the SHAKAI MINSHUTŌ, Japan's first socialist-democratic party, which was quickly outlawed. Kōtoku published *Nijisseiki no kaibutsu teikoku shugi* (1901, Imperialism: The Specter of the 20th Century) and *Shakai shugi shinzui* (1903, The Quintessence of Socialism).

Faced with the growing threat of war with Russia, Kōtoku joined UCHIMURA KANZŌ and other writers in a pacifist campaign. He organized the weekly HEIMIN SHIMBUN to protest the RUSSO-JAPANESE WAR (1904–05). It was in this paper that he and fellow socialist SAKAI TOSHIHIKO published the first Japanese translation of Karl Marx's *Communist Manifesto* in 1904. In 1907 he brought his program of anarchist "direct action" to the second convention of the JAPAN SOCIALIST PARTY. Kōtoku's stand split the party and led to its dissolution.

Kōtoku was tried for high treason in 1910 for participating in a plot to assassinate the emperor. In 1911 Kōtoku and 11 others were executed. See HIGH TREASON INCIDENT OF 1910.

kōtō semmon gakkō →technical colleges

kōtō shōgakkō 高等小学校

(higher elementary schools). A system of supplemental four-year elementary schools established in 1886 for students who had completed the four-year compulsory elementary schools (*jinjō shōgakkō*). When the *jinjō shōgakkō* became six-year schools in

1907, the *kōtō shōgakkō* program was shortened to two years. Thereafter, until the pre-World War II elementary school system was replaced by the wartime KOKUMIN GAKKŌ with their eight years of compulsory schooling, the *kōtō shōgakkō* represented the final preparation for adult life for children unable to advance to secondary schools.

Kōtō Ward 江東区

(Kōtō Ku). One of the 23 wards of Tōkyō. Between the rivers Sumidagawa and Arakawa; part of the Kōtō Delta area. The reclaimed land along Tōkyō Bay is now the site of large factories, housing complexes, and parks. Pop: 385,159.

kotowaza→proverbs

kotoyōka 事八日

("small eighth day"). Annual ceremonies of agrarian origin held on the 8th day of the 2nd and 12th months. Originally entailing a period of abstinence during which temporary lodgings (*yorishiro*) were set up to receive beneficent Shintō spirits, *kotoyōka* was later transformed·into a ceremonial warding off of evil deities. The initial ceremony is called *koto hajime* and the final ceremony *koto osame*. Rites vary widely, but in the Kantō area woven baskets are placed atop poles, their meshes (*me*) thought to prevent visitations by HITOTSUME KOZŌ, goblins with one eye (*me*). HARI KUYŌ, a ceremony to honor used sewing needles, is observed on the same day.

kouta 小唄

(literally, "short songs"). Also known as Edo *kouta*. Type of popular song with SHAMISEN accompaniment. The *shamisen* is plucked with the fingernails instead of with a plectrum, the pitch is high, and the music is too fast for dancing. The Edo *kouta* has antecedents going back to the 16th century; but it derives immediately from *hauta*, a *shamisen* song type that flourished first in the Fukagawa district of Edo (now Tōkyō) in the early 19th century, and was performed mainly by GEISHA. Edo *kouta* of the mid-19th century were often performed by singers of KIYOMOTO-BUSHI, who left their own imprint on its style; but in the early Meiji period (1868–1912) separate lines of *kouta* singers were established by one Kumame and her male successor Masajusai (b 1839; succeeded 1875 or 1876). After Masajusai's death the interest of such literati as OZAKI KŌYŌ, NAGAI KAFŪ, SASAKI NOBUTSUNA, and KUBOTA MANTARŌ, as well as the composer Yamada Shōtarō (1899–1970), helped give new directions to the genre. At present Edo *kouta* are sung mainly by geisha.

kōwaka-mai 幸若舞

Genre of musical ballads dating from the 15th century, also known as *kuse-mai* and *mai-mai*. *Kōwaka-mai* consist mainly of accounts of military episodes from warrior tales such as the HEIKE MONOGATARI recited to a musical chant. *Kōwaka-mai* were connected with NŌ and other medieval entertainments and provided material for later literary and dramatic works. There are 36 pieces in the traditional repertoire, but 50 extant texts, called *mai no hon* (dance books), are now known. *Kōwaka-mai* had been largely forgotten by the end of the 17th century, but performances that had continued in one locality were discovered by scholars early in the 20th century.

Kōwaka-mai are performed by three men standing side by side and reciting the texts in a highly stylized way to the beat of a fan or, at the most, to the accompaniment of two small drums and a flute. The *kōwaka-mai* pieces were composed in narrative form and are now declaimed in chorus or in turn by the three performers.

Koyama Keizō 小山敬三

(1897–1987). Western-style painter. Born in Nagano Prefecture. Studied under the Western-style painter FUJISHIMA TAKEJI and at the Japan Fine Arts Academy (Nihon Bijutsuin). In 1936 he helped to found the Issuikai painter's group. In 1958 he won the Japan Art Academy Award (Geijutsuin Shō). There is a museum devoted to his work in Komoro, Nagano Prefecture. His traditional, realistic landscapes display great compositional acuity. He received the Order of Culture in 1975.

Koyama Yūshi 小山祐士

(1906–82). Playwright. Born in Hiroshima Prefecture. A graduate of Keiō University, he studied drama under KISHIDA KUNIO. His plays are uniformly set against the local color of the Inland Sea region. His later plays look closely at individuals scarred by World War II. Two of his best plays are *Seto Naikai no kodomora* (1934, Children of the Inland Sea) and *Nihon no yūrei* (1965, Ghosts of Japan).

Kōyasan 高野山

(Mt. Kōya). Mountain in the north-central Kii Peninsula, northern Wakayama Prefecture, central Honshū. On the south bank of the river Kinokawa. The mountain is famous as the location of the temple KONGŌBUJI, constructed by the priest KŪKAI in 816 and the head temple of the SHINGON SECT of Buddhism; more than 110 other related temples are also located here. (The name Kōyasan refers to Kongōbuji and the other temples here as well as the large mountain itself.) It has long attracted a large number of pilgrims, but women were prohibited from climbing the mountain until 1872. It forms part of the Kōya-Ryūjin Quasi-National Park. Height: approximately 1,000 m (3,300 ft).

Kōyasan 高野山

General name for the Buddhist monastic complex of the SHINGON SECT on Mt. Kōya (Kōyasan), Wakayama Prefecture. With KONGŌBUJI as its head temple, Kōyasan has more than 110 temples and monasteries. (Kongōbuji was originally a name for all the temples on the mountain, but in 1869 it was adopted as the name of a single large temple.) Regarded as one of the most sacred places in Japan, Kongōbuji traditionally has been associated with KŪKAI (founder of Shingon ESOTERIC BUDDHISM) and contrasted with HIEIZAN (the Tendai sect complex near the city of Kyōto, which centers on ENRYAKUJI).

Kōyasan is believed to have been a sacred mountain for ascetics even before Kūkai obtained imperial permission in 816 to found a religious community there, far from the capital of Kyōto. The main temple complex was built under the second abbot, Shinzen (804–891). During the 10th century Kōyasan was temporarily eclipsed by the temple TŌJI in Kyōto and was ravaged by fire (994). It was fully restored under Meizan (1021–1106) and patronized by the retired emperors SHIRAKAWA and TOBA, whose visits set a precedent for future sovereigns.

KAKUBAN's reform movement around 1132 gave momentum to Buddhist studies at Kōyasan. As evidenced by Kakuban's at-

tempts to integrate the belief in the Pure Land into Shingon teachings, Kōyasan at the time attracted a number of Pure Land Buddhists, who formed communities in the area. Called HIJIRI, these people included Kyōkai (1001–93), Myōhen (1142–1224), and Chōgen (1121–1206), who made Kōyasan a center of PURE LAND BUDDHISM almost rivaling Hieizan. Especially from the late 12th century, in the wake of the TAIRA-MINAMOTO WAR, aristocrats and warriors, such as KUMAGAI NAOZANE and SAIGYŌ, took refuge at Kōyasan, many of them joining the *hijiri* group.

Kōyasan continued to flourish under the patronage of successive shogunates, although there were setbacks, such as the massacre of hundreds of *hijiri* and other members of Kōyasan by the hegemon ODA NOBUNAGA and threats of invasion by TOYOTOMI HIDEYOSHI (both in the late 16th century), as well as occasional fires. In 1872 a traditional ban on women's entry to Kōyasan was lifted (see NYONIN KINZEI; MURŌJI). — *See photos, next page.*

Kōyasan Treasure House 高野山霊宝館

(Kōyasan Reihōkan). Located at Mt. Kōya (KŌYASAN), in the town of Kōya, Wakayama Prefecture. Built in 1921, it preserves and displays important art of the Heian (794–1185) and Kamakura (1185–1333) periods owned by the temples on Kōyasan. Its holdings include paintings, calligraphy, sutras, sculpture, and Buddhist ritual objects. The collection also contains copies of the *Issaikyō* (the entire Buddhist canon), writings of KŪKAI, letters of the warriors MINAMOTO NO YORITOMO and MINAMOTO NO YOSHITSUNE, mandalas, and portraits of priests.

Kōyasan University 高野山大学

(Kōyasan Daigaku). A coeducational private university in Ito District, Wakayama Prefecture. The university traces its origins to a school founded in 1886 by the older division (*kogi*) of the Shingon sect of Buddhism. It became a university in 1949. Its objective is to develop the character of its students according to the spirit of Buddhism. It maintains a faculty of letters, which includes departments of esoteric Buddhism, Buddhism, sociology, and the humanities. Enrollment in 1989 was 1,016.

Kōyō gunkan 甲陽軍鑑

A 20-volume military treatise dating from the early Edo period (1600–1868), probably

835
Kōyō gunkan

around 1625. Focusing on the illustrious military careers of two warrior generals, TAKEDA SHINGEN and his son TAKEDA KATSUYORI, the work presents a picture of the accomplishments, battle tactics, and government practices of the warrior class (*bushi*) of Kai Province (now Yamanashi Prefecture). It is the oldest existing document to use the term BUSHIDŌ ("the Way of the warrior") in examining the psychology and ideals of the warrior class. The most reliable studies single out Obata Kagenori (1572–1663), a military strategist, as compiler.

koyori 紙縒

String or cord formed by twisting thin strips of Japanese paper (WASHI). Also called *kanze-yori*. *Koyori* are traditionally used for binding notebooks, wrapping gifts, tying up Japanese-style hairdos, and cleaning pipes. They may be woven together and then lacquered to make items such as trays, cigarette cases, and pillboxes (INRŌ).

Kōyō Seikō Co, Ltd 光洋精工[株]

(Kōyō Seikō). Manufacturer of quality ball and roller bearings and automotive steering gears. Incorporated in 1935. The company has diversified its product line to include automotive hub units, ceramic bearings, hard disk drive units, machine tools, precision spindle units, drive shafts, and industrial furnaces. It has seven plants in Japan, two in the United States, and one each in Brazil and Thailand, as well as sales subsidiaries in 15 countries. Sales for the fiscal year ending March 1991 totaled ¥259.0 billion (US $1.9 billion), and the company was capitalized at ¥25.9 billion (US $188.8 million). Headquarters are in Ōsaka.

Kōzaha 講座派

("Lectures" faction). Group of Marxist theorists who supported the JAPAN COMMUNIST PARTY line, as expressed in the seven-volume NIHON SHIHON SHUGI HATTATSU SHI KŌZA (1932–33, Lectures on the History of the Development of Japanese Capitalism). In the 1930s the Kōzaha was engaged in a dispute with members of the rival RŌNŌHA (Labor-Farmer faction) over the nature of Japanese capitalism and of the coming revolution in Japan. The Kōzaha argued that the MEIJI RESTORATION of 1868 had been an incomplete revolution and had resulted in the establishment of an absolutist emperor system based on a semifeudal land system. Therefore, the group asserted, Japan's impending revolution would be a "bourgeois-democratic" upheaval, aimed at abolishing feudal land-ownership and overthrowing the emperor system, which would serve as prelude to the proletarian revolution that was their ultimate goal. In contrast to this two-stage theory of revolution, the Rōnōha emphasized the bourgeois character of Japanese capitalism and claimed that Japan's coming revolution would be a socialist one. Suspended when members of both groups were arrested in 1937 and early 1938, the dispute was resumed after World II in Japanese academic circles as an analytical issue and remains unresolved to this day. See also NIHON SHIHON SHUGI RONSŌ.

Kozai Yoshihide 古在由秀

(1928–). Scholar of celestial mechanics and geodesy. Born in Tōkyō. Graduate of Tōkyō University. From 1958 to 1962 he was a research fellow at the Smithsonian Astrophysical Observatory in Washington, DC, where he completed work on the Kozai equation, which was employed in the United States to calculate the orbits of artificial satellites. Using data based on variation in the orbits of satellites, he also succeeded in determining irregularities in the shape of the earth with a high degree of accuracy. His work provided the foundation for geodesy by means of artificial satellites. In 1966 he was appointed professor at the Tōkyō Astronomical Observatory (since 1988, the NATIONAL ASTRONOMICAL OBSERVATORY), and he became its director in 1981.

Kozaki Hiromichi 小崎弘道

(1856–1938). Christian leader and educator. Born in the Kumamoto domain (now Kumamoto Prefecture). After graduating

from Dōshisha (now Dōshisha University) in Kyōto in 1879, he went to Tōkyō, where he contributed to the founding of the Reinanzaka Church, the Japan YMCA (1880), and the magazine *Rikugō zasshi* (1880–1921, The Universe), an important forum for Christian and socialist thought. He became president of Dōshisha in 1890 and served as pastor of Reinanzaka Church (1899–1931). Kozaki also served as chairman of the Japan Council of Churches.

Kōzanji 高山寺

Temple in Ukyō Ward, Kyōto, belonging to the Omuro branch (see NINNAJI) of the SHINGON SECT of Buddhism. Also called Toganoodera. It is first mentioned in a biography of Son'i (866–940), the abbot of ENRYAKUJI. After it fell into disrepair the celebrated monk MONGAKU sought to restore the temple but illness forced him to entrust the task to the great KEGON SECT scholar MYŌE, who obtained authorization from the retired emperor Go-Toba (r 1183–98) for its reconstruction. Many of the present buildings date from another major reconstruction, in 1636. The temple's treasures include a group of ink paintings called the CHŌJŪ GIGA (Scrolls of Frolicking Animals and Humans).

Kōzen gokoku ron 興禅護国論

(On Promoting Zen and Protecting the Nation). A three-volume treatise expounding the legitimacy of ZEN Buddhism and asserting that Zen alone could protect Japan. The earliest Japanese work on Zen; written in 1198 by the monk EISAI, founder of the RINZAI SECT. Eisai had returned from China in 1191, advocating the revival of Buddhism through the Zen practices he had studied while abroad. Although he quickly found a following among the warrior class, he encountered opposition from the older, established Buddhist sects, which denounced his teachings as heretical and urged their suppression by the imperial court. Eisai wrote his treatise in order to counter these attacks.

Kōzuke monuments 上野三碑

(Kōzuke *sampi*). Stone monuments in Gumma Prefecture (historically known as Kōzuke Province) dating from the 7th and 8th centuries. They are the Yamanoue (or Yamana) Monument and the Kanaizawa Monument, both in the city of Takasaki, and the Tago Monument in Yoshii Machi, Tano District. The Yamanoue Monument was erected by Chōri, a priest of the temple Hōkōji, as a gravestone for his mother in either 681 or 741, depending on the calculation of the sexagenary calendric dates (see JIKKAN JŪNISHI). The Tago Monument commemorates the establishment in 711 of Tago no Kōri (Tago District), an event also recorded in the chronicle *Shoku nihongi* (797). The Kanaizawa Monument was erected in 726 to commemorate a pledge to the Buddhist faith taken by nine residents of the area.

kū → emptiness

kubō   公方

A contraction of the honorific term *kuge no kata* (the character *kata* also being read *hō* or *bō*) and sometimes read *ōyakekata*, the word *kubō* originally referred to the emperor and his court. From the Kamakura period (1185–1333) through the Edo period (1600–1868) it was used by *samurai* to refer to the shōgun. During the Muromachi period (1333–1568) the term referred to the Ashikaga shōguns and to their deputies in the Kantō region who were members of the Ashikaga family (e.g., KOGA KUBŌ and HORIKOSHI KUBŌ). See also KANTŌ KANREI.

Kubo Kakutarō   久保角太郎

(1892–1944). Founder of the REIYŪKAI, one of Japan's largest contemporary lay religious organizations (see NEW RELIGIONS). Born in Chiba Prefecture. In his mid-twenties Kubo joined the Bussho Gonenkai, a Nichiren Buddhist lay movement. He was strongly influenced by the Lotus Sutra, from which he developed the idea of ancestor veneration as the key to national salvation and social harmony. He also devised an ancestral ritual to be performed by lay believers rather than priests. Enlisting the help of his sister-in-law KOTANI KIMI, who excelled in proselytization and organization, Kubo founded the Reiyūkai in 1925. The organization developed significantly between the 1930s and 1960s and is now, along with the SŌKA GAKKAI, one of the most influential new religions in Japan.

Kubokawa Tsurujirō   窪川鶴次郎

(1903–74). Literary critic. Born in Shizuoka Prefecture. Attended the Fourth Higher School (now part of Kanazawa University) in the city of Kanazawa, Ishikawa Prefecture. Kubokawa wrote for the literary magazine *Roba*. He was active in the PROLETARIAN LITERATURE MOVEMENT and was imprisoned in 1932 for being a member of the Communist Party. His works include *Gendai bungaku ron* (1939) and *Saisetsu gendai bungaku ron* (1944), both critical essays on modern literature. He was married to the writer SATA INEKO.

Kubo Ryōgo   久保亮五

(1920–). Physicist known for his early research on the statistical mechanics of rubber elasticity and for his later work in solid-state physics, particularly on magnetic resonance absorption. Born in Tōkyō, he graduated from Tōkyō University in 1941. After doing research at the University of Chicago, he became a professor at Tōkyō University in 1954. He served as dean of science from 1968 to 1971 and received the Order of Culture in 1973. His publications include *Gomu dansei* (1947, Rubber Elasticity).

Kubo Sakae   久保栄

(1901–58). Playwright, producer, and novelist. Born in Hokkaidō. He studied German literature at Tōkyō University. In 1926 he joined the Tsukiji Shōgekijō (Tsukiji Little

Theater) and studied drama under OSANAI KAORU. He was influenced by German expressionism. Kubo was active in the prewar proletarian theater movement (see PROLETARIAN LITERATURE MOVEMENT). Two of his best plays date from this time: *Goryōkaku kessho* (1933) and *Kazan baichi* (1937). He later turned to stage production and theater studies. His major postwar achievement was *Noborigama* (1951), a historical novel.

Kubo Shumman   窪俊満

(1757–1820). UKIYO-E woodblock-print designer, writer, poet, painter, and craftsman in lacquer and shell work. Central figure in the development and production of the privately published prints called SURIMONO. Born into the Kubota family. His first teacher was KATORI NAHIKO (1723–82) who gave him the name Shumman. He studied *ukiyo-e* with KITAO SHIGEMASA and designed a few elegant prints in *ukiyo-e* style, most of them with a narrowly limited range of colors, in the late 1780s. He then studied KYŌKA ("mad verse") with Rokujuen and later became a leader in the Bakuro Group.

From the late 1790s he became interested in *surimono*, his name or seal appearing on the works of TOTOYA HOKKEI, UTAGAWA TOYOKUNI, and other artists in addition to his own.

Kubota Corporation   ［株］クボタ

(Kubota). Manufacturer of farm and industrial equipment, pipe, industrial castings and machinery, and building materials. Founded in 1890 by Kubota Gonshirō; incorporated in 1930. Kubota's more than 2,000 products are sold in some 130 countries. The company's production network comprises 18 plants in Japan, a subsidiary in Brazil, and affiliates in the United States, Spain, Taiwan, Indonesia, Thailand, and the Philippines. There are also sales and service networks in Canada, France, the United Kingdom, Germany, Australia, and Singapore. The company's net sales were ¥709.0 billion (US $5.2 billion) in the fiscal year ending March 1991. The sales breakdown in that year was as follows: farm and industrial equipment, 39 percent; pipe, 27 percent; industrial castings and machinery, 19 percent; and building materials and other products, 15 percent. The company was capitalized at ¥77.8 billion (US $567.1 million) in 1991. Headquarters are in Ōsaka.

Kubota Mantarō   久保田万太郎

(1889–1963). Novelist, playwright, and HAIKU poet. Born in Tōkyō; graduate of Keiō University, where his first stories and plays were published. In 1931 he became director of the drama and music department of the Tōkyō Broadcasting Station (now NHK). Kubota lived all his life in the old downtown area of Tōkyō (SHITAMACHI), and his writing reflects the pathos, humor, and speech patterns of its denizens. Notable works are the novels *Uragare* (1917) and *Shundei* (1928), the short story "Hanabie" (1938), and the play *Ōdera gakkō* (1927).

Kubota Utsubo   窪田空穂

(1877–1967). TANKA poet, author, and scholar of Japanese literature. Real name Kubota Michiharu. Born in Nagano Prefecture. Graduate of Tōkyō Semmon Gakkō (now Waseda University), where he later taught Japanese classics. Kubota became an early member of YOSANO TEKKAN's New Poetry Society (Shinshisha). His many poetry collections contain both new-form poems (SHINTAISHI) and CHŌKA. *Rohen* (1911), a collection of his short stories, shows the influence of

Japanese NATURALISM (*shizen shugi*). He also published criticism and commentaries on classical works such as the MAN'YŌSHŪ and the ISE MONOGATARI.

kubunden   口分田

(personal field allotment). The share of rice land granted by the central government to an individual in the land distribution system (HANDEN SHŪJU SYSTEM) under the RITSURYŌ SYSTEM that developed in the late 7th century. For male commoners (RYŌMIN) aged six years or more, the allotment was two *tan* (1 *tan* = about 0.12 hectare or 0.3 acre); for females it was two-thirds of that amount; for servants (KENIN) and private slaves (*shinuhi*; see NUHI) it was one-third of the regular allotment for male or female commoners. Apart from government servants (*kanko*) and government slaves (*kannuhi* or *kunuhi*), who received the same amount of land as commoners, all grantees were obligated to pay taxes on the land (see SO, YŌ, AND CHŌ). By the early 10th century the *kubunden* system had decayed because of irregular enforcement of the law, and most of these lands were eventually absorbed by private landed estates (SHŌEN).

Kubushiro Ochimi   久布白落実

(1882–1972). Feminist and Christian social reformer. Born in Kumamoto Prefecture, the daughter of a Christian minister; maiden name Ōkubo. Graduate of Joshi Gakuin. In 1916 she joined the KYŌFŪKAI (Japan Woman's Christian Temperance Union) led by her great-aunt YAJIMA KAJIKO and became especially active in its campaigns against prostitution. As a member of the FUSEN KAKUTOKU DŌMEI she was a major organizer of the first Zen Nihon Fusen Taikai (All-Japan Women's Suffrage Conference) in 1930.

kuchiei and kuchimai   口永と口米

(*kuchiei to kuchimai*). A kind of miscellaneous surcharge, usually of 2 to 3 percent, added to the annual land tax (see HONTO MONONARI) during the Edo period (1600–1868). When collected in rice, it was called *kuchimai;* when collected in cash, it was called *kuchiei, kuchigin,* or *kuchizeni.* The tax originated in the Kamakura period (1185–1333) to compensate for loss or damage to tax rice during shipment, but did not become a common form of taxation until the late 16th century. In the Edo period it became a regularized tax to cover the expenses of tax collectors' offices. The assessment of *kuchimai* and *kuchiei* was discontinued with the enactment of the LAND TAX REFORM OF 1873–1881.

kuchinashi → gardenia

Kudamatsu   下松［市］

City in southeastern Yamaguchi Prefecture, western Honshū, on the Suō Sea. Once a flourishing port town, it now has chemical and other heavy industries. Pop: 53,030.

Kudara → Paekche

Kudaradera remains   百済寺跡

(Kudaradera *ato*). Site of a temple affiliated with the Kudaraō family, descendants of the royal house of PAEKCHE who migrated to Japan in the 7th century. Located in what is now Nakamiya, in the city of Hirakata, Ōsaka Prefecture, the temple flourished from the Nara period (710–794) into the Heian period (794–1185). Excavations in 1932 and 1965 revealed that the buildings

Kubota Mantarō
A shop owner's son from Tōkyō's Asakusa district, this writer produced stories and plays that reflect the manners and speech of the old mercantile middle class.

Kūkai Detail of an idealized 14th-century portrait of the itinerant Buddhist priest who founded the Shingon sect of Buddhism in the 9th century and who was also known as a poet, calligrapher, and lexicographer.

were arranged in the manner of YAKUSHIJI in an area of about 4 hectares (9.9 acres). The pagodas were encircled with stones and the main hall with rows of tiles. Recovered artifacts include numerous ROOF TILES, gilt bronze ornaments, and BUDDHA TILES.

kudashibumi   下文

A type of document used to convey orders from a superior official or office to a subordinate one. The *kudashibumi* originated in the Heian period (794–1185), replacing the more complicated *fu* stipulated by the YŌRO CODE. Usually *kudashibumi* had the word *kudasu* ("ordered") at the beginning of the text, but this form was not always followed. See also DIPLOMATICS.

Kudō Heisuke   工藤平助

(1734–1800). Administrator and medical doctor. The son of a physician, he was adopted by Kudō Jōan, a doctor of the Sendai domain (now Miyagi Prefecture). Heisuke served as a doctor of the Sendai domain from his station in Edo (now Tōkyō), where he studied Japanese and Chinese classics and WESTERN LEARNING through friendships with KATSURAGAWA HOSHŪ, NAKAGAWA JUN'AN, AOKI KON'YŌ, and MAENO RYŌTAKU. His report AKA-EZO FŪSETSU KŌ, which stressed the need for colonization of EZO (now Hokkaidō) to defend it from Russian encroachment, presaged the ideas of later advocates of national defense such as HAYASHI SHIHEI and HONDA TOSHIAKI.

kudzu → kuzu

Kuga Katsunan   陸羯南

(1857–1907). Journalist of the Meiji period (1868–1912). Real name Nakada Minoru. Born in the Tsugaru domain (now part of Aomori Prefecture), he was adopted into the Kuga family. Katsunan was a pen name. He attended the law school (Hōgakkō) of the Ministry of Justice and became an official in the Meiji government in 1881. In 1888 he resigned in opposition to the Westernization policy of government leaders eager to secure revision of the Unequal Treaties (see UNEQUAL TREATIES, REVISION OF). In the same year he founded the newspaper *Tōkyō dempō* (Tōkyō Telegram). He discontinued its publication in 1889 and started another newspaper, *Nihon* (Japan). More than 20 issues of *Nihon* were suppressed by the government because Kuga's editorials criticized cliquism (see HAMBATSU) in the government and called for a nationalism based upon the united will of the Japanese people (*kokumin shugi*). *Kinji seiron kō* (1891, Thoughts on Recent Politics) is his major work.

kugatachi   盟神探湯

Also called *kukatachi; kukadachi.* A kind of trial by ordeal, recorded in the NIHON SHOKI (720), in which a suspect was forced to take a small stone out of a pot of boiling water, and his guilt or innocence was determined by whether or not his hand blistered. A somewhat similar practice, called *yugishō,* is recorded in the Muromachi period (1333–1568).

kuge   公家

Term used to refer to the imperial court nobility. Originally the word was pronounced *kōke* or *kōka* and signified the emperor or the court itself. However, from the late Heian period (794–1185) onward, with the rise of the great military houses and religious establishments to positions of power and prominence, the word *kuge* came to be used more broadly to refer to the noble families with administrative responsibilities within the imperial court and its bureaucracy, as distinct from these other social groups. Status distinctions within the *kuge* were determined by an elaborate system of court ranks and attendant duties, which from the Kamakura period (1185–1333) onward tended to rigidify to the extent that certain noble families became hereditarily specialized in particular aspects of court affairs— political administration, law, religion, or the arts. With the turmoil of the Sengoku period (1467–1568) and the establishment of the Tokugawa shogunate (1603–1867), the *kuge* lost almost all that remained of their former authority, retaining only certain formalized and ceremonial functions, as well as some prominence in artistic and religious matters. In the social reforms that followed the Meiji Restoration, the status of *kuge* and the traditional system of court ranks were abolished in 1869. They were replaced by a new PEERAGE, called the *kazoku,* which was created out of a fusion of the former court nobility with the highest stratum of the former *samurai* class. After World War II, the new constitution adopted in 1947 abolished the *kazoku,* and the nobility as a historical institution was finally eliminated.

Kūge nikkushū   空華日工集

Full title *Kūge nichiyō kufū ryakushū* (Instructions on Monastic Life by Kūge). Journal kept by GIDŌ SHŪSHIN (pen name Kūge; 1325–88), a ZEN priest of the period of the Northern and Southern Courts (1337–92). Of 48 volumes, only four chapters of excerpts survive, but they provide useful information on the monastic and cultural life of the leading Zen temples of his day as well as on political events, of which Shūshin, as an adviser to the Muromachi shogunate, was a close observer.

kugyō   公卿

Also called *kandachime.* The highest-ranking officials, numbering about 20, at the imperial court in Kyōto during the Heian period (794–1185). Essentially the title was restricted to officials of the third rank and higher (see COURT RANKS), but it was also applied to councillors (SANGI) who had not achieved the third rank. The term refers to the grand minister of state (*dajō daijin*), regents (*sesshō, kampaku*), ministers of the left and right (*sadaijin, udaijin*), great and middle counselors (*dainagon, chūnagon*), and *sangi.* Although political power passed into other hands after the Heian period, the offices were often filled and the term designating their holders remained in use until early in the Meiji period (1868–1912).

Kuhara Fusanosuke   久原房之助

(1869–1965). Mining magnate and conservative politician. His Kuhara Mining Company eventually became Nippon Sangyō (Nissan), largest of the newer ZAIBATSU (financial combines) that started in the 1920s and 1930s. Born in what is now Yamaguchi Prefecture, Kuhara graduated from Keiō Gijuku (now Keiō University) and joined the Fujita-Gumi, a mining company. In 1905 Kuhara purchased and modernized an old mine at Hitachi in Ibaraki Prefecture. Buying other copper mines, he formed the Kuhara Mining Company in 1912 and profited greatly from the World War I copper boom. However, the financial crisis of the 1920s slowed company growth, and Kuhara turned to politics. In 1928 Kuhara transferred company management to AIKAWA YOSHISUKE, who reorganized the administration to create Nissan.

Kuhara was a major contributor to the RIKKEN SEIYŪKAI party. In 1928 he was named communications minister in the TANAKA GIICHI cabinet. Kuhara strongly supported the 1931 movement to form a coalition government with the rival RIKKEN MINSEITŌ party. In 1940, as president of the Seitō faction of the Seiyūkai, he played a willing role in its absorption by the IMPERIAL RULE ASSISTANCE ASSOCIATION. Kuhara was purged by Occupation authorities, but after purge restrictions were lifted in 1955 he became active in negotiations for reopening relations with China.

kuiawase   食い合わせ

The term *kuiawase* (also called *tabeawase;* literally, "eating together") refers to combinations of certain foods traditionally believed to cause food poisoning or illness and the prohibitions surrounding these combinations of foods. Although there were some local variations, taboos concerning such combinations as eel and pickled plum (UMEBOSHI), TEMPURA and watermelon, eel and watermelon, and crab and persimmon were widespread.

kuina → rails

Kuji   久慈[市]

City in northeastern Iwate Prefecture, northern Honshū, on the Pacific Ocean. Kuji is the center of thriving lumber and marine-products-processing industries. Pop: 38,743.

kuji   公事

(literally, "public matters"). Term variously used to mean political affairs, court ceremonies, or legal proceedings but mainly to indicate a major tax under the SHŌEN (private estate) system of land tenure from the 9th through the 15th centuries. Tax requirements for these *shōen* were broadly divided into *kuji* and NENGU (rice tax); the *kuji* category was subdivided into corvée labor (BUYAKU) and miscellaneous goods (*zōkuji*). *Kuji* taxes, levied mainly on independent landholders (MYŌSHU), were collected by estate proprietors (RYŌSHU) and the shogunate-appointed military governors (SHUGO) and estate stewards (JITŌ).

Kujigawa 久慈川

River in Ibaraki Prefecture, central Honshū, originating at the mountain Yamizosan and emptying into the Pacific Ocean south of the city of Hitachi. The port of Hitachi is located at its mouth. Scenic gorges are found on the upper reaches of the river, and sweetfish (*ayu*) are plentiful. Length: 124 km (77 mi); area of drainage basin: 1,490 sq km (575 sq mi).

Kujikata Osadamegaki 公事方御定書

(Official Provisions). Important legal code of the Tokugawa shogunate (1603–1867); issued in 1742, it remained in effect until the Meiji Restoration (1868). It was compiled at the command of the shōgun TOKUGAWA YOSHIMUNE and consisted of two parts. The first outlined administrative procedures and civil regulations in 81 articles; the second set forth criminal laws and penalties in 103 articles (popularly called the Hyakkajō, or Hundred Articles). The code, which was in principle secret and issued only to designated officials, served as a guide for commissioners in passing judgments in both civil and criminal cases. Although it was directed primarily at commoners in the shogunate's own domains (TENRYŌ), some of its regulations were applicable to lesser *samurai*. The code was also enforced in domains held by the shogunate's direct retainers (HATAMOTO and GOKENIN) and was adopted, with some modifications, by several other *daimyō* for use as their own domainal code.

Kuji kongen 公事根源

(Origins of Court Ritual). Book on ancient practices and precedents of the imperial court (YŪSOKU KOJITSU), written about 1422 and attributed to the noble and scholar ICHIJŌ KANEYOSHI. Drawing on such sources as the KEMMU NENCHŪ GYŌJI, it lists the annual events observed by the imperial court in monthly order and explains their origins and historical development.

Kujō family 九条家

(Kujōke). One of the five houses (GOSEKKE) of the Northern Branch (Hokke) of the FUJIWARA FAMILY whose members were eligible for the post of imperial regent (SESSHŌ; KAMPAKU). The Kujō were descended from Fujiwara no Tadamichi's (1097–1164) third son, KUJŌ KANEZANE, who took the name of his Kyōto residence as his family name. The Kujō were closely linked with the Kamakura shogunate (1192–1333), and after the murder of MINAMOTO NO SANETOMO, the regent HŌJŌ FAMILY installed Kujō Yoritsune (1218–56) and Kujō Yoritsugu (1239–56) as the fourth and fifth shōguns. After the Meiji Restoration (1868), the Kujō were given the rank of prince (*kōshaku*) in the new peerage. A Kujō became the chief consort of Emperor TAISHŌ and the mother of Emperor SHŌWA.

Kujō Kanezane 九条兼実

(1149–1207). Also known as Fujiwara no Kanezane. Courtier of the Kamakura period

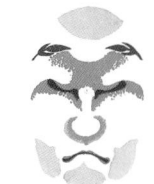

kumadori

This style of *kabuki* makeup comprises some 70 masklike patterns, categorized by the dominant color employed.

The striking *sujiguma* pattern augments the forceful style of kabuki acting known as *aragoto*.

Asagaoguma is a mixture of the red and blue styles.

Mukimiguma, one of the red styles.

The *chaguma* or *taishaguma* style of brown makeup.

Kijoguma, one of the blue styles.

(1185–1333). Third son of the imperial regent (KAMPAKU) Fujiwara no Tadamichi (1097–1164); an elder brother of the scholar-priest JIEN. Kanezane founded the Kujō family (one of the GOSEKKE, or five regent families), named after his residence in Kyōto. In 1186 he was appointed SESSHŌ (regent for a minor sovereign) and five years later, *kampaku*. Kanezane attempted to restrain retired emperors (see INSEI) from intervening in politics, but he fell from power in 1196. He spent the rest of his life as a Buddhist priest, becoming a patron-disciple of HŌNEN. A number of his poems are included in the anthologies SENZAI WAKASHŪ and SHIN KOKINSHŪ. His informative diary is titled GYOKUYŌ (or *Gyokukai*).

Kujū Kōgen 久住高原

Grassy highland on the slopes of the Kujū Volcanic Group, west central Ōita Prefecture, Kyūshū. It is a lava highland, with abundant pumice. It is used for cattle grazing and hay production and is part of Aso-Kujū National Park. Elevation: 600–1,100 m (2,000–3,600 ft).

Kujūkurihama 九十九里浜

Sandy coastal area in northeastern Chiba Prefecture, central Honshū. Situated on the Pacific seaboard. The nearby seas provide good fishing grounds for sardines. It is designated a prefectural natural park, with numerous swimming resorts along the coast. Length: approximately 60 km (37 mi).

Kujūsan 九重山

Volcanic group in western Ōita Prefecture, Kyūshū. The highest peak in the group is Nakadake (1,791 m; 5,876 ft). Kujūsan is part of Aso-Kujū National Park.

Kūkai 空海

(774–835). Also known as Kōbō Daishi. Buddhist priest of the early Heian period (794–1185); founder of the SHINGON SECT of Buddhism. Born at Byōbugaura in Sanuki province (now Zentsūji, Kagawa Prefecture) in Shikoku, into a declining aristocratic family. At age 18 he entered the national college in the capital with the aim of becoming a statesman but withdrew after a few years. He justified his action by denouncing Confucianism and Taoism and extolling Buddhism in a provocative work entitled *Sangō shiiki* (798, Principles of the Three Teachings). Kūkai then pursued his Buddhist studies while wandering about the country as an itinerant hermit practicing meditation.

In 804 he sailed to China as a student monk. In Chang'an (Ch'ang-an), he studied under Huiguo (Hui-kuo; J: Keika), the patriarch of esoteric Buddhism, and returned to Japan in 806 a master of esoteric Buddhist teachings. In 809 he assumed the abbacy of Takaosanji (now called JINGOJI), a temple in the suburbs of Kyōto. In 819 Kūkai initiated construction of a monastic center on Mt. Kōya (KŌYASAN) for the practice of esoteric Buddhist meditation. This and systematization of the Shingon doctrine were Kūkai's major concerns during the remainder of his life. In 823 the emperor SAGA (r 809–823) presented him with TŌJI, the most important temple at the southern entrance to Kyōto, which became the headquarters for Shingon Buddhism.

Credited with the invention of the KANA syllabary, Kūkai is considered the father of Japanese culture. He is remembered as the originator of the pilgrimage circuit of 88 temples on Shikoku (see PILGRIMAGES), a builder of lakes, and a wandering saint who engaged in severe ascetic practices. He was also known as a poet, calligrapher, sculptor, and lexicographer who compiled the *Tenrei banshō meigi*, the oldest extant dictionary in Japan. He founded the SHUGEI SHUCHIIN school in Kyōto. Two of Kūkai's most significant writings are *Sokushin jōbutsu gi* (Meanings of Attaining Enlightment in This Very Existence) and JŪJŪSHIN RON (Treatise on the Ten Stages of the Development of Mind).

Kuki 久喜[市]

City in northeastern Saitama Prefecture, central Honshū. A market town during the Edo period (1600–1868), it is now an industrial and residential area. Pop: 66,852.

Kuki Shūzō 九鬼周造

(1888–1941). Philosopher. Born in Tōkyō. After graduation from the philosophy department of Tōkyō University in 1912, Kuki went to Europe in 1922 to study with Heinrich Rickert, Henri Bergson, and Martin Heidegger. Returning to Japan in 1929, he taught the history of philosophy at Kyōto University. He engaged in a phenomenological, hermeneutical study of *iki* (see IKI AND SUI), a key concept in Japanese aesthetics. He also studied the notion of the "accidental," which he considered to be a concept essential to existentialist philosophy and which was little developed in Western existentialism. Kuki's works include *Iki no kōzō* (1930, The Structure of *Iki*) and *Gūzensei no mondai* (1935, The Problem of the Accidental).

kumadori 限取り

Style of makeup used in KABUKI. The term *kumadori* refers to the red, blue, brown, and black cosmetics painted on an actor's face to emphasize the nature of the character he plays. The basic patterns of *kumadori* were established by the kabuki actor Ichikawa Danjūro I (1660–1704; see ICHIKAWA DANJŪRO). The 60 to 70 *kumadori* patterns can be divided into two general categories: *beniguma* (red makeup), expressing passion, virtue, or superhuman power, and *aiguma* (blue makeup), expressing jealousy, fear, and other negative traits. This exaggeration of facial features developed alongside the exaggeration of gesture found in the *aragoto* ("rough business") style of kabuki acting.

kumagaisō Japan's largest wild orchid grows in clusters in shaded forest areas. The plant's name derives from the similarity between the flower's sac-shaped corolla and the hood worn by the famous *samurai* Kumagai Naozane.

Kumagai Gumi Co, Ltd　[株]熊谷組

(Kumagai-Gumi). General construction firm specializing in large-scale public works projects. Incorporated in 1938. The company is noted for its achievements in the construction of high-rise buildings and housing tracts. It has subsidiaries and branch offices in 21 countries, including the United States, the United Kingdom, and Australia, as well as China, Hong Kong, and other Asian countries. Net sales for the fiscal year ending March 1991 totaled ¥1.2 trillion (US $8.7 billion), of which public works projects accounted for 24 percent; general construction projects, 71 percent; and real estate, 5 percent. The company was capitalized at ¥81.9 billion (US $597.0 million) in the same year. Headquarters are in Tōkyō.

Kumagai Naoyoshi　熊谷直好

(1782–1862). WAKA poet of the late Edo period (1600–1868). Born in Suō Province (now part of Yamaguchi Prefecture). Kumagai studied under KAGAWA KAGEKI. In his forties he moved to Ōsaka to write and teach poetry. Regarded along with KINOSHITA TAKAFUMI as one of Kageki's leading disciples, he elaborated his master's theories in such works as *Ryōjin kōshō* (1860).

Kumagai Naozane　熊谷直実

(1141–1208). Military commander who joined the Minamoto faction during the TAIRA-MINAMOTO WAR (1180–85). He took a leading part in the Minamoto victory at Ichinotani (near modern Kōbe) in 1184. Naozane became a disciple of HŌNEN, patriarch of the JŌDO SECT of Buddhism. In 1192 Naozane himself became a priest, taking the religious name Renshō. In an incident recounted in the 13th-century war romance HEIKE MONOGATARI, Naozane, tempted to spare TAIRA NO ATSUMORI, is forced by the arrival of other Minamoto warriors to kill the youth; his remorse leads him to the priesthood. This moving story, which is probably fictional, became the basis of such classic dramas as the Nō play *Atsumori* (ca 15th century; tr *Atsumori*, 1920) and the *bunraku* and *kabuki* play *Ichinotani futaba gunki* (1751; tr *Chronicle of the Battle of Ichinotani*, 1975).

Kumamoto Prefecture Location and Prefectural Crest

kumagaisō　熊谷草

Cypripedium japonicum. Perennial herb belonging to the group called "lady's slippers" of the orchid family (Orchidaceae). It grows wild in mountain woods and sometimes in bamboo forests throughout Japan. It is also highly prized as a garden flower. The straight stem grows 30–40 centimeters (12–16 in) high. Fan-shaped, alternate leaves grow nearly opposite. From April to May a flower stalk (15 cm; 6 in) bears a yellowish white flower surrounded by a sac-shaped corolla. The *kumagaisō* was introduced to Europe by the Swedish botanist

Carl Peter THUNBERG. The closely related species *atsumorisō* (*C. macranthum*), a reddish flower, is also widely found in Japan.

Kumagai Taizō　熊谷岱蔵

(1880–1962). Medical scientist. Born in Nagano Prefecture; graduate of Tōkyō University. Kumagai is noted for his research on tuberculosis—its process of infection, its pathology, and the BCG vaccine. He served as professor and president of Tōhoku University. A member of the Japan Academy from 1943, he received the Order of Culture in 1952.

Kumagawa　球磨川

River in southern Kumamoto Prefecture, Kyūshū, flowing through the Kyūshū Mountains into the Yatsushiro Sea. It is the third longest river in Kyūshū and one of Japan's swiftest. Its water is used for irrigation, electric power, and industry. The 18 km (11 mi) Kumagawa *kudari* (boating down the river) offers a memorable experience. Length: 115 km (71 mi); area of drainage basin: 1,880 sq km (725 sq mi).

Kumagaya　熊谷[市]

City in northern Saitama Prefecture, central Honshū, on the river Arakawa. A post-station town in the Edo period (1600–1868), it is now an important business and transportation center in the region. Principal industries are nonferrous metal, steel, and electrical machinery. Of interest are the Uchiwa (fan) Festival at the Yasaka Shrine in July, the Ebisu Festival in November, and the temple Yūkokuji. Pop: 152,124.

Kumai Kei　熊井啓

(1930–). Film director. His films are known for their documentarylike realism. Born in Nagano Prefecture. After graduating from Shinshū University Kumai got a job at NIKKATSU CORPORATION, assisting Hisamatsu Seiji (1912–90), TASAKA TOMOTAKA, Abe Yutaka (1895–1977), and other directors on various films through the 1950s. In 1964 he made his debut as a director with *Teigin jiken: Shikeishū* (The Long Death), a fictional re-creation of a sensational post–World War II crime (see TEIGIN INCIDENT). Both his *Shinobugawa* (1972, The Long Darkness) and *Sandakan hachiban shōkan: Bōkyō* (1974, Sandakan #8 or Brothel #8) won the Kinema Jumpō Prize as best film of the year. Kumai's *Honkakubō ibun Sen no Rikyū* (1989, Death of the Tea Master) won the Silver Lion at the 1989 Venice Film Festival.

Kumamoto　熊本[市]

Capital of Kumamoto Prefecture, Kyūshū. A provincial center since the 7th century, it flourished with the construction of Kumamoto Castle by KATŌ KIYOMASA in 1601. It later came under the rule of the HOSOKAWA FAMILY. It was the site of a garrison (*chindai*) from the Meiji period (1868–1912) until the end of World War II. Principal industries are electronics and foodstuffs. Attractions are Kumamoto Castle; Suizenji Park; Tatsuta Park, with the grave of HOSOKAWA GRACIA; and the grave of MIYAMOTO MUSASHI, in the city's Tatsutamachi section. Pop: 579,306.

Kumamoto Plain　熊本平野

(Kumamoto Heiya). Located in western Kumamoto Prefecture, Kyūshū. It extends from the diluvial uplands on the slopes of Asosan, a mountain to the east, where fruits and vegetables are grown, to the alluvial lowlands that border Shimabara Bay to the

west, where large rice crops are produced. The major city in the area is Kumamoto. Area: approximately 780 sq km (300 sq mi).

Kumamoto Prefectural Art Museum　熊本県立美術館

(Kumamoto Kenritsu Bijutsukan). Located in the city of Kumamoto. One of the handsomest of the prefectural museums, it was designed by MAEKAWA KUNIO and opened in 1976. It has an active program of temporary exhibitions and special activities. Its permanent collection contains excellent objects of the Kofun period (ca 300–710) as well as contemporary paintings and prints. In spring and autumn the museum houses a special exhibition of objects from the collection of the EISEI BUNKO MUSEUM in Tōkyō.

Kumamoto Prefecture　熊本県

(Kumamoto Ken). Located in western Kyūshū and bounded to the north by Fukuoka Prefecture, to the northeast by Ōita Prefecture, to the east by Miyazaki Prefecture, to the south by Kagoshima Prefecture, and to the west by the Amakusa Sea. The southern and northeastern sections of the prefecture are mountainous, and the north-central area forms a large plain that contains most of the population. Southwest of the capital of KUMAMOTO, the AMAKUSA ISLANDS extend toward the East China Sea. The climate is generally mild.

Formerly known as Higo Province, it was strongly influenced by continental culture, as evidenced by the great number of ORNAMENTED TOMBS found here. The area fell under the control of a succession of warlords from the end of the Heian period (794–1185). Peasants and Christians from the Amakusa Islands took part in the great SHIMABARA UPRISING of 1637. The prefecture's present boundaries were established in 1876.

Agriculture remains the principal occupation. The main crop is rice, but a wide variety of fruits and vegetables are also grown, with mandarin oranges as the best-known specialty crop. Stock and dairy farming and forestry are important. Industrial development has been hampered by the prefecture's remoteness from major economic centers, and large factories are limited to a few of the major cities. Industrial development, however, has accelerated in recent years.

Tourist attractions include ASOSAN, a large active volcano in the northeastern part of the prefecture, and the unspoiled coastal scenery of the Amakusa Islands, both of which are designated as national parks. The city of KUMAMOTO features a restored feudal castle, one of the largest in Japan, and the garden of Suizenji. Area: 7,408 sq km (2,860 sq mi); pop: 1,840,326; capital: Kumamoto. Other major cities include YATSUSHIRO, ARAO, and HITOYOSHI.

Kumamoto University　熊本大学

(Kumamoto Daigaku). A coeducational national university located in the city of Kumamoto, Kumamoto Prefecture. Founded in 1949, the university maintains faculties of letters, education, law, science, medicine, pharmaceutical sciences, and engineering. The faculty of medicine has made great strides in both research and treatment of Minamata disease (see POLLUTION-RELATED DISEASES). Enrollment in 1989 was 7,616.

Kumamoto Yōgakkō　熊本洋学校

School in Kumamoto established in 1871. Staffed by foreign teachers (all classes were given in English), its curriculum emphasized

Western science. In 1876 some 40 students, having converted to Christianity under the influence of the teacher Leroy Lansing JANES, formed the "Kumamoto Band" and signed an oath to preach the gospel. Displeased conservatives in Kumamoto had the school closed later that year, and the Kumamoto Band transferred to the Dōshisha (now Dōshisha University) in Kyōto.

Kumano 熊野[市]

City in southern Mie Prefecture, central Honshū, on the Kumano Sea. Fishing, forestry, and horticulture are its principal industries. It is the gateway to Yoshino-Kumano National Park. Pop: 23,718.

Kumanogawa 熊野川

River in Nara, Mie, and Wakayama prefectures, central Honshū. It originates in the Ōmine Mountains, in southern Nara Prefecture, and flows south along the border of Mie and Wakayama prefectures to empty into the Kumano Sea at the city of Shingū. The upper reaches are known as TOTSUKAWA. A sharply winding river, it has carved its way through granite porphyry. The gorge of DOROKYŌ is located on the Kitayamagawa, a tributary. Length: 183 km (114 mi); area of drainage basin: 2,360 sq km (911 sq mi).

Kumano Sanzan Shrines 熊野三社

(Kumano Sansha). Collective name for three Shintō shrines located in the Kumano district of Wakayama Prefecture: Kumano Hongū Taisha in Hongū, dedicated to Ketsumiko no Kami (i.e., SUSANOO NO MIKOTO); Kumano Hayatama Taisha in Shingū, dedicated to Kumano Hayatama no Kami; and Kumano Nachi Taisha in Nachi Katsuura, dedicated to Kumano Fusumi no Kami. From earliest times Kumano, a mountainous area overlooking the sea, was believed to be a dwelling place of the gods (KAMI), and the Kumano shrines became a popular pilgrimage site. Kumano was also a center of SHUGENDŌ mountain asceticism. In medieval times, the cult of the Kumano Sansha was spread by wandering monks (HIJIRI), shrine maidens (MIKO), and mountain ascetics (YAMABUSHI). Each of the Kumano Sanzan Shrines holds an annual festival—the Kumano Hongū Taisha on 15 April, the Kumano Hayatama Taisha on 15-16 October, and the Kumano Nachi Taisha on 14 July.

Kumano Sea 熊野灘

(Kumano Nada). Inlet of the Pacific Ocean on the eastern coast of the Kii Peninsula (Mie and Wakayama prefectures), central Honshū. It extends approximately 140 km (87 mi) from the Shima Peninsula to the cape SHIONOMISAKI. The warm KUROSHIO (Japan Current) makes it an important fishing area.

Kumashiro Tatsumi 神代辰巳

(1927–). Film director. Born in Saga Prefecture. After graduating from Waseda University in 1952, he entered SHŌCHIKU CO, LTD's Kyōto studios as an assistant director. In 1955 he moved to the NIKKATSU CORPORATION as an assistant director. He made his debut as a director with *Kaburitsuki jinsei* (1968, Life on the Front Row). When Nikkatsu began producing pornographic films (ROMAN PORUNO) in 1971, Kumashiro worked in the genre. His *Yojōhan fusuma no urabari* (1973, The Paper Lining of the Sliding Doors of a Four-and-a-Half-Mat Room) was chosen the best film of the year by Japanese movie magazines and praised as a masterpiece that transcended the genre of mere pornography.

Since 1974 he has also turned his hand to film adaptations of contemporary novels such as *Beddo taimu aizu* (1987, Bedtime Eyes).

Kumashiro Yūhi 熊代熊斐

(1713–72). Artist of the Edo period (1600–1868). Real name Kumashiro Hi. Also known as Kamashiro Shūkō; he sometimes used the signature Yū Hi, an imitation of a Chinese name. Born into a family that served as hereditary translators (*tsūji*) for Chinese merchants in Nagasaki. Kumashiro studied painting with Watanabe Shūseki and then with Shen Nanpin (Shen Nan-p'in) from China, who taught him a new Chinese technique of painting directly from life. Kumashiro is known for his use of strong colors and also for his vigorous monochrome ink paintings.

Kumaso 熊襲

A tribe mentioned in early Japanese writings such as the chronicles KOJIKI (712) and NIHON SHOKI (720). The Kumaso are believed to have inhabited the southern parts of Kyūshū. Some scholars believe that the Kumaso were identical with or racially related to the HAYATO tribe. The early chronicles contain accounts of a rebellion of the Kumaso against the YAMATO COURT, the best-known episode being their defeat by Prince YAMATOTAKERU. Although these episodes, which supposedly took place during the 4th century, are questionable as history, they are an important part of Japan's early heroic literature.

Kumazawa Banzan 熊沢蕃山

(1619–91). Important Confucian thinker of the Edo period (1600–1868). Born the son of a *rōnin* (masterless *samurai*) in Kyōto, Banzan entered the service of IKEDA MITSUMASA, the *daimyō* of Bizen Province (now part of Okayama Prefecture), in 1634 but resigned in 1639. In 1641–42 he studied under NAKAE TŌJU, founder in Japan of the Wang Yangming school of Neo-Confucianism (see YŌMEIGAKU), becoming his leading disciple. He reentered Mitsumasa's service in 1645 and was instrumental in bringing about domain governmental reforms before resigning in 1656 to teach and study. He was primarily an eclectic popularizer rather than a systematic philosopher. Banzan's voluminous writings almost all date from the last period of his life. Most important are two collections of dialogues and letters (the *Shūgi washo*, primarily concerned with moral philosophy, and the *Shūgi gaisho*, concerned with social problems and politics); a treatise on contemporary strategic, political, social, and economic problems entitled *Daigaku wakumon* (Questions on the Great Learning); commentaries on the Confucian classics; and a commentary on the *Genji monogatari* (TALE OF GENJI).

Kumejima 久米島

Volcanic island approximately 100 km (60 mi) west of Okinawa. The chief activity is sugarcane production. The special product of the island is Kumejima *tsumugi*, a handspun silk with a distinctive KASURI pattern. Area: 55.7 sq km (21.5 sq mi).

Kume Keiichirō 久米桂一郎

(1866–1934). Western-style painter. Born in Saga Prefecture. In 1886 he went to Paris and, with KURODA SEIKI, studied under Raphaël Collin (1850–1916). Returning to Japan in 1893, he and Kuroda opened a studio called

Kumano Sanzan Shrines The existing buildings (pictured) of the Kumano Hongū Taisha, said to be the oldest of the three Kumano Sanzan Shrines, were constructed in the early 18th century.

Tenshin Dōjō, where he taught OKADA SABURŌSUKE, WADA EISAKU, and others. In 1896 with Kuroda he organized a Western-style painting association, the HAKUBAKAI (White Horse Society). Two years later he began teaching at Tōkyō Bijutsu Gakkō (now TŌKYŌ UNIVERSITY OF FINE ARTS AND MUSIC), and from that time on he rarely painted, devoting himself to education and administration of the arts.

Kume Kunitake 久米邦武

(1839–1931). Historian. Born in the Saga domain (now part of Saga Prefecture). After studying at the Shōheikō, the shogunal academy in Edo (now Tōkyō), he assisted in administrative reform in Saga. In 1871 he joined the IWAKURA MISSION to Europe and the United States to observe Western institutions. As private secretary to IWAKURA TOMOMI, he compiled a five-volume account of the journey, *Tokumei zenken taishi: Beiō kairan jikki* (1878). He was appointed professor at Tōkyō University in 1888; he also assisted in the compilation of the *Dai Nihon hennenshi*, a comprehensive history of Japan. Reaction to his article "Shintō wa saiten no kozoku" (Shintō Is an Outmoded Custom of Worshiping Heaven), published in the history journal *Shigakukai zasshi* (1891; reprinted the following year in *Shikai*), obliged him to resign from the university. Kume continued to write and lecture at Tōkyō Semmon Gakkō (now Waseda University).

Kume Masao 久米正雄

(1891–1952). Novelist and playwright. Born in Nagano Prefecture. Graduate of Tōkyō University. With his classmates AKUTAGAWA RYŪNOSUKE and KIKUCHI KAN, Kume participated in the literary coterie that published the magazine SHINSHICHŌ. His play *Gyūnyūya no kyōdai*, staged in 1914, was very popular. In 1933 he wrote the melodramatic novel *Tsuki yori no shisha* and soon became a best-selling author. He is also known as a HAIKU poet, under the pen name Santei.

kumi 組

Neighborhood groups of households bound together by residential proximity and reciprocal aid. Consisting of up to 15 households, *kumi* function as joint work and assistance subunits of the village. Together the members of a *kumi* plant rice, prepare for festivals and ceremonies, handle funerals, build and repair homes and roads, and often provide capital, credit, and especially labor for one another. In the Edo period (1600–1868), with the growth of cities, urban *kumi* called GONINGUMI were institutionalized to handle neighborhood functions. During World War II, the *kumi* were officially reorganized as

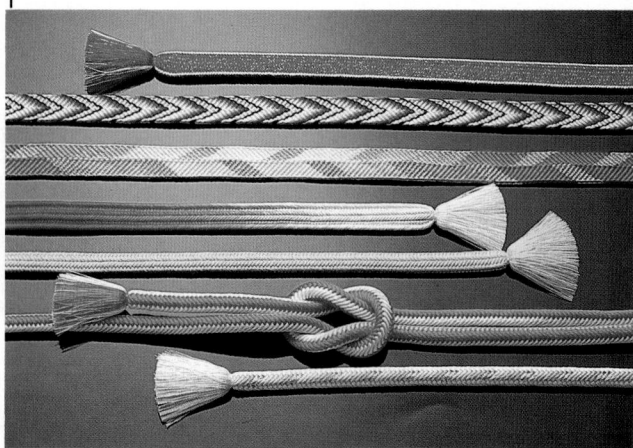

kumihimo
1 Some of the many different *kumihimo* designs used for *obijime* (the cords that secure the *obi* worn with women's *kimono*).
2 An expert braider can move the weighted strands used in making *kumihimo* around the outside of the *marudai* stool at amazing speed.
3 The most common current use of *kumihimo* is as *obijime*.

TONARIGUMI and played a role in civil defense, rationing, and other activities.

Kumiai Chemical Industry Co, Ltd
クミアイ化学工業[株]

(Kumiai Kagaku Kōgyō). Manufacturer of agrochemicals. Incorporated in 1949. It manufactures and markets herbicides, fungicides, insecticides, plant-growth regulators, and other chemicals. The key products, Saturn (herbicide) and Kitazin (fungicide), are exported to more than 40 countries. The company has 14 sales offices, 7 factories, 2 research institutes, and 3 experimental stations. Its overseas affiliated companies are located in the United States, Thailand, and Brazil. Sales for the fiscal year ending October 1990 totaled ¥54.9 billion (US $423.2 million), and capitalization stood at ¥4.5 billion (US $34.7 million). Headquarters are in Tōkyō.

kumihimo
組紐

(braiding). Silk cords or bands handcrafted by the weighted-bobbin braiding technique of the same name. The strands of *kumihimo* are interlaced obliquely in prescribed sequences to produce a wide variety of patterns. The number of component strands runs from 3 to over 100, with each strand consisting of up to several hundred fine silk threads. *Kumihimo* was highly developed as early as the 7th century. It has traditionally been used as sword belts; wrapping for sword hilts; trim for amulet cases, ritual banners, and priestly vestments; and in armor as lacing, trim, shoulder straps, and belts. Today women use it in the form of the *obijime*, a decorative as well as functional band worn on OBI. Over the past four centuries, the principal tools for the craft have been weighted bobbins and, depending on the structure of the *kumihimo*, various types of stands or looms. Recent research has shown, however, that in earlier times a free-hand braiding technique, generally known as loop manipulation, was used.

Kunikida Doppo After gaining a reputation as a romantic poet and short-story writer, Doppo developed a realistic style that influenced the development of naturalism in Japan.

Kumoi Tatsuo
雲井竜雄

(1844–70). Political activist of the Edo (1600–1868) and Meiji (1868–1912) periods. Real name Kojima Moriyoshi. After the overthrow of the Tokugawa shogunate in 1868, Kumoi, who was of *samurai* lineage, helped form a league of northeastern domains (see ŌUETSU REPPAN DŌMEI) against the new Meiji government. The coalition was short-lived, and in 1869 Kumoi became a representative to the Shūgiin, the newly established legislative body. He soon resigned and gathered around him samurai discontented with the new government. Suspected of fomenting a plot to assassinate government officials in order to restore feudal government, he was executed.

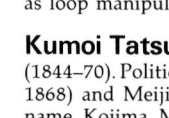

kumon
公文

(official documents; clerks). A general term for documents, especially census and tax records, during the 7th and 8th centuries, when the RITSURYŌ SYSTEM of government was evolving. In the Heian (794–1185) and Kamakura (1185–1333) periods *kumon* came to mean the functionaries in noble houses and religious institutions who were in charge of drawing up and keeping documents and records and of assigning tax burdens. See also KUMONJO; SHŌKAN.

kumonjo
公文所

Originally departments within provincial headquarters (*kokuga*) for keeping documents under the RITSURYŌ SYSTEM of government from the 7th century onward. By the middle of the Heian period (794–1185) *kumonjo* had come to refer to offices in noble households, religious institutions, and private landed estates (SHŌEN) charged with keeping records. The most famous Kumonjo (known in English as the Public Documents Office) was that established by MINAMOTO NO YORITOMO in 1184 at his headquarters in Kamakura. He appointed ŌE NO HIROMOTO to head the office, with Nakahara no Chikayoshi (1143–1208), Fujiwara (Nikaidō) no Yukimasa (dates unknown), and several other scholars working under him. After 1191 the Kumonjo was absorbed into the Administrative Board (MANDOKORO). See also KUMON.

kumosuke
雲助

Hired carriers of freight and palanquins on major highways during the Edo period (1600–1868). The master of each post station (*shukueki*) was required to make available a specified number of porters for hire by imposing a labor-service requirement (SUKEGŌ) on the local peasantry. When this was commuted to a cash payment, the post stations turned to hired labor, often unruly types who were called *kumosuke* (literally, "cloud men") because they drifted like clouds with no fixed residence.

Kunaichō→ Imperial Household Agency

Kunashiri
国後

Volcanic island approximately 20 km (12 mi) off the eastern coast of Hokkaidō. This long, narrow island is southwest of the Kuril Islands and separated from Hokkaidō by the Nemuro Strait. The fishing ports of Tomari and Furukamappu are located on the southwestern side of the island. Ships once ran regularly between Tomari and Nemuro on Hokkaidō, but the island was occupied by the Soviet Union in 1945 and, as of early 1992, was still under occupation by the Russian Federation (see TERRITORY OF JAPAN). Area: 1,500 sq km (580 sq mi).

kuni ikki
国一揆

Provincial uprisings of the Muromachi period (1333–1568). Led by local landowners and warriors (KOKUJIN) against the military governors (SHUGO), they differed from other uprisings in their large scale and political goals. *Shugo* often lacked the territorial base and military following needed to dominate their provinces (*kuni*), and so they tried to enlist the *kokujin* as vassals. The aim of the *kokujin*, however, was to increase their own power, which they did by forming leagues (IKKI). Though *kokujin* leagues were normally temporary responses to military threats, they could be used to resist or supersede the *shugo*'s authority; such leagues were especially effective when supported by the peasantry, cooperating in order to avoid taxation by the *shugo*. In 1429 *kokujin* and peasants rose against the *shugo* of Harima Province (now part of Hyōgo Prefecture) in the first important *kuni ikki*. In Yamashiro Province (now part of Kyōto Prefecture) in 1485, a similar league expelled the *shugo* HATAKEYAMA FAMILY from the southern half of the province and ruled it for the next eight years through a *kokujin* council (see YAMASHIRO NO KUNI IKKI). *Kuni ikki* hastened the rise of local political power, in which many *kokujin* emerged as autonomous territorial lords (SENGOKU DAIMYŌ). See also TSUCHI IKKI.

Kunikida Doppo
国木田独歩

(1871–1908). Poet and novelist. One of the important forerunners of Japanese NATURALISM, he was nevertheless basically a romantic. Real name Kunikida Tetsuo. Born in Chōshi, Chiba Prefecture, and raised in Yamaguchi Prefecture. He enrolled in the English-language department at Tōkyō Semmon Gakkō (now Waseda University) when he was 19 years old and already well read in literature. Three years later he was baptized by UEMURA MASAHISA and became a Christian. In November 1895 he married Sasaki Nobuko, on whom ARISHIMA TAKEO is thought to have based his well-known novel *Aru onna* (1919; tr *A Certain Woman*, 1978), but their marriage broke up five months later. Deserted by his wife, Doppo wrote *Azamukazaru no ki* (1908–09, An Honest Diary) in which he expressed his mental anguish over his separation from Nobuko, an incident that was to color all his subsequent writing.

Doppo made his literary debut as a romantic poet with *Doppo gin* (Doppo's Poems), a group of poems influenced by Wordsworth that appeared in *Jojōshi* (Lyric

Poems), an anthology he coauthored in 1897 with TAYAMA KATAI and Matsuoka Kunio (later known as YANAGITA KUNIO). In these poems he sang of his love of nature. Doppo enjoyed continuous literary success until his death from tuberculosis in 1908.

Doppo's writing career can be roughly divided into three short periods. From 1897 to 1901 he attempted to discover the meaning of life in nature, producing such romantic short stories as "Gen Oji" (1897; tr "Uncle Gen," 1946) and "Musashino" (1898). In the second period, 1901 to 1904, Doppo focused on man's fate in the universe; realistic elements became more pronounced, but the romantic undertones were not yet lost. A representative work of this period is "Gyūniku to bareisho" (1901; tr "Meat and Potatoes," 1957). During the third period, 1906 to 1908, Doppo moved toward naturalism. Although he is often called the forerunner of naturalism, it may be argued that Doppo produced naturalistic works not because he himself desired to move in that direction, but because his romantic spirit gradually ebbed.

Kunimidake　　　　国見岳
Also known as Ōkunimi. Mountain on the border of Kumamoto and Miyazaki prefectures, Kyūshū. The second highest peak of the KYŪSHŪ MOUNTAINS. Height: 1,739 m (5,705 ft).

Kuninaka no Muraji Kimimaro
国中連公麻呂
(?–774). Preeminent Nara-period (710–794) sculptor of Buddhist images. He supervised the making of the DAIBUTSU or great Buddha for the temple TŌDAIJI in Nara, a project completed in 752. In 761 he was given administrative responsibility for the construction of the Tōdaiji itself; he retired from all official activities in 767.

Kuni no Miya　　　　恭仁京
Capital of Japan from 741 to 744; situated at what is now Kamomachi Mikanohara in the southern part of Kyōto Prefecture. After the rebellion of FUJIWARA NO HIROTSUGU, Emperor SHŌMU took the advice of TACHIBANA NO MOROE and moved the capital from HEIJŌKYŌ (Nara) to Kuni, but in 744, before its completion, he decided to move the capital to NANIWAKYŌ.

kuni no miyatsuko　　　　国造
Local chieftains of the 6th and 7th centuries who governed small territories (kuni) under the jurisdiction of the YAMATO court. They were often given the honorific cognomens (KABANE) kimi or atae, while a few received the more prestigious cognomen omi (see UJI-KABANE SYSTEM). At the time of the TAIKA REFORM of 645, new officials called kuni no mikotomochi or KOKUSHI were appointed to oversee local administration. Between this time and the late-7th-century establishment of the KOKUGUN SYSTEM by the centralizing ritsuryō government, the older kuni no miyatsuko system was abandoned. The title kuni no miyatsuko was retained, however, designating one who exclusively presided over the Shintō rites of each kuni or province. The latter type of kuni no miyatsuko are often called shin kokuzō (new kuni no miyatsuko, kokuzō being an alternate pronunciation of the Chinese characters used to write kuni no miyatsuko) to distinguish them from the former.

Kunisada →Utagawa Kunisada

Kunisaki Peninsula　　　　国東半島
(Kunisaki Hantō). Located in northeastern Ōita Prefecture, northeastern Kyūshū, bounded to the north by the Suō Sea, to the east by the Iyo Sea, and to the south by Beppu Bay. This rich agricultural region yields rice, mandarin oranges, tobacco, and vegetables. Many ancient temples and stone statues of the Buddha are on the peninsula. The major cities are Bungo Takada and Kitsuki.

Kunitachi　　　　国立[市]
City in west-central Tōkyō Prefecture. It is primarily a campus town and residential district, with Hitotsubashi University and Kunitachi College of Music. Pop: 65,833.

Kunitachi College of Music
国立音楽大学
(Kunitachi Ongaku Daigaku). A coeducational private college in the city of Tachikawa, Tōkyō Prefecture. It originated as the Tōkyō Kōtō Ongaku Gakuin (Tōkyō School of Music) in 1926 and became a university in 1950. Its only academic division is its School of Music. Enrollment in 1989 was 3,553.

kuniyaku　　　　国役
(literally, "provincial levies"). Also called kokuyaku or kuniyakukin. Taxes imposed by a provincial governor, domainal lord, or shogunate on a province or domain. These levies originated in the Heian period (794–1185) in the form of corvée labor for palaces, landed estates (shōen), and public-works projects such as roads and irrigation facilities. The Kamakura (1192–1333) and Muromachi (1338–1573) shogunates imposed these taxes for similar purposes in the form of cash levies and labor service.

During the Edo period (1600–1868) kuniyaku was an irregular tax collected to meet extraordinary expenses. The Tokugawa shogunate established kuniyaku regulations for its own domains (tenryō) in 1720. It was not levied nationwide. A different tax, also called kuniyaku, was assessed on craftsmen in Edo (now Tōkyō), the administrative seat of the Tokugawa shogunate.

Kuniyoshi →Utagawa Kuniyoshi

Kuniyoshi, Yasuo　　　　国吉康雄
(1893–1953). Painter. Born in the city of Okayama, Okayama Prefecture, he came to the United States in 1906. He studied at the Los Angeles School of Art and Design and later at the National Academy of Design and the Art Students League in New York City. In 1929 his work was included in the Museum of Modern Art's "Nineteen Living American Artists" exhibition. In Kuniyoshi's mature work, such as I Think So (1938) and Somebody Tore My Poster (1943), languorous women predominate, drawn in melancholy moods and dark shades. His work was presented in 1948 at the Whitney Museum of American Art's first major retrospective of a living artist.

Kuno Yasu　　　　久野寧
(1882–1977). Physiologist. Specialist in the physiology of human perspiration. Also known as Kuno Yasushi. Born in Aichi Prefecture. After graduating from the Aichi Igakkō, a medical college, he studied at Tōkyō University. Kuno gained recognition after publishing The Physiology of Human Per-

Yasuo Kuniyoshi *Girl Thinking.* 1935. Oil on canvas. 128 × 102 cm. Yasuo Kuniyoshi Museum.

spiration (1934) in English (the Japanese version appeared in 1946). He taught at Nagoya University from 1937 to 1955. He received the Order of Culture in 1963.

Kunōzan　　　　久能山
Hill in the eastern part of the city of Shizuoka, Shizuoka Prefecture, central Honshū. On the summit is the shrine Tōshōgū, dedicated to TOKUGAWA IEYASU, the first Tokugawa shōgun. The hill is known for its strawberries, which are grown along stone walls built into its slopes. Height: 219 m (718 ft).

kun readings　　　　訓読み
(kun yomi). One of the two basic types of pronunciation of Chinese characters (kanji) as they are used in the Japanese writing system. Whereas ON READINGS are Japanese approximations of the original Chinese pronunciations and occur when the characters are used to write words of Chinese origin, kun readings consist of native Japanese words that translate the meaning of the characters (the Chinese character used to write kun originally meant "to interpret the meaning"). Some characters have no established kun readings, being used exclusively to write words of Chinese origin. There are also many native compound words written with two or more characters, and most have only on or only kun readings, but a few may be read both ways. An example is 食物 "food," which can be pronounced shokumotsu (two on readings) or tabe-mono (two kun readings). There are also a few instances of the joining of on and kun readings: 団子 dan-go (a confection) follows the order on + kun, and 古本 furu-hon (used book) the order kun + on.

Kuo Mo-jo →Guo Moruo (Kuo Mo-jo)

Kuonji →Minobusan

Kuo Sung-ling →Guo Songling (Kuo Sung-ling)

Kurashiki Now a tourist information center, this Western-style building beside the river Kurashikigawa served as this city's town hall from 1914 to 1928.

Kurabō Industries, Ltd 　倉敷紡績[株]

(Kurashiki Bōseki). Textile firm possessing a high level of technology in the spinning and weaving of cotton and synthetic threads. Incorporated in Kurashiki, Okayama Prefecture, in 1888. Through mergers and acquisitions it moved into production of woolen yarn and cloth. It established a unified system for knitwear production from manufacture of raw thread to sale of the finished product. The firm aggressively diversified, developing new products such as chemical products, information systems, environmental protection equipment, and electronic equipment. It has joint ventures in Brazil, Thailand, Indonesia, and the United Kingdom. Sales for the fiscal year ending March 1991 totaled ¥140.8 billion (US $1.0 billion). Capitalization was ¥22.0 billion (US $160.3 million) in the same year. Headquarters are in Ōsaka.

kurabu katsudō 　クラブ活動

(school club activities). The activities of groups of students with common interests (such as sports, music, or art) who meet on campus. These clubs have been a part of Japanese middle and high school life since the late 19th century, but they were not formally incorporated into elementary and secondary school education until the educational reforms of 1947. Since the late 1960s the SCHOOL COURSE GUIDELINES have mandated that each student take part in at least one club meeting per week. Joining additional clubs is optional.

Kurahara Korehito 　蔵原惟人

(1902–91). Literary critic. Born in Tōkyō. He studied Russian at Tōkyō Foreign Language School (now Tōkyō University of Foreign Studies). After returning from study in Russia, he worked as the leading theorist for BUNGEI SENSEN, a literary magazine that led the PROLETARIAN LITERATURE MOVEMENT of the 1920s. His advocacy of "proletarian" realism in literature greatly influenced such writers as KOBAYASHI TAKIJI. He joined the then-illegal Japan Communist Party and published underground essays on the application of Marxist principles to art. During the 1930s he spent several years in prison for his activities. After World War II, he became an active leader in the Japan Communist Party.

Kurahara Shinjirō 　蔵原伸二郎

(1899–1965). Poet. Real name Kurahara Korekata. Born in Kumamoto Prefecture. Graduate of Keiō University. Kurahara began composing poetry under the influence of HAGIWARA SAKUTARŌ. In 1939 he published his first poetry collection, *Tōyō no mangetsu* (Full Moon in the East), in which he strove to give expression to the primal consciousness and visionary nature of the East. During World War II, Kurahara published war poetry in such collections as *Sentōki* (1943, Fighter Plane). After the war his work expressed a sense of desolation, emptiness, and spiritual longing. Kurahara's other works include *Rekijitsu no oni* (1946, Calendar Day Demon), which won the Japan Poetry Prize, and *Iwana* (1964, Char), which won the Yomiuri Literary Prize.

Kurahashijima 　倉橋島

Island in the western Inland Sea, southwestern Hiroshima Prefecture. Separated from the city of Kure on the mainland by the Ondo Strait. Composed of granite, but almost entirely under cultivation. Chief activities are mandarin orange (*mikan*) cultivation, shipbuilding, and granite quarrying. Area: 69 sq km (27 sq mi).

Kurahashi Yumiko 　倉橋由美子

(1935–). Writer. Born in Kōchi Prefecture. Graduate of Meiji University. She first gained recognition for her short story on political alienation, "Parutai" (1960; tr "Partei," 1961). She is known as an antirealist, influenced by Kafka and other modern European writers. Later works include the essay collection *Watashi no naka no kare e* (1970, To Him Inside Me), the story collection *Hanhigeki* (1971, Anti-Tragedies), and the novels *Sumiyakisuto Q no bōken* (1969, The Adventures of Q the Charcoalist), *Yume no ukihashi* (1971, The Bridge of Dreams), and *Kōkan* (1989, Exchange of Courtesies).

kuramai 　蔵米

(granary rice). Tax rice collected from peasants by the shogunate or by *daimyō* during the Edo period (1600–1868) and stored in their granaries to be dispensed to their retainers as stipends (see KIRIMAI). The term also refers to the portion of such rice sent to various domainal warehousing offices (KURAYASHIKI) in major cities and sold on the commercial market, as distinct from *nayamai*, or rice that was handled exclusively by merchants. The largest suppliers of *kuramai* were the granaries of the domains of Kuroda (now part of Fukuoka Prefecture), Hosokawa (now Kumamoto Prefecture), Chōshū (now Yamaguchi Prefecture), and Asano (now part of Hiroshima Prefecture), all in southwestern Japan and known collectively as "the four granaries" (*shikura*).

Kuramayama 　鞍馬山

Hill in the northern part of the city of Kyōto. Kuramadera, a temple founded in 796, is located on its slopes. The annual Hi Matsuri (Torch Festival) held in October is widely known. Height: 570 m (1,870 ft).

Kuramoto Sō 　倉本聡

(1935–). Film and television scriptwriter. Real name Yamaya Kaoru. Born in Tōkyō; graduated from Tōkyō University. Known for his wistfully poetic depiction of the sorrows and joys of life. His works include the film *Eki* (1981, Station), the television series *Kita no kuni kara* (broadcast 1981–82, From the North Country) and *Kinō, Kanashibetsu de* (broadcast 1984, Kanashibetsu Graffiti), and the essay collection *Tōmin no mori* (1987, The Hibernating Forest).

Kuraray Co, Ltd 　[株]クラレ

(Kurare). Manufacturer of synthetic fiber, synthetic leather, and resin film. Founded in 1926 as Kurashiki Kenshoku, it assumed its present name in 1970. The firm was the first in the world to initiate commercial manufacture of polyvinyl alcohol fiber, establishing an integrated production system. The firm has sold its polyvinyl alcohol technology to foreign firms and since 1963 has exported three production plants to China. It has seven overseas subsidiaries, situated in the United States, the Middle East, and Southeast Asia. Adapting the technology of polymer chemistry, the company has moved into the fields of fine chemicals, chiefly isoprene derivatives, and medical products, such as kidney dialysis machines. Sales for the fiscal year ending March 1991 totaled ¥276.5 billion (US $2.0 billion), of which sale of textiles constituted 45 percent. Its export rate was 18 percent and capitalization stood at ¥37.0 billion (US $269.7 million) in the same year. Headquarters are in Ōsaka.

Kurashiki 　倉敷[市]

City in southwestern Okayama Prefecture, western Honshū. The city flourished in the Edo period (1600–1868) as a commercial center and river port. The center of a textile industry since 1888, it also has steel and petrochemical industries. The Ōhara Art Museum, the Kurashiki Folk Craft Museum, the Kurashiki Archaeology Museum, and the Edo-period warehouses on the banks of the Kurashikigawa attract tourists. WASHŪZAN, a nearby hill, commands a view of the Inland Sea. Pop: 414,693.

Kurata Chikara 　倉田主税

(1889–1969). Businessman. Second president of HITACHI, LTD. Born in Fukuoka Prefecture, he graduated from Sendai Higher Technical School (now Tōhoku University). Kurata joined Hitachi, then a machinery repair division of the Hitachi mine owned by Kuhara Kōgyōsho. He became Hitachi's president in 1947 when company founder ODAIRA NAMIHEI was purged by Allied Occupation authorities. During Kurata's 20-year term as president and chairman, Hitachi became an important international firm widely known for its innovative technology.

Kurata Hyakuzō 　倉田百三

(1891–1943). Playwright and essayist on religious subjects. Born in Hiroshima Prefecture. Influenced by the philosophical writings of NISHIDA KITARŌ, he became interested in religious thought. In 1917 he published *Shukke to sono deshi* (1917; tr *The Priest and His Disciples*, 1922), a best-selling play about the early-13th-century Buddhist priest SHINRAN. His best work is *Ai to ninshiki to no shuppatsu* (1921, The Beginning of Love and Understanding). This collection of essays on such subjects as love, sex, and faith remained something of a classic among young people for over a quarter century.

Kuratsukuri no Tori 　鞍作止利

(fl early 7th century). Sculptor of Buddhist images. Born into a saddle-making (*kuratsukuri*) family; grandson of the naturalized Chinese craftsman SHIBA TATTO (Ch: Sima Dadeng or Ssu-ma Ta-teng) and son of the Buddhist sculptor Kuratsukuri no Tasuna. He was patronized by Prince SHŌTOKU, who commissioned many of his works. In 606 he completed a large image of the Buddha Shaka (Śākyamuni), commissioned for the temple ASUKADERA by the empress SUIKO. He is best known for his Shaka Triad in the main hall of the temple HŌRYŪJI in Nara, which was dedicated in 623 for the repose of the souls of Prince Shōtoku and the prince's wife and mother. This masterpiece, in the style of the Chinese Northern Wei dynasty (386–535), is representative of the Tori style: lips upturned at the corners in an enigmatic, archaic smile; flat, rectilinear layers of pleats in the garment; and wide-open almond-shaped eyes.

kurayashiki 蔵屋敷

Business offices established in the Edo period (1600–1868) by the shogunate, *daimyō*, vassals (*hatamoto*), domainal officials, and temples in major transport and market centers. Tax rice (KURAMAI) was the main commodity traded, but other important products that were traded included sugar, indigo, paper, and *tatami* covers.

The number of *kurayashiki* increased as domains needed to convert more goods to cash. These trading activities were first conducted at daimyō residences in major cities, with leading merchants handling the transactions. Later, domain officials were appointed to supervise the activities of the *kurayashiki*. The senior official (*myōdai*) represented the *kurayashiki* and oversaw transactions. His deputies, the *kuramoto*, supervised the arrival and departure of goods. Agents called *kakeya* handled accounts. Those domains not having *kurayashiki* sometimes appointed *kuramoto* and lesser clerks to transact business for them.

Kurayoshi 倉吉[市]

City in Tottori Prefecture, western Honshū. It was the seat of the provincial capital and temple from the 8th century on. A castle town of the Yamana family in the 14th century, it later became known for its *kasuri* (cotton ikat cloth) and rice-threshing machines. Textile, machinery, and food industries flourish. Pop: 51,834.

Kurayoshi Plain 倉吉平野

(Kurayoshi Heiya). Alluvial plain located in central Tottori Prefecture, western Honshū. Bordering the Sea of Japan, this fertile grain-producing area also grows pears in the highlands in the east and grapes in the sandy soil by the sea. The plain has several hot springs. The major city is KURAYOSHI. Area: 50 sq km (20 sq mi).

Kure 呉[市]

City in southwestern Hiroshima Prefecture, western Honshū, on Hiroshima Bay. With an excellent natural harbor, Kure was an important naval base until the end of World War II. Shipbuilding, steel, and pulp industries have been established. The ONDO STRAIT is popular with visitors. Pop: 216,723.

Kureha Chemical Industry Co, Ltd
呉羽化学工業[株]

(Kureha Kagaku Kōgyō). General chemical firm producing and selling synthetic resin, organic and inorganic chemicals, agricultural chemicals, plastic packaging materials, medicines, and carbon products. Incorporated in 1944, it later expanded to include petrochemicals and in 1977 initiated production of pharmaceuticals. The basis of the firm's growth has been the development of technology, an area in which it continues to be strong. Sales for the fiscal year ending March 1991 totaled ¥101.5 billion (US $739.8 million), and capitalization was ¥12.5 billion (US $91.1 million). Headquarters are in Tōkyō.

Kure Ken 呉健

(1883–1940). Internist. Born in Kyōto Prefecture. Graduate of Tōkyō University. Professor at Kyūshū and Tōkyō universities. Known for his studies on the autonomic nervous system, Kure discovered and determined the nature of the efferent (or centrifugal) spinal parasympathetic system in the spinal posterior root. He also confirmed that the nervous system exerts control over the tension and nutrition of voluntary muscles and added to the knowledge of progressive muscular dystrophy. He received the Japan Academy Prize in 1939. Kure's publications include *Jiritsu shinkeikei* (1934, The Autonomic Nervous System).

Kurihama 久里浜

District in the southeastern part of the city of YOKOSUKA, Kanagawa Prefecture, central Honshū. An industrial district facing the port of Kurihama, it has a thermoelectric power plant and factories for processing seafood products. Commodore PERRY landed here in 1853, an event commemorated annually.

Kurikara Pass 俱利伽羅峠

(Kurikara Tōge). Located on the border of Toyama and Ishikawa prefectures, central Honshū. The highway Hokurikudō ran through the pass in ancient times; tunnels now carry the JR (Japan Railways) Hokuriku Main Line and National Route No. 8. The surrounding regions are known as old battlefields of the wars between the Minamoto and Taira families. Altitude: 277 m (909 ft).

Kurikara Pass, Battle of
俱利伽羅峠の戦い

(Kurikara Tōge no Tatakai). Battle in 1183 during the TAIRA-MINAMOTO WAR that took place at KURIKARA PASS in the Tonamiyama Mountains. MINAMOTO NO YOSHINAKA was marching against the Taira regime in Kyōto; an army under Taira no Koremori (dates unknown) was dispatched to intercept him, and they met at the pass. According to the military chronicle GEMPEI SEISUIKI, Yoshinaka mounted a surprise attack under the cover of night; driving a herd of oxen with torches attached to their horns, he terrified and overwhelmed the superior Taira forces. He then proceeded on to Kyōto.

Kurikomayama 栗駒山

Also known as Sukawadake. Stratovolcano situated at the junction of the borders of Akita, Iwate, and Miyagi prefectures, northern Honshū. Northwest of the summit is the central cone, Tsurugiyama. Alpine flora abound. Sukawa Hot Spring is located on the northwest slopes. Height: 1,628 m (5,341 ft).

Kuril Current→Oyashio

Kuril Islands 千島列島

(Chishima Rettō). Group of islands extending from south of the Kamchatka Peninsula, northeastern Siberia, to Hokkaidō. They form the boundary between the Sea of Okhotsk to the northwest and the Pacific Ocean to the southwest. Of volcanic origin, the group of more than 30 large and small islands includes many active volcanoes and hot springs. Surrounded by rich fishing grounds for salmon and codfish, the islands also have active forestry, hunting, and trapping industries; grains and vegetables are cultivated in the southern islands. Under the terms of the SAN FRANCISCO PEACE TREATY of 1951, Japan renounced all claims to the Kuril Islands, which had been Japanese territory since 1875 (see ST. PETERSBURG, TREATY OF). However, Japan still claims the islands of ETOROFU, KUNASHIRI, and SHIKOTAN and the HABOMAI ISLANDS, which were occupied by the Soviet Union in 1945 (they were still occupied by the Russian Federation in early 1992) and which Japan maintains are not part of the Kuril Islands. See TERRITORY OF JAPAN.

Kurimoto Joun 栗本鋤雲

(1822–97). Shogunate official of the late Edo period (1600–1868); later active as a journalist. Real name Kurimoto Kon; also known as Kurimoto Hōan. Born in Edo (now Tōkyō). In 1872 Kurimoto joined Japan's first daily Japanese-language newspaper, the YOKOHAMA MAINICHI SHIMBUN. In 1873 he became chief editor of the YŪBIN HŌCHI SHIMBUN. A collection of his essays, *Hōan ikō* (1900), was published posthumously.

Kurimoto Kaoru 栗本薫

(1953–). Novelist. Real name Imaoka Sumiyo. Other pen name Nakajima Azusa. Born in Tōkyō; graduated from Waseda University. Recipient of the Gunzō Prize for New Talent for the critique *Bungaku no rinkaku* (1974, Contours of Literature), Kurimoto writes mysteries, science fiction, historical novels, and reviews. Her works include the mystery *Bokura no jidai* (1978, Our Era) and the heroic fantasy *Guin sāga*, which began publication in 1979 and is scheduled to contain a total of 100 volumes.

Kurimoto, Ltd [株]栗本鉄工所

(Kurimoto Tekkōsho). Manufacturer of cast-iron pipes, industrial machinery, castings, and valves; also engaged in construction of floodgates and bridges and in manufacture of plastic products. Incorporated in 1909, it assumed its present organization in 1934. Sales for the fiscal year ending March 1991 totaled ¥129.8 billion (US $946.1 million). In the same year capitalization stood at ¥27.1 billion (US $197.5 million). Headquarters are in Ōsaka.

Kurishima Sumiko 栗島すみ子

(1902–87). Movie actress. She starred at age 19 in the enormously popular *Gubijinsō* (1921, Red Poppy) directed by Henry Kotani. Ikeda Yoshinobu, her husband and a director at Shōchiku Kinema Co (see SHŌCHIKU CO, LTD), provided her with many roles—*Hototogisu* (1922, Nightingale), *Sendō kouta* (1923, Boatman's Song), *Shinju fujin* (1927, Madam Pearl), and *Onna no isshō* (1928, A Woman's Life), among others. After retiring from acting, Kurishima became head of the Mizuki school of traditional Japanese dancing.

Kuriyagawa Hakuson 厨川白村

(1880–1923). Literary critic and scholar of English literature. Real name Kuriyagawa Tatsuo. Born in Kyōto; graduate of Tōkyō University. Professor at Kyōto University. He lectured on 19th-century Western literary trends but later turned from literary to social concerns, criticizing Japanese ideas of human nature and love. Among his writings are *Kindai bungaku jukkō* (1912, Ten Aspects of Modern Literature), *Zōge no tō o dete* (1920, Leaving the Ivory Tower), and *Kindai no ren'aikan* (1922, Modern Views of Love).

Kuriyama Sempō 栗山潜鋒

(1671–1706). Real name Kuriyama Gen. Confucian scholar and historian of the MITO school. Born in Yodo, near Kyōto. At 18 he wrote *Hoken taiki*, an account of events from the HŌGEN DISTURBANCE of 1156 to the ap-

Kuroda Seiki By the Lake, a portrait of the artist's wife. 1897. Oil on canvas. 68 × 83 cm. National Cultural Property Research Institute, Tōkyō.

pointment of MINAMOTO NO YORITOMO as shōgun in 1192. In 1697 TOKUGAWA MITSUKUNI, the scholar-daimyō of the Mito domain (now part of Ibaraki Prefecture), invited Sempō to become head of the domain's research facility, SHŌKŌKAN, in Edo (now Tōkyō). He assisted in compilation of the DAI NIHON SHI, a monumental history of early Japan.

Kurobe   黒部[市]

City in northwestern Toyama Prefecture, central Honshū; on the lower reaches of the river Kurobegawa. The city is a commercial and industrial center with lead-refining and lumber plants, as well as a large zipper factory. Rice and watermelons are grown on the outskirts. Pop: 36,493.

Kurobe Dam   黒部ダム

(Kurobe Damu). Electric-power-generating dam located on the upper reaches of the river KUROBEGAWA, southeastern Toyama Prefecture, central Honshū. Commonly called Kurobe Daiyon Damu or Kuroyon Damu. Completed in 1963, this arch-type dome dam created Lake Kurobe. An electric power plant is located about 10 km (6 mi) below the dam and has a maximum output of 335,000 kilowatts. Height: 186 m (610 ft); length of embankment: 492 m (1,614 ft); storage capacity: 149 million cu m (5.3 billion cu ft).

Kurobegawa   黒部川

River in eastern Toyama Prefecture, central Honshū, originating in the central Hida Mountains and flowing north to empty into the Sea of Japan. It is a swift river, and the lower reaches below Kurobeko, a man-made lake, form gorges with steep cliffs. Some gorges, designated Scenic Natural Monuments, have more than a million visitors an-

nually. The KUROBE DAM and electric power plants are located along the river. Length: 85 km (53 mi).

Kurobe Kyōkoku   黒部峡谷

Gorge on the upper and middle reaches of the river Kurobegawa, eastern Toyama Prefecture, central Honshū. It is one of Japan's deepest gorges. Part of Chūbu Sangaku National Park, Kurobe Kyōkoku is surrounded by rugged mountains with scenic spots, including granite rock formations, towering cliffs, waterfalls, and rapids. Numerous hotspring resorts located near the gorge include Kuronagi, Unazuki, and Babadani.

Kuroda Hisao   黒田寿男

(1899–1986). Politician. Born in Okayama Prefecture; graduate of Tōkyō University. He worked for the FARMERS' MOVEMENT and in 1948 helped form the Labor-Farmer Party (RŌDŌSHA NŌMINTŌ). After the party merged with the JAPAN SOCIALIST PARTY in 1957, Kuroda aligned himself with its extreme left faction. Except for the war years and his imprisonment in connection with the POPULAR FRONT INCIDENT in 1937, he served in the House of Representatives from 1936 to 1972.

Kuroda Kiyotaka   黒田清隆

(1840–1900). Politician and elder statesman of the Meiji period (1868–1912); prime minister from 1888 to 1889. Born in Kagoshima, Satsuma domain (now Kagoshima Prefecture). In 1874 Kuroda became director of the Hokkaidō Colonization Office (Kaitakushi) and a sangi (councillor) in the central government, reorganized the colonist-militia (TONDENHEI) system in order to develop Hokkaidō agriculture, and was promoted to lieutenant general in the imperial army. Kuroda was dispatched as an envoy to Korea in 1875, and in 1876 the Treaty of KANGHWA was concluded. In 1877 Kuroda served in the force that subdued the SATSUMA REBELLION.

Kuroda was a central figure in the HOKKAIDŌ COLONIZATION OFFICE SCANDAL of 1881, part of the POLITICAL CRISIS OF 1881. At a time when the government had decided to sell off many of its enterprises to private entrepreneurs (see KAN'EI JIGYŌ HARAISAGE), Kuroda proposed to sell the Colonization Office's Hokkaidō assets to a trading consortium led by a colleague from the former Satsuma domain. The cost was nominal. When the terms of the sale were leaked to the press a scandal ensued; the sale was canceled.

In 1887 he became minister of agriculture and commerce and in 1888 prime minister. The most troublesome problem facing his cabinet was revision of the Unequal Treaties (see UNEQUAL TREATIES, REVISION OF). Foreign Minister ŌKUMA SHIGENOBU drafted a revised treaty; the ensuing controversy split the cabinet and led to its resignation. In 1892 Kuroda became minister of communications and in 1895 president of the Privy Council. He was a member of the GENRŌ (elite elder statesmen).

Kuroda Kiyoteru → Kuroda Seiki

Kuroda Nagamasa   黒田長政

(1568–1623). Daimyō of the Azuchi-Momoyama period (1568–1600) and the early Edo period (1600–1868); son of the CHRISTIAN DAIMYŌ Dom Simeão KURODA YOSHITAKA and himself baptized Damião. When his father, a provincial baron of Harima (now part of Hyōgo Prefecture), adhered to ODA NOBUNAGA in 1577, Nagamasa was sent as hostage to Nobunaga's general

TOYOTOMI HIDEYOSHI. He served Hideyoshi in the Battle of SHIZUGATAKE (1583) against SHIBATA KATSUIE and was active in Hideyoshi's conquest of Kyūshū four years later. Nagamasa inherited the 180,000-koku (see KOKUDAKA) domain of Nakatsu in Buzen (now Ōita Prefecture) in 1589. He participated in Hideyoshi's INVASIONS OF KOREA IN 1592 AND 1597; after Hideyoshi's death he drew close to TOKUGAWA IEYASU. At the Battle of SEKIGAHARA in 1600 Nagamasa was instrumental in the crucial defection of KOBAYAKAWA HIDEAKI to Ieyasu's side. Ieyasu rewarded him with a 523,100-koku domain at Fukuoka. His last exploit was participation in Ieyasu's Ōsaka Campaign of 1614–15 (see ŌSAKA CASTLE, SIEGES OF).

Kuroda Seiki   黒田清輝

(1866–1924). Western-style painter who introduced impressionism to Japan. Also known as Kuroda Kiyoteru. Born in what is now Kagoshima Prefecture. In 1884 he went to Paris to study both law and art, eventually devoting himself to painting. In recognition of his artistry, he was admitted to several French fine-arts societies. He returned to Japan in 1893. With Kume Keiichirō (1866–1934) he opened the Tenshin Dōjō, a studio patterned on the French system. In 1896 he and his followers left the Meiji Fine Arts Society (Meiji Bijutsukai) to form an independent association of Western-style painters called the White Horse Society (HAKUBAKAI). He joined the faculty of the Tōkyō Bijutsu Gakkō (now Tōkyō University of Fine Arts and Music) and by the turn of the century was the undisputed leader of progressive Western-style painters. In 1910 he was appointed an artist for the imperial household (teishitsu gigeiin) and was elected in 1919 to the Imperial Fine Arts Academy (Teikoku Bijutsuin), becoming its president in 1922. In 1920 he was elected to the House of Peers. Through his bequest the Institute for Art Research (now TŌKYŌ NATIONAL RESEARCH INSTITUTE OF CULTURAL PROPERTIES) was established in Tōkyō in 1930. By the Lake (1897) is perhaps his best-known work.

Kuroda Yoshitaka   黒田孝高

(1546–1604). Also known as Kuroda Josui; Christian name, Simeão. Daimyō of the Azuchi-Momoyama period (1568–1600). The Kuroda family, prominent provincial barons of Harima (now part of Hyōgo Prefecture), supported ODA NOBUNAGA, and Yoshitaka distinguished himself in several campaigns, serving under Nobunaga's general TOYOTOMI HIDEYOSHI. Yoshitaka retired in 1589, to be succeeded by his son KURODA NAGAMASA. Yoshitaka had become a Christian in 1585, and when he sided with TOKUGAWA IEYASU in the great conflict of 1600 that led to the founding of the Tokugawa shogunate, he may have influenced Ieyasu's initially positive attitude toward Christianity.

Kurōdo-dokoro   蔵人所

(Bureau of Archivists, or Chamberlains' Office). An extrastatutory office (RYŌGE NO KAN) established by Emperor SAGA in 810 during the conflict culminating in the so-called KUSUKO INCIDENT. Saga required secrecy and security, and he staffed this private office—separate from the formal bureaucracy—with loyal men to handle his most important documents. The office later became permanent and expanded to other court functions. Because they were in close attendance upon the emperor, Kurōdo-

Kuroda Kiyotaka
A Meiji-period politician who was prime minister from 1888 to 1889.

dokoro officials came to exercise great political influence. Control of these appointments is thought to have been one important basis of the power of the FUJIWARA FAMILY. By the end of the 10th century, retired emperors (see INSEI) as well as the Fujiwara and other great families had established their own private offices modeled on the Kurōdo-dokoro (see MANDOKORO).

kurofune 黒船
("black ships"). Term used to refer to all Western ships that visited Japan from the 16th century to the end of the Edo period (1600–1868) and also to Western-style ships and warships built in Japan during this time. These ships were called *kurofune* because they were painted black, unlike the ships from China and Southeast Asia.

Kurohimeyama 黒姫山
Stratovolcano in the Fuji Volcanic Zone, northern Nagano Prefecture, central Honshū. It is covered by primeval forests of beech trees and black pines. Kagami Pond is a crater lake on the mountain. Popular with skiers in winter, the mountain is a major peak in JŌSHIN'ETSU KŌGEN NATIONAL PARK. Height: 2,053 m (6,735 ft).

kurohon →kusazōshi

Kuroi ame 黒い雨
(tr *Black Rain*, 1969). Novel by IBUSE MASUJI (1898–1993); published 1965–66. *Kuroi ame* tells of Shizuma Shigematsu; his wife, Shigeko; and their niece Yasuko, residents of Hiroshima at the time of the atomic bombing. The novel opens several years after World War II with marriage negotiations for Yasuko under way. Past proposals have ended in failure, her suitors having feared that Yasuko might develop radiation sickness. To dispel such suspicions, Shigematsu, a victim of the illness, copies out portions of Yasuko's diary and his own that will prove Yasuko, unlike himself, was far from the site of the bombing at the time of the explosion. These entries, recounting the chaos and horror of Hiroshima, constitute the bulk of the novel. The family's hopes, however, are shattered when Yasuko, who was caught in a shower of seemingly harmless "black rain" soon after the bombing, falls desperately ill with radiation sickness. Ibuse based his novel on actual diaries and on interviews with survivors. Avoiding sentimentality and heavy-handed judgments, *Kuroi ame* is probably the finest example of atomic bomb literature.

Kuroi Senji 黒井千次
(1932–). Novelist. Real name Osabe Shunjirō. Born in Tōkyō. Graduate of Tōkyō University. While working for an automobile company, Kuroi published the short story "Jikan" (1969, Time). A primary theme of his work is the white-collar worker's alienation from his true self in highly industrialized contemporary society. Works include *Hashiru kazoku* (1971, Family on the Road) and *Gunsei* (1984, Herd Life).

Kuroishi 黒石[市]
City in central Aomori Prefecture, northern Honshū. An Edo-period (1600–1868) castle town, it is known for its rice, apples, and hot springs. It is also a gateway to Lake Towada. Pop: 39,213.

Kuroiso 黒磯[市]
City in northern Tochigi Prefecture, central Honshū. It is a gateway to the Nasu Hot

kurofune The stylized representation of a Dutch steamer in this woodblock print typifies the premodern Japanese image of a Western "black ship."

Spring resort and the Nikkō National Park. Principal activities are rice cultivation and dairy farming. Pop: 52,344.

Kuroita Katsumi 黒板勝美
(1874–1946). Historian and a founder of the discipline of DIPLOMATICS in Japan. Born in Nagasaki Prefecture, he graduated from Tōkyō University. With TAGUCHI UKICHI he contributed to the publication of several landmark historical works, including KOKUSHI TAIKEI and the reedition of GUNSHO RUIJŪ. He later became a professor at Tōkyō University and was a pioneer in the ESPERANTO movement in Japan.

Kuroiwa Jūgo 黒岩重吾
(1924–). Novelist. Born in Ōsaka. Graduate of Dōshisha University. His military service during World War II and subsequent battle with polio influenced his work, which portrays the ambition and vanity of human egoism in modern society. He was awarded the Naoki Prize for *Haitoku no mesu* (1960). Since the 1970s most of his works have dealt with early historical themes, including *Shōtoku Taishi* (1985–86, Prince Shōtoku).

Kuroiwa Ruikō 黒岩涙香
(1862–1920). Journalist, critic, translator, and novelist. His real name was Kuroiwa Shūroku, but he published under various pen names. Born in what is now Kōchi Prefecture, he entered Keiō University in Tōkyō. He soon became involved in political activities and withdrew from school. After publishing a book on politics, he became editor of the newspaper *Dōmei kaishin shimbun* in 1883; when the newspaper went bankrupt, Kuroiwa moved from one publisher to another. In 1892 he launched YOROZU CHŌHŌ, a newspaper that earned its popularity through serializations of Western novels and sensational reportage on social issues. He associated with many educators, religious leaders, and writers and widely influenced the general public. His works include *Gankutsuō* (1901–02), an adaptation of Alexandre Dumas's *Le Comte de Monte-Cristo*, and *Aa mujō* (1902–03), an adaptation of Victor Hugo's *Les Misérables*.

Kurokawa Kishō 黒川紀章
(1934–). Architect and urban planner. Born in Aichi Prefecture; graduated from Kyōto University in 1957. In 1960 he joined the architect KIKUTAKE KIYONORI and others in organizing the Metabolist group, whose designs sought to express the cyclical quality of urban growth. His buildings include Anderson Memorial Hall (1965) and the Takara Group Pavilion, both for Ōsaka EXPO '70; the Nakagin Capsule Tower Building (1971); the Sony Tower Building in Ōsaka (1976); the National Museum of Ethnology (1978); the National Bunraku Theater (1984); and the Roppongi Prince Hotel (1984). He received the Grand Prize for Architecture from the French Academy of Architecture in 1986.

His "New Tōkyō Plan, 2025" (1987), which proposed relocation of the city's center onto reclaimed land in Tōkyō Bay, gained wide notice.

Kurokawa Takeshi 黒川武
(1928–). Trade union leader. Born in Gumma Prefecture. Graduated from Chūō University in 1948. Kurokawa became the leader of the TEITO RAPID TRANSIT AUTHORITY union and also the chairman of SHITETSU SŌREN (General Federation of Private Railway Workers' Unions of Japan), a leading union within the SŌHYŌ organization. He was appointed chairman of Sōhyō in 1983 and led it through increasingly difficult times as the power of more moderate labor unions grew. He played a decisive role in combining Sōhyō with RENGŌ and was appointed adviser of the new organization.

Kurokawa Toshio 黒川利雄
(1897–1988). Internist. Born in Hokkaidō. Graduated from and later president of Tōhoku University. Kurokawa is noted for his contributions in diagnosing diseases of the digestive organs, involving, for example, X-ray examination of the digestive tract and cytological confirmation of gastric cancer. The author of *Shōkakan no rentogen shindan* (1936, Roentgenological Diagnosis of the Digestive Tract) and *I oyobi jūnishichō kaiyō no shindan* (1942, Diagnosis of Gastric and Duodenal Ulcers), he received the Order of Culture in 1968.

kuromoji 黒文字
(Japanese spicebush). *Lindera* or *Benzoin umbellatum*. Deciduous shrub of the laurel family (Lauraceae). It is indigenous to Japan and grows wild in Shikoku, Kyūshū, and western Honshū to a height of 2–3 meters (7–10 ft). Its bark bears distinctive black spots resembling Chinese characters, hence the name *kuromoji* (literally, "black character"). The leaves are alternate and narrowly elliptical. In spring yellow or yellowish green flowers appear before or accompanying the appearance of the leaves. *Kuromoji* is dioecious, with male flowers slightly bigger and more numerous than female flowers. Its globular fruits ripen into black berries, usually in October. Oil extracted from the leaves is used to make perfume and soap, and the wood is used to make toothpicks.

Kuropatkin, Aleksei Nikolaevich クロパトキン, A. N.
(1845–1925). Commander in chief of the Russian Far Eastern forces during the RUSSO-JAPANESE WAR of 1904–05. A graduate of the General Staff Academy (1874), he saw active service and then was on the General Staff from 1883 to 1890. He served as minister of war from 1898 until 1904, when he was ap-

Kurokawa Kishō This architect's unconventional use of space and bold modeling are evident in the entrance hall of the Hiroshima City Museum of Contemporary Art (1988), shown here.

Kuroiwa Ruikō Founder of the popular newspaper *Yorozu chōhō* in 1892, Kuroiwa appealed to readers with a mixture of scandalmongering, reformist politics, and adaptations of Western novels.

kuromoji This fragrant, deciduous shrub has been considered a sacred plant since ancient times. Pictured are the yellow-green flowers.

847

Kurosawa Akira The works of this director won a worldwide audience for Japanese film. **1** Kurosawa on location for *Kagemusha* (1980, The Shadow Warrior). **2** A scene from *Kagemusha* in which warlord Takeda Shingen's double, or "shadow warrior," reviews his troops. **3** Manifestations of peach tree spirits, these dolls come to life in "The Peach Orchard," one of the eight vignettes making up *Yume* (1990, Akira Kurosawa's Dreams).

pointed commander in chief of the Manchurian Army of Operations. Like most of his countrymen Kuropatkin underestimated the strength and resolution of the Japanese. Unable to rout the Japanese forces, he was replaced following the Battle of MUKDEN but stayed on as commander of the First Army. During World War I, Kuropatkin commanded the northern front and then was governor-general of Turkestan.

Kurosawa Akira　　　黒沢明

(1910–). Film director and scriptwriter. Born in Tōkyō. He first sought success as a painter but abandoned that career, joining PCL Studios (a company that later merged with others to form TŌHŌ CO, LTD) as an assistant director in 1936. He worked under director YAMAMOTO KAJIRŌ and developed his scriptwriting skills before directing his first film, *Sugata Sanshirō* (1943), for Tōhō Co, Ltd. This highly entertaining story of a gifted young devotee of JŪDŌ was a great success and established Kurosawa's reputation. As its hero defeats challengers from many different schools of martial arts in exciting action sequences, he learns from his teacher that *jūdō* requires more than physical strength; his spiritual growth prepares him for a final life-and-death duel.

Four films he made soon after the war further strengthened Kurosawa's reputation in Japan. *Waga seishun ni kui nashi* (1946, No Regrets for Our Youth) was the first antiwar film of real quality to be made in Japan, while *Subarashiki nichiyōbi* (1947, One Wonderful Sunday), *Yoidore tenshi* (1948, Drunken Angel), and *Norainu* (1949, Stray Dog) capture the devastation of Tōkyō after the war. With RASHŌMON (1950) Kurosawa turned to a story set in medieval Japan. Based on two stories by AKUTAGAWA RYŪNO-SUKE, its plot revolves around a murder case in which four involved parties—among them a murderer, his victim, and a witness—present different descriptions of the crime, each of them insisting that his or her self-serving version is "the truth." With each sequence filmed to accord perfectly with its narrator's version of the facts, this chilling meditation on how human subjectivity shapes reality was awarded the grand prize at the 1951 Venice Film Festival, becoming the first Japanese film to win an international award.

The director's next two films were *Hakuchi* (1951, The Idiot), based on the Dostoevsky novel, and IKIRU (1952, To Live). Both exemplify Kurosawa's ongoing preoccupation with the question of how man ought to live, an issue that assumes crisis proportions for the latter film's rather ordinary protagonist, a middle-aged civil servant who learns he will die of cancer within six months.

His next film, *Shichinin no samurai* (1954, SEVEN SAMURAI), may be the best-known Jap-

anese film ever made. The human dimensions of the story, in which the residents of a village besieged by bandits hire seven masterless samurai to protect them, are handled with humor and moral insight, while the battle scenes are among the most exciting ever filmed. *Ikimono no kiroku* (1955, Record of a Living Being) is a powerful rendition of the anxiety provoked by nuclear weapons, while *Kumonosujō* (1957, shown abroad as *Throne of Blood*) uses Japan's civil wars of the Sengoku period (1467–1568) as the backdrop for a highly pictorial version of Shakespeare's *Macbeth*. Another masterful reworking of a foreign classic is *Donzoko* (1957, The Lower Depths), based on the Maksim Gorky play.

Kurosawa, who had made most of his films to this point for Tōhō, now formed Kurosawa Production, Inc, to coproduce subsequent projects with Tōhō and other entities. *Yōjimbō* (1961) and *Tsubaki Sanjūrō* (1962, shown abroad as *Sanjuro*) feature spectacular samurai fight scenes, while *Warui yatsu hodo yoku nemuru* (1960, The Bad Sleep Well) and *Tengoku to jigoku* (1963, shown abroad as *High and Low*) are crime thrillers blending psychological insight with serious social comment. In *Akahige* (1965, Red Beard), an arrogant young doctor of the Edo period (1600–1868) gets an education in humanistic values, as does the protagonist of the Soviet-sponsored *Derusu Uzāra* (1975, Dersu Uzala), who learns truths about man and nature from a native guide while leading an expedition into the undeveloped province of Siberia early in this century. Set in the Sengoku period, *Kagemusha* (1980, The Shadow Warrior) and RAN (1985), the latter produced with foreign capital, are epic war films in which the pathos and horror unleashed by the lust for power are unflinchingly portrayed. In *Yume* (1990, shown abroad as *Akira Kurosawa's Dreams*), made for Warner Brothers Pictures, Inc, the director re-creates eight of his dreams in a film that is informed by his nostalgia for childhood and his fear of the destruction of nature.

In 1990, at the 62nd annual Academy Awards ceremony in Los Angeles, Kurosawa received a special honorary Oscar for his lifetime achievements as a cinematic artist. He received the Order of Culture in 1985.

Kuroshima Denji　　　黒島伝治

(1898–1943). Author. Born in Kagawa Prefecture. He studied at Waseda University until he was drafted to participate in Japan's SIBERIAN INTERVENTION (1919). He became ill and was discharged in 1922. His experience in the army was the basis for his antiwar fiction, such as the short stories "Sori" (1927) and "Uzumakeru karasu no mure" (1928). He was a contributor to the magazine BUNGEI SENSEN and a participant in the PROLETARIAN LITERATURE MOVEMENT. His diary during his stay in Siberia was published posthumously

in 1955 under the title *Guntai nikki*. Another of his works is *Busō seru shigai* (1930), a novel.

Kuroshio　　　黒潮

(Black Stream). Also known as the Japan Current. The largest ocean current in the seas off Japan. A warm current, originating in the area east of the Philippines, the Kuroshio flows northward between Taiwan and the island of Ishigakijima into the East China Sea. After passing along the Ryūkyū Islands, it splits into two currents just south of Kyūshū. The main current proceeds between the islands of Yakushima and Amami Ōshima, flowing northeastward along Japan's Pacific coast. It turns east off northeastern Honshū, where it meets the cold southbound current known as OYASHIO. The branch current, known as the TSUSHIMA CURRENT, flows west of Kyūshū and enters the Sea of Japan through the Tsushima Strait. Southwesterly winds blowing up to Japan over the Kuroshio contribute to Japan's muggy summers. The SANRIKU COAST, where the Kuroshio meets the Oyashio, is a rich fishing ground.

Kuroyanagi Tetsuko　　　黒柳徹子

(1933–). Television personality. Born in Tōkyō. Graduated from Tōyō College of Music (now Tōkyō College of Music). Kuroyanagi joined the NHK Radio Theater in 1954, making her broadcasting debut in IIZAWA TADASU's radio drama series for children, *Yambō, Nimbō, Tombō* (1954–57). In television she is known chiefly as a master of ceremonies. In 1981 Kuroyanagi published a book of reminiscences about her elementary school years entitled *Madogiwa no Totto chan* (tr *Little Girl at the Window*, 1982), which sold 6 million copies. She was appointed as a UNICEF goodwill ambassador in 1984.

Kurozumikyō　　　黒住教

A Shintō-oriented religious sect founded by Kurozumi Munetada (1780–1850) in the late Edo period (1600–1868), with headquarters in the city of Okayama. It originated in 1814 when Kurozumi, a Shintō priest, experienced a divine union with the sun goddess AMATERASU ŌMIKAMI, in which he received a "direct bestowal of the Heavenly Decree."

Kurozumikyō holds that Amaterasu Ōmikami is the deity of the creation of the universe and nurtures all things and that man partakes of that divinity. It emphasizes such virtues as sincerity, selflessness, hard work, and gratitude and affirms the established social order. Formally organized in 1846, it developed as a religion centered upon the acquisition of worldly benefits, emperor worship, and semifeudal ethics. In 1876 it became one of the SECT SHINTŌ groups, and in 1885 the Munetada Shrine was established in Okayama. However, from the latter Meiji period (1868–1912), it stagnated because of its inability to cope with modernization. Kurozumikyō, a regional religion centered in Okayama, had about 295,000 followers in 1989.

Kurume　久留米[市]

City in southern Fukuoka Prefecture, Kyūshū. An Edo-period (1600–1868) castle town, it was an army base until the end of World War II. It is known for rubber goods, Kurume ikat cloth (KASURI), and flower nurseries. Pop: 228,347.

Kurusu Saburō　来栖三郎

(1886–1954). Diplomat; born in Kanagawa Prefecture. A graduate of Tōkyō Kōtō Shōgyō Gakkō (now Hitotsubashi University), he joined the Ministry of Foreign Affairs in 1909. He became ambassador to Germany in 1939 and helped negotiate the TRIPARTITE PACT of 1940. In 1941, on the eve of Japan's entry into World War II, he was sent as a special envoy to Washington, DC, where he assisted Ambassador NOMURA KICHISABURŌ in striving unsuccessfully to ease the growing tensions between Japan and the United States. In an exchange of diplomats in 1942 he was returned to Japan, where his American wife and their children had remained; their son died as a pilot fighting for Japan.

Kurutta ippeiji　狂った一頁

(Page of Madness). A 1926 film directed by KINUGASA TEINOSUKE. Scripted by KAWABATA YASUNARI, at the time an emerging writer, the film stars Inoue Masao (1881–1950) and Nakagawa Yoshie (1886–1953). Set in a mental institution, the film attempts to portray the inner life of the patients. Made before the era of sound, it foregoes the use of titles and relies entirely on visual imagery to convey its meaning. It was the first Japanese avant-garde experimental film.

Kuruwa bunshō　廓文章

(A Story of the Pleasure Quarters). Also known as *Yūgiri Izaemon*. KABUKI play of the *sewa-mono* (domestic play) category derived from the "Yoshidaya" scene of the puppet play *Yūgiri Awa no Naruto* (1712) by CHIKAMATSU MONZAEMON; first performed as kabuki in 1808. Izaemon, the son of a wealthy Ōsaka merchant, is disinherited for his dalliance with the courtesan Yūgiri, who then accepts a new patron. The destitute Izaemon, reduced to wearing a paper *kimono* even on New Year's Eve, comes to rebuke Yūgiri for her unfaithfulness. The two are reunited even as news arrives that Izaemon has been reinstated to his former position of wealth. The role of Izaemon is a parade piece for the Ōsaka-type *nimaime* (beau-actor), a lovable type.

kusaboke → quince, dwarf Japanese

Kusaka Genzui　久坂玄瑞

(1840–64). *Samurai* of the Chōshū domain (now Yamaguchi Prefecture) and a leading figure in the proimperial, antishogunate movement of the early 1860s. A disciple and brother-in-law of YOSHIDA SHŌIN, Kusaka was much influenced by his radical loyalist doctrines. Impatient with Chōshū's moderate political policy (see MOVEMENT FOR UNION OF COURT AND SHOGUNATE), in 1862 Kusaka decided to join other imperial loyalists in plans to expel foreigners from Japan. Early in 1863 he and fellow activist TAKASUGI SHINSAKU set fire to the British legation at Shinagawa; returning to Chōshū, he participated in the bombardment of Western ships in the Shimonoseki Strait. He then went to Kyōto, but with the expulsion of

activists by the forces of Satsuma (now Kagoshima Prefecture) and Aizu (now part of Fukushima Prefecture) in the COUP D'ETAT OF 30 SEPTEMBER 1863, Kusaka returned once more to Chōshū and helped to formulate its new antiforeign, antishogunate policy. In the summer of 1864 he joined a Chōshū expeditionary force in an attempt to retake the Imperial Palace (see HAMAGURI GOMON INCIDENT). His contingent was defeated; Kusaka was wounded and later committed suicide.

Kusama Naokata　草間直方

(1753–1831). Also known as Kusama Isuke. Ōsaka merchant and writer. Employed by the KŌNOIKE FAMILY, who adopted him. Kusama was an accomplished calligrapher and practitioner of the tea ceremony. He is best known for his *Sanka zui* (Illustrated Encyclopedia of Coins). Kusama's other writings include *Chaki meibutsu zui* (Illustrated Encyclopedia of Treasured Tea Utensils); his notes, *Kusama Isuke hikki;* and *Shinden kaihatsu jiryaku* (A Brief Outline of Land Reclamation). Kusama also extended financial aid to the blind scholar HANAWA HOKIICHI.

Kusano Shimpei　草野心平

(1903–88). Poet. Born in Fukushima Prefecture; studied at Lingnan University in Guangzhou (Canton). He started to write poetry in the late 1920s, heavily influenced by the anarchist poetry movement. His verse is vigorous and uses colloquial speech patterns. Kusano is especially known for his poems describing human life and feelings through a frog's eyes. These were collected in *Teihon kaeru* (1948, The Frog Poems), which won the first Yomiuri Literary Prize. He was awarded the Order of Culture in 1987.

kusarigama　鎖鎌

A sickle-shaped weapon with a metal weight and chain attached to the neck of the handle; during the Edo period (1600–1868) its use developed into a martial art form known as *kusarigamajutsu.* The shaft was made of hard wood and ranged in length from 20 to 60 centimeters (8 to 24 in). The chain was 2 to 3 meters (6.5 to 10 ft) in length. Holding the sickle in one hand and the chain in the other, the weight was swung in a circular motion at the opponent's head or neck. The chain could be used to lasso the opponent or to wrap around his weapon so that he could be pulled into a position to be beheaded with a sickle. See also MARTIAL ARTS.

Kusatsu　草津[市]

City in southern Shiga Prefecture, central Honshū. The river Kusatsugawa runs through its center. Kusatsu prospered in the Edo period (1600–1868) as a post-station town, at the junction of the highways Tōkaidō and Nakasendō. It has numerous knitted-goods and electrical-appliance factories. Pop: 94,767.

Kusatsu　草津[町]

Town in northwestern Gumma Prefecture, central Honshū, on the southeastern foothills of SHIRANESAN. Known for its hot springs since the 12th century, Kusatsu holds a hot-spring festival in August. A part of the JŌSHIN'ETSU KŌGEN NATIONAL PARK, it is the base for skiing and climbing in such mountain areas as SHIGA KŌGEN, Shiranesan, and ASAMAYAMA. Pop: 8,620.

kusazōshi　草双紙

Type of popular fiction of the Edo period (1600–1868), published in books known as

Kusatsu Attendants at one of the Kusatsu hot springs sing traditional songs as they stir and cool the hot water with wooden paddles. This colorful ritual has become a tourist attraction.

akahon, kurohon, aohon, KIBYŌSHI, and GŌKAN; they were essentially picture books with narrative and dialogue written in phonetic characters in the blank spaces of full-page illustrations. The pictures were of central importance, and at first the artists composed the texts as well. *Kusazōshi* were produced in Edo (now Tōkyō) on cheap paper in the form of slim booklets, each containing five double pages measuring about 19 by 13 centimeters (7.5 by 5.1 in) and stitched together at the cut edges.

Akahon (red books), so called because of their covers, first appeared around 1662 and derived their content from didactic children's folktales. *Kurohon* (black books) were first published in 1744, almost concurrently with *aohon* (green books), which they closely resembled in content. In addition to plots adapted from popular dramas, they presented stories of folk heroes and great battles as well as miracle tales from Buddhist and Shintō literature. *Kibyōshi* (yellow covers), which first appeared in the 1770s, normally ran to two or three booklets. Specifically intended for a sophisticated adult readership, they treated contemporary social life satirically, especially the ways of the licensed quarter. They were followed in 1804 by *gōkan*, volumes bound from as many as six booklets, which were longer, more literary works and featured greater depth of characterization and intricacy of plot.

Kusha school　俱舎宗

(Kushashū). A school of Buddhist studies; one of the six schools of NARA BUDDHISM. The Kusha school was based upon the *Abhidharmakośa-bhāṣya* (J: *Abidatsuma kusha ron;* shortened to *Kusharon*), attributed to the Indian thinker Vasubandhu (ca 320–400), and similar scriptures. It was introduced, along with the HOSSŌ SECT, from China by the monk DŌSHŌ and others in the late 7th century. As a systematic exposition of Buddhist doctrine on being, the *Kusharon* has been widely studied by Buddhists of all denominations.

Kushida Tamizō　櫛田民蔵

(1885–1934). Marxist economist and a founder of academic Marxism in Japan. Born in Fukushima Prefecture, he majored in economics at Kyōto University. In 1917 Kushida joined the staff of the newspaper *Ōsaka asahi shimbun*, where he met ŌYAMA IKUO and HASEGAWA NYOZEKAN, two of the leading liberal journalists of their day. After serving as head of the Faculty of Law of Dōshisha University in Kyōto (1918–20), Kushida returned to Tōkyō to teach economics at Tōkyō University. He soon resigned in protest over the forced resignation of MORITO TATSUO (see also MORITO INCIDENT) and joined the newly established ŌHARA INSTITUTE FOR

Kusano Shimpei This poet is admired for his vigorous, colloquial style and his lyrical treatment of nature and everyday life.

849

Kushida Tamizō

Kushiro Shitsugen National Park The park in October. About 60 percent of Japan's total marshland is contained in this Hokkaidō park.

SOCIAL RESEARCH. Kushida was a theoretician who developed his views by criticizing leading economists of the 1920s, such as KOIZUMI SHINZŌ and especially his own mentor KAWAKAMI HAJIME. He helped found the school of Marxist historical analysis called the RŌNŌHA (Labor-Farmer Faction). His writings are collected in *Kushida Tamizō zenshū* (5 vols, 1935).

Kushikino   串木野[市]

City in Kagoshima Prefecture, Kyūshū. A gold-producing area since the Edo period (1600–1868), it is still the leading producer of gold in Japan. It is also a fishing port. Local products include *kamaboko* (boiled fish paste), ham, and bacon. Pop: 29,385.

Kushima   串間[市]

City in southern Miyazaki Prefecture, Kyūshū, on Shibushi Bay. It is mainly a farming area, producing rice, tomatoes, cucumbers, and other vegetables. The cape TOIMISAKI and the island of KŌJIMA are popular attractions. Pop: 26,734.

Kushimoto   串本[町]

Town in southern Wakayama Prefecture, central Honshū. Principal industries are

Kusunoki Masashige This 17th-century painting by Kanō Tan'yū depicts the legendary warrior bidding farewell to his son before the Battle of Minatogawa, which ended in his death and the collapse of the imperial restoration he supported.

fishing and tourism. Excursion ships ply between Kushimoto and the island of Ōshima. Scenic attractions include the cape SHIONOMISAKI and HASHIKUIIWA, an interesting rock formation in the sea. Pop: 17,385.

Kushimoto Marine Park 串本海中公園

(Kushimoto Kaichū Kōen). Marine park in the town of Kushimoto, Wakayama Prefecture, central Honshū. Established in 1971. Due to the influence of the KUROSHIO current, there is an abundance of stone coral and tropical fish on the coast near Kushimoto. These can be viewed from glass-bottomed boats, from an undersea observatory, or by snorkeling. The park also has a research station and a marine pavilion where sharks and rays swimming in a long tunnellike tank can be seen close up by visitors.

Kushiro   釧路[市]

City in eastern Hokkaidō, at the mouth of the river Kushirogawa, on the Pacific Ocean. First settled early in the Meiji period (1868–1912), Kushiro is the administrative and commercial center of eastern Hokkaidō, as well as the main base for fishing in the northern seas. The paper, seafood-processing, and lumber industries are also important. The Kushiro Coal Mine is situated in the eastern part of the city. Kushiro Shitsugen National Park is known for *tanchō* (a type of Japanese crane). Pop: 205,639.

kushiro→bracelets, ancient

Kushirogawa   釧路川

River in eastern Hokkaidō, originating in Lake KUSSHARO and flowing through the Kushiro Plain into the Pacific Ocean. The upper reaches are a part of AKAN NATIONAL PARK. The port of Kushiro is located at the river's mouth. Length: 154 km (96 mi); area of drainage basin: 2,510 sq km (970 sq mi).

Kushiro Shitsugen National Park
釧路湿原国立公園

(Kushiro Shitsugen Kokuritsu Kōen). National park centered on Kushiro Marsh (Kushiro Shitsugen) in eastern Hokkaidō. Japan's largest marsh, it extends across the Kushiro Plain and is fed by the waters of the river Kushirogawa. Reeds grow in the wettest areas, which are surrounded by grasslands, encircled in turn by dense stands of alder. Approximately 600 plant species have been identified in the park. It offers habitats for many birds, including the Japanese crane

Kushimoto Marine Park The tunnellike design of this marine park's aquarium allows visitors to view sea life from an unusual perspective.

(*tanchō*); birds migrating to other areas also stop here. Area: 269 sq km (104 sq mi).

Kussharo, Lake   屈斜路湖

(Kussharoko). Also known as Lake Kutcharo. Caldera lake in eastern Hokkaidō. Located within the Kussharo caldera and part of Akan National Park. An island called Nakajima, a composite volcano, is situated in the center of the lake. The water is acid, and fish are practically nonexistent. Area: 79.7 sq km (30.8 sq mi); circumference: 58 km (36 mi); depth: 117.5 m (385.5 ft); altitude: 121 m (397 ft).

kussō→flexed burials

Kusube Yaichi   楠部弥弌

(1897–1984). Potter. Born in Kyōto. In 1920 he helped found the pottery organization Sekido (Red Earth). He won high honors at the 1933 Teiten (Exhibition of the Imperial Fine Arts Academy). His white porcelains are distinguished by patterns sculpted in low relief with a stylus. He received the Order of Culture in 1978.

Kusuko Incident   薬子の変

(Kusuko no Hen). An attempted usurpation in 810. Pleading illness, Emperor Heizei (774–824; r 806–809) abdicated in favor of his younger brother Emperor SAGA. Fujiwara no Kusuko (d 810; daughter of the powerful court official Fujiwara no Tanetsugu [737–785] of the Shikike branch of the Fujiwara family and the favorite of Heizei) persuaded Heizei to reclaim the throne. Heizei secretly assembled a military force for that purpose, but the plot was discovered. Kusuko poisoned herself, and Heizei took Buddhist orders. After the incident the Hokke branch of the family, represented by FUJIWARA NO FUYUTSUGU, outstripped the Shikike in power and prestige.

Kusumi Morikage   久隅守景

(ca 1620–ca 1690). KANŌ SCHOOL painter born in Kaga (now part of Ishikawa Prefecture). He studied painting with KANŌ TAN'YŪ at the Kajibashi atelier in Edo (now Tōkyō), married one of Tan'yū's nieces, and assisted in such important commissioned painting projects as the TŌSHŌGŪ in Nikkō, an honor that should have secured his position in the Edo Kanō school. However, it is generally believed that, for reasons unknown, he was dismissed from the Kajibashi atelier. According to one account, in the mid-1670s he was summoned to the city of Kanazawa by the head of the Kaga domain to make designs for KUTANI WARE potters. A few years later it seems that he went to Kyōto, where he spent the rest of his life. Morikage is best known for his genre painting of rural life executed in a fluid ink style with restrained color. His most famous work of this type, *Nōryōzu* (A

Peasant Family Beneath a Hanging Gourd Trellis), is a National Treasure housed in the Tōkyō National Museum.

kusunoki → camphor tree

Kusunoki Masashige　楠木正成

(?–1336). Warrior chieftain from Kawachi Province (now part of Ōsaka Prefecture) who died supporting the ill-fated KEMMU RESTORATION (1333–36) of Emperor GO-DAIGO. In later centuries Masashige was depicted in folk mythology and school textbooks before World War II as the supreme paragon of imperial loyalty.

Knowledge of Masashige's career is derived mainly from passages in the TAIHEIKI—a chronicle covering the civil strife of 1318–67—that seem to be more literarily fanciful than historically convincing. The chronicle introduces Masashige as a supporter of Go-Daigo who was involved in guerrilla warfare during Go-Daigo's two-year exile to the Oki Islands. In 1333 the shogunate dispatched an army under ASHIKAGA TAKAUJI, who changed allegiance and proclaimed his support for Go-Daigo. The shogunate collapsed, and the Kemmu Restoration became a reality. Masashige was appointed governor (kokushi) and military governor (shugo) of Kawachi Province and military governor of Izumi Province (now part of Ōsaka Prefecture). In 1335 Takauji was driven into revolt against the restoration government. The decisive battle was fought in July 1336 at the river Minatogawa, near what is now Kōbe, between the Ashikaga and loyalist forces that included Masashige and NITTA YOSHISADA (see MINATOGAWA, BATTLE OF). After many hours of ferocious combat, Masashige and his brother withdrew from the battle and committed suicide.

Kutani ware　九谷焼

(kutani-yaki). Name given to a variety of porcelain wares, both for everyday and TEA CEREMONY use, made in Kaga Province (now part of Ishikawa Prefecture) during the late 17th century and again from 1807 to the present. The Old Kutani kiln is best known for its boldly designed tableware in dark, restrained overglaze enamels—mostly dishes and bowls. Their bodies are grayish and coarse-grained. The white glazes vary from dull white to a shiny, even white with a bluish tinge; the underglaze blue decoration, when present, varies from pale indigo to sooty, dark blue. Their color schemes emphasize green and yellow. The colorful, vigorously brushed designs draw on late Ming (1368–1644) and early Qing (Ch'ing; 1644–1912) dynasty porcelains of China, KANŌ SCHOOL and TOSA SCHOOL paintings, and textiles. In the 19th century the Old Kutani style was revived at a number of kilns, most notably in Kutani at the Yoshidaya kiln (1823–31). The name Kutani has also been applied to the red and gold pieces popular in the West, and during the 19th century numerous kilns (some still operative) were built in Kaga Province to produce them.

Kutchan　倶知安[町]

Town in southwestern Hokkaidō on the river Shiribetsugawa. Kutchan is the administrative and cultural center of the surrounding area. It was first settled in 1892. The economy is based on dairy farming and the cultivation of rice and potatoes. Pop: 18,030.

Kutcharo, Lake → Kussharo, Lake

Kūya An early-13th-century statue of this Buddhist monk invoking the name of the Buddha Amida (represented by the small figures issuing from his mouth). Rokuharamitsuji, Kyōto.

Kutsuki Masatsuna　朽木昌綱

(1750–1802). Daimyō of the Fukuchiyama domain (now part of Kyōto Prefecture) and scholar of WESTERN LEARNING; also known as Kuchiki Masatsuna. He translated a Dutch version of a geographical treatise by the German scholar Johann Hübner (1668–1731) and published it as Taisei yochi zusetsu (1789, Illustrated Account of the Western World).

Kuttara, Lake　倶多楽湖

(Kuttarako). In southwestern Hokkaidō. Located to the east of Noboribetsu Hot Spring, this lake was created when the volcano Kuttaradake erupted, forming a round caldera that filled with water. Area: 5 sq km (1.9 sq mi); circumference: 8 km (5 mi); depth: 148 m (486 ft); altitude: 258 m (846 ft).

kuwa　鍬

(hoes). The use of kuwa (hoes) in Japan goes back as far as the Yayoi period (ca 300 BC–ca AD 300), although it was not until the Kofun period (ca 300–710) that it became widespread. Different types of hoes have gradually developed in different regions, and there are distinct local names for each. Some examples are the itaguwa for furrowing and plowing fields, the small karaguwa with a thick blade for clearing land, the three-pronged bitchūguwa for rice cultivation, and the kusakezuri kuwa for weeding.

Kuwabara Takeo　桑原武夫

(1904–88). Scholar of French literature and critic. Born in Fukui Prefecture. Graduate of Kyōto University. After World War II, Kuwabara wrote extensive criticism on traditional Japanese culture. He was also known as an alpinist. Kuwabara's main works include "Daini geijutsu: Gendai haiku ni tsuite" (1946), a controversial criticism of HAIKU as a modern art form, and Nakae Chōmin no kenkyū (1966), a critical biography of NAKAE CHŌMIN. He received the Order of Culture in 1987.

Kuwada Yoshinari　桑田義備

(1882–1981). Cytologist. Born in Ōsaka. A graduate of Tōkyō University, he later taught at Kyōto University. Kuwada conducted research concerning the structure of the chromosome and contributed to development in this area. He received the Order of Culture in 1962. His works include Kakubun-

retsu no shinka (1954, The Evolution of Mitosis).

Kuwaki Gen'yoku　桑木厳翼

(1874–1946). Philosopher. Born in Tōkyō. A graduate of Tōkyō University, he studied in Germany and was particularly influenced by Neo-Kantian philosophy and by the philosophy of critical realism. As a professor at Tōkyō University from 1914 to 1935 and through his articles in the Tetsugaku zasshi (Journal of Philosophy), he worked for the spread of "culturalism," a movement based on German idealist philosophy. His writings include Tetsugaku gairon (1900, Outline of Philosophy) and Kanto to gendai no tetsugaku (1917, Kant and Contemporary Philosophy). See also MODERN PHILOSOPHY.

Kuwana　桑名[市]

City in northern Mie Prefecture, central Honshū, 25 km (15 mi) southwest of Nagoya. Kuwana prospered in the Edo period (1600–1868) as a castle town, a post-station town, and a port on the river Ibigawa. It is a residential and industrial suburb of Nagoya, with iron-casting, steel, and machine industries. Pop: 97,909.

Kūya　空也

(903–972). Also known as Kōya. Along with GYŌGI (668–749), one of the prototypes of the HIJIRI, charismatic itinerant Buddhist monks. Kūya is best known for his popularization of PURE LAND BUDDHISM. By traditional accounts he was a scion of the imperial family. In his twenties he privately took religious vows at the provincial temple (KOKUBUNJI) in Owari

Kutani ware This Old Kutani dish is decorated with a fanciful pair of flying rabbits, an allusion to an episode in Japanese mythology. Ca 17th century. Diameter 43 cm.

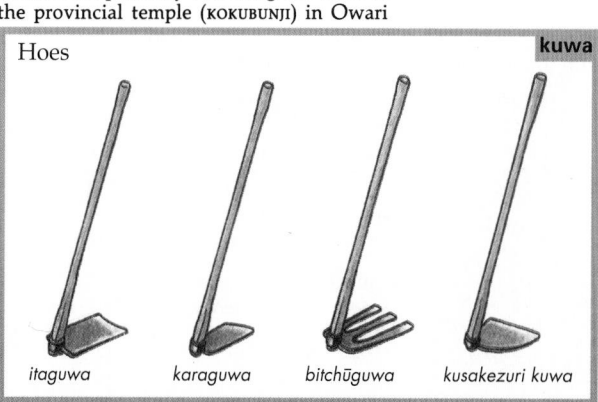

Hoes　　　　　　　　　　　　　　　　kuwa

itaguwa　karaguwa　bitchūguwa　kusakezuri kuwa

kuzu The *kuzu* root (right), long used as a food in Japan, is about 20 percent starch. The root of a single plant can weigh more than 30 kg. Leaves, left; flower cluster, center.

Province (now part of Aichi Prefecture), adopting the Buddhist name Kūya. Thereafter he spent some years in study at the temple Mineaidera in Harima Province (now part of Hyōgo Prefecture) and underwent a period of ascetic discipline and devotion to the bodhisattva KANNON of Yushima (now Ishima) in Awa (now Tokushima Prefecture) on Shikoku. Following a period of evangelization in the far northeastern provinces of Mutsu (now Fukushima, Miyagi, Iwate, and Aomori prefectures) and Dewa (now Akita and Yamagata prefectures), he returned to Kyōto in 938 and took up the role of a mendicant monk, distributing the alms he received among the poor and the sick. He came to be known as Ichi no Shōnin (or Ichi no Hijiri), "Saint of the Marketplace," and his popular following grew. In 948 he ascended Mt. Hiei (HIEIZAN) and for the first time underwent formal ordination. In 951, seeking divine relief from an epidemic, Kūya constructed an image of the Eleven-Headed Kannon (still housed at Saikōji, later renamed ROKUHARA-MITSUJI, founded by Kūya in 963).

Kuze Hirochika   久世広周

(1819–64). *Daimyō* of the Sekiyado domain (now part of Chiba Prefecture) and senior councillor (*rōjū;* 1852–58; 1860–62) of the Tokugawa shogunate (1603–1867). Born in Edo (now Tōkyō). Kuze worked to promote cooperation between the imperial and military governments (see MOVEMENT FOR UNION OF COURT AND SHOGUNATE) and helped arrange the marriage of Emperor KŌMEI's sister Princess KAZU to the shōgun TOKUGAWA IEMOCHI. His efforts to extend the deadline for opening Japanese ports to the West under the ANSEI COMMERCIAL TREATIES were criticized, and in 1862 he was placed under house arrest for having been "disrespectful" to the court.

kuzu   葛

(kudzu). *Pueraria thunbergiana.* Perennial herbaceous climbing vine of the pea family (Leguminosae). Large and strong, it grows wild in fields and mountains all over Japan. It is one of the seven flowers of autumn (*aki no nanakusa*). The vines are covered with brown hairs and may reach 10 meters (33 ft) in length. The stems are woody at the base. Large, compound leaves composed of three nearly round leaflets alternate on the vine. In autumn inflorescences (15–18 cm; 6–7 in) bear reddish purple, butterfly-shaped flowers in clusters.

Starch from pounded *kuzu* roots has long been used by the Japanese as a food; root fibers were also used to make cloth for work clothes. In China dried *kuzu* root is used in preparing a medicine to treat colds. The leaves are used for livestock feed in the United States as well as Japan.

Kuzuryūgawa   九頭竜川

River in eastern Fukui Prefecture, central Honshū, originating in the mountains between Fukui and Gifu prefectures and flowing through the Fukui Plain into the Sea of Japan. Length: 116 km (72 mi); area of drainage basin: 2,930 sq km (1,130 sq mi).

Kwaidan   怪談

(*Kaidan*). A film released in 1964, directed by KOBAYASHI MASAKI. MIZUKI YŌKO wrote the screenplay based on Lafcadio HEARN's collection of Japanese ghost stories. Divided into four tales of the supernatural, the film stars

Kwanggaet'o monument This inscribed stone monument, erected in 414 in what is now the Chinese province of Jilin, is an important source of information on early Korean history and Korean-Japanese relations.

Aratama Michiyo (b 1930), Nakamura Kan'emon (1901–82), Nakamura Katsuo (b 1938), and Kishi Keiko (b 1932). Although it features ghosts and supernatural characters, the film aims to depict the beauty in unfathomable mystery rather than to induce terror. It won a special judges' prize at Cannes in 1965.

Kwanggaet'o monument   広開土王陵碑

(J: Kōkaido Ō *ryō hi;* also known as Kōtai Ō *hi*). A stone tablet, a little over 6 meters (20 ft) high, that was erected in 414 to commemorate the deeds of King Kwanggaet'o (J: Kōkaido Ō or Kōtai Ō), ruler of the Korean kingdom of KOGURYŎ from 391 to 413. Located on the Manchurian (Chinese) side of the Yalu River in Ji'an (Chi-an) County, Jilin (Kirin) Province, it was unearthed in 1880. It is an important source of information on early Korean history and Korean-Japanese relations. In about 1,800 elegantly carved Chinese characters, its text celebrates the king's wars of conquest in Manchuria and the Korean peninsula as well as his campaigns against the Japanese-dominated state of KAYA in the south. Considerable disagreement persists among scholars concerning portions of the text pertaining to the WA, or Japanese people.

Kwangju Student Resistance Movement   光州学生運動

(J: Kōshū Gakusei Undō). Nationwide explosion of violent anti-Japanese sentiment that swept Korea during the winter of 1929–30. It began when Japanese male students ridiculed Korean female students at the Naju train station located just west of Kwangju, capital of South Chŏlla Province in southwestern Korea. On 3 November 1929 some 600 Japanese and Korean middle and high school students clashed in the streets of Kwangju. Harsh treatment of Korean girls by Japanese police and the involvement of the patriotic Korean group SIN'GANHOE led to a bloody five-month series of demonstrations against Japanese prejudice and colonial rule, in which more than 54,000 students at 194 schools participated. The brutality of police suppression made it the last outburst for independence until Korea's liberation from Japanese rule in 1945. See also KOREA AND JAPAN.

Kwantung Army →Guandong
(Kwantung) Army

Kwantung Territory →Guandong
(Kwantung) Territory

kyahan   脚絆

Leggings traditionally worn for outdoor work or when traveling to protect the legs from cold. They are still used by farmers and others who must work long hours outdoors. Leggings made from cotton, hemp, silk, and other cloth materials have been worn since the Muromachi period (1333–1568). There are three different types of *kyahan. Ōtsukyahan* are fan-shaped pieces of cloth strapped to the leg with cord. *Edokyahan* are cloth pieces fit to the calf, cut to size, and secured with cord and clasps. *Tsutsukyahan* are cylindrically shaped pieces of single cloth that are slipped snugly onto the lower leg.

Kygnus Sekiyu KK   キグナス石油[株]

(Kigunasu Sekiyu). Company engaged in the sale, export, and import of oil and petro-

chemical products. Incorporated in 1972. Sales for the fiscal year ending March 1990 totaled ¥242.7 billion (US $1.6 billion), of which volatile oils and naphtha accounted for 60 percent; kerosene and light oil, 19 percent; and heavy oil and other products, 21 percent. Capitalization stood at ¥2.0 billion (US $13.1 million) in the same year. Headquarters are in Tōkyō.

Kyōbushō   教部省

(Ministry of Religion). Government ministry of the early Meiji period (1868–1912). It replaced the Jingikan (Office of Shintō Worship) and the Jingishō (Ministry of Shintō Religion), two earlier institutions that had been created to implement the Meiji state's initial policy of a fusion of religion and government (*saisei itchi*). The creation of the Kyōbushō in 1872 signaled a retreat from this policy and the abandonment of an exclusive emphasis on Shintō affairs. The new ministry took charge of Buddhist temples as well as Shintō shrines, the ordination of both Shintō and Buddhist priests, and the care of the imperial tombs. It was abolished in turn in 1877 in a further liberalization of religious policy, and its administrative duties were assumed by the Home Ministry.

Kyōcera Corporation   京セラ[株]

(Kyōsera). Manufacturer and seller of ceramic material for electronic parts and industrial machines as well as of semiconductor parts, electronic components, electronic equipment, and optical and precision instruments. Incorporated in 1959 as Kyōto Ceramic Co, Ltd, it merged with four other companies in 1982, assuming its present name. In 1983 Kyōcera merged with Yashica Co, Ltd. Sales for the fiscal year ending March 1991 totaled ¥330.9 billion (US $2.4 billion), and capitalization stood at ¥101.6 billion (US $740.5 million). Headquarters are in Kyōto.

Kyōdo kenkyū   郷土研究

(Local Studies; literally, "native place studies," i.e., studies on local traditions). The first journal in Japan devoted exclusively to FOLKLORE STUDIES; founded in 1913 by the noted folklorist YANAGITA KUNIO and Takaki Toshio (1876–1922). In addition to articles and essays, the journal published reports from various parts of Japan on folklore research materials and sources. Among its contributors were such leading folklore scholars as ORIKUCHI SHINOBU, MINAKATA KUMAGUSU, and KINDAICHI KYŌSUKE. Although it ceased publication in 1917, it was revived in 1931 by Okamura Chiaki (1884–1941) and was continued until 1934.

kyōdo kumiai →cooperative
associations

Kyōdo News Service   共同通信社

(Kyōdō Tsūshinsha). One of Japan's largest cooperative news agencies. Its membership is composed of the 63 most influential national and local newspapers and Nippon Hōsō Kyōkai (NHK; Japan Broadcasting Corporation), Japan's public broadcasting company. Kyōdō News Service began operation in 1945 when the news agency DŌMEI TSŪSHINSHA disbanded after World War II. Over the years it has become one of the world's major wire services and now exchanges news with 68 international agencies, including the Associated Press, Reuters, Deutsche Presse Agentur, and Tass. Each day the agency offers domestic and foreign news, feature stories, stock market reports, and wirephotos to the nation's newspapers and broadcasting stations. Kyōdō also operates 33 foreign bureaus, deploys special correspondents, and has 103 participating and associate news media providing services to national and foreign subscribers.

Kyōdō Oil Co, Ltd   共同石油[株]

(Kyōdō Sekiyu). Company engaged in the sale and distribution of oil products. Kyōdō Oil was incorporated in 1965 when the marketing divisions of three independent oil companies (Nippon Mining, Asia Oil, and Tōa Sekiyu) were integrated with the support of the Japanese government. Subsequently, FUJI OIL CO, LTD, became the fourth member of the Kyōdō Oil group (1966) and was soon followed by Kashima Oil (1967). In response to the growing demand for oil products, Kyōdō Crude Oil of Japan, Ltd, was incorporated in 1970 to promote and stabilize the group's crude oil procurement and tanker-chartering operations. Together with the group's refiners, Kyōdō Oil has been operating domestically and internationally to expand capacities in all fields of the oil business. As a result, Kyōdō Oil is now the fourth largest oil company in the nation. Total sales for the fiscal year 1990 were ¥1.3 trillion (US $8.5 billion). Capitalization stood at ¥18.0 billion (US $117.6 million) in the same year. Headquarters are in Tōkyō.

Kyōdō Printing Company strike   共同印刷争議

(Kyōdō Insatsu sōgi). Major labor dispute in 1926 between the Kyōdō Printing Company in Tōkyō and its employees. A reduction of working hours triggered a massive strike by workers, many of whom belonged to the Kantō Publishing Industry Labor Union (Kantō Shuppan Rōdō Kumiai). The company dismissed all 2,142 striking union members. The 57-day strike, marked by some 1,500 cases of arrest or detention by military police, ended in defeat for the union, but spurred the development of new strike tactics, and so marked a turning point in the history of the Japanese labor movement. The strike was the subject of the novel Taiyō no nai machi (1929, Streets without Sun) by TOKUNAGA SUNAO.

Kyōdō Shiryō Co, Ltd   協同飼料[株]

(Kyōdō Shiryō). Manufacturer and vendor of poultry and swine feeds and animal husbandry products. Incorporated in 1946. Through its nationwide distribution network, the company provides its customers with feed, bull semen, and embryos, along with technical expertise. Sales for the fiscal year ending March 1991 totaled ¥106.4 billion (US $775.5 million). In the same year capitalization stood at ¥5.1 billion (US $37.2 million). Headquarters are in Yokohama.

Kyōei Life Insurance Co, Ltd   協栄生命保険[株]

(Kyōei Seimei Hoken). Life insurance company specializing in annuities for individuals. Established in 1946. The company has a subsidiary in São Paulo. In the fiscal year ending March 1990 the company received premiums totaling ¥765.0 billion (US $5.0 billion), and total assets stood at ¥3.0 trillion (US $19.6 billion). Headquarters are in Tōkyō.

Kyōfūkai   矯風会

(Abbreviation of Nihon Kirisutokyō Fujin Kyōfūkai; Japan Woman's Christian Temperance Union). Inspired by the visit of American WCTU campaigner Mary Leavitt (1830–1912), YAJIMA KAJIKO and some 50 other Japanese women started the Tōkyō Kirisutokyō Fujin Kyōfūkai in 1886. Reorganized on a national scale in 1893, the Kyōfūkai became Japan's largest women's organization in the 1890s. The group campaigned against alcohol, tobacco, and legalized prostitution, including the practice of sending Japanese prostitutes abroad (see KARAYUKI SAN). In 1894 it established the Jiaikan, a Tōkyō settlement to rehabilitate prostitutes and other women in trouble. In 1901–02 the group also called attention to the pollution victims of the ASHIO COPPER MINE INCIDENT. The Kyōfūkai's official magazine Fujin shimpō (Women's News) still helps to publicize such causes.

Kyō-ganoko musume Dōjōji   京鹿子娘道成寺

(The Dancing Girl at the Temple). Popular title Musume Dōjōji. KABUKI dance by Fujimoto Tobun and others; first performed in 1753. A shosagoto (dance piece) based upon the NŌ play Dōjōji, it recounts the outcome of the maiden Kiyohime's unrequited love for Anchin, a priest of the temple Dōjōji. As a new temple bell is being dedicated at Dōjōji, a beautiful dancer named Hanako appears at the gate and begs permission to enter. There she performs a series of brilliant dances. At the climax she leaps inside the bell, only to reappear metamorphosed into a horrible serpent, the true form of the spurned Kiyohime. In the finale a superhuman figure appears who quells this demon. The dazzling sequence of dances, coupled with the rapid changes of magnificent costume, make this piece a showcase for the accomplished onnagata (female impersonator).

kyōgen   狂言

A form of comic drama that evolved, as did NŌ, in the earlier tradition of SARUGAKU, flourished from the mid-14th century, and is still performed today. The word kyōgen can be used to refer to comic roles within a single Nō play, of which the most common are those known as AIKYŌGEN (intermission kyōgen), but generally it refers to the independent comic pieces that are traditionally performed between two separate Nō plays.

Although the relationship between kyōgen and Nō is one of complementary development, kyōgen is the opposite of Nō in almost every respect. It is straightforward and colloquial, drawing on the real world for its material. Instead of idealizing characters as does Nō, kyōgen portrays their weaknesses, usually with compassion, subtlety, and humor. In its largest sense, however, Nō includes kyōgen.

History — The roots of kyōgen go back to the 8th century. At that time one of the many cultural imports from Tang (T'ang; 618–907) China was an entertainment called

in Japanese sangaku ("scattered [i.e., miscellaneous] entertainments"), or later sarugaku, which featured such aspects as acrobatics, juggling, magic, and comic imitations. Throughout its history, sarugaku was performed as an entertainment at shrines and temples. As a result, it came into close contact with religious rituals and ceremonies and with other forms of entertainment given on similar occasions. It seems likely that professional sarugaku players were gradually called upon to take over the performance of some of these other entertainments because, between the 10th and 14th centuries, sarugaku came to have two main and distinct elements: on the one hand, the original kyōgen-type comic pieces, and, on the other, serious plays based on music and dance — i.e., Nō plays — developed from the Buddhist temple entertainments.

In spite of its temple connections, sarugaku remained primarily a popular entertainment until at least the end of the 14th century, dependent on its appeal to audiences in country towns and villages, who gathered to watch performances by touring groups of players. By the early 14th century, however, a clear distinction was being made between the performers of Nō and the kyōgen players, with the serious and literary Nō plays becoming the overwhelmingly dominant element in sarugaku performances.

The association of sarugaku with the most powerful leaders in the land began in the Muromachi period (1333–1568) with the supreme military ruler ASHIKAGA YOSHIMITSU and his patronage of KAN'AMI and in particular of his son ZEAMI. Most of what is known about sarugaku at this time comes from Zeami who, in 1400, began an invaluable series of writings on the art of Nō. He was greatly concerned to elevate the literary and aesthetic standards of Nō performances to conform to the tastes of his patrons among the military rulers. His references to his reluctance to take kyōgen players to perform with him before the nobility because of the embarrassment they sometimes caused by their largely impromptu dialogue is a good indication of the continued existence of the element of earthy humor in kyōgen.

The patronage of such sarugaku groups by the richest and most powerful families in Japan continued right up until the Meiji Restoration in 1868 and had far-reaching effects on the development of Nō and kyōgen. During the 16th century, patrons adopted various skilled performers as their favorites and came to treat them and their followers as part of their retinue. As a result, the first independent kyōgen school, the ŌKURA SCHOOL, was established in the latter part of the century, and around the turn of the century it was followed by the emergence of two others, the Sagi school and the IZUMI SCHOOL.

Minor groups of kyōgen players were either absorbed into these three main schools

Kyō-ganoko musume Dōjōji The actor Onoe Kikugorō VII, playing the title role, dances atop a temple bell at the climax of this kabuki dance piece.

Although typical *kyōgen* do not use masks, 20 types of masks are available for the portrayal of special characters.

▲ The *kitsune* (fox) mask represents both the servant of the deity Inari and a fox that assumes human form.

▲ The *buaku* mask is used to portray a comical and ineffectual devil character.

▲ The *saru* (monkey) mask is worn by the messenger of the deity Sannō Gongen.

◀ As part of the Nō ceremonial piece *Okina* (Old Man), the *kyōgen* character Sambasō (played by Nomura Mansaku) performs a dance as supplication for a good harvest and prosperity.

▼ In the play *Bōshibari* (Tied to a Pole), Tarō-kaja (played by Nomura Mannojō, foreground) and Jirō-kaja (Nomura Mansaku) try to steal their lord's *sake*.

▶ A local administrator (played by Nomura Kōsuke, center) intervenes in a fight between a country bumpkin (Nomura Mansaku, right) and a robber (Nomura Mannojō). The robber had tried to steal the bumpkin's tea in this scene from the play *Chatsubo* (The Tea Jar).

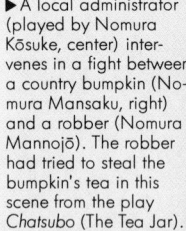

◀ In the play *I-danuki* (Hunting Tanuki), a *tanuki* (raccoon dog) transforms itself into a nun (played by Yamamoto Tōjirō, right) in order to persuade a hunter (Yamamoto Noritada) to stop killing *tanuki*.

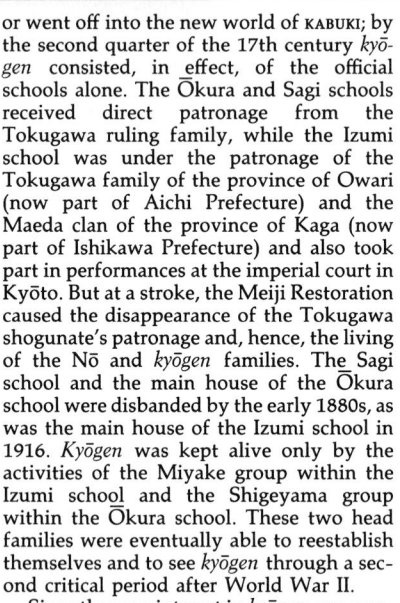

or went off into the new world of KABUKI; by the second quarter of the 17th century *kyōgen* consisted, in effect, of the official schools alone. The Ōkura and Sagi schools received direct patronage from the Tokugawa ruling family, while the Izumi school was under the patronage of the Tokugawa family of the province of Owari (now part of Aichi Prefecture) and the Maeda clan of the province of Kaga (now part of Ishikawa Prefecture) and also took part in performances at the imperial court in Kyōto. But at a stroke, the Meiji Restoration caused the disappearance of the Tokugawa shogunate's patronage and, hence, the living of the Nō and *kyōgen* families. The Sagi school and the main house of the Ōkura school were disbanded by the early 1880s, as was the main house of the Izumi school in 1916. *Kyōgen* was kept alive only by the activities of the Miyake group within the Izumi school and the Shigeyama group within the Ōkura school. These two head families were eventually able to reestablish themselves and to see *kyōgen* through a second critical period after World War II.

Since the war, interest in *kyōgen* as a popular drama form has been stimulated in Japan by successful tours to Europe and the United States. Traditionally all professional *kyōgen* players were men, but in recent years a few female *kyōgen* players have emerged, as well as foreign students of the art. In spite of these developments, the main unit in *kyōgen* is still the extended family group and the Izumi and Ōkura schools remain dominant.

Content and Texts—Although some *kyōgen* use songs and dances, these are not key constituents as they are in Nō, but only

occur naturally within the action of a play. *Kyōgen* are essentially spoken plays and, having no literary pretensions, are meant to be performed rather than read. Performances depended on an oral tradition that allowed the players great freedom for impromptu dialogue until standard texts began to be recorded for private use by the Ōkura and Izumi schools toward the middle of the 17th century and by the Sagi school around 1700. The earliest published texts, in the *Kyōgen ki* (Records of Kyōgen) of 1660, were unattributable versions apparently derived from a number of sources. It was not until the Meiji period (1868–1912) and later that the official texts of the professional schools were published.

Kyōgen Roles within Nō Plays—*Kyōgen* roles in Nō plays vary in the extent of their integration with the plot. The most notable example of an inseparable role is found in the auspicious, ceremonial piece called *Okina* (Old Man), a set of songs, chants, and dances that has its roots in ancient folk beliefs and that is performed only on very special occasions. The two characters Okina and Sambasō are of more or less the same importance in the piece as a whole, but, whereas Okina is played by a Nō actor, the role of Sambasō is taken by a *kyōgen* player who, in the later part of the piece, performs a dance, parodying that of Okina, as a supplication for a good harvest and prosperity. In a certain, especially congratulatory type of *Okina* production, a number of colorfully dressed *kyōgen* players perform roles known as FURYŪ.

Although *Okina* is clearly a unique case, there are plenty of examples of *kyōgen* roles that have a direct connection with the action in Nō plays, such as the two temple servants in *Dōjōji* or the boatman in *Funa Benkei*

(Benkei in the Boat). Finally, in the *aikyōgen* the player has the scene all to himself during the interval between two acts as he comments on, or explains, the action of the Nō play in colloquial language.

Independent Plays—The two current schools of *kyōgen* have between them about 260 honkyōgen (main, i.e., independent, *kyōgen*) in their repertoires, 174 of them being common to both. Traditionally, an independent *kyōgen* was given between each pair of Nō plays in a full program of five Nō (*gobandate*)—some of them are parodies of particular Nō plays—but nowadays, when there are only two or three Nō in an ordinary program, only one *kyōgen* is usually given. Most *kyōgen* use two or three players, although a few require nine or so.

Classification and Content—There are various ways of grouping the plays, but the following classification is based on the play's main role or defining characteristics.

1. *Waki kyōgen* (auspicious plays). These convey an atmosphere of felicitation, centering on gods, rich men, or farmers; e.g., *Fuku no kami* (The God of Good Fortune). (35 plays.)

2. *Daimyō* (feudal lord) plays. The main character is usually a lord who, although haughty and overbearing, is basically stupid and is therefore always worsted by his subordinates; e.g., *Futari* (or *Ninin*) *daimyō* (The Two Lords). (16 plays.)

3. *Tarō-kaja*, or *shōmyō* ("small landowner"), plays. Tarō-kaja is a retainer who, although something of a drunkard and coward, always manages to outwit his master; e.g., *Bōshibari* (Tied to a Pole). (45 plays.)

4. *Muko* (bridegroom, son-in-law) plays. These center on a young, newly married man and his embarrassing experiences with his wife's family, which arise typically from

his naïveté and weak character; e.g., *Kuchimane muko* (The Mimicking Bridegroom). (19 plays.)

5. *Onna* (woman) plays. Included in this category are plays that might be called husband-and-wife pieces. Since the wife is often the more overbearing and strong-willed, there grew up a comic genre of "terrifying wife tales"; e.g., *Hanago.* (28 plays.)

6. *Oni* (devil) plays. These show devils to be, not frightening, but as weak and vulnerable as humans and often as pitiable; e.g., *Setsubun* (The Eve of Spring). (9 plays.)

7. *Yamabushi* (mountain ascetic) plays. These priests were supposed to have fearsome mystical powers, but in the plays they appear to be as foolish and human as anyone else; e.g., *Kani yamabushi* (The Crab and the Mountain Priest). (9 plays.)

8. *Shukke* (Buddhist priest) plays. The priests in these plays are usually revealed as worldly, ignorant, and self-seeking; e.g., *Fuse nai kyō* (A Sermon with No Donation). (25 plays.)

9. *Zatō* (blind man) plays. These plays depict men who are blind or otherwise handicapped, and they either make cruel fun of them or treat them with pathos; e.g., *Tsukimi zatō* (The Moon-Viewing Blind Man). (8 plays.)

10. *Mai* (dance, i.e., Nō-type) plays. These are closely based on particular Nō plays or follow the Nō style in their composition; e.g., *Tsūen.* (7 plays.)

11. *Zatsu* (miscellaneous) plays. A general group for plays not covered by the preceding categories, it includes a few newly written *kyōgen*; e.g., *Susugigawa.* (62 plays.)

Stage Properties and Sound Effects — *Kyōgen* uses the same stage as Nō, and similarly few properties, but of the props used, some are the same as in Nō and others, like the "horse" or "ox," consisting essentially of tufted canes, are unique to *kyōgen*. The fan is widely used in both to represent a variety of objects and actions. *Kyōgen* also uses as stage props a range of small, realistic everyday objects such as tools and kitchen utensils. It is one of the humorous and unaffected aspects, peculiar to *kyōgen*, that, when sound effects become necessary, the actor makes his own as he is performing.

Costumes and Masks — *Kyōgen* costume is markedly different from the rich and lavish brocades so characteristic of Nō. Although it contains many varied types, *kyōgen* costume is based on the dress of the ordinary people of medieval Japan, as typified by the dress of its two stock characters: the servant Tarō-kaja, who wears a bold-check underrobe, a wide-shouldered sleeveless top robe (*kataginu*), and *hakama* trousers (*kyōgenbakama*), and his master, who dresses in a bold-striped underrobe, *kataginu*, *hakama* trousers with the legs trailing along the ground, and a sword. *Kyōgen* players are further distinguished from Nō performers by their use of yellow socks (*tabi*) instead of the usual white ones.

The most typical *kyōgen* plays do not use masks, even when the role is that of a woman. There are, though, some 20 types of mask — some that were adapted from Nō masks — available for special characters: supernatural beings, some humans, and animals. Some animal masks are used along with imitation skins to cover the player completely.

Importance of Kyōgen — *Kyōgen* has always been overshadowed by Nō, which consciously strove to reach the highest levels of aesthetic development, and it is easy to underrate *kyōgen*'s value and the difficulty of its performance. If its players do not need to have quite the same degree of slow precision as the main actors in Nō and do not perform in the same kind of tense and solemn atmosphere, they must instead have a wider range of talent. At times their performances include singing and dancing similar to that in Nō, and they must always have in addition the indefinable qualities needed for an effective comic performance.

With a history that shows it to be centuries older even than Nō, *kyōgen* is important on another level for the linguistic value of its texts, its portrayal of many aspects of life in medieval Japan, its preservation of a variety of popular songs and musical styles, and its uses as a rich source of material and comic inspiration by many later forms of literature and drama, especially kabuki. *Kyōgen* has survived and has, in recent years, gained international acclaim as a dramatic form with settings and characters that, although of a specific time in Japanese history, have a humor and humanity that make their appeal universal.

Kyōgoku family　京極氏

(Kyōgokushi). Warrior family active from the Kamakura (1185–1333) through the Edo (1600–1868) periods (not to be confused with the courtier family that produced such outstanding poets as KYŌGOKU TAMEKANE). An offshoot of the Sasaki family of the Uda Genji branch of the MINAMOTO FAMILY, it was founded by Sasaki Nobutsuna's (1180–1242) fourth son, Ujinobu, who was appointed military governor (SHUGO) of the northern half of Ōmi Province (now Shiga Prefecture) by the Kamakura shogunate. Ujinobu took the name Kyōgoku from his place of residence in Kyōto; his brother Yasutsuna, who took the name Rokkaku, was appointed *shugo* of the southern half of Ōmi (see ROKKAKU FAMILY). The family prospered for several generations, but after the ŌNIN WAR (1467–77) fell into decline and lost most of its domains. In the Azuchi-Momoyama period (1568–1600) Kyōgoku Takatsugu (1563–1609) served the national unifiers ODA NOBUNAGA and TOYOTOMI HIDEYOSHI, and the family's fortunes revived.

Kyōgoku Tamekane　京極為兼

(1254–1332). Poet; courtier. Tamekane belonged to the Kyōgoku, one of the rival poetic branches of the Fujiwara family descended from FUJIWARA NO SADAIE (Fujiwara no Teika) through his son FUJIWARA NO TAMEIE, Tamekane's grandfather. Both poetic and political activities brought Tamekane into conflict with NIJŌ TAMEYO (1250?–1338), another grandson of Tameie. Their disagreement over plans for an imperial anthology led to a Nijō polemic against Tamekane, *Nomori no kagami* (Mirror of the Watchman of the Fields).

In 1311 Tamekane was commanded by the abdicated emperor Fushimi to compile the 14th imperial anthology, which he entitled GYOKUYŌ WAKASHŪ (*Gyokuyōshū;* Collection of Jeweled Leaves). Tamekane, an innovative poet, took the opportunity to include as much poetry as possible from his supporters and as little as possible from Nijō's supporters. The resulting anthology of 2,796 poems is the largest of all 21 imperial collections. Of the many poems Tamekane is thought to have written, only the 132 poems preserved in imperial anthologies survive.

Kyōgyōshinshō　教行信証

(full title: *Ken jōdo shinjitsu kyōgyōshō monrui;* A Collection of Passages Revealing the True Teaching, Practice, and Attainment of the Pure Land). The major work of SHINRAN (1173–1263), the founder of the JŌDO SHIN SECT of Buddhism. The *Kyōgyōshinshō* consists of six chapters structured on the most significant of the 48 vows fulfilled by the Buddha AMIDA. Chapter 1 reveals the *Muryōjukyō* (The Scripture of Immeasurable Life) as the "True Teaching" among the Mahāyāna sutras, for expounding the Primal Vow of Amida which affirms the enlightenment of all sentient beings. Chapter 2, on "True Practice," elaborates upon the name of Amida (see NEMBUTSU) and encourages its recitation as the supreme religious act. Chapter 3, "True Faith," demonstrates the working of Amida in releasing beings from blind passion to an openness to the world. Chapter 4, entitled "True Attainment," discusses the ultimate goal of the Buddhist life as *nirvāna*, which liberates beings to work for the salvation of all existence. Chapter 5, on the "True Land and True Buddha," shows their content as being inconceivable light and immeasurable life, metaphors for wisdom and compassion. Chapter 6 criticizes false and incomplete teachings under the title "Provisional Land and Provisional Buddha." The contrast between the first five chapters, revealing true reality, and this final chapter highlights the significance of Shinran's religious thought.

Kyōhō Famine　享保の飢饉

(Kyōhō no Kikin). The first of three major famines during the Edo period (1600–1868); it occurred in southwestern Japan in 1732 (Kyōhō 17) as a result of a severe locust plague and an unseasonably cold and wet summer. Stricken farmers flocked to the cities to seek relief, further adding to the misery of urban residents, and early in 1733 a large riot (UCHIKOWASHI) broke out in the shogunal capital of Edo (now Tōkyō). The Tokugawa shogunate organized relief efforts, emptying its own grain reserves and granting loans and tax remissions to the most severely afflicted areas. It issued directives prohibiting rice hoarding, limiting *sake* production, and exhorting wealthy individuals and religious institutions to provide food for the starving. In the domains a total of 1,990,000 were affected, and more than 12,000 died of starvation. Relief finally came with the bumper crops of 1734 and 1735. See also TEMMEI FAMINE; TEMPŌ FAMINE.

Kyōhō Reforms　享保の改革

(Kyōhō no Kaikaku). A series of reforms and retrenchments carried out by the Tokugawa shogunate during the Kyōhō era (1716–36) and the following decade under the direction of the eighth shōgun, TOKUGAWA YOSHIMUNE. The Kyōhō Reforms have traditionally been regarded as the most successful of the three great retrenchments of the Edo period (1600–1868) and as the model for the KANSEI REFORMS of the 1780s and 1790s and the TEMPŌ REFORMS of the 1840s.

The immediate intent of the Kyōhō reforms was to resolve the financial crisis facing the shogunate and the *samurai* class as a result of the increasing disparity between the theoretical socioeconomic power of the

Kyō Machiko This actress's inspired performances in a number of internationally acclaimed Japanese films have assured her place in Japanese cinema history.

samurai and the structural reality that had evolved since the founding of the shogunate. The reforms sought both to increase the financial resources available to the shogunate and to make it possible for the shogunate and samurai class to live within their means.

Although the reforms were basically economic, they had important political repercussions. These included the further enhancement and institutionalization of the personal authority of the shōgun; the expansion and development of bureaucratic offices, particularly those under the aegis of the commissioners of finance (KANJŌ BUGYŌ); and closer control of the intendants (DAIKAN) responsible for local governance of shogunate territories (TENRYŌ).

According to one historical analysis, the initial stage of the reform (1716–22) concentrated on retrenchment through curbing of expenditures and restoration of the currency. Such measures failed to solve the financial crisis, however, and in 1721–22 the shogunate was unable to pay its retainers' stipends in full. Under such pressures, the reform entered a more active phase (1722–36). To meet its immediate financial needs, the shogunate levied a series of forced loans on the *daimyō* in return for which it relaxed the SANKIN KŌTAI regulations, which required the daimyō to spend approximately half their time in Edo (now Tōkyō). The shogunate also instituted measures such as the shift to the JŌMEN system of tax levy designed to increase its absolute tax yield. The tax income of the shogunate began to rise steadily, enabling it to abolish the forced loans and restore the *sankin kōtai* regulations in 1731. Thereafter, however, the shogunate's tax income again declined in the face of peasant protests, demands for tax relief, and economic stagnation.

These problems were surmounted only by the fundamental shift in direction that marked the third stage of the reform (1736–45). The shogunate again adopted an expansionary financial policy, reverting to the debasement of gold and silver. Simultaneously the shogunate resumed a hard-line policy on increasing the tax yield, balanced by greater tolerance of the penetration of the countryside by urban merchant capital. These trends laid the groundwork for the commercial development and close shogunate-merchant ties characteristic of the ensuing Tanuma period of the 1760s to 1780s.

Kyōiku Chokugo→Imperial Rescript on Education

kyōiku kanji 教育漢字

(literally, "education *kanji*"). Popular name for the Chinese characters (KANJI) that Japanese students are expected to have learned to read and write by the end of elementary school. In 1946, 1,850 characters out of the existing thousands were named *tōyō kanji* (Chinese characters for daily use). Of these, 881 were designated in 1948 as the most essential characters, which are supposed to be learned within the six years of elementary school. In 1968, 115 more *tōyō kanji* were added, increasing the *kyōiku kanji* to 996. In 1981 the *tōyō kanji* were increased to 1,945 characters and the name changed to JŌYŌ KANJI (Chinese characters for common use), but the number of *kyōiku kanji* remained 996, with the remaining *jōyō kanji* to be learned by the ninth grade.

Kyōiku Kihon Hō→Education, Fundamental Law of

kyojin legends 巨人伝説

(*kyojin densetsu*). In Japan there are many legends linking giants (*kyojin*) to the creation of mountains, lakes, marshes, and islands. The 8th-century chronicles KOJIKI and NIHON SHOKI both contain stories in which the giant male and female deities IZANAGI AND IZANAMI create the Japanese islands. Later giants were no longer worshiped as deities; stories of them came to be passed down in legends throughout Japan, depicting them as superhuman creatures with extraordinary powers. See also ONI; YAMAMBA; TENGU.

kyōka 狂歌

(literally, "mad verse"). A comic variant of the 31-syllable WAKA. *Kyōka* depended heavily on the KAKEKOTOBA (pivot word) and *engo* (related word) techniques of *waka* but often used vocabulary and subject matter foreign to that genre for parodic effect. Although various theories exist concerning its origins, *kyōka* as a genre did not come into its own until the Edo period (1600–1868).

In Kyōto it was developed by the poet MATSUNAGA TEITOKU, who published a volume of "mad verse" in 1636. NAGATA TEIRYŪ became the first poet to make a living by writing *kyōka* and in the process established the "Naniwa," or Ōsaka, variant of the genre. His anthology *Kyōka iezuto* (1729) established his fame and the future of the form.

The Edo, or Temmei, style (named after the period 1781–89) was developed by the disciples of the *waka* poet Uchiyama Gatei (1723–88), notably KARAGOROMO KISSHŪ and ŌTA NAMPŌ, and flourished during the 1770s and 1780s. The excitement created by the Edo *kyōka* reached throughout Japanese society—it was popular among *samurai* and commoners alike—and brought its practitioners adulation and prestige. *Kyōka* poets were sought out by UKIYO-E artists, who published many of their works on special small-edition prints called SURIMONO. The appeal to poets and readers of all classes, however, proved too unsettling to a state that had always preferred clear separation among classes and was not fond of satire; during the KANSEI REFORMS (ca 1787–93), *kyōka* became a significant target for suppression. The form survived, but never again regained the popularity it once enjoyed.

kyōkaku 侠客

General term for gangsters during the Edo period (1600–1868). The common Japanese usage of the term, meaning "righteous" or "valiant" (*kyō*) and "outsider" (*kaku*), dates from the 19th century. The early-17th-century equivalent was *kabukimono* or *otokodate*. The *kyōkaku* organization was much like that of the modern YAKUZA, composed of a head man and his followers (OYABUN-KOBUN) and known as a gang (KUMI). Major *kyōkaku* groups in Edo (now Tōkyō) included those in the service of the shōgun's bannermen (HATAMOTO YAKKO) and unattached town groups (MACHI YAKKO). There were also numerous *kyōkaku* groups in provincial towns who were primarily gamblers. Some *kyōkaku* have become legendary heroes through glorification in KABUKI plays, modern KŌDAN and NANIWA-BUSHI, and films.

Kyokutei Bakin→Bakin

Kyokuyō Co, Ltd ［株］極洋

(Kyokuyō). Japan's fourth largest fishing company. Incorporated in 1937. Kyokuyō originally operated factory ships in Atlantic whaling operations. Today it is engaged in trawling and other types of fishing and in the importation and processing of various types of seafood. The company also operates refrigerator ships and freezing warehouses. Sales for the fiscal year ending March 1991 totaled ¥191.3 billion (US $1.4 billion). Capitalization stood at ¥5.7 billion (US $41.5 million) in the same year. Headquarters are in Tōkyō.

Kyō Machiko 京マチ子

(1924–). Film actress. Real name Yano Motoko. Born in Ōsaka. Kyō's first featured role was in *Saigo ni warau otoko* (1949, He Who Laughs Last). Her talent was recognized after an acclaimed performance as the bride in RASHŌMON (1950), director KUROSAWA AKIRA's elaborately woven tale of rape and murder. Her glamour and starring roles in such award-winning films as MIZOGUCHI KENJI's UGETSU MONOGATARI (1953, shown abroad as *Ugetsu*) and KINUGASA TEINOSUKE's *Jigokumon* (1953, Gate of Hell) made her a leading performer in Japanese motion pictures for almost two decades and brought her international recognition.

Her other outstanding pictures include NARUSE MIKIO's *Ani imōto* (1953, Older Brother, Younger Sister), ICHIKAWA KON's *Kagi* (1959, The Key; shown abroad as *Odd Obsession*), and YOSHIMURA KŌZABURŌ's *Onna no kunshō* (1961, Women's Prize). She is known to Western audiences for her role in Daniel Mann's *Teahouse of the August Moon* (1956).

Kyōō Gokokuji→Tōji

Kyōritsu Women's University 共立女子大学

(Kyōritsu Joshi Daigaku). A private university for women in Chiyoda Ward, Tōkyō. Originally established in 1886 as the Kyōritsu Joshi Shokugyō Gakkō (Kyōritsu Women's Vocational School) to educate self-reliant women for the modern age, it achieved university status in 1949. The university maintains faculties of home economics, arts and letters, and international studies. Enrollment in 1989 was 2,961.

kyoryūchi 居留地

Restricted areas for foreign residence and commerce established by the Japanese government after the ANSEI COMMERCIAL TREATIES of 1858 opened Japan to trade with Western nations. The *kyoryūchi* were self-governing units and the only places in the country where foreigners were allowed to live and move about freely. Entrance by Japanese and exit by foreigners were strictly controlled. The first of these settlements was built in Yokohama in 1859; it was followed by others in Nagasaki, Kōbe, Ōsaka, and Edo (now Tōkyō). With the revision of the Ansei Treaties in 1899 (see UNEQUAL TREATIES, REVISION OF), restrictions on foreigners within Japan were lifted, and the *kyoryūchi* were abolished. See also NAICHI ZAKKYO.

kyōsai nenkin→mutual aid association pensions

kyōsei shikkō 強制執行

(execution of judgment). Judicial proceeding to enforce obligations embodied in a judgment or other document given executory force under the law (such as notarial deed, record of settlement, or record of conciliation) and also to foreclose contractual or other liens (such as a mortgage) for the benefit of a lien creditor. This proceeding is now regulated by the Civil Judgment Execution Law (Minji Shikkō Hō) of 1979, effective 1 October 1980. There are different kinds of execution of judgment: (1) execution to enforce monetary obligations; (2) execution to enforce an obligation to deliver a certain object; (3) execution to enforce an obligation to do or to refrain from doing a certain act; and (4) lien foreclosure proceedings.

kyōshi and kyōbun 狂詩と狂文

(*kyōshi to kyōbun*). Written from about 1770 to 1885, *kyōshi* (literally, "wild Chinese-style poetry") was poetry composed entirely in Chinese characters by poets who, though often observing the formal rules governing the composition of poetry in Chinese, would deliberately disregard accepted standards of decorum in language and subject matter. In form, *kyōshi* spans the range of *kanshi* (poetry written in Chinese). With a poetic line of either five or seven words, *kyōshi* could be as short as 4 lines or longer than 100. *Kyōbun* (literally, "wild prose") was Chinese prose that, much like *kyōshi*, treated unconventional themes in a mock-serious classical style.

Chinese poetry was the quintessential cultural embellishment of the ruling class, its practice according to accepted norms demonstrating commitment to shared cultural values and to the philosophy that shaped the lives of the upper-class *samurai*. *Kyōshi*, on the other hand, was primarily written by members of the lower samurai class, and by 1800 it had been taken up by relatively uneducated samurai as well as by members of the *chōnin* (townsman) class with pretensions to upper-class culture. *Kyōshi* can thus be seen as a response to a particular social and cultural milieu. Though short-lived as a poetic genre, *kyōshi*'s use of new language and themes hitherto thought unsuited to the poetic tradition had the effect of pushing *kanshi* in a perceptibly new direction.

Among the most highly accomplished *kyōshi* poets were Ōta Tan (1749–1823), more familiar for his work in the KYŌKA genre of humorous verse under the name ŌTA NAMPO, and Hatanaka Tanomo (1752–1801), best known under the pen name Dōmyaku Sensei.

kyōtaku 供託

(public deposit). Deposits of money or materials made by a party (obligor) with a public deposit office (*kyōtakusho*) in order to discharge an obligatory duty with respect to the obligee and to obtain release from said obligatory duty. The public deposit system may be utilized for both monetary and nonmonetary obligations, but in actual practice it is most frequently used for the former. A public deposit is made under such circumstances as when the obligee has refused to accept payment or when the obligor is unable to identify the obligee.

Kyōtaru Co, Ltd [株]京樽

(Kyōtaru). Restaurant chain and take-out food service operator based in the Kantō area. Incorporated in 1950. The company has 2 branches in China and 47 branches in the United States. Sales for the fiscal year ending December 1990 totaled ¥76.3 billion (US $571.3 million), and capitalization was ¥12.3 billion (US $92.1 million). Headquarters are in Tōkyō.

Kyōto This early-17th-century folding screen depicting Kyōto city life, including a number of well-known landmarks, exemplifies the genre of decorative art known as *rakuchū rakugai zu*, or "scenes in and around the capital."

Kyōto 京都[市]

City in southern KYŌTO PREFECTURE, central Honshū, in the northern part of the Kyōto fault basin. The ancient capital of Japan and home of the imperial court from 794 to 1868, Kyōto, rich in historical sites and relics, is today the seat of the prefectural government and one of Japan's largest cities. Kyōto is renowned for its fine textiles and traditional products and is also a thriving center for industry.

Natural Features—The low Tamba Mountains surround the city to the north, east, and west. Two peaks, HIEIZAN and Atagoyama, dominate the northeast and northwest of the city. The rivers Kamogawa and Katsuragawa flow through the central and western districts of the city to join the Yodogawa in the south before draining into Ōsaka Bay. Kyōto's landlocked location accounts for its cold winters and hot summers. The annual average temperature is 15.2°C (59.4°F) and annual precipitation is 1,600 mm (63 in).

History—The Kyōto fault basin was first settled in the 7th century by the HATA FAMILY, immigrants from Korea. In 603 KŌRYŪJI, the family temple of the Hata, was constructed at Uzumasa in the western part of the basin. In 794 Kyōto, then called HEIANKYŌ, became the capital of Japan. The plan of the new city, like that of Heijōkyō in Nara, was patterned after China's Tang (T'ang) dynasty (618–907) capital of Chang'an (Ch'ang-an; modern Xi'an or Sian). Its rectangular shape measured 4.5 kilometers (2.8 mi) east to west and 5.2 kilometers (3.2 mi) north to south. During the Heian period (794–1185) residences of the powerful FUJIWARA FAMILY and TAIRA FAMILY were built in central Kyōto.

Kyōto was temporarily eclipsed as the center of national power by Kamakura during the Kamakura period (1185–1333), but during the Muromachi period (1333–1568) a shogunate was established in Kyōto, and the city regained its status as the nation's political center. Many major temples were built, including TENRYŪJI, NANZENJI, KINKAKUJI, and GINKAKUJI. During the ŌNIN WAR (1467–77), which signaled the end of the Muromachi shogunate, a large part of the city was destroyed.

During the Edo period (1600–1868) the Tokugawa shogunate was firmly established in Edo (now Tōkyō) and the political focus of the country again shifted away from Kyōto. However, the city still prospered as an artistic, economic, and religious center. Particularly notable were fabrics such as NISHIJIN-ORI and *yūzen-zome* (see YŪZEN), pottery (see KYŌTO CERAMICS), lacquer ware, doll making, and fan making. The city received a great blow when the capital was transferred to Tōkyō after the Meiji Restoration (1868), but responded with a rapid program of modernization.

Kyōto Today—Lacking a harbor and surrounding open land, Kyōto was slow in developing modern industries, but today, as part of the HANSHIN INDUSTRIAL ZONE, Kyōto has numerous electrical, machinery, and chemical plants. Its traditional industries continue to flourish. The city is also an educational and cultural center. There are some 37 universities and private institutes of higher learning, including Kyōto and Dōshisha universities. Kyōto has 24 museums, including the KYŌTO NATIONAL MUSEUM, and it possesses a total of 202 NATIONAL TREASURES (20 percent of the country's total) and 1,684 Important Cultural Properties (15 percent). In addition the city itself is a veritable historical storehouse. The KYŌTO IMPERIAL PALACE and the NIJŌ CASTLE are both remarkable examples of Japanese architecture. The KATSURA DETACHED PALACE with its lovely pond and teahouses, and the SHUGAKUIN DETACHED PALACE, famed for its fine garden, draw visitors from afar. Located close to Kyōto Station are two temples of the Jōdo Shin sect, NISHI HONGANJI and HIGASHI HONGANJI, both imposing examples of Buddhist architecture, as well as TŌJI, noted for its five-tiered pagoda.

East of the Kamogawa are the temple KIYOMIZUDERA, with its wooden platform built out over a deep gorge; the YASAKA SHRINE, where the annual GION FESTIVAL is held in July; and HEIAN SHRINE, where the annual JIDAI FESTIVAL is held in October. Other noted temples include CHION'IN; GINKAKUJI, built in 1482 and famed for its garden; and NANZENJI, situated in a pine grove east of Heian Shrine. In the northern part of the city are the KAMO SHRINES, where the AOI FESTIVAL is held in May each year. To the northwest are the Zen temple DAITOKUJI, with its priceless art objects; KINKAKUJI, with its three-story golden pavilion; NINNAJI, renowned for its cherry blossoms; and KŌRYŪJI. The natural beauty of the Honzukyō gorge, the Sagano district, and the hills of Takao also attracts visitors. Kyōto is the national center for the tea ceremony and flower arrangement and is the birthplace of NŌ, KYŌGEN, KABUKI, and other traditional performing arts. Area: 610.6 sq km (235.7 sq mi); pop: 1,461,140. ➡ *See map, next two pages.*
860–863 *864–865*

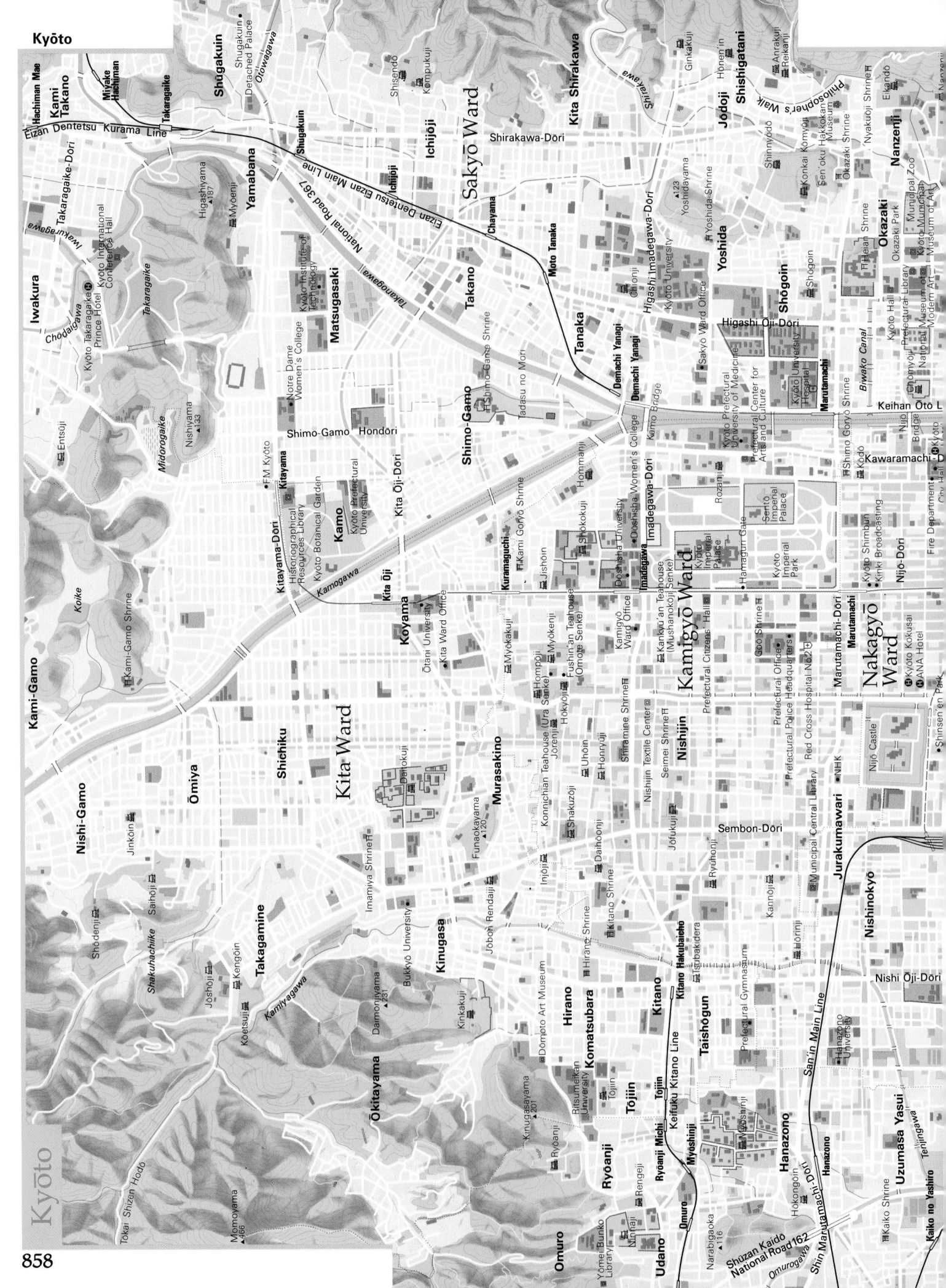

Kyōto

858

1:30,000

1mile

1km

Ukyō Ward

Higashiyama Ward

Yamashina Ward

Shimogyō Ward

Fushimi Ward

Minami Ward

Nishikyō Ward

Hinooka
Kujōyama
Zushioku
Awadaguchi
Kita Kazan
Kami Kazan
Kawata
Nishinoyama
Kanshūji
Seikanji
Kiyomizu
Inariyama
Shōren-in
Chion-in
An'yōji
Kyōto University
Kwazan Observatory
221 Kazan
Seikanji
Inariyama
Kyoto University Kwazan Observatory

Yasaka Shrine
Maruyama Park
Minamiza Theater
Chōrakuji
Higashi Ōtani
Kaburenjō Hall
Gion Kōbu
Ninenzaka
Kōdaiji
Kiyomizuzaka
Sannenzaka
Kiyomizudera
Kwazan Tunnel
Tomb of Toyotomi Hideyoshi
Higashiyama Tunnel
Kannonji
233 Inariyama
Fushimi Inari Shrine
Sekihōji
Hōtōji
Zuikōji

Gion Kōbu
Kenninji
Nishi Ōtani
Shōrinji
Kyōto Women's College
Tōkaidō Shinkansen
Higashiyama Ward Office
Myōhōn
Shin Hie Shrine
Imakumano
Sennyūji
Tōfukuji
Sennyūji
Nara Line

Shijō
Gion
Kawaramachi
Hōkoku Shrine
Chōshakuji
Yōgen-in
Red Cross Hospital No.1
Inari
Fukakusa
Biwako Canal
Keihan Main Line
Fujinomori

Shin Seiganji
Shijō
Shijō
Bridge
Hankyū
Dept-Store
Rakutō Hospital
Hōkōji
Kyōto National Museum
Sanjūsangendō
Fukuine
Ryūkoku University
National Road 24
Keihan Main Line
Takasegawa

Shin Kyōgoku
Nishiki Market
Fuji Daimaru
Dept. Store
Takashimaya Dept. Store
Shōkōji
Bukkōji
Hōkoku Shrine
Shōseien Garden
Kintetsu Dept. Store
Kyōto Tower
Central Post Office
Fukakusa
Tōfukuji
Takeda Kaidō
Fushimi Inari
Kami Tobaguchi
Kuinabashi

Rokkakudō
Daimaru Dept. Store
Byōdōji
Higashi Honganji
Kyōto
Higashi Kujō
Kujō
Takeda Kaidō
Jūjō
Fushimi Ward

Kawaramachi Sanjō
Sanjō
Keihan Sanjō
Keihan Keishin Line
Zushioku

Karasuma-Dōri
Karasuma
Karasuma Line
Higashi Honganji
Shichijō-Dōri
Kyōto Grand
Shimogyō Ward Office
Shichijō
Nishi Kujō
Kujō-Dōri
Kujō
Jūjō-Dōri
Jūjō
Kami Tobaguchi
Takeda

Horikawa-Dōri
Gojō-Dōri
Gojōten Shrine
Ōmiya-Dōri
Shimabara
Sumiya
Tambaguchi
Nishi Honganji
Kōshōji
Tōji
Rokusonō Shrine
Hachijō
Nishi Kujō
Daitsūji
Tōji
National Road 171
Karahashi
Minami Ward Office
Minami Ward
Kami Toba
National Road 1

Ōmiya
Shijō
Ōmiya
Shimogyō Ward

Mibu
Chūdōji
Kyōto Research Park
Umekōji Steam Locomotive Museum
Municipal Hospital
Sujaku
Nishi Shichijō
Central Wholesale Market
Shimabara
Toba Kaidō
Nishi Takasegawa
Kuzebashi-Dōri
Kichishōin Shima

Saiin
Sai
Saiin
Hankyū Kyōto Line
Nishi Shichijō
Shichijō Goshonouchi
Hachijō-Dōri
Hachijō
Karahashi
Toba Kaidō
Kichishōin Ishihara
Kichishōin
Kichishōin Shinden

Yamanouchi
Yamanouchi
Kyōto University of Foreign Studies
Nishi Kyōgoku Sports Center
Kōka Women's College
Nishi Kyōgoku
Kichishōin Nakagawara
Nishi Ōji
Kichishōin Shinden
Kichishōin

Nishi Kyōgoku
National Road 9
Nishi Kyōgoku Sports Center
Tenjingawa
Kuze Bridge
Katsuragawa

Katsura Detached Palace
Katsura Bridge
Katsura
Tenjingawa
Ushigase
Kuze
Kōfukuji
Nishikyō Ward

Katsuragawa
Kamogawa
National Road 1

Business and Commercial District	Residential Area
Hotel	Hospital	Temple

Governmental or Public Facility
Cultural Facility
Historical Site
Shrine
Cultural Facility
Industrial or Transport Facility
Meishin Expressway
Railway
Subway
Ward Boundary
Subway Under Construction

859

The Four Seasons of Kyōto

There are few places on this earth where people and nature commingle as gracefully as in Kyōto, the city that reigned as Japan's capital for a millennium. Because Kyōto is surrounded on three sides by steep, wooded hills that reflect the cycle of the seasons, its residents have a heightened awareness of the time of year. They need only lift their eyes from the narrow back streets lined with *machiya*, or traditional townhouses, to take in the panorama of a distant ridge bedecked in autumn foliage, a blanket of snow, or the bright green of early spring. The passage of seasons is also evident in the peaceful gardens of Kyōto's nearly 2,000 temples and shrines and in the colorful festivals and celebrations held throughout the year.

The arts, crafts, and cuisine for which Kyōto is famous consistently refer to seasonal motifs. So too do many of the masterpieces of Japanese literature that were created in the ancient capital. In classic works like the *Genji monogatari* (Tale of Genji), the *Makura no sōshi* (The Pillow Book), and the *Kokinshū* (Collection from Ancient and Modern Times), the four seasons of Kyōto are preserved in enduring form.

Spring

Kyōto's March winds usher in three months of spring rituals and celebrations, including the Hina Matsuri (Doll Festival), *hanami* (cherry-blossom viewing), the traditional dances known as Miyako Odori, and the Aoi Festival. Cherry blossoms are perhaps the most vivid feature of spring in Kyōto, and the city abounds in historic sites renowned for their trees. The glorious spectacle at Maruyama Park, the temple Kiyomizudera, or the river Shirakawa may have inspired the 9th-century monk Sosei when he wrote of letting "my eyes roam over / the swirl of willows and cherries / as the capital puts on her spring best."

A cherry tree in flower over the river Shirakawa in the Gion district.

Dolls on display at the temple Hōkyōji during the Hina Matsuri (Doll Festival) in March. Female members of the imperial family often cloistered themselves here, and the temple's collection includes several hundred *hina* dolls from the Imperial Palace.

During the Miyako Odori festival of traditional dance held throughout April in the Gion district, lanterns are hung beneath the eaves of teahouses, signaling that the *geisha* and their apprentices (*maiko*) are dancing.

A palanquin carries the figure of an *itsukinomiko*, an unmarried female relative of the emperor, in a 500-person procession held in May as part of the Aoi Festival.

Summer

Weeks of rain herald the hot and humid weather that typifies Kyōto summers. Along the banks of the Kamogawa, diners take their evening meal on platforms above the cool riverbed. Sprinkling water on rock-lined floors or retreating behind rattan blinds are other ways Kyōto residents seek relief from the heat. By mid-July music fills the streets as the Gion Festival slowly builds to its tumultuous climax. When candles are lit at the temple Adashino Nembutsudera to console the dead, Kyōto's summer has come to an end.

夏

Tiny alleyways such as this one in Nishijin wind their way through older neighborhoods. Splashing water on the stone-lined paths and placing wooden grates over the windows help Kyōto residents stay cool.

Kimono, byōbu (screen paintings), and other household treasures are aired out and displayed in a family's parlor during the Byōbu Festival in mid-July, part of the monthlong Gion Festival. The public usually views displays such as this through latticed windows.

As the heat peaks, geisha and their apprentices (*maiko*) make the rounds on 1 August to pay their respects to the masters who have trained them and the teahouses that employ their services.

Floats called yamaboko move in a long procession down Shijō, Kawaramachi, Oike, and other major Kyōto thoroughfares as part of the Gion Festival held in July.

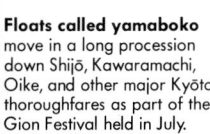

861

Autumn

In the *Kokinshū*, the poet Fujiwara no Toshiyuki observes, "The eye may not clearly see when autumn comes / but we are alerted to it by the sound of the wind." Autumn moon viewing, or *tsukimi*, a September ritual, is followed in October by the Jidai Festival at the Heian Shrine and the Hi Matsuri (Torch Festival) on Kuramayama. Before long, a rich carpet of fallen leaves covers the mountain paths through Sagano and Arashiyama. As the ensuing rains bring the colors of the leaves into full luster, the Kyōto autumn reaches its culmination.

Autumn colors stand out against the thatched roof of the Sagano area's Hiranoya teahouse, renowned for such specialties as *ayu*, or sweetfish, for over 400 years.

The Hi Matsuri (Torch Festival) at Yuki Shrine on Kuramayama, a hill in the northern part of the city. Participants light their torches in bonfires along the parade route and march up the hill.

On September nights on Ōsawa Pond at the temple Daikakuji, people reenact a Heian-period tradition by taking part in moon-viewing (*tsukimi*) banquets. They ride in paired boats that have dragon heads or mythical water birds carved on their prows.

The garden of a *ryokan*, or inn, near the Nishiki shopping district. The cluster of yellow flowers blooming on the *tsuwabuki* plants indicates that it is late autumn.

The sound reverberates throughout the city as monks at the temple Chion'in heave their weight against Japan's largest bell 108 times; this is known as *joya no kane*, the New Year's Eve tolling.

Ceramics and other goods are sold on the grounds of the temple Tōji on Kōbō feast days—the 21st day of every month. The January observance, which draws especially big crowds, is known as Hatsu Kōbō.

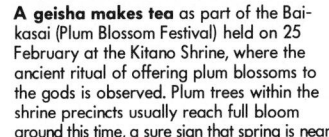

Winter

Winter in Kyōto begins in December, when the *kabuki* actors at the theater Minamiza "show their faces" (*kaomise*) to the public. Geisha in full dress add a dash of color to the streets as they make their year-end rounds visiting the people who trained them. The tolling of temple bells on New Year's Eve and the stream of visitors pouring into the Yasaka Shrine signal the onset of the city's chilliest season. As snow dances in the sky surrounding Mt. Hiei, yearly rituals are observed, such as the New Year's festivities, the Hatsu Kōbō feast day, and the Setsubun ceremony to dispel demons. After these events enliven the winter days, the plum blossoms at the Kitano Shrine begin to open, hinting that once again spring is on its way.

A geisha makes tea as part of the Baikasai (Plum Blossom Festival) held on 25 February at the Kitano Shrine, where the ancient ritual of offering plum blossoms to the gods is observed. Plum trees within the shrine precincts usually reach full bloom around this time, a sure sign that spring is near.

Snow falls on the bridge Tatsumibashi in the Gion district. On a bleak winter day, a colorfully clad woman makes her way through this neighborhood of historic teahouses.

Kyōto:
A Cultural Legacy

*Although 20th-century modernization steadily encroaches,
the aura of classical Japan still lingers in the ancient capital of Kyōto.*

Down through the dark cypress forests of Mt. Hiei, the call of a solitary cuckoo (*hototogisu*) awakens the poet Bashō from a restless sleep. From his hut on the mountainside overlooking the city of Kyōto, the 17th-century *haiku* master holds the ancient valley in his view. He lights the lamp and fumbles for his brush:

> Though I am in Kyōto
> I long for Kyōto . . .
> Song of the *hototogisu*.

What was this longing the wandering poet felt? Perhaps a vague sense of loss, nostalgia for a golden era and a city whose name was once synonymous with peace and tranquillity. Bashō's sentiment may have reflected a desire we all share to return to an enlightened place or moment in time. In Japan, that special place is Kyōto.

For more than a thousand years, from 794 to 1868, Kyōto reigned as capital of Japan and home of the imperial court. Poets, pilgrims, priests, tea masters, artists, and craftsmen all gathered there, and despite the city's turbulent history, Kyōto has remained the Japanese ideal of traditional culture and refinement.

History and legend hide within the walls of every villa and temple. Hundreds of inconspicuous stone markers on street corners and in alleys designate the sites of famous incidents from Japan's past. You may find one in memory of a warlord's vanished pleasure palace while another may mark the spot where a famous *samurai* died. And art can still be found outside museum walls—gilded tiger screens, Zen scroll paintings, dragon ceilings, and sculpted Buddhas—in the half-light of the ancient temples and villas for which they were intended.

Although its modern thoroughfares and crowded back streets may appear bereft of greenery, Kyōto is a garden city. Its exquisite moss gardens are hidden from public view within the precincts of temples and shrines or within the inner recesses of traditional Kyōto houses.

There are almost 2,000 Buddhist temples and Shintō shrines in Kyōto. The enigmatic rock garden of Ryōanji—presumed to be the creation of the monk Sōami in the 16th century—is an invitation to contemplation. In its mysterious gathering of stones, you may see tigers and dragons and islands afloat on a sea of raked sand, or perhaps a quiet landscape of the inside of your own mind.

Kyōto's monuments do not boast their presence—they are wooden, man-sized, and contained. The beauty of Kyōto is quiet—the spirit of simplicity. Its greatest gardens are miniature landscapes. Its modest, raked sand-and-stone enclosures may depict great jutting crags in mid-sea or symbolize the ideal of austerity. Kyōto is potted, trimmed, and trained. It is a city like no other; it must be courted, engaged.

Go to Kinkakuji, Temple of the Golden Pavilion, at the foot of Kinugasayama. It was built by order of the shōgun Ashikaga Yoshimitsu in the late 14th century.

A *machiya* in the Gion Shimbashi district.

Yoshimitsu remarked to his retainers one hot summer day that he would like to see the mountain covered in snow. So powerful was he that his men covered the entire hill with pure white silk to please him—hence the legend of Kinugasayama ("Silk Hat Mountain").

Spared the bombings of World War II, the narrow streets of Kyōto still follow the original checkerboard pattern designed in the 8th century after the great Chinese capital, Chang'an. Kyōto holds the last of the handcrafted, tile-roofed town houses, although their number dwindles as each new high rise pierces the sky. Nicknamed the "bedrooms of eels," the long narrow *machiya*, or traditional town houses of Kyōto, share wooden walls with their concrete neighbors in this densely populated city.

Small neighborhood establishments—*tōfu* makers, *sake* stores, and public baths—and craftsmen's workshops housing lacquerers, candle makers, and fan painters can still be found on tiny back streets throughout the city. Inside these shops there are still many glimpses of an elegant past—in the luster of a hand-painted lacquer bowl, in the delicate shape of a sweet bean cake, or in the intricately woven pattern of colored threads that bind a common house broom. Kyōto has always attracted the finest craftsmen. The appellation "Kyō" before a product was a guarantee of the highest quality: Kyō *ningyō* (Kyōto dolls), Kyō *sensu* (Kyōto fans), Kyō *yūzen* (Kyōto dyeing), and a dozen others. Kyō *ryōri* is the name of the famed local cuisine, a multicourse meal carefully prepared and exquisitely arranged.

But today Kyōto belongs to the 20th century as surely as it belongs to the past. First-time visitors are startled by the city's eclectic face. The old wooden houses with their tile rooftops and quiet, handcrafted beauty are dwarfed by the new additions to the modern cityscape. Faced with a tower striped like a bowling pin and a liberal sprinkling of concrete and steel, a visitor can lose track of the thread that binds present to past. The famed classical beauty of Kyōto exists now only in pockets. The movement to preserve what is left of the city's traditional character struggles on against developers and their bulldozers.

Exploring Old Kyōto

"Kyōto is Eastern; its beauty is concealed, a secret to be wrested from it little by little," wrote Fosco Maraini, a 20th-century Florentine scholar. To discover the hidden treasures of this ancient city, you must explore on foot the narrow byways among the famous tourist destinations.

If you have just one day, follow the Philosopher's Walk (Tetsugaku no Michi) beside the stream in the eastern district (Rakutō), from the Temple of the Silver Pavilion (Ginkakuji) in the north to the temple Eikandō, and from there to the temple Nanzenji and the Yasaka Shrine. Culturally, this area is the most compact, including everything from Zen temples to the famous *geisha* quarters of Gion.

The central district (Rakuchū) has the densest concentration of shops old and

A bamboo grove in rural Sagano.

new—there, the Nishiki Market Street (Nishiki Kōji) is a colorful path to take. South of this street lie the temples Nishi Honganji and Higashi Honganji. The western region (Rakusei) contains the mountain district of Arashiyama, with its placid river and bamboo forests. The northern sector (Rakuhoku) holds the Kami-Gamo Shrine and some of the last vestiges of Kyōto countryside, with Ōhara, Kurama, and Kibune villages in the mountains beyond. Located in the southern district (Rakunan) are the Fushimi Inari Shrine, a shrine with the famous One Thousand Gateways (Sembon Torii) lining its path, and Fushimi Momoyama, a former castle town where *sake* has been made for more than 400 years.

Historic Preservation Districts

Amid the bustle and traffic of modern Kyōto, a movement has begun to protect some of the *machinami*, the traditional districts of row houses, before they disappear. To date, four small neighborhoods have been protected by law. A grass-roots movement, worthy of international support, is struggling to preserve the historic character of other parts of the city as well. The four designated areas, which I will describe here, are best explored on foot.

Kiyomizu Sanneizaka—This area in eastern Kyōto was designated for protection in the 1970s. A sloping cobblestone path leads to the famous 1,000-year-old temple Kiyomizudera. Tea shops along the way have been serving pilgrims to the temple for centuries. Since the 1500s the surrounding hills have also been famous for the colorfully painted Kiyomizu ware crafted there.

Start at the south gate of the Yasaka Shrine and walk a few blocks to Ishibe Kōji, a quiet, narrow passageway that turns toward the mountains and leads past stone-walled villas and teahouses (*ochaya*) to the road in front of the temple Kōdaiji. From there continue southeast to Ninenzaka, the first of two cobblestone slopes that wind up the hill to Kiyomizudera. There are many fine traditional restaurants and sweetshops there, as well as along Sanneizaka (or Sannenzaka), where you'll find shops selling antiques, ceramics, and local crafts. Kiyomizudera crowns the hill, and the view from its grand platform should not be missed.

Gion Shimbashi—The heart of Kyōto's most famous geisha quarter is a five-minute walk from the center of town. Starting at the *kabuki* theater Minamiza on Shijō-Dōri, walk north on Nawate-Dōri to the canal and turn right. The triangular "island" that clings to the edge of the river Shirakawa here is named Shimbashi, after the bridge in front of little Tatsumi Shrine at the point of the triangle. The wooden-slatted, tile-roofed teahouses that line the streets belong to the romantic "floating world" of geisha depicted in *ukiyo*-e prints. At dawn, the quiet streets are deserted, but in the evening when the lanterns are lit, shadows move behind the night air. The *sake* and laughter have begun to flow, and geisha and their elaborately gowned *maiko* apprentices rustle past to disappear behind the sliding doors.

This world of traditional entertainment exists nowhere else in Japan today; it belongs to an age of elegance that has long since faded. Shops in the area sell items used by geisha: hair ornaments, fans, parasols, wooden clogs, and *kimono* accessories. Nearby Shimmonzen-Dōri is lined with antique shops, as is Nawate-Dōri north of Shijō.

Saga Toriimoto—Beside the vermilion *torii* gateway that leads to the Atago Shrine in western Kyōto is a stretch of thatch-roofed houses to remind visitors that within living memory this whole area consisted of rice paddies and farmhouses. Saga Toriimoto, as this district at the foot of the western mountains is called, is nearly all that is left of rural Kyōto. The walls of the old houses that line this slope have a heavier, more rustic character than the thinly slatted houses in the city center. Most of the old homes now function as shops and restaurants, set up to serve the many visitors who wend their way from temple to temple. A walking course that begins at the Togetsukyō, a bridge on the river Hozugawa in the Arashiyama district, leads through a bamboo forest and past a number of shops and smaller temples on its way up to Toriimoto.

Kami-Gamo Shake Machi—Founded in the 7th century, the Kami-Gamo Shrine is one of the oldest and most revered shrines in Kyōto. The neighborhood outside its gates has been known for centuries as Kami-Gamo *shake machi*, a town that housed the *shake*, or families of the priests, who tended this famous Shintō shrine. The stream that runs through the shrine precincts is sacred, and the priests built their homes outside the shrine along its banks. There were once more than 200 *shake machi* households in Kami-Gamo. If you follow the sacred stream down the narrow road that runs east of Kami-Gamo, you pass these clay-walled *shake machi* homes, one of which, the Nishimurake (Nishimura House), is a historic landmark. The gardens of these homes have streams, using water channeled from the sacred canal, and the priests used to bathe in these before attending official ceremonies held at the shrine. Records from the 17th century tell of a tightly knit township that had formed around the shrine to defend it in times of trouble. A system of moats encircled the town to help protect it from fire and warfare. The moats were also used to irrigate the fields. Compared with houses in downtown Kyōto, where the population was dense, the rural homes near the northern mountains were more spacious and airy. Today, pickled vegetables (*tsukemono*) are sold in several shops in this area.

There are other old neighborhoods that are not protected by law and are now rapidly changing. Walk through Nishijin, the weavers' district northwest of the Kyōto Imperial Palace. Visit Shimabara (northwest of Kyōto Station) or Kami Shichiken (near the Kitano Shrine) for a glimpse of two other old Kyōto geisha districts. Or wander the side streets between the temples Nishi Honganji and Higashi Honganji (directly north of Kyōto Station) to peek into the workshops of craftsmen making candles, lanterns, prayer beads, and elaborate Buddhist altars for the patrons of the two popular temples that border their neighborhood.

Three hundred years after his death, the aura Bashō longed for in Kyōto persists—behind the slatted windows of a fan shop, or the *noren* (split curtain) of an old-fashioned confectionery, or in the tiny interior gardens of a traditional inn. The spirit lives on in the hearts of the poets, pilgrims, and townspeople. With the help of those who love it, Kyōto may survive today's fashion for concrete and live on another thousand years.

Diane Durston

The bridge Togetsukyō leads to the hill district of Arashiyama.

Kyōto Basin 京都盆地

(Kyōto Bonchi). In southern Kyōto Prefecture, central Honshū. One of several fault
basins in the central Kinki (Kyōto-Nara-
Ōsaka) region, it consists of the floodplains
of the rivers Katsuragawa, Ujigawa, and
Kizugawa (all of which flow into the
Yodogawa). At the basin's north end lies the
city of Kyōto. Rice is cultivated on the lowlands in the south, where numerous industrial plants are also found. Area: approximately 270 sq km (104 sq mi).

Kyōto ceramics 京焼

(kyō-yaki). The ceramics produced in and
around the city of Kyōto, with the exception
of RAKU WARE. Sometimes called kiyomizu-
yaki, after the kilns in the Kiyomizu area of
Kyōto. Kyōto ceramics generally display a
high standard of technical proficiency and
decoration, including overglaze enamel
work. Three-colored lead-glazed wares
seem to have been made in Kyōto in the 8th
century and monochrome green wares from
the 9th to the 11th centuries. The next ware
known to have been produced there is
Oshikōji ware in the late 16th century. It
was probably colored and fired at low temperatures.

The first kyō-yaki kilns were probably established in the late 16th century. Potters
began to use stamps and seals for identification from about the mid-17th century.
Kyōto potters first used underglaze iron
oxide and cobalt for decoration. The most
characteristic kyō-yaki is probably overglaze
enameled ware. Kyōto potters were as
skilled at slab-building, reticulation, carving, and sprigging as they were precise at
throwing, and they frequently used glazes in
a special way. Some typical kyō-yaki is covered in a thick glaze of one color, often dark
blue or green, with additional decoration in
a restricted area. The decorative motif is
often built up in thick layers of enamel, giving a three-dimensional effect. Brown, gold,
and red were also used.

The history of Kyōto ware is punctuated
with the names of such famous potters as
NONOMURA NINSEI, Ogata KENZAN, OKUDA EISEN,
AOKI MOKUBEI, NIN'AMI DŌHACHI, and EIRAKU
HOZEN. The contemporary industry is generally flourishing, although oil, gas, and electric kilns have almost entirely replaced the
old wood-burning kilns.

Kyōto City University of Arts
京都市立芸術大学

(Kyōto Shiritsu Geijutsu Daigaku). A coeducational public university in the city of
Kyōto, Kyōto Prefecture. It maintains a faculty of arts and a faculty of music. The former can be traced back to the Kyōto Fu
Gagakkō (Kyōto Prefecture School of Arts)
founded in 1880, the oldest art school in
Japan. It was established as a university in
1950, and the faculty of music was added in
1969. Enrollment in 1989 was 749.

Kyōto Gozan →Gozan

Kyōto Imperial Palace 京都御所

(Kyōto Gosho). The former official residence
of Japanese emperors (the present IMPERIAL
PALACE is in Tōkyō). Situated in Kamigyō
Ward, Kyōto, on grounds occupying 11.3
hectares (27.8 acres). The palace, which was
originally one of the "provisional palaces"
(see SATODAIRI), became the official imperial
residence in 1331. It has been ravaged by fire
several times, undergoing numerous restorations, and was fully reconstructed in 1855.
After the Meiji Restoration of 1868, the
Kyōto Imperial Palace lost its status as the
official imperial residence; the capital of
Japan was relocated to Tōkyō, and in 1869
the former EDO CASTLE became the imperial
palace. The principal buildings on the Kyōto
Palace grounds, the Shishinden (main ceremonial hall) and Seiryōden (main palace
building), are in the architectural style of the
Heian period (794–1185). There are a number of other structures on the palace grounds,
including six traditional-style gates (the
principal gate is the Kenreimon). The facilities are managed by the Imperial Household
Agency and are open to public view every
spring and autumn.

Kyōto Institute of Technology
京都工芸繊維大学

(Kyōto Kōgei Sen'i Daigaku). A coeducational national university. Established in
1949 by a merger of the Kyōto College of Industry (founded 1902) and the Kyōto College of Textile Fibers (founded 1899). Kyōto
Institute of Technology maintains a faculty
of engineering and design and a faculty of
textile science. It engages in extensive teaching and research in such areas as electronics
and information science and polymer engineering. Enrollment in 1989 was 2,637.

Kyōto Municipal Museum of Art
京都市美術館

(Kyōto Shi Bijutsukan). Located in the city
of Kyōto. Opened in 1933, it was one of the
first public art museums established in Japan.
Works on exhibit are chiefly Japanese paintings, ceramics, and sculpture, dating from
the Meiji period (1868–1912) to the present,
by artists with connections to Kyōto, such as
TAKEUCHI SEIHŌ, UEMURA SHŌEN, and ASAI CHŪ.

Kyōto National Museum
京都国立博物館

(Kyōto Kokuritsu Hakubutsukan). Located
in Higashiyama Ward, Kyōto. First opened
in 1897 as the Imperial Kyōto Museum
(Teikoku Kyōto Hakubutsukan), it was originally built to house and display art treasures
owned by temples and shrines and items
donated by the Imperial Household Ministry. The museum's collection is divided into
three parts: fine arts, which includes sculpture, painting, and calligraphy; handicrafts,
which includes pottery, fabrics, lacquer
ware, and metalwork; and archaeology,
which includes objects of archaeological and
historical interest. The fine arts division has
especially impressive holdings, containing
more than 230 items that have been classified
as National Treasures (Kokuhō) or Important Cultural Properties (Jūyō Bunkazai). In
its especially valuable Japanese art collection
are such well-known items as a 12th-century
Gakizōshi (Scroll of Hungry Ghosts) and
SESSHŪ TŌYŌ's famous painting Amanohashidate.

Kyōto Prefectural University of
Medicine 京都府立医科大学

(Kyōto Furitsu Ika Daigaku). A coeducational public medical school in Kamigyō
Ward, Kyōto. The university originated in a
teaching hospital established in 1872. It became a university in 1921 and is one of the
oldest medical schools in Japan. Enrollment
in 1989 was 631.

Kyōto Prefecture 京都府

(Kyōto Fu). Located in central Honshū,
bounded by Fukui, Shiga, and Mie prefectures on the east, Nara Prefecture on the
south, and Hyōgo and Ōsaka prefectures on
the west. It faces the Sea of Japan to the
north. Kyōto Prefecture is divided roughly
into two parts, north and south, by the TAMBA
MOUNTAINS. The southern part, formerly
called Yamashiro Province, is centered on the
KYŌTO BASIN, and the northern part, formerly
called Tamba and Tango provinces, is composed of the TANGO MOUNTAINS. The southern
part flourished after the imperial capital was
moved in 794 to HEIANKYŌ, as Kyōto was then
known. The southern part of the prefecture,
of which the center is Kyōto, is part of the
TŌKAIDŌ MEGALOPOLIS and is undergoing continuous urbanization. The center of the
northern part is the port city of MAIZURU on
the Sea of Japan.

Geography and Climate—Kyōto Basin,
located in the southern part of the prefecture, is a graben basin. The horst mountains
surrounding the basin are generally low. Mt.
Hiei (HIEIZAN), located northeast of Kyōto, is
only 848 meters (2,782 ft) high. The mountains of Tango and Tamba in the northern
part of the prefecture are also not high; part
of the Tango Mountains forms the Tango
Peninsula and juts out into the Sea of Japan.
WAKASA BAY to the east forms a heavily indented coast with a number of good natural
harbors. The principal rivers of the prefecture are the UJIGAWA, the KATSURAGAWA, and
the KAMOGAWA, all in the southern part of the
prefecture and all of which flow into the
YODOGAWA. The only notable river in the
northern part is the YURAGAWA. The temperature tends to run to extremes in the Kyōto
Basin. Because of the Tsushima Current the
coastal regions on the Sea of Japan are
warmer in winter. Precipitation is heavier in
the north.

History— Remains from the Jōmon (ca
10,000 BC–ca 300 BC) and Yayoi (ca 300 BC–
AD 300) periods have been discovered in the
prefecture. After the 3rd century, the Kyōto
Basin was settled by naturalized immigrants
(KIKAJIN) from Korea and China. Under the
ancient provincial system (see KOKUGUN SYS-

TEM), Kyōto Prefecture was known as Yamashiro, Tamba, and Tango provinces. The prefectural system was established in 1871, and the boundaries of the prefecture were fixed in 1876.

Industries— Commerce, traditional industries, and tourism support the economy. Representative products include NISHIJIN-ORI and YŪZEN silks, Kiyomizu ware (see KYŌTO CERAMICS), lacquer wares, fans, dolls, and other crafts. The manufacture of these traditional wares is concentrated in the city of Kyōto. The northern part of the prefecture is renowned for its Tango *chirimen* silk and Fushimi *sake*. Modern industries include machinery, metal, and synthetic fiber industries. The southern part of the prefecture, an extension of the HANSHIN INDUSTRIAL ZONE, has highly developed industries. Farming is centered on rice cultivation, but vegetables are produced in the suburban districts surrounding Kyōto. Tea is grown on the highlands surrounding the Kyōto Basin, centering on the city of UJI. Cryptomeria and cypress grow from north of the city of Kyōto to the southern part of the Tamba Mountains. Fish such as yellowtail, mackerel, and sardine are caught off the coast of the Sea of Japan.

Tourism and Culture— As the capital region for over 1,000 years, Kyōto Prefecture has many historical sites. Each year more than 38 million people visit the city of Kyōto, whose attractions include the Imperial Palace, NIJŌ CASTLE, HEIAN SHRINE, and temples such as HONGANJI, KIYOMIZUDERA, NINNAJI, DAITOKUJI, KINKAKUJI, GINKAKUJI, KŌRYŪJI, and SAIHŌJI. The temple BYŌDŌIN in Uji, the gorge Hozukyō on the upper reaches of the river HOZUGAWA between Kameoka and ARASHIYAMA, and such places as Ōhara, Kurama, Sagano, and Takao on the outskirts of Kyōto are also well known. On the Sea of Japan coast are AMANOHASHIDATE and other scenic spots that belong to Wakasa Bay Quasi-National Park and SAN'IN COAST NATIONAL PARK. Area: 4,613 sq km (1,781 sq mi); pop: 2,602,460; capital: Kyōto. Other major cities include Uji, Maizuru, Jōyō, and NAGAOKAKYŌ. See also KYŌTO.

Kyōto Sangyō University
京都産業大学

(Kyōto Sangyō Daigaku). A coeducational private university established in 1965 in the city of Kyōto, Kyōto Prefecture. It maintains faculties of business administration, economics, engineering, foreign languages, law, and science. Enrollment in 1989 was 11,375.

Kyōto shoshidai
京都所司代

(Kyōto deputy). Originally a deputy (*dai*) to the head (*shoshi*) of the Board of Retainers (SAMURAI-DOKORO) of the Muromachi shogunate (1338–1573) after the Ōnin War (1467–77). Later the hegemons ODA NOBUNAGA and TOYOTOMI HIDEYOSHI appointed *shoshidai* to govern the populace of Kyōto. During the first half-century of the Tokugawa shogunate (1603–1867) the post was held in succession by three influential shogunal vassals: Okudaira Nobumasa (1556–1615), ITAKURA KATSUSHIGE, and the latter's son Shigemune (1586–1656). The Kyōto deputies oversaw the affairs of the imperial court and were responsible for the administration of justice in the adjacent provinces. They also supervised the city commissioners (MACHI BUGYŌ) of Kyōto, Fushimi, and Nara, and together with the keeper of Ōsaka Castle they were charged with surveillance of the *daimyō* of western

Japan. After Shigemune's retirement in 1654, 58 men served in the post; because of its political importance, they were usually middle-ranking FUDAI daimyō who were later promoted to senior councillors (RŌJŪ).

Kyōto shugoshoku
京都守護職

(military commissioner for Kyōto). A post established in September 1862 by the Tokugawa shogunate (1603–1867) to counteract the growing SONNŌ JŌI (Revere the Emperor, Expel the Barbarians) movement, which was centered in Kyōto. The new commissioner assumed full police powers in the Kyōto and Ōsaka areas. Except during the brief tenure of MATSUDAIRA YOSHINAGA, the post of Kyōto *shugoshoku* was held by MATSUDAIRA KATAMORI from its inception until the overthrow of the shogunate in 1867–68. The office should not be confused with that of military governor of Kyōto (Kyōto *shugo*), established in 1185 by the Kamakura regime (see KAMAKURA SHOGUNATE) to oversee Kamakura vassals stationed in Kyōto.

Kyōto University
京都大学

(Kyōto Daigaku). A national, coeducational university located in Sakyō Ward, Kyōto. The second national university in Japan, it was founded in 1897 as Kyōto Imperial University and renamed Kyōto University in 1949. Since its inception it has been known for its tradition of academic freedom. It maintains faculties of letters, education, law, economics, science, medicine, pharmacology, engineering, and agriculture. Kyōto University has the following research institutes: Yukawa Institute for Theoretical Physics, Research Institute for Mathematical Sciences, Research Reactor Institute, Primate Research Institute, Institute for Chemical Research, Research Institute for Humanistic Studies, Chest Diseases Research Institute, Institute of Atomic Energy, Wood Research Institute, Research Institute for Food Science, Disaster Prevention Research Institute, Institute for Virus Research, and Institute of Economic Research. Enrollment in 1989 was 12,495.

Kyōto University Incident
京大事件

(Kyōdai Jiken; abbreviation of Kyōto Daigaku Jiken). Term used to refer to a number of incidents involving the issues of university autonomy and academic freedom at Kyōto University.

The first, known as the Sawayanagi Incident after the name of the president of the university at that time, occurred in 1913; it involved protests by the faculty in order to gain autonomy in the hiring and firing of their colleagues (previously carried out by the university president at the behest of the Ministry of Education).

The Gakuren Incident witnessed the first use by the government of the new PEACE PRESERVATION LAW OF 1925 to suppress militant students associated with the Marxist-Leninist group Gakuren (Gakusei Shakai Kagaku Rengōkai, or Student Social Science Federation). The "incident" consisted of a series of arrests in December 1925 and January through April 1926 that marked the beginning of efforts by the government and university officials to eliminate the radical student movement.

The Takikawa Incident of 1933 signaled the spread of the prewar thought control system to affect even moderate liberals: a Kyōto University law professor, TAKIKAWA YUKITOKI, was forced to resign and two of his widely used textbooks on criminal law were banned

Kyōto University
A view of the university's main gate and, behind it, the clock tower constructed in 1924.

because of the favor he had supposedly shown to leftist students. A nationwide campaign by students and intellectuals to defend Takikawa had little success in the face of the hard-line stance taken by Education Minister HATOYAMA ICHIRŌ.

Postwar incidents in 1949, 1951, and 1955 carried on this prewar tradition of conflict between radical students and government and university officials. Although Takikawa was restored to his faculty post in 1946 and became president of the university in 1953, the limits of his prewar type of liberalism were revealed in his own attempts to contain the postwar student movement; Hatoyama, who had engineered Takikawa's ouster in 1933, became Japan's prime minister in 1954.

Kyōto University Research Institute for Humanistic Studies
京都大学人文科学研究所

(Kyōto Daigaku Jimbun Kagaku Kenkyūjo). Established in 1939, incorporating in 1949 the Institute of Oriental Culture (est 1929) and the private Research Institute of Western Culture (est 1946). It is composed of a Documentation Center for Oriental Studies and 17 research sections grouped under 3 departments focusing on the West, Japan, and the rest of Asia. Journals published include *Tōhō gakuhō*, *Jimbun gakuhō*, and *Zimbun* (an English journal for scholars abroad); library resources number about 420,000 volumes.

kyōtsūgo
共通語

(common Japanese). The term *kyōtsūgo* refers to linguistic usage common in Japanese society, in contrast to regional DIALECTS (*hōgen*) and other specialized forms. In general, *kyōtsūgo* is based on the language of the Tōkyō area. Because *kyōtsūgo* is rooted in actual linguistic practice, a conceptual distinction is made between it and *hyōjungo* (standard Japanese), which is a more normative term indicating the ideal standards for Japanese usage approved by scholars and other authorities on the language. In actuality, however, the two concepts are frequently confused. Before World War II, the teaching of *hyōjungo* was compulsory in the schools, but today it is *kyōtsūgo* that is emphasized, and there is even some consideration given to dialect forms as well. In daily life the majority of Japanese still generally use a mixture of *kyōtsūgo* and regional dialect, with the balance between the two being situationally determined. In recent years, however, partly as a result of the pervasive influence of the mass media, dialect forms have been weakening and *kyōtsūgo* has moved even further in the direction of becoming a truly "common language."

Kyōwa Hakkō Kōgyō Co, Ltd
協和醱酵工業[株]

(Kyōwa Hakkō Kōgyō). Manufacturer of pharmaceuticals, chemicals, alcohol, alco-

kyūdō After the introduction of firearms in the 16th century, Japanese archery gradually became more a means of physical and spiritual discipline than a practical martial art.

holic beverages, food, food additives, and cosmetics. Incorporated in 1949. In 1956 the company developed a fermentation process for the production of amino acids. Kyōwa Hakkō is also engaged in research on the use of alcohol as an alternative energy source. The company has 14 subsidiaries and representative offices overseas, including 4 in the United States. Sales for the fiscal year ending December 1990 were ¥288.5 billion (US $2.2 billion), distributed as follows: pharmaceuticals, 44 percent; chemicals, 26 percent; food and food additives, 19 percent; and alcohol and alcoholic beverages, 11 percent. The company was capitalized at ¥26.7 billion (US $199.9 million) in the same year. Headquarters are in Tōkyō.

Kyōwakai → Concordia Society

kyōyujo   教諭所
(literally, "place of instruction"). Educational facilities for commoners during the mid-Edo period (1600–1868); often established together with GŌGAKU. They offered lectures on the Confucian classics, everyday conduct, housekeeping, penmanship, and farming methods. They were dissolved at the time of the Meiji Restoration (1868).

kyōzuka → sutra mounds

kyū → moxa treatment

Kyūchū Bō Jūdai Jiken
宮中某重大事件
(literally, "Grave Incident in the Imperial Palace"). Dispute over the betrothal of Crown Prince Hirohito (later Emperor SHŌWA), lasting from 1919 to 1921. In June 1919 the imperial court officially announced its choice of a fiancée for the crown prince: Princess Nagako, daughter of Prince Kuni no Miya Kunihiko and granddaughter of Shimazu Tadayoshi (1840–97), the last *daimyō* of Satsuma (now Kagoshima Prefecture). YAMAGATA ARITOMO, the leader of the rival Chōshū (now Yamaguchi Prefecture) political clique, opposed the match. The incident was symptomatic of the continuing

rivalry between the Satsuma and Chōshū cliques (see HAMBATSU). In February 1921 the Imperial Household Ministry and the Home Ministry jointly declared that the betrothal was final. Yamagata's protégé Nakamura Yūjirō (1852–1928) took full responsibility for the incident and resigned from his position as imperial household minister. Prince Hirohito and Princess Nagako were married in 1924.

kyūdō   弓道
Japanese archery; literally, "the Way of the bow." *Kyūjutsu*, the technique of the bow, was the term more commonly used until well into the 19th century. Under the influence of Chinese culture from the 6th century, Japanese archery was divided into military and civil archery. Military archery was primarily mounted archery, while civil archery was shooting in the standing position, with emphasis on form and etiquette. Over the centuries the rules of archery became systematized, and schools began to proliferate. Those of the Ogasawara school, the Heki school, and the Honda school dominate modern *kyūdō*.

The bow is usually 2 meters 21 centimeters (7 ft 3 in) in length. It is an eccentric bow; that is, two-thirds of its length is above the grip and one-third below. Two target distances are used in modern *kyūdō* competition. Usually the archer stands 28 meters (92 ft) from a circular target 36 centimeters (14 in) in diameter. In contrast to Western archery, in *kyūdō* the emphasis is on form rather than accuracy. Certain schools are strongly influenced by Zen. The Amateur Archery Federation of Japan was formed in 1949; membership in 1990 was about 300,000.

Kyūji   旧辞
Also known as *Kuji*. An ancient collection of myths and legends, said to have been completed in the first half of the 6th century but no longer extant. *Kyūji*, along with the TEIKI, an imperial genealogy, is believed to have formed the basis for the KOJIKI (712) and NIHON SHOKI (720), Japan's oldest chronicles.

kyūsei kōtō gakkō → higher schools

Kyūshū Electric Power Co, Inc
九州電力[株]
(Kyūshū Denryoku). One of the nine Japanese electric companies. Incorporated in 1951, it supplies electricity to the island of Kyūshū. In the fiscal year ending March 1991 the firm had total revenue of ¥1.2 trillion (US $8.7 billion). In the same year capitalization stood at ¥236.3 billion (US $1.7 billion). Headquarters are in Fukuoka, Fukuoka Prefecture.

Kyūshū Institute of Technology
九州工業大学
(Kyūshū Kōgyō Daigaku). A coeducational national university. Founded as a private school, the Meiji College of Technology, in 1909, it became a national college in 1921 and was reorganized as a university in 1949. The university maintains faculties of engineering and of computer science and systems engineering. Enrollment in 1989 was 4,063.

Kyūshū Matsushita Electric Co, Ltd
九州松下電器[株]
(Kyūshū Matsushita Denki). Manufacturer of telecommunications products, business machines, and precision components. A member of the Matsushita Group. Incorporated in 1955. The company produces a vari-

ety of products, including electronic data terminals, computer printers, word processors, and home appliances. Sales for the fiscal year ending March 1990 totaled ¥242.7 billion (US $1.6 billion), 48 percent of which was derived from exports, and capitalization stood at ¥24.0 billion (US $156.8 million). Headquarters are in Fukuoka.

Kyūshū Mountains   九州山地
(Kyūshū Sanchi). Mountain range running northeast to southwest through central Kyūshū, dividing the island in two. The highest peak is Sobosan (1,757 m; 5,764 ft). It is the source of the rivers Ōnogawa, Kumagawa, and Mimikawa. The Kami Shiiba Dam, located on the Mimikawa, is Japan's first arch-type dam and a hydroelectric power source for Kyūshū. There are vast virgin forests of hemlock-spruce, fir, and beech. The village of Gokanoshō is said to have been settled by survivors of the TAIRA FAMILY after its defeat in the TAIRA-MINAMOTO WAR of the 12th century.

Kyūshū Railway Co
九州旅客鉄道[株]
(Kyūshū Ryokaku Tetsudō). Passenger railway company. Incorporated in 1987 after the privatization of the former Japan National Railways. It is engaged in passenger railway service in Kyūshū, as well as freight railway transport, bus transport, travel agency services, and warehouse services. Sales for the fiscal year ending March 1990 totaled ¥144.0 billion (US $970.7 million), and capitalization stood at ¥16.0 billion (US $104.5 million). Headquarters are in Fukuoka, Fukuoka Prefecture.

Kyūshū region   九州地方
(Kyūshū chihō). Region consisting of Kyūshū, the third largest and southernmost of the four major islands of Japan, and surrounding islands. The island of Kyūshū comprises Fukuoka, Nagasaki, Ōita, Kumamoto, Miyazaki, Saga, and Kagoshima prefectures. Okinawa Prefecture is included in the term Kyūshū when the latter is considered as a wide-area administrative unit. Geographically divided into north, central, and south Kyūshū, the region has a mountainous interior with numerous coastal plains, volcanoes, and hot springs. The climate is subtropical with heavy precipitation.

Rice, tea, tobacco, sweet potatoes, and citrus fruit are the major crops, and stock farming, hog raising, and fishery also flourish. Coal is mined, but its production is rapidly decreasing. Heavy and chemical industries are concentrated in northern Kyūshū. The major cities are Kita Kyūshū and FUKUOKA. Area (including Okinawa Prefecture): 44,420 sq km (17,150 sq mi); pop: 14,518,257.

Kyūshū University   九州大学
(Kyūshū Daigaku). A national, coeducational university whose main campus is in the city of Fukuoka. It was founded in 1910 as Kyūshū Imperial University. It became Kyūshū University in 1949. It maintains faculties of letters, education, law, economics, science, medicine, dentistry, pharmacology, engineering, and agriculture. Research institutes include the following: the Research Institute of Balneotherapeutics, Research Institute of Applied Mechanics, Research Institute of Industry and Labor, and Research Institute of Industrial Science. Enrollment was 10,570 in 1989.

labor 労働

(*rōdō*). Organized labor in Japan traces its beginnings to the late 19th century, when industrialization first took hold and an industrial working class began to emerge. However, many decades passed before unions became firmly established, and it was not until after 1945 that Japan developed a durable labor movement.

Emergence of an Industrial Labor Force——At the time of the MEIJI RESTORATION (1868), the Japanese economy was primarily nonindustrial, with as much as 80 percent of the working population engaged in farming and fishing. There was no rationally organized labor market that could provide the labor force necessary for further industrialization. As a result there were constant shortages of workers in Japan's new industries, despite the existence of a large pool of surplus labor engaged in small-scale agricultural activities.

In the heavy industries the supply of skilled labor initially centered on craftsmen from traditional trades who received technical training from FOREIGN EMPLOYEES OF THE MEIJI PERIOD, and eventually from the inflow of labor from the excess agricultural population. During this early period of industrialization, semiskilled workers set themselves up as labor "bosses" (*oyakata*), each with his own group of client workers (*kokata*). Typically, these labor gangs would move from one work site to another, offering services to the highest bidder. The *oyakata* not only provided work for his clients, he also managed and supervised them in the work performed. The labor boss institution remained entrenched in parts of Japanese industry up to the end of World War II, when it was legally abolished as an undemocratic practice under the reforms of the Allied OCCUPATION. Before its abolition, however, it had already been on the wane for some 30 years.

As Japan's industrialization progressed, it became clear to the increasingly professional managers and technical personnel of large corporations that the *oyakata* and their clients did not possess the skills and discipline needed to cope with rapidly changing technology. These companies preferred to have direct control over their work forces and to be able to train the workers themselves. In their desire to eliminate inefficiencies and hold down labor costs, firms built up "closed," or internal, employment systems; this was the origin of the practice of "lifetime," or career-long, employment in large organizations. Another factor that underlay management's promotion of closed employment systems was the rise of labor unrest in Japan during the 1920s. In response, companies sought to appease workers by stressing corporate paternalism, an adaptation of premodern notions drawing on traditional Japanese family relationships and the social and political organization of the feudal period (see IE). Companies took in workers as members of the corporate family, and secured their loyalty within a tight superior-subordinate hierarchical structure in exchange for company welfare facilities and a stable livelihood. The corporate family, lifetime employment, and the seniority wage system, all with roots in the 1920s and 1930s, are practices that continue to the present.

Direct control of the labor force developed first in the textile industry, where employees were all factory workers. The great majority of these workers were young unmarried girls from rural areas. Obliged to work for a fixed period according to the terms of the contracts between their families and employers, they were called *dekasegi jokō* (female workers who returned home on termination of employment). They lived mostly in company dormitories and their freedom was severely restricted during their period of employment.

Working conditions for factory employees gradually improved after the passage of the FACTORY LAW OF 1911, but poor rural families continued to send their daughters away to work for low wages in the factories until the post–World War II labor reforms. Other industries also drew their workers from among the second and third sons of farming families who left their villages to become low-paid industrial workers. This was the basic pattern of labor supply throughout the process of Japanese industrialization.

Given labor market conditions, the early organization of labor unions remained limited and short-lived. In addition, political obstacles were also difficult to overcome as the 1889 CONSTITUTION OF THE EMPIRE OF JAPAN included no guarantees of workers' rights. Furthermore, out of a desire to sustain rapid industrialization based on low wages, the government severely repressed any signs of growing militancy among the working class. Class consciousness was slow to develop among the workers themselves, and a modern labor movement based on collective action made only slow and sporadic progress.

The first continuing unions emerged among skilled workers in the late 1890s. In 1897 TAKANO FUSATARŌ and KATAYAMA SEN, both of whom had studied the American labor movement firsthand, set up the Rōdō Kumiai Kiseikai (Society for Formation of Labor Unions) and began to advocate the development of a genuine organized-labor movement in Japan. The result was the formation of unions of skilled workers, all organized on American models, including the Tekkō Kumiai for metalworkers, the Kappankō Kumiai for printers, and the Nittetsu Kyōseikai for engineers working for the Japan Railway Company. However, these early unions were mutual benefit associations set up to provide workers' compensation rather than organizations for collective bargaining and strike action. None of them survived beyond 1901, due to financial difficulties and police harassment following the passage of the PUBLIC ORDER AND POLICE LAW OF 1900.

The labor movement also turned to direct political action. With the formation of the Social Democratic Party (SHAKAI MINSHUTŌ) in 1901, union organizers aimed at the establishment of political rights. This movement was also banned by the government, so the only outlets for the opposition were sporadic violence and protests. During World War I, however, workers' awareness of their lack of rights grew, and the movement for democracy gradually linked up with the labor movement. In 1912, SUZUKI BUNJI formed the YŪAIKAI, Japan's first lasting national labor federation. This organization adopted an exceedingly moderate posture in order to gain acceptance by employers and government. The Yūaikai eventually developed into the Dai Nippon Rōdō Sōdōmei (Japan Federation of Labor) in 1919. Sōdōmei engaged in increasingly active organizing campaigns. Its peak year was 1921, when labor disputes broke out in the Kawasaki and Mitsubishi

Workers by Industry

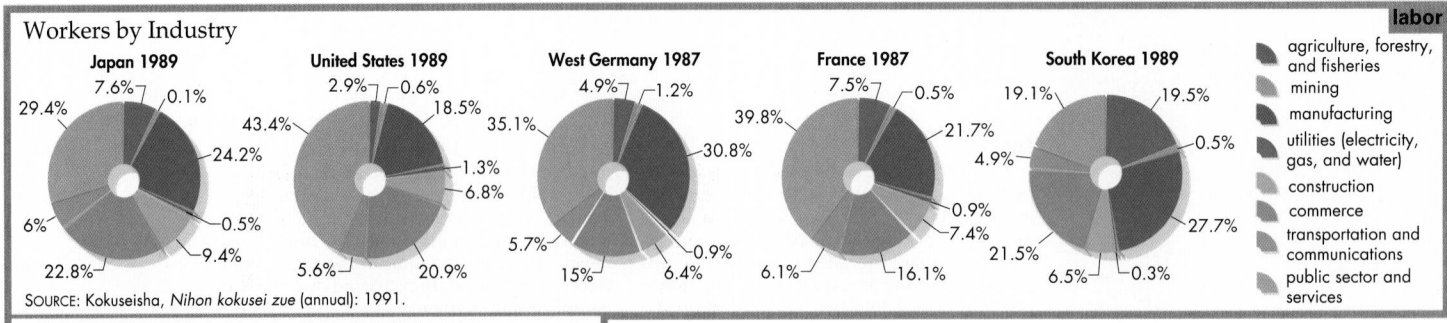

	agriculture, forestry, and fisheries
	mining
	manufacturing
	utilities (electricity, gas, and water)
	construction
	commerce
	transportation and communications
	public sector and services

Japan 1989: 29.4%, 7.6%, 0.1%, 24.2%, 0.5%, 9.4%, 22.8%, 6%

United States 1989: 2.9%, 0.6%, 18.5%, 1.3%, 6.8%, 20.9%, 5.6%, 43.4%

West Germany 1987: 4.9%, 1.2%, 35.1%, 0.9%, 6.4%, 15%, 5.7%, 30.8%

France 1987: 7.5%, 0.5%, 21.7%, 0.9%, 7.4%, 16.1%, 6.1%, 39.8%, 4.9%

South Korea 1989: 19.1%, 19.5%, 0.5%, 27.7%, 0.3%, 6.5%, 21.5%, 4.9%

SOURCE: Kokuseisha, *Nihon kokusei zue* (annual): 1991.

Hourly Wages in the Manufacturing Industry

Country	Hourly wages (national currency/hour)			US dollars/hour[1]	Index (Japan=100)
	Unit	1970	1990	1990	1990
Japan	yen	336	1,603*	11.62	100
West Germany	Mark	5.96	20.07	12.42	107
Sweden	Krone	12.17	73.20	12.37	106
Canada	Canadian dollar	3.01	14.30	12.26	105
United States	US dollar	3.35	10.84	10.84	93
United Kingdom	Pound sterling	0.55	5.38	9.61	83
Netherlands	Guilder	4.82	17.67†	8.94	77
Ireland	Irish pound	0.42	5.33	8.84	76
Belgium	Belgian franc	—	327.13*	8.30	71
New Zealand	New Zealand dollar	—	13.43	8.02	69
France	French franc	5.92	40.97‡	6.82	59

[1]US dollar figures are calculated according to the annual average exchange rates for that year published in IMF, *International Financial Statistics*.
*Figure for 1989.   †Figure for 1988.   ‡Figure for 1987.
SOURCE: Keizai Kōhō Center, *Japan 1992: An International Comparison* (annual):1991.

Japanese Workers by Age and Gender, 1987

Type of employment	Age 15–24		25–34		35–54		Over 55	
	Men	Women	Men	Women	Men	Women	Men	Women
	(in percentages)							
Full-time:								
Managerial[1]	0.4	0.1	2.6	1.4	9.5	4.1	21.9	12.2
Other employees[2]	81.5	81.6	93.2	70.4	86.3	50.5	57.1	47.5
Part-time[3]	16.0	15.8	2.1	24.4	1.2	41.7	6.2	31.4
Other	2.1	2.5	2.1	3.8	3.0	3.7	14.8	8.9

[1]Private-sector management-level employees.
[2]Other private-sector employees and all public-sector employees.
[3]Includes both public and private sectors.
SOURCE: Ministry of Labor, *Rōdō hakusho* (annual): 1991.

shipyards in Kōbe over the right to bargain collectively. The disputes ended in failure for the labor movement, however, due to pressure from the authorities.

Unity in the Japanese labor movement did not last long. Sharp ideological competition, turning on the desirability of change through violence versus parliamentary action, fatally split the labor movement into radical and moderate wings. Although the radical wing was virtually destroyed by governmental suppression in the pre–World War II period, the ideological split within organized labor persisted and, to a degree, has continued to exist up to the present. In the late 1930s the militarists gained direct state control over labor with the establishment of Sampō (Sangyō Hōkoku Kai, or the Industrial Patriotic Association). An independent labor movement was no longer tolerated and by 1941 unions had dissolved or gone underground. Sampō organizations heavily emphasized traditional loyalty, family-centeredness, and ultranationalism and strengthened closed employment systems, reducing status distinctions between white- and blue-collar employees. Because of the tight unity they created among workers at the enterprise

level, the Sampō organizations provided an important base for the rapid growth of enterprise unions after 1945.

The Post–World War II Labor Movement—Labor reform was an important part of Allied efforts to democratize during the postwar Occupation. Among the earliest decrees issued by the supreme commander for the Allied powers (SCAP) in the fall of 1945 were guarantees of fundamental labor rights for all workers, including the right to organize labor unions, the right to bargain collectively, and the right to strike. These decrees were implemented by labor laws that went into effect the following spring. The 1946 Labor Union Law (Rōdō Kumiai Hō) and the 1947 Labor Standards Law (Rōdō Kijun Hō) were instrumental in securing these new labor rights and protections (see LABOR LAWS). Together with new provisions for social welfare, workers' compensation, social security, and the like, they amounted to a considerable increase in workers' rights. The 1947 CONSTITUTION OF JAPAN explicitly included labor rights and guarantees, and for the first time in Japanese history a MINISTRY OF LABOR was established to administer most of the new labor legislation.

Given SCAP's encouragement, unionization grew rapidly, rising from a membership of zero in August 1945 to more than 3 million a year later. Never in the history of any industrial nation had labor unions spread so rapidly. By and large, these unions were spontaneous attempts by workers to exercise their newly received rights and to protect their employment and income within the closed enterprise systems in the context of a highly unstable economy. There was little drive at the grass-roots level to form strong unions on a "horizontal" or industry-wide basis, with chapters in several companies. As there had been little use of external labor markets among the large firms, in the prostrated postwar economy prospects for labor market mobility became even dimmer, and employment security lay in becoming permanently attached to a large firm. This drive for security was the fundamental reason for the spread of unionism at the enterprise level, which has come to characterize Japan's postwar labor movement.

However, the standard of living for most workers had fallen so low due to the economic chaos caused by the war that the new labor movement was soon involved in energetic and often violent campaigning. Both public and private unions engaged in an increasing number of strikes and other direct actions, some involving violence. Spreading labor unrest culminated in a call by national labor organizations for a nationwide strike in February 1947. SCAP's immediate reaction was to prohibit this GENERAL STRIKE OF 1947. SCAP thereafter began to modify labor union rights, for instance by prohibiting strikes by public sector employees. It also purged the communists who had dominated the labor movement since the end of the war (see RED PURGE) and, under pressure from NIKKEIREN (the Japan Federation of Employers' Associations), strengthened the rights of

employers.

At the same time, various anticommunist groups within the labor movement joined together to form a new labor center, SŌHYŌ (the General Council of Trade Unions of Japan). Labor relations rapidly turned in the direction of cooperation between labor and management. However, with the outbreak of the Korean War, Sōhyō veered toward the political left. It proclaimed neutrality for Japan, condemned Japanese rearmament, adopted a stance of political activism, and campaigned vigorously for collective bargaining. In reaction to this, a bloc of unions more favorable to cooperation with employers broke away from Sōhyō in 1954 to form their own organization, Zenrō (later named Dōmei; the Japanese Confederation of Labor). Thus the prewar split between the radical and moderate wings of the labor movement reasserted itself in postwar organized labor.

Although major strikes and labor protests continued sporadically in the 1960s (see MIIKE STRIKE), this period was one of relative labor-management stability. The annual spring wage offensive (SHUNTŌ) began in 1955 and led to substantial improvements in working conditions and wages throughout the ensuing period of high economic growth, which continued, with minor interruptions, until the early 1970s. At the company level, unions tended to cooperate with management in pursuing modernization and rationalization programs, in the hope of achieving the long-term benefits that were assumed to follow. This pattern of industrial relations was widespread throughout the private sector and was an important cause of the remarkable increases in labor productivity achieved by Japanese industry. Companies responded to their continuing shortages of labor by introducing merit-oriented principles of management, and individual workers were encouraged to raise personal standards of achievement to gain promotion and improved status. At the same time, workers were subsumed within cooperative systems, for instance as symbolized by quality-control circles (see QC CIRCLES). The combination of these individually oriented and cooperative methods came to be recognized as a distinctly Japanese pattern of industrial relations.

However, the OIL CRISIS OF 1973 brought Japan's high economic growth period to an end, and as the business climate stagnated it became more difficult to maintain increases both in productivity and wages. Certain heavy and basic industries went into structural recession and were unable to avoid substantial labor cuts. Some firms were able to retrain and reassign excess workers to others parts of the company or else to other related companies. Firms also cut overtime work, held wage increases to a minimum, sought voluntary resignations from redundant workers, and, as a last resort, fired workers. The enterprise unions were not in a position to prevent cutbacks and could only negotiate to prevent too great a burden from being placed on particular groups of workers. The labor market in Japan today is complex and changeable. The shift in the INDUSTRIAL STRUCTURE toward the tertiary sector has increased the volatility of the labor market. Compared to the old-line manufacturing industries, labor mobility in service-related industries such as banking and securities tends to be much higher. The recovery of the economy in the 1980s, among other things, led to an increase in the number of short-term workers and housewives working part time. In recent years, the rise of nominal wages in Japan has served to attract increasing numbers of FOREIGN WORKERS to Japan, mainly in the construction and service industries.

Against the background of growing volatility in the labor market, the enterprise unions, whose ranks consist entirely of full-time employees, have been unable to increase their membership. The percentage of organized workers has continued to drop, as has the influence of the unions themselves. In an effort to unify and strengthen the political influence of organized labor, in 1987 various labor organizations cooperated in establishing a national labor federation. These efforts led to the creation of RENGŌ (Japanese Trade Union Confederation), an organization consisting of unions in the private sector and, after the dissolution of Sōhyō in November 1989, public sector unions as well. However, this development has drawn the criticism of communist-aligned unions, which argue that Rengō has been promoted by moderate unions seeking cooperation with management. The communist-aligned unions, together with some public sector unions, have therefore broken away to form their own organization, ZENRŌREN (the National Confederation of Trade Unions). The ideological division of the labor movement seems destined to continue.

labor dispute resolution procedures 労働争議の調整

(rōdō sōgi no chōsei). Procedures for the resolution of LABOR DISPUTES in Japan are governed by the Labor Relations Adjustment Law of 1946 (Rōdō Kankei Chōsei Hō). There are three types of resolution procedures. Conciliation (assen) is conducted through conciliators designated by one of the nation's LABOR RELATIONS COMMISSIONS. Mediation (chōtei) is performed by a mediation committee established by a labor relations commission. Settlement proposals developed in either mediation or conciliation have no binding power over the parties to the dispute. Arbitration (chūsai) results in settlement decisions binding on the parties. Arbitration is performed by an arbitration committee, which is established by a labor relations commission. Compulsory arbitration is not practiced in Japan. The Labor Relations Adjustment Law also provides for emergency reconciliation (kinkyū chōsei). The prime minister is authorized to suspend a dispute for up to 50 days if there is danger that the strike will seriously damage the national interest.

labor disputes 労働争議

(rōdō sōgi). Most Japanese labor disputes involve scheduled one- or two-day strikes during the annual spring labor offensive (SHUNTŌ). Although the level of strike activity in Japan is comparable to that of other industrialized nations, the short duration of strikes and their predictability significantly reduce their economic impact. Strikes that occur during wage negotiations are not a result of a breakdown in the negotiation process, but are more a ceremonial means of

hastening that process.

Labor disputes over issues other than wage negotiations often extend over a longer period of time and sometimes result in a lockout by the employer. Since the employment system and labor-management relations are based largely on the promise of guaranteed employment, the discharge of employees often results in bitter, prolonged disputes. Almost all of the major disputes in Japan have been of this kind (see, for example, ASHIO COPPER MINE LABOR DISPUTE; MIIKE STRIKE). Many cases are resolved by LABOR DISPUTE RESOLUTION PROCEDURES. Agreements are often reached before a final decision is handed down, indicating that negotiations continue even while official hearings are taking place.

Prolonged disputes often result in a split in the labor union and the formation (often with the assistance of company management) of a second union more sympathetic to the employer. This occurs primarily from the strikers' fear that further extension of the dispute will cause irreparable harm to the business and thus undermine their future employment security. This fear gives Japanese management a strong advantage in collective bargaining and serves to limit the length of strikes during wage negotiations. Another limiting factor is that unions do not generally accumulate large strike funds.

There have been a few notable strikes carried out for political purposes; for example, to win the right to strike for public employees (these are known as suto ken suto) or to put pressure on the Diet. Such strikes are usually led by public-employee unions, which tend to be more radical than private-

Major Japanese Labor Disputes

Dispute	Dates	Remarks
Amamiya silk mill	14–16 June 1886	Strike by women silk-mill workers; the first strike by factory workers in Japan.
Ashio Copper Mine labor dispute*	4–7 February 1907	A dispute that turned violent; military forces called out.
Kawasaki and Mitsubishi shipyards	25 June–9 August 1921	Simultaneous strikes at two Kōbe shipyards; largest dispute prior to World War II.
Kyōdō Printing Company strike*	19 January–18 March 1926	Led by a Japan Communist Party–related national federation.
Noda Soy Sauce	16 September 1927–20 April 1928	The longest prewar strike.
Kanegafuchi spinning mills	5 April–6 June 1930	Four mills strike over a 40-percent reduction in wages.
Yomiuri Shimbun	23 October–11 December 1945; 13 June–16 October 1946	Successful strike for democratization of the newspaper company's management through use of production-control strategy; management reasserts control in 1946, causing second strike.
General Strike of 1947*	scheduled for 1 February 1947	Planned general strike of all government and public workers; suspended by order of the Allied Occupation authorities.
Tōhō Co, Ltd (Tōhō Strike*)	8 April–19 October 1948	Dispute over dismissals and the abolition of the management council of the motion picture company; intervention by the Occupation authorities.
Tōshiba Corporation	10 February–16 November 1949	Strike over dismissals during industrial reorganization.
Electrical Workers' Union (Densan)	14 April–18 December 1952	Long dispute leads to a September strike that halts production of electricity, resulting in the 1953 enactment of restrictions against strikes in the electric power and coal industries.
Japan Coal Miners' Union (Tanrō)	13 August–17 December 1952	Long dispute coordinated with Densan; strike begins in October and is ended in December through use of the national emergency provision of the Labor Relations Adjustment Law.
Nissan Motor Co, Ltd	25 May–21 September 1953	Dispute over management prerogatives and regulation of union activities.
Japan Steel Works, Ltd, Muroran factory	17 June–26 December 1954	Strike over dismissals involving members of the local community as well as the employees themselves.
Mitsui Mining Co, Ltd, Miike Coal Mines (Miike strike*)	25 January–1 November 1960	Strike over the dismissal of workplace activists; a representative workplace struggle.
Kōrōkyō (Council of Public Corporation and National Enterprise Workers' Unions)	26 November–13 December 1975	A series of strikes demanding restoration to public employees of the right to strike (suto ken suto).

*See individual entries on these disputes.

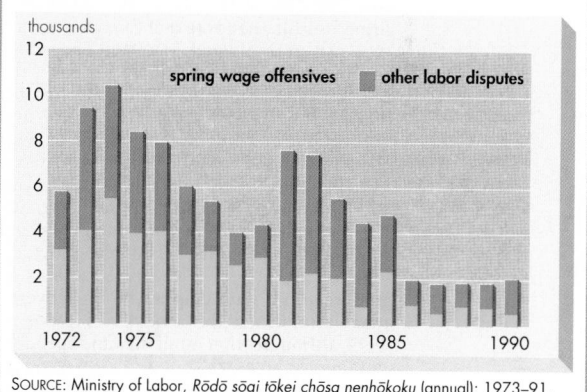

Spring Wage Offensives and Other Labor Disputes

SOURCE: Ministry of Labor, Rōdō sōgi tōkei chōsa nenhōkoku (annual): 1973–91.

sector unions. See also LABOR; STRIKES AND OTHER FORMS OF LABOR DISPUTE; RIGHT TO STRIKE.

Labor-Farmer Party → Rōdō Nōmintō

labor force → employment structure

labor laws 労働法

(rōdōhō). Since 1945 Japan has adopted a comprehensive legal framework dealing with labor conditions, based on far-reaching labor reforms instituted at the direction of the Allied OCCUPATION. See LABOR REFORMS OF 1945–1947.

Prewar Labor Legislation—Prior to 1945 the development of labor law in Japan was exceedingly slow. In the 1890s, special legislation was adopted to improve working conditions for miners, but by and large, the Meiji government left responsibility for employment conditions to employers. The most important exception was the passage of the FACTORY LAW OF 1911, effective from 1916, which stipulated minimum conditions for the employment of women and children in industrial plants and regulated apprenticeships.

In 1926 the Labor Dispute Mediation Law (Rōdō Sōgi Chōtei Hō) provided for tripartite government, employer, and worker commissions for settling strikes and other conflicts between management and employees in industry. However, the PUBLIC ORDER AND POLICE LAW OF 1900 (Chian Keisatsu Hō) and its replacement, the PEACE PRESERVATION LAW OF 1925 (Chian Iji Hō), had effectively curbed union activity through government surveillance. The question of labor union legitimacy was swept aside with the establishment of the government-controlled "labor front" or "Sampō" (Sangyō Hōkoku Kai) as part of wartime mobilization in the late 1930s. The only other notable labor law in the prewar period was the establishment of retirement pension systems and health and work-accident insurance plans for certain limited groups of employees.

Reforms during the Occupation—One of the first steps taken by the supreme commander for the Allied powers (SCAP) was initiation of wholesale legal reforms to establish industrial democracy. In the fall of 1945, SCAP required the Japanese government to adopt the Labor Union Law (Rōdō Kumiai Hō), and in 1946 the Labor Relations Adjustment Law (Rōdō Kankei Chōsei Hō). Also by 1947 the government put into effect the Labor Standards Law (Rōdō Kijun Hō) as well as a host of other new laws providing a basis for worker safety and regulation of conditions of work. These laws were reaffirmed within the context of the CONSTITUTION OF JAPAN promulgated in 1946. The wide-ranging Labor Standards Law has been the basis of regulating minimum protection for workers in industry. The law of 1947 and subsequent enactments not only deal with the establishment of minimum wages, maximum hours of work, rest and holidays, plant safety and worker health, apprentice training, employment of women and minors, and other working conditions, but also provide a "bill of rights" for individual workers in their relations with employers. The government established the MINISTRY OF LABOR in 1947, although other ministries and agencies, notably the MINISTRY OF HEALTH AND WELFARE, are responsible for specialized labor legislation. See RIGHT TO ORGANIZE LABOR UNIONS; COLLECTIVE BARGAINING RIGHT; UNFAIR LABOR PRACTICES; LABOR DISPUTES; LABOR DISPUTE RESOLUTION PROCEDURES; WORK REGULATIONS.

Following the threatened GENERAL STRIKE OF 1947, the National Civil Service Law (Kokka Kōmuin Hō) was enacted, and the following year the law was revised to deny to national government employees the right to organize provided under the Labor Union Law, although it did permit civil servants to form "associations" within their individual agencies. The NATIONAL PERSONNEL AUTHORITY (Jinjiin) governs civil service employment. A parallel law, the Local Civil Service Law (Chihō Kōmuin Hō), was promulgated in 1950 for local government civil servants and provides for separate regional personnel

commissions. The second major change was the adoption in 1948 of the Public Corporations and Government Enterprises Labor Relations Law (Kōkyō Kigyōtai Tō Rōdō Kankei Hō; revised in 1952), which defined conditions of employment in government-owned industrial operations and expressly denied the right to strike. In the early 1950s similar laws were enacted for local-government-operated enterprises. See PUBLIC EMPLOYEES.

Subsequent Revisions of Labor Relations Laws—In a revision of the Labor Union Law in 1949, management personnel with clear supervisory responsibility were forbidden to join unions, although this exclusion did not extend to foremen and other workshop supervisors. A 1952 amendment to the Labor Relations Adjustment Law empowered the prime minister, after consultation with the CENTRAL LABOR RELATIONS COMMISSION (Chūō Rōdō Iinkai), to obtain a 50-day injunction against any strike that the government felt would seriously threaten national economic activities or the daily life of the nation. In 1953, after prolonged stoppages in the previous year, the government adopted a special law, commonly known as the Suto Kisei Hō, prohibiting wide-scale strikes in the electric power and coal mining industries.

Recent major changes have resulted from the divestment by the government of its three public corporations and one of its five government enterprises. By 1986 the Japan Tobacco and Salt Public Corporation, the Japan Telegraph and Telephone Public Corporation, and the JAPANESE NATIONAL RAILWAYS, as well as the Government Alcohol Monopoly, had passed into private hands, necessitating replacement of the Public Corporation and Government Enterprises Labor Relations Law. Prohibition of the right to strike has been preserved in the NATIONAL ENTERPRISE LABOR RELATIONS LAW (1986), which establishes conditions of employment for the four remaining government enterprises. See also LABOR; JUVENILE WORKERS, PROTECTIVE LEGISLATION FOR; WOMEN WORKERS, PROTECTIVE LEGISLATION FOR.

labor market 労働市場

(rōdō shijō). There are three main types of employment relationships in the Japanese labor market: regular employees hired on a permanent basis, temporary employees hired for a fixed period only, and workers who are assigned to a particular company by subcontractors or by an employment agency and who are formally employed by those agents. The main body of workers is usually hired on a permanent basis, and major companies regularly select these employees from among recent secondary school and university graduates, who then continue with the company until retirement. The large-company labor market is therefore a closed one, and few employees are hired in midcareer. This trend is also evident in smaller companies, but there the employment structure is more fluid.

Since the quality of an employee's working conditions tends to depend on the size of the company rather than on skills or job differentials, the Japanese labor market could be described as forming strata according to company size. Workers employed by companies with under 100 employees receive on the average only 70 percent of the pay of workers doing the same job in companies with 1,000 or more employees. In the large companies, workers' status and wages in-

crease in line with length of service, although regular achievement assessments are also important. Employees' promotion prospects are more or less determined by their educational backgrounds. Consequently, obtaining a good job requires, above all, graduation from a good university.

The working conditions of temporary employees, who account for some 20 percent of employees (specifically, 10 percent of male employees and 37 percent of female employees) in large companies, are markedly inferior to those of regular employees. The variety of jobs and employment configurations makes an accurate comparison difficult, but temporary workers certainly receive less than half the rate paid to regular employees for the same job. In many cases temporary employment does not entitle workers to receive retirement gratuities or company welfare benefits and cannot be described as a stable occupation.

The normal pattern of company employment practice has been affected by recent trends in the labor market: the aging of the population, young people staying longer in institutions of higher education, and the increased number of women, especially married women, entering the labor market. Imbalances in labor demand and supply owing to different job types and areas of company operation have also begun to increase to the point that there now sometimes occur extreme shortages of labor as well as striking surpluses. See also CORPORATE RECRUITMENT; EMPLOYMENT STRUCTURE.

labor mobility 労働移動

(rōdō idō). It has long been the normal pattern for Japanese companies to hire employees right after their graduation from school and to train them within the company by giving them experience in various areas of company work. For this reason labor mobility has not been seen as a very desirable element in the Japanese LABOR MARKET, and the usual understanding of a good employment opportunity has been that an employee continues to work for a single company throughout his working life. This was because Japanese industrialization developed in response to pressure from the international environment in accordance with central government policies without waiting for the appropriate establishment of a domestic labor force. As a result, there were frequent imbalances between the needs of manufacturing industries and the available labor supply, leading to constant shortages of workers for skill-intensive jobs. Companies responded by creating industrial relations environments based on lengths of service, the intention being to guarantee stable work forces.

Because smaller businesses cannot guarantee stability for the main bodies of their work forces and larger firms readily shed TEMPORARY WORKERS to adjust to fluctuations in the market, labor mobility is actually quite brisk and frequently is associated with instability of employment. Labor mobility also can result in a fall into a lower-level labor market. It used to be the norm for women to leave their jobs to marry or have children, but in recent years this is less often the case. Today many young workers change jobs when they are dissatisfied with their choice of employment, and those with a poor educational track record tend to move the most. In a 1989 survey of regular workers who had been employed for more than one month by companies with more than 30 employees, 1.8

percent of employees were new entrants and 1.7 percent had left or been discharged recently.

However, with the diversification of the job market due to the development of technology and the consequent increased demand for particular skills, it is no longer possible for companies to train their own employees to the requisite levels, and there is a growing trend toward recruiting from external labor markets. The number of skilled people recruited in midcareer by labor scouts and headhunters is still small, but the trend is attracting attention, and specialized recruiting companies have been established to meet the demand. Reflecting this trend, more and more workers are choosing jobs that will stretch their abilities. The number of workers wanting to change their jobs has increased rapidly, from 4.0 percent in 1969 to 12.2 percent in 1990. Consequently, employment agencies and recruitment companies that hire out workers for a specified period have become widespread, and in 1985 the Labor Services Temporary Assignment Bill (Rōdōsha Haken Hō) was enacted to regulate such companies. See also EMPLOYMENT SYSTEM, MODERN.

labor reforms of 1945–1947
　　　　　　　　　　　　　　　労働改革

(rōdō kaikaku). Legal framework for the organization of labor unions and for collective bargaining established by the Japanese government under the direction of SCAP (headquarters of the Allied OCCUPATION of Japan). Occupation authorities considered the development of an organized labor movement, along with land reform and educational reform, one of the primary means of preventing the resurgence of militarism in post–World War II Japan. The fundamental legislation enacted during this period comprised the Rōdō Kumiai Hō (Labor Union Law, 1945), the Rōdō Kankei Chōsei Hō (Labor Relations Adjustment Law, 1946), and the Rōdō Kijun Hō (Labor Standards Law, 1947).

The Labor Union Law extended the right to strike to all workers except prison guards, fire fighters, and police officers; protected workers from discharge because of labor activities; and established LABOR RELATIONS COMMISSIONS composed of labor, management, and public representatives to apply and enforce the law.

By late 1946 there were some 17,000 labor unions with 4.8 million members. The largest national labor organization, the militant SAMBETSU KAIGI, was organized in August 1946 and represented 21 affiliated unions controlling about 40 percent of the organized labor force; it had close ties with the JAPAN COMMUNIST PARTY and was particularly strong among public employees. Occupation authorities issued a number of warnings against militant labor activity, and finally, in September 1946, the government enacted the Labor Relations Adjustment Law. This law banned strikes by public employees and ordered the arbitration of disputes by public utility workers during a mandatory 30-day cooling-off period. Furthermore the government was empowered to declare any important industry a "public utility." Widespread worker discontent with the new law led to a call for the GENERAL STRIKE OF 1947, planned for 1 February. At the last minute, however, it was banned by General Douglas MACARTHUR, the head of the Occupation. The Labor Standards Law of 1947 set the

maximum workday at eight hours and established the principle of equal pay for equal work. In 1948 the Labor Union Law was revised to democratize the leadership of unions and to depoliticize the labor movement. The so-called RED PURGE eliminated much of the communist leadership of the movement and accelerated the demise of Sambetsu. In short, the Occupation-period labor reforms reestablished both the minimum rights of workers and the political limits of the labor union movement in postwar Japan. See also LABOR LAWS.

labor relations commissions
　　　　　　　　　　　　　　　労働委員会

(rōdō iinkai). Administrative boards with responsibility to resolve LABOR DISPUTES, remedy UNFAIR LABOR PRACTICES, and oversee the affairs of LABOR UNIONS. Regional labor relations commissions (chihō rōdō iinkai) in each prefecture have jurisdiction over all nonmaritime employees in the private sector, employees of local government-operated enterprises, and nonclerical local government employees. The CENTRAL LABOR RELATIONS COMMISSION (Chūō Rōdō Iinkai) has authority over labor disputes of a national scale and serves as an administrative court of second hearing for appeals of decisions of the local commissions. It also exercises jurisdiction over labor disputes of public corporations, which were under the jurisdiction of the National Enterprise Labor Relations Commission (Kokuei Kigyō Rōdō Iinkai) until it was abolished in 1988. Local and central labor relations commissions for seafarers (chihō, chūō sen'in rōdō iinkai) have jurisdiction over maritime workers and employers. See also LABOR LAWS.

labor standards inspection offices
　　　　　　　　　　　　　　　労働基準監督署

(rōdō kijun kantokusho). Local offices of the MINISTRY OF LABOR charged with enforcement of the Labor Standards Law, the Labor Safety Law, the MINIMUM WAGE LAW, and the Workers' Accident Compensation Law (see LABOR LAWS). There are about 350 such offices, including one in each prefecture and major city. The inspection offices are under the authority of the Labor Standards Bureau of the Ministry of Labor and the prefectural labor standards offices and are staffed by superintendents, labor standards inspectors, and other employees. The inspectors are employees of the national government who supervise the enforcement and expose violations of the above laws. They have the authority to investigate labor conditions and safety standards in all industries and act as judicial police officers to expose and provide remedies for violations of the law.

Labor Standards Law → labor laws

Labor Union Law → labor laws

labor unions
　　　　　　　　　　　　　　　労働組合

(rōdō kumiai). Japan's first labor unions were organized in the 1890s among skilled workers (metalworkers, printers, etc); all prewar unions, however, were disbanded by the government during World War II. Fundamental labor rights were codified in the postwar constitution, and the rights of workers to organize, to bargain collectively, and to strike were guaranteed for the first time. Nearly all Japanese trade unions are organized on a company basis, and civil servants and workers in public enterprises also belong to unions with memberships restricted to their own place of work.

Origins of the Enterprise Union—The notion of the company, or any organization, as a form of hierarchically ordered family has its roots deep in Japanese culture and was consciously utilized by Japanese managers to win the loyalty of workers in the volatile labor market of the early period of industrialization (1890–1930; see CORPORATE CULTURE). The concrete forms which the managers' efforts took led to the development of the lifelong employment system (shūshin koyō), which offered workers the security of a job for life, and the SENIORITY SYSTEM (nenkō joretsu), which linked promotion and benefits strictly to age and length of service. New technological imperatives necessitated a stable source of skilled labor, and the difficulty of securing such labor in a fluid labor market led companies to employ and train workers themselves rather than leave hiring and training to labor contractors. Gradually, more and more workers' careers (hiring, training, and promotion) became circumscribed within a single company instead of being subject to the conditions of an open and fluid labor market. The habit of hiring employees immediately after graduation from school or university, which began before World War II, was to become particularly entrenched in the postwar period (see CORPORATE EDUCATION AND TRAINING PROGRAMS). All these factors tended to restrict labor mobility and encourage the development of closed employment systems (see LABOR MARKET; LABOR MOBILITY).

During World War II the government, appealing to the traditional company-as-family concept, abolished unions entirely and organized the national labor force along strict company lines in order to allocate workers to the industries deemed most necessary for military purposes (see LABOR). By closely identifying the worker with his or her employing firm, this had the effect of further consolidating the tendencies, already strong in the prewar period, toward the development of closed employment systems. All these factors predisposed the Japanese to organize unions on an enterprise, rather than an industrywide, basis when the OCCUPATION authorities encouraged the formation of trade unions after 1945.

The Enterprise Union Today—Most regular full-time employees automatically become members of the enterprise union on joining their company, and their union dues are automatically deducted from their wages. They also automatically cease to be union members as soon as employment is terminated or if they are promoted above a certain level. All workers in the same company, both white and blue collar, are organized in the same union. There is no distinction between skilled or unskilled workers or between higher- or lower-ranking employees; all belong equally to the workplace branch of their enterprise union.

As all employees apart from those of top-management rank belong to the same union, collective bargaining negotiations are wide-ranging and usually result in a yearly agreement on pay and working conditions that is negotiated every spring (see SHUNTŌ). At such times management supplies the union with a great deal of information about the current state of the company, which is then passed on to the members. Such collective bargaining negotiations are, in effect, a joint labor-management conference. Joint discussions

Japanese Labor Federations and Their Affiliated Unions

Organization	Number of members
Japanese Trade Union Confederation (Rengō)	7,614,000
All-Japan Prefectural and Municipal Workers' Union (Jichirō)	1,061,000
Confederation of Japan Automobile Workers' Unions (Jidōsha Sōren)	728,000
Japanese Federation of Electrical Machine Workers' Unions (Denki Rōren)	720,000
The Japan Federation of Textile Industry Workers' Unions (Zensen Dōmei)	529,000
National Federation of Life Insurance Workers' Unions (Seiho Rōren)	457,000
Japan Teachers' Union (Nikkyōso)	440,000
Japanese Metal Industrial Workers' Unions (Zenkin Rengō)	321,000
Federation of Telecommunications' Electric Information and Allied Workers (Jōho Rōren)	280,000
Confederation of Electric Power Industry Workers' Unions of Japan (Denryoku Sōren)	222,000
Japan Federation of Steel Workers' Unions (Tekkō Rōren)	197,000
General Federation of Private Railway Workers' Unions of Japan (Shitetsu Sōren)	191,000
National Metal and Machinery Workers' Union of Japan (Kinzoku Kikai)	190,000
Japan Postal Workers' Union (Zentei)	160,000
Japan Confederation of Railway Workers' Unions (JR Sōren)	132,000
All-Japan Federation of Transport Workers' Unions (Un'yu Rōren)	128,000
Japan Confederation of Shipbuilding and Engineering Workers' Unions (Zōsen Jūki Rōren)	128,000
National Federation of General Workers' Unions (Ippan Dōmei)	115,000
Japan Federation of Commercial Workers' Unions (Shōgyō Rōren)	112,000
Japan Federation of Transport Workers' Unions (Kōtsū Rōren)	103,000
National Confederation of Trade Unions (Zenrōren)	835,000
Japan Federation of Prefectural and Municipal Workers' Unions (Jichi Rōren)	179,000
Japan Federation of Medical Workers' Unions (Nihon Irōren)	152,000
All-Japan Teachers and Staff Union (Zenkyō)	139,000
Japan Federation of National Public Service Employees (Kokkō Rōren)	139,000
National Trade Union Council (Zenrōkyō)	290,000
Federation of Tōkyō Municipal Workers' Unions (Torōren)	184,000
Other large unions not affiliated with the above groups	1,295,000
National Federation of Construction Workers' Unions (Zenken Sōren)	481,000
Federation of City Bank Employees' Unions (Shiginren)	144,000

NOTE: Only unions with more than 100,000 members are listed. Membership figures are as of 1990.
SOURCE: Ministry of Labor, *Nihon no rōdō kumiai no genjō* (annual): 1991.

Union Participation

Labor union memberships, 1990

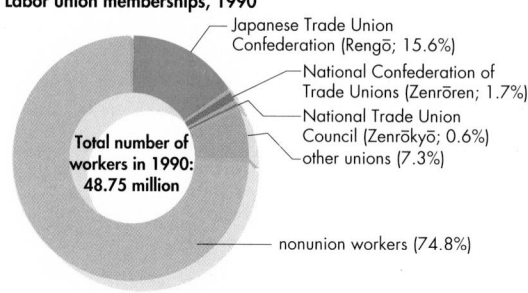

- Japanese Trade Union Confederation (Rengō; 15.6%)
- National Confederation of Trade Unions (Zenrōren; 1.7%)
- National Trade Union Council (Zenrōkyō; 0.6%)
- other unions (7.3%)

Total number of workers in 1990: 48.75 million

- nonunion workers (74.8%)

Unionization rates since World War II

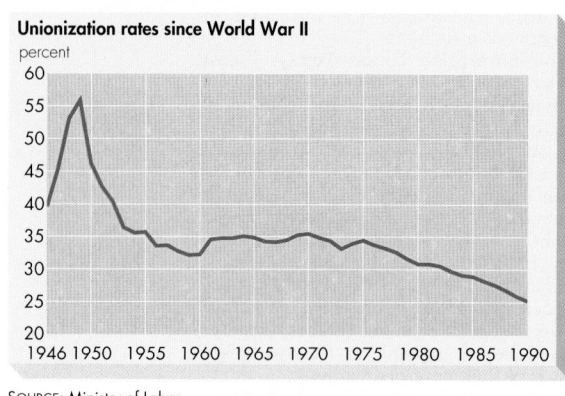

SOURCE: Ministry of Labor.

are held between the union and management both before the actual collective bargaining sessions and also after the negotiations to monitor the implementation of the terms reached. Such cooperation is often seen as signifying both the manipulation of Japanese enterprise unions by their companies and the loss of their independence, but it can also be regarded as resembling the cooperation seen in the German example of labor-management councils.

Labor Federations—Many enterprise unions are affiliated with industrywide labor federations, but it is the enterprise unions that actually negotiate with management and draw up agreements on a company-by-company basis. All decisions as to executive appointments, finances, and union objectives are determined by the enterprise unions themselves. The federations are able to do no more than consolidate and coordinate the activities of their member unions. An important function of the federations in wage-bargaining negotiations is to keep the single-enterprise unions in touch with developments in other companies, so that they do not become too narrowly focused on conditions prevailing within their own company. The most typical example of such coordination is seen in the annual *shuntō* wage offensive.

Until recently there were four competing national labor federations: SŌHYŌ (General Council of Trade Unions of Japan), aligned with the former JAPAN SOCIALIST PARTY (now renamed the Social Democratic Party of Japan); Dōmei (Japanese Confederation of Labor), which is linked with the DEMOCRATIC SOCIALIST PARTY; and two politically neutral organizations, CHŪRITSU RŌREN (Federation of Independent Unions) and Shinsambetsu (National Federation of Industrial Labor Organizations). In 1987 a fifth national labor federation, RENGŌ (Japanese Trade Union Confederation), was formed when Dōmei, Chūritsu Rōren, and Shinsambetsu all agreed to dissolve themselves and join forces. Two years later, Sōhyō also disbanded itself and joined Rengō. With about 7 million members, Rengō has become Japan's largest federation of labor unions. In opposition to Rengō, those unions under the influence of the JAPAN COMMUNIST PARTY formed a national labor organization of their own, ZENRŌREN (National Confederation of Trade Unions), in November 1989. The following month a group of unions centering on

the National Railway Workers' Union and supported by the left wing of the Japan Socialist Party formed a third rival organization, Zenrōkyō (National Trade Union Council). See also EMPLOYMENT SYSTEM, PREMODERN; EMPLOYMENT SYSTEM, MODERN; CORPORATE RECRUITMENT.

lacquer tree 漆

(*urushi*). *Rhus verniciflua*. A deciduous tree of the sumac family (Anacardiaceae), cultivated as a source of lacquer since ancient times. Indigenous to China, India, and Tibet, it reaches more than 10 meters (33 ft) in height and 30–50 centimeters (12–20 in) in diameter. The bark of young trees is grayish white, and that of older ones is dark gray. The branches are thick and grow from the main trunk in a regular pattern. The compound leaves are odd-pinnate and cluster alternately at the ends of branches. Trees bear either male or female flower clusters in panicles at the leaf axils. The many small yellowish green blossoms flower in May and June. The fruit is a spheroid drupe.

The tree is suited to cool, sunny places with a deep layer of moist, fertile soil. Similar species found in Japan include *tsutaurushi* (*R. ambigua*) and *nurude* (*R. javanica*). The sap of these trees contains an oily toxic irritant, urushiol. The lacquer sap is usually gathered when the tree is 10 years old and its trunk is at least 10 centimeters (4 in) in diameter. The sap oozes naturally out of the tree from mid-June through late October. Once the sap is out, the tree is cut down. Lacquer is made by removing water and impurities from the raw sap, after which dehydrating agents and dye are added. Today Japan imports most of its lacquer from China. See also LACQUER WARE.

lacquer ware 漆器

(*shikki*). Containers, utensils, furniture, and other useful objects employing lacquer as a protective varnish and often as a decorative medium as well. It ranks among the most distinctive achievements of traditional Japanese crafts.

Lacquer (*urushi*) is prepared by evaporation and filtration of sap collected by cutting through the bark of the LACQUER TREE (J: *urushi*; *Rhus verniciflua*). One of the most durable natural adhesives and varnishes known in the premodern world, lacquer appears to have been recognized as a useful substance in China and Japan by the second millennium BC. Lacquer penetrates and seals porous surfaces, taking on an amber to deep brown color and a glossy sheen as it hardens. An application of lacquer increases the durability and utility of materials such as wood, the most common material for the construction of lacquer ware. Basketry, woven textiles, bamboo, pottery, metal, paper, and leather have also been used in making lacquer ware.

Lacquer's decorative appeal can be enhanced by the addition of certain pigments to produce opaque colors. Red and black lacquer occur in some of the earliest extant fragments of Chinese and Japanese lacquer, and these have remained the most common colors. Yellow, green, and brown occur in Japanese lacquer prior to the Meiji period (1868–1912). Within the past century blue, violet, and white lacquer have been successfully produced. Hardened lacquer may be polished with abrasives to achieve a brilliant, mirrorlike finish. If the lacquer veneer is sufficiently thick—the result of numerous separate applications of thin layers of lac-

lacquer ware

A lacquer-ware banquet set from the Edo period, typical of those used by feudal *daimyō* for special occasions. Black lacquer with gold *maki-e* designs.

A Kōdaiji *maki-e* portable cabinet and its case from the late 16th century. Made for holding poetry anthologies, it was part of the household furnishings of Toyotomi Hideyoshi's wife. 38 × 32 × 22 cm. Kōdaiji, Kyōto.

Peony patterns decorate this modern tray made with *kamakura-bori*, a technique in which lacquer is applied to a carved wooden base.

quer—it can be carved, incised, or inlaid with metals, mother-of-pearl, and other materials.

Outstanding among Japanese decorative techniques is MAKI-E, literally, "sprinkled-picture." This term encompasses a variety of techniques employing gold or silver powder or particles sprinkled on areas defined by liquid lacquer.

History——Archaeological excavations of Jōmon-period (ca 10,000 BC–ca 300 BC) sites have yielded numerous remains of lacquered objects made of wood, woven bamboo, or pottery. Both red and black lacquer appear, sometimes in combination. Lacquer ware of the Nara period (710–794) reveals a rich variety of materials and decorative techniques, including MOTHER-OF-PEARL INLAY (*raden*), inlay of sheet silver and gold (*heidatsu* or *hyōmon*), and lacquer painting (URUSHI-E) using colored lacquer or lacquer mixed with powdered silver and gold. The *maki-e* technique was introduced during the Nara period. Other types of lacquer ware, such as NEGORONURI and KAMAKURA-BORI, both influenced by Chinese lacquer ware, were produced for use in Buddhist temples during the Kamakura (1185–1333) and the Muromachi (1333–1568) periods.

The Azuchi-Momoyama period (1568–1600) saw the growth of KŌDAIJI MAKI-E, characterized by simplified, bold patterns often based on the theme of flowering autumn grasses (*akikusa*). Japanese lacquerers also produced numerous items specifically for export to Europe. The surviving lacquer ware of the Edo period (1600–1868) suggests a significant broadening of usage, especially among the prosperous merchant class. In the Meiji period, the industry was stimulated by a renewed domestic and foreign demand for lacquer ware. Today, Japanese lacquer ware maintains a high standard of quality.

Ladybird Incident　レディーバード号事件

(*Redībādo gō Jiken*). An international incident that occurred early in the SINO-JAPANESE WAR OF 1937–1945 when the Japanese were advancing on Nanjing (Nanking). On 12 December 1937 the British gunboat *Ladybird* and several commercial vessels were fired upon by the Japanese army while cruising the Yangzi (Yangtze) River near Wuhu, Anhui (Anhwei) Province. Casualties included one dead and several injured. The British gunboats *Cricket*, *Scarab*, and *Bee* and the American gunboat *Panay* (see PANAY INCIDENT) were attacked by Japanese naval planes on the same day. On 14 December the Japanese government issued an official

apology, promising to make financial reparations for the incident and to punish those responsible. It was accepted by the British government. Testimony after the war indicated that the local Japanese commander had ordered that all non-Japanese boats moving toward Nanjing be sunk.

Lady Chatterley's Lover case　チャタレー裁判

(*Chatarē saiban*). Landmark Supreme Court decision on OBSCENITY, 1957. The publisher Oyama Hisajirō (1905–84) and the translator ITŌ SEI (novelist and D. H. Lawrence specialist) were charged in 1950 under the obscenity provisions of the Criminal Code (art. 175) for translating, publishing, and distributing *Lady Chatterley's Lover*. Courtroom and mass media debate attending the trials was generally critical of both the indictments and the general distribution of the unexpurgated translation. In an unusual procedure, the Tōkyō District Court, at the request of both defense and prosecution, heard the divided opinions of 24 witnesses (professors of medicine, literary critics, psychiatrists, high school principals) as to the charge of obscenity. The Supreme Court unanimously found both defendants guilty (G. B., 13 March 1957; 11 Keishū [no. 3] 997 [1957]) and held that the 12 passages at issue infected the entire work with obscenity. The *Chatterley* decision and the later DE SADE CASE remain the most influential obscenity holdings under the 1947 constitution.

laity　平信徒

(*hirashinto*). The term *hirashinto* refers to the body of lay followers of the various sects of SHINTŌ and BUDDHISM. In Shintō, parishioners of a community shrine devoted to the local deity (UJIGAMI) are called UJIKO. In Buddhism, parishioners are called *dan'otsu*, *danna*, or DANKA. The custom of patronizing a particular Buddhist temple developed in the Kamakura period (1185–1333) with the rise of the Pure Land or JŌDO SECT, the NICHIREN SECT, and ZEN. Because it is common to be affiliated with both Shintō and Buddhism, an individual may be both an *ujiko* and a *danka*. Some lay Buddhist movements have developed into independent religious organizations, such as the REIYŪKAI, RISSHŌ KŌSEIKAI, and SŌKA GAKKAI (see NEW RELIGIONS).

land improvement　農地造成

(*nōchi zōsei*). Land improvement works in Japan include land reclamation, dredging, irrigation of dry fields, drainage, improvement of soils, and land readjustment. Japa-

nese agricultural and horticultural activities have long been hampered by the limited areas and often irregular shapes of arable land plots. Therefore, adjustment and realignment of arable land have received top priority in the government's plans to improve agricultural structure. The creation of new arable land through land reclamation was actively promoted during and after World War II, a period of chronic food shortages in Japan. As a result, some 400,000 hectares (990,000 acres) of new farmland were created. One of Japan's largest reclamation projects is in HACHIRŌGATA, a giant lagoon in Akita Prefecture.

Various hydrologic projects to upgrade irrigation facilities in paddy and dry field areas are under way. Land improvement projects, which once centered on paddy fields, have now been extended to dry fields as well. For improvement of soils, soil dressing is being conducted on paddies in peat-bog areas as well as on exhausted and polluted paddies, while soil-improving agents and trace elements are applied to dry fields. By 1990 some 18,000 hectares (44,000 acres) of farmland were being reclaimed in Japan each year. However, the government has begun to play down the creation of new farmland through reclamation in favor of modern techniques of improving existing farmland.

landlordism　地主制

(*jinushisei*). The land tenure system whereby tenants tilled a landlord's fields and paid him a heavy annual rent. Having first appeared in the 18th century, it flour-

lacquer tree
1 The process of making lacquer begins with the collection of sap from scores made in the trunk of an *urushi* tree.
2 The compound leaves of the tree are odd-pinnate with 9 to 13 leaflets. The fruit forms on panicles.

Land and Dwellings in Selected Countries land problem

	Japan		United Kingdom		West Germany		United States	
Total land area (in hundreds of square kilometers)	3,777	(1990)	2,441	(1988)	2,486	(1989)	93,726	(1988)
Agricultural land	534		1,855		1,336		43,138	
Forest	2,524		241		740		26,519	
Developed land	101		289		329		3,129	
Land value per square meter (in US dollars)*	293	(1985)	37	(1986)	39	(1985)	25	(1984)
Percentage of households which own dwelling	61.3	(1988)	64.1	(1987)	39.3	(1987)	64.0	(1987)
Average number of years' salary required to buy dwelling	5.7	(1988)	4.4	(1987)	4.6	(1986)	3.4	(1987)

*Figures converted into dollars at corresponding annual rates.
SOURCES: National Land Agency, *Tochi hakusho* (annual): 1991 and 1992; Kokuseisha, *Nihon kokusei zue* (annual): 1990; Bandō Mariko, *Sekai no naka no Nihon no kurashi* (1991); US Department of Commerce, *Statistical Abstract of the USA* (1992).

Survey of Land Ownership and Use in Selected Tōkyō Wards

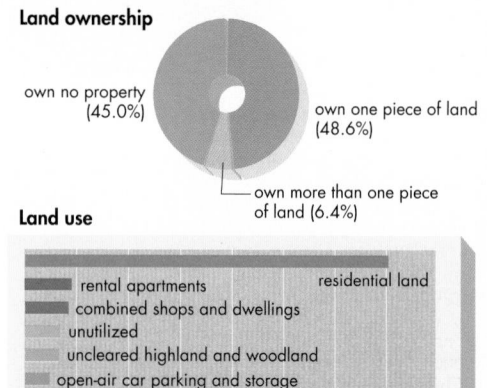

Land ownership

own no property (45.0%)

own one piece of land (48.6%)

own more than one piece of land (6.4%)

Land use

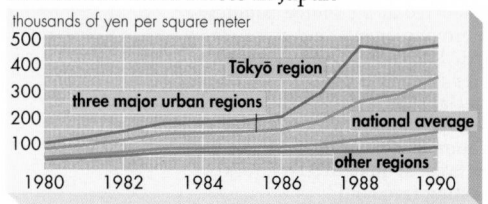

rental apartments
combined shops and dwellings
unutilized
uncleared highland and woodland
open-air car parking and storage
combined factories and dwellings
combined offices and dwellings

residential land

percentage of land owners

NOTE: Data is based on a December 1990 survey of people aged 30 and over residing in 9 of Tōkyō's 23 wards.
SOURCE: National Land Agency, *Tochi hakusho* (annual): 1991.

Residential Land Prices in Japan

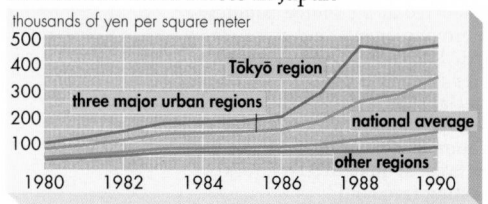

thousands of yen per square meter

Tōkyō region
three major urban regions
national average
other regions

NOTE: The Tōkyō region comprises the prefectures of Tōkyō, Kanagawa, Chiba, and Saitama. The three major urban regions are those of Tōkyō, Ōsaka (Ōsaka, Kyōto, and Hyōgo prefectures), and Nagoya (Aichi and Mie prefectures). "Other regions" includes all of Japan except the three major urban regions.
SOURCE: Diamond, Inc, *Tochi kakaku no suii to bunseki* (annual): 1986 and 1991.

Average Number of Years' Salary Required to Buy a Newly Built Dwelling in Japan

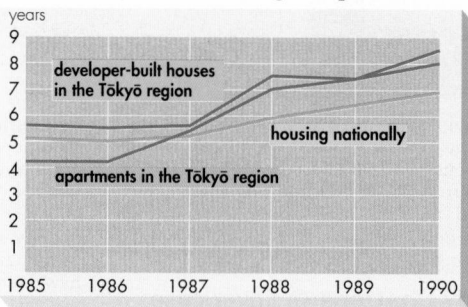

years

developer-built houses in the Tōkyō region

housing nationally

apartments in the Tōkyō region

NOTE: Housing prices given are the average prices of developer-built houses and apartments put on the market that year. In the data for developer-built houses, the Tōkyō region consists of Tōkyō, Kanagawa, Chiba, and Saitama prefectures and the southern part of Ibaraki Prefecture. Ibaraki Prefecture is omitted from the Tōkyō region data for apartments.
SOURCE: National Land Agency, *Tochi hakusho* (annual): 1992.

Population Distribution within Fifty Kilometers of the Center of Tōkyō

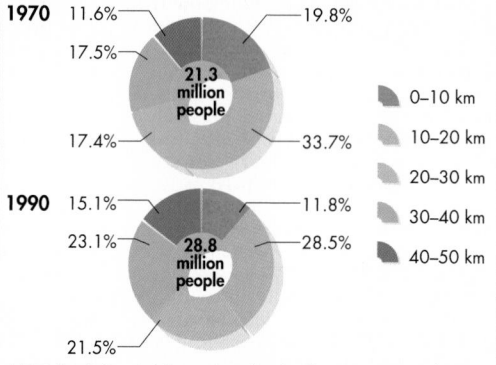

1970 11.6% — 19.8%
17.5%
21.3 million people
17.4% — 33.7%

1990 15.1% — 11.8%
23.1%
28.8 million people
21.5% — 28.5%

0–10 km
10–20 km
20–30 km
30–40 km
40–50 km

NOTE: Population statistics are based on local-government population registers (*jūmin kihon daichō*), which include only Japanese citizens.
SOURCE: Ministry of Home Affairs, *Jūmin kihon daichō ni motozuku zenkoku jinkō setaisū hyō jinkō dōtai hyō* (annual): 1970 and 1990.

ished in the Meiji period (1868–1912) and lasted until the LAND REFORMS OF 1946.

Because of increasing agricultural productivity combined with the fixed levels of domainal land taxes under the Tokugawa shogunate's (1603–1867) BAKUHAN SYSTEM, some 18th-century peasant landholders (HOMBYAKUSHŌ) came to enjoy agricultural surpluses and to raise commercial crops. A number of these *hombyakushō* became landlords by acquiring agricultural land from less successful peasants, who became their tenant farmers in a relationship known as *shitchi kosaku*. The Meiji government based its industrialization program on tax revenues from private landownership, and the LAND TAX REFORM OF 1873–1881 hastened the spread of landlordism.

The deflation brought on by the MATSUKA-

TA FISCAL POLICY of 1881–85 affected peasant households so severely that by 1887 some 39.4 percent of agricultural land was worked by tenant farmers, and 67 percent of all peasant families were tenants or tenant-owners; by 1902 the former figure had risen to 44.5 percent. Since tenants on average paid half of their rice crop as rent, they were often forced to send their wives and daughters to work in textile mills, usually for subsistence wages.

After the RICE RIOTS OF 1918 many peasants fell under the influence of the urban labor movement, and large-scale tenant-landholder disputes broke out. In the pre–World War II capitalist system, under which the imperial family and the ZAIBATSU (giant financial combines) were the major landholders, opposition to the land tenure system represented a radical attack on the state. As men of wealth, landlords were an important faction in the lower house of the Diet—until 1928 an

income-tax payment requirement severely limited the right to vote—and the wealthiest were appointed to the upper house. All the powers of the land were in league against the tenant farmers and their demands for lower rents and tenant rights.

However, the portion of total arable land tilled by tenants reached its peak in 1920, and the continued growth of urban industry subsequently caused the gradual relaxation of the landlords' hold over the rural economy. When the SHŌWA DEPRESSION and the development of Japan's wartime economy made it evident that landlordism impeded agricultural production, such laws as the Kosakuryō Tōsei Rei (1939, Tenant Rent Control Ordinance) were passed. These reforms helped pave the way for the abolition of landlordism after World War II. See also INDUSTRIAL REVOLUTION IN JAPAN.

land problem 土地問題

(*tochi mondai*). A blanket term comprising a number of serious interrelated social problems, including overly concentrated urbanization and high land prices resulting from extremely intensive land utilization in Japan's mountainous terrain. Japan's total land area is 377,688 square kilometers (145,825 sq mi), but 66.8 percent consists of uninhabitable mountains and forests. Farmland constitutes 14.1 percent of the archipelago; urban areas, 4.3 percent; roads, 3.0 percent; rivers, lakes, and canals, 3.5 percent; and other areas, 8.3 percent. Of the urban land area, 62.0 percent is residential; 12.0 percent, industrial; and 26.0 percent, commercial and other. Comparisons with other countries regarding the ratio of land area to population and economic activity show the extreme density of population in Japan and a dramatically high concentration of economic activity in a limited land area.

Postwar increases in urban land prices in Japan began in the mid-1950s and accompanied the subsequent decades of rapid economic growth. Price increases were also related to the improvement of TRANSPORTATION services in urban and suburban areas, as well as of residential amenities. Other factors were also involved: when land price increases were accepted as normal, companies began to think of land as a profitable investment option, encouraging a snowball effect. As a result, the relative percentage of land as part of Japan's NATIONAL WEALTH (domestic tangible fixed assets plus NET EXTERNAL ASSETS) became extremely high. On a practical level, the land price increases caused a growing social cleavage between people who became wealthy through landownership and people who possessed no land and could never hope to do so.

Land prices in Japan are, however, marked by extreme regional differentials. Housing land prices are highest in Tōkyō, averaging ¥858,600 (US $5,930) per square meter (10.76 sq ft) in 1990. The lowest housing land prices that year were in Shimane Prefecture, where they averaged ¥22,300 (US $154) per square meter. The discrepancy between land prices in the TŌKYŌ METROPOLITAN AREA and those in other cities increased significantly in the second half of the 1980s. As a result, in Tōkyō it has become increasingly costly to maintain and develop public facilities such as parks and roads. It has also become increasingly difficult for the average worker to buy a house, even in suburbs more than 90 minutes' commuting time from the central city. Furthermore, serious problems are developing in outlying areas because facilities such as schools and waterworks are unable to cope with population shifts out of Tōkyō.

Since differences in land prices are a reflection of regional imbalances in economic development and population distribution, in the 1980s the government took up population and industrial decentralization as a key policy issue in an effort to balance the use of the nation's land resources. To date, however, it has been unable to achieve substantial results.

land reclamation 土地造成

(*tochi zōsei*). Land reclamation in Japan covers a wide range of activities, including the conversion of wasteland into fertile fields, the transformation of shallow coastal waters into industrial land, and, especially in recent years, the opening of land for residential housing and urban development.

The largest Japanese land reclamation project in the premodern era was the early 17th century reclaiming of a vast landmass out of Edo Bay (now Tōkyō Bay) for the construction of EDO (now Tōkyō). After 1900, large areas of land were purchased in rural areas and turned into factory sites at the same time that land readjustment programs were carried out. The largest drainage reclamation project of this period was that of KOJIMA BAY in Okayama Prefecture.

After World War II, urban reconstruction and modernization was one of the many areas government officials targeted in an attempt to put the country back on its feet. During the period of rapid economic growth after 1950, large amounts of land were secured for industry by dredge reclamation of coastal areas and the utilization of interior land.

By the 1980s, increased population in urban areas had created a demand for more land for housing and recreation areas, and land for industrial use was also in demand. Among the many projects underway or near completion in the early 1990s were the Tōkyō Bay Frontier Project, a landfill project that includes plans for new urban centers on the Ariake and Daiba sites in Tōkyō Bay; Port Island and Rokkō Island, the artificial islands in Kōbe Bay; and the KANSAI INTERNATIONAL AIRPORT, which is being built on an artificial island in Ōsaka Bay.

land reforms of 1946 農地改革

(*nōchi kaikaku*). An effort to redistribute land holdings that was one of the most successful reform measures of the post–World War II Allied OCCUPATION of Japan. It aimed at establishing a US-style democracy through the creation of a broad class of independent yeoman farmers. Welcomed by the many Japanese who were troubled by the problems of the tenant farmer prior to the war, land reform was implemented with relatively little opposition. It brought substantial changes to the countryside but was dependent for its ultimate success upon industrial policy and other seemingly unrelated factors.

Old Land Practices—At the end of World War II, close to 50 percent of Japan's 72 million people still lived in largely rural surroundings. Of these, 27 percent owned less than 10 percent of their land. Tenants paid rents in kind that averaged as much as 60 percent of the crop; many were bound by strong communal rights to paternalistic landlords, but they had few contractual rights and little incentive to undertake technological innovations. See TENANT FARMER DISPUTES; LANDLORDISM.

Most US officials agreed that land legislation was needed, although some worried that too radical a restructuring of the traditional order might lead to social chaos. Other more-influential officials stressed that elimination of tenant farming was essential to the destruction of MILITARISM. Thus, by 9 December 1945, SCAP (the supreme commander for the Allied powers) had issued a public pronouncement listing the kinds of reform measures needed.

Reforms—A 30 April 1946 proposal by the Russian delegate General Derevyanko to the third session of the ALLIED COUNCIL FOR JAPAN led to discussions among Japanese, SCAP bureaucrats, and William MacMahon BALL of Australia, the British Commonwealth representative. Under the leadership of Prime Minister YOSHIDA SHIGERU, the Japanese government incorporated the main features of Ball's proposals into its own bill, which passed the Diet on 21 October 1946.

This bill permitted the government to buy all the land of absentee landlords, as well as all land that might be cultivated but was not. Landlords resident in villages were permitted to lease small amounts of land. Such landlords were now forced to grant their tenants substantial contractual rights, to limit their rents to money payments of no more than 25 percent of annual paddy crop and 15 percent of field crop values, and to limit the total size of their rented land under cultivation to an average of 12 *chō* (12 hectares or 29.6 acres) in Hokkaidō and an average of 3 *chō* (3 hectares or 7.4 acres) on the other three main islands of Japan. Excess land was to be purchased by the state and sold to the tenants through 30-year mortgages at 3.2 percent interest.

Aided in part by a 4 February 1948 SCAP statement that stressed that land reform had become "one of the foremost objectives of the Japanese people as well as the Allied Occupation," land transfers significantly altered economic relationships in rural Japan. The percentage of paddy land owned by the cultivator increased from 55.7 in 1947 to 88.9 in 1949, and that of dry field land from 66.5 to 91.2. The percentage of tenant farmers who owned less than 10 percent of the lands they cultivated dropped from 27 in 1947 to 5 in 1950. In 1938, 47 percent of farmland was cultivated by tenant farmers, but by 1949 the figure had been reduced to 13 percent. The steep inflation that took place during the late 1940s also helped make land reform effective by reducing the real cost of the 30-year mortgages, allowing tenants to pay back their obligations with plenty of cash to spare. Inflation also created new opportunities for social mobility in the countryside. The land reforms of the Allied Occupation of Japan were one of the most ambitious and most consistently applied reform policies of the entire period. Popular both because they addressed long-standing social problems and because they benefited far more people than they harmed, the reforms were effectively implemented without violence and carefully maintained throughout the postwar period.

landscape painting, traditional

→ sansuiga

land tax 土地税制

(*tochi zeisei*). The Japanese land tax consists of the national taxes on capital gains and inheritance and a local (municipal) fixed assets tax. In the capital gains tax on land, rates for long-term ownership (over five years), which range from 26.0 to 32.5 percent, are lower than those for short-term ownership (less than five years), which range from 52.0 to 71.5 percent. In an attempt to halt recent rampant land speculation, exceedingly high rates have been imposed since 1988 on the gains from land owned for less than two years.

A current problem affecting the Japanese inheritance tax and the fixed assets tax is that in most cases the appraised value of land is lower than the present price at which it is being sold. This results in inequity in the tax burden between financial assets and land ownership. Consequently, the holding of vacant land is thwarting effective land use in many places. See also TAXES.

Land Tax Reform of 1873–1881 地租改正

(Chiso Kaisei). Thorough revision of the land tax system carried out by the government from 1873 to 1881. One of the most important reforms of the early Meiji period (1868–1912), it was the basis for Japan's subsequent modernization.

The early Meiji government had to finance its developing civil and military administration and continued to pay hereditary stipends to *samurai* of the former Tokugawa shogunate (1603–1867). It relied initially on paper money and domestic and foreign loans to supplement ordinary land tax revenues, but it found that such short-term measures were insufficient.

Under the so-called Unequal Treaties (see ANSEI COMMERCIAL TREATIES), protective tariffs were out of the question. An increase in internal revenues, including excise taxes and stamp taxes, however, depended on the growing prosperity of domestic commerce and industry, and signs were not encouraging. The only solution seemed to lie in a nationwide standardization of the land tax system based on land values and an equalization of its burden.

Reforms—On 28 July 1873 the government issued the Land Tax Reform Law. Assuming that levying an amount equal to the total annual tax revenue of the Edo period (1600–1868) would not overburden the public, once uniformity and equity were realized, the government decided on a tax rate of 3 percent of the land value for land tax and 1 percent of land value for local surtax. Evaluation of land was left to the landowners, who were instructed to follow the "Examples for Investigation" of the Land Tax Reform Law and submit a figure for approval. The farmers' evaluations were accepted if they were less than 10 percent below official calculations.

Rational as the law might have seemed, its actual application required amendments. Article 8 added to the Land Tax Reform Law (12 May 1874) established that the land value determined at the time of the reform would be the official value for tax assessment, irrespective of subsequent changes in market values. The government ordered the initial values frozen for five years. The so-called Proclamation 68 was issued (12 May 1876), stipulating that disputed land values should follow those of neighboring lands for which official values had already been fixed. A Land Tax Reform Agency was established to implement the reform.

Toward the end of 1876 rural uprisings protesting the tax reform increased, and these, coupled with rebellions by former sa-

Japanese larch
Although a member of the pine family, the larch loses its needles yearly. The bright green needles lighten to a brilliant yellow before falling.

murai in several regions, persuaded the government to make compromises. On 4 January 1877 the government reduced the 3-percent land tax and 1-percent local surtax to 2.5 percent and 0.5 percent respectively.

Rice prices under the deflationary MATSUKATA FISCAL POLICY (1881–85) were not at all advantageous to small farmers. Nevertheless, farmers' incomes did increase because of the spread of commercial crops, more efficient agricultural techniques, and new by-employments, making the burden of fixed taxes a relatively smaller portion of total income. Many farmers were unable to pay their taxes, and lands were confiscated in lieu of tax payments. Together with an increase in debt and mortgage foreclosures, this resulted in a noticeable rise in tenancy, a trend that continued until the early 1920s.

Lansing-Ishii Agreement
石井・ランシング協定

(Ishii-Ranshingu Kyōtei). Name commonly given to the diplomatic notes exchanged on 2 November 1917 in which Japan and the United States enunciated the principles that were to guide their conduct in dealings with a China torn by war and revolution. In the published texts, ISHII KIKUJIRŌ, the distinguished career diplomat who led a special mission to the United States, and Secretary of State Robert LANSING affirmed the intent of their two nations to uphold a basic principle of the OPEN DOOR POLICY—to respect China's independence and its territorial and administrative integrity. The US government also professed to recognize that "territorial propinquity creates special relations between countries and consequently . . . that Japan has special interests in China, especially the part to which her possessions are contiguous." Finally, in a secret protocol that was attached to the public notes, the two governments agreed not to take "advantage of the present [World War I] conditions to seek special rights or privileges in China which would abridge the rights of the subjects or citizens of other friendly states."

These products of some two months of high-level talks were presented to the world as evidence of an understanding that laid to rest an increasingly troublesome Japanese-American rivalry over China. The hard fact, however, was that the notes were filled with ambiguities and therefore offered no far-reaching solutions. In April 1923, following still another definition of international conduct in the NINE-POWER TREATY (signed in Washington, 6 February 1922), Japan and the United States agreed to annul the Lansing-Ishii Agreement.

Historians have generally agreed that the Lansing-Ishii Agreement was a landmark in Japanese-US relations. During the years between World Wars I and II the agreement seemed important because it spoke to the

continuing US-Japanese duel over China. In recent years, however, the histories of US-Japanese relations tended to be more critical of the agreement. They were more inclined than they once had been to question the wisdom of the two nations' having settled for its limited accomplishments.

Lansing, Robert
ランシング, R.

(1864–1928). American specialist in international law. Lansing was appointed by President Woodrow Wilson as US secretary of state in 1915. In an era of American-Japanese tensions, he sought amicable relations that resulted in the 1917 LANSING-ISHII AGREEMENT. Lansing was determined that Japan's growing influence in East Asia should be directed toward economic rather than territorial expansions. To this end he secretly advocated a settlement in which the United States would recognize Japan's claims to a special position in Manchuria in return for explicit Japanese pledges to respect the territorial and administrative integrity of the remainder of China, and to accede to American treatment of Japanese residing in the United States.

Later, convinced that Japan's military was gaining undue influence on Japanese foreign policy, Lansing became an opponent of Japan's imperial designs. At the 1919 Paris Peace Conference he urged Wilson to risk Japan's withdrawal from the proceedings rather than accede to its demands that its prior acquisition of German privileges in Shandong (Shantung) be formally recognized. Wilson rejected Lansing's proposed bargain; he also rejected Lansing's subsequent plea for a firm stand on the SHANDONG (SHANTUNG) QUESTION, because it would rob the League of Nations of Japanese support.

lanterns
灯籠・行灯・提灯

(tōrō; andon; chōchin). The lantern, originating from an Indian prototype, was introduced to Japan along with Buddhism in the 6th century. The most distinctive form of lantern is the ishi-dōrō, or stone lantern, which is used widely on the grounds of temples and shrines and as a garden ornament. Ishi-dōrō are usually made of granite or syenite. They come in a variety of shapes and sizes, but all have an upper section hollowed out to hold a candle or oil lamp that is lighted on special occasions. The most famous ishi-dōrō are the 2,000 that line the approaches of the KASUGA SHRINE in Nara. These are lighted twice a year, in February and August. The secular use of ishi-dōrō dates from the Azuchi-Momoyama period (1568–1600), when masters of the TEA CEREMONY began to use them to decorate tea gardens. Bronze or iron tōrō are also widespread. The most famous of these is the large (4 m; 13 ft), octagonal bronze lantern in front of the main hall of the temple Tōdaiji in Nara. The lantern dates from the Nara period (710–794) and is decorated with pierced metal carvings in low relief. Hanging lanterns, usually bronze, are called tsuri-dōrō; there are some 1,000 of these on the precincts of the Kasuga Shrine. Smaller standing lanterns of wood or iron are known as andon. They became popular during the Edo period (1600–1868) for interior illumination. They usually rest on four legs and have cut-out designs decorating their sides. Traditionally andon burned oil or candles, but now they are often wired for electricity. The finest andon are sought after by collectors of folk art. The bombori is a portable lantern, though it is sometimes used as a permanent fixture in the home. It is carried by means of

a pole attached horizontally at the base. The distinctive hexagonal shade of the bombori is often made of a delicate wood or metal frame covered with paper or glass. Paper lanterns used outside the house are called chōchin. They are hung from the eaves of a building, often a restaurant, or are carried in processions to light the way. The frame is a collapsible structure of bamboo hoops covered with tough paper. Chōchin come in a variety of colors and are often decorated with crests, inscriptions, or names of restaurants. During the BON FESTIVAL, chōchin are lighted in Buddhist memorial services. ☎879

Laos and Japan
ラオスと日本

(Raosu to Nihon). Before World War II, relations between Laos and Japan were indirect since Laos was under French rule. Direct relations began with Japan's occupation of Indochina during the war. In March 1945, the Japanese ousted the French administration from Indochina and in April proclaimed the independence of Laos. Immediately after Japan's defeat in August 1945, the French returned and restored colonial rule. After Laos gained full independence in 1953, a civil war broke out, which eventually resulted in the seizure of power by the communist Pathet Lao and the establishment of the Lao People's Democratic Republic in 1975. Before the communist takeover, Japan, together with the United States and Australia, provided financial support to the Laotian government. Japan also paid war reparations based on an agreement concluded in 1958.

Due to economic difficulties, the Laotian government eventually came to look to noncommunist countries, including Japan, as new economic partners. In 1988 the Laotian vice-president visited Japan and expressed interest in building contacts with Japan. In 1990 Japan exported products valued at US $19.6 million to Laos and imported goods totaling US $4.6 million from that country. Although Japan is one of the major exporters to Laos, trade volume remains low.

LARA
アジア救済連盟

(Licensed Agencies for Relief in Asia; J: Rara; Ajia Kyūsai Remmei). A group of American private charitable and religious agencies that contributed food, clothing, and medical supplies to Japan and other Asian nations after World War II. LARA was organized in 1946 after permission had been granted by the supreme commander for the Allied powers (SCAP). By 1950 it had contributed to Japan supplies worth $6.5 million.

larch, Japanese
落葉松

(karamatsu). Larix leptolepis. Deciduous tree of the family Pinaceae that mainly grows wild in volcanic regions of central Japan, especially at the foot of Mt. Fuji (Fujisan), and is also planted widely. The tree grows to 30 meters (100 ft) and has a conical crown. The bright green needles (3 cm; 1 in) grow in clusters of 20 to 30 on short branches; they turn brilliant yellow and are shed in late autumn. The tree's straight-grained, water-resistant wood is used in construction, toolmaking, and for pulp. The bark serves as the source of a dye and the resin as material for turpentine.

In the United States karamatsu is prized as an ornamental tree, and a dwarf subspecies (L. leptolepis var. minor) has been developed. Another subspecies (L. leptolepis var. murrayana) with golden-variegated leaves was developed in Germany.

Varieties of the Japanese Lantern

Before the age of electricity, Japan dispelled the dark primarily with candles and with lamps fueled by animal or vegetable fat. The use of lamp oil spread rapidly during the Asuka (593–710) and Nara (710–794) periods. For outdoor lighting, stone lanterns called *ishi-dōrō* came into use, although these were found almost exclusively on the grounds of Buddhist and Shintō sanctuaries until the 16th century. *Chōchin*, the portable, collapsible paper lanterns widely known outside Japan, and wood-frame *andon*, or standing lanterns, did not become popular until the Edo period (1600–1868). Both *ishi-dōrō* and *chōchin* eventually appeared in a wide variety of styles. These and other traditional lanterns have been almost entirely replaced by modern lighting fixtures, but their characteristic forms have been faithfully preserved in the designs of many contemporary lamps.

Hanging lanterns (*tsuri-dōrō*). Electric light shines through the Japanese paper lining these bronze *tsuri-dōrō*, revealing ornate pierced-metal carving. Hung from the eaves of the Nigatsudō (Second Month Hall) of the temple Tōdaiji, they frame the temple's great Buddha hall.

odawara-jōchin
(collapsible paper lantern)

yumihari-jōchin
(paper lantern with bow-shaped handle)

gifu-jōchin
(Gifu-style paper lantern)

tsuri-dōrō
(hanging lantern)

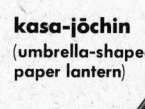

kasa-jōchin
(umbrella-shaped paper lantern)

kaku andon
(box-shaped standing lantern)

kago chōchin
(basket-frame paper lantern)

ishi-dōrō
(stone lantern)

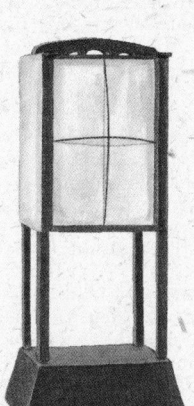
bajō chōchin
(horseman's lantern)

Stone lanterns (*ishi-dōrō*). The Mandōe ("ten-thousand-lantern-lighting" ceremony) at the temple Tōkōji, Yamaguchi Prefecture. During this mid-August memorial service to comfort the souls of returning ancestors, the path to the temple is bathed in candlelight from hundreds of lanterns. This time exposure reveals one candlelighter's route. The lanterns were donated by the retainers of several *daimyō* of the Chōshū domain during the Edo period.

bombori teshoku
(hand-held candle lantern)

kaku andon
(four-legged standing lantern)

bombori
(lantern stands)

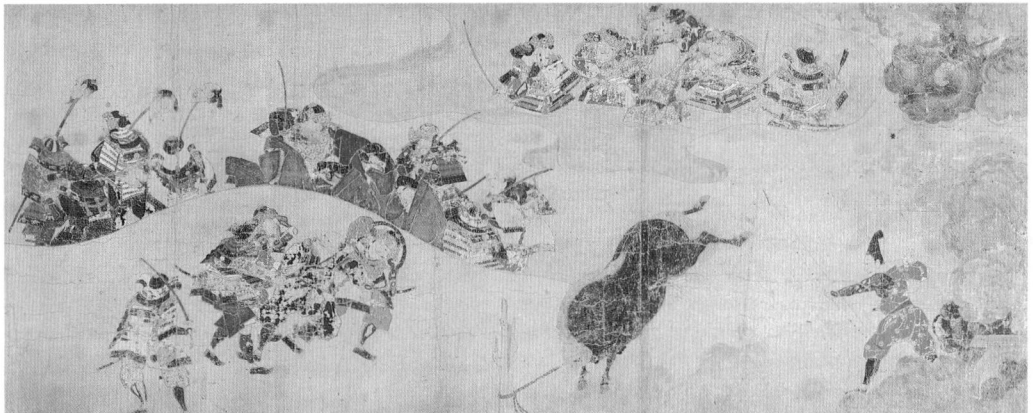

**Later Three Years'
War** Detail from a
14th-century scroll
depicting this early-
11th-century conflict.
Shown here is the scene
after the forces of
Minamoto no Yoshiie
have captured a
stockade defended by
Kiyohara warriors.

Large-Scale Earthquake Countermeasures Law

大規模地震対策特別措置法

(Daikibo Jishin Taisaku Tokubetsu So-
chihō). Law empowering the Japanese prime
minister to take special preparatory measures in the event of prediction of a major
earthquake. Enacted in 1978, the law in-
structs the prime minister to issue an emergency warning upon receiving a prediction
of an impending earthquake from the
Meteorological Agency. Local government
authorities then become responsible for putting disaster prevention systems into effect.
The law also allows for certain central-
government-imposed emergency limitations
on private rights, as well as the dispatching
of the Self Defense Forces as necessary.

Large-Scale Retail Stores Law

大規模小売店舗法

(Daikibo Kouri Tempo Hō). Law enacted in
1973 to protect small-scale stores from unrestricted competition from larger retail stores.
The law requires that companies notify public officials of their intention to build any
new store with floor space greater than 500
square meters (5,380 sq ft). A conference
among the store and local retailers, consumers, and other interested parties is then convened to discuss the store's plans and to
reach consensus on such issues as the store's
opening date, operating hours, number of
holidays, and floor space. If these issues cannot be resolved, the minister of international
trade and industry or the governor of the
prefecture involved will mediate disagreements. However, the process from notification to final resolution of all problems is so
time-consuming and expensive that the law
is tantamount to an outright restriction on
the- opening of large stores. Western distributors, claiming that the law prevents
them from effectively entering the Japanese
market, are strongly urging Japan to revise it.
Within Japan as well, many critics who claim
that the law hinders the revitalization of the
retail industry are calling for its thorough revamping.

larks

雲雀

(hibari). In Japanese, hibari is the general
name for small birds of the family Alaudidae. It is also used specifically for the skylark (Alauda arvensis). This bird is about 17
centimeters (7 in) in length and is colored
golden brown with vertical black stripes on
the breast and back. It has a small crest. The
bird resides in meadows and fields throughout Japan north from Kyūshū. The male
sings as he flies over his territory. Widely
distributed through central Eurasia, the
family Alaudidae also includes the hama-
hibari (shore lark or horned lark; Eremo-
phila alpestris) and the himekōtenshi (short-
toed lark; Calandrella cinerea) in Japan.

The song of the lark has been loved and
celebrated since ancient times in Japan. Larks
were also prized as pets. There was a type of
amusement called agehibari in which tame
larks were released to see how long they
would sing in flight and which bird would
return most quickly to its cage after descending.

Later Three Years' War 後三年の役

(Gosannen no Eki). Military campaign in
which MINAMOTO NO YOSHIIE subdued the
fractious Kiyohara family of northeastern
Japan between 1083 and 1087 (only three of
these years saw actual fighting). The
Kiyohara were hereditary commanders in
Dewa Province (now Akita and Yamagata
prefectures) who had helped court forces to
crush ABE NO SADATŌ in the EARLIER NINE YEARS'
WAR (1051–62), thus becoming masters of
Mutsu Province (now Aomori, Iwate,
Miyagi, and Fukushima prefectures) as well.
In 1083 Yoshiie became governor of Mutsu
and commander of court forces in the northeast. Though not supported by the court, he
put an end to the violence that was disrupting the region. Through this victory Yoshiie
created a strong Minamoto power base in
eastern Japan.

lathes → rokuro

Latin America and Japan

ラテンアメリカと日本

(Raten Amerika to Nihon). The first recorded contact between Japan and Latin
America dates to the late 16th century,
when the Spanish established a transpacific
trade route between Acapulco in Nueva España (now Mexico) and the Philippines. In
the early 17th century the founder of the
Tokugawa shogunate, TOKUGAWA IEYASU,
negotiated with the governor of Manila and
the viceroy of Nueva España in the hope of
establishing trade relations. A number of
Japanese sailed to Nueva España during this
period: more than 20 Japanese traveled with
Rodrigo VIVERO Y VELASCO, the governor ad
interim of Manila who had been shipwrecked on the Japanese coast; in addition,
some 140 sailed to Acapulco with HASEKURA
TSUNENAGA, an envoy sent to the Vatican by
the daimyō DATE MASAMUNE.

This early contact, however, was disrupted in 1624 with the adoption of Japan's
NATIONAL SECLUSION policy. Despite the closing of the country, information about the
American continent still managed to reach
Japan. Reports by Japanese shipwreck survivors became the first written Japanese accounts of Latin America.

Reestablishment of Contact—Of the
many Latin American nations that had
become independent by the time of the Meiji
Restoration of 1868, Peru was the first to establish diplomatic ties with Japan, as an aftermath of the MARIA LUZ INCIDENT. In 1888, a
similar treaty with Mexico was concluded,
which is known as the first "equal" treaty
signed by Japan (see UNEQUAL TREATIES, REVI-
SION OF). Subsequently, diplomatic relations
were established with Brazil (1895), Argentina (1898), Panama (1904), Chile (1906), and
Colombia (1908).

The most important aspect of relations
between Japan and Latin America before
World War II was Japanese immigration. The
number of Japanese immigrants to Latin
America from 1897 to 1941 was 244,536, of
which more than 75 percent went to Brazil.

Post–World War II Relations—During
World War II, virtually all Latin American
countries sided with the Allies, although
they did not actually do battle with Japanese
forces. The SAN FRANCISCO PEACE TREATY of
1951 led to restored diplomatic ties and to the
resumption of Japanese immigration. Between 1952 and 1981, 66,189 Japanese immigrants came to Latin America, of whom approximately 80 percent immigrated to Brazil.
As of 1986 there were about 144,000 Japanese permanently residing in Latin America
and the number of people of Japanese ancestry was about 622,000.

Economic relations between Japan and
Latin America became increasingly close
after 1945. In the 1960s the rapid growth of
the Japanese economy led to increased demand for imports of raw materials and foodstuffs from Latin America. The balance of
trade during the decades after the war was
generally in favor of the Latin American
countries. In the 1970s, however, Japanese
exports expanded greatly, tipping the balance of trade in Japan's favor. Major export
items included steel, machinery, automobiles, and ships.

The growth in Japanese exports was
slowed by the debt crisis that beset many of
the Latin American countries beginning in
1982. Japan's exports to those countries
dropped sharply in 1983 but largely recovered in the late 1980s. Bilateral trade volume
in 1989 was the highest since the debt crisis,
with Latin America exporting goods valued
at US $8.9 billion to Japan and importing US
$9.4 billion. During the 1980s Latin America
greatly increased its exports to Japan; major
exports included petroleum and manufactured goods as well as foodstuffs and raw
materials.

Japanese investments in Latin America
started as early as the 1950s, when the countries of the region embarked on ambitious industrialization programs designed to increase their self-sufficiency. Japanese
investments in the region totaled US $36.9
billion between 1951 and 1989, accounting
for 14.5 percent of total Japanese overseas investments. Japanese investors have been active in the development of natural resources
in Brazil, Venezuela, Peru, and Mexico. Most
investments in the manufacturing sector
have occurred in Brazil.

Latin American countries were also major
recipients of foreign loans by Japan's commercial banks in the 1970s. Loans outstanding to Latin America in 1986 totaled US $36.4
billion, accounting for about 25 percent of
the total Japanese private loans made that
year. It is estimated that Japan accounts for
16–17 percent of the total debt accumulated
by Brazil and Mexico.

In the area of economic cooperation,
Japan's contributions to Latin America have
been relatively small, in part because of the
comparatively high level of economic development in the region. In 1989 Latin American countries received only 8.3 percent of

Japan's official development assistance (ODA). Technical cooperation has come to be a very important area of assistance, especially in the areas of agriculture, manufacturing, and medical services. Measures to ease the debt crisis are another important area of cooperation. Japan has provided Latin American and Caribbean nations with financial aid amounting to US $5.58 billion (as of April 1990) under a fund recycling scheme aimed at providing relief to debtor nations. See also ARGENTINA AND JAPAN; BRAZIL AND JAPAN; CHILE AND JAPAN; MEXICO AND JAPAN; PERU AND JAPAN; BRAZIL, JAPANESE IMMIGRANTS IN.

Laurel, José Paciano ラウレル, J. P.

(1891–1959). President of the Republic of the Philippines during the Japanese occupation and an influential politician before and after World War II. Born in Batangas, Luzon, he studied law at Yale University. Practicing and teaching law intermittently, he formed connections with members of the local Japanese community, many of whom were his clients, in the years before World War II. During the Japanese occupation (1942–45) Laurel was made president of an "independent" Republic of the Philippines, the existence of which he proclaimed on 14 October 1943. His cautious collaboration with the Japanese served substantially to relieve Filipino hardships. Laurel left the Philippines in March 1945 and later lived in exile in Nara, Japan. He was arrested and imprisoned on war crimes charges by the Allied authorities in September and subsequently released. After his repatriation in 1946, he successfully defended himself against a charge of treason and in 1948 was granted complete amnesty by President Manuel Roxas. He later served in the senate, where he promoted the restoration of amicable relations with Japan. See also PHILIPPINES AND JAPAN.

Laures, Johannes ラウレス, J.

(1891–1959). German scholar and Jesuit missionary who wrote widely about the early Christian mission in 16th- and 17th-century Japan. Born at Fleringen in the Rhineland, he entered the Society of Jesus in 1913. After receiving his doctorate at Columbia University, he joined the staff of Jōchi Daigaku (Sophia University), Tōkyō, in 1928. Laures wrote extensively about early Japanese Christians, particularly TAKAYAMA UKON and HOSOKAWA GRACIA. He made a special study of the JESUIT MISSION PRESS and wrote *Kirishitan Bunko: A Manual of Books and Documents on the Early Christian Mission in Japan* (1940; rev ed, 1941, 1957).

law→legal system; hōritsu

law, attitudes toward 法意識

(*hōishiki*). The use of mediation and CONCILIATION, both involving the relatively informal intervention by a third party into a dispute, is much more common than litigation and preferred by many Japanese. The Japanese have often been said to possess an aversion to open hostility and a corresponding desire for the preservation of social harmony, which would be perceived as shattered by the spectacle of a public trial. The concept of harmony and the importance of submission to social superiors in Confucian philosophy are cited as both evidence and cause for these attitudes, as are the economic and social patterns of the traditional Japanese village, with its basis in the cooperative

spirit necessary for wet rice cultivation.

Conscious government policies to discourage litigation have worked to reinforce these traditions and may be the real cause for the prevalence of informal means of dispute resolution. These policies include maintaining the number of lawyers and judges at an extremely low level, so that litigation is both expensive and time-consuming, while simultaneously establishing administrative alternatives to litigation. See also DISPUTE RESOLUTION SYSTEMS OTHER THAN LITIGATION; JUDICIAL SYSTEM; LAWYERS; LEGAL EDUCATION.

Law concerning Health and Medical Services for the Aged 老人保健法

(Rōjin Hoken Hō). Law providing medical care for people aged 70 and above, as well as other health-care services for people aged 40 and above. The law was enacted in 1982 and became effective the following year. It replaced the system of free government health care for the aged that had been in effect since 1973 and stipulated that costs were to be covered partly by fixed-rate contributions from prefectures, municipalities, the National Health Insurance program, and employee insurance plans and partly by the individual. Health-care services established for people aged 40 and above included the distribution of "health notebooks," in which a person's medical history was to be recorded; health education and advice; and medical consultation and diagnosis.

Law concerning the Control of Important Industries 重要産業統制法

(Jūyō Sangyō Tōsei Hō). Enforced by the HAMAGUCHI OSACHI cabinet in 1931, this law legitimized government control over private cartels to encourage monopolization of important industries (more than 20 altogether) in order to aid Japan's recovery from the world economic crisis of the early 1930s. It was voided in 1941. See SHŌWA DEPRESSION.

law examination 司法試験

(*shihō shiken*). A national examination designed to select those with legal knowledge and ability appropriate to service as a judge, public prosecutor, or practicing lawyer. It is given under the direction of the Shihō Shiken Kanri Iinkai (National Bar Examination Administration Commission) of the Ministry of Justice. The *shihō shiken* is open to university graduates, university students credited with general education subjects at a university, and all other persons who wish to take it. Applicants in the first two categories are exempt from the first examination, but those in the third category must pass it before applying for the second examination. The second examination is comprised of a multiple-choice test, an essay examination, and an oral test.

In 1989 there were 23,202 applicants for the second examination. The final success rate was only 2.2 percent. Successful candidates complete a two-year period of special study at the LEGAL TRAINING AND RESEARCH INSTITUTE (Shihō Kenshūjo) of the Supreme Court.

law of evidence 証拠法

(*shōkohō*). In Japan, as in most modern nations, legal findings of fact must be based on evidence, as required by the principle of trial by evidence. In both criminal and civil cases, evaluation of the probative force of the evidence is left to the free determination of the

judge, except in the case of a defendant's CONFESSION, where there may be no finding of guilt unless there is corroborative evidence. The burden of proving guilt rests unilaterally on the public prosecutor.

The accused may refuse to testify on grounds of self-incrimination or because testimony would incriminate certain relatives. A doctor or lawyer may refuse to reveal confidences relating to his or her professional duties. Involuntary confessions are not admissible. Hearsay evidence is, as a general rule, inadmissible. A person may refuse to allow seizure of evidence on the grounds that it contains official or business secrets. Illegally obtained evidence may not be admitted. See also CRIMINAL PROCEDURE; CIVIL PROCEDURE, CODE OF.

Law on the Applicability of Laws →Hōrei

lawyers 弁護士

(*bengoshi*). Largest and only private branch of the legal profession. Compared with judges and prosecutors, Japanese lawyers have long had a reputation for independence and separation from government.

Representation of parties to civil litigation was recognized in 1872. However, it was not until 1880 that *daigennin* (advocates), the forerunners of the present *bengoshi*, were allowed to participate in criminal defense. In 1893 the Attorneys Law (Bengoshi Hō) required a demonstration of legal knowledge for qualification as an attorney. The recruitment and training of lawyers remained distinct from that of the other branches of the legal profession, and their legal competence, social position, and role in the judicial system were generally considered inferior to those of judges and prosecutors.

This situation was drastically altered by post–World War II reforms. Recruitment and training were consolidated for all three branches, and private practice has now become the first choice of career for most graduates of the LEGAL TRAINING AND RESEARCH INSTITUTE. As is the case with judges and public prosecutors, lawyers must pass first the national LAW EXAMINATION and then attend a two-year course at the Legal Training and Research Institute. The Attorneys Law of 1949 and the 1947 constitution have guaranteed both the autonomy of the bar and the fundamental position of civil rights and the rule of law in the Japanese polity. Private attorneys have in turn become effective advocates of those values.

As of December 1990, there were 14,106 lawyers (including 810 women), less than 5 percent of the number in the United States on a per capita basis. Sixty percent of all practicing attorneys are registered in Tōkyō and Ōsaka. Most Japanese lawyers concentrate on litigation, and most are sole practitioners or members of firms with two to four attorneys. In Japan, many legal functions are performed by nonlawyers, including nonlawyer graduates of university law faculties, and by quasi-legal professionals. There is a very low rate of litigation in Japan, possibly because the Japanese often exhaust more conciliatory methods of dispute resolution before bringing suit. In 1986 the Diet enacted special legislation concerning the practice of law by FOREIGN ATTORNEYS in an effort to open Japan's legal system to foreign lawyers. See also LAW, ATTITUDES TOWARD.

Laxman, Adam Erikovich

ラクスマン, A. E.

(1766–96?). Russian army lieutenant who headed the Russian expedition of 1792–93 to Japan. The mission was dispatched by the empress Catherine the Great under the pretext of returning Japanese castaways, but actually Laxman had been instructed to collect information about Japan and to explore the possibility of establishing commercial relations between the two countries. In spite of Japan's NATIONAL SECLUSION policy Laxman and his companions were hospitably received at Nemuro, Hokkaidō. In July 1793 they sailed to Hakodate and proceeded overland to Matsumae to confer with Ishikawa Shōgen and Murakami Daigaku, who had been sent there by the TOKUGAWA SHOGUNATE (1603–1867) to forestall a visit by the Russians to the capital.

The Japanese officials accepted the castaways and formally exchanged gifts with the Russians, but they returned Laxman's credentials and the letters he had transmitted and refused to discuss the question of trade. Not until 1804 did another Russian, Nikolai Petrovich REZANOV, attempt to establish commercial relations with Japan.

lay Buddhist movement

仏教信徒運動

(Bukkyō shinto undō). Lay men and women played important roles in the early Buddhist community in India. Although MONASTICISM was normative in southern (Hīnayāna, Theravāda) Buddhism, both monastic and lay paths were accepted in the Mahāyāna tradition of East Asia.

Government sponsorship and control of monasticism in 7th- and 8th-century Japan did not curtail the popularity of the unorthodox shamanistic Buddhists called UBASOKU (Skt: upāsaka), who combined pre-Buddhist indigenous folk piety with simple faith in Buddha. The resultant path of the holy man (J: HIJIRI) strongly influenced subsequent lay Buddhist movements.

From the late 10th century, belief in the imminence of the millennium, the Period of the Latter Day of Buddha's Law (J: mappō; see ESCHATOLOGY), stimulated the growth of devotional confraternities outside of temples and monasteries. Established Buddhism later came under the rigid control of the Tokugawa shogunate (1603–1867); however, the lay movement survived in numerous devotional associations (KŌ).

The modern period has seen vigorous lay activity in a number of Buddhist movements and sects. See also NEW RELIGIONS.

Lay, Horatio Nelson

レイ, H. N.

(1833–98). British government employee in China who was commissioned by the Meiji-period (1868–1912) government to raise its first foreign loan, aimed at financing the construction of Japan's first railways. Born in London, Lay became commissioner of the Chinese Imperial Maritime Customs in 1859. In 1869 he went to Japan with an offer to supply the Japanese government with funds for railway and telegraph construction. By December 1869 government leaders had commissioned him to raise a loan of £1 million. Having led the government to believe that he would raise the money privately, Lay floated Japanese national bonds on the London stock exchange, arranging the interest on the bonds to leave himself a large profit. The Jap-

anese government canceled his commission, appointing the British Oriental Bank Corporation to replace him as its agent.

Leach, Bernard Howell

リーチ, B. H.

(1887–1979). English potter and author who introduced the aesthetics and standards of Japanese ceramics to the West and was one of the major guiding influences in modern studio pottery. Born in Hong Kong and educated in England, he lived in Japan from 1909 to 1920 and made numerous subsequent visits. During those 11 years Leach came in contact with members of the SHIRAKABA SCHOOL, a literary group, and became close to TOMIMOTO KENKICHI, YANAGI MUNEYOSHI (Sō-etsu), and HAMADA SHŌJI. Leach was the first to build a climbing kiln in the West; his work centered around reduction-fired stoneware, with glazes ranging from celadon to tem-moku; he also worked in porcelain with underglaze cobalt. Leach reached a wide audience through his books, particularly A Potter's Book (1940).

League for Establishing a National Assembly

国会期成同盟

(Kokkai Kisei Dōmei). National political organization formed from the AIKOKUSHA (Society of Patriots) in 1880 to petition for a national assembly; the immediate predecessor of the JIYŪTŌ (Liberal Party). The league's campaign for political reform contributed to the POLITICAL CRISIS OF 1881. The Jiyūtō was formed after the government agreed to establish a parliamentary system by 1890. See also FREEDOM AND PEOPLE'S RIGHTS MOVEMENT.

League of Blood Incident

血盟団事件

(Ketsumeidan Jiken). Assassinations of INOUE JUNNOSUKE, former finance minister and a leader of the RIKKEN MINSEITŌ (Constitutional Democratic Party), and DAN TAKUMA, director-general of the MITSUI holding company, by the civilian terrorist organization Ketsumeidan (League of Blood) on 9 February and 5 March 1932. The arrest of the two assassins led to the discovery of the group formed by the ultranationalist INOUE NISSHŌ. Under the slogan ichinin issatsu ("one person, one death"), the group had drawn up a list of more than 20 important figures as targets. Inoue and the two assassins were sentenced to life imprisonment; the 11 remaining members were given sentences from 3 to 15 years. The incident was closely related to the MAY 15TH INCIDENT of the same year, in which navy officers (similarly influenced by Inoue) murdered Prime Minister INUKAI TSUYOSHI.

League of Nations and Japan

国際連盟と日本

(Kokusai Remmei to Nihon). Headquartered at Geneva, Switzerland, the League of Nations was an organization for international cooperation established in 1920 in the aftermath of World War I. Japan was one of the founding members of the league and had permanent membership in the league's council, its central organization. Japan possessed the right to attend all council meetings, to act as a member of the executive board of the league's assembly (its general meeting), and to take part in international conferences. Japan was also empowered to dispatch a judge to the Permanent Court of International Justice, a related organization. NITOBE INAZŌ occupied the post of under secretary–general of the league and director-

general of its international bureau. ISHII KIKUJIRŌ and Matsui Keishirō (1868–1946) were active in council meetings and in the assembly. Sugimura Yōtarō (1884–1939) succeeded Nitobe as under secretary–general and also took the position of director of political affairs. In 1930 Adachi Mineichirō (1869–1934) became a judge in the Court of International Justice.

In the early 1930s the Sino-Japanese problem became an issue in Geneva, and the MANCHURIAN INCIDENT of 1931 compelled the league to examine the Japanese occupation of Chinese territory. Despite strong opposition from YOSHIZAWA KENKICHI, a council member, the council dispatched the LYTTON COMMISSION to make an on-the-spot investigation. The SHANGHAI INCIDENT of 1932 and the establishment of the puppet state of MANCHUKUO by the Japanese military aroused further criticism from league members, and Japanese representatives SATŌ NAOTAKE and Nagaoka Harukazu (1877–1949) had great difficulty in defending Japanese policies. The findings of the Lytton Commission were submitted to the assembly, which issued a report criticizing both China and Japan but naming Japan as the aggressor. The Japanese delegation, headed by MATSUOKA YŌSUKE, cast a negative vote on the adoption of the report and walked out. Japan notified the league of its withdrawal on 27 March 1933. Later, Japan announced that it would cooperate with the league on peace programs but would not participate in the league's political activities. When the second Sino-Japanese War broke out in July 1937, China appealed to the league, and the issue of Japanese aggression was once again formally addressed. The council invited Japan to participate in league discussions, but Japan refused. The council applied sanctions against Japan, and soon afterward Japan notified the league of its decision to break all ties on 2 November 1938. The League of Nations ceased its activities during World War II and was replaced in 1946 by the United Nations (see UNITED NATIONS AND JAPAN).

learned societies

学会

(gakkai). Along with the introduction of European learning and the establishment of universities in the Meiji period (1868–1912), learned societies were formed in the various academic disciplines. Those in the field of the natural sciences were established early on: the Japan Mathematical Society (1877), the Japan Physics Society (1877), the Japan Chemical Society (1878), and the Japan Zoological Society (1879). During the period of rapid growth of learned societies—the second and third decades of the 20th century—many societies in the social sciences and humanities represented only a single university or research group. It was not until after World War II that societies in these fields became national in scope.

The majority of Japanese learned societies are informal groups rather than registered legal corporations. As a result, it is difficult to determine the exact number. According to a survey by the SCIENCE COUNCIL OF JAPAN, however, in 1988 there were around 1,300 national academic societies in Japan. Japanese learned societies use the Science Council of Japan as their line of communication with societies abroad.

leased house rights

借家権

(shakuyaken). The rights of a tenant, based on a building lease contract, to use the leased building either for habitation as a

Bernard Howell Leach This influential English potter introduced the techniques and aesthetics of Japanese ceramics to the West.

dwelling or for business purposes such as a shop or factory in the manner set forth in the contract. These rights are protected by the Leased House Law (Shakuya Hō), enacted in 1921. The law provides the following rights: (1) A tenant may, if he is using the building, claim leased house rights against any new owner to whom the building is assigned or any hypothecator of the building. (2) If, upon expiration of the term of the lease set forth in the lease contract, the tenant wishes to continue to rent the building, the landlord may not refuse to renew the contract except when he has a "justifiable reason" for doing so. (3) If the lease contract does not set forth the term of the lease, the contract may be canceled at any time upon three months' advance notice by the tenant or six months' advance notice by the landlord. Cancellation by the landlord is not recognized, however, unless he has a justifiable reason. The contract may be canceled if the tenant commits an act that violates the trust of the landlord, such as being several months in arrears on the rent. (4) If the rent is set forth in the contract but there is an increase in commodity prices or taxes, the landlord may unilaterally raise the rent. However, courts are empowered to determine whether the size of such an increase is legally justified.

leased land rights   借地権

(*shakuchiken*). The rights of a renter to use the land of another and own a building on it in return for paying rent. These rights are protected by the Leased Land Law (Shakuchi Hō), enacted in 1921. The Japanese CIVIL CODE provides for two types of leased land right: superficies and lease. Under Japanese law, land and the structures on it are legally distinct, so that land leases in which one rents the land of another but owns the buildings on it are frequently used.

Under the principles of the Civil Code, a leased land right must be recorded in order for the renter to assert this right against a third party who might claim a right to the land. The Law for Protection of Buildings (Tatemono Hogo Hō) of 1909 provides that after the holder of a leased land right has recorded ownership of the buildings on the rented land, he or she may claim a right to the land itself against the claims of a third party.

The Leased Land Law provides for the protection of leased land rights as follows: (1) The term of the leased land right must, if stipulated by contract, be at least 20 years; if not stipulated, it is 30 years for a wooden structure and 60 years for a steel-frame or other structure of similar durability. (2) If there is a building on the land after the leased land right has expired, the holder of the leased land right may demand that it be renewed, and the land owner may not refuse to do so except for a "justifiable reason." (3) If the holder of a leased land right assigns a building on the land to a third party, he or she must also, with the owner's consent, simultaneously assign the leased land right.

leeches   蛭

(*hiru*). In Japanese, *hiru* is the common name for segmented worms of the class Hirudinea, phylum Annelida. The *chisuibiru* (*Hirudo nipponica*) lives in ponds and swamps throughout Japan and was once used in the medical treatment of boils. The largest Japanese leech, the *umabiru* (*Whitmania pigra*), does not suck blood. The *umibiru* (genus *Pontobdella*) lives in the sea and attaches itself to fish; the *kaibiru* (*Hemiclepsis kas-*

miana) is parasitic on freshwater bivalves. The land leech *yamabiru* (*Haemadipsa zeylanica japonica*) lives in mountainous areas of southern Japan and is a source of annoyance to hikers in summer.

In the accounts given in the ancient chronicles KOJIKI (712) and NIHON SHOKI (720), a mistake in the order of the rituals at the marriage of the deities IZANAGI AND IZANAMI leads to the birth of a *hiruko* ("leech baby"), who is put into a boat woven of reeds and abandoned.

Lee Hwe-song   李恢成

(1935–   ; also spelled Yi Hoe-sŏng; J: Ri Kaisei). Author. One of the first of the second-generation Koreans in Japan to win literary acclaim for fiction written in Japanese. He was born on Sakhalin and relocated to a refugee camp in Kyūshū in 1947. He worked his way through Waseda University and received a degree in Russian literature in 1961. Lee's early works tended toward short but complex semiautobiographical accounts, structured along the lines of the traditional Korean oral narrative (*p'ansori*). Among the most highly regarded are the 1972 Akutagawa Prize–winning "Kinuta o utsu onna" (tr "The Woman Who Ironed Clothes," 1977) and *Warera seishun no tojō nite* (1969). In 1979 he completed a six-volume novel, *Mihatenu yume*, in which he articulates his utopian vision and his dreams of a unified Korea. *Saharin e no tabi* (1983) is a record of a journey to Sakhalin.

left wing   左翼

(*sayoku*). The Japanese left wing dates back to the early 20th century. The 1920s and early 1930s saw an upsurge of left-wing activity in Japan, including the birth of the leftist STUDENT MOVEMENT (see also SHINJINKAI) and the founding of both legal "proletarian" parties (see RŌDŌ NŌMINTŌ; NIHON RŌNŌTŌ; SHAKAI MINSHŪTŌ) and the illegal JAPAN COMMUNIST PARTY (JCP). Ruthlessly suppressed from the late 1920s through the war years under the provisions of the PEACE PRESERVATION LAW OF 1925, the left wing revived after World War II, led by the JCP and the radical wing of the JAPAN SOCIALIST PARTY. Over the years, as the major leftist parties have gradually adopted a more moderate and reformist stance, the term *sayoku* has tended to be replaced by the gentler *kakushin* ("progressive"). At the same time, since the 1950s small but vociferous New Left groups, usually originating in the student movement (see ZENGAKUREN), have continued to call for violent, revolutionary change in Japanese society and to reject what they see as the enfeeblement of the established left-wing parties.

legal education   法学教育

(*hōgaku kyōiku*). In Japan almost every university has a faculty of law (*hōgakubu*), which offers an undergraduate concentration leading to a bachelor's degree in the study of law but not leading directly to entry into the legal profession. In order to become qualified lawyers, law graduates must first pass the national LAW EXAMINATION and then complete two years of additional study at the national LEGAL TRAINING AND RESEARCH INSTITUTE. Since only a very small number of law graduates enter the legal profession per se, the course of study at law faculties is intended to provide a broad general knowledge of law useful to those students who will enter government service or become company employees. See also LAWYERS.

League of Nations and Japan On 24 February 1933 the chief of Japan's delegation, Matsuoka Yōsuke, repudiates the Lytton Commission report criticizing Japan's seizure of Manchuria. Japan formally withdrew from the league a month later.

legal scholarship   法学

(*hōgaku*). During the first decade following the Meiji Restoration of 1868, French law and scholarship strongly influenced Japanese law. Progressivism and the natural law philosophy prevailed in Japan. From the 1880s, when the CONSTITUTION OF THE EMPIRE OF JAPAN, based on German models, was adopted (1889), legal scholarship turned more toward German sources. Under the banner of universalism Japanese legal scholarship endeavored for a long time to do away with feudalistic status discrimination inherited from the past, though with little success.

Legal scholarship from the 1860s until about 1926 favored modernization to attain civil liberties and equality. With the help of such imported legal concepts as "general welfare" from the US constitution and *Gerechtigkeit* from the Weimar constitution, modern legal scholarship in Japan has promoted social equality by adapting Western scholarship to Japan's needs.

In constitutional law, MINOBE TATSUKICHI, with his theory of the emperor as an organ of the state (TENNŌ KIKAN SETSU), interpreted the 1889 constitution to strengthen the power of the elective Diet. His opponent, UESUGI SHINKICHI, argued in favor of the mythical history of Japan and its "national polity" (KOKUTAI), supporting the quasi-absolutist theory of the power of the emperor.

In criminal law there was antagonism between the old school (objectivist theory), represented by TAKIKAWA YUKITOKI, who believed that criminal law must require criminals to pay objectively determined penalties for crimes, and the new school (subjectivist theory), represented by MAKINO EIICHI, who advocated the rehabilitation of criminals. There was also a new school in the field of civil law: in judging a case, interpretations of abstract legal regulations were thought to be less important than analyses of the social relationships involved. Such analysis of social relationships should lead to concrete, appropriate, and rational solutions compatible with positive laws. This pragmatic approach was applied by SUEHIRO IZUTARŌ. There was also a school that advocated a "Japanese philosophy of law" (Nihon *hōri*). This was supported by nationalists and disappeared from scholarship with the collapse of the empire in 1945.

Post–World War II legal scholarship has become more influenced by sociological methods. Until the end of World War II there were no nationwide academic associations of legal science, but at present there are more than 40 academic organizations of law registered with the Science Council of Japan. Some are small and highly specialized, and others focus on broad areas of law such as public law (the Nihon Kōhō Gakkai) and private law (the Nihon Shihō Gakkai). All of these learned societies as well as a great many university faculties of law (altogether 105 national, public, and private universities have faculties of law) publish scholarly journals, making for diverse and highly developed legal scholarship in modern Japan.

legal system 法律制度

(*hōritsu seido*). The law in Japan provides, along with the ethical imperatives of society, the framework of general and specific rules within which citizens carry on their social, political, and economic lives and settle disputes in a reasonably predictable manner. Japan's present legal system is the heir of centuries of development and a complex history of adaptation of foreign legal models (Chinese in earlier times and Western more recently) to meet the needs of a changing society and polity.

LAW IN CONTEMPORARY JAPAN

Japan's present legal system is a blend of civil law (adopted in the late 19th century from the European tradition), judicial common law, and customary law. In its civil law, Japan operates under very comprehensive codes, called the Six Codes (Roppō). Of these, the constitution has been the primary document governing legal and political relationships, its democratic principles forming the basis for continuing modifications of society, law, and government since it came into effect in May 1947 (see CONSTITUTION OF JAPAN). The constitution established popular sovereignty, an emperor whose sole function was to serve as a symbol of the nation, human rights, a unique ban on war and unfettered armament, a strong bicameral legislature (the Diet), an independent judiciary, and limited local autonomy. The other five codes (the CIVIL CODE, the Code of Civil Procedure, the Penal Code, the Code of Criminal Procedure, and the COMMERCIAL CODE) are quasi-constitutional in nature and add to the constitutional foundations the outlines of various parts of the legal structure, the details of which are filled in by statutes, cabinet orders, local ordinances, various types of administrative regulations, and judicial decisions.

Judicial holdings became an important source of law under American influence during the Allied OCCUPATION (1945–52). Although Japan's judges have enjoyed independence in deciding cases since the late 19th century, the courts were limited under the Constitution of 1889 (CONSTITUTION OF THE EMPIRE OF JAPAN) in the kinds of cases they could decide and were administered by the Ministry of Justice. Under the present constitution, "the whole judicial power is vested in a Supreme Court," which administers, independently from other government branches, 8 high courts with 6 branches, 50 district courts with 201 branches, 50 family courts with 201 branches and 79 subbranches, and 452 summary courts. The power of judicial review extends to judging the validity of all laws and official acts, but it has been used against government acts sparingly, in part because of civil law deference to the democratically elected Diet. Japanese jurists also take into account the judicial decisions of other countries, especially the United States and Germany, when resolving legal issues.

A great body of Japanese statutes and other official rules has been accumulated, refined, and added to for decades, but in addition, customary law influences the way statutory law is understood and applied. For example, under the Civil Code, when the father of a family dies, the widow is accorded special rights of inheritance and all children have a right to claim equal shares of an inheritance. Custom, however, recognizes the special place of the eldest son, mainly by giving him primary responsibility for settling the affairs of the deceased on behalf of the family.

Disputes and Their Settlement—The Japanese legal system facilitates out-of-court problem resolution. Under special laws and procedures, disputes are very often resolved by compromise on one or both sides in the presence of an empathetic and conciliating third party, whose task is to draw the opposing sides closer together on the issues in as civil an atmosphere as possible and confirm any agreement that has been reached. Such a mediator may be a friend or relative of a disputing party, or someone with official status, such as a conciliation commissioner, a family court counselor, or a judge. Lay civil liberties commissioners and local administrative counselors also play a role in dealing with local human rights problems. The various modes of adjustment and conciliation of differences between parties somewhat alleviate the problem of Japan's small number of judges and supplement the litigation proceedings of courts. See DISPUTE RESOLUTION SYSTEMS OTHER THAN LITIGATION; LAW, ATTITUDES TOWARD.

Perceptions and Uses of Law—The preference for conciliation does not mean that the Japanese are less prone to argument or litigation than other peoples, or that disputants usually settle for less than they would receive if they asserted their rights in court. However, most Japanese seem more comfortable in a group context, such as that created by mediation, than in a situation in which they must face an adversary, a superior, an official, or the public alone.

A substantial number of Japan's officials, cultural leaders, and business leaders majored in law as undergraduates at university faculties of law, and they refer to the written law on a regular basis in conducting their affairs. Members of the local and national higher civil service tend to be legalistic in their approach to problems. In foreign and domestic business matters, the bureaucracy's customary ADMINISTRATIVE GUIDANCE has been quite influential, but Japan generally follows common international law practices in its trade relations.

Well-used copies of the Six Codes and of a wide array of pertinent laws and regulations will be found not only in law offices and judicial chambers but also in the offices of Japan's private organizations, government units, mass media companies, schools, and scholars. In addition, many companies have their own codes, which may best be classified as customary law.

The Legal Profession and the Public—Virtually all judges, prosecutors, and lawyers have been trained since 1947 in the same postgraduate education program at the Supreme Court's LEGAL TRAINING AND RESEARCH INSTITUTE in Tōkyō, entrance to which is only by severely competitive national law examinations.

Synopses of the law in special-interest areas and popularized treatments of the law and famous cases appear in books, maga-zines, and newspapers for the general reader, which also give information about consumer rights and the intricacies of real estate and tax law. Both legislative disputes and major judicial decisions receive substantial coverage in the mass media. Thus there is ready access to information about law and legal problems.

Criminal Justice—Japan's crime rate is low, due in part to a lenient yet effective criminal justice system. A high proportion of offenders turn themselves in; most other suspects apprehended by the police confess their wrongdoing. A coerced confession is not evidence admissible in court, but judges and officials tend to weigh heavily confession and a contrite attitude. Relatively few cases reach the courts, because the prosecutors have quasi-judicial powers and often avoid indictment even where guilt is clear. Of the defendants who are tried by summary courts (for minor crimes) and district courts, over 99 percent are convicted, but most penalties are small fines. Of the few defendants sentenced to prison, about two-thirds have their sentences suspended.

Compassion for offenders who obey the customary laws of repentance and apology is characteristic. For example, in private law, a magazine sued for defamation may pay smaller damages if it publishes a retraction or apology. Japan's human rights record is generally good; remaining problems, however, include pre-indictment detention practices and insufficient access to defense attorneys.

As in all rule-of-law systems, the task of law in Japan is to provide generally operative guidelines and procedures for making and implementing formal agreements and for approximating justice in a civilized settlement of disputes and criminal cases. In pursuing these ends, the legal system of Japan nudges society toward perceptions and practices ever more in keeping with the principles in the constitution of Japan while respecting its rich legal heritage.

HISTORY OF JAPANESE LAW

Surviving legal codes allow a division of the history of Japanese law into five major stages, beginning with the late-7th-century establishment of a centralized government organized on the basis of a Chinese-style legal code (see RITSURYŌ SYSTEM). This body of law was concerned with state operations under a theoretically supreme EMPEROR and a centralized, hereditary bureaucracy subordinate to him. Its framework served as the theoretical basis for delegation of political authority until the issuance of the first modern constitution in 1889. Nonetheless, its administrative apparatus and substance fell into disuse, and its administrative sections were used by de facto powerholders to legitimize their rule. Thus, the second period of Japanese legal history can be dated from the 9th to the late 15th century, a time in which political organization was characterized by the gradual decentralization of jurisdiction and reliance upon local legal procedures.

The third stage of legal history developed between the late 15th century and 1868, during which time an absolutist military government grafted new forms of law onto the roots of the *ritsuryō* system's delegation of authority. The fourth stage of legal development lasted from 1868 to 1945, a period in which Japan implemented governmental reform and economic modernization with the aid of a modified emperor system and the European concept of an absolute state. The application then of the radically new principle of separation of legislative and judicial, if not executive, powers provided a useful precedent for the constitutional and judicial reforms instituted in Japan's fifth stage of legal development, from 1945 to the present.

Law and the Early State (600–800) — In 604 the SEVENTEEN-ARTICLE CONSTITUTION was issued by the YAMATO state. Although it may not, as some claim, have been written by Prince SHŌTOKU, the general character of this constitution's Chinese-inspired injunctions embodied his vision of political centralization, a plan that entailed integration of the chieftains of previously independent UJI (clans) into an aristocracy that would function as an imperial bureaucracy subordinate to the emperor. Actual codification of law began with the TAIHŌ CODE (Taihō Ritsuryō) of 701 and the YŌRŌ CODE of 718 (promulgated 757). The Yōrō Code, parts of which survive, comprehensively regulated the central administration of the growing national government. As the name *ritsuryō* implies, these articles consisted of criminal law provisions (*ritsu*) and administrative statutes (*ryō*). Supplements and revisions to the criminal laws and statutes, called *kyaku* and *shiki*, were issued until about 927 (see ENGI SHIKI).

Principles of criminal law. The Japanese criminal code, like its Chinese model, was intended to correct and edify the criminal by application of punishments appropriate to his crime. The seriousness of a crime was determined by the degree to which it had upset the Confucian moral order, which was embodied in the legal code. The formal provisions of criminal law underwent very little revision, but its administration did change considerably. The decentralization of authority encouraged the application of native norms for criminal procedures.

The judicial function. The *ritsuryō* government was not divided into judiciary and executive branches. Rather, administrative officers generally held judicial authority over their subordinates. Procedure followed the Chinese pattern, with little differentiation between civil and criminal cases. The court procedure adhered to an inquisitorial, as opposed to an adversary, system. A party in disagreement with the court's decision could appeal, but only after obtaining from the original court a document authorizing the appeal.

Throughout the Heian period (794–1185) many statutory offices gradually lost their authorized duties and powers to the increasingly numerous extrastatutory offices (RYŌGE NO KAN). The result was increasing devolution and fragmentation of central government authority.

Land law. Under *ritsuryō* law the state owned most land. With the exception of officials' "salary land" (*shikiden*), it equally distributed all cultivated rice land to the peasantry and granted the use of forest lands to their communities. Residential land, however, was not "nationalized," and its sale was unrestricted. Such sales could be made in perpetuity once the parties drew up contracts (KOKEN) and petitioned local officials, usually at the district level, for authorization.

In order to encourage private reclamation of uncultivated lands, the Nara period (710–794) government issued edicts authorizing exemptions from taxation as a reward—for three generations (SANZE ISSHIN NO HŌ) in 723, and for perpetuity (KONDEN EISEI SHIZAI HŌ) in 743. Religious institutions, high-ranking aristocratic households, and other landhold-

ing enterprises already exempt from taxes because of their special status were thereby able to develop huge landed estates. The ensuing commendation of land by the peasantry to these powerful landlords for tax evasion purposes resulted eventually in a shift of control over the land from the central government to the estate (SHŌEN) proprietors.

The Shōen Period: Decentralized Jurisdictions (800–1500) — During this period, state power over the land assumed more and more the function of a tax-collecting institution, delegating administrative authority over the land to managers of *shōen*. Since the state also granted other kinds of authority over the land to many other levels of social organization, the political system began to function in terms of private rights over productive land and its residents—an arrangement that the legal system had theoretically denied. By the middle of the 9th century, decentralization of government had reached the point where peasants had no direct contact with the state legal apparatus and were governed instead by the *shōen* proprietors.

Shōen law. After *shōen* proprietors—either court aristocrats or religious institutions—acquired land management rights, they appointed managers to administer their *shōen* independent of state control. Furthermore, upon receipt of state exemptions from tax payment and from intrusion by provincial government police (FUYU AND FUNYŪ), the proprietors effectively barred government officials from their *shōen*. Consequently, the legal process there was detached from the confines of *ritsuryō* statutes. *Shōen* law varied considerably from place to place, but one commonly shared feature was that court procedure began to show elements of an adversary, as opposed to an inquisitorial, system. Uncodified norms recognizing precedent also developed over generations in local communities and came to be the core of "private" land law.

Military law. Exercise of political authority by military leaders (*buke*) was legitimized by legal procedures stemming from the *ritsuryō* code. After the KAMAKURA SHOGUNATE (1192–1333) acquired the right to exercise nationwide control over all police and military agents, it set up the Board of Inquiry (MONCHŪJO) to make and apply rules for the resolution of land disputes among its own retainers.

In 1232 the shogunate issued a legal code, the GOSEIBAI SHIKIMOKU (also called the Jōei Shikimoku), which institutionalized and rationalized shogunate organization after the death of the charismatic leaders of the founding period. In essence, this new military code was meant to handle conflicts over private property, problems the old *ritsuryō* code had no reason to treat. Regulations were issued by the Council of State (HYŌJŌSHŪ), but scholars have found that the Hyōjōshū relied increasingly on precedent rather than on statute and allowed at times the use of an adversary system in civil law cases.

The legal system of the Goseibai Shikimoku and its supplementary regulations endured until the end of the medieval period (mid-12th–16th centuries). Both the Kamakura and Muromachi shogunate (1338–1573) legal systems issued regulations mainly concerned with the affairs of their own *samurai* retainers. Especially from the late Muromachi period (1333–1568), after the ŌNIN WAR (1467–77), these military men performed an even wider range of civilian administrative functions. Samurai control of all civilian affairs and direct application of

military law to all nonmilitary sectors, including religious communities, farmers, artisans, and merchants, brought Japan in the 16th century to an absolutist government that lasted through the three succeeding centuries.

Absolutist Government under Military Law (ca 1500–1868) — During the Warring States (Sengoku) period (1467–1568), SENGOKU DAIMYŌ (territorial warlords) issued legal codes (BUNKOKUHŌ) to govern the areas they had seized. These codes regulated the property dealings, marriage relations, and alliances of a daimyō's retainers. They taxed merchants, artisans, and the agricultural population, circumscribing the power of the landlords to charge rent and administer judicial and police affairs. They also prescribed litigation procedures and all forms for financial transactions. As is evident from such concerns, these legal codes were intended to regulate tightly the social and economic activities of all inhabitants within a daimyō's territory. The comprehensive character of these codes thus significantly distinguished them from earlier shogunate law with its almost exclusive concern with the affairs of its military retainers. The predominant basis of jurisdiction and military rule became territorial, and, when the Sengoku daimyō eventually yielded to the Tokugawa shogunate (1603–1867), this principle of territorial jurisdiction was adopted by the new regime for the entire nation.

Foundation of the Tokugawa shogunate. There were three major stages of legal development during the Edo period (1600–1868). The first and most successful stage (1600–1640) saw the establishment of political regulations for the state's transition to the relatively centralized BAKUHAN SYSTEM. The new government's first body of national law, the BUKE SHOHATTO (1615), consisted of abstract principles to guide daimyō in the independent administration of their domains (HAN). But the major provisions of its second body of law, issued in 1635, were far more specific and restrictive, dictating to the daimyō their conduct and responsibilities.

The KINCHŪ NARABI NI KUGE SHOHATTO regulated the imperial court and Kyōto aristocracy and barred the emperor from taking part in political activity. Temples and shrines were controlled by a series of regulations collectively known as the Shoshū Jiin Hatto and the Shosha Negi Kannushi Hatto.

The second stage of Tokugawa legal development (ca 1640–1853) saw the Confucian refinement and rationalization of the shogunate's political control. Shogunate jurists, influenced by studies of Ming dynasty (1368–1644) Chinese statutes, created new *ritsuryō*-type provisions, the best known of which is the KUJIKATA OSADAMEGAKI, issued in 1742. In addition, shogunate proclamations to the general public were issued and collected (see OFUREGAKI SHŪSEI) after 1744.

Many of the conflicts that arose from growing commercialization and social change remained unresolvable. Social legislation became more repressive. In the final stage of Tokugawa legal development, 1853–67, the shogunate was faced with foreign aggression as well as economic instability and domainal independence. Insurgents joined to crush its regime and establish the Meiji government in 1868.

Institutionalization of Absolutist Monarchy (1868–1945) — During the 1870s jurists still depended on Chinese models of

leisure industry
Reflecting Japan's expanding leisure industry, the establishment of theme parks is increasing. Opened in 1990, Space World, in the city of Kita Kyūshū, Fukuoka Prefecture, is billed as the world's first space theme park.

law, but during the 1880s they abandoned them in favor of Western legal systems in order to persuade the Western powers to revise the so-called Unequal Treaties (see UNEQUAL TREATIES, REVISION OF). They rejected English law with its liberal common-law tradition as a model for the Meiji-period codes, because Japan's legal heritage consisted of a mixture of codified law based on the Chinese legal framework and Japanese authoritarian practices. Instead, Japanese lawmakers initially showed a preference for French law and, after a period of intense translation of five Napoleonic codes, invited Gustave Emile BOISSONADE DE FONTARABIE, a French scholar of criminal law, to assist in drafting a new penal code.

By the time the Penal Code was issued in 1880 (see CRIMINAL LAW), however, Japanese leaders had begun to shift their attention to German models. Sharing with Tokugawa law the conception of law as a system imposed by an absolute monarch, and not as the embodiment of justice, German law provided a model of a "constitutional state" (*Rechtsstaatprinzip*), which the Japanese authorities adapted in a severely restricted manner.

Public law. From the first, public law remained the most conservative part of the new legal system. In the 1870s the government declared that it was dedicated to developing a legal system based upon the separation of powers and the guarantee of human rights. When actually promulgated, however, the 1889 CONSTITUTION OF THE EMPIRE OF JAPAN did not guarantee even rule by law. Its drafters described it as a gift of the emperor to the people, with the legislature, cabinet, and judiciary all under his authority. When the emperor delegated this authority to government officials, they were beholden not to the constitution but to him. In fact, since the constitution did not explicitly subordinate military and civil administration to law, authoritarian groups in the army and cabinet used their imperially delegated powers to thwart the process of liberalization evident in Japan after World War I. Indeed, the legislature, anxious to restrict civil rights, passed the PEACE PRESERVATION LAW OF 1925, which stipulated punishment for anyone who organized, participated in an organization, or induced participation in action against the private property system or the state polity (KOKUTAI).

The Meiji oligarchs who drafted the 1889 constitution were far less concerned with establishing a rule of law than with achieving military and economic modernization. Law

was little more than a tool for implementing the reforms they desired.

Development of a Rule of Law (1945 to the Present)——The constitution of 1947 superseded the 1889 constitution with a wholesale revision, removing those features that had seriously hampered the development of a rule of law. First, it finally established the principle of the separation of powers by abolishing the ADMINISTRATIVE COURT. Second, it formally introduced a system of JUDICIAL REVIEW similar to that of the United States by granting the courts supreme judicial power. The growing strength of judicial review, along with a strong consciousness of judicial independence nurtured since the Meiji period (1868–1912), indicates that the public law field is a fertile ground for the growth of rights consciousness. Third, the new constitution provided for extensive protection of civil liberties. This reform entailed the complete revision of the Code of Criminal Procedure and the enactment of new laws protecting workers' rights, such as the Labor Standards Law, Labor Union Law, and Labor Relations Adjustment Law (see LABOR LAWS).

In the area of public law, the most radical feature of the current constitution is article 9, on the RENUNCIATION OF WAR, which states that "the Japanese people forever renounce war as a sovereign right of the nation. . . . The right of belligerency of the state will not be recognized."

Private law. Legal practices concerning private transactions and litigation have a tradition different from that of public law. In the early Meiji period litigation and formal judicial decisions were found not to work in many social settings, and in 1876 the government recognized informal resolution methods by reinstating conciliation. In 1922 mediation was recognized for the resolution of land and house lease disputes, pecuniary debts, and domestic relations. Increasingly, however, in present-day Japan disputants seek resolution by litigation, hoping to obtain judgments made in accordance with universal standards.

One problem with the present Civil Code, still basically the 1898 Civil Code, is the ever-widening gap between legal needs and legal codification. For example, there are only a few articles covering torts. Attorneys must represent clients, such as industrial pollution victims, by means of only one tort provision. Case law has developed since Meiji times, but it is not the principal source of law as it is in the Anglo-American tradition.

Anglo-American influence was most strongly felt in the post–World War II era. The OCCUPATION government, under American direction, paid strict attention to regulating economic and political organizations that it believed had contributed to national militarization in the 1930s. To dissolve permanently the huge business combines known as ZAIBATSU, the ANTIMONOPOLY LAW and the Fair Trade Commission were instituted; these are two of the most significant legal reforms outside constitutional law. The American influence in business-related fields can also be seen in the partial revision of company law, which emphasizes the protection of shareholders and the fiduciary duties of management, and in the newly enacted CORPORATE REORGANIZATION LAW.

Japan's present legal system is an intricately woven fabric of codes, whose design has been often modified in the past century. Its warp of traditional political concepts and woof of social and economic change are pro-

ducing a continually new blend of law. The jury system, for example, has been tried (1928) and discarded (1943) as inappropriate. On the other hand, other principles like judicial review (1947) have been slowly nurtured and appear likely to survive.

Legal Training and Research Institute　司法研修所

(Shihō Kenshūjo). A national educational institution that provides professional legal training. It was established by law in 1947 in Tōkyō as an agency of the Supreme Court. Its major functions are to provide legal apprentices with comprehensive professional training in civil and criminal jurisprudence and to offer judges continuing advanced legal education.

About 500 applicants annually successfully pass the national LAW EXAMINATION (*shihō shiken*); almost all of them are admitted to the Legal Training and Research Institute as legal apprentices called *shihō shūshūsei*. Upon successfully completing the two-year training program and the final qualifying law examination, apprentices may either be appointed assistant judges or public prosecutors, or they may register as practicing lawyers. See also LEGAL EDUCATION.

Le Gendre, Charles William
ル・ジャンドル, C. W.

(1830–99). American general and diplomat; as an adviser to the Japanese Ministry of Foreign Affairs from 1872 to 1875, he played an important role in the TAIWAN EXPEDITION OF 1874. In 1866 Le Gendre was appointed US consul at the Chinese treaty port of Xiamen (Amoy) and led a punitive expedition against Taiwan aborigines who had massacred the crew of a shipwrecked American vessel. In 1872 Le Gendre visited Japan and was hired by Foreign Minister SOEJIMA TANEOMI as an adviser. At that time the Japanese government was considering an expedition to Taiwan to avenge the murder of shipwrecked Ryūkyū Islanders in 1871, and Le Gendre helped organize the expedition. For this he was confined briefly at the US consulate, but the Japanese government showed its appreciation in 1875 by awarding him the Order of the Rising Sun. He was the first foreigner so honored. He remained in Japan until 1890, working in a private capacity for the political party leader ŌKUMA SHIGENOBU. He was the author of *Progressive Japan: A Study of the Political and Social Needs of the Empire* (1878).

leisure industry　レジャー産業

(*rejā sangyō*). Japan's leisure industry is expanding due to an increase in the average person's free time caused by changes such as the move to a five-day workweek by government offices and financial institutions. According to the Leisure Development Center, leisure spending in 1989 accounted for 28.8 percent of total private expenditures, or ¥63.5 trillion (US $460.3 billion). The Japanese leisure industry has expanded to include such areas as fitness clubs, restaurants, rental cars, cultural education courses, theater, and concerts. Traditional leisure businesses such as travel, hotels, Japanese inns, amusement parks, and movies remain popular.

In the early 1990s some companies in Japan were concentrating on developing large-scale domestic resorts for long-term stays. One special characteristic of this new resort development is that the key players include not just companies from leisure-

Spectators at the Tōkyō Race Course waiting for the running of the Japan Derby, a major horse-racing event.

Fans watching a professional baseball night game at Tōkyō's Jingū Stadium, home field of the Yakult Swallows.

This detail from a pair of Edo-period folding screens depicts warriors and spectators gathered to enjoy *inuoumono*, a sport in which mounted warriors shot arrows at dogs.

related businesses, such as railways, housing developers, and tourism, but also many participants from heavy industries, such as iron and steel, shipbuilding, and mining.

leisure-time activities　余暇活動

(*yoka katsudō*). The significance and variety of leisure activities have changed as different social classes achieved prominence during the course of Japanese history. Today many of the pastimes once restricted to the upper classes, as well as leisure activities imported from the West, are enjoyed by all levels of society.

The Early Historical Period: Courtly Pastimes—With the establishment of the RITSURYŌ SYSTEM of government at the end of the 7th century, noblemen of the imperial court constituted the principal leisure class of the time. Favorite pastimes in the imperial court included poetry composition; music; indoor games such as GO, SUGOROKU, and SHŌGI; sports such as KEMARI and FALCONRY; and seasonal excursions of various kinds, including SNOW VIEWING and cherry-blossom viewing (HANAMI).

Medieval Period: Warrior Pastimes—During the Kamakura (1185–1333) and Muromachi (1333–1568) periods, the warriors, who replaced the noblemen as the rulers of the country, became the principal leisure class. Their favorite pastimes were active outdoor sports such as YABUSAME, KASAGAKE, and INUOUMONO. SUMŌ wrestling, which had existed as a sport in the imperial court, was encouraged and became increasingly popular.

The more elegant courtly pastimes of poetry and music were also taken up by the higher ranks of warriors and popularized. It was during the Kamakura period that RENGA (linked verse) developed from WAKA (court poetry). During the Muromachi period, the intricate practices of the TEA CEREMONY were established. Board games continued to be very popular throughout the medieval period.

The Early Modern Period: The Leisure Pursuits of the Townspeople—During the Azuchi-Momoyama (1568–1600) and Edo (1600–1868) periods, the merchant classes, or CHŌNIN, who were economically powerful, became the core of the new leisure class. The growth of the cities led to the de-

velopment of entertainment quarters reflecting every level of taste, from sophisticated drama such as KABUKI and JŌRURI (puppet plays) to more popular art forms such as RAKUGO and *kōshaku*, which were forms of storytelling.

Introduction of Western Leisure Activities—During the Meiji (1868–1912) and Taishō (1912–26) periods, many Western pastimes, such as card games, billiards, and ballroom dancing, were imported. A more significant development was the introduction of Western sports, such as TENNIS, BASEBALL, TRACK AND FIELD EVENTS, TABLE TENNIS, soccer, rugby, basketball, VOLLEYBALL, and boating. Many of these sports became part of school curricula and thus took root in Japan. The mass media also assumed growing importance. By the Taishō period, motion pictures (see FILM, JAPANESE) were the main source of entertainment for the masses.

Leisure Pursuits since World War II—During the difficult days that immediately followed World War II, the radio was an important source of entertainment. Songs, *rakugo*, MANZAI (comic dialogue), and radio dramas helped many people to forget the hardships they were facing daily. Partly encouraged by the Occupation forces, various sports were revived, although such martial arts as JŪDŌ and KENDŌ were forbidden for some time. Among the revived sports, baseball was the most popular.

Although Japan's traditionally long working hours have, in theory, decreased somewhat with the adoption of the five-day workweek by some companies, the growth of the country's economy that began in the 1960s still tends to demand long hours on the job. As a result, leisure in Japan is generally centered on activities that require only small amounts of time; these activities also tend to be costly. Fitness and relief from work-related stress became important leisure-time pursuits in the 1970s.

Traditional leisure activities, such as the tea ceremony, FLOWER ARRANGEMENT, and CALLIGRAPHY, have remained popular. There has been a significant increase in the number of CULTURE CENTERS, which offer courses in subjects such as art, foreign languages, and dance.

Sports events, plays, concerts, and films continue to be popular forms of entertain-

ment. Traditional board games such as *go*, *shōgi*, and MAH-JONGG are still enjoyed both at home and in clubs. Gambling, in the form of PACHINKO, and betting sports, such as horse, bicycle, and speedboat racing, show no sign of disappearing.

Travel continues to gain in popularity as a leisure-time activity for the Japanese. Spurred in part by the favorable yen-dollar exchange rate, overseas travel has continued to flourish. The Japanese view of leisure has shifted, with leisure being seen increasingly as an end in itself rather than merely as a means of renewing one's physical energies for work.

Lelang (Lolang)　楽浪郡

(J: Rakurō Gun; Kor: Nangnang). A Former (206 BC–AD 8) and Later (25–220) Han dynasty Chinese colony established in northwestern Korea, in the area surrounding what is now the city of P'yŏngyang, by Emperor Wu-ti (Wudi) in 108 BC. According to the Chinese chronicle WEI ZHI (*Wei chih*), HIMIKO, the ruler of the Japanese state of Yamatai, sent tribute to Lelang. The colony submitted to forces of the Korean kingdom of KOGURYŌ in AD 313.

Lenin and Japan　レーニンと日本

(Rēnin *to* Nihon). Vladimir Il'ich Lenin (1870–1924), the founder of the modern Soviet state and a major contributor to the theory of communism, studied the history of Japan in depth. His statements about Japan contain an economic and political description of Japan at various stages of its development, starting in the late 1860s and early 1870s. In "An Attempt at the Summary of the Data of World History after 1870," Lenin saw the Meiji Restoration of 1868 as revolutionary in character. Lenin's greatest contribution in his discussion of Japan was to identify the military-feudal nature of Japanese imperialism.

In the early 1920s he had a number of meetings with prominent figures in the Japanese socialist movement, notably with KATAYAMA SEN (1860–1933; three times), Taguchi Unzō (1892–1933), and Yoshida Hajime (dates unknown). Between 1921 and 1937, 292 separate editions of the works of Lenin

Battle of Leyte Gulf
The aircraft carrier *Zuihō*, shown here under attack by American warplanes, was one of the many Japanese ships lost during this decisive naval battle off the Philippines in October 1944.

were published in Japan; between 1945 and 1967, 134 separate editions and 32 collections of his writings appeared. In 1969 a 45-volume translation of the complete works of Lenin was completed.

Lerch, Theodor von レルヒ, T.

(1869–1945). Austrian officer who introduced skiing to Japan. Posted to Japan in 1910 as a military attaché at the Austrian embassy, in the following year he taught skiing to members of the Takada 58th Infantry Regiment. He later taught skiing to the Asahikawa army division. He returned to Austria in 1912.

lese majesty 不敬罪

(*fukeizai*). Crime against the dignity of the emperor or a member of the imperial family. Lese majesty was recognized under the CONSTITUTION OF THE EMPIRE OF JAPAN of 1889 but is not included in the 1947 CONSTITUTION OF JAPAN. The latter establishes the principles of equality under the law and prohibits any discrimination on the basis of social status or family origin (art. 14), thus eliminating the special status of the emperor and the imperial family. Consequently, the current Penal Code, as revised under the 1947 constitution, does not contain the crime of lese majesty.

Leyte Gulf, Battle of レイテ沖海戦

(Reite Oki Kaisen; also known in Japan as Firipin Oki Kaisen, Battle off the Philippines; not to be confused with the Battle of the PHILIPPINE SEA). Largest naval engagement in the Pacific in World War II; a decisive defeat for the Japanese forces. It was fought near the Philippine Islands from 23–26 October 1944. The Combined Fleet of the Imperial Japanese Navy was divided into three groups, with the final objective of attacking the US landing craft assembled in Leyte Gulf for the invasion of Leyte Island. The Japanese lost many ships, including the MUSASHI, and hundreds of aircraft, leaving the Combined Fleet incapable of any further large-scale naval operations. See also WORLD WAR II.

liability based on negligence 過失責任

(*kashitsu sekinin*). Legal term that refers to the principle that no liability is incurred without negligence. The principle of liability based on negligence is set forth clearly in article 709 of the CIVIL CODE: "A person who by willful intent or negligence infringes the rights of another shall be responsible for indemnifying the injury which is thereby incurred."

In contrast to other types of tort liability in which the burden of proof concerning negligence is on the offending party, this re-

sponsibility is not, as a matter of course, imposed on businesses for injury to human life or health resulting from chemicals, medicines, food products, and air or water pollution. The development of modern industry inevitably entails a measure of pollution to which the attribution of liability based on negligence has been deemed contradictory to the intent of the law. However, in a series of lawsuits involving damages of this nature, the courts have imposed a duty on enterprises to foresee such consequences and have recognized their responsibility to compensate for damages. Thus, the liability of enterprises, although subject to the principle of negligence liability, virtually amounts to liability without fault. See also STRICT LIABILITY.

liability without fault→strict liability

Liang Qichao (Liang Ch'i-ch'ao) 梁啓超

(1873–1929; J: Ryō Keichō). Influential Chinese intellectual leader and advocate of reform and constitutionalism; leading disciple of KANG YOUWEI (K'ang Yu-wei). Following the failure of the Hundred Days' Reform in 1898, Liang escaped to Tōkyō, where he was befriended by the politician INUKAI TSUYOSHI. During his years in Japan, he published a series of influential journals emphasizing the importance of individualism. Although his political stance fluctuated, Liang continued to support Kang Youwei's constitutional monarchy movement against the revolutionary, anti-Manchu movement of SUN YAT-SEN and the Tōkyō-based revolutionary United League (Tongmeng Hui; T'ung-meng Hui). After the fall of the Qing (Ch'ing) dynasty in 1912, Liang returned to China, where he was involved in politics until his retirement in 1917.

Liao Chengzhi (Liao Ch'eng-chih) 廖承志

(1908–83; J: Ryō Shōshi). Chinese communist official active in Sino-Japanese relations. Born in Tōkyō. The son of Liao Zhongkai (Liao Chung-k'ai; 1878–1925), a revolutionary associate of SUN YAT-SEN then in exile in Japan, Chengzhi studied at Waseda University. He negotiated the repatriation of Japanese nationals from China in 1953. In 1962 Liao and Takasaki Tatsunosuke (1885–1964), a Japanese Diet member, signed an agreement that increased Sino-Japanese trade. See also CHINA AND JAPAN.

Libel Law of 1875 讒謗律

(Zambōritsu). Law enacted on 28 June 1875 to control the press and limit freedom of expression. It provided varying penalties for publicly misrepresenting or defaming a person in writing, print, or drawing. Along with the PRESS ORDINANCE OF 1875 and the PUBLICATION ORDINANCE OF 1869, it was used by the Meiji government to stifle public political discussion stimulated by the FREEDOM AND PEOPLE'S RIGHTS MOVEMENT.

Liberal Democratic Party 自由民主党

(LDP; J: Jiyū Minshutō). Political party. Japan's ruling party since its establishment in November 1955 through the merger of the LIBERAL PARTY (Jiyūtō) and the Japan Democratic Party (see NIHON MINSHUTŌ), both of which had been founded by conservative Diet members formerly affiliated with the pre–World War II parties RIKKEN SEIYŪKAI and RIKKEN MINSEITŌ. As their predecessors had dominated party politics in prewar Japan, the

Liberals and Democrats had dominated politics in the first decade of the postwar period, except during the short tenure of a coalition government led by a Socialist prime minister in 1947–48. After its formation, the LDP inherited their dominant role in Japanese politics and has since enjoyed nearly 40 years of uninterrupted power at the national level. By the summer of 1991, 14 successive LDP presidents had served as prime ministers of Japan.

The LDP has established a wide base of support among farmers, businessmen, professionals, upper- and middle-level civil servants, and nonunionized workers. Until the late 1960s the party won every DIET election and the majority of local elections with substantial margins. During the 1970s, however, the LDP's popularity at the polls declined steadily. Both the LOCKHEED SCANDAL, which tarnished the reputation of the LDP, and the formation of the breakaway New Liberal Club (Shin Jiyū Kurabu) led to an erosion of the LDP majority in the HOUSE OF REPRESENTATIVES in the 1976 and the 1979 elections. The party temporarily managed to reverse this trend by making substantial gains in simultaneous elections for both the House of Representatives and the HOUSE OF COUNCILLORS in June 1980. However, in the general election of December 1983, the LDP again suffered losses in the House of Representatives, due in large part to voter reaction to the sentencing of former Prime Minister TANAKA KAKUEI to prison for his role in the Lockheed Scandal. As a result, the LDP was forced to form a coalition cabinet with the New Liberal Club in order to maintain a narrow majority in the lower house. More recently, in July 1989, the LDP lost control of the House of Councillors when the JAPAN SOCIALIST PARTY won a major election victory, capitalizing on voter dissatisfaction with the LDP stemming from its members' involvement in the RECRUIT SCANDAL and their role in passing the unpopular CONSUMPTION TAX. During lower-house elections the following year the LDP was able to retain its majority in the House of Representatives, but due to the loss of its majority in the House of Councillors, the party was forced to collaborate with both the KŌMEITŌ and the DEMOCRATIC SOCIALIST PARTY.

Ideology and Policies—The LDP is a conservative party in the sense that the majority of its leaders uphold such traditional political and civic values as patriotism, deference to authority, respect for the institution of the family, and belief in law and order. Even in such basic ideological commitments, however, the party is by no means monolithic. On particular policy issues, opinion in the party has almost always been divided. In most cases consensus is achieved by compromise. As a result, eclectic and often contradictory positions have been propounded as official party lines.

While the LDP has advocated individual initiative, free enterprise, and the sanctity of private property, it has also supported government-sponsored medical insurance, old-age pensions, and social welfare programs; it has defended the right of management to profits, but also the right of labor to a minimum wage and improved working conditions; it has called for academic freedom, but also for government control of school textbooks and teachers. The party has supported a United Nations–centered diplomacy, while also promoting special ties with the industrialized West, especially the United States, and with the nations of Asia; it has called for development of a substantial independent self-defense capability, but within the framework of mutual defense arrangements with the United States; and it has espoused free trade, but also the attainment of self-sufficiency in staple agricultural products.

Party Organization——The president (*sōsai*) is the top party official and serves concurrently and almost automatically as the prime minister of each LDP cabinet. The president is assisted by a secretary-general (*kanjichō*) who directs the management of the party secretariat, including bureaus of budget and personnel. The most important among the standing committees of the party are the Executive Council (Sōmukai) and the Political Affairs Research Committee (Seimu Chōsakai). Since 1964 the Executive Council has consisted of 30 LDP Diet members and functions as a substitute for the annual party conference, which is formally the highest decision-making body. Along with the secretary-general, the chairmen of the two councils constitute a triumvirate that acts as the ultimate arbiter of disputes between the party and such various groups outside the party as government agencies and private interest groups, as well as among groups within the party.

Factions——Because of the extensive powers and prerogatives vested in his office as the leader of the party and the government, the election of an LDP president breeds intense competition among candidates and their factional followers. Since even the largest faction has not controlled more than about one-quarter of the voting delegates, competing alliances of several factions have formed in support of rival candidates. Following each presidential election, the winning coalition becomes the "mainstream" and the losing bloc the "opposition." The competition and campaigning continues into periods between elections and has become a constant preoccupation of both the incumbent officeholders and their opponents.

From the time of founding of the LDP to the present day, a half-dozen major factions with up to about 100 affiliated Diet members have fought, bargained, and compromised with one another for control of high party and government posts. In the process, large amounts of money have routinely changed hands among candidates for such posts and their supporters.

Money Politics——Funds expended in the never-ending electioneering activities of rival LDP factions are supplied mainly by conservative businessmen associated with particular faction leaders. A successful candidate for LDP president has usually been the leader of a large faction or coalition of factions with access to the wealthiest and most generous businessmen. Intimate personal relationships have developed between influential LDP politicians and corporate executives.

Funds are needed by the LDP as a whole in order to finance periodic Diet election campaigns, parliamentary activities of members, and even the regular maintenance of party offices and their staffs. These funds as well are raised mainly from corporate sources through the medium of a donor consortium, the Kokumin Kyōkai (not to be confused with the two prewar organizations of the same name). The bulk of the money is expended to support the LDP candidates in Diet ELECTIONS, to pay the wages and benefits of the party office staff, and, occasionally, to bribe opposition members during Diet de-

bates on controversial bills. The generous contributions of the consortium, however, have not prevented faction leaders and other Diet members from soliciting additional donations from individual businessmen and firms. All these funds made available by the business community have contributed to the rise of "money politics," seriously damaging the LDP's public image.

Party Reform——The public image of the LDP as a party dominated by a few hundred conservative Diet members, internally fragmented by factionalism, and beholden to big business interests has long impeded the party's efforts to build strong grass-roots organizations and recruit members. With a view to correcting the situation and improving the party's public image, the LDP leadership has undertaken time and again to purge the factions and "modernize" the party structure. But the changes have always been merely temporary.

The serious defeat suffered by the LDP in July 1989, however, had a major impact on the party. Voter dissatisfaction with "money politics," as symbolized by the Recruit Scandal, was clearly manifested in the election results. In response to voter demands for "money-free politics" and an end to the LDP's lock on political power, the LDP leadership resolved to embark on the first large-scale electoral reforms of the postwar period.

The main thrust of the proposed reforms is to institute an electoral system based on a combination of single-member constituencies and proportional representation, in place of the medium-constituency system (CHŪ SENKYOKU SEI) that has been in effect since 1946 and has been blamed for both the dominance of money politics and the monolithic power of the LDP. However, since by their very nature these reforms threaten a long-established structure of party power as well as the individual positions of a number of LDP party members, they have been met with vociferous opposition. Continued LDP dominance of the Japanese political scene may well depend on how successfully the necessity of reform can be reconciled with entrenched interests within the ruling party.

liberalism 自由主義

(*jiyū shugi*). Movement or set of beliefs generally supporting individual freedom. The concept was introduced from the West in the latter half of the 19th century after the MEIJI RESTORATION (1868). The term *jiyū*, introduced through Chinese Buddhist writings in which it means "as one pleases," was used by the advocate of Westernization FUKUZAWA YUKICHI to translate the English word "liberty"; however, because of its emphasis upon personal interests, it was often disparaged.

Japanese liberalism before 1945 must be understood within the context of the Japanese national polity (KOKUTAI). The CONSTITUTION OF THE EMPIRE OF JAPAN placed the emperor at the pinnacle of power; in his name every form of civil liberty, including freedom of thought and speech, was put under the constraints of the state. The constitution was based on the assumption that the state is more important than the individual.

Opposed by imperialists and capitalists on the right and by socialists on the left, liberalism never developed as a system of thought that could contend with other systems, nor was it internalized as a norm for action. The few who enlisted in its cause were leaders of the FREEDOM AND PEOPLE'S

RIGHTS MOVEMENT in the early 1880s such as UEKI EMORI, NAKAE CHŌMIN, and TANAKA SHŌZŌ, who opposed the new authoritarian government, and academics such as MINOBE TATSUKI-CHI, KAWAI EIJIRŌ, and YOSHINO SAKUZŌ in the 1920s and 1930s, who stressed the supremacy of rule by law and freedom of speech. In addition, a small number of intellectuals, including Kawai and HANI GORŌ, struggled against the rising tide of fascism and militarism during World War II. Their examples had a profound influence on new developments in Japanese liberalism in the postwar years. See also DEMOCRACY.

liberalization of capital investment 資本自由化

(*shihon jiyūka*). The relaxation or removal of government restrictions on direct foreign investment in Japan. Investments can be for the purpose of acquiring stock in an existing enterprise or the outright purchase of that enterprise, the establishment of a wholly owned subsidiary or a joint-venture corporation, or the acquisition of physical assets necessary for business operations (for instance to set up a business office or factory). The liberalization of capital investment was not originally established as a principle of postwar economic organizations such as the IMF or GATT, but came to be regarded as an obligation of developed countries under the capital investment liberalization policies of the Organization for Economic Cooperation and Development (OECD). Although this principle was not implemented by Japan when it joined the OECD in 1964, the Japanese government took its first steps to liberalize capital investments in July 1967. Between then and May 1973 Japan undertook four other rounds of investment liberalizations. The number of industries considered to be liberalized (including partially liberalized industries in which foreign participation of up to 50 percent received automatic government approval) increased from 50 in July 1967 to 204 in March 1969 and to 524 in September 1970. Subsequently, the definition of a liberalized industry was tightened to cover only those industries in which projects with up to 100 percent foreign participation received automatic government approval. This figure increased from 77 in August 1971 to 228 in May 1973. In 1980 the government finally accepted the principle of complete liberalization by replacing the former licensing system for new foreign-capitalized enterprises with a simple registration system (although projects in the agriculture, forestry, fishery, oil, and leather industries are still designated on a case-by-case basis). In the early 1980s there was a rush by foreign companies to take advantage of the new liberalization, and the annual average number of companies applying to register exceeded 400, over 40 percent of them American. In 1990 some 37 percent of total foreign capital investment had entered the country since 1985 and 57 percent since 1980. The rush peaked in 1987; since then there has been overall a slight decline, but the fundamentally sound characteristics of the Japanese market—its growth potential, its social and economic stability, and the quality of its labor force—are reasons to expect continued high levels of investment in the future. Nevertheless, opinions in Japan are sharply divided on whether hostile takeover bids should remain unrestricted. See also FOREIGN INVESTMENT IN JAPAN.

Liberal Party　　　自由党

(Jiyūtō). Political party formed on 1 March 1950. Not to be confused with a party of the same name formed in 1881 (see JIYŪTŌ). Its forerunner was the Minshu Jiyūtō (Democratic Liberal Party; March 1948–March 1950), which was formed through a merger of the Nihon Jiyūtō, founded by HATOYAMA ICHIRŌ in November 1945, with dissidents from the MINSHUTŌ.

The Liberal Party was in power until December 1954. In 1951 Hatoyama, who had been barred from public office under the Occupation purge, gathered party members opposed to the party's president and prime minister YOSHIDA SHIGERU and seceded from the party in March 1953. Hatoyama's anti-Yoshida faction united with the Kaishintō (Reform Party) and other parties to form the NIHON MINSHUTŌ in November 1954. As a result, Liberal Party seats in the Diet sharply declined, forcing the Yoshida cabinet to resign on 7 December 1954. The next cabinet was formed by Hatoyama, president of the Nihon Minshutō. On 15 November 1955 the Liberal Party and the Nihon Minshutō merged to form the LIBERAL DEMOCRATIC PARTY (Jiyū Minshutō). See also POLITICAL PARTIES.

libraries　　　図書館

(toshokan). There exists in Japan today a full range of public and private libraries and information services, including many that are devoted to special subjects or serve limited constituencies. Library associations, educational and training programs, and interlibrary book loan systems provide further services. Among nationwide systems of information sharing, the most prominent are in the sciences, where the Japan Information Center of Science and Technology (JICST) plays a leading role.

History— A library, believed to be the first in Japan, was located in the palace of Prince SHŌTOKU (574–622). Promulgation of the TAIHŌ CODE in 701 led to the establishment of the ZUSHORYŌ (Bureau of Books and Charts), which, among other functions, served as Japan's first archival library. In the Nara period (710–794), schools financed by the aristocracy to educate their scions created their own libraries, known as *kuge bunko*, to house Buddhist scriptures, Chinese classics, family genealogies, and local histories. One such library, the UNTEI, built by ISONOKAMI NO YAKATSUGU (792–781), was open to scholars upon application. The establishment in the medieval period (mid-12th–16th centuries) of warrior libraries (*buke bunko*) reflected the dominance, and protected the secrets, of the warrior class. However, the best-known *buke bunko*, the KANAZAWA BUNKO, established in 1275 by Hōjō Sanetoki (1224–76), made both Japanese and Chinese books available to scholars and priests. It is maintained today as the Kanagawa Prefectural

Kanazawabunko Museum and is situated in the city of Yokohama. The Ashikaga Bunko was already a noted library when in 1439 UESUGI NORIZANE (1411–66) formally established ASHIKAGA GAKKŌ with the library as its centerpiece. It exists today in the city of Ashikaga as the Ashikaga School Historic Site Library. The Momijiyama Bunko is a collection of books that were assembled at Edo (now Tōkyō) by the Tokugawa shogunate (1603–1867). Libraries built during the Edo period (1600–1868) by *daimyō* for the use of retainers include, among others, the SONKEIKAKU LIBRARY established by the Maeda family and the ASAKUSA BUNKO assembled by Itazaka Bokusai (1578–1655).

FUKUZAWA YUKICHI (1835–1901), who had inspected libraries while serving as a member of shogunal missions to the United States (1860) and Europe (1862), wrote a study of Western culture, SEIYŌ JIJŌ (1867–70), in which he reported, with some display of wonder, that libraries in the West were open to all, regardless of social status. In 1872 Japan's first modern public library, the Shojakukan, was constructed in Tōkyō. Laws were promulgated to enable the establishment of libraries throughout the country, and in 1892 the Japan Library Association was founded. However, as the development of public libraries was an imposed priority of modern Japan's leaders and conflicted with the traditional emphasis on the private ownership of books, their acceptance was slow. The NATIONAL DIET LIBRARY, Japan's counterpart to the United States Library of Congress, was not founded until 1948.

Since the mid-1960s, however, there have been enormous budget increases for cultural institutions at the regional level, with libraries a high priority. The number of public libraries grew from 791 in 1965 to 1,843 in 1989. In order to train staff to operate these and other information-dispensing facilities, the University of Library and Information Science (see LIBRARY AND INFORMATION SCIENCE, UNIVERSITY OF) was established in 1979. By 1989 computerization of catalogs and circulation had been instituted at about 35 percent of public libraries and 60 percent of university libraries. In 1986 the Ministry of Education set up the NATIONAL CENTER FOR SCIENCE INFORMATION SYSTEMS, a facility to maintain academic data bases for scholars and bibliographers, and, as of 1989, 20 percent of university libraries in Japan had joined the system. Establishment of a computer network to link regional libraries is a current priority.

Types of Libraries and Information Services— The national government has played a major role in the establishment and funding of libraries. The National Diet Library is maintained by the government, as are national university libraries and, to a limited extent, institutions like the National Center for Science Information Systems. In 1989, 67 out of 97 braille libraries received subsidies from the Ministry of Health and Welfare. The government also funds the library facilities of its constituent agencies, as well as those of national hospitals and prisons and certain research institutes. Government and corporate special libraries, coordinated by the Japan Special Libraries Association, have assumed the major part of the burden of supplying specialized information. The chief institutions of this kind are the Japan Information Center for Science and Technology, the Institute of Developing Economies, the Nomura Research Institute, and the NATIONAL ARCHIVES.

The 67 prefectural libraries maintain reference services and form the nucleus of regional library systems. Local public libraries in cities, wards, towns, and villages receive support from all levels of government, including, under provision of the Library Law of 1950, the national government. Services offered by regional libraries include storytelling for children, reading for the blind, and the dispatch of bookmobiles.

Library facilities for elementary, middle, and high schools are provided for under the School Library Law of 1953 (see SCHOOL LIBRARIES). Virtually all of Japan's 96 national universities, 39 prefectural and municipal universities, and 364 private universities have substantial library holdings. As of 1982 the number of volumes per student at national universities averaged 128.9; at prefectural and municipal universities, 126.0; and at private universities, 43.4. To redress this disparity the national government initiated a program under which financial assistance is provided to the libraries of private universities, and as a result their holdings have increased dramatically over the last decade. In 1990 the library of Tōkyō University, the largest national university, possessed 6.3 million volumes; its holdings increase by some 200,000 volumes every year. The TENRI CENTRAL LIBRARY at the private Tenri University is noted for its collection of rare Japanese, Chinese, and Western books.

Classification and Cataloging— Most of the school, university, and public libraries in Japan today use the Nippon Jisshin Bunruihō (1929, Nippon Decimal Classification; NDC), a version of the Dewey Decimal System altered to meet the different range of topics in Sino-Japanese publications. Special libraries generally use the Universal Decimal Classification. The introduction of a standard approach to cataloging has been hampered by the Chinese and Japanese custom of cataloging by title rather than by author. The Nippon Mokuroku Kisoku (1943, Nippon Cataloging Rules; NCR) emphasizes the feasibility of cataloging main entries by author for all works, both Eastern and Western, but the tendency has been toward separate catalogs for foreign and domestic publications. Advances in the development of data bases, specialized bibliographies, and the retrieval of catalog information have resulted in a movement toward standardization spearheaded by the National Diet Library. While these efforts have largely focused on scientific and technological information, the call for standardization is having a great impact on the organizational structure, staffing, and budgets of libraries throughout the country, including libraries specializing in the humanities and social sciences.

Library and Information Science, University of　　　図書館情報大学

(Toshokan Jōhō Daigaku). A coeducational national university in the city of Tsukuba, Ibaraki Prefecture. Founded in 1979, the institution is devoted to the training of librarians and specialists who work in information centers. It has only one department, the School of Library and Information Science. Enrollment in 1988 was 613.

Liefde　　　リーフデ号

(*Rīfude gō*). First Dutch ship to reach Japan. The *Liefde*, belonging to a Rotterdam trading firm, was disabled and arrived in Usuki Bay in Bungo Province (now Ōita Prefecture) on 29 April 1600 (Keichō 5.3.16). Of the original crew of 110, only 24 survived, including Captain Jacob Quaeckernaeck, the English pilot William ADAMS, and Second Mate Jan JOOSTEN VAN LODENSTIJN. They were received at Ōsaka Castle by the future shōgun TOKUGAWA IEYASU. Through the efforts of Adams, trade was initiated between Japan and the Netherlands. See also NETHERLANDS AND JAPAN; DUTCH TRADE.

life cycle   ライフサイクル

(*raifu saikuru*). Society's schedule of stages for an individual's life. The cycle is generally thought to extend from birth to death, although an individual is considered a social entity before birth, and many religions posit continuing life for the soul after death. Stages of the cycle mark a person's readiness to participate in social roles and institutions. The schedule has evolved over time and has been altered radically by the institutions of 20th-century mass society and by the greater longevity of modern populations.

Age Reckoning—For social purposes age is reckoned in both relative and absolute terms. Relative age is set by order of birth: one is senior, peer, or junior to someone else. Japanese often claim that theirs is a uniquely "vertical" society, pervaded by rules of seniority. Seniority rules, however, are common to modern institutions such as schools, corporations, and bureaucracies in all societies.

The most important measure of age in absolute terms is that of years of life. Premodern Japan counted age by calendar years: an infant was "one" in the year of birth and became "two" on the first day of the next year. Technically, an infant born on the last day of December would be counted as two years old on the next day. Today, however, age ordinarily is counted from one's day of birth, and it is common to celebrate personal birthday anniversaries.

Certain ages traditionally have been considered favorable, others dangerous. The most favorable years—60, 70, 77, and 88—mark successful aging. The danger years (*yakudoshi*) occur earlier: 19 and 33 for women, 25 and 42 for men. Although most Japanese scorn the danger years as superstition, many continue to observe them. To ward off danger, people obtain protective amulets and purifications at Shintō shrines and avoid new ventures during the year.

The following outline depicts life stages as a typical individual might pass through them.

Infancy—In Japan it is common for an expectant mother to don an abdominal sash in the fifth month of pregnancy (see OBI IWAI): this is society's first overt recognition of a new individual. One month after birth the infant is taken to a local Shintō shrine to be introduced to the guardian gods and symbolically to all of society (see MIYAMAIRI). Annual celebrations for children occur on 3 March for girls (DOLL FESTIVAL), 5 May for boys (CHILDREN'S DAY), and on 15 November for girls aged seven and three and boys aged five (SHICHIGOSAN).

Childhood (about 7–13 years)—In the past, when children reached the age of seven they were expected to help their parents with household tasks and to assume community duties as members of the children's group (*kodomo-gumi*). Today, however, a child's first duty is to study. Under the modern school system in Japan the most important rites of passage are matriculation and graduation. During this stage of life one's "age" is reckoned more by years-in-school than by years-since-birth.

Youth (about 13–25 years)—In the past, coming of age was recognized between the ages of 13 and 17, depending on the locality, by changes in clothing and hairstyle (see GEMPUKU). Young people were considered eligible for marriage and were expected to perform a full day's work on community projects. Youth groups (WAKAMONO-GUMI) often had important social responsibilities, such as organizing festivals or fighting fires. Village youth and apprentices in the cities often moved away from home to live in single-sex dormitories. Today other institutions have taken over most of the functions once performed by these groups.

Although only nine years of schooling are required, more than 90 percent of Japanese young people complete high school, and 40 percent enter college. In middle school and high school many students also attend special tutoring academies (JUKU) to prepare for entrance examinations for the next level of schooling. The demands of this "examination hell" have had a great impact on the daily lives not only of students but of their families and friends as well. See ENTRANCE EXAMINATIONS.

Today one attains legal maturity at age 20 (see AGE, LEGAL DEFINITION OF), and municipal governments celebrate Coming-of-Age Day (Seijin no Hi) for 20-year-olds on 15 January. Job recruitment is formalized, mainly through employment agencies and school placement offices. Mate selection, by contrast, is a task for informal social networks. Two out of three married couples now define their marriage as a "love marriage" (meaning that they found each other on their own), but the go-between (NAKŌDO) continues to play an important role, at least ceremonially, during engagement and wedding rites. The marrying age, as well as the age of full-fledged adulthood (*ichinimmae*), has steadily risen in Japan. The increase in number of years of education has delayed the entrance of many into adult society, and the economic burden of maintaining a household separate from one's parents means that many young people work and save for years before getting married. The average marrying age is around 25 or 26 for women and 28 or 29 for men, with many marrying later. See also MARRIAGE; WEDDINGS.

Maturity (about 26–60 years)—Most adults move through the phases of the family cycle at a uniform pace, establishing households, rearing children, and taking care of aging parents. Schedules for occupational careers, however, are diverse: a *sumō* wrestler may be "old" at 35, but a Diet member "young" at 45. Male and female schedules diverge more widely during the mature years than at any other stage, and the gap seems to have widened during industrialization. Before, a man could gradually yield craft tasks and household leadership to his eldest son, and a woman could train her son's wife in domestic duties and slowly shift to her the responsibility for them. Today men are expected to work full time throughout their years of maturity, and, for all but a fraction of men who have farms, crafts, or small shops, this means paid employment away from home. A man's pace of life and focus of ambition are caught up in promotions, raises, and occupational skills, and less in the family dynamics. Most women find paid work after leaving school, but few are able to sustain long-term occupational careers because social expectation dictates that they attend to housekeeping and child-rearing duties. In contrast to a century ago, however, today the typical woman gives birth to only two or three children, spaced closely together, so that she has completed the period of intensive child care within about a decade after marriage. Many women later take up paid employment, though they are at a disadvantage in the labor market. Lately the trend toward "life-long learning" has expanded educational opportunities for adults, and women may become busy with many such activities outside the home. One is responsible, in these years of middlehood, for the life passage of aging seniors and growing juniors. Much of one's own life passage is marked by events in those other lives, such as the retirement of a parent or the school graduation of a child.

Old Age (about 61 and over)—The 60th birthday, when the zodiac signs complete a full cycle, was the traditional beginning of old age (see KANREKI); today many Japanese celebrate this birthday with family and friends. In some organizations, retirement (*teinen*) occurs before age 60, and long-term employees receive pension benefits. Most men and many women, however, take other jobs and remain in the labor force for another 10 years. Often this is because retirement incomes are thought to be inadequate. See also INKYO.

After Death—In Buddhist tradition, at death an individual is given a posthumous name by the priest of the family temple. This is inscribed on the tombstone and on a personal memorial tablet (*ihai*) kept in the home. In the early weeks and months after death, frequent rites are held to comfort the soul. Thereafter, deathday anniversaries are honored for up to 50 years (see also FUNERALS). After that, one's individuality dissolves into the collective body of the household ancestors, and, except for the famous or notorious, social recognition ceases.

Change and Conflict—Under the impact of modernization different parts of the life-cycle schedule have changed in ways that may often be contradictory. Legal maturity is granted at age 20, but popular opinion regards anyone as immature until married or embarked on a working career. Family versus work is a serious issue for many men and women. Retirement before 60 seems unduly early when life expectancy is now 80 years.

Options have widened at some stages of the cycle and narrowed at others. There are now no legal barriers to the choice of spouse or occupation, but schooling and retirement have become compulsory at fixed times. Japanese social critics in the 1970s began calling on individuals and the state to build into all institutions and programs a life-cycle perspective relevant to the changes in modern society. See also FAMILY; SOCIETY.

life insurance   生命保険

(*seimei hoken*). The life insurance business in Japan began in 1881 with the establishment of the MEIJI MUTUAL LIFE INSURANCE CO. Following World War II, the life insurance business recovered quickly and expanded vigorously during the years of rapid economic growth. As of 1988 there were 26 companies (10 incorporated companies and 16 mutual companies) licensed to operate by the minister of finance under the Insurance Businesses Law. Their total assets at the end of 1988 amounted to ¥90.7 trillion (US $733.6 billion), while the total contracted balance was as much as ¥1.2 quadrillion (US

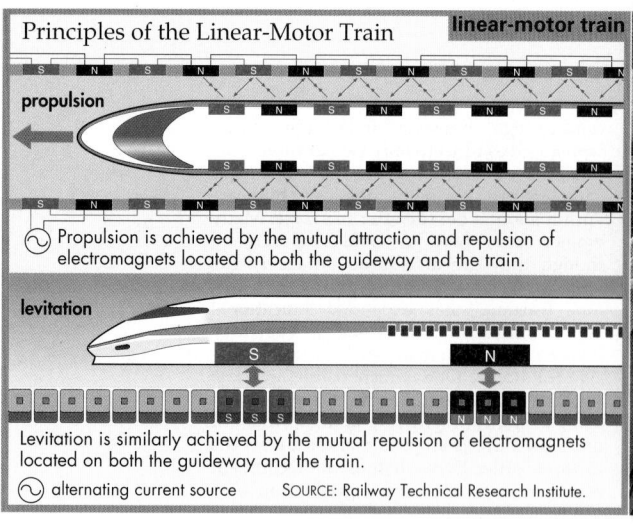

Principles of the Linear-Motor Train

linear-motor train

propulsion

Propulsion is achieved by the mutual attraction and repulsion of electromagnets located on both the guideway and the train.

levitation

Levitation is similarly achieved by the mutual repulsion of electromagnets located on both the guideway and the train.

⊙ alternating current source   SOURCE: Railway Technical Research Institute.

linear-motor train Test passengers board a computer-operated prototype of the magnetically levitated train popularly known as the "Maglev."

$9.7 trillion). In 1988, on the basis of total population, Japanese were insured for an average of ¥11 million (US $89,000) per person, while the average in the United States was $33,200 and in the United Kingdom $16,200. Life insurance companies absorb and manage a massive amount of long-term capital, which makes them the largest institutional investors in Japan. At the end of 1988, life insurance companies had invested ¥42.1 trillion (US $340.5 billion) in stocks and bonds, of which ¥18.4 trillion (US $148.8 billion) was in limited company shares.

lifelong learning
生涯学習

(*shōgai gakushū*). An alternative term for adult education that has gained wide currency in Japan since the concept was discussed by UNESCO in 1965. In 1988 a PROVISIONAL COUNCIL ON EDUCATIONAL REFORM report urged that a major aspect of such reform should be the shift to a lifelong learning system wherein COMMUNITY EDUCATION plays a role comparable to that of school-based education in Japan. The Ministry of Education created the Lifelong Learning Bureau later that year as a first step.

lifetime employment→employment system, modern

lighting, traditional
灯火

(*tōka*). The oldest lighting sources in Japan were the hearth, the torch, and the bonfire. In addition to providing light and heat, fire had religious significance in its association with purification. With the introduction of Buddhism to Japan in the 6th century, various kinds of oil lamps came into use, at first for temples but later for homes and public buildings. The earliest lamps in Japan burned plant oil. The oil was placed in a saucer with a wick of hemp or cotton and was either used as is or placed in a lampstand (*tōdai*). An early lampstand known as *tankei* consisted of a single pole attached to a large base, often made of metal. To this was added a reflector, at first a round shield affixed behind the oil cup, later a movable piece allowing control over the direction of the light.

The first Japanese candles (*rōsoku*) were made of hardened pine resin wrapped in bamboo leaves. Later candles were made of the wax of a kind of sumac. Wicks were made of twisted paper, then cotton, and later rush. Candlestands and candlesticks (*shokudai*) were generally similar in shape to the oil-lamp stands and were much used in temples. Many candlestick designs employed Buddhist symbols. Perhaps the best-known and most artistically developed Jap-

anese lighting devices are *tōrō* (see LANTERNS). During the Edo period (1600–1868) the most widespread light source for the home was the *andon*, a small standing lantern.

With Western influences reaching Japan during the Edo period, a Western-style metal or ceramic lamp known as *kantera* became popular. The kerosene lamp, a later Western import, quickly caught on and remained the chief source of light until the introduction of electricity in the 20th century.

Li Hongzhang (Li Hung-chang)
李鴻章

(1823–1901; J: Ri Kōshō). Chinese statesman and diplomat who dominated China's foreign relations in the last quarter of the 19th century. From 1870 to 1895 he was governor-general of the capital district of Zhili (Chihli) and superintendent of trade for the north. He promoted the development of economic enterprises and the adoption of Western technology. Representing the Chinese government, Li negotiated the SINO-JAPANESE AMITY TREATY OF 1871, the first modern treaty between Japan and China.

In the spring of 1885 Li met Japanese leader ITŌ HIROBUMI in Tianjin (Tientsin) to discuss disturbances in the tribute state of Korea, where Japan was pushing for modern commercial and diplomatic relations. The TIANJIN (TIENTSIN) CONVENTION of 1885 acknowledged equality between China and Japan in relation to Korea.

After China's defeat in the SINO-JAPANESE WAR OF 1894–1895, Itō and Li met once again to negotiate an armistice. Li refused the harsh terms that Itō presented. On 24 March 1895 a Japanese fanatic shot and wounded Li, and amidst the public reaction Itō granted an armistice on 30 March. Li's nephew and adopted son, Li Jingfang (Li Ching-fang; d 1934), continued the negotiations, which resulted in the Treaty of SHIMONOSEKI. Li Hongzhang died shortly after signing the protocol concluding the antiforeign BOXER REBELLION (1900–1901).

lilies
百合

(*yuri*). *Lilium* spp. *Yuri* is a general term for plants of the family Liliaceae, genus *Lilium*. Bulbous perennials that grow wild in mountain fields and on coastal cliffs, they are also cultivated as ornamentals. Fifteen species grow wild in Japan. The *yamayuri* (*L. auratum*) grows to a height of 100–150 centimeters (3–5 ft). Its funnel-shaped flowers, 15–20 centimeters (6–8 in) in diameter, are white with purplish brown spots. It is fragrant and has an edible bulb. The *sakuyuri* (*L. platyphyllum*) resembles the *yamayuri* but grows to a greater height with broader leaves and larger yellow-spotted flowers.

The *teppōyuri* (*L. longiflorum*), or the Easter lily, has white or pale red trumpet-shaped flowers. The *himesayuri* (*L. rubellum*) grows to a height of 30–50 centimeters (12–20 in), with soft leaves. The flower is 5 centimeters (2 in) in diameter and gracefully shaped; hence the name "princess lily" (*himesayuri*) or "maiden lily" (*otomeyuri*). The *sasayuri* (*L. japonicum*) grows to a height of 50–100 centimeters (1.5–3 ft) and has pink flowers. The *oniyuri* (*L. lancifolium*) has a deep red, purple-spotted flower, about 10 centimeters (4 in) in diameter. The petals curl backward toward the base. The *oniyuri* is widely cultivated for its edible bulb. The flowers of the *kanokoyuri* (*L. speciosum*) are white, blending into pink at the center, with red spots. They measure 10 centimeters (4 in) and the petals curl backward. Cultivated extensively as an ornamental with many varieties, it is exported. The *sukashiyuri* (*L. maculatum*) has flowers that measure 10 centimeters (4 in) in diameter and grow erect, the petals narrowing at the base. Many horticultural varieties have been developed. The *kurumayuri* (*L. medeoloides*) is a small species with deep red flowers measuring 5–6 centimeters (2–2.5 in). Lilies of foreign origin are also cultivated in Japan. See also DAY LILIES.

limited liability company
有限会社

(*yūgen kaisha*). Type of association incorporated for the purpose of profit making under the provisions of the Limited Liability Company Law (Yūgen Kaisha Hō) of 1938. The capital of a limited liability company consists of many equal contribution units, and all its members (limited by law to fewer than 50) are obliged to contribute to the capital of the company. Individual members are not personally liable for corporate obligations. The *yūgen kaisha* is a corporate form especially suitable for small and medium enterprises that are not in need of contributions of capital from the general public and wish to avoid many of the onerous requirements imposed on joint-stock companies. Next to the joint-stock company, the limited liability corporation is the most common corporate form in Japan. See JOINT-STOCK COMPANY; LIMITED PARTNERSHIP COMPANY; UNLIMITED PARTNERSHIP COMPANY.

limited partnership company
合資会社

(*gōshi kaisha*). Type of company incorporated under the COMMERCIAL CODE that is composed of both limited and unlimited liability partners. It is similar to a limited partnership in Anglo-American law. Unlimited partners not only have a duty to contribute a specific amount of capital to the company but also jointly and severally bear direct and unlimited liability to the company's creditors. Limited partners jointly and severally bear direct and limited liability to the company's creditors up to the specified amount of their contributions. Limited partners do not, as a general principle, have the right to administer the affairs of the company or to represent it. See also JOINT-STOCK COMPANY; LIMITED LIABILITY COMPANY; PARTNERSHIP; UNLIMITED PARTNERSHIP COMPANY.

linear-motor train
リニアモーターカー

(*riniamōtākā*). A superconductive, magnetically levitated railway system propelled by a linear electric motor. The JAPANESE NATIONAL RAILWAYS (JNR) began studying the feasibility of developing a linear-motor train in 1962. In 1977 the Ministry of Transport agreed to the development of such a

lilies Found in the wild throughout most of Japan, lilies are also cultured as ornamentals and for their edible bulbs.
1 The mountain lily (*yamayuri*) in bloom (left) and its edible bulb, which grows up to 10 cm in diameter.
2 The tiger lily (*oniyuri*) in bloom (left) and its edible bulb.

1

2

system, and by 1986 manned and unmanned trains were regularly making experimental runs at speeds of about 300 kilometers (186 mi) per hour. After the privatization of the JNR in 1987 (see JR), the development of the linear-motor train was transferred to the RAILWAY TECHNICAL RESEARCH INSTITUTE, which made successful manned test runs at about 400 kilometers (249 mi) per hour.

With an eye toward putting the linear-motor train technology to practical use in relieving congestion on the Tōkaidō SHINKANSEN ("bullet train"), the CENTRAL JAPAN RAILWAY CO (JR Tōkai) has announced plans for the construction of the Chūō Linear Express, a train line that will take passengers from Tōkyō to Ōsaka in one hour. The company plans to lay some 42 kilometers (26 mi) of experimental track in 1994 and begin construction of the main line in 1998.

JAPAN AIRLINES CO, LTD, is developing another type of linear-motor train that is powered electromagnetically. Test runs have been conducted between 200 and 300 kilometers (124 and 186 mi) per hour. Experts are studying the economic feasibility of applying this technology to the Tōkyō metropolitan transportation network.

Lion Corporation　ライオン[株]

(Raion). Leading manufacturer of toothpaste and detergent. Also manufactures and markets household and personal care products, pharmaceuticals, food products, and industrial chemicals. Established in 1980 by the merger of two sister companies, Lion Dentifrice Co (founded in 1891) and Lion Fat & Oil Co (founded in 1919). Lion Corporation is engaged in joint ventures in Japan with such companies as Bristol-Meyers-Squibb and McCormick & Co of the United States, Akzo Chemie b.v. of the Netherlands, and Henkel KGaA of Germany. It has subsidiaries and affiliated companies in Southeast Asia, Europe, and the United States. It also exports finished or intermediate products to more than 50 countries. Sales for the fiscal year ending December 1990 totaled ¥299.2 billion (US $2.2 billion) and the company was capitalized at ¥23.4 billion (US $175.2 million). Headquarters are in Tōkyō.

Lions Club　ライオンズ・クラブ

(Raionzu Kurabu). Lions Club activities in Japan began in 1952 when the Tōkyō chapter was organized. The club is an organization for business people and professionals, devoted to providing community services and promoting international relations. As of 1989, there were 2,950 chapters, with a total membership of 163,739.

literacy rate　識字率

(shikijiritsu). Japan achieved a relatively high rate of literacy during the Edo period (1600–1868) through the proliferation of educational institutions. By 1870, 40 to 45 percent of boys and 15 percent of girls were found able to read and write Japanese. A modern educational system was instituted under the EDUCATION ORDER OF 1872, and within 30 years the school attendance rate had reached 90 percent. Currently, the attendance rate is about 99.9 percent with the literacy rate assumed to be parallel.

literary criticism, modern
近現代の文芸批評

(kingendai no bungei hihyō). Although the basic concept of modernity and its application to literature are difficult to define clearly, it is, nevertheless, generally ac-

cepted that the Meiji Restoration (1868) marks the starting point of Japan's modernization in various fields, including literature. During the latter half of the 19th century, "modernization" was synonymous with "Westernization," and naive but serious attempts were made to learn the terms, framework, and standards of Western literary criticism and apply them to Japanese works. However, as a tradition of literary criticism arises from a canon distinct to a culture, attempts to criticize by Western standards proved unreasonable. Too frequently literary critiques of this early modern period were procrustean beds, completely unrelated to the actual literary works and the psychology of their authors.

With the self-reflection that accompanied a reaction against hasty Westernization, there appeared critics who began to place great emphasis on reevaluation of Japan's own literary traditions. It became gradually clear that the fundamental issue of Japan's modern literature lay in the relationship between the imported idea of modernity and native traditions, and efforts were made to find a common ground from which both Western and Japanese literature could be studied.

The First Modernists—Most literary historians agree that the first work of modern Japanese literary criticism was TSUBOUCHI SHŌYŌ's (1859–1935) Shōsetsu shinzui (1885–86, The Essence of the Novel), a pamphlet written when Shōyō was young, his scholarship shallow, and his critical judgment immature. In this work—which, despite its weaknesses, strongly influenced the contemporary literary community—Shōyō clearly states that the novel is the leading genre of modern literature and, furthermore, that "human nature is the nucleus of the novel, and social conditions and popular morals are next in importance." Although his criticism was directed largely against the early-19th-century writer Takizawa BAKIN (1767–1848), whose works were struck through with Confucian didacticism, he deserves credit for adumbrating the principles of modern realism and for championing the novel as an art form at a time when theoretical criticism of the genre was only beginning in the West.

Another pioneering Westernizer was MORI ŌGAI (1862–1922), who engaged Shōyō in a literary dispute when the latter praised Shakespeare for his "rejection of ideals" (botsu risō). What Shōyō intended was to draw attention to Shakespeare's dramatic objectivity, but Ōgai misunderstood this and attempted to refute him from the standpoint of German idealist aesthetics. An even more idealistic critic was KITAMURA TŌKOKU (1868–94), who participated in the radical FREEDOM AND PEOPLE'S RIGHTS MOVEMENT and was strongly attracted to the American transcendentalist Ralph Waldo Emerson. Tōkoku attacked the Edo-period (1600–1868) idea that sensual love did not bear upon the relationship of husband and wife—a belief upon which much of Edo literature was founded—and, coining the word ren'ai (love from the heart), he urged upon his readers the Western ideal of romantic love.

The Advent of Traditionalists—In the early 1890s there emerged a nationalistic reaction to the first major wave of Westernization in Japan. The most notable publications carrying articles by critics of this bent were the magazine Nihonjin and the newspaper Nihon. During this period voluminous col-

lections of Japanese classical literature appeared, and an interest in the literary past was also reflected in the adaptation of certain stylistic features of the writings of Ihara SAIKAKU (1642–93) in the novels of OZAKI KŌYŌ (1867–1903) and HIGUCHI ICHIYŌ (1872–96). There was also a revival of the traditional short-verse forms HAIKU and TANKA. The leading organizer and critic of this movement was MASAOKA SHIKI (1867–1902), who was a regular contributor to Nihon. Both traditionalist and iconoclast, Shiki revived the short-verse forms while challenging conventional viewpoints: he criticized the revered master Matsuo BASHŌ (1644–94) and acclaimed the long-ignored Yosa BUSON (1716–84). Stimulated by Western-style painters of the day, Shiki insisted on a realistic photographic element (shasei) in poetry, and it remains an important stylistic feature of modern haiku and tanka.

TAKAYAMA CHOGYŪ (1871–1902), another traditionalist critic, attacked Shōyō's advocacy of a literature free from moralizing and decried his call for realism as "antinationalistic." A traditionalist critic of another type was OKAKURA KAKUZŌ (1862–1913). In such works as The Ideals of the East (1903) and The Book of Tea (1906), which were originally written in English, he attempted to explain what he saw as the superior values of oriental arts and Japanese culture. Bold generalizations can be found in his writings, but his perspective was broad and his style of writing, with its striking paradoxes and skillful anecdotes, appealed greatly to his readers.

Second Wave of Westernization—Japan's victory in the Russo-Japanese War of 1904–05 brought relief from the tensions created by the Meiji Restoration. A renewed confidence in the nation's ability to compete on an equal footing with the Western powers was accompanied by another wave of Westernizing. Literature of the period was primarily characterized by the emergence of novels and criticism from the Japanese school of NATURALISM, which focused on the dark and seamy aspects of life and shocked a society still bound by Confucian morality. In parallel with this trend there appeared young writers who leaned toward aestheticism (tambi). There also appeared the so-called SHIRAKABA SCHOOL of novelists and critics, who glorified the West's artistic geniuses and sought to imitate their expression of extreme individuality. Far more cosmopolitan than critics during the initial period of borrowing from the West, writers of the early 20th century embraced a wide range of interests.

SHIMAMURA HŌGETSU (1871–1918), UEDA BIN (1874–1916), NATSUME SŌSEKI (1867–1916), and ISHIKAWA TAKUBOKU (1886–1912) were among the leading literary critics of this era. Hōgetsu, who studied drama in both England and Germany, committed himself to establishing a new theater in Japan. Initially interested in European symbolism and the relationship between Christianity and Western literature, he later came to appreciate the realism of the Japanese naturalists.

Ueda Bin, whose translations of the French symbolists inspired Japanese poets, studied English literature under Lafcadio HEARN and became one of the first generation of Japanese who could truly appreciate Western literature. Natsume Sōseki, who was more famous for his novels than his criticism, wrote Bungakuron (1907, Theory of Literature), the first systematic and comprehensive work of literary criticism in modern Japan. Though it contains psychological interpretations that could be said to anticipate those of I. A. Richards, its excessive ambitiousness made it resemble a colossal building of unfinished rooms. Ishikawa Takuboku produced fragmentary criticism but was primarily a poet; his *tanka*, full of unconventional colloquialisms, are still popular despite their sentimentality. While recognizing the importance of the Japanese naturalist novelists' contributions, he complained that their works dealt only with their private lives and failed to analyze or resolve social problems.

Practical Critics—Japan's long tradition of criticism by novelists and other creative writers became particularly important from about 1920. Novelist-critics such as MASAMUNE HAKUCHŌ (1879–1962), TANIZAKI JUN'ICHIRŌ (1886–1965), and later KAWABATA YASUNARI (1899–1972) and NAKANO SHIGEHARU (1902–79) produced impressionistic criticism that lacked theoretical consistency but was enjoyable to read. Particularly perceptive is Hakuchō's *Bundan jimbutsu hyōron* (1932), a collection of essays on practically all major modern Japanese writers from the Meiji period until his own time. Tanizaki wrote essays on traditional Japanese culture and on the BUNRAKU puppet theater. Kawabata, who was essentially a lyrical novelist, displayed broad appreciation, sharp critical intuition, and sensitivity in a long series of monthly critical studies on the current literary scene.

Professional Critics—The first professional critics were SAITŌ RYOKUU (1867–1904) and UCHIDA ROAN (1868–1929), who was active in introducing Western literature to Japan. Literary criticism as an independent profession, however, did not really come into its own until the field of journalism was firmly established. In the late 1920s and early 1930s a group of committed critics well read in Western literary criticism emerged. Among them was the brilliant KOBAYASHI HIDEO (1902–83), who became Japan's most influential literary critic. Others included KAWAKAMI TETSUTARŌ (1902–80), KAMEI KATSUICHIRŌ (1907–66), the leftist critic AONO SUEKICHI (1890–1961), and later NAKAMURA MITSUO (1911–88) and HIRANO KEN (1907–78). Kobayashi's essays of the 1940s dealing with the Japanese classics are short and fragmentary but wonderfully evocative and poetic. One of his most important works is *Motoori Norinaga* (1965–76), a perceptive analysis of the scholar of National Learning MOTOORI NORINAGA (1730–1801). Nakamura used the modern European novel as his criterion and sharply criticized what he considered to be the weaknesses and distortions of Japan's modern novels. Hirano studied the I-NOVEL, a peculiarly Japanese genre, with strong sympathy, concentrating on the relationship between the literary work and the private life of the author.

The two men who were most influential in reevaluating the Japanese literary heritage in terms of the native tradition itself were the poet-scholar ORIKUCHI SHINOBU (1887–1953) and the folklorist YANAGITA KUNIO (1875–1962). Among critics who pursued this theme in regard to modern literature were YASUDA YOJŪRŌ (1910–81) and YAMAMOTO KENKICHI (1907–88).

With Japan's rapid economic growth since the 1960s, the literary market expanded and the demand for literary criticism increased. The number of critics active in the 1980s far

surpassed any previous period. As standards of criticism have diversified, the tendency to look to the West for critical models has weakened in favor of reevaluating modern Japanese works in terms of their relationship to the native literary tradition or examining them from the viewpoint of comparative literature. Noteworthy are recent efforts by younger scholars and critics to place Japanese literature within a broader Asian context and to reevaluate its oriental heritage.

literary criticism, premodern
前近代の文芸批評

(*zenkindai no bungei hihyō*). Literary criticism in premodern Japan comprises critical and theoretical writings on WAKA, *haikai* (see HAIKU), NŌ, and other literary forms that evolved over a span of more than 10 centuries. Since major critics were usually themselves poets, playwrights, and novelists, they focused on providing practical advice to fellow artists rather than systematic analysis.

The earliest anthology of Japanese poetry, the MAN'YŌSHŪ (ca 759), includes prefatory notes to individual poems, such as "Allegorical Poem" or "Pouring Forth Emotion," which imply a conscious use of technique and an underlying concept of poetry as emotional expression. Such ideas originated in China, where literary criticism developed early. Given the strength of that country's influence, it was only natural that the first treatise on Japanese poetics, *Kakyō hyōshiki* (772) by Fujiwara no Hamanari (724–790), was written in Chinese and drew heavily on Chinese poetics.

Japanese poets became increasingly aware of their national identity in the Heian period (794–1185). Following a 9th-century vogue for Chinese verse, native *waka* enjoyed new prestige, and the first major piece of literary criticism in Japanese, the *kana* (Japanese syllabary) preface to the KOKINSHŪ, appeared in the early 10th century. Its author, KI NO TSURAYUKI (872?–945), stressed spontaneity as well as harmony between emotion (*kokoro*) and expression (*kotoba*). These became the standard ideals for *waka* throughout the Heian period, although later critics stressed the creation of beauty over the expression of emotion and, while emphasizing freshness and novelty, valued indirection and understatement (YOJŌ) in diction.

The Heian period also saw the rise of fictional tales (MONOGATARI BUNGAKU) designed primarily for the entertainment of leisured court ladies. Considered morally deficient by both Buddhist and Confucian critics, prose fiction was defended by MURASAKI SHIKIBU (fl ca 1000), author of the TALE OF GENJI, a masterpiece of the genre, as being more valuable than history in treating the internal realities of life and, in an imaginative guise, as capable as scripture in presenting truth.

Moralistic attacks on fiction intensified as Buddhism grew more influential in the medieval period (mid-12th–16th centuries), but the focus of literary criticism shifted back to *waka*. FUJIWARA NO TOSHINARI (1114–1204), a court noble who had watched the Heian aristocracy collapse, evolved an aesthetic of melancholy. Some of his poetic ideals, such as MONO NO AWARE ("pathos") and SABI ("loneliness"), reflect disillusionment with society, while others such as YŪGEN ("mystery and depth") suggest romantic longing for glories past. His son, Fujiwara no Teika (FUJIWARA NO SADAIE; 1162–1241), preferred *yōen*, an unearthly beauty that lay beyond the realities of

human life. The writings of these and other medieval critics rendered the Japanese concept of poetry vastly more complex and subtle, yet eventually led to academicism and factional rivalries.

Another form of criticism was the UTA-AWASE, or poetry contest, a practice that peaked in the early Kamakura period (1185–1333). In it, two *waka* on the same theme were paired in a round and submitted for judging, usually by respected poets. Judges often wrote comments on the poems, and the need for specificity in justifying decisions helped sharpen critical acumen.

By the 14th and 15th centuries criticism of poetry focused increasingly on RENGA (linked verse). The creation of a lengthy chain of stanzas had evolved into a serious artistic endeavor with intricate rules. Since successive stanzas were normally composed by different poets and since artful linkage and progression were of preeminent importance in *renga*, no other type of literary criticism explored in such detail compositional conventions and techniques that were conducive to structural unity.

Dramatic criticism began to appear during the 14th century with the maturation of NŌ. A number of treatises were written by actors, such as ZEAMI (1363–1443) and KOMPARU ZENCHIKU (1405–70?), who wished to hand down the secrets of their trade to their heirs. Zeami's writings on the art of Nō centered on the importance of verisimilitude in acting as well as on its aesthetic effect, or "flower." In his day, leading actors also composed the plays in which they performed, so Zeami wrote on the art of the playwright as well. In structure he favored an "introduction" (*jo*), "development" (*ha*), and "finale" (*kyū*), a three-part pattern borrowed from GAGAKU court music.

The treatises of Zenchiku attempt to integrate the art of Nō with both Buddhism and *waka*. To Zenchiku, a Nō performance of the highest quality was as transparent and tasteless as water, yet inclusive of all colors and tastes on earth, much like the Buddhist concept of the void; while an actor's movements were a form of emotional expression, or "wordless *waka*."

By the mid-Edo period (1600–1868), *haikai* poetics had become well established as a branch of literary criticism, although much writing on the craft was pedagogical or polemical. Matsuo BASHŌ (1644–94) laid the foundation, although he produced no treatise himself. According to his disciple MUKAI KYORAI (1651–1704), Bashō's poetry centered on the lonely beauty of *sabi*, which entails a sadly resigned recognition of man's mortality. The poet BUSON (1716–84), on the other hand, placed poetry in a realm far removed from quotidian reality and urged "detachment from the mundane." Through reading the Chinese and Japanese classics, he argued, poets could roam distant worlds, forgetting the frustrations of life.

By the Edo period, dramatic criticism dealt almost exclusively with JŌRURI and KABUKI. However, these were evaluations of players and performances and did not deal with the nature of the art itself. More valuable are the casual remarks of actors or of playwrights, such as CHIKAMATSU MONZAEMON (1653–1754), who observed that "art lies in the narrow realm between the real and the unreal."

Didactic views of literature gained prominence in the Edo period, due mainly to the government's endorsement of Neo-Confucianism (see SHUSHIGAKU). Takizawa BAKIN

(1767–1848) remarked that in prose fiction the writer's aim lay "simply in presenting the truth about human feelings so as to promote virtue," and most writers of popular Edo fiction accepted this viewpoint. Knowing that the masses required entertaining edification, they embraced a literary theory that conveniently accommodated their profession as tellers of tales to their obligation to point a moral.

National Learning (KOKUGAKU), which developed in the 17th and 18th centuries, profoundly affected the evolution of literary criticism in Japan. Kokugaku scholars' interest in ancient Japanese classics promoted the study of historical linguistics, which helped develop textual criticism, while their predilection for primitive culture led them to emphasize the role of emotion in creative writing, in contrast to the Chinese emphasis on intellect. Under the influence of scholars such as KAMO NO MABUCHI (1697–1769) and MOTOORI NORINAGA (1730–1801), literary criticism became noticeably more humanistic.

Premodern Japanese concepts of literature tended to be antirealistic and antirational, owing largely to Buddhist influence, which encouraged representation of invisible essence rather than visible surface. Lacking the West's Hellenistic tradition, Japanese theorists adopted a mystical approach, often centered around vague, ethereal qualities. The penchant for ambiguity also resulted in a fondness for brevity of form and expression. Clear delineation was eschewed as shallow, and logically conceived structure was avoided in favor of a unity achieved through tone, imagistic association, and mood.

literary prizes　　　　　文学賞

(*bungakushō*). Literary prizes are awarded in various categories by publishing companies, newspapers, and literary organizations. The best-known awards are those for writers of fiction. Many, such as the Akutagawa Ryūnosuke Shō (AKUTAGAWA PRIZE) and the Naoki Sanjūgo Shō (NAOKI PRIZE), are specifically designated for works by new authors, while the Nihon Geijutsuin Shō (Japan Art Academy Award) is given in recognition of a writer's lifelong contribution to literature. The Noma Bungei Shō (NOMA LITERARY PRIZE), the Mishima Yukio Shō (Mishima Literary Prize), the Yamamoto Shūgorō Shō (Yamamoto Literary Prize), and the Tanizaki Jun'ichirō Shō (Tanizaki Prize) are given for outstanding works by active leading writers. There are also prizes for companies that have published works of outstanding literary value.

The oldest and most prominent of the several annual poetry awards is the H-Shi Shō (H-Shi Prize), established in 1951 to recognize new poets. The Yomiuri Bungaku Shō (Yomiuri Literary Prize) is awarded in several literary categories. The most important prize for mystery fiction is the Edogawa Rampo Shō (Edogawa Rampo Prize), established and funded in 1954 by the writer EDOGAWA RAMPO to celebrate his 60th birthday. The most important nonfiction prize is the Ōya Sōichi Nonfiction Prize, established to commemorate ŌYA SŌICHI's contributions to the field of mass communications.

literati painting —→ bunjinga

literature　　　　　日本文学

(Nihon *bungaku*). The written literature of Japan is one of the more venerable of the literary traditions of the Orient. Moreover,

the oldest works in the standard canon, the histories KOJIKI and NIHON SHOKI (early 8th century), provide in their myths, legends, and songs ample evidence of an ancient tradition of oral literature that, for the lack of a native system of writing, was not recorded until the introduction of Chinese characters.

Contact with the Asian mainland, the source of much of the material culture of the Yayoi period (ca 300 BC–ca AD 300) of Japanese history, became increasingly close during the 4th and 5th centuries. By the late 6th or early 7th century a small number of Japanese had gained an incipient mastery of Chinese writing and had developed the rudiments of a system whereby the Japanese language could be transcribed, using Chinese characters semantically to denote corresponding Japanese words or phonetically by the assignment of a Japanese sound value to individual characters. The pervasive influence of Chinese literature and its system of writing persisted until the mid-19th century, and most educated men considered it the literary language of Japan. Consequently over the course of more than a millennium a vast number of literary works were written in classical Chinese; these, as well as writings in high-classical Japanese and in hybrid forms of Sino-Japanese, of which modern Japanese is one, are all considered by the Japanese people to be elements of their literary heritage. For a discussion of aspects of the tradition of Japanese oral literature, see FOLKTALES.

Early and Heian Literature—Official embassies to Sui (589–618) and Tang (T'ang; 618–907) dynasty China, initiated in 600, were the chief means by which Chinese culture, technology, and methods of government were introduced on a comprehensive basis in Japan. The *Kojiki* and the *Nihon shoki*, the former written in hybrid Sino-Japanese and the latter in classical Chinese, were compiled under the sponsorship of the government for the purpose of authenticating the legitimacy of its polity. However, among these collections of myths, genealogies, legends of folk heroes, and historical records there appear a number of songs—largely irregular in meter and written with Chinese characters representing Japanese words or syllables—that offer insight into the nature of preliterate Japanese verse.

The first major collection of native poetry, again written with Chinese characters, was the MAN'YŌSHŪ (late 8th century), which contains verses, chiefly the 31-syllable WAKA, that were composed in large part between the mid-7th and mid-8th centuries. The earlier poems in the collection are characterized by the direct expression of strong emotion but those of later provenance show the emergence of the rhetorical conventions and expressive subtlety that dominated the subsequent tradition of court poetry. Although the *Man'yōshū* is today considered the great monument of early Japanese verse, contemporary literati, invariably men, chose to write their public verse in Chinese, and between the mid-8th century and the early years of the Heian period (794–1185) four imperial anthologies of Chinese poetry written by Japanese were compiled.

A revolutionary achievement of the mid-9th century was the development of a native orthography (*kana*) for the phonetic representation of Japanese. Employing radically abbreviated Chinese characters to denote Japanese sounds, the system contributed to a deepening consciousness of a native literary tradition distinct from that of China. The *waka*, now written with *kana*, was an

indispensable element of social relations, and the practice arose of holding poem contests (*uta-awase*) at which pairs of verses were set against one another. Poets compiled collections (*shikashū*) of their verses, and, drawing in part on these, the KOKINSHŪ, the first of 21 imperial anthologies of native poetry, was assembled in the early 10th century.

The introduction of *kana* also led to the development of a prose literature in the vernacular, early examples of which are the UTSUBO MONOGATARI, a work of fiction; the ISE MONOGATARI, a collection of vignettes centered on poems; and the diary TOSA NIKKI. From the late 10th century the ascendancy of the Fujiwara regents, whose power over emperors depended on the reception of their daughters as imperial consorts, resulted in the formation of literary coteries of women in the courts of empresses, and it was these women who produced the great prose classics of the 11th century. Written in high-classical Japanese with only the rare intrusion of Chinese characters, such works as the TALE OF GENJI, a fictional narrative by MURASAKI SHIKIBU, and the MAKURA NO SŌSHI, a collection of essays by SEI SHŌNAGON, are considered by Japanese to be a watershed in the development of the native literary tradition. A distinctive feature of these and of many of the best of later Japanese prose works is their tendency to disregard formal structure in favor of a series of discrete scenes or discourses that present in the aggregate a comprehensive and richly detailed vision of a time and place.

The hybrid variety of Sino-Japanese that was used by aristocrats in their diaries of court events contributed to the development in the 12th century of a type of literary Japanese that employed numerous Chinese words, and from which modern Japanese evolved. The KONJAKU MONOGATARI, a voluminous collection of anecdotes, a number of which touch on the lives of commoners, is an early example of works written in this style. See also EARLY LITERATURE; HEIAN LITERATURE.

Medieval Literature—The establishment of a warrior government at the end of the 12th century and its arrogation of political power from the Yamato emperors led to the development of literary genres that were grounded in other classes of society. Although the eighth imperial anthology of Japanese verse, the SHIN KOKINSHŪ, contains some of the finest of court poetry, the verse of the succeeding 13 collections was increasingly bound by convention and added little to the tradition. The chief development in poetry

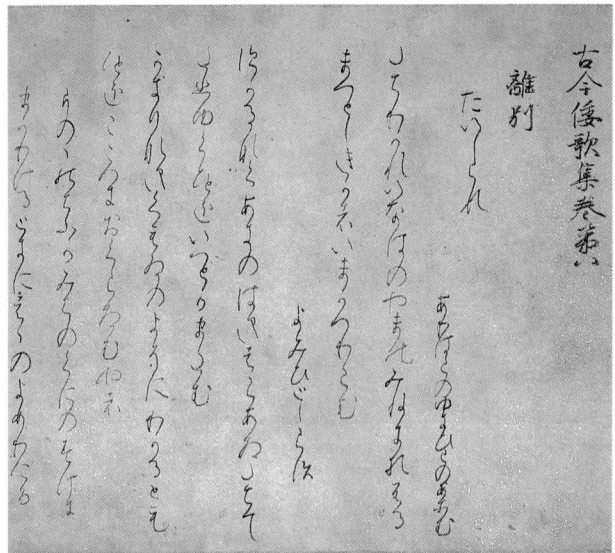

literature The *Kokinshū* is the first of 21 imperial anthologies of *waka* poetry and one of the most celebrated collections of Japanese literature. Pictured here is a page from the earliest extant manuscript copy, which dates to the middle of the 11th century.

Little Tōkyō Many of the Japanese restaurants and souvenir shops in this Los Angeles district are located in and around the Japanese Village Plaza (pictured).

during the medieval period (mid-12th–16th centuries) was linked verse (*renga*). Arising from the court tradition of *waka*, *renga* was cultivated by the warrior class as well as by courtiers, and some among the best *renga* poets, such as SŌGI, were commoners. The court romance, of which the *Genji* is the paradigm, became increasingly imitative and schematic and gave way in the 15th century to short tales known as *otogi-zōshi*, which deal largely with the lives of the common people.

A major development in prose literature of the medieval era was the war tale (GUNKI MONOGATARI). The HEIKE MONOGATARI relates the events of the war between the Taira and Minamoto families that brought an end to imperial rule; it was disseminated among all levels of society by itinerant priests who chanted the story to the accompaniment of a lutelike instrument, the *biwa*. An increase in travelers along the highway connecting Kamakura, the seat of the military government, with the old capital of Kyōto gave rise to a number of travel diaries, such as the IZAYOI NIKKI, and the social upheaval of the early years of the era led to the appearance of works deeply influenced by the Buddhist notion of the inconstancy of worldly affairs (*mujō*). Not only does the theme of *mujō* provide the ground note of the *Heike monogatari* and the essay collections HŌJŌKI and TSUREZUREGUSA, it is also an element of the theoretical framework of the historical work GUKANSHŌ. The writing of literary works in Chinese continued in the hands of aristocrats and Zen Buddhist priests of the Gozan temples (see GOZAN LITERATURE).

In the latter part of the medieval era the poetic form *haikai* (now called HAIKU) arose from *renga*, and works in the genre of the war tale, the finest of which was the SOGA MONOGATARI, were now character studies of war heroes. In the field of the performing arts, KAN'AMI and ZEAMI allied themes of classical origin with folk theatrical conventions to produce the Nō drama. The related comedic form *kyōgen* was staged in the intervals between Nō performances. See also MEDIEVAL LITERATURE.

Edo Literature—The formation of a stable central government in Edo (now Tōkyō), after some 100 years of turmoil, and the growth of a market economy based on the widespread use of a standardized currency led to the development in the Edo period (1600–1868) of a class of wealthy townsmen. General prosperity contributed to an increase in literacy, and literary works became marketable commodities, giving rise to a publishing industry. Humorous fictional studies of contemporary society by Ihara SAIKAKU and EJIMA KISEKI were huge commercial successes, and prose works, often elaborately illustrated, that were directed toward a mass audience became a staple of Edo-

period literature. Commercial playhouses, patronized by commoner and *samurai* alike, were established for the performance of puppet plays (*jōruri*) and *kabuki*, whose plots often centered on conflicts arising from the rigidly hierarchical social order that was instituted by the Tokugawa shogunate and underpinned by Neo-Confucian moral precepts.

The 17-syllable form of light verse known as *haikai*, whose subject matter was drawn from nature and the lives of ordinary people, was raised to the level of great poetry by Matsuo BASHŌ, who applied to its composition the standards of classical aesthetics. Some of the most evocative of native poetry in Chinese appeared during the Edo period; moreover, government adherence to the principles of Neo-Confucianism led to the writing in Chinese of a great number of prose works that dealt with the Neo-Confucian philosophical system. The *waka*, long stultified by functionless compositional conventions, was given new life when it was taken up by townsmen. A number of philologists, among them KEICHŪ, KAMO NO MABUCHI, and MOTOORI NORINAGA, wrote scholarly studies on early literary texts, such as the *Kojiki*, the *Man'yōshū*, and the *Tale of Genji*, in which they attempted to elucidate the native Japanese world view as it existed before the introduction of Buddhism and Confucianism. See also EDO LITERATURE.

Modern Literature—The imperial restoration of 1868 was followed by the wholesale introduction of Western technology and culture, which largely displaced Chinese culture. As a result the novel, which during the Edo period had been considered a base form of literature appropriate only for the titillation or, in some instances, the moral edification of the masses, became established as a serious and respected genre of the literature of Japan. A related development was the gradual abandonment of the literary language in favor of the usages of colloquial speech, fully achieved for the first time in UKIGUMO by FUTABATEI SHIMEI. Although the *tanka* and the haiku remained viable poetic forms, notably in the hands of ISHIKAWA TAKUBOKU, YOSANO AKIKO, MASAOKA SHIKI, and TAKAHAMA KYOSHI, there developed under the influence of Western poetry a genre of free verse, the first great achievement of which was the collection *Wakanashū* by SHIMAZAKI TŌSON. Early stylistic influences on Japanese literature were romanticism, introduced in the 1890s by MORI ŌGAI; symbolism, introduced in UEDA BIN's *Kaichōon* (1905), a collection of translations of French poems; and naturalism, which reigned supreme from 1905 to 1910 and out of which developed the enduring genre of the confessional novel (I-NOVEL or *watakushi shōsetsu*).

Until the 1950s a distinctive feature of the Japanese literary community was the publication of coterie magazines by writers of like mind. The humanist Shirakaba school of writers, including MUSHANOKŌJI SANEATSU and SHIGA NAOYA, published the journal *Shirakaba* from 1910; the early writings of YOKOMITSU RIICHI and KAWABATA YASUNARI appeared in *Bungei jidai* (1924–27), the organ of the modernist Shinkankaku school; and works of the proletarian writers KOBAYASHI TAKIJI and SATA INEKO were published in *Senki* (1928–31), a Marxist-oriented periodical. The serial publication of novels in newspapers has also been a common practice, and some of the best Japanese novelists, from NATSUME SŌSEKI to NAGAI KAFŪ, TANIZAKI JUN'ICHIRŌ, and Kawabata Yasunari, have written

for the newspapers. Translations of Japanese literary works have appeared in rapidly increasing numbers since the 1970s, and the best creations of Sōseki, Ōgai, Kafū, AKUTAGAWA RYŪNOSUKE, Shiga, Tanizaki, Kawabata, IBUSE MASUJI, DAZAI OSAMU, ENCHI FUMIKO, and MISHIMA YUKIO are available in English versions. Among the foremost writers of fiction in the early 1990s were ŌE KENZABURŌ, ABE KŌBŌ, ENDŌ SHŪSAKU, TSUSHIMA YŪKO, MURAKAMI RYŪ, NAKAGAMI KENJI, and MURAKAMI HARUKI. See also MEIJI LITERATURE; TAISHŌ LITERATURE; SHŌWA LITERATURE.

little-theater movement→ shōge-kijō undō

Little Tōkyō リトルトウキョウ

(Ritoru Tōkyō). The social, cultural, and economic center of the Japanese-American community in the Los Angeles area. The origins of Little Tōkyō date to 1885, when an ex-seaman from Japan opened a small restaurant. The small section of downtown Los Angeles soon became the home for numerous Japanese-style shops, restaurants, and shrines. Little Tōkyō's size belies its rich tradition and symbolic importance as a focal point of Japanese-American culture. The area remains a center for community activities for residents and a popular attraction for visitors to Los Angeles. Little Tōkyō was commercially renovated during the 1970s and 1980s, spurred on by considerable investment by Japanese corporations.

Liutiaogou (Liu-t'iao-kou) Incident 柳条溝事件

(Ryūjōkō Jiken). Bombing incident staged by the Japanese military at Liutiaogou just north of Mukden (now Shenyang), Manchuria, in September 1931; it was a pretext for Japan's subsequent seizure of Manchuria in what is known as the MANCHURIAN INCIDENT. As planned by Colonel ITAGAKI SEISHIRŌ and Lieutenant Colonel ISHIWARA KANJI of the Japanese GUANDONG (KWANTUNG) ARMY, Japanese troops detonated a bomb on the rails of the South Manchuria Railway on 18 September. Itagaki accused Chinese troops in Mukden of planting the bomb, seized the Mukden army barracks and arsenal, and by dawn on 19 September was in control of the city. The General Staff of the army in Tōkyō knew in advance of the plot but, thinking it premature, sent General TATEKAWA YOSHITSUGU to prevent it. However, HASHIMOTO KINGORŌ cabled Itagaki and Ishiwara to speed up their plans, and it is believed that Tatekawa purposely delayed delivering his message.

Liu Yongfu (Liu Yung-fu) 劉永福

(1837–1917; J: Ryū Eifuku). Chinese military leader. He was most famous for commanding the "Black Flags" irregulars against the French seizure of Annam (Vietnam), beginning in 1873. With the conclusion in 1885 of the treaty between the French and the Qing (Ch'ing) dynasty (1644–1912) terminating this conflict, Liu returned to China and became a military official. With the outbreak of the SINO-JAPANESE WAR OF 1894–1895, Liu went to Taiwan, where he led local Taiwanese resistance against the Japanese occupation even after China's defeat. After the cession of Taiwan to Japan in the Treaty of SHIMONOSEKI, the Taiwanese elite established a short-lived, independent Taiwan Republic. It collapsed, however, with the arrival of Japanese governor-general KABAYAMA SUKENORI and Japanese troops, and Liu escaped to the Chinese mainland.

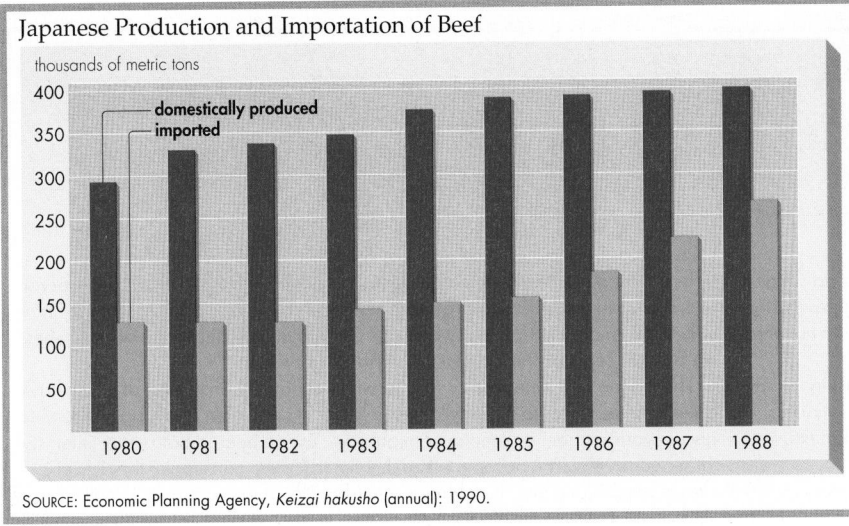

Japanese Production and Importation of Beef

thousands of metric tons

domestically produced
imported

(Bar chart, years 1980–1988, y-axis from 50 to 400)

SOURCE: Economic Planning Agency, *Keizai hakusho* (annual): 1990.

Livestock Production

Year	Dairy cattle	Beef cattle	Hogs	Chickens, layers	Chickens, broilers
			(millions of animals)		
1960	0.82	2.34	1.92	54.63	—
1965	1.29	1.89	3.98	88.09	18.28
1970	1.80	1.79	6.34	118.20	53.74
1975	1.79	1.86	7.68	116.42	87.66
1979*	2.07	2.08	9.49	123.72	125.62
1985	2.11	2.59	10.72	127.60	150.22
1990	2.06	2.70	11.82	136.96	150.45

*The survey was not conducted in 1980.
SOURCE: Ministry of Agriculture, Forestry, and Fisheries, *Nōgyō hakusho fuzoku tōkeihyō* (annual): 1990.

Livelihood Protection Law
生活保護法

(Seikatsu Hogo Hō). Law based on the provisions of article 25 of the constitution that provides for the right to live (SEIZONKEN), whereby the state is to provide necessary care to all citizens living in poverty, according to the extent of their impoverishment. The objective of the law is to ensure a minimum means of livelihood while promoting the independence of the aid recipients. The original law was enacted in 1946 and the present law in 1950.

It provides that all citizens who fulfill the requirements of the law may receive the care provided (principle of equality without prejudice). It guarantees a healthy, civilized, minimum standard of living (guarantee of minimal lifestyle). It also provides that impoverished recipients must take self-help measures using their own resources and abilities. Furthermore, support by parties obliged under the Civil Code to provide support must precede any care provided by this law (principle of supplementary care).

livestock
畜産

(*chikusan*). Farmers engaged in animal husbandry in Japan are relatively few, and herd size per family is small as is the total area devoted to pasturage (about 834,000 hectares or 2,060,000 acres). Grass is harvested abundantly in summer, but high-quality hay is difficult to obtain. Many areas have volcanic-ash soils unsuitable for growing leguminous plants such as alfalfa. The limited amount of grazing land also causes high fixed material costs and labor costs, factors that result in high livestock production costs.

Although the Japanese ate animal flesh in ancient times, they hunted game rather than raise livestock. The livestock introduced from the Asian mainland were employed as a source of muscle power rather than of food, and domestic fowl were kept as pets. Horses were valued mainly for their military role. In ancient times milk was drunk for medicinal purposes at the imperial court, but consumption of products of four-footed beasts was strictly prohibited after the introduction of Buddhism to Japan in the 6th century. In the Meiji period (1868–1912) the consumption of animal products began under the influence of the West but was small in volume. During the agricultural depression, which lasted from the end of the Taishō period (1912–26) through the early years of the Shōwa period (1926–89), animal husbandry was encouraged nationwide, but livestock were still used primarily for work and as a source of manure for crop farming.

A temporary shortage of rice immediately after World War II led to an increased consumption of wheat flour, milk, meat, and eggs, a trend that has continued ever since. In response, the number of farmers raising livestock has also grown. In recent years the breeding of dairy cattle, beef cattle, hogs, and chickens has increased; in 1990 dairy cattle numbered 2.1 million head; beef cattle, 2.7 million; hogs, 11.8 million; and chickens (broilers), 150.5 million. The demand for beef and pork far exceeds domestic production.

Living National Treasures
人間国宝

(Ningen Kokuhō). Term popularly used to refer to the men and women in the fields of traditional crafts and performing arts who have been designated Bearers of Important Intangible Cultural Assets (Jūyō Mukei Bunkazai Hojisha) by the government. These designations are part of a government plan administered by the Agency for Cultural Affairs of the MINISTRY OF EDUCATION since 1950 to preserve and pass on to future generations cultural skills necessary for the preservation of certain traditional arts.

An effort to nurture traditional crafts and performing arts on a national basis resulted in the promulgation of the 1950 Law for the Protection of Cultural Assets (Bunkazai Hogo Hō), amended and expanded in 1954 and 1970. The 1950 law covered certain intangible assets (*mukei bunkazai*) as well as tangible objects. By 1990, a total of 97 individuals in the fields of NŌ, BUNRAKU, KABUKI, traditional music, and *buyō* (see DANCE, TRADITIONAL) had been singled out for their particular skills in the performing arts. In traditional crafts, by that year, 92 individuals had been designated for their work in CERAMICS, weaving, stenciling, dyeing (see TEXTILES; DYES AND DYE COLORS), lacquer, metal, wood and bamboo, DOLLS, and paper (WASHI).

The first such persons were designated by the government on 15 February 1955. The public immediately transferred the word *kokuhō* ("national treasure"), from a 1929 law referring to the preservation of important objects, to these individuals, calling them Ningen Kokuhō, or Living (literally, "human") National Treasures. The term has been used ever since. Eighty-five specific skills under the general heading of traditional performance or craft have been recognized under this program. An updated list usually appears each spring.

loanwords
外来語

(*gairaigo*). Foreign loanwords and phrases that are extensively used in Japanese and normally written in the *katakana* syllabary (see KANA) are called *gairaigo*. Loanwords from China are not normally treated as *gairaigo*, since they are not only numerous but written in Chinese characters and hence are not easily distinguishable from native words. The most important *gairaigo* are American and European loanwords. According to a 1956 survey conducted by the NATIONAL LANGUAGE RESEARCH INSTITUTE, *gairaigo* constitute approximately 10 percent of the language, a proportion that is increasing. Arakawa Sōbei's *Kadokawa gairaigo jiten* (1977, Kadokawa Dictionary of Foreign Loanwords) contains 27,000 headings.

Foreign words were introduced along with new things and new ideas from foreign cultures; many of these, such as the large number of technical terms, had no adequate Japanese equivalent. Even when Japanese had equivalent expressions, foreign words were in many cases employed for their novelty or the sense of prestige they gave the speaker. A foreign word is often substituted as a euphemism for a Japanese word, as in the case of "WC" and *toire* (from "toilet").

The earliest foreign loanwords, many from Sanskrit, Ainu, or Korean, are hardly recognized as such by present-day Japanese speakers. Most of them are written in Chinese characters rather than *katakana*. Many were introduced quite early in Japanese history and often refer to things closely associated with everyday Japanese life. After the arrival of the Portuguese in 1543, Christian and commercial terms were borrowed from Portuguese. *Kurusu* is derived from *cruz* (cross), *pan* from *pão* (bread), and *tempura* from *tempero* (batter-fried foods). When Christianity was banned and the NATIONAL SECLUSION policy adopted in 1639, borrowing from Portuguese stopped. These words are often written in Chinese characters, and most Japanese people believe they are original Japanese words.

The Spanish also entered Japan about the same time as the Portuguese, but the number of Spanish words that remained in Japanese is limited. The Dutch arrived in 1600 and continued to have limited access to Japan even during National Seclusion, bringing a number of Dutch words into the language. Some commercial, scientific, and nautical terms are still widely employed. *Gomu* is derived from *gom* (rubber), *koppu* from *kop* (cup, glass), and *dokku* from *dok* (dock).

In the late Edo period (1600–1868), English, French, and Russian words began to arrive. At present English loanwords outnumber all others; among the countless ex-

Continued on page 900➤

Japanese-Style English:
For Business and Pleasure

*Whether it is used to impress, persuade, seduce, or sell, the brand of English
utilized in Japan is far removed from its origins.*

One evening, the conversation among company managers took a sudden plunge into sensitive waters. Someone mentioned the sales figures for the company's latest venture, which were sinking fast. An unspoken question hovered on everybody's lips: "Who should take the blame?"

After several moments of listening to the bubbling *sukiyaki* cooking on the table, Yamanishi, the most senior member of the group, took the initiative.

"I was of the impression, Sugimoto, that it is not you but Director Tanaka who must take responsibility."

Sugimoto's head hung low. Fixing his eyes on a spot between his chopstick rest and his beer glass, he composed a reply that, in one breath, paid homage to both the grammar of correct English and the distortive phonetics of Japanese.

"*Nō. Aimu in chāji.*" (No. I'm in charge.)

Sugimoto was confessing his guilt—that much was obvious. Yet was he contrite? Nobody could tell. His feelings remained concealed behind the strangeness of his words. He had gambled on a sense of confusion to take his listeners by surprise. It worked. The topic was dropped, and Sugimoto, unscathed, was able to continue his ascent up the corporate ladder.

As used by the Japanese—in advertising copy, consumer product names, technical jargon, and media-coined buzzwords—English is one of the country's most powerful and beguiling tools. It is used to perplex, persuade, cajole, seduce, and, most often, to impress. To native English speakers, it is an Alice-in-Wonderland universe of strangeness and familiarity, in which the connection between words and their original meanings is sometimes obscured.

Translations and Transliterations

The Japanese fascination with the English language can be traced to the Meiji period (1868–1912), when a cabal of intellectuals proposed making English the lingua franca of commerce and government. Although the plan failed, English words were still imported at a heady pace. Some, like *sutēshon* (for "station"), were simply rendered syllable by syllable into *katakana*, the Japanese script used for transliterating foreign terms. Other more abstract words, such as "logic," "science," "optics," and "chemistry," were translated into easily understandable combinations of Chinese ideograms, or *kanji*. Meiji wordsmiths looked for groupings that best conveyed the spirit of the original word. Indeed, *ronri*, a combination of the ideograms for "discourse" and "reason," seems to impart more meaning than the English word "logic."

In dense, technical articles, like those making the rounds of Japan's universities, more than 75 percent of the terms used may be English-based *yakugo* (literally, "translation words"). While people don't usually think of them as being English, these words are the most ubiquitous, enduring examples of the type of English hammered out on the Japanese anvil.

Although Meiji neologists preferred ideograms for difficult English words, Meiji writers, ever on the lookout for ways to add intellectual gloss to their prose, took to larding their work with abstruse English words in *katakana* (or, in extreme examples, in the original Roman alphabet). "If you don't know the meaning," they reasoned, "then you're too backward (or Japanocentric) to be reading our books." These terms were adopted into Japanese, forming a duplicate lexicon of words already in existence. Thus, there are two words for "freedom" in Japanese—*jiyū*, a combination of the ideograms meaning "myself" and "basis," and *furīdamu*. The first word means freedom in the English sense; that is, the absence of constraint in choice or action. The second word, which also means freedom, connotes an air of optimism—freedom with a capital F. ("This is a 'Freedom' appliance," the ad for a word processor might read.) In turn, *furīdamu* has spawned the word *furī*, which itself has three meanings. The statement *Kanojo wa furī da* (She is free) can mean variously, "She is open with her opinions," or "She has no steady boyfriend," or "She is a free-lance worker." The speaker's meaning is drawn from the context.

A huge litany of English words have been shorn of vital elements after making the crossover into Japanese. The resulting words can mean something completely different in English. Who would guess that *basuketto* or *basuke* (basket), *barē* (volley), and *shinkuro* (synchro) are sports terms referring, respectively, to basketball, volleyball, and synchronized swimming? Or that *kyasutā* (caster) is not the wheel on a chair leg but the contracted form of "newscaster"?

The jargon of businessmen is littered with truncated words, most of which have been whittled down to three syllables or less. "Let's make an *apo* (appointment) to discuss your career," an employer might say. "You've been a *pāto* (part-timer) for three years. Why not become a *furu* (full-timer)?" "We can't make the delivery as our shipping division is having a *suto* (short for *sutoraiki*, strike)." "What kind of retail outlet should we open—a *kombini* (convenience store) or a *sūpā* (supermarket)?" "You'd better dismiss Matsumoto. We don't want a *sekuhara* litigation on our hands." Nothing could be more chilling to most executives than this last example, *sekuhara*. It is the result of grafting *hara* of *harasumento* (harassment) onto *seku* of *sekusharu* (sexual), to form a double-barreled compound that bears no resemblance to anything in English. Tight and laconic, the new word is a solution to the problem faced by Japanese tongues not used to pronouncing English words.

The practice of taking two English words and welding them into a compound became fashionable in the 1920s, when Japan was enamored of the modernity of the West. The era ushered in challenges of both a social and a semantic nature. We need a new word, opined the bob-haired Japanese flappers of the day, to set us apart from our *kimono*-clad, tradition-bound sisters. The solution was to borrow a word from English, one so clipped, staccato, and up-to-date that it sounded like code: *moga*. Only the truly initiated could see that these throaty syllables were a contraction of *modan gāru* (modern girl) or that *mobo* meant "modern boy." Soon, both *moga* and *mobo* followed the path of other compound loanwords. Their origins in two English words were forgotten, and they took on an intoxicating glamour of their own.

Wielded by the media—or *masukomi* (mass + communication), as they have dubbed themselves—compound words have enjoyed great popularity. *Amerikan futtobōru* (American football), for example, has become *amefuto*. And *purofesshonaru resuringu* (professional wrestling) has been condensed to *puroresu*. The same is true for a number of other spectator sports.

"Business English"

To advertising agencies charged with keeping Japan's consumer economy on an even keel, compound loanwords are particularly appealing because they add a sugary coating to the most humdrum of products. *Pansuto*, *rajikase*, and *wāpuro* sound fresh, dynamic, and inviting. But if you look at the origins of these words, you will see that they refer to ordinary merchandise. *Pansuto* (*pantsu* + *sutokkingu*) means "panty stocking," or panty hose; *rajikase* (*rajio* + *kasetto*) is a portable cassette deck with radio; *wāpuro* (*wādo* + *purosessā*) is a word processor.

Compound loanwords are almost mantralike in the way they impress themselves on the minds of consumers. A whole flotilla of such words end with the

syllable *kon*: *pasokon* (personal computer), *bodikon* ("body conscious," for body-hugging women's fashions), *misukon* ("miss contest," or beauty contest), *eakon* (air conditioner), and *rimokon* (the "remote control" device for TV and stereo sets) are notable examples. You would think that most Japanese would have had enough of them by now, but the opposite seems to be the case. A vocabulary studded with compound loanwords (or English words of any stripe) can be worn like a badge, especially if the words are *au courant*.

It is in business contexts that the crowning possibilities of Japan's version of English are evident. The species of Japanese-English used in these situations is sometimes called *katakanago* (*katakana* language), because it consists mainly of words spelled out in the *katakana* syllabary. A speaker will occasionally make an attempt at the English pronunciation, but for the most part these words are pronounced as written in *katakana*, each syllable given the same emphasis, such as *kō-po-rē-to a-i-de-n-ti-tī*, for "corporate identity." Some words sound completely unfamiliar but refer to commonplace things. Others, recognizable to English speakers, have been wrenched out of context and given subtle shades of meaning almost impossible to discern. Heading the list is *imēji*, or "image," a word that is as inseparable from business Japanese as rice is from a Japanese meal. In Japan, *imēji* turns up in a variety of pseudo-English expressions used to gauge a company's reputation in the eyes of the public. Take, for instance, the imaginary company AAA, Ltd. For almost a decade this much-heralded rising star of the computer software industry had been the company of choice for college graduates with its dynamic and innovative *kigyō imēji*, or corporate image (*kigyō* means "corporation"). Led by a flamboyant young president and housed in a gleaming glass-and-steel office tower, AAA had been a beacon of hope for aspiring entrepreneurs as well as a target of envy within the industry. However, when its large-scale bribery scandal surfaced in the press last year, AAA suffered a devastating *imēji daun* ("image down," or fall in reputation).

Last month, in a desperate attempt to repair the *mainasu imēji* ("minus image," or bad reputation) afflicting his company, the once-invincible president announced his resignation in a solemn speech before the press. This public act of contrition seems to have triggered an initial *imēji appu* ("image up," or boost in reputation) for the beleaguered company, as stock prices and sales have now finally begun to show healthy gains.

Other English words that often spring up in business banter include *aidia* (idea), *konseputo* (concept), and *bijon* (vision). If a coworker says, "I need better vision," recommending a diet with plenty of vitamin A is not what he wants to hear.

Another group of words in the lexicon of Japanese "business English" seems to have been copied straight out of an encyclopedia entry on plumbing. Consider, for example, *paipu* (pipe) and *channeru* (channel). "We need to extend a channel to his office," a *sararīman* (salaried worker) might say. "We're constructing a pipe to that firm." Non-Japanese minds might picture bulldozers and jackhammers, but these words are used to express the intricacies of Japanese business connections. Such words demonstrate the speaker's command of English and make him or her appear up-to-date on the latest parlance.

| **Buzzwords** | The value of contemporaneity has been especially apparent in the past few decades and is inextricable from the world of *ryūkōgo* |

("trend words")—neologisms that suddenly pop into the language, enjoy a brief spate of popularity, and vanish.

In the fall of 1989, on the eve of the Persian Gulf War, the *New York Times* quoted a Western official who talked about the "linkage" Iraq was making between its actions and the Palestinian issue. This section of the article was included in news broadcasts, and within 24 hours the Japanese media had adopted the word "linkage" (*rinkēji*) as their own. Journalists raged over the "Iraqi/Soviet weapon linkage"; political analysts decried the "Liberal Democratic Party/US Republican Party linkage." Businessmen, not to be left out in the cold, began talking about the "low cost/low quality linkage" or the "bad service/unhappy customer linkage." Then the war ended, and "linkage" was banished to the cold realm of buzzword obsolescence.

The origins of most buzzwords adopted by the media are not as easy to pin down. *Taimu toraberu* (time travel), *taimu surippu* (time slip), and *taimu wāpu* ("time warp," sometimes shortened to *wāpu*) are obviously from American science-fiction movies, but what does it mean when somebody says, "Bob Dylan records make you feel a warp"? (Answer: they make you feel nostalgic.) Some words sound mysterious and exotic until you realize that they are abbreviations of longer terms scaled down to bite size. "AV" and "SFX" slide off the tongue more cleanly than "audiovisual" and "special effects"; they take up less space on billboards and in movie ads, too.

Some buzzwords have developed under unusual circumstances. One example is *obatarian*, a binational merger of the Japanese word *obasan* (middle-aged woman) and the English word "battalion." An *obatarian* is a self-serving middle-aged lady, the type who, according to one source, "fights her way to a seat on a crowded train with liberal plying of umbrella, handbag, and elbows." Rightly lambasted by feminists for its unabashed *sekuhara* overtones, the word derives from *The Return of the Living Dead*, a 1985 Dan O'Bannon film about zombies. As often happens, the Japanese distributor rechristened the film with a shorter, less daunting English title: *Battalion*. A strange word to choose, maybe, judging from the dictionary definition. But the sound is bold, trenchant, meaty! Unfortunately, Japanese viewers thought that "battalion" was the word for the zombies—ill-humored, havoc-wreaking beings with no regard for propriety or the feelings of others. A little wordsmithing, a little word alchemy, and *obatarian*, a word whose value should be measured in gold, was accepted into the ranks of today's argot. How long will it last? Your guess is as good as mine.

Glenn Sullivan

amples are *sutoraiki* (labor strike), *depāto* (department store), and *karē raisu* (curried rice). French words are especially numerous in fashion, cooking, foreign affairs, and politics. Russian has supplied words for foods and things Russian. After Japan reopened to foreign countries in the second half of the 19th century, a great number of German words also entered. They are most numerous in medicine and the humanities and among mountaineering and skiing terms. Italian words were also introduced beginning in the Meiji period (1868–1912), especially for music and food.

Some argue that the borrowing of foreign words enriches the Japanese vocabulary and makes foreign languages more accessible. Others find it a sign of cultural backwardness, or object to it on the grounds that enlarging a vocabulary insufficiently comprehensible to them reinforces the Japanese people's ambiguous attitude toward the meaning of words.　▣▷898–899

lobsters →shrimps, prawns, and lobsters

local autonomy　　　　　地方自治

(*chihō jichi*). The concept of local autonomy in government involves the right of local entities, such as prefectures, cities, towns, and villages, to decide and administer a range of public policies on their own initiative, with relative freedom from supervision ("corporate autonomy"), and the right of local citizens to participate, directly or indirectly, in the formation of such policies ("civic autonomy"). Although the term *chihō jichi* had been widely used ever since the Meiji period (1868–1912), little local autonomy in either sense existed before 1945. The 1947 constitution contains a chapter on "local autonomy," implemented by the Local Autonomy Law (Chihō Jichi Hō) of the same year. The HOME MINISTRY, which had been the fulcrum of centralization, was also abolished in 1947, but in 1949 a successor, the Local Autonomy Agency (Chihō Jichi Chō), was created and became a full-fledged ministry (see MINISTRY OF HOME AFFAIRS) in 1960. Education and police, decentralized under the OCCUPATION, were recentralized to some extent thereafter. Many functions that could be considered local are governed by national laws. The administration of these laws is often delegated to governors and mayors as agents of the national government.

The types and standard rates of local taxes are determined by the Local Tax Law (Chihōzei Hō). Local taxes account for about one third of total revenues, the rest being transfers of funds from the national government. The transfers often fall short of local requirements, and financial dependence and financial stringency limit local autonomy. Demands for reforms for fuller implementation of the constitutional "principle of local autonomy" have increased with the emergence of progressive governors and mayors since the late 1960s.

local government　　　　地方政治

(*chihō seiji*). Subnational executive and legislative institutions responsible for the delivery of basic services and the implementation of central-government policy on a local level. The general trend in local government since the MEIJI RESTORATION (1868) has been for the expansion of local decision-making authority in areas of local concern and the fuller participation of citizens in the local process. The World War II years stand out as an interlude during which this trend was reversed in order to effect the total mobilization of the populace for war, but since 1945 development has mostly followed prewar trends.

Establishment of the Prefectural System—Following the Meiji Restoration, the government began replacing the approximately 260 domains (*han*) and local administrative organs of the BAKUHAN SYSTEM with a centralized administrative structure consisting primarily of prefectures (*ken*) and urban prefectures (*fu*). In 1871 the government instituted a nationwide administrative system consisting of 72 prefectures with prefectural governors appointed by the central government to provide administration on a subnational level. Local administration within prefectures was provided by large and small census districts. The Home Ministry, created in 1873, had the authority to sanction or disapprove of the actions of prefectural governors and became the central administrative element in state control of local government. See PREFECTURAL SYSTEM, ESTABLISHMENT OF.

In 1878, legislation known as the Three New Laws (Sanshimpō) was promulgated to eliminate local variations in administrative organization and governance. The first law called for the institution of districts (*gun*) in rural areas and wards (*ku*) in populous urban areas to replace large census districts as units of local administration. Prefectural governors appointed and supervised the chief officers of *gun* and *ku*, while citizens selected ruling chiefs on a more local level, such as town or village. The second law established representative deliberative assemblies in all prefectures, but reserved for the governors the power to originate bills. Less than 5 percent of the population was enfranchised to vote in these elections—fewer still were eligible for election—nevertheless, prefectural assemblies marked the establishment of elective representative institutions in Japanese government. The third law established rules for the collection of taxes at the prefectural and subprefectural levels. Amalgamations reduced the number of prefectures to 47 (3 *fu*, 43 *ken*, and 1 administrative province or *dō*) by 1888, further promoting uniformity in subnational governance.

In 1888 the Local Autonomy System (Chihō Jichi Seido) superseded the first of the Three New Laws and established a Municipal Code (Shisei) and Town and Village Code (Chōsonsei) declaring that these units of local government were juristic persons that should administer their own affairs "subject to the supreme control of the central government." The codes provided for the establishment of a mayorship and elected assemblies on the local level and specified that male citizens who met certain criteria of age, family, financial condition, and taxpaying status could vote or hold elective office. In 1890 the Prefectural Code (Fukensei) and District Code (Gunsei) made further revisions to the structure of local government. Prefectural councils (*ken sanjikai*) were created to handle business delegated to them by the prefectural assemblies. The District Code made the district a unit of local government with a chief (appointed by the governor), an elected district assembly, and a district council.

Districts were abolished as local govern-

ment entities in 1923 and as state administrative units in 1926. Universal male suffrage, adopted in 1925, expanded citizen participation in local government, as it did in national affairs. In 1929 local self-government powers were strengthened when the home minister lost the authority to make peremptory cuts in prefectural budgets and local and prefectural assemblies were given more legislative authority.

Wartime Centralization of Government Authority—Following the outbreak of conflict with China in 1937, the government required localities to take on more delegated tasks in an attempt to strengthen the state through centralization. In 1940 the Home Ministry ordered that community councils (CHŌNAIKAI) be organized in city block areas and villages, with mayors and town and village chiefs as heads. Neighborhood associations (TONARIGUMI) were made responsible for the policing and welfare of their areas. Laws enacted in 1943 reduced the powers of prefectural assemblies and enlarged the power of the governorship. The last modification in the local government system before the end of World War II came in July 1943 when the government created nine Regional Administrative Councils (Chihō Gyōsei Kyōgikai) to coordinate the action of local bodies and further strengthen central authority.

Postwar Local Government System—Decentralization of governmental authority and the strengthening of local government emerged early in the Allied OCCUPATION as a central goal of the democratization program of the headquarters of the supreme commander for the Allied powers (SCAP). The new system of local government was intended to break up concentrated bureaucratic power revolving around Home Ministry–appointed governors, increase citizen participation and control, assure fairness in the conduct of local affairs, and expand the scope of autonomous local jurisdiction. SCAP decentralized or abolished what it believed to be authoritarian structures that had limited basic liberties in the prewar years and eliminated the Home Ministry in December 1947. It placed educational and police affairs largely in local hands. The new CONSTITUTION OF JAPAN (1947) in essence guaranteed the decentralization of political authority by confirming the "principle of local autonomy" and by establishing such basic features of the new system as the separation of local from national administration and the direct popular election of prefectural governors and of mayors, as well as local assemblies. The latter provision gave voters the potential for controlling the executive authority, thereby providing incentives for governors and mayors to address the concerns of the local electorate. SCAP further sought to deconcentrate authority at the local level by creating prefectural and municipal commissions in charge of public safety, election management, and inspection of local administration. Local assemblies were given the jurisdiction to approve executive appointments to the commissions and certain other offices.

These reforms did not provide as solid a base for local autonomy as intended by Occupation authorities. Consequently there was a strong bureaucratic resistance to administrative and financial decentralization and skepticism on the part of conservative governments concerning the administrative capacity of local authorities. Resistance was further compounded by SCAP's failure to tackle early and strongly enough problems of local finance and division of administrative functions among the three levels of government—national, prefectural, and municipal.

Post-Occupation Evolution—The legacy of SCAP's local governmental reforms was a mixed system combining aspects of prewar centralized administration with postwar norms of local autonomy, an institutional separation between levels of government, and an intensified need for local governmental responsiveness to popular constituencies. During the first postwar decade, controversy centered on the relative merits of the Occupation reforms and on the efforts of central government bureaucracies and conservative parties to recentralize administrative authority. Recentralization of the police and educational systems, completed by 1956, stirred strong opposition from socialists, labor unionists, and intellectuals fearful of a reversion to prewar authoritarianism. On the other hand, central government elites encouraged amalgamations of municipalities to avoid waste of scarce resources, upgrade the overall quality of public administration, and facilitate the implementation of economic plans and national functions delegated to local authorities.

Beginning in the mid-1950s, local governments became participants in the national drive for economic growth. National authorities created a legal framework and a variety of national and regional development banks to promote public financing and investment in new industrial sites, water resources, transportation, harbors, and industrial infrastructure. Local authorities joined this effort at industrial expansion by trying to attract industry with ordinances that provided for corporate tax breaks and other incentives for industrial development. Furthermore, new national laws for regional development were established in the early 1960s. In response, local authorities competed with each other to receive national government designation as target areas for development, thereby furthering the nationwide spread of the petrochemical, steel, nonferrous metals, machinery, and other heavy and chemical industries.

By the late 1960s and early 1970s, many local governments began reordering their priorities. Economic growth encouraged a rapid URBANIZATION of the population and urban land prices spiraled, making the provision of an adequate social infrastructure difficult. At the same time, new urban problems such as POLLUTION-RELATED DISEASES, traffic congestion, and uncontrolled urban sprawl proliferated. Urbanization also created the need for additional social services.

The intensity of such problems resulted in substantial grass-roots protests and efforts by citizens to seek ameliorative policies from local government. Local politics became more competitive as opposition representation in assemblies increased and coalitions of opposition parties formed around new urban issues succeeded in backing reformist candidates for major mayoral and gubernatorial posts. Under these circumstances, local authorities began to pioneer new forms of communication with residents, pollution-control measures, SOCIAL WELFARE programs, planning mechanisms, and public corporations. As a result, local priorities diverged significantly from national ones and contributed to the eventual shift in national priorities from unrestricted economic growth to establishing a higher quality of life.

Moreover, government reform efforts of the late 1970s and early 1980s led to an increased reliance on local authorities for the implementation of national social and environmental programs. There emerged, in effect, a broad recognition that local governments had matured in their administrative competence, had a unique role in setting local priorities and coordinating public programs, and were necessary partners of the national government in creating livable communities and responding to new social and public policy challenges.

local history 地方史

(*chihōshi*). The generic term for historical studies of a region and its people, as opposed to more conventional studies of the rule of a centralized state. Full-scale research into local history in Japan began after World War II.

Before World War II, an author's historical account of his native place (*kyōdoshi*) served to chronicle and explain the national government's relation with a particular region and the characteristics peculiar to that region's political history. The underlying values found in such studies included an agrarian nationalism (NŌHON SHUGI). In contrast, postwar *chihōshi* had its start from criticism of this type of agrarian thinking and marks an attempt to restructure the historical study of the state's relationship with its people from the standpoint of the local area.

The tradition of local history in Japan began with the Nara-period (710–794) regional gazetteers (FUDOKI). These were compiled on order of the central government for the purpose of gaining information about local areas. Gazetteers were also compiled in the Edo period (1600–1868) to help the central government control the people and exploit the resources of the provinces. In the Meiji period (1868–1912) the writing of state-centered histories promoting patriotism was increasingly encouraged at the expense of histories describing regional characteristics. However, under the influence of Prussian gazetteers (*Heimatkunde*), an increased emphasis was placed on local natural history.

The folklorist YANAGITA KUNIO (1875–1962), together with NITOBE INAZŌ (1862–1933), called for study of the lore of rural areas, which he felt to be endangered by state-sponsored rural improvement programs. In his studies of folk culture Yanagita developed the idea of *jōmin*, the "unchanging" people, who throughout history had supplied the productive energy of Japan. He considered it crucial that rural people continue to transmit their traditional wisdom.

In the postwar period local governments have provided funds for research and publication of their regional histories and have offered scholars full access to public documents. There has also been a concerted effort by local organizations to collect and preserve regional cultural artifacts.

local ordinances 条例

(*jōrei*). The word *jōrei* refers in a broad sense to any law enacted under the authority of a local public body (*chihō kōkyō dantai*) and more specifically to laws enacted by local assemblies. The 1947 CONSTITUTION OF JAPAN emphasizes local self-government and commits a wide range of matters to the management of local public bodies. The Local Autonomy Law (Chihō Jichi Hō) permits punishment (including imprisonment for up to two years) for violation of a local ordinance. Citizens have the right to seek the revision or repeal of local ordinances as distinguished from statutes (HŌRITSU) passed by the national Diet. An ordinance may not conflict with a statute or an order (*meirei*). In this sense, ordinances occupy the bottom rank among laws, but, in fact, a large part of a citizen's daily life is regulated by ordinances. Examples of important ordinances include those concerned with antipollution measures and consumer protection.

Lo Chen-yü → Luo Zhenyu (Lo Chen-yü)

Lockheed Scandal ロッキード事件

(Rokkīdo Jiken). A political scandal that occurred in 1976 with the purchase by a Japanese civil airline of planes manufactured by Lockheed Aircraft Corporation. Involving bribes and kickbacks, it led to the prosecution of 17 people, including former prime minister TANAKA KAKUEI. In February 1976 the US Senate subcommittee on multinational industries announced that Lockheed Aircraft had spent large sums of money to sell its military and civilian aircraft in several foreign countries, including Japan. Investigations revealed collusion between the Liberal Democratic Party (LDP; Jiyū Minshutō) and business sectors that resulted in government corruption and, with the high growth rate of the Japanese economy during the 1960s, the emergence of a kind of plutocracy (*kinken seiji*) within the LDP. Tanaka was found guilty in his first two trials but appealed to the Supreme Court, where the case was still pending in 1992.

locusts 稲子

(*inago*). A general term for insects of the family Acrididae, genus *Oxya*. From about July to September, the adult insects, about 4 centimeters (1.6 in) long, appear in rice paddies and feed on rice plants, but the damage is insignificant. Crop failure said to be caused by locusts is often caused by plant hoppers (*unka*) and other harmful insects. Locusts are often eaten in farm villages. They are rapidly decreasing because of the widespread use of insecticide.

Loew, Oscar ロイブ, O.

(1844–1941). German agricultural chemist. Twice instructor at what is now Tōkyō University between 1893 and 1907. Succeeding Oskar KELLNER, he taught agricultural chemistry. Among his students were SUZUKI UMETARŌ and many other Japanese agrochemists. His research studies include work on the effect of lime on acid soils. With Kellner, he was instrumental in introducing agricultural chemistry to Japan.

London, Jack ロンドン, J.

(1876–1916). US author of 50 books ranging from stories of adventure to essays on cultural and political ferment. Real name John Griffith London. Born in San Francisco, at age 17 he joined a sealing expedition to the Pacific, which provided the material for his first published story, "A Typhoon Off the Coast of Japan" (1893). He helped William Randolph Hearst exploit fear of the "YELLOW PERIL" as a correspondent during the Russo-Japanese War of 1904–05. His major works include *The Call of the Wild* (1903), *The Sea Wolf* (1904), and the more autobiographical *Martin Eden* (1909) and *John Barleycorn* (1913).

London Naval Conferences

ロンドン軍縮会議

(Rondon Gunshuku Kaigi). Conferences held in London in 1930 and 1935–36 to extend the Five-Power naval arms limitation system established at the WASHINGTON CONFERENCE (1921–22). The first London conference imposed limits on submarines and auxiliary surface craft such as cruisers and destroyers. The second ended in failure.

A Geneva meeting on naval armaments in 1927 degenerated into an Anglo-American quarrel. At a new conference at London, opening on 21 January 1930, Japanese proposals for a 10:10:7 ratio (for US, British, and Japanese auxiliary surface craft, respectively) were unacceptable to the US and British delegates. A compromise accepted by the cabinet of HAMAGUCHI OSACHI on 14 March 1930 limited the Imperial Japanese Navy to a 10:10:6 ratio in eight-inch-gun cruisers but gave it the desired 70 percent strength ratio in other cruisers and destroyers and parity in submarines. The treaty embodying these terms was to last for five years and was signed on 22 April 1930.

After much criticism of the Washington and London treaties, on 30 December 1934 the OKADA KEISUKE cabinet announced its intention to abrogate the Washington Naval Treaty of 1922. British, US, and Japanese delegates met at London in December 1935 in an effort to prevent the collapse of the naval arms limitation system. Japan's representatives, Ambassador Nagai Matsuzō (1877–1957) and Admiral NAGANO OSAMI,

lotus In the photo, a lotus flower of the species ōgahasu blooms amid its leaves and seed receptacles. The flowers appear for only a few days between mid-July and mid-August. Below, the seed receptacle and edible rhizome.

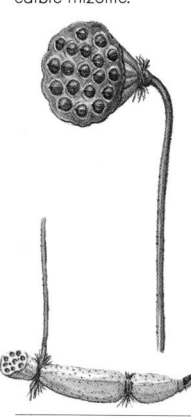

sought full parity with the US and British navies. When this proposal was rejected, Japan withdrew from the conference, but the remaining delegates concluded an agreement that preserved limits on the size and armaments of individual vessels and required exchange of information on building programs. While it did not immediately touch off an arms race, the failure of the second London conference ended an arms control system that had moderated naval rivalry in the Pacific for 15 years.

Long-Term Credit Bank of Japan, Ltd

[株]日本長期信用銀行

(Nippon Chōki Shin'yō Ginkō). Private bank that specializes in long-term credit loans to businesses. The Long-Term Credit Bank of Japan was incorporated in 1952 and now ranks second in the nation among such banks. Its aim was to provide financial aid for the Japanese economy, seeking recovery from its devastation after World War II. Initially the bank financed chiefly the steel, coal, electric, and ocean transport industries, but, keeping pace with the rapid growth of the economy, it provided long-term loans to the electric machinery and shipbuilding industries and to the chemical and other heavy industries for investment in equipment and factories. In the 1970s the bank expanded its operations to include real estate, wholesale, retail, service, and other tertiary industries. The bank has wholly owned subsidiaries in the United Kingdom, Switzerland, Hong Kong, and Curaçao and joint financial institutions in Belgium, Thailand, and other countries. At the end of March 1991 it had funds of ¥30.7 trillion (US $223.8 billion). In the same year it was capitalized at ¥322.0 billion (US $2.3 billion). Headquarters are in Tōkyō.

looms

織機

(shokki). The earliest evidence of spinning and weaving in Japan is found in textile imprints on pottery of the late Jōmon period (ca 10,000 BC–ca 300 BC) and early Yayoi period (ca 300 BC–ca AD 300). Fibers were made into yarn by hand-knotting and twisting. Garments were made by netting, twining, braiding, and weaving with simple looms. A primitive loom used for weaving bast fibers (fibers taken from tree bark, plant stems, etc) is still extant in the form of the Ainu backstrap loom used to weave attush in Hokkaidō. The kappeta loom of the island of Hachijōjima is also of primitive construction.

During the Kofun period (ca 300–710) new techniques of weaving and dyeing were introduced from China and Korea. The type of ancient backstrap loom brought from Korea at that time is called jibata or izaribata and is still used in Japan. The jibata was used for weaving hemp, ramie, banana fiber,

homespun silk, and cotton fabrics. The floor loom and the technique of weaving fine silk are said to have been brought to Japan in the 4th century, but it was not until the 19th century that the floor loom became dominant. Compound silk weaving using intricate patterns was done on a draw loom (hanabata). In the early Meiji period (1868–1912) the first jacquard loom was introduced. Other types of looms used in Japan are twining frames for matting, frames for braiding (KUMIHIMO), and a vertical loom with a heavy beater-heddle used for making straw mats.

lord keeper of the privy seal→

naidaijin

Loti, Pierre

ロチ, P.

(1850–1923). French naval officer and novelist. Real name Louis Marie Julien Viaud. Loti's portrayals of exotic characters and settings won him great popularity. His visits to Japan in 1885 and 1900–1901 provided him with material for several books, including Madame Chrysanthème (1887) and Japoneries d'automne (1889); the former is one of the earliest successful treatments of Japan as a setting by a Western author.

Lotte Co, Ltd

[株]ロッテ

(Rotte). Leading Japanese confectioner. Incorporated in 1948. Lotte manufactures chewing gum, chocolate, candies, cookies, fruit drinks, and ice cream. Subsidiaries include the fast-food chain Lotteria, the delicatessen chain Mutter Rosa, Lotte Electronics, and the Chiba Lotte Marines, a professional baseball team. For the fiscal year ending March 1990, sales of the parent company totaled ¥210.0 billion (US $1.4 billion) and capitalization stood at ¥217.0 million (US $1.4 million). Headquarters are in Tōkyō.

lotteries, public

宝くじ

(takara kuji). Public lotteries were introduced in 1945 in order to provide a source of revenue for the national and local governments. Both the central and local governments operated public lotteries until 1954; since then only local governments (prefectural governments and designated city governments) have done so. Under the law, these local governments are required to appropriate the proceeds from public lotteries to public works projects. The proportion of monies from public lotteries in local government finance was only about 0.2 percent in 1988.

lotus

蓮

(hasu). Nelumbo nucifera. Perennial water plant of the family Nymphaeaceae found in ponds, marshes, and paddy fields throughout Japan. Its flowers are admired for their beauty, and its rhizomes (underground stems) are used for food. This species of lotus is believed to have originated in India and to have come to Japan from China in ancient times.

The white, multiple-jointed rhizomes lie under water in the mud. In late fall the tip of the rhizome grows large enough to be harvested for the food called renkon. Leaves grow straight up to the surface of the water. In summer the lotus produces large, fragrant flowers about 20 centimeters (8 in) across on long, straight stalks rising above the water surface; they are red, pink, or white in color. The flowers bloom for a few days, opening each day at dawn and closing in mid-afternoon. The fruit is oval, and its receptacle, which contains the seeds, looks like a beehive. The seeds are extremely long-lived; some believed to be more than 2,000 years old have been successfully germinated.

The lotus flower is an important symbol in the Buddhist tradition. Because it rises above the mud to bloom, the lotus symbolizes the human capacity to rise above the world's impurities and attain enlightenment. See also WATER LILY.

Lotus Sutra 法華経

(J: *Hokekyō; Hokkekyō;* Skt: *Saddharmapuṇḍarīka-sūtra*). Early Mahāyāna sutra that provided a doctrinal basis for Buddhist devotional cults of the 1st and 2nd centuries. The Lotus Sutra advocates simple devotion as a means of enlightenment. The sutra attempted to subsume the two contending traditions among the Hīnayāna (Lesser Vehicle) of disciples or "listeners" and self-enlightened ones and the Mahāyāna (Greater Vehicle) of the BODHISATTVA (J: *bosatsu*) under the Ekayāna (J: Ichijō) or One Vehicle.

The Lotus Sutra in a 5th-century translation into Chinese was influential in Japan from an early date, as indicated by its inclusion among 7th-century commentaries on three sutras (see SANGYŌ GISHO) by Prince SHŌTOKU. Later, SAICHŌ introduced the teachings of Tiantai (T'ien-t'ai; J: Tendai) patriarch Zhiyi (Chih-i; J: Chigi; 538–597) on the Lotus Sutra and established the Japanese TENDAI SECT with this sutra as its canonical basis. The 25th chapter of this translation exalts the salvific grace of the bodhisattva Avalokiteśvara (J: KANNON). In the Kamakura period (1185–1333) it was the sutra of primary importance to DŌGEN and NICHIREN, who defended the Lotus Sutra and advocated chanting its *daimoku* (title), the invocation NAMU MYŌHŌ RENGE KYŌ, as the ultimate act of devotion. The Lotus Sutra has remained a major influence in Japanese Buddhism, serving as the canon for such modern lay religious movements as SŌKA GAKKAI, RISSHŌ KŌSEIKAI, and REIYŪKAI.

Lowell, Percival ローエル, P.

(1855–1916). US astronomer and writer. Born in Boston; brother of the poet Amy Lowell. After graduating from Harvard College in 1876, he entered business. From 1883 to 1893 he traveled extensively in Asia and related his experiences in a series of books, including *The Soul of the Far East* (1888). In *Occult Japan* (1895), he described the practices and rites of SHINTŌ. Lowell developed an interest in astronomy and founded the Lowell Observatory in Flagstaff, Arizona, in 1894.

loyalty 忠

(*chū*). The Confucian concept of loyalty was introduced to Japan from China early in the historical period. In the feudal period it provided an ideological basis for the relationship of a warrior to his lord. Loyalty required service to one's lord, even at the risk of death, in return for rewards that the lord gave. One's immediate superior was the primary object of loyalty, so that large-scale organizations involving hundreds or thousands of people, such as the Kamakura or Tokugawa governments, were actually constructed from smaller groups tied together through an ascending series of loyalty relationships. In the Meiji period (1868–1912) the concept of loyalty was extended to apply to the emperor and to the state as a nonpersonal entity in an attempt to adapt feudal relationships to the modern world of nation-states. See also FILIAL PIETY.

Lucky Dragon Incident 第五福竜丸事件

(*Daigo fukuryū maru* Jiken). Nuclear incident that sparked a massive outcry in Japan against US testing of nuclear weapons. On 1 March 1954 a 141-ton Japanese fishing boat operating in the central Pacific, the *Daigo fukuryū maru* (*Lucky Dragon V*), was sprayed by a cloud of radioactive ash caused by a US thermonuclear weapon test on Bikini Island (part of the Marshall Islands), 135 kilometers (85 mi) to the west of the boat. US authorities had issued a general warning defining a danger zone around Bikini, but no specific warning had been given as to the timing or location of tests. The United States donated ¥1 million (US $2,800) as a gesture of sympathy to the widow of one crew member who died. The remaining crew members all recovered with no apparent aftereffects.

Following extended negotiations the United States made a payment of $2 million to the Japanese government, without admitting legal liability, to compensate for all injuries and damages resulting from the five nuclear tests it had conducted in the Marshall Islands, including the damages and injuries sustained by the crew of the *Daigo fukuryū maru*. The *Lucky Dragon* Incident exacerbated deep-rooted Japanese concern that the United States was insensitive to Japanese feelings and unduly preoccupied with development of nuclear weapons. See ATOMIC WEAPONS, MOVEMENT TO BAN.

Lu Hsün →Lu Xun (Lu Hsün)

Luo Zhenyu (Lo Chen-yü) 羅振玉

(1866–1940; J: Ra Shingyoku). Eminent Chinese classical scholar, antiquarian, and bibliographer. Luo Zhenyu was a Manchu loyalist who served in the government of the Japanese-sponsored puppet state of MANCHUKUO during the 1930s. Luo first visited Japan in 1901 to study its educational system. After the collapse of the Manchu (Qing or Ch'ing) dynasty (1644–1912), he went to Kyōto and did research on Chinese archaeology. Returning to Tianjin (Tientsin) in 1919, Luo became one of three main advisers to PUYI (P'u-i), the dethroned Manchu emperor.

He frequently disagreed with ZHENG XIAOXU (Cheng Hsiao-hsü), Puyi's other main adviser. Zheng's acceptance of Japan's proposal for the creation of a republic in Manchuria prevailed over Luo's insistence on a monarchy, and Manchukuo was established on 1 March 1932, with Puyi as chief executive. After serving in the Manchukuo government (1933–38), Luo retired to Dairen (Ch: Dalian or Talien), disappointed by Japanese control of Manchukuo.

Lutheran Church ルーテル派教会

(Rūteruha Kyōkai). The history of the Lutheran churches in Japan began in 1892 with the arrival of missionaries from the United States and later from Finland. After World War II, joined by other groups, they formed the Japan Evangelical Lutheran Church. There are, in addition, the Japan Lutheran Church and two groups in the Kansai (Kyōto–Ōsaka–Kōbe) area. The church has its own educational and social service institutions. In the late 1980s there were about 25,000 Lutheran church members in Japan.

Lu Xun (Lu Hsün) 魯迅

(1881–1936; J: Ro Jin). The most influential writer and social critic in modern China. Real

Lucky Dragon Incident The boat that gave this 1954 US nuclear-test incident its name, in a photograph from the early 1970s. The *Lucky Dragon V* was later restored and put on display in Tōkyō.

name Zhou Shuren (Chou Shu-jen). Lu Xun went to Japan in 1902 to study medicine but gave up his medical studies in 1906. Convinced that only a basic alteration of the Chinese spirit could effect the changes necessary in China, he spent the next three years in Tōkyō writing, translating, and trying to introduce the literature of other countries to China.

Lu Xun's most productive period was between the second decade of the 20th century (see MAY FOURTH MOVEMENT)—when his first vernacular story, "Kuangren riji" ("K'uang-jen jih-chi," 1918; tr "A Madman's Diary," 1954), appeared in the radical monthly *Xin qingnian* (*Hsin ch'ing-nien;* New Youth)—and the repression of the leftists in 1927. Like his brother ZHOU ZUOREN (Chou Tso-jen), Lu Xun was a leading figure in the Wenxue Yanjiu Hui (Wen-hsüeh Yen-chiu Hui; Literary Research Society; founded 1921) and the Yusi She (Yü-ssu She; Tatler Society; founded 1924). These groups encouraged humanism and realism in literature against the romanticism of the Chuang-zao She (Ch'uang-tsao She; Creation Society), founded in 1921 by GUO MORUO (Kuo Mo-jo).

Lyman, Benjamin Smith ライマン, B. S.

(1835–1920). American geologist. Born in Massachusetts. In 1872 he was invited by the Japanese government to survey the coal and oil fields in Hokkaidō and along the Sea of Japan coastline. Until his return to the United States in 1881, he educated many Japanese and introduced them to modern techniques for the survey of natural resources. He published the first geologic map of Hokkaidō, called *Nihon Ezo chishitsu yōryaku no zu* (Geological Sketch Map of the Island Yesso, Japan), in 1876.

Lytton Commission リットン調査団

(Ritton Chōsadan). Commission appointed by the League of Nations in December 1931 to determine the causes of the incident near Mukden (now Shenyang) on 18–19 September 1931 that led to Japan's seizure of Manchuria (see MANCHURIAN INCIDENT). After visiting government leaders in Japan and China, the five-man commission, headed by the second Earl of Lytton, spent six weeks in Manchuria in the spring of 1932. In September the Japanese government recognized MANCHUKUO, the puppet state created by the GUANDONG (KWANTUNG) ARMY in Manchuria. On 2 October the commission announced that Japan had been the aggressor. When in February 1933 the General Assembly of the League of Nations adopted the Lytton Report, the Japanese delegate, MATSUOKA YŌSUKE, walked out. In March Japan announced its withdrawal from the organization. See also LEAGUE OF NATIONS AND JAPAN.